BLACKSTONE'S

CIVIL PRACTICE

BLACKSTONE'S

CIVIL PRACTICE

2014

EDITOR-IN-CHIEF

THE RT HON LORD JUSTICE MAURICE KAY

EDITORS

STUART SIME

DEREK FRENCH

EDITORIAL ADVISORY BOARD

STUART BRIDGE

MICHAEL WALKER

IVOR WEINTROUB

CONTRIBUTORS

EVAN ASHFIELD, JULIE BRANNAN

JULIE BROWNE, PETER JOLLY, ADRIAN KEANE

LISA LAURENTI, ANDREW LIDBETTER, ALAN OWENS

ANNA PERTOLDI, WILLIAM ROSE, CHARLES SCOTT

MATTHEW WEINIGER

OXFORD

UNIVERSITY PRESS

OXFORD
UNIVERSITY PRESS

Great Clarendon Street, Oxford, OX2 6DP,
United Kingdom

Oxford University Press is a department of the University of Oxford.
It furthers the University's objective of excellence in research, scholarship,
and education by publishing worldwide. Oxford is a registered trade mark of
Oxford University Press in the UK and in certain other countries

First Edition published by Blackstone Press in 2000
Fourteenth Edition published in 2013

Impression: 1

Published in the United States of America by Oxford University Press
198 Madison Avenue, New York, NY 10016, United States of America

British Library Cataloguing in Publication Data
Data available

ISBN 978–0–19–968065–8

Printed in Italy by
L.E.G.O. S.p.A.—Lavis TN

Preface

NEW TO THE 2014 EDITION

Blackstone's Civil Practice 2014 is up to date to 31 July 2013, and includes rule changes which came into effect then, together with all the civil justice reforms of 2013 that came into force on 1 April 2013 implementing the Jackson reforms. The commentary incorporates rule amendments up to the Civil Procedure (Amendment No. 6) Rules 2013 and the 65th Update. The rules and practice directions in the Appendices include revisions up to the Civil Procedure (Amendment No. 4) Rules 2013 and the 63rd Update. It has not been possible to deal with the new Part 82 of the Civil Procedure Rules, which came into force on 27 June 2013. Among the revisions to *Blackstone's Civil Practice* for this edition are:

- Abolition of recoverability of success fees and additional liabilities
- Damages-based agreements
- Legal aid under LASPO 2012 replacing the Community Legal Service
- Overriding objective revised to include ensuring litigation proceeds at proportionate cost
- Small claims track limit raised
- Allocation questionnaires replaced with directions questionnaires
- Provisional track allocation
- Standard directions for multi-track claims
- Direct judicial contact with legal representatives
- Docketing
- Menu option disclosure
- Disclosure reports
- Costs budgets
- Costs management
- Restrictions on witness statements
- Costs estimates for experts
- Concurrent expert evidence ('hot-tubbing')
- Proportionality: replacement test
- Proportionality, necessity and reasonableness
- Qualified one-way costs shifting
- Part 36: additional amount where there is a successful claimant's Part 36 offer
- Costs rules and costs practice directions completely replaced
- Provisional assessment of costs
- Appeals practice directions completely replaced
- ADR: enhanced importance, and the ADR Handbook
- Contempt of court: the new Part 81

These changes have resulted in the need for three new chapters, and for the chapter on legal aid to be completely replaced, as well as extensive amendments throughout the book.

An online resource centre for *Blackstone's Civil Practice 2014* will also be available with regular updates and useful reading. This can be found at: www.oup.com/blackstones/civil.

Blackstone's Civil Practice 2014 provides the civil litigation practitioner with a comprehensive and authoritative work covering every topic which the practitioner can reasonably expect to encounter in everyday practice. The objective of the publishers and the editorial team has been to produce a single volume of manageable size and expense.

Blackstone's Civil Practice occupies a unique place in the civil litigation practitioner's library. It is a complete treatise on all aspects of the law and practice relating to the progress of a civil claim, from funding the litigation to enforcing the judgment. It provides a complete commentary on the Civil Procedure Rules and practice directions, the text of which is set out in appendix 1. There are chapters providing comprehensive but condensed summaries of the law of evidence, judicial review, human rights, sale of goods and unfair contracts. There is commentary on specialist proceedings including arbitration, mortgage possession, company, insolvency and director disqualification.

A team of highly experienced and respected authors has ensured that each subject is given authoritative and specialist attention. The authors and editors have sought to provide a text which is sufficiently comprehensive, clear and up to date to enable a practitioner easily to assimilate a topic on which he or she may have little knowledge, whilst at the same time providing a depth of analysis and information which will enable those with greater experience of a subject to research in greater detail.

Comprehensive and up-to-date appendices include not only the Civil Procedure Rules, practice directions and pre-action protocols, but also the court fees orders and some of the statutes most commonly needed in civil litigation. Procedural checklists, which are step-by-step guides to various aspects of civil procedure, can be found at the front of the book, beginning on page 1. These provide quick and practical guidance on how to comply with the requirements of the rules.

It has been the foresight and enthusiasm of its publishers which has enabled this work to come to fruition. The editors would, in particular, like to thank Heather Saward and Jeremy Stein, and remember the late Alistair MacQueen, of Blackstone Press, because this work would not have seen the light of day without their vision and enthusiasm. We also extend our thanks to Vicky Pittman and Andy Redman of Oxford University Press for their guidance, encouragement and total support. We also warmly thank the contributors who have provided authoritative material on their subjects and met a tight schedule notwithstanding their other important commitments.

This edition states the law as it was known to the editors and contributors at 31 July 2013 and includes changes to the Civil Procedure Rules and practice directions, which took effect on 31 July 2013 (except that it has not been possible to deal with the new Part 82 of the CPR). Court fees are those in effect from 1 July 2013.

The editors
31 July 2013

Contributors

Evan Ashfield, LLB, Barrister (original contributor of chapters 4, 89 and 90). Until his death in 2011, Evan Ashfield was Head of Chambers, Temple Chambers. He was co-author of *Sale of Goods and Consumer Credit in Practice,* a contributor to Inns of Court School of Law Manuals and former Chairman of the Free Representation Unit.

Julie Brannan, MA (Oxon), Solicitor (non-practising) (chapters 2, 3, 11, 12, 13, 15, 17, 18 and 20). Julie Brannan is Director of Education and Training at the Solicitors Regulation Authority. She was formerly the Director of the Oxford Institute of Legal Practice and before that was a litigation partner at Herbert Smith.

Stuart Bridge, MA (Cantab), Barrister (editorial advisory board). Stuart was a Lecturer in Law at the University of Cambridge from 1990 until 2012. He served as a Law Commissioner for England and Wales from 2001 until 2008, and he has been one of Her Majesty's Circuit Judges, based on the South Eastern Circuit, since 2012. He is a Bencher of the Middle Temple and a Life Fellow of Queens' College, Cambridge. He has recently co-authored the eighth edition of *Megarry and Wade's Law of Real Property.*

Julie Browne, LLB, Barrister (chapters 14 and 88). Julie Browne is a deputy course director of the bar vocational course at the City Law School, where she teaches advocacy, civil litigation, drafting, company law and commercial law. She was called to the Bar in 1989 and during 10 years in full-time practice, she undertook a wide variety of general civil and commercial work, including insolvency, company and property litigation. She is the series editor of the 14 bar vocational manuals, published by Oxford University Press. She is also an experienced CPD trainer in advocacy, evidence, case preparation, drafting and litigation.

Derek French, BSc (editor; chapters 81 to 86, 90 and 92 and appendices). Derek French is co-author of *Mayson, French and Ryan on Company Law* and *Blackstone's Guide to the Civil Justice Reforms 2013* and author of *Applications to Wind Up Companies, Model Articles of Association for Companies* and *How to Cite Legal Authorities.* He is editor of *Blackstone's Statutes on Company Law* and has also written on insolvency law, accountancy and management.

Peter Jolly, MA (Oxon) (chapter 87). Peter Jolly was a district judge from 1993 to 2012, latterly sitting full time at Portsmouth Combined Court, dealing with a mixed civil and family caseload. Before appointment he was a partner in a provincial high street practice with offices in Surrey and Hampshire.

The Right Honourable Lord Justice Maurice Kay (editor-in-chief). Sir Maurice Kay is a Lord Justice of Appeal and Vice President of the Court of Appeal (Civil Division). He was a professor of law before being called to the bar in 1975 where he practised until becoming a High Court Judge in 1995.

Professor Adrian Keane, LLB, Barrister (chapters 49 and 53). Adrian Keane is Professor of Law at The City Law School, City University. Previously, he was Dean of the Inns of Court School of Law. He is a contributor to *Blackstone's Criminal Practice* and his many publications include *The Modern Law of Evidence.*

Lisa Laurenti, LLB, Solicitor (non-practising) (chapters 23 to 30). Lisa Laurenti is a deputy course director of the bar vocational course at the City Law School, teaching civil litigation, professional negligence and drafting. When in practice, she was a partner in a Legal 500 firm where she specialised in professional indemnity and civil fraud work.

Andrew Lidbetter, MA (Oxon), BCL, Solicitor (chapters 77, 78 and 91). Andrew Lidbetter is a litigation partner at Herbert Smith specialising in public law including judicial review and human rights. He is the author of *Company Investigations and Public Law,* is on the advisory board of *Judicial Review* and frequently writes and speaks on public law.

Alan Owens, LLB, Solicitor (chapters 5 and 6). Alan Owens is a partner in the commercial litigation and arbitration department at the London Office of Morrison & Foerster, with extensive international experience across a wide range of contentious matters. He has lectured widely on civil procedure and is an editor of the *Civil Court Service Newsletter.*

Anna Pertoldi, LLB, LLM, Solicitor (chapters 16 and 19). Anna Pertoldi is a litigation partner at Herbert Smith with responsibility for know-how management in the central litigation team. She is a solicitor advocate and editor of Herbert Smith's litigation summary ebulletin as well as the author and editor of other Herbert Smith litigation publications. She has wide-ranging experience of commercial litigation, particularly in the context of international fraud, and has lectured on both substantive and procedural law.

His Honour Judge William Rose, Circuit Judge (former editor-in-chief; original contributor of chapters 23 to 30 and 88). William Rose was appointed a circuit judge in 1998 and was the resident circuit judge at Wandsworth County Court in south-west London from 2001 until his death in 2007. He was the author of *Pleadings Without Tears* and a contributor to the Inns of Court School of Law Manuals on *Remedies* and *Opinion Writing.* He was a Member of the Board of Examiners of the Inns of Court School of Law between 1990 and 2001. He was Director of Studies at the Judicial Studies Board from 2002 to 2004 and was appointed a Judicial Member of the Parole Board in 2004.

Charles Scott, LLB, Barrister (chapter 4). Charles Scott practises in civil law in the Chambers of Nicholas Syfret QC at 13 Kings Bench Walk. He edits chapter 4 authored by the late Evan Ashfield and is a contributor to the bar vocational manuals published by Oxford University Press.

Professor Stuart Sime, LLB, Barrister (editor; chapters 1, 7, 8, 9, 10, 21, 22, 31 to 48, 50, 51, 52, 54 to 71, 74, 75, 76, 79 and 89). Stuart Sime is the course director of the full-time bar professional training course at the City Law School, where he teaches civil litigation, commercial and company law. He was a practising barrister until 2005. In his early career he spent a number of years in the litigation department of the Treasury Solicitor's Office. He is the author of *A Practical Approach to Civil Procedure* and co-author of *A Practical Approach to ADR*, the *Jackson ADR Handbook* and *Blackstone's Guide to the Civil Justice Reforms 2013.*

District Judge Michael Walker, CBE (consultant editor). Michael Walker was appointed a district judge in April 1994. Before his appointment to the bench he was a partner in a South London firm of high street, legal aid, solicitors. From 1994 to 2007 he sat full time at Wandsworth County Court with a mixed workload of civil and family cases but since September 2007 he has been seconded to the Senior Presiding Judge's office at the Royal Courts of Justice. Between 2000 and 2011 he was Honorary Secretary of the Association of Her Majesty's District Judges. In April 2008 he became one of the judicial members of the board of what is now known as Her Majesty's Courts and Tribunals Service.

Matthew Weiniger, MA (Cantab), Solicitor Advocate (chapters 72, 73 and 80). Matthew Weiniger is a partner at Herbert Smith practising in the international arbitration group. He specialises in international arbitration and alternative dispute resolution (particularly in banking, investment and joint venture disputes). He also advises on matters relating to public and private international law.

Ivor Weintroub, LLB (editorial advisory board). Ivor Weintroub is a Civil and Family Recorder of the Crown and County Courts and previously sat as a district judge in Bournemouth County Court. He is also an Honorary Visiting Lecturer to the Business and Law department of

Bournemouth University LPC course. He has lectured and been a tutor judge on civil and family courses for the Judicial Studies Board. Before appointment as a district judge he was a partner in a High Street practice with offices in Southampton and Hampshire and was a member of the Law Society Child Care and Mental Health Review Tribunal Panels.

The tables and index were compiled by Moira Greenhalgh BSc MCLIP FSI and updated by Penny Dickman (index) and Margaret Hibbert (tables).

Contents Summary

Contents

A GENERAL MATTERS

B FUNDING LITIGATION

D COMMENCEMENT

S ANTI-SOCIAL BEHAVIOUR AND HARASSMENT

T SALE OF GOODS AND UNFAIR CONTRACTS

U HUMAN RIGHTS AND CIVIL PROCEDURE

V TERMINOLOGY

APPENDICES

Guide to *Blackstone's Civil Practice*

CHAPTERS AND APPENDICES

Blackstone's Civil Practice has 92 chapters and four appendices. The chapters are grouped into 20 parts, A to V. For a list of the parts, chapters and appendices see the **Contents** starting on page xiii.

Chapters are divided up by numbered headings. The first heading in chapter 1 is numbered **1.1**, the second is **1.2** and so on. The number of a heading is printed in the margin against the first line of text after the heading. Each chapter begins with a list of its numbered headings. The numbers are used for cross-references throughout the book.

ORGANISATION OF THE SUBJECT MATTER

Subject-focused chapters

The chapters of *Blackstone's Civil Practice* are subject-focused, dealing with all the law on a topic, wherever the source of the law may be in statutes, rules, practice directions or cases. General points are discussed in part A (**chapters 1** to 4), then parts B to P (**chapters** 5 to 81) describe the progress of a civil claim in a county court or the High Court in England and Wales, from consideration of how to fund it (part B) to the methods of enforcing judgment (part P). Part Q (**chapters 82** to 86) deals with procedure in insolvency proceedings and companies matters in the county courts and High Court. Other special procedures in the county courts and High Court are considered in **chapter** 72 (arbitration claims), **chapter** 77 (judicial review, which is conducted in the High Court only), **chapter** 87 (mortgage possession claims) and **chapter 88** (anti-social behaviour and harassment, which are dealt with in county courts only). Parts T and U of *Blackstone's Civil Practice* contain compact summaries of some topics of particular importance to practitioners: sale of goods and unfair contracts (part T) and human rights (part U). Part V lists the changes of terminology in civil proceedings which have occurred from 1998 onwards.

Blackstone's Civil Practice does not deal with family proceedings or with civil proceedings ancillary to criminal matters.

Procedural checklists

Starting on page 1 there are 38 procedural checklists which summarise the steps to be taken in the most commonly encountered stages of a civil claim.

Source-focused appendices

Appendices 1 to 4 of *Blackstone' s Civil Practice* are source-focused. **Appendix 1** gives the complete, up-to-date text of the Civil Procedure Rules and supplementing practice directions. Pre-action protocols are in **appendix** 2. **Appendix 3** is court fees orders. **Appendix** 4 gives the up-to-date text of the principal statutes relating to civil procedure. Each appendix begins with a list of its contents.

If the title of a legislative provision is set in **bold type** in chapters 1 to 92, the text of the provision will be found in the appropriate appendix to the book.

Contents, index, cross-references and useful references section

Research in *Blackstone's Civil Practice* can be started either from a subject focus or a source focus, because of the comprehensive indexing and cross-referencing of the book.

The index at the end of *Blackstone's Civil Practice* is an in-depth subject index of chapters 1 to 92 and of the Civil Procedure Rules and practice directions. The index is usually the best way of finding where a particular topic is discussed in chapters 1 to 92 of *Blackstone's Civil Practice* and which rules or practice directions are concerned with that topic.

In **appendix 1**, after the heading of each Part of the Civil Procedure Rules, and after the title of each rule, cross-references are given to the headings (by number) in chapters 1 to 92 under which the Part or rule is mentioned. There is a similar system of cross-referencing for the practice directions in **appendix 1. Appendix 1** is usually the best place to start to find commentary on a particular rule or practice direction.

At the beginning of *Blackstone's Civil Practice* there is a **Table of Cases**, a **Table of Statutes** and a **Table of Rules, Practice Directions, Protocols, Other Secondary Legislation and Court Guides**. These tables list all the headings (by number) under which each case, statute etc. is mentioned.

On the front inside cover there is a **Useful References** section. This comprises a list of important and useful paragraphs which often need to be accessed in a hurry.

There is a **Calendar** on the back inside cover.

ONLINE RESOURCE CENTRE

This will alert practitioners to key developments taking place during the life cycle of this edition. It will be available to all *Blackstone's Civil Practice 2014* subscribers. Please visit <www.oup.com/blackstones/civil> and bookmark the site.

Abbreviations

ADR	alternative dispute resolution
ATE	after-the-event
Brussels I Regulation	Regulation (EC) No. 44/2001
CCA 1974	Consumer Credit Act 1974
CCR	County Court Rules 1981 (SI 1981/1687) as amended, or as re-enacted in CPR, sch. 2
CDDA 1986	Company Directors Disqualification Act 1986
CFA	conditional fee agreement
CJEU	Court of Justice of the European Union
CJJA 1982	Civil Jurisdiction and Judgments Act 1982
CLS	Community Legal Service
CPFO	Civil Proceedings Fees Order 2008 (SI 2008/1053)
CPR	Civil Procedure Rules 1998 (SI 1998/3132)
CRU	Compensation Recovery Unit
DCS	debtor-creditor-supplier
ECHR	European Court of Human Rights
EEO	European enforcement order
EL/PL Protocol	Pre-Action Protocol for Low Value Personal Injury (Employers' Liability and Public Liability) Claims
EOP	European order for payment
ESCP	European small claims procedure
Final Report	Lord Woolf, *Access to Justice. Final Report* (London: HMSO, 1996)
GLO	group litigation order
Interim Report	Lord Woolf, *Access to Justice. Interim Report* (London: Lord Chancellor's Department, 1995)
IR 1986	Insolvency Rules 1986 (SI 1986/1925)
IVA	individual voluntary arrangement
Jackson Report	Sir Rupert Jackson's *Review of Civil Litigation Costs: Final Report* (London: TSO, 2010)
LA 1980	Limitation Act 1980
LAA	Legal Aid Agency
LEI	legal expenses insurance
LSC	Legal Services Commission
MF	McKenzie friend
MIB	Motor Insurers' Bureau
ord.	order
para.	paragraph
paras	paragraphs

PD	Practice Direction. PD followed by a number is a practice direction supplementing the Part of the CPR with that number.
PD Directors Disqualification Proceedings	Practice Direction — Directors Disqualification Proceedings
PD Insolvency Proceedings	Practice Direction — Insolvency Proceedings
PD Pre-action Conduct	Practice Direction — Pre-action Conduct
r.	rule
RCJ	Royal Courts of Justice
RLSC	regional legal services committee
rr.	rules
RSC	Rules of the Supreme Court 1965 (SI 1965/1776) as amended, or as re-enacted in CPR, sch. 1
RTA	road traffic accident
RTA Protocol	Pre-action Protocol for Low Value Personal Injury Claims in Road Traffic Accidents
s.	section
SCCO	Senior Courts Costs Office
sch.	schedule
SCR	Supreme Court Rules 2009 (SI 2009/1603)
Service Regulation	Regulation (EU) No. 1348/2000
SoGA 1979	Sale of Goods Act 1979
SoGITA 1973	Supply of Goods (Implied Terms) Act 1973
SoGSA 1982	Supply of Goods and Services Act 1982
ss.	sections
Taking of Evidence Regulation	Regulation (EC) No. 1206/2001
TCC	Technology and Construction Court
TFEU	Treaty on the Functioning of the European Union
WFO	worldwide freezing order
Woolf Report	Lord Woolf, *Access to Justice: Final Report* (London: HMSO, 1996)

Table of Cases

Table of Statutes

(including European and International legislation)

Table of Rules, Practice Directions, Protocols, Other Secondary Legislation and Court Guides

Procedural Checklists

Procedural checklist 1 Pre-action Protocol for Personal Injury Claims

See **8.16** to **8.27**.

All references are to the **Pre-action Protocol for Personal Injury Claims** unless otherwise indicated.

Soon after being retained	Solicitor should consider whether an informal notification of the possible claim should be made to the defendant. This will not start the protocol timetable (**para. 2.6**).
Letter before claim	This should be sent at least 6 months before the expiry of limitation period to give time for compliance before limitation expires. Two copies of the letter should be sent to the defendant, or one to the defendant and one to the insurer (**paras 2.7** and **3.1**). For detailed contents of the letter, see **paras 3.2** to **3.5** and **annex A**.
21 days from letter before claim	Defendant should reply with name of insurer, or the insurer should acknowledge (**para. 3.6**). The period is up to 42 days if the accident was outside England and Wales (**para. 3.8**).
Failure to acknowledge	If there is no acknowledgment within 21 days, proceedings may be issued (**para. 3.6**).
3 months from acknowledging letter before claim	Defendant should have completed investigations. Defendant must reply stating if liability is admitted or denied (**paras 2.12** and **3.7**). If liability is denied or if contributory negligence is alleged, the defendant should give reasons and provide documents on liability (**paras 3.7**, **3.10** to **3.12**). Standard disclosure lists are in **annex B**. No charge is to be made for providing copy documents (**para. 3.13**).
Before issuing proceedings	If contributory negligence has been alleged, the claimant should respond to those allegations (**para. 3.12**).
As soon as possible after defendant's response	Claimant sends defendant a schedule of special damages and documents in support. This is particularly important where liability has been admitted (**para. 3.14**). Both sides must consider the claimant's rehabilitation needs (**para. 4.1**).
No time limit, but usually shortly after the defendant's response	Either party may send the other a list of suggested experts for each field of expertise (**para. 3.15**). The letter should also state the basis of the proposed instruction (otherwise this procedure results in the joint selection of experts rather than joint instruction, see **54.19**).
No time limit	Claimant organises access to relevant medical records (**para. 3.16**).
14 days after list of experts	Other side may raise objections to the suggested experts (**para. 3.17**).
Objection to all suggested experts	Both parties are free to instruct their own experts. This may be penalised in costs later if either side has acted unreasonably (**para. 3.18**).
No complete objection	First party selects an expert from those left, and sends a letter of instruction in accordance with the standard letter (**annex C**).
Receipt of report	First party decides whether to send copy to the other side (see **54.19**). Both parties consider sending questions to clarify the report to the expert. The second party should send its questions via the first party's solicitors (**para. 3.20**).
Before proceedings	Both parties should consider sending Part 36 offers to the other side. Both parties should also consider whether mediation or ADR might be appropriate (**paras 2.16**, **5.2**, and **8.7**; see **68.19** and **73.23**).
14 days before issue	Claimant should ask the defendant's insurers to nominate solicitors, and both parties should carry out a stocktake of the issues and evidence (**para. 2.17**).

Procedural checklist 2 Pre-action procedure where no protocol applies

See **8.12** to **8.15**.

All references are to **PD Pre-action Conduct.**

Letter before claim	Letter before claim is sent to the defendant stating the basis of the claim and other matters set out in **annex A, paras 2.1** to **2.3**, including time for a full response

	('reasonable period of time'). This is usually 14 days in straightforward matters, 30 days where there are issues about evidence, and up to 90 days if particularly complex (**para. 7.2**). The letter must list the essential documents the claimant relies upon. If the defendant is not represented, the letter must refer to **PD Pre-action Conduct**, draw attention to the court's power to impose sanctions under **para. 4**, and inform the defendant that ignoring the letter before claim may result in proceedings being issued and increase the defendant's liability for costs (**annex A, para. 2.3**).
Within next 14 days	Defendant acknowledges letter before claim, stating when a detailed response will be sent, and reasons for any extra time required (**annex A, paras 3.1** to **3.3**). No need to acknowledge if a full response is sent within this time.
Reasonable time from letter before claim	Defendant provides full written response accepting the claim and making proposals for settlement, or denying the claim with detailed reasons, listing essential documents and stating other matters set out in **annex A, para. 4.2**.
Promptly thereafter	The parties should consider ADR and engage in appropriate genuine and reasonable negotiations with a view to settling the claim economically and without court proceedings (**paras 8.1** to **8.3**).
Expert evidence	If expert evidence is required, the parties should if possible engage a single joint expert or an agreed expert (**annex C, para. 3**).

Procedural checklist 3 Issue and service where service of the claim form is to be effected by the court

See chapters 12 and 15.

Where the court is to effect service the procedure is as follows:

(a)	The claimant sends or takes to court one copy of the claim form and, if necessary, a notice of funding of claim or copy LSC certificate for the court, and a copy for each defendant to be served, together with the issue fee (**CPFO, fee 1**). Claimants in the RCJ can get the court to seal a 'claimant's copy' claim form, if convenient.
(b)	The court issues the claim form by entering the issue date on the claim form, affixing the court seal to the claim form and allocating a number to the claim. It creates a case management file, in which it files its copy of the claim form and, if supplied, notice of funding of claim. The claimant's copy of the claim form (if any) will be returned.
(c)	The court serves the claim form and, if supplied, notice of funding of claim. It is for the court to decide which method of service to choose, although the method will normally be by first-class post (**CPR, r. 6.4(2); PD 6A, para. 8.1**).
(d)	Where particulars of claim are contained in the claim form or are to be served with it, court staff will add to the documents for service a response pack consisting of forms for admitting and for defending the claim and for acknowledging service (**CPR, r. 7.8(1)**). Where the particulars of claim are to be served later, these documents do not accompany the claim form.
(e)	The court will send the claimant a notice of issue (form N205A, N205B or N205C), which will include the date when the claim form is deemed to be served under **r. 6.14** (**r. 6.17(1)**).
(f)	Where the court sends the claim form by post and it is returned to the court, or where there is an unsuccessful attempt to effect bailiff service, it must notify the claimant (**rr. 6.18(1)** and **6.19**).
(g)	A claimant who receives a notice of ineffectual bailiff service should take steps to effect service of the claim form himself. If the court sent the claim form by first-class post to the correct address for service, there is an irrebuttable presumption of due service (**r. 6.18(2)**).

Procedural checklist 4 Issue and service where service of the claim form is to be effected by the claimant

See **chapters 12 and 15**.

Where the claimant is to effect service the procedure is as follows:

(a) The claimant sends or takes to court one copy of the claim form for the court, and a copy for each defendant to be served, together with the issue fee. Claimants in the RCJ can get the court to seal a 'claimant's copy' claim form, if convenient. There must be a notification to the court that the claimant wishes to effect service. If applicable, a notice of funding of claim must be filed.

(b) The court issues the claim form by entering the issue date on the claim form, affixing the court seal to the claim form and allocating a number to the claim. It creates a case management file, which will include the court's copy of the claim form and, if supplied, copy of public funding certificate.

(c) The claimant's copy of the claim form (if any) and the copies for service on the defendants will be returned.

(d) The claimant will effect service, in one of the ways specified in **CPR, r. 6.3**. If a notice of funding of claim form N251 was filed, it must be served with the claim form. Where particulars of claim are contained in the claim form or are to be served with it, the claimant must also serve the forms for acknowledging service, for admitting and for defending the claim (**r. 7.8(1)**). Where the particulars of claim are to be served later, these documents do not accompany the claim form.

(e) The claimant must file a certificate of service (form N215) within 21 days of service of the particulars of claim, unless all defendants have acknowledged service. The certificate must give the details set out in **r. 6.17(3)** (**r. 6.17(2)(a)**).

Procedural checklist 5 Claim under standard Part 8 procedure

See **chapter 13**.

Issue	Issue claim on form N208 (**PD 8A, para. 4.2**). At same time, file evidence in support of claim (**CPR, r. 8.5(1); PD 8A, para. 7.1**).
Fee	Part 8 claims are likely to be non-money claims for which the fee is £465 in the High Court, £175 in a county court (**CPFO, fee 1.5**).
Service	Serve claim form (form N208), form for acknowledging service (form N210), and evidence in support of claim (**CPR, r. 8.5(4)**). Forms for defending or admitting the claim are not required (**rr. 7.8(2)** and **8.9(b)(ii)**). Usual rules for service, set out in **Part 6** apply.
Time for service	The claim must be served within four months after issue, if it is served in the jurisdiction, or six months after issue, if it is served out of the jurisdiction (**r. 7.5**).
Acknowledgment	Defendant should file acknowledgment (form N210), verified by a statement of truth (**r. 22.1(1)(d)**) within 14 days after service of claim form, and serve copies of form N210 on other parties at the same time (**r. 8.3(1)**).
Objecting to Part 8 procedure	At same time as filing acknowledgment, defendant may file and serve statement of reasons for objecting to Part 8 procedure (**CPR, r. 8.8(1); PD 8A, para. 5.3**).
Responding to claim	At the same time as acknowledging service, the defendant should file and serve evidence in opposition to the claim (**CPR, r. 8.5(3)** and **(4)**). If he fails to do this, he may participate in the hearing only if the court gives permission. However, judgment in default may not be entered against him (**rr. 8.1(5)** and **8.4**).
Evidence in reply	Within 14 days after service of defendant's evidence, claimant may file and serve evidence in reply (**r. 8.5(5)** and **(6)**).

Form of evidence	Evidence may be in the form of an affidavit or witness statement, or in the case of the claimant's evidence in support, in the claim form itself, provided it is verified by a statement of truth (**PD 8A, para. 7.2**).
Extending time for service of evidence	Parties may agree in writing to extensions of time for service of the defendant's evidence, and of the claimant's evidence in reply, of up to 14 days. A copy of the agreement to extend time for the defendant's evidence must be filed with the defendant's acknowledgment (**PD 8A, para. 7.5(2)(a)**). Any longer extensions may only be granted by the court (**PD 8A, para. 7.4**).
Case management	Part 8 claims are automatically allocated to the multi-track and parties do not need to complete directions questionnaires (**CPR, r. 8.9(c)**). No allocation fee is payable in a Part 8 claim (**CPFO, notes following fee 2.2**). Directions (including fixing a hearing date) will be given by the court either when the claim is issued or after the acknowledgment has been filed (**PD 8A, para. 6**).
Listing and hearing fees	A listing fee of £110 is payable (**CPFO, fee 2.2**) together with a multi-track hearing fee of £1,090 (**CPFO, fee 2.3(a)**). Usually these fees are payable by the claimant on filing the pre-trial checklist. They are not payable if the hearing date was fixed on issue of the claim.
Hearing	Most claims will be disposed of at a hearing based on the written evidence.

Procedural checklist 6 Approval of settlement or compromise involving a child or protected party, where sole purpose of claim is to obtain court approval

See 14.22.

Part 8 claim form	Issue Part 8 claim form, including request for approval of the settlement and either set out the terms of the settlement or attach a draft consent order in form N292 (**PD 21, para. 5.1**).
Contents of Part 8 claim form	The claim form must include the following information (**PD 21, para. 5.1**): • whether and to what extent the defendant admits liability; • the age and occupation (if any) of the child or protected party; • the litigation friend's approval of the proposed settlement; • in a personal injury case only, the circumstances of the accident, any medical reports, a schedule of damages, any evidence or police reports in any related criminal proceedings or inquest and details of any prosecution; • where the settlement provides for periodical payments, the terms of the settlement or compromise. Alternatively the draft consent order should be attached to the claim form.
Part 8 Procedure	See **procedural checklist 5**.
Opinion on the merits	An opinion on the merits by counsel or solicitor should be supplied to the court (**PD 21, para. 5.2**).
Hearing	In proceedings involving a child, the application will normally be heard by a master or district judge (**PD 21, para. 5.6(1)**). In proceedings involving a protected party, the proceedings will normally be heard by a master, designated civil judge or his nominee (**PD 21, para. 5.6(2)**). In the Chancery Division, the application will be heard by a judge if the amount exceeds £100,000 (**PD 2B, para. 5.1 (a)**).
Privacy	The hearing of the application to approve the settlement may be in private where it involves the interests of a child or protected party (**CPR, r. 39.2(3)(d); PD 39A, para. 1.6**).

Procedural checklist 7 Interpleader proceedings: High Court

See 14.75 to 14.79.

(a) Enforcement officer's interpleader: preliminary steps

Notice to enforcement officer	The person claiming ownership of goods taken or intended to be taken by the enforcement officer should notify the enforcement officer of his claim, and give his address for service (**RSC, ord. 17, r. 2(1)** in **CPR, sch. 1**).

Enforcement officer's notice to judgment creditor	Enforcement officer must notify judgment creditor immediately of claim (**RSC, ord. 17, r. 2(2)** in **CPR, sch. 1**).
Response from judgment creditor	Within seven days, judgment creditor must inform the enforcement officer whether he admits or disputes the claim (**RSC, ord. 17, r. 2(2)** in **CPR, sch. 1**). Where the claim is disputed, the enforcement officer may apply for interpleader relief.

(b) Interpleader application

Application	Application for interpleader relief in existing proceedings is made by application notice (form N244) or, where there are no pending proceedings, by Part 8 claim form (form N208) (**RSC, ord. 17, r. 3(1)** in **CPR, sch. 1**).
Fee	£80 where claim is made by application notice (**CPFO, fee 2.6**); £465 where claim is made by Part 8 claim form (where claim is for goods, not proceeds of sale) (**CPFO, fee 1.5**).
Evidence in support	Where the enforcement officer is interpleader claimant, no evidence in support is required. Otherwise, evidence must be filed and served showing that the interpleader claimant: • claims no interest in the subject matter in dispute, other than for charges or costs; • does not collude with any of the claimants to the subject matter; and • is willing to pay or transfer that subject matter into court or to dispose of it as the court may direct (**RSC, ord. 17, r. 3(4)** in **CPR, sch. 1**).
Service	The claim form or application notice must be served on all persons asserting a claim to the property.
Claimant's response	Where the claim relates to goods seized in execution, the claimant then has 14 days in which to serve a witness statement or affidavit on the enforcement officer and the judgment creditor. This must identify the property claimed and the grounds for asserting rights in the property (**RSC, ord. 17, r. 3(6)** in **CPR, sch. 1**).

Procedural checklist 8 Interpleader proceedings: county court

See 14.75 and 14.80 to 14.82.

(a) Bailiff's interpleader

Notice to bailiff	The person claiming ownership of goods taken or intended to be taken in execution (the 'interpleader claimant') should notify the bailiff of his claim, give his address for service, and the grounds for the claim (**CCR, ord. 33, r. 1(1)** in **CPR, sch. 2**).
Security	Except where the claim is for the value or proceeds of goods, the interpleader claimant must make a deposit or provide security for the claim (**CCR, ord. 33, r. 1(2)(b)** in **CPR, sch. 2**).
Notice to judgment creditor	Court will notify judgment creditor of claim (**CCR, ord. 33, r. 1(2)(a)** in **CPR, sch. 2**).
Response from judgment creditor	Within four days, judgment creditor must inform the court whether he admits or disputes the claim (**CCR, ord. 33, r. 2** in **CPR, sch. 2**).
Issue of interpleader proceedings	Where the claim is disputed, the court will issue an interpleader notice (form N88 or N88(1)), fix a date for the hearing and serve the notice on the judgment creditor and the interpleader claimant at least 14 days before the hearing date (**CCR, ord. 33, r. 4** in **CPR, sch.2**).

(b) Stakeholder's interpleader

Jurisdiction	A person ('the applicant'), who is being, or expects to be, sued by two or more persons (the 'interpleader claimant') making opposing claims to a debt, money or goods for which the applicant is liable, may apply for interpleader relief (**CCR, ord. 33, r. 6(1)** in **CPR, sch. 2**).

Application	Application is made by filing a witness statement or affidavit showing that the applicant: • claims no interest in the subject matter in dispute, other than for charges or costs; • does not collude with any of the interpleader claimants; and • is willing to pay or transfer that subject matter into court or to dispose of it as the court may direct (**CCR, ord. 33, r. 6(3)** in **CPR, sch. 2**).
Number of copies	One copy of the affidavit or witness statement should be filed for the court together with an additional copy for each competing interpleader claimant (**CCR, ord. 33, r. 6(3)** in **CPR, sch. 2**).
Time for application	Where the applicant is a defendant in a pending claim, the application should be filed within 14 days after service of the claim form.
Interpleader notice	Where there are no pending proceedings, the court will issue an interpleader notice (form N89).
Pre-trial review	The court will fix a date for a pre-trial review on receipt of the application.
Service	The court will serve notice of the application, form N89 (where appropriate) and copies of the affidavit or witness statement on all parties and interpleader claimants at least 21 days before the date for the pre-trial review.
Interpleader claimant's response	Within 14 days after service, the interpleader claimant must either file a notice that no interpleader claim is to be made or file particulars of the grounds for a claim. Copies for all parties should be filed. The court will serve the parties (**CCR, ord. 33, r. 10** in **CPR, sch. 2**).

Procedural checklist 9 Application for joinder

See **14.86** to **14.89**.

Timing	If joinder is sought before service of claim form, the court's permission is not required. If joinder is sought after service of the claim form, application must be made for the court's permission.
Application notice	Form N244. Apply for new party to be added as claimant/defendant, or for new party to be substituted for existing party, or for existing party to be removed and also, in each case, for permission to amend statement of case. Attach draft of order sought and draft of proposed amended statement of case. Set out brief reasons for application.
Consent of new party	Where party to be added or substituted is a claimant, file and serve, with the application notice, the signed written consent of the new party (**PD 19A, para. 2.1**).
Evidence	Application to add or substitute a party must be supported by evidence setting out the proposed new party's interest in or connection with the claim (**PD 19A, para. 1.3**). The evidence must be filed and served with the application notice.
Fee	£80 (**CPFO, fee 2.6**); for consent application £45 (**CPFO, fee 2.7**).
Service	The application notice, attachments and evidence in support must be served on all existing parties and any proposed new party as soon as practicable after filing and at least three clear days before the hearing date (**CPR, r. 23.7**).
Costs	In contested applications, parties should file and serve costs schedules in form N260 24 hours before hearing (**PD 44, para. 9.5**).
Hearing	Consent applications may be dealt with without a hearing.
After the hearing	Comply with directions. If permission is given, these will normally require the applicant to file the amended claim form and particulars of claim within 14 days of the order (a fee of £45 is payable (**CPFO, fee 1.6**)), to serve the new defendant with the existing statements of case, the amended claim form and particulars of claim, a response pack and a copy of the order.
Limitation	A new defendant does not become a party to the proceedings for the purpose of the Limitation Act 1980 until served with the claim form (**PD 19A, para. 3.3**).

Procedural checklist 10 Application to extend time for service of claim form

See **15.30**.

Application notice	Form N244. The application is for the period within which the claim form may be served to be extended to a specific date. Brief reasons for the application should be included in form N244.
Evidence in support	Evidence in support must be filed with form N244 and will usually either be set out in the notice of application itself or in a witness statement. The evidence must state all the circumstances relied on; the date of issue of the claim; the expiry date of any extension already granted under **CPR, r. 7.6**; and a full explanation of why the claim form has not been served (**PD 7A, para. 8.2**). Where the application is without notice, the evidence must also state why notice has not been given (**CPR, r. 25.3(3)**).
Without notice	Application will usually be made without notice, as the defendant is not yet on the record (**CPR, r. 7.6(4)(b)**). Because the application is without notice to the defendant, the claimant must make full and frank disclosure of all relevant facts.
Fee	£45 (**CPFO, fee 2.7**).
Hearing	As the application is made without notice, there will not normally be a hearing. However, where the application is made shortly before expiry of the period for service of the claim form and where the cause of action has become time-barred since the date of issue of the claim form, it is desirable that the application should be dealt with by an urgent hearing.
Service of order	A copy of any order made without notice to the defendant, whether extending time for service of the claim form or refusing to do so, must be served on the defendant, together with form N244 and any evidence in support. The order should contain a statement of the defendant's right to apply to set aside or vary the order within seven clear days of service of the order (**CPR, r. 23.9**).

Procedural checklist 11 Application for permission to serve claim form out of jurisdiction

See **16.43**.

Claim form	Claimant has the choice of whether to issue the claim form before or after seeking permission to serve outside the jurisdiction (see **16.43**).
Application	If a claim form is issued first, the application is for permission to serve outside the jurisdiction, and **fee 2.7** (see 'Fee' below) is payable on the application. If a claim form is not issued first, the application is for permission to issue and to serve the claim form, and **fee 1.8** (see 'Fee' below) is payable on the application.
Application notice	Form N244. Apply for permission under **CPR, r. 6.36**, to serve the defendant at his address out of the jurisdiction because [state grounds of **PD 6B, Para. 3.1**, relied on; claimant believes his claim has a reasonable prospect of success; state defendant's address, or where it is believed he is, or it is likely he may be. Where **PD 6B, para. 3.1(3)**, is relied on state also that it is believed that there is a real issue which it is reasonable for the court to try between the claimant and an existing defendant]. Indicate that the claimant wishes to have the matter dealt with without a hearing, and that no notice should be given to the defendant.
Evidence in support	Evidence in form of witness statement must be filed with form N244. Evidence must show which paragraph of **PD 6B, para. 3.1** applies to the claim; that the claimant has a reasonable prospect of success; why England and Wales is the proper place to bring the claim and state the defendant's address, or at least the country in which he may be found. Where **PD 6B, para. 3.1(3)**, is relied on set out evidence for belief that there is a real issue which it is reasonable for the court to try between the claimant and an existing defendant (**CPR, r. 6.37**).
Without notice to defendant	Application will be made without notice to the defendant. In the RCJ, leave the application notice and supporting evidence in the Master's Secretary's Department, room E16.The papers will be placed before a master or district judge, who will note the order on the papers and on the court file. Because the application is made without notice to the defendant, the claimant must make full and frank disclosure of all relevant facts.

Fee	£45 (**CPFO, fees 1.8(a)** and **2.7**).
Hearing	As the application is made without notice, there will not normally be a hearing.

Procedural checklist 12 Admitting a claim and requesting time to pay

See **chapter 17**.

Type of claim and admission	Step to be taken by defendant	Step to be taken by claimant where claimant accepts defendant's offer	Step to be taken by claimant where claimant rejects defendant's offer
Specified sum. Admitted in whole; defendant seeking time to pay (**CPR, r. 14.9**).	Return form N9A to claimant (**r. 14.4(2)**) within 14 days after service of the particulars of claim (**r. 14.2**).	File request for judgment, form N225, reflecting defendant's offer for payment. No fee is payable (**CPFO, notes to fee 2.7**). Court will enter judgment for the amount of the claim and costs, and for payment at the time and rate specified in defendant's request for time to pay (**r. 14.9**).	File request for judgment form N225, and N9A giving notice that claimant does not accept defendant's offer. No fee is payable (**CPFO, notes to fee 2.7**). Court will enter judgment for the amount of the claim and decide time and rate for payment (**r. 14.10(2)** and **(4)**), and will issue decision on form N30(2). Either party can object to the determination within 14 days after receipt of form N30(2).
Specified sum. Admitted in whole; defendant not seeking time to pay (**r. 14.4**).	Return form N9A to claimant (**r. 14.4(2)**) within 14 days after service of the particulars of claim (**r. 14.2**).	Claimant files request for judgment (form N225) and specifies the times and rates for payment. No fee is payable (**CPFO, notes to fee 2.7**). The court enters judgment as requested by claimant (**r. 14.4(4)** to **(6)**).	
Specified sum. Admitted in part, but defendant seeks time to pay (**r. 14.5**).	Return forms N9A and N9B to the court (**r. 14.5(2)**) within 14 days after service of the particulars of claim (**r. 14.2**). Court sends forms N9A, N9B and N255A to claimant, requiring claimant to notify response to the court within 14 days (**r. 14.5(3)**). If defendant does not reply within 14 days, claim stayed (**r. 14.5(5)**).	Within 14 days of receipt of forms N9A, N9B and N255A, from court, file request for judgment (form N255A), reflecting defendant's offer for payment. Court will enter judgment for the amount admitted and costs, and for payment at the time and rate specified in defendant's request for time to pay (**r. 14.9**).	Within 14 days of receipt of court notice, file request for judgment (form N255A), giving notice either: • that claimant does not accept defendant's partial admission, in which case the claim will proceed as a defended claim, or • that claimant accepts the partial admission in settlement of the claim but does not accept defendant's proposals for payment. The court will then enter judgment for the amount admitted and will calculate a rate of payment. It will notify the parties of its decision in form N30(2). Either party can object to the determination within 14 days after receipt of form N30(2) (**rr. 14.10** to **14.13**).

Specified sum. Admitted in part; defendant does not seek time to pay (**r. 14.5**).	Return forms N9A and N9B to the court (**r. 14.5(2)**) within 14 days after service of the particulars of claim (**r. 14.2**). Court sends forms N9A, N9B and N255A, requiring claimant to notify response to court within 14 days (**r. 4.5(3)**). If defendant does not reply within 14 days, claim stayed (**r. 14.5(5)**).	Within 14 days of receipt of forms N9A, N9B and N255A, file request for judgment (form N225A), reflecting defendant's offer for payment. No fee is payable (**CPFO, notes to fee 2.7**). Court enters judgment for amount offered by defendant and costs to be paid by the date or at the rate specified in form N255A (**r. 14.5(7)** to **(9)**).	File form N255A at court, indicating that partial admission is rejected and case will proceed as a defended claim.
Unspecified sum. Defendant admits liability without saying how much is admitted (**r. 14.6**).	Return form N9C to court (**r. 14.6(2)**) within 14 days after service of the particulars of claim (**r. 14.2**). Court will forward form N9C to claimant, together with form N226 (notice of admission) (**r. 14.6(3)**). If claimant does not respond within 14 days, claim will be stayed (**r. 14.6(5)**).	Within 14 days of receipt of forms N9C and N226, file completed N226 asking the court to enter judgment for an amount to be decided by the court and costs. No fee is payable (**CPFO, notes to fee 2.7**). Court will enter judgment and give directions, either allocating the claim to the small claims track or directing a disposal hearing (**r. 14.6(6)**).	–
Unspecified sum. Defendant admits liability and offers a fixed sum in settlement of it, without seeking time to pay (**r. 14.7**).	Return form N9C to court (**r. 14.7(2)**) within 14 days after service of the particulars of claim (**r. 14.2**). Court will forward form N9C to claimant, together with form N226 (notice of admission).	Within 14 days of receipt of notice from the court, file form N226, accepting the offer. No fee is payable (**CPFO, notes to fee 2.7**). Court will enter judgment in accordance with the offer (**r. 14.7(6)** to **(8)**). Failing to file N226 results in a stay (**r. 14.7(4)**).	Within 14 days of receipt of notice from the court, file form N226, notifying court that offer of sum in settlement of claim rejected. No fee is payable (**CPFO, notes to fee 2.7**). Judgment will be entered for an amount to be decided by the court and costs. The court will give case management directions (**rr. 14.7(9) and 14.8**).
Unspecified sum. Defendant admits liability, offers a fixed sum in settlement and asks to pay by instalments or at a future date (**r. 14.7**).	Return form N9C to court (**r. 14.7(2)**) within 14 days after service of the particulars of claim (**r. 14.2**). Court will forward form N9C to claimant, together with form N226 (notice of admission). If claimant does not respond within 14 days, claim will be stayed (**r. 14.7(4)**).	If the offer is accepted in full, including the proposals for payment, file request for payment (form N226) and court will enter judgment for amount offered and costs at the time and rate specified in defendant's request for time to pay (**r. 14.9**). No fee is payable (**CPFO, notes to fee 2.7**).	If claimant rejects the amount offered, file request for judgment form N226. No fee is payable (**CPFO, notes to fee 2.7**). Court enters judgment for an amount to be decided by the court and costs (**r. 14.7(9)**). If claimant accepts the amount offered, but not the proposals for payment, file form N226. The court will enter judgment and calculate the rate of payment, and will notify the parties of its decision in form N30(2). Either party can object within 14 days after receipt of form N30(2) (**r. 14.10**).

Procedural checklist 13 Time limits for responding to claim by acknowledging service and/or filing a defence

See **chapter 18**.

Step to be taken	Place of service of claim form	Time limit
Acknowledgment to be filed at court	Within the jurisdiction.	14 days after service of particulars of claim (whether or not particulars of claim served with claim form) (**CPR, r. 10.3(1)**).
	Out of the jurisdiction under **r. 6.32** or **6.33** in Scotland or Northern Ireland, or in a Convention territory within Europe or a member State.	21 days after service of particulars of claim (**r. 6.35(2)** and **(3)**).
	Out of the jurisdiction under **r. 6.33** in a Convention territory outside Europe.	31 days after service of particulars of claim (**r. 6.35(4)**).
	Out of the jurisdiction with permission under **r. 6.36**.	Court will specify the time for acknowledging service, calculated by reference to the table at the end of **PD 6B** (**CPR, r. 6.37(5); PD 6B, para. 6.2**).
Filing of defence at court, where no acknowledgment filed	Within the jurisdiction.	14 days after service of particulars of claim (**CPR, r. 15.4(1)(a)**).
	Out of the jurisdiction under **r. 6.32** or **6.33** in Scotland or Northern Ireland, or in a Convention territory within Europe or a member State.	21 days after service of particulars of claim (**r. 6.35(2)** and **(3)**).
	Out of the jurisdiction under **r. 6.33** in a Convention territory outside Europe.	31 days after service of particulars of claim (**r. 6.35(4)**).
	Out of the jurisdiction with permission under **r. 6.36**.	Court will specify the time for acknowledging service, calculated by reference to the table at the end of PD **6B** (**CPR, r. 6.37(5); PD 6B, para. 6.2**).
Filing of defence at court, following filing of acknowledgment	Within the jurisdiction.	28 days after service of particulars of claim (**CPR, r. 15.4(1)(b)**).
	Out of the jurisdiction under **r. 6.32** or **6.33** in Scotland or Northern Ireland, or in a Convention territory within Europe or a member State	35 days after service of particulars of claim (**r. 6.35(2)** and **(3)**).
	Out of the jurisdiction **r. 6.33** in a Convention territory outside Europe.	45 days after service of particulars of claim (**r. 6.35(4)**).
	Out of the jurisdiction with permission under **r. 6.36**.	Court will specify the time for acknowledging service, calculated by reference to the table at the end of **PD 6B**, plus an additional 14 days (**CPR, r. 6.37(5); PD 6B, para. 6.2**).

Procedural checklist 14 Procedure for disputing the court's jurisdiction

See **chapter 19**.

Acknowledgment	File acknowledgment of service within 14 days after service of particulars of claim, if served in the jurisdiction, within 21 days after service of the particulars of claim, if served in Europe under **CPR, r. 6.33**, or within the period given in the court order, if served out of the jurisdiction with the court's permission, under **r. 6.36 (r. 11(2))** Tick only the 'intention to contest the jurisdiction' box. See **procedural checklist 13**.

Application — time	Within 14 days after filing an acknowledgment make an application under **Part 23** for an order that the court has no jurisdiction to try the claim (**r. 11(4)**).
Extension of time	If more time is needed, apply under **r. 3.1(2)(a)** for an extension of the time limit laid down in **r. 11(4)**. An extension of time for service of the defence will not carry with it an extension of time for an application to dispute the jurisdiction (*Montrose Investments Ltd v Orion Nominees Ltd* [2001] CP Rep 109).
Application notice	Form N244. Where service out of the jurisdiction is contested, application is for any order giving permission for service out of the jurisdiction under **r. 6.36** to be set aside, for service of the claim form to be set aside and for the proceedings to be stayed.
Evidence in support	Must be filed and served with form N244.
Fee	£80 (**CPFO, fee 2.6**).
Service	On defendant as soon as practicable after filing application notice, and at least three days before hearing (**CPR, r. 23.7(1)**).
Costs	Both parties should file and serve costs schedules in form N260 24 hours before hearing (**PD 44, para. 9.5**).
Defence	Do not file defence before hearing (**CPR, r. 11(9)(a)**). If the application is unsuccessful, the defendant must file a further acknowledgment of service if intending to take part in the proceedings, and then the court must give directions for filing and service of the defence (**r. 11.7(c)**). Claimant cannot enter default judgment (**r. 12.3**).

Procedural checklist 15 Request for entry of judgment in default

See **chapter 20**, especially **20.3** to **20.6**.

Claim form	Serve claim form on defendant in accordance with **CPR, r. 6.3**.
Certificate of service of claim form	If claim form is served by claimant rather than court, file certificate of service of claim form, within 21 days after service of claim form (**r. 6.17(2)(a)**), unless all defendants have filed acknowledgments within that time, in which case there is no need to file a certificate of service.
Particulars of claim	Serve particulars of claim, either with claim form or within 14 days after service of claim form, and within period of validity of the claim form (**r. 7.4(1)** and **(2)**).
Filing particulars of claim	Where the particulars of claim are served separately from the claim form, within seven days of service of the particulars on the defendant, file a copy of the particulars (**r. 7.4(3)**).
Failure to respond: request for judgment	Wait 14 days after service of particulars of claim (whether served with claim form or later) (**rr. 10.3** and **15.4**). (For time limits where service effected out of the jurisdiction, see **procedural checklist 13**.) If neither acknowledgment of service nor defence filed by then, file request for default judgment in form N205A or N225 (for specified sum) or N205B or N227 (for unspecified sum) (**r. 12.4(1)(a)**; **PD 12, para. 3**). No fee is payable (**CPFO, notes to fee 2.7**).
Failure to file defence: request for judgment	If acknowledgment filed within 14 days after service of particulars of claim, wait until 28 days after service of particulars of claim (**CPR, rr. 10.3** and **15.4**). (For time limits where service effected out of the jurisdiction, see **procedural checklist 13**.) If defence not filed by then, file request for default judgment inform N205A or N225 (for specified sum) or N205B or N227 (for unspecified sum) (**r. 12.4(1)(b)**; **PD 12, para. 3**). No fee is payable (**CPFO, notes to fee 2.7**).
Calculating time	The periods of 14 and 28 days above should be calculated to exclude the date of service of the particulars of claim but to include the date of filing of the acknowledgment or service of the particulars of claim (**CPR, r. 2.8(3)(b)**), and must take into account the deemed dates of service in **rr. 6.14** and **6.26** (see **15.36** and **15.42**).

Procedural checklist 16 Application for entry of judgment in default

See **chapter 20**, especially **20.8** to **20.9**.

When required	Claims for costs (other than fixed costs); claims for delivery up (where the defendant has not offered the alternative of paying the value of the goods claimed); claims by one spouse or civil partner against the other in tort and claims against children and protected parties. Also, the following cases where the defendant has not filed an acknowledgment: claims where service has been effected out of the jurisdiction under **CPR, r. 6.32** or **6.33**, or on a defendant domiciled in a Convention territory or Regulation State; claims against States, diplomats and bodies granted immunity under the International Organisations Acts 1968 and 1981.
Preliminary steps	• Serve claim form and particulars of claim and file certificate of service **(procedural checklist 15)**. • In an application against a child or protected party, apply for a litigation friend to be appointed under **CPR, r. 21.6**.
Time	Wait 14 days after service of particulars of claim (whether served with claim form or later) (**rr. 10.3** and **15.4**). If neither acknowledgment of service nor defence filed by then, make application under **Part 23**. If acknowledgment filed within 14 days after service of particulars of claim, wait until 28 days after service of particulars of claim (**rr. 10.3** and **15.4**) before making application under **Part 23**. Time limits to be calculated as in **procedural checklist 15**. (For time limits where service effected out of the jurisdiction, see **procedural checklist 13**).
Application notice	Form N244. Application is for judgment to be entered against the defendant on the ground that he has not filed an acknowledgment of service or defence, as the case may be. Where application not on notice, state on form N244 that claimant wishes to have the matter dealt with without a hearing. Where the defendant is an individual, state his/her date of birth, if known.
Evidence in support	An application must be supported by evidence if it is for default judgment • against a child or protected party; • in a claim in tort between spouses or civil partners; • against a State; • against a defendant who was served outside the jurisdiction, or inside the jurisdiction when domiciled in a Convention territory or Regulation State, and who has not acknowledged service (see **r. 12.11(4)(a)**) (**r. 12.11(3)** and **PD 12, para. 4**).
Service of evidence	Evidence in support need not be served on defendant who failed to file an acknowledgment of service (**CPR, r. 12.11(2)**).
Notice	Generally the application is with notice, but will be without notice where the claim was served under the **Civil Jurisdiction and Judgments Act 1982** or the **Brussels I Regulation** or where application is made against a State and in either case the defendant has failed to file an acknowledgment (**CPR, r. 12.11(4)** and **(5)**).
Fee	£80 for application on notice (**CPFO, fee 2.6**); £45 where application without notice (**CPFO, fee 2.7**).
Service of N244	Where application on notice, serve defendant as soon as practicable after filing application notice, and at least three days before hearing (**CPR, r. 23.7(1)**).
Costs	Where application on notice, both parties should file and serve costs schedules in form N260 24 hours before hearing (**PD 44, para. 9.5**). The court will not summarily assess the costs of a child or protected party, unless the solicitor acting for the child or protected party has waived the right to further costs (**PD 44, para. 9.9(1)**).
Hearing	Normally before master or district judge. Where the application is made without notice, there will not normally be a hearing.

Procedural checklist 17 Counterclaim (Part 20)

See chapter 28.

Timing	Generally, at the same time as filing the defence in order to avoid the need for permission (**CPR, r. 20.4(2)**). Can be made up to trial, but obtaining permission gets progressively more difficult.
Forms	N211. Simple counterclaims can be made on forms N9B or N9D.
Title	Must comply with **PD 20, paras 7.1** to **7.11**.
Issue	Issue fee is payable when the counterclaim is filed (**CPFO, fee 1.7**).
Pleading	Particulars of the counterclaim, verified by a statement of truth, can be set out in a counterclaim, but if the defendant also intends to defend the main proceedings, the defence and counterclaim should normally form one document with the counterclaim following the defence (**PD 20, para. 6.1**).
Counterclaim against a person other than the claimant	Most counterclaims are made against the claimant, but it is possible to bring a counterclaim against a person other than a claimant (**CPR, r. 20.5**). Permission is always required (**r. 20.5(1)**), and, unless the court otherwise directs, the application is made without notice (**r. 20.5(2)**). The new party is added as an additional party (**r. 20.5(1)**).
Permission to issue	Required if a defendant wishes to file a counterclaim after filing a defence (**r. 20.4(2)**). Issue application notice with written evidence in support: • stating the stage the main proceedings have reached; • stating the nature of the counterclaim; • summarising the facts on which the counterclaim is based; • stating the name and address of the defendant to the counterclaim; • explaining any delay where this is a factor; and • providing a timetable of the steps in the claim to date. As **rr. 20.5(2)** and **20.7(5)** do not apply to this situation, the application is made on notice to the claimant.
Documents to be served	Claim form; counterclaim or defence and counterclaim.
Service	**CPR, Part 6**, applies (**chapter 15**).
Response	Acknowledgment of service (**Part 10**) does not apply (**r. 20.4(3)**). The claimant should file and serve a defence to counterclaim or a reply and defence to counterclaim within 14 days of deemed service of the counterclaim (**rr. 15.4(1), 20.3(1)**).
Default judgment	May be entered (**CPR, r. 12.3(2)**; **PD 20, para. 3**).
Directions	The effect of **rr. 20.3(2)(c)** and **20.13**, together with **PD 20, para. 5.1**, is that the relevant directions governing counterclaims are (unless the court gives special directions for the counterclaim) those given in the main proceedings.

Procedural checklist 18 Additional claim (against third party)

See chapter 29.

Timing	Generally, before or at the same time as filing the defence in order to avoid the need for permission (**CPR, r. 20.7(3)**). Can be made up to trial, but obtaining permission gets progressively more difficult.
Form	Additional claim form, form N211.
Title of claim	Must comply with **PD 20, paras 7.1** to **7.11**.
Issue	Issue fee is the same as for Part 7 claim forms (see **CPFO, fee 1**). Issue takes place when the claim form is sealed and on the date entered by the court on the claim form (**CPR, r. 20.7(2)** and **r. 7.2(2)**).

Pleading	Particulars of the additional claim must be contained in or served with the claim form (**r. 20.7(4)**), and must be verified by a statement of truth in the form '[I believe] [the defendant believes] that the facts stated in this statement of case are true.' (**PD 20, para. 4.2**).
Permission to issue	Required if a defendant wishes to issue an additional claim after filing a defence (**CPR, r. 20.7(3)**). Issue application notice (see **procedural checklist 19**) with written evidence in support: • stating the stage the main proceedings have reached; • stating the nature of the additional claim, question or relief; • summarising the facts on which the additional claim is based; • stating the name and address of the third party; • explaining any delay where this is a factor; and • providing a timetable of the steps in the claim to date. Unless the court otherwise directs, the application is made without notice (**r. 20.7(5)**).
Documents to be served on third party	Additional claim form (N211);notes for defendant on replying to the additional claim form (N211C); particulars of the additional claim (either contained in or served with the claim form) (**r. 20.7(4)**); forms for defending and admitting the claim (forms N9A and N9B or N9C and N9D as appropriate); form for acknowledging service (form N213) (**r. 20.12(1)**); copies of every statement of case previously served (**r. 20.12(1)(d)(i)**); and such other documents as the court may direct (**r. 20.12(1)(d)(ii)**).
Service	**CPR, Part 6**, applies (**chapter 15**).
Time to serve	An additional claim issued without permission must be served within 14 days after the additional claim is issued by the court (**r. 20.8(1)(b)**).Any order for permission will give directions for service (**r. 20.8(3)**).
Effect of service	Third party becomes a party to the proceedings on being served (**r. 20.10(1)**).
Service on other parties	Copies of the additional claim form must be served on all existing parties (**r. 20.12(2)**).
Response	Third party must acknowledge service or file a defence within 14 days of deemed service (**rr. 6.14, 7.5, 9.2, 10.3, 14.2, 15.4** and **20.3(1)**).
Defence	A defence to the additional claim must be filed within 14 days of deemed service of the additional claim, or within 28 days if an acknowledgment of service is filed (**r. 15.4**). Time may be extended by consent for up to 28 days (**r. 15.5**). A copy of the defence to the additional claim must be served on every other party (**r. 15.6**). It must be verified by a statement of truth (**PD 15, paras 2.1, 2.2**).
Default judgment	Subject to **r. 20.11(2)**, default judgment is not available (**r. 20.3(3)**). Instead, if there is no response within the prescribed period, the third party is deemed to admit the additional claim and is bound by any judgment or decision in the main proceedings (**r. 20.11(2)(a)**). If default judgment is given against the defendant and if the defendant satisfies that judgment, the defendant can enter default judgment for a contribution or indemnity against the third party by filing a request (**r. 20.11(3)**). Otherwise, default judgment against a third party is possible only with permission (**r. 20.11(3), (4)**).
Directions	After a defence to an additional claim is filed the court will list the matter for case management directions (**r. 20.13(1)** and **PD 20, para. 5.1**). The court: • will ensure, so far as practicable, that the main proceedings and additional claim are managed together (**r. 20.13(2)**); • may treat the hearing as a summary judgment hearing (**PD 20, para. 5.3**); • may dismiss the additional claim; • may require the additional claim to be dealt with separately from the main proceedings (**CPR, r. 20.9(1)(c)**); • may give directions about the way the claim should be dealt with (**PD 20, para. 5.3**); • may give directions as to the third party's involvement at trial; and • may give directions about the extent to which the third party will be bound by any judgment or decision in the main proceedings.

Procedural checklist 19 Interim application without notice

See **chapter 32**, especially 32.7 to 32.11

Application notice	Issue and file form N244, stating whether a hearing is sought (**CPR, r. 23.6**). Interim injunction applications should be on form N16A.
Evidence in support	Normally required. In addition to covering evidence required for the order sought (**PD 25A, para. 3.3**), written evidence must: • state reasons why notice was not given (**CPR, r. 25.3(3)**); • where secrecy is not essential, state what steps have been taken to give informal notice to the respondent (**PD 25A, para. 4.3(3)**). Usually in the form of witness statements, but affidavits are required for freezing and search orders (**PDA 25A, para. 3.1**). Applicant is under a duty of full and frank disclosure, which includes a duty to disclose adverse matters which could be discovered on making reasonable inquiries.
Fee	£45 (**CPFO, fee 2.7**).
Draft order	Usually required for without notice applications as most are complex. If application is for an interim injunction, use form PF 39 CH (intended actions) or PF 40 CH (after issue). Freezing and search orders should follow the standard forms in **PD 25A**.
Undertakings	Should be incorporated into the order as required (e.g. to issue and serve a claim form (**CPR, r. 25.2(3)**), to file and serve written evidence, to pay damages (injunctions)).
Skeleton argument	Required for most High Court applications dealt with by judges. Should state how the requirements for the relief sought are satisfied. File two clear days before the hearing (if possible).
Arrange hearing	Urgent applications: emergency telephone number for the High Court is (020) 7947 6000. See **37.6** and **PD 25A, para. 4.5**.
Hearing	Explain, among other things: • why without notice; • whether any informal notice has been given, and why; • points relevant to the duty of full and frank disclosure; • any variations on standard-form orders.
Note of hearing	Advocate should produce note of the hearing (see **32.8**).
Order	Should include a statement of the respondent's right to apply to set aside (**CPR, r. 23.9(3)**). It also often provides for listing a hearing to review to be heard on notice. Application notice, evidence in support and note of the hearing should be served with the order (see **32.8**).

Procedural checklist 20 Interim application with notice

See **chapter 32**, especially **32.12** to **32.31**.

Timing	As soon as it becomes apparent that it is desirable or necessary (**PD 23A, para. 2.7**).Other than urgent applications, they can only be made once applicant has come on the record. Applications can be made after judgment (**CPR, r. 25.2**).
Application notice	Form N244, which must be filed (**r. 23.3**). It must state the order sought and the reason for applying (**r. 23.6**) and provide a time estimate. Interim injunction applications should be on form N16A.
Draft order	Not required for simple applications. Drafts of more complex orders should be brought to the hearing (**PD 23A, para. 12.1**) together with a copy on electronic storage device.
Evidence in support	Consider whether evidence is required. If so, consider whether to use the box in question 10 of N244, witness statements, affidavits or statements of case. Must be served and filed (if not already done) with the N244.

Combined applications	Are encouraged (**CPR, r. 1.4(2)(i)**), and should be combined with any existing case management hearing (**PD 23A, para. 2.8**).
Fee	£80 (**CPFO, fee 2.6**).
Service	On respondent as soon as practicable after N244 is filed, and at least three clear days before hearing (**CPR, r. 23.7(1)**) (unless some other period is prescribed, such as for summary judgment and interim payments).
Cross-applications	Respondent may issue a cross-application returnable at the same hearing date as the applicant's application. This may require relisting of both applications if the original time estimate is insufficient for both.
Directions	Sometimes directions are made for filing and serving evidence and skeleton arguments in the application (**PD 23A, para. 9.2**).
Respondent's written evidence	Serve and file in accordance with directions, if any, or as soon as possible (**PD 23A, para. 9.4**) and in sufficient time to avoid the need to adjourn.
Applicant's evidence in reply	Serve and file in accordance with directions, if any, or as soon as possible (**PD 23A, para. 9.5**) and in sufficient time to avoid the need to adjourn.
Application bundles	In substantial applications bundles of material documents should be prepared (usually at least two clear days before the hearing, see **32.17**).
Skeleton arguments	Not mandatory for applications before circuit judges, masters and district judges, but if used should be served and filed the day before the hearing. Usually required for applications before High Court judges, where they should be filed two clear days before the hearing (see **32.18**).
Costs schedules	Both parties should file and serve costs schedules in form N260 24 hours before the hearing (**PD 44, para. 9.5**). (But see **paras 9.8** and **9.9**, where the receiving party is publicly funded, or a child or protected party.)
Hearing	Most applications should be listed for hearing by a master or district judge. Injunctions should usually be heard by judges. Freezing and search orders should normally be dealt with by High Court judges. Most applications are heard in chambers even if technically they are dealt with in public. The court may review the case and give case management directions (**PD 23A, para. 2.9**).
Costs orders	If the hearing is less than a day, usually there will be a summary assessment (**PD 44, para. 9.2**).

Procedural checklist 21 Application for striking out

See **chapter 33**.

General procedure	Follow **procedural checklist 20**.
Application notice	E.g.: 'for an order that the particulars of claim be struck out under **CPR, r. 3.4**, and judgment be entered for the defendant with costs because the particulars of claim disclose no reasonable grounds for bringing the claim [is an abuse of the court's process] [is likely to obstruct the just disposal of the proceedings]'
Combined application	It is common to combine the various grounds in **CPR, r. 3.4**, in a single application, and also to seek summary judgment in the alternative.
Fee to Costs orders	See **procedural checklist 20**.
Claim totally without merit	If the court strikes out a claimant's statement of case and considers it is totally without merit, it must record that fact in the order (**r. 3.4(5)**), and consider making a civil restraint order (see **14.55**).

Procedural checklist 22 Application by party for summary judgment

See **chapter 34**.

Timing	After acknowledgment of service or filing defence (**34.2**). Generally before filing directions questionnaire (**PD 26, para. 5.3(1)**).
Application notice	Form N244. Apply for 'summary judgment under **CPR, Part 24**, and costs because the [claimant has no real prospect of succeeding on the claim/issue] or [defendant has no real prospect of successfully defending the claim/issue] and the applicant knows of no other reason why disposal of the claim or issue should await trial' (**PD 24, para. 2(3)**). If the application relates to specific issues, these must be identified (**CPR, r. 24.4(3)(b)**). Also add to the N244: 'Take notice that if the respondent wishes to rely on written evidence at the hearing, he must file and serve the written evidence at least 7 days before the summary judgment hearing' (**PD 24, para. 2(5)**).
Evidence in support	Must be served and filed with the N244.
Combined applications	It is common to combine a summary judgment application with an application for striking out under **CPR, r. 3.4**, or for interim payment under **r. 25.7**.
Fee	£80 (**CPFO, fee 2.6**).
Service	On respondent at least 14 days before hearing (**CPR, r. 24.4(3)**).
Respondent's written evidence	Serve and file at least seven days before hearing (**r. 24.5(2)**).
Applicant's evidence in reply	File and serve at least three days before the hearing (**r. 24.5(2)**).
Main proceedings	No need to file defence (**r. 24.4(2)**). Claimant cannot enter default judgment if defendant is applying for summary judgment (**r. 12.3(3)(a)(ii)**). Court will not normally allocate to a track before hearing application to strike out (**PD 26, para. 5.3(2)**).
Costs	Both parties should file and serve costs schedules in form N260 24 hours before the hearing (**PD 44, para. 9.5**).
Hearing	Normally before master or district judge (**PD 24, para. 3(1)**). In addition to determining the application, the court usually gives directons (**CPR, r. 24.6**).

Procedural checklist 23 Proposal by court for order for summary judgment

See **34.5**.

Notice of date for hearing	At least 14 days before the hearing.
Written evidence	Both side file and (unless the court otherwise orders) serve written evidence at least seven days before the hearing (**CPR, r. 24.5(3)(a)**).
Evidence in reply	Both sides may file and (unless the court otherwise orders) serve written evidence in reply at least three days before the hearing (**r. 24.5(3)(b)**).
Costs	Both parties should file and serve costs schedules in form N260 24 hours before the hearing (**PD 44, para. 9.5**).

Procedural checklist 24 Application for an order for interim payment

See **chapter 36**.

Timing	After period for filing acknowledgment of service (**CPR, r. 25.6(1)**). More than one application can be made (**r. 25.6(2)**).
Application notice	Form N244. Apply for 'an interim payment under **CPR, r. 25.7**, and costs because the [defendant has admitted liability] [the claimant has obtained judgment for damages to be assessed] [if the claim went to trial the claimant would obtain judgment for a substantial amount of money (other than costs) against the defendant] [the claim is for possession of land and if the claim went to trial the defendant would be held liable to pay the claimant a sum of money for occupation and use of the land while the claim is pending]'.
Evidence in support	Must be served and filed with the N244. It must deal with the matters set out in **PD 25B, para. 2.1**, and exhibit all documents in support, including (in personal injuries claims) medical reports (**para. 2.2**).
Combined applications	Interim payment applications are commonly combined with applications for summary judgment.
Fee	£80 (**CPFO, fee 2.6**).
Service	On respondent at least 14 days before hearing (**CPR, r. 25.6(3)**).
Respondent's written evidence	Serve and file at least seven days before hearing (**r. 25.6(4)**).
Applicant's evidence in reply	File and serve at least three days before the hearing (**r. 25.6(5)**).
Costs	Both parties should file and serve costs schedules in form N260 24 hours before the hearing (**PD 44, para. 9.5**).
Hearing	Normally before master or district judge (**PD 24, para. 3(1)**). In addition to determining the application, the court may give directions (**PD 23A, para. 2.9**).
Instalments	If an interim payment is payable by instalments, the order must comply with **PD 25B, para. 3**.
Trial	The fact that an interim payment has been made should not be mentioned to the trial judge until all questions on liability and quantum have been decided (**CPR, r. 25.9**), unless the defendant agrees.
Final judgment	Where an interim payment has previously been made, the final judgment must include details in a preamble, deduct the interim payments from the amount of the judgment, and make any necessary adjustments or orders for repayment (**PD 25B, para. 5**; **PD 40B, para. 6**).

Procedural checklist 25 Standard disclosure

See **chapter 50**, especially **50.4** to **50.9**.

When first retained	Inform clients of their duty to retain disclosable documents (*Rockwell Machine Tool Co. Ltd v E. P. Barrus (Concessionaires) Ltd* [1968] 1 WLR 693; **PD 31B, para. 7**).
Pre-action	Preliminary disclosure of documents should often take place in accordance with **PD Pre-action Conduct** and any pre-action protocol applicable to the claim (**chapter 8**). This is not standard disclosure, but a means of providing the other side with the key documents to inform them of the nature and strength of the case.

NE 95194509

Before first case management conference	Parties and legal representatives discuss use of technology in managing electronic documents (**PD 31B, para. 8**) and disclosing them (**para. 9**).
Timing for standard disclosure	In accordance with directions made by the court. In most fast track and multi-track claims directions are made when the claim is allocated to a track (**CPR, rr. 28.2(1)**, **28.3**, **29.2(1)(a)** and **PD 29, para. 4**) or at the first case management conference (**CPR, r. 29.2(1)(b)**). These typically include directions for standard disclosure in fast track claims and personal injuries claims on the multi-track.
Normal directions	(1) Standard disclosure by 4 weeks after directions (**PD 28, para. 3.12**). (2) Requests for inspection of listed documents within 7 days thereafter (**CPR, r. 31.15(a)**). (3) Inspection of documents, or provision of copies, within 7 days thereafter (**r. 31.15(b)** and **(c)**).
Documents to be disclosed	Standard disclosure covers (**r. 31.6**) documents in a party's control (**r. 31.8**): (a) on which the disclosing party relies; (b) which adversely affect his own case; (c) which adversely affect another party's case; (d) which support another party's case; and (e) which are specified by a PD.
Documents	Anything on which information of any description is recorded (**r. 31.4**). Includes papers (whether written, pictures or photographs); video and sound recordings; computer records, files, mobile phone texts and emails; metadata; inscriptions on metal, wood and stone.
Control	A document is in a party's control (**r. 31.8**) if: (a) it is or was in his physical possession; (b) he has or has had a right to possession of it; or (c) he has or has had a right to inspect or take copies of it.
Search	Each party must make a reasonable search for disclosable documents (**r. 31.7**).
Method of giving disclosure	Usually by serving a list of documents (**r. 31.10(2)**, form N265).Parties may agree in writing to give disclosure without making a list or without a disclosure statement (**r. 31.10(8)**).Parties may agree in writing, or the court may direct, that disclosure and/or inspection should take place in stages (**r. 31.13**).Parties may use the electronic documents questionnaire (**PD 31B, paras 10** to **13**).
List of documents	The list (N265) must (**r. 31.10**): (a) Identify the documents concisely and in a convenient order, (b) Identify privileged documents, stating the grounds on which it is claimed there is a right or duty to withhold inspection (**r. 31.19(3)**). (c) Identify documents no longer in the party's control, stating what has happened to them. (d) Include a disclosure statement in the form set out in the **annex to PD 31A** (**PD 31A, para. 4.1**).
Signing disclosure statement	(a) Should normally be signed by the party (**r. 31.10(6)**: exceptions are set out in **r. 31.10(7)** to **(9)**). (b) Legal representative must ensure person signing understands the duty of disclosure in **Part 31** (**PD 31A, para. 4.4**). (c) Companies, firms etc. sign by a duly authorised officer. The disclosure statement must include that person's name and address, the office or position held, and explain why he or she is an appropriate person to make the statement (**CPR, r. 31.10(7)** and **PD 31A, para. 4.3**). (d) An insurer, or the Motor Insurers' Bureau, may sign if they have a financial interest in the claim (**PD 31A, para. 4.7**). An electronic documents questionnaire has a statement of truth (**PD 31B, para. 11**).

Inspection	The party seeking to inspect must give written notice (by letter) (**CPR, r. 31.15(a)**), which must be complied with within 7 days. (a) Inspection may take place by attendance at the other side's offices or solicitor's office (**r. 31.15(b)**). (b) Inspection usually takes place by making a written request for photocopies, with the inspecting party undertaking to pay reasonable copying costs (**r. 31.15(c)**). Electronic documents should be provided in native format, preserving metadata (**PD 31B, para. 33**).
Continuing duty	Each party has a continuing duty to disclose documents subsequently coming into their control. If this happens they must immediately notify the other parties (**r. 31.11**) by serving a supplemental list (**PD 31A, para. 3.3**).

Procedural checklist 26 Specific disclosure

See **chapter 50**, especially **50.40 and 50.42.**

Timing	Usually after standard disclosure. A request for the documents to be sought in the application should be made first by letter.
Application	Application notice (form N244). Wording for question 3: 'An order that the [claimant/defendant] do give specific disclosure of documents because [the claimant/defendant] [has failed to give full standard disclosure] [further disclosure is necessary in order to investigate this claim fully]'.
Form of order	(1) The [claimant/defendant] do give specific disclosure of documents by filing and serving a supplementary list of documents in form N265 by 4 p.m. on [date] specifying whether each of the [documents] and/or [classes of documents] specified in the schedule to this order are presently in its control, and if not, specifying which of those [documents] and/or [classes of documents] are no longer in its control (and indicating what has happened to such documents), and also specifying which of those [documents] and/or [classes of documents] it claims a right or duty to withhold inspection of. (2) The [claimant/defendant] do make any request for inspection in writing within 7 days after service of the list of documents. (3) The [claimant/defendant] do provide the [claimant/defendant] with copies of the requested documents within 7 days of receipt of the request. A schedule attached to the application, or to a draft order, should set out concisely and in a convenient order the documents and classes of documents sought from the other side.
Written evidence	Is required (**PD 31A, para. 5.2**), and is typically given in a witness statement (although the box in question 10 of the N244 can be used). The evidence should: (a) Exhibit the lists of documents provided by the other side. (b) Exhibit relevant correspondence. (c) Deal with each document or class of document in the schedule to the application: (i) Explaining why it is believed to be in the control of the other side; and (ii) Explaining why it should be disclosed (because it is relevant to an issue in the case, and should have been disclosed under standard disclosure, or because it is a 'train of inquiry' document, explaining the value of the document in investigating the claim).
Issue application	See **procedural checklist 20**, and **CPR, Part 23**. Fee £80 (**CPFO, fee 2.6**).
Serve application	At least 3 clear days before the return day (**CPR, rr. 23.7(1)** and **2.8(3)**).

Procedural checklist 27 Non-party disclosure

See **50.90** to **50.95**.

Timing	At any time after proceedings are issued (Senior Courts Act 1981, s. 34(2); County Courts Act 1984, s. 53(2); **CPR, r. 31.17(1)**). A request for the documents to be sought in the application should be made first by letter.
Application	Application notice (form N244). Wording for question 3: 'An order pursuant to the [Senior Courts Act 1981, s. 34(2)] [County Courts Act 1984, s. 53(2)] that [name of person with the documents] give non-party disclosure of documents because it has in its control documents which are likely to support the [claimant's/defendant's] case and disclosure is necessary in order to dispose fairly of the claim or to save costs'.
Form of order	(1) [Name of person with the documents] do by 4 p.m. on [date] serve on the [claimant's/defendant's] solicitors a list of documents in form N265 specifying whether each of the [documents] and / or [classes of documents] specified in the schedule to this order are presently in its control, and if not, specifying which of those [documents] and/or [classes of documents] are no longer in its control (and indicating what has happened to such documents), and also specifying which of those [documents] and/or [classes of documents] it claims a right or duty to withhold inspection of. (2) The [claimant/defendant] do make any request for inspection of the documents disclosed by [name of person with the documents] in writing within 7 days after service of the list of documents. (3) [Name of person with the documents] do provide the [claimant/defendant] with copies of the requested documents within 7 days of receipt of the request. A schedule attached to the application, or to a draft order, should set out concisely and in a convenient order the documents and classes of documents sought from the non-party.
Written evidence	Is required (**r. 31.17(2)**), and is typically given in a witness statement (although the box in question 10 of the N244 can be used). The evidence should: (a) Exhibit relevant correspondence. (b) Deal with each document or class of document in the schedule to the application: (i) explaining why it is believed to be in the control of the non-party; (ii) explaining how it is likely to support the case of the applicant or adversely affect the case of another party (**r. 31.17(3)(a)**); (iii) explaining why disclosure is necessary in order to dispose fairly of the claim or to save costs (**r. 31.17(3)(b)**).
Issue application	See **procedural checklist 20**, and **Part 23**. Fee £80 (**CPFO, fee 2.6**).
Serve application	At least 3 clear days before the return day (**rr. 23.7(1)** and **2.8(3)**).

Procedural checklist 28 Trial preparation

See **chapter 61**.

Item	Timing	Action
Witness availability	Before listing for trial	Communicate with lay and expert witnesses, and also counsel, to obtain available dates (and reasons). See **61.8**.

Witness abroad or incapacitated	Several months before trial	Consider best means of adducing evidence from the witness: (a) Hearsay statement (**chapter 53**). (b) Letter of request (**58.8** to **58.12**). (c) Video link (**58.11**). (d) Deposition (**58.2** to **58.7**).
Listing for trial	In accordance with case management directions	See **61.2** to **61.6**.
Inform witnesses	Receipt of trial date or window	Write to lay and expert witnesses confirming trial date or window and seeking confirmation of the witness's availability.
Pre-trial review (if directed in case management directions)	8–10 weeks before trial	Most common in multi-track claims Brief trial advocate to attend. May result in further directions, settling a statement of issues, and fixing a trial timetable (see **47.23**).
Statement of issues	As directed	May need to be settled and agreed between the parties after a pre-trial review (see **61.13**).
Brief counsel	Sufficient time before trial	Prepare counsel's brief and supporting trial bundles or papers for the trial bundle. Agree fees with counsel's clerk. Even for simple cases counsel should be briefed at least a week in advance because counsel has to prepare a skeleton argument. In complex claims a period of months may be required. Counsel will also often advise on further pre-trial preparation that may be required.
Witness summonses	At least 2 weeks before trial	Issue witness summonses for unwilling witnesses (see **57.2**, form N20). Fee £40 (**CPFO, fee 2.8**). Serve at least 7 clear days (**rr. 2.8(2)** and **34.5(1)**) before the date the witness is required to attend, bearing in mind deemed dates of service (**r. 6.26**). Include witness expenses (see **57.6**).
Reading guide and time estimate	Before lodging trial bundle	In QBD and ChD reading lists and time estimates signed estimate by counsel must be lodged with trial bundles (Practice Direction (Royal Courts of Justice: Reading Lists and Time Estimates) [2000] 1 WLR 208), see **59.8**.
Trial bundles	c. 14 days before trial	Defendants should notify claimant of documents they wish to be included.
	3 to 7 days before trial	Copies for judge, witness box and all parties.
	At least 7 days before ChD trials	Paginated and prepared in accordance with **PD 39A**, see **chapter 59**.
Skeleton argument (required in the High Court, often directed or desirable in the county courts)	As directed 2 clear days before HC trials	Usually simultaneous exchange, but directions may provide for sequential exchange (see **32.17** and **61.13**). Lodge at list office (Queen's Bench Guide, para. 7.11.11) or with judge's clerk (Chancery Guide, para. 7.26).

Statement of costs (fast track trials)	2 days before trial	Form N260. **PD 44, para. 9.2**, see **71.4**.
Authorities	4 p.m. day before trial	Advocates should exchange lists of authorities (e.g. Chancery Guide, para. 7.34).
	9 a.m. trial day	Provide usher with list of authorities (Queen's Bench Guide, para. 7.11.8; Chancery Guide, para. 7.33).
Adjournment	As soon as need arises	Immediately inform court and other parties in writing, seeking adjournment. If not dealt with administratively, issue application in accordance with **Part 23** (see **r. 3.1(2)(b)** and **61.7**).

Procedural checklist 29 Offer to settle (from 6 April 2007)

See **chapter 66**.

Timing	Can be made before or after issue of proceedings. Should be made once an appraisal has been made of the merits and value of the claim. Should be made, if possible, more than 21 days before the trial.
Method	Form N242A is the prescribed form, but is not obligatory, and the offer can be made by letter.
Relevant period	Normally, this is the period of not less than 21 days after the offer is made specified as the period within which the defendant will be liable for the claimant's costs if the Part 36 offer is accepted. If the offer is made less than 21 days before trial, the relevant period ends with the end of the trial or such other period as the court determines (**CPR, r. 36.3(1)(c)**).
Form	(a) Must be in writing (**r. 36.2(2)(a)**). (b) Must state on its face that it is intended to have the consequences of **Part 36** (**r. 36.2(2)(b)**). (c) If made at least 21 days before trial, it must specify a period of not less than 21 days within which the defendant will be liable for the claimant's costs in accordance with **r. 36.10** if the offer is accepted (**r. 36.2(2)(c)**). (d) Must state whether it relates to the whole claim or part or to an issue, and if so, which (**r. 36.2(2)(d)**). (e) Must state whether it takes into account any counterclaim (**r. 36.2(2)(e)**). (f) Needs to state the proposed terms of compromise.
Additional requirements	(a) Money claims. Must offer a single sum of money (**r. 36.4(1)**), which is treated as inclusive of interest until the end of the relevant period (**r. 36.3(3)**, see **66.9**). (b) Personal injury claims. Must set out the position on deductible amounts/State benefits and lump sum payments under the Social Security (Recovery of Benefits) Act 1997 (see **r. 36.15** and **66.10**), unless the offer is made after the certificate of benefits has been requested but before it arrives. In the latter situation, the defendant is required to clarify the offer within 7 days after receipt of the certificate (**r. 36.15(7)**). (c) Personal injury claims for future pecuniary loss. There are additional requirements in **r. 36.5**, see **66.11**. (d) Provisional damages claims. There are additional requirements in **r. 36.6**, see **66.12**.
Making a Part 36 offer	A Part 36 offer is made when it is served on the offeree (**r. 36.7(1)**). The offer should be served on the legal representative of a person who is legally represented (**PD 36A, para. 1.2**). A certificate of service in form N215 should be filed.
Clarification	*Can be sought*, using the **Part 23** procedure (see **66.21**). See **procedural checklist 20**.

Withdrawal	Permission is required to withdraw or reduce a **Part 36** offer during the relevant period (**r. 36.3(5)**). Thereafter, permission is not required, but the offer can be withdrawn or reduced only if it has not been accepted (**r. 36.3(6)**). Notice of withdrawal must be in writing (**r. 36.3(7)**) and should clearly identify the offer being withdrawn (Gibbon v Manchester City Council [2010] EWCA Civ 726, [2010] 1 WLR 2081).
Acceptance	By serving written notice of acceptance on the offeror (**r. 36.9(1)**) and filing notice of acceptance at court (**PD 36A, para. 3.1**).
Late acceptance	If a Part 36 offer has not been withdrawn, it may be accepted even after the relevant period (**r. 36.9(2)**).
Effect of acceptance	(a) The claim is stayed (**r. 36.11(1)**). (b) If accepted within the relevant period, the defendant is liable to pay the claimant's standard-basis costs to the date of acceptance (**r. 36.10(1)** and **(3)**). This is subject to four exceptions, see **66.24** to **66.27**. (c) If accepted after the relevant period, the parties may agree costs, but if they do not, the court will make an order for costs (**r. 36.10(4)(b)**).
Trial	A Part 36 offer is treated as 'without prejudice save as to costs' (**r. 36.13(1)**). It must not be communicated to the trial judge, and must not be included in the trial papers, until the case has been decided (**r. 36.13(2)**).
Non-acceptance	The question is whether the offeree can obtain a result on judgment which is more advantageous than the terms of the offer (**r. 36.14**). If not: (a) if the offer was made by the defendant, the claimant will normally be ordered to pay the defendant's costs from the end of the relevant period (**r. 36.14(2)**); (b) if the offer was made by the claimant, the court has a discretion to order enhanced interest at up to 10 per cent above base rate, indemnity-basis costs, and enhanced interest on those costs, from the end of the relevant period (**r. 36.14(3)**).
Appeal proceedings	Need a separate **Part 36** offer. A **Part 36** offer made in the proceedings at first instance only relates to the proceedings at first instance (**r. 36.3(4)**).

Procedural checklist 30 Summary assessment of costs

See 71.4 to 71.6.

When required	Unless the court orders otherwise, costs will be assessed summarily (**PD 44, para. 9.2**): (1) At the conclusion of a trial on the fast track; (2) At the conclusion of an interim hearing lasting no more than one day. In these cases the summary assessment covers the interim costs only, unless the whole proceedings are disposed of, in which event the summary assessment may deal with the costs of the whole claim; and (3) At the conclusion of interim hearings within appeals and appeals listed for one day or less.
Statement of costs	Form N260. Should be filed and served 24 hours before the hearing (**PD 44, para. 9.5(4)**).
Failure to serve statement of costs 24 hours in advance	Court may (see **32.30**): (1) give the paying party a brief (minutes or hours) adjournment, and then proceed with the summary assessment; (2) stand over for a detailed assessment; (3) stand over for a summary assessment at a later date; (4) if both sides agree, stand over for a summary assessment to be dealt with in writing.

Procedural checklist 31 Arbitration claim

See **chapter 72**.

Commence an arbitration claim under **CPR, Part 62**, using arbitration claim form N8.	Claim form must: • include a concise statement of remedy claimed; • include any questions on which the claimant seeks the decision of the court; • give details of any arbitration award challenged by the claimant; • show statutory requirements have been met; • specify under which section of the Arbitration Act 1996 the claim is made; • identify against which (if any) defendants a cost order is sought; • specify either: – the persons on whom the arbitration claim form is to be served, stating their role in the arbitration and whether they are to be defendants; or – that the claim is made without notice under the Arbitration Act 1996, s. 44(3), and the grounds relied on. (**CPR, r. 62.4(1)**). Where required, evidence in support must be filed with the arbitration claim form.
Issue	Claim form may be issued in one of the following courts: • Admiralty and Commercial Registry at the Royal Courts of Justice (Commercial List); • Technology and Construction Court Registry (TCC List); • district registry of the High Court (where a Mercantile Court is established) (Mercantile List); • district registry of the High Court (arbitration claim form must be marked 'Technology and Construction Court' in the top right-hand corner) (TCC List). (**PD 62, para. 2.3(1)**). Claim form relating to a landlord and tenant or partnership dispute must be issued in the High Court, Chancery Division (**PD 62, para. 2.3(2)**).
Service	Claim form must be served by the claimant within one month from the date of issue unless court orders otherwise (**CPR, r. 62.4(2)**). Once served, the claimant must file the certificate of service within seven days of service (**PD 62, para. 3.2**).
Service out of the jurisdiction	The court can give permission to serve a claim form out of the jurisdiction in the following circumstances: • When a claimant seeks to challenge an arbitration award or appeal on a question of law arising out of an award made within England and Wales. • The claim is for an order under the Arbitration Act 1996, s. 44. The court can give permission for service out of the jurisdiction notwithstanding the only remedy sought is in respect of proceedings taking place outside England and Wales. • Any other situation where the claimant seeks a remedy or requires a question to be determined by the court which affects an arbitration (pending or anticipated), an arbitration agreement or an arbitration award. Seat of the arbitration must be in England and Wales. Where the seat is not in England and Wales the court can still give permission as long as the seat has not been designated or, by reason of connection with England and Wales or Northern Ireland, the court is satisfied it is appropriate to do so. (**CPR, r. 62.5(1)**). Application must be supported by written evidence and: • state the grounds on which the application is made; • show in what place or country the person to be served is, or probably may be, found (**CPR, r. 62.5(2)**). **CPR, rr. 6.40** to **6.46** (which regulate service of claim forms abroad), apply to the service of arbitration claim forms out of the jurisdiction (**r. 62.5(3)**). The order giving permission to serve out of the jurisdiction must specify the period within which the defendant has to file the acknowledgment of service (**r. 62.5(4)**).

Acknowledgment of service	Generally within 14 days after service of the arbitration claim form (**r. 10.3(1)(b)**) by using form N15 or, alternatively in the commercial court, form N210(CC) (Admiralty and Commercial Courts Guide, para. O5.1(b)).
Defendant's written evidence	Must be filed and served within 21 days after the date by which the defendant is required to acknowledge service or, if not required to file an acknowledgment, within 21 days after the service of the arbitration claim form (**PD 62, para. 6.2**).
Claimant's written evidence in reply	Evidence in reply to the defendant's written evidence must be filed or served within seven days after service of the defendant's evidence (**PD 62, para. 6.3**).
Preparation for hearing	Agreed indexed and paginated bundles of all evidence and other documents to be used at the hearing should be prepared by the claimant (**PD 62, para. 6.4**). Estimates for length of the hearing and a complete set of documents should be filed no later than five days before the hearing date (**PD 62, para. 6.5**).
Main hearing	The claimant must file and serve no later than 2 days before the hearing: • chronology of relevant events cross-referenced to a bundle of documents; • list of persons involved; and • skeleton argument (**PD 62, para. 6.6**). The defendant must file and serve its skeleton argument not later than the day before the hearing date. The skeleton argument must list: • issues which arise for decision; • the grounds for relief to be relied upon; • submissions of fact to be made with references to the evidence; and • submissions of law with references to the relevant authorities (**PD 62, para. 6.7**). Hearing generally in private save for claims to determine a preliminary point of law (Arbitration Act 1996, s. 45) or appeal on a question of law arising out of an award (Arbitration Act 1996, s. 69) (**CPR, r. 62.10(3)**).

Procedural checklist 32 Appeals within the county courts and High Court

See **chapter** 74.

Timing	At the end of the hearing in the lower court, permission to appeal should be sought (see **74.13**). An appellant's notice in form N161 must be filed (unless time is extended, see **71.20**) no later than 21 days from the date of the decision of the lower court (**CPR, r. 52.4(2)(b)**).
Permission	Required for all civil appeals (**r. 52.3**) other than those involving personal liberty and from decisions of authorised court officers in detailed assessments (see **71.12**).
Seeking permission	Initially sought orally from the lower court (**r. 52.3(2)**) If refused, can renew application for permission to the appeal court (**r. 52.3(3)**).Permission from the appeal court is initially sought in the appellant's notice (form N161), and is normally considered without a hearing (**PD 52A, para. 4.2**).
Reconsideration of permission	Where the appeal court refuses permission without a hearing, it may reconsider granting permission at a hearing (**CPR, r. 52.3(4)**). There is no jurisdiction to consider an appeal from an appeal court's refusal to grant permission (**Access to Justice Act 1999, s. 54(4)**).

Appeal court	(1) From county court district judge appeal to circuit judge. (2) From county court circuit judge appeal to High Court judge. (3) From High Court master, district judge or registrar appeal to High Court judge. See **74.4**. The above applies equally to deputies and part-time judges fulfi lling the above roles. By way of exceptions to the above (a) Final decisions in multi-track claims are appealed to the Court of Appeal (**Destination of Appeals Order, art. 4**). (b) Final decisions in specialist claims are appealed to the Court of Appeal (**Destination of Appeals Order, art. 4**). (c) Second appeals are appealed to the Court of Appeal (**Destination of Appeals Order, art. 5**). This applies where a county court district judge's decision is appealed to the circuit judge, whose decision is subject to a second appeal (which is taken to the Court of Appeal).
Extending time to appeal	Can only be granted by the appeal court (not by consent) (**CPR, r. 52.6**), although the lower court can direct some period other than 21 days for filing the appellant's notice (**r. 52.4(2)(a)**). Applications to extend time are made in the appellant's notice (**PD 52B, para. 3.2**).
Appellant's notice	Form N161. Must be filed with the appeal court no more than 21 days after the decision of the lower court (or as directed or extended) (**CPR, r. 52.4(2)(b)**). It must: (a) set out the grounds of the appeal; (b) give reasons why the lower court's decision is wrong or unjust through serious procedural or other irregularity and state whether each ground is on a point of law or against a finding of fact (**PD 52B, para. 4.2(d); PD 52C, para. 5.1**); (c) include any application for permission to appeal (**PD 52A, para. 4.2**); (d) include any application to appeal out of time (**PD 52B, para. 3.2**); (e) include any application for a transcript of the judgment of the lower court at public expense (**PD 52B, para. 4.3**); (f) include information about any issue raised or remedy sought under the Human Rights Act 1998 (**PD 16, para. 15.1**). The N161 may include applications for interim relief (**PD 52B, para. 4.3**), including any stay of execution.
Fee	£115 for small claims appeal; £135 for other appeals in the county courts (**CPFO, fee 2.5**); £235 for appeals in the High Court (**CPFO, fee 2.4**).
Documents to be filed	At the same time as filing the appellant's notice, the appellant must file (**PD 52B, para. 4.2; PD 52C, para. 3(3)**): (a) two additional copies of the appellant's notice for the court and one for each respondent; (b) the same number of copies of the appellant's skeleton argument; (c) a sealed copy of the order of the court below; (d) any orders giving or refusing permission to appeal together with the reasons for each decision; (e) any written evidence in support of any interim application within the appeal; (f) a paginated appeal bundle complying with **PD 52B, para. 6.3**; and (g) a transcript (or agreed note, see **71.30**) of the judgment under appeal (**PD 52B, para. 6.2**). Where it is not possible to file any of the above, the appellant must state which items are not being filed and why.

Skeleton argument	Form N163. Should be filed with the appellant's notice, or, if impractical, within 14 days of filing the notice. Only required if issues are complex or if skeleton will assist in respects not readily apparent from the papers in the appeal (see **PD 52B, para. 8.3**).
Transcripts of evidence	Are requested, if required, after permission to appeal is granted (see **74.30**). Transcripts of judgments are required before permission.
Service of appellant's notice	As soon as practicable, and within 7 days of being filed the appellant must serve the appellant's notice and skeleton argument on the respondents (**CPR, r. 52.4(3)**). The appellant must then file a certificate of service (form N215).
Service of supporting documents	Appeal bundles, orders in the court below and for permission etc. (a) where permission to appeal is being sought, need not be served unless and until permission is given; (b) where permission is granted by the lower court (or not required), supporting documents must be served with the appellant's notice (**PD 52B, para. 6.5(a)**). Where permission is granted by the appeal court, service is required within 7 days of receiving the order granting permission (**para. 6.5(b)**).
Permission granted	Court sends order and any directions to the parties (**PD 52C, para. 15(1)**) together with date for the appeal hearing or listing window. The appellant must add the order and other documents to the appeal bundle. Appeal questionnaires are optional in the High Court.
Respondent's notice	Respondent's notice (form N162) is required (**r. 52.5(2)**) where the respondent: (a) seeks permission to appeal against the decision in the court below; (b) wishes the appeal court to uphold the decision of the court below for different or additional reasons to those given by the court below. In circumstances (a) and (b), there is a fee of £115 for a small claims appeal or £135 for any other appeal in the county court (**CPFO, fee 2.5**); £235 in the High Court (**CPFO, fee 2.4**).
Filing respondent's notice	As directed, otherwise within 14 days of: (a) service of appellant's notice if permission to appeal was not required or if permission was given to the appellant by the court below; (b) service of notification of permission to appeal; or (c) service of notification that permission and the substantive appeal are to be heard together. With the respondent's notice, the respondent must file two additional copies of the notice for the court and one for every other party (**PD 52C, para. 10**).
Additional documents	The respondent must make every effort to agree any additional documents for the appeal bundle with the appellant. If they cannot agree, the respondent should prepare a supplementary bundle, to be served and filed with the respondent's notice (**PD 52B, para. 8.2**).
Service of respondent's notice	As soon as practicable, and within 7 days of being filed (**r. 52.5(6)**).
Respondent's skeleton argument	May be included in the respondent's notice, or served within 14 days of filing the respondent's notice (**PD 52C, para. 9; but see PD 52B, para. 8.3**).
Authorities	In the county court authorities must be brought to the hearing. In the High Court lists of authorities must be provided to the head usher by 5.30 p.m. on the working day before the hearing (see **71.51**) or copies should be included in the appeal bundles (Queen's Bench Guide, para. 7.11.9).
Summary assessment of costs	In appeals from case management decisions and appeals listed for one day or less, statements of costs should be filed 24 hours before the appeal hearing (**PD 52, para. 14.1**).

Procedural checklist 33 Appeals to the Court of Appeal

See **chapter** 74.

Timing	At the end of the hearing in the lower court, permission to appeal should be sought (see **74.13**). Any request for the provision of a transcript at public expense (on the ground of poor financial circumstances) should be made at the hearing. An appellant's notice in form N161 must be filed (unless time is extended, see **74.20**) no later than 21 days from the date of the decision of the lower court (**CPR, r. 52.4(2)(b)**).
Permission	Required for all civil appeals (**r. 52.3**) other than those involving personal liberty and from decisions of authorised court officers in detailed assessments (see **74.12**).
Fee	£235 if permission and/or an extension of time is required (**CPFO, fee 13.1(a)**); £465 if permission is not required or was granted by the lower court (**CPFO, fee 13.1(b)**).
Seeking permission	Initially sought orally from the lower court (**r. 52.3(2)**). If refused, can renew application for permission to the appeal court (**r. 52.3(3)**). Except that in second appeals to the Court of Appeal permission can only be sought from the Court of Appeal (**r. 52.13(1)**). Permission from the Court of Appeal is initially sought in the appellant's notice (form N161), and is normally considered without a hearing (**PD 52C, para. 15**).
Reconsideration of permission	Where the Court of Appeal refuses permission without a hearing, it may reconsider granting permission at a hearing (**CPR, r. 52.3(4)**). If represented, the appellant's advocate must file and serve a brief written statement at least 4 days before the hearing identifying the points proposed to be raised and his reasons why permission should be granted (**PD 52C, para. 14**). There is no jurisdiction to consider an appeal from a refusal by the Court of Appeal to grant permission (**Access to Justice Act 1999, s. 54(4)**).
Appeals taken to the Court of Appeal	(a) Final decisions in multi-track claims (**Destination of Appeals Order, art. 4**). (b) Final decisions in specialist claims (**Destination of Appeals Order, art. 4**). (c) Second appeals in the county courts (**Destination of Appeals Order, art. 5**). This applies where a county court district judge's decision is appealed to the circuit judge, whose decision is subject to a second appeal (which is taken to the Court of Appeal). See **74.15**. (d) Appeals from High Court judges.
Extending time to appeal	Can only be granted by the appeal court (not by consent) (**CPR, r. 52.6**), although the lower court can direct some period other than 21 days for filing the appellant's notice (**r. 52.4(2)(a)**). Applications to extend time are made in the appellant's notice (**PD 52C, para. 4(1)(b)**).
Appellant's notice	Form N161. Must be filed with the appeal court no more than 21 days after the decision of the lower court (or as directed or extended) (**CPR, r. 52.4(2)(b)**). It must: (a) set out the grounds of the appeal; (b) identify as concisely as possible the respects in which the lower court's decision is wrong or unjust through serious procedural or other irregularity and state whether each ground is on a point of law or against a finding of fact (**PD 52C, para. 5(1)**); (c) include any application for permission to appeal (**PD 52A, para. 4.2**); (d) include any application to appeal out of time (**PD 52C, para. 4(1)(b)**); (e) include information about any issue raised or remedy sought under the Human Rights Act 1998 (**PD 16, para. 15.1**). The N161 may include applications for interim relief (**PD 52B, para. 4.3**), including any stay of execution.

Documents to be filed	At the same time as filing the appellant's notice, the appellant must file (**PD 52C, para. 3(3)**): (a) three copies of the appellant's notice for the court and one for each respondent; (b) a sealed copy of the order of the court below; (c) any orders giving or refusing permission to appeal together with the reasons for each decision; (d) any written evidence in support of any interim application within the appeal; and (e) in a second appeal, the first-instance order, reasons and appellant's notice; (f) a copy of the order allocating the case to a track (if any) (g) the appellant's skeleton argument; (h) approved transcript of the judgment Where it is not possible to file any of the above, the appellant must state which items are not being filed and why (**PD 52C, para. 6**).
Skeleton argument	Form N 163. Should be filed with the appellant's notice
Transcripts	Transcripts of evidence are requested, if required, after permission to appeal is granted (see **74.30**). Transcripts of judgments are required before permission.
Service of appellant's notice	As soon as practicable, and within 7 days of being filed (**CPR, r. 52.4(3)**). Served by the appellant (**PD 52C, para. 7.1**), who must file a certificate of service (**PD 52B, para. 6.1**).
Permission granted	Court sends order and any directions to the parties (**PD 52C, para. 21**), together with listing window notification.
Proposed appeal bundle index	Served by appellant 7 days after date of listing window notification (**PD 52C, paras 21 and 27**).
Respondent's notice	Form N162. Fee of £235 (**CPFO, fees 13.1(a)** and **13.2**). Required if (**CPR, r. 53.5(2)**) the respondent: (a) Seeks permission to appeal against the decision below (in which event the time for the respondent's notice is 21 days from the lower court's decision). (b) Wishes the appeal court to uphold the decision of the court below for different or additional reasons to those given by the court below (in which event it is required 14 days after the grant of permission to appeal to the appellant).
Respondent's skeleton argument	Respondent who has filed a respondent's notice must lodge and serve its skeleton argument within 14 days of filing a respondent's notice (**PD 52C, para. 9**).
Appeal questionnaire	Filed and served on every respondent 14 days after date of listing window notification (**PD 52C, paras 21** and **23**).
Disagreement with time estimate	If a respondent disagrees with the appellant's time estimate, 7 days after service of the appeal questionnaire the respondent must file and serve its own time estimate (**PD 52C, paras 21** and **24**).
Appeal skeleton	Appellant serves appeal skeleton on each respondent 21 days after listing window (**PD 52C, paras 21** and **31**).
Agree bundle	21 days after date of listing window notification (**PD 52C, paras 21** and **27**). If there is no agreement in relation to particular documents, they must be placed in a supplementary bundle.
Respondent's skeleton argument (no respondent's notice)	Respondent who has not filed a respondent's notice must lodge and serve its skeleton argument within 42 days of filing a respondent's notice (**PD 52C, paras 13** and **21**).
Lodge appeal bundles	Not later than 42 days before the appeal hearing (**PD 52C, paras 21** and **27**).
Appellant's replacement skeleton argument	Not later than 14 days before the appeal hearing (**PD 52C, paras 21** and **31**).

Respondent's replacement skeleton argument	Not later than 7 days before the appeal hearing (**PD 52C, para. 21**).
Bundles of authorities	Not later than 7 days before the appeal hearing (**PD 52C, paras 21** and **29**).
Every document needed for the appeal	If not already lodged or filed, every document needed for the hearing must be lodged or filed not later than 7 days before the appeal hearing (**PD 52C, para. 21**).
Summary assessment of costs	For appeal hearings estimated at no more than one day, statements of costs (form N260) should be filed 24 hours before the appeal hearing (**PD 44, paras 9.2(b)** and **9.5(4)**).

Procedural checklist 34 Claim for judicial review

See **chapter** 77.

Pre-action protocol	The **Pre-action Protocol for Judicial Review** requires that, where applicable, before making a claim, the claimant should send a letter to the defendant identifying issues in dispute and establishing whether litigation can be avoided. Copies of the letter should be sent to all interested parties for information. Defendant should normally respond within 14 days to the letter before claim. Response should be sent to all interested parties identified by claimant and contain details of any other parties who the defendant considers also have an interest.
Timing	Claim form must normally be filed promptly and in any event not later than three months after the grounds to make the claim first arose (**CPR, r. 54.5(1)**), although case law disapplies promptness but not three months when advancing European Union law grounds. In planning and procurement cases, the time limit is six weeks from when the grounds first arose and 30 days from when the claimant first knew or ought to have known about the grounds respectively (**r. 54.5(5)** and (**(6)**). There must be good reason before this time limit will be extended. This time limit may not be extended by agreement between the parties (**r. 54.5(2)**).
Claim form	Form N461. The claim form must specify: • the name and address of any person considered to be an interested party, • that permission is sought to proceed with a judicial review claim, and • any remedy (including any interim remedy) being claimed. The claim form must include or be accompanied by: • a detailed statement of the claimant's grounds for bringing the claim, • a statement of facts relied on, • any application to extend the time limit for filing the claim form, and • any application for directions (**PD 54A, para. 5.6**). In addition the claim form must be accompanied by: • any written evidence in support of the claim or application to extend time, • a copy of any order that the claimant seeks to have quashed, • where the claim relates to a decision of a court or tribunal, an approved copy of the reasons for reaching that decision, • copies of any relevant statutory material, and • a list of essential documents for advance reading by the court (with page references to the passages relied on) (**PD 54A, para. 5.7**). Where it is not possible to file all the above documents, the claimant must indicate which documents have not been filed and the reasons why they are not currently available (**PD 54A, para. 5.8**).
Urgent procedure	Form N463. Claimant must state the reasons for urgency, the proposed timescale for consideration of the permission application, and the date by which the full hearing of the merits should take place if permission is granted. A claimant who applies for an interim *injunction must* also provide a draft order and a statement of the grounds on which the injunction is sought. The application must be served by fax and post, along with the claim form, on the defendant and interested parties. The defendant and interested parties must be advised that they may make representations on the application.

Fee	£60 when claim form is issued and a further £215 if permission to proceed is granted (**CPFO, fee 1.9**).
Service	The claim form must be served on the defendant and any person the claimant considers to be an interested party within seven days of issue (**CPR, r. 54.7**).
Acknowledgment of service	Form N462. Any person served with the claim form who wishes to take part in the proceedings must file an acknowledgment of service (A/S) in the Administrative Court Office within 21 days after service of the claim form. Where person filing A/S intends to contest the claim, the A/S must set out a summary of his grounds for doing so. The A/S must also be served on the claimant and interested persons named on the claim form not later than seven days after it is filed (**CPR, r. 54.8**).
Permission	The court's permission to proceed is required in a judicial review claim (**CPR, r. 54.4**). If permission is granted, the court may give directions (**r. 54.10**). The court will serve the permission decision on the claimant and defendant and on any other person who filed an A/S (**r. 54.11**).
Defendant's and other interested parties' detailed grounds of opposition/ support	The defendant and any other interested person has 35 days after service of the permission order to file detailed grounds for contesting the claim or supporting it on additional grounds and any written evidence (**CPR, r. 54.14**).
Skeleton arguments	The claimant must file and serve a skeleton argument not less than 21 working days before the date of the hearing (or the warned date) (**PD 54A, para. 15.1**). The defendant and other relevant parties wishing to make representations must file and serve a skeleton argument not less than 14 working days before the hearing (or warned date) (**PD 54A, para. 15.2**).
Substantive hearing	Substantive judicial review applications in civil matters are generally heard by a single judge sitting in open court. The court may determine the claim without a hearing where all parties agree (**CPR, r. 54.18**).

Procedural checklist 35 Application by a creditor whose debt is presently payable to wind up a company incorporated in England and Wales

See **chapter 82**.

Pre-action	Check that the amount of the creditor's claim is at least £750 and that there is no substantial dispute about the amount or about whether it is due and payable. Check that there is no substantial cross-claim which would reduce the balance owed to the creditor to less than £750. Check that an appropriately clear demand for payment has been made and that no payment has been received. Consider whether serving a statutory demand (form 4.1) or other action short of petitioning might induce payment.
Preparation	Check the company's correct name and details required for the petition (form 4.2) at Companies House. Check at the Central Registry of Winding-up Petitions that no other petition has been presented (go to the RCJ Companies Court General Office or telephone (020) 7947 7328). If a petition has already been presented, do not present a second petition, but notify the existing petitioner of intention to support. In order to complete the petition, ascertain whether the company appears to be an insurance undertaking, credit institution, investment undertaking providing services involving the holding of funds or securities for third parties, or a collective investment undertaking, and ascertain whether the company's centre of main interests is outside the United Kingdom.

Appropriate court	High Court, or, if company's paid-up capital is £120,000 or less, the county court with insolvency jurisdiction for the district where the company's registered office is located. In the London area, only the High Court has jurisdiction. If the company's centre of main interests is in another EU State (apart from Denmark) and it has no establishment in the United Kingdom (see **82.9** to **82.13**), proceedings must be started in the country where the centre of main interests is located, not in England and Wales.
Form of petition	Form 4.2, which must be verified by statement of truth complying with IR 1986, r. 4.12. For details see **82.19** to **82.25**. At least three copies will be required for filing (one for the court, one for service on the company, one for the petitioner). Extra copies are required if the company has a liquidator in a voluntary winding up, an administrator, an administrative receiver or a supervisor of a voluntary arrangement.
Fees	A court fee of £220 (**CPFO, fee 3.3**) and a deposit of £1,165 for the official receiver's fee must be paid when filing.
Filing	All required copies are sealed and endorsed with the venue for hearing the petition. One copy is retained by the court, the others are returned to the petitioner.
Service	On the company at its registered office: • by handing it to a person who there and then acknowledges him or herself to be, or to the best of the server's knowledge, information and belief is, a director or other officer, or employee, of the company, or • by handing it to a person who there and then acknowledges him or herself to be authorised to accept service on the company's behalf, or • if no individual meeting these criteria is available, by depositing it at or about the registered office in such a way that it is likely to come to the notice of a person attending at the office. • If service at the registered office is not practicable, see **82.37** and **82.38**. Copies of the petition must also be sent (by post or personal delivery) to the company's voluntary liquidator, administrator, supervisor of a voluntary arrangement or administrative receiver.
Certificate of service	Certificate of service (see **82.39**) on company must be filed as soon as reasonably practicable after service and not less than five business days before the hearing.
Notice	Petition must be advertised in the London Gazette, but not until seven business days after service on the company. There must be no other publicity for the petition until this advertisement appears. Advertisement must appear at least seven days before the date appointed for hearing the petition.
Track	Automatically multi-track.
Provisional liquidator	An application may be made for the appointment of a provisional liquidator (see **82.46** to **82.55**).
Evidence	The petition and verifying statement of truth will usually be the only evidence in the case. The company may file evidence in opposition, a copy of which must be sent to the petitioner, not less than five business days before the hearing. No further evidence may be filed unless the court directs.
Certificate of compliance	Certificate of compliance (form 4.7) must be filed, with a copy of the advertisement, by 4.30 p.m. on Friday before hearing (at least five days before hearing in county courts).

List of persons appearing	Form 4.10 must be completed and handed to the court before the hearing commences.
Heard by	Registrar or district judge in public.
Decision	Court may make order applied for, dismiss the petition, adjourn (conditionally or unconditionally), make an interim order, or any other order it thinks fit. Registrar or district judge may refer case to judge.
Perfection	If court makes winding-up order, it will notify the official receiver, who becomes liquidator. All documents necessary to enable the order to be completed must be left at the court by the next business day. Court draws up the order. Official receiver notifies the order in the *London Gazette*.

Procedural checklist 36 Application by a creditor whose debt is presently payable for a bankruptcy order

See **chapter 83**.

Pre-action	Check that the amount of the creditor's claim is at least £750 and that there is no substantial dispute about the amount. Check that the claim is unsecured and is for a liquidated debt payable immediately and there is no substantial dispute that it is due and payable. Check that there is no substantial cross-claim which would reduce the balance owed to the creditor to less than £750. Check that an appropriately clear demand for payment has been made and that no payment has been received. If judgment has been obtained for the debt, consider whether to execute: partly or wholly unsatisfied execution is a ground for a bankruptcy petition.
Statutory demand	Unless there is a partly or wholly unsatisfied execution for the debt, a statutory demand must be served on the debtor. Prescribed form is form 6.1, or form 6.2 if the debt is a judgment debt for which execution has not been issued. If practicable, there must be personal service of a statutory demand, by leaving it with the debtor (**CPR, r. 6.5(3)**). Steps specified in **PD Insolvency Proceedings, para. 13.3.4(1)** must be followed. If that fails to effect service, the steps specified in **para. 13.3.4(2), (3)** and **(4)**, which may involve substituted service by first-class post or insertion through a letter box, must be followed. If the debt is a judgment debt, service may be by newspaper advertisement if the debtor has absconded or is avoiding service and there is no real prospect of successful execution. Evidence of service, using form 6.11 or, for substituted service, 6.12, must be filed with the petition. The debtor has three weeks to comply with the statutory demand and may apply for it to be set aside, see **83.8**. A petition may be presented before the three weeks expire if there is a serious possibility that the debtor's property or the value of any of it will be significantly diminished during the three weeks. The petition must state that possibility.
Preparation	In order to complete the petition, ascertain whether the debtor appears to be carrying on business as an insurance undertaking, credit institution, investment undertaking providing services involving the holding of funds or securities for third parties, or a collective investment undertaking, and ascertain whether the debtor's centre of main interests is outside the United Kingdom.
Appropriate court	County court which has insolvency jurisdiction for the district in which the debtor resided or carried on business in the previous six months. All petitions assigned to the London insolvency district are dealt with at the RCJ, either in the Central London County Court if the petition debt is less than £50,000 or in the High Court if it is £50,000 or more. See **83.4**.

	If the debtor's centre of main interests is in another EU State (apart from Denmark) and the debtor has no establishment in the United Kingdom (see **82.9** to **82.12**), proceedings must be started in the country where the centre of main interests is located, not in England and Wales.
Form of petition	Form 6.7, or form 6.9 if the petition is based on partially or wholly unsatisfied execution. The petition must be verified by witness statement or affidavit in form 6.13. See **83.9** and **83.10**. Three copies will be required for filing (one for the court, one for service on the debtor, one to be exhibited to the affidavit of service).
Fees	A court fee of £220 (**CPFO, fee 3.1(b)**) and a deposit of £700 for the official receiver's fee must be paid when filing.
Filing	Three copies of the petition must be filed and, if the petition relies on non-compliance with a statutory demand, written evidence of service of the demand. All three copies of the petition are sealed and endorsed with the venue for hearing the petition. One copy is retained by the court, the others are returned to the petitioner.
Service	Personal service of the petition by leaving it with the debtor (**CPR, r. 6.5(3)**) is required. **PD Insolvency Proceedings, para. 13.3.4**, sets out the steps which should be taken before concluding that personal service cannot be effected so that an application for substituted service is justified.
Certificate of service	Certificate of service on the debtor (form 6.17A for personal service; form 6.18A for substituted service) must be filed as soon as reasonably practicable after service, and not less than five business days before the hearing of the petition.
Track	Automatically multi-track.
Interim receiver	An application may be made by the debtor or any creditor for the appointment of an interim receiver (see **83.16**).
Evidence	The petition and verifying statement of truth will usually be the only evidence in the case. If the debtor intends to oppose the petition, he or she must, not later than five business days before the hearing, file in court a notice specifying the grounds of objection and send a copy to the petitioner.
List of persons appearing	Form 6.20 must be completed and handed to the court before the hearing commences.
Decision	Court may make order applied for if satisfied that the statements in the petition are true, and that the debt on which it is founded has not been paid, or secured or compounded for.
Perfection	The court settles a bankruptcy order. Two sealed copies are sent to the official receiver, who sends one to the bankrupt. Official receiver notifies the order in the London Gazette.

Procedural checklist 37 Residential mortgage possession claims

See **chapter 87**.

Protocol	**Pre-Action Protocol for Possession Based on Mortgage or Home Purchase Plan Arrears in Respect of Residential Property**: required behaviour of mortgage lenders includes initial pre-proceedings letter giving the borrower regulatory information sheet or equivalent and the following account information: amount of arrears, the outstanding balance and what interest charges are to be added to the account (**para. 5.1**). If an agreement for repayment is made, 15 business days' notice must be given of intention to commence court action (**para. 5.7**). Consideration to be given to postponing possession claim (**paras 6, 7 and 8**).

Which court	County court for district of property address (**CPR, r. 55.3(1)**); Unless exceptionally High Court (**CPR, r. 55.3(2)** and **(3)**; **PD 55A, paras 1.3, 1.4, 1.6**; **County Courts Act 1984, s. 21**); Or online (see below).
Intended parties	All parties to mortgage deed: consider status of persons with overriding interests.
Commencement	Claim form (N5) and particulars of claim (N120) filed and served together. See **CPR, rr. 55.3**, **55.4**, and **PD 55A, para. 2.5**; and **PD 16, para. 7.3**. Specific contents of particulars of claim (**PD 55A, paras 2.1, 2.5, 2.5A**). Fee is £175 in the county court, £465 in the High Court (**CPFO, fees 1.4(a)** and **(b)**).
Online	PCOL system. Combined claim form and particulars of claim. See **CPR, r. 55.10A**, and **PD 55B**. No filing of mortgage deed (**PD 55B, para. 6.2**). Specific contents of online form (**PD 55B, paras 6.3, 6.3A, 6.3B**). Fee is £100 (**CPFO, fee 1.4(c)**). Deemed served 5th day after issue. Not more than 7 days after issue, claimant serves full arrears history if online form had only a summary (**PD 55B, para. 6.3C**).
Defence	Form N11M. Must be filed within 14 days after service of particulars of claim (**CPR, rr. 15.4** and **55.7(3)**). In Consumer Credit Act 1974 case may apply for time order in defence (**PD 55A, para. 7.1**) or can make later **Part 23** application.
Notices to tenants and others	Within 5 days of receiving hearing date, claimant sends notice of hearing to tenants/occupiers at the property, to local housing authority and other mortgagees (**CPR, r. 55.10(2)**).
Evidence	Witness statements served at least 2 days before hearing updating figures to hearing date (**CPR, r. 55.8(4)**).
Pre-hearing adjournment	Application by consent. No fee if made more than 14 days pre-hearing, otherwise £45 (**CPFO, fee 2.7**).
Hearing	Date fixed at issue. Is 28 days or more after issue and 21 days or more after service (**CPR, r. 55.5**), unless time abridged under **CPR, r. 3.1(2)(a)** or **(b)**. At hearing claimant produces office copy Land Registry entries and search, Protocol checklist (N123) with copy for defendant and, if not already filed, copy mortgage, conditions and certificate of service of **CPR, r. 55(10)**, notice (unless in witness statement). Oral update of key figures.
Allocation	If substantial dispute, allocation to track (**CPR, Part 26** and **rr. 55.8(2)** and **55.9**) — potentially proceeds to multi-track trial. Fee of £220 (**CPFO, fee 2.1(b)**).

Procedural checklist 38 Enforcement of possession orders

See 87.49 to 87.58.

Warrant of possession	14 days' notice to tenants etc. (**CCR, ord. 26, r. 17(2A)** in **CPR, sch. 2**). Request for warrant of possession (within 6 years of order) (**CCR, ord. 26, r. 17** in **CPR, sch. 2**). Form N325. Fee is £110 (**CPFO, fee 8.6**).
Stay or suspension	Defendant's application to stay, suspend or vary possession order, or application by unauthorised tenant to stay or suspend order for two months. Form N244. See **CPR, Part 23**. Fee is £40 (**CPFO, fee 2.9**). Hearing listed.
Forcible re-entry	Application for permission for warrant of restitution (and witness statement) (**CCR, ord. 26, r. 17(4)** and **(5)** in **CPR, sch. 2**). Form N244. Fee is £45 for the application (**CPFO, fee 1.8(a)**) plus £110 for the warrant (**CPFO, fee 8.6**).

Chapter 1 The Overriding Objective and Sources of Procedural Law

INTRODUCTION

This chapter will consider the various sources of the law governing civil proceedings, and will also give general guidance on the interpretation of the main source, the Civil Procedure Rules 1998 ('CPR'). Specific consideration of the detailed provisions of the CPR and related statutory sources and case law can be found in **chapters 2** to **81**. These are supplemented by the procedural checklists starting on page 1. The full text of the CPR, and their related practice directions, can be found in **appendix 1**. Pre-action protocols are in **appendix 2**. Court fees orders are in **appendix 3**. Statutes governing civil proceedings are in **appendix 4**. **Chapters 82** *to 91 contain text on:* 1.1

(a) insolvency proceedings and companies matters (82 to 86);
(b) mortgage possession claims (**chapter 87**);
(c) anti-social behaviour and harassment (**chapter 88**);
(d) sale of goods (**chapter 89**);
(e) unfair contracts (**chapter 90**); and
(f) human rights law (**chapter 91**).

Commentary

SOURCES OF PROCEDURAL LAW

Inherent jurisdiction

1.2 Being the successor to the pre-1875 common law courts, the High Court has inherent jurisdiction to control its procedures to ensure its proceedings are not abused to achieve injustice. As Lord Diplock said in *Bremer Vulkan Schiffbau und Maschinenfabrik v South India Shipping Corporation Ltd* [1981] AC 909 at p. 977, the High Court has:

> a general power to control its own procedure so as to prevent its being used to achieve injustice. Such a power is inherent in its constitution as a court of justice….it would stultify the constitutional role of the High Court as a court of justice if it were not armed with power to prevent its process being misused in such a way as to diminish its capability of arriving at a just decision of the dispute.

Before the introduction of the CPR, much of the law relating to striking out as a sanction, and the initial development of the jurisdiction to grant freezing injunctions and search orders, was based on the High Court's inherent jurisdiction. Once an area has been codified, the need for recourse to the inherent jurisdiction recedes or disappears, see *Harrison v Tew* [1990] 2 AC 523, in which it was held that the inherent jurisdiction to order the assessment by the court of a solicitor's bill of costs had been ousted by subsequent statutory codification. Likewise, there is no residual inherent discretion where there are express provisions of the CPR (*Raja v Van Hoogstraten (No. 9)* [2008] EWCA Civ 1444, [2009] 1 WLR 1143). In his Hamlyn lecture, 'The inherent jurisdiction of the court' ([1970] Current Legal Problems 23, 50–1), Sir Jack Jacob said the powers of the court under its inherent jurisdiction: 'are complementary to its powers under rules of court; one set of powers supplements and reinforces the other….where the usefulness of the powers under the rules ends, the usefulness of the powers under the inherent jurisdiction begins.' Professor Dockray ('The inherent jurisdiction to regulate civil proceedings' (1997) 113 LQR 120, 128) said: 'the inherent jurisdiction may supplement but cannot be used to lay down procedure which is contrary to or inconsistent with a valid rule of [court]'. See also *Moore v Assignment Courier Ltd* [1977] 1 WLR 638 at pp. 644–5; *Langley v North West Water Authority* [1991] 1 WLR 697 at p. 709; *Raja v Van Hoogstraten (No. 9)* at [74]–[78]). As a new procedural code (**CPR, r. 1.1(1)**), the CPR are intended to be comprehensive. If there is any lacuna, any exercise of the inherent jurisdiction should be in a way which is consistent with the rules (*Raja v Van Hoogstraten (No. 9)* at [85]).

In *Al Rawi v Security Service* [2011] UKSC 34, [2012] 1 AC 531, the defendant applied for permission to use a 'closed material procedure' that would have permitted the defendant to set out part of its case in an open defence, and to deploy a substantial amount of material in closed statements of case, witness statements and oral evidence at trial which would be kept secret from the claimants but made available to special advocates representing the claimants' interests. Similar processes are permitted by **CPR, Part 80**, for proceedings under the Terrorism Prevention and Investigation Measures Act 2011, and the Supreme Court has held that use of a statutory closed material procedure under the Employment Tribunals (Constitution and Rules of Procedure) Regulations 2004 (SI 2004/1861) in proceedings before an employment tribunal does not contravene the European Convention on Human Rights, **art. 6(1)**, in the **Human Rights Act 1998, sch. 1** (*Tariq v Home Office* [2012] UKSC 35, [2012] 1 AC 452). In *Al Rawi v Security Service* [2010] EWCA Civ 482, [2012] 1 AC 531, the Court of Appeal felt that a closed material procedure was impermissible in the absence of express statutory authority because it would be inconsistent with various provisions of the CPR. In the Supreme Court ([2011] UKSC 34, [2012] 1 AC 531), Lord Dyson JSC regarded this as an insufficient justification: a closed material procedure would not contravene the CPR. A more fundamental justification for refusing the use of closed material procedures in civil proceedings, which commended itself to the Supreme Court, is that it would infringe the principles of natural justice that underpin civil justice, particularly the right to a fair trial, the right to be confronted by one's accusers, and the right to know the reasons for the outcome (per Lord Hope of Craighead DPSC at [72]). Further reference was made to Professor Dockray's article on the court's inherent jurisdiction, where the point is made that in some circumstances procedure is as important as substantive law. As Professor Dockray said:

> Major innovations in procedural law should therefore be recognised as an institutional responsibility, not a matter on which individual judges should respond to the pleas of particular litigants. Procedural revolutions should appear first in statutes or in the Rules of Court, not in the law reports.

It is probably the case that the county court, being the creature of statute, has no inherent jurisdiction. There is direct authority to the contrary in *Langley v North West Water Authority* [1991] 1 WLR 697, in which it was held (before the enactment, in the Civil Procedure Act 1997, of the County Courts Act 1984, s. 74A) that a county court had inherent jurisdiction to issue a local practice direction. See also the family cases of *D v D (County Court Jurisdiction: Injunctions)* [1993] 2 FLR 802 and *Devon County Council v B* [1997] 1 FLR 591, which probably turn on the effect of the Children Act 1989. The wide scope of the legislation governing county court proceedings now allows practically no scope or necessity for the exercise of the county court's inherent jurisdiction even if it has one.

Statutory sources

The primary source of law governing procedure in the High Court and Court of Appeal is the Senior Courts Act 1981 (formerly the Supreme Court Act 1981). County courts are governed by the County Courts Act 1984. These statutes are the primary source of the jurisdiction exercised by the civil courts in England and Wales. Both statutes are often expressed in very wide terms, leaving the detailed mechanics of many of the procedures used in the courts to be set out in rules of court. The power to make court rules is granted by the Civil Procedure Act 1997. The **Access to Justice Act 1999** made provision for funding litigation, and also contains provisions dealing with appeals, courts, judges and civil proceedings. Various other statutes also govern aspects of civil procedure. For example, the Administration of Justice Act 1969 provides for leapfrog appeals to the Supreme Court, certain enforcement procedures are governed by the Charging Orders Act 1979 and the Attachment of Earnings Act 1971, and limitation is governed by the Limitation Act 1980. **1.3**

There are a number of important statutory instruments. The main source of procedural law is the **Civil Procedure Rules 1998 (SI 1998/3123)** (which are amended several times each year), see **1.5**. Jurisdiction between the High Court and county courts is mainly dealt with by the **High Court and County Courts Jurisdiction Order 1991 (SI 1991/724)** (see **appendix** 4). Court fees are laid down by the **Civil Proceedings Fees Order 2008 (SI 2008/1053)** (CPFO) (see **appendix** 3).

The international dimension is becoming increasingly important in civil procedure. A fundamental change in the approach to many issues, such as the right to a fair trial, has been brought in by the **Human Rights Act 1998**, which incorporates the provisions of the European Convention on Human Rights into English law (see **chapter 91** and **appendix** 4). Also important are European Community Regulations dealing with jurisdiction and service of proceedings. Extracts from **Regulation** (EC) **No. 44/2001** and the **Civil Jurisdiction and Judgments Act 1982** can be found in **appendix 4**.

Former Rules of the Supreme Court and County Court Rules

Until April 1999, rules governing civil procedure were the Rules of the Supreme Court 1965 (RSC) which covered proceedings in the High Court and the Civil Division of the Court of Appeal (these were an extensively revised version of rules set out in sch. 1 to the Supreme Court of Judicature Act 1875, which were themselves in part distilled from pre-existing procedures), and the County Court Rules 1981 (CCR) which covered proceedings in the county **1.4**

Commentary

courts. The fact that the CCR differed in many respects from the RSC added to the complexity of the old civil justice system, and the production of a unified set of rules is one of the main improvements introduced by the **Civil Procedure Rules 1998.**

Civil Procedure Rules

1.5 By the Civil Procedure Act 1997, s. 2, a Civil Procedure Rule Committee was established, with the power to make rules governing the practice and procedure to be followed in:

(a) the civil division of the Court of Appeal;
(b) the High Court; and
(c) the county courts.

The committee is required, by **s. 1(3)**, to exercise its power to make rules 'with a view to securing that the civil justice system is accessible, fair and efficient'. Pursuant to this power, with effect from 26 April 1999, civil proceedings in England and Wales have been governed by a unified set of procedural rules, the **Civil Procedure Rules 1998 (SI 1998/3123)**. These rules brought into effect the proposals for reform of the civil justice system set out in the *Final Report* compiled by Lord Woolf (Access to Justice. Final Report (London: HMSO, 1996)). They embody the most radical reform of civil litigation since the Judicature Acts 1873 to 1875. The full text of the CPR, as amended (apart from rules concerning civil proceedings which are ancillary to criminal proceedings and investigations), can be found in **appendix 1**.

Schedule rules

1.6 When the CPR were introduced, quite substantial sections of the old RSC and CCR were retained (with minor revisions) in **CPR, sch. 1** (the preserved provisions of the RSC) and **sch. 2** (the preserved provisions of the CCR). These provisions continue in force by virtue of **CPR, Part 50**. Since 1998 many provisions of the old rules in the schedules have been replaced by new rules in the main body of the CPR. So the number of Parts of the CPR has increased, with corresponding deletions from the schedules.

The rules re-enacted in the schedules are of two general types. First, a number of general procedural rules are retained, such as some of the rules on enforcement of judgments. Secondly, there are provisions from the old rules dealing with the county courts' special jurisdiction under three statutes (see **CCR, ord. 44** and **ord. 49** in **CPR, sch 2**) and rules concerning proceedings, under various statutes, which are ancillary to criminal proceedings and investigations, which are not considered in *Blackstone's Civil Practice*. **CPR, r. 50(2)**, provides that the CPR apply in relation to the proceedings to which the schedules apply, subject to the provisions in the schedules and the relevant practice directions. This means that the overriding objective (see **1.12**) applies to applications made under these re-enacted provisions from the old rules.

Practice directions

1.7 As permitted by the Civil Procedure Act 1997, ss. 1 and 5, and sch. 1, para. 6, the CPR are supplemented by practice directions (PDs). The general scheme is that individual areas of civil procedure are governed by Parts of the CPR, with almost every Part being supplemented by one or more PDs. Practice directions set out details of procedure that it is felt do not need to be set out in statutory instruments (as required for amendments to the CPR), which allows for flexible amendment in the light of experience. The full text of the PDs can be found in **appendix 1**. Each PD is printed after the Part of the CPR which it supplements.

Practice directions may be given either in accordance with the Constitutional Reform Act 2005, sch. 2, part 1, or with the approval of either the Lord Chancellor or Lord Chief Justice (Civil Procedure Act 1997, s. 5). Judges are bound to follow, and have no power to alter, PDs made under s. 5. Judges have no authority to lay down PDs which change rules laid down in the CPR or PDs promulgated by the Ministry of Justice, and any such purported practice direction has no effect (*Bovale Ltd v Secretary of State for Communities and Local Government* [2009] EWCA Civ 171, [2009] 1 WLR 2274). Practice directions are 'directions as to the practice and procedure of any court' (s. 9(1) and (2)). Guidance on the application and interpretation of the law (which is often given in judicial decisions, and often includes guidance on how the rules and PDs work) does not come within this definition (s. 9(5)). A judgment of the court which suggests a procedure to fill a gap in the rules was held not to be a practice direction in *Bovale Ltd v Secretary of State for Communities and Local Government*.

Pre-action protocols

Pre-action protocols have been formulated for clinical negligence, disease and illness, personal injury, construction and engineering, housing disrepair, rent arrears, mortgage repossession, defamation, professional negligence and judicial review claims, and low value personal injury claims arising from road traffic accidents. Each protocol contains detailed rules for stating the allegations being made and the reasons for any denial of liability, and for disclosure of documents. **PD Pre-action Conduct, paras 6.1** to **8.4** and **annex A**, set out the similar approach required in cases not covered by specific pre-action protocols. The protocols are intended to enable parties to obtain relevant information at an early stage, and to promote settlement of the dispute (see **chapter 8**). The CPR enable the court to take into account compliance or non-compliance with **PD Pre-action Conduct** or any relevant protocol when giving directions for the management of proceedings (**CPR, rr. 3.1**(4) and (5) and **3.9**(1)(e)) and when making orders for costs (**r. 44.3**(5)(a)). The text of the relevant protocols can be found in **appendix** 2. **1.8**

Court guides

Practical guidance on the conduct of proceedings in the specialist courts and in the main Divisions of the High Court have been published. Court guides were first published before the introduction of the CPR. The first edition of the Chancery Guide, for example, was issued in April 1995. The present editions of the guides have been written so as to comply with the provisions of the CPR and relevant PDs. They can be seen at the Ministry of Justice website, http://www.justice.gov.uk. **1.9**

The court guides draw attention to important matters of practice, common errors and failings, give detailed information about forms to use, provide courtroom and telephone numbers for the use of practitioners, and generally supplement the provisions of the CPR and PDs. Court guides have no formal status, and provide no more than guidance (*Bovale Ltd v Secretary of State for Communities and Local Government* [2009] EWCA Civ 171, [2009] 1 WLR 2274; *Brown v Innovatorone plc* [2009] EWHC 1376 (Comm), [2010] 2 All ER (Comm) 80 at [30]). They are not designed to define the court's jurisdiction, are not to be taken as replacements for the CPR, and are not to be read as if they were statutes (*Vitpol Building Service v Samen* [2008] EWHC 2283 (TCC), [2009] Bus LR D65). Nor can they override the PDs (*Carnegie v Giessen* [2005] EWCA Civ 191, [2005] 1 WLR 2510 at [20]).

Forms

Numerous standard forms have been promulgated to assist practitioners and court users. Many are prescribed forms, made under the authority of statutory instruments, and can be identified by the letter 'N' in their designations (e.g. form N244 is the standard application notice). Others are 'practice forms', issued under the authority of the masters of the High Court, which can be identified by the letters 'PF' in their designations. Some PDs contain important precedents, such as the standard-form freezing injunctions and search orders in the annex to **PD 25A**. Forms that are to be completed by parties can be downloaded, in versions that can be completed on-screen, from the Court Form Finder at http://hmctsformfinder.justice.gov.uk/HMCTS/FormFinder.do. **1.10**

Commentary

THE CIVIL PROCEDURE RULES 1998

Scope of the Civil Procedure Rules

1.11 The general rule is that the Civil Procedure Rules 1998 apply to all proceedings in the county courts, the High Court and the Civil Division of the Court of Appeal (**r. 2.1(1)**). Seven types of civil proceedings are taken outside the scope of the CPR by **r. 2.1(2)**. These cover insolvency, non-contentious probate, Prize Court, Court of Protection, family, adoption and election proceedings. The exceptions are mostly covered by their own specific procedural rules, such as the Insolvency Rules 1986 (SI 1986/1925), the Court of Protection Rules 2007 (SI 2007/1744) and the Family Procedure Rules 2010 (SI 2010/2955).

The CPR established an entirely new procedural code (**CPR, r. 1.1(1)**). As a result authorities under the old rules must be applied with considerable caution when interpreting the CPR (see **1.21**). At one level this is because all procedural decisions made under the CPR have to be in accordance with the overriding objective of dealing with cases justly (see **1.12**), whereas there was no specific statement to this effect in the old rules of court. While superficially attractive, this is not the real reason why old cases are not authoritative under the CPR. Making the CPR a new 'code' means that a new start was made. The CPR are not merely a more modern restatement of the old rules, but a complete replacement of those rules. **Rule 1.1(1)** specifically refers to the CPR as being a 'procedural' code. However, there is a clear distinction between procedure (or how the court system operates) and practice (the principles applied when dealing with procedural problems). **Rule 1.1(1)** does not say, perhaps deliberately, that the CPR are to be regarded as being a new codification of the practice to be adopted by the courts when making procedural decisions. Nor does **r. 1.1** override existing rules of evidence (see *McPhilemy v Times Newspapers Ltd (No. 2)* [2000] 1 WLR 1732).

While r. 2.1(1) provides that the CPR apply to all proceedings in the county courts, High Court and the Civil Division of the Court of Appeal, they derive their authority as subordinate legislation, and therefore do not oust the effect of Acts of Parliament. This is sometimes stated in terms in the CPR (such as **r. 6.1(a)**, which says Part 6 applies except where any other enactment makes other provision), but also applies generally as a matter of principle (*Mucelli v Government of Albania* [2009] UKHL 2, [2009] 1 WLR 276 at [74]).

Overriding objective

1.12 The ethos of the CPR is encapsulated in **r. 1.1**, which provides:

(1) These Rules are a new procedural code with the overriding objective of enabling the court to deal with cases justly and at proportionate cost.
(2) Dealing with a case justly and at proportionate cost includes, so far as is practicable—
  (a) ensuring that the parties are on an equal footing;
  (b) saving expense;
  (c) dealing with the case in ways which are proportionate—
    (i) to the amount of money involved;
    (ii) to the importance of the case;
    (iii) to the complexity of the issues; and
    (iv) to the financial position of each party;
  (d) ensuring that it is dealt with expeditiously and fairly;
  (e) allotting to it an appropriate share of the court's resources, while taking into account the need to allot resources to other cases; and
  (f) enforcing compliance with rules, practice directions and orders.

The court is required to give effect to this overriding objective of dealing with cases justly when exercising any power under the rules, or when interpreting any rule (**r. 1.2**). Modifications are made to the overriding objective in three situations. In these exceptional cases the overriding objective has to be read and applied in ways that are compatible with the duty to ensure that information is not disclosed contrary to the public interest (see **50.69** to **50.71** for public interest immunity). The prescribed situations where the overriding objective is modified in this way are:

(a) control order proceedings under the Prevention of Terrorism Act 2005 (which are governed by CPR, Part 76, and in particular r. 76.2 — the Prevention of Terrorism Act 2005 was repealed by the Terrorism Prevention and Investigation Measures Act 2011, s. 1, subject to transitional provisions in s. 29 and sch. 8);
(b) financial restrictions proceedings under the Counter-Terrorism Act 2008 (which are governed by CPR, Part 79, and in particular r. 79.2); and
(c) terrorism prevention and investigation measures proceedings (known as 'TPIM proceedings') under the Terrorism Prevention and Investigation Measures Act 2011 (which are governed by CPR, Part 80, and in particular r. 80.2).

Parties to litigation are required to help the court to further the overriding objective (**r. 1.3**).

Interpretation

The CPR have been promulgated in a statutory instrument, so they must be interpreted in accordance with the provisions of the Interpretation Act 1978 (Interpretation Act 1978, ss. 5 and 11; *Collier v Williams* [2006] EWCA Civ 20, [2006] 1 WLR 1945 at [32]). Reference can be made to the headings to the rules as an aid to interpretation (*Brown v Innovatorone plc* [2009] EWHC 1376 (Comm), [2010] 2 All ER (Comm) 80). Headings may be taken into account in interpreting primary legislation provided due account is taken of the fact that headings are intended to provide brief but necessarily inexact guides to the contents of the relevant provisions and that headings in legislation are not included in a Bill for debate but for ease of reference (*R v Montila* [2004] UKHL 50, [2004] 1 WLR 3141 at [34]). However, headings are available for consideration by the Civil Procedure Rule Committee, so the last point does not apply when considering headings in the CPR (*Brown v Innovatorone plc* at [17]). **1.13**

By **CPR, r. 1.2**, the CPR must be interpreted so as to give effect to the overriding objective (in **r. 1.1**, see **1.12**) of enabling the court to deal with cases justly and at proportionate cost. This is subject, in control order proceedings under the Prevention of Terrorism Act 2005 and financial restrictions proceedings under the Counter-Terrorism Act 2008, to **CPR, rr. 76.2** and **79.2**, respectively (see **1.12**). Where there are no express words in the CPR dealing with a situation, the court is bound to consider which interpretation best reflects the overriding objective when construing the rules (*Totty v Snowden* [2001] EWCA Civ 1415, [2002] 1 WLR 1384 at [34]). As a result, the old 'quasi-statutory' approach to interpretation, based upon a close analysis of the language used in an attempt to find the true intention of the rules, might be thought to be a thing of the past. Lord Woolf commented in the *Final Report*, ch. 14, para. 5, that:

> judges exercising appellate functions will have a significant part to play in giving effect to the new system of case management...by laying down principles to be followed in exercising the new powers of case management. It should be borne in mind, however, that management decisions are pre-eminently matters of discretion with which an appeal court would seldom interfere.

Purposive interpretation

Lord Woolf himself made clear in the *Final Report* how the overriding objective must be used to interpret the rules. At paras 10–11 of ch. 20 he stated: **1.14**

> Every word in the rules should have a purpose, but every word cannot sensibly be given a minutely exact meaning. Civil procedure involves more judgment and knowledge than the rules can directly express. In this respect, rules of court are not like an instruction manual for operating a piece of machinery. Ultimately their purpose is to guide the court and the litigants towards the just resolution of the case.

Although the rules can offer detailed directions for the technical steps to be taken, the effectiveness of those steps depends upon the spirit in which they are carried out. That in turn depends on an understanding of the fundamental purpose of the rules and of the underlying system of procedure.

In order to identify that purpose at the outset, I have placed at the very beginning of the rules a statement of their overriding objective.

In other words, interpretation is to be purposive rather than a matter of close analysis of the meaning of individual words without taking into account their context.

Plain meaning of the rules

1.15 The CPR have been deliberately drafted in a plain English style in order to make them intelligible to lay people using the courts. When construing the rules the courts primarily seek to find the natural meaning of the words used. Although the court must seek to give effect to the overriding objective when interpreting any rule (**CPR, r. 1.2(b)**), this does not enable the court to hold that provisions of the CPR which have a plain meaning should be construed contrary to that meaning, nor that the plain meaning should be ignored (*Vinos v Marks and Spencer plc* [2001] 3 All ER 784 at [20]). The court cannot, therefore, assume a discretion in order to assist a deserving case where there is no jurisdiction to make an order, even by resorting to the overriding objective (*Godwin v Swindon Borough Council* [2001] EWCA Civ 1478, [2002] 1 WLR 997 at [45]).

May, must and should

1.16 There is a clear distinction between a rule that says a court 'may' do something, thereby giving the court a discretion (which ought to be exercised in accordance with the overriding objective), and a rule which says something 'must' be done (which is obligatory). An example is **CPR, Part 13**. Where a default judgment has been entered prematurely or otherwise in circumstances where the claimant is not entitled to judgment, **r. 13.2** provides that the default judgment must be set aside. On the other hand, where there has been compliance with the rules relating to entering a default judgment, setting aside the judgment is a matter of discretion, **r. 13.3** providing that the court 'may' set it aside. Most of the powers given to the courts under the CPR are given in discretionary form.

Most of the steps to be taken by the parties in the course of proceedings are expressed in mandatory terms. This is frequently made clear by use of the word 'must'. For example, **PD 7A, para. 3.5**, which applies where a claim is to be served outside the jurisdiction under **Regulation (EC) No. 44/2001**, provides that a prescribed endorsement 'must' be included on the claim form. In the past 'should' or 'shall' have been used interchangeably with the word 'must' in a number of provisions in the CPR, but most of these were changed to 'must' by the Civil Procedure (Amendment) Rules 2008 (SI 2008/2178). Subsequent amendments to the CPR, and Ministry of Justice updates to the practice directions, have made various changes such as 'may' to 'will', and 'shall' to 'will', with the intention of ensuring the relevant requirements are treated as mandatory. These changes were made after cases such as *Choudhury v Kingston Hospital NHS Trust* [2006] EWHC 90057 (Costs), LTL 7/9/2006, and *Metcalfe v Clipston* [2004] EWHC 9005 (Costs) held that 'should' is not mandatory.

Problems with mandatory and discretionary language

1.17 The word 'may' is, in certain contexts, used in a mandatory rather than a discretionary sense. An example is **CPR, r. 24.4(1)**, which provides that a claimant 'may' not apply for summary judgment until the defendant has filed an acknowledgment of service or a defence.

Sometimes there are problems in determining who has the power to exercise a discretion created by use of the word 'may'. An example is **r. 32.5(5)**, which provides that if a party who has served a witness statement does not call the witness or use the statement at trial, 'any other party may put the witness statement in as hearsay evidence'. A natural reading of the rule would indicate that the discretion is vested in the other party to the proceedings. Remarkably, in *McPhilemy v Times Newspapers Ltd (No. 2)* [2000] 1 WLR 1732 it was held that the court has a discretion to refuse permission to use such a statement (see **51.23**).

Sometimes the word 'should' is interpreted to mean 'ought, but may do something else'. The prime example of this is *Bloomsbury Publishing Group Ltd v News Group Newspapers Ltd* [2003] EWHC 1205 (Ch), [2003] 1 WLR 1633, in which it was held that it is possible to issue a claim against 'person or persons unknown'. **PD 7A, para. 4.1(3)**, provides that the title of a claim form must contain a title which 'should' state the full name of each party. Use of the word 'should' was contrasted by the court with the word 'must', and was held to justify an interpretation allowing proceedings to be issued against persons unknown.

Different meanings given to different expressions

In a number of cases the courts have held that different expressions appearing in a single rule have to be given different meanings. An example is the difference between 'day' and 'business day' where they appear in **CPR, r. 6.26**. 'Business day' is defined by **r. 6.2(b)** as excluding Saturdays, Sundays and bank holidays (including Christmas Day and Good Friday). In *Anderton v Clwyd County Council (No. 2)* [2002] EWCA Civ 933, [2002] 1 WLR 3174 it was held that 'day' had to bear a different meaning, and was interpreted as meaning any calendar day, including weekends and bank holidays etc. **1.18**

This is based on a literalistic approach to interpretation, and is hard to reconcile with the intended purposive approach advocated by Lord Woolf (see **1.14**).

Commentary

Interpretation and human rights

The **Human Rights Act 1998, s. 3(1)**, provides that, so far as it is possible to do so, primary legislation and subordinate legislation (which includes the CPR) must be read and given effect in a way which is compatible with the rights set out in the European Convention on Human Rights. In *Goode v Martin* [2001] EWCA Civ 1899, [2002] 1 WLR 1828, s. 3(1) of the Act and **art. 6(1)** of the Convention were used by the court as a basis for reading additional words into **CPR, r. 17.4**, so that it would not prevent the claimant bringing her real claim to trial. The **Human Rights Act 1998, s. 2(1)** provides that a court determining a question which arises in connection with a Convention right must take into account any judgment, decision, declaration or advisory opinion of the European Court of Human Rights. Although lawyers must take a responsible attitude to raising human rights points (*Daniels v Walker* [2000] 1 WLR 1382), such points do arise on occasion when courts are considering procedural applications, and the CPR and practice directions have been drafted with a view to being compatible with the Convention. **1.19**

Reliance on court staff

In *Sayers v Clarke Walker* [2002] EWCA Civ 645, [2002] 1 WLR 3095, the appellant's solicitors said that a breach of the rules had occurred because they had relied on misleading advice given by court staff. It was held to be wrong for solicitors to attempt to rely on conversations with court staff for the purpose of interpreting civil practice, and that being solicitors they should be expected to know such matters themselves. Likewise, no reliance can be placed on indications given by court staff as to the decision to be made by a judge (*City and General (Holborn) Ltd v Structure Tone Ltd* [2009] EWHC 2139 (TCC), [2009] BLR 541. **1.20**

Old case law: generally redundant

As a general rule, advocates should not resort to decisions under the old rules for assistance in interpreting the CPR. In *Biguzzi v Rank Leisure plc* [1999] 1 WLR 1926 the Court of Appeal (Lord Woolf MR, Brooke LJ, Robert Walker LJ) held that the pre-CPR cases on abuse of process in **1.21** the form of wholesale disregard of court rules (such as *Arbuthnot Latham Bank Ltd v Trafalgar Holdings Ltd* [1998] 1 WLR 1426) are not binding or persuasive authorities on the exercise of the court's discretion under the CPR. The Court of Appeal said the position under the CPR is fundamentally different from under the old system. It pointed out that under **r. 1.1** the CPR are a 'new procedural code', and compliance with court orders would be regarded as more important than under the previous system. Lord Woolf made it clear that, 'Earlier authorities are no longer generally of any relevance once the CPR applies' ([1999] 1 WLR 1926 at p. 1934). Counsel in *Vinos v Marks and Spencer plc* [2001] 3 All ER 784 had made submissions by reference to authorities under the old rules. May LJ said, at [17]:

> these submissions are not in point. The CPR are a new procedural code, and the question for this court in this case concerns the interpretation and application of the relevant provisions of the new procedural code as they stand untrammelled by the weight of authority that accumulated under the former Rules.

In *SSQ Europe SA v Johann & Backes OHG* [2002] 1 Lloyd's Rep 465 the court commented that decisions under similar (but not identical) provisions of the RSC should be treated 'with caution'. While this is the position in all courts up to and including the Court of Appeal, the Supreme Court frequently reviews case law of some antiquity when deciding important points of principle (see for example, *Summers v Fairclough Homes Ltd* [2012] UKSC 26, [2012] 1 WLR 2004).

Old cases as a guide to exercise of discretion

1.22 Where the CPR and previous rules have similar or identical wording, and where it can be shown that the operation of old authorities is consistent with the requirement to further the overriding objective as it applies in the particular case, the court may be prepared to take them into account or at least be persuaded by arguments based on principles established in pre-CPR cases. In *Purdy v Cambran* [1999] CPLR 843 May LJ stated:

> Lord Woolf in *Biguzzi v Rank Leisure plc* [1999] 1 WLR 1926 was not saying that the underlying thought processes of previous decisions should be completely thrown overboard. It is clear in my view, that what Lord Woolf was saying was that reference to authorities under the former rules is generally no longer relevant. Rather it is necessary to concentrate on the intrinsic justice of a particular case in the light of the overriding objective.

Previous jurisprudence, for example, on the exercise of the court's discretion to discharge orders for service out of the jurisdiction made without notice, is not binding, although it may still be illuminating (*Bua International Ltd v Hai Hing Shipping Co. Ltd* [2000] 1 Lloyd's Rep 300). Likewise, although prejudice is no longer an essential prerequisite for an order to strike out for delay — as the decision depends on the justice in all the circumstances of the individual case — the courts will consider prejudice as part of the general enquiry into what is just in the circumstances (*Axa Insurance Co. Ltd v Swire Fraser Ltd* [2000] CPLR 142; *Annodeus Entertainment Ltd v Gibson* (2000) *The Times*, 3 March 2000). When dealing with excusing delay in filing a defence, in *Thorn plc v Macdonald* [1999] CPLR 660, Brooke LJ and Robert Walker LJ applied the pre-CPR principles established in *Mortgage Corporation Ltd v Sandoes* [1997] PNLR 263 and *Finnegan v Parkside Health Authority* [1998] 1 WLR 411 (although it ought to be mentioned that these cases were decided with a view to the forthcoming implementation of the Woolf reforms).

Pre-CPR cases were applied as authoritative on striking out a claim with no basis (*Nomura International plc v Granada Group Ltd* [2007] EWHC 642 (Comm), [2008] Bus LR 1), on pleading practice (*Taranissi v British Broadcasting Corporation* [2008] EWHC 2486 (QB), LTL 24/10/2008), on the principles to be applied on applications for permission to amend (*Swain-Mason v Mills and Reeve LLP* [2011] EWCA Civ 14, [2011] 1 WLR 2735) and on the question whether a judge should withdraw after a premature disclosure of a Part 36 offer (*Garratt v Saxby* [2004] EWCA Civ 341,

[2004] 1 WLR 2152). The Court of Appeal in *Nasser v United Bank of Kuwait* [2001] EWCA Civ 556, [2002] 1 WLR 1868, said that the coming into force of the CPR meant that applications for security for costs are now governed by different principles, whereas in *Vedatech Corporation v Seagate Software Information* [2001] EWCA Civ 1924, LTL 29/11/2001, a differently constituted Court of

Appeal held that the judge below had been wrong in not applying a principle derived from pre-CPR case law.

Old cases as a guide to principle

Sometimes, it is entirely sensible to have regard to the old authorities. In *Harrison v Bloom Camillin* (1999) *The Independent*, 28 June 1999, Neuberger J said that although the court had to be careful in relying on old cases, in the context of the application he was dealing with (to set aside a witness summons) some regard was to be paid to the authorities under the old rules. Another example is *Hertfordshire Investments Ltd v Bubb* [2000] 1 WLR 2318, in which the Court of Appeal held that the principles set out in *Ladd v Marshall* [1954] 1 WLR 1489, concerning the reception of new evidence on appeal, continue to be relevant as factors which must be considered, rather than as strict rules (the court must also consider the overriding objective, *Gillingham v Gillingham* [2001] EWCA Civ 906, LTL 8/6/2001). 1.23

In *Nomura International plc v Granada Group Ltd* [2007] EWHC 642 (Comm), [2008] Bus LR 1, the claim form had been issued merely to protect the claimant's position at a time when the claimant had not decided to pursue a claim against the defendant. Cooke J reiterated the point that while pre-CPR authorities are not generally of relevance under the CPR, it is different where a CPR provision follows the same form and has the same intention as a provision in the RSC. In that situation the court should have regard to the principles that had informed the case law on the equivalent provision in the RSC. A similar approach was taken in *Adelson v Associated Newspapers Ltd* [2007] EWCA Civ 701, [2008] 1 WLR 585, in the context of an application to substitute a party after the expiry of limitation under **CPR, r. 19.5(3)(a)**. This gives effect to the Limitation Act 1980, s. 35, with the same intention as the old provision in RSC, ord. 20, r. 5. Post-CPR cases (*Morgan Est (Scotland) Ltd v Hanson Concrete Products Ltd* [2005] EWCA Civ 134, [2005] 1 WLR 2557; *Weston v Gribben* [2006] EWCA Civ 1425, [2007] CP Rep 10), which sought to lay down principles free of the pre-CPR case law, were doubted, and the court followed the principles laid down by the pre-CPR authorities. To the same effect is *City and Country Properties Ltd v Kamali* [2006] EWCA Civ 1879, [2007] 1 WLR 1219, in relation to the address for service of a defendant while temporarily out of the jurisdiction. The Court of Appeal overruled *Chellaram v Chellaram (No. 2)* [2002] EWHC 632 (Ch), [2002] 3 All ER 17, para. [47], as inconsistent with *Rolph v Zolan* [1993] 1 WLR 1305.

Reference to old rules and other procedural rules

Because the CPR are a new procedural code, the courts usually refuse to look at equivalent provisions in the RSC or CCR as an aid to interpretation. *Omega Engineering Inc. v Omega SA* [2003] EWHC 1482 (Ch), *The Times*, 29 September 2003, is an exception. **CPR, r. 3.1(2)(a)**, which provides a general power to extend or abridge time, was construed by reference to the equivalent provision in the RSC, to avoid an unnecessarily restrictive interpretation being placed on the present rule. A more striking example is *Carnegie v Giessen* [2005] EWCA Civ 191, [2005] 1 WLR 2510. In this case the Court of Appeal said that the pre-CPR **Queen's Bench Masters' Practice Direction (11)** (see **63.18**) is to be treated as remaining in effect, because the CPR do not contain express reference to the enforcement of judgments in foreign currency. 1.24

Adopting practice from family proceedings, which have a different procedural framework, is generally unsound (see *Roult v North West Strategic Health Authority* [2009] EWCA Civ 444, [2010] 1 WLR 487).

Rules of practice

1.25 As mentioned at **1.11**, there is a distinction between matters of procedure and matters of practice. Quite a few areas of practice have developed in a way that reflects the substantive law (such as the 'cheque rule' and the rules relating to set-offs in summary judgment applications, see **34.40** to **34.44**) or statutory provisions (such as the Senior Courts Act 1981, s. 37, on injunctions) which have not been changed by the introduction of the CPR. The practice in such areas has not been changed by the introduction of the CPR.

Unreported, unopposed and first-instance decisions

1.26 An important point is the extent to which the courts should look at unreported first-instance decisions on the procedure under the CPR and similar decisions reported in the legal periodicals. Often such reports are very short, they are often misleading when compared with the full transcripts, and there is also a worrying tendency for cases which are in fact contrary to the rules to be the subject of such reports. The danger in citing such cases, especially when they are at first instance, is that they can distract the court from applying the overriding objective and the spirit and intention of the CPR in general and the provisions that directly apply to a case. To combat this, Practice Direction (Citation of Authorities) [2001] 1 WLR 1001 prohibits the use of reports of applications attended by one party only, applications for permission to appeal, applications to decide whether the application is arguable, and county court cases (other than to illustrate damages or where no higher authorities are available). Excessive citation of authorities and reliance on summaries of cases which may not have been prepared by professional lawyers will not be tolerated (*Hamblin v Field* (2000) *The Times*, 26 April 2000).

APPLICATION OF THE OVERRIDING OBJECTIVE

Dealing with cases justly

1.27 The main concept in the overriding objective (**CPR, r. 1.1**) is that the primary concern of the court is to do justice. Ultimately the function of the court is to resolve issues between the parties. It does not have the power to dismiss a claim simply on the ground that the claim (or the issue left in a claim) has a relatively trivial value which will inevitably be exceeded by the costs (*Devaraja v Roy* [2008] EWHC 464 (QB), LTL 3/6/2008). Before the Jackson Reforms, shutting a litigant out through a technical breach of the rules was not regarded as consistent with doing justice, because the primary purpose of the civil courts is to decide cases on their merits, not to reject them for procedural default. An example of this is *Jones v Telford and Wrekin Council* (1999) *The Times*, 29 July 1999, where service had been delayed beyond the period of validity because the claimant's solicitors had problems in obtaining psychiatric reports for service with the particulars of claim. The Court of Appeal upheld an extension of time largely because there were no previous authorities dealing with this situation, Lord Woolf MR commenting that the court must not lose sight of the fact that its primary concern is doing justice.

In *Gilbart v Thomas Graham* [2008] EWCA Civ 897, LTL 24/6/2008, the Court of Appeal overturned a decision to refuse an adjournment of the trial date, in order to give effect to the overriding objective. The defendant had applied for the adjournment 21 days before the date for the trial, on realising that the claimant had not disclosed crucial documents. 21 days was an unrealistically short time for the defendant to obtain specific disclosure from the claimant and to instruct an expert on a loss of profits claim. In *Ratiopharm (UK) Ltd v Alza Corporation* [2008] EWHC 1182 (Ch), LTL 1/5/2008, six months was regarded as enough time to prepare a patent infringement claim for trial (the party seeking to avoid the trial date having received a letter with the allegations in the litigation 13 months before the trial date). Firmer case management control is called for where litigation has taken longer than might otherwise have been hoped for, and where there is a danger that costs will become disproportionate (*Multiplex Construction (UK) Ltd v Cleveland Bridge UK Ltd* [2008] EWHC 231 (TCC), LTL 9/5/2008). A stronger stance is expected following the reforms introduced on 1 April 2013, and there will be cases which are dismissed for procedural default, because courts do not exist for the purpose of providing justice at disproportionate cost.

In *Adan v Securicor Custodial Services Ltd* [2004] EWHC 394 (QB) [2005] PIQR P79 the claimant asked the court to use **r. 3.1(2)(i)** so that his claim for medical expenses in a personal injuries claim could be dealt with at a later date if and when the claimant was discharged from long-term hospital care. The application was refused as contrary to the overriding objective. It would have exposed the defendant's insurers to an uncertain liability for an indefinite period, which was oppressive and undesirable. Standing down witnesses in advance of an application for an adjournment was regarded as failing to act justly in *Albon v Naza Motor Trading Sdn Bhd (No. 5)* [2007] EWHC 2613 (Ch), [2008] 1 WLR 2380, because it precluded the court from determining the merits of the application.

In *Chilton v Surrey County Council* [1999] CPLR 525 the Court of Appeal indicated that dealing with a claim justly involved dealing with the real claim, and allowed the claimant to rely on a revised statement of past and future loss and expense quantifying the claim at about £400,000 rather than the original statement, which indicated a claim value of about £5,000.

In *Cala Homes (South) Ltd v Chichester District Council* (1999) 79 P & CR 430, the principle of dealing with cases justly was invoked in refusing to strike out a claim which was wrongly started in the Central Office of the High Court instead of in the Crown Office. A party who starts a claim using the wrong form, or relying on the wrong statutory provision, is likely to be granted permission to amend in order to deal with the claim justly (particularly if the defendants are not misled by the mistake) (*Thurrock Borough Council v Secretary of State for the Environment, Transport and the Regions* [2001] 1 PLR 94). In *Hannigan v Hannigan* [2000] 2 FCR 650, it was held that although proceedings were instituted using the wrong form, and although the form used contained numerous defects, the substance of the claim was fully known to the defendant. The administration of justice would have been better served had the defendants' solicitors pointed out the defects rather than attempted to take a technical point. *Re Osea Road Camp Sites Ltd* [2004] EWHC 2437 (Ch), [2005] 1 WLR 760, where proceedings were struck out because the claimant issued a claim form rather than presenting a petition, turns on the different code governing unfair prejudice petitions.

Even where one of a number of joint claimants makes a fraudulent claim, unless the fraud makes the trial unfair, dealing with the claim justly means that the other claimants should be awarded remedies in accordance with the evidence, rather than having their claims struck out (*Summers v Fairclough Homes Ltd* [2012] UKSC 26, [2012] 1 WLR 2004, and see the cases discussed at **33.14**). When a case is being considered on appeal, dealing with the case justly includes giving weight to the public interest in the finality of the decision at trial, see *Evans v Tiger Investments Ltd* [2002] EWCA Civ 161, [2002] 2 BCLC 185.

Proportionality: the rule

The overriding objective of dealing with cases justly is defined in terms that include ensuring **1.28**
that justice is achieved at proportionate cost. This is expanded by **CPR, r. 1.1(2)**, which provides that dealing with a case justly and at proportionate cost includes dealing with it in ways which are proportionate to the importance of the case (**r. 1.1(2)(c)(ii)**) and allotting to it an appropriate share of the court's resources, while taking into account the need to allot resources to other cases (**r. 1.1(2)(e)**). An assessment of the importance of the case appears to require consideration of factors other than the amount of money involved and the complexity of the issues, which are mentioned separately (**r. 1.1(2)(c)(i)** and **(iii)**) Proportionality in relation to costs includes considering any additional work generated by the conduct of the other party, and any wider factors, such as reputation and public importance (**r. 44.3(5)(d)** and **(e)**). It is

submitted that the importance which is to be considered may be either an exceptional significance to one of the parties or an importance to the public in general or a section of the public (for example, if it is a test case). The court resources to be considered will include not merely available finance but also the availability of judiciary or judicial time to deal with a case.

Proportionality and costs

1.29 With effect from 1 April 2013 a number of measures may be used by the courts to ensure litigation is conducted at proportionate cost as required by **CPR, r. 1.1(1)**. These include:

(a) making prospective costs capping orders (see **chapter 44**);
(b) making protective costs orders (see **chapter 44**);
(c) costs management in most multi-track claims (see **chapter 43**);
(d) the agreement or approval of costs budgets in most multi-track claims (see **chapter 43**);
(e) having regard to costs budgets when making case management decisions (see **chapter 42**);
(f) having regard to, or holding parties to, agreed or approved costs budgets when assessing costs (see **chapter 71**);
(g) assessing costs on the standard basis in accordance with **r. 44.3**, and disallowing or reducing costs which are disproportionate even if they were reasonably or necessarily incurred; and
(h) making wasted costs orders (see **68.64**).

Examples of case management decisions made before 1 April 2013 which were designed to keep costs proportionate include:

(i) permitting a defendant to file and serve a single defence to two related claims in order to save costs (*Rosenberg v Nazarov* [2008] EWHC 812 (Ch), LTL 10/4/2008);
(ii) making summary assessments of both sides' costs in a low-value case to avoid the costs that would have been incurred on a detailed assessment (*Gould v Armstrong* [2002] EWCA Civ 1159, LTL 23/7/2002).

Proportionality: examples

1.30 Proportionality lies at the heart of the rules on sanctions (see **chapter 48**), where the court aims to impose punishments which fit the crime. Thus, striking out for failing to file a pre-trial checklist and being late for a case management hearing was regarded as disproportionate in *Lambeth London Borough Council v Onayomake* [2007] EWCA Civ 1426, *The Times*, 2 November 2007. Setting aside an order granting permission to serve outside the jurisdiction on the ground that the claim form and witness statement were not signed was regarded as disproportionate in *Colliers International Property Consultants v Colliers Jordan Lee Jafaar Sdn Bhd* [2008] EWHC 1524 (Comm), [2008] 2 Lloyd's Rep 368. Proportionality may influence various case management decisions, such as limiting the issues to be tried, or even disallowing some issues entirely (see **42.43**). Likewise, proportionality may be taken into account in deciding to restrict the expert evidence the parties may call at trial (see **54.12**).

The need to conduct litigation efficiently and proportionately requires that routine case management decisions and other routine applications should be disposed of without hearings under **CPR, r. 23.8** (*Collier v Williams* [2006] EWCA Civ 20, [2006] 1 WLR 1945, at [29]). Pursuing allegations on collateral matters and events relied upon as similar fact evidence (see **49.74**) may, depending on the circumstances of the case and the probative value of the evidence, be disproportionate (*Guerrero v Monterrico Metals plc* [2010] EWHC 3228 (QB), LTL 20/12/2010).

The concept of proportionality will not be applied to prevent a party from instructing lawyers chosen by that party, even if it means one side is represented by far more eminent lawyers than the other (*Maltez v Lewis* (1999) *The Times*, 4 May 1999). Neuberger J said that the right to choose a legal representative, although not absolute, was a fundamental and well-established ingredient in any free society. In *Ali v Naseem* (2003) *The Times*, 3 October 2003, it was held that a writ *ne exeat regno* (see **38.42**) would only be granted if proportionate and necessary to secure the ends of justice. The importance of the proportionality principle was underlined by *South Bucks District Council v Porter* [2003] UKHL 26, [2003] 2 AC 558, where the House of Lords used the expression 'just and proportionate' to describe the circumstances in which an interim injunction should be granted rather than the conventional 'just and convenient' formula.

Equal footing

Ensuring the parties are on an equal footing is primarily concerned with the unfair exploitation of superior resources, rather than issues such as a failure to provide information (*Henry v News Group Newspapers Ltd* [2013] EWCA Civ 19, [2013] CP Rep 20). The case management powers of the court will be exercised so as to ensure, so far as possible, that where the parties have very different financial means the costs thought to be unreasonably incurred by the more affluent party should be paid by that party in any event. In *Maltez v Lewis* (1999) *The Times*, 4 May 1999, it was held that the court had the power to ensure a 'level playing field' by using its case management powers to allow a smaller firm more time, or to require a larger firm to prepare court bundles even though the responsibility would otherwise be that of the smaller firm. However, the fact that one party is better informed or better advised, or has stronger evidence than the other, will not normally justify a conclusion that a fair trial is not possible, or that there is an inequality of arms, unless the inequality is very substantial and very prejudicial (*Henley v Bloom* [2010] EWCA Civ 202, [2010] 1 WLR 1770). **1.31**

In *McPhilemy v Times Newspapers Ltd* [1999] 3 All ER 775 Lord Woolf MR said that a party which wanted the court to restrain the activities of another party with the object of achieving greater equality must demonstrate that it is itself conducting the proceedings with a desire to limit expense so far as practical. However, the powers of the court to restrain excess do not extend to preventing a party from putting forward allegations which are central to its case. That said, it is open to the court to attempt to control how those allegations are litigated with a view to limiting costs.

Ensuring the parties are on an equal footing is not an absolute requirement. For example, the tests on striking out and summary judgment will not be adjusted even where one party is suffering from an inequality of arms (*Bank of Tokyo-Mitsubishi UFJ Ltd v Baskan Gida Sanayi ve Pazarlama AS* [2008] EWHC 659 (Ch), LTL 17/4/2008). The requirement applies so far as practicable, and may be displaced by other considerations, such as proportionality or dealing with the case justly. This may result, for example, in one party being given permission to call more expert witnesses than the other side (*Kirkman v Euro Exide Corporation (CMP Batteries Ltd)* [2007] EWCA Civ 66, [2007] CP Rep 19). Putting the parties on an equal footing may mean that the court ought to allow a party to call more than one expert in a single area of expertise where the other side is able to deploy an independent witness and a number of factual witnesses who are professionally qualified (*ES v Chesterfield and North Derbyshire Royal Hospital NHS Trust* [2003] EWCA Civ 1284, [2004] Lloyd's Rep Med 90).

It is an elementary rule of the administration of justice that none of the parties to proceedings can communicate with the court without simultaneously alerting other parties to that fact (*R (Mohamed) v Secretary of State for Foreign and Commonwealth Affairs (No. 2)* [2010] EWCA Civ 158, [2011] QB 218 at [6]). Not providing the opposite party with a letter sent to the judge, and thereby failing to give the other side an opportunity to respond to it, was a serious procedural irregularity within the meaning of **CPR, r. 52.11(3)**, and a breach of the *audi alteram partem* principle (*National Westminster Bank plc v Rushmer* [2010] EWHC 554 (Ch), [2010] 2 FLR 362).

The case management powers of the court will be exercised so as to ensure, so far as possible, that where the parties have very different financial means the costs thought to be unreasonably incurred by the more affluent party should be paid by that party in any event. In *Maltez v Lewis* (1999) *The Times*, 4 May 1999, it was held that the court had the power to ensure a 'level playing field' by using its case management powers to allow a smaller firm more time, or to require a larger firm to prepare court bundles even though the responsibility would otherwise be that of the smaller firm. However, the fact that one party is better informed or better advised, or has stronger evidence than the other, will not normally justify a conclusion that a fair trial is not possible, or that there is an inequality of arms, unless the inequality is very substantial and very prejudicial (*Henley v Bloom* [2010] EWCA Civ 202, [2010] 1 WLR 1770).

In *McPhilemy v Times Newspapers Ltd* [1999] 3 All ER 775 Lord Woolf MR said that a party which wanted the court to restrain the activities of another party with the object of achieving greater equality, must demonstrate that it is itself conducting the proceedings with a desire to limit expense so far as practical. However, the powers of the court to restrain excess do not extend to preventing a party from putting forward allegations which are central to its case. That said, it is open to the court to attempt to control how those allegations are litigated with a view to limiting costs.

Dealing with cases expeditiously and saving expense

1.32 In *Cadogan Properties Ltd v Mount Eden Land Ltd* (1999) LTL 29/6/99 the court at first instance had made an order for substituted service in circumstances where there were no grounds for doing so. That order was set aside on appeal, with the result that proceedings had not been served and the period of validity had expired. The Court of Appeal relied on **CPR, r. 1.1(2)(d)**, and the need to deal with cases fairly and expeditiously, and also on the need for proportionality (**r. 1.1(2)(c)**), to justify making an order extending the validity of the originating process. The defendant was aware of the proceedings, and suffered no significant prejudice by the course adopted by the court. A court may refuse to hear the merits of an application on the ground of dealing with the case justly, expeditiously and economically where the application will bring no proportionate benefit to the claim as a whole (*Norwich Union Linked Life Assurance Ltd v Mercantile Credit Co. Ltd* [2003] EWHC 3064 (Ch), LTL 6/1/2004). Where appropriate and available, parties should use technology, such as videoconferencing, to reduce costs (*Black v Pastouna* [2005] EWCA Civ 1389, [2006] CP Rep 11). In *Re Hoicrest Ltd* [2000] 1 WLR 414 it was held that, because there was a dispute about crucial facts, the claimant's application under what is now the Companies Act 2006, s. 125, for rectification of a company's register of members, could not proceed under **CPR, Part 8**. The claimant had known all along about the factual dispute and it was his fault for starting the proceedings in the wrong way. The Court of Appeal held that the overriding objective would be furthered by actively managing the case, with appropriate directions, which would be likely to be more cost-effective than striking it out and requiring the claimant to start fresh proceedings. The court may, under its inherent jurisdiction, decline to continue with a trial which has been delayed by the court's own fault (*Re Rocksteady Services Ltd* [2001] BCC 467).

Allotting an appropriate share of the court's resources

1.33 In *S. B. J. Stephenson Ltd v Mandy* [1999] CPLR 500 the defendant appealed against an interim order restraining him from breaching a restrictive covenant in his contract of employment. The appeal against the interim order came before the Court of Appeal on 30 June, but the trial of the main proceedings had been fixed for 20 July. Given the short period before the trial and the fact that the claimant had given the usual undertaking in damages, the court decided that considering the merits of the appeal would not be in accordance with the overriding objective. Expense would not be saved by hearing the appeal, and, given the short time to trial, hearing the appeal would not be a good use of the court's resources.

An appeal was also dismissed (with costs on the indemnity basis) in *Adoko v Jemal* (1999) *The Times*, 8 July 1999, in very different circumstances, on the ground of allotting to it no more than an appropriate share of the court's resources. In this case the appellant had failed to correct the notice of appeal despite a warning from the respondent that it was seriously defective, and had failed to comply with the directions relating to appeal bundles. The Court of Appeal spent over an hour trying to sort out the position, and then decided it was inappropriate that any further share of the court's resources should be allocated to the appeal.

Cooperating

In *Chilton v Surrey County Council* [1999] CPLR 525, referred to above at **1.27**, the Court of Appeal decided against the defendant partly because it seemed to be attempting to take tactical advantage of a mistake by the claimant's solicitors in overlooking to serve the revised statement of past and future loss and expense rather than cooperating with the claimant's solicitors to put matters right. Similar reasoning informed *Hertsmere Primary Care Trust v Administrators of Balasubramanium's Estate* [2005] EWHC 320 (Ch), [2005] 3 All ER 274. The claimant made a Part 36 offer, and was then told by counsel for the defendant that the offer was defective. Despite requests, the defendant declined to explain why. Solicitors for the claimant wrote to ask why, but got no reply. It transpired there was an obvious, but technical, defect. The defendant's conduct was held to be a refusal to cooperate, and the court treated the offer as if it had been in the proper form. **1.34**

Even in litigation with serious allegations it is essential that the parties and their legal teams put to one side their understandable feelings of outrage and hostility and cooperate in the process of preparing the case for trial (*Lexi Holdings v Pannone and Partners* [2010] EWHC 1416 (Ch), LTL 21/6/2010). In *Hateley v Morris* [2004] EWHC 252 (Ch), [2004] 1 BCLC 582, a striking-out order made by the registrar was overturned on appeal despite an eight-month delay when neither side applied to relist a case management conference. One of the reasons given by the court was that either side could have relisted the matter, and both sides have a duty to cooperate in progressing proceedings.

PRACTICAL IMPACT

Culture

The civil justice system is essentially adversarial in nature, with the legal profession performing its traditional adversarial role in a managed environment governed by the courts. The CPR encourage cooperation between the parties in the preparation of cases for trial. The rules discourage the taking of technical points and obstructive tactics, and promote the identification and speedy trial of relevant issues only. The parties are required to exhibit openness and cooperation from the outset, to assist the expeditious resolution of their dispute. This requirement is supported by pre-action protocols, the need to consider ADR, and a system of judicial case management to scrutinise the conduct, cost, and progress of litigation. **1.35**

Case management

Judicial case management effectively removes control of the timescale of litigation from the parties. Procedural judges seek to identify the relevant issues at an early stage, and control the extent to which a party can inflate the costs of the litigation. Particular issues are the curtailment of the rights of parties to adduce expert evidence and to require others to disclose documents. The CPR require the parties to do a substantial amount of work investigating and disclosing information and documents early in the litigation process, and this results in the front-loading of costs. **1.36**

The cost of litigation should be affordable, predictable and proportionate to the value, or to the complexity, of individual cases. Proceedings are therefore allocated by the court to the small claims track, the fast track or the multi-track, depending on the complexity of the matters to be tried, and the amount in issue. These tracks have different timetables and pre-trial procedures. Small claims track cases (see **chapter 45**) are generally given directions requiring minimal pre-trial preparation, and early trial dates. In non-complex proceedings involving between £10,000 and £25,000 (which are allocated to the fast track, **chapter 46**), there are fixed timetables of no more than 30 weeks between track allocation and trial. Strict sanctions are normally applied to parties who do not comply with the procedures or timetables. More complex cases (assigned to the multi-track, **chapter** 47) usually require more judicial attention during the preparation stages, and there are usually a number of case management hearings to ensure they are prepared in an efficient manner. They are usually tried at civil trial centres which have the required resources, including specialist judges.

Active management of the more complex and substantial cases assigned to the multi-track requires practitioners to investigate the facts, research the legal principles and identify the issues at an earlier stage. At case management conferences the judge can ask searching questions about a party's case with the objective of narrowing the issues to be tried, and may eliminate minor issues which are of little or no relevance to the substance of the dispute. In all cases, litigation practitioners must comply with a rigorous timetable, with a regime of real sanctions on default.

Role of the client

1.37 Even if a solicitor is retained, clients have a number of rights and obligations under the CPR. All statements of case must be verified by a statement of truth, declaring the belief of the party that the contents are true and accurate (see **23.13** to **23.17**). A party giving disclosure (**chapter 50**) is required to make a statement setting out the extent of the search which has been made to locate documents which he is required to disclose, and certifying that he understands his duty to disclose and that to the best of his knowledge he has complied with that duty (**CPR, r. 31.10(6)**). The court may order that a judgment or order be served on a party in person as well as any solicitor acting for the party (**r. 40.5**). A solicitor is under a duty to notify a client against whom a costs order is made, if the client was not present when the costs order was made (**r. 44.2**). When deciding what order to make in respect of costs, the court should have regard not only to which party succeeded, but also to the conduct of the parties, including the manner in which a claim was pursued or defended, and whether a claim was exaggerated (**r. 44.3(4)**). Additionally, the conduct of the parties before, as well as during, the proceedings, and efforts made, if any, before or during the proceedings to resolve the dispute, are factors to be taken into account in deciding the amount of costs (**r. 44.3(5)**).

Close involvement of clients in solicitors' work is one of the objectives of the SRA Code of Conduct 2011. A solicitor is obliged to ensure clients are in a position to make informed decisions about the services they need and the options open to them (O 1.12) and receive the best possible information about the likely overall cost of a case (O 1.13). Solicitors should also discuss with the client whether the likely outcome justifies the expense or risk (including the risk of paying the other side's costs). Solicitors must also give their clients a clear explanation of the issues raised, and keep them properly informed about progress in the case.

Role of the solicitor

1.38 The Legal Services Act 2007, s. 188(2), provides that any person exercising a right of audience before any court has 'a duty to the court to act with independence in the interests of justice' and that the duty 'shall override' any other obligation with which it is inconsistent (other than an obligation under the criminal law) (s. 188(3)). Further, the SRA Code of Conduct 2011, O 5.1, requires that a solicitor must not attempt to deceive or knowingly or recklessly mislead the court. If a solicitor is instructed by a client to conduct a case without regard to the overriding objective of the CPR (such as a well-heeled client instructing his solicitor to incur dis*proportionate expenditure* when acting against a client of limited means), the solicitor must warn the client of the potential sanctions in costs that may be incurred as a result. There will be an infringement of the duty in **CPR, r. 1.3**, to assist the court to further the overriding objective if a solicitor advances a case which the solicitor does not regard as properly arguable (*Richard Buxton v Mills-Owen* [2010] EWCA Civ 122, [2010] 1 WLR 1997). If the client insists on the unarguable case being advanced, the solicitor will have a good reason for terminating the retainer (see **22.6**).

Role of the barrister

A barrister is under a similar duty to 'assist the court in the administration of justice and must not deceive or knowingly or recklessly mislead the court' (Code of Conduct of the Bar of England and Wales, para. 302). **1.39**

Confidentiality and the overriding objective

Conflict may occur between the overriding objective and the duty of a practitioner not to disclose confidential information. For example, **CPR, r. 29.3(2)**, provides for a representative to attend a case management conference 'with sufficient authority to deal with any issues that are likely to arise'. During a case management conference, it is possible that the court may seek information, the disclosure of which would involve a waiver of privilege. The court may well ask about the costs expended to date, the relative financial standing of the parties (one of the issues to be taken into account in meeting the overriding objective), and details of the funding arrangements for the litigation. It is clear the court does not have power to order a representative to disclose privileged information (see **50.53**), but there is an obvious tension between obtaining information for active case management purposes and client confidentiality. If the client is not to attend the case management conference, specific authority will be required to disclose the information which is likely to be sought. **1.40**

Advice to clients

It is important that every client should be advised at an early stage, not only about the general duties to promote the overriding objective, but also other matters, including: **1.41**

(a) the wide-ranging costs and interest sanctions available to the court (see **chapter 48**);
(b) the client's duty in relation to a statement of truth (see **23.15**);
(c) the client's duties of search in relation to disclosure of documents (see **50.4**, **50.13** and **50.15**);
(d) the duties to the court of an expert witness (see **54.10**).

Chapter 2 Court Organisation

INTRODUCTION

2.1 Civil proceedings in England and Wales may be conducted in magistrates' courts, county courts and the High Court. Magistrates' courts have only limited jurisdiction in relation to civil matters, and will not be considered further in *Blackstone's Civil Practice.* Appeals in civil matters are taken to the Court of Appeal, Civil Division, and the Supreme Court of the United Kingdom (before October 2009, the House of Lords). Appeals are considered in **chapters** 74 to 76. A wide range of civil disputes are also determined by various tribunals, including employment tribunals and the various chambers of the First-Tier Tribunal, which have their own rules of procedure and will not be considered further in this book.

This chapter looks at the composition and organisation of the High Court and the county courts and considers the different court personnel and their powers. The rules governing venue, allocation of business and transfer between the High Court and the county courts are dealt with in **chapter 11**.

COUNTY COURTS

2.2 The county courts derive their jurisdiction and powers from statute, principally the County Courts Act 1984. There are about 180 county courts in England and Wales, each exercising its powers for a limited geographical district (County Courts Act 1984, s. 1). The Court Finder at the Ministry of Justice website, https://courttribunalfinder.service.gov.uk/, provides a complete list of all county courts with contact details and location maps. For administrative purposes, certain county courts have been designated as civil trial centres at which multi-track cases for their areas will be heard. County courts within the group area which are not civil trial centres are called satellite courts. Each civil trial centre is presided over by a designated civil judge, who is a circuit judge responsible for the effective organisation of each civil trial centre and its satellite courts. Although it was originally envisaged that all multi-track cases would be remitted from satellite courts to the civil trial centre for case management and hearing, some multi-track cases, in particular, possession cases, will remain with the satellite court.

The Crime and Courts Act 2013, s. 17 and sch. 9, amend the County Courts Act 1984 to create a single County Court for England and Wales. It is expected that this will be brought into force in 2014–15.

The principal judicial officers of the county courts are circuit judges and district judges. Circuit judges must be solicitors or barristers of at least seven years' standing and with at least seven years' relevant legal experience (see Courts Act 1971, s. 16). Most (but not all) circuit judges sit in the Crown Court as well as the county courts, and may be supplemented by recorders, who are part-time judges and who, with limited exceptions, exercise the full powers of a circuit judge (County Courts Act 1984, s. 5(3)). Circuit judges conduct most county court trials, sitting alone, and also hear appeals from decisions of district judges. It is preferred for such appeals to be heard by a full-time rather than part-time judge, but this is not always possible.

A circuit judge or recorder may be specifically requested (or 'ticketed'), under the Senior Courts Act 1981, s. 9, to sit in the High Court (see **2.7**) or, under s. 68, in the Technology and Construction Court (see **2.16**). Where a circuit judge, without being aware she was not duly authorised, heard a High Court case which had not been properly released to her for trial, there was an error of procedure falling within **CPR, r. 3.10** (*Fawdry and Co. v Murfitt* [2002] EWCA Civ 643, [2003] QB 104). The court applied the de facto doctrine, which is that a person who has acted as a judicial tribunal while believing him or herself to have the necessary judicial authority, and who is believed by the parties to have that authority, is regarded in law as possessing the authority. This meant the error could be remedied, and the result of the trial would stand unless the appeal court so ordered. The result would have been different if the judge had known she was not authorised to hear the case. *Fawdry and Co. v Murfitt* was applied in *Coppard v Commissioners of Customs and Excise* [2003] EWCA Civ 511, [2003] QB 1428, in which it was held that the de facto doctrine does not offend against the European Convention on Human Rights, **art. 6(1)**. *Fawdry and Co. v Murfitt and Coppard v Commissioners of Customs and Excise* were both applied in *Baldock v Webster* [2004] EWCA Civ 1869, [2006] QB 315, in which the de facto doctrine was invoked to uphold the decision of a recorder at the trial of a High Court case which he had not been authorised to hear under the Senior Courts Act 1981, s. 9, and which he had dealt with in the mistaken belief that it was proceeding in the county court.

District judges, who must be solicitors or barristers of at least five years' standing and with at least five years' relevant legal experience (County Courts Act 1984, s. 9), deal with most interim applications made in the county courts, and normally try all small claims track, and many fast track cases. The allocation of business to different levels of judiciary in the county courts is dealt with in **2.3** to **2.6**.

The correct mode of address for circuit judges and recorders is 'Your Honour'. District judges are addressed as 'Sir' or 'Madam'. Full-time judiciary are addressed as 'Judge', when not formally sitting in court, or in private.

The administrative staff of the county courts are civil servants. They are headed by the court manager and correspondence with the court is usually addressed to that official. The administrative staff draw up and issue court documents, and arrange for them to be served. They also maintain court records.

The county court bailiff is responsible for enforcing judgments by process of execution and serving documents personally. Unlike the High Court enforcement officer, a county court bailiff is a civil servant.

County courts are usually open to the public between 10.00 a.m. and 4.00 p.m., although precise times do vary. Exact times are published in the Court Finder section of Her Majesty's Courts and Tribunals Service website http://hmctscourtfinder.justice.gov.uk/HMCTS/FormFinder.do. The county courts are open every day of the year except weekends, bank holidays and one or two other days specified in **PD 2A, para. 3.2** (the same days as those on which the Senior Courts are closed; see 2.7).

Allocation of business to levels of judiciary in the county courts

2.3 **Trials** Circuit judges may exercise the full powers of the county court. By **PD 2B, para. 11.1**, district judges can deal with all small claims and fast track cases, and may also hear cases for the recovery of land, the assessment of damages, and Part 8 claims allocated to the multi-track (with some exceptions listed in **PD 2B, para. 11.1(a)**). Other claims may be allocated to a district judge only with the permission of the designated civil judge (**PD 2B, para. 11.1(d)**). Cases allocated to the small claims track may only be assigned to a circuit judge with his or her consent (**PD 2B, para. 11.2**). A district judge may not try a case in which an allegation of indirect discrimination is made against a public authority under the Race Relations Act 1976, s. 19B (which made it unlawful for a public authority to perform a discriminatory act in carrying out its functions but has been repealed and replaced by the Equality Act 2010) (**PD 2B, para. 15**).

2.4 **Injunctions, anti-social behaviour injunctions and committal** A district judge may grant an injunction:

(a) in any proceedings which he or she has jurisdiction to hear under **PD 2B, para. 11.1** (see 2.3) (**PD 2B, para. 8.1(a)**);
(b) in a money claim which has not yet been allocated to a track, provided the amount claimed is not greater than the fast track limit of £25,000 (**PD 2B, para. 8.1(b); CPR, r. 26.6(4)(b)**);
(c) in terms agreed by the parties (**PD 2B, paras 2.3(a)** and **8.1(c)**);
(d) in connection with or ancillary to a charging order (**PD 2B, paras 2.3(b)** and **8.1(c)**);
(e) in connection with or ancillary to an order appointing a receiver by way of equitable execution (**PD 2B, paras 2.3(c)** and **8.1(c)**);
(f) in proceedings under **CPR, r. 66.7** (an order restraining a person from receiving a sum due from the Crown) (**PD 2B, paras 2.3(d)** and **8.1(c)**);
(g) under the Housing Act 1996, ss. 153A, 153B or 153D (anti-social behaviour injunctions), the Protection from Harassment Act 1997, s. 3 (an order restraining a person from conduct which amounts to harassment) or the Policing and Crime Act 2009, ss. 34, 40 or 41 (injunctions to prevent gang-related violence) (**PD 2B, para. 8.1(d)**).

Otherwise only a circuit judge may grant an injunction in a county court (**PD 2B, para. 8.1**).

A district judge cannot make a committal order to punish breach of an injunction unless authorised by statute (**PD 2B, para. 8.3**, which lists provisions giving such authority; see also **85.11**). It is preferable for committal applications to be heard by a circuit judge rather than a recorder, but this is not always possible.

The limited statutory powers to attach a power of arrest to certain types of injunction, and to remand persons arrested, can be exercised by a district judge where authorised by the relevant enactment (**PD 2B, para. 8.3**; see, e.g., **88.11**).

A district judge may also make anti-social behaviour orders under the Crime and Disorder Act 1998, s. 1B or 1D, parenting orders under the Anti-social Behaviour Act 2003, s. 26A, 26B or 26C and drinking banning orders under the Violent Crime Reduction Act 2006, s. 4 or 9 (**PD 2B, para. 8.1A**).

A district judge will normally hear a claim brought under **PD 8B** and the **Pre-action Protocol for Low Value Personal Injury Claims in Road Traffic Accidents** (**PD 8B, para. 1.2**).

Distribution of business between circuit and district judges Where both circuit and district judges have jurisdiction, the designated civil judge may make arrangements distributing business between them, including assigning particular cases to individual district judges (**PD 2B, paras 13 and 14**). 2.5

Case management By virtue of **PD 29, para. 3.10**, a district judge or a circuit judge may deal with case management issues in respect of cases proceeding in the county courts. 2.6

HIGH COURT

With the introduction of the United Kingdom Supreme Court to take over the judicial work of the House of Lords on 1 October 2009, the former Supreme Court of England and Wales is now known as the Senior Courts of England and Wales. 2.7

The High Court is one part of the Senior Courts of England and Wales. The other parts are the Crown Court, the Senior Courts Costs Office and the Court of Appeal. The High Court's main administrative offices and court facilities are located at the Royal Courts of Justice (RCJ), Strand, London. In addition, there are about 130 district registries, which are established by the Senior Courts Act 1981, ss. 99 to 102. Each registry serves the districts of the county courts listed in the Civil Courts Order 1983 (SI 1983/713), as amended.

Most trials in the High Court are conducted by High Court judges (puisne judges), who must either be practitioners of at least seven years' standing and with at least seven years' relevant legal experience or have been a circuit judge for at least two years (Senior Courts Act 1981, s. 10). Most interim applications are dealt with in the RCJ by judicial officers known as masters, or by district judges in cases proceeding in the district registries. The allocation of business to different levels of judiciary in the High Court is dealt with in detail in **2.8** to **2.13** below.

Under the Senior Courts Act 1981, s. 9(1) and (2), the Lord Chief Justice may request a circuit judge or recorder to act as a High Court judge: when so acting such a judge is informally known as a section 9 judge. A request may be made only after consulting the Lord Chancellor (s. 9(2B)) and only with the concurrence of the Judicial Appointments Commission (s. 9(2D)). The Lord Chief Justice, after consulting the Lord Chancellor, may appoint as a deputy High Court judge, for a certain period or to sit on certain occasions, any person who is qualified for appointment as a puisne judge (s. 9(4)).

High Court district judges often also hold the office of district judge for the local county court. Masters and district judges must be practitioners of at least five years' standing and with at least five years' relevant legal experience (Senior Courts Act 1981, s. 88 and sch. 2).

The correct mode of address for a High Court judge is 'My Lord' or 'My Lady'. Masters are addressed as 'Master'. District judges are addressed as 'Sir' or 'Madam'.

As in the county court, the administrative work of the High Court is performed by civil servants. Enforcement is conducted by enforcement officers who are self-employed practitioners.

The High Court consists of three Divisions, namely the Chancery Division, the Family Division and the Queen's Bench Division. Each High Court judge is attached to a particular Division, by direction of the Lord Chief Justice under the Senior Courts Act 1981, s. 5(2), but may occasionally act as an additional judge of another Division, by direction of the Lord Chief Justice under s. 5(3). Under s. 5(1)(a), the Chancellor of the High Court is president of the Chancery Division. Under s. 5(1)(b), the Lord Chief Justice is a judge of the Queen's Bench Division by virtue of his office and there are also a president and a vice-president of that Division. There is a president of the Family Division (s. 5(1)(c)). Each

Commentary

Division has its own administrative offices for issuing claim forms, arranging interim hearings and trials and for dealing with enforcement. Further, specialist courts exist within the Queen's Bench Division and the Chancery Division to deal with particular classes of cases. These include the Admiralty Court, the Commercial Court, and the Technology and Construction Court in the Queen's Bench Division and the Companies Court and the Patents Court in the Chancery Division (see further **2.15** to **2.21**). Each of these specialist courts also has its own judges and administrative offices. In addition, public law matters, particularly applications for judicial review, are dealt with separately in the Administrative Court (see **2.22**).

By **PD 2A, para. 2.1(1)**, the offices of the Senior Courts are open on every day of the year except:

(a) Saturdays and Sundays;
(b) Good Friday;
(c) Christmas Day;
(d) a further day over the Christmas period determined in accordance with the table annexed to **PD 2A** which is based on the day of the week on which Christmas Day falls and is designed to ensure consistency between the various civil courts round the country;
(e) Bank Holidays in England and Wales under the Banking and Financial Dealings Act 1971; and
(f) such other days as the Lord Chancellor, with the concurrence of the Heads of Division, may direct.

Opening hours for the offices of the Senior Courts at the Royal Courts of Justice and Rolls Building are 10.00 a.m. to 4.30 p.m. and such other hours as the Lord Chancellor, with the concurrence of the Heads of Division may direct (**PD 2A, para. 2.1(2)**). Opening hours for a district registry are (in the absence of any specific direction from the Lord Chancellor) the same as those for the county court offices of which it forms part (see **2.2**) (**PD 2A, para. 2.1(3)**).

Allocation of cases to different levels of the judiciary in the High Court

2.8 **Paragraphs** 2 to 7A of **PD 2B** state how hearings are allocated between the different levels of the judiciary in the High Court. **PD 2B** does not apply to proceedings in the Family Division, save to the extent that they can also be dealt with in the Chancery Division (**PD 2B, para. 3.2**).

2.9 **Trials** Masters and district judges have the power to try Part 8 claims (subject to **PD 2B, para. 5.1(d)** — see **2.11**), but may not try other cases allocated to the multi-track, or determine a preliminary issue in a multi-track claim, except with the consent of the parties (**PD 2B, para. 4.1**). This does not prevent masters and district judges from hearing applications for summary judgment, or from assessing damages (**PD 2B, paras 4.1** and **4.2**). A bankruptcy registrar has jurisdiction to make third party debt orders (*Thakerar v Lynch Hall and Hornby (No. 2)* [2005] EWHC 2752 (Ch), [2006] 1 WLR 1513).

Deputy High Court judges, masters and district judges cannot try claims under the **Human Rights Act 1998** in respect of judicial acts or for declarations of incompatibility (**PD 2B, para. 7A**).

2.10 **Injunctions and interim remedies** Applications for injunctions, orders for specific performance, freezing injunctions (including orders for disclosure of assets which may become the subject of an application for a freezing injunction), search orders and orders authorising entry on to land to recover, inspect or sample property must be made to a judge (**PD 2B, paras. 2.1 and 2.2**). Masters and district judges may grant ordinary injunctions in terms agreed by the parties, or connected to charging orders or a receivership by way of equitable execution or in proceedings under **CPR, r. 66.7(3)**, (an order restraining a person from receiving a sum due from the Crown) (**PD 2B, para. 2.3**). Examinations made under freezing orders will usually be dealt with by a master or district judge, or before an examiner they have appointed (**PD 2B, para. 7**). **PD 2B, para. 3.1**, lists a number of orders a master or district judge may not make. These include orders relating to the liberty of a subject, and relating to judicial review claims (except that Queen's Bench Division masters may make orders on interim applications in judicial review claims).

Masters of the Crown Office or Administrative Court have power under **PD 2B, para 3.1A** to make interim orders in judicial review proceedings (including judicial review proceedings relating to criminal cases, extradition appeals, and applications to vary bail conditions provided in the latter case the prosecutor consents), costs orders in judicial review cases and orders in applications under the Senior Courts Act 1981, s. 42, for permission to start or continue a judicial review claim.

Chancery proceedings **PD 2B, para. 5.1**, contains a list of Chancery applications that must be dealt with by a judge rather than a master or district judge, unless the Chancellor of the High Court consents. These include approving compromises on behalf of a person under a disability, where the value of the claim exceeds £100,000; hearing Part 8 claims to determine a question of law or the construction of a document; and making final orders under the Landlord and Tenant Acts 1927 and 1954, except by consent or for interim rents under ss. 24A to 24D of the 1954 Act. The list also includes orders in Patents Court proceedings, except for a number of largely procedural matters such as orders for extensions of time (**PD 2B, para. 5.1(k)**). 2.11

Assignment of claims to masters and transfers between masters **PD 2B, para. 6**, empowers the Senior Master and Chief Master to assign claims in the RCJ to individual masters, or to transfer an assigned case from one master to another. The fact that a case has been assigned to one master does not prevent it being dealt with by another master, where necessary. 2.12

Case management By virtue of **PD 29, para. 3.10**, masters will generally deal with case management issues in respect of cases proceeding in the RCJ, and district judges in respect of cases proceeding in the district registries. 2.13

High Court Divisions

Business is allocated between the three High Court Divisions by the Senior Courts Act 1981, s. 61 and sch. 1. However, the jurisdiction of the High Court is exercisable by all three Divisions alike (Senior Courts Act 1981, s. 5(5)). Thus, business not specifically allocated to a particular Division may be dealt with by any. In practice, the Divisions have developed their own areas of expertise. The broad position is as follows: 2.14

(a) The Queen's Bench Division is usually the most appropriate Division for dealing with claims seeking common law remedies (debt, damages, recovery of land, recovery of goods), including most claims in contract and tort. It will deal, for example, with all personal injury and clinical negligence claims proceeding in the High Court. The Queen's Bench Division has been assigned all cases involving applications for writs of habeas corpus (save those relating to a child, which would be dealt with by the Family Division), applications for judicial review, the proceedings specified in s 30(1)c of the Terrorism Prevention and Investigation Measures Act 2011, financial restrictions proceedings under the Counter-Terrorism Act 2008, s. 65, and Admiralty claims and claims being dealt with in the Commercial Court (Senior Courts Act 1981, sch. 1).

(b) The Chancery Division sits in the Rolls Building. It has been assigned all cases involving the sale, exchange or partition of land; mortgages; execution of trusts; administration of estates; bankruptcy; taking of partnership accounts; rectification etc. of deeds; probate; intellectual property; the appointment of a guardian of a child's estate; and applications under the enactments relating to companies (Senior Courts Act 1981, sch. 1). It can also deal with other areas, such as actions in contract and tort not specifically assigned to other divisions. Any claim which raises an issue under the EC Treaty, art. 81 (anti-competitive agreements) or art. 82 (abuse of a dominant market position) (now the Treaty on the Functioning of the European Union, arts 101 and 102), or the equivalent United Kingdom statutory provisions, chapter 1 or chapter 2 of part 1 of the Competition Act 1998, which is not proceeding in the Commercial or Admiralty Court must be transferred to the Chancery Division at the RCJ (**CPR, r. 30.8**). For more information on Chancery business see **11.6**.

(c) The Family Division has been assigned all matrimonial matters; matters relating to children, such as adoption, legitimacy and guardianship; non-contentious probate business; and application for parental orders under the Human Fertilisation and Embryology Act 1990, s. 30, or under the Human Fertilisation and Embryology Act 2008 (Senior Courts Act 1981, sch. 1). Proceedings which invoke the jurisdiction of the High Court to grant declarations as to the best interests of incapacitated adults (such as permanent vegetative state cases and sterilisation of persons unable to give consent) are civil proceedings to which the CPR apply. Although they are not allocated to any Division, they are more suitable for the Family Division (Practice Direction (Declaratory Proceedings: Incapacitated Adults) [2002] 1 WLR 325). Cases about the best interests of children are also to be litigated by claims for declaratory relief in the Family Division (*A v A Health Authority* [2002] EWHC 18 (Fam/Admin), [2002] Fam 213). Cases which only involve issues of public law, even though they are concerned with the welfare of children or incompetent adults, are properly litigated by way of a claim for judicial review in the Administrative Court (*A v A Health Authority*). Human rights challenges to care plans and placements of children should be heard in the Family Division, preferably by judges with experience of administrative law (*C v Bury Metropolitan Borough Council* [2002] EWHC 1438 (Fam), [2002] 2 FLR 868). The procedure relating to family matters is not considered in this book.

SPECIALIST COURTS

2.15 Within the High Court there are several specialist courts which deal with special types of claim. Some of these courts have issued guides to their own procedure. These court guides can be seen at the Ministry of Justice website, http://www.justice.gov.uk.

The jurisdiction of these specialist courts is dealt with at **11.7**. The types of case suitable for the specialist courts, and a brief outline of the procedure to be followed in them is set out below.

Technology and Construction Court

2.16 The Technology and Construction Court (TCC) sits in the Rolls Building. It consists of judges and other officers nominated under the Senior Courts Act 1981, s. 68, to exercise the jurisdiction of the High Court in TCC claims, as defined in **CPR, r. 60.1**. Nomination is by the Lord Chief Justice after consulting the Lord Chancellor. **CPR, Part 60**, and **PD 60** set out the practice relating to TCC claims. They are supplemented by the Technology and Construction Court Guide, revised on 1 October 2010. All TCC cases started in or transferred to London will be classified as suitable for determination either by a High Court judge or a senior circuit judge, and will be allocated accordingly (Technology and Construction Court Guide, para 3.7). Parties may make brief representations by letter as to the appropriate classification (para. 3.7.3). The TCC deals with technically complex matters, with particular emphasis on construction cases. TCC claims in the High Court outside London may be issued in any district registry, but preferably in one where a TCC judge will usually be available, namely, Birmingham, Bristol, Cardiff, Chester, Exeter, Leeds, Liverpool, Manchester, Mold, Newcastle upon Tyne and Nottingham (**PD 60, para. 3.3**). The county courts in which a TCC claim may be issued are Birmingham, Bristol, Cardiff, Central London, Chester, Exeter, Leeds, Liverpool, Manchester, Mold, Newcastle upon Tyne and Nottingham (**PD 60, para. 3.4**).

A claim in the TCC will be assigned to a named TCC judge who will have primary responsibility for the case management of the claim (**PD 60, para. 6.1**). The trial will usually be conducted by the assigned judge (**para. 11.1**).

Commercial Court

The Commercial Court is part of the Queen's Bench Division and sits in the Rolls Building. The judges of the Commercial Court are High Court judges who are nominated to be commercial judges (Senior Courts Act 1981, s. 6). Nomination is by the Lord Chief Justice after consulting the Lord Chancellor. **CPR, Part 58**, and **PD 58** govern proceedings in the Commercial Court. The Commercial Court hears commercial claims, as defined in **CPR, r. 58.1** (Senior Courts Act 1981, s. 62(3)). Claim forms should be marked with the words 'Queen's Bench Division, Commercial Court' (**PD 58, para. 2.3**). All claims in the commercial list are allocated to the multi-track and therefore the rules relating to directions questionnaires and track allocation do not apply to them (**CPR, r. 58.13(1)**), and generally all pre-trial applications are dealt with by a High Court judge, rather than by a master or district judge (**PD 58, para. 1.3**). The Admiralty and Commercial Courts have published a guide which is designed to ensure effective management of proceedings in the Commercial Court, without prejudice to provisions of the CPR and practice directions. A new edition of the Admiralty and Commercial Courts Guide was published in April 2011. **2.17**

Admiralty Court

The Admiralty Court, which sits in the Rolls Building, is the part of the Queen's Bench Division which exercises the High Court's Admiralty jurisdiction, as defined in the Senior Courts Act 1981, s. 20, and the High Court's jurisdiction as a prize court (s. 62(2)). The judges of the Admiralty Court are High Court judges who are nominated to be Admiralty judges (s. 6). Nomination is by the Lord Chief Justice after consulting the Lord Chancellor. All Admiralty proceedings must be commenced in the High Court (Civil Courts (Amendment) (No. 2) Order 1999 (SI 1999/1011)). **CPR, Part 58** (Commercial Court), applies to claims in the Admiralty Court except where **Part 61** provides otherwise (**r. 61.1(3)**). **CPR, Parts 58** and **61**, and **PD 61**, are the principal sources for the practice of the Admiralty Court and are supplemented by the Admiralty and Commercial Courts Guide. A new edition of the Admiralty and Commercial Courts Guide was published in April 2011. **2.18**

Mercantile Courts

A commercial or business claim, in a broad sense, not specifically required to be brought in the Chancery Division or another specialised court may be brought in one of the Mercantile Courts (**CPR, r. 59.1(2)**), but only if it will benefit from the expertise of one of the judges (known as Mercantile judges: **r. 59.1(3)**) authorised to sit in Mercantile Courts (**PD 59, para. 2.1**). Thus, the ambit of mercantile claims is wider than that of commercial claims. There are Mercantile Courts in the Birmingham, Bristol, Cardiff, Chester, Leeds, Liverpool, Manchester, Mold, and Newcastle upon Tyne district registries of the High Court. There is also a Mercantile List in the Commercial Court of the Queen's Bench Division at the Royal Courts of Justice, **2.19** called the London Mercantile Court. A claim proceeding in a Mercantile Court is known as a mercantile claim (**CPR, r. 59.1(3)**). Procedure in the Mercantile Courts is governed by **CPR, Part 59**, and **PD 59**. The Mercantile Courts have published an overall guide to their procedure (*The Mercantile Court Guide* 2012). This largely adopts the Admiralty and Commercial Courts Guide, although the procedure is simpler as befits the size, value and type of case commonly heard in the Mercantile Courts. It is available at the Ministry of Justice website, http://www.justice.gov.uk. (The guide is incorrectly referred to as the 'London Mercantile Court Guide' in the link on the Ministry of Justice website. In fact it applies to Mercantile Court proceedings both in and outside London.)

Companies Court

2.20 The Companies Court, which sits in the Rolls Building, is part of the Chancery Division and exercises the High Court's jurisdiction under the enactments relating to companies, including petitions and applications under the Companies Acts and the Insolvency Act 1986 (see **chapters 82, 84, 85** and **86**).

Patents Court

2.21 The Patents Court sits in the Rolls Building. It hears patents cases within the jurisdiction conferred on it by the Patents Act 1977 (Senior Courts Act 1981, s. 62(1)). Patents and other intellectual property claims are governed by **CPR, Part 63**, and **PD 63**, supplemented by the Patents Court Guide. Patents cases are dealt with either in the Patents Court of the Chancery Division or a patents county court (**CPR, r. 63.2(2)**). Claims under the Trade Marks Act 1994 and other intellectual property rights set out in **PD 63, para. 16.1**, must be started in the Chancery Division, a patents county court or a county court where there is also a Chancery district registry. (These are the courts at Birmingham, Bristol, Caernarfon, Cardiff, Leeds, Liverpool, Manchester, Mold, Newcastle upon Tyne, and Preston, although the courts at Caernarfon, Mold, and Preston have no jurisdiction in relation to registered or Community trade marks.) The judges of the Patents Court in the Chancery Division are High Court judges who are nominated to be patents judges (Senior Courts Act 1981, s. 6). Nomination is by the Lord Chief Justice after consulting the Lord Chancellor.

Administrative Court

2.22 The Administrative Court is the part of the Queen's Bench Division which hears judicial review proceedings, which are governed by **CPR, Part 54**, and **PD 54A**, **PD 54C** and **PD 54D**. There is detailed consideration of judicial review proceedings in **chapter 77**. The Administrative Court also hears habeas corpus applications and some appeals in criminal cases.

Chapter 3 Computing Time

APPLICATION OF THE RULES

CPR, rr. 2.8 to **2.11**, deal with calculating time. **Rule 2.8** (see 3.2, 3.3 and 3.5) applies to periods of time specified by the CPR, any practice direction or any judgment or order of the court. **Rules 2.9** (see 3.6) and **2.10** (see 3.4) apply to any judgment, order, direction or document, but not to the CPR or to practice directions. **Rule 2.11** (see 3.7) applies to a time specified in the CPR or by the court, but is not relevant to practice directions. 3.1

Rules 2.8 and **2.9** apply when calculating the time for 'doing any act' specified in the documents or court orders to which they apply. It was held in *Anderton v Clwyd County Council (No. 2)* [2002] EWCA Civ 933, [2002] 1 WLR 3174, that they do not apply when calculating a time which is not a time by which an act is to be done. **Rules 2.8** and **2.9** therefore apply to calculations of time for doing acts such as filing statements of case, serving application notices, complying with mandatory orders, and most other steps required by the CPR, practice directions and court orders. They do not, however, apply to calculating deemed dates of service, because nothing is to be 'done' by the deemed date.

Rules 2.8 and **2.9** also do not apply to the computation of statutory time limits (see, for example, *Hinde v Rugby Borough Council* [2011] EWHC 3684 (Admin), LTL 3/11/2011). The construction of the time limit will depend on the exact wording of the statute. Thus it was held in *Barker v Hambleton District Council* [2012] EWCA Civ 610, [2012] CP Rep 36, that a statutory time limit which read that an application 'must be made within six weeks from the relevant date' meant that the first day to be counted was the day after the relevant date. This was to be distinguished from a period for doing an act 'starting with' the relevant day, in which case the first day to be counted was the relevant day itself.

DAYS

Clear days

A period of time, for doing an act, expressed as a number of days must be computed as 'clear days' (**CPR, r. 2.8(2)**). This means that if an act must be done a specified number of days before an event occurs, the day on which the act is done and the day on which the event occurs are not counted when calculating whether the required period has elapsed (**r. 2.8(3)**). 3.2

For example, if service must be effected at least three days before a hearing on Friday, 18 October, the last date for service is Monday, 14 October.

Five days or less

If the period of time for doing any act is five days or less, the following days within the period do not count: Saturday, Sunday, a bank holiday, Christmas Day, Good Friday (**CPR, r. 2.8(4)**). 3.3

For example, if service must be effected at least three days before a hearing on Monday, 21 October, the last date for service is Tuesday, 15 October.

Rule 2.8(4)(b), which excludes Saturdays, Sundays and bank holidays when calculating periods of five days or less, does not apply when calculating the deemed date for service of a claim form under **r. 6.14** or of other documents under **r. 6.26** (*Anderton v Clwyd County Council (No. 2)* [2002] EWCA Civ 933, [2002] 1 WLR 3174, applied in *R (Frezghi Semere) v Asylum and Immigration Tribunal* [2009] EWHC 335 (Admin), LTL 4/3/2009). This is because the deemed dates of service as set out in **rr. 6.14** and **6.26** for these methods of service are not periods 'for doing any act' as required for **r. 2.8(1)** to apply. What **rr. 6.14** and **6.26** do is to lay down rules for calculating artificial dates when those documents will be taken as having been received by the other party as a matter of law (**rr. 6.14** and **6.26** create an irrebuttable presumption of law), and so fall outside of **r. 2.8**.

MONTHS

3.4 In the CPR, 'month' means calendar month (Interpretation Act 1978, ss. 5 and 22 and sch. 1) and **CPR, r. 2.10**, applies the same definition to any judgment, order, direction or other document.

COURT OFFICE CLOSED

3.5 Where a period for doing any act at the court office, such as filing a document, ends on a day when the office is closed, the act will be done in time if done on the next day on which the office is open (**CPR, r. 2.8(5)**). **Rule 2.8(5)** is expressed to apply to a period specified by the CPR, a practice direction, a judgment or a court order. It does not apply to a time limit prescribed by statute (*Adesina v Nursing and Midwifery Council* [2012] EWHC 2615 (Admin), LTL 1/10/2012). However, there is a common law rule to the same effect, which applies, for example, if the court office is closed on the day when a limitation period under the Limitation Act 1980 expires (*Pritam Kaur v S. Russell and Sons Ltd* [1973] QB 336) or the day when a statutory time limit for bringing an appeal expires (*Mucelli v Government of Albania* [2009] UKHL 2, [2009] 1 WLR 276, approving *Pritam Kaur v S. Russell and Sons Ltd*) or the day when a statutory time limit for making an application expires (*R (Modaresi) v Secretary of State for Health* [2011] EWCA Civ 1359, LTL 23/11/2011). This common law rule is not limited to acts, such as issuing a claim form, which require something to be done by court staff to make them complete (*R (Modaresi) v Secretary of State for Health*).

When the period specified for doing an act at a court office ends on a day on which the office is open, the act may be done after office hours on that day, provided nothing has to be done by court staff to make the act complete (*Van Aken v Camden London Borough Council* [2002] EWCA Civ 1724, [2003] 1 WLR 684, where the relevant act was filing a document at court, which does not require any action by court staff).

If a claim form is filed during office hours on the last day of a limitation period, it does not matter that the court staff do not issue the claim until a later day (see *Barnes v St Helens Metropolitan Borough Council* [2006] EWCA Civ 1372, [2007] 1 WLR 879, discussed at **12.5**).

PD 2A, paras 2.1 and **3.2** to **3.3**, give details of the opening days and times of the RCJ, the district registries of the High Court and of the county courts.

These rules are irrelevant to electronic filing, as described in **PD 5C**. This is because electronic filing operates 24 hours a day, all year round, subject only to planned downtime for system maintenance and unplanned downtime caused by unforeseen problems such as power failure. A party may therefore issue claim forms and file documents electronically at any time, including when the court offices are closed (**PD 5C, para. 1.2**). Claim forms received by the court before midnight on any given day will bear that date as the issue date (**PD 5C, para. 6.4(1)**).

Additionally, a document filed at court by fax or email after 4 pm is treated as filed on the next day the court office is open (**PD 5B, para. 8** and **PD 5A, para. 5.3(6)**).

TIME LIMITS IN COURT ORDERS

In a court order, judgment or direction which imposes a time limit for doing any act, the last date for compliance must, wherever practicable, be expressed as a calendar date and include a time on that date by which the act must be done (**CPR, r. 2.9(1)**). For example, an order should be drafted to state that an act must be done 'by 4 p.m. on 27 February 2014', rather than 'no later than 14 days after the date of this order'. **3.6**

When the date by which an act must be done is inserted in any document, the date must, wherever practicable, be expressed as a calendar date (**r. 2.9(2)**).

VARIATION BY CONSENT

CPR, r. 2.11, makes clear that parties may, by written agreement, vary any deadline specified in the CPR or by the court, unless forbidden to do so by a court order, the CPR or a practice direction. This extends to agreements for extensions of time for service of the claim form (*Thomas v Home Office* [2006] EWCA Civ 1355, [2007] 1 WLR 230). **Rule 3.8(3)** forbids extension of time by agreement of a deadline if the consequence of failure to comply with the deadline is specified in the rule or court order creating it. **Rule 3.8(3)** also applies to deadlines set in practice directions, implying that a practice direction deadline which does not specify the consequence of failure to comply can be varied by agreement. However, authority to vary practice direction deadlines is not given expressly by **r. 2.11**, unless they can be taken to be covered by the phrase 'specified…by the court'. **3.7**

The meaning of a 'written agreement of the parties' was considered by the Court of Appeal in *Thomas v Home Office*. The court held that there must be a document, or exchange of documents, which is intended to constitute the agreement or to confirm or record an oral agreement. An oral agreement between two solicitors recorded in a letter sent by one solicitor to the other but not replied to by the other cannot constitute a 'written agreement of the parties'. Similarly, an oral agreement between two solicitors, evidenced by an internal confirmatory note by one solicitor, or even by each of the solicitors, cannot constitute a written agreement unless the internal notes are exchanged (or in some way confirmed in writing to each other). On the facts of the case, an oral agreement confirmed by one party in writing to the other and by that party in writing to their expert witness (even though this letter was copied to the first party) could not constitute a 'written agreement of the parties' under **r. 2.11**.

An example of the CPR restricting agreement by the parties is **r. 15.5(1)**, which allows an agreement to extend the time for service of a defence by a maximum of 28 days.

The date specified in a notice of proposed allocation for compliance with specified matters (including filing directions questionnaires) cannot be varied by agreement between the parties (**r. 26.3(6A)**). In a fast track claim, the parties are not allowed to vary by consent the date for the return of pre-trial checklists, the trial date or trial window, or any other directions which would impinge on these dates (**r. 28.4**). In a multi-track claim, the parties are not allowed to vary by consent the dates for any case management conference, pre-trial review, the return of pre-trial checklists, the trial date or trial period, or any other directions which would impinge on these dates (**r. 29.5**).

Where parties agree changes to the case management timetable under **r. 2.11**, they need not file the written agreement at court (**PD 28, para. 4.5; PD 29, para. 6.5**).

Commentary

VARIATION BY THE COURT

3.8 The court has power under **CPR, r. 3.1(2)(a)**, to extend or shorten the time for compliance with any rule, practice direction or court order. This power does not extend, however, to statutory time limits, such as the time for filing notices of appeal to the High Court under the many provisions listed in **PD 52D** (*Mucelli v Government of Albania* [2009] UKHL 2, [2009] 1 WLR 276, applied in *Mitchell v Nursing and Midwifery Council* [2009] EWHC 1045 (Admin), LTL 28/5/2009, *Harrison v General Medical Council* [2011] EWHC 1741 (Admin), LTL 8/6/2011, and *Reddy v General Medical Council* [2012] EWCA Civ 310, [2012] CP Rep 27, which confirms that *Mucelli* is of general application, not just of relevance to extradition cases).

Chapter 4 Remedies

INTRODUCTION

Many kinds of remedy may be asked for in civil proceedings, with the aim of establishing or changing a legal status, determining legal rights and duties, or rectifying an infringement or denial of legal rights. The remedy which the court decides to grant is embodied in its judgment, which is usually phrased as, and is often called, an 'order'. The remedy sought by a claimant must be specified in the claim form (**CPR, r. 16.2(1)(b)**), though this statement does not limit the remedies which the court may award (**r. 16.2(5)**) (see **23.7**). There is nothing to prevent the court giving a merely declaratory judgment stating what parties' rights are without giving any other remedy (**r. 40.20**) (see **4.19**). **4.1**

Pending a court's decision on what its judgment may be at the trial or final hearing of a claim, it may make interim orders providing what are usually called 'interim remedies', which are discussed in **chapters 32** and **36** to **41**.

Remedies can be granted only in accordance with established principles of law or under statutory authority: the court does not have an inherent jurisdiction to make any order necessary to ensure that justice is done (*Wicks v Wicks* [1999] Fam 65 at pp. 76–8 and 88–9).

The principal remedies which are available in civil proceedings generally are examined in this chapter, consisting of legal remedies (debt and damages), which are available as of right on proof of infringement of the claimant's legal rights, and equitable remedies (injunction, specific performance, rectification and account), which the court may award, at its discretion, when a legal remedy would be inadequate or unavailable. The discretion to award equitable remedies is exercised in accordance with established principles. In particular, an equitable remedy will not be awarded where it would be inequitable to do so, for example, in the light of the claimant's previous bad behaviour in relation to the subject matter of the claim (the rule that the claimant must come to the court with clean hands), or where the claimant has delayed in claiming the remedy, to the defendant's detriment (the rule against laches, see **10.40**).

Numerous other remedies are available in special types of proceedings, such as the discretionary remedies available in judicial review proceedings (see **chapter** 77), the discretionary remedy of rescission of contract, and many orders created by statute (see 4.23).

In claims concerning sale of goods to consumers the court now has statutory powers to require the seller to repair or replace the goods (see **89.36**).

Methods of enforcing judgments are considered in **chapters 79** to **81**.

EFFECT OF JUDGMENTS

4.2 A judgment or order of a court in civil proceedings takes effect from the day when it is given or made (**CPR, r. 40.7(1)**) and this means from the first moment of that day (*Shelley's Case* (1582) 1 Co Rep 93b). The court may specify a later date on which its judgment or order is to take effect (**r. 40.7(1)**). There are special rules in **r. 40.10** concerning default judgments against foreign States.

It is in the public interest that legal proceedings brought to resolve a dispute should result in a final answer to that dispute. The parties must put their whole case before the court and are not permitted to relitigate the questions which the court decides (see **33.15** to **33.20**).

Judgments are traditionally divided into:

(a) those which are *in personam*, that is, determinative of the rights of the parties to the proceedings, and not challengeable by those parties in other proceedings, but not binding on anyone else, and
(b) those which are *in rem*, that is, determinative of legal status and not challengeable in any proceedings before any tribunal which recognises the jurisdiction of the court which gave the judgment (though it may be possible to question the court's jurisdiction).

A judgment by a court of competent jurisdiction binds the parties even if a judgment of a higher court in other proceedings shows that it was wrong in law (*Watt v Ahsan* [2007] UKHL 51, [2008] 1 AC 696).

The finality of a judgment or order is subject to three qualifications:

(a) A person who was not a party to the proceedings in which the judgment or order was made, but who is directly affected by it, may apply under **r. 40.9** for it to be set aside or varied.
(b) Any accidental slip or omission in a judgment or order may be corrected by the court under **r. 40.12** (see **63.42**).
(c) It may be possible to appeal against the judgment or order, see **chapters** 74 to 77.
(d) In insolvency proceedings, the court may be asked to review, rescind or vary its order (see **84.6** to **84.10**).

Merger of cause of action into judgment

4.3 When judgment is given, the original cause of action is treated as merged with the judgment, so that no further proceedings can be brought on that cause of action. Where an event gives rise to more than one cause of action, not all of which are litigated, the ones which have not been litigated do not merge in the judgment given on those that were. For example, a claim in contract will not merge with a judgment on a tortious claim which arose from the same event. Merger does not apply to successive causes of action, so that judgment for specific instalments of debt or rent will not bar a claim for further instalments. Merger does apply where the court gives judgment on the merits on one of two mutually exclusive alternative bases for the claim (*Balgobin v South West Regional Health Authority* [2012] UKPC 11, [2013] 1 AC 582).

Res judicata

4.4 The parties to a claim that is determined by a judgment of the court on the merits of the claim are estopped from bringing further similar claims. This estoppel, known as *res judicata* (a thing or matter that has been decided), takes three distinct forms. First, there is a narrow form of estoppel flowing from the merger of the cause of action in the judgment which provides that the issues between the parties which were actually adjudicated by the court have been finally resolved between them. Second, there is a wider form of estoppel known as cause of action estoppel, which is founded on the rule in *Henderson v Henderson* (1843) 3 Hare 100. This rule is based on encouraging finality in litigation and (unless the decision was secured by fraud or collusion) prevents any party to a claim in which judgment has been given from raising in other proceedings any issue which was resolved or could have been raised and resolved in the adjudicated claim (see *Arnold v National Westminster Bank* [1991] 2 AC 93 and *R (Coke-Wallis) v Institute of Chartered Accountants in England and Wales* [2011] UKSC 1, [2011] 2 AC 146, and **33.16**). The third form of estoppel, known as issue estoppel, is based on the same public policy (see **33.17**). The doctrine of issue estoppel is that if, after judgment is delivered in civil proceedings, two of the parties to those proceedings, or their successors in title, are parties to further civil proceedings, then one of those parties cannot repeat, as against the other, in the second proceedings, an assertion which was found to be incorrect by the court in the first proceedings (*Mills v Cooper* [1967] 2 QB 459 per Diplock LJ at pp. 468–9). The doctrine applies only to an assertion — whether of fact, opinion (*Humberclyde Finance Group Ltd v Hicks* (2001) LTL 19/11/2001) or the legal consequences of facts or opinions — which was an essential element of the asserting party's cause of action or defence in the first proceedings. The doctrine affects a party whether the party was an original claimant or defendant in the first proceedings or was joined to those proceedings, but it only affects parties who appear in the same capacity in both sets of proceedings (*Humberclyde Finance Group Ltd v Hicks*). Issue estoppel does not prevent a party repeating an assertion if further material, which is relevant to the correctness or incorrectness of the original assertion in the previous proceedings, has become available and it could not in the exercise of reasonable diligence have been deployed in the previous proceedings.

Where a claimant brings proceedings against more than one defendant, entering summary judgment against one defendant may amount to an election to abandon the claim against the other defendants (*Morel Brothers and Co. Ltd v Earl of Westmorland* [1903] 1 KB 64). A default judgment is entered without investigating the merits, unlike summary judgment. Consequently, entering a default judgment against one defendant does not, without more, amount to an election to abandon the claim against the other defendant (*Pendleton v Westwater* [2001] EWCA Civ 1841, LTL 28/11/2001). In order to make an effective election to abandon a claim against another defendant, a claimant claiming two or more remedies must decide to follow one of them at the expense of the others and must communicate that choice to the defendant against whom the remedy is claimed in terms which make clear a deliberate preference for that remedy over any other. Those requirements were not satisfied where the claimant entered judgment in default against D2 for damages to be assessed for personal injury in reliance on an allegation by D1 that D2 was the claimant's employer at the same time as pursuing her claim that D1 was in truth her employer (*Balgobin v South West Regional Health Authority* [2012] UKPC 11, [2013] 1 AC 582).

In *Johnson v Gore Wood and Co.* [2002] 2 AC 1 the House of Lords reviewed the circumstances in which public policy permitted a second claim (in this case brought by the majority shareholder of a company after the claim by the company had been compromised) to proceed. The test is whether, taking into account all the public and private interests involved and the facts of the case, a claimant is misusing or abusing the process of the court (see **33.16** to **33.19**).

MONEY JUDGMENTS

The most common judgment given is for payment of a sum of money. The money due will **4.5**
usually be a debt (or other liquidated sum) or damages. The distinction between a debt (or other liquidated claim) and damages is no longer as important as it was in the past, as is reflected in the CPR by the distinction drawn in several places between claims for specified amounts and claims for unspecified amounts. Interest may be awarded on a money judgment (see **chapter 64**), but this is relief ancillary to the principal remedy of a money judgment, rather than an independent remedy (*Bank voor Handel en Scheepvaart NV v Slatford* [1953] 1 QB 248 at p. 278).

Set-off

4.6 If two parties to proceedings make monetary claims against each other (a claim and a cross-claim), and both claim and cross-claim are upheld, the court will deduct the smaller of the amounts found due from the larger and give only one judgment for the balance, if the claim and the cross-claim can be set off. There are two sets of rules governing whether a claim and a cross-claim can be set off: one creates a legal set-off, the other an equitable set-off.

In a claim for a liquidated sum the defendant can assert a legal set-off of any liquidated debt or money demand cross-claimed by it from the claimant, whether or not the mutual debts arise from the same transaction, provided both the claimant's claim and the defendant's cross-claim can be quantified with certainty at the time of filing a defence (see *Hanak v Green* [1958] 2 QB 9 per Morris LJ at p. 17; *Axel Johnson Petroleum AB v MG Mineral Group AG* [1992] 1 WLR 270; *B. Hargreaves Ltd v Action 2000 Ltd* [1993] BCLC 1111; **CPR, r. 16.6**).

Equitable set-off (also called equitable defence) permits a cross-claim by the defendant to be set off against the claimant's claim if it arises out of the same transaction or is closely connected with that transaction and is so closely connected with those demands that it would be manifestly unjust to allow the claimant to enforce payment without taking the defendant's claim into account (per Lord Denning MR in *Federal Commerce and Navigation Co. Ltd v Molena Alpha Inc.* [1978] QB 927 at pp. 974–5 and Goff LJ at p. 987, point not considered on appeal; *Geldof Metaalconstructie NV v Simon Carves Ltd* [2010] EWCA Civ 667, [2010] 4 All ER 847). Equitable set-off is not available against a claim for freight (*Aries Tanker Corporation v Total Transport Ltd* [1977] 1 WLR 185) or for payment of a bill of exchange (*Nova (Jersey) Knit Ltd v Kammgarn Spinnerei GmbH* [1977] 1 WLR 713).

A defendant who has an unquantified cross-claim against the claimant which is not connected with the claimant's claim is not entitled to either legal or equitable set-off.

It is possible for the contract governing payment of a debt to prevent the debtor from exercising a right of set-off against the creditor even in legal proceedings brought to enforce payment of the debt (*Coca-Cola Financial Corporation v Finsat International Ltd* [1998] QB 43; *Re Kaupthing Singer and Friedlander Ltd* [2009] EWHC 740 (Ch), [2009] 2 Lloyd's Rep 154).

For more on set-off see **34.37** to **34.39**.

DAMAGES

4.7 Damages are a monetary payment as the legal remedy for infringement of legal rights. The amount to be paid primarily reflects the compensation required by the claimant for loss caused by the defendant's wrongdoing (compensatory damages), though the court may increase this compensation because of the additional hurt caused by the objectionable way in which the defendant acted (aggravated damages). In limited circumstances the court, representing the public interest, may mark its disapproval of the defendant's behaviour by adding a penalty element to the damages (exemplary damages). Where there has been a breach of contract, the contract itself may provide how damages for the breach are to be calculated (liquidated damages). An infringement of a legal right which has caused no compensable loss may result in only nominal damages.

Nominal damages

4.8 Nominal damages are awarded where there has been an infringement of a legal right but it has not resulted in any loss for which compensation may be claimed (*The Mediana* [1900] AC 113).

If actual damage to the claimant is an essential element of a cause of action (as it is, for example, for tortious negligence) then failure to prove any damage to the claimant will result in the dismissal of the claim. If actual damage to the claimant is not an essential element of a cause of action (as is the case, for example, with breach of contract or trespass to land), the claimant will be given judgment on proof of the matters that are essential, but cannot be awarded damages beyond a nominal amount.

Aggravated damages

Aggravated damages are defined in the CPR Glossary as 'Additional damages which the court may award as compensation for the defendant's objectionable behaviour'. A claim for aggravated damages must be made separately in the particulars of claim (**CPR, r. 16.4(1)(c)**). Aggravated damages compensate for injury to feelings caused by the manner in which the wrong was committed, and cannot be awarded to a company, which has no feelings to be injured (*Collins Stewart Ltd v Financial Times Ltd* [2005] EWHC 262 (QB), [2006] EMLR 5). Aggravated damages are quite distinct from exemplary damages and in a suitable case both may be awarded. The most common situation in which both are awarded is unlawful eviction (if statutory damages are not claimed or awarded). **4.9**

Exemplary damages

Exemplary damages are defined in the CPR Glossary as 'Damages which go beyond compensating for actual loss and are awarded to show the court's disapproval of the defendant's behaviour'. A claim for exemplary damages must be made separately in the particulars of claim (**CPR, r. 16.4(1)(c)**). Exemplary damages can be awarded only in very limited circumstances. The House of Lords in *Rookes v Barnard* [1964] AC 1129 recognised only three categories. They are: **4.10**

(a) oppressive, arbitrary or unconstitutional behaviour by government servants;
(b) cases where the conduct of the defendant is calculated to make a profit which will be in excess of the compensatory damages which are payable; and
(c) where an award of exemplary damages is expressly authorised by statute.

In *Kuddus v Chief Constable of Leicestershire Constabulary* [2002] 2 AC 122 the House of Lords overruled the decision of the Court of Appeal in *AB v South West Water Services Ltd* [1993] QB 507 with the result that the categories of claim which can give rise to an award of exemplary damages are not now limited to those in which awards were made prior to 1964. It now seems that it is the behaviour complained of rather than the precise cause of action which the court must consider. Awards of exemplary damages are certainly available in claims for trespass to the person or property, defamation, false imprisonment and private nuisance. It is now arguable that awards may be made in other categories of case such as misfeasance in public office (the cause of action in *Kuddus*).

Damages may be awarded as exemplary damages even though they have been quantified by reference to specific losses by the claimant (*Borders (UK) Ltd v Commissioner of Police of the Metropolis* [2005] EWCA Civ 197, *The Times*, 15 April 2005).

Liquidated damages

A claim for liquidated damages is a claim for the sum agreed in a contract between the parties as payable in the event of a specified breach of that contract which has in fact occurred. In many cases the amount payable has to be calculated by reference to the circumstances of the breach, such as the number of days' delay in performance. A sum which is a genuine pre-estimate by the parties of the loss occasioned by the breach of contract will be recoverable as liquidated damages, but any other sum will be an irrecoverable penalty (*Dunlop Pneumatic Tyre Co. Ltd v New Garage and Motor Co. Ltd* [1915] AC 79). The circumstances in which a term in a written contract can be challenged so as to avoid this consequence are considered at **89.25**. **4.11**

Compensatory damages

4.12 Compensatory damages can be divided into pecuniary and non-pecuniary damages. Pecuniary damages compensate the claimant for measurable financial losses caused by the defendant's wrongdoing. Non-pecuniary damages (often called 'general' damages) are awarded in recognition of suffering which that wrongdoing has caused the claimant. The amount to award as non-pecuniary damages must be assessed according to the court's sense of what would be appropriate in the case before it, in the light of what has been awarded in comparable cases. Information about appropriate awards for pain, suffering and loss of amenity in personal injuries claims is given by the Judicial College in *Guidelines for the Assessment of General Damages in Personal Injury Cases*, 12th ed. (Oxford University Press, 2013). Conventionally a claimant does not specify the amount sought as non-pecuniary damages, though an estimate of what is likely to be awarded must be made in order to decide which court to start the claim in (see **11.4**). In personal injury claims, pecuniary damages sought must be specified in a schedule of past and future expenses and losses attached to the particulars of claim (**PD 16, para. 4.2**; see **chapter 25**).

Traditionally, an award for pecuniary loss is based on the loss which the claimant has sustained and not on what it would be fair or reasonable for the defendant to pay (*General Tire and Rubber Co. v Firestone Tyre and Rubber Co. Ltd* [1975] 1 WLR 819). However, in exceptional cases, where it is just to do so, the court may make orders to ensure that the defendant in a claim for breach of contract retains no benefit from the breach (*Attorney-General v Blake* [2001] 1 AC 268), or, in cases of misuse of property, to award a sum which it would be reasonable for the defendant to pay for that use (*Experience Hendrix LLC v PPX Enterprises Inc.* [2003] EWCA Civ 323, [2003] 1 All ER (Comm) 830).

In tortious claims the aim is to award a sum of money which will restore the claimant's position to what it would have been but for the wrong for which the damages are being awarded (*Livingstone v Rawyards Coal Co.* (1880) 5 App Cas 25). Compensatory damages in tort can include heads of loss which have been aggravated by the claimant's impecuniosity (*Lagden v O'Connor* [2003] UKHL 64, [2003] 1 AC 1067, overruling *Liesbosch Dredger (Owners of) v Owners of SS Edison* [1933] AC 449 on this point).

Claims for damages for breach of contract may be made on two different bases:

(a) to restore the claimant's position to what it would have been had the contract been properly performed (loss of bargain); or
(b) to compensate for expenditure rendered futile by the breach (reliance loss).

The claimant can choose the basis on which to claim (*CCC Films (London) Ltd v Impact Quadrant Films Ltd* [1985] QB 16).

DELIVERY UP OF GOODS

4.13 A final judgment ordering delivery up of goods may take one of the three forms permitted by the Torts (Interference with Goods) Act 1977, s. 3(2):

(a) an order for the delivery of the goods and payment of any consequential damages;
(b) an order for delivery of the goods but giving the defendant the alternative of paying the stated value of the goods together, in either case, with the consequential damages; or
(c) judgment for damages.

An order in form (a) is discretionary (s. 3(3)(b)), and tends to be made only where the goods are rare or have some special value, or where they are not readily available on the market (*Howard E. Perry and Co. Ltd v British Railways Board* [1980] 1 WLR 1375). If an order in form (a) is obtained but not complied with, the person in whose favour the judgment was given can return to court and the court can revoke the order and make an order for the payment of damages by reference to the value of the goods (s. 3(4)). Payment of a judgment for the value of the goods extinguishes the claimant's title to those goods (s. 5).

INJUNCTIONS

An injunction may be either mandatory (requiring some act to be done) or prohibitory (requiring some conduct to stop, or prohibiting threatened conduct). Injunction is an equitable remedy awarded at the court's discretion where a legal remedy would be inadequate (see **4.1**). **4.14**

The general power to grant injunctions has been given statutory form in the Senior Courts Act 1981, s. 37 (which applies also in the county courts by virtue of the County Courts Act 1984, s. 38). This provides that injunctions, whether final or interim, 'may' (emphasising that this is a discretionary power) be granted where it is 'just and convenient'. In cases where rights under the European Convention on Human Rights may be engaged, the test may better be expressed as 'just and proportionate' (see *South Bucks District Council v Porter* [2003] UKHL 26, [2003] 2 AC 558). There are also specific statutory powers to grant injunctions, for example, in the Housing Act 1996, ss. 153A and 153B (see **88.2** to **88.11**). Power to grant an injunction in judicial review claims is conferred by the Senior Courts Act 1981, s. 31(2) (see **77.58**).

The discretion to grant an injunction must be exercised judicially, taking into account all the relevant circumstances. Factors include the importance of curbing the defendant's activities, whether breaches of the claimant's rights or the law will continue unless restrained, whether the court would be prepared to impose the sanctions available for breach of the injunction (fining and imprisonment, see **chapter 84**), and, in the case of specific statutory powers to grant injunctions, the purpose for which the power was given (*South Bucks District Council v Porter* at [29] and [32]). The inability to order imprisonment is the reason why injunctions are rarely imposed against children (*G v Harrow London Borough Council* [2004] EWHC 17 (QB), LTL 23/1/2004). When granting an injunction the court does not contemplate that it will be disobeyed (*Castanho v Brown and Root (UK) Ltd* [1981] AC 557 at p. 574). Concern that a defendant might disobey an injunction should not therefore deter a court from granting it. As Lord Bingham of Cornhill said in *South Bucks District Council v Porter* at [32], there is not one law for the law-abiding and another for the lawless and truculent. Consequently, a final injunction was granted in *Mid Bedfordshire District Council v Brown* [2004] EWCA Civ 1709, [2005] 1 WLR 1460, where the defendants had moved on to land in breach of an interim order, because the public interest in upholding court orders far outweighed the factors favouring suspension of the injunction.

When a public body applies for an injunction in pursuance of its public functions, one factor which the court may take into account is the lawfulness of the decision to make the application. But this is not the only factor to be taken into account and, in deciding whether to grant the injunction, the court is exercising an original rather than a supervisory jurisdiction (*South Bucks District Council v Porter* at [27]).

The court may award damages in addition to or in lieu of an injunction (Senior Courts Act 1981, s. 50; County Courts Act 1984, s. 38). It is possible to award both an injunction ordering cessation of a breach of the claimant's rights and damages for injury to those rights during the time that the injunction will be in force, for example, where it is clear that the injunction will be evaded (*Brazier v Bramwell Scaffolding (Dunedin) Ltd* [2001] UKPC 59, LTL 20/12/2001). However, if the claimant has established that the claim is one in which the court would usually grant an injunction, the court may not, of its own motion, instead award nominal damages (*Nelson v Nicholson* (2000) LTL 1/12/2000).

When drafting a final injunction it is important that the wording is clear and specific. The order must state what is to be done and when, or what is not to be done from a particular date and time. This is because disobedience of an injunction is contempt of court, for which punishments such as committal and sequestration may be imposed (see **81.7**). Injunction orders should be endorsed with a penal notice (see **81.6**) and follow any relevant form in the **CPR**, practice directions or court guides. Forms for a final injunction order can be based on the interim injunction forms with the omission of the parts that are relevant to an interim injunction.

SPECIFIC PERFORMANCE

4.15 An order for specific performance requires the performance of the obligations of a party to a contract. An order for specific performance is an equitable remedy awarded at the court's discretion where a legal remedy would be inadequate (see **4.1**). In most cases an order for specific performance is asked for as a remedy for a breach of an obligation, but it is also possible to make an order for specific performance in anticipation of a breach. Specific performance is asked for most often in claims for the enforcement of agreements relating to land, but it can also be ordered for the sale of goods, particularly those which are rare or unique such as an original work of art or an heirloom.

Certain obligations will not be specifically enforced, including illegal contracts, unenforceable contracts (e.g. sale of land without the necessary written contract), voluntary obligations, contracts for personal skill or work, and obligations which require constant supervision (*Ryan v Mutual Tontine Westminster Chambers Association* [1893] 1 Ch 116). The claimant must show that he is ready, willing and able to perform his part of the obligation or contract. Specific performance may be refused where there has been a misrepresentation by the claimant, where there has been a serious mistake or misdescription, and in cases of severe hardship.

The court may award damages in addition to or in lieu of specific performance (Senior Courts Act 1981, s. 50; County Courts Act 1984, s. 38).

An order for specific performance must state what is to be done and when. The contract or obligation does not merge completely into the order, but further performance is subject to the control of the court.

RECTIFICATION

4.16 Rectification (alteration of a document to reflect the parties' true intentions) is a discretionary equitable remedy (see **4.1**). It is not the bargain which is rectified, but the written record of the transaction. Rectification is not required where the true meaning is revealed by the ordinary rules of construction of written agreements. Where applying those rules of construction to the document shows that it does not reflect the agreement of the parties, the document may be rectified. An order for rectification has retrospective force so that the document is treated as if it was in the rectified form from the date it was signed or created. Rectification will not be ordered in the absence of convincing evidence of what the parties agreed or intended and of the erroneous recording of their agreement or intention in the written document.

RESCISSION

4.17 Rescission is a discretionary equitable remedy (see **4.1**) by which a party may be entitled to set aside a contract or other transaction entered into with another party in reliance on a misrepresentation or in consequence of a breach of a fiduciary duty on the part of that other party. Under the Misrepresentation Act 1967, s. 2(2), the court may affirm the contract or transaction and award damages in lieu of rescission where the misrepresentation was innocent or negligent. The damages awarded are compensatory. In the case of fraudulent misrepresentation the claimant is entitled to rescission as of right. There is no general right to relief by way of rescission simply because it would be equitable to do so. A contract terminated by the acceptance of a repudiatory breach may often be said to have been 'rescinded' but that is not a proper use of the true meaning of the word or the relevant remedy.

ACCOUNTS

The power of the court to order an account to be taken is considered at **63.36**. Accounts are a common remedy in claims between principal and agent, claims between partners and claims involving jointly owned property. The first stage is to establish that an account should be taken by the court. An account will not be ordered where the parties have already settled the balance between themselves by an account stated or a settled account. As an account is an equitable remedy, the court may refuse to order an account if it would be unjust to do so, for example where the party in default was entirely innocent or the claimant has unjustifiably delayed in bringing the claim (*Hollister Inc. v Medik Ostomy Supplies Ltd* [2012] EWCA Civ 1419, [2013] Bus LR 428). If the limitation period for the claim has expired, an account will not be ordered to avoid that limitation period. At the second stage, the court should give directions for the taking of the account, which may involve disclosure and inspection. The party liable to account will usually be ordered to prepare the first account. The receiving party can then raise objections to items in that account. Those disputed items can then be determined by the court. **4.18**

In cases of jointly owned real property where one party has left the property and the other has remained in occupation until sale, the court may try to avoid taking detailed accounts as the cost of doing so can exceed the sums involved. The party remaining in occupation will have to pay an occupation rent assessed as the fair rental value of the property. If, as is often the case, that person has paid all the outgoings, those will have to be credited. The result in many cases is that the court will refuse to order an account on the ground that the outgoings paid will be broadly the same as the occupation rent (*Bernard v Josephs* [1982] Ch 391; *Dennis v McDonald* [1982] Fam 63).

An account may also be sought (as an alternative to damages) where there has been an infringement of a proprietary right (e.g. misuse of confidential information, or intellectual property rights). A claimant must elect whether to seek damages (based on the loss he can show he has suffered) or an account (based on the net profits made by the defendant). Proving damage is often extremely difficult, so that an account of the profit made by the defendant may be a more attractive remedy. An account of profits does not involve a consideration of the loss suffered by the innocent party as a result of the unlawful conduct giving rise to the obligation to account. In assessing the new profit made by the party in default, the court should disregard general overheads or expenditure incurred by the defaulting party, but may have regard to overheads or expenditure directly referable to the defaulting party's unlawful conduct. The burden of proof lies on the defaulting party (*Hollister Inc. v Medik Ostomy Supplies Ltd*). The claimant may elect between two alternative remedies, such as an account of profits or damages, at any time before judgment is entered for the claimant. The claimant ought not to be required to elect between the two until he has been provided with all the available information required for him to make an informed choice (*Island Records Ltd v Tring International plc* [1996] 1 WLR 1256; *Ramzan v Brookwide Ltd* [2011] EWCA Civ 985, [2011] 2 P & CR 22).

DECLARATIONS

Final declarations

The power to make binding final declarations can be found in **CPR, r. 40.20**, and the power to make interim declarations is in **r. 25.1(1)(b)**. Power to make a declaration in judicial **4.19** review claims is conferred by the Senior Courts Act 1981, s. 31(2) (see 77.59). When deciding whether to make a declaration the court should take into account justice to the claimant, justice to the defendant, whether the declaration will serve a useful purpose, and any special reasons affecting the decision (*Financial Services Authority v Rourke* (2001) *The Times*, 12 November 2001). A declaration about the lawfulness of future conduct will not be granted unless the circumstances are truly exceptional (*R (Rusbridger) v Attorney-General* [2003] UKHL 38, [2004] 1 AC 357). In deciding whether this test is met, according to *Blackland Park Exploration Ltd v Environment Agency* [2003] EWCA Civ 1795, [2004] Env LR 33, the court will consider the following criteria:

(a) the absence of any genuine dispute about the subject matter;
(b) whether the case is fact-sensitive; and
(c) whether there is a cogent public or individual interest that will be advanced by making the declaration.

A declaration may make findings of fact as well as declaring legal rights (*Compagnie Noga d'Importation et d'Exportation SA v Abacha (No. 3)* [2002] EWCA Civ 1142, LTL 31/7/2002).

Interim declarations

4.20 The inclusion of the power to grant an interim declaration in **CPR, r. 25.1(1)(b)**, means that such an order is no longer 'a contradiction in terms'. It was recognised in *NHS Trust v T (Adult Patient: Refusal of Medical Treatment)* [2004] EWHC 1279 (Fam), [2005] 1 All ER 387, that there are still difficulties, but:

(a) the power to grant interim declarations is not restricted to judicial review claims;
(b) interim declarations can be granted for a one-off medical procedure, for example, a Caesarean section or an amputation (at [44]);
(c) a material change of circumstances can found a reconsideration.

In the case of interim relief in relation to medical treatment of a person said to lack mental capacity, Charles J said the patient should be given an opportunity to make representations. It is for the judge to decide on capacity, then to decide on the best interests of the patient applying the usual civil standard on the best evidence then available.

RESTITUTION

4.21 Claims for restitution can be made at law and in equity and are based on the principle of unjust enrichment. The claim is for repayment of the benefit received by the defendant and not the loss suffered by the claimant. The claim will be particularly important where the claimant's damages are less than the benefit received by the defendant, where the claimant may have difficulty proving his damages and where the claimant made a bad bargain. Thus, where a car is purchased without obtaining good title, the purchaser will normally prefer to reclaim the entire purchase price rather than damages based on the lower value of the car when the defect in title is discovered.

Where a claimant seeks restitution of something given to the defendant in return for something received, there is no principle or rule of practice which requires the claim to include an offer of full counter-restitution. It is for the court to decide at trial what form of counter-restitution should be ordered so as to do practical justice between the parties (*Halpern v Halpern (Nos. 1 and 2)* [2007] EWCA Civ 291, [2008] QB 195; *Ruttle Plant Ltd v Secretary of State for the Environment and Rural Affairs* [2007] EWHC 2870 (TCC), [2008] 2 All ER (Comm) 264).

The most common claims in restitution are for repayment of money had and received which covers both money paid under a mistake and money paid where there has been a total failure of consideration. A claim in restitution may also be made in some tortious actions, particularly those involving interference with proprietary rights. If a defendant takes the claimant's goods and sells them for an advantageous price, it will be more attractive to claim the money received by the defendant rather than the value of the goods. The remedy in tort and the restitutionary remedy are alternatives and the claimant must elect which remedy he seeks. If a claimant seeks restitution he waives the commission of the tort.

POSSESSION

The court may order a person who has ceased to be entitled, or never has been entitled, to occupation or possession of land or property to give up possession to the person who is entitled to it. This may happen on the termination of a lease or licence, or other right of occupation or possession, e.g., as a mortgagor, or where the defendant occupies land or property as a trespasser (**chapter 35**). An order for possession is an order *in rem*. It relates to the land or property and can be expressly assigned or transferred by the claimant with his title to the land or property. A person in occupation or possession who was not a party to the claim may apply to the court to have the order set aside. Enforcement of the order may be stayed or suspended (see, for example, **87.36** and **87.50** in the context of mortgage possession proceedings). In the absence of such an application the order for possession may be enforced against a non-party occupier in the same way as any party named in the order. **4.22**

STATUTORY REMEDIES

A large number of statutory provisions allow the court to grant special statutory remedies in specified circumstances. In each case the requirements to be satisfied before the court has any special power and the criteria for the exercise of that power have to be considered. Statutory remedies include: **4.23**

(a) winding-up and administration orders (**chapter 82**);
(b) bankruptcy orders (**chapter 83**);
(c) orders regulating the affairs of companies (**chapter 85**);
(d) director disqualification orders (**chapter 86**);
(e) various orders and injunctions to control anti-social behaviour and harassment (**chapter 88**);
(f) orders to repair or replace goods in consumer contracts for sale of goods (**89.36**);
(g) orders remedying unfair relationships arising out of credit agreements (**90.27** to **90.30**);
(h) orders declaring that legislative provisions are incompatible with the European Convention on Human Rights (**91.4**).

Chapter 5 Funding Litigation

INTRODUCTION[1]

5.1 There is no doubt that civil litigation, particularly in England and Wales, is expensive. Potential parties to a claim have to consider their solicitors' fees (which in England are some of the highest in the world), their barristers' fees, court fees and, depending on the case, experts' fees. An unsuccessful party can end up paying legal fees twice over or more if he also has to meet a substantial proportion of his opponent's costs. What that means in practice is that every hour spent pursuing a claim can cost one or more of the parties many hundreds, or even thousands, of pounds.

That cumulative cost means that, aside from the relatively rich, few can afford to bring cases unless they receive some type of financial support from a third party. For those with very low income and limited savings, the State might be prepared to assist through the provision of legal aid, although that has been restricted to only certain types of litigation. Other options are for clients to share the financial risk of litigation with their lawyers or with an insurer, or with a third-party funder.

Conditional fee agreements (CFAs) enable lawyers to share the risk of the litigation with their clients by offering a number of variations on 'no win, no fee' arrangements. Essentially, the lawyer agrees not to charge the client if the claim fails, but will charge at their normal hourly rates, usually with an additional 'success fee' calculated as a percentage of those normal fees, if the claim succeeds. Damages-based agreements (DBAs) are similar, in that they are no win, no fee agreements, but the success element is based on a percentage of the amount recovered in the proceedings rather than on the normal fees of the lawyer. The private insurance market can assist parties by underwriting some or all of the costs of litigation in return for a premium.

CFAs and various insurance products now dominate personal injury litigation. In other civil proceedings the use of CFAs and insurance products has risen steadily, particularly following the **Access to Justice Act 1999**. That Act restricted the scope of public funding but encouraged the use of CFAs, backed by insurance, in a number of ways. In particular, the uplift on the lawyer's fees which becomes payable by the party if the case is won, and which is intended to cover the cost of unsuccessful CFA cases run by the same lawyer, could be recovered from the losing party. Further, any insurance premiums paid to cover the party's risk of paying his opponent's costs could also be recovered from the opponent.

[1] The author, Alan Owens, is grateful to Gemma Anderson, Senior Associate at Morrison & Foerster, for her assistance in compiling the material used in chapters 5 and 6.

It is perhaps not surprising that when CFAs led to both an increase in the number of claims and the level of costs, a substantial body of satellite litigation relating to the enforceability of CFAs and the recoverability of success fees and insurance premiums followed. While solicitors and clients became more familiar both with the concept and practical requirements of 'risk sharing', the consequent uncertainty caused considerable disquiet among practitioners, judges, insurance companies and claims management companies. Ongoing reform, aimed at ensuring that CFAs are workable, led to the introduction of 'predictable costs' in bulk litigation markets, the revocation of the Conditional Fee Agreements Regulations 2000 (SI 2000/692) in 2005, and changes to the Solicitors' Practice Rules 1990.

Of course the question 'Who pays?' is quickly followed by 'How much?' Retrospective assessment of the level of costs is becoming increasingly influenced, and sometimes circumscribed, by prospective, court-approved, budgeting and by predictable and fixed cost regimes (for costs budgeting see **chapter 43**, and for fixed costs see the now revoked CPR, rr. 45.15 to 45.22).

The ever increasing cost of litigation in the English courts has attracted criticism from the judiciary and insurers, and has prompted a number of reviews. The most significant and comprehensive review was Sir Rupert Jackson's *Review of Litigation Costs: Final Report* (2009), which was commissioned by the Ministry of Justice. That report proposed a 'coherent package of interlocking reforms, designed to control costs and promote access to justice'.

Commentary

JACKSON FUNDING REFORMS

The essential elements of the civil justice reforms of 2013, which were introduced on 1 April 2013, are: **5.2**

- Elimination of recoverable CFA success fees and recoverable ATE premiums. This is subject to some technical savings, for example in relation to mesothelioma claims, insolvency proceedings, and publication and privacy claims. These areas are the subject of further reviews. Details of the transitional provisions can be found in *Blackstone's Guide to the Civil Justice Reforms 2013*, Sime and French (Oxford: OUP, 2013), chapter 2.
- Extension of the range of funding mechanisms available to parties, by use of:
  - contingency fees ('damages-based agreements'), where:
    - in personal injury claims, there is a 25 per cent cap (excluding damages for future care and loss); and
    - for all non-personal injury claims (excluding employment tribunal cases), there is a 50 per cent cap.
  - third-party funding; and
  - 'contingent legal aid funds'.
- Banning of referral fees, at least in personal injury cases.

Primary legislation giving effect to these reforms was enacted in the Legal Aid, Sentencing and Punishment of Offenders Act 2012. The primary legislation is supplemented by a number of statutory instruments, and extensive amendments to the CPR and practice directions, all of which came into force on 1 April 2013.

GLOSSARY OF KEY FUNDING TERMS

after-the-event (ATE) insurance. Insurance which is purchased when litigation is contemplated or started and which covers the risk of having to pay the opponent's costs. It can be extended to include cover for the insured's own legal costs and expenses. **5.3**

before-the-event (BTE) insurance, also known as legal expenses insurance (LEI). An insurance product (often linked to other insurance, such as a household or motor policy) which is purchased on a subscription basis prior to any litigation being contemplated or started and which usually pays all of the insured's legal costs and the risk of having to pay the opponent's costs, subject to a financial limit written into the policy. The limit for non-business cases is usually between £15,000 and £50,000.

conditional fee agreement (CFA). A written agreement between a solicitor and his client, or between a barrister and a solicitor, relating to a particular claim, typically providing that if the case is lost, no fees are payable, but if the case is won, the costs will be calculated by reference to a normal hourly rate plus a percentage uplift (a success fee) which is agreed at the outset. For example, a 100 per cent success fee will double the agreed hourly rate. 100 per cent is the maximum success fee allowed and is the appropriate uplift for a case with a 50–50 chance of success.

contingency fee agreement, also known as a damages-based agreement (DBA). An agreement between a solicitor and his client, typically providing that the solicitor's fees for a claim will be calculated by reference to a pre-agreed percentage of the damages recovered. The amount of time the solicitor may spend on the case is irrelevant. Until 1 April 2013 this type of agreement was illegal for court proceedings, but lawful for non-contentious work and tribunal proceedings (see 5.19). DBAs became lawful across a wide range of civil litigation on 1 April 2013.

detailed assessment. A line-by-line assessment by the court, at the end of a case, of the level of legal costs of a party. This is often undertaken by specialist costs judges.

disbursements. The expenses in a claim, including court fees, travel costs, experts' fees etc.

indemnity principle. The principle that a party who is ordered to pay another party's costs does not have to pay amounts which the receiving party has no enforceable obligation to pay to his own lawyers.

payment. The amount the client has to pay his legal representatives under a DBA if the claim is successful, usually calculated as a percentage of the damages awarded.

public funding (also known as legal aid). Funding by the State of a person's legal costs, subject to reimbursement from what is recovered in the proceedings. In England and Wales public funding of civil claims is now very restricted. An assisted party has substantial protection against having to pay his opponent's costs even if the case is lost.

ready reckoner. The usual formula for calculating success fees, namely, the chances of losing divided by the chances of winning. For example, in a case where the chances of winning are 50 per cent, the success fee would be 100 per cent, and in a case where the chances of winning are 75 per cent, the success fee would be 33 per cent.

statutory charge. A charge on property or damages recovered or preserved in publicly funded legal proceedings, as security for the payment of costs which are not recovered from the losing party.

success fee. The percentage uplift payable under a CFA on top of a solicitor's (or barrister's) base hourly rate costs in the event of a successful outcome.

third-party funding (TPF). A funding arrangement under which commercial third parties fund the costs of litigation in return for a percentage of damages recovered, most readily obtained for high-value cases with good prospects of success.

DUTY TO ADVISE CLIENTS ON FUNDING

5.4 Solicitors are under a professional duty to ensure their clients know the funding options available to them and that they understand the main features of different funding methods.

The SRA Code of Conduct sets out 'outcomes-focused' conduct requirements, providing greater flexibility for individual firms to decide how best to meet and 'uphold the intention' of the Code, with reference to 'indicative behaviours'. In funding matters the Code provides as follows:

Outcomes

You must achieve these outcomes...

O(1.6) you only enter into fee agreements with your clients that are legal, and which you consider are suitable for the client's needs and take account of the client's best interests;...

O(1.12) clients are in a position to make informed decisions about the services they need, how their matter will be handled and the options available to them;

O(1.13) clients receive the best possible information, both at the time of engagement and when appropriate as their matter progresses, about the likely overall cost of their matter;

O(1.14) clients are informed of their right to challenge or complain about your bill and the circumstances in which they may be liable to pay interest on an unpaid bill;

O(1.15) you properly account to clients for any financial benefit you receive as a result of your instructions;

Indicative behaviours

Acting in the following way(s) may tend to show that you have achieved these outcomes and therefore complied with the Principles:

Dealing with the client's matter

...IB(1.4) explaining any arrangements, such as fee sharing or referral arrangements, which are relevant to the client's instructions;

IB(1.5) explaining any limitations or conditions on what you can do for the client, for example, because of the way the client's matter is funded;...

Fee arrangements with your client

IB(1.13) discussing whether the potential outcomes of the client's matter are likely to justify the expense or risk involved, including any risk of having to pay someone else's legal fees;

IB(1.14) clearly explaining your fees and if and when they are likely to change;

IB(1.15) warning about any other payments for which the client may be responsible;

IB(1.16) discussing how the client will pay, including whether public funding may be available, whether the client has insurance that might cover the fees, and whether the fees may be paid by someone else such as a trade union;

IB(1.17) where you are acting for a client under a fee arrangement governed by statute, such as a conditional fee agreement, giving the client all relevant information relating to that arrangement;

IB(1.18) where you are acting for a publicly funded client, explaining how their publicly funded status affects the costs;

IB(1.19) providing the information in a clear and accessible form which is appropriate to the needs and circumstances of the client;

IB(1.20) where you receive a financial benefit as a result of acting for a client, either:

(a) paying it to the client;

(b) offsetting it against your fees; or

(c) keeping it only where you can justify keeping it, you have told the client the amount of the benefit (or an approximation if you do not know the exact amount) and the client has agreed that you can keep it;

IB(1.21) ensuring that disbursements included in your bill reflect the actual amount spent or to be spent on behalf of the client;...

Commentary

Acting in the following way(s) may tend to show that you have not achieved these outcomes and therefore not complied with the Principles:

Accepting and refusing instructions

...IB(1.27) entering into unlawful fee arrangements such as an unlawful contingency fee.

Practical advice on funding

5.5 A client must be told about the potential liability for the other side's costs if the claim is unsuccessful. The usual rule is that the unsuccessful party in proceedings is ordered to pay the successful party's costs (**CPR, r. 44.2(2)**). The other side's costs generally have to be paid out of the losing party's personal resources. It may be possible to arrange ATE insurance to cover the other side's costs (see **5.15**).

A solicitor must consider whether a client's claim could be funded by someone else's legal expenses insurance, for example, that of the householder where the client lives or the driver of a vehicle in which the client was a passenger. A solicitor should always ask a client to bring to the first consultation all relevant insurance policies, if obtaining them is reasonably practicable. The solicitor's duty may extend to making thorough enquiries and reviewing the relevant insurance documentation (*Garrett v Halton Borough Council* [2006] EWCA Civ 1017, [2007] 1 WLR 554). The nature of the client, the claim and the cost of any ATE policy are relevant to the depth of inquiry required (see also *White v Revell* [2006] EWHC 90054 (Costs), LTL 15/9/2006, and *Choudhury v Kingston Hospital NHS Trust* [2006] EWHC 90057 (Costs), LTL 7/9/2006). If the client's claim is against the policyholder, and both might be funded by the same insurer, the solicitor must advise whether the degree of control given to the intended defendant's insurer makes it unreasonable to rely on the policy; and this will depend on the size and difficulty of the claim. A failure to follow this practice could mean that the claimant's additional liabilities under a pre-April 2013 funding arrangement, such as an ATE insurance premium and/or success fee under a CFA, cannot be recovered. That is on the basis that any additional liability may have been unreasonably incurred and hence not recoverable on an assessment between parties (*sarwar v Alam* [2001] EWCA Civ 1401, [2002] 1 WLR 125; see also *Barlow v Perks* (2007) SCCO 0606555, LTL 31/10/2007).

Information about funding should be given to the client not only at the outset of litigation but at appropriate stages throughout. A solicitor should tell his or her client how much the costs are at regular intervals and in appropriate cases the solicitor should deliver interim bills at agreed intervals. The solicitor should explain to the client and confirm in writing any change in circumstances which will, or which are likely to, affect the amount of the costs, the degree of risk involved or the ratio of cost to benefit to the client of continuing with the matter. The client should be informed in writing as soon as it appears that a cost estimate or agreed upper limit may or will be exceeded. There is an ongoing obligation to consider the client's eligibility for public funding if a material change in the client's means comes to the solicitor's attention.

Standard information sent out with solicitors' terms of business has an important role to play in ensuring compliance with the requirements of the Code, but attention must be given to the particular circumstances of each case for each client. Assumptions should not be made, and the solicitor and client should regularly discuss how the litigation is to be funded and whether it deserves funding at all. Not only does that ensure compliance with the Code but it is an essential part of basic client care, and can prevent complaints arising. The unexpectedly large bill at the end of litigation remains a fertile source of client dissatisfaction.

Hourly rates

5.6 Private funding is the traditional method of paying for litigation. Usually, the client will pay the solicitor's costs of conducting the case at an agreed hourly rate. Charge-out rates are based on the salaries of the staff and fee earners working at the solicitor's office together with an element representing the firm's overheads and profit margins. The usual approach is to fix a single hourly rate for each fee earner (or grade of fee earner) in the firm taking these factors into account. Guideline hourly rates for different grades of fee earners for different parts of the country can be seen in **tables 71.2 to 71.4**.

The client should be informed if the solicitor's charges are likely to be substantially more than a client can expect to recover on an assessment between parties. In *MacDougall v Boote Edgar Esterkin* (2000) SCCO Case Summary No. 15 of 2000 the client agreed to pay the solicitors at the rate of £300 per hour for work done in Manchester from 1992 onwards. Holland J sitting with assessors found that the consent of the client to that rate was not an informed consent. The solicitor had failed to explain the relationship between party and party and solicitor/own client costs and misrepresented what the approach of the costs officer might be. Notwithstanding that the solicitor was held to have given the client 'devoted skilled service on a sustained basis', on a solicitor/own client assessment his hourly rate was substantially reduced.

Disbursements

In addition to the legal representative's hourly rates, the client will be expected to pay for disbursements. These are sums paid by the firm during the course of litigation such as court, experts' and counsel's fees, travel costs, copies of photographs, and similar expenditure. **5.7**

Fixed fees

Hourly rates are not the only basis for charging. Fixed fees, especially for small claims or fast track litigation, can be agreed. They do, however, require a substantial amount of overall management by the solicitor both in terms of client expectations and the uncertainty of the defendant's conduct. **5.8**

Following work by the Civil Justice Council, a regime of predictable costs for various classes of personal injury claims has applied to road traffic accidents from 6 October 2003 (and has been retained in the current **CPR, rr. 45.9 to 45.15**). Similar schemes applied to accidents at work from 1 October 2004, and to employers' liability disease claims from 1 October 2005, but these have been revoked with effect from 1 April 2013. A streamlined claims process for low-value road traffic accident personal injury claims between £1,000 and £10,000 where liability is admitted (the RTA Protocol) was introduced from 30 April 2010 (see **8.30** to **8.60**) with fixed costs (now to be found in **CPR, rr. 45.16** to **45.28**). The RTA Protocol aims to reduce both costs and the time to admission of liability. Lord Young of Graffham's report, *Common Sense Common Safety* (2010), recommended that the scheme be expanded, and it is likely that similar schemes will be implemented for employers' liability and public liability personal injuries claims, and that an extension of the existing RTA Protocol upper limit to £25,000 will be implemented at the same time.

Discounted fees

Practitioners must take particular care with private funding arrangements which offer discounted fees. It is not uncommon, especially when acting for commercial clients, for solicitors to agree, in writing or otherwise, to reduce their normal hourly rate in the event that the litigation is ultimately unsuccessful. Such arrangements are likely to be construed as CFAs and so, to be enforceable, they must comply with the requirements discussed at **6.6**. **5.9**

Costs forecasts and budgets

Forecasting fees can be extremely difficult, but the Code requires the solicitor to give the 'best information possible'. That can include giving a forecast within a possible range of costs or **5.10** explaining to the client the reasons why it is not possible to fix or give a realistic estimate of the overall costs, and giving instead the best information possible about the costs of the next stage. In cases where proceedings are issued, fees will in any event need to be accurately forecast and budgeted for case management purposes. Particularly in multi-track claims, cost budgets will need to be served and filed as part of usual case management (see **chapter 43**). The client can also be invited to set an upper limit on the firm's costs not to be exceeded without further authority.

Where there is a difference of 20 per cent or more between the costs claimed by a receiving party on a detailed assessment and the costs shown in a costs budget filed by that party, the receiving party will need to be able to provide reasons for the difference (**PD 44, paras 3.5** to 3.7). If there is no satisfactory explanation for the difference, the court may regard the difference between the costs claimed and the costs shown on the budget as evidence that the costs claimed are unreasonable or disproportionate (**para. 3.7**).

Under the pre-Jackson version of these rules, the difference of 20 per cent was taken as a starting point only, and the extent to which the court had regard to any such difference was a matter for its judgment in the individual case (*Mastercigars Direct Ltd v Withers LLP* [2007] EWHC 2733 (Ch), [2009] 1 WLR 881). A solicitor who gave no estimate at all might be able to recover his fees free of any such restriction (*Garbutt v Edwards* [2005] EWCA Civ 1206, [2006] 1 WLR 2907). However, if a complaint of inadequate professional service in not giving an estimate was upheld, the Legal Ombudsman could (and still can) vary the fee to what was appropriate and impose a fine.

Client care letter

5.11 A client care letter, which should include the funding arrangements and, if possible, an estimate of the future costs, should be sent to the client promptly after the firm is retained. It may be appropriate to ask for a sum on account of costs at this stage, and it is sensible to agree to periodical billing of the client (which avoids the client being taken by surprise by a large bill at the end of the case, and also assists with the firm's cash flow).

PUBLIC FUNDING (LEGAL AID)

5.12 Public funding of legal proceedings (legal aid) is administered on behalf of the Lord Chancellor (see **chapter 7**). The introduction of contracting has reduced the number of solicitors who can undertake publicly funded work. Further restrictions on the scope of public funding were introduced by the Legal Aid, Sentencing and Punishment of Offenders Act 2012.

Publicly funded cases are subject to strict procedural and cost limits which the solicitor must have regard to and advise the client accordingly. When acting for a publicly funded client, a solicitor's compliance with the Principles of the SRA Code of Conduct 2011 is indicated by explaining to the client how their publicly funded status affects costs (IB 1.18).

CONDITIONAL FEE AGREEMENTS

5.13 From 1 April 2013, funding under a CFA continues to be an option (see **chapter 6**), but success fees and additional liabilities under CFAs entered into from 1 April 2013 cease to be recoverable from the unsuccessful party.

In *Sibthorpe v Southwark London Borough Council* [2011] EWCA Civ 25, [2011] I WLR 2111, the Court of Appeal held that a CFA containing an indemnity given by the solicitors against any adverse costs order made in favour of their client did not amount to maintenance or champerty. Lord Neuberger of Abbotsbury MR acknowledged that the indemnity meant that the solicitors had a financial interest in the outcome of the litigation (being the risk of having to pay the defendant's costs if the claim failed, whilst not enjoying any gain if the claim succeeded). However, Lord Neuberger went on to note that there were no cases in which such an arrangement had been held to be champertous and that judicial definitions of champerty all envisaged a gain if the claim succeeded. Lord Neuberger held that it was not appropriate to extend the law of champerty at a time when both the judicial and legislative trends were in favour of its scope being curtailed. Further, public policy favoured such an indemnity being valid, at the very least where it permits access to justice in small cases where ATE insurance is unavailable or prohibitively expensive (such as the instant case). Arrangements such as that in *Sibthorpe v Southwark London Borough Council* are therefore legal.

BEFORE-THE-EVENT INSURANCE

Before-the-event (BTE) insurance or legal expenses insurance (LEI) provides the policyholder with an indemnity for the cost of legal fees if the policyholder becomes involved in litigation. It is generally considered a relatively inexpensive mechanism for resolving a range of problems and legal disputes, primarily for consumers. 5.14

The Market for 'BTE' Legal Expenses Insurance, a research report by Fwd thinking communications on behalf of the Ministry of Justice, dated July 2007, revealed that there is a considerable lack of information about the product both in the public domain in general and at the point of sale. Awareness among lower socio-economic groups is particularly low even though people in these groups appear more likely to benefit from LEI.

The report also revealed that despite low awareness overall, market penetration of LEI has increased to 59 per cent of the population (this compares with 50 per cent penetration revealed by Mintel in their report published in December 2006). The research estimates that 28 million adults currently have LEI, most often as an add-on to another insurance policy (usually a motor or buildings policy).

Sir Rupert Jackson's *Review of Civil Litigation Costs: Final Report* (Ministry of Justice, December 2009) recommended that positive efforts should be made to encourage the take up of BTE insurance by small and medium-sized enterprises in respect of business disputes and by householders as an add-on to insurance policies. Lord Young of Graffham's report, *Common Sense Common Safety* (2010), also endorses extending BTE insurance as a possible solution to the problem of access to justice. Lord Young proposes to consult with the insurance industry on developing stand-alone BTE policies for individuals, as well as on how best to develop policies for small businesses.

Legal expenses cover is usually broadly limited to the subject matter of the main policy and to claims of merit, although it is surprising how widely some policies are worded. The level of cover is usually limited to an agreed figure (£25,000 to £50,000 is not unusual) and will cover both the policyholder's liability for their own legal costs, and their liability for an opponent's costs if a case is lost. Legal expenses insurers often require the client's lawyers to provide advice on the merits of the claim from time to time so they can assess whether continuing the litigation can be justified under the terms of the insurance.

Most policies insist that, before the issue of proceedings, the policyholder uses a solicitor selected from a panel appointed by the insurer, who can then retain control over its terms of business with the panel firms. After proceedings have begun the policyholder has a right to instruct a solicitor of his or her choice (Insurance Companies (Legal Expenses Insurance) Regulations 1990, SI 1990/1159). The narrow interpretation of 'proceedings' to exclude pre-issue work, including working through a pre-action protocol, has been endorsed by the Financial Ombudsman Service in a policy statement issued in March 2003 *Ombudsman*

News, issue 26). However, in a different context (when considering costs-only proceedings in *Crosbie v Munroe* [2003] EWCA Civ 350, [2003] 1 WLR 2033) Brooke LJ commented, obiter, at [37]:

> lower courts are encountering...difficulties over the meaning of the word 'proceedings' as used in PD Protocols, para. 4A.2....it appears to me that...for instance, the dealings between the parties which lead up to the disposal of a clinical negligence claim are to be treated as 'proceedings' for the purposes of that paragraph even if the dispute is settled without the need to issue a claim form.

AFTER-THE-EVENT INSURANCE

5.15 ATE insurance policies are taken out to help cover the cost of litigation once a dispute has already arisen. If the premium is affordable, it can provide some peace of mind against the possibility of having to pay the total litigation costs if the case is lost. A fixed or predictable premium can also provide a certainty of cost exposure which is otherwise missing for a client involved in litigation.

Cover can be obtained to insure both the client's own legal costs, including disbursements, and those of opposing parties. They are commonly, but not exclusively, used in conjunction with CFAs so that there is risk sharing between both the insurance company and the solicitor. An application for insurance can normally be made at any time in the litigation but many insurance companies encourage applications to be made as early as possible, and preferably before the issue of proceedings.

Whether or not insurance is offered by a particular provider and at what premium will depend primarily on the strength of the case and the level of cover required. As a very rough guide, insurance is generally available for cases with prospects of success greater than 65 per cent. In matters other than personal injury, premiums tend to be about 20 to 30 per cent of the amount of cover required.

The practitioner must exercise caution before assuming any responsibility to give 'best or suitable advice' in relation to the products which may be available. Although it may be incumbent upon the solicitor to suggest to the client a suitable policy, the solicitor should not guarantee that the means of funding adopted will necessarily be the most appropriate to the client's needs. A list of insurance providers is updated quarterly in the Law Society's publication, *Litigation Funding*. Specialist ATE insurance brokers exist, and may charge a fee for their service (often refundable when a policy is taken out). Several different types of policy are available. Some providers offer policies which defer payment of the premium until the conclusion of the case and which rebate the premium if the client is unsuccessful. In *Tilby v Perfect Pizza Ltd* (2002) LTL 28/3/2002 Senior Costs Judge Hurst held that there is no reason why an ATE policy premium must be paid when the policy is taken out. Accordingly an ATE policy can provide for payment of the premium on the conclusion of proceedings without being regarded as providing credit and so subject to the Consumer Credit Act 1974. Other policies do specifically offer credit schemes allowing clients to borrow money to pay ongoing disbursements or the insurance premium itself.

A non-party costs order under the Senior Courts Act 1981, s. 51, may be made against an ATE funder, though the liability may be capped to the level of funding provided to the opposing party (*Arkin v Borchard Lines Ltd (Nos. 2 and 3)* [2005] EWCA Civ 655, [2005] 1 WLR 3055). Such an order is much less likely to be made if the funder is a 'pure funder' — one with no commercial or financial interest in the outcome — such as those who made donations towards the legal expenses of the unsuccessful claimant in *Hamilton v Al Fayed (No. 2)* [2002] EWCA Civ 665, [2003] QB 1175. An ATE insurer may avoid a policy for material misrepresentation and non-disclosure (*Persimmon Homes Ltd v Great Lakes Reinsurance (UK) plc* [2010] EWHC 1705 (Comm), LTL 13/7/2010). In that case, the successful defendant in the underlying proceedings claimed directly against the insolvent claimant's ATE insurer for its costs under the Third Parties (Rights against Insurers) Act 1930. The ATE insurer successfully avoided the policy for material misrepresentations and non-disclosure, based largely on findings in the underlying proceedings, meaning that the defendant was unable to rely on the ATE insurance obtained by the claimant. The decision confirms that ATE insurance is not to be treated differently from any other type of insurance with respect to the impact of material misrepresentations and non-disclosure.

In *Guerrero v Monterrico Metals plc* [2009] EWHC 2475 (QB), LTL 26/10/2009, the court held that the amount to be frozen in respect of a worldwide freezing order could include a sum to reflect part of an ATE insurance premium, but it refused to permit the entire premium (which was close to the defendants' agreed costs limit) to be frozen on the basis that this would shift the preponderance of the litigation risk on to the defendant.

Recoverability of ATE insurance premiums paid before 1 April 2013

Provided the policy was entered into before 1 April 2013, or relates to proceedings in which **5.16**
recoverability is still allowed, a successful party may claim the premium paid for ATE cover from the other side as part of the costs of the proceedings (**Access to Justice Act 1999, s. 29**, which has been repealed from 1 April 2013 by the Legal Aid, Sentencing and Punishment of Offenders Act 2012, s. 46, subject to some savings). In accordance with the usual rules on the quantification of costs by the court (now to be found in **CPR, rr. 44.3** and **44.4**), to be recoverable in full the premium must have been reasonably incurred and reasonable and proportionate in amount. There is a considerable body of case law, discussed in **71.61**, on the circumstances in which such a premium can be recovered and what amount is reasonable and proportionate.

In considering whether a premium is recoverable at all, the principal factor is whether there were any real risks against which it was proper to insure at the time of entering into the insurance policy (*Burgess v J. Breheny Contracts Ltd* [2009] EWHC 90131 (Costs)). A premium on an ATE policy taken out at a late stage may be recoverable depending on the circumstances of the case (*Kris Motor Spares Ltd v Fox Williams LLP* [2010] EWHC 1008 (QB), LTL 13/5/2010). Where the policy was entered into after the defendant made an admission of liability, there may still be real risks against which it was reasonable to insure, including the risk of failing to equal a Part 36 offer (*Burgess v J. Breheny Contracts Ltd*). In considering whether a premium is reasonable, the court must have regard to such evidence as there is, or knowledge that experience has provided, of the relationship between the premium and the risk, and the cost of alternative cover (*Callery v Gray (No. 2)* [2001] EWCA Civ 1246, [2001] 1 WLR 2142, at [69]).

In straightforward road traffic claims, only a modest premium is likely to be allowed. Thus in *Callery v Gray (No. 2)* the court allowed a premium of £367.50. Account has also been taken of the predictable cost regime for smaller personal injury cases (see **5.8**). The courts have taken care when considering premiums charged by claims management companies, where the payment described as the 'premium' might cover a basket of services only one of which was the ATE insurance cover. In *Sharratt v London Central Bus Co. Ltd (No. 2)* [2004] EWCA Civ 575, [2004] 3 All ER 325, the Court of Appeal approved the costs judge's approach of investigating how much of the payment in fact related to the cost of the ATE cover. The fees charged by claims management companies for the referral or introduction of a client or potential client attracted criticism in both the *Jackson Report* (2009) and Lord Young of Graffham's report, *Common Sense Common Safety* (2010). Sir Rupert Jackson recommended that referral fees be banned in personal injury claims and this was implemented by the Legal Aid, Sentencing and Punishment of Offenders Act 2012, ss. 56 to 60.

Fixed staged premiums (which increase at defined stages in the litigation process) in large-volume, low-value cases have also been approved. In *Rogers v Merthyr Tydfil County Borough*

Council [2006] EWCA Civ 1134, [2007] 1 WLR 808, the Court of Appeal rejected arguments that the proportionality of a staged premium in an individual case should be tested against the damages recovered. Instead the court held that if it is necessary to incur a staged premium, then it should be found to be a proportionate expense. Necessity could be demonstrated 'by the application of strategic considerations which travel beyond the dictates of the particular case and may include the unavoidable characteristics of the market in insurance of this kind'. In *Rogers v Merthyr Tydfil County Borough Council* the Court of Appeal expressly recognised that due regard should be had to an underwriter's ability to rate the risk the insurer faced as judges do not have the expertise to judge the reasonableness of a premium except in very broad-brush terms, and the viability of the ATE insurance market could be undermined if they were to behave as if they did. In *Parker v Seixo* [2010] EWHC 90162, BAILII, Master Wright reiterated that without the assistance of expert evidence the court could not regard itself as better qualified than the underwriter to assess an ATE insurer's financial risk. This meant that the courts were reluctant to interfere with the amount of a premium even if it appeared at first blush to be disproportionate (*Burgess v J. Breheny Contracts Ltd*).

It is nonetheless important for the parties to provide clear evidence of the reasonableness of a premium, and equally a paying party wishing to challenge the level of a premium should be prepared to adduce evidence of the level which they claim is appropriate (*Burgess v J. Breheny Contracts Ltd*). In *Kris Motor Spares Ltd v Fox Williams LLP* [2010] EWHC 1008 (QB), LTL 13/5/2010, the paying party failed to adduce any evidence that a premium of £95,550 for £130,000 cover (a rate of 73.5 per cent) was unreasonable and, accordingly, its appeal on the grounds that the premium was unreasonable was dismissed.

In *Redwing Construction Ltd v Wishart* [2011] EWHC 19 (TCC), [2011] BLR 186, Akenhead J commented that on a summary assessment, particularly in a relatively low value claim, it may be disproportionate to expect in effect expert evidence to be adduced as to the unreasonableness of the premium, and that the court should be able to look at the amount of the premium compared to the amount of cover provided and form some realistic view of the assessment of risk which must have been taken by the insurer. In doing so, Akenhead J concluded that a premium of £8,480 for cover of £20,000 (i.e. 42 per cent of the insured amount) was 'substantially excessive' and only allowed recovery of 20 per cent of the premium.

Although in most cases there is an evidential burden on the paying party to produce some evidence that the premium is unreasonable, this does not reverse the burden of proof. If following evidence and argument there is still a doubt about the reasonableness of the charge, that doubt must be resolved in favour of the paying party (*kris Motor Spares Ltd v Fox Williams LLP*; *Rogers v Merthyr Tydfil County Borough Council*).

For difficult litigation, premiums can be substantial. In *Sarwar v Alam* (2003) LTL 23/3/2003 the claim was an important test case. A premium of £62,500 subject to a 50 per cent no-claims bonus was allowed in full. The costs judge, Master Rogers, commented that although the premium was high, it was unlikely that a lower quotation could have been obtained. In practice, solicitors may have to show they considered more than one insurer if a very large premium is to be recovered in full from the other side.

Former requirement to notify other side

5.17 Until 1 April 2013, the fact that a party had taken out an ATE insurance policy had be notified to the court and every other party (former CPR, r. 44.15; PD 43–48, para. 19, in force before 1 April 2013). Form N251 had to be used. A party was potentially prohibited from recovering the CFA success fee and any ATE insurance premium for any period in the proceedings during which they failed to provide details in connection to the funding arrangement (former CPR, r. 44.15; PD 43–48, para. 19 in force before 1 April 2013). This was illustrated in *Kutsi v North*

Middlesex University Hospital NHS Trust [2008] EWHC 90119 (Costs), in which the claimant was unable to recover an ATE insurance premium where her solicitors had mistakenly failed to notify the defendant of the existence of an ATE policy, and only did so after the claim had settled.

THIRD-PARTY 'CONTINGENCY' FUNDING

For high-value cases, third-party funding (TPF) has emerged, in which commercial third parties fund the costs of litigation, in return for a percentage of damages recovered. The risk undertaken by the funder is reflected in the percentage of damages which the funder is entitled to receive in the event of success. TPF is most readily obtained for high-value cases with good prospects of success. For instance in *Arkin v Borchard Lines Ltd (Nos. 2 and 3)* [2005] EWCA Civ 655, [2005] 1 WLR 3055, the funder agreed to pay for the claimants' substantial expert accountants' fees (expected to be £600,000 but which ended up at circa £1.3 million) in return for any recovery of the experts' fees from the other party plus 25 per cent of any damages recovered up to £5 million, and 23 per cent of any sum above that. Although the claimant lost, the Court of Appeal approved the arrangement in principle, finding that it was not champertous. The funder was, however, additionally exposed to a non-party costs order in favour of the defendant equal to the amount of the financial assistance given to the claimant, i.e. £1.3 million. The market for this kind of funding continues to develop. 5.18

A product comparison table of third-party litigation funders and brokers is updated quarterly by the Law Society's publication, *Litigation Funding*.

A prominent example of the operation of TPF is *Stone and Rolls Ltd v Moore Stephens* [2009] UKHL 39, [2009] 1 AC 1391, in which the claimant company brought a substantial (£106 million) professional negligence claim against its former auditors using funding provided by commercial third-party funders (who reportedly stood to receive some 40 per cent of the proceeds if the claim succeeded). The claim was ultimately unsuccessful and the third-party funders accepted liability for the defendant's costs (reported to be in the region of £2.5 million).

The issue whether third-party funders should be liable for adverse costs has been a matter of debate. In *Arkin v Borchard Lines Ltd (Nos. 2 and 3)* Lord Phillips of Worth Matravers MR suggested that potential liability for adverse costs would discourage third-party funders. Sir Rupert Jackson's *Review of Civil Litigation Costs: Final Report* (Ministry of Justice, December 2009) considered this issue and concluded that there is no evidence that full liability for adverse costs would stifle TPF and that it is possible for litigation funders to have business models which encompass such liability (as illustrated by *Stone and Rolls Ltd v Moore Stephens*). Sir Rupert therefore recommended that third-party funders should potentially be liable for the full amount of adverse costs, subject to the discretion of the judge.

The growth of TPF in recent years has also led to debate about whether third-party funders should be regulated or subscribe to a voluntary code. The *Jackson Report* concluded that statutory regulation was not currently necessary, but that a satisfactory voluntary code should be drawn up, to which all litigation funders should subscribe, containing (among other things) effective capital adequacy requirements and restrictions on funders' ability to withdraw support for ongoing litigation.

The Civil Justice Council published a voluntary Code of Conduct for Litigation Funders in November 2011.

TPF has sometimes been viewed as a more expensive funding option than a combination of CFAs and ATE insurance (where both the success fee and the ATE premium are potentially recoverable from an unsuccessful opponent). However, with removal of recoverability from 1 April 2013, the overall cost to a funded party of TPF may be comparable.

DAMAGES-BASED AGREEMENTS

5.19 Lawyers can share in the risk of litigation with their clients by agreeing to link the recovery of their fees with the outcome of the litigation. These fee agreements are known as 'contingency fees' — the lawyers' fees are contingent on the result obtained.

Contingency fees strictly encompass all types of CFA (where the solicitor charges an uplift on fees if the case is won, and a reduced fee or no fee at all if the case is lost) but generally refer to agreements to charge fees equivalent to a percentage of the damages awarded (known as damages-based agreements (DBAs), which are common in the USA).

Contingency fee agreements have been generally unenforceable in litigation because they are champertous arrangements, contrary to public policy and the common law. However, that position has developed radically in recent years. First, specific statutory authority has been provided for the use of CFAs in litigation. The whole topic is considered further in **chapter 6**. Secondly, DBAs have not been unlawful for funding mediations and First-tier Tribunal cases as these are non-contentious matters for the purposes of the Solicitors Act 1974, s. 57(2). Thirdly, the Legal Aid, Sentencing and Punishment of Offenders Act 2012, s. 45, which came into force on 1 April 2013, extends the use of DBAs to all proceedings (whether issued or not) for resolving disputes.

Requirements for DBAs

5.20 A DBA will be legal and enforceable if:

(a) it is in writing (Courts and Legal Services Act 1990, s. 58AA(4)(a));
(b) it does not relate to proceedings which cannot be the subject of an enforceable CFA (see **chapter 6**) or to proceedings of a description prescribed by the Lord Chancellor (Courts and Legal Services Act 1990, s. 58AA(4)(aa));
(c) it does not provide for a payment above a prescribed amount or for a payment above an amount calculated in a prescribed manner (Courts and Legal Services Act 1990, s. 58AA(4)(b));
(d) its terms and conditions comply with any prescribed requirements (Courts and Legal Services Act 1990, s. 58AA(4)(c)). As provided by the Damages-Based Agreement Regulations 2013 (SI 2013/609), reg. 3, these terms must specify:
  (i) the claim or proceedings or parts of them to which the agreement relates;
  (ii) the circumstances in which the representative's payment, expenses and costs, or part of them, are payable; and
  (iii) the reason for setting the amount of the payment at the level agreed;
(e) the person providing services under the agreement has complied with any prescribed requirements concerning the provision of information (Courts and Legal Services Act 1990, s. 58AA(4)(d)). Requirements to provide information in SI 2013/609, reg. 5 apply only to employment matters.

Prescribed amounts and payments for the purposes of point (c) apply only to claims at first instance (SI 2013/609, reg. 4(4)). First-instance matters fall into two categories in non-employment proceedings:

(a) In respect of non-personal injuries claims, a DBA must not require an amount to be paid by the client other than costs and expenses which are net of any costs and expenses which have been paid by another party to the proceedings (reg. 4(1)). The amount to be paid by the client must not exceed an amount which, including VAT, is equal to 50 per cent of the sums ultimately recovered by the client (reg. 4(3)). These costs and expenses may include disbursements in respect of counsel's fees as well as other types of disbursements (regs 1(2) and 4(1)(a)(ii)). 'Costs' means the total of the representative's time reasonably spent, in respect of the claim or proceedings, multiplied by the reasonable hourly rate of remuneration of the representative (reg. 1(2)).

(b) In a claim for personal injuries (which, by SI 2013/609, reg. 1(2), has the same meaning as in **CPR, r. 2.3**) a DBA must not provide for a payment above an amount which, including VAT, is equal to 25 per cent of the combined sums of:
(i) general damages for pain, suffering and loss of amenity; and
(ii) damages for pecuniary loss other than future pecuniary loss,
which are ultimately recovered by the client (SI 2013/609, reg. 4(2)).

The only sums recovered by the client from which the payment may be met are those damages net of any sums recoverable by the Compensation Recovery Unit of the Department for Work and Pensions (reg. 4(2)(a)).

The validity of contingency fee agreements in non-employment First-tier Tribunal cases was confirmed by Senior Costs Judge Master Hurst in *Tel-Ka Talk Ltd v Commissioners of HM Revenue and Customs* [2010] EWHC 90175 (Costs), BAILII.

ASSIGNMENT OF CAUSES OF ACTION

Sometimes someone in whom a cause of action is vested will assign it to another person who **5.21**
may be better placed to fund the litigation. Doing so, if effective, will allow that other person to bring (or continue) proceedings based on that cause of action. There may be practical reasons for doing this. For example, a cause of action may be vested in a trustee in bankruptcy, who may be unwilling to prosecute the claim.

Assignments are sometimes attacked on the ground that they are tainted by champerty or maintenance, particularly in cases involving the assignment of a large number of small claims to a claims management company in exchange for a substantial success fee in the event of a successful claim (see, e.g., *Claims Group Direct Ltd v Lloyds TSB Bank plc* (2009) LTL 11/11/2009, in which such a scheme was found to be champertous). The subject is dealt with in more detail at **14.6 to 14.9**.

Assignments by companies intended to obtain the benefit of public funding and to avoid the risk of having to provide security for costs were upheld by the House of Lords in *Norglen Ltd v Reeds Rains Prudential Ltd* [1999] 2 AC 1. However, 'matters arising out of the carrying on of a business' are now excluded from the scope of public funding by the Legal Aid, Sentencing and Punishment of Offenders Act 2012, sch. 1, part 2, para. 14, and it is difficult to envisage circumstances where public funding will be available following an assignment of this type.

Chapter 6 Conditional Fee Agreements

INTRODUCTION[1]

6.1 A conditional fee agreement (CFA) is defined by the **Courts and Legal Services Act 1990, s. 58(2)(a)**, as an agreement for advocacy or litigation services which provides that the lawyer's fees and expenses, or any part of them, will be payable only in specified circumstances. The basic nature of CFAs, including this definition, is unchanged by the Legal Aid, Sentencing and Punishment of Offenders Act 2012.

CFAs with success fees are the more familiar arrangements whereby the legal representative charges nothing if the case is lost but the full fee plus an enhancement — calculated as a percentage uplift on the fee — if the case is won. Removing the recoverability of success fees from the unsuccessful party was the main change effected by the Legal Aid, Sentencing and Punishment of Offenders Act 2012, and applies to CFAs entered into on or after 1 April 2013. Recoverability of success fees and after-the-event (ATE) premiums, were important elements contributing to the popularity of CFAs, particularly with claimants and claims companies. It is possible that the use of CFAs will decline in favour of damages-based agreements (DBAs), which are permitted from 1 April 2013 (see **5.19**).

CFAs without success fees effectively replace what were *Thai Trading Co. v Taylor* [1998] QB 781 agreements, i.e. agreements where the client is charged nothing, or a reduced fee, if the case is lost but the full fee where the case is won.

CFAs can be extremely flexible. If the case is lost, the agreement may be that the client will pay nothing at all, or will pay the solicitor's charges at a reduced hourly rate or even a fixed fee depending on the stage reached in the litigation. If the case is won, the agreement can provide for the payment of the solicitor's basic costs without any enhancement, or a percentage uplift on those fees. CFAs can use any combination of these provisions, and, within certain boundaries, set basic hourly rates and the level of discounts and enhancements.

[1] The author, Alan Owens, is grateful to Gemma Anderson, Senior Associate at Morrison & Foerster, for her assistance in compiling the material used in chapters 5 and 6.

Since 30 July 1998 (Conditional Fee Agreements Order 1998 (SI 1998/1860)) it has been possible to enter into CFAs in all types of civil litigation with the exception of family work. By the **Courts and Legal Services Act 1990, s. 58A(4)**, 'proceedings' for the purposes of CFAs includes any sort of proceedings for resolving disputes and is not limited to proceedings in court. Nor is the term limited to cases where proceedings are commenced as opposed to contemplated, and it may include pre-action matters, such as enforcing compliance with a pre-action protocol and an application for pre-action disclosure (*Connaughton v Imperial College Healthcare NHS Trust* [2010] EWHC 90173 (Costs), LTL 2/12/2010). CFAs can be used for many kinds of dispute resolution, including arbitration and tribunal matters.

CFAs and champerty

The concern that it might be possible for an unsuccessful defendant to avoid paying the costs of a claimant on the basis that the legal representative's retainer under a CFA was illegal on the ground of maintenance or champerty (see **14.7**) was removed by *Hodgson v Imperial Tobacco Ltd* [1998] 1 WLR 1056. The Court of Appeal has confirmed in *Sibthorpe v Southwark London Borough Council* [2011] EWCA Civ 25, [2011] 1 WLR 2111, that a CFA containing an indemnity by the instructed solicitors in favour of their client against any adverse costs order does not amount to maintenance or champerty (see **5.13**). An argument that taking a weak case on a CFA is an abuse of process was rejected in *King v Telegraph Group Ltd* [2003] EWHC 1312 (QB), LTL 9/6/2003. In *Tinseltime Ltd v Roberts* [2012] EWHC 2628 (TCC), [2012] 6 Costs LR 1094, the court held that it was not appropriate to make a non-party costs order against a solicitor who acted for an impecunious claimant under a CFA, where the solicitor funded the disbursements and where there was no ATE policy in place. **6.2**

The **Courts and Legal Services Act 1990, s. 58**, permits the recovery of success fees from unsuccessful opponents. But recoverability has been abolished by the Legal Aid, Sentencing and Punishment of Offenders Act 2012, s. 44, for CFAs entered into on or after 1 April 2013.

CFAs and freedom of expression

Even before the Legal Aid, Sentencing and Punishment of Offenders Act 2012, the European Court of Human Rights (ECHR) held that the requirement that MGN pay success fees to the supermodel Naomi Campbell on costs awarded in respect of proceedings brought by her for breach of confidence violated its right to freedom of expression under the European Convention on Human Rights, **art. 10** in the **Human Rights Act 1998, sch. 1** (*MGN Ltd v United Kingdom* (application 39401/04) (2011) 53 EHRR 5). Ms Campbell had been successful at first instance, but the decision was overturned by the Court of Appeal before being reinstated by a majority of the House of Lords (*Campbell v MGN Ltd* [2004] UKHL 22, [2004] 2 AC 457). MGN was subsequently served with a bill in respect of Ms Campbell's costs for just over £1 million, made up of £850,000 base costs and £365,000 success fees payable under CFAs entered into by Ms Campbell with her solicitors and counsel for the first and second appeals, which provided for success fees of 95 per cent and 100 per cent respectively. MGN appealed to the House of Lords on the basis that its liability to pay the success fees was so disproportionate as to infringe its **art. 10** rights. The House of Lords dismissed the appeal, holding that the CFA regime (including the recoverability of success fees against defendants) was proportionate to the legitimate aim of providing litigants with access to justice, notwithstanding the possible effects on **art. 10** rights (*Campbell v MGN Ltd (No. 2)* [2005] UKHL 61, [2005] 1 WLR 3394). In contrast, the ECHR found that the requirement that MGN pay success fees was disproportionate, exceeding even the broad margin of appreciation accorded to the government in such matters, and constituted a violation of **art. 10**. In support of this conclusion, the ECHR pointed to 'the depth and nature of the flaws in the [current CFA] system', as reflected in Sir Rupert Jackson's *Review of Litigation Costs: Final Report* (2009), which flaws were borne out by the facts of the **6.3** case, Ms Campbell being wealthy and therefore not in the category of persons who would be excluded from access to justice for financial reasons.

The decision of the ECHR is binding on the UK government, who will be obliged to introduce legislation to cure the unlawfulness, at least in defamation and privacy cases where **art. 10** is engaged. However, publication and privacy cases are one of the areas where implementation of the non-recoverability provisions of the Legal Aid, Sentencing and Punishment of Offenders Act 2012 has been delayed (**CPR, r. 48.2(1)(b)** and **PD 48, para. 3.2**).

PRACTICAL CONSIDERATIONS

6.4 Although most CFAs are entered into by claimants, there is no reason to prevent defendants from using them. The definition of 'win' for the purposes of the agreement is a matter for negotiation between the lawyer and the client. When acting for a claimant 'win' will almost always mean an award (but not recovery of) damages. Lawyers who represent a defendant may agree to a definition of 'win' that relates to the amount of damages paid by the defendant at the conclusion of the claim, whether by settlement or trial. The level of those damages could be set at nil, or a figure relating to the claim put in the claimant's statement of case. A successful defendant will be able to benefit from the rules on recovery of a success fee and insurance premium in the same way as a successful claimant, although there is much less of a market for after-the-event insurance for defendants than for claimants.

CFAs are most prevalent in personal injury litigation where they are commonly used in conjunction with ATE insurance (see **5.15**). They are also popular in libel claims. However, concern has been expressed regarding the effect of the recoverability of success fees and ATE premiums on costs in defamation proceedings. The previous government's plans to reduce the maximum success fee in defamation proceedings from 100 per cent to 10 per cent were abandoned due to lack of Parliamentary time. Following the decision in *MGN Ltd v United Kingdom* (application 39401/04) (2011) 53 EHRR 5 (discussed at **6.3**), it is likely that the pressure for reform in this area will be renewed and, at least, the end of the recovery of 100 per cent success fees in defamation cases is nigh. The use of CFAs in commercial litigation is increasingly led by client demand and is supported by a wide choice of ATE providers and third-party funders. Although many commercial clients do not insist on CFAs now, it is likely that more and more clients will enquire about their use and will increasingly ask their lawyers to give serious consideration to them.

Since the removal of public funding for business-related disputes, CFAs offer a route to funding and progressing meritorious cases when a client may be unable to raise sufficient funds to pay privately. However, disbursements will need funding during the conduct of the claim and there is no statutory protection (unlike in public funding cases) against an adverse order for costs if the claim is unsuccessful. This means that obtaining suitable ATE insurance is often crucial, as is an assessment of the likelihood of being able to recover base costs from the unsuccessful opponent.

CFAs have a potentially important part to play in the effective management of litigation. Entering into a CFA (and paying for insurance against an adverse costs order) can have significant tactical advantages to a client. Until 1 April 2013, the client's risk of having to pay legal fees at all could be substantially reduced, or even extinguished. In *Sousa v Waltham Forest London Borough Council* [2011] EWCA Civ 194, [2011] 1 WLR 2197 the court clarified that a claimant who has had the benefit of a full indemnity of costs from his insurer (and was therefore never at risk as to costs) is nonetheless entitled to rely on a CFA with a success fee. CFAs with pre-April 2013 recoverable success fees have the effect of raising the stakes in terms of costs while shifting some of the risk away from the client and sending the message to the opponent that the case is strong enough to attract risk-sharing from the solicitor and often an insurer too.

ENTERING INTO A CFA

The SRA Code of Conduct 2011 sets out 'outcomes-focused' conduct requirements, providing greater flexibility for individual firms to decide how best to meet and 'uphold the intention' of the Code, with reference to 'indicative behaviours'. For CFAs a solicitor must achieve the following outcome: 6.5

O(1.6) you only enter into fee agreements with your clients that are legal, and which you consider are suitable for the client's needs and take account of the client's best interests;...

Acting in the following way(s) may tend to show that you have achieved these outcomes and therefore complied with the Principles:

...IB(1.4) explaining any arrangements, such as fee sharing or referral arrangements, which are relevant to the client's instructions;...

IB(1.17) where you are acting for a client under a fee arrangement governed by statute, such as a conditional fee agreement, giving the client all relevant information relating to that arrangement;

IB(1.18) where you are acting for a publicly funded client, explaining how their publicly funded status affects the costs;

IB(1.19) providing the information in a clear and accessible form which is appropriate to the needs and circumstances of the client.

It is clear from *Callery v Gray* [2001] EWCA Civ 1117, [2001] 1 WLR 2112, that the fact that proceedings have not been issued is not a bar to entering into a valid CFA, and that it may be reasonable to enter into a CFA at the outset of the retainer, before the defendant has been approached or has clarified its position. In *Forde v Birmingham City Council* [2009] EWHC 12 (QB), [2009] 1 WLR 2732, Christopher Clarke J held that there is no prohibition against retrospective CFAs and that a retrospective success fee is not contrary to public policy. The case departs from the previous position that retrospective success fees were contrary to public policy (following the decision of Senior Costs Judge Hurst in *King v Telegraph Group Ltd* [2005] EWHC 90015 (Costs)).

It is not unreasonable to enter into a CFA after admissions have been made on liability and causation, provided a proper risk assessment is made for the purposes of setting the success fee (*Thornley v Ministry of Defence* [2010] EWHC 2584 (QB), [2011] 3 Costs LR 335).

Requirements for validity of CFAs before 1 April 2013

A CFA entered into on or after 1 November 2005 must comply with the **Courts and Legal Services Act 1990, ss. 58 and 58A**. This means that a CFA must: 6.6

(a) be in writing (s. 58(3)(a));
(b) relate to a type of case that the statute allows to be run on a CFA (s. 58(3)(b)); and
(c) specify the success fee, which must not exceed 100 per cent (s. 58(4); Conditional Fee Agreements Order 2000 (SI 2000/823), art. 4).

A failure to comply with any of these basic elements is likely to mean that the CFA is unenforceable.

An additional fee which depends on success but does not form part of the success fee may be allowed even where the success fee is 100 per cent. In *Morris v John Dennis (Barnsley) Ltd* [2008] EWHC 90112 (Costs), an 'administration charge' of £150, payable only in the event of success, was held not to be part of a 100 per cent success fee and did not, therefore, infringe the **Courts and Legal Services Act 1990, s. 58(4)**. The court held that the use of such charges could be policed in the usual way through seeking an assessment of the solicitors' costs under the Solicitors Act 1974, s. 70. In *Hanley v Smith* [2009] EWHC 90144 (Costs) the court confirmed that entering into a CFA will not of itself prevent a party from being awarded interest on costs from the date of judgment under the Judgments Act 1838, s. 17 (on the basis that a party operating under a CFA has not actually had to pay any costs). The decision clarifies that the right to interest on costs under s. 17 exists whether or not a party has a contractual obligation to pay, or has paid, interest on costs to his lawyers.

By the **Courts and Legal Services Act 1990, s. 58A(1)**, the only proceedings which cannot be the subject of an enforceable CFA are criminal proceedings and family proceedings, as defined in **s. 58A(2)**, apart from proceedings under the Environmental Protection Act 1990, s. 82 (proceedings in a magistrates' court to abate a statutory nuisance).

From 1 April 2000 to 30 October 2005, a CFA was not effective unless it complied with the and **Courts and Legal Services Act 1990, ss. 58** and **58A**, and complied with the Conditional Fee Agreements Regulations 2000 (SI 2000/692). Those Regulations have been revoked and do not apply to CFAs entered into on or after 1 November 2005.

Requirements for validity of CFAs from 1 April 2013

6.7 A CFA that complies with the requirements of the **Courts and Legal Services Act 1990, s. 58**, shall not be unenforceable by reason only that it is a CFA, but any other CFA is unenforceable. The requirements that must be satisfied for a CFA to be effective if entered into on or after 1 April 2013 are laid down by amended **s 58(3), (4A)** and **(4B)**, and fall into two categories: those for non-personal injury CFAs and those for personal injury CFAs.

6.8 **Non-personal injury CFAs** There are no changes to the requirements for CFAs concerning claims other than for personal injury (nor for personal injury claims where the CFA does not include a success fee). In these cases CFAs must, by the **Courts and Legal Services Act 1990, s. 58(3)** and **(4)**, comply with the following conditions:

(a) The agreement must be in writing (**s. 58(3)(a)**).
(b) It must not relate to proceedings which cannot be the subject of an enforceable CFA (**s. 58(3)(b)**). The only type of civil proceedings which cannot be the subject of an enforceable CFA are family proceedings (**s. 58A(1)(b)**). For the purposes of these provisions, the term 'proceedings' includes any sort of proceedings (whether commenced or contemplated) for resolving disputes, and not just proceedings in a court (**s. 58A(4)**).
(c) It must comply with any requirements which may be prescribed by the Lord Chancellor (**s. 58(3)(b)**). At present there are none.
(d) If the agreement includes a success fee, it must:
  (i) relate to proceedings of a description specified by statutory instrument (**s. 58(4)(b)**; all civil proceedings which can be the subject of an enforceable CFA are currently specified, see the Conditional Fee Agreements Order 2013 (SI 2013/689), art. 2); and
  (ii) state the percentage uplift ('success fee'), which must not exceed the percentage prescribed by statutory instrument (**Courts and Legal Services Act 1990, s. 58(4)(b)** and **(c)**), which is currently 100 per cent (SI 2013/689, art. 3).

6.9 **Personal injury CFAs** A CFA in a claim for personal injuries must comply with the following conditions:

(1) The agreement must be in writing (**Courts and Legal Services Act 1990, s. 58(3)(a)**).
(2) It must not relate to proceedings which cannot be the subject of an enforceable CFA (**s. 58(3)(b)**; see **6.8**).
(3) It must comply with any requirements which may be prescribed by the Lord Chancellor (**s. 58(3)(c)**). At present there are none.
(4) If the agreement includes a success fee, it must:
  (a) relate to proceedings of a description specified by statutory instrument (**s. 58(4)(a)**); all civil proceedings which can be the subject of an enforceable CFA are currently specified (Conditional Fee Agreements Order 2013 (SI 2013/689), art. 2);

(b) state the percentage uplift ('success fee'), which must not exceed the percentage prescribed by statutory instrument (**Courts and Legal Services Act 1990, s. 58(4)(b)** and (**c**)), which is currently 100 per cent (SI 2013/689, art. 3);
(c) provide that the success fee is subject to a maximum limit, which must be expressed as a percentage of the descriptions of damages awarded in the proceedings that are specified in the agreement (**Courts and Legal Services Act 1990, s. 58(4A)** and (**4B**)(**a**) and (**b**)). Those descriptions of damages may only include descriptions of damages specified by order made by the Lord Chancellor in relation to the proceedings (**s. 58(4B)(d)**), which by virtue of SI 2013/689, art. 5(2), are:
  (i) general damages for pain, suffering and loss of amenity; and
  (ii) damages for pecuniary loss, other than future pecuniary loss,
  net of any sums recoverable by the Compensation Recovery Unit of the Department for Work and Pensions; and
(d) the maximum limit must not exceed 25 per cent in respect of first-instance proceedings (**Courts and Legal Services Act 1990, s. 58(4A)** and (**4B**)(**c**); SI 2013/689, art. 5(1)(a)) or 100 per cent in respect of appeal proceedings (art. 5(1)(b)).

'Personal injuries' for this purpose has the same meaning, by SI 2013/689, art. 1(2), as it does in **CPR, r. 2.3**. This provides that a 'claim for personal injuries' means proceedings in which there is a claim for damages in respect of personal injuries to the claimant or any other person or in respect of a person's death, and 'personal injuries' includes any disease and any impairment of a person's physical or mental condition.

Commentary

Setting the success fee

Setting the success fee in a CFA is primarily about risk assessment. Claims with very good prospects of success only justify low-level success fees, whereas claims with approximately 50:50 prospects of success justify success fees of about 100 per cent. The former PD 43–48, paras 11.7 to 11.10, in force before 1 April 2013, govern the assessment of what is a 'reasonable' amount for a success fee in a pre-April 2013 CFA. The guidance given is as follows: 6.10

(a) The court will have regard to the facts and circumstances as they reasonably appeared to the solicitor or counsel at the time the funding arrangement was entered into or varied (para. 11.7).
(b) The court will assess the level of the success fee by reference to the risk of non-payment of the costs, fees or expenses, the legal representative's liability for any disbursements and what other methods of financing were available (para. 11.8).
(c) The court will not reduce the success fee simply because, when added to otherwise reasonable base costs, the total becomes disproportionate (para. 11.9). In other words, proportionality for the purposes of costs under the CPR is assessed net of any success fee.

Complexity is not to be equated with risk: a complex case may justify a higher hourly rate, not a higher success fee (*Thornley v Ministry of Defence* [2010] EWHC 2584 (QB), [2011] 3 Costs LR 335).

Risk assessment To fix a success fee, the solicitor needs to undertake a risk assessment of the case before him and record that assessment carefully. There are broadly two approaches to assessing risk in litigation claims. Risk can be assessed on case-by-case basis by looking at the particular features of the individual case and assessing those which have a risk of being lost. The alternative approach is to look at generic types of case and consider statistically how many of each type are successful. 6.11

Generic risk assessment In high-volume, low-value claims a proportionate way of assessing risk is by using a generic model. The generic model fits with the concept of staged success fees, which the Court of Appeal was attracted to in *Callery v Gray* [2001] EWCA Civ 1117, [200] 1 WLR 2112, and which it endorsed later in *Halloran v Delaney* [2002] EWCA Civ 1258, [2003] 1 WLR 28. Lord Woolf in *Callery v Gray* said, 'by way of example the uplift might be 100 per cent, 6.12

subject to a reduction to 5 per cent should the claim settle before the end of the protocol period'.

In *Halloran v Delaney* the court applied the reduction to 5 per cent to pre-proceedings settlement, subject to a district judge's discretion to exceed 5 per cent in appropriate cases. Both cases concerned road traffic accident claims. Brooke LJ, who gave the leading judgment in *Halloran v Delaney*, later clarified that the 5 per cent figure only applies to straightforward road traffic accident cases (see *Re Claims Direct Test Cases* [2003] EWCA Civ 136, [2003] 4 All ER 508, at [99]–[101]). He went on to say that it did not require any research evidence or submissions from other parties in the industry to persuade the court that in this type of extremely simple claim a success fee of over 5 per cent was no longer tenable in all the circumstances. He then made it clear that in straightforward road traffic accident cases the prospects of success are virtually 100 per cent and that the 5 per cent is 'to cater for the wholly unexpected risk lurking below the limpid waters of the simplest of claims'.

From 30 April 2010, the RTA Protocol claims process applies in respect of personal injury claims worth between £1,000 and £10,000 resulting from road traffic accidents where liability is admitted (see **8.30 to 8.60**). The applicable success fees for pre-April 2013 CFAs were set out in r. 45.31.

Until 1 April 2013 employers' liability accident cases were also subject to fixed success fees, albeit that (again based on statistical research) the levels are higher than those in road traffic accident cases. Former rr. 45.20 to 45.22 provided that the CFA success fee in personal injury claims against an employer (save for disease and road traffic accident claims: r. 45.20(2)(a)(i) and (iii)) were fixed at 25 per cent for both solicitors and counsel. If a membership organisation provided ATE cover, the percentage was increased to 27.5 per cent.

6.13 **Case-by-case assessment** In non-routine cases it is usually proportionate to undertake individual risk assessment. For each case common risk areas, such as limitation, evidence, liability, causation, loss and recovery can be identified and assessed. There is necessarily a large element of subjectivity in assessing the risk in any given case, but the more detailed the list of risk factors identified the more likely it is the court will uphold the level of success fee claimed. Complexity does not necessarily increase risk, although it may increase the unknown and therefore unquantifiable factors at the time of assessment. It remains true that even the simplest cases can be lost, for example, because of evidential difficulties.

Risk factors identified as justifying success fees should be real and not fanciful. For instance, if a simple telephone call will resolve any doubt about the identity of a driver, the call should be made before the success fee is fixed (*Atack v Lee* [2004] EWCA Civ 1712, [2005] 1 WLR 2643).

Probability can be a useful tool in assessing risk. For instance, to succeed at trial a claimant will have to succeed on liability and causation and be able to show a loss. To evaluate the probability of succeeding, the chance of proving all of those elements must be assessed.

If the chance of proving liability in a particular case is 70 per cent and, because of different evidential issues, the chance of proving causation and loss is 80 per cent, the chance of winning the case is 70 per cent multiplied by 80 per cent, that is, 56 per cent.

If there is a further 5 per cent chance of the defendant becoming insolvent, win or lose, the chance of recovering damages is reduced to 53.2 per cent.

What may have appeared at first to be a strong case can, with proper analysis, be shown to have prospects hardly better than predicting the outcome of a tossed coin.

A success fee is ordinarily calculated as: the chances of losing divided by the chances of winning. In a case with 60 per cent prospects, the success fee is 40 per cent divided by 60 per cent, which is 66 per cent. An 80 per cent case will have a success fee of 25 per cent (20/80). The Law Society has published a table for easy reference.

Modest percentages (usually 5 per cent per year) can be added to the success fee to take into account the fact that the solicitor cannot bill the client on an interim basis for costs or disbursements. This additional sum can be claimed against the client, but not between the parties.

There is no need to make a separate assessment of the risk relating to the possible need for a detailed assessment of costs when entering into a CFA. The costs of assessment will, in the (probable) absence of a separate success fee, be dealt with in the same way as other base costs in the case (*Crane v Canons Leisure Centre* [2007] EWCA Civ 1352, [2008] 1 WLR 2549).

C v W [2008] EWCA Civ 1459, LTL 19/12/2008, concerned assessment of an appropriate success fee under a CFA where liability had already been admitted in a road traffic accident case. The Court of Appeal found that the risk of losing was very small but the CFA provided for a success fee of 98 per cent. The Court of Appeal found that there was no more than a 5 per cent risk of losing which, when applying the ready reckoner, gave a basic success fee of 5 per cent. The Court of Appeal found that the real difficulty was in assessing the risk that the solicitors might lose the right to recover part of their fees should the client fail to beat a Part 36 offer rejected on the advice of the solicitors. It was acknowledged that making a proper assessment of that risk was difficult and Moore-Bick LJ concluded that the best solicitors can hope to do is to make a broad assessment of the risks associated with a Part 36 offer based on their own experience. However, given the difficulty of making such an assessment, he wondered whether solicitors should consider including in the CFA a two-stage success fee in the form of a provision giving them the right to review the success fee if a Part 36 offer is made. Thomas LJ also suggested that a new regime may be required for cases where liability is admitted. In the result, the Court of Appeal accepted that a reasonable assessment of the risk in overall terms would be 17 per cent, leading to a success fee of 20 per cent.

In *Redwing Construction Ltd v Wishart* [2011] EWHC 19 (TCC), [2011] BLR 186, the court considered the role of CFAs and ATE insurance in adjudication enforcement cases, in which the vast majority of claims are successful and the prospects of success thus inherently very high. Akenhead J noted that, whilst parties are entitled to enter into such funding arrangements in these cases, the court 'will think long and hard about allowing substantial CFA mark-ups, particularly when there is a summary judgment application by the party with the CFA'. Akenhead J reduced the allowable success fee from 100 per cent to 20 per cent on the basis that, at the time the CFA was entered into the claimant was 'virtually bound substantially to "win"' and its solicitors must have been aware of this in pursuing a summary judgment application.

The Court of Appeal has strongly criticised the use of success fees in CFAs entered into in circumstances involving no risk to the instructed solicitors. In *Pankhurst v White* [2010] EWCA Civ 1445, [2011] 3 Costs LR 392, it considered a CFA entered into two months after a judgment on liability had been obtained, but prior to a separate trial on quantum, which provided for a success fee of 22.5 per cent if the case settled pre-trial and 100 per cent if it went to trial. Success was defined in the CFA as 'any recovery of damages'. Jackson LJ commented that in the circumstances the CFA 'involved no risk whatsoever to the solicitors' and described the arrangement as 'grotesque'.

In *Grant v Bragg* [2009] EWCA Civ 1228, [2010] 1 All ER (Comm) 1166, the Court of Appeal considered the appropriate success fee for an appeal which has a more than real prospect of success. The court acknowledged that the prospects of success on appeal are always 'somewhat speculative', and that the setting of a success fee for appeal proceedings is a 'tickish issue'. However, a 100 per cent uplift is not appropriate where an appeal always has a good prospect of success. The appropriate uplift in such circumstances was assessed to be 60 per cent. The decision is an indication that it is likely to be difficult to justify a success fee of 100 per cent (generally considered appropriate for cases with a 50 per cent prospect of success) whilst at the same time arguing the appeal has a real prospect of success (being one of the grounds on which permission to appeal may be granted). This is particularly so in cases where the success fee is set after permission to appeal has been granted, and the reasons for granting it suggest that the appeal has a very good chance of success.

In *Oliver v Whipps Cross University Hospital NHS Trust* [2009] EWHC 1104 (QB), 108 BMLR 181, Jack J confirmed that a solicitor is entitled to enter into a CFA at an early stage, even though the prospects of success may be uncertain. In that case, the court upheld a success fee of 100 per cent where the solicitor had not had the opportunity to test the credibility of the evidence or assess the relevant facts or expert witnesses at the time the CFA was entered into, and it was therefore impossible to assess the percentage chance of success with any mathematical precision.

In *Hanley v Smith* [2009] EWHC 90144 (Costs) the court assessed the success fees contained in CFAs entered into by a claimant who had suffered serious head injuries in a motorcycle accident. The CFAs for the claimant's solicitors and junior counsel had been entered into at a time when the liability of the first defendant (uninsured) driver had been established, but not the extent of liability in percentage terms, quantum, or the question of whether the claimant was eligible for cover by the second defendant (the Motor Insurers' Bureau). The court rejected an argument put by the defendants that there had already been a 'win' at this stage simply because the issue of liability against the first defendant had been resolved, as there was still every chance that the second defendant could defend the case on the eligibility point. The court held that a 'win' in this case would mean the final disposal of the case in the claimant's favour as against both defendants (rather than obtaining a worthless (but necessary) judgment against the driver). In the result, the court held that the appropriate success fees were 82 per cent for the solicitors (for the risk element only) and 50 per cent for junior counsel (rising to 100 per cent if a trial brief had been delivered). The court reduced the success fee for leading counsel from 82 per cent to 54 per cent on the ground that, by the time that CFA was concluded, the overall risk had declined.

There is a limited amount of guidance from the courts on appropriate success fees in particular cases. The following list may be illustrative, but each case should be considered with reference to its particular facts:

Claim for industrial injury where the employer's liability for negligence is already established and solicitors' fees are covered by the claim handling agreement (*Beresford v Solicitors Regulation Authority* [2009] EWHC 3155 (Admin), LTL 2/12/2009)	0 per cent
Road traffic accident (pre-trial) (former CPR, rr. 45.15 to 45.19 in force before 1 April 2013)	12.5 per cent
Road traffic accident case where settlement occurs before trial, but application is subsequently made to the court to clarify one aspect of an agreed order (for example, in relation to the frequency of periodic payments) (*Hosking v Smallshaw* [2009] EWHC 90137 (Costs), LTL 6/4/2009)	12.5 per cent
Appeal to the Court of Appeal (where it is 'almost certain' that the client will successfully resist the appeal) (*Alfa Begum v Supin Klarit* [2005] EWCA Civ 210, [2005] 3 Costs LR 452)	15 per cent
Straightforward clinical negligence (*Bensusan v Freedman* (2001) LTL 6/11/2001; *Metcalfe v Clipston* [2004] EWHC 9005 (Costs))	20 per cent
Road traffic accident case where liability is admitted but there is a reasonable risk of the rejection of an effective Part 36 offer (*C v W* [2008] EWCA Civ 1459, *[2009] 4 All ER 1129; Gandy v King* [2010] EWHC 90177 (Costs), LTL 2/12/2010)	20 per cent
Personal injury claim against an employer (pre-trial) (former CPR, rr. 45.20 to 45.22 in force before 1 April 2013)	25 per cent

Mesothelioma claim where the claimant does not have a complicated history of employment (*Holliday v E C Realisations Ltd* [2008] EWHC 90103 (Costs))	33.3 per cent
Slip and trip (*Abrew v Tesco Stores Ltd* (2003) LTL 18/6/2003)	50 per cent
Personal injury claim where the claimants have sustained serious injuries and liability was uncertain (*Burton v Kingsley* [2005] EWHC1034 (QB), [2006] PIQR P2)	50 per cent
Appeal to the Court of Appeal (where the prospects of success are good, particularly where the success fee is set after permission to appeal has been granted and the reasons for granting permission suggest that the appeal has a very good chance of success) (*Grant v Bragg* [2009] EWCA Civ 1228, [2010] 1 All ER (Comm) 1166)	60 per cent
Accident at work (with evidential and causation difficulties) (*Chalk v Hightown Praetorian Housing Association* (Cambridge County Court 1 October 2002))	63 per cent
Asbestosis claims (*Smiths Dock Ltd v Edwards* [2004] EWHC 1116 (QB), LTL 20/5/2004)	87 per cent
Road traffic accident (which is tried) (former CPR, rr. 45.15 to 45.19 in force before 1 April 2013, and *Callery v Gray* [2001] EWCA Civ 1117, [2001] 1 WLR 2112)	100 per cent
Fatal accident claim against employer (*Peto-Williamson v Ivan Housley Poultry Ltd* (Nottingham County Court 10 September 2002))	100 per cent
Intellectual property case lost in the Court of Appeal, successful in the House of Lords (*Designer Guild Ltd v Russell Williams (Textiles) Ltd (No. 2)* (HL, 20 February 2003, SCCO Case Summaries No. 4 of 2003))	100 per cent
Clinical negligence claim where CFA entered into at an early stage and the prospects of success are uncertain (*Oliver v Whipps Cross University Hospital NHS Trust* [2009] EWHC 1104 (QB), 108 BMLR 181)	100 per cent

Commentary

Staged success fees

Staged success fees, starting low and increasing as the case progresses, or starting high and decreasing if admissions of liability are made during the proceedings, are consistent with practical experience of how cases are resolved. Inherently strong claims (generically or by reference to the individual case facts) settle early; the weaker, and therefore riskier, claims often find their way to trial. 6.14

Staged success fees have been encouraged by the Court of Appeal since *Halloran v Delaney* [2002] EWCA Civ 1258, [2003] 1 WLR 28, and were adopted in the fixed success fee schemes for road traffic accident and employers' liability claims. The court does not have the power to impose a staged success fee retrospectively (*U v Liverpool City Council* [2005] EWCA Civ 475, [2005] 1 WLR 2657). This is so even after the risks have been substantially reduced, after admissions or on a detailed assessment of costs following the success of the main claim.

A different version of staged success fees was approved in *Benaim (UK) Ltd v Davies Middleton and Davies Ltd* [2004] EWHC 737 (TCC), LTL 29/3/2004, in which the success fee was linked to the amount awarded to the claimant. The definition of the success fee varied the percentage uplift by stages from 40 per cent if the recovery was up to £200,000, to 100 per cent if more than £1 million was recovered.

A CFA with a discounted success fee provides for a basic fee at a stated hourly rate, which is discounted to a lower rate if the client loses, but with the CFA (usually) providing that the basic fee plus any success fee will be payable if the client is successful. In deciding whether the success fee is within the maximum 100 per cent uplift, the court compares the success fee with the basic fee, not the discounted fee (*Gloucestershire County Council v Evans* [2008] EWCA Civ 21, [2008] 1 WLR 1883).

NOTIFICATION OF FUNDING ARRANGEMENT

6.15 From 1 October 2009 to 31 March 2013, a potential party to proceedings who, before proceedings are issued, entered into a CFA that provided for a success fee had to inform the other parties of the funding arrangement as soon as possible (**PD Pre-action Conduct, para. 9.3**).

Once proceedings were started, a party who had retained solicitors under a CFA was under a duty to file and serve notice to that effect in form N251 (former CPR, r. 44.15(1); PD 43–48, para. 19.2; both in force before 1 April 2013).

A success fee associated with a funding arrangement was not recoverable where a party failed to notify the other parties of the arrangement in accordance with a practice direction requirement (former CPR, r. 44.3B(1)(d)). Relief from sanctions was granted by the courts in certain circumstances (**CPR, r. 3.9**; former PD 43–48, para. 10.1, in force before 1 April 2013; *Supperstone v Hurst* [2008] EWHC 735 (Ch), LTL 23/4/2008; *Montlake v Lambert Smith Hampton Group Ltd* [2004] EWHC 1503 (Comm), LTL 16/7/2004).

In *Montlake v Lambert Smith Hampton Group Ltd* [2004] EWHC 1503 (Comm), LTL 16/7/2004, the claimant failed to serve a form N251 notice of funding in respect of a CFA and ATE insurance policy on the defendant or its solicitors. However, the letter before claim stated that 'this claim is now being funded by a conditional fee agreement which provides for a success fee'. In fact the CFA was not finally entered into until a month later and costs were claimed only after that date. The court was informed of the existence of the CFA at the first case management conference. The court found that the defendant had from the outset the information (albeit in an irregular form) to which it was entitled and the court could not see any conceivable prejudice to the defendant from the breaches of the rule and practice directions. Accordingly the court granted relief (pursuant to **r. 3.9**) from the sanction provided for by r. 44.3B(1)(c), ordering that the claimant was not to be deprived of the opportunity in principle to recover the agreed success fee. In *Kutsi v North Middlesex University Hospital NHS Trust* [2008] EWHC 90119 (Costs) relief against sanctions for failing to provide details of an ATE insurance premium was refused on the ground that the claimant had failed to provide a good explanation for its failure to comply with the notice requirement. Notably, relief was refused despite the fact that the claimant's insurers had requested that the claimant not provide details of the insurance policy to the defendant and the fault for the failure to comply fell squarely with the claimant's solicitor (who had agreed to this request without checking whether this was permitted under the CPR).

There was no requirement for a party to inform the opponent of a funding arrangement made between the solicitor and counsel or the solicitor and a quasi-expert. If notice of a CFA was given at first instance, there was no requirement to give separate notice in respect of an appeal (*Beer v BexBes LLP* [2009] EWCA Civ 628, LTL 26/6/2009). It was therefore safest to assume (unless expressly informed otherwise) that parties funded by a CFA at first instance would also be funded on a CFA basis on appeal.

ASSESSMENT OF CFA COSTS

General

6.16 For a CFA entered into before 1 April 2013, assessment by the court of CFA costs is governed by the former CPR, r. 44.3A and 44.3B, and PD 43–48, paras 11.4 to 11.10 (party-and-party assessments), and CPR, r. 48.8(3) and (4), and PD 43–48, paras 54.5 to 54.8 (solicitor-and-client assessments), in force before 1 April 2013. For the procedure on assessment of costs generally see **71.10** to **71.29**.

In a successful conditional fee case the solicitor will calculate his or her fees (referred to in the Law Society's model agreement as 'basic costs') and the barrister's fees at the rates set out in the CFA with the client. The solicitor will seek to recover 100 per cent of the basic costs plus the barrister's fees and disbursements from the unsuccessful paying party. The solicitor may in addition recover from the client:

(a) any part of the solicitor's basic costs, counsel's fees and disbursements not recovered from the paying party;
(b) the agreed success fee (which cannot be more than 100 per cent) calculated as a percentage of the basic costs (and as a separate percentage of the barrister's fees).

When a client receives from the solicitor a bill calculated on the above basis the client is entitled to challenge:

(a) the shortfall in full recovery of the solicitor's basic costs and the barrister's fees,
(b) the solicitor's and barrister's success fees.

The procedure to facilitate such a challenge by the client is set out in **PD 46, paras 6.4 and 6.5**.

Assessment of basic costs

For CFAs entered into both before and after 1 April 2013, as the basic costs in a CFA are the costs which would have been charged whether or not the solicitor was retained on a conditional fee basis, detailed assessment of them, as between solicitor and client, is governed by the same rules as apply to detailed assessment of any other solicitor's bill, namely, **CPR, r. 46.9. Rule 46.9(3)** provides that costs are to be assessed on the indemnity basis, in which costs are presumed: 6.17

(a) to have been reasonably incurred if they were incurred with the express or implied approval of the client;
(b) to be reasonable in amount if their amount was expressly or impliedly approved by the client;
(c) to have been unreasonably incurred if:
   (i) they are of an unusual nature or amount and
   (ii) the solicitor did not tell the client that as a result he might not recover all of them from the other party.

Assessment of basic costs between the parties is usually on the standard basis unless an indemnity basis costs order has been made.

The standard-form CFA Conditions published by the Law Society define the basic charges as 'our charges for the legal work we do on your claim for damages'. This is wide enough to cover generic work done for clients on claims covered, or intended to be covered, by a group litigation order (GLO), and there is no need for any collateral agreement between the solicitor and client for such generic costs (*Brown v Russell Young and Co.* [2007] EWCA Civ 43, [2008] 1 WLR 525).

In *Crane v Canons Leisure Centre* [2007] EWCA Civ 1352, [2008] 1 WLR 2549, a collective CFA defined base costs as 'charges for work done by or on behalf of the Solicitors which would have been payable if this agreement did not provide for a success fee, calculated on the basis of the fees allowable for that work in the court in which the [claim] in question is conducted or would be conducted *if proceedings were to be issued*'. The costs of the detailed assessment, which was actually conducted by costs consultants engaged by the solicitors, were held to be part of the solicitors' base costs, and to attract the success fee on the same footing as the base costs on the substantive claim.

Assessment of additional liabilities between the parties

For CFAs entered into before 1 April 2013, the **Courts and Legal Services Act 1990, s. 58A(6)**, allowed the CPR to provide that costs orders could include provision requiring the 6.18

paying party to pay the success fee as well as the basic costs. The **Access to Justice Act 1999, s. 29**, also enabled insurance premiums to be recovered. The insurance premium could be one paid alongside a CFA but the rules were drafted so as to provide for other 'additional liabilities' including stand-alone insurance policies, such as ATE insurance, and even the cost of membership (perhaps of a trade union) as the case may be. The relevant rules are the former CPR, r. 44.3A (costs orders relating to funding arrangements) and r. 44.3B (limits on recovery under funding arrangements), as amplified by PD 43–48, paras 11.4 to 11.10, in force before 1 April 2013.

The effect of these rules, taken together, is that an 'additional liability' (whether a success fee or insurance premium or both) may be recovered provided that:

(a) the success fee relates to the risk of losing and not to compensating the legal representative for delayed payment (this, incidentally, is why it is crucial for the CFA to split the success fee);
(b) the additional liability does not relate to a period where information about the funding arrangement has not been provided as required by PD 43–48, para. 19.2, in force before 1 April 2013;
(c) the reasons justifying the success fee have been disclosed;
(d) the additional liability is reasonable.

The assessment of the success fee is considered at **6.10** to **6.14**.

In *Abeles v Equitable Life Assurance Society* (2009) LTL 20/4/2009, an application by the defendant for disclosure of the claimants' CFAs following the settlement of litigation and prior to any request for a detailed assessment of costs was refused on the basis that it had been made prematurely and was not necessary to enable the defendant, as the paying party, to properly formulate its points of dispute. The application could be renewed after an application for a detailed assessment hearing had been made.

The Court of Appeal has indicated that it should be the usual practice for a CFA, redacted where appropriate, to be disclosed for the purposes of costs proceedings in which a success fee is claimed. From 6 April 2010, if the CFA is not disclosed, a receiving party is nonetheless required to disclose details of the CFA (including the definition of 'win' and 'lose' and details of the receiving party's liability to pay costs if it wins or loses or fails to obtain a judgment more advantageous than a Part 36 offer), so as to enable the paying party and the court to determine the level of risk undertaken by the solicitor (PD 43–48, para. 32.5(1), in force before 1 April 2013).

Assessment of additional liabilities between solicitor and client

6.19 For CFAs entered into both before and after 1 April 2013, in a detailed assessment of solicitor-and-client costs under a CFA, when the court is considering the percentage increase, it will have regard to all the relevant factors as they reasonably appeared to the solicitor or counsel when the agreement was entered into or varied (current **CPR, r. 46.9(4)**).

SPECIAL ISSUES RELATING TO CONDITIONAL FEES UNDER THE CPR

Interim costs in CFA cases before 1 April 2013

6.20 A special difficulty in a case with a pre-April 2013 CFA is the summary assessment of costs for interim hearings of less than one day.

The former PD 43–48, paras 14.1 to 14.4, in force before 1 April 2013, provided that the existence of a conditional fee or other funding arrangement was not of itself a reason for declining to assess costs summarily, but that an order for payment of those costs would not be made unless the court was satisfied that in respect of the costs claimed, the receiving party was at the time liable to pay to his legal representative an amount equal to or greater than the costs claimed. The effect of this was that the order for payment would be postponed until the conclusion of the case unless the client was already liable to his solicitor for the costs, for example, because the client had acted outside the terms of the CFA, perhaps by acting unreasonably. Whether or not the client was liable could be proved by the solicitor filing a statement with the court (para. 14.3).

At the end of the case, if the conditional fee client's case was unsuccessful then the costs summarily assessed would form a part of the total costs payable and would generally be paid by the insurer. If the case was won then it would depend on the terms of the policy. However, most insurance policies provide that costs summarily assessed against the client earlier in the case will not be met by the insurer unless those costs exceed the damages recovered. Then, the insurer would pay the difference. Otherwise, the client would have to pay the costs out of the damages.

When summarily assessing costs in conditional fee cases at an interim stage the court should not assess the amount of any additional liability (CPR, r. 44.3A) and the statement of costs filed by the receiving party need not say what the amount of that liability is (PD 43–48, para. 13.5(5)).

In *Arkin v Borchard Lines Ltd* (2001) LTL 19/6/2001 Colman J permitted the claimant to set off his interim costs liability against costs owed to him by the defendant. The set-off effectively extinguished the claimant's liability and was important to him because without it, under the terms of his CFA, he would have been liable to reimburse his solicitors and counsel. Colman J rejected the defendant's argument that no set-off could arise because the costs under the CFA were not immediately payable. On the proper construction of the CFA, he said, 'winning' meant recovering an enforceable payment order — including a pre-trial costs order — not receiving payment.

Colman J then went on to consider what happened when parties sought set-off in cases where there were a number of costs orders going both ways and providing for both summary assessment and detailed assessment. Here, he said, the court should generally preserve the principle of set-off by either delaying the 14-day payment requirement for the costs summarily assessed, otherwise postponing compliance with the summary assessment costs order or having the summarily assessed costs paid into court.

Commentary

Children, protected parties and conditional fees

An omission from the statutory and regulatory framework that established conditional fees in 1995 was the lack of special provisions required for conditional fee cases conducted on behalf of children or protected parties. **CPR, Part 21**, sets out the basis for court approval of an award of damages to a child or protected party. Under the old RSC, ord. 80, at the settlement, approval or award of damages to a child or patient the court was also required to approve costs. This caused a problem in conditional fee cases. The solicitor who had entered into a CFA with the litigation friend of a child or patient was vulnerable to the court disapproving the level of the success fee at the approval stage without the protection of the conditional fee taxation procedure under the old RSC, ord. 62, r. 15A (for the assessment procedure before 1 April 2013 see **6.16**). From 3 July 2000, this anomaly was corrected by the former CPR, r. 48.9(6), which provided that in a case where the client in a CFA was a child or a patient, the court could not vary the percentage increase except in accordance with r. 48.9(5). Rule 48.9 was revoked as from 26 March 2001. Although the current **r. 46.9(4)** makes much the same provision as r. 48.9(5) (and, immediately before 1 April 2013, r. 48.8(3)) did, there is now no provision corresponding to the former r. 48.9(6). **6.21**

In *Dunn v Mici* [2008] EWHC 90115 (Costs) the court considered a CFA entered into by a 17-year-old claimant 'by his mother and litigation friend'. The CFA had been signed by the claimant's mother at a time when she could only have been a 'proposed litigation friend' (given that a litigation friend is not formally appointed until proceedings are issued). Nonetheless, the court concluded that the mother had been acting as agent for her son, and that the solicitors had correctly inquired about pre-existing legal expenses insurance relating to the claimant, not his mother. The court pointed out that the CFA should make clear on its face that it is made with a child, if necessary acting through an agent. The child may subsequently ratify the CFA (preferably expressly) after turning 18.

A CFA can also be adopted and ratified by a litigation friend in a case of supervening mental incapacity. In *Findley v Jones* [2009] EWHC 90130 (Costs) the claimant had entered into two CFAs with his solicitors and was later found to lack capacity within the meaning of the Mental Capacity Act 2005. The claimant's sister agreed to act as his litigation friend, but did not formally sign a CFA or ratify either of the existing CFAs. Master Hurst held that a litigation friend could adopt the retainer (the simplest course being to formally adopt the CFA). Although the CFA was strictly required to be signed to be enforceable (meaning it could not be adopted by the conduct of the litigation friend), Master Hurst nonetheless concluded that the CFA was enforceable on the basis that to allow the defendant to avoid liability would 'adversely affect the administration of justice'.

BARRISTERS AND CONDITIONAL FEES

6.22 In a claim where the client has entered into a CFA with the solicitor, it is usual for the solicitor to invite any barrister who may be instructed to enter into a CFA on a similar basis. A high level of mutual understanding is necessary between solicitors and barristers working together as a team on a case where both are acting on a conditional-fee basis. Whilst firms and sets of chambers have developed good working relationships on conditional fee cases, the fact remains that barristers are at a disadvantage because, typically, the greatest financial risk is run in claims that have to be determined at trial and much more work is generally required to be done by counsel in cases as they approach trial than at earlier stages. By the time a case reaches this point the solicitor will still be at risk, but may at the same time have spread that risk by settling large numbers of other cases being run on a conditional-fee basis. Even if the barrister has been involved earlier in the case, he or she will tend to have far fewer cases that succeed through negotiation. Some solicitors prefer counsel not to be on a CFA to avoid any conflict when, for instance, an offer of settlement is made. 'Hybrid' agreements may be an acceptable compromise. In *Designer Guild Ltd v Russell Williams (Textiles) Ltd (No. 2)* (HL 20 February 2003, SCCO Case Summaries No. 4 of 2003) counsel was guaranteed half his fees regardless of the outcome. Accordingly his success fee was approved at 50 per cent, where his solicitors were entitled to a 100 per cent success fee.

To assist with uniformity, a model CFA for barristers in personal injury cases has been produced by collaboration between the Association of Personal Injury Lawyers and the Personal Injury Bar Association. This model agreement has also received the approval of the Bar Council and the Law Society, and is known as APIL/PIBA. In addition the Bar Council has produced a guideline manual about conditional fees. This has been distributed to all sets of chambers and is available at www.barcouncil.org.uk. The Chancery Bar Association has produced its own model CFA.

EXPERTS AND CONDITIONAL FEES

6.23 A solicitor must not make or offer to make payments to witnesses dependent upon their evidence or the outcome of the case (SRA Code of Conduct 2011, O 5.8). It is permissible to make a deferred fee arrangement by which the expert (particularly one who does a lot of work for a firm of solicitors) agrees not to render a fee note until the end of the case when, if it is lost, the expert may decide to waive the fee. Provided there is no antecedent agreement that the expert will not charge if the case is lost, the deferred arrangement does not breach the professional conduct rules.

In *R (Factortame Ltd) v Secretary of State for Transport, Local Government and the Regions (No. 8)* [2002] EWCA Civ 932, [2003] QB 381, the enforceability of a contingency arrangement made between a quasi-expert and solicitors was considered. At a relatively late stage of the litigation, accountants had been instructed to provide forensic accountancy services to the claimants' fishing industry experts. This support included the assessment of the claimants' financial losses. The accountants had agreed to act in return for 8 per cent of the final settlement achieved (not in fact a CFA, but a contingency fee arrangement — the losses being calculated not by an uplift on costs incurred, but by reference to the award of damages). Perhaps surprisingly the court held that the arrangement was enforceable. The Courts and Legal Services Act 1990 was held not to apply as that Act only deals with agreements between clients and 'litigators'. The court was quick to emphasise that this was a 'very rare' case and that the court would not normally consent to an expert being instructed on a contingency fee basis. It noted that experts are frequently in a position to influence litigation in a manner that neither the client nor the lawyer can. To allow an expert to have a financial interest in the outcome of a case carries great dangers for the administration of justice. However, in this case the accountants took care to restrict their role to the provision of support services to the experts who were to be called. Accordingly, their conduct did not offend public policy. The court observed that the accountants' prospect of receiving 8 per cent of the recoveries might have provided a motive for them to inflate the calculation of damages, although not to the extent that a larger percentage might have done. However, there were no grounds for suspecting that the accountants, as reputable members of a respectable profession subject to regulation would do anything other than perform their duties in an honest manner. The court also took some comfort from the fact that, in part at least, the accountants were involved in a joint exercise with the defendant's experts.

In *Papera Traders Co. Ltd v Hyundai Merchant Marine Co. Ltd (No. 2)* [2002] EWHC 2130 (Comm), [2002] 2 Lloyd's Rep 692, the claimant sought to recover as part of its damages fees payable to a firm of marine loss adjusters based on 5 per cent of the recovery made in respect of vehicles which were destroyed in a fire on board the defendant's vessel. The loss adjusters were instructed initially on a fee basis to carry out salvage and general average work and then instructed to carry out recovery services on a percentage basis. The defendant's argument that the agreement was champertous was unsuccessful. The court did agree that the claim was not properly categorised as damages, being too remote, but that the loss adjusters' costs could be assessed on the standard basis, with reference to the amount of time spent on each item.

COLLECTIVE CONDITIONAL FEE AGREEMENTS

Collective conditional fee agreements (collective CFAs) are intended to help bulk users of CFAs and their solicitors, by allowing the users to enter into a single agreement with solicitors to allow them to run their members' cases. The agreement need not refer to specific proceedings, but will provide for fees to be payable on a common basis in relation to a class of proceedings. Agreements entered into before 1 November 2005 are subject to the Collective Conditional Fee Agreements Regulations 2000 (SI 2000/2988). 6.24

A collective CFA is an agreement between a solicitor and a bulk provider of work. If the provider is also the claimant (as in debt recovery work) there is no difficulty in establishing the terms of the retainer between the party to the litigation and the solicitor. That is not the case

Commentary

if the work provider is a referrer of work, such as a trade union or insurance company. In this situation there is an implied retainer between the solicitor and the client, alternatively, the client will be regarded as having ratified the appointment of the solicitor by the funder (*Thornley v Lang* [2003] EWCA Civ 1484, *The Times*, 31 October 2003, applying *Adams v London Improved Motor Coach Builders Ltd* [1921] 1 KB 495). This means the client is under a legal obligation to pay the solicitor's bill, even though in practice this may never happen. Consequently, provided there is compliance with the regulations, where they apply, costs incurred under a collective CFA are recoverable from the opposite party.

A clause in a collective CFA requiring the claimants' solicitors to prepare and retain written risk assessments was held to be an innominate term. The Collective Conditional Fee Agreements Regulations 2000 (SI 2000/2988) required compliance with the specified particulars in the form of the agreement, but did not require the actual performance of those specifications (see *Various Claimants v Gower Chemicals Limited* (Cardiff County Court, 8 March 2007) LTL 8/3/2007).

Collective CFAs are often commercially sensitive documents and the parties to them are unlikely to consent to their disclosure in costs assessment proceedings. In *Hollins v Russell* [2003] EWCA Civ 718, [2003] 1 WLR 2487, the Court of Appeal considered CFAs to be generally disclosable unless no success fee is claimed. There is nothing in the judgment which suggests any distinction will be made between CFAs and collective CFAs if the paying party or the court seeks sight of the agreement. However, in practice many collective CFAs do not provide for a success fee, but instead are discounted fee arrangements (see **5.9** and **6.1**).

The Collective Conditional Fee Agreements Regulations 2000 (SI 2000/2988) were revoked on 1 November 2005, leaving no statutory reference to collective CFAs although it is possible that individual cases will continue to be brought under a collective CFA entered into before 1 November 2005. Collective CFAs continue to be a valid form of CFA, so there is no reason why parties should not continue to enter into collective CFAs where appropriate.

Chapter 7 Legal Aid

Commentary

INTRODUCTION

The Legal Aid, Sentencing and Punishment of Offenders Act 2012 (LASPO 2012), s. 39(1) 7.1 and sch. 5, para. 51, repeal the provisions in the Access to Justice Act 1999 on the Community Legal Service. Those provisions are replaced by a new system of legal aid which is administered on behalf of the Lord Chancellor by a civil servant known as the Director of Legal Aid Casework (LASPO 2012, ss. 1 and 4). Many of the concepts of the old legal aid and Community Legal Service systems are retained in the new provisions. The most notable change is that legal aid for clinical negligence has largely been removed (s. 9 and sch. 1). In relation to clinical negligence, legal aid under LASPO 2012 will only be available for claims for severely disabled infants (as defined in sch. 1, para. 23).

It might be thought that the legal aid provisions in LASPO 2012 are part of the Jackson reforms, not least because they appear in the same statute that makes the necessary legislative changes needed for the funding changes recommended by the *Jackson Report*. In fact it was simply legislative convenience that put the legal aid and Jackson reforms into the same statute, a point made by Sir Rupert Jackson in his first implementation lecture (Cambridge Law Faculty, Legal Aid and the Costs Review Reforms (Legal Aid etc Lecture 5), a talk by Lord Justice Jackson to the Cambridge Law Faculty on 5 September 2011). As was made clear in that lecture, abolition of public funding for most clinical negligence claims runs counter to the views expressed in the *Jackson Report*, which were to the effect that maintenance of legal aid at no less than the existing levels makes sound economic sense and is in the public interest (*Jackson Report*, ch. 7, para. 4.2).

Nevertheless, the changes to the legal aid system did come into force on 1 April 2013 at the same time as the Jackson reforms. Public funding has traditionally played an important role in promoting access to justice. With modern constraints on the public finances, that role will be an attenuated one for the foreseeable future.

ABOLITION OF THE LEGAL SERVICES COMMISSION

Following the recommendations of the *Magee Report* (Sir Ian Magee, *Review of Legal Aid Delivery and Governance* (March 2010)), the Legal Services Commission is abolished (LASPO 7.2 2012, s. 38(1)) and, with effect from 1 April 2013, is replaced by the Legal Aid Agency. This is an executive agency of the Ministry of Justice. The day-to-day administration of legal aid is transferred to the Lord Chancellor (ss. 1 to 3), who is required to designate a civil servant as the Director of Legal Aid Casework (s. 4(1)). The Director is obliged to comply with directions from, and must have regard to guidance given by, the Lord Chancellor about the carrying out of the Director's functions under the Act, but the Lord Chancellor is not permitted to give directions or guidance in relation to individual cases (s. 4(4)).

CIVIL LEGAL AID

7.3 The Lord Chancellor is under a duty to secure that legal aid ('civil legal services') is made available in accordance with LASPO 2012, part 1 (s. 1(1)). This does not include a duty to provide those services by the means selected by the legally aided person (s. 27(1)), so services could be provided by telephone or electronic means (s. 27(2)). Likewise, in civil cases there is no general obligation for the legal services to be provided by the lawyer selected by the legally aided person (s. 27(3)), who will usually, in effect, be forced to accept the services from a provider who has entered into a contract with the Legal Aid Agency.

Individuals

7.4 Legal aid is available only to individuals (LASPO 2012, s. 9(1)). Consequently, it is not generally available to limited liability companies. It may be available to partnerships, though not on matters of partnership law or relating to the carrying on of the firm's business. Corporations may be covered if the Director has made an exceptional case determination (s. 31 and sch. 3, para. 3).

Exclusions

7.5 Civil legal services are to be made available to individuals for cases covered by LASPO 2012, sch. 1, part 1, unless excluded or modified by sch. 1, parts 2, 3 or 4 (s. 9). Schedule 1 runs to 31 pages, and covers various family, immigration and other categories of proceedings, often with detailed exclusions. Included within the scheme are judicial review claims (sch. 1, para. 19), habeas corpus (sch 1, para. 20), abuse of position or power by public authorities (sch. 1, para. 21), breach of rights under the European Convention on Human Rights by public authorities (sch. 1, para. 22), clinical negligence claims for severely disabled infants (sch. 1, para. 23), and various other categories (sch. 1, paras 24 to 46). Most of these are subject to specific exclusions. There continues to be a list of general excluded services (sch. 1, part 2), including the familiar exclusions for claims relating to personal injuries and death, defamation, and matters relating to company and partnership law, but now joined by most clinical negligence claims.

Exceptional case determination

7.6 There is provision for civil legal services to be made available on an exceptional case determination by the Director of Legal Aid Casework where this must be done to avoid a breach of an individual's rights under the European Convention on Human Rights, or where any rights of the individual to the provision of legal services are enforceable EU rights (LASPO 2012, s. 10). An exceptional case determination must be made in accordance with the provisions of the Civil Legal Aid (Procedure) Regulations 2012 (SI 2012/3098), which apply to the form of civil legal services which is the subject of the application (reg. 66(2)).

Financial qualifications

7.7 There continue to be financial qualifications for legal aid (LASPO 2012, ss. 11(1)(a) and 21). Regulations may, as with the Community Legal Service, provide for the payment of contributions, or even the whole cost of the services (s. 23(2)), by way of periodical payments, one or more lump sums, and out of income or capital (s. 23(8)).

Powers to request information about financial resources are contained in the Legal Aid (Information about Financial Resources) Regulations 2013 (SI 2013/628). Detailed rules for determining financial eligibility for legal aid are contained in the Civil Legal Aid (Financial Resources and Payment for Services) Regulations 2013 (SI 2013/480). These contain rules for determining an individual's income and capital, and for determining contributions. The basic rules are that an individual is not eligible for legal aid if their gross monthly income exceeds £2,657 (reg. 7(4)) or if their capital exceeds £8,000 (reg. 6(4)). There are complex rules on the resources that are to be treated as the individual's resources for this purpose. There are also waivers for certain types of proceedings.

There are also rules dealing with determining the financial eligibility of legal persons in the rare cases where legal aid is available to artificial persons as opposed to individuals (Legal Aid (Financial Resources and Payment for Services) (Legal Persons) Regulations 2013 (SI 2013/512)).

Protection against supplementary payment

Individuals continue to be protected from having to pay for the provision of legal services which are provided under the Act other than as provided in regulations (LASPO 2012, s. 23(1)). 7.8

Criteria for funding

There are detailed rules setting out the criteria for granting the different forms of civil legal services (LASPO 2012, s. 11). These criteria are based on factors such as cost-benefit considerations, the availability of resources to provide legal services, and the importance of the matter (s. 11(3)). These are intended to reflect the requirements of the different levels of service (see 7.11), and also to ensure that public money is targeted at the cases that deserve or need it. 7.9

Merits of the case

The prospects of success criterion is divided into four categories (Civil Legal Aid (Merits Criteria) Regulations 2013 (SI 2013/104), reg. 43): 7.10

(a) 'very good', meaning 80 per cent or more;
(b) 'good', meaning 60 per cent to 80 per cent;
(c) 'moderate', meaning 50 per cent to 60 per cent;
(d) 'borderline', meaning that, because of difficult disputes of fact, law, or expert evidence, it is not possible to say that the prospects of success are better than 50 per cent, but they are not so weak that the claim is likely to fail.

In borderline cases, the merits criterion will not be met unless the case is also of significant wider public interest, or if the case has overwhelming importance to the individual.

FORMS OF CIVIL LEGAL SERVICES

Different forms of publicly funded legal services have been developed. The purpose is to ensure that the amount of public funding given to a case should be commensurate with its needs, so that limited funding will be given if that is all that is needed, but full public funding will be given to the most deserving cases. Civil legal services may therefore take any of the following forms (Civil Legal Aid (Procedure) Regulations 2012 (SI 2012/3098), reg. 3): 7.11

(a) legal help;
(b) help at court;
(c) family help;
(d) family mediation;

(e) help with family mediation;
(f) legal representation; and
(g) other legal services.

Legal help

7.12 This is the lowest level of service, and includes providing advice and legal assistance on things like how the law applies to a particular case. It is intended for people on low incomes who need initial advice and to assist with the early investigation of claims, and is intended to provide a limited amount of legal help at a modest cost to the taxpayer.

Help at court

7.13 This authorises legal representation for the purposes of a particular hearing, without the lawyer becoming the client's legal representative in the proceedings. Again, the intention is that limited legal assistance will be given, covering no more than is necessary, so as to keep the cost to the taxpayer to the minimum.

Legal representation

7.14 This covers individuals contemplating legal proceedings or who are parties to particular proceedings. This will fund 'investigative representation' or 'full representation'. Investigative representation is limited to investigating the strength of contemplated proceedings, issuing proceedings, and conducting proceedings broadly up to obtaining information relevant to advising on the prospects of success. Full representation means legal representation other than investigative representation.

Family help

7.15 Family help may be provided in relation to family disputes, and may include assistance in resolving a dispute through negotiation or otherwise. It does not cover representation at a contested final hearing or appeal. It encompasses two levels of service. Family help (lower) is limited to all steps up to issue of proceedings. Family help (higher) can be used to issue proceedings and for representation in such proceedings other than at a contested final hearing.

Specific directions

7.16 Other services are not strictly forms of service covered by the main legal aid scheme, but there is some public funding of other cases if a specific order or direction is made. This may happen in important test cases and possibly also in group litigation.

APPLYING FOR AND WITHDRAWING LEGAL AID

7.17 Different procedures apply for making and withdrawing different categories of public funding, as set out in the Civil Legal Aid (Procedure) Regulations 2012 (SI 2012/3098). For example, applications for legal representation that is not controlled work or special case work come within what is known as licensed work, and are governed by regs 29 to 49. Applications must be made in the prescribed form, which must be signed by the individual and the proposed provider (reg. 31). There are detailed requirements to be followed. If the Director makes a determination that an individual qualifies for licensed work, the Director is under a duty to issue and send a certificate recording the determination to the individual with a copy to the provider (reg. 37(1)). The determination must specify any contributions payable by the individual (reg. 36), and the certificate must specify the proceedings to which the determination relates and any conditions or limitations on the cover (reg. 37(2)).

Individuals have a reporting obligation if there is any change in circumstances which might affect their qualification for civil legal services (reg. 40(1)). Providers have duties to report various matters, such as any refusal to accept an offer to settle or an offer to use ADR, or any information which might affect the client's continued qualification for civil legal services (reg. 40(3)).

REMUNERATION FOR PROVIDERS

7.18 The Lord Chancellor must pay remuneration to a provider of civil legal services in accordance with the provisions of the Civil Legal Aid (Remuneration) Regulations 2013 (SI 2013/422). These provide for remuneration in accordance with the relevant provider contract, or the fees and rates set out in sch. 1 to the Regulations (reg. 6(2); Civil Legal Aid (Statutory Charge) Regulations 2013, SI 2013/503).

FIRST CHARGE

7.19 By virtue of LASPO 2012, s. 25, the amounts expended by the Lord Chancellor in securing the provision of the services to the client constitute a first charge on any property recovered or preserved in the proceedings or by any settlement or compromise of the dispute. This means that any money, costs or other property recovered in a publicly funded claim automatically become the subject of an unwelcome charge in favour of the State, which can use the damages recovered to reimburse itself for the costs incurred on behalf of the publicly funded client. Regulations may provide for exceptions (s. 25(3)).

The underlying principle is to place a publicly funded party in a similar position to a party privately funding litigation, whose primary responsibility at the end of proceedings is to pay the costs incurred by his or her own solicitors in bringing or defending the claim.

The charge applies only if there is a net liability to the Legal Aid Agency. This means that it is first necessary to calculate the total costs incurred on behalf of the publicly funded client, then deduct any contributions paid by the publicly funded client, and also deduct any costs paid by the other side. The statutory charge will be for the amount, if any, of the balance. The charge attaches to any property recovered or preserved in the claim. This includes, in the case of proceedings concluded by a court order, any property or money which was the subject matter of the proceedings, and in the case of proceedings concluded by a settlement, any property or money received under the settlement, even if it was not claimed in the proceedings (*Van Hoorn v Law Society* [1985] QB 106). Property is 'recovered' if the publicly funded client gains ownership or possession of it through the proceedings. It is 'preserved' if another's claim to ownership or possession is defeated.

Whenever property is recovered or preserved for a publicly funded person, it is the duty of that person's solicitor to inform the Legal Aid Agency immediately so that the charge can be registered and enforced. It can be enforced in the same way as other charges. Enforcement can be postponed if immediate repayment would be unreasonable and if the charge relates to property to be used as a home for the client or his dependants, or, where the relevant proceedings are family proceedings, it relates to money to pay for such a home.

Solicitors have professional duties to advise clients who apply for public funding of the effects of the statutory charge. This should be done both personally and in writing.

COSTS PROTECTION

7.20 LASPO 2012, s. 26, substantially reproduces the costs protection rules in favour of assisted individuals previously found in the Access to Justice Act 1999, s. 11. Costs ordered against an individual in relevant civil proceedings must not exceed the amount (if any) which it is reasonable for the individual to pay having regard to all the circumstances, including:

(a) the financial resources of all of the parties to the proceedings; and
(b) their conduct in connection with the dispute to which the proceedings relate.

For this purpose, the term 'relevant civil proceedings' means the whole or part of proceedings for which civil legal services have been made available to an individual under LASPO 2012, part 1 (s. 26(2)). The principles are discussed in more detail at **68.53** to **68.55**.

LEGAL AID COSTS ORDERS AND ASSESSMENTS

7.21 Regulations may make provision about costs in relation to proceedings for the purposes of which civil legal services are made available under LASPO 2012, part 1 (s. 26(5)). Such regulations may specify the principles to be applied in determining the amount of costs which may be awarded to a party with the benefit of civil legal services (s. 26(6)(d) and (e)). Three situations have been provided for:

(a) Costs orders in favour of a successful legally aided party are made in the same way as if the party was not publicly funded. The amount of costs to be paid under a legally aided party's costs order must be determined as if they were not legally aided (Civil Legal Aid (Costs) Regulations 2013 (SI 2013/611), reg. 21(1)).
(b) Legal representatives acting for a publicly funded party need to obtain an order for the court to assess the amount payable to them out of public funds. See **71.21**.
(c) There is jurisdiction to make an order requiring the payment by the Lord Chancellor of the whole or part of any costs incurred by an unassisted party. This is a very exceptional power, which is discussed at **68.56** to **68.59**.

Chapter 8 Pre-action Protocols

Commentary

The following procedural checklists, which are at the front of the book, are relevant to this chapter:

Procedural checklist 1 Pre-action Protocol for Personal Injury Claims
Procedural checklist 2 Pre-action procedure where no protocol applies

INTRODUCTION

8.1 The conduct the court will normally expect of prospective parties prior to the start of proceedings is set out in **PD Pre-action Conduct** and a number of protocols published with the approval of the Head of Civil Justice. There are currently 12 protocols for specific types of dispute. The full text of these protocols is set out in **appendix 2. table 8.1** shows where commentary of each protocol can be found in this book.

PD Pre-action Conduct lays down general guidance on pre-action conduct forming the background to the specific protocols, and also sets out principles governing disputes falling outside the scope of the specific protocols. The current version of **PD Pre-action Conduct**, discussed in this chapter, came into effect on 6 April 2009. It replaced an earlier version, PD Protocols, commentary on which can be found in **chapter 8A** at http://www.oup.com/blackstones/civil.

Objectives of the protocols are to encourage the exchange of early and full information about prospective legal claims and to enable the parties to avoid proceedings by settling their dispute before a claim is issued. If a dispute is settled through use of a pre-action protocol, the usual expectation is that the defendant will pay the claimant's reasonable costs assessed, if not agreed, on the basis of the case management track which would have been appropriate for the claim had proceedings been issued (*Birmingham City Council v Lee* [2008] EWCA Civ 891, [2009] HLR 15. If settlement is not achieved, the protocols should assist with the efficient case management of the proceedings (**PD Pre-action Conduct, para. 1.1(2)**).

Table 8.1 Pre-action protocols

Protocol	In force	*Blackstone's Civil Practice 2014*
Personal Injury Claims	26 April 1999	8.16–8.29
Clinical Disputes	26 April 1999	8.61–8.63
Construction and Engineering Disputes	2 October 2000	8.86–8.87
Defamation	2 October 2000	8.88
Professional Negligence	16 July 2001	8.89–8.97
Judicial Review	4 March 2002	77.31
Disease and Illness Claims	8 December 2003	8.64–8.70
Housing Disrepair Cases	8 December 2003	8.71–8.77
Dilapidations (Commercial Property)	1 January 2012	8.78–8.80
Possession Claims Based on Rent Arrears	2 October 2006	8.81–8.83
Possession Claims Based on Mortgage Arrears	19 November 2008	8.84–8.85
Low Value Road Traffic Accidents	30 April 2010	8.30–8.60
Claims Not Covered by Specific Protocols	26 April 1999	8.12–8.15

Each protocol includes a description of its own aims, consistent with the introduction to the overall objectives set out above, but tailored to meet the particular type of proceedings covered. For example, **para 1.2** of the **Pre-action Protocol for Personal Injury Claims** summarises its aims as encouraging:

- more pre-action contact between the parties
- better and earlier exchange of information
- better pre-action investigation by both sides
- putting the parties in a position where they may be able to settle cases fairly and early without litigation
- enabling proceedings to run to the court's timetable and efficiently, if litigation does become necessary
- promoting the provision of medical or rehabilitation treatment (not just in high-value cases) to address the needs of the claimant.

Procedural checklist 1 at the front of this book describes how to comply with the **Pre-action Protocol for Personal Injury Claims.** It, like the **Pre-action Protocol for the Resolution of Clinical Disputes** and the **Pre-action Protocol for Disease and Illness Claims,** provides for disclosure before the commencement of proceedings and is designed to avoid the necessity for applications to the court for pre-action disclosure. While disclosure of documents is a common feature of most of the protocols, there are variations. For example, pre-action disclosure is not one of the requirements of the **Pre-action Protocol for Defamation.**

When following a pre-action protocol, care must be taken to observe the time prescribed for the commencement of the proceedings by the Limitation Act 1980 (for example, three years for personal injury claims) or other legislation (see **chapter 10**). This is because statutory limitation periods take precedence over the time needed for compliance with the protocols. If instructions are received late, making it impossible to comply with the requirements of the relevant protocol before the need to issue a claim, the claim must be issued. **PD Pre-action Conduct, para. 9.6,** states that if for any reason proceedings are commenced before the protocol procedures are complied with, the parties are encouraged to agree to apply to the court for a stay of proceedings while they comply with the requirements.

Sir Rupert Jackson's *Review of Civil Litigation Costs: Final Report* (Ministry of Justice, December 2009) recommended:

- revoking the general provisions in **PD Pre-action Conduct** dealing with cases not covered by specific protocols (see **8.12** to **8.15**) (recommendation 73);
- using those provisions as the basis for a new debt claims protocol (recommendation 73);
- including financial penalties for not providing medical notes under the **Pre-action Protocol for the Resolution of Clinical Disputes** (see **8.63**) (recommendation 26);
- amending the **Pre-action Protocol for Possession Claims based on Rent Arrears** (**8.82** and **8.83**) to ensure it is consistent with the European Convention on Human Rights, **art. 8(1)**, in the **Human Rights Act 1998, sch. 1** (recommendation 46);
- revising the **Pre-action Protocol for Construction and Engineering Disputes** (see **8.86** and **8.87**) to make it less prescriptive (recommendation 72);
- pre-action applications being available for breaches of the protocols (recommendation 85).

Implementation of these recommendations was not included in the civil justice reforms of 2013.

EXPECTATION OF COMPLIANCE WITH THE PROTOCOLS

8.2 The court will expect the parties to have complied in substance with the protocol relevant to the claim (**PD Pre-action Conduct, para. 4.2**). The expectation of compliance is explained in **para. 4.3**, where it is said the court will be concerned about whether the parties have complied in substance with the relevant principles and requirements in **PD Pre-action Conduct**, and is not likely to be concerned with minor or technical shortcomings. Circumstances, such as preparing for mediation, may mean that the parties reasonably depart from the letter of the protocol, and should not be penalised for doing so (*Roundstone Nurseries Ltd v Stephenson Holdings Ltd* [2009] EWHC 1431 (TCC), [2009] 5 Costs LR 787).

The overall aims of the protocols are to enable the parties to settle their disputes without the need to start proceedings, and to support the efficient management by the court of matters where proceedings cannot be avoided (**para. 1.1**). Particular matters the court will consider are whether the parties have exchanged information about the dispute and considered using a form of ADR (**para. 1.2**). The court will also consider the proportionality of the steps taken compared to the size and importance of the matter (**para. 4.3(2)**). It will take account of any urgency, and in such cases will expect the parties to comply only to the extent that it is reasonable to do so (**para. 4.3(3)**). What the court will look for is the impact of non-compliance on the other party before imposing sanctions (**para. 4.5**).

Strict compliance with the relevant protocol is not insisted on in living mesothelioma claims (see 47.15), on account of the limited time for getting these cases to trial (**PD 3D, para. 9**). Other situations where the principles in **PD Pre-action Conduct** do not apply include (**para. 2.2**):

(a) applications for consent orders;
(b) applications where there is no other party for the applicant to engage with;
(c) most applications for directions by a trustee or other fiduciary;
(d) applications where informing the other potential party in advance would defeat the purpose of the application (such as freezing injunctions).

The protocols apply to additional claims under **CPR, Part 20**, as well as to normal claims under **Part 7** (*Daejan Investments Ltd v Park West Club Ltd* [2003] EWHC 2872 (TCC), [2004] BLR 223). However, a pragmatic approach is taken, with due leeway being given to the parties bearing in mind that directions may have been given in the main claim fixing the trial date or window (*Orange Personal Communications Services Ltd v Hoare Lea* [2008] EWHC 223 (TCC), [2009] Bus LR D24).

Examples of non-compliance are given in **PD Pre-action Conduct, para. 4.4**. They include not having supplied sufficient information to the defendant and not following the procedure set out by the relevant protocol. A defendant may be found to have failed to comply by failing to give a preliminary reply to the letter before claim, or not making a full response within the relevant time prescribed by the particular protocol, or not supplying documents required to be disclosed by the relevant protocol. Careful consideration needs to be given to the relevant protocol that applies (e.g. personal injury or clinical disputes) and the requirements of that protocol.

Procedural Checklist 2 sets out the requirements in a non-protocol case. Consideration is given to non-protocol cases at **8.12** to **8.15**.

Whether a sanction should be imposed

The CPR enable the court to take into account compliance or non-compliance with an applicable protocol when giving directions for the management of proceedings (**CPR, rr. 3.1**(4) and (5) and **3.9(1)(e)**) and when making orders for costs (**r. 44.2(5)(a)**). A failure to send a letter of claim was taken into account in *Zambia v Meer Care and Desai* [2008] EWCA Civ 754, LTL 9/7/2008, on an application to set aside judgment for non-attendance under **r. 39.3** (see **62.2**). Sanctions, whether in costs or otherwise, should not be imposed where there has been substantial compliance with the relevant protocol (*T. J. Brent Ltd v Black and Veatch Consulting Ltd* [2008] EWHC 1497 (TCC), 119 Con LR 1). Failing to give an adequate response, or giving an evasive response, to the letter before claim may be reflected in the court's order for the costs of the proceedings (*Fox Gregory Ltd v Hamptons Group Ltd* [2006] EWCA Civ 1544, LTL 4/10/2006). **PD Pre-action Conduct, para. 4.6** sets out orders which the court may make if, in its opinion, there has been non-compliance. **8.3**

Sanctions and orders following non-compliance

The court has a general power to impose sanctions under **CPR, r. 3.1**, where a party has failed to comply with any relevant pre-action protocol, and those sanctions remain effective unless the party in default applies for and obtains relief from sanctions (**rr. 3.8** and **3.9**, see **chapter 48**). According to **PD Pre-action Conduct, para. 4.6**, the court has power to make a variety of orders, which include: **8.4**

(a) imposing a stay of the proceedings until steps which ought to have been taken are taken—this may simply allow the parties to catch up with the requirements of the protocols, but may also be desirable to improve the prospects of settling the dispute (*Cundall Johnson and Partners v Whipps Cross University Hospital NHS Trust* [2007] EWHC 2178 (TCC), [2007] BLR 520);
(b) an order that the party at fault pay the costs of the proceedings, or part of those costs, of the other party or parties;
(c) an order that the party at fault pay those costs on an indemnity basis;
(d) if the party at fault is the claimant in whose favour an order for the payment of damages or some specified sum is subsequently made, an order depriving that party of interest on such sum and in respect of such period as may be specified, and/or awarding interest at a lower rate than that at which interest would otherwise have been awarded;
(e) if the party at fault is a defendant and an order for the payment of damages or some specified sum is subsequently made in favour of the claimant, an order awarding interest on such sum and in respect of such period as may be specified at a higher rate, not exceeding 10 per cent above base rate, than the rate at which interest would otherwise have been awarded.

Commentary

This list is not exhaustive. General sanctions which the court may impose include:

(a) costs, which may be ordered to be paid forthwith;
(b) an order refusing permission to call evidence from an expert who has been instructed by one or other party without compliance with the relevant protocol;
(c) under **CPR, r. 3.1(5)**, the court may order any party to pay a sum of money into court if that party has without good reason failed to comply with a rule, practice direction or relevant pre-action protocol. If applied to a claimant, this sanction could amount to giving security for costs, and in the case of a defendant, a payment into court in respect of the whole or part of the claim. The court is reluctant to use this sanction unless breaches have been repeated or there has been lack of good faith (*Mealey Horgan plc v Horgan* (1999) *The Times*, 6 July 1999).

The court will look at the overall effect of non-compliance on the other party when deciding whether to impose a sanction (**PD Pre-action Conduct, para. 4.5**). For example, in *Paul Thomas Construction Ltd v Hyland* [2001] CILL 1748 the court ordered the claimant to pay the defendant's costs on the indemnity basis after finding that the claimant had ignored repeated requests for further information and proposals for resolution of the matter by some form of ADR and had commenced wholly unnecessary proceedings.

CPR, r. 44.2(4), lists factors to be taken into account by the court when deciding to make an order for costs. One of them is the conduct of the parties, which is defined in **r. 44.2(5)** to include 'conduct, before, as well as during the proceedings and in particular the extent to which the parties followed any relevant pre-action protocol'. In *Straker v Tudor Rose* [2007] EWCA Civ 368, [2008] 2 Costs LR 205 (discussed further at **68.5**), the court in effect imposed a 10 to 15 per cent reduction in the costs of the proceedings awarded to the claimant for failing to consider negotiations, in breach of the protocol. This was regarded as a proportionate sanction to reflect the breach.

In *King v Telegraph Group Ltd* [2004] EWCA Civ 613, [2005] 1 WLR 2282, one of the factors which inclined the court towards making a prospective cost-capping order (see **44.2**) was that the letter before claim was written in a vituperative tone calculated to raise the temperature and inflate the parties' costs.

COSTS OF MATTERS DROPPED AT THE PRE-ACTION STAGE

8.5 It has always been clear that costs incurred in complying with pre-action protocols (and general pre-action work) are recoverable as 'incidental to' proceedings if a claim is subsequently issued (Senior Courts Act 1981, s. 51; *Callery v Gray* [2001] EWCA Civ 1117, [2001] 1 WLR 2112). The costs of such work are therefore recoverable as part of the general costs of the proceedings. In the absence of agreement between the parties, it has always been the case that costs are not recoverable between parties in dispute if proceedings are not issued.

In *McGlinn v Waltham Contractors Ltd* [2005] EWHC 1419 (TCC), [2005] 3 All ER 1126, it was argued that a successful claimant who raised a number of issues in pre-action correspondence, but abandoned some of them before issuing proceedings, was to be treated as only partially successful. A partially successful party is usually awarded just a percentage of the costs of the claim (see **68.10**). It was held that save in exceptional circumstances (such as where there is unreasonable conduct) the costs of the abandoned issues will not be 'incidental to' the subsequent proceedings. It would be contrary to the whole purpose of the pre-action protocols if claimants were routinely penalised if they dropped matters included in their letters before claim. The protocols are designed to narrow the issues, and allow a defendant to persuade a claimant that claims would not succeed.

ALTERNATIVE DISPUTE RESOLUTION

PD Pre-action Conduct, paras 8.1 to **8.3** remind parties that starting proceedings usually should be the last resort. Lord Dyson, MR, in January 2013 wrote that the effective promotion of ADR is unquestionably in the public interest. Recommendation 76 in the *Jackson Report* was that there should be a single authoritative handbook explaining clearly and concisely what ADR is, which was implemented by the publication of the *Jackson ADR Handbook*, Blake, Browne and Sime (Oxford: OUP, 2013), which has been issued to all the civil judges to ensure effective and consistent use of ADR. 8.6

While it is recognised that no party can or should be forced to enter into any form of ADR, there is a warning that a failure to consider ADR may be taken into account on the issue of costs. Specific types of ADR referred to in **para 8.2** are:

- discussion and negotiation,
- early neutral evaluation by an independent third party,
- mediation, which is a facilitated negotiation assisted by an independent neutral person,
- arbitration.

It says that parties may be required to provide evidence that alternative means of dispute resolution were considered. ADR is considered in detail in **chapter 73**.

Whether ADR costs are incidental to litigation

A key issue is whether alternative dispute procedures adopted by the parties form part of 'the costs of or incidental to the litigation' within the meaning of the Senior Courts Act 1981, s. 51(1) (and so potentially recoverable under a costs order), or whether the ADR procedure is to be treated as a separate process for costs purposes. It is clear that the general costs of complying with a pre-action protocol may be recoverable as costs incidental to the litigation (*McGlinn v Waltham Contractors Ltd* [2005] EWHC 1419 (TCC), [2005] 3 All ER 1126). Recoverability of mediation costs may be expressly agreed between the parties. An agreement that each side shall bear its own costs of mediation makes it clear that the mediation costs are not part of the main litigation costs (*Lobster Group Ltd v Heidelberg Graphic Equipment Ltd* [2009] EWHC 1919 (TCC), LTL 6/8/2009). In the absence of express agreement, the court will have to consider the circumstances and decide whether the parties have implicitly agreed or accepted that the costs of mediation form part of the costs of the proceedings (*Roundstone Nurseries Ltd v Stephenson Holdings Ltd* [2009] EWHC 1431 (TCC), [2009] 5 Costs LR 787). Only the **Pre-action Protocol for Construction and Engineering Disputes** requires a pre-action meeting between the parties (**paras 5.1** to **5.7**; see **8.87**). This meeting is occasionally swept up in a formal mediation process. 8.7

NOTIFICATION OF FUNDING ARRANGEMENT

Whether or not the dispute is governed by a pre-action protocol, the parties should inform each other in the pre-action stages whether they have the benefit of public funding under legal aid or the Community Legal Service. Likewise, a party who is being funded under a conditional fee arrangement should notify the other potential parties of this fact, although there is no obligation to give details of the level of 'success fee' that has been agreed (see **6.15**; **PD Pre-action Conduct, para. 9.3** and **form** N251). 8.8

DOCUMENTS: COLLATERAL USE

Documents disclosed pursuant to a specific protocol or the general provisions in **PD Pre-action Conduct** must not be used for any purpose other than resolving the matter, unless the disclosing 8.9

party agrees in writing (**PD Pre-action Conduct, para. 9.2**). This is a slight variation on the usual implied undertaking applicable to disclosed documents in litigation (see **50.45** to **50.48**).

EXPERTS

8.10 Where the evidence of an expert is necessary, the parties should consider how best to minimise expense (**PD Pre-action Conduct, para. 9.4**). Guidance on instructing experts is set out in **PD Pre-action Conduct, annex C**. This refers to **CPR, Part 35, PD 35** and the protocol to PD 35 (see **chapter 54**). **PD Pre-action Conduct, annex C** particularly encourages the use of single joint experts or agreed experts (**annex C, para. 3**).

STATEMENTS OF CASE

8.11 Where proceedings are started, the claim form or the particulars of claim should state whether the parties have complied with the general provisions of **PD Pre-action Conduct** or any relevant protocol (**PD Pre-action Conduct, para. 9.7**). The defendant will need to respond to this in the defence. The purpose appears to be to ensure that allegations of non-compliance are raised in the early stages of proceedings, rather than being saved until trial.

CASES NOT SUBJECT TO SPECIFIC PRE-ACTION PROTOCOLS

8.12 **PD Pre-action Conduct, paras 6.1** to **8.4** and **9.1** to **9.7** (which apply to all cases) and **annex A**, lay down principles and guidance on reasonable pre-action conduct in cases not governed by any of the specific protocols. The general approach is that parties should exchange sufficient information to allow them to understand each other's position and to make informed decisions with a view to settling the matter. They should also make appropriate attempts to settle the dispute, and should consider whether to use ADR (**para. 6.1**).

The parties should act in a reasonable and proportionate manner in all their dealings with each another (**para. 6.2**). In particular, the costs incurred in complying should be proportionate to the complexity of the matter and any money at stake. The detailed guidance applies to cases which are likely to be disputed, and does not apply to debt claims where there is no dispute that the money is owed and where the claimant follows a statutory or other formal pre-action procedure (**annex A, para. 1.1**). There is an express statement in **para. 6.2** that **PD Pre-action Conduct** must not be used as a tactical device to secure an unfair advantage for one party or to generate unnecessary costs.

Letter before claim

8.13 The claimant should send a detailed letter before claim enclosing copies of the essential documents and asking for an acknowledgment within 14 days and a full response within a stated period (**PD Pre-action Conduct, para. 7.1**). The period given for the full response depends on the nature of the dispute (**para. 7.2**). In undisputed debt claims this will normally be the same 14 days as for the acknowledgment (**para. 7.2(2)**). Matters involving an insurer or third party will usually merit 30 days for the full response (**para. 7.2(3)**). If the matter is complex or requires specialist advice, a longer period should be allowed, although it is only in exceptional cases that the period should exceed 90 days (**para. 7.2(4)** and **(5)**).

The letter before claim should give concise details about the matter sufficient to enable the defendant to understand and investigate the issues without needing to request further information (**annex A, para. 2.1**). The letter should include:

(a) the claimant's full name and address;

(b) the basis on which the claimant alleges the defendant is liable;
(c) a clear summary of the facts on which the claim is based;
(d) what the claimant wants from the defendant;
(e) if financial loss is claimed, an explanation of how the amount has been calculated;
(f) details of any funding arrangement (see **8.8**) that has been entered into by the claimant;
(g) a list of the essential documents on which the claimant intends to rely;
(h) the form of ADR (if any) that the claimant considers the most suitable and an invitation to the defendant to agree to this;
(i) the date by which the claimant considers it reasonable for a full response to be provided by the defendant;
(j) details of any relevant documents not in the claimant's possession which the claimant wishes the defendant to provide;
(k) unless the defendant is known to be legally represented, an express reference to **PD Pre-action Conduct** and in particular to **para. 4** concerning the court's powers to impose sanctions for failure to comply; and
(l) a warning to the defendant that ignoring the letter before claim may lead to the claimant starting proceedings and may increase the defendant's liability for costs.

It is generally inappropriate to commence proceedings without at the very least a letter before claim, unless the matter is one of extreme urgency. A claimant who brings and loses a claim without having sent a letter before claim may be ordered to pay costs on the indemnity basis, even if the claim is not covered by a specific protocol (*Phoenix Finance Ltd v Fédération Internationale de l'Automobile* [2002] EWHC 1242 (Ch), *The Times*, 27 June 2002). In *Reid v Capita Group plc* [2005] EWHC 2448 (Ch), LTL 17/10/2005, the claimant brought proceedings to obtain documents relating to a commercial transaction without having sent a letter before claim, and without having identified the documents sought. It was held the proceedings were premature, and the claimant was ordered to pay the defendant's costs of the proceedings.

In *King v Telegraph Group Ltd* [2004] EWCA Civ 613, [2005] 1 WLR 2282, solicitors who sent a 10-page letter before claim, settled by junior counsel (at [60]), failed to comply with the spirit of cooperation required by the protocols. Among other things it accused the newspaper of cant, reckless falsehood, and a malicious agenda of incriminating misrepresentation. Its effect was to remove the prospect of conciliation between the parties, making litigation almost inevitable.

Subsequent formal letters

The defendant's full response should say whether liability is accepted in full or in part or denied (**PD Pre-action Conduct, annex A, para. 4.1**). If liability is denied, the response must give detailed reasons and the basis of any factual dispute (**annex A, para. 4.2(1)**). It must include details of any counterclaim or allegation of contributory negligence (**annex A, para. 4.2(2)** and **(3)**). It must state whether the defendant agrees with the claimant's proposals for ADR (**annex A, para 4.2(4)**). It must also list the essential documents on which the defendant intends to rely, enclose copies of the documents requested by the claimant, or explain why they will not be provided, and request any documents the defendant wishes the claimant to provide (**annex A, para 4.2(5)** to **(7)**). The claimant must provide the documents requested by the defendant in as short a period of time as is practicable, or explain why they will not be provided (**annex A, para. 5.1**). If the defendant raises a counterclaim, the defendant's letter should include details equivalent to a letter before claim, and the claimant's response must be the equivalent of a defendant's full response (**annex A, paras 4.2(2)** and **5.2**). **8.14**

Other requirements in general cases

PD Pre-action Conduct, annex B sets out a number of requirements where the claimant is a business and the defendant is an individual. The requirements may be complied with at any **8.15**

time between the claimant first intimating the possibility of court proceedings and the claimant's letter before claim. Where expert evidence is required, **annex C** should be complied with (see **8.10**). Consideration should be given to some form of ADR once the parties are able to make informed decisions about liability and remedies (**paras 6.1** and **8.1** to **8.3**). At the very least it should be possible to narrow the issues (**annex A, para. 6.1**). Before starting proceedings the parties should undertake a further review of their respective positions to see if proceedings can be avoided (**annex A, para. 6.2**).

PERSONAL INJURY CLAIMS PROTOCOL

8.16 The **Pre-action Protocol for Personal Injury Claims** is primarily drafted for road traffic, slipping and tripping and accident at work claims on the fast track (**para. 2.3**). The protocol is intended to assist in the preparation of a claim, which, on the fast track, must be ready to be tried within 30 weeks of allocation. It also applies generally to all claims for personal injuries, whatever their value (**para. 2.2**; note to **PD 14, para. 1.1**). It does not apply to claims covered by the clinical disputes or disease and illness protocols.

The spirit, if not the letter, of the **Pre-action Protocol for Personal Injury Claims** should be followed in multi-track claims, where the protocol should be complied with so far as possible, particularly regarding letters before claim, exchanging information and documents, and agreeing experts (**para. 2.4**).

The protocol applies to the whole of a claim, not just the personal injury element (**para. 2.2**). The protocol lays down a timetable for the pre-action period but **para. 2.3** envisages that there may be claims where some flexibility in the timetable will be necessary. Arrangements for disclosure and expert evidence may need to be varied to suit the particular circumstances of individual cases. There may be difficulties, for example, in a claim with a modest personal injury element, which is easily resolved, but a substantial claim for vehicle repairs, where the claimant may wish to move expeditiously to have the vehicle examined and repaired or scrapped and replaced. It may well be considered reasonable for the claimant to give the defendant's insurers much less notice of his or her intention in relation to the vehicle, and to insist on an inspection far more quickly than the timescale indicated by the protocol. It is undesirable for a claimant to be put in the position of wondering whether a defendant's dilatory insurer will or will not accept the claimant's figures for repairs particularly when an alternative vehicle may have to be hired. It is submitted that common sense must prevail in allowing for variations of the timetable set by the protocol.

If it is considered, by either or both parties to a claim, that the detail of the protocol is not appropriate to it, and proceedings are subsequently issued, the court will expect an explanation of why the protocol has not been followed or has been varied (**para. 2.5**). A space is provided in the directions questionnaire for giving such an explanation.

The steps required by the protocol are summarised in **procedural checklist 1**, which is at the front of the book, and are discussed in detail in **8.17** to **8.27**.

Early notification

8.17 The **Pre-action Protocol for Personal Injury Claims** promotes early notification of the possibility of a claim to the person against whom it may be made. **Paragraph 2.6** recognises that it may not be possible to provide all the relevant details immediately but that it may be best to put the potential defendant on notice by writing an initial letter as soon as it is apparent *that a claim is likely* to be made. An early notification of this kind will not start the timetable for responding.

Letter before claim

The timetable set by the **Pre-action Protocol for Personal Injury Claims** is initiated by the letter before claim. This should be as detailed as possible and a specimen letter appears at annex A to the protocol. The letter should concentrate on providing sufficient information for the defendant to assess liability. It should also provide sufficient information to enable the defendant to estimate the likely size of the claim (**para. 2.9**). In a road traffic claim the letter should provide the name and address of the hospital where the claimant was treated, and, if available, the claimant's hospital reference number (**para. 2.8**). In low-impact road traffic accident cases the claimant's advisers should offer access to the claimant's vehicle and give early disclosure of the claimant's general practitioner and other relevant medical notes (suitably redacted to remove irrelevant passages). This is to enable the defendant's advisers to get hold of the most important evidential material expeditiously and inexpensively, see *Kearsley v Klarfeld* [2005] EWCA Civ 1510, [2006] 2 All ER 303. Normally two copies of a letter before claim are sent to the defendant, who is asked to pass one copy to the insurers responsible (**paras 3.1** and **3.4**). If the insurers are already known, the second copy should be sent direct to them (**para. 3.4**). After sending a letter before claim the claimant should do no more work on investigating liability until the defendant responds indicating whether liability is accepted or denied (**para. 2.10**). 8.18

Defendant's acknowledgment

The defendant is required to acknowledge receipt of the letter before claim within 21 days of posting, identifying the insurers, if any (**Pre-action Protocol for Personal Injury Claims, para. 3.6**). If the defendant or the insurers fail to respond within 21 days, the claimant is entitled to issue proceedings (**para. 3.6**). Bearing in mind the spirit of reasonable pre-action behaviour, if the defendant delays passing the letter before claim on to the insurers, it would be reasonable to allow the insurers additional time for responding to it (**para. 2.7**). 8.19

Commentary

Investigation and response

Having acknowledged the letter before claim, the defendant (or insurer) then has three months to investigate and to reply stating whether liability is denied and, if it is, giving reasons for denial and any alternative version of the events relied upon (**Pre-action Protocol for Personal Injury Claims, para. 3.7**). In low-impact road traffic accident cases the defendant's advisers should make it clear whether they intend to allege that the claimant's injuries could not possibly have been caused by the accident, see *Kearsley v Klarfeld* [2005] EWCA Civ 1510, [2006] 2 All ER 303. 8.20

Proceedings should not be issued in this three-month period. For some claims this may not be possible. For example, if the claimant consults a solicitor towards the end of a relevant limitation period, a protective claim form will have to be issued, so as not to deprive the claimant of a remedy. In these circumstances, the protocol recommends, at **para. 2.11**, that the claimant's solicitor should give as much notice as is practicable and the parties should consider whether the court might be invited to extend the time for service of the claimant's supporting documents and the service of any defence, or alternatively to stay the proceedings while the recommended steps in the protocol are followed. This may only be done where there is an expectation that there is a valid claim to be pursued. In *West Bromwich Building Society v Mander Hadley and Co.* [1998] CLC 814 the Court of Appeal held that the issue of protective proceedings, when a claimant had no intention of prosecuting the claim and was unaware of any valid basis for it, was an abuse of process.

Status of letters before claim and response

Although a letter before claim and its response should be as full as possible, in order to meet the 'cards on the table approach', it is not intended that they should bear the same status as 8.21

formal statements of case (**Pre-action Protocol for Personal Injury Claims, para. 2.12**). It is recognised that various matters may well come to light as a result of investigations after the letter before claim has been sent or after the defendant has responded, especially in a situation where the disclosure of documents takes place outside the recommended three-month period. Circumstances such as these could mean that particulars of claim and/or the defence may present a party's case in a slightly different way than in the letter before claim and/or response, and it would be inconsistent with the spirit of the protocol for a party to take a point on this in the proceedings, provided there was no deliberate intention to mislead (**para. 2.12**). Indeed it is clear from the comments of Lord Woolf MR in *McPhilemy v Times Newspapers Ltd* [1999] 3 All ER 775 that contests over the terms of statements of case are to be avoided.

Disclosure of documents and schedule of special damages

8.22 The **Pre-action Protocol for Personal Injury Claims, para. 3.10** provides for pre-action disclosure of documents where the defendant denies liability. The defendant should enclose documents material to the issues with the letter of reply. Annex B to the protocol lists documents likely to be material in different types of claim. No charge is to be made for supplying documents under the protocol (**para. 3.13**). The claimant is required to send the defendant a schedule of special damages with supporting documents as soon as practicable (**para. 3.14**). This is particularly important where the defendant has admitted liability, where the schedule should be sent to the defendant at least 21 days before proceedings are issued to give the defendant a chance to make a Part 36 offer (**para. 5.3**).

The aim of early disclosure of documents is not to encourage 'fishing expeditions' by the claimant but to promote an early exchange of relevant information to assist in clarifying or resolving the issues in dispute (**para. 2.13**). The claimant's solicitors can assist by identifying in the letter before claim or in a subsequent letter the particular categories of documents which they consider are relevant (**para. 2.13**).

Experts

8.23 The **Pre-action Protocol for Personal Injury Claims** encourages the joint selection of, and access to, experts (**para. 2.14**). The expectation is that the selection and instruction of experts will be largely or wholly accomplished before proceedings are issued (*Edwards-Tubb v J. D. Wetherspoon plc* [2011] EWCA Civ 136, [2011] 1 WLR 1373 at [27]). In most claims this will apply to medical experts, but there may be occasions when it will also apply to others, such as engineers. The protocol also promotes the practice of the claimant obtaining a medical report, disclosing it to the defendant, who then has the opportunity to ask questions on the report and/or agree it without the need to obtain a second report (**para. 2.14**). At **para. 3.15**, the protocol suggests that before instructing any expert a party should provide the other party with a list of names of experts in the relevant area who are considered suitable to instruct. The court has some (or a great deal of) control over experts instructed pursuant to a protocol (see below and **chapter 54**). Such an expert produces a report which has to be addressed to the court, and is to be contrasted with an expert instructed pre-protocol purely to advise a client and at the client's expense. That kind of expert falls outside the definition in **CPR, r. 35.2**, their report remains privileged in the hands of the client and cannot in usual circumstances be made the subject of an *Edwards-Tubb* order (*Edwards-Tubb v J. D. Wetherspoon plc* at [31], and see 54.19).

It is often the case that the claimant will wish the medical practitioner who provided the medical treatment to be retained as the expert in the claim. In most cases this is best avoided, as the court may well reach the conclusion that the medical expert is no longer sufficiently objective, because, first, he or she will have developed a relationship with the patient/claimant and secondly, may regard his or her views on prognosis as unchallengeable. It is suggested that the procedure for the joint selection of experts set out in **paras 3.15** to **3.19** of the protocol is preferable in order that a mutually acceptable expert can be instructed.

Claimants who choose to instruct their own expert unilaterally may well discover that the court will later refuse permission to call that expert and insist that an expert be jointly instructed (**CPR, r. 35.7**). The consequence of this is that the costs of the first expert will not be recoverable, regardless of the outcome of the case. The question relating to experts in the directions questionnaire asks whether reports have been disclosed and whether it is proposed to use a joint expert. This allows arguments to be put for a separate defence expert and for the court to enquire whether the defendant's position cannot be protected by simply delivering written questions to the claimant's expert.

Furthermore, the protocol does maintain the flexibility for either party to obtain their own expert's report, if necessary, once proceedings have been commenced, but with the permission of the court. It is also for the court to decide whether the costs of more than one expert report should be recoverable (see **CPR, r. 35.4(4)**).

It is clear from the foregoing that the provisions of the CPR and those of the protocol do not lie easily with each other. However, with cooperation between practitioners together with appropriate judicial intervention, common sense should prevail. In applying the overriding objective, the court will decide whether it is more efficient to order a report from a second expert for the opposing side and will probably determine the question of costs at a later stage. Whether the costs of the additional expert will be recoverable will depend upon the degree and extent to which the protocol was complied with, or whether it would have been more advantageous to instruct a new joint expert.

Joint selection **Paragraphs 3.15** to **3.21** of the **Pre-action Protocol for Personal Injury Claims** lay down the procedure for the joint selection of experts. Joint selection of an expert means that one party's choice of expert to be instructed is agreed by the other party, but it does not mean that the expert is jointly instructed by both parties. At least initially, only the party who instructed the jointly selected expert is entitled to see the expert's report, which is protected by legal professional privilege unless the instructing party chooses to disclose it (*Carlson v Townsend* [2001] EWCA Civ 511, [2001] 1 WLR 2415). Conditions requiring the disclosure of such reports are considered at **54.17**. In contrast, if an expert is jointly instructed, both parties are entitled to see his or her report. The party who instructed a jointly selected expert is solely liable to pay the expert's fee, but both parties are liable to pay a jointly instructed expert. **8.24**

Medical agencies Some solicitors have adopted the practice of obtaining medical reports via medical agencies rather than directly from a specific doctor or hospital (**Pre-action Protocol for Personal Injury Claims, para. 2.15**). The protocol does not discourage this but emphasises that in such a case, the defendant's prior consent should be sought and, if the defendant so requests, the agency should be asked to provide in advance the names of the doctors whom they are considering instructing (**para. 2.15**). **8.25**

Negotiation, rehabilitation and settlement

Paragraph 2.16 of the **Pre-action Protocol for Personal Injury Claims** requires the parties to consider whether some form of ADR would be more suitable than litigation. Both sides may be required to provide the court with evidence that ADR was considered. Litigation is regarded as a last resort, and proceedings should not be issued while settlement is being actively explored. It is expressly recognised that the parties cannot be forced to mediate or enter into any form of ADR (**para. 2.19**), but a failure to comply with the aim of **para. 2.16** may be taken into account on costs. **8.26**

As early as possible both sides should consider whether the claimant has reasonable needs that could be met by rehabilitation treatment or other measures (**para. 4.1**). Annex D to the protocol is a Rehabilitation Code which gives guidance on how to identify the claimant's needs. This may involve obtaining a report assessing the claimant's rehabilitation needs. An assessment report should be produced using the seven headings set out in **para. 5.2** of the **Rehabilitation Code**. It will not deal with diagnostic criteria, causation or long-term care requirements (**Code, para. 5.3**). Instead it must deal with short- and medium-term rehabilitation treatment, its likely benefits, and cost (**Code, para. 5.2**). The defendant's insurer will pay for the report within 28 days of receipt (**Code, para. 6.5**). It is for the parties to agree that any particular regime of rehabilitation or treatment shall be put in place (**Code, para. 6.4**). Any funds laid out by the insurer for treatment are treated as voluntary interim payments (**Code, para. 7.2**). Provided the claimant uses such funds for the recommended purpose, the insurer warrants it will not dispute the reasonableness or the agreed cost of the treatment in subsequent proceedings (**Code, para. 7.2**). Any assessment report must not be used in the litigation except by consent (**Pre-action Protocol for Personal Injury Claims, para. 4.4**). Any notes and reports created in connection with the assessment process shall not be disclosed in any litigation, and any person involved in the preparation of the assessment report shall not be a compellable witness (**Code, para. 6.3**).

Preparation for proceedings

8.27 Where a claim is not resolved, even though the parties have followed the protocol, they might wish to carry out a 'stocktake' of the issues in dispute and the evidence that the court is likely to require to resolve those issues, prior to the commencement of proceedings (**Pre-action Protocol for Personal Injury Claims, para. 2.17**).

If the pre-action steps on the defendant's side have been taken by insurers, the protocol recommends that, seven to 14 days before the intended issue date, the claimant's solicitor should invite the insurers to nominate solicitors to act in the proceedings.

Application to the small claims track

8.28 Strictly, **PD Pre-action Conduct** (see **8.12** to **8.15**), applies to small-value personal injuries claims rather than the **Pre-action Protocol for Personal Injury Claims**. Acting reasonably may involve adopting some features from the **Pre-action Protocol for Personal Injury Claims**, but much will depend on the circumstances of the case. In particular, it may be appropriate to rely on a short report from a general practitioner rather than obtaining a jointly selected consultant's report. **PD Pre-action Conduct, para. 7.2(3)**, suggests that 30 days will usually be sufficient time for the defendant to investigate and respond. Further, it is submitted that, given the restricted costs regime on the small claims track, solicitors representing claimants in small-value claims should not be criticised for issuing proceedings soon after receiving a response, save where there has been the most flagrant disregard of the need for cooperation provided for in the protocols.

Personal injury claims worth more than the fast track limit

8.29 The strict requirements, and timetables, laid down in the **Pre-action Protocol for Personal Injury Claims** apply to personal injury claims up to the fast track limit (**para. 2.3**). In claims worth more than the fast track limit the courts will expect to see reasonable pre-action behaviour (**para. 2.4**). This is likely to mean that the parties must comply with the protocol as far as possible, particularly in respect of letters before claim, exchanging information and agreeing experts (**para. 2.14**). Where a claim is initially believed to have a value under £25,000, but on investigation appears to have a value exceeding that figure, the claimant should notify the defendant as soon as possible (**para. 3.9**).

RTA PROTOCOL

The **Pre-action Protocol for Low Value Personal Injury Claims in Road Traffic Accidents** (the **RTA Protocol**) has to be read together with a number of related provisions in the CPR. The protocol and related provisions are designed to provide a streamlined and swift process for settling by agreement road traffic personal injury claims where liability is admitted and damages are in the range of £1,000 to £10,000. It is likely that the upper limit will be raised to £25,000 in 2013–14, and that the scheme will be extended to employer's liability and public liability claims. 8.30

The system provided for dealing with these claims is highly regulated, with short, fixed periods for most of the necessary steps, prescribed interim payments, and a regime of fixed costs. The process under the **RTA Protocol** is divided into three stages, which are shown in general terms in **figure 8.1**.

Cases covered by the RTA Protocol

A claim will be covered by the RTA Protocol if: 8.31

(a) the claim is for damages arising from a road traffic accident (**RTA Protocol, para. 4.1(1)**);
(b) the accident was on or after 30 April 2010 (**para. 4.1(1)**);
(c) the defendant was a road user (**para. 4.4(1)**);
(d) the claim includes damages in respect of personal injury (**para. 4.1(2)**);

Stage 1
Claimant sends Claim Notification Form (CNF) to defendant's insurer. D has 15 days to decide whether to admit liability.
C's fixed Stage 1 costs: £400 (before 30 April 2013); £200 (from 30 April 2013)

↓

Stage 2
Claimant obtains medical reports.
Claimant then sends D's insurer relevant documents on quantum with a Stage 2 Settlement Pack.
35-day negotiation period to agree quantum.
C's fixed Stage 2 costs: £800 (before 30 April 2013); £300 (from 30 April 2013)

↓

Stage 3
Part 8 claim for the court to determine quantum where:
(a) the parties are unable to agree quantum;
(b) the claimant is a child; or
(c) proceedings have been started to avoid the claim being time-barred.

C's fixed Stage 3 costs: Type A – solicitors' costs £250
Type B – advocate's fee £250
Type C – advice on quantum where C is a child £150

Figure 8.1 RTA Protcol: the three stages

Commentary

(e) the claimant values the claim between £1,000 and £10,000 on a full liability basis (**para. 4.1(3) and (4)**); and
(f) the claim does not fall into any of the excluded categories (**para. 4.4**).

Financial condition

8.32 A claim will not be covered by the **RTA Protocol** if the small claims track would be the normal track for that claim (**RTA Protocol, para. 4.1(4)**). This is the case where the total value of the claim is not more than £5,000, and where the value of the claim for pain, suffering and loss of amenity is not more than £1,000 (**CPR, r. 26.6(1)**). These claims are excluded from the **RTA Protocol** because the no-costs rule in small claims track cases (see **CPR, r. 27.14**) is inconsistent with the fixed costs regime under the **RTA Protocol**. In deciding whether the claim exceeds the £10,000 upper limit the claimant should:

(a) include pecuniary losses;
(b) exclude the value of vehicle-related damage (**para. 4.3**); and
(c) exclude interest (**para. 4.1(3)**).

Excluded cases

8.33 The **RTA Protocol** does not apply (**para. 4.4**) to claims:

(a) made to the MIB pursuant to the Untraced Drivers' Agreement 2003 (see **9.5**);
(b) where the claimant or defendant is deceased (see **14.12**);
(c) where the claimant or defendant is a protected party (see **14.15**);
(d) where the claimant is bankrupt (see **14.25**); or
(e) where the defendant's vehicle is registered outside the United Kingdom.

Stage 1: Claim notification

8.34 **Starting the RTA Protocol process** **Figure 8.2** is a flow diagram showing the steps that have to be followed in Stages 1 and 2 of the **RTA Protocol.**

The **RTA Protocol** procedure is commenced by the claimant completing a claim notification form (CNF), which is available on Her Majesty's Courts and Tribunals Service website at http://www.hmcourts-service.gov.uk/ as form RTA 1. All boxes in the CNF that are marked as mandatory must be completed before it is sent. The claimant must make a reasonable attempt to complete the boxes that are not marked as mandatory (**RTA Protocol, para. 6.3**). Details of rehabilitation, following the principles in the Rehabilitation Code in the **Pre-action Protocol for Personal Injury Claims**, must be included in the CNF (**RTA Protocol, para. 6.7**). There is an obligation to state whether any vehicle damage claim is being dealt with separately by third parties, or, if not, to include details of the vehicle damage claim together with relevant invoices and receipts (**para. 6.4**). The CNF must be verified by a statement of truth. When completed electronically this requirement is satisfied by entering the name of the person verifying the form in the signature box (**para. 6.6**).

The CNF must be sent electronically to the defendant's insurer. The relevant address should be available on the RTA PI Claims Process website (http://www.rtapiclaimsprocess.org.uk/). To make use of this website it is necessary to register online. At the same time as the CNF is sent to the insurer, or as soon as practicable thereafter, a defendant only CNF (form RTA 2) must be sent to the defendant by first class post (**para. 6.2**).

Apart from the defendant only CNF, all communications under the **RTA Protocol** must be sent electronically (**para. 5.1**). There is an obligation on the claimant to include electronic contact details on the CNF. The obligation to use electronic communications presumably means that supporting documents need to be scanned before being sent (although this is not spelt out in the **RTA Protocol**).

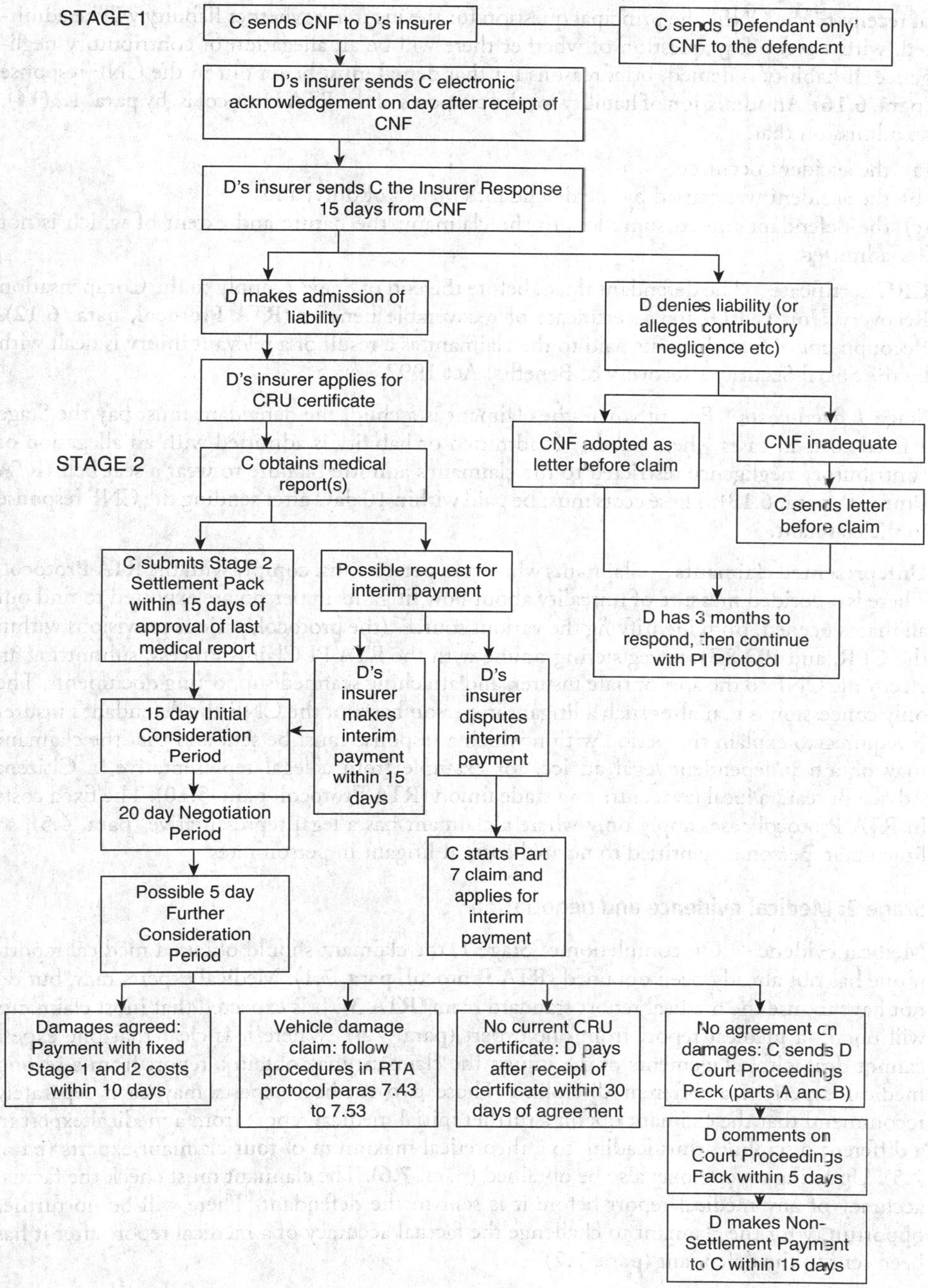

Figure 8.2 Flow diagram of Stages 1 and 2 under the RTA Protocol

Response by defendant's insurer An electronic acknowledgment must be sent by the defendant's insurer on the next business day after receipt of the CNF (**RTA Protocol, para. 6.10**). The insurer has 15 days to investigate liability, and must complete the 'Insurer Response' section of the CNF (the CNF response) and send it to the claimant within 15 business days **8.35**

of receipt of the CNF. The principal question for the insurer is whether liability will be admitted, with a secondary question of whether there will be an allegation of contributory negligence. If liability is denied, brief reasons for that denial must be set out in the CNF response (**para. 6.16**). An admission of liability for the purposes of the RTA Protocol is, by **para. 1.1(14)**, an admission that:

(a) the accident occurred;
(b) the accident was caused by the defendant's breach of duty; and
(c) the defendant caused some loss to the claimant, the nature and extent of which is not admitted.

8.36 **CRU certificate** The defendant must, before the end of Stage 1, apply to the Compensation Recovery Unit (CRU) for a certificate of recoverable benefits (**RTA Protocol, para. 6.12**). Recoupment of State benefits paid to the claimant as a result of a relevant injury is dealt with by the Social Security (Recovery of Benefits) Act 1997.

8.37 **Stage 1 fixed costs** Except where the claimant is a child, the defendant must pay the Stage 1 fixed costs in cases where liability is admitted or liability is admitted with an allegation of contributory negligence restricted to the claimant's admitted failure to wear a seat belt (**RTA Protocol, para. 6.18**). These costs must be paid within 10 days after sending the CNF response to the claimant.

8.38 **Unrepresented claimants** Claimants who act in person must comply with the **RTA Protocol**. There is a decided measure of unreality about how litigants in person are expected to find out all that is needed, from identifying the various sources (the protocol, various provisions within the **CPR**, and **PD 8B**), to registering online with the RTA PI Claims Process, submitting an electronic CNF to the appropriate insurer, and attaching scanned supporting documents. The only concession is that after such a litigant in person has sent the CNF, the defendant's insurer is required to explain the period within which a response must be sent and that the claimant may obtain independent legal advice, for example from a legal representative, a Citizens Advice Bureau, a local law centre or a trade union (**RTA Protocol, para. 5.10**). The fixed costs in RTA Protocol cases apply only where a claimant has a legal representative (**para. 4.5**), so litigants in person are entitled to normal costs at litigant in person rates.

Stage 2: Medical evidence and negotiation

8.39 **Medical evidence** On completion of Stage 1, the claimant should obtain a medical report, if one has not already been obtained (**RTA Protocol, para. 7.1**). Medical experts may, but do not have to, use the medical report standard form (**RTA 3**). It is expected that most claimants will obtain a medical report from one expert (**para. 7.4**). Where it is clear that one expert cannot deal with all elements of the injury, the claimant may obtain a report from a second medical expert in a different discipline. Those two medical experts may each separately recommend that the claimant obtain a further initial medical report from a medical expert in a different discipline, thus leading to a theoretical maximum of four claimant experts (**para. 7.5**). Updating reports may also be obtained (**para. 7.6**). The claimant must check the factual accuracy of any medical report before it is sent to the defendant. There will be no further opportunity for the claimant to challenge the factual accuracy of a medical report after it has been sent to the defendant (**para. 7.2**).

8.40 **Stay for updating reports** Where subsequent medical reports need to be obtained, the parties should agree to stay the protocol process for a suitable period (**RTA Protocol, para. 7.7**).

8.41 **Interim payment** Where there is a stay for updating reports, the claimant can request an interim payment of £1,000, which generally the defendant's insurer must pay within 10 days (**RTA Protocol, paras 7.7 to 7.10**). A claimant may make a request for an interim payment exceeding £1,000, in which case the defendant's insurer has 15 days to consider the matter. If the defendant fails to make the interim payment, or if the claimant is not satisfied with the defendant's response to the request, the claimant has 10 days to give notice that the claim will no longer be governed by the **RTA Protocol**.

Stage 2 settlement pack After obtaining the necessary medical reports, the claimant must send the defendant's insurers a Stage 2 settlement pack within 15 days of the claimant approving the final medical report and agreeing to rely on the prognosis in that report (**RTA Protocol, para. 7.26**). This pack consists of: 8.42

(a) the Stage 2 settlement pack form (form RTA 5). This includes space for the claimant to make an offer of what they will accept in settlement of the claim. Where the defendant alleges contributory negligence because of the claimant's failure to wear a seat belt, the form must give the claimant's suggested percentage reduction (which may be 0 per cent);
(b) a medical report or reports;
(c) evidence of pecuniary losses; and
(d) evidence of disbursements (for example the cost of any medical report).

Consideration of claim and negotiation There is a 35-day period (which can be extended by agreement) for consideration of the Stage 2 settlement pack by the defendant (this is called 'the total consideration period': **RTA Protocol, para. 7.29**). The total consideration period includes an initial period of up to 15 days for the defendant to consider the documents and make an offer. Within this period the defendant must either accept the offer made by the claimant on the Stage 2 settlement pack form or make a counter-offer using that form (**para. 7.31**). When making a counter-offer the defendant must propose an amount for each head of damage. Where the defendant has obtained a CRU certificate, the counter-offer must state the name and amount of any deductible amount (**para. 7.35**). If there is no current CRU certificate, a fresh certificate will be needed (**paras 7.41, 7.42, 7.54 and 7.65**). The defendant must also explain in the counter-offer why a particular head of damage is less than the amount claimed by the claimant. The explanation will assist the claimant when negotiating a settlement and will allow both parties to focus on the areas of the claim that remain in dispute (**para. 7.34**). 8.43

Once the initial consideration period has elapsed, the defendant can withdraw the admission of liability only with the claimant's consent (**CPR, r. 14.1B(2)(a)**).

The remaining 20 days of the total consideration period are for any further negotiation between the parties ('the negotiation period'). If there is an offer within five days of the end of the 35-day period, there is an automatic five-day extension to give time for the other side to consider whether to accept the offer (**RTA Protocol, para. 5.30**).

Terms of offers Any offer to settle made at any stage by either party will automatically include, and cannot exclude (**RTA Protocol, para. 7.37**): 8.44

(a) the Stage 2 fixed costs in **CPR, r. 45.15**;
(b) an agreement in principle to pay disbursements.

Payment after acceptance of offer Where the claimant is an adult and the claim is settled during Stage 2, under the **RTA Protocol, para. 7.40**, the defendant must pay: 8.45

(a) the agreed damages less any deductible amount which is payable to the CRU and any interim payment;
(b) any unpaid Stage 1 fixed costs;
(c) the Stage 2 fixed costs; and
(d) the disbursements allowed in accordance with **CPR, r. 45.19(2)(a)**.

These sums must be paid within 10 days of the end of the initial consideration period or negotiation period during which the parties agreed the settlement (**RTA Protocol, para. 7.40**).

Failure to compromise If the parties do not reach agreement in the total consideration period, the claimant is required by **RTA Protocol, para. 7.55**, to send the defendant's insurer 8.46

the court proceedings pack (parts A and B) (forms **RTA 6** and **RTA 7**), which must contain:

(a) in part A, the schedule of the claimant's losses and the defendant's responses, comprising only the figures for the original and additional damages, together with supporting comments and evidence from both parties on any disputed heads of damage; and
(b) in part B, the final offer and counter-offer from the Stage 2 settlement pack form and, where relevant, the offer and any final counter-offer made under **para. 7.45**.

The court proceedings pack (part A) must not raise anything that has not been raised in the Stage 2 settlement pack form (**para.** 7.57). The defendant has five days to make any comments on this pack (**paras 5.58** and **5.60**), and can nominate a solicitor to accept service of court proceedings (**para.** 5.59).

8.47 **Stage 2 payment** Where the claimant is an adult, the defendant must within 15 days of receipt of the court proceedings pack make a payment to the claimant of:

(a) the final offer of damages made by the defendant in the court proceedings pack, less any deductible amount which is payable to the CRU and any interim payment;
(b) any unpaid Stage 1 fixed costs;
(c) the Stage 2 fixed costs; and
(d) any agreed disbursements.

Stage 3: Part 8 claim to determine quantum

8.48 **Procedure under Stage 3** **Figure 8.3** is a flow diagram showing the steps that have to be followed in Stage 3 in cases governed by the **RTA Protocol**. Stage 3 involves a Part 8 claim and the court assessing damages where the claim has not been settled in Stages 1 or 2. The procedure is governed by **PD 8B**, which is a substantially modified version of the normal Part 8 procedure. Most of the provisions of **CPR, Part 8** are disapplied (**PD 8B, para. 2.2**), except for **rr.** 8.2 (the Part 8 claim form), 8.4 (consequences of not acknowledging service) and 8.9(a) and (b) (CPR provisions on statements of case and entering judgments on admissions do not apply).

8.49 **Filing and service** By **PD 8B, para. 6.1**, the claimant must file with the claim form and serve on the defendant:

(a) the court proceedings pack (part A);
(b) the court proceedings pack (part B) (the claimant and defendant's final offers) in a sealed envelope. These are treated as modified Part 36 offers, and must not be communicated to the court until the claim is determined (**CPR, r. 36.20(1)**);
(c) copies of medical reports;
(d) evidence of special damages;
(e) evidence of disbursements; and
(f) any notice of funding.

The claimant can only use documents that have already been sent to the defendant under the **RTA Protocol** (**para.** 6.3).

8.50 **Acknowledgment of service** The defendant must file and serve an acknowledgment of service in form N210B not more than 14 days after service of the claim form (**PD 8B, para. 8.1**). At the same time the defendant must file any notice of funding and a current CRU certificate (**para.** 8.2).

Where the defendant opposes the claim because the claimant has either not followed the **RTA Protocol** or has filed and served additional or new evidence with the claim form that had not been provided under the protocol, the court will dismiss the claim and the claimant may start proceedings under **CPR, Part 7** (**PD 8B, para. 9.1**).

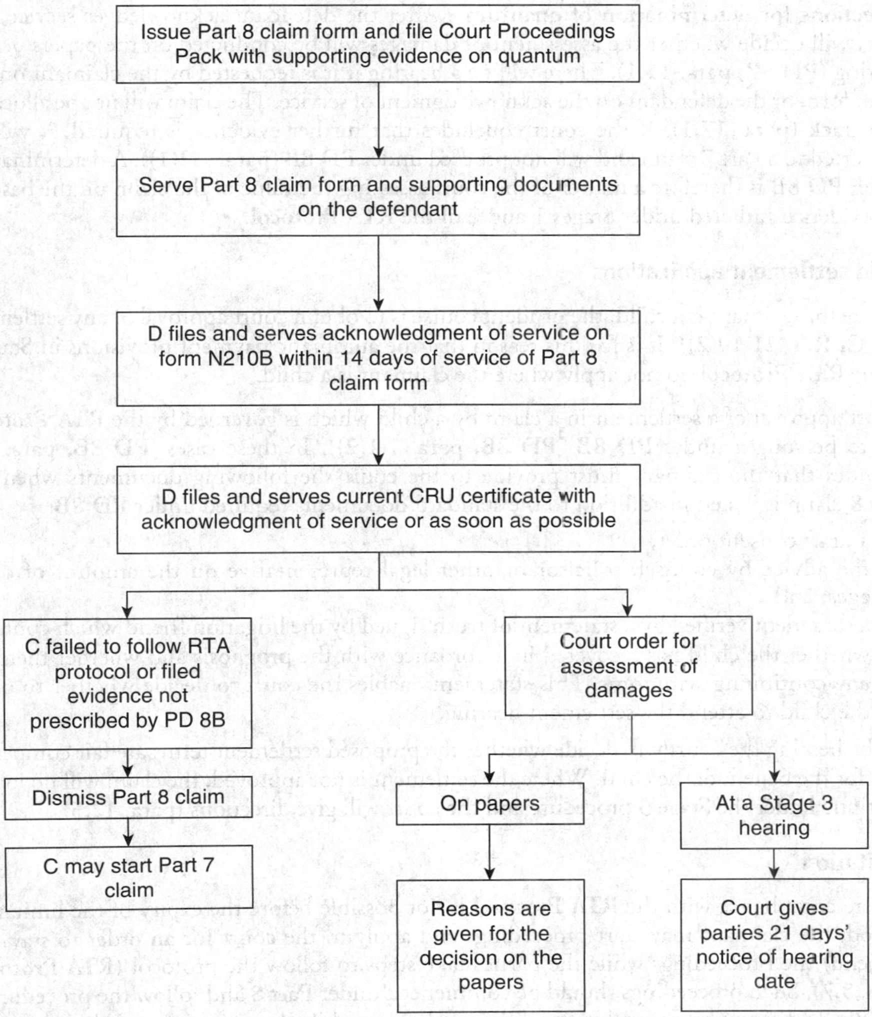

Figure 8.3 Flow diagram of Stage 3 under the RTA Protocol

Changing to or from the PD 8B procedure The court can order a Part 7 claim to proceed as if it was governed by the Stage 3 procedure in **PD 8B (PD 8B, para. 4.1)**. It may also order a **PD 8B** claim which is unsuitable for the **PD 8B** procedure to continue as if it were a Part 7 claim **(PD 8B, para. 7.2(2))**. 8.51

Withdrawal of RTA Protocol admissions and offers Once the Part 8 claim under **PD 8B** has been issued, the defendant can only withdraw an admission made under the **RTA Protocol** with the consent of all the other parties or with the court's permission **(CPR, r. 14.1B(2)(b))**. An application for permission is made using the Part 23 procedure. 8.52

A party may withdraw an RTA Protocol offer after proceedings have started only with the court's permission **(PD 8B, para. 10.1)**. Where the court gives permission, the claim will no longer continue under the Stage 3 procedure and the court will give directions. The court will give permission only where there is good reason for the claim not to continue under Stage 3.

Commentary

8.53 **Directions for determination of quantum** After the defendant acknowledges service, the court will decide whether the assessment of damages will be conducted on the papers or at a hearing (**PD 8B, para. 11.1**). There will be a hearing if it is requested by the claimant on the claim form or the defendant on the acknowledgment of service. The claim will not be allocated to a track (**para. 17.1**). If the court concludes that further evidence is required, it will be converted to a Part 7 claim and will not proceed under **PD 8B (para. 7.2(1))**. A determination under **PD 8B** is therefore a matter of the court assessing the value of the claim on the basis of the evidence gathered under Stages 1 and 2 of the **RTA Protocol**.

Child settlement applications

8.54 Where the claimant is a child, the prudent course is to obtain court approval of any settlement (see **CPR, r. 21.10(2)**). It is for this reason that the automatic payment provisions in Stage 2 of the **RTA Protocol** do not apply where the claimant is a child.

Court approval of a settlement in a claim by a child which is governed by the **RTA Protocol** has to be sought under **PD 8B (PD 8B, para. 1.1(2))**. In these cases, **PD 8B, para. 6.5** provides that the claimant must provide to the court the following documents when the Part 8 claim is issued in addition to the standard documents required under **PD 8B**:

(a) a draft consent order;
(b) the advice by counsel, solicitor or other legal representative on the amount of damages; and
(c) a statement verified by a statement of truth signed by the litigation friend which confirms whether the child has recovered in accordance with the prognosis and whether there are any continuing symptoms. This statement enables the court to decide whether to order the child to attend the settlement hearing.

At the hearing the court will decide whether the proposed settlement terms are fair compensation for the benefit of the child. Where the settlement is not approved, the claim will no longer continue under the Stage 3 procedure and the court will give directions (**para. 12.5**).

Limitation

8.55 Where compliance with the **RTA Protocol** is not possible before the expiry of the limitation period, the claimant may start proceedings and apply to the court for an order to stay (i.e. suspend) the proceedings while the parties take steps to follow the protocol (**RTA Protocol, para. 5.7**). Such proceedings should be commenced under **Part 8** and follow the procedure in **PD 8B**. If the parties are unable to reach a settlement while the claim is stayed by the end of Stage 2 of the protocol, the claimant must, in order to proceed to Stage 3, apply to lift the stay and request directions in the existing proceedings (**para. 5.8**).

Fixed costs under the RTA Protocol

8.56 There is a detailed system of fixed costs in RTA Protocol claims. The basic amounts are included in **figure 8.1**. The detailed rules are in **CPR, rr. 45.16** to **45.27**.

RTA Protocol offers

8.57 There are adjustments to the rules relating to Part 36 offers for RTA claims being dealt with under the **RTA Protocol**, see **CPR, rr. 36.16** to **36.22**. An offer to settle in an RTA Protocol case must be set out in the court proceedings pack (part B) form (**CPR, r. 36.17(2)(a)**). It should contain the final total amount of the offers from both sides (in accordance with the **RTA Protocol, para. 7.55**). These amounts are treated as exclusive of all interest (**CPR, r. 36.19(a)**). An RTA Protocol offer is deemed to be made on the first business day after the court proceedings pack (parts A and B) is sent to the defendant. It must not be communicated to the court until the claim is determined, at which point the court will examine the RTA

Protocol offer (r. 36.20). There is an absolute prohibition on any other form of offer being communicated to the court at all (r. 36.20(b)).

Failing to obtain a judgment more advantageous than an RTA Protocol offer Costs consequences for non-acceptance of RTA Protocol offers are set out in **CPR, r. 36.21(1)**, and arise in three different situations: 8.58

(a) where the determination of the court is less than or equal to the amount of the defendant's RTA Protocol offer (**r. 36.21(1)(a)**). In this case the court will order the claimant to pay the fixed costs under **r. 45.26** and interest on those fixed costs from the first business day after the deemed date of the RTA Protocol offer (**r. 36.21(2)**); or

(b) where the determination of the court is more than a defendant's RTA Protocol offer, but less than the claimant's RTA Protocol offer (**r. 36.21(1)(b)**). In this case the court will order the defendant to pay the fixed costs under **r. 45.20** (**r. 36.21(3)**); or

(c) where the determination of the court is equal or more than the claimant's RTA Protocol offer (**r. 36.21(1)(c)**). In this case the court will order the defendant to pay interest on the whole of the damages at a rate not exceeding 10 per cent above base rate for all or part of the period from the deemed date of the RTA Protocol offer, fixed costs under **r. 45.20**, and interest on those costs at a rate not exceeding 10 per cent above base rate.

Success and deductible amounts **CPR, r. 36.22**, is similar to **r. 36.15(8)** and provides that the amount of a judgment is less than an RTA Protocol offer where the judgment is less than the offer once deductible amounts identified in the judgment are deducted. 8.59

Cases where the RTA Protocol ceases to apply

The **RTA Protocol** ceases to apply in the following situations: 8.60

(a) where, at any stage, the claimant notifies the defendant that the claim has now been revalued at more than £10,000 (**RTA Protocol, para. 4.2**);

(b) where the defendant notifies the claimant that it considers that inadequate mandatory information has been provided in the CNF (**paras 6.8** and **6.15(4)(a)**);

(c) where the defendant alleges contributory negligence (other than in relation to the claimant's admitted failure to wear a seat belt) (**para. 6.15(1)**);

(d) where the defendant does not admit liability within the 15 days allowed for sending the CNF response (**para. 6.15(3)**);

(e) where the defendant does not complete and send the CNF response within the 15 days allowed (**para. 6.15(2)**);

(f) where the defendant notifies the claimant that the defendant considers that if proceedings were issued the small claims track would be the normal track for that claim (**para. 6.15(4)(b)**);

(g) where the defendant fails to pay the Stage 1 fixed costs within the 10-day period specified in **para. 6.18**, and, within 10 days thereafter, the claimant gives the defendant written notice that the claim will no longer continue under the protocol (**para. 6.19**);

(h) where the claimant is not satisfied with the defendant's response to a request for an interim payment in Stage 2 (**paras 7.21** and **7.22**);

(i) where the defendant gives notice to the claimant, within the initial 15-day consideration period after receiving the Stage 2 settlement pack, that the defendant considers that the small claims track would be the normal track for that claim (**para. 7.32(a)**);

(j) where the defendant gives notice to the claimant, within the initial 15-day consideration period after receiving the Stage 2 settlement pack, withdrawing the admission of causation (**para. 7.32(b)**);

(k) where the defendant does not respond within the initial 15-day consideration period (**para. 7.33**);

(l) where a party withdraws an offer made in the Stage 2 settlement pack form after the total consideration period (**para. 7.39**);

(m) where the defendant fails to make the Stage 2 payment (**para. 7.66**); and

(n) where the claimant gives notice to the defendant that the claim is unsuitable for the protocol (for example, because there are complex issues of fact or law in relation to the vehicle-related damages) (**para. 7.67**).

Where a claim drops out of the RTA Protocol in Stage 1, pre-action conduct should continue under the **Pre-action Protocol for Personal Injury Claims** where appropriate (**RTA Protocol, para. 6.17**). Generally, the CNF will stand as the letter before claim for the purposes of the Personal Injury Protocol (**Pre-action Protocol for Personal Injury Claims, para. 2.10A**), unless the CNF is regarded as inadequate. Where a case drops out of the RTA Protocol in Stage 2, further progress is often through starting a Part 7 claim (**RTA Protocol, paras 7.21, 7.22, 7.32, 7.39** and **7.66**). Claims which drop out of the protocol cannot subsequently re-enter the process (**para. 5.11**).

CLINICAL NEGLIGENCE PROTOCOL

8.61 The **Pre-action Protocol for the Resolution of Clinical Disputes** came about following detailed investigation by the Clinical Disputes Forum, a body formed in 1997 following Lord Woolf's Access to Justice Inquiry. One of the aims of the Forum is to establish less adversarial and more cost-effective ways of resolving disputes relating to healthcare and medical treatment. According to the **Executive Summary, para. 3**, the **Clinical Negligence Protocol**:

(a) encourages a climate of openness when something has 'gone wrong' with a patient's treatment or the patient is dissatisfied with that treatment and/or the outcome;
(b) provides general guidance on how this more open culture might be achieved when disputes arise;
(c) recommends a timed sequence of steps for patients and healthcare providers, and their advisers, to follow when a dispute arises. This should facilitate and speed up exchanging relevant information and increase the prospects that disputes can be resolved without resort to legal action.

It is recognised in **paras 1.3** and **1.4** of the protocol that, in the past, there has been mistrust on both sides, patient and healthcare provider, meaning that patients fail to raise their concerns regarding treatment as early as possible and that healthcare providers are reluctant to be honest with patients, fail to provide prompt and clear explanations and tend to 'close ranks' once a claim has been made. Despite having complaints about treatment, patients often wish to maintain their relationships with medical practitioners. Thus the general aims of the protocol are (**para. 2.1**):

(a) to maintain or restore the patient-healthcare provider relationship;
(b) to resolve as many disputes as possible without litigation.

The specific objectives are (**para. 2.2**):

(a) to encourage early communication of perceived problems between patients and their healthcare providers;
(b) to encourage patients to voice their concerns regarding treatment;
(c) to encourage healthcare providers to develop systems of early reporting and investigation for serious adverse treatment outcomes and to provide full and prompt explanations to dissatisfied patients;
(d) to ensure that sufficient information is disclosed by both parties to enable each to understand the other's perspective and case, and to encourage early resolution.

The protocol encourages a timely approach to investigation by recommending that any investigations are carried out promptly and that all relevant medical records are provided to patients or their advisers on request, to a realistic timetable, by healthcare providers (**para. 2.2**).

The protocol does not attempt to usurp the function of the National Health Service Litigation Authority by providing any detailed guidance to healthcare providers on clinical risk management, or adverse outcome reporting (**para. 2.3**). Nor does the protocol recommend changes to the codes of conduct of healthcare professionals, or derogate from the guidance given by the GMC in *Good Medical Practice* (2006) on the duty of doctors to be honest and trustworthy when completing documents and to cooperate fully with any formal inquiry.

Code of good practice

The protocol does not set out to be a comprehensive code governing all the steps which need to be taken in a clinical dispute but attempts to set out a code of good practice which parties should follow where litigation is contemplated (**para. 3.1**). There is a 'commitments' section (**para. 3.4**) which sets out some guiding principles both to healthcare providers and patients and their advisers, which each side is invited to endorse when dealing with potential complaints and claims. This includes encouraging healthcare providers to ensure that key staff are appropriately trained and have some knowledge of healthcare law, that they set up adverse outcome reporting systems, and use the results as a guide to improving their services in the future. Patients should be given clear and comprehensible information on how to raise concerns and complaints. They should also be advised of serious adverse outcomes, and provided, on request, with explanations of what happened. **8.62**

Patients should consider the full range of options for dealing with adverse outcomes, not only litigation (**para. 3.5**). A patient must inform the healthcare provider when satisfied that the matter has been concluded, and legal advisers should notify the provider when they are no longer instructed, particularly if proceedings have not started.

Steps required by the Clinical Negligence Protocol

Paragraphs 3.6 to 3.27 of the **Pre-action Protocol for the Resolution of Clinical Disputes** set out the sequence of actions to be followed if litigation is a prospect. There is an illustrative flowchart at **annex A**. **8.63**

The first step is the request by the patient or his or her legal advisers for records. That request should be made in standard form as provided at **annex B** to the protocol. Records should be provided within 40 days of the request. If there is a failure by the healthcare provider to make records available and no explanation has been given, the potential claimant can apply to the court for an order for pre-action disclosure. Sanctions are also likely to be imposed where there is an unreasonable delay in providing records.

The letter before claim will follow and it should be as detailed as possible. A template for the recommended contents is provided at **annex C1** to the protocol.

A template for the letter of response appears at **annex C2**. The letter before claim should be acknowledged by the healthcare provider within 14 days of receipt. The healthcare provider should identify who will be dealing with the matter. The healthcare provider then has four months in which to provide a 'reasoned answer'. Thus proceedings should not be issued until after four months from the letter before claim, unless there is a limitation problem or the patient's position needs to be protected by early issue.

The parties are encouraged to resolve their dispute without recourse to litigation and **para. 5.2** of the protocol provides details of a number of forms of alternative dispute resolution.

DISEASE AND ILLNESS PROTOCOL

The **Pre-action Protocol for Disease and Illness Claims** applies to all personal injuries claims where the injury takes the form of an illness or disease rather than a physical injury (**para. 2.1**). These tend to be complex cases, and are usually suitable for the multi-track regardless of the **8.64** value of the claim. The protocol applies to any illness, whether physical or psychological, any disorder, ailment, affliction, complaint, malady or derangement, other than a physical or psychological injury caused solely by an accident or other similar single event (**para. 2.2**). It covers diseases and illnesses occurring in the workplace, and also those caused by, for example, the occupation of premises (where there may be an overlap with the **Pre-action Protocol for Housing Disrepair Cases**) or the use of products (including medications). The Disease and Illness Protocol is not intended to cover cases dealt with as group or class claims (**para. 2.4**). If the claimant's life expectancy is short, it may not be possible to follow the protocol and the defendant is expected to treat the claim with urgency (**para. 2.7**).

Disclosure of occupational and health records, and product data

8.65 Before sending a letter before claim, under the **Pre-action Protocol for Disease and Illness Claims**, the potential claimant is permitted to request copies of any relevant occupational or health records, and also to request copies of product data which may be relevant to a causation issue. The potential defendant should provide copies of the claimant's records within 40 days (**para. 4.3**), and the protocol says it is good practice to provide product data. If a defendant is in difficulties in providing the documents in time, this should be explained, with a reasonable time estimate for compliance (**para. 4.4**). Failure to comply may provide grounds for an application for pre-action disclosure (**para. 4.5**, and see **chapter 50**).

Records with third parties

8.66 Employment records with previous employers, and general practitioner and hospital records, should, if relevant, be sought by the claimant (**Pre-action Protocol for Disease and Illness Claims, para. 5.1**). If, on considering the records, the claimant decides not to pursue the claim, this decision should be communicated in writing to any defendants previously notified of the claim (**para. 5.3**).

Letter before claim, chronology and schedule of damages

8.67 Two copies of a letter before claim, primarily addressing liability issues, should be sent to the defendant (one copy is for any insurer) (**Pre-action Protocol for Disease and Illness Claims, paras 6.1 to 6.4**). The standard format for the letter is laid down in **annex B of the protocol**. It should identify relevant documents (**para. 6.6**) and identify any other potential defendants (**para. 6.7**). A chronology, including dates of exposure to the substance alleged to be the cause of the complaint, should be sent with the letter before claim (**para. 6.5**). A schedule of special damages, with copies of supporting documents, should be sent to the defendant as soon as practicable, particularly where the defendant admits liability (**para. 8.1**).

Response

8.68 The defendant should send an acknowledgment identifying any liability insurer within 21 days of posting of the letter before claim (**Pre-action Protocol for Disease and Illness Claims, para. 7.1**). The response should make clear which insurer is dealing with the claim where there may be multiple defendants, and should give the names of any additional insurers during a work career, which can be important in cases concerning diseases such as asbestosis. The defendant will need to investigate the claim, and must provide a reasoned answer to the letter before claim, stating a number of matters including the extent to which the claim is admitted or denied, within 90 days of the date of the acknowledgment letter (**para. 7.3**). Copies of documents material to the issues should be sent with the reply. If 90 days is insufficient time, the defendant may seek an agreed extension if there is a reasonable justification (**para. 7.5**). If the claimant's life expectancy is short, it may not be possible to follow the protocol and the defendant is expected to treat the claim with urgency (**para. 2.7**).

Experts in disease and illness claims

Expert evidence may be required dealing with: 8.69

(a) knowledge, fault, causation and apportionment;
(b) the claimant's condition and prognosis; and
(c) valuing aspects of the claim.

The **Pre-action Protocol for Disease and Illness Claims** recognises that it is important to adopt a flexible approach to the decisions that have to be made about obtaining expert evidence in these claims (**paras 9.2** and **9.3**). Joint selection, joint instruction, separate experts, and claimants disclosing medical evidence before defendants take a view on causation are all canvassed in the protocol. Different approaches may be appropriate for different issues within a claim. Care must be taken before the parties decide on instructing their own experts, because the court may subsequently rule that doing so was unreasonable (**para. 9.7**).

Commencing proceedings and negotiations

Proceedings should not be commenced within the three-month investigation period unless there is a limitation problem or some other reason for needing to protect the claimant's position (**Pre-action Protocol for Disease and Illness Claims, paras 6.10** and **6.11**). Further, the defendant should be given 21 days from disclosure of reports to allow for attempts to settle the claim without the need for proceedings (**paras 10.1** and **10.3**). **Paragraph 2A.1** requires the parties to consider whether some form of ADR would be more suitable than litigation. Both sides may be required to provide the court with evidence that ADR was considered. Litigation is regarded as a last resort, and proceedings should not be issued while settlement is being actively explored. It is expressly recognised that the parties cannot be forced to mediate or enter into any form of ADR (**para. 2A.4**), but a failure to comply with the aim of **para. 2A.1** may be taken into account on costs. 8.70

Before proceedings are commenced the parties should carry out a 'stocktake' of the issues in dispute and the evidence required (**para. 10.2**). If an insurer is acting for the defendant, it is good practice to give the insurer seven to 14 days' notice to nominate solicitors to accept service of the proposed proceedings (**para. 10.5**).

HOUSING DISREPAIR PROTOCOL

The **Pre-action Protocol for Housing Disrepair Cases** applies to all civil claims arising from the condition of residential premises (**para. 3.1**), except when raised as a counterclaim or set-off (because, by definition, a claim has already commenced, see **para. 4.2**). Where housing disrepair is raised by a counterclaim or set-off, the landlord and tenant will still be expected to act reasonably in exchanging information and trying to settle the claim at an early stage (**para. 4.2(a)**). 8.71

The protocol is aimed primarily at claims with a value between £1,000 and the fast track limit (**para. 4.2(b)**), but applies also to claims which are likely to be allocated to the small claims track and multi-track. It applies to disrepair claims brought by tenants, members of the *tenant's family* (**para. 3.1(c)**), and to 'lessees', which is presumably a typographical error for licensees. The Housing Disrepair Protocol applies where the claim includes a personal injury element, and in these claims the **Pre-action Protocol for Personal Injury Claims** should be followed as well, unless the personal injury is relatively minor and suitable for being dealt with by reliance on a general practitioner's letter (**Pre-action Protocol for Housing Disrepair Cases, para. 4.4(d)**).

Early notification

8.72 As a matter of substantive law (see *O'Brien v Robinson* [1973] AC 912), the tenant must show that the landlord has received sufficient information about the alleged defects to put a reasonable person on inquiry as to whether repairs are necessary. Nothing in the **Pre-action Protocol for Housing Disrepair Cases** avoids this requirement, the protocol being aimed at seeking to resolve cases where the problem persists despite notice (**para. 4.3(a)**).

Under the protocol, where the landlord fails to remedy the situation despite knowing of the defects, the claimant should send an early notification letter to the landlord as soon as possible (**para. 3.2(a)**). Detailed requirements for this letter, which should include all the alleged defects, are set out in **para. 3.2(a)**, with a template letter at **annex A** and a template schedule of defects at **annex G**. It should request a copy of the tenancy agreement and copies of the landlord's documents dealing with notice of the defects and work done (**para. 3.2(b)**). **Paragraph 3.2** says that an early notification letter is not required in every case, but is a helpful tool.

Letter before claim

8.73 A letter before claim should be sent at the earliest reasonable opportunity (**Pre-action Protocol for Housing Disrepair Cases, para. 3.3(a)**). Detailed requirements for the information to be included in this letter, in so far as it has not been given in an early notification letter, are set out in **para. 3.3(a)**, with template letters at **annex B**, a template schedule of special damages at **annex E**, and a template schedule of defects at **annex G**. A letter before claim should identify the proposed expert, and enclose a proposed letter of instruction (in the form of the template at **annex C**). Copies of documents the tenant relies upon should also be enclosed, together with a list of the documents the tenant wishes the landlord to disclose.

Landlord's response

8.74 The landlord should provide a written response within 20 working days of receipt of the first letter from the tenant (**Pre-action Protocol for Housing Disrepair Cases, para. 3.5.1**). The letter should include copies of the landlord's disclosure documents and a response on appointing an expert (**para. 3.5.1**). This letter may state whether liability is admitted, take any point about lack of notice or difficulty in gaining access, include a full schedule of intended works, and any offer of compensation or costs, although a response on these points may be delayed until up to 20 working days from receipt of the report of a single joint expert (**para. 3.5.2**).

Evidence

8.75 The **Pre-action Protocol for Housing Disrepair Cases** reminds tenants that photographic and video evidence may be useful in disrepair claims (**para. 3.6(a)**).

Experts

8.76 There will be some cases where no expert evidence is required (**Pre-action Protocol for Housing Disrepair Cases, para. 3.6(a)**), but generally it is expected that the parties will agree on a single joint expert (**para. 3.6(d)**). The expert should be asked to report on all the defects the landlord ought reasonably to have known, or which the expert should reasonably report on, and should be asked to prepare a schedule of works and an estimate of the costs of repair, and to list any urgent works (**para. 3.6(b)**). If the parties cannot agree on a jointly instructed expert, the landlord should send the tenant a copy of its letter of instruction (the tenant having already done so, see **8.73**), and the parties should attempt to agree to a joint inspection of the premises (**para. 3.6(d), (e)**). The tenant should give reasonable access for inspection (and repairs) (**para. 3.6(k)**).

Costs, negotiations and proceedings

If the tenant's claim is settled without proceedings on terms that justify raising the claim, the landlord 'will' pay the tenant's reasonable costs or out-of-pocket expenses (**Pre-action Protocol for Housing Disrepair Cases, para. 3.7(a)**). These costs should be calculated according to the track which the claim would have been allocated to if litigation had been started (*Birmingham City Council v Lee* [2008] EWCA Civ 891, [2009] HLR 15). The appropriate order to make is one for costs on the appropriate basis up to the date the repair work is done (*Birmingham City Council v Lee*). **Annex F to the protocol** is a standard statement of costs for this purpose. **8.77**

The purpose of the protocol is to prevent unnecessary proceedings, so the parties are required to consider whether some form of ADR would be more suitable than litigation (**para. 4.1(a)**. Both sides may be required to provide the court with evidence that ADR was considered. A number of different ADR procedures that might be appropriate are set out in **para. 4.1(b)**. It is expressly recognised that the parties cannot be forced to mediate or enter into any form of ADR (**para. 4.1(d)**), but a failure to comply with the aim of **para. 4.1(a)** may be taken into account on costs. The parties will be expected to have attempted to agree a schedule of works, a timetable for implementation, and any claim for compensation before a claim is issued. If limitation is an issue, the tenant should ask for an extension of the limitation period in the first letter to the landlord. If this is refused, the court will decide whether this was reasonable (**para. 4.8**).

DILAPIDATIONS (COMMERCIAL PROPERTY) PROTOCOL

Claims for damages for dilapidations against tenants at the termination of commercial tenancies are governed by the **Pre-action Protocol for Claims for Damages in Relation to the Physical State of Commercial Property at Termination of a Tenancy**, the 'Dilapidations Protocol', which came into effect on 1 January 2012. The nature and extent of the work that may have to be done to demised premises at the end of a lease will depend on the terms of the lease, so expressions such as 'dilapidations', 'repair', 'reinstatement' and 'redecoration' are not defined by the protocol. **8.78**

Schedule of dilapidations and quantified demand

A schedule of dilapidations should be compiled by the landlord setting out what the landlord considers to be the breaches, the works required, and the landlord's costings (**Dilapidations Protocol, para. 3.1**). This takes the form of a Scott schedule, with an additional column for the tenant's responses. Slightly different versions of the schedule can be found in **annexes B** and **C** to the **Dilapidations Protocol**. **Annex B** is for use where the schedule is compiled by the landlord's surveyor, and **Annex C** is where it is compiled by the landlord. In compiling and signing the schedule, a surveyor should have regard to the principles laid down in the Royal Institute of Chartered Surveyors' Guidance Note on Dilapidations (**Dilapidations Protocol, para. 3.5**). The schedule of dilapidations should be sent to the tenant electronically (**para. 3.7**) within 56 days of the termination of the lease (**para. 3.3**). Also within 56 days of the termination of the lease, the landlord should send the tenant a quantified demand setting out all aspects of the dispute and substantiating the monetary sum sought as damages (**paras 4.2.1 and 4.2.3**) supported by invoices or detailed estimates (**para. 4.3**). The quantified demand should confirm the landlord and/or its surveyor will attend a meeting or meetings on a without-prejudice basis to seek to agree as many items as possible (**paras 4.2.2 and 7**), and should specify a period, usually within 56 days, by which the tenant should respond. **8.79**

Commentary

Response and subsequent steps

8.80 The tenant's response should be set out by using the additional column in the schedule of dilapidations (**Dilapidations Protocol, para. 5.3**). The entries must be in sufficient detail to enable the landlord to understand clearly the tenant's views on each item, and must comply with the principles laid down in the Royal Institute of Chartered Surveyors' Guidance Note on Dilapidations (**Dilapidations Protocol, para. 5.4**). If the tenant considers that items in the schedule of dilapidations are likely to be superseded by works to be carried out by the landlord or by the landlord's intentions for the property, this should be stated in the response with particulars (**para. 5.6**).

The landlord and tenant and/or their respective surveyors should meet within 28 days after the tenant's response on a without-prejudice basis to seek to agree as many items as possible (**para. 7**). They should also consider whether some form of ADR would be more suitable than litigation (**para. 8.1**), and may have to provide evidence that ADR was considered. If proceedings are to be issued, the landlord should quantify its loss by providing a detailed breakdown of the issues and consequential losses to the tenant (**para. 9.1**). If a formal diminution valuation is required, it should be prepared by a valuer (**para. 9.2**). Details of the landlord's intentions must be supplied to the tenant if remedial works have not been carried out (**para. 9.3**). Any diminution valuation from the tenant should be supplied by the tenant to the landlord within 56 days of the landlord's detailed breakdown of issues (**para. 9.6**). A final stocktake, reviewing their respective positions, the state of the papers, the evidence, and any possible narrowing of the issues, should be undertaken before proceedings are issued (**para. 10**).

POSSESSION CLAIMS BASED ON RENT ARREARS PROTOCOL

8.81 The **Pre-action Protocol for Possession Claims Based on Rent Arrears** applies to residential possession claims by social landlords where possession is sought solely on the ground of rent arrears. It does not apply to tenancies involving long leases or where there is no security of tenure.

Pre-action steps under the Possession Claims Based on Rent Arrears Protocol

8.82 Where a tenant falls into arrears of rent, the landlord is required to contact the tenant as soon as reasonably possible to discuss the cause of the arrears, the tenant's financial circumstances, the tenant's entitlement to benefits (including housing benefit), and how the arrears are to be paid (**Pre-action Protocol for Possession Claims Based on Rent Arrears, para. 1**). Pre-action contact is encouraged, with the aim of seeking to achieve agreement on affordable sums for the tenant to pay towards the arrears (**para. 2**). It is recognised that rent arrears cases are often part of a wider debt problem (**para. 8**). Where appropriate the landlord should offer to assist the tenant with any claim for housing benefit (**para. 6**) and should advise the tenant to seek assistance from citizens' advice or debt advice agencies (**para. 8**). Extra care should be taken where the tenant is under 18, unable to read or otherwise vulnerable (**para. 4**).

Pre-action correspondence should set out clearly any time limits the landlord wants the tenant to comply with (**para. 2**). Upon request, the landlord should provide the tenant with copies of rent statements in a comprehensible form from the date when arrears first arose, and in all cases should provide the tenant with quarterly rent statements covering the previous 13 weeks (**para. 3**). Possession proceedings should not be commenced (**para. 7**) against a tenant who can demonstrate that:

(a) all the evidence required to process a housing benefit claim has been provided to the local authority;
(b) there is a reasonable expectation of eligibility for housing benefit; and
(c) other sums not covered by housing benefit have been paid.

After service of a statutory notice, the landlord should make reasonable attempts to contact the tenant to discuss the amount of arrears, its causes, repayment and the housing benefit position (**para.** 9). Proceedings should be postponed for so long as the tenant keeps to any agreement to pay the current rent and a reasonable amount towards the arrears (**para. 10**). If the tenant breaks such an agreement, the landlord should warn the tenant of the intention to bring proceedings, and give the tenant clear time limits within which to comply (**para. 10**). ADR should be considered, and litigation should be a last resort (**para. 11**).

Litigation steps under the Possession Claims Based on Rent Arrears Protocol

Possession hearings are often marked by the non-attendance of tenants, so the **Pre-action Protocol for Possession Claims Based on Rent Arrears** requires landlords to inform tenants of the date and time of any court hearing, and to have evidence available that they have done so (**para. 13(a)**). Another common problem is confusion at the hearing over the exact amount of arrears, so **para.** 12 requires landlords to provide their tenants with up-to-date rent statements and any information available to the landlord on the housing benefit position at least 10 days before the hearing. The landlord should agree to postpone court proceedings if the tenant complies with any agreement to pay current rent and a reasonable amount towards the arrears (**para. 13(b)**). 8.83

Failure by a landlord to comply with the protocol may result in costs sanctions, and may be taken into account when considering whether (if the case is brought on a non-mandatory ground) to adjourn, strike out or dismiss the claim (**para.** 14). Unreasonable non-compliance by the tenant may be taken into account in deciding whether it is reasonable to make a possession order (**para.** 15).

Commentary

POSSESSION CLAIMS BASED ON MORTGAGE OR HOME PURCHASE PLAN ARREARS PROTOCOL

The **Pre-action Protocol for Possession Claims Based on Mortgage or Home Purchase Plan Arrears in Respect of Residential Property** applies to potential money and/or possession claims based on: 8.84

(a) first charge mortgages and home purchase plans regulated by the Financial Services Authority under the Financial Services and Markets Act 2000;
(b) second charge mortgages over residential property and other secured loans regulated under the Consumer Credit Act 1974 on residential property; and
(c) unregulated residential mortgages.

Where a borrower falls into arrears the lender should provide the borrower with information on the amount of arrears, the total capital outstanding, and whether interest or charges will be added (with an estimate) (**Pre-action Protocol for Possession Claims Based on Mortgage or Home Purchase Plan Arrears in Respect of Residential Property, para.** 5.1(2)). Where appropriate the lender must also provide the required regulatory information sheet or the National Homelessness Advice Service booklet on mortgage arrears (**para. 5.1(1)**). The lender must advise the borrower to make early contact with the housing department and, where necessary, refer the borrower to appropriate sources of independent debt advice (**para. 5.3**). The parties or their representatives must take all reasonable steps to discuss the causes of the arrears, the borrower's financial circumstances, whether the causes of the arrears are temporary or long term, and whether the borrower may be able to pay the arrears in a reasonable time (**para. 5.2**).

A possession claim should normally be a last resort. The parties should instead consider whether it is reasonable and appropriate (**para 7.1**) to:

(a) extend the term of the mortgage;

(b) change the type of mortgage;
(c) defer payment of interest due under the mortgage;
(d) capitalise the arrears; or
(e) make use of any government forbearance initiatives in which the lender chooses to participate.

The lender must respond promptly to any proposal for payment, and should give written reasons for any refusal of an offer within 10 business days of the proposal (**para. 5.5**). If the lender makes a proposal for payment, it must include sufficient details to enable the borrower to understand the implications of the proposal, and the borrower must be given a reasonable time to consider the proposals (**para. 5.6**). If the borrower fails to comply with an agreement, the lender should give the borrower 15 business days' notice of intention to start a possession claim unless the borrower remedies the breach (**para. 5.7**).

Postponing the start of a mortgage possession claim

8.85 A lender must consider postponing the commencement of a possession claim where the borrower has submitted a claim under a mortgage payment protection policy or to the Department for Work and Pensions ('DWP') for support for mortgage interest. The borrower will need to demonstrate that all the necessary evidence required to process the claim has been provided to the insurer or DWP, that there is a reasonable expectation of eligibility, and that the borrower is able to pay instalments not covered by the policy or scheme (**Pre-action Protocol for Possession Claims Based on Mortgage or Home Purchase Plan Arrears in Respect of Residential Property, para. 6.1**).

Similarly, the lender must consider postponing the start of possession proceedings if the borrower can demonstrate taking reasonable steps to market the property at an appropriate price (**para. 6.2**). The borrower should provide the lender with a copy of the particulars of sale, the energy performance certificate and details of any purchase offers. The borrower should also provide details of the estate agent dealing with the sale, and authorise the agent to communicate with the lender about the progress of any sale and the borrower's conduct during the process (**para. 6.3**).

If the lender decides not to postpone possession proceedings despite a claim under a payment protection policy, support for mortgage interest, mortgage rescue scheme or proposed sale, the lender must inform the borrower of the reasons at least five business days before starting proceedings (**para. 6.4**). The lender must complete a mortgage pre-action protocol checklist, form N123. Two completed copies of this form will be required for the hearing (**PD 55A, para. 5.5**).

CONSTRUCTION AND ENGINEERING DISPUTES PROTOCOL

8.86 The **Pre-action Protocol for Construction and Engineering Disputes** applies to all construction and engineering disputes, including professional negligence claims against architects, engineers and quantity surveyors. It applies to additional claims under **CPR, Part 20** (*Daejan Investments Ltd v Park West Club Ltd* [2003] EWHC 2872 (TCC), [2004] BLR 223), although a pragmatic approach has to be taken as there will often be limited time in which to comply with the protocol, issue the claim and get the case ready for any trial (*Alfred McAlpine Capital Projects Ltd v SIAC (UK) Ltd* [2005] EWHC 3139 (TCC), [2006] BLR 139). It applies to claims for the payment of an engineering firm's fees, even though such a claim could be characterised as a debt recovery case (*Cundall Johnson and Partners v Whipps Cross University Hospital NHS Trust* [2007] EWHC 2178 (TCC), [2007] BLR 520). However, a claimant is not expected to follow the protocol where the proposed proceedings:

(a) are for the purpose of enforcing an adjudicator's decision under the Housing Grants, Construction and Regeneration Act 1996, s. 108;
(b) include a claim for an interim injunction;

(c) are expected to proceed to an application for summary judgment; or
(d) relate to the same or substantially the same issues as have been the subject of a recent adjudication under the 1996 Act or some other formal ADR procedure.

In additional claims under **CPR, Part 20**, care should be taken before granting a stay of the main proceedings to enable full compliance with the protocol by the parties to the additional claim if that will mean breaking trial directions (*Orange Personal Communications Services Ltd v Hoare Lea* [2008] EWHC 223 (TCC), [2009] Bus LR D24).

The **Pre-action Protocol for Construction and Engineering Disputes** must not be used as a tactical device to secure advantage or to generate unnecessary costs (**para. 1.5**). This means that in lower-value claims the letter before claim and response should be simple, and the costs of both sides should be kept to a modest level.

Requirements of the Construction and Engineering Disputes Protocol

The protocol timetable starts with a letter before claim being sent by the claimant to the proposed defendants (**Pre-action Protocol for Construction and Engineering Disputes, para. 3**). This should include details of all the proposed defendants, a clear summary of the facts on which the claim or claims are based, and the allegations forming the basis of each claim. This will include reference to the contractual terms and statutory provisions relied upon, the nature of the relief claimed, and a breakdown of how any damages are quantified or liquidated claim is calculated. It does not have to identify every detail on liability, or the exact amount claimed (*T. J. Brent Ltd v Black and Veatch Consulting Ltd* [2008] EWHC 1497 (TCC), 119 Con LR 1). If a claim has previously been made and rejected, the claimant must explain the reasons for disagreeing with the rejection of the claim. If any experts on whom the claimant wishes to rely have already been instructed, the letter before claim must include their names and state the issues to which the experts' evidence is directed. **8.87**

The defendants should acknowledge receipt of the letter before claim within 14 days (**para. 4.1**). If there is no response, the claimant becomes entitled to issue proceedings. It may also be necessary for a claimant to issue proceedings at an early stage if the expiry of the limitation period is approaching (**para. 6**).

If a defendant intends to dispute the court's jurisdiction, or allege that the claim should be referred to arbitration, or allege that the wrong defendant has been identified, this should be made clear by a letter of objection which should be sent within 28 days after the letter before claim (**para. 4.2.1**). In *Bovis Homes Ltd v Kendrick Construction Ltd* [2009] EWHC 1359 (TCC), [2009] 5 Costs LR 778, failure to mention a preference for arbitration in the letter of objection resulted in an order that the defendant should pay the costs thrown away when it later sought a stay of proceedings under the Arbitration Act 1996, s. 9. If a letter of objection is sent, there is no need to make a substantive response to the letter before claim (**para. 4.2.2**). If there is no letter of objection, the defendants have to send a letter of response (**para. 4.3.1**). This should normally be sent within 28 days after the letter before claim, although the parties may agree to a longer period of up to four months. A letter of response will set out in detail which parts of the claim are agreed, which parts are rejected and why. If a defendant raises an allegation of contributory negligence, a summary of the facts relied on should be included in the letter of response and the claimant should reply with detailed responses within 28 days (**para. 4.4**). Neither the letter before claim nor the defendant's response are required to resemble pleadings, either in their length or in their detail (*Cundall Johnson and Partners v Whipps Cross University Hospital NHS Trust* [2007] EWHC 2178 (TCC), [2007] BLR 520).

Within 28 days of completion of this correspondence, the parties should normally arrange a without-prejudice meeting to seek to agree what are the main issues, identify the root problem and consider how to resolve matters without recourse to litigation (**para. 5.2**). If litigation cannot be avoided, the parties should seek to agree the steps they should take in accordance

Commentary

with the overriding objective, including how best to obtain any expert evidence that might be necessary, the extent of the disclosure of documents required, and how best to minimise costs and prevent delay (**para. 5.5**). In respect of specific issues, or the dispute as a whole, the parties should consider whether some form of ADR would be more suitable than litigation. It is expressly recognised that no party can, however, be forced to mediate or adopt any other form of ADR (**para. 5.4**). Although pre-action meetings are 'without prejudice', this does not prevent any of the parties disclosing that meetings did or did not take place, any refusal to attend and the result of any agreements made (**para. 5.6**).

DEFAMATION PROTOCOL

8.88 Since the primary limitation period for defamation claims is only one year, it is recognised that time is of the essence regarding pre-action skirmishing in this area. The claimant is, under the protocol, required to notify the defendant in writing of the claim at the earliest reasonable opportunity (**Pre-action Protocol for Defamation, para. 3.1**). The letter before claim should include as much detail as possible, including an identification of the publication or broadcast containing the words complained of, factual inaccuracies, where relevant, any facts tying the claimant to the alleged defamatory statement and any special facts relevant to interpretation, and the nature of the remedies sought (**para. 3.2**). The defendant is required to respond as soon as reasonably possible, and normally within 14 days (**para. 3.4**). The letter of response should say whether or the extent to which the claim is accepted. If the claim is rejected, the defendant should explain why, indicating any facts relied upon in support of any substantive defence. If more information is sought, this should be stated in the response (**para. 3.5**). Both parties are expected to act reasonably so as to keep costs proportionate, and should consider whether the matter could be referred to ADR (**paras 3.6 to 3.9**).

PROFESSIONAL NEGLIGENCE PRE-ACTION PROTOCOL

Introduction

8.89 The **Professional Negligence Pre-action Protocol** applies to any claim against a professional, other than a construction professional or healthcare provider, as a result of that professional's alleged negligence or breach of fiduciary duty, although there may be other types of claim for which the protocol is appropriate (**para. A1**). This protocol is not intended to replace existing alternative forms of dispute resolution, such as the Surveyors and Valuers Arbitration Scheme (**para. A3**). Indeed, parties are encouraged to use these procedures where available but to use the protocol where alternative procedures fail and prior to litigation (**para. A3**). The standards set in this protocol will be treated by the courts as the normal, reasonable approach in professional negligence cases (**para. A4**). The protocol contains no definition of 'professional'. Should it become an issue whether a defendant is or is not a professional, the parties are reminded of the overriding need to act reasonably and rather than argue about the definition of 'professional', it is recommended that they use the protocol, adapting it where appropriate (**para. C2.3**).

Preliminary notice

8.90 Immediately there is a reasonable chance that a claim will be brought against a professional, the potential claimant is encouraged to notify the professional by letter, referred to as a preliminary notice (**Professional Negligence Pre-action Protocol, para. B1.1**) informing the recipient of the claimant's identity, a brief outline of the complaint against the professional and, if possible, an indication of the financial value of the claim (**para. B1.2**). The letter should also request the professional to notify his or her professional indemnity insurers, if any (**para. B1.3**). Receipt of the letter is required to be acknowledged by the professional within 21 days (**para. B1.4**). At this stage there is no obligation on the professional to take any further action (**para. B1.4**).

Letter before claim

As soon as the claimant considers that there are grounds for a claim against the professional a detailed letter before claim should be sent (**Professional Negligence Pre-action Protocol, para. B2.1**). Normally a letter before claim should not be expressed to be without prejudice and it should include (**para. B2.2**): 8.91

(a) the identity of any other parties to the dispute;
(b) a chronological summary of the facts on which the claim is based identifying and enclosing copies of key documents;
(c) acts and omissions alleged against the professional;
(d) explanation of how the error has caused the loss claimed;
(e) estimate and calculation of the loss together with documentary evidence in support or an explanation of why details of the loss cannot be supplied, if this is the case;
(f) whether the claimant seeks any form of non-financial redress;
(g) confirmation of whether or not an expert has been appointed and if so, the identity of the expert, his or her discipline and the date of appointment;
(h) request that the letter before claim is immediately forwarded to the professional's insurers.

Although the letter before claim is not intended to have the same status as a statement of case, if it differs materially from a statement of case in subsequent proceedings, the court may decide to impose sanctions (**para. B2.3**). Where the claimant has sent other letters before claim to other parties in relation to this or a related dispute, those letters should also be copied to the professional (**para. B2.4**). The letter before claim should be acknowledged by the professional in a letter of acknowledgment within 21 days of receipt (**para. B3.1**). If the claimant is claiming against a person to whom the protocol does not apply, there are a number of potential problems recognised in **para. C4.2**. It is possible that different protocols will apply to different defendants, that defendants will claim against each other, and that other parties will be drawn into the dispute. It is possible that the protocol timetable against one party will not be synchronised with the protocol timetable against a different party. Parties are expected to act reasonably, which will depend on the individual facts of each case (**para. C4.3**). The protocol does not provide solutions to specific problems but encourages parties to cooperate and to discuss how problems might be resolved.

Investigations

The professional will have three months from the date of the letter of acknowledgment to investigate the claim (**Professional Negligence Pre-action Protocol, para. B4.1**). Any difficulty in complying with that period should be notified to the claimant as soon as possible, together with an explanation of what is being done to resolve the problem and when the professional expects to complete the investigations. The claimant should agree to any reasonable request for an extension of the three-month period (**para. B4.2**). During this stage and throughout, the parties should provide each other with whatever relevant information or documentation is reasonably requested (**para. B4.3**). As with the other protocols, the early exchange of information is considered conducive to early settlement. 8.92

Letter of response and letter of settlement

As soon as the professional has completed his investigations, the claimant should be sent: 8.93

(a) a letter of response, or

(b) a letter of settlement, or
(c) both.

These may be contained within a single letter (**Professional Negligence Pre-action Protocol, para. B5.1**).

The letter of response will normally not be expressed to be without prejudice (**para. B5.2**). It should be a reasoned answer to the claimant's allegations. If the claim is admitted, the letter of response should say so.

If only part of the claim is admitted, the letter of response should make clear which parts of the claim are admitted and which are denied.

If the claim is denied in whole or in part, the letter of response should include specific comments on the allegations against the professional and, if the claimant's version of events is disputed, the professional should provide his or her version of events.

If the professional is unable to admit or deny the claim, any further information which is required should be identified.

If the professional disputes the estimate of the claimant's financial loss, the letter of response should set out the professional's estimate. If an estimate cannot be provided, the professional should explain why and should state when it will be possible to provide an estimate. This information should be sent to the claimant as soon as reasonably possible.

Where additional documents are relied upon in the letter of response, copies should be provided.

The letter of response is not intended to have the same formal status as a defence. However, if it differs materially from the defence in subsequent proceedings, the court may decide to impose sanctions (**para. B5.3**).

A letter of settlement will normally be a without-prejudice letter and should be sent if the professional intends to make proposals for settlement (**para. B5.4**). It should contain the professional's views on the claim identifying those issues which the professional believes are likely to remain in dispute and those which are not. This information is not required if the professional has sent a letter of response. The letter of settlement should contain a settlement proposal or identify any further information which is required before the professional can formulate proposals. Copies of additional documents should be provided where these are relied upon.

Effect of letter of response and/or letter of settlement

8.94 Where the letter of response denies the claim in its entirety and there is no letter of settlement, it is open to the claimant to commence proceedings (**Professional Negligence Pre-action Protocol, para. B5.5**). Otherwise, the professional and the claimant should begin negotiations with the aim of reaching a conclusion within six months of the date of the letter of acknowledgment (not from the date of the letter of response) (**para. B5.6**). If the claim cannot be resolved within this period, the parties should agree within 14 days of the end of the period whether the period should be extended and, if so, by how long (**para. B5.7**). They should also identify the issues which remain in dispute and those which are agreed. If an extension of time for settlement negotiations cannot be agreed, the claimant may commence proceedings.

Alternative dispute resolution

8.95 The **Professional Negligence Pre-action Protocol, para. B6.1** requires the parties to consider whether some form of ADR would be more suitable than litigation. Both sides may be required to provide the court with evidence that ADR was considered. Litigation is regarded as a last resort, and proceedings should not be issued while settlement is being actively explored. It is expressly recognised that the parties cannot be forced to mediate or enter into any form of ADR (**para. B6.4**), but a failure to comply with the aim of **para. B6.1** may be taken into account on costs.

Experts

If the claimant has obtained expert evidence prior to sending the letter before claim, the professional will have an equal right to obtain expert evidence prior to sending the letter of response and/or letter of settlement (**Professional Negligence Pre-action Protocol, para. B7.1**). If the claimant has not previously obtained expert evidence, the parties are encouraged to appoint a joint expert (**para. B7.2**). If they do so, they should seek to agree the identity of the expert and the terms of the expert's appointment (**para. B7.2**). In the event that such agreement cannot be reached, all parties are free to appoint their own experts (**para. B7.3**). The protocol recognises the range of complexity and amounts of financial loss that may be involved in professional negligence cases and is thus very flexible on the issue of experts, leaving it to the parties to reach agreement on the instruction of experts, their payment and how and to whom the expert should report. **8.96**

Proceedings

Unless it is necessary, for example, to obtain protection against the expiry of a relevant limitation period, court proceedings should not be commenced until the letter of response denies the claim in its entirety and there is no letter of settlement, or the period for negotiation has come to an end (**Professional Negligence Pre-action Protocol, para. B8.1**). If the claimant does intend to institute proceedings, where possible 14 days' written notice should be given to the professional, indicating the court within which the claimant is intending to commence litigation (**para. B8.2**). Proceedings should be served on the professional, unless the professional's solicitor has notified the claimant in writing that he or she is authorised to accept service on the professional's behalf (**para. B8.3**). If proceedings are commenced prior to the parties following the procedures in the protocol, they are encouraged to agree to apply to the court for a stay of proceedings while the protocol procedures are followed (**para. C7.2**). **8.97**

Commentary

Chapter 9 Notices before Action

LETTER BEFORE CLAIM

9.1 Whether a claim is governed by a specific pre-action protocol or by the general requirements in **PD Pre-action Conduct**, generally a letter before claim should be sent before starting proceedings. The matters to include in the letter before claim will be laid down either in the specific protocol, or in **PD Pre-action Conduct, annex A**. Exceptional cases where a letter before claim are dispensed with are where an application needs to be made urgently or secretly, where there is no other party to engage with, or where the matter is agreed or non-contentious (see **8.2** and **PD Pre-action Conduct, para. 2.2**). The court has a discretion to order a claimant who issues proceedings without giving warning to the other side to pay indemnity-basis costs (*Phoenix Finance Ltd v Fédération Internationale de l'Automobile* [2002] EWHC 1242 (Ch), *The Times*, 27 June 2002; and see **8.13**).

ROAD TRAFFIC CASES

Introduction

9.2 A person who sustains injury in a road traffic accident has a cause of action against a negligent driver but not against his or her insurers. Damages may be recovered direct from the insurers provided the claimant gives the insurers notice of the proceedings against the defendant driver either before or within seven days after the commencement of the proceedings (Road Traffic Act 1988, s. 152). The phrase 'commencement of proceedings' has its ordinary meaning (*Silver v Goodall* [1997] PIQR P451). The **Pre-action Protocol for Personal Injury Claims, para. 3.4**, states that a letter before claim should ask a potential defendant for insurance details.

Notice must be something more formal than a casual mention of proceedings in conversation (*Herbert v Railway Passengers Assurance Co.* [1938] 1 All ER 650). However, notice given in a telephone conversation, dealing mainly with obtaining details of the insured driver, with a secretary employed by the insurer was held to be sufficient in *Nawaz v Crowe Insurance Group* [2003] EWCA Civ 316, *The Times*, 11 March 2003. A loosely written letter may not be sufficient notice (*Weldrick v Essex and Suffolk Equitable Insurance Society Ltd* (1949) 83 Ll L Rep 91, in which the letter which purported to give notice was found to be no more than an intimation that proceedings might be brought).

A pre-action protocol letter before claim is insufficient notification of the proceedings for the purposes of the Road Traffic Act 1988, s. 152(1)(a) (*Wylie v Wake* [2000] RTR 291). Lack of notice may be raised as a defence at any stage of the proceedings and the fact that a claim has been defended on its merits does not constitute a waiver of lack of notice (*Wylie v Wake*).

Motor Insurers' Bureau

It sometimes happens that a claimant sustains injury in a road traffic accident arising out of the negligence of a driver who is uninsured or untraceable. In return for the business generated by compulsory motor insurance, the insurance industry has set up the Motor Insurers' Bureau (MIB) to enable claimants to obtain compensation in circumstances in which they would be unable to bring effective proceedings. There are two agreements between the MIB and the Minister for Transport, one dealing with uninsured drivers and the other with untraced drivers. The question whether the MIB is an emanation of the State (which is relevant in cases on whether these agreements are a sufficient compliance with the Second Council Directive (84/5/EEC), see below) has been referred to the Court of Justice of the European Union by the Court of Appeal (*McCall v Poulton* [2008] EWCA Civ 1313, [2009] PIQR P8). See also Donald B. Williams, *Guide to Motor Insurers' Bureau Claims*, 9th edn. (London: Law Society, 2003). 9.3

Uninsured drivers

Under the Motor Insurers' Bureau (Compensation of Victims of Uninsured Drivers) Agreement 1999, the claimant must satisfy a number of conditions in order for the MIB to pay an award of damages in respect of an uninsured driver. Provided the claim is one that the MIB is obliged to satisfy and the claimant fulfils the requisite conditions, the MIB will pay any award of damages if the judgment is not satisfied within seven days. Two conditions of the agreement are particularly relevant to pre-action conduct. First, under cl. 13(a) of the agreement, the claimant must have demanded the information, and where appropriate, the particulars, specified in the Road Traffic Act 1988, s. 154, in accordance with that section or, if so required by MIB, have authorised MIB to do so on the claimant's behalf. Section 154 requires the person against whom a claim is made to provide the claimant with details of the name and address of his insurers, details of his insurance and the policy number. This can be dealt with very simply in the letter before claim. The MIB does not have to wait for a judgment to be obtained before intervening in a case. Claimants may wish to apply to the MIB before the commencement of proceedings, but any claim must comply with cl. 7 of the agreement. This means that the claim must be in the form required by the MIB and must give such information about the proceedings and other relevant matters and be accompanied by such documents as the MIB may require. Wherever possible, claims should be made on the MIB application form, accompanied by supporting documents. Using the correct forms is likely to avoid delays occurring in the claim being processed. 9.4

A further condition is that the claimant must give written notice of proceedings to the MIB or identified insurer not later than 14 days after commencement of proceedings and that such notice should be accompanied by a copy of the sealed claim form, particulars of claim, schedule of past and future loss and expense, medical report and any other relevant documents, for example, correspondence with the defendant. A pre-action protocol letter before claim is insufficient notification of the proceedings for these purposes (*Wylie v Wake* [2000] RTR 291, a case under the Road Traffic Act 1988, s. 152(1)(a)). The particulars of claim, schedule and medical report may, alternatively, be served within seven days after service on the defendant (cl. 9(3)). Furthermore, notice of service of the claim form must be given to the MIB or identified insurer within seven days of notification by the court (or 14 days of deemed service) (see cl. 10). It is recommended that the claimant's notice, if sent by post, be sent by recorded delivery, which will provide confirmation to the claimant that the notice has in fact been received by the MIB. The MIB does, however, prefer service by fax because it is speedy and can be confirmed equally quickly. Service of documents by DX is not permitted.

A common problem is failing to give the required notice in MIB cases. The purpose of requiring notice is to ensure the MIB is informed so it can intervene and prevent judgment being entered by default (*Richardson v Watson* [2006] EWCA Civ 1662, [2007] RTR 247), although the MIB

Commentary

believes the reason is to prevent stale claims. Until about 2000, it was common for the MIB to ignore the notice point. More recently, the MIB has been raising want of notice when it arises. A claimant who fails to give notice should, if the point is taken by the MIB, discontinue the defective claim, and issue a second claim giving the necessary notice. Taking this approach is certainly not an abuse of process if the primary limitation period has not expired. *Richardson v Watson* held that issuing a second claim is not an abuse of process even if the primary limitation period has expired. *Horton v Sadler* [2006] UKHL 27, [2007] 1 AC 307, held that in this situation there is jurisdiction under the Limitation Act 1980, s. 33, to make an order disapplying the primary limitation period to the second claim (see **10.19**), and such an order was made in *Richardson v Watson*.

Under cl. 6(1)(e)(ii) of the uninsured drivers' agreement, the MIB is absolved from liability where the injured passenger 'knew or ought to have known' that the vehicle was uninsured. Article 1(4) of the Second Council Directive (84/5/EEC) (to which the uninsured drivers' agreement is intended to give effect) entitles member States to exclude liability only if the injured person 'knew' the vehicle was uninsured. This was held by the House of Lords in *White v White* [2001] 1 WLR 481 to include actual knowledge and cases where the injured party deliberately refrained from asking questions about the insured status of the vehicle. It does not cover cases where the passenger was careless or negligent about whether the vehicle was insured. This exception of the MIB from liability does not apply unless the passenger's presence in the vehicle was voluntary. A passenger who knows the driver is uninsured on entering a vehicle will continue being voluntarily in the vehicle until he or she either gets out or unequivocally requests the driver to stop (*Pickett v Roberts* [2004] EWCA Civ 6, [2004] 1 WLR 2450). The exception only applies to 'the claimant'. In a fatal accident case this is the dependant making the claim, so if he or she was unaware that the driver was not insured the exception does not apply (*Phillips v Rafiq* [2007] EWCA Civ 74, [2007] 1 WLR 1351).

Untraced drivers

9.5 The MIB's other agreement with the Minister of Transport seeks to provide compensation for any victim of any untraced driver. The current agreement relating to untraced drivers was concluded in 2003 and applies to accidents on or after 14 February 2003. The Court of Justice of the European Union has decided that the untraced drivers' agreement broadly complies with Council Directive 84/5/EEC (*Evans v Secretary of State for the Environment, Transport and the Regions* (case C-63/01) [2005] All ER (EC) 763). The court pointed out, however, that art. 1(4) of the Directive has to be interpreted to mean that compensation awarded under the agreement must take account of the passage of time between the accident and payment. This is now provided for by cl. 9 of the 2003 agreement. Costs need not be included in the scheme, unless reimbursement of costs is necessary to safeguard the rights derived from the Directive (see cl. 10 of the 2003 agreement).

An application arising out of an accident alleged to have been caused by an untraced driver must be made within three years of the accident where the application includes a claim for compensation for personal injuries or death, or within nine months of the accident where the claim is limited to compensation for damage to property (cl. 4(3)(a)). In order to comply with Directive 84/5/EEC, this has to be taken as subject to a similar extension to the time limit for bringing a claim as that contained in the Limitation Act 1980, s. 28. The result is that time does not run against a child until he or she reaches the age of 18 (*Byrne v Motor Insurers' Bureau* [2008] EWCA Civ 574, [2009] QB 66). The applicant must, unless this was not reasonably possible, have reported the accident to the police within 14 days of the accident (within five days if limited to damage to property (cl. 4(3)(c)). When it receives the application, the MIB makes a *preliminary investigation* (cl. 7(1)(a)) to decide whether the case is one to which the agreement applies and whether there is, in addition to the untraced driver, a second person partly liable for the accident (for which see cl. 13). If the preliminary investigation indicates that the agreement applies and that cl. 13 does not apply, the MIB may notify the applicant that it is using the accelerated procedure in cl. 26 and make an offer to settle the claim. The offer will include reasons for the assessment of the award. The applicant then has six weeks to notify the MIB whether the offer is accepted or rejected. If the offer is accepted, the MIB has to pay the compensation within the next 14 days, and is discharged from all liability under the agreement (cl. 27).

If the accelerated procedure is not adopted by the MIB, or if the applicant rejects an offer made under that procedure, the MIB arranges for a full investigation to be made of the accident by a delegated member of the Bureau. The subsequent report enables the MIB to decide whether an award will be made and if so, the amount of that award. Decisions are based on ordinary principles of negligence and quantification of damage, but with some minor adjustments regarding quantum, as they would apply to the accident (cl. 8).

Under the normal procedure, the MIB's decision is sent, together with reasons, to the claimant (cl. 16). If the claimant does not disagree with the decision or the amount of any award within the period of six weeks from the notice of the decision, the MIB will pay the award to the claimant. An applicant who is unwilling to accept the MIB's decision or determination has six weeks from being notified by the MIB of its decision to send a written notice of appeal to the MIB (cl. 19(1)). The matter will then be referred to arbitration in accordance with cll. 19 to 25 of the agreement.

Commentary

Procedure on Motor Insurers' Bureau claims

The agreements are between the MIB and the Minister of Transport. Claimants are not parties 9.6
to the agreements, though the agreements were clearly made for their benefit and the MIB has never tried to rely on the lack of privity of a claimant as a defence to a claim, because doing so would make the agreements pointless. In *Albert v Motor Insurers' Bureau* [1972] AC 301 Lord Donovan said:

> The question immediately suggests itself as to how the appellant as a third party can claim the benefit of this agreement. The point was looked at in *Hardy v Motor Insurers' Bureau* [1964] 2 QB 745 where, at p. 757, Lord Denning MR remarks that the agreement is on the face of it a contract between two parties for the benefit of a third, and that no point was taken by the Bureau that the agreement was not enforceable by the third person.

Diplock LJ also considered the matter in *Gurtner v Circuit* [1968] 2 QB 587, saying that on a number of occasions the court had turned a blind eye to the position and that unless the point were specifically raised the court was 'entitled to proceed upon the assumption that the Bureau has, before action is brought, contracted for good consideration with the [claimant] to perform the obligations specified in its contract with the Minister or has by its conduct raised an estoppel which would bar it from relying on absence of privity of contract'.

As the uninsured drivers agreement was made before the Contracts (Rights of Third Parties) Act 1999 was passed it is not covered by the Act, but it is clear that when it is renewed it will be.

The effective paying party in uninsured drivers cases is the MIB, but the named defendant will be the driver, who will often play no active role in the litigation. It is therefore common practice for the court to grant permission for the MIB to be added as a defendant under what is now **CPR, r. 19.2(2)(a)** (see *Gurtner v Circuit* [1968] 2 QB 587). The same does not apply to untraced drivers (see *White v London Transport Executive* [1971] 2 QB 721).

There is no formal procedure for making claims to the MIB under either of the agreements. The notification of the claim may usually be made in a letter to the MIB from the claimant or the claimant's legal representatives, after which the MIB sends out a claim form which should be completed and returned. The rest is up to the MIB, either in the case of untraced drivers to appoint a member to investigate or in the case of uninsured drivers to make enquiries of anyone such as witnesses and experts who may be able to piece together the accident. In cases where the driver is untraced, there is little a victim can do but apply to the MIB for assistance. In the case of the uninsured driver, however, claimants and those representing them would do well to make their own enquiries to ensure that there was no insurance cover at the time of the accident. The MIB should not be notified unless and until the claimant is aware of the true position, in order to avoid time being wasted and unnecessary expense.

FOURTH MOTOR INSURANCE DIRECTIVE

9.7 Directive 2000/26/EC on the approximation of laws of the member States relating to insurance against civil liability in respect of the use of motor vehicles ('the Fourth Motor Insurance Directive') provides the victim of a road traffic accident with a mechanism for dealing with his claim in his own country and in his own language, even though the applicable law may remain that of the country where the accident happened. It applies when a person who is resident in an EU State suffers loss or damage resulting from an accident in another member State and the responsible vehicle is registered and insured with an insurer established in a member State other than his own. It can also apply when the accident is in a non-EU green card signatory country if the offending vehicle is registered and insured in another EU State.

The Directive requires every motor insurer authorised in an EU State to appoint a claims representative in every other member State capable of responding to road traffic claims and paying them where necessary. Every EU State has established an 'information centre' so a victim can, by reference to the registration number of a vehicle, obtain details of its insurance, or the name and address of the owner or user. The Directive is implemented in the United Kingdom by the Motor Insurance (Compulsory Insurance) (Information Centre and Compensation Body) Regulations 2003 (SI 2003/37), and the Motor Insurers' Information Centre is the information centre for the United Kingdom (reg. 3(1)). This should result in the identification of the correct insurer. A claim can then be made, and the insurer's representative must provide a reasoned reply within three months. Under the Fourth Motor Insurance Directive there has to be a direct right of legal action available against insurers. This has been implemented by the European Communities (Rights against Insurers) Regulations 2002 (SI 2002/3061) (see 14.4). A claim is dealt with in accordance with the law of the country where the accident occurred.

Where there is no reasoned response within the three-month period the MIB is the compensation body for the United Kingdom for the purposes of the Fourth Motor Insurance Directive (SI 2003/37, reg. 10). If the insurer's representative corrects the omission, it can continue to handle the claim. Otherwise the claim will be dealt with by the MIB. The MIB will also deal with the claim (reg. 13) where it has proved impossible:

(a) to identify the vehicle the use of which is alleged to have been responsible for the accident; or
(b) within a period of two months after the date of a request, to identify an insurance undertaking which insures the use of the vehicle.

In claims governed by reg. 13, liability is dealt with in accordance with the law where the accident happened, but quantum is governed by English law (*Jacobs v Motor Insurers' Bureau* [2010] EWCA Civ 1208, [2011] 1 WLR 2609).

LANDLORD AND TENANT NOTICES

9.8 Various pre-action notices must be given in landlord and tenant disputes. These include:

(a) *Notice to quit.* This is a means of terminating a periodic tenancy. At common law, notice to quit could be given orally, but had to be of the correct length (generally that corresponding to a period of the tenancy, although for tenancies from year to year, only six months' notice was required). Difficulties of proof have resulted in notices to quit invariably being given in writing. In relation to residential premises, the notice must set out certain prescribed information.

(b) *Statutory notices in claims for possession of residential property.* There are different statutory codes dealing with security of tenure for residential tenants. Before possession proceedings can be brought, various forms of notice must be served on the tenant.

(c) *Business tenancies.* There is a regime of serving pre-action notices and counter-notices in relation to the termination of business tenancies and seeking new business leases under the Landlord and Tenant Act 1954, part 2.

(d) *Law of Property Act 1925, s. 146.* This section provides that where the landlord seeks to enforce a right of re-entry or forfeiture for breach of covenant or condition (other than non-payment of rent), the landlord must first serve a notice specifying the breach; requiring it to be remedied (if capable of remedy) within a reasonable, specified, time; and requiring the payment of any compensation. For further details, see works on landlord and tenant law.

(e) *Notice of disrepair.* In a claim for housing disrepair, whether brought for breach of the tenancy agreement or in tort, the tenant must show that the landlord has received sufficient information about the alleged defects to put a reasonable person on inquiry as to whether repairs are necessary (*O'Brien v Robinson* [1973] AC 912). A landlord will be assumed to have notice of defects in the common parts of a building as these areas are under the landlord's care and control (*British Telecommunications plc v Sun Life Assurance plc* [1996] Ch 69).

BILLS OF EXCHANGE

Notice of dishonour

A claim against a person for liability on a bill of exchange which has been dishonoured by non-acceptance or non-payment cannot be made unless notice of dishonour has been given (Bills of Exchange Act 1882, s. 48). Notice must be sent off on the day after dishonour, or, if there is no convenient post on that day, by the next post, unless the person giving, and the person to be given, the notice reside in the same place, in which case notice must be sent off in time to reach the latter on the day after dishonour (s. 49(12)). 9.9

Section 50(2) provides several exceptions from the requirement to give notice of dishonour. In particular, it dispenses with the need to give notice of dishonour in practically all instances where a cheque (which is a bill of exchange drawn on a banker payable on demand: s. 73) is dishonoured by non-payment. (There is no need to present a cheque for acceptance: s. 39.) Normally the only person liable on a dishonoured cheque is the drawer and usually it is not necessary to give notice of dishonour to the drawer of a cheque because s. 50(2)(c)(4) provides that notice is dispensed with if the drawee (the bank) is under no obligation (as between drawee and drawer) to pay the cheque, and normally this is the only reason why a cheque is dishonoured. A bank has no obligation to pay its customer's cheque if, for example, there are insufficient funds in the account on which the cheque is drawn, or the customer has countermanded (stopped) payment (ss. 50(2)(c)(5) and 75) or the bank has notice that the customer has died (s. 75). The answer given on the cheque when it is returned by the paying bank will indicate whether any of these apply.

If notice of dishonour of a bill of exchange is not dispensed with by s. 50(2), the notice, in order to be valid and effectual, must be given in accordance with the rules in s. 49.

Notice can be given only by or on behalf of the holder of the bill, or by or on behalf of an endorser who is at the time liable on the bill (s. 49(1)), but written notice need not be signed (s. 49(7)). Notice may be given to a duly authorised agent of the party sought to be made liable (s. 49(8)).

There is no prescribed form of notice, which need not even be written, but it must sufficiently identify the bill and state whether the dishonour was by non-acceptance or non-payment (s. 49(5)). If notice is given of non-acceptance, it is unnecessary to give a further notice of non-payment, unless the bill has been accepted in the meantime (s. 48, proviso (2)). In fact there is no need to present a non-accepted bill for payment (s. 43(2)). Misdescription of the bill does not vitiate the notice unless the recipient of the notice has in fact been misled by it (s. 49(7)). Simply returning the bill to the drawer or an endorser is sufficient notice (s. 49(6)), but in practice it is usual to retain possession of the bill for the purposes of taking proceedings on it.

Notice of dishonour must be given within a reasonable time after the dishonour (s. 49(12)). In the absence of special circumstances, notice is not deemed to have been given within a reasonable time, unless (s. 49(12)):

(a) where the person giving, and the person to receive, notice reside in the same place, the notice is given or sent off in time to reach the latter on the day after the dishonour;
(b) otherwise, the notice is sent off on the day after the dishonour, unless there is no post at a convenient time on that day, in which case it must be sent by the next post.

Whether persons are in the same place for the purposes of s. 49(12)(a) seems to be determined by facilities for travel rather than administrative boundaries (*Hamilton Finance Co. Ltd v Coverley Westry Walbaum and Tosetti Ltd* [1969] 1 Lloyd's Rep 53, in which Upper Brook Street, London W1 and Seething Lane EC3 were held to be in the same place as they are 'a modest bus or tube journey apart, both in the central area').

Where a notice of dishonour is duly addressed and posted, the sender is deemed to have given due notice of dishonour, 'notwithstanding any miscarriage by the post office' (s. 49(15)).

Where a bill which has been dishonoured is in the hands of an agent, for example, a bank collecting payment for its customer, notice of dishonour may be given by the agent either direct to the person liable on the bill or to the agent's principal, who then has a reasonable time (as specified in s. 49(12), see above) to give notice to the person liable (s. 49(13)).

Delay in giving notice of dishonour is excused where the delay is caused by circumstances beyond the control of the party giving notice (s. 50(1)).

Section 50(2) lists circumstances in which notice of dishonour is not required. They are:

(a) when, after the exercise of reasonable diligence, notice as required by the Act cannot be given or does not reach the drawer or endorser sought to be made liable;
(b) where it has been waived (waiver may be express or implied and may be after notice should have been given).

Notice to the drawer is not required where (s. 50(2)(c)):

(a) drawer and drawee are the same person (as with a bank draft);
(b) the drawee is fictitious or has no capacity to contract;
(c) presentation was to the drawer;
(d) as between drawee/acceptor and drawer, the drawee/acceptor is under no obligation to pay/accept the bill (see above, in relation to cheques);
(e) the drawer has countermanded payment.

Notice to an endorser is not required where (s. 50(2)(d)):

(a) at the time of endorsing the bill the endorser was aware that the drawee was fictitious or had no capacity to contract;
(b) presentation was to the endorser;
(c) the bill was drawn or accepted for the accommodation of the endorser.

Notice given by or on behalf of the holder of a bill enures for the benefit of all prior endorsers who have a right of recourse against the person notified, and also for the benefit of any subsequent holder (s. 49(3)). Notice given by or on behalf of an endorser enures for the benefit of the holder and all subsequent endorsers (s. 49(4)).

Protesting foreign bills

A foreign bill which has been dishonoured by non-acceptance must be protested for non-acceptance, and a foreign bill which is dishonoured by non-payment must be protested for non-payment, unless it has been previously dishonoured by non-acceptance (Bills of Exchange Act 1882, s. 51(2)). A foreign bill is a bill of exchange which is not an inland bill (s. 4) and an inland bill is one which is either (a) both drawn and payable within the British Islands or (b) drawn within the British Islands upon some person resident in the British Islands. The British Islands are the United Kingdom, the Isle of Man and the Channel Islands (s. 4(1)). Failure to protest a foreign bill discharges the liability of the drawer and endorsers. A protest is made by a notary public in the form prescribed in s. 51(7). It is usual to ask a notary to note a dishonoured bill, which must be done on the day of dishonour or the next business day (s. 51(4)), so that a later protest will take effect, under s. 51(4), as from the date of noting. Protest is required in addition to notice of dishonour and is dispensed with in the same circumstances (s. 51(9)). **9.10**

Letter before claim on a bill of exchange

Even if a statutory notice of dishonour of a bill of exchange is not required, in a letter before claim sent before proceedings are started, the dishonoured bill should be identified and a photocopy provided, the nature of the dishonour should be stated and the amount claimed should be set out in detail. **9.11**

DEMANDS IN MONEY CLAIMS

In the case of a bank owing money to a customer (perhaps being money held to the customer's credit on a current or deposit account), subject to contrary agreement, a demand from the customer is a condition precedent to repayment (*N. Joachimson v Swiss Bank Corporation* [1921] 3 KB 110) and the demand must be made at the branch where the account is kept (*Clare and Co. v Dresdner Bank* [1915] 2 KB 576). In all other situations where money has been borrowed with no time specified for repayment, including lending repayable on demand (such as bank overdrafts, which, subject to contrary agreement, are repayable on demand: *Paget's Law of Banking*, 11th edn. (1996), p. 167, citing *Titford Property Co. Ltd v Cannon Street Acceptances Ltd* (ChD, 22 May 1975)), at common law the demand was not regarded as a condition precedent to repayment (*Re Brown's Estate* [1893] 2 Ch 300; *Bradford Old Bank v Sutcliffe* [1918] 2 KB 833). This meant that the limitation period ran from the time of making the loan. However, the effect of the Limitation Act 1980, s. 6, is that in relation to loans which are not for a fixed term, time only starts running for limitation purposes from the making of a demand. Demands have a further importance in lending cases, because under the terms of any security agreements (such as guarantees and mortgages), resort to the security or the right to appoint a receiver is usually only possible after a demand has been made. **9.12**

To be effective, a demand must be a clear intimation that payment is required. It must be peremptory in character and unconditional, but the language used is immaterial, and the word 'demand' need not be used (*Re Colonial Finance, Mortgage, Investment and Guarantee Corporation Ltd* (1905) 6 SR (NSW) 6, followed in *Re a Company* [1985] BCLC 37). A demand need not state the amount to be repaid (*Bank of Baroda v Panessar* [1987] Ch 335).

In England and Wales the rule is that a borrower of money repayable on demand must have the money ready to repay at all times, so that the only time that need be allowed between making a demand and regarding the borrower as being in default is the time necessary to effect the mechanics of payment, and if it is known that the borrower has not got the money then no time at all need be allowed (*Sheppard and Cooper Ltd v TSB Bank plc* [1996] 2 All ER 654). The commercially unrealistic mechanics-of-payment test has been rejected in Canada in favour of a reasonable-time test, and may be due for re-examination at appellate level in England (see *Lloyds Bank plc v Lampert* [1999] BCC 507).

A claim for restitution after rescission of a contract cannot be made until notice of rescission has been given, but no demand is necessary before claiming restitution in a case of unjust enrichment (*Fuller v Happy Shopper Markets Ltd* [2001] 1 WLR 1681).

NOTICE OF ASSIGNMENT

9.13 Where there has been a legal assignment of a debt or other thing in action, express written notice must be given to the debtor or other person against whom the right can be enforced. See the Law of Property Act 1925, s. 136, and **14.96**.

DIRECTOR DISQUALIFICATION

9.14 For pre-action notification of disqualification proceedings see **86.9**.

Chapter 10 Limitation

INTRODUCTION

Expiry of a limitation period provides a defendant with a complete defence to a claim. Lord Griffiths in *Donovan v Gwentoys Ltd* [1990] 1 WLR 472 said, 'The primary purpose of the 10.1

Commentary

limitation period is to protect a defendant from the injustice of having to face a stale claim, that is a claim with which he never expected to have to deal'. If a claim is brought a long time after the events in question, the likelihood is that evidence which may have been available earlier may have been lost, and the memories of witnesses who may still be available will inevitably have faded or become confused. Further, it is contrary to general policy to keep people perpetually at risk.

Most limitation periods are laid down in the Limitation Act 1980 (LA 1980) as amended. Several other statutes lay down limitation periods, and some procedural rules impose time limits which act rather like limitation periods (see **table 10.1** and **10.64** to **10.67**). The usual rule is that no objection can be taken to a claim started on the last day of the limitation period, but there is a complete defence if proceedings are brought one day late.

There has been a move in recent legislation towards flexible limitation periods for some types of cases, which will be considered in this chapter in the context of the limitation rules affecting different causes of action. Examples are the Latent Damage Act 1986, which provides for limitation to apply as a defence only from the date when a negligence claim was discoverable, and LA 1980, s. 33, which allows the court to disapply the three-year personal injuries time limit where the court considers it equitable to do so. Where flexibility of this kind is available the LA 1980 may be seen as seeking to achieve a balance of justice between the claimant and the defendant.

Limitation is usually a procedural defence (the exceptions relate to limitation periods operating outside the LA 1980). Limitation will not be taken by the court of its own motion, but must be specifically set out in the defence (**PD 16, para. 13.1**). Time-barred cases rarely go to trial. If the claimant is unwilling to discontinue the claim (see **chapter 55**), it is usually possible for the defendant to apply successfully for the claim to be struck out (see **chapter 33**) as an abuse of the court's process.

Normally, the only consequence of the expiry of a limitation period is that the defendant acquires a technical defence to the claim. The claimant still has a cause of action, but one that cannot be enforced. In cases of adverse possession of land and conversion, expiry of the limitation period has the additional consequence of extinguishing the party's title to the land or goods.

Main concepts

10.2 When a limitation issue arises in a claim, the following concepts need to be considered:

(a) The date the cause of action accrued (see **10.4**). Accrual starts time running.
(b) Whether time did not start running when the cause of action accrued. This might be because the cause of action is subject to 'date of knowledge' provisions, which apply to personal injuries claims (see **10.12** to **10.18**) and latent damage claims (see **10.30** to **10.32**), or because the claimant was under a disability (see **10.51**), or because the claimant can take advantage of the provisions dealing with acknowledgments, fraud, concealment or mistake (see **10.55** to **10.58**).
(c) The applicable limitation period (see **10.5**).
(d) The date time stopped running. This is the date the claim is brought, see **10.6**.
(e) Whether the claim is subject to rules analogous to limitation, albeit outside the LA 1980.

Issuing a second claim

10.3 *Where proceedings are* issued and come to naught through inactivity on the part of the claimant, they can be abandoned or discontinued, and, provided the limitation period has not expired, fresh proceedings can be commenced in respect of the same cause of action. There are exceptions where the original proceedings are struck out as an abuse of process or as a sanction for non-compliance with the rules or directions (see *Janov v Morris* [1981] 1 WLR 1389 and **33.13**). *Horton v Sadler* [2006] UKHL 27, [2007] 1 AC 307, held that there is jurisdiction to make an order under LA 1980, s. 33, to disapply the primary personal injury limitation period in a second claim after an earlier claim has been discontinued or struck out. The House of Lords applied Practice Statement (Judicial Precedent) [1966] 1 WLR 1234 and reversed the decision in *Walkley v Precision Forgings Ltd* [1979] 1 WLR 606, which had held there is no such jurisdiction. Issuing a second claim in these circumstances is not an abuse of process (*Aktas v Adepta* [2010] EWCA Civ 1170, [2011] QB 894).

ACCRUAL OF CAUSE OF ACTION

Time runs from the day following the day on which the cause of action arose, as parts of a day are ignored (*Marren v Dawson Bentley and Co. Ltd* [1961] 2 QB 135). **10.4**

The rules on accrual fix the date from which time begins to run for limitation purposes. Lindley LJ in *Reeves v Butcher* [1891] 2 QB 509 said: 'it has always been held that the statute runs from the earliest time at which an action could be brought'. In *Read v Brown* (1888) 22 QBD 128 Lord Esher MR defined 'cause of action' as encompassing 'every fact which it would be necessary for the [claimant] to prove, if traversed, in order to support his right to the judgment of the court'. In other words, time runs from the point when facts exist establishing all the essential elements of the cause of action.

Commentary

A distinction is drawn between the substantive elements and mere procedural requirements. Thus, a solicitor can commence a claim to recover costs from a client only if at least a month has elapsed since a bill for those costs has been delivered to the client (Solicitors Act 1974, s. 69(1)). In *Coburn v Colledge* [1897] 1 QB 702 it was held that the requirement to furnish a bill was only a procedural matter, and time ran from completion of the work as opposed to delivery of the bill. Sometimes this can be a difficult distinction to draw. A 'misfeasance' claim for a summary remedy against a delinquent director for breach of duty to a company under the Insolvency Act 1986, s. 212, accrues with the breach of duty, not when the liquidator is appointed (*Re Eurocruit Europe Ltd* [2007] EWHC 1433 (Ch), [2008] Bus LR 146), because s. 212 is only procedural in nature. Conversely, a claim against a former director under the Insolvency Act 1986, s. 213 (fraudulent trading), which only comes into effect when a company is being wound up, accrues on the date the company is ordered to be wound up (*Re Overnight Ltd* [2009] EWHC 601 (Ch), [2009] Bus LR 1141). *Sevcon Ltd v Lucas CAV Ltd* [1986] 1 WLR 462 concerned the Patents Act 1949, s. 13(4), which contained a proviso: 'Provided that an applicant shall not be entitled to institute any proceedings for infringement until the patent has been sealed'. It was held that the cause of action accrued on the date of the infringement, but could not be enforced until the procedural requirement of sealing was met.

In addition to the elements of the cause of action being present, there must be a party capable of suing and a party liable to be sued. So, if goods are converted after the owner has died intestate, time would run only from the date letters of administration were taken out (*Thomson v Lord Clanmorris* [1900] 1 Ch 718 per Vaughan Williams LJ). However, if it is necessary to restore to the register of companies a company against which a claim is to be made, the date of accrual remains based on the date of the breach (or other element of the cause of action), not on the date of restoration (*Smith v White Knight Laundry Ltd* [2001] EWCA Civ 660, [2002] 1 WLR 616). Although the court has power under the Companies Act 2006, s. 1032(3), to direct that the period between dissolution and restoration shall not count for the purposes of limitation, a direction under this provision should not normally be made unless notice of the application has been served on all parties who could be expected to oppose it. Time continues running during a period in which the defendant is an undischarged bankrupt (*Anglo Manx Group Ltd v Aitken* [2002] BPIR 215.

LIMITATION PERIODS

10.5 Time runs from accrual of the cause of action until the claim form is filed, or, as it is put in the LA 1980, when the claim is brought. **Table 10.1** sets out the limitation periods for the most important classes of cases.

The relevant claim form is the one issued in the present proceedings. An earlier claim form based on the same alleged cause of action which is not proceeded with does not affect the question whether the claim form in the present claim was issued before limitation expired (*Markfield Investments Ltd v Evans* [2001] 1 WLR 1321).

Table 10.1 Limitation periods

	Class of claim	Limitation period	Blackstone's Civil Practice 2014
1	Fraudulent breach of trust	None (LA 1980, s. 21(1))	**10.36**
2	Recovery of land	12 years (LA 1980, s. 15(1))	**10.41**
3	Recovery of money secured by mortgage	12 years (LA 1980, s. 20(1))	**10.44**
4	Specialty	12 years (LA 1980, s. 8(1))	**10.46**
5	Defective product claims	10 years (Consumer Protection Act 1987, s. 11A(3))	**10.27**
6	Recovery of a sum due under statute	6 years (LA 1980, s. 9(1))	**10.47**
7	Enforcement of a judgment	6 years (LA 1980, s. 24(1))	**10.50**
8	Contract	6 years (LA 1980, s. 5)	**10.35**
9	Recovery of trust property and breach of trust	6 years (LA 1980, s. 21(3))	**10.36**
10	Recovery of arrears of rent	6 years (LA 1980, s. 19)	
11	Enforcement of awards not under seal	6 years (LA 1980, s. 7)	**10.62**
12	Tort (except those listed below)	6 years (LA 1980, s. 2)	**10.7**
13	Defective Premises Act 1972 claims	6 years (Defective Premises Act 1972, s. 1(5))	
14	Personal injuries claims	3 years (LA 1980, s. 11(4))	**10.12**
15	Fatal Accidents Act 1976 claims	3 years (LA 1980, s. 12(2))	**10.29**
16	Personal injuries or damage to property claims under the Consumer Protection Act 1987	3 years (LA 1980, s. 11A)	**10.27**
17	Carriage by Air Act 1961 claims	2 years (Carriage by Air Act 1961, sch. 1)	
18	Claims for personal injuries or damage to vessel, cargo or property or personal injuries to passengers at sea	2 years (Merchant Shipping Act 1995, s. 190(3) and sch. 6, part 1, art. 16)	
19	Disqualification of company directors under the Company Directors Disqualification Act 1986, s. 6	2 years (Company Directors Disqualification Act 1986, s. 7(2))	**86.8**
20	Contribution under the Civil Liability *(Contribution) Act 1978*	2 years (LA 1980, s. 10(1))	**10.45**
21	Contribution under the Maritime Conventions Act 1911	1 year (Merchant Shipping Act 1995, s. 190(4))	

Table 10.1 (Continued)

	Class of claim	Limitation period	Blackstone's Civil Practice 2014
22	Carriage of Goods by Road Act 1965 claims	1 year (Carriage of Goods by Road Act 1965, sch., art. 32)	
23	Cargo claims under the Hague–Visby Rules	1 year (Hague–Visby Rules, art. III, rule 6)	
24	Defamation and malicious falsehood	1 year (LA 1980, s. 4A)	**10.33**
25	Applications for judicial review	3 months (CPR, r. 54.5)	**77.36**
26	Unfair dismissal under the Employment Rights Act 1996	3 months (Employment Rights Act 1996, s. 111(2))	
27	Applications for new business tenancies under the Landlord and Tenant Act 1954, part 2	If made by the tenant, not before 2 months after the tenant's request for a new tenancy under s. 26 (s. 29A(3)), and whether by the tenant or landlord, not after the date specified in any s. 25 notice or the day before the date specified in any s. 26 request (s. 29A(2))	
28	Claims for an account	Period applicable to claim on which account is based (LA 1980, s. 23)	

Commentary

DATE A CLAIM IS BROUGHT

10.6 A claim is time-barred under LA 1980 if proceedings are not 'brought' (which is the word used in most of the provisions in the Act) before the expiry of the stated limitation period. Traditionally it was thought that a claim was brought for limitation purposes 'when the [claim form] or other originating process is issued by the central office of the High Court and not when it is brought to the knowledge of the defendant by service upon him' (per Lord Diplock in *Thompson v Brown* [1981] 1 WLR 744). *Barnes v St Helens Metropolitan Borough Council* [2006] EWCA Civ 1372, [2007] 1 WLR 879, drew a distinction between the date a claim is 'brought' and the date it is 'issued'. The result is that time stops running for limitation when the claim form and issue fee are delivered to the court (this is the date the claim is 'brought'), which is in the claimant's control, rather than on the date of issue, which the claimant does not control. The same result was achieved for the two-year limitation period under the Company Directors Disqualification Act 1986, s. 6, in *Secretary of State for Trade and Industry v Vohora* [2007] EWHC 2656 (Ch), [2008] Bus LR 161. Likewise, in relation to laying of informations in the magistrates' courts (*Rockall v Department for Environment, Food and Rural Affairs* [2007] EWHC 614 (Admin), [2007] 1 WLR 2666) and the presentation of petitions (*Re Blights Builders Ltd* [2006] EWHC 3549 (Ch), [2007] Bus LR 629). Part 20 proceedings are brought for limitation purposes on the date the Part 20 claim is commenced (LA 1980, s. 35(1)(a)).

A claimant may send a claim form to the court office for issue. Letters requesting the issue of claim forms will be date-stamped on receipt, and the date of receipt will stop time running for limitation purposes if the court does not issue the claim form on the same day (**PD 7A, paras 5.1 and 5.2**). An enquiry as to the date on which a claim form was received by the court should be directed to a court officer (**para 5.3**). **Paragraph 5.4** goes on to say that parties should recognise the importance of establishing the date of receipt if a limitation period is approaching, and should take steps to record the date of receipt. To avoid difficulties in cases where limitation might be a problem, it is usually best to make a personal attendance at court to issue the proceedings.

If the court office is closed on the final day of the limitation period, proceedings are deemed to be in time if they are issued on the next day the court office is open (*Pritam Kaur v S. Russell and Sons Ltd* [1973] QB 336).

TORT

General claims in tort

10.7 LA 1980, s. 2, provides:

2. Time Limit For Actions Founded on Tort

An action founded on tort shall not be brought after the expiration of six years from the date on which the cause of action accrued.

The general rule is that in addition to proving the defendant is guilty of some wrongful conduct, liability in tort can only be established on proof of damage. Usually, damage is the final matter to come into existence, so the usual rule is that time runs in tort from the date when damage is sustained. In most situations this is the first date on which the claimant has suffered a measurable loss. This means that a claim against a structural engineer for negligent advice in relation to remedial works required on a building project will accrue when the remedial works failed (*Renwick v Simon and Michael Brooke Architects* [2011] EWHC 874 (TCC), [2011] PNLR 31).

In *Law Society v Sephton and Co.* [2006] UKHL 22, [2006] 2 AC 543, it was alleged that accountants had negligently prepared solicitors' accounts which failed to find misappropriations of clients' money which might have been prevented if the accounts had been prepared properly. Various clients of the solicitors made claims against the Solicitors' Compensation Fund based on the misappropriations. It was held that each misappropriation gave rise to a contingent liability against the Fund, and that the cause of action accrued when the contingency occurred. This was the date each client made a claim against the Fund, because it was at that point that a loss or damage was sustained by the Fund. *Law Society v Sephton and Co.* should not be understood as laying down a general rule that damage only occurs when a claim is made against the party who is now the claimant as a result of the alleged negligence of the defendant. The date when damage is suffered is a fact-specific question. In a claim by an ATE insurer against a solicitor, based on negligent vetting of the prospects of success of personal injuries claims, the insurer suffered measurable loss when the ATE policies were entered into, as this was the time at which the insurer valued the policies erroneously in reliance on the defendant's negligent vetting (*AXA Insurance Ltd v Akther and Darby Solicitors* [2009] EWCA Civ 1166, [2010] 1 WLR 1662).

A claim for damages under the principle in *Francovich v Italy* (cases C-6 and 9/90) [1995] ICR 722) based on an alleged failure of the government to implement EU law accrued when the claimants suffered their personal injuries (*Spencer v Secretary of State for Work and Pensions* [2008] EWCA Civ 750, [2009] QB 358). A similar result was achieved in a claim by Lloyd's underwriters against the Treasury in *Poole v Her Majesty's Treasury* [2006] EWHC 2731 (Comm), [2007] 1 All ER (Comm) 255. There is a principle that time does not run until there has been full implementation of a Directive, but this applies only where the conduct of the member State was responsible for the lapse of time which brought the relevant time bar into operation such as to make it inequitable for the State then to rely on the time bar.

Time will not start running until the claimant has suffered some damage. In *Rothwell v Chemical and Insulating Co. Ltd* [2007] UKHL 39, [2008] 1 AC 281, the claimants had developed pleural plaques, which proved that the claimants' lungs had been penetrated by asbestos fibres. The evidence was that pleural plaques cause no symptoms and do not increase susceptibility to other asbestos-related diseases or shorten life expectancy. Their presence did not amount to an injury such as to set time running.

The important date is the date damage was sustained, not the date on which the claimant discovered the damage (*Cartledge v E. Jopling and Sons Ltd* [1963] AC 758). There are, of course, many cases where measurable damage and its discovery coincide (*Abbott v Will Gannon and Smith Ltd* [2005] EWCA Civ 198, [2005] BLR 195). In *Pirelli General Cable Works Ltd v Oscar Faber and Partners* [1983] 2 AC 1 it was held that a cause of action for negligent design of a chimney arose when cracking in the structure first developed, and not when the damage could have been or was in fact discovered. Likewise, where additional damage is suffered after the tortious act complained of, time continues to run from the original tortious act (*Iqbal v Legal Services Commission* [2005] EWCA Civ 623, LTL 10/5/2005). Latent damage is considered at **10.30**.

Continuing torts

The decision in *Darley Main Colliery v Mitchell* (1886) 11 App Cas 127 on continuing torts is probably confined to subsidence claims (*Iqbal v Legal Services Commission* [2005] EWCA Civ 623, LTL 10/5/2005). Conversely, it was held in *Phonographic Performance Ltd v Department of Trade and Industry* [2004] EWHC 1795 (Ch), [2004] 1 WLR 2893, that where the tort is one which is not actionable per se, there is a continuing breach of duty and a fresh cause of action every time the claimant suffers loss. Where work done by a developer is defective, and the developer does further work intended to rectify defects but which is also defective, the further work is a fresh cause of action and time starts running again (*Alderson v Beetham Organization Ltd* [2003] EWCA Civ 408, [2003] 1 WLR 1686). **10.8**

Professional negligence

In a claim against a solicitor for negligent advice, actual damage is suffered when the advice is acted upon, such as by executing a document (*Forster v Outred and Co.* [1982] 1 WLR 86) or entering into an agreement (*McCarroll v Statham Gill Davis* [2003] EWCA Civ 425, [2003] PNLR 509). Thus, in *Pegasus Management Holdings SCA v Ernst and Young* [2008] EWHC 2720 (Ch), [2009] PNLR 11, a claim against accountants based on alleged failure to advise the client to incorporate a company with subsidiaries accrued when the client acquired shares in the company. A claim against financial advisers, arising from advice to transfer benefits from an occupational pension scheme to a personal pension fund, accrues when the benefits are transferred (*Shore v Sedgwick Financial Services Ltd* [2008] EWCA Civ 863, [2009] Bus LR 42; *Williams v Lishman, Sidwell, Campbell and Price Ltd* [2010] EWCA Civ 418, [2010] PNLR 25). In a claim based on alleged negligence in a conveyancing transaction, if the property is diminished in value on completion due to the negligence, accrual occurs at that point rather than on registration of the transfer (*Nouri v Marvi* [2010] EWCA Civ 1107, [2011] PNLR 7, although there are cases where the cause of action accrues on exchange, such as *Edehomo v Edehomo* [2011] EWHC 393 (Ch), [2011] 1 WLR 2217). **10.9**

A claim against a solicitor based on alleged negligent advice on inheritance tax accrues when the client relies on the advice (*Daniels v Thompson* [2004] EWCA Civ 307, [2004] PNLR 33). In *Watkins v Jones Maidment Wilson* [2008] EWCA Civ 134, [2008] PNLR 23, negligent advice resulted in an immediate measurable loss because the claimant lost the chance of negotiating a better agreement, which meant the claim was time-barred. Even if the advice given by the solicitor should have included advice to renegotiate the contract, there was a single event amounting to the breach of duty. Where a claimant seeks to sue a solicitor for negligently allowing a claim to be struck out as a sanction for breach of directions or the requirements of the CPR, time runs from the date when the claimant had no arguable basis for avoiding the claim being struck out, not from the date on which it was actually struck out (*Khan v R. M. Falvey and Co.* [2002] EWCA Civ 400, [2002] PNLR 28; *Hatton v Chafes* [2003] EWCA Civ 341, [2003] PNLR 24, disapproving *Hopkins v MacKenzie* (1994) 6 Med LR 26). A related, but different point, was considered in *Cohen v Kingsley Napley* [2006] EWCA Civ 66, [2006] PNLR 22. Pill LJ at [19] said that even if the original claim would have been struck out if an application had been made by the original opponent at the point six years before the present claim was issued against the solicitors, the claim against the solicitors will not be time-barred if:

(a) on the evidence the original opponent would not have applied to strike out at that time;
(b) with the result that the original claim still had some value at the point six years before the current proceedings.

There are not many cases where the first point will be satisfied. *Cohen v Kingsley Napley* was a strike-out application, and the Court of Appeal said it was a matter that could be argued at trial. The court was swayed by the fact the original claim was a counterclaim, so the original opponent was a claimant, and so may have been reluctant to strike out the counterclaim for delay given the claim would also be in danger of being struck out.

Applying the rule that a claim accrues when actual damage is sustained, a professional negligence claim against solicitors based on failing to serve a claim form in time, or based on wrongly relying on an order (later set aside) extending time for service, accrues when the original period of validity of the claim form expires (*Polley v Warner Goodman and Street Solicitors* [2003] EWCA Civ 1013, [2003] PNLR 784). A continuing duty on a solicitor to advise will continually renew the accrual of limitation until the duty to advise ends, usually on termination of the retainer (*Workman v Pannone and Partners* [2002] EWHC 2366 (QB), LTL 18/11/2002).

Where a claim is in respect of a transaction entered into through a breach of duty owed by the defendant to the claimant (such as a loan agreement entered into in reliance on a negligent property valuation), time will run from the date the transaction was entered into if the claimant suffered a loss there and then. If there was no immediate loss, such as where the security for a loan was worth more than the loan when it was first advanced (albeit not as much as the defendant's valuation), time will start running only when the value of the security falls below the amount of the loan (see the discussion in *First National Commercial Bank plc v Humberts* [1995] 2 All ER 673).

The principle that a judicial decision stating what the common law is has retrospective effect meant, in *Awoyomi v Radford* [2007] EWHC 1671 (QB), [2008] QB 793, that time had started running in a claim against a barrister from before the decision in *Arthur J. S. Hall and Co. v Simons* [2002] 1 AC 615, which had removed the immunity from suit previously enjoyed by advocates.

Trespass

10.10 Trespass claims are actionable per se, so time runs from the wrongful act since there is no requirement to prove damage.

Conversion

10.11 Time runs from the date the goods were converted. A number of special rules apply:

(a) where goods are converted more than once, the original six-year period continues to run and is not renewed (LA 1980, s. 3(1));
(b) at the end of the original six-year period the true owner's title is extinguished (s. 3(2));
(c) subject to (d) below, there is no time limit where goods are stolen (s. 4);
(d) where goods are converted (but not stolen) and are then stolen at a later date, proceedings in respect of the theft are barred once the true owner's title is extinguished under s. 3(2) by virtue of the original conversion (s. 4(1)).

Personal injuries claims

10.12 Subsections (1) to (4) of LA 1980, s. 11, provide:

11. Special Time Limit For Actions in Respect of Personal Injuries

(1) This section applies to any action for damages for negligence, nuisance or breach of duty (whether the duty exists by virtue of a contract or of provision made by or under a statute or independently of any contract or any such provision) where the damages claimed by the plaintiff for the negligence, nuisance or breach of duty consist of or include damages in respect of personal injuries to the plaintiff or any other person.

(1A) This section does not apply to any action brought for damages under section 3 of the Protection from Harassment Act 1997.

(2) None of the time limits given in the preceding provisions of this Act shall apply to an action to which this section applies.

(3) An action to which this section applies shall not be brought after the expiration of the period applicable in accordance with subsection (4) or (5) below.

(4) Except where subsection (5) below applies, the period applicable is three years from—
(a) the date on which the cause of action accrued; or
(b) the date of knowledge (if later) of the person injured.

Claims for personal injuries (class 14 in **table 10.1**) comprise all claims in negligence, nuisance and breach of duty (including contractual and statutory duties) where the claim to relief consists of or includes damages in respect of personal injuries to the claimant or any other person (LA 1980, s. 11(1)). Under s. 11(4) the basic limitation period for such claims is three years. An attempt was made to avoid this limitation period in *Letang v Cooper* [1965] 1 QB 232. The claimant was injured when the defendant drove his car over her legs while she was sunbathing on the grass in the car park of a hotel. Proceedings were issued four years afterwards, but the cause of action was pleaded both in negligence and in trespass to the person. The Court of Appeal overruled the trial judge and held the claim was time-barred. Two reasons were advanced. One was that where an injury is inflicted negligently rather than intentionally, the only cause of action is in negligence, so the claimant is unable to rely on the six-year limitation period in trespass (class 12 in **table 10.1**). The second reason was that the phrase 'breach of duty' in what is now s. 11(1) covered a breach of any duty under the law of tort.

A claim by an employee against an employer for failing to advise on the benefits available after suffering a personal injury is a claim for negligent advice (class 12), see *Gand v Leeds Health Authority* (1999) *The Times*, 14 May 1999. On the other hand, a claim in professional negligence against a solicitor arising out of the firm's handling of a divorce ancillary relief claim, which included a claim for anxiety and stress arising out of the firm's alleged mishandling of her claim, became, for that reason, a claim in respect of personal injuries and subject to a three-year limitation period (class 14) rather than the usual six-year period in claims in tort and breach of contract (*Oates v Harte Reade and Co.* [1999] PIQR P120). A negligent failure by an education authority to improve the consequences of the claimant's dyslexia by appropriate teaching, or a negligent failure to treat a physical injury, are both claims for personal injuries (*Adams v Bracknell Forest Borough Council* [2004] UKHL 29, [2005] 1 AC 76).

In *Ackbar v C. F. Green and Co. Ltd* [1975] QB 582 a claim against an insurance broker for damages for breach of contract for failing to effect cover for a passenger who later suffered personal injuries in a road accident was held to be a claim in contract (class 8). A claim for breach of statutory duty to insure a motor vehicle on the road was, in contrast, held to be a claim for personal injuries in *Norman v Ali* [2000] RTR 107.

Deliberate trespass to the person

There is no distinction in LA 1980, s. 11, between negligent breaches of duty resulting in personal injuries (as discussed at **10.12**) and cases involving deliberate trespass to the person. Consequently, civil claims arising out of assaults, battery, rape and indecent assaults etc. are governed by the same three-year limitation period (and the rules in ss. 14 and 33) as claims **10.13** arising through negligence (*A v Hoare* [2008] UKHL 6, [2008] 1 AC 844). *Stubbings v Webb* [1993] AC 498 (which was confirmed by the European Court of Human Rights in *Stubbings v United Kingdom* (applications 22083/93 and 22095/93) (1996) 23 EHRR 213) was departed from in accordance with Practice Statement (House of Lords: Judicial Precedent) [1966] 1 WLR 1234.

Personal injuries claims: date of knowledge

10.14 Time runs in personal injuries claims from the date the cause of action accrued, or, if later, the date of the claimant's date of knowledge (LA 1980, s. 11(4)). Date of knowledge is defined by s. 14, which provides:

14. Definition of Date of Knowledge for Purposes of Sections 11 and 12

(1) Subject to subsection (1A) below, in sections 11 and 12 of this Act references to a person's date of knowledge are references to the date on which he first had knowledge of the following facts—
(a) that the injury in question was significant; and
(b) that the injury was attributable in whole or in part to the act or omission which is alleged to constitute negligence, nuisance or breach of duty; and
(c) the identity of the defendant; and
(d) if it is alleged that the act or omission was that of a person other than the defendant, the identity of that person and the additional facts supporting the bringing of an action against the defendant;

and knowledge that any acts or omissions did or did not, as a matter of law, involve negligence, nuisance or breach of duty is irrelevant.

[*Subsection (1A) deals with claims for death caused by defective products.*]

(2) For the purposes of this section an injury is significant if the person whose date of knowledge is in question would reasonably have considered it sufficiently serious to justify his instituting proceedings for damages against a defendant who did not dispute liability and was able to satisfy a judgment.

(3) For the purposes of this section a person's knowledge includes knowledge which be might reasonably have been expected to acquire—
(a) from facts observable or ascertainable by him; or
(b) from facts ascertainable by him with the help of medical or other appropriate expert advice which it is reasonable for him to seek;

but a person shall not be fixed under this subsection with knowledge of a fact ascertainable only with the help of expert advice so long as he has taken all reasonable steps to obtain (and, where appropriate, to act on) that advice.

The provision for time to run from date of knowledge was first introduced in July 1963 by the Limitation Act 1963 and has no application to any claim already time-barred before it was introduced (*McDonnell v Congregation of Christian Brothers Trustees* [2003] UKHL 63, [2003] 1 AC 1101, applying *Arnold v Central Electricity Generating Board* [1988] AC 228).

10.15 **Constructive knowledge** Time will start running before a claimant has actual knowledge within LA 1980, s. 14(1), if the claimant has constructive knowledge under s. 14(3). A claimant is taken to know facts observable or ascertainable by him or her, and also facts ascertainable with the help of expert advice which it would have been reasonable to obtain (s. 14(3)). The burden of proof under s. 14(3) rests on the defendant (*Norton v Corus UK Ltd* [2006] EWCA Civ 1630, LTL 13/11/2006). Despite this, the issue continues to be argued (*Whiston v London Strategic Health Authority* [2009] EWHC 956 (QB), [2009] LS Law Med 355, in which it was said, at [6], the burden of proof rests on the claimant).

Defining the test for constructive knowledge has proved difficult. Authorities suggesting a substantially subjective test concentrating on the characteristics of the individual claimant (*Davis v City and Hackney Health Authority* (1998) 2 Med LR 366 and *KR v Bryn Alyn Community (Holdings) Ltd* [2003] EWCA Civ 85, [2003] QB 1441) should be treated with caution. A substantially objective test was said to be applicable under s. 14(3)(b) in *Adams v Bracknell Forest*

Borough Council [2004] UKHL 29, [2005] 1 AC 76. However, in *AB v Ministry of Defence* [2012] UKSC 9, [2013] 1 AC 78, it was held that time will start running against a claimant who believes their injury was attributable to the relevant act or omission 'with sufficient confidence to justify embarking on the preliminaries to the issue of a claim form, such as submitting a claim to a proposed defendant, taking legal and other advice, and collecting evidence'. While suspicion is not knowledge within the meaning of s. 14, reasonable belief normally suffices.

In *Forbes v Wandsworth Health Authority* [1997] QB 402, the Court of Appeal doubted the relevance of the claimant's individual characteristics in what is expressed to be an objective test. This means that personal characteristics of the claimant, such as a lack of confidence or wishing to avoid contention, are irrelevant under s. 14. Rather, the court has to consider how a reasonable person in the claimant's situation, suffering from the claimant's medical condition, would have acted. It is to be expected that claimants who have suffered significant injuries will seek professional advice on the cause of their problems, even if they have serious difficulties with reading and writing (*Adams v Bracknell Forest Borough Council*). The way it was put in *Whiston v London Strategic Health Authority* [2010] EWCA Civ 195, [2010] 1 WLR 1582, was that a person who knows he has a significant injury is to be judged against an objective expectation of heightened curiosity to find out what happened. This might include asking his parents about what happened at his birth. The question is whether, having regard to the symptoms the claimant was experiencing, it would have been reasonable to expect him to seek specific advice from his doctor (*White v Eon* [2008] EWCA Civ 1463, LTL 26/11/2008).

A claimant will not have constructive knowledge over a period where her post-operation symptoms are consistent with what she was told before the operation, where she trusts her doctors, and there is nothing to put her on notice that something may have gone wrong (*Rogers v East Kent Hospitals NHS Trust* [2009] EWHC 54 (QB), [2009] LS Law Med 153). Time will, however, run against a claimant from the moment he had information demonstrating a real possibility that his working conditions caused his symptoms, even without information establishing causation (*Kew v Bettamix Ltd* [2006] EWCA Civ 1535, [2007] PIQR P210).

The *Forbes* approach was applied in *Parry v Clwyd Health Authority* [1997] PIQR P1, where in context the knowledge of the 'reasonable man' was regarded as being that of a person who knew no more of the subject than what might have been learnt at school, from parents or friends or the media. A claimant who is clear in her own mind that there was a connection between the defendant's conduct and her injury has sufficient knowledge even if other people would want to get expert advice before making up their minds (*Spargo v North Essex District Health Authority* [1997] PIQR P235). In *Ali v Courtaulds Textiles Ltd* [1999] Lloyd's Rep Med 301 the Court of Appeal held that the claimant in an industrial deafness case could not be said to know his deafness was attributable to his working conditions, as opposed to being age-induced, until after he had been advised by his doctors. A claimant who eventually makes a claim against a drug company in respect of the effects of an allegedly defective drug may well have consulted a doctor at an early stage when possibly drug-related symptoms first became apparent. A doctor is likely to concentrate on a solution to the patient's problems rather than give advice on attributing blame. Therefore, whether the doctor's knowledge about the cause of the claimant's symptoms should be attributed to the claimant depends on whether in the circumstances it would have been reasonable to expect the claimant to have asked the doctor about cause as well as cure (*Nash v Eli Lilly and Co.* [1993] 1 WLR 782).

In *Henderson v Temple Pier Co. Ltd* [1998] 1 WLR 1540 the claimant was injured as she boarded a moored ship. She did not know the identity of the owners. She instructed solicitors about a month after the accident. If they had acted competently, they could have discovered the identity of the defendant from the General Register of Shipping and Seamen fairly soon after they were retained, but in the event they only discovered the defendant's identity about 18 months after the accident. Proceedings were issued 4 years and 3 months after the accident. It was held that the proviso to s. 14(3) was not intended to give an extended period to a person whose

Commentary

solicitor acted in a dilatory manner in obtaining information which is obtainable without particular expertise, and the claimant was fixed with constructive knowledge which her solicitors ought to have acquired. The same reasoning applies where a solicitor fails to identify a defendant through failing to request a copy of a police road accident report (*Copeland v Smith* [2000] 1 WLR 1371), or through declining to see relevant care records (*Pierce v Doncaster Metropolitan Borough Council* [2008] EWCA Civ 1416, [2009] 1 FLR 1189).

10.16 **Significant injury** The 'injury in question' for the purposes of LA 1980, s. 14(1)(a), is the injury for which the claim is brought (*McManus v Mannings Marine Ltd* [2001] EWCA Civ 1668, LTL 29/10/2001). Therefore, where a claimant sues for the exacerbation of a previous injury following further exposure to hazardous working conditions, time runs from the date the claimant knew the exacerbated injury was significant. It has been held that it is legitimate for a claimant to restrict a claim to post-traumatic stress disorder which arose in a delayed form, and not to include a claim for the alleged underlying (and earlier) physical abuse. In such a case the 'injury in question' for the purposes of s. 14 is the post-traumatic stress disorder, for which the claimant's date of knowledge may be later than for the underlying abuse (*H v Northampton County Council* [2004] EWCA Civ 526, [2005] PIQR P87, per Pill LJ at [18]). The cases relied on, *KR v Bryn Alyn Community (Holdings) Ltd* [2003] EWCA Civ 85, [2003] QB 1441, at [39] and *Stubbings v Webb* [1992] QB 197 at p. 208, have not survived *A v Hoare* [2008] UKHL 6, [2008] 1 AC 844, and so it is unlikely that *H v Northampton County Council* remains good law.

An injury is 'significant' for the purposes of s. 14(1)(a) if the claimant would have considered it sufficiently serious to justify proceedings against a defendant who does not dispute liability and is able to satisfy any judgment (s. 14(2)). The burden of proof on this question rests on the defendant (*Furniss v Firth Brown Tools Ltd* [2008] EWCA Civ 182, LTL 12/3/2008). It could be objected that any injury will satisfy this test. However, it was held in *Stephen v Riverside Health Authority* (1989) *The Times*, 29 November 1989, that the early symptoms of cancer arising from excessive radiation received from a medical X-ray did not amount to a significant injury. A person who alleges rape, whether vaginal or anal, must know objectively, at the time of the assault, that he or she has suffered a significant injury (*Albonetti v Wirral Metropolitan Borough Council* [2008] EWCA Civ 783, LTL 7/7/2008).

Reasons for not bringing proceedings outside the merits of the claim, such as reluctance to sue an employer, have been held to be irrelevant under s. 14, although they can be relevant under s. 33 (see **10.19**) (*McCafferty v Metropolitan Police District Receiver* [1977] 1 WLR 1073). To a similar effect is *McCoubrey v Ministry of Defence* [2007] EWCA Civ 17, [2007] 1 WLR 1544. The key question is whether the claimant knew he or she had suffered a significant injury. The effect of the injury on the claimant's career or private life is irrelevant under s. 14.

The test in s. 14(2) is only 'subjective' to the limited extent that it is applied to what the claimant knows of his or her injury, rather than the injury as it actually is. The claimant's knowledge may have to be supplemented by constructive knowledge under s. 14(3). Otherwise, the test in s. 14(2) sets an entirely impersonal standard. The question is not whether the claimant considered his or her injury was sufficiently serious, but whether the claimant reasonably would have done so. The court needs to find what the claimant knew about the injury, then add any constructive knowledge under s. 14(3). The court must then consider whether a reasonable person with that knowledge would have considered the injury sufficiently serious to justify commencing proceedings against a defendant who did not dispute liability and who was able to satisfy a judgment (*A v Hoare* [2008] UKHL 6, [2008] 1 AC 844, per Lord Hoffmann at [34]). It is not a case of considering whether someone with the claimant's intelligence would have been reasonable if he did not consider the injury sufficiently serious to justify proceedings (*B v Nugent Care Society* [2009] EWCA Civ 827, [2010] 1 WLR 516, at [9]). Once the court has ascertained what the claimant knew and should have known, the characteristics of the actual claimant (such as intelligence or vulnerability) drop out of the picture.

There is a difference between s. 14(3), which turns on what the claimant ought reasonably to have done, and s. 14(2), which sets a standard for whether the injury suffered was significant. Under s. 14(3) the court must take into account the injury the claimant has suffered. For example, the court will not assume a claimant who has been blinded could reasonably have acquired knowledge by seeing things. Under s. 14(2), on the other hand, the effect of the injuries on what the claimant could reasonably be expected to do is irrelevant (*A v Hoare* at [39]). Where the injury suffered has impeded the claimant in bringing a claim (for example, repressed memories following sexual abuse), the correct approach is to consider the effect under s. 33, not s. 14 (at [44], [45]).

James v East Dorset Health Authority (1999) *The Times*, 7 December 1999, is a relatively rare case where a patient who underwent an unsuccessful operation did not realise he might have suffered an injury until he was put on notice that this was a possibility by an independent consultant five years later. Time did not start running against the claimant over the subsequent 17 months either, because it was not unreasonable for him to have taken at least that time to obtain confirmation that the original operation had caused him injury. In *Field v British Coal Corporation* [2008] EWCA Civ 912, LTL 31/7/2008, time did not run against a claimant who alleged he had suffered industrial deafness while he followed medical advice that his hearing loss was due to wax or an infection.

Attributable to defendant's conduct The knowledge mentioned in LA 1980, s. 14(1)(b), is not knowledge detailed enough to enable the claimant's advisers to draft particulars of claim, and there is no requirement that the claimant must be aware that the defendant's conduct is actionable. To hold that this is the case would be contrary to the final words of s. 14(1) that knowledge that any acts or omissions do or do not constitute negligence as a matter of law is irrelevant. In *Spargo v North Essex District Health Authority* [1997] PIQR P235, Brooke LJ laid down the following four principles: **10.17**

(a) The knowledge required to satisfy s. 14(1)(b) is a broad knowledge of the essence of the causally relevant act or omission to which the injury is attributable.
(b) 'Attributable' in this context means 'capable of being attributed to' in the sense of being a real possibility.
(c) An injured person has the requisite knowledge when he or she knows enough to make it reasonable to begin to investigate whether or not there is a case against the person responsible. This will be the case if the injured person so firmly believes that his condition is capable of being attributed to an act or omission which he can identify (in broad terms) that he goes to a solicitor to seek advice about making a claim for compensation.
(d) An injured person will not have the requisite knowledge if he thinks he knows of acts or omissions which he should investigate, but in fact is barking up the wrong tree; or if his knowledge is so vague or general that he cannot fairly be expected to know what he should investigate; or if his state of mind is such that he thinks his condition could be attributable to the act or omission alleged to constitute negligence, but he is not sure about this, and would need to check with an expert before he could properly be said to know that it was.

In *Broadley v Guy Clapham and Co.* [1994] 4 All ER 439 the claimant had gone into hospital for a knee operation, and left suffering from a condition known as foot drop. It was held that time started to run when the claimant had both a 'broad knowledge' that the operation had caused an injury to her foot, and specific knowledge that the operation had been carried out in such a way as to damage a nerve in her leg (the cause of her foot drop condition). She had the requisite broad knowledge shortly after the operation, and should have had the specific knowledge within a few months after the operation if she had taken the appropriate expert advice. In *Dobbie v Medway Health Authority* [1994] 1 WLR 1234 it was alleged that a hospital carried out a mastectomy without conducting the usual tests, and that the operation was entirely unnecessary. The surgeon was alleged to have told the claimant afterwards that at least she was fortunate that there was no malignancy. It was held that within days of the operation the claimant had the requisite broad knowledge that she had suffered a significant injury, and time started running from that point, even though it was not until several years later that she realised she could make a claim. In *Whiston v London Strategic Health Authority* [2010] EWCA Civ 195, [2010] 1 WLR 1582, the relevant knowledge in a clinical negligence claim based on being deprived of oxygen at birth was not merely that the claimant knew he had a forceps delivery, but whether he knew his injury was due to a junior doctor's persistence in attempting a forceps delivery, his use of the wrong forceps, and delay in seeking assistance.

Whether the relevant facts could only be known after obtaining an expert's report depends on the complexity of the case (*Hendy v Milton Keynes Health Authority* (1991) 3 Med LR 114). Thus, in *Forbes v Wandsworth Health Authority* [1997] QB 402 the claimant was admitted to hospital for an operation to cure circulation problems in his leg. The operation was not a success, and a fortnight later his leg was amputated. He did not obtain actual knowledge of the default of the hospital that he later relied on in proceedings for medical negligence until he received advice from a consultant 10 years later. It was held that, where an operation was expected to be successful, but ended up with disappointing results, the patient had to be allowed a reasonable time in which to get over the shock and to take stock of the situation before being expected to seek advice for the purpose of bringing a claim. Where the results were serious, as in this case, the taking-stock period would be in the region of 12 to 18 months. From that point the patient would be fixed with constructive knowledge, and time would start running for limitation purposes. The claimant in *Secretary of State for Trade and Industry v Mackie* [2007] EWCA Civ 642, LTL 28/6/2007, was a miner, who took a hearing test in 1992 and was informed he had suffered a 9.98 dB hearing loss. He was aware that other miners were making noise exposure claims based on hearing losses exceeding 10 dB. He was informed by a union official that he did not have a claim. He did not bring proceedings until consulting solicitors in 2003. It was held that time ran from 1992, as the original hearing test was plainly arranged with a view to bringing a claim for damages, and showed an injury which was attributable to his working conditions. Even if the misinformation provided by the union official had displaced that knowledge, it was unreasonable, for the purposes of s. 14(3), for the claimant to do nothing for the next 10 years.

10.18 **Defendant's identity** Typical cases where time is postponed under LA 1980, s. 14(1)(c), are hit-and-run accidents and cases where claimants are rendered unconscious and have no recollection of the accident. Claimants injured at work almost always have immediate knowledge of the identity of their employer. However, there are cases where the exact identity of the claimant's employer does not become clear until some time after an accident. In *Simpson v Norwest Holst Southern Ltd* [1980] 1 WLR 968 time was postponed where the claimant's employer 'hid' (to use the word used by Lawton LJ at p. 974) its identity by calling itself 'Norwest Holst Group'. Time was also postponed in *Cressey v E. Timm and Son Ltd* [2005] EWCA Civ 763, [2005] 1 WLR 3926, where the actual employer was one company in the group (Holdings), but the claimant's pay slips were issued by another company (Limited). Rix LJ made the point (at [29]) that application of s. 14(1)(c) does not depend on deliberate 'hiding' of the defendant's identity. At [35] Rix LJ said that knowing the defendant's 'identity' in s. 14(1)(c) requires something specific enough to enable a person to be identified for the purposes of a claim form. This in turn means that time will run against a claimant who knows who the defendant is, but does not have the defendant's correct name (at [33]).

Personal injuries claims: discretion to disapply limitation period

A wide discretion is given to override the usual three-year limitation period in personal injuries claims by LA 1980, s. 33, which in part provides: 10.19

33. Discretionary Exclusion of Time Limit for Actions in Respect of Personal Injuries or Death

(1) If it appears to the court that it would be equitable to allow an action to proceed having regard to the degree to which—
- (a) the provisions of section 11 or 11A or 12 of this Act prejudice the plaintiff or any person whom he represents; and
- (b) any decision of the court under this subsection would prejudice the defendant or any person whom he represents;

the court may direct that those provisions shall not apply to the action, or shall not apply to any specified cause of action to which the action relates....

(3) In acting under this section the court shall have regard to all the circumstances of the case and in particular to—
- (a) the length of, and the reasons for, the delay on the part of the plaintiff;
- (b) the extent to which, having regard to the delay, the evidence adduced or likely to be adduced by the plaintiff or the defendant is or is likely to be less cogent than if the action had been brought within the time allowed by section 11, by section 11A or (as the case may be) by section 12;
- (c) the conduct of the defendant after the cause of action arose, including the extent (if any) to which he responded to requests reasonably made by the plaintiff for information or inspection for the purpose of ascertaining facts which were or might be relevant to the plaintiff's cause of action against the defendant;
- (d) the duration of any disability of the plaintiff arising after the date of the accrual of the cause of action;
- (e) the extent to which the plain tiff acted promptly and reasonably once he knew whether or not the act or omission of the defendant, to which the injury was attributable, might be capable at that time of giving rise to an action for damages;
- (f) the steps, if any, taken by the plaintiff to obtain medical, legal or other expert advice and the nature of any such advice he may have received.

Interpretation of s. 33 The leading authority on LA 1980, s. 33, is *Thompson v Brown* [1981] 1 WLR 744, in which the House of Lords held that the court has a discretion unfettered by any rules of practice, that the court must consider all the circumstances of the case, and is not restricted to the matters specifically set out in s. 33(3). Lord Diplock said in that case that a direction under s. 33 is always prejudicial to the defendant, but the extent of the prejudice is related to the strength or otherwise of the claim or defence. 'Equitable' in s. 33 means doing what is fair and just. A tortfeasor only deserves to have his obligation to pay damages removed if the passage of time has significantly compromised his ability to defend the claim (*Cain v Francis* [2008] EWCA Civ 1451, [2009] QB 754). 10.20

While the analysis of s. 14 in *KR v Bryn Alyn Community (Holdings) Ltd* [2003] EWCA Civ 85, [2003] QB 1441, is no longer good law given the decision in *A v Hoare* [2008] UKHL 6, [2008] 1 AC 844, Auld LJ's statement of the principles to be applied in applications under s. 33 at [74] remains broadly good law, albeit in need of adjustment to take into account subsequent decisions, in particular *A v Hoare* (*B v Nugent Care Society* [2009] EWCA Civ 827, [2010] 1 WLR 516, at [11]–[26]). As adjusted, Auld LJ's principles on the substantive aspects of applications under s. 33 are as follows:

(a) [In cases where there is more than one claimant], a judge should consider the exercise of his discretion separately in relation to each claim.

(b) The burden of showing that it would be equitable to disapply the limitation period lies on the claimant. [How easy or difficult it is for the claimant to persuade the court to exercise its discretion depends on the facts of the particular case (*Sayers v Hunt* [2012] EWCA Civ 1715, [2013] 1 WLR 1695). In *B v Nugent Care Society* at [20] Lord Clarke of Stone-cum-Ebony MR said that 'it is correct to describe the exercise of the discretion as an exceptional indulgence to the claimant because, but for the exercise of the discretion, his claim will be time-barred.

But it is only exceptional for that reason. The cases stress that the discretion is wide and unfettered.']

(c) Depending on the issues and the nature of the evidence going to them, the longer the delay the more likely, and the greater, the prejudice to the defendant.
(d) Where a judge is minded to grant a long 'extension' he should take meticulous care in giving reasons for doing so.
(e) A judge should not reach a decision effectively concluding the matter on the strength of any one of the circumstances specified in s. 33(3), or on one of any other circumstances relevant to his decision, or without regard to all the issues in the case. He should conduct the balancing exercise at the end of his analysis of all the relevant circumstances and with regard to all the issues, taking them all into account.
(f) [Auld LJ's sub-para. (vii)] Where a judge determines the s. 33 issue along with the substantive issues in the case, he should take care not to determine the substantive issues, including liability, causation and quantum, before determining the issue of limitation and, in particular, the effect of delay on the cogency of the evidence….To rely on his findings on those issues to assess the cogency of the evidence for the purposes of the limitation exercise would put the cart before the horse. Put another way, it would effectively require the defendant to prove a negative, namely, that the judge could not have found against him on one or more of the substantive issues if he had tried the matter earlier and without the evidential disadvantages resulting from the delay.
(g) [Auld LJ's sub-para. (viii).] This deals with the merits of the claim. Auld LJ, relying on *Hartley v Birmingham City District Council* [1992] 1 WLR 968 at pp. 979–80, said the merits are usually a neutral factor. Auld LJ pointed to the exception identified by *Nash v Eli Lilly and Co.* [1993] 1 WLR 782 at p. 804E, that weak claims on liability brought by impecunious claimants do cause prejudice to defendants, which should be taken into account. In *B v Nugent Care Society* the Master of the Rolls at [23] explained that *Hartley v Birmingham City District Council* had been misunderstood. All that Parker LJ intended to say in that case was that the prejudice to the defendant of losing a limitation defence is not the relevant prejudice to be addressed. The relevant prejudice is that which affects the defendant's ability to defend (confirmed by *Cain v Francis* [2008] EWCA Civ 1451, [2009] QB 754). Lord Clarke MR in *B v Nugent Care Society* at [23] said in terms that: 'Clearly the strength of the claimant's case is relevant and was relevant to the decision of Parker and Leggatt LJJ in *Hartley v Birmingham City District Council*.']

The circumstances set out in s. 33(3) are those which experience had indicated were of real importance in considering where the balance of prejudice was likely to lie. The delay referred to in point (a) is the same as that referred to in point (b), namely, the delay after the expiry of the primary limitation period as extended, if appropriate, by the claimant's date of knowledge under s. 14 (*Long v Tolchard and Sons Ltd* (1999) *The Times*, 5 January 2000). Overall delay is also relevant as part of all the circumstances of the case (s. 33(3); *McDonnell v Walker* [2009] EWCA Civ 1257, LTL 24/11/2009). The reasons for the delay to be considered are those of the claimant: it is a subjective test (*Coad v Cornwall and Isles of Scilly Health Authority* [1997] 1 WLR 189). Having found what the reason is for the delay, the court must then decide whether the reason is good or bad. The general rule is that the longer the delay, the more likely it is that the balance of prejudice will move away from granting relief to the claimant. While it has been said to be wrong to concentrate mainly on the claimant's reasons for the delay, without sufficient emphasis on the length of the delay (*Buckler v Sheffield City Council* [2004] EWCA Civ 920, [2005] PIQR P36), this was in a case decided before *A v Hoare*. The current approach is to give greater emphasis than formerly, especially in childhood abuse claims, to the 'reasons' for the delay under s. 33(3)(a) (*B v Nugent Care Society*).

The question of cogency in point (b) is only concerned with the loss or adverse effect on evidence through the passage of time. A court is not entitled in an application under s. 33 to find prejudice to the defendant by assuming that omissions or contradictions in the claimant's evidence may be excused by the trial judge (*Nash v Eli Lilly and Co.* [1993] 1 WLR 782). Any prejudice to contribution proceedings, such as tracing witnesses, has to be taken into account under s. 33(3)(b) (*Buckler v Sheffield City Council* [2004] EWCA Civ 920, [2005] PIQR P36).

The period of disability referred to in point (d) is one of mental disability arising after the accrual of the cause of action, and hence one which does not prevent time running (see 10.51).

Cross-claims against solicitor One factor not mentioned in LA 1980, s. 33(3), but of considerable importance, is whether the claimant has an alternative claim in negligence against his or her solicitor for failing to issue proceedings in time (*Thompson v Brown* [1981] 1 WLR 744). Possibly negligent discontinuance of the first claim tended towards dismissing an application under s. 33 (*Williams v Johnstone* [2008] EWHC 1334 (QB), LTL 26/6/2008). This factor can be discounted if there is real doubt about the strength of the claim against the solicitor, and in any event the claimant will suffer some prejudice through further delay, instructing unknown solicitors to pursue the new claim, the old solicitors knowing the weaknesses of the original claim, and possible restrictions in obtaining disclosure against the original defendants (see disclosure against non-parties in **chapter 50**). In *Steeds v Peverel Management Services Ltd* [2001] EWCA Civ 419, *The Times*, 16 May 2001, the claimant's solicitors had, through oversight, issued proceedings 49 days after the expiry of limitation. The Court of Appeal held that the judge at first instance had erred in law in assuming that the solicitors' failings were those of the claimant, and in criticising a period of delay after the solicitors were instructed. Despite the strong claim in negligence against the solicitors, if the claim were defeated by the expiry of the limitation period, greater prejudice would be suffered by the claimant than the defendant, and the claim was allowed to proceed. **10.21**

Date of notification and forensic prejudice A second factor not mentioned in LA 1980, s. 33(3), which is always regarded as being of considerable importance, is the delay between the accident and the defendant being informed of the claim. The reason is that a defendant who is informed of the potential claim at an early stage has the opportunity to investigate the facts while the events are still fresh in witnesses' memories, even if proceedings are issued rather late, and hence cannot complain of significant prejudice under s. 33(3)(b). This seems to have been a significant factor in *Thompson v Brown* [1981] 1 WLR 744 and also in *Hartley v Birmingham City District Council* [1992] 1 WLR 968. In early notification cases where there is no defence on liability, financial prejudice to the defendant should not be taken into account (*Cain v Francis* [2008] EWCA Civ 1451, [2009] QB 754). It is unclear whether the court should disregard financial prejudice to the defendant in other cases, although the principle is stated in general terms. *Cain v Francis*, where the limitation period was disapplied despite a one-year delay, must be regarded as a case where there was no forensic prejudice (*McDonnell v Walker* [2009] EWCA Civ 1257, LTL 24/11/2009). **10.22**

The length of time since the accident (in *McDonnell v Walker* it was seven years), substantial changes in the nature of the alleged claim since first notification, or the death of witnesses, may mean there is forensic prejudice. In these cases *McDonnell v Walker* says the court must consider:

(a) the cause of the delays (often it is necessary to split the delay into different periods);
(b) whether the delays are excusable;
(c) the effects of the delays in effectively being able to investigate the evidence; and
(d) whether it is still possible to have a fair trial.

In *Donovan v Gwentoys Ltd* [1990] 1 WLR 472 there was a delay in excess of six years before the defendants were given full details of the claim. In fact proceedings were issued only six months late, as the claimant was a child at the date of the accident. She instructed solicitors 19 days before her eighteenth birthday, so she had an alternative claim against her solicitors. It was held that the delay in notifying the defendants was an extremely important consideration, that

Commentary

it would be inequitable to require the defendants to meet such a stale claim, and the claimant would suffer only the slightest prejudice in being required to sue her solicitors. Permission was refused. See also *Kamar v Nightingale* [2007] EWHC 2982 (QB), [2008] PNLR 15. In sexual abuse claims, the date of notification of the claim and, where the claim is brought many years after the alleged events, the possibility of having a fair trial, are important factors (*A v Hoare* [2008] UKHL 6, [2008] 1 AC 844).

10.23 **Merits of substantive claim** Parker LJ in *Hartley v Birmingham City District Council* [1992] 1 WLR 968 expressed the view that the merits of the claimant's case are of little importance, on the ground that the stronger the merits the greater the prejudice to both the claimant and the defendant of the decision under LA 1980, s. 33, going against them. This is inconsistent with Lord Diplock's speech in *Thompson v Brown* [1981] 1 WLR 744, and contrary to subsequent cases. These include *Nash v Eli Lilly and Co.* [1993] 1 WLR 782, where a finding that the claims were weak was regarded as an important factor in refusing to make orders under s. 33, and *Long v Tolchard and Sons Ltd* (1999) *The Times*, 5 January 2000, where it was said that if the claimant has a strong, or even a cast-iron, case against the original tortfeasor, that is an important factor to place into the balance that has to be struck. Unless the claim has no realistic prospect of success (in which event the application should be refused: *TCD v Harrow London Borough Council* [2008] EWHC 3048 (QB), [2009] 1 FLR 719), the strength of the case is not determinative of the application. Where the question of the merits arises at an interim hearing, all the court should do is determine the overall prospects (*Dale v British Coal Corporation (No. 2)* (1992) *The Times*, 2 July 1992), although a determination to the usual civil standard may be appropriate where the matter is raised as a preliminary issue.

10.24 **Second claim cases** When finding the balance of prejudice under LA 1980, s. 33, in a 'second claim' case, the court has to consider the degree of prejudice in that second claim. In *Richardson v Watson* [2006] EWCA Civ 1662, [2007] RTR 247, following *Horton v Sadler* [2006] UKHL 27, [2007] 1 AC 307, the court disapplied the limitation period. In this case the first claim was brought within the three-year limitation period, but had to be discontinued because of a failure to give the requisite notice under the Uninsured Drivers Agreement (see **9.4**). In *Adams v Ali* [2006] EWCA Civ 91, [2006] 1 WLR 1330, the first claim was started a week outside the three-year limitation period, and was struck out for failure to serve particulars of claim. Liability was not in dispute, and the delay was the fault of the claimant's solicitors. It was held to be equitable to disapply the limitation period under s. 33 in a second claim issued about 13 months after the expiry of limitation.

10.25 **Other factors** In *Das v Ganju* [1999] PIQR P260 the Court of Appeal held that delays caused by incorrect advice given by the claimant's lawyers should not be laid at the claimant's door, and allowed a claim to continue despite a delay of many years. Conversely, a delay of almost a year after the law was changed by *Horton v Sadler* [2006] UKHL 27, [2007] 1 AC 307 (see **10.3**), tended against disapplying limitation in *Williams v Johnstone* [2008] EWHC 1334 (QB), LTL 26/6/2008. In *Whiston v London Strategic Health Authority* [2010] EWCA Civ 195, [2010] 1 WLR 1582, the judge was held to have placed far too much weight on the claimant's decision not to sue when he was younger and not so badly affected by his cerebral palsy. Once he acquired actual knowledge of the alleged negligence there was no basis for finding he had made a decision not to sue. A fair trial was still possible, and he had a substantial claim which gave him a prospect of having his future needs provided for. It was therefore equitable to allow the claim to proceed.

As mentioned at **10.16**, many reasons for not bringing a claim, such as a reluctance to sue one's present employer, are irrelevant under LA 1980, s. 14. However, they can be important factors under s. 33. So, in *McCafferty v Metropolitan Police District Receiver* [1977] 1 WLR 1073 *Lawton LJ said, in relation* to an application under s. 33, 'the court should be understanding of men who, after taking an overall view of their situation, come to the conclusion that they would prefer to go on working rather than become involved in litigation'. Also relevant is the defendant's ability to satisfy a judgment, such as by winning the lottery. Claimants should not feel obliged to sue indigent defendants in the hope they might at some later stage become rich enough to pay (*A v Hoare* [2008] UKHL 6, [2008] 1 AC 844; the limitation period was disapplied on the facts when the matter was considered by Coulson J in *A v Hoare* [2008] EWHC 1573 (QB), LTL 15/7/2008). Limitation was disapplied in the sexual abuse claim of *Raggett v Society of Jesus Trust 1929 for Roman Catholic Purposes* [2009] EWHC 909 (QB), 108 BMLR 147, despite a delay of 28 years, whereas a fair trial was felt to be impossible 40 years after the event in the otherwise similar case of *Albonetti v Wirral Metropolitan Borough* [2009] EWHC 832 (QB), LTL 12/5/2009.

Discretionary disapplication of the limitation period under s. 33 has no application in cases governed by the two-year limitation period under the Convention relating to the Carriage of Passengers and their Luggage by Sea (as enacted by the Merchant Shipping Act 1995; class 18 in **table 10.1**), see *Higham v Stena Sealink Ltd* [1996] 1 WLR 1107.

Procedure In *KR v Bryn Alyn Community (Holdings) Ltd* [2003] EWCA Civ 85, [2003] QB 1441, at [74(vi)], Auld LJ suggested that wherever the judge considers it feasible to do so, decisions under LA 1980, s. 33, should be made at preliminary hearings by reference to the statements of case and written witness statements, together with the documents provided through standard disclosure. In *B v Nugent Care Society* [2009] EWCA Civ 827, [2010] 1 WLR 516, at [21], Lord Clarke of Stone-cum-Ebony MR said that in many cases (probably of childhood abuse) the judge may conclude that it is desirable that oral evidence should be heard, because the strength of the claimant's evidence is relevant to the way the discretion under s. 33 should be exercised. It is incumbent on the claimant to disclose all relevant circumstances at the hearing of the application, and if this is breached, the decision may be set aside (*Long v Tolchard and Sons Ltd* (1999) *The Times*, 5 January 2000). **10.26**

Defective products

Claims under the Consumer Protection Act 1987 in respect of personal injuries or damage to property accrue on the date of damage or the 'date of knowledge' (LA 1980, s. 11A(4)). By s. 11A(3), proceedings must be instituted against the producer of an allegedly defective product within 10 years. Section 11A provides in part: **10.27**

11A. Actions in Respect of Defective Products

(3) An action to which this section applies shall not be brought after the expiration of the period of ten years from the relevant time, within the meaning of section 4 of the said Act of 1987; and this subsection shall operate to extinguish a right of action and shall do so whether or not that right of action had accrued, or time under the following provisions of this Act had begun to run, at the end of the said period of ten years.

(4) Subject to subsection (5) below, an action to which this section applies in which the damages claimed by the plaintiff consist of or include damages in respect of personal injuries to the plaintiff or any other person or loss of or damage to any property, shall not be brought after the expiration of the period of three years from whichever is the later of—
 (a) the date on which the cause of action accrued; and
 (b) the date of knowledge of the injured person or, in the case of loss of or damage to property, the date of knowledge of the plaintiff or (if earlier) of any person in whom his cause of action was previously vested.

(5) If in a case where the damages claimed by the plaintiff consist of or include damages in respect of personal injuries to the plaintiff or any other person the injured person died before the expiration of the period mentioned in subsection (4) above, that subsection shall have effect as respects the cause of action surviving for the benefit of his estate by virtue of section 1 of the Law Reform (Miscellaneous Provisions) Act 1934 as if for the reference to that period there were substituted a reference to the period of three years from whichever is the later of—
 (a) the date of death; and
 (b) the date of the personal representative's knowledge.

For substitution of a party after the expiry of the ten-year period under s. 35 see **14.90**.

Fatal accidents: accrual of cause of action

10.28 If a person injured in an accident later dies as a result of those injuries, the cause of action vesting in the injured person's estate under the **Law Reform (Miscellaneous Provisions) Act 1934** accrued at the date of the accident. However, the related cause of action for the benefit of the injured person's beneficiaries under the **Fatal Accidents Act 1976, s. 1**, accrues on the date of death, with the result there are two limitation periods (*Reader v Molesworths Bright Clegg* [2007] EWCA Civ 169, [2007] 1 WLR 1082).

Fatal accidents and death: date of knowledge

10.29 In proceedings brought for the benefit of the deceased's estate under the **Law Reform (Miscellaneous Provisions) Act 1934** time runs from the date of death or the personal representative's 'date of knowledge' (LA 1980, s. 11(5)). Section 11(5) provides:

> If in a case where the damages claimed by the plaintiff consist of or include damages in respect of personal injuries to the plaintiff or any other person the injured person died before the expiration of the period mentioned in subsection (4) above, that subsection shall have effect as respects the cause of action surviving for the benefit of his estate by virtue of section 1 of the Law Reform (Miscellaneous Provisions) Act 1934 as if for the reference to that period there were substituted a reference to the period of three years from whichever is the later of—
> (a) the date of death; and
> (b) the date of the personal representative's knowledge.

Time runs in claims brought by dependants under the **Fatal Accidents Act 1976** from the date of death or the 'date of knowledge' (as set out in **10.14**) of the person for whose benefit the proceedings are brought (LA 1980, s. 12). Section 12(1) and (2) provide:

> **12. Special Time Limit for Actions under Fatal Accidents Legislation**
>
> (1) An action under the Fatal Accidents Act 1976 shall not be brought if the death occurred when the person injured could no longer maintain an action and recover damages in respect of the injury (whether because of a time limit in this Act or in any other Act, or for any other reason).
> Where any such action by the injured person would have been barred by the time limit in section 11 or 11A of this Act, no account shall be taken of the possibility of that time limit being overridden under section 33 of this Act.
>
> (2) None of the time limits given in the preceding provisions of this Act shall apply to an action under the Fatal Accidents Act 1976, but no such action shall be brought after the expiration of three years from—
> (a) the date of death; or
> (b) the date of knowledge of the person for whose benefit the action is brought;
> whichever is the later.

Latent damage

10.30 It follows from the decision in *Pirelli General Cable Works Ltd v Oscar Faber and Partners* [1983] 2 AC 1 noted at **10.7** that it is possible for a claim in tort to be statute barred before the claimant knows that damage has been sustained, because time runs from the date of damage rather than discovery. To mitigate this position the Latent Damage Act 1986 inserted ss. 14A and 14B into the LA 1980:

> **14A. Special Time Limit for Negligence Actions Where Facts Relevant to Cause of Action are Not Known at Date of Accrual**
>
> (1) This section applies to any action for damages for negligence, other than one to which section 11 of this Act applies, where the starting date for reckoning the period of limitation under subsection (4)(b) below falls after the date on which the cause of action accrued.
>
> (2) *Section 2 of this Act shall* not apply to an action to which this section applies.
>
> (3) An action to which this section applies shall not be brought after the expiration of the period applicable in accordance with subsection (4) below.

(4) That period is either—
 (a) six years from the date on which the cause of action accrued; or
 (b) three years from the starting date as defined by subsection (5) below, if that period expires later than the period mentioned in paragraph (a) above.

(5) For the purposes of this section, the starting date for reckoning the period of limitation under subsection (4)(b) above is the earliest date on which the plaintiff or any person in whom the cause of action was vested before him first had both the knowledge required for bringing an action for damages in respect of the relevant damage and a right to bring such an action.

(6) In subsection (5) above 'the knowledge required for bringing an action for damages in respect of the relevant damage' means knowledge both—
 (a) of the material facts about the damage in respect of which damages are claimed; and
 (b) of the other facts relevant to the current action mentioned in subsection (8) below.

(7) For the purposes of subsection (6)(a) above, the material facts about the damage are such facts about the damage as would lead a reasonable person who had suffered such damage to consider it sufficiently serious to justify his instituting proceedings for damages against a defendant who did not dispute liability and was able to satisfy a judgment.

(8) The other facts referred to in subsection (6)(b) above are—
 (a) that the damage was attributable in whole or in part to the act or omission which is alleged to constitute negligence; and
 (b) the identity of the defendant; and
 (c) if it is alleged that the act or omission was that of a person other than the defendant, the identity of that person and the additional facts supporting the bringing of an action against the defendant.

(9) Knowledge that any acts or omissions did or did not, as a matter of law, involve negligence is irrelevant for the purposes of subsection (5) above.

(10) For the purposes of this section a person's knowledge includes knowledge which he might reasonably have been expected to acquire—
 (a) from facts observable or ascertainable by him; or
 (b) from facts ascertainable by him with the help of appropriate expert advice which it is reasonable for him to seek;

but a person shall not be taken by virtue of this subsection to have knowledge of a fact ascertainable only with the help of expert advice so long as he has taken all reasonable steps to obtain (and, where appropriate, to act on) that advice.

14B. Overriding Time Limit for Negligence Actions Not Involving Personal Injuries

(1) An action for damages for negligence, other than one to which section 11 of this Act applies, shall not be brought after the expiration of fifteen years from the date (or, if more than one, from the last of the dates) on which there occurred any act or omission—
 (a) which is alleged to constitute negligence; and
 (b) to which the damage in respect of which damages are claimed is alleged to be attributable (in whole or in part).

(2) This section bars the right of action in a case to which subsection (1) above applies notwithstanding that—
 (a) the cause of action has not yet accrued; or
 (b) where section 14A of this Act applies to the action, the date which is for the purposes of that section the starting date for reckoning the period mentioned in subsection (4)(b) of that section has not yet occurred;

before the end of the period of limitation prescribed by this section.

These provisions apply to claims for negligence other than for personal injuries (s. 14A(1)). They do not apply while the claimant can rely on the defendant's concealment under s. 32 (*Williams v Lishman, Sidwell, Campbell and Price Ltd* [2010] EWCA Civ 418, [2010] PNLR 25). They are restricted to claims in tort, and do not extend to claims for 'contractual negligence' (*Société Commerciale de Réassurance v ERAS (International) Ltd* [1992] 2 All ER 82).

Latent damage: starting date Two alternative periods of limitation are provided by LA 1980, s. 14A(4), namely, six years from accrual and three years from the 'starting date'. The first of these periods is simply the usual period for claims in tort. Where the claimant was under a disability on the starting date, the period of three years in s. 14A(4)(b) runs from when he **10.31**

Commentary

ceased to be under a disability or died (s. 28A). The 'starting date' is the earliest date the claimant knew:

(a) that the relevant damage was sufficiently serious to justify proceedings; and
(b) that the damage was attributable to the alleged negligence; and
(c) the defendant's identity.

These concepts are very similar to those in s. 14 (see **10.14** to **10.18**) and it was accepted in *Hallam-Eames v Merrett* (1995) *The Times*, 25 January 1995, that the authorities on s. 14 apply to applications under s. 14A. 'Knowledge' in s. 14A means knowing with sufficient confidence to justify embarking on the preliminaries to issuing proceedings (*Haward v Fawcetts* [2006] UKHL 9, [2006] 1 WLR 682s). Regarding condition (b), it is clear the claimant does not need to know he has a cause of action, or that the defendant's acts would be characterised by the law as negligence. It is enough if the claimant has broad knowledge of the facts on which the complaint is based, and knows there is a real possibility that the defendant's acts or omissions caused the damage under condition (a) (*Haward v Fawcetts*). In *Gravgaard v Aldridge and Brownlee* [2004] EWCA Civ 1529, [2005] PNLR 19, the defendant solicitors negligently failed to advise the claimant that it was not necessary for her to transfer the matrimonial home into joint names with her husband before charging it as security to pay her husband's debts. It was held that the claimant did not have actual knowledge for the purposes of condition (b) until she knew that the exposure of her husband's share of the home to her husband's creditors was caused by the solicitors' wrongful advice. In *3M United Kingdom plc v Linklaters and Paines* [2006] EWCA Civ 530, [2006] PNLR 30, which was a negligence claim by a tenant against its solicitors complaining that an assignment of a lease had caused the loss of a break clause, it was held that the tenant had the relevant knowledge when, during negotiations with the landlord, it came to light that the break was no longer exercisable.

The knowledge of a loss adjuster appointed by the claimant's insurer in a subrogated claim can be attributed to the claimant for the purposes of s. 14A(5) (*Graham v Entec Europe Ltd* [2003] EWCA Civ 1177, [2003] 4 All ER 1345).

Section 14A(9) provides that knowledge that any acts or omissions did or did not, as a matter of law, involve negligence is irrelevant for the purposes of the provisions on date of knowledge in s. 14A. In *Bowie v Southorns* [2002] EWHC 1389 (QB), 152 NLJ 1240, it was held that this covers both knowledge of breach and knowledge that the defendant owed a duty of care, both of which are irrelevant for the purposes of date of knowledge under s. 14A(5).

A claimant is fixed with constructive knowledge by LA 1980, s. 14A(10). Knowing there had been large erosions in the capital in a pension scheme should have put the claimants in *Williams v Lishman, Sidwell, Campbell and Price Ltd* [2009] EWHC 1322 (QB), [2009] PNLR 34, on notice of possibly negligent advice by their pension adviser. In s. 14A(10), 'expert advice' means advice from an independent expert rather than one of the parties whose conduct is being called into question (*Williams v Lishman, Sidwell, Campbell and Price Ltd*).

10.32 **Latent damage: longstop** In order to give some protection to defendants who might otherwise be perpetually at risk, LA 1980, s. 14B, provides a longstop or overriding time limit for bringing proceedings of 15 years from the act or omission alleged to constitute the negligence causing the claimant's damage. *Financial Services Compensation Scheme Ltd v Larnell (Insurances) Ltd* [2005] EWCA Civ 1408, [2006] QB 808, held that the principle in *Re General Rolling Stock Co., Joint Stock Discount Co.'s claim* (1872) LR 7 Ch App 646 (see **10.59**) is not defeated by the longstop provision in s. 14B. The longstop is merely a procedural bar to bringing a claim.

Defamation

10.33 **Libel: accrual** Libel claims are actionable per se, so time runs from publication. Knowledge of the identity of the publisher is not an essential element of the cause of action (*Edwards v Golding* [2007] EWCA Civ 416, *The Times*, 22 May 2007).

Defamation: discretion to disapply Where defamation or malicious falsehood proceedings are not commenced within the one-year time limit, the court may direct that the limitation period shall not apply if it appears equitable to allow the claim to proceed, having regard to the balance of prejudice between the claimant and the defendant (LA 1980, s. 32A, as substituted by the Defamation Act 1996, s. 5). LA 1980, s. 32A, is modelled on s. 33, which provides a similar discretion in personal injuries cases, and which is considered in some detail at **10.19** to **10.26**. Permission was granted in *Wood v Chief Constable of West Midlands Police* [2004] EWCA Civ 1638, *The Times*, 13 December 2004, to add an alternative claim for slander four years after the event by way of an amendment at the close of evidence in a libel trial. Permission was also granted in *Gentoo Group Ltd v Hanratty* [2008] EWHC 627 (QB), LTL 11/4/2008, to include claims arising from material published on a website five days beyond the one-year limitation period. The court took into account the connection between the material published outside the limitation period and material published on the same website which came within the primary limitation period, the fact that the relevant evidence was no less cogent through the five-day delay, the seriousness of the alleged libels, and conduct of the defendant in seeking to deflect suspicion that he was responsible for some of the publications. **10.34**

The discretion was exercised against the claimant in *Hinks v Channel 4 Television Corporation* (2000) LTL 3/3/2000, principally because the claimant's solicitor had missed the one-year limitation period by relying, in April 1999, on a textbook written in 1994, which was before the limitation period was reduced from three years to one year in 1996. Another case where solicitors overlooked the one-year limitation period is *Steedman v British Broadcasting Corporation* [2001] EWCA Civ 1534, [2002] EMLR 17, in which it was held that an absence of prejudice to the ability to defend by reason of the delay is simply a factor, and in this case it was outweighed by the strong claim against the solicitors. *Steedman v British Broadcasting Corporation* should not be regarded as inconsistent with *Cain v Francis* [2008] EWCA Civ 1451, [2009] QB 754, discussed at **10.22**. Instead, there are different considerations in defamation and personal injuries claims, which are reflected in the shorter limitation period in defamation and an enhanced need to pursue any claim speedily (*Brady v Norman* [2011] EWCA Civ 107, [2011] EMLR 16).

CONTRACT

LA 1980, s. 5, provides: **10.35**

5. Time Limit for Actions Founded on Simple Contract

An action founded on simple contract shall not be brought after the expiration of six years from the date on which the cause of action accrued.

Time runs from the breach of contract. When this is depends on the nature of the obligation sued on and the terms of the contract, and also on whether a repudiatory breach is accepted by the claimant. Applying the general rule, causes of action in breach of contract will accrue as follows:

(a) In claims for breach of the implied terms about satisfactory quality etc. in the **Sale of Goods Act 1979** (SoGA 1979), time normally starts running on delivery of the goods (*Battley v Faulkner* (1820) 3 B & Ald 288).
(b) In claims for late delivery of goods, time runs from the contractual date for delivery.
(c) In claims based on the implied terms about title to goods sold, time runs from the date of the contract, or, in the case of an agreement to sell, from the date title was to pass (see **SoGA 1979, s. 12(1)**).
(d) Claims for the price of goods sold accrue on the contractual date for payment (**SoGA 1979, s. 49(2)**), failing which on the date property in the goods passes to the buyer (**s. 49(1)**) or the date the buyer is informed that the seller is ready and willing to deliver (**s. 28**).

(e) In a construction contract where the price is payable by stated instalments at the end of each month, time runs in respect of each instalment from the end of the relevant month (*Henry Boot Construction Ltd v Alstom Combined Cycles Ltd* [2005] EWCA Civ 814, [2005] 1 WLR 3850, at [60]).

(f) In a construction contract where stage and final payments are payable after certification by an architect or engineer, the certificate is a condition precedent to payment, so time runs from the date the certificate is issued or ought to be issued (*Henry Boot Construction Ltd v Alstom Combined Cycles Ltd* [2005] EWCA Civ 814, [2005] 1 WLR 3850, at [23] to [28] and [50]). This case also pointed out that there are separate causes of action based on interim and final certificates, even if the amounts certified are the same (at [56]).

(g) In claims based on defective building work, time usually starts running on practical or substantial completion (*Tameside Metropolitan Borough Council v Barlow Securities Group Services Ltd* [2001] BLR 113).

(h) Claims for the price of entire contracts for work and services accrue on completion of the work (*Emery v Day* (1834) 1 Cr M & R 245). In many building contracts the parties agree to stage payments, and time starts running in relation to these at the contractual date for payment.

(i) Claims by banks to recover overdrafts from customers normally accrue on service of a demand in writing (LA 1980, s. 6). There is an exception in s. 6 relating to loans where the debtor also enters into a collateral obligation to pay, such as by delivering a promissory note, but most bank overdrafts fall into the main category.

(j) Claims against sureties and guarantors usually accrue on default by the principal debtor (*Parr's Banking Co. v Yates* [1898] 2 QB 460).

(k) Accrual in the case of negotiable instruments is somewhat complicated. Claims against acceptors and makers based on non-payment accrue on the maturity of the instrument, unless it is a bill of exchange which is accepted after maturity, in which case time runs from the date of acceptance (Bills of Exchange Act 1882, s. 10(2)). Bills of exchange often mature on fixed dates, but if they mature (say) a fixed period of time after sight, time starts running that fixed period after acceptance (or after noting or protesting if it is not accepted) (s. 14(3)). A claim against a drawer or endorser after dishonour by non-payment accrues when the bill is duly presented for payment and payment is refused or cannot be obtained, or, if presentment is excused, when the bill is overdue and unpaid (s. 47(2)).

(l) Accrual in claims against insurers depends on the terms of the policy. The general rule is that time starts running at the date of the loss. For example, claims for constructive total loss accrue on the date of the casualty (*Bank of America National Trust v Chrismas* [1994] 1 All ER 401). However, it is open to the parties to displace the general rule by creating conditions precedent to the insured's right to payment. For example, in *Virk v Gan Life Holdings plc* [2000] Lloyd's Rep IR 159 critical illness benefit became payable under a policy if the insured survived 30 days after suffering a stroke. It was held that time started running 30 days after the stroke. Liability under an indemnity policy does not accrue unless and until the existence and amount of the liability to the third party is established (*Post Office v Norwich Union Fire Insurance Society Ltd* [1967] 2 QB 363).

In cases where the claimant has accepted an anticipatory breach as a repudiation, time starts running from the date of acceptance rather than the contractual date for performance of the obligation in question (*Reeves v Butcher* [1891] 2 QB 509). Claims for consequential losses, such as salvage charges arising out of a claim against an insurer based on the loss of a ship, are not separate causes of action, so accrual turns on the date of the underlying cause of action (the casualty) not on the date the consequential loss was incurred (*Bank of America National Trust v Chrismas* [1994] 1 All ER 401). There are several types of contractual obligation that give rise to continuing or repeated breaches. An example of a continuing breach is a failure to comply with a covenant to keep in repair (*Spoor v Green* (1874) LR 9 Ex 99 at p. 111), and an example of a repeated breach is a failure to pay rent (*Archbold v Scully* (1861) 9 HL Cas 360). In these cases the claimant will be able to succeed in respect of the consequences of breach over the six-year period (12 years for claims on a specialty) before the claim form is issued.

BREACH OF TRUST

Breach of trust: limitation periods

LA 1980, s. 21, provides: 10.36

21. Time Limit for Actions in Respect of Trust Property

(1) No period of limitation prescribed by this Act shall apply to an action by a beneficiary under a trust, being an action—
 (a) in respect of any fraud or fraudulent breach of trust to which the trustee was a party or privy; or
 (b) to recover from the trustee trust property or the proceeds of trust property in the possession of the trustee, or previously received by the trustee and converted to his use.

(2) Where a trustee who is also a beneficiary under the trust receives or retains trust property or its proceeds as his share on a distribution of trust property under the trust, his liability in any action brought by virtue of subsection (1)(b) above to recover that property or its proceeds after the expiration of the period of limitation prescribed by this Act for bringing an action to recover trust property shall be limited to the excess over his proper share. This subsection only applies if the trustee acted honestly and reasonably in making the distribution.

(3) Subject to the preceding provisions of this section, an action by a beneficiary to recover trust property or in respect of any breach of trust, not being an action for which a period of limitation is prescribed by any other provision of this Act, shall not be brought after the expiration of six years from the date on which the right of action accrued.
For the purposes of this subsection, the right of action shall not be treated as having accrued to any beneficiary entitled to a future interest in the trust property until the interest fell into possession.

(4) No beneficiary as against whom there would be a good defence under this Act shall derive any greater or other benefit from a judgment or order obtained by any other beneficiary than he could have obtained if he had brought the action and this Act had been pleaded in defence.

The main limitation periods are six years in claims for breach of trust and to recover trust property (LA 1980, s. 21(3)), and the unlimited period for bringing claims in respect of any fraud or fraudulent breach of trust to which the trustee was party or privy (s. 21(1)(a)) and for claims to recover from a trustee trust property in the possession of the trustee or which was previously received by the trustee and converted to the trustee's use (s. 21(1)(b)). A claim for an account of profits against a director following a deliberate non-disclosure of an interest was held in *Gwembe Valley Development Co. Ltd v Koshy (No. 3)* [2003] EWCA Civ 1478, [2004] 1 BCLC 131, to be a fraudulent breach of trust within s. 21(1)(a), so there was no period of limitation. It was held that a breach of trust is fraudulent if it was dishonest. *J. J. Harrison (Properties) Ltd v Harrison* [2001] EWCA Civ 1467, [2002] 1 BCLC 162, in which it was held that a claim to recover property conveyed to a director who was in breach of fiduciary duty came within s. 21(1)(b) (also resulting in there being no limitation period), was distinguished in *Gwembe Valley Development Co. Ltd v Koshy (No. 3)*. In *Re Pantone 485 Ltd, Miller v Bain* [2002] 1 BCLC 266 it was held that use of a beneficiary's money for the benefit of the fiduciary amounts to a conversion for the use of the fiduciary, and thereby brings the claim within s. 21(1)(b) (so there is no limitation period). Likewise, a claim for an account and payment of amounts found due to the estate from a personal representative were held to fall within s. 21(1)(b) in *Green v Gaul* [2006] EWCA Civ 1124, [2006] 4 All ER 1011.

A trustee who had negligently left trust money with a solicitor, who then embezzled it, but who was not a party to or privy to the solicitor's fraud, was held in *Thorne v Heard* [1894] 1 Ch 599 to be entitled to rely on a limitation defence after six years (class 9 in **table 10.1**). *Halton International Inc. v Guernroy Ltd* [2006] EWCA Civ 801, [2006] WTLR 1241 concerned a voting agreement between shareholders under which one shareholder was given power of attorney to act, in its absolute discretion, as the agent of and to vote the shares of the other shareholders. This was

Commentary

held to give rise to a bare promise, not a trust. A claim based on allegations of a failure to exercise those powers in good faith and not to make secret profits was therefore governed by the usual six-year limitation period, and did not come within LA 1980, s. 21(1)(b).

Breach of fiduciary duty

10.37 In *Nelson v Rye* [1996] 1 WLR 1378 it was held that a claim for breach of fiduciary duty *simpliciter* is outside the provisions of LA 1980, and so is not subject to any limitation period. This case has been called into question by subsequent decisions, particularly *Paragon Finance plc v D. B. Thakerar and Co.* [1999] 1 All ER 400. In *Nelson v Rye* the claimant was a musician and sought accounts from his former manager stretching back 11 years before proceedings were issued. Millett LJ in *Paragon Finance plc v D. B. Thakerar and Co.* pointed out that every agent owes fiduciary duties to his principal, and without something more the claim would have been subject to the usual six-year limitation period. The defendant in *Nelson v Rye* was no more than an accounting party who had failed to account. To have been entitled to a longer limitation period, the claimant would have had to show, among other things, that the defendant owed fiduciary duties in relation to the money.

Constructive trusts

10.38 Millett LJ in *Paragon Finance plc v D. B. Thakerar and Co.* [1999] 1 All ER 400 (and followed in *Coulthard v Disco Mix Club Ltd* [1999] 2 All ER 457) pointed out that there is a distinction between two categories of constructive trust claim:

(a) Where the constructive trustee, although not expressly appointed as a trustee, has assumed the duties of a trustee before the events which are alleged to constitute the breach of trust. In this category the defendant is a real trustee, and the provisions of the LA 1980, s. 21(1), may apply if the other conditions of the subsection are satisfied, with the result that there may be an unlimited period for bringing proceedings. It also applies to a constructive trustee who has given dishonest assistance (*Central Bank of Nigeria v Williams* [2012] EWCA Civ 415, [2013] QB 499). In *James v Williams* [2000] Ch 1 it was held on the facts that an executor de son tort, who was one of three surviving adult children of an intestate parent, became a constructive trustee, and consequently there was no limitation period by virtue of s. 21(1).

(b) Where the constructive trust is merely the creation of the court as a remedy to meet the alleged wrongdoing. It includes claims alleging knowing and dishonest assistance in the fraudulent breach of trust of another (*Cattley v Pollard* [2006] EWHC 3130 (Ch), [2007] Ch 353). In this category there is no real trust, and usually no prospect of a proprietary remedy. The defendant is merely said to be liable to account as a constructive trustee. In this category the other provisions of LA 1980 apply, with the result that the period will usually be six years from accrual. An example is *Halton International Inc. v Guernroy Ltd* [2006] EWCA Civ 801, [2006] WTLR 1241, discussed at **10.36**.

When considering the boundary between cases where the defendant is a true trustee under an express or constructive trust, and those where he is not, the key factor is whether there is trust property (*Clarke v Marlborough Fine Art (London) Ltd* (2001) *The Times*, 5 July 2001).

Beneficiaries

10.39 Different types of claims by beneficiaries have no time limits, 12-year and six-year time limits, see LA 1980, ss. 21 and 22. A right of action for non-fraudulent breach of trust does not accrue until a future interest falls into possession (LA 1980, s. 21(3)). Claims to the personal estate of a deceased person accrue on 'the date on which the right to receive the share or interest accrued'. Time was held to run from the end of the executor's year (one year from death) in *Re Loftus* [2005] EWHC 406 (Ch), [2005] 1 WLR 1890.

EQUITABLE REMEDIES, LACHES AND ACQUIESCENCE

LA 1980, s. 36, provides: 10.40

36. Equitable Jurisdiction and Remedies

(1) The following time limits under this Act, that is to say—
  - (a) the time limit under section 2 for actions founded on tort;
  - (aa) the time limit under section 4A for actions for libel or slander, or for slander of title, slander of goods or other malicious falsehood;
  - (b) the time limit under section 5 for actions founded on simple contract;
  - (c) the time limit under section 7 for actions to enforce awards where the submission is not by an instrument under seal;
  - (d) the time limit under section 8 for actions on a specialty;
  - (e) the time limit under section 9 for actions to recover a sum recoverable by virtue of any enactment; and
  - (f) the time limit under section 24 for actions to enforce a judgment;

  shall not apply to any claim for specific performance of a contract or for an injunction or for other equitable relief, except in so far as any such time limit may be applied by the court by analogy in like manner as the corresponding time limit under any enactment repealed by the Limitation Act 1939 was applied before 1st July 1940.

(2) Nothing in this Act shall affect any equitable jurisdiction to refuse relief on the ground of acquiescence or otherwise.

Claims for equitable damages or equitable compensation are claims to which s. 36 applies the six-year limitation periods in ss. 2 and 5 by analogy (*Companhia de Seguros Imperio v Heath (REBX) Ltd* [2001] 1 WLR 112). In such cases the question is whether prior to 1 July 1940 a court facing such a case would have applied a limitation period by analogy. However, trawling through ancient authorities to find actual instances where this had been done in the past is deprecated.

In *Clarke v Marlborough Fine Art (London) Ltd* (2001) *The Times*, 5 July 2001, it was said that it is probable that in undue influence claims the only time-related defences available are laches and acquiescence (and presumably, affirmation). The defences of laches and acquiescence are preserved by s. 36(2).

Laches is an equitable doctrine under which delay can bar a claim to equitable relief. Some form of detrimental reliance is usually an essential ingredient, which has to be considered together with the period of the delay and the nature of the acts done during the interval, with the court considering the balance of justice or injustice in either allowing or disallowing the continuation of the proceedings (*Fisher v Brooker* [2009] UKHL 41, [2009] 1 WLR 1764 at [62], [64]). It can only bar equitable relief (at [79]), so on the facts did not bar the claim which was for a declaration as to the long-term existence of a property right despite the passage of 38 years. Further, laches only applies where the defendant can establish prejudice, and even then only if that prejudice is not outweighed by any benefits obtained by the defendant through the delay.

The essence of the defence of acquiescence is that there has been an encouragement or allowance of a party to believe something to his detriment. Principles dealing with this defence were laid down in *Jones v Stones* [1999] 1 WLR 1739, which considered the older cases of *Willmott v Barber* (1880) 15 ChD 96 and *Habib Bank Ltd v Habib Bank AG Zurich* [1981] 1 WLR 1265. The first question is whether one party, by its action or inaction, has encouraged the other party to believe a certain state of affairs. The second question is whether there was reliance on that encouragement. Thirdly, whether in all the circumstances of the case it would be unconscionable for the first party to then insist on its legal right. It is incorrect to concentrate on the period of delay as being enough of itself. Lord Neuberger of Abbotsbury in *Fisher v Brooker* took the view at [62] that acquiescence does not add anything to the established equitable doctrines of laches and estoppel. The classic example of proprietary estoppel (standing by whilst a neighbour builds on one's land believing it to be his property) can be characterised as acquiescence. Similarly, laches (failing to raise or enforce an equitable right for a long period) can also be characterised as acquiescence.

The period of delay likely to give rise to these equitable defences depends on the nature of the relief claimed and the facts of the case. Delay in the context of interim injunctions is considered in **37.59**. For claims to redeem mortgages, a period of 20 years was said to be a convenient guide in *Weld v Petre* [1929] 1 Ch 33. Laches was held to be a defence in *Lynch v James Lynch and Sons (Transport) Ltd* (2000) LTL 8/3/2000 where a shareholder failed to assert his rights for 24 years.

LAND

Accrual in claims for the recovery of land

10.41 For recovery of land cases not governed by the Land Registration Act 2002 (see **10.42**), there are detailed rules dealing with accrual in LA 1980, sch. 1. For adverse possession against Crown land, and the 30-year period in LA 1980, sch. 1, para. 10, see *Hill v Transport for London* [2005] EWHC 856 (Ch), [2005] Ch 379. Broadly, time runs from the taking of adverse possession where the person bringing the claim has a present interest in the land but will be delayed until the determination of the preceding interest in the case of future interests. Use of the phrase 'adverse possession' is well established, but was regretted by the House of Lords in *J. A. Pye (Oxford) Ltd v Graham* [2002] UKHL 30, [2003] 1 AC 419 because it may be misleading. The question is whether the squatter dispossessed the paper owner by going into ordinary possession of the land for the requisite 12 years without the consent of the owner. There are two elements:

(a) Factual possession. This requires an appropriate degree of physical control, which depends on the circumstances, such as the nature of the land and the manner in which such land is commonly used. It has to be shown that the squatter has dealt with the land as an occupying owner might be expected to do, and that no one else has done so. Parking vehicles and delivering goods on the disputed land amounted to no more than use of the land in *Tennant v Adamczyk* [2005] EWCA Civ 1239, [2006] 1 P & CR 28. Anchoring a vessel in a tidal river may be sufficient (*Port of London Authority v Ashmore* [2009] EWHC 954 (Ch), [2009] 4 All ER 665).

(b) Intention to possess. What must be proved is an intention to possess, not a more extensive intention to own, or to acquire ownership, or to exclude the true owner. Lord Browne-Wilkinson described as heretical and wrong the concept, stemming from *Leigh v Jack* (1879) 5 ExD 264, that it must be shown that acts have been done which were inconsistent with the true owner's enjoyment of the land for the purposes for which he intended to use it. What is required is proof of an intention, in the squatter's own name and on his own behalf, to exclude the world at large, including the paper owner so far as was reasonably practicable and so far as the processes of the law would allow. Consequently, evidence that the squatter was willing to pay for his occupation if asked by the paper owner does not prevent time running against the paper owner.

The principles for establishing adverse possession laid down in *J. A. Pye (Oxford) Ltd v Graham* apply in all claims to recover land (*Ofulue v Bossert* [2008] EWCA Civ 7, [2009] Ch 1 (not affected by the further appeal); *Ashe v National Westminster Bank plc* [2008] EWCA Civ 55, [2008] 1 WLR 710). This includes claims by legal mortgagees against mortgagors in possession (*Ashe v National Westminster Bank plc*) and cases where the person claiming adverse possession believed he was a tenant because he had been let into the property by a former tenant (*Ofulue v Bossert*). It also applies in favour of the Crown (Limitation Act 1980, s. 37; *Roberts v Swangrove Estates Ltd* [2008] EWCA Civ 98, [2008] Ch 439). In *Ashe v National Westminster Bank plc* a mortgagee's legal charge was extinguished under the Limitation Act 1980, s. 17, 12 years after the last payment made by the mortgagor.

Registered land The provisions of the LA 1980 as regards registered land were replaced as from 13 October 2003 by the Land Registration Act 2002, sch. 6 and sch. 12. These support the principle under the 2002 Act that the register is to be a complete and accurate record of the state of the title to registered land at any given time, so that it will be possible to investigate title to land online and with the absolute minimum of additional enquiries and inspections. A person claiming adverse possession of registered land for at least 10 years is allowed to apply for registration. The usual evidence of adverse possession is required. Notice of the application is then served on the registered owner, and any chargees and other interested persons, and they may serve counter-notice. If they fail to do so, the applicant will be registered as the registered proprietor in place of the former proprietor, and free from former charges. If counter-notice is served, the application is dismissed unless one of three grounds is established. These are that it would be unfair to dispossess the applicant because of an equity by estoppel; that the applicant has an independent right which suggests he ought to be registered as the owner; or that there has been a reasonable mistake over boundaries. If an exception applies, the applicant is registered in place of the registered proprietor, and this happens notwithstanding objections from registered chargees. However, charges will continue to apply unless as a matter of general law the applicant's rights have priority over the charge. Where prior charges continue to apply, the applicant can apply for an apportionment of the charges between the land acquired by adverse possession and the remainder of the original title. 10.42

If an application under the 2002 Act is dismissed, the registered owner then has two years to take action to evict the person claiming adverse possession or otherwise regularise the position. If this is not done, once the two-year period has elapsed the person claiming adverse possession may reapply for registration, and, if still in possession, will be automatically registered in place of the existing registered owner. If this happens, the applicant is registered with a new, separate title, and takes free of any former registered charges.

Commentary

Extinction of title and the European Convention on Human Rights

The Grand Chamber of the European Court of Human Rights in *J. A. Pye (Oxford) Ltd v United Kingdom* (application 44302/02) (2007) 46 EHRR 45 held that the extinction of title under the Land Registration Act 1925 and LA 1980 after 12 years' adverse possession does not infringe **art. 1** of the First Protocol to the European Convention on Human Rights in the **Human Rights Act 1998, sch. 1** (no one shall be deprived of his possessions except in the public interest). The 12-year rule is part of general land law, and is intended to regulate the use and occupation of land between individuals. Similar rules, also without payment of compensation, apply in a large number of other European countries, so the rules cannot be said to be manifestly without reasonable foundation. It was held that a fair balance had been struck between the demands of the general interest and the interests of the individuals concerned. This was so even though the land in question was extremely valuable. Limitation periods, if they are to fulfil their purpose, have to apply regardless of the size of the claim. 10.43

Mortgages and deeds

LA 1980, s. 20, provides: 10.44

20. Time Limit for Actions to Recover Money Secured by a Mortgage or Charge or to Recover Proceeds of the Sale of Land

(1) No action shall be brought to recover—
(a) any principal sum of money secured by a mortgage or other charge on property (whether real or personal); or
(b) proceeds of the sale of land;

after the expiration of twelve years from the date on which the right to receive the money accrued.

(2) No foreclosure action in respect of mortgaged personal property shall be brought after the expiration of twelve years from the date on which the right to foreclose accrued.But if the mortgagee was in possession of the mortgaged property after that date, the right to foreclose on the property which was in his possession shall not be treated as having accrued for the purposes of this subsection until the date on which his possession discontinued.

(3) The right to receive any principal sum of money secured by a mortgage or other charge and the right to foreclose on the property subject to the mortgage or charge shall not be treated as accruing so long as that property comprises any future interest or any life insurance policy which has not matured or been determined.

(4) Nothing in this section shall apply to a foreclosure action in respect of mortgaged land, but the provisions of this Act relating to actions to recover land shall apply to such an action.

(5) Subject to subsections (6) and (7) below, no action to recover arrears of interest payable in respect of any sum of money secured by a mortgage or other charge or payable in respect of proceeds of the sale of land, or to recover damages in respect of such arrears shall be brought after the expiration of six years from the date on which the interest became due.

(6) Where—

(a) a prior mortgagee or other encumbrancer has been in possession of the property charged; and

(b) an action is brought within one year of the discontinuance of that possession by the subsequent encumbrancer;

the subsequent encumbrancer may recover by that action all the arrears of interest which fell due during the period of possession by the prior encumbrancer or damages in respect of those arrears, notwithstanding that the period exceeded six years.

(7) Where—

(a) the property subject to the mortgage or charge comprises any future interest or life insurance policy; and

(b) it is a term of the mortgage or charge that arrears of interest shall be treated as part of the principal sum of money secured by the mortgage or charge;

interest shall not be treated as becoming due before the right to recover the principal sum of money has accrued or is treated as having accrued.

A claim for the recovery of the principal due under a mortgage, even after the property has been repossessed and sold, is governed by the 12-year period in LA 1980, s. 20 (class 3 in **table 10.1**), but claims for interest are subject to a six-year limitation period as set out in s. 20(5) (*Bristol and West plc v Bartlett* [2002] EWCA Civ 1181, [2003] 1 WLR 284). A claim to enforce a charge by deed securing moneys guaranteed by the defendant is a claim on a specialty and governed by the 12-year limitation period (*Securum Finance Ltd v Ashton* [2001] Ch 291). It seems from *Global Financial Recoveries Ltd v Jones* (1999) *The Times*, 23 February 2000, that whether a claim for any shortfall after the realisation of mortgaged property (the mortgage being by deed) is one based on simple contract or specialty depends on whether the terms of the mortgage include the consequences of any shortfall.

In *West Bromwich Building Society v Wilkinson* [2005] UKHL 44, [2005] 1 WLR 2303, the defendants bought a property with a loan secured by a legal charge. The charge contained a proviso for redemption in conventional form. It also provided for a power of sale which was exercisable on demand of the money advanced or on five other events of default, including non-payment. Only two of the monthly instalments were paid. Default on the monthly payments, and obtaining and execution of an order for possession, occurred more than 12 years before the present proceedings, which sought judgment on the shortfall after sale of the property. Sale of the property was less than 12 years before the claim was issued. The building society argued that under the charge it had no right to recover the mortgage advance until the shortfall was quantified, which was when the property was sold. The House of Lords held that on the true construction of the charge, the principal money outstanding became payable when the power of sale became exercisable. Although the relevant clause did not in terms say this, the natural meaning of the clause was that the money became payable on making the demand or on the occurrence of any of the other events of default (at [19]). This was more than 12 years before the date of issue, so the claim was time-barred under LA 1980, s. 8.

A charge on a bankrupt's dwelling house in favour of the trustee in bankruptcy created by an order under the Insolvency Act 1986, s. 313, secures a future obligation, with no immediate right to receive any principal sum. Accordingly, time cannot run under LA 1980, s. 20(1), until an order has been made for the sale of the property (*Gotham v Doodes* [2006] EWCA Civ 1080, [2007] 1 WLR 86). Enforcement of a charging order (see **79.23** to **79.28**) is not an 'action brought to recover any principal sum secured by a...charge on property' within LA 1980, s. 20, and is not subject to any limitation period (*Ezekiel v Orakpo* [1997] 1 WLR 340; *Yorkshire Bank Finance Ltd v Mulhall* [2008] EWCA Civ 1156, [2009] 2 All ER (Comm) 164).

INDEMNITY AND CONTRIBUTION CLAIMS

At common law, an indemnity accrued on actual payment to the third party rather than on the event giving rise to the liability to the third party (*Huntley v Sanderson* (1833) 1 Cr & M 467). Equity, on the other hand, allowed a party to preserve its position by claiming an indemnity as soon as the liability was incurred, and to recover once the liability was established or quantified (*British Union and National Insurance Co. v Rawson* [1916] 2 Ch 476). The leading modern case is *Telfair Shipping Corporation v Inersea Carriers SA* [1985] 1 WLR 553. Accrual depends on the construction of the indemnity clause. The key question is usually whether the clause gives rise to the indemnity once primary liability to the third party has been ascertained or established, or whether the indemnity arises only after payment to the third party (*Socony Mobil Oil Co. Inc. v West of England Ship Owners Mutual Insurance Association (London) Ltd (No. 2)* [1989] 1 Lloyd's Rep 239). **10.45**

A contribution claim accrues on the date the amount of the underlying liability is fixed, disregarding any possible appeal. If the amount of underlying liability is determined by the court, time runs from judgment (LA 1980, s. 10(3)), which means judgment on quantum, not merely liability (see *Aer Lingus v Gildacroft Ltd* [2006] EWCA Civ 4, [2006] 1 WLR 1173). If the amount of the underlying liability is fixed by agreement, time runs from the date of settlement (s. 10(4)). Where a firm agreement to settle the primary claim is made, time starts running immediately under s. 10(4), and does not start again if the agreement is subsequently recorded in a consent order (*Knight v Rochdale Healthcare NHS Trust* [2003] EWHC 1831 (QB), [2004] 1 WLR 371). However, if the agreement requires the making of a consent order before it takes effect, time starts running from the consent order (*Knight v Rochdale Healthcare*).

STATUTES AND SPECIALTIES

A claim for damages for infringement of a right conferred by EU law amounts to a claim for damages for breach of statutory duty. It is therefore founded on tort and subject to a six-year limitation period under LA 1980, s. 2 (*R v Secretary of State for Transport, ex parte Factortame Ltd (No. 7)* [2001] 1 WLR 942). A claim to recover rent due under a lease under seal is governed by the six-year limitation period in class 10, not the 12 years in class 4 (*Romain v Scuba TV Ltd* [1997] QB 887). Although statutes are specialties, money claims pursuant to statute are governed by the six-year period in s. 9 (class 6) (see *Central Electricity Board v Halifax Corporation* [1963] AC 785 and *Re Farmizer (Products) Ltd* [1997] 1 BCLC 589), whereas claims for other remedies pursuant to statute will be governed by the 12-year period in s. 8 (class 4). Consequently, a claim to reopen an extortionate credit bargain under the Consumer Credit Act 1974, s. 139 has a 12-year limitation period running from the date of the agreement (*Rahman v Sterling Credit Ltd* [2001] 1 WLR 496 confirmed in *Nolan v Wright* [2009] EWHC 305 (Ch), [2009] 3 All ER 823). Direct claims against insurers under the Third Parties (Rights against Insurers) Act 1930, s. 1, are governed by the same limitation period, accruing on the same date, as is applicable against the original tortfeasor (*Matadeen v Caribbean Insurance Co. Ltd* [2002] UKPC 69 [2003] 1 WLR 670). Claims to recover unpaid council tax are subject to the six-year period in the Council Tax **10.46**

Commentary

(Administration and Enforcement) Regulations 1992 (SI 1992/613), reg. 34(3), which runs from the date the tax fell due (*Bolsover District Council v Ashfield Nominees Ltd* [2010] EWCA Civ 1129, [2011] Bus LR 492).

Money due under statute

10.47 In *Swansea City Council v Glass* [1992] QB 844 the council brought a claim to recover the cost of repairing a house owned by the defendant and let to a tenant where the defendant had failed to effect necessary repairs. The claim was brought under the Housing Act 1957, s. 10(3), and was commenced over six years after the work was done, but less than six years after a demand for payment. It was held that time ran from completion of the work, so the claim was statute barred. A claim to recover sums owed after revocation of a legal aid certificate under the Civil Legal Aid (General) Regulations 1989 (SI 1989/339), reg. 86, accrues on the date of revocation, not the date when the amount to be recovered has been quantified (*Legal Services Commission v Rasool* [2008] EWCA Civ 154, [2008] 1 WLR 2711).

Compulsory purchase compensation claims

10.48 In *Hillingdon London Borough Council v ARC Ltd* [1998] 1 WLR 174 it was held that a cause of action in respect of a claim for compensation under the Compulsory Purchase Act 1965, s. 9, accrues on the date of the acquiring authority's entry on the land. In *Halstead v Manchester City Council* [1998] 1 All ER 33 it was held that the statutory right to recover interest on compensation under the 1965 Act did not accrue until the amount on which interest became due was awarded or agreed.

Competition claims

10.49 A claim under the Competition Act 1998, s. 47A, accrues for the purposes of the Competition Appeal Tribunal Rules 2003 (SI 2003/1372), r. 31, on the 'relevant date', which is the end of the period for appealing to the Court of First Instance against a Commission decision, or, if such an appeal is lodged, the time when the appeal proceedings are determined. Decisions on infringement and the amount of any fine are separate for this purpose, so an appeal against the fine only does not postpone the relevant date (*BCL Old Co. Ltd v BASF SE* [2009] EWCA Civ 434, [2009] Bus LR 1516).

JUDGMENTS

10.50 By LA 1980, s. 24(1), an action may not be brought upon any judgment after the expiration of six years from the date on which the judgment became enforceable. A judgment for costs to be assessed is not enforceable for the purposes of s. 24(1) until the costs have been assessed (*Chohan v Times Newspapers Ltd* [2001] EWCA Civ 964, [2001] 1 WLR 1859). Insolvency proceedings, whether personal or corporate, are not 'actions' within the meaning of s. 24(1). Accordingly, a winding-up petition based on a judgment for costs obtained more than six years before the winding-up petition was held not to be time-barred in *Ridgeway Motors (Isleworth) Ltd v ALTS Ltd* [2005] EWCA Civ 92, [2005] 1 WLR 2871. Similarly, bringing an 'action' on a judgment does not include proceedings by way of execution (*Lowsley v Forbes* [1999] 1 AC 329), or by enforcement of a charging order (*Yorkshire Bank Finance Ltd v Mulhall* [2008] EWCA Civ 1156, [2009] 2 All ER (Comm) 164) or third party debt order (*Westacre Investments Inc. v Yugoimport SDPR* [2008] EWHC 801 (Comm), [2009] 1 All ER (Comm) 780.

A judgment creditor is entitled to bring a second claim seeking a judgment upon an earlier *unsatisfied judgment*. The juridical basis for the second claim is an implied contract to honour the first judgment (*Kuwait Oil Tanker Co. SAK v Al Bader* [2008] EWHC 2432 (Comm), LTL 23/10/2008). The only defence is that the second claim is an abuse of process. Requiring a fresh judgment to avoid problems in enforcing a judgment more than six years old is not an abuse. The court will impose a condition on the second judgment that permission to enforce it must be sought under **RSC, ord. 46, r. 2** in CPR, sch 1. If enforcement proceedings are brought more than six years after judgment, LA 1980, s. 24(2), will limit the interest that can be claimed on the judgment debt to that accrued over six years.

DISABILITY

Subsections (1), (2) and (6) of LA 1980, s. 28, provide: 10.51

28. Extension of Limitation Period in Case of Disability

(1) Subject to the following provisions of this section, if on the date when any right of action accrued for which a period of limitation is prescribed by this Act, the person to whom it accrued was under a disability, the action may be brought at any time before the expiration of six years from the date when he ceased to be under a disability or died (whichever first occurred) notwithstanding that the period of limitation has expired.

(2) This section shall not affect any case where the right of action first accrued to some person (not under a disability) through whom the person under a disability claims.

(6) If the action is one to which section 11 or 12(2) of this Act applies, subsection (1) above shall have effect as if for the words 'six years' there were substituted the words 'three years'.

There are two categories of persons under disability: children and persons who lack capacity (within the meaning of the Mental Capacity Act 2005) to conduct legal proceedings (LA 1980, s. 38(2)). By virtue of LA 1980, s. 28, time does not run against a child until his or her 18th birthday. Also by virtue of s. 28, time does not run against a person who lacks capacity if that person was under disability at the date the cause of action accrued. Thus, an adult who is immediately deprived of capacity by an accident is not subject to limitation until he or she recovers. The same applies to a child who, though not lacking capacity when a cause of action arises, loses capacity before reaching the age of majority. However, time will continue to run during a period of lack of capacity where a cause of action accrues to an adult who did not lack capacity at the date of accrual.

A potential defendant who is concerned that delay in bringing a claim by a person under disability may prejudice the trial through the evidence becoming stale may force the issue by bringing a claim for a negative declaration as to liability. The person under disability may choose to bring the substantive claim as a counterclaim to those proceedings. The court's decision whether to grant such a negative declaration is a matter of discretion rather than jurisdiction (*Messier Dowty Ltd v Sabena SA* [2000] 1 WLR 2040 as applied in *Eidha v Toropdar* [2008] EWHC 1219 (QB), LTL 6/6/2008).

ACKNOWLEDGMENTS AND PART PAYMENTS

Renewal of limitation period

Under LA 1980, s. 29, acknowledging title to land, acknowledging a debt and making part payments have the effect of renewing the limitation period from the date of acknowledgment or payment. Subsections (1) to (4) deal with acknowledgments relating to land and mortgages. Subsections (5) to (7) provide: 10.52

(5) Subject to subsection (6) below, where any right of action has accrued to recover—
  (a) any debt or other liquidated pecuniary claim; or
  (b) any claim to the personal estate of a deceased person or to any share or interest in any such estate;

and the person liable or accountable for the claim acknowledges the claim or makes any payment in respect of it the right shall be treated as having accrued on and not before the date of the acknowledgment or payment.

(6) A payment of a part of the rent or interest due at any time shall not extend the period for claiming the remainder then due, but any payment of interest shall be treated as a payment in respect of the principal debt.
(7) Subject to subsection (6) above, a current period of limitation may be repeatedly extended under this section by further acknowledgments or payments, but a right of action, once barred by this Act, shall not be revived by any subsequent acknowledgment or payment.

Section 29(5) applies to claims for debts and liquidated pecuniary claims. It does not apply to claims for damages (*City and General (Holborn) Ltd v Royal and Sun Alliance Insurance plc* [2010] EWCA Civ 911, [2010] BLR 639).

Acknowledgments

10.53 A statement of case can amount to an acknowledgment for the purpose of LA 1980, s. 29(5) (*Ofulue v Bossert* [2009] UKHL 16, [2009] 1 AC 990). An acknowledgment must, however, be precisely focused on the disputed right (*Surrendra Overseas Ltd v Sri Lanka* [1977] 1 WLR 565). A letter in which the defendant said he was 'happy to confirm that you suggest the following amounts are owed by me to you' was held to be a sufficient acknowledgment in *Ross v McGrath* [2004] EWCA Civ 1054, LTL 14/7/2004. *Bradford and Bingley plc v Rashid* [2006] UKHL 37, [2006] 1 WLR 2066, was essentially the same as *West Bromwich Building Society v Wilkinson* [2005] UKHL 44, [2005] 1 WLR 2303 (discussed at **10.44**). To avoid the claim being time-barred the lender sought to rely on letters sent on behalf of the defendant, one saying: 'at present, he is not in a position to repay the outstanding balance owed to you', and the other saying: 'He is willing to pay approximately £500 towards the outstanding amount as a final settlement'. It was held that both letters amounted to acknowledgments of the debt under s. 29, and started time running again. It did not matter that neither letter acknowledged the amount owed by the debtor. It was sufficient that they acknowledged the liability. It was said in *City and General (Holborn) Ltd v Royal and Sun Alliance Insurance plc* that it was not immediately obvious that an open offer in a small sum in response to a claim for a much larger amount could amount to an acknowledgment of the larger sum. An acknowledgment of a claim without an admission of liability is ineffective to start time running again under s. 29(5). It may amount to an estoppel by convention, for which see *Commissioners of HM Revenue and Customs v Benchdollar Ltd* [2009] EWHC 1310 (Ch), [2009] STC 2342.

Under s. 30 any acknowledgment must be in writing and signed by the person liable or by that person's agent. A typed signature on a telex is a sufficient signature for this purpose (*Good Challenger Navegante SA v Metalexportimport SA* [2003] EWCA Civ 1668, [2004] 1 Lloyd's Rep 67).

Part payments

10.54 Acknowledgments and part payments are explicitly separated and given equal status by LA 1980, s. 29(5). Part payments are not merely a subspecies of acknowledgments (*Ashcroft v Bradford and Bingley plc* [2010] EWCA Civ 223, [2010] 2 P & CR 13). Whether a part payment is 'in respect of' the sum owed is a question of fact. Once it is established that a payment has been made, if there is no other debt owed by the defendant to the claimant, it is permissible to infer that the payment was in respect of the debt sued for. It may be different where the part payment is clearly referable to an admitted part of a debt (*Surrendra Overseas Ltd v Sri Lanka* [1977] 1 WLR 565). All that s. 29(5) does is to enlarge the time for bringing a claim, it does not fix the amount of the debt (*Ashcroft v Bradford and Bingley plc*). The part payment of rent or interest due at any time does not extend the time for claiming the balance (s. 29(6)). However, a payment made outside a repayment schedule has the effect of renewing the limitation period (*International Finance Corporation v Utexafrica sprl* [2001] CLC 1361).

FRAUD, CONCEALMENT AND MISTAKE

The commencement of a limitation period may be postponed under the LA 1980, s. 32, where there is fraud, concealment or mistake. Section 32 provides: 10.55

32. Postponement of Limitation Period in Case of Fraud, Concealment or Mistake

(1) Subject to subsections (3) and (4A) below, where in the case of any action for which a period of limitation is prescribed by this Act, either—
 (a) the action is based upon the fraud of the defendant; or
 (b) any fact relevant to the plaintiff 's right of action has been deliberately concealed from him by the defendant; or
 (c) the action is for relief from the consequences of a mistake;
 the period of limitation shall not begin to run until the plaintiff has discovered the fraud, concealment or mistake (as the case may be) or could with reasonable diligence have discovered it.
 References in this subsection to the defendant include references to the defendant's agent and to any person through whom the defendant claims and his agent.

(2) For the purposes of subsection (1) above, deliberate commission of a breach of duty in circumstances in which it is unlikely to be discovered for some time amounts to deliberate concealment of the facts involved in that breach of duty.

(3) Nothing in this section shall enable any action—
 (a) to recover, or recover the value of, any property; or
 (b) to enforce any charge against, or set aside any transaction affecting, any property;
 to be brought against the purchaser of the property or any person claiming through him in any case where the property has been purchased for valuable consideration by an innocent third party since the fraud or concealment or (as the case may be) the transaction in which the mistake was made took place.

(4) A purchaser is an innocent third party for the purposes of this section—
 (a) in the case of fraud or concealment of any fact relevant to the plaintiff 's right of action, if he was not a party to the fraud or (as the case may be) to the concealment of that fact and did not at the time of the purchase know or have reason to believe that the fraud or concealment had taken place; and
 (b) in the case of mistake, if he did not at the time of the purchase know or have reason to believe that the mistake had been made.

(4A) Subsection (1) above shall not apply in relation to the time limit prescribed by section 11A(3) of this Act or in relation to that time limit as applied by virtue of section 12(1) of this Act.

(5) Sections 14A and 14B of this Act shall not apply to any action to which subsection (1)(b) above applies (and accordingly the period of limitation referred to in that subsection, in any case to which either of those sections would otherwise apply, is the period applicable under section 2 of this Act).

Fraud

In claims based on fraud, the limitation period does not begin to run until the claimant discovers the fraud or could with reasonable diligence have discovered it (LA 1980, s. 32(1)(a)). Time does not run while a claimant merely suspects the defendant is dishonest (*Barnstaple Boat Co. Ltd v Jones* [2007] EWCA Civ 727, [2008] 1 All ER 1124). Section 32(1)(a) applies only where fraud is the essence of the claim. An action in conversion where the defendant has incidentally been guilty of fraud or dishonesty does not bring the provision into effect (*Beaman v ARTS Ltd* [1949] 1 KB 550). 10.56

Concealment

Where any fact relevant to a claim has been deliberately concealed by the defendant, time does not run until the concealment is discovered or with reasonable diligence could have been discovered (LA 1980, s. 32(1)(b)). The normal test for whether a fact is 'relevant' for this purpose is whether that fact should be pleaded in the particulars of claim, although it may be 10.57

that this test should be modified (*Williams v Lishman, Sidwell, Campbell and Price Ltd* [2010] EWCA Civ 418, [2010] PNLR 25). A concealment may be 'deliberate' even if the defendant is not dishonest (*AIC Ltd v ITS Testing Services (UK) Ltd* [2006] EWCA Civ 1601, [2007] 1 All ER (Comm) 667). For the purposes of s. 32(1)(b), deliberate commission of a breach of duty in circumstances in which it is unlikely to be discovered for some time amounts to deliberate concealment of the facts involved in that breach of duty (s. 32(2)). 'Breach of duty' within the meaning of s. 32(2) includes executing a document to defraud a debtor's creditors contrary to the Insolvency Act 1986, s. 423 (*Giles v Rhind (No. 2)* [2008] EWCA Civ 118, [2009] Ch 191). At one time, LA 1980, s. 32(2), was interpreted by a number of authorities as meaning that time did not run where a professional person deliberately provided a service, even if the professional did not realise that the service was being provided in a negligent way (*Brocklesby v Armitage and Guest* [2002] 1 WLR 598 and *Liverpool Roman Catholic Archdiocese Trustees Inc. v Goldberg* [2001] 1 All ER 182). This line of authorities was overruled by *Cave v Robinson Jarvis and Rolf* [2002] UKHL 18, [2003] 1 AC 384, in which it was held that s. 32(1)(b) deprives a defendant of a limitation defence:

(a) where the defendant has taken active steps to conceal his breach of duty after he has become aware of it; and
(b) where the defendant is guilty of deliberate wrongdoing and conceals or fails to disclose it in circumstances where the wrongdoing is unlikely to be discovered for some time.

However, the mere fact that the defendant intended to do the act complained of does not mean that s. 32(1)(b) applies to prevent time running. If the defendant is unaware of his alleged error or that he may have failed to take proper care, there is nothing for the defendant to disclose, and time is not prevented from running by s. 32(1)(b). Consequently, to use examples referred to in *Cave v Robinson Jarvis and Rolf*, time will run where a surgeon negligently leaves a swab inside a patient; and where an anaesthetist negligently administers the wrong drug; and where a solicitor gives a client negligent advice. Time will not run if the surgeon deliberately left the swab inside the patient, or if the lawyer after giving negligent advice fails to disclose other facts which he is under a duty to disclose to the client which would have alerted the client to the negligent nature of the advice. Thus, there was concealment by a solicitor sued for the negligent conduct of litigation who failed to inform the client that the claim had been compromised and failed to tell the client he had agreed to a consent order (*Williams v Fanshaw Porter and Hazelhurst* [2004] EWCA Civ 157, [2004] 1 WLR 3185). Likewise, time did not run in favour of a testing services company when it failed to reveal to its principal the results of retesting of samples in *AIC Ltd v ITS Testing Services (UK) Ltd* [2006] EWCA Civ 1601, [2007] 1 All ER (Comm) 667.

In *Sheldon v R. H. M. Outhwaite (Underwriting Agencies) Ltd* [1996] AC 102 the claim was governed by a six-year limitation period and was allowed to continue although it was commenced 10 years after accrual. The defendants were alleged to have deliberately concealed material facts two years after accrual, and it was held that s. 32(1)(b) applies both where the concealment of the relevant facts was contemporaneous with the accrual of the cause of action and where it occurred subsequently. Concealment, for the purposes of s. 32(1)(b), will almost inevitably occur after the cause of action has arisen. In *Skerratt v Linfax Ltd* [2003] EWCA Civ 695, LTL 6/5/2003, it was held that there had not been concealment for the purposes of s. 32(1)(b) when, before allowing the claimant to take part in the activity which injured him, the defendant required him to sign a document which misled him to believe that he could not make a claim, and more than three years elapsed before a solicitor advised him that this was not so.

Mistake

10.58 Where a claim is for relief from the consequences of a mistake, time does not run until the mistake is, or could with reasonable diligence have been, discovered (LA 1980, s. 32(1)(c)). In *Kleinwort Benson Ltd v Lincoln City Council* [1999] 2 AC 349 the House of Lords held that LA 1980,

s. 32(1)(c), applies to all mistakes, whether of fact or of law, so that it could apply where the claimant had paid money to the defendant under a mistake of law. Conversely, a restitutionary claim made by a person who makes a payment to HM Revenue and Customs pursuant to an unlawful demand (see *Woolwich Equitable Building Society v Commissioners of Inland Revenue* [1993] AC 70) accrues when the payment is made. These cases were considered in *Deutsche Morgan Grenfell Group plc v Commissioners of Inland Revenue* [2006] UKHL 49, [2007] 1 AC 558, which held that s. 32(1)(c) applies where a taxpayer makes a mistake of law and as a result wrongly pays tax. Time ran against the taxpayer on its restitutionary claim from the date it discovered the mistake, which on the facts was the date of a decision of the Court of Justice of the European Union which clarified the relevant tax law. Lord Hoffmann at [20]–[30] dealt with the question of whether the taxpayer had made a mistake within s. 32(1)(c), or merely had a doubt as to the legal position (the latter does not come within s. 32(1)(c)). Even after the taxpayer became aware that there was a challenge to the English tax provision, the taxpayer took the view that the existing tax statute had to be complied with, which was held to be properly characterised as a mistake.

What amounts to 'reasonable diligence' is a question of fact. In *Peco Arts Inc. v Hazlitt Gallery Ltd* [1983] 1 WLR 1315, a case involving an alleged mistake over whether a 19th-century drawing was an original signed by the artist, it was held that the term meant doing what an ordinary prudent buyer of a valuable work of art would do. Depending on the facts, this might include taking suitable expert advice. See also *West Sussex Properties Ltd v Chichester District Council* (2000) LTL 28/6/2000. By way of exception, none of the provisions in s. 32 applies to the time bar on interest on judgment debts in s. 24(2) (see **10.50**), because execution of a judgment is not an 'action' within the meaning of s. 32 (*Lowsley v Forbes* [1999] 1 AC 329).

Commentary

COMMENCEMENT OF INSOLVENCY

A claim against a company which is not time-barred when the company goes into liquidation remains alive no matter how much time elapses thereafter (*Re General Rolling Stock Co., Joint Stock Discount Co.'s claim* (1872) LR 7 Ch App 646). In other words, limitation periods cease running from the date of the winding-up order (*Re General Rolling Stock Co.; Re Cases of Taffs Well Ltd* [1992] Ch 179) or resolution for voluntary winding up (*Re Northern Ontario Power Co. Ltd* [1954] 1 DLR 627; *Re Mixhurst Ltd* [1994] 2 BCLC 19). The same applies to claims against an individual when a bankruptcy order is made. Time ceases to run no matter which provision of LA 1980, including the latent damage provisions in ss. 14A and 14B, preserve the claim at the date of going into liquidation or bankruptcy (*Financial Services Compensation Scheme Ltd v Larnell (Insurances) Ltd* [2005] EWCA Civ 1408, [2006] QB 808). Lloyd LJ's remark in *Financial Services Compensation Scheme Ltd v Larnell (Insurances) Ltd* that the principle in *Re General Rolling Stock Co.* applies in 'all types of insolvency' is obiter and is, it is submitted, a dubious generalisation. The *Re General Rolling Stock Co.* principle cannot apply to administrative receivership and, depending on what the rationale for the rule is, it probably does not apply to any insolvency procedure other than bankruptcy, voluntary winding up and winding up by the court. **10.59**

AGREEMENT TO EXTEND

An agreement to extend time for commencing proceedings will be interpreted by applying the principles from *Investors Compensation Scheme Ltd v West Bromwich Building Society* [1998] 1 WLR 896, discussed at **89.22**, see *Gold Shipping Navigation Co. SA v Lulu Maritime Ltd* [2009] EWHC 1365 (Admlty), [2009] 2 Lloyd's Rep 484. **10.60**

ARBITRATION AND ADR

Arbitration and limitation

10.61 The normal limitation periods under the LA 1980 apply to arbitration (Arbitration Act 1996, s. 13(1)). In determining when a cause of action accrued, any provision that an award is a condition precedent to the bringing of legal proceedings (a *Scott v Avery* (1856) 25 LJ Ex 308 clause) is to be disregarded (s. 13(3)). In arbitration proceedings the parties are entitled to agree when the arbitration is to be regarded as having commenced for limitation purposes (s. 14(1)). If there is no such agreement, s. 14(3) to (5), set out three rules for when the arbitration is to be regarded as having commenced depending on how the arbitral tribunal is to be appointed. These are:

(a) where the arbitrator is named or designated in the arbitration agreement, arbitral proceedings are commenced when one party serves on the other party or parties a notice in writing requiring him or them to submit the dispute to the person so named or designated (s. 14(3));

(b) where the arbitrator or arbitrators are to be appointed by the parties, arbitral proceedings are commenced when one party serves on the other party or parties notice in writing requiring him or them to appoint an arbitrator or to agree to the appointment of an arbitrator in respect of the dispute (s. 14(4)); and

(c) where the arbitrator or arbitrators are to be appointed by a person other than a party to the proceedings, arbitral proceedings are commenced when one party gives notice in writing to that person requesting him to make the appointment in respect of the dispute (s. 14(5)).

If an arbitral award is set aside or declared to be of no effect, the court can direct that the period between the commencement of the arbitration and the relevant order is to be excluded (s. 13(2)).

Enforcement of arbitral awards

10.62 Enforcement of an arbitration award under the Arbitration Act 1996, s. 66, or bringing an ordinary claim on an award, are both subject to the six-year limitation period in the LA 1980, s. 7 (class 11 in **table 10.1**) (*National Ability SA v Tinna Oils and Chemicals Ltd* [2009] EWCA Civ 1330, [2010] Bus LR 1058).

ADR and limitation

10.63 Where there is a dispute, making use of ADR processes such as negotiation and mediation does not stop time running. **PD Pre-action Conduct, para. 9.6,** recommends that where it is not possible to complete the stages required by the protocols (which may include ADR) before the expiry of limitation, proceedings should be commenced to avoid the claim becoming time-barred, and the parties should seek to agree to apply to the court for a stay so that the remaining steps can be completed.

Limitation periods apply in respect of litigation and arbitration, so probably do not apply to non-adjudicative ADR processes or ADR processes where there is no dispute, such as expert determination (*Braceforce Warehousing Ltd v Mediterranean Shipping Company (UK) Ltd* [2009] EWHC 3839 (QB), LTL 4/6/2009).

CASES OUTSIDE THE LIMITATION ACT 1980

10.64 *The LA 1980 does not* apply to any action or arbitration for which a period of limitation is prescribed by or under any other enactment, whether passed before or after the passing of LA 1980 (LA 1980, s. 39). Warsaw Convention claims (class 17 in **table 10.1**) and cargo claims under the Hague–Visby Rules (class 23) are subject to substantive as opposed to procedural time bars (*Aries Tanker Corporation v Total Transport Ltd* [1977] 1 WLR 185). The same applies to defective product claims (class 5: *O'Byrne v Aventis Pasteur SA* (case C-358/08) [2010] 1 WLR 1375; *O'Byrne v Aventis Pasteur MSD Ltd* [2010] UKSC 23, [2010] 1 WLR 1412). In these cases the right of action ceases to exist after the expiry of the relevant time bar, which is not suspended, interrupted or extended by anything in the LA 1980 (*Laroche v Spirit of Adventure (UK) Ltd* [2009] EWCA Civ 12, [2009] QB 778, at [70]).

A claim which is outside the provisions of the LA 1980 (or other enactment creating a time bar) is not subject to a strict period of limitation (*Nelson v Rye* [1996] 1 WLR 1378). It may, however, be subject to a time limit by analogy to the LA 1980 (see s. 36 and *Coulthard v Disco Mix Club Ltd* [1999] 2 All ER 457), or it may be subject to the defences of laches and acquiescence (as in *Nelson v Rye* [1996] 1 WLR 1378, but see the discussion at **10.36**). For example, a claim against a mortgagee for failing to obtain a proper price on the sale of mortgaged property was held to be governed by a six-year limitation period by analogy with s. 2 in *Raja v Lloyds TSB Bank plc* (2000) *The Times*, 16 May 2000. In *Companhia de Seguros Imperio v Heath (REBX) Ltd* [2001] 1 WLR 112 a six-year limitation period was imposed on a claim for breach of fiduciary duty, by analogy with ss. 2 and 5.

By way of contrast, the court refused to apply any limitation period (other than laches and acquiescence) to a claim for specific performance of a contract in *P and O Nedlloyd BV v Arab Metals Co. (No. 2)* [2006] EWCA Civ 1717, [2007] 1 WLR 2288. Undue influence claims fall outside LA 1980 (*Clarke v Marlborough Fine Art (London) Ltd* (2001) *The Times*, 5 July 2001, but see **10.40**). Further, if there is no limitation period, the court may still strike out the proceedings as an abuse of process. In *Taylor v Ribby Hall Leisure Ltd* [1998] 1 WLR 400 an application to commit was delayed by about five years. It was struck out, the court taking into account factors such as the prospects of the court exercising its supervisory powers at the hearing, and the public interest in the efficient administration of justice and the compliance with court orders and undertakings.

Commentary

Agreement extending Landlord and Tenant Act 1954, part 2, time limits

The statutory period for commencing applications by landlords or tenants for new business tenancies under the Landlord and Tenant Act 1954, s. 24, and by landlords for orders terminating part 2 tenancies under s. 29(2), is set out in s. 29A(2). Where the landlord has given a notice under s. 25, the statutory period ends on the date specified in that notice, and where the tenant has made a request for a new tenancy under s. 26, it ends immediately before the date specified in the request. **10.65**

In the period between the landlord's notice under s. 25 or the tenant's request under s. 26 and the expiry of the statutory period, the parties may agree to extend the time for bringing an application under the Act for a specified period (s. 29B(1)). The parties may from time to time agree further, specified, extensions, but such agreements must be made before time has expired under the current agreement (s. 29B(2)).

Judicial review: discretionary extension

The three-month time limit for bringing a claim for judicial review can be extended if good reasons are shown, see **77.36**. **10.66**

Foreign limitation periods

Where, in accordance with the rules of private international law, the law of any other country is to be taken into account in any claim in England and Wales, the law of that other country relating to limitation must be applied (Foreign Limitation Periods Act 1984, s. 1(1)). When applying the foreign limitation period the question is whether the defendant can establish on **10.67** the balance of probabilities that the foreign court would have dismissed the claim on the ground of limitation (*Harley v Smith* [2010] EWCA Civ 78, [2010] CP Rep 33). If so, the claimant may seek to rely on the exceptions in s. 2, which include conflicts with public policy (s. 2(1)) and causing undue hardship (s. 2(2)), for which see *OJSC Oil Co. Yugraneft v Abramovich* [2008] EWHC 2613 (Comm), LTL 3/11/2008. In considering whether a claimant will suffer undue hardship under s. 2(2), problems caused by the fact the claimant's lawyer did not appreciate there was a short foreign limitation period are irrelevant (*Harley v Smith*). It is hardship caused by the application of the foreign limitation period that is relevant, not the effect of wrong legal advice. Further, uncertainty over how limitation is calculated in the foreign jurisdiction is not relevant hardship. In a case where there is uncertainty of this type it behoves those advising the claimant to issue proceedings promptly to avoid the difficulty.

Chapter 11 Where to Start Proceedings

JURISDICTION OF THE HIGH COURT AND THE COUNTY COURTS

Concurrent jurisdiction

The High Court and the county courts have concurrent jurisdiction over most claims. These include claims: 11.1

(a) in contract and tort (County Courts Act 1984, s. 15);
(b) for the recovery of land (s. 21);
(c) under the Inheritance (Provision for Family and Dependants) Act 1975 (County Courts Act 1984, s. 25);
(d) for relief from forfeiture (s. 139); and
(e) under the Landlord and Tenant Act 1954, part 2, in relation to the security of tenure of business tenants (Landlord and Tenant Act 1954, s. 63).

Cases where the jurisdiction of the county courts is limited

The jurisdiction of the county courts is limited in certain cases to claims which fall below 11.2
particular financial limits. For example, county courts have jurisdiction over claims in equity where the estate, fund or value of property does not exceed £30,000 (County Courts Act 1984, s. 23) (parties can in certain cases agree to vary this limit: s. 24). Other limits to the jurisdiction of county courts are set out in the **High Court and County Courts Jurisdiction Order 1991 (SI 1991/724), art. 2.**

Further, the following claims may not be conducted in a county court, whatever their financial value, unless (in the case of paragraphs (c) and (d)) the parties agree in writing:

(a) a claim for judicial review, as a county court does not have the power to make any of the orders asked for in judicial review claims (County Courts Act 1984, s. 38(3)(a)) except on a claim under the Equality Act 2010 (see 11.3(d)): judicial review is assigned to the Queen's Bench Division by the Senior Courts Act 1981, sch. 1, para. 2(b) (referred to in **PD 7A, para. 2.6**), and claims are dealt with in the Administrative Court (**PD 54A, para. 2.1**; **PD 54D, para. 2.1**);
(b) an application for a writ of habeas corpus, which must be made in the Queen's Bench Division (Senior Courts Act 1981, sch. 1, para. 2(a); **PD 7A, para. 2.6**), unless it is an application by a parent or guardian of a child in relation to the custody care or control of the child, in which case it must be made in the Family Division (**RSC, ord. 54, r. 11 in CPR, sch. 1**);
(c) a claim for libel or slander (County Courts Act 1984, s. 15(2)(c); **PD 7A, para. 2.9**);

(d) a claim in which the title to any toll, fair, market or franchise is in question (County Courts Act 1984, s. 15(2)(b); **PD 7A, para. 2.9**);
(e) applications concerning the decisions of local authority auditors (**High Court and County Courts Jurisdiction Order 1991, art. 6**).

A claim under the **Human Rights Act 1998**, s. 7(1)(a), in respect of a judicial act may only be brought in the High Court. Any other claims under that section may be brought in any court (**CPR, r.** 7.11).

County courts no longer have Admiralty jurisdiction as defined in the County Courts Act 1984, s. 27 (Civil Courts (Amendment) (No. 2) Order 1999 (SI 1999/1011)). Most Admiralty claims must be started in the Admiralty Court in the Queen's Bench Division (**CPR, r.** 61.2).

Cases which must be brought in a county court

11.3 Certain claims must be brought in a county court:

(a) Claims under the Consumer Credit Act 1974 may only be brought in a county court, normally the county court where the debtor resides or carries on business (**PD 7B, para.** 4).
(b) A mortgage possession claim must be brought in the county court for the district in which the land is situated unless circumstances such as complex factual disputes or points of law of general importance justify starting a claim in the High Court (**CPR, r. 55.3; PD 55A, para.** 1).
(c) Applications under the Access to Neighbouring Land Act 1992, s. 1, must be started in a county court (**High Court and County Courts Jurisdiction Order 1991, art. 6A**).
(d) Proceedings under the Equality Act 2010 to enforce claims of discrimination arising in the context of premises, education, associations or the provision of services must be brought in a county court (Equality Act 2010, s. 114). In any such proceedings, a county court has power make any of the orders which could be granted by the High Court in tort or in judicial review claims (s. 119(2)).
(e) Claims brought under **PD 8B** and the **Pre-action Protocol for Low Value Personal Injury Claims in Road Traffic Accidents** (**PD 8B, para. 1.2**).

ALLOCATION OF BUSINESS BETWEEN THE HIGH COURT AND COUNTY COURTS

11.4 Where the High Court and the county courts have concurrent jurisdiction, business is allocated according to the following rules:

(a) A claim for damages or for a specified sum may be issued in the High Court only where the value of the claim is more than £25,000 (increased from the old limit of £15,000 on 6 April 2009) (**PD 7A, para. 2.1**).
(b) **PD 29, para.** 2.2, restricts a claimant's right to continue proceedings issued in the Central Office or Chancery Chambers of the Royal Courts of Justice (RCJ). Although any money claim worth over £25,000 may be issued in the RCJ, claims with an estimated value less than £50,000 will generally be transferred to a county court, unless one of the following exceptions applies:
  (i) The claim is required by statute to be tried in the High Court.
  (ii) The claim falls within a specialist list as defined in **CPR, r.** 2.3(2). The specialist lists are the lists of proceedings in the Commercial Court (**r.** 58.2(1)), Mercantile Courts (*r. 59.1(3)(a)*) and the Technology and Construction Court (**r.** 60.2(1)). Claims falling within Part 63, Section I (see **r.** 63.2(1)), must be started in the Patents Court

or a patents county court (**r. 63.2(2)**) and form specialist lists (**r. 63.3**) for the purpose of **r. 30.5** (transfers are ordered by judge dealing with specialist claims), but other intellectual property claims within Part 63 do not. A county court may be designated as a patents county court under the Copyright, Designs and Patents Act 1988, s. 287(1).

(iii) The claim falls into one of the following categories: professional negligence, fraud or undue influence, defamation, malicious prosecution or false imprisonment, claims against the police, claims under the Fatal Accidents Act 1976, or contentious probate claims (**PD 29, para. 2.6**).

(iv) The claim is otherwise 'within the criteria of art. 7(5) of the **High Court and County Courts Jurisdiction Order 1991**' (SI 1991/724). This article has in fact now been repealed by the High Court and County Courts Jurisdiction (Amendment) Order 1999 (SI 1999/1014). It stated the following criteria: the financial substance of the action; its importance, and in particular whether it raises questions of importance to non-parties or the general public; its complexity; and whether transfer is likely to result in a more speedy trial of the action (although transfer may not be ordered on this ground alone).

(c) A claim for personal injuries must not be started in the High Court unless the value of the claim is £50,000 or more (**PD 7A, para. 2.2**).

(d) A claim must be issued in the High Court or in a county court, as appropriate, where an enactment requires it (**PD 7A, para. 2.3**).

(e) Subject to paragraphs (a) and (c) above, a claim should be started in the High Court if the claimant believes it should be tried by a High Court judge because of the financial value of the claim and the amount in dispute, its complexity or its importance to the general public (**PD 7A, para. 2.4**). In other words, the £25,000 and £50,000 limits are the lowest thresholds for issuing a claim in the High Court. But, even where a case is worth more than these amounts, the claimant should not issue automatically in the High Court but should go on to consider the factors listed in **para. 2.4** in deciding whether trial by a High Court judge is really necessary.

By **PD 7A, para. 2.2**, the value of a claim is determined in accordance with the **High Court and County Courts Jurisdiction Order 1991, art. 9**. This simply cross-refers to **CPR, r. 16.3(6)**. Thus, the following must all be disregarded:

(a) interest;
(b) costs;
(c) any reduction for contributory negligence against the claimant;
(d) the value of any counterclaim or set-off; and
(e) the recoupment of benefits under the Social Security (Recovery of Benefits) Act 1997.

Table 11.1 Summary of the rules on allocation of business where both the High Court and the county courts have jurisdiction

Nature of claim	Venue
Money claim (i.e. claim for debt or liquidated demand or damages)	May be commenced in the High Court only if the claimant expects to recover more than £25,000.
Money claim issued in the RCJ	May be commenced in the RCJ, but will generally be transferred to a county court if worth less than £50,000, unless one of the exceptions stated in **PD 29, para. 2.2**, applies.
Claim for personal injuries	May be commenced in the High Court only if the value of the claim is £50,000 or more.

Commentary

ALLOCATION OF BUSINESS TO THE QUEEN'S BENCH DIVISION OF THE HIGH COURT

11.5 The following claims must be issued in the Queen's Bench Division of the High Court:

(a) applications for a writ of habeas corpus (Senior Courts Act 1981, sch. 1, para. 2(a); **PD 7A, para. 2.6**) except applications by a parent or guardian in relation to a child (see **11.2**);
(b) applications for judicial review (Senior Courts Act 1981, sch. 1, **para. 2(b); PD 7A, para. 2.6**);
(c) the proceedings specified in s. 30(1) of the Terrorism Prevention and Investigation Measures Act 2011 (Senior Courts Act 1981, sch. 1, para. 2(bd));
(d) all financial restrictions proceedings within the meaning of the Counter-Terrorism Act 2008, part 6, chapter 2 (Senior Courts Act 1981, sch. 1, para. 2(bb));
(e) matters involving the exercise of the High Court's jurisdiction as a prize court (Senior Courts Act 1981, sch. 1, para. 2(c));
(f) Commercial Court claims (Senior Courts Act 1981, sch. 1, para. 2(d); see further **11.7(d)**).

A claim in the High Court ordered to be tried by jury will be transferred to the Queen's Bench Division, if not already being conducted there (**PD 7A, para. 2.8**).

CHANCERY BUSINESS

11.6 Claims involving Chancery business may be dealt with either in the High Court or in a county court (**PD 7A, para. 2.5**). The claim form must be marked 'Chancery Division' in the top right corner, if issued in the High Court, and 'Chancery Business' if issued in the county court (**PD 7A, para. 2.5**). The county court's jurisdiction over equity claims is limited to £30,000 (County Courts Act 1984, s. 23), though parties may agree to vary this in certain types of proceedings (s. 24).

PD 7A, para. 2.5, defines 'Chancery business' as including any of the matters specified in the Senior Courts Act 1981, sch. 1, para. 1. Those matters are:

(a) the sale, exchange or partition of land, or the raising of charges on land;
(b) the redemption or foreclosure of mortgages;
(c) the execution of trusts;
(d) the administration of the estates of deceased persons;
(e) bankruptcy;
(f) the dissolution of partnerships or the taking of partnership or other accounts;
(g) the rectification, setting aside or cancellation of deeds or other instruments in writing;
(h) probate business, other than non-contentious or common form business;
(i) patents, trade marks, registered designs, copyright or design right;
(j) the appointment of a guardian of a minor's estate;
(k) all causes and matters involving the exercise of the High Court's jurisdiction under the enactments relating to companies.

Within the £30,000 limit in the County Courts Act 1984, s. 23, any county court can deal with any Chancery business claim except that:

(a) county court probate claims must be brought in a court where there is a Chancery district registry or in the Central London County Court (**CPR, r. 57.2(3)**);
(b) county court claims falling within **Part 63, Section I** (see **r. 63.2(1)**), must be started in a patents county court (**r. 63.2(2)**; see **11.4**);
(c) other county court intellectual property claims may be brought either in a patents county court or in a county court where there is a Chancery district registry (**r. 63.13; PD 63, para. 16.2**); and

(d) insolvency and companies matters in county courts may only be brought in courts designated for those purposes in the Civil Courts Order 1983 (SI 1983/713) — in Greater London, such matters must be brought in the High Court (see **82.8** and **83.4**).

There are ten Chancery district registries, at Birmingham, Bristol, Caernarfon, Cardiff, Leeds, Liverpool, Manchester, Mold, Newcastle upon Tyne and Preston (**PD 63, para. 16.2**). The county courts at Caernarvon, Mold and Preston do not have jurisdiction in relation to registered or Community trade marks.

This means that there will be claims designated as Chancery business which are commenced in county courts with no Chancery expertise. Detailed guidance on transferring these cases, and also claims from the Chancery Division to an appropriate county court (and in particular to the Central London County Court, Chancery List), is given in the Chancery Guide, paras 13.4 to 13.11.

Any claim which raises an issue under the EC Treaty, art 81 (anti-competitive agreements) or art. 82 (abuse of a dominant market position) (now the Treaty on the Functioning of the European Union, arts 101 and 102), or the equivalent United Kingdom statutory provisions, chapter 1 or chapter 2 of the Competition Act 1998, must be transferred to the Chancery Division at the RCJ if commenced in any court other than the Commercial and Admiralty Court (**CPR, r. 30.8**). If a commercial claim, as defined in **r. 58.1(2)**, which raises a competition issue is commenced in the Queen's Bench Division or a Mercantile Court, any party may apply for the claim to be transferred to the Commercial Court instead of the Chancery Division. If the application to transfer to the Commercial Court is refused, the claim must be transferred to the Chancery Division at the RCJ in the usual way (**r. 30.8(4)**).

Commentary

SPECIALIST CLAIMS

Various rules and practice directions regulate the place where the specialist proceedings to which they relate should be started. In brief, the position is as follows: **11.7**

(a) Probate claims: **CPR, Part 57**, and **PD 57**. A probate claim to be conducted in the High Court must be issued in the Chancery Division, that is, either Chancery Chambers of the Royal Courts of Justice, or a Chancery district registry. (Chancery district registries are to be found at Birmingham, Bristol, Caernarfon, Cardiff, Leeds, Liverpool, Manchester, Mold, Newcastle upon Tyne and Preston.) A probate claim may be issued in a county court, but only where the value of the estate does not exceed £30,000 (County Courts Act 1984, s. 32). A probate claim in the county court can only be brought in a county court where there is also a Chancery district registry or in the Central London County Court (**CPR, r. 57.2(3)**).
(b) Companies Acts applications: **PD 49A**. Applications under the Companies Acts, and related legislation (see **85.3**), to be conducted in the High Court must be issued in the Companies Court of the Chancery Division, in the Royal Courts of Justice, or in a Chancery district registry. Applications under the Companies Acts and related legislation in county courts may only be brought in courts designated for those purposes in the Civil Courts Order 1983 (SI 1983/713) — in Greater London, such matters must be brought in the High Court.
(c) Technology and Construction Court (TCC): **CPR, Part 60**, and **PD 60**. Claims that involve issues or questions which are technically complex, or for which a trial by a judge of the TCC is desirable, may be issued in the TCC. TCC claims may be brought either in the High Court or certain county courts. In the High Court outside London, they may be issued in any district registry, but preferably in a district registry where a TCC judge will usually be available. These are: Birmingham, Bristol, Cardiff, Chester, Exeter, Leeds, Liverpool, Manchester, Mold, Newcastle upon Tyne and Nottingham (**PD 60, para. 3.3**). TCC claims may be issued only in the following county courts: Birmingham, Bristol,

Cardiff, Central London, Chester, Exeter, Leeds, Liverpool, Manchester, Mold, Newcastle upon Tyne and Nottingham (**PD 60, para. 3.4**). In recent years, there has been a significant increase in the work of the TCC in London and the TCC judges wish to ensure that only the most substantial cases are heard at the High Court in London. Accordingly in *West Country Renovations Ltd v McDowell* [2012] EWHC 307 (TCC), [2012] 3 All ER 106 Akenhead J, following consultation with the other TCC judges, stated that TCC claims worth less than £250,000 should be commenced in the county courts or High Court centres outside London that have TCC-designated judges instead of in the TCC in Fetter Lane in London. A non-exhaustive list of exceptions to this general rule is identified, including international claims, adjudications, public procurement cases, claims for an injunction or for a declaration, Part 8 claims, cases involving new or difficult points of law, test cases and complex nuisance claims.

(d) Commercial Court: **CPR, Part 58**, and **PD 58**. Commercial claims as defined by **CPR, r. 58.1(2)**, may be conducted in the commercial list in the Royal Courts of Justice and, if they are, they should be issued out of the Admiralty and Commercial Registry (**PD 58, para. 2.1**). By **CPR, r. 58.1(2)**, any case arising out of trade and commerce in general may be commenced in the Commercial Court, including any case relating to:

(i) a business document or contract;
(ii) the export or import of goods;
(iii) the carriage of goods by land, sea, air or pipeline;
(iv) the exploitation of oil and gas reserves or other natural resources;
(v) insurance and reinsurance;
(vi) banking and financial services;
(vii) the operation of markets and exchanges;
(viii) the purchase and sale of commodities;
(ix) the construction of ships;
(x) business agency; and
(xi) arbitration.

(e) Mercantile Courts: **CPR, Part 59**, and **PD 59**. Claims which are broadly commercial in nature, and which are not required to proceed in the Chancery Division or in any other specialist list may be issued in a Mercantile Court (**CPR, r. 59.1(2); see 2.19**). By **PD 59, para. 2.1**, a claim should only be started in a Mercantile Court if it would benefit from the expertise of a Mercantile judge.

(f) Patents etc.: **CPR, Part 63**, and **PD 63**. The jurisdiction of the Patents Court and the Patents County Court is conferred by the statutes concerning intellectual property rights. The Patents County Court is designed to deal with simpler and lower-value intellectual property disputes in a more cost-effective way.

(g) Admiralty proceedings: **CPR, Part 61**, and **PD 61**. An Admiralty claim listed in **CPR, r. 61.2(1)**, must be commenced in the Admiralty Court. County courts no longer have Admiralty jurisdiction (Civil Courts (Amendment) (No. 2) Order 1999 (SI 1999/1011)).

(h) The business assigned to the Family Division is listed in **2.14**.

An application to transfer a claim from one specialist list to another specialist list can be made to a judge dealing with claims in either list (**CPR, r. 30.5(3)**, *Natl Amusements (UK) Ltd v White City (Shepherds Bush) LP* [2009] EWHC 2524 (TCC), [2010] 1 WLR 1181).

APPLICATIONS BEFORE ISSUE

11.8 Applications made before a claim has started should be made to the court where it is likely that the claim to which the application relates will be issued, unless there is good reason to make the application to a different court (**CPR, r. 23.2(4)**). There is no explanation in the rules of what is meant by 'good reason' but one circumstance in which it would be appropriate to make an application in a different court is where a freezing injunction or search order (which may be made only by the High Court or a duly authorised judge, see 37.2) is sought in relation to a claim to be issued in a county court.

A pre-issue application in a designated money claim may be made in any county court (**r. 23.2(4A)**). See **11.9** for the definition of a designated money claim.

DESIGNATED MONEY CLAIMS

From 19 March 2012, the administrative functions of the county courts in the early stages of straightforward money claims have been centralised at the National Civil Business Centre ('the Business Centre'). **11.9**

Claims which fall within the new procedure are called 'designated money claims' and are defined in **CPR, r. 2.3(1)**, as any claim which is started in a county court under **Part 7**, for either or both of a specified or unspecified amount of money, and to which no special procedures apply. By **PD 7A, para. 4A.1**, in all designated money claims, the claim form (form N1) must be sent to the County Court Money Claims Centre, PO Box 527, M5 0BY. The claim will then be issued in the Northampton County Court.

The claimant must specify their 'preferred court' in the claim form (**PD 7A, para 4A.2**). The preferred court is the county court to which the proceedings will be transferred 'if necessary' (**CPR, r. 2.3(1)**). Broadly, it is the court to which the claim will be sent if it requires attention beyond routine processing, or if it proceeds beyond allocation stage and the parties have not specified any alternative court.

Designated money claims remain in the Northampton County Court until the 'relevant time' as defined by **r. 26.2A(6)**. This is broadly when all parties have returned their directions questionnaires. A designated money claim is transferred to the preferred court if:

(a) the claimant files a request for default judgment under **rr. 12.4** and **12.5** which includes an amount of money to be decided by the court (**r. 12.5A**);
(b) a defendant who is not an individual applies under **r. 13.4** to set aside or vary a default judgment on a claim for a specified sum (**r. 13.4(1B)**);
(c) the claimant files a request for judgment on an admission by the defendant under **r. 14.6** or **14.7**, for an amount of money to be decided by the court (**r. 14.7A**);
(d) a judge is to determine the time and rate of payment under **r. 14.12** on a judgment entered following an admission of liability and a request from the defendant for time to pay — automatic transfer under this rule will take place where the claim is for a specified sum only, the defendant is not an individual and the claim has not already been transferred to another court (**r. 14.12(2A)**); or
(e) a judge, or a court officer, has determined the time and rate of payment under **r. 14.11** or **14.12** without a hearing and either party makes an application under **r. 14.13** for the decision to be redetermined by a judge. Automatic transfer under this rule will take place where the claim is for a specified sum only, the defendant is not an individual and the claim has not already been transferred to another court (**r. 14.13(3A)**).

In each case, the transfer will happen automatically upon receipt of the request for judgment or application by the Business Centre. Automatic transfer to the defendant's home court is dealt with at **42.7**, and transfer to the claimant's preferred court is discussed at **42.8**.

COMMENCING IN THE WRONG COURT AND TRANSFER

Generally, when proceedings are commenced in the wrong court, they will be transferred to the correct court using the power under the County Courts Act 1984, ss. 40 to 42, and **CPR, r. 30.2**. The High Court has power under the County Courts Act 1984, s. 40(2), to order **11.10**

Commentary

transfer of a claim to the county court. Both the High Court and the county courts have power under the County Courts Act 1984, ss. 41 and 42, to order transfer from the county court to the High Court. An application to transfer a claim from one county court to another should be made to the court in which the claim is proceeding, not the court to which transfer is sought (**CPR, r. 30.2**). Applications for transfer between district registries of the High Court or from a district registry to the RCJ should also be made in the court where the claim is proceeding (**r. 30.2(6)**). Applications under **r. 30.5(1)** for transfer from one division to another may be made in either division (*Natl Amusements (UK) Ltd v White City (Shepherds Bush) LP* [2009] EWHC 2524 (TCC), [2010] 1 WLR 1181). Application for a transfer to or from a specialist list must be made to a judge dealing with claims in that list (**r. 30.5(3)**).

However, **r. 30.5(3)** does not govern transfers of copyright and passing off claims falling within Part 63, Section II from the Patents Court in the High Court to the Patents County Court. This is because the Patents County Court is a specialist list only for the purposes of Section I of Part 63. For cases falling within Section II, transfer is instead governed by s. 40 of the County Courts Act 1984. Application should therefore be made to the sending court and can be made to a master rather than being referred to a judge (*DKH Retail Ltd v Republic (Retail) Ltd* [2012] EWHC 877, [2012] Bus LR 1363). The High Court has no power to order the transfer of proceedings within the special jurisdiction of a Patents County Court from the county court to the High Court (Copyright, Designs and Patents Act 1988, s. 289(1)). The factors to be taken into account in deciding whether to transfer a case to or from a Patents County Court are set out at **PD 30, para. 9** and the Copyright, Designs and Patents Act 1988, s. 289(2)).

The criteria to which the court must have regard when considering whether or not to transfer a case are set out at **r. 30.3**. An example of the application of these criteria, in this case to a claim being transferred from the county court to the TCC, is to be found in *Collins v Drumgold* [2008] EWHC 584 (TCC), [2008] CILL 2585. In deciding whether or not to make an order for transfer from one High Court division to another, the court does not have to decide that it is inappropriate for a case to remain in the division in which it has been issued, although the suitability of the expertise of its judges is the single most important consideration. Where the differences in the suitability of different courts for the particular type of case are less marked, factors such as cost and speed can be taken into account (*Natl Amusements (UK) Ltd v White City (Shepherds Bush) LP*).

It was held in *National Westminster Bank plc v King* [2008] EWHC 280 (Ch), [2008] Ch 385, that the High Court has power to transfer a case under the County Courts Act 1984, s. 40(2), even if the value of the case exceeds the county court limit. This case involved the enforcement of a charging order for £39,356, where the county court's jurisdiction is limited to £30,000. In making an order for the claim to be transferred to the county court, the High Court held that the county court's jurisdiction effectively derived from the order of transfer. This decision was followed by the Court of Appeal in *Wallace v Crossley* [2009] EWCA Civ 896, LTL 26/8/2009.

The claimant will usually be penalised by being ordered to pay the costs involved in the transfer. In addition, where proceedings which, in the court's opinion, should have been commenced in a county court have been commenced in the High Court, the court may reduce any award of costs by up to 25 per cent (Senior Courts Act 1981, s. 51(8) and (9)). However, if a claimant brings a claim in the High Court in breach of a requirement that it should be in a county court (or vice versa), the court may either transfer the claim, or, if it is satisfied that the person bringing the claim knew or ought to have known of the requirement, strike out the proceedings (County Courts Act 1984, ss. 40(1)(b) and 42(1)(b); see *Adshead v Royal Bank of Scotland plc* [2002] EWHC 192 (Ch), LTL 25/2/2002). According to *Restick v Crickmore* [1994] 1 WLR 420, striking out is inappropriate for bona fide mistakes, but would be a proper response to instances where starting in the wrong court was a deliberate attempt to harass a defendant, or a deliberate attempt to run up unnecessary costs, or was done despite the claimant being told by the defendant where the claim should be commenced.

Where a claimant seeks to issue proceedings, and the court manager believes they are being issued in the wrong court, the court should nevertheless accept the papers. Court officials have no power to make judicial determinations as to whether they should accept a claim (*Gwynedd County Council v Grunshaw* [2000] 1 WLR 494). Once the claim is issued, an order for transfer may be made.

It is desirable to give notice to the court from which transfer is sought of the making of an application under **CPR, r. 30.2.** However, in *Neath Port Talbot County Borough Council v Currie and Brown Project Management Ltd* [2008] EWHC 1508 (TCC), [2008] BLR 464, this procedural irregularity did not prevent the TCC from determining an application for the claim to be transferred to it from a county court. **PD 60, para 5**, makes provision for the transfer of cases between the TCC in the High Court and County Courts, but provides no criteria for transfer. *Neath* also provides guidance for the factors to be considered on making applications for transfer to and from the TCC in London. See also *West Country Renovations Ltd v McDowell* [2012] EWHC 307, [2012] 3 All ER 106 (discussed in **11.7**).

Chapter 12 Issuing Proceedings

The following procedural checklists, which are at the front of the book, are relevant to this chapter and **chapter 15**:

Procedural checklist 3 Issue and service where service of the claim form is to be effected by the court

Procedural checklist 4 Issue and service where service of the claim form is to be effected by the claimant

METHODS OF COMMENCING CIVIL PROCEEDINGS

12.1 Lord Woolf's *Final Report* commented that 'A prime example of [the complexity of the old rules] is the fact that there are four different ways of starting proceedings in the High Court, and another four in the county courts' (ch. 12, para. 1). In order to further the aim of achieving simplicity in civil proceedings, Lord Woolf recommended that there should be a single claim form which could be used for every case (ch. 2, para. 3).

This radical simplification has not worked out in practice. First, during the drafting of the CPR it was realised that it is possible to use a simplified procedure (now in **CPR, Part 8**; see **chapter 13**) for certain classes of proceedings in which it is normal for there to be no disputes over facts. Secondly it was decided to create a special form of process for third-party and other subsidiary claims (**CPR, Part 20**; see **chapters 28** and **29**). Thirdly it was not possible, in time for the introduction of the CPR in April 1999, to assimilate the numerous varieties of specialist proceedings for which special forms of originating process existed under the old rules, and at present they remain exceptions under the CPR. Some of these exceptional procedures are prescribed by statute and some were excluded from the terms of reference of Lord Woolf's inquiry.

The result is that there are still at least 15 different ways of commencing claims in civil courts. These are by:

(a) Claim form (form N1; see **chapter 23**), which is the standard method under the CPR. Three special claim forms are prescribed for use in Admiralty claims (ADM 1, ADM 1A and ADM 15); there is a special version of form N1 for use in the Commercial Court (form N1(CC)); and a special claim form (N461) is prescribed for judicial review proceedings.

(b) Part 8 claim form (form N208), for use in proceedings in which there are no substantial factual disputes and where required by a practice direction (see **chapter 13**). There is a special version of form N208 for use in the Commercial Court (form N208(CC)) and a special Part 8 claim form (N500) has been prescribed for director disqualification proceedings. There is also a special claim form (N501) for applications under the Company Directors Disqualification Act 1986, s. 8A.

(c) Claim form (form N211) for additional claims under **CPR, Part 20** (see **chapters 28** and **29**). There is a special version of form N211 for use in the Commercial Court (form N211(CC)).
(d) Arbitration claim form (form N8), which is used in arbitration applications (see **72.2** and **72.3**).
(e) Special claim forms for starting a claim for possession of land (N5 and N5B), for relief against forfeiture of a lease (N5A) and for demotion of tenancy (N6).
(f) Special claim form (N2) for use in probate claims.
(g) A control order claim form relating to proceedings under the Prevention of Terrorism Act 2005, s. 11.
(h) A European Small Claims Procedure claim form, which is required for claims under Regulation (EC) No. 861/2007 (see **45.33**) and a European Order Payment application form, for claims under Regulation (EC) No. 1896/2006 (see **12.11**).
(i) Petition, which is required by statute or statutory instrument for various proceedings, such as divorce and judicial separation (which are not considered in this work), winding up of companies (see **chapter 82**) and bankruptcy (see **chapter 83**).
(j) Administration application, to obtain an order appointing an administrator of a company (see **82.102** to **82.117**).
(k) Application notice, which is required for an application under the Insolvency Act 1986 or the Insolvency Rules 1986 (SI 1986/1925) if it is not in pending proceedings (see **chapter 84**).
(l) Interpleader notice, which is used in certain circumstances in county court interpleader proceedings (**CCR, ord. 33** in CPR, sch. 2), but is not used in the High Court.
(m) Summons in respect of alleged offences contrary to the County Courts Act 1984, ss. 14, 92, and 124 (**CPR, r. 81.34**), which is a procedure more of a criminal nature than civil.
(n) Request, such as under the rules for enforcing parking penalties under the Road Traffic Act 1991 (**CPR, r. 75.3**).
(o) Some cases can be brought very informally simply by making an application by witness statement or affidavit, examples being an application under the Deeds of Arrangement Act 1914, s. 7 (**PD 8A, para. 12A**, which states that an application may be made either by Part 8 claim form or by witness statement), and an application for confirmation of a creditors' voluntary winding up of a company (Insolvency Rules 1986 (SI 1986/1925), r. 7.62).

Commentary

The point is made in **PD Pre-action Conduct, para 8.1**, and in most of the pre-action protocols themselves, that litigation is a last resort (see **chapter 8**). Complaints procedures and other forms of alternative dispute resolution should at least be considered before most forms of litigation are started: even if the whole dispute cannot be resolved by these means, the parties and their legal advisers should resolve the dispute as far as possible without litigation (*R (Cowl) v Plymouth City Council* [2001] EWCA Civ 1935, [2002] 1 WLR 803).

Use of incorrect form

A party who commences proceedings using the incorrect form is likely to be given permission, **12.2**
under **CPR, r. 3.10**, to rectify the error, applying the principle in **r. 1.1** of dealing with cases justly. Thus, in *Hannigan v Hannigan* [2000] 2 FCR 650, the court allowed the claimant to rectify an error in using the wrong form on the grounds that all the information the defendant needed to understand the case had been provided. Similarly, use of the wrong form to bring an application in insolvency proceedings (see **84.2**) is a formal defect or irregularity which does not invalidate the application unless it has caused substantial injustice which cannot be remedied by any order of the court (Insolvency Rules 1986, r. 7.55). For example, in *Phillips v McGregor-Paterson* [2009] EWHC 2385 (Ch), LTL 8/10/2009, use of a claim form instead of an insolvency ordinary application was excused because it had not caused injustice even though it meant that an insolvency application for summary judgment was not heard by a registrar but

by a master, whose decision was reversed on appeal. In *Re Osea Road Camp Sites Ltd* [2004] EWHC 2437 (Ch), [2005] 1 WLR 760, however, an application which had incorrectly been brought by claim form rather than by petition under what is now the Companies Act 2006, s. 994 (see **85.10**), was struck out on the grounds that **CPR, r. 3.10**, gives the court power to cure a defect in procedure under the CPR only.

In *Islam v Secretary of State for Communities and Local Government* [2012] EWHC 1314 (Admin), [2012] JPL 1378, the claimant incorrectly brought an appeal against the refusal of planning permission under s. 288 of the Town and Country Planning Act instead of s. 289. The court refused to permit an appeal under s. 289 out of time because to do so would have the effect of substituting a new claim. (For further discussion of using the incorrect form to initiate proceedings, see **1.27** and **23.4**.)

ISSUING A CLAIM FORM

12.3 Under the CPR, unless another method of commencing proceedings is required or permitted (see **12.1**), proceedings are started when the court issues, at the request of the claimant, a claim form (form N1) prepared by or on behalf of the claimant (**r. 7.2(1)**).

Issue, rather than service, is the relevant date for the purposes of the supply of court records of proceedings under **r. 5.4(1)** (*Advance Specialist Treatment Engineering Ltd v Cleveland Structural Engineering (Hong Kong) Ltd* [2000] 1 WLR 558). The date the claim is brought (i.e., the date on which the request for issue is delivered to the court office), as opposed to issued, is the relevant date for limitation (*Barnes v St Helens Metropolitan Borough Council* [2006] EWCA Civ 1372, [2007] 1 WLR 879; see **12.5**).

An issue fee is payable in accordance with the CPFO (see **appendix 3**). The court will issue the claim form by affixing the court seal (**CPR, r. 2.6(1)**), which it may do by hand or by printing a facsimile of the seal on the document, electronically or otherwise (**r. 2.6(2)**). There is nothing to prevent a claim being issued with a stated value well below the full value of the damage done, even though the effect may be that a lower issue fee will be payable (*Khiaban v Beard* [2003] EWCA Civ 358, [2003] 1 WLR 1626). The procedure for issuing and serving a claim is summarised in **procedural checklist 3** and **procedural checklist 4**, at the front of the book. Those procedural checklists should be read in conjunction with **chapter 15**.

Number of copies required

12.4 In order to have a claim form issued, the claimant must take or send to court one copy of the completed claim form for the court and one for each defendant (**CPR, r. 6.4(3)**). The rules do not mention a copy for the claimant's own use. However, a claimant who wants a file copy of the claim form as issued will be required to provide a further copy of the claim form which the court will seal and return to the claimant marked 'claimant's copy' (Queen's Bench Guide, para. 4.1.5).

Time of issue

12.5 For the purposes of the CPR, proceedings are started when the claim form is issued by the court (**CPR, r. 7.2(1)**). The date of issue is entered on the form by the court (**r. 7.2(2)**). For the purposes of the Limitation Act 1980 and other statutes a claim is 'brought' when the claimant's request for the issue of a claim form (together with the court fee) is delivered to the court office. That is also when the court is seised of the claim for the purposes of **Regulation (EC) No. 44/2001** (the **Brussels I Regulation**) (see **16.37**). The Court of Appeal confirmed in *Barnes v St Helens Metropolitan Borough Council* [2006] EWCA Civ 1372, [2007] 1 WLR 879, that the guidance in **PD 7A, para. 5.1**, clarifying **CPR, r. 7.2**, is correct, for the reason that the claimant is not responsible for any shortcomings of the court in failing to issue the claim form promptly and so should not be at risk of his claim being time-barred once the claim form is in the hands of the court (*Page v Hewetts Solicitors* [2012] EWCA Civ 805, [2012] CP Rep 40). In *Barnes v St Helens Metropolitan Borough Council*, the claim form was received by the court office on 4 November 2004 and date stamped by the court with that date. The limitation period expired the following day. Because of industrial action at the court offices, the claim form was not issued until Monday 8 November. The court held that the claim was not time-barred. Where, as here, a claim form is received in the court office on a date earlier than the date on which it is issued by the court, the claim is brought for the purposes of the Limitation Act 1980 on the earlier date (see **3.5** and **10.6**). Court officials will record the date of receipt of the claim form either on the claim form itself, or on its covering letter (**PD 7A, para. 5.2**). However **PD 7A, para. 5.4**, enjoins claimants for whom the date of receipt is crucial to make their own arrangements for recording it.

Notice of issue

Once the court has issued a claim form, it will assign the claim a number, create a case management file and send a notice of issue to the claimant, using form N205A, N205B or N205C, depending on whether the claim is for a specified or unspecified amount of money or whether it is a non-money claim. **12.6**

Issue by fax in the Admiralty and Commercial Registry

Appendix A to **PD 58** provides a procedure for claimants to make a request by fax for the issue of a claim form in the Admiralty and Commercial Registry in the RCJ when that registry is closed. Provided the procedure is followed, the claim form is treated as issued at the time when the fax is recorded by the registry as having been received. **12.7**

The electronic working scheme which permitted the electronic issue of claim forms in the Rolls Building jurisdictions and to which **PD 5C** applied has ceased to function because of a low take-up and technical problems.

CLAIM PRODUCTION CENTRE

Claim forms in debt recovery claims may be issued and served in bulk from the Production Centre in Northampton. The Centre issues and serves claim forms electronically either in the name of the Northampton County Court or in the name of any other county court whose name appears on the claim form, in accordance with **PD 7C**. Proceedings may be issued using the Centre only by persons, known as 'centre users', permitted to use it, such as credit card companies and public utilities. Any rule or practice direction requiring documents to be filed is complied with in claim production cases by delivering to the Production Centre data for the document in computer readable form (**PD 7C, para. 1.4(1)**). A code of practice provides for the forms of magnetic media that may be used when delivering data. **12.8**

Claims that may be issued at the Production Centre are restricted to county court claims for specified sums, in pounds sterling, up to £100,000 brought against only one defendant (or two if the same sum is claimed from each of them), none of whom has an address for service out of the jurisdiction, where the claimant is not publicly funded and does not have an address for service outside the United Kingdom, and where none of the parties is a child or protected party. The Centre will not deal with claims against the Crown, nor will it issue Part 8 claims. The Centre can deal with cases issued in the name of the Northampton County Court from issue, service, entry of default judgment and judgment on admissions, and to the registration of judgment and issuing warrants of execution. When a defence is filed the Centre will send a notice to the claimant requiring a reply within 28 days stating whether the claimant wishes the claim to proceed. If no such notification is given the claim will be stayed. If, however, notification is received that the claim is to continue, the proceedings will be transferred to (if the defendant is an individual) the defendant's home court (defined in **CPR, r. 2.3(1)**), or (if the defendant is not an individual) to the court for the area of the claimant's address (or that of the claimant's solicitors) (**PD 7C, paras 1.3(2)(e)** and **5.3**). A claim will also be transferred to the defendant's home court where an order for oral examination or enforcement (other than by warrant of execution, charging order or third party debt order) is made (**PD 7C, para. 1.3(2)(f)**).

The claimant can serve particulars of claim separately, once the Centre has issued and served the claim form. But in this case the claim form must state that the particulars will follow and include a brief summary of the claim. The claimant must file a certificate of service (form N215) at the Centre within 14 days of service. There is no requirement to file particulars of claim, unless the defendant files a defence and the claim is transferred to the defendant's home court, in which case the claimant must file a copy of the particulars at the court to which the claim is transferred. The requirement in **PD 16, para.** 7.3, to attach contractual documents to the particulars of claim in breach of contract cases does not apply to claims issued in the Production Centre, unless the particulars of claim are served separately under **PD 7C, para. 5.2** (**PD 7C, para. 1.4(3A)**).

CLAIMS UNDER THE CONSUMER CREDIT ACT 1974: FIXED-DATE CLAIMS

12.9 The court may in certain cases fix a date for a hearing upon issue of a claim form (**CPR, r. 7.9**). The claims for which the court will adopt this procedure are listed in **PD 7B, para. 3**. They are all claims under specified sections of the Consumer Credit Act 1974. A modified procedure applies to these claims, as set out in **PD 7B, para. 5**. It is as follows:

(a) The court will fix a hearing date on the issue of the claim form. Each party must be given at least 28 days' notice of the hearing date. Notice of the hearing date must be served at the same time as the claim form, unless the hearing date is specified in the claim form.

(b) The claimant must serve particulars of the claim with the claim form.

(c) The defendant should not file an acknowledgment of service. A defendant who wishes to defend the claim should file a defence, within 14 days after service of the claim form.

(d) Where the defendant fails to file a defence within 14 days, the claimant may not apply for judgment in default: **CPR, Part 12**, does not apply where the claimant is using the **PD 7B** procedure. The defendant may file a defence after the expiry of the 14-day time limit, but the court may take account of the delay in the costs order it makes.

(e) The court will usually dispose of the claim at the hearing, provided the defendant has not served a defence. If a defence has been served, the court may allocate the claim to a track and give directions.

MONEY CLAIM ONLINE

12.10 A claimant may start a claim electronically at the Money Claim Online website, http://www.moneyclaim.gov.uk, where a request can be made for the issue of a claim form by Northampton County Court (**CPR, r. 7.12; PD 7E, paras 1.2(1)** and **1.4**). Once a claim has been started in this way, the claimant can also file electronically a request for judgment in default, or judgment on acceptance of an admission of the whole of the amount claimed or the issue of a warrant of execution (**para. 1.2(2)**). The claimant can also view an electronic record of the progress of the claim. The record of each claim will be reviewed and, where necessary, updated every day until the claim is either transferred from the Northampton County Court or a party files a defence, or a part admission or an application notice requiring a hearing (**para. 13.2**).

By **para. 4**, Money Claim Online may only be used for money claims in sterling which are for less than £100,000. It may not be used where the claimant is a child or protected party, or is funded by the Legal Services Commission. Nor may it be used against more than one defendant (or more than two, where the claim is for a single amount against each of them) or where the defendant is the Crown or a child or protected party. The defendant's address for service must be within England and Wales, and the claimant's address for service must be within the United Kingdom.

The claimant requests the issue of a claim form by completing and sending an online claim form and electronically paying the appropriate issue fee at http://www.moneyclaim.gov.uk (**para. 5.1**). The claim is brought for the purposes of the Limitation Act 1980 on the date on which the online claim form is received by the court's computer system (**PD 7E, para. 5.4**). The court will serve a hard copy of the claim form on the defendant, and will also send the claimant notice of issue by post (**para. 5.5**). The claim form is deemed to be served on the fifth day after issue, whether that day is a business day or not (**para. 5.7**). The claim form includes a unique customer identification number or password to enable the defendant to gain access to the claim at the website.

The claimant may file particulars of claim with the claim form or serve particulars of claim separately to the claim form, provided they comply with the requirements set out at **para. 6.1**. The requirement in **PD 16, para. 7.3**, to attach contractual documents to the particulars of claim in breach of contract cases does not apply to Money Claim Online cases unless the particulars of claim are served separately under **PD 7E, para. 5.2** (**PD 7E, para. 5.2A**). The defendant may then acknowledge service or file a defence and/or counterclaim in the conventional way or by completing and sending the relevant online form.

By **para. 12**, where the Northampton County Court is not the defendant's home court, the court will transfer the claim to the defendant's home court (or, where the defendant is not an individual, the court for the district in which the claimant's address for service is situated) if:

(a) the defendant applies to set aside or vary judgment under **CPR, r. 13.4**;
(b) there is to be a hearing for a judge to determine the time and rate of payment under **r. 14.12**;
(c) a defence is filed to all or part of the claim under **r. 26.2**; or
(d) either party makes an application which cannot be dealt with without a hearing.

EUROPEAN ORDER FOR PAYMENT

Regulation (EC) No. 1896/2006 of 12 December 2006 (the 'EOP Regulation') has created a **12.11**
European order for payment ('EOP') procedure with effect from 12 December 2008. The purpose of the Regulation is to simplify, speed up and reduce the costs of litigation in cross-border cases concerning uncontested pecuniary claims by creating the EOP procedure, and to permit the free circulation of EOPs throughout the member States by laying down a common procedure for establishing liability to pay. Compliance with the EOP procedure renders unnecessary any intermediate proceedings in the member State of enforcement prior to recognition and enforcement (recital 9). The procedure established by the EOP Regulation is intended to serve as an additional and optional means for the claimant, who remains free to resort to a procedure provided for by national law. Accordingly, the Regulation neither replaces

nor harmonises the existing mechanisms for the recovery of uncontested claims under national law (recital 10).

The EOP Regulation applies to civil and commercial matters in cross-border cases, whatever the nature of the court or tribunal, but with various exceptions set out in art. 2(1) and (2). For this purpose, a cross-border case is one in which at least one of the parties is domiciled or habitually resident in a member State other than the member State of the court seised (art 3(1)).

The EOP Regulation lays down detailed procedural rules, and EOP applications are primarily governed by the EOP Regulation. Where the EOP Regulation is silent, the CPR apply with necessary modifications (**PD 78, para. 1.1**). When deciding which courts are to have jurisdiction to issue an EOP, member States should take due account of the need to ensure access to justice (EOP Regulation, recital 12). The procedure is based, to the largest extent possible, on the use of standard forms in any communication between the court and the parties in order to facilitate its administration and enable the use of automatic data processing.

An EOP application form A must be completed in English or accompanied by a translation into English, and filed at court in person or by post (**PD 78, para. 2.1**). An EOP application made to the High Court will be assigned to the Queen's Bench Division, but that will not prevent the application being transferred where appropriate (**para. 2.2**). The court seised of an EOP application must examine, as soon as possible and on the basis of the application form, whether the requirements set out in the EOP Regulation, arts 2, 3, 4, 6 and 7, are met and whether the claim appears to be founded (art. 8). The application will be rejected if the requirements are not met (art. 11). If the requirements are met, the court must issue, as soon as possible and normally within 30 days of the lodging of the application, an EOP using standard form E as set out in annex 5 to the EOP Regulation (art. 12(1)). The 30-day period does not include the time taken by the claimant to complete, rectify or modify the application. In the EOP, the defendant is advised of his options to:

(a) pay the amount indicated in the order to the claimant; or
(b) oppose the order by lodging with the court of origin a statement of opposition, to be sent within 30 days of service of the order on him.

Articles 13 to 15 of the EOP Regulation contain rules on service. Where the EOP Regulation is silent on service, the Service Regulation (Regulation (EC) No. 1393/2007) and the CPR apply as appropriate (**PD 78, para. 4**).

The defendant may lodge a statement of opposition to the EOP with the court of origin using standard form F (as set out in the EOP Regulation, annex 6), which must be supplied to him together with the EOP (art. 16(1)). A statement of opposition has to be sent within 30 days of service of the order on the defendant (art. 16(2)). If a statement of opposition is entered within the time limit laid down in art. 16(2), the proceedings continue before the competent courts of the member State of origin in accordance with the rules of ordinary civil procedure unless the claimant has explicitly requested that the proceedings be terminated in that event (art. 17(1)).

Detailed further provisions can be seen in the EOP Regulation, **CPR, Part 78** and **PD 78**.

Chapter 13 Part 8 Claims

The following procedural checklist, which is at the front of the book, is relevant to this chapter:

Procedural checklist 5 Claim under standard Part 8 procedure

TYPES OF CLAIM TO WHICH PART 8 APPLIES

Introduction

The Part 8 procedure is intended for cases where the nature of the relief or remedy sought, or the lack of factual dispute, would make the standard procedure unnecessarily cumbersome. It provides a speedy mechanism for disposing of claims without the need for particulars of claim (**CPR, rr. 8.9(a)(i)** and **16.1**), a defence (**rr. 8.9(a)(ii)** and **15.1**), or a directions questionnaire (because all Part 8 claims are allocated to the multi-track: **r. 8.9(c)**). Judgment in default is not available (**r. 12.2(b)**). By **r. 8.1(2)** and **(6)**, and **PD 8A, paras** 3.1 to 3.3, a claimant may use the Part 8 procedure to seek the court's decision on a question which is unlikely to involve a substantial dispute of fact (see **13.2**), or where a rule or practice direction requires or permits use of the procedure (see **13.3** and **13.4**). **13.1**

PD 8B, which came into force on 30 April 2010, sets out the procedure to be followed in certain situations covered by the **Pre-action Protocol for Low Value Personal Injury Claims in Road Traffic Accidents** (the **RTA Protocol**). See further **13.4**.

General claims unlikely to involve a substantial dispute of fact

Claims for which the Part 8 procedure may be used on the ground that they are unlikely to involve a substantial dispute of fact include claims which turn on a question of law, claims relating to the construction of a document or statute and applications for a declaration. However, Part 8 proceedings are wholly unsuitable for a disputed issue of estoppel, because estoppel requires careful pleading. Further, because the issue will be fact sensitive, it will not comply with the requirement in **r. 8.1(2)(a)** that the case should be unlikely to involve a substantial dispute of fact (*ING Bank NV v Ros Roca SA* [2011] EWCA Civ 353, [2012] 1 WLR 472). In some cases, the claimant will have the choice between (a) invoking the Part 8 procedure, and (b) issuing a Part 7 claim form and applying for summary judgment. However, as the Part 8 procedure does not permit the exchange of particulars of claim or defences, it will not be **13.2** suitable for claims where the parties need to set out their respective cases in complicated or lengthy statements of case. Nor will Part 8 be suitable for a claim where the claimant does not know until the defence is available whether the defendant admits the factual basis of the claim. But where a claim is suitable for determination under Part 8, the claimant may well find it a speedier mechanism for disposing of the claim than issuing proceedings under Part 7, even where these are dealt with by way of summary judgment.

Part 8 is the appropriate procedure for an application for a mediation settlement enforcement order under **r. 78.24(1)(b)(1)** where there are no existing proceedings in the jurisdiction (**PD 78, para. 22.2**). These provisions permit the enforcement of commercial mediation agreements in cross-border disputes under Directive 2008/52/EC.

Part 8 is also the appropriate mechanism to use where a party wishes to obtain court orders or declarations in relation to a disputed adjudication, although such applications should be the exception rather than the norm and orders should only be made in clear-cut cases (*Dorchester Hotel Ltd v Vivid Interiors Ltd* [2009] EWHC 70 (TCC), [2009] Bus LR 1026). The courts have been prepared to hear such cases under the Part 8 procedure even where there are disputed facts between the parties, provided these are facts which do not require oral evidence to determine. Where oral evidence is required on a limited factual dispute, the court is prepared to be flexible, to the extent of making orders for a hybrid Part 7 and Part 8 procedure which can accommodate oral evidence at the final hearing (*Vitpol Building Service v Samen* [2008] EWHC 2283 (TCC), [2009] Bus LR D65). This hybrid procedure is only suitable where the disputed issue of fact can be determined by a short hearing with a narrow focus and without the need for disclosure (*Forest Heath District Council v ISG Jackson Ltd* [2010] EWHC 322 (TCC), LTL 29/3/2010).

PD 8A, para. 3.1, gives the following examples where the Part 8 procedure may be used:

(a) Where a claim by or against a child or protected party has been settled before the commencement of proceedings and the sole purpose of issuing the claim form is to obtain the approval of the court to the settlement. **CPR, r. 21.10(2)**, says that **Part 8** must be used in these circumstances.

(b) Where a claim for provisional damages has been settled before the commencement of proceedings and the sole purpose of the claim is to obtain a consent judgment.

The Part 8 procedure must be used for the claims and applications listed in the table in **PD 8A, Section B**, as well as for any claim or application required by an Act, rule or practice direction to be commenced by originating summons, originating motion or originating application (**PD 8A, paras 3.2** and **3.3**).

Landlord and tenant claims under **PD 56, para. 2.1** are conducted under a Part 8 procedure, modified by **Part 56** and **PD 56**.

It is the claimant, or the claimant's legal advisers, who must choose whether to use the Part 8 procedure, but the rules enable the court to weed out claims for which the chosen procedure appears to be inappropriate. Where the court receives a Part 8 claim form, a court officer who believes it may not be appropriate for the claim may refer it to a judge for consideration (**PD 8A, para. 3.4**). The court may at any stage order a Part 8 claim to continue using the standard procedure, and give appropriate directions (**CPR, r. 8.1(3)**).

Claims and applications that must be made under Part 8

13.3 **PD 8A, Section B** sets out a table listing the claims and applications which must be made using the Part 8 procedure. The claims and applications fall into three categories:

(a) Applications and claims to which special provisions set out in **PD 8A, Section C**, apply, *modifying the usual Part 8 procedure*. The table cross-refers to the relevant paragraphs of **PD 8A, Section C**. There is no longer a standard, modified Part 8 procedure. Rather, different provisions apply to different applications in this category.

(b) Applications and claims dealt with in schedules 1 and 2 to the CPR (the re-enacted pro-visions of the RSC and CCR, respectively). The table cross-refers to the relevant schedule rules which modify the usual Part 8 procedure.
(c) Other claims and applications for which the Part 8 procedure must be used, without modification.

The table also specifies the Division to which the application is assigned.

The RTA Protocol and PD 8B

The **RTA Protocol** covers road traffic claims for personal injury worth no more than £10,000 arising out of accidents occurring on or after 30 April 2010. It provides a mechanism for the settlement of claims and the recovery of fixed legal costs under **CPR Part 45, Section III**, without the need for court proceedings. The pre-action processes which the parties are expected to follow are set out in detail at **8.34** to **8.47**, and are divided into two consecutive stages, Stage 1 and Stage 2. Following an admission of liability under Stage 1 and a negotiation over the amount to pay in Stage 2, the amount of the defendant's final offer, plus disbursements and fixed costs, the ('non-settlement payment') should be paid to the claimant, who may or may not accept it. Where there is no admission of liability, or there is an admission but the defendant fails to make a non-settlement payment, the claimant may issue proceedings under **Part** 7 in the usual way, exposing the defendant to the risk of Part 7 costs. Proceedings should be issued under **Part 8** where: **13.4**

(a) parties have complied with the terms of the **RTA Protocol**, but have not agreed quantum; or
(b) the court's approval is sought of a settlement of a claim under the **RTA Protocol** brought by a child; or
(c) it is not possible to follow the terms of the **RTA Protocol** before the expiry of the limitation period.

In each of these three cases, the procedure to be followed is set out at **8.48** to **8.55**. A settlement offer under the **RTA Protocol** takes effect as a type of Part 36 offer (see **8.57** to **8.59**).

Where proceedings are issued because of the imminent expiry of the limitation period, there is no need to include the documents required under the **RTA Protocol**. Instead, the claimant should issue a claim form in which he states that his claim is for damages and that a stay of proceedings is sought in order to comply with the **RTA Protocol** (**PD 8B, para. 16.2**). The court will issue the claim and order an immediate stay which can be lifted in due course if liability is admitted under the RTA Protocol but damages need to be determined by the court (**PD 8B, para. 16.5**).

PART 8 PROCEDURE

The Part 8 procedure is straightforward (see **procedural checklist** 5). The claim is begun by the issue of a Part 8 claim form. Evidence in support must be filed and served at the same time as the claim form is issued and served. The defendant responds by filing and serving an acknowledgment of service and evidence in opposition, but not a defence. The claimant may then serve evidence in reply. The court will automatically allocate the case to the multi-track, and will give directions for the disposal of the case. In most cases there will be a hearing, usually on written evidence only (but see **13.2** on cases for which a hybrid Part 7 and Part 8 procedure is appropriate). **13.5**

Issue and service of Part 8 claim

The claim is issued on claim form N208. The rules on issue and service contained in **CPR, Parts 6** and 7 (see **chapters 12** and **15**), apply to Part 8 claims, save that the only form which should be served with the claim form when it is served on the defendant is the form for **13.6** acknowledging service (form N210). Forms for defending or admitting the claim are not required (**rr.** 7.8(2) and **8.9(a)(iv)** and **(b)(ii)**).

As with any other claim form, a Part 8 claim form must be served within four months after issue, or six months where it is served out of the jurisdiction (**r.** 7.5). The provisions of **r.** 7.6 permitting a claimant to apply for an extension of time for service of the claim form apply also to Part 8 claims (*Barker v Casserly* (2000) LTL 24/10/2000).

Forms N208(CC) and N210(CC) are special versions of the Part 8 claim and acknowledgment forms for use in the Commercial Court (**PD 58, paras** 2.4 and 5.2).

Contents of Part 8 claim form

13.7 The following requirements for Part 8 claim forms are made by **r. 8.2**:

(a) The form must state that **Part 8** applies to the claim.
(b) The form must set out the question which the claimant wants the court to decide or the remedy the claimant is seeking, and the legal basis for the remedy claimed.
(c) If the claim is being made under an enactment, the claimant must identify the enactment.
(d) If the claimant is claiming, or the defendant is being sued, in a representative capacity, the claim form must state that fact and state what the capacity is.

In *Szekeres v Alan Smeath and Co.* [2005] EWHC 1733 (Ch), LTL 2/8/2005, a Part 8 claim form which was intended to seek an order for detailed assessment of a solicitor's bills failed to state the question to be decided, did not state the remedy sought, did not refer to the Solicitors Act 1974, did not state that **CPR, Part 8**, applied and did not contain a statement of truth. Despite these defects, it was held that the claim form contained enough information to convey the nature of the claim. That being so, the claim form was sufficient to commence the proceedings and there was no basis on which the court could decline putting the document into formal order.

Because of the nature of the procedure, it is not necessary in a claim started by a Part 8 claim form to serve particulars of claim, and **Part 16** does not apply to Part 8 claims (**r. 8.9(a)(i)**). Instead, any written evidence on which a Part 8 claimant intends to rely must be filed and served with the Part 8 claim form (**r. 8.5(1)** and **(2)**). Written evidence will usually be in the form of a witness statement or affidavit, but the matters included in the claim form may stand as the claimant's evidence, where the claim form is verified by a statement of truth (which it must be by virtue of **Part 22**) (**PD 8A, para.** 7.2).

Under **CPR, r. 8.2A**, a Part 8 claim form may be issued without naming a defendant, provided the court's permission is obtained first by issuing an application notice, with a copy of the draft claim form. This enables proceedings to be issued under **Part 8** where there is no defendant to a claim, or where the defendant is unascertained. Claim forms which do not name a defendant may be issued for certain proceedings without the court's permission. See the provisions of **PD 49A** discussed at 85.6; **PD 64A, para.** 5; and **PD 78, para.** 22.2.

Acknowledgment of service

13.8 The defendant responds to service of a Part 8 claim form by filing an acknowledgment of service, and serving a copy on the claimant and any other parties (**CPR, r. 8.3(1)**). Acknowledgment must be made in the appropriate form (N210) (**PD 8A, para.** 5.2).

An acknowledgment of service in a Part 8 claim must be verified by a statement of truth (**CPR, r. 22.1(1)(d)**).

The acknowledgment must be filed no more than 14 days after service of the claim form (**CPR, r. 8.3**) (unless **r. 10.3(2)** applies: see **18.2**). It is in the nature of the sort of claims which are suitable for determination by the Part 8 procedure, that a pleaded defence is inappropriate. Accordingly, the rules state that the defendant should not file a defence. Rather, any points which the defendant wishes to rely on in reply to the claim should be set out in a witness statement or affidavit. The provisions of **Part 15** in relation to defences do not apply to Part 8 claims (**r. 8.9(a)(ii)**) nor do **rr. 14.4** to **14.7** in relation to judgments on an admission (**r. 8.9(b)(i)**).

In the acknowledgment of service the defendant must:

(a) indicate whether he contests the claim (**r. 8.3(2)(a)**);
(b) if he seeks a different remedy from that set out in the claim form, state what remedy he seeks (**r. 8.3(2)(b)**);
(c) include his address for service (**r. 10.5**).

The acknowledgment must be signed by the defendant or his legal representative (**r. 10.5**). **Paragraphs 4.2** to **4.4** of **PD 10** specify who should sign the acknowledgment where the defendant is a company, corporation or partnership.

Consequences of failure to file an acknowledgment

Due to the nature of the proceedings, in a Part 8 claim the claimant may not obtain default judgment under **CPR, Part 12**, if the defendant fails to acknowledge service in time, or at all (**r. 8.1(5)**). However, a defendant who has not acknowledged service may not take part in the hearing of the claim unless the court gives permission, although he may attend the hearing (**r. 8.4**). Clearly the likelihood of permission being granted will depend on the reasons for the failure, the circumstances of the claim, the nature of the defendant's interest and the speed with which the claimant and the court were notified of the wish to be heard. **13.9**

In an application under the Town and Country Planning Act, 1990, s. 280, to which **PD 8A**, Section C, **para. 22**, applies, the rules make no provision for an acknowledgment of service to be served or filed by the respondent. Accordingly, in *Morris v Secretary of State for Communities and Local Government* [2009] EWHC 2302, LTL 8/10/2009, the fact that the respondent had not served an acknowledgment did not provide grounds for refusing to hear him. He had served a skeleton argument and copies of relevant documents so it could not be said that the applicant had not had time to consider the respondent's case.

Defendant's evidence

A defendant to a Part 8 claim who wishes to rely on written evidence (which by **PD 8A, para.** 7.2, may be in the form either of a witness statement or affidavit) should file and serve it when filing and serving the acknowledgment of service (**CPR, r. 8.5(3)** and **(4)**). If the deadline is missed, the case may proceed without the defendant's evidence. See *Clanbrassil Trust Co. v Clanbrassil (Nominees) Ltd* [2011] EWHC 1163 (Ch), LTL 28/3/2011, for an example of an application for permission to serve evidence late under **r. 8.5** and the court's approach to the exercise of its discretion under **r. 3.9** to grant relief from sanctions. **13.10**

In practice, 14 days may not be long enough to prepare evidence in opposition to the claim. After filing the acknowledgment, a party may apply to the court for an extension of time for filing and service of evidence, or for permission to serve additional evidence (**r. 8.6(1)(b)**; **PD 8A, para.** 7.4). Alternatively, parties can agree an extension of up to 14 days for filing and serving the defendant's evidence. The agreement must be in writing, and a copy of the agreement must be filed at court at the same time as the acknowledgment (**PD 8A, para.** 7.5(1) and (2)).

Commentary

For a Part 8 claim in the Commercial Court, the rule is modified to provide that the defendant's evidence must be filed and served within 28 days after filing an acknowledgment of service (**CPR, r. 58.12**).

In *Bovale Ltd v Secretary of State for Communities and Local Government* [2009] EWCA Civ 171, [2009] 1 WLR 2274, it was held that although courts have very wide powers to make directions in individual cases (see at [69]), they cannot declare that rules made by delegated legislation are to be disapplied or varied in future cases (in this case the court had sought to declare that time limits for service of evidence under **PD 8A, para. 22**, would be varied in future). See **1.7** on the power to make practice directions.

In *Kensington and Chelsea Royal London, Borough Council v Secretary of State for Communities and Local Government* [2012] EWHC 1785 (Admin), 162 NLJ 963, an interested party to Part 8 proceedings was allowed the costs of filing and serving Grounds of Defence as well as an Acknowledgement of Service, even though there is no requirement in **Part 8** to file a defence. There was no objection in principle to the party being awarded costs and it was appropriate in this case because it had a separate interest to the defendant and its defence clarified the issues.

Contesting jurisdiction

13.11 A defendant to a Part 8 claim may contest the jurisdiction of the English courts in the usual way provided for in **CPR, Part 11** (see **chapter 19**), by filing an acknowledgment of service, completing section C, and proceeding to make an application for an order that the court does not have jurisdiction. Any such application must be made within 14 days after filing the acknowledgment of service (**r. 11(4)(a)**).

Objecting to use of the Part 8 procedure

13.12 A defendant to a Part 8 claim who believes that the Part 8 procedure should not be used, should file an acknowledgment of service, completing section D, but at the same time should file and serve a statement of reasons for opposing the procedure (**CPR, r. 8.8(1)**).

The court has power to order the claim to continue as if it were an ordinary claim not governed by **Part 8**, and give appropriate directions (**CPR, r. 8.1(3)**). Upon receipt of the defendant's acknowledgment and evidence opposing the procedure, the court will consider how the claim should continue, and will give directions as to its future management (**r. 8.8(2)**).

Claimant's evidence in reply

13.13 If the defendant to a Part 8 claim files evidence, the claimant may file and serve evidence in reply within 14 days (**CPR, r. 8.5(5)** and **(6)**). Evidence may be served after this deadline with the permission of the court (**CPR, r. 8.6(1)(b); PD 8A, para. 7.5**). Alternatively, parties can agree an extension of up to 28 days for service of the claimant's evidence in reply. Any such agreement must be in writing (**PD 8A, para. 7.5(1)** and **(3)**).

Parties may also apply to the court for permission to serve and file additional evidence (**CPR, r. 8.6(1); PD 8A, para. 7.4**).

Case management of a Part 8 claim

13.14 Part 8 claims to which the usual procedure applies are automatically allocated to the multi-track (**CPR, r. 8.9(c)**) and there is no need to complete directions questionnaires. Part 26 does not apply. This implies that Part 8 proceedings will be treated as allocated to the multi-track and so fixed costs will not be restricted to small claims track costs, even when the amount at issue falls within the small claims track financial threshold (see *JR v Turner* (2009) LTL 3/11/2009, following *W v Robinson* [2002] CLY 389, for an application of this principle in child settlement cases). However, at a hearing of a Part 8 claim, the court has power under **PD 8A, para. 8.2**, to allocate a Part 8 claim to any specific track, in which case **CPR, rr. 26.5(3)** to **(5)** and **26.6** to **26.10**, apply. Also, under **r. 46.13(3)** the court may restrict the recoverable costs to those that would have been allowed on the track to which the claim would have been allocated if allocation had taken place.

The court may give directions immediately a Part 8 claim form is issued, either upon application of a party or on its own initiative (**PD 8A, para. 6.1**). The directions can include fixing a hearing date either where there is no dispute (for example, in child and protected party settlements) or where there is a dispute but it is convenient to give a hearing date (for example, in mortgage possession claims or applications for the appointment of trustees). If it has not fixed a hearing date earlier, the court will give directions for the disposal of the claim as soon as practicable after the defendant has acknowledged service and filed any written evidence or after the time has expired for this to be done (**PD 8A, para. 6.2**).

CPR, Part 29, applies to Part 8 claims automatically allocated to the multi-track and, as in all multi-track claims, the parties should try to agree appropriate directions for the management of the claim. Parties should submit these to the court either at the same time as filing the acknowledgment or at the latest by the time any case management conference is fixed.

Hearing of a Part 8 claim

On the hearing date, the court may proceed to hear the case and dispose of the claim or give case management directions (**PD 8A, para. 8.1**). **13.15**

Evidence at the hearing of a Part 8 claim will normally be adduced in written form. A party may only rely on evidence served after the time limits specified in **CPR, r. 8.5** (i.e. at the time of service of the claim form or acknowledgment of service, or in reply 14 days thereafter), with the court's permission (**r. 8.6(1)(b)**).

However, the court has power to require or permit oral evidence or to require a witness who has given written evidence to attend for cross-examination (**r. 8.6(2)** and **(3)**). Such an order may be appropriate where there is a limited factual dispute (*Vitpol Building Service v Samen* [2008] EWHC 2283 (TCC), [2009] Bus LR D65).

Additional claims and the Part 8 procedure

Counterclaims and other additional claims do not sit easily with Part 8 claims. A defendant to a Part 8 claim who wishes to bring any other claim may do so only with the permission of the court (**CPR, r. 8.7**). (See **chapters 28** and **29** on additional claims.) **13.16**

Chapter 14 Joinder and Parties

Commentary

The following procedural checklists, which are at the front of the book, are relevant to this chapter:

Procedural checklist 6	Approval of settlement or compromise involving a child or protected party, where sole purpose of claim is to obtain court approval
Procedural checklist 7	Interpleader proceedings: High Court
Procedural checklist 8	Interpleader proceedings: county court
Procedural checklist 9	Application for joinder

IDENTIFYING PARTIES WHEN COMMENCING A CLAIM

Description of parties

Under the CPR the party who makes a claim is known as 'the claimant' (**r. 2.3(1)**). The party against whom proceedings are brought is 'the defendant' (**r. 2.3(1)**). Parties to applications are referred to as 'applicant' and 'respondent' (**r. 23.1**). Parties to petitions are known as the 'petitioner' and the 'respondent'. Before 6 April 2006, parties to additional claims under **Part 20** were known as the 'Part 20 claimant' and 'Part 20 defendant'. From 6 April 2006, parties to additional claims are known by their titles as they appeared in the original claim (if they were claimants or defendants: **PD 20, para. 7.3**), but if they have been brought in under **CPR, Part 20**, they are known as the 'third party', 'fourth party' etc. (**PD 20, para. 7.4**). **14.1**

The heading of a claim form must include the full name of each party (**PD 16, para. 2.6**). The name of a party who is an individual must include the title by which he or she is known (**para. 2.6(a)**).

The form of words to be used in describing different types of parties in the headings of statements of case and other court documents is considered at **14.10** to **14.50** and in **table 14.1**.

Joinder of causes of action and parties

14.2 The Senior Courts Act 1981, s. 49(2), requires the court to exercise its discretion to ensure that:

as far as possible, all matters in dispute between the parties are completely and finally determined, and all multiplicity of legal proceedings with respect to any of those matters is avoided.

This is reflected in **CPR, r. 7.3**, which states that a single claim form may be used to start all claims which can be conveniently disposed of in the same proceedings. This does not require a claimant to include in his pleaded case all the heads of damage he could possibly argue against a defendant (*Khiaban v Beard* [2003] EWCA Civ 358, [2003] 1 WLR 1626). **Rule 19.1** states that any number of claimants or defendants may be joined as parties to one claim. There must, however, be a cause of action against all those joined (*Douihech v Findlay* [1990] 1 WLR 269, but see *Individual Homes Ltd v Macbream Investments Ltd* (2002) *The Times*, 14 November 2002, where a bank was joined as a party to enable it to recover the costs of complying with a witness summons). Joint claimants must have the same interest in the claim and must be represented by the same solicitors and counsel. The particulars of claim must be contained in or served with the claim form or served on the defendant within 14 days after service of the claim form but no later than the latest time for serving a claim form (**CPR, r. 7.4(1)** and **(2)**). In *Tetra Pak Ltd v Biddle and Co.* [2010] EWHC 54 (Ch), [2010] 1 WLR 1466, it was held that it would not be inconsistent with the CPR, and in particular **rr. 7.4** and **16.4**, for a claimant to serve separate particulars of claim on different defendants within the same claim.

Rule 19.3 (which does not apply to probate claims: **r. 19.3(3)**) deals with claims in respect of rights held by two or more persons jointly (as opposed to severally held rights, alternative claims and related claims). All persons jointly entitled to a remedy must be parties to the claim, either as joint claimants, if they are willing, or as defendants, if they are not (**r. 19.3(1)** and **(2)**). When claiming to recover land it is good practice, though not a legal requirement, to name as co-claimants, all the persons in whom title to possession is vested (*Dearman v Simpletest Ltd* (1999) *The Times*, 14 February 2000).

The court may consider the constitution of proceedings, and make appropriate orders of its own initiative, as part of its duty to manage a case. The case management powers given to the court expressly include power to direct that part of a claim (such as a counterclaim) be dealt with separately, power to consolidate (i.e. to order two separate claims to continue and be tried as if they were a single claim), and power to try two or more claims on the same occasion (**r. 3.1(2)**).

No guidance is provided about which claims it might be considered convenient to dispose of in the same proceedings. However, the court will take into account the overriding objective in coming to its decision, in particular the objectives of saving expense and of ensuring that cases are dealt with expeditiously and fairly. Thus claims involving common questions of law or fact between different parties, or different causes of action involving the same parties, should be dealt with in the same proceedings.

Persons unknown

14.3 **PD 7A, para. 4.1**, provides that a claim form must be headed with the title of the proceedings and that the title should include the full name of each party and each party's status in the proceedings (e.g. claimant, defendant, third party). All known forenames and the surname should be used. But a claimant who does not know the identity or name of a defendant may use a description rather than a name, or sue 'Persons Unknown', provided the description is *sufficiently clear to identify* who is included within it and who is not (*Bloomsbury Publishing Group Ltd v News Group Newspapers Ltd* [2003] EWHC 1205 (Ch), [2003] 1 WLR 1633; approved by the Court of Appeal in *South Cambridgeshire District Council v Persons Unknown* [2004] EWCA Civ

1280, *The Times*, 11 November 2004). This is of particular application in intellectual property claims where there is a clear case for an injunction against a defendant whose identity is not known to the claimant. For possession claims against squatters see **chapter 35**.

Rights against insurers in road traffic cases

Under the European Communities (Rights against Insurers) Regulations 2002 (SI 2002/3061), a claimant who is resident in an EEA country (the EU plus Iceland, Liechtenstein and Norway) bringing proceedings in tort arising out of a road accident may issue proceedings against the insurer of the vehicle alleged to be responsible for the accident (reg. 3). An 'accident' for the purposes of the Regulations means an accident on a road or other public place in the United Kingdom caused by, or arising out of, the use of any insured vehicle (reg. 2(1)). A 'vehicle' is any vehicle normally based in the United Kingdom intended for travel on land which is propelled by mechanical power, but not running on rails, and includes any trailer whether or not it is coupled (reg. 2(1)). A vehicle is 'insured' if there is a policy of insurance in force fulfilling the requirements of the Road Traffic Act 1988, s. 145 (SI 2002/3061, reg. 2(3)). If the Regulations apply, the insurer is directly liable to the claimant (reg. 3(2)), and the right to sue the insurer is in addition to the existing right of action against the driver (reg. 3(2)). **14.4**

Claims for wrongful interference with goods

A claimant bringing a claim for wrongful interference with goods must state in the particulars of claim the name and address of every person who, to the claimant's knowledge, has or claims an interest in the goods, but who is not a party to the claim (**CPR, r. 19.5A**). The defendant may then apply to the court for any person named to be made a party to the claim. If the defendant makes such an application, but the person sought to be joined fails to attend the hearing of the application or to comply with any directions made, the court may order that person to be deprived of any claim against the defendant in respect of the goods. **14.5**

This rule gives effect to the provisions of the Torts (Interference with Goods) Act 1977, ss. 7 and 8. These sections deal with the potential wrong of a defendant being doubly liable in damages to competing owners of goods. They deal with this wrong in two ways:

(a) Section 7 of the Act requires any order for relief in proceedings for wrongful interference to which two or more persons interested in goods are parties to be such as to avoid the double liability of the wrongdoer as between those persons. Where only one of two or more persons interested in goods is a party, and receives more from the wrongdoer than is properly due, the overpayment must be passed on to other persons interested or repaid to the defendant.

(b) Section 8 of the Act entitles the defendant to show that a third party has a better right to the goods which are the subject matter of the claim, and to rely on this as a defence to the claim or in reduction of the damages claimed.

ASSIGNMENT OF CAUSES OF ACTION: MAINTENANCE AND CHAMPERTY

Introduction

It sometimes happens that a litigant's rights and liabilities in a claim are voluntarily transferred to a non-party before judgment has been obtained. Whether such a transfer can be validly made depends on whether the transaction is tainted by maintenance or champerty (see **14.7** to **14.9**). Assignment of a cause of action arising from a contract may be forbidden by the **14.6**

Commentary

terms of the contract (*Ruttle Plant Ltd v Secretary of State for the Environment and Rural Affairs* [2007] EWHC 2870 (TCC), [2008] 2 All ER (Comm) 264). For a case on a defective assignment, see *Smith v Henniker-Major and Co.* [2002] EWCA Civ 762, [2003] Ch 182 (applied in *Finlan v Eyton Morris Winfield* [2007] EWHC 914 (Ch), [2007] 4 All ER 143).

Maintenance and champerty

14.7 Maintenance is the support of litigation by a stranger without just cause. Champerty is an aggravated form of maintenance. The distinguishing feature of champerty is the support of litigation by a stranger with a financial interest in their outcome, such as a share of the proceeds (*Giles v Thompson* [1994] 1 AC 142). Until 1967 champerty and maintenance gave rise to both criminal and tortious liability. The Criminal Law Act 1967 abolished champerty and maintenance as crimes and torts. But s. 14(2) of the Act expressly preserved the common law rule that contracts which are tainted by champerty or maintenance are 'to be treated as contrary to public policy or otherwise illegal'.

The doctrines of maintenance and champerty must be reappraised in light of current notions of public policy (*Trendtex Trading Corporation v Credit Suisse* [1982] AC 679; see also Sir Rupert Jackson's *Review of Civil Litigation Costs* (Ministry of Justice, December 2009)). The bounds of justification for supporting litigation by others have greatly widened in the last 50 years. Support of legal proceedings based on a bona fide community of pecuniary interest, religion, principle, problems or mutual protection is not likely to constitute maintenance (*Martell v Consett Iron Co. Ltd* [1955] Ch 363; *Hill v Archbold* [1968] 1 QB 686).

A contract of maintenance is unenforceable between the parties to it. However, the illegal maintenance of a claim does not give rise to a defence to the claim, or lead to it being stayed or dismissed, unless the proceedings are an abuse of process (*Abraham v Thompson* [1997] 4 All ER 362; *Murphy v Young and Co.'s Brewery plc* [1997] 1 WLR 1591). An order for costs can be made against the maintainer under the Senior Courts Act 1981, s. 51 (see *Germany v Flatman* [2011] EWHC 2945 (QB), LTL 10/11/2011). In *Media CAT Ltd v Adams* [2011] EWPCC 10, [2011] FSR 29, the court considered that there was a good arguable case that a wasted costs order should be made against solicitors who entered into champertous contingency revenue-sharing agreements which underpinned the whole case and without which the other party to the litigation would not have been sued.

There are two circumstances in which the rule against champerty and maintenance continues to be of relevance:

(a) The rule may still invalidate agreements whereby a stranger to litigation provides funding to enable a party to bring or continue a claim. Historically, this has precluded solicitors from entering into contingency fee arrangements with their clients. The decision of the Court of Appeal in *Thai Trading Co. v Taylor* [1998] QB 781 appeared to remove the prohibition against the type of contingency fee arrangement in which the solicitor agrees with the client not to charge if the claim fails, but to seek costs from the other side if the claim succeeds. Subsequent decisions (*Hughes v Kingston upon Hull City Council* [1999] QB 1193; *Awwad v Geraghty and Co.* [2001] QB 570) preserved the original rule. In *Sibthorpe v Southwark London Borough Council* [2011] EWCA Civ 25, [2011] 1 WLR 2111, the court held that a CFA agreement that included an indemnity clause preventing a party from being liable to pay the opponent's costs if the claim were unsuccessful and if insurance could not be obtained against that risk was not void for champerty and did not undermine the public interest or undermine justice. The court applied *Wallersteiner v Moir (No. 2)* [1975] QB 373 and *Awwad v Geraghty and Co.* [2001] QB 570 and doubted the decision in *Thai Trading Co. v Taylor* [1998] QB 781 as it was per incuriam. A licence agreement permitting a person to act on behalf of others in relation to alleged breaches of copyright was not an agreement to conduct litigation within the meaning of the *Sibthorpe* case, but was rather a commercial agreement which did not jeopardise the administration of justice (*Golden Eye (International) Ltd v Telefonica UK Ltd* [2012] EWCA Civ 1740, [2013] Bus LR 414). In *Ahmed v Powell* [2003] PNLR 22 it was held that the basis on which costs negotiators charged fees was champertous. In an arrangement with the defendant's insurers, the costs negotiators were to receive a percentage of the reduction in the amount of costs which they achieved. On the other hand, in *Benaim (UK) Ltd v Davies Middleton and Davies Ltd* [2004] EWHC 737 (TCC), LTL 29/3/2004, the court upheld a CFA which provided for an uplift of up to 100 per cent depending upon the amount of damages recovered. For discussion of the current rules on CFAs, see **chapter 6**. In *Westlaw Services Ltd v Boddy* [2010] EWCA Civ 929, [2011] PNLR 4, it was held that a fee-sharing arrangement whereby individuals who obtained work for the firm were to obtain a percentage of the net fees received for that work was void and unenforceable.

(b) The rule may invalidate some assignments of causes of action.

Scope of maintenance and champerty The scope of the rule against champerty and maintenance, in so far as it affects both funding of litigation and assignments of causes of action, has been progressively narrowed. The current position can be summarised as follows: **14.8**

(a) Liquidated claims in contract, such as the right to sue for the price of goods sold and delivered for which the defendant had failed to pay, can be assigned (*County Hotel and Wine Co. Ltd v London and North Western Railway Co.* [1918] 2 KB 251).

(b) The fruits of litigation can be validly assigned (*Glegg v Bromley* [1912] 3 KB 474; *Ruttle Plant Hire Ltd v Secretary of State for the Environment, Food and Rural Affairs (No. 2)* [2008] EWHC 238 (TCC), [2009] 1 All ER 448). An assignment of the benefit of a costs order (which required the costs to be assessed) from one party to the other is not likely to be champertous (*Zabihi v Janzemini* [2009] EWHC 3471 (Ch), LTL 29/1/2010).

(c) Assignments of property are permissible (*Dawson v Great Northern and City Railway* [1905] 1 KB 260), as are assignments which are designed to support or enlarge a property interest which the assignee already possesses (*Compañia Colombiana de Seguros v Pacific Steam Navigation Co.* [1965] 1 QB 101). An assignment of a bare right to litigate is also permissible if it is incidental and subsidiary to a transfer of property (*Williams v Protheroe* (1829) 3 Y & J 129; *Offer-Hoar v Larkstore Ltd* [2006] EWCA Civ 1079, [2006] 1 WLR 2926). See also *Pegasus Management Holdings SCA v Ernst & Young* [2012] EWHC 738 (Ch), [2012] PNLR 24.

(d) The status of the assignment of a damages claim in contract or tort is more complex. The current approach of the courts is set out in *Giles v Thompson* [1994] 1 AC 142. The first question the court will ask is whether the contract of assignment has the characteristics of champerty or maintenance and is therefore prima facie unlawful. In other words, has a stranger to the dispute agreed to involve itself in litigation (maintenance) in a way which yields it a financial benefit from a successful outcome (champerty)? If it does, the court will then inquire whether the transaction is validated by the legitimate interest of the person supporting the action in its outcome. A proprietary interest in the subject matter of the litigation has been held to be a sufficient interest (*Alabaster v Harness* [1894] 2 QB 897), as has a genuine commercial interest in the outcome of the litigation (*Trendtex Trading Corporation v Credit Suisse* [1982] AC 679). A bare right to litigate that was not supported by any collateral interest sufficient to justify the pursuit of the proceedings by the third party for its own benefit was champertous and contrary to public policy (*Skywell (UK) Ltd v Commissioners of HM Revenue and Customs* [2012] UKFTT 611 (TC), [2012] STI 3030). A member of a family has been held justified in maintaining a claim by another member of the family (*Bradlaugh v Newdegate* (1883) 11 QBD 1). An agreement granting a company's former majority shareholder the right to bring a claim for damages for breach of contract in the name of the company, on the basis that he received a percentage of damages as additional consideration for the sale of his shares, was not champertous (*Eurocall Ltd v Energis Communications Ltd* [2010] EWHC 1730 (QB), LTL 12/8/2010).

In *Simpson v Norfolk and Norwich University Hospital NHS Trust* [2011] EWCA Civ 1149, [2012] QB 640, the Court of Appeal held that a claim for damages for personal injury is a legal thing in action which is capable of being assigned, but the assignee did not have a sufficient legitimate interest of a kind that the law would recognise as justifying the pursuit of the proceedings for her own benefit. The assignment was therefore void on the grounds of champerty. The assignee's objective was primarily to mount a campaign against the NHS Trust to implement procedures to prevent and control infection. The court noted that the law on maintenance and champerty was open to further development and it was not possible to state definitely what might constitute a sufficient interest to support the assignment of a cause of action in tort for personal injury. Each case will therefore be decided, to some extent, on its own facts.

The court will also look at public policy considerations. It will examine the question of maintenance and champerty in the light of their 'origins as a principle of public policy designed to protect the purity of justice and the interests of vulnerable litigants' (*Giles v Thompson*, per Lord Mustill).

(e) An administrator, administrative receiver or liquidator of a company has a statutory power under the Insolvency Act 1986, sch. 1, para. 2, and sch. 4, para. 6, to sell the company's property, which includes assigning the fruits of a cause of action on terms that the assignees, by way of consideration, will return a share of the recoveries (*Glegg v Bromley* [1912] 3 KB 474; *Grovewood Holdings plc v James Capel and Co. Ltd* [1995] Ch 80; *Norglen Ltd v Reeds Rain Prudential Ltd* [1999] 2 AC 1). A liquidator may assign the fruits of litigation, but not the right to prosecute it, because that is not an asset of the company, but a right conferred on the liquidator by the Insolvency Act 1986 (*Ruttle Plant Hire Ltd v Secretary of State for the Environment, Food and Rural Affairs (No. 2)* [2008] EWHC 238 (TCC), [2009] 1 All ER 448). Property which could be acquired for the company's estate by the exercise of a statutory power to bring proceedings given to a liquidator or administrator by the Insolvency Act 1986, ss. 127, 213, 214, 238, 239, 244 or 245, is not the company's property and cannot be assigned in return for funding the proceedings (*Re Oasis Merchandising Services Ltd* [1998] Ch 170). A trustee in bankruptcy has a similar power under the Insolvency Act 1986, sch. 5, para. 9 (*Grovewood Holdings plc v James Capel and Co. Ltd* [1995] Ch 80). These powers must be exercised in the best interests of the creditors. So, for example, in *Faryab v Smith* [2001] BPIR 246 a trustee in bankruptcy was ordered not to assign a right of action of the bankrupt to the potential defendant without evaluating the claim.

(f) The right to litigate about purely personal claims (e.g. slander) is not assignable (*Trendtex Trading Corporation v Credit Suisse* [1980] QB 629).

14.9 **Examples** *Giles v Thompson* [1994] 1 AC 142 involved car insurance arrangements, whereby the insurance company loaned its insured a replacement vehicle at no charge in return for the assignment of the insured's right to claim hire charges against the defendant. The House of Lords considered whether such arrangements would harm the administration of justice or the interests of the motorist. It concluded that they did not, and therefore, that even though the insurance companies had no interest in the outcome of the litigation, the arrangements were not champertous.

This approach was upheld by the Court of Appeal in *R (Factortame Ltd) v Secretary of State for Transport, Local Government and the Regions (No. 8)* [2002] EWCA Civ 932, [2003] QB 381. The question in that case was whether the provision of expert accounting services to the claimants in return for an assignment of 8 per cent of the damages to be received by the claimants was champertous. Lord Phillips of Worth Matravers MR said that:

> It is necessary to look at the agreement under attack in order to see whether it tends to conflict with existing public policy that is directed to protecting the due administration of justice with particular regard to the interests of the defendant.

The court held first that the agreement was not in breach of the **Courts and Legal Services Act 1990, s. 58** (which invalidates any conditional fee agreements outside its ambit), as the section applies only to the provision of litigation services by a legal representative, not by an expert. Secondly, the court held that giving evidence on a contingency fee basis gives an expert a significant financial interest in the outcome of the case, which is undesirable. The court would only rarely permit an expert to operate under a contingency fee agreement. However, the court concluded that in this case the agreement was not champertous and did not put justice in jeopardy. The accountants did not perform the role of expert witnesses. Their involvement was limited to assisting the quantification of damages. They had no involvement in the court's decision on the merits of the claim.

In *Stocznia Gdanska SA v Latreefers Inc.* [2001] 2 BCLC 116 the Court of Appeal considered the status of an agreement to fund litigation where the funder had a clear commercial interest in the litigation, but the funding agreement gave it a substantial profit in the form of a division of the damages which was in excess of its preceding loss. Morritt LJ considered the circumstances in which the court would stay a claim on the grounds of champerty or maintenance. He stated that the court was concerned with abuses of the court's process, but that not every abuse will result in a stay. The court was concerned to prevent 'trafficking in litigation'. He declined to define 'trafficking', but continued:

> it seems to us to connote unjustified buying and selling of rights to litigation where the purchaser has no proper reason to be concerned with the litigation.... A large mathematical disproportion between any pre-existing financial interest and the potential profit of funders may in particular cases contribute to a finding of abuse, but is not bound to do so.

In this case, the funding agreement did not constitute trafficking in litigation, and there was no abuse of process.

In *Papera Traders Co. Ltd v Hyundai Merchant Marine Co. Ltd (No. 2)* [2002] EWHC 2130 (Comm), [2002] 2 Lloyd's Rep 692, the court considered whether an agreement to pay 5 per cent of the amount recovered in litigation against insurers to a firm of marine loss adjusters was champertous. Again, the question for the court was whether the agreement impugned the integrity of the English legal system and in coming to a decision the court had to consider the precise nature of the loss adjusters' interest in the outcome of the litigation. In this case, the agreement was not champertous as their activities were subject to the control of solicitors and counsel, the agreement was not exclusively concerned with litigation and there was a good commercial reason to retain them.

In *Mansell v Robinson* [2007] EWHC 101 (QB), LTL 9/2/2007, it was held that an agreement to provide investigative services in return for 1 per cent of the proceeds of litigation plus a weekly salary was not champertous. The agreement could not realistically be said to have a tendency to corrupt public justice. In some meritorious cases, it could be a real barrier to justice to insist on an absolute rule preventing a skilled researcher or inquiry agent, whose services were sought by a person with a potential claim, from making an enforceable contract under which he would be partly remunerated by reference to sums recovered.

In *Lediaev v Vallen* [2008] EWHC 1271 (Ch), LTL 1/8/2008, reversed on other grounds, [2009] EWCA Civ 156, LTL 5/3/2009, the court considered whether it could make a finding of champerty of its own motion, when no such claim had been pleaded and neither party had invited the court to hold the agreement illegal. It concluded that it did have the power to do so, as champerty is a matter of public policy. However, it could only make a finding where it could clearly see that it had all the relevant facts and was in a position to take a close look at the circumstances of the individual case, as envisaged by *R (Factortame Ltd) v Secretary of State for Transport, Local Government and the Regions (No. 8)* [2002] EWCA Civ 932, [2003] QB 381. In the present case the court did have access to the facts and it was satisfied that the agreement was not champertous. The fact that the success fee came from a third party and was not a share of the proceeds of the litigation made no difference to whether or not the agreement was illegal.

Properly structured litigation funding agreements by professional funders are not likely to infringe the rules relating to maintenance or champerty (*Arkin v Borchard Lines* [2005] EWCA Civ 655, [2005] 1 WLR 3055). Such funders will usually comply with the Code of Conduct for Third Party Funders and be members of and comply with the Rules of the Association of Litigation Funders in England and Wales. Litigation funders are likely to have a greater role to play under the reformed system of civil litigation costs operating from 1 April 2013.

NAMING PARTIES IN STATEMENTS OF CASE

14.10 A claim form must be headed with the title to the proceedings, including the full name of each party (**PD 16, para. 2.6**). **Paragraph 2.6** continues with more detailed rules for different classes of party, which are summarised in **table 14.1** and at **14.11** to **14.50**. The rules on serving different classes of party are discussed at **15.45** to **15.53**.

Table 14.1 Names of parties

Class of party	Form of words
An individual	His or her full unabbreviated name and the title by which he or she is known, e.g. Mr Richard John Brown
An individual carrying on business in a name other than his own name	The full unabbreviated name of the individual, together with the title by which he is known and the full trading name (e.g. John Smith T/as JS Autos)
A child under 18	Miss Jane Mary Brown (a child by Mr Joe Bloggs her litigation friend)
A child under 18 who is conducting proceedings on his or her own behalf	Master Tim Brown (a child)
A child reaching full age	Ms Jane Mary Brown (formerly a child but now of full age)
An individual who is a protected party within the meaning of the Mental Capacity Act 2005	Mrs Jane Mary Brown (by Mr Joe Bloggs, her litigation friend)
An individual who is trading under another name	Mr John Smith, trading as (or T/as) 'Smith's Groceries'
An individual who is suing or being sued in a representative capacity	Miss Jane Mary Brown, as the representative of Hilda Marion Brown (deceased)
An individual who is suing or being sued in the name of a club or other unincorporated organisation	Miss Jane Mary Brown, suing/sued on behalf of the Northtown Under 16 Football Club
A firm (other than a limited liability partnership)	(a) where partners are being sued in the name of the partnership, the full name by which the partnership is known and the words '(a firm)', e.g. 'Brown & Co. (A Firm)'; (b) where the partners are being sued as individuals, the full unabbreviated name and title of each partner.
A corporation (other than a company)	The full name of the corporation by which it is known, including indication of legal form ('Corporation', 'Incorporated', etc.), where appropriate
A company, whether registered in England and Wales, or an overseas company, or a limited liability partnership	The full registered name, including indication of legal form (plc, Ltd, LLP, etc.)

DECEASED PARTIES

Survival of causes of action

Under the **Law Reform (Miscellaneous Provisions) Act 1934, s. 1(1)**, most causes of action subsisting against or vested in an individual survive his or her death, against or for the benefit of his or her estate. Even a claim for unlawful racial discrimination survives the claimant's death (*Lewisham and Guys Mental Health NHS Trust v Andrews* [2000] 3 All ER 769). The principal exception to this is that a defamation claim comes to an end upon the claimant's death. **14.11**

Death of party before claim issued

If an individual who has a claim dies before the claim is started, it must be brought by the personal representatives of the deceased if they have been granted probate or letters of administration. The capacity of the executor or administrator must be made clear in their description in the claim form, for example, 'Mr Joe Bloggs as the executor of Mrs Sharon Bloggs (deceased)' (**PD 7A, para. 5.5; CPR, r. 19.8(3)(a)**). A claim brought against a person who was in fact dead at its commencement will be treated as if it had been commenced against his or her estate (**r. 19.8(3)(b)**). However, the irregularity must be corrected by the making of an application for a person to represent the deceased for the purposes of the claim. Until that happens there is no defendant with legal personality (*Piggott v Aulton* [2003] EWCA Civ 24, [2003] RTR 540; *Millburn-Snell v Evans* [2011] EWCA Civ 577, [2012] 1 WLR 41). **14.12**

Where a defendant against whom a claim could have been brought has died, and a grant of probate or administration has been made, the claim must be brought against the persons who are the personal representatives of the deceased (**r. 19.8(2)(a)**). A claimant who wishes to start proceedings against the estate of a deceased defendant before there has been a grant of probate or letters of administration should bring a claim against 'the estate' of the deceased (**r. 19.8(2)(b)(i)**). A claim is treated as having been brought against 'the estate of' the deceased where it is brought against the 'personal representatives' of the deceased but a grant of probate or administration has not been made (**r. 19.8(3)(a)**). However, the claim form may not be served in this form, because it does not identify the defendants upon whom it should be served. So the next step in the claim is for the claimant to apply, within the time limited for service of the claim form (which is four months within the jurisdiction, six months outside), for an order appointing a person to represent the estate of the deceased person for the purpose of the claim and for the action to continue against the representative (**PD 7A, para. 5.5; CPR, r. 19.8(2)(b)(ii)**).

Before making an order, the court may direct notice of the application to be given to any other person with an interest in the claim (**r. 19.8(4)**). Where an order is made, any judgment or order made in the claim is binding on the estate of the deceased (**r. 19.8(5)**).

Before the grant of letters of administration there is a limited power for a person to take essential steps to preserve and protect the deceased's estate. Unless proceedings are necessary for that purpose, a claimant has no right to commence proceedings before the grant, and the court will refuse to give relief to the claimant in such proceedings (*Caudle v LD Law Ltd* [2008] EWHC 374 (QB), [2008] 1 WLR 1540).

Death of party after claim issued

Where a claimant or defendant dies after the claim has been issued, an order may be obtained under **CPR, r. 19.2(4)**, for the claim to be carried on by or against his or her personal representatives. Application should be made by application notice, with evidence in support, in accordance with the procedure set out **CPR, Part 19**, and **PD 19A** (see 14.83 to 14.96). **14.13**

Where a party who has an interest in a claim has died but has no personal representatives, the court may order the claim to proceed in the absence of a person representing the estate, or may order the appointment of a person to represent the estate for the purpose of the proceedings (**CPR, r. 19.8(1)**). This enables the court to dispense with the need for a formal grant of probate or letters of administration. In *Re Berti* [2001] EWCA Civ 2079, LTL 16/11/2001 the Court of Appeal emphasised that a person who wishes to represent a deceased's estate may obtain a representation order under **r. 19.8(1)(b)** as an alternative to being granted probate or letters of administration, and the court should not insist on such a person going to the expense of obtaining probate or administration, especially where the estate is small. **Rule 19.8(1)** does not permit the court to correct deficiencies in the manner in which proceedings were instituted. It only enables the court to make directions for the continued prosecution of proceedings where a person who had an interest in the claim had died. So an action brought by a claimant purportedly as administrator, when he did not have that capacity, was a nullity (*Milbum-Snell v Evans* [2011] EWCA Civ 577, [2012] 1 WLR 41).

The court will require notice of an application under **r. 19.8(1)** to be given to anyone who may have an interest in the deceased's estate (**r. 19.8(4)**). Any judgment or order made in the claim will then bind the estate (**r. 19.8(5)**).

An application for an order to carry on existing proceedings, which were brought before the expiry of limitation in the name of the personal representatives following the death of a party, raises no issues under the Limitation Act 1980, whether the death or application occurs before or after the expiry of limitation (*Roberts v Gill and Co.* [2010] UKSC 22, [2011] 1 AC 240, at [103]–[104]). **CPR, r. 19.5(3)(c)**, therefore probably has no real function (see **14.93**).

Notice of claim to non-parties

14.14 In a claim relating to the estate of a deceased person, the court has power under **CPR, r. 19.8A**, to require notice of the claim or a judgment or order in it to be given to any person who is not a party but who may be affected by any judgment. An application for an order under this rule may be made without notice but must be supported by written evidence which includes the reasons why the person to be served should be bound by the judgment in the claim. Notice must be given in form 52, accompanied by a copy of the claim form, a form for acknowledging service and any affidavits, witness statements or statements of case ordered by the court to be served. Once the person served acknowledges service, that person becomes a party to the claim. Even if there is no acknowledgment of service, the person will be bound by any judgment or order made in the claim. If after service of notice of a claim, the claim form is substantially amended so as to alter the relief claimed, the court can direct that a judgment will not bind the notified person unless a further notice, together with the amended claim form, is served on him (**r. 19.8A(7)**).

Any person served with a notice of a judgment or order under **r. 19.8A** is bound by it as if he had been a party to the claim, but may, provided he acknowledges service, apply to the court within 28 days of service, to set aside or vary the judgment or order and take part in any proceedings relating to it (**r. 19.8A(8)**).

CHILDREN AND PROTECTED PARTIES

Introduction

14.15 **CPR, Part 21**, contains special provisions governing proceedings involving children (defined as persons under 18: **r. 21.1(2)**) and protected parties. This latter term replaces the old term 'patient' following the entry fully into force on 1 October 2007 of the Mental Capacity Act 2005. The 2005 Act makes wide-ranging changes designed better to protect the interests of individuals who lack mental capacity. The new law is reflected in the new **CPR, Part 21**, and **PD 21**, which also came into force on 1 October 2007.

Protected parties

The term 'protected party' means a party, or an intended party, who lacks capacity within the meaning of the Mental Capacity Act 2005, s. 2(1), to conduct proceedings (**CPR, r. 21.1(2)**). Thus the statutory definition in the Mental Capacity Act 2005 is to be used to decide whether a person is a protected party (*Saulle v Nouvet* [2007] EWHC 2902 (QB), [2008] LS Law Medical 201). The Mental Capacity Act 2005, s. 2(1), states that a person lacks capacity if at the material time he or she is unable to make a decision for him or herself in relation to a matter because of an impairment of, or a disturbance in, the functioning of the mind or brain. The disturbance could be permanent or temporary, and could cover a range of problems such as psychiatric illness, learning disability, dementia and brain damage. **14.16**

Section 1 establishes a number of fundamental principles. The most important is a presumption of capacity. A person must be assumed to have capacity unless it is established that he lacks capacity (s. 1(2)). A person must be presented with all of the options so that his or her capacity to weigh up those options can be fairly assessed. A person who understands the salient features of the available options may have capacity even if there is a lack of understanding of every nuance or point of detail of each respective option (*CC v KK* [2012] EWHC 2136, (COP), BAILII). A person is not to be treated as unable to make a decision unless all practicable steps to help him to do so have been taken without success (s. 1(3); *Re W (Children)* [2008] EWHC 1188 (Fam), LTL 2/6/2009). A person is not to be treated as unable to make a decision merely because he makes an unwise decision (s. 1(4)). Any act done or decision made under the Act for or on behalf of a person who lacks capacity must be done, or made, in his best interests (s. 1(5)), and s. 4 sets out factors which must be applied in deciding what is in a person's best interests. When determining the best interests of a person lacking capacity pursuant to s. 4, the substituted judgment of the court as to what the decision of the protected person would have been had he not lacked capacity is a relevant factor (*Re G* [2010] EWHC 3005 (Fam), [2011] WTLR 231). Before the act is done or the decision is made, regard must be had to whether the purpose can be achieved in a way that is less restrictive of a person's rights and freedom of action (s. 1(6)).

The court has power to make declarations about capacity (s. 15) and decisions on the person's behalf (ss. 16, 17 and 18). The powers of the court are subject to s. 1 (principles) and s. 4 (best interests). Some decisions are excluded (see ss. 27, 28 and 29).

There is a two-stage test to be applied to assess capacity. First, does the individual have an impairment of the mind or brain? Secondly, is this impairment such as to prevent him or her from being able to make the decision in question at the time it needs to be made. In order to assess the individual's ability to make the decision, the test set out in s. 3(1) must be satisfied. This is that a person lacks capacity if he or she is unable:

(a) to understand information relevant to a decision;
(b) to retain the information;
(c) to use or weigh that information as part of the process of making the decision; or
(d) to communicate the decision (by any means).

A lack of capacity cannot be established merely by reference to a person's age or appearance, or a condition of his, or an aspect of his behaviour, which might lead others to make unjustified assumptions about his capacity (s. 2(3)). A person should not be regarded as unable to understand information if he is able to understand an explanation of it given to him in a way that is appropriate to his circumstances (e.g. using simple language, by visual aids or other means), and he should not be regarded as unable to make a decision because he can only retain information for a short period of time (s. 3(2) and (3)). Profound loss or impairment of memory might be compatible with capacity to make a decision provided the person could retain relevant information for a sufficient period of time to enable him to understand and evaluate it and to form and communicate his decision (*Re S* [2010] EWHC 2405 (COP), BAILLI, at [37]–[39]).

The definition of capacity in the Mental Capacity Act 2005 reflects the common law position (see *Re C (Adult: Refusal of Treatment)* [1994] 1 WLR 290 and *Masterman-Lister v Brutton and Co. (Nos. 1 and 2)* [2002] EWCA Civ 1889, [2003] EWCA Civ 70, [2003] 1 WLR 1511).

Mental capacity is a matter of fact. See *Assessment of Mental Capacity: Guidance for Doctors and Lawyers* (2004) published jointly by the Law Society and the British Medical Association before the entry into force of the Mental Capacity Act 2005. There is a presumption of capacity and the burden of proof (which, by s. 2(4), is on the balance of probabilities) rests on the party asserting incapacity (*Masterman-Lister v Brutton and Co. (Nos. 1 and 2)* [2002] EWCA Civ 1889, [2003] EWCA Civ 70, [2003] 1 WLR 1511; see also *Phillips v Symes* [2004] EWHC 1887 (Ch), LTL 18/8/2004). The question is whether the litigant is capable of understanding, with assistance from his legal representatives and other experts, the issues on which his consent or decision is likely to be necessary in the course of the proceedings. Similar issues arise when considering whether a party has the mental capacity to approve a settlement of liability or quantum, where the enquiry has to be directed to the transaction which is to be approved, and the question is whether the party is able to understand the proceedings and make an informed decision, with the help of any explanation from his or her advisers (*Bailey v Warren* [2006] EWCA Civ 51, [2006] WTLR 753). In determining whether a party had the capacity to enter into a compromise agreement, the proper question was not the narrow one of whether the party had capacity to enter into that compromise but the broader question of whether the party had the capacity to litigate. A compromise agreement is not a self-contained transaction but rather an inseparable part of the proceedings as a whole (*Dunhill v Burgin* [2012] EWCA Civ 397, [2012] PIQR P15).

The overarching principle under the Act is that decisions must be made in the best interests of the protected person. This is not the same as asking what that person would have decided if he or she had full capacity, and care must be taken not to conflate the assessment of capacity with the best interests analysis (*CC v KK* [2012] EWHC 2136 (COP), BAILII). The decision-maker must consider all relevant circumstances, follow the steps set out in the Act (including consideration of s. 1(6)), then form a value judgment of his or her own giving effect to the paramount statutory principle that the decision has to be made in the person's best interests. Although the wishes of the protected person must be given great weight, together with the protected person's beliefs, values and other factors that would have influenced his or her own decision, they are simply part of the balance (see *A London Local Authority v JH* [2011] EWHC 2420 (Fam), LTL 28/10/2011). The 'best interest' test in s. 4 requires a person-centred approach rather than considering, in general terms, what is best for a certain group of the population (*AH v Hertfordshire Partnership NHS Foundation Trust* [2011] EWHC 276 (Fam), 14 CCL Rep 301). An unwise decision cannot be made by the decision-maker simply because the protected person would have made it (*Re P* [2009] EWHC 163 (Ch), [2009] 2 All ER 1198; *Re S and S* [2009] LS Law Medical 97).

Where apparently irrational comments and instructions lead legal representatives to suspect there is a real risk that their client lacks legal capacity, it is right to take steps (including bringing the matter before the court if there is an impending trial) to ascertain whether it is necessary to appoint a litigation friend (*McFaddens v Platford* [2009] EWHC 126 (TCC), [2009] PNLR 26; *V v R* [2011] EWMC 822 (QB), LTL 23/1/2012).

The court will almost certainly require a medical report before being able to find a party to be under a mental incapacity. In cases where no one recognises the fact that one of the parties is under a mental incapacity, the court can regularise the position retrospectively, provided everyone is acting in good faith. The rules on capacity are not designed to allow a party to reopen litigation which has apparently been conducted properly (*Phillips v Symes*).

Alongside the Mental Capacity Act 2005, the court has an inherent jurisdiction to protect vulnerable adults who, while not suffering from mental incapacity within the meaning of that Act, are nevertheless unable to make relevant decisions because of vitiating factors such as coercion or undue influence (*Re L (Vulnerable Adults with Capacity: Court's Jurisdiction) (No.2)* [2012] EWCA Civ 253, [2013] Fam 1).

Litigation friends

Both protected parties and children (subject, in the latter case to any order by the court to the contrary, see **14.20**) must have a litigation friend to conduct proceedings on their behalf (**CPR, r. 21.2**). The title to a claim where one of the parties is a protected party should read 'AB (a protected party by CD his litigation friend)'. In the case of a child, it should read 'AB (a child, by CD his litigation friend)' (**PD 21, paras 1.1** and **1.2**). **14.17**

A claimant who sues a child or protected party who has no litigation friend may take no step in a claim without the court's permission, other than issuing and serving the claim form, or making an application for the appointment of a litigation friend (**CPR, r. 21.3(2)**). If a party lacks capacity to continue to conduct proceedings, no further step in the claim may be taken without the court's permission until he or she has a litigation friend (**r. 21.3(3)**). Any step taken before the appointment of the litigation friend has no effect, subject to any order by the court to the contrary (**r. 21.3(4)**).

Default judgment may be entered against a child or protected party only with the court's permission (**r. 12.10(a)(i)**) and only after a litigation friend has been appointed by the court (**PD 12, para. 4.2(1)**). It would seem that a litigation friend appointed out of court under **CPR, r. 21.5** (see **14.19**), is not acceptable.

Commentary

Who may be a litigation friend?

By **CPR, rr. 21.4(3)** and **21.6**, a litigation friend may be: **14.18**

(a) a person appointed by the court (see **14.19**);
(b) a 'deputy' appointed under the Mental Capacity Act 2005, s. 16(2), with power to conduct specified legal proceedings on the protected party's behalf; or
(c) a person who can fairly and competently conduct proceedings on behalf of the child or protected party and who has no adverse interest in the claim.

A litigation friend who acts for a claimant (but not a defendant) must undertake to pay any costs which the claimant may be ordered to pay (subject to any right that the friend may have to be repaid from the claimant's assets) (**CPR, r. 21.4(3)**). A litigation friend who incurs expenses on behalf of a child or protected party in the course of proceedings is entitled to recoup them out of any money recovered from the opposing party or from a payment into court, provided the expenses are of a reasonable amount and were reasonably incurred (**r. 21.12**). By **r. 21.12(6)**, where the child or protected party recovers £5,000 or less from the proceedings, the litigation friend may not recoup more than 25 per cent of the sum recovered to cover expenses, unless the court orders otherwise. Even with a court order, the amount recouped may not exceed 50 per cent.

Where the litigation friend's expenses are recoverable as *inter partes* costs, the claim for expenses should be made at the detailed assessment hearing. If they are not recoverable as costs, the application should be made either at the hearing under **Part 21** to approve a settlement of the claim or, where no approval is necessary, by separate application under **Part 23**.

Whatever its form, the application must be supported by a witness statement setting out the nature and amount of the expense being claimed and the reason it was incurred (**PD 21, para. 11.2**).

In practice, a child's litigation friend will normally be a parent, guardian or other relative who can comply with these requirements. A protected party's litigation friend may be a deputy under the Mental Capacity Act 2005 (particularly where there are assets to be administered) or, where no such person has been appointed, the person with whom the protected party lives or who is caring for the party. If no one is available to be a litigation friend, application can be made to the Official Solicitor for him to act.

In *Nottinghamshire County Council v Bottomley* [2010] EWCA Civ 756, [2010] Med LR 407, the local authority's director of social care was acting as the claimant's litigation friend. It was held she had a conflict of interest between achieving the best outcome for the claimant and the interest of her employer in achieving a result on the question of periodical payments that favoured the local authority. Accordingly, she could not continue in the role of litigation friend.

How is a litigation friend appointed?

14.19 There are two methods in the CPR whereby a litigation friend may be appointed.

First, a person may become a litigation friend without a court order, under **r. 21.5**, by filing either:

(a) in the case of a deputy under the Mental Capacity Act 2005, an official copy of the order of the Court of Protection which confers the deputy's power to act; or
(b) in the case of any other person, a certificate of suitability in form N235. The details of what the certificate must state are set out at **PD 21, para. 2.2.**

These documents must be filed when proceedings are first issued (where the litigation friend acts on behalf of the claimant) or when the litigation friend first takes a step in the proceedings (where acting on behalf of the defendant). A copy of the certificate of suitability must, by **CPR, r. 21.5(4)**, be served on every person on whom the claim form must be served under **r. 6.13** (see **15.45**) and a certificate of service must be filed with the certificate of suitability.

Alternatively, a litigation friend may be appointed by court order under **r. 21.6**. An application for an order under this rule may be made by any person who wishes to be appointed as litigation friend or by any party to the action (**r. 21.6(2)**). The application should be made under the Part 23 procedure. It must, by **PD 21, para. 3.3**, be supported by evidence that the person proposed for appointment:

(a) consents to act;
(b) can conduct proceedings fairly and competently;
(c) has no adverse interest to the child or protected party; and
(d) in the case of a claimant, undertakes to pay any costs order (subject to any right to be repaid from the assets of the child or protected party).

The last three of these conditions are also specified in **CPR, r. 21.4(3)**. Where it is sought to appoint the Official Solicitor as the litigation friend, provision must be made for payment of his charges (**PD 21, para. 3.4**). The courts are reluctant to permit the question of whether a party has the mental capacity to conduct litigation to become unnecessary satellite litigation, and the Court of Appeal has held in *Folks v Faizey* [2006] EWCA Civ 381, *The Independent*, 12 April 2006, that the question is not suitable for determination as a preliminary issue. Although the court must have evidence to support any application for an order appointing a litigation friend, where the protected party and the litigation friend both consent to the appointment, where there is adequate evidence to support the application and where there is no evidence to suggest that the application is anything but a bona fide one, the court should make the order.

The Court of Appeal in *Folks v Faizey* also cast doubt on the need to serve a copy of the notice applying for the appointment of a litigation friend on other parties to the litigation.

It commented that an application notice under **CPR, Part 23**, need only be served on the person against whom the order is sought and any other person as the court may direct and that this therefore might not include parties other than the child or protected party. However, in making these comments, it seems to have overlooked the express requirement in **r. 21.8(1)** that an application to appoint a litigation friend must be served on every person on whom the claim form should be served under what is now **r. 6.13** (see **15.45**). An application to appoint a litigation friend for a protected party must also be served on the protected party, unless the court orders otherwise (**r. 21.8(2)**).

On an application under **r. 21.6** the court may, under **r. 21.8(4)** appoint the person proposed in the application or any other person who complies with the conditions in **r. 21.4(3)**.

When may a child conduct proceedings without a litigation friend?

In the case of a child (but not a protected party) the court has a discretion to make an order permitting the child to conduct proceedings without a litigation friend (**CPR, r. 21.2(3)**). The order may be made on application by the child, on notice to the litigation friend if the child already has one. The court has power to rescind any such order (**CPR, r. 21.2(3) to (5)**). **14.20**

The court will only authorise a child to conduct proceedings without a litigation friend where it is satisfied that the child is of sufficient maturity and understanding (*Gillick v West Norfolk and Wisbech Area Health Authority* [1986] AC 112).

Where a child is conducting proceedings on his or her own behalf, the claim should be headed 'A. B. (a child)' (**PD 21, para. 1.2(2)**).

Terminating the appointment of a litigation friend

The court may direct that a person may not act as a litigation friend, or may substitute or remove a litigation friend (**CPR, r. 21.7**). An application for an order under **r. 21.7** must be supported by evidence (**r. 21.7(2)**). **14.21**

By **r. 21.8(1)** and **(3)**, an application to substitute or remove a litigation friend must be served on every person on whom the claim form should be served (see **15.45**) and on the person acting, or purporting to act, as litigation friend. A person proposed for substitution as a litigation friend must comply with the conditions specified in **r. 21.4(3)** (see **14.19**) (**r. 21.7(3)**) and must be served with the application, unless he or she is the applicant (**r. 21.8(3)**).

By **r. 21.8(4)**, on an application for substitution the court may appoint the person proposed in the application or any other person who complies with the conditions in **r. 21.4(3)**.

When a child (who is not a protected party) reaches 18, the appointment of his or her litigation friend ceases (**r. 21.9(1)**). No application to the court to terminate the appointment is necessary. The individual for whom the friend has been acting must serve a notice under **PD 21, para. 4.2**, stating that he or she has reached full age and that the litigation friend's appointment has ceased, giving an address for service and stating whether he or she intends to continue the proceedings. The heading in the action then becomes: 'A. B. (formerly a child but now of full age)' (**para. 4.3**). Alternatively, the litigation friend may serve a notice under **para. 4.4**.

When a protected party recovers, an application to court must be made in order to terminate the appointment of the litigation friend (**CPR, r. 21.9(2)** and **(3)**). The application can be made by the former protected party, the litigation friend or a party (**r. 21.9(3)**). The application must be supported by medical or other suitable expert evidence that the protected party has regained or acquired capacity to conduct the proceedings, a copy of any relevant order of

Commentary

the Court of Protection, and (if the application is made by the protected party) a statement whether or not he or she intends to continue to pursue or defend the proceedings (**PD 21, para. 4.6**). The former protected party must file in court a notice that the litigation friend's appointment has ceased, giving an address for service and stating whether he or she intends to continue to pursue or defend the proceedings (**para. 4.7; CPR, r. 21.9(4)**). If a child or protected party does not serve such a notice within 28 days after the day on which the appointment of the litigation friend ceases, the court may, on application, strike out the claim (or defence) of the child or the protected party (**r. 21.9(5)**). The litigation friend's liability for costs continues until the notice has been served by the child or protected party or the litigation friend serves notice on the parties that his or her appointment has ceased (**r. 21.9(6)**). Any order made must be served on other parties to the proceedings.

Court approval of settlement of a claim involving a child or protected party

14.22 In a claim by, or on behalf of, or against a child or protected party, no settlement, compromise or payment, and no acceptance of money paid into court, is valid without the court's approval (**CPR, r. 21.10(1)**). **CPR, Part 21** invalidates a consent judgment involving a protected party reached without the appointment of a litigation friend and the approval of the court, even where the individual's lack of capacity was unknown to anyone acting for either party at the time of the compromise (*Dunhill v Burgin* [2012] EWHC 3163 (QB), [2012] 1 WLR 3739). Whether proceedings have been started or not, until a proposed settlement is approved by the court there is no binding contract, and either party may renege on it (*Dietz v Lennig Chemicals Ltd* [1969] 1 AC 170; *Drinkall v Whitwood* [2003] EWCA Civ 1547, [2004] 1 WLR 462). **Rule 21.10(1)** is intended to enable a defendant to obtain a valid discharge from a claim, and to ensure that any settlement etc. is fair on the child or protected party. The court will weigh the claimant's prospects of success against the likely level of damages, assuming full liability, and decide whether the proposed settlement etc. is in the interests of the child or protected party. **Paragraphs 6.2** and **6.3** of **PD 21** set out the procedure to be used where the parties have agreed that damages are to be paid periodically. The court must be supplied with an opinion on the merits from counsel or a solicitor, and, except in a very clear case, a copy of any financial advice (**PD 21, para. 6.4**).

An application for approval of a settlement etc. in proceedings is made using the Part 23 procedure (see **chapter 32**). In the Chancery Division the application will be heard by a judge, not a master, where the claim exceeds £100,000 or is in respect of absent, unborn or unascertained persons (**PD 2B, para. 5.1(a)**). The court cannot use its power to vary or revoke an order under **CPR, r. 3.1(7)**, to vary or revoke an approved settlement order as this would, in effect, permit a judge to hear an appeal from himself (*Roult v North West Strategic Health Authority* [2009] EWCA Civ 444, [2010] 1 WLR 487).

It is possible to bring proceedings solely for the purpose of obtaining the court's approval for a settlement of a claim before it has been issued. Court approval of a settlement reached in these circumstances is necessary to prevent a defendant repudiating the settlement at a later stage (*Drinkall v Whitwood* [2003] EWCA Civ 1547, [2004] 1 WLR 462). Such proceedings should be brought using the Part 8 procedure (see **chapter 13**) (**CPR, r. 21.10(2); PD 8A, para. 3.1**). For a summary of the approval procedure see **procedural checklist 6** at the front of the book. The Part 8 claim form should set out the details of the claim and request the court's approval of the settlement. A draft consent order in form N292 must be attached (**PD 21, para. 5.1(1)**). The court must satisfy itself that the parties have considered whether payment in instalments is appropriate (**para. 5.4**). Where periodic payments are included in the settlement, **para. 5.5** sets out further information which the parties should provide.

PD 21, para. 5.1, *sets out* details of other information which must be included in the claim form. This includes whether and to what extent the defendant admits liability, the age and occupation (if any) of the child or protected party, the litigation friend's approval of the proposed settlement, a copy of any relevant financial advice, and, in a personal injury case arising from an accident, the circumstances of the accident, any medical reports, schedules of damages, and details of any relevant criminal proceedings. A legal opinion on the merits of the settlement (including the instructions on which it is given) must be provided to the court **(para. 5.2)**.

The apportionment of any claim brought on behalf of dependent children under the **Fatal Accidents Act 1976** must be approved by the court. See **PD 21, para. 7.4**, for the additional information which must be provided to the court in such a claim.

Where the only remedy which a claimant is seeking against a child or protected person is the payment of money, judgment cannot be entered by the claimant on an admission by the defendant **(CPR, r. 14.1(4)(a))**.

Where a child or protected person makes a claim in which the only remedy sought is the payment of money, judgment cannot be entered by the claimant on an admission if it is only an admission under **r. 14.5** of part of the claim for a specified amount or it is an admission under **r. 14.7** of liability for an unspecified amount with an offer of a sum in satisfaction **(r. 14.1(4)(b))**.

For limitations on default judgments see **14.17**.

When making an order approving a settlement, the court can also make an order under the Children and Young Persons Act 1933, s. 39, prohibiting any newspaper report of the proceedings from revealing the name, address or school attended by the child or the inclusion of any information that would lead to the identification of the child. This is regarded as being more acceptable than an anonymity order as it interferes less with the principle of open justice and freedom of expression. The court made such an order in *A (A child) v Cambridge University Hospitals NHS Foundation Trust* [2011] EWHC 454 (QB), [2011] EMLR 18. See also *U v Sarker* (2011) LTL 24/6/2011.

Investment of money recovered for a child or protected party

Any money recovered by or on behalf of a child or protected party, including an accepted payment into court, may be dealt with only as directed by the court **(CPR, r. 21.11)**. Before giving directions under **r. 21.11(2)** for the investment or otherwise of that money the court must consider whether the protected party is a protected beneficiary **(r. 21.11(3))**. This is a protected party who lacks capacity to manage and control money he or she recovers in the proceedings **(r. 21.1(2)(e))**. The court has power to appoint the Official Solicitor a guardian of a child's estate **(r. 21.13)**. **Paragraphs 8 to 13 of PD 21** set out details concerning how money recovered for a child or protected party should be applied. 14.23

In *Brennan v Eco Composting Ltd* [2006] EWHC 3153 (QB), [2007] 1 WLR 773, the court held that the claimant's entitlement to interest on money paid into court under CPR, old Part 36, which ran from the date of acceptance of the payment in, and no earlier, applied equally to parties under a disability even though the requirement for the payment in to be approved by the court inevitably delayed the date upon which the money could be accepted.

Control of litigation in mental health matters

The Mental Health Act 1983, s. 139(2), provides that no civil proceedings shall be brought against any person in any court in respect of any act purporting to have been done under the Act without the leave of the High Court. *Seal v Chief Constable of South Wales Police* [2007] UKHL 31, [2007] 1 WLR 1910, held that a failure to obtain leave under s. 139(2), before commencing proceedings based on police action in removing the claimant to a place of safety under s. 136 rendered the proceedings a nullity. 14.24

BANKRUPTCY

14.25 A bankrupt's estate becomes vested in the trustee in bankruptcy immediately on the trustee's appointment taking effect (Insolvency Act 1986, s. 306(1)). Property vests in the trustee without the need for any conveyance, assignment or transfer (s. 306(2)). By s. 283, a bankrupt's estate comprises all property belonging to or vested in the bankrupt at the commencement of the bankruptcy, and property which by virtue of the Insolvency Act 1986 is treated as belonging to the bankrupt. There are certain exceptions, such as tools and basic domestic belongings. By s. 436, 'property' includes money, goods, things in action, land and every description of property, and every description of interest in property. Consequently, most causes of action vested in an individual become vested in the trustee in bankruptcy once the trustee is appointed. Even in cases where a trustee in bankruptcy has not yet been appointed and therefore the assets remain vested in the bankrupt, the bankrupt has no interest in the assets and therefore no standing to make an application for a stay of execution pending an appeal (*Dadourian Group International Inc. v Simms* [2008] EWHC 723 (Ch), [2008] BPIR 508). However, personal claims, and in particular claims for defamation and personal injuries, remain vested in the bankrupt notwithstanding the appointment of a trustee in bankruptcy (*Heath v Tang* [1993] 1 WLR 1421), provided the claim is solely of a personal nature (*Ord v Upton* [2000] Ch 352). An appeal against self-assessment which had been settled by agreement between the trustee in bankruptcy and HMRC was not a personal right which remained vested in the bankrupt (*McNulty v Commissioners of HM Revenue & Customs* [2012] UKUT 174 (TCC), [2012] STC 2110). Where a claim in negligence gives rise to heads of damage personal to the bankrupt (such as for pain, suffering and loss of amenity) and others which have vested in the trustee (such as for loss of earnings up to the date of discharge from bankruptcy or for loss of reputation), the whole cause of action vests in the trustee, who is therefore the proper claimant. The trustee does not hold such a mixed cause of action on a bare trust for the bankrupt alone, but for the benefit of both the bankrupt and the creditors (*Mulkerrins v PricewaterhouseCoopers* [2001] BPIR 106, point not considered on appeal). However, in such a case the trustee will hold the damages recovered in respect of the personal heads on a constructive trust for the bankrupt (*Ord v Upton* [2000] Ch 352; see also *Simpson v Norfolk and Norwich University Hospital NHS Trust* [2011] EWCA Civ 1149, [2012] QB 640).

Where the trustee refuses to bring proceedings on a cause of action in which part of the damages will be held on trust for the bankrupt, one solution is for the bankrupt (after discharge) to negotiate an assignment of the cause of action from the trustee. It appears there may be jurisdiction for the court to give directions for such an assignment (*Smith and Williamson v Sims Pipes* (2000) LTL 17/3/2000). The bankrupt could also apply to the court under the Insolvency Act 1986, s. 303, for review of the trustee's decision.

For control of litigation against individuals subject to insolvency procedures, see **84.16** and **84.23** to **84.37**.

COMPANIES

14.26 A company registered under the Companies Act 2006 or an earlier Companies Act must sue and be sued using the full, registered company name. Where the company is in liquidation, the words '(in liquidation)' should be included in the heading. A company which is not required to end its name with 'Ltd' or 'plc' (or their Welsh equivalents) should be referred to by its name followed by an appropriate description, such as '(a company limited by guarantee)'. The full name of a foreign company should be followed, if helpful, by '(a company incorporated under the law of...)'.

The articles of association of a registered company usually confer on its directors a general power to manage the business of the company (see, for example, the Companies (Model Articles) Regulations 2008 (SI 2008/3229), sch. 1, art. 3 (private companies limited by shares), and sch. 3, art. 3 (public companies)).The power to litigate in the name of a company is part of this general power of management and so may be exercised by the directors, not the members (shareholders) (*John Shaw and Sons (Salford) Ltd v Shaw* [1935] 2 KB 113; *Breckland Group Holdings Ltd v London and Suffolk Properties Ltd* [1989] BCLC 100; *Mitchell and Hobbs (UK) Ltd v Mill* [1996] 2 BCLC 102). The members may be able to take a decision to litigate in the company's name only if there is no board of directors capable of acting (*Alexander Ward and Co. Ltd v Samyang Navigation Co. Ltd* [1975] 1 WLR 673).

If a company has more than one director, they must take decisions collectively. No one director has authority to act for the company unless the authority arises by implication from his office or the board has delegated authority in accordance with the company's constitution (*Smith v Butler* [2012] EWCA Civ 314, [2012] Bus LR 1836). All actions by the directors of a company must be taken in accordance with their duties to the company which are set out in the Companies Act 2006, ss. 171 to 177.

If directors of a company, in breach of their duty to the company, refuse to agree to it taking legal proceedings, the other directors, even if they do not have a majority of votes in directors' decision-making, may cause the proceedings to be brought in the company's name, and the court will treat the proceedings as properly authorised (*Fusion Interactive Communication Solutions Ltd v Venture Investment Placement Ltd (No. 2)* [2005] EWHC 736 (Ch), [2005] 2 BCLC 571). Alternatively, assuming that the directors who are blocking proceedings cannot be removed from office, a member of the company may:

(a) commence the proceedings as a derivative claim under the Companies Act 2006, ss. 260 to 264 (see **14.27**); or
(b) petition under s. 996 on the ground that the failure to bring the proceedings is unfairly prejudicial conduct of the company's affairs (see **85.9** to **85.20**); or
(c) apply to the court, under the Senior Courts Act 1981, s. 37(1) and (2), for the appointment of a receiver of the company's cause of action.

If a company is in administration, or an administrative receiver has been appointed, the administrator or receiver has a power to bring or defend any claim in the name and on behalf of the company (Insolvency Act 1986, s. 42, sch. B1, para. 60, and sch. 1, para. 5). During administration, any power of the company or its officers, including the power to litigate, that could be exercised in such a way as to interfere with the administrator's exercise of his or her powers is not exercisable except with the consent of the administrator (sch. B1, para. 64).

In *Newhart Developments Ltd v Cooperative Commercial Bank Ltd* [1978] QB 814 it was held that the appointment of a receiver does not divest the directors of their power to institute proceedings in the company's name, provided they do not interfere with the receiver's work of realising the charged assets (cf. *Shanks v Central Regional Council* 1987 SLT 410, affirmed 1988 SLT 212). In *Tudor Grange Holdings Ltd v Citibank NA* [1992] Ch 53 Browne-Wilkinson V-C said that he had substantial doubts that *Newhart Developments Ltd v Cooperative Commercial Bank Ltd* was correctly decided, and thought that, at present, it should only be followed in cases where, as in the *Newhart Developments* case, the directors proposing litigation undertook to meet any award of costs against the company if the litigation should fail. In *Sutton v GE Capital Commercial Finance Ltd* [2004] EWCA Civ 315, [2004] 2 BCLC 662, the Court of Appeal, following the *Newhart Developments* case, held that it was open to the company, acting by its directors, to bring proceedings notwithstanding the appointment of administrative receivers, so long as the proceedings did not impinge prejudicially on the position of the debenture holder.

It is likely that directors do have power to bring proceedings in the company's name to challenge the appointment of the receiver, sue the receiver for breach of duty, or oppose a petition to wind up the company (*Watts v Midland Bank plc* [1986] BCLC 15; *Re Reprographic Exports (Euromat) Ltd* (1978) 122 SJ 400). The directors also retain their office notwithstanding the appointment of a receiver, and they retain their powers and functions in relation to the assets

Commentary

which are not under the control of the receiver, provided this does not prejudice the course of the receivership.

If a company is in voluntary liquidation, its liquidator has a power to bring or defend any claim in the name and on behalf of the company (Insolvency Act 1986, s. 165(3) and sch. 4, para. 4), but in a compulsory liquidation (a winding up by the court) the liquidator must obtain the permission of the court or of the liquidation committee (Insolvency Act 1986, s. 167(l)(a) and sch. 4, para. 4).

For control of litigation against companies subject to insolvency proceedings see **84.16** to **84.22** and **84.27** to **84.37**.

Derivative claims

14.27 Normally, it is not possible for a company's rights to be enforced in proceedings brought in the name of a member of the company (*Foss v Harbottle* (1843) 2 Hare 461), because the company is the proper claimant to enforce its own rights. As an exception to this proper claimant principle, a court may permit proceedings in the name of a member of the company if the company will not commence a claim. The member's claim derives from the company's cause of action and is called a 'derivative claim', which is defined in the Companies Act 2006, s. 260(1), as a proceeding by a member of a company:

(a) in respect of a cause of action vested in the company, and
(b) seeking relief on behalf of the company.

In this provision, 'member' includes a person to whom shares in the company have been transferred, or have been transmitted by operation of law (that is, to a personal representative of a deceased member or the trustee of a bankrupt member), but who is not a member of the company (because of not being registered as the holder of the shares) (s. 260(5)(c)).

A derivative claim may be brought only under the Companies Act 2006, part 11, chapter 1 (ss. 260 to 264), or in pursuance of a court order under s. 996(2)(c) (protection of members against unfair prejudice) (s. 260(2)). The procedure on a derivative claim is governed by **CPR, rr. 19.9** to **19.9F**, but those rules do not apply to a claim authorised by the court under the Companies Act 2006, s. 996(2)(c) (**CPR, r. 19.9(1)(b)**). A derivative claim must be commenced by claim form (**r. 19.9(2)**), which must be headed 'Derivative claim' (**PD 19C, para. 2(1)**). The company must be joined as a co-defendant so that if its rights are vindicated it will be able to enforce the judgment (**CPR, r. 19.9(3)**). Other reasons why the company must be named as a co-defendant in a derivative claim are in order for it to be bound by any judgment (otherwise it could bring its own proceedings in respect of the same wrong), to receive the fruits (if any) of the judgment, and because the claim has not been authorised by its board or general meeting (*Roberts v Gill and Co.* [2010] UKSC 22, [2011] 1 AC 240, at [57]). It is not a requirement that the delinquent director should have profited or benefited from his misconduct.

A statutory derivative claim under the Companies Act 2006, ss. 260 to 264, may be brought only in respect of a cause of action specified in s. 260. The cause of action must be vested in the company (s. 260(1)). It must arise from an actual or proposed act or omission which involves negligence, default, breach of duty or breach of trust by a director, former director or shadow director of the company (s. 260(3) and (5)(a) and (b)). The cause of action may be against the director, or another person or both (s. 260(3)). It may have arisen before the claimant became a member of the company (s. 260(4)).

A member of a company who brings a statutory derivative claim under ss. 260 to 264 must apply to the court for permission to continue it (s. 261(1)). Section 263 gives guidance on how the court should approach deciding whether to give permission. The principal matters to be taken into account are:

(a) the good faith of the derivative claimant (s. 263(3)(a));

(b) the importance that a person acting in accordance with the duty to promote the success of the company would attach to continuing it (s. 263(3)(b));
(c) whether there has been, or could be, authorisation or ratification of the act or omission giving rise to the claim (s. 263(2)(b) and (c) and (3)(c) and (d));
(d) whether the company has decided not to pursue the claim (s. 263(3)(e));
(e) whether the claim is one which the member could pursue in his own right rather than on behalf of the company (s. 263(3)(f));
(f) the views of disinterested members (s. 263(4));
(g) whether the claim would promote the company's success (s. 263(2)(a) and (3)(b)).

The fact that the claimant's primary motivation is to enhance the value of its own shareholding rather than the prosperity of the company does not show that it is acting in bad faith. Permission to continue a derivative claim may be refused if appropriate remedies could be obtained by pursuing an unfair prejudice petition under s. 994 (*Franbar Holdings Ltd v Patel* [2008] EWHC 1534 (Ch), [2009] 1 BCLC 1; *Stimpson v Southern Private Landlords Association* [2009] EWHC 2072 (Ch), [2010] BCC 387; *Kleanthous v Paphitis* [2011] EWHC 2287 (Ch), LTL 21/9/2011), but this is not inevitable, particularly where the applicant is not seeking to be bought out (see *Wishart v Castlecroft Securities Ltd* [2009] CSIH 65, 2010 SC 16; *Stainer v Lee* [2010] EWHC 1539 (Ch), [2011] 1 BCLC 537). There is no need for a derivative claim if the persons bringing it could bring a private claim for their own loss and the claim cannot be regarded as a corporate asset (*Certain Limited Partners in Henderson PFI Secondary Fund II LLP v Henderson PFI Secondary Fund LP* [2012] EWHC 3259 (Comm), LTL 23/11/2012). Although it cannot be said that it would never be appropriate for a derivative claim to be brought by a majority shareholder in control of a company, permission to do so would be given only in very exceptional circumstances and it is difficult to imagine what those might be (*Cinematic Finance Ltd v Ryder* [2010] EWHC 3387 (Ch), LTL 21/10/2010). A derivative claim can be brought and may be allowed to continue where the applicant and proposed respondent are each 50 per cent shareholders in the company (*Parry v Bartlett* [2011] EWHC 3146 (Ch), LTL 11/1/2012). Although there is no rule that a derivative action can only be brought where the alleged wrongdoers remain in control, the potential of the company itself to commence proceedings was a relevant consideration. An application for permission to continue a derivative claim may be refused if a procedure exists for instituting a claim on the company's behalf under a company's shareholder agreement (*Bamford v Harvey* [2012] EWHC 2858 (Ch), *The Times*, 7 December 2012).

The court may take into account other factors, but must pay particular regard to the listed factors (*Franbar Holdings Ltd v Patel*). In *Kiani v Cooper* [2010] EWHC 577 (Ch), [2010] 2 BCLC 427, the court granted permission to continue a derivative claim where the director alleged to be in breach of fiduciary duty had failed to produce any evidence which corroborated his defence to the allegations against him (see also *Phillips v Fryer* [2013] BCC 176). Although it was possible for the applicant to bring a petition under the Companies Act 2006, s. 994, instead of the derivative claim, the existence of this alternative remedy was only one factor which the court should consider. A notional director, acting in accordance with his duties under s. 172 of the Act, would wish to continue with the claim, at least to the stage of disclosure, where corroborative documents might be produced by the respondent. In contrast, in *Kleanthous v Paphitis* [2011] EWHC 2287 (Ch), LTL 21/9/2011, the court refused permission to allow the derivative claim to continue as it was not of such a size and strength (there being a number of limitation and other difficulties) to make it appropriate to grant permission when this was opposed by the companies and the applicant could obtain his preferred remedy (a share buy-out) by the more appropriate course of an Unfair Prejudice petition under the Companies Act, s. 994.

Section 263(3)(b) asks the court to take into account, in particular, the importance that a person (called, in the cases, the 'hypothetical director') acting in accordance with s. 172 (duty to promote the success of the company) would attach to continuing the claim. Section 263(2)(a) requires the court to refuse permission if satisfied the hypothetical director would not seek

Commentary

to continue the claim. The claimant does not have to show that the hypothetical director would undoubtedly continue the claim (*Franbar Holdings Ltd v Patel*). If the hypothetical director would not attach much importance to the claim, permission to continue it will be refused (*Mission Capital plc v Sinclair* [2008] EWHC 1339 (Ch), [2008] BCC 866; *Iesini v Westrip Holdings Ltd* [2009] EWHC 2526 (Ch), LTL 26/10/2009; *Stimpson v Southern Private Landlords Association*).

The relationship between s. 263(2)(a) and s. 263(3)(b) was considered in *Iesini v Westrip Holdings Ltd.* Section 263(2)(a) applies only where the court is satisfied that no director acting in accordance with s. 172 would seek to continue the claim. If some directors would, and others would not, seek to continue the claim, then s. 263(3)(b) should be applied, when many of the same considerations will apply.

Permission must be refused where the cause of action arises from an act or omission yet to occur, and that act or omission has been ratified by the company, or is in relation to past acts or omissions which were authorised by the company before they occurred or have been subsequently ratified by the company (s. 263(2)(b) and (c)).

Section 261 requires the court to consider an application for permission to continue a derivative claim in two stages. At the first stage it considers only the evidence presented by the claimant and must dismiss the application if this evidence does not disclose a prima facie case for giving permission (s. 261(2)). The prima facie case to which s. 261(1) refers is a prima facie case for giving permission. There must be a prima facie case that the company has a good cause of action and that cause of action arises out of a director's default, negligence, breach of duty or breach of trust (*Iesini v Westrip Holdings Ltd*). If the court decides that there is a prima facie case, it will give directions for evidence to be provided by the company and for a contested hearing of the application (s. 261(3)). Both stages may be taken together if the parties agree (*Mission Capital plc v Sinclair*; *Franbar Holdings Ltd v Patel*).

In *Stainer v Lee* [2010] EWHC 1539 (Ch), [2011] 1 BCLC 537, the court considered the standard to be applied when considering the provisional merits of the cause of action against the respondents. If the case seemed very strong, it might be appropriate to continue it even if the sums at stake were not large, as such a claim is likely to be settled or result in summary judgment being awarded. On the other hand if the sums at stake were very large, it might be in the company's interests for the claim to be continued even if the court formed the provisional view that the claim was not a strong one. See also *Hughes v Weiss* [2012] EWHC 2363 (Ch), LTL 28/9/2012.

When the claim form for a derivative claim is issued, the claimant must file an application notice under **CPR, Part 23**, for permission to continue the claim, together with written evidence in support (Companies Act 2006, s. 261(1); **CPR, r. 19.9A(2)**). The claimant must not take any further step in the proceedings (other than pursuing the permission application) without the court's permission, except for an urgent application for interim relief (r. 19.9(4)).

At the first stage the company must not be made a respondent to the permission application (**r. 19.9A(3)**) but must be given notice of it in accordance with **r. 19.9A(4)**, (5) and (6), and **PD 19C, para.** 4. A witness statement must be filed by the claimant confirming that the company has been notified (**r. 19.9A(6)**). The court may, on a without-notice application by the claimant, order that the company need not be notified of the permission application, if notification would be likely to frustrate some part of the remedy sought (**r. 19.9A(7)** and (8)). An application for an order under **r. 19.9A(7)** must state the reasons for the application and any written evidence in support must be filed with it (**PD 19C, para. 3**).

A permission application in the High Court is assigned to the Chancery Division and will be decided by a judge. In a county court it will be decided by a circuit judge (**PD 19C, para. 6**).

At the first stage, the court must dismiss the permission application if it appears that the application and the supporting evidence do not disclose a prima facie case for giving permission (Companies Act 2006, s. 261(2)). A permission application may be dismissed on this basis without a hearing (**CPR, r. 19.9A(9)**), but if it is, the claimant may, within seven days of being notified of the decision, request an oral hearing to reconsider it (**r. 19.9A(10)**). Such a request must be in writing and must be notified to the company in writing, unless the court orders otherwise (**r. 19.9A(10)**).

A decision at the first stage will normally be made without submissions from the company. If, without invitation by the court, the company volunteers a submission, or appears at an oral hearing, it will not normally be allowed its costs (**PD 19C, para. 5**).

If the court does not dismiss for failure to disclose a prima facie case, it will order that the company, and any other appropriate party, must be made respondents to the application, and give directions for service (**CPR, r. 19.9A(12)**) so that there can be a full hearing.

On a full hearing, the court may give permission to continue the derivative claim on such terms as it thinks fit, or refuse permission and dismiss the claim, or adjourn the proceedings and give such directions as it thinks fit (Companies Act 2006, s. 261(4)).

A person making a derivative claim on behalf of a company may seek indemnification by the company for the costs of the claim (**CPR, r. 19.9E**; see **44.7**). For an example see *Stainer v Lee* [2010] EWHC 1539 (Ch), [2011] 1 BCLC 537.

If a claim vested in a company arises out of facts which also disclose unfairly prejudicial conduct of the company's affairs, a petition by a member under the Companies Act 2006, s. 994 (see **85.9** to **85.20**), may be used as an alternative to a derivative claim (*Re a Company (No. 005287 of 1985)* [1986] 1 WLR 281; *Lowe v Fahey* [1996] 1 BCLC 262; *Clark v Cutland* [2003] EWCA Civ 810, [2004] 1 WLR 783).

The proper claimant principle applies to any association which is capable of suing or being sued in its own name, and **CPR, r. 19.9**, is expressed to apply not only to companies but also to other bodies corporate and trade unions (**r. 19.9(1)(a)** and **r. 19.9C**). A derivative claim may be brought in relation to a foreign company as well as a company incorporated in England and Wales. However, the appropriate forum for such a claim is likely to be the country of incorporation (*Konamaneni v Rolls-Royce Industrial Power (India) Ltd* [2002] 1 WLR 1269; *Music Sales Ltd v Shapiro Bornstein and Co. Inc.* [2005] EWHC 759 (Ch), [2006] 1 BCLC 371; *Reeves v Sprecher* [2007] EWHC 117 (Ch), [2007] 2 BCLC 614; see **16.53**).

A derivative claim can also be brought in respect of a limited partnership. However, there was no need for a derivative claim to be made by limited partners against the general partner of a limited partnership where the claim was not a partnership asset and each limited partner had its own claim for its own loss. However, a claim against the manager of the partnership was a partnership asset and could not be pursued by any limited partner individually. It was just to allow the derivative claim to be brought because the partnership had no realistic prospects of obtaining redress by any other route (*Certain Limited Partners in Henderson PFI Secondary Fund II LLP v Henderson PFI Secondary Fund LP* [2012] EWHC 3259 (Comm), LTL 23/11/2012).

Derivative claims may also be made by beneficiaries of a trust or beneficiaries under a will. However, a beneficiary under a will may bring a derivative claim only if the circumstances of the case are sufficiently special to make it just for the beneficiary to have the remedy rather than the personal representatives. If a beneficiary is entitled to bring a derivative action, the personal representatives should also be joined at the outset of the proceedings (*Roberts v Gill and Co.* [2010] UKSC 22, [2011] 1 AC 240).

Commentary

Continuation of a company's claim as a derivative claim or of a derivative claim with a different claimant

14.28 If those with authority to conduct a company's litigation fear a derivative claim, they may try to block it by causing the company to bring a claim but with no intention of genuinely pursuing it. The Companies Act 2006, s. 262, therefore permits a member of a company to apply to the court for permission to take over a claim brought by the company and continue it as a derivative claim on the grounds that:

(a) the manner in which the company commenced or continued the claim amounts to an abuse of the process of the court;
(b) the company has failed to prosecute the claim diligently; and
(c) it is appropriate for the member to continue the claim as a derivative claim.

There is a similar provision in s. 264 for an existing derivative claim to be taken over by a new claimant on the same grounds.

An application for permission under s. 262 or s. 264 follows the same two-stage process as an application under s. 261 (see **14.27**). **CPR, r. 19.9B**, applies **r. 19.9A** with necessary modifications.

Permission to continue a derivative claim may be given on condition that the claim is not to be discontinued, settled or compromised without the court's permission (**r. 19.9F**). This will be appropriate to ensure that other members of the company are given an opportunity to continue the derivative claim themselves (**PD 19C, para. 7**).

Reflective loss

14.29 It follows from the proper claimant principle (**14.27**) that a member holding shares in a company cannot claim any compensation for the diminution in value of those shares which merely reflects a loss which the company could recover (the 'no reflective loss principle'). The diminution in value of the shares due to the company's loss will be reversed when the company recovers compensation for that loss (*Prudential Assurance Co. Ltd v Newman Industries Ltd (No. 2)* [1982] Ch 204 at pp. 222–3; *Johnson v Gore Wood and Co.* [2002] 2 AC 1). A member of the company also cannot sue for any other losses which merely reflect losses which the company could recover, such as lost dividends and any other payments which the shareholder might have obtained from the company if it had not been deprived of its funds, including payments which might have been made in the shareholder's capacity as an officer or employee of the company. See also *Webster v Sandersons Solicitors* [2009] EWCA Civ 830, [2009] 2 BCLC 542.

The no reflective loss principle ensures that a defendant can only be sued once for the same loss. It prevents a person other than the company suing even if that person has a cause of action against the defendant and even if that cause of action differs from the company's (*Day v Cook* [2001] EWCA Civ 592, [2002] 1 BCLC 1, at [79]). It applies whether the cause of action lies in common law or equity, and whether the remedy is damages or restitution (*Gardner v Parker* [2004] EWCA Civ 781, [2004] 2 BCLC 554). It applies to prevent a member suing whether the member has a controlling or a minority interest (*Gardner v Parker*, rejecting doubts expressed in *Humberclyde Finance Group Ltd v Hicks* (2001) LTL 19/11/2001 and in *Floyd v John Fairhurst and Co.* [2004] EWCA Civ 604, [2004] PNLR 41, at [77]). See also *Mellor v Partridge* [2013] EWCA Civ 477, LTL 3/5/2013.

The no reflective loss principle is not an infringement of the European Convention on Human Rights, **protocol 1, art. 1** (protection of property), in the **Human Rights Act 1998, sch. 1** (*Humberclyde Finance Group Ltd v Hicks* (2001) LTL 19/11/2001).

Practice relating to reflective loss

If a company with a right to sue a person, D, to recover a loss fails to recover all or part of that loss, for example, because it settles the claim before trial, or refuses to take any action at all, then all or part of members' reflective losses will not be recovered. This does not give the members a right to sue D for the unrecovered amount of the reflective losses, because the shortfall in recovery is caused by the company, not D (*Johnson v Gore Wood and Co.* [2002] 2 AC 1). There is an exception if it is D's wrongdoing which has caused the company to be unable to sue, for example, because that wrongdoing has left it without enough money to fund litigation (*Giles v Rhind* [2002] EWCA Civ 1428, [2003] Ch 618). **14.30**

The mere fact that D has caused a company to suffer loss does not give a holder of shares in that company a right of action to sue for the diminution in share value resulting from that loss. However, it is possible for a company to suffer loss because of something done by D but have no right of action against D while a shareholder does have a right of action against D. In such a case, the shareholder is permitted to claim for loss in value of the shareholding due to a loss which the company itself has no cause of action to recover (*George Fischer (Great Britain) Ltd v Multi Construction Ltd* [1995] 1 BCLC 260; *Gerber Garment Technology Inc. v Lectra Systems Ltd* [1997] RPC 443).

It is possible, when both company and shareholder have causes of action against the same defendant, that some of the shareholder's claims are not for reflective losses and can be pursued by the shareholder personally (see, for example, *R. P. Howard Ltd v Woodman Matthews and Co.* [1983] BCLC 117; *Giles v Rhind*). A secured debenture holder's claim against an administrative receiver it had appointed over the company did not offend the rule against reflective loss. The administrative receiver's primary duty was to the appointing debenture holder and not the company. A secured debenture holder's position was different to that of a shareholder who sought to sue for loss suffered by a company (*International Leisure Ltd v First National Trustee Co UK Ltd* [2012] EWHC 1971 (Ch), [2013] 2 WLR 466).

It has been suggested that a defendant applying to strike out a claim, on the ground that it reflects a loss which a company could have sued for, but did not, must show that the supposed claim by the company would have been likely to succeed (*Perry v Day* [2004] EWHC 1398 (Ch), LTL 18/6/2004, per Rimer J at [65]).

By analogy with the no reflective loss principle, if a defendant's wrongful act is found to have caused both a loss to a claimant and a gain to a company in which the claimant is a shareholder, the claimant's loss and the company's gain must be set off, at least where the claimant effectively owns all the shares in the company (*Floyd v John Fairhurst and Co.* [2004] EWCA Civ 604, [2004] PNLR 41).

If a company has been injured by a breach of the European Convention on Human Rights, a member of the company is not a victim of that breach and so has no standing to apply to the European Court of Human Rights or to bring proceedings under the **Human Rights Act 1998, s. 7** (*Agrotexim v Greece* (application 14807/89) (1995) 21 EHRR 250; *Weir v Secretary of State for Transport* [2005] EWHC 2192 (Ch), LTL 14/10/2005, at [294]–[298]). The European Court of Human Rights has, however, allowed a form of derivative claim, in which a member of a company presents an application in the company's name, where it is clear that it is not possible for those responsible for the company's litigation to make the application (*Credit and Industrial Bank v Czech Republic* (application 29010/95) ECHR 2003-XI at paras 46–52).

PARTNERSHIPS

Name

14.31 By **PD 7A, para. 5A.3**, claims by and against partners carrying on business within the jurisdiction at the time when the cause of action accrued must be brought in the partnership name, unless it is inappropriate to do so (as to which, no guidance is provided). The name to be used is that at the date of accrual of the cause of action, not at the date when proceedings are issued. For the purpose of para. 5A, 'partners' includes persons claiming to be entitled as partners and persons alleged to be partners (**para. 5A.2**). Partners in a firm which was not carrying on business in England and Wales at the time the cause of action accrued may only sue or be sued individually in their own names.

Where partners are being sued in the name of the partnership the full name of the partnership and the words '(A Firm)' should appear in the title of the claim. Where they are being sued as individuals, the full unabbreviated name of each partner and the title by which he is known should appear (**PD 16, para. 2.6**). It is arguable that bringing proceedings against a named partner and also against the firm in which he was a partner at the relevant time is an irregularity because the partner is effectively being sued twice in the same claim (*Brown v Innovatorone plc* [2009] EWHC 1376 (Comm), [2010] 2 All ER (Comm) 80, at [12]).

Disclosure of partners' names

14.32 Any party to a claim may serve a request asking for the partners to provide a partnership membership statement, providing details of the names and last known places of residence of all the partners at the time when the cause of action accrued (PD 7A, **paras. 5B.1** and **5B.2**). It is for the party making the request to specify the date when the relevant cause of action accrued (**para. 5B.3**). If the partners are requested to provide a copy of the partnership membership statement by any party to the claim, the partners must do so within 14 days of receipt of the request (**PD 7A, para. 5B.2**). However, presumably an application for disclosure could be made under **CPR, Part 23**.

Enforcement of a judgment debt against partnership property is dealt with at **79.38**.

Limited liability partnerships

14.33 A limited liability partnership is a body corporate with legal personality separate from that of its members (Limited Liability Partnerships Act 2000, s. 1(2)). It should be sued in its full registered name, including the expression 'limited liability partnership' or the abbreviation 'llp' or LLP' (or their Welsh equivalents), which must be at the end of the registered name (Limited Liability Partnerships Act 2000, sch. 1, para. 2).

SOLE TRADERS

14.34 By **PD 7A, para. 5C**, where a claim is brought against an individual carrying on business in the jurisdiction under a business name, the claim may be brought against the business name as if it were the name of a partnership. The provision therefore enables proceedings to be issued against a business even if the name of the person running it is not known. However, if the full name of the sole trader is known, the claim form should state the individual's full *unabbreviated name and title*, and the full trading name (for example, John Smith trading as (or T/as) JS Autos) (**PD 16, para. 2.6(b)**).

OTHER INCORPORATED AND UNINCORPORATED ASSOCIATIONS

Building societies

A building society must be incorporated under the Building Societies Act 1986 and can sue or be sued in its corporate name. **14.35**

Charities

A charitable corporation, which may sue or be sued in its own name, may be created in a number of ways: by royal charter, by the Charity Commission under the Charities Act 2011, or as an industrial and provident society, company or community interest company registered at Companies House. Part 11 of the Charities Act 2011 contains provisions for the constitution and registration of charitable incorporated organisations (CIOs). These provisions came into force on 2 January 2013. Where a CIO is constituted and entered on the register of charities maintained by the Charity Commission under Part 4 of the Charities Act 2011, it becomes, by virtue of the registration, a body corporate (Charities Act 2011, s. 210). **14.36**

Where a charitable institution is unincorporated, proceedings may be brought against it by suing an officer of the charity 'on behalf of the charity [naming it]'. Alternatively, the charity's trustees may be named as parties (*Muman v Nagasena* [2000] 1 WLR 299).

Proceedings under the court's jurisdiction with respect to charities, or with respect to trusts in relation to the administration of a trust for charitable purposes, cannot be brought without the permission of the Charity Commission (Charities Act 2011, s. 115). The Commission will not give permission without special reasons if, in its opinion, it can deal with the matter itself under the 2011 Act (s. 115(3)). If the Commission refuses to give permission, it may be given instead by a judge of the Chancery Division (s. 115(5)). For the approach to be followed in applications for permission under s. 115(5), see *Rai v Charity Commission for England and Wales* [2012] EWHC 1111 (Ch), [2012] WTLR 1053. These rules do not apply to proceedings brought by the Commission itself or by the Attorney-General (s. 115(6)).

Applications to the High Court to start charity proceedings, following refusal by the Charity Commission to authorise them, must be brought in accordance with **CPR, Part 64**. Although **CPR, Part 64** continues to refer to the repealed Charities Act 1993, this should be construed as a reference to the Charities Act 2011. An application for permission to start charity proceedings must be made within 21 days after the Commission's refusal to do so (**r. 64.6**). The application is made by issuing a Part 8 claim form, containing the information specified in **PD 64A, para. 9.1**. The Commission must be made a defendant to the claim, and the judge may direct it to file a written statement of the reasons for its decision (**CPR, r. 64.6**). If the commissioners have given reasons, a copy of those reasons must be filed with the claim form (**PD 64A, para. 9.2**). The judge may give permission without a hearing or fix a hearing (**r. 64.6(6)**). The Attorney-General is a necessary party to all charity proceedings, other than any commenced by the Charity Commission, and must be joined as a defendant if he or she is not the claimant (PD 64A, para. 7).

Applications for permission to appeal against an order of the Charity Commission are governed by **CPR, Part 52**, and **PD 52, para. 23.8A** (see **PD 64A, para. 10**).

Trade unions and employers' associations

A trade union which is not a special register body under the Trade Union and Labour Relations (Consolidation) Act 1992, s. 117, is not a body corporate. However, even if unincorporated, **14.37**

Commentary

a trade union is capable of suing or being sued in its own name (Trade Union and Labour Relations (Consolidation) Act 1992, s. 10(1)(b)). It may not, however, unless it is a special register body and therefore a body corporate, sue in its own name for damages for defamation. This is because a libel is a wrong to the person and therefore no claim may be brought unless the trade union has a legal personality (*Electrical, Electronic, Telecommunication and Plumbing Union v Times Newspapers Ltd* [1980] QB 585).

An employers' association may be either a body corporate or an unincorporated association. However, even where unincorporated, it may sue or be sued in its own name (Trade Union and Labour Relations (Consolidation) Act 1992, s. 127(2)(b)).

Central government departments

14.38 Most central government departments may sue or be sued in their own name: see **14.44** to **14.46**.

Local government bodies

14.39 London boroughs (London Government Act 1963, s. 1), metropolitan districts and non-metropolitan counties and districts (Local Government Act 1972, s. 2) are bodies corporate, and may sue or be sued by name.

A local authority (which includes a county council, a district council, a London borough council and a parish council: Local Government Act 1972, s. 270) may institute civil proceedings where it considers it expedient for the promotion or protection of the interests of the inhabitants of its area (Local Government Act 1972, s. 222).

Quasi-governmental public bodies

14.40 There are numerous quasi-governmental public bodies which are not formal departments of State. These bodies will usually have an implicit power to bring proceedings to protect their special interests in the performance of their functions (*Broadmoor Special Health Authority v Robinson* [2000] QB 775). See also *R v Rollins* [2010] UKSC 39, [2010] 1 WLR 1922.

Clubs

14.41 An unincorporated members' social or sporting club is not a separate legal entity and may not sue or be sued in the name of the club. Thus, in *Oxford University v Webb* [2006] EWHC 2490 (QB), LTL 20/10/2006, it was held that the Animal Liberation Front, an unincorporated association, could not sue or be sued in its own name because it was not a legal person. It could only be joined through representative proceedings under **CPR, r. 19.6.** Nor can the secretary or any other officer of such a club sue or be sued on behalf of the club. Where proceedings are necessary, there are two main options:

(a) Bring proceedings against individual members of the club. However, members who are not made parties will have no direct interest in the claim, and any judgment obtained may not be enforced against them.

(b) Bring representative proceedings (see **14.62**) (*Campbell v Thompson* [1953] 1 QB 445; *Artistic Upholstery Ltd v Art Forma (Furniture) Ltd* [1999] 4 All ER 277). A judgment in a representative action binds the members represented, but may not be enforced against any member who is not a party to the proceedings, without the court's permission.

A proprietary club is one where the property and funds of the club belong to the proprietor, who usually conducts it with a view to profit. Where such a club is unincorporated, the proprietor may sue or be sued, either in his or her own name or in the name of the club (*Firmin and Sons Ltd v International Club* (1889) 5 TLR 694). Where it is incorporated, it should sue and be sued in its corporate name.

A costs order against 'London Animal Action', an unincorporated association, was enforced against a bank account in the association's name by a third party debt order. An appeal by London Animal Action, arguing that an order can only be enforced against persons with legal identity, was rejected (*Huntingdon Life Sciences Group plc v Cass* [2005] EWHC 2233 (QB), [2005] 4 All ER 899).

TRUSTS AND TRUSTEES

A claim by or against a trust is brought by joining its trustees. Trustees should act jointly and all should be named in any proceedings (as defendants, if they will not consent to act as claimants). 14.42

It is provided in **CPR, r. 19.7A**, that beneficiaries need not be joined as parties to a claim brought by or against a trust. Any judgment or order made in the claim will bind the beneficiaries unless the court orders otherwise. The predecessor to this rule (RSC, ord. 15, r. 14(1)) empowered the court to order otherwise only because the trustees could not or did not represent the beneficiaries' interests. In practice this is likely to remain the principal reason for ordering that a judgment is not binding on beneficiaries.

In a claim, judgment or order relating to trust property, the court has power under CPR, **r. 19.8A**, to order notice of the claim to be given to anyone who is not a party but who may be affected by it. An application for an order under this rule may be made without notice but must be supported by written evidence which includes the reasons why the person to be served should be bound by the judgment in the claim. Notice must be given in form No. 52, accompanied by a copy of the claim form, a copy of the judgment or order (if relevant), all other statements of case, including written evidence as the court may direct and a form for acknowledging service. The person served becomes a party to the claim on acknowledging service. Even if there is no acknowledgment of service, the person will be bound by any judgment or order made in the claim.

Derivative claim by beneficiaries

While claims involving the assets of an estate or *inter vivos* trust are ordinarily brought by or against the personal representatives or trustees, in special circumstances it may be possible for beneficiaries to bring a derivative claim. Typical examples of special circumstances are fraud on the part of the trustees, or collusion between the trustees and third parties, or the insolvency of the trustee, although the categories are not closed (*Roberts v Gill and Co.* [2010] UKSC 22, [2011] 1 AC 240, at [45]). The availability of public funding to the beneficiary that might not be available to the trustees is not a special circumstance (*Roberts v Gill and Co.* at [75]). 14.43

If there are special circumstances, it is necessary to name the trustees or personal representatives as defendants (*Roberts v Gill and Co.* at [56]). The claimant's representative capacity has to be set out in the claim form (**CPR, r. 16.2(3)**), and the special circumstances have to be set out in the particulars of claim (*Roberts v Gill and Co.* at [103]). The detailed rules on company derivative claims in **rr. 19.9** to **19.9F** do not technically apply to derivative claims by beneficiaries, but it is suggested that an application for permission to continue the claim and for directions should be issued at an early stage, perhaps after the acknowledgment of service.

CROWN PROCEEDINGS

Introduction

Proceedings by and against the Crown are governed by the Crown Proceedings Act 1947 and **CPR, Part 66**. The intention behind the Crown Proceedings Act 1947 is that proceedings 14.44

involving the Crown should be governed by broadly the same procedure as between private litigants. **CPR, Part 66**, has removed some of the procedural advantages which the Crown had under earlier rules. There are still special rules for Crown proceedings concerning the content of a claim form (see **23.18**), service (**15.52**), venue (**14.45**), forms of relief (**14.47**), default judgment (**20.7**), counterclaims (**28.2**) and enforcement (**79.40**). Crown proceedings cannot be undertaken through the Claim Production Centre (**12.8**) or Money Claim Online (**12.10**).

Venue

14.45 The Crown Proceedings Act 1947, s. 20(2), provides that the usual rules on transfer from a county court to the High Court, or the transfer of proceedings from the High Court to a county court, apply in relation to proceedings against the Crown. However, **CPR, r. 30.3(2)(h)**, adds to the factors to which the court must have regard in considering whether or not to transfer the claim 'the location of the relevant government department or officers of the Crown and, where appropriate, any relevant public interest that the matter should be tried in London'. A note by the Attorney-General to assist judges and practitioners with matters relevant to the venue of Crown proceedings is annexed to **PD 66**. The note points out that whilst a number of government departments have offices outside London, central government bodies are based in London and the Government Legal Service is geared towards processing claims in the RCJ. Where there is a High Court claim, many witnesses as well as lawyers and officials are London based and there may be a disproportionate cost in transferring them to a venue outside London. However, the Crown will not oppose transfer away from the RCJ where it is appropriate, for example, in personal injury disputes.

Parties to the proceedings

14.46 Only authorised government departments may sue or be sued in their own name (Crown Proceedings Act 1947, s. 17(2) and (3)). Where a department is not authorised under the Act, proceedings by or against it may be instituted in the name of the Attorney-General. **CPR, r. 19.4(4A)**, provides that the Commissioners for HM Revenue and Customs may be added as a party to proceedings only if they consent in writing. The Cabinet Office publishes a list of government departments authorised for the purposes of the Act. The list is annexed to **PD 66**. See also **15.52**.

In a claim against the Crown, the claim form must give the names of the government departments and officers of the Crown concerned, and brief details of the circumstances in which the alleged liability of the Crown arose (**CPR, r. 16.2(1A)**).

Forms of relief available against the Crown

14.47 Apart from the cases set out below, the court has power to grant the same relief against the Crown as it has in proceedings between private litigants. By the Crown Proceedings Act 1947, s. 21, the court may not, however, make an order for any of the following against the Crown:

(a) an injunction (although the court may require the Crown to provide a cross-undertaking in damages in support of an application for an interim injunction: *F. Hoffmann-La Roche & Co. AG v Secretary of State for Trade and Industry* [1975] AC 295);
(b) specific performance; or
(c) an order for the recovery of land or other property.

In these cases, the court will instead make a declaration against the Crown.

There are procedural restrictions on applications for default judgments (**CPR, r. 12.4(4)**) and summary judgment (**r. 24.4(1A)**) against the Crown.

Human rights: joining minister

The court cannot make a declaration of incompatibility under the **Human Rights Act 1998, s. 4**, unless 21 days' notice has been given to the Crown (**CPR, r. 19.4A(1)**). The minister, or other person permitted by the Act, is entitled to be joined on giving notice to the court. Where a claim is made for damages in respect of a judicial act under the Human Rights Act 1998, s. 9, notice must again be given to the Crown (**CPR, r. 19.4A(3)**), but in this situation, if the appropriate person does not apply to be joined within 21 days or such other time as may be allowed by the court, the court may join that person as a party (**r. 19.4A(4)**). A notice to the Crown under **r. 19.4A** must be served on the person named in the list published under the **Crown Proceedings Act 1947, s. 17** (**PD 19A, para. 6.4(1)**; the list is annexed to **PD 66**; for more on service on the Crown see **15.52**). In *Poplar Housing and Regeneration Community Association Ltd v Donoghue* [2001] EWCA Civ 595, [2002] QB 48 the Court of Appeal said that, in addition to the formal notice required under **r. 19.4A**, the party intending to raise the issue of incompatibility should also give informal notice of its intention to do so, both to the court and to the Crown, at the earliest possible opportunity. Directions under these provisions will usually be made at the case management conference (**PD 19A, paras 6.2 and 6.6**). **14.48**

FOREIGN STATES AND DIPLOMATS

Foreign States

The State Immunity Act 1978 gives foreign States immunity from the jurisdiction of the United Kingdom courts for acts of a governmental nature. The Act applies to any foreign or Commonwealth State, and to its government, head of State and governmental departments (s. 14(1)). Entities which are distinct from the executive organs of State are also immune if the proceedings relate to something done by the separate entity in the exercise of sovereign authority and the circumstances are such that a State would have been immune under the Act (s. 14(2)). A certificate issued by the Secretary of State of the Foreign and Commonwealth Office is conclusive evidence as to whether a territory is a State, and as to the person or persons to be regarded as the head of the government or State (s. 21(a)). **14.49**

The 1978 Act sets out the categories of claims for which a foreign State is not immune. Acts which could be performed by a company or a private individual will not enjoy immunity. These include where the proceedings relate to a commercial transaction (s. 3, the application of which is discussed in *NML Capital Ltd v Argentina* [2011] UKSC 31, [2011] 2 AC 495), to a contract of employment made or to be performed within the United Kingdom (s. 4), to death or personal injury, or damage to or loss of tangible property, caused by an act or omission in the UK (s. 5), to immovable property within the United Kingdom (s. 6), or to intellectual property rights (s. 7). The House of Lords has held in *Jones v Ministry of the Interior of Saudi Arabia* [2006] UKHL 26, [2007] 1 AC 270, that State immunity extends to the officials, servants and agents of the State. Immunity extended to a State's central bank which was acting to maintain the State's currency reserves, and was therefore to be considered the agent of the State (*Koo Golden East Mongolia v Bank of Nova Scotia* [2007] EWCA Civ 1443, [2008] QB 717).

The European Court of Human Rights has accepted that a plea of State immunity does in principle interfere with rights under **art. 6** of the European Convention on Human Rights in the **Human Rights Act 1998, sch. 1** (e.g. *McElhinney v Ireland* (application 31253/96) (2001) 34 EHRR 13, para. 26; *Fogarty v United Kingdom* (application 37112/97) (2001) 34 EHRR 12, para. 28; and *Al-Adsani v United Kingdom* (application 35763/97) (2001) 34 EHRR 273, para. 52). However, the House of Lords cast doubt on this proposition in *Jones v Ministry of the Interior of Saudi Arabia*. It stated that the rule of international law to which the State Immunity Act 1978 gives effect is that one State has no jurisdiction over another State and therefore a State cannot be said to deny access to its court if it has no access to give. The case involved an allegation of

Commentary

torture against the Kingdom of Saudi Arabia, alleged to have occurred in Saudi Arabia, in respect of which the Kingdom claimed State immunity. The court held that the application of state immunity to a torture claim did not infringe the claimants' rights under the European Convention of Human Rights, **art. 6** in the **Human Rights Act 1998, sch. 1**, as it could not be shown that the prohibition of torture is a preremptory norm which takes precedence over State immunity or a disproportionate restriction on access to a court.

A claim may be brought against a State where it has submitted voluntarily to the jurisdiction. It may do this by filing an acknowledgment of service and not taking any step to contest jurisdiction, or by prior written agreement, or by instituting, or intervening in, proceedings (s. 2).

Foreign diplomats

14.50 Both at common law, and under the provisions of the Diplomatic Privileges Act 1964, foreign diplomats, their families and their servants are immune from civil or criminal proceedings. A certificate of immunity issued by the Secretary of State will be conclusive (s. 4). Accordingly, service of a claim form on a person with diplomatic immunity is null and void, unless immunity is waived by the defendant filing an acknowledgment of service, and not following it up by an application under **CPR, Part 11**.

VEXATIOUS LITIGANTS

Means of restraining vexatious litigants

14.51 A small minority of litigants misuse the freedom of access to the courts by launching large numbers of unmeritorious claims or numerous interim applications, wasting court resources and causing a great deal of anxiety, trouble and expense to the persons they litigate against. Following amendments to the CPR made as a consequence of the decision in *Bhamjee v Forsdick* [2003] EWCA Civ 1113, [2004] 1 WLR 88, there are now two mechanisms for restraining the activities of a vexatious litigant. They are:

(a) Civil proceedings and all proceedings orders under the Senior Courts Act 1981, s. 42, made by the Divisional Court on the application of the Attorney-General, preventing a vexatious litigant issuing proceedings without permission of the court for an indefinite period (see **14.52**).

(b) One of three kinds of civil restraint orders, as defined in **CPR, r. 2.3(1)**. The procedure for making these is simpler than for orders under the Senior Courts Act 1981, s. 42, and does not require the involvement of the Attorney-General. Civil restraint orders can be made by the court acting on its own initiative (**CPR, r. 3.3(7)**). See **14.55** to **14.60**.

The Court of Appeal considered the relationship between the new rules and the court's inherent jurisdiction to regulate its own affairs in *R (Kumar) v Secretary of State for Constitutional Affairs* [2006] EWCA Civ 990, [2007] 1 WLR 536. Here, a general civil restraint order had been made despite the fact that there was no extended civil restraint order in place, contrary to the requirements of **PD 3C, para. 4.1**. The Court of Appeal held that there was no power, under either the CPR or the court's inherent jurisdiction, to make an order in these circumstances. Although the court's inherent jurisdiction to protect its process from abuse has been preserved alongside the powers conferred on it by the CPR, it would be a very rare case in which a judge could rely on the inherent jurisdiction in an area which appears to have been comprehensively covered in the rules.

However, the court also has relevant case management powers under **r. 3.1** which it can invoke to restrain disproportionate and unnecessary litigation. In *Phillips v Symes* [2006] EWHC 2595 (Ch), LTL 17/10/2006, the court upheld an order for a stay of proceedings in order to avoid the costs of litigation and to give the parties an opportunity to negotiate, thereby furthering the overriding objective.

Civil proceedings orders and all proceedings orders

Where it is proved that a litigant has 'habitually and persistently and without any reasonable ground' instituted vexatious proceedings or applications, whether in the High Court or any inferior court, and this includes tribunals such as the Leasehold Valuation Tribunal (which has now been abolished) (*Attorney General v Singer* [2012] EWHC 326 (Admin), LTL 25/1/2012), the High Court is given power under the Senior Courts Act 1981, s. 42, to make: **14.52**

(a) a civil proceedings order; or
(b) an all proceedings order applying both to all civil proceedings and applications and specified criminal proceedings.

A person subject to either order is prevented from continuing or commencing a civil claim, or making applications in a civil claim, without the permission of the High Court. The order will remain in force indefinitely, unless it is expressed to be for a specific period.

An order under the Senior Courts Act 1981, s. 42, does not violate the European Convention on Human Rights, **art. 6(1), in the Human Rights Act 1998, sch. 1** (*Attorney-General v Covey* [2001] EWCA Civ 254, *The Times*, 2 March 2001). The Convention requires a fair and reasonable opportunity to address the court, not an unlimited and uncontrolled opportunity.

In considering an application by the Attorney-General, the court will not go behind the previous adjudications made on the vexatious litigant's claims. The total litigation picture may merit a civil proceedings order being made under s. 42 with a penal notice attached so that defendants are protected from claims that disclose no intelligible grounds or are abusive (*Attorney-General v Ali* [2008] EWHC 1452 (Admin), LTL 25/7/2008; *Attorney-General v Ford* [2008] EWHC 2066 (Admin), LTL 28/8/2008). A civil proceedings order under the Senior Courts Act 1981, s. 42, covers proposed judicial review proceedings relating to a criminal cause or matter because the judicial review proceedings are civil (*Ewing v Director of Public Prosecutions* [2010] EWCA Civ 70, [2010] ACD 48).

Applying for orders under the Senior Courts Act 1981, s. 42

Application for an order under the Senior Courts Act 1981, s. 42, must be made by the Attorney-General and is heard by a Divisional Court (**PD 8A, para. 16**). The claim form must be filed at the Administrative Court. It should be accompanied by a witness statement in support and served on the person against whom the order is sought. **14.53**

Where a vexatious litigant (despite a civil proceedings order being made against him) is likely to conduct litigation in the names of others, acting as a litigation friend, but perhaps using the litigation as a vehicle for his own claims, an order (a '*Noueiri*' order) may be made restraining him from acting or purporting to act for others in legal proceedings unless he has obtained permission from a judge of the High Court or Court of Appeal (*Paragon Finance plc v Noueiri* [2001] EWCA Civ 1402, [2001] 1 WLR 2357; *Attorney-General v Branch* [2008] EWHC 2872 (Admin), LTL 7/11/2008).

Once an order is made under s. 42, it will not usually be appropriate to allow the person subject to the order to reopen the earlier proceedings even if he wishes to rely on facts that arose in those proceedings in his defence to a fresh claim brought against him by the other party (*University of Southampton v Mohtasham* [2011] EWHC 3979 (QB).

Permission applications by vexatious litigants

Permission to institute or continue or make an application in any civil proceedings by a person subject to a civil proceedings order will not be granted unless the High Court is satisfied **14.54**

Commentary

that the proceedings or application are not an abuse of the process of the court and that there are reasonable grounds for bringing the proceedings or application (Senior Courts Act 1981, s. 42(3)). The jurisdiction under s. 42(3) should be exercised with due care and caution or carefully and sparingly. In considering whether the applicant can show that there are reasonable grounds for bringing a claim, the court normally has to consider whether or not the claim has a real prospect of success. Deciding whether a claim is an abuse of process involves a careful consideration of all the likely issues as well as proportionality and the overriding objective. On an application for permission, the court should take into account all of the information before it, which includes evidence of conduct before and after being categorised a vexatious litigant (*Ewing v News International Ltd* [2008] EWHC 1390 (QB), LTL 29/7/2008).

The procedure whereby a litigant against whom an order has been made under the Senior Courts Act 1981, s. 42, makes an application for permission to commence or continue a claim is set out in **PD 3A, para. 7**. An application notice should be issued in the High Court and signed by the litigant who is subject to the order. The application notice must state:

(a) the title and reference number of the proceedings in which the order was made;
(b) the full name and address of the litigant;
(c) the order the litigant is seeking; and
(d) briefly, why the order is sought.

Written evidence may be filed in support of the application. Either in the application notice, or the supporting evidence, the litigant must list the previous occasions on which he or she has made an application for permission.

The application will then be placed before a High Court judge, who may:

(a) make an order granting or dismissing the application without the attendance of the applicant;
(b) ask for further written evidence from the litigant; or
(c) give directions for there to be a hearing of the application. Such directions may include an order that the application notice be served on the Attorney-General and on anyone against whom the litigant wishes to bring the new claim.

No appeal is possible against a decision refusing permission (Senior Courts Act 1981, s. 42(4)).

If permission is given for a vexatious litigant to commence a new claim, at a hearing of which the proposed defendant was not given notice, the defendant to the new claim may apply to set it aside (**PD 3A, para. 7.9**).

In *R (Ewing) v Office of the Deputy Prime Minister* [2005] EWCA Civ 1583, [2006] 1 WLR 1260, the court considered concurrent applications by a vexatious litigant under the Senior Courts Act 1981, s. 42, for permission to bring proceedings and for permission to seek judicial review. The court stated that a vexatious litigant should not allow his name to be included in a claim form (even as a 'proposed' claimant) unless and until he has obtained the necessary permission, and went on to give guidance on dealing with an application for permission under s. 42 in the context of a proposed judicial review claim. It also held that the procedure under s. 42 is designed to provide a mechanism to ensure that a vexatious litigant has access to the court to pursue his own genuine legal grievances, not to set himself up as a public champion. Where the court considers that the vexatious litigant does not have sufficient standing in the substantive action, it should refuse permission under s. 42 to bring the claim.

Civil restraint orders

14.55 *By virtue of* **CPR, r. 3.11**, and **PD 3C**, the court has power to make civil restraint orders. These provisions give effect to the recommendations in *Bhamjee v Forsdick* [2003] EWCA Civ 1113, [2004] 1 WLR 88, extending the old '*Grepe v Loam*' orders which restrained a party from making further applications in current proceedings (*Grepe v Loam* (1887) 37 ChD 168). **CPR, r. 2.3(1)**, defines three kinds of civil restraint orders:

(a) a limited civil restraint order, restraining a party from making any further applications in current proceedings (see **14.56**);
(b) an extended civil restraint order, restraining a party from issuing particular claims or making particular applications in specified courts (see **14.57** and **14.58**); and
(c) a general civil restraint order, restraining a party from issuing any claim or making any application in specified courts (see **14.59** and **14.60**).

Court orders must record whether any application (including an application for permission to appeal or for permission to apply for judicial review), statement of case or appeal has been struck out or dismissed as being totally without merit. Whenever it makes any such order, the court must go on to consider whether to make a civil restraint order (**rr. 3.3(7), 3.4(6), 23.12** and **52.10(6)**). However, the court is entitled to take into account any proceedings and applications made by the respondent which the court considers to be totally without merit. It is not restricted to proceedings and applications where there was at the time an express finding of a total lack of merit (*R (Kumar) v Secretary of State for Constitutional Affairs* [2006] EWCA Civ 990, [2007] 1 WLR 536). **Rule 3.3(7)** gives the court power to make a civil restraint order on its own initiative. In this case, the procedure in **r. 3.3** must be followed. Alternatively, a party to the litigation may make an application for an order using the procedure in **Part 23** (**PD 3C, paras 5.1** and **5.2**). Examples of limited, extended and general restraint orders are annexed to **PD 3C**. In *R (Kumar) v Secretary of State for Constitutional Affairs* [2006] EWCA Civ 990, [2007] 1 WLR 536, the Court of Appeal stressed that where the history of the litigation is complicated, the court should not make an order without giving the litigant an opportunity to prepare resistance to the order. Here, an order had been applied for by the defendant without filing any Part 23 notice, and the claimant against whom the order was sought had not had three clear days' notice of the application. The court held that the application should have been adjourned to give the claimant more time to prepare his case. Where the court is considering making a civil restraint order of its own initiative immediately upon striking out or dismissing a statement of case as being without merit (under **CPR, rr. 3.3(7), 3.4(6), 23.12** or **52.10(6)**) it will need to consider whether the party against whom an order is being considered has had adequate time to prepare opposition to the order. Similarly, in *R (Webster) v West Yorkshire Police* [2008] EWHC 2594, LTL 21/11/2008, the court declined to make a civil restraint order of its own motion and 'on the hoof', even though it had dismissed an application for judicial review as wholly without merit, because it did not have enough information before it to be satisfied that the claimant had persistently issued claims without merit. It required a formal application to be made so that full details of previous applications and claims made by the defendant could be considered with care.

Sometimes the court must go further and protect its staff from a litigant who persists in wasting their time and disturbing the orderly conduct of court business. The appropriate way of doing this is by an injunction prohibiting the litigant from entering the court building unless summoned by the court (*Attorney-General v Ebert* [2001] EWHC Admin 695, [2002] 2 All ER 789). See also *Mahajan v Department for Constitutional Affairs* [2004] EWCA Civ 946, *The Times*, 13 July 2004, in which an order was made restraining the claimant from addressing or corresponding with court staff in a rude or abusive manner.

In *Ebert v Venvil* [2000] Ch 484 the Court of Appeal made an extended civil restraint order restraining a party from taking any steps, including the issuing of new proceedings, in any Division of the High Court or any county court, arising out of the same matter. It rejected an argument that this would be contrary to the European Convention on Human Rights, **art. 6**, or the common law approach indicated in *R v Lord Chancellor, ex parte Witham* [1998] QB 575. The same view was taken in *Mahajan v Department for Constitutional Affairs* [2004] EWCA Civ 946, *The Times*, 13 July 2004, in which the Court of Appeal confirmed that, so long as the right of access to the court is not being extinguished, the court is entitled to regulate its affairs so as to protect its process and the interests of other parties against whom vexatious litigation is persistently brought.

An important factor in exercising the discretion to make a civil restraint order once the necessary preconditions are satisfied is whether the unmeritorious applications have been made as part of a vendetta (or similar motivation) or merely through ignorance or lack of funds (*R (Austin) v Portsmouth City Council* [2009] EWHC 1339 (Admin), LTL 22/6/2009).

CPR, r. 3.11, applies to High Court and county court proceedings only. It does not confer jurisdiction on the High Court to make an order in respect of tribunal proceedings, even though it can take into account unmeritorious claims in a tribunal when deciding whether to make a civil restraint order in the High Court or county courts. Where an inferior court lacks jurisdiction to make a restraint order, the High Court has a power to make a general restraint order which extends to tribunal proceedings under its inherent jurisdiction (*Law Society v Otobo* [2011] EWHC 2264 (Ch), LTL 20/4/2011). An employment tribunal has power to strike out an application where the applicant has acted vexatiously (*Fariba v Pfizer Ltd* UKEAT/0605/10/CEA, LTL 29/7/2011). The Employment Appeal Tribunal can also make a restriction of proceedings order against a vexatious litigant (see Employment Tribunals Act 1996, s. 33; *Attorney General v Bentley* (2012) LTL 14/6/2012).

Limited civil restraint orders

14.56 A limited civil restraint order restrains a party from making any further applications in current proceedings without obtaining the permission of a particular judge specified in the order (**PD 3C, para. 2.2(1)**). An order may be made by a judge of any court, where a party has made two or more applications which are totally without merit (**para. 2.1**). The order will remain in force for the duration of the proceedings (**para. 2.9**). This is the only form of civil restraint order which may be made by a master, circuit judge or district judge under **PD 3C**. For the position before **PD 3C** came into force see *Wickramaratna v Cambridge University Chemistry Department* [2004] EWCA Civ 1532, LTL 2/11/2004.

A party subject to a limited civil restraint order may apply to vary or discharge the order only with the permission of the judge specified in the order (**para. 2.2(2)**). The restrained party may also appeal against the order, but again only with permission (**para. 2.2(3)**). Making an application without permission will result in automatic dismissal (**para. 2.3(1)**). Where a person who is subject to a civil restraint order makes repeated applications for permission which are totally devoid of merit, by **para. 2.7**, a Court of Appeal judge, a High Court judge or master, or a designated civil judge or his deputy may make a further order refusing any further right of appeal unless the judge who refused permission to appeal now grants it (**para. 2.3(2)**).

Notice of an application, by a party who is subject to a limited civil restraint order, for permission under **para. 2.2(1)** or **(2)** must be served by that party on any other parties to the proceedings, setting out the nature and grounds of the application and giving the other parties at least seven days in which to respond. The application must be in writing, must include the other parties' written responses and will be determined without a hearing (**para. 2.6**). Any appeal against the refusal of permission under **para. 2.2(1)** or **(2)** must also be in writing and will also be determined without a hearing (**para. 2.8**).

Extended civil restraint orders

14.57 An extended civil restraint order restrains a party from issuing claims or applications in specified courts which involve, relate to, touch upon or lead to the proceedings in which the order is made (**PD 3C, para. 3.2(1)**). By **para. 3.1** a Court of Appeal judge, a High Court judge or a designated civil judge or his deputy may make such an order where a party has persistently issued claims or applications which are totally without merit in more than one set of proceedings (*Supperstone v Hurst* [2009] EWHC 1271 (Ch), [2009] 1 WLR 2306). The fact that the party has also made some successful, or partially successful, applications is relevant to the exercise of the discretion to grant an extended civil restraint order, but is not a bar (*Thakerar v Lynch Hall and Hornby* [2005] EWHC 2751 (Ch), [2006] 1 WLR 1511). There is a greater willingness to make these orders in light of the steadily increasing nuisance represented by vexatious litigants (*Bhamjee v Forsdick* [2003] EWCA Civ 1113, [2004] 1 WLR 88). An extended civil restraint order cannot curtail a person's communications with others. The order is designed to prevent abuse of the court's process, not harassment of persons (which can be prevented under the Protection from Harassment Act 1997) (*Supperstone v Hurst* [2009] EWHC 1271 (Ch), [2009] 1 WLR 2306). Masters, circuit judges and district judges have no power to make such an order. If they consider that an order should be made in a case before them, they must transfer it to a High Court or designated civil judge (**para. 3.11**). An extended civil restraint order can also be imposed on a non-party to proceedings if that person has been the driving force behind unmeritorious legal proceedings and there is a risk of such litigation occurring in the future (*Hurst v Denton-Cox* (2011) LTL 24/2/2011).

An extended civil restraint order will apply to claims or applications in:

(a) any court, where the order is made by a Court of Appeal judge;
(b) the High Court or the county court, where the order is made by a High Court judge; or
(c) any county court where the order is made by a designated civil judge or his deputy.

An extended civil restraint order will remain in force for a specified period not exceeding two years, although it may be extended for periods of up to two years at a time (**paras 3.9** and **3.10**).

Commentary

Applications by persons subject to extended civil restraint orders

A person subject to an extended civil restraint order may apply to vary or discharge the order only with the permission of the judge specified in the order (**PD 3C, para. 3.2(2)**). The restrained person may also appeal against the order, but again only with permission (**para. 3.2(3)**). Issuing a claim or making an application without permission will result in automatic striking out or dismissal (**para. 3.3(1)**). Where a person who is subject to an extended civil restraint order makes repeated applications for permission which are totally devoid of merit, by **para. 3.7**, a Court of Appeal judge, a High Court judge or a designated civil judge or his deputy may make a further order refusing any further right of appeal unless the judge who refused permission to appeal now grants it (**para. 3.3(2)**). 14.58

Notice of an application, by a party who is subject to an extended civil restraint order, for permission under **para. 3.2(1)** or **(2)**, must be served by that party on any other parties to the proceedings, setting out the nature and grounds of the application and giving the other parties at least seven days in which to respond. The application for permission must be in writing, must include the other parties' written responses and will be determined without a hearing (**para. 3.6**). Any appeal against the refusal of permission under **para. 3.2(1)** or **(2)** must also be in writing and will be determined without a hearing (**para. 3.8**). In *Forrester Ketley and Co. v Brent* [2008] EWHC 3150 (Ch), LTL 9/1/2009, the court considered the test to be applied in applications under **PD 3C, para. 3.2(2)**. It held that whilst it was not possible to provide a comprehensive list of factors, usually permission would not be granted unless the claim, application or step in the action for which permission was sought had a realistic prospect of success. Where a civil restraint order has been made against a vexatious litigant, the requirement to pay a fee in accordance with the Civil Proceedings Fees Order 2008, sch. 2 for permission to appeal against the order is not incompatible with **art. 6** of the European Convention on Human Rights (*Senior-Milne v Secretary of State for Justice* [2012] EWHC 3062 (Admin), LTL 14/11/2012).

As an alternative to making any form of civil restraint order, the court may accept an appropriate assurance from the litigant. In *Wilkes v Ballam Delaney Hunt* [2005] EWCA Civ 1104, the court declined to order an extended civil restraint order against a litigant who had given an assurance to the court not to commence fresh proceedings against specified individuals and had kept to his assurance.

An undertaking which is accepted by the court as an alternative to making a civil restraint order should be limited to the same period as a civil restraint order, namely, two years (*R (Austin) v Portsmouth City Council* [2009] EWHC 1339 Admin), LTL 22/6/2009).

General civil restraint orders

14.59 A general civil restraint order restrains a person from issuing any claim or making any application in specified courts without obtaining the permission of a particular judge specified in the order (**PD 3C, para. 4.2(1)**). By **paras 4.2(1)** and **4.1** a Court of Appeal judge, a High Court judge, or a designated civil judge or his deputy may make an order where a person has persistently issued claims or applications which are totally without merit and where an extended civil restraint order would not be sufficient or appropriate. Masters, circuit judges and district judges have no power to make general civil restraint orders. If they consider that an order should be made in a case before them, they must transfer it to a High Court or designated civil judge (**para. 4.11**).

Where a litigant had repeatedly breached an extended civil proceedings order and there was no indication that the extended order had effectively limited his activities, it was appropriate to make a general civil proceedings order against him. This was particularly so, given that he had made applications in relation to third parties to the main litigation (*Carroll v Kynaston* [2005] EWHC 927, LTL 2/6/2005).

The court can make a civil restraint order of its own initiative under **CPR, r. 3.11**. Where an extended civil restraint order cannot deal with the issues raised by the respondent because the court would have to speculate about what the next cause of action might be, a general civil restraint order can be made (*R (Salmon) v Secretary of State for the Home Department* [2009] EWHC 760 (Admin), LTL 5/5/2009).

A general civil restraint order will apply to claims or applications in:

(a) any court, where the order is made by a Court of Appeal judge;
(b) the High Court or the county court, where the order is made by a High Court judge; or
(c) any county court where the order is made by a designated civil judge or his deputy (**para. 4.2(1)**).

A general civil restraint order will remain in force for a specified period not exceeding two years, although it may be extended for periods of up to two years at a time (**paras 4.9** and **4.10**). In *Bar Mutual Indemnity Fund v Sheikh* [2011] EWHC 1946 (QB), LTL 28/7/2011, the court extended a general civil restraint order for a further two years as the respondent's behaviour clearly required the order to be continued.

Applications by persons subject to general civil restraint orders

14.60 A person subject to a general civil restraint order may apply to vary or discharge the order only with the permission of the judge specified in the order (**PD 3C, para. 4.2(2)**). The restrained person may also appeal against the order, but again only with permission (**para. 4.2(3)**). Issuing a claim or making an application without permission will result in automatic striking out or dismissal (**para. 4.3(1)**). Where a person who is subject to a general civil restraint order makes repeated applications for permission which are totally devoid of merit, by **para. 4.7**, a *Court of Appeal judge*, a High Court judge or a designated civil judge or his deputy may make a further order refusing any further right of appeal unless the judge who refused permission to appeal now grants it (**para. 4.3(2)**).

Notice of an application, by a party who is subject to a general civil restraint order, for permission under **para. 4.2(1)** or (2), must be served by that party on any other parties to the proceedings, setting out the nature and grounds of the application and giving the other parties at least seven days in which to respond. The application for permission must be in writing, must include the other parties' written responses and will be determined without a hearing (**para. 4.6**). Any appeal against the refusal of permission under **para. 4.2(1)** or (2) must also be in writing and will also be determined without a hearing (**para. 4.8**).

CONSOLIDATION

The court may order closely connected claims to be consolidated (**CPR, r. 3.1(2)(g)**). After consolidation the claims continue as if they were a single claim. Consolidation is only likely to be ordered where there is a strong overlap of issues of fact or law, or where there is a risk of irreconcilable judgments. Where there is minimal overlap, consolidation is inappropriate (*Law Debenture Trust Corporation (Channel Islands) Ltd v Lexington Insurance Co.* (2001) LTL 12/11/2001). The court will refuse consolidation, even where there is a sufficient overlap, if an order would lead to procedural unfairness and difficulties in case management. In *IXIS Corporate and Investment Bank v WestLB AG* [2007] EWHC 1748 (Comm), LTL 30/7/2007, the court refused an application to consolidate because the two cases concerned were at very different stages: a trial date had been fixed in one whereas the other had not reached the defence stage. **14.61**

A consolidation order can only be made if all the claims are before the court on the same occasion. Therefore applications will have to be made in each of the claims returnable in the same court (perhaps after some of the claims are transferred) at the same time. Alternatively, a single application can be issued (again after ensuring all claims are proceeding in the same court and Division) stating the titles of all the claims proposed to be consolidated. If the order is made, one of the claims is nominated as the lead claim. After consolidation, the usual rule is that all claimants (if legally represented) must have the same solicitors and counsel.

Where consolidation is inappropriate, similar case management objectives can be achieved by ordering trials of related claims to be listed together. In *Actavis UK Ltd v Eli Lilly and Co. Ltd* [2010] EWCA Civ 43, LTL 13/1/2010, the claimant in the first claim applied for the revocation of the defendant's patent. The claimant in the second claim, being concerned that the parties in the first claim might reach a settlement which would adversely affect its market position, commenced its own proceedings also seeking the revocation of the patent on the same grounds as those set out in the first claim. Case management directions in both claims provided that they be heard simultaneously before the same judge pursuant to r. 3.1(2)(h), and that the expert evidence, experiments and evidence at trial in the first claim would serve as the evidence in the second claim. The Court of Appeal upheld an order that the costs of both claims be split equally because it was impossible to distinguish between the two claims.

REPRESENTATIVE PARTIES

Principles

Where it is difficult or impossible for all persons affected by a claim to be parties to the proceedings, the court may, under **CPR, rr. 19.6** and **19.7**, order one or more persons to be made party to the claim as representative of persons who are not parties and direct that orders made in the claim are to bind represented persons. **Rule 19.6** also permits a claim to be commenced by or against a representative party without a court order. **Rule 19.6** applies to any kind of claim (but not to claims governed by **r. 19.7**). **Rule 19.7** (see 14.64) is available only in the **14.62**

Commentary

kinds of claims listed in **r. 19.7(1)**. The rules provide for two different sorts of 'representative proceedings':

(a) representation under **r. 19.6** of one person by another with the same interest in the claim (see below); and
(b) representation under **r. 19.7** of one person by another, where the person represented cannot be identified (see **14.63**).

An alternative method of dealing with the interests of several persons is by a group litigation order, or 'GLO' (see **14.66**).

It is provided in **CPR, r. 19.6(1)**, that:

> Where more than one person has the same interest in a claim—
> (a) the claim may be begun; or
> (b) the court may order that the claim be continued,
> by or against one or more of the persons who have the same interest as representatives of any other persons who have that interest.

In *Duke of Bedford v Ellis* [1901] AC 1 (followed in *Independiente Ltd v Music Trading On-Line (HK) Ltd* [2003] EWHC 470 (Ch), LTL 25/3/2003) it was held that there are three elements to be satisfied in deciding whether the representative party and the persons represented have the same interest:

(a) a common interest;
(b) a common grievance; and
(c) a remedy beneficial to all.

For a review of authorities and principles relevant to **r. 19.6** see *Millharbour Management Ltd v Weston Homes Ltd* [2011] EWHC 661 (TCC), [2011] 3 All ER 1027.

A representation order in respect of a defendant may be made only where everyone within the class has a common interest in the claim. Where different defendants have different defences there is no common interest within **r. 19.6(1)** (*London Association for Protection of Trade v Greenlands Ltd* [1916] 2 AC 15). However, in *Oxford University v Webb* [2006] EWHC 2490 (QB), LTL 20/10/2006, Irwin J held that the fact that different members of a defendant class have different defences will not prevent a representative order being made in all cases. There are two safeguards available to a member of the class affected by a representative action. First, the existence of the representation order and the fact that it binds them should be drawn to the attention of all those in the class. Any person wishing to argue a difference of interest and/or to run a different defence could apply to the court to be joined as a party and run that different defence. Secondly, by **r. 19.6(4)(b)**, a judgment or order may not be enforced against a person who is not a party to the claim without the permission of the court. It was concluded in this case that the Animal Liberation Front was a sufficiently consistent and coherent organisation, even though it deliberately lacked the 'trappings' of an organisation, to make it capable of being represented under **r. 19.6** by its public spokesman.

The court must also take account of the overriding objective. In *National Bank of Greece SA v R. M. Outhwaite 317 Syndicate at Lloyd's* [2001] Lloyd's Rep IR 652 it was held in the Commercial Court that it was proper to begin proceedings against one individual as representative of all members of 39 Lloyd's syndicates which had subscribed an insurance policy, even though the chosen individual was a member of only one of the syndicates and there was no leading underwriter clause in the policy. Andrew Smith J said that the phrase 'the same interest in a claim' in **r. 19.6** is to be interpreted with a view to giving effect to the overriding objective in the CPR. Specifically, it should be interpreted in a way that makes representative proceedings available in cases where they would save expense and enable a matter to be dealt with expeditiously.

The class the claimant seeks to represent must have a common interest in the claim and a common grievance, which must have existed when the claim was begun. If it is impossible to say whether any given person was a member of the class at the time the claim form was issued and throughout the proceedings because the criteria for inclusion in the class depend on the outcome of the litigation itself, then no representation order can be made under **r. 19.6** (*Emerald Supplies Ltd v British Airways plc* [2010] EWCA Civ 1284, [2011] Ch 345).

It is not a purpose of representative orders to shut out a person who is ready and willing to conduct his own case in the litigation, and such a person should ordinarily be added in his own right (*Irish Shipping Ltd v Commercial Union Assurance Co. plc* [1991] 2 QB 206; *Re PD Teesport Ltd* [2009] EWHC 1693 (Ch), LTL 16/7/2009).

Procedure

The representative capacity of the claimant or defendant, and the class of persons represented, must be made clear in the description of the parties in the claim form. For example, 'AB, as representing himself and all other members of the British Phonographic Industry Ltd'. **14.63**

It is not necessary for a representative claimant to obtain the authority of the represented persons to bring the claim. The authority to bring the proceedings is provided by **CPR, r. 19.6**, itself, *Independiente Ltd v Music Trading On-Line (HK) Ltd* [2003] EWHC 470 (QB), LTL 25/3/2003; *Howells v Dominion Insurance Co. Ltd* [2005] EWHC 552 (QB), LTL 8/4/2005. Nor is it necessary for a claimant to obtain the court's permission to issue a claim form either as a representative of other claimants, or against a representative defendant. But the court is expressly empowered by **CPR, r. 19.6(2)**, to order that a person may not act as a representative. Any party may make an application for such an order.

The representative claimant is fully empowered to choose how to run the litigation on behalf of the class. However, those represented are not parties to the litigation, so, for example, disclosure may be ordered against them only as non-parties (*Ventouris v Mountain* [1990] 1 WLR 1370, QBD). Nor are the persons represented individually liable for costs (*Howells v Dominion Insurance Co. Ltd*), though the representatives may be (*SmithKline Beecham plc v Avery* [2009] EWHC 1924 (QB), LTL 26/8/2009).

By virtue of **r. 19.6**, unless the court orders otherwise, any judgment or order is binding on the persons represented. However, it may not be enforced by or against a person who is not a named party without the court's permission (**r. 19.6(4)(b)**). The requirement for permission is an important protection and the court will consider whether it should be enforced on a case-by-case basis (*Howells v Dominion Insurance Co. Ltd*). Permission to enforce an order may not be granted in advance, without identifying the represented party or parties against whom the order could be enforced. Such a person should have an opportunity to make submissions before any enforcement could occur (*SmithKline Beecham plc v Avery* [2007] EWHC 948 (QB), LTL 9/5/2007; *Huntingdon Life Sciences Group plc v Stop Huntingdon Animal Cruelty (SHAC)* [2007] EWHC 522 (QB), LTL 19/4/2007). A judgment may be enforced against a person represented whether or not that person authorised the litigation (*Howells v Dominion Insurance Co. Ltd*).

Representation of unascertained persons

In claims involving: **14.64**

(a) the estate of a deceased person,
(b) trust property, or
(c) the meaning of a document (including a statute),

the court has power to appoint a representative for another person or class, for the purposes of the claim (**CPR, r. 19.7**). The court may exercise the power where:

(a) the person or persons to be represented are unborn, or cannot be found or easily ascertained; or

(b) in the case of a class, the members of the class have the same interest in the claim and:
 (i) one or more members are unborn, or cannot be found or easily ascertained; or
 (ii) appointing a representative would further the overriding objective.

An application for a representation order may be made by any person who seeks to be appointed under the order or by any party to the claim. The application can be made at any time before or after the issue of the claim form (**r. 19.7(3)**). The application must be served on all parties to the claim if it has started, and the person to be appointed (if that person is not already a party to the claim), and any other person directed by the court (**r. 19.7(4)**).

Court approval must be sought to settle a claim in which a party is acting as a representative under **r. 19.7** (**r. 19.7(5)**), and the settlement will be approved only if it is for the benefit of all the represented parties (**r. 19.7(6)**).

If the court does appoint such a representative, any judgments or orders made in the action are binding on the person(s) represented, but may only be enforced by or against a person who is not a party with the permission of the court (**r. 19.7(7)**). It is unlikely that the fact that parties who have no opportunity to be heard personally can be bound by a judgment made against them under **r. 7.7** gives rise to any issue under the European Convention on Human Rights, **art. 6**, in the **Human Rights Act 1998, sch. 1** (*Smithson v Hamilton* [2008] EWCA Civ 996, [2009] ICR 1; *Re PD Teesport Ltd* [2009] EWHC 1693 (Ch), LTL 16/7/2009). Nevertheless, in *Smithson v Hamilton*, the court ordered that the judgment should not be enforced until 28 days after notification to parties who would be affected by it, with liberty to apply in the meantime.

INTERVENTION

14.65 In cases where there is no effective respondent and which raise issues likely to be of wider importance than the immediate interests of the parties, the court may adjourn so that a suitable person, or advocate to the court (*amicus curiae*), be appointed to ensure arguments are raised in the public interest. The Pensions Ombudsman was invited to appear on this basis in *Legal and General Assurance Society Ltd v CCA Stationery Ltd* [2003] EWHC 1491 (Ch), LTL 11/6/2003.

Applications to intervene are made under **CPR, r. 19.2** (see **14.83**). Unmeritorious applications will be dismissed in the court's discretion. In *Nottinghamshire County Council v Bottomley* [2010] EWCA Civ 756, [2010] Med LR 407, the local authority was given permission to intervene. It had a financial interest in the form of the award in the case (whether it should be a lump sum or periodical payments, see **63.29**), which made it desirable to make the order under both **r. 19.2(2)(a)** and **(b)**.

GROUP LITIGATION

Group litigation orders

14.66 Until May 2000, no special provision was made in rules of court for multi-party group litigation, or class actions. Representative proceedings under **CPR, r. 19.7** (see **14.62** to **14.64**) are one way of dealing with multi-party actions, but are not designed for group litigation. In particular, they do not provide an effective mechanism for managing group litigation, for identifying generic issues applicable to the entire group or for resolving cases at a cost which is proportionate to the value of an individual claim. By the early 1990s there was wide agreement that a new approach was needed (see *Nash v Eli Lilly and Co.* [1993] 1 WLR 782). Recommendations by Lord Woolf in ch. 17 of his *Final Report* for a new framework for multi-party actions led (albeit with some differences) to the introduction of **CPR, r. 19.11**, and **PD 19B**. The court may, under **CPR, r. 19.11**, make a 'group litigation order' or 'GLO', where a number of claims give rise to common or related, issues of fact or law. The order may be made upon the application of any party, or by the court acting of its own initiative (**PD 19B, paras 3.1** and 4). The types of cases suitable for a GLO include mass product liability claims, claims arising out of a public transport disaster, and housing claims involving similar claims by numerous tenants.

The key features of the rules on GLOs are:

(a) Either before or after the commencement of litigation, a party may apply for a GLO.
(b) The GLO will identify the issues to be managed as part of the group litigation (the 'GLO issues'). Any individual claim (a 'GLO claim') must raise these issues to fall under the terms of the order. In *Hobson v Ashton Morton Slack Solicitors* [2006] EWHC 1134 (QB), LTL 26/5/2006, a GLO was refused in part because no group litigation issue had been sufficiently or precisely identified. The GLO issues cannot be phrased so as to exclude the individual circumstances of some of the parties from the scope of the litigation. The GLO issues must properly encapsulate the issues that arise in the litigation (*Tew v BOS (Shared Appreciation Mortgages) No. 1 plc* [2010] EWHC 203 (Ch), LTL 30/4/2010). The case concerned a GLO relating to challenges to the fairness of certain mortgages under the Consumer Credit Act 1974 and the Unfair Terms in Consumer Contracts Regulations 1994 (SI 1994/3159) (see **90.18**). As questions of fairness involve a one-stage inquiry based on the facts of particular situations, it was decided that the appropriate case management directions would be for the taking of lead cases, rather than trying to identify common issues.
(c) A register will be established for the GLO claims, and a specified court will be given responsibility for managing them.
(d) The managing court is given wide powers to give case management directions to ensure the effective coordination and resolution of the GLO claims (see **14.71**).
(e) Any judgment made on a GLO issue will bind all the GLO claimaints (see **14.73**).

Preliminary steps

Solicitors acting for potential applicants for a GLO should contact the Law Society's Multi-Party Action Information Service (telephone 0870 606 2522) to identify other potential claims giving rise to the same issues (**PD 19B, para. 2.1**). (Members of the public should ring Law Society Information Services on 0870 606 2555.) Consideration should also be given to forming a solicitors' group and to identifying a solicitor to lead the application for a GLO and the litigation of the GLO issues. **PD 19B, para. 2.2**, advises that the lead solicitor's role and relationship with other members of the solicitors' group should be defined in writing. In any event, the lead solicitor will be subject to any directions given by the court. **14.67**

PD 19B, para. 2.3, advises that the applicant should consider whether it would be more appropriate to seek any other order, in particular, an order for claims to be consolidated or for a representative to be appointed under **CPR, rr. 19.6** to **19.9**. In *Hobson v Ashton Morton Slack Solicitors* [2006] EWHC 1134 (QB), LTL 26/5/2006, a GLO was refused in part because insufficient consideration had been given to more cost-efficient means of resolving the dispute, such as bringing a test case, or consolidating the claims.

The Law Society publishes practice guidelines for those conducting or wishing to conduct disaster litigation under a GLO. A copy is available on the Law Society website (www.lawsociety.org).

Applying for a GLO

Application for a GLO, whether before or after issue of the claim, is made by the Part 23 procedure (see **chapter 32**), and can be made by any party to the claim (**PD 19B, para. 3.1**). **14.68**

Alternatively the court may make an order of its own motion (**PD 19B, para. 4**). The application should be made to the Senior Master in the Queen's Bench Division of the High Court, or the Chief Chancery Master in the Chancery Division. For claims likely to proceed in a specialist list (see **11.4**), the application should be made to a senior judge of that list. For claims likely to proceed in a district registry, application should be made to the presiding judge, or to the supervising Chancery judge. County court applications should be made to the designated civil judge for the area in which the court is situated (**PD 19B, paras 3.5 to 3.7**).

By **PD 19B, para. 3.2**, either the application notice itself, or the written evidence in support should include the following information:

(a) a summary of the nature of the litigation;
(b) the number and nature of claims already issued;
(c) the number of parties likely to be involved;
(d) the common issues of fact or law ('the GLO issues'); and
(e) whether there are any matters that distinguish smaller groups of claims within the wider group.

The decision whether to make a GLO is a matter for the court's discretion. A GLO requires substantial resources of both the parties and the court and it should not be made unless it is clear that there is a sufficient number of claimants and that they clearly intend to proceed (*Austin v Miller Argent (South Wales) Ltd* [2011] EWCA Civ 928, [2011] Env LR 32, in which it was not established that a sufficient number of claimants intended to proceed).

A GLO may not be made without the consent of the Lord Chief Justice, in the case of claims proceeding in the Queen's Bench Division, or the Vice-Chancellor, in the case of claims proceeding in the Chancery Division, or the Head of Civil Justice in the case of claims proceeding in a county court (**PD 19B, para. 3.3**). It is for the court, not the parties, to seek such consent, by sending to the Lord Chief Justice, or the Vice-Chancellor, or the Head of Civil Justice, as appropriate, a copy of the application notice, any relevant written evidence in support and a written statement of the reasons a GLO is thought to be desirable. This step may be taken before or after hearing the application. Indeed, in the county court, the applicant should request the court to refer the application notice to the designated civil judge as soon as possible to enable him or her to consider seeking the consent of the Head of Civil Justice prior to the hearing of the application (**PD 19B, para. 3.8**).

Nature of the order

14.69 A GLO must, by **CPR, r. 19.11(2)**:

(a) identify the issues which a claim must raise if it is to be managed under the order (the 'GLO issues');
(b) set up a register for such claims; and
(c) specify the court that will manage the claims (the 'management court').

The management court is the court to which any application to vary the GLO should be made (**PD 19B, para. 12.2**).

Once a GLO has been made, a copy should be supplied to the Law Society and to the Senior Master of the Queen's Bench Division (**PD 19B, para. 11**). There is a list of GLOs at http://www.justice.gov.uk/courts/rcj-rolls-building-queens-bench/group-litigation-orders with a link to archived details of lead solicitors and defined issues.

Group register

14.70 The group register of claims managed under a GLO is normally maintained by the management court, but that court may direct it to be kept by a solicitor for one of the parties to a case entered on it (normally the lead solicitor) (**PD 19B, para. 6.5**). In this case, the solicitor must permit the register to be inspected by the public during business hours, upon reasonable notice and upon paying an appropriate fee (**PD 19B, para. 6.6(2)**).

Any party to a case may apply to be entered on or removed from a group register (**PD 19B, paras 6.2 and 9.2; CPR, r. 19.14**). An order for a case to be entered may be made where the case raises at least one of the GLO issues (**PD 19B, para. 6.3**). A claim must be issued before it can be entered on the group register (**PD 19B, para. 6.1A**). However, even where a case does raise a GLO issue, the court has a discretion to refuse registration (or to order the removal of a case from the register) on the grounds that it cannot conveniently be managed with the other cases on the register, or that its inclusion would adversely affect the management of the other cases (**PD 19B, para. 6.4**).

The management court may specify a cut-off date after which no claim may be added to the register without the court's permission (**CPR, r. 19.13; PD 19B, para. 13**). In *Taylor v Nugent Care Society* [2004] EWCA Civ 51, [2004] 1 WLR 1129, the claimant issued separate proceedings arising out of alleged abuse in a children's home, an issue which was the subject of a GLO. He applied unsuccessfully to join the group litigation, some two and a half years after the cut-off date set by the court. The defendant made an application to strike out the claim. The Court of Appeal refused the application on the grounds that it was a disproportionate reaction to the claimant's delay and there were other steps, such as staying the claimant's action pending case management directions, which adequately protected the defendant's interests. The Court of Appeal also considered the relationship between a GLO and a claim on the same issue not included in the group. The court stated that although there is no requirement in **CPR, Part 19**, for a claimant to join a GLO, if he chooses not to do so he is still subject to the management powers of the court. If he brings proceedings in parallel to a GLO, the court is entitled to manage those separate proceedings in a way which takes account of the position of those who have joined the GLO. Those who have joined the GLO are entitled to have their interests given a higher priority than those of a defendant who has not joined. This is partly because of their number but also because by joining the GLO they are cooperating with the proper management of the claim.

Commentary

Managing the GLO claims

After a GLO is made, all existing claims which raise any of the GLO issues will, where necessary, be transferred to the management court, be listed on the group register and, where appropriate (for example, where one claim is proceeding as a test claim or to await group case management directions), be stayed pending further order (**CPR, r. 19.11(3)**). Every claim entered on the group register will automatically be allocated to the multi-track. Any case management directions already given will be set aside and any hearing date already fixed other than for the purpose of the group litigation will be vacated (**PD 19B, para. 7**). 14.71

The management court will normally require all new claims to be commenced in it. Failure to comply with any such order will not invalidate a claim, but the claim should be transferred to the management court and entered on the group register as soon as possible after issue (**PD 19B, para. 9**).

A GLO claim will be managed by a single assigned judge, assisted by an assigned district judge or master and a costs judge (**PD 19B, para. 8**). Case management directions may be given when the GLO is made, or subsequently. Such directions may include orders for one claim to proceed as a test claim, appointing a lead solicitor and specifying a cut-off date for joining the group, and provision for allocation of costs (**CPR, r. 19.13; PD 19B, paras 12 and 13**).

Directions will normally also address the form that the particulars of claim should take. In particular, **PD 19B, para. 14**, makes provision for the service of 'group particulars of claim' — i.e. one statement of case which sets out details of all the claims on the group register at the time it is filed. **PD 19B** suggests that the particulars should contain details of the general allegations common to all claims and a schedule (or a series of questionnaires, in a form approved by the court) setting out specific facts relating to particular claimants on the group register (**paras 14.1** and **14.3**).

PD 19B, para. 12, does not give the court power to order disclosure and inspection of group litigation claimants' ATE insurance policies, the terms of which are privileged (*Arroyo v BP Exploration Co. (Colombia) Ltd* (2010), LTL 4/6/2010).

The management court may give directions for the trial of the action, addressing how the issues common to the group claims and those raised by particular claims should be dealt with (**PD 19B, para. 15.1**). While common issues will normally be tried in the management court, the separate issues raised by individual claims may be tried at a court which suits the convenience of the parties to that particular claim (**PD 19B, para. 15.2**).

Test claims

14.72 If one claim on the group register proceeding as a test claim is settled, the management court may order that another claim on the group register be substituted as the test claim. If such an order is made, any order made in the test claim before the date of substitution is binding on the substituted claim unless the court otherwise orders (**CPR, r. 19.15**). The court can make an interim payment in favour of a party to group litigation provided the relevant conditions are satisfied and the fact that the applicant is not a test claimant in the group litigation is not a reason for refusing to do so (*Commissioners of HM Revenue & Customs v GKN Group* [2012] EWCA Civ 57, [2012] 1 WLR 2375).

Judgment

14.73 Subject to any court order to the contrary, any judgment or order made by the court in relation to a GLO issue is binding on the parties to all the other claims which are by then already on the GLO register (**CPR, r. 19.12(1)(a)**). An appeal against the judgment or order may only be made with the permission of the court (**CPR, r. 19.12(2)**).

The court may also direct to what extent any order or judgment should bind parties to claims entered subsequently on the GLO register (**CPR, r. 19.12(1)(b)**). However, in this case, an affected party may apply to the court for an order that the judgment or order is not binding on him (**CPR, r. 19.12(3)**).

Any document disclosed by a party to any claim on the GLO register is disclosed to all parties to claims on the GLO register at the time disclosure is made and to those subsequently entered (**CPR, r. 19.12(4)**).

Costs

14.74 In assessing costs, the court will need to apportion costs between those relating to common issues and those which relate to issues in particular cases. The question of costs in group actions is governed by **CPR, r. 46.6**, and is considered more fully at **68.51**. While recognising that complex funding and costs issues arise in applications in GLO cases, the starting point on interim costs decisions is that the usual single party costs order should be made (adjusted as appropriate) (*AB v Ministry of Defence* [2009] EWHC 1421 (QB), LTL 6/7/2009). A proportionate costs order can be made in group litigation if the claimants do not win on all issues (*Jones v Secretary of State for Energy & Climate Change* [2012] EWHC 3647 (QB), [2013] 2 Costs LR 230).

INTERPLEADER PROCEEDINGS

Introduction

Interpleader proceedings are used to determine ownership of disputed property in two circumstances: 14.75

(a) where a person ('the stakeholder') owes a debt, or has possession of goods or money, and does not claim the property personally, but is being, or expects to be, sued by competing claimants to the property;
(b) where a High Court enforcement officer or county court bailiff has seized goods in execution which a person other than the judgment debtor claims to own.

The stakeholder, enforcement officer or bailiff in effect calls on the competing claimants to claim against each other (to 'interplead') so that title to the property can be decided by the court. The stakeholder, enforcement officer or bailiff may then dispose of the property in accordance with the court's order, safe from being sued by the competing claimants.

The rules governing interpleader proceedings are to be found in **RSC, ord. 17 in CPR, sch. 1**, and **CCR, ord. 33 in CPR, sch. 2**. The two sets of rules are similar, but not identical. Regrettably, the opportunity to unify the procedure has not yet been taken. The procedure is summarised in **procedural checklist 7** (High Court) and **procedural checklist 8** (county court), at the front of the book, and there is detailed commentary in **14.76 to 14.82**.

In a county court, the district judge is technically responsible for bailiffs. So the rules refer to the district judge being in possession of the goods seized, when in practice it will be the bailiff who has custody of them.

Participation by a property holder as an applicant in interpleader proceedings does not ordinarily amount to a submission to the jurisdiction, because the purpose of interpleader proceedings is to gain the protection of the court from the competing claimants (*Australia v Peacekeeper International FZC UAE* [2008] EWHC 1220 (QB), LTL 9/6/2008).

Procedure in the High Court

Goods seized in execution A person who claims to own goods seized in execution by a High Court enforcement officer should notify the enforcement officer of the claim, and provide details of an address for service (**RSC, ord. 17, r. 2(1) in CPR, sch. 1**). The enforcement officer must notify the judgment creditor immediately of the claim. The judgment creditor then has seven days to inform the enforcement officer whether the claim is admitted or disputed. If the claim is admitted, the judgment creditor will not be liable for any fees or expenses incurred by the enforcement officer after receipt of the notice of admission (**RSC, ord. 17, r. 2(2) in CPR, sch. 1**) and the enforcement officer must withdraw from the goods, and may apply to the court for an order restraining the bringing of a claim against the enforcement officer for having taken possession of the goods (**RSC, ord. 17, r. 2(4) in CPR, sch. 1**). Where the judgment creditor disputes the claim, or fails to respond within the seven days, and the third party does not withdraw the claim, the enforcement officer may issue interpleader proceedings in order to have the court resolve the question of ownership. The interpleader application may be made either in the court where the underlying claim was proceeding, or in the court where the judgment is being executed, if different (**RSC, ord. 17, r. 2(3) and 4 in CPR, sch. 1**). 14.76

Claim in respect of goods protected from seizure **RSC, ord. 17, r. 2A in CPR, sch. 1**, sets out the procedure where a judgment debtor makes a claim in relation to goods that would be exempt from seizure by an enforcement officer. Until 15 March 2004, the exemptions were specified in the Senior Courts Act 1981, s. 138(3A), to which **RSC, ord. 17, r. 2A**, still refers. Since 15 March 2004, the Senior Courts Act 1981, s. 138(3A), has been repealed and replaced by the Courts Act 2003, sch. 7, para. 9(3), which **RSC, ord. 17, r. 2A**, must now be construed 14.77

as referring to (Interpretation Act 1978, ss. 17(2)(a) and 23(1)). The items excluded from seizure by the Courts Act 2003, sch. 7, para. 9(3), are:

(a) such tools, books, vehicles and other items of equipment as are necessary to the execution debtor for use personally by him in his employment, business or vocation; and
(b) such clothing, bedding, furniture and household equipment and provisions as are necessary for satisfying the basic domestic needs of the execution debtor and his family.

A judgment debtor whose goods have been, or are intended to be, seized by an enforcement officer under a writ of execution, but who claims that the goods are protected from execution, must, within five days of the seizure, give notice in writing to the enforcement officer identifying those goods and the grounds of the claim in respect of each item (**RSC, ord. 17, r. 2A(1)**). The enforcement officer should immediately give notice of the debtor's claim to the execution creditor and any other person who has made a claim in respect of the goods under **RSC, ord. 17, r. 2(1)**, and those persons must, within seven days, inform the enforcement officer in writing whether the claim in respect of each item is admitted or disputed (**RSC, ord. 17, r. 2A(2)**).

If the judgment debtor's claim is admitted, or no notice is given by the execution creditor or other person claiming title to the goods under **RSC, ord. 17, r. 2(1)**, the enforcement officer must withdraw from possession of the goods, and inform the parties of this fact in writing (**RSC, ord. 17, r. 2A(3)**). However, if the enforcement officer receives notice that the claim is disputed, he must, by an application under **CPR, Part 23**, seek directions, which may include an order restraining the bringing of a claim against him for having seized those goods or having failed to do so (**RSC, ord. 17, r. 2A(4) in CPR, sch. 1**). The court will determine the judgment debtor's claim summarily or give directions for its determination (**RSC, ord. 17, r. 2A(5)** and **(6)**).

14.78 Application for interpleader relief Application for interpleader relief other than in existing proceedings is made by Part 8 claim form (**PD 8A, Section B**). An application in existing proceedings should be made by issuing an application notice under **CPR, Part 23 (RSC, ord. 17, r. 3(1) in CPR, sch. 1)**.

It is required by **RSC, ord. 17, r. 3(4) in CPR, sch. 1** that, save where the application is brought by an enforcement officer, the claim form or application notice must be supported by evidence (in the form permitted under **CPR, rr. 32.6 and 32.15**) that the applicant:

(a) claims no interest in the subject matter in dispute, other than for charges or costs;
(b) does not collude with any of the claimants to the subject matter; and
(c) is willing to pay or transfer that subject matter into court or to dispose of it as the court may direct.

Under the old version of this rule, the evidence had to be given by the applicant personally, rather than by a solicitor, save where there were practical difficulties, such as the applicant being abroad (*Wood v Lynne* (1850) 4 De G & Sm 16). Under the CPR, if the evidence is adduced in the form of a witness statement, it should still be that of the applicant rather than the applicant's solicitor, as the applicant will have the first-hand knowledge of the matters about which evidence is being given.

Once issued, the claim form or notice must be served on all claimants to the property (*Lambert v Townsend* (1832) 1 LJ Ex 113; **RSC, ord. 17, r. 3(2) in CPR, sch. 1**).

Where the claim relates to goods seized in execution, the claimant then has 14 days in which to serve a witness statement or affidavit on the enforcement officer and the judgment creditor. This must identify the property claimed and the grounds for asserting rights in the property ***(RSC, ord. 17, r. 3(6) in CPR, sch. 1)***.

14.79 Powers of the court hearing the claim In interpleader proceedings the court has a wide discretion to make any order, including any order as to costs, which it thinks just (**RSC, ord. 17,**

r. 8 in CPR, sch. 1). Where there are several different existing claims, even in different divisions of the High Court, the court may make an order which binds the parties to all of them (RSC, ord. 17, r. 9 in CPR, sch. 1).

Trial of the interpleader issue. The court may order the trial of an interpleader issue. In this case, at the first return date, it will give directions dealing with the constitution of the action, for example, directing which of the competing claimants is to be claimant and which is to be defendant. In relation to an existing claim concerning the disputed property, in which the applicant is the defendant:

(a) the court may order a person claiming the property to become the defendant, in substitution for or in addition to the applicant (RSC, ord. 17, r. 5(1)(a) in CPR, sch. 1);
(b) the court may stay all further proceedings in the claim (RSC, ord. 17, r. 7 in CPR, sch. 1).

Where appropriate, the court may also order disclosure under CPR, Part 31, or the provision of further information under CPR, Part 18. The trial itself will take place in the usual way and CPR, Part 39, will apply (RSC, ord. 17, rr. 10 and 11(1) in CPR, sch. 1).

Orders in relation to the property. The court may also give directions as to the safe custody of the property in dispute, pending trial. If the property is money, the court will usually order it to be paid into court. If it is goods, the court may make orders for its safe custody or sale. Where the applicant is an enforcement officer and the claimant alleges that the property is security for a debt, the court may order the sale of the property and the application of the proceeds of sale as it thinks just (RSC, ord. 17, r. 6 in CPR, sch. 1).

Summary judgment. Where the applicant is an enforcement officer, or with the consent of all claimants, or at the request of any of them, or if the case turns on a question of law, the court may order the summary determination of the claim (RSC, ord. 17, r. 5(2) in CPR, sch. 1).

Barring a claimant. Where a claimant to the property does not appear at the hearing, or fails to comply with an order in the proceedings, the court may make an order barring that claimant from making any future claim against the applicant. This order does not affect any rights the interpleader claimants have as between themselves (RSC, ord. 17, r. 5(3) in CPR, sch. 1).

County court procedure

Goods seized in execution A person who claims to own goods seized by a county court bailiff **14.80**
must give notice to the bailiff of the claim or file notice of the claim in court. The notice must include the claimant's name and address, the grounds of the interpleader claim, and, where the claim is for rent, particulars of the amount of rent in arrears and the period in respect of which it is due, as required by the County Courts Act 1984, s. 102(2) (CCR, ord. 33, r. 1(1) in CPR, sch. 2). Except where the claim is for the proceeds or value of goods, the court will require the claimant to make a deposit or provide security for the claim, in accordance with the County Courts Act 1984, s. 100 (CCR, ord. 33, r. 1(2)(b) in CPR, sch. 2). The court will also notify the judgment creditor of the claim (CCR, ord. 33, r. 1(2)(a)) in CPR, sch. 2).

The judgment creditor must notify the court, within four days of receipt of the notice of claim, whether the claim is disputed or admitted or whether the district judge (i.e. the bailiff, see 14.75) is requested to withdraw from possession of the disputed property. If the claim is admitted or the district judge is requested to withdraw from possession, the judgment creditor will not be liable for any fees or expenses incurred by the district judge after receipt of the notice (CCR, ord. 33, r. 2 in CPR, sch. 2). In addition, the district judge can apply to the circuit judge for an order restraining the bringing of a claim against the district judge for having taken possession of the goods (CCR, ord. 33, r. 3 in CPR, sch. 2).

Where the judgment creditor gives notice disputing a claim, or fails to give a notice within four days whether he admits or disputes the claim, the court will issue an interpleader notice in form N88 or N88(1). A hearing date will be fixed, and the court will serve the notice on the judgment creditor and the interpleader claimant at least 14 days before the return date.

14.81 **Claims by stakeholders** A stakeholder who is defending a claim should apply for interpleader relief to the court in which the claim is proceeding, and one threatened with a claim should apply to the court where the claim might be brought (**CCR, ord. 33, r. 6(2)** in **CPR, sch. 2**).

Whether in a pending action or not, by **CCR, ord. 33, r. 6(3)** in **CPR, sch. 2**, the stakeholder makes an application for interpleader relief by filing a witness statement or affidavit showing that the applicant:

(a) claims no interest in the subject matter in dispute other than for charges or costs;
(b) does not collude with any of the interpleader claimants; and
(c) is willing to pay or transfer the subject matter into court or to dispose of it as the court may direct.

One copy of the witness statement or affidavit should be filed for the court, together with an additional copy for each competing interpleader claimant (**CCR, ord. 33, r. 6(3)** in **CPR, sch. 2**).

The witness statement or affidavit of a stakeholder who is a defendant in a pending claim must be filed within 14 days after service of the claim form on the stakeholder. On receipt of this evidence, the court will fix a date for a pre-trial review and will send notice of the application to all parties to the pending claim. These notices will be served at least 21 days before the return date. Each must be accompanied by a copy of the affidavit or witness statement together with the claim form and particulars of claim in the underlying action (**CCR, ord. 33, r. 7** in **CPR, sch. 2**).

Where the stakeholder is not a defendant in a pending claim, the court will fix a date for a pre-trial review, will issue an interpleader notice in form N89 and will serve the notice together with a copy of the witness statement or affidavit on each of the competing claimants at least 21 days before the return date (**CCR, ord. 33, r. 8** in **CPR, sch. 2**).

In either case, each interpleader claimant must, within 14 days after service of the notice under **r. 7** or **r. 8**, either file a notice that no interpleader claim is to be made, or file particulars of the grounds for a claim. The claimant should file copies for service on all other parties. The court will forward these documents (**CCR, ord. 33, r. 10** in **CPR, sch. 2**).

14.82 **Powers of the court** At the final hearing, the court will give judgment determining the rights and claims of the competing parties (**CCR, ord. 33, r. 11(3)** in **CPR, sch. 2**). The court also has the power to make an order barring and striking out the claim of an interpleader claimant who does not appear at a pre-trial review or at the final hearing (**CCR, ord. 33, r. 11(1)** and **(2)** in **CPR, sch. 2**). The court may also bar the claim of an interpleader claimant who fails or refuses to comply with an order made in the proceedings (**CCR, ord. 33, r. 11(1)** in **CPR, sch. 2**).

ADDITION AND SUBSTITUTION OF PARTIES

Addition of parties

14.83 The court is given a wide discretion under the CPR to order that a person be added, removed or substituted as a party to a claim, provided that (in the case of adding a party) the limitation period has not yet expired. The court's attitude is permissive, provided the other party can be appropriately protected in costs. The court's power may be exercised upon application by a party, or by a person who wishes to intervene in proceedings to become a party, or by the court acting on its own initiative (**CPR, r. 19.4(2); PD 19A, para. 1.1**). Addition of a party after the expiry of a limitation period is considered at **14.89** to **14.94**.

The Administrative Court held in *River Thames Society v First Secretary of State* [2006] EWHC 2829 (Admin), LTL 22/9/2006, that the provisions of **CPR, Part 19**, do not apply to public law cases. The power to substitute parties in public law cases depends on the inherent jurisdiction of the court. In this case it permitted the vice-president of the claimant society to be substituted for the society itself, which wished to withdraw a challenge under the Town and Country Planning Act 1990, s. 288, because it had adopted a policy of non-involvement in litigation. The court allowed the substitution, applying *Eco-Energy (GB) Ltd v First Secretary of State* [2004] EWCA Civ 1566, LTL 10/1/2005, on the ground that there was sufficient identity of interest between the society and its vice-president so that the substitution would not undermine the principles of s. 288. Where substitution cannot take place because proceedings have been discontinued, the court may allow fresh judicial review proceedings to be brought out of time where they are in substantially the same terms as the original claim (*R (SDR) v Bristol City Council* [2012] EWHC 859 (Admin), LTL 5/4/2012).

The court is empowered by **CPR, r. 19.2(2)**, to add a party where it is desirable:

(a) to enable it to resolve all the matters in dispute in the proceedings; or
(b) to resolve an issue between an existing party and a proposed new party, which is connected to the matters in dispute in the claim.

Adding a person as a claimant may not be done without the person's written consent, which must be filed at court (**CPR, r. 19.4(4)**). Any order made by the court joining a new claimant will not take effect unless and until the signed, written consent of the person joined has been filed (**PD 19A, para. 2.2**). The Commissioners for HM Revenue and Customs may be added as a party only if they consent (**CPR, r. 19.4(4A)**).

Commentary

Discretion

In *United Film Distribution Ltd v Chhabria* [2001] EWCA Civ 416, [2001] 2 All ER (Comm) 865, the Court of Appeal stated that the discretion to add a party under **CPR, r. 19.2(2)**, is as wide as under the predecessors to that paragraph, namely, RSC, ord. 15, rr. 4 and 2(b). **CPR, r. 19.2**, is not to be construed in a narrow way. Accordingly, where a party cannot bring himself within **r. 19.2(4)** (substitution where the existing party's interest or liability has passed to a new party), an order for substitution may nevertheless be made under **r. 19.2(2)** and (3) because the language of those rules achieves in two steps what could be achieved in a single step under **r. 19.4(2)**. To limit the power to substitute to circumstances where an interest or liability has passed from the party to the new party under **r. 19.4** would be to read the whole of **r. 19.2** in a way which would not do justice to a number of other situations where it would clearly be desirable to permit a change of party (*Hounslow London Borough Council v Cumar* [2012] EWCA Civ 1426, LTL 7/11/2012). However, claims that are quite separate will not be joined (*Turner v Haworth Associates* [2001] EWCA Civ 370, LTL 23/2/2001). The Court of Appeal confirmed in *Davies v Department of Trade and Industry* [2006] EWCA Civ 1360, [2007] 1 All ER 518, that the court has a very wide discretion to consider joinder under **r. 19.2(2)**. In this case, the interests of existing parties in keeping costs to a minimum outweighed the possible injustice to parties who wished to be added as additional defendants, which might arise from their being prevented from participating in the trial in circumstances when Part 20 proceedings might be brought against them at a later date. A party may be added to a claim under **r. 19.2(2)** even if none of the existing parties to the litigation could assert a substantive claim against the new party (*Dunlop Haywards (DHL) Ltd v Erinaceous Insurance Services Ltd* [2009] EWCA Civ 354, [2009] Lloyd's Rep IR 464). The court's power to add a new defendant is not limited to joining a person against whom the claimant wishes to make a claim or who is needed to complete the claimant's cause of action. **Rule 19.2(2)(b)** is wider than that. For the rule to **14.84** be engaged, all that is necessary is that there is an 'issue' to be determined, which is 'connected to the matters in dispute in the proceedings', not that the issue forms part of a claim for relief against the new party (*Shetty v Al Rushaid Petroleum Investment Co.* [2011] EWHC 1460 (Ch), LTL 14/6/2011).

Where an application is made to re-join a defendant against whom a claim in the same action has previously been struck out, the court should exercise its discretion under **r. 19.2**, in accordance with the test for bringing a second claim on the same facts as a claim struck out, established in *Securum Finance Ltd v Ashton* [2001] Ch 291 (see **33.25**) (*Kent v M and L Management and Legal Ltd* [2005] EWHC 2546 (Ch), LTL 28/11/2005). In *Kent v M and L Management and Legal Ltd* the court refused permission to re-join the defendant because it was no longer possible for him to have a fair trial. He had become mentally ill and could not give live evidence. Further, part of the evidence against him was contained in written statements from his mother who had since died.

In *Kooltrade Ltd v XTS Ltd* (2001) IPD 25018 doubt was cast on whether the power to substitute a new party under **r. 19.2** could be exercised after judgment, because it related to 'matters in dispute in the proceedings'. The Court of Appeal has now clarified the point. In *Dunwoody Sports Marketing v Prescott* [2007] EWCA Civ 461, [2007] 1 WLR 2343, it was held (following *C Inc. plc v L* [2001] 2 Lloyd's Rep 459 and *The Selby Paradigm* [2004] EWHC 1804 (Admlty), [2004] 2 Lloyd's Rep 714) that the power under **r. 19.2** to substitute a new party for an existing party does exist after judgment as well as before. On the facts of the case, the transferee of the claimant's business was substituted even though a final injunction had already been granted. See also *Starlight Shipping Co. v Allianz Marine and Aviation Versicherungs AG* [2011] EWHC 3381 (Comm), LTL 3/1/2012, where permission was granted under **r. 19.2(2)(b)** to add a party to a claim after it had been settled by Tomlin orders which the original defendant was seeking to enforce and which the new party wished to take advantage of.

Under **r. 19.2(2)** the court will add a person who is bound to satisfy any judgment given in the claim, for example, the Motor Insurers' Bureau (*Gurtner v Circuit* [1968] 2 QB 587). But it will not substitute a person who runs the risk of being ordered to pay costs, for example, a person funding one of the parties (see *Hamilton v Al Fayed* (2000) *The Times*, 13 October 2000) or a professional body such as the Medical Defence Union.

Substitution and removal of parties

14.85 The court may, by **CPR, r. 19.2(3)**, remove a party if it is not desirable for that person to be a party to the proceedings.

The court may, by **r. 19.2(4)**, substitute a new party for an existing one if:

(a) the existing party's interest or liability has passed to the new party; and
(b) it is desirable to substitute the new party so that the court can resolve the matters in dispute in the proceedings.

If proceedings were commenced, before the expiry of the relevant limitation period, by a party whose cause of action has since been assigned following insolvency or transmitted on death, an application for an order under **r. 19.2(4)** does not involve raising a new claim under the Limitation Act 1980, s. 35, whether the assignment, death, bankruptcy or application occurs before or after the expiry of limitation (*Roberts v Gill and Co.* [2010] UKSC 22, [2011] 1 AC 240, at [103]–[104]).

Procedure

14.86 *A party may only be added*, removed or substituted with the permission of the court, unless the claim form has not been served. Thus where an existing party, or the proposed new party, wishes to change the parties to a claim, an application for permission to do so must be made under **CPR, Part 23 (r. 19.4(1); PD 19A, para. 1.4)**. The procedure is summarised in **procedural checklist 9**, at the front of the book, and there is detailed commentary at **14.87** to **14.89**.

Application Application is made by filing an application notice in accordance with **CPR, r. 23.3 (PD 19A, para. 1.4)**. The application must be made on notice (except in the case of the substitution of a party following a transfer of interest or liability) and, where it is on notice, a copy of the application notice must be filed and served in accordance with **CPR, rr. 23.3** and **23.4 (PD 19A, para. 1.4)**. An application to add or substitute a party must be supported by evidence setting out the proposed new party's interest in or connection with the claim (**PD 19A, para. 1.3**). Where the application is to substitute a party following the transfer of an interest or liability, the evidence in support must show the stage reached by the proceedings and set out the change which has occurred to cause the transfer of interest or liability (**PD 19A, para. 5.2**). The rules contain no requirement for evidence to be submitted in support of an application to remove a party. The party applying for the amendment will usually be ordered to pay the costs of the application and any additional costs arising from the amendment. **14.87**

Where the party to be added or substituted is a claimant, a copy of the proposed amended claim form and particulars of claim and the signed written consent of the new party must be filed with the application notice (**PD 19A, para. 2.1**).

Hearing Where all parties (and the proposed new party) agree the change, the application may be dealt with without a hearing (**PD 19A, para. 1.2**). The application must still be approved by a judicial officer, and the procedural judge has a discretion to refuse or allow an agreed order. **14.88**

Order and consequential directions Where the court makes an order adding or substituting a party it will normally also make consequential directions (**CPR, r. 19.4(6)**). In addition to directions about the management of the proceedings, these will normally include orders that: **14.89**

(a) the claimant or the party who made the application file the amended claim form and particulars of claim within 14 days (**PD 19A, paras 2.3(3)** and **3.2(1)**);
(b) the new party be served with a copy of the existing statements of case (and documents referred to in them) (**paras 2.3(2)** and **3.2(3)**);
(c) any new defendant (and, unless the court orders to the contrary, any other defendants) be served with the amended claim form and particulars of claim and the usual response pack (forms for admitting, defending and acknowledging the claim) (**para. 3.2(3)**); and
(d) a copy of the order be served on the parties, and any other person affected by it (**CPR, r. 19.4(5); PD 19A, paras 2.3(1)** and **3.2(2)**).

A new defendant does not become a party to the proceedings until served with the amended claim form (**PD 19A, para. 3.3**). Thus it is this step (not the making of the application) which will interrupt the running of the limitation period against that person (*Ketteman v Hansel Properties Ltd* [1987] AC 189).

When a party is removed, the claimant must file in court an amended claim form and particulars of claim, and a copy of the order must be served on every party and on any other person affected (**CPR, r. 19.4(5); PD 19A, para. 4**). The court may give consequential directions about the management of the proceedings (**CPR, r. 19.4(6)**).

The procedure for amending a statement of case is dealt with in **PD 17, para. 2** (see **chapter 31**).

An order giving permission to amend should normally be drawn up. The court will serve it, unless the parties wish, or the court orders them, to do so (**PD 19A, para. 1.5**).

Commentary

Addition or substitution of a party after the expiry of the limitation period

14.90 The addition or substitution of parties after the expiry of a limitation period is considered at **14.90** to **14.95**. For the related topic of adding new causes of action after a limitation period has expired see **31.24** to **31.28**. The starting point is the Limitation Act 1980, s. 35, which provides:

35. New Claims in Pending Actions: Rules of Court

(1) For the purposes of this Act, any new claim made in the course of any action shall be deemed to be a separate action and to have been commenced—
  (a) in the case of a new claim made in or by way of third party proceedings, on the date on which those proceedings were commenced; and
  (b) in the case of any other new claim, on the same date as the original action.

(2) In this section a new claim means any claim by way of set-off or counterclaim, and any claim involving either—
  (a) the addition or substitution of a new cause of action; or
  (b) the addition or substitution of a new party;

and 'third party proceedings' means any proceedings brought in the course of any action by any party to the action against a person not previously a party to the action, other than proceedings brought by joining any such person as defendant to any claim already made in the original action by the party bringing the proceedings.

(3) Except as provided by section 33 of this Act or by rules of court, neither the High Court nor any county court shall allow a new claim within subsection (1)(b) above, other than an original set-off or counterclaim, to be made in the course of any action after the expiry of any time limit under this Act which would affect a new action to enforce that claim.

For the purposes of this subsection, a claim is an original set-off or an original counterclaim if it is a claim made by way of set-off or (as the case may be) by way of counterclaim by a party who has not previously made any claim in the action.

(4) Rules of court may provide for allowing a new claim to which subsection (3) above applies to be made as there mentioned, but only if the conditions specified in subsection (5) below are satisfied, and subject to any further restrictions the rules may impose.

(5) The conditions referred to in subsection (4) above are the following—
  (a) in the case of a claim involving a new cause of action, if the new cause of action arises out of the same facts or substantially the same facts as are already in issue on any claim previously made in the original action; and
  (b) in the case of a claim involving a new party, if the addition or substitution of the new party is necessary for the determination of the original action.

(6) The addition or substitution of a new party shall not be regarded for the purposes of subsection (5)(b) above as necessary for the determination of the original action unless either—
  (a) the new party is substituted for a party whose name was given in any claim made in the original action in mistake for the new party's name; or
  (b) any claim already made in the original action cannot be maintained by or against an existing party unless the new party is joined or substituted as plaintiff or defendant in that action.

(7) Subject to subsection (4) above, rules of court may provide for allowing a party to any action to claim relief in a new capacity in respect of a new cause of action notwithstanding that he had no title to make that claim at the date of the commencement of the action.

This subsection shall not be taken as prejudicing the power of rules of court to provide for allowing a party to claim relief in a new capacity without adding or substituting a new cause of action.

(8) Subsections (3) to (7) above shall apply in relation to a new claim made in the course of third party proceedings as if those proceedings were the original action, and subject to such other modifications as may be prescribed by rules of court in any case or class of case.

Section 35 and **CPR, r.19.5** restrict the circumstances in which parties can be added or substituted after the limitation period has expired. The addition or substitution has to be necessary to cure some defect, namely an error in the constitution or formality of the action relating to the parties joined, or the capacity in which the parties sue or are sued (*Nameti v Sabre Insurance Co Ltd* [2012] EWHC 3355 (QB), LTL 28/11/2012). Substitution after expiry of the 10-year limitation period in the Limitation Act 1980, s. 11A(3), is not generally permitted (*O'Byrne v Aventis Pasteur SA* (case C-358/08) [2010] 1 WLR 1375; *O'Byrne v Aventis Pasteur MSD Ltd* [2010] UKSC 23, [2010] 1 WLR 1412).

The Supreme Court had to interpret a passage in the decision of the Court of Justice which said that Council Directive 85/374/EEC, art. 11, did not preclude a national court from allowing substitution after the 10-year limitation period if a claim had been instituted in time against a wholly owned subsidiary of the producer and the putting into circulation of the product had in fact been determined by the parent company which manufactured it. The Supreme Court held that this meant substitution was permitted only if the supplier could itself be sued as a producer within art. 3(1). As that was not the case on the facts, substitution was not permitted. In claims other than for personal injury, the court may grant permission only where the limitation period had not expired when the claim was issued, and the addition or substitution is necessary. It will be 'necessary' only if one of the circumstances discussed in **14.91** to **14.95** exists. In *Martin v Kaisary* [2005] EWCA Civ 594, [2006] PIQR P5, the court held that whether it is 'necessary' to add a defendant depends on whether the claim against the existing defendant can be determined without the addition of the new defendant. Adding an alternative claim against a new defendant is not 'necessary' within the meaning of the rule.

In *Tetra Pak Ltd v Biddle and Co.* [2010] EWHC 54 (Ch), [2010] 1 WLR 1466, it was held that serving separate particulars of claim on different defendants within the same claim did not involve raising a 'new claim' within the meaning of the Limitation Act 1980, s. 35(2) (at [71]), and involved no amendments to the particulars of claim served on the first defendants (at [88]).

Correcting a mistake Under **CPR, r. 19.5(3)(a)**, which implements the Limitation Act 1980, s. 35, the court may substitute a new party for an existing party, after the expiry of a relevant limitation period, where the existing party was named in mistake for the new party. **CPR, r. 19.5(3)(a)**, allows the substitution of a new party for an existing party named in error, but not the addition of a new party, and so contemplates only a change in the persons named as parties, not an increase in their number. *Broadhurst v Broadhurst* [2007] EWHC 1828 (Ch), LTL 10/4/2007, makes the point (which must be right, and contradicts *Morgan Est (Scotland) Ltd v Hanson Concrete Products Ltd* [2005] EWCA Civ 134, [2005] 1 WLR 2557 — see below) that the use of 'substituted' in **r. 19.5(3)(a)** as opposed to 'added or substituted' in **r. 19.5(3)(b)** is significant. It means that a pure addition of a party is not permitted under **r. 19.5(3)(a)**. However, if there are two or more distinct claims against a party, substitution is possible under **r. 19.5(3)(a)** in respect of only some of the claims, leaving the others to continue against the original party (*Procter and Gamble (Health and Beauty Care) Ltd v Carrier Holdings Ltd* [2003] EWHC 83 (TCC), [2003] BLR 255; *Ultra Furniture Ltd v KPMG Audit plc* [2003] All ER (D) 302). **14.91**

The Court of Appeal has stated in *Adelson v Associated Newspapers Ltd* [2007] EWCA Civ 701, [2008] 1 WLR 585, that it is necessary to have regard to the pre-CPR principles in applying **r. 19.5(3)(a)** as the provision is intended to replicate RSC, ord. 20, r. 5. It doubted *Morgan Est (Scotland) Ltd v Hanson Concrete Products Ltd* [2005] EWCA Civ 134, [2005] 1 WLR 2557, and *Weston v Gribben* [2006] EWCA Civ 1425, [2007] CP Rep 10, which sought to lay down principles free of the pre-CPR case law.

It held that in allowing applications under **CPR, r. 19.5(3)(a)**:

(a) The court must be satisfied that the person who makes the mistake, directly or through an agent, was the person responsible for issuing the claim form (**r. 19.5(3)(a)**).
(b) The applicant has to show that, had the mistake not been made, the new party would have been named in the claim form.
(c) The mistake must be about the name of the party rather than the identity of the party (*The Sardinia Sulcis* [1991] 1 Lloyd's Rep 201). Such a mistake in name may exist where the statements of case provided a description of the party, but gave the party the wrong name. A key question to ask is whether it is possible to identify the party by reference to a description more or less specific to the particular case. If the right description is given, but the wrong name is used, there is unlikely to be any doubt about the identity of the party

Commentary

to be sued, but if the wrong description is used, there is likely to be doubt about identity, and an order for substitution is unlikely to be made under **r. 19.5(3)(a)**. That a mistake is about name rather than identity may be demonstrated, for example, if a mistake is made about the group structure or the roles played by members of the group of companies in which the defendant and the new party operate. Often there will be a connection between the party named in the claim form and the party to be substituted (although this is not a requirement), and often the party intended to be substituted will have been aware of the proceedings (again this is not a formal requirement). If the party to be substituted was unaware of the claim, the court is likely to exercise its discretion against granting the application (*Horne-Roberts v SmithKline Beecham plc* [2001] EWCA Civ 2006, [2002] 1 WLR 1662). An application to substitute a director for the company, as it was the former rather than the latter which was the contracting party, failed under **r. 19.5(3)(a)**, because the mistake was as to the identity not the name of the party (*Dewrace Ltd v Brown* [2007] EWHC 3100 (TCC), LTL 20/2/2008).

In *Lockheed Martin Corp v Willis Group Ltd* [2010] EWCA Civ 927, [2010] PNLR 34, a claimant sued the wrong defendant by mistake and applied under **r. 19.5(3)(a)** and the Limitation Act 1980, s. 35(6)(a), to substitute a new party as defendant on the basis that the original party was named in mistake for the new defendant. An appeal was dismissed against an order refusing substitution on the ground that there was no cause of action against the proposed substituted defendant. It could not be said to be necessary to substitute the new party for the existing party when the claimant had no cause of action against the new party. The Court of Appeal also considered whether it was necessary to show that the original party was aware of the identity of the true intended party. It considered the status of the supposed second condition in genuine mistake cases that the true intended party had to be reasonably apparent to the original defendant. It held that this was not an additional formal condition of **CPR, r. 19.5**. This requirement was really an aspect of discretion. In many cases, the justice of the matter would militate against a successful application under **r. 19.5** unless the correct defendant was aware of the complaint before the limitation period expired, although this cannot be stated too firmly as a principle, and may be inconsistent with *Horne-Roberts v SmithKline Beecham plc* [2001] EWCA Civ 2006, [2002] 1 WLR 1662. The element of the test from *The Sardinia Sulcis* [1991] 1 Lloyd's Rep 201 that *Adelson v Associated Newspapers Ltd* [2007] EWCA Civ 701, [2008] 1 WLR 585 requires the court to apply is whether it is possible to identify the intended new party 'by reference to a description which was more or less specific to the particular case'. This phrase has to be interpreted as a reference to what description of the intended party was material, from a legal point of view, to the claim made (*Insight Group Ltd v Kingston Smith* [2012] EWHC 3644 (QB), [2013] PNLR 13).

Rule 19.5(3)(a) should be read in conjunction with **r. 17.4(3)**, which provides that the court may make an amendment to correct a mistake as to the name of a party, but only where the mistake was genuine and not one which would cause reasonable doubt as to the identity of the party in question. Whether a mistake would cause reasonable doubt about the identity of the party intending to sue must be determined objectively having regard to what is said in the claim form in the light of what was known by the defendant and the context in which the claim was made (*ABB Asea Brown Boveri Ltd v Hiscox Dedicated Corporate Member Ltd* [2007] EWHC 1150 (Comm), LTL 24/5/2007). A description of the role played by the claimant in the particulars of claim attached to the claim form may be sufficiently clear to avoid such doubt (*International Bulk Shipping and Services Ltd v Minerals and Metals Trading Corporation of India* [1996] 1 All ER 1017). In *Gregson v Channel Four Television Corporation* (2000) *The Times*, 11 August 2000 (approved in *Adelson v Associated Newspapers Ltd*), the Court of Appeal considered the relationship between **r. 17.4(3)** and **r. 19.5(2)** and **(3)**. It held that **r. 19.5** deals with cases where the claimant mistakenly names the wrong person as defendant, whereas **r. 17.4** deals with cases where the claimant misnames the defendant. The court made clear that there is no significant conflict between the two rules, thus confirming the decision in *International Distillers and Vintners Ltd v*

J. F. Hillebrand (UK) Ltd (1999) *The Times*, 25 January 2000. In *Lockheed Martin Corp v Willis Group Ltd* [2010] EWCA Civ 927, [2010] PNLR 34, the Court of Appeal also noted that there is no further jurisdictional requirement in **r. 19.5(3)(a)** that the mistake was not misleading to the other party or had not caused reasonable doubt as to the identity of the party intended to be sued. Even if such a test had to be applied, it had to be judged objectively by the court.

Claim cannot properly be continued The court may add or substitute a new party as claim- 14.92
ant or defendant after the expiry of a relevant limitation period if the claim cannot properly be continued without the addition or substitution of the new party (**CPR, r. 19.5(3)(b)**). This rule gives effect to the Limitation Act 1980, s. 35(6)(b). The operation of the equivalent provision in the old rules (RSC, ord. 15, r. 6(6)) was limited to five categories of case in which, for technical reasons, claims were liable to be defeated for want of the correct parties. These were where: the claim concerned property vested in the new party at law or in equity and the claimant had an equitable interest in the property; the claim was vested in the claimant and the new party jointly but not severally; the new party was the Attorney-General and the proceedings should have been brought as relator proceedings in his name; the new party was a company in which the claimant was a shareholder whose claim was liable to be defeated by the proper claimant principle (see **14.27**); and the claim should have been brought against new party and the existing defendant jointly. It remains to be seen whether **CPR, r. 19.5(3)(b)**, will be interpreted in a similar, restrictive way, but it is submitted that it should be, so as to accord with the policy of the Limitation Act 1980, s. 35. This view is supported by *Merrett v Babb* [2001] EWCA Civ 214, [2001] QB 1174, where permission to add the claimant's mother as second claimant was granted after the expiry of the limitation period on the ground that the cause of action was vested in them jointly, so the claim could not be maintained by the original claimant without joining her mother. In *Martin v Kaisary* [2005] EWCA Civ 594, [2006] PIQR P5, joinder of a new defendant was not permitted as it was not necessary to establish the liability of the original defendant. The addition of a party could not be said to be necessary within the meaning of **CPR, r. 19.5(2)** and **(3)(b)**, where it was not needed to maintain an existing claim but rather to enable the bringing of a new claim outside the limitation period (*Roberts v Gill and Co.* [2010] UKSC 22, [2011] 1 AC 240).

In *Parkinson Engineering Services plc v Swan* [2009] EWCA Civ 1366, [2010] Bus LR 857, the Court of Appeal distinguished *Adelson v Associated Newspapers Ltd* [2007] EWCA Civ 701, [2008] 1 WLR 585, and *Roberts v Gill and Co.*, and upheld an order permitting a liquidator to be substituted as claimant, instead of the company in liquidation, in proceedings brought against administrators for negligence. The substitution was made so as to prevent the administrators relying on a statutory defence under what is now the Insolvency Act 1986, sch. B1, para. 98, which the court could not disapply in a claim brought by the company, but could, and did disapply in an application brought by the liquidator under s. 212 (sch. B1, para. 75(6)). The Court of Appeal held that the order for substitution was necessary in the terms of the Limitation Act 1980, s. 35(5)(b), and **CPR, r. 19.5(3)(b)**. The original claim could not properly be carried on by the original party (the company) as it was bound to fail or be struck out because of the statutory defence, but it could be maintained and carried on if the liquidator was substituted.

While the Supreme Court dismissed the appeal in *Roberts v Gill and Co.* [2010] UKSC 22, [2011] 1 AC 240, the unanimous ground was that there were no special circumstances justifying a derivative claim by the beneficiary. A majority (Lord Collins of Mapesbury JSC, Lord Rodger of Earlsferry JSC and Lord Walker of Gestingthorpe JSC) also held that it would be an abuse of process to allow changes in capacity (from the claimant's personal capacity as a beneficiary to a representative capacity) and the addition of the personal representative of the estate in stages as a device to get around the provisions of the Limitation Act 1980, s. 35 (see [70]–[72], [85] and [95]).

An order substituting a company in place of the company's administrator under **CPR, r. 19.5(3)(b)**, was made in *Irwin v Lynch* [2010] EWCA Civ 1153, LTL 6/10/2010, in a misfeasance claim against its directors. Such a claim cannot be brought by an administrator (Insolvency Act 1986, s. 212(3)), so the claim could not be continued without substituting the company. The court commented that it would not allow the jurisdiction under **r. 19.5(3)(b)** to be used to circumvent the restrictions in **rr. 17.4** and **19.5(3)(a)** where the case really involves a mistake if the additional requirements in those provisions for curing mistakes cannot be satisfied.

14.93 **Death and bankruptcy** If a party to a claim dies or is adjudicated bankrupt, the court may, even if a relevant limitation period has expired, add or substitute as a party the person to whom the deceased or bankrupt party's interest or liability has passed (**CPR, r. 19.5(3)(c)**). In *Morgan Est (Scotland) Ltd v Hanson Concrete Products Ltd* [2005] EWCA Civ 134, [2005] 1 WLR 2557, the court used **r. 19.5(3)(c)** to permit the addition of a claimant to whom the claim had been assigned, despite the fact that the rule does not refer to transmission by assignment. **Rule 19.5(3)(c)** was included in **Part 19** in order to provide for situations referred to in *Yorkshire Regional Health Authority v Fairclough Building Ltd* [1996] 1 WLR 210, at p. 218. As discussed at **14.85**, this is unnecessary because the transmission of a cause of action following assignment, death or bankruptcy does not raise a new claim under the Limitation Act 1980, s. 35, and these situations should be dealt with under **r. 19.2(4)**. Lord Walker of Gestingthorpe JSC described **r. 19.5(3)(c)** as an 'oddity' in *Roberts v Gill and Co.* [2010] UKSC 22, [2011] 1 AC 240, at [104].

14.94 **Alteration of capacity** The court may, after a relevant limitation period has expired, allow an amendment to alter the capacity in which a party claims, if the new capacity is one which that party had when the proceedings started or has since acquired (**CPR, r. 17.4(4)**). In *Haq v Singh* [2001] EWCA Civ 957, [2001] 1 WLR 1594 the court held that 'capacity' in **r. 17.4(4)** has the same meaning as it has in the Limitation Act 1980, s. 35. Thus the alteration in capacity referred to is an alteration from a representative capacity or personal capacity to another representative capacity, or (in the case of a representative claim) from a representative capacity to a personal capacity. The claimant could not take advantage of **CPR, r. 17.4(4)**, to cure her lack of standing by taking an assignment of the cause of action which had previously been vested in her trustee in bankruptcy. The reality was that the claim was being brought by her in her personal capacity both before and after the assignment. If an amendment after the limitation period requires the addition of a new party as well as a change of capacity, the requirements of **r. 19.5(3)** must be satisfied as well as those of **r. 17.4** (*Roberts v Gill and Co.* [2010] UKSC 22, [2011] 1 AC 240).

The final words in **r. 17.4(4)** ('or has since acquired') give effect to a recommendation of the Law Reform Commission to avoid the anomaly that while the title of an executor relates back, on the grant of probate, to the date of the testator's death, the title of an administrator only relates back to the date of the grant of letters of administration. These words therefore allow alterations in the case of administrators as well as executors (*Roberts v Gill and Co.* [2010] UKSC 22, [2010] 1 AC 240, at [34]).

14.95 **Personal injury claims** **CPR, r. 19.5(4)**, gives the court an additional power in a personal injuries case to add a new party after the expiry of the limitation period:

(a) where it has exercised its discretion under the Limitation Act 1980, s. 33, to override the usual three-year limitation period for a personal injuries claim (Limitation Act 1980, s. 11) or a claim under the fatal accidents legislation (Limitation Act 1980, s. 12); or

(b) where it directs that this issue should be decided at trial.

Procedure for substitution following assignment

CPR, r. 19.2(4), provides that: 14.96

The court may order a new party to be substituted for an existing one if—
(a) the existing party's interest or liability has passed to the new party; and
(b) it is desirable to substitute the new party so that the court can resolve the matters in dispute in the proceedings.

An application for such an order may be made without notice but must be supported by evidence (r. 19.4(3)) showing the stage the claim has reached and setting out details of the transfer of interest or liability (**PD 19A, para. 5.2**).

A new claimant must consent in writing to being added as a claimant, and the consent must be filed at court (**CPR, r. 19.4(4)**). The order substituting the new party must then be served on all parties and any other person affected by it (**r. 19.4(5)**). The court will order service of the existing statements of case on the new party.

Chapter 15 Filing and Service

The following procedural checklists, which are at the front of the book, are relevant to this chapter and **chapter 12**:

Procedural checklist 3 Issue and service where service of the claim form is to be effected by the court
Procedural checklist 4 Issue and service where service of the claim form is to be effected by the claimant

The following procedural checklist is relevant to this chapter:

Procedural checklist 10 Application to extend time for service of claim form

INTRODUCTION

Service is the process by which one party seeks to bring a document to the attention of another party. The document may be the claim form, service of which notifies the defendant that proceedings have been issued against him, or any other document in the proceedings. As has been stated in previous editions of this book, the rules on service in the CPR were initially among the least successful of the Woolf reforms and generated a large volume of new case law. In *Collier v Williams* [2006] EWCA Civ 20, [2006] 1 WLR 1945, Dyson LJ noted that the rules were proving difficult to understand and apply. He commented with dismay that the intention of reducing cost, complexity and delays in litigation by the introduction of rules which were simple, straightforward and not susceptible to satellite litigation had not been achieved in this area. **15.1**

For this reason, and because of the fundamental importance of the service rules, the Civil Procedure Rule Committee conducted a comprehensive review of **CPR, Part 6**, leading to the introduction, with effect from 1 October 2008, of a new **CPR, Part 6**, and associated practice directions, **PD 6A** and **PD 6B**. The new rules have been effective in reducing the quantity of satellite litigation on the question of service.

SERVICE OF CLAIM FORM

CPR, Part 6, distinguishes between service of claim forms and service of other documents. **Part 6, Section II**, sets out the rules for service of the claim form in the jurisdiction. The rules governing the service of other documents in the United Kingdom are contained in **Part 6, Section III**, and are dealt with at **15.37** to **15.44**. In practice, there are few differences between the two regimes, the most important being those relating to the rules for deemed service (see **15.36** and **15.42**). **Part 6, Section IV**, governs service of the claim form and other documents out of the jurisdiction (see **chapter 16**). Service of claim forms in Scotland and Northern Ireland is governed by **r. 6.32**. Service of other documents in Scotland and Northern Ireland is covered by **Part 6, Section III** (see **r. 6.38(3)**). **15.2**

Definition of 'claim form'

'Claim form' is defined to include petitions and other documents used to commence proceedings as well as documents used to bring pre-action applications (**CPR, r. 6.2(c)**). Thus an *application notice* for pre-action disclosure under **r. 31.16**, for example, must be served in accordance with **Part 6, Section II**, and **r. 6.14** will determine its deemed date of service. **15.3**

In *Weston v Bates* [2012] EWHC 590 (QB), [2013] 1 WLR 189, the court considered whether service of a printout of a scan of a photocopy of a claim form was valid, or whether the original, sealed copy of the claim form was required for service. It held that under the CPR what constituted a claim form was a matter of substance and that the words 'claim form' were not a reference to a particular hard copy of the document. Nevertheless, although the court upheld service in this case, practitioners were strongly advised to serve the original, sealed copy to avoid questions being raised about the validity of service. Although the case concerned service out of the jurisdiction, the court's reasoning applies equally, it is submitted, to service within the jurisdiction.

Documents to be served

15.4 In most cases, the only document which must be served on the defendant is the claim form itself. Where the Part 8 procedure is being used, the claim form must be accompanied by a form for acknowledging service (**CPR, r. 7.8(2)**) as well as any written evidence on which the claimant intends to rely (**r. 8.5(1) and (2)**).

The particulars of claim may be included in the claim form, served at the same time but in a separate document, or served subsequently, although **PD 16, para. 3.1**, exhorts practitioners to include the particulars of claim in the claim form if practicable. The response pack required under **CPR, r. 7.8(1)**, accompanies the particulars of claim not the claim form, and so is not needed if the particulars are not included in or served with the claim form. However, in this case the claim form must contain a statement that particulars of claim will follow (**PD 7A, para. 6.2; PD 16, para. 3.3**). Where particulars of claim are served with the claim form, and so must be accompanied by the response pack, failure to include the response pack will not invalidate service. Failure to include the response pack is a matter for the court to take into account under **CPR, r. 13.3(1)(b)**, in considering whether or not to set the judgment aside (*Hart Investments Ltd v Fidler* [2006] EWHC 2857 (TCC), [2007] BLR 30). A similar approach was taken in *Hughes v Alan Dick and Co. Ltd* [2008] EWHC 2695 (QB), LTL 8/1/2009; see further **20.13**).

There are exceptions in specialised proceedings. For example, in possession claims the particulars of claim must be filed and served with the claim form (**CPR, r. 55.4**). In Commercial Court cases, the documents for responding to the claim must be served with the claim form (**r. 58.5(1)(b)**).

For the documents required to be served with the particulars of claim, see **15.40**.

Who may serve the claim form?

15.5 Unless the claimant is required to serve the claim form by a rule, court order or practice direction, the claimant may either serve it himself or ask the court in which it is issued to do so (**CPR, r. 6.4(1)**). The court will not serve particulars of claim unless they are to be served with the claim form (**r. 6.21(1)**).

For several specialist proceedings, the option of court service is not available. The Commercial Court will not serve documents or orders (**PD 58, para. 9**). Neither the High Court nor county courts will serve documents in insolvency proceedings, except where otherwise provided by the Insolvency Rules 1986 or required under Regulation (EU) No 1393/2007 (**PD Insolvency Proceedings, para. 6.2**). Those courts will not serve documents in proceedings under the Companies Acts and related legislation (**PD 49A, para. 28**) or claim forms in directors disqualification proceedings (**PD Directors Disqualification Proceedings, para. 7.1**).

The Civil Appeals Office will not serve documents relating to proceedings before the Court of Appeal (**PD 52C, para 7.1**).

15.6 **Service by the court** A claimant who wishes the court to serve the claim form must file in court a *copy* of it for service on each defendant, as well as a copy for the court (**CPR, r. 6.4(3)**). Copies should also be filed of any notice of funding, which the court will serve with the claim form (**PD 6A, para. 8.2**). It is then for the court to decide which method of service to use (**CPR, r. 6.4(2)**). The method will normally be first class post (**PD 6A, para. 8.1**).

The court will notify the claimant that the claim form has been served in the notice of issue, which will also indicate the deemed date of service (**CPR, r. 6.17(1)**).

The court will notify the claimant if a claim form which the court has served on the defendant by post is returned undelivered (**r. 6.18**). **Rule 6.18(2)** provides that the claim form will nevertheless be deemed to have been served, unless the defendant's address on the claim form is not the right address under **rr. 6.7–6.10**. The court must also notify the party who requested service of a document by the bailiff if the bailiff has been unable to serve it (**r. 6.19**).

Where the court file contains no record that service has taken place, there can be no presumption that service has indeed been effected by the court (*Patel v Smeaton* [2000] WL 1675263). Where a court fails to effect service within the period for service of the claim form, the claimant may apply for an extension of time for serving the claim form under **r. 7.6(3)(a)**.

The procedure is summarised in **procedural checklist 3**, at the front of the book.

Service by a party It is always open to a claimant to make its own arrangements to serve the claim form, instead of using the option of court service. Many practitioners prefer to serve documents themselves, either to retain control over the process, for example, because they do not wish to serve the claim form immediately upon issue, or to take advantage of the wider methods of service available when a party serves. **15.7**

The claimant should notify the court that it intends to serve the claim form when it files the claim form (**CPR, r. 6.4(1)(b)**). The rules do not specify the form that notification should take. In practice, a party may notify the court informally by letter that it wishes to effect service. In the RCJ, solicitors are invited to indicate at the commencement of proceedings whether they wish to effect service themselves, and if this is done, the file will be marked accordingly and no further application will be necessary.

The claimant must file a certificate of service of the claim form (form N215) within 21 days of service of the particulars of claim, giving the particulars required by **r. 6.17(3)**, unless the defendants have all filed acknowledgments by then, in which case no notification to the court is required (**r. 6.17(2)(a)**). A claimant may not obtain judgment in default under **Part 12** unless a certificate of service has been filed (**r. 6.17(2)(b)**). Failure to file a certificate of service will not automatically lead to a default judgement being set aside, but it may constitute a good reason under **r. 13.3(1)(b)** why the court may set aside judgement (*Henriksen v Pires* [2011] EWCA Civ 1720, LTL 14/2/2012). In this case, as the claimant had held an affidavit of service containing all the information requested by form N215 it was not appropriate to set aside the default judgement.

Service out of the jurisdiction through the Senior Master and through diplomatic channels is service by the claimant and not service by the court (*Chare v Fairclough* [2003] EWHC 180 (QB), LTL 20/01/2003).

The procedure is summarised in **procedural checklist 4**, at the front of the book.

On whom may a claim form be served?

Service on the defendant A claim form should be served on the defendant except where the defendant has nominated a solicitor or European lawyer to accept service on his behalf, in which case service must be effected on the solicitor or European lawyer (see **15.9**). Subject to any requirement for personal service (see **15.11**), service on the defendant may be at the address for service specified (before service) by the defendant. For this purpose, a defendant may specify an address in any part of the United Kingdom or any other EEA State where the **15.8**

Commentary

defendant resides or carries on business (**r. 6.8**, which is subject to any contrary provision in any rule or practice direction). Service outside England and Wales is subject to the provisions of **Part 6, Section IV**, on service out of the jurisdiction (see **16.55** to **16.66**). Before 6 April 2011, the address had to be within the United Kingdom. Before 1 October 2008, it had to be within England and Wales.

There are special rules specifying the individuals who may validly be served on behalf of companies, partnerships, limited partnerships, children and protected parties. These are dealt with in **15.45** to **15.51**.

15.9 **Service on the defendant's solicitor or European lawyer** Unless personal service on the defendant is required (see **15.11**), a claim form must (**CPR, r. 6.7(1)**) be served at the business address within the jurisdiction of the defendant's solicitor if:

(a) the defendant has given written notification that that address is his address for service of the claim form; or
(b) the solicitor has notified the claimant that he has the defendant's instructions to accept service at that address.

Unless personal service on the defendant is required (see **15.11**), a claim form must (**r. 6.7(2)**) be served at the business address in another part of the United Kingdom or in another EEA State of the defendant's solicitor if:

(a) the defendant has given written notification that that address is his address for service of the claim form; or
(b) the solicitor has notified the claimant that he has the defendant's instructions to accept service at that address.

Unless personal service on the defendant is required (see **15.11**), a claim form must (**r. 6.7(3)**) be served on the defendant's solicitor or European lawyer at that lawyer's business address anywhere in the EEA if:

(a) the defendant has given written notification that that address is his address for service of the claim form; or
(b) the European lawyer has notified the claimant that he has the defendant's instructions to accept service at that address.

Service outside England and Wales is subject to the provisions of **Part 6, Section IV**, on service out of the jurisdiction (see **16.55** to **16.66**).

For the purposes of **Part 6**, 'solicitor' has an extended definition, which includes any person who, under the Legal Services Act 2007, is authorised to conduct litigation (**CPR, r. 6.2(d)**). The term 'European lawyer' is defined in the European Communities (Services of Lawyers) Order 1978 (SI 1978/1910), art. 2 (applied by **CPR, r. 6.2(e)**).

Sending the claim form to a solicitor who has been involved in pre-action correspondence with the claimant will not be good service if notification under **r. 6.7** has not been given, even though it will probably result in the claim form coming to the attention of the defendant (*Brown v Innovatorone plc* [2009] EWHC 1376 (Comm), [2010] 2 All ER (Comm) 80).

The wording of **r. 6.7** neatly avoids the confusion under the old rules which had led to the Court of Appeal holding that, in the case of personal service, notification of the nomination of a solicitor for service had to come from the solicitor not the defendant. The result of this was that personal service on a defendant was valid even where the defendant had notified the claimant that service should be effected on his solicitor, although no other forms of service on the defendant were permitted once such notification had been made (see *Collier v Williams* [2006] EWCA Civ 20, [2006] 1 WLR 1945).

It is likely that jurisprudence under what was then r. 6.5, requiring the solicitor's authority to accept service to relate to the specific claim in which the claim form has been issued, remains valid (*Nagusina Naviera v Allied Maritime Inc.* [2002] EWCA Civ 1147, LTL 10/7/2002; *Firstdale Ltd v Quinton* [2004] EWHC 1926 (Comm), [2005] 1 All ER 639; *Peacocks Ltd v Chapman Taylor* [2004] EWHC 2898 (TCC), LTL 18/4/2005). Practitioners acting for a claimant should seek written instructions to accept service of each specific claim form, rather than relying on the fact that the defendant's solicitors have accepted service in related proceedings, or have been involved in pre-action correspondence.

METHODS OF SERVING A CLAIM FORM

Prescribed methods of service of the claim form

The methods of service permitted under **CPR, Part 6**, are listed in **r. 6.3**. They are: **15.10**

(a) personal service in accordance with **r. 6.5**;
(b) first class post, document exchange or other service which provides for delivery on the next business day, in accordance with **PD 6A**;
(c) leaving the claim form at a place specified in **rr. 6.7, 6.8, 6.9** or **6.10**;
(d) fax or other means of electronic communication in accordance with **PD 6A**; or
(e) any method authorised by the court under **r. 6.15**.

Rule 6.3 lists the methods of service of a claim form in the jurisdiction. Alternative methods of service are considered at **15.17** to **15.21**. Whether the list in **r. 6.3** is exhaustive is considered at **15.22**.

The CPR do not define what is meant by service other than prescribing how it may be done. In *Asia Pacific (HK) Ltd v Hanjin Shipping Co. Ltd* [2005] EWHC 2443 (Comm), [2005] 2 CLC 747, the question arose whether a claim form which had been transmitted to a defendant by fax, and therefore in a manner provided for under the rules, was intended to be served or was for information only. The court held that when a claim form was delivered to the recipient in a manner provided for by the rules, it was served unless it was made clear by the person who delivered it that whilst he was delivering the form by such a method he was not in fact serving it. The facts that no response pack was served, that the claim form was marked 'Claimant's copy' and that the fax did not state that the claim form was faxed by way of service did not demonstrate that no service was intended at all.

General provisions about methods of service are considered at **15.10** to **15.15**.

There are special rules for service on the Crown (see **15.52**) and service in proceedings for the recovery of land and mortgage possession claims (**Part 55**). There are also special guidelines for service on members of the US Air Force and members of HM Forces in the annex to **PD 6A**.

Personal service

Personal service has to be used to serve a claim form where a statute, a rule, practice direction or order requires it (**CPR, r. 6.5(1)**). An example of a claim form which is required by a rule to be served personally is a Part 8 claim form for permission to make a committal application (**r. 81.14(2)**). **15.11**

In other cases, an individual may be served personally except where notice has been given under **r. 6.7** that a solicitor has instructions to accept service on the defendant's behalf. For service on a party's solicitor, see **15.9**.

A document is served personally on an individual by leaving it with that individual (**r. 6.5(3)(a)**). The meaning of 'personal service' was considered in *Ener-G Holdings plc v Hormell* [2012] EWCA Civ 1059, [2012] CP Rep 47. The question arose in the context of the construction of a contract which required a notice to be served by 'delivering it personally'. The court held that this phrase meant personal service, and that personal service required that the notice should be handed to the intended recipient personally. It did not mean delivery in person by a process server (or anyone else) who simply left the notice at the address for service to be found by the defendant.

Personal service may be effected on the defendant wherever he or she happens to be found in the jurisdiction. It is likely that personal service on a reluctant defendant is effective if the individual to be served is informed of what the document is and it is left as nearly as possible in his or her possession or control (*Thompson v Pheney* (1832) 1 Dowl Pr Cas 441). Once a document which is to be served on an individual has been handed to that individual and the individual knows what it is, the document is served and it makes no difference that the individual gives it back to the process server (*Nottingham Building Society v Peter Bennett and Co.* (1997) *The Times*, 26 February 1997).

Leaving the claim form with a third party who has no authority to accept it on behalf of the defendant does not amount to personal service (*Cherney v Deripaska* [2007] EWHC 965 (Comm), [2007] 2 All ER (Comm) 785). This is so even if the third party hands the documents to the defendant, unless the third party agrees to become the claimant's agent for the purpose of effecting service of the claim form (*Kenneth Allison Ltd v A. E. Limehouse and Co.* [1992] 2 AC 105).

Postal service

15.12 Under **CPR, r. 6.3(1)(b)**, service of a claim form within the jurisdiction may be effected by first class post, document exchange or other service which provides for delivery on the next business day. Postal service is no longer limited to Royal Mail first class post, as the Royal Mail's postal service monopoly came to an end in 2006.

Exactly how service is effected by post, document exchange (DX) or other service is defined in **PD 6A, para. 3.1**, as:

(a) placing the claim form in a postbox;
(b) leaving it with or delivering it to the relevant service provider; or
(c) having it collected by the relevant service provider.

In addition, by **PD 6A, para. 2.1**, service by DX is only allowed if:

(a) the address at which the party is to be served includes a numbered box at a DX; or
(b) the writing paper of the party who is to be served or of the solicitor acting for that party sets out a DX box number; and (in either case)
(c) the party or the solicitor acting for that party has not indicated in writing that they are unwilling to accept service by DX.

The claim form should be posted to:

(a) the address of the defendant's solicitor or European lawyer under **CPR, r. 6.7**; or
(b) if the defendant has not instructed a solicitor or European lawyer to accept service for him, the address (in the UK or any other EEA State) for service which the defendant has provided under **r. 6.8**; or
(c) if the defendant has provided no address for service, as a last resort, the address specified in the table at **r. 6.9(2)** (see **15.14**). Postal service at this address is valid even if the defendant is out of the jurisdiction at the time of service (*Kamali v City and Country Properties Ltd* [2006] EWCA Civ 1879, [2007] 1 WLR 1219).

Service by leaving the claim form at an address

15.13 Service of a claim form may be effected under **CPR, r. 6.3(1)(c)**, by leaving it at the defendant's solicitor's address, or if he has not instructed a solicitor to accept service for him, at the address for service he has provided, or, if he has provided no such address, as a last resort, at the address specified in the table at **r. 6.9(2)**. See **15.14**.

Where the claim form must be served

Personal service may be effected on an individual defendant wherever he or she is found within the jurisdiction. Service on a defendant's solicitor should be effected at the solicitor's business address within the United Kingdom or within an EEA State (**CPR, r. 6.7**). **15.14**

The position in relation to postal service or service by leaving the claim form at an address is more complicated.

In order to identify an address where service may safely be effected, the claimant should ask the defendant for his or her address for service within the United Kingdom or any other EEA State, under **r. 6.8(a)**. Although the rules do not expressly require a claimant to make this enquiry, in *Mersey Docks Property Holdings v Kilgour* [2004] EWHC 1638 (TCC), [2004] BLR 412, the court concluded that the claimant had not taken all reasonable steps to ascertain the defendant's whereabouts because it had taken no steps to communicate with the defendant directly.

If a defendant does not provide any address in response to this enquiry, service should be effected at the address specified in the table in **r. 6.9(2)** (see **table 15.1**). In the case of an individual, the address in the table is that of his or her usual or last known residence. Where the individual is being sued in the name of a business, service may alternatively be effected at the principal or last known place of business. Where the individual is being sued in the name of a partnership, the individual may alternatively be effected at the principal or last known place of business of the partnership.

Service at the address specified in **r. 6.9(2)** is effective even though the defendant does not receive the claim form (*Collier v Williams* [2006] EWCA Civ 20, [2006] 1 WLR 1945). To mitigate against this potential unfairness, **r. 6.9(3)** provides that where the claimant has reason to believe that the defendant may no longer reside or carry on business from his or her usual, principal or last known address, the claimant must take reasonable steps to ascertain the address of the defendant's current residence or place of business ('current address'), confirming *Mersey Docks Property Holdings v Kilgour*. In *Re Broadside Colours and Chemicals Ltd* [2012] EWHC 195 (Ch), LTL 22/2/2012, the court decided that a claimant was entitled to rely on the address for a defendant director of a company revealed by a Companies House search, even though the details of the address had been filed six years before the date of service, as the claimant had no reason to believe that the published address was not current. The requirement under **r. 6.9(3)** to make further enquiries was not triggered. As a result, service at that address was good service, even though the defendant no longer lived there and the proceedings did not thereby come to his attention. Where, having taken the reasonable steps required by **r. 6.9(3)**, the claimant ascertains the defendant's current address, the claim form must be served at that address (**r. 6.9(4)(a)**).

Where the claimant, having made reasonable enquiries, cannot ascertain the defendant's current address, the claimant must consider whether the defendant could be served at an alternative place or by an alternative method, and if so make an application under **r. 6.15**.

If all these steps have failed (i.e. the defendant has failed to provide an address for service; the claimant has reason to believe the defendant no longer resides or carries on business at the address specified in the table at **r. 6.9(2)** but reasonable enquiries have not revealed the defendant's current address; service by an alternative method or at an alternative place is not possible), the claimant may effect valid service on the defendant at the address specified in the table at **r. 6.9(2)** even though the claimant knows the defendant no longer resides or carries on business there.

The meaning of 'reasonable steps' in **r. 6.9(3)** is not defined in the rules or practice directions, and will inevitably vary from case to case. It is likely that taking reasonable steps would include checking the defendant's address for service with him (*Mersey Docks Property Holdings v Kilgour*). A rather more difficult judgment is the extent of the steps which should be taken

Table 15.1 Service of claim form if the defendant does not give an address (CPR, r. 6.9(2))

Nature of defendant to be served	Place of service
1. Individual	Usual or last known residence.
2. Individual being sued in the name of a business	Usual or last known residence of the individual; or principal or last known place of business.
3. Individual being sued in the business name of a partnership	Usual or last known residence of the individual; or principal or last known place of business of the partnership.
4. Limited liability partnership	Principal office of the partnership; or any place of business of the partnership within the jurisdiction which has a real connection with the claim.
5. Corporation (other than a company) incorporated in England and Wales	Principal office of the corporation; or any place within the jurisdiction where the corporation carries on its activities and which has a real connection with the claim.
6. Company registered in England and Wales	Principal office of the company; or any place of business of the company within the jurisdiction which has a real connection with the claim.
7. Any other company or corporation	Any place within the jurisdiction where the corporation carries on its activities; or any place of business of the company within the jurisdiction.

where the defendant's whereabouts are not known, or where the defendant is not cooperating. Of all the new rules in force from 1 October 2008, this perhaps leaves the most scope for uncertainty, in that the claimant will not know when he effects service whether the steps he has taken to ascertain the defendant's current address are reasonable, and so whether service at what he believes to be the defendant's usual or last known address will be treated as good service by the court.

The meaning of 'residence' in the table at **r. 6.9(2)** has proved problematic. In *Varsani v Relfo Ltd* [2010] EWCA Civ 560, [2010] 3 All ER 1045, the Court of Appeal considered the meaning of 'residence' in the context of an international businessman with more than one home. The claim form was left by way of service on the defendant at an address in Middlesex where the defendant's wife, children and extended family lived. The evidence before the court was that the defendant worked in Kenya and visited his family at this address once a year for several weeks. There was no evidence that he was estranged from his family. The court held that it was possible for a person to reside in more than one place at the same time, and that the question before it was whether the quality of occupation was as a home. On the basis that the defendant's address in Middlesex was the home of his wife and children, which he could not share because of his work in Kenya but to which he returned regularly each year, the court held that the address was the defendant's residence. The test to be applied in determining a defendant's usual residence is his pattern of life, taking into account the nature of the use of the premises as well as the duration of the periods of occupation. The facts were to be distinguished from cases such as *Cherney v Deripaska* [2007] EWHC 965 (Comm), [2007] 2 All ER (Comm) 785, and *OJSC Oil Co. Yugraneft v Abramovich* [2008] EWHC 2613 (Comm), LTL 3/11/2008, where the defendants owned several houses in different countries and their visits to their London houses were sporadic, often for single nights only and for the purpose of business. For a case applying the test in *Varsani v Reflo Ltd* see *Moloobhoy v Kanani* [2012] EWHC 1670 (Comm), LTL 9/7/2012.

Service by fax or other electronic means

Service by fax or other electronic means is only permitted in accordance with **PD 6A, para. 4.1**. This provides that the party who is to be served or the solicitor acting for that party must previously have indicated in writing to the party serving: **15.15**

(a) that the party to be served or the solicitor is willing to accept service by fax or other electronic means. The following are sufficient written indications for the purpose:
   (i) a fax number set out on the writing paper of the solicitor acting for the party to be served;
   (ii) an email address set out on the writing paper of the solicitor acting for the party to be served but only where it is stated that the email address may be used for service; or
   (iii) a fax number, email address or electronic identification set out on a statement of case or a response to a claim filed with the court; and

(b) the fax number, email address or other electronic identification to which it must be sent.

The fax number must be either that of the address for service provided by the defendant under **CPR, r. 6.8**, or as set out in the table in **r. 6.9**, or that of the defendant's solicitor instructed to accept service under **r. 6.7**.

Where the claimant wishes to serve the claim form electronically (other than by fax) he must first check whether there are any restrictions on the format in which the claim form may be sent or as to the maximum size of attachments (**PD 6A, para. 4.2**). There is no need to send a hard copy of the claim form (**PD 6A, para. 4.3**).

In *Thorne v Lass Salt Garvin* [2009] EWHC 100 (QB), LTL 5/2/2009, service by fax on a defendant firm of solicitors without their prior consent was not valid service. The fact that they were solicitors and that their fax number appeared on their letterhead did not bring them within **PD 6A, para. 4.1(2)(a)**, as they were not acting for themselves. Nor was the case sufficiently exceptional to justify an order dispensing with service under what is now **CPR, r. 6.16**.

A solicitor is 'acting for' a party within the meaning of **PD 6A, para. 4.1**, only where either the defendant has given written notification that his address for service is that of his solicitor, or the solicitor has notified the claimant that he has the defendant's instructions to accept service (**CPR, r. 6.7**). Faxing a copy of the claim form to the address of a solicitor who has been involved in pre-action correspondence will not be valid service unless notice under **r. 6.7** has been given (*Brown v Innovatorone plc* [2009] EWHC 1376 (Comm), [2010] 2 All ER (Comm) 80). The reference in **PD 6A, para. 4.1**, to 'the solicitor acting for the party' is to a solicitor whose authority to accept service has been notified to the claimant under **CPR, r. 6.7**. In other words, the requirement of **PD 6A, para. 4.2(a)**, simply makes clear that a solicitor is willing to accept service by fax, as a method of service. It does not constitute any representation that a solicitor has the defendant's authority to accept service.

Where a document other than a claim form is served by fax, it must be served at the party's address for service (**CPR, r. 6.23(5)**). This will be the defendant's solicitor's address only if that is the address for service specified by the defendant under **r. 6.23(1)**.

Where a claimant is entitled to serve a defendant out of the jurisdiction under **Part 6, Section IV**, service may be effected by email, provided the defendant's permission for service by this method has been obtained under **PD 6A, para. 4.1**. Where this requirement is not met, an order for service by an alternative method will be needed under **r. 6.15** (*Bacon v Automattic Inc.* [2011] EWHC 1072 (QB), [2011] 2 All ER (Comm) 852). In either case, service by email must be permitted under local law as required by **r. 6.40(3)**.

Service by contractually agreed method

15.16 Where a contract contains a provision for service, a claim form containing a claim in respect only of that contract may be served at the place or by the method specified in it (**CPR, r. 6.11(1)**). By **r. 6.11(2)**, the claim form may not be served at a contractually agreed place out of the jurisdiction unless either permission is obtained under **r. 6.36**, or service can be effected without permission under **rr. 6.32** or **6.33**. Only parties to the contract, their transferees and assignees can take advantage of a contractual method of service (*Argo Capital Investors Fund SPC v Essar Steel Ltd* [2005] EWHC 2587, LTL 28/11/2005).

SERVICE BY AN ALTERNATIVE METHOD

15.17 The court may authorise service of a claim form or any other document by an alternative method, or at a place not otherwise permitted by **CPR, Part 6,** where 'there is a good reason' to do so (**rr. 6.15(1)** and **6.27**). Authorisation can be applied for before or after service has been unsuccesfully attempted (**PD 6A, paras 9.1** and **9.2**). It is not a prerequisite for the making of an order under **CPR, rr. 6.15** or **6.27** (as it was under RSC, ord. 65, r. 4), that service in accordance with the rules is impracticable: it is only necessary that there is a good reason (*Albon v Naza Motor Trading Sdn Bhd (No. 2)* [2007] EWHC 327(Ch), [2007] 1 All ER (Comm) 813). In deciding whether a good reason has been shown, the court will take into account the overriding objective and whether the making of the order will enable the court to deal with the case fairly (*Albon v Naza Motor Trading Sdn Bhd (No. 2)*). The phrase 'good reason' is less stringent than the 'exceptional circumstances' required for the court to make an order dispensing with service under **CPR, r. 6.16** (*Brown v Innovatorone plc* [2009] EWHC 1376 (Comm), [2010] 2 ALL ER (Comm) 80). The court must examine with some care the reason why it is being asked to make an order. The power in **r. 6.15** should not be exercised over-readily, and the mere absence of prejudice to the defendant is unlikely to be enough to justify an order. On the facts of this case, where the claimant's solicitors had left service very late, and no explanation was offered for the lateness, there was no 'good reason' to justify an order. If the court finds that there is a good reason to justify making an order, it will go on to consider whether it should excercise its discretion to do so, having regard to all the facts including the parties' conduct (*Albon v Naza Motor Trading Sdn Bhd (No. 2)*). In that case it had been right to make an order for service by an alternative method as there was evidence of non-cooperation by the defendant with the claimant's attempts to effect service. Further, making the order saved expense and time and promoted the objective of dealing with the case justly.

The desirability of serving a defendant in the jurisdiction in order to ensure that England is the jurisdiction first seised of proceedings for the purposes of the Brussels Convention, art. 21, does not constitute a good reason (*Knauf UK GmbH v British Gypsum Ltd* [2001] EWCA Civ 1570, [2002] 1 WLR 907; see also the comments in *Albon v Naza Motor Trading Sdn Bhd (No. 2)* [2007] EWHC 327 (Ch), [2007] 1 All ER (Comm) 813).

Service by an alternative method or at an alternative place on a defendant who is abroad

15.18 The court's power to order service by an alternative method applies to service both within and outside the jurisdiction, despite the fact that **CPR, r. 6.15** appears in **Section II of Part 6** (the rules for service within the jurisdiction). This is because **r. 6.37(5)(b)(i)**, which authorises the court to give directions about the method of service when it gives permission to serve a claim out of the jurisdiction enables it to make orders for alternative service under **r. 6.15** (*Bacon v Automattic Inc.* [2011] EWHC 1072 (QB), [2011] 2 All ER (Comm) 852, following *Cecil v Bayat* [2011] EWCA Civ 135, [2011] 1 WLR 3086, and overturning previous decisions in *Brown v Innovatorone plc* [2009] EWHC 1376 (Comm), [2010] 2 All ER (Comm) 80, and *Amalgamated Metal Trading Ltd v Baron* [2010] EWHC 3207, LTL 4/1/2011).

Two further considerations apply where it is sought to serve a defendant who is abroad pursuant to an order under **r. 6.15**. First, the order may not be used to circumvent the rules on service out of the jurisdiction. So service abroad must be permitted under **Regulation (EC) No. 44/2001**, the Lugano Convention or the common law rules on jurisdiction (see **chapter 16**). Secondly, save in exceptional circumstances, the method of service ordered must comply with the law of the country in which service is to be effected (*Cecil v Bayat* [2011] EWCA Civ 135, [2011] 1 WLR 3086, and *Abela v Baadarani* [2011] EWCA Civ 1571, [2012] CP Rep 11). Cases which might justify an order for service abroad by an alternative method are where there are grounds for believing that the defendant is avoiding personal service by the only method permitted by the foreign law, or where there is a need for urgency, although speed of itself will not in general be a sufficient reason for an order. In *Bitumex (HK) Co. Ltd v IRPC Public Co. Ltd* [2012] EWHC 1065, [2012] 2 All ER (Comm) 1131, the court was prepared to make an order under **r. 6.15(2)** retrospectively authorising service by a method which did not comply with Thai law. The reason was not only that service under the Hague Convention would take substantially longer but that the order was justified in order to assist the progress of an international arbitration in London which the defendants were seeking to delay by failing to join in the appointment of an arbitrator.

Questions of the legality of service under foreign law do not arise if the court exercises power under **r. 6.15** to order service by an alternative method on a foreign defendant in England (provided of course the relevant jurisdictional gateway is satisfied) *BNP Paribas SA v OJSC 'Russian Machines'* [2012] EWCA Civ 644, [2012] 1 Lloyd's Rep, 649.

Commentary

Examples of orders which may be made under r. 6.15

PD 6A, para. 9.3, gives some examples of the alternative methods which may be used to serve a document, and the additional evidence required. Where an application is made to serve a third party who knows the person to be served (such as a friend, relative or solicitor acting for the defendant but without instructions to accept service), the application must include evidence that the claim form is likely to reach the person to be served by this method. An application to serve by sending a text message or leaving a voicemail message with details of the place where the claim form, or other document, can be found must be accompanied by evidence that the person to be served uses the relevant telephone number and is likely to receive the message. An application to serve a company by email (other than in accordance with **PD 6A, para 4.1**) must include evidence that the email is likely to come to the attention of a person holding a senior position in that company. **15.19**

Other commonly ordered alternatives include newspaper advertisement and service at a place the defendant is known to frequent. An order can be made for service by an alternative method on the insurers of drivers of motor vehicles who have disappeared but are not 'untraced drivers' for the purposes of the Motor Insurers' Bureau agreements (see *Gurtner v Circuit* [1968] 2 QB 587). Similarly, in a claim for professional negligence against a solicitor who had disappeared, service was allowed at the address of the Solicitors' Indemnity Fund in *Abbey National plc v Frost* [1999] 1 WLR 1080. In *South Cambridgeshire District Council v Persons Unknown* [2004] EWCA Civ 1280, *The Times*, 11 November 2004, a case involving the eviction of squatters from an illegal caravan site, the court permitted service by documents placed in plastic bags nailed to posts in prominent positions on the site. This reflects one of the methods of service provided for in possession claims under **CPR, r. 55.6**.

Retrospective order for alternative service

The court is given express power by **CPR, r. 6.15(2)**, to make an order that steps already taken to bring the claim form to the attention of the defendant by an alternative method or at an alternative place are good service. This reverses the effect of the decisions in *Nanglegan v Royal Free Hampstead NHS Trust* [2001] EWCA Civ 127, [2002] 1 WLR 1043, and *Elmes v Hygrade Food* **15.20**

Products plc [2001] EWCA Civ 121, LTL 27/2/2001, to the effect that the court had no retrospective power under the former **r. 6.8** to cure defects in service. Although **r. 6.15** appears in **Section II of Part 6**, it applies to service both within and outside the jurisdiction (*Bacon v Automattic Inc.* [2011] EWHC 1072 (QB), [2011] 2 All ER (Comm) 852, following *Cecil v Bayat* [2011] EWCA Civ 135, [2011] 1 WLR 3086).

In the case of service out of the jurisdiction, the claimant will also have to show, save in exceptional circumstances, that the method of service which is to be retrospectively validated is good service under local law (*Abela v Baadarani* [2011] EWCA Civ 1571, [2012] CP Rep 11; see further the discussion in **15.18**).

The applicant for a retrospective order under **r. 6.15** will have to satisfy the court that there is a 'good reason' under **r. 6.15(1)** to make an order in the circumstances. **PD 6A, para. 9.2,** requires retrospective applications for an order to include evidence showing why the order is sought, what alternative method or place was used, when service was attempted by this method, and why the applicant believes that the document in question is likely to have reached the person to be served by the steps taken.

Application for order permitting alternative service

15.21 An application for an order permitting service by an alternative method should be made using the Part 23 procedure. The application may be made without notice to other parties (**CPR, r. 6.15(3)(b)**). The application must be supported by evidence (**r. 6.15(3)(a)**), including evidence showing why the order is sought, what alternative order or place is proposed and why the applicant believes the alternative steps are likely to enable the document to reach the person to be served (**PD 6A, para. 9.1**). Where the court makes an order permitting such service, it will specify the method of service, the deemed date of service and the date for filing an acknowledgment, admission or defence (**CPR, r. 6.15(4)(c)**).

Service by means outside the CPR

15.22 Under the RSC it was possible to effect service by a method outside the rules, provided the defendant had agreed to accept service by the method chosen. In *Kenneth Allison Ltd v A. E. Limehouse and Co.* [1992] 2 AC 105 a process server effected service on the defendant partnership by leaving the writ with the receptionist, who took it only after she had consulted one of the partners and he had authorised her to accept it. The House of Lords held that although service by this method was outside the rules, it was nevertheless valid as it had been effected pursuant to an ad hoc agreement. The decision was followed in *Finn v Girobank plc* (2000) LTL 19/1/2000, which was a case on the old RSC, ord. 10.

The Court of Appeal in *Anderton v Clwyd County Council (No. 2)* [2002] EWCA Civ 933, [2002] 1 WLR 3174, appears to have held that the list of methods for service in what is now **CPR, r. 6.3**, is exhaustive and that provision of the claim form to the defendant by any other method, even where it is effective to bring the existence of the claim to the defendant's attention, does not constitute service under the rules. In that case, the Court of Appeal did not consider the effect of an agreement by the defendant to the use of an alternative method of service. In *Cranfield v Bridgegrove Ltd* [2003] EWCA Civ 656, [2003] 1 WLR 2441, though, it approved, obiter, *Kenneth Allison Ltd v A. E. Limehouse and Co.* as authority for the proposition that an ad hoc agreement for service in a manner outside the CPR is legally effective.

COURT'S POWER TO CURE DEFECTS IN SERVICE

15.23 The court has power to make orders retrospectively under **CPR, r. 3.10**, to cure a procedural defect in service, and there are no material differences between this rule and RSC, ord. 2, r. 1 (*Phillips v Symes (No. 3)* [2008] UKHL 1, [2008] 1 WLR 180). Attempting to serve at the wrong address is an 'error of procedure' within the meaning of **CPR, r. 3.10**, and the court has power under this rule, and alternatively under **r. 3.1(2)(m)**, to make an order remedying the error (*Nelson v Clearsprings (Management) Ltd* [2006] EWCA Civ 1252, [2007] 1 WLR 962). The type of situation where the court might exercise this power is where no question of limitation arises and there is no benefit to the defendant in requiring the claimant to reissue. In these circumstances, it cannot be said that it is in the interests of the overriding objective for the claimant to be required to reissue proceedings for no good purpose.

DISPENSING WITH SERVICE

The court may dispense with service of a claim form in exceptional circumstances (**CPR, r. 6.16(1)**). An application for an order to dispense with service may be made at any time and without notice (**r. 6.16(2)(b)**). It must be supported by evidence (**r. 6.16(2)(a)**). **15.24**

Under the predecessor to this rule in force before 1 October 2008 (**r. 6.9**), the court granted orders dispensing with service both before and after the period for service of the claim form had expired. However, orders would only be made in exceptional circumstances where the time for service of the claim form had expired before the order was sought (*Godwin v Swindon Borough Council* [2001] EWCA Civ 1478, [2002] 1 WLR 997; *Anderton v Clwyd County Council (No. 2)* [2002] EWCA Civ 933, [2002] 1 WLR 3174). The version of the rule now in force preserves the power to make orders at any time, but extends the requirement for exceptional circumstances to all cases. This is a more stringent test than the requirement in **r. 6.15** to show 'good reason' (*Bethell Construction Ltd v Deloitte and Touche* [2011] EWCA Civ 1321, LTL 13/11/2011).

The jurisprudence on the old r. 6.9 sheds light on what is meant by 'exceptional circumstances'. The court's approach under the old rule was strict. The fact that the defendant had actually received the claim form, albeit in a manner which did not comply with the rules, was not of itself exceptional (e.g. *Nathoo v Ashford and St Peter's Hospital Trust* [2004] EWHC 1571 (QB), LTL 24/11/2003). Nor were simple errors in service by the claimant's solicitors likely to amount to exceptional circumstances (e.g. *Kuenyehia v International Hospitals Group Ltd* [2006] EWCA Civ 21, *The Times*, 17 February 2006, service by fax when the defendant's solicitors had not consented to it). However, the Court of Appeal upheld the decision to dispense with service under the old r. 6.9 in *Olafsson v Gissurarson (No. 2)* [2008] EWCA Civ 152, [2008] 1 WLR 2016, where it did consider that the circumstances were truly exceptional. The facts were that the claimant had sought to serve the defendant in Iceland and had requested service through the appropriate channels. The correct documents were given to the defendant in Iceland, but were not served in accordance with Icelandic law because the defendant was not asked to and did not sign a declaration confirming his receipt of them. The claimant had not taken steps in time to cure the defect by re-serving the proceedings, because he had received a certificate from the British Embassy in Reykjavik stating that the relevant documents had been served.

The court will not make an order dispensing with service in circumstances in which this would enable a party to circumvent the rules on service out of the jurisdiction (*Cherney v Deripaska* [2007] EWHC 965 (Comm), [2007] 2 All ER (Comm) 785, applying *Shiblaq v Sadikoglu* [2004] EWHC 1890 (Comm), [2004] 2 All ER (Comm) 596).

The House of Lords has held in *Mucelli v Government of Albania* [2009] UKHL 2, [2009] 1 WLR 276, that the CPR do not apply to, and so there is no power to dispense with service of documents in, the procedures under the Extradition Act 2003.

The fact that the defendant happens to be a firm of solicitors does not make the case an exceptional one such as to justify dispensing with service under **CPR, r. 6.16** (*Thorne v Lass Salt Garvin* [2009] EWHC 100 (QB), LTL 5/2/2009). Attempting service on the final day of validity, and attempting to serve without prior notification to the defendant, are powerful factors against dispensing with service.

DEFENDANT REQUIRING SERVICE

15.25 Where the claimant has issued but not yet served the claim form, the defendant can serve a notice under **CPR, r. 7.7**, requiring the claimant either to do so, or to discontinue the claim by a date which is at least 14 days after the date of service of the notice. If the claimant fails to comply, the defendant may apply to the court for an order dismissing the claim. This rule enables the defendant to require the claimant to proceed with the claim, rather than wait for the four or six months during which the claim form may be served. In practice, the provision is rarely used.

TIME FOR SERVING A CLAIM FORM IN THE JURISDICTION

Period of validity

15.26 Proceedings are started when the court issues a claim form (see **chapter 12**) at the request of the claimant, on the date entered on the form by the court (**CPR, r. 7.2**). Before 12.00 midnight on the calendar day four months after the date of issue of the claim form, the claimant must take the relevant step specified in **table 15.2** to dispatch or deliver the claim form in the jurisdiction (**r. 7.5**).

The effect of this rule is to give the claimant complete control over compliance with **r. 7.5**, provided he is satisfied he knows the defendant's address. He need not concern himself about whether the claim form gets to the defendant on time. Two business days after the relevant step has been taken, the defendant is deemed served (**r. 6.14**; see **15.36**).

Calculating the period of validity

15.27 It is clear from the precise wording used in **CPR, r. 7.5**, that for a claim form issued on 21 July 2010, the relevant step must be taken before midnight on 21 November 2010. When there is no corresponding date in the month in which the period ends it will end on the last day of the month, using the corresponding date rule (*Dodds v Walker* [1981] 1 WLR 1027). So, for a claim form issued on 30 October 2011, the relevant step must be taken before midnight on 29 February 2012. The relevant step may therefore be taken on any day, including Saturdays, Sundays and bank holidays and at any time of day or night.

Effect on period of validity of applying to serve outside the jurisdiction

15.28 Under the pre-October 2008 version of the CPR, the court had power to grant permission for service out of the jurisdiction of a claim form originally issued as one not for service out of the

Table 15.2 Service of a claim form within the jurisdiction: steps to be completed before 12.00 midnight on the calendar day four months after the date of issue of the claim form (CPR, r. 7.5)

Method of service	Step required
First class post, document exchange or other service which provides for delivery on the next business day	Posting, leaving with, delivering to or collection by the relevant service provider
Delivery of the document to or leaving it at the relevant place	Delivering to or leaving the document at the relevant place
Personal service under **r. 6.5**	Completing the relevant step required by **r. 6.5(3)**
Fax	Completing the transmission of the fax
Other electronic method	Sending the email or other electronic transmission

jurisdiction even where the application was made more than four months after the date of issue. In this case the provisions of **CPR, r. 7.6(3)**, did not apply, provided that the application for permission was made no later than six months from the date of issue (*Anderton v Clwyd County Council (No. 2)* [2002] EWCA Civ 933, [2002] 1 WLR 3174). It is unlikely the changes to the CPR have affected this.

Failure to serve a claim form in time

The consequences of failure to take the relevant steps within the time limits in **CPR, r. 7.5**, particularly when the limitation period for the claim has expired, are extremely dangerous for the claimant and for the claimant's legal advisers. The claim form will have expired and the cause of action will by then be time-barred. Now that control of compliance with the deadline in **r. 7.5** has been given to the claimant, there will be few (if any) acceptable excuses for failure to do so. 15.29

Practitioners can expect little sympathy from the court where they delay service of proceedings, particularly where the claim form was itself issued at the end of the limitation period. The usual position is that the court will not grant an extension of time for service of the claim form if to do so deprives the defendant of a limitation defence (*Cecil v Bayat* [2011] EWCA Civ 135, [2011] 1 WLR 3086; see the discussion in **15.32**).

Negligent failure to serve the claim form within the period stipulated in **r. 7.5** does not render the subsequent issue of a second claim form an abuse of process where either the limitation period has not yet expired (see, for example, *Hoddinott v Persimmon Homes (Wessex) Ltd* [2007] EWCA Civ 1203, [2008] 1 WLR 806, at [54]) or, in a personal injury case, in order to seek an extension to the primary limitation period under the Limitation Act 1980, s. 33 (*Aktas v Adepta* [2010] EWCA Civ 1170, [2011] QB 894).

EXTENDING TIME FOR SERVING A CLAIM FORM

Procedure

If it is not possible to comply with the time limit set out in **CPR, r. 7.5**, the claimant can apply under **r. 7.6** for an extension. (For Part 8 claim forms see **13.6**.) The procedure is summarised in **procedural checklist 10**, at the front of the book, and there is detailed commentary from here to **15.35**. Practitioners should beware, however, of relying on this provision where they know time for service of the claim form is running out, but they are not yet ready to proceed. In these circumstances, the appropriate procedure is to serve proceedings and then apply for a stay or an extension of time for the next steps in the action rather than applying for an extension of time to serve the claim form. See, for example, *Hoddinott v Persimmon Homes (Wessex) Ltd* [2007] EWCA Civ 1203, [2008] 1 WLR 806, a case where the particulars of claim were not yet ready, or *Cecil v Bayat* [2011] EWCA Civ 135, [2011] 1 WLR 3086, where the claimants were seeking funding for the litigation. 15.30

An application for extending time for serving a claim form should be made using the Part 23 procedure (see **chapter 32**). It may be made without serving a copy of the application notice on the defendant (or any other respondent) (**r. 7.6(4)(b)**). A defendant who is served with an order made without notice, extending time for service of a claim form, has seven days in which to apply for it to be set aside (**r. 23.10**).

The application must be supported by evidence (**r. 7.6(4)(a)**). The evidence will either be set out in the application notice (which must then be verified by a statement of truth) or be in the form of a witness statement (which must also be verified by a statement of truth) (**r. 32.6**).

Commentary

Alternatively, evidence may be in affidavit form, although any additional cost of producing the evidence in this form may not be recovered from any other party without a court order (**r. 32.15(2)**).

PD 7A, para. 8.2, requires the evidence to include the following details:

(a) all the circumstances relied on;
(b) the date of issue of the claim;
(c) the expiry date of any extension already granted under **CPR, r. 7.6**; and
(d) a full explanation of why the claim form has not been served.

In stating the circumstances relied on the evidence should cover both those relating to the cause of action and the reasons for seeking an extension. The former will include the dates of accrual and expiry of the limitation period. As an application for extending time for service is made without notice, the applicant has a duty of full and frank disclosure, which includes an obligation to make reasonable inquiries into the matters relevant to the application.

An applicant who wishes to have the application dealt with without a hearing should request this in the application notice (**PD 23A, para. 2.1(5)**). The court has the power to dispense with a hearing where it does not consider a hearing appropriate (**CPR, r. 23.8(c)**), for example, where there are clear grounds for granting an extension. In practice, it is very common for these applications to be considered without a hearing and without notice to the defendant. However, in *Collier v Williams* [2006] EWCA Civ 20, [2006] 1 WLR 1945, the Court of Appeal stated that courts should consider whether that is an appropriate way of proceeding. Where the application is made shortly before expiry of the period in **r. 7.5** and where the cause of action has become time-barred since the date on which the claim form was issued, the application is potentially crucial. It is highly desirable that applications of this type, where time is running out, should normally be dealt with by an urgent hearing. Where pressure of business means it is not possible to deal with the application other than on paper, consideration should be given to dealing with it by telephone. In *Hoddinott v Persimmon Homes (Wessex) Ltd* [2007] EWCA Civ 1203, [2008] 1 WLR 806, the Court of Appeal made clear that a claimant who applies for and obtains an extension of time for service of the claim form, without giving notice to the defendant, bears the risk that the order may subsequently be set aside.

Order extending time for serving

15.31 There is no limit on the length of any extension, or on the number of extensions which a court may grant. It will be for the applicant to justify the length of extension sought. Bearing in mind the court's duty as part of the overriding objective to ensure that cases are dealt with expeditiously it is unlikely that the court will be prepared to grant long or multiple extensions in the absence of good reason (see **15.32**). Under the old rules in the RSC and CCR, the maximum period of any extension was 12 months at a time (this was renewable), but the courts insisted on a justification for the period of any extension sought.

Where an order is made (whether granting or dismissing the application) without notice to the defendant, a copy of the order, the application notice and any evidence in support must be served on the defendant, unless the court orders to the contrary (**CPR, r. 23.9**). The order must contain a statement of the defendant's right to apply to have the order set aside or varied (**r. 23.9(3)**). The defendant has seven days from the date of service to apply to the court for the order to be varied or set aside (**r. 23.10**).

Grounds on which the court will grant an extension

15.32 A new version of **CPR, r. 7.6**, came into operation on 1 October 2008. It is reworded for consistency with the new **r. 7.5**, but is unchanged in substance. It is likely, therefore, that the jurisprudence on the old version of this rule, which is considered below, will continue to be of relevance, even though the full control given to the claimant to comply with **r. 7.5** will make it harder for orders extending time for service to be obtained. The crucial enquiry will relate to the relevant steps under **r. 7.5** for dispatching the claim form. Dates of deemed service are no longer of any relevance.

The general rule is that an application to extend the time for taking the relevant steps under **r. 7.5** should be made within the usual period of service (or that period as already extended by the court) (**r. 7.6(2)**). The application is 'made' when the notice is received by the court, not when it is heard (**r. 23.5**; *Collier v Williams* [2006] EWCA Civ 20, [2006] 1 WLR 1945). The CPR are silent on the test to be applied in deciding whether to allow an extension under **r. 7.6(2)**, but guidance was given in *Hashtroodi v Hancock* [2004] EWCA Civ 652, [2004] 1 WLR 3206, in which the Court of Appeal made clear that the authorities on extending the period of validity of a writ under RSC, ord. 6, r. 8, no longer apply. *Hashtroodi v Hancock* was clarified by *Collier v Williams*. The approach of the court to applications under **r. 7.6(2)** should now be as follows:

The crucial enquiry the court must undertake is to evaluate why the claimant did not take the relevant steps under **r. 7.5** within the specified period. Whereas under the RSC a plaintiff who was unable to show a good reason for not serving in time failed to satisfy the former threshold condition (*Kleinwort Benson Ltd v Barbrak Ltd* [1987] AC 597), under the CPR a more calibrated approach is adopted, albeit in the context of a generally strict regime, especially where limitation is involved. A defendant should not be deprived of a limitation defence by an extension of time for serving a claim form, save in exceptional cicumstances (*Cecil v Bayat* [2011] EWCA Civ 135, [2011] 1 WLR 3086). If there is a good reason for the failure to take the relevant steps within the specified period, an extension of time will usually be granted. The weaker the reason, the readier the court will be to refuse the application and where there is no reason or only a very weak reason the court is most unlikely to grant an extension of time. The fact that the claimant has taken all reasonable steps to try to effect service will be a strong reason to grant the application. Where service has not been effected because of the incompetence of the claimant's legal advisers, that will be a strong reason to refuse the application, even if not an absolute bar.

The good reason must be a difficulty in serving the claim form on the defendant, not other problems which the claimant might have, such as needing more time to prepare the claim. In the latter circumstances, as stated at **15.30**, the appropriate procedure is to issue the claim form and apply for a stay or an extension of time for taking the next steps in the action (*Cecil v Bayat*).

In *Collier v Williams*, the reason for the failure to serve in time was the claimant's erroneous belief as to the whereabouts of the defendant's usual or last known residence. So the court needed to consider the reasonableness of that belief. If the claimant had been misled by the defendant as to his residence, the court would be likely to hold that the claimant had reasonable grounds for his belief, that there was a very good reason for the claimant's failure to serve in time and would grant an extension of time under **r. 7.6(2)**. But it is always incumbent on the claimant to take reasonable steps to ascertain the defendant's last known residence. What is reasonable must depend on the circumstances of the case. The claimant in this case had made an assumption about the defendant's address based on little evidence and so there was no good reason to extend the period for service of the claim form. The discretion must be exercised in accordance with the overriding objective. However, the exercise of going through the checklist of factors set out in **r. 1.1(2)** will often not be necessary. Where there is no good reason justifying the failure to serve the claim form in time (or, now, to take the relevant steps), there should normally be no need to go further. On the facts of the case, the court refused to grant an extension because the reason for failing to serve within the period of validity was the incompetence of the claimant's advisers. The requirement to take reasonable steps to ascertain the defendant's usual or last known residence is now enshrined in **r. 6.9(3)**.

Collier v Williams was applied in *Hoddinott v Persimmon Homes (Wessex) Ltd* [2007] EWCA Civ 1203, [2008] 1 WLR 806. The court again articulated the principle that where there is no good reason for the failure to serve the claim form within the four-month period, the court still has a discretion to grant an extension of time, but is unlikely to do so. In this case, the reason for non-service was that full particulars of the claim were not ready by the last date for service of the claim form. The court held that this was not a good reason. The correct course of action would have been for the claim form to have been served and then agreement obtained from the defendant, or an order from the court, that no further steps be taken in the litigation until the claimant was able to produce particulars of claim. However, the case was not yet time-barred, so if the order were set aside the claimant could simply reissue. The fact that a claim was clearly not time-barred was a relevant consideration, albeit not determinative, to be taken into account in favour of the claimant when the court decided whether to grant an extension of time under **r. 7.6(2)** (but not **r. 7.6(3)**, where the list of factors specified is exhaustive). Further, the claimant had sent a copy of the claim form to the defendant for information. These two facts together were sufficiently exceptional to justify the extension.

The Court of Appeal has made clear in *Collier v Williams* that while the **r. 7.6(3)** requirements (see **15.33**) are relevant to the exercise of the discretion given by **r. 7.6(2)**, there is a clear difference between the two paragraphs and the fact that the preconditions stated in **r. 7.6(3)** are not satisfied is not necessarily determinative of the outcome of an application under **r. 7.6(2)**. In particular, in deciding whether to grant an extension under **r. 7.6(2)**, the court is required to make a judgment about how good a reason there is for the failure to serve in time (assuming that the application is being dealt with after the expiry of the four-month period for service). Under **r. 7.6(3)** the position is that unless all reasonable steps have been taken, the court cannot extend time. However, more recently, in *Cecil v Bayat*, the Court of Appeal stated that it would be curious if the test to be applied in applications under **r. 7.6(2)** where the limitation period has expired should be different to applications under **r. 7.6(3)** where the period of validity of the claim form has expired. At the very least, even if he has not taken *all* reasonable steps, the claimant should have to show that he has taken reasonable steps. Generally, where the limitaion period has expired, an extension will not be granted save in exceptional circumstances. This requires the claimant to show that the good reason for failing to serve the claim form in time directly impacts on the limitation problem, as for instance where the claimant can show that he has been delayed in service for reasons for which he does not bear responsibility. In *JSC BTA Bank v Ablyazov* [2011] EWHC 2988 (Comm), LTL 29/11/2011, the long period of time (up to two years) required to effect service under the Hague Convention in Russia was a good reason justifying an extension under **r. 7.6(2)** notwithstanding a small period of delay on the part of the claimants' solicitors. The long delay also surmounted the expiry of the limitation period during this time.

The view taken by the court of the conduct of the claimant's solicitors can be an important factor. In *Imperial Cancer Research Fund v Ove Arup and Partners Ltd* [2009] EWHC 1453 (TCC), LTL 25/6/2009, the court granted an extension where a claim form supported by a statement of truth could not properly be served without expert evidence and the claimant's solicitors had been acting responsibly. This case looks surprising in the light of *Cecil v Bayat*. However, it was not clear that there was a limitation defence. In *City and General (Holborn) Ltd v Structure Tone Ltd* [2010] EWCA Civ 911, [2010] BLR 458, the court set aside an extension obtained without notice where the claim form could in fact have been served, even if loss and damage could not be fully particularised in the particulars of claim. In *F. G. Hawkes (Western) Ltd v Beli Shipping Co. Ltd* [2009] EWHC 1740 (Comm), [2010] 1 Lloyd's Rep 449, an extension was refused when the claimant's solicitors did not make enquiries of the defendant about its address for service until the last month of the six-month period for service of the claim form out of the jurisdiction. The defendant had refused to cooperate with the claimant's enquiries, had notice of the claimant's intention to bring proceedings and would not be prejudiced by a short extension. Further, the claimant had a good arguable case. But none of these factors outweighed the fault of the claimant's advisers in not taking steps to effect service until too late. In *Duckworth v Coates* [2009] EWHC 1936 (Ch), LTL 4/8/2009, five applications were made under **r. 7.6(2)** for extensions totalling 12 months. All the applications were made without notice and without a hearing. None of the applications after the first drew the court's attention to the fact that previous orders had been made. The applications also contained other errors of fact. Although it was the claimant's responsibility to ensure that all relevant information was brought to the court's attention, the court declined to set the orders aside on the ground that the claimant had failed to comply with its duty to make full and frank disclosure. It did set the orders aside on the ground that it could not find any good reason for the extensions. Although for much of this period the claimant's solicitors were trying to effect service through diplomatic channels (at, it transpired, the wrong address), they had let matters drift. Once they properly instructed a local process server to locate and serve the relevant defendant, service took place within a matter of two weeks.

It is clear from these cases that neither the defendant nor the defendant's solicitors are under any obligation to assist the claimant's solicitors' attempts to serve the defendant, provided that they do not actually obstruct service.

In *Steele v Mooney* [2005] EWCA Civ 96, [2005] 1 WLR 2819, the Court of Appeal considered the relationship between **r. 3.10** (the power to cure an irregularity) and **r. 7.6(2)**. In this case, an application to extend time for service of the particulars of claim had by mistake failed to refer to the claim form, so an application to extend time for service of the claim form had not been made within the four-month period for service. The court held that the error was procedural in nature and did fall within the ambit of **r. 3.10**, which should not be given an artificially restrictive meaning. However, **r. 3.10** should not be used to circumvent something that is prohibited under another rule (an application of the decision in *Vinos v Marks and Spencer plc* [2001] 3 All ER 784 — see **15.34**). The application now fell to be considered under the provisions of **r. 7.6(2)** (not **r. 7.6(3)**, see **15.34**) as the original application for an extension had been made within the usual time limit for service. The application would have succeeded under **r. 7.6(2)** if it had been made correctly, so **r. 3.10** could be used to correct the error now and extend time for service of the claim form.

Commentary

Applications made after the usual period of service has expired

The rules permit the making of an application after the expiry of time for service of the claim form. But in this case, an order may be made only if (**CPR, r. 7.6(3)**): **15.33**

(a) the court has failed to serve the claim form, or
(b) the claimant has taken all reasonable steps to comply with **r. 7.5** but has been unable to do so, and
(c) in either case the claimant has acted promptly in making the application.

The application may be made without notice, but must be supported by evidence (**r. 7.6(4)**). For the distinction between this test and the test under **r. 7.6(2)**, see **15.32**. Because of the requirement in applications under **r. 7.6(3)(b)** that the claimant must have taken *all* reasonable steps to comply with **r. 7.5**, it is difficult to see, in practice, how extensions will now be justified, save where the defendant is evading service or where the court has failed to serve the claim form. It is clear from *Latreefers Inc. v Hobson* [2002] EWHC 1586 (Ch), LTL 31/7/2002 (a case on the old version of **r. 7.6(3)**), that parties will be expected to have used the whole period of **r. 7.5** to attempt to take the relevant steps and that if they wait until the last moment, the court will not be sympathetic.

'Promptly' is to be construed in accordance with the ordinary meaning of the word, 'readily, quickly, at once' (*Chare v Fairclough* [2003] EWHC 180 (QB), LTL 20/1/2003).

The phrase 'the court has failed to serve the claim form' in **r. 7.6(3)(a)** includes a case where the court overlooks the claim form and makes no attempt to serve it (*Cranfield v Bridgegrove Ltd*

[2003] EWCA Civ 656, [2003] 1 WLR 2441). In most cases of court neglect it will be appropriate to grant an extension of time provided the claimant has acted promptly. However, if failures on the part of the claimant or his solicitors are the real reason why the claim form is not served within the period of validity, it will often be inappropriate to grant an extension.

In *Hoddinott v Persimmon Homes (Wessex) Ltd* [2007] EWCA Civ 1203, [2008] 1 WLR 806, the Court of Appeal held that in applications made under **r. 7.6(3)**, the fact that a claim is clearly not yet time-barred (and so the claimant can reissue if the extension is denied) is irrelevant.

Only steps taken within the period of validity of the claim form — not afterwards — are relevant in deciding whether the claimant has taken all reasonable steps to serve the claim form, for the purposes of **r. 7.6(3)(b)** (*Drury v British Broadcasting Corporation* [2007] EWCA Civ 497, [2007] EMLR 24).

Attempts to evade r. 7.6(3)

15.34 Under the old version of **CPR, r. 7.6(3)**, in force before 1 October 2008, attempts to use **rr. 3.1** (extending time), **3.9** (relief from sanctions) and **3.10** (correcting errors of procedure) to evade the operation of **r. 7.6** were all rejected by the court (see *Vinos v Marks and Spencer plc* [2001] 3 All ER 784; *National Bank of Greece SA v R. M. Outhwaite 317 Syndicate at Lloyd's* [2001] Lloyd's Rep IR 652 and *Kaur v CTP Coil Ltd* (2000) LTL 10/7/2000). Although it now appears, following the decision of the House of Lords in *Phillips v Symes (No. 3)* [2008] UKHL 1, [2008] 1 WLR 180, that the court does have power to make orders retrospectively under **r. 3.10** to cure a procedural defect in service, that case was not one which involved attempted service of a claim form after the expiry of the period for service of the claim form under **r. 7.6**.

The rules in force since 1 October 2008 do, however, offer two possible avenues of relief to claimants who have been unable to comply with **r. 7.5** (changing the position which operated previously — see *Elmes v Hygrade Food Products plc* [2001] EWCA Civ 121, LTL 27/2/2001; *Godwin v Swindon Borough Council* [2001] EWCA Civ 1478, [2002] 1 WLR 997; and *Anderton v Clwyd County Council (No. 2)* [2002] EWCA Civ 933, [2002] 1 WLR 3174). First, claimants may make a retrospective application under **r. 6.15(2)** for an order that steps they have already taken are good service. Secondly, they may in exceptional circumstances make an application under **r. 6.16** to dispense with service. See **15.20** and **15.24**.

Agreeing extensions of time for service of the claim form

15.35 In *Thomas v Home Office* [2006] EWCA Civ 1355, [2007] 1 WLR 230, the Court of Appeal considered the question, on which there was no previous authority, of whether the parties could agree extensions of time for service of the claim form under **CPR, r. 2.11**, or whether this rule was effectively excluded by the provisions of **r. 7.6**. The court held that parties could indeed agree extensions of time for service of the claim form under **r. 2.11** and rejected the submission that this enabled parties to extend time virtually indefinitely and meant the court had no mechanism to prevent proceedings stagnating. Rather it was persuaded by the fact that **rr. 7.5** and **7.6** are not included in the list set out at **r. 2.11** of the provisions in the CPR which cannot be varied by agreement between the parties. See **3.7** for what constitutes a 'written agreement of the parties'.

DEEMED DATES OF SERVICE

15.36 Under **CPR, r. 6.14**, a claim form served in the UK in accordance with **Part 6** is deemed served on the second business day after completion of the relevant step set out in the table in **r. 7.5(1)** (see **table 15.2**). This applies to all forms of service, with the effect that leaving a *document with an individual* by way of personal service under **r. 6.5(3)** is no longer deemed served immediately. 'Business day' is defined in **r. 6.2(b)** to mean any day except Saturday, Sunday, a bank holiday, Good Friday or Christmas Day. 'Bank holiday' means a bank holiday under the Banking and Financial Dealings Act 1971 in the part of the United Kingdom where service is to take place (**r. 6.2(a)**). **Rule 2.8** (which excludes weekends and public holidays when calculating periods of five days or less) does not apply here (*Anderton v Clwyd County Council (No. 2)* [2002] EWCA Civ 933, [2002] 1 WLR 3174), because nothing is 'done'.

The phrase 'is deemed to be served' in **r. 6.14** creates an irrebuttable presumption that service occurred on the deemed day of service. The presumption cannot be displaced by proving the actual day of receipt (*Godwin v Swindon Borough Council* [2001] EWCA Civ 1478, [2002] 1 WLR 997; *Anderton v Clwyd County Council (No. 2)* [2002] EWCA Civ 933, [2002] 1 WLR 3174; *Cranfield v Bridgegrove Ltd* [2003] EWCA Civ 656, [2003] 1 WLR 2441).

The function of the deemed date of service is to compute with certainty the next steps to be taken in the claim. It is no longer the case that service needs to be deemed to have taken place within the four-month period for service of the claim form in the jurisdiction (**r. 7.5**). The effect of **rr. 7.5(1)** and **6.14** is that, in dispatching or delivering the claim form for service within the period of validity, the claimant does not have to be concerned with how long it takes for the claim form to reach the defendant, or even if it ever does reach the defendant. Also, full use of the periods available means that a claim form may be validly served where deemed service takes effect four months and two business days after issue.

There are different rules for calculating the deemed dates of service of documents other than the claim form (**r. 6.26**, see **15.42**).

Commentary

SERVICE OF DOCUMENTS OTHER THAN THE CLAIM FORM IN THE UNITED KINGDOM

The rules relating to service of documents other than the claim form are set out in **CPR, Part 6, Section III**. The term 'other documents' excludes not just claim forms but other documents used to commence proceedings, such as petitions, as well as documents used to issue pre-action applications. These documents are included in the definition of 'claim form' in **r. 6.2(c)** and therefore their service is governed by **Part 6, Section II**. 'Other documents' therefore refers primarily to documents generated in the course of litigation. **15.37**

The geographical area within which a defendant's nominated address for service can be located has been expanded from England and Wales (before 1 October 2008) to anywhere in the United Kingdom (from 1 October 2008) and now to anywhere in the EEA where the defendant resides or carries on business or where the defendant's solicitor or European lawyer has a business address (from 6 April 2011).

Who may serve documents?

Service by the court The court will serve documents it has prepared, unless a rule or practice direction provides otherwise, the court orders otherwise or the party on whose behalf it is to be served informs the court it wishes to effect service (**CPR, r. 6.21(2)**). This notification may be made at the start of the case, informally by letter. In the RCJ, solicitors are invited to indicate at the commencement of proceedings whether they wish to effect service themselves, and if this is done, the file will be marked accordingly and no further applications will be necessary. **15.38**

The court will decide which method of service to use (**r. 6.21(3)**). It will usually be first class post (**PD 6A, para. 8.1**). In the minority of cases where the court is serving a document prepared by a party, the party must provide a copy for the court and for each party to be served (**r. 6.21(4)**).

Where the court delivers a defence to a claimant or notifies a claimant that the defendant has filed an acknowledgment of service, the court will also serve a copy of any notice of funding, provided that copies for service were filed at the same time as the defence or acknowledgment (**PD 6A, para, 8.2**).

The **CPR** do not require the court to give notice of service in the case of documents other than the claim form (as defined in **r. 6.2(c)**). Nor do the rules contain any provision requiring the court to notify a party that a document it has served (other than the claim form, as defined) has been returned undelivered.

15.39 **Service by a party** Parties are required to serve documents they have prepared, unless a rule or practice direction provides otherwise or the court orders otherwise (**CPR, r. 6.21(1)**). There is no requirement to notify the court of service of any document other than the claim form (as defined in **r. 6.2(c)**). However, the rules make provision for many documents, including statements of case, to be filed as well as served.

Service of particulars of claim

15.40 Particulars of claim must be served within 14 days after serving the claim form (**CPR, r. 7.4(1)**) and no later than the latest time for serving the claim form (**r. 7.4(2)**). Where a claimant is late in serving the particulars of claim, the court has a general discretion under **r. 3.1(2)(a)** to extend time. Thus, in *Rogers v East Kent Hospitals NHS Trust* [2009] EWHC 54 (QB), [2009] LS Law Med 153, an objection that particulars had been served out of time, because they were faxed one minute after the last time for service (under the current **r. 6.26**, this is 4.30 p.m.) on the last day on which they should have been served, was regarded as being unmeritorious in the absence of prejudice to the defendant. The court exercised its discretion to order a retrospective extension of time for service of the particulars of claim. The court's discretion applies even where the delay extends beyond the period of validity of the claim form, and such applications are not bound by the requirements in **r. 7.6(3)** (see **15.33**) (*Totty v Snowden* [2001] EWCA Civ 1415, [2002] 1 WLR 1384).

When the particulars of claim are served separately there is nothing in the CPR which requires a claimant to include all claims against different defendants in a single set of particulars (*Tetra Pak Ltd v Biddle and Co.* [2010] EWHC 54 (Ch), [2010] 1 WLR 1466).

In a case of any complexity, before the Jackson reforms in April 2013, it was held that when a court was considering an application for an extension of time made after the time prescribed for the taking of a step in proceedings has expired, the court had to follow the checklist given in r. 3.9 as it was before 1 April 2013 (*Sayers v Clarke Walker* [2002] EWCA Civ 645, [2002] 1 WLR 3095; see **48.34**). It is not necessary for the court to apply the **r. 3.9** criteria (either before or since 1 April 2013) in an application for an extension of time made before the deadline for service has expired: the court's discretion should be exercised simply by having regard to the overriding objective and the factors listed in **r. 1.1(2)** (*Robert v Momentum Services Ltd* [2003] EWCA Civ 299, [2003] 1 WLR 1577).

Totty v Snowden and *Sayers v Clarke Walker* were applied in *Price v Price* [2003] EWCA Civ 888, [2003] 3 All ER 911, in which the Court of Appeal signalled that the courts should take care not to relax the disciplinary framework created by the CPR. In this case an extension of time for service of particulars of claim was granted, but subject to a condition restricting the value of the claim, using the case management powers under **r. 3.1(2)(a)** and **(3)(a)**.

An intentional delay in serving particulars of claim would, if made out, be highly significant if not determinative of whether to grant relief (*Bournemouth and Boscombe Athletic Football Club Ltd v Lloyds TSB Bank plc* [2003] EWCA Civ 1755, LTL 10/12/2003).

In summary, the effect of these authorities is that applications for extensions of time for service of particulars of claim after the period of validity of the claim form has expired appears to be governed by *r. 3.9*, not *r. 7.5*. Where application is made before the period of validity of the claim form has expired, the application is governed by the overriding objective and the list of factors in **r. 1.1(2)**.

The particulars of claim must be accompanied by the response pack, which consists of forms for acknowledging service, and for admission, defence and counterclaim (**CPR, r. 7.8(1)**). Where the claim is for a specified sum, forms N9A and N9B should be used. Where the claim is for an unspecified sum, or is a non-money claim, forms N9C and N9D should be used. A default judgment entered where a claimant has failed to serve a response pack may be set aside under **r. 13.3(1)(b)** (*Rajval Construction Ltd v Bestville Properties Ltd* [2010] EWCA Civ 1621, [2011] CILL 2994).

In personal injury claims, the particulars of claim must be accompanied by a medical report and schedule of past and future loss and expense (**PD 16, paras 4.2** and **4.3**). In a claim based upon a written contract, a copy of the contract or documents constituting the agreement, or any relevant general conditions of sale should accompany the particulars of claim (**PD 16, para. 7.3**).

If particulars of claim are served separately from the claim form, a copy of the particulars must be filed within seven days of service on the defendant, unless the claim is proceeding in the bulk claim production centre in the Northampton county court or through Money Claim Online (**CPR, r. 7.4(3)**).

Method

The methods of service of other documents are prescribed by **CPR, r. 6.20**. In essence, they are the same as those to be used for serving claim forms (see **15.10**). As with claim forms, other documents must be served personally where a statute, practice direction or court order requires it (**r. 6.22(1)**). Examples include orders endorsed with a penal notice under **CPR, r. 81.4** and search orders under **PD 25A, para. 7.4(1)**. Personal service cannot be used for service on a party that has provided an address for service under **CPR, r. 6.23**, unless it is required by an enactment, practice direction or court order (**r. 6.22(1)** and **(2)(a)**). **15.41**

After proceedings are started, every party to the proceedings must give an address at which that party may be served with documents relating to the proceedings (**r. 6.23(1)**). **Rule 6.23(2)** requires a party's address for service to be within the EEA and to be:

(a) the business address of a solicitor acting for the party; or
(b) the business address of a European lawyer nominated to accept service of documents; or
(c) where there is no solicitor acting for the party or no European lawyer nominated to accept service of documents, an address at which the party resides or carries on business. For the definitions of 'solicitor' and 'European lawyer' see **15.9**.

Where a party has indicated (or is deemed to have indicated) willingness to accept service by fax or email, the fax number must be at the address for service (**r. 6.23(5)**) and the email address is deemed to be there (**r. 6.23(6)**).

If he has not already done so, the defendant will provide an address for service when he completes the acknowledgment of service. Parties must notify the court and all other parties in writing immediately if their address for service changes (**r. 6.24**).

Deemed dates of service

The deemed dates of service of other documents are different for those of claim forms, and are set out at the table in **CPR, r. 6.26**, which is reproduced in **table 15.3**. The table uses the expression 'day' (which means a calendar day) and 'business day', which is defined in **r. 6.2(b)** as any day except Saturday, Sunday, a bank holiday, Good Friday or Christmas Day. 'Bank holiday' means a bank holiday under the Banking and Financial Dealings Act 1971 in the part of the United Kingdom where service is to take place (**r. 6.2(a)**). **Rule 2.8** (which excludes weekends and public holidays when calculating periods of five days or less) does not apply **15.42**

Table 15.3 Deemed dates of service of other documents within the UK (CPR, r. 6.26)

Method of service	Deemed date of service
1. First class post (or other service which provides for delivery on the next business day)	The second day after it was posted, left with, delivered to or collected by the relevant service provider provided that day is a business day; or if not, the next business day after that day.
2. Document exchange	The second day after it was left with, delivered to or collected by the relevant service provider provided that day is a business day; or if not, the next business day after that day.
3. Delivering the document to or leaving it at a permitted address	If it is delivered to or left at the permitted address on a business day before 4.30 p.m., on that day; or in any other case, on the next business day after that day.
4. Fax	If the transmission of the fax is completed on a business day before 4.30 p.m., on that day; or in any other case, on the next business day after the day on which it was transmitted.
5. Other electronic method	If the email or other electronic transmission is sent on a business day before 4.30 p.m., on that day; or in any other case, on the next business day after the day on which it was sent.
6. Personal service	If the document is served personally before 4.30 p.m. on a business day, on that day; or in any other case, on the next business day after that day.

here (*Anderton v Clwyd County Council (No. 2)* [2002] EWCA Civ 933, [2002] 1 WLR 3174), because nothing is 'done'.

Examples of how to calculate the deemed dates of service in **r. 6.26** are provided in **PD 6A, para. 10**. Example 6 makes clear that the words 'provided that day is a business day' refer only to the deemed date of service, not to the date of dispatching. Example 6 says: 'Where the document is posted (by first class post) on a bank holiday Monday, the day of deemed service is the following Wednesday (a business day)'.

These deeming provisions apply only where service is effected in the United Kingdom (**CPR, r. 6.26**).

The decision in *Godwin v Swindon Borough Council* [2001] EWCA Civ 1478, [2002] 1 WLR 997, that the deemed dates of service create an irrebuttable presumption that service occurred on the deemed date applies to other documents just as much as to the claim form (*Joyce v West Bus Coach Services Ltd* [2012] EWHC 404 (QB), [2012] 3 Costs LR 540).

Alternative service and dispensing with service

15.43 The court has the power to make an order for service of other documents by an alternative method or at an alternative place under **CPR, r. 6.15**, as well as to make an order dispensing with service (**rr. 6.27** and **6.28**). In both cases, the application must be supported by evidence and may be made without notice (**rr. 6.15(3)** and **6.28(2)**).

Certificate of service

15.44 A table at **CPR, r. 6.29**, sets out the information to be included in a certificate of service, where one is required for a document other than a claim form.

PARTICULAR TYPES OF PARTY

Children and protected parties

Claim form and application for appointment of litigation friend by court order Where proceedings are begun against a child (who is not also a protected party), the claim form must be served on one of his or her parents or guardians, or, if there is no such person, on the person with whom the child resides or who has care of the child (**CPR, r. 6.13(1)**). 15.45

In the case of a protected party, the claim form must be served on a person with authority in relation to the protected party by virtue of being that party's attorney under a registered enduring power of attorney, the donee of a lasting power of attorney or the protected party's deputy appointed by the Court of Protection. Where there is nobody so authorised, the claim form should be served on an adult with whom the protected party resides or in whose care the protected party is (**r. 6.13(2)**).

There is no requirement for the child or the protected party to be served, or given any other form of notification of the existence of the proceedings, although the court has a discretion to make an order to that effect (**r. 6.13(4)**). Where the court has made an order allowing a child to conduct proceedings without a litigation friend, the usual rules for service on an individual apply (**r. 6.13(7)**).

An application for the appointment of a litigation friend by court order under **r. 21.8**, must be served on every person on whom a claim form must be served, under **r. 6.13** (**r. 21.8(1)**). An application made before proceedings have started falls within the definition of claim form in **r. 6.2(c)** and will have to be served in the same way as a claim form, under **Part 6, Section II**. If the application is made after the claim has started, it will be served in accordance with the provisions of **Part 6, Section III**.

Other documents Once proceedings have been commenced with a litigation friend acting on behalf of the child or protected party, any document which would otherwise be served on the child or protected party should be served on his or her litigation friend (**CPR, r. 6.25(2)**). 15.46

These rules are subject to any order to the contrary made by the court (**r. 6.25(3)**). Such an order may be made without notice (**r. 6.25(4)**). Where a document has been served on some other person, the court may make an order that service should stand (**r. 6.25(5)**). Where the court has made an order allowing a child to conduct proceedings without a litigation friend, the usual rules for service on an individual apply (**r. 6.25(6)**).

Companies

Service of a claim form in the jurisdiction on a company is governed by **CPR, r. 6.3(2)**. It is clear that, in **r. 6.3(2)**, 'company' includes a company registered under the Companies Act 2006 and an overseas company whose particulars have been registered under s. 1046 of the 2006 Act, as express provision for these companies is made in **r. 6.3(2)(b)** (see below and **15.48**). There is separate provision for limited liability partnerships in **r. 6.3(3)**. Elsewhere in **Part 6**, a distinction is made between companies and other corporations (table in **r. 6.9(2)**). 15.47

By **CPR, r. 6.3(2)(a)**, a company may be served by any of the methods permitted under **Part 6** (see **15.10**).

Personal service on a company is effected by leaving a document with a person holding a senior position within the company (**r. 6.5(3)(b)**). The following hold a senior position for the purpose of the CPR: a director, secretary, treasurer, chief executive, manager or other officer of the company (**PD 6A, para. 6.2(1)**). Whether a person falls within the ambit of **CPR, r. 6.5(3)(b)**, and **PD 6A, para. 6.2(1)**, is a matter of fact (*Lakah Group v Al Jazeera Satellite Channel* [2003] EWHC 1231 (QB), *The Times* ,18 April 2003, [2003] EWCA Civ 1781, LTL 9/12/2003).

The word 'company' in **CPR, r. 6.5(3)(b)**, means a company that is carrying on business within the jurisdiction. Thus serving a claim form on a director of a foreign company not carrying on business in the jurisdiction when he happens to be temporarily visiting, purportedly under **r. 6.5(3)(b)**, is not good service on the company (*SSL International plc v TTK LIG Ltd* [2011] EWCA Civ 1170, [2012] 1 WLR 1842).

If a company registered in England and Wales has not instructed a solicitor or European lawyer to accept service under **r. 6.7** or provided an address for service under **r. 6.8**, service, by any method permitted by **Part 6** other than personal service, may be effected at its principal office or at any place of business of the company within the jurisdiction which has a real connection with the claim (**r. 6.9(2)**).

As an alternative to service under the CPR, a company may be served by any of the methods of service permitted under the Companies Act 2006 (**CPR, r. 6.3(2)(b)**). The Companies Act 2006, s. 1139(1), provides that: 'A document may be served on a company registered under this Act by leaving it at, or sending it by post to, the company's registered office'. A document is sent by post by a person if that person posts a prepaid envelope containing the document (Companies Act 2006, sch. 4, paras 1(1) and 3(2)). This definition is wide enough to cover first and second class post, registered post or the use of postal services other than those provided by the Royal Mail. Unless the contrary is proved, service is deemed to be effected at the time when the letter would be delivered in the ordinary course of post (Interpretation Act 1978, s. 7). Service on a registered company at its registered office takes effect under the Companies Act 2006, s. 1139, and not under the CPR. Service under the Companies Act 2006 and under the CPR are true alternatives. There are the following differences between the two methods. If service of a document is effected by post under the Companies Act 2006, the document will be deemed to have been served, unless the contrary is proved, when the letter would have been delivered in the ordinary course of post (Interpretation Act 1978, s. 7; *Cranfield v Bridgegrove Ltd* [2003] EWCA Civ 656, [2003] 1 WLR 2441). Service by second class post is allowed by the Companies Act 2006, but not by the CPR because second class post does not provide for delivery on the next business day as required by **r. 6.3(1)(b)**. Under the Companies Act 2006 the deemed date of delivery depends on which day the letter is posted and whether first or second class is used, and the deemed date can be displaced by evidence to the contrary.

Service on a company registered in Northern Ireland or Scotland at its registered office will be service outside the jurisdiction (see **chapter 16**). English court process may be served on a Northern Irish or Scottish company by leaving it at, or posting it to, the company's principal place of business in England and Wales, if it carries on business here (Companies Act 2006, s. 1139(4)). The process must be addressed to the manager or other head officer in England and Wales of the company (s. 1139(4)) and a copy must be sent by post to the company's registered office (s. 1139(4)).

Overseas companies

15.48 By **CPR, r. 6.3(2)**, a claim form may be served in the jurisdiction on a company incorporated outside the United Kingdom (known as an 'overseas company': see the Companies Act 2006, s. 1044), whose particulars have been registered under s. 1046. Registration under s. 1046, is governed by the Overseas Companies Regulations 2009 (SI 2009/1801). Whenever an overseas company establishes a branch or other place of business in the UK, it must, within one month, deliver a return to Companies House complying with part 2 of the Regulations (reg. 4). The return must state the name and service address of every person resident in the UK authorised to accept service of documents on behalf of the company in respect of the establishment, or a statement that there is no such person (reg. 7(1)(e)). This information is available for inspection at Companies House. In addition, any person with whom the company deals in the course of business may make a written request to the company for the address of any person resident in the UK authorised to accept service of documents on its behalf (reg. 65(1)). The company must send a written response within five working days of receiving the request (reg. 65(2)). The company may be served:

(a) by any of the methods permitted under **CPR, Part 6** (see **15.10**), including personal service under **r. 6.5(3)(b)** on its directors who happen to be visiting the jurisdiction (*SSL International plc v TTK LIG Ltd* [2011] EWCA Civ 1170, [2012] 1 WLR 1842), or, where the company has not provided an address for service, at any place in the jurisdiction where the company carries on its activities or any place of business of the company in the jurisdiction (**r. 6.9(2)**; *Sea Assets Ltd v PT Garuda Indonesia* [2000] 4 All ER 371); or
(b) under the provisions of the Companies Act 2006, s. 1139(2).

Service will not be valid under **CPR, r. 6.9(2)**, at an address with which the company has no more than a transient or irregular connection (*Lakah Group v Al Jazeera Satellite Channel* [2003] EWHC 1231, *The Times*, 18 April 2003, [2003] EWCA Civ 1781, LTL 9/12/2003).

Whether a company has a place of business in the jurisdiction, and where that place of business is, are questions of fact (*Rakusens Ltd v Baser Ambalaj Plastik Sanayi Ticaret AS* [2001] EWCA Civ 1820, [2002] 1 BCLC 104, at [8]; *Matchnet plc v William Blair and Co. LLC* [2002] EWHC 2128 (Ch), [2003] 2 BCLC 195). A place may be a company's place of business even if only an ancillary part of the company's business is carried on there (*South India Shipping Corporation Ltd v Export-Import Bank of Korea* [1985] 1 WLR 585). A place in the jurisdiction where a person takes orders for a company incorporated outside the United Kingdom, without authority to decide whether to accept or reject them, is not the company's place of business (*Rakusens Ltd v Baser Ambalaj Plastik Sanayi Ticaret AS*; *Harrods Ltd v Dow Jones and Co. Inc.* [2003] EWHC 1162 (QB), LTL 29/5/2003). In *Harrods Ltd v Dow Jones and Co. Inc.* the criteria used to determine whether the place of business of an agent of a foreign company was that company's place of business were the criteria suggested by the Court of Appeal in *Adams v Cape Industries plc* [1990] Ch 433 at pp. 530–1 for determining whether the activities of an agent here of a foreign company make the company subject to the jurisdiction of the courts here. The same approach was taken in *Reuben v Time Inc.* [2003] EWHC 1430 (QB), LTL 3/7/2003.

The Companies Act 2006, s. 1139(2), provides that a document may be served on an overseas company whose particulars are registered under s. 1046:

(a) by leaving it at, or sending it by post to, the registered address of any person resident in the United Kingdom who is authorised to accept service of documents on the company's behalf; or
(b) if there is no such person, or if any such person refuses service or service cannot for any other reason be effected, by leaving it at or sending by post to any place of business of the company in the United Kingdom.

The rules on postal service under s. 1139 are discussed at **15.47**.

If the only address given by an overseas company of a UK resident authorised to accept service is in Northern Ireland or Scotland, service under the Companies Act 2006, s. 1139(2), will be service outside the jurisdiction (see **chapter 16**).

To be served in accordance with s. 1139(2), a document must be addressed to the person resident in the United Kingdom who is authorised to accept service — addressing it to the company and leaving it at the authorised person's address is not sufficient (*Boocock v Hilton International Co.* [1993] 1 WLR 1065).

In *Harrods Ltd v Dow Jones and Co. Inc.* [2003] EWHC 1162 (QB), LTL 29/5/2003, at [32] and [33], it was held that an overseas company that was not required to register under what is now the Companies Act 2006, s. 1046, could not be served either under what is now s. 1139(2) or by any of the methods permitted by **CPR, Part 6**. In particular, it cannot be served, under **r. 6.9(2)**, at a place in the jurisdiction where its activities are carried on. In *Reuben v Time Inc.*

Commentary

[2003] EWHC 1430 (QB), LTL 3/7/2003, Morland J said, at [31], that he agreed with this statement of the law. In *Lakah Group v Al Jazeera Satellite Channel* Gray J, at first instance, thought that **Part 6** allows for service on a wider range of foreign companies than those which can be served under the Companies Act 2006. However, when refusing permission to appeal against Gray J's decision, the Court of Appeal found it unnecessary to discuss the point.

Other corporations

15.49 A corporation, incorporated in England and Wales, which cannot be served under the Companies Act 2006, s. 1139(1) (see **15.47**), must be served by one of the methods listed in **CPR, r. 6.3(1)** (see **15.10**). This applies to entities such as building societies and incorporated friendly societies.

Personal service on a corporation is effected by leaving the document to be served with a person holding a senior position within the corporation (**r. 6.5(3)(b)**). The following hold a senior position for this purpose: a director, the treasurer, secretary, chief executive, manager or other officer of the corporation, the mayor, chairman, president, town clerk or similar officer (**PD 6A, paras 6.1** and **6.2**).

Service by any other method under the CPR on a corporation incorporated in England and Wales, which has not instructed a solicitor to accept service under **CPR, r. 6.7**, or provided an address for service under **r. 6.8**, may be effected at either the principal office of the corporation or any place within the jurisdiction where the corporation carries on its activities and which has a real connection with the claim (**r. 6.9(2)**).

Rule 6.9(2) names the place of service (other than personal service) for a company not registered in England and Wales and a corporation (other than a company) not incorporated in England and Wales where no solicitor is acting and no address for service in the jurisdiction has been given. This is 'any place within the jurisdiction where the *corporation* carries on its activities; or any place of business of the *company* within the jurisdiction' (emphasis added).

Partnerships

15.50 Service on a partnership may be effected by any of the methods permitted by **CPR, r. 6.3(1)** (see **15.10**).

Where partners are sued in the firm name, personal service is effected by leaving the document to be served with a partner, or, alternatively, at the firm's principal place of business, with a person having, at the time of service, control or management of the partnership business (**r. 6.5(3)(c)**). Postal service at the usual or last known residence of one partner constitutes good service on the firm, and therefore on his co-partners (*Lexi Holdings plc v Luqman* (2007) LTL 30/10/2007).

Where a firm has not instructed a solicitor to accept service under **r. 6.7** or provided an address for service under **r. 6.8**, service on it by any method other than personal service should be effected by sending the claim form either to the usual or last known residential address of a partner, or to the principal or last known place of business of the firm (**r. 6.9(2)**).

Partners sued in their individual names must be served as individual defendants. This will now be rare, as **PD 7A, para. 5A.3**, requires proceedings by or against a partnership to be brought in the name of the partnership at the time the cause of action accrued 'unless it is inappropriate to do so'. Proceedings against a foreign partnership, however, will still be brought against the individual partners, as **PD 7A, para. 5A.3**, applies only to partnerships 'carrying on business *within the jurisdiction*' (**PD 7A, para. 5A.1**). When a claim is made against a partnership, any party to the claim may require the partners to provide a 'partnership membership statement', which is a written statement of the names and last known places of residence of all the persons who were partners in the partnership at the time when the cause of action accrued (**PD 7A, para. 5B.1**). The statement must be provided within 14 days of the date of the request (**PD 7A, para. 5B.2**).

By **PD 10, para. 4.4**, where a claim is brought against a partnership, service must be acknowledged in the name of the partnership on behalf of all the partners at the time the cause of action accrued. The acknowledgment may be signed by anyone who was a partner at the time the cause of action accrued or any other person authorised to do so by such a partner.

The mechanism formerly set out in RSC, ord. 81, r. 4(2) in **CPR, sch. 1**, enabling a person who denied he or she was a partner at the time the cause of action accrued to sign an acknowledgment under protest and then apply to have the acknowledgment set aside has been abolished. Someone in this position must now take the point in his or her defence. The CPR also make no provision for the situation where a partner has no actual authority to sign the acknowledgment on behalf of another partner — where, for example, the other partner wishes to conduct his or her defence separately. The problem was recognised in *Brooks v A. H. Brooks and Co.* [2010] EWHC 2720 (Ch), [2011] 3 All ER 982. The court accepted that, although there is no express provision in the CPR, it must still be possible for a partner to acknowledge service on behalf of only some of the partners at the time the cause of action accrued. But it also held that, by virtue of **PD 10, para. 4.4(2)**, an acknowledgment signed by a partner at the time the cause of action accrued (or by a person authorised by any such partner) is effective on behalf of all partners at the relevant time, regardless of whether the person signing has actual authority from his or her partners.

For the effect of acknowledging service on enforcement against the assets of individual partners see **79.38**.

Commentary

Limited liability partnerships

By **CPR, r. 6.3(3)**, a limited liability partnership (LLP) may be served by any of the methods permitted under **Part 6** or by any method permitted under the Companies Act 2006, s. 1139(1) (see **15.47**), as applied to LLPs in modified form by the Limited Liability Partnerships (Application of Companies Act 2006) Regulations 2009 (SI 2009/1804), reg. 75. SI 2009/1804, reg. 75 also applies the Companies Act 2006, s. 1139(2) (in modified form) to Scottish or Northern Irish LLPs, with the effect that where such LLPs carry on business in England and Wales, service of court process can be effected by leaving the document to be served at, or posting it to, the LLP's principal place of business in England and Wales, addressed to the manager or a designated member of the LLP. A copy must then be sent to the registered office of the LLP. **15.51**

Where a limited liability partnership has not instructed a solicitor to accept service under **CPR, r. 6.7**, or provided an address for service under **r. 6.8**, service by any method other than personal service should be effected by sending the claim form either to the principal office of the partnership or any place of business of the partnership within the jurisdiction which has a real connection with the claim (**r. 6.9(2)**).

Crown proceedings

By **CPR, r. 6.5(2)(b)**, documents required to be served on the Crown may not be served personally. Further, **r. 6.10** stipulates that service on the Attorney-General must be effected on the Treasury Solicitor and service on a government department must be effected on the solicitor acting for that department as required by the Crown Proceedings Act 1947, s. 18. The method of service in **CPR, r. 6.10**, applies both to claim forms, as defined in **r. 6.2(c)**, and to other documents (**r. 6.23(7)**). The list published under the Crown Proceedings Act 1947, s. 17, is annexed to **PD 66**. **15.52**

Agent of a principal who is overseas

15.53 By **CPR, r. 6.12**, a claimant may, with the court's permission, serve a claim form on the agent of a defendant who is out of the jurisdiction, where:

(a) the claim relates to a contract entered into within the jurisdiction, with or through the agent; and
(b) at the time of the application for permission, the agent's authority has not been terminated or the agent is still in business relations with the defendant.

Application for permission should be made in accordance with the Part 23 procedure. No notice need be given, but the application must, by **r. 6.12(2)**, be supported by evidence setting out details of the contract, confirming that it was entered into in the jurisdiction or through an agent who is in the jurisdiction and providing the other information specified in **r. 6.12(2)(a)**. Any order made under the rule must give a time limit within which the defendant must respond to the particulars of claim (not the claim form) (**r. 6.12(3)**). For cases proceeding in the Commercial Court or the Mercantile Courts, the court must specify a period for the defendant to respond which runs from the date of service of the claim form, not the particulars of claim (**CPR, rr. 58.6(3)** and **59.5(3)**). A copy of the order and of the claim form must be served on the defendant (**r. 6.12(4)**). **Rule 6.12(5)** makes clear that **r. 6.12** does not exclude the court's power to make an order for alternative service under **r. 6.15**.

A Practice Direction (1920) 150 LT Jo 388 was issued in relation to an earlier version of this rule. It contains the following guidance for practitioners, which the courts may still take into account:

(a) The court's power to make an order under the rule is discretionary, and to be exercised with caution. It should not be used where there is no difficulty in getting an order and serving out of the jurisdiction in the usual way.
(b) The court will look at the nature of the agency relationship. If it is 'casual', the court will be less ready to make an order.

FILING DOCUMENTS

15.54 The CPR distinguish between serving a document, which is the procedure whereby a document is brought to the attention of another party and filing a document, which is the procedure whereby the court receives a copy of a document. 'Filing' is defined in **r. 2.3(1)** as: 'delivering [a document], by post or otherwise, to the court office'. A document sent by post is filed when it is delivered to the court, not when it is posted (*Morshead Mansions Ltd v Langford* [2003] EWHC 2023 (QB), LTL 29/8/2003). Filing takes effect immediately documents are put through the court's letter box, even if the court is then closed to the public and there are no officials to take delivery of the document (*Van Aken v Camden London Borough Council* [2002] EWCA Civ 1724, [2003] 1 WLR 684). The problem with this approach is that it will be impossible for court officials to establish the time (and therefore the date) of filing without making further enquiry of the person who delivered the document.

The deeming rules discussed at **15.36** and **15.42** only apply to service, so for filing it is the actual delivery date that counts. The Interpretation Act 1978, s. 7, applies (by s. 23(1) and (2)), so a document filed by post is deemed to be filed at the time at which the letter containing it would be delivered in the ordinary course of post, unless the contrary is proved.

The CPR make clear which documents must be filed, and when. The detailed requirements are addressed at relevant points in this work. The general rule is that a copy of most formal documents generated in the course of a claim must be filed at court. Thus, all statements of case must be filed, and witness statements and experts' reports may be ordered to be filed. The purpose of the requirement is clear: it is only by having access to information about the case as it progresses that the court is able to exercise its case management powers.

Officials will record the date and time when a document was received at court for filing in court records and/or computer systems (**PD 5A, para. 5.2**). The actual date of filing will be stamped on the document itself (**PD 5A, para. 5.1**).

Filing by email or fax

Under **CPR, r. 5.5**, practice directions may provide for filing by fax or other electronic means. Filing by fax is covered by **PD 5A, para. 5.3**, which provides that a fax received after 4 p.m. is treated as filed on the next day that the court office is open. Any court which has published an email address for the filing of documents on Her Majesty's Courts and Tribunals Service website, http://hmctscourtfinder.justice.gov.uk/HMCTS/FormFinder.do, will accept electronic filing (**PD 5B, para. 2.1**). Many courts now accept filing by email, see **PD 5B**. Electronic filing is used in Money Claim Online (**PD 7E**; see **12.10**). **PD 5B, para. 8.9**, makes clear that emailing a judge direct does not constitute filing by email in accordance with the rules. 15.55

HM Courts and Tribunals Service has published guidance (http://www.justice.gov.uk/courts/email-guidance) about emailing the civil and family courts, which includes information about what may be emailed to which courts and also technical information about which file types the courts will accept. A particular scheme runs in the Preston Combined Court, permitting court users to file applications electronically under the terms of the Preston E-mail Application Service User Guide and Protocols, also published on the Courts and Tribunals Service website (http://www.justice.gov.uk/courts/email-guidance/prema-email-guidance) (**PD 5B, paras 3.2A and 3.3A**).

The electronic working scheme launched in 2010, to which PD 5C relates, is no longer functioning and the eWorking Service mailbox is no longer available, due to the very low take-up of the service and technical problems.

Commentary

Inspecting the court file

Public right of access to court register and to court documents In accordance with the principle of open justice, the CPR make provision for members of the public or the press to be able to apply for copies of particular court documents. Under **CPR, r. 5.4(1)**, the Queen's Bench and Chancery Divisions and the Admiralty and Commercial Court registry in the RCJ keep a register of the claims which they have issued (**PD 5A, para. 4.1**). The register is open to members of the public to search upon payment of the prescribed fee (**CPR, r. 5.4(2)**). There are no registers of claims in any district registries or other offices of the High Court or any county courts (**PD 5A, para. 4.2**). 15.56

The Attorney-General may search, inspect and copy any document on a court file with a view to making an application under the Senior Courts Act 1981, s. 42, or the Employment Tribunals Act 1966, s. 33, for a person to be declared a vexatious litigant (**CPR, r. 5.4A(1)**). The Attorney-General must make his request in writing, pay the prescribed fee and name the person who would be the subject of the application (**r. 5.4A(2)**).

A non-party is entitled, under **r. 5.4C**, to obtain from court records:

(a) a copy of a statement of case, but not any documents filed with or attached to it or intended to be served with it (**r. 5.4C(1)(a)**);
(b) a judgment or order given or made in public (whether made at a hearing or not) (**r. 5.4C(1)(b)**);
(c) a copy of any other document filed by a party, or communication between the court and a party or another person, but only if the court gives permission (**r. 5.4C(2)**).

Statements of case are defined in **CPR, r. 2.3(1)** as meaning a claim form, particulars of claim, defence, Part 20 claim or reply as well as any further information given in relation to them either voluntarily or under **CPR, r. 18.1**. It was held in *Various Claimants v News Group Newspapers Ltd* [2012] EWHC 397 (Ch), [2012] 1 WLR 2545, that the reference to statements of case in **r. 5.4C(1)(a)** covers generic particulars of claim, including amended particulars of claim. A notice to admit and a response to that notice were not within the definition. An application for a copy of these documents fell under **r. 5.4C(2)** and could only be granted with the permission of the court. However, the right of access to statements of case under **r. 5.4C(1)(a)** does include the acknowledgment of service and detailed grounds for contesting a claim for judicial review, although not the documents annexed to the acknowledgment or grounds (*R (Corner House Research) v Director of the Serious Fraud Office* [2008] EWHC 246 (Admin), LTL 20/2/2008).

The distinction between private and public hearings is addressed in **PD 39A, para. 1**.

Various documents listed in **CPR, r. 5.4C(1B)**, relating to mediated cross-border disputes subject to Directive 2008/52/EC and **CPR, rr. 78.23** to **78.28**, may be inspected only with the court's permission.

The right to a copy of a statement of case, judgment or order only arises once the defendant has filed an acknowledgment of service or defence (or, where there is more than one defendant, all have done so or at least one has and the court gives permission), or the claim has been listed for hearing or judgment has been entered (**r. 5.4C(3)**). The rules include a measure of protection for those mentioned in statements of case, but not judgments or orders under **r. 5.4C(1)(b)** because they have been given or made in public and the rules reflect the principle of open justice. A party or person identified in a statement of case (which may not have been referred to in open court) has the right under **r. 5.4C(4)** to apply for an order that a non-party may not obtain a copy of a statement of case, or that the categories of person who may obtain a copy should be restricted or that the statement of case should be provided only in edited form, or any other appropriate restriction. However, the presumption is that the public should be entitled to see any statement of case in unredacted form. A restriction may be ordered under **r. 5.4C(4)** where, for example, there is a risk that disclosure of unredacted statements of case will prejudice a criminal trial. The presumption is reversed in relation to documents which are the subject of an application under **r. 5.4C(2)** which can only be disclosed with the permission of the court. Here, there is no presumption in favour of disclosure, although the court will lean in favour of allowing disclosure of documents which have been read out in open court or documents which have been read by the judge in the course of the decision-making process. The court will look at the reason why the documents are sought, the use to which they will be put and whether they are truly required to understand and report the court proceedings to which they relate (*Various Claimants v News Group Newspapers Ltd* [2012] EWHC 397 (Ch), [2012] 1 WLR 2545 and *Chan U Seek v Alvis Vehicles Ltd* [2004] EWHC 3092 (Ch), [2005] 1 WLR 2965). No distinction can be drawn between documents used at trial and those used at the interim stages of a case (*Various Claimants v News Group Newspapers Ltd* [2012] EWHC 397 (Ch), [2012] 1 WLR 2545, and *Cleveland Bridge UK Ltd v Multiplex Constructions (UK) Ltd* [2005] EWHC 2101 (TCC), LTL 31/8/2005).

For statements of case filed before 2 October 2006, the former **r. 5.4(5)** to **(9)** continue to apply and are reproduced in full in **PD 5A, paras 4A.1** to **4A.9**. Under the old rules, a non-party was entitled to obtain a claim form, subject to a court order to the contrary. However, an application for permission had to be made in order to obtain a statement of case other than the claim form.

A witness statement which stands as the evidence-in-chief of a witness is open for inspection by the public during the trial unless the court directs otherwise (**CPR, r. 32.13**).

In *Dian AO v David Frankel and Mead* [2004] EWHC 2662 (Comm), [2005] 1 WLR 2951, the court considered an application by a non-party for permission to inspect and copy the entire court file. It held that the applicant must identify with reasonable precision the documents or class of documents it wished to search for and explain why it wanted them. The principle of open justice which lies behind the rules must be borne in mind in any application for access to the court file. The court granted permission for specified documents only to be copied and inspected on the grounds that the relevance of those documents on the court file to proceedings in which the applicant was involved abroad constituted a legitimate reason for seeking access to the court file. The principle stated in this case remains good law despite the revision of the rules in 2006 (*ABC Ltd v Y* [2010] EWHC 3176 (Ch), [2011] 4 All ER 113; *Pfizer Health AB v Schwarz Pharma AG* [2010] EWHC 3236 (Pat), [2011] FSR 14).

Rule r. 5.4C applies both to private law and public law claims. If either a claimant or a defendant wishes to keep matters out of the public domain, they should make a positive application to this effect either in the claim form or acknowledgment (*R (Corner House Research) v Director of the Serious Fraud Office* [2008] EWHC 246 (Admin), [2008] ACD 63). An order for disclosure under **r. 5.4C** may be made where the documents are sought for the purpose of collateral litigation. It is in the interests of justice for disclosure to be made of any documents which will be relevant to the collateral litigation (*R (Taranissi) v Human Fertilisation and Embryology Authority* [2009] EWHC 130 (Admin), LTL 2/2/2009).

In *Glidepath BV v Thompson* [2005] EWHC 818 (Comm), [2005] 2 Lloyd's Rep 549, the court refused to order disclosure of documents filed in court proceedings which had subsequently been stayed pursuant to the Arbitration Act 1996, s. 9. The private and confidential character of proceedings ancillary to the arbitral process ought to be protected. Disclosure should be granted only if all parties consented or if there were an overriding reason in the interests of justice.

The presumption in favour of inspection under the CPR does not apply to documents in bankruptcy proceedings in respect of which an application is made under the Insolvency Rules 1986 (SI 1986/1925), **r. 7.31(4)** (*Mansell v Acton* [2005] EWHC 3048 (Ch), LTL 3/2/2006). The principle of open justice extends to criminal cases. In cases where documents have been placed before a judge and referred to in the course of proceedings, the default position should be that access should be permitted on the open justice principle. The case for allowing access will be particularly strong where it is sought by the press for a proper journalistic purpose (*R (Guardian News and Media Ltd) v City of Westminster Magistrates' Court* [2012] EWCA Civ 420, [2012] 3, WLR 1343).

Parties' right of access to court documents Subject to an order to the contrary, **CPR, r. 5.4B(1)**, and **PD 5A, para. 4.2A**, give parties to proceedings the right to obtain copies of the following documents from the court file: **15.57**

(a) a certificate of suitability of a litigation friend;
(b) a notice of funding;
(c) a claim form or other statement of case, together with any documents filed with, or attached to, or intended by the claimant to be served with, it;
(d) an acknowledgment of service, together with any documents filed with, or attached to, or intended by the party acknowledging service to be served with, it;
(e) a certificate of service, other than a certificate of service of an application notice or order in relation to a type of application mentioned in sub-paragraph (h)(i) or (ii) below;
(f) a notice of non-service;
(g) a directions questionnaire;
(h) an application notice, other than in relation to:
  (i) an application by a solicitor for an order declaring that he has ceased to be the solicitor acting for a party; or
  (ii) an application for an order that the identity of a party or witness should not be disclosed;
(i) any written evidence filed in relation to an application, other than a type of application mentioned in sub-paragraph (h)(i) or (ii);

Commentary

(j) a judgment or order given or made in public (whether made at a hearing or without a hearing);
(k) a statement of costs;
(l) a list of documents;
(m) a notice of payment into court;
(n) a notice of discontinuance;
(o) a notice of change; or
(p) an appellant's or respondent's notice of appeal.

Provision of a copy of any other document filed at court, or of any communication between the court and a party or any other person, requires the court's permission (**CPR, r. 5.4B(2)**).

A party is entitled to copies of documents on the court file not in order to enable the case to be dealt with fairly (it is not a question of disclosure) but in order to ensure the open and transparent administration of justice (*R (Riseborough) v Lands Tribunal* [2009] EWHC 1135 (Admin), LTL 9/6/2009).

Procedure

15.58 A person who wishes to obtain a copy of a document from court records must pay a fee and either file a written request for the document (if the court's permission is not required) or an application notice under **CPR, Part 23** (if the court's permission is required) (**r. 5.4D(1)**). Applications for permission by a party under **r. 5.4B(2)** or a non-party under **r. 5.4C** and applications for restrictions on access under **r. 5.4C** may be made without notice. An application by a non-party under **r. 5.4C(6)** for access to a document on which restrictions have been placed under **r. 5.4C(4)** must be on notice to the person who requested the restrictions (**r. 5.4C(6)**).

Inspecting a document without the court's permission is an interference with the administration of justice, and is a criminal contempt of court if done in the knowledge that the court's permission is required (*Dobson v Hastings* [1992] Ch 394).

Although the new version of **Part 5** no longer makes this explicit, the CPR do contain provisions which restrict access to certain documents. These include:

(a) **r. 57.5(5)**, which provides that, unless the court gives permission, a party to a probate claim may not inspect testamentary documents or written evidence filed by any other party until he has filed his own testamentary documents and evidence;
(b) **PD 62, para. 5.1**, which states that an arbitration claim form may only be inspected with the permission of the court (reflecting the privacy of arbitration proceedings);
(c) PD Application for a Warrant under the Competition Act 1998, paras 3.3 and 3.4, and PD Application for a Warrant under the Enterprise Act 2002, paras 3.3 and 3.4, under which no Part 8 claim form issued on an application by the Office of Fair Trading for a warrant under the Competition Act 1998 or the Enterprise Act 2002 may be inspected by a member of the public unless a High Court judge grants permission.

Chapter 16 Service outside the Jurisdiction

Commentary

The following procedural checklist, which is at the front of the book, is relevant to this chapter:

Procedural checklist 11 Application for permission to serve claim form out of the jurisdiction

INTRODUCTION

16.1 Inevitably, there are a number of complexities where the intended defendant to proceedings is outside the jurisdiction. At common law, an action *in personam* (i.e. an action against a legal person as opposed to an action *in rem* against a ship or other property) could only be brought against a defendant served with process while in England or Wales. This, at least superficially, had the merit of ensuring the courts of this country did not purport to exert an exorbitant jurisdiction over defendants who were not amenable to the coercive powers of the courts. The superficiality stemmed from the fact that jurisdiction could be established by service on a defendant while on a temporary visit to this country (**16.2**) or by a foreign defendant submitting to the jurisdiction (**16.3**). In any event, the restrictive common law rule has been subject to a discretionary power to allow English proceedings against defendants outside the jurisdiction since the enactment of the Common Law Procedure Act 1852. This discretionary power is governed by **CPR, r. 6.36**, and is discussed at **16.41** to **16.53**. These rules will be referred to in this chapter as the common law rules.

If a defendant is domiciled in another EU country, the common law rules are replaced by **Regulation (EC) No. 44/2001** on jurisdiction and the recognition and enforcement of judgments in civil and commercial matters (the '**Brussels I Regulation**', referred to in **CPR, Part 6**, as the 'Judgments Regulation'). This lays down a general rule that a defendant domiciled in an EU State must be sued in the courts of that State (**16.16**). This is subject to a number of wide-ranging exceptions, which are discussed in **16.17** to **16.35**.

The text of the **Brussels I Regulation** is based on, and is substantially the same as, an earlier treaty which all the then member States of the EU agreed to. This was the Brussels Convention on Jurisdiction and the Enforcement of Judgments in Civil and Commercial Matters (the 'Brussels Convention'). Unlike a Regulation, which has direct effect, the Brussels Convention had to be incorporated into United Kingdom law by an Act of Parliament: the **Civil Jurisdiction and Judgments Act 1982** ('CJJA 1982'). The Brussels Convention is set out in sch. 1 to the **CJJA 1982**. The Brussels Convention continues to determine questions of jurisdiction between EU States and Aruba and the French overseas departments (recital (23)). However, the States which joined the EU after 2000 have never been parties to the Brussels Convention. The EU States in which the **Brussels I Regulation** takes effect are listed in **table 16.1**.

For legal proceedings instituted on or after 10 January 2015, **Regulation (EC) No. 44/2001** is replaced by Regulation (EU) No. 1215/2012, the 'recast Brussels I Regulation' (for the commencement date see art. 66). The key changes are referred to in the relevant paragraphs of this chapter.

As between EU States and the EFTA States, Norway, Switzerland and Iceland, questions of jurisdiction and the enforcement of judgments are governed by two versions of the Lugano Convention: the original 1988 Convention, which is in practically the same terms as the Brussels Convention, and the revised 2007 Convention, which is in practically the same terms

Table 16.1 EU States in which the Brussels I Regulation takes effect

Until 30 April 2004	As from 1 May 2004	As from 1 January 2007 or later
Austria	Austria	Austria
Belgium	Belgium	Belgium
		Bulgaria
		Croatia (from 1 July 2013)
	Cyprus	Cyprus
	Czech Republic	Czech Republic
		Denmark (from 1 July 2007)
	Estonia	Estonia
Finland	Finland	Finland
France	France	France
Germany	Germany	Germany
Greece	Greece	Greece
	Hungary	Hungary
Republic of Ireland	Republic of Ireland	Republic of Ireland
Italy	Italy	Italy
	Latvia	Latvia
	Lithuania	Lithuania
Luxembourg	Luxembourg	Luxembourg
	Malta	Malta
Netherlands	Netherlands	Netherlands
	Poland	Poland
Portugal	Portugal	Portugal
		Romania
	Slovakia	Slovakia
	Slovenia	Slovenia
Spain	Spain	Spain
Sweden	Sweden	Sweden
United Kingdom	United Kingdom	United Kingdom

as the **Brussels I Regulation**. Norway, Switzerland and Iceland moved to the revised Lugano Convention on 1 January 2010, 1 January 2011 and 1 May 2011 respectively. Proceedings commenced on or after those dates will be governed by the 2007 Convention whilst proceedings commenced before those dates will be governed by the 1988 Convention.

The States which joined the EU after 1988, apart from Poland, never became parties to the original Lugano Convention but are parties to the revised one. Poland became a party to the original Lugano Convention on 1 February 2000.

Until 1 July 2007, Denmark opted out of the **Brussels I Regulation** and questions of jurisdiction between Denmark and other EU States continued to be determined by the Brussels Convention. As from 1 July 2007 the **Brussels I Regulation** applies to Denmark under an agreement (OJ L299, 16/11/2005, pp. 62–7) which was approved on behalf of the EU by Council Decision 2006/325/EC (OJ L120, 5/5/2006, p. 22).

This chapter concentrates on discussing the **Brussels I Regulation**. We will not consider the Brussels and Lugano Conventions separately in this chapter.

Within the United Kingdom, separate jurisdiction is exercised by the courts of England and Wales, Scotland and Northern Ireland. Under the **CJJA 1982** these three areas are known as 'parts' of the United Kingdom. Allocation of jurisdiction between the courts of the various parts of the United Kingdom is regulated by a modified form of the Brussels I Regulation, which can be found in the CJJA 1982, sch. 4. The substantive provisions of the Brussels Convention are applied as between Gibraltar and the United Kingdom by the Civil Jurisdiction and Judgments Act 1982 (Gibraltar) Order 1997 (SI 1997/2602).

Where a claim can be brought in the courts of more than one country, there is a general concern that it should be brought in the courts of the most appropriate country. The courts are also concerned that the same dispute should not be litigated in several countries at the same time, with the risk of irreconcilable judgments and difficulties regarding the recognition of judgments for enforcement purposes. These problems are addressed under the common law rules by the courts' powers to stay English proceedings on the ground of *forum non conveniens* (**16.68** to **16.73**) and to grant injunctions to restrain foreign proceedings (**16.74**).

Similar problems in **Brussels I Regulation** cases are dealt with by requirements that courts other than the one first seised of the matter must either decline jurisdiction or stay their proceedings (see **16.36** and **16.38**). Determining the system of law to be applied to resolve an action where one or more of the parties is foreign is a matter of private international law. As such it is outside the scope of this book, and specialist works should be consulted.

SERVICE ON THE FOREIGN DEFENDANT WITHIN THE JURISDICTION

16.2 Under the common law rules, a foreign defendant is amenable to the jurisdiction of the courts in this country if process is served upon the defendant within the jurisdiction. Applying this rule, jurisdiction was established in *Maharanee Seethaderi Gaekwar of Baroda v Wildenstein* [1972] 2 QB 283, where the proceedings were served on the defendant while on a temporary visit to this country to attend the Ascot Races. This rule has been abolished for cases governed by the **Brussels I Regulation**, which by **art. 3** provides that jurisdiction against EU defendants can no longer be founded by service during the defendant's temporary presence in this country. The old provision entitling a claimant to issue a claim form marked 'not for service out of the jurisdiction' which used to be found in **PD 6B, para. 1.4**, is not replicated in the new version of **Part 6, PD 6A** and **PD 6B**, which came into force on 1 October 2008. However, the practice is still that a claim form with a foreign defendant will be marked 'not for service out of the jurisdiction', unless it is filed with form N510 or an order permitting service abroad is obtained. The intention when this is done is usually either to effect service on the defendant during a temporary visit to this country (unless the defendant lives in the EU) or to secure the defendant's agreement to service within the jurisdiction (often on English solicitors). The period of validity of an originating process intended to be served within the jurisdiction is four months, not six (**CPR, r. 7.5**).

If a domestic claim form has been issued, and it is later discovered that the defendant is outside the jurisdiction, the proper procedure is to apply for permission to issue a concurrent claim form for service outside the jurisdiction. Although the CPR contain no provision for issuing concurrent claim forms, this practice has continued and express reference is made to it in the Admiralty and Commercial Courts Guide, app. 15, para. 4.

It is no longer the case that the defendant must be present in the jurisdiction at the time of actual or deemed service for service to be effective (*Kamali v City and Country Properties Ltd* [2006] EWCA Civ 1879, [2007] 1 WLR 1219, overturning *Chellaram v Chellaram (No. 2)* [2002] EWHC 6323 (Ch), [2002] 3 All ER 17).

A foreign company which does not carry on business within the jurisdiction is not effectively served by purporting to serve on a director within the jurisdiction (*SSL International plc v TTK LIG Ltd* [2011] EWCA Civ 1170, [2012] 1 WLR 1842).

Despite having jurisdiction over a foreign defendant through service within England and Wales, the English court may decide not to exercise that jurisdiction and to grant a stay of proceedings if there is another more appropriate forum to hear the dispute (see **16.68** to **16.73**).

SUBMISSION TO THE JURISDICTION

Regardless of whether the court would otherwise have jurisdiction, a defendant may submit to the jurisdiction of the courts of this country. It may be, for example, to save the costs of disputing jurisdiction, that a defendant will agree to English proceedings being served at the offices of a solicitor in England. Alternatively, a domestic claim form may be sent to a defendant outside the jurisdiction in breach of the rules requiring permission to serve (**16.41** to **16.52**) and the defendant may proceed to contest the action on its merits without objecting to the defect in service. In the absence of any express agreement to submit to the jurisdiction, it is a question of whether the defendant's conduct, when viewed objectively in the context of all the circumstances of the case, is inconsistent with maintaining an objection to the jurisdiction of the court. It is always dangerous to do anything more than to acknowledge service and to make an application under **CPR, Part 11**, to contest the jurisdiction (see **chapter 19**). It is easy to submit to the jurisdiction inadvertently by, for example: **16.3**

(a) instructing a solicitor to accept service in the jurisdiction (*Manta Line Inc. v Sofianites* [1984] 1 Lloyd's Rep 14); or
(b) appearing to contest the merits. An example is *Marc Rich & Co. AG v Società Italiana Impianti PA* (No. 2) [1992] 1 Lloyd's Rep 624, where the defendant was held to have submitted to the jurisdiction of the courts in Italy by delivering a statement of case disputing the merits of the claim. See, also, *SSQ Europe SA v Johann & Backes OHG* [2002] 1 Lloyd's Rep 465, and *Global Multimedia International Ltd v ARA Media Services* [2006] EWHC 3612 (Ch), [2007] 1 All ER (Comm) 1160, which are discussed in **19.3** and **19.4**.

A claimant who has commenced proceedings thereby submits not just the determination of the claim itself to the jurisdiction of the court, but also the incidents of the litigation (*Liberia v Gulf Oceanic Inc.* [1985] 1 Lloyd's Rep 539). Most commonly, this principle means that the court has jurisdiction over a counterclaim brought against the claimant. But a costs order, and an application to commit for contempt for failing to comply with it, are also ordinary incidents of the claim, and as such the court has jurisdiction over them so that the court's permission is not needed to serve the application out of the jurisdiction (*Marketmaker Technology Ltd v CMC Group plc* [2008] EWHC 1556 (QB), LTL 4/9/2008).

A similar principle applies in **Brussels I Regulation** cases, where **art. 24** provides that the courts of a member State have jurisdiction where the defendant 'enters an appearance' unless the appearance is entered solely to contest jurisdiction. The reference to entering an appearance is to acknowledging service or filing a defence. From *Elefanten Schuh GmbH v Jacqmain* (case 150/80) [1981] ECR 1671, it appears that a defence contesting jurisdiction and the merits in the alternative does not constitute a submission to the jurisdiction (there is no equivalent to the word 'solely' in the French text of the Convention). It is not possible to submit to the jurisdiction of a court where the courts of another country have exclusive jurisdiction under **art. 22**. It is possible to submit even if there is a jurisdiction clause in favour of another State, or the proceedings have been brought in a jurisdiction other than those provided for to protect the weaker party in **arts 8** to **21** (insurance, employment and consumer claims) (*Česká podnikatelská pojišťovna as, Vienna Insurance Group v Bilas* (case C-111/09) [2010] ECR I-4545).

CASES OUTSIDE THE GENERAL RULES

Certain types of proceedings affect rights *in rem*. Both under the common law rules and under the **Brussels I Regulation** special rules govern where many of these types of proceedings must be litigated. The main policy consideration justifying these special rules is that rights *in rem* are often protected by detailed national laws, and the courts of the country in question are in the best position to apply them. These special rules are considered at **16.5** to **16.13**. **16.4**

Under the common law rules

16.5 **Land disputes** Claims founded on a dispute as to the title to, or possession of, land must be brought in the courts of the country where the land is situated. The authority for this is *British South Africa Co. v Companhia de Moçambique* [1893] AC 602 as interpreted by later decisions. Where a question as to the title of foreign land is no more than a collateral issue in a claim, the rule does not prevent the courts in this country exercising jurisdiction (see *St Pierre v South American Stores (Gath and Chaves) Ltd* [1936] 1 KB 382 and, in relation to claims for trespass, CJJA 1982, s. 30). It was established by *Penn v Lord Baltimore* (1750) 1 Ves Sen 444 that the rule can be circumvented if the defendant is subject to the general jurisdiction of the courts in this country, such as through presence here, and if the claim can be framed so as to impose a personal obligation on the defendant. An example is a claim for rent due under a lease of foreign land (*St Pierre v South American Stores (Gath and Chaves) Ltd* [1936] 1 KB 382).

16.6 **Intellectual property** Claims alleging breach of foreign copyright are justiciable in the UK where the court has personal jurisdiction over the defendant (*Lucasfilm Ltd v Ainsworth* [2011] UKSC 39, [2012] 1 AC 208). It is unclear from the Supreme Court's decision, however, whether cases involving other foreign IP rights are justiciable. Following the approach under the **Brussels I Regulation**, claims involving validity of rights which are required to be deposited or registered are unlikely to be justiciable whereas claims of infringement will be. Of particular difficulty will be cases which involve consideration of both validity and infringement.

16.7 **Insolvency proceedings** The **Brussels I Regulation** does not apply to bankruptcy, proceedings relating to the winding up of insolvent companies or other legal persons, judicial arrangements, compositions and analogous proceedings (**art. 1(2)(b)**). Jurisdiction over insolvency proceedings in EU States (apart from Denmark) is subject to Regulation (EC) No. 1346/2000 (see **82.9** to **82.12** and **83.3**). Service outside the jurisdiction of any document in proceedings under the Insolvency Act 1986 or the Insolvency Rules 1986 is governed by the Insolvency Rules 1986 (SI 1986/1925), r. 12A.20 (see **84.5**). The intention is that the **Brussels I Regulation** and Regulation (EC) No. 1346/2000 dovetail completely (*Polymer Vision R&D Ltd v Van Dooren* [2011] EWHC 2951 (Comm), LTL 28/11/2011), but there are some difficulties of classification. Not all claims by or against liquidators or trustees in bankruptcy are excluded from the **Brussels I Regulation** by **art. 1(2)(b)**. In order to be excluded by **art. 1(2)(b)**, a claim must derive directly from the bankruptcy or winding up and be closely connected with the insolvency proceedings (*Gourdain v Nadler* (case 133/78) [1979] ECR 733). Claims based on pre-insolvency rights, such as a retention of title clause, are unlikely to be excluded (*German Graphics Graphische Maschinen GmbH v Van der Schee* (case C-292/08) [2009] ECR I-8421). Whereas claims brought by or against liquidators exercising their powers for the general body of creditors are likely to be excluded (*Seagon v Deko Marty Belgium NV* (case C-339/07) [2009] ECR I-767). Claims assigned by a liquidator, where the validity of the assignment is not in question, will not come within the exception (*F-Tex SIA v Lietuvos-Anglijos UAB 'Jadecloud-Vilma'* (case C-213/10) [2013] Bus LR 232).

Under the Brussels I Regulation

16.8 **Exclusive jurisdiction** **Article 22** of the **Brussels I Regulation** allocates exclusive jurisdiction, regardless of the domicile of the parties, over five categories of cases. The courts of the member States are required, of their own motion, to declare they have no jurisdiction in these cases (**art. 25**). The words 'shall have exclusive jurisdiction, regardless of domicile' at the beginning of **art. 22** have been interpreted as applying only as between the courts of member States (*Choudhary v Bhatter* [2009] EWCA Civ 1176, [2010] 2 All ER 1031). They do not create an 'extra-EU jurisdiction' or 'universal international jurisdiction' in the subject-matter jurisdiction cases set out in **art. 22** (*Lucasfilm Ltd v Ainsworth* [2009] EWCA Civ 1328, [2010] Ch 503, at [129], [183]). For legal proceedings instituted on or after 10 January 2015, changes are made in the recast Brussels I Regulation (see Regulation (EU) No. 1215/2012, art. 24 and recital 14).

Land Article 22(1) of the **Brussels I Regulation** provides that proceedings which have as their object rights *in rem* in immovable property or tenancies of immovable property are subject to the exclusive jurisdiction of the courts of the Regulation State in which the property is situated. This is subject to an exception in respect of actions concerning tenancies between natural persons domiciled in the same country for temporary private use for periods of up to six months, which may be brought in the country where the defendant is domiciled. **16.9**

Regarding rights *in rem*, the article has been interpreted by the Court of Justice of the European Union (CJEU) in *Reichert v Dresdner Bank* (case C-115/88) [1990] ECR 27 as being restricted to actions to determine the extent, content, ownership or possession of immovable property, or the existence of other rights *in rem* therein. In *Webb v Webb* (case C-294/92) [1994] QB 696 an apartment in France had been bought in the defendant's name with money provided by the claimant. An action was brought in England claiming a declaration that the property was held on an express or resulting trust for the claimant. It was held, by reasoning analogous to that in *Penn v Lord Baltimore* (1750) 1 Ves Sen 444 (see **16.5**), that the claim affected the defendant's obligations *in personam* and did not have as its object rights *in rem*, and so was outside the scope of **art. 22**.

Conversely, the provision regarding tenancies has been construed widely. It covers cases where the existence of a lease is disputed (*Sanders v Van der Putte* (case 73/77) [1977] ECR 2383) and to any dispute concerning the respective obligations of the parties under a lease (*Rösler v Rottwinkel* (case 241/83) [1986] QB 33). It therefore applies to claims in respect of unpaid rent and other breaches of covenant under a lease. There are limits, however. In *Jarrett v Barclays Bank plc* [1999] QB 1, claims by consumers against the bank under the Consumer Credit Act 1974 arising out of loans to purchase timeshares in properties in Portugal did not have as their object tenancies in immovable property. The foundation of the claims was the loan agreement, and so the claims were not prevented by **art. 22** from being commenced in England.

Commentary

Companies and associations Article 22(2) of the **Brussels I Regulation** provides that proceedings having as their object the validity of the constitution, nullity or dissolution of companies or associations of legal or natural persons, or of their organs, must be brought in the country where the relevant body has its 'seat'. Under the Regulation a court in a member State determines where a company has its seat by applying its rules of private international law (see also **art. 60**). In *Choudhary v Bhatter* [2009] EWCA Civ 1176, [2010] 2 All ER 1031, the Court of Appeal held that the English court had jurisdiction against a company formed in England in 1872, but which had its entire operations in India. It did not have jurisdiction, however, under **art. 22(2)** against a director who was not domiciled in a member State. **16.10**

Problems have arisen in practice where there are a number of issues in the case, not all of which come within **art. 22(2)**. The CJEU has clarified the position in *Berliner Verkehrsbetriebe (BVG), Anstalt des öffentlichen Rechts v J. P. Morgan Chase Bank NA, Frankfurt Branch* (case C-144/10) [2011] 1 WLR 2087. For **art. 22(2)** to be engaged, the validity of a company's decision must form the subject matter of the dispute, not merely be an ancillary question. **Article 22(2)** therefore does not apply to proceedings in which a company pleads that a contract cannot be relied upon against it because a decision of its organs which led to the conclusion of the contract is supposedly invalid on account of infringement of its statutes.

Public registers Article 22(3) of the **Brussels I Regulation** gives exclusive jurisdiction over proceedings concerning the validity of entries in a public register to the courts of the State where the register is kept. **16.11**

Intellectual property Article 22(4) of the **Brussels I Regulation** gives exclusive jurisdiction over proceedings concerning the registration or validity of patents, trade marks, designs and similar rights to the courts of the State where the property in question has been registered or where registration has been applied for. This does not extend to claims for infringement, which are claims in tort and may be brought in accordance with **art. 5(3)** (see **16.27**). **16.12**

Article 22(4) provides that the courts of a member State have exclusive jurisdiction in proceedings concerned with the registration or validity of a European patent granted for that State. This does not prevent courts in other member States granting interim relief under **art. 31** (*Solvay SA v Honeywell Fluorine Products Europe BV* (case C-616/10) CJEU judgment 12 July 2012).

16.13 **Enforcement of judgments** **Article 22(5)** of the **Brussels I Regulation** gives exclusive jurisdiction in enforcement proceedings to the courts of the State in which the judgment is to be enforced.

JURISDICTION UNDER THE BRUSSELS I REGULATION

16.14 The **Brussels I Regulation** is designed to determine the international jurisdiction of the courts of the member States, to facilitate recognition, and to introduce a simple procedure for securing the international enforcement of judgments. Enforcement under the Regulation is considered in **chapter 80**.

The main rule (**16.16**) is that a claim must be brought in the courts of the country where the defendant is domiciled. However, there are many types of claim that can be brought in other countries (**16.17** to **16.35**). Where the other country is England, English proceedings may be issued and served out of the jurisdiction without permission. As there is a possibility that the courts of more than one country may have jurisdiction over a case, provision has been made for jurisdiction being declined or subsequent claims being stayed (**16.36** and **16.38**).

As the **Brussels I Regulation** is an act of the institutions of the Union, the CJEU may give preliminary rulings on its interpretation under the Treaty on the Functioning of the European Union, art. 267 (see **chapter 78**).

Under the 1971 Protocol on the interpretation of the Brussels Convention by the European Court, questions of interpretation of the Brussels Convention can also be referred to the CJEU.

It is important that the Regulation and Convention are interpreted in the same way in all the contracting States. Obviously, there are many differences in the domestic laws applied in the various contracting States, particularly between the civil and common law systems. The CJEU has therefore regularly decided that legal concepts used in the Regulation and the Convention must be given a 'Community meaning'. This involves attempting to discover shared principles, a far from simple task. Many of the CJEU cases involve interpretation of the Brussels Convention. It may be assumed that the CJEU will interpret the Regulation in the same way as it interpreted the Brussels Convention.

Scope of the Brussels I Regulation

16.15 The **Brussels I Regulation** applies to civil and commercial proceedings whatever the nature of the court or tribunal (**art. 1**). It does not apply to revenue, customs, social security, insolvency (see **16.7**), arbitration or administrative matters, nor to proceedings relating to the status or legal capacity of natural persons, rights in property arising out of a matrimonial relationship, wills and succession. Arbitration matters were excluded from the scope of the Brussels Convention because they were already covered by international conventions, particularly the New York Convention, 1958. However, a number of the provisions in the **Brussels I Regulation**, as interpreted by the CJEU, have undermined the exclusion of arbitration. Most significantly, proceedings relating to the incorporation or validity of an arbitration clause have been held to be within the scope of the Regulation (*National Navigation Co. v Endesa Generaciün SA* [2009] EWCA Civ 1397, [2010] 1 Lloyd's Rep 193, applying *West Tankers Inc. v Allianz SpA* (case C-185/07) [2009] AC 1138, where the CJEU held that a preliminary ruling on the applicability of an arbitration clause in proceedings in which the main subject of the proceedings was within the Regulation was itself to be categorised as within the Regulation). For legal proceedings instituted on or after 10 January 2015, changes made in the recast Brussels I Regulation seek to reverse this gradual encroachment (see in particular Regulation (EU) No. 1215/2012, recital 12).

A claim which is brought by or against a public body acting in the exercise of its public powers is not a 'civil [or] commercial matter' within the meaning of the **Brussels I Regulation, art. 1** (*Grovit v De Nederlandsche Bank NV* [2007] EWCA Civ 953, [2008] 1 WLR 51). In this case a decision by the central bank to refuse registration of a money transaction business was held to be a public law decision. Where a fine is imposed to ensure compliance with an order or judgment given in a civil or commercial matter, the fine is also civil and commercial in nature (*Realchemie Nederland BV v Bayer CropScience AG* (case C-406/09) [2012] Bus LR 1825).

Domicile: the general rule

The general rule laid down by the **Brussels I Regulation** is that proceedings must be brought in the courts of the country where the defendant is domiciled. **Article 2** provides: **16.16**

Subject to this Regulation, persons domiciled in a member State shall, whatever their nationality, be sued in the courts of that member State.

Domicile is determined by reference to the internal law of the State concerned (**art. 59**). In the United Kingdom it is defined for the purposes of the Regulation by the Civil Jurisdiction and Judgments Order 2001 (SI 2001/3929), sch. 1, paras 9 to 12. The domicile of individuals is governed by SI 2001/3929, sch. 1, para. 9, which provides in sub-para. (2):

An individual is domiciled in the United Kingdom if and only if—

(a) he is resident in the United Kingdom; and
(b) the nature and circumstances of his residence indicate that he has a substantial connection with the United Kingdom.

By sub-para. (6) an individual is presumed to have a substantial connection with the United Kingdom after being resident in the United Kingdom for three months unless the contrary is proved. It is domicile at the time of the proceedings which is relevant not domicile at, for example, the time of contracting (*Sherdley v Nordea Life and Pension SA* [2012] EWCA Civ 88, [2012] 2 All ER (Comm) 725).

An individual may have more than one domicile, but ownership of property and business interests in the jurisdiction will not be sufficient to establish domicile here if there is no settled or usual place of abode (*High Tech International AG v Deripaska* [2006] EWHC 3276 (QB), [2007] EMLR 15; *Cherney v Deripaska* [2007] EWHC 965 (Comm), [2007] 2 All ER (Comm) 785; *OJSC Oil Co. Yugraneft v Abramovich* [2008] EWHC 2613 (Comm), LTL 3/11/2008).

Where the defendant's whereabouts are unknown, in spite of attempts to locate him, his last known domicile may be sufficient in some circumstances (*Hypoteční banka as v Lindner* (case C-327 /10) CJEU judgment 17 November 2011).

Article 60 of the **Brussels I Regulation** provides that a corporation is domiciled where it has its 'statutory seat', central administration or principal place of business. A company's statutory seat is its registered office or, if it does not have one, the place where it was incorporated. The 'principal place of business' of a company within **art. 60** is the place at the heart of its operations (*King v Crown Energy Trading AG* [2003] EWHC 163 (Comm), [2003] ILPr 28)). In *Ministry of Defence and Support for the Armed Forces of Iran v FAZ Aviation Ltd* [2007] EWHC 1042 (Comm), [2008] 1 All ER (Comm) 372, the court stated that the principal place of business is likely to be the place where the corporate authority (shareholders and directors) is to be found and to be the place from which the company is controlled and managed. The place where the company's day-to-day activities are conducted may not be the principal place of business if those activities are subject to the control of senior management located elsewhere. The central administration of a company is where decisions are made and where the entrepreneurial management takes place (*Flatela Vava v Anglo American South Africa Ltd* [2012] EWHC 1969 (QB), [2012] 2 CLC 684).

A corporation may be domiciled in more than one State under the rules in **art. 60**.

A dispute about where a company has its seat is determined on the basis of establishing a good arguable case, meaning that one side has a much better argument on the material available (*889457 Alberta Inc. v Katanga Mining Ltd* [2008] EWHC 2679 (Comm), [2009] 1 BCLC 189; *OJSC Oil Co. Yugraneft v Abramovich* [2008] EWHC 2613 (Comm), LTL 3/11/2008).

The time for judging whether there is a defendant domiciled within the jurisdiction for the purposes of **art. 60** is the date of issue, not the date of service (*Canada Trust Co. v Stolzenberg (No. 2)* [2002] 1 AC 1).

Exceptions to the rule that jurisdiction is based on domicile

16.17 Although **art.** 2 of the **Brussels I Regulation** lays down the general rule, a claimant often has a choice of forum under the Regulation. This is because, in a wide variety of cases, the claimant is given the option of suing in another country. **Article 3** provides that 'Persons domiciled in a member State may be sued in the courts of another member State only by virtue of the rules set out in sections 2 to 7 of this Chapter'. These sections encompass **arts 5 to 24** of the Regulation. **Article 22** was considered at **16.8** to **16.13. Articles 5, 6, 8** to **21** and **23** will be considered at **16.18** to **16.35**.

The basic scheme, as confirmed by **CPR, r. 6.33(2)**, is that the courts of England and Wales will have jurisdiction to hear and determine a claim under the Regulation if:

(a) the case falls within one of the provisions set out in **arts 5** to **24**;
(b) there are no proceedings pending involving the same claim in another part of the United Kingdom or another member State; and
(c) the defendant is domiciled in a member State. This requirement is modified in cases within **art. 23(1)** (jurisdiction clauses, see **16.24**), where the requirement is that *any* one of the parties must be domiciled in a member State. Where there is a jurisdiction agreement between parties, none of whom is domiciled in a member State, **art. 23** provides that courts in other member States have no jurisdiction until the chosen court has declined jurisdiction (see **16.25**). For the position in exclusive jurisdiction cases under **art. 22** see **16.8**.

Similar provision is made in relation to Aruba, French overseas departments, Iceland, Norway and Switzerland by **CPR, r. 6.33(1)**.

Contract

16.18 **Main provision** **Article** 5(1) of the **Brussels I Regulation** provides in part that a person domiciled in one member State may alternatively 'be sued in matters relating to a contract, in the courts for the place of performance of the obligation in question'.

16.19 **Scope of article** 5(1) In *Arcado SPRL v Haviland SA* (case 9/87) [1988] ECR 1539 the CJEU confirmed that, in the **Brussels I Regulation, art.** 5(1), the phrase 'matters relating to a contract':

> is to be regarded as an independent concept which, for the purpose of the application of the Convention, must be interpreted by reference principally to the system and objectives of the Convention in order to ensure that it is fully effective.

A claim brought under the Contracts (Rights of Third Parties) Act 1999 is a matter relating to a contract within the **Brussels I Regulation, art.** 5(1) (*WPP Holdings Italy SRL v Benatti* [2007] EWCA Civ 263, [2007] 1 WLR 2316).

In *Kalfelis v Bankhaus Schröder, Münchmeyer, Hengst & Co.* (case 189/87) [1988] ECR 5565 the CJEU laid down the general principle that the special jurisdiction given by **art. 5** must be interpreted restrictively as it derogates from the principle that jurisdiction is vested in the courts of the country where the defendant is domiciled. An earlier decision of the CJEU, *Martin Peters Bauunternehmung GmbH v Zuid Nederlandse Aannemers Vereniging* (case 34/82) [1983] ECR 987, decided that as membership of an association creates close links between members of the same kind as those between the parties to a contract, jurisdiction over a dispute between an association and one of its members could be given by **art. 5(1)**.

The effect is that **art.** 5(1) can be invoked where either there is a contractual relationship giving rise to an actual contract, or there is a consensual obligation similar to a contract giving rise to a comparable obligation.

In *Kleinwort Benson Ltd v Glasgow City Council* [1999] 1 AC 153, the House of Lords held that restitutionary claims based on void contracts did not fall within **art. 5(1)**. Where the only connection with this country is an alleged non-disclosure or misrepresentation in relation to the making of a contract, jurisdiction may be given by **art. 5(1)**. This is because the word 'obligation' in **art. 5(1)** is not limited to contractual obligation, and in suitable cases the objects of the Convention can be achieved by bringing proceedings where the negotiations in a matter related to a contract were conducted (*Agnew v Länsförsäkringsbolagens AB* [2001] 1 AC 223).

In *Effer SpA v Kantner* (case 38/81) [1982] ECR 825 the CJEU held that **art. 5(1)** applies even where the existence of the contract on which the claim is based is disputed by the defendant. Otherwise, a defendant could oust the jurisdiction granted by **art. 5(1)** merely by saying there is a dispute. This decision was interpreted by the Court of Appeal in *Tesam Distribution Ltd v Schuh Mode Team GmbH* [1990] ILPr 149 as meaning that a court cannot accept jurisdiction under **art. 5(1)** on the mere assertion or pleading of the claimant. There must be evidence from which it would be proper to conclude that a contract existed and that the place of performance was the country in which the action was brought. This concept was also applied by the Court of Appeal in *Boss Group Ltd v Boss France SA* [1997] 1 WLR 351 where Saville LJ's judgment is to the effect that a claimant relying on **art. 5(1)** does not have to establish finally and conclusively that the place of performance of the obligation was in England, but does have to establish a 'good arguable case that that was so'.

Article 5(1) can confer jurisdiction where the relief sought is a negative declaration (as can **art. 5(3)** in relation to tort claims: *Folien Fischer AG v Ritrama SpA* (case C-133/11) [2013] 2 WLR 373).

Place of performance of obligation If the **Brussels I Regulation, art. 5(1)**, applies, proceedings may be brought in the courts of 'the place of performance of the obligation in question'. 16.20
In *Etablissements A. de Bloos SPRL v SCA Bouyer* (case 14/76) [1976] ECR 1497 the CJEU held that the 'obligation' in **art. 5(1)** refers to the contractual obligation forming the basis of the legal proceedings. Regard must be had to the contractual obligation under consideration, and not to the contract as a whole. The place of performance is not necessarily the same as the place where breach occurred. In *Medway Packaging Ltd v Meurer Maschinen GmbH & Co. KG* [1990] 2 Lloyd's Rep 112 an English claimant brought an action in England against a German defendant alleging the defendant had repudiated an exclusive distribution agreement without giving reasonable notice. It was held, first, that the defendant's alleged obligation to give due notice terminating the contract had to be performed at the claimant's place of business in England. Secondly, the agreement granting the claimant exclusive rights to distribute the defendant's machines was essentially negative in character, and could be broken in either England or Germany. That was held to be sufficient to give the courts in England jurisdiction under **art. 5(1)**. In *MBM Fabri-Clad Ltd v Eisen und Hüttenwerke Thale AG* (1999) LTL 3/11/99, the Court of Appeal held that in a claim for damages for breach of a contract to design, manufacture and

supply goods, the obligation in question was the obligation to supply goods which met the contractual specification, rather than the defendant's acts and omissions in Germany which led to the goods failing to meet the specification. Since the goods were to be supplied to the claimant in England, the English courts had jurisdiction under **art. 5(1)**.

Where a claimant brings a claim concerning a number of obligations under a single contract, it is the principal obligation that determines jurisdiction under **art. 5(1)** (*Shenavai v Kreischer* (case 266/85) [1987] ECR 239). This was applied in *Union Transport plc v Continental Lines SA* [1992] 1 WLR 15, where the claimant had claims under a voyage charter for failing to nominate a vessel (which was to be performed in England) and for failure to provide a vessel (which was to be performed in the USA). It was held that nominating a vessel was the principal obligation as it triggered the other contractual obligations, and therefore proceedings had validly been brought in England. The place of performance of a warranty as to an existing state of affairs is the place where that state of affairs was required to exist (*Crucial Music Corporation v Klondyke Management AG* [2007] EWHC 1782 (Ch), [2008] Bus LR 327).

The Regulation goes on to provide that the place of performance of the obligation in question shall be, in the case of the sale of goods, the place in a member State where, under the contract, the goods were delivered or should have been delivered, and in the case of the provision of services, the place in a member State where, under the contract, the services were provided or should have been provided (**art. 5(1)(b)**). There is no equivalent provision in the Brussels Convention. The revision was introduced by the Regulation to counter criticism that the operation of art. 5(1) of the Brussels Convention tended to give jurisdiction to the courts of the claimant's domicile not the courts of the country with the closest connection to the dispute.

In a claim relating to the sale of goods where the contract provides for delivery to a number of locations, the place of delivery under the **Brussels I Regulation, art. 5(1)**, is the place with the closest link with the contract. In general this is the principal place of delivery determined on the basis of economic criteria, which is a matter to be decided by the domestic court seised of the proceedings. If there is no principal place of delivery, each of the delivery points can found the basis for jurisdiction under **art. 5(1)**, giving the claimant a choice of where to litigate (*Color Drack GmbH v Lexx International Vertriebs GmbH* (case C-386/05) [2008] 1 All ER (Comm) 169). In a case involving carriage of goods, the place where the goods were delivered or should have been delivered should be determined on the basis of the provisions of the contract. Where it is impossible to do so, the place of delivery is where the physical transfer of the goods took place, as a result of which the purchaser obtained or should have obtained actual power of disposal over those goods at the final destination of the sales transaction (*Car Trim GmbH v KeySafety Systems Srl* (case C-381/08) [2010] Bus LR 1648). In an FOB contract, risk and property pass to the buyer on shipment, and delivery as a result is effected on shipment by virtue of the **Sale of Goods Act 1979, s. 32(1)** (*Scottish and Newcastle International Ltd v Othon Ghalanos Ltd* [2008] UKHL 11, [2008] Bus LR 583). Contracts for the manufacture of goods will usually be contracts for the sale of goods within the **Brussels I Regulation, art. 5(1)** (*Car Trim GmbH v KeySafety Systems Srl*).

In a claim relating to services provided in different member States, the place of provision is the place with the closest link to the contract, in particular, the place where the main provision of services is to be carried out. Where this is in more than one country, the claimant has a choice of where to sue (*Rehder v Air Baltic Corporation* (case C-204/08) [2009] ILPr 44). In the case of a commercial agency contract, the main place of provision of services depends on the provisions in the contract or, in the absence of such provisions, the actual place of performance or, failing that, the place where the agent is domiciled (*Wood Floor Solutions Andreas Domberger GmbH v Silva Trade SA* (case C-19/09) [2010] 1 WLR 1900).

16.21 **Contracts of employment** Articles 18 to 21 of the **Brussels I Regulation** deal with jurisdiction over individual contracts of employment and have no equivalent in the Brussels

Convention. The Regulation provides that the employee may be sued only in the courts of the member State in which the employee is domiciled (save that a counterclaim may be brought against an employee in the courts where the original claim is pending) (**art. 20**). The employer, on the other hand, under **art. 19**, may be sued either in:

(a) the courts where the employer is domiciled; or
(b) in the courts for the place where the employee habitually carries out his or her work, or last did so; or
(c) if the employee does not or did not habitually carry out his or her work in any one country, in the courts for the place where the business which engaged the employee is or was situated.

In any disputes with its employees, an employer who is not domiciled in a member State is deemed to be domiciled in the member State where it operates any branch or agency (**art. 18**, overriding the provisions of **arts 4** and **5(5)**). This includes an embassy of a non-member State (*Mahamdia v Algeria* (case C-154/11) [2013] ICR 1). For legal proceedings instituted on or after 10 January 2015, the recast Brussels I Regulation will extend the application of (b) and (c) to employers not domiciled in the EU (see Regulation (EU) No. 1215/2012, art. 21(2) and recital 14).

The rights given to employees in the Regulation are in accordance with one of the policies of the Convention, carried forward in the Regulation, namely, the protection of the weaker party in contractual relationships. This was emphasised by *Mercury Publicity Ltd v Wolfgang Loerke GmbH* (1991) *The Times*, 21 October 1991, where the Court of Appeal said the rule was restricted to relationships of master and servant of a personal nature, and refused to extend the rule to a contract of commercial agency. Where proceedings are brought by an employer against an employee, the claim is likely to relate to the contract of employment. There is no test that the defendant's status as an employee has to be 'legally relevant' to the claims (*Alfa Laval Tumba AB v Separator Spares International Ltd* [2012] EWCA Civ 1569, [2013] 1 WLR 1110).

Consumer contracts **Articles 15** to **17** of the **Brussels I Regulation** apply to consumer contracts, ousting the special jurisdiction granted by **art. 5(1)**. Again, these provisions are designed to protect the weaker party to certain contracts. A restrictive meaning has been given by **art. 15** to the term 'consumer contract'. To qualify as a consumer a party must not have entered into the contract in the course of a trade or profession. The contract must then be either: **16.22**

(a) for the sale of goods on instalment credit terms; or
(b) for a loan repayable by instalments, or for any other form of credit, made to finance the sale of goods; or
(c) concluded with a person who pursues commercial or professional activities in the member State of the consumer's domicile or, by any means, directs such activities to that member State or to several States including that member State, and the contract falls within the scope of such activities.

The circumstances in which a website which can be accessed from a member State amounts to directing commercial activities to that State has been considered by the CJEU in *Pammer v Reederei Karl Schlüter GmbH & Co. KG* (case C-585/08) [2010] ECR I-12527. It is not necessary that the sales contract was entered into at a distance (*Mühlleitner v Yusufi* (case C-190/11) CJEU judgment 6 September 2012).

By **art. 16** a consumer acting as a claimant may bring proceedings in the courts where either party is domiciled, but a consumer may only be sued in the courts of the country in which he or she is domiciled. For legal proceedings instituted on or after 10 January 2015, the recast Brussels I Regulation will permit a consumer to bring proceedings in the courts of his or her domicile regardless of whether the trader is domiciled in another member State (see Regulation (EU) No. 1215/2012, art. 18(1) and recital 14).

Commentary

16.23 **Insurance contracts** Jurisdiction in insurance matters is governed by **arts 8** to **14** of the **Brussels I Regulation** and **art.** 5(1) is ousted. These provisions are designed to protect the insured, who is regarded as being the weaker party in insurance matters. It is not always the case that an insured will be in a weaker negotiating position than the insurer, especially where the insured is a large commercial corporation. Nevertheless, the Court of Appeal held in *New Hampshire Insurance Co. v Strabag Bau AG* [1992] 1 Lloyd's Rep 361 that the concept of 'matters relating to insurance' in these provisions has to be given a literal interpretation, and is not restricted to insurance for domestic or private purposes. However, contract claims between insurers are outside the scope of the provisions (*Youell v La Réunion Aérienne* [2009] EWCA Civ 175, [2009] Bus LR 1504), as are reinsurance contracts (*Universal General Insurance Co. v Group Josi Reinsurance Co. SA* (case C-412/98) [2001] QB 68).

By **arts 9** and **10** an insurer domiciled (or having a branch, agency or establishment) in a member State may be sued:

(a) in the courts of the State where it is domiciled; or
(b) in the courts of the State where the policyholder, insured or beneficiary is domiciled, provided that State is a member State; or
(c) if there are co-insurers, in the courts of a member State where proceedings have been brought against the leading insurer; or
(d) if the case involves liability insurance or insurance over immovable property, in the courts for the place where the harmful event occurred.

The insured is protected by **art. 12**, which provides that an insurer may bring proceedings only in the courts of the country where the insured is domiciled.

16.24 **Jurisdiction agreements** Article 23(1) of the **Brussels I Regulation** provides:

> If the parties, one or more of whom is domiciled in a member State, have agreed that a court or the courts of a member State are to have jurisdiction to settle any disputes which have arisen or which may arise in connection with a particular legal relationship, that court or those courts shall have jurisdiction. Such jurisdiction shall be exclusive unless the parties have agreed otherwise. Such an agreement conferring jurisdiction shall be either—
> (a) in writing or evidenced in writing; or
> (b) in a form which accords with practices which the parties have established between themselves; or
> (c) in international trade or commerce, in a form which accords with a usage of which the parties are or ought to have been aware and which in such trade or commerce is widely known to, and regularly observed by, parties to contracts of the type involved in the particular trade or commerce concerned.

Article 23(2) goes on to provide that any communication by electronic means which provides a durable record of the agreement shall be equivalent to 'writing'.

It is for the party who is relying on **art. 23** to prove the existence of an agreement which satisfies the requirements of **art. 23** (*Konkola Copper Mines v Coromin Ltd* [2006] EWCA Civ 5, [2006] 1 Lloyd's Rep 410). However, as jurisdictional questions are resolved at an interim stage, the standard of proof must be moderated. The general rule is that any fact or matter on which the assumption of jurisdiction by the court depends has to be shown to exist by reference to the test of 'a good arguable case' (*Canada Trust Co. v Stolzenberg (No. 2)* [1998] 1 WLR 547). In the case of **art. 23**, 'good arguable case' means the party invoking **art. 23** must show it has much the better of the argument that the requirements as to form are met and that the jurisdiction clause was the subject of consensus between the parties (*Bols Distilleries BV v Superior Yacht Services Ltd* [2006] UKPC 45, [2007] 1 WLR 12).

16.25 **Application of article 23(1)** General words of incorporation might be effective to incorporate a jurisdiction clause for the purposes of the **Brussels I Regulation, art. 23(1)(a)**, but will do so only if they clearly and precisely demonstrate the existence of a consensus to that effect (*AIG Europe SA v QBE International Insurance Ltd* [2001] 2 All ER (Comm) 622; *Tradigrain SA v Siat SpA* [2002] CLC 574).

In order for **art. 23** to apply the parties must have 'agreed' to give jurisdiction to the courts of a member State. *Dresser UK Ltd v Falcongate Freight Management Ltd* [1992] QB 502 concerned a jurisdiction clause in a bill of lading relied on by a bailor of goods against a sub-bailee. As that relationship does not depend on agreement, the clause did not satisfy the requirements of **art. 23**. In *Powell Duffryn plc v Petereit* (case C-214/89) [1992] ECR I-1745 the CJEU held that a jurisdiction clause in the articles of association of a company was to be regarded as being part of a contract for the purposes of **art. 23** as between the company and the shareholders and also between the shareholders *inter se*. A jurisdiction clause will generally only apply to the parties to the contract. It is not possible to pierce the corporate veil and make non-parties subject to the jurisdiction provisions (*VTB Capital plc v Nutritek International Corporation* [2013] UKSC 5, [2013] 2 WLR 398). The position may be different where the contract is made for the benefit of a non-party (*Gerling Konzern Speziale Kreditversicherungs-AG v Amministrazione del Tesoro dello Stato* (case 201/82) [1983] ECR 2503).

Article 23 may still apply where there is an allegation that the contract is vitiated by mistake, misrepresentation, illegality, lack of authority or lack of capacity. In *Deutsche Bank AG v Asia Pacific Broadband Wireless Communications Inc.* [2008] EWCA Civ 1091, [2009] 2 All ER (Comm) 129, the claimant brought proceedings for breach of a credit facility containing a widely drafted English exclusive jurisdiction clause. The defendants alleged that the agreement was void as it had been entered into as part of a large-scale fraud perpetrated against them by their officers. The Court of Appeal held that the requirements of form were met in that the relevant agreements were signed by all the parties and the only question was whether the agreements were authorised. A jurisdiction clause is severable from the main contract. This means that it is only where the clause itself is under attack that jurisdiction may be lost.

Article 23(1) of the **Regulation** also lays down certain requirements as to the form of jurisdiction clauses. A distinction is drawn between international trading and commercial contracts and, on the other hand, more general contracts. A jurisdiction clause in a general contract must be in writing or evidenced in writing, or else accord with the practices of the parties. The CJEU held in *Colzani v Rüwa* (case 24/76) [1976] ECR 1831 that if the jurisdiction clause is contained in written standard terms, the contract must contain an express reference to those standard terms. In *7E Communications Ltd v Vertex Antennentechnik GmbH* [2007] EWCA Civ 140, [2008] Bus LR 472, jurisdiction under **art. 23** was conferred by a jurisdiction clause contained in standard terms and conditions which were referred to in a contract, even though the defendant had not seen those terms and the reference to the standard terms and conditions did not refer expressly to the jurisdiction clause. It is more difficult to demonstrate that a jurisdiction clause in a separate contract has been incorporated (*Seitz GmbH & Co. KG v Brunner SpA* [2009] ILPr 31; *Africa Express Line Ltd v Socofi SA* [2009] EWHC 3223 (Comm), [2010] 2 Lloyd's Rep 181). Similarly, in *SSL International plc v TTK LIG Ltd* [2011] EWCA Civ 1170, [2012] 1 WLR 1842, there was no evidence of any consensus where the jurisdiction clause was contained in supply conditions which were only mentioned on a website and in purchase orders which were not sent to the defendants. In international trade or commerce, a jurisdiction clause may alternatively be in a form which accords with a widely known usage in that trade or commerce of which the parties are or ought to have been aware.

Problems arise in practice where there are a number of different but connected agreements between the parties containing conflicting provisions in respect of jurisdiction. This has arisen on a number of occasions in recent years, in particular in cases concerning international finance. In these circumstances the court has to undertake a commercially minded construction of the agreements. If a dispute clearly comes within the scope of a particular agreement then effect will be given to this even if this results in a fragmentation of disputes (*Sebastian Holdings Inc. v Deutsche Bank AG* [2010] EWCA Civ 998, [2011] 1 Lloyd's Rep 106). The position is different where a claim involves a number of agreements and commercial parties would not have intended more than one jurisdiction to apply. In those circumstances the parties may be taken to have agreed to refer the dispute to the jurisdiction provided for in the jurisdiction agreement at the commercial centre of the claim (*UBS AG v HSH Nordbank AG* [2009] EWCA Civ 585, [2009] 2 Lloyd's Rep 272).

International finance agreements also commonly include unilateral jurisdiction options, whereby jurisdiction is given to a particular court but the finance parties have the option to bring proceedings in another country, or refer the dispute to arbitration. It is possible that some member States will not give effect to such clauses (see for example the decision of the Cour de cassation in France in *Société Banque privée Edmond de Rothschild Europe v Mme X* (11-26.022) 26 September 2012 Bull civ I No. 176). It is unlikely the English courts would adopt this interpretation.

Article 23(3) of the Regulation provides:

> Where such an agreement is concluded by parties, none of whom is domiciled in a member State, the courts of other member States shall have no jurisdiction over their disputes unless the court or courts chosen have declined jurisdiction.

Jurisdiction given by **art. 23** does not take precedence over the rules on *lis pendens* and related actions in **arts 27** and **28** (see **16.36** to **16.38**), even where there is excessive delay in the first court (*Erich Gasser GmbH v MISAT Srl* (case C-116/02) [2005] QB 1). This can give rise to problems in practice, as considerable delay can be caused by the need to wait for the court first seised to determine that it does not have jurisdiction as a result of a jurisdiction agreement in favour of a court in another member State. For legal proceedings instituted on or after 10 January 2015, this problem has been addressed in the recast Brussels I Regulation (see **16.37**). The **Brussels I Regulation, art. 23**, does take precedence over the provisions of **art. 6(2)** (see **16.34**) (*Hough v P and O Containers Ltd* [1999] QB 834).

16.26 **Restrictions on jurisdiction clauses** Parties are not completely free to confer jurisdiction by means of jurisdiction clauses. The following restrictions should be noted:

(a) a jurisdiction clause cannot override exclusive jurisdiction conferred by the **Brussels I Regulation, art. 22** (for which, see **16.8** to **16.13**);
(b) a jurisdiction clause inserted for the benefit of one party may be waived by that party;
(c) in actions relating to individual contracts of employment, consumer contracts and insurance contracts, jurisdiction agreements are only effective (in broad terms) if entered into after the dispute has arisen or if invoked by the employee, consumer or insured (see **arts 13, 14, 17** and **21**); *Sherdley v Nordea Life and Pension SA* [2012] EWCA Civ 88, [2012] 2 All ER (Comm) 725);
(d) submission to the jurisdiction (**16.3**) overrides a jurisdiction clause (*Elefanten Schuh GmbH v Jacqmain* (case 150/80) [1981] ECR 1671).

Tort

16.27 A claim in tort may be brought where the harmful event occurred or may occur (**Brussels I Regulation, art. 5(3)**).

On the same lines as jurisdiction in contract under **art. 5(1)**, the Court of Appeal in *Mölnlycke AB v Procter and Gamble Ltd* [1992] 1 WLR 1112 held that the court has power to filter off frivolous or vexatious use of the jurisdiction given by **art. 5(3)** by insisting that the claimant must establish a good arguable case on the merits. This test was applied in *Bank of Tokyo-Mitsubishi Ltd v Baskan Gida Sanayi ve Pazarlama AS* [2004] EWHC 945 (Ch), [2004] 2 Lloyd's Rep 395.

16.28 **Meaning of 'tort'** Like matters relating to contract (**16.18**), it is important that the **Brussels I Regulation, art. 5(3)**, should be construed consistently in all the member States despite differences in the types of conduct regarded as tortious in the various countries. Accordingly, the CJEU in *Kalfelis v Bankhaus Schröder, Münchmeyer, Hengst & Co.* (case 189/87) [1988] ECR 5565 decided that 'tort' must be regarded as an autonomous concept.

As to what is meant by the independent concept of tort, the CJEU in the *Kalfelis* case said:

> the term 'matters relating to tort, delict or quasi-delict' within the meaning of article 5(3) of the Convention must be regarded as an independent concept covering all actions which seek to establish the liability of a defendant and which are not related to a 'contract' within the meaning of article 5(1).
>
> ... it must be observed ... that the 'special jurisdictions' enumerated in articles 5 and 6 of the Convention constitute derogations from the principle that jurisdiction is vested in the courts of the State where the defendant is domiciled and as such must be interpreted restrictively. It must therefore be recognised that a court which has jurisdiction under article 5(3) over an action in so far as it is based on tort or delict does not have jurisdiction over that action in so far as it is not so based.

The first half of this passage has been frequently misunderstood as meaning that **art. 5(3)** is a catch-all provision. Such an interpretation is inconsistent with the second half of the quotation. In fact, the word 'liability' in the first passage must be understood as connoting liability within the scope of **art. 5(3)**. 'Mainstream' torts, such as negligence, nuisance, defamation and patent infringement, all come within the definition. A claim that the defendant was constructive trustee of money which, with the dishonest assistance of the defendant, had been taken from the claimant by a senior employee in breach of duty was held to be a matter 'relating to tort, delict or quasi-delict' within **art. 5(3)** in *Casio Computer Co. Ltd v Kaiser* [2001] EWCA Civ 661, [2001] ILPr 43. Likewise a claim for a contribution under the **Civil Liability (Contribution) Act 1978, s. 1**, also fell within **art. 5(3)** (*Hewden Tower Cranes Ltd v Wolffkran GmbH* [2007] EWHC 857 (TCC), [2007] 2 Lloyd's Rep 138).

Harmful event It was held by the CJEU in *Handelskwekerij G. J. Bier BV v Mines de Potasse d'Alsace SA* (case 21/76) [1978] QB 708 that **art. 5(3)** of the Brussels Convention gives the claimant the option of commencing proceedings either in the country where the wrongful act or omission took place, or in the country where the damage occurred. The place where the harmful event occurred in the case of negligent misstatement is where the misstatement originated and not where it was received and acted upon (*Domicrest Ltd v Swiss Bank Corporation* [1999] QB 548; *Sunderland Marine Mutual Insurance Co. Ltd v Wiseman* [2007] EWHC 1460 (Comm), [2007] 2 Lloyd's Rep 308). In *Future Investments SA v FIFA* [2010] EWHC 1019 (Ch), [2010] ILPr 34, a case concerning causing loss by unlawful means, the place where the harmful event occurred was the place where the contract complained of was signed. 16.29

The place where the damage occurred is not the place where the damage was quantified or where steps were taken to mitigate the effects of the wrongful conduct of the defendant (*Netherlands v Rüffer* (case 814/79) [1980] ECR 3807). It was held in *London Helicopters Ltd v Heliportugal LDA-INAC* [2006] EWHC 108 (QB), [2006] 1 All ER (Comm) 595, that in order to determine the place where the damage had occurred the court needed to establish where the event giving rise to the damage had produced its initial, direct, immediate or physical harmful effect. This was a claim for negligent misstatement arising out of certificates of airworthiness issued by the defendant, in reliance on which the claimant had bought a helicopter. The claimant had subsequently resold the helicopter and had been sued by the purchaser on the ground that the aircraft's engine was neither of satisfactory quality nor fit for purpose. The court held that the initial and direct damage had occurred when the certificates were received and relied upon by the claimant in England. Further, it had suffered loss and incurred expense in England when it was sued in respect of the engine.

In *Dolphin Maritime and Aviation Services Ltd v Sveriges Ångfartygs Assurans Förening* [2009] EWHC 716 (Comm), [2009] 2 Lloyd's Rep 123, claims for procuring or inducing a breach of contract and conspiracy to use unlawful means came within **art. 5(3)**. They could be brought in England as the damage occurred in England because that is where the claimant would have received money if the underlying contract had been performed. In *Crucial Music Corporation v Klondyke Management AG* [2007] EWHC 1782 (Ch), [2008] Bus LR 327, a case concerning misrepresentation, damage occurred where the contract was entered into, as the agreed price was greater than the price would have been if the true facts had been known.

In *Shevill v Presse Alliance SA* (case C-68/93) [1995] 2 AC 18 (CJEU); [1996] AC 959 (HL), the claimants commenced proceedings in England against a French defendant complaining that they had been libelled in one of the defendant's newspapers. The newspaper had a daily circulation of 200,000 copies in France, and about 250 copies in England. The particulars of claim relied only on publication in England. It was held that as the 'harmful event' in **art.** 5(3) included the place where the damage was suffered, the action had been validly brought in England, although the English courts had jurisdiction solely in respect of the harm caused in England. An action to recover in respect of all the harm caused could alternatively have been brought before the courts of the defendant's domicile or the place where the publisher of the defamatory publication was established. In *eDate Advertising GmbH v X* (case C-509/09) [2012] QB 654 the CJEU held that the publication of harmful content on the Internet needed to be treated differently to the circulation of printed media. The wronged party had the option of bringing a claim in respect of all the damage caused either before the courts of the member State in which the publisher of the content was established or before the courts of the member State in which the publisher's centre of interests was based. Alternatively, claims could be brought in the courts for each State in which online content was or had been accessible, but only in respect of damage caused in that territory. An action for trade mark infringement based on an adword (advertising keyword) can be brought in the country of registration or the member State in which the advertiser is established (*Wintersteiger AG v Products 4U Sondermaschinenbau GmbH* (case C-523/10) [2013] Bus LR 150).

In *Henderson v Jaouen* [2002] EWCA Civ 75, [2002] 1 WLR 2971, the claimant was injured in a road accident in France, and obtained a final award of damages from the civil courts in France. Under French law he was entitled to bring a fresh action, which was regarded in French law as a fresh cause of action, if his injuries subsequently deteriorated. His injuries did deteriorate, and by this time the claimant was living in England. He brought English proceedings based on this deterioration, alleging that the deterioration was a 'harmful event' engaging **art.** 5(3). The Court of Appeal held that this second claim had to be brought in France, because the 'harmful event' was the original 'tort, delict or quasi-delict', which was the original road traffic accident in France. That was a single event, which had no extraterritorial effect.

The court should adopt a restrictive approach to the application of **art.** 5 (*Kleinwort Benson Ltd v Glasgow City Council* [1999] 1 AC 153). Applying this principle, it is the place where the tortious event takes place that matters for **art.** 5(3), not the place where the decision is made to commit the tort (*Anton Durbeck GmbH v Den Norske Bank ASA* [2002] EWHC 1173 (Comm), LTL 17/6/2002, point not considered on appeal). Although the decision (in this case, to arrest a ship in Panama, which was alleged to be wrongful interference with goods), which was made in England, was a connecting factor with England, it was not a 'particularly close connecting factor'.

Article 5(3) confers jurisdiction in an action seeking a declaration of non-liability in tort (*Folien Fischer AG v Ritrama SpA* (case C-133/11) [2013] 2 WLR 373).

Criminal compensation

16.30 Where a civil claim is made based on an act giving rise to criminal proceedings, jurisdiction is given by **art.** 5(4) of the **Brussels I Regulation** to the courts of the country dealing with the criminal proceedings.

Branches, agencies and establishments

16.31 **Article** 5(5) of the **Brussels I Regulation** provides that alternative jurisdiction is given as regards disputes arising out of the operations of a branch, agency or other establishment to the courts for the place in which the branch, agency or other establishment is situated. This provision has been restrictively interpreted. From the Jenard Report and the opinion of the advocate general in *Etablissements A. de Bloos SPRL v SCA Bouyer* (case 14/76) [1976] ECR 1497 it is accepted that the branch, agency or other establishment referred to must be that of the proposed defendant, and the claimant's arrangements in this respect are irrelevant. Further, the mere fact that some person in the country where the claimant wishes to commence proceedings acted as the proposed defendant's agent for the purposes of the law of agency is not enough, on its own, to satisfy **art. 5(5)**. 'Agency' must be interpreted *eiusdem generis* with 'branch' and 'establishment'. The effect is that **art. 5(5)** is dealing with emanations of the defendant's business which are subject to the defendant's control and which give the defendant a corporate presence within the relevant jurisdiction. Even if the defendant does have a branch, agency or establishment within the meaning of **art. 5(5)**, it is further necessary that the dispute must arise out of the activities of that branch, agency or establishment. This will comprehend, according to *Somafer SA v Saar-Ferngas AG* (case 33/78) [1978] ECR 2183, the following types of activities by the branch, agency or establishment:

(a) management matters, such as the local engagement of staff;
(b) contractual undertakings given in the name of the parent;
(c) tortious and other non-contractual liability.

If a dispute arises out of the operations of a branch, there is no further requirement that the obligation in question must be performed in the State where the branch is situated. So, in *Lloyd's Register of Shipping v Société Campenon Bernard* (case C-439/93) [1995] ECR I-961 the claimant entered into a contract with the French branch of the defendant under which the defendant agreed to do certain work in Spain. The work was carried out by the defendant's Spanish branch. A dispute arose, and proceedings were commenced in France, the claimant relying on **art. 5(5)**. The CJEU held the proceedings had been validly commenced in France, and there was no requirement in **art. 5(5)** for performance to be in the State where proceedings were commenced.

It was held in *Anton Durbeck GmbH v Den Norske Bank ASA* [2003] EWCA Civ 147, [2003] QB 1160, applying *Lloyd's Register of Shipping v Société Campenon Bernard* (case C-439/93) [1995] ECR I-961, that there has to be a nexus between the operations of the branch and the dispute to render it natural to describe the dispute as arising out of the operations of the branch. It is, however, unnecessary for the activities of the branch to bring about the harmful event giving rise to the dispute. In contract claims the nexus required could be derived from the negotiations giving rise to the contract. Tort claims vary widely, so whether the necessary nexus exists depends on the facts of the particular case.

Trusts

A settlor, trustee or beneficiary of a trust created by the operation of a statute, or by a written instrument, or created orally and evidenced in writing, may be joined as a party to proceedings brought in the courts of the country where the trust is domiciled (**Brussels I Regulation, art. 5(6)**. This form of wording excludes implied and constructive trusts. The word 'trustee' in **art. 5(6)** has to be restrictively construed. It does not extend to persons such as appointors, or protectors, or to any other person with fiduciary powers who does not come within the normal meaning of the expression 'trustee' (*Gómez v Gómez-Monche Vives* [2008] EWCA Civ 1065, [2009] Ch 245). The Court of Appeal in this case also considered the mechanism for determining the domicile of a trust. It held that the court had to apply its rules of private international law (**art. 60(3)**). The relevant rule is that a trust is domiciled in England if English law is the system of law with which the trust has its closest and most real connection (Civil Jurisdiction and Judgments Order 2001 (SI 2001/3929), sch. 1, para. 12(3)). Although a choice of English law might not be conclusive, it was very difficult to see what other circumstances would be sufficient to outweigh it, because of the close connection between a trust and its governing law. Here, the fact that the trust had no other connection with England, that it was 16.32

Commentary

administered elsewhere, that the trustees and beneficiaries were resident elsewhere and that the assets were located elsewhere did not outweigh the connection made by virtue of the choice of law.

Salvage and freight

16.33 Under **art. 5(7)** of the **Brussels I Regulation** claims for freight or salvage of cargo may be brought where the freight or cargo has been or could be arrested.

Co-defendants

16.34 It is provided by **art. 6(1)** of the **Brussels I Regulation** that a person domiciled in a member State may also be sued, 'where he is one of a number of defendants, in the courts for the place where any one of them is domiciled'. This is followed by a proviso that the claims must be so closely connected that it is expedient to hear and determine them together to avoid the risk of irreconcilable judgments resulting from separate proceedings. In order to use this provision to join persons domiciled outside England and Wales to a claim against a person domiciled in England and Wales there must, first of all, be a valid claim against the defendant domiciled within the jurisdiction (the 'anchor defendant') (*The Rewia* [1991] 2 Lloyd's Rep 325) and the proposed co-defendant (*Brown v Innovatorone plc* [2010] EWHC 2281 (Comm), [2011] ILPr 9). The anchor defendant must have been domiciled here at the time the claim was issued (*Canada Trust Co. v Stolzenberg (No. 2)* [2002] 1 AC 1). It is then necessary to consider whether the joinder is valid. The nature of the connection justifying joinder of a defendant not domiciled in England is given an independent Community meaning, and it is not necessarily enough that the joinder satisfies **CPR, r. 7.3** (for which see **14.2**) (*Kalfelis v Bankhaus Schröder, Münchmeyer, Hengst & Co.* (case 189/87) [1988] ECR 5565). According to the CJEU, the proper use of art. 6(1) of the Brussels Convention is to avoid the risk of irreconcilable judgments and to prevent related actions proceeding in different contracting States. The proviso added to the Regulation makes this principle explicit. In order for decisions to be regarded as contradictory, it has been held that it is not sufficient that there be a divergence in the outcome of the dispute, that divergence must also arise in the context of the same situation of law and fact (*Roche Nederland BV v Primus* (case C-539/03) [2006] ECR 1-6335). A difference in legal basis between the claims brought against a number of defendants is, however, just one factor, it does not preclude the application of the **Brussels I Regulation, art. 6(1)** (*Painer v Standard VerlagsGmbH* (case C-145/10) CJEU judgment 1 December 2011).

The Court of Appeal held in *Masri v Consolidated Contractors International (UK) Ltd* [2005] EWCA Civ 1436, [2006] 1 WLR 830, that there is nothing in **art. 6(1)** which requires the close connection to be in relation to a single set of proceedings. In this case, there were two separate sets of proceedings: claim 1, against English domiciled defendants, and claim 2, against a number of defendants who were not domiciled in England. The Court of Appeal upheld the decision of the judge at first instance that the two claims were so closely connected that it was expedient to hear them together and that this was a sufficient basis for **art. 6(1)** to apply and for the two claims to be consolidated.

The CJEU has held in *Freeport plc v Arnoldsson* (case C-98/06) [2008] QB 634) that **art. 6(1)** applies to claims based on different causes of action (e.g. contract and tort). All that is required is that the claims are sufficiently close to make it expedient to determine them together in order to avoid the risk of irreconcilable judgments. The court went on to hold that, provided the necessary connection exists, there is no need for the claimant to establish that the claims have not been brought in order to oust the jurisdiction of the courts where any of the defendants is domiciled. In *Cooper Tire and Rubber Co. v Shell Chemicals UK Ltd* [2009] EWHC 2609 (Comm), [2009] 2 CLC 619, Teare J noted that it was alleged that three of the defendants in a claim had been selected as a tactical device to establish jurisdiction against other defendants. He said that appeared to be likely, but the question was whether it was a tactic which succeeded. On the facts, there was a good arguable case against the anchor defendants, so jurisdiction was established. Alternate or contingent claims also fall within **art. 6(1)**. **Article 6(1)** requires an examination of the claim as a whole and where a contingent or alternate claim is inextricably linked with the anchor claim, it is right to hear them together in order to avoid the risk of inconsistent judgments (*FKI Engineering Ltd v De Wind Holdings Ltd* [2008] EWCA Civ 316, [2009] 1 All ER (Comm) 118).

Article 6(1) does not apply where the claimant seeking to invoke it does not have a claim against the anchor defendant, but another claimant with a similar claim is suing both the anchor defendant and the defendant challenging jurisdiction (*Madoff Securities International Ltd v Raven* [2011] EWHC 3102 (Comm), [2012] 2 All ER (Comm) 634).

In *Gard Marine and Energy Ltd v Tunnicliffe* [2009] EWHC 2388 (Comm), [2010] Lloyd's Rep IR 62, it was held that it did not matter that the defendant domiciled in England had been added subsequently to the proceedings.

The court also has a discretion whether to permit a party to be joined to proceedings, because **arts 6** and **24** do not give an absolute right (see **14.84**; **CPR, r. 19.2**; *Dornoch Ltd v Westminster International BV* [2009] EWHC 201 (Admlty), [2009] Lloyd's Rep IR 540).

Commentary

Counterclaims and Part 20 proceedings

By **art. 6(2)** and **(3)** of the **Brussels I Regulation**, counterclaims arising from the same contract or facts as those founding the claim, and third-party proceedings, may be brought in the court in which the claimant's claim is pending. In the case of third-party proceedings, this does not apply if the initial proceedings were instituted solely with the object of removing the third-party claim from the jurisdiction of the court which would otherwise be competent. The nexus required for bringing claims under **CPR, Part 20** (see **chapter 29**), is likely to be sufficient to justify the special jurisdiction granted by **art. 6(2)** (*Kinnear v Falconfilms NV* [1996] 1 WLR 920) but this will not always be the case (*Waterford Wedgwood plc v David Nagli Ltd* [1998] CLC 1011). It needs to be demonstrated that there is a close connection between the original proceedings and the third-party proceedings so as to fulfil the objective of **art. 6(2)** of securing the rational and efficient disposal of trials and the avoidance of the risk of irreconcilable judgments (*Barton v Golden Sun Holidays Ltd* [2007] EWHC 3455 (QB), [2007] ILPr 57; *Shetty v Al Rushaid Petroleum Investment Co.* [2011] EWHC 1460 (Ch), LTL 14/6/2011). A cross-claim made by a party who was not an original defendant to the claim is not within the definition of **art. 6(3)** (*Dollfus Mieg et Cie v CDW International Ltd* (2003) [2004] ILPr 12). **16.35**

At first instance, it has been held that a contribution notice under **CPR, r. 20.6**, is not a claim form and cannot be served outside the jurisdiction (*Knauf UK GmbH v British Gypsum Ltd* [2002] EWHC 739 (Comm), [2002] 2 Lloyd's Rep 416). Further, a contribution notice will be set aside if the defendant served with the notice ceases to be a defendant by an order setting aside service on that defendant (*Knauf UK GmbH v British Gypsum Ltd*).

Lis pendens

Article 27 of the **Brussels I Regulation** provides: **16.36**

(1) Where proceedings involving the same cause of action and between the same parties are brought in the courts of different member States, any court other than the court first seised shall of its own motion stay its proceedings until such time as the jurisdiction of the court first seised is established.

(2) Where the jurisdiction of the court first seised is established, any court other than the court first seised shall decline jurisdiction in favour of that court.

This article is designed to prevent parallel proceedings before the courts of different contracting States, and to avoid the conflicts that might otherwise result. It is to be interpreted broadly, and covers all situations of *lis pendens,* irrespective of the parties' domicile (*Overseas Union Insurance Ltd v New Hampshire Insurance Co.* (case C-351/89) [1992] QB 434; *West Tankers Inc. v Allianz SpA* (case C-185/07) [2009] AC 1138). **Article 27** envisages that the court will stay the proceedings as a whole, rather than deal with each claim separately (*WMS Gaming Inc. v B Plus Giocolegale Ltd* [2011] EWHC 2620 (Comm), [2012] ILPr 5). The phrase 'proceedings involving the same cause of action' must be given an independent Community meaning (*Gubisch Maschinenfabrik KG v Palumbo* (case 144/86) [1987] ECR 4861). The article obviously covers the situation where a claimant brings identical proceedings in two countries. It also covers the situation where a claimant brings proceedings in one country for a declaration that there has been no breach of a contract and the defendant to that action brings proceedings in another country claiming damages for breach of that contract (see *The Maciej Rataj* (case C-406/92) [1994] ECR I-5439). It even covers a case where one party to a contract brings an action for rescission of a contract and the other party to the contract brings proceedings in another country to enforce the same contract. The key question is whether the two claims have the same cause and object. Competing claims in England and Greece arising out of the same facts but with a different cause of action (breach of contract on the one hand, and tort and breach of statutory duty on the other) did not come within **art. 27** (*Underwriting Members of Lloyd's Syndicate 980 v Sinco SA* [2008] EWHC 1842 (Comm), [2008] 2 CLC 187). However, **art. 27** only operates to the extent that the parties to the second claim are the same as those in the first. The term 'the same parties' in **art. 27** has an independent Community meaning and in considering whether two entities are the same party, the court will look to the substance, not the form. The same parties can include separate legal entities. Whether they are the same parties for this purpose may depend on whether a judgment against one of them would have the force of *res judicata* as against the other. It will also depend on whether their interests are identical and indissociable. It is for the national court to ascertain whether this is the case (*Kolden Holdings Ltd v Rodette Commerce Ltd* [2008] EWCA Civ 10, [2008] Bus LR 1051; *Cooper Tire and Rubber Co. v Shell Chemicals UK Ltd* [2009] EWHC 2609 (Comm), [2009] 2 CLC 619; *UBS Ltd v Regione Calabria* [2012] EWHC 699 (Comm), [2012] ILPr 22).

16.37 **Court first seised** Priority under the **Brussels I Regulation, art. 27,** is given to the court 'first seised'. An English court becomes seised when a claim form (or other originating process) is lodged at court for issue, unless the claimant fails to effect service (**art. 30(1)**). There is no obligation to serve 'forthwith' or 'as soon as practicable'. The claimant simply has to serve within the time allowed under **CPR, r. 7.5** (*UBS AG v Kommunale Wasserwerke Leipzig GmbH* [2010] EWHC 2566 (Comm), [2010] 2 CLC 499).

Slightly different rules apply in some other Regulation States (**art. 30(2)**) where domestic law requires the originating process to be served before being lodged in court. In such cases the court becomes seised when the document is received by the authority responsible for service, provided the claimant has not subsequently failed to take any required steps to lodge the document with the court. It is not the case that for a court to be seised of a claim under **art. 30(2)** the defendant must have been validly served (*WPP Holdings Italy SRL v Benatti* [2007] EWCA Civ 263, [2007] 1 WLR 2316). All that is required is that a document capable of being served has been lodged at court, so as to institute proceedings. Thus, the fact that an Italian writ was lodged at the court office for service without the requisite translation did not prevent the Italian court being seised for the purposes of **art. 30(2)** on the date it was filed at court. Non-payment of a court fee can, however, amount to a failure to take a step required for effective service (*Debt Collect London Ltd v SK Slavia Praha-Fotball AS* [2010] EWCA Civ 1250, [2011] 1 WLR 866). Where proceedings are amended or a party is added, the court will consider the court in which that particular claim was first brought or that party was first sued to be the court first seised, even if the proceedings overall were first commenced in a different State. The position is different under **art. 28** (see **16.38**) (*Striborg Ltd v FKI Engineering Ltd* [2011] EWCA Civ 622, [2011] Bus LR 1410).

The court has power to make an order in relation to service under **CPR, r. 3.10** (power to remedy an error) and/or **r. 6.16** (power to dispense with service), even if the effect is to give the English court priority (*Phillips v Symes (No. 3)* [2008] UKHL 1, [2008] 1 WLR 180). Such an order is not retrospective validation of service, but a declaration that the previous service was valid and effective. The facts of the case were that the claim form (but not the translation into German) was removed from the service pack by the Swiss court, because it was mistakenly marked 'not for service out of the jurisdiction'. The Swiss defendant challenged service and issued proceedings before the Swiss court for a negative declaration. The House of Lords held that as the error was that of the Swiss court, and had resulted in no prejudice to the defendant, who was able to read the German translation of the claim form, it was appropriate to exercise its discretion under **rr. 3.10** and **6.16** with the result that the English court was seised of the proceedings on the date of service, before proceedings were issued in Switzerland.

Where an action is brought in one country, and the defendant to that action brings a second action in another country and alleges that the courts of the country first seised have no jurisdiction under the **Brussels I Regulation**, the second court may either decline jurisdiction or stay its proceedings to await the outcome of any challenge made to the jurisdiction of the first court. What the second court is not allowed to do is to investigate the jurisdiction of the first court (*Overseas Union Insurance Ltd v New Hampshire Insurance Co.* (case C-351/89) [1992] QB 434; *West Tankers Inc. v Allianz SpA* (case C-185/07) [2009] AC 1138). This is so even where there is a choice-of-forum clause conferring jurisdiction on the second court, and even where there are excessive delays in the first court (*Erich Gasser GmbH v MISAT Srl* (case C-116/02) [2005] QB 1). There is a possible exception if the second court has exclusive jurisdiction under **art. 22** (*Speed Investments Ltd v Formula One Holdings Ltd (No. 2)* [2004] EWCA Civ 1512, [2005] 1 WLR 1936).

This has given rise to problems in practice as considerable delay can be caused by the need to wait for the court first seised to determine whether it has jurisdiction, particularly where proceedings have been started in a country where there is no mechanism for jurisdiction to be considered as a preliminary issue. For legal proceedings instituted on or after 10 January 2015, the recast Brussels I Regulation will resolve this issue. Where there is an exclusive jurisdiction clause in favour of a member State, proceedings brought in another member State must be stayed until the chosen court has ruled upon its jurisdiction. This is regardless of which proceedings are commenced first in time, although proceedings must have actually been commenced before the chosen court. Where there is an agreement to arbitrate, each member State will have the right to refer parties to arbitration, stay or dismiss proceedings and examine whether an arbitration agreement is null, void or inoperative or incapable of being performed. This is regardless of whether it is the court first seised. (See Regulation (EU) No. 1215/2012, art. 31 and recitals 22 and 12.)

Commentary

Related actions

Article 28 of the **Brussels I Regulation** provides: **16.38**

(1) Where related actions are pending in the courts of different member States, any court other than the court first seised may stay its proceedings…

(3) For the purposes of this article, actions are deemed to be related where they are so closely connected that it is expedient to hear and determine them together to avoid the risk of irreconcilable judgments resulting from separate proceedings.

Article 28 deals with the area between situations where two claims are the same (where the second claim must be stayed under **art. 27**) and situations where it is right for two claims to proceed at the same time. In considering whether to grant a stay, the court must apply the test set out in the article, which is designed to cover a range of circumstances. The purpose of **art. 28** is to harmonise courts' jurisdiction and avoid irreconcilable judgments (*Sarrio SA v Kuwait Investment Authority* [1999] 1 AC 32).

The court is given a discretion under **art. 28** to assess the degree of connection between the two claims and the risk of inconsistent judgments. The fact that there is some measure of risk does not mean that proceedings are inevitably related. **Article 28** leaves it open to a court to acknowledge a connection, or a risk of inconsistent judgments, but to say that the connection is not sufficiently close, or the risk is not sufficiently great, to make the actions related for the purposes of the article (*Research in Motion UK Ltd v Visto Corporation* [2008] EWCA Civ 153, [2008] 2 All ER (Comm) 560). It would cover a claim *in rem* and a claim *in personam* in respect of the same loss, where technically the parties are not the same (*The Sylt* [1991] 1 Lloyd's Rep 240). It was conceded in *Dresser UK Ltd v Falcongate Freight Management Ltd* [1992] QB 502 that it would cover proceedings for limitation of liability for loss of cargo at sea and a claim for damages for the loss of the same cargo. Once it is held that proceedings are related, the court has a discretion whether to grant a stay.

It is unclear whether an action which is subject to the **Brussels I Regulation** and an action subject to Regulation (EC) No. 1346/2000 on insolvency proceedings can be related for the purposes of the **Brussels I Regulation, art. 28** (see *Rahman v GMAC Commercial Finance Ltd* [2012] EWCA Civ 1467, [2013] ILPr 5).

In *Cooper Tire and Rubber Co. v Shell Chemicals UK Ltd* [2009] EWHC 2609 (Comm), [2009] 2 CLC 619, there was a clear risk of conflicting decisions by the English and Italian courts. The court declined, however, to grant a stay under **art. 28** having examined three matters relevant to the exercise of the discretion:

(a) the extent of the relatedness and the risk of mutually irreconcilable decisions (the Italian proceedings had been dismissed at first instance although experts agreed an appeal was likely to succeed);
(b) the stage reached in each set of proceedings (the Italian proceedings were no further advanced and English proceedings were likely to be determined more quickly); and
(c) the proximity of the courts to the subject matter of the case (there was a significant connection with Italy, connections with England were slight but the centre of gravity of the case was not in Italy — the case concerned a cartel allegedly operating in several countries).

Where proceedings become related by amendment, the court first seised for the purposes of **art. 28** will be the court where the proceedings first in time were commenced. The position is different under **art. 27** (see **16.37**) (*Striborg Ltd v FKI Engineering Ltd* [2011] EWCA Civ 622, [2011] Bus LR 1410). In *Striborg* proceedings were commenced in Germany and then subsequently in England. The German proceedings did not include a claim for the purchase price of certain assets when commenced, but were subsequently amended so as to put the payment of the purchase price in issue. This took place after the commencement of the English proceedings which claimed payment of the purchase price. The Court of Appeal decided that the test is not which court was first seised of the issue which makes the claims related as at the date of the application. The test is whether the claims were related as at the date of the application. If so, which action was commenced first in time? Adopting this approach the German court was the court first seised and the English court therefore had the power to stay its proceedings. *Striborg* did not involve a new cause of action or new party, so it is not clear whether the same principles would apply in those circumstances.

It is unclear whether there is a power to stay proceedings in favour of a non-member State where an identical or related action is pending there, i.e. whether **arts 27** and **28** can be given so-called reflexive effect. See **16.73** for further consideration of this issue.

Interim relief

16.39 The **CJJA 1982, s. 25(1)** and the Civil Jurisdiction and Judgments Act 1982 (Interim Relief) Order 1997 (SI 1997/302) confer on the High Court in England power to grant interim relief in the absence of substantive proceedings, provided proceedings have been or will be commenced in another jurisdiction (see **38.6**).

Section 25 is not confined to freezing injunctions, **subsection** (7) defining 'interim relief' as relief of any kind which the court has power to grant in proceedings within its jurisdiction other than warrants for arrest and orders for obtaining evidence.

PROCEDURE ON COMMENCING PROCEEDINGS PURSUANT TO THE REGULATION OR CONVENTIONS

A claim form may be served on a defendant out of the jurisdiction, without the court's permission, if each claim being made against that defendant can be determined by the court under **CJJA 1982** or the Lugano Convention (**CPR, r. 6.33(1)**), or the **Brussels I Regulation** (**CPR, r. 6.33(2)**) or any other enactment (**r. 6.33(3)**). **Rule 6.32** makes separate provision for service of the claim form without permission in Scotland and Northern Ireland. **16.40**

The only formality is that the claimant must file and serve with the claim form a notice (form N510) containing a statement of the grounds on which the claimant is entitled to serve out of the jurisdiction (**r. 6.34(1); PD 6B, para. 2.1**). This statement replaces the jurisdiction endorsement which until October 2008 was required to be included on a claim form for service out of the jurisdiction. The claim form may not be served out of the jurisdiction until the statement of grounds is filed, unless the court gives permission (**CPR, r. 6.34(2)**). Regard should also be had to the provisions in the Queen's Bench Guide (para. 4.4) and the Commercial Court Guide when the proceedings have been or are to be issued in those courts. Incorrect completion of form N510 will not necessarily mean the claimant is unable to rely on the relevant provisions of the Regulation (*DSG International Sourcing Ltd v Universal Media Corporation (Slovakia) sro* [2011] EWHC 1116 (Comm), [2011] ILPr 33).

JURISDICTION UNDER THE COMMON LAW RULES

The rules discussed at **16.42** to **16.54** deal with the situation where it is desired to serve English proceedings on a defendant outside the jurisdiction in proceedings outside the scope of the **Brussels I Regulation** or the Brussels and Lugano Conventions. Permission is required from the court in those circumstances. A claimant may either issue his claim form for service abroad first and then apply for permission to serve (in which case the court will stamp the claim form on issue 'not for service out of the jurisdiction' and a concurrent claim form must be issued when permission is granted) or he may apply for permission both to issue the claim form and to serve it out of the jurisdiction (Queen's Bench Guide, para. 4.4.11). **16.41**

Basic principles governing applications for permission

The requirements that need to be satisfied if the English courts are to grant permission to serve proceedings outside the jurisdiction under the court's assumed jurisdiction were set out by Lord Collins in *AK Investment CJSC v Kyrgyz Mobil Tel Ltd* [2011] UKPC 7, [2011] 4 All ER 1027. The intending claimant must establish that: **16.42**

(a) There is a serious issue to be tried on the merits, i.e., a substantial question of fact or law or both. The current practice in England is that this is the same test as for summary judgment, namely, whether there is a real (as opposed to a fanciful) prospect of success (e.g., *Carvill America Inc. v Camperdown UK Ltd* [2005] EWCA Civ 645, [2005] 2 Lloyd's Rep 457). Where a question of law goes to the existence of jurisdiction, the court will normally decide it, rather than treating it as a question of whether there is a good arguable case (*E. F. Hutton and Co. (London) Ltd v Mofarrij* [1989] 1 WLR 488; *Chellaram v Chellaram (No. 2)* [2002] EWHC 632 (Ch), [2002] 3 All ER 17).

(b) There is a good arguable case that the claim falls within one or more classes of case in which permission to serve out may be given, i.e., it falls within one of the 20 grounds set out in **PD 6B, para. 3.1**. These are discussed at **16.44** to **16.52**. In this context, good arguable case connotes that one side has a much better argument than the other (*Canada Trust Co. v Stolzenberg (No. 2)* [1998] 1 WLR 547, [2002] 1 AC 1; *Bols Distilleries BV v Superior Yacht Services Ltd* [2006] UKPC 45, [2007] 1 WLR 12).

(c) In all the circumstances England is clearly or distinctly the appropriate forum for the trial of the dispute and that in all the circumstances the court ought to exercise its discretion to permit service of the proceedings out of the jurisdiction. This is considered further at **16.53**.

Obviously, putting a foreigner to the inconvenience of defending an action in this country is a serious matter, so the courts have always exercised the power to allow service abroad with caution.

Procedure on seeking permission

16.43 An application for permission to serve a claim form out of the jurisdiction, or to issue a claim form for service out of the jurisdiction, should be made without notice under **CPR, Part 23**. There will be no hearing. The papers are lodged in the appropriate court office and the claimant is later notified of the court's decision. A refusal to grant permission can be appealed. If permission is granted and the defendant considers that it should not have been, he can challenge the court's jurisdiction (see **chapter 19**).

The evidence in support of the application for permission must state, according to **CPR, r. 6.37**:

(a) which ground in **PD 6B, para. 3.1** is relied on;
(b) that the claimant believes that the claim has a reasonable prospect of success;
(c) the defendant's address, or, if that is not known, in what place the defendant is or is likely to be found;
(d) where the application is made under **PD 6B, para. 3.1(3)** (that the defendant is a necessary or proper party), the grounds for believing that there is a real issue between the claimant and the existing defendant which it is reasonable for the court to try.

The procedure is summarised in **procedural checklist 11**, at the front of the book.

Because service out of the jurisdiction is an assertion of extraterritorial jurisdiction which could have international repercussions, it was the rule under RSC, ord. 11, that irregularities should be cured only in exceptional cases (*Camera Care Ltd v Victor Hasselblad* AB [1986] 1 FTLR 348). In *Ophthalmic Innovations International (UK) Ltd v Ophthalmic Innovations International Inc.* [2004] EWHC 2948 (Ch), LTL 4/1/2005, Lawrence Collins J stated that the same principle applies under the CPR.

As the application is made initially without notice, the claimant is under an obligation to make full and frank disclosure of all material facts. In deciding whether that duty has been complied with, the primary question is whether in all the circumstances the effect of the evidence in support of the application is such as to mislead the court in any material respect concerning its jurisdiction and the discretion under the rules (*BP Exploration Co. (Libya) Ltd v Hunt* [1976] 1 WLR 788). The existence of overlapping proceedings in a foreign jurisdiction between the same or related parties (whether pending or prospective) is likely to be a particularly relevant matter which in normal circumstances must be disclosed, and the non-disclosure of which may well lead to the order for permission being set aside (*Konamaneni v Rolls-Royce Industrial Power (India) Ltd* [2002] 1 WLR 1269). The failure fully to disclose concurrent proceedings in the United States in the witness statement in support of the claimant's application to serve out of the jurisdiction was one reason why service was ordered to be set aside in *Ophthalmic*

Innovations International (UK) Ltd v Ophthalmic Innovations International Inc. [2004] EWHC 2948 (Ch), LTL 4/1/2005.

It seems it is possible to apply retrospectively under the CPR for permission to serve out of the jurisdiction, after service has been effected without permission and even after the six-month time limit for service has expired (*Nesheim v Kosa* [2006] EWHC 2710 (Ch), [2007] WTLR 149). Although the CPR are silent on the point, the court held that authority is to be found in the pre-CPR case of *National Justice Compania Naviera SA v Prudential Assurance Co. Ltd (No. 2)* [2000] 1 WLR 603.

Grounds for granting permission

General interpretation The grounds in **PD 6B, para. 3**, were formerly in RSC, ord. 11, r. 1(1), and have been amended several times over the years. The grounds were reformulated in 1983 and again in 2000, so some caution is necessary with earlier case law. However, it is likely that case law on the basic principles governing applications for permission to serve a claim form out of the jurisdiction remains valid. **16.44**

As **PD 6B, para. 3**, allows the court to exercise an exorbitant jurisdiction, its provisions are to be strictly construed in favour of the foreigner (*The Hagen* [1908] P 189). It appears that in order to establish one of the grounds it is not necessary to come within the 'spirit' as well as the letter of the rule, although this may be relevant to the exercise of discretion if one of the grounds is established (*Sharab v Prince Al-Waleed bin Talal bin Abdal-Aziz-Al-Saud* [2009] EWCA Civ 353, [2009] 2 Lloyd's Rep 160; *Johnson v Taylor Bros and Co.* [1920] AC 144; *Beck v Value Capital Ltd (No. 2)* [1975] 1 WLR 6). Service out is not allowed unless each claim falls into one or other of the grounds set out in the rule (*Holland v Leslie* [1894] 2 QB 346). Although the claimant can choose which ground or grounds to rely on (*Matthews v Kuwait Bechtel Corporation* [1959] 2 QB 57), the claimant must specifically state those grounds in the evidence in support of the application.

Before the CPR came into force, a claimant could not rely on alternative causes of action to sustain an order for service out of the jurisdiction in addition to the causes of action relied upon to obtain permission, unless, possibly, the alternative basis had been specifically referred to in affidavit evidence (*Metall und Rohstoff AG v Donaldson Lufkin and Jenrette Inc.* [1990] 1 QB 391). The Supreme Court has, however, disapproved of this approach in *NML Capital Ltd v Argentina* [2011] UKSC 31, [2011] 2 AC 495, albeit obiter. In *VTB Capital plc v Nutritek International Corporation* [2011] EWHC 3107 (Ch), LTL 5/12/2011, Arnold J considered he was not bound by post-CPR cases which suggested *Metal und Rohstoff* remained good law (*E. D. and F. Man Sugar Ltd v Lendoudis* [2007] EWHC 2268 (Comm), [2008] 1 All ER 952; *Pacific International Sports Clubs Ltd v Soccer Marketing International Ltd* [2009] EWHC 1839 (Ch), LTL 30/7/2009) but his comments were also obiter.

An application, made before the end of the six months allowed for service of a claim form, for permission to serve it out of the jurisdiction is governed by **CPR, r. 6.33**, and **PD 6B, para. 3**, not by **CPR, r. 7.6(3)** (*Anderton v Clwyd County Council (No. 2)* [2002] EWCA Civ 933, [2002] 1 WLR 3174).

Domicile (PD 6B, para. 3.1(1)) A claim form may be served out of the jurisdiction if the claim is for a remedy against a person domiciled within the jurisdiction (**PD 6B, para. 3.1(1)**). **Article 2** of the **Brussels I Regulation** permits a person to be sued where domiciled, and, by **CPR, r. 6.31(1)(i)**, domicile for the purposes of **Part 6, Section IV**, is to be determined: **16.45**

(a) in relation to EU States, in accordance with the **Brussels I Regulation** and the Civil Jurisdiction and Judgments Order 2001 (SI 2001/3929), sch. 1, paras 9 to 12, and
(b) in relation to Aruba, French overseas departments, Iceland, Norway and Switzerland, by the rules in the **CJJA 1982, ss. 41 to 46**.

This provision is of little practical significance as in cases coming within the **Brussels I Regulation** or the Brussels or Lugano Conventions permission to serve outside the jurisdiction on defendants domiciled within the jurisdiction is not required.

16.46 **Injunctions and interim relief (PD 6B, para. 3.1(2) and (5))** The injunction referred to in **PD 6B, para. 3.1(2)**, has to be final as opposed to interim (*The Siskina* [1979] AC 210). The injunction must be the real form of relief sought, and must not simply be tacked on in order to found jurisdiction (*Rosler v Hilbery* [1925] Ch 250).

However, the **CJJA 1982, s. 25(1)** (see **16.39**), enables the court to grant interim relief in the absence of substantive proceedings, regardless of whether the defendant is domiciled in a country which is a party to the **Brussels I Regulation** or the Brussels or Lugano Conventions. Since **PD 6B, para. 3.1(2)**, applies only to final injunctions, **para. 3.1(5)** enables the court to permit service out of the jurisdiction in such cases where the defendant is not resident in an EU or Convention country.

16.47 **Necessary or proper party** **PD 6B, para. 3.1(3)**, may be compared with **art. 6(1)** of the **Brussels I Regulation** (**16.34**). It is no longer a requirement, as it was under RSC, ord. 11, that the claim form be served before making the application to join a defendant as a necessary or proper party. The ground in **PD 6B, para. 3.1(3)**, applies where 'a claim is made against a person... on whom the claim form has been or will be served (otherwise than in reliance on this paragraph)'. The words in parentheses were added with effect from 1 October 2004. They make clear that **PD 6B, para. 3.1(3)**, only permits the claimant to join a defendant to proceedings brought against another defendant against whom jurisdiction can be established in reliance on some other provision. The claimant's evidence must depose to the grounds for believing that there is an arguable case that there is a real issue which it is reasonable for the court to try between the claimant and the defendant (see **16.43**). Once this has been established, the claimant must further show that the second defendant is a necessary or proper party to the action. There is particular reluctance to allow service under this paragraph given its anomaly (in relation to the other grounds) in not being founded upon any territorial connection between the claim and the jurisdiction of the English courts (*Multinational Gas and Petrochemical Co. v Multinational Gas and Petrochemical Services Ltd* [1983] Ch 258). However, a claim against a foreign defendant could be brought under the old RSC, ord. 11, provided it was bona fide and constituted a good cause of action, even if the predominant reason for including the English defendant was to found an application against a foreign defendant (*Multinational Gas and Petrochemical Co. v Multinational Gas and Petrochemical Services Ltd* [1983] Ch 258). This approach was followed under the CPR by *Credit Agricole Indosuez v Unicof Ltd* [2003] EWHC 2676 (Comm), [2004] 1 Lloyd's Rep 196. In *AK Investment CJSC v Kyrgyz Mobil Tel Ltd* [2011] UKPC 7, [2011] 4 All ER 1027, the Privy Council stated that the fact that the anchor defendant is sued only for the purpose of adding the foreign defendants is a factor in the exercise of discretion and not an element in the question whether the action was properly brought against the anchor defendant, provided there is a viable claim against him.

In *United Film Distribution Ltd v Chhabria* [2001] EWCA Civ 416, [2001] 2 All ER (Comm) 865, the Court of Appeal held that the ground for serving a defendant out of the jurisdiction, that it is a necessary or proper party, is the same as would justify adding a party to existing proceedings under **CPR, r. 19.2**. The court's power to add a party under **r. 19.2** is no narrower than it was under its predecessors, RSC, ord. 15, rr. 4.4(1) and 6(2)(b). Where, as in this case, the claims give rise to common questions of fact and arise out of the same series of transactions, permission would be granted. The decision in *United Film Distribution Ltd v Chhabria* has been followed in *Trumann Investment Group Ltd v Societe Generale SA* [2004] EWHC 1769 (Ch), LTL 3/9/2004, and in *Philips Domestic Appliances and Personal Care BV v Salton Europe Ltd* [2004] EWHC 2092 (Ch), (2004) LTL 30/7/2004. However, in *Konkola Copper Mines plc v Coromin Ltd (No. 2)* [2006] EWHC 1093 (Comm), [2006] 2 Lloyd's Rep 446, the Commercial Court refused to permit service out of the jurisdiction, even though the claims against the party sought to be served arose out of the same facts and series of transactions, where to do so would be in contradiction of a foreign jurisdiction agreement. The case arose out of a mining disaster in Zambia, following which the mine owners made a claim against their Bermudan insurers, under a policy containing an English law and jurisdiction clause. It then obtained an order to serve local Zambian insurers out of the jurisdiction, on the grounds that they were a necessary or proper party under what is now **PD 6B, para. 3.1(3)**, although the relevant insurance policy contained a Zambian law and jurisdiction clause. The court set aside the order for service out of the jurisdiction, holding that the risk of conflicting decisions was not a strong enough reason for overriding the Zambian jurisdiction clause when the claim against the Zambian insurers had no connection with the jurisdiction.

By **PD 6B, para. 3.1(4)**, permission may be given to serve a claim form under **CPR, Part 20**, on persons who are necessary or proper parties to the claim or additional claim.

Contract Claims under **PD 6B, para. 3.1(6)** and (7), presuppose the existence of a contract between the claimant and the defendant. Claims seeking a declaration that such a contract never existed fall instead under **PD 6B, para. 3.1(8)**. **16.48**

PD 6B, para. 3.1(6)(a) (a claim in respect of a contract made within the jurisdiction), has no equivalent in the **Brussels I Regulation** or the Brussels and Lugano Conventions. Whether a contract was made within the jurisdiction depends on general contractual principles (see *Brinkibon Ltd v Stahag Stahl und Stahlwarenhandelsgesellschaft mbH* [1983] 2 AC 34). This case involved an exchange of telexes between parties in different countries. It was held that the contract was made in the country where the telex accepting the offer was received. A contract made within the jurisdiction which is subsequently amended outside the jurisdiction still comes within **PD 6B, para. 3.1(6)**, unless the amendment substitutes a new contract (*BP Exploration Co. (Libya) Ltd v Hunt* [1976] 1 WLR 788; *Sharab v Prince Al-Waleed bin Talal bin Abdal-Aziz-Al-Saud* [2009] EWCA Civ 353, [2009] 2 Lloyd's Rep 160). The words 'in respect of a contract' in **PD 6B, para. 3.1(6)**, do not require that the claim arose under a contract. They require only that the claim relates to or is connected with the contract. The rule therefore includes a claim in restitution for recovery of alleged overpayments under an oral agreement (*Albon v Naza Motor Trading Sdn Bhd* [2007] EWHC 9 (Ch), [2007] 1 WLR 2489). It also includes a claim for a contribution under the **Civil Liability (Contribution) Act 1978, s. 1**, even where the claimant is not a party to a contract and the claim is not brought for breach of contract. A claim (such as for a contribution) will be a claim 'in respect of a contract' within the meaning of **PD 6B, para. 3.1(6)** and (7), if it has a connection with a contract having one of the attributes in **para. 3.1(6)(a)** to **(d)** or a contract broken in England within **para. 3.1(7)**. There is no requirement that the claim has to be in respect of a contract between the claimant and the defendant, because that would be adding words to the rules which are not there (*Greene Wood and McLean v Templeton Insurance Ltd* [2009] EWCA Civ 65, [2009] 1 WLR 2013). A claim to enforce a trust which arose from a contract is also a claim in respect of a contract within **PD 6B, para. 3.1(6)** (*Cherney v Deripaska* [2009] EWCA Civ 849, [2009] 2 CLC 408). Claims 'in respect of a contract' probably do not include *quantum meruit* claims if they are restitutionary and do not derive from a contract (*Sharab v Al-Saud* [2012] EWHC 1798 (Ch), [2012] 2 CLC 612). Where there is more than one contract, the court needs to consider which contract the claim is made in respect of. It is not sufficient that a connected contract meets the jurisdictional gateway (*Global 5000 Ltd v Wadhawan* [2012] EWCA Civ 13, [2012] 2 All ER (Comm) 18).

Unlike the **Brussels I Regulation, art. 5(5)** (see **16.31**), **PD 6B, para. 3.1(6)(b)** (contract made by or through an agent trading or residing within the jurisdiction), is given a wide interpretation, and even includes a case where the defendant's London agent merely sent the claimant the defendant's price list and forwarded the claimant's order to the defendant (*National Mortgage and Agency Co. of New Zealand Ltd v Gosselin* (1922) 38 TLR 832). The 'agent', however, must be that of the defendant, not the claimant (*Union International Insurance Co. Ltd v Jubilee Insurance Co. Ltd* [1991] 1 WLR 415).

There is no equivalent to **PD 6B, para. 3.1(6)(c)**, that the contract is governed by English law, in the **Brussels I Regulation** or the Brussels and Lugano Conventions. The law governing the contract will generally be determined in respect of contracts entered into on or after 17 December 2009 by Regulation (EC) 593/2008 (Rome I). For contracts entered into before that date the rules in the Rome Convention apply, incorporated into UK law by the Contracts (Applicable Law) Act 1990. An express choice of English law clause should not cause difficulties in most cases.

An express jurisdiction clause granting jurisdiction to the English courts (**PD 6B, para. 3.1(6)(d)**) will almost always be given effect by the courts (compare **16.24**), but there are sometimes questions as to whether the dispute arises under a particular agreement where there are a number of interlocking contracts. See *Satyam Computer Services Ltd v Upaid Systems Ltd* [2008] EWCA Civ 487, [2008] 2 All ER (Comm) 465; *UBS AG v HSH Nordbank AG* [2009] EWCA 585, [2009] 2 Lloyds Rep 272; *Sebastian Holdings Inc. v Deutsche Bank AG* [2010] EWCA Civ 998, [2011] 1 Lloyd's Rep 106; *PT Thiess Contractors Indonesia v PT Kaltim Prima Coal* [2011] EWHC 1842 (Comm), LTL 7/2/2012.

PD 6B, para. 3.1(7), breach within the jurisdiction, should be compared with **art. 5(1)** of the **Brussels I Regulation** (see **16.18**). Where the breach consists of a failure to perform a contractual obligation, it is necessary to find the place where performance should have taken place (*Brinkibon Ltd v Stahag Stahl und Stahlwarenhandelsgesellschaft mbH* [1983] 2 AC 34).

16.49 **Tort** Jurisdiction in tort under **PD 6B, para. 3.1(9)** has been modelled on the Regulation and Conventions, **art. 5(3)** (see **16.27**). Jurisdiction may be founded either on the basis of damage being suffered in England or through the tortious act being committed in England. In a case on the meaning of RSC, ord. 11, r. 1(1)(f), predecessor to **PD 6B, para. 3.1(9)**, the Court of Appeal held that it was sufficient if the cause of action in substance arose in England. If separate acts constituting a single tort were committed here and abroad, the question was whether the tort was in substance committed within the jurisdiction (*Metall und Rohstoff AG v Donaldson Lufkin and Jenrette Inc.* [1990] 1 QB 391). In *Booth v Phillips* [2004] EWHC 1437 (Comm), [2004] 1 WLR 3292, the court considered the meaning of the word 'damage' in what is now **PD 6B, para. 3.1(9)**, and stated that it should be given its natural and ordinary meaning. It referred to harm which had been sustained by the claimant, whether physical or economic, and it was sufficient if some damage (not necessarily all of the damage) was sustained within the jurisdiction. There was no requirement that the damage sustained within the jurisdiction should be that which completed the cause of action. *Booth v Phillips* has been followed in *Cooley v Ramsey* [2008] EWHC 129 (QB), [2008] ILPr 27, in which the claimant, a British citizen, had suffered economic loss. He had been left handicapped and unable to work after an accident in Australia. This consequential economic loss in England and Wales was enough to found jurisdiction. Where a computer server located in London was hacked into from outside the jurisdiction, the damage was sustained and the act was committed within the jurisdiction, satisfying both heads of **PD 6B, para. 3.1(9)** (*Ashton Investments Ltd v OJSC Russian Aluminium (RUSAL)* [2006] EWHC 2545 (Comm), [2007] 1 All ER (Comm) 857).

16.50 **Enforcing judgment or arbitral award** **PD 6B, para. 3.1(10)** permits service out of the jurisdiction to enforce a judgment or arbitral award. There is no requirement that assets should be located in the jurisdiction as a prerequisite to an order for service out of the jurisdiction under the rule, although the claimant must show some benefit, even if only an indirect or prospective benefit, accruing to it from the granting of permission (*Tasarruf Mevduatı Sigorta Fonu v Demirel* [2007] EWCA Civ 799, [2007] 1 WLR 2508). Here, the Court of Appeal held that a benefit could be made out by the fact that, unless permission were granted, the defendant would be free to transfer assets into the jurisdiction with impunity after late 2007 when the Turkish judgment which the claimant sought to enforce would become time-barred.

Property **PD 6B, para. 3.1(11)** permits service out of the jurisdiction where the whole subject matter of a claim relates to property located within the jurisdiction. 'Property' is not restricted to land. **16.51**

Trusts The equivalent to **PD 6B, para. 3.1(12)**, in the **Brussels I Regulation** is **art. 5(6)** (see **16.32**). **PD 6B, para. 3.1(12)** may be used against an absconding trustee even after trust assets have been removed from the jurisdiction. Like **art. 5(6)**, **PD 6B, para. 3.1(12)** is restricted to trusts under written instruments. The provision now in **PD 6B, para. 3.1(15)** was added in 1990 to allow claims arising from acts committed within the jurisdiction to be brought in England against constructive trustees who cannot be served within the jurisdiction. There is some uncertainty over the acts needed within the jurisdiction to found jurisdiction under this head (see *NABB Brothers International Ltd v Lloyds Bank International (Guernsey) Ltd* [2005] EWHC 405 (Ch), [2005] ILPr 506). **16.52**

The proper place to bring the claim (*forum conveniens*)

It is provided in **CPR, r. 6.37(3)**, that the court will not give permission for service out of the jurisdiction 'unless satisfied that England and Wales is the proper place in which to bring the claim', i.e. is the *forum conveniens*. The leading case is *Spiliada Maritime Corporation v Cansulex Ltd* [1987] AC 460. The claimant shipowner sought permission to serve English proceedings on Canadian sulphur exporters, claiming damages in respect of severe corrosion to the hold of the claimant's ship, the *Spiliada*, allegedly caused by a cargo of wet sulphur. An almost identical claim, *The Cambridgeshire*, had just reached trial in England. The defendants in both claims were the same, and the claimants in both claims had the same insurer (through subrogation, the insurer rather than the nominal claimants had the real interest in bringing the actions). *The Cambridgeshire* was in the nature of a test case. The scientific investigations made approached the limits of scientific knowledge. The claimant's experts came from England, whereas the defendant had instructed two English and four foreign experts. A total of 15 counsel were instructed, each being armed with 75 files of evidence and documents, and the trial was estimated for six months. Many of the potential witnesses of fact would be Canadian, but many witnesses would come from other places (the *Spiliada* was registered in Liberia). **16.53**

Lord Goff of Chieveley laid down the general principle that the court has to identify the forum in which the case can be most suitably tried in the interests of all the parties and for the ends of justice. The burden of proof rests on the claimant to show that England is clearly the most appropriate place for the trial of the action. Factors to be considered by the court when deciding whether to exercise its discretion to grant permission include the residence or place of business of the parties, the ground invoked by the claimant, the applicable law and the residence and availability of factual and expert witnesses. The weight to be attached to the relevant factors depends on all the circumstances of the case. As Lord Goff said:

> the defendant's place of residence may be no more than a tax haven to which no great importance should be attached. It is also significant to observe that the circumstances specified in ord. 11, r. 1(1), as those in which the court may exercise its discretion to grant leave to serve proceedings on the defendant outside the jurisdiction, are of great variety, ranging from cases where, one would have thought, the discretion would normally be exercised in favour of granting leave (e.g. where the relief sought is an injunction ordering the defendant to do or refrain from doing something within the jurisdiction) to cases where the grant of leave is far more problematical. In addition, the importance to be attached to any particular ground invoked by the plaintiff may vary from case to case. For example, the fact that English law is the putative law of the contract may be of very great importance (as in *BP Exploration Co. (Libya) Ltd v Hunt* [1976] 1 WLR 788, where, in my opinion, Kerr J rightly granted leave to serve proceedings on the defendant out of the jurisdiction); or it may be of little importance as seen in the context of the whole case.

On the facts, the extent and depth of preparation undertaken in *The Cambridgeshire* proceedings, and the fact that English law was the proper law of the contract, meant that England was the appropriate forum, and permission to serve outside the jurisdiction was granted. The doctrine of *forum non conveniens* will be considered further at **16.68** to **16.73**.

An English court may have jurisdiction to hear a derivative claim concerning a foreign company in an appropriate case, and if so, it will give permission for the claim form to be served on the company out of the jurisdiction, because the company is a necessary party to the claim (**PD 6B, para. 3.1(3)**; *Konamaneni v Rolls-Royce Industrial Power (India) Ltd* [2002] 1 WLR 1269). However, the courts of the place of incorporation of a company will almost invariably be the most appropriate forum for determining whether a shareholder may sue on behalf of the company (*Konamaneni v Rolls-Royce Industrial Power (India) Ltd*). In *SMAY Investments Ltd v Sachdev* [2003] EWHC 474 (Ch), [2003] 1 WLR 1973, the court held, following *Konamaneni*, that the appropriate forum for the resolution of a dispute about the ownership of, and investment in, an Indian company was India, despite the existence of an agreement made in England to provide financial assistance to the company. The sort of case where English courts may have jurisdiction to hear a derivative claim concerning a foreign company, are where the company has assets within the jurisdiction, or the acts giving rise to the claim occurred within the jurisdiction. The fact that the claimant lived within the jurisdiction was insufficient to displace the normal rule (*Reeves v Sprecher* [2007] EWHC 117 (Ch), [2007] 2 BCLC 614).

In *King v Lewis* [2004] EWCA Civ 1329, [2005] EMLR 4, the court considered the appropriate forum to hear a claim in relation to a libel published on the Internet. For a tort claim, the starting point for ascertaining the most appropriate forum is to identify the place where the tort was committed. The alleged defamation had occurred in England when the libel had been viewed on a computer here, and permission to serve out had been obtained on the basis of publication here. But the more tenuous the claimant's connection with this jurisdiction (and the more substantial the publication abroad) the weaker this consideration would become. Whilst every case would depend on its own circumstances, the court's discretion would have to be more open-textured in order to give effect to the publisher's choice of a global medium.

In *Novus Aviation Ltd v Onur Air Taşımacılık AŞ* [2009] EWCA Civ 122, [2009] 1 Lloyd's Rep 576, England was held, in 'a finely balanced case' to be the appropriate forum where the only connecting factor was that the contract was governed by English law. The issues in the case included construction of an English language document and evidence of negotiations in English conducted by people who did not have English as their first language. Generally, the existence of agreements governed by English law will be a factor but not a major factor in favour of English jurisdiction (see *Alliance Bank JSC v Aquanta Corporation* [2012] EWCA Civ 1588, [2013] 1 All ER (Comm) 819).

The English courts were to be preferred where the competing forum was not one which was able to exercise jurisdiction over the defendant as of right and to which, at the time of the hearing, he had not agreed voluntarily to submit, where there was a risk that any judgment from the competing jurisdiction could not be enforced against the defendant's assets in the jurisdiction and where the claimant was entitled to the benefit of having started the proceedings in the jurisdiction (*Sharab v Prince Al-Waleed bin Talal bin Abdal-Aziz-Al-Saud* [2009] EWCA Civ 353, [2009] 2 Lloyd's Rep 160). England was the forum where a claim could be most suitably tried, despite Russia being the natural forum, where there were risks that the claimant would be arrested on trumped-up charges and would not get a fair trial of his claim in Russia (*Cherney v Deripaska* [2009] EWCA Civ 849, [2009] 2 CLC 408). By contrast in *OJSC Oil Co. Yugraneft v Abramovich* [2008] EWHC 2613 (Comm), LTL 3/11/2008, and *Pacific International Sports Clubs Ltd v Soccer Marketing International Ltd* [2009] EWHC 1839 (Ch), LTL 30/7/2009, it was held that a fair trial in Russia and Ukraine respectively would be possible. According to the Privy Council, the claimant needs to show a real risk that justice will not be obtained in the foreign court by reason of incompetence, or lack of independence or corruption (*AK Investment CJSC v Kyrgyz Mobil Tel Ltd* [2011] UKPC 7, [2011] 4 All ER 1027). There is no rule that the court will not consider whether a foreign court or court system is corrupt or lacking in independence based on act of

State doctrine or judicial restraint. Otherwise the paradoxical result would follow that the worse the system of justice, the less it would be permissible to make adverse findings on it. Considerations of international comity will, however, militate against any such finding in the absence of cogent evidence.

Where the proceedings concern a claim for negative declaratory relief, it is necessary to demonstrate that they serve a useful purpose (contrast *Faraday Reinsurance Co. Ltd v Howden North America Inc.* [2012] EWCA Civ 980, [2012] Lloyd's Rep IR 631, with *Howden North America Inc. v Ace European Group Ltd* [2012] EWCA Civ 1624, LTL 6/12/2012).

The court does not have the power to stay proceedings against a defendant domiciled in the jurisdiction in favour of a court in a non-Regulation State (*Owusu v Jackson* (case C-281/02) [2005] QB 801; see **16.73**). Where permission is sought to join non-EU defendants to the proceedings (or a stay is sought of claims against non-EU defendants) the court has had to consider in recent cases what relevance this has to its decision. A refusal to grant permission to serve out (or the granting of a stay) will inevitably result in two sets of proceedings, with the risk of inconsistent judgments and duplication of time and costs. In *Pacific International Sports Clubs Ltd v Surkis* [2010] EWCA Civ 753, LTL 2/7/2010, the court ordered a stay against all defendants other than an English domiciled company as the Ukraine was the proper forum for a dispute over control of a stake in a Ukrainian football team. The English company had a minor role in the dispute and, as Blackburne J put it at first instance (*Pacific International Sports Clubs Ltd v Soccer Marketing International Ltd* [2009] EWHC 1839 (Ch), LTL 30/7/2009), this would be allowing the tail to wag the dog. In contrast, in *JSC BTA Bank v Granton Trade Ltd* [2010] EWHC 2577 (Comm), [2011] 2 All ER (Comm) 542, a case which concerned an alleged fraud on a Kazakhstan bank carried out in Kazakhstan by two Kazakhstan nationals, the court refused to set aside orders granted for service out of the jurisdiction on non-EU defendants. The English courts had jurisdiction under the **Brussels I Regulation, art. 2**, over the two individuals who were the alleged architects of the fraud as they had since moved to England, so in this case it would, continuing Blackburne J's metaphor, be allowing the dog to wag the tail.

Recast Brussels I Regulation The initial proposals for revision of the Brussels I Regulation put forward by the EU Commission in December 2010 included a proposal to extend it to non-EU defendants, thereby replacing the common law rules in most cases. This proposal was rejected during the course of the negotiations, although there are limited extensions to non-EU defendants in some areas (e.g. in favour of employees and consumers, see **16.21** and **16.22**). **16.54**

SERVICE ABROAD

Effecting service abroad

It is provided in **CPR, r. 6.40**, that service abroad must be effected either: **16.55**

(a) in accordance with the provisions of the EU Service Regulation (Regulation (EU) No. 1393/2007; see **16.59**) (**CPR, r. 6.40(3)(a)(i)**); or
(b) by a method permitted by the law of the country in which it is to be served (**r. 6.40(3)(c)**); or
(c) through foreign governments, judicial authorities or British consular authorities (see **16.60**) (**r. 6.40(3)(a)(ii)**); or
(d) by a method permitted by a civil procedure convention (see **16.61**) (**r. 6.40(3)(b)**).

Rule 6.40(4) goes on to provide that nothing in the CPR, or a court order, authorises or requires any person to do anything which is contrary to the law of the country where the claim form or other document is to be served. But service does not have to be valid under that law (*Abela v Baadarani* [2013] UKSC 44, [2013] 1 WLR 2043).

It is unclear whether the provisions of the EU Service Regulation are mandatory, or whether other methods of service are permitted. The first instance decision in *Hornan v Baillie* [2012] EWHC 285, [2012] ILPr 29, suggests the provisions of the Regulation are mandatory. The safest course is therefore to serve in accordance with the Regulation where it applies (see **16.59**). Where there is a service of process clause in a contract which does not accord with the service provisions in the Service Regulation, it may be advisable to serve twice, once in accordance with the terms of the contractual provision and again in accordance with the Service Regulation.

To decide on the appropriate method of service in any particular case, it may be necessary to consult lawyers in the jurisdiction where service is to be effected and the Foreign Process Section at the RCJ (telephone (020) 7947 6691). The following factors may need to be considered:

(a) The methods available for service in that country (there will usually be a choice).
(b) The speed with which service will be effected. Service can be very slow through governments and consular authorities in particular.
(c) The cost involved. Instructing local lawyers to effect service, where permitted, will be relatively speedy but is likely to cost more than the other methods.
(d) Whether the defendant is likely to seek to evade service. Personal service is likely to be most effective in those circumstances if permitted.
(e) Whether the defendant is likely to appear in the proceedings. If he is not, then proof of service in order to obtain judgment in default of acknowledgment will be of key importance. This may be difficult where service has been effected by post.

16.56 **Alternative service** It was controversial for a period of time whether there was any jurisdiction to order alternative service of proceedings outside the jurisdiction (*Bacon v Automattic Inc.* [2011] EWHC 1072 (QB), [2011] 2 All ER (Comm) 852, sets out the reasons). That controversy has been resolved in favour of the existence of such a jurisdiction (*Cecil v Bayat* [2011] EWCA Civ 135, [2011] 1 WLR 3086; *Abela v Baadarani* [2013] UKSC44, [2013] 1 WLR 2043). **CPR, r. 6.37(5)(b)(i)** therefore authorises the court to make an order for alternative service pursuant to **r. 6.15(1)** and also to make an order with retrospective effect pursuant to **r. 6.15(2)**. In cases where service cannot be effected under the Hague Convention, the EU Service Regulation or a bilateral service treaty, the claimant needs to show 'good reason' for the order to be made. There is no requirement to show 'exceptional circumstances' (*Abela v Baadarani*). For further information on alternative service see **15.17**.

16.57 **Scotland** Proceedings can be served in Scotland and Northern Ireland by the same methods permitted for service in England (**CPR, r. 6.40(2)**).

16.58 **Service on a foreign State** Service of a claim form or any other document on a foreign State must be effected in the manner set out in **r. 6.44**. A request for service, a copy of the claim form or other document and any translation of it required under **r. 6.45** must be filed in the Central Office of the Royal Courts of Justice. The Senior Master will send the documents filed to the Foreign and Commonwealth Office to be transmitted to the Ministry of Foreign Affairs of the State which is to be served. Service is deemed to have been effected when the claim form or other document is received at the Ministry (State Immunity Act 1978, s. 12(1)).

A foreign State may agree to an alternative method of service. Where it does, service may be effected either under the provisions of **CPR, r. 6.44**, or by the agreed method (**r. 6.44(7)**).

Service under the EU Service Regulation

16.59 The Service Regulation (Regulation (EU) No. 1393/2007) came into force on 13 November 2008. It repeals Regulation (EU) No. 1348/2000 and binds all EU member States (including *Denmark, see* OJ L331, 10.12.2008, p. 21). The Service Regulation applies to service between member States of documents in civil and commercial matters. As between EU States, the Service Regulation supersedes all earlier treaties including any earlier bilateral conventions and the Hague Convention (Service Regulation, art. 20). It is unclear whether the provisions of the Service Regulation are mandatory, or whether other methods of service can be used if they are permitted by the State in which service is to be effected. The safest course is therefore to serve in accordance with the Service Regulation where it applies.

The Service Regulation requires member States to establish transmitting and receiving agencies to effect service of judicial documents (art. 2(1) and (2)). Under the Service Regulation, documents are transmitted directly between courts, without going through a central authority as under the Hague Convention. For England and Wales the transmitting and receiving agency is the Senior Master, Foreign Process Section, room E10, in the RCJ (telephone (020) 7947 6691; fax (020) 7947 6237). To achieve service under the Service Regulation the claimant must file with the claim form, or other document, any translations and other documents required by the Service Regulation (**CPR, r. 6.41(2)**). The court officer will then seal the copy of the claim form and forward the documents to the Senior Master (**r. 6.41(3)**). The documents will then be transmitted to the receiving agency in the State where they are to be served and that agency will serve them. The CJEU has held in *Leffler v Berlin Chemie AG* (case C-443/03) [2005] ECR I-9611, that where a claim form is served without a proper translation, and the defendant has accordingly refused to accept service, the defect may be remedied by sending the translation through the channels established by the Service Regulation as soon as possible. It may not be necessary to translate annexes to a document if they have an evidentiary function and are not necessary to understand the subject matter of the claim and the cause of action (*Ingenieurbüro Michael Weiss und Partner GbR v Industrie- und Handelskammer Berlin* (case C-14/07) [2009] ILPr 24).

The Service Regulation attempts to deal with the delays which are often inherent in other methods of service through formal channels by providing that the receiving agency must send a receipt for any document it receives to the transmitting agency as soon as possible, and in any event within seven days of receipt (art. 6(1)). All steps necessary to effect service must be taken as soon as possible, and the receiving agency must notify the transmitting agency if it has not proved possible to effect service within one month of receipt (art. 7(2)).

Article 9 establishes a mechanism for calculating the date of service of a document served under the Service Regulation. Where the document has to be served within a particular time under the law of the sending State, the rules of the sending State will determine the date of service. Otherwise, the date of service will be determined by the law of the receiving State.

Article 19 sets out the conditions which must be satisfied before judgment in default of acknowledgment can be entered against a defendant served under the provisions of the Service Regulation. See **16.66**.

The European Union publishes a manual containing details of the receiving agencies established by the member States under the terms of the Service Regulation, the geographical areas in which they have jurisdiction, the means of receipt of documents available and the languages that may be used for the completion of the standard form for service. It also publishes a glossary, for information purposes only, of the documents which may be served. An updated version of this manual is maintained online at the website of the European Judicial Atlas in Civil Matters, http://ec.europa.eu/justice_home/judicialatlascivil/html/ds_information_en.htm. The necessary forms are available at that website for completion on-screen.

Service under the Hague Convention

The United Kingdom is one of the 68 contracting States to the Hague Convention on the Service Abroad of Judicial and Extra-judicial Documents in Civil or Commercial Matters (1965) ('the Hague Convention'). The member States of the EU (apart from Austria) are also parties to the Hague Convention, but as between all of the EU States the provisions of the EU **16.60**

Service Regulation (Regulation (EU) No. 1393/2007, see **16.59**) prevail over the provisions of the Hague Convention (Service Regulation, art. 20). The Service Regulation also applies to the French overseas departments of French Guiana, Guadeloupe, Martinique and Réunion, which are part of the EU territory. The Netherlands and the United Kingdom have extended the operation of the Hague Convention to some of the overseas countries and territories for which they are responsible and which are not part of the EU territory, so that the Service Regulation does not apply to them. The countries in which English process may be served under the Hague Convention are listed in **table 16.2**. The text of the Convention and the declarations of the contracting States on the details of how it applies in their territories can be seen on the website of the Hague Conference on Private International Law: http://www.hcch.net.

The main method of service under the Hague Convention is through a central authority. Under art. 2, each contracting State is obliged to designate a central authority which will undertake to receive requests for service coming from other contracting States. In the UK the central authority is the Senior Master, the Foreign Process Section, Royal Courts of Justice (telephone: (020) 7497 6691). Effect is given to this method of service by **CPR, r. 6.42(1)(a)**.

The Hague Convention also permits service in some circumstances through a contracting State's diplomatic or consular agents, through consular channels or through diplomatic channels (arts 8 and 9). The procedure is then as set out in **CPR, r. 6.43**.

The Hague Convention does not prevent certain other informal methods of service provided the State of destination does not object (art. 10, see **16.63**).

By **CPR, rr. 6.43, 6.45** and **6.46**, and **PD 6B, paras 4.1** and **4.2**, the following documents should be filed at the Foreign Process Section, RCJ, room E02 for onward transmission to the central authority in the receiving country:

(a) request for service;
(b) the claim form, plus a duplicate for every defendant to be served;
(c) particulars of claim, and any documents accompanying them, where these are to be served with the claim form, plus a duplicate of these documents;
(d) the response pack (form N9), or form N1C (notes for defendants) where the claim form is served without particulars of claim — both form N9 and N1C must be amended to show the relevant deadline for filing the acknowledgment and/or the defence;
(e) unless the claim form is to be served in a country where English is an official language or on a British citizen, a certified translation into the language of the jurisdiction where service is to be effected of the claim form, particulars of claim and form N9 or N1C;
(f) an undertaking to be responsible for the expenses incurred by the Foreign and Commonwealth Office; and
(g) any documents required by the country where service is to be effected (e.g. legalisation of documents is required in some countries). Further information is available from the Foreign Process Section, Room E02 at the RCJ.

Where permission to serve out of the jurisdiction has been granted, the order giving permission, and a translation of it where necessary, will also need to be served.

Service under a bilateral civil procedure convention

16.61 The United Kingdom has entered into bilateral conventions for service of proceedings with a number of countries. Details can be found on the Foreign and Commonwealth Office website, http://www.fco.gov.uk. It is also advisable to check with the Foreign Process Section at the RCJ.

A claim form may be served in such countries either through the judicial authorities of that country or through a British consul, subject to any provisions of the applicable convention governing the nationality of a person who may be served by a British consul (**CPR, r. 6.42(1)(b)**).

As in Hague Convention cases (see **16.60**), the documents to be served should be filed in the Foreign Process Section for onward transmission. The documents are the same as in Hague Convention cases.

Service through diplomatic channels where there is no civil procedure convention

It is possible for service to be effected through diplomatic channels even where there is no civil procedure convention between the United Kingdom and the country where it is sought to effect service. By **CPR, r. 6.42(2)**, in such cases, provided the law of the relevant jurisdiction permits it, the claim form may be served either: **16.62**

(a) through the government of that country, where that government is willing to effect service; or

(b) through a British consular authority in that country.

However, given that the receiving country has not bound itself by international treaty to permit service through these channels, there is no guarantee that service will be effective under local law. In practice, the advice of a local lawyer must be sought.

The same documents as in Hague Convention cases must be filed at the Foreign Process Section (**r. 6.43(1)**; see **16.59**).

Service cannot be effected through judicial authorities, consular authorities or diplomatic channels in the Isle of Man, the Channel Islands, or any United Kingdom Overseas Territory. Service in any of these places can be effected by the claimant or his agent (**r. 6.42(3)**).

The United Kingdom Overseas Territories are listed in **PD 6B, para.** 5.2: the Hague Convention has been extended to most of them (see **table 16.2**).

The same is generally true of Commonwealth States which are not a party to the Hague Convention, save that some do require service to be through judicial authorities. A list of these countries can be obtained from the Foreign Process Section at the RCJ (**CPR, r. 6.42(3)(a); PD 6B, para. 5.1**).

Service by informal methods

In practice, service through diplomatic channels is usually a slow and laborious process. It is often quicker, where permitted under local law, for the claimant to effect service by an informal method, for example, by instructing a local process server to effect service personally on the defendant. **16.63**

Personal service by the claimant's agent is permitted in most common law countries. The position in civil law countries, where service is seen as a judicial act, is more problematic. However, even here, it is possible in some countries to use a local agent to transmit documents direct to the court official responsible for effecting service of court documents. For service in Scotland and Northern Ireland see **16.57**.

The EU Service Regulation permits service directly through judicial officers, officials or other competent persons of the member State addressed, where such direct service is permitted under the law of that member State (Regulation (EU) No. 1393/2007, art. 15). The Hague Convention has similar provisions in art. 10. Where service is pursuant to another civil procedure convention the terms of that bilateral convention would need to be checked.

Table 16.2 Countries in which English process may be served under the Hague Convention. In case of doubt contact the Foreign Process Section, RCJ, room E10 (telephone (020) 7947 6691; fax (020) 7947 6237), or consult the Hague Conference website, www.hcch.net

Albania, Anguilla, Antigua and Barbuda, Argentina, Armenia, Aruba, Australia (including Australian external territories), Bahamas, Barbados, Belarus, Belize, Bermuda, Bosnia and Herzegovina, Botswana, British Virgin Islands, Canada, Cayman Islands, China, Egypt, Falkland Islands and dependencies, Gibraltar, Guernsey, Hong Kong SAR, Iceland, India, Israel, Isle of Man, Japan, Jersey, Republic of Korea, Kuwait, Macau SAR, Macedonia, Malawi, Mexico, Moldova, Monaco, Montenegro, Montserrat, Morocco, Norway, Pakistan, Pitcairn, Russian Federation, San Marino, Serbia, Seychelles, Sri Lanka, St Helena and dependencies, St Vincent and the Grenadines, Switzerland, Turkey, Turks and Caicos Islands, Ukraine, United States of America, Venezuela, Virgin Islands.

As regards service by post, the EU Service Regulation permits member States to effect service of judicial documents directly by post on persons residing in another member State by registered letter with acknowledgment of receipt or equivalent (art. 14). It is unclear whether this permits postal service by the claimant or requires service by the member State, but it is probably the latter. In view of this, the courts have put in place a special procedure for service through the Aldwych Post Office. The documents for service are provided by the claimant to the Foreign Process Section. If all documents are present and translated (including the covering letter), they are sealed by the court in an envelope addressed to the defendant. The documents are then collected by the claimant's solicitors who sign an undertaking to pay all costs and to post the documents. The solicitors in compliance with the undertaking take the documents directly to the Aldwych Post Office and post them by recorded post. The original receipt of posting is then provided to the court with a copy retained by the solicitors.

Service by post is also permitted under the Hague Convention provided the State of destination does not object (art. 10(a)). The Aldwych Post Office system can also be used in such cases. In the case of a bilateral convention, the specific terms of the convention would need to be checked.

Although service by post is not costly and is quick, problems can arise in establishing whether service has taken place and if so when, for the purposes of entering judgment in default. It may be possible to obtain the necessary information from the equivalent in the country of service of the Royal Mail's Track and Trace system, but this is by no means straightforward. A further question is whether service abroad by the electronic methods now permitted under **CPR, Part 6**, would be good service. In theory, provided that electronic methods of service are not contrary to local law, and in particular to the provisions of any relevant convention, the answer should be yes. In *Molins plc v GD SpA* [2000] 1 WLR 1741 it was held that service by fax effected by an Italian litigant on a defendant in England could have been good service under art. 15 of the Hague Convention if the requirements of what is now **PD 6A, para. 4.1** had been met.

For service on a defendant who is abroad under **CPR, r. 6.37** (service by an alternative method or at an alternative place) see **15.17**.

Responding to service

16.64 Where a court in England and Wales has jurisdiction under **Regulation (EC) No. 44/2001** (the **Brussels I Regulation**) or the Brussels or Lugano Convention, or the modified Regulation *which applies* within the United Kingdom, over a claim against a defendant out of the jurisdiction and the claim form is served on the defendant in a European territory of a contracting State or a Regulation State (or in Scotland or Northern Ireland), the defendant must acknowledge service or file a defence within 21 days after service of the claim form, or, where the claim form states that particulars of claim are to follow, of the particulars (**CPR, r. 6.35(2)** and (3)). The defendant is not obliged to acknowledge service at all, but where an acknowledgment is filed, the period for filing a defence is extended by 14 days (**PD 6B, para. 6.4(2)**). **Rule 6.35(4)** prescribes a response period of 31 days where a claim form is served in 'a Convention territory outside Europe' (i.e. other than European territory, which is covered in **r. 6.35(3)**). It seems that **r. 6.35(4)** can only ever have referred to the French overseas departments (French Guiana, Guadeloupe, Martinique and Réunion) and the African territories of Portugal (Madeira) and Spain (Canary Islands, Ceuta and Melilla), so that it should refer to Regulation States rather than Convention territories.

Where proceedings are served on a defendant outside the jurisdiction who resides outside the territories of contracting States (either where permission to serve has been obtained, or where arts 16 or 17 of the Conventions apply and the defendant is not in the territory of a contracting State), the period for acknowledging service is set out in the table at the end of **PD 6B**. The periods for acknowledging service or filing an admission in the response pack included with particulars of claim served outside the jurisdiction have to be amended accordingly (**PD 6B, para. 6.6**). After service of the particulars of claim the defence must be served within the number of days set out in the table. But a defendant who has acknowledged service is given an extra 14 days to file the defence (**PD 6B, para. 6.4(2)**).

Commentary

Service abroad of documents other than a claim form

Where permission is required to serve a claim form out of the jurisdiction, the claimant must apply for permission to serve any other document in the proceedings which he needs to serve abroad (**CPR, r. 6.38(1)**). Permission is not required, however, to serve particulars of claim abroad where permission has been given to serve a claim form out of the jurisdiction which states that particulars are to follow (**r. 6.38(2)**), or where the defendant has given an address for service in Scotland or Northern Ireland (**r. 6.38(3)**). In practice, as parties will usually provide an address for service within the United Kingdom (no longer just England and Wales) under **r. 6.23**, the necessity to apply for permission will be limited. As regards the method of service, if there is an address for service within the jurisdiction, no special considerations arise. In rare circumstances there may not be such an address. This might be because a defendant has not acknowledged service but the claimant has decided not to seek default judgment (e.g. in a multi-party case with interlinking issues). It may also occur because a party has given as his address for service the address of a solicitor in another EEA State, as permitted under **r. 6.23(2)(a)**. Such cases will need to be considered and dealt with on an individual basis, by agreement or court order. **16.65**

Where an application notice or order is served out of the jurisdiction, the period for responding is seven days less than the number of days listed in the table set out at the end of **PD 6B** (**PD 6B, para. 7.1**).

Proof of service

Where service is effected through the central authority designated under the Hague Convention or through consular, government or judicial channels, the claimant will be provided with an official certificate of service (which is evidence that service has been effected) and with a note of the expenses incurred (**CPR, r. 6.43(5)**). It is important to check that service has been carried out correctly and in a permitted manner (see *Olafsson v Gissurarson (No. 2)* [2008] EWCA Civ 152, [2008] 1 WLR 2016). **16.66**

Where service is effected through informal methods, service should be evidenced by a certificate of service (or affidavit or witness statement of service) from the person who effected service.

JUDGMENT IN DEFAULT

16.67 No special rule applies in cases of assumed jurisdiction regarding entering judgment in default other than the need for waiting the enhanced period laid down by **PD 6B**.

Where service outside the jurisdiction has been effected without permission under **CPR, rr. 6.32** and **6.33**, and the defendant has failed to file an acknowledgment of service, judgment in default can only be entered by application under **CPR, Part 12** (**CPR, r. 12.10(b)(i)** and **(ii)**). These provisions give effect to **art. 26** of the **Brussels I Regulation**, which requires the courts of contracting States to declare of their own motion that they have no jurisdiction where that is the case and the defendant has failed to 'enter an appearance' (i.e. acknowledge service).

Where a hearing date is fixed when a claim is issued, and a defendant who is served with the claim form outside the jurisdiction does not appear at the hearing, the claimant may not take any further step without filing written evidence of service of the claim form (**CPR, r. 6.47**). **Rule 6.47** does not apply where service has been effected under the EU Service Regulation (see **16.59**) (**r. 6.41(4)**).

Where service is effected under the Service Regulation, judgment in default cannot be given until it is established that service was effected by a method prescribed by the internal law of the receiving State or that the documents were actually delivered to the defendant or to the defendant's residence by another method provided by the Regulation and that, in either case, the defendant had sufficient time to defend the claim (Service Regulation, art. 19).

STAYS ON THE GROUND OF *FORUM NON CONVENIENS*

General

16.68 English proceedings can be served under the common law as of right on a defendant within the jurisdiction irrespective of the degree of connection with this country of the defendant or the cause of action (see **16.2**). A claim form for an Admiralty claim *in rem* may be served within the jurisdiction on a ship or sister ship while at port in the country, even if there is absolutely no other connection with this country.

To prevent completely unsuitable actions proceeding, the courts have a discretion in common law cases to stay English proceedings on the principle of *forum non conveniens*. The leading case is *Spiliada Maritime Corporation v Cansulex Ltd* [1987] AC 460 (see **16.53**). The principles applied are similar to those on applications for permission under **CPR, r. 6.36** (see **16.41** to **16.53**), but the burden of proof is reversed. In an application for a stay there is a two-stage test. The defendant has to show there is another forum which is prima facie the appropriate forum. If he does so, the court considers whether there are special circumstances by reason of which justice requires the trial should take place in England. In contrast, in an application for permission under **CPR, r. 6.36**, or a challenge to permission granted under that rule, the court must be satisfied by the claimant that England is clearly or distinctly the appropriate forum (*VTB Capital plc v Nutritek International Corporation* [2012] EWCA Civ 808, [2012] 2 Lloyd's Rep 313, at [131]).

The court will not grant a stay on the ground of *forum non conveniens* on the application of the claimant, where there has been no challenge to the court's jurisdiction by the defendant, unless there are exceptional circumstances (*Ledra Fisheries Ltd v Turner* [2003] EWHC 1049 (Ch), LTL 15/4/2003). In *Ledra Fisheries Ltd v Turner* the court also refused the claimant's application for stay of a counterclaim by the defendant.

Appropriate forum

In *Spiliada Maritime Corporation v Cansulex Ltd* [1987] AC 460 Lord Goff of Chieveley said: 16.69

The basic principle is that a stay will only be granted on the ground of *forum non conveniens* where the court is satisfied that there is some other available forum, having competent jurisdiction, which is the appropriate forum for the trial of the action, i.e. in which the case may be tried more suitably for the interests of all the parties and the ends of justice.

The burden of proof rests on the defendant to show there is some other clearly more appropriate forum. If there is no other more suitable forum, the stay should usually be refused. So, for example, in *The Vishva Abha* [1990] 2 Lloyd's Rep 312 the owners of cargo on board a ship named the *Dias* made a claim *in rem* against the owners of a ship named the *Vishva Apurva*. The collision happened on the high seas. The only connection with England other than the fact that the defendant's ship was arrested here was that the defendant's ships regularly docked in this country. The suggested alternative forum was South Africa, on the ground that the *Dias* had been arrested there in litigation between the owners of the two ships. The only connection with South Africa was that proceedings had been served there while the *Dias* was in port. It was pure chance that litigation was pending in South Africa over the same collision as opposed to any other country, so there was no other distinctly more appropriate forum. In *Catlin Syndicate Ltd v Adams Land and Cattle Co.* [2006] EWHC 2065 (Comm), [2005] 2 CLC 425, the court considered the effect of jurisdiction clauses on the question of *forum conveniens.* The claim arose out of an insurance policy, where the parties had on the face of the insurance slip agreed to English law and jurisdiction, but at the same time they had agreed to an option in the policy itself enabling the insured to require the underwriters to submit to the jurisdiction of the US courts. Thus, the appropriateness of both the English and US courts had been accepted by the parties. The insured had exercised its right to issue proceedings in Nebraska and this gave rise to duplication of proceedings and brought into play the question of *forum conveniens.* The court held that the specific election and the provision which provided for it took precedence over the general law and jurisdiction clause in the context of deciding the appropriate forum.

Commentary

Real and substantial connection

In considering whether there is an alternative forum, the court will look for the country 'with which the action has the most real and substantial connection' (*The Abidin Daver* [1984] AC 398 per Lord Keith of Kinkel). Sometimes, the natural forum of the action will be obvious. In *MacShannon v Rockware Glass Ltd* [1978] AC 795, a Scots employee sued his employer, which was registered in England, in respect of an accident in Scotland. All the witnesses lived in Scotland. Clearly, Scotland was the natural forum. *Gulf Oil Belgian SA v Finland Steamship Co. Ltd* [1980] 2 Lloyd's Rep 229 arose from a collision between two ships in Swedish waters caused by a misunderstanding between two Swedish pilots speaking in Swedish by VHF radio. It was patently obvious that the case should be tried in Sweden. The places of residence or business of the parties must be considered. A stay will be more readily granted if service was effected during a temporary visit to England and Wales. On the other hand, where the defendant has an established place of business within the jurisdiction, very clear and weighty grounds must be shown for refusing to exercise jurisdiction (*Banco Atlantico SA v British Bank of the Middle East* [1990] 2 Lloyd's Rep 504). The court will also consider the availability of factual and expert witnesses, the law governing the dispute and whether the parties have conferred jurisdiction on any particular court. The law governing the dispute will be particularly significant if the case involves an issue where the application of that law is not straightforward (*Golden Ocean Group Ltd v Salgaocar Mining Industries Pvt Ltd* [2011] EWHC 56 (Comm), [2011] 1 WLR 2575). An alternative forum which simply applies its own laws irrespective of the generally accepted rules on the 16.70

conflict of laws is unlikely to be regarded as a suitable alternative (*Banco Atlantico SA v British Bank of the Middle East* [1990] 2 Lloyd's Rep 504). Convincing reasons must usually be shown before the court will go behind an express agreement between the parties as to jurisdiction (*Kuwait Oil Co. (KSC) v Idemitsu Tankers KK* [1981] 2 Lloyd's Rep 510; *Deutsche Bank AG v Sebastian Holdings Inc.* [2009] EWHC 3069 (Comm), [2009] 2 CLC 949).

Reasons of justice

16.71 If there is some more appropriate forum, the court may refuse a stay if, in all the circumstances of the case, justice requires that a stay should not be granted (*Spiliada Maritime Corporation v Cansulex Ltd* [1987] AC 460). The burden of proof regarding showing some reason for not granting a stay despite there being some more suitable forum is on the claimant. A stay may be refused, for example, where the claimant can provide cogent evidence of a real risk that justice will not be done in the foreign jurisdiction, by reason of incompetence, lack of independence or corruption (*The Abidin Daver* [1984] AC 398; *Cherney v Deripaska* [2009] EWCA Civ 849, [2009] 2 CLC 408; *AK Investment CJSC v Kyrgyz Mobil Tel Ltd* [2011] UKPC 7, [2012] 1 WLR 1804). In a group action, the lack of established procedures for handling such claims together with the strong likelihood that funding will be unavailable in the foreign jurisdiction to investigate complex factual and legal issues may mean that substantial justice would not be done there (*Lubbe v Cape plc* [2000] 1 WLR 1545).

Legitimate personal or juridical advantage

16.72 There are many cases where a claimant can secure some advantage by commencing proceedings in one jurisdiction rather than another. Examples include the measure of damages, the vigour of the procedures on disclosure, the power to award interest, the enforceability of the judgment and the length of the limitation period. Generally, an advantage to the claimant will give rise to an equal disadvantage to the defendant. Stays have been granted in cases where doing so deprives the claimant of some advantage, as in *Trendtex Trading Corporation v Credit Suisse* [1982] AC 679. Generally, the court seeks to do 'practical justice' between the parties (see Lord Goff of Chieveley in *Spiliada Maritime Corporation v Cansulex Ltd* [1987] AC 460), being less worried about depriving a claimant of a benefit secured by 'forum shopping'. Any injustice that may be caused by granting a stay may be avoided by making the order subject to conditions. For example, a stay may be granted in favour of a jurisdiction with a shorter limitation period on condition that the defendant waives any limitation defence. Indeed, the parties may try to pre-empt arguments along these lines by voluntarily undertaking not to take advantage of procedural differences in advance of the hearing for the stay.

Brussels I Regulation cases

16.73 Generally, the **Brussels I Regulation** provides a complete code, so a stay in favour of the courts of another member State in circumstances not specifically provided for in the Regulation (e.g. **art. 27**) would be inconsistent with it. The English courts initially took the approach, in the context of the Brussels Convention, that where the defendant is domiciled in England, but the dispute about jurisdiction was between the courts of this country and the courts of a non-contracting State, English proceedings could be stayed on the ground of *forum non conveniens* (*Re Harrods (Buenos Aires) Ltd* [1992] Ch 72).

In *Owusu v Jackson* [2002] EWCA Civ 877, LTL 19/6/2002, however, the Court of Appeal referred to the CJEU the following question:

(a) whether it is inconsistent with the Brussels Convention, where a claimant contends that jurisdiction is founded on art. 2, for a court of a contracting State to exercise a discretionary power, available under its national law, to decline to hear proceedings brought against a person domiciled in that State in favour of the courts of a non-contracting State if: (i) the

jurisdiction of no other contracting State under the Convention is in
proceedings have no connecting factors with any other contracting Stat and (ii) the
(b) if the answer to (a)(i) or (a)(ii) is yes, whether it is inconsistent in all circu
in some, and if so, which. s or only

The CJEU held (*Owusu v Jackson* (case C-281/02) [2005] QB 301) in answer to (
mandatory and can be derogated from only by express provision in the Conven
therefore no power to stay in those circumstances. The court declined to answer 2 is
question, which has left it unclear whether there can be a stay in other circu is
Ferrexpo AG v Gilson Investments Ltd [2012] EWHC 721 (Comm), [2012] 1 Lloyd's Rep 5
Smith J held that the **Brussels I Regulation, art. 22** (which gives exclusive juri
particular EU courts in specified cases) should be applied by analogy or 'reflexivel
giving the English court a discretion to stay its proceedings in favour of the c
non-contracting State in appropriate circumstances. On the facts, the proceeding
English domiciled companies were stayed in favour of the Ukrainian courts as the
their object the validity of resolutions of a Ukrainian company.

There are conflicting first-instance decisions on whether **arts 27** and **28** (stays where id
or related proceedings are on foot) can be given reflexive effect, so as to allow a stay in
of proceedings in a non-member State which are identical or related. Andrew Smith
Ferrexpo AG v Gilson Investments Ltd and Deputy Judge Theis QC in *JKN v JCN* [2010] EWHC
(Fam), [2011] 1 FLR 826, considered that to be the case; Barling J in *Catalyst Investment Group v Lewinsohn* [2009] EWHC 1964 (Ch), [2010] Ch 218, reached the opposite conclusion.

For legal proceedings instituted on or after 10 January 2015, the recast Brussels I Regulation gives courts in member States the power to stay proceedings in favour of non-member States in certain circumstances (see Regulation (EU) No. 1215/2012, recitals 23 and 24 and art. 34).

The court also has a general power to order a temporary stay on case management grounds. But the burden on the defendant is heavy and stays will be granted only in rare and compelling cases (*Reichhold Norway ASA v Goldman Sachs International* [2000] 1 WLR 173; *Equitas Ltd v Allstate Insurance Co.* [2008] EWHC 1671 (Comm), [2009] 1 All ER (Comm) 1137; *Citigroup Global Markets Ltd v Amatra Leveraged Feeder Holdings Ltd* [2012] EWHC 1331 (Comm), [2012] 2 CLC 279). A stay on the grounds of abuse of process is also possible, it seems, where the proceedings pointlessly duplicate other proceedings (*Ferrexpo AG v Gilson Investments Ltd*).

INJUNCTIONS TO RESTRAIN FOREIGN PROCEEDINGS (ANTI-SUIT INJUNCTIONS)

In rare circumstances, an English court may grant an injunction restraining the institution or continuance of foreign proceedings. Such an injunction is only granted when it is required for the ends of justice (*Castanho v Brown and Root (UK) Ltd* [1981] AC 557). The injunction is directed to a party, not to the foreign court, so is only available against a party who is amenable to the jurisdiction of the English courts. It is a jurisdiction which must be exercised with a great deal of caution. There are two main categories of case in which an anti-suit injunction will be awarded. First, where the pursuit of the foreign proceedings is vexatious and oppressive (see further below) and second, in order to restrain proceedings brought in a foreign country in breach of either a jurisdiction or an arbitration agreement between the parties (see *Continental Bank NA v Aeakos Compania Naviera SA* [1994] 1 WLR 588; *Aggeliki Charis Compania Maritima SA v Pagnan SpA* [1995] 1 Lloyd's Rep 87; *Skype Technologies SA v Joltid Ltd* [2009] EWHC 2783 (Ch), [2011] ILPr 8). 16.74

The leading case concerning the first of these categories is now *Société Nationale Industrielle Aérospatiale v Lee Kui Jak* [1987] AC 871. The principle laid down was that where a remedy for a particular wrong is available both in England and in a foreign country, an injunction will

… to restrain the foreign proceedings if pursuit of those proceedings would be …ressive or unconscionable. This presupposes that England is the natural forum … Account must be taken of the balance of injustice to the parties depending on … injunction is either granted or refused, bearing in mind the possibility of remov-… ustice by the imposition of suitable terms or the giving of undertakings.

…s were that the deceased, who had lived in Brunei, was killed in a helicopter crash in … A government report on the accident concluded that the accident was caused by metal … in the rotating assembly. The administrators of the deceased's estate started proceed-… *inter alia*, against the manufacturer of the helicopter and the maintenance company in …n Brunei and Texas. The maintenance company had been served with a contribution …otice in Brunei where they did not object to the jurisdiction of the court, but were vigorously …esisting the jurisdiction of the court in Texas. Brunei was obviously the natural forum for the action, but an injunction could only be granted if the proceedings in Texas were vexatious or oppressive. Vexation on the ground that under Texan law there was strict liability and punitive damages was neutralised by undertakings by the claimants that neither of these would be pursued. However, there was a distinct possibility that the defendants would be unable to claim contribution from the maintenance company in Texas, whereas they could in Brunei, with the result that the proceedings in Texas could be described as oppressive. An injunction was granted.

The existence of two concurrent proceedings in different jurisdictions is not of itself 'vexatious and oppressive' and will not alone justify the granting of an anti-suit injunction (*Dornoch Ltd v Mauritius Union Assurance Co. Ltd* [2005] EWHC 1887 (Comm), LTL 30/8/2005; *Deutsche Bank AG v Highland Crusader Offshore Partners LP* [2009] EWCA Civ 725, [2010] 1 WLR 1023).

A litigant's reliance on the availability of enhanced or punitive damages in a jurisdiction having no connection with a dispute may be an indicator that he is acting oppressively, as might misinforming a foreign court about the status of English proceedings (*Royal Bank of Scotland plc v Hicks* [2011] EWHC 287 (Ch), LTL 21/2/2011).

An application for an anti-suit injunction does not have to be made by a formal claim or counterclaim (*Glencore International AG v Exter Shipping Ltd* [2002] EWCA Civ 528, [2002] 2 All ER (Comm) 1). In this case it was held there was territorial, *in personam* jurisdiction to grant the injunction against a party who had submitted to the jurisdiction, and on the facts there was a clear need to protect the English proceedings.

An application for an anti-suit injunction should be made promptly. It is unlikely to be granted once judgment has been obtained in the foreign claim, or where it has been allowed to continue almost to the point of judgment (*Toepfer International GmbH v Molino Boschi Srl* [1996] 1 Lloyd's Rep 510). On the other hand, the foreign action must be more than merely anticipated (*Pan American World Airways v Andrews* 1992 SLT 268). Delay also needs to be considered viewed against the stage the proceedings have reached (*REC Wafer Norway AS v Moser Baer Photo Voltaic Ltd* [2010] EWHC 2581 (Comm), [2011] 1 Lloyd's Rep 410).

If a company is in compulsory liquidation in England and Wales, the winding-up court may restrain any person subject to its jurisdiction from taking proceedings outside the jurisdiction which would distort the distribution of the company's assets in accordance with English law (*Re Oriental Inland Steam Co., ex parte Scinde Railway Co.* (1874) LR 9 Ch App 557; *Re Vocalion (Foreign) Ltd* [1932] 2 Ch 196). This may be applied to a voluntary winding up on an application under the Insolvency Act 1986, s. 112 (*Re Jenkins and Co. Ltd* (1907) 51 SJ 715). An anti-suit injunction may also be granted where an administration order has been made (*Bloom v Harms Offshore AHT 'Taurus' GmbH & Co. KG* [2009] EWCA Civ 632, [2010] Ch 187).

An anti-suit injunction is not a substantive cause of action requiring a separate basis of jurisdiction. Once the court has jurisdiction over the underlying claim, it has power to make ancillary orders, including anti-suit injunctions, in order to protect the process of the English court (*Masri v Consolidated Contractors International (UK) Ltd (No. 3)* [2008] EWCA Civ 625, [2009] QB 503).

In *OT Africa Line Ltd v Hijazy* [2001] 1 Lloyd's Rep 76 the court considered whether an anti-suit injunction restraining proceedings before a foreign court was a breach of **art. 6** of the European Convention on Human Rights in that it would prevent a party's case being considered by an independent and impartial tribunal established by law. The court held that **art. 6** does not give a person an unfettered choice of tribunal in which to pursue or defend civil rights. **Article 6** does not deal with the place where the right to a fair trial is to be exercised by a litigant: it simply requires a fair trial to be available somewhere. Accordingly **art. 6** does not prevent an anti-suit injunction being granted.

An anti-suit injunction may be refused if the applicant does not have clean hands, applying general equitable principles (*Royal Bank of Scotland plc v Highland Financial Partners LP* [2012] EWHC 1278 (Comm), [2012] 2 CLC 109).

Brussels I Regulation cases

An anti-suit injunction can be obtained to restrain proceedings in a non-EU State where the **16.75**
English courts have jurisdiction under the **Brussels I Regulation** (*Royal Bank of Scotland plc v Hicks* [2011] EWHC 287 (Ch), LTL 21/2/2011). In *Samengo-Turner v J. and H. Marsh and McLennan (Services) Ltd* [2007] EWCA Civ 723, [2007] 2 CLC 104, employers had started proceedings in New York against employees under bonus agreements. The New York court, applying its rules, held it had exclusive jurisdiction over the claim. The employees applied to the English courts for an anti-suit injunction restraining the New York proceedings. The Court of Appeal held that the claim related to an employment contract and granted an injunction on the grounds that under the **Brussels I Regulation, art. 18**, claims relating to a contract of employment had to be brought before the English courts as the employees' courts of domicile. Granting the anti-suit injunction was the only way to give effect to the claimants' statutory rights.

It is not possible, however, to obtain an anti-suit injunction from the English courts to prevent proceedings continuing in another member State, even where they have been brought in breach of a jurisdiction or arbitration clause.

The CJEU held, in *Turner v Grovit* (case C-159/02) [2005] AC 101, that a court in a country which is a party to the Brussels Convention may not issue an injunction prohibiting another party from commencing or continuing proceedings in another Convention State on the ground that the proceedings are vexatious and oppressive. The reasoning was that an anti-suit injunction constitutes an interference with the jurisdiction of the foreign court and is therefore inconsistent with the system of the Convention. The position is no different in relation to the **Brussels I Regulation.** In *West Tankers Inc. v Allianz SpA* (case C-185/07) [2009] AC 1138 the CJEU held that it is also incompatible with the **Brussels I Regulation** for an English court to grant an anti-suit injunction to restrain proceedings in another member State on the ground that those proceedings are inconsistent with an arbitration agreement. It is exclusively for the courts of the member State seised of the original proceedings to determine any objection to its jurisdiction.

This clearly opens up the possibility of tactical use of proceedings: beginning proceedings in country B in breach of a jurisdiction clause in favour of country A or in breach of an arbitration clause in order to delay the substantive consideration of a dispute. It may be possible to claim equitable damages in these circumstances (*West Tankers Inc. v Allianz SpA* [2012] EWHC 854 (Comm), [2012] 2 Lloyd's Rep 103). It may also be possible to prevent the recognition of any

Commentary

inconsistent foreign judgment in England by enforcing a declaratory arbitral award under the Arbitration Act 1996, s. 66 (*West Tankers Inc. v Allianz SpA* [2012] EWCA Civ 27, [2012] Bus LR 1701).

For legal proceedings instituted on or after 10 January 2015, the recast Brussels I Regulation addresses the problems caused by tactical use of proceedings in this way (see **16.37**). It is likely, however, that an anti-suit injunction will still be unavailable where proceedings in another member State are concerned.

Chapter 17 Admitting the Claim and Requesting Time to Pay

The following procedural checklist, which is at the front of the book, is relevant to this chapter:

Procedural checklist 12 Admitting a claim and requesting time to pay

DEFENDANT'S OPTIONS ON RECEIVING PARTICULARS OF CLAIM

A defendant to a claim is not required by the CPR to do anything until particulars of claim are served. On receipt of particulars of claim, **Part 9** provides for three alternative responses: **17.1**

(a) A defendant who wishes to admit the claim should file a form of admission (see **17.4** to **17.10**).
(b) A defendant who wishes to contest the claim should file a defence within 14 days of service of the particulars of claim (see **18.4** to **18.8**).
(c) A defendant who wishes to contest the claim but needs more than 14 days to prepare the defence, or who wishes to contest the jurisdiction of the court, should file an acknowledgment of service (see **18.1** to **18.3**).

ADMISSIONS MADE BEFORE COMMENCEMENT OF PROCEEDINGS

It was held in *Sowerby v Charlton* [2005] EWCA Civ 1610, [2006] 1 WLR 568, that the provisions of **CPR, Part 14**, did not apply to an admission of liability made before proceedings were commenced. This decision was followed in *Walley v Stoke-on-Trent City Council* [2006] EWCA Civ 1137, [2007] 1 WLR 352. Brooke LJ, however, added a recommendation that **Part 14** should be extended to cover pre-action admissions in claims governed by a pre-action protocol. **17.2**

Accordingly, a new **r. 14.1A** has been introduced, which applies to pre-action admissions made on or after 6 April 2007. The new rule enables a party who wishes to admit the truth of the whole or any part of another party's case before the commencement of proceedings to do so by giving notice in writing (**r. 14.1A(1)**).

In proceedings to which the **Pre-action Protocols** for **Personal Injury Claims**, for the **Resolution of Clinical Disputes**, and for **Disease and Illness Claims** apply, a pre-action admission may be withdrawn or judgment entered on it if the admission is made after the party making it has received a letter before claim under the protocol or it is made before receipt of any letter before claim and the party making the admission states it to be made under **CPR, Part 14** (**r. 14.1A(2)**). The rules refer to a 'letter before claim' even though the pre-action protocol refers to a 'letter of claim'. Accordingly, the Association of British Insurers, the Association of Personal Injury Lawyers, the Forum of Insurance Lawyers and the Motor Accident Solicitors Society entered into a memorandum of understanding on 2 April 2009 agreeing that the reference to 'letter before claim' in **CPR, r. 14.1A**, should be interpreted as a reference to 'letter of claim' in a protocol. A pre-action admission may only be withdrawn before commencement of proceedings if the person to whom the admission was made agrees or after proceedings have been commenced if all parties consent or with the permission of the court (**r. 14.1A(3)**).

See 17.4 for the court's approach in granting permission to withdraw an admission.

ADMISSION AFTER COMMENCEMENT OF PROCEEDINGS

17.3 Any party may admit the truth of the whole or any part of another party's case at any stage after the commencement of the proceedings (**CPR, r. 14.1(1)**), by giving notice in writing either in a statement of case or by letter (**r. 14.1(2)**). Where a defendant makes an admission by notice under **r. 14.1**, the claimant is then entitled to apply for judgment (**r. 14.3(1)**). The court will enter such judgment as it appears to the court that the applicant is entitled to on the admission (**r. 14.3(2)**).

WITHDRAWAL OF AN ADMISSION

17.4 There are four sets of rules regulating the withdrawal of an admission:

(a) Admissions made under **CPR, r. 14.1**, after commencement of proceedings may be amended or withdrawn only with the permission of the court (**r. 14.1(5)**).

(b) Pre-action admissions made after 6 April 2007 in cases to which **r. 14.1A(2)** applies may be withdrawn before commencement of proceedings only with the consent of the relevant party and after commencement only with all parties' consent or the court's permission (**r. 14.1A(3)**).

(c) Pre-action admissions made before 6 April 2007, or after that date in cases not covered by **r. 14.1A(2)**, continue to be ruled by the decision in *Walley v Stoke-on-Trent City Council* [2006] EWCA Civ 1137, [2007] 1 WLR 352, with the effect that the withdrawal of the admission does not require court approval and can only be challenged by an application to strike out a defence, or part of it, under **r. 3.4(2)** as an abuse of process, for which the claimant will have to demonstrate bad faith on the part of the defendant. (See below.)

(d) Pre-action admissions made in cases covered by the **Pre-action Protocol for Low Value Personal Injury Claims in Road Traffic Accidents** have their own separate rules (**CPR, r. 14.1B**). See further 17.5.

On any application for permission to withdraw an admission, the court must consider the factors listed at **PD 14, para. 7.2**:

(a) the grounds on which the applicant seeks to withdraw the admission, including whether or not new evidence has come to light which was not available at the time the admission was made;

(b) the conduct of the parties, including any conduct which led the party making the admission to do so;
(c) the prejudice that may be caused to any person if the admission is withdrawn, or, conversely, if the application to withdraw is refused;
(d) the stage in the proceedings at which the application is made, and in particular the proximity of the trial;
(e) the prospects of success, if the admission is withdrawn, of the claim or part of the claim in relation to which the offer was made; and
(f) the interests of the administration of justice.

The approach the court should take in applying the factors in **PD 14, para. 7.2**, has been considered by the Court of Appeal in *Woodland v Stopford* [2011] EWCA Civ 266, [2011] Med LR 237. The existence of fresh evidence is not a threshold test which applies to all applications for permission to withdraw a pre-action admission, and it cannot be said that without new evidence a pre-action admission cannot be withdrawn. The court will need to consider all the factors in **PD 14, para. 7.2.** They are not listed in any hierarchical order and the weight to be given to them will vary from case to case. Thus, the overriding importance attached by the court in *American Reliable Insurance Co. v Willis Ltd* [2008] EWHC 2677 (Comm), LTL 20/11/2008, to the need for fresh evidence, whilst appropriate in that case, is not of general application.

The regime set out in **PD 14, para. 7.2**, applies only to the withdrawal of admissions during rather than after the final determination of proceedings (*Kojima v HSBC Bank plc* [2011] EWHC 611, [2011] 3 All ER 359). Where the admission has resulted in a final judgment, the finality principle means that it cannot be revoked under the power given the court by CPR, r. 3.1(7), to vary or revoke an order (*Roult v North West Strategic Health Authority* [2009] EWCA 444, [2010] 1 WLR 487).

The provisions of **CPR, Part 14**, relating to the withdrawal of admissions do not affect the law relating to the compromise of a claim. The distinction between a bare admission and a binding compromise depends on whether the requirements for the creation of a contract (consideration, intention to create legal relations and clarity as to the terms of the contract) are met. Where they are, the agreement is binding and the provisions of **Part 14** have no application (*Burden v Harrods Ltd* [2005] EWHC 410 (QB), [2005] PIQR P17, in which the acceptance of an admission of liability in return for a 25 per cent reduction in damages for contributory negligence was held to be a binding contract). In *Telling v OCS Group Ltd* (2008) LTL 2/6/2008 (Sheffield County Court), the court held that an admission of liability by the defendant in consideration for which the claimant ended her investigations into the claim was sufficient to create a binding compromise to which **Part 14** did not apply.

There is some authority that the provisions of **Part 14** relating to the withdrawal of an admission do not apply to cases proceeding on the fast track. In *Green v Brunel and Family Housing Association Ltd* (2008) LTL 6/6/2008 (Bradford County Court), the judge struck out sections of a defence which sought to resile from a pre-action admission. The court drew a distinction between fast track claims (where the Pre-action Protocol for Personal Injury Claims then in force created a presumption that such admissions would be binding) and multi-track claims. However, the relevant provision no longer appears in the **Pre-action Protocol for Personal Injury Claims. Paragraph 2.12** of the current protocol envisages clearly that investigations between the date of pre-action correspondence and statements of case may result in parties' cases being put differently.

In *White v Greensand Homes Ltd* [2007] EWCA Civ 643, [2007] 1 CLC 1001 (a case to which **CPR, r. 14.1A**, did not apply), the Court of Appeal clarified the approach to a difference between a party's pleaded case and that set out in pre-action correspondence. There are two different circumstances to which different principles apply. The first is where a party seeks to amend a statement of case under **CPR, r. 17.1(2)(b)**, where the amendment will have the effect of

Commentary

withdrawing an admission made in an earlier response letter sent under a pre-action protocol. In this circumstance, the court must have regard to the factors listed above in **PD 14, para.** 7.2.

The second situation is where an admission is made in pre-action correspondence but not repeated in a statement of case, and the question is whether the statement of case which did not repeat the admission can stand. Here, (as **CPR, r. 14.1A**, did not apply) the court should follow the approach set out in *Walley v Stoke-on-Trent City Council* [2006] EWCA Civ 1137, [2007] 1 WLR 352. An application should be brought under **CPR, r. 3.4(2)(b)**, to strike out the statement of case on the ground that it is an abuse of the court's process or is otherwise likely to obstruct the just disposal of the proceedings. In order to show abuse, the claimant would normally have to show that the defendant had acted in bad faith.

In *Gunn v Taygroup Ltd* [2010] EWHC 1665 (TCC), LTL 8/7/2010, the court held that where there is no assertion of bad faith, so that it cannot strike out parts of the defence on the grounds of an abuse of process within **r. 3.4(2)(b)**, the court's decision must be founded on the principles of equity and estoppel. The admission cannot be withdrawn if it was relied upon by the party to whom it was made to its substantial detriment. On the facts in this case, there was no prejudice to the claimant. The court rejected the argument that key evidence may have been lost or deteriorated over the passage of time. Further, it would be unfair to hold the defendant to its pre-admission decision in the face of a fivefold increase in the value of the claim between the pre-action admission and the denial of liability in the defence.

There must be good reason why it is in the interests of justice for an admission to be withdrawn close to trial. This will usually be that there is good evidence that the admission is in fact false. The court should go on to consider other factors such as prejudice to the parties caused by permitting the admission to stand only where there is also counter-evidence of the truth of the facts admitted (*Les Laboratoires Servier v Apotex Inc.* [2007] EWHC 591 (Pat), IPD 30030).

Withdrawal of an admission made under the RTA Protocol

17.5 The **Pre-action Protocol for Low Value Personal Injury Claims in Road Traffic Accidents** (**'the RTA Protocol'**) covers road traffic claims for personal injury worth no more than £10,000 arising out of accidents occurring on or after 30 April 2010. It provides a mechanism for the settlement of claims and the recovery of fixed legal costs without the need for court proceedings. **CPR, r. 14.1B**, sets out the position relating to the withdrawal of admissions made under Stage 1 or Stage 2 of the **RTA Protocol**. It distinguishes between admissions of causation and other admissions. Withdrawal of an admission of causation may be made before proceedings are issued during the initial consideration period (defined in the **RTA Protocol, para.** 7.28, as the period of 15 days which the defendant has for consideration of the Stage 2 settlement pack sent by the claimant) or at any time up to the commencement of the claim if the person to whom it was made agrees (**CPR, r. 14.1B(2)(a)**). After issue of proceedings, an admission of causation, or any pre-action admission, may be withdrawn with all parties' consent or court permission (**r. 14.1B(2)(b)** and **(3)**). An application for permission must be made under **Part 23** (**r. 14.1B (4)**).

ADMISSION OF A MONEY CLAIM WITHIN 14 DAYS OF SERVICE OF THE PARTICULARS OF CLAIM

17.6 In money claims (whether for a specified sum or not), the CPR contain a procedure for the admission of the claim at an early stage. This procedure (which is in addition to the procedure described in 17.3) is aimed primarily at individual defendants in debt claims (though it is not actually restricted to such defendants). It provides a mechanism whereby the rate and time by which the admitted claim is to be paid can be agreed between the parties or fixed by the court.

There are separate rules for four different categories of admission:

(a) admission of the whole of a claim for a specified sum (r. 14.4; see 17.7);
(b) admission of part of a claim for a specified sum (r. 14.5; see 17.8);
(c) admission of liability to pay the whole of a claim for an unspecified amount of money (r. 14.6; see 17.9); and
(d) admission of liability to pay the whole of a claim for an unspecified amount of money, where the defendant offers a sum in satisfaction of the claim (r. 14.7; see 17.10).

The claimant may not enter judgment in default under these rules against a child or a protected party, nor may a claimant who is a child or protected party enter judgment where the admission has been made under **r. 14.5** or **r. 14.7** (**r. 14.1(4)**).

Any admission by the defendant under **rr. 14.4** to **14.7** must be made within 14 days after service of the claim form, or, where the claim form states that particulars of claim will follow, within 14 days after service of the particulars of claim (**r. 14.2**). **Rule 14.2(2)** extends this deadline in two cases:

(a) Where the claim form has been served out of the jurisdiction in circumstances where the court's permission is not required, in which case the time limits set out in **r. 6.35** apply. (Where the court's permission is required for service out of the jurisdiction the court's order will specify the time for filing or serving an admission (**PD 6B, para. 6.2**) calculated by reference to the table at the end of **PD 6B** (**PD 6B, para. 6.2**).)
(b) Where the court makes an order for service on an agent of an overseas principal under **CPR, r. 6.12(3)**, in which case the deadline for filing the acknowledgment will be that specified in the order.

In any event, the defendant may return an admission under **rr. 14.4** to **14.7** after the dead-line specified in **r. 14.2**, provided judgment in default has not already been entered (**r. 14.2(3)**).

When particulars of claim are served on a defendant, the response pack will include a series of forms for responding to the claim. These will include forms for making an admission (**r. 7.8(1)**; **PD 14, para. 2.1**). The defendant will need to choose the correct form from the pack for making his admission.

Admission of the whole of a claim for a specified sum

Under **CPR, r. 14.4**, a defendant who admits the whole of a claim for a specified sum has three options: **17.7**

(a) If he is able, he may simply pay the sum claimed in full (together with interest, and the amount of fixed costs (see **chapter 69**) and issue fee endorsed on the claim form) direct to the claimant in full within 14 days after service.
(b) Alternatively, the defendant may ask for time to pay, or ask to pay by instalments (**r. 14.9**), by returning form N9A to the claimant having completed the details sought about his means (**r. 14.4(2)**). Where the claimant accepts the defendant's proposals, he may obtain judgment by filing request form N225 (**r. 14.9(4)**). The court will then enter judgment for payment at the time and rate specified in the defendant's request (**r. 14.9(5)**). If the claimant does not accept the defendant's proposals, he should still file request form N225, but give notice that he does not accept the proposals (**r. 14.10(2)**). The court will then decide the time and rate at which payment should be made (**r. 14.10(4)**).
(c) The defendant may simply admit the claim without seeking time to pay, by returning form N9A to the claimant. In this case, the claimant may obtain judgment by filing a request for judgment in form N225 (**r. 14.4(3)**). The claimant may specify the date by which the judgment should be paid or the times and rates at which it is to be paid by instalments (**r. 14.4(4)**). Judgment will then be entered by the court in the terms specified by the claimant (**r. 14.4(5)** and **(6)**).

Admission of only part of a claim for a specified sum

17.8 A defendant who, under **CPR, r. 14.5**, admits part of a claim for a specified sum should complete forms N9A and N9B and return them to the court within 14 days after service. The claimant then has the choice of accepting the partial admission and entering judgment, or refusing the admission altogether, in which case the claim will continue as a defended claim.

On receipt of the defendant's admission, the court will serve notice on the claimant requiring notification to the court within 14 days of whether the claimant wishes to accept the defendant's offer, reject it or accept the amount of the offer but reject the proposals for payment (**r. 14.5(3)**). If the claimant does not reply within 14 days, the claim will be stayed until the reply is filed (**r. 14.5(4)** and **(5)**).

The defendant may or may not have asked for time to pay. Where the claimant has accepted the partial admission in principle, the procedure in **17.7(b)** and **(c)** then applies in relation to proposals for payment (except that form N225A is used instead of N225).

The provisions of **r. 14.5** do not apply to claims in the Commercial Court (**r. 58.9(1)**). Instead the claimant should simply apply for judgment on the admission under **r. 14.3**.

Admission of liability on a claim for an unspecified sum

17.9 A defendant who, under **CPR, r. 14.6**, admits liability for the whole of a claim for an unspecified sum should complete form N9C and return it to the court within 14 days after service. This form is then sent by the court to the claimant, who may request the court to enter judgment on liability, with damages to be assessed. If the claim is a designated money claim (i.e. a claim started in any county court under **Part** 7 for a specified or unspecified amount of money, **r. 2.3(1)**), receipt of a request from the claimant for judgment to be entered for an amount to be decided by the court under **r. 14.6** will trigger the automatic transfer of the claim to the preferred court (this is the court specified by the claimant in the claim form under **PD 7A, para. 4A.2**) (**r. 14.7A**). That court will then enter judgment and give directions for the assessment of damages. If appropriate, the case may be allocated to a track (**r. 14.8**). The procedure for assessing damages is considered at **42.46** to **42.49**.

If the claimant does not file a request for judgment within 14 days after service of the admission on him, the claim is stayed until the request is filed (**r. 14.6(5)**).

Admission of liability for a claim for an unspecified sum and offer of an amount to satisfy the claim

17.10 A defendant who, under **CPR, r. 14.7**, admits liability for a claim for an unspecified sum and offers an amount of money to satisfy the claim should complete form N9C and send it to the court within 14 days after service. The court will forward it to the claimant. The claimant may then either accept the amount offered and request judgment to be entered in that amount, or reject the amount offered and request judgment to be entered for an amount to be decided by the court and costs. The claimant's choice must be notified to the court within 14 days of being served with a notice of request. If the claimant does not reply within 14 days, the claim will be stayed until the reply is filed. If the claim is a designated money claim (i.e. a claim started in any county court under **Part** 7 for a specified or unspecified amount of money, **r. 2.3(1)**), receipt of a request from the claimant for judgment to be entered for an amount to be decided by the court under **r. 14.7** will trigger the automatic transfer of the claim to the preferred court (this is the court specified by the claimant in the claim form under **PD 7A, para. 4A.2**) (**r. 14.7A**).

The defendant may or may not ask for time to pay under **r. 14.9**. Where the claimant accepts the admission in principle, the procedure in **17.7(b)** and **(c)** then applies in relation to proposals for payment (except that form N226 is used instead of N225).

Court's discretion to postpone payment under r. 14.10

The nature of the court's jurisdiction under **CPR, r. 14.10**, to postpone payment or to order payment by instalments was considered in *Gulf International Bank v Al Ittefaq Steel Products Co.* [2010] EWHC 2601 (QB), LTL 1/11/2010, there having previously been no authority on the point. The case was an unusual one for the application of the Part 14 rules on admitting a claim and seeking time to pay, in that it involved commercial parties seeking to restructure major loan debt. The defendants admitted the claim under **r. 14.4** and then made a request under **r. 14.9** for postponement of the normal 14-day period for payment, on the basis that there was a real prospect of a rescheduling agreement of its indebtedness, which would benefit all creditors. The court took the view that the same considerations applied as to applications under **r. 40.11** for extensions of time to pay a judgment debt (e.g. *Amsalem v Raivid* [2008] EWHC 3226 (TCC), LTL 27/3/2009). Applying these principles, it refused the application, holding that mere inability to pay would not usually justify the postponement of the normal period for payment, particularly where the parties were business entities. The court will extend time under **r. 14.10** only exceptionally and then only where the judgment debtor is solvent and for a relatively short period of time. **17.11**

Chapter 18 Acknowledging Service and Filing a Defence

The following procedural checklist, which is at the front of the book, is relevant to this chapter:

Procedural checklist 13 Time limits for responding to claim by acknowledging service and/ or filing a defence

ACKNOWLEDGING SERVICE

18.1 When particulars of claim are served on the defendant, the response pack will include a form (form N9) for acknowledging service of the claim (**CPR, r. 7.8(1)**). Except in the case of Part 8 claims (see **chapter 13**), contentious probate claims and claims issued in the Commercial and Mercantile Courts (see below), a defendant is under no obligation to file an acknowledgment, even if there is an intention to defend the claim. Instead of filing an acknowledgment, a defendant may proceed immediately to file and serve a defence.

By **r. 10.1(3)**, an acknowledgment may be filed in any case where:

(a) the defendant is not able to file a defence within 14 days after service of the particulars of claim; or

(b) the defendant wishes to dispute the court's jurisdiction.

In the latter case, filing an acknowledgment indicating an intention to contest the jurisdiction will not constitute a submission to the jurisdiction (**r. 11(3)**) (see further **chapter 19** on disputing the court's jurisdiction). However, by signing an acknowledgment without indicating an intention to challenge jurisdiction, a party waives any defects in service (see, e.g., *Brooks v A. H. Brooks and Co.* [2010] EWHC 2720 (Ch), [2011] 3 All ER 982).

If the claim has been brought under the Part 8 procedure (in which case the claim form must state that **Part 8** applies), the claim form is accompanied only by a form of acknowledgment of service (**r. 7.8(2)(b)**). The defendant must then file and serve an acknowledgment within 14 days after service of the claim form (**r. 8.3**). See further **chapter 13**.

The general provisions for acknowledging service are modified for claims issued in the Commercial and Mercantile Courts. In those courts the defendant must always file an acknowledgment of service (**rr. 58.6(1)** and **59.5(1)**) within 14 days after service of the claim form (whether or not it is accompanied by particulars of claim) (**rr. 58.6(2)** and **59.5(2)**). An adapted version of N9 has been approved for use in the Commercial Court (form N9(CC)). The period for acknowledging service is extended in the situations listed in **rr. 58.6(3)** and **59.5(3)**. There are special rules for Admiralty claims in **rr. 61.3** and **61.4**.

For acknowledging service in cases under the **Pre-action Protocol for Low Value Personal Injury Claims in Road Traffic Accidents** see **8.50**.

TIME FOR FILING THE ACKNOWLEDGMENT

An acknowledgment of service must, by **CPR, r. 10.3(1)**, be filed: **18.2**

(a) within 14 days after service of the particulars of claim, where the particulars of claim are served after the claim form; or
(b) within 14 days after service of the claim form, where the particulars of claim are included in or served with the claim form.

In contentious probate proceedings, the time limits are 28 days after service of the claim form or particulars of claim, where the particulars are served after the claim form (**r. 57.4**).

In *Coll v Tattum* (2001) *The Times*, 3 December 2001, Neuberger J held that, although the CPR are silent on the point, a defendant who wishes to acknowledge service or file a defence after these time limits have expired but before judgment in default is entered needs either the other side's consent or the court's permission. Granting permission is a matter for the court's discretion, which will normally be exercised in favour of extending time where there is a defence which is apparently bona fide and arguable (see **20.9**). *Coll v Tattum* has been followed in *Boeing Capital Corporation v Wells Fargo Bank Northwest* [2003] EWHC 1364 (Comm), LTL 17/7/2003 and *Lexi Holdings plc v Luqman* [2007] EWHC 2497 (Ch), LTL 26/11/2007. In *ESR Insurance Services Ltd v Clemons* [2008] EWHC 2023 (Comm), LTL 2/9/2008, the court gave permission to a defendant to file an acknowledgment late, and extended time for him to do so, on the grounds that it would be unfair to the defendant to enter default judgment where he had in fact filed an acknowledgment by the time of the application for judgment in default and needed time to take legal advice. However, at the same time it gave permission to the claimant to make a summary judgment application, on the strength of the existing evidence. See further **18.6**.

These deadlines are extended where the claim form has been served out of the jurisdiction (**r. 10.3(2)(a)**). Where service out of the jurisdiction has been effected without the court's permission, under **rr. 6.32** and **6.33**, the time limits set out in **r. 6.35** apply. Where an order for service out of the jurisdiction has been obtained, it will include the date by which acknowledgment should be filed (**PD 6B, para. 6.2**) calculated by reference to the table at the end of **PD 6B (PD 6B, para. 6.2)**. In contentious probate proceedings, the time limits for service out of the jurisdiction without permission under **CPR, rr. 6.32** and **6.33**, are extended by a further 14 days (**CPR, r. 57.4(3)**).

Where the court makes an order under **r. 6.12**, for service on an agent of an overseas principal, any acknowledgment of service must be filed within the period specified by the court under **r. 6.12(3)** for responding to particulars of claim (**r. 10.3(2)(b)**).

In judicial review cases, acknowledgment of service must be filed within 21 days after service of the claim form, and must be served on the claimant and any other person named in the claim form (**r. 54.8(2)**).

Naturally, time for filing the acknowledgment does not run during the period of a stay (*Roundstone Nurseries Ltd v Stephenson Holdings Ltd* [2009] EWHC 1431 (TCC), [2009] 5 Costs LR 787).

The court must notify the claimant in writing that an acknowledgment has been filed (**r. 10.4**).

CONTENTS OF THE FORM OF ACKNOWLEDGMENT

The form of acknowledgment of service (form N9) requires the defendant: **18.3**

(a) to indicate the intention to defend all or part of the claim;
(b) to state whether it is intended to contest the jurisdiction; and
(c) if an individual, to state his or her date of birth (**PD 16, para. 10.7**).

If a party seeks to challenge the jurisdiction of the court, the most prudent course is to tick only the second box. See further the discussion at **19.2**.

The acknowledgment must give the defendant's full name, if it is different from the name given on the claim form. It must give an address for service (**CPR, r. 10.5(b)**). If the defendant's legal representative has signed the acknowledgment, the representative's business address will be the defendant's address for service (**PD 10, para. 3.2**).

The acknowledgment must be signed either by the defendant or by the defendant's legal representative (**CPR, r. 10.5(a)**). In the case of a company or other corporation, the acknowledgment must be signed by a person in a senior position. Persons who fall into this category are set out at **PD 10, para. 4.3**. Where the defendant is a partnership, the acknowledgment must be signed in the name of the partnership on behalf of all partners at the time the cause of action accrued. It may be signed by any partner or a person authorised by any partner to sign it (**PD 10, para. 4.4**) (see further **15.50** for a fuller discussion of acknowledging service on behalf of a partnership, and **79.38** for the effect of acknowledgment on enforcement against the personal assets of a partner). A child or protected party may sign an acknowledgment only through his or her litigation friend or solicitor, unless the court orders to the contrary (**PD 10, para. 4.5**).

An acknowledgment of service in a claim begun using the CPR, Part 8, procedure (but not other types of claim) must be verified by a statement of truth (**r. 22.1(1)(d)**).

The same form may be used for two or more defendants, if they are represented by the same solicitor (**PD 10, para. 5.3**).

If the defendant has entered into a funding arrangement (as defined in **r. 43.2(1)(k)**), a notice of funding of case (form N251) must be filed at court with the acknowledgment of service and a copy served on every other party (**PD 43–48, para. 19.2(3)**).

An acknowledgment of service may be amended or withdrawn only with permission of the court (**PD 10, para. 5.4**).

Where an acknowledgment is returned by a defendant with the 'I do not intend to defend this claim' box ticked, the proper course for the defendant is to issue an application for judgment to be entered, rather than a request for judgment. This means that the acknowledgment can be considered by the court, rather than being dealt with as an administrative act (*Northern Rock (Asset Management) plc v Chancellors Associates Ltd* [2011] EWHC 3229, [2012] 2 All ER 501).

FILING A DEFENCE

18.4 Save in the case of Part 8 claims (**CPR, r. 15.1**), a defendant who wishes to defend all or part of a claim must file a defence (**r. 15.2**). A defendant's privilege against self-incrimination does not give rise to a right not to plead a defence in civil proceedings (*Versailles Trade Finance Ltd v Clough* [2001] EWCA Civ 1509, [2002] CP Rep 8, and affirmed by the Court of Appeal in *Coogan v News Group Newspapers Ltd* [2012] EWCA Civ 48, [2012] 2 WLR 848; *Phillips v News Group Newspapers Ltd* [2012] UKSC 28, [2013] 1 AC 1). If a defence is not filed within the specified period, default judgment (see **chapter 20**) may be entered (**r. 15.3**). A copy of the defence must be served on every other party (**r. 15.6**). **Rule 15.6** does not explicitly state whether it is the court's or the defendant's responsibility to serve the defence, but **r. 6.21(1)** makes clear that the party who has prepared a document must serve it, except where a rule, practice direction or court order provides otherwise.

If the defendant has entered into a funding arrangement (as defined in **r. 43.2(1)(k)**) and the defence is the first document to be filed by the defendant, a notice of funding of case (form N251) must be filed at court with the defence and a copy served on every other party (**PD 43–48, para. 19.2(3)**).

None of the rules relating to the filing of defences applies to Part 8 claims (**r. 15.1**). They do, however, apply to cases where a defence is filed to a counterclaim (**r. 20.3**).

Period for filing a defence

The general rule is that a defence must be filed within 14 days after service of the particulars of claim (**CPR, r. 15.4(1)(a)**). Where a claim form is served which does not include, and is not accompanied by, particulars of claim, the defendant should wait for the particulars, which should be served by the claimant within 14 days after service of the claim form (**r. 7.4**). **18.5**

If more time is needed in which to file and serve a defence, the defendant may file an acknowledgment of service under **Part 10**. The time for filing a defence is then extended until 28 days after service of the particulars of claim (**r. 15.4(1)(b)**).

There are different time limits for filing a defence where the claim form is served out of the jurisdiction without the court's permission, under **rr. 6.32** and **6.33** (see **r. 6.25**). Where an order for service out of the jurisdiction has been obtained, it will include the date by which a defence should be filed (**PD 6B, para. 6.2**) calculated by reference to the table at the end of **PD 6B** (**PD 6B, para. 6.2**). Where a claim form is served on the agent of a principal who is overseas the court will, under **CPR, r. 6.12(3)**, specify the period for responding to the particulars of claim.

There are two further exceptions to the general rule:

(a) A defendant who makes an application disputing the jurisdiction of the court (see **chapter 19**) need not file a defence before the hearing of the application (**r. 11(9)**). However, if any such application is abandoned, the protection of **r. 11(9)** is lost (*Flame SA v Primera Maritime (Hellas) Ltd* [2009] EWHC 1973 (Comm), LTL 29/9/2009).

(b) Where the claimant makes an application for summary judgment under **Part 24** (see **chapter 34**) before the defendant has filed a defence, the defendant need not then do so before the hearing of the application (**r. 24.4(2)**).

If either application is unsuccessful, and the claim continues, the court will make a direction for filing and service of the defence within a stated period. **Rules 11(9)** and **24.4(2)** do not prevent a defendant filing a defence in the period before the hearing of the application.

Naturally, time for filing a defence does not run during the period of a stay (*Roundstone Nurseries Ltd v Stephenson Holdings Ltd* [2009] EWHC 1431 (TCC), [2009] 5 Costs LR 787).

Late filing of the defence

Under **CPR, r. 15.4**, the general rule is that the period for filing a defence is 14 days after service of the particulars of claim. This period can be extended by filing an acknowledgment of service, obtaining the claimant's consent, or obtaining an order for an extension. Once this period has elapsed, the claimant is usually entitled to enter a default judgment under **Part 12**, and the only consequence stated in the CPR as flowing from not filing a defence within the stated time is the danger that the claimant might enter judgment in default (**r. 15.3**). A default judgment may only be entered where the defendant has failed to file an acknowledgment of service or a defence (**r. 12.1**). This means that if the claimant delays in entering judgment in default, the question is which side then acts first. If the claimant enters judgment first, all the defendant can do is to apply to set the judgment aside under **Part 13**. If the defendant files a defence first, it is no longer open for the claimant to enter judgment in default because of **r. 12.1**. In this situation, the claim proceeds as normal, but the delay by the defendant may be taken into account on costs or in general case management. **18.6**

In a number of situations, judgment in default can only be entered after the claimant issues an application for permission to enter judgment (see **20.8** and **20.9**). Typically, these are claims where the relief sought includes equitable remedies. What is the position if the

Commentary

defendant purports to acknowledge service or file a defence in the period between the claimant issuing an application for the entry of default judgment and the hearing of the application? In *Coll v Tattum* (2001) *The Times*, 3 December 2001, Neuberger J said that as the defendant was seeking to file the defence outside the time limit, he needed either the consent of the claimant or the permission of the court. Permission would normally be granted where there was a genuine defence. A similar result was achieved in *Boeing Capital Corporation v Wells Fargo Bank Northwest* [2003] EWHC 1364 (Comm), LTL 17/7/2003, a case like *Coll v Tattum* where the claimant needed permission because the claim was for equitable relief. In *Lexi Holdings plc v Luqman* [2007] EWHC 2497 (Ch), LTL 26/11/2007, the court followed *Coll v Tattum*, and held that a defence which was on its face apparently bona fide and arguable should be permitted to be served out of time after an application for judgment in default had been made. The test applied by the court in deciding whether to enter judgment in default was different to the wider question of whether the defence was susceptible to an application for summary judgment, which should normally be left over to a further application, should the claimant wish to pursue it. However, this approach was a rule of thumb rather than an invariable rule. On the facts of this case, where the defence had been filed late, and it could be shown it was bound to fail in part, judgment in default would be entered on that part (see **34.10**).

Extending the time for service of a defence

18.7 Under CPR, r. 15.5, the defendant and the claimant may agree an extension of the time for filing a defence of up to 28 days only. Where they do so, they must notify the court in writing (**r. 15.5(2)**).

A defendant who requires additional time beyond this must make an application, using the Part 23 procedure, under **r. 3.1(2)(a)**. Guidance on the exercise of the court's discretion when making orders under **r. 3.1(2)(a)** is to be found in *Sayers v Clarke Walker* [2002] EWCA Civ 645, [2002] 1 WLR 3095, and *Robert v Momentum Services Ltd* [2003] EWCA Civ 299, [2003] 1 WLR 1577 (see **15.40**). However, the court will expect the parties to be reasonable in agreeing appropriate extensions. A court hearing, involving the preparation of witness statements and exhibits, to determine whether an extension should be final or not was inappropriate and a wholly disproportionate waste of time. A future judge could decide if the defendant had had ample time to prepare its defence by the end of the agreed extension, should further time be necessary (*TIP Communications LLC v Motorola Ltd* [2009] EWHC 212 (Pat), LTL 23/2/2009).

Filing and serving a defence in the Commercial Court

18.8 The Commercial Court no longer has special rules on filing and serving defences.

Chapter 19 Disputing the Court's Jurisdiction

The following procedural checklist, which is at the front of the book, is relevant to this chapter:

Procedural checklist 14 Procedure for disputing the court's jurisdiction

Commentary

INTRODUCTION

CPR, Part 11, makes provision for the defendant to challenge the jurisdiction of the English court, or to argue that the court should not exercise any jurisdiction which it may have. The rule is not confined to challenges over the court's geographic jurisdiction. It may be invoked where there is any dispute over the court's power or authority to try a claim, including disputes over the bringing of litigation despite an arbitration clause in an agreement between the parties or over service of a claim form after it has expired (*Hoddinott v Persimmon Homes (Wessex) Ltd* [2008] EWCA Civ 1203, [2008] 1 WLR 806). **Part 11** does not, however, extend to disputes over possible limitation defences, whether under the Limitation Act 1980 or under the **Human Rights Act 1998, s. 7(5)** (*Dunn v The Parole Board* [2008] EWCA Civ 374, [2009] 1 WLR 728; *M v Ministry of Justice* [2009] EWCA Civ 419, LTL 19/5/2009). The rules on jurisdiction are considered in **chapter 16**. The procedure for disputing the court's jurisdiction is considered below. 19.1

ACKNOWLEDGMENT OF SERVICE

The defendant must first file an acknowledgment of service within the usual time limit (i.e. within 14 days after service of the claim form, or of the particulars of claim, if served later, or, where served out of the jurisdiction, the time limits given under **CPR, r. 6.35**, and **PD 6B, para. 6.2**) stating an intention to contest the jurisdiction (**CPR, r. 11(2)**). To avoid any ambiguity about submitting to the jurisdiction, the defendant should tick only the 'intention to contest the jurisdiction' box and not also tick the 'intention to defend' box (see **19.4**). In *Hoddinott v Persimmon Homes (Wessex) Ltd* [2007] EWCA Civ 1203, [2008] 1 WLR 806, the defendant applied to set aside an order extending time for service of the claim form, made without notice to it. Before the application was heard, the claimant served the claim form. In response, the defendant filed an acknowledgment of service in which it ticked the box 'I intend to defend all of this claim', and not the box 'I intend to contest the jurisdiction'. However, it made no application under **Part 11**. The Court of Appeal held that it had abandoned its application to set aside the order extending the time for service. It was reinforced in its conclusion by the fact that the defendant had indicated in the acknowledgment of service that it did not intend to contest jurisdiction and did intend to defend the claim. 19.2

APPLICATION DISPUTING JURISDICTION

Within 14 days after filing an acknowledgment of service, the defendant should make an application for the order sought, using the Part 23 procedure (**CPR, r. 11(4)(a)**). In the 19.3

Commercial and Mercantile Courts the time limit is 28 days after filing an acknowledgment (**rr. 58.7** and **59.6**). Failure to make the application within this time limit will be taken as a submission to the jurisdiction (**r. 11(5)(b)**). The application must be supported by evidence (**r. 11(4)(b)**). No defence need be served before the hearing of the application (**r. 11(9)**). Indeed, serving a defence may constitute a voluntary submission to the jurisdiction (see **19.4**).

As originally drafted, **r. 11(4)** expressed the time limit for making an application as 'the period for filing a defence'. It became clear in *Monrose Investments Ltd v Orion Nominees Ltd* [2001] CP Rep 109 that it was confusing to express the time limit in this way as the reference was to the time limit in **r. 15.4**, not the time as it might have been extended by the court. The current wording of **r. 11(4)** deals with this problem. It was also held in *Monrose Investments v Orion Nominees* that if a party needs additional time to make an application to contest the jurisdiction, it should make an application for an extension of the time limit laid down in **r. 11(4)** and the court has a discretion under **r. 3.1(2)(a)** to extend it. The decision on this point was followed in *SSQ Europe SA v Johann & Backes OHG* [2002] 1 Lloyd's Rep 465, in which the court confirmed that an extension of time for service of a defence does not carry with it an extension of time for an application to challenge the court's jurisdiction.

The application for an extension of time in which to challenge jurisdiction should be made within the time limit (14 days or 28 days in the Commercial and Mercantile Courts) as a failure to do so may be taken as a submission to the jurisdiction (*Maple Leaf Macro Volatility Master Fund v Rouvroy* [2009] EWHC 257 (Comm), [2009] 2 All ER (Comm) 287, at [187]).

In *Sawyer v Atari Interactive Inc.* [2005] EWHC 2351 (Ch), LTL 9/11/2005, Lawrence Collins J held that he had discretion under **r. 3.1(2)(a)** retrospectively to extend the period for making an application to dispute the jurisdiction. It was appropriate to exercise the discretion where the application was made promptly, there was no prejudice to the claimant and the solicitor's error in not making the application in time was understandable, if not excusable in that he erroneously believed the relevant time limit to be the period for filing the defence.

Applications disputing jurisdiction should, as a matter of principle, be decided at the earliest reasonable opportunity (*Cooper Tire and Rubber Co. v Shell Chemicals UK Ltd* [2009] EWHC 1529 (Comm), LTL 7/7/2009, where an adjournment was refused, despite a risk that the costs of a complex jurisdictional challenge could prove to be wasted depending on the result of pending appeals in Italy). The court in that case also rejected an argument that the procedural time limits laid down in the CPR were inconsistent with the **Brussels I Regulation, art. 28** (which gives the court a discretion to stay its proceedings if it is not the court first seised and a related action is pending in the court of another member State).

The time limits in **CPR, part 11**, do not apply where a party is seeking a stay under the Arbitration Act 1996, s. 9 (*Bilta (UK) Ltd v Nazir* [2010] EWHC 1086 (Ch), [2010] Bus LR 1634).

A non-party served out of the jurisdiction with an application notice may apply to contest the jurisdiction in relation to the application notice, by virtue of **r. 6.39(2)**.

SUBMISSION TO JURISDICTION

19.4 Acknowledging service does not affect any right the defendant might have to contest the jurisdiction of the court (**CPR, r. 11(3)**). Although the CPR do not address the point explicitly, taking any step in the claim other than acknowledging service and applying under **Part 11** to contest the court's jurisdiction is extremely dangerous. Any such action may constitute a voluntary submission to the jurisdiction of the English courts. It was held in *Monrose Investments Ltd v Orion Nominees Ltd* [2001] CP Rep 109 (applying Sage v Double A Hydraulics Ltd (1992) *The Times*, 2 April 1992) that applying for an extension of time for service of a defence, without any reference to an intention to contest the jurisdiction, constituted a submission to the jurisdiction. In *Global Multimedia International Ltd v ARA Media Services* [2006] EWHC 3612 (Ch), [2007] 1 All ER (Comm) 1160, the defendant filed an acknowledgment of service indicating an intention to defend the claim, but not to contest the jurisdiction. The defendant's solicitors also entered into correspondence with solicitors for the claimant over a five-week period seeking an extension of time for service of the defence and entering into discussions as to the merits of the defence. The court held that the test to be applied in considering whether such conduct amounted to a submission was an objective one, and that on the facts this conduct was consistent with an acceptance of the jurisdiction of the English courts. The court advised solicitors who may have little time to decide whether or not to challenge the jurisdiction to tick the box indicating an intention to contest the jurisdiction and then apply for an extension of time under **r. 11(4)**. In *SSQ Europe SA v Johann & Backes OHG* [2002] 1 Lloyd's Rep 465 it was held that service of a defence and counterclaim accompanied by an express challenge to the jurisdiction did not constitute a submission. It did not amount to the unconditional entry of an appearance or unequivocal conduct required by art. 18 of the Brussels Convention (now **Brussels I Regulation, art. 24**) (*Elefanten Schuh GmbH v Jacqmain* (case 150/80) [1981] ECR 1671). In *SMAY Investments Ltd v Sachdev* [2003] EWHC 474 (Ch), [2003] 1 WLR 1973 (followed by *Massey v Glover* [2006] EWHC 2323 (Ch)), it was held that neither (a) ticking both the 'intention to defend' and the 'intention to contest the jurisdiction' boxes on the acknowledgment of service nor (b) obtaining an extension of time for service of the defence and offering undertakings to the court accompanied by an intention to contest the jurisdiction constituted an unequivocal intention to submit to the jurisdiction. Attending before a judge to challenge a freezing injunction obtained without notice does not amount to submitting to the jurisdiction, unless the party agrees to an order regulating his position pending trial (*SMAY Investments Ltd v Sachdev*). See further **16.3**. Participation by a property holder as an applicant in interpleader proceedings does not ordinarily amount to a submission to the jurisdiction because the purpose is to gain the protection of the court from the competing claimants (*Australia v Peacekeeper International FZC UAE* [2008] EWHC 1220 (QB), LTL 9/6/2008).

SUSPENSION OF TIME IN MAIN CLAIM

Making an application to contest the jurisdiction suspends time in the main claim. Thus, a defendant need not file a defence (**CPR, r. 11(9)(a)**); a defendant to a Part 8 claim need not file evidence in opposition (**r. 11(9)(b)**) and in claims in the Commercial or Mercantile Courts where the application has been made before service of the particulars of claim, the claimant need not file particulars of claim (**rr. 58.7** and **59.6**). **19.5**

ORDERS

The court may make a declaration that it has no jurisdiction over the claim, or that it will not exercise its jurisdiction. Under **CPR, r. 11(6)**, the order may also: **19.6**

(a) set aside the claim form;
(b) set aside service of the claim form;
(c) discharge any order made before the claim was commenced or the claim form served;
(d) stay the proceedings.

SECOND ACKNOWLEDGMENT

Where the court does not make any declaration that it does not have, or should not exercise, jurisdiction, the acknowledgment of service already filed by the defendant will cease to have effect and the defendant should, if it intends to take part in the proceedings, complete and file **19.7** another form within 14 days or such period as the court may order (**CPR, r. 11(7)**). This acknowledgment will be treated as a submission to the jurisdiction (**r. 11(8)**). The court will give directions for the filing and service of the defence, in a Part 7 claim, or for the filing of evidence in a Part 8 claim (**r. 11(7)(c)**).

In very rare cases the court may, however, hear a summary judgment application immediately following an unsuccessful challenge to the jurisdiction (*Moloobhoy v Kanani* [2013] EWCA Civ 600, LTL 30/5/2013).

Chapter 20 Default Judgment

Commentary

The following procedural checklists, which are at the front of the book, are relevant to this chapter:

Procedural checklist 15 Request for entry of judgment in default
Procedural checklist 16 Application for entry of judgment in default

INTRODUCTION

Failure to file an acknowledgment or a defence within the time limits laid down in the CPR may result under **Part 12** in the claimant entering judgment in default, that is, judgment without a trial of the claim. In most cases the entry of judgment in default is a purely administrative act, not involving any judicial determination of the merits of the claim. Nevertheless, a default judgment is a final judgment which can be enforced in the usual way. It is a final judgment for the purposes of the Housing Act 1996, s. 81 (*Church Commissioners for England v Koyale Enterprises* (2011) LTL 30/11/2011). 20.1

There are two mechanisms under the rules for entering default judgment:

(a) A simple request-for-judgment procedure under **Part 12** is available in money claims (**r. 12.4(1)**), which include claims for specified sums, claims for unquantified damages and some other types of claim. Under this procedure, judgment is entered over the counter on filing a request for default judgment, without any consideration of the merits of the claim. (See **20.4 to 20.7**.) This will apply in the overwhelming majority of cases.
(b) In a claim for a remedy other than a money claim, in a claim only for costs (other than fixed costs) and in certain other cases set out in **r. 12.10**, an application for judgment must be made using the Part 23 procedure (see **chapter 32**). On an application for the entry of a default judgment there will be a hearing and the court will give 'such judgment as it appears to the court that the claimant is entitled to on his statement of case' (**r. 12.11(1)**). This does not mean that the court will consider the merits of the particular claim. Rather, the court's role is to ensure that the claimant is entitled, procedurally, to the relief

sought (*Football Dataco Ltd v Smoot Enterprises Ltd* [2011] EWHC 973 (Ch), [2011] 1 WLR 1978). (See **20.8** and **20.9**.)

A default judgment obtained using the request procedure in error instead of the application-for-judgment procedure was irregular and capable of being set aside as of right under **r. 13.2** (*Intense Investments Ltd v Development Ventures Ltd* [2005] EWHC 1726 (TCC), [2005] BLR 478 (see further **20.12**).

There is no objection in EU law to issuing a default judgment against a defendant where service has been effected by public notice under local law because the claimant is unable to locate him, provided that all the investigations required by the principles of diligence and good faith to trace the defendant have been undertaken and there is no firm evidence that the defendant is domiciled outside the European Union (*G v de Visser* (case C-292/10), CJEU judgment 15 March 2012).

CASES WHERE DEFAULT JUDGMENT MAY NOT BE ENTERED

20.2 CPR, **r. 12.2**, and **PD 12, para. 1.2**, provide that judgment in default may not be entered:

(a) on a claim where the Part 8 procedure has been used (see further **13.9**);
(b) on a claim for 'delivery of goods' (i.e. delivery up of goods) subject to an agreement regulated by the Consumer Credit Act 1974; and
(c) in any case where a practice direction provides that a claimant may not obtain a default judgment.

Default judgment cannot be obtained in a possession claim to which **CPR, Part 55** applies (**r. 55.7(4)**) or in a probate claim (**r. 57.10(1)**). In the Admiralty Court the procedure is modified by **r. 61.9** and **PD 61, para. 8.1**. In the Commercial Court, the procedure is modified by **CPR, r. 58.8**, and **PD 58, para. 6**. Default judgment cannot be obtained in arbitration claims under **CPR, Part 62**, because they are brought under the Part 8 procedure (**rr. 62.3(1)** and **62.13(1)**). Nor can default judgment be entered in a case involving a claim for provisional damages, unless the claimant abandons the claim for provisional damages. If the defendant does not file his acknowledgment or defence in time, and the claimant does not wish to abandon the claim for provisional damages, he should apply to the court for directions under **Part 23** (**PD 41A, para. 5.1**).

Where a defendant has made an admission, the correct response is for the claimant to proceed under **CPR, Part 14** (see **chapter 17**), rather than by way of entry of judgment in default.

CONDITIONS FOR ENTERING JUDGMENT IN DEFAULT

20.3 In order to enter judgment in default, the court is required by **CPR, r. 12.3**, and **PD 12, paras 4.1** and **4.2**, to be satisfied:

(a) that the particulars of claim have been served (a certificate of service on the court file will be sufficient evidence where service was effected by the claimant);
(b) that either the defendant has not filed an acknowledgment of service or has not filed a defence, and, in either case, time for doing so has expired;
(c) that the defendant has not satisfied the claim;
(d) that the defendant has not filed or served an admission together with a request for time to pay;
(e) that the defendant has not made an application to strike out the claim or for summary judgment which has not been disposed of; and
(f) where it is sought to enter judgment in default against a child or protected party, that a litigation friend has been appointed.

Point (a) does not have to be satisfied in the Commercial and Mercantile Courts, where default judgment may be entered before the claimant has served particulars of claim (**CPR, rr. 58.8** and **59.7**). However, in the Mercantile Courts it is necessary to make an application, rather than a request, for default judgment in these circumstances.

If the claimant (rather than the court) served the claim form, judgment in default cannot be obtained unless a certificate of service of the claim form has been filed (**r. 6.17**). The purpose of the rule is to ensure there is satisfactory evidence that the claim form has been served, and it was held in *Lombard North Central plc v Hussein* (2011) LTL 7/3/2011 that it would not be in accordance with the overriding objective for a default judgment to be set aside because the certificate of service had been filed one day late, but before the entry of the judgment in default. The court therefore extended time retrospectively under **r. 3.1(2)** in order to validate the certificate of service.

For the purpose of (b) above, the filing of any document purporting to be a defence will prevent the claimant obtaining judgment in default (**PD 12, para. 1.1**). If a purported defence discloses no substantial grounds of defence, the claimant may consider applying to strike it out (see **chapter 33**) or may seek summary judgment (see **chapter 34**).

For the position where service has been effected under Regulation (EC) No. 1393/2007 (the Service Regulation) see **20.19**.

Commentary

REQUEST FOR DEFAULT JUDGMENT

The procedure for requesting entry of judgment in default is summarised in **procedural checklist 15**, which is at the front of the book. **20.4**

By **CPR, r. 12.4**, a claimant may obtain judgment in default by filing a form requesting judgment to be entered where the claim is for:

(a) a specified sum of money (save where the claim is only for costs other than fixed costs);
(b) an amount of money to be decided by the court;
(c) delivery of goods where the claim form gives the defendant the alternative of paying their value; or
(d) any combination of these remedies.

The claimant is not required to give the defendant notice of making a request for default judgment.

Judgment in default can be obtained under **r. 12.4** for a claim which includes a claim or claims for a remedy other than money provided the non-money claims are abandoned in the request form (**r. 12.4(3)**). However, where this is done and default judgment is entered only to be later set aside, the abandoned claim will be restored when judgment is set aside (**r. 13.6**). The court will require a direct and explicit statement that a non-money claim has been abandoned before it permits the entry of default judgment if the claim form includes an application for an injunction. This requirement will not be satisfied simply by completion of the standard wording in the request for judgment form that 'judgment be entered for an amount including costs to be decided by the court' (*Media CAT Ltd v A* [2010] EWPCC 17, BAILII).

The forms used for requesting judgment in default (forms N205A, N205B, N225 and N227) require the claimant to provide the date of birth (if known) of the defendant, where the defendant is an individual (**PD 12, para. 3.2**). This is because the request procedure applies only where the defendant is an adult. Permission must be sought if the defendant is a child (**CPR, r. 12.10(a)(i)**).

Claim for specified sum

20.5 To obtain judgment in default on a claim for a specified sum, the claimant files a request for judgment in form N205A (part of the notice of issue) or N225.

Judgment will be entered for the amount sought in the claim form, plus fixed costs (set out in **table 2** at **CPR, r. 45.4**, and see **chapter 69**). Alternatively, the claimant may give the defendant time to pay or permit the defendant to pay in instalments. This is done by setting out the rate and times of payment acceptable in the request for judgment form. Judgment will then be entered on this basis (**r. 12.5**).

By **r. 12.6**, the default judgment will include interest on claims for specified sums which has accrued due up to the date on which the default judgment was entered, provided that:

(a) full particulars of interest were set out in the particulars of claim;
(b) on a claim for statutory interest, the rate sought is no higher than that payable on judgment debts (currently 8 per cent); and
(c) the request for judgment sets out a calculation of the interest claimed between the date to which interest has been calculated in the claim form, and the date of the request for judgment.

Otherwise, judgment will be entered for interest to be decided by the court (**r. 12.6(2)**).

Claim for unspecified sum

20.6 To obtain judgment in default on a claim for an unspecified sum, the claimant files form N205B (part of the notice of issue) or N227 and judgment will be for an amount to be decided by the court, plus costs (**CPR, r. 12.5(3)**). If the claim is a designated money claim (i.e. a claim started in any county court under **Part 7** for a specified or unspecified amount of money, **r. 2.3(1)**), receipt of a request from the claimant under **rr. 12.4** and **12.5** for judgment to be entered for an amount to be decided by the court will trigger the automatic transfer of the claim to the preferred court (this is the court specified by the claimant in the claim form under **PD 7A, para. 4A.2**) (**r. 12.5A**). A default judgment on liability for an amount to be decided by the court is conclusive on liability in respect of all matters pleaded. But all questions going to quantification of the damage remain open. Any point may be raised by the defendant at the assessment of damages, provided it is consistent with the judgment on liability. Thus it is not open to the defendant to say that its acts or omissions had not caused any damage, but it could say that its acts or omissions had not caused certain individual items of damage (*Lunnun v Singh* (1999) *The Times*, 19 July 1999, followed in *Pugh v Cantor Fitzgerald International* [2001] EWCA Civ 307, *The Times*, 19 March 2001) and approved by the Privy Council in *Strachan v Gleaner Co. Ltd* [2005] UKPC 33, [2005] 1 WLR 3204). A defendant who wishes to dispute liability must appeal or apply to set aside the judgment.

In any case where the court enters judgment for:

(a) an amount to be decided by the court,
(b) the value of goods to be decided by the court, or
(c) interest to be decided by the court,

it will also give any directions it considers appropriate and may allocate the case to a track (**r. 12.7**). However, it will normally only allocate the case (other than in small claims track cases) where there is a substantial dispute between the parties as to the amount payable (**PD 26, para. 12.3**).

The detailed procedure governing the assessment of damages is set out in **PD 26, para. 12**. On the entry of the default judgment, the court will fix an appointment for a disposal hearing, at which it may either give case management directions, or, where it has sufficient information, quantify the claim immediately. Where the value of the claim is below the limit for the small claims track, the court will allocate the case to that track and may treat the disposal hearing as the final hearing of the case (**PD 26, para. 12.4(3)**). The types of case management orders the court may make are set out in **PD 26, para. 12.2**, and include the filing of directions questionnaires and stays for the purpose of ADR. The court may also fix further hearings, and, to enable it to come to a decision on quantum, it might order disclosure, the filing of expert evidence and the exchange of witness statements on the issues which remain live between the parties.

Claims against the Crown

Default judgment in claims against the Crown may now be entered upon filing a request for judgment. An application is no longer necessary. However, a request for a default judgment against the Crown must be considered by a master or district judge, who must be satisfied that the claim form and particulars of claim have been properly served on the Crown in accordance with the Crown Proceedings Act 1947, s. 18, and **CPR, r. 6.10** (**CPR, r. 12.4(4)**). **20.7**

APPLICATION FOR DEFAULT JUDGMENT

The procedure for applying for entry of judgment in default is summarised in **procedural checklist 16**, which is at the front of the book. **20.8**

CPR, rr. 12.9(1)(b) and **12.10**, and **PD 12, para. 2.3**, specify certain types of claim on which default judgment may only be obtained by making an application under **CPR, Part 23**. Cases where the claimant must make an application are where:

(a) the claim is:
   (i) not a money claim (**r. 12.4(2)**);
   (ii) a claim against a child or protected party;
   (iii) a claim in tort by one spouse or civil partner against the other;
   (iv) a claim for costs other than fixed costs;
   (v) for delivery up of goods where the defendant will not be allowed the alternative of paying their value; or

(b) the defendant is:
   (i) a person who has been served with the claim out of the jurisdiction without the court's permission under **rr. 6.32** and **6.33** or is a person domiciled in Northern Ireland, Scotland or any other country to which **Regulation (EC) No. 44/2001** applies or an EU State;
   (ii) a State;
   (iii) a diplomatic agent who enjoys diplomatic immunity by virtue of the Diplomatic Privileges Act 1964;
   (iv) a person or organisation which enjoys immunity from civil claims under the International Organisations Acts 1968 and 1981.

A claimant who has served a claim form and particulars of claim on a child or protected party cannot apply immediately for default judgment, because no step may be taken in the proceedings (other than issuing and serving a claim form) until a litigation friend has been appointed for the defendant (**CPR, r. 21.3(2)**). Therefore, the correct procedure is to apply for the appointment of a litigation friend under **r. 21.6** before applying for default judgment (**PD 12, para. 4.2(1)**).

Where an acknowledgment is returned by a defendant with the 'I do not intend to defend this claim' box ticked, the proper course for the defendant is to issue an application for judgment to be entered, rather than a request for judgment. This means that the acknowledgment can be considered by the court, rather than being dealt with as an administrative act (*Northern Rock (Asset Management) plc v Chancellors Associates Ltd* [2011] EWHC 3229, [2012] 2 All ER 501).

Application procedure

20.9 A notice of application for default judgment must be filed in accordance with the procedure in **CPR, Part 23**. Where the defendant is an individual, the claimant must provide the defendant's date of birth (if known) at para. 10 of the application notice, for use in the registration of judgments (**r. 12.4(2)**). Notice of the application must be given to the defendant, unless the defendant has not acknowledged service and the claim was either served under **r. 6.32** or **r. 6.33** (service out of the jurisdiction for which permission is not required) or is a claim against a foreign State (**r. 12.11(4); PD 12, para. 5.1**).

A defendant who seeks to prevent judgment being entered in default by filing an acknowledgment of service or a defence at or just before the hearing must apply for an extension of time. Whether permission will be granted is a matter for the court's discretion, but normally it will be exercised in favour of extending time where, in the case of late acknowledgment, it is a genuine preliminary to a defence to the claim (*Coll v Tattum* (2001) *The Times*, 3 December 2001, followed in *Boeing Capital Corporation v Wells Fargo Bank Northwest* [2003] EWHC 1364 (Comm), LTL 17/7/2003). Thus a defence which is on its face apparently bona fide and arguable will normally be permitted to be served out of time after the making of an application for judgment in default. The wider question of whether the defence is susceptible to an application for summary judgment will normally be left over to a further application, should the claimant wish to pursue it. In *Lexi Holdings plc v Luqman* [2007] EWHC 2497 (Ch), LTL 26/11/2007, however, the court held that this principle was a rule of thumb rather than an invariable rule. Here, the court entered judgment in default on part of the claim, because not only had the defence been filed late, but it could be shown it was bound to fail on that part.

There will be a hearing, and judgment will be entered for what it appears to the court that the claimant is entitled to on the statement of case (**CPR, r. 12.11(1)**). The meaning of **r. 12.11(1)** was considered in *Football Dataco Ltd v Smoot Enterprises Ltd* [2011] EWHC 973 (Ch), [2011] 1 WLR 1978. It was held that the rule does not require the court to consider the legal foundation of the cause of action. Rather, the purpose of the requirement is to enable the court to consider the aspects of the case which prompted the need for an application for default judgment instead of a request, e.g., whether the conditions for service out of the jurisdiction have been fully and properly satisfied or what the precise terms of a non-monetary remedy should be. In any event, the existence of an adjourned appeal of a related claim, pending reference to the CJEU, would not be sufficient to prevent entry of the judgment in default.

On an application for default judgment against a child or a protected party or a claim in tort between spouses or civil partners, evidence must be produced to satisfy the court that the claimant is entitled to the judgment claimed (**r. 12.11(3); PD 12, para. 4.2**).

On an application for default judgment in a claim where service was effected under the Civil Jurisdiction and Judgments Act 1982, the Lugano Convention or **Regulation (EC) No. 44/2001** or a claim against a foreign State, evidence must establish the points listed in **PD 12, paras 4.3** or **4.4**, respectively, and must be given by affidavit (**para. 4.5**).

TWO OR MORE DEFENDANTS

20.10 If there are two or more defendants, the claimant may obtain a judgment on request against one defendant and proceed with the claim against any other defendants (**CPR, r. 12.8(1)**). However, where a claimant applies for default judgment against some defendants and not others, the court will only enter default judgment where the claim can be dealt with separately from the claim against other defendants (**r. 12.8(2)**). Otherwise, the court must deal with the application for default judgment at the same time as it disposes of the claim against the other defendants (**r. 12.8(2)(b)**).

Rule 12.8 enables the court to deal with the complications that can arise from the common law doctrine of election, whereby judgment against one defendant severally liable with another defendant can discharge the other defendant's liability (*Morel Brothers and Co. Ltd v Earl of Westmoreland* [1903] 1 KB 64). The doctrine has been abolished in the case of joint liability by the Civil Liability (Contribution) Act 1978, s. 3. Entry of a default judgment against one defendant in a case which has been pleaded on a number of different bases does not necessarily amount to an election, because the judgment is entered without an investigation of the merits (*Pendleton v Westwater* [2001] EWCA Civ 1841, LTL 28/11/2001). This approach has been confirmed by the Privy Council in *Balgobin v South West Regional Health Authority* [2012] UKPC 11, [2013] 1 AC 582. For an unequivocal election to have been made, there must be a decision by the person making the election to follow one remedy out of a range of two or more and that choice must be communicated to the other side in a way which will make it clear that there has been a deliberate preference of the chosen alternative over any other. It was not correct to say that the entry of a default judgment could never amount to an unequivocal election, and it was relevant that the judgment had been obtained without any consideration of the merits. The court should be slow to regard the entry of a default judgment as constituting an unequivocal election where, as in this case, it was not intended to be the abandonment of a primary cause of action.

Rule 12.8 is not confined to cases involving truly alternative claims. It applies to any case where the effect of entering a default judgment would be that the claim could not be pursued separately against another defendant (*Crown Aluminium Ltd v Northern and Western Insurance Co. Ltd* [2011] EWHC 277 (TCC), [2011] BLR 355).

Having obtained the default judgment, a claimant may enforce it against only some defendants, save where it is for the possession of land or delivery of goods. Here, the defendant may enforce only after obtaining judgment against all defendants, or where the court gives its permission (**r. 12.8(3)**).

Commentary

SETTING ASIDE A DEFAULT JUDGMENT

Principles upon which a default judgment will be set aside

A defendant against whom judgment in default has been entered may apply for it to be varied or set aside under **CPR, Part 13**. **20.11**

A judgment which has been entered wrongly (as defined in the CPR) must be set aside by the court. In other cases, the court has a discretion to set the judgment aside and it will normally require the defendant to show a real prospect of successfully defending the claim before it will do so.

In any case where the court sets aside a default judgment, it may attach conditions, such as the payment of money into court (**r. 3.1(3)**). See 20.21.

Where the default judgment was entered wrongly

The court must set aside any judgment entered wrongly (**CPR, r. 13.2**). The phrase 'entered wrongly' is defined precisely under the rules. By **r. 13.2(a)** to (c), it is limited to the following cases: **20.12**

(a) time for acknowledging service, or for serving a defence (as the case may be) had not expired by the time the default judgment was entered;
(b) a summary judgment application or an application to strike out the claim made by the defendant was pending when the default judgment was entered; or
(c) the defendant had satisfied the whole claim or, on a money claim, filed an admission and a request for time to pay at the time the default judgment was entered.

It is, therefore, a condition for entering judgment in default that service has been effected. Thus, judgment was set aside as of right under **r. 13.2(a)** in *Credit Agricole Indosuez v Unicof Ltd* [2003] EWHC 77 (Comm), LTL 4/2/2003. The claimant purported to serve the claim form by leaving it with the defendant's company secretary in Kenya, whereas service in Kenya had to be by leaving the claim form at the company's registered office. For a full discussion of the rules on service within and out of the jurisdiction see **chapters 15 and 16**.

Time for acknowledging service or filing a defence does not run for the purposes of **r. 13.2(a)** during the period of a stay (*Roundstone Nurseries Ltd v Stephenson Holdings Ltd* [2009] EWHC 1431 (TCC), [2009] 5 Costs LR 787).

A default judgment obtained using the request procedure in error instead of the application for judgment procedure was irregular and capable of being set aside as of right under r. **13.2** (*Intense Investments Ltd v Development Ventures Ltd* [2005] EWHC 1762 (TCC), [2005] BLR 478). It is submitted that this decision ignores the constraints of **r. 13.2** which specifies precisely the circumstances in which the court must set aside a default judgment. These do not include using the wrong procedure to enter the default judgment.

What about the case where a judgment has been entered incorrectly, in circumstances other than those set out at **r. 13.2**? In *Northern Rock (Asset Management) plc v Chancellors Associates Ltd* [2011] EWHC 3229, [2012] 2 All ER 501, an acknowledgment was returned to the claimant with the 'I do not intend to defend this claim' box ticked in error. The claimant submitted a request for judgment form to court instead of making an application for judgment in default, and, incorrectly, judgment was entered by the court as an administrative act without any judicial consideration of the case. The circumstances clearly fell outside the situations envisaged by **r. 13.2**. The court held that it had jurisdiction under **r. 3.1(2)(m)** to set the judgment aside if it was fair and just to do so, on the grounds that the overriding objective would normally demand that a judgment should be set aside, where it had been obtained irregularly on the basis of an obviously mistaken admission, where there was a properly arguable defence, where the application to set aside was brought reasonably promptly and where there was no prejudice caused by the setting aside.

WHERE THE DEFAULT JUDGMENT WAS NOT ENTERED WRONGLY

20.13 The court has a discretion to set aside a default judgment which was not entered wrongly. It may exercise its discretion if (**CPR, r. 13.3(1)**):

(a) the defendant has a real prospect of successfully defending the claim; or
(b) it appears to the court that there is some other good reason why:
   (i) the judgment should be set aside or varied; or
   (ii) the defendant should be allowed to defend the claim.

In considering whether to set aside or vary a judgment entered under **Part 12**, the matters to which the court must have regard include whether the person seeking to set aside the judgment made an application to do so promptly (**r. 13.3(2)**).

Discretion to set aside

20.14 In *Rahman v Rahman* (1999) LTL 26/11/99 the court considered the nature of the discretion to set aside a default judgment under **CPR, r. 13.3**. It concluded that the elements the judge had to consider were the nature of the defence, the period of delay (i.e. why the application to set aside had not been made before), any prejudice the claimant was likely to suffer if the default judgment was set aside, and the overriding objective.

In *Thorn plc v Macdonald* [1999] CPLR 660 the Court of Appeal approved the following principles:

(a) while the length of any delay by the defendant must be taken into account, any pre-action delay is irrelevant;
(b) any failure by the defendant to provide a good explanation for the delay is a factor to be taken into account, but is not always a reason to refuse to set aside;
(c) the primary considerations are whether there is a defence with a real prospect of success, and that justice should be done; and
(d) prejudice (or the absence of it) to the claimant also has to be taken into account.

An application to set aside a default judgment is a decision about whether or not to relieve a party from a sanction imposed on its failure to comply with a rule and so the factors listed in **r. 3.9(1)** must be considered (*Hussain v Birmingham City Council* [2005] EWCA Civ 1570, LTL 25/11/2005; but see *Mullock v Price* [2009] EWCA Civ 1222, [2010] CP Rep 10, discussed at **20.15**).

The Privy Council has held in *Strachan v Gleaner Co. Ltd* [2005] UKPC 33, [2005] 1 WLR 3204, that the court is not deprived of its jurisdiction to set aside a default judgment by the fact that final judgment on quantum has been entered and damages assessed. These factors are, however, relevant to the exercise of the court's discretion in deciding whether to set aside the default judgment as an aspect of, but separate from, the question of delay.

In *Continuity Promotions Ltd v O'Connor's Nenagh Shopping Centre Ltd* [2005] EWHC 3462 (QB), [2006] All ER (D) 39 (Feb), the court considered the impact on the exercise of its jurisdiction to set aside a default judgment of the fact that it did not have jurisdiction over the claim under **Regulation (EC) 44/2001**. It held that only in an exceptional case should an English court decline to set aside a default judgment entered against a defendant without jurisdiction. However, it declined to do so here, holding that the fact that the defendant had made no application to challenge the jurisdiction despite being advised by solicitors and the delay in bringing the application to set aside amounted to exceptional circumstances.

In *Law v St Margarets Insurance Ltd* [2001] EWCA Civ 30, LTL 18/1/2001, the Court of Appeal allowed judgment in default to be set aside despite the defendant's solicitors' procedural errors in failing to file an acknowledgment of service and in failing to ensure that the statement of truth in relation to the evidence in support of the application was signed by the right person. The overriding objective required that the default judgment be set aside in order to enable the merits of the defence to be determined.

Making the application promptly

In *Mullock v Price* [2009] EWCA Civ 1222, [2010] CP Rep 10, the Court of Appeal held that 'promptly' in **CPR, r. 13.3(2)**, is an ordinary English word with a plain and obvious meaning. It adopted the definition given in *Regency Rolls Ltd v Carnall* (2000) LTL 16/10/2000, that 'promptly' means to act 'with all reasonable celerity'. **20.15**

It is clear from the wording of **r. 13.3** that promptness is not an absolute requirement for the making of an order withdrawing a default judgment. But it is also clear that an application to set aside default judgment may fail simply on the ground of significant delay in bringing the application, notwithstanding the existence of a defence with a realistic prospect of success (*Standard Bank plc v Agrinvest International Inc.* [2010] EWCA Civ 1400, *The Times*, 10 January 2011). Similarly, in *Mullock v Price* [2009] EWCA Civ 1222, [2010] CP Rep 10, the existence of a defence with a real prospect of success did not prevent the failure of the application to set aside judgment. The obligation in **r. 13.1** to bring the application promptly is personal to the defendant. The provision in r. 3.9(1)(f) enabling the court to take into account on an application for relief from sanctions that the default was that of a party's legal representative, not their own, does not apply to an application to set aside a default judgment (though the other circumstances listed in **r. 3.9(1)** should be considered: *Hussain v Birmingham City Council* [2005]

EWCA Civ 1570, LTL 25/11/2005). In *Mullock v Price*, the defendant had delayed for two years in making an application to set aside judgment, in the mistaken belief that his insurers were dealing with the claim. The defendant could not shield behind his representatives' inaction to excuse this period of delay.

In unusual circumstances, though, delay may not necessarily be fatal. In *Hussain v Birmingham City Council* [2005] EWCA Civ 1570, LTL 25/11/2005, the Court of Appeal held that the defendant had not acted promptly in making an application to set aside a default judgment. But it considered it appropriate for the judgment to be set aside on the grounds that the defendant had a real prospect of successfully defending the claim and full participation by the defendant at trial was necessary in order to determine where liability lay between a number of defendants. Similarly, in *Berezovsky v Russian Television and Radio Broadcasting Co.* [2009] EWHC 1733 (QB), LTL 20/7/2009, the court accepted that the defendant had not acted promptly but still set the judgment aside, holding that the delay was outweighed by the need to avoid any suggestion of a 'cover-up' and to investigate the defence fully, which constituted a 'good reason' under **r. 13.3(1)(b)**. In *Wuxi Suntech Power Co. Ltd v Tittmann Solar GmbH* [2011] EWPCC 17, LTL 15/7/2011, the court went further still and allowed default judgment to be set aside despite a delay of six months in making the application, for three months of which there was no proper explanation. It did this despite sufficiently serious reservations about the existence of a defence with a reasonable prospect of success that it made the order conditional upon the defendant paying into court a sum by way of security for the claimant's costs.

If the investigations for the evidence required for an application to set aside are not straightforward, such as where evidence has to be sought from a distant country, an application may be prompt within the meaning of **r. 13.3(2)** even if it is issued some weeks after the default judgment (*Shandong Chenming Paper Holding Ltd v Saga Forest Carriers Intl AS* [2008] EWHC 1055 (Comm), LTL 16/5/2008).

Reasonable prospect of success

20.16 The wording of **CPR, r. 13.3(1)(a)**, mirrors the test established in *Alpine Bulk Transport Co. Inc. v Saudi Eagle Shipping Co. Inc.* [1986] 2 Lloyd's Rep 221, that the defendant must have a case with a reasonable prospect of success, and it is not enough to show a merely arguable defence. The approach to be taken by the court was summarised by Moore-Bick J in *International Finance Corporation v Utexafrica Sprl* [2001] CLC 1361: 'A person who holds a regular judgment, even a default judgment, has something of value and in order to avoid injustice he should not be deprived of it without good reason. Something more than a merely arguable case is needed to tip the balance of justice in favour of setting the judgment aside... the expression "realistic prospect of success" in this context means a case which carries a degree of conviction.' In *E. D. and F. Man Liquid Products Ltd v Patel* [2003] EWCA Civ 472, [2003] CPLR 384, the Court of Appeal confirmed that the test is the same as the test for summary judgment. The only significant difference is that in a summary judgment application the burden of proof rests on the claimant to show that the defendant has no real prospect of success whereas in an application to set aside a default judgment it is for the defendant to show that his defence has a real prospect of success. For this reason it might be harder for a defendant to succeed in an application to set aside than to resist an application for summary judgment. The test was considered in detail in *Swain v Hillman* [2001] 1 All ER 91 (see **34.10**).

In *Lloyds Investment (Scandinavia) Ltd v Ager-Hansen* (2001) LTL 7/11/2001 a default judgment was set aside on the ground that the defendant had a real prospect of success. Although the claimant had raised serious questions about the defendant's credibility, no finding could be made without oral evidence and cross-examination.

Where summary judgment had been refused against defendants who appeared on the application but default judgment had been entered against a defendant who did not appear, the court subsequently set aside the default judgment, because there had been no examination of the evidence against that defendant. Given that the question of a real prospect of successfully defending the claim had been determined in favour of the defendants who had filed defences, it would have been wrong to come to a different conclusion in relation to the defendant who had not participated (*Huntingdon Life Sciences Ltd v Stop Huntingdon Animal Cruelty* [2004] EWHC 3145 (QB), LTL 11/11/2004).

The privilege against self-incrimination does not afford an excuse for failing to serve a defence with a realistic prospect of success, and will not provide grounds for setting aside a judgment in default (*Versailles Trade Finance Ltd v Clough* [2001] EWCA Civ 1509, [2002] CP Rep 8).

There was a real prospect of success in establishing a time-bar defence where there was some documentary evidence in support of an argument that the cause of action accrued just outside the relevant time limit (*Shandong Chenming Paper Holding Ltd v Saga Forest Carriers Intl AS* [2008] EWHC 1055 (Comm) LTL 16/5/2008).

The provisions governing default judgments in Admiralty claims are in **CPR, r. 61.9.** Although **r. 61.9(5)** gives the court power to set aside a default judgment, it does not prescribe the criteria. It was held in *The Selby Paradigm* [2004] EWHC 1804 (Admlty), [2004] 2 Lloyd's Rep 714, that the burden on the defendant is to show that it has a real prospect of success in defending the claim, and is not akin to that imposed on an appellant.

Some other good reason

There is no definition of what constitutes 'some other good reason' under **CPR, r. 13.3(1)(b).** **20.17**
However, the authorities establish that the parties' conduct may be relevant (*Hart Investments Ltd v Fidler* [2006] EWHC 2857 (TCC), [2007] BLR 30). In *Roundstone Nurseries Ltd v Stephenson Holdings Ltd* [2009] EWHC 1431 (TCC), [2009] 5 Costs LR 787, the court held that a claimant's unreasonable conduct in taking advantage of a mutual failure to extend a stay in order to enter judgment in default was a good reason under **r. 13.3(1)(b)** for judgment to be set aside. In the same case, Coulson J also commented that a claimant should not enter judgment in default because he is technically entitled to, where he knows the defendant has a good defence and so would be entitled to set judgment aside. A claimant who enters judgment in these circumstances is at risk of an adverse costs order on the application to set aside. *Roundstone* has been followed in *APP Wholesale plc v Adlink UK Ltd* [2012] EWHC 1806 (QB), LTL 14/5/2012. Here, the defendant posted an acknowledgment of service to the court, but it was never received. The claimant entered judgment in default without notice to the defendant, even though it knew (or could have checked by a simple phone call) that there was a substantial dispute between the parties. Entering judgment in these circumstances was a waste of time and money and was set aside under **r. 13.3(1)(b).**

In *Berezovsky v Russian Television and Radio Broadcasting Co.* [2009] EWHC 1733 (QB), LTL 20/7/2009, the court set aside the judgment where, although it was not established on the evidence that the defendant had a case with a real prospect of success, it did consider that there was a defence which was not bound to fail and the nature of the allegations (involving fraud and vindication of the claimant's reputation) provided 'some other good reason' for allowing the defendant to defend the claim. However, this decision should not be read as creating a rule that in the event of serious allegations there must be a trial. The existence of such allegations is a relevant consideration, but must be regarded in the light of the other factors in the case. Where the defendant was unable to establish a realistic prospect of successfully defending the claim, had not taken steps open to him to ask for documents so as to be able to investigate and challenge the claim, and it was unlikely that he would be able to defend the claim even if he were able to go into the witness box to deny the allegations made against him, judgment should not be set aside (*Defty v Hirani* [2012] EWHC 1812, LTL 25/5/2012).

In *Latmar Holdings Corp v Media Focus Ltd* [2012] EWHC 262 (Comm), LTL 13/12/2012, the court exercised its discretion under **r. 13.3(1)(b)** to set a judgment aside on the grounds that although the defendants did not reach the threshold required for **r. 13.3(1)(a)** of being able to show a defence with a realistic prospect of success, nevertheless the allegations involved serious allegations of fraud and the value of the claim was relatively large. Further, the period of delay was not inordinate.

In *Messer Griesheim GmbH v Goyal MG Gases Pvt Ltd* [2006] EWHC 79 (Comm), *The Times*, 14 February 2006, there was a good reason for setting aside a default judgment under **r. 13.3(1)(b)** where the default judgment was not capable of being enforced in the foreign jurisdiction in which the defendant's assets were located, and so the claim would effectively be lost. As the defendant had no prospect of successfully defending the claim, the court entered summary judgment instead, which was capable of enforcement. Another good reason for setting aside under **r. 13.3(1)(b)** was where a judgment in default had been entered which had the effect of discharging an injunction and the master who had ordered the entry of the default judgment had no power under **PD 2B, para. 2.2**, to discharge the injunction (*Richmond v Burch* [2006] EWHC 921 (Ch), [2007] 1 All ER 658).

The failure by the claimant to include a response pack with the particulars of claim is a matter which may result in a default judgment being set aside under **r. 13.3(1)(b)**, even where the defendant has not shown that they have a reasonable prospect of defending the claim. The requirement to serve the response pack, which includes the acknowledgment of service and guidance for the defendant as to how to proceed next, is an important omission. In *Rajval Construction Ltd v Bestville Properties Ltd* [2010] EWCA Civ 1621, [2011] CILL 2994, and in *Gulf International Bank BSC v Ekttitab Holding Co. KSCC* (2010) LTL 15/11/2010 the default judgment was set aside under **r. 13.3(1)(b)** on the ground that no response pack had been filed regardless of whether the defendant could show it had a reasonable prospect of defence. However, setting aside a default judgment under **r. 13.3(1)(b)** is a matter of discretion, and so other factors, such as delay and the strength of any possible defence, will weigh in the court's decision. In *Henriksen v Pires* [2011] EWCA Civ 1720, LTL 14/2/2012, the Court of Appeal held that the failure of the claimant to include a response pack did not justify the making of an order under **r. 13.3**. In this case, the failure to include a response pack emerged as a possible ground upon which to seek to set aside judgment only very late in the day and the merits of the defence were not sufficiently strong to justify setting aside the judgment.

In *Henriksen v Pires* [2011] EWCA Civ 1720, LTL 14/2/2012, the Court of Appeal also considered the effect on the default judgment of the claimant's failure to file a certificate of service under **r. 6.17(2)**. It held that this was a free-standing requirement, independent of **r. 12.3**. The failure to file a certificate of service would not lead to a mandatory order setting aside the default judgment but it could constitute a good reason under **r. 13.3(1)(b)** why the court might set aside judgment. Where, as here, the claimant had filed an affidavit of service which contained all the information required of a certificate of service, even if it was not in the relevant practice form (N215), the defendant had not suffered any prejudice and it was not appropriate to make an order setting aside judgment.

In *Paseana Ltd v Lextrex Holdings Ltd* [2010] EWCA Civ 1539, LTL 30/11/2010, the Court of Appeal set aside a default judgment even though there was evidence that the defendants had put forward inaccurate or dishonest statements about the circumstances in which the default judgments had come to be entered. There had been no delay in making the application and the defendants had a defence with a real prospect of success. Applying the overriding objective, it was in the interests of justice that the defendants should be given an opportunity to defend the claim.

Defendant unaware that service has been deemed to have occurred

20.18 Once it is proved (such as by a certificate of service) that proceedings have been served by one of the methods prescribed by the CPR, service is deemed to take effect on the date laid down by **r. 6.14**, and evidence to prove the contrary is not admissible (see *Anderton v Clwyd County Council (No. 2)* [2002] EWCA Civ 933, [2002] 1 WLR 3174). Where a default judgment has been entered after the expiry of 14 days from the deemed date of service in a case where the defendant did not in fact receive the proceedings, setting aside is subject to the court's discretion rather than as of right (*Godwin v Swindon Borough Council* [2001] EWCA Civ 1478, [2002] 1 WLR 997). The decisions in *Anderton v Clwyd County Council (No. 2)* and *Godwin v Swindon Borough Council* concerned the effect of the deeming provisions on a claimant who delays serving a claim form until the end of the period for service. However, in *Akram v Adam* [2004] EWCA Civ 1601, [2005] 1 WLR 2762, the Court of Appeal looked at the position of a defendant who says that he had no notice of the proceedings at all until after he heard of the default judgment. The court dismissed the contention that a defendant in this situation should be entitled to have the judgment set aside as of right on the grounds that he had received no notification of the proceedings and was therefore a stranger to them. It also held that the deeming provisions on service in the CPR did not contravene the European Convention on Human Rights, **art. 6** in the **Human Rights Act 1998, sch. 1**. It confirmed that a judgment entered on a claim served in accordance with the rules, but of which the defendant had no notice, has not been entered wrongly and the defendant can have it set aside only on the grounds specified in **CPR, r. 13.3(1)** (see **20.13**). Such a defendant will therefore either have to show a defence with a real prospect of success, or rely on non-service as 'some other good reason' for setting aside the judgment. According to May LJ in *Godwin v Swindon Borough Council* at [49] this may arise where a defendant would have paid instead of having an embarrassing judgment entered, and it may give grounds for departing from the usual rule of the defendant being ordered to pay the costs thrown away (see **table 68.1** at **68.29**). In *Manx Electricity Authority v J P Morgan Chase Bank* [2002] EWHC 867 (Comm), LTL 16/5/2002, the court agreed that a judgment entered in this situation should be set aside under **r. 13.3(1)(b)**. Doubts about the effectiveness of alternative service in the circumstances of the case appear to have been treated as a factor in setting aside a default judgment in *Black Arrow Finance Ltd v Orderdaily Co. Ltd* [2002] EWCA Civ 289, LTL 31/1/2002.

Setting aside under the Service Regulation

Where service is effected under Regulation (EC) No. 1393/2007 (the Service Regulation), judgment in default cannot be given until it is established that service was effected by a method prescribed by the internal law of the receiving State or that the documents were actually delivered to the defendant or to the defendant's residence by another method provided by the Service Regulation and that, in either case, the defendant had sufficient time to defend the claim (**art. 19**). See **16.67**. **20.19**

Procedure

A defendant must apply for judgment in default to be varied or set aside under the Part 23 procedure (see **chapter 32**). An application to set aside a default judgment which has not been entered wrongly must be supported by evidence (**CPR, r. 13.4(3)**). Commonly, a draft defence is attached to a witness statement in support of the application. **20.20**

Where the claim is for a specified sum of money, has not been started in a specialist list and the judgment is entered against an individual in a court which is not the defendant's home court (defined in **r. 2.3(1)**), the court will automatically transfer the application there (**r. 13.4(1)**).

If the claim is a designated money claim (i.e. a claim started in any county court under **Part 7** for a specified or unspecified amount of money, **r. 2.3(1)**), receipt of an application to set aside judgment will trigger the automatic transfer of the claim to the preferred court (this is the court specified by the claimant in the claim form under **PD 7A, para. 4A.2**) (**CPR r. 13.4(1B)**).

Setting aside on conditions

20.21 The court may attach conditions to an order to set aside judgment (**CPR, r. 3.1(3)**). In most cases the defaulting defendant will be ordered to pay the claimant's costs thrown away. In appropriate cases, the court may also require the defendant to pay money into court to await the final disposal of the claim. Such a condition is commonly imposed where, although the defendant has satisfied the court that it has a defence with a real prospect of success, the defence is 'shadowy' (see **34.34**). However, conditions imposed on setting aside a default judgment are not intended to punish the defendant but to ensure that justice is achieved between the parties (*Hussain v Birmingham City Council* [2005] EWCA Civ 1570, LTL 25/11/2005). Security for costs should not be imposed as a condition unless the requirements in **r. 25.13** are satisfied (*Camden London Borough Council v Makers UK Ltd* [2009] EWHC 605 (TCC), 124 Con LR 32). Nor should the court impose a condition barring the defendant from exercising its statutory right to make use of the adjudication process under the Housing Grants, Construction and Regeneration Act 1996 (see **34.20**) save in exceptional cases (*Camden London Borough Council v Makers UK Ltd*).

FORMER DUTY OF CLAIMANT TO SET ASIDE A WRONGLY ENTERED DEFAULT JUDGMENT

20.22 The provision formerly in **CPR, r. 13.5**, which placed a duty on a claimant who had entered default judgment, but subsequently became aware that the particulars of claim had not reached the defendant before judgment was entered, to request that the default judgment be set aside or apply for directions, has been revoked. It was inconsistent with the policy that there is an irrevocable presumption of service on the date in what are now **rr. 6.14** and **6.26** (**r. 6.7** before 1 October 2008) on proof of service by one of the methods permitted by **Part 6**. See **15.36** and *Anderton v Clwyd County Council (No. 2)* [2002] EWCA Civ 933, [2002] 1 WLR 3174.

An application to set aside a judgment entered after a trial which a defendant failed to attend is not governed by **Part 13** at all. It should be made under **r. 39.3(5)** (if the defendant has been served and so is properly a party to the proceedings) or (where he has not been properly served) in accordance with the procedure set out by the Court of Appeal in *Nelson v Clearsprings (Management) Ltd* [2006] EWCA Civ 1252, [2007] 1 WLR 962 (see **62.3**).

DEFAULT JUDGMENT ON AN ADDITIONAL CLAIM

20.23 There are special rules which apply in relation to entering judgment in default on an additional claim. These are dealt with in **29.10**.

Chapter 21 Acting by a Solicitor

Commentary

INTRODUCTION

This chapter deals with a number of issues that arise when litigation is conducted, as it often is, by solicitors. A solicitor is an officer of the court, and is therefore under certain duties to the court and subject to the disciplinary jurisdiction of the High Court. Once proceedings are issued by a solicitor on behalf of a client, or acknowledged by a solicitor on behalf of a client, the solicitor will be regarded as being on the record. All further steps taken on behalf of that client should be taken by that solicitor, and all further documents served on that client should be served on that solicitor, until formal notice of change has been served. While on the record the solicitor will have apparent authority (and often actual authority) to take all steps on behalf of the client, who will be bound by the action taken. A number of other topics are also considered. **21.1**

OFFICER OF THE COURT

The Solicitors Act 1974, s. 50, provides as follows: **21.2**

(1) Any person duly admitted as a solicitor shall be an officer of the Senior Courts.
(2) Subject to the provisions of this Act, the High Court, the Crown Court and the Court of Appeal respectively, or any division or judge of those courts, may exercise the same jurisdiction in respect of solicitors as any one of the superior courts of law or equity from which the Senior Courts were constituted might have exercised immediately before the passing of the Supreme Court of Judicature Act 1873 in respect of any solicitor, attorney or proctor admitted to practise there.
(3) An appeal shall lie to the Court of Appeal from any order made against a solicitor by the High Court or the Crown Court in the exercise of its jurisdiction in respect of solicitors under subsection (2).

As officers of the court, solicitors are under duties not to mislead the court, to bring to the court's attention authorities relevant to the case which may go against their clients, and various other duties conveniently summarised in *Cordery on Solicitors*, 9th edn. (London: Butterworths, 1995) and the SRA Code of Conduct 2011. Counsel owe similar duties under the Code of Conduct of the Bar of England and Wales. Solicitors and counsel must, moreover, be regarded as owing a duty to assist the court in achieving the overriding objective by reason of **CPR, r. 1.3** (which in fact places the duty on the legal representatives' clients), and the fact that solicitors are officers of the court. A solicitor who receives a request from another party for pre-action disclosure of its records has no obligation to explain why electronic or paper records have been destroyed. The solicitor's only obligation is to tell the truth (*Beckett Bemrose and Hagen Solicitors v Future Mortgages Ltd* [2010] EWHC 1997 (QB), LTL 12/7/2010).

The High Court has a summary disciplinary jurisdiction over solicitors. In *Myers v Elman* [1940] AC 282 Lord Wright said that the underlying principle of the summary jurisdiction is that the High Court has a right and a duty to supervise the conduct of solicitors, and to impose penalties where the conduct of a solicitor is of such a nature as to tend to defeat justice. The jurisdiction is compensatory rather than punitive, but does have a disciplinary slant. There was formerly a body of case law dealing with applications for costs orders against solicitors pursuant to the court's inherent jurisdiction over them. This particular area is now covered by the detailed rules on wasted costs applications, which are considered further in **chapter 68**.

Disciplinary proceedings against solicitors are currently mainly investigated by the Solicitors Regulation Authority (SRA) under the SRA Disciplinary Procedure Rules 2011 and, where appropriate, are brought before the Solicitors Disciplinary Tribunal under r. 10 of those Rules. The tribunal's procedures are governed by the Solicitors (Disciplinary Proceedings) Rules 2007 (SI 2007/3588) and the Solicitors Disciplinary Tribunal (Appeals and Amendment) Rules 2011 (SI 2011/2346). Powers still exist, however, to apply to the High Court to strike the name of a solicitor off the roll of solicitors, or to answer certain allegations, under the Solicitors Act 1974, ss. 50 to 55. An independent Legal Ombudsman service has been set up under the Legal Services Act 2007. They act as a point of entry for reports of alleged breaches of the SRA Code of Conduct 2011, and work with consumers and very small businesses to resolve legal complaints in a fair and independent way. Members of the Chartered Institute of Legal Executives (CILEx) are subject to the disciplinary procedures laid down by ILEX Professional Standards Ltd (IPS), which carries out on behalf of CILEx its functions and responsibilities as an approved regulator under the Legal Services Act 2007. All members of CILEx must comply with its Code of Conduct. Disciplinary hearings are conducted before the Institute of Legal Executives Appeal Tribunal, whose decisions are amenable to judicial review (*R (Kaur) v Institute of Legal Executives Appeal Tribunal* [2010] EWHC 3321 (Admin), [2011] ACD 25).

SOLICITOR ON THE RECORD

21.3 Every party to litigation must provide an address for service within the United Kingdom (**CPR, r. 6.23(2)**), which, where a solicitor is acting for a party, will be the business address of the party's solicitor (**r. 6.23(2)(a)**). The claim form will identify whether the claimant is acting by a solicitor, and the acknowledgment of service form, defence, or defence and counterclaim, will similarly identify whether the defendant is acting by a solicitor.

Once a solicitor is on the court record as acting for a party, by **rr. 42.1** and **42.2(5)**, that solicitor will be considered to be continuing to act for that party until due notice is given or an order is made in accordance with **Part 42**. The rules on giving notice of change are considered further in **chapter 22**.

ACTING FOR JOINT CLAIMANTS

21.4 Before the introduction of the CPR, the usual rule where there were joint claimants was that they were not allowed to take inconsistent steps (such as by just one of them making an interim application within the proceedings), they had to act by a common firm of solicitors, and be represented at trial and other hearings by the same counsel (*Re Wright* [1895] 2 Ch 747; *Re Mathews* [1905] 2 Ch 460; *Lewis v Daily Telegraph Ltd (No. 2)* [1964] 2 QB 601). Pearson LJ in *Lewis v Daily Telegraph Ltd (No. 2)* said that there may be scope for making a special order for separate representation of joint claimants, but indicated a distinct reluctance to do this. The disinclination against separate representation of joint claimants must be stronger under the CPR, given the elements of the overriding objective relating to saving expense and ensuring that cases are dealt with expeditiously. A defendant faced with separately represented claimants should consider applying for a stay (**chapter 56**).

DUTY OF CONFIDENTIALITY

A solicitor has a duty of single-minded loyalty to his client's interests, and a duty to respect his client's confidences (*Hilton v Barker Booth and Eastwood* [2005] UKHL 8, [2005] 1 WLR 567 at [30]). **21.5**
These duties arise primarily from the contractual retainer between the solicitor and client, but there is also usually a fiduciary relationship between the solicitor and client arising from the fact that the client reposes trust and confidence in the solicitor (per Lord Walker of Gestingthorpe at [28] and [29]). This means that the solicitor's duty of confidence need not be coterminous with the retainer (*Conway v Ratiu* [2005] EWCA Civ 1302, [2006] 1 All ER 571 at [71]). The nature of the solicitor's fiduciary duty may have to be moulded and informed by the terms of the retainer, because it has to be consistent and in conformity with the terms of the contract between the parties (*Conway v Ratiu* at [73]). Depending on the facts, a solicitor's fiduciary duty may extend beyond the termination of the retainer (*Longstaff v Birtles* [2001] EWCA Civ 1219, [2002] 1 WLR 470), and may arise without a retainer at all (*Conway v Ratiu* at [73]).

CONFLICTS BETWEEN CLIENTS

No-conflict rule

A solicitor will be unable to act for two or more clients in the same matter (whether as claimants or defendants) where there is a conflict of interest between the clients. If the **21.6**
clients whose interests are in conflict are intending claimants, the best course is for them all to go to new solicitors and, if proceedings are necessary, to bring separate proceedings so that they can be separately represented. The original solicitor will have to consider carefully whether he or she is able to act for one of the parties in view of the initial contact with another party, bearing in mind the outcomes and indicative behaviour set out in the SRA Code of Conduct 2011, chapter 3. A solicitor who discovers a conflict of interest in representing a client must inform the client of his or her inability to act, and that the client should seek legal advice from other solicitors, starting afresh and not relying on any advice already given by the solicitor (*Hilton v Barker Booth and Eastwood* [2005] UKHL 8, [2005] 1 WLR 567).

Nor can a solicitor generally act for a client where that client's interests conflict with those of a former client. For example, in *Saminadhen v Khan* [1992] 1 All ER 963 Lord Donaldson of Lymington MR said he could conceive of no circumstances in which it would be proper for a solicitor who had acted for one defendant in criminal proceedings, in which a cut-throat defence had been advanced between two defendants, to act subsequently for the other defendant after the first retainer had terminated. However, the full position is more complicated than this, because the courts dealing with this problem are in fact seeking to balance two conflicting public interests:

(a) The public interest in enabling the client to repose the fullest confidence in the solicitor he retains, and ensuring there is no risk or perception of a risk that confidential information relating to a client will be conveyed to anyone else. The information that the court will seek to protect will have the following characteristics:

(i) It was originally communicated to the solicitor in confidence.

(ii) It is still confidential, and reasonably capable of being considered capable of being recalled. It might lose this characteristic by becoming common knowledge, or (in certain circumstances) if it has been communicated to an opponent during the course of litigation. Alternatively, it might be so eminently forgettable that it should not be protected. A client complaining that confidential information might be at risk must identify it with some particularity, but the degree of particularity required depends on the facts of the case (*Re a Firm of Solicitors* [1997] Ch 1).

(iii) It is relevant to the subject matter of the subsequent retainer.

(b) The public interest in the freedom of the solicitor to obtain instructions from any member of the public, and for all members of the public to instruct the solicitor of their choice.

A solicitor who continues to act without disclosing a conflict between duty of loyalty to the first client and duty of confidentiality to a second client, is liable for any loss suffered by the first client. The duty of loyalty to the first client is not modified by the fact that complying with it will involve breaching the duty of confidentiality to the second client: the predicament is the solicitor's own fault in allowing the conflict to arise (*Hilton v Barker Booth and Eastwood* [2005] UKHL 8, [2005] 1 WLR 567).

Further, a solicitor cannot simultaneously act for two clients in separate matters if the clients have potentially conflicting interests and there is a reasonable relationship between the two transactions (*Marks and Spencer plc v Freshfields Bruckhaus Deringer* [2004] EWHC 1337 (Ch), [2004] 1 WLR 2331).

As a matter of practice, it is wise for solicitors to run computer conflict checks when instructed and when parties are added to existing proceedings.

Restraining a solicitor from acting

21.7 A solicitor who is possessed of relevant confidential information will be restrained from acting against the former client (*Re a Firm of Solicitors* [1992] QB 959). In the case of a firm previously retained by a client, the partners and employees who are in possession of confidential information may be restrained from acting against the former client, and this extends to them if they change firms. Members and employees of the firm who never had possession of relevant confidential information are in a rather more complex position. While they remain with the firm they will, generally, be precluded from acting against the former client of the firm, but it is possible they may be allowed to act if there is no real (as opposed to fanciful) risk that relevant confidential information may have been communicated to them (*Re a Firm of Solicitors* [1992] QB 959).

Real risk of disclosure

21.8 In *Bolkiah v KPMG* [1999] 2 AC 222 the claimant had retained the defendant firm of accountants in his private capacity to provide extensive litigation support services of a kind commonly provided by solicitors in relation to proceedings he was involved in. In the course of this retainer the defendants became privy to detailed information relating to the claimant's financial affairs, and no less than 168 of the defendants' employees were involved. Some months after the conclusion of the claimant's action, the defendants were retained by the claimant's former employer (the Brunei Investment Agency, BIA) to investigate the location of substantial funds that had been transferred during his period of employment. Aware of a possible conflict of interest, the defendants erected an information barrier (also known as an 'ethical wall' or 'Chinese wall') around the department conducting the BIA investigation. The defendants did not, however, ask for the claimant's consent to them acting for the BIA. It was held that the claimant was entitled to an injunction restraining the defendants from continuing to act in the BIA investigation. Such injunctions will be granted unless the firm produces clear and convincing evidence that effective measures have been taken to ensure that no disclosure of the former client's affairs will be made to the department acting for the new client, and that there is no risk of the former client's information reaching the department acting for the new client. Although, in some cases, ethical walls may be sufficient protection, there is a very heavy burden on the firm to prove this, and it will be very difficult for the firm to do so unless those measures were an established part of the firm's organisational structure. Institution of an ethical wall system and various other precautions to protect the client's confidential information from risk of disclosure were sufficient in *Gus Consulting GmbH v LeBoeuf Lamb Greene and MacRae* [2006] EWCA Civ 683, [2006] PNLR 32, to enable solicitors to act against a former client in an arbitration.

Following *Bolkiah v KPMG* the question is whether there is a real, as opposed to a fanciful, risk of disclosure. Whether there is such a risk is a question of fact. Where a solicitor acted for a party many years before, but neither the solicitor nor the client have any material recollection of the previous matter, there is no material conflict (*Re T and A (Children) (Risk of Disclosure)* [2000] 1 FLR 859). Each case turns on its own facts. There was no real risk of disclosure in *Re Bloomsbury International Ltd, Bloomsbury International Ltd v Holyoake* [2010] EWHC 1150 (Ch), LTL 24/5/2010, where the issue concerned the company's administrators who had previously acted for the company in relation to its tax affairs. The retainer relating to its tax affairs had been terminated, and there was an information barrier between the two teams dealing with the administration and the company's tax affairs. In *Koch Shipping Inc. v Richards Butler* [2002] EWCA Civ 1280, [2003] PNLR 11, it was held that fears of inadvertent disclosure of confidential information by the solicitor formerly with day-to-day conduct of a case for one side who then joined the firm representing the other side (where she had no dealings with the case) were fanciful.

In *Bodle v Coutts and Co.* [2003] EWHC 1865 (Ch), LTL 17/7/2003, Farrer and Co. ('the solicitors') had acted for the claimant some years previously in matrimonial proceedings. Subsequently, the claimant sued the defendant bank, who were now represented by the solicitors. The claimant had not paid the solicitors, who exerted a lien over her matrimonial papers. An application was made to restrain the solicitors from acting for the bank. The court directed the solicitors to produce the papers (which were not shown to the claimant), and the judge concluded they contained nothing relevant to the present proceedings. This procedure was held not to infringe the European Convention on Human Rights, art. 6(1), as production had been directed by the court, rather than the papers being voluntarily deployed by the solicitors. On the solicitors giving undertakings restricting access to the papers and discussion of their contents, the claimant's application was refused.

Staff moving to new firms

Once members or employees, who never had possession of confidential information about a former client of a firm, move to new firms, they will be free from constraint. To come into this more favoured class, the burden is on the solicitor to prove not only that he or she did not have possession of relevant confidential information, but that there is no real risk that he or she has such information (*Re a Firm of Solicitors* [1997] Ch 1). **21.9**

Other examples

A different problem was considered in *Re Schuppan* [1996] 2 All ER 664. A well-known firm of solicitors had acted for the judgment creditor in hard-fought High Court proceedings involving allegations of fraud and a detailed investigation of the assets of the judgment debtor. The judgment was not satisfied, and the debtor was declared bankrupt. The trustee in bankruptcy retained the solicitors who had been acting for the judgment creditor to act in the bankruptcy. **21.10**

Commentary

It was held that having a blanket rule that it is never allowable for a creditor's solicitors to act for the trustee in bankruptcy was a counsel of perfection, and this could be allowed if no difficulty was expected in quantifying the provable debts (which generally is the most obvious area of possible conflict of interest), provided there were good reasons for retaining the creditor's solicitors. In this case there were good reasons, as they already had a good grasp of the bankrupt's finances, and it would have been very expensive for any new firm to read into the case. In addition, there were further unresolved issues arising from the original litigation, including a wasted costs application against the creditor's solicitors and an inquiry based on the creditor's undertaking in damages in respect of a discharged freezing order. These issues did give rise to a possible conflict of interest, but it was held that the risk could be averted by a division of responsibility (with another firm being retained to deal with these issues), and then a balancing exercise would be undertaken (which on the facts favoured allowing the creditor's solicitor to act).

In *Re L (Minors) (Care Proceedings: Solicitors)* [2001] 1 WLR 100 Wilson J in the Family Division made a declaration that the solicitor acting for the local authority in care proceedings was not so acting, thus removing her from the record, because the fact of her cohabiting with the solicitor for two of the seven respondents to the proceedings could give rise to an apprehension of bias by lay persons.

There may be a conflict of interest where a solicitor has a financial interest in a transaction which may conflict with the interests of a client (*Hilton v Barker Booth and Eastwood* [2005] UKHL 8, [2005] 1 WLR 567).

Orders available

21.11 Where a party establishes a conflict of interest, the most the court can do is to grant an injunction forbidding the solicitor from continuing to act for the other party and, if necessary, a stay unless and until new solicitors are instructed. There is no power to order a party to instruct new solicitors (*SMC Engineering (Bristol) Ltd v Fraser* (2000) *The Times*, 26 January 2001).

MONEY LAUNDERING

21.12 Where the matter involves a financial or real property transaction, the solicitor must apply customer due diligence measures when establishing a business relationship with the client (Money Laundering Regulations 2007 (SI 2007/2157), regs 3, 5 and 7). There is a similar obligation when an occasional transaction is to be entered into with a value of €15,000 or more. Customer due diligence means identifying the customer and verifying the customer's identity on the basis of documents, data or information obtained from a reliable and independent source, such as a passport, or photo-card driving licence, or birth certificate, and keeping a record of the identification evidence.

AUTHORITY OF SOLICITORS

21.13 A solicitor retained by a client is, of course, the client's agent, and has actual or apparent authority to do all things that may reasonably be expected to arise in litigation being conducted for the client (*Prestwich v Poley* (1865) 18 CB NS 806). As against an opposing litigant, the only limitation on the apparent authority of a solicitor to compromise litigation is that it cannot be taken to include the compromise of matters collateral to the proceedings. A matter will only be regarded as collateral where it really is extraneous to the proceedings (*Waugh v H. B. Clifford and Sons Ltd* [1982] Ch 374). A solicitor with general authority to act for a client may have authority to defend the client against disparagement in the media based on information from the solicitor's own experience rather than being limited to direct instructions from the client (*Regan v Taylor* [2000] EMLR 549; *Khader v Aziz* [2010] EWCA Civ 716, [2010] 1 WLR 2673).

However, as between solicitor and client, there will be a breach of authority by the solicitor unless any action taken (particularly compromising the claim) is within his or her express or implied authority. It may well be that a proposed compromise of a claim will be within the apparent authority of the solicitor as against the other side (because it does not include anything collateral to the claim), but will be outside the actual authority of the solicitor as between himself and his client. The solicitor will generally only be safe in concluding the proposed compromise if the client gives express instructions. See *Waugh v H. B. Clifford and Sons Ltd. Fusion Interactive Communication Solutions Ltd v Venture Investment Placement Ltd (No. 2)* [2005] EWHC 736 (Ch), [2005] 2 BCLC 571, dealt with the effect on a defendant where conflicting letters before claim are sent by different firms of solicitors instructed by the same client. On the facts, compliance with one letter before claim meant that there was no default in respect of the second (and wider) claim as set out in the other letter.

In general, death of a client will terminate a solicitor's authority. However, where the client is a company, death of its sole shareholder and director will not have this effect, as the company will continue to exist (*Donsland Ltd v Van Hoogstraten* [2002] EWCA Civ 253, [2002] PNLR 26). A solicitor with a 'general retainer' in litigation is required to act for the client to the end and to take all necessary steps to bring the claim to a conclusion. Difficulties in obtaining instructions do not affect the authority of solicitors acting under a general retainer (*Euroafrica Shipping Lines Co. Ltd v Żegluga Polska SA* [2004] EWHC 385 (Comm), [2004] 2 BCLC 97).

Commentary

AUTHORITY OF COUNSEL

In *Swinfen v Lord Chelmsford* (1860) 5 Hurl & N 890 Pollock CB said that a barrister has complete authority over the conduct of litigation and all that is incidental to it, but not over matters which are collateral to the case. In *Matthews v Munster* (1887) 20 QBD 141 Lord Esher MR said, at p. 143: **21.14**

> when the client has requested counsel to act as his advocate... he thereby represents to the other side that counsel is to act for him in the usual course, and he must be bound by that representation so long as it continues.... The request does not mean that counsel is to act in any other character than that of advocate or to do any other act than such as an advocate usually does. The duty of counsel is to advise his client out of court and to act for him in court, and until his authority is withdrawn he has, with regard to all matters that properly relate to the conduct of the case, unlimited power to do that which is best for his client.

In *Worldwide Corporation Ltd v Marconi Communications Ltd* (1999) *The Times*, 7 July 1999, an application for permission to amend to set up a different cause of action, leading counsel for the claimant had abandoned the cause of action originally pleaded, in a strategy to try to obtain permission to amend. Permission was refused, with the result that, as the original claim had been abandoned, the claim was dismissed. An attempt was then made on behalf of the claimant to resuscitate the original claim, and new leading counsel was briefed. Although it left open the possibility that there may be exceptional cases, the Court of Appeal held that the court had to be able to rely on counsel, and the client was not able to retreat from the abandonment of the original claim.

WARRANTY OF AUTHORITY

Breach of warranty of authority

By issuing proceedings a firm of solicitors warrant that they have authority from the claimant to do so. Similarly, by filing a defence or taking any other step in the proceedings a firm **21.15** purporting to act for a defendant warrant that they have authority to act for the defendant. According to Buxton LJ in *SEB Trygg Liv Holding AB v Manches* [2005] EWCA Civ 1237, [2006] 1 WLR 2276, the solicitor warrants:

(a) that he has a client; and
(b) that the client has instructed him to assert or deny the claims made in the proceedings.

There is no warranty that the solicitor's client has the same name as that used in the proceedings. Otherwise the solicitor would be liable for every misnomer, including typographical errors and changes in company names (*SEB Trygg Liv Holding AB v Manches*).

If solicitors do not have authority to issue proceedings, they will be in breach of warranty of authority and liable to the other parties. This rarely occurs through the deliberate action of the solicitors. However, the cases show that it is no defence that the solicitors acted perfectly innocently and without knowledge of the defect in their authority. Solicitors have been held to be in breach of warranty of authority in the following circumstances:

(a) where the claimant is a child or under a mental disability (*Geilinger v Gibbs* [1897] 1 Ch 479; *Yonge v Toynbee* [1910] 1 KB 215);
(b) where the claimant does not exist (*Simmons v Liberal Opinion Ltd* [1911] 1 KB 966);
(c) where the claimant is a limited company which has no directors or officers with authority to give instructions to the solicitors (*West End Hotels Syndicate Ltd v Bayer* (1912) 29 TLR 92);
(d) where the claimant has died before proceedings were commenced (*Tetlow v Orela Ltd* [1920] 2 Ch 24);
(e) where the claimant is a company that has been dissolved (*Babury Ltd v London Industrial plc* (1989) 139 NLJ 1596).

Being without instructions

21.16 There is a difference between a solicitor being without instructions and being without authority. It is only in the latter case that damages may be awarded against the solicitor for breach of warranty of authority (*Donsland Ltd v Van Hoogstraten* [2002] EWCA Civ 253, [2002] PNLR 26). Where a sole director and shareholder of a company died during the course of proceedings, the company's solicitors, acting under a general retainer, continued to have authority to make applications in those proceedings even though they did not have anyone to give them specific instructions (*Donsland Ltd v Van Hoogstraten*).

Practice after a breach of warranty of authority

21.17 Where a breach of warranty of authority occurs, the court has jurisdiction to make a summary order against the solicitor where the issues are reasonably clear, but where there are real issues of fact or law the injured party should be left to bring the claim by issuing separate proceedings (*Skylight Maritime SA v Ascot Underwriting* [2005] EWHC 15 (Comm), [2005] PNLR 25). In both cases the jurisdiction is compensatory rather than punitive, so proof of loss is essential (*Skylight Maritime SA v Ascot Underwriting*). Where the summary procedure is used, the innocent party should make an application using form N244 seeking an order striking out the claim (or the defence) and that the solicitor should be ordered to pay the costs on the indemnity basis. (The principles established in the old cases are unlikely to have been altered in this respect by the introduction of the CPR. The earlier cases indicate that the solicitor in breach should be ordered to pay its client's costs on the indemnity basis.) The application should be served on the solicitors and on the party (if it exists) for whom the solicitor has purported to act.

There are some breaches that can be cured, such as by the appointment of a litigation friend (*Cooper v Dumnett* [1930] WN 248) or the passing of necessary company resolutions and ratification of the actions of the solicitors (*East Pant Du United Lead Mining Co. Ltd v Merryweather* (1864) 2 Hem & M 254), and in these cases the court may be prepared to grant a stay for these steps to be taken. In some cases there may be a dispute of fact as to whether there was a want of authority. For example, it may be disputed whether the claimant lacks capacity. In these cases the court may dismiss or adjourn the application, and leave the applicant to bring separate proceedings for damages for breach of warranty of authority (*Yonge v Toynbee* [1910] 1 KB 215). Otherwise, an order dismissing the claim (or defence) and for indemnity basis costs follows almost as a matter of course.

SOLICITORS' AGENTS

It is common practice for solicitors to appoint local agents to deal with court hearings, particularly simple interim applications and short trials. There is also a common practice for provincial firms to appoint London agents for trials and important hearings at the Royal Courts of Justice. In these situations the London or local agent's principal is the firm of solicitors originally retained by the lay client, subject to contrary express agreement. The local or London agents must therefore look to their principals for payment of their costs, rather than the client (*Collins v Griffin* (1734) Barnes 37; *Scrace v Whittington* (1823) 2 B & C 11). If the agent is negligent, the client is able to sue the principal, who will be liable for the acts and omissions of the agent (*Re Ward* (1862) 31 Beav 1). In most such cases the principal could seek a contribution or indemnity from the agent by issuing an additional claim under **Part 20**. As regards the other side, the solicitor agent has apparent authority within the scope of the application under consideration. If that is the trial, the agent has apparent authority to compromise the claim (*Re Newen* [1903] 1 Ch 812), and if an application, to agree terms relevant to the application. **21.18**

ENFORCING SOLICITORS' UNDERTAKINGS

Binding nature of undertakings

Undertakings are regularly given by solicitors in a variety of circumstances, and include undertakings that payments will be made, or that things will or will not be done. Holding money on a solicitor's undertaking may give rise to a stakeholder relationship, typically involving two contracts, one between the principals, and the other being a tripartite contract with the stakeholder agreeing terms. Alternatively, such money may be held on trust. The actual relationship depends on the facts and wording of the undertaking (*Tradegro (UK) Ltd v Wigmore Street Investments Ltd* [2011] EWCA Civ 268, LTL 16/3/2011, in which it was held there was no security provided by an undertaking given in place of a freezing injunction). An undertaking will bind not only the individual solicitor giving it, but also his or her firm, if it is made by a partner in the usual way of business of the kind carried on by the firm (see Partnership Act 1890, and *United Bank of Kuwait Ltd v Hammoud* [1988] 1 WLR 1051). Where the underlying transaction is unusual, the other partners will be bound only if they expressly consent (*see Hirst v Etherington* (1999) 149 NLJ 1110). **21.19**

Failing to implement a solicitor's undertaking is regarded by the courts and the Solicitors Disciplinary Tribunal as professional misconduct, even if the solicitor has not been guilty of dishonourable conduct. As solicitors are officers of the court, the High Court has a general jurisdiction to enforce undertakings given by solicitors in their capacities as solicitors (*United Mining and Finance Corporation Ltd v Becher* [1910] 2 KB 296). This jurisdiction is not limited to undertakings given in the course of litigation. The court also has the power to grant a solicitor relief from an undertaking on sufficient cause being shown (*John Fox v Bannister, King and Rigbeys*

[1988] QB 925). It may do so, for example, to give relief from a mistake or where there has been impropriety by the other side.

Practice on enforcing solicitors' undertakings

21.20 In *Udall v Capri Lighting Ltd* [1988] QB 907 Balcombe LJ said there are three ways in which a party seeking to enforce a solicitor's undertaking can proceed:

(a) by an action at law;
(b) by an application to the High Court to exercise its inherent supervisory jurisdiction over solicitors; and
(c) by reporting the solicitor to the SRA or the Legal Ombudsman for disciplinary action.

A claim against the solicitor (option (a)) may be capable of being framed as a breach of trust, such as where the solicitor has not applied money in the way specified in the undertaking (*Global Marine Drillships Ltd v Landmark Solicitors LLP* [2011] EWHC 2685 (Ch), LTL 25/10/2011, applying *Twinsectra Ltd v Yardley* [2002] UKHL 12, [2002] 2 AC 164). The drawback in taking this course is that there may be defences available to the solicitor which will make it difficult to obtain summary judgment (this was the problem in *Global Marine Drillships Ltd v Landmark Solicitors LLP*), whereas invoking the inherent jurisdiction (option (b)) will in many cases produce a simple claim for the enforcement of the solicitor's obligations in the undertaking.

In *Rooks Rider v Steel* [1994] 1 WLR 818 the claimant solicitors acted for a company based in Louisiana in a complex transaction under which the Louisiana company agreed to lend money to a hotel company. The hotel company's solicitors undertook in writing to pay the claimant's fees in connection with the transaction 'whether the matter proceeds to completion or not'. The transaction was never completed, and it transpired the Louisiana company did not have the funds to make the loan, and used the proposed transaction for fraudulent purposes. The defendant solicitors refused to honour their undertaking, relying on the fraud as absolving them from liability. It was found that the claimant solicitors were not involved in their client's fraud. It was accordingly held there was no lawful justification for not complying with the undertaking, and an order was made requiring the defendants to comply. In *Bentley v Gaisford* [1997] QB 627 it was held to be a breach of an undertaking given by the defendant firm to hold documents, which were the subject of a lien against unpaid fees, to the order of the claimant firm, when a partner in the defendant firm, acting in good faith and in what he regarded as his duty to his client, copied all the documents to the client. Doing so rendered the lien worthless.

Where on an application under the supervisory jurisdiction over solicitors it is shown that there has been a breach of an undertaking by a solicitor, the court will usually make an order requiring the solicitor to comply with the undertaking (*Re a Solicitor* [1966] 1 WLR 1604). On the breach by a solicitor of the standard undertaking in a residential property transaction to redeem or discharge existing mortgages or charges, the solicitor is liable to pay any sums required to discharge those instruments at the time redemption is sought (*Angel Solicitors v Jenkins O'Dowd and Barth* [2009] EWHC 46 (Ch), [2009] 1 WLR 1220). There may be a defence if the demand on the undertaking is wholly unreasonable or outside the solicitor's contemplation (*Clark v Lucas Solicitors LLP* [2009] EWHC 1952 (Ch), [2010] PNLR 2). If compliance with the undertaking will be impossible (perhaps because it involves actions which are not within the control of the solicitor), the court may order the solicitor to pay compensation to any person who suffers loss as a result of the breach of undertaking (*Udall v Capri Lighting Ltd* [1988] QB 907). In *Bentley v Gaisford* [1997] QB 627 the court refused to order the defendant solicitors to pay compensation despite their breach of undertaking because the partner who had copied the documents to the client was not guilty of inexcusable conduct meriting reproof.

Option (c), taking disciplinary action, has the drawback that there are limited remedies. There is no disciplinary power to order specific performance, although returning money to clients can be included as part of a regulatory settlement agreement. The SRA may alternatively refer the conduct to the Solicitors Disciplinary Tribunal, which has the disciplinary powers set out in the Solicitors Act 1974, s. 47, which include striking off, suspension and the imposition of penalties.

Chapter 22 Change of Solicitor

TERMINATION OF RETAINER

22.1 A retainer to conduct litigation is generally regarded as an entire contract, with the effect that a solicitor once retained must see the litigation through to its conclusion. However, the retainer is subject to an implied term that the solicitor may withdraw if there is good cause and provided reasonable notice is given to the client. The client may terminate the retainer without cause at any time. When a party changes solicitors, or retains a solicitor having previously been acting in person, or starts acting in person having previously retained a solicitor, the other parties and the court need to be informed so that future correspondence and court applications, orders and other documents can be sent to the correct address.

SOLICITOR ON THE RECORD

22.2 **CPR, Part 6**, contains general rules on service of documents. Although there are several refinements (see **chapter 15**), some of the basic rules on where litigation documents should be served are:

(a) Under **r. 6.23**, each party to litigation must provide an address for service within the United Kingdom or any other EEA State.

(b) **Rules 6.7** and **6.23(2)** in effect provide that where a solicitor or European lawyer is acting for a party, that party's address for service is the business address of the solicitor or European lawyer. The address of the solicitor or European lawyer may be anywhere in the United Kingdom or any other EEA State.

(c) The address for service of a party who is acting in person is usually the party's residential address or place of business (**rr. 6.8, 6.9(2)** and **6.23(2)(c)**).

(d) Any change of address of a party or of a party's solicitor (without changing the identity of the person acting for that party) must be notified in writing to the court and to other parties as soon as the change takes place (**r. 6.24**).

(e) In recent times the practice has been that if one solicitor acts for a number of parties in a claim, it is sufficient to serve on that solicitor a single copy of any documents that need to be served (see, for example, **PD 10, para. 5.3**).

The claim form will identify whether the claimant is acting by a solicitor or in person, and the defence or defence and counterclaim will similarly identify whether the defendant is acting in person or by a solicitor. **CPR, Part 42**, contains rules dealing with giving notice of changes relating to representation by solicitors.

PRESUMED CONTINUANCE

22.3 Where the address for service of a party is the business address of the party's solicitor, by **CPR, rr. 42.1** and **42.2(5)**, that solicitor will be considered to be continuing to act for that party until due notice is given or an order is made in accordance with **Part 42**. However, a solicitor appointed solely for the purpose of acting as an advocate at a hearing is not considered to be acting for the client for the purposes of **Part 42** (**PD 42, para. 1.3**).

NOTICE OF CHANGE

By **CPR, r. 42.2**, notice of change stating the change and the new address for service (which must be within the United Kingdom or another EEA State, see **r. 6.23(2)**) must be filed at court and served on all other parties whenever: **22.4**

(a) a party who has been acting by a solicitor changes solicitor;
(b) a party who has been acting in person appoints a solicitor; or
(c) a party who has been acting by a solicitor intends to act in future as a litigant in person.

In the circumstances set out in (a) and (c) above the notice of change must also be served on the former solicitor. The form of notice of change of solicitor is form N434. It should not be filed until every other party has been served (**PD 42, para. 1.2**), and should be filed in the court office in which the claim is proceeding (**para. 2.5**). Where the claim is the subject of an appeal to the Court of Appeal, the notice should also be filed in the Civil Appeals Office (**para. 2.7**). The copy of the notice filed at court must state that it has also been served on the other parties, and, if appropriate, the former solicitor.

REVOCATION OR DISCHARGE OF PUBLIC FUNDING

The retainer of any solicitor acting on behalf of a publicly funded client determines forthwith upon receipt of a notice of revocation or discharge (Civil Legal Aid (General) Regulations 1989 (SI 1989/339), reg. 83; Community Legal Service (Costs) Regulations 2000 (SI 2000/ 441), reg. 4; Civil Legal Aid (Procedure) Regulations 2012 (SI 2012/3098), reg. 14). As soon as the retainer of a solicitor is ended under these regulations, the solicitor is required by **CPR, r. 42.2(6)(a)**, to cease acting for the formerly funded or assisted litigant. If the litigant wishes to continue the litigation despite the cessation of public funding, a notice of change (see **22.4**) must be given (**r. 42.2(6)(b)**; **PD 42, para. 2.2**), even if the same solicitor is retained (because the previous solicitor is deemed by **CPR, r. 42.2(6)(a)**, to have ceased to act and **r. 42.2(6)(b)(i)** treats the litigant as previously having acted in person). Where a solicitor is appointed the notice of change does not have to be served on the former solicitor (again because **r. 42.2(6)(b)(i)** treats the litigant as previously having acted in person). The notice must give the last known address of the formerly funded or assisted person (**PD 42, para. 2.2**). **22.5**

COMING OFF THE RECORD

A solicitor's retainer may be terminated by the solicitor if there is a 'good reason' within the meaning of the Solicitors' Practice Rules 1990, r. 12.12, and the SRA Code of Conduct 2011, O 1.3, and on giving reasonable notice to the client. There is no comprehensive definition of what amounts to a good reason for this purpose, the question being fact-sensitive. There may be a good reason where the client fails to give instructions, acts unreasonably, or fails or refuses to pay a reasonable sum on account of the past and future costs of the litigation within a reasonable time of a request for payment (Solicitors Act 1974, s. 65(2); *Underwood, Son and Piper v Lewis* [1894] 2 QB 306). The test will be satisfied if the client insists on advancing a case which the solicitor does not regard as properly arguable (*Richard Buxton v Mills-Owen* [2010] EWCA Civ 122, [2010] 1 WLR 1997). This may arise through the use of documents containing contentions that are not properly arguable, or through instructing counsel to advance such contentions. It is recognised that it is difficult to draw the line between weak **22.6** cases which are and are not properly arguable. A solicitor who withdraws in the absence of good reason is in breach of the contract of retainer, and, as it is an entire contract, will be unable to recover any fees from the client (and may be required to refund fees previously paid).

When a solicitor ceases to act for a client, whether or not there is a breach of contract as between the solicitor and client, the change ought to be entered in the court records by one means or another. In most cases this will be done by the client or any new solicitor retained by the client giving notice of change as discussed in **22.4**. If this does not happen, the former solicitor will in practical terms be obliged to take steps to come off the record. To do this it is necessary to apply for an order under **CPR, r. 42.3**. It is reasonably clear from *Plenty v Gladwin* (1986) 67 ALR 26 (High Court of Australia) that such an application has nothing to do with whether or not the solicitor was right to withdraw, but is simply a matter of ensuring the court's record accords with the reality of whether the solicitor is continuing to act for the client. Unless there are special circumstances to the contrary, orders that a solicitor has ceased to act are generally made as a matter of course when it is shown that the solicitor is no longer acting for the party, and that no notice of change has been given.

An application under **r. 42.3** is made by application notice, which must be served on the client unless the court directs otherwise, and must be supported by evidence, usually by witness statement (see **r. 42.3(2)** and **Part 23**). The application and evidence must not be served on the other parties as it will often contain information which is confidential between the solicitor and client (*Re Creehouse Ltd* [1983] 1 WLR 77).

If an order is made under **r. 42.3** that a solicitor has ceased to act, the order must be served on all the parties to the proceedings, and if the order is not served by the court, the serving party or solicitor must also file a certificate of service in form N215 (**r. 42.3(3)**).

REMOVAL OF SOLICITOR ON APPLICATION OF ANOTHER PARTY

22.7 Where a solicitor has died, become bankrupt, ceased to practise or gone missing, the court and other parties should be informed and the client's address for service duly altered. Although this is not expressly provided by the CPR, ceasing to practise covers a multitude of circumstances, including retirement, changing professions, and also being struck off the roll of solicitors, failing to take out a practising certificate and being suspended from practising. In the circumstances mentioned in this paragraph there is a strong likelihood of the Solicitors Regulation Authority intervening in the solicitor's practice, under the Solicitors Act 1974, s. 35 and sch. 1.

Normally the client will appoint a new solicitor who will serve and file the appropriate notice of change. However, if no notice of change is served, the position can be regularised on the application of any other party under **CPR, r. 42.4**, for an order declaring the solicitor has ceased acting for the relevant party. Under the RSC the phrase 'any other party', which appeared in a number of contexts in the old rules and also appears in **CPR, r. 42.4(1)**, was until recently interpreted restrictively by cases such as *Shaw v Smith* (1886) 18 QBD 193 as limited to opposite parties, with the result that a co-defendant was not included. More recently, in *Manatee Towing Co. v Oceanbulk Maritime SA* [1999] 1 Lloyd's Rep 876, a decision under the old rules, it was held that this restrictive interpretation of the phrase no longer applied to the latest version of the old rules. There is no prospect of the old restrictive interpretation being carried forward into the CPR. The result is that an application under **r. 42.4** may be made by any party other than the party whose solicitor is no longer available.

An application notice seeking a declaration under r. 42.4 must be supported by evidence (**PD 42, para. 4.2**) and, unless the court otherwise directs, must be served on the client whose solicitor is unavailable. If the declaration is made, a copy of the order must be served on all the other parties, and if the order is not served by the court, the serving party must also file a certificate of service in form N215 (**CPR, r. 42.4(3)**).

Chapter 23 Statements of Case and Claim Forms

INTRODUCTION

23.1 The standard method of starting a claim under the CPR is by the court issuing a claim form (form N1), prepared for or by the claimant (the other methods and the circumstances in which they are used are summarised in **12.1**). A claim form is required by the CPR to set out essential details of the claim, including a concise statement of the nature of the cause of action and a statement of the remedy sought. The CPR also require the claimant to provide rather fuller particulars of claim (see **chapter 24**), which must include, among other prescribed matters, a concise statement of the facts on which the claimant relies. If practicable the particulars of claim should be set out in the claim form, though they may be in a separate document either accompanying the claim form or served and filed separately (see **15.40**).

STATEMENTS OF CASE

23.2 Claim forms and separate particulars of claim are examples of what the CPR calls 'statements of case', a term which applies to all documents in which a party's case is set out for the other parties and for the court. The former term for statements of case, 'pleadings', is still commonly used. **CPR, r. 2.3(1)**, includes the following definition:

'statement of case'—
(a) means a claim form, particulars of claim where these are not included in a claim form, defence, Part 20 claim, or reply to defence; and
(b) includes any further information given in relation to them voluntarily or by court order under rule 18.1.

This definition excludes winding-up petitions. Although they are not strictly 'statements of case', this does not prevent the court from striking them out under **r. 3.4** (*Investment Invoice Financing Ltd v Limehouse Board Mills Ltd* [2006] EWCA Civ 9, [2006] 1 WLR 985).

The term 'statement of case' within **r. 2.3** extends to the acknowledgment of service and detailed grounds for contesting a claim for judicial review (*R (Corner House Research) v Director of the Serious Fraud Office* [2008] EWHC 246 (Admin), [2008] ACD 63). Scott schedules are also treated as statements of case (*Easygroup IP Licensing Ltd v Easyjet Airline Co. Ltd* [2009] EWHC 1386 (Ch), LTL 13/7/2009, at [2]–[3]).

Every statement of case, including a claim form and particulars of claim, must be verified by a statement of truth (see **23.12**). A person who makes a false statement in a document verified by a statement of truth, without an honest belief in its truth, is guilty of a contempt of court (**r. 32.14(1)**). See *Nield v Loveday* [2011] EWHC 2324 (Admin), LTL 14/9/2011, where a claimant who had brought a personal injury claim following a road traffic accident was committed to prison for nine months for contempt as he had verified his statement of claim and witness statement despite knowing that they contained false information which tended to exaggerate the value of his claim. His wife, who had verified false statements to support his claim, admitted her contempt and was given a suspended six-month sentence. Thus there is now a degree of consanguinity between statements of case, witness statements and affidavits.

Statements of case exceeding 25 pages

There are cases which, on account of their complexity, have to be pleaded at length. Where, exceptionally, a statement of case exceeds 25 pages (excluding schedules), an appropriate short summary must also be filed and served (**PD 16, para. 1.4**). Lengthy statements of case can contribute to excessive costs, as recognised by the Jackson Review of Civil Costs. In the Admiralty and Commercial Courts, statements of case should be limited to 25 pages (Admiralty and Commercial Courts Guide, para. C1.1(b)). This is backed by prohibitions against setting out evidence (para. C1.1(a)) and substantial quotations from documents (para. C1.1(c): where this is necessary the quotations should be included in a schedule). A party seeking to rely on a statement of case exceeding 25 pages in these courts must apply on paper for permission to do so, including a brief statement of the reasons for exceeding the 25-page limit (para. C1.1(b)). The Chancery Guide does not require permission for statements of case exceeding 25 pages, but does require the document to be as brief and concise as possible and includes guidance on not pleading evidence or lengthy extracts from documents (app. 2). **23.3**

CONTENTS OF A CLAIM FORM

Form N1 is the form used to start most proceedings under **CPR, Part** 7. There is a special version of form N1 for use in the Commercial Court (form N1(CC)). There are also special claim forms for Admiralty claims (ADM 1, ADM 1A and ADM 15), arbitration applications (N8, see **chapter 72**), claims for possession of land (N5 and N5B), claims for relief against forfeiture of a lease (N5A), claims for demotion of tenancy (N6), judicial review claims (N461, see **chapter 74**) and probate claims (N2). Part 8 claims (see **chapter 13**) are generally commenced by form N208, but form N208(CC) is used in the Commercial Court, and N500 and N501 are used in director disqualification proceedings (see **chapter 86**). For additional claims under **Part 20** see **chapters 28** and **29**. This chapter is principally concerned with form N1. **23.4**

It is not appropriate to strike out a claim merely because the wrong form has been used to bring it, even if important elements such as the royal arms have been omitted, provided it is clear to the defendant (or, at least, the defendant's lawyers) what case has to be met and what type of proceedings are being brought (*Hannigan v Hannigan* [2000] 2 FCR 650). In *Hannigan v Hannigan* the mistake was made by the claimant's professional advisers and the Court of Appeal indicated that its judgment was not to be taken as giving general permission to practitioners not to bother about using correct forms. However, a claimant using the wrong form of originating process may well be granted permission to correct the position in the interests of dealing with the case justly (see *Thurrock Borough Council v Secretary of State for the Environment, Transport and the Regions* [2001] 1 PLR 94). The court does not have any power under the CPR to waive a failure to use a form (such as a petition) prescribed by Act of Parliament (*Re Osea Road Camp Sites Ltd* [2004] EWHC 2437 (Ch), [2005] 1 WLR 760, see **1.27**).

Heading

23.5 On page 1 of form N1 there must be stated:

(a) The court in which the claimant wishes to issue the claim. If the claim is to be issued in the High Court, the form must specify (a) the Division and (b) whether the claim is to be issued in the Royal Courts of Justice or a named district registry. The name of the court must be stated on the claim form for a claim in the Commercial Court (**PD 58, para. 2.3**), a Mercantile Court (**PD 59, para. 2.2**) or the Technology and Construction Court (**PD 60, para. 3.2**). In patent **claims, PD 63, para. 3.1(a)**, requires that claim forms must be marked 'Chancery Division Patents Court' or 'Patents County Court' in the top right-hand corner below the title of the court, and must state the number of any patent or registered design to which the claim relates. Claims within **CPR, Part 63, Section II**, must be marked 'Intellectual Property' in the top right-hand corner below the title of the court, unless it is started in the Patents County Court (**PD 63, para. 17.1**).

(b) Following the establishment of the National Civil Business Centre, designated money claims must be sent to the County Court Money Claims Centre, PO Box 527, and are all issued in the Northampton County Court (**PD 7A, para 4A.1**). This type of claim is defined in **r. 2.3(1)** as being (a) any claim which is started in a county court under **Part 7**; (b) only a claim for either or both a specified amount of money or an unspecified amount of money; and (c) not a claim for which special procedures are provided in the rules, e.g. no equitable remedy such as an injunction is being sought. The claimant must also specify their preferred court (**PD 7A, para. 4A.2**), and this will be considered by the court if transfer to a local county court is necessary, e.g. if the matter is contested.

(c) The parties, who should be described as in **table 14.1**. The full unabbreviated names and titles must be given of parties who are individuals (see **PD 16, para. 2.6**). If the claimant is claiming in a representative capacity, the claim form must state what that capacity is (**CPR, r. 16.2(3)**). If the defendant is sued in a representative capacity, the claim form must likewise state what that capacity is (**r. 16.2(4)**).

(d) The addresses of all parties, as specified in **table 15.1** in **15.14**. An address for service must include a full postcode unless the court orders otherwise (**r. 6.6(2)**). Postcode information can be obtained from http://www.royalmail.com. The claimant's address goes under the heading 'Claimant' on page 1. This address must be that at which the claimant resides or carries on business, even if the business address of the claimant's solicitor is the claimant's address for service (**PD 16, para. 2.2**). If the claimant's address for service is different from the address on page 1, it should be entered on page 2 in the box headed 'Claimant's or claimant's solicitor's address'. The defendant's name and address go in the space provided at the foot of page 1. Where the defendant is an individual, the claimant should (if the information is available) include the address at which the defendant resides or carries on business, even though solicitors may have agreed to accept service on the defendant's behalf (**para. 2.3**). A separate claim form must be prepared for each defendant, giving that defendant's name and address in this box.

If a claim form does not include full addresses for either the claimants or defendants, it will still be issued, but will be retained by the court and will not be served (**para. 2.5**). The court will notify the claimant, and will retain the claim form until the claimant provides full addresses including postcodes, or until the court dispenses with the requirement to provide full addresses (**para. 2.5**).

In clinical negligence claims the words 'clinical negligence' must be inserted at the top of every statement of case (**para. 9.3**).

Brief details of claim

23.6 Every claim form must contain a concise statement of the nature of the claim (**CPR, r. 16.2(1)(a)**). This should be inserted in page 1 of form N1 under the heading 'Brief details of claim'. It is suggested that, save in the most straightforward cases where the particulars of claim will be included in the claim form, this will be a simple statement such as:

The claimant's claim is for damages for personal injuries and interest arising out of a collision caused by the defendant's negligence when driving a motor car along Regent Street, London W1 on 1 July 2013.

More precise details of the allegations and issues will be contained in the particulars of claim (see **chapter 24**), and from a drafting standpoint, it would perhaps not be amiss to state that in the brief details. Particulars of claim should be included in the claim form (page 2 of form N1), if practicable (**PD 16, para. 3.1**), but may be in a separate document. If particulars of claim are not set out in the claim form for a claim issued through the Claims Production Centre or Money Claim Online, the claim form must state that the particulars of claim will follow and must include a brief summary of the claim (**PD 7C, para, 5.2(1); PD 7E, para. 5.2(2)**). It is an abuse of process to issue a claim for which no basis is known to the claimant (*Nomura International plc v Granada Group Ltd* [2007] EWHC 642 (Comm), [2008] Bus LR 1). The claim form had been issued at a time when the claimant had not decided to pursue a claim against the defendant, and had issued the claim form merely to protect its position. Cooke J said that **r. 16.2(1)** followed the same form and had the same intention as RSC, ord. 6, r. 2. Therefore, he had regard to the principles that had informed the pre-CPR cases of *Sterman v E. W. and W. J. Moore* [1970] 1 QB 596 and *Marshall v London Passenger Transport Board* [1936] 3 All ER 83. These decided that failing to include a concise statement on what is now the claim form could only be cured if the claimant had a known and genuine cause of action when the claim was issued. Gaining such knowledge by the time the application to strike out was heard was not enough, and the claim was struck out.

In probate cases, the claim form must contain a statement of the nature of the interest that the claimant and each defendant has in the estate (**CPR, r. 57.7(1)**); *O'Brien v Seagrave* [2007] EWHC 788 (Ch), [2007] 1 WLR 2002).

Remedy sought

Every claim form must specify the remedy which the claimant seeks (**CPR, r. 16.2(1)(b)**). **23.7**
There is no separate heading for this statement in form N1 and so the remedies sought should be included in the section of the claim form dealing with the brief details of claim.

Failure to specify a particular remedy will not limit any power of the court to grant such a remedy if the claimant is entitled to it (**r. 16.2(5)**). Likewise, in *Slater v Buckinghamshire County Council* [2004] EWCA Civ 1478, LTL 10/11/2004, it was held that the trial judge was entitled to make a finding of fact on an issue which had not been specifically pleaded, but which the parties clearly regarded as live and crucial to the case, and which they adequately dealt with at trial. Thus it should not be possible for a defendant to rely on a technical but unmeritorious defence that a particular remedy has not been set out, in order to escape the full scope of the court's powers (but see the cases discussed at **31.10**). It is suggested that the best practice is to set out all the remedies that are being claimed against the defendant, and there may be costs penalties if this is not done.

STATEMENT OF VALUE

Where the claimant is making a claim for money, the claim form must contain a statement of **23.8**
value (**CPR, r. 16.2(1)(c)**). The term 'claim for money' includes both a claim for a debt or liquidated demand and a claim for damages.

The clear objective of this rule is not merely to ensure precision and avoid ambiguity, but also to enable the court to allocate the case to the appropriate court and track. A statement of value

Commentary

on a claim form does not, however, limit the power of the court to give judgment for the amount to which it considers the claimant to be entitled (**r. 16.3(7)**).

By **r. 16.2(1)(c)**, a statement of value must be in accordance with **r. 16.3**, and additional requirements are set out in **PD 7A, para. 3**. On page 1 of form N1 there is a space headed 'Value'. By **CPR, r. 16.3(2)**, a statement of value must specify:

(a) the amount of money claimed;
(b) that the claimant expects to recover:
  (i) not more than £5,000, or
  (ii) more than £5,000 but not more than £25,000, or
  (iii) more than £25,000 (these are the basic delineations between cases on the small claims track, the fast track, and the multi-track); or
(c) that the claimant cannot say how much is likely to be recovered.

If the claim is one for personal injuries, the claimant must state whether the amount that he or she expects to recover as general damages for pain, suffering and loss of amenity is not more than £1,000 or more than £1,000 (**r. 16.3(3); PD 7A, para. 3.8**). This declaration is in addition to the statement of the overall expected value of the claim required by **CPR, r. 16.3(2)**, as it relates solely to the general damages aspect of the claim value. This may be important if the overall value of the claim is less than £5,000 (in which event it would normally fall to be tried on the small claims track) but where the general damages aspect of the case is expected to be over £1,000, the claim will normally be dealt with on the fast track, by virtue of **r. 26.6(1)(a)**. Curiously, the 'notes for claimant' (form N1A) only require the statement of value for the personal injury claim to be inserted in a case where the overall value does not exceed £5,000, but this guidance does not accord with the requirements of **r. 16.3(3)**.

If the claim includes a claim by a tenant of residential premises against his or her landlord seeking an order requiring the landlord to carry out repairs or other work to the premises, the claimant must state whether the estimated cost of those repairs or other work is not more than £1,000 or more than £1,000; and whether or not the claimant expects to recover more than £1,000 in respect of any other claim for damages (**r. 16.3(4); PD 7A, para. 3.9**). This will determine whether the claim can be allocated to the small claims track (see **CPR, r. 26.6(1)(b)**).

For other matters concerning claim forms in specialist jurisdictions, or using special procedures, see **23.18**.

Reason for starting claim in High Court

23.9 If the claim form is to be issued in the High Court, it must include an explanation of why it is being filed there, by stating (**CPR, r. 16.3(5)**):

(a) that the claimant expects to recover more than £25,000; or
(b) that some other enactment provides that the claim may be commenced only in the High Court (stating the relevant enactment); or
(c) if the claim is one for personal injuries, that the claimant expects to recover £50,000 or more; or
(d) that the claim needs to be in one of the specialist High Court lists, stating which list.

The way in which the financial details are to be entered in the claim form is set out in the notes for claimant on form N1A.

Computation of values

23.10 In calculating how much it is expected to recover, the following matters should be disregarded (**CPR, r. 16.3(6)**):

(a) interest;
(b) costs;

(c) any potential finding of contributory negligence;
(d) any potential counterclaim or defence of set-off;
(e) any potential payments that the defendant may have to make, out of any award to the claimant, to the Secretary of State for Social Security under the Social Security (Recovery of Benefits) Act 1997, s. 6.

Foreign currency claim

Where a claim is for a sum of money expressed in a foreign currency, the claim form should expressly state (**PD 16, para. 9.1**): **23.11**

(a) that the claim is for payment in a specified foreign currency;
(b) why it is for payment in that currency;
(c) the sterling equivalent of the sum at the date of the claim; and
(d) the source of the exchange rate used in calculating the sterling equivalent.

STATEMENT OF TRUTH

Requirements

By **CPR, r. 2.3(1)**, a claim form and, if separate, the particulars of claim are classified as statements of case. **Rule 22.1(1)(a)** requires every statement of case to be verified by a statement of truth, that is, a statement that the party putting forward the document believes the facts stated in the document are true (**r. 22.1(4)**). The basic format of a statement of truth is (**PD 22, para. 2.1**): **23.12**

I believe that the facts stated in this [name of document being verified] are true.

It is possible for the legal representative of a party to make a statement of truth verifying a document put forward by that party (**CPR, r. 22.1(6)**), in which event the basic format of the statement is:

The [claimant/defendant] believes that the facts stated in this [name of document being verified] are true.

There is a pro forma statement of truth on form N1 for use when the particulars of claim are included in the claim form.

A statement of truth may be contained in the document it verifies, or it may be in a separate document served subsequently (**PD 22, para. 1.5**). If it is in a separate document, the formalities set out in **PD 22, para. 2.3**, must be observed.

Who may sign a statement of truth

A statement of truth verifying a document put forward by a party must be signed by the party or his or her litigation friend (**CPR, r. 22.1(6)(a)(i)**). Alternatively it can be signed by the party's legal representative (**r. 22.1(6)(a)(ii)**), provided the capacity in which the representative signs and the name of his or her firm are stated (**PD 22, para. 3.7**). The term 'legal representative' is defined by **CPR, r. 2.3**, as a person who: **23.13**

(a) has been instructed to act for a party in relation to proceedings; and
(b) is a barrister, solicitor, solicitor's employee, manager of a body recognised under the Administration of Justice Act 1985, s. 9, or a person who, for the purposes of the Legal Services Act 2007, is an authorised person in relation to an activity which constitutes the conduct of litigation (within the meaning of that Act).

A statement of truth signed by a legal representative will refer to the client's belief and not the representative's but must be signed in the representative's own name and not that of his or her firm or employer (**PD 22, para. 3.10**). The individual who signs a statement of truth must print his or her full name clearly beneath the signature (**PD 22, para. 3.9**).

In the case of a company or other corporation, the statement of truth must be signed by one of the persons 'holding a senior position' listed in **PD 22, para. 3.5**, giving his or her position in the organisation (**PD 22, para. 3.4**). The list in **para. 3.5** includes 'manager or other officer of the company or corporation'. A footnote in **para. 3.4** refers to **PD 6A, para. 6.2**, which, however, defines persons holding a senior position in a company or corporation in precisely the same terms as **PD 22, para. 3.5**. A manager signing a statement of truth must be someone who has personal knowledge of the contents of the document being verified or is responsible for managing those who have that knowledge. In a large company this may be the manager of a claims, insurance or legal department. In a small company it may be that the only persons who hold senior positions are the directors. An employee of a company who works in a legal department managed by an employed solicitor is employed by the company, not by the solicitor, and so cannot qualify as the company's legal representative, though, depending on his or her responsibilities, such an employee might be regarded as holding a senior position.

If an insurer or the Motor Insurers' Bureau has a financial interest in the result of the proceedings for which the document is created, the insurer or Bureau may sign the statement of truth verifying the document (**PD 22, para. 3.6A**). A claims manager may be a person holding a senior position who can sign for the insurer (**para. 3.11**). Signature of a statement of truth when insurers are conducting proceedings on behalf of several claimants or defendants, is dealt with in **para. 3.6B**.

When the claimant is a partnership, the statement of truth may be signed by any of the partners or a person having the control or management of the partnership business (**para. 3.6**). It is not thought that there is any significance in the difference between the word 'must' used in **para. 3.4** and 'may' used in **para. 3.6**.

An agent who manages property or investments for a party cannot sign a statement of truth to verify that party's documents (**para. 3.11**).

It is stated in **para. 3.11** that 'Where some or all of the trustees [of a trust] comprise a single party one, some or all of the trustees comprising the party may sign a statement of truth. The legal representative of the trustees may sign it.' It seems that this permits one trustee to sign on behalf of all.

Mechanically reproduced signatures

23.14 It is submitted that it is not good practice for a statement of truth to be signed otherwise than by the hand of the person making the statement. If a mechanically reproduced signature is added by the person making the statement and is an assertion that the signatory's mind has been applied to the contents of the verified document, it is highly arguable that **CPR, r. 22.1(6)**, has been complied with, but it is difficult to see why the signature could not have been written. If a mechanically reproduced signature is applied by someone other than the purported signatory, **r. 22.1(6)** has not been complied with (*Birmingham City Council v Hosey* 2002 Legal Action 20). Although the defect is an irregularity which could be cured by order of the court under **r. 3.10**, until that is done, the statement of case cannot be relied on as evidence of any of the matters set out in it (**r. 22.2(1)**; see **23.17**).

In *Goodman v J. Eban Ltd* [1954] 1 QB 550 it was held that a solicitor's bill of costs accompanied by a letter, on which the solicitor's signature had been rubber-stamped, was 'signed by' the solicitor, as required by what is now the Solicitors Act 1974, s. 69(2), the rubber stamp having been applied by the solicitor himself, but the practice was disapproved by the court. In *Birmingham City Council v Hosey* a statement of truth was rubber-stamped with the name of an employee in the council's legal services department who had never seen the papers, checked the facts or read any of the source documents. He had merely authorised more junior employees to apply the rubber stamp. Judge MacDuff QC held that the statement had not been properly signed, saying that the requirement in **CPR, r. 22.1(6)**, was not a mere technicality or a matter of form only. **Rule 5.3**, which allows a document to be signed by 'computer or other mechanical means' did not apply, because a statement of truth is not a document but a statement in a document.

Liability for a statement of truth

A person who makes a false statement in a document verified by a statement of truth, or who causes such a statement to be made, without an honest belief in its truth, is guilty of contempt of court (**CPR, r. 32.14(1)**). It must be shown that the person knew (a) that the statement was false, (b) that it was likely to interfere with the course of justice (*Malgar Ltd v R. E. Leach (Engineering) Ltd* [2000] FSR 393; *KK Sony Computer Entertainment v Ball* [2004] EWHC 1984 (Ch), LTL 11/8/2004). Proceedings for such contempt can only be brought by the Attorney-General or with the permission of the court (**r. 81.18; PD 81, para. 5**). This is to ensure that proceedings are brought only when required in the public interest. **23.15**

A request for an allegation of falsity of a statement of truth to be referred to the Attorney-General must be made to the court dealing with the case in which the statement of truth or disclosure statement was made (**PD 32, para. 28.1(1)**). Despite the language of **CPR, r. 32.14(2)**, and **PD 32, para. 28**, a party in county court proceedings can go straight to the Divisional Court (but not a single judge of the High Court) for an order for committal under **RSC, ord. 52 in CPR, sch. 2**, against a person alleged to have made a false statement of truth (*Barnes v Seabrook* [2010] EWHC 1849 (Admin), [2010] ACD 87). The written evidence in support of an application for permission under **r. 32.14(2)** should include a chronology of events (*Barnes v Seabrook*). An additional factor in deciding whether to give permission to proceed under r. 32.14(2) is whether there has been any delay in seeking permission (*Barnes v Seabrook*).

The obligatory language in **para. 28.1(1)** is inconsistent with the permissive approach (albeit with a strong direction that requests should be made through the court) in **para. 28.2(2)**, which states:

> The Attorney-General prefers a request that comes from the court to one made direct by a party to the claim in which the alleged contempt occurred without prior consideration by the court. A request to the Attorney-General is not a way of appealing against, or reviewing the decision of the judge.

A request to the Attorney-General must be made in writing and sent to the Attorney-General's Office at 20 Victoria Street, London SW1H 0NF (**PD 32, para. 28.2(1)**). The request must be accompanied by a copy of the order directing that the matter be referred to the Attorney-General and must:

(a) identify the statement said to be false;
(b) explain:
 (i) why it is false; and
 (ii) why the maker knew the statement to be false at the time it was made; and
(c) explain why contempt proceedings would be appropriate in the light of the overriding objective in **Part 1**.

PD 32, para. 28.3, says that where a party makes an application to the court for permission to commence proceedings for contempt of court, the application must be supported by written evidence of the facts and matters specified in **para. 28.2(1)** and the result of the request to the Attorney-General made by the applicant.

A party who intends to ask for an allegation of falsity to be referred should warn the maker of the statement at the earliest suitable opportunity (*KJM Superbikes Ltd v Hinton* [2008] EWCA Civ 1280, [2009] 1 WLR 2406). If the maker of the statement of truth is likely to be a witness at the trial of the claim in which the statement was made, such notification should be delayed

Commentary

until after that evidence has been given, so as to avoid imposing improper pressure on the witness.

In deciding whether to give permission under **CPR, r. 32.14(2)**, the only question is whether the complaint has sufficient gravity to make it in the public interest for committal proceedings to be brought (*KJM Superbikes Ltd v Hinton*). Permission should be given in serious examples of false statements, because otherwise parties and witnesses will regard the statement of truth as a mere formality. Factors to be taken into account in deciding whether it is in the public interest to proceed include:

(a) the strength of the evidence tending to show the statement was false;
(b) the strength of the evidence showing the maker of the statement knew it was false when the statement was made;
(c) the circumstances in which the statement was made;
(d) the significance of the document in the proceedings;
(e) any evidence of the maker's state of mind, including his understanding of the significance of the document in the proceedings;
(f) the length of time the false statements were persisted in (*Kirk v Walton* [2008] EWHC 1780 (QB), [2009] 1 All ER 257).

Settling the claim does not remove the jurisdiction to bring proceedings for contempt of court under **r. 32.14** (*Kirk v Walton* [2008] EWHC 1780 (QB), [2009] 1 All ER 257).

It was held in *Kirk v Walton* [2009] EWHC 703 (QB), LTL 9/4/2009, that contempt of court will only be found if it is established beyond reasonable doubt that the respondent:

(a) made or caused to be made a false statement;
(b) in a document verified by a statement of truth (which includes documents exhibited to a document verified by a statement of truth); and
(c) without an honest belief in its truth.

It is not enough to find discrepancies between a document verified by a statement of truth and other objectively verifiable evidence. It is the degree of difference and/or the circumstances in which the verified statement was made that matter (*Kirk v Walton* [2009] EWHC 703 (QB), LTL 9/4/2009).

The belief stated in a statement of truth (and the consequent responsibility for making a false statement) is that of the party putting forward the document, save in the case where a party is conducting proceedings with the aid of a litigation friend, in which event the statement of belief is that of the litigation friend (**r. 22.1(5)**). Although it could possibly be argued that both a litigation friend and the party on whose behalf such friend is acting, could be jointly or independently responsible for the accuracy of the statement of truth in the (possibly rare) circumstances where it could be shown that the party was aware that the statement was false, this seems to be precluded by the terms of **r. 22.1(5)**.

When a statement of truth verifying a document is signed by a legal adviser of the party putting forward the document, its contents and the consequences of signing it are deemed, by virtue of the signature, to have been explained to the claimant, and the signature will be taken by the court as meaning that the client has authorised the representative to sign (**PD 22, para. 3.8**).

For the position of an insurer or the Motor Insurers' Bureau signing a statement of truth see **PD 22, paras 3.6A** and **3.6B**.

The effect of this rule is to rest the responsibility for the contents of the document squarely on the shoulders of the person putting forward the facts. It is not sufficient for a legal representative to put forward matters in the belief (however genuine) that what his client has told him is the truth — it is incumbent on him to ensure that he has received direct instructions to that effect. This is particularly important in view of the explanation deemed to have been made to the client by **PD 22, para. 3.8**, which, if not actually given, could well lead to an allegation of professional misconduct. Provided that such instructions have been given, the legal representative signing a statement should not incur personal liability in respect of any default, unless he is aware that the contents are false, notwithstanding his instructions to the contrary.

Use of a verified statement of case as evidence

23.16 The principal reason for the requirement for a statement of case to be verified by a statement of truth is to ensure that litigants do not lightly put forward false cases. A secondary purpose is to enable a statement of case to be used as evidence in interim proceedings. By **r. 32.6(2)**, at hearings other than the trial, matters set out in a party's statement of case or application notice may be relied on in support of that party's application, provided that the statement or notice is verified by a statement of truth.

Consequence of failure to verify a statement of case

23.17 If a statement of case is not verified by a statement of truth, it will remain effective unless struck out, but the party putting it forward may not rely on it as evidence of any of the matters set out in it (**CPR, r. 22.2(1)**). The omission simply means that the statement of case cannot be used for the purpose of supporting an application under **r. 32.6(2)**.

Where a statement of case remains unverified, any party may apply either:

(a) under **r. 22.4** for an order that the statement be verified within such period as the court may specify, or be struck out in default (**PD 22, para. 4.2**); or
(b) under **r. 22.2(2)** for an order that the statement be struck out.

The costs of such an application will normally be ordered to be paid by the defaulting party in any event, and forthwith (**PD 22, para. 4.3**). It is probable that the majority of such applications will be as a result of oversight on the part of the party putting forward the document, rather than as a result of any deliberate intention to avoid the rule.

The usual order on failing to verify a statement of case is to allow the defaulting party a limited period of time to file a verified statement of case. Setting aside an order granting permission to serve outside the jurisdiction on the ground that the claim form and witness statement were not signed was regarded as disproportionate in *Colliers International Property Consultants v Colliers Jordan Lee Jafaar Sdn Bhd* [2008] EWHC 1524 (Comm), [2008] 2 Lloyd's Rep 368.

OTHER MATTERS TO BE SET OUT IN THE CLAIM FORM

23.18 Special rules concerning claims against the Crown are set out in **CPR, r. 16.2(1A)**.

A claim form must contain such other matters as may be set out in a practice direction (**CPR, r. 16.2(1)(d)**).

For entering fixed costs on a claim form see **70.6**. Where fixed costs do not apply, the words 'to be assessed' should be entered in the box for Solicitor's costs.

Paragraphs 14 and 15 of **PD 16** specify matters which must be included in a claimant's statement of case and so could either be in the claim form or in the particulars of claim. **Paragraph 14** is concerned with certain proceedings under the Competition Act 1998, and specifies information which must be presented by a claimant intending to rely on a determination of the Office of Fair Trading. **Paragraph 15** specifies what must be set out in a statement of case by a claimant who seeks to rely on any provision of, or right arising under, the **Human Rights Act 1998**, or seeks a remedy under that Act.

PD Pre-action Conduct, para. 9.7, says that a claimant should state, either in the claim form or in particulars of claim, whether there has been compliance with **Sections III** and **IV** of the

Commentary

practice direction, or any relevant protocol. In most cases this is likely to be a positive statement concerning both parties' conduct and it ought to be in the claim form. However, where the defendant is in default, the claimant may wish to set out the defendant's failure in the particulars of claim so that the defendant is obliged to respond to the allegation when drafting the defence.

NOTICES TO BE FILED WITH THE CLAIM FORM

23.19 If a claim form, which is to be served out of the jurisdiction, is one which the court has power to deal with under the **Civil Jurisdiction and Judgments Act 1982** and the **Brussels I Regulation**, it must be filed and served with form N510 (**CPR, r. 6.34; PD 6B, para. 2.1; PD 7A, para. 3.5**).

Chapter 24 Particulars of Claim

REQUIREMENT

Particulars of claim are required by **CPR, r. 7.4(1)**. They must include the matters specified in **r. 16.4**, the first of which is a concise statement of the facts on which the claimant relies (see **24.3**). Particulars of claim should, if practicable, be set out in the claim form (**PD 16, para. 3.1**). Page 2 of form N1 has a space headed 'Particulars of Claim'. If it is not practicable to state the particulars of claim on the claim form, they may be in a separate document accompanying the claim form, or they may be served and filed separately within the time limits stated in **15.40**. In the **PD 7B** procedure, which applies to most claims under the Consumer Credit Act 1974, particulars of claim must be served with the claim form (**PD 7B, para. 5.2**). In Money Claim Online there is a limit of 1080 characters (including spaces) for particulars of claim in the claim form (**PD 7E, para. 5.2(1)**). If particulars of claim are not set out in a claim form issued through the Claims Production Centre or Money Claim Online, the claim form must state that the particulars of claim will follow and must include a brief summary of the claim (**PD 7C, para, 5.2(1)**; **PD 7E, para. 5.2(2)**). **24.1**

In *Tetra Pak Ltd v Biddle and Co.* [2010] EWHC 54 (Ch), [2010] 1 WLR 1466, it was held that it would not be inconsistent with the CPR, and in particular **rr. 7.4** and **16.4**, for a claimant to serve separate particulars of claim on different defendants within the same claim.

CPR, Part 8, provides an alternative procedure for bringing claims, and specifically excludes the provisions in **Part 16** on statements of case (**r. 8.9(a)(i)**).

POWER TO DISPENSE WITH STATEMENTS OF CASE

If a claim form has been properly issued and served on a defendant, the court has the power under **CPR, r. 16.8**, to order that the claim will then continue without any statements of case having to be filed. This will presumably be reserved for cases of considerable urgency where the matter can be dealt with expeditiously without formal disclosure of the respective parties' cases, or matters where the issue is extremely simple, and where the service of statements of case would only add to the delay and expense of the proceedings. **24.2**

CONTENT

24.3 Where the particulars of claim are served separately from the claim form, they must state (**PD 16, para. 3.8**):

(a) the name of the court in which the claim is proceeding;
(b) the claim number;
(c) the title of the proceedings (parties should be described as in **table 14.1**); and
(d) the claimant's address for service.

The body of the particulars of claim must include:

(a) A concise statement of the facts on which the claimant relies (**CPR, r. 16.4(1)(a)**). Particulars of claim extending to 109 pages with 162 numbered paragraphs could not be regarded as concise (*Diamantides v J. P. Morgan Chase Bank* [2005] EWHC 263 (Comm), LTL 5/3/2005, at [10]). The rules should not be read or interpreted as suggesting that the particulars of claim should contain evidence. The distinction between material facts (relevant), and the evidence by which those facts are to be proved (irrelevant) still remains good practice.

The purpose of statements of case is to elucidate the facts. A party is not obliged to particularise or explain its legal arguments in its statements of case (that is the function of skeleton arguments) (*Trader Publishing Ltd v Autotrader.Com Inc.* [2010] EWHC 142 (Ch), LTL 12/3/2010).

In *Petromec Inc. v Petróleo Brasileiro SA* [2007] EWCA Civ 1371, [2008] 1 Lloyd's Rep 305, the claimant was seeking to recover reasonably incurred extra costs pursuant to contractual clauses for extra work carried out to upgrade an oil production platform for the defendant beyond the original specifications and for alterations specified by the defendant. The claimant could not just assert the final costs from which the reasonable extra costs could be calculated, instead it was necessary to identify the work required to effect the changes from the original specification, particularise what the defendant instructed it to do, the cost incurred and where necessary a causal nexus.

(b) Details of any interest claimed (**CPR, r. 16.4(1)(b) and (2)**). A claimant who is seeking interest must state whether it is being claimed under the terms of a contract, or under a specified enactment, or for some other (defined) reason (**r. 16.4(2)(a)**). If the claim is for a specified sum of money, the particulars of claim should state the percentage rate claimed, the date from which interest is claimed, the date to which it is calculated (being not later than the date of issue of the claim form), the amount claimed up until that date, and the daily rate of interest accruing after that date (**r. 16.4(2)(b)**). Thus, on a specified sum, a claim for interest 'pursuant to statute' or 'at such rate and for such period as the court shall deem fit' will not comply with the rule.

(c) Where appropriate, a statement to the effect that aggravated or exemplary damages (or both) are being claimed; together with the grounds on which they are claimed (**r. 16.4(1)(c)**).

(d) Where appropriate, a statement to the effect that provisional damages are being claimed, together with the grounds on which they are claimed (**r. 16.4(1)(d)**).

(e) Where a claim is brought to enforce a right to recover possession of goods, a statement showing the value of the goods (**PD 16, para. 7.2**).

(f) Where a claim is based upon a written agreement, a copy of the contract or contractual documents should be attached to or served with the particulars of claim; together with relevant parts of the contract or documents incorporating any general conditions of sale (**PD 16, para. 7.3**). The requirement to attach contractual documents to the particulars of claim in breach of contract cases does not apply in Claims Production Centre or Money Claim Online cases (**PD 7C, para. 1.4(3A); PD 7E, para. 5.2A**), unless the particulars of claim are served separately in accordance with **PD 7C, para. 5.2, or PD 7E, para. 5.2(2)**. In trespass and injunction cases it is often helpful to illustrate the facts with plans annexed to the particulars of claim. The original documents should be available at the hearing.

(g) Where a claim is based upon an oral agreement, the contractual words relied upon, including by whom, to whom, when and where they were spoken (**PD 16, para. 7.4**).
(h) Where a claim is based upon an agreement by conduct, particulars of the conduct relied on, stating by whom, when and where the acts constituting the conduct were done (**PD 16, para. 7.5**).
(i) In a claim issued in the High Court relating to a Consumer Credit Act 1974 agreement, a statement that the action is not one to which s. 141 of the Act applies (**PD 16, para. 7.6**).
(j) Any other matters required by practice directions to be included in respect of certain types of claim (**CPR, r. 16.4(1)(e); PD 16, para. 3.6(2)**).
(k) Where a party seeks to raise a human rights point, the particulars of claim (and any other type of statement of claim or appeal notice filed on behalf of that party) must set out precise details of the Convention right relied upon. It must also give details of the alleged infringement and it must state the relief sought (**PD 16, para. 15.1**).
(l) In a claim for wrongful interference with goods the particulars of claim must state the name and address of every person (who is not a party) who the claimant knows claims an interest in the goods (**CPR, r. 19.5A(1)**).

Additionally, the following specific matters are required by **PD 16, para. 8.2**, to be set out in particulars of claim, if the claimant wishes to rely on them:

(a) any allegation of fraud (see *Rigby v Decorating Den Systems Ltd* [1999] EWCA Civ 986 BAILII, LTL 15/3/99; Chancery Guide, **paras 2.8** and **2.9**);
(b) the fact of any illegality;
(c) details of any misrepresentation;
(d) details of all breaches of trust;
(e) notice or knowledge of a fact;
(f) details of unsoundness of mind or undue influence;
(g) details of wilful default;
(h) any facts relating to mitigation of loss or damage.

A statement of compliance with requirements concerning pre-action conduct (**PD Pre-action Conduct, para. 9.7**) will normally be in the claim form, but, if it alleges default by the defendant, may be better placed in the particulars of claim (see **23.18**).

Signature when drafted by legal representative

Statements of case and other documents drafted by a legal representative must be signed. Documents drafted by counsel must bear counsel's signature, and those drafted by a solicitor must be signed in the name of the firm (**PD 5A, para. 2.1**). In practice, counsel's handwritten signature appears only on the draft as settled by counsel. The version of the document used for service and filing simply has the barrister's name typed in capitals. For the use of mechanically reproduced signatures see **23.14**. **24.4**

Statement of truth

The particulars of claim, being a statement of case, must be verified by a statement of truth (**CPR, r. 22.1(1)(a)**; see **23.12** to **23.17**). The purpose of requiring a statement of truth is to eliminate claims in which a party has no honest belief and to discourage the pleading of claims unsupported by evidence and which are put forward in the hope that something may turn up on disclosure or at trial (*Clarke v Marlborough Fine Art (London) Ltd* [2002] 1 WLR 1731). **24.5**

Special rules for certain types of claim

For special requirements in: **24.6**

(a) personal injury claims, see **PD 16, para. 4**;
(b) fatal accident claims, see **PD 16, para. 5**;

(c) possession claims, see **PD 55A, paras 2.1** to **2.7**;
(d) hire-purchase claims, see **PD 16, para. 6**;
(e) claims under the Consumer Credit Act 1974 to which **PD 7B** applies, see **PD 7B, para. 7**;
(f) defamation claims, see **PD 53, para. 2**;
(g) claims made for an injunction or declaration in respect of land or its possession, see **PD 16, para. 7.1**;
(h) claims for recovery of goods, see **PD 16, para. 7.2**;
(i) cases where a claimant wishes to rely on the provisions of the Civil Evidence Act 1968, s. 11 or s. 12, concerning evidence of conviction of an offence, or a finding of adultery or paternity, see **PD 16, para. 8.1**;
(j) a claim for infringement of a patent or registered design, or an application in which the validity of a patent or registered design is challenged, see **CPR, r. 63.6**, and **PD 63, para. 4**.

Paragraphs 14 and **15** of **PD 16** specify matters which must be included in a claimant's statement of case and so could either be in the claim form or in the particulars of claim. **Paragraph 14** is concerned with certain proceedings under the Competition Act 1998 and specifies information which must be presented by a claimant intending to rely on a determination of the Office of Fair Trading. **Paragraph 15** specifies what must be set out in a statement of case by a claimant who seeks to rely on any provision of, or right arising under, the Human Rights Act 1998, or seeks a remedy under that Act.

Points of law, witnesses and documents

24.7 **PD 16, para. 13.3**, states that a statement of case may include:

(a) a reference to any point of law on which the party's claim or defence is based;
(b) the name of any witness whom the party proposes to call; and
(c) (by way of service or attachment) a copy of any document which the party considers is necessary to the claim or defence (including any expert's report to be filed in accordance with **Part 35**).

It is interesting that there is no reference to this option in the guidance notes on drafting particulars of claim which are given to claimants on form N1A.

STRUCTURE OF PARTICULARS OF CLAIM

24.8 It is not intended to provide precedents of statements of case in this work, as some of the worst excesses of the previous system came about as a result of over-reliance on formulaic pleading, to the detriment of clear and objective thought. It is suggested that the basic objective of particulars of claim should be to inform the court and the other side what the case is all about, including (in the vast majority of cases) the duty that was allegedly owed, the fact that it was broken, how it was broken, and the remedies sought as a result. It is hoped that the following advice on structure will be of assistance.

Identification of the parties

24.9 It is, of course, essential to ensure that the correct parties appear as claimant(s) and defendant(s). Although in most cases these may be self-evident, there are instances in which the correct parties may only be ascertained by reference to the cause of action (for example, where there are special rules as to the parties entitled to claim relief, or against whom relief can be claimed). It may be necessary to sue *'persons unknown'*, who are identified by description rather than name (see **14.3**).

The manner in which a claim form, and every other statement of case should be headed, is now set out specifically in **PD 7A, paras 4.1** and **4.2**, and **PD 16, para. 2.6**. The title should state:

(a) the number of proceedings (i.e. the case number);
(b) the court or Division in which they are proceeding;
(c) each party's full unabbreviated name and title by which he is known;
(d) each party's status in the proceedings (i.e. claimant or defendant).

Where there is more than one claimant and/or defendant, the parties should be described in the title as:

(1) Mr AB
(2) Miss CD
(3) Mrs EF Claimants
— and —
(1) Mr GH
(2) Ms IJ
(3) Master KL Defendants

Although it may be helpful for some description of the parties to be given in the first paragraph of the particulars of claim, it is not necessary to do this when their business, profession or relationship to the other parties is not relevant to the claim. If, however, it is necessary to assert the identity and status of the claimant or defendant in order to set out the legal basis on which the claim is being brought, this should be done. Thus, it may be necessary to state the nature of a company's business where a claim is being brought by or against a company arising out of matters concerning its business. Similarly it may be important to set out the fact that a party is a landlord or tenant of premises, or the owner of a particular chattel, or an employer or employee.

Background

Before turning to the precise nature of the duty owed, it will often (but not invariably) be necessary to 'set the scene', by giving a short description of the circumstances in which the duty came about. This should be done with sufficient precision to enable the defendant precisely to identify what will subsequently be alleged, and to put it into context. This may vary from a short description of the circumstances in which an accident occurred, to the events which ultimately gave rise to a concluded agreement between the parties. In many cases, the **CPR** or **PDs** will require the insertion of material here, such as supporting documentation, or particulars of words spoken. **24.10**

Duty alleged

The vast majority of claims involve allegations of breaches of duty. It is thus essential first to state what the duty is (and if necessary how it is alleged to have arisen) before alleging the breach or breaches relied on. Often this will be no more than stating the fact that a contract has come into being with various terms. Sometimes the relationship between the parties has given rise to a duty. In road traffic cases, it is conventional not to allege the fact that the presence of a motor vehicle on a road gave rise to a duty of care towards other road users, because that is taken for granted. **24.11**

Breach of duty

Once the existence and nature of the duty have been alleged, it is necessary to set out precisely the manner in which it is alleged that the duty has been breached. Inserting 'stock' particulars, which tell little or nothing about the real nature of the claim, is to be avoided. A specimen of such unsatisfactory particulars appears in example 24.3 in **24.20**. Such particulars will almost inevitably be struck out today. **24.12**

Commentary

It must be remembered that the objectives of particulars of breach are twofold — first to describe the nature of the breach, and secondly to do so in such a way that it is clear to the defendant and the court how the breach actually took place. In particulars of negligence, for example, it is essential that each particular should not only describe a breach of the duty, but set out the manner and circumstances (singly or collectively) in which that breach occurred. See example 24.1 for an annotated description of properly drafted particulars.

Example 24.1 Properly drafted particulars

PARTICULARS OF NEGLIGENCE

The defendant was negligent in that he:

1. Drove his car along Litigation Avenue towards the junction with Blackstone Road, at a speed that was excessive in the circumstances.

(The conventional phrase 'drove too fast', says very little if anything about the breach, and often appears to be inserted as a matter of form. It is often incorrectly thought that this allegation means that the defendant was exceeding the speed limit. The duty is to drive at a safe speed in the circumstances. The manner in which the particulars are set out makes this clear, and also starts to build up the picture which, when all the particulars are complete, will properly identify the claimant's case, so that it can be answered by the defendant.)

2. Failed to keep a proper lookout.

(This is a straightforward example of an allegation of breach of a generic duty. It should later be qualified by particulars of how precisely it is alleged that the breach took place.)

3. Failed to see or heed the presence of the claimant's vehicle, which was in the process of entering into Litigation Avenue from Blackstone Road into the path of the defendant's car.

(This paragraph comprises specific particulars of the generic allegation made in paragraph 2, and adds further details which, in conjunction with paragraph 1, clarifies the circumstances in which the accident took place. Essentially, this paragraph could be silently prefaced by the words, 'because he failed to keep a proper lookout, he…'.

4. Failed to brake, steer or otherwise manoeuvre his car in order to avoid colliding with the claimant.

(Again, this paragraph runs logically on from the last one: 'Because he failed to see the claimant, he failed to brake etc.'. Once again, specific breaches of duty are alleged here in the context of the events that are being described.)

5. Caused his car to collide with that of the claimant.

(Often, and wrongly, omitted in many particulars, this is the actual breach of duty which gives rise to the claim.)

The above example not merely describes the alleged breaches of duty, but puts them in a context which enables the claimant's case to be understood, so that an appropriate response can be made. This does not, of course mean that the case is unassailable — the defence in the above example may well be to the effect that the claimant was emerging from a minor road and that the defendant had the right of way. He would not, however, be in a position to assert this had the context of the claim not been fully particularised.

In *Uren v First National Home Finance Ltd* [2005] EWHC 2529 (Ch), *The Times*, 17 November 2005, the claim simply pleaded a sequence of events and stated that as a result of those events the defendant had been unjustly enriched. This was struck out. It failed to set out facts which were capable of bringing the claim within one of the established restitutionary categories, or some justifiable extension of them. However, in *Sinclair Investment Holdings SA v Versailles Trade Finance Ltd* [2005] EWCA Civ 722, [2006] 1 BCLC 60, in a claim for breach of fiduciary duty based on an assumption of a duty of loyalty with an alternative claim in constructive trust, although the *assumption of loyalty* was not expressly pleaded, it was held to be sufficiently pleaded by allegations that the defendant controlled the exercise, or was in a position to control the exercise, of powers over the claimant's money.

While the court will be slow to strike out for failing to give sufficient particulars of negligence, where the claimant has been given the opportunity to provide those particulars and fails to do so, striking out may be appropriate (*S v Chapman* [2008] EWCA Civ 800, [2008] ELR 603). Indeed, the court in *Spencer v Barclays Bank plc* (2009) LTL 30/10/2009 struck out the claim as an abuse of process because the particulars failed to include a concise statement of the facts upon which the claimants were relying, such that neither the court nor the defendant could see the case the defendant was to meet, and further, the claimants clearly had no intention of trying to amend their statement of case to put forward a coherently pleaded and intelligible claim.

Particulars of claim expressed in a general non-specific way may be struck out. See *English, Welsh and Scottish Railway Ltd v Goodman* [2007] EWHC 3463 (QB), LTL 21/8/2007, which was a claim for breach of restrictive covenants against a former employee. The particulars of claim were struck out as far too broad in making claims and allegations which were unfocused and unparticularised. See also *Dunn v Glass Systems (UK) Ltd* [2007] EWHC 1901 (QB), LTL 23/7/2007, in which particulars of claim running to 221 pages were struck out. They were excessively long, which was oppressive, and contained details irrelevant to the cause of action, a large number of terms that were incomprehensible and privileged material.

Where a company director is alleged to have failed to disclose to the board conflicts of interest, it is essential that the transactions affected by the conflicts of interest be pleaded and clearly identified (*Towler v Wills* [2010] EWHC 1209 (Comm), LTL 27/5/2010).

A party is obliged to plead its positive case on an issue, even if the burden of proof rests with the other side (*Baxter Healthcare Corporation v Abbott Laboratories* [2005] EWHC 2878 (Pat), LTL 6/12/2005).

Commentary

Loss suffered

Although the claim form N1 contains a section into which the value of the claim has to be inserted (the 'statement of value', see **23.8**), it will normally be necessary to set out what loss has been suffered in consequence of the breaches alleged in the previous paragraph(s). Without this, logically, there will be no sustainable claim, as there is no formal averment that the relief being sought is as a result of the breach previously alleged. Such particulars may well include, for example, brief details of any injury suffered (attaching or serving any evidence from a medical practitioner on which reliance is made: **PD 16, para. 4.3**) as well as details of the effect of the breaches on the claimant, in support of the relief sought at the end of the particulars of claim. Where there is a money claim, it will be necessary to make clear whether it is a claim for general and/or special damages. In many cases it will be necessary to deal with the amount of special damages by means of a schedule attached to the particulars of claim. This must be done when the claim is for personal injury, where the claimant is claiming past and future expenses and losses (**PD 16, para. 4.2**), and in all cases where the damages claimed are anything other than short and straightforward. **24.13**

Pleading the number of hours worked multiplied by the applicable hourly rates in a claim for unpaid building work was regarded as perfectly clear in *Clancy Consulting Ltd v Derwent Holdings Ltd* [2010] EWHC 762 (TCC), LTL 21/4/2010. However, a claim for lost management time in dealing with the defendant's breach of contract must show the alleged causal link between the cost incurred and the alleged default, and also how the claimant's normal trading routine was disturbed (and hence why additional money had to be spent). See *Clancy Consulting Ltd v Derwent Holdings Ltd*.

Failing to plead losses flowing from specific transactions alleged to have been affected by conflicts of interest was held to be defective in *Towler v Wills* [2010] EWHC 1209 (Comm), LTL 27/5/2010. Similarly, where a claimant relied not on actual damage but on probable damage under the Defamation Act 1952, s. 3(1), he had to give particulars of the nature of the alleged probable damage and the grounds relied on for saying that it was more likely than not. In *Tesla Motors Ltd v British Broadcasting Corporation* [2011] EWHC 2760 (QB), LTL 1/11/2011, a claim for damages for malicious falsehood under s. 3(1) was so lacking in particularity that it could not be allowed to proceed.

As a matter of law, a claimant is not required to give credit against a debt claim for sums saved through not having to complete a contract after the defendant is in repudiatory breach. Such credit is only required for damages claims (*Ram Media Ltd v Ministry of Culture for the Hellenic Republic (Secretariat of Sport)* [2009] EWCA Civ 528, LTL 16/6/2009).

Other relevant matters

24.14 Many types of claim require certain information to be inserted in the particulars of claim, and care should be taken to ensure that these requirements are complied with. For example, claims for aggravated or exemplary damages must be specifically set out together with the grounds for claiming them (**CPR, r. 16.4(1)(c)**). Claims for interest must comply with **r. 16.4(2)**.

In many cases some of this information will have to be given in previous paragraphs or particulars. In others, it will be sufficient to set them out formally in separate paragraphs. Often it will be a combination of the two (see, for example, the required matters in claims for the recovery of land in **PD 55A, para. 2**, where it is clear that the special requirements will have to be inserted at various places in the particulars of claim). Further special rules are set out in **24.6**.

Names of persons which are known to the claimant who play a significant part in the narrative relating to the claim (such as persons to whom a libel is alleged to have been published) should be included in the particulars of claim (*Freer v Zeb* [2008] EWHC 212 (QB), LTL 21/2/2008). Particulars must be pleaded of any assignment of the cause of action sufficient to show that it is vested in the claimant (*Pickthall v Hill Dickinson LLP* [2008] EWHC 3409 (Ch), [2009] PNLR 10).

General allegations must be supported by particulars. Commonly occurring examples are particulars of negligence, of breach of statutory duty, of breach of contract, and of loss and damage. An allegation of 'systematic overcharging' had to be supported by particulars of the supposed system (*Clyde and Co. LLP v New Look Interiors of Marlow Ltd* [2009] EWHC 173 (QB), LTL 13/2/2009).

Although there is no express requirement for a statement of value to be included in the particulars of claim (**CPR, r. 16.3**, referring specifically to it being set out in the claim form), it may nevertheless be good practice to repeat it in the particulars of claim, particularly when that document is likely to be the principal one referred to in the course of the trial.

Alternative and contradictory claims

24.15 The purpose of requiring statements of truth is to deter parties from advancing cases which are inherently untrue or wholly speculative. Nevertheless, if it would further the overriding objective, a party should be allowed to rely on more than one version of the facts (*Binks v Securicor Omega Express Ltd* [2003] EWCA Civ 993, [2003] 1 WLR 2557). There is, therefore, no objection to a claimant advancing alternative claims, provided the alternative sets of facts are clearly set out. Examples are where:

(a) The claimant advances one set of facts, and the defence advances a different set of facts. The claimant seeks to amend, saying that even on the defendant's version of the facts liability is established.

(b) The claimant, perhaps because of injuries suffered in the accident, has no personal re-collection of the material events, and has to rely on independent witnesses, who give different versions of those events, each of which is consistent with liability being established.

(c) The claimant, perhaps through having honestly convinced himself of the truth of his version of events as set out in the particulars of claim, gives evidence, but a different version of events emerges from the body of evidence at the trial. Permission may be sought to amend at trial to adopt the version that has emerged at trial.

Subject to the court's discretion based on the overriding objective, a claimant in each of these situations may be given permission to rely on the alternative or new versions of events (*Binks v Securicor Omega Express Ltd*). The claimant's statement of truth has the effect of stating the claimant's honest belief that on either one set of facts or the other the claim is made out (*Clarke v Marlborough Fine Art (London) Ltd* [2002] 1 WLR 1731). It may be necessary to seek the court's permission in cases like the examples set out above to amend without verifying the amended statements of case with a new statement of truth, or to use an amended statement of truth making clear that the primary case is not an assertion of the truth (say) of the defendant's alternative version, but that the defendant's version is relied on as an alternative basis for liability if the court finds the facts to be as pleaded by the defendant (*Binks v Securicor Omega Express Ltd*).

A claimant cannot make a unified claim relying on contradictory allegations of fact, because in such a case the claimant cannot honestly sign a statement of truth (*Clarke v Marlborough Fine Art (London) Ltd*).

Commentary

Allegations of abuse of process and anti-suit injunctions

Any allegation of abuse of process should be fully pleaded in the statements of case so that the true nature of the issue can be identified and considered in advance of the trial (*Conlon v Simms* [2006] EWCA Civ 1749, [2008] 1 WLR 484, at [151], [166] and [176]). There is probably a similar obligation to plead any claim for an anti-suit injunction in the particulars of claim (*Albon v Naza Motor Trading Sdn Bhd (No. 4)* [2007] EWCA Civ 1124, [2008] 1 All ER (Comm) 351, at [9]). 24.16

It is necessary for allegations of fraud to be separately and distinctly pleaded in order to comply with **CPR, r. 16.2(1)(a)** (*Berezovsky v Abramovich* [2008] EWHC 1138 (Comm), LTL 30/5/2008).

Foreign law

CPR, Part 16, does not have an express requirement, unlike RSC, ord. 18, r 8(1)(b), to plead any allegation of foreign law. However, **CPR, r. 16.4(1)(a)**, provides that particulars of claim must include a concise statement of the facts on which the claimant relies. It was held in *Global Multimedia International Ltd v ARA Media Services* [2006] EWHC 3612 (Ch), [2007] 1 All ER (Comm) 1160, that a requirement to plead foreign law that is relied upon can be read into the CPR through **r. 16.4(1)(a)** or through the application of the overriding objective. A party relying on foreign law must plead the relevant point of foreign law, and must expressly state which system of foreign law is alleged to give rise to the point. 24.17

Relief claimed

The CPR do not require a summary of the relief claimed in particulars of claim. The claim form contains a box for 'brief details of the claim' and another for the value, but it is suggested that it is good practice to provide a list of remedies sought at the end of particulars of claim so that the extent of the claim can be seen at a glance. It is unnecessary to include a claim for costs in this list. 24.18

EFFECT OF THE CPR ON DRAFTING STYLE

Is evidence required in a claim form or particulars of claim?

The requirement set out in **CPR, r. 16.2(1)(a)**, that the claim form must contain a concise statement of the nature of the claim, has led some to take the view that some evidence must 24.19

be set out in the claim form, and if such evidence is omitted, it would be possible to have the claim struck out for containing insufficient particulars. Support for this argument is gained by the fact that the claim form is required to be verified by a statement of truth (see **23.12**), which, by its very nature, implies that the claim form is to contain matters of evidence.

Nevertheless, it is submitted that the CPR do not impose any additional *requirement* to include evidence in a statement of case, but in making it clear that the claim form must contain a concise statement of the nature of the claim (**r. 16.2(1)(a)**) and that particulars of claim must include a concise statement of the facts on which the claimant relies (**r. 16.4(1)(a)**), the principles of pleading are reaffirmed in mandatory form. In practice, there appear to be few instances of statements of case containing much evidential matter.

The fact that there is no direct rule to the effect that evidence should *not* be contained in a statement of case does not mean that a statement of case is automatically defective if evidence is not included. If that was the intention of the rules, **r. 16.2(1)** would surely say so. Furthermore, although statements of case are required to be verified by a statement of truth, and when so verified can stand as the evidence on interim applications, the notice of application (form N244) provides space for evidence to be inserted separately or attached as witness statements or affidavits, which would be unnecessary if the evidence was required already to have been fully incorporated into the statement of case. It may of course be that in some instances a verified statement of case will contain all the particulars and evidence necessary to entitle an applicant to the remedy sought, but there will be many instances in which it will not.

There has always been a grey area between 'material facts' and 'evidence'. A situation in which particulars would be sufficient to support an interim application, without necessarily involving the inclusion of evidence, is set out in example 24.2.

Example 24.2

1. The claimant is and was at all relevant times the owner of residential premises known as 1 Acacia Gardens, Boggle, Kent. The premises comprise a house together with a 100 foot back garden.

2. On at least 3 occasions per week since 1 March 2013, the defendants have unlawfully entered into the claimant's garden and remained there for periods of up to 2 hours, using the same for football practice. The last 3 occasions on which the defendants have trespassed into the garden were [a], [b] and [c].

3. Despite being orally requested to leave the garden by the claimant on several occasions, the defendants have refused to do so, and the claimant fears that unless an injunction is granted restraining such acts of trespass, they will be frequently repeated.

4. Further, by reason of the acts of trespass described in paragraph 2, the claimant has suffered damage to his garden plants and furniture... [particulars etc.].

If the statement of case in example 24.2 was verified by a statement of truth, there seems little doubt that it would be sufficient, on its own, to support an application made in the case (e.g. for an interim injunction under **CPR, Part 25**), yet it would be hard to argue that the statement of case actually contains any evidence. Put another way, the example sets out the relevant material such that the defendants are made aware of the nature and extent of the claimant's case, but not the means by which he intends to prove it. Verification of the particulars by a statement of truth will suffice for the purposes of an interim application, but for a final hearing, the claimant's case must be proved in the conventional manner.

True purpose of statements of case

24.20 A good claim or defence should enable the parties and the court to narrow down and identify the central issues in dispute. This has always been the case. For example, a defendant is

Example 24.3 Unsatisfactory drafting

IN THE NORTHAMPTON COUNTY COURT Claim No. 3YL 3456

BETWEEN:

Mr ADAM BROWN Claimant

— and —

Mr CHARLES DAVIS Defendant

Brief details of claim: The Claimant claims damages for loss and personal injuries caused in a road traffic accident on 21 May 2012.

Value: more than £5,000 but not more than £25,000. The claim includes a claim for personal injuries and the amount expected to be recovered exceeds £1,000.

Particulars of claim: On 21 May 2012 an accident occurred at the junction of Fairfax Road and Grove Hill, London SW99 between the Claimant's Renoir Nicole RN 59 ABC and a Bergman P 456 JKL driven by the Defendant.

The accident was caused by the Defendant's negligence, in that he:

(a) drove too fast;

(b) failed to keep a proper lookout;

(c) failed to brake in time or at all to avoid the accident.

As a result, the Claimant suffered injuries and loss.

(Particulars etc.)

(Statement of truth etc.)

entitled to know not merely the cause of action against him, but also the manner in which it is alleged that he was in breach of his duty, thereby causing the claimant to seek redress against him. To achieve that objective requires no more than a properly detailed set of particulars (as opposed to evidence), thereby allowing him to set out his case in response.

Thus a claim or defence which discloses little or nothing about the party's case is liable to be (and almost certainly will be) struck out. Example 24.3 shows a common type of defective claim, which will almost certainly be struck out (relevant parts of the claim only are illustrated).

Similarly a 'block and parry' defence, confining itself merely to admitting, requiring proof of or denying the allegations in the claim, but not containing any particulars of the defendant's case, will also be liable to be struck out.

The ultimate purpose of a party's statement of case is to inform the other party of the case against them. In *Conticorp SA v Central Bank of Ecuador* [2007] UKPC 40, LTL 20/6/2007, the issues were convoluted but were not in doubt; partly because further and better particulars (equivalent to further information under **CPR, Part 18**) had been provided.

Similarly, in *MMI Research Ltd v CellXion Ltd* [2007] EWHC 2611 (Pat), LTL 8/11/2007, a patents case, Warren J, applying *Visx Inc. v Nidek Co. Ltd (No. 2)* [1999] FSR 91, held that whilst a claimant should make real efforts to comply with **PD 63**, a pleading which did not do so to the letter would not necessarily be struck out. Whilst there had to be sufficient particularity, it was a question of degree whether it was a genuine ground for objection to a patent and raised an issue in a way that the other party knew what he had to meet.

Length on its own is not a reason for striking out a statement of case. Complex claims inevitably need to be pleaded with care. If a statement of case is too long, the proper course is for the court to order the party to produce a summary, possibly in schedule form, by reference to the relevant paragraphs in the pleading (*Waite v Denby* [2009] EWCA Civ 592, LTL 29/6/2009). See also **23.3** for the requirement in **PD 16, para. 1.4**, to produce a short summary of any statement of case exceeding 25 pages.

A proposed amendment to include a defence of justification in a libel claim was refused in *Al Rajhi Banking and Investment Corporation v Wall Street Journal Europe Sprl* [2003] EWHC 1358 (QB), LTL 24/6/2003, because the draft amended statement of case lacked clarity and precision.

Good drafting involves the concise and clear identification of the subject matter of the claim, the issues in the case, and the parties' respective positions in respect of those issues.

Drafting language

24.21 There is little doubt that the aims and objectives of the CPR militate against much of the previously conventional and archaic language of pleadings. Not only is the use of Latin terms now obsolete, but many of the more 'old-fashioned' English words such as 'hereinbefore' and 'thereafter' are thought to be inconsistent with the objectives of the CPR, though the price of drafting in modern language is frequently a lack of elegance and an increase rather than saving in verbiage.

Court procedure is designed for use by laypersons as well as lawyers, however, the CPR are not intended to encourage sloppy drafting. Although it is clear that the overriding objective does not permit cases to be won or lost on purely technical points of pleading, the need for precision in the drafting of statements of case (particularly in more complex matters) is still paramount.

A short list of some of the conventional Latin and English phrases previously used (and still to be found in some precedents), and possible modern counterparts, appears in **table 24.1**.

Table 24.1 Suggested replacements for traditional legal language

Old term	Suggested equivalent
Aforesaid	Above
Aver	Contend
By reason of the matters aforesaid	Due to the above matters, or As a result of the above
Due to (meaning 'because of')	Because of
Hereinafter set out	Set out below
Hereinbefore set out	Set out above
In the premises	In the circumstances
In so far (or insofar)	To the extent that
Inter alia	Among other things
Material	Relevant
Mutatis mutandis	With all necessary changes
Notwithstanding	Despite (the fact that)
Pursuant to	In consequence of, or as a result of, or in the course of, or under
Seriatim	Individually
Without prejudice to the generality of the foregoing	Without prejudice to the matters set out above

MEANINGS OF COMMON DRAFTING TERMS

At all material times

'At all material times' is perhaps the most commonly used stock phrase in drafting statements of case. When used in relation to breach by the defendant, it means 'material to the period of the breach' as detailed in the particulars of claim (*Convergence Group plc v Chantrey Vellacott* [2005] EWCA Civ 290, *The Times*, 25 April 2005). **24.22**

Include, but not limited to

Where a statement of case is drafted when inquiries are incomplete, it is common to plead such particulars as are known, but prefaced by a phrase such as 'include but are not limited to' the particulars that immediately follow or which are set out in a schedule. This device is used at various times when giving particulars of breach and particulars of loss. Its use prevents the statement of case being treated as deliberately excluding details not specifically set out (*Deutsche Morgan Grenfell Group plc v Commissioners of Inland Revenue* [2005] EWCA Civ 78, [2006] Ch 243, at [257], approved in the House of Lords [2006] UKHL 49, [2007] 1 AC 558, by Lord Walker of Gestingthorpe at [148]). If used, the statement of case should be amended to include the full particulars when these become known. A defendant faced with such an allegation should make a request for further information (see **chapter 30**), rather than applying to strike it out (Lord Walker of Gestingthorpe at [148]). **24.23**

Commentary

UNPLEADED ALLEGATIONS

A judge should not normally make a finding of fact on an issue which depends on evidence and which has not been raised in statements of case, so that all parties did not have a proper opportunity to address it, even if it was raised in correspondence after statements of case have been served (*Sivanandan v Executive Committee of Hackney Action for Racial Equality* [2002] EWCA Civ 111, LTL 25/1/2002). However, if a factual issue has been adequately dealt with at trial and is clearly regarded by all parties as a live issue which is crucial to the case, the judge is entitled to make a finding of fact, even if the issue was not raised in the statements of case, which could have been amended during the trial (*Slater v Buckinghamshire County Council* [2004] EWCA Civ 1478, LTL 10/11/2004). In *Strover v Strover* [2005] EWHC 860 (Ch), [2005] NPC 64, it was held that where the essential allegations to establish proprietary estoppel had not been pleaded, but had formed the central planks in the evidence of the claimant in support of his original plea, the court could grant the relief flowing from the estoppel. An allegation which is not included in the particulars of claim cannot provide a sustainable ground for an appeal (*Dunnett v Railtrack plc* [2002] EWCA Civ 303, [2002] 1 WLR 2434). **24.24**

While a court should give a fair reading to a statement of case, it was not open to the court below in *Lawrence v Poorah* [2008] UKPC 21, LTL 9/4/2008, to read allegations of undue influence or unconscionable bargain into an imprecisely drawn statement of case. There are limits on the degree to which a judge can intervene, even with the scope of the active case management powers granted by **CPR, Part 1**, in defining a case for a party. Ultimately, the judge must remain scrupulously impartial, and it is wrong to conclude, while giving judgment, that the claimant should succeed on an unpleaded basis.

In *Lombard North Central plc v Automobile World (UK) Ltd* [2010] EWCA Civ 20, LTL 26/1/2010, it was held that the onus is on the party to amend its statement of case if it wishes to advance an unpleaded point. In this case not only was the issue not pleaded, but the defendant also failed to raise it when invited to summarise its main points when the trial started. It was raised for the first time after all the evidence had been taken. The Court of Appeal decided that the trial judge had not made a substantial procedural error in not allowing the defendant to raise the unpleaded point at the trial.

In *JN Dairies Ltd v Johal Dairies Ltd* [2010] EWCA Civ 348, LTL 31/3/2010, the claim was based on an alleged breach of confidence by a former employee. Shortly before the trial the defendant disclosed an affidavit to the effect that the claimant had sought to bribe the former employee to commit perjury, which the claimant responded to by disclosing witness statements to the effect that the former employee had confessed to being paid £40,000 by the defendant to steal confidential documents from the claimant. It was held that both sides should have pleaded these allegations, and both should have applied to the court to list a pre-trial review to deal with amendments, further disclosure and other directions. Both sides had been willing to proceed with the pleadings in their unamended form, so trying the case on that basis was not unfair. In *Investec Bank (UK) Ltd v Zulman* [2010] EWCA Civ 675, LTL 18/5/2010, the court decided whether a written contract had been varied by an oral agreement, even though the issue was not pleaded, because it had surfaced in cross-examination and was covered by closing speeches. If this is not the result that is wanted, an objection must be made at the time.

An appeal against a decision on an unpleaded basis may therefore be dismissed if there is no real injustice in that the evidence would be the same on the new basis of the claim (*Whitecap Leisure Ltd v John H. Rundle Ltd* [2008] EWCA Civ 429, [2008] 2 Lloyd's Rep 216).

Chapter 25 Schedule of Loss and Damage

INTRODUCTION

The purpose of a schedule of loss and damage is to display, in concise and digestible form, the extent of the special damage that the claimant wishes to obtain from the defendant. This is not merely to enable the value of the claim to be appreciated, but also to allow the defendant to agree with or dispute the contents (independently of whether or not liability is admitted), and to draft a counter-schedule indicating any areas of contention. As a result, the parties and court will know the degree and extent to which damages are disputed, and the areas of dispute should clearly be defined. This is, of course, precisely what the system of statements of case is intended to achieve. 25.1

In *Tomer v Atlantic Cleaning Service Ltd* [2008] EWHC 1652 (QB), LTL 25/7/2008, particulars of claim which stated that a schedule of past and future loss and expense was 'to follow' were held to include a claim for special damages (which could accordingly be attacked by way of striking out or a request for further information).

CONTENTS OF THE SCHEDULE

No format for a schedule of loss and damage is prescribed by the CPR or any practice direction. Logic dictates that different heads of damage should be separately calculated in the body of the schedule, and that subtotals should be calculated wherever possible. This will normally cause no problems where specific amounts have already been expended or loss of earnings incurred, but items of alleged future loss may be more difficult to set out. The appropriate manner in which to do this is by reference to the multiplier that it is alleged is appropriate in the particular case, thus making the basis of the calculation quite clear, and enabling the preparation of a counter-schedule in similar format on the defendant's side. 25.2

A schedule or counter-schedule must be verified by a statement of truth (**PD 22, para. 1.4(3)**).

EXAMPLES

Two examples of a schedule of loss and damage are given below, showing how different heads of loss should be set out. 25.3

Example 25.1

IN THE NORTHAMPTON COUNTY COURT — Claim No. 3YL 1234

BETWEEN:

Ms ANNA BRIGHT — Claimant

and

(1) Mr CHARLES DAVIS
(2) Mrs ELEANOR FOWKES — Defendants

SCHEDULE OF PAST AND FUTURE LOSS AND EXPENSE

The calculations in this Schedule are calculated up to 8 February 2013.

A) Past Losses

1. Earnings

Prior to the accident, which occurred on 4 June 2010, the Claimant, who is an Auxilary Nurse, worked for the Loganberry Nursing Home, Beresford Road, Blackstone BL5 lAB. At the time of the accident the Claimant's average net weekly earnings were £230.61. Since the accident the Claimant has been unable to return to work, and has received no pay from her previous (or any other) employer. The Claimant claims loss of income as follows:

4.6.2010 to 31.12.2010, being 30 weeks at £230.61 per week	£6,918.30
1.1.2011 to 31.12.2011, being 52 weeks at £235.83 per week	£12,263.16
1.1.2012 to 31.12.2012, being 52 weeks at £241.26 per week	£12,542.52
1.1.2013 to 8.2.2013, being 6 weeks at £246.91 per week	£1,481.46
Total claim under this part	£33,208.44

2. Medication

(a) Prescriptions, 2 at £7.20 each	£14.40
(b) Paracetamol. The Claimant takes four paracetamol tablets a day, and has done since the accident. Estimated cost	£100.00
Total claim under this paragraph	£114.40

3. Taxi fares

As a result of her injuries the Claimant has not been as mobile as she was before the accident, and has had to travel by taxi or minicab, whereas before being injured she would have walked or travelled by public transport. The Claimant claims the taxi and minicab fares and/or the difference in costs between the fares and the costs of travel by public transport. The Claimant walks to the supermarket once a week, but has to take a minicab back home with her shopping. This minicab fare is paid out once a week and has been since March 2011.

25.3.2011 to 8.2.2013, being 97 weeks at £5.00 per week	£485.00

4. Care and Assistance

Since the accident the Claimant has received considerable care and assistance from her husband. The Claimant's husband does all the vacuum cleaning in the house. He assists with the washing. The Claimant puts washing in the washing machine a piece at a time but her husband has to empty the machine and hang out the washing. The Claimant is unable to do gardening and her husband now spends about one hour per week keeping weeds under control. He also strips the beds, does the cooking and a little shopping for the Claimant. This assistance amounts to 8 hours per week at £6.04 per hour and the Claimant claims for the period from 4.6.2010 to 8.2.2013, being 140 weeks:

£6,764.80

Summary of Past Losses

Para. 1	£33,208.44
Para. 2	£114.40
Para. 3	£485.00
Para. 4	£6,764.80
Total	£40,572.64

Together with interest to be assessed

B) Future Losses

1. Earnings

(a) The Claimant will not be able to return to her job or to ever undertake any form of paid employment. Her loss of earnings will continue until the date she would have retired had she not been injured in the accident. The Claimant contends that but for the accident she would have retired on 24 May 2013. From 9 February 2013 her net loss of earnings will be £246.91 per

9.2.2013 to 24.5.2013, being 15 weeks at £246.91 per week	£3,703.65

week. The Claimant claims:

(b) The Claimant would have worked part-time from 25 May 2013 for a period of 5 years earning approximately half her pre-retirement income, being £123.45 net per week. Her annual loss of income during this period is therefore £6,419.40. The appropriate multiplier is 4.94 and amounts to: £31,711.84

The Claimant therefore claims total future loss of earnings of £35,415.49

2. Medication

This loss will continue at the approximate rate of £1.50 per week, equivalent to £78.00 per annum. The appropriate multiplier is 20.3 and the Claimant claims £1,583.40

3. Taxi Fares

This loss continues at the rate of £5.00 per week, and will continue for the rest of her life. The annual loss is £260.00, and the appropriate multiplier is 20.3. The Claimant therefore claims; £5,278.00

4. Care and Assistance

The Claimant will need assistance for 8 hours per week at an hourly rate of £6.04 for the rest of her life. The annual loss is £2,512.64 and the appropriate multiplier is 20.3. The Claimant therefore claims: £51,006.59

Summary of Future Losses

Para. 1	£35,415.49
Para. 2	£1,583.40
Para. 3	£5,278.00
Para. 4	£51,006.59
Total	£93,283.48

TOTAL CLAIM UNDER THIS SCHEDULE

A) Past Losses	£40,572.64
B) Future Losses	£93,283.48
Total	£133,856.12

STATEMENT OF TRUTH etc.

DATED 8 February 2013

Messrs O'Reilly & Mackman, Bank Chambers, Edinburgh Road, Blackstone BL3 8GC,

Solicitors for the Claimant.

Example 25.2

In this example, various heads of damage are claimed which cannot presently be quantified. The Claimant is aged 30

IN THE NORTHAMPTON COUNTY COURT Claim No. 3YL 4753

BETWEEN:

Mr GARTH HOPKINS Claimant

and

Mr IAN JACKS Defendant

SCHEDULE OF PAST AND FUTURE LOSS AND EXPENSE

The calculations in this Schedule are made to 21 January 2013

Past Losses

Loss of Earnings

1. At the time of the accident the Claimant was employed by Closestaff Limited as a trainee manager. He was paid at his standard salary rates despite a protracted period off work as a result of his injuries. On 31 January 2011 he was made redundant. His gross average monthly earnings at the time he was made redundant were £1,250, with deductions of £167.83 for tax and £94.00 for National Insurance (net £988.17 per month). Thereafter he was unemployed for 6 months 19 days until he commenced work on 19 August 2011 with Opendoors Limited. He was offered another job with Final Position Limited on 23 August 2012, which he accepted and commenced work on 10 September 2012. His current annual salary is £18,500, so there is no continuing loss of earnings while he remains in this employment.

2. By reason of his injuries the Claimant was unable to apply for jobs in the period between his redundancy and August 2011 which involved an element of manual work and had to restrict himself to office-based jobs. He also would have been able to put more energy into his job search but for the accident. If he had not been injured he would have commenced work about 3 months earlier than he did.

Total claim for loss of earnings:

3 months at £988.17 net per month £2,964.51

Care and Assistance

3. Before the accident the Claimant lived in his own house. On being discharged from hospital on 21 June 2010 he moved in with his parents because he was totally reliant on them. In particular he needed assistance with washing, shaving and personal hygiene, with dressing and drinking and eating. In the period until 1 November 2010 he was unable to wash or iron his clothes, do his shopping or cooking, and was reliant entirely on his parents. 1 November 2010 was the first occasion on which he was able to assist his mother with preparing meals and some washing-up. The Claimant was unable to drive until 20 December 2010. Until then he was dependent on his parents for lifts to hospital and physiotherapy sessions and for all other purposes. From the beginning of November 2010 until the end of January 2011 the Claimant was given reducing levels of assistance, until he was able to cope with most domestic tasks by himself by the beginning of February 2011. The Claimant required additional assistance in late October and November 2011 when he returned to hospital for removal of the plate and screws in his elbow. The Claimant claims for the care and assistance he has been given.

Damages to be assessed

Gardening, DIY etc.

4. As a result of his injuries the Claimant has been unable to carry out gardening or domestic jobs requiring heavy lifting, and has had to obtain assistance from members of his family. He has also been unable to do any decorating, and will have to seek assistance from his family for decorating and DIY work at his own property and will be restricted in assistance he can give to his parents. He has also been unable to continue doing maintenance work on his car, and has had to seek the help of his brother-in-law. All these are continuing. The annual values for these are:

(a) Gardening	£100.00
(b) Heavy domestic work	£50.00
(c) Decorating	£250.00
(d) DIY	£100.00
(e) Assistance to parents	£50.00
(f) Car maintenance	£100.00
Total	£650.00

5. The Claimant therefore claims under this head the value to date of gardening, heavy domestic work, decorating, DIY, assistance to parents and car maintenance from 21 June 2010 to 21 January 2013 (2 years 7 months) at £650.00 per annum: £1,679.16

Accidental Damage

6. Excess	£450.00
7. Loss of use of car and inconvenience from 14 June 2010 to 16 August 2010	£750.00
8. Damage to clothing	£87.00
Total claim under this head	£1,287.00

Other Out-of-pocket Expenses

9. Loss of deposit for holiday	£115.00
10. Loss of deposit for railway ticket	£23.00
11. Miscellaneous expenses for telephone, letters and the like	£70.00
Total claim under this head	£208.00

Travel Costs

12. Taxis

(a) Before 20 November 2010	£39.00
(b) 20 November 2010	£10.00
(c) 11 January 2011	£10.00
(d) 14 November 2011	£5.00
Subtotal	£64.00

13. Driving to hospital, physiotherapy etc. at £0.35 per mile

(a) To Blackstone General Hospital up to 20 November 2010 (13 visits)	£50.00
(b) 7 January 2011 (6 miles)	£2.10
(c) 11 January 2011 (6 miles)	£2.10
(d) 4 February 2011 (6 miles)	£2.10
(e) 28 April 2011 (6 miles)	£2.10

Commentary

(f) 7 June 2011 (6 miles)	£2.10
(g) 7 July 2011 (6 miles)	£2.10
(h) Parking on 7 July 2011	£1.40
(i) 12 July 2011 (6 miles)	£2.10
(j) 18 July 2011 (6miles)	£2.10
(k) 9 September 2011 (6 miles)	£2.10
(l) 27 October 2011 (20 miles)	£7.00
(m) 2 December 2011 (10 miles)	£3.50
(n) 6 January 2012 (6 miles)	£2.10
(o) 6 June 2012 (20 miles)	£7.00
(p) 5 visits for physiotherapy (the Claimant walked for the other 26 sessions) at 3 miles each round trip	£5.25
(q) Additional trips to physiotherapy (78 miles)	£27.30
(r) 8 August 2012 (24 miles)	£8.40
Subtotal	£130.85
Total claim under this head	£194.85

Medication

19. To November 2010	£21.60
20. From November 2010 to January 2013 at £12.00 a year	£24.00
Total for this head	£45.60
Total quantified Past Losses	**£6,379.12**
Together with Interest to be assessed	

Future Losses

Disadvantage on the Labour Market

21. The Claimant has a 12-month contract in his current employment ending on 13 September 2013.

22. By reason of his elbow injury the Claimant has been left with residual pain and restricted movements which compromise the overall function of his dominant right arm. This substantially limits the amount of physical work he can do with his arms, and also interferes with his driving in that he finds it difficult to steer. He is therefore effectively restricted to purely clerical work, whereas before the accident he could take jobs which included physical work. He is also going to be unable to take jobs involving any substantial amount of driving. He is consequently disadvantaged if he needs to look for work in the future, and he claims:

Damages to be assessed

Gardening, DIY etc.

23. Future value of gardening, heavy domestic work, decorating, DIY, assistance to parents and car maintenance from 21 January 2013 @ £650 per annum with a multiplier of 29.6

Total claim under this head	£19,240.00

Power Steering

24. By reason of his elbow injury the Claimant needs to buy cars with power steering. His car at the *time of the accident* was a Kurosawa Benidorm 1.1, which was replaced by another Benidorm 1.1 registration number LG53 DAB. These cars do not come with power-assisted steering, and there is

no practical method of converting them to power steering. In order to buy cars with power steering the Claimant will have to buy cars which are more expensive than if he did not have this restriction. The Claimant estimates the price difference to be about £1,000, and that he will replace his vehicles approximately every 3 years until age 70. His annual loss is therefore about £330.Additional annual cost of buying cars with power steering, with a multiplier of 25.42:

£8,388.60

Future Surgery

25. There is an approximately 30% chance that the Claimant will require either elbow replacement surgery or an arthrodesis of his elbow within the next 30 years. Such an operation is likely to cost about £5,000 to £6,000. The Claimant will give credit for advanced receipt as appropriate.

To be assessed

26. There is an approximately 30% chance that the Claimant will require an arthrodesis of his great toe within the next 30 years. Such an operation is likely to cost about £2,000 to £2,500. The Claimant will give credit for advanced receipt as appropriate.

Medication

27. Continuing need for medications at £12.00 a year, with a multiplier of 29.6. Total claim under this head: £355.20

STATEMENT OF TRUTH etc.

DATED 21 January 2013

Messrs O'Reilly & Mackman, Bank Chambers, Edinburgh Road, Blackstone BL3 8GC,

Solicitors for the Claimant.

Commentary

Chapter 26 Defending a Claim

INTRODUCTION

26.1 The principal rules concerning the drafting of the defence can be found in **CPR, Parts 15** and **16**, and their associated practice directions.

The matters discussed below do not apply where the claimant uses the Part 8 procedure, and apply with limited effect to specialist claims. They do, however, apply to cases where a defence is drafted to a counterclaim.

Although it is not mandatory, form N9B (specified amount) or N9D (unspecified amount or non-money claims) may be used for the purpose of setting out a defence (**PD 15, para. 1.3**). Copies of the forms are included in the response pack served on the defendant with the particulars of claim.

WHEN A DEFENCE IS REQUIRED

26.2 A defendant who wishes to defend all or part of a claim must file a defence (**CPR, r. 15.2**). If a defence is not filed, default judgment (see **chapter 20**) may be entered if the conditions set out in **Part 12** have been met (**r. 15.3**). The consequences therefore of failing to file a defence are grave. At best the defendant will incur unnecessary expense in applying to set aside the judgment but he risks being unable to persuade a judge to allow him to defend the claim, or only on satisfaction of conditions. A copy of the defence must be served on every other party (**r. 15.6**).

PERIOD FOR FILING A DEFENCE

26.3 The general rule is that a defence must be filed within 14 days after service of the particulars of claim (**CPR, r. 15.4(1)(a)**). Therefore, no defence need be filed where a claim form is served which does not include, and is not accompanied by, particulars of claim (which can be served within 14 days thereafter: see **15.40**). As the particulars of claim can be contained within the body of the claim form (as opposed to served with it, or at a later date) care should therefore be taken to ensure whether the claim form contains the full particulars of claim, or merely the basic information required.

The defendant is allowed to gain an additional 14 days for filing the defence simply by filing the acknowledgment of service form included in the response pack (see **chapter 18**). If this is done, the time for filing a defence is extended to 28 days after service of the particulars of the claim (**r. 15.4(1)(b)**).

There are different periods for filing a defence where the claim form is served out of the jurisdiction (see **r. 15.4(2)(a)**). If the court grants permission for a claim form to be served on the agent of a principal who is overseas, the court will, at the same time, under **r. 6.12(3)**, specify the period for responding.

There are three further exceptions to the above rules:

(a) Where the defendant makes an application disputing the jurisdiction of the court under **Part 11** (see **chapter 19**), the defence need not be filed before the hearing of the application (**r. 11(9)**).

(b) Where the claimant applies for summary judgment under **Part 24** (see **chapter 34**) before the defendant has filed a defence, the defendant need not file a defence before the summary judgment hearing (**r. 24.4(2)**).

(c) Where the defendant has applied for summary judgment under **Part 24**, or for the claimant's statement of case to be struck out under **r. 3.4**, default judgment may not be entered for the claimant until that application has been disposed of (**r. 12.3(3)(a)**).

The words of **r. 15.4** do not appear to prohibit the filing of a defence in the exceptional circumstances should the defendant wish. Where an application for summary judgment has been made by the claimant under **Part 24**, the defendant would appear to have a choice:

(a) His response may be supported by evidence, usually by witness statement, which may exhibit a draft defence. In practice this is usually the simplest and best approach.

(b) Alternatively, under **r. 32.6(2)**, a party may rely on his statement of case in hearings other than the trial, provided that it is verified by a statement of truth. Thus it appears, should the defendant wish to file his defence, he may do so, and then rely on it in addition to any witness statement he may wish to file.

EXTENDING THE TIME FOR SERVICE OF A DEFENCE

The defendant and the claimant may, under **CPR, r. 15.5**, agree that the period for filing a defence shall be extended by up to 28 days. Where this is done, the defendant must notify the court in writing (**r. 15.5(2)**). Thus there is a strict limit to the degree of 'slippage' which the parties may, by consent, allow. The principle of judicially led case management precludes the parties from agreeing further (or even open-ended) extensions of time. Any party wishing a further extension of time (whether by consent or otherwise) will have to make an application to the court under **r. 3.1(2)(a)**. **26.4**

STAY OF CLAIM WHERE NO ACTION TAKEN

Where at least six months have expired since the end of the period for filing a defence, and no defendant has served or filed any admission, defence or counterclaim, and the claimant has not entered or applied for default judgment under **CPR, Part 12**, or summary judgment under **Part 24**, the claim shall be stayed, although any party can apply for such stay to be lifted (**r. 15.11**). The evidence in support of an application to lift the stay must give the reason for the delay in proceeding with or responding to the claim (**PD 15, para. 3.4**). **26.5**

CONTENTS OF A DEFENCE — GENERAL MATTERS

26.6 The defence of a defendant who is an individual must include the defendant's residential or business address, unless it has been correctly given on the claim form (**PD 16, para. 10.4**). The address must include the postcode unless the court orders otherwise (**para. 10.6**). Postcode information can be obtained from www.royalmail.com. This address determines which court is the defendant's home court and must be established even if it is not the defendant's address for service (**para. 10.5**).

A defendant who is an individual must provide his or her date of birth (if known) in the defence (or acknowledgment of service, admission, defence and counterclaim, or reply or other response) (**para. 10.7**). This is primarily to identify the defendant if a judgment is to be registered (see **63.49**).

Admit, require to prove, deny

26.7 A defence to a claim must say which of the allegations in the particulars of claim are admitted, which are denied and which allegations the defendant is unable to admit or deny, but requires the claimant to prove (**CPR, r. 16.5(1)**). Every allegation made in a claim should be dealt with in the defence (**PD 16, para. 10.2**).

It may be useful to restate the established principles behind the three possible responses to an allegation in particulars of claim, and their consequences so far as the claimant is concerned.

If an allegation is *admitted*, the claimant is absolved from any obligation to bring any further evidence in support of that allegation. This is apart from any other consequences that may flow from the admission made. Allegations should be admitted if they are accepted by the defendant or if they make no material difference. A defendant who wishes to admit the truth of all or part of the other party's case may adopt the admissions procedure set out in **CPR, Part 14** (see **17.3**). The principles governing applications for permission to withdraw admissions are considered at **34.31**.

A defendant may *require the claimant to prove* an allegation which the defendant is unable to admit or deny (**r. 16.5(1)(b)**), usually because the defendant does not have sufficient information on the point. Often this will be because the evidence relevant to the allegation is in the possession of another party or person, or has been lost. Allegations which the claimant is required to prove are still in issue, but the defendant will not be making a positive alternative case on the point.

Where an allegation is *denied*, this normally implies that the defendant intends to put up a positive case to the contrary. Indeed, **r. 16.5(2)** specifically provides that where the defendant denies an allegation, he must state his reasons for doing so; and if he intends to put forward a different version of events from that given by the claimant, he must state his own version.

Where a paragraph in a statement of case sets up a contention followed by a number of sub-paragraphs, each containing allegations of fact, a general response to the main allegation without responding to the individual sub-paragraphs may be inadequate, depending on the circumstances and how important the allegations are (*Ciccone v Associated Newspapers Ltd* [2009] EWHC 1108 (Ch), LTL 12/6/2009, where further particulars were required).

It is inappropriate to require a claimant to prove a matter of which the defendant must have personal knowledge. Such a matter must either be admitted or denied with reasons (*Ciccone v Associated Newspapers Ltd*, where it was alleged the defendant 'knowingly and deliberately infringed [certain copyrights]'). If a party can plead to a matter they should. There is no concept that general non-admissions can be used when a defendant has made all the admissions they want to (**r. 16.5(1)**; *Ciccone v Associated Newspapers Ltd*).

A defendant who fails to answer a specific allegation will nevertheless be taken to require that allegation to be proved, provided that in his defence, he has set out the nature of his case in relation to the issue to which that allegation is relevant (**r. 16.5(3)**). In such an event, it will presumably be open to the claimant to apply to the court that the defendant give further information under **Part 18**, or for the court to order it of its own volition. However if the defendant totally fails to deal with an allegation, he shall be taken to have admitted it (**r. 16.5(5)**), unless it is an allegation relating to the value of a money claim, in which case he shall be taken to require that any allegation relating to the amount of money claimed by proved, unless he expressly admits the allegation (**r. 16.5(4)**).

Stand-alone defences and positive case

In addition to responding to the particulars of claim by admitting, requiring proof and denying the allegations made by the claimant, the defendant is obliged to set out his own case in sufficient detail to ensure the claimant can prepare for trial and understand the case which has to be met. This is the effect of **PD 18, para. 1.2**. The obligation extends beyond stating reasons and any alternative version where the defence uses denials (see 26.7). It means the defence must give full details of: **26.8**

(a) Any stand-alone defence relied upon. Examples are reliance on limitation periods, exemption and limitation of liability clauses in contracts, and equitable and legal defences, such as laches, delay, consent, illegality, lack of writing etc. The obligation is to set out sufficient facts to establish the elements of the defence based on the circumstances of the case.

(b) Any positive case relied upon by the defendant on an issue, even if the burden of proof rests with the claimant (*Baxter Healthcare Corporation v Abbott Laboratories* [2005] EWHC 2878 (Pat), LTL 6/12/2005). In a building case where there is a claim based on hours worked multiplied by alleged rates, it is for the defendant to set out a positive case in its defence if it wishes to dispute the reasonableness of the claimed rates (*Clancy Consulting Ltd v Derwent Holdings Ltd* [2010] EWHC 762 (TCC), LTL 21/4/2010).

CONTENTS OF A DEFENCE — SPECIFIC MATTERS

Dispute about statement of value

A claim form is required by **CPR, r. 16.3**, to contain a statement of value (see 23.8). If this statement is disputed, the defendant must state why he disputes it, and if he can, give his own statement of the value of the claim (**r. 16.5(6)**). **26.9**

Claims already paid

Where (apart from costs and interest) the only claim against a defendant is for a specified sum of money, and a defence is filed stating that the sum has been paid to the claimant, the special procedure in **CPR, r. 15.10** applies. **26.10**

Defendant in representative capacity

A defendant who is defending in a representative capacity must state that fact in the defence, and also say what that capacity is (**CPR, r. 16.5(7)**). **26.11**

Address for service

CPR, r. 16.5(8), requires a defence to contain an address for service, within the United Kingdom (**r. 6.23**), to which documents can be sent to the defendant, if no acknowledgment of service has been filed. **26.12**

Commentary

Personal injury claim

26.13 Where a defended claim is one in respect of personal injury, and the claimant has attached a medical report in respect of his or her alleged injuries, **PD 16, para. 12.1**, provides that the defence should state whether the defendant:

(a) agrees with the medical report; or
(b) disputes it (in which event the reasons for doing so should be stated (**para. 12.1(2)**); or
(c) neither agrees nor disputes it, but has no knowledge of the matters contained in the medical report.

If a medical report has been obtained by the defendant, on which the defendant intends to rely, it should be attached to the defence (**para. 12.1(3)**). It is submitted that 'should' in **PD 16, para. 12.1**, has the same mandatory force as 'must' in **CPR, r. 16.5**, and that no technical distinction should be drawn between the two.

Thus, there is an obligation on a defendant who disputes medical evidence served with the particulars of claim to attach his own medical report to his defence, when it has been obtained by the time the defence is drafted. There is, interestingly, no mandatory requirement to attach a medical report to a defence *whenever* the claimant's report is in dispute, but only where the defendant has already obtained his own medical report at the time of drafting the defence. However, it may well be difficult to dispute the claimant's report (particularly when reasons have to be given) save on grounds obtained as a result of a defence medical report, which is frequently not predicated upon a defence medical examination of the claimant, but upon an examination of medical records. If a defence medical report is not attached to a defence when detailed reasons for dispute are given, it would almost certainly prompt the claimant to question the basis for the response and apply for disclosure of the report. If the defendant has not had the opportunity to obtain his own expert evidence by the time the defence is drafted, it is likely that he would then have to state that he had 'no knowledge of the matters contained in the [claimant's] medical report', under **PD 16, para. 12.1(1)(c)**. Such a situation should be rare. In the vast majority of personal injury claims, and particularly when the amount of damages claimed is less than £25,000 and consequently allocated to the fast track, the parties will have been expected to have complied with the **Pre-action Protocol for Personal Injury Claims** (**paras 2.2** and **2.3** of the Protocol). By **para. 2.14** of the Protocol, the joint selection of experts is encouraged, and is an almost invariable requirement in fast track cases. Thus it is likely that if the Protocol has been complied with, and proceedings are then issued, the medical report will have been agreed or obtained on a joint basis, and it is unlikely that the defendant will have obtained one of his own. If separate experts are instructed, it will be for the court ultimately to decide whether either party had acted unreasonably (**para. 3.18** of the Protocol). For detailed discussion of the pre-action protocols, see **chapter 8**.

Where, in a personal injuries case, the claimant has included a schedule of past and future expenses and losses, the defendant must include in or attach to his defence a counter-schedule stating which items are agreed, in dispute, or neither agreed nor disputed, because of lack of knowledge (**PD 16, para. 12.2(1)**). Where items are disputed, alternative figures, where appropriate, should be supplied (**para. 12.2(2)**). The counter-schedule must be verified by a statement of truth (**PD 22, para. 1.4(3)**).

Whole claim alleged to be fraudulent

26.14 There are occasions where the defendant alleges the whole claim is fraudulent or fabricated. A typical example is a low velocity impact road traffic accident. The argument is that the two vehicles collided at such a low speed that it is impossible for the injuries alleged by the claimant to have been caused by the collision. In such a case there is no burden on the defendant to prove fraud, and no obligation on the defendant to plead fraud or fabrication in the defence (*Kearsley v Klarfeld* [2005] EWCA Civ 1510, [2006] 2 All ER 303). It is sufficient simply to set out in the defence the facts from which the defendant will invite the judge to infer that the claimant had not suffered the injuries being claimed (*Cooper v P and O Stena Line Ltd* [1999] 1 Lloyd's Rep 734). In these cases the court will expect the parties to be particularly open and cooperative on matters such as access to the vehicles for expert examination and access to medical notes, and these claims are likely to be suitable for the multi-track even if below the usual threshold (*Kearsley v Klarfeld*).

Limitation defence

A defendant who relies on the expiry of any limitation period, must give in his defence details of the date on which it is alleged the relevant limitation period expired (**PD 16, para. 13.1**). 26.15

Human Rights Act 1998

A defendant who seeks to rely on any provision of, or right arising under, the **Human Rights Act 1998**, or seeks a remedy under that Act, must state in the defence the matters set out in **PD 16, para. 15.1**. 26.16

Defamation

For particular rules in cases of defamation etc., see **PD 53, para. 2**. 26.17

Tender

For particular rules where the defence is one of tender before claim see **PD 16, para. 13.2, CPR, r. 37.2**, and **PD 37, para. 2**. 26.18

Competition Act 1998

In certain proceedings under the Competition Act 1998, a defendant who intends to rely on a determination of the Office of Fair Trading must comply with **PD 16, para. 14**. 26.19

SET-OFFS

A defendant who wishes to rely wholly or in part on a defence of set-off (see **34.37**) may, by **CPR, r. 16.6**, include this in the defence, whether or not it will also form the subject of a counterclaim under **Part 20**. Interestingly, the rule does not *require* this to be done, but set-offs continue to be pleaded in the defence. 26.20

STATEMENT OF TRUTH

A defence must be verified by a statement of truth (see **23.13** to **23.17**). The form of statement is (**PD 16, para. 11.2**): 26.21

[I believe] [the defendant believes] that the facts stated in the defence are true.

DRAFTING STYLE

It is as incumbent upon a defendant to state full particulars of his case as it is for the claimant. In addition to stating his position with regard to the allegations made against him, the defendant, when denying an allegation, must state his reasons for doing so, and if he intends to put forward a different version of events from that given by the claimant, he must state his own version (**CPR, r. 16.5(2)**). Defences that concentrate point by point on the allegations set out 26.22

in the claim, stating whether they are admitted, denied or not admitted, but then wholly neglect to set out the defendant's own case on the issues are in grave danger of being struck out. The incorrect and correct approaches are illustrated in example 26.1.

Example 26.1

Insufficiently set out

It is denied that the defendant was negligent as alleged or at all.

Insufficiently set out

It is denied that the defendant drove along Litigation Avenue at an excessive speed, and/or failed to keep a proper lookout, and/or failed to brake or steer his car so as to avoid colliding with the claimant, as alleged or at all.

Correctly set out

It is denied that the defendant was negligent in any of the ways set out in the particulars of negligence, or at all. The defendant was driving at a safe speed down Litigation Avenue, which is a major road. The accident was caused when the claimant drove his car out of Blackstone Road, which was a minor road, into the path of the defendant's car, giving the defendant no opportunity to avoid the collision. In the circumstances, the collision was wholly caused by the negligence of the claimant, as set out below:

PARTICULARS OF NEGLIGENCE

etc.

Chapter 27 Reply and Subsequent Statements of Case

GENERAL AND PROCEDURAL REQUIREMENTS

Although a claimant may file a reply to a defence, he does not have to do so, and failure to file a reply must not be taken as an admission of any of the matters raised in the defence (**CPR, r. 16.7(1)**). If a reply is filed, but fails to deal with a matter raised in the defence, the claimant shall nevertheless be taken to require that matter to be proved. Thus, strictly speaking, it is unnecessary for the reply to commence with a statement joining issue with the defendant upon all matters not specifically admitted in the defence, as there is an implied joinder of issue. Where, however, the defence includes a counterclaim to which it is intended to file a defence, it is suggested that a formal reply should also be filed in the conventional manner, joining issue with the defendant on his defence and counterclaim, although the rules do not specifically provide for, or require, this to be done. **27.1**

When a claimant intends to file a reply, this must be done when he files his directions questionnaire under **r. 26.3(6)**, and the reply must be served on the other parties at the same time as it is filed (**r. 15.8**).

Commentary

CONTENTS OF A REPLY

Conventionally, a reply may respond to any matters raised in the defence which were not, and which should not have been, dealt with in the particulars of claim, and exists solely for the purpose of dealing disjunctively with matters which could not properly have been dealt with in the particulars of claim, but which require a response once they have been raised in the defence. It has always been a cardinal principle of pleading (which has certainly not been altered by the CPR) that a claim should not anticipate a potential defence (popularly known as 'jumping the stile'). Once, however, a defence has been raised which requires a response so that the issues between the parties can be defined, a reply becomes necessary for the purpose of setting out the claimant's case on that point. The reply is, however, neither an opportunity to restate the claim, nor is it, nor should it be drafted as, a 'defence to the defence'. **27.2**

Where the defence takes issue with a fact set out in the particulars of claim, and the claimant accepts that the fact is incorrect, the proper course should be for the claimant to seek to amend his statement of case accordingly (see **chapter 31**), and not to deal with the matter in a reply (**PD 16, para. 9.2**). Thus where, for example, the particulars of claim contain an error as to the quantity of goods ordered, and the correct quantity is set out in the defence, the error should be corrected by way of amendment, rather than reply.

A reply must be verified by a statement of truth (see **23.13 to 23.17**; **CPR, r. 22.1(1)(a)**).

SUBSEQUENT STATEMENTS OF CASE

A party may not file or serve any statement of case beyond a reply, without the permission of the court (**CPR, r. 15.9**). Such permission should rarely be required, and presumably **27.3** will rarely be granted. Save in the most exceptional cases the supposed need for additional pleadings normally evidences a failure to plead the case properly in the first place. Problems of this kind can be resolved either by amendment or by requests for further information.

Chapter 28 Counterclaims

The following procedural checklist, which is at the front of the book, is relevant to this chapter:
Procedural checklist 17 Counterclaim (Part 20)

INTRODUCTION

The rules governing counterclaims are contained in **CPR, Part 20**, and **PD 20**. For claims against co-defendants and other parties (which are also covered by **Part 20**) see **chapter 29**. **28.1**

Any claim other than a claim by a claimant against a defendant, is classed as an 'additional claim', an expression which includes a counterclaim by a defendant (whether against the claimant or against the claimant and some other person) (r. 20.2(2)).

The ability to bring a counterclaim within existing proceedings allows a defendant to wrest some of the initiative away from the claimant. Its main purpose, however, is to promote the general policy of ensuring that, so far as convenient, all issues between the parties are resolved together, with a view to saving costs, avoiding a multiplicity of claims, and avoiding the risk of irreconcilable judgments. Under **CPR, r. 3.1(2)(e)** and **(j)**, the court has general case management powers to order part of proceedings to be dealt with as separate proceedings, and to decide the order in which issues are tried. Specific factors that the court should take into account in making such decisions in the context of additional claims like counterclaims are set out in **r. 20.9**.

PERMISSION TO MAKE A COUNTERCLAIM

Provided it is filed with the defence, the court's permission is not required to make a counterclaim (**CPR, r. 20.4(2)(a)**). However, permission is required for filing a counterclaim after service of the defence (**r. 20.4(2)(b)**), and the procedure and conditions laid down in **Part 20** and **PD 20** will have to be followed. A copy of the proposed counterclaim must be filed together with the application notice seeking permission (**PD 20, para. 1.2**). The evidence in support must state the stage reached in the main proceedings, the nature of the additional claim, a summary of the facts on which the additional claim is based, and the name and address of any proposed additional party (**para. 2.1**). Where possible the applicant should provide a timetable of the proceedings to date (**para. 2.3**). **28.2**

The permission of the court is required for a counterclaim against the Crown if:

(a) the proceedings were brought in the name of a government department and the counterclaim does not relate to that department (**CPR, r. 66.4(4)**); or
(b) the proceedings were brought in the name of the Attorney-General (**r. 66.4(3)**).

A defendant who wishes to counterclaim against a person other than the claimant must apply to the court for an order adding that person as a defendant to the counterclaim (**r. 20.5(1)**). An application for such an order may be made without notice, unless the court directs otherwise (**r. 20.5(2)**), and if the order is made, the court will at the same time give directions for the management of the case (**r. 20.5(3)**).

The court will refuse permission to add a counterclaim which shows no reasonable prospects of success (*K/S Victoria Street v House of Fraser (Stores Management) Ltd* [2011] EWHC 3179 (Ch), LTL 1/12/2011).

PROCEDURE

28.3 A defendant may make a counterclaim against a claimant by filing particulars of the counterclaim (**CPR, r. 20.4(1)**). The counterclaim will attract an additional fee, equal to that of starting fresh proceedings (**CPFO, fee 1.7**). A fee of £45 is payable if a party is added to the claim (**CPFO, fee 1.6**). If the issue fee is not paid after due warning by the court, the counterclaim will be struck out automatically (**CPR, r. 3.7A**).

The defence and counterclaim should normally form one document with the counterclaim following on from the defence (**PD 15, para. 3.1; PD 20, para. 6.1**).

The usual rule once judgment has been obtained and fully satisfied is that it is not possible to bring a counterclaim, because there is no subsisting claim against which the counterclaim can be brought. This rule has been held to be subject to an exception where the claim is for possession of land, see *Laib v Aravindan* [2003] EWHC 2521 (QB), *The Times*, 13 November 2003.

In a claim by the Crown for taxes, duties or penalties, the defendant cannot bring a counterclaim or raise a set-off (**CPR, r. 66.4(1)**). Similarly, in a claim by the Crown, the defendant cannot bring a counterclaim or raise a set-off based on a claim for repayment of taxes, duties or penalties (**r. 66.4(2)**).

Where the permission of the court to make a counterclaim is not required, the counterclaim should also be served on every other party when a copy of the defence is served (**r. 20.8(1)(a)**), or within 14 days after the date on which the counterclaim was issued by the court, if it is to be served on a person who is not an existing party (**r. 20.8(1)(b)**). **Rule 20.8(1)(a)** refers to a counterclaim against an 'additional' party only. This is an obvious drafting error (a counterclaim against an additional party only is not a counterclaim at all, but a third party claim), and should refer to a counterclaim against an 'existing' party only. Where the permission of the court is required, the court will give directions as to service (**r. 20.8(3)**). If a counterclaim is made against an additional party, the copy served on that additional party must be accompanied by forms for admitting and defending the counterclaim, and for acknowledging service. Also, that additional party must be served with copies of all statements of case which have been served in the proceedings, together with any other documents which the court may direct (**r. 20.12(1)**). A copy of the additional claim form must be served on every existing party (**r. 20.12(2)**).

28.4

HEADING A COUNTERCLAIM

Example 28.1

<u>IN THE BLACKSTONE COUNTY COURT</u> Claim No. BP13 12345

BETWEEN

AB <u>Claimant</u>

— and —

CD <u>Defendant</u>

— and —

EF <u>Third Party</u>

PD 20 adopts the practice set out in example 28.1. This provides that claimants and defendants in the original claim should always be referred to as such in the title to the proceedings, even if they subsequently acquire an additional procedural status (**para.** 7.3). In a simple counterclaim there is no change in the parties, with the counterclaim being brought by the defendant against the claimant. Where the defendant brings a counterclaim against the claimant and an additional party, the additional party is called the 'third party' (**para.** 7.4(c)), unless there has been an earlier additional claim within the proceedings. In that event there will already be a third party, so the additional party on the counterclaim will be the 'fourth party' (or whatever in accordance with the order in which this person is added to the proceedings, see **para.** 7.4).

A counterclaim brought against the original claimant is simply described as the counterclaim, see example 28.2. A counterclaim brought against the claimant and an additional party has to be described in the title as such. For example, 'Defendant's Counterclaim against Claimant and Third Party' (see **para** 7.10).

Example 28.2

IN THE HIGH COURT OF JUSTICE — Claim No. HQ13X 12345

QUEEN'S BENCH DIVISION

BETWEEN:

Mr. EDWARD GLOVER — Claimant

— and —

Mr. RICHARD BULMORE — Defendant

DEFENDANT'S DEFENCE AND
COUNTERCLAIM AGAINST CLAIMANT

Commentary

STATUS OF A COUNTERCLAIM

Save where **CPR, Part 20**, states to the contrary, the provisions of the CPR apply to counterclaims as if they were claims (**r. 20.3(1)**). In particular, as **PD 20, para. 3**, points out, the provisions relating to any failure to respond will apply as much to a counterclaim as they do to a claim. **CPR, Part 15**, applies to a defence to a counterclaim. Thus it is, for example, open to a defendant to obtain judgment in default of a defence to a counterclaim, subject to the conditions and procedure laid down in **Part 12**. However, a claimant wishing to defend a counterclaim is not permitted to file an acknowledgment of service (**r. 20.4(3)**), and various consequential rules pertaining to time limits, statements of value for the purposes of issue in the High Court, and preliminary case management under **Part 26** also do not apply (see **r. 20.3(2)** for details). **28.5**

CONTENTS OF A COUNTERCLAIM

As a counterclaim is treated as if it was a claim for the purposes of the CPR, it should be set out in the same format, and with the same particularity as particulars of claim. Consequently, counterclaims which do not disclose a reasonable cause of action are liable to be struck out **28.6**

(*Ikea Ltd v Brown* [2009] EWHC 955 (Comm), LTL 13/5/2009; *RGI International Ltd v Synergy Classic Ltd* [2011] EWHC 3166 (Comm), LTL 8/12/2011).

For the features which are required of a cross-claim if it is to qualify as a set-off see **34.37**.

The contents of a counterclaim must be verified by a statement of truth (see **23.13** to **23.17**; **CPR, r. 22.1(1)(a)**; **PD 20, para. 4.1**). The form of statement is (**PD 20, para 4.2; PD 22, para. 2.1**):

[I believe] [the defendant believes] that the facts stated in this counterclaim are true.

DEFENCE TO COUNTERCLAIM

General and procedural requirements

28.7 A claimant who files a reply and a defence to a counterclaim should normally put them in one document, with the reply followed by the defence to counterclaim (**PD 20, para. 6.2**).

Where a defence is filed to a counterclaim, the court must consider the future conduct of the proceedings and give appropriate directions, in the course of which it must ensure that both the main claim and the counterclaim are managed together, so far as is practicable (**CPR, r. 20.13**). For this purpose the court will arrange a case management conference. Normally this will be fixed for the same time as a case management hearing for the original claim and any other additional claims (**PD 20, para. 5.1**).

Contents of defence to counterclaim

28.8 A defence to a counterclaim is governed by the same rules as a defence to a claim (see **chapter 26**) and must be verified by a statement of truth (see **23.13** to **23.17**).

Chapter 29 Additional Claims under Part 20

The following procedural checklist, which is at the front of the book, is relevant to this chapter:

Procedural checklist 18 Additional claim (against third party)

Commentary

INTRODUCTION

CPR, Part 20, concerns both counterclaims and claims against third parties. Counterclaims have already been discussed in **chapter 28**. This chapter considers claims made by a defendant, either against a co-defendant, seeking a contribution or indemnity, or against a third party. Together with counterclaims, these are generically known as 'additional claims'. **29.1**

An indemnity is an obligation to reimburse someone, i.e. it is a claim for the fulfilment of an obligation, not for damages for breach of one. A contribution is essentially a partial indemnity.

CONTRIBUTION

A right to a contribution can arise as between joint tortfeasors, debtors or contractors, or by statute, for example, under the **Civil Liability (Contribution) Act 1978, s. 1(1)**, which provides that where two or more persons are liable to the same claimant for the same damage, each may claim contribution towards that liability from the others. The 'damage' referred to in s. 1(1) is the wrong causing the injury: it is not the injury itself (*Jameson v Central Electricity Generating Board* [1998] QB 323). Note also that the word used is 'damage' rather than 'damages' (see *Birse Construction Ltd v Haiste Ltd* [1996] 1 WLR 675). There is no limit or restriction on this concept. For example, a building contractor who remedies defective building work at no cost to the employer can claim a contribution from a consulting engineer based on the value of the remedial work (*Baker and Davies plc v Leslie Wilks Associates* [2005] EWHC 1179 (TCC), [2005] 3 All ER 603). The 1978 Act extends the reach of the contribution principle to cover cases whatever the legal basis of the liability, whether in tort, breach of contract, breach of trust or otherwise (see s. 6(1)). **29.2**

In deciding whether the defendant and the third party are 'liable for the same damage', the words from s. 1(1) must be given their natural and ordinary meaning, without any restrictive or expansive gloss (*Royal Brompton Hospital NHS Trust v Hammond* [2002] UKHL 14, [2002] 1 WLR 1397). The words do not cover damage which is merely substantially or materially similar (per

Lord Steyn). The defendants in *Royal Brompton Hospital NHS Trust v Hammond* were architects who were sued by the hospital for negligently issuing certificates to building contractors, the effect of which was to give the contractors a defence to a claim the hospital had against the contractors for breach of contract for delays in completing building work. It was held that the hospital's claims against the contractors and against the architects were different, so the architects could not claim a contribution against the contractors. If the third party has no liability to the claimant, such as through a term in a contract absolving the third party from liability, the defendant cannot claim contribution from the third party (*Cooperative Retail Services Ltd v Taylor Young Partnership Ltd* [2002] UKHL 17, [2002] 1 WLR 1419).

Nationwide Building Society v Dunlop Haywards (DHL) Ltd [2009] EWHC 254 (Comm), [2010] 1 WLR 258, involved a claim by the lender against two defendants, in fraud against a valuer and in negligence against solicitors. In a claim by the solicitors for a contribution from the valuer, it was necessary to leave out of account the losses that arose only because one defendant was fraudulent when identifying the foreseeable losses for which both defendants were liable. For the purposes of the **Civil Liability (Contribution) Act 1978, ss. 1** and **2**, the 'same damage' (also the 'damage in question') in the contribution proceedings was therefore limited to the net amount advanced and lost interest on alternate advances, less the value of the property, and was not the value of the total liability. The 'damage in question' could not mean, as the solicitors asserted, the amount for which they were liable by agreement, having regard to their defences of limitation of liability and contributory negligence, or there would be no scope for the operation of **s. 2(3)**. The court went on to make a reduction for contributory negligence by the claimant to reach the final amount to be apportioned between the defendants. In *Cook v Green* [2009] BCC 204, in apportioning contributions between parties who had personally benefited from the wrong to the claimant and those who had not, the court added the whole of the value of the personal benefit to the amount of the contribution required from those taking that benefit.

A relevant liability under **s. 1** includes a liability under a court order, even if the amount of that liability has not been determined (*Abbey National plc v Matthews and Son* [2003] EWHC 925 (Ch), [2003] 1 WLR 2042, applying *R. A. Lister and Co. Ltd v E. G. Thomson (Shipping) Ltd (No. 2)* [1987] 1 WLR 1614).

An overall settlement, including a sum attributed by the paying party to costs, can found a contribution claim under **s. 1(1)** and **(4)**. A 'contribution' is not limited to a contribution in respect of damages, but includes one based on 'liability for damage' (*Mouchel Ltd v Van Oord (UK) Ltd (No. 2)* [2011] EWHC 1516 (TCC), [2011] BLR 492).

An additional claim under **CPR, Part 20**, was struck out in *Abbey National plc v Matthews and Son* on the ground of circularity. The building society sued solicitors for failing to disclose material relevant to a loan agreement, and the solicitors issued an additional claim against surveyors seeking a contribution on the ground of an alleged negligent valuation. The solicitors settled with the building society, and assigned their additional claim to the building society. By virtue of the settlement arrangements, the building society, using the assigned additional claim, could only claim a contribution from the surveyors if the solicitors were liable to the building society, but the solicitors were only liable to the building society if and to the extent that the building society obtained a contribution order from the surveyors.

The personal innocence of a person vicariously liable for the acts of an employee or partner is not relevant for the purpose of contribution proceedings between that person and another wrongdoer (*Dubai Aluminium Co. Ltd v Salaam* [2002] UKHL 48, [2003] 2 AC 366).

A claim in breach of trust or fiduciary duty is a claim for compensation in respect of any damage within the meaning of the **Civil Liability (Contribution) Act 1978, ss. 1(1)** and **6(1)**, if it is a claim to make good the claimant's loss, whereas a claim for an account of profits falls outside the statute (*Charter plc v City Index Ltd* [2007] EWCA Civ 1382, [2008] Ch 313).

In *Charter plc v City Index Ltd* a claim that a company's auditors and directors had allowed unauthorised transactions to continue in breach of duty to the company was held to be in respect of the same damage as a claim in breach of trust or fiduciary duty against a manager who used the company's funds to finance his personal betting transactions.

A contribution could be claimed under s. 1(1) from the company in fact liable to a former employee where a residuary body mistakenly paid compensation to the former employee (*BRB (Residuary) Ltd v Connex South Eastern Ltd* [2008] EWHC 1172 (QB), [2008] 1 WLR 2867).

INDEMNITY

Entitlement to an indemnity can arise by contract, under statute, or by virtue of the relationship between the parties. It is reasonably common for commercial and standard-form contracts to include provisions requiring one party to indemnify the other in specified circumstances, such as where one party incurs a liability to another person through the fault or breach of the other contracting party. General principles of contract law apply to such terms. **29.3**

The principal purpose of a contract of insurance is to provide an indemnity to the assured. It has long been the practice not to allow a defendant to join its insurer as a third party in claims where the defendant is insured against the potential liability. Traditionally this has been because jurors were thought to be unduly influenced by the presence of insurance (*Harman v Crilly* [1943] KB 168), but even today joining an insurer can only be justified in accordance with the overriding objective if the insurer is denying liability under the insurance contract.

Indemnities arising by statute are mostly of a specialised nature.

Indemnities arising out of the relationship between the parties depend on the substantive law. For example, a principal is required to indemnify an agent in respect of liabilities incurred by the agent when acting within the agent's authority (*Adamson v Jarvis* (1827) 4 Bing 66; *Frixione v Tagliaferro and Sons* (1856) 10 Moo PC 175). Similarly, a surety who is sued may claim an indemnity against the principal debtor (*Ascherson v Tredegar Dry Dock and Wharf Co. Ltd* [1909] 2 Ch 401; *Thomas v Nottingham Incorporated Football Club Ltd* [1972] Ch 596).

A contractual clause giving an indemnity for all actions, claims, costs, proceedings and demands was considered in *Lomax Leisure Ltd v Fabric London Ltd* [2003] EWHC 307 (Ch), LTL 19/3/2003.

REQUIREMENT FOR PERMISSION

The permission of the court is not required in order to bring an additional claim, save in the following circumstances: **29.4**

(a) where a defendant wishes to counterclaim against a claimant after having already filed his defence (**CPR, r. 20.4(2)(b)**; see **chapter 28**);
(b) where a defendant wishes to counterclaim against a person other than the claimant (**r. 20.5(1)**; see **chapter 28**);
(c) where a defendant wishes to make a claim for contribution or indemnity against a co-defendant, but does not file the notice of claim with his defence (**r. 20.6**);
(d) where a defendant who has already filed a defence wishes to make a claim for contribution or indemnity against a co-defendant added to the proceedings after the defence was filed, but does not file the notice of claim within 28 days of the filing of the new defendant's defence (**r. 20.6**); and

(e) where a defendant wishes to make a claim (whether for a contribution or indemnity or otherwise) against a person who is not a co-defendant, and where the claim is not a counterclaim, and where such claim is not issued before or at the same time as he files his defence (**r. 20.7(1)** and (3)).

It follows that the permission of the court to make an additional claim is not required:

(a) where a defendant wishes to counterclaim against the claimant at the same time that he files his defence (see **chapter 28**);
(b) where a defendant wishes to make a claim against a co-defendant for a contribution or an indemnity at the same time as filing his own defence (**r. 20.6**);
(c) where a defendant who has filed a defence wishes to make a claim for a contribution or an indemnity against a new co-defendant added after the defence was filed and does so within 28 days of the filing of the new co-defendant's defence (**r. 20.6**);
(d) where a defendant wishes to make any claim against a third party before or at the same time as he files his defence (**r. 20.7(3)(a)**). The expression 'defendant' in **r. 20.7(3)** is presumably intended to apply to a third (or fourth) party wishing to make a further claim against a person not already a party. This was perfectly clear on the pre-6 April 2006 wording of **r. 20.7(3)**, because at that time a third party brought in by the original defendant was known as the 'Part 20 defendant'. It is not so clear under the present version of **r. 20.7(3)**, because it is worded on the basis that the 'defendant' means the defendant to the original claim (see **PD 20, paras 7.3** and **7.4**), and the person brought in by the defendant is known as the 'third party'. However, this should not prevent a third party who acts quickly being allowed to issue a fourth party claim without permission. This is because **CPR, r. 20.3(1)**, provides that an additional claim is to be treated as if it were a claim for the purposes of the CPR, and there is no reason to read **r. 20.7(3)** as derogating from that for this purpose.

PROCEDURE FOR COMMENCING AN ADDITIONAL CLAIM WHEN PERMISSION IS NOT REQUIRED

29.5 The claim and particulars must be served on the person against whom it is made within 14 days after the date on which the additional claim is issued by the court (**CPR, r. 20.8(1)(b)**). There is no express provision that copies must also be served on every other party, which apparently only has to be done, under **r. 20.12(2)**, when an additional claim is served on a person who is not already a party (**r. 20.12(2)** refers to 'the additional claim form', referring to the form which is the subject of **r. 20.12(1)**). However, it is suggested that it would be good practice to do so. **Rule 20.8(1)** does not apply to a defendant's claim against a co-defendant for contribution or indemnity, for which see **29.11** (**r. 20.8(2)**).

PROCEDURE FOR FILING AN ADDITIONAL CLAIM WHEN PERMISSION IS REQUIRED

29.6 A party requiring permission to make an additional claim may apply without notice unless the court directs otherwise (**CPR, r. 20.7(5)**). The application notice should be filed together with a copy of the proposed additional claim (**PD 20, para. 1.2**), and the evidence in support should set out (**PD 20, para. 2.1**):

(a) the stage which the proceedings have reached;
(b) the nature of the additional claim, or details of the question or issue which needs to be decided;

(c) a summary of the facts on which the additional claim is based; and
(d) the name and address of any proposed additional party.

Where there has been delay which has caused or contributed to the need to apply for permission an explanation of the delay should be given in the evidence in support (**PD 20, para. 2.2**). Additionally, where possible, the evidence should include a timetable of the proceedings to date (**PD 20, para. 2.3**).

Relevant considerations in applications for permission to file an additional claim

When considering whether or not to give permission for the filing of an additional claim, the court clearly has the power either to grant the application, dismiss it, or, under **CPR, r. 3.1(2)(e)**, require the additional claim to be dealt with separately from the claim by the claimant against the defendant. Apart from the question of whether or not it would be proper to allow the claim to be filed on its merits, or when there has been any delay, the court may also, by **r. 20.9(2)**, have regard to: **29.7**

(a) the connection between the additional claim and the claim made by the claimant against the defendant;
(b) whether the party making the additional claim is seeking substantially the same remedy which some other party is claiming from him;
(c) whether the party making the additional claim wants the court to decide any question connected with the subject matter of the proceedings not only between existing parties, but between existing parties and a third party; or against an existing party in some different capacity in which he may stand, as well as in the capacity in which he is already a party.

There is no reason to believe that the approach of the courts in deciding whether or not to grant permission to bring an additional claim will differ substantially from the manner in which discretion was exercised under the old rules. In *Chatsworth Investments Ltd v Amoco (UK) Ltd* [1968] Ch 665 Russell LJ held that the court had to take a wide approach in exercising its discretion, and had to ask whether the third-party claim accorded with the general functions of third-party proceedings. In *Barclays Bank Ltd v Tom* [1923] 1 KB 221 Scrutton LJ identified these functions as safeguarding against differing results, ensuring the third party is bound by the decision between the claimant and the defendant, ensuring the additional claim is decided close in time to the proceedings commenced by the claimant, and to save the expense of having two trials.

Essentially, therefore, the establishment of some factual, legal or personal connection between the additional claim and the original claim will be helpful in ensuring the success of the application.

In *Angel Solicitors v Jenkins O'Dowd and Barth* [2009] EWHC 46 (Ch), [2009] 1 WLR 1220, permission to bring in a third party was refused when the application was heard at the same time as a summary judgment application which resulted in judgment against the only defendant. As the main claim had come to an end, it was more convenient for the third party claim to be brought in fresh proceedings (see [18]).

Permission to make an additional claim for contribution will be refused if no court would order the contribution claimed (*African Strategic Investment (Holdings) Ltd v Main* [2011] EWHC 2223 (Ch), LTL 30/8/2011).

Permission to issue an additional claim may be refused if the application is made after an unjustified delay. In *Borealis AB v Stargas Ltd* [2002] EWCA Civ 757, LTL 9/5/2002, there was a counterclaim against the claimant, and the claimant had sought to bring an additional claim against a non-party, SA, to contribute towards any liability on the counterclaim. The claimant's additional claim was set aside by the House of Lords in March 2001. In September 2001

Commentary

there was a case management conference and a trial was fixed for July 2002. In March 2002 the defendant, for the first time, sought to bring its own additional claim against SA to contribute towards any liability the defendant might have. Although it was held that the defendant had a good arguable case on its additional claim, permission was refused because there was an inexcusable delay of a year after the House of Lords decision, and granting permission would have resulted in the trial being vacated.

Being a discretionary decision, an appeal court can only interfere with a decision on permission to file an additional claim where the judge either fails to apply the correct principles or makes a decision outside the generous ambit of the discretion (*Walbrook Trustees (Jersey) Ltd v Fattal* [2008] EWCA Civ 427, LTL 11/3/2008).

CONTENTS OF AN ADDITIONAL CLAIM

29.8 An additional claim under **CPR, Part 20**, must contain particulars, or particulars must be served with the claim (**r. 20.7(4)**). **Rule 20.7** does not apply to a defendant's claim against a co-defendant for contribution or indemnity, for which see **29.11** (**r. 20.7(1)**). The title of an additional claim should, where there are additional parties, comprise a list of all the parties, describing them by giving each party a separate identification (**PD 20, para 7.2**). This identification should be used throughout. Claimants and defendants in the original claim should be described as such, a position that does not change even if they acquire an additional procedural status (**para.** 7.3). The first party added under **CPR, Part 20**, is called the 'third party'. Subsequently added parties are the 'fourth party', 'fifth party', etc., in the order in which they are joined to the proceedings (**PD 20, para.** 7.4). If an additional claim is brought against more than one party jointly, they are known as the 'first named third party' and 'second named third party' (etc.) (**para.** 7.5). If an additional party ceases to be a party, all the remaining parties retain their existing nominal status (**para.** 7.9).

The description of an additional claim (traditionally set out in tramlines beneath the names of the parties in the title) must reflect the nature of the document and its relation to the parties. Thus:

(a) A 'defendant's additional claim against third party' is an additional claim brought by the defendant against a single additional party, the third party.
(b) A 'third party's defence to defendant's additional claim' would be the defence filed by the third party in the previous example.

It is established drafting practice to set out in the opening paragraphs of the particulars of an additional claim summaries of the original and any existing additional claims, to state that copies of the previous statements of case are being served with the present statement of case (in compliance with **CPR, r. 20.12**), and a denial of the claim made against the drafting party. This provides a context for the rest of the draft against the new additional party, and also allows certain terms to be defined for use in the rest of the draft. See example 29.1.

In proceedings where there are fourth or subsequent parties, they should be referred to in the text of statements of case, witness statements etc. by name, suitably abbreviated if appropriate (**PD 20, para.** 7.11). If parties have similar names, suitable distinguishing abbreviations should be used.

An additional claim should be verified by a statement of truth (see **23.13** to **23.17**; **CPR, r. 22.1(1)(a)**; **PD 20, para.** 4.1). The form of statement is (**PD 20, para 4.2**; **PD 22, para. 2.1**):

[I believe] [the [defendant] believes] that the facts stated in this additional claim are true.

PROCEDURE AND CASE MANAGEMENT AFTER FILING

Although **CPR, Part 12** (obtaining judgment in default of a defence), applies to counterclaims (see **28.3**), it does not apply to other additional claims (**r. 20.3(3)**). Instead, the procedure where no acknowledgment of service or defence is filed to an additional claim is set out in **r. 20.11** (see **29.10**) (which does not apply to a defendant's claim against a co-defendant for contribution or indemnity: **r. 20.11(1)(a)**). **29.9**

Part 14 (admissions) also does not apply (**r. 20.3(4)**), save for the provisions relating to the ability to admit in writing the truth of another party's case (under **r. 14.1(1)** and **(2)**), so that the other party can obtain judgment under **r. 14.3**.

Where the court gives permission to make an additional claim it will at the same time give directions as to its service (**r. 20.8(3)**). Service is effected in accordance with **Part 6**, see **r. 20.3(1)** and **chapter 15**.

Example 29.1

IN THE HIGH COURT OF JUSTICE Claim No. ....

QUEEN'S BENCH DIVISION

BETWEEN:

Mr ALAN BEST Claimant

— and —

Miss CATHERINE DAY Defendant

— and —

Ms ELAINE FRASER Third Party

— and —

Ms GAIL HARVEY Fourth Party

THIRD PARTY'S ADDITIONAL CLAIM AGAINST FOURTH PARTY

1. In his claim against the Defendant the Claimant claims damages and interest for alleged breach of a contract in writing dated 14 June 2011 ('the third contract') for the sale of a Bergman car registration number ML03 TYS ('the car'). Copies of the third contract, Claim Form and Particulars of Claim are served with these particulars of additional claim.

2. The Defendant denies she is liable to the Claimant on the grounds set out in the Defence, a copy of which is served with these particulars of additional claim.

3. In her additional claim against the Third Party, the Defendant claims damages and interest for alleged breach of a contract in writing dated 3 June 2011 ('the second contract') for the car. Copies of the second contract, Additional Claim Form and Defendant's Additional Claim against Third Party are served with these particulars of additional claim.

4. The Third Party denies she is liable to the Defendant on the grounds set out in the Third Party's Defence to Defendant's Additional Claim, a copy of which is served with these particulars of additional claim. If, contrary to the Third Party's Defence to Defendant's Additional Claim, the Third Party is held liable in whole or in part to the Defendant, the Third Party claims against the Fourth Party ('Ms Harvey') [to be indemnified against] [, alternatively, a contribution towards] [her liability, if any, to the Defendant] [damages and interest for alleged breach of a contract in writing dated 26 May 2011 ('the first contract') for the car] for the reasons set out below.

5. [*Continue with details of the claim against the Fourth Party as in normal particulars of claim.*]

Once an additional claim is served on a person, he either becomes a party if he is not one already, or if he is already a party but the additional claim is served on him for the purpose of requiring the court to decide a question against him in a further capacity, he also becomes a party in such further capacity (**r. 20.10**).

If an additional claim form is served on a person who is not already a party, **r. 20.12(1)** requires it to be accompanied by:

(a) a form for defending the claim (form N9B (specified amount) or form N9D (unspecified amount));
(b) a form for admitting the claim (form N9A (specified amount) or form N9C (unspecified amount));
(c) a form for acknowledging service (form N213);
(d) a copy of every statement of case which has already been served in the proceedings; and
(e) such other documents as the court may direct.

A copy of the additional claim form must also be served on every existing party (**r. 20.12(2)**).

Where a defence is filed to an additional claim, the court must consider the future conduct of the proceedings and give appropriate directions (**r. 20.13(1)**). In order to do so, the court will arrange a hearing to consider case management of the additional claim, and will give notice of the hearing to each party likely to be affected by any order made at the hearing (**PD 20, paras 5.1** and **5.2**). When giving directions, the court must ensure that, so far as practicable, the additional and the main claims are managed together (**CPR, r. 20.13(2)**). An additional claim which is unsuitable for hearing with the main claim may be filtered out at an earlier stage if it requires the court's permission before it can be made (see **29.7**). However, if the permission of the court was not required, the question of the best means by which the two matters should be heard will be decided at this stage.

At the hearing, the court may (**PD 20, para. 5.3**):

(a) treat the matter as a summary judgment hearing (whether on the application of the defendant, third party, or of its own volition);
(b) order that the additional claim be dismissed (presumably as an outcome of (a) above);
(c) give directions as to the manner in which any matter set out in or arising from the additional claim should be dealt with, and as to the part, if any, that the third party will take at the trial of the claim, and the extent to which he is to be bound by any judgment or decision to be made in the claim.

It would be wrong, however, for a judge to conclude that a third party does not require representation at the main trial because he shared a common intention with the defendant. The third party is not just a witness: he is at risk and he needs to be represented by his own lawyers (*Tantera v Moore* [2009] EWCA Civ 1393, LTL 29/10/2009).

Any of the above orders can be made either before or after any judgment in the claim has been entered by the claimant against the defendant (**PD 20, para. 5.4**).

Where an additional claim had proceeded to trial without an order expressly stating that permission had been granted, contrary to **CPR, r. 20.7(3)**, it was held in *Lloyds Bank plc v Ellicott* [2002] EWCA Civ 1333, [2003] BPIR 632, to have been wrong to have struck out the additional claim. Rather, the judge should have exercised his case management powers under **r. 3.10** to cure the irregularity and proceeded on the basis that permission had been granted.

Where third parties were added at a late stage in a case where there were good reasons for not granting an adjournment of the trial of the main claim, the judge was held to have been entitled to order that the third parties would not be added to the trial between the claimant and the defendant (*Powell v Pallisers of Hereford Ltd* [2002] EWCA Civ 959, LTL 1/7/2002). The Court of Appeal in this case also advised the parties to reach a consensual agreement whereby the third parties were given an opportunity (such as by being allowed to ask questions at trial) to test the defendant's witnesses, with a view to reducing the costs caused by duplication at the later trial of the additional claim.

DEFAULT JUDGMENT IN ADDITIONAL CLAIMS

Where no acknowledgment of service or defence is filed in respect of an additional claim, the procedure is governed by **CPR, r. 20.11**. The provisions for judgment in default under **Part 12** are not applicable, except in respect of a counterclaim, because a default judgment in an additional claim may depend on the success or otherwise of the principal claim against the defendant. **29.10**

A failure to file an acknowledgment of service or defence will be deemed to be an admission of the additional claim, and, to the extent that it is relevant, the third party will be bound by any judgment or decision in the main proceedings (**r. 20.11(2)(a)**). The consequences of default are set out in the notes for the third party which are sent with the additional claim.

If a default judgment under **Part 12** is given against a defendant who has made an additional claim, then, if no acknowledgment of service or defence has been filed by the third party, the defendant may, in turn, obtain judgment in respect of the additional claim, by filing a request in the relevant practice form (**r. 20.11(2)(b)**). Until Her Majesty's Courts and Tribunals Service issues a form it is suggested that form N227 may be adapted for this purpose. This may be done without the court's permission, provided that the defendant has satisfied the default judgment against himself, and does not wish to obtain judgment against the third party for any other remedy than a contribution or indemnity (**r. 20.11(3)**). However, if he has not satisfied the judgment against himself, or if he wishes to obtain judgment for some remedy other than a contribution or indemnity, the permission of the court has to be obtained, on an application which can be made without notice, unless the court otherwise directs (**r. 20.11(4)**). Such a judgment can be set aside or varied by the court at any time (**r. 20.11(5)**). The rule requiring prior payment (unless the court's permission is obtained) is presumably to ensure that a defendant does not profit by a default judgment against him, by keeping the proceeds of a default judgment against the third party, and failing to pass it on to the claimant. **Rule 20.11(3)(b)** does not appear to preclude the obtaining of a default judgment against a third party where a claim has been made against him for a remedy in addition to that of a contribution or indemnity, provided that it is not intended to pursue that part of the claim — the rule uses the words 'he wishes to obtain judgment for any remedy' rather than 'the claim is for any remedy'.

DEFENDANT'S CLAIM AGAINST A CO-DEFENDANT FOR CONTRIBUTION OR INDEMNITY

Under **CPR, r. 20.6**, a defendant may make an additional claim against a co-defendant for contribution or indemnity by: **29.11**

(a) filing a notice containing a statement of the nature and grounds of the claim; and
(b) serving that notice on the co-defendant against whom the claim is to be made.

Unless this notice is filed with the defendant's defence, the court's permission is required. If the only reason for not filing the notice with the defence is that the co-defendant was not added to the claim until after the defence was filed, the court's permission is not required if the notice is filed and served within 28 days after the new co-defendant's defence is filed.

Rules 20.7 to **20.12** are either irrelevant to or are expressed not to apply to a defendant's claim against a co-defendant for contribution or indemnity. There is apparently no provision for any

Commentary

form of judgment in default of defence. The co-defendant against whom the claim is made will presumably remain a party to the main action (unless he fails to file a defence to that action, in which event judgment in default will presumably be obtained in the main action), and thus all issues will be heard together.

At first instance, it has been held that a contribution notice under **r. 20.6** is not a claim form and cannot be served outside the jurisdiction (*Knauf UK GmbH v British Gypsum Ltd* [2002] EWHC 739 (Comm), [2002] 2 Lloyd's Rep 416). Defendants who are outside the jurisdiction, once they come on the record by acknowledging service or filing a defence, are obliged to provide an address for service within the jurisdiction (**r. 6.23**), which is the address to be used for serving contribution notices.

RESOLVING CLAIMS BETWEEN A DEFENDANT AND A THIRD PARTY

29.12 There will be occasions when a claim by a claimant against a defendant is intimately connected with a dispute between the defendant and a third party which involves the same facts or a common point of law, but does not affect the defendant's liability to the claimant. In such an event, the defendant has a choice of either commencing separate proceedings against the third party, or applying that the third party be joined to the existing claim under **CPR, r. 19.2(2)(b)**, on the ground that there is an issue between the defendant and the new party which is connected to the matters in dispute, and that it is desirable to add the new party to resolve that issue.

The advantage of the latter procedure is that bringing the claim within existing proceedings will normally provide a speedier and more cost-effective means of resolving the dispute, and will also avoid the potentially difficult situation of different tribunals arriving at different conclusions on what are essentially the same facts and issues. See also **chapter 14**.

Chapter 30 Further Information

PRINCIPLES

CPR, Part 18, and **PD 18** provide procedures by which, subject to any rule of law or procedure to the contrary, one party to proceedings can obtain from any other party: **30.1**

(a) clarification of any matter which is in dispute in the proceedings; and/or
(b) additional information in relation to any such matter.

Initially this is to be done by making a request directly to the other party, under **PD 18**, without the court's involvement. If the other party does not respond to the request, or the response is considered inadequate, an application may be made to the court for an order under **CPR, r. 18.1**, to give further information.

The doctrine of proportionality and the approach to statements of case generally, should mean that requests for further information are used with some caution. Although they can be used to advantage in some claims, considerable care must be taken in selecting the areas to be investigated by a request, and in formulating the questions to be put. Where the responding party's statement of case is already sufficiently pleaded, requests for further information designed for:

(a) tactical reasons;
(b) obtaining further explanation of matters clearly put in issue on the existing statements of case;
(c) an explanation of the responding party's legal arguments; or
(d) obtaining information that might be useful for bringing separate claims against other persons,

are abuses of **Part 18** and will not be allowed (*Trader Publishing Ltd v Autotrader.Com Inc.* [2010] EWHC 142 (Ch), LTL 12/3/2010). Before making a request for further information a party should consider the other side's statement of case very carefully, and avoid making requests concerning matters that are already adequately particularised or are otherwise unnecessary (*Trader Publishing Ltd v Autotrader.Com Inc.*). The tests of necessity and proportionality in **PD 18, para. 1.2**, mean the procedure is more restrictive than the old procedure for further and better particulars. There is no need to make a request for further information on matters of evidence (statements of case should deal with facts, not evidence) or points which are for argument at trial (these should be in the skeleton arguments), or where the information is readily available (*Lexi Holdings v Pannone and Partners* [2010] EWHC 1416 (Ch), LTL 21/6/2010).

On the other hand, a request for further information may be the proportionate and best way of dealing with a statement of case by an opponent which does not provide full information, rather than the more drastic approach of applying to strike out (*Deutsche Morgan Grenfell Group plc v Commissioners of Inland Revenue* [2006] UKHL 49, [2007] 1 AC 558, at [148]).

REQUEST FOR FURTHER INFORMATION

A party should not make an application to the court for an order under **CPR, r. 18.1**, without having first served a written request on the party from whom the information or clarification is sought. The request must give a reasonable time to respond, and set a date by which the **30.2**

Commentary

response should be served (**PD 18, para. 1.1**). Such request should be made, as far as possible, in a single comprehensive document, and not piecemeal (**para. 1.3**). It should be concise, and strictly confined to matters which are reasonably necessary and proportionate to enable the party requesting the information to prepare his own case or to understand the case he has to meet (**para. 1.2**). The requirement of proportionality is, of course, to ensure compliance with the overriding objective in **Part 1**, and provides the recipient with a new ground for refusing to give further information (although, it is suggested, not clarification) even though the request might otherwise be legitimate.

In patent infringement claims, it is unusual for the court to order a party to answer a request for further information to clarify the construction which that party proposes to put on the terms of the patent (*Lux Traffic Controls Ltd v Staffordshire Public Works* [1991] RPC 73). This is not an invariable rule, and it may save costs to order further information where the answers will assist in defining the issues before experts are instructed (*Novartis AG v Johnson and Johnson Medical Ltd* [2008] EWHC 293 (Pat), LTL 5/3/2008).

What constitutes 'a matter in dispute' was liberally construed in relation to requests for information concerning the nature and extent of insurance cover available to meet the claimant's claim in *Harcourt v Griffin* [2007] EWHC 1500 (QB), [2007] PIQR Q177. That claim was likely to be worth over £8 million against an unincorporated association with limited assets. Disclosure was ordered as it would be irrational to devote a great deal of expense to maximise damages if the resources available were limited.

However, this was not followed in *West London Pipeline and Storage Ltd v Total UK Ltd* [2008] EWHC 1296 (Comm), [2008] 1 CLC 935, where it was held there is no jurisdiction to order a party to disclose its insurance position, where it is not a matter in dispute in the proceedings. It is submitted that this is the appropriate line for the court to take. *Arroyo v BP Exploration Co. (Colombia) Ltd* (2010) LTL 4/6/2010 followed this line in refusing a request for the disclosure of the claimant's ATE cover. There is no general right to be informed of an opponent's ability to satisfy a judgment or pay an order for costs. Similarly, a request for further information about the number of times a judge had acted for a particular client while the judge was at the Bar was refused as fishing and failing to relate to any issue in the case in *Mireskandari v Associated Newspapers Ltd* [2010] EWHC 967 (QB), 160 NLJ 695.

Form and content of request

30.3 There is no requirement that a request for further information should be in a particular form, save that a party who has indicated willingness to be served by email (see **15.15**) should be served with a request by email (**PD 18, para. 1.7**). If the text is brief, and the reply likely to be so as well, it may be made by letter (**PD 18, para. 1.4**). Such a letter should expressly state that it contains a request made under **CPR, Part 18**, and should deal with no matters other than the request (**PD 18, para. 1.5**). It is required to contain the same formalities as a request made in a separate document (**para. 1.6**). These requirements tend to blur the distinction between the two formats to the extent that there seems little advantage in making the request other than by way of a formal separate document.

Whether made by letter or in a separate document, the request must (**PD 18, para. 1.6(1)**):

(a) be headed with the name of the court and the title and number of the claim;
(b) state in its heading that it is a request made under **Part 18**;
(c) identify the party making the request and the party to whom the request is made (referred to in **PD 18** as the 'first party' and the 'second party');
(d) set out in a separate numbered paragraph, each request for information or clarification;
(e) *identify* any *document* referred to in the request, and (if relevant) the paragraph or words to which the request relates;
(f) state the date by which the response is expected.

A further advantage of making the request by way of a separate document rather than by letter is that, if convenient, it may be prepared with the numbered paragraphs set out on the left-hand half of each sheet, leaving room for the response to appear on the same document on the right. Thus the entire request and response would appear on the same document. If the request is prepared in this manner, an extra copy should be served for the use of the recipient (**PD 18, para. 1.6(2)**). It may well be, however, that, save in straightforward cases, limitations of space, and word-processing difficulties may make it easier for the 'second party' to adopt the alternative response procedure, where the text of the request is repeated, followed by the response (**PD 18, para. 2.3(1)(c)**) (as was formerly the case when responding to a request for further and better particulars).

Example 30.1 provides some suggestions as to the manner in which a request could be approached. The request need not be verified by a statement of truth, although the response must be (see **23.12** to **23.17**; **CPR, r. 22.1(1)(a)**; **PD 18, para. 3**).

Example 30.1

IN THE BLACKSTONE COUNTY COURT — Claim No. BK13 1234

BETWEEN

AB — Claimant

— and —

CD — Defendant

REQUEST FOR FURTHER INFORMATION
ABOUT THE CLAIMANT'S CASE UNDER PART 18

Sought on behalf of the Defendant (the first party) from the Claimant (the second party), and made on 19 March 2013.

[*Example of a straightforward request for clarification of the claim*]

Under Paragraph 2 of the Particulars of Claim

Of: 'It was a term of the agreement between the parties that the propellers would be delivered to the Claimant within 7 working days of receipt of the order by the Defendant'.

Request

1. Please state whether the alleged term was made orally or in writing. If the term was made orally, please give full information as to the parties agreeing the term, the date, time and place that it was allegedly agreed, and the gist of all words spoken. If it is alleged that the term was made in writing, please give the above information with all necessary changes, identifying any document or documents relied on, and attaching a copy of the same to the response.

[*Example of a request not directly referable to the particulars of claim*]

2. Is it not the case:

(a) that on 20 May 2011 the Claimant was handed a cheque for £2,350 by the Defendant, in the course of a meeting at the Defendant's premises, being a refund in respect of propellers that the Defendant was unable to supply?

(b) that the Claimant, or some other person on his behalf, subsequently presented the cheque and that it was duly met and cleared through the Defendant's bank account on 3 June 2011?

(c) that such sum falls therefore to be deducted from the Claimant's claim against the Defendant?

[*Example of a request referable to a document attached to the particulars of claim*]

Please look at the letter dated 17 May 2011 from the Claimant to the Defendant, attached to the Particulars of Claim.

Request

3. Please state whether it is the Claimant's case:

(a) that the propellers referred to in the final paragraph on page 1 are of model PDG 234, or PDG 236, or some other, and if so, which model?

(b) that the signature on the letter is that of the Claimant, or some other person (and if so, please identify the alleged signatory)?

Take notice that these requests must be answered no later than 4.00 p.m. on 9 April 2013

Dated 19 March 2013

FORM AND CONTENT OF RESPONSE

30.4 The response to a request for further information must be in writing and must be dated and signed by the second party or his legal representative (**PD 18, para. 2.1**). It must be verified by a statement of truth (see **23.12 to 23.17; CPR, r. 22.1(1)(a); PD 18, para. 3**). Where the request is made by letter, the response may be in like form, or in a formal reply (**para. 2.2(1)**), but if the response is made in a letter it should identify itself as a response, and deal with no matters other than the response (**para. 2.2(2)**). To this extent the format of the letter will be similar to that containing the original request. By analogy, it is submitted, a response to an email request should be sent by email.

If the original request was prepared in the form set out in **para. 1.6(2)** (so that the response could be made on the same form as the request), the second party may choose whether to use it, or to reply in a separate document. If he uses the original form, no additional formalities are required (save for the date, signature and statement of truth). However, if the response is made in a formal document, it must (**para. 2.3(1)**):

(a) be headed with the name of the court and the title and number of the claim;

(b) in its heading, identify itself as a response to the request;

(c) repeat the text of each separate paragraph of the request and set out under each paragraph the response to it;

(d) refer to and have attached to it, a copy of any document not already in the possession of the first party, which forms part of the response.

A second or supplementary response must identify itself as such in its heading (**para. 2.3(2)**).

It seems clear from the practice direction, that where the original request is made in a formal document, the response should not be by way of letter.

The response must be served on all parties (in addition to the first party), and a copy should be filed with the court together with a copy of the request (**para. 2.4**).

OBJECTIONS TO RESPONDING

30.5 The second party appears to be allowed five principal grounds on which to object to part or all of a request:

(a) that it is a request for information or clarification that is unnecessary, irrelevant or improper;

(b) that he is unable to provide the information or clarification requested;
(c) that insufficient time has been given to him to formulate a reply;
(d) that the request can only be complied with at an expense which is disproportionate to the claim, or is otherwise contrary to the overriding objective;
(e) that he is protected from answering by privilege.

In the event of an objection being taken, the second party must inform the first party promptly, and in any event within the time stipulated in the request (**PD 18, para. 4.1(1)**). Such information may be by letter, or by way of a formal response in a separate document, but in either event must be accompanied by reasons for the objection, and, where relevant, a date by which he expects to be able to comply with the request (**para. 4.1(2)**). Presumably, there is no reason why such objection(s) could not be taken in the course of a response that does answer other requests, although this is not specifically dealt with in **PD 18**.

Where the objection is one of disproportionate expense, it seems that it will not be sufficient for the second party to adopt the above course. Instead, he must serve a reply, and explain in it briefly why he has taken the view (**para. 4.2(2)**). Where the objection is founded on privilege, a reply should be served setting out the nature of the privilege relied upon.

Once the second party has indicated his objection(s) in the appropriate format, there is no need for him to make any application to the court (**para. 4.2(1)**). Upon receipt of the response or objection, it will be for the first party to decide whether or not to make an application to the court for an order that the information be provided.

A 'fishing' request will be improper. A request is fishing where the party making the request does not have evidence supporting the cause of action or defence being put forward, but is hoping that something may turn up in response to the request (*Best v Charter Medical of England Ltd* [2001] EWCA Civ 1588, *The Times*, 19 November 2001).

In *English, Welsh and Scottish Railway Ltd v Goodman* [2007] EWHC 3463 (QB), LTL 21/8/2007, the claim was pleaded in a general and non-specific way. It was struck out partly because the claimant refused to answer a request for further information, on the ground, regarded as inadequate in the circumstances, that the answers would be found in the exchanged witness statements.

COURT ORDER TO PROVIDE FURTHER INFORMATION

Under **CPR, r. 18.1**, a party to proceedings may ask the court to order another party: **30.6**

(a) to clarify any matter which is in dispute in the proceedings; or
(b) to give additional information in relation to any such matter.

This may be done whether or not the matter is contained in or referred to in a statement of case. The court may exercise the power to make an order under **r. 18.1(1)** at any time, but the power is expressed by **r. 18.1(2)** to be subject to any rule of law to the contrary.

If a party makes no response to a request (in whole or in part) or it is considered that such response as is made is inadequate, an application can be made to the court in the manner laid down in **CPR, Part 23** (see **chapter 32**) for an order under **r. 18.1**. The application notice should set out, or have attached to it, the text of the order sought, and in particular should specify the matter or matters in respect of which the clarification or information is sought (**PD 18, para. 5.2**). In practice, it would presumably be helpful to set out or attach the request (or that part of it that is said still to be unanswered) in the format in which it was originally sent to the 'second party'. If no request had originally been sent to the 'second party', an explanation for this should be set out in the application notice (**PD 18, para. 5.3(1)**), as should any response made by the 'second party' to any request that had been made (**PD 18, para. 5.3**).

If a request has been served, and no response received, the party making the application need not serve the application notice on the second party, and the court may deal with the application without a hearing, provided that at least 14 days have passed since the request was served, and the time stated in it for a response has expired (**PD 18, para. 5.5**). In all other cases, the application notice must be served on the second party and on all other parties to the claim (**PD 18, para. 5.6**).

Both parties to the application (or just the first party if an application notice is not served) should consider whether evidence in support of or in opposition to the application is required (**PD 18, para. 5.4**).

Where an order is made, the party required to provide the clarification or information must file his response and serve it on the other parties within the time specified (**CPR, r. 18.1(3)**). The order itself must be served on all parties to the claim (**PD 18, para. 5.7**), regardless of whether or not notice of the application was originally given. The order may also make a summary assessment of costs (**PD 18, para. 5.8**). If the order makes no reference to costs, no party is entitled to claim them (**PD 18, para. 5.8(2)**).

RESTRICTIONS ON THE USE OF FURTHER INFORMATION

30.7 Whether or not further information is given voluntarily or following an order of the court, the court may direct that such information must not be used for any purpose except for that of the proceedings in which it is given (**CPR, r. 18.2**).

Chapter 31 Amendments to Statements of Case

INTRODUCTION

Generally, statements of case can be amended without seeking permission before they are served. After service, amendments are generally either by consent or with permission. Permission is generally granted where there is no prejudice to other parties, and in general there is no prejudice if the other parties are adequately protected by the usual order that the costs of and occasioned by the amendments are paid by the amending party. For the documents that are statements of case see 23.2. Amendments involving the addition or substitution of parties are considered at 14.83 to 14.96, and this chapter will consider amendments not involving changes in the parties. There are particular restrictions on amendments sought after the expiry of limitation, see 14.90 to 14.95 and 31.21 to 31.28. **31.1**

WHEN PERMISSION IS NOT REQUIRED FOR AMENDMENT

A party may amend a statement of case at any time before it has been served on any other party (CPR, r. 17.1(1)), and in such an event, the permission of the court is not required. However, such an amendment can subsequently be disallowed by the court (r. 17.2(1)) on the application, within 14 days of service of the amended statement of case, by the party on whom it is served (r. 17.2(2)). The rules do not presently state any specific matters that the court will take into consideration when deciding whether or not to grant such an application, but it is almost certain that the overriding objective and general principles of case management will be applied. **31.2**

If a statement of case has been served, an amendment can be made without permission of the court, provided the written consent of all the other parties has been obtained (r. 17.1(2)(a)).

It will not be sufficient under this rule simply to obtain the consent of the party to whom the statement of case has been directed.

If, however, the application is to amend by removing, adding or substituting a party, the application must be made in accordance with **r. 19.4** (which deals more specifically with the addition and substitution of parties; see **14.83** to **14.89**).

Where an amended statement of case is filed without the need for the permission of the court, it should be endorsed in the following manner (**PD 17, para. 2.1(2)**):

Amended [particulars of claim/defence (or as may be)] under CPR, [rule 17.1(1) or 17.1(2)(a)], dated...

For the format of an amended statement of case, see **31.20**.

APPLICATION FOR PERMISSION TO AMEND

31.3 Where a statement of case has been served, and the written consent of all the other parties has not been obtained, or is not forthcoming, a party may apply to the court for permission to make an amendment (**CPR, r. 17.1(2)(b)**). The applicant should file the application notice with the court, together with a copy of the statement of case with the proposed amendments (**PD 17, para. 1.2**). By **PD 17, para. 2.2**, the statement of case in its amended form need not show the original text (see **31.20**), but it is difficult to see how the court will be assisted in making a decision on an application to amend, if the original text is not shown in the copy to be filed with the application.

The application may be dealt with at a hearing, or, where all parties consent, without a hearing (i.e. on written submissions) (**PD 17, para. 1.1**). If permission to amend is given, the court may (not must) give directions as to amendments to be made to any other statement of case, and service of any amendments (**CPR, r. 17.3(1)**). Thus provision can (and it is suggested normally will) be made by the court for the service of any amendments that will have to be made by other parties consequent upon the service of the amended statement of case on them. In any event, the amended statement of case should be filed by the applicant within 14 days of the date of the order, unless the court directs otherwise (**PD 17, para. 1.3**). A copy of the amended statement of case and the order should be served on every party to the proceedings unless the court directs otherwise (**PD 17, para. 1.5**). The court's power to give permission is subject to the rules on change of parties, both before and after the end of a relevant limitation period, set out in **CPR, rr. 19.2** and **19.5**, and to **r. 17.4** dealing with amendments after the expiry of a relevant limitation period (**r. 17.3(2)**).

One of the conditions considered on an application for permission is whether the proposed amended case has a real prospect of success (see **31.13**). This should be addressed in the written evidence in support of the application. The judge may consider the evidence in support and decide that the amended case has a real prospect of success. Alternatively, the judge may grant permission to amend conditionally on supporting evidence being adduced at trial, with permission to amend being subject to disallowance if such evidence is not adduced (*Swain-Mason v Mills and Reeve LLP* [2011] EWCA Civ 14, [2011] 1 WLR 2735 at [81]). Another alternative is to disallow amendments which are not at the time of the application supported by evidence establishing a real prospect of success, but to allow the application to be renewed at trial once the evidence is complete (*Bleasdale v Forster* [2011] EWHC 596 (Ch), LTL 17/3/2011).

Where an amended statement of case is filed with the permission of the court, it should be endorsed in the following manner (**PD 17, para. 2.1(1)**):

Amended [particulars of claim/defence (or as may be)] by order of [Master.../District Judge...or as may be] dated...

PRINCIPLES ON WHICH PERMISSION IS GRANTED

General principles applied on applications to amend

No criteria are laid down in **CPR, rr. 17.1, 17.3** and **19.4**, to govern applications for permission to amend. In accordance with the overriding objective, as a general statement of principle, it can be said that amendments should be allowed where this is just and proportionate. There are two distinct lines of authority on how this should be applied (see **31.5** and **31.6**). **31.4**

Amendments which introduce a new cause of action after the expiry of limitation raise special problems which are considered at **31.21** to **31.28**. For addition and substitution of parties see **14.83** to **14.96**. For withdrawal of admissions see **17.4**. On amending to withdraw an offer of amends under the Defamation Act 1996, s. 2, see **66.28**.

Traditional approach

Under the RSC a permissive approach was taken to applications to amend, which was based on the principle that at trial the court should determine the real issues between the parties. Thus, in *Cropper v Smith* (1883) 26 ChD 700 at pp. 710–11 Bowen LJ said: **31.5**

> It is a well-established principle that the object of the court is to decide the rights of the parties, and not to punish them for mistakes they make in the conduct of their cases by deciding otherwise than in accordance with their rights.... I know of no kind of error or mistake which, if not fraudulent or intended to overreach, the court ought not to correct, if it can be done without injustice to the other party. Courts do not exist for the sake of discipline, but for the sake of deciding matters in controversy, and I do not regard such amendment as a matter of favour or grace.... It seems to me that as soon as it appears that the way in which a party has framed his case will not lead to a decision of the real matter in controversy, it is as much a matter of right on his part to have it corrected if it can be done without injustice, as anything else in the case is a matter of right.

The rule on the traditional approach was encapsulated by Brett MR in *Clarapede and Co. v Commercial Union Association* (1883) 32 WR 262 at p. 263 as follows:

> However negligent or careless may have been the first omission, and however late the proposed amendment, the amendment should be allowed if it can be compensated by costs.

It is the latter phrase in this quotation that is the guiding concept in the traditional approach. It is the reason why the opening words of **PD 17** and of **PD 19A** are that: 'A party applying for an amendment will usually be responsible for the costs of and arising from the amendment' (see further **31.18**). *Cropper v Smith* and *Clarapede and Co. v Commercial Union Association* have been applied, expressly or by implication, in numerous post-CPR cases. They were described as laying down timeless principles in *Charlesworth v Relay Roads Ltd* [2000] 1 WLR 230. They were restated in a more modern form in *Cobbold v Greenwich London Borough Council* (1999) LTL 24/5/2001. Peter Gibson LJ said that in considering an application to amend the court has to apply the overriding objective of dealing with cases justly, which includes ensuring that cases are dealt with both expeditiously and fairly. His Lordship said:

> Amendments in general ought to be allowed so that the real dispute between the parties can be adjudicated upon provided that any prejudice to the other party or parties caused by the amendment can be compensated for in costs, and the public interest in the efficient administration of justice is not significantly harmed.... There is always prejudice when a party is not allowed to put forward his real case, provided that that is properly arguable.

On this approach the key questions are whether there is any injustice or prejudice that cannot be compensated in costs, and whether the party seeking to amend can pay the usual costs order. Inconvenience in investigating the amended case after the passage of time since the original pleading is not normally relevant prejudice for this purpose (*P and O Nedlloyd BV v Arab Metals Co.* [2006] EWCA Civ 1300, [2007] 1 WLR 2483 at [22]). Loss of evidence through the death or disappearance of witnesses might be.

Balancing factors approach

31.6 The second line of authorities on permission to amend stems from *Worldwide Corporation Ltd v GPT Ltd* [1998] EWCA Civ 1894 (BAILII), LTL 2/1/98, and the cases referred to in the judgment, such as *Ketteman v Hansel Properties Ltd* [1987] AC 189 and *Ashmore v Corporation of Lloyd's* [1992] 1 WLR 446. In *Worldwide Corporation Ltd v GPT Ltd* counsel for the claimant realised that the claim could not succeed on the pleaded basis, so the defendant was notified 11 days before the trial that permission would be sought at the trial to rely on amended points of claim which abandoned large parts of the pleaded case and inserted a different case. Permission was refused. After referring to the passage from *Cropper v Smith* (1883) 26 ChD 700 set out at **31.5**, Waller LJ said:

> In the modern era it is more readily recognised that in truth the payment of costs of an adjournment may well not adequately compensate someone who is desirous of being rid of a piece of litigation which has been hanging over his head for some time, and may not adequately compensate him for being totally (and we are afraid there are no better words for it) 'mucked around' at the last moment. Furthermore, the courts are now much more conscious that in assessing the justice of the case the disruption caused to other litigants by last-minute adjournments and last-minute applications have also to be brought into the scales.

Worldwide Corporation Ltd v GPT Ltd was approved in *Savings and Investment Bank Ltd v Fincken* [2003] EWCA Civ 1630, [2004] 1 WLR 667, where Rix LJ said it gives better effect to the overriding objective by requiring the court to have greater regard to all the circumstances before granting permission to amend. In *Swain-Mason v Mills and Reeve LLP* [2011] EWCA Civ 14, [2011] 1 WLR 2735, *Worldwide Corporation Ltd v GPT Ltd* was held to be the correct modern approach, and reliance on *Cobbold v London Borough of Greenwich* was held to be wrong in law (at [85]). According to Lloyd LJ in *Swain-Mason v Mills and Reeve LLP* at [72], the decision whether to grant permission to amend is always one of balancing the relevant factors.

Swain-Mason v Mills and Reeve LLP was applied at first instance in *Capita Alternative Fund Services (Guernsey) Ltd v Drivers Jonas* [2011] EWHC 1228 (Comm), LTL 25/5/2011, and, in relation to raising a new point of mixed law and fact, on an appeal in *Jones v Environcom Ltd* [2011] EWCA Civ 1152, [2012] PNLR 5.

Choice between the two approaches

31.7 It is not entirely clear from *Swain-Mason v Mills and Reeve LLP* [2011] EWCA Civ 14, [2011] 1 WLR 2735, whether the court intended to say that the *Cobbold v Greenwich London Borough Council* (1999) LTL 24/5/2001 approach is always wrong in law (this seems to be the meaning of paras [72] and [85]), or whether it was wrong in law in the circumstances of the case. Like *Worldwide Corporation Ltd v GPT Ltd* [1998] EWCA Civ 1894 (BAILII), LTL 2/1/98, *Swain-Mason v Mills and Reeve LLP* was a late amendment case, where permission to amend was sought on the second effective date of the trial to make a fundamental change to the nature of the claim, albeit one that was not so radical as the change sought in *Worldwide Corporation Ltd v GPT Ltd*. The various cases, including Court of Appeal decisions, that have applied *Cobbold v Greenwich London Borough Council* were not considered in the judgment. *Worldwide Corporation Ltd v GPT Ltd* was expressly decided on the basis of being a late amendment case.

It is submitted that late amendments are the most prominent of a group of situations where proposed amendments have the effect of overreaching the other parties. It is where there is a good arguable case that an amendment will have the effect of overreaching other parties that the balancing of factors approach should be used. In *P and O Nedlloyd BV v Arab Metals Co.* [2006] *EWCA Civ 1300, [2007] 1 WLR 2483* at [23], Thomas LJ said it is only where there is some express prejudice that the court has to balance the prejudice against the reasons why the applicant did not advance their new case at the correct time. Overreaching may arise in any of the following circumstances:

(a) the amendment is sought at a very late stage;
(b) the amendment raises a radically different case than that originally pleaded;
(c) the amended case will be difficult to investigate due to the passage of time or the loss of evidence;
(d) the costs incurred in investigating the original case have been substantial and are unlikely to be recoverable from the party seeking to amend;
(e) the amendment is sought for tactical reasons; and
(f) the amendment seeks to replace a case that has been taken to the point of defeat.

Each of these situations involves a value judgment, and the situations will often overlap. *Ketteman v Hansel Properties Ltd* [1987] AC 189 was a case where the amendment was sought during closing speeches to substitute a completely new defence where the case had reached the point where the defence appeared to have been defeated. Permission to amend was refused. Lateness in itself is not a reason for refusing permission to amend, and it is extremely common for amendments to be made at the start and even the end of trials. Where the purpose is to correct the statements of case to ensure that they reflect the way the evidence emerges at the trial, permission is usually granted as this accords with the overriding objective (*Binks v Securicor Omega Express Ltd* [2003] EWCA Civ 993, [2003] 1 WLR 2557).

Where an amendment does not have the effect of overreaching the other parties, it is submitted that the traditional approach of granting permission, almost as a matter of right, but subject to payment of the costs of and arising from the amendment, should continue to apply. This is reflected in the Admiralty and Commercial Courts Guide, para C5.3, which says that questions of amendment, and consequential amendment, should wherever possible be dealt with by consent. A party should consent to a proposed amendment unless he has substantial grounds for objecting to it.

Commentary

Factors in making the balance

Where permission to amend is being approached by balancing the relevant factors to find where justice lies (see **31.6** and **31.7**), Lord Griffiths in *Ketteman v Hansel Properties Ltd* [1987] AC 189 at p. 220 said that many and diverse factors will bear upon the exercise of the court's discretion, and that it is not possible or wise to attempt to enumerate them all. Justice cannot always be measured in terms of money. Nevertheless, factors regarded as relevant include: **31.8**

(a) the strain of litigation, particularly for personal litigants (*Ketteman v Hansel Properties Ltd*);
(b) anxieties caused by needing to face fresh issues (*Ketteman v Hansel Properties Ltd*);
(c) the legitimate expectation that the trial will finally determine the dispute (*Ketteman v Hansel Properties Ltd*);
(d) how late the application is made (*Ketteman v Hansel Properties Ltd*);
(e) the effect on other litigants, and the delays caused to them (*Ketteman v Hansel Properties Ltd*; *Worldwide Corporation Ltd v GPT Ltd* [1998] EWCA Civ 1894 (BAILII), LTL 2/1/98);
(f) whether the need to amend arose from some recent disclosure or other good reason explaining the delay (*Worldwide Corporation Ltd v GPT Ltd*; *Hussain v Sarkar* [2010] EWCA Civ 301, LTL 16/4/2010). A reappraisal by the lawyers of the merits of the case is not regarded as a good reason (*Swain-Mason v Mills and Reeve LLP* [2011] EWCA Civ 14, [2011] 1 WLR 2735);
(g) the earlier history of amendment in the case (*Swain-Mason v Mills and Reeve LLP*);
(h) whether the amending party can pay the usual costs order (*Swain-Mason v Mills and Reeve LLP*);
(i) the length of any adjournment of the trial (*Swain-Mason v Mills and Reeve LLP*);
(j) the effect on the length of the trial (*Swain-Mason v Mills and Reeve LLP*);

(k) whether the amendment will prevent the trial taking place on a false or artificial basis (*Swain-Mason v Mills and Reeve LLP*); and
(l) the size or importance of the claim (*Swain-Mason v Mills and Reeve LLP*).

Late amendments

31.9 In the case of last-minute amendments, there is a heavy onus on the party seeking permission to show the strength of the new case and why justice both to him, his opponent and other litigants requires him to be able to pursue it (*Worldwide Corporation Ltd v GPT Ltd* [1998] EWCA Civ 1894 (BAILII), LTL 2/1/98; *Swain-Mason v Mills and Reeve LLP* [2011] EWCA Civ 14, [2011] 1 WLR 2735). The degree to which lateness should influence the decision in part depends on the extent to which the amended case is a surprise to the other side. An amendment at trial to adopt allegations in the other side's statement of case against them should cause no such surprise, so delay ought not to be a ground for refusing permission (*Bleasdale v Forster* [2011] EWHC 596 (Ch), LTL 17/3/2011).

Amendments can be made during the course of the trial, and even during closing speeches (see **31.10**), Lateness is often combined with related factors, such as impact on the trial date, and whether the party seeking to amend can be criticised for failing to apply earlier because they have known for some time of the material forming the basis of the amended case. In *National Westminster Bank plc v Rabobank Nederland* [2006] EWHC 2108 (Comm), LTL 29/1/2007, the defendant was ordered to serve a correcting statement of case because its original defence and counterclaim was inadequately pleaded. The defendant then sought to incorporate the improved pleading by amending its defence and counterclaim. The original defence was based on misrepresentation, but the amended pleading included both misrepresentation and negligent misstatement, and made wider allegations of misrepresentation than those included in the original defence. The trial was imminent when the application was heard. Permission was granted to amend the misrepresentation allegations on conditions as to the service of additional witness statements. Permission was refused to add the negligent misstatement allegations as contrary to the overriding objective as they would have resulted in delay and disruption to the trial timetable. Lateness, combined with a weak case, albeit one with some prospect of success (see **31.13**), resulted in permission being denied in *Savings and Investment Bank Ltd v Fincken* [2003] EWCA Civ 1630, [2004] 1 WLR 667. Permission to make an apparently small amendment, which in fact amounted to a complete volte-face by the defendant, sought two weeks before trial in a substantial claim, was refused in *Calenti v North Middlesex NHS Trust* (2001) LTL 10/4/2001.

An amendment sought at a late stage in an attempt to save a claim that would otherwise have been struck out as disclosing no reasonable claim was refused in accordance with the overriding objective in *Christofi v Barclays Bank plc* [2000] 1 WLR 937. It is not clear how late the application was made, but it may have been during the appeal hearing itself. On the other hand, amendments were allowed in accordance with the overriding objective in *Finley v Connell Associates* (1999) *The Times*, 23 June 1999. In *Mark v Associated Newspapers Ltd* (2002) LTL 6/2/2002 permission to make amendments was granted even though the amendments represented a complete change of tack and involved allegations which were always open and obvious to the claimant, because permission was sought at an early stage in the proceedings (even though there had been delay before issue) and the amendments would not prejudice the defendant. A careless error resulting in the wrong defendant being named was allowed to be corrected by amendment under what is now **CPR, r. 19.5**, in *Virk v Gan Life Holdings plc* [2000] Lloyd's Rep IR 159 as there was no suggestion of prejudice to the defendant being brought in by the amendment.

A very late amendment was allowed in *Les Laboratoires Servier v Apotex Inc.* [2010] EWCA Civ 279, LTL 12/2/2010, primarily because refusing permission to amend would have given the claimant a large financial windfall. In *Hussain v Sarkar* [2010] EWCA Civ 301, LTL 16/4/2010, permission to amend the defence in an RTA claim to plead that the accident had been staged was sought one week before trial. It had not been possible to amend earlier because it was not until three weeks before trial that the defendant had sufficient evidence to enable counsel to plead fraud in accordance with the Bar Code of Conduct. Permission to amend was granted.

Where a claimant had failed to file an amended schedule of special damages and this had clearly been an obvious mistake and had been foreshadowed, the overriding objective meant that the parties should have cooperated with each other to allow a late amendment at a time where the mistake could have obviated satellite litigation (*Chilton v Surrey County Council* [1999] CPLR 525). Refusal of permission to amend was held to have been wrong in *Kelly v Chief Constable of South Yorkshire Police* [2001] EWCA Civ 1632, LTL 25/10/2001, even though it was sought at the end of the trial and changed the basis of the case against the defendant. Where proposed amendments had been raised in earlier statements of case and affidavits, delay in applying to amend should not, of itself, preclude permission being granted (*Stansburys v Pashley* (2000) LTL 6/4/2000).

Changing basis of case at trial

A not infrequent occurrence is that a party will seek to rely on a secondary case at trial that is **31.10**
not fully reflected in the way that party's case was previously put in its statement of case. Where this is done to reflect a version of the facts that only emerges with the evidence at the trial, an amendment is generally permitted as this accords with the overriding objective (*Binks v Securicor Omega Express Ltd* [2003] EWCA Civ 993, [2003] 1 WLR 2557). Where the party seeking to amend is aware of the alternative version in advance of the trial, an application to amend should be made a reasonable time before the trial. Likewise, seeking permission to argue a point which is raised for the first time at or shortly before the hearing will generally be granted, as refusing may be an unduly harsh penalty and represent a windfall to the other side (*E. I. Du Pont de Nemours and Co. v S. T. Dupont (No. 2)* [2002] EWHC 2455 (Ch), *The Times*, 23 November 2002). Neuberger J in this case said that permission may be refused if there are special factors, such as the point being raised at a late stage combined with:

(a) the other side needing a significant adjournment to adduce evidence in response; or
(b) the point being new and difficult, again requiring a long adjournment.

An example of a party seeking to amend to rely on a secondary case is *Sturton v Sutherland Holdings plc* (2000) LTL 27/10/2000, in which the counterclaim set out a claim for damages for breach of warranty, relying on one set of accounts. At trial, the defendant sought to rely on a fallback case based on amended accounts, which had not been mentioned in the counterclaim (although they had been referred to in the defence). It was held that the defendant had been under a duty to make clear it was relying on the fallback case well in advance of trial, so that the claimant could answer that case and call appropriate evidence.

Permission to amend the particulars of claim was granted on the first day of the trial in *Airways Aero Associations Ltd v Wycombe District Council* [2010] EWHC 1774 (Ch), LTL 10/8/2010, despite the amendment being very substantial, largely because the amended case was important both within the context of the case and as raising a point of some general importance in other claims. In *Bowerbank v Amos* [2003] EWCA Civ 1161, LTL 31/7/2003, a re-re-re-re-re-amendment was allowed during the course of the trial changing the case from one pleaded in breach of trust to one pleaded in breach of contract. It was held that this was permissible, especially as otherwise a meritorious claim would have been defeated on a pleading point. Once such an amendment was allowed, the judge had to be scrupulous to minimise any prejudice to the other party. The judge had refused permission to recall the claimant for further cross-examination after the amendment was made, so the case was remitted back to the judge to hear the further cross-examination and to reconsider his findings.

In *Hall v Motor Sport Vision Ltd* (2002) LTL 1/5/2002 an appeal was dismissed against a refusal of permission sought at trial to allow amendments and additional evidence. These had the effect of raising certain allegations as separate breaches of the defendant's obligations, whereas in the original particulars of claim they were pleaded only as particulars of breach.

A judge is not permitted to give judgment on the basis of a claim that is not included in the statements of case. If this is done, there may be no option but to order a retrial (*Rosengrenstann Ltd v Ayres* (2001) LTL 22/6/2001).

Substantial amendments

31.11 In *Cook v News Group Newspapers Ltd* [2002] EWHC 1070 (QB), LTL 21/6/2002, permission to make substantial amendments to the defences in a libel claim was sought five months before trial. The amendments would have entailed substantial amendments to the replies, together with extensive further disclosure and additions to the witness statements. In such cases the court needed to have regard to the public interest in enabling the defendant to deploy the defences it wished to use, while fulfilling the overriding objective. Such applications are therefore considered with great care, being astute to avoid granting permission to allegations which failed to address (in the context of a libel claim) the real sting of the publication. The court would be more accommodating where the proposed amendments related to matters which had only emerged at a late stage with the discovery of evidence which previously had been genuinely unavailable. On the facts, permission was granted restricted to allegations genuinely supporting the central allegations. A similar case, *Morris v Bank of America National Trust and Savings Association* (2001) LTL 11/1/2002, resulted in all the substantial proposed amendments being disallowed, with permission being granted only for one amendment, which narrowed the issues. Late permission to add a single, but important, paragraph to a defence was allowed in *Electronic Data Systems Ltd v National Air Traffic Services Ltd* [2002] EWCA Civ 13, LTL 15/1/2002.

Case management considerations

31.12 An amendment may be refused where it will only enlarge the litigation with little potential benefit (*Clarke v Bain* [2008] EWHC 2636 (QB), LTL 26/11/2008). Amendments were refused in *Multiplex Construction (UK) Ltd v Cleveland Bridge UK Ltd* [2008] EWHC 231 (TCC), LTL 9/5/2008, in the interests of firm case management. In particular Jackson J disallowed non-essential amendments to the pleadings which either imperilled the trial date or would cause material prejudice to either party in maintaining that date. It is incumbent on a party, particularly in complex litigation, to state clearly the nature of his case (*Law Debenture Trust Corporation (Channel Islands) Ltd v Lexington Insurance Co.* [2002] EWCA Civ 1824, LTL 13/12/2002). It is preferable as a matter of case management to allow amendments which set out details of a party's allegations, rather than simply let matters take their natural course at trial based on general allegations (*Three Rivers District Council v Bank of England* [2003] EWHC 1269 (Comm), LTL 9/6/2003).

An amendment order should not require a party to plead its case in accordance with the judge's view of the law where the party has a different view which is at least arguably correct (*Coflexip SA v Stolt Offshore MS Ltd* [2003] EWCA Civ 296, [2003] FSR 728).

Amendments with no real prospect of success

31.13 A proposed amendment will be refused where the amended case has no real prospect of success (*Oil and Mineral Development Corporation Ltd v Sajjad* (2001) LTL 6/12/2001; *Savings and Investment Bank Ltd v Fincken* (2001) *The Times*, 15 November 2001; *Clarke v Slay* [2002] EWCA Civ 113, LTL 25/1/2002). **CPR, Part 24**, can properly be relied upon to establish this (*Flexitallic Group Inc. v T. and N. Ltd* (2001) LTL 9/1/2002; *Findlay v Cantor Index Ltd* [2007] EWHC 643 (QB), LTL 20/4/2007). Permission to amend a pleading in a way which was speculative, pleading every conceivable cause of action in a scattergun approach, and which sought to reverse the burden of proof, was refused in *Clyde and Co. LLP v New Look Interiors of Marlow Ltd* [2009] EWHC 173 (QB), LTL 13/2/2009. Amendments will not be allowed if they seek to introduce matters covered by issue estoppel, or which will be an abuse of process (see **33.14** to **33.16**) (*Seele Austria GmbH & Co. KG v Tokio Marine Europe Insurance Ltd* [2009] EWHC 255 (TCC), [2009] BLR 261).

In *Hussain v Sarkar* [2010] EWCA Civ 301, LTL 16/4/2010, the first-instance judge had described the evidence in support of a proposed amended case that an RTA had been staged as no more than 'fishing'. This was criticised on appeal. Fishing implies a lack of a factual basis for an allegation which it is hoped will be strengthened either through disclosure or cross-examination. What the first-instance judge had in mind was that there was no hard evidence of the fraud. The Court of Appeal pointed out that there rarely is any direct hard evidence of fraud: it is far more common for fraud to be established by the assembly of circumstantial evidence pointing to the probability of guilt.

Permission to amend was refused in *Groveholt Ltd v Hughes* [2010] EWCA Civ 538, LTL 20/5/2010, because there was an insufficient basis for implying terms into a commercial contract. In *Giles v Rhind* [2007] EWHC 687 (Ch), [2007] Bus LR 1470, the claimant sought to amend the particulars of claim to change the alleged date of a deed which he said set out the proportions held by the parties in certain property. The defence had alleged that the deed as originally pleaded was a sham, or was in fact made six years later, and after the relevant dispute arose. It was held that while there were serious questions as to the reliability and credibility of the claimant's evidence, this was not a case where the amended case was incredible, so permission to amend was granted. In *Hussain v Cuddy Woods and Cochrane* (1999) LTL 19/10/99 an application to amend particulars of claim was refused where the claimant had no prospect of success against the solicitor and barrister defendants in his claim that a settlement reached was inadequate. Similarly, permission will be refused to make an amendment adding a claim which cannot succeed (*Laws v Society of Lloyd's* [2003] EWCA Civ 1887, *The Times*, 23 January 2004; *Collier v Blount Petre Kramer* [2004] EWCA Civ 467, LTL 1/4/2004). In *Multiplex Constructions (UK) Ltd v Cleveland Bridge UK Ltd* [2008] EWHC 569 (TCC), LTL 30/5/2008, the court refused permission to make certain amendments which were regarded as being incomprehensible.

Cause of action accruing after issue

The modern approach is flexible, with amendments being granted in accordance with the **31.14**
justice of the case. There is no longer any absolute rule of law or practice which precludes an amendment to rely on a cause of action which has arisen after the commencement of the proceedings where otherwise the claim would fail (*Maridive and Oil Services (SAE) v CNA Insurance Co. (Europe) Ltd* [2002] EWCA Civ 369, [2002] 2 Lloyd's Rep 9). Likewise, amendments may be allowed adding heads of claim which have arisen after the proceedings were commenced (*British Credit Trust Holdings v UK Insurance Ltd* [2003] EWHC 2404 (Comm), LTL 28/10/2003). In *Finlan v Eyton Morris Winfield* [2007] EWHC 914 (Ch), [2007] 4 All ER 143, an amendment was allowed after the expiry of limitation to substitute an assignment of the cause of action which was executed after the claim form was issued.

Abandonment

In *British Credit Trust Holdings v UK Insurance Ltd* [2003] EWHC 2404 (Comm), LTL 28/10/2003, the **31.15**
claim form sought damages and declaratory relief. The original particulars of claim only sought damages. It was held that the particulars of claim could be amended to include the declaratory relief, which had not been abandoned. There was no intention to abandon and no detriment.

Deemed amendment

31.16 While generally contrary to principle and fraught with difficulties, there are occasions where a court deems the pleadings to have been amended without actual production of amended pleadings. An example is *Khan v Rehman* [2008] EWCA Civ 1407, LTL 24/11/2008.

AMENDING IN AN APPEAL COURT

31.17 In *Islington London Borough Council v Uckac* [2006] EWCA Civ 340, [2006] 1 WLR 1303, Dyson LJ at [36] to [41] said that an appeal court has the power to allow a party to amend in order to deal with a point raised during the course of an appeal. This power may be used, for example, on an appeal from a strike-out application, even if permission to amend had not been sought in the court of first instance. An appeal court should not grant permission to amend if it would have been refused had the point been raised at trial (*Jones v Environcom Ltd* [2011] EWCA Civ 1152, [2012] PNLR 5).

COSTS OF AMENDING

31.18 Normally, amendments are allowed with the party making the amendment being ordered to pay the costs of and arising from the amendments (**PD 17, introduction; PD 19A, introduction**). Costs arising from an amendment may include the costs of any extension to the length of the trial (*Airways Aero Associations Ltd v Wycombe District Council* [2010] EWHC 1774 (Ch), LTL 10/8/2010). A party who ought to have consented to proposed amendments was ordered to pay the costs of the amendments in *La Chemise Lacoste SA v Sketchers USA Ltd* [2006] EWHC 3462 (Ch), LTL 24/5/2006. Strictly, where consent is unreasonably refused, the correct approach is to order that party to pay the costs of the application to amend, but the costs of and occasioned by the amendments themselves should still be paid by the party seeking to amend. Despite *La Chemise Lacoste SA v Sketchers USA Ltd*, the normal rule is that the applicant should pay the costs of the application to amend (*Lidl UK GmbH v Davies* [2008] EWCA Civ 976, LTL 10/7/2008). Even if costs will not adequately compensate the other party, amendments will be allowed if they are required in the interests of justice (*Gabriel v Hayward* [2004] EWHC 2363 (TCC), LTL 29/10/2004).

CHANGING TRACK AT TRIAL

31.19 There are no additional problems if an amendment at trial involves changing between the small claims and fast tracks, or from the multi-track to the fast track. However, an amendment involving changing from the fast track to the multi-track may involve having to change judges, because multi-track claims cannot be tried by district judges without the consent of the designated civil judge (**PD 2B, para. 11.1(a) and (d)**). Having to adjourn (for example, where the new value of the claim is substantially above the normal fast track limit of £25,000) may be a sufficient reason for refusing permission to amend (*Maguire v Molin* [2002] EWCA Civ 1083, [2002] 4 All ER 325). Another option is for the district judge to allow the amendment without changing tracks (*Maguire v Molin*), but this may lead to an inappropriate fast track costs limitation (see 71.7).

FORMAT OF AN AMENDED STATEMENT OF CASE

31.20 The amended form of the statement of case need not show the original text, unless the court thinks that it is desirable for it to do so, in which event it may direct that the amendments should be shown either by coloured amendments (either manuscript or computer-generated) or by use of a numerical code in a monochrome computer-generated document (**PD 17, para. 2.2**). (Many word processing packages include the facility to print an amended text automatically showing corrections and deletions.) Where colour is used, the deleted text should be struck through in colour, and any replacement text should be inserted or underlined in the same colour (**PD 17, para. 2.3**). The order for successive amendments is, as has always been the case: red for the first amendment, green for the second, violet for the third, and yellow for the fourth (**PD 17, para. 2.4**).

The court will normally direct whether the original text should be shown together with the amendment at the time that it gives the permission for the amendment to be made. However, if no such permission is required, such a direction would have to be given after service. The principal purpose of displaying the original text has always been to enable the parties and the court to see the degree and extent to which a party has departed from its original stated case. Obviously, if the amendment is comparatively minor, and has been undertaken under **CPR, r. 17.1(1)**, the case for showing the original text is far less persuasive. In cases where it is wished to amend a statement of case after it has been served, there seems no reason why, as a precondition of giving written consent, the other party should not require the amendment to display the original text as well, failing which the 'amending party' will have to apply to the court, which may well be persuaded by the opposing party to order that the original text be shown.

If the substance of the statement of case is changed by reason of the amendment, the statement of case should be re-verified by a statement of truth (**PD 17, para. 1.4**). When a statement of case is amended, the court has a power in **r. 22.1(2)** to dispense with the need to re-verify with another statement of truth. This power may be exercised, or a suitably drafted statement of truth may be used making it clear that there is a primary and a secondary case, where a party relies on the facts asserted by the other side (which are inconsistent with the primary case) as an alternative basis for a finding in his favour (*Binks v Securicor Omega Express Ltd* [2003] EWCA Civ 993, [2003] 1 WLR 2557, and see **24.15**).

Commentary

AMENDMENT AFTER A RELEVANT LIMITATION PERIOD HAS EXPIRED

Effect of expiry of limitation

For the purposes of the Limitation Act 1980 (LA 1980), an amendment to add or substitute a new party (a situation discussed at **14.83** to **14.96**) or a new cause of action is deemed to be a separate claim and to have been commenced on the same date as the original claim (LA 1980, s. 35(1) and (2)). Consequently, if the original claim was commenced within the relevant limitation period, and an amendment is allowed adding a party or cause of action after the expiry of the limitation period, the defendant will be deprived of the limitation defence, and will usually suffer injustice not compensable by an order for costs. The usual rule, therefore, is that such amendments are not permitted (LA 1980, s. 35(3)). There are, however, a number of exceptions which are considered below. It seems that if there is a dispute about whether a limitation period has expired, the test is whether the claim is unarguably time-barred (*Leicester Wholesale Fruit Market Ltd v Grundy* [1990] 1 WLR 107), although in *BP plc v Aon Ltd* [2005] EWHC 2554 (Comm), [2006] 1 Lloyd's Rep 549 at [57], Colman J said the question is whether there is a reasonably arguable case that the claim is time-barred. **31.21**

The statutory relation back in the LA 1980, s. 35(1), only applies to the procedural time bars in the LA 1980. It does not apply to contractual or substantive time limits, like that in the Hague–Visby Rules, art. III, rule 6 (Carriage of Goods by Sea Act 1971, sch.), which have the effect that on expiry of the period laid down the claimant's cause of action ceases to exist (*Payabi v Armstel Shipping Corporation* [1992] QB 907).

Permission to amend after expiry of limitation

31.22 Provision is made in **CPR, r. 17.4**, for the problem which can arise when a party wishes to amend a statement of case after a period of limitation has expired. The rule is expressed to apply where a party applies to amend a statement of case under **Part** 17, and a period of limitation has expired under the LA 1980, the Foreign Limitation Periods Act 1984 or other statutory provision (**CPR, r. 17.4(1)**). No provision is made in **r. 17.4** for a situation in which no application is made because a party is entitled to amend without permission. Clearly, if the statement of case has been served, it is unlikely that the other party will give written permission under **r. 17.1(2)(a)**, and an application would have to be made to the court. However, if proceedings are filed immediately before the expiry of the limitation period, but have not been served, and the claimant wishes to amend them before service, no application would ordinarily be made to the court. Of course, the court may disallow the amendment on an application under **r. 17.2**, but it is suggested that **r. 17.4** implies that such an amendment should only be made upon application to the court.

Rule 17.4(1) makes it clear that **r. 17.4** is merely procedural and does not give a power to add or substitute a new case after the expiry of limitation where this is not allowed by the governing statute. Consequently, while such amendments may be made in prescribed circumstances under the LA 1980 (see **14.83** to **14.95** and **31.23** to **31.27**) and the Foreign Limitation Periods Act 1984, they are not permitted under the Hague–Visby Rules (see **31.21**).

New cause of action

31.23 In assessing whether proposed amendments in fact amount to a new cause of action for the purposes of LA 1980, s. 35 (rather than a clarification of the existing cause of action), it is necessary to consider the statement of case as a whole (*Leeds and Holbeck Building Society v Ellis* (2000) LTL 5/10/2000). To determine whether a proposed amendment introduces a new cause of action for the purposes of LA 1980, s. 35(5)(a), it is necessary to compare the essential factual elements of the existing cause of action with the essential factual elements of the proposed cause of action (*Aldi Stores Ltd v Holmes Buildings plc* [2003] EWCA Civ 1882, [2005] PNLR 9; *Commissioners of HM Revenue and Customs v Noorasa Begum* [2010] EWHC 1799 (Ch), LTL 15/7/2010). In making this assessment the court may take into account any further information provided under **CPR, Part 18** (*Boake Allen Ltd v Commissioners of HM Revenue and Customs* [2006] EWCA Civ 25, [2006] STC 606).

According to Brett J in *Cooke v Gill* (1873) LR 8 CP 107 at p. 116:

> 'Cause of action' has been held from the earliest time to mean every fact which is material to be proved to entitle the [claimant] to succeed — every fact which the defendant would have a right to traverse.

Robert Walker LJ in *Smith v Henniker-Major and Co.* [2002] EWCA Civ 762, [2003] Ch 182, said that in identifying a new cause of action, it is necessary to compare the bare minimum of essential facts abstracted from the original statement of case with the minimum facts required to constitute the cause of action in the amended statement of case. As Millett LJ said in *Paragon Finance plc v D. B. Thakerar and Co.* [1999] 1 All ER 400 at p. 405, this has to be done 'at the highest level of abstraction'.

In *Evans v Cig Mon Cymru Ltd* [2008] EWCA Civ 390, [2008] 1 WLR 2675, the claimant had contemplated bringing a claim against his former employer for damages following an accident at work together with a claim based on workplace bullying. He decided to pursue only the accident claim, and issued a claim form shortly before the expiry of limitation. After limitation it was noticed that the claim form described the claim as for 'loss and damage arising out of abuse at work'. The supporting medical report and particulars of claim were based on the accident. It was held to be permissible to read the claim form together with the particulars of claim and medical report to determine what the claim was intended to cover. In context, the words 'of abuse' were an obvious clerical error for the phrase 'of an accident', and permission to amend was granted as the amendment did not involve introducing a new claim within the meaning of s. 35(5)(a).

It is necessary to examine the duty alleged, the nature and extent of the breach alleged, and the nature and extent of the damage claimed. Where the only difference between the original case and the case set out in the proposed amendments is a further instance of breach, or the addition of a new remedy, there is no addition of a new cause of action (*Savings and Investment Bank Ltd v Fincken* [2001] EWCA Civ 1639, *The Times*, 15 November 2001). An amendment to plead consequential loss in a professional negligence claim was interpreted as simply adding a new head of damage, so was not a new cause of action in *Harland and Wolff Pension Trustees Ltd v Aon Consulting Financial Services Ltd* [2009] EWHC 1557 (Ch), [2010] ICR 121. Changing from alleging the claimant had a beneficial interest in shares (a concept unknown in Russian law) to an interest based on a joint activity or *sui generis* contract was regarded as just applying a different label, and not to involve a new cause of action, in *Berezovsky v Abramovitch* [2011] EWCA Civ 153, [2011] 1 WLR 2290.

However, making an amendment to justify a claim on a different factual basis amounts to making a new claim even if the sum claimed remains unchanged (*Seele Austria GmbH & Co. KG v Tokio Marine Europe Insurance Ltd* [2009] EWHC 2066 (TCC), [2009] BLR 481). Amendments changing page references from the American edition of a magazine to the European page references were held not to involve making a new claim in *Reuben v Time Inc.* [2003] EWCA Civ 6, LTL 22/1/2003. An amendment adding a new duty or obligation usually raises a new cause of action, whereas pleading additional facts, or better particulars, allegedly constituting a breach of the duty already pleaded usually will not (*Darlington Building Society v O'Rourke James Scourfield* [1999] PNLR 365). An amendment to plead a claim under the law of a different State raises a new claim within s. 35 (*Latreefers Inc. v Hobson* [2002] EWHC 1586 (Ch), LTL 31/7/2002). In *Abbey National plc v John Perry and Co.* [2001] EWCA Civ 1630, LTL 24/10/2001, it was held that deleting the word 'constructive' from a claim, thereby altering the basis of the claim from one in constructive trust to one in implied trust, was a matter of semantics and did not involve the substitution of a new cause of action.

Where a claimant has brought proceedings as an assignee of a claim, a valid assignment is an essential element of the cause of action (*Smith v Henniker-Major and Co.* [2002] EWCA Civ 762, [2003] Ch 182 at [99]). An amendment after limitation to plead an assignment can therefore only be allowed if it comes within s. 35(5)(a). In *Smith v Henniker-Major and Co.* the claim as originally formulated relied on an invalid assignment from a company purportedly signed at an inquorate board meeting. After limitation expired, the claimant procured a resolution from the company purporting to ratify parts of the invalid assignment. Although the amendment to plead the ratification arose out of substantially the same facts as the original claim, permission was refused, because a party seeking to ratify a transaction had to adopt it in its entirety, and because of prejudice to the defendant caused by the delays.

Amendment of causes of action after expiry of limitation

Amendment after a limitation period has expired is governed by LA 1980, s. 35, the text of which can be found at **14.90**. A new cause of action (as opposed to a new party) may be added to an existing claim after the relevant period of limitation has expired in three situations: **31.24**

(a) Where the claim is in respect of personal injuries and the court makes a direction under the LA 1980, s. 33 (see **10.19**), that the usual limitation period shall not apply (LA 1980, s. 35(3)).
(b) Where the new cause of action is an original set-off or counterclaim (LA 1980, s. 35(3)). An original set-off or counterclaim is one made by an original defendant

who has not previously raised any counterclaim under **CPR, Part 20**, in the claim, and the counterclaim must be made against the original claimant (see *Kennett v Brown* [1988] 1 WLR 582, which is still good law on this point). All that is required to engage this exception is that the party proposing to make the counterclaim has not previously counterclaimed and is on the opposite side of the record to the defendant to the proposed counterclaim (*Law Society v Shah (No. 2)* [2008] EWHC 2515, [2009] 1 WLR 2254). Section 35(3) may be regarded as a procedural quirk, and amendments under this provision may be refused in the court's discretion, for example, where the counterclaim is being used as an offensive weapon, or if it is radically different to the existing causes of action (*Law Society v Shah (No. 2)*). See also *Ernst and Young v Butte Mining plc (No. 2)* [1997] 1 WLR 1485. If bringing a counterclaim in effect evades an accrued limitation period, the claimant should consider making an application to strike out the counterclaim under **CPR, r. 3.4**.

(c) Where the new cause of action arises out of the same facts or substantially the same facts as are already in issue in the original claim (LA 1980, s. 35(5)(a); see **31.25**).

Same or substantially the same facts

31.25 **Raised by either party** The LA 1980, s. 35 (5)(a), permits rules of court to allow a claimant to add, after a limitation period has ended, a new claim which arises out of the same facts as are already in issue on any claim previously made in the original claim. This includes facts which are put in issue in the defence to the original claim (*Goode v Martin* [2001] EWCA Civ 1899, [2002] 1 WLR 1828; *Lidl UK GmbH v Davies* [2008] EWCA Civ 976, LTL 10/7/2008). It also allows a claimant to adopt facts after the expiry of limitation which had been pleaded by one defendant by amending the particulars of claim against another defendant (*Charles Church Developments Ltd v Stent Foundations Ltd* [2006] EWHC 3158 (TCC), [2007] 1 WLR 1203).

CPR, r. 17.4(2), is expressed to allow a new claim to be added only if it arises out of the same facts as the original claim, but it must be read as also allowing a new claim which arises out of the same facts as 'are already in issue on' the original claim, because otherwise the rule would impede a claimant's access to a court for determination of civil rights, contrary to the European Convention on Human Rights, art. 6 (*Goode v Martin*). The court held that words in quotation marks in the previous sentence must be read into **r. 17.4(2)** under the **Human Rights Act 1998, s. 3**. The wording of the rule has not been amended to reflect this. In *Goode v Martin* the claimant had originally alleged that the defendant had negligently caused personal injuries to the claimant in the factual circumstances set out in the claim. The defendant served a defence asserting that the personal injuries happened in different circumstances. After the limitation period had expired the claimant was allowed to add a claim that, even if the defendant's version of events was true, the injuries were caused by the defendant's negligence.

31.26 **The test** Whether amendments involve the same or substantially the same facts as those already in issue is largely a matter of impression (*Darlington Building Society v O'Rourke James Scourfield* [1999] PNLR 365). In deciding whether the new cause of action arises out of substantially the same facts as those originally pleaded it is necessary to identify 'the bare minimum of essential facts abstracted from the original pleading [and to compare them] with the minimum as it would be constituted under the amended pleading' (*P and O Nedlloyd BV v Arab Metals Co.* [2006] EWCA Civ 1300, [2007] 1 WLR 2483 at [14], applying the similar test from *Smith v Henniker-Major and Co.* [2002] EWCA Civ 762, [2003] Ch 182). In *Hoechst UK Ltd v Commissioners of Inland Revenue* [2003] EWHC 1002 (Ch), LTL 11/4/2003, it was held that it is not enough that the background facts of the two claims are the same: the central facts of both causes of action must be the same or based on substantially the same facts. In making this assessment the judge must not confine himself to the original statements of case, but must consider the facts that would have had to be litigated on the original statements of case (*Hemmingway v Roddam* [2003] EWCA Civ 1342, LTL 18/9/2003).

Examples Spanish fishermen were refused permission to amend their claim to add further claims for compensation for breach of EU law (in being prevented from fishing by unlawful UK legislation) in respect of additional vessels. This was because the facts they needed to prove were largely specific to each boat, and so the additional claims did not arise out of substantially the same facts as were already in issue (*R v Secretary of State for Transport, ex parte Factortame Ltd (No. 7)* [2001] 1 WLR 942). A claim in negligent misrepresentation, which focused on what the defendant should have done, was held in *Law v Society of Lloyd's* [2003] EWCA Civ 1887, *The Times*, 23 January 2004, not to arise out of substantially the same facts as the original case pleaded in fraud (which was based on an allegation that the defendant knew the representations were false). In *BP plc v Aon Ltd* [2005] EWHC 2554 (Comm), [2006] 1 Lloyd's Rep 549, a claim for breach of an insurance contract did not arise out of substantially the same facts as a claim pleaded in negligence. In *Del Grosso v Payne and Payne* [2007] EWCA Civ 340, LTL 1/3/2007, the original claim against the defendant solicitors was based on alleged negligence in failing to advise the client on the effect of a break clause in a lease. It was held that a wide-ranging amendment to the particulars of claim, alleging new beaches of duty, issues relating to the scope of the retainer, and the basis of the alleged financial losses, did not arise out of the same or substantially the same facts as the original claim. 31.27

In *Senior v Pearsons and Ward* (2001) LTL 26/1/2001 the claim originally alleged that the defendant solicitors had acted contrary to their instructions. The claimant was permitted to amend the particulars of claim after the expiry of limitation to add allegations of failing to advise fully, as the additional allegations arose out of the same facts, or substantially the same facts, as those originally pleaded. In *Brickfield Properties Ltd v Newton* [1971] 1 WLR 862 the general endorsement on the writ (the equivalent of a claim form giving just a concise statement of the nature of the claim under **CPR, r. 16.2(1)(a)**) claimed damages against an architect for negligent supervision of certain building works. The particulars of claim were served after the expiry of the limitation period, and contained claims both for negligent supervision and negligent design. It was held that the negligent design claim arose substantially out of the same facts as the negligent supervision claim and in its discretion the court allowed the amendment. In *Hancock Shipping Co. Ltd v Kawasaki Heavy Industries Ltd* [1992] 1 WLR 1025, permission to amend the particulars of claim was sought three years after service of the original statement of case and after the limitation period had expired. In considering whether it is just to allow an amendment in such circumstances, the court held that it had to take into account that granting permission will deprive the defendant of an accrued limitation defence, but could exercise its discretion to allow the amendment in the light of all the relevant factors. An important factor is the degree to which the defendant is prejudiced in being unable to investigate the facts of the new claim through the disappearance of evidence. The Court of Appeal in *Hancock Shipping Co. Ltd v Kawasaki Heavy Industries Ltd* disallowed certain of the proposed amendments on the ground that the defendant would be prejudiced through the loss of evidence, but allowed certain other amendments which were closely related to the claim already made as there was likely to be little prejudice through the loss of evidence.

Amendments after the limitation period affecting accrued rights

A defendant will not be given permission to amend where the effect of the proposed amendment is to transfer responsibility for the claim on to a non-party who cannot be sued by the claimant as a result of the expiry of the relevant limitation period. An example is *Steward v North Metropolitan Tramways Co.* (1886) 16 QBD 556, where the claimant sued the tramway for personal injuries. After the expiry of the limitation period, the defendant sought to amend its defence. The effect of the proposed amendment was to transfer the defendant's liability for the claimant's injuries to the local road authority. Permission to amend was refused, because even 31.28

an order for costs could not put the claimant into the same position as if the proposed defence had been pleaded at the proper time. This approach was confirmed by *Cluley v R. L. Dix Heating* [2003] EWCA Civ 1595, LTL 31/10/2003, where the court dismissed an argument that the prejudice was caused by the claimant having failed to identify the proper person to bring proceedings against rather than by the defendant seeking, after the expiry of limitation, to withdraw an admission of having entered into a contract with the claimant.

Much depends on whether the defendant has been at fault in not pleading the proposed defence at the proper time. In *Weait v Jayanbee Joinery Ltd* [1963] 1 QB 239, through no fault of their own, the defendants discovered after the expiry of the limitation period that the claimant's injuries were probably worse than they should have been through the intervening negligence of the doctor who treated the claimant. An amendment to the defence to plead the doctor's negligence was allowed despite the fact that the claimant could not make a claim against the doctor as that claim was time-barred. Further, an amendment blaming a non-party may be allowed if it alleges facts within the knowledge of the claimant, since in such a case the prejudice to the claimant arises from the claimant's own failure to sue the non-party in time, rather than by some line of defence being made known at a late stage. An example is *Turner v Ford Motor Co. Ltd* [1965] 1 WLR 948. The claimant sued the occupier and a building contractor (but not his own employer) for injuries suffered when he was struck by a falling brick. After disclosure of documents by the first defendant, and after the expiry of the limitation period, the second defendant discovered that the claimant had not been wearing a safety helmet at the relevant time, and sought to amend its defence to allege contributory negligence on the part of the claimant. The claimant opposed the amendment on the ground that he was now out of time in suing his employer for failing to provide him with a helmet. The amendment was allowed, because the claimant must have known whether he was wearing a safety helmet at the time of the accident, so the amendment told him nothing he did not know in order to commence his claim. If the first defendant, who had knowledge of the claimant not wearing a helmet, had sought an amendment to plead contributory negligence after the expiry of the limitation period, permission would have been refused.

Chapter 32 Applications and Interim Orders

The following procedural checklists, which are at the front of the book, are relevant to this chapter:

Procedural checklist 19 Interim application without notice
Procedural checklist 20 Interim application with notice

INTRODUCTION

Interim applications are made when a party to proceedings seeks an order or directions from the court prior to the substantive hearing of the claim. Parties seeking interim orders or directions in general have to issue an application notice in form N244, pay a court fee, and often have to provide written evidence in support. The application notice and evidence must in general be served at least three clear days before the return date. Generally, service will be effected by the applicant where the applicant prepares the application notice (CPR, r. 6.21(1)). 32.1

Commentary

Chapters 33 to 41 deal with various types of interim application, such as for summary judgment, interim injunctions, freezing injunctions and search orders. Applications for disclosure orders, such as specific disclosure and pre-action disclosure, are dealt with in **chapter 50**. Various other types of application are considered elsewhere, such as applications for alternative service in **15.19** and **15.43**, setting aside default judgments in **20.11** to **20.18**, for further information in **30.6** and for amendment in **chapter 31**. There is a separate code of procedure for applications in insolvency proceedings, which is considered in **chapter 84**.

In most cases there should be a limited need for making interim applications because of the level of involvement of the judiciary in case management. Part of the obligation placed on the courts in furthering the overriding objective is to consider whether the likely benefits of taking a particular step will justify the cost of taking it (**r. 1.4(2)(h)**). The court is also required to deal with as many aspects of the case as is practicable on the same occasion (**r. 1.4(2)(i)**).

In fast track and multi-track cases the procedural judge will scrutinise defended claims shortly after defences are filed, and there will be further judicial consideration of the case at the listing for trial stage (see **chapters 42**, **46** and **47**). A party contemplating a particular order may ask the court to consider it during the scrutiny process.

Whenever the parties are notified that an interim hearing, such as a case management conference or listing hearing, has been fixed, they must consider and make any application which may be appropriate for the court to deal with at the hearing (**PD 23A, para. 2.8; PD 28, para. 2.5** (fast track cases); **PD 29, para. 3.5** (multi-track cases)).

Consequently, most interim orders are made as part of the regular case management system. Further, there is a general obligation to make all interim applications as soon as it becomes apparent they are necessary or desirable (**PD 23A, para. 2.7**).

The CPR permit the court to make interim orders on its own initiative, and to hold hearings by telephone or other direct means of communication. Solicitors should keep correspondence with masters and district judges to a minimum, and must ensure that opposing parties receive copies (Chancery Guide, para. 5.54). The ordinary rule is that interim hearings are in public, although there are significant exceptions (see **61.21**).

A distinction needs to be drawn between applications for directions and applications for interim remedies. A somewhat more formal approach is taken with applications for interim remedies, which should in almost all cases be supported by written evidence (see **CPR, r. 25.3(2)**). The distinction is between:

(a) case management matters, such as standard disclosure of documents, exchange of factual and expert evidence, and trial directions; and
(b) applications for specific remedies, such as specific disclosure, interim injunctions, interim payments and striking out.

There is a further important distinction between interim applications made without giving notice to any other parties, and those made on notice. This distinction will be considered further at **32.7** and **32.12**.

TO WHICH COURT SHOULD AN APPLICATION BE MADE?

32.2 In general an application must be made to the court where the claim is presently being dealt with. This will be the court where the proceedings were commenced (**CPR, r. 23.2(1)**), unless:

(a) the claim has been transferred (**r. 23.2(2)** and see **42.6**);
(b) the claim has been listed for trial at another court, in which event the application should be made to the trial court (**r. 23.2(3)**); or

(c) the application is made after judgment, in which event the application may need to be made to the court dealing with enforcement (**r. 23.2(5)**).

An application for pre-action remedies (such as some injunction, freezing injunction and search order applications) should be made to the court where the substantive proceedings are likely to be brought, unless there is a good reason for applying to another court (**r. 23.2(4)**). An application in relation to a designated money claim (as defined in **r. 2.3(1)**) may be made in any county court (**r. 23.2(4A)**).

Rule 2.7 gives the court a general power to deal with a case at any place that it considers appropriate. This power may be used in courts with shared listing arrangements, and where a court with congested lists arranges to release some cases to another court to reduce listing delays.

WHICH JUDGE SHOULD DEAL WITH AN APPLICATION?

Unless otherwise provided for by an Act, rule or practice direction, interim applications can be **32.3**
dealt with by judges, masters and district judges (**CPR, r. 2.4**). The most significant exceptions are freezing injunctions and search orders, which are dealt with by High Court judges, and ordinary interim injunctions, which are generally dealt with by a judge who would have jurisdiction to try the claim (see **PD 25A, para. 1.3; PD 2B, para. 2**). In the county courts this means that circuit judges will deal with interim injunction applications in most multi-track claims, but district judges may hear such applications in small claims and fast track cases (see **2.4**), and also in a number of other types of claim (**PD 2B, para. 11.1**). High Court masters and district judges may grant interim injunctions by consent, in connection with charging orders and receivers and in aid of execution (see **2.10**). Apart from injunctions, most applications are dealt with by masters and district judges, but they may refer particular applications to be dealt with by a judge (**PD 23A, para. 1**).

Applications to a High Court judge in the Chancery Division are made to the interim applications judge (Chancery Guide, paras 5.8 and 5.9). An application notice must be used, which should usually state that it is to be heard by 'the interim applications judge'.

In the Chancery and Queen's Bench Divisions there are arrangements for assigning claims to individual masters. Once assigned a claim may be transferred to another master, and the fact that a claim has been assigned does not prevent it being dealt with by another master (**PD 2B, para. 6.2**). However, the usual rule is that once a claim is assigned all applications in that claim will be dealt with by the assigned master.

TIMING AND EXPEDITION

The basic rules are that interim applications should be made as early as possible (**PD 23A**, **32.4**
para. 2.7), but after the party making the application has come on to the court record. For a claimant this is after proceedings are issued, and for a defendant it is after service is acknowledged or a defence is filed (**CPR, r. 25.2(2)**). Applications for interim relief should be dealt with expeditiously, because delay might frustrate the purpose for which the application was made (*E. E. and Brian Smith (1928) Ltd v Hodson* [2007] EWCA Civ 1210, LTL 23/11/2007). In the case of an interim injunction, a delay of three or four weeks in announcing the decision or giving reasons was regarded as too long.

PRE-ACTION INTERIM REMEDIES

A claimant may exceptionally make an application for an interim order before the commence- **32.5**
ment of proceedings (see **CPR, r. 25.2(2)(b)**) if either:

(a) the matter is urgent; or

(b) it is otherwise desirable to grant the interim remedy before the claim is brought in the interests of justice.

The courts may thus entertain pre-commencement applications for urgent interim injunctions (such as some libel cases where publication is threatened within hours of the applicant finding out about the matter) and some applications for freezing injunctions and search orders. If the application is to be served, the rules on service of claim forms apply (**r. 6.2(c)**).

If a pre-action interim remedy is granted, the court should give directions requiring a claim to be commenced (**r. 25.2(3)**). **Rule 25.2(4)** points out that such directions need not be given where an order is made for pre-action disclosure or inspection under the Senior Courts Act 1981, s. 33, or the County Courts Act 1984, s. 52 (see **50.84**). This is because such an order may result in the applicant deciding not to bring substantive proceedings at all, as recognised in *Dunning v United Liverpool Hospitals' Board of Governors* [1973] 1 WLR 586. The same can be said for *Norwich Pharmacal orders* (see **50.97**), which may not result in the true wrongdoer being identified. Normally directions for bringing substantive proceedings are made in other types of pre-action order.

OBLIGATION TO APPLY EARLY

32.6 The obligation to apply early for an interim remedy stems from the overriding objective, which includes ensuring that cases are dealt with expeditiously (**CPR, r. 1.1(2)(d)**).

Parties should normally notify the court of any intention to apply for interim remedies when they file their directions questionnaires (**PD 26, para. 2.2**).

In multi-track cases the appropriate time to consider most forms of interim relief, if possible, is the first case management conference. A party that wishes to invite the court to make directions or orders of types not usually dealt with on case management conferences, and which are likely to be opposed, is required by **PD 29, para. 5.8**, to issue and serve an application returnable at the same time as that set for the case management conference (with a time estimate if it is clear that the time originally allowed for the case management conference will be insufficient, so a fresh date can be fixed). **Paragraph 3.8** expressly says that applications in multi-track cases must be made as early as possible so as to minimise the need to change the directions timetable, and an application to vary a directions timetable laid down by the court (perhaps on its own initiative) must ordinarily be made within 14 days of service of the directions (**para. 6.2**).

There are some express restrictions in the CPR about when some types of application can be made. Examples include summary judgment, which can be applied for only after the defendant has acknowledged service or entered a defence (**r. 24.4(1)**), and interim payments, where a similar restriction applies (**r. 25.6(1)**). Nevertheless, summary judgment (and striking-out) applications should normally be made on or before filing of directions questionnaires (**PD 26, para. 5.3(1)**).

Of course the need for an interim remedy may not become apparent until some later stage. **CPR, r. 25.2(1)(b)**, provides that applications can be made even after final judgment has been given. Where it becomes necessary to make an application shortly before trial, it should be dealt with on the pre-trial review if there will be one (there is a pre-trial review about eight to 10 weeks before the trial in some multi-track cases, see **47.23**). If this is not possible, another option is to make the application at the start of the trial itself.

APPLICATIONS WITHOUT NOTICE

32.7 *The general rule is that all* applications must be made on notice to the other parties (**CPR, r. 23.4(1)**). Exceptions to this rule are only allowed where permitted by a provision in the CPR, a practice direction, or a court order (**r. 23.4(2)**). For example, applications to extend the time for serving a claim form (renewal of process) are permitted without notice (**r. 7.6(4)**), as are applications for permission to issue additional claims after filing of the defence (**r. 20.7(5)**). These are both examples of applications where the opposite party will not be on the court record when the application is made. Other situations where applications may be made without giving notice to the other parties are:

(a) Where the application arises in urgent circumstances, so there is no practical possibility of giving the required minimum of three clear days' notice to the other side. In cases of this sort informal notification should be given to the other parties unless the circumstances require secrecy (**PD 23A, para. 4.2**). Delay by the applicant cannot make an application urgent (*Bates v Lord Hailsham of St Marylebone* [1972] 1 WLR 1373). Giving only one hour's notice for no good reason, combined with a failure to give full and frank disclosure, resulted in an interim injunction being discharged in *Kulkarni v Milton Keynes Hospital NHS Trust* [2008] EWHC 1861 (QB), [2008] LS Law Medical 494. See also the cases at **37.4**. An alternative is to combine the main application with an application to abridge time under **r. 3.1(2)(a)**. Abridging time may be appropriate where a defendant is repeating behaviour previously adjudicated upon (*Secretary of State for the Environment, Food and Rural Affairs v Meier* [2009] UKSC 11, [2009] 1 WLR 2780, at [82]).
(b) Where a party decides to make an application at a hearing that has already been fixed, but there is insufficient time to serve an application notice. In cases of this sort the applicant should inform the other parties and the court (preferably in writing) as soon as possible of the nature of the application, the reason for it, and then make the application orally at the hearing (**PD 23A, para. 2.10**).
(c) Where the application depends on secrecy for its efficacy, such as most applications for freezing injunctions and search orders.

Commentary

Procedure on applications without notice

The procedure for an interim application without notice is summarised in **procedural checklist 19**, which is at the front of the book. **32.8**

Like applications on notice, applications without notice should normally be made by filing an application notice (**CPR, r. 23.3(1)**) in form N244, which must state the order being sought and the reasons for seeking the order (**r. 23.6**). Letters must not be used in place of formal application notices (Chancery Guide, para. 5.54). The prescribed fee is £45 (**CPFO, fee 2.7**). The application notice must also be signed, and include the title of the claim, its reference number and the full name of the applicant. If the applicant is not already a party it should also give the applicant's address for service. If the applicant wants a hearing, that too must be stated (**PD 23A, para. 2.1**). The application should normally be supported by evidence, which should, in addition to setting out the evidence in support of the relief sought, state the reasons why notice was not given (**CPR, r. 25.3(3)**).

By virtue of **r. 39.2**, which applies to all types of hearings, including interim hearings and trials, applications made without notice will in general be held in public. However, sometimes one of the exceptions may apply, such as publicity defeating the object of the application (as in applications for freezing injunctions and search orders) or the application being made without notice and it being unjust to the respondent for there to be a public hearing (**r. 39.2(3)(a) and (e)**). In any event, most applications will be heard in chambers even if technically they are being dealt with in public.

Legal representatives acting for the applicant are under a duty to provide full notes of the hearing to all parties affected by the order (*Interoute Telecommunications (UK) Ltd v Fashion Gossip Ltd* (1999) *The Times*, 10 November 1999, freezing injunctions and search orders; *Cinpres Gas Injection Ltd v Melea Ltd* [2005] EWHC 3180 (Pat), *The Times*, 21 December 2005, interim injunctions). This is to ensure other parties know exactly what happened, the basis and material on which the order was made, and so they can make an informed decision whether to apply to discharge the order. Applications to set aside or vary are normally made back to the judge who made the original order.

Duty of full and frank disclosure

32.9 Any application made without notice is subject to a duty of full and frank disclosure of matters adverse to the application. These include matters which are known to the applicant and matters which the applicant should have known on making reasonable inquiries. Proper disclosure requires advocates to identify specially all relevant documents for the judge, taking the judge to the particular passages in those documents, and ensuring the judge is aware of the legal significance of the material (*R (Lawer) v Restormel Borough Council* [2007] EWHC 2299 (Admin), [2008] HLR 20). The burden on counsel to ensure that this duty is discharged is all the more onerous on urgent telephone applications (**PD 25A, para. 4.2; 37.6**) where the judge will not have any papers and will know nothing in advance about the case.

The duty is to disclose facts relevant to the matter being decided on the application. What is material depends on the nature of the application. Facts going to granting permission to serve outside the jurisdiction are not relevant on an application for permission to serve by an alternative method (*Albon v Naza Motor Trading Sdn Bhd (No. 2)* [2007] EWHC 327 (Ch), [2007] 1 All ER (Comm) 813 at [47]). While the duty of full and frank disclosure might mean that a without-prejudice document, or the fact it existed, must be disclosed, it was held that failure to make such a disclosure was not a breach of the duty in *Linsen International Ltd v Humpuss Sea Transport Pte Ltd* [2010] EWHC 303 (Comm), LTL 1/3/2010. The defendant had deliberately chosen to withhold information about the without-prejudice negotiation, and neither the fact of the meeting nor what was discussed had any real bearing on the risk of dissipation of assets. The duty is a continuing one, continuing until the application is renewed on notice or until the without notice order is acted upon (*Network Telecom (Europe) Ltd v Telephone Systems International Inc* [2003] EWHC 2890 (QB), LTL 21/10/2003). This duty, and the question of discharging for material non-disclosure, has frequently been an issue in applications for freezing injunctions (see **38.35** for a full discussion), but the principles apply to all applications made without notice.

Applications to set aside or vary

32.10 Where an application is made for an order to be made against a person without notice to that person, the order made on the application must be served on the person together (unless the court orders otherwise) with the application notice and any evidence in support (**CPR, r. 23.9(2)**). The order must, by virtue of **r. 23.9(3)**, contain a statement to the effect that the person against whom it is made has a right to apply to set aside or vary the order within seven clear days of service of the order (**rr. 23.9(3)** and **23.10**). In *Dadourian Group International Inc. v Simms* [2005] EWHC 268 (Ch), [2005] 2 All ER 651, affirmed [2006] EWCA Civ 399, [2006] 1 WLR 2499, a without-notice order was not served in accordance with **r. 23.9(2)** and did not contain the notice required by **r. 23.9(3)**. The defendant was a solicitor. It was held at [24] that while the parties must not flout the CPR, the court had to retain a sense of balance in deciding the consequences of any breach, and refused to discharge the order on this ground.

Rules 23.9 and **23.10** apply to applications to set aside without-notice orders whether or not the original application was supported by an application notice (*Raja v Van Hoogstraten (No. 9)* [2008] EWCA Civ 1444, [2009] 1 WLR 1143). The headnote in this case says that under the court's inherent jurisdiction a party affected by 'an order made without notice' is entitled to have it set aside *ex debito justitiae*, in the sense that the order will be set aside unless the right has been lost, for example, by waiver or estoppel. The relevant part of the judgment (at [79]–[85], and particularly [83]) is focused on orders and judgments which ought to have been applied for on notice, but which (perhaps through being misaddressed) did not come to the attention of the respondent before the hearing (or before a default judgment was entered). References to 'affecting the rights of parties' (e.g. at [84]) should be understood as meaning adversely affecting non-parties served with an order. *Raja v Van Hoogstraten (No. 9)* must not be understood as meaning that legitimately obtained orders made under without-notice applications are set aside as of right. A literal application of the comments in *Raja v Van Hoogstraten (No. 9)* would destroy the essential role played by without-notice orders in providing urgent relief, protection where secrecy is essential, and savings in costs on certain (usually) non-controversial applications as prescribed by the CPR.

Renewing without-notice applications

There are cases where an applicant initially asks the court to consider an application without notice on the papers, and then, being disappointed with the resulting order, wishes to challenge that order. Rather than bringing an appeal, the applicant may ask the same court for an order setting aside or varying that order at a renewed application with a hearing. See *Collier v Williams* [2006] EWCA Civ 20, [2006] 1 WLR 1945, discussed at **32.43**. **32.11**

APPLICATIONS WITH NOTICE

The general rule is that all other parties should be given three clear days' notice of any interim application that may be made (**CPR, rr. 23.4(1)** and **23.7(1)**). While pre-action applications are treated as claim forms for the purposes of the rules on service (**r. 6.2(c)**), applications in pending proceedings are governed by **rr. 6.20 to 6.29**. Advance notice should be given of the grounds on which an interim order is sought. A particular example is an application to discharge a freezing injunction on the ground of material non-disclosure, where specific notice of the grounds of the application must be given (*Bracken Partners Ltd v Gutteridge* (2001) LTL 16/1/2002). The procedure for an interim application with notice is summarised in **procedural checklist 20**, which is at the front of the book, and there is a detailed discussion in **32.13** to **32.31**. Even if an application is misconceived or hopeless, the respondent should not cross-apply to strike out the first application, but should simply oppose it, as issuing such a cross-application wastes costs (*Arkin v Borchard Lines Ltd (No. 2)* (2001) LTL 21/6/2001). **32.12**

There is no requirement to give three days' or any other notice to a party of conditions or orders in the nature of sanctions which the court decides to impose after hearing an application (*Anglo-Eastern Trust Ltd v Kermanshahchi* [2002] EWCA Civ 198, [2002] CP Rep 36; *Olatawura v Abiloye* [2002] EWCA Civ 998, [2003] 1 WLR 275 at [29]).

Documentation

An interim application should normally be made by filing an application notice stating the order being sought and the reasons for seeking the order (**CPR, rr. 23.3(1)** and **23.6**). The application notice must be signed, and should include the title of the claim, its reference number and the full name of the applicant. If the applicant is not already a party it should also give the applicant's address for service. If the applicant seeks a hearing, that must be stated (**PD 23A, para. 2.1**). If the applicant wants the application dealt with by a telephone hearing, that must also be stated (**para. 6.1A**). The application should normally be supported by written evidence setting out the facts justifying the relief sought (**CPR, r. 25.3(2)**). The notice must be filed at court together with the prescribed fee (£80, **CPFO, fee 2.6**), and served as soon as possible thereafter (**r. 23.7(1)**). The standard form of application notice is form N244. **32.13**

On receipt of the application notice the court may either notify the parties of the time and date of the hearing, or notify them that it proposes to consider the application without a hearing (**PD 23A, para. 2.3; CPR, r. 23.8(c)**).

Any application for a court order requires an application notice unless this is dispensed with (**r. 23.3(2)(b)**) or where a rule or practice direction permits an application without an application

Commentary

notice (**r. 23.3(2)(a)**). Unless these exceptions apply it is impermissible to apply by letter (*R (Simmons) v Bolton Metropolitan Borough Council* [2011] EWHC 2729 (Admin), LTL 14/11/2011).

Applications by persons who are not parties

32.14 Persons who are not parties may make applications in existing proceedings in a number of circumstances. These include applications to intervene in the proceedings (see **14.65**) and applications by third parties to vary the terms of injunctions (see **38.31**). In urgent cases an intending claimant may apply for injunctive relief before a claim form is issued (see **37.4** and **37.5**).

A person who is not already a party who issues an application notice must include a postcode in his address for service on the application notice (**PD 23A, para. 2.1(4)**).

Evidence in support

32.15 The general rule is that applications for interim remedies must be supported by evidence (**CPR, r. 25.3(2)**), but evidence in support is not required when applying for case management directions. Some judgment is required from lawyers when deciding whether they need evidence for their applications. **PD 23A, para. 9.1**, specifically mentions that, as a practical matter, the court will often need to be satisfied by evidence of the facts that are relied on in support of, or for opposing, an application. Sometimes the matter will be put beyond doubt if the court gives directions for filing evidence when it fixes a hearing.

The evidence in support must be filed at court, although the exhibits should not be filed unless the court otherwise directs (**PD 23A, para. 9.6**). The evidence (including exhibits) in support must be served with the application (**CPR, r. 23.7(3)**). The comment by Floyd J in *Re Names at Lloyd's* [2008] EWHC 2960 (Ch), *The Times*, 22 December 2008, that it is sufficient if the evidence in support of an interim application is filed by the time 'it is needed' (relying on **rr. 13.4(3)** and **21.6(4)**) was made without reference to **r. 23.7(3)**. However, it echoes the provisions in the court guides that documents must be served on other parties in sufficient time to enable them to be prepared (Queen's Bench Guide, para. 9.8.6; Chancery Guide, para. 5.50(3)). Any evidence which a respondent wishes to rely upon must be served as soon as possible, and in any event in accordance with any directions the court may have given (**PD 23A, para. 9.4**). The court will not take kindly to respondents who serve evidence in response at the last minute, particularly if this results in a wasted hearing and a need to adjourn.

Four options are available to the applicant regarding the format of the evidence to be used in support of an interim application. They are:

(a) To provide sufficiently full factual information in support of the application in the body of the application notice itself (**CPR, rr. 22.1(3)** and **32.6(2)(b)**), and include a statement of truth in the notice. This is a signed statement that the applicant believes that any facts stated in the application are true (**r. 22.1(4)** and **(6)**; **PD 22, para. 2.1**). A statement of truth of an application notice which did not disclose any facts on which the application (to strike out or give summary judgment on a claim) could be based was regarded as insufficient in *Vectone Services Ltd v Transport Media Ltd* (2011) LTL 10/6/2011.

(b) To rely on the facts stated in a statement of case filed in the proceedings, provided it contains a statement of truth (**CPR, r. 32.6(2)(a)**). This will usually have been previously served and filed, and if so there is no need to reserve or refile (**r. 23.7(5)**).

(c) To rely on witness statements each with statements of truth signed by the witnesses (**rr. 22.1(4)** and **32.6(1)**). The witness statements used may be ones drafted specifically for the interim application, or it may be possible to rely on the main witness statements that have been disclosed on the substantive issues in the case. The general rule is that any fact that needs to be proved at any hearing other than the trial should be proved by the evidence of witnesses in writing (**r. 32.2(1)**), and it is further provided by **r. 32.6(1)** that at hearings other than the trial evidence is to be by witness statement unless the court, a practice direction or any other enactment requires otherwise. Consequently, evidence by witness statement is the primary means of adducing evidence at interim hearings.

(d) To rely on affidavit evidence. **Rule 32.15(2)** allows a witness to give evidence by affidavit at any hearing other than a trial if he or she chooses to do so. This also allows the use of affirmations (**PD 32, para. 1.7**). However, using affidavits may result in the loss of the additional costs over and above the cost of using an ordinary witness statement. There are situations where affidavit evidence is required either by specific court order, or by virtue of a practice direction or other enactment. Affidavits are required, for example, in applications under the Protection from Harassment Act 1997, s. 3(5)(a) (see **88.36**); for certain applications relating to confiscation and forfeiture in connection with criminal proceedings; under the environmental control legislation; and in director disqualification proceedings. **PD 32** and **PD 25A** require affidavit evidence in support of applications for:
   (i) search orders,
   (ii) freezing injunctions,
   (iii) orders to require an occupier to permit another to enter land, and
   (iv) orders for contempt of court.

Affidavits are not used in applications for other types of interim injunction unless specifically ordered by the court.

Unless the form which the evidence in support has to take is prescribed, a party to an interim application may choose the method of adducing evidence in support from the above options. This allows flexibility, and should assist in ensuring applications are prepared in a cost-efficient manner. Form N244 requires the applicant to indicate which type of evidence will be relied upon by ticking an appropriate box. It may on occasion be appropriate to use a combination of these methods. It may also be important to place the background facts of the case before the court (which could be done by use of the statement of case), as well as facts relevant solely to the application in hand (which could be adduced by a specifically drawn-up witness statement or affidavit).

Commentary

Time estimates and judicial pre-reading

A time estimate has to be included on the N244 when an application is issued. This should cover the entire hearing (submissions by both sides, giving any judgment, and applications for costs and permission to appeal, see Chancery Guide, para. 5.51). For hearings likely to exceed two hours the estimate should be discussed between the parties. Where extensive judicial pre-reading is required the parties must inform the court in advance (*Jacobs UK Ltd v Skidmore Owings and Merrill LLP* [2008] EWHC 2847 (TCC), LTL 1/12/2008). **32.16**

Bundles of documents

Sometimes it is appropriate to prepare bundles of documents for interim applications. Often it is sufficient to rely on the application notice, written evidence and exhibits without the need to go to the expense of compiling formal bundles. It is stated in the Chancery Guide, para. 7.9, and the Queen's Bench Guide, para. 7.11.7, that bundles should be prepared for applications heard by judges whenever more than 25 pages are involved, although it must be said that even in straightforward applications it is easy to exceed this. In the Chancery Division, bundles are also required for case management conferences and any interim hearing likely to last at least an hour (Chancery Guide, para. 7.41). The whole point of compiling bundles is to save time and expense (as recognised in the paragraphs of the court guides just cited). If they are used, the general guidance discussed in **chapter 59** should be followed, but bearing in mind that for an interim application it ought to be possible to restrict the number of documents that need to be included. There are plenty of interim applications that do not need all the statements of case, witness statements, etc. **32.17**

All parties should cooperate in agreeing bundles (see, for example, Chancery Guide, para. 7.12), and should make clear whether they are simply agreeing which documents should be included in the bundles, or whether they are also agreeing that the included documents are to be treated as evidence of the facts stated in them and/or that the documents to be included are agreed to be authentic (Chancery Guide, para. 7.13; **CPR, r. 32.19**).

For applications, the applicant should ensure that one copy of the bundle is lodged at court at least two clear days before the hearing (though for a Queen's Bench master's appointment, the bundle should be brought to the hearing, unless the master otherwise directs: Queen's Bench Guide, para. 7.11.8), and that all parties and the court have identical bundles.

Skeleton arguments

32.18 Skeleton arguments are not often used on interim applications before district judges, masters and bankruptcy and Companies Court registrars, but are usually required for hearings before High Court judges and are often used for interim hearings before county court judges. It depends on the complexity of the application. Failing to provide a skeleton argument on a striking-out application was described as 'regrettable' in *Vectone Services Ltd v Transport Media Ltd* (2011) LTL 10/6/2011. Even before High Court judges they are not insisted on if the application is likely to be short or if it is so urgent that preparation of a skeleton argument is impracticable. For applications estimated at one hour or more (Chancery Guide, para. 7.49) skeletons should be delivered to the court with the bundles (see **32.17**). For shorter applications, or urgent applications, they may be delivered the day before the hearing or at the hearing.

According to the Chancery Guide, app. 7, a skeleton argument should provide a concise summary of the party's submissions on the issues raised by the application, and should be as brief as the nature of the case allows. There is a general ceiling of 20 pages of double-spaced A4 paper. It should cite the main authorities relied upon, be divided into numbered paragraphs, be paginated, make use of abbreviations (such as 'C' for claimant, 'A/345' for page 345 of bundle A) and give dates in the form '26.4.2013'. It should not go so far as to argue the case on paper. In more substantial applications it should have a reading list for the judge of the core documents. See also **61.18** and **74.29**. In *Khader v Aziz* [2010] EWCA Civ 716, [2010] 1 WLR 2673, the Court of Appeal deprecated the tendencies:

(a) to produce skeleton arguments that are not skeletal; and
(b) to produce bundles of authorities with unnecessary cases.

The costs of preparing these materials may be disallowed if the guidelines are not followed.

Authorities in skeleton arguments

32.19 Practice Direction (Citation of Authorities) [2001] 1 WLR 1001 provides that the following types of authorities should not be cited unless they establish a new principle or extend the law:

(a) law reports of applications attended by one party only;
(b) applications for permission to appeal;
(c) applications that only decide the application is arguable; and
(d) county court cases (other than to illustrate damages in personal injuries claims or to illustrate current authority where no higher authorities are available).

Lawyers were criticised in *Bank of Scotland v Henry Butcher and Co.* [2003] EWCA Civ 67, [2003] 2 All ER (Comm) 557, for using the *All England Law Reports* and *All England Law Reports Reprint* rather than the *Weekly Law Reports* and *English Reports*. BAILII (British and Irish Legal Information Institute) transcripts of judgments, with neutral citations (which are assigned by BAILII if they have not been given by the court), should only be used if no recognised reports are available and then only if the case really needs to be cited (*A City Council v T* [2011] EWCA Civ 17, [2011] 1 WLR 819).

Practice Direction (Citation of Authorities) [2001] 1 WLR 1001 says that skeleton arguments will have to justify reliance on decisions that merely apply decided law to the facts, and also decisions from other jurisdictions. Decisions of the Court of Justice of the European Union and organs of the European Convention on Human Rights are treated as domestic authorities for this purpose. For each authority cited, the skeleton must state the proposition of law the case demonstrates, and refer to the passages in support. Any bundle or list of authorities must contain a certificate by the advocate that these requirements have been complied with.

Practice Direction (Judgments: Form and Citation) [2001] 1 WLR 194 and Practice Direction (Judgments: Neutral Citations) [2002] 1 WLR 346 introduced a method of neutral citation in the format *Smith v Jones* [2001] EWCA Civ 10 at [30], [2001] QB 124. 'EWCA' stands for England and Wales, Court of Appeal. 'Civ 10' stands for Civil Division, 10th case of 2001. 'At [30]' stands for paragraph 30 of the judgments (with the paragraph numbering continuing into the second and subsequent judgments). This is designed to assist publication of judgments on the Internet. Reports cited in court should be taken from the official *Law Reports*, and only from other series if unavailable from the *Law Reports*. **Practice Direction (Citation of Authorities) (2012)** also provides that it is permissible to cite judgments by means of copies reproduced from electronic sources. Such copies should preferably be in 12-point fonts (although 10- or 11-point fonts are acceptable), and the advocate presenting the report must be satisfied that it has not been reproduced in a garbled form. More detailed guidance on the use of author-ities in appeals, including the use of *Hansard*, which should also be followed in first-instance skeleton arguments, can be found at **74.51** to **74.52**.

Commentary

Chronologies

Skeleton arguments are often accompanied by chronologies. Good chronologies have short entries for the material events, phrased in a non-contentious way to promote agreement with the other parties. **32.20**

Draft orders

Paragraph 12.1 of **PD 23A** says that except in the most simple applications the applicant should bring to the hearing a draft of the order sought. The standard form N244 asks whether a draft of the order sought has been attached. If the order is unusually long or complex, the draft should be supplied on disk as well as on hard copy (**PD 23A, para. 12.1**). Preparing draft orders is particularly important in all types of interim injunction applications, and (although strictly this is turning **PD 23A** on its head) whenever the order is at all complicated or unusual. Draft orders are also useful if a detailed directions timetable needs to be laid down. For almost all other types of application the short particulars of the orders sought normally inserted in the N244 will be sufficient. **32.21**

Service and three days' notice

Where the applicant prepares the application notice, as is usual, the applicant must serve it and evidence in support, except where a rule or practice direction provides that the court will serve, or the court orders otherwise (**CPR, r. 6.21(1)**). The usual methods of service may be used (personal service, service through first class post, document exchange or other delivery service that provides for next-day delivery, leaving it at the address for service, fax or electronic service where allowed by **PD 6A**, and alternative service, see **CPR, r. 6.27**). An irrebuttable presumption of due service applies where one of these methods is used in accordance with the table in **r. 6.26** (*Anderton v Clwyd County Council (No. 2)* [2002] EWCA Civ 933, [2002] 1 WLR 3174). **32.22**

Where the court prepares the application notice, the court will serve it, unless a rule or practice direction provides that a party must serve the document, or the party on whose behalf the document is to be served notifies the court that the party wishes to serve it, or the court orders otherwise (**r. 6.21(2)**). Where the court is to serve a document, it is for the court to decide which method of service is to be used (**r. 6.21(3)**). When the court is to effect service, the applicant must file with the court copies of the evidence in support for service on the respondents and a copy of any draft order prepared on behalf of the applicant. There is no requirement to refile or re-serve documents which have already been filed or served at an earlier stage (**CPR, r. 23.7(5)**).

Service must be effected as soon as possible after the application is issued, and in any event not less than three days before it is to be heard (**r. 23.7(1)**). In accordance with the general rules on computing time in **r. 2.8**, this means clear days (excluding the date of effective service and the date of the hearing), and, because the period is less than five days, also excluding weekends, bank holidays, Christmas and Good Friday. Take, for example, a hearing which is listed for Wednesday 13 March 2013. Assume the solicitor for the applicant decides to serve the application and evidence in support by document exchange. The three clear days before the hearing are Friday 8 March, Monday 11 March and Tuesday 12 March. The documents must therefore arrive on Thursday 7 March, and given the provision in **r. 6.26** that documents transmitted by DX are deemed to be served on the second day after being left at the document exchange, the latest the documents could be left at the document exchange would be Tuesday 5 March 2013.

Disposal without a hearing

32.23 **CPR, r. 23.8**, provides that the court may deal with an interim application without a hearing if:

(a) the parties agree the terms of the order; or
(b) the parties agree that the court should dispose of the application without a hearing (the applicant's view on whether there should be a hearing should be stated in the application notice); or
(c) the court does not consider that a hearing would be appropriate.

A party dissatisfied with any order or direction made without a hearing is able to apply to have it set aside, varied or stayed (**r. 3.3(5)(a)**). Such an application must be made within seven days after service of the order, and the right to make such an application must be stated in the order (**r. 3.3(5)(b)** and **(6)**). See also renewing interim applications at **32.44**.

In *Irwin Mitchell Solicitors v Patel* [2003] EWCA Civ 633, LTL 15/4/2003, an application for disclosure of documents, which resulted in an 'unless order', was marked to be dealt with without a hearing. Although the respondent should have been served with the application, this was not done. Ultimately, all the orders flowing from the application notice were set aside because of the procedural irregularity.

Hearings by telephone

32.24 Active case management in accordance with the overriding objective includes dealing with cases without the parties needing to attend court, and by making use of technology (**CPR, r. 1.4(2)(j)** and **(k)**). Both may be achieved by dealing with some applications by telephone conference calls, which is specifically provided for by **r. 3.1(2)(d)**. The rule enables the court to hold a hearing by telephone or any other method of direct oral communication, so other means of electronic communication may be used as technology develops.

District Registries of the High Court and county courts in which telephone conferencing facilities are available are termed 'telephone conference enabled courts' (**PD 23A, para. 6.1**). Contact details for these courts are given in the Court Finder at the Ministry of Justice website, http://www.justice.gov.uk. At a telephone conference enabled court, the following hearings will be conducted by telephone unless the court orders otherwise:

(a) allocation hearings;
(b) listing hearings; and
(c) interim applications, case management conferences and pre-trial reviews with time estimates of less than one hour (**para. 6.2**).

Even in the above cases, telephone hearings will not be used if the application is made without notice, or if all the parties are unrepresented, or if there are more than four parties who wish to take part (**para. 6.3**). A request for a hearing to take place in the normal way rather than by telephone can be made by letter, which should arrive at court at least seven days before the appointed day (**para. 6.4**). Where there is to be a telephone hearing the application notice must be served as soon as practicable after it has been issued and in any event at least five days before the date of the hearing (**para. 4.1A**).

Where **para. 6.2** does not apply, the court may order an application to be dealt with by telephone either of its own initiative or at the request of the parties (**para. 6.5**). The applicant should state in the application notice whether he seeks an order for a telephone hearing (**para. 6.6**). Orders under **para. 6.5** will not normally be made unless all the parties consent (**para. 6.7**).

If an application is to be heard by telephone, normally the directions set out in **para. 6.10** will apply (and see also **para. 6.8**). There will be a 'designated legal representative', who is usually the solicitor for the applicant (**para. 6.1**), who is responsible for setting up the telephone hearing. In multi-track claims, and in other cases if the court so directs, the designated legal representative is required to file and serve a case summary and draft order no later than 4 p.m. two days before the hearing (**paras 6.11** and **6.12**). Any other documents relied upon must be filed and served by the party relying on them within the same time limit (**para. 6.13**). The conference call for the hearing should be fully connected at least 10 minutes before the time for the hearing (**para. 6.10(5)**), with the call being set up with the designated legal representative (and counsel) being called first, then the other parties and their counsel, and finally the judge (**para. 6.10(4)**). No party or representative may attend in person unless every other party agrees (**para. 6.9**).

Commentary

Orders made on the court's own initiative

As part of the ethos of active case management, the courts are encouraged to exercise their powers on their own initiative where this is appropriate, and to this end **CPR, r. 3.3(1)**, gives the court the power to make orders of its own initiative. This power is intended to be exercised for the purpose of managing the case and furthering the overriding objective (see **r. 3.1(2)(m)**). Orders made in this way must, by virtue of **r. 3.3(5)(b)** and **(6)**, include a statement that parties who are affected may apply within seven days (or such other period as the court may specify) after service for the order to be set aside, varied or stayed. Failing to make an application to vary or set aside is likely to result in the court assuming the orders or directions made were correct in the circumstances then existing (**PD 28, para. 4.2(2)**, for fast track cases; **PD 29, para. 6.2(2)**, for multi-track cases). **32.25**

There is a related power enabling the court to make orders on its own initiative after giving the parties an opportunity of making representations on the matter. Where the court proposes to make such an order it will specify a time within which the representations must be made (**CPR, r. 3.3(2)**). If the court on its own initiative strikes out a statement of case or application, and it considers the claim or application was totally without merit, that fact must be recorded in the court's order, and the court must consider whether to make a civil restraint order (see **r. 3.3(7)** and **14.55**).

Hearings convened on the court's own initiative

In addition, the court has power to fix a hearing for the purpose of deciding whether to make any order it might propose to make of its own initiative. For example, in order to reduce the issues in a case it might convene a summary judgment hearing. Unless some other period is specified in the rules regarding notice, any application convened by the court must be notified to parties likely to be affected by the proposed order at least three clear days in advance (**CPR, r. 3.3(3)**). **32.26**

Court hearing

32.27 The general rule is that interim hearings will be in public (**CPR, r. 39.2**). In practice the public do not attend most hearings before masters and district judges, even if notionally they are heard in public, because most interim applications are conducted in chambers, with limited facilities for accommodating the public. It is sufficient if the door is open, or if there is no sign on the door indicating that the hearing is in private (**PD 39A, para. 1.10**). There is no obligation to provide space for the public, although the judge may, if he or she thinks it appropriate, adjourn to a larger room or court (**para. 1.10**).

In addition to dealing with the specific application that has been made, the court may wish to review the conduct of the case as a whole and give any necessary case management directions. The parties will therefore have to be prepared for this and be able to answer any questions the court may ask (**PD 23A, para. 2.9**). The procedural judge will keep, either by way of a note or a tape recording, brief details of all proceedings, including a short statement of the decision taken at each hearing (**PD 23A, para. 8**).

In most courts applications are given specific hearing times, and are called in one at a time. The main exception are judge's applications in the Chancery Division (see Chancery Guide, para. 5.14). For these the judge sitting has a discretion as to the order in which applications are heard. However, urgent applications and applications affecting the liberty of the subject are given priority, followed by ineffective applications (those which are to be adjourned or have settled), then effective applications usually in order of their time estimates, with the shortest applications being heard earliest. Applications estimated for more than two hours are usually made applications by order. In these cases the applications judge may make a temporary order to preserve the position pending a full hearing of the application. Solicitors or counsel's clerks must then apply to the Chancery Judges' Listing Officer for a date for the hearing of the application. There is also a procedure for interim applications by order by consent. See Chancery Guide, paras 5.15 and 5.20.

Adjournment of applications

32.28 An application may be adjourned (**CPR, r. 3.1(2)(b)**). This power is exercised in accordance with the overriding objective, and similar considerations to those applicable on applications to adjourn trials (see **61.9** to **61.14**) are taken into account. Dealing with an application justly may make it appropriate to adjourn an application so that a party has the time needed to recover its files (*Financial Services Authority v Anderson* [2010] EWHC 308 (Ch), LTL 1/3/2010).

Standard of proof on disputed facts on interim applications

32.29 Imposing the trial standard of proof (on the balance of probabilities) on an issue at an interim hearing is erroneous, and in effect would require the premature trial of the issue or premature expression of the court's view on the merits (*Seaconsar Far East Ltd v Bank Markazi Jomhouri Islami Iran* [1994] 1 AC 438). It would require at least the cross-examination of the makers of the witness statements, which is strongly discouraged on interim hearings (per Lord Steyn in *Canada Trust Co. v Stolzenberg* (No. 2) [2002] 1 AC 1 at p. 13 and Waller LJ in the same case in the Court of Appeal [1998] 1 WLR 547). The comment of Aikens LJ in *Test Claimants in FII Group Litigation v Commissioners of HM Revenue and Customs (No. 2)* [2012] EWCA Civ 57, [2012] 1 WLR 2375 at [33] that 'whatever conditions have to be satisfied must be to the usual standard of proof in civil proceedings unless there is express indication in a statute or rule of court to the contrary' can only be right if it is referring to conditions and issues at trial and other final decisions. The example given by Aikens LJ in footnote 18 is the express requirement to prove civil contempt of court beyond reasonable doubt (see **81.15**). However, the context of Aikens LJ's remarks was an application for an interim payment, which of course is an interim application. The explanation is almost certainly that interim payment applications under **CPR, r. 25.7(1)(c)**, are a special case, given that the rule demands that the court must be 'satisfied' that the claimant 'would obtain judgment', both of which point towards the trial standard being required (see **36.8**).

The normal standard of proof in interim applications is therefore whether any disputed fact is established by a good arguable case (per Lord Nicholls in *Re H (Minors) (Sexual Abuse: Standard of Proof)* [1996] AC 563). An applicant must show a good arguable case that the matter falls within one of the grounds for granting permission to serve outside the jurisdiction (**CPR, r. 6.37**), and it applies to disputes on the grounds giving jurisdiction under the **Brussels I Regulation** (*Kolden Holdings Ltd v Rodette Commerce Ltd* [2008] EWCA Civ 10, [2008] Bus LR 1051). It applies to the merits of the substantive claim in freezing injunction applications (*Ninemia Maritime Corporation v Trave Schiffahrtsgesellschaft mbH & Co. KG* [1983] 1 WLR 1412), and the maximum amount that can be frozen (*Pacific Maritime (Asia) Ltd v Holystone Overseas Ltd* [2007] EWHC 2319 (Comm), [2008] 1 Lloyd's Rep 371).

The 'good arguable case' test is intended to encapsulate the crucial rule that the court must be as satisfied as it can be, given the limitations of an interim application, that factors exist which give the court jurisdiction or justify the exercise of that jurisdiction. Inevitably, the way the test is applied must vary from case to case (*WPP Holdings Italy Srl v Benatti* [2007] EWCA Civ 263, [2007] 1 WLR 2316).

What amounts to a good arguable case depends on what is required to be shown in any particular situation (*Bols Distilleries BV v Superior Yacht Services Ltd* [2006] UKPC 45, [2007] 1 WLR 12 at [28]). There will be a good arguable case where the judge is able to reach a provisional or tentative conclusion on all the admissible evidence that the claimant is probably right on the disputed facts (*Attock Cement Co. Ltd v Romanian Bank for Foreign Trade* [1989] 1 All ER 1189). A good arguable case is one which is better than barely capable of serious argument, yet not necessarily one which the judge believes to have a better than 50 per cent chance of success (*Ninemia Maritime Corporation v Trave Schiffahrtsgesellschaft mbH & Co. KG* [1983] 2 Lloyd's Rep 600 at p. 605). If the argument on one side is clearly better than the argument on the other, that will normally be sufficient to resolve an issue on this test (*Masri v Consolidated Contractors International (UK) Ltd (No. 2)* [2008] EWCA Civ 303, [2009] QB 450 at [88] per Lawrence Collins LJ). To similar effect, in *Bols Distilleries BV v Superior Yacht Services Ltd* Lord Rodger of Earlsferry said at [28] that the applicant has to show it has a much better argument than the respondent on the material available at the hearing on the matter. See also *Deutsche Bank AG v Asia Pacific Broadband Wireless Communications Inc.* [2008] EWCA Civ 1091, [2009] 2 All ER (Comm) 129 at [16].

For various types of application, or issues in applications, case law, or occasionally provisions in the CPR, lay down different standards of proof. Examples are:

(a) serious question on merits (*American Cyanamid Co. v Ethicon Ltd* [1975] AC 396, see **37.21**);
(b) real prospect of success: see **CPR, r. 6.37** (merits in applications for permission to serve outside the jurisdiction), **r. 13.3(1)(a)** (setting aside default judgment), **r. 24.2(a)** (summary judgment), and **r. 52.3(6)(a)** (applications for permission to appeal);
(c) real possibility or grave danger of destruction of evidence (search orders, see **39.9**);
(d) much better argument on the material available, which is used where an issue is effectively determinative of whether the court has jurisdiction (*Canada Trust Co. v Stolzenberg (No. 2)* [1998] 1 WLR 547);
(e) extremely strong prima facie case, which is used in relation to the merits of the substantive claim in applications for search orders, see **39.7**;
(f) high degree of assurance (the merits of the claim in applications for interim mandatory injunctions: *Shepherd Homes Ltd v Sandham* [1971] Ch 340);
(g) overwhelming case, which is on occasions applied on interim injunction applications which finally dispose of the case (*Cayne v Global Natural Resources plc* [1984] 1 All ER 225).

On an interim application it is generally inappropriate for an English court to examine the strength of a proposed claim in a different jurisdiction (*Sybron Corporation v Barclays Bank*

Commentary

plc [1985] Ch 299). All that is required is that the overseas claim is not obviously unsustainable (*Vitol SA v Capri Marine Ltd* [2010] EWHC 458 (Comm), [2011] 1 All ER (Comm) 366 at [40]).

Weight attached to written evidence

32.30 The courts will give the same weight to all forms of written evidence whether they have statements of truth or are sworn. It has always been the case that, unless deponents are called for cross-examination, written evidence adduced on an interim application will usually be accepted as correct for the purposes of the application. A court will not normally go behind a witness statement on an interim hearing except in a clear case (*Vestergaard Frandsen A/S v Bestnet Europe Ltd* [2009] EWHC 2662 (Ch), LTL 25/11/2009). Most applications are dealt with on the basis of facts which are not disputed by the respondent, together with the respondent's version of any disputed facts (*Prince of Wales v Associated Newspapers Ltd* [2006] EWCA Civ 1776, [2008] Ch 57). Cases such as *National Westminster Bank plc v Daniel* [1993] 1 WLR 1453 established that the court would only go behind written evidence if its contents are incredible. In *Shyam Jewellers Ltd v Cheeseman* [2001] EWCA Civ 1818, LTL 29/11/2001, it was stated that choosing between witnesses is the function of the trial judge, and it is only permissible for a judge to go behind a witness statement in an interim application if there is some inherent improbability being asserted or there is extraneous evidence contradicting it.

Facts may be inferred on an interim application from a failure to deal adequately with an issue in response to correspondence or the written evidence in an interim application. In *Pattihis v Jackson* [2002] EWHC 2480 (QB), LTL 22/11/2002, an assistant solicitor left his employment with the claimant to work for the second defendant, taking with him a large number of the claimant's client files. The fact of the removal of the files, and the second defendant's failure to demonstrate a right to the files in the two days following demands for the return of the files, enabled the court to find the files were unlawfully in the second defendant's possession. Evidence from a defendant, who had set up a rival business, to the effect he had not opened certain emails was disregarded in *World Trade Group Ltd v Basanez* (2008) LTL 22/10/2008 given the lack of an explanation of why he had not opened any of his email accounts, and the fact that when examined all the emails in his accounts had been deleted.

Written evidence may be rejected where it is inconsistent with unchallengeable contemporaneous documentation (*Three Rivers District Council v Bank of England (No. 3)* [2001] UKHL 16, [2003] 2 AC 1), or where there has been a failure to include exhibits where the narrative would be expected to be supportable with documentary evidence. Whether exhibits are required depends on the circumstances (*Congentra AG v Sixteen Thirteen Marine SA* [2008] EWHC 1615 (Comm), [2008] 2 Lloyd's Rep 602, where the court regarded an argument that there was no good arguable case on quantum because it was not supported by documents as hopeless).

In *Zappia Middle East Construction Co. Ltd v Clifford Chance* [2001] EWCA Civ 946, in an application for security for costs, there was a conflict of evidence on the claimant's place of residence. The court refused to accept unparticularised second-hand evidence from the claimant's solicitor, the claimant obviously being able to give first-hand and detailed evidence on the matter, and decided the point in a summary way in favour of the applicant.

Facts can also be inferred from the nature of the situation. In *Aims Asset Management Sdn Bhd v Kazakhstan Investment Fund Ltd* [2002] EWHC 3225 (Ch), LTL 23/5/2002, the court found, based on the respondent's location in Kazakhstan but no further evidence, that there was a very substantial, but unquantifiable, risk that enforcement in that country of an English judgment would be extremely difficult and expensive, if not impossible. This comes close to taking judicial notice (see **49.27** to **49.34**) of such facts.

The power to order cross-examination of a witness in an interim application pursuant to **CPR, r. 32.7**, tends to be used only in extreme cases (see *West London Pipeline and Storage Ltd v Total UK Ltd* [2008] EWHC 1729 (Comm), [2008] 2 CLC 258). In an application for a non-party costs order, it was held in *Dweck v Forstater* [2010] EWHC 1874 (QB), LTL 28/7/2010, that a finding that witnesses were, in effect, lying in their witness statements should only have been made after cross-examination of the witnesses.

Summary determination of interim costs

Where an interim application is disposed of in less than a day (which will cover the vast majority of such applications), the court will normally make a summary assessment of the costs of the application immediately after making its order (**PD 44, para. 9.2**). In the absence of a specific order to the contrary, costs assessed summarily are payable within 14 days of the order (**CPR, r. 44.7**). To assist the judge in assessing costs the parties are required by **PD 44, para. 9.5**, to file and serve not less than 24 hours before the interim hearing signed statements of their costs for the interim hearing in form N260 setting out: **32.31**

(a) the number of hours to be claimed;
(b) the hourly rate to be claimed;
(c) the grade of the earner;
(d) the amount and nature of any disbursements other than counsel's fee for attending the hearing;
(e) the amount of the legal representative's costs for attending or appearing at the hearing;
(f) counsel's fees; and
(g) VAT on the above.

Any failure to file or serve a statement of costs, without reasonable excuse, will be taken into account in deciding the costs order to be made on the application (**PD 44, para. 9.6**). In the absence of any aggravating factors, mere failure to serve a statement of costs in compliance with **para. 9.5** should not result in the successful party being deprived of its costs. Instead, the court should consider whether the failure has resulted in any prejudice to the paying party and decide on a proportionate response which will deal with any prejudice found (*MacDonald v Taree Holdings Ltd* [2001] CPLR 439). Options are:

(a) giving the paying party a brief adjournment to consider the statement of costs, then proceeding with the summary assessment, with the judge erring towards a lighter figure;
(b) standing the matter over for a detailed assessment;
(c) standing the matter over for a summary assessment at a later date; and
(d) provided all the parties agree, standing the matter over for the summary assessment to be dealt with in writing.

Immediate summary assessment of costs will be appropriate only where the court decides to order costs in any event. Where the interim costs are to be in the case, assessment will almost certainly be left to the conclusion of the case. In cases where costs are awarded in any event, the court should make a summary assessment there and then, but may decide to give directions for a further hearing to deal with the costs (**PD 44, para. 9.7**). Summary assessment will be unnecessary in cases where the parties have agreed the amount of costs (**para. 9.4**). The court must not make a summary assessment of the costs of a publicly funded party (**para. 9.8**). Nor may it make a summary assessment of the costs of a party under a disability, unless that party's solicitor has waived the right to further costs (**para. 9.9(1)**). These last two sentences do not prevent the court making a summary assessment of any interim costs which it decides are payable by an assisted party or a party under a disability (as reflected in **para. 9.9(2)**), although the court should not make such costs payable immediately (in the case of an assisted paying party) unless it also makes a determination under the **Access to Justice Act 1999, s. 11(1)**, or the Legal Aid, Sentencing and Punishment of Offenders Act 2012, s. 26(1) (for which, see **68.56**).

Non-attendance

The court may proceed in the absence of any party to an application (**CPR, r. 23.11(1)**). When this happens the court has a general discretion to relist the application (see **62.1**). **32.32**

GENERAL POWERS REGARDING INTERIM RELIEF AND ORDERS

32.33 CPR, r. 3.1(2), sets out a non-exhaustive list of orders that may be made for the purpose of managing cases, and **r. 25.1(1)** sets out a non-exhaustive list of interim remedies that may be granted by the court. The **r. 3.1(2)** list includes orders:

(a) extending or shortening time for compliance with rules, orders and practice directions (see **48.23**)
(b) adjourning or bringing forward hearing dates (see **61.7** and **61.9**);
(c) requiring a party or a legal representative to attend court;
(d) directing part of proceedings, such as a counterclaim, to be dealt with as separate proceedings;
(e) dealing with part of a case as a preliminary issue (see **61.57**);
(f) staying all or part of the proceedings generally or to a specified date or event (see **chapter 56**);
(g) consolidating two or more claims, or trying two or more claims on the same occasion (see **14.61**);
(h) deciding the order in which issues are to be tried;
(i) excluding an issue from consideration (see **42.43**); and
(j) to require any party to file and serve a statement of costs (form N260) (see **65.19**).

The **r. 25.1(1)** list of interim remedies includes:

(a) Interim injunctions (see **chapter 37**).
(b) Interim declarations (see **4.20**).
(c) Freezing injunctions, which may also include ancillary disclosure orders (see **chapter 38**).
(d) Search orders (see **chapter 39**).
(e) Orders for the detention, custody, preservation, inspection or sale of, taking samples from or carrying out of experiments on relevant property, or for the payment of income from relevant property (see **41.2**, **41.3**). The order may include authority to enter land in the possession of a party to the proceedings for one of these purposes. 'Relevant property' means property which is the subject of a claim, or as to which any question may arise in a claim.
(f) Orders for interim delivery up of goods pursuant to the Torts (Interference with Goods) Act 1977, s. 4 (see **chapter 40**).
(g) Orders for pre-action disclosure and inspection pursuant to the Senior Courts Act 1981, s. 33, or the County Courts Act 1984, s. 52. For the application of these provisions to disclosure of documents, see **chapter 50**. For their application to inspection of property, see **chapter 41**.
(h) Disclosure or inspection orders against non-parties pursuant to the Senior Courts Act 1981, s. 34, or the County Courts Act 1984, s. 53. For the application of these provisions relate to disclosure of documents, see **chapter 50**. For their application to inspection of property, see **chapter 41**.
(i) Interim payment orders (see **chapter 36**).
(j) An order that a specified fund be paid into court or otherwise secured (see **41.4**).
(k) An order permitting a party seeking to recover personal property to pay money into court pending the outcome of the case, and directing that if this is done, the property shall be given to the party (see **chapter 40**).
(l) An order directing a party to prepare and file accounts relating to the dispute or directing an account to be taken or inquiry to be made by the court (see **CPR, r. 25.1(1)(n)** and **(o)**) (see **34.49** and **chapter 63**).
(m) *An order in intellectual* property proceedings under Directive (EC) 2004/48, art. 9, making the continuation of an alleged infringement subject to the lodging of guarantees (see **CPR, r. 25.1(1)(p)**).

Care has to be taken when the court is asked to use its general powers under **r. 3.1** to make orders equivalent to specific orders which are governed by principles laid down elsewhere in the CPR. Generally, the principles governing the specific procedure should be adopted, although it may be appropriate to adjust the strict requirements of the specific procedure. See *Quest Advisors Ltd v McFeely* [2011] EWCA Civ 1517, LTL 9/12/2011, at **36.7** in relation to interim payments, and *Olatawura v Abiloye* [2002] EWCA Civ 998, [2003] 1 WLR 275, and *Huscroft v P and O Ferries Ltd* [2010] EWCA Civ 1483, [2011] 1 WLR 939, at **48.20** in relation to security for costs.

Where an order imposes a time limit for doing any act, the date for compliance must be expressed as a calendar date, and must include the time of day by which the act must be done (**r. 2.9(1)**). Orders may be made subject to conditions, and may, at the court's discretion, specify the consequences of failing to comply (**r. 3.1(3)**).

If the court dismisses an application, and it considers the application was totally without merit, that fact must be recorded in the court's order, and the court must consider whether to make a civil restraint order (see **r. 23.13** and **14.55**).

Relief where there are proceedings in another jurisdiction

The High Court has power under the **Civil Jurisdiction and Judgments Act 1982, s. 25(1)**, to grant interim relief where proceedings have been or are to be commenced in another jurisdiction. This is discussed in relation to freezing injunctions at **38.6**. The principle underpinning s. 25 is that the High Court should be willing to assist the courts of other jurisdictions by providing interim relief on the same basis as if the High Court was itself seised of the substantive claim (*Kensington International Ltd v Republic of Congo* [2007] EWCA Civ 1128, [2008] 1 WLR 1144). **32.34**

CONSENT ORDERS

Consent orders are divided into those which can be entered on a purely administrative basis, without seeking the approval of a judicial officer, and those that need approval. The court may deal with an application without a hearing if the parties agree on the terms of the order sought (**CPR, r. 23.8(a)**). **32.35**

Administrative consent orders

Administrative entry of consent orders is only permitted where none of the parties is a litigant in person (**CPR, r. 40.6(2)(b)**). By **r. 40.6(3)** only the following types of orders may be entered by this process: **32.36**

(a) judgments and orders for the payment of money;
(b) judgments and orders for the delivery up of goods with or without the option of paying the value of the goods or an agreed value;
(c) orders for the dismissal of the whole or part of proceedings;
(d) Tomlin orders (for the stay of proceedings on agreed terms, which are usually set out in a schedule to the order) and other stays on agreed terms disposing of the proceedings;
(e) orders for the stay of enforcement of a judgment, either unconditionally or on condition that the money due under the judgment be paid by specified instalments;
(f) orders setting aside unsatisfied default judgments;
(g) orders for the payment out of money paid into court;
(h) orders for the discharge from liability of any party; and
(i) orders for the payment, assessment or waiver of costs.

Approved consent orders

Proposed orders or directions which are agreed between the parties must be submitted to the court for scrutiny if either (a) one or more of them is a litigant in person, or (b) any of the **32.37**

Commentary

orders or directions fall outside the list set out at **32.3**. The procedural judge has a discretion to allow or refuse agreed orders and directions. The court will be particularly concerned to ensure that orders and directions that may have been agreed between the parties are consistent with the overriding objective and with the case management structure for the case. The parties may agree the terms for interim orders at or shortly before a hearing, and to submit them to the court for approval. As at present the court will usually expect the agreed terms to be reduced into writing before being submitted to the court, which is often done in a fairly informal manner. If there is time, it may be possible to draw up a formal Tomlin order or other suitable order for approval by the court.

Costs in consent orders

32.38 Where the parties agree to an order by consent in an interim application, they should also agree a figure for costs to be inserted in the consent order, or agree that there should be no order for costs (**PD 44, para. 9.4**). If they cannot agree on a figure for costs, they will need to attend on the appointment. If this happens, costs are unlikely to be allowed for the attendance unless good reason can be shown for the failure to agree the figure for the costs.

DRAWING UP INTERIM ORDERS

Drawing up consent orders

32.39 A consent order must be drawn up in the terms that have been agreed, must be expressed to be 'by consent', and must be signed by the legal representatives of all parties (or, if approved by the court, any litigant in person) affected by the order (**CPR, r. 40.6(7)**). Letters sent to the court by the respective parties signifying their consent to a draft order are sufficient (**PD 23A, para. 10.2**). The order is then filed with the court, which will arrange for it to be sealed, entered in the court records, and sent out to the parties.

Drawing up non-consent interim orders

32.40 CPR, rr. 40.2(2) and 40.3(1)(c), provide that all interim orders have to be drawn up and sealed by the court, unless the court dispenses with the need to do so. Normally the court will take responsibility for drawing up, but:

(a) unless otherwise ordered, every judgment or order in the Queen's Bench Division (including the Admiralty, Commercial, and Technology and Construction Courts, but excluding the Administrative Court) must be drawn up by the parties (**rr. 40.3** and **63.37**);
(b) in any court, the court may order a party to draw up an order; or
(c) a party may, with the permission of the court, agree to draw up an order; or
(d) the court may direct a party to draw up the order subject to checking by the court before it is sealed; or
(e) the court may direct the parties to file an agreed statement of the terms of the order before the court itself draws up the order; or
(f) the order may be entered administratively by consent, in which event the parties will submit a drawn-up version of their agreement for entry.

A party who is required to draw up a judgment is allowed seven days to file it, together with sufficient copies for all relevant parties, failing which any other party may draw it up and file it for sealing (**rr. 40.3(3)** and **40.4(1)**).

Every judgment (apart from judgments on admissions, default judgments and consent judgments) must state the name and judicial title of the judge who made it (**r. 40.2(1)**).

Once an order has been drawn up the court will serve sealed copies on the applicant and respondent, and also on any other person the court may order to be served (**r. 40.4(2)**).

(Service will not be by the court if one of the exceptions set out in **r. 6.21(2)** applies.) The court is given a specific power by **r. 40.5** to order service on a litigant as well as the litigant's solicitor.

Judgments and orders normally take effect from the day they are given or made, not from the time they are drawn up, sealed or served (**r. 40.7**). However, the court is given the power to specify some later date from which the order shall take effect.

REVIEW OF INTERIM DECISIONS

Additional submissions before judgment

Once a hearing has ended, exceptional circumstances should be shown before advocates seek to add to their submissions or introduce additional evidence. It is a long-standing rule of natural justice not to hear one side behind the back of the other. There are exceptions, principally where an advocate has to bring a matter to the court's attention in compliance with the advocate's duty to the court (e.g. so as to ensure the court is not misled, or is aware of an adverse authority, or in compliance with the continuing duty of full and frank disclosure in without-notice applications). Where any post-hearing communication takes place with the judge, the usual principle should be that the other side are provided with copies, and given an opportunity to address the court on those matters. **32.41**

This is an area on which the CPR are silent. It is a potential source of problems, as illustrated by *Albon v Naza Motor Trading Sdn Bhd (No. 2)* [2007] EWHC 327 (Ch), [2007] 1 All ER (Comm) 813, where counsel sent a plethora of emails to the judge after he had commenced writing his judgment.

Reconsideration

The court has a power to reconsider its decision in an interim application at any point up to the time the order is drawn up (*Pittalis v Sherefettin* [1986] QB 868; *Charlesworth v Relay Roads Ltd* [2000] 1 WLR 230). This jurisdiction will only be exercised in exceptional cases where it is in the interests of justice to do so (*Re Blenheim Leisure (Restaurants) Ltd (No. 3)* (1999) *The Times*, 9 November 1999). Circumstances where it may be appropriate to ask the court to reconsider the matter include cases where there has been a plain mistake on the part of the court; a failure to draw to the court's attention facts or points of law that are plainly relevant; the discovery of new facts; and being taken by surprise in circumstances where a party did not have a fair opportunity to present its arguments. **32.42**

Varying and revoking orders

The court has the power to vary or revoke a previous order made under a power conferred by the CPR (**CPR, r. 3.1(7)**). It is suggested that this power should only be used in relation to an interim order where: **32.43**

(a) there has been a material change of circumstances (see **47.32**) — this should be established by evidence, or possibly argument (*Edwards v Golding* [2007] EWCA Civ 416, *The Times*, 22 May 2007);
(b) the original order was made on a without notice application (see **37.71**);
(c) where a party does not attend (see **62.1**);
(d) where a third party is adversely affected by an order made in his absence (see **37.71** and **38.31**); or
(e) where the judge at the earlier hearing was misled in some way, whether innocently or otherwise, about the correct factual position. This would include cases of material non-disclosure on without notice applications.

Collier v Williams [2006] EWCA Civ 20, [2006] 1 WLR 1945, where Dyson LJ at [39], said the only situations where **r. 3.1(7)** can be employed are situations (a) and (e) above, is too narrow. What is clear is that **r. 3.1(7)** cannot be used to have a second attempt relying on the same evidence as on the first application, or where additional evidence or submissions are to be deployed which were available but for whatever reason not used on the first application (*Collier v Williams* at [39]–[40]). In such a case the only available route is to appeal.

Rule 3.1(7) can be used to vary a final costs order to include a non-party costs order (see **68.60**) if it is discovered after judgment that a litigant's costs were being funded by another person (*Latimer Management Consultants Ltd v Ellingham Investments Ltd* [2006] EWHC 3662 (Ch), [2007] 1 WLR 2569).

It is probable that the specific power to revoke given by **r. 3.1(7)** only applies to orders made since the CPR came into force (*DEG-Deutsche Investitions- und Entwicklungsgesellschaft mbH v Koshy (No. 2)* [2004] EWHC 2896 (Ch), [2005] 1 WLR 2434). It applies to case management decisions, not to final orders and judgments such as orders to approve settlements of persons under a disability (*Roult v North West Strategic Health Authority* [2009] EWCA Civ 444, [2010] 1 WLR 487). An order was revoked under **r. 3.1(7)** in *Edwards v Golding* [2007] EWCA Civ 416, *The Times*, 22 May 2007, rather than requiring an appeal by a misjoined party. Where an order is set aside, the court has a discretion to preserve the effect or protection of steps taken between the original order and setting aside (*Raja v Van Hoogstraten (No. 9)* [2007] EWHC 1743 (Ch), *The Times*, 23 August 2007, [2008] EWCA Civ 1444, [2009] 1 WLR 1143 at [104]–[105]).

While there is no jurisdictional ban on using **r. 3.1(7)** to revoke or vary a final order, the public interest in finality in litigation will generally mean that something more than a material change of circumstances or the judge having been misled will be needed before the power is exercised (*Kojima v HSBC Bank plc* [2011] EWHC 611, [2011] 3 All ER 359). Great caution is needed if the court is asked to vary an order made at trial (*Mid Suffolk District Council v Clarke* [2006] EWCA Civ 71, [2006] Env LR 38).

Renewing interim applications

32.44 The general principle is that it is incumbent on the parties to bring their whole case to the court at the relevant hearing. If they choose to hold back some of their evidence or arguments, they are not, generally, permitted to have a second attempt, deploying further arguments. There are limits to this general principle:

(a) Most decisions can be reviewed on appeal (see **chapter 74**). There are restricted grounds on which an appeal can be brought (see **75.6**), and generally permission must be sought if an appeal is to be brought (see **74.12**). Although sometimes fresh evidence can be adduced on an appeal, there are severe restrictions on when this will be permitted (see **75.16**).

(b) Interim orders can be varied or revoked by a court at the same level as the court that made the original order where there has been a change of circumstances (see **32.42**).

(c) Where the court makes an order of its own initiative, without hearing the parties or giving them an opportunity to make representations, a party affected by the order may apply, within seven days of being served with it, for it to be set aside, varied or stayed (**CPR, r. 3.3(4)** and **(5)**). Where an application notice includes a request for the application to be dealt with without a hearing, and the court accedes to that request, it is **r. 23.8(c)** that applies rather than **r. 23.8(b)** (*Collier v Williams* [2006] EWCA Civ 20, [2006] 1 WLR 1945 at [30]–[37]). This is because the agreement referred to in **r. 23.8(b)** is one between the parties, rather than an agreement with the court. Consequently, the court will treat this situation as if the eventual order were an order the court made on its own initiative (**PD 23A, para. 11.2**), which means either party may apply to have the order varied or set aside under **r. 3.3(5)** (*Collier v Williams* at [30]). The proper practice is to decide any application under **r. 3.3(5)** at a hearing rather than on paper, to prevent repeat applications (*Collier v Williams* at [37]). In situations where the parties agree the terms of the order (**r. 23.8(a)**) or agree to the application being disposed of without a hearing (**r. 23.8(b)**), it is only the respondent who may apply to have the order set aside or varied (under **r. 23.10**).

(d) The court has power to adjourn a hearing under **CPR, r. 3.1(2)(b)**, which it can use while a hearing is part-heard to allow a party to return on a future date with additional evidence.

Beyond this, it is submitted, the court should not go. A first-instance decision, *Laemthong International Lines Co. Ltd v ARTIS* [2004] EWHC 2226 (Comm), [2004] 2 All ER (Comm) 797, appears to have taken an additional, forbidden step. Colman J held that a judge has jurisdiction to hear a without notice application for a freezing injunction despite the same application having been heard and dismissed on two previous occasions by two different judges. Plainly, the duty of full and frank disclosure requires an applicant who is renewing an application to disclose to the court all previous unsuccessful attempts (see **32.9**). While Colman J said that another judge will normally dismiss a renewed application, this is not strong enough, and the correct position is that the renewed application must be dismissed unless there has been a material change of circumstances.

Chapter 33 Striking Out

The following procedural checklist, which is at the front of the book, is relevant to this chapter:

Procedural checklist 21 Application for striking out

INTRODUCTION

33.1 By **CPR, r. 3.4**, the court has the power to order the whole or any part of a statement of case to be struck out. This power may be resorted to on an application by a party seeking to attack the statement of case drafted by the other side. It may also be used by the court of its own initiative. This may be because of failure to comply with the requirement to give a concise statement of the facts on which the claimant relies (**r. 16.4(1)(a)**) or the requirement to give the reasons for any denial in a defence (**r. 16.5(2)(a)**). A related use of the power is where it is alleged that a statement of case, even if its contents are assumed to be true, does not amount to a sustainable claim or defence as a matter of law. Striking out is also used to prevent the misuse of the right to issue proceedings, on the ground that proceedings are an abuse of process. These facets of the jurisdiction to strike out will be considered in this chapter.

Striking out is also used as a means of enforcing compliance with the general provisions of the CPR, practice directions and court orders and directions as part of the court's case management functions. This aspect of striking out will be considered in **chapter 48**.

Once a claim is struck out there are no subsisting proceedings that can provide a platform for making interim applications (*Mireskandari v Associated Newspapers Ltd* [2010] EWHC 967 (QB), 160 NLJ 695). All that can be done after a claim is struck out is to appeal, assess damages, assess *costs, enforce judgment* or deal with false statement of truth.

It is recognised in several places in the CPR that striking out under **r. 3.4** is closely related to the jurisdiction to enter summary judgment under **Part 24**, discussed in **chapter 34** (see, for example, **PD 3A, paras 1.2, 1.7** and **6.1**; the note to **CPR, r. 24.2**; and **PD 26, para. 5.2**). Both powers are used to achieve the active case management aim of summarily disposing of issues that do not need full investigation at trial (**CPR, r. 1.4(2)(c)**). As they are closely related, it is very common for parties to make applications in suitable cases for striking out and summary judgment in the alternative, although in *Clarke v Davey* [2002] EWHC 2342 (QB), LTL 11/11/2002, it was said that the right course is to apply only for summary judgment. In *Three Rivers District Council v Bank of England (No. 3)* [2001] UKHL 16, [2003] 2 AC 1, Lord Hope of Craighead said, that under **r. 3.4** the court generally is only concerned with the statement of case which it is alleged discloses no reasonable grounds for bringing or defending the claim. In *Monsanto plc v Tilly* [2000] Env LR 313 Stuart-Smith LJ said that **r. 24.2** gives a wider scope for dismissing a claim or defence. The court should look to see what will happen at the trial and, if the case is so weak that it has no reasonable prospects of success, summary judgment should be entered. There is an inevitable overlap between the two concepts. Some allegations will be factually weak and aptly described as disclosing no reasonable grounds within the meaning of **r. 3.4**. Procedural judges are under a duty to narrow the issues as part of their case management functions under **Part 1** and have the power to treat an application to strike out as one for summary judgment in order to dispose of issues or claims that do not deserve full investigation at trial (*Three Rivers District Council v Bank of England (No. 3)* at [88]).

THE MAIN RULE

CPR, r. 3.4(2), provides: **33.2**

The court may strike out a statement of case if it appears to the court—

(a) that the statement of case discloses no reasonable grounds for bringing or defending the claim;
(b) that the statement of case is an abuse of the court's process or is otherwise likely to obstruct the just disposal of the proceedings; or
(c) that there has been a failure to comply with a rule, practice direction or court order.

By **r. 3.4(1)** references in **r. 3.4(2)** to a statement of case include references to part of a statement of case. A claim may fall within **r. 3.4(2)(b)** where it is vexatious, scurrilous or obviously ill-founded (**PD 3A, para. 1.5**).

In addition, the High Court retains its power to strike out under its inherent jurisdiction, as **CPR, r. 3.4(5)**, provides that **r. 3.4(2)** does not limit any other power of the court to strike out a statement of case (*Re Abermeadow Ltd* [2000] 2 BCLC 824).

PROCEDURE ON APPLICATIONS MADE BY PARTIES

An application to strike out made by a party should be brought by issuing an application notice in accordance with the procedure in **CPR, Part 23** (see **chapter 32**). **PD 3A, para. 5.2**, says that while many applications to strike out can be made without evidence in support (the poor drafting of the statement of case may be self-evident, or the point may be one of law on which no evidence would be required), the applicant should always consider whether facts need to be proved. If so, evidence in support should usually be filed and served, unless the facts relied upon have already been adequately evidenced in, say, a statement of case which included a statement of truth. However, careful consideration should be given before relying on a statement of case in this way. **33.3**

In accordance with **PD 23A, para. 2.7**, any application to strike out should be made as soon as it becomes apparent that it is desirable to make it. Applications to strike out should normally be made in the period between acknowledgment of service and filing of directions questionnaires (**PD 26, para. 5.3(1)**, and see also **PD 3A, para. 5.1**).

Commentary

There will be cases where it may be appropriate to seek striking out or summary judgment in the alternative (**PD 3A, para. 1.7**; see **33.1**).

Effect on default and summary judgment and allocation

33.4 If a striking-out application is issued before the defence is filed, default judgment cannot be entered until the striking-out application has been disposed of (**CPR, r. 12.3(3)**). If a striking-out application is dealt with before allocation and the claim survives, the court may be in a position to dispense with the need to file directions questionnaires, and may allocate the case and make case management directions at the end of the striking-out hearing (**PD 26, para. 2.4**). If a striking-out application is contemplated, but has not been dealt with by the time directions questionnaires have to be returned, the intention to make the application should be included as extra information provided when the questionnaire is returned (**PD 26, para. 2.2(3)(a)**).

PD 26, para. 5.3(2), provides that where a party makes an application to strike out before the claim has been allocated to a track the court will not allocate the claim before hearing the application. By **PD 26, para. 5.3(3)** and **(4)**, where a party files a directions questionnaire and states an intention to strike out but has not yet done so, the judge will usually direct that an allocation hearing is listed. The striking-out application may be heard at the allocation hearing if the application notice has been issued and served in sufficient time.

REFERENCES BY COURT OFFICERS

33.5 A claim form that has been lodged for issuing may be referred by a court official to the judge (**CPR, r. 3.2**), and this power may be exercised where it is felt that the claim form (which in context means the particulars of claim) is amenable to being struck out under (see **PD 3A, para. 2.1**). The judge may then make an order designed to ensure that the claim is disposed of, or proceeds, in a way that accords with the rules. The judge has a discretion whether to hear the claimant before making such order as may be appropriate (**para. 2.3**). If an order is made without giving notice to the claimant, **CPR, rr. 23.9** and **23.10**, apply, so that the order has to include a statement that the claimant has the right within seven days after service of the order to apply to vary or set it aside.

One option available to the judge is to order a stay to allow the claimant an opportunity of putting the claim on a proper footing. This may take the form of a simple stay until further order, or an order that the claim form shall not be served until the stay is lifted, or an order that no application to lift the stay shall be made until the claimant files specified further documents, such as amended particulars of claim or a witness statement (**PD 3A, para. 2.4**). If the claimant does what the judge requires, and the stay is lifted, the judge may give directions regarding service of the order and any other documents on the court file (**para. 2.5**). The fact that the judge allows the claim to proceed does not preclude the defendant from making an application to strike out or for summary judgment once proceedings are served (**para. 2.6**).

Similar powers are available where a court official believes a document purporting to be a defence is amenable to being struck out (**para. 3**). A stay would be inappropriate in this situation, but the judge may strike out the defence on his or her own initiative, or allow the defendant an opportunity to file an amended defence, or may require the defendant to provide further information to clarify the defence within a stated time, failing which the judge may order the defence to be struck out. The fact that a judge does not strike out a defence under this power does not prejudice the claimant's right to apply for such an order or any other order.

GENERAL TEST

Under the old rules it was well settled that the jurisdiction to strike out was to be used sparingly. The reason was, and this has not changed, that the exercise of the jurisdiction deprives a party of its right to a trial, and of its ability to strengthen its case through the process of disclosure and other court procedures such as requests for further information. Further, it has always been true that the examination and cross-examination of witnesses often changes the complexion of a case. It was accordingly the accepted rule that striking out was limited to plain and obvious cases where there was no point in having a trial. **33.6**

Under the CPR it is part of the court's active case management role to identify the issues at an early stage and to decide which issues need full investigation at trial, and to dispose summarily of the others (**CPR, r. 1.4(2)(b)** and **(c)**). In *Swain v Hillman* [2001] 1 All ER 91 (a summary judgment case), Lord Woolf MR said that Part 24 applications had to be kept within their proper limits, and were not meant to be used to dispense with the need for a trial where there were issues which should be considered at trial. The same could be said in relation to striking out under **r. 3.4**. In the same vein, before using **r. 3.4** to dispose of 'side issues', care should be taken to ensure that a party is not deprived of the right to trial on issues essential to its case. In *McPhilemy v Times Newspapers Ltd* [1999] 3 All ER 775, one of the first cases decided under the CPR, the Master of the Rolls said that the powers of the court to restrain excess do not extend to preventing a party from putting forward allegations which are central to its case. That said, it is open to the court to attempt to control how those allegations are litigated with a view to limiting costs.

Commentary

The leading case under the old rules was *Williams and Humbert Ltd v W. and H. Trade Marks (Jersey) Ltd* [1986] AC 368. The claimant's application to strike out the defence took seven days to argue before the judge, six days in the Court of Appeal, and four days in the House of Lords. The case reiterated the point that striking out was only appropriate in plain and obvious cases. Sometimes, a case would only become clear after protracted argument. Lord Templeman said that:

> if an application to strike out involves a prolonged and serious argument the judge should, as a general rule, decline to proceed with the argument unless he not only harbours doubts about the soundness of the pleading but, in addition, is satisfied that striking out will obviate the necessity for a trial or will substantially reduce the burden of preparing for trial or the burden of the trial itself.

A judge may therefore refuse to hear a striking-out application if: (a) the application is unlikely to succeed; or (b) the application will not be decisive or appreciably simplify the eventual trial (see *Morris v Bank of America National Trust* [2000] 1 All ER 954). It is generally improper to conduct what is in effect a mini-trial involving protracted examination of the documents and facts as disclosed in the written evidence on a striking-out application (*Wenlock v Moloney* [1965] 1 WLR 1238), although such a detailed analysis is sometimes appropriate in striking-out applications in relation to unfair prejudice petitions under the Companies Act 2006, s. 994 (*Morris v Bank of America National Trust*).

The principles from *Williams and Humbert Ltd v W. and H. Trade Marks (Jersey) Ltd*, *Wenlock v Moloney* and *Morris v Bank of America National Trust* were approved in *Three Rivers District Council v Bank of England (No. 3)* [2001] UKHL 16, [2003] 2 AC 1 at [96]–[97]. No adjustment is made to the test where one party is suffering from an inequality of arms (*Bank of Tokyo-Mitsubishi UFJ Ltd v Baskan Gida Sanayi ve Pazarlama AS* [2008] EWHC 659 (Ch), LTL 17/4/2008).

If an application to strike out is unsuccessful, the claim will proceed towards trial. In such cases it may be considered undesirable for the judge or master to express any reasons as to why that decision has been made (*Re Baltic Real Estate Ltd (No. 1)* [1993] BCLC 498).

NO REASONABLE GROUNDS FOR BRINGING OR DEFENDING THE CLAIM

33.7 Applications under **CPR, r. 3.4(2)(a)**, may be made on the basis that the statement of case under attack fails on its face to disclose a sustainable claim or defence. Traditionally this has been regarded as restricted to cases which are bad in law, or which fail to plead a complete claim or defence. In practice the rule is regarded as shading into applications for summary judgment, which have traditionally been regarded as a means for attacking cases which are weak on the evidence. For example, in *Freer v Zeb* [2008] EWHC 212 (QB), LTL 21/2/2008, a claim that the defendant was vicariously liable for the actions of certain people was struck out, because all the evidence pointed to them being employed not by the defendant but by a company of which the defendant was a director.

On hearing such an application it will be assumed that the facts alleged by the respondent are true (see *Morgan Crucible Co. plc v Hill Samuel and Co. Ltd* [1991] Ch 295 per Slade LJ). For purists it ought to be unnecessary to seek to undermine the claim or defence with evidence in support of the application. The rules do not, however, contain any express ban on adducing evidence in support: **r. 25.3(2)** provides that applications must be supported by evidence unless the court otherwise orders, and **PD 3A, para. 5.2**, leaves open the option of adducing evidence in support. In claims for breach of written contracts, including cases where the contractual obligations are contained in more than one document, the courts have always been willing to consider the contractual documents to decide whether there is an arguable case on a strike-out application. A counterclaim was struck out on this basis in *Al-Dawood Shipping Lines Ltd v Dynastic Maritime Inc.* [2010] EWCA Civ 104, LTL 19/2/2010.

In deciding whether to strike out, the judge should consider the effect of the order. In *Watson v Ian Snipe and Co.* [2002] EWCA Civ 293, LTL 21/2/2002, there were parallel proceedings against two firms of solicitors, which had successively been retained by the claimants in an unsuccessful claim. It was held to have been inconsistent with sound case management principles to have struck out the claim against one of the firms, because this added to the overall complexity of the proceedings.

A number of examples of statements of case open to attack under **CPR, r. 3.4(2)(a)**, are given by **PD 3A**. A claim may be struck out if it sets out no facts indicating what the claim is about (such as a claim simply saying it is for 'Money owed £5,000'), or if it is incoherent and makes no sense, or if the facts it states, even if true, do not disclose a legally recognisable claim against the defendant. A defence may be struck out if it consists of a bare denial or otherwise fails to set out a coherent statement of facts, or if the facts it sets out, even if true, do not amount in law to a defence to the claim. Many institutional defendants have been in the habit of filing short defences making blanket denials without stating any positive case. These defences ought to be a thing of the past. See **chapters 24** and **26**.

Some prospects of success

33.8 Under the old rules, a cause of action with some prospects of success would not be struck out. Provided the statement of case raised some question fit to be tried, it did not matter that the case was weak or unlikely to succeed (*Wenlock v Moloney* [1965] 1 WLR 1238), one of the leading cases under the old rules, and *Chan U Seek v Alvis Vehicles Ltd* [2003] EWHC 1238 (Ch), *The Times*, 16 May 2003, which adopted the same test under the CPR). Judges often apply the test of *whether the claim is bound to fail*, so that even a case 'fraught with difficulty' will not be struck out (*Smith v Chief Constable of Sussex* [2008] EWCA Civ 39, [2008] PIQR P12; *K v Central and North West London Mental Health NHS Trust* [2008] EWHC 1217 (QB), [2008] PIQR P19). The apparent implausibility of a case on paper is not in itself enough to justify striking it out (*Merelie v Newcastle*

Primary Care Trust [2004] EWHC 2554 (QB), *The Times*, 1 December 2004). Nor is it appropriate to strike out a claim where the central issues are in dispute (*King v Telegraph Group Ltd* [2003] EWHC 1312 (QB), LTL 9/6/2003). In *Top Layers Interior Ltd v Azure Maritime Holdings SA* [2007] EWHC 2844 (QB), LTL 10/12/2007, a statement of case alleging the parties had orally agreed a term that time was of the essence was regarded as having no prospect of success where there had been no complaints at the time.

According to Potter LJ in *Partco Group Ltd v Wragg* [2002] EWCA Civ 594, [2002] 2 Lloyd's Rep 343 at [46], cases where striking out under **CPR, r. 3.4(2)(a)**, is appropriate include:

(a) where the statement of case raises an unwinnable case where continuing the proceedings is without any possible benefit to the respondent and would waste resources on both sides (*Harris v Bolt Burdon* [2000] CPLR 9); and
(b) where the statement of case does not raise a valid claim or defence as a matter of law (*Price Meats Ltd v Barclays Bank plc* [2000] 2 All ER (Comm) 346).

A cause of action that is unknown to the law will be struck out, such as a claim alleging abuse of civil proceedings (*Ustimenko v Prescot Management Co. Ltd* [2007] EWHC 1853 (QB), LTL 20/8/2007). Subject to the court giving permission to amend, a statement of case will be struck out that omits some material element of the claim or defence. A statement of case ought also to be struck out if the facts set out do not constitute the cause of action or defence alleged, or if the relief sought would not be ordered by the court. A defence may be struck out if it does not answer the claim being made. However, purely technical objections to the form of statements of case will not be entertained, provided the statement of case is sufficient to allow the other side to have a fair trial (*Morris v Bank of America National Trust* [2000] 1 All ER 954).

Sinclair Investment Holdings SA v Versailles Trade Finance Ltd [2005] EWCA Civ 722, [2006] 1 BCLC 60, was a claim for breach of fiduciary duty based on an assumption of a duty of loyalty (as opposed to the more usual director and trustee situations) with an alternative claim in constructive trust. It was held that the assumption of loyalty element was sufficiently pleaded by allegations that the defendant controlled, or was in a position to control, the exercise of powers over the claimant's money. The constructive trust claim was pleaded in novel circumstances, but there was no authority against liability being established on the pleaded facts (which included actual fraud), so this was allowed to proceed.

In *Taylor v Inntrepreneur Estates (CPC) Ltd* (2001) LTL 7/2/2001 the claimant brought a claim seeking a declaration that a lease agreement had come into force, damages for breach of the lease, and damages for misrepresentation resulting from having entered into the alleged lease. On the documents it was clear that throughout the parties had negotiated on a 'subject to contract' basis. It was held that as no written agreement had been signed, no lease had been entered into. It followed that there was no reasonable cause of action, and the claim was struck out. Conversely, in *Cornelius v Hackney London Borough Council* [2002] EWCA Civ 1073, [2003] LGR 178, an application to strike out a misfeasance claim was dismissed because liability turned on whether an official had abused his public office, which was a question of fact. In *Kirk v London Borough of Brent* [2005] EWCA Civ 1701, LTL 8/12/2005, the Court of Appeal said it had been wrong to strike out a nuisance claim which alleged the claimant's property had been damaged by tree roots. While the defendant had been notified of the claim very late, a letter about a similar problem involving a neighbouring property written a year after the damage to the claimant's property had been discovered raised implications about the defendant's state of knowledge which meant the claim was not suitable for striking out.

Points of law

Where the argument involves a substantial point of law which does not admit of a plain and obvious answer, it may be best not to have it determined on a striking-out application. One thing the courts are anxious to avoid is expensive satellite litigation. Instead, sensible case 33.9

management may indicate that it would be better dealt with as a preliminary issue, although dealing with issues in this way sometimes increases costs and delay — see **61.59**.

Where the law is in a state of development, it will usually be inappropriate to decide questions, such as whether a duty of care exists in a novel situation, on hypothetical facts. Such questions are usually best dealt with at trial (*D v East Berkshire Community Health NHS Trust* [2005] UKHL 23, [2005] 2 AC 373, per Lord Bingham of Cornhill at [4]; *Brooks v Commissioner of Police of the Metropolis* [2005] UKHL 24, [2005] 1 WLR 1495, per Lord Bingham of Cornhill at [3]; *Hughes v Richards* [2004] EWCA Civ 266, [2004] PNLR 35).

Claim meriting further investigation

33.10 A similar approach is taken in striking-out applications to that adopted in summary judgment applications (see **34.22**) where the strength of a case may not be clear because it has not been fully investigated. Where there is a real possibility that, on a full investigation of the factual background, any uncertainty on the merits might be remedied, striking out should be refused (*Kyrris v Oldham* [2003] EWCA Civ 1506, [2004] 1 BCLC 305).

Amendment, rectifying errors and disclosure

33.11 The court may allow a party to amend rather than striking out. There have been cases where amendments have been allowed at a very late stage (see, under the old rules, *CBS Songs Ltd v Amstrad Consumer Electronics plc* [1987] RPC 417). An amendment may be allowed on an appeal, even if the amendment has not been raised in the court below (*Islington London Borough Council v Uckac* [2006] EWCA Civ 340, [2006] 1 WLR 1303 at [39]. The power to amend will be exercised in accordance with the overriding objective, and this may militate against giving permission depending on the circumstances of the case (see *Finley v Connell Associates* (1999) *The Times*, 23 June 1999, where permission to amend was granted, and *Christofi v Barclays Bank plc* [2000] 1 WLR 937, where permission was refused). An amendment should only be permitted as an alternative to striking out if there is a real prospect of establishing the amended case (*Charles Church Developments plc v Cronin* [1990] FSR 1; *Savings and Investment Bank Ltd v Fincken* (2001) *The Times*, 15 November 2001).

Where the problem is an error of procedure, the judge has to consider whether to cure the irregularity, which may avoid a striking-out order (*Firth v Everitt* [2007] EWHC 1979 (Ch), LTL 25/9/2007).

Where a claim is arguably so speculative that it discloses no reasonable cause of action or amounts to an abuse of process, instead of striking out the court may be prepared to allow the claim to proceed to enable the claimant to obtain disclosure from the defendant to see whether there is evidence substantiating the claim. If it does not, the defendant would be allowed to reapply for striking out (*Arsenal Football Club plc v Elite Sports Distribution Ltd* [2002] EWHC 3057 (Ch), [2003] FSR 26, where the circumstances pointed towards the defendant having committed some tort, but it was unclear which one).

ABUSE OF PROCESS

33.12 The first half of **CPR, r. 3.4(2)(b)**, gives the court power to strike out a statement of case which is an abuse of the court's process. This is a power 'which any court of justice must possess to prevent misuse of its procedure in a way which, although not inconsistent with the literal application of its procedural rules, would nevertheless be manifestly unfair to a party to litigation before it, or would otherwise bring the administration of justice into disrepute among right-thinking people' (per Lord Diplock in *Hunter v Chief Constable of the West Midlands Police* [1982] AC 529 at p. 536). Applications to strike out for abuse of process should be made shortly after service. Once the defendant has filed a defence and defended on the merits he is taken to have acquiesced, and it is too late to take the point (*Johnson v Gore Wood and Co.* [2002] 2 AC 1; *Coca-Cola Co. v Ketteridge* [2003] EWHC 2488 (Ch), [2004] FSR 29).

Whether there is an abuse of process is a question of judgment to which there is only one correct answer, even though many factors will usually have to be weighed in coming to that judgment. It is not a matter of discretion (*Aldi Stores Ltd v WSP Group plc* [2007] EWCA Civ 1260, [2008] 1 WLR 748).

The court has the power to strike out even a valid claim where there has been an abuse of process, but it is not always correct to do so. Striking out should be the last option. If the abuse can be addressed in some less draconian way, it should be (*Reckitt Benckiser (UK) Ltd v Home Pairfum Ltd* [2004] EWHC 302 (Pat), [2004] FSR 37).

Some striking-out applications are brought on the basis that it is an abuse of process to litigate a very weak claim. It is submitted that this is a misuse of the term 'abuse of process', and that weak claims should be dealt with either as disclosing no reasonable grounds for bringing or defending the claim (see **33.7** to **33.10**) or on an application for summary judgment (**chapter 34**). In so far as there is any validity in striking out on this basis, it was held in *Barrett v Universal-Island Records Ltd* [2003] EWHC 625 (Ch), *The Times*, 24 April 2003, that the court needed to have a high degree of confidence that the claim or defence would not succeed before striking it out as an abuse of process.

Commentary

General examples of abuse of process

A claim that is issued after the expiry of limitation may be struck out as an abuse of process **33.13** (alternatively, the limitation point may be determined as a preliminary issue, or at trial, or by way of an application for a direction under the LA 1980, s. 33), but cannot be struck out on the ground of there being no reasonable cause of action. The reason is that limitation is a procedural defence, so does not prevent there being a cause of action. See *Ronex Properties Ltd v John Laing Construction Ltd* [1983] QB 398.

Issuing a claim form merely to protect the claimant's position at a time when the claimant had not decided to pursue a claim against the defendant is an abuse of process (*Nomura International plc v Granada Group Ltd* [2007] EWHC 642 (Comm), [2008] Bus LR 1). The relevant provision in the CPR (**r. 16.2(1)**) follows the same form and has the same intention as RSC, ord. 6, r. 2. In these circumstances the court properly had regard to the principles behind the pre-CPR case-law. *Sterman v E. W. and W. J. Moore* [1970] 1 QB 596 and *Marshall v London Passenger Transport Board* [1936] 2 All ER 83 decided that failing to include a concise statement on what is now the claim form could only be cured if the claimant had a known and genuine cause of action when the claim was issued. Gaining such knowledge by the time the application to strike out is heard does not cure the abuse. Generally it is an abuse of process to have simultaneously two active, identical, claims against the same defendant. This is because it is oppressive to force a defendant into defending the same claim in multiple proceedings. A claim is active for this purpose once it is served, and it is a common precaution where there is a technical problem with proceedings to issue a second, protective, claim (which is not served) pending resolution of the objections to the first claim. In *Rosenberg v Nazarov* [2008] EWHC 812 (Ch), LTL 10/4/2008, there were two active claims against the defendant, the only difference between the two particulars of claim being two paragraphs. The court declined to strike out the first claim because it was issued eight months before the second, and there were potential limitation problems with the second claim which would not affect the first, and the court took the view that consolidation would avoid any oppression to the defendant.

In *Jameel v Dow Jones and Co. Inc.* [2005] EWCA Civ 75, [2005] QB 946, the claimant brought a defamation claim in respect of an alleged internet libel which had been accessed (apparently) by five people. While there was a reasonable cause of action because of the presumption of damage, the claim was struck out as an abuse of process. The court sought to keep a balance between the right of freedom of expression under the European Convention on Human Rights, **art. 10**, in the **Human Rights Act 1998, sch. 1**, and the need to protect individual rights. As there was only minimal publication and insignificant damage to the claimant's reputation, it was held there was no 'real and substantial tort', with the result that the claim was disproportionate and an abuse of process. *Jameel v Dow Jones and Co. Inc.* has been followed in a number of other defamation claims which engage **art. 10** (*Lonzim plc v Sprague* [2009] EWHC 2838 (QB), LTL 13/11/2009; *Williams v MGN Ltd* [2009] EWHC 3150 (QB), LTL 4/12/2009, where a claimant with convictions for serious offences was held to have no reputation capable of protection by a claim in libel). It will be interesting to see whether this approach will be adopted in cases which do not directly engage Convention rights on the part of the defendant, but which are little more than technical torts, such as many neighbour disputes and claims for minor nuisances.

Withdrawing in bad faith a pre-action admission of liability may be an abuse of process (*Walley v Stoke-on-Trent City Council* [2006] EWCA Civ 1137, [2007] 1 WLR 352, and see the discussion at **34.30**).

Generally, it is an abuse of process for a claimant complaining about a public authority's infringement of the claimant's public law rights to seek redress by way of an ordinary claim rather than by way of judicial review (see *O'Reilly v Mackman* [1983] 2 AC 237). In considering whether to strike out on this ground, the court will take into account whether the claimant has used the ordinary procedure to obtain some advantage not available in judicial review proceedings, and generally whether striking out accords with the overriding objective (*Clark v University of Lincolnshire and Humberside* [2000] 1 WLR 1988). The prohibition is limited to bringing claims, so there is no restriction on raising public law issues in a defence (*Rhondda Cynon Taff County Borough Council v Watkins* [2003] EWCA Civ 129, [2003] 1 WLR 1864).

In *Barton Henderson Rasen v Merrett* [1993] 1 Lloyd's Rep 540 Saville J said that, as courts exist to determine claims in contentious matters, starting a claim with no intention of pursuing it is an abuse of process. Protracted delay combined with a legitimate concern to avoid costs in the hope of settlement do not amount to this (*Artibell Shipping Co. Ltd v Markel International Insurance Co. Ltd* [2008] EWHC 811 (Comm), LTL 2/5/2008). Similarly, issuing a claim for which the claimant knows no basis is an abuse of process (*Nomura International plc v Granada Group Ltd* [2007] EWHC 642 (Comm), [2008] Bus LR 1), as is advancing a claim making serious charges involving bad faith without adequate particulars (*RGI International Ltd v Synergy Classic Ltd* [2011] EWHC 3166 (Comm), LTL 8/12/2011). 'Parking' proceedings in an attempt to achieve a settlement with other defendants justified striking out with indemnity costs in *Sodeca SA v NE Investments Inc.* [2002] EWHC 1700 (QB), LTL 27/8/2002. Litigating for the purpose of causing expense, harassment or commercial prejudice beyond that normally encountered in the course of properly conducted litigation justifies striking out as an abuse of process (*Wallis v Valentine* [2002] EWCA Civ 1034, [2003] EMLR 8). A claim based on comments made in without-prejudice communications is an abuse of process (*Unilever plc v Procter and Gamble Co.* [2000] 1 WLR 2436).

In *Raja v Van Hoogstraten* [2006] EWHC 1315 (Ch), LTL 20/6/2006, a finding on the trial of a preliminary issue was that the defendant had arranged for the killing of the claimant in order to prevent him giving evidence. Bearing in mind the European Convention on Human Rights, **art. 6**, in the **Human Rights Act 1998, sch. 1**, the defence and counterclaim were struck out. Arranging for the killing of an opponent was a grave form of abuse of process.

According to *McDonald's Corporation v Steel* [1995] 3 All ER 615, it is an abuse of process where the statement of case is incurably incapable of proof. The fact that a party's case may be incapable of proof may become apparent after disclosure of documents or after exchange of witness statements. However, in *McDonald's Corporation v Steel* it was said that striking out on this basis will be fairly unusual, as there are few cases which are sufficiently clearly and obviously hopeless that they deserve the draconian step of being struck out. A clinical negligence claim commenced five years after the event and which was not supported by the medical experts instructed for the claimant was regarded as unwinnable in *Harris v Bolt Burdon* [2000] CPLR 9.

Commencing proceedings knowing that the cause of action is vested in someone else is an abuse of process, as it is only the person with the vested right of action who can bring a claim (*Pickthall v Hill Dickinson LLP* [2009] EWCA Civ 543, [2009] PNLR 31).

Framing a claim in malicious falsehood rather than the more natural cause of action in libel, in order to gain the benefit of public funding for the claim, was not regarded as an abuse of process in *Joyce v Sengupta* [1993] 1 WLR 337. In *R v Richmond upon Thames London Borough Council, ex parte C* [2001] LGR 146, bringing judicial review proceedings relating to obtaining a place for a child in a preferred school in the name of the child rather than his parent in order to obtain public funding was regarded by Kennedy LJ as an abuse of process.

Where a claimant has two reasons for bringing a claim, one legitimate, and one illegitimate, it was held in *JSC BTA Bank v Ablyazov (No. 6)* [2011] EWHC 1136 (Comm), [2011] 1 WLR 2996, that there is no abuse of process. Teare J recognised there is an argument that there would be an abuse of process if the illegitimate reason for bringing the claim was the predominant reason (at [23(iii)] and [53], citing *Metall und Rohstoff AG v Donaldson Lufkin and Jenrette Inc.* [1990] 1 QB 391).

Fraudulent claims

Making a claim tainted by dishonesty can amount to an abuse of process, but it will rarely result in a claim being struck out. In *Arrow Nominees Inc. v Blackledge* one of the parties admitted tampering with a number of material documents. It was held that where a litigant was guilty of conduct which put the fairness of the trial in jeopardy and prevented the court doing justice, striking out may be appropriate. *Arrow Nominees Inc. v Blackledge* was considered in two Court of Appeal decisions with differing results. In *Ul-Haq v Shah* [2009] EWCA Civ 542, [2010] 1 WLR 616 one of a number of co-claimants made a fraudulent claim with the assistance of the other co-claimants. While the fraudulent claim was dismissed, the other claimants were awarded damages in accordance with the evidence. However, where a party's conduct (such as perjury or presenting fraudulent evidence) so damages the integrity of the case being presented that its continuation would be an affront to justice, it may be struck out as an abuse of process (*Masood v Zahoor* [2009] EWCA Civ 650, [2010] 1 WLR 746). These cases were considered in *Summers v Fairclough Homes Ltd* [2012] UKSC 26, [2012] 1 WLR 2004, where *Masood v Zahoor* was preferred. In *Summers v Fairclough Homes Ltd* the claimant suffered genuine injuries, but gave false evidence about his date of recovery, and signed false statements of truth on his schedules of special damages. It was held that in theory a striking-out order could be made, even at the end of the trial, in such a case. However, this power is likely to be used only rarely for two reasons. First, it will be more appropriate at that stage of the proceedings for the judge to make the necessary findings (probably with wide adverse inferences being drawn against the dishonest party) and for judgment to follow in the usual way. Secondly, the judgment on the genuine part of the claim is a possession within the meaning of the European Convention on Human Rights, Protocol 1, art. 1, in the **Human Rights Act 1998, sch. 1**, so should only be lost if striking out performs a legitimate aim and is a proportionate means of achieving that aim. It was held that while this was a case of a serious abuse of process, it would have been wrong to strike it out. 33.14

Destruction of evidence before proceedings are commenced in an attempt to pervert the course of justice may result in a claim or defence being struck out. Destruction of evidence after proceedings are issued may be visited by striking out if a fair trial is no longer achievable (*Douglas v Hello! Ltd (No. 2)* [2003] EWHC 55 (Ch), [2003] 1 All ER 1087).

Relitigation amounting to an abuse of process

Several cases have considered whether a claim which is inconsistent with an earlier claim or evidence given by the claimant in earlier proceedings (such as an affidavit used in an 33.15

application to discharge a freezing injunction) should be struck out as an abuse of process. Further, a party to litigation must bring forward his whole case, and is generally not permitted to bring later proceedings raising matters that could have been resolved in the earlier proceedings (*Henderson v Henderson* (1843) 3 Hare 100). It is clear from cases such as *Bradford and Bingley Building Society v Seddon* [1999] 1 WLR 1482 that there are two main elements:

(a) that the second claim is one that could have been brought in the first claim, or is in conflict with an earlier claim or evidence; and
(b) an additional element, such as a collateral attack on the earlier decision, or dishonesty, election, or unjust harassment.

Thus, in *Hunter v Chief Constable of the West Midlands Police* [1982] AC 529 a claim against the police was struck out as it was held to be no more than a collateral attack upon the decision of another court of competent jurisdiction. The same principle applies where the earlier decision is a disciplinary finding of a professional regulator (*Baxendale-Walker v Middleton* [2011] EWHC 998 (QB), LTL 20/4/2011). In *Calzaghe v Warren* [2010] EWHC 71 (QB), LTL 9/4/2010, the claimant had brought a first claim against a boxing promoter's company, and in winning that claim had established at trial that the promoter's evidence was dishonest. The company was put into administration, so the judgment on the first claim remained unsatisfied. A second claim was then brought, this time against the promoter in his individual capacity, based on the same facts as the first claim, and alleging that the company was the promoter's alter ego. As the defendants were different in the two claims this was not a case of issue estoppel. Nevertheless it was held to be an abuse of process for the promoter to seek to put in issue the facts found against him as a witness in the first claim, including the finding that his evidence had been dishonest. Summary judgment was entered for the claimant. See also *Taylor Walton v Laing* [2007] EWCA Civ 1146, (2007) 47 EG 169 (CS), where the claim was in substance a complete relitigation of a previous decision at trial.

33.16 **Issue estoppel** Where the issues raised in an earlier claim are identical to those raised in a later claim, there is an absolute bar on the later proceedings unless fraud or collusion is alleged (*Arnold v National Westminster Bank plc* [1991] 2 AC 93). Where an issue decided in a previous claim between the parties is central to a second claim between the same parties, the whole second claim will be struck out (*Kennecott Utah Copper Corporation v Minet Ltd* [2002] EWHC 1622 (Comm), [2003] PNLR 18). Issue estoppel, like cause of action estoppel, only applies to matters finally decided in litigation. It applies where an order is made, whether by consent or after argument (*Lennon v Birmingham City Council* [2001] EWCA Civ 435, LTL 27/3/2001). While a consent order is treated like a judgment, if it does not in terms set out the issues compromised, the court needs to consider the circumstances to find the issues implicitly compromised for the purposes of issue estoppel (*South Somerset District Council v Tonstate (Yeovil Leisure) Ltd* [2009] EWHC 3308 (Ch), LTL 14/12/2009). Issue estoppel also prevents a party reopening a liability issue after a judgment for damages to be decided by the court on the assessment of damages (*Item Software (UK) Ltd v Fassihi* (2003) LTL 28/1/2003).

Issue estoppel does not apply where the court declines jurisdiction, or if a claim is struck out as a sanction, or if a claim is discontinued (*Pople v Evans* [1969] 2 Ch 255). Nor does it apply to rulings on interim applications or hearings for directions, because these are not designed to be conclusive (*Autofocus Ltd v Accident Exchange Ltd* [2010] EWCA Civ 788, LTL 14/7/2010). There is no issue estoppel if there is no definitive decision on the issue in the first claim (*Tannu v Moosajee* [2003] EWCA Civ 815, LTL 20/6/2003). Issue estoppel does not apply in criminal proceedings (*Director of Public Prosecutions v Humphreys* [1977] AC 1), subject to a limited exception relating to habeas corpus (*R v Governor of Brixton Prison, ex parte Osman* [1991] 1 WLR 281). Judicial review proceedings cannot found an issue estoppel (*R v Secretary of State for the Environment, ex parte Hackney London Borough Council* [1983] 1 WLR 524). The facts on which a prosecution for murder was based but which resulted in an acquittal can be relied upon in the First-tier Tribunal (Immigration and Asylum) when considering a deportation order to show that the individual facing deportation had in fact committed the murder (*R (V (Colombia)) v Asylum and Immigration Tribunal* [2010] EWCA Civ 491, LTL 27/5/2010). However, where subsequent proceedings are a collateral attack on the findings in judicial review proceedings, they can be struck out as an abuse of process based on relitigating matters found in the judicial review proceedings (*Eco-Power UK Ltd v Transport for London* [2010] EWHC 1683 (Admin), [2010] ACD 69, and see **33.15**).

Where the parties in two claims are not the same, issue estoppel does not apply (*Sweetman v Nathan* [2003] EWCA Civ 1115, *The Times*, 1 September 2003), and the factual findings in the first claim are not admissible evidence in the second (*Hollington v F. Hewthorn and Co. Ltd* [1943] KB 587; see **49.95** and **49.100**). A person claiming title to property is treated as being privy to the interests of those through whom title is claimed, and so will be bound by the decision in proceedings in which any predecessor in title was a party, but only if judgment in those proceedings was given before the presently claimed title was acquired. A person who purchased title before judgment is not regarded as a privy (*Powell v Wiltshire* [2004] EWCA Civ 534, [2005] QB 117).

Issue which should have been raised in earlier proceedings It is an abuse of process to raise in a second claim an issue which should have been raised against someone who was a party to earlier proceedings (*Henderson v Henderson* (1843) 3 Hare 100; *Talbot v Berkshire County Council* [1994] QB 290). Where it is alleged that an issue was or should have been raised in earlier proceedings, it is first necessary to consider whether issue estoppel applies, which can only be negatived by fraud or collusion (see **33.16**). It is only if there is no such estoppel that it is appropriate to consider whether raising the issue now would be an abuse of process under the principle in *Henderson v Henderson* (see *Coflexip SA v Stolt Offshore MS Ltd* [2004] EWCA Civ 213, [2004] FSR 34; *Kennecott Utah Copper Corporation v Minet Ltd* [2003] EWCA Civ 905, [2004] 1 All ER (Comm) 60; *Bim Kemi AB v Blackburn Chemicals Ltd* [2004] EWCA Civ 1490, [2005] EuLR 176). The judge dealing with such an application has to make a decision involving the assessment of a large number of factors to which there is only one answer: it is not a matter of discretion (*Aldi Stores Ltd v WSP Group plc* [2007] EWCA Civ 1260, [2008] 1 WLR 748). An appellate court will be reluctant to allow an appeal where the judge below had balanced the relevant factors (*Stuart v Goldberg* [2008] EWCA Civ 2, [2008] 1 WLR 823; *Challinor v Staffordshire County Council* [2011] EWCA Civ 90, LTL 9/2/2011). There is no distinction between situations where the earlier case is concluded either by settlement or trial (*Aldi Stores Ltd v WSP Group plc*). There can be cases, like *Kotonou v National Westminster Bank plc* [2010] EWHC 1659 (Ch), [2011] 1 All ER (Comm) 1164, where it is an abuse of process to put forward assertions of fact which are contrary to findings in earlier proceedings concerning the same factual matters. In *Johnson v Gore Wood and Co.* [2002] 2 AC 1 the House of Lords held that when considering whether a second claim is an abuse of process a broad, merits-based judgment has to be made, taking into account all the public and private interests involved, and all the facts. A second claim should be struck out only if, in all the circumstances, it should, rather than merely could, have been brought in the first claim. Mr Johnson was a shareholder in a company which had sued the defendant solicitors. That first claim was settled, with the compromise agreement containing a clause seeking to limit the defendants' liability to Mr Johnson personally. Mr Johnson then sued the solicitors in his personal capacity, and the defendants applied to strike out his personal claim as an abuse. Certain heads of claim were struck out, as they merely reflected losses suffered by the company in which Mr Johnson held shares, but others were arguably recoverable by Mr Johnson in his own right, and it was held that even though his personal claim could have been joined with the first claim by the company, it was not on the facts an abuse to have brought the personal claim by separate proceedings. Contrast *Giles v Rhind* [2002] EWCA Civ 1428, [2003] Ch 18, where a shareholder's claim was allowed to proceed because it was not reflective of the company's loss. The question of reflective losses is discussed further at **14.29** and **14.30**. **33.17**

In *Dexter Ltd v Vlieland-Boddy* [2003] EWCA Civ 14, 147 SJLB 117, the defendant in the second claim was the brother of the defendant in an earlier claim based on the same facts. It was held that the burden was on the defendant to show that the second claim was abusive. Applying a broad

Commentary

merits-based approach, taking into account the fact the defendants were different and that the first claim resulted in an unsatisfied judgment, the second claim was allowed to proceed. In *De Crittenden v Bayliss* [2005] EWCA Civ 1425, LTL 13/10/2005, the claimant became aware of an alternative cause of action after issuing the first claim, and issued a second claim form. It was held that the second claim should have been brought by amending the first claim, so issuing separate proceedings was an abuse of process. Where permission to amend to claim an account of profits was refused in a first action, it was an abuse of process to bring a second claim for damages under the principle in *Wrotham Park Estate Co. Ltd v Parkside Homes Ltd* [1974] 1 WLR 798 (*WWF-World Wide Fund for Nature v World Wrestling Federation Entertainment Inc.* [2007] EWCA Civ 286, [2008] 1 WLR 445).

It will only be an abuse of process to challenge the findings in the earlier claim if it would be manifestly unfair to a party in the later claim for the issues to be relitigated, or if relitigating will bring the administration of justice into disrepute (*Secretary of State for Trade and Industry v Bairstow* [2003] EWCA Civ 321, [2004] Ch 1), or if the later proceedings amount to unjust harassment or oppression of the defendant (*Meretz Investments NV v ACP Ltd* [2006] EWHC 74 (Ch), [2007] Ch 197). *Secretary of State for Trade and Industry v Bairstow* provides a means of circumventing the rule in *Hollington v F. Hewthorn and Co. Ltd* [1943] 1 KB 587 (see 33.16) on the theory that, if an abuse of process is established, the party against whom the previous finding was made is prevented from asserting facts contrary to the previous finding (*Conlon v Simms* [2006] EWCA Civ 1749, [2008] 1 WLR 484 at [177] per Ward LJ). In applying the principles in *Secretary of State for Trade and Industry v Bairstow* the court should be slower in preventing a party from continuing to deny serious charges after a previous adverse finding by way of defence, than in preventing a party from initiating proceedings for the purpose of launching a collateral attack on such a previous finding (*Conlon v Simms*). In *Conlon v Simms* the court refused to strike out a solicitor's defence in a claim by the solicitor's former partners which alleged they had been induced to enter into partnership with him by fraudulent misrepresentations. It would have been unfair to allow the claimant to raise findings of the Solicitors Disciplinary Tribunal in previous disciplinary proceedings against the solicitor without having to prove its case, which would have been the position if the defence had been struck out as an abuse of process. Where an issue, which is raised on taking accounts following judgment, was before the trial judge, but was not decided definitively, the question is whether a party is misusing or abusing the process of the court in raising the issue again (*Tannu v Moosajee* [2003] EWCA Civ 815, LTL 20/6/2003). Keeping a second claim secret while prosecuting the first claim may well be an abuse. In assessing the balance to be struck it is not significant that large parts of the particulars of claim have been adopted from the first claim. Delay in bringing the second claim is not in itself relevant, nor is weakness on the merits not coming within the test for summary judgment (*Stuart v Goldberg*).

Where the first and second claims are of a different nature, compelling reasons are required before the later claim will be struck out (*Specialist Group International Ltd v Deakin* [2001] EWCA Civ 77, LTL 23/5/2001). In *Heffernan v Grangewood Securities Ltd* [2001] EWCA Civ 1082, LTL 19/6/2001, proceedings were commenced by a mortgagee which were compromised in 1995 on terms that the mortgagors would pay the arrears over the remaining term of the mortgage. In 1997 the mortgagors commenced their own claim seeking a declaration that the original mortgage was not binding. This second claim was struck out because the mortgagors should have raised this issue in the first claim.

33.18 **Estoppel preventing application to strike out** In *Johnson v Gore Wood and Co.* [2002] 2 AC 1 the House of Lords considered whether a court should refuse to strike out a second claim, which is alleged to be an abusive relitigation of an earlier claim, because of the defendant's previous conduct, in particular where the second claim was taken into consideration when reaching a settlement of the first claim. This is best considered as an estoppel by representation, with the key question being whether it would be unconscionable for the defendant to apply for striking out.

Fresh evidence Claims have been allowed even though they involve questioning the decision of a court of competent jurisdiction if fresh evidence has come to light since the earlier decision, or where the second claim is a professional negligence claim against the solicitors acting for the claimant in the first claim, see *Walpole v Partridge and Wilson* [1994] QB 106. A damages claim was permitted to proceed, subject to stringent conditions, in *Sweetman v Shepherd* (2000) *The Times*, 29 March 2000, despite the fact that it could have been brought by contribution proceedings in an earlier claim. 33.19

Reviving earlier claim In *Buckland v Palmer* [1984] 1 WLR 1109 it was held to be an abuse of process to commence a second claim in respect of the same cause of action as was raised in an earlier claim. The claimant's car had been damaged in a motor accident. Repairs cost £1,142. She claimed on her insurance, and brought proceedings against the defendant claiming the £50 excess not paid by her insurer. This claim was stayed when she accepted a payment into court. The insurer then commenced a second claim in the name of the claimant claiming £1,092, and this claim was struck out as an abuse of process. However, it was possible for the insurer to apply for the first claim to be revived (as it had not proceeded to judgment) and for the original claim to be amended to include the full costs of repairs. A comment was made in *Bradford and Bingley Building Society v Seddon* [1999] 1 WLR 1482 that abuse of process cases of this nature will perhaps be less frequent under the CPR, because of the requirement that the claimant must sign a statement of truth in relation to the second claim, which might be difficult given an earlier, inconsistent, claim. 33.20

Commentary

Settlement acting as a bar to later proceedings

Settling a claim can act as a bar to later proceedings. In *Jameson v Central Electricity Generating Board* [2000] 1 AC 455, the deceased accepted £80,000 from his former employer in 'full and final settlement and satisfaction of all the causes of action' set out in his statement of claim against his employer in respect of asbestos-related disease. After his death his widow brought a claim against the Board as the owner of premises where the deceased had been exposed to asbestos. It was held, on the assumption that the employer and the Board were concurrent and not joint tortfeasors, and as the settlement could not be construed as only a partial settlement, that the compromise with the employer operated to extinguish the claims against all the tortfeasors. The claim against the Board was therefore struck out. *Jameson v Central Electricity Generating Board* was interpreted by the House of Lords in *Heaton v AXA Equity and Law Life Assurance Society plc* [2002] UKHL 15, [2002] 2 AC 329, as laying down the following principles: 33.21

(a) A claim for unliquidated damages, whether in contract or tort, is capable of being fixed in a specific sum of money either on judgment or by agreement.
(b) Although a judgment invariably fixes the full measure of the claimant's loss, whether a compromise fixes the full measure depends on the proper construction of the compromise agreement. Lord Bingham of Cornhill said that in construing a compromise agreement for this purpose one significant factor is whether the claimant has expressly reserved the right to sue other persons, although the absence of such a reservation is by no means conclusive in favour of an argument that other claims are extinguished.
(c) If a compromise, on its proper construction, fixes the full measure of the claimant's loss, the compromise extinguishes the claim so that other claims for the same damage cannot be pursued against other persons, whether in contract or tort.

The question for the court is whether on its true construction the settlement agreement applies to claims of the type raised in the subsequent proceedings (*Satyam Computer Services Ltd v Upaid Systems Ltd* [2008] EWCA Civ 487, [2008] 2 All ER (Comm) 465). In *Steenberg v Enterprise Inns plc* [2010] EWCA Civ 201, LTL 10/3/2010, a nuisance claim arising out of the use of the kitchen and an extractor fan at a public house was compromised in 2001 with a consent order which provided it was 'in full and final settlement of all claims by either party howsoever arising of which either party are aware at the date hereof'. The present claim involved the use of the kitchen and compressors located outside the kitchen at the same public house. The parties were also the same as in the earlier claim. The actual nuisances complained of, however, all post-dated the 2001 consent order, so they could not have been claims that the claimants were 'aware of' when they signed the consent order, and so the present claim was not barred by the consent order. In *Henley v Bloom* [2010] EWCA Civ 202, [2010] 1 WLR 1770, a consent order 'in full and final settlement' of any claim the claimant might have in respect of improvements he made to a leased flat was held not to act as a bar to a disrepair claim.

Following *Heaton v AXA Equity and Law Life Assurance Society plc*, in *Cape and Dalgleish v Fitzgerald* [2002] UKHL 16, LTL 25/4/2002, it was held that a settlement between the original claimant and the defendant was not intended or understood to represent full compensation, so the original claimant had been able to commence a second claim against another party (Cape). The consequence was that Cape was then entitled, in a third claim, to seek a contribution against the defendant in respect of the damages Cape was ordered to pay the claimant in the second claim.

Although a party can agree to release claims or rights of which he is unaware if appropriate language is used in the agreement, the court will be very slow to accept that this is the effect of a release (*Capital Trust Investments Ltd v Radio Design TJ AB* [2002] EWCA Civ 135, [2002] 2 All ER 159). Express words are required before a settlement agreement will be construed as applying to fraud claims (*Satyam Computer Services Ltd v Upaid Systems Ltd*).

In *Minton v Kenburgh Investments (Northern) Ltd* [2000] CPLR 551 liquidators brought misfeasance proceedings under the Insolvency Act 1986, s. 212, against former directors alleging breach of fiduciary duty, which were compromised with sums payable in full and final settlement of the proceedings. The liquidators then brought proceedings against the company's former solicitors arising out of the same transaction as had formed the basis of the first claim for breach of their duties to the company. It was held that as the causes of action were different in the two claims the *Jameson* principle did not apply.

Impossible to have a fair trial

33.22 In *Al Rawi v Security Service* [2011] UKSC 34, [2012] 1 AC 531, the Supreme Court held that in the absence of statutory authority, or possibly consent by the parties, there is no inherent jurisdiction to permit a closed material procedure (as discussed at 1.2). This arose in a case where a claim was made by claimants who alleged the defendants were complicit in their detention and ill-treatment at Guantánamo Bay. The defendants said a great deal of the material relevant to their defence was protected by public interest immunity. It was held there is no inherent jurisdiction to permit material protected in the public interest to be deployed without disclosure to the other side. In such cases both sides are faced with three possibilities:

(a) proceeding with the case without the material protected by public interest immunity;
(b) abandoning the claim or conceding liability (depending on which side's case is more severely damaged by the absence of the material); or
(c) applying to the court to stay or strike out the claim on the ground that through neither side's fault a fair trial is not possible. This alternative was recognised by *Carnduff v Rock* [2001] EWCA Civ 680, [2001] 1 WLR 1786 (where a claim by a police informer for contractual payments was struck out because it would have required evidence of special police operations which were protected by public interest immunity), and approved by Lord Clarke of Stone-cum-Ebony JSC in *Al Rawi v Security Service* at [159].

OBSTRUCTING THE JUST DISPOSAL OF THE PROCEEDINGS

33.23 The second half of **CPR, r. 3.4(2)(b)**, allows the court to strike out a statement of case which obstructs the just disposal of the proceedings. This is expanded upon by **PD 3A, para. 1.5**, which provides that a claim may come within **r. 3.4(2)(b)** if it is vexatious, scurrilous or obviously ill-founded. Generally, the court will know a claim of this kind when it sees it.

Whether a statement of case is vexatious depends 'on all the circumstances of the case: the categories are not closed and the considerations of public policy and the interests of justice may be very material' (per Stuart-Smith LJ in *Ashmore v British Coal Corporation* [1990] 2 QB 338). The applicant in *Ashmore v British Coal Corporation* was one of 1,500 women claiming they were employed on less favourable terms than certain male comparators. Fourteen cases were selected for determination, and the eventual finding was in favour of the employer. The applicant then sought to proceed with her claim. Although the previous determination was not strictly binding, the applicant's claim was struck out as being frivolous and vexatious. Pleadings under the old system have also been struck out on this ground where a party has been joined merely to obtain disclosure of documents or costs (*Burstall v Beyfus* (1884) 26 ChD 35) or where a claim is a disguised action for gaming debts (*Day v William Hill (Park Lane) Ltd* [1949] 1 KB 632).

Poor drafting

A party confronted with a poorly drafted statement of case cannot insist on it being amended, but can take the initiative by applying to have the whole or offending parts of the statement of case struck out. If the statement of case fails to comply with the principles discussed in **chapter 24**, it is likely to obstruct the just disposal of the claim. Statements of case which fail to inform the other side of the case it will have to meet tend to be described as 'embarrassing' (a term that does not appear in the CPR). A statement of case that was unreasonably vague and incoherent was struck out as an abuse of process and for obstructing the just disposal of the claim in *Towler v Wills* [2010] EWHC 1209 (Comm), LTL 27/5/2010. **33.24**

Rassam v Budge [1893] 1 QB 571 concerned a claim for damages for slander. Instead of pleading to the words alleged by the claimant, the defence set out the defendant's rather different version of what he had said, and alleged the words he alleged he had spoken were true. These allegations were struck out as tending to prejudice the fair trial of the claim, because they left it unclear whether the issue was whether the words complained of by the claimant were spoken and published, or whether those words were true.

In *Philipps v Philipps* (1878) 4 QBD 127 Cotton LJ said, at p. 139:

> in my opinion it is absolutely essential that the pleading, not to be embarrassing to the defendants, should state those facts which will put the defendants on their guard and tell them what they have to meet when the case comes on for trial.

Deutsche Morgan Grenfell Group plc v Commissioners of Inland Revenue [2006] UKHL 49, [2007] 1 AC 558, was a claim for restitution of money paid to the Inland Revenue. The particulars of claim sought repayment of sums which 'include but are not limited to' certain payments set out in a schedule. As this only stated part of the sum actually sought, Lord Walker of Gestingthorpe said it was imprecise and unsatisfactory, but the defect could be cured by a request for further information (at [148]). Bearing in mind the overriding objective, an overly pedantic approach should be avoided. As Millett LJ said in *Paragon Finance plc v D. B. Thakerar and Co.* [1999] 1 All ER 400 at p. 405:

> The pleading of unnecessary allegations or the addition of further instances or better particulars do not amount to a distinct cause of action. The selection of the material facts to define the cause of action must be made at the highest level of abstraction.

A defence will be struck out if it does not make clear how much of the claim is admitted and how much is denied (*British and Colonial Land Association Ltd v Foster* (1887) 4 TLR 574). Mere prolixity or setting out of inconsistent claims or defences would be unlikely to result in striking out (see, for example, *Re Morgan* (1887) 35 ChD 492), although costs sanctions may be imposed if the case is protracted as a result.

POWERS AFTER A STRIKING-OUT APPLICATION

33.25 When a court strikes out a statement of case it may enter such judgment as the successful party appears entitled to (**PD 3A, para.** 4.2) and make any consequential order it considers appropriate (**CPR, r.** 3.4(3)). If the court strikes out a claimant's statement of case, and it considers the claim was totally without merit, that fact must be recorded in the court's order, and the court must consider whether to make a civil restraint order (see **r. 3.4(6)** and **14.55**). An appeal was designated as being totally without merit where the appellant was seeking to relitigate an issue that had repeatedly been decided against him in *Shepherd v Official Receiver* [2010] EWHC 681 (Ch), LTL 24/3/2010. If a claim survives a striking-out application, the court may dispense with the need to file directions questionnaires, may allocate the claim to a track, and make case management directions (**PD 26, para.** 2.4).

Loss of QOCS protection

33.26 Costs protection under qualified one-way costs shifting (see **chapter 69**) is lost if the claim is struck out as disclosing no reasonable grounds for bringing the proceedings, or if the proceedings are an abuse of process or if the conduct of the claimant or those acting on the claimant's behalf is likely to obstruct the just disposal of the proceedings (**CPR, r. 44.15**). Loss of costs protection under **r. 44.15** is obligatory (unlike the discretionary loss of costs protection under **r. 44.16** for claims that are fundamentally dishonest).

COMMENCING A SECOND CLAIM

33.27 In *Janov v Morris* [1981] 1 WLR 1389 it was held to be an abuse of process to commence a second claim after a first claim based on the same cause of action had been struck out for failing to comply with an unless order where no explanation was advanced for the failure to comply with the unless order. As explained by Dunn LJ, the second claim could be an abuse where there had been intentional and contumacious default, for example, disobedience of a peremptory order, or where there had been inordinate and inexcusable delay. Intentional and contumacious default can also be established where there has been a wholesale disregard of court orders (*Arbuthnot Latham Bank Ltd v Trafalgar Holdings Ltd* [1998] 1 WLR 1426).

Where a claim is struck out for delay, the claimant is entitled to issue fresh proceedings based on the same cause of action, which will not have been determined on its merits. Such a second claim may be met by an application to strike out if the limitation period has expired. Even if the limitation period has not expired, the court has the power to strike out the second claim as an abuse of process if doing so accords with the overriding objective, particularly on the ground that it constitutes a misuse of the court's resources. See *Securum Finance Ltd v Ashton* [2001] Ch 291, where the second claim raised a different cause of action, and was allowed to continue. In *Collins v CPS Fuels Ltd* [2001] EWCA Civ 1597, LTL 9/10/2001, the first claim was struck out for repeated breaches of orders for disclosure of documents, and because the claimant's solicitors failed to attend two case management conferences. A second claim was then issued, making the same allegations. There were no limitation difficulties because the claimant was a child. The judge balanced the prejudice to the claimant in having to sue her solicitors and the possibility of the original allegations being fairly dealt with, against the conduct giving rise to the first claim being struck out and the effect of the delays, and concluded that the second claim should be struck out. This decision was approved on appeal, where it was held that the decision to strike out has to be made by balancing all the competing arguments and reasons. Putting a gloss on this exercise, by saying (as previous authorities have said) that the claimant has to establish 'special reasons', grounds that are 'good enough' or 'sufficient reasons', was regarded as unhelpful.

It was argued for the defendants in *Aktas v Adepta* [2010] EWCA Civ 1170, [2011] QB 894, that the above principles should, under the CPR, also apply to situations where the claimant failed to serve the first claim in time. Reliance was placed on *Securum Finance Ltd v Ashton* where Chadwick LJ at [34] said:

> The position, now, is that the court must address the application to strike out the second action with the overriding objective of the Civil Procedure Rules in mind — and must consider whether the claimant's wish to have a 'second bite of the cherry' outweighs the need to allot its own limited resources to other cases.... It is an abuse because it is a misuse of the court's limited resources.

This was rejected in *Aktas v Adepta*, where Rix LJ concluded that a mere failure to serve a claim form in time is not an abuse of process, and never has been. Real abuse of process cases in the *Janov v Morris* sense require intentional and contumacious default, inordinate and inexcusable delay, or possibly a wholesale disregard of court orders. Negligence in the first claim is not an abuse of process, and to hold otherwise would have been to disregard the decision in *Horton v Sadler* [2006] UKHL 27, [2007] 1 AC 307, that in a personal injuries claim it is possible for the court to disapply the primary limitation period under the Limitation Act 1980, s. 33, in a second claim form case.

Endorsing the rule laid down in *Gardner v Southwark London Borough Council (No. 2)* [1996] 1 WLR 561, **CPR, r. 3.4(4)**, provides that where a claim is struck out and the claimant is ordered to pay the defendant's costs, if the claimant commences a second claim (within the limitation period) arising out of substantially the same facts as those forming the basis of the struck-out claim, the defendant may apply for a stay of the second claim until the costs of the first claim have been paid. In *Investment Invoice Financing Ltd v Limehouse Board Mills Ltd* [2006] EWCA Civ 9, [2006] 1 WLR 985, a creditor company presented a winding-up petition against the present defendant based on unpaid invoices, which was dismissed with an order for costs against the creditor company. The costs order was never paid. The creditor company assigned some of the invoices to the claimant, which brought the present claim against the defendant. This was regarded as equivalent to the situation in *Gardner v Southwark London Borough Council (No. 2)*. The present claim was therefore an abuse of process, and was stayed until the costs of the earlier proceedings were paid. A stay will not be granted where the two sets of proceedings do not have a sufficient degree of similarity (*Star Reefers Pool Inc. v JFC Group* [2011] EWCA Civ 1052, LTL 13/9/2011, a case on **r. 52.9(1)(c)**).

Commentary

Chapter 34 Summary Judgment

The following procedural checklists, which are at the front of the book, are relevant to this chapter:

Procedural checklist 22 Application by a party for summary judgment
Procedural checklist 23 Proposal by court for order for summary judgment

INTRODUCTION

34.1 In cases where the defendant fails to defend it is usually possible to enter a default judgment (see **chapter 20**). Where there is no real defence, a defendant may go through the motions of defending in order to delay the time when judgment may be entered. It is possible for defendants to put up the pretence of having a real defence to such an extent that some cases run all the way through to trial before judgment can be entered. The CPR provide several ways of preventing this happening. The court can use its power to strike out (see **chapter 33**) to knock out hopeless defences, such as those that simply do not amount to a legal defence to a claim. Entering summary judgment is a related procedure, and is used where a purported defence can be shown to have no real prospect of success and there is no other compelling reason why the case should be disposed of at trial. Indeed, **PD 3A, para. 1.7**, recognises that there will be cases where applications for summary judgment and striking out may be sought in the alternative. Where a defence includes bare denials, it may be appropriate to strike out the offending paragraphs under **CPR, r. 3.4(2)(a)**, and to grant summary judgment under **r. 24.2** on the parts of the claim denied (*Clancy Consulting Ltd v Derwent Holdings Ltd* [2010] EWHC 762 (TCC), LTL 21/4/2010).

The procedure for entering summary judgment is not limited to use by claimants against defendants. Defendants may apply for summary judgment to attack weak claims brought by claimants. Further, summary judgment can be used by the court of its own initiative to perform the important function of stopping weak cases from proceeding. The procedure can also be used for the purpose of obtaining a summary determination of some of the issues in a case, thereby reducing the complexity of the trial.

Many applications under the Companies Acts are made on a summary basis, usually on the substantive hearing of a Part 8 claim (see **chapter 85**). It is also possible for these applications to be made by way of summary judgment applications (*Oxford Legal Group Ltd v Sibbasbridge Services plc* [2008] EWCA Civ 387, [2008] Bus LR 1244).

Commentary

TIME AT WHICH THE APPLICATION MAY BE MADE

Summary judgment can be applied for by a claimant or a defendant (see **procedural checklist 22** at the front of the book) or can be proposed by the court of its own initiative (see **34.5** and **procedural checklist 23**). **34.2**

A claimant may apply for summary judgment only after the defendant has filed either an acknowledgment of service or a defence (**CPR, r. 24.4(1)**). If the defendant fails to do either of these within the time limited by the CPR, the claimant may enter a default judgment, which, depending on the nature of the claim, may require the court's permission (see **chapter 20**). By analogy with **r. 25.2(2)(c)**, a defendant likewise can only apply for summary judgment after either filing an acknowledgment of service or a defence.

Where the claimant has failed to comply with **PD Pre-action Conduct** or any relevant pre-action protocol, an application for summary judgment will not normally be entertained before the defence has been filed, or the time for doing so has expired (**PD 24, para. 2(6)**).

Applications for summary judgment should normally be made in the period between acknowledgment of service and filing of the applicant's directions questionnaire (**PD 26, para. 5.3(1)**). This is normally the appropriate time, because, if the other side have no realistic prospects of success, entering summary judgment early prevents unnecessary costs being incurred. Question D in the directions questionnaire (form N181) specifically asks whether there is any intention of making an application for summary judgment. If for any reason the application is not made before allocation, there is still a general obligation to apply as soon as it becomes apparent that it is desirable to do so (**PD 23A, para. 2.7**).

Under the old rules there was nothing to prevent a late application for summary judgment (see, for example, *Brinks Ltd v Abu-Saleh (No. 1)* [1995] 1 WLR 1478), but as a practical matter the judge dealing with a late application might well have felt there was a lack of conviction on the part of the applicant if the application was significantly delayed. For summary judgment at trial, see **61.37**.

Summary judgment applications made before filing the defence

34.3 If the application is made after filing an acknowledgment of service, but before filing of the defence, there is no need to file a defence before the hearing (**CPR, r. 24.4(2)**). At that stage the court will give directions, which will include providing a date for filing the defence. The permissive wording of the rule confirms *Natural Resources Inc. v Origin Clothing Ltd* [1995] FSR 280, in which it was held that there is nothing to prevent a defendant from serving a defence in the period before the hearing if the defendant chooses to do so.

Summary judgment applications made before allocation to a track

34.4 PD 26, **para.** 5.3(2), provides that where a party makes an application for summary judgment before the claim has been allocated to a track the court will not allocate the claim before hearing the application. If a party files a directions questionnaire stating an intention to apply for summary judgment but has not yet made an application, the judge will usually direct the listing of an allocation hearing (**para.** 5.3(3) and (4)). The summary judgment application may be heard at the allocation hearing if the application notice has been issued and served in sufficient time.

Hearings fixed by the court of its own initiative

34.5 The rules specifically mention that the court may fix a summary judgment hearing of its own initiative (**CPR, r. 24.4(3)**), and doing so may further the overriding objective, which includes deciding promptly which issues need full investigation and trial, and accordingly disposing summarily of the others (**r. 1.4(2)(c)**). If the court is minded to make use of this power, it is most likely to do so on the initial scrutiny at the track allocation stage shortly after filing of the defence. If the court uses the power, it will not allocate the case to a track, but instead it will fix a hearing, giving the parties 14 days' notice and informing them of the issues it proposes to decide (**PD 26, para. 5.4**).

DEFENDANT'S APPLICATION FOR SUMMARY JUDGMENT: NO DEFAULT JUDGMENT

34.6 Where a defendant has applied for summary judgment against a claimant, the claimant cannot obtain a default judgment until the summary judgment application has been disposed of (**CPR, r. 12.3(3)(a)**).

EXCLUDED PROCEEDINGS

34.7 Under **CPR, r. 24.3(2)**, an application for summary judgment cannot be brought against the defendant in:

(a) residential possession proceedings against a mortgagor or a tenant or person holding over whose occupancy is protected by the Rent Act 1977 or the Housing Act 1988; or
(b) Admiralty claims *in rem*.

The Crown's exemption from summary judgment was repealed by the Civil Procedure (Modification of Crown Proceedings Act 1947) Order 2005, SI 2005/2712, art. 8.

In applications against claimants there are no excluded types of proceedings (**CPR, r. 24.3(1)**).

PROCEDURE

34.8 The general rules on making interim applications (see **chapter 32**) apply on making an application for summary judgment, with certain refinements. The application is made by application notice, which must be supported by evidence (**CPR, r. 25.3(2)**). The evidence in support is most likely to be contained either in the application notice, or in a separate witness statement.

The facts supporting the claim will have been verified by a statement of truth included in the particulars of claim. The evidence in support of an application by a claimant will have to state a belief that there is no defence with a reasonable prospect of success. It may be prudent to go further and to give details of the background facts and to exhibit relevant documentation to show there is no reasonable defence. On an application by the defendant there may or may not be a filed defence. If not, clearly the evidence will have to explain why the claim is unlikely to succeed, and will probably have to go into the background in some detail.

Instead of the usual notice period of three clear days which applies to most types of interim application, the notice period in applications for summary judgment is 14 clear days (**r. 24.4(3)**). The 14-day period of notice may be varied by practice directions (**r. 24.4(4)**), and has been shortened for specific performance claims (see **34.48**).

The respondent must file and serve any evidence in reply at least seven clear days before the hearing (**r. 24.5(1)**). The application notice must inform the respondent of this time limit (**PD 24, para. 2(5)**). If the applicant wishes to respond to the respondent's evidence, the further evidence must be served and filed at least three clear days before the hearing of the application (**CPR, r. 24.5(2)**).

In cases where the hearing is fixed by the court on its own initiative, all parties must file and serve their evidence at least seven clear days before the return day, and if they want to respond to their opponents' evidence, that must be done at least three clear days before the return day (**r. 24.5(3)**).

Commentary

ORDERS AVAILABLE

Paragraph 5.1 of **PD 24** says that the range of orders available on a summary judgment application include: **34.9**

(a) giving judgment on the claim;
(b) striking out or dismissal of the claim — the court cannot dismiss the claim unless the claimant has been given notice and an opportunity to address the court and place before it any relevant material (*P and O Nedlloyd BV v Arab Metals Co. (No. 2)* [2006] EWCA Civ 1717, [2007] 1 WLR 2288, per Moore-Bick LJ at [67]);
(c) dismissal of the application; and
(d) making a conditional order (see **34.34**).

This is not a comprehensive list (note the use of the word 'include' in **PD 24, para. 5.1**), and the court can make other orders. These include:

(e) allowing the claim to continue to trial on condition that a party pay money into court as security for costs (*Olatawura v Abiloye* [2002] EWCA Civ 998, [2003] 1 WLR 275, relying on **r. 3.1(3), (5) and (6)**);
(f) making summary declarations (*BBC Worldwide Ltd v Bee Load Ltd* [2007] EWHC 134, *The Times*, 15 March 2007);
(g) entering summary judgment subject to a stay of execution. This may be ordered where there is a counterclaim (not amounting to a set-off) which is linked to the claim (see **34.36**, sub-paragraph (b)). More generally, there needs to be some unresolved matter which may mean it is unjust for payment to be required immediately, particularly where the party required to make the payment may not be able to recover it, for example, because of the likely insolvency of the party receiving the payment. In *Mead General Building Ltd v Dartmoor Properties Ltd* [2009] EWHC 200 (TCC), [2009] BCC 510, it was held that the court

could order a stay of execution of summary judgment on a claim to enforce an adjudicator's award (see **34.20**) if the claimant has solvency difficulties (these cases proceed on the principle 'pay now, argue later', so there is always the possibility that the money will have to be paid back). The nature of the claimant's financial difficulties is relevant, as is the question of the extent to which those difficulties have been caused by the defendant's failure to pay on the contract in question;

(h) entering summary judgment for such part of the sum for which there is no defence, with dismissal of the application as to the balance; and

(i) entering summary judgment on particular issues under **CPR, r. 24.2**. This is most appropriate where resolving the issue or issues will resolve or help to resolve the litigation (*Kent v Griffiths (No. 3)* [2001] QB 36 at p. 51). The court must apply the overriding objective, and may consider that where there are connected issues, some of which should go to trial, summary judgment should be refused on the others as well (*Redevco Properties v Mount Cook Land Ltd* [2002] EWHC 1647 (Ch), LTL 30/7/2002). The court should be slow to entertain an application for summary judgment on certain issues where there is going to be a full trial in any event, particularly where dealing with such an application may delay (because of possible appeals) the final disposal of the claim (*Partco Group Ltd v Wragg* [2002] EWCA Civ 594, [2002] 2 Lloyd's Rep 343 at [27]).

In *Costain Ltd v Wilson* [2007] EWHC 713 (QB), LTL 12/4/2007, it was held there was no real prospect of success on D2's defence on a claim to recover sums obtained from the claimant on false invoices, where the proceeds had been divided equally between D1 and D2. The claimant was in the process of negotiating a settlement with D1. In order to avoid double recovery, while the claimant was strictly entitled to judgment in the full amount against D2, summary judgment was entered for half that amount in order to set a realistic unarguable recovery target. It is doubtful whether this is legitimate. Once a decision has been made that there is no prospect of success, the applicant should be given the whole of the remedy that follows as a matter of law.

TEST FOR ENTERING SUMMARY JUDGMENT

34.10 CPR, r. 24.2, provides:

> The court may give summary judgment against a claimant or defendant on the whole of a claim or on a particular issue if—
> (a) it considers that—
> (i) that claimant has no real prospect of succeeding on the claim or issue; or
> (ii) that defendant has no real prospect of successfully defending the claim or issue; and
> (b) there is no other compelling reason why the case or issue should be disposed of at a trial.

An application for summary judgment is decided applying the test of whether the respondent has a case with a real prospect of success, which is considered having regard to the overriding objective of dealing with the case justly. This has been said to be consistent with the need for a fair trial under **art. 6(1)** of the European Convention on Human Rights (*Three Rivers District Council v Bank of England (No. 3)* [2001] UKHL 16, [2003] 2 AC 1). Whether there is a real prospect of success is the same test as that applied in applications to set aside default judgments (see **20.13** and *E. D. and F. Man Liquid Products Ltd v Patel* [2003] EWCA Civ 472, [2003] CPLR 384). No adjustments are made to the test for summary judgment where one party is suffering from an inequality of arms (*Bank of Tokyo-Mitsubishi UFJ Ltd v Baskan Gida Sanayi ve Pazarlama AS* [2008] EWHC 659 (Ch), LTL 17/4/2008).

In *Swain v Hillman* [2001] 1 All ER 91 Lord Woolf MR said that the words 'no real prospect of succeeding' did not need any amplification as they spoke for themselves. The word 'real' directed the court to the need to see whether there was a realistic, as opposed to a fanciful, prospect of success. The phrase does not mean 'real and substantial' prospect of success. Nor does it mean that summary judgment will only be granted if the claim or defence is 'bound to be dismissed at trial'. Nor does it require compelling evidence, but simply enough evidence to raise a real prospect of a contrary case (*Korea National Insurance Corporation v Allianz Global Corporate and Specialty AG* [2007] EWCA Civ 1066, LTL 30/10/2007).

In *Bee v Jenson* [2006] EWHC 2534 (Comm), [2007] RTR 115, the court adopted the approach explained by Potter LJ in *E. D. and F. Man Liquid Products Ltd v Patel* [2003] EWCA Civ 472, [2003] CPLR 384 at [8]:

> I regard the distinction between a realistic and fanciful prospect of success as appropriately reflecting the observation in the *Saudi Eagle* that the defence sought to be argued must carry some degree of conviction. Both approaches require the defendant to have a case which is better than merely arguable, as was formerly the case under RSC ord. 14.

A claim may be fanciful where it is entirely without substance, or where it is clear beyond question that the statement of case is contradicted by all the documents or other material on which it is based (*Three Rivers District Council v Bank of England (No. 3)*). The judge should have regard to the witness statements and also to the question of whether the case is capable of being supplemented by evidence at trial (*Royal Brompton Hospital NHS Trust v Hammond* [2001] BLR 297). Where the respondent's evidence, taken at its highest, does not raise a possibility of a defence, but is in the realm of a mere (and distinctly improbable) possibility, it is right to enter summary judgment (*Akinleye v East Sussex Hospitals NHS Trust* [2008] EWHC 68 (QB), [2008] LS Law Medical 216). Conversely, where there is some prospect of success, summary judgment should be refused, and the court should not conduct a mini-trial into disputed questions of fact (*Cotton v Rickard Metals Inc.* [2008] EWHC 824 (QB), LTL 25/4/2008).

The question of whether there is a real prospect of success is not approached by applying the usual balance of probabilities standard of proof (*Royal Brompton Hospital NHS Trust v Hammond*). Many cases will succeed at trial, but will be unsuitable for summary judgment because there are complexities, disputes of fact, or further inquiries that need to be resolved through case management and trial before it can be said that the applicant should win on the balance of probabilities. Rather, summary judgment should only be entered where, on the untested written evidence, and whatever further evidence may be found in the future, there is no real prospect of success. Comments in *Director of the Assets Recovery Agency v Woodstock* [2006] EWCA Civ 741, LTL 18/5/2006, to the effect that the onus on the applicant is to establish its version on the balance of probabilities have to be understood in this context. This need for a case which will succeed no matter what further work is done on behalf of the respondent explains why summary judgment was refused in *Director of the Assets Recovery Agency v Woodstock* despite obvious weaknesses in the respondent's case because that case was not bound to be disbelieved. Applying a test of whether the claim is arguable will give grounds for appeal (*Sinclair v Chief Constable of West Yorkshire* (2000) LTL 12/12/2000).

In *E. D. and F. Man Liquid Products Ltd v Patel* Potter LJ at [6] regarded the terms 'real prospect' and 'realistic prospect, as interchangeable. Lord Woolf MR in *Swain v Hillman* said that summary judgment applications have to be kept within their proper role. They are not meant to dispense with the need for a trial where there are issues which should be considered at trial. Further, summary judgment hearings should not be mini-trials. They are simply summary hearings to dispose of cases where there is no real prospect of success. Without allowing the application to become a mini-trial, there are occasions when the court has to consider fairly voluminous evidence in order to understand the facts that are in issue (*Miles v ITV Networks Ltd* [2003] EWHC 3134 (Ch), LTL 9/12/2003).

Burden of proof

In *E. D. and F. Man Liquid Products Ltd v Patel* [2003] EWCA Civ 472, [2003] CPLR 384, Potter LJ said **34.11**
at [9] that the burden of proof is on the applicant to show the respondent's case has no real

prospect of success. Strictly this is no more than an *obiter dictum*, because the learned judge was dealing with an application to set aside a default judgment, and was contrasting his view of the burden of proof on the two types of application. A similar approach was taken in *Director of the Assets Recovery Agency v Woodstock* [2006] EWCA Civ 741, LTL 18/5/2006, where the Court of Appeal said that the onus is on the applicant. Tuckey LJ said that where the applicant establishes a prima facie case against the respondent, there is an evidential burden on the respondent to show a case answering that advanced by the applicant. A respondent who shows a prima facie case in answer should ordinarily be allowed to take the matter to trial.

Complex claims

34.12 Complex claims, cases relying on complex inferences of fact, and cases with issues involving mixed questions of law and fact where the law is complex are likely to be inappropriate for summary judgment (*Three Rivers District Council v Bank of England (No. 3)* [2001] UKHL 16, [2003] 2 AC 1; *Arkin v Borchard Lines Ltd (No. 2)* (2001) LTL 21/6/2001). The high standard of proof required at trial in fraud claims means that it will be difficult to succeed on a summary judgment application in such a case (*Allied Dunbar Assurance plc v Ireland* [2001] EWCA Civ 1129, LTL 12/6/2001).

If an application for summary judgment involves prolonged serious argument, the court should, as a rule, dismiss it without hearing the argument, unless it harbours doubt about the soundness of the statement of case and is satisfied that granting summary judgment would avoid the need for a trial or would substantially reduce the burden of the trial (*Three Rivers District Council v Bank of England (No. 3)*; *Partco Group Ltd v Wragg* [2002] EWCA Civ 594, [2002] 2 Lloyd's Rep 343, at [28]; *Equitable Life Assurance Society v Ernst and Young* [2003] EWCA Civ 1114, [2003] 2 BCLC 603). Despite this, judges do on occasion fully investigate complex applications for summary judgment, particularly where there is a suspicion that the respondent has overloaded the court with documents in an attempt to escape judgment (*Jacobs UK Ltd v Skidmore Owings and Merrill LLP* [2008] EWHC 2847 (TCC), LTL 1/12/2008, where the application took three days). The general rule, however, is that the court cannot expect a party to bring forward its entire case at an interim hearing such as for summary judgment, which is one of the reasons why it may not be appropriate to enter summary judgment in a complicated case (*Groveholt Ltd v Hughes* [2010] EWCA Civ 538, LTL 20/5/2010). Summary judgment was refused in *Apvodedo NV v Collins* [2008] EWHC 775 (Ch), LTL 29/4/2008, where the respondent raised a defence of common mistake which turned on a detailed analysis of a complex factual matrix. Summary judgment is also inappropriate in cases in areas of developing jurisprudence (*Farah v British Airways plc* (1999) *The Times*, 26 January 2000; *Barrett v Enfield London Borough Council* [2001] 2 AC 550), unless the claim is doomed to failure (*K v Central and North West London Mental Health NHS Trust* [2008] EWHC 1217 (QB), [2008] PIQR P19).

Defence on the merits

34.13 In most summary judgment applications the applicant presents its case to the court in the form of witness statements and exhibits, and seeks to persuade the court there is no conceivable defence to the claim. Defendants are invariably invited to state the basis of any dispute they may wish to raise during the course of pre-action correspondence. This is particularly so where the parties are following one of the pre-action protocols. If a defendant has failed to state a defence in pre-action correspondence, or if the purported defence is viewed as merely spurious, the claimant may well be justified in seeking summary judgment.

When faced with an application for summary judgment by a claimant, the defendant may seek to show a defence with a real prospect of success by setting up one or more of the following:

(a) a substantive defence, e.g. *volenti non fit injuria*, frustration or illegality;
(b) a point of law destroying the claimant's cause of action;

(c) a denial of the facts supporting the claimant's cause of action;
(d) further facts answering the claimant's cause of action, e.g. an exclusion clause, or that the defendant was an agent rather than a principal, or that a dispute has been settled by a compromise agreement.

An example under the old rules was *Mercer v Craven Grain Storage Ltd* [1994] CLC 328. The claimant was a farmer who deposited a quantity of grain with the defendant storage company. Later, the claimant requested redelivery, but the defendant was only able to deliver a small fraction of the grain. The defendant alleged that the claimant had entered into an agreement with a marketing company, and that the missing grain had been withdrawn from the store with the authority of the marketing company. By a bare majority it was held that this defence raised triable legal and factual issues, and leave to defend was given. With the change in the test, this case would now perhaps result in a conditional order being made.

Points of law and construction

Although summary judgment applications should not be allowed to turn into mini-trials, where the case turns on an issue of construction of a term in a contract the court will usually determine the point and give judgment accordingly (*Wootton v Telecommunications UK Ltd* (2000) LTL 4/5/2000). In *ICI Chemicals and Polymers Ltd v TTE Training Ltd* [2007] EWCA Civ 725, LTL 13/6/2007, it was held that where a short point of construction arises on a summary judgment application and the parties are ready to argue it, the judge should decide the point, unless there is likely to be other evidence available at trial which will shed light on it. This is particularly so where the disputed phrase can be readily construed applying the principles in *Investors Compensation Scheme Ltd v West Bromwich Building Society* [1998] 1 WLR 896 (see **89.22**) (*Gaetano Ltd v Obertor Ltd* [2009] EWHC 2653 (Ch), LTL 29/10/2009, where the words 'at any time' were given their ordinary meaning). Likewise where there is a short point on whether a disputed term can legitimately be implied into a written contract (*Omega SA v Omega Engineering Inc.* [2011] EWCA Civ 645, [2011] ETMR 40). **34.14**

Where a clear-cut issue of law is raised by way of defence in an application for summary judgment, the court should decide it immediately. This is so even if the question is, at first blush, of some complexity and therefore will take some time to argue fully (see Lord Greene MR in *Cow v Casey* [1949] 1 KB 474). Not deciding a case once full argument has been addressed to the court on the issue will result in the case going to trial, where the argument will be rehearsed again, with consequent delay and unnecessary expense. Summary judgment may be given where the dispute is largely one of law and any disputed questions of fact are largely peripheral (*Jenson v Faux* [2011] EWCA Civ 423, [2011] 1 WLR 3038). A misconceived 'legal' point does not amount to a triable issue (*National Commercial Bank Jamaica Ltd v Olint Corporation Ltd* [2009] UKPC 16, [2009] 1 WLR 1405, at [7], an injunction case). In *GMAC Commercial Credit Ltd v Dearden* (2002) LTL 31/5/2002 it was held that defences of economic duress had no real prospect of success, the claimant having acted in good faith and its conduct not going beyond what was normal and legitimate in commercial arrangements.

However, it is quite a different matter, per Lord Donaldson of Lymington MR in *R. G. Carter Ltd v Clarke* [1990] 1 WLR 578:

> if the issue of law is not decisive of all the issues between the parties or, if decisive of part of the [claimant's] claim or of some of those issues, is of such a character as would not justify its being determined as a preliminary point, because little or no savings in costs would ensue. It is an a fortiori case if the answer to the question of law is any way dependent upon undecided issues of fact.

Summary judgment should also be refused where the point requires protracted argument (*Home and Overseas Insurance Co. Ltd v Mentor Insurance Co. (UK) Ltd* [1990] 1 WLR 153). Summary judgment was refused in *System Control plc v Munro Corporate plc* [1990] BCLC 659, in which it was held that whether the claimants had irrevocably elected to treat a contract as discharged,

Commentary

or whether they could enforce it, was an issue which should be decided at trial. In *I-Way Ltd v World Online Telecom Ltd* [2002] EWCA Civ 413, LTL 8/3/2002, the claimant sued to recover the benefits it alleged were due to it under an oral variation of a written contract. The defendant resisted the claim relying on a clause of the written contract that there was to be no addition or amendment to the contract unless it was in writing and signed by both parties. An application by the defendant for summary judgment against the claimant was dismissed, because there was no direct authority on the issue whether the parties could prevent oral variations of a contract by use of such a clause, and an important point of principle such as the one in issue needed to be tried rather than determined by summary judgment.

Disputes of fact

34.15 Many summary judgment applications are made after a defence has been filed by the defendant. Most of these applications are decided on the basis of the facts which are not disputed by the respondent, together with the respondent's version of the disputed facts (*Prince of Wales v Associated Newspapers Ltd* [2006] EWCA Civ 1776, [2008] Ch 57). Judgment may be entered if there is no, or no real, prospect of the defendant establishing facts sufficient to justify the key elements pleaded in the defence (*P. and S. Amusements Ltd v Valley House Leisure Ltd* [2006] EWHC 1510 (Ch), LTL 4/7/2006). Where there is no dispute of fact, in that the evidence on liability is either admitted or is derived from matters adduced by the respondent, summary judgment may be entered (*Wrexham Association Football Club Ltd v Crucialmove Ltd* [2006] EWCA Civ 237, [2008] 1 BCLC 508). A defence that consists mainly of denials with no explanations may lead the court into concluding the defence has no real prospect of success (*Broderick v Centaur Tipping Services Ltd* (2006) LTL 22/8/2006).

Where there are issues of fact, which, if decided in the respondent's favour, would result in judgment for the respondent, it is inappropriate to enter summary judgment, even if there is substantial evidence in support of the applicant's case (*Munn v North West Water Ltd* (2000) LTL 18/7/2000). Primarily the court will consider the written evidence adduced by the parties, and if it discloses a dispute with a real prospect of success, the summary judgment application will be dismissed. However, there is no rule that summary judgment must always be refused where the respondent puts in written evidence to support its case (*Miller v Garton Shires* [2006] EWCA Civ 1386, LTL 31/10/2006). The court is not always obliged to accept written evidence at face value, and may disregard evidence which is incredible (see **32.30**). There has to be some basis for going behind the respondent's written evidence, and it is not permissible for the judge on a summary judgment application simply to disbelieve the respondent's account (*Mentmore International Ltd v Abbey Healthcare (Festival) Ltd* [2010] EWCA Civ 761, LTL 7/7/2010). Where the respondent's assertion that he retained a beneficial interest in property was unsupported by documentary evidence and where the circumstances (such as no provision for any rental income or how his interest was to be realised) was regarded as fantastic, summary judgment was entered (*Sandhar v Sandhar and Kang Ltd* [2008] EWCA Civ 238, LTL 14/2/2008). It is generally unsafe to base a summary judgment application on second- and third-hand evidence. Such evidence frequently takes on a different character when subjected to cross-examination (*Radiocomms Systems Ltd v Radio Communications Systems Ltd* [2010] EWHC 149 (Ch), LTL 25/2/2010). It is also a risky course to rely on facts set out in a statement of case without more detailed witness statement evidence, particularly in support of an alleged oral agreement (*Korea National Insurance Corporation v Allianz Global Corporate and Specialty AG* [2007] EWCA Civ 1066, LTL 30/10/2007).

In *Public Trustee v Williams* (2000) LTL 10/2/2000 the claimant sought to recover for a deceased's estate the sum of £74,000 which was received by one of the defendants and used by her to buy a house. The evidence of the recipient filed in response to an application for summary judgment was at its best unclear and at its worst confusing as to where she thought the money had come from. However, there was no clear evidence that the money had come from the estate, and it was held it was not a suitable case for summary judgment. In *Bates v Microstar Ltd* (2000) LTL 4/7/2000 summary judgment had been granted based on a purported contract written on hotel notepaper. There were two other documents purporting to be the contract between the parties, and a number of the terms in the hotel notepaper document were arguably too vague. The judgment was set aside on appeal. In *Mehdi v Bates* [2001] EWCA Civ 1948, LTL 3/12/2001, the contractual documentation was unclear on the issue of whether the contract had been entered into by the defendant personally or by the defendant's company. It was held that the judge had not been justified in entering summary judgment against the claimant on the basis that it was unlikely that a businessman would have entered into this contract personally.

Cases involving disputes over whether employers are vicariously liable for the tortious acts of employees who might not be acting in the course of their employment are fact-sensitive and inappropriate for summary judgment (*Cercato-Gouveia v Kiprianou* [2001] EWCA Civ 1887, LTL 30/11/2001).

Where the applicant has the burden of proving a disputed issue, such as the reasonableness of an exclusion clause under the **Unfair Contract Terms Act 1977**, it will be difficult for the applicant to establish that the respondent has no real prospect of success (see, for example, *Lalji v Post Office Ltd* [2003] EWCA Civ 1873, LTL19/12/2003).

In a proprietary estoppel claim, where the context and meaning of the words used needs to be investigated, summary judgment is inappropriate (*Century (UK) Ltd SA v Clibbery* [2003] EWCA Civ 1374, LTL 17/7/2003). Where there is no arguable evidence on an essential element of the claim (or defence), or where a claimant will be unable to establish any loss flowing from a breach not actionable per se, summary judgment should be entered (*Morshead Mansions Ltd v Langford* [2003] EWHC 2023 (QB), LTL 29/8/2003). In *Shamil Bank of Bahrain EC v Beximco Pharmaceuticals Ltd* [2003] EWHC 2118 (Comm), [2003] 2 All ER (Comm) 849, a defence to a claim by the bank for repayment of moneys lent was that there was an oral agreement suspending payment until a further agreement had been reached. This was dismissed as fanciful, as it made no commercial sense for a bank to enter such an arrangement, because if the parties failed to reach a further agreement the defendants would be released from liability (different issues were raised on the appeal, [2004] EWCA Civ 19, [2004] 1 WLR 1784).

Defamation

Summary judgment will not be granted in a libel claim where there is a material issue of fact between the parties, because such issues must be decided by the jury (Senior Courts Act 1981, s. 69; *Safeway Stores plc v Tate* [2001] QB 1120). However, where the evidence, taken at its highest, is such that no properly directed jury could reach a verdict contended for by one of the parties, summary judgment is available (*Alexander v Arts Council of Wales* [2001] EWCA Civ 514, [2001] 1 WLR 1840). **34.16**

Claims involving the investigation of the respondent's state of mind, such as the issue of malice in a defence of qualified privilege in a defamation claim, are not suitable for summary judgment (*Hayter v Fahie* [2008] EWCA Civ 1336, LTL 28/10/2008).

In *Creative Resins International Ltd v Glasslam Europe Ltd* [2005] EWHC 777 (QB), LTL 11/5/2005, the claimant sued the second defendant (the solicitors acting for the first defendant) in libel based on a letter sent by the solicitors to one of the claimant's customers. The second defendant applied for summary judgment, arguing that the letter was protected by qualified privilege. The first defendant had not at this point waived legal professional privilege in respect of solicitor and client communications leading up to the allegedly libellous letter. The possibility that legal professional privilege might be waived before trial, combined with the complexity surrounding cases raising qualified privilege, meant this was not a suitable case for summary judgment.

Fraud, deceit and misconduct

34.17 Claims involving allegations of fraudulent or deceitful misconduct which are not admitted and which are not capable of being substantiated by inference from the documentary or written evidence are inappropriate for summary judgment (*Esprit Telecoms UK Ltd v Fashion Gossip Ltd* (2000) LTL 27/7/2000). Conversely, where a challenge to a fraud claim has no real prospects of success, summary judgment may be appropriate (*Sinclair Investment Holdings SA v Cushnie* [2006] EWHC 219 (Ch), LTL 6/2/2006). *Costain Ltd v Wilson* [2007] EWHC 713 (QB), LTL 12/4/2007, was a claim to recover sums obtained from the claimant on false invoices, where the proceeds had been divided equally between a subcontractor and the claimant's accountants. The subcontractor sought to avoid summary judgment by alleging that four of the claimant's employees, whom the subcontractor refused to name, had also benefited from the fraud, and were the alter ego of the claimant. The fact these allegedly corrupt employees were not named, the absence of evidence that they had gained from the fraud, and the fact that it was not a defence to the subcontractor's own wrongdoing, meant this was a hopeless argument.

There is no rule that summary judgment is not available where this involves a finding adverse to the integrity of the respondent (*Wrexham Association Football Club Ltd v Crucialmove Ltd* [2006] EWCA Civ 237, [2008] 1 BCLC 508, where summary judgment was entered in a claim based on a director being in breach of his duty of good faith to his company).

Negligence claims and previous convictions

34.18 Although there is nothing in principle preventing a claimant from applying for summary judgment in claims seeking damages for negligence, such cases invariably involve disputed factual issues, so it is rare for a court to find there is no real defence once liability is denied. It is unlikely to be appropriate to grant summary judgment to a defendant on the basis there was no duty of care in a novel situation (*Bishara v Sheffield Teaching Hospitals NHS Trust* [2007] EWCA Civ 353, LTL 26/3/2007). The question of whether a duty of care is owed often has to be decided in the light of all the facts and evidence (*Caparo Industries plc v Dickman* [1990] 2 AC 605; *Capital and Counties plc v Hampshire County Council* [1997] QB 1004).

An exception was *Dummer v Brown* [1953] 1 QB 710, where summary judgment was given against the defendant, a coach driver, who had previously pleaded guilty of dangerous driving in respect of the accident giving rise to the claim. Even if there is a conviction, summary judgment may be refused if there are good reasons for believing the conviction was erroneous (*McCauley v Vine* [1999] 1 WLR 1977).

Previous disciplinary proceedings

34.19 Adverse findings in disciplinary proceedings against a solicitor may mean the solicitor has no real prospect of success in related proceedings (*Simms v Law Society* [2005] EWCA Civ 849, [2005] ACD 98).

Housing Grants, Construction and Regeneration Act 1996 claims

34.20 The Housing Grants, Construction and Regeneration Act 1996, part 2, provides for the speedy resolution of construction industry disputes. It applies only where the contract is in writing (s. 107) and it does not apply to contracts with residential occupiers (s. 106). A party to a contract to which the Act applies has the right to refer a dispute arising under the contract for adjudication under a procedure that complies with s. 108. To the extent that a construction contract does not do this, the adjudication provisions contained in the Scheme for Construction Contracts (England and Wales) Regulations, SI 1998/649, apply (see s. 108(5)). By s. 108(2) an adjudicator is required to reach a decision within 28 days after a referral, or such longer term as may be agreed by the parties. A clause in a construction contract that provided that the adjudicator's decision was valid even if issued out of time meant that the Housing Grants,

Construction and Regeneration Act 1996, s. 108(2)(c) and (d), had not been complied with. This meant that the provisions in the Scheme for Construction Contracts applied to the dispute (*Aveat Heating Ltd v Jerram Falkus Construction Ltd* [2007] EWHC 131 (TCC), 113 Con LR 13). By s. 108(3) the construction contract must provide that the adjudicator's decision is binding until the dispute is finally determined by legal proceedings, by arbitration or agreement. The parties may agree to accept the decision of the adjudicator as finally determining the dispute.

Adjudications are intended to be provisional, but binding, decisions (*Macob Civil Engineering Ltd v Morrison Construction Ltd* [1999] BLR 93 at [14]). The policy is 'pay now, argue later' (*RJT Consulting Engineers Ltd v DM Engineering (Northern Ireland) Ltd* [2002] EWCA Civ 270, [2002] 1 WLR 2344). A party with the benefit of an adjudicator's decision may bring enforcement proceedings by issuing a Part 8 claim form, and then entering default judgment (*Coventry Scaffolding Co. (London) Ltd v Lancsville Construction Ltd* [2009] EWHC 2995 (TCC), LTL 3/12/2009), if there is no acknowledgment of service, or otherwise applying for summary judgment. In most cases it is to be expected that summary judgment will be entered in accordance with the policy of the Act.

Summary judgment will be refused, however, if the defendant advances a properly arguable jurisdictional objection, such as a dispute about whether there was a written construction contract between the parties (*Pegram Shopfitters Ltd v Tally Weijl (UK) Ltd* [2003] EWCA Civ 1750, [2004] 1 WLR 2082), or a dispute that the defendant was a party to the relevant contract (*Estor Ltd v Multifit (UK) Ltd* [2009] EWHC 2108 (TCC), 126 Con LR 40). An issue as to whether an implied term existed does not impact on the question of whether the contract was in writing for the purposes of s. 107 (*Connex South Eastern Ltd v MJ Building Services Group plc* [2004] EWHC 1518 (TCC), [2004] BLR 333). A list of nine questions which are relevant where there is a dispute over an adjudicator's jurisdiction was suggested in *McAlpine PPS Pipeline Systems Ltd v Transco plc* [2004] EWHC 2030 (TCC), [2004] BLR 352. Summary judgment was refused in *Lead Technical Services Ltd v CMS Medical Ltd* [2007] EWCA Civ 316, [2007] BLR 251, because there was a real prospect that the defendant could prove that the original agreement between the parties had been supplanted by a signed deed of appointment which had the effect of depriving the adjudicator of jurisdiction. If the defendant has agreed that the adjudicator can rule on the issue of jurisdiction and that he will be bound by the adjudicator's decision, summary judgment will be entered even if the adjudicator is wrong (*Thomas-Fredric's (Construction) Ltd v Wilson* [2003] EWCA Civ 1494, [2004] BLR 23 at [20]). Summary judgment may also be entered if the defendant has not submitted to the adjudicator's jurisdiction, provided the adjudicator's decision is plainly right (*Thomas-Fredric's (Construction) Ltd v Wilson*).

Summary judgment will also be entered where the defendant has not paid the amount due under an architect's certificate, unless the defendant has given an effective notice of intention to withhold payment under s. 111. This is so even if the certificate might be wrong (*Rupert Morgan Building Services (LLC) Ltd v Jervis* [2003] EWCA Civ 1563, [2004] 1 WLR 1867).

Performance bonds

A bank which has given a performance bond must honour that obligation according to its **34.21**
terms. The bank cannot rely on issues relating to the relations between the supplier and the customer, or whether the supplier has performed its obligations, or with any question of whether the supplier is in default. The bank must pay according to its guarantee, on demand if so stipulated, without proof or conditions. The only exception is where there is clear fraud of which the bank has notice at the date when payment was due (*Edward Owen Engineering Ltd v Barclays Bank International Ltd* [1978] QB 159 at p. 171). The fraud exception applies where there is clear evidence both of the fraud and the bank's knowledge. There must be a real prospect on the material available that the only realistic inference is that the beneficiary could not have honestly believed in the validity of its demand on its performance bond (*United Trading Corporation SA v Allied Arab Bank Ltd* [1985] 2 Lloyd's Rep 554 as interpreted by *Solo Industries UK Ltd v Canara Bank* [2001] EWCA Civ 1041, [2001] 1 WLR 1800 at [32]). In applying this test the court

must be careful not to upset what is in effect a strong presumption in favour of fulfilment of the bank's obligation under a performance guarantee (*Czarnikow-Rionda Sugar Trading Inc. v Standard Bank London Ltd* [1999] 1 All ER (Comm) 890 at p. 913). The effect is that there is a heightened test in relation to the fraud exception in an application for summary judgment against a bank (*Banque Saudi Fransi v Lear Siegler Services Inc.* [2006] EWCA Civ 1130, [2007] 1 All ER (Comm) 67 at [16]).

Conversely, in an application for summary judgment by a bank which has honoured a performance bond against a person who has given the bank a counter-indemnity, the normal 'real prospect of success' test applies (*Banque Saudi Fransi v Lear Siegler Services Inc.* at [18]).

Evidence not yet investigated

34.22 Where the contractual position between the parties needs to be investigated, and disclosure has not taken place, summary judgment should be refused (*Groveholt Ltd v Hughes* [2008] EWHC 1358 (Ch), LTL 27/6/2008). Summary judgment was regarded as inappropriate in *Derksen v Pillar* (2002) LTL 17/12/2002 because evidence was still being acquired or investigated and the claim raised complex issues.

Where an issue requires the court to consider conduct over a period of time, it is unlikely that the issue can be disposed of on an application for summary judgment (*Celador Productions Ltd v Melville* [2004] EWHC 2362 (Ch), 28(1) IPD 10). In *Microsoft Corporation v P4 Com Ltd* [2007] EWHC 746 (Ch), LTL 23/4/2007, the claimant alleged trade mark and copyright infringement during a specific 14-month period. The defendant sought summary judgment, relying on documentary evidence supporting its allegation that it had been a dormant company during that period. Summary judgment was refused, because the evidence adduced was simply that chosen by the defendant. Disclosure and cross-examination could be revelatory and could completely change the picture, and there was evidence that the defendant had operated a website during the relevant period which could have been used for allegedly infringing activities. On the other hand, in *Mancini v Telecommunications UK Ltd* [2003] EWHC 211 (Ch), LTL 16/1/2003, the lack of evidence produced by the claimant resulted in the claim being struck out. It was reasonable to expect the claimant to have numerous documents, and to be able to produce witnesses, to explain what had happened in relation to the key issue. The court was not impressed by the explanation, first raised on appeal, that the documents had been destroyed in a flood, and there was no explanation for not adducing witness statements dealing with the facts.

Case management reasons

34.23 Case management decisions, or the failure to comply with them, may make it plain that one side has no real prospect of success. For example, various paragraphs might be struck out of a statement of case, and the court might grant summary judgment because the remainder may mean there is no real prospect of success. In *Wright v Basildon and Thurrock Hospital NHS Trust* (2011) LTL 8/12/2011, the claimant in a clinical dispute was debarred from relying on all the medical evidence other than a written report, and did not apply to vary or set aside that order. On an application for summary judgment heard three days before the trial it was held the claimant had no real prospect of success, given the heavy burden on a claimant in a clinical dispute, and the fact the report would be untested by cross-examination.

In complex and borderline cases there may be sound case management reasons for adjourning an application for summary judgment to trial. In some cases an appeal against the summary judgment decision will jeopardise the trial date. This may mean it is better to adjourn the summary judgment application to trial (*Monsanto Technology LLC v Cargill International SA* (2006) LTL 13/11/2006; *Doncaster Pharmaceuticals Group Ltd v Bolton Pharmaceutical Co. 100 Ltd* [2006] EWCA Civ 661, [2007] FSR 3).

Conduct in the litigation

In *Penningtons v Abedi* (1999) LTL 13/8/99 there had been ongoing litigation in which the defendant had advanced a series of defences, each of which had been shown to be false. An application was made for summary judgment, and it was held that the defendant's conduct of the litigation was such that there was no realistic prospect of her successfully defending the claim. 34.24

Contemporaneous documentation

There are cases where the contemporaneous documentation shows that the respondent will never be able to establish its case at trial, and in those cases, such as *Collins v Union Bank of Switzerland* (2000) LTL 25/5/2000, summary judgment will be entered. In *Abelene Ltd v Cranbrook Finance Inc.* (2000) LTL 25/8/2000 it was held that although it was open to a court to accept documents produced at the last moment by a respondent to an application for summary judgment, if there was no explanation as to the circumstances in which the documents were executed or why they were not produced at the proper time, it would also be open to the court to be sufficiently suspicious of their genuineness to disregard them. Summary judgment was entered in *Musical Fidelity Ltd v Vickers* [2002] EWCA Civ 1989, LTL 2/12/2002, where the contents of the defendant's website established a clear case of infringement of the claimant's trade mark. Likewise, in *National Westminster plc v Szirtes* (2003) LTL 27/6/2003, the cumulative effect of all the evidence, and in particular the correspondence between the parties, strained the credibility of the defendants' evidence that they were unaware of the guarantees relied upon by the bank to such an extent that they had no real prospect of success. A slightly different formulation was applied in *Hussain v Cuddy Woods and Cochrane* [2001] Lloyd's Rep PN 134, where it was said in a professional negligence claim against a barrister that, from a consideration of the voluminous documentation available, it was 'difficult to see how the claimant could establish' his claim, and summary judgment was entered in favour of the defendant. 34.25

In *Vaseeharan v Uthayaranjan* [2010] EWHC 1083 (Ch), LTL 24/5/2010, the key issue between the parties was whether the defendant was an employee (as contended by the claimant) or a partner (as contended by the defendant) of the claimant. There was no contemporaneous documentation of either a contract of employment or a partnership deed or agreement. That was not regarded as surprising in what was plainly an informal arrangement. What made a difference was the complete lack of evidence to show the defendant asked for any annual accounts or payment of his share of the alleged partnership profits for a period of almost five years. Summary judgment was entered for the claimant on this part of the claim.

Amendment

It is inappropriate to subject a pleading to too close a syntactical analysis on an application for summary judgment where it is clear on the pleadings overall what the real issues are, and where any defects in the respondent's pleaded case can be saved by amendment (*Landfast (Anglia) Ltd v Cameron Taylor One Ltd* [2008] EWHC 343 (TCC), LTL 23/5/2008). As it was put by Moore-Bick LJ in *P and O Nedlloyd BV v Arab Metals Co. (No. 2)* [2006] EWCA Civ 1717, [2007] 1 WLR 2288 at [62], a respondent to an application for summary judgment cannot be strictly confined to matters set out in his existing statement of case. If the problem with the respondent's case is one of how the case is put rather than of substance, the court has a wide power to allow an amendment to correct the problem, which can be exercised at the hearing (*Stewart v Engel* [2000] 1 WLR 2268) or on an appeal (*Islington London Borough Council v Uckac* [2006] EWCA Civ 340, [2006] 1 WLR 1303 at [39]). 34.26

ADMISSIONS

In *E. D. and F. Man Liquid Products Ltd v Patel* [2003] EWCA Civ 472, [2003] CPLR 384, a defence which might have had a real prospect of success was destroyed by clear, written admissions made by 34.27

the defendant. Likewise, in *Soir Contracting and General Trading Co. v Desai* [2006] EWCA Civ 245, LTL 14/2/2006, despite a lack of documentary evidence substantiating the claim, and an allegation that the defendant was the victim of a dishonest fabrication, clear, signed acknowledgments of the debt by the defendant meant the defence had no real prospect of success. In *Equant SAS v Ives* [2002] EWHC 1992 (Ch), LTL 4/10/2002, the defendant was permitted to resile from an admission in the defence, and on the amended case there were disputes of fact which resulted in summary judgment being refused. A defendant seeking to avoid summary judgment being entered on an admission has to issue an application for permission to amend, otherwise the court is entitled to enter judgment on the unamended statement of case (*Loveridge v Healey* [2004] EWCA Civ 173, *The Times*, 27 February 2004).

Whether an apparent admission is binding on a party and such as to justify the entry of summary judgment is considered further at **34.29** to **34.33**.

Whether the admission binds the other party

34.28 In the case of parties which are artificial bodies, such as registered companies, an issue arises as to whether the individual said to have made the admission was authorised in fact or in law to bind the party in question in this way. Much depends on the seniority of the individual within the body in question, and on the nature of the relationship between the individual and that body. So, a limited company's directors or solicitor would have authority to bind it when making an admission, whereas an ordinary employee would not in the absence of express authority from the directors. Questions of actual, apparent or ostensible and usual authority of agents may arise, for which see the general works on agency.

Under the general law of evidence, binding admissions can sometimes be made by persons connected with a party. Typical examples are admissions made by partners (see the Partnership Act 1890, s. 15), predecessors in title and referees.

A related question is the extent to which a party is bound by an admission once it has been made. The following distinctions must be drawn between:

(a) formal and informal admissions (see **34.29**). Any fact which is formally admitted is no longer in issue, whereas an informal admission is merely an item of evidence;
(b) admissions made before and after proceedings are issued (see **34.30**). Admissions made before proceedings are issued can only be informal admissions;
(c) pre-action admissions made in fast track personal injuries claims and in other types of claims (see **34.30**). A pre-action admission in a fast track personal injury claim made before 6 April 2007 may bind the person making it;
(d) admissions made in certain personal injuries claims from 6 April 2007, when **CPR, r. 14.1A**, came into force. It restricts the ability of a party to withdraw pre-action admissions in these claims (see **34.30**); and
(e) admissions made with and without a proper understanding of the situation (see **34.32**).

Formal and informal admissions

34.29 Admissions may be formal or informal. As discussed in **chapters 17, 26** and **27**, the statements of case, and in particular the defence and any reply, may well contain admissions. These reduce the area of dispute, and can be very helpful in summary judgment applications. Admissions in statements of case are one example of formal admissions, which have the effect of establishing the facts admitted without the need to call evidence, and which can only be withdrawn with the permission of the court. Other examples of formal admissions are admissions made and recorded at a case management conference or pre-trial review, admissions made in reply to a notice to admit facts (see **49.9**) and admissions made by counsel at trial (for which see *Worldwide Corporation Ltd v Marconi Communications Ltd* (1999) *The Times*, 7 July 1999).

Informal admissions, on the other hand, are merely items of evidence and may be disproved or explained away by other evidence at trial. Informal admissions may be oral statements made by a party or person connected to a party which are at least partially adverse to that party's case, or may be made in correspondence. Admissions made in statements of case in other proceedings, or by witnesses called by a party in other proceedings, are not binding as informal admissions in the present proceedings (*British Thomson-Houston Co. Ltd v British Insulated and Helsby Cables Ltd* [1924] 2 Ch 160). Rather inconsistently, it was held in the old case of *Brickell v Hulse* (1837) 7 Ad & El 454 that reliance on written evidence in earlier proceedings can amount to an informal admission of anything contained in that evidence. Possibly this can be explained on the basis that by relying on written evidence the party is to be taken as adopting it, whereas the details of oral testimony are uncertain until the evidence has been called, and that statements of case are delivered for the purposes of the present litigation only. Admissions made in answers to requests for further information in the present action are probably formal admissions because of the need to include a statement of truth.

Withdrawing and amending admissions

A party may withdraw a pre-action admission if it was made before 6 April 2007 as of right, and court permission is not required (*Sowerby v Charlton* [2005] EWCA Civ 1610, [2006] 1 WLR 568). *Gale v Superdrug Stores plc* [1996] 1 WLR 1089, which held that the court could investigate the defendant's explanation for a decision to withdraw a pre-action admission, is no longer good law. *Sowerby v Charlton* was followed by *Walley v Stoke-on-Trent City Council* [2006] EWCA Civ 1137, [2007] 1 WLR 352. A withdrawn pre-action admission is merely an item of evidence. Exceptionally, summary judgment may be available even after a pre-action admission is withdrawn if the other facts in the case mean that any defence has no real prospects of success. It may also be possible to strike out the defence if the withdrawal of the pre-action admission was made in bad faith (*Walley v Stoke-on-Trent City Council*). **34.30**

Commentary

Restrictions on withdrawing pre-action admissions are made by **CPR, r. 14.1A**, with effect from 6 April 2007. These restrictions apply if the pre-action admission:

(a) was made after 5 April 2007 (Civil Procedure (Amendment No. 3) Rules 2006 (SI 2006/3435), r. 5);
(b) was made by a notice in writing (**CPR, r. 14.1A(1)**);
(c) was made in one of the types of proceedings listed in **PD 14, para. 1.1(2)**; and
(d) was made either:
    (i) after the party making it had received a letter before claim written in accordance with **PD Pre-action Conduct** or any relevant pre-action protocol (**CPR, r. 14.1A(2)(a)**); or
    (ii) before receipt of a letter before claim, but is stated to be made under **Part 14** (**r. 14.1A(2)(b)**).

The proceedings listed in **PD 14, para. 1.1(2)** are claims governed by either the **Pre-action Protocol for Personal Injury Claims** (see **8.16**); the **Pre-action Protocol for the Resolution of Clinical Disputes** (see **8.61**); or the **Pre-action Protocol for Disease and Illness Claims** (see **8.64**). The reference to **PD Pre-action Conduct** in **CPR, r. 14.1A(2)(a)**, only describes the nature of the letter before claim. It does not extend the types of relevant proceedings to cases not covered by specific protocols. A note to **PD 14, para. 1.1(2)**, makes it clear that for this purpose the **Pre-action Protocol for Personal Injury Claims** applies to all personal injury claims regardless of the value of the claim.

If these conditions are satisfied, such an admission may be withdrawn before proceedings are issued only with the consent of the person to whom the admission was made (**r. 14.1A(3)(a)**). After proceedings are issued, such an admission may only be withdrawn if all parties consent or if the court gives permission (**r. 14.1A(3)(b)**). Once proceedings are issued, any party may apply for judgment on the pre-action admission, and the party who made it may apply (or cross-apply) for permission to withdraw it (**r. 14.1A(4)** and **(5)**).

Withdrawal and amendment of post-issue admissions is governed by **r. 14.1(5)**, see **34.31**, and by the rules on amendment of statements of case (see **chapter 31**).

Permission to withdraw or amend admissions

34.31 Once proceedings have been issued, a party seeking to amend or withdraw a pre-action admission made after 5 April 2007 or a post-issue admission should either:

(a) obtain the consent of all the other parties (**CPR, r. 14.1A(3)(b)** for pre-action admissions; **r. 17.1(2)(a)** for admissions in statements of case); or
(b) apply or cross-apply for permission (**r. 14.1A(3)(b)** for pre-action admissions; **rr. 14.1(5)** and **17.3** for admissions in statements of case).

In deciding whether to give permission to withdraw an admission, the court is required by **PD 14, para.** 7.2, to have regard to all the circumstances of the case, including:

(a) the grounds upon which the applicant seeks to withdraw the admission, including whether or not new evidence has come to light which was not available at the time the admission was made;
(b) the conduct of the parties, including any conduct which led the applicant into making the admission;
(c) any prejudice that may be caused to any person if the admission is withdrawn;
(d) the prejudice that may be caused to any person if the application is refused;
(e) the stage in the proceedings at which the application to withdraw is made, and in particular in relation to the trial date or window;
(f) the prospects of success (if the admission is withdrawn) of the claim or part of the claim in relation to which the admission was made; and
(g) the interests of the administration of justice.

Brooke LJ in *Sowerby v Charlton* [2005] EWCA Civ 1610, [2006] 1 WLR 568, a decision before **para.** 7.2 was introduced on 6 April 2007, endorsed a number of guidelines suggested by Sumner J in *Basildon and Thurrock University NHS Trust v Braybrook* [2004] EWHC 3352 (Fam), LTL 7/1/2005. These may be of continuing importance. They include seeking to give effect to the overriding objective, whether the application to withdraw the admission is made in good faith, whether any party has been the author of any prejudice he might suffer, and the need to avoid satellite litigation and the disproportionate use of court resources.

In *White v Greensand Homes Ltd* [2007] EWCA Civ 643, [2007] 1 CLC 1001, the defendant consulting engineers admitted an allegation that they had designed the foundations for a building, and defended the claim on other grounds. After reviewing the matter, the engineers found that the design work had been done by another contractor (a company that was dissolved three years before the current application), and applied to amend by withdrawing the admission. The admission in the defence repeated one that had been made in earlier correspondence. The admission in the letter was before the expiry of limitation, the original defence was after the expiry of limitation. If there had been no letter, the amendment would simply have been allowed, because there would have been no claim lost because of the admission. With the letter, there was potential prejudice to the claimant. The amendment should only be allowed if the claimant could be left in no worse a position than if the amended defence had been served at the time of the original defence, and in no better position than if the claimant had applied to strike it out under **CPR, r. 3.4(2)(b)**. Taking into account the risk of finding liability on a false basis, the chances of the claimant bringing a claim against the other contractor relying on the latent damage provisions, and the risk the other contractor may have been unable to pay at all stages, the balance favoured granting permission to withdraw the admission.

Admissions of limited evidential value

An 'admission' made without knowledge of the facts said to have been admitted has little if any evidential value (see *Comptroller of Customs v Western Lectric Co. Ltd* [1966] AC 367). Also, the 'admission' must be one of fact, not law. In *Ashmore v Corporation of Lloyd's* [1992] 1 WLR 446 the House of Lords held that statements made by members of the Committee of Lloyd's said to be admissions that the defendants owed a duty of care to 'names' (members of underwriting syndicates) concerned a question of law and so the statements were neither relevant nor admissible. **34.32**

Obtaining judgment on admissions

There is rarely any doubt about formal admissions, although occasionally points of construction are taken in respect of admissions said to have been made in statements of case. Informal admissions, on the other hand, need to be proved. In *Re Beeny* [1894] 1 Ch 499 judgment was entered on the basis of informal oral admissions made by the defendant to the claimant's solicitor. The admissions were proved by an affidavit sworn by the solicitor, the court having to decide whether the admissions were sufficiently proved and sufficiently clear. As North J said in this case: **34.33**

> No doubt, if the alleged admission is only verbal, there is more difficulty in treating it as sufficient, if there be any dispute as to the fact of its having been made.

Commentary

CONDITIONAL ORDERS

PD 24, para. 4, provides that where it appears to the court possible that a claim or defence may succeed but improbable that it will do so, the court may make a conditional order. **Paragraph 5.2** provides that a conditional order is an order which requires a party: **34.34**

(a) to pay a sum of money into court (which is complied with if a cheque is lodged with the Court Funds Office by the final date specified in the order, even if the cheque does not clear until later: *Petróleo Brasileiro SA v Ene Kos 1 Ltd* [2009] EWCA Civ 1127, [2010] 1 All ER 1099); or
(b) to take a specified step in relation to his claim or defence, as the case may be, and which provides that that party's claim will be dismissed or his statement of case will be struck out if he does not comply.

Conditional orders are appropriate for cases in the grey area between granting judgment and dismissing the application. A conditional order was appropriate where the prospects of success on a defence of *force majeure* or frustration were felt to be remote in *Classic Maritime Inc. v Lion Diversified Holdings Bhd* [2009] EWHC 1142 (Comm), [2010] 1 Lloyd's Rep 59. A conditional order was made against the claimant in *Olatawura v Abiloye* [2002] EWCA Civ 998, [2003] 1 WLR 275, where the claim, which was based on an oral contract, had limited prospects of success. A similar case was *Allen Wilson Joinery Ltd v Privetgrange Construction Ltd* [2008] EWHC 2802 (TCC), 123 Con LR 1, where there were issues as to whether any oral agreement was superseded by a quotation in an email, and whether the eventual contract required working drawings. In *Homebase Ltd v LSS Services Ltd* [2004] EWHC 3182 (Ch), LTL 28/6/2004, the claimant made a claim against the defendant seeking five months' licence fees for occupying a site. The defendant filed a witness statement to the effect that the claimant had orally agreed that the defendant need pay nothing until the claimant had obtained consent from its landlord to assign the land to the defendant. The claimant denied there was any such agreement. Despite the absence of contemporaneous documents, it could not be said that the defendant's version of events was incredible. Entering summary judgment was therefore inappropriate, but because of the justifiable doubts about the defendant's version, a conditional order was made requiring the whole sum claimed to be paid into court.

Amount to be paid in

34.35 If the court decides to make the respondent to the application pay money into court under a conditional order, it must decide how much should be paid in. The starting point has traditionally been the full amount of the claim. However, the court has a discretion, which it will exercise in accordance with the overriding objective. Obviously, the more uncertain the defence, the more likely it is that the court will order the full amount to be paid in. Another factor is the defendant's ability to pay. Under the old rules (and similar principles are applied under the CPR, see *Sweetman v Shepherd* (2000) *The Times*, 29 March 2000), Lord Diplock in *M. V. Yorke Motors v Edwards* [1982] 1 WLR 444 endorsed the following principles:

(a) Defendants seeking to limit a financial condition must make full and frank disclosure of their finances. This is done on affidavit or witness statement. It is common for defendants who realise that a conditional order may be made to produce such written evidence in advance of the summary judgment hearing, and to disclose it to the claimant on the claimant undertaking not to refer to it unless a conditional order is made.
(b) Reliance on a legal aid certificate as evidence of impecuniosity is not enough.
(c) The test is whether it will be impossible for the defendant to comply with the financial condition, as opposed to merely finding it difficult. An impossible condition is tantamount to entering judgment.

M. V. Yorke Motors were suing Mr Edwards for breach of warranty of title in relation to a contract for the sale of a car for £23,520. Conditional leave to defend was given, because the court was sceptical about his defence that he was only acting as the agent for a foreign buyer. By the time of the hearing Mr Edwards was unemployed, living with his father, and in receipt of legal aid with a nil contribution. The House of Lords substituted a condition of bringing £3,000 into court. The 'impossibility' test on the amount to pay in is sometimes modified for the purpose of avoiding a conditional order stifling the defence (see *Kazeminy v Siddiqi* [2010] EWHC 201 (Comm), LTL 2/3/2010).

A claimant who intends to invite the court to make a conditional order if summary judgment is not granted should give the defendant notice of that intention in advance of the hearing. If this is not done, the judge should not make such an order without giving the defendant an opportunity to be heard (and adduce evidence) on questions such as whether the defendant has the means to pay the amount contemplated (*Anglo-Eastern Trust Ltd v Kermanshahchi* [2002] EWCA Civ 198, [2002] CP Rep 36).

Where money is paid into court in compliance with a conditional order, the claimant is a secured creditor for that amount in the event of the defendant's bankruptcy (*Re Ford* [1900] 2 QB 211).

CROSS-CLAIMS

34.36 Cross-claims fall into three categories. Where the only answer to the claim is a cross-claim, the nature and effect of the three types are as follows:

(a) Cross-claims unconnected with the claim. Here, summary judgment should be entered. An example is *Rotheram v Priest* (1879) 41 LT 558, where the claimant claimed arrears of rent, and the defendant counterclaimed in libel. It was held that the counterclaim was totally foreign to the claim, so summary judgment was given to the claimant. The result would be the same under the CPR.
(b) Counterclaims linked to the claim. The appropriate order used to be for judgment subject to a stay of execution pending trial of the counterclaim. In *Drake and Fletcher Ltd v Batchelor* (1986) 130 SJ 285 Sir Neil Lawson said that in considering whether to grant a stay of execution, 'The question is whether the two contracts are so closely linked that it would be fair

and equitable to deprive the [claimant] of the fruits of its judgment until resolution of the counterclaim'. The judge said there were three matters which needed to be considered:

(i) The degree of connection between the claim and the counterclaim.
(ii) The strength of the counterclaim. The weaker it was, the weaker the case for granting a stay.
(iii) The claimant's ability to satisfy any judgment on the counterclaim. Any doubt on this matter strengthened the case for granting a stay.

There is some doubt about how cases where the only matter raised by the defendant is a connected counterclaim should be dealt with under the CPR. There is no longer any equivalent to the former RSC, ord. 14, r. 3(2), which provided for a stay of execution in summary judgment applications where there was a connected counterclaim. Early drafts of the CPR had a directly equivalent provision, and the probable consequence of removing it from the final version of the rules is that the court should simply enter judgment for the claimant. If this is correct, there is no longer any practical difference between this type of counterclaim and totally unconnected cross-claims.

(c) Set-offs. Where a counterclaim amounts to a set-off it is a defence to the claim and any summary judgment application should be dismissed, provided the value of the set-off is at least equal to the value of the claim. Where a set-off is not worth as much as the claim, the appropriate order is for summary judgment for the undisputed balance. The nature of set-offs is considered in **34.37**.

Commentary

Set-offs

The following are established set-off situations: **34.37**

(a) Mutual debts. By virtue of the 18th-century Statutes of Set-off, mutual debts owed between the claimant and the defendant can be set off against each other. There is no need for the transactions giving rise to the debts to be connected other than through the parties. They need not be debts, strictly so-called, but may sound in damages provided they are capable of being ascertained with precision at the time of the application (*Morley v Inglis* (1837) 4 Bing NC 58, applied in *Axel Johnson Petroleum AB v MG Mineral Group AG* [1992] 1 WLR 270). A former partner was held in *Hurst v Bennett* [2001] 2 BCLC 290 to be unable to set off claims for money allegedly owed to him on the taking of partnership accounts against the claim of certain of the former partners to be indemnified against expenses they had incurred on the ground of lack of mutuality.
(b) Sale of goods. By virtue of the **Sale of Goods Act 1979, s. 53(1)**, a buyer may set off counterclaims for breach of the statutory implied conditions about satisfactory quality, fitness for purpose and correspondence to description against a claim by the seller for the price.
(c) On a claim for the price of services, for example, where a builder is suing for the price of building work done, the defendant can set off a counterclaim for damages for poor workmanship in respect of the contract the claimant is suing on (*Basten v Butler* (1806) 7 East 479).
(d) Arrears of rent. Where a landlord brings a claim for arrears of rent, the tenant is allowed to set off a counterclaim for damages against the landlord for breach of a covenant in the lease in respect of which the landlord is claiming (*British Anzani (Felixstowe) Ltd v International Marine Management (UK) Ltd* [1980] QB 137, not following *Hart v Rogers* [1916] 1 KB 646, confirmed by *Agyeman v Boadi* (1996) 28 HLR 558). A tenant does not have a similar right of set-off in respect of a counterclaim for breach of repairing obligations against a claim for service charges as against a manager appointed by the court under the Landlord and Tenant Act 1987, s. 24(1) (*Taylor v Blaquiere* [2002] EWCA Civ 1633, *The Times*, 21 November 2002), nor where the tenant's failure to pay has the intended consequence that the landlord will be unable to meet the repairing covenant (*Bluestorm Ltd v Portvale Holdings Ltd* [2004] EWCA Civ 289, [2004] HLR 49).
(e) Equitable set-off.

Mutual debts amount to set-offs whether or not the relevant transactions are connected, but they must be liquidated. Set-offs in categories (b) to (d) above involve liquidated claims and unliquidated cross-claims arising from the same transaction. A defendant relying on an unliquidated cross-claim also has to establish a case with at least a real prospect of success on quantum. An alleged set-off will be ineffective if its value cannot be quantified (*Eilon and Associates Ltd v Easygroup IP Licensing Ltd* (2011) LTL 15/4/2011). If the amount to be set off is less than the amount claimed, it can be effective as a partial defence.

The authorities on equitable set-off were reviewed in *Geldof Metaalconstructie NV v Simon Carves Ltd* [2010] EWCA Civ 667, [2010] 4 All ER 847. There has for a long time been a lack of clarity over when a cross-claim will amount to an equitable set-off (*Aries Tanker Corporation v Total Transport Ltd* [1977] 1 WLR 185). One test, which can be traced back to *Rawson v Samuel* (1841) Cr & Ph 161 (per Lord Cottenham at p. 178), and which was applied in modern authorities such as *Federal Commerce and Navigation Co. Ltd v Molena Alpha Inc.* [1978] QB 927 at pp. 974–5 (not affected by the appeal to the House of Lords), was whether there was an equity which went to impeach the claimant's demands ('the impeachment of title test'). Rix LJ in *Geldof Metaalconstructie NV v Simon Carves Ltd* at [28]–[31] applied Lord Brandon of Oakbrook's reasoning from *Bank of Boston Connecticut v European Grain and Shipping Ltd* [1989] AC 1056 at pp. 1106–10 in concluding that the impeachment of title test has been rejected as of continuing use in the modern world.

The test for whether a cross-claim amounts to an equitable set-off used by Lord Brandon in *Bank of Boston Connecticut v European Grain and Shipping Ltd* was whether the cross-claim 'flows out of and is inseparably connected with the dealings and transactions giving rise to the subject of the claim'. In *Geldof Metaalconstructie NV v Simon Carves Ltd* at [43(vi)] Rix LJ preferred a test based on the discredited passage of Lord Denning MR's judgment in *Federal Commerce and Navigation Co. Ltd v Molena Alpha Inc.*, but with the offending reference to the impeachment of title test removed, as the best modern statement of the test, namely whether the cross-claim is 'so closely connected with [the claimant's] demands that it would be manifestly unjust to allow him to enforce payment without taking into account the cross-claim'.

Care also needs to be taken with this formulation, because 'manifest injustice' was omitted from the formulation of Lord Brandon in *Bank of Boston Connecticut v European Grain and Shipping Ltd*, a matter considered important by Potter LJ in *Bim Kemi v Blackburn Chemicals Ltd* [2001] EWCA Civ 457, [2001] 2 Lloyd's Rep 93 at [38]. Rix LJ in *Geldof Metaalconstructie NV v Simon Carves Ltd* at [43(iv)] concluded that Lord Brandon did not intend to remove the manifest injustice element of the test, which has been emphasised in all the modern cases, including *Bim Kemi v Blackburn Chemicals Ltd* itself. The reason Lord Brandon did not refer to manifest injustice was that in *Bank of Boston Connecticut v European Grain and Shipping Ltd* Lord Brandon was focusing on dethroning the impeachment of title test.

In applying the modern test in *Geldof Metaalconstructie NV v Simon Carves Ltd*, Rix LJ at [43(ii)–(iv)] said there are two elements:

(a) A formal requirement of close connection between the claim and cross-claim. This is to ensure the doctrine of equitable set-off is based on principle and not discretion. There have been various ways in which this has been expressed in the cases: 'so closely connected with [the claimant's] demands that it would be manifestly unjust to allow him to enforce payment without taking into account the cross-claim' (*Federal Commerce and Navigation Co. Ltd v Molena Alpha Inc.*); 'flowing out of and inseparably connected with the dealings and transactions which also give rise to the claim' (*Government of Newfoundland v Newfoundland Railway Co.* (1888) 13 App Cas 199); 'inseparably connected so that the one ought not to be enforced without taking into account the other' (*Dole Dried Fruit and Nut Co. v Trustin Kerwood Ltd* [1990] 2 Lloyd's Rep 309). These should not be regarded as competing tests, but as different ways of expressing the broad concept that there has to be a close connection. This is an area where the courts have wisely refused to get bogged down in nuances of formulation (*Bim Kemi v Blackburn Chemicals Ltd* per Potter LJ at [38] and *Geldof Metaalconstructie NV v Simon Carves Ltd* per Rix LJ at [43(iii)]).

(b) A functional requirement whereby it needs to be unjust to enforce the claim without taking into account the cross-claim. This is the 'manifestly unjust' element of Lord Denning's formulation. Ultimately the rationale of the principle is equity.

At [43(v)] Rix LJ expressly said these requirements are not to be regarded as establishing a two-stage test. Instead, he preferred to say that there is both a formal element in the test and a functional element.

In one-contract cases (where the cross-claim arises out of the alleged breach of the same contract on which the claim is based) the claim and cross-claim will almost certainly have a close connection. A counterclaim for breach of a financial consultant's fiduciary and contractual duties to act in the client's best interests was regarded as capable of being set off against a claim for the consultant's fees in *Eilon and Associates Ltd v Easygroup IP Licensing Ltd* (2011) LTL 15/4/2011 because both claims arose from the same contract. There is, nevertheless, high authority for the proposition that 'there is no universal rule that claims arising out of the same contract may be set off against each other in all circumstances' (per Lord Hobhouse in *Government of Newfoundland v Newfoundland Railway Co.* at p. 212). The exceptions, which in most cases should be regarded as not fulfilling the functional requirement of the test, are probably limited to the traditional categories where the court has taken the strict view that the claimant has the right to be paid a liquidated sum free from any set-off. These were identified by Potter LJ in *Bim Kemi v Blackburn Chemicals Ltd* at [38], including claims for rent, freight and sums due under bills of exchange. To these should be added claims for a solicitor's fees (*Templer v M'Lachlan* (1806) 2 Bos & P NR 136) and cases where there is an effective 'no set-off' clause in the contract (see **34.39**). Other than in these established exceptions, it is difficult to justify refusing to accept a one-contract cross-claim as an equitable set-off.

Commentary

Lord Denning's principle uses the expression 'without taking into account' the cross-claim. This is deliberately stated in non-quasi-statutory language (Rix LJ in *Geldof Metaalconstructie NV v Simon Carves Ltd* at [43]) to avoid spurious arguments that the doctrine is restricted to one-contract cases. There are various examples of two-contract cases where the doctrine has been applied in the past (examples include *Bankes v Jarvis* [1903] 1 KB 549; *Dole Dried Fruit and Nut Co. v Trustin Kerwood Ltd; Bim Kemi v Blackburn Chemicals Ltd*). As Lord Denning said in *Federal Commerce and Navigation Co. Ltd v Molena Alpha Inc.* at pp. 974–5, an equitable set-off may be based on a cross-claim that arises out of the same transaction or which is closely connected with it.

Geldof Metaalconstructie NV v Simon Carves Ltd itself was a two-contract case. Both contracts were between the same parties and related to the construction of a bioethanol plant. One was for goods to be supplied by the claimant ('the supply contract'), and the other for installation work to be done by the claimant ('the installation contract'). The dispute arose after the defendant alleged the claimant was in breach of the installation contract and issued a notice of default, and did not pay the claimant's invoice under the supply contract. The claimant then informed the defendant it would not continue with the installation work until the defendant paid all its outstanding invoices, including the invoice under the supply contract. The defendant then terminated the installation contract. The claimant issued proceedings for part of the contract price of the goods that became payable following delivery, and the defendant cross-claimed for damages for repudiation of an installation contract. It was held that the cross-claim amounted to an equitable set-off. While there were two contracts, they were both dedicated to the construction of the bioethanol plant. Any doubts about the degree of connection were dispelled by the claimant's conduct in insisting on payment of the supply contract invoice as a precondition for its continued performance of the installation contract. While the cross-claim did not arise from the supply contract or the claim for non-payment of the price, it did arise from the use to which the claimant sought to put its supply contract claim.

Geldof Metaalconstructie NV v Simon Carves Ltd was applied in *Addax Bank BSC v Wellesley Partners LLP* [2010] EWHC 1904 (QB), LTL 26/7/2010, where it was held there was a close connection between a claim for a liquidated sum payable under an investment contract and a cross-claim for unpaid invoices raised under an earlier consultancy contract which met the requirements for the cross-claim to amount to an equitable set-off. *Crastvell Trading Ltd v Bozel SA* [2010] EWHC 166 (Comm), LTL 10/3/2010, should be treated with caution. It applies a test of whether the cross-claim actually impugns the claim itself, which is probably a variant on the discredited impeachment of title test.

See also **63.19** on final judgments where there is an effective set-off.

34.38 **Parties to set-off** Although set-offs usually arise between the immediate parties to a transaction, this is not always the case. A defendant who has guaranteed payment of a debt owed to the claimant by a principal debtor can rely on set-offs and cross-claims available to the debtor. This principle extends to certain types of bonds entered into in building contracts (whereby the party giving the bond promises to pay a specified sum to the claimant if one of the contractors fails to perform) provided the bond is construed as a guarantee, see *Trafalgar House Construction (Regions) Ltd v General Surety and Guarantee Co. Ltd* [1996] AC 199.

Unliquidated damages claims which can be set off as between the original parties can also be set off against an assignee (*Hanak v Green* [1958] 2 QB 9), because an assignee of a chose in action takes subject to all rights of set-off available against the assignor (*Roxburghe v Cox* (1881) 17 ChD 520). A tenant is therefore entitled to set off any damages for disrepair due from the original landlord against a claim for arrears of rent brought by the landlord's assignee (*Smith v Muscat* [2003] EWCA Civ 962, [2003] 1 WLR 2853).

34.39 **Excluding rights of set-off** It is open to the parties to a contract to exclude any right to set-off by an express term to that effect (*Hong Kong and Shanghai Banking Corporation v Kloeckner & Co. AG* [1990] 2 QB 514), but it is possible that such a term may be unreasonable and rendered ineffective by virtue of the Unfair Contract Terms Act 1977, as happened in *Stewart Gill Ltd v Horatio Myer and Co. Ltd* [1992] QB 600. Where there is a dispute over the reasonableness of a contractual term excluding the right of set-off the court should either determine whether the clause is effective on the summary judgment application, or order its effectiveness to be tried as a preliminary issue (*Stewart Gill Ltd v Horatio Myer and Co. Ltd* at p. 604G). Making a conditional order is inappropriate because the purpose of such a clause is to enable the claimant to be treated almost as a cash seller, and delaying the issue until trial deprives the claimant of the benefit of the clause.

An example of the opposite of a 'no set-off' clause was a clause in the contract in *Geldof Metaalconstructie NV v Simon Carves Ltd* [2010] EWCA Civ 667, [2010] 4 All ER 847, which provided that the purchaser: 'shall be entitled from time to time to set off against the purchase order price any amounts lawfully due from the supplier to the purchaser whether under this purchase order or otherwise'. Such a clause should be given effect in accordance with its terms, and was regarded as effective in *Geldof Metaalconstructie NV v Simon Carves Ltd* (at [48]–[54]).

The cheque rule

34.40 Cheques are one form of bill of exchange. Where goods or services are paid for by cheque, two contracts are entered into by the parties. The first contract is the underlying contract for the sale of goods or for the provision of services. The second contract is contained in the cheque, whereby the drawer of the cheque undertakes to pay the payee the sum stated. If a cheque is dishonoured, the seller has the option of suing on the underlying contract or on the cheque.

If the seller sues on the underlying contract, the buyer is entitled to rely on any set-off that may be available in respect of that contract by way of defence to an application for summary judgment. However, if the seller sues on the cheque, the buyer is only permitted to raise defences relating to the cheque itself. The reason probably stems from the unconditional nature of a bill of exchange, as provided by the Bills of Exchange Act 1882, s. 3(1). As Lord Wilberforce said in *Nova (Jersey) Knit Ltd v Kammgarn Spinnerei GmbH* [1977] 1 WLR 713, bills of exchange 'are taken as equivalent to deferred instalments of cash. Therefore English law does not allow cross-claims or defences to be made.' The rule is regarded as being of considerable importance to the business community, and the courts will not 'whittle away [the] rule of practice by introducing unnecessary exceptions to it under influence of sympathy-evoking stories' (per Sachs LJ in *Cebora SNC v SIP (Industrial Products) Ltd* [1976] 1 Lloyd's Rep 271). It is only in exceptional circumstances that the court will allow a stay of execution when entering summary judgment for non-payment of a cheque. The fact the claimant is a company in administration is not an exceptional circumstance (*Isovel Contracts Ltd v ABB Building Technologies Ltd* [2002] 1 BCLC 390).

The cheque rule applies to:

(a) cheques and bills of exchange;
(b) direct debits (*Esso Petroleum Co. Ltd v Milton* [1997] 1 WLR 938);
(c) letters of credit (*SAFA Ltd v Banque du Caire* [2000] 2 All ER (Comm) 567); and
(d) performance bonds (*Solo Industries UK Ltd v Canara Bank* [2001] EWCA Civ 1041, [2001] 1 WLR 1800) (see **34.21**).

The cheque rule does not apply in the context of statutory demands (*Hofer v Strawson* [1999] 2 BCLC 336, a case which turns on the wording of the Insolvency Rules 1986 (SI 1986/1925), r. 6.5(4)).

There are some exceptional cases where summary judgment will not be given in a claim on a bill of exchange (see **34.42** to **34.44**). Before looking at these it is necessary to consider the nature of the claimant's title to the bill of exchange.

Types of holder of a bill of exchange Under the Bills of Exchange Act 1882 there are four types of holder of a bill of exchange. A mere holder is a person in possession of the bill. Although a mere holder can sue on the bill and give a valid discharge (s. 38), any claim is prone to be defeated for want of consideration. A holder for value is a person in possession of a bill who has given consideration sufficient to support a simple contract, or who derives title directly or indirectly from a previous holder who gave value for the bill (s. 27). A holder for value cannot be defeated on the ground of want of consideration. A holder in due course is broadly a holder of a complete and regular bill who gave value for it in good faith without notice of any defect in the title of the person who negotiated it (s. 29). A holder in due course obtains title to the bill free from equities and defects in the title of the transferor. The fourth type of holder is one who derives title through a holder in due course, and who broadly has all the rights of a holder in due course (s. 29(3)). **34.41**

An application for summary judgment by a mere holder will always be defeated by a plea of want of consideration, whereas an application by a holder in due course should always succeed as such a holder takes free of equities. If the claimant's title as a holder in due course is challenged by the defendant, judgment will only be given for the claimant if the claim to be a bona fide holder for value is supported by unchallenged or unchallengeable contemporary documents (*Bank für Gemeinwirtschaft AG v City of London Garages Ltd* [1971] 1 WLR 149). Holders for value are the most problematic category. They are also the most numerous, given that an immediate party to a bill cannot be a holder in due course (*R. E. Jones Ltd v Waring and Gillow Ltd* [1926] AC 670).

Fraud, duress and illegality To amount to a defence against a holder for value, an allegation of fraud, duress or illegality must be supported by evidence. A mere allegation in the **34.42**

Commentary

defendant's written evidence is insufficient (*Bank für Gemeinwirtschaft AG v City of London Garages Ltd* [1971] 1 WLR 149). Such a defence will not, however, avail against a holder in due course (see the Bills of Exchange Act 1882, s. 30(2)).

34.43 **No consideration** As explained in **34.40**, there will be a defence where the claimant is a mere holder who has given no consideration for the bill sued on. A total failure of consideration arises where a buyer lawfully rejects goods sold, the buyer being entitled to recover the price from the seller. Again summary judgment should be refused. Likewise, a liquidated partial failure of consideration is a defence *pro tanto* (*Thoni GmbH & Co. KG v RTP Equipment Ltd* [1979] 2 Lloyd's Rep 282). In *Isovel Contracts Ltd v ABB Building Technologies Ltd* [2002] 1 BCLC 390 the defendant countermanded a cheque given to a subcontractor in payment of the sum due under an interim certificate in a building project. The certificate had been issued by the main contractor, and, before payment of the cheque, had been shown to be wrong, because later certificates showed no money at all was due at the time the cheque was given. The subcontract provided that in this event any overpayment would be deducted from the amounts payable under subsequent interim certificates. It was held that in these circumstances the defendant could not rely on failure of consideration as a defence to an application for summary judgment.

34.44 **Misrepresentation** In *Clovertogs Ltd v Jean Scenes Ltd* [1982] Com LR 88 the Court of Appeal held that an allegation that the claimant had procured two cheques by misrepresentation amounted to a defence in an application for summary judgment. This decision was described as surprising in *Famous Ltd v Ge Im Ex Italia SRL* (1987) *The Times*, 3 August 1987, and should be regarded as wrongly decided as it is inconsistent with other cases on bills of exchange. Following *SAFA Ltd v Banque du Caire* [2000] 2 All ER (Comm) 567 and *Solo Industries UK Ltd v Canara Bank* [2001] 1 WLR 1800, a distinction needs to be drawn between:

(a) Cases where there is a misrepresentation by a beneficiary which was made directly to induce the execution of the bill of exchange (or other payment obligation covered by the cheque rule). In such cases, provided there is a real prospect of establishing the misrepresentation, summary judgment on the cheque (or other payment obligation) should be refused.
(b) Cases where an allegation of misrepresentation is in reality an allegation relating to the underlying contract of services or sale on which the payment obligation is based. In these cases summary judgment should be entered on the cheque (or other payment obligation), with no stay of execution. The courts need to be particularly astute in ensuring the cheque rule is not diluted by treating cases in this category as ones affecting the cheque or other payment obligation.

International trade

34.45 Irrevocable letters of credit are treated as cash and must be honoured. If the bank refuses to honour such a transaction, the court will grant summary judgment to the claimant (*Power Curber International Ltd v National Bank of Kuwait SAK* [1981] 1 WLR 1233). See also **34.21** on performance bonds. Summary judgment will also be given on a claim for freight even if there is a cross-claim relating to the cargo (*Aries Tanker Corporation v Total Transport Ltd* [1977] 1 WLR 185).

SOME OTHER COMPELLING REASON

34.46 Summary judgment will be refused if there is some other compelling reason why the case should be disposed of at a trial (**CPR, r. 24.2(b)**). An assertion that pleading a defence would infringe the defendant's *privilege against self-incrimination* does not amount to a compelling reason for a trial, nor for staying or adjourning a summary judgment application (*Versailles Trade Finance Ltd v Clough* [2001] EWCA Civ 1509, [2002] CP Rep 8). The privilege does not amount to a defence in civil proceedings, nor does it provide a right not to plead a defence. It does not, therefore, provide any basis for resisting an application for summary judgment (although the defendant in *Versailles Trade Finance Ltd v Clough* was allowed 14 days to file a full defence). Seeking an adjournment to negotiate with the claimant was not regarded as a compelling reason in *Phonographic Performance Ltd v Planet Ice (Peterborough) Ltd* [2004] EWHC 436 (Ch), LTL 2/2/2004. Reasons for going to trial include:

(a) The respondent is unable to contact a material witness who may provide material for a defence.
(b) The facts are wholly within the applicant's hands. In such a case it may be unjust to enter judgment without giving the respondent an opportunity of establishing a defence in the light of disclosure or after serving a request for further information (*Harrison v Bottenheim* (1878) 26 WR 362). However, summary judgment will not necessarily be refused in cases where the evidence for any possible defence could only lie with the applicant if there is nothing devious or artificial in the claim *State Trading Corporation of India v Doyle Carriers Inc.* [1991] 2 Lloyd's Rep 55).
(c) The case is highly complicated such that judgment should only be given after mature consideration at trial.
(d) Strange factual situations which call for further investigation. An example is *Global Marine Drillships Ltd v Landmark Solicitors LLP* [2011] EWHC 2685 (Ch), LTL 25/10/2011, where £7 million was deposited with a solicitor to pay an insurance premium on a policy that involved the services of a shadowy overseas broker.
(e) The applicant has acted harshly or unconscionably, or the facts disclose a suspicion of dishonesty or deviousness on the part of the applicant such that judgment should only be obtained in the light of publicity at trial. An example is *Miles v Bull* [1969] 1 QB 258, where possession proceedings had the appearance of a device to evict the defendant.

Commentary

DIRECTIONS ON SUMMARY JUDGMENT HEARING

If a summary judgment application is dismissed or otherwise fails finally to dispose of the claim, the court will give case management directions for the future conduct of the case (**PD 24, para. 10**), which may include directions for filing and service of a defence (**CPR, r. 24.6**), and may dispense with directions questionnaires and allocate the case to a case management track. **34.47**

SPECIFIC PERFORMANCE, RESCISSION AND FORFEITURE IN PROPERTY CASES

An even speedier process for obtaining summary judgment is available by virtue of **PD 24, para.** 7, in claims for specific performance and similar claims arising out of the sale, purchase, exchange, mortgage or charge of any property, or for the grant or assignment of a lease or tenancy of any property. Specific performance as a remedy requires an exceptional case (*Cooperative Insurance Society Ltd v Argyll Stores (Holdings) Ltd* [1998] AC 1), and the same applies on an application for summary judgment. Summary judgment for specific performance of a share purchase agreement was ordered in *Gaetano Ltd v Obertor Ltd* [2009] EWHC 2653 (Ch), LTL 29/10/2009, damages not being an adequate remedy for an obligation to transfer shares in an unquoted company due to the lack of a ready market in the shares. The judge is not entitled to enter into a mini-trial on an application for summary judgment, and it is wrong to attempt to resolve disputes of fact on such an application on the balance of probabilities (*North East Lincolnshire Borough Council v Millenium Park (Grimsby) Ltd* [2002] EWCA Civ 1719, *The Times*, 31 October 2002). Summary judgment was not appropriate in *Greenacre Properties Ltd v Tower* **34.48**

Hamlets London Borough Council (2002) LTL 24/7/2002 where it was arguable that the sale of land was beyond the council's power as it had not obtained ministerial consent.

Where there is no defence, summary judgment can be sought at any time after the claim is served, rather than having to wait until after acknowledgment or defence, and the application can be made even in the absence of particulars of claim. The application notice, evidence in support and a draft order must be served no less than four clear days before the hearing.

SUMMARY ORDERS FOR ACCOUNTS AND INQUIRIES

34.49 By **CPR, r. 25.1(1)(o)**, the court may make an interim order directing accounts to be taken or inquiries to be made. The application notice seeking such an order should ask:

(a) for specified accounts to be taken or specified inquiries to be made;
(b) for directions for the taking of the account or for making the inquiries; and
(c) for payment of the amount found to be due on taking the accounts.

Written evidence is not always required in support, but if the matter is at all contentious such evidence should be filed and served with the application. The court may refuse to make the order if there is a preliminary question that ought to be tried, such as whether the defendant is under a duty to account.

The practice on taking accounts and conducting inquiries is dealt with by **PD 40A**. When making an order for accounts and inquiries the court may also at the same time or later give directions as to how the account is to be taken or the inquiry conducted (**PD 40A, para. 1.1**). Among the directions that may be made are the following:

(a) that the relevant books of account shall be evidence of their contents, subject to the parties having the right to make objections (**para. 1.2**);
(b) that an accounting party must make out his account and verify it by exhibiting it to an affidavit or witness statement (**para. 2(1)**); and
(c) that, if appropriate, and at any stage in the proceedings, the parties must serve points of claim and points of defence (**para. 5**).

A party alleging that an account drawn by an accounting party is inaccurate (or making similar allegations) must give written notice of the objections to the accounting party (**para. 3.1**). These objections must give full particulars, specify the grounds on which it is alleged the account is inaccurate, and be verified by a statement of truth (or exhibited to an affidavit or witness statement).

Unless the court orders otherwise, accounts and inquiries are conducted by a master or district judge (**para. 9**). Detailed provisions dealing with inquiries into estates, trusts and for beneficiaries and next of kin can be found in **paras 10** to **15**.

SUMMARY DETERMINATION OF CONSTRUCTION OF WILLS

34.50 The High Court may make an order authorising trustees or personal representatives to act in reliance on an opinion of counsel of 10 years' call on the construction of a will or trust (Administration of Justice Act 1985, s. 48). Applications under s. 48 are made in the Chancery Division without notice supported by written evidence stating the names of all persons who may be affected by the order sought; all admissible surrounding circumstances; counsel's call and experience; the value of the fund; and details of any known dispute. Instructions to counsel, counsel's opinion, and draft minutes of the order sought must be exhibited to the evidence in support. The papers are considered by a judge without hearing argument, who will make the order sought if that order is appropriate and if there appears to be no tenable argument contrary to counsel's opinion.

Claims by trustees seeking orders approving any sale, purchase, compromise or other transaction by a trustee, including a case where the remedy sought is approval of a transaction affected by conflict of interests or duties (**PD 64A, para. 1(2)(b)**), may be determined without a hearing (**para. 1A.1**). Detailed procedural requirements can be found in **para. 1A.3**.

Chapter 35 Possession Claims against Trespassers

INTRODUCTION

35.1 Machinery for obtaining possession orders without undue delay against trespassers and similar categories of unauthorised occupiers is provided by **CPR, Part 55**. Landowners seeking possession against squatters frequently do not know the identity of those on their land. One of the main objects of the rules governing claims against trespassers is to avoid the need for the claimant to investigate the identities of the people in unauthorised occupation, and to allow possession orders to be made even against 'persons unknown'. Where the summary procedure against trespassers is not available, ordinary possession proceedings (see **35.15**) should be used.

POLICE

35.2 There are occasions when trespassers enter on to land and refuse to leave. A person entitled to possession who attempts to turn trespassers off the land without the sanction of a court order risks a breach of the peace and may incur civil or criminal liability for doing so. A court order is not needed, however, if the person entitled to the land can make use of the Criminal Law Act 1977, s. 7, as substituted by the Criminal Justice and Public Order Act 1994, s. 73. This makes it an offence for any person who is on premises as a trespasser to fail to leave on being required to do so by the residential occupier or a protected occupier. A constable in uniform may arrest such a trespasser without a warrant. The section only applies to residential property, and not to commercial property or open land.

PROCEDURE ON POSSESSION CLAIMS AGAINST TRESPASSERS

Definition

35.3 Possession claims against trespassers are claims for the recovery of land which is alleged to be occupied by persons who entered or remained on the land without the consent of a person entitled to possession of the land (**CPR, r. 55.1(b)**). They do not include claims against tenants or sub-tenants, whether the defendant's tenancy has terminated or not. These claims can include claims against licensees who remain in occupation after the termination of their licences.

In addition to the obvious situation of the owner in fee simple in possession claiming against a squatter, the summary procedure against trespassers may be used:

(a) By the owner of the premises against a person who had gone into possession as a licensee, but whose licence has expired (*Greater London Council v Jenkins* [1975] 1 WLR 155). This also applies where the occupant is a former employee whose right to remain was terminated on dismissal, even where the employee has applied to an employment tribunal for reinstatement if the employer has expressed an intention not to reinstate in any event (*Whitbread West Pennines Ltd v Reedy* [1988] ICR 807). It can also apply to a claim against a former freehold owner who sold the premises to the claimant and who did not give vacant possession in accordance with the terms of a licence granted by the claimant (*Pritchard v Teitelbaum* [2011] EWHC 1063 (Ch), [2011] 2 EGLR 1).

(b) By a tenant of premises against a person who, while the tenant was absent, was let into occupation with the consent of the landlord (*Borg v Rogers* (1981) 132 NLJ 134).

(c) By a licensee who was not in occupation of the land against a trespasser where possession was necessary to give effect to the licensee's contractual rights of occupation (*Manchester Airport plc v Dutton* [2000] QB 133). The land in this case was owned by the National Trust, and the airport was given a licence in order to fell some trees for purposes connected with the construction of a second runway. The trespassers were protesters. It was held that an order for possession would not interfere with the prior rights of the National Trust.

Situations not amounting to claims against trespassers

The summary procedure in claims against trespassers cannot be used against a tenant or sub- **35.4**
tenant or a former tenant or sub-tenant holding over at the end of the tenancy (see **CPR, r. 55.1(b)**). In addition, the following situations have been considered by the courts:

(a) Where the defendant was allowed into the premises by a tenant, the landlord was held not to be entitled to use the summary procedure unless the tenancy had been determined or surrendered (*Auto Finance Ltd v Pugh* (unreported, 10 June 1985)).

(b) A number of cases have considered claims brought by councils which may be in breach of statutory duty to provide accommodation for the defendants. It has been held that the fact that the council is in breach of its statutory duty, and that the breach has caused the presence of the defendants on the council's land, does not by itself provide the defendants with any defence (*Southwark London Borough Council v Williams* [1971] Ch 734). However, if the decision to use the summary procedure against trespassers is void on the ground of unreasonableness in the *Wednesbury* sense (see *Associated Provincial Picture Houses Ltd v Wednesbury Corporation* [1948] 1 KB 223), then the defendants can seek to have the possession proceedings struck out (*Bristol District Council v Clark* [1975] 1 WLR 1443). In *Cannock Chase District Council v Kelly* [1978] 1 WLR 1 Megaw J said that overwhelming proof of the unreasonableness would be required. A case in which possession was refused on this basis is *West Glamorgan County Council v Rafferty* [1987] 1 WLR 457.

(c) Where a complicated issue arises as to title (*Cudworth v Masefield* (1984) *The Times*, 16 May 1984) or as to whether there has been a surrender of a tenancy by operation of law (*Cooper v Vardari* (1986) 18 HLR 299), the summary procedure against trespassers may be inappropriate.

(d) A doubtful situation is where a head landlord seeks possession against unlawful sub-tenants. This was held to be a situation where summary possession could be ordered under the old rules (*Moore Properties (Ilford) Ltd v McKeon* [1976] 1 WLR 1278), but the words 'or sub-tenant' in **r. 55.1(b)** may be regarded as extending even to an unlawful sub-tenant, with the effect that the summary procedure will not be available in such a claim.

County court or High Court

Possession claims must normally be started in the county court for the district in which the **35.5**
land is situated (**CPR, r. 55.3(1)**). The High Court may be appropriate where there

Commentary

are complicated issues of fact, points of law of general importance, or the claim is against trespassers and there is a substantial risk of public disturbance or of serious harm to persons or property which require immediate determination (**PD 55A, para. 1.3**). If the claim is started in the High Court when it should have been started in a county court, the claim will either be struck out or transferred (**PD 55A, para. 1.2**).

Claim form, particulars of claim and evidence in support

35.6 A special claim form (form N5) must be used in claims against trespassers. The claim form should name as defendants all the persons in occupation whose identities are known to the claimant. Where the claimant does not know the names of all the occupiers, the claim is brought against 'persons unknown' in addition to any named defendants. There is nothing to be gained, therefore, by making inquiries as to who might be in occupation, but there will be extra people to serve if some of those in occupation become known to the claimant. Where the claimant is a large organisation, it is important for the solicitor conducting the case to find out what may be known by any of the employees of the claimant, as there have been cases where delays have occurred through the need to amend by adding extra defendants when it later becomes clear that some of the occupiers were known to local employees of the claimant.

The particulars of claim must be in form N121, which is specifically for claims against trespassers. This must identify the land, state whether it is residential property, state the claimant's interest in the property or the basis for claiming possession, the circumstances in which it has been occupied without the claimant's licence or consent, and give details of every person who, to the best of the claimant's knowledge, is in possession of the property (**PD 55A, paras 2.1** and **2.6**). Particulars of claim and witness statements in support must be filed when the claim is issued (**CPR, rr. 55.4** and **57.8(5)**). When the claim is issued the court will fix a date for the hearing, which will usually be just a few days after issue.

Service

35.7 No acknowledgment of service form is required (**CPR, r. 55.7(1)**), so the only documents that need to be served are the claim form, particulars of claim, any additional evidence in support, and any notice of the return day. Service copies of the claim form must be sealed (see **12.3**).

Individually named defendants must be served in accordance with the normal rules on service (see **chapter 15**). Service by the means described below for 'persons unknown' will not suffice for individually named defendants (*Greater London Council v Tully* (1976) 120 SJ 555).

Where the claim is against, or includes, persons unknown, in addition to serving the named defendants in the normal way, the documents must, by **r. 55.6**, be served by:

(a) attaching copies to the main door or some other part of the land so they are clearly visible, and, if practicable, by inserting another set of the documents through the letter box in a sealed transparent envelope addressed to 'the occupiers'; or

(b) attaching copies, contained in sealed transparent envelopes addressed to 'the occupiers', to stakes placed in the land in places where they are clearly visible. This method is used where the trespassers are on open land. Where service is to be effected by the court, the claimant must provide sufficient transparent envelopes and stakes (**PD 55A, para. 4.1**).

In *Westminster City Council v Chapman* [1975] 1 WLR 1112, the county court bailiff served the proceedings, but did not affix a copy to the main door or other conspicuous part of the premises. The defendants learnt of the matter by reading the copy inserted through the letter box. It was held that service was irregular (rather than a nullity), and as there was no prejudice to the defendants, the irregularity was cured under what is now **CPR, r. 3.10**.

Service must be effected not less than five days before the hearing in the case of residential property, and not less than two days before the hearing in respect of commercial property and open land (**r. 55.5(2)**). Time is calculated from service on each of the various defendants. Time may be shortened under **r. 3.1(2)(a)** and **(b)** where the occupiers have threatened to assault the claimant or to cause serious damage to the property or other property in the locality (**PD 55A, para. 3.2**).

Defence

The form for a defence in a possession claim against trespassers (form N11) simply provides a space for giving the reasons for disputing the claim and a statement of truth. However, in possession claims against trespassers, **CPR, r. 15.2**, does not apply, and there is no need for a defendant to file a defence (**r. 55.7(2)**). The provisions on default judgment do not apply (**r. 55.7(4)**). **35.8**

Application by occupier to be made a party

By **CPR, r. 19.4**, an occupier who is not named as a defendant and who wishes to be heard on the return day may apply at any stage to be joined as a defendant. An application notice should be filed and served in accordance with **Part 23** (**PD 19A, para. 1.4**). Such applications are often heard on the day of the hearing. All that need be shown is that the occupier wishes to be heard on whether an order for possession should be made, so permission to join is usually granted quite readily. **35.9**

Hearing in claims against trespassers

Summary possession hearings are generally heard by masters in the Royal Courts of Justice and by district judges in the county courts. Unless the court orders otherwise, the facts are placed before the court at the hearing by relying on the evidence in the witness statements served with the claim form (**CPR, r. 55.8(3)**). The fact of service is proved by producing a certificate of service (**r. 55.8(6)** and form N215). **35.10**

If the defendants need an opportunity to file evidence in reply, the first hearing may be used for giving directions (particularly where there is not much time between service and the return date). If the necessary five or two clear days have not elapsed since service, the court should ordinarily adjourn the hearing to enable the proper time to elapse (*Westminster City Council v Monahan* [1981] 1 WLR 698). If the maker of a witness statement does not attend the hearing, and another party disputes material evidence contained in the statement, the court will normally adjourn the hearing so that oral evidence can be given (**PD 55A, para. 5.4**). Adjournments are usually very short, as the whole point of the procedure is to provide an expeditious means of obtaining possession orders where there is no defence.

The summary procedure against trespassers is only appropriate where the defendants have no real defence. If the court takes the view that the case is not suitable for summary possession, it may dismiss the claim (particularly where it does not come within the scope of the procedure). If the defendants attend and adduce evidence showing a substantial defence, the claim is usually converted into an ordinary possession claim.

Possession orders against trespassers

Normally, if the court is satisfied that there are grounds for granting possession of the land, the order will be for possession forthwith. It has been held that where the defendants' original entry on to the land was unlawful, the court has no discretion to make a suspended order in the absence of consent from the landowner (*Swordheath Properties Ltd v Floydd* [1978] 1 WLR 550) and this is not affected by the Housing Act 1980, s. 89 (*Boyland and Son Ltd v Persons Unknown* [2006] EWCA Civ 1860, [2007] HLR 24). Even in this situation it may be necessary to consider whether it is proportionate to make the possession order, and to do so separately against **35.11** different defendants, under the European Convention on Human Rights, **arts 10 and 11**, in the **Human Rights Act 1998, sch. 1** (*Mayor of London v Hall* [2010] EWCA Civ 817, [2011] 1 WLR 504). If the original occupation was lawful, such as under a service agreement, the court may exercise any power which it could have exercised if possession had been sought in an ordinary possession claim.

Area orders

35.12 Usually the order will grant possession of the land actually occupied by the defendants. This may not provide sufficient protection for the claimant, who may fear (often based on experience) the defendants will simply relocate to a site nearby. Where only part of a single piece of land is occupied by the trespassers, the order can cover the whole piece of land, particularly where it is unrealistic to require the claimant to identify different parts of the land occupied by different trespassers (*Mayor of London v Hall* [2010] EWCA Civ 817, [2011] 1 WLR 504). What the court cannot do is to make an order covering similar areas of land also owned by the claimant but which are wholly detached and separate from the land occupied by the defendants (*Secretary of State for the Environment, Food and Rural Affairs v Meier* [2009] UKSC 11, [2009] 1 WLR 2780). The order made may be supported by an injunction forbidding the defendants from re-entering the occupied site or from entering other sites.

Warrant of possession

35.13 A warrant of possession to enforce a possession order against a trespasser may be issued immediately after the order is made. However, permission to issue a warrant of possession is required if the warrant is not issued within the next three months (**CCR, ord. 24, r. 6, in CPR, sch. 2**). Orders for permission to enforce out of time are made on application to the master or district judge without notice (unless the court otherwise directs). If permission is granted, the defendants may apply to vary or set it aside by making an application within seven days of service of the order granting permission (**CPR, r. 23.10**).

Interim possession orders

35.14 An interim order for possession can be sought in a claim for possession against trespassers by following the procedure in **CPR, rr. 55.20** to **57.28**. Such an order is available if the following conditions are satisfied:

(a) the only claim in the proceedings is for possession so there can be no money claim;
(b) the claim is in respect of premises (and not open land); and
(c) the claim is made within 28 days of the claimant knowing (or reasonably being able to know) of the wrongful occupation.

The claim must be brought by issuing an application for possession in form N130, supported by written evidence in the prescribed form, and a notice of application for an interim possession order must also be issued (in form N131). Once the proceedings have been issued the court will fix a date for consideration of the application, which must be not less than three days after the proceedings were issued. Service must be effected by the applicant within 24 hours after issue. Service is effected by fixing one set of copies to the main door or other conspicuous part of the premises, and inserting a second set through the letter box in a transparent envelope addressed to 'the occupiers'.

The defendant is permitted to file written evidence in reply, and a standard form for this must be used (form N133). If the court decides to make an interim possession order, the claimant is required to give a number of undertakings set out in **CPR, r. 55.25(1)** including a promise to reinstate the defendant if the court later holds that the interim possession order should not have been made. An interim possession order requires the defendant to vacate within 24 hours of service (**r. 55.25(3)**). A defendant who does not comply commits an offence contrary to the

Criminal Justice and Public Order Act 1994, s. 76, punishable by imprisonment for up to six months and/or a fine not exceeding level 5 on the standard scale. The only means of enforcement is under the 1994 Act, which requires the involvement of the police.

After an interim possession order is made there is a second return date when the court will consider whether to make a final order for possession, or to dismiss the claim for possession.

OTHER POSSESSION PROCEEDINGS

Ordinary possession claims

Ordinary possession claims, like possession claims against trespassers, are governed by **CPR, Part 55**, and **PD 55A**. The court has a power to allocate these claims to the fast track or multi-track (**CPR, r. 55.8(2)**), may give case management directions, and may require the facts to be proved by calling witnesses at the trial. **35.15**

The claim form to be used in possession claims is form N5; the claim form for relief against forfeiture is form N5A; the form for particulars of claim in claims in respect of rented residential premises is form N119; the form for particulars of claim in claims for possession of mortgaged residential premises is form N120; the form for a defence in mortgage possession claims is form N11M; and the form for a defence in claims in respect of rented residential premises is form N11R.

ACCELERATED PROCEDURE FOR ASSURED SHORTHOLD TENANCIES

CPR, rr. 55.11 to 57.19, provide an accelerated procedure for obtaining possession orders to recover possession of residential properties let under assured shorthold tenancies. There are prescribed claim forms and defence forms, and the papers are referred to a district judge or judge, who may strike out the claim if it discloses no reasonable grounds (**r. 55.16(1)(c)**), or may make an order for possession without requiring the attendance of the parties (**r. 55.17**). Although an application can be made to set aside such an order (**r. 55.19**), the procedure is intended to provide a speedy and inexpensive means of obtaining possession orders in cases where there is unlikely to be any defence. **35.16**

There is a special claim form (form N5B) for use in accelerated procedure claims in respect of assured shorthold property and it includes the particulars of claim. The form for a defence to such a claim is form N11B.

Chapter 36 Interim Payments

The following procedural checklist, which is at the front of the book, is relevant to this chapter:

Procedural checklist 24 Application for an order for interim payment

ORDERS FOR INTERIM PAYMENT

36.1 An order for interim payment is defined in **CPR, r. 25.1(1)(k)**, as an order for payment of a sum of money by a defendant on account of any damages, debt or other sum (except costs) which the court may hold the defendant liable to pay. Such orders are likely to be made in claims where it appears the claimant will achieve at least some success, and where it would be unjust to delay, until after the trial, payment of the money to which the claimant appears to be entitled. The purpose behind this procedure is to alleviate the hardship that may otherwise be suffered by claimants who may have to wait substantial periods of time before they recover any damages in respect of wrongs they may have suffered. In addition to providing resources to the claimant, sometimes making an interim payment will enable the claimant to pay for treatment, or to save assets which would otherwise be lost, or to have an asset repaired earlier than might otherwise be the case, and may thereby reduce the amount of the claim. Further, making an early interim payment will reduce the defendant's liability to pay interest.

Cases on the small claims track are unlikely to be large enough to justify the expense of applications for interim payments, and small claims and fast track cases, unless delayed, are likely to proceed to final hearing with such speed that there will be little point in making an application, unless the hearing results in a judgment for damages to be assessed. Most applications for interim payments are therefore likely to be made in multi-track cases (or cases likely to be allocated to the multi-track when track allocation is considered).

Voluntary interim payments and rehabilitation

36.2 There is nothing to prevent the parties agreeing to voluntary interim payments, and these are quite common in cases where liability is not in dispute but where quantum is still being investigated. Payments made by insurers for intervention or treatment pursuant to the Rehabilitation Code (**Annex D to the Pre-action Protocol for Personal Injury Claims**) are treated as interim payments on account of damages (**Code, para. 7.2**). The permission of the court must be obtained if a voluntary interim payment is being considered where the claimant is a child or protected party (**PD 25B, para. 1.2**).

EU law and informal interim payments under CPR, r. 25.1

In *R (Teleos plc) v Commissioners of Customs and Excise* [2005] EWCA Civ 200, [2005] 1 WLR 3007, the company brought judicial review proceedings to challenge a VAT assessment which the Commissioners had levied through a set-off. The Commissioners refused to make an interim payment to the company under the Value Added Tax Act 1994, and it was clear there were no grounds for granting an interim payment under **CPR, r. 25.7**. The company applied for interim relief under **r. 25.1** and/or the court's inherent jurisdiction for an interim payment of 50 per cent of the assessed VAT. Dyson LJ said at [23] that if there were no mechanism for a taxpayer in these circumstances to obtain an interim payment of VAT withheld by the Commissioners, there would be an infringement of the principle of proportionality (see *Garage Molenheide BVBA v Belgium* (cases C-286/94, C-340/95, C-401/95 and C-47/96) [1997] ECR I-7281). This did not apply to the present case, given the Commissioners' power to make interim payments and the right to challenge their decisions through judicial review. Accordingly, it was unnecessary to give a strained interpretation of **CPR, r. 25.1**, to provide such a power, nor did the court need such a power as a consequence of EU law (at [33]). **36.3**

PROCEDURE

Who may apply

The rules (**CPR, rr. 25.1(1)(k)** and **25.6(1)**) refer to interim payments being applied for by claimants against defendants. This should be interpreted as meaning that interim payments may also be applied for by claimants in additional claims, so that defendants may bring interim payment applications against the defendants to their counterclaims, and defendants may seek interim payments against additional parties. **36.4**

Time for applying

An application for an order for an interim payment cannot be made until the period for filing an acknowledgment of service has expired (**CPR, r. 25.6(1)**). However, voluntary interim payments may be made at any time, including the period before proceedings are issued. It is possible to make several applications for interim payments during the life of a claim (**r. 25.6(2)**). **36.5**

Application and evidence

The procedure for applying for an interim payment is summarised in **procedural checklist 24**, which is at the front of the book. Applications for interim payments are made on notice, and must be served at least 14 clear days before the hearing of the application (**CPR, rr. 2.8(2)** and **25.6(3)(a)**). Rather unnecessarily, it is specifically stated as a requirement by **r. 25.6(3)(b)**, that applications for interim payments must be supported by evidence which must be served with the application (**r. 23.7(2)** and **(3)**). **PD 25B, para. 2.1**, provides that the evidence in support should set out all relevant matters including: **36.6**

(a) the amount sought by way of interim payment;
(b) what the money will be used for (see **36.15**);
(c) the likely amount of money that will be awarded;
(d) the reasons for believing the relevant ground (see **36.7**) is satisfied;
(e) in a personal injuries claim, details of special damages and past and future loss; and
(f) in a claim under the **Fatal Accidents Act 1976**, details of the persons on whose behalf the claim is made and the nature of the claim.

All relevant documents in support should be exhibited. In personal injuries claims these will include the disclosed medical reports.

Respondents who wish to rely on written evidence in reply must file and serve their evidence at least seven clear days before the hearing. In personal injuries claims and claims in which damages in respect of a disease for which a lump sum payment within the definition of the Social Security (Recovery of Benefits) Act 1997, s. 1A(2), has been, or is likely to be made, the respondent will need to obtain a certificate of recoverable benefits from the Secretary of State. This is needed for the purposes of framing the order. If the applicant wants to respond to the respondent's evidence, any further evidence must be filed and served at least three clear days before the return day (**CPR, r. 25.6(4)** and **(5)**).

GROUNDS

36.7 The conditions which must be satisfied before an interim payment order can be made are set out in **CPR, r. 25.7**. Under **CPR, r. 25.7(1)**, an interim payment may be ordered against a specific defendant only if:

(a) the defendant has admitted liability to pay damages or some other sum of money to the claimant (**r. 25.7(1)(a)**); or

(b) the claimant has obtained judgment against the defendant for damages or some other sum (other than costs) to be assessed (**r. 25.7(1)(b)**); or

(c) the court is satisfied that, if the claim went to trial, the claimant would obtain judgment against the defendant from whom the interim payment is sought for a substantial sum of money (other than costs) whether or not that defendant is the only defendant or one of a number of defendants to the claim (**r. 25.7(1)(c)**); or

(d) the claimant is seeking possession of land, and the court is satisfied that if the case went to trial the defendant would be held liable to pay the claimant a sum of money for use and occupation of the land while the claim is pending (**r. 25.7(1)(d)**).

Where there are two or more defendants and the court, though satisfied that the claimant will obtain judgment, cannot determine which of the defendants will be found liable, **r. 25.7(1)(e)**, which is discussed in **36.11**, provides an alternative ground for granting an interim payment.

There is probably no basis for making an interim payment order outside these categories (*Quest Advisors Ltd v McFeely* [2011] EWCA Civ 1517, LTL 9/12/2011).

Standard of proof

36.8 On an application under **CPR, r. 25.7(1)(c)**, the court has to be satisfied on the balance of probabilities that if the claim went to trial, the claimant would obtain judgment for a substantial amount of money from the respondent (*Test Claimants in FII Group Litigation v Commissioners of HM Revenue and Customs (No. 2)* [2012] EWCA Civ 57, [2012] 1 WLR 2375 at [36]). 'Substantial' has to be considered in the context of the total claim made, and is to be contrasted with negligible rather than nominal damages (at [39]). It may be that in small claims an applicant can never satisfy the 'substantial amount of money' condition (at [39]). Similar principles, with the necessary changes, should apply to applications under **r. 25.7(1)(d)** and **(e)**, which also apply where the court is satisfied either that the defendant would be liable or that the claimant would obtain judgment.

Establishing the claim would succeed

36.9 In an application under **CPR, r. 25.7(1)(c)**, the judge has to put himself in the hypothetical position of being the trial judge, and, on the material before him on the interim payment *application*, *decide* whether the claimant would actually succeed on the claim, and that the claimant would actually obtain judgment for a substantial amount of money (*Test Claimants in*

FII Group Litigation v Commissioners of HM Revenue and Customs (No. 2) [2012] EWCA Civ 57, [2012] 1 WLR 2375 at [36], [38]). It is open for the court to make an interim payment in respect of only part of the claim (at [48]). In *O2 (UK) Ltd v Dimension Data Network Services Ltd* (2007) LTL 8/11/2007 summary judgment was refused as there was a real prospect that a defence of overcharging and a counterclaim might succeed. However, the court found that the defendant was bound to have to pay something for the services provided by the claimant, and an interim payment was made on that basis.

Under the old rules before the CPR there were several reported cases that considered the question of whether it was possible to make an interim payment order if a summary judgment application was unsuccessful (see, for example, *Schott Kem Ltd v Bentley* [1991] 1 QB 61 and *Andrews v Schooling* [1991] 1 WLR 783). The better view under the old rules was that an interim payment order would not be made in such cases, although it was possible to make an interim payment order if conditional leave to defend (the old equivalent to a conditional order) was granted. With the increased availability of summary judgment under the CPR, there can be no doubt that if summary judgment is refused it would be inconsistent for the court then to decide that the claimant 'would' succeed so as to give grounds for an interim payment. There may even be a little doubt about whether making an interim payment order can be consistent with making a conditional order, again because of the change in the test for summary judgment. If the defence is on the border of having a real prospect of success (the situation where conditional orders are appropriate), it is difficult to see how the court can simultaneously find that the claimant will win for the purposes of making an interim payment order.

MULTIPLE DEFENDANTS

Where the court is satisfied a specific defendant is liable

An interim payment order can be made against a specific defendant if the claimant establishes one of the conditions in **CPR, r. 25.7(1)(a)** to **(d)** to the required standard against that specific defendant. Where this can be done there is no need to satisfy the additional requirements of **CPR, r. 25.7(1)(e)** described at **36.11**. **36.10**

Where the court cannot determine which defendant is liable

By **CPR, 25.7(1)(e)**, an interim payment may be ordered where all the following conditions are satisfied: **36.11**

(a) there are two or more defendants;
(b) the court is satisfied that if the claim went to trial the claimant would obtain judgment for a substantial sum of money (other than costs) against at least one of the defendants;
(c) the court cannot determine under **r. 25.7(1)(c)** which of the defendants will lose; and
(d) all the defendants are either insured, public bodies, or are defendants whose liability will be met by an insurer under the Road Traffic Act 1988, s. 151, or an insurer acting under the Motor Insurers' Bureau Agreement or by the Motor Insurers' Bureau itself.

In **r. 25.7(1)(e)** the term 'defendants' (see points (b) and (d) above) means the defendants against whom the interim payment is sought (*Berry v Ashtead Plant Hire Co. Ltd* [2011] EWCA Civ 1304, [2012] PIQR P6). The provision in **r. 25.7(1)(e)(ii)(b)** (see (d) above) should be construed as including cases where liability will be met by an insurance company under the Domestic Regulations Agreement between the Motor Insurers' Bureau and its members pursuant to the Uninsured Drivers' Agreement (*Sharp v Pereira* [1991] 1 WLR 195, considering a provision in the same form).

If it transpires that the wrong defendant was required to make the interim payment, the requirement that all the defendants must be insured etc. means it should be possible to make effective adjustments (see **36.16**) after the final determination of the case.

EFFECT OF COUNTERCLAIMS AND DEFENCES

36.12 When deciding on an order for interim payment the court 'must take into account' any relevant set-off or counterclaim and any contributory negligence (**CPR, r. 25.7(5)**). From the context of this provision it clearly applies at the second stage of an interim payment application when the court is considering the amount to be ordered by way of an interim payment. Counterclaims and allegations of contributory negligence with reasonable prospects of success obviously affect the likely amount of the final judgment. **Rule 25.7(5)**, however, has no express restriction to quantum. Unlike unconnected cross-claims, set-offs are also defences. Consequently, the existence of a set-off with a reasonable prospect of success should also be taken into account at the first stage when the court is considering the grounds for granting an interim payment, and may prevent the court being satisfied that the claimant will obtain judgment for the purposes of **r. 25.7(1)(c)**. This was the position under the previous rules (see *Shanning International Ltd v George Wimpey International Ltd* [1989] 1 WLR 981).

COMBINED WITH SUMMARY JUDGMENT

36.13 It is quite common to combine applications for summary judgment under **CPR, Part 24** (see **chapter 34**) with applications for interim payments. Summary judgment is available where the defence has no real prospect of success, and interim payments are available where the claimant can show that liability will be established. Obviously these are similar concepts. Further, on the summary judgment application the court may make a 'relevant order' (**PD 26, para. 12.1**) entering judgment for damages to be assessed, which would itself provide grounds for making an order for an interim payment. Another possibility is that the court may make a conditional order on the summary judgment application, with the condition being compliance with an interim payment order.

DISCRETION

36.14 Even if the claimant establishes a ground for making an interim payment, the court retains a discretion whether to make an order. As a general proposition, once an applicant satisfies the conditions in **CPR, r. 25.7**, the court should order an interim payment unless there is a sufficient specific reason not to do so (*Test Claimants in the FII Group Litigation v Revenue and Customs Comrs (No. 2)* [2012] EWCA Civ 57, [2012] 1 WLR 2375 at [47]). The discretion is exercised in accordance with the overriding objective, bearing in mind the policy behind the jurisdiction conferred by the Senior Courts Act 1981, s. 32, and the County Courts Act 1984, s. 50, to make interim payment orders. This is essentially to alleviate the hardship that can occur when a claimant is kept out of his money for a protracted period of time. Relevant factors include the time that has elapsed since the cause of action accrued and the estimated time to trial (*Spillman v Bradfield Riding Centre* [2007] EWHC 89 (QB), LTL 13/2/2007), and the effect on the claimant of being kept out of what may turn out to be his money. In one of the old cases (*British and Commonwealth Holdings plc v Quadrex Holdings Inc.* [1989] QB 842) it was said that the court may take into account the respondent's lack of means in either refusing to make an order or in fixing its amount.

AMOUNT TO BE ORDERED

The court is not permitted to order an interim payment of more than a reasonable proportion of the likely amount of any final judgment, taking into account any contributory negligence and any relevant set-off or counterclaim (**CPR, r. 25.7(4)** and **(5)**). The judge is obliged to assess the likely amount of the final judgment, and is not permitted to take short cuts such as basing the assessment on offers made by the defendant (*Eeles v Cobham Hire Services Ltd* [2009] EWCA Civ 204, [2010] 1 WLR 409). The issues need to be considered individually, and the judge has to decide whether there is an irreducible minimum sum the claimant will recover in any event (*Chiron Corporation v Murex Diagnostics Ltd (No. 13)* [1996] FSR 578). While most judges err on the side of caution, a reasonable proportion may in an appropriate case be a high proportion, provided the assessment of the likely final award is conservative. The amount payable should not expose the defendant to the risk that the eventual damages would be less than the interim payments that are made (*Osunde v Guy's and St Thomas' Hospital* [2007] EWHC 2275 (Fam), LTL 26/11/2007). In *Spillman v Bradfield Riding Centre* [2007] EWHC 89 (QB), LTL 13/2/2007, 75 per cent of the likely total award was regarded as a 'reasonable proportion' of the likely award in a personal injuries case. The interim payment of £1.7 million (part of which had already been paid voluntarily) which was ordered in a claim with an estimated value of £1.8 million in *FP v Taunton and Somerset NHS Trust* [2009] EWHC 1965 (QB), [2009] LS Law Medical 598, should be regarded as either exceptional or wrong. In a personal injuries claim the amount ordered is not limited to the likely lump sum award, but also includes the capitalised value of any likely award for periodical payments (for which, see **63.29**) (*Braithwaite v Homerton University Hospital NHS Foundation Trust* [2008] EWHC 353 (QB), [2008] LS Law Medical 261). In deciding how much to order by way of interim payment in a personal injuries claim where the claimant had suffered catastrophic injuries, the court in *Mealing v Chelsea and Westminster Healthcare NHS Trust* [2007] EWHC 3254 (QB), [2008] LS Law Medical 236, took into account: **36.15**

(a) whether there was any likelihood that the amount ordered would pre-empt any decision by the trial judge on any of the issues between the parties;
(b) that ordering too much by way of interim payments could act as a disincentive to the claimant in progressing the claim to trial; and
(c) that if too much were ordered by way of interim payments the amount left to be awarded at trial may be too little to make an effective periodical payments order, or too little to make an effective lump sum award for the necessary capital expenses for the claimant's care.

In the non-personal injuries field, the pre-CPR case of *Andrews v Schooling* [1991] 1 WLR 783 is helpful. This was a claim for damages against builders under the Defective Premises Act 1972. The court ignored the claimant's quantification of the claim at £12,000, but made an order for an interim payment of £7,500 given an estimate of £10,000 for necessary remedial works.

PD 25B, para. 2.1(2), states that the evidence in support of the application must deal with the items or matters in respect of which the interim payment is sought. In general, the claimant's intended use of the money if an interim payment is awarded is irrelevant to the court's decision. As stated in *Schott Kem Ltd v Bentley* [1991] 1 QB 61, commercial people always have a need for money for the purposes of their business interests. Once an interim payment is made they will invest it somewhere. It is generally the same in personal injuries claims (*Stringman v McArdle* [1994] 1 WLR 1653), particularly where the interim payment is limited to an amount based on the damages alleged to have been suffered to the date of the application (*Eeles v Cobham Hire Services Ltd*). The court is not concerned with how a claimant of full capacity spends a final award in damages, and should not try to prescribe what an interim payment is spent on either. Despite the general principle, the rule in *Stringman v McArdle* must not be applied in a mechanistic way, and there are cases where the proposed use of the interim payment has a significant bearing on the decision of the court (*Tinsley v Sarkar* [2004] EWCA Civ 1098, LTL 23/7/2004). The intended use of the money may be relevant where the payment may prejudice the trial or the position of the defendant in the proceedings or pre-judge an issue to be determined at the trial (Thorpe LJ at [48]). In periodical payments cases it is essential to establish a real need for the money, and an award will be made only if the judge can confidently predict the trial judge will wish to award a capital sum greater than past special damages and damages for pain, suffering and loss of amenity (*Eeles v Cobham Hire Services Ltd*). Where an interim payment may effectively preclude a periodical payments order at trial, it should be ordered only where the court is satisfied to a high degree of confidence that the interim payment is reasonably necessary (*Preston v City Electrical Factors Ltd* [2009] EWHC 2907 (QB), LTL 16/11/2009). Information on the claimant's proposed use of the money may assist the court in deciding whether the money is needed urgently, or in deciding how much to order.

Judges applying these principles have tended, in cases of catastrophic personal injuries, to award interim payments coming close to the likely lump sum award at trial and covering the likely cost of suitable accommodation and other expenditure which is felt ought not to be postponed until after trial (*Brewis v Heatherwood and Wrexham Park Hospitals NHS Trust* [2008] EWHC 2526 (QB), LTL 3/11/2008; *Pitcher v Headstart Nursery Ltd* [2008] EWHC 2681 (QB), LTL 17/11/2008).

There is a standard interim payment for mesothelioma claims (**PD 3D**), which is currently £50,000.

In personal injuries and lump sum disease claims the defendant will need to obtain a certificate of recoverable benefits from the Secretary of State under the Social Security (Recovery of Benefits) Act 1997. A copy of the certificate should be filed at the hearing, and any order made must set out the amount by which the payment to be made to the claimant has been reduced in accordance with the Act and the Social Security (Recovery of Benefits) Regulations 1997 (SI 1997/2205) (**PD 25B, paras 4.1 to 4.4; PD 40B, paras 5.1 and 5.1A**).

CPR, r. 25.6(7), allows an interim payment order to require payment by instalments. Where this happens, the order should set out the total amount of the interim payment, the amount of each instalment, the number of instalments and the date they are to be paid, and to whom the payments should be made (**PD 25B, para. 3**).

Undertaking for repayment

36.16 In *Ultraframe (UK) Ltd v Eurocell Building Plastics Ltd* [2005] EWHC 2111 (Ch), LTL 30/8/2005, as a condition for granting an interim payment, the claimant and its holding company were required to give a cross-undertaking to repay the interim payment, and to provide a guarantee. Such undertakings are comparatively rare.

FURTHER APPLICATIONS

36.17 The claimant is permitted to make more than a single application for an interim payment (**CPR, r. 25.6(2)**). In practice, a second or subsequent application will have to be justified by a change in circumstances or other cause being shown, such as an increase in the special damages claim through additional loss of income or expenses being incurred, or through unforeseen delays in determining the claim.

NON-DISCLOSURE

36.18 The fact that a defendant has made an interim payment must not be disclosed to the trial judge until all questions of liability and quantum have been determined (**CPR, r. 25.9**), unless the defendant agrees. This is important, as the trial judge may (unwittingly) be influenced by knowing that the court has previously decided that the claimant will win, and that the claim is worth more than the amount of the interim payment. In advance of trial a request should be made to the court office to remove all references to interim payments (and Part 36 offers) from the court file to avoid accidental disclosure to the trial judge. Where a claimant (usually through ignorance) does disclose this information prematurely, the judge will usually abort the trial and consider making a wasted costs order against the lawyer responsible (but compare **66.3**).

ADJUSTMENT

The court has powers to order all or part of an interim payment to be repaid, to vary or discharge an interim payment order, and to order a co-defendant to reimburse a defendant who has made an interim payment (provided the defendant who made the interim payment has claimed a contribution, indemnity or other remedy against the co-defendant being ordered to reimburse) (**CPR, r. 25.8**). Reimbursement can also be ordered between co-claimants (*Trebor Bassett Holdings Ltd v ADT Fire and Security plc* [2012] EWHC 3365 (TCC), 145 Con LR 147). Interest may be ordered in favour of the defendant on any overpaid interim payment. These powers are usually exercised, if at all, at trial. **36.19**

PD 25B, para. 5, and **PD 40B, para. 6**, contain detailed rules on recording the effect of interim payments and any order for adjustment on the final award for damages. **Paragraphs 6.1** and **6.3** of **PD 40B** say that the amount and dates of any interim payments should be set out in a preamble to the judgment whether or not the interim payments exceed the amount awarded at trial, together with the total amount awarded by the judge. If the interim payments are less than the judgment, the total award has to be reduced by the interim payments, with an order for payment of the balance (**para. 6.2**). Where the interim payments exceed the amount awarded at trial, the judgment has to provide for repayment, reimbursement, variation or discharge under **CPR, r. 25.8(2)**, and for interest on the overpayment under **r. 25.8(5)** (**PD 40B, para. 6.4**).

Chapter 37 Interim Injunctions

INTRODUCTION

Interim injunctions are temporary orders made with the purpose of regulating the position between the parties to an action pending trial. Imposing an interim injunction is a serious matter, and should be restricted to appropriate cases. Such an order is particularly useful where there is evidence that the respondent's alleged wrongdoing will cause irreparable damage to the applicant's interests in the period between issue of process and trial. **37.1**

Interim injunctions should be distinguished from perpetual injunctions, which are final orders, usually made at trial (but see 37.56) and which continue with no limitation of time. Further distinctions are:

(a) Injunctions made without notice. These are a form of interim injunction, usually made in circumstances of urgency, which are expressed to continue in force for a limited period, usually a few days, sufficient for the application to be renewed on a hearing with notice being given to the respondent.
(b) Mandatory injunctions require the other side to do specified acts (such as to deliver up documents or to demolish a wall), whereas prohibitory injunctions require the other side to refrain from doing specified acts (such as publishing a libel or breaching a confidence). It is the substance of the order (rather than its wording) which makes it mandatory or prohibitory. Both types of injunction can be granted on an interim basis, but the courts are more wary of granting mandatory orders (see 37.61).
(c) Where the other side have not yet committed a civil wrong, but have threatened to do so in the future, it is possible to obtain an interim injunction on a *quia timet* basis.

Interim injunctions can be applied for even in claims allocated to the small claims track (**CPR, r. 27.2(1)**).

Any party to proceedings can apply for an interim injunction, and can do so whether or not a claim for the injunction was included in that party's originating process or statement of case (**CPR, r. 25.1(4)**).

JUDGES ABLE TO GRANT INJUNCTIONS

Given the serious nature of injunctions and the consequences of breach, subject to the following exceptions, all applications for interim injunctions must be made to a judge rather than a master or district judge. **37.2**

There are several exceptions and restrictions. The detailed rules are to be found in **PD 25A, paras 1.1 to 1.4**, which have to be read together with **PD 2B**. The effect of the various rules is set out in **table 37.1**.

Table 37.1 Power to grant interim injunctions

Type of order	Judges with power to grant
Search order	High Court judge and any other 'duly authorised' judge.
Freezing injunction	High Court judge and any other 'duly authorised' judge.
Other High Court interim injunction	Generally, only High Court judges. However, masters and district judges have power to grant injunctions: (a) in terms agreed by the parties; (b) in connection with charging orders and appointment of receivers; and (c) restraining a person receiving a sum due from the Crown.

Type of order	Judges with power to grant
County court interim injunctions	Judge with trial jurisdiction. Generally this will be the circuit judge, but may be the district judge in claims on the small claims and fast tracks, where the terms have been agreed by the parties, in relation to charging orders and the appointment of receivers, and certain Housing Act 1996 and harassment claims.
Variation of interim injunctions	Generally by a judge of the same level as the judge who granted the original injunction. Masters and district judges have jurisdiction as well if all parties consent to the variation or discharge.

PRE-ACTION APPLICATIONS FOR INTERIM INJUNCTIONS

37.3 CPR, r. 25.2(1), empowers the court to grant an interim injunction before a claim form has been issued. An application for an interim injunction at that stage must be made under **Part 23** (**PD 23A, para. 5**). By **CPR, r. 25.2(2)**, an interim injunction can be obtained prior to issue of proceedings provided:

(a) no rule or practice direction prohibits the granting of the order;
(b) the matter is urgent or it is otherwise desirable to make the order in the interests of justice;
(c) in the less common circumstance in which the applicant is an intended defendant, the defendant has obtained the court's permission to make the application. The defendant cannot without this permission apply for an interim remedy prior to the filing of an acknowledgment of service or defence (which can only happen after issue). It seems that the defendant could apply for permission and for the injunction in the same application and at the same hearing.

Urgent cases

37.4 A case is 'urgent' where there is a true impossibility in giving the requisite three clear days' notice or in arranging for the issue of process. There has to be an element of threatened damage, requiring the immediate intervention of the court, which may occur between the without-notice hearing and the hearing of an effective application (*Mayne Pharma (USA) Inc. v Teva UK Ltd* [2004] EWHC 3248 (Ch), LTL 3/12/2004). An 'impossibility' resulting from delay on the part of the claimant will not suffice (*Bates v Lord Hailsham of St Marylebone* [1972] 1 WLR 1373).

Reasons for applying without notice have to be given to the judge. It is especially important to give notice where grave allegations are to be made on the application. Thus, in *Cinpres Gas Injection Ltd v Melea Ltd* [2005] EWHC 3180 (Pat), *The Times*, 21 December 2005, a without-notice interim injunction to restrain the defendant from threatening, intimidating or harassing any witnesses was set aside because it should have been made on notice. Although the court will not usually consider an application made without notice where there is no true impossibility in notifying the defendant, there is a suggestion in *Bates v Lord Hailsham of St Marylebone* that the court may do so if the case is overwhelming on the merits. The relief sought on a without-notice application must be necessary and proportionate to the reasons for applying without notice (*Moat Housing Group-South Ltd v Harris* [2005] EWCA Civ 287, [2006] QB 606).

Where a case is urgent, the usual procedural requirements are relaxed in so far as is necessary to do justice between the parties. For example:

(a) The application may be made before issue of process.
(b) The application may be made without notice. However, it is still incumbent on the applicant to give the other side such notice as is possible, such as by telephone or by fax, and it will be rare that short notice cannot be given (*National Commercial Bank Jamaica Ltd v Olint Corporation Ltd* [2009] UKPC 16, [2009] 1 WLR 1405). The exception is where secrecy is

essential (such as on applications for search orders and freezing injunctions). A defendant who is notified in this way may decide to attend the hearing, a situation which is known as an 'opposed hearing without notice'.
(c) Informal evidence may be relied on. This may be in the form of an unsworn draft affidavit, or a witness statement, correspondence or even simply facts related to the court by counsel on instructions.
(d) Although very much a last resort, the court may make an order without a draft having been prepared by counsel on behalf of the applicant. It is very rare for there to be no time for anything to be drafted in advance of appearing before the judge.
(e) In particularly urgent cases it is possible to interrupt the judge's list, or even to see the judge out of normal hours or to apply to the judge over the telephone.

Procedure on pre-action applications

For a summary of the procedure, see **procedural checklist 19** at the front of the book. **37.5**

The application itself will normally be in a written application notice (**CPR, r. 23.3(1)**), the general requirement for which is that it should set out the order sought and why the order is being sought (**r. 23.6**). In the High Court form N244 should usually be used for the application notice, but in the county court there is a special form for applying for injunctions (form N16A) which must be used. It must include the title of the proposed claim, the full name of the applicant, and, as the applicant is not yet a party, the applicant's address for service. It should contain a request for a hearing or ask that the application be dealt with without a hearing (**PD 23A, para. 2.1**). It will be very rare for injunctions to be sought without hearings. Dispensing with a hearing is only permissible if the parties agree to the terms of the order sought, or agree that the court should dispose of the application without a hearing, or if the court does not consider a hearing would be appropriate (**CPR, r. 23.8**). None of these is very likely in the case of pre-action injunctions. **PD 25A, para. 2.1**, provides that an application notice for an interim injunction should:

(a) state the order sought, and
(b) give the date, time and place of the hearing.

It is good practice to annex a draft order to the application notice where time allows. Form PF 39 CH must be used for pre-action applications.

Many pre-action applications for injunctions are made in cases of real urgency. Drafting and issuing an application notice may delay matters to the detriment of the applicant, and the court may in such cases exercise its power in **CPR, r. 23.3(2)(b)**, to dispense with the requirement for an application notice. If the court dispenses with the application notice, it will usually only do so for the purposes of the initial hearing. **PD 25A, para. 5.1(4)**, provides that in these circumstances the court will, unless it orders otherwise, require an undertaking from the applicant to file an application notice and pay the appropriate fee on the same or the next working day.

An application for an interim remedy must be supported by evidence, unless the court orders otherwise (**CPR, r. 25.3(2)**). The evidence required is discussed further in **37.13**.

The application should be made in the court in which the substantive proceedings are likely to be issued unless 'there is good reason to make the application to a different court' (**CPR, r. 23.2(4)**).

Especially where the terms of the injunction sought are complex, it is good practice to attach a draft of the order to the application notice and to provide it on computer disk (**PD 25A, para. 2.4**).

If the court is to serve the application on the respondent, a suitable number of copies of the application notice and evidence in support must be filed with the court. Unless the court orders otherwise, or an application without service of an application notice can be justified, the application notice should be served as soon as practicable and in any event at least three clear days before the hearing (**CPR, r. 23.7**). Pre-action applications are treated as claim forms for the purposes of the rules on service (**r. 6.2(c)**). Obviously, if three days' notice can be given of an application for an interim injunction, there will be time to issue proceedings. Pre-action applications will therefore always be made without full notice to the respondent. This can only be justified if there are 'good reasons for not giving notice' (**r. 25.3(1)**). Urgency and/or the need for secrecy will be accepted as good reasons.

Arrangements for pre-action injunction hearings

37.6 Pre-action interim injunction applications will almost always be considered at a hearing but without full (or any) notice to the respondent. Such applications will almost certainly be of an urgent nature. If they arise during or shortly before the ordinary times when the court is sitting, the hearing will take place in court as soon as the circumstances permit. This means that generally such applications are heard before other matters that are listed, either as soon as the court sits in the morning or immediately after lunch. The necessary arrangements must be made with the court staff, who will invariably do all they can to ensure urgent applications are dealt with at the first available opportunity. Solicitors should therefore contact the court by telephone as soon as they know they will need to make an urgent application, so as to allow the court time to make the necessary arrangements. Sometimes urgent applications arise during the course of the morning or afternoon in circumstances where it is not possible to wait to the beginning of the next session. If the case is sufficiently urgent the court will invariably interrupt whatever it is doing at a convenient moment so that it can hear the urgent application.

On other occasions the need for a pre-action interim injunction may arise at a time when it is not possible to wait until the next occasion when the court will be sitting. If the application is of extreme urgency it may be dealt with by telephone (**PD 25A, para. 4.2**). If the problem has arisen during business hours, but in circumstances where it will not be possible to go before a judge before the close of business, initially it is necessary to telephone the court (either the High Court on (020) 7947 6000 or the appropriate county court) asking to be put in touch with a High Court judge of the appropriate division or county court judge available to deal with an emergency application (**PD 25A, para. 4.5(1)**).

If the problem has arisen outside office hours, the applicant should telephone either the High Court (on the same number as above) asking to be put in touch with the clerk to the appropriate duty judge (or the appropriate area circuit judge where known), or should telephone the urgent court business officer of the appropriate circuit, who will contact the local duty judge.

If the facilities are available, a draft of the order sought will usually be required to be sent by fax to the duty judge who will be dealing with the application.

Telephone hearings are only available if the applicant is acting by solicitors or counsel (**PD 25A, para. 4.5(5)**).

The pre-action order and related matters

37.7 The order should be in form PF 39 CH. If the order is granted, the court may give directions requiring a claim to be commenced (**CPR, r. 25.2(3)**). **PD 25A, para. 5.1(5)**, gives effect to this by providing that an order made before issue of the claim form will, unless the court orders otherwise, *include* 'an undertaking to issue and pay the appropriate fee on the same or next working day' or contain directions for the commencement of the claim. In other respects the order will follow the same form as other interim injunctions, see **37.63**.

As the application will invariably have been made without notice to the respondent, the order must, by **PD 25A, para.** 5.1(2) and (3), include, unless the court orders otherwise:

(a) an undertaking by the applicant to the court to serve the respondent with the application notice, evidence in support and any order made, as soon as practicable; and
(b) a return date for a further hearing at which the other party can be present.

Counsel and solicitors have a responsibility to take a full note of what is said on a hearing where the respondent is not present, so the respondent can know the case that was made against him. There are too many technical problems in the recording system at the Royal Courts of Justice for lawyers to rely on official transcripts for this purpose (*Cinpres Gas Injection Ltd v Melea Ltd* [2005] EWHC 3180 (Pat), *The Times*, 21 December 2005).

Service of pre-action interim injunctions

Generally, pre-action applications for interim injunctions are made without notice to the respondent. Therefore, **CPR, r. 23.9**, applies. This requires a copy of the application notice and any evidence in support to be served with the injunction order on all parties and persons against whom the order was sought or made. The order must contain a statement of the right to apply under **r. 23.10** to set aside or vary the order within seven days after it is served. **37.8**

Where possible the claim form should be served with the injunction order (**PD 25A, para.** 4.4(2)).

APPLICATIONS FOR INTERIM INJUNCTIONS DURING THE COURSE OF PROCEEDINGS

Time for applying for general interim injunctions

An application for an interim injunction in proceedings must be made after the claim form commencing the proceedings is issued if applying before issue is prevented by the conditions laid down in **CPR, r. 25.2(2)** (see 37.3). This will be the case where a pre-action application is prohibited by a rule or practice direction, or the matter is not urgent and it is not desirable to grant an injunction before issue in the interests of justice, or the applicant is an intended defendant and the court refuses permission. **Paragraphs 2.7** and **2.8** of **PD 23A** say that any application during proceedings should be made as soon as it becomes apparent that it is necessary or desirable, but should preferably be made at a hearing for which a date has already been, or is about to be, fixed. In many cases this means that the right time to apply for an interim injunction will be at the allocation stage, but an earlier, separate hearing would be justified if delay would make it more difficult to preserve the status quo. **37.9**

If the applicant is a defendant who has yet to file either an acknowledgment or a defence, the applicant must obtain the court's permission to make the application (**CPR, r. 25.2(2)(c)**).

Procedure on applications during proceedings

The procedure will be as described in 37.5 for pre-action applications except that: **37.10**

(a) The application notice need not give the applicant's address for service.
(b) The application will be made:
    (i) to the court in which the substantive proceedings were started (**CPR, r. 23.2(1)**), or
    (ii) to the court in which the proceedings were subsequently transferred (**r. 23.2(2)**), or
    (iii) if a date has been fixed for trial, to the court where the trial is to take place (**r. 23.2(3)**), or
    (iv) if after enforcement proceedings have been started, to the court dealing with enforcement 'unless any rule or practice direction provides otherwise' (**r. 23.2(5)**).

Commentary

(c) The rules for service of documents other than claim forms apply (**rr. 6.20** to **6.29**).
(d) It is good practice to annex a draft order to the application notice where time allows. Form PF 40 CH must be used for applications made after a claim has been issued.

For a summary of the procedure, see **procedural checklist 19** and **procedural checklist 20** at the front of the book.

Where the court is to serve, sufficient copies of the application notice and evidence in support should be provided for the court and each respondent (**PD 25A, para. 2.3**). Service should be effected as soon as possible, and in any event not less than three clear days before the hearing.

Although **PD 23A, para. 2.8**, provides that 'Applications should wherever possible be made so that they can be considered at any other hearing for which a date has already been fixed or for which a date is about to be fixed', clearly an application for an injunction, even where both parties are to appear at the hearing, will very often be of sufficient urgency to make it inappropriate to wait to make it until, say, the case management conference. Given the requirement to save expense (**CPR, r. 1.1(2)(b)**) and to allot to the case an appropriate share of the court's resources, while taking into account the need to allot resources to other cases (**r. 1.1(2)(e)**), an applicant should expect to be called on to justify the need for a separate hearing.

Respondents to applications made on notice are not under any specific duty under the rules to disclose their evidence in reply in advance of the hearings. However, deliberately holding back evidence in reply to the last minute will be a clear breach of the overriding objective. If the minimum of three clear days' notice was given by the applicant, it might be difficult or impossible for a respondent to compile and serve evidence in reply, which is why the CPR require the applicant to serve the application notice and evidence in support as soon as practicable after issue. The greater the notice given to the respondent, the greater is the effective obligation on the respondent to serve evidence in advance of the hearing. The rules seek to avoid multiple hearings (**CPR, r. 1.4(2)(i)**), and although the court may be prepared to give directions as to the service of evidence on the first hearing, it may well impose sanctions if it considers the need to give directions was caused by the default of either party.

Hearing of interim injunction applications in pending proceedings

37.11 Normally the hearing of an application for an interim injunction will be listed in the usual way for disposal in public (see **CPR, r. 39.2**). There are exceptional circumstances in which the hearing will be in private, such as where the hearing involves confidential information, the interests of children or protected parties, or where it would be unjust to proceed in public because the respondent has not been given due notice.

If the application is of an urgent nature justifying giving less than the usual three clear days' notice (see 37.4), unless secrecy is essential, the applicant should give the respondents informal notice (**PD 25A, para. 4.3(3)**), which should be explained in the evidence in support. If the urgency justifies making the application without first issuing an application notice, a draft order (at least) should be provided at the hearing. Normally the court will direct that an application notice and evidence in support must be filed with the court on the same or the next working day (**PD 25A, para. 4.3(2)**). If possible, even in the case of urgent applications, the application notice, evidence in support and draft order should be filed with the court at least two hours before it is intended to go before the judge (**PD 25A, para. 4.3(1)**).

In cases of extreme urgency, the court may interrupt its list, or conduct the hearing by telephone with the duty judge, in the same way as extremely urgent pre-action applications (see 37.6).

Where there is to be a hearing, then with consent of all parties (and provided no party is acting in person), the court can order the hearing to be dealt with by telephone (**PD 23A, para. 6.1**) or by video conference (**PD 23A, para. 7**).

Both parties should be prepared to deal with the future case management of the action. **PD 23A, para. 2.9**, warns them that: 'at any hearing the court may wish to review the conduct of the case as a whole and give any necessary case management directions. They should be ready to assist the court in doing so and to answer questions the court may ask for this purpose.' Indeed if the application takes place before allocation, the court may deal with allocation at the hearing (**PD 26, para. 2.4**).

Order obtained without notice

When an interim injunction is obtained in the course of proceedings without notice to the respondent, **CPR, rr. 23.9** and **23.10**, apply as they do to pre-action injunctions (see 37.8). Lawyers acting for the applicant have to make and serve on the respondent a note of what was said at the without-notice hearing (*Cinpres Gas Injection Ltd v Melea Ltd* [2005] EWHC 3180 (Pat), *The Times*, 21 December 2005). **37.12**

EVIDENCE IN SUPPORT OF AN APPLICATION FOR AN INTERIM INJUNCTION

An application for an interim injunction must be supported by evidence unless the court orders otherwise (**CPR, r. 25.3(2)**). The evidence must cover the substantive issues and also, if the application is without notice, explain why notice has not been given (**r. 25.3(3)**; **PD 25A, para. 3.4**). If the application is made before the issue of a claim form, the evidence should also address the urgency of the application or why it is 'desirable…in the interests of justice' to make the order (**CPR, r. 25.2(2)(b)**). The evidence should also address the relevant principles for granting injunctive relief (see below). **37.13**

PD 25A, para. 3.2, states that unless the court or an Act requires evidence by affidavit, evidence is to be:

(a) by witness statement;
(b) set out in the application, provided it is verified by a statement of truth; or
(c) set out in a statement of case, provided it is verified by a statement of truth.

The provision whereby a statement of case can be relied on as evidence is more likely to be of use where an application for an interim injunction is made during the course of proceedings.

PD 25A, para. 3.3, provides that 'The evidence must set out the facts on which the applicant relies for the claim being made against the respondent, including all material facts of which the court should be made aware.' This provision is not restricted to applications without notice. It appears to import at least some of the concepts of the previous duty of full and frank disclosure in relation to *ex parte* applications. The extent to which there is any duty, in any applications on full notice, to make reasonable inquiries remains obscure. Further, the 'material facts of which the court should be made aware' are likely to be more wide-ranging in an application made without notice than one made with the required three clear days' notice. Nevertheless, this paragraph of the practice direction is clearly intended to make parties address adverse facts in their evidence, even where the application is on notice and the respondent has a clear ability to file evidence and make representations at the hearing.

Where the application is on notice the respondent may, of course, file evidence in opposition (**PD 23A, para. 9.4**).

STATUTORY AUTHORITY

37.14 Like all forms of equitable relief, the granting of interim injunctions is a matter within the discretion of the court. The fundamental principle is contained in the Senior Courts Act 1981, s. 37(1), which (using pre-CPR terminology) provides:

> The High Court may by order (whether interlocutory or final) grant an injunction or appoint a receiver in all cases in which it appears to the court to be just and convenient to do so.

The same principle applies in the county courts, where the County Courts Act 1984, s. 38, provides in part:

> (1) Subject to what follows, in any proceedings in a county court the court may make any order which could be made by the High Court if the proceedings were in the High Court.
> (2) Any order made by a county court may be—
> (a) absolute or conditional;
> (b) final or interlocutory.

With the introduction of the **Human Rights Act 1998**, the test to be applied may be whether granting relief is just and proportionate rather than just and convenient (*South Bucks District Council v Porter* [2003] UKHL 26, [2003] 2 AC 558).

SUBSTANTIVE CAUSE OF ACTION

37.15 Injunctions are only remedies, so can usually only be granted if the applicant has a substantive cause of action. As stated by Lord Diplock in *The Siskina* [1979] AC 210:

> A right to obtain an [interim] injunction is not a cause of action. It cannot stand on its own. It is dependent upon there being a pre-existing cause of action against the defendant arising out of an invasion, actual or threatened by him, of a legal or equitable right of the [claimant] for the enforcement of which the defendant is amenable to the jurisdiction of the court. The right to obtain an [interim] injunction is merely ancillary and incidental to the pre-existing cause of action.

In *The Siskina* the claimant had a cause of action against the defendant, but it was only actionable in a foreign country. It was therefore held that the English courts had no jurisdiction to grant an interim injunction to protect the applicant's position. This principle was restated by Lord Brandon of Oakbrook in *South Carolina Insurance Co. v Assurantie Maatschappij 'De Zeven Provincien' NV* [1987] AC 24, where he said that, apart from freezing injunctions and injunctions to restrain foreign proceedings, the court has discretion to grant injunctions in only two situations:

(a) where a party has invaded or threatened to invade a legal or equitable right of another party which is amenable to the jurisdiction of the court;
(b) where a party has behaved or threatened to behave in an unconscionable manner.

Point (a) above has been largely overtaken by well-known exceptions. Lord Brandon himself referred to the established jurisdiction to grant injunctions to restrain foreign proceedings. Further, the High Court has a wide power to grant injunctions in support of overseas proceedings.

Civil Jurisdiction and Judgments Act 1982, s. 25

37.16 The **CJJA 1982, s. 25**, as extended by the Civil Jurisdiction and Judgments Act 1982 (Interim *Relief) Order 1997, SI 1997/302*, enables the High Court to grant interim relief where proceedings have been or are to be commenced in an overseas jurisdiction. The principle underpinning **CJJA 1982, s. 25**, is that the court should assist the courts of other jurisdictions by providing such interim relief as would be available if it were itself seised of the substantive proceedings (*Refco Inc. v Eastern Trading Co.* [1999] 1 Lloyd's Rep 159; *Kensington International Ltd v Republic of Congo* [2007] EWCA Civ 1128, [2008] 1 WLR 1144). Two key restrictions in the original s. 25 (that the overseas jurisdiction had to be in the EU, and that the substantive proceedings had to come within the scope of what is now the **Brussels I Regulation, art. 1**) were removed by the 1997 Order. The only remaining limitation is under **CJJA 1982, s. 25(2)**, that the court may refuse relief if, in the opinion of the court, the fact that the court has no jurisdiction apart from **s. 25** makes it inexpedient for the court to grant the interim relief that is sought.

Examples

Lord Browne-Wilkinson in *Channel Tunnel Group Ltd v Balfour Beatty Construction Ltd* [1993] AC 334 in the House of Lords expressed doubt on whether the law as stated in *The Siskina* [1979] AC 210 (see **37.15**) was correct in restricting the power to grant injunctions to certain exclusive categories. The question was, however, reserved for consideration when it arises. **37.17**

The *South Carolina Insurance Co.* principles (see **37.15**) were applied in *Ali v Westminster City Council* [1999] 1 WLR 314, in which it was held that the county court had no jurisdiction to grant an injunction in favour of applicants seeking interim mandatory injunctions to require their local housing authorities to provide them with accommodation pending the resolution of their appeals against decisions that they were not homeless persons within the meaning of the Housing Act 1996.

A company law claim for relief of unfairly prejudicial conduct (see **85.9**) is not in itself a substantive cause of action, and it is only if there is a claim that the directors are in breach of fiduciary duty or some other established cause of action that an injunction can be granted in such proceedings (*Re Premier Electronics (GB) Ltd* [2002] 2 BCLC 634).

A judge should not be deterred from granting an interim injunction on the correct basis where, through the incompetent presentation of the applicant's case, the underlying legal cause of action has not been identified by the applicant's representatives (*Watson v Durham University* [2008] EWCA Civ 1266, LTL 24/10/2008).

Person unknown as defendant

Under the pre-CPR rules it was an almost invariable rule that proceedings and orders could only be granted against named parties (*Friern Barnet Urban District Council v Adams* [1927] 2 Ch 25). The only exception related to claims for summary possession of land. **37.18**

In a radical decision, *Bloomsbury Publishing Group Ltd v News Group Newspapers Ltd* [2003] EWHC 1087 Ch, [2003] 1 WLR 1633, the claimant was allowed to join 'person or persons unknown' as second defendants to a claim where an interim injunction was granted restraining disclosure of the contents of, or information from, a book prior to its publication date. Laddie J said that if somebody could be identified clearly enough, a court should do what it could to allow injunctive relief to be ordered against him even if it was not possible to identify him by name. **PD 7A, para. 4.1**, merely says that the defendant 'should' be named. If proceedings are started against an unnamed person, they can be remedied under **CPR, r. 3.10**, unless the court thinks otherwise. On the facts, the injunction would be effective against people who, knowing of the order, assisted in its breach or nullified the purpose of a trial. The significance attached in this decision to the use of the word 'should' instead of 'must' in **PD 7A, para. 4.1**, while highly technical, may have been confirmed by the retention of the word 'should' in **para. 4.1** when many other occurrences of the word in the CPR and practice directions were changed to 'must' as from 1 October 2008. *Bloomsbury Publishing Group Ltd v News Group Newspapers Ltd* has been approved by the Court of Appeal in *South Cambridgeshire District Council v Persons Unknown*

[2004] EWCA Civ 1280, *The Times*, 11 November 2004; and *South Cambridgeshire District Council v Gammell* [2005] EWCA Civ 1429, [2006] 1 WLR 658.

Generally, media groups that might be affected by the injunction should be given prior notice of the application. The extent of any prior notification depends on the facts of each case. It may be appropriate to limit prior notification to organisations that are believed to have shown an interest in publishing (*TUV v Person or Persons Unknown* [2010] EWHC 853 (QB), [2010] EMLR 19).

INJUNCTIONS IN SUPPORT OF THE CRIMINAL LAW

37.19 The High Court has jurisdiction to grant injunctions in support of the criminal law. In *Attorney-General v Chaudry* [1971] 1 WLR 1614 Lord Denning MR said:

> There are many statutes which provide penalties for breach of them—penalties which are enforceable by means of a fine—or even imprisonment—but this has never stood in the way of the High Court granting an injunction. Many a time people have found it profitable to pay a fine and go on breaking the law. In all such cases the High Court has been ready to grant an injunction...
>
> Whenever Parliament has enacted a law and given a particular remedy for the breach of it, such remedy being in an inferior court, nevertheless the High Court always has reserve power to enforce the law so enacted by way of an injunction or declaration or other suitable remedy. The High Court has jurisdiction to ensure obedience to the law whenever it is just and convenient so to do.

These injunctions are exceptional. The main questions are whether criminal proceedings are likely to be effective to achieve the public-interest purposes of the legislation and whether there are good grounds for believing that compliance would not be secured by prosecution (*Guildford Borough Council v Hein* [2005] EWCA Civ 979, *The Times*, 21 September 2005).

In the 1980s there were cases (*Chief Constable of Kent v V* [1983] QB 34; *West Mercia Constabulary v Wagener* [1982] 1 WLR 127; *Chief Constable of Hampshire v A Ltd* [1985] QB 132; *Chief Constable of Leicestershire v M* [1989] 1 WLR 20) dealing with applications for injunctions brought by chief constables to freeze suspected proceeds of crime in advance of any conviction for the crime in question. In *Chief Constable of Leicestershire v M* it was said that the detailed interventions by Parliament in part 6 of the Criminal Justice Act 1988 (now in the Proceeds of Crime Act 2002) suggested that the civil courts should not indulge in parallel creativity by extension of the common law principles. In *Attorney-General v Blake* [2001] 1 AC 268 the claimant sought an injunction restraining the defendant from receiving any payment from a publisher resulting from the defendant's criminal conduct as a spy. The defendant had escaped to Moscow in 1966 and there was no realistic prospect of him returning to the United Kingdom. It was held that there was no common law power to confiscate property (the royalties) without compensation and no statutory confiscatory powers applied, so the court had no jurisdiction to grant the injunction.

THE *AMERICAN CYANAMID* GUIDELINES

37.20 In *American Cyanamid Co. v Ethicon Ltd* [1975] AC 396 Lord Diplock laid down guidelines on how the court's discretion to grant interim injunctions should be exercised in the usual types of cases. They most typically apply in applications for interim prohibitory injunctions. Particular examples of where they apply include applications for interim injunctions in unfair prejudice petitions under the Companies Act 2006, s. 994 (*Re Canterbury Travel (London) Ltd, Collins v Collins [2010] EWHC 1464 (Ch)*, LTL 12/7/2010) and to applications relating to the Public Contracts Regulations 2006 (SI 2006/5) (*Exel Europe Ltd v University Hospitals Coventry and Warwickshire NHS Trust* [2010] EWHC 3332 (TCC), LTL 4/1/2011). Although these guidelines are of great authority, they must not be read as if they were statutory provisions, and in practice they are applied with some degree of flexibility. However, it is not unknown for judges to give reasoned judgments in interim injunction cases following the sequence of steps set out by Lord Diplock (for example, *Rottenberg v Monjack* [1993] BCLC 374). The court must also be careful to apply the overriding objective, and to grant an injunction only if it is 'just and convenient'.

The underlying purpose of the guidelines is to enable the court to make an order that will do justice between the parties, whichever way the decision goes at trial, while interfering with the parties' freedom of action to the minimum extent necessary (see *Polaroid Corporation v Eastman Kodak Co.* [1977] RPC 379 per Buckley LJ at p. 395). The guidelines are described in **37.21** to **37.33**, but there are exceptions, which are discussed in **37.34** to **37.53**.

Serious question to be tried

Before *American Cyanamid Co. v Ethicon Ltd* [1975] AC 396, the courts would only grant an interim injunction if the applicant could establish a prima facie case on the merits. Consequently, the courts needed to consider the respective merits of the parties' cases in some detail. This encouraged the filing of detailed written evidence supported by voluminous exhibits, and resulted in lengthy interim hearings. As Lord Diplock said at p. 407: **37.21**

> It is no part of the court's function at this stage of the litigation to try to resolve conflicts of evidence on affidavits as to facts on which the claims of either party may ultimately depend nor to decide difficult questions of law which call for detailed argument and mature consideration.

Therefore, the court only needs to be satisfied that there is a serious question to be tried on the merits. A cause of action that can be described as hopeless will not satisfy this test (*National Commercial Bank Jamaica Ltd v Olint Corporation Ltd* [2009] UKPC 16, [2009] 1 WLR 1405 at [11]–[12]). The result is that the court is required to investigate the merits to a limited extent only. All that needs to be shown is that the claimant's cause of action has substance and reality. Beyond that, it does not matter if the claimant's chance of winning is 90 per cent or 20 per cent (*Mothercare Ltd v Robson Books Ltd* [1979] FSR 466 per Megarry V-C at p. 474; *Alfred Dunhill Ltd v Sunoptic SA* [1979] FSR 337 per Megaw LJ at p. 373). Having a weak case does not mean there is no serious issue to be tried (*B2net Ltd v HM Treasury* [2010] EWHC 51 (QB), 128 Con LR 53).

However, if there is no merit in the substantive cause of action, the application does not get past the first stage of the *American Cyanamid* guidelines (*APCOA Parking (UK) Ltd v Westminster City Council* [2010] EWHC 943 (QB), LTL 30/4/2010).

Examples Convincing the court that the claim brought by an applicant for an interim injunction raises a serious question to be tried is not a difficult hurdle to surmount. In *Porter v National Union of Journalists* [1980] IRLR 404, the issue was whether a strike instruction by the union affected a majority of its members. If it did, the union's rule book required a ballot. Neither party adduced accurate figures of the total numbers in the union, nor of the numbers affected by the strike instruction. It was held there was a serious question to be tried. **37.22**

In *Les Laboratoires Servier v KRKA Polska Sp zoo* [2006] EWHC 2453 (Pat), LTL 3/10/2006, the claimant owned a patent for a pharmaceutical product which it alleged was about to be infringed by the defendant. There was evidence that the patented form of the product had been sold by the claimant before the priority date for the patent, thus potentially depriving the patent of its novelty. This did not mean that the claimant had no case, and it was held there was a serious issue to be tried.

On the other hand, if there is no serious question to be tried on the substantive claim, the injunction must be refused. *Morning Star Co-operative Society Ltd v Express Newspapers Ltd* [1979]

FSR 113 should be regarded as not having passed this hurdle. At the time of the case, the *Daily Star* newspaper was about to be launched. The claimant alleged that it was going to be passed off as the established *Morning Star* newspaper. Apart from the fact that they were both newspapers and had the word 'Star' in their names, they were different in about every other respect. As Foster J commented, 'Only a moron in a hurry would be misled' into thinking that the *Daily Star* was the *Morning Star*, so the claimant had failed to show a serious issue to be tried on the alleged cause of action. A weak claim on the merits combined with relatively little financial harm to the claimant through the defendant's alleged infringement of intellectual property rights resulted in a refusal of relief in *GMG Radio Holdings Ltd v Tokyo Project Ltd* [2005] EWHC 2188(Ch), LTL 21/10/2005.

In *Boobyer v David Holman and Co. Ltd* [1993] 1 Lloyd's Rep 96 the claimant, a name at Lloyd's, applied for an interim injunction to restrain the defendant underwriting agent from paying cash calls on the claimant for being a member of a number of syndicates. Saville J refused the injunction without considering the balance of convenience as the claimant had failed to show even a serious issue to be tried. In *News Datacom Ltd v Satellite Decoding Systems* [1995] FSR 201 the claimant alleged that the defendant was selling a computerised 'smart card' for decoding satellite television programmes by copying the computer program supplied by the claimant to its customers. It was accepted that the defendant's card enabled its customers to decode the claimant's satellite broadcasts. In its application for an interim injunction the claimant exhibited an expert's report in which the expert stated an opinion that the defendant's product must have been copied from the claimant's program. This opinion was based on the complexity of the program and the implausibility of the defendant's product not being a copy, and not on a comparison of the two products. The High Court of Ireland held that as the claimant had failed to adduce evidence comparing the two products it had failed to show a serious question to be tried.

Sometimes there are arguments about whether the claimant's allegations amount to a cause of action known to the law. An example was *Khorasandjian v Bush* [1993] QB 727, in which it was held by a majority that the tort of harassment exists, and on the facts the judge had been entitled to grant an interim injunction restraining the defendant from 'harassing, pestering or communicating' with the claimant. In a related case, it was held in *Burris v Azadani* [1995] 1 WLR 1372 that, when granting an interim injunction to restrain future assaults or harassment, the court has power to impose an exclusion zone at the same time. An injunction to prevent cybersquatting was granted in *Lifestyle Management Ltd v Frater* [2010] EWHC 3258 (TCC), LTL 7/1/2011.

Adequacy of damages to the applicant

37.23 If there is a serious question to be tried on the merits of the substantive claim, the court should then consider whether the applicant will be adequately compensated by an award of damages at trial. The test was stated in the following way by Lord Diplock in *American Cyanamid Co. v Ethicon Ltd* [1975] AC 396 at p. 408:

> If damages in the measure recoverable at common law would be an adequate remedy and the defendant would be in a financial position to pay them, no [interim] injunction should normally be granted.

The question is whether it is just that the claimant be confined to its remedy in damages (*Evans Marshall and Co. Ltd v Bertola SA (No. 1)* [1973] 1 WLR 349). Damages will often be an adequate remedy for the claimant in claims for breach of contract, including contracts of employment (see *Ali v Southwark London Borough Council* [1988] ICR 567, but the position regarding claims in respect of contracts of employment is not completely free from doubt, see *Powell v Brent London Borough Council* [1988] ICR 176). A term providing for liquidated damages with damages at large in the alternative was regarded as being an adequate remedy in *Araci v Fallon* [2011] EWHC 1621 (QB), LTL 3/6/2011, where the applicant sought an injunction to restrain a jockey riding for another owner in breach of contract. Liquidated damages will be lower than the probable loss caused by a breach of the contract (*Bath and North East Somerset District Council v Mowlem plc* [2004] EWCA Civ 115, [2004] BLR 153). A claimant bringing an action for breach of copyright or confidence may (depending on the facts) be refused injunctive relief on the ground that damages would be an adequate remedy (*Hubbard v Vosper* [1972] 2 QB 84). However, damages will be inadequate if:

(a) The defendant is unlikely to be able to pay the sum likely to be awarded at trial.
(b) The wrong is irreparable, e.g. suspension from a professional post (*Watson v Durham University* [2008] EWCA Civ 1266, LTL 24/10/2008), loss of the right to vote.
(c) The damage is non-pecuniary, e.g. breach of an arbitration clause (*Starlight Shipping Co. v Tai Ping Insurance Co. Ltd, Hubei Branch* [2007] EWHC 1893 (Comm), [2008] 1 All ER (Comm) 593), libel, nuisance, trade secrets.
(d) There is no available market. In *Howard E. Perry and Co. Ltd v British Railways Board* [1980] 1 WLR 1375 the defendant refused to allow the claimant to remove a consignment of steel during a steelworkers' dispute. The claimant sought an order that the defendant permit the claimant to remove it. As steel was otherwise unobtainable at the time, damages were not an adequate remedy.
(e) Damages would be difficult to assess. Examples are loss of goodwill (*Foseco International Ltd v Fordath Ltd* [1975] FSR 507), disruption of business (*Evans Marshall and Co. Ltd v Bertola SA* [1973] 1 WLR 349) and where the defendant's conduct has the effect of killing off a business before it is established (*Mitchelstown Co-operative Society Ltd v Société des Produits Nestlé SA* [1989] FSR 345). Damages following being excluded from a public procurement exercise were held to be readily capable of calculation in *B2net Ltd v HM Treasury* [2010] EWHC 51 (QB), 128 Con LR 53.

As where the claimant fails to show a serious question to be tried, if damages would be an adequate remedy, that is the end of the matter and the injunction must be refused.

Undertakings in damages

Subject to some limited exceptions, an undertaking in damages is always required when an interim injunction is granted. The court has a discretion to order an interim injunction subject to a limited undertaking in damages (*RBG Resources plc v Rastogi* (2002) LTL 31/5/2002). By the undertaking the claimant is required to compensate the defendant for any loss incurred by the defendant during the currency of the injunction if it later appears that the injunction was wrongly granted. Its purpose is to provide a safeguard for the defendant who may be unjustifiably prevented from doing something it was entitled to do. As stated in *Wakefield v Duke of Buccleugh* (1865) 12 LT 628, this assists the court 'in doing that which was its great object, viz. abstaining from expressing any opinion on the merits of the case until the hearing'. 37.24

Undertakings in damages are not required where the Crown or a local authority is seeking an interim injunction to enforce the law (*Kirklees Metropolitan Borough Council v Wickes Building Supplies Ltd* [1993] AC 227), nor from the Financial Services Authority (*Securities and Investments Board v Lloyd-Wright* [1993] 4 All ER 210) or a foreign regulator (*United States Securities and Exchange Commission v Manterfield* [2009] EWCA Civ 27, [2010] 1 WLR 172) performing its regulatory functions, unless the defendant shows a strong prima facie case that its conduct is lawful (*F. Hoffmann-La Roche & Co. AG v Secretary of State for Trade and Industry* [1975] AC 295).

The modern approach is to require an undertaking in damages in applications for freezing injunctions in aid of enforcement in the same way as other applications (*Banco Nacional de Comercio Exterior SNC v Empresa de Telecommunicaciones de Cuba SA* [2007] EWCA Civ 662, [2008] 1 WLR 1936). Like other injunctions, the undertaking is usually dispensed with in freezing injunctions sought by public authorities to enforce the law (*Financial Services Authority v Sinaloa Gold plc* [2011] EWCA Civ 1158, [2012] CP Rep 4, where the absence of an express provision about cross-undertakings in the Financial Services and Markets Act 2000 was held not to change the position). In *Customs and Excise Commissioners v Anchor Foods Ltd* [1999] 1 WLR 1139 the Commissioners applied to restrain the disposal of certain assets by the defendant. The purpose of the application was to protect funds which the Commissioners contended should be paid to them. Neuberger J said that in these circumstances the presence or absence of an undertaking in damages was a factor to be weighed when considering the balance of convenience, and was only prepared to grant an injunction if the Commissioners gave an undertaking in damages.

An undertaking is also dispensed with where the injunction is in the nature of final relief (*Fenner v Wilson* [1893] 2 Ch 656), and where an injunction is granted in aid of execution after judgment (*Gwembe Valley Development Co. Ltd v Koshy (No. 4)* (2001) *The Times*, 28 February 2002).

37.25 **Fortifying the undertaking in damages** Where there is doubt about the claimant's solvency and hence the value of the usual undertaking in damages, the claimant may be required to 'fortify the undertaking' by bringing money into court or by providing security. A defendant seeking an order that the claimant must fortify an undertaking needs to satisfy the court that the injunction is likely to cause the defendant significant loss and there must be satisfactory evidence that the claimant may be unable to pay (*Bhimji v Chatwani (No. 2)* [1992] BCLC 387). See also **38.16**.

37.26 **Whether the undertaking in damages is an adequate protection for the defendant** In *American Cyanamid Co. v Ethicon Ltd* [1975] AC 396 Lord Diplock said at p. 408:

> If... damages would not provide an adequate remedy for the [claimant] in the event of his succeeding at the trial, the court should then consider whether, on the contrary hypothesis that the defendant were to succeed at the trial in establishing his right to do that which was sought to be enjoined, he would be adequately compensated under the [claimant's] undertaking as to damages for the loss he would have sustained by being prevented from doing so between the time of the application and the time of the trial. If damages in the measure recoverable under such an undertaking would be an adequate remedy and the [claimant] would be in a financial position to pay them, there would be no reason upon this ground to refuse an [interim] injunction.
>
> It is where there is doubt as to the adequacy of the respective remedies in damages available to either party or to both, that the question of balance of convenience arises.

It is clear from this that, unlike the question whether the claimant would be adequately compensated in damages, the adequacy of the undertaking will rarely be determinative of the application. If it is an adequate protection, that is 'no reason' for refusing the injunction. The court will then consider the balance of convenience, but the fact that the defendant is adequately protected will be a substantial factor in favour of granting the injunction (see *Bunn v British Broadcasting Corporation* [1998] 3 All ER 552). If there is a serious issue to be tried, and the claimant could be prejudiced by the acts or omissions of the defendant pending trial, and the claimant's undertaking in damages would provide the defendant with an adequate remedy if it transpires that his freedom of action should not have been restrained, an interim injunction should ordinarily be granted (*National Commercial Bank Jamaica Ltd v Olint Corporation Ltd* [2009] UKPC 16, [2009] 1 WLR 1405, at [16]). If the undertaking does not adequately protect the defendant, although that is a reason for refusing the injunction, normally the court will go on to consider the balance of convenience.

Even a freezing injunction has been granted in favour of a legally aided claimant (who obviously could not give a valuable undertaking in damages) where otherwise it was a proper case for granting the injunction (*Allen v Jambo Holdings Ltd* [1980] 1 WLR 1252). If the claimant is unable to give an undertaking in damages, care must be exercised before granting an injunction. It was said in *Belize Alliance of Conservation Non-Governmental Organisations v Department of the Environment* [2003] UKPC 63, 63 WIR 42, that it is particularly important to form a view on the merits of the claim in such cases, and to grant an injunction only if the claimant has a strong case. Where defendants in an application for a freezing injunction had failed to put in any evidence of the sort of loss they might suffer as a result of the order, it was held in *Bracken Partners Ltd v Gutteridge* (2001) LTL 16/1/2002 that there was no present basis for regarding the claimant's undertaking in damages as being insufficient.

Refusal of injunction in extreme cases In extreme cases where the claimant cannot give an adequate undertaking in damages, the court will refuse the injunction without considering the balance of convenience. *Morning Star Co-operative Society Ltd v Express Newspapers Ltd* [1979] FSR 113 was such a case, referred to at 37.22. In addition to the weak cause of action, the claimant had assets of £170,000 and liabilities of £260,000, so there was no realistic chance of it being able to honour the undertaking, especially as the defendants were likely to suffer appreciable, unquantifiable, damages. In *Merrell Dow Pharmaceuticals Inc. v N. H. Norton and Co. Ltd* [1994] RPC 1 a patentee would probably have had to make a permanent reduction in its prices as a result of an alleged infringement, which was an ascertainable loss, whereas the defendant had an unascertainable loss represented by the possible market share it would not achieve if the injunction was granted. On this basis the injunction was refused. **37.27**

Balance of convenience Most injunction cases are determined on the balance of convenience. In *American Cyanamid Co. v Ethicon Ltd* [1975] AC 396 Lord Diplock said, at p. 408: **37.28**

> it would be unwise to attempt even to list all the various matters which may need to be taken into consideration in deciding where the balance lies, let alone to suggest the relative weight to be attached to them. These will vary from case to case.

In other cases, such as *Cayne v Global Natural Resources plc* [1984] 1 All ER 225, the courts have insisted that it is not mere convenience that needs to be weighed, but the risk of doing an injustice to one side or the other. This is often an exercise in seeking to determine whether granting or refusing the injunction will cause irremediable prejudice, and to what extent (*National Commercial Bank Jamaica Ltd v Olint Corporation Ltd* [2009] UKPC 16, [2009] 1 WLR 1405 at [17]–[18]). Among the matters the court may take into account are:

(a) The prejudice the claimant may suffer if no injunction is granted or the defendant may suffer if it is. A claimant can reduce the potential injustice to the defendant by drafting the terms of the injunction as narrowly as is consistent with preserving the claimant's interests, or by offering undertakings to provide extra safeguards for the defendant.
(b) The likelihood of such prejudice actually occurring.
(c) The extent to which it may be compensated by an award of damages or enforcement of the undertaking in damages. Lord Diplock in *American Cyanamid Co. v Ethicon Ltd* said the extent to which the disadvantages to each party would be incapable of being compensated in damages is always a significant factor in assessing where the balance of convenience lies. In *Dyrlund Smith A/S v Turberville Smith Ltd* [1998] FSR 774 the apparent inability of the defendants to meet an award of damages was regarded as the decisive factor in favour of granting an interim injunction.
(d) The likelihood of either party being able to satisfy such an award.
(e) The likelihood that the injunction will turn out to have been wrongly granted or withheld (i.e. the court's view of the relative strengths of the parties' cases). It is submitted that this last matter should only be considered if the other matters are evenly balanced, or where it is possible to form such a view on facts which are clear or not in dispute. The main purpose behind the decision in *American Cyanamid Co. v Ethicon Ltd* [1975] AC 396 was to avoid contentious disputes over the merits of the case on applications for interim injunctions, which is the reason why the threshold is for a serious question to be tried, rather than the earlier prima facie case test.

Commentary

The fact a court may have decided to order a speedy trial is no more than a factor in assessing the balance of convenience (*Talaris (Sweden) AB v Network Controls International Ltd* [2008] EWHC 2930 (TCC), LTL 5/12/2008).

37.29 **Examples** The claimants in *American Cyanamid Co. v Ethicon Ltd* [1975] AC 396 sought an interim injunction to prevent the defendants marketing a surgical suture alleged to be in breach of patent. The claimants' patented suture had recently been introduced, and the claimants were expanding their market. The defendants' product had not at that time been introduced. They asserted that their product did not infringe the claimants' patent, alternatively, that the patent was invalid. If the injunction had been granted no factories would have closed, but if refused the claimants might have failed to increase their market and would effectively have lost the benefit of their patent. Therefore, the balance favoured the claimants. In *Douglas v Hello! Ltd* [2001] QB 967 an interim injunction to restrain a magazine from publishing wedding photographs alleged to infringe the first two claimants' rights of privacy was refused. If the event had been more intimate and private, the court would have been more willing to assist, but the first two claimants had already sold the rights to their wedding photographs to the third claimant, and the third claimant was adequately protected by an award of damages. On the other side, an injunction would have prevented publication of an issue of the defendant's magazine.

Each case turns on its own facts, but matters found to be important include:

(a) being deprived of employment (*Fellowes and Son v Fisher* [1976] QB 122);
(b) damage to business through picketing (*Hubbard v Pitt* [1976] QB 142);
(c) damage to the goodwill of a business (*Associated Newspapers plc v Insert Media Ltd* [1991] 1 WLR 571);
(d) closing down a factory, which was described as being catastrophic in *Potters-Ballotini Ltd v Weston-Baker* [1977] RPC 202;
(e) long-term effects on the price of the claimant's patented products if the defendant and other competitors are able to copy them (*Les Laboratoires Servier v KRKA Polska Sp zoo* [2006] EWHC 2453 (Pat), LTL 3/10/2006);
(f) whether complying with its mandate would put a bank in breach of the Proceeds of Crime Act 2002 (*K Ltd v National Westminster Bank plc* [2006] EWCA Civ 1039, [2007] 1 WLR 311);
(g) although the fact that an injunction may result in a company being wound up is a weighty matter, in *Astor Chemicals Ltd v Synthetic Technology Ltd* [1990] BCLC 1 this was outweighed by other considerations, particularly the fact that the company wanted to continue trading on a very speculative venture while hopelessly insolvent;
(h) interim relief seeking to prolong a state of affairs that is unsustainable in the long term is likely to be refused (*Re Canterbury Travel (London) Ltd, Collins v Collins* [2010] EWHC 1464 (Ch), LTL 12/7/2010, an unfair prejudice case);
(i) disruption to non-parties (*B2net Ltd v HM Treasury* [2010] EWHC 51 (QB), 128 Con LR 53, an application to suspend a public procurement exercise);
(j) preserving confidential information (*X AG v A Bank* [1983] 2 All ER 464);
(k) the public interest in keeping a drug with life-saving qualities on the market (*Roussel-Uclaf v G. D. Searle and Co. Ltd* [1977] FSR 125);
(l) preserving a substantial financial investment (*Catnic Components Ltd v Stressline Ltd* [1976] FSR 157);
(m) a failure by the claimant to respond to a letter from the defendant frankly stating its plans and enclosing sample containers, use of which is alleged by the claimant to amount to passing off (*Dalgety Spillers Foods Ltd v Food Brokers Ltd* [1994] FSR 504).

Status quo

37.30 In *American Cyanamid Co. v Ethicon Ltd* [1975] AC 396 Lord Diplock said at p. 408 that, in considering the balance of convenience: 'Where other factors appear to be evenly balanced it is a counsel of prudence to take such measures as are calculated to preserve the status quo'. From

Garden Cottage Foods Ltd v Milk Marketing Board [1984] AC 130, it appears that the status quo ante is the state of affairs before the defendant started the conduct complained of, unless there has been unreasonable delay, when it is the state of affairs immediately before the application. Therefore, it behoves the claimant to act quickly. An apparently unreasonable delay may be excused if sufficiently explained by the claimant.

Special factors

As Lord Diplock said in *American Cyanamid Co. v Ethicon Ltd* [1975] AC 396 at p. 409, 'there may be many special factors to be taken into consideration [in the balance of convenience] in the particular circumstances of individual cases'. If American Cyanamid Co. had been refused interim relief, but had established its claim at trial, it was probable that it would have been commercially impracticable for it to have insisted on Ethicon's sutures then being withdrawn, as doctors would have by then become used to using Ethicon's new sutures. **37.31**

Merits of the claim

In *American Cyanamid Co. v Ethicon Ltd* [1975] AC 396 Lord Diplock said at p. 409 that, as a last resort: **37.32**

> it may not be improper to take into account in tipping the balance the relative strength of each party's case as revealed by the affidavit evidence adduced on the hearing of the application. This, however, should be done only where it is apparent upon the facts disclosed by evidence as to which there is no credible dispute that the strength of one party's case is disproportionate to that of the other party. The court is not justified in embarking upon anything resembling a trial of the action upon conflicting affidavits in order to evaluate the strength of either party's case.

An example of a case where the merits were considered under this principle is *Cambridge Nutrition Ltd v British Broadcasting Corporation* [1990] 3 All ER 523. The merits were considered, because the incompensable damage to each party did not differ widely.

Less formal approaches

Although the *American Cyanamid* principles are well established, there are occasions where judges adopt slightly different approaches when deciding whether it is just and convenient (the Senior Courts Act 1981, s. 37, test, see **37.14**) to grant an injunction. There are some judges who, in exceptional cases, will weigh the respective merits of the parties' cases as disclosed in the written evidence and exhibits in deciding whether or not to grant interim injunctive relief. This approach finds expression in the judgment of Laddie J in *Series 5 Software Ltd v Clarke* [1996] 1 All ER 853. In his judgment Laddie J said the following were the guidelines to be adopted on a proper analysis of the *American Cyanamid* decision: **37.33**

(a) that interim injunctions are discretionary and all the facts of the case must be considered;
(b) there are no fixed rules, and the relief must be kept flexible;
(c) the court should rarely attempt to resolve complex issues of disputed fact or law;
(d) important factors in exercising the jurisdiction to grant interim injunctions are:
  (i) the extent to which damages are likely to be an adequate remedy to either side, and the ability of the other party to pay;
  (ii) the balance of convenience;
  (iii) maintaining the status quo; and
  (iv) any clear view the court may reach about the relative strength of the parties' cases.

In *Carlisle Cumbria United Independent Supporters Society Ltd v Courtray* (2005) LTL 25/11/2005 the questions asked by Sir Donald Rattee in considering whether to continue an injunction restraining the defendant from acting contrary to an agreement between the parties (a case close to the negative covenant exception discussed at 37.51) were:

(a) whether the claimant had shown a good arguable case on the merits; and
(b) whether the continuation of the injunction would better preserve the court's ability to do justice between the parties at trial than a refusal to continue the injunction.

EXCEPTIONAL CASES

37.34 There are some well-settled categories of cases where the *American Cyanamid* guidelines (see 37.20 to 37.33) are not applied. The usual difference is that in these cases the courts will investigate the merits of the cause of action. How these various cases can be reconciled with *American Cyanamid Co. v Ethicon Ltd* [1975] AC 396 is a question of some theoretical controversy. Suggestions are that they are examples of the 'special factors' mentioned by Lord Diplock; that the *American Cyanamid* guidelines only apply where the facts are in dispute; that *American Cyanamid* only applies where a trial is likely; and that the existence of some or all of the categories were not directly considered by Lord Diplock.

Final disposal of the claim

37.35 In *NWL Ltd v Woods* [1979] 1 WLR 1294 Lord Diplock said at p. 1306:

> *American Cyanamid Co. v Ethicon Ltd* [1975] AC 396...was not dealing with a case in which the grant or refusal of an injunction at that stage would, in effect, dispose of the action finally in favour of whichever party was successful in the application, because there would be nothing left on which it was in the unsuccessful party's interest to proceed to trial.

Two questions arise (see *Cayne v Global Natural Resources plc* [1984] 1 All ER 225; *Channel Tunnel Group Ltd v Balfour Beatty Construction Ltd* [1993] AC 334). First, on the assumption that the injunction is refused, and taking into account the likely length of time it will take to get to trial and the probable factual situation at that time, is there any realistic possibility that the claimant will wish to proceed to trial? Assertions by claimants that they will in any event proceed to trial to recover damages may be disregarded if in reality a trial would be a meaningless gesture (*Lansing Linde Ltd v Kerr* [1991] 1 WLR 251). Secondly, on the assumption that the injunction is granted, is there any realistic prospect of the defendant insisting on going to trial to vindicate its defence and having the injunction discharged? Where neither party has a real interest in going to trial, the interim application will finally determine the claim. In such a case, Lord Diplock in *NWL Ltd v Woods* [1979] 1 WLR 1294, said at p. 1307:

> the degree of likelihood that the [claimant] would have succeeded in establishing his right to an injunction if the action had gone to trial, is a factor to be brought into the balance by the judge in weighing the risks that injustice may result from his deciding the application one way rather than the other.

The degree to which the claimant must establish the merits of the case vary with the circumstances. Thus, in *Cayne v Global Natural Resources plc* [1984] 1 All ER 225, the claimants, who were shareholders in the defendant company, sought injunctions, *inter alia*, to restrain the company from implementing a merger transaction without first obtaining the approval of the company in general meeting. There was no realistic prospect of a trial, because by the time the claim could be tried either the deal would have been implemented or the general meeting would have taken place. The claimants alleged the purpose of the transaction was to maintain the directors in office. The defendants served evidence which, if true, completely destroyed the claimants' case. Instead of applying the *American Cyanamid* guidelines the court had to apply the broad principle of doing its best to avoid injustice. Eveleigh LJ said, at *p. 233*:

> it would be wrong to run the risk of causing an injustice to a defendant who is being denied the right to trial where the defence put forward has been substantiated by affidavits and a number of exhibits.

Accordingly, an injunction would only have been granted if the claimants' case was overwhelming on its merits. It was not, so the injunction was refused. The actual standard of proof demanded in final disposal cases depends on the circumstances of each case. The 'high degree of assurance' test (the usual test for interim mandatory injunctions, see **37.61**) was applied in the final disposal case of *Chambers v British Olympic Association* [2008] EWHC 2028 (QB), LTL 18/7/2008. *Lansing Linde Ltd v Kerr* [1991] 1 WLR 251 concerned an application for an injunction to enforce a covenant in restraint of trade. It was not possible for the claim to be tried before the expiry of the period of the restraint; the claimants were not realistically interested in pursuing their claim for damages; so there was no prospect of a trial. Staughton LJ said that in the circumstances justice simply required 'some assessment of the merits. . .more than merely a serious issue to be tried'. A case just on the other side of the line regarding final disposal was *Astor Chemicals Ltd v Synthetic Technology Ltd* [1990] BCLC 1. The main issue on this aspect of the case was whether the defendant had any real interest in taking the case to trial if the injunction was granted, given that the effect of the injunction was almost certainly to force it into liquidation. It was held that there was some prospect of the liquidator taking the claim to trial for the defendant, so *American Cyanamid Co. v Ethicon Ltd* had to be applied.

Defamation claims at common law

Since *Bonnard v Perryman* [1891] 2 Ch 269, it has been held that interim injunctions will not generally be granted in defamation cases if the defendant intends to plead justification. In *Bestobell Paints Ltd v Bigg* [1975] FSR 421 it was held that this principle is unaltered by *American Cyanamid Co. v Ethicon Ltd* [1975] AC 396, because of the overriding public interest in protecting the right to free speech. In *Greene v Associated Newspapers Ltd* [2004] EWCA Civ 1462, [2005] QB 972, it was held that the rule in *Bonnard v Perryman* is also unaltered by the **Human Rights Act 1998, s. 12(3)** (see **37.37**) or by the **Human Rights Act 1998, s. 6** (which requires public authorities to act in ways compatible with the Convention, see **91.6**). The defamation rule does not, however, apply to trade mark infringement cases, even where the trademark is used in comparative advertising (*Boehringer Ingelheim Ltd v Vetplus Ltd* [2007] EWCA Civ 583, [2007] Bus LR 1456). **37.36**

For the *Bonnard v Perryman* exception to apply there are two conditions:

(a) The defendant must state in the evidence in reply that it is intended to set up the defence of justification.
(b) The alleged libel must not be obviously untruthful. The claimant may accordingly adduce evidence to prove the falsity of the words published. However, the burden on the claimant is a heavy one (*Holley v Smyth* [1998] QB 726).

In *Holley v Smyth* the claimants could not discharge the burden of proving that the alleged libel was obviously untruthful, but argued that an injunction should nevertheless be granted on account of the defendant's motive. The defendant alleged that the first two claimants were guilty of fraud and that the third and fourth claimants were guilty of negligence in relation to the fraud. He wrote to the claimants enclosing copies of press releases he proposed publishing if the sums he alleged had been lost were not repaid. It was accepted in the Court of Appeal that his motive was not so much to publish the truth, but the less high-minded one of obtaining the sum he considered he was owed by the claimants. It was held that this was insufficient to allow the court to go behind the principle in *Bonnard v Perryman*. However, if the defendant's conduct had gone further and amounted to the crime of blackmail, an injunction would have been granted.

Similar principles apply where the defendant intends to plead fair comment on a matter of public interest (*Fraser v Evans* [1969] 1 QB 349) and where the publication is privileged, unless, in the case of qualified privilege, there is overwhelming evidence of malice (*Harakas v Baltic*

Mercantile and Shipping Exchange Ltd [1982] 1 WLR 958). There is even greater reluctance to restrain publication of an expression of opinion. The rule in *Bonnard v Perryman* cannot be evaded by pleading the claim in both libel and breach of confidence, where it is clear that the main claim is in libel (*Woodward v Hutchins* [1977] 1 WLR 760). However, the rule in *Bonnard v Perryman* is ousted where the publication amounts to a contempt of court as well as a libel (*Attorney-General v News Group Newspapers Ltd* [1987] QB 1).

Right to freedom of expression

37.37 Article 10(1) of the European Convention on Human Rights provides that everyone has the right to freedom of expression. This right is subject to safeguards in **art. 10(2)**, which include restrictions for the protection of the reputation or rights of others. The **Human Rights Act 1998**, sets out three interlocking provisions to protect the primacy of the right to freedom of expression. First, the applicant is under a duty to take all practical steps to inform the respondent of the application (**s. 12(2)**). Secondly, **s. 12(3)** provides that no relief to restrain publication before trial which might affect the **art. 10(1)** right is to be allowed 'unless the court is satisfied that the applicant is likely to establish that the publication should not be allowed'. In *Cream Holdings Ltd v Banerjee* [2004] UKHL 44, [2005] 1 AC 253, the House of Lords rejected an argument that **s. 12(3)** simply required the applicant to show a 'real prospect of success', even one convincingly established. Instead, a flexible approach has to be taken. To satisfy the test in **s. 12(3)** the applicant must in most cases advance a case which will probably ('more likely than not') succeed at trial (Lord Nicholls of Birkenhead at [22]). The threshold that the applicant needs to pass is a high one (*Viscount Monckton of Brenchley v British Broadcasting Corporation* (2011) LTL 3/2/2011). While the cases may appear to lay down clear principles, applying them is far more difficult. Eady J in *CDE v MGN Ltd* [2010] EWHC 3308 (QB), LTL 11/2/2011, commented that the guidance given in *Cream Holdings Ltd v Banerjee* does not make the task any easier: there are no hard and fast rules, and it is a question of weighing up competing Convention rights and forming a judgment based on the unique facts of each case. The court will then exercise its discretion, taking into account the jurisprudence on **art. 10** and any other relevant matters.

Where this approach does not achieve the legislative intention behind **s. 12(3)**, or fails to give effect to countervailing Convention rights, a lesser degree of likelihood will suffice to satisfy the test. Exceptional cases suggested by Lord Nicholls in *Cream Holdings Ltd v Banerjee* were where the potential adverse consequences of disclosure are particularly grave, and where a short-term injunction is needed to enable the court to give proper consideration to an application for an interim injunction. Damage to reputation is not in itself enough to make a case exceptional for this purpose (*Boehringer Ingelheim Ltd v Vetplus Ltd* [2007] EWCA Civ 583, [2007] Bus LR 1456).

Thirdly, **s. 12(4)** provides that the court must have particular regard to the importance of the Convention right to freedom of expression, and in particular:

(a) whether the material is available to the public; and
(b) whether it is in the public interest for material to be published.

In considering whether a publication is in the public interest for the purposes of **s. 12(4)(b)** the court is obliged to consider any relevant privacy code (*TSE v News Group Newspapers Ltd* [2011] EWHC 1308 (QB), LTL 26/5/2011). Under the Press Complaints Commission Editors' Code of Practice, 'Editors will be expected to justify intrusions into any individual's private life without consent' (cl. 3(ii)). Such intrusions can be justified only where they 'can be demonstrated to be in the public interest'. It is frequently the case that stories newspapers may wish to publish are of great interest to the public, but are not in the public interest (*K v News Group Newspapers Ltd* [2011] EWCA Civ 439, [2011] 1 WLR 1827).

Privacy: new or extended torts

Interim injunctions in proceedings to restrain newspapers from publishing articles that invade the claimant's privacy should normally be governed by the *American Cyanamid* guidelines (see **37.20** to **37.33**), as adapted by the **Human Rights Act 1998, s. 12(3)** (see **37.37**). *Douglas v Hello! Ltd* [2001] QB 967, which is discussed at **37.29**, was widely interpreted as opening the door to a new cause of action to protect individual privacy based on the European Convention on Human Rights, **art. 8**, in the **Human Rights Act 1998, sch. 1**. The House of Lords has made clear there is no common law tort of invasion of privacy, with or without the **Human Rights Act 1998** (*Wainwright v Home Office* [2003] UKHL 53, [2004] 2 AC 406). The absence of a legally binding requirement to notify the subject in advance of any publication in the media does not breach **art. 8** (*Mosley v United Kingdom* (application 48009/08) (2011) 53 EHRR 30). **37.38**

Despite the decision in *Wainwright v Home Office* the courts have been concerned to develop a law of privacy that provides protection of the rights of an individual to 'private and family life, his home and his correspondence' as recognised by **art. 8**. Among the high-profile reported cases are *Prince of Wales v Associated Newspapers Ltd* [2006] EWCA Civ 1776, [2008] Ch 57; *Douglas v Hello! Ltd (No. 3)* [2007] UKHL 21, [2008] 1 AC 1; *Campbell v MGN Ltd* [2004] UKHL 22, [2004] 2 AC 457; *Murray v Express Newspapers plc* [2008] EWCA Civ 446, [2009] Ch 481; and *Donald v Ntuli* [2010] EWCA Civ 1276, [2011] 1 WLR 294. As Lord Neuberger MR said in his *Report of the Committee on Super-Injunctions: Super-Injunctions, Anonymised Injunctions and Open Justice, Judiciary* (20 May 2011) the courts have:

(a) developed the pre-existing tort of breach of confidence; and
(b) started to develop a new tort of misuse of private information.

Confidentiality

Confidentiality cases broadly fall into three categories: those where there is an express prior confidentiality agreement; those involving conduct which is inconsistent with a pre-existing relationship; and those involving purloining of private information. An express contractual duty of confidentiality should be given more weight than an implied duty arising from the general principles of equity (*London Regional Transport v Mayor of London* [2001] EWCA Civ 1491, [2003] EMLR 4). Stolen private information is more likely to be protected than confidential information arising from a pre-existing relationship (*McKennitt v Ash* [2006] EWCA Civ 1714, [2008] QB 73 at [8]). **37.39**

Where no Convention rights are engaged, applications to restrain confidential information are decided applying the usual *American Cyanamid* principles (*Lock International plc v Beswick* [1989] 1 WLR 1268). An additional question is whether the information is in the public domain, in which event there will not be a serious question to be tried.

Applications to restrain the use of confidential information often engage either or both of **arts 8** and **10** of the European Convention on **Human Rights in the Human Rights Act 1998, sch. 1**. Where **art. 10** is engaged, the applicant has to satisfy the merits test set out in the **Human Rights Act 1998, s. 12(3)** (see 37.37). In these cases three issues arise:

(a) whether the information is in principle protected (*McKennitt v Ash*) (if not, there is no case);
(b) whether the information is already in the public domain, so that it has lost its private or confidential nature (*Attorney-General v Guardian Newspapers Ltd (No. 2)* [1990] 1 AC 109); and
(c) whether the interest in keeping the information private or confidential should yield to the public interest in freedom of expression (*McKennitt v Ash*).

Protection of private or confidential information

A duty of confidence may arise by statute (such as the Official Secrets Acts 1911 to 1989) or through the obligations imposed by a person's professional rules (such as the SRA Code of Conduct 2011 and the Bar Code of Conduct: see also the Legal Services Act 2007, ss. 176 and 188). **37.40**

Commentary

Employees, purchasers of businesses, parties involved in arbitrations and mediations, and parties in numerous other situations, may enter into contractual obligations of confidentiality. In these situations there may be little doubt over the duty of confidentiality. The more difficult question may be whether the relevant information or circumstances come within the duty.

There may be a duty of confidentiality where sensitive information is communicated in a letter marked 'private and confidential' (see *Prince of Wales v Associated Newspapers Ltd* [2006] EWCA Civ 1776, [2008] Ch 57).

In other cases the duty arises only if the information is of such a nature and obtained in such circumstances that any reasonable person in the position of the recipient ought to recognise that it should be treated as confidential (*Napier v Pressdram Ltd* [2009] EWCA Civ 443, [2010] 1 WLR 934). This will be satisfied where a reasonable person in the position of the subject of the disclosure would find the publication offensive (*Campbell v MGN Ltd* [2004] UKHL 22, [2004] 2 AC 457). The result of a disciplinary inquiry is not confidential information, nor is the identity of the parties (*Napier v Pressdram Ltd*). The court must bear in mind the jurisprudence under **art. 8**, including *Hannover v Germany* (application 59320/00) (2005) 40 EHRR 1, which decided that activities such as family holidays and sporting activities are part of a person's private recreation time and are protected by **art. 8**. Factors to take into account in deciding whether there was a reasonable expectation of privacy include the attributes of the claimant, what he was doing at the time, where, the nature of the intrusion, whether there was consent, the effect on the claimant and the circumstances of the proposed publication (*Murray v Express Newspapers plc* [2008] EWCA Civ 446, [2009] Ch 481). Depending on the facts, this may mean that photographs taken of a child in a public place may be protected. In *Mosley v News Group Newspapers Ltd* [2008] EWHC 1777 (QB), [2008] EMLR 20, it was held that the clandestine recording of sexual activity on private property engaged **art. 8**. Photographs taken at a private wedding were held to be protected in *Douglas v Hello! Ltd (No. 3)* [2007] UKHL 21, [2008] 1 AC 1. A finding that the information is untrue is not a defence (*McKennitt v Ash* [2006] EWCA Civ 1714, [2008] QB 73).

Information in the public domain

37.41 Once information has become available to the public it loses its confidential nature *Attorney-General v Guardian Newspapers Ltd (No. 2)* [1990] 1 AC 109). An injunction will not be granted to restrain disclosure of information which is already in the public domain (*D v L* [2003] EWCA Civ 1169, LTL 31/7/2003). The 'springboard doctrine' (that an injunction might be granted to restrain continued use of confidential information once the information has ceased to be confidential) has been laid to rest (*Vestergaard Frandsen A/S v Bestnet Europe Ltd* [2009] EWHC 1456 (Ch), [2010] FSR 2). Whether dissemination of the information has resulted in it losing its confidential nature is a qualitative and not merely a quantitative question (*Northern Rock plc v Financial Times Ltd* [2007] EWHC 2677 (QB), LTL 26/11/2007). Publication of the material on some remote or expert website not generally available to the public without a great deal of effort, may mean confidentiality is not lost (*Barclays Bank plc v Guardian News and Media Ltd* [2009] EWHC 591 (QB), LTL 27/3/2009).

Balancing art. 8 and art. 10 rights

37.42 If information is private, the question is whether the interest of its owner, under the European Convention on Human Rights, **art. 8**, in the **Human Rights Act 1998, sch. 1**, should in all the circumstances yield to the right of freedom of expression which the publisher has under **art. 10**. Four principles were extracted from *Campbell v MGN Ltd* [2004] UKHL 22, [2004] 2 AC 457, by Lord Steyn in *Re S (A Child) (Identification: Restrictions on Publication)* [2004] UKHL 47, [2005] 1 AC 593 at [17]:

(a) neither **art. 8** nor **art. 10** has precedence over the other;
(b) where the values under the two articles are in conflict, an intense focus on the comparative importance of the specific rights being claimed in the individual case is necessary;

(c) the justifications for interfering with or restricting each right must be taken into account; and
(d) the proportionality test must be applied to each (also known as the ultimate balancing test).

In *Campbell v MGN Ltd* details of the claimant's drug addiction therapy went beyond the level of detail required to give credibility to the story published in the newspaper. Taking into account all the circumstances, the claimant's right to respect for her private life under **art. 8** outweighed the newspaper's right to freedom of expression under **art. 10**. In *Donald v Ntuli* [2010] EWCA Civ 1276, [2011] 1 WLR 294, it was held there was a reasonable expectation of privacy over salacious details and other details of an intimate nature about a past personal relationship, unless it could be shown that there was a countervailing public interest (such as the relationship between a politician and someone they have appointed to public office).

At this stage the court takes into account whether the publication would be highly offensive to an objective, reasonable person (*Murray v Express Newspapers plc* [2008] EWCA Civ 446, [2009] Ch 48). A particularly weighty factor is the **art. 8** rights of any children who might be harmed by a publication (*K v News Group Newspapers Ltd* [2011] EWCA Civ 439, [2011] 1 WLR 1827). In *Mosley v News Group Newspapers Ltd* [2008] EWHC 1777 (QB), [2009] EMLR 20, it was held that a particularly serious reason was required before clandestine recordings could be published under **art. 10**.

A distinction is drawn between cases where there is and is not a breach of confidence (*Prince of Wales v Associated Newspapers Ltd* [2006] EWCA Civ 1776, [2008] Ch 57, per Lord Phillips of Worth Matravers LCJ). Where there is no breach of confidence, the balance between **arts 8** and **10** usually involves weighing the nature and consequences of the breach of privacy against the public interest, if any, in the disclosure of the information. In cases where there is a breach of confidence, that is in itself a factor capable of justifying restrictions on freedom of expression under **art. 10(2)**. The question is whether a fetter on the right of freedom of expression is in the particular circumstances necessary in a democratic society. A significant element in reaching a proportionate decision on this issue is the importance attached in a democratic society to upholding duties of confidence, as well as considering the nature of the information and the nature of the relationship giving rise to the duty of confidentiality. In *Re A Local Authority (Inquiry: Restraint on Publication)* [2003] EWHC 2746 (Fam), [2004] Fam 96, the balance came down in favour of granting an injunction to restrain publication of a report on fostering children as the **art. 8** rights of the children and vulnerable adults identified in the report outweighed the local authority's right to publish under **art. 10**.

Super-injunctions

The term 'super-injunction' was first used by *The Guardian* newspaper when describing the injunction granted in the *Trafigura* case (*RJW v Guardian News and Media Ltd* [2009] EWHC 2540 (QB)). A super-injunction clause uses words that prohibit the publication or disclosure of the court proceedings and also the fact that an interim injunction has been applied for, to anyone other than the respondent's lawyers. In the *Trafigura* case Maddison J granted an injunction against the newspaper and persons unknown preventing them from publishing or disclosing a privileged report on alleged dumping of toxic waste in the Ivory Coast. The application: 37.43
(a) was made without notice; and
(b) was dealt with at a hearing conducted in private.

The order included clauses which:

(a) anonymised the claimant's name by changing it to a sequence of letters, 'RJW';
(b) adjusted all references to people and places to conceal the identity of the claimant;

(c) contained a super-injunction clause;
(d) contained a further clause that 'sealed' the court file for the purposes of **CPR, r. 5.4C**; and
(e) prevented the respondent from disclosing court papers to anyone other than for the purpose of obtaining legal advice.

Detailed guidance on the procedures to be followed, together with precedents for the draft order, can be found in Practice Guidance (Interim Non-disclosure Orders) [2012] 1 WLR 1003. It is the cumulative effect of the above clauses, combined with making the application without notice and at a private hearing, that make super-injunctions controversial. It is the lack of public scrutiny that has caused the main concern. To assess the extent of the problem **PD 40F** requires judges to provide data on all injunctions that involve a derogation from the principle of open justice, and is not restricted to super-injunctions.

The complete abrogation of the open justice principle inherent in strict super-injunction orders means they should only be granted in extremely exceptional situations. This may be the case if it is necessary to ensure the ultimate vindication of the claimant's rights at trial is not undermined by the way the court has processed the interim application (*Donald v Ntuli* [2010] EWCA Civ 1276, [2011] 1 WLR 294). Any restrictions, however, must be the minimum that can be imposed to give the claimant the protection to which they are entitled (at [54]).

Hearing super-injunction applications in private

37.44 The general rule is that litigation is conducted in public (European Convention on Human Rights, **art. 6(1)**, in the **Human Rights Act 1998, sch. 1; CPR, r. 39.2(1)**; *Scott v Scott* [1913] AC 417). There are recognised exceptions, a list of which appears in **r. 39.2(3)**. They principally cover situations where it is necessary to depart from the general rule to avoid frustrating or rendering impracticable the administration of justice (*Attorney-General v Leveller Magazine Ltd* [1979] AC 440 per Lord Diplock at p. 450).

Where the hearing involves reference to confidential material the parties and the court need to make arrangements to ensure justice is done in as open a manner as is practicable. For example, confidential material could be placed in an annex or separate file in the application bundle, which will allow it to be readily identified by the court and assist in ensuring clarity if the court orders it not to be disclosed (*Ambrosiadou v Coward* [2011] EWCA Civ 409, [2011] 2 FLR 617). When giving judgment the court should consider the extent to which details need to be included which would directly or indirectly reveal confidential information. A carefully constructed judgment may mean there is no need to deliver judgment in private (*Donald v Ntuli* [2010] EWCA Civ 1276, [2011] 1 WLR 294). If the court permits the identity of the applicant to be revealed, it will almost certainly mean that less detail should be included in the judgment than if an anonymity order is made (*H v News Group Newspapers Ltd* [2011] EWCA Civ 42, [2011] 1 WLR 1645). If an order is made permitting only a redacted version of a document to be made public, the parties must ensure the redaction is effective (*Ambrosiadou v Coward*, where the redacted copy could be unredacted using fairly easily available software).

Anonymity orders

37.45 A true super-injunction will invariably include an anonymity clause, but an injunction without the super-injunction clause is not a super-injunction even if it has anonymity provisions. An anonymity order will remove the claimant's name from the court papers and replace them with initials. The initials chosen, for example 'CTB', bear no relation to the actual name of the litigant. This is sometimes referred to as 'alphabet soup'. Anonymity and reporting restriction orders cannot be made by consent, because the parties cannot waive the rights of the public (*H v News Group Newspapers Ltd* [2011] EWCA Civ 42, [2011] 1 WLR 1645).

Anonymising judgments is considered at **63.35**. Questions of necessity and proportionality similar to those relevant to the decision to hold the hearing in private are taken into account when considering whether to anonymise the parties to an interim injunction application (*Donald v Ntuli* [2010] EWCA Civ 1276, [2011] 1 WLR 294, where the application was refused; *CDE v MGN Ltd* [2010] EWHC 3308 (QB), LTL 11/2/2011, where the application was granted). It is necessary to balance the competing interests under **arts 8** and **10**, and the facts and circumstances of the case have to be sufficiently strong to justify encroaching on the cardinal principle of open justice (*H v News Group Newspapers Ltd*). Careful writing up of the judgment may ensure it is in a form suitable for publication (*Donald v Ntuli* at [55]).

Hyper-injunctions

Hyper-injunctions are injunctions which appear to go further than a super-injunction, and prohibit discussion of the case or the order with a constituent's Member of Parliament. They are exceptionally rare. Lord Neuberger MR (*Report of the Committee on Super-Injunctions: Super-Injunctions, Anonymised Injunctions and Open Justice*, Judiciary 20 May 2011) made the point that hyper-injunctions are unnecessary. The standard super-injunction clause prevents publication or disclosure of the order or proceedings to anyone, which includes Members of Parliament (at least outside the Chamber of the House of Commons, because the courts have no jurisdiction to restrain anything said in either Chamber of the Houses of Parliament by virtue of the Bill of Rights 1689, art. 9). The law on discussing cases subject to super-injunctions with Members of Parliament was found to be undeveloped by Lord Neuberger MR when this was discussed in his report. However, a clear view was expressed that a super-injunction order would prevent any such discussion or disclosure, but that such a restriction does not infringe the Bill of Rights, art. 9, because it is not a direct restraint on Parliamentary debates. **37.46**

Anonymising judgments is considered at **63.35**. Similar questions of necessity and proportionality are taken into account when considering whether to anonymise the parties to an interim injunction application (*Donald v Ntuli*, where the application was refused; *CDE v MGN Ltd* [2010] EWHC 3308 (QB), LTL 11/2/2011, where the application was granted). Careful writing up of the judgment may ensure it is in a form suitable for publication (*Donald v Ntuli* at [55]).

Copyright

In *Hubbard v Vosper* [1972] 2 QB 84 Lord Denning MR said that in copyright claims defendants with reasonable defences of fair dealing under what is now the Copyright, Designs and Patents Act 1988, s. 30, should not be restrained by injunctions. The reason is that a defendant with such a defence 'is entitled to publish it: and the law will not intervene to suppress freedom of speech except when it is abused'. **37.47**

Industrial disputes

After *American Cyanamid Co. v Ethicon Ltd* [1975] AC 396, whenever an interim injunction was sought against a trade union that claimed it was acting in contemplation or furtherance of a trade dispute, the courts refused to investigate the respective merits of the case on each side, and tended to concentrate on the balance of convenience. Unions could rarely point to significant inconvenience if they were restrained from striking, whereas employers could readily identify their continuing financial losses. The result was that injunctions were invariably granted against unions involved in trade disputes despite the statutory defences. Legislation was accordingly passed to ensure the merits of the statutory defences are considered before injunctions are granted against trade unions. This legislation is now contained in the Trade Union and Labour Relations (Consolidation) Act 1992, s. 221(2), which provides: **37.48**

Where—

(a) an application for an interlocutory injunction is made to a court pending the trial of an action, and
(b) the party against whom it is sought claims that he acted in contemplation or furtherance of a trade dispute,

the court shall, in exercising its discretion whether or not to grant the injunction, have regard to the likelihood of that party's succeeding at the trial of the action in establishing any matter which would afford a defence to the action under section 219 (protection from certain tort liabilities) or section 220 (peaceful picketing).

Differing views have been expressed on the interpretation of this section. The approach favoured by Lord Scarman in *NWL Ltd v Woods* [1979] 1 WLR 1294 was that the court must consider:

(a) whether the cause of action against the union discloses a serious action to be tried;
(b) the balance of convenience; and
(c) the likelihood of the union establishing the statutory defence.

Lord Fraser of Tullybelton in the same case pointed out that the word 'likelihood' is a word of degree, and the weight to be given to establishing the trade dispute defence varies according to the degree of the likelihood. Where it is highly probable that a trade union will persuade the court that it has complied with the requirements for strike balloting laid down in the Trade Union and Labour Relations (Consolidation) Act 1992, an interim injunction to restrain strike action will be refused (*British Airways plc v Unite the Union* [2010] EWCA Civ 669, [2010] ICR 1316).

Claims against public authorities

37.49 *Smith v Inner London Education Authority* [1978] 1 All ER 411 is authority for the proposition that public authorities should not be restrained from exercising their statutory powers and duties unless the claimant has an extremely strong case on the merits. If the evidence indicates that the authority is exceeding the law, often upholding the rule of law will prevail over administrative inconvenience (*Bradbury v Enfield London Borough Council* [1967] 1 WLR 1311). Most cases of this nature should now be brought by proceedings for judicial review (**chapter** 77). Where interim injunctions are sought in judicial review proceedings, the *American Cyanamid* principles (see **37.20** to **37.33**) will be applied (see *R v Ministry of Agriculture, Fisheries and Food, ex parte Monsanto plc* [1999] QB 1161). The *Monsanto plc* case also considered how those principles ought to be applied in a public law case. An interim injunction may be granted to restrain the enforcement of a UK statute where there are strong grounds for finding that the statute contravenes EU law (*R v Secretary of State for Transport, ex parte Factortame Ltd (No. 2)* (case C-213/89) [1991] 1 AC 603).

In considering an application to disapply national legislation by injunction pending a reference to the CJEU, the Court of Appeal in *R v Her Majesty's Treasury, ex parte British Telecommunications plc* [1994] 1 CMLR 621 said the following factors must be taken into account:

(a) The apparent strength of the Community right asserted. This is not to be considered in depth, as this is a matter for the CJEU. However, if the English court is almost persuaded that the applicant will succeed before the CJEU, albeit having enough doubt to refer the point to the CJEU, an injunction is far more likely to be granted than where the Community right is more speculative.
(b) The importance, in political terms, of the impugned legislation. An injunction is more likely to be granted where the legislation is obscure than where it is a major piece of legislation on which an election was fought.
(c) Other factors include whether the economic survival of the applicant depends on injunctive relief being granted, and the degree to which the applicant can be compensated in damages.

Town and Country Planning Act 1990 injunctions

For the factors to be taken into account in applications for injunctions under the Town and Country Planning Act 1990, s. 187B, including the personal circumstances of the persons in occupation, see *South Bucks District Council v Porter (No. 2)* [2004] UKHL 33, [2004] 1 WLR 1953, and *South Cambridgeshire District Council v Gammell* [2005] EWCA Civ 1429, [2006] 1 WLR 658. **37.50**

Negative covenants and covenants in restraint of trade

A perpetual injunction has been held to issue 'as of course' where it is established that the defendant is in breach of a valid express negative covenant (*Doherty v Allman* (1878) 3 App Cas 709). The same principle applies to applications for interim injunctions (*Attorney-General v Barker* [1990] 3 All ER 257), which means the balance of convenience test does not apply (*Araci v Fallon* [2011] EWHC 1621 (QB), LTL 3/6/2011). **37.51**

As a matter of competition law, a negative covenant which is in restraint of trade will not be enforced unless it is in a contract of employment or a contract for the sale of a business and its terms relating to activities restrained, duration and geographical limits are reasonably required to protect the covenantee's legitimate interests. In *Office Overload Ltd v Gunn* [1977] FSR 39, the defendant was the branch manager of the claimant's employment agency in Croydon. In his contract of employment he covenanted not to work for or set up a competing business in the Croydon area for one year after ceasing to work for the claimant. After giving notice the defendant immediately started competing. The claimant applied for an interim injunction. Given that to be valid a covenant has to be for a limited period of time, refusal of interim relief will usually deprive a claimant of the benefit of the covenant. Lord Denning MR accordingly said:

> Covenants in restraint of trade are in a special category...if they are prima facie valid and there is an infringement the courts will grant an injunction.

A covenant will be prima facie valid if:

(a) all the facts are before the court; and
(b) the covenant is reasonable in ambit, area and duration.

Restraint of trade cases to which the *American Cyanamid* guidelines apply The rule that an interim injunction will be issued to prevent breach of a valid covenant in restraint of trade (*Office Overload Ltd v Gunn* [1977] FSR 39) applies only where there is no sustainable dispute concerning the claimant's cause of action. If there is real doubt about the claimant's case, the *American Cyanamid* guidelines apply. Thus, in *Lawrence David Ltd v Ashton* [1991] 1 All ER 385, the claimant had dismissed the defendant from his employment, and there was a real issue as to whether that amounted to a repudiatory breach of the employment contract (and if so, it could not insist on the covenant being observed). Further, the terms of the covenant were perhaps too wide. Given those two matters, the case was not an open-and-shut one in favour of the claimant, and the *American Cyanamid* guidelines were applied. **37.52**

As the foundation of this exception is the effective deprivation of the employer of the benefit of the covenant due to the effluxion of time before trial, the exception does not apply if a trial can be arranged before the period of the covenant expires (for example, through ordering a speedy trial) (*Dairy Crest Ltd v Pigott* [1989] ICR 92). An example of what can be done with co-operation from all sides is *Symphony Group plc v Hodgson* [1994] QB 179, where the action was tried six weeks after the employee gave his notice.

Injunctions to restrain breaches of covenants in employment contracts are often combined with injunctions to restrain the misuse of confidential information obtained during the defendant's employment. Injunctions to restrain breach of confidence are decided in accordance with *American Cyanamid* guidelines, see *Lock International plc v Beswick* [1989] 1 WLR 1268, or the guidelines in *McKennitt v Ash* [2006] EWCA Civ 1714, [2008] QB 73, and **37.38**.

37.53 **Enforced inactivity ('garden leave')** If a covenant in a contract of employment against working for competitors is too wide and therefore void, the employer may still be able to obtain some injunctive relief if the employee resigns and starts working for a competitor under the principle in *Evening Standard Co. Ltd v Henderson* [1987] ICR 588. In this case the Court of Appeal found that a newspaper production manager, whose contract provided that he had to give a year's notice, was in clear breach of his contract of employment when he purported to give two months' notice after which he intended to work for a competitor. The claimant refused to accept the defendant's repudiation of his contract, and undertook to pay the defendant his full normal salary during his period of notice. Applying the *American Cyanamid* guidelines, an injunction was granted restraining the defendant from working for any competitor for his contractual period of notice, thereby giving the defendant a period of 'garden leave'. It is not always possible to obtain a 'garden leave' injunction even if the employee fails to give the contractual period of notice. The cases fall into two categories (see *Langston v Amalgamated Union of Engineering Workers (No. 2)* [1974] ICR 510). In the first, the employment contract extends to an obligation to permit the employee to do the contractual work. Theatrical engagements usually fall into this category. In these cases the employer needs a provision in the employment contract entitling the employer to send the employee home on garden leave. There will be little scope for implying such a term into the contract. Without such a term, no injunction will be granted. In the second category the employment contract is confined to the employer agreeing to pay wages for the work done. In this category the employer is entitled to send the employee home on garden leave even in the absence of an express or implied term, because there is no contractual obligation to prevent this. Garden leave injunctions are therefore far more likely to be granted in this category. See *William Hill Organisation Ltd v Tucker* [1999] ICR 291. Other decisions have shown that enforcing a period of idleness on the defendant is a factor to be taken into account in the balance of convenience against granting such an injunction (*Euro Brokers Ltd v Rabey* [1995] IRLR 206), and it may be appropriate to impose the injunction for a period shorter than the contractual period of notice where other 'defectors' are on shorter periods of notice than the defendant (*GFI Group Inc. v Eaglestone* [1994] IRLR 119).

Injunction equivalent to specific performance

37.54 The House of Lords in *Scandinavian Trading Tanker Co. AB v Flota Petrolera Ecuatoriana* [1983] 2 AC 694 held that specific performance will not be ordered of a non-demise time charter. Under this type of charterparty the owner provides the ship and the crew, and the charterer provides the cargo. It is therefore a contract for services, which the law never enforces by specific performance. In *Lauritzencool AB v Lady Navigation Inc.* [2005] EWCA Civ 579, [2005] 1 WLR 3686, it was held that nevertheless the court could grant an interim injunction prohibiting a shipowner from employing the vessel in a manner inconsistent with a charterparty. Such an order does not juristically amount to an order for specific performance, even if in practical reality it compels the owner to perform the charterparty.

Arbitration Act 1996 injunctions

37.55 The Arbitration Act 1996, s. 44, provides:

(1) Unless otherwise agreed by the parties, the court has for the purposes of and in relation to arbitral proceedings the same power of making orders about the matters listed below as it has for the purposes of and in relation to legal proceedings.

(2) Those matters are—
   (a) the taking of the evidence of witnesses;
   (b) the preservation of evidence;
   (c) making orders relating to property which is the subject of the proceedings or as to which any question arises in the proceedings...;

(d) the sale of any goods the subject of the proceedings;
(e) the granting of an interim injunction or the appointment of a receiver.

(3) If the case is one of urgency, the court may, on the application of a party or proposed party to the arbitral proceedings, make such orders as it thinks necessary for the purpose of preserving evidence or assets.

Econet Wireless Ltd v Vee Networks Ltd [2006] EWHC 1568 (Comm), [2006] 2 Lloyd's Rep 428, held that the purpose of the power to grant injunctions under s. 44 is to provide protection for the period before an arbitrator can be appointed. Nevertheless, there may be jurisdiction to grant an anti-suit injunction even if there are no pending or contemplated arbitral proceedings under the principle in *Turner v Grovit* [2001] UKHL 65, [2002] 1 WLR 107 (*AES Ust-Kamenogorsk Hydropower Plant LLP v Ust-Kamenogorsk Hydropower Plant JSC* [2010] EWHC 772 (Comm), [2010] 2 Lloyd's Rep 493; **CPR, r. 62.5(1)(c)**). The steps being taken to appoint an arbitrator must be set out in the evidence in support, and there must be an undertaking to appoint an arbitrator without delay. It was held to be inappropriate to seek an interim injunction in England under s. 44 when the arbitration is to take place in another jurisdiction. In *Cetelem SA v Roust Holdings Ltd* [2005] EWCA Civ 618, [2005] 1 WLR 3555, a dispute arose between parties to a share sale contract containing a London arbitration clause. A condition precedent under the contract was that approval had to be given by the Russian Central Bank. Five weeks before the expiry of the time for obtaining approval, no action had been taken by the defendant, so the claimant applied for an urgent mandatory interim injunction requiring the defendant to lodge the necessary papers in Russia. It was held that such an order could only be made if it was necessary for the preservation of evidence or assets, and there was no jurisdiction to make the order on any wider basis. Nevertheless the injunction satisfied the test. 'Assets' to be preserved under s. 44(3) could include choses in action. In this case the injunction was necessary to preserve the claimant's contractual right to purchase the shares, because the right to purchase them would be lost if no application was made for Russian Central Bank approval.

Commentary

An application to the court for a freezing injunction in support of arbitration proceedings under the Arbitration Act 1996, s. 44, has the advantages that the court's order will bind third parties and is buttressed by sanctions (*Pacific Maritime (Asia) Ltd v Holystone Overseas Ltd* [2007] EWHC 2319 (Comm), [2008] 1 Lloyd's Rep 371).

Apart from the Arbitration Act 1996, s. 44, the High Court also has an inherent jurisdiction to grant interim injunctions. This jurisdiction can be invoked even if there is an arbitration clause in the contract underlying the dispute which might be invoked at a later stage and lead to a stay of the court proceedings (*Glidepath Holding BV v Thompson* [2004] EWHC 2234 (Comm), [2005] 1 All ER (Comm) 434).

No defence

In *Official Custodian for Charities v Mackey* [1985] Ch 168 Scott J said that the *American Cyanamid* principles: 'are not, in my view, applicable to a case where there is no arguable defence to the [claimant's] claim'. The court will not consider the balance of convenience, but will grant the relief claimed subject to the usual equitable considerations. Injunctions have been granted on this basis in cases of clear trespass (*Patel v W.H. Smith (Eziot) Ltd* [1987] 1 WLR 853) and of clear breach of contract (*Sheppard and Cooper Ltd v TSB Bank plc* [1996] 2 All ER 654). Similarly, if all that is at issue on the merits is a simple point of construction, the court will resolve it and dismiss or grant the application accordingly (*Associated British Ports v Transport and General Workers Union* [1989] 1 WLR 939 at p. 979). **37.56**

Alternatively, where there is no defence with real prospects of success the claimant may apply for summary judgment including a final order for an injunction, instead of applying for an interim order (*Viscount Chelsea v Muscatt* [1990] 2 EGLR 48). Summary judgment was entered and an injunction granted in *WWF-World Wide Fund for Nature v World Wrestling Federation Entertainment Inc.* [2002] EWCA Civ 196, [2002] FSR 504, in a claim to enforce a settlement of an earlier trade mark dispute. A settlement is presumed to represent a reasonable division of the parties' trading interests for the purposes of the restraint-of-trade doctrine, and it is for the party seeking to go behind the settlement to show grounds for doing so, such as the settlement being contrived, or there being no reasonable basis for the rights claimed, or the settlement being otherwise contrary to the public interest.

Restraint of legal proceedings

37.57 *American Cyanamid* principles do not govern the exceptional jurisdiction of the courts to restrain the commencement of legal proceedings. This commonly arises in relation to preventing the presentation of petitions to wind up companies (see **82.28** to **82.32**). An injunction may also be sought to restrain foreign proceedings to prevent 'forum shopping', if it can be established that the foreign proceedings would be vexatious or oppressive (*Société Nationale Industrielle Aérospatiale v Lee Kui Jak* [1987] AC 871, see **16.74**). Anti-suit injunctions can also be sought to enforce 'no-action' clauses (prohibiting proceedings other than by a named person) (*Elektrim SA v Vivendi Holdings 1 Corporation* [2008] EWCA Civ 1178, [2009] 1 Lloyd's Rep 59) or to restrain unreasonable or oppressive adjudication proceedings under the Housing Grants, Construction and Regeneration Act 1996, s. 110 (*Mentmore Towers Ltd v Packman Lucas Ltd* [2010] EWHC 457 (TCC), [2010] BLR 393).

According to *Glencore International AG v Exter Shipping Ltd* [2002] EWCA Civ 528, [2002] 2 All ER (Comm) 1 at [42]–[43], the principles applicable when deciding whether an injunction to restrain foreign proceedings should be granted are:

(a) whether the defendant is amenable to the English territorial and personal jurisdiction; and
(b) whether it is just and convenient to grant the injunction under the Senior Courts Act 1981, s. 37(1).

In exercising the discretion factors the court will consider include:

(a) whether the threatened conduct is unconscionable, which primarily refers to conduct which is oppressive, vexatious or unconscionable, or which interferes with the due process of the court;
(b) whether injunctive relief is necessary to protect the applicant's legitimate interest in proceedings in England; and
(c) whether England is the natural forum for the litigation.

The same principles were applied on an application to restrain arbitration proceedings in *Albon v Naza Motor Trading Sdn Bhd (No. 4)* [2007] EWCA Civ 1124, [2008] 1 All ER (Comm) 351. In applying these principles in an arbitration case, Jackson J in *J. Jarvis and Sons Ltd v Blue Circle Dartford Estates Ltd* [2007] EWHC 1262 (TCC), [2007] BLR 439, said at [40]:

(a) the discretion to grant such an injunction is exercised very sparingly and with due regard to the principles on which the Arbitration Act 1996 is expressly based (for which see **72.1**); and
(b) delay by the applicant is material to the court's exercise of its discretion, and in some cases will be fatal to the application.

Worldwide injunctions

37.58 In exceptional cases the courts may make injunctive orders having a worldwide effect. Such orders have been made in a small number of freezing injunction cases (see **38.9**), and also in an application to enforce a covenant of confidentiality against a former employee of the Royal household (*Attorney-General v Barker* [1990] 3 All ER 257).

Medical treatment

37.59 In *Re J (A Minor) (Child in Care: Medical Treatment)* [1993] Fam 15 an application was made for an interim injunction to compel doctors to give a child in an intensive care unit a specific form of medical treatment. It was held that there was absolutely no room in such a case for the application of the *American Cyanamid* principles. The proper approach was to consider the options available to the court, and in the proper exercise of its inherent powers to make such orders as would best serve the interests of the child pending a final decision. In future these applications will be dealt with under the Mental Capacity Act 2005.

Anti-social behaviour

It is not just and convenient to grant interim injunctions under the Senior Courts Act 1981, s. 37, in circumstances where an anti-social behaviour order (see **chapter 88**) might be available. Such applications have to be brought under the relevant anti-social behaviour legislation, to ensure the prescribed checks and balances are applied (*Birmingham City Council v Shafi* [2008] EWCA Civ 1186, [2009] PTSR 503). **37.60**

INTERIM MANDATORY INJUNCTIONS

In *National Commercial Bank Jamaica Ltd v Olint Corporation Ltd* [2009] UKPC 16, [2009] 1 WLR 1405 at [19], Lord Hoffmann said there is no underlying difference in principle between interim applications for prohibitory and mandatory injunctions. His Lordship's view is that it is often more likely that there will be irremediable prejudice to the defendant if the injunction is mandatory in nature. If the injunction is likely to cause irremediable damage to the defendant, the court should be reluctant to grant the injunction unless it is satisfied that the chances that it will turn out to have been wrongly granted are low. It is for this reason that Megarry J in the leading case of *Shepherd Homes Ltd v Sandham* [1971] Ch 340 said, at p. 351, that such injunctions should be granted only if the court felt a 'high degree of assurance' that at trial it will turn out that the injunction was rightly granted. **37.61**

In *Leisure Data v Bell* [1988] FSR 367, a dispute arose about the copyright in a computer program developed by the defendant for the claimant. The claimant was granted a mandatory injunction despite the merits being equally arguable either way. Partly this was because the claimant was prepared to give wide-ranging undertakings to protect the defendant's position, and partly because the practical reality of the situation was that of the two parties only the claimant was in a position to make commercial use of the program.

The importance of taking the course carrying the least risk of injustice was emphasised in *Nikitenko v Leboeuf Lamb Greene and Macrae* (1999) *The Times*, 26 January 1999. Pumfrey J in *Incasep Ltd v Jones* (2001) LTL 26/10/2001 said that an application for an interim mandatory injunction requiring a company to reinstate the claimant as an executive director pending the outcome of his unfair prejudice petition (see the Companies Act 2006, s. 994) was governed by the *American Cyanamid* guidelines, albeit having regard to particular factors concerning the potential injustice that such injunctions could cause. On the facts the injunction was refused.

DEFENCES

Any of the following equitable defences and bars to relief may be raised on an application for an interim injunction: **37.62**

(a) Acquiescence. This arises where the claimant's conduct (usually inactivity) induces the defendant to believe something to his detriment (*Davies v Marshall* (1861) 10 CB NS 697; *Jones v Stones* [1999] 1 WLR 1739; see **10.40**).
(b) Delay or laches. Simply allowing time to elapse may persuade a court to refuse injunctive relief even if the conduct does not amount to acquiescence. Delay is a more significant

factor in interim applications than at trial (*Johnson v Wyatt* (1863) De G J & S 18). The length of delay meriting refusal of relief depends on the nature of the case and whether the defendant has been prejudiced, but usually will need to be measured in months. See, for example, *Century Electronics Ltd v CVS Enterprises Ltd* [1983] FSR 1 and *Newport Association Football Club Ltd v Football Association of Wales Ltd* [1995] 2 All ER 87, where the facts were sufficiently exceptional to excuse a two-year delay. Furthermore, what may appear to be an unreasonable delay may be justified by the claimant (*Carroll v Tomado Ltd* [1971] FSR 218). On the other hand, a delay of 20 days was held to bar relief in *Bunn v British Broadcasting Corporation* [1998] 3 All ER 552, where an application to restrain the broadcast of confidential information was made just two working days before the intended date of the broadcast. Delay of over a year was fatal to an application for an interim injunction to restrain trademark infringement and passing off in *Blinkx UK Ltd v Blinkbox Entertainment Ltd* [2010] EWHC 1624 (Ch), LTL 27/10/2010. Delay interrelates with the status quo (for which, see **37.30**).

(c) Hardship. This is taken into account in the balance of convenience.
(d) Clean hands. Inequitable conduct by the claimant may be a bar to equitable relief (*Hubbard v Vosper* [1972] 2 QB 84).
(e) Equity does not act in vain. In *Attorney-General v Guardian Newspapers Ltd (No. 2)* [1990] 1 AC 109 an injunction to restrain breach of confidence was refused where there had already been widespread publication.
(f) 'The court will not and ought not to make an order performance or obedience to which it cannot enforce' (per Astbury J in *Amber Size and Chemical Co. Ltd v Menzel* [1913] 2 Ch 239). Injunctions are therefore rarely granted against children, because they cannot be committed to prison and can rarely pay a fine (*G v Harrow London Borough Council* [2004] EWHC 17 (QB), LTL 23/1/2004).
(g) An injunction will be refused if its effect is to enforce an agreement for personal services (e.g. *Warren v Mendy* [1989] 1 WLR 853).
(h) Difficulty in compliance. An injunction was refused in *Unique Pub Properties Ltd v Licensed Wholesale Co. Ltd* (2003) LTL 13/10/2003 as it would have imposed on the defendant a serious obligation to check information given to it by its tenants, any error constituting a breach.

THE ORDER

37.63 There are currently four standard forms for interim injunction orders:

(a) PF 39 CH, order for an injunction (intended action) (introduced in March 2005);
(b) PF 40 CH, order for interim injunction (for use where substantive proceedings have been issued) (introduced in March 2005);
(c) Freezing injunction order (**PD 25A, Annex**, revised 1 October 2005);
(d) Search order (**PD 25A, Annex**, revised 1 October 2005).

All these forms are for use in the county courts and High Court, and both the Queen's Bench Division and the Chancery Division.

An injunction order may only be enforced by committal proceedings under **CPR, r. 81.4**, if a penal notice is prominently displayed on the front of the copy of the order served on the defendant (**r. 81.9(1)**). A penal notice should be in form N77, and is a warning that disobedience of the order is a contempt of court punishable by imprisonment, a fine or sequestration of assets. For undertakings in lieu of injunctions, see **61.10**.

Undertakings

37.64 Undertakings may be required from either party to ensure there is no injustice as a result of the decision on an application for an interim injunction. Subject to the exceptions referred to at

37.24, the applicant will always be required to give an undertaking in damages. An impecunious claimant may be required to fortify the undertaking in damages by providing security or paying money into court (**37.25**). The general principle is that the amount of security should be based on the highest arguable figure for the likely damage to the defendant that is supported by the evidence (*Business Online Group plc v MCI Worldcom Ltd* [2001] EWCA Civ 1399, LTL 9/8/2001).

Until the standard form injunctions were changed in March 2005, there was no need in most interim injunctions, other than freezing injunctions, to include an undertaking to pay the reasonable costs of any third party incurred as a result of the order (*Miller Brewing Co. v Ruhi Enterprises Ltd* [2003] EWHC 1606 (Ch), [2004] FSR 5). In *SmithKline Beecham plc v Apotex Europe Ltd* [2006] EWCA Civ 658, [2007] Ch 71, the claimant obtained an interim injunction in the pre-2005 form against alleged infringement of patented pharmaceuticals by the original defendants. These defendants were supplied by related companies based in Canada (the additional defendants). The additional defendants were made parties two days before the injunction was discharged, and then sought to recover on the claimant's undertaking in damages. As this was a pre-2005 injunction there was no express undertaking to compensate third parties. At first instance it was held that the additional defendants only took the benefit of the undertaking from the day they were joined, not retrospectively, which was regarded as *de minimis*. It was also held that the injunction could not be corrected under the slip rule (**CPR, r. 40.12**) to include an undertaking to compensate third parties. The slip rule can only be used to correct mistakes on matters which the court or party had in mind. Here no one had thought of including an undertaking to compensate third parties until after the new standard forms were introduced. On appeal it was also held that the third-party companies were not entitled to any remedy against the claimant in restitution or through any estoppel.

Forms PF 39 CH and PF 40 CH contain undertakings to compensate both parties and third parties who suffer loss caused by the order. The additional protection for third parties is not always needed. Under **PD 25A, para. 5.1A**, when the court makes an order for an injunction, it should consider whether to require an undertaking by the applicant to pay any damages sustained by a person other than the respondent, including another party to the proceedings or any other person who may suffer loss as a consequence of the order.

Other undertakings include without-notice undertakings to serve and file evidence etc. (see **37.7**), and other undertakings designed to reduce the possible prejudice to the other side. For example, in *Travel Intelligence v Townsend* [2009] EWHC 726 (QB), LTL 30/4/2009, the defendant was permitted to continue running a business on undertaking to provide the other party with monthly financial statements. In *Watson v Durham University* [2008] EWCA Civ 1266, LTL 24/10/2008, an employee undertook not to attend the employer's premises until the dispute was determined.

Undertakings given by a party may be released or modified if there are special or exceptional circumstances (*Warren v Random House Group Ltd* [2008] EWCA Civ 834, [2009] QB 600). These include:

(a) the context of the agreement in which the undertaking was given;
(b) whether the undertaking was given to the court independently of the agreement of the other party or as part of a collateral agreement; and
(c) whether there are circumstances so different from those contemplated or intended to be governed by the undertaking when it was given that the party should be released.

Operative provisions

The operative part of the order for an interim injunction should not be in terms wider than is necessary to do justice between the parties. In *Moat Housing Group-South Ltd v Harris* [2005] EWCA Civ 287, [2006] QB 606, Brooke LJ said that the relief granted must be limited to that which is necessary and proportionate as a means of avoiding the apprehended harm. In *E. E. and Brian Smith (1928) Ltd v Hodson* [2007] EWCA Civ 1210, LTL 23/11/2007, the order as drawn was too wide in that it prevented the company from fulfilling contracts already entered into, and there was no sufficient definition of **37.65**

Commentary

the information caught by the restrictions, nor any exclusion of information in the public domain. *Hall v Save Newchurch Guinea Pigs (Campaign)* [2005] EWHC 372 (QB), *The Times*, 7 April 2005, was an application under the Protection from Harassment Act 1997, s. 3, for an injunction and an exclusion zone of seven parishes, covering 200 square kilometres. Although there had been extreme conduct in the past, only a prohibitory injunction was granted. The judge said that an exclusion zone might be added later if the initial injunction was not effective.

The injunction should be worded so that the defendant can know with certainty what is and what is not permitted (**PD 25A, para. 5.3**). An injunction to restrain publication must be to the highest degree clear and precise so that no publisher can be in any doubt whether he is infringing or not (*Times Newspapers Ltd v MGN Ltd* [1993] EMLR 443). A provision in an injunction will be too uncertain if there would be issues of fact over whether particular conduct would be a breach (*Staver Co. Inc. v Digitext Display Ltd* [1985] FSR 512). Thus, an order which restrained, among other things, the defendant 'from otherwise infringing' a patent lacked sufficient specificity (*Hepworth Plastics Ltd v Naylor Bros (Clayware) Ltd* [1979] FSR 521). The fact that there is an overlap between different words used in an order does not necessarily establish there is any ambiguity or lack of clarity. There is nothing objectionable about injunctions that restrain 'publishing, communicating or disclosing' or restraining publication of 'any intimate, personal or sexually explicit' details (*Donald v Ntuli* [2010] EWCA Civ 1276, [2011] 1 WLR 294). It is usually best to avoid using legal terms of art, especially the names of torts, which often include matters of degree with the result that the defendant will often not know whether specific conduct will breach the order. A proposed order restraining disclosure of 'confidential information' is oppressive, excessively general and wide. Instead, it needs to be limited to defined confidential information (*Raks Holdings AS v TTPCom Ltd* [2004] EWHC 2137 (Ch), LTL 29/7/2004). An injunction may adopt the precise wording of a contractual provision, because in such a case the order simply requires the defendant to comply with its contractual obligation (*Parallel Media Group plc v Lagardère SCA* [2010] EWHC 27 (QB), LTL 17/2/2010). In *Mid Suffolk District Council v Clarke* [2006] EWCA Civ 71, [2006] Env LR 38, an undertaking was given by a defendant to restrain a nuisance in defined ways whether by himself, his employees or agents 'or otherwise howsoever'. These three words were not too imprecise or uncertain, but were aimed at ensuring the defendant would not carry out the prohibited acts in any way, directly or indirectly. In *Huntingdon Life Sciences Group plc v Stop Huntingdon Animal Cruelty* [2007] EWHC 522 (QB), LTL 19/4/2007, a final injunction was granted restraining animal rights protestors from harassing the claimant's employees. This was done by establishing exclusion zones, imposing a maximum number of protestors, permitting use of megaphones for a maximum of one hour at medium to low amplification for verbal sound, and a protest procession to be allowed every three months. For this purpose 'protestor' was defined as meaning the defendants, whether by themselves, their employees or agents, any other person, whether by himself, his employees or agents, who was acting in concert with the defendant. The order was not to be enforceable against any individual without the express permission of the court.

The judge will have regard to the draft prepared by the claimant, and may initial the draft without amendment. Ultimately, however, the choice of wording is a matter within the discretion of the judge (*Khorasandjian v Bush* [1993] QB 727). It will not usually be appropriate to qualify the terms of an injunction to protect the defendant from the consequences of any misbehaviour by its employees (*British Telecommunications plc v Nextcall Telecom plc* [2000] FSR 679). Where the order is made in the presence of all relevant parties (or at least at a hearing of which they had notice even if they did not attend), it may be expressed to last 'until trial or further order' (**PD 25A, para. 5.2**).

Injunctions affecting third parties

37.66 For undertakings to compensate third parties see 37.64. Where an injunction will affect a third party who was not present at the hearing, that person may request copies of any materials read by the judge, any documents prepared after the hearing in compliance with directions of the judge, and the note of the hearing (**PD 25A, para. 9.2**). The applicant is required to comply with such a request promptly, unless the court orders otherwise. It may be appropriate to include a restriction in an order that documents requested under **para. 9.2** will be provided only on the third party giving a written undertaking to use the documents only for the purposes of the proceedings (*TUV v Person or Persons Unknown* [2010] EWHC 853 (QB), [2010] EMLR 19).

Suspending the operation of an injunction

The court has the power to suspend the operation of an injunction. This is generally exercised where it is necessary to ensure injunctions operate in a just and convenient (or just and proportionate, see **37.14**) manner. See *Waverley Borough Council v Lee* [2003] EWHC 29 (Ch), LTL 14/1/2003. An injunction was postponed until the end of a school term when otherwise it would have interfered with the defendant's children's schooling in *Tewkesbury Borough Council v Brown* [2006] EWHC 2697 (QB), LTL 7/11/2006. **37.67**

INQUIRY AS TO DAMAGES

Where it transpires that an interim injunction should not have been granted (for example, if the claimant loses at trial) the defendant may seek to enforce the undertaking in damages by applying for an order for an inquiry as to damages. If a claimant discontinues (for which, see **chapter 55**), the court should consider the circumstances and the reasons why this has been done before ordering an inquiry as to damages (*Goldman Sachs International Ltd v Lyons* (1995) *The Times*, 28 February 1995). **37.68**

Excessive, inexcusable delay may result in an application for an inquiry as to damages being dismissed (*Barratt Manchester Ltd v Bolton Metropolitan Borough Council* [1998] 1 WLR 1003). An order for an inquiry is not penal and does not depend on fault on the part of the claimant.

Where an interim injunction is discharged before trial, the court has a number of options on an application for an inquiry as to damages. These were identified in *Cheltenham and Gloucester Building Society v Ricketts* [1993] 1 WLR 1545, as being:

(a) To accede to the application and immediately proceed to determine the question of damages. This should be done only in the most straightforward cases. In *Fourie v Le Roux* [2007] UKHL 1, [2007] 1 WLR 320, it was held to have been wrong in principle to order an immediate inquiry into damages on the discharge of a freezing injunction before trial. A second, replacement, injunction had been granted, and there was evidence that the frozen money was either itself, or the proceeds from, assets which had been fraudulently obtained by the defendant. The question of whether to order an inquiry was postponed to trial.
(b) To allow the application, and to order the inquiry by a master or district judge. The judge making the order will give directions for the inquiry.
(c) To stand the application over (that is, adjourn it) to a specified time. This is perhaps the usual order where an injunction is discharged during the interim stages of a claim. It is the most appropriate option where matters material to the question whether it is just to order an inquiry are still in issue and will only be determined at trial. The application is most frequently stood over to trial, when all the facts should be known.
(d) To order an inquiry and to direct that the question of liability on the undertaking be determined at the inquiry. This is unusual.
(e) To refuse the application. This is only done in straightforward cases where, for example, it is clear the defendant has suffered no loss as a result of the injunction.
(f) To make an order setting off the sum found on making an inquiry against an earlier judgment. Such an order was made in *Keller v Cowen* [2001] EWCA Civ 1704, LTL 6/11/2001, where the earlier judgment was obtained in a foreign court, and despite there being no mutuality of debts.

Example 37.1 High Court interim injunction (form PF 40 CH)

IN THE HIGH COURT OF JUSTICE Claim No. HQ13X 73635

QUEEN'S BENCH DIVISION

BEFORE the Honourable Mr Justice Collier (judge in private) Monday the 20th day of January 2014

BETWEEN

CASPKEELER PRODUCTS LIMITED <u>Claimants</u>

— and —

LOAMER TECHTRONICS LIMITED <u>Defendants</u>

ORDER FOR AN INJUNCTION

Important

NOTICE TO THE DEFENDANTS

(1) This Order prohibits you from doing the acts set out in this Order. You should read it carefully. You are advised to consult a Solicitor as soon as possible. You have a right to ask the Court to vary or discharge this Order.

(2) If you disobey this Order you may be guilty of Contempt of Court [and any of your directors may be sent to prison or fined] and you may be fined or your assets may be seized.

Include the words in square brackets in the case of a corporate defendant. This notice is not a substitute for the endorsement of a penal notice

An Application was made on 20 January 2014 by Counsel for the Claimants to the Judge and was attended by Counsel for the Defendants. The Judge heard the Application and read the witness statements listed in Schedule 1 and accepted the undertakings in Schedule 2 of this Order.

IT IS ORDERED that

THE INJUNCTION

(1) Until after final judgment in this claim the Defendants must not:

(a) license the right to distribute the Loamer Techtron Capacitor anywhere in the world in the term of six years from 16 September 2010 granted to the Claimants Caspkeeler Products Limited under an agreement between the Claimants and the Defendants dated 16 September 2010;

(b) sell Loamer Techtron Capacitors otherwise than through the Claimants Caspkeeler Products Limited;

(c) assert or represent to customers that the Claimants Caspkeeler Products Limited are not the sole distributors of the Loamer Techtron Capacitor.

Costs of the Application

(2) [The Defendant shall pay the Claimant's costs of this Application.] [The costs of this Application are reserved to be dealt with by the Judge who tries this Claim.] [The costs of this Application are to be costs in the case.] [The costs of this Application are to be the Claimant's costs in the case.]

Variation or Discharge of This Order

The Defendants may apply to the Court at any time to vary or discharge this Order, but if they wish to do so they must first inform the Claimants' Solicitors in writing at least 48 hours beforehand.

Name and Address of Claimants' Solicitors

The Claimant's Solicitors are:
Collins, Brown and Heath, of 7 Ingrave Road, Birmingham B5 8EP
Ref: JGB/4663, Telephone: 01212158349.

Interpretation of This Order

(1) In this Order the words 'he' 'him' or 'his' include 'she' 'her' or 'hers' and 'it' or 'its'.
(2) Where there are two or more Defendants then (unless the contrary appears):
  (a) references to 'the Defendant' mean both or all of them;
  (b) an Order requiring 'the Defendant' to do or not to do anything requires each Defendant to do or not to do it.

The Effect of This Order

(1) A Defendant who is an individual who is ordered not to do something must not do it himself or in any other way. He must not do it through others acting on his behalf or on his instructions or with his encouragement.
(2) A Defendant which is a corporation and which is ordered not to do something must not do it itself or by its directors, officers, employees or agents or in any other way.

Service of This Order

This Order shall be served by the Claimants on the Defendants.

SCHEDULE 1

Witness Statements

The Judge read the following witness statements before making this Order:

(1) Rachel Helen Radcliffe, made on 14 January 2014.
(2) Daniel Jordan Loamer, made on 15 January 2014.

SCHEDULE 2

Undertaking given to the Court by the Claimants

If the Court later finds that this Order has caused loss to the Defendants or any other Party served with or notified of this Order and decides that the Defendant or other Party should be compensated for that loss, the Claimants will comply with any Order the Court may make.

All communications to the Court about this Order should be sent to Room 307, Royal Courts of Justice, Strand, London WC2A 2LL quoting the case number. The office is open between 10 a.m. and 4.30 p.m. Monday to Friday. The telephone number is (020) 7936 6148.

Quantification of damages

An application for an inquiry as to damages made by a successful defendant at the end of the trial will normally only be refused if it is unlikely that the defendant has suffered any provable loss (*McDonald's Hamburgers Ltd v Burgerking (UK) Ltd* [1987] FSR 112). Ordinary contractual principles are applied on causation and quantum, though it is possible for aggravated or exemplary damages to be awarded in cases where the claimant has acted oppressively. Where defendants had sought enormous damages and failed, the court was justified in refusing any order rather than seeking out a smaller loss (*Tyco European Metal Framing Ltd v New Systems Ltd* (2001) LTL 7/12/2001). As a term for granting permission to discontinue, the court in *FSL Services Ltd v MacDonald* [2001] EWCA Civ 1008, LTL 21/6/2001, had made a direction that there be an inquiry as to damages in respect of a freezing injunction that had previously been granted. The losses claimed by the defendant were the costs incurred by the defendant and ordered to be paid to the claimant by the defendant in contesting the injunction at the earlier stage. The claimant applied for an order striking out the inquiry. It was held that although there is jurisdiction to strike out an inquiry, on the facts it was inappropriate to do so, as the objections to the recovery of the costs were matters that could best be raised on the inquiry itself. Inquiries are normally conducted by masters and district judges. 37.69

UNDERTAKINGS GIVEN BY THE DEFENDANT

37.70 Instead of contesting an application for an interim injunction, a defendant may give undertakings in similar terms to the injunction sought by the claimant. Such undertakings have the same force as an injunction ordered by the court, with the result that the defendant will be in contempt of court if the undertakings are broken. Where undertakings are given by a defendant and incorporated into a consent order, the undertakings may be construed as having contractual effect between the parties. In such a case breach of the undertakings may be enforced as breaches of contract, resulting in a claim for damages (*Independiente Ltd v Music Trading On-Line (HK) Ltd* [2007] EWCA Civ 111, [2008] 1 WLR 608). The claimant will be required to give a cross-undertaking in damages to safeguard the defendant.

A defendant can be released from an undertaking only in special circumstances and where this will not occasion an injustice (*Eronat v Tabbah* [2002] EWCA Civ 950, LTL 10/7/2002). In the absence of special circumstances, a claim commenced in breach of an undertaking will be struck out as an abuse of process, unless striking out would not further the overriding objective (*Di Placito v Slater* [2003] EWCA Civ 1863, [2004] 1 WLR 1605).

DISCHARGE

37.71 Applications to vary or discharge injunctions are made by application notice to a judge, often the same judge who granted the initial injunction. The normal practice where there are cross-applications to continue an interim injunction and to discharge the original interim injunction is for both applications to be heard at the same time. However, the court could hear the applications separately (*Network Multimedia Television Ltd v Jobserve Ltd* (2000) *The Times*, 25 January 2001) applying the following factors: the likely delay if they are heard together; prejudice to the defendant if the injunction were to be discharged after being renewed; prejudice to the claimant if the injunction is discharged and later reimposed; the grounds relied upon for discharging the injunction; the interrelationship of the two applications; the circumstances in which the injunction was obtained; and any special facts. Grounds for varying or discharging injunctions include:

(a) Material non-disclosure if the injunction was granted without notice. The importance of the issue, the nature of the undisclosed evidence and the extent of the non-disclosures have to be considered in deciding whether non-disclosures are material (*Millhouse Capital UK Ltd v Sibir Energy plc* [2008] EWHC 2614 (Ch), [2009] Bus LR D33). In *Network Multimedia Television Ltd v Jobserve Ltd (No. 2)* (2001) LTL 9/4/2001 it was found there were non-deliberate material non-disclosures. The injunction obtained without notice was therefore discharged. On a full consideration of the *American Cyanamid* factors (see **37.20** to **37.33**) the judge decided that it was an appropriate case for reimposing an injunction, albeit recognising that this discretion should be used sparingly after a previous injunction had been discharged.
(b) The particulars of claim being inconsistent with the written evidence on an application without notice.
(c) The facts not justifying relief without giving notice.
(d) The claimant's failure to comply with the undertakings incorporated into the order.
(e) The order having an oppressive effect.
(f) Unreasonable interference with the rights of innocent third parties. Affected third parties are entitled to apply for a variation of the order. All the circumstances have to be considered, and it is sometimes within the court's powers to grant an injunction to restrain a defendant from fulfilling a contract already entered into with an innocent third party. An example is where this is necessary in order to protect the claimant's trade secrets (*PSM International plc v Whitehouse* [1992] IRLR 279).

(g) Material change in the circumstances.
(h) A failure to prosecute the substantive claim with due speed.
(i) If the claim is stayed other than by agreement between the parties, any interim injunction, other than a freezing injunction, will be set aside unless the court orders that it should continue in force (**CPR, r. 25.10**).
(j) If the claim is struck out for non-payment of the fees payable at allocation or listing, the interim injunction will lapse 14 days after the claim is struck out. However, if within that 14-day period the claimant applies to reinstate the claim, the injunction will remain in force until the hearing of that application (unless the court otherwise orders) (**r. 25.11**).

Non-disclosure at on-notice hearing

Traditionally, material non-disclosure has only been a ground for discharging an injunction granted without notice (see 37.71). In *DEG-Deutsche Investitions- und Entwicklungsgesellschaft mbH v Koshy (No. 2)* [2005] EWHC 2896 (Ch), [2005] 1 WLR 2434, a freezing injunction (granted before the introduction of the CPR) was continued after an on-notice hearing. The defendant argued that the facts found by the trial judge showed there had been material non-disclosure by the claimant. It was held that, apart from provision made by rules of court, there is no jurisdiction to discharge a freezing injunction based on alleged non-disclosure at an on-notice hearing. **CPR, r. 3.1(7)**, provides, 'A power of the court under these Rules to make an order includes a power to vary or revoke the order'. As the case was decided under the old rules, Hart J did not express an opinion on whether the wording of **r. 3.1(7)** has changed the position. It is doubtful whether it has. The rule is expressed as conferring a jurisdiction to vary or revoke, but does not deal in terms with the grounds for doing so. A provision more likely to assist the argument is **PD 25A, para. 3.3**, which says that the evidence in support of applications for interim injunctions must include 'all material facts of which the court should be made aware'. The counter-argument is that what the court should be made aware of depends on the nature of the application. 37.72

Commentary

BREACH

Breach of an injunction is a contempt of court punishable by imprisonment or sequestration. Contempt must be proved beyond reasonable doubt. Punishment for contempt of court is considered in more detail in **chapter 81**. 37.73

Clearly, the person against whom the order was made will be in contempt if he or she acts in breach of an injunction after having notice of it (*Z Ltd v A-Z and AA-LL* [1982] QB 558 per Eveleigh LJ). A non-party who aids and abets the defendant in breaching the terms of an injunction, or who acts with the intention of impeding the administration of justice, will also be in contempt of court (*Attorney-General v Times Newspapers Ltd* [1992] 1 AC 191). The Attorney-General had obtained interim injunctions against a number of national newspapers restraining them from publishing materials from a book (*Spycatcher*) pending trial. The substantive action was based on alleged breach of confidence. The present defendants were not named in the injunction. They obtained serialisation rights in the book, and published their first instalment. The purpose of the injunctions was to prevent publication pending trial. Publication nullified the purpose of the trial by putting into the public domain what was alleged to be confidential material, and thereby impeded or interfered with the administration of justice. As the defendants had acted knowingly, they were in contempt of court. To establish a contempt by a non-party it must be demonstrated both that the non-party's acts defeated, in whole or in part, the court's purpose in granting the injunction, and that the non-party appreciated that what he was doing was what the injunction was intended to prevent. There is no need to prove an intention to thwart the court's purpose (*Attorney-General v Punch Ltd* [2002] UKHL 50, [2003] 1 AC 1046).

Attorney-General v Times Newspapers Ltd and the Court of Appeal's decision in *Attorney-General v Punch Ltd* [2001] QB 1028 were interpreted in *Jockey Club v Buffham* [2002] EWHC 1866 (QB), [2003] QB 462, as only protecting from interference with pending proceedings. On that basis it was held that the *Spycatcher* principle does not extend to final injunctions. *Jockey Club v Buffham* might have been decided differently if the committal had been brought on the basis that the third party had aided and abetted a breach of the injunction rather than on the basis of interfering with the administration of justice (see *Attorney-General v Punch Ltd* [2002] UKHL 50, [2003] 1 AC 1046).

EFFECT OF NOT APPLYING FOR INTERIM RELIEF

37.74 Failing to apply for interim relief is a factor in considering at trial whether the claimant is guilty of acquiescence (*Shaw v Appelgate* [1977] 1 WLR 970). It may also provide grounds for awarding damages in lieu of an injunction (*Jaggard v Sawyer* [1995] 1 WLR 269). Delay in issuing proceedings after the claimant is aware of the defendant's breach, and deciding not to apply for an interim injunction to avoid giving an undertaking in damages, were considered by the Court of Appeal in *Mortimer v Bailey* [2004] EWCA Civ 1514, [2005] 2 P & CR 9. These are both matters to be taken into account in considering whether to grant a final injunction, but do not bar granting such an injunction where the claimant has made clear his objection to the defendant's conduct. *Blue Town Investments Ltd v Higgs and Hill plc* [1990] 1 WLR 696, which said that continuing proceedings was an abuse of process after failing to apply for an interim injunction to avoid having to give an undertaking in damages, should be regarded as wrongly decided. (Another first-instance decision, *Oxy-Electric Ltd v Zainuddin* [1991] 1 WLR 115, reached the opposite conclusion.)

Chapter 38 Freezing Injunctions

Commentary

NATURE OF A FREEZING INJUNCTION

A freezing injunction is an interim order restraining a party from removing assets located within the jurisdiction out of the country, or from dealing with assets whether they are located within the jurisdiction or not (CPR, r. 25.1(1)(f)). Usually the order will be restricted to assets not exceeding the value of the claim. Until the CPR came into force on 26 April 1999 this form of order was known as a *Mareva* injunction, taking its name from *Mareva Compania Naviera SA v International Bulkcarriers SA* [1980] 1 All ER 213. **38.1**

The purpose of a freezing injunction is to prevent the injustice of a defendant's assets being salted away so as to deprive the claimant of the fruits of any judgment that may be obtained. However, as Ackner LJ said in *A. J. Bekhor and Co. Ltd v Bilton* [1981] QB 923, the jurisdiction to grant freezing injunctions has not rewritten the law of insolvency, and the imposition of such an order does not give the claimant any priority or security if the defendant becomes insolvent. It is a relief *in personam* which simply prohibits certain acts in relation to the assets frozen.

In *Mareva Compania Naviera SA v International Bulkcarriers SA* [1980] 1 All ER 213 the Court of Appeal refused to consider itself bound by *Lister v Stubbs* (1890) 45 ChD 1, which had held that a defendant could not be compelled to give security before judgment, and decided that what is now the Senior Courts Act 1981, s. 37(1), is wide enough to permit the court to grant an interim injunction restraining the dissipation of assets. Parliament has subsequently acknowledged the jurisdiction in the Senior Courts Act 1981, s. 37(3), the County Court Remedies Regulations 1991 (SI 1991/1222) and **CPR, r. 25.1(1)(f)**.

It has always been recognised that freezing orders are draconian measures, and they will be granted only if a number of onerous conditions are fulfilled (see **38.4** to **38.29**). The most significant of these conditions is that there must be a real risk that the defendant will dissipate assets to frustrate any judgment the claimant may obtain.

Although freezing injunctions are most commonly sought by claimants, they may be sought by any party, such as a counterclaiming defendant or a defendant against a third party.

PROCEDURE

38.2 For a summary of the procedure, see **procedural checklist 19** at the front of the book.

County courts do not generally have jurisdiction to grant freezing injunctions, so applications must usually be made in the High Court (County Court Remedies Regulations 1991, regs 2 and 3). Freezing injunctions may be granted by a county court where a High Court or Court of Appeal judge sits, in Business List and Patents County Court cases, certain family proceedings, and in aid of execution (reg. 3(2) and (3)(a), (c) and (d)). Another exception where a freezing injunction can be ordered by a county court is where the proposed order seeks to preserve or detain property which is or may form the subject-matter of the proceedings or proposed proceedings (reg. 3(3)(b)). Where a freezing injunction is sought in a county court claim (and none of the exceptions in the County Court Remedies Regulations 1991 applies), the application for the freezing injunction must be made in the High Court (**High Court and County Courts Jurisdiction Order 1991 (SI 1991/724), art. 3**). The application must be made returnable to a judge, and the application notice must (see *Schmidt v Wong* [2005] EWCA Civ 1506, [2006] 1 WLR 561) carry the following endorsement:

> This application is being made in the course of [in anticipation of] proceedings in the [] county court pursuant to article 3 of the High Court and County Courts Jurisdiction Order 1991. The county court has no jurisdiction to grant the relief sought by reason of regulation 3(1) of the County Court Remedies Regulations 1991.

Given that a freezing injunction can only be ordered against an unscrupulous defendant who is prepared to dissipate assets to prevent the claimant recovering on any judgment obtained, the application is, in practice, made without informing the defendant to ensure the injunction is effective. They are often sought on an urgent basis (see **37.4**) before proceedings are issued, in which event directions should be given for instituting proceedings for substantive relief (*Fourie v Le Roux* [2007] UKHL 1, [2007] 1 WLR 320 at [36]). Where the claimant had been pursuing the defendant for some time, and there had been other applications for relief in other jurisdictions, it was not wrong to refuse to deal with an application for a freezing order without notice (*Kensington International Ltd v Republic of Congo* [2003] EWCA Civ 709, LTL 13/5/2003). The application is made to a judge sitting in private and is made before service of the claim form so as not to alert the defendant.

Papers in support

38.3 An application for a freezing injunction must be supported by an affidavit making full and frank disclosure of all material facts, including those going against the grant of the order. This type of application is one of the exceptions where affidavits must be used (**PD 25A, para. 3.1**). The affidavit must be clear and fair, and claimants should avoid the temptation to flood the court with voluminous exhibits, particularly where this will tend to obscure the real issues.

A draft claim form, or its overseas equivalent, must be produced in order to identify the substantive claim against the defendant (*Fourie v Le Roux* [2007] UKHL 1, [2007] 1 WLR 320). Counsel must produce a draft minute of the order sought. The form of the order is considered at **38.15** to **38.29**. In urgent cases the application can be made before issue of the proceedings, and may be supported by evidence in draft or referred to orally on instructions, but in such cases the applicant will be required to confirm on affidavit all the evidence presented at the hearing (*Flightwise Travel Services Ltd v Gill* [2003] EWHC 3082 (Ch), *The Times*, 5 December 2003).

The papers must, wherever possible, be delivered to the court at least two hours before the hearing to allow the judge to read them in advance (**PD 25A, para. 4.3(1)**). Further, even on applications without notice and especially where 'worldwide' freezing injunctions (see **38.9**) are sought, counsel should consider drafting a skeleton argument indicating how the requirements for granting the order are made out (see *ALG Inc. v Uganda Airlines Corporation* (1992) *The Times*, 31 July 1992). Judges dealing with freezing injunctions applications made without notice to the respondents must be astute to ensure the provisions of **PD 25A** are complied with, and must be sure that the evidence adduced by the applicant justifies the order in the terms sought (*Thane Investments Ltd v Tomlinson* [2003] EWCA Civ 1272, LTL 29/7/2003).

Paragraph 3 of the standard-form freezing injunction order in the annex to **PD 25A** provides for a return day for a further hearing on notice, which is normally a few days after the without-notice hearing. The respondent must be fully informed of the case against him well in advance of the hearing on notice, including being provided with the evidence and being told of the arguments used (and, if appropriate, any observations made by the judge) at the without-notice hearing (*Flightwise Travel Services Ltd v Gill* [2003] EWHC 3082 (Ch), *The Times*, 5 December 2003). Consequently, a full note of the hearing must be provided to all parties affected by the order to ensure they know exactly what happened, the basis and material on which the order had been made (*Interoute Telecommunications (UK) Ltd v Fashion Gossip Ltd* (1999) *The Times*, 10 November 1999). Full notes must be provided without respondents needing to ask for them (*Thane Investments Ltd v Tomlinson* [2002] EWHC 2972 (Ch), *The Times*, 10 December 2002). A failure to provide notes of the without-notice hearing was not regarded as a strong enough reason to justify discharging the freezing order in *Thane Investments Ltd v Tomlinson*.

A third party who did not attend the hearing at which a freezing injunction was made, but who is served with the order, may request copies of the materials read by the judge, material prepared at the direction of the judge, and the note of the hearing (**PD 25A, para. 9.2**). Unless the court otherwise orders, the applicant must comply promptly with the request.

CONDITIONS FOR GRANTING FREEZING INJUNCTIONS

The jurisdiction to grant freezing injunctions derives from the Senior Courts Act 1981, s. 37(1). This section enables the court to grant interim injunctions on such terms and conditions as the court thinks just where it appears 'just and convenient' to do so. The requirements laid down by the courts for granting freezing injunctions are: **38.4**

(a) a cause of action justiciable in England and Wales;
(b) a good arguable case;
(c) the defendant having assets within the jurisdiction;
(d) a real risk that the defendant may dissipate those assets before judgment can be enforced;
(e) that the defendant will be adequately protected by the claimant's undertaking in damages (the discussion at **37.26** applies equally to freezing injunctions).

These principles cover the general run of cases. Because injunctions are granted where it is just and convenient, the court retains a discretion to refuse relief, and has power to stretch the usual rules in the interests of justice. This power is used only in truly exceptional cases.

Otherwise, the above requirements must be established, and it is not sufficient to say that a freezing injunction would involve no immediate and obvious prejudice to the defendant (*Flightwise Travel Services Ltd v Gill* [2003] EWHC 3082 (Ch), *The Times*, 5 December 2003).

Claim justiciable in England and Wales

38.5 Since the jurisdiction was first recognised, it has been stated the first condition for granting a freezing injunction is that there is a cause of action justiciable in England and Wales (*The Siskina* [1979] AC 210). Traditionally that meant the defendant had to be available for service within the jurisdiction, or otherwise amenable to the jurisdiction of the High Court through the rules on service outside the jurisdiction (now **CPR, r. 6.36**) or submission to the jurisdiction. Today, the High Court has such a wide jurisdiction to grant injunctions in aid of overseas proceedings (see **38.6**) under the **CJJA 1982, s. 25**, that this requirement is satisfied provided there is a claim for substantive relief which can be formulated against the defendant somewhere in the world.

Injunctions in support of foreign proceedings

38.6 If proceedings have been, or are to be, commenced in another jurisdiction, the High Court is empowered by the **Civil Jurisdiction and Judgments Act 1982, s. 25**, and the Civil Jurisdiction and Judgments Act 1982 (Interim Relief) Order 1997 (SI 1997/302) to grant interim relief, including freezing injunctions, in support of those foreign proceedings (see **16.39**). *The Siskina* [1979] AC 210 was decided before the **CJJA 1982**, so could be decided differently today if its facts were to reoccur. The result is that jurisdiction, in the sense of whether the court has power to deal with the application, is no longer an issue. Instead, the focus is on whether the claimant can identify a cause of action against the defendant, which means there must be a formulated claim for substantive relief against the defendant. It does not matter if the substantive claim is to be brought in England and Wales or an overseas jurisdiction (*Fourie v Le Roux* [2007] UKHL 1, [2007] 1 WLR 320 at [35]). Particular caution is shown before granting freezing injunctions under **s. 25** (*Crédit Suisse Fides Trust SA v Cuoghi* [1998] QB 818), because this can result in the English freezing order overlapping with similar orders made in other countries, which can lead to double jeopardy for the defendants and the opportunity for forum shopping by the claimants (*Ryan v Friction Dynamics Ltd* (2000) *The Times*, 14 June 2000).

ICSID arbitration proceedings are not 'proceedings' for the purpose of **s. 25**. This is because the power in **s. 25(3)(c)**, to extend **s. 25** to arbitration proceedings was repealed by the Arbitration Act 1996, and while the Arbitration Act 1996 contains a power to extend the Arbitration Act 1996, s. 44, that power has not been exercised in relation to ICSID arbitration proceedings (*ETI Euro Telecom International NV v Bolivia* [2008] EWCA Civ 880, [2009] 1 WLR 665). Further, the foreign proceedings have to be on the substance of the dispute, so foreign attachment proceedings, being interim in nature, do not come within **s. 25** (*ETI Euro Telecom International NV v Bolivia*).

A court in England and Wales can grant interim relief in aid of foreign courts unless the fact the court has no jurisdiction over the case apart from **s. 25** 'makes it inexpedient' (**s. 25(2)**) for the court to grant relief. According to *Motorola Credit Corporation v Uzan (No. 2)* [2003] EWCA Civ 752, [2004] 1 WLR 113, the following factors are relevant in deciding expediency:

(a) whether making the order would interfere with the management of the case in the primary court;
(b) whether it is the policy in the primary jurisdiction to refuse to make worldwide freezing or disclosure orders;
(c) whether there is a danger that the order would give rise to disharmony or confusion and/or the risk of conflicting, inconsistent or overlapping orders in other jurisdictions;

(d) whether at the time the order is sought there is likely to be potential conflict as to jurisdiction; and
(e) whether the worldwide order could be enforced. In such cases each defendant falls to be considered separately.

It will rarely if ever be expedient to make an order under **s. 25** where the relevant defendants have no connection with the jurisdiction and the relevant assets are not located here either (*Belletti v Morici* [2009] EWHC 2316 (Comm), LTL 28/9/2009). In *Banco Nacional de Comercio Exterior SNC v Empresa de Telecomunicaciones de Cuba SA* [2007] EWCA Civ 662, [2008] 1 WLR 1936, the court made a domestic freezing injunction in support of a judgment obtained in Turin, but refused to make a worldwide order. It is not the policy of the Italian courts to grant worldwide freezing orders. A worldwide order was inexpedient because the judgment debtor was outside the jurisdiction, the original judgment was granted in Italy, any assets within the jurisdiction were covered by the domestic freezing injunction, and granting a worldwide order would be likely to give rise to disharmony and confusion. It was also held that there is no jurisdiction under **Regulation (EC) No. 44/2001, art. 47**, to grant a worldwide freezing injunction. All this provision says is that a person with a judgment which must be recognised is not prevented from applying for protective measures before registration. By way of contrast, in *Amedeo Hotels Ltd Partnership v Zaman* [2007] EWHC 295 (Comm), LTL 14/6/2007, the non-availability of worldwide freezing orders in New York was regarded as a reason in favour of granting an English worldwide order, rather than as a reason against doing so.

Of course the other basic requirements must also be satisfied (*Refco Inc. v Eastern Trading Co.* [1999] 1 Lloyd's Rep 159). Where it is appropriate to grant a freezing order that overlaps with an order from a foreign court, it is sensible to state in the order which court is to have the primary role in enforcing the overlapping orders, and for the English order, if it is a secondary order, to be in substantially the same terms as the primary foreign order (*Ryan v Friction Dynamics Ltd*).

Lawyers in England and Wales have to exercise extreme caution when instructed to apply for freezing injunctions in aid of foreign proceedings under the **Civil Jurisdiction and Judgments Act 1982, s. 25**. These applications often involve copious and complex financial or commercial information which is difficult to digest, and because the lawyers in this jurisdiction will not be as familiar with the case as the foreign lawyers, it can mean that important features of the case are not covered in the evidence or otherwise not disclosed to the judge (see *Lewis v Eliades* [2002] EWHC 335 (QB), *The Times*, 28 February 2002).

Good arguable case

Regarding the merits of the substantive claim, the minimum threshold for the exercise of the discretion is the establishment of a 'good arguable case' (*Ninemia Maritime Corporation v Trave Schiffahrtsgesellschaft mbH & Co.* [1983] 1 WLR 1412). This imposes a higher merits requirement than the 'serious issue to be tried' test commonly used in applications to amend and in applications applying the *American Cyanamid* principles (*Fiona Trust Holding Corporation v Privalov* [2007] EWHC 1217 (Comm), LTL 30/5/2007). According to Mustill J in *Ninemia Maritime Corporation v Trave Schiffahrtsgesellschaft mbH & Co.* [1983] 2 Lloyd's Rep 600 at p. 605, the expression means 'a case which is more than barely capable of serious argument, and yet not necessarily one which the judge believes to have a better than 50 per cent chance of success'. In *Attock Cement Co. Ltd v Romanian Bank for Foreign Trade* [1989] 1 All ER 1189 (a case on service outside the jurisdiction), it was said that a judge considering whether there is a good arguable case must reach a provisional or tentative conclusion on all the admissible material that the claimant is probably right on the disputed question of fact. This test will not be satisfied if the claimant does not have the evidence to substantiate the case relied upon, or if the case is likely to be struck out, and may not be satisfied if there is an arguable defence. Experts' reports supporting the claim, or a body of documentary evidence, might satisfy the test. In *Fiona Trust Holding Corporation v Privalov* matters pointing to a good arguable case included a lack of negotiations in allegedly fraudulent **38.7** transactions, unconvincing evidence from the defendants to explain their conduct, a letter referring to 'the delicate nature of our exchanges', and attempts to prevent outsiders finding out. Freezing injunctions against directors were refused in an unfair prejudice case (see **85.9**), where there was no personal cause of action against the directors (*Re Premier Electronics (GB) Ltd* [2002] 2 BCLC 634). The courts have on occasion been reluctant to find there is a good arguable case where fraud is alleged, as in *Cheltenham and Gloucester Building Society v Ricketts* [1993] 1 WLR 1545, given the difficulty of proving this particular allegation. An arguable set-off may be taken as reducing or extinguishing the value of the claim. Anticipation that the defendant will be in breach of contract in the future has been held to be insufficient to satisfy this part of the test (*Veracruz Transportation Inc. v VC Shipping Co. Inc.* [1992] 1 Lloyd's Rep 353, overruling *A v B* [1989] 2 Lloyd's Rep 423).

In *Softwarecore Ltd v Pathan* [2005] EWHC 1845 (Ch), LTL 1/8/2005, Pumfrey J used a 'triable issue' test for the merits of the claim, rather than the traditional 'good arguable case' test. This was satisfied on the facts, where the issue was whether the defendant was knowingly involved in certain alleged frauds. The judge took into account the pattern of trading, the lack of any formal written terms of agreement, the lack of investigations into the other parties' creditworthiness, and suspicious figures for profits in various transactions.

Assets

38.8 The requirement of proving that the defendant has assets within the jurisdiction stems from the principle that equity will not act in vain so that if an injunction will not be effective it will not be granted. The claimant must show 'some grounds for believing' that the defendant has assets within the jurisdiction. 'Assets' includes money, shares, securities, insurance money, bills of exchange, motor vehicles, ships, aircraft, trade goods, office equipment, jewellery and paintings. Ownership may be legal or beneficial, but must be in the same capacity as the defendant is or will be a party to the claim.

The existence of an overdrawn bank account was held in one case, *Third Chandris Shipping Corporation v Unimarine SA* [1979] QB 645, to be some evidence of assets within the jurisdiction. This is so particularly where the court can infer that the account is likely to be secured in some way.

Assets in the name of a third party will not usually be included in a freezing injunction unless the claimant establishes a good arguable case that the assets are beneficially owned by the defendant (*TSB Private Bank International SA v Chabra* [1992] 1 WLR 231; approved by the Court of Appeal in *Yukong Line Ltd v Rendsburg Investments Corporation* [2001] 2 Lloyd's Rep 113). In *TSB Private Bank International SA v Chabra* it was clear that the claimant had a good cause of action against the first defendant, and equally clear there was no independent cause of action against the second defendant, a company owned by the first defendant and/or his wife. As there was credible evidence that the assets apparently owned by the second defendant in fact belonged to the first defendant, Mummery J granted a freezing injunction against the second defendant on the ground that it was ancillary and incidental to the claim against the first defendant. See also the discussion on freezing injunctions against third parties at **38.26**.

Worldwide freezing injunctions

38.9 A worldwide freezing order (WFO) operates against assets located outside of England and Wales (with or without a clause covering assets within the jurisdiction). Such an order should not be made where the defendant has sufficient assets within the jurisdiction to satisfy the claim. In any event, it should only be granted in an exceptional case. Typically, exceptional cases are those having the three following characteristics:

(a) the defendant has acted dishonestly or fraudulently on a large scale;
(b) the defendant has the ability to transfer large sums of money around the world quickly; and

(c) the defendant is able to hide assets behind companies or in countries where they are unlikely to be found.

Examples are *Derby and Co. Ltd v Weldon (No. 1)* [1990] Ch 48, and *Republic of Haiti v Duvalier* [1990] 1 QB 202. The power to grant WFOs in support of domestic proceedings or domestic judgments derives from the Senior Courts Act 1981, s. 37(1), not the **Civil Jurisdiction and Judgments Act 1992, s. 25**, or the **Brussels I Regulation, art. 31** (*Masri v Consolidated Contractors International (UK) Ltd (No. 2)* [2007] EWHC 3010 (Comm), [2008] 1 All ER (Comm) 305 at [53]; [2008] EWCA Civ 303, [2009] QB 450 at [92]–[107]). WFOs are readily made against defendants incorporated in the jurisdiction or with a significant presence in the jurisdiction where there is cogent evidence of international fraud (*Mediterranean Shipping Co. v OMG International Ltd* [2008] EWHC 2150 (Comm), LTL 25/9/2008). A WFO may be granted even where the defendant has no assets within the jurisdiction (*Derby and Co. Ltd v Weldon (Nos. 3 and 4)* [1990] Ch 65).

A WFO may be granted under the **Civil Jurisdiction and Judgments Act 1992, s. 25** (see **38.6**), in support of foreign proceedings (*Credit Suisse Fides Trust SA v Cuoghi* [1998] QB 818). A WFO in aid of foreign proceedings affecting assets outside the jurisdiction will only be granted where the respondent or the dispute has a sufficiently strong link with the jurisdiction, or if there is some other factor justifying the court's intervention despite the lack of such a link (*Mobil Cerro Negro Ltd v Petróleos de Venezuela SA* [2008] EWHC 532 (Comm), [2008] 1 Lloyd's Rep 684).

WFO undertakings WFOs must include a *Babanaft* proviso that the order will not affect third parties outside the jurisdiction until, and to the extent that, it has been recognised, registered or enforced by a foreign court. See *Babanaft International Co. SA v Bassatne* [1990] Ch 13 and clause 19 of the standard-form freezing injunction in **PD 25A**. They must also include a 'Baltic' proviso to the effect that third parties served with the order may comply with what they reasonably believe to be their civil and criminal obligations in the country where the assets are located (*Bank of China v NBM LLC* [2001] EWCA Civ 1933, [2002] 1 WLR 844, and clause 20 of the standard-form freezing injunction). The claimant is further required to undertake not to enforce the order in a foreign court without first obtaining permission from the English court (*Derby and Co. Ltd v Weldon (No. 1)* [1990] Ch 48 and sch. B, para. 10, of the standard-form freezing injunction). **38.10**

In *Re Bank of Credit and Commerce International SA* [1994] 1 WLR 708 the English liquidators of foreign companies had obtained WFOs in proceedings brought against two individuals alleging fraud in connection with the companies' affairs. The defendants sought an undertaking that the liquidators would not commence criminal proceedings against them outside the jurisdiction without the court's permission, but the court refused to impose such an undertaking, because it would impede investigation of the companies' affairs by regulatory and prosecuting authorities which the liquidators had a duty to assist.

Schedule B, para. 10, of the standard-form freezing injunction is an undertaking by the applicant not to seek to enforce the order outside the jurisdiction without the permission of the court. This undertaking takes effect as if it were an injunction, and can be replaced by an express injunction to the same effect (*Grupo Torras SA v Al Sabah* [2005] EWCA Civ 1370, LTL 24/8/2005). In deciding whether to release the claimant from an undertaking not to use information obtained from another party under a WFO in contempt proceedings, the court should consider whether it would be just and convenient to permit use of that information for the purpose of policing or enforcing the WFO (*Dadourian Group International Inc. v Simms (No. 2)* [2006] EWCA Civ 1745, [2007] 1 WLR 2967) (slightly different formulations were given by the three members of the court).

Seeking permission to enforce outside the jurisdiction Guidance on the procedure to be followed on an application for permission to enforce a WFO outside the jurisdiction was given in *Dadourian Group International Inc. v Simms* [2006] EWCA Civ 399, [2006] 1 WLR 2499: **38.11**

(a) Normally the application should be made on notice to the respondent, but in cases of urgency, where it is just to do so, the permission may be given without notice to the party against whom relief will be sought in the foreign proceedings, but that party should be given the earliest opportunity of having the matter reconsidered by the court at a hearing on notice (Arden LJ's guideline 8).

(b) The evidence in support of the application for permission should contain all the information (so far as it can reasonably be obtained in the time available) necessary to enable the judge to make an informed decision. This should include evidence of the applicable law and practice in the foreign court; evidence as to the nature of the proposed proceedings to be commenced; evidence as to the assets believed to be located in the jurisdiction of the foreign court; and the names of the parties by whom such assets are held (Arden LJ's guideline 5).

Arden LJ laid down the following guidelines for deciding whether to grant permission to enforce a WFO:

1. The principle applying to the grant of permission to enforce a WFO abroad is that the grant of that permission should be just and convenient for the purpose of ensuring the effectiveness of the WFO, and in addition that it is not oppressive to the parties to the English proceedings or to third parties who may be joined to the foreign proceedings.
2. All the relevant circumstances and options need to be considered. In particular consideration should be given to granting relief on terms, for example terms as to the extension to third parties of the undertaking to compensate for costs incurred as a result of the WFO and as to the type of proceedings that may be commenced abroad. Consideration should also be given to the proportionality of the steps proposed to be taken abroad, and in addition to the form of any order.
3. The interests of the applicant should be balanced against the interests of the other parties to the proceedings and any new party likely to be joined to the foreign proceedings.
4. Permission should not normally be given in terms that would enable the applicant to obtain relief in the foreign proceedings which is superior to the relief given by the WFO.
5. [Deals with evidence in support, see above.]
6. The standard of proof as to the existence of assets that are both within the WFO and within the jurisdiction of the foreign court is a real prospect, that is the applicant must show that there is a real prospect that such assets are located within the jurisdiction of the foreign court in question.
7. There must be evidence of a risk of dissipation of the assets in question.
8. [Deals with applying on notice, see above.]

The court will also consider whether granting permission is appropriate in the interests of justice, and whether information obtained under the injunction is intended to be used for a purpose which is not a purpose of the worldwide injunction (*Bates v Microstar Ltd* [2003] EWHC 661 (Ch), *The Times*, 15 April 2003).

Risk of disposal

38.12 The claimant must establish that there is a real risk that the defendant will dissipate assets if unrestrained (*Ninemia Maritime Corporation v Trave Schiffahrtsgesellschaft mbH & Co. KG* [1983] 1 WLR 1412). There has to be 'solid evidence' of the risk of disposal (*Ninemia Maritime Corporation v Trave Schiffahrts GmbH & Co. KG*; *Dean and Dean v Grinina* [2008] EWHC 927 (QB), LTL 13/5/2008). In *Customs and Excise Commissioners v Anchor Foods Ltd* [1999] 1 WLR 1139 Neuberger J said that what is required is a good and arguable case for a risk of dissipation. This was found to be so where the defendant proposed to dispose of its entire business at a price which had been independently verified by a partner in a leading accountancy firm, because the purchaser was a company controlled by the same people who controlled the defendant and there was contrary valuation evidence (also from very eminent experts) indicating that the price was too low. A real risk of disposal of assets may be established by reference either to previous conduct which tends to show a want of probity or to a course of dealing suggesting the defendant will deal with his assets to make himself judgment-proof, or by raising an inference that such is the case by other evidence (*Re Industrial Services Group Ltd (No. 1)* [2003] BPIR 392). While it may be difficult to establish a real risk of dissipation if the respondent is a well-established business (*Vinprom Rousse v Bulgarian Vintners Co. Ltd* (2000) LTL 8/5/2001), there is a real risk of disposal where even an apparently financially solid company transfers its assets outside the jurisdiction if enforcement overseas would cause extra costs and delays (*Stronghold Insurance Co. Ltd v Overseas Union Insurance Ltd* [1996] IRLR 13). The risk of dissipation has to involve a risk of impairing the claimant's ability to enforce a judgment (*Mobil Cerro Negro Ltd v Petróleos de Venezuela SA* [2008] EWHC 532 (Comm), [2008] 1 Lloyd's Rep 684). It is sufficient if the defendant's actions are unjustifiable (*Ketchum International plc v Group Public Relations Holdings Ltd* [1997] 1 WLR 4 at p. 10) and will have this effect. It is not necessary to show the defendant intends to produce this effect (*Mobil Cerro Negro Ltd v Petróleos de Venezuela SA* at [40]). However, being short of money is not to be equated with an intention to dissipate assets (*Midas Merchant Bank plc v Bello* [2002] EWCA Civ 1496, LTL 14/10/2002).

In *Oaktree Financial Services Ltd v Higham* [2004] EWHC 2098 (Ch), LTL 11/5/2004, one of the solicitors involved in the case wrote to the defendant unwittingly but in effect warning him of the possibility of an application being made for a freezing injunction. Laddie J was almost minded to refuse the injunction on this ground alone, as there was a strong prospect that any funds would have been dissipated once the defendant was put on notice.

At one time it was thought that freezing injunctions could only be granted against foreign defendants. The Senior Courts Act 1981, s. 37(3), now provides that the jurisdiction to grant these orders 'shall be exercisable in cases where [the defendant] is, as well as in cases where he is not, domiciled, resident or present within [the] jurisdiction'. Lord Denning MR in *Third Chandris Shipping Corporation v Unimarine SA* [1979] QB 645 said, at p. 669:

> The mere fact that the defendant is abroad is not by itself sufficient . . . But there are some foreign companies whose structure invites comment. We often see in this court a corporation which is registered in a country where the company law is so loose that nothing is known about it—where it does no work and has no officers and no assets . . . Judgment cannot be enforced against it. There is no reciprocal enforcement of judgments . . . In such cases the very fact of incorporation there gives some ground for believing there is a risk that, if judgment or an award is obtained, it may go unsatisfied.

Reciprocal enforcement of judgments is considered in **chapter 80**.

Assessing risk Factors relevant to the question of risk of dissipation include: 38.13

(a) the nature of the assets: the more easily disposed of, the easier it is to establish a real risk of disposal;
(b) the location of the respondent's assets. There will be less risk if the respondent has substantial assets within the jurisdiction. If the respondent's assets are overseas, an important factor is whether English judgments are enforceable in the country where those assets are situated (*Montecchi v Shimco (UK) Ltd* [1979] 1 WLR 1180). There will be less risk if the assets are in an EU country on account of the ease of enforcement under the **Brussels I Regulation**;
(c) the nature and financial standing of the respondent's business, and the time it has been in existence;
(d) any intentions expressed by the respondent about dealings with its assets;
(e) whether the respondent is reputable and accustomed to paying its debts (*Barclay-Johnson v Yuill* [1980] 1 WLR 1259);
(f) whether the respondent is domiciled or incorporated in a tax haven or country with lax company law;
(g) whether the evidence supporting the substantive cause of action discloses dishonesty or a suspicion of dishonesty on the part of the respondent. This is a weighty factor when it is present, and this is so whether or not it is pleaded as fraud (*Guinness plc v Saunders* (1987)

The Independent, 15 April 1987). Alleged or admitted dishonesty is not of itself enough: all the circumstances must be considered (*Thane Investments Ltd v Tomlinson* [2003] EWCA Civ 1272, LTL 29/7/2003). There was a real risk of disposal in *Lawson v Mizzi* [2010] EWHC 55 (Ch), LTL 19/2/2010, where the respondent was an admitted fraudster who misapplied funds over a considerable period, and who had admitted destroying evidence. The fact she made admissions after being caught out did not remove the risk. Lesser allegations, such as of negligence, breach of contract and breach of fiduciary duty, rarely make it appropriate to infer risk of disposal of assets from the nature of the allegation in the substantive cause of action (*Renewable Power and Light plc v Renewable Power and Light Services Inc.* [2008] EWHC 1058 (Ch), LTL 23/5/2008);

(h) any pattern of evasiveness (*Linsen International Ltd v Humpuss Sea Transport Pte Ltd* [2010] EWHC 303 (Comm), LTL 1/3/2010), the raising of thin defences, or total silence, in the face of the claimant's claim. A good arguable case of perjury was significant in *Congentra AG v Sixteen Thirteen Marine SA* [2008] EWHC 1615 (Comm), [2008] 2 Lloyd's Rep 602;

(i) whether there is evidence that the respondent has been dishonest, outside the actual cause of action. This includes matters such as contrivances designed to generate an appearance of wealth;

(j) past incidents of debt default by the respondent, although it is not essential for the claimant to have such evidence (*Third Chandris Shipping Corporation v Unimarine SA* [1979] QB 645);

(k) evidence that the respondent has already taken steps to remove or dissipate its assets (*Aiglon Ltd v Gau Shan Co. Ltd* [1993] 1 Lloyd's Rep 164);

(l) any history of non-compliance with court orders and other action by the respondent taken in total disregard of court orders (*Great Future International Ltd v Sealand Housing Corporation* (2002) LTL 16/5/2002).

Discretion

38.14 In its discretion, the court can refuse a freezing injunction even if the usual requirements are made out. In *Rasu Maritima SA v Perusahaan Pertambangan Minyak Dan Gas Bumi Negara* [1978] QB 644 the Court of Appeal refused to grant an order partly because the 'cleanliness' of the claimant's hands was open to question, and partly in the exercise of its discretion. The assets frozen were parts for a fertiliser plant, and were valued at $12 million in the hands of the defendants, but were only worth $0.35 million as scrap. This was regarded as only a 'drop in the ocean' in comparison with the size of the claim.

A freezing order against a defendant bank was discharged in the exercise of the court's discretion in *Polly Peck International plc v Nadir (No. 2)* [1992] 4 All ER 769. The claimants claimed the bank, the fourth defendant, was liable as a constructive trustee in respect of money allegedly misapplied by the first defendant. The freezing injunction covered 60 per cent of the bank's assets, and would almost certainly have severely damaged its day-to-day banking business, and also was likely to result in a loss of confidence among investors with the possibility of a run on its deposits. In those circumstances, the granting of the order was inimical to the purpose for which the freezing injunction jurisdiction existed. Lord Donaldson of Lymington MR said that the judgments in this case should not be taken as meaning that it will never be possible to obtain a freezing injunction against a bank, but the circumstances would have to be unusual. At the other end of the scale, freezing injunctions will not be granted where the assets in question are relatively modest. The defendant in *Indosuez International Finance BV v National Reserve Bank* [2002] EWHC 774 (Comm), LTL 26/4/2002, applied to discharge a freezing injunction in support of a foreign judgment on the ground that sufficient funds had been frozen under a Belgian order also in support of that judgment.

The application was refused, partly because the defendant was strenuously resisting enforcement in Belgium, and partly because the value of the Belgian assets (bonds) was highly volatile, so the Belgian assets were not adequate protection. In *Sions v Price* (1988) *The Independent*,

19 December 1988, an order was refused where the claim was £2,000. The current small claims limit of £5,000 may be a good guide to where the line should be drawn.

CONTENTS OF A FREEZING INJUNCTION

Undertakings

The following undertakings by the claimant must be given to the court and incorporated into the order (see the standard order in **PD 25A** at sch. B): **38.15**

(a) as with other interim injunctions, to pay damages to the defendant if it transpires that the order should not have been granted. The court has a discretion to order a freezing injunction subject to a limited undertaking in damages (*RBG Resources plc v Rastogi* [2005] EWHC 994 (Ch), [2005] 2 BCLC 592);
(b) to notify the defendant forthwith of the terms of the order, often by telex or fax, and to serve the defendant with the affidavit and exhibits in support. This is a consequence of applying without notice;
(c) to pay the reasonable costs and expenses incurred by third parties in complying with the order;
(d) to indemnify third parties in respect of any liability incurred in complying with the order.

In urgent cases, the following further undertakings may be required:

(e) to issue a claim form in the terms of the draft used on the application;
(f) to swear and file affidavits deposing to the facts relied on before the judge.

Financial undertakings ((a) and (c) in the above list) are not normally required if the applicant is a public body acting under a public duty (*Financial Services Authority v Sinaloa Gold plc* [2013] UKSC 11, [2013] 2 WLR 678).

Under the Senior Courts Act 1981, s. 37(2), interim injunctions can be granted on such terms and conditions as the court thinks fit. A little latitude is permissible. So, in *Allen v Jambo Holdings Ltd* [1980] 1 WLR 1252 the Court of Appeal continued a freezing injunction in favour of a legally aided claimant who could not give a valuable undertaking in damages. The case was unusual in that the defendants had sworn an affidavit blatantly exaggerating the effects of the order and had been less than forthcoming on a number of points. Also, in any event, the defendants could have obtained the release of their frozen aeroplane by providing security.

In the event that the order is discharged, the defendant is entitled to both special and general damages arising from the effects of the order. Special damages might include disruption to the defendant's business and management time in dealing with the order. The scale of the order (particularly if combined with a search order) may of itself be sufficient for the court to be satisfied that there was significant disruption to the defendant's business (*Aerospace Publishing Ltd v Thames Water Utilities Ltd* [2007] EWCA Civ 3, [2007] Bus LR 726; *Al-Rawas v Pegasus Energy Ltd* [2008] EWHC 617 (QB), [2009] 1 All ER 346). In most circumstances evidence is required to support an award for general damages; damages for emotional distress are not recoverable; and exemplary damages are unlikely to be appropriate (*Al-Rawas v Pegasus Energy Ltd*).

Fortifying the undertaking in damages In appropriate cases the court can order the applicant to fortify the undertaking in damages by paying money into court or providing other security. In deciding whether to make such an order the court will take into account whether there is a realistic risk that the order might cause significant harm to the defendant. In making that assessment it is important to distinguish between the harm caused by the litigation and the harm caused by the freezing injunction (*Al-Rawas v Pegasus Energy Ltd* [2008] EWHC 617 (QB), [2009] 1 All ER 346). Practical difficulties can also be taken into account: it may be difficult for an administrator to obtain suitable security in cases where a company has a large number of small creditors, whereas the position may be different if the company has a small number of large creditors (*Re Bloomsbury International Ltd, Bloomsbury International Ltd v Holyoake* [2010] EWHC **38.16**

1150 (Ch), LTL 24/5/2010). The usual undertaking is intended to provide a means of compensating for potential loss, and the court should consider whether it is an adequate protection. A respondent may apply for the order to be varied to include a requirement to fortify the undertaking, and in such a case it is for the respondent to establish a sufficient risk of loss (*Sinclair Investment Holdings SA v Cushnie* [2004] EWHC 218 (Ch), LTL 23/3/2004). Factors that the court should consider are similar to those on applications for security for costs (see **67.16** to **67.24**). Therefore, the court should not usually take into account the merits of the claim, but should consider whether requiring the applicant to fortify the undertaking may stifle a genuine claim (*Sinclair Investment Holdings SA v Cushnie*).

Assets covered by the order

38.17 Considered in relation to the assets they cover, freezing injunctions can be divided into three types:

(a) General orders, which cover all the defendant's assets.
(b) Maximum-sum orders, which cover the defendant's assets up to the highest amount, including interest and costs, for which the claimant has a good arguable case (*Pacific Maritime (Asia) Ltd v Holystone Overseas Ltd* [2007] EWHC 2319 (Comm), [2008] 1 Lloyd's Rep 371). An appropriate sum should be included for the applicant's estimated costs (*Fourie v Le Roux* [2005] EWCA Civ 204, [2006] 2 BCLC 531, point not considered on appeal). A slightly different test applies in applications to enforce WFOs outside the jurisdiction, see *Dadourian Group International Inc. v Simms* [2006] EWCA Civ 399, [2006] 1 WLR 2499, in which Arden LJ at [47] said that the applicant must show a real prospect that the assets are located within the jurisdiction of the foreign court.
(c) Orders attaching to specific assets, such as a ship, a cargo or an aeroplane.

Often, orders attaching to specific assets are combined with either general or maximum-sum orders. The choice between general and maximum-sum orders was considered in *Z Ltd v A-Z and AA-LL* [1982] QB 558. Maximum-sum orders are the norm. A general order is likely to provoke an application for a variation down to a maximum-sum order. One drawback with maximum-sum orders is that banks will not necessarily know if they can honour transactions on the defendant's accounts as they will not know the total value of the defendant's assets covered by the order at any particular time. Where such practical difficulties result in a larger sum being 'frozen' than the sum stated in the order, the claimant may be held liable on its undertakings in damages. General orders may accordingly be used where the defendant's assets are not fully known by the claimant, and are also appropriate in fraud cases where the amount of the claim may be unknown.

Where the claimant asks for a freezing injunction to cover assets which the defendant or some third party alleges belong to someone other than the defendant, the court has a wide power to do whatever is just and convenient, including ordering the question of ownership to be tried as an issue between the claimant and the third party (*SCF Finance Co. Ltd v Masri* [1985] 1 WLR 876). Unless specifically excluded, the defendant's assets subject to a freezing order will include assets over which the defendant claims to have only legal title (for example, as executor or bare trustee) as well as assets in respect of which the defendant is beneficial owner (*Federal Bank of the Middle East Ltd v Hadkinson* [2000] 1 WLR 1695). The extended definition of 'his assets' in para. 6 of the standard freezing injunction order in **PD 25A** is designed to preserve the decision in *Federal Bank of the Middle East Ltd v Hadkinson*, but to make it clear that such assets include assets controlled by the defendant or in which the respondent has beneficial ownership but which are held by third parties (*JSC BTA Bank v Solodchenko* [2010] EWCA Civ 1436, [2011] 1 WLR 888). These may include assets held by a foreign trust or a Liechtenstein *Anstalt*. It is possible to include assets of which the respondent is the legal owner for the benefit of someone else by including words such as 'whether the respondent is interested in them legally, beneficially or otherwise' (*JSC BTA Bank v Solodchenko*; see **38.26**). Any dispute about whether the defendant is only a legal owner can be dealt with by trying an issue, as suggested in *SCF Finance Co. Ltd v Masri*. In *C Inc. plc v L* [2001] 2 Lloyd's Rep 459, the claimant obtained judgment against the defendant, and sought a freezing injunction in aid of execution against both the defendant and her husband. On the facts the defendant had an arguable right to an indemnity from her husband in respect of the judgment, and it was held that in those circumstances it was right to add the husband as a party and to extend the freezing injunction to cover his assets.

Bank accounts

Bank accounts are one of the most common assets covered by freezing injunctions. The following points should be noted: 38.18

(a) A joint account will not be affected by a freezing injunction unless it is specifically covered by the wording of the order (*SCF Finance Co. Ltd v Masri* [1985] 1 WLR 876).
(b) If the defendant has an account containing money over which the claimant asserts a proprietary interest, mixed with the defendant's own money and/or money held by the defendant on behalf of a third party, the court has jurisdiction to freeze the entire account (*Chief Constable of Kent v V* [1983] QB 34).
(c) The claimant must give the fullest possible details (bank, branch, account name and number) in the affidavit in support. If it is necessary to ask the bank to search for an account, the number of branches involved should be as limited as possible. The claimant will be required to pay the costs of such searches immediately, which may or may not be recoverable from the defendant as costs of the action.
(d) The bank should honour transactions entered into before the order is made. The bank must also honour cheques backed by guarantee cards and irrevocable letters of credit, see, for example, *Cretanor Maritime Co. Ltd v Irish Marine Management Ltd* [1978] 1 WLR 966, and *Lewis and Peat (Produce) Ltd v Almatu Properties Ltd* (1992) *The Times*, 14 May 1992. Cheque cards should be recalled once the order has been served on the bank. Transferring money from a current account to a deposit account is a breach by the bank (*R (Revenue and Customs Prosecution Office) v R* [2007] EWHC 2393 (Admin), LTL 22/11/2007).
(e) A freezing injunction can apply to the *proceeds* of a letter of credit when received (*Z Ltd v A-Z and AA-LL* [1982] QB 558).
(f) A provision must be incorporated into the order to allow any bank served with the order to exercise any right of set-off it may have in respect of facilities given to the defendant before the order (*Oceanica Castelana Armadora SA v Mineralimportexport* [1983] 1 WLR 1294).

Duty owed by banks to the claimant The negligence liability of banks after being notified of freezing orders was considered by the House of Lords in *Commissioners of Customs and Excise v Barclays Bank plc* [2006] UKHL 28, [2007] 1 AC 181. Under its usual practice, the bank would have frozen the defendant's accounts on being notified of a freezing injunction. Due to human error it allowed the defendant to withdraw £2 million two hours after notification. Shortly afterwards the bank wrote to the claimant confirming it would comply with the order. The Court of Appeal ([2004] EWCA Civ 1555, [2005] 1 WLR 2082) held that the three-fold test of foreseeability, proximity and fairness pointed to the imposition of a duty of care, which was not displaced by the apparent lack of any assumption of responsibility, and that the incremental approach supported liability (at [48]). This was reversed by the House of Lords which held the bank did not owe a duty of care. Lord Bingham of Cornhill at [17] to [23] gave six reasons why the reasoning of the Court of Appeal would not be upheld. These include the fact that freezing injunctions do not warn third parties that there might be liability, and that it is illogical to impose a duty of care on a third party when it is already established that a litigant owes no duty of care to an opponent. The imposition of a duty of care in a novel situation turns on a careful analysis of the circumstances of the case. Lord Hoffmann in particular made it clear that deciding whether a duty of care is owed in novel situations cannot be answered by a mechanical application of any of the established tests. 38.19

Port authorities

38.20 Where a freezing injunction affects a ship in harbour, the claimant will be required to undertake to reimburse the port authority for lost income, and a proviso will be incorporated into the order giving the port authority a discretion to move the ship for operational reasons (*Clipper Maritime Co. Ltd v Mineralimportexport* [1981] 1 WLR 1262).

Land

38.21 Freezing injunctions can be granted over land, although it may be difficult to prove there is a 'risk of disposal'. An order, if granted, would not be made for the purpose of enforcing a judgment, so would not be registrable as a land charge (*Stockler v Fourways Estates Ltd* [1984] 1 WLR 25).

Living expenses

38.22 A freezing injunction must allow an individual defendant to use a reasonable sum each week or month to pay his or her ordinary living expenses. As decided in *PCW (Underwriting Agencies) Ltd v Dixon* [1983] 2 All ER 158, a defendant is not dissipating his assets by living as he has always lived. It is a misuse of the jurisdiction to grant freezing injunctions to seek to apply pressure on the defendant (perhaps with a view to obtaining a favourable settlement) by unreasonably limiting the money available for ordinary living expenses. A provision requiring an account of expenditure on living expenses does not require the submission of receipts, although that may be the most convenient way of complying. Such a clause does not control the relevant person's expenditure, but merely monitors that expenditure, and is a proportionate invasion of rights under the European Convention on Human Rights, **art. 8(1)**, and the **First Protocol, art. 1**, in the **Human Rights Act 1998, sch. 1** (*R (K) v HM Treasury* [2009] EWHC 1643 (Admin), LTL 22/5/2009).

Living expenses money must not, however, be spent on extraordinary items, such as expensive motor cars (see *TDK Tape Distributor (UK) Ltd v Videochoice Ltd* [1986] 1 WLR 141). More caution must be shown before allowing a defendant to use frozen assets where the claim is a proprietary one, because the allegation is that the frozen assets belong to the claimant (*Halifax plc v Chandler* [2001] EWCA Civ 1750, [2002] CPLR 41). Spending in excess of the living expenses clause is not a breach of the injunction if it is funded by borrowing from another source (*Cantor Index Ltd v Lister* (2001) LTL 23/11/2001). Retrospective variation to allow frozen assets to be used to pay for substantial living expenses is unlikely to be allowed (*Cantor Index Ltd v Lister*).

Trade debts

38.23 A freezing injunction must allow a defendant who is engaged in trade to pay any legitimate trade debts as they would be paid in the ordinary and proper course of the defendant's business (cl. 11(2) of the standard freezing injunction order in **PD 25A**). The philosophy behind this is that a freezing injunction is not intended to confer priority over other trade creditors. A defendant should be allowed to pay a trade debt, if the defendant is acting in good faith and in the ordinary course of business, even if the debt is not strictly enforceable (*Iraqi Ministry of Defence v Arcepey Shipping Co. SA* [1981] QB 65). Ordinary business expenses may usually be paid from frozen funds, and, in the event of a dispute, the court does not usually consider whether the business venture is reasonable nor whether the business expenses are reasonable. Further, it does not balance the strength of the defendant's case against that of the claimant, nor does it take into consideration that money will not be available to the claimant if it gets judgment (*Halifax plc v Chandler* [2001] EWCA Civ 1750, [2002] CPLR 41). The standard trade debts clause only covers transactions which are consistent with the way the defendant's business has been carried on in the past (*Abbey Forwarding Ltd v Hone* [2010] EWHC 1532 (Ch), LTL 5/7/2010). Payments falling outside this concept require the court's permission. In deciding whether to grant permission the court in *Abbey Forwarding Ltd v Hone* took into account:

(a) the fact this was a conventional freezing injunction rather than an injunction giving effect to a proprietary claim. In conventional freezing injunctions the frozen assets still belong to the defendant;
(b) the prospects of the defendant succeeding at trial;
(c) restrictions on the defendant's related business activities by any insolvency procedures or other practical matters which made it difficult for the defendant to make the payment from other sources.

Whether the defendant should use assets not covered by the order where such are available depends ultimately on the defendant's motive (*Campbell Mussels v Thompson* (1984) 81 LS Gaz 2140, interpreting *A v C (No. 2)* [1981] QB 961). A payment by a defendant as an agent to its principal was accepted as amounting to an abuse of a freezing injunction in *Atlas Maritime Co. SA v Avalon Maritime Ltd (No. 1)* [1991] 4 All ER 769, where the relationship of principal and agent was held not to exist on the facts.

The 'ordinary course of business' proviso is inappropriate in a post-judgment freezing order in respect of bank accounts (*Soinco SACI v Novokuznetsk Aluminium Plant* [1998] QB 406), although it was regarded as appropriate for a post-judgment receivables freezing injunction in *Masri v Consolidated Contractors International Co. SAL* [2008] EWHC 2492 (Comm), LTL 28/10/2008 and for a freezing injunction to enforce an arbitral award in *Mobile Telesystems Finance SA v Nomihold Securities Inc.* [2011] EWCA Civ 1040, [2012] 1 All ER (Comm) 223.

Commentary

Costs of litigation

A freezing injunction should normally also allow the defendant to pay the ordinary costs of the present proceedings if no other funds are available. Even substantial expenditure, and expenditure on VAT advice which is necessary for the defendant's solicitor to formulate the defence, may be allowed under this proviso (*Furylong Ltd v Masterpiece Technology Ltd* [2004] EWHC 3103 (Ch), LTL 13/7/2004). It does not cover the costs of unnecessary legal advice (*Chantrey Vellacott v Convergence Group plc* (2008) LTL 23/6/2008). A case where the Court of Appeal held there were other funds available to pay the defendant's costs was *Atlas Maritime Co. SA v Avalon Maritime Ltd (No. 3)* [1991] 1 WLR 917. In this case it was found that the defendants' parent company operated the defendants in such a way that all funds received by the defendants were immediately paid to the parent company, and any sums payable by the defendants were paid by the parent company. **38.24**

The permission to use money to pay reasonable legal costs (or living expenses or trade debts) does no more than to permit the expenditure without the defendant being in contempt of court. Thus, where the underlying cause of action asserts a proprietary claim against the defendant, the permission to use money to pay reasonable legal expenses is no guarantee that the recipients of that money will escape a later claim in constructive trust for knowing receipt should the claim be established (*United Mizrahi Bank Ltd v Doherty* [1998] 1 WLR 435).

A freezing injunction should not prevent, and may be varied if it does, bona fide expenditure on the legal costs of litigation other than the case in hand, where the other case has a reasonable prospect of success and was on foot when the freezing injunction was granted (*Halifax plc v Chandler* [2001] EWCA Civ 1750, [2002] CPLR 41).

Disclosure of assets orders

The court has power under **CPR, r. 25.1(1)(g)**, to make ancillary orders for disclosure and answers to requests for further information to ensure the effectiveness of the main freezing injunction. Such an order can be granted where there is a reasonable possibility, based on credible evidence, that a freezing injunction application might be made (*Lichter v Rubin* [2008] EWHC 450 (Ch), *The Times*, 18 April 2008). While there is no free-standing power to grant this type of order, it can be made where there is a likelihood of a freezing injunction application (*Parker v* **38.25**

CS Structured Credit Fund Ltd [2003] EWHC 391 (Ch), [2003] 1 WLR 1680). Clause 9(1) of the standard freezing injunction order in **PD 25A** requires the defendant to provide information confirmed on affidavit giving details of all his assets exceeding a specified value. The figure inserted in clause 9(1) in *Cinar Corporation v Panju* [2006] EWHC 2557 (QB), [2007] 1 All ER (Comm) 373, was £1,000. Clause 18 of the standard search order requires the defendant to provide information confirmed on affidavit of the whereabouts of all listed items, the names and addresses of the persons who supplied them or to whom they have been supplied, and dates and quantities of each transaction. Orders may be made requiring disclosure of the nature and whereabouts of all the defendant's assets within the jurisdiction. An order for a company to disclose its assets does not extend to disclosure of the assets of its subsidiaries (*Linsen International Ltd v Humpuss Sea Transport Pte Ltd* [2010] EWHC 303 (Comm), LTL 1/3/2010). A proposed variation on the asset disclosure order in *Intercontinental Bank plc v Akingbola* [2010] EWHC 35 (QB), LTL 3/2/2010, which would have limited the disclosure to the applicant's London-based lawyers, was refused. The practical effect of the proposed variation would have been to prevent the lawyers obtaining effective instructions from the applicant, rendering the order unworkable.

Grupo Torras v Fahad [2004] EWCA Civ 60 held that the court has a discretion to make such an order even if there is a pending application disputing the court's jurisdiction over the substantive claim. *JSC BTA Bank v Ablyazov (No. 3)* [2010] EWCA Civ 1141, [2011] Bus LR D119, went further, and held that it is even possible to make an unless order, with judgment to be entered in default, to secure compliance with a disclosure order in a freezing injunction while there is a pending application challenging the court's jurisdiction.

At the post-judgment stage a disclosure of assets order serves two purposes. One is to assist in the identification of assets which may be covered by the freezing order, and the other is to assist the judgment creditor in locating assets against which enforcement may be sought (*Vitol SA v Capri Marine Ltd* [2010] EWHC 458 (Comm), [2011] 1 All ER (Comm) 366). Post-judgment it is usually just and convenient for the judgment creditor to have full information to assist with execution of the judgment anywhere in the world (*Gidrxslme Shipping Co. Ltd v Tantomar-Transportes Marítimos Lda* [1995] 1 WLR 299). Use in this way is not a collateral purpose within the meaning of **CPR, r. 31.22**, and does not need prior permission from the court (*Vitol SA v Capri Marine Ltd* at [23]).

Defendants should be given a realistic time for compliance (*Oystertec plc v Davidson* [2004] EWHC 627 (Ch), LTL 7/4/2004, where four working days was regarded as extremely short). Seven working days may be reasonable, depending on the circumstances. A judge may be justified in refusing to extend a seven-day order despite a pending application to discharge the injunction (*VTB Capital plc v Malofeev* [2011] EWCA Civ 1252, LTL 4/10/2011). In addition, the defendant's bank may be ordered, even if not a party, to give disclosure of documents relating to the defendant's bank account (*A v C* [1981] QB 956).

Orders requiring disclosure of the nature and whereabouts of all the defendant's assets within the jurisdiction are a standard requirement in freezing injunctions, and are generally required if freezing injunctions are to be effective (*Motorola Credit Corporation v Uzan* [2002] EWCA Civ 989, *The Times*, 10 July 2002, in which the defendant was required to disclose the whereabouts of his assets notwithstanding a pending application to set aside the freezing order). They can require disclosure before the hearing of an appeal challenging the granting of the freezing injunction (*JSC BTA Bank v Ablyazov* [2009] EWCA Civ 1125, [2010] 1 All ER (Comm) 1029). They are nevertheless regarded as intrusive in that they override the defendant's privacy, and compliance can be burdensome. In the case of freezing injunctions in support of foreign proceedings, they should be used sparingly. Factors are the interests of justice, the nature of the claim against the defendant, whether making the order would be proportionate to the interference with the defendant's rights, and whether it would be oppressive (*Cinar Corporation v Panju*).

There are three major limits on the jurisdiction to make ancillary disclosure orders. First, as with other forms of disclosure, such orders will not be granted if they are merely 'fishing' (see *Faith Panton Property Plan Ltd v Hodgetts* [1981] 1 WLR 927). Essentially, an application for disclosure will be 'fishing' if it is based on no more than suspicion as opposed to some evidence.

Secondly, similar problems arise in relation to the privilege against self-incrimination as can arise in relation to search orders (see **chapter 39**).

Thirdly, there is no free-standing power under **r. 25.1(1)(g)** to order the disclosure of information which might be of assistance in seeking a freezing injunction if the applicant has no material at present justifying an application for a freezing injunction (*Parker v CS Structured Credit Fund Ltd* [2003] EWHC 391 (Ch), [2003] 1 WLR 1680).

Freezing injunction against third party

There is an undoubted jurisdiction to make a freezing injunction against a third party where there is good reason to believe that assets in the name of the third party are really those of the principal defendant (*SCF Finance Co. Ltd v Masri* [1985] 1 WLR 876). This power is ancillary to para. 6 of the standard-form freezing injunction order, which states the order covers assets over which the respondent has a direct or indirect power to dispose of or deal with as if they were his own. Assets held on a bare trust can be frozen up to the amount of the principal defendant's assets (*TSB Private Bank International SA v Chabra* [1992] 1 WLR 231). Likewise, ancillary freezing orders can be made where there is a good arguable case that the principal defendant has hidden assets in offshore trusts and companies in tax havens (*International Credit and Investment Co. (Overseas) Ltd v Adham* [1998] BCC 134). Even where the principal defendant has no strict legal or equitable right to the assets, such as where assets are held under a discretionary trust, an ancillary freezing injunction can be made if the principal defendant has some right in respect of the assets, or has control over them, or other rights of access to them (*Dadourian Group International Inc. v Azuri Ltd* (2005) LTL 26/7/2005), for example, where the defendant has a degree of control over the third party's assets amounting to ownership in all but name (*Yukos Capital Sàrl v OJSC Rosneft Oil Co.* [2010] EWHC 784 (Comm), [2001] 1 All ER (Comm) 172). 38.26

In *Her Majesty's Revenue and Customs v Egleton* [2006] EWHC 2313 (Ch), LTL 20/9/2006, HMRC presented a winding-up petition against a company for unpaid VAT, alleging there had been a large-scale carousel fraud. It was held there was jurisdiction to grant freezing injunctions not only against the company but also against persons alleged to be liable to the company. It was not alleged that HMRC had any direct cause of action against those persons, but that a liquidator appointed in the liquidation of the company would have causes of action against them under the Insolvency Act 1986. An argument that *Her Majesty's Revenue and Customs v Egleton* was inconsistent with *Yukong Line Ltd v Rendsburg Investments Corporation* [2001] 2 Lloyd's Rep 113 was rejected in *Yukos Capital Sàrl v OJSC Rosneft Oil Co.* because when Potter LJ used the phrase 'beneficially entitled' ([2001] 2 Lloyd's Rep 113 at [44]) all he was doing was briefly describing the Chabra-style jurisdiction, and was not limiting it to cases where the principal defendant was beneficially entitled. In fact, the decision in *Yukong Line Ltd v Rendsburg Investments Corporation* showed there is a wider jurisdiction, because it held that specific assets did not have to be identified, and thus no question of beneficial ownership arose (*Yukos Capital Sàrl v OJSC Rosneft Oil Co.* at [17]). In such cases the court has to consider whether it would be just and convenient to freeze the assets held by the further defendants.

Cross-examination as to assets

It is only in exceptional circumstances that cross-examination will be ordered on an affidavit of assets sworn pursuant to a freezing order. However, where the claimant has justifiable concerns as to whether the defendant has made a full disclosure as required by the order, the court may order the defendant to be cross-examined (*Den Norske Bank ASA v Antonatos* [1999] QB 271). 38.27

Following *Den Norske Bank ASA v Antonatos*, while it is legitimate for claimants to have information in order to enable them to trace their money, ancillary orders cannot require the defendant to reveal whether he has obtained bribes other than those identified by the claimant. The purpose of the cross-examination is solely to discover what assets the defendant has, with a view to freezing them, and so will be unnecessary if sufficient assets are known to meet the value of the claim (*Great Future International Ltd v Sealand Housing Corporation* [2001] CPLR 293). It must not be undertaken for an ulterior purpose (*Jenington International Inc. v Assaubayev* [2010] EWHC 2351 (Ch), LTL 17/2/2011).

In the absence of an express order to the contrary, the information gained on the cross-examination is covered by the same undertaking given by the applicant on being granted the freezing injunction not to use the information for the purpose of any civil or criminal proceedings, either in England and Wales or any other jurisdiction, other than the present claim (*British Sky Broadcasting Group plc v Digital Satellite Warranty Cover Ltd* [2011] EWHC 3062 (Ch), [2012] 1 WLR 219).

Where a third party is to be cross-examined as to the assets of a defendant, it is likely to be appropriate to require the claimant to give a cross-undertaking not to use the answers for collateral purposes. In *Dadourian Group International v Simms* [2008] EWHC 186 (Ch), LTL 19/5/2008, an undertaking not to use the answers for the purposes of 'any criminal or committal proceedings, or for the trial of the actions' was held to cover use in a summary judgment application. Similar considerations to those laid down in *Dadourian Group International Inc. v Simms (No. 2)* [2006] EWCA Civ 1745, [2007] 1 WLR 2967 (see **38.10**) were applied in deciding whether to release the claimant from this undertaking. It was also held that two defendants had no standing to object to the lifting of the undertaking as it was given to protect the third party, not them.

The examination will be conducted by a master or district judge unless the judge making the order otherwise directs (**PD 2B, para. 7**).

Duration

38.28 A freezing injunction made without notice will remain in force for a limited period until the 'return date', which will be fixed by the judge when the order is granted. So far as practicable, any application to discharge or vary the injunction should be dealt with on the return date. The standard forms of freezing injunction in **PD 25A** contain a clause enabling the defendant or any third party notified of the order to apply to the court at any time (i.e. less than the usual three clear days' notice), but must first notify the claimant's legal representatives. The standard-form freezing injunctions in the annex to **PD 25A** say the orders are to continue 'until further order'. This is a reference to an order which expressly or impliedly discharges the freezing injunction. A freezing injunction does not therefore lapse when final judgment is entered against the defendant (*Cantor Index Ltd v Lister* (2001) LTL 23/11/2001).

Standard-form orders

38.29 A combined standard-form freezing injunction order for domestic freezing injunctions and worldwide freezing injunctions can be found in the annex to **PD 25A**. The current form was revised with effect from 1 October 2005, with minor amendments with effect from 2 October 2006 and 6 April 2010. This form should always be used, with only such modifications as are essential to fit the circumstances of the case. Any substantial variation from the form should be brought to the attention of the judge at the hearing. Wherever possible, a draft of the order sought should be filed with the application notice, with a copy on disk ***(PD 25A, para. 2.4)***.

EFFECT OF THE ORDER

A defendant or anyone else with notice of a freezing injunction will be in contempt of court if they dispose or assist in the disposal or dissipation of enjoined assets (*Z Ltd v A-Z and AA-LL* [1982] QB 558 at p. 572 per Lord Denning MR). A non-party who hands an asset covered by a freezing injunction back to the defendant does not thereby dissipate or dispose of it (*Law Society v Shanks* [1988] 1 FLR 504), unless the non-party knows of a probability that after receiving it the defendant will dispose of it in breach of the order (*Bank Mellat v Kazmi* [1989] 1 QB 541). **38.30**

A freezing injunction covering unspecified assets has an ambulatory effect (see *Cretanor Maritime Co. Ltd v Irish Marine Management Ltd* [1978] 1 WLR 966 per Buckley LJ). Assets acquired by the defendant after the order is granted will be covered by it, up to the maximum sum (if any) stated in the order (*TDK Tape Distributor (UK) Ltd v Videcchoice Ltd* [1986] 1 WLR 141).

VARIATION OR DISCHARGE OF A FREEZING INJUNCTION

Procedure on application to vary or discharge

Applications to vary or discharge freezing injunctions are made to a judge, either pursuant to the liberty to apply provision in the order itself, or on the claimant's application to renew the order on the return date. The application will be made in accordance with **CPR, Part 23** (see **chapter 32**). It is inappropriate to entertain an application to discharge a freezing injunction where a defendant has given no warning of an intention to argue that it should be discharged on the ground of material non-disclosure (*Bracken Partners Ltd v Gutteridge* (2001) LTL 16/1/2002). **38.31**

A non-party who is affected by the terms of a freezing injunction can apply to intervene in the proceedings under **CPR, r. 19.2(2)**, and for the terms of the order to be varied. However, formal intervention may be unnecessary, as Buckley LJ in *Cretanor Maritime Co. Ltd v Irish Marine Management Ltd* [1978] 1 WLR 966 said that a non-party may apply for a variation of a freezing injunction order without intervening provided the non-party had a clear interest. Provided the intervention (whether formal or on the lines indicated by Buckley LJ) is justified, the non-party should be entitled to its costs on the indemnity basis (see *Project Development Co. Ltd SA v KMK Securities Ltd* [1982] 1 WLR 1470).

Where it is clear that the order should be varied or discharged, the parties may agree to this in the form of a consent order. A master or district judge can deal with a variation or discharge by consent (**PD 2B, para. 2.4**).

Grounds for variation

Variations of freezing injunctions may be allowed where the original order is more onerous to the defendant than is necessary, or if it imposes unnecessary obligations on a non-party. Examples are failures to include necessary provisos, such as for ordinary living expenses, paying trade debts, allowing banks the usual set-off, or making a general order when a maximum-sum order is appropriate. Hardship to third parties may also give grounds for a variation. In *Camdex International Ltd v Bank of Zambia (No. 2)* [1997] 1 WLR 632 a freezing injunction had caught a large quantity of banknotes for issue in Zambia. It was varied to allow the release of the bank- notes, to prevent serious damage being inflicted on the general population of the country. **38.32**

Discharge where the claim is not one in which a freezing injunction order may be made

A freezing injunction may be discharged on the ground that one of the usual requirements has not been made out. This may be on the basis, for example, that the claimant does not have a **38.33** good arguable case, as in *Cheltenham and Gloucester Building Society v Ricketts* [1993] 1 WLR 1545. Alternatively, what may have appeared to be a good arguable case on the application without notice may be wiped out by an arguable defence or set-off. It may be that evidence concerning the defendant's financial status, business history or links with this country (or other countries where an English judgment would be enforceable) will persuade the court that there is no real risk of the defendant dissipating the enjoined assets in order to frustrate any judgment the claimant may obtain. Further, a change in the management of a company defendant may remove the risk of dissipation and merit a freezing injunction being discharged (*Capital Cameras Ltd v Harold Lines Ltd* [1991] 1 WLR 54).

Discharge on provision of security

38.34 A freezing injunction will cease to have effect where the defendant provides sufficient security for the claim (cl. 11(4) of the standard freezing injunction order). Security can be provided by bond or guarantee, paying money into an account in the joint names of the parties' solicitors or by paying money into court. The standard security provision in a freezing injunction in cl. 11(4) only gives 'security' against the risk of dissipation of assets. It does not confer priority over the defendant's other creditors (*Technocrats International Inc. v Fredic Ltd* [2004] EWHC 2674 (QB), [2005] 1 BCLC 467). Likewise, a payment into a bank account in the joint names of the parties' solicitors was held not to confer any security rights in *Flightline Ltd v Edwards* [2003] EWCA Civ 63, [2003] 1 WLR 1200. For an equitable charge to be created it is necessary for the terms on which the 'security' is given to include an obligation on the debtor to pay the debt out of the fund (*Palmer v Carey* [1926] AC 703). This can be done by including a clause that the respondent has to satisfy any judgment obtained by the applicant out of the moneys in the joint account. Giving security can be to the advantage of the defendant, since it may be that the order 'freezes' an asset worth more to the defendant than the cost of the security being offered, and in any event it is often important for defendants for freezing injunctions to be discharged as such orders carry a significant financial stigma, and usually result in banking facilities being withdrawn.

Discharge on the basis of material non-disclosure

38.35 A consequence of freezing injunction applications being made without notice is that a claimant applying for a freezing injunction is under a duty to give full and frank disclosure of any defence or other facts going against the grant of the relief sought. This duty extends both to facts within the actual knowledge of the claimant, and to facts which would have been known on the making of reasonable inquiries. It also extends to breaches of an advocate's duty to the court (*Memory Corporation plc v Sidhu (No. 2)* [2000] 1 WLR 1443).

To determine whether there has been a material non-disclosure, it is first necessary to consider the affidavit in support to see whether any adverse facts which the applicant either knew or could have discovered have been omitted. All material facts must appear in the affidavit itself, not in documents exhibited to it (see *National Bank of Sharjah v Dellborg* (1992) *The Times*, 24 December 1992). Second, it is necessary to consider whether anything omitted was 'material' in the sense that it would have affected the judgment of a reasonable tribunal when deciding whether to grant the freezing injunction in question (*Lloyds Bowmaker Ltd v Brittania Arrow Holdings plc* [1988] 1 WLR 1337). Facts are material if they are necessary to enable the court to exercise its discretion on a proper basis, bearing in mind the need to act fairly between the parties, the fact that the defendant has not been heard, and the inherent hardship and inconvenience caused by a freezing injunction. There is obviously a distinction between what are material facts and documents for the purposes of the application for the injunction and those which will be relevant at the trial of the action, and a claimant should not feel it is necessary to exhibit more than a few key documents to the affidavit in support of the application without notice (*National Bank of Sharjah v Dellborg* (1992) *The Times*, 24 December 1992). Instances where omitted facts have been held to be material include:

(a) mistakes in framing the cause of action (*Bank Mellat v Nikpour* [1985] FSR 87);
(b) failing to disclose the existence of proceedings in another country (*Behbehani v Salem* [1989] 1 WLR 723) or this country (*Elvee Ltd v Taylor* [2001] EWCA Civ 1943, [2002] FSR 48);
(c) misstating the source of information (*St Merryn Meat Ltd v Hawkins* [2001] CP Rep 116, where the affidavit said that information about the defendants' activities was obtained using a bugged telephone in the claimants' offices, whereas in fact it was obtained using an interception device at one of the defendant's homes);
(d) failing to correct an assertion that the defendant was outside the jurisdiction once the claimant knew that was wrong (*Lombard North Central plc v Bradley* [2002] EWHC 121 (QB), LTL 3/2/2002, but this was an innocent non-disclosure and did not justify discharging a worldwide freezing injunction);
(e) a series of independent breaches which, taken together, result in the court being given a misleading picture of the case against the defendant (*Complete Retreats Liquidating Trust v Logue* [2010] EWHC 1864 (Ch), LTL 27/7/2010);
(f) failing to disclose weaknesses in the claimant's financial position, which are relevant to the value of the claimant's undertaking in damages and to the undertaking to indemnify third parties;
(g) failing to disclose the application is a 'trap' application (where a buyer obtains a without-notice freezing injunction shortly before executing a contract, so the seller in effect walks into a trap when executing the contract) (*Swift-Fortune Ltd v Magnifica Marine SA* [2007] EWHC 1630 (Comm), [2008] 1 Lloyd's Rep 54). If the fact the application is a trap application is disclosed, the court is very unlikely to grant the order.

Delay in objecting to an alleged non-disclosure can be a reason in itself for dismissing an application to discharge (*Indicii Salus Ltd v Chandrasekaran* [2008] EWCA Civ 67, LTL 12/2/2008, a search order case).

Continuing duty of disclosure

The duty to make full and frank disclosure is a continuing one until the first hearing on notice, so the applicant has a duty to bring to the attention of the court any material changes in the circumstances after a freezing injunction has been granted (*Commercial Bank of the Near East plc v A* [1989] 2 Lloyd's Rep 319). There is a continuing duty on the claimant to draw the defendant's attention to any material change in the claimant's financial position (*Staines v Walsh* [2003] EWHC 1486 (Ch), *The Times*, 1 August 2003). **38.36**

Discretion to forgive a non-disclosure

Finding a material non-disclosure is not necessarily the end of the matter. As Lord Denning said in *Bank Mellat v Nikpour* [1985] FSR 87 at p. 90, 'It is not for every omission that the injunction will be automatically discharged. A *locus poenitentiae* may sometimes be afforded.' The court has a discretion to continue the order, or to make a new order on terms (such as on costs or payment of damages) 'if the original non-disclosure was innocent and if an injunction could properly be granted even had the facts been disclosed' (per Glidewell LJ in *Lloyds Bowmaker Ltd v Brittania Arrow Holdings plc* [1988] 1 WLR 1337). 'Innocence' in this connection depends on whether the omission was made intentionally, but, of course, there are degrees of culpability. Much depends on the quality of the facts that have not been disclosed. **38.37**

In *Millhouse Capital UK Ltd v Sibir Energy plc* [2008] EWHC 2614 (Ch), [2009] Bus LR D33, Christopher Clarke J approved the following principles, which were formulated by Alan Boyle QC sitting as a deputy judge in *Arena Corporation Ltd v Schroeder* [2003] EWHC 1089 (Ch), LTL 15/5/2003 at [213]:

(a) if the court finds that there have been breaches of the duty of full and fair disclosure on the without-notice application, the general rule is that it should discharge the order obtained in breach and refuse to renew the order until trial;
(b) notwithstanding that general rule, the court has jurisdiction to continue or re-grant the order;
(c) that jurisdiction should be exercised sparingly, and should take account of the need to protect the administration of justice and uphold the public interest in requiring full and fair disclosure;
(d) the court should assess the degree and extent of the culpability with regard to non-disclosure. It is relevant that the breach was innocent, but there is no general rule that an innocent breach will not attract the sanction of discharge of the order. Equally, there is no general rule that a deliberate breach will attract that sanction;
(e) the court should assess the importance and significance to the outcome of the application for an injunction of the matters which were not disclosed to the court. In making this assessment, the fact that the judge might have made the order anyway is of little importance;
(f) the court can weigh the merits of the claimant's claim, but should not conduct a simple balancing exercise in which the merits of the claimant's case is allowed to undermine the policy objective of the principle;
(g) the application of the principle should not be carried to extreme lengths or be allowed to become an instrument of injustice;
(h) the jurisdiction is penal in nature and the court should therefore have regard to the proportionality between the punishment and the offence; and
(i) there are no hard and fast rules as to whether the discretion to continue or re-grant the order should be exercised, and the court should take into account all relevant circumstances.

Some facts are so important that the court will readily infer that the non-disclosure was deliberate. For example, in *St Merryn Meat Ltd v Hawkins* [2001] CP Rep 116 the claimants stated in the affidavits in support of the without notice application that certain information was obtained using a bugged telephone in the claimants' offices. It later transpired that the conversations were taped using an interception device at one of the defendant's homes. The order was discharged and not re-granted to mark the gravity of the claimants' conduct. Others, being material but not central to the application, will be more readily forgiven. See the judgment of Woolf LJ in *Behbehani v Salem* [1989] 1 WLR 723. Three incidents of non-disclosure were regarded as not very serious in *Caring Together Ltd v Bauso* [2006] EWHC 2345 (Ch), LTL 13/7/2006, where the injunction was continued because overall there had been a serious and sustained process of frank disclosure.

In deciding what sanctions, if any, to impose for any breach of duty, it is necessary to take into account all the relevant circumstances, including the gravity of the breach, the excuse or explanation offered, the severity and duration of any prejudice occasioned, and whether the consequences of the breach were remediable and had been remedied. The court must also apply the overriding objective and the need for proportionality (*Memory Corporation plc v Sidhu (No. 2)* [2000] 1 WLR 1443). A past record on the part of the defendant of breaking court orders and assisting others to do so for financial gain is a reason for reimposing freezing injunctive relief despite material non-disclosure (*Amedeo Hotels Ltd Partnership v Zaman* [2007] EWHC 295 (Comm), LTL 14/6/2007). It is important that the rule against material non-disclosure does not itself become an instrument of injustice (*Brink's Mat Ltd v Elcombe* [1988] 1 WLR 1350).

Discharge on the basis of unfair conduct

38.38 In *Negocios Del Mar SA v Doric Shipping Corporation SA* [1979] 1 Lloyd's Rep 331 the claimants had agreed to buy a ship from the defendants. Before paying the agreed price, they discovered it was damaged. So they obtained a freezing injunction, which they served immediately on the exchange of the ship for the price. The effect was that the proceeds of the sale were immediately frozen in the hands of the sellers. On appeal, this was regarded as being unfair conduct on the part of the claimants, and the injunction was discharged.

Discharge on the basis of delay

It was stated by Glidewell LJ in *Lloyds Bowmaker Ltd v Brittania Arrow Holdings plc* [1988] 1 WLR 1337 that: **38.39**

a plaintiff who succeeds in obtaining a Mareva injunction is in my view under an obligation to press on with his action as rapidly as he can so that if he should fail to establish liability in the defendant the disadvantage which the injunction imposes upon the defendant will be lessened so far as possible.

A failure to press on with the substantive action will therefore provide grounds for discharging a freezing injunction. A fully and sufficiently explained delay will not result in the injunction being discharged (*Walsh v Deloitte and Touche Inc.* [2001] UKFC 58, 59 WIR 30).

FREEZING INJUNCTIONS AFTER JUDGMENT

There is nothing in the decision in *Lister v Stubbs* (1890) 45 ChD 1 to prevent an injunction being granted *after* judgment to restrain a judgment debtor from disposing of assets in order to prevent the judgment creditor enforcing the judgment that has been obtained. Indeed, it was expressly held in *Orwell Steel (Erection and Fabrication) Ltd v Asphalt and Tarmac (UK) Ltd* [1984] 1 WLR 1097 that a freezing injunction may be granted in aid of the execution of a judgment debt, and in *Faith Panton Property Plan Ltd v Hodgetts* [1981] 1 WLR 927, that a freezing injunction may be granted to restrain the disposal of assets to frustrate the enforcement of an order for costs. In the latter case, the proceedings for the assessment of costs were likely to take about four or five months to complete, but the Court of Appeal held that it was appropriate to grant the injunction under principles established before *Mareva Compania Naviera SA v International Bulkcarriers SA* [1980] 1 All ER 213. **38.40**

Freezing injunctions after judgment, like freezing injunctions in support of pending proceedings, operate *in personam* rather than *in rem* (*Masri v Consolidated Contractors International (UK) Ltd (No. 2)* [2007] EWHC 3010 (Comm), [2008] 1 All ER (Comm) 305 at [64]–[75]; [2008] EWCA Civ 303, [2009] QB 450 at [92]).

Regarding the principles to be applied on a post-judgment application, provided the judgment is enforceable in England and Wales, the requirements that the claimant must have a cause of action justiciable in England and Wales and a good arguable case are satisfied by the judgment itself. Consequently, the only requirements are that the defendant has assets within the jurisdiction and there is a real risk of those assets being dissipated before judgment can be enforced. A freezing injunction in aid of execution should operate in the same way as a freezing injunction granted in the course of proceedings. So, for example, a bank served with an order freezing a customer's account should still honour routine banking transactions such as bills of exchange or letters of credit (see *Lewis and Peat (Produce) Ltd v Almatu Properties Ltd* (1992) *The Times*, 14 May 1992).

In *Banco Nacional de Comercio Exterior SNC v Empresa de Telecomunicaciones de Cuba SA* [2007] EWCA Civ 662, [2008] 1 WLR 1936, it was held that a domestic freezing injunction granted after registration of a foreign judgment should be varied to include an undertaking in damages. Earlier cases indicating that such an undertaking is not required in post-judgment freezing injunctions (*Gwembe Valley Development Co. Ltd v Koshy (No. 4)* (2001) *The Times*, 28 February 2002; *Oystertec plc v Davidson* [2004] EWHC 2004 (Ch), LTL 6/8/2004) are therefore to be treated as overruled. Whether this is good practice is another matter. The reason why such undertakings are not insisted upon after judgment is that the risk of the injunction being discharged is minimal, as the claimant has already won, whereas in pre-judgment freezing injunctions all the claimant will have shown is a good arguable case. In these cases there is a substantial risk that the claim will not succeed at trial.

TRACING CLAIMS

38.41 Unlike a claim for damages, an equitable tracing claim is a claim of a proprietary character. The only interim protection that can be sought in a damages claim is a freezing injunction. On the other hand, the sum subject to a tracing claim may be protected by an ordinary interim injunction, which will be granted on the usual *American Cyanamid Co. v Ethicon Ltd* [1975] AC 396 principles (for which, see **chapter 37**) (*Polly Peck International plc v Nadir (No. 2)* [1992] 4 All ER 769).

WRIT *NE EXEAT REGNO*

38.42 The writ *ne exeat regno* (also called a tipstaff order) is directed to the tipstaff, who is required to bring a named person before a High Court judge for the purpose of examination. Its effect is to prevent that person from leaving the jurisdiction. It originated in the thirteenth century as a prerogative writ, but was subsequently adapted by equity as a means of coercing a defendant to give bail on pain of arrest in cases where the defendant owed a debt that was equitable (so that the defendant was not liable under the old procedure of arrest on mesne process). It may be granted where the defendant may leave the jurisdiction to the damage of a claimant to whom the defendant is indebted until he or she gives security for the debt. A good deal of caution is applied before the writ will be issued (*Allied Arab Bank Ltd v Hajjar* [1988] QB 787), and the court must be satisfied that issuing the writ is proportionate and necessary to secure the ends of justice (*Ali v Naseem* (2003) *The Times*, 3 October 2003). The requirements for such a writ were stated by Megarry J in *Felton v Callis* [1969] 1 QB 200 as being:

(a) The claim must be one in which the defendant would formerly have been liable to arrest at law.
(b) A good cause of action for at least £50 must be established.
(c) There must be good probable cause for believing the defendant is about to leave the jurisdiction unless he or she is arrested.
(d) It must be shown that the absence of the defendant from the jurisdiction will materially prejudice the claimant in the prosecution of the claim.
(e) The claim must be an equitable one.

In *Allied Arab Bank Ltd v Hajjar* [1988] QB 787 a writ *ne exeat regno* was discharged on a number of grounds, one of them being that it had been obtained for the primary purpose of requiring the defendant to identify his assets for the purposes of a freezing injunction, rather than prejudicing the prosecution of the claim (condition (d)). Freezing injunctions are remedies in aid of execution, and are therefore distinct from prosecuting the substantive claim. It also follows from this condition that the writ is only available before trial, and not in aid of execution (*Hume v Druyff* (1873) LR 8 Ex 214).

The related passport order requires the defendant to deliver up his passports and restrains him from leaving the jurisdiction until execution of the freezing or search order (*Bayer AG v Winter* [1986] 1 WLR 497). The jurisdiction is derived from the Senior Courts Act 1981, s. 37(1), rather than the restrictive rules governing writs *ne exeat regno*. In *B v B (Injunction: Jurisdiction)* [1997] 1 WLR 329 Wilson J held the power to restrain a party from leaving the jurisdiction and to surrender his passport exists where the applicant has established a right to interim relief (such as a freezing order) which would otherwise be rendered nugatory and where a hearing is shortly to take place. The power to make such an order would be exercised with considerable caution, and only for a short period. It certainly would not be granted in order to pressurise a defendant into paying a claim. A passport order was justified in *Lawson v Mizzi* [2010] EWHC 55 (Ch), LTL 19/2/2010, where the defendant was an admitted fraudster, and her behaviour was on any view erratic and extremely evasive, so there was a serious risk that she might try to leave the country.

Passport orders are available in aid of all the court's procedures and are also available after judgment (*B v B (Injunction: Jurisdiction)*). After judgment was obtained against the claimant in *Robinson v Robinson* [2003] EWHC 2473 (Ch), LTL 16/10/2003, an order for the surrender of his passport was made for the purpose of ensuring that he complied with an order to swear an affidavit of assets in support of a freezing injunction. It was feared that he would leave for his home in the USA.

Commentary

Chapter 39 Search Orders

NATURE OF A SEARCH ORDER

39.1 A search order is a bundle of interim orders which require the respondent to admit another party to premises for the purpose of preserving evidence which might otherwise be destroyed or concealed by the respondent (see **CPR, r. 25.1(1)(h)**). Statutory authority for the jurisdiction is given by the Civil Procedure Act 1997, s. 7. Prior to the introduction of the CPR this form of order was commonly known as an Anton Piller order, taking its name from *Anton Piller KG v Manufacturing Processes Ltd* [1976] Ch 55.

A search order is both injunctive and mandatory in nature. It requires the intended defendant to allow a named supervising solicitor from an independent firm, a partner from the claimant's own solicitors, and a limited number of additional people to enter on to the defendant's premises, and any vehicles in the defendant's control in the vicinity of those premises, so that they can search for, inspect, take photocopies and remove specified items and documents. The specified items and documents are those likely to be probative in the proceedings. The order will also often require the intended defendant to deliver up relevant documents not located at the premises searched, and to verify information on affidavit. The potential oppression inherent in such an order is recognised by the courts, and a search order is regarded as at the extremity of the court's powers. Although the jurisdiction to make search orders may be invoked in any type of claim, it is most frequently encountered in claims for infringement of intellectual property rights in the entertainment industry.

PROCEDURE ON APPLICATIONS FOR SEARCH ORDERS

Court

39.2 Search orders are, by virtue of the County Court Remedies Regulations 1991 (SI 1991/1222 as amended by SI 1995/206), available:

(a) In the High Court, which is the usual venue. Intellectual property claims, which form the bulk of the cases where this type of application is likely to be made, are assigned to the

Chancery Division (Senior Courts Act 1981, sch. 1, para. 1(i)). If an application for a search order in an intellectual property case is not made in the Chancery Division, the applicant should tell the court that applications should normally be made in the Chancery Division and explain why the present application is not being made there (*Elvee Ltd v Taylor* [2001] EWCA Civ 1943, [2002] FSR 48).

(b) In the patents county court.

(c) In any county court, provided the judge dealing with the application is a High Court or Court of Appeal judge.

Where a search order is sought in a county court claim (and none of the exceptions in the County Court Remedies Regulations 1991 applies), the application for the search order must be made in the High Court (**High Court and County Courts Jurisdiction Order 1991 (SI 1991/724), art. 3**). Such an application is deemed to include an application for the transfer of the proceedings to the High Court (County Court Remedies Regulations 1991, reg. 4). The application must be made returnable to a judge, and the application notice must (see *Schmidt v Wong* [2005] EWCA Civ 1 506, [2006] 1 WLR 561) carry the following endorsement:

This application is being made in the course of [in anticipation of] proceedings in the [ ] county court pursuant to article 3 of the High Court and County Courts Jurisdiction Order 1991. The county court has no jurisdiction to grant the relief sought by reason of regulation 3(1) of the County Court Remedies Regulations 1991.

Commentary

Procedure

Search orders are only obtainable against defendants who are likely to destroy relevant evidence if an application on notice were to be made (see **39.9**). Consequently, secrecy is essential, so the application will be made without notice and the court will sit in private. Many applications are also urgent, and many are made before proceedings are issued. The general procedure for applications for interim injunctions applies, for which see **37.5** to **37.13** and **procedural checklist 19** at the front of the book. Essentially, the claimant must: **39.3**

(a) have issued a claim form in respect of the substantive cause of action, unless the application is too urgent to wait for this to be done;

(b) issue an application notice in form N244;

(c) provide affidavit evidence in support (witness statements are not acceptable: **PD 25A, para. 3.1**);

(d) provide a draft order, together with a copy on disk;

(e) provide a skeleton argument in support; and

(f) after the hearing, provide all affected parties with a full note, for which they do not have to ask, of what happened at the hearing, including the basis and materials on which the order was made (*Interoute Telecommunications (UK) Ltd v Fashion Gossip Ltd* (1999) *The Times*, 10 November 1999).

It is very common to combine applications for search orders with other forms of urgent interim relief. It is not unknown, to use the old terminology, to 'pile *Piller* upon *Mareva*' in fraud and pirating claims.

Full and frank disclosure

As the application is made without notice, the claimant has the usual duty of full and frank disclosure. The courts have insisted that this is especially important in applications for search orders, and the claimant should err on the side of excessive disclosure. The supporting affidavit must disclose in very full terms the reason for seeking the order, including the probability that relevant material will disappear if the order is not made (**PD 25A, para. 7.3**). **39.4**

Supervising solicitor

39.5 The affidavit supporting an application for a search order must state the name and experience of the proposed supervising solicitor, and give the name and address of his or her firm. The proposed supervising solicitor must be someone experienced in the operation of search orders (**PD 25A, para. 7.2**) and must not be a member or employee of the claimant's solicitors (**para. 7.6**). Names of suitable supervising solicitors can be obtained through the Law Society and (for the London area) the London Solicitors Litigation Association. If the court orders that a search order need not be served by the supervising solicitor, the reason for so ordering must be set out in the order (**para. 7.7**). Various undertakings given by the supervising solicitor appear in the standard-form search order in **sch. E**. These include an undertaking by the supervising solicitor to keep the existence of the removed items confidential.

Documents to third parties

39.6 A third party who did not attend the hearing at which a search order was made, but who is served with the order, may request copies of the materials read by the judge, materials prepared at the direction of the judge, and the note of the hearing (**PD 25A, para. 9.2**). Unless the court otherwise orders, the applicant must comply promptly with the request.

PRINCIPLES

39.7 Ormrod LJ in *Anton Piller KG v Manufacturing Processes Ltd* [1976] Ch 55 laid down the following preconditions for granting search orders:

(a) There must be an extremely strong prima facie case on the merits. It is worth contrasting this with the requirement of merely showing a good arguable case in applications for freezing orders.
(b) The defendant's activities must be proved to result in very serious potential or actual harm to the claimant's interests.
(c) There must be clear evidence that incriminating documents or materials are in the defendant's possession.
(d) There must be a real possibility that such items may be destroyed before any applications on notice can be made. This is considered at **39.9**.
(e) The defendant will be adequately protected by the claimant's undertaking in damages (the discussion at **37.26** applies equally to search orders).

Insistence on strict compliance

39.8 In the early 1980s it was thought that the conditions set out in **39.7** had been relaxed by *Yousif v Salama* [1980] 1 WLR 1 540 and *Dunlop Holdings Ltd v Staravia Ltd* [1982] Com LR 3. In the former it was inferred that there was a real risk of the defendant disobeying any orders made on applications on notice from evidence that he had forged a signature on a cheque. In the latter, Oliver LJ said:

> it has certainly become customary to infer the probability of disappearance or destruction of evidence where it is clearly established on the evidence before the court that the defendant is engaged in a nefarious activity which renders it likely that he is an untrustworthy person. It is seldom that one can get cogent or actual evidence of a threat to destroy material or documents.

The claimant's solicitors in *Columbia Picture Industries Inc. v Robinson* [1987] Ch 38 had applied for some 300 search orders between 1974 and 1985, and none of their applications had been refused.

Since *Booker McConnell plc v Plascow* [1985] RPC 425 there has been a marked change in judicial attitude, and nowadays the courts insist on strict compliance with the principles enunciated by Ormrod LJ in *Anton Piller KG v Manufacturing Processes Ltd* [1976] Ch 55. The order is regarded as a serious stigma on the defendant's commercial reputation, and will often result in banks refusing further credit or even calling in loans. The order itself often allows the claimant's representatives to remove the defendant's stock-in-trade, and the net result is often to drive the defendant out of business. Accordingly, the order is regarded as a remedy of last resort, and should be made only 'when there is no alternative' (per Ormrod LJ in *Anton Piller KG v Manufacturing Processes Ltd*). As Dillon LJ explained in *Booker McConnell plc v Plascow*:

> the courts have always proceeded, justifiably, on the basis that the overwhelming majority of people in this country will comply with the court's order, and that defendants will therefore comply with orders to, for example, produce and deliver up documents without it being necessary to empower the [claimants'] solicitors to search the defendant's premises.

Putting the matter slightly differently, Hoffmann J in *Lock International plc v Beswick* [1989] 1 WLR 1268 said at p. 1281: 'there must be ***proportionality*** between the perceived threat to the [claimant's] rights and the remedy granted'. Before embarking on an application for a search order, it is therefore necessary to consider whether some less draconian measure, such as applying on notice for negative injunctions or for an order that the documents be delivered up to the defendant's solicitor, or even awaiting disclosure in the usual way, would adequately protect the claimant.

REAL RISK OF DESTRUCTION

In *Anton Piller KG v Manufacturing Processes Ltd* [1976] Ch 55 it was said that a search order would not be made unless there is 'real possibility' that material evidence will be destroyed if an application for disclosure were to be made on notice to the defendant. This formula has been adopted in numerous cases since then. It is possible that the CPR have made a slight alteration in this requirement. **PD 25A, para.** 7.3(2), referring to the evidence needed in support of an application for a search order, says it must cover 'the probability' that relevant material would disappear if the order were not made. There is a slight difference between a 'real possibility' and a 'probability', in that the latter expression means that the risk of destruction has to be proved on the balance of probabilities, whereas the earlier expression can be satisfied by evidence coming a little distance short of establishing the risk on the balance of probabilities. However, it is doubtful that **para.** 7.3(2), which is a provision dealing with the evidence required in support of an application, can have been intended to alter the established conditions for the remedy. **39.9**

The requirement of showing there is a real risk that the defendant will destroy vital evidence lies at the heart of the jurisdiction to grant search orders. Sometimes it is possible to infer this risk from the nature of the defendant's alleged conduct, for instance, in video pirating claims and commercial fraud actions. Even in these cases, however, the claimant is still obliged to give full and frank disclosure of anything known about the defendant, including past responsible conduct or other matters which tend to show the defendant would obey the court's orders.

Outside the area of actions based directly on dishonesty, it will be rare for the claimant to have evidence of a real risk of destruction. An example is *Lock International plc v Beswick* [1989] 1 WLR 1268, where the claimant alleged the defendants, who were former employees now competing with the claimant, were making use of its trade secrets and confidential information. A search order was executed, and the defendants successfully applied to discharge the order. Hoffmann J said the claimant's evidence:

> came nowhere near [establishing]...a 'grave danger' or 'real possibility' that the defendants might destroy evidence...these defendants were no fly-by-night video pirates. They were former long-service

employees with families and mortgages, who had openly said that they were entering into competition and whom the plaintiff knew to be financed by highly respectable institutions.

FORM OF THE ORDER

39.10 A standard form of search order is provided in the annex to **PD 25A** (as refined from time to time). This form is described in **PD 25A, para. 7.11**, as an 'example', and should be used with such modifications as are necessary to fit the circumstances of the case. Any substantial variation from the form should be brought to the attention of the judge at the hearing. All the standard wording should be retained even where the privilege against self-incrimination has been removed by statute (see **39.16**, and **PD 25A, para. 7.9**).

The main provision is clause 6, which provides that the defendant 'must permit [certain named people, referred to as "the search party"] to enter' the defendant's premises. Other clauses in the order are designed to give effect to the basic purpose of the order, which is to allow the search party to enter the defendant's premises and to take documents which might be disclosable in the proceedings or otherwise be relevant, while providing suitable safeguards for the defendant. These include the appointment of an independent supervising solicitor to ensure the order is not misused by the claimant. Clause 22 may be used to set out prohibitory injunctions ancillary to the main part of the order. Schedule B sets out the items that may be seized, and must extend no further than the minimum necessary to preserve the evidence which might otherwise be concealed or destroyed (*Columbia Picture Industries Inc. v Robinson* [1987] Ch 38).

Service of the order

39.11 Since *Universal Thermosensors Ltd v Hibben* [1992] 1 WLR 840 execution of search orders has been subject to oversight by supervising solicitors who are independent of the claimant's usual solicitors. Before this case there was mounting concern about the execution of search orders by enthusiastic but inexperienced persons. Execution by a solicitor related to the claimant or by one of the claimant's directors was deprecated in *Manor Electronics Ltd v Dickson* [1988] RPC 618.

The order must be served personally by the supervising solicitor, unless the court otherwise orders. Together with the order there must be served an application notice for a hearing on notice in respect of the search order (see **39.21**). The affidavits in support and any exhibits capable of being copied must be served at the same time as the order (**PD 25A, para. 7.4(1)**). Confidential exhibits need not be served, but they must be made available for inspection by the defendant in the presence of the claimant's solicitors while the order is being executed. Copies of confidential exhibits may be retained by the defendant's solicitors on their undertaking not to permit the defendant to see them except in their presence, nor to allow the defendant to make or take away any note or record of them (**para. 7.4(2)**). Unless the court otherwise orders, service may only be effected between 9.30 a.m. and 5.30 p.m. Monday to Friday (**para. 7.4(6)**). The reason for this is that the defendant is entitled to seek legal advice, and this will only be effective if the order is executed during office hours. It is recognised that mistakes (on both sides) are less likely to occur if these orders are executed during office hours (for an example, see *Adam Phones Ltd v Goldschmidt* [1999] 4 All ER 486).

Planning is essential for effective execution. If several addresses are included in the order, it is important that execution is simultaneous. To reduce its oppressive effect the order will limit the number of persons who can assist with its execution at each address specified. Further, if the defendant is a woman living alone, a woman must accompany those executing the order (**para.** 7.4(5)). The police will be informed beforehand if there is any prospect of a breach of the peace.

Gaining access and explaining the order

A search order is not a search warrant, and does not authorise the use of force to gain access. In cases where the defendant has committed both a civil wrong against the claimant and a criminal offence, a search order must not be executed at the same time as a police search warrant (**PD 25A, para.** 7.8; cl. 8 of the standard form of search order). Clause 6 is a mandatory order that the defendant 'must permit' access to the supervising solicitor. But before entering, the supervising solicitor must explain the terms and effect of the order in everyday language and must inform the defendant that legal advice may be sought before entry is permitted and of the defendant's right to apply to vary or discharge the order. **39.12**

By **PD 25A, para.** 7.4(4), the supervising solicitor must also advise the respondent that he may avail himself of:

(a) legal professional privilege; and
(b) the privilege against self-incrimination. Situations where the privilege against self- incrimination do not apply are listed in **para. 7.9** (see **39.16** and **39.17**).

A solicitor who negligently failed to explain the effect of the order to the defendant in a fair and accurate manner was held to be in contempt of court in *VDU Installations Ltd v Integrated Computer Systems and Cybernetics Ltd* [1989] FSR 378. The right to seek legal advice means that the obligation to give permission for entry only arises after a reasonable period of time has elapsed for legal advice to be obtained (*Bhimji v Chatwani* [1991] 1 WLR 989). Thereafter, the defendant must give permission, or else will be in contempt of court. Even if there are grounds for seeking an order for the immediate discharge of the search order, while it subsists it is an order of the court and must be obeyed (*Wardle Fabrics Ltd v G. Myristis Ltd* [1984] FSR 263). However, if entry is refused and the order is successfully discharged shortly thereafter, that will give the court grounds for imposing no penalty on an application to commit for contempt of court. Matters to be taken into account include whether an application to discharge is merely a device to delay the search, and whether the defendant has interfered with the evidence during the delay (*Bhimji v Chatwani*).

Executing the order

There is a heavy duty on the supervising solicitor to comply strictly with the terms of the order as to the premises which can be searched and the items which can be removed. **39.13**

The defendant's premises must not be searched, and no items may be removed, except in the presence of the defendant or a person who appears to be a responsible employee of the defendant (**PD 25A, para.** 7.5(2)). If any of the items covered by the order exist only in computer-readable form, the defendant must immediately give the claimant's solicitors effective access, including any necessary passwords, and arrange for the material to be printed out. The claimant must take all reasonable steps to ensure that no damage is done to the defendant's computer system, and must ensure that the person searching the defendant's system has sufficient expertise to avoid causing damage (**para.** 7.5(8) to (10)). Items seized must be recorded by the supervising solicitor in a list, and must be retained by the claimant's solicitors for the minimum time necessary to take copies and in any case for no more than two days, after which they must be returned to their owner (**para.** 7.5(3) and (6)). Nothing should be removed until the defendant has had a reasonable opportunity to check it against the list (**para.** 7.5(7)). Where ownership of the material seized is in dispute, the claimant's solicitors should place it in the custody of the defendant's solicitors pending trial on the defendant's solicitors undertaking to retain it in safekeeping and to produce it to the court when required (**para. 7.5(4)**). It may be appropriate for the order to require the claimant to insure the materials seized (**para. 7.5(5)**).

Execution of a search order in an excessive or oppressive manner will render the claimant liable under the undertaking in damages. Seizing documents not specified in the order may be penalised by an award of aggravated damages. An award of £10,000 against the claimant was made on this ground in *Columbia Picture Industries Inc. v Robinson* [1987] Ch 38.

It is important that neither the claimant nor the claimant's employees are allowed to conduct searches for documents belonging to a trade competitor. Safeguards must be built into the order to protect the confidentiality of the defendant's trade secrets.

Additional powers and duties of the supervising solicitor

39.14 It may become apparent that it is impracticable to comply fully with the requirement that the defendant be allowed to check the claimant's list of materials before anything is removed from the premises, or the conditions for accessing material stored on computer. If the supervising solicitor is satisfied that compliance is impracticable, he or she may permit the search to proceed and for items to be removed without full compliance (**PD 25A, para. 7.5(13)**).

Once the search has been completed, the supervising solicitor must provide the claimant's solicitors with a report on the carrying out of the order. The claimant's solicitors must then serve a copy on the defendant and file a copy with the court (**PD 25A, para. 7.5(11) and (12)**).

Contempt by the defendant

39.15 In *Alliance and Leicester Building Society v Ghahremani* (1992) 142 NLJ 313 a search order was executed at the premises of a firm of solicitors. The order required the defendant solicitor to disclose 'documents' of various categories. There was evidence that the defendant erased information stored on computer while the order was being executed. Hoffmann J held that the word 'document' in the order was, in the light of the earlier decision of *Derby and Co. Ltd v Weldon (No. 9)* [1991] 1 WLR 652, wide enough to include information stored on computer, and that the defendant was guilty of contempt of court. It is probable that if the defendant had not been a lawyer the court would have held that the wording was insufficiently clear to found an application for committal. It is for this reason that the standard search order contains specific provision in cl. 17 for copying information stored on computer. In addition to being a contempt of court, 'the refusal to comply may be the most damning evidence against the defendant at the subsequent trial' (per Ormrod LJ in *Anton Piller KG v Manufacturing Processes Ltd* [1976] Ch 55).

On the other hand, a petty breach of a search order in circumstances where the defendant had honestly tried to obey it should be ignored by the parties. Under the CPR, given the emphasis on proportionality, an application to commit for no more than a technicality is likely to be dismissed with costs (*Adam Phones Ltd v Goldschmidt* [1999] 4 All ER 486).

PRIVILEGE AGAINST SELF-INCRIMINATION

39.16 The House of Lords in *Rank Film Distributors Ltd v Video Information Centre* [1982] AC 380 held that where a criminal charge was more than a contrived, fanciful or remote possibility, the defendant could refuse to provide information by relying on the privilege against self-incrimination. In many cases where the evidence is strong enough for a search order, it will also amount to a breach of the criminal law. The privilege applies in relation to any piece of information or evidence on which the prosecution might wish to rely in establishing guilt or in deciding whether to prosecute or not (*Den Norske Bank ASA v Antonatos* [1999] QB 271). The precise scope of the privilege has been modified as a result of the incorporation into UK law of the European Convention on Human Rights by the **Human Rights Act 1998**. Consequently, in *C plc v P* [2007] EWCA Civ 493, [2008] Ch 1, it was held that free-standing evidence (in this case images of children found on a computer which had been imaged under the terms of a search order) which was not created in compliance with the terms of the search order could be passed to the police. The scope of the privilege is discussed at **50.51**.

The *Rank* decision threatened to destroy the utility of many search orders, and was swiftly reversed by the Senior Courts Act 1981, s. 72. This is not the only provision making inroads into the privilege against self-incrimination (see **PD 25A, para. 7.9**), the relevant provisions being:

(a) the Senior Courts Act 1981, s. 72, which focuses on the civil cause of action, applying to intellectual property and passing-off civil claims, and removes the privilege in respect of 'related offences' and the recovery of 'related penalties';
(b) the Theft Act 1968, s. 31(1), which removes the privilege in civil proceedings for the recovery or administration of any property, for the execution of any trust, or for an account, notwithstanding that compliance may expose the witness or his spouse to a charge under the Theft Act 1968;
(c) the Fraud Act 2006, s. 13, which operates in a similar way to the Theft Act 1968, s. 31;
(d) the Children Act 1989, s. 98, which removes the privilege in applications relating to the care, supervision or protection of a child;
(e) various statutes and statutory instruments where the privilege has been impliedly removed (see *Bank of England v Riley* [1992] Ch 475).

In cases where the privilege against self-incrimination still applies, it was held in *Tate Access Floors Inc. v Boswell* [1991] Ch 512 that the privilege entitles a defendant served with a search order to refuse:

(a) permission to enter;
(b) to deliver up documents covered by the order; and
(c) to verify information about suppliers and customers.

However, as was also held in *Tate Access Floors Inc. v Boswell*, it is a privilege against *self*-incrimination. The privilege may be relied on by persons ordered to give information whether they are natural persons or artificial persons such as limited companies (for which see *Triplex Safety Glass Co. Ltd v Lancegaye Safety (1934) Glass Ltd* [1939] 2 KB 395) provided they do so on their own behalf. However, one person cannot refuse to give information which might incriminate another, except where the other is the person's spouse. In *Tate Access Floors Inc. v Boswell* the court left open the question whether the connection between the controller of a company and the company might be so strong that they should be allowed to refuse to incriminate each other. In *Sociedade Nacional de Combustiveis de Angola UEE v Lundqvist* [1991] 2 QB 310 the court said that a company officer nominated to transmit the company's information (which in that case was information about assets subject to a freezing injunction) could refuse to transmit evidence which might incriminate him or her, but that the court would immediately nominate another person to transmit the information.

The above problems can be avoided if the risk of the information supplied being used in criminal proceedings can be removed. This can be achieved if the Crown Prosecution Service indicate in writing that they will not make use of the information for the purposes of any criminal prosecution against the defendant or the defendant's spouse, and if a clause stating that no disclosure made in compliance with the order will be used in evidence in the prosecution or any offence committed by the defendant of the defendant's spouse is included in the order (*AT and T Istel Ltd v Tully* [1993] AC 45).

Commentary

Privilege and terms of the search order

39.17 Until *Den Norske Bank ASA v Antonatos* [1999] QB 271 an attempt was sometimes made to add a clause to a search order to the effect that a defendant who claimed to be entitled to the benefit of the privilege against self-incrimination still had to provide the allegedly privileged information to the supervising solicitor, who would hold the information to the order of the court. It was held in *Den Norske Bank ASA v Antonatos* that such a clause is inconsistent with the privilege if it applies, and should no longer be used.

A respondent who wishes to claim that listed documents are protected by privilege may gather them together and hand them over to the supervising solicitor to assess whether they are privileged as claimed (standard search order, cl. 11(1)). On assessing the materials, the supervising solicitor may:

(a) Decide they are privileged (standard search order, cl. 11(2)). In such a case the materials will be excluded from the search. The supervising solicitor will list them for inclusion in his report, and return them to the respondent.
(b) Decide they may be privileged (standard search order, cl. 11(3)). In such a case the supervising solicitor will exclude the material from the search, but will retain it in his possession pending further order of the court.

Clause 11(3) of the standard search order states the same procedure as in (b) above applies 'if the respondent claims to be entitled to withhold production on [the grounds that the documents may be privileged or incriminating]'. It is probable, but not clear from cl. 11(1) and (3), that this applies only where the respondent does not hand the documents over to the supervising solicitor to assess whether they are privileged (under cl. 11(1)). It is possible to read cl. 11(3) as applying also where cl. 11(1) has been invoked and the supervising solicitor has decided the documents are clearly not privileged, but the respondent then claims to be entitled to withhold them.

DISCHARGE AND VARIATION OF SEARCH ORDERS

Discharge of search orders

39.18 Applications to discharge or vary search orders are largely governed by the principles already discussed in relation to freezing injunctions at **38.32** to **38.39**. However, if a search order has been executed, there is a strong argument that it is an unjustified waste of costs and of the court's time to seek its discharge before trial. Doing so was said by Browne-Wilkinson V-C in *Dormeuil Frères SA v Nicolian International (Textiles) Ltd* [1988] 1 WLR 1362 to be little more than an empty gesture, and that the right course was normally to adjourn an application to set aside the order to be dealt with at trial. Where the order had not been complied with at the time of the application to set aside, as in *Arab Monetary Fund v Hashim* [1989] 1 WLR 565, it was necessary to consider whether the order would be made in the light of the full facts. In *Tate Access Floors Inc. v Boswell* [1991] Ch 512 the Vice-Chancellor reconsidered his decision in *Dormeuil Frères SA* in the light of the freezing injunction case of *Behbehani v Salem* [1989] 1 WLR 723. There is a conflict between the public interest in ensuring that applications made without notice are made in good faith, and the public interest in ensuring the courts are not clogged up with long interim hearings. The Vice-Chancellor suggested the solution may be that the circumstances in which an order without notice was obtained should only be investigated at the pre-trial stage if it is clear there has been a material non-disclosure or where the nature of the alleged non-disclosure is so serious as to demand immediate investigation. If the ground for seeking to have the order discharged is that the claimant is guilty of material non-disclosure over a matter relevant to the granting of relief without notice, being a matter which has no relevance to the merits of the substantive action (such as the value of the claimant's undertaking in damages), it may be more appropriate to determine the matter immediately rather than waiting until trial.

Further, it is sometimes argued that even if the original order was granted on insufficient grounds, the fruits of the search may indicate that justice was done in the event. Such an argument was rejected in *Manor Electronics Ltd v Dickson* [1988] RPC 618 in the face of a clear material non-disclosure.

A search order was discharged in *Gadget Shop Ltd v Bug.Com Ltd* [2001] FSR 26, for multiple breaches of procedure. Small variations in the standard form of order had not been drawn to the attention of the judge on the initial application; the lack of experience of the supervising solicitor had not been adequately explained in the evidence in support; and the evidence in support did not give adequate full and frank disclosure, for example, that some of the allegedly confidential material said to have been taken by the defendants had been published on the applicant's own website. Conversely, in *Indicii Salus Ltd v Chandrasekaran* [2008] EWCA Civ 67, LTL 12/2/2008, it was held that the fact the applicant's accountants had reservations about its ability to pay their fees did not have to be disclosed on an application for a search order, and that a statement that an asset had a substantial but uncertain value had not been false.

Exclusion of evidence obtained under a discharged search order

The question of whether any documents seized under a search order which is subsequently **39.19** discharged should be held to be inadmissible at trial was left open by the Vice-Chancellor in *Tate Access Floors Inc. v Boswell* [1991] Ch 512. The general rule has been that there is no exclusionary discretion in civil cases, and if the documents are otherwise relevant and admissible it should not matter how they were obtained. This has been changed by **CPR, r. 32.1**, as decisively held in *Grobbelaar v Sun Newspapers Ltd* (1999) *The Times*, 12 August 1999. The defendant also has a remedy under the claimant's undertaking in damages.

Variation on grounds of intimidation

One of the defendants in *Coca-Cola Co. v Gilbey* [1995] 4 All ER 711 argued that he should not be **39.20** required to disclose the identities of other persons involved with him in a highly organised passing-off operation, and other information, as required by a search order, on the ground that doing so might expose himself and his family to physical violence from those other persons. It was held that, although violence or threats of violence would be legitimate grounds if put forward by innocent parties, when put forward by actual participants, public policy and the interests of the victim carried more weight, and disclosure was ordered forthwith.

AFTER EXECUTION

After executing the order, the supervising solicitor is required to compile a report of what hap- **39.21** pened (see **39.14**). The report is served on the defendant. Clause 3 of the model form of search order specifies a return date when there will be a second hearing, this time on notice to the defendant. The applicant's solicitors are required to provide the supervising solicitor with an application for hearing on the return date (sch. D, para. 1(iii)), which will be served on the defendant when the main order is executed by the supervising solicitor.

On the hearing the court will consider the supervising solicitor's report and the defendant may apply to discharge the order. Once a search order has been executed, there is an enhanced duty on the claimant to prosecute the main action without delay. In *Hytrac Conveyors Ltd v Conveyors International Ltd* [1983] 1 WLR 44, the claimant delayed for 10 weeks after obtaining a search order without serving a statement of claim. The claim was dismissed, Lawton LJ saying that claimants 'must not use [search] orders as a means of finding out what sort of charges they could make'.

If the claim was transferred to, or commenced in, the High Court for the purposes of applying for a search order, but is otherwise more suitable for the county court, after the application for the search order has been disposed of the claim will be transferred down to the county court (County Court Remedies Regulations 1991 (SI 1991/1222), reg. 5). The application is not treated as disposed of until any application to set the order aside has been heard, or until the expiry of 28 days during which no such application is made.

COLLATERAL USE OF MATERIAL

39.22 As with other forms of disclosure (see **chapter 50**), the claimant gives an implied undertaking not to use items seized under a search order for any collateral purposes. The court may sanction a relaxation of this undertaking in a proper case. The leading case is *Crest Homes plc v Marks* [1987] AC 829. In 1984 the claimant brought a claim against the defendant seeking injunctions to restrain breach of copyright in certain house designs. In the course of that claim a search order was obtained and executed. In 1985 the claimant commenced a second copyright claim against the defendant in relation to another house design, and obtained and executed a second search order. Some of the documents seized under the second search order were alleged by the claimant to show the defendant had not given full disclosure under the first search order. The claimant therefore sought to use those documents in contempt proceedings in relation to the first search order. The House of Lords held that although there were technically two separate actions, in substance they were a single set of proceedings. As the defendant would suffer no injustice by lifting the implied undertaking, permission was given to allow the claimant to use the documents in the contempt proceedings.

Chapter 40 Interim Delivery Up of Goods

INTRODUCTION

An order for the interim delivery up of goods operates in a similar way to freezing injunctions, but instead of merely restraining the defendant from disposing of or otherwise dealing with the goods covered by the order, actually requires the defendant to deliver up the goods to the claimant or someone else specified in the order. In the primary legislation the term used is 'delivery up' (see **40.2**), whereas in the CPR it is 'giving up' (see **40.3**). In this chapter 'delivery up' will be used. These orders are only available in proceedings for wrongful interference with goods. **40.1**

Commentary

JURISDICTION

The jurisdiction to make orders for interim delivery up is conferred by the Torts (Interference with Goods) Act 1977, s. 4, which provides: **40.2**

(1) In this section 'proceedings' means proceedings for wrongful interference.
(2) On the application of any person in accordance with rules of court, the High Court shall, in such circumstances as may be specified in the rules, have power to make an order providing for the delivery up of any goods which are or may become the subject matter of subsequent proceedings in the court, or as to which any question may arise in proceedings.
(3) Delivery shall be, as the order may provide, to the claimant or to a person appointed by the court for the purpose, and shall be on such terms and conditions as may be specified in the order.

By the Torts (Interference with Goods) Act 1977, s. 4(5), orders under s. 4 can be made in county court claims on the same basis as equivalent orders in the High Court. The power to make s. 4 orders is listed among the interim remedies available to the court under **CPR, r. 25.1(1)(e)**.

'Wrongful interference', for the purpose of the Torts (Interference with Goods) Act 1977, s. 4(1), is defined by s. 1 to mean:

(a) conversion of goods (a claim in conversion is expanded by s. 2(2) to cover the loss or destruction of goods which a bailee has allowed to happen in breach of his duty to his bailor, to balance the abolition of detinue, see (d) below);
(b) trespass to goods;
(c) negligence so far as it results in damage to goods or to an interest in goods; and
(d) any other tort so far as it results in damage to goods or to an interest in goods (but the tort of detinue was abolished by s. 2(1)).

By the Torts (Interference with Goods) Act 1977, s. 14, for the purposes of the Act the term 'goods' includes all chattels personal other than things in action and money.

PROCEDURE

Among the interim remedies listed in **CPR, r. 25.1**, is an interim order permitting a party seeking to recover personal property to pay money into court pending the outcome of the case, and **40.3** directing that if this is done, the property shall be given up to the party (**r. 25.1(1)(m)**). The procedure in **Part 23**, should be followed on making an application under the Torts (Interference with Goods) Act 1977, s. 4 (see **chapter 32** and **procedural checklist 20** at the front of the book). An application notice in form N244 should be issued seeking delivery up of the goods, which must be specified, usually in a schedule to the application notice. It is not uncommon to combine the application with requests for orders for the detention, custody or preservation of the goods under **CPR, r. 25.1(1)(c)**, in the alternative. The application will need to be supported by written evidence (**r. 25.3(2)**).

Usually, applications for the interim delivery up of goods will be made on notice in the course of pending proceedings. However, if the case is of an urgent nature, the application may be made before the claim form is issued (as recognised in the Torts (Interference with Goods) Act 1977, s. 4(2) itself). If there is reason to believe the defendant may destroy or otherwise dispose of the goods if notice is given, the application may be made without giving notice, but the need for this will have to be justified in the evidence in support, and the usual duty of full and frank disclosure will apply to any application without notice.

Hearings for orders for interim delivery up of goods are usually dealt with by masters and district judges (see **CPR, r. 2.4**, and **PD 2B**). However, if the order will require permission to enter land, it is submitted that the hearing should be dealt with by a judge, as is required by **PD 2B, para. 2.1**, in the case of other types of interim orders involving entry on to land.

PRINCIPLES

40.4 A court considering an application for interim delivery up must first decide whether the goods are or may become the subject matter of proceedings for wrongful interference with goods (see **40.2**), and then consider whether to exercise its discretion to make the order. All that is required at the first stage is an arguable case. In *Pattihis v Jackson* [2002] EWHC 2480 (QB), LTL 22/11/2002, an assistant solicitor left his employment with the claimant to work for the second defendant, taking with him a large number of the claimant's client files. It was held that the second defendant had converted the files when it failed to return them by the third day after receiving a request for their return.

Once it is established that there is an arguable case for one of the forms of wrongful interference with goods, the court has a discretion whether to make an interim delivery-up order. There is no need to show that there is an urgent need for the order, or that there might be a danger or risk that the goods might be lost or destroyed if the order is not made (*Howard E. Perry and Co. Ltd v British Railways Board* [1980] 1 WLR 1375). However, the order may be refused in the court's discretion where there would be no grounds for making an order for specific delivery (for which, see the Torts (Interference with Goods) Act 1977, s. 3, and **4.13**), because the order in effect gives an advance order for specific delivery (*Howard E. Perry and Co. Ltd v British Railways Board*).

The discretion is exercised by the balancing of considerations from each side (*Howard E. Perry and Co. Ltd v British Railways Board*).

If the order is refused, the court may make an order for the detention or preservation of the goods, falling short of delivery up, if the application includes this in the alternative. Normally, orders in this form are very readily made, as there are usually few reasons why the subject matter of the claim should not be preserved so it can be available at the trial. Countervailing considerations may be that the defendant has some legitimate reason for selling the goods for business reasons or because the goods are of a perishable nature.

Solicitors' and accountants' liens

The court will not usually order the delivery up of documents over which an accountant or solicitor is asserting a lien for unpaid fees, but it has a discretion to do so, particularly where there is a lack of evidence in support of the work alleged to have been done and which is said to give rise to the lien (*Thaper v Singh* 1987 FLR 369). **40.5**

If a solicitor discharges himself, it is clear there is jurisdiction to make an order under **CPR, r. 25.1(1)(m)**, for the delivery up of the client's papers (*Ismail v Richards Butler* [1996] QB 711, where the client was required to pay the full amount of the solicitor's fees into court). The order should be limited to documents which are the property of the applicant. It will not include memoranda, calculations, draft plans and other documents which a professional person has prepared to assist in carrying out his professional duties (*Gwelhayl Ltd v Midas Construction Ltd* [2008] EWHC 2316 (TCC), [2008] CILL 2637). In *Paragon Finance plc v Rosling King* (2000) LTL 26/5/2000, where the client terminated the retainer, the court refused the order in the exercise of its discretion.

THE ORDER

The order may provide for delivery up to the claimant or to anyone else appointed by the court for the purpose (Torts (Interference with Goods) Act 1977, s. 4(3)). The order may have to make provision for how delivery up is to be effected, and whether the claimant is to be allowed to collect the goods himself. The court must consider whether to include in the order similar provisions to those specified in **PD 25A, paras 5.1** to **5.3** (ordinary injunctions) and **paras 7.1** to **7.11** (search orders) for the benefit or protection of the parties (**PD 25A, para. 8.2**). Suitable provisions may well include undertakings in damages, and provisions dealing with the listing, insurance and custody of the goods to be delivered up. The order should provide that the applicant must pay money into court pending the outcome of the proceedings, and direct that if he does so, the property shall be given up to him (**CPR, r. 25.1(1)(m)**). **40.6**

HYBRID DELIVERY-UP ORDERS

According to the Court of Appeal in *CBS United Kingdom Ltd v Lambert* [1983] Ch 37, the court has a power deriving from either its inherent jurisdiction or from the Senior Courts Act 1981, s. 37(1), to order the interim delivery up of assets as an adjunct to a freezing order. The defendant had admitted his involvement in the large-scale counterfeiting of musical recordings, and the evidence pointed to the defendant having deliberately put the proceeds of his activities into easily disposable chattels such as expensive motor cars. It was held to be a clear case for ordering delivery up of his assets. A number of guidelines were laid down for this type of order: **40.7**

(a) There should be clear evidence that the defendant is likely, unless restrained by order, to dispose of or otherwise deal with the goods in order to deprive the claimant of the fruits of any judgment which may be obtained. The court will be slow to order the delivery up of property belonging to the defendant unless there is some evidence or inference that the property has been acquired as a result of the defendant's alleged wrongdoing.
(b) No order should be made for the delivery up of a defendant's clothes, bedding, furnishings, tools of his trade, farm implements, livestock or machinery (including motor vehicles) or stock-in-trade which it is likely that the defendant uses for the purposes of a lawful business. However, furnishings consisting of *objets d'art* of substantial value which the evidence indicates were bought with the fruits of the wrongdoing may be included in the order.

Commentary

(c) The order should specify as clearly as possible the goods or classes of goods to be delivered up. If the claimant is unable to identify the goods in question, that points towards refusing an order.
(d) The order must not authorise the claimant to enter the defendant's premises or to seize the defendant's property save with the defendant's permission.
(e) The order should not require delivery up to anyone other than the claimant's solicitor or a receiver appointed by the court. The court will need to be satisfied that the claimant's solicitor, if to be the person taking possession of the goods, has facilities for suitable safe custody.
(f) Suitable safeguards should be built into the order for the protection of the defendant along the lines of freezing injunctions. These will include an undertaking in damages, and provision for the defendant's living expenses.
(g) The order should give the defendant liberty to apply to stay, vary or discharge the order.

Chapter 41 Inspection of Property

INTRODUCTION

By **CPR, r. 25.1(1)(c)**, the High Court and county courts have powers to make orders, on the application of one party to proceedings, for the inspection and preservation of property in the possession of another party. There are ancillary powers to authorise the taking of samples, and conducting experiments on and with property in the possession of the other party. There is a further power to authorise entry on to any land or building in the possession of the other party where the property that needs to be inspected is located (**r. 25.1(1)(d)**). These powers are useful for ensuring that the subject matter of the claim is still in existence when the proceedings reach trial. They are also used to give all sides a fair and proper opportunity to obtain informed expert evidence relevant to the issues in the claim. For example, in a claim arising out of an accident at work it may be necessary for the claimant's engineering expert to be able to inspect and test the machinery involved in the accident, which is likely to be located in the defendant's premises. In a claim arising out of the sale of goods it may be necessary for the seller's expert to take a sample of the goods in question and to test them or comment on their quality, and the goods may well be in the possession of the buyer. In a claim for negligence against a valuer the defendant's expert will almost inevitably have to inspect the claimant's property for the purposes of considering both liability and quantum. **41.1**

The most usual situation arises where the property that needs to be inspected is in the possession of an opposite party, and the request for inspection arises during the course of proceedings. However, the rules also make provision for inspection (and related orders) before the claim is issued, and for orders for inspection against persons who are not parties to the proceedings.

When making an order for the preservation of property the court must consider whether to include in the order similar provisions to those specified in **PD 25A, paras 5.1** to **5.3** (ordinary injunctions) and **paras 7.1** to **7.11** (search orders) for the benefit or protection of the parties (**PD 25A, para. 8.2**). Suitable provisions are likely to include undertakings in damages, and provisions dealing with the listing, insurance and custody of the property to be preserved.

INSPECTION DURING THE COURSE OF PROCEEDINGS AGAINST A PARTY

CPR, r. 25.1(1)(c), provides that the courts have power to make orders for: **41.2**

(a) the detention, custody or preservation of relevant property (for the purpose of ensuring that the property is still available at trial); and

(b) the inspection of, taking samples of, carrying out of experiments on or with relevant property (for the purpose of ensuring that experts can provide informed evidence at the trial, and to ensure fairness to both sides).

The order may include authority to enter land in the possession of a party to the proceedings for any of these purposes (**r. 25.1(1)(d)**).

Detention and preservation orders are usually sought where there is some risk that the other side may deliberately or accidentally get rid of the property before trial. If there is some risk, the order should be made quite readily as, unless there is some legitimate reason for the party with possession of the property wishing to sell it or use it up, justice points strongly towards it being preserved for the purposes of the proceedings.

Regarding orders for inspection etc., it is usually unarguably in the interests of justice and in accordance with the overriding objective for such orders to be made. It is usual, given the requirement of cooperation (**r. 1.3**), for the parties to seek consent to any necessary inspections before resorting to the assistance of the court. An order should only be sought if the other side do not respond in a reasonable time, or refuse their consent, or insist on unreasonable conditions.

Meaning of 'property'

41.3 'Relevant property' for the purposes of **CPR, r. 25.1(1)(c)**, means property which is the subject of a claim, or as to which any question may arise in a claim (**r. 25.1(2)**). It covers land and physical items and processes which might need to be preserved, inspected, sampled or experimented upon for the purposes of the litigation. An identified fund or money subject to a trust might be 'property' for this purpose if it is the subject matter of the claim, but money claimed by way of damages, compensation or debt is not (*Sports Network Ltd v Calzaghe* [2008] EWHC 2566 (QB), LTL 3/11/2008 at [49] to [51]). Before the introduction of the CPR it was held that the rules allowing inspection of 'property' did not extend to inspecting the defendant's manufacturing process (*Tudor Accumulator Co. Ltd v China Mutual Steam Navigation Co. Ltd* [1930] WN 200). Nevertheless, under the old system it was held that there was inherent jurisdiction to make such an order (*Ash v Buxted Poultry Ltd* (1989) *The Times*, 29 November 1989). Technical limitations like those identified in *Tudor Accumulator Co. Ltd v China Mutual Co.* are precisely the sorts of restrictions the CPR were intended to sweep away, and inspection of a manufacturing process is almost certainly included within the meaning of 'relevant property' as set out in **r. 25.1(2)**. In *Huddleston v Control Risks Information Services Ltd* [1987] 1 WLR 701 (a case on the related pre-action procedure in the Senior Courts Act 1981, s. 33(1), discussed at **41.6**) it was held that a document could be an item of 'property' for these purposes, but whether it was depended on whether the application sought inspection or detention of the physical document. If the application in substance sought the disclosure of the information recorded on the document, it was a disclosure application (for which, see **chapter 50**) rather than an application relating to 'property'.

Payment into court or securing a specified fund

41.4 The court can make an interim order that a specified fund be paid into court or otherwise secured (**CPR, r. 25.1(1)(l)**). This power is limited to money which forms all or part of a 'specified fund'. This phrase is not a term of art, and is capable of a number of meanings depending on the context. It can include the proceeds from the sale of property, but an order may only be appropriate if the claimant has a proprietary interest in those proceeds. The power cannot be used to order the payment into court of a sum merely representing a debt owed to the claimant (*Myers v Design Inc. (International) Ltd* [2003] EWHC 103 (Ch), [2003] 1 WLR 1642). The opposite conclusion was reached in *Sports Network Ltd v Calzaghe* [2008] EWHC 2566 QB), LTL 3/11/2008 at [53], relying on *Polly Peck International plc v Nadir (No. 2)* [1992] 4 All ER 769.

An order can be made where the claimant establishes a serious issue to be tried on the merits, and if the balance of convenience favours granting the order (*Sports Network Ltd v Calzaghe* at [53]).

Procedure on applications for inspection etc. during proceedings

Where an order for the preservation, detention or inspection of relevant property is required, the proper time for seeking it is at the track allocation stage, if the need for the order can be identified at that time. If so, the terms of the order sought should be provided to the court in the form of a draft order and sent to the court with the directions questionnaire (see **PD 26, para. 2.2(3)(d); PD 28, paras 3.4** and **3.5; PD 29, para. 4.7**). The parties should seek to agree suitable directions, but failing that, the minimum is that the party seeking inspection etc. should send details of the proposed orders to the other side no later than the time the questionnaire is sent to the court. **41.5**

There are cases where the need for preservation, detention or inspection orders only becomes apparent at a later stage. If so, the application should be made at a case management conference or pre-trial review or other hearing, and having a hearing just for this purpose is a last resort. In the latter situation an application notice in form N244 will need to be issued. If a hearing is necessary because of the default of a party, sanctions may be imposed (**PD 28, para. 2.3; PD 29, para. 3.6**).

Written evidence in support is required unless the court otherwise orders (**CPR, r. 25.3(2)**). There will be some cases where the need for the order is so self-evident that no evidence is required.

Generally, these orders may be granted by a master or district judge. However, where the order seeks authorisation of entry on to land to recover, inspect or sample property, it must be made to a judge (**PD 2B, para. 2.3**).

INSPECTION BEFORE COMMENCEMENT OF PROCEEDINGS

There is jurisdiction to make orders for the inspection, detention and preservation of relevant property even before proceedings are issued, under the Senior Courts Act 1981, s. 33(1), and the County Courts Act 1984, s. 52(1). The Senior Courts Act 1981, s. 33(1), provides: **41.6**

> On the application of any person in accordance with rules of court, the High Court shall, in such circumstances as may be specified in the rules, have power to make an order providing for any one or more of the following matters, that is to say—
> (a) the inspection, photocopying, preservation, custody and detention of property which appears to the court to be property which may become the subject matter of subsequent proceedings in the High Court, or as to which any question may arise in such proceedings; and
> (b) the taking of samples of any such property as is mentioned in paragraph (a), and the carrying out of any experiment on or with any such property.

The County Courts Act 1984, s. 52(1), is in essentially the same terms, but refers to the power being vested in the county court.

The only condition laid down by the statutory provisions is that an order for inspection etc. must be in respect of 'property which may become the subject matter of subsequent proceedings'. The discussion of what constitutes 'property' in **41.3** also applies for the purposes of these sections. However, the importance of *Huddleston v Control Risks Information Services Ltd* [1987] 1 WLR 701 has all but disappeared since the jurisdiction to make pre-commencement orders for disclosure of documents (see **chapter 50**) was widened by the Civil Procedure

(Modification of Enactments) Order 1998 (SI 1998/2940) to extend these orders to all types of proceedings (and not just personal injuries claims).

There are no other restrictions, apart from the application of the overriding objective. An order may be refused on the grounds of proportionality and saving expense if it is not necessary to obtain the order until after proceedings are issued, or if no attempt has been made to obtain the inspection by consent. Also, it is less likely that the court will be prepared to make an order against someone who is not likely to be a party to the substantive proceedings than a respondent who is the likely opposite party.

Procedure on pre-commencement application for inspection

41.7 The general rules governing applications made before the commencement of proceedings are considered in **chapter 32**, particularly at **32.2** and **32.5**. Pre-commencement inspection orders are applied for by issuing an ordinary application notice in form N244 in the anticipated proceedings, supported by written evidence. **CPR, r. 25.5(2)**, requires the evidence in support of the application to show, if practicable by reference to any statement of case prepared in relation to the anticipated proceedings, that the property:

(a) is or may become the subject matter of such proceedings; or
(b) is relevant to the issues that will arise in relation to such proceedings.

A copy of the application and a copy of the evidence in support must be served on the person against whom the order is sought (**r. 25.5(3)**). If the order is made, the court will probably decide against giving directions requiring a claim to be commenced, as the decision to commence will usually turn on the nature of the evidence gathered from the inspection (see **r. 25.2(3)** and **(4)**).

INSPECTION AGAINST NON-PARTIES

41.8 There is jurisdiction to make orders in pending proceedings for the inspection, detention and preservation of relevant property against persons who are not parties to the substantive claim, under the Senior Courts Act 1981, s. 34(3), and the County Courts Act 1984, s. 53(3). The Senior Courts Act 1981, s. 34(3), provides:

> On the application, in accordance with rules of court, of a party to any proceedings, the High Court shall, in such circumstances as may be specified in the rules, have power to make an order providing for any one or more of the following matters, that is to say—
>
> (a) the inspection, photographing, preservation, custody and detention of property which is not the property of, or in the possession of, any party to the proceedings but which is the subject matter of the proceedings or as to which any question arises in the proceedings;
> (b) the taking of samples of any such property as is mentioned in paragraph (a) and the carrying out of any experiment on or with any such property.

The County Courts Act 1984, s. 53(3), is in essentially the same terms, but refers to the power being vested in the county court. Before amendment by the Civil Procedure (Modification of Enactments) Order 1998 (SI 1998/2940), the provisions applied only to personal injuries claims, but now they cover all types of proceedings.

There are two conditions:

(a) substantive proceedings must have been issued before the application is made; and
(b) the property must be the subject matter of the proceedings, or a question relating to the property must arise in the proceedings. The discussion of what constitutes 'property' in **41.3** also applies for the purposes of these sections.

If the conditions are satisfied, the court has a discretion whether to make the order, which will be exercised in accordance with the overriding objective.

Procedure on application for inspection against a non-party

An order for inspection of property against a non-party is sought by issuing an application notice in form N244 supported by evidence during the course of the proceedings. The fact that such an application is contemplated should be mentioned in further information filed with the directions questionnaire. If possible the application should be made returnable at any case management hearing that may already have been listed. The evidence in support of an application for inspection against a non-party must, by **CPR, r. 25.5(2)**, show, if practicable by reference to any statement of case prepared in relation to the proceedings, that the property in question is the subject matter of the proceedings, or is relevant to the issues that will arise in relation to the proceedings. **41.9**

A copy of the application notice and a copy of the evidence in support must be served on the person against whom the order is sought and every party to the proceedings other than the applicant (**r. 25.5(3)**).

ORDERS FOR SALE AND IN RELATION TO INCOME

Power is conferred on the civil courts by **CPR, r. 25.1(1)(c)(v)** and (vi), to make orders: **41.10**

(a) for the sale of relevant property which is of a perishable nature, or which for any other good reason should be sold quickly; and
(b) for the payment of income from relevant property until the claim is decided.

'Relevant property' means property which is the subject of a claim, or as to which any question may arise in a claim (**r. 25.1(2)**). In *On Demand Information plc v Michael Gerson (Finance) plc* [2002] UKHL 13, [2003] 1 AC 368, an interim order for sale of the subject matter of the proceedings was made under the equivalent provisions of the old rules (RSC, ord. 29, r. 4). The claimants had leased video and editing equipment from the defendants on three-year lease agreements which provided that after expiry of the three-year term the claimants could sell the equipment and retain 95 per cent of the price. The claimants went into receivership, which under the terms of the leases allowed the defendants to terminate the leases. The receiver wished to sell the claimants' business as a going concern, together with the leased equipment, and brought a claim seeking relief from forfeiture (so as to preserve the claimants' right to retain 95 per cent of the proceeds of sale). An interim order was made under what would now be **CPR, r. 25.1(1)(c)(v)**, allowing the equipment to be sold on the ground that there was good reason for it to be sold quickly. At trial it was held that because the equipment had been sold under the interim order, the court no longer had jurisdiction to grant relief from forfeiture, such relief only being available if the relevant asset remained unsold. In the House of Lords it was said that the whole purpose of this type of interim order is to preserve the value of the parties' rights. Once the equipment was sold the proceeds of sale stood in the place of the equipment for the purposes of the litigation, and although relief from forfeiture was no longer possible (because of the sale), the court could still give effect to the respective rights of the parties by formulating an order deciding the proportions in which the parties were entitled to the proceeds of sale.

A party seeking an order under **r. 25.1(1)(c)(v)** or (vi) should issue an application notice in form N244 supported by written evidence. The application should, if possible, be listed with any subsisting pending case management hearing.

Chapter 42 Case Management

INTRODUCTION

42.1 Judicial case management of civil litigation is one of the central planks of the CPR. The *Woolf Report* stressed the idea that ultimate responsibility for the control of litigation should move from the litigants and their advisers to the court. Under the CPR, the legal profession is intended to perform its traditional adversarial role in a managed environment governed by the courts. One of the purposes behind the CPR is to require the parties to focus their efforts on the key issues rather than allowing every issue to be pursued regardless of expense and time. Case management is seen as the principal means by which the judiciary will ensure this happens.

Active case management: *Woolf* and *Jackson*

42.2 As explained by the former Senior Master, Robert Turner in '"Actively": the word that changed the civil courts' in *The Civil Procedure Rules Ten Years On*, ed. Déirdre Dwyer (OUP, 2009), 77–88, including active case management as part of the court's overriding objective effected a revolution in English civil procedure. This single change wrested control of litigation from the parties, and gave it to the judiciary. Instead of judges influencing litigation in a reactive way, under the CPR judges have been expected to intervene in a proactive way. One of the conclusions reached by Sir Rupert Jackson's *Review of Civil Litigation Costs* (2009) was that the revolution had not gone far enough, and an even more radical change of ethos was needed, with judges adopting a robust approach to case management (see *Blackstone's Guide to the Civil Justice Reforms 2013* (OUP), paras 5.01 to 5.06). The change of ethos demands:

(a) a proactive judiciary who engage with the litigation from a very early stage; and
(b) lawyers who are prepared to put aside during the pre-trial stages the adversarial attitudes of the old regime and adopt a cooperative stance with the courts and with their opponents.

Robust case management has three elements:

(a) delivery of effective case management directions by a judge with relevant expertise who is on top of the case;
(b) moving the claim along swiftly to settlement or trial; and
(c) firm enforcement of directions once they are given, applying a 'no nonsense' approach.

Case management and the overriding objective

In exercising their powers to manage cases, the courts seek to secure the overriding objective **42.3**
of ensuring that cases are dealt with justly and at proportionate cost. **CPR, r. 1.1(2)**, provides that this includes ensuring cases are dealt with expeditiously and fairly, allotting to them an appropriate share of the court's resources, and ensuring they are dealt with proportionately bearing in mind factors such as the importance and complexities of the issues and the monetary value of the claim. Conducting litigation expeditiously includes taking steps to enforce compliance with rules, practice directions and court orders (**r. 1.1(2)(f)**).

Rule 1.3, which is discussed at **1.12** and **1.38**, requires the parties to assist the court in furthering the overriding objective. This means that the parties must ensure the court has the information required if effective directions are to be made, and must inform the court of events which may affect directions previously made which cannot be dealt with by the consent of the parties. Examples are case management hearings, permission to call experts, pre-trial checklist dates and the trial date or window. Failure to do so may result in sanctions being imposed, including costs sanctions for any resulting applications and even striking out under **r. 3.4(2)(c)**.

The *Woolf Report*, ch. 1, para. 4, envisaged there would be active case management by the courts, with procedural judges identifying the issues in the case, summarily disposing of some issues and deciding the order in which other issues are to be resolved, fixing timetables for the procedural steps in preparing cases for trial, and limiting evidence, particularly documentary and expert evidence. These ideas are put into effect by **r. 1.4(1)**, which provides that the court must further the overriding objective by actively managing cases. The rule goes on to list 12 methods that may be adopted to achieve this, a number of which adopt the ideas listed at the beginning of this paragraph. It is accordingly intended that procedural judges should be willing to intervene during the early stages of proceedings to ensure that the issues are narrowed, that cases are prepared economically and speedily, and disposed of fairly and without undue delay or expense.

Proportionate case management

To ensure that case management is proportionate the *Woolf Report* envisaged there would be **42.4**
active judicial intervention only in cases which would require and repay it. Basic management, with a fixed timetable and standard procedure, is used wherever possible, on the multi-track as well as on the fast track. Standard directions are laid down for the small claims track (**PD 27, app. A**), fast track (**PD 28, app.**) and multi-track (**CPR, r. 29.1(2)**). Keeping case management proportionate can, however, prove quite difficult, particularly on the multi-track,

or where the parties fail to identify the issues or fail to consider properly the expert evidence required to prove the case. Directions may be given without hearings and by consent (see **32.23** and **32.35**). The CPR give the courts powers to hold five types of procedural hearing (allocation hearings, case management conferences, costs management conferences, pre-trial reviews and hearings under **rr. 28.5(4)** and **(5)** and **29.6(4)**), which, unless kept under control, could result in substantial increases in the use of court resources and expense to the parties. The overall result is that the majority of defended cases proceed between the filing of a defence and trial with directions in a more or less standard form, but tailored to the needs of the particular case.

Recommendations made by Sir Rupert Jackson's *Review of Civil Litigation Costs* (Ministry of Justice, December 2009, the *Jackson Report*) and implemented with effect from 1 April 2013 include:

- measures to assign more cases to designated judges (recommendation 81).
- a menu of standard paragraphs for directions in different types of cases (recommendation 82).
- case management conferences and pre-trial reviews to be more effective, and dealt with on the papers where appropriate (recommendation 83).
- less tolerance of delays, with court monitoring of progress (recommendation 86).
- a standard costs management procedure (recommendation 91, see **chapter 43**).

PROCEDURAL JUDGES

42.5 Case management decisions are generally dealt with by masters for cases proceeding in the Royal Courts of Justice, and by district judges in High Court district registry and county court cases. The governing rule (**CPR, r. 2.4**) in fact gives the courts a great deal of flexibility, allowing performance by any judicial officer, whether a district judge, master or judge, subject to any specific contrary provision in any enactment, rule or practice direction. However, **PD 29, para. 3.10**, says (in relation to multi-track cases) that masters will in general perform case management functions in the Royal Courts of Justice, district judges in district registry matters, and either district judges or circuit judges in county court cases. Much the same is said, in effect, by **PD 2B, para. 1.1**. **PD 2B** enables masters and district judges to deal with all types of application, but with express exceptions set out in the practice direction. Exceptions include most interim injunction applications, and applications affecting the liberty of the subject, which must be dealt with by a High Court or circuit judge. Detailed lists of exceptions can be seen in **para. 3.1** (Queen's Bench Division), **para. 5.1** (Chancery Division) and **paras 8** and **9** (county courts). A county court district judge can deal with interim injunctions (see **para. 8.1**) before allocation where the claim has a monetary limit not exceeding the fast track limit, also in cases where district judges have trial jurisdiction as listed in **para. 11.1**, and under the legislation on protection from harassment and anti-social behaviour (see **chapter 88**).

Cases in the Chancery and Queen's Bench Divisions are assigned to individual masters (**PD 2B, para. 6.1**), although from time to time hearings may be dealt with by other masters or deputies as the circumstances may require, and cases may be transferred from one master to another.

References to circuit judges include recorders and references to masters and district judges include deputies (**PD 2B, para. 1.1**).

TRANSFER TO APPROPRIATE COURT

42.6 The Business Centre at Northampton County Court is the sole court of issue for all non-specialist county court money claims issued under **CPR, Part 7** (**r. 7.10**; **PD 7C**). Designated money claims as defined by **CPR, r. 2.3(1)**, must be started through the County

Court Money Claims Centre, and are issued in Northampton County Court (**PD 7A, para. 4A.1**). There are also detailed rules on the allocation of business between the High Court and county courts (see **11.4**). Subject to these rules, a claimant has a free choice of which court to use when commencing a civil claim. The first case management intervention may be to transfer the case to the most appropriate court. General powers to order transfers can be found in the County Courts Act 1984, ss. 40 to 42. The High Court has unlimited power under s. 40(2) to transfer cases to the county court regardless, in a suitable case, of whether the case is outside the monetary limits of the county court (*National Westminster Bank plc v King* [2008] EWHC 280 (Ch), [2008] Ch 385). An application for a transfer from a county court to a specialist list should be made to the receiving court under **CPR, r. 30.5**, with notice to the relevant county court (*Collins v Drumgold* [2008] EWHC 584 (TCC), [2008] CILL 2585), because transfers to and from specialist lists can only be made by judges dealing with claims in the specialist list (**r. 30.5(2)** and **(3)**). Comments in *Natl Amusements (UK) Ltd v White City (Shepherd Bush) LP* [2009] EWHC 2524 (TCC), [2010] 1 WLR 1181, to the effect that **r. 30.5** gives any division of the High Court jurisdiction to order transfers are too wide, given that **r. 30.5(3)** requires applications for transfers to and from specialist lists to be made to the specialist court. Allocation of cases to Divisions and specialist courts is discussed in **chapter 11**.

Commentary

Automatic transfers

Transfer to home court Where automatic transfer to the preferred county court under **CPR, r. 26.2A**, does not apply (see **42.8(f)**), defended claims for specified sums of money against individuals are automatically transferred to the defendant's home court on receipt by the court of a defence (**CPR, r. 26.2**). A claim for a specified amount of money will also be automatically transferred to the defendant's home court if the defendant is an individual and applies to set aside a default judgment (**r. 13.4(1)**), or if the court is to determine or redetermine the rate of payment following an admission by a defendant who is an individual (**rr. 14.12(2)** and **14.13(3)**). **42.7**

Where the claim is a designated money claim (see **42.8**) for a specified amount and the defendant is an individual, at the 'relevant time':

(a) the claim will be transferred automatically to the defendant's home court, or, where there are two or more defendants who are individuals, to the home court of the defendant who first files a defence (**r. 26.2A(3)**); unless
(b) the defendant specifies another court in their directions questionnaire, in which case the transfer will be to that specified court (**r. 26.2A(5)**).

For this purpose the 'relevant time' is defined by **r. 26.2A(6)**. With the exception of claims for the recovery of taxes and duties, this is when all the parties have filed their directions questionnaires, or any stay ordered by the court or period to attempt settlement through mediation has expired.

A designated money claim will be automatically transferred to the court where the defendant resides or carries on business for the purposes of any application to obtain further information from the judgment debtor and any other form of enforcement (**rr. 71.2(2)(b)(ii)**, **72.3(b)(ii)** and **73.3(2)(e)**; **CCR, ord. 27, r. 3(4)**, in CPR, sch. 2; **PD 70, paras 8.1** to **11.1**).

In county court claims the defendant's home court is the county court for the district in which the defendant resides or carries on business. For High Court claims, the home court is the district registry for the district where the defendant resides or carries on business or, where there is no such registry (such as where the defendant is outside the jurisdiction), the Royal Courts of Justice (**CPR, r. 2.3(1)**).

Transfer to preferred court From 19 March 2012, county court Part 7 money claims are 'designated money claims' if the only remedies sought are either specified or unspecified amounts of money, and the claim is not a specialist claim (**CPR, r. 2.3(1)**). Designated **42.8**

money claims are issued in the County Court Money Claims Centre at Northampton County Court. When such a claim is issued, the claimant is required to specify a 'preferred court' on the claim form to which the proceedings should be transferred if necessary (**r. 2.3**; **PD 7A, para. 4A.2**). A designated money claim will be transferred automatically to the preferred court where:

(a) the claimant files a request for judgment following an order striking out a statement of case where the request includes an amount of money to be decided by the court in accordance with **CPR, r. 3.5** (**r. 3.5A**); or
(b) the claimant files a request for the entry of judgment in default where the request includes an amount of money to be decided by the court in accordance with **rr. 12.4** and **12.5** (**r. 12.5A**); or
(c) the defendant, not being an individual, applies to set aside a default judgment in a claim for a specified amount of money (**r. 13.4(1A)**); or
(d) the claimant files a request for judgment following an admission of liability where the request includes an amount of money to be decided by the court in accordance with **r. 14.6** or **r. 14.7** (**r. 14.7A**); or
(e) the court is to determine or redetermine the rate of payment following an admission by a defendant who is not an individual (**rr. 14.12(2A)** and **14.13(3A)**); or
(f) the defendant is not an individual or the claim is not for a specified amount (**r. 26.2A(1)**, (3) and (4)). Transfer under **r. 26.2A(4)** occurs at the 'relevant time' defined by **r. 26.2A(6)** (see 42.7) and is to the preferred court, unless the claimant specifies another court in his directions questionnaire, in which case the transfer will be to that specified court (**r. 26.2A(5)**).

Discretionary transfers

42.9 Transfers in other cases are governed by **CPR, Part 30**, with criteria for deciding whether to transfer being set out in **r. 30.3(2)**. These criteria include the financial value of the claim, and whether it would be more convenient to try the case in another court. The convenience of the defendant is always a strong factor, because the defendant has not chosen to be sued (*Pepin v Taylor* [2002] EWCA Civ 1522, LTL 10/10/2002). Simply inserting a high value on the claim form does not ensure the claim will not be transferred to a county court (*Kohanzad v Derbyshire Police Authority* [2004] EWCA Civ 1387, LTL 8/10/2004, where the amount was £5 million). For transfers to the Royal Courts of Justice where the Crown is a party, see the Attorney-General's note annexed to **PD 66**.

Guidance was given on the allocation of cases between the county courts and the Technology and Construction Court of the High Court by *West Country Renovations Ltd v McDowell* [2012] EWHC 307 (TCC), [2013] 1 WLR 416. Claims with a value up to £250,000 should usually be commenced in the county court, or will be transferred down if they are commenced in the TCC. The judgment includes a lengthy but non-exhaustive list of exceptions to the general rule. General factors listed by Coulson J in *Collins v Drumgold* [2008] EWHC 584 (TCC), [2008] CILL 2585 were:

(a) whether the dispute arose out of or was connected with a claim of a type set out in **PD 60, para. 2.1**;
(b) the value of the claim and its complexity;
(c) the convenience of the parties;
(d) any costs implications in proceeding in the High Court rather than the county court (sometimes transferring to a specialist list will save costs).

Transfer to civil trial centre

42.10 Cases commenced in courts that are not civil trial centres (such courts are described as 'feeder courts') are considered by a procedural judge when defences are filed. If it appears that the case is suitable for allocation to the multi-track, the district judge will normally make an order allocating the case to the multi-track, will give case management directions, and transfer the claim to a civil trial centre (**PD 26, para. 10.2(5)**). A case may be allocated to the multi-track and be retained in a feeder court, if it is envisaged that there may need to be more than one case management conference and the parties or their legal advisers are located inconveniently far from the designated civil trial centre (**PD 26, para. 10.2(10)**) or where pressure of work in the trial centre has led to the designated civil judge approving retention of the case by the feeder court. If it is not possible to decide whether a case should be allocated to the fast or multi-track, the procedural judge will either hold an allocation hearing at the feeder court, or transfer the case to a civil trial centre for the allocation decision to be made there (**paras 10.2(6)** and **(8)**). Once a case is transferred, a judge will consider the file when it is received at the civil trial centre and give any further directions that appear necessary or desirable (**para. 10.2(9)**).

ALLOCATION

Every defended claim must be allocated to one of the three tracks (small claims track, fast track, multi-track). The underlying purpose is to ensure a proportionate amount of resources is devoted to each case based on its value and complexity. **42.11**

Provisional allocation

With effect from 1 April 2013, under **CPR, r. 26.3(1)**, if a defendant files a defence, a court officer will provisionally decide the track which appears to be most suitable for the claim, and will serve on each party a notice of proposed allocation. **42.12**

The notice of proposed allocation will:

(a) specify any matter to be complied with by the date specified in the notice;
(b) require the parties to file a completed directions questionnaire and serve copies on all other parties;
(c) state the address of the court or the court office to which the directions questionnaire must be returned;
(d) inform the parties how to obtain the directions questionnaire; and
(e) if a case appears suitable for allocation to the fast track or multi-track, require the parties to file proposed directions by the date specified in the notice.

There are three forms of notice of proposed allocation:

(i) N149C, notice of proposed allocation to the small claims track;
(ii) N149A, notice of proposed allocation to the fast track; and
(iii) N149B, notice of proposed allocation to the multi-track.

The effect of **r. 26.3(2)** is that where there are two or more defendants the court will serve the notice of proposed allocation under **r. 26.3(1)** when all the defendants have filed a defence, or when the period for filing the last defence has expired, whichever is the sooner. Where either **r. 14.5** (admission of part of a claim for a specified amount of money) or **r. 15.10** (claimant's notice where the defence is that the money claimed has been paid) applies, **r. 26.3(4)** says the court will not serve the notice of proposed allocation under **r. 26.3(1)** until the claimant has filed a notice requiring the proceedings to continue. Where there is an interim hearing the court has the power to fix a date for filing directions questionnaires and may give other directions (**PD 26, para. 2.4(b)**).

Unrepresented parties

The court will serve unrepresented parties with the appropriate directions questionnaire (**CPR, r. 26.3(1B)**). The time when the court does so may be varied by a practice direction in respect of claims issued by the Production Centre (**r. 26.3(7)**), although at present no such variation has been made in **PD 7C**. **42.13**

Commentary

DIRECTIONS QUESTIONNAIRES

42.14 There are three forms of directions questionnaire:

(a) N180 Directions questionnaire (small claims track);
(b) N181 Directions questionnaire (fast track and multi-track); and
(c) N151 Directions questionnaire (amount to be decided by the court).

The questionnaire asks for details of whether the relevant pre-action protocol procedure was complied with. Unjustified failure to follow the protocol may result in sanctions being imposed (see **8.2** to **8.4**). It also asks whether a stay is sought for settlement (see **42.42**), about possible transfer to another court, for the party's view on the appropriate track for the case, for details about disclosure of electronic documents, experts and factual witnesses, and for details of any contemplated application for summary judgment. It should provide information to enable the judge to gauge the value of the claim, to see how many expert witnesses are required, and how long the trial is likely to take. A costs budget (see **chapter 43**) will have to be filed in accordance with **r. 3.13** if the claim is likely to be allocated to the multi-track. The questionnaire is obviously an important document, and care in completing it will assist the court in deciding whether to transfer the case to a more appropriate venue, on the appropriate track for the case, on the nature of any directions that may be appropriate, and whether a case management conference will be required if the case is allocated to the multi-track. The parties are encouraged to consult one another and cooperate in completing their directions questionnaires, and also in deciding on any additional information, which may include suggested directions (see **42.15**), they may send to the court with their questionnaires (**PD 26, para. 2.3**).

Completion of directions questionnaires

42.15 The parties should consult one another and cooperate in completing the directions questionnaires and giving other information to the court (**PD 26, para. 2.3(1)**). They must try to agree the case management directions which they will invite the court to make (**para. 2.3(2)**). The process of consultation must not delay the filing of the directions questionnaire or, where required, the proposed directions (whether or not agreed) (**para. 2.3(3)**). Specimen directions for multi-track claims should be used where applicable (**CPR, r. 29.1(2)**), and are available on the Ministry of Justice website at: www.justice.gov.uk/courts/procedure-rules/civil.

If a party wishes to give the court further information which is believed to be relevant to allocation or case management it shall be given when the party files the directions questionnaire and must be copied to all other parties (**para. 2.2(1)**). The general rule is that the court will not take such information into account unless the document containing it either confirms that all parties have agreed that the information is correct and that it should be put before the court, or confirms that the party who has sent the document to the court has delivered a copy to all the other parties (**para. 2.2(2)**). Examples of information likely to assist the court are given by **para. 2.2(3)**, and include:

(a) whether any of the parties intends to apply for summary judgment or to strike out or for some other order that might dispose of the case or reduce the amount in dispute or the issues to be decided;
(b) whether any of the parties intends to make an additional claim or to apply to add another party;
(c) information about the steps taken and intended to be taken regarding preparing the evidence for trial; and
(d) suggested case management directions for the case.

FILING DIRECTIONS QUESTIONNAIRES

The date for filing directions questionnaires will be specified in the notice of proposed allocation served by the court under **CPR, r. 26.3(1)**. Once a notice of proposed allocation has been served, by **r. 26.3(6)**: **42.16**

(a) each party must file at court, and serve on all other parties, the relevant directions questionnaire by no later than the date specified in it; and
(b) the date specified will be:
  (i) if the notice relates to the small claims track, at least 14 days; or
  (ii) if the notice relates to the fast track or multi-track, at least 28 days,

  after the date when it is deemed to be served on the party in question.

The parties are not permitted to vary the date for complying with the notice of proposed allocation by agreement (**r. 26.3(6A)**).

Allocation fee

On filing a directions questionnaire the claimant is required to pay a fee, which is £40 if the claim is on the small claims track and has a value exceeding £1,500, and £220 if the claim is on the fast track or multi-track (**CPFO, fee 2.1**). If the court dispenses with the need to file directions questionnaires, the fee is payable within 14 days of the dispatch of the notice of allocation to a track. In cases which are automatically allocated to a track, the fee is payable within 28 days of the filing of the last defence. In claims proceeding only on a counterclaim the fee is payable by the defendant. No fee is payable in a Part 8 claim, or a claim managed under a group litigation order (GLO) or in proceedings in the county court in which the only claim is to recover a sum of money which does not exceed £1,500. Rules on remission and part remission of court fees can be found in **CPFO, sch. 2**. **42.17**

Failing to pay allocation etc. fee

CPR, r. 3.7, provides that claims will be struck out automatically if allocation or listing or hearing fees are not paid after due warning, which the court gives by sending the claimant a form N173. Automatic striking out after due warning also covers non-payment of the issue, allocation, listing and hearing fees for counterclaims, and dishonouring cheques used to pay fees (**rr. 3.7A** and **3.7B**). **PD 3B** says that if a claim is struck out, the court will send the defendant a notice which will explain the effect of **CPR, r. 25.11**, which provides that any interim injunction will cease having any effect after 14 days unless the claimant applies to reinstate the claim. This notice will prompt most defendants to apply for their costs against the defaulting claimant. Once the claim has been struck out the court retains a power to reinstate it (**r. 3.7(7)**), and on such an application the court will apply the criteria set out in **r. 3.9** relating to applications for relief from sanctions (see **chapter** 48). However, any order for reinstatement will be made conditional on either paying the fee or filing evidence of remission or part remission, of the fee (**r. 3.7(7)**). The time limit for payment or filing such evidence is two days from the date of the order if the claimant is present or represented, otherwise seven days from the date of service of the order (**r. 3.7(8)**). **42.18**

Dispensing with directions questionnaires

Where a court hearing takes place (for example, on an application for an interim injunction or for summary judgment under **CPR, Part 24**) before the claim is allocated to a track, the court may at that hearing dispense with the need for the parties to file directions questionnaires, treat the hearing as an allocation hearing, make an order for allocation and give directions for case management (**PD 26, para. 2.4(a)**). **42.19**

Commentary

Cases where directions questionnaires are not used

42.20 Directions questionnaires are not used in Part 8 claims, because these cases are automatically allocated to the multi-track (see **42.25(f)** and Chancery Guide, para. 2.16(3)). Nor are they, in general, used in specialist cases automatically allocated to the multi-track (the types of cases automatically allocated to the multi-track are mentioned at **42.25(g)**, and see, for example, **CPR, r. 60.6**, for claims in the TCC). Each specialist court has its own procedure dealing with case management at the allocation stage. In the TCC, for example, the court will send the parties a case management information sheet and a case management directions form (see **PD 60, para. 8.2** and **app. A** and **B**). In the Commercial Court, within 14 days after service of the defence, the claimant must apply for a case management conference (**PD 58, para. 10.2**). The legal representatives for each party must liaise for the purpose of preparing a short case memorandum and an agreed list of important issues (with a separate section dealing with matters which are common ground between all or some of the parties), and the claimant's solicitors must prepare a case management bundle (**PD 58, para. 10.8**). Seven days before the case management conference each party must file a completed case management information sheet, in the form set out in the Admiralty and Commercial Courts Guide, app. 6, and it is this form that takes the place of the directions questionnaire (**PD 58, para. 10.7**). On the other hand, directions questionnaires are used in Chancery Division cases (Chancery Guide, para. 3.8), although the vast majority will be allocated to the multi-track (para. 2.7).

FAILING TO FILE DIRECTIONS QUESTIONNAIRES

Designated money claims: automatic striking out

42.21 The **CPR, r. 26.3(7A)**, provides that if a claim is a designated money claim and a party does not comply with the notice served under **r. 26.3(1)** by the date specified:

(a) the court will serve a further notice on that party requiring them to comply, within 7 days of service; and
(b) if that party fails to comply with the notice served under subparagraph (a), the party's statement of case will be struck out without further order of the court.

This is not the same as the notorious CCR, ord. 17, r. 11(9), under the pre-CPR rules, in that under **r. 26.3(7A)** there are two reminders from the court before striking out takes effect. However, there are obvious risks of satellite litigation over exactly when automatic striking out under **r. 26.3(7A)** takes effect, and on when it would be appropriate to grant relief from the sanction.

Rule 26.3(7A) is also likely to attract attention over whether it complies with the European Convention on Human Rights, **art. 6(1)**, on two grounds:

(a) whether it is both necessary and a proportionate response to the perceived public need; and
(b) striking out under **r. 26.3(7A)(b)**, without any judicial involvement, may be difficult to justify under the European Convention on Human Rights, **art. 6**.

The answer to these points may be that because striking out under **r. 26.3(7A)**, takes place without a hearing, the defaulting party may apply to set aside or vary the striking out of their statement of case. This is plainly what is assumed by **r. 26.3(10)**, see below. There are a number of problems with this. One is that there is no 'order' under **r. 26.3(7A)**. Striking out takes effect automatically, with no judge making any order, so there is no order to set aside or vary. The wording of **r. 26.3(10)**, although plainly aimed at **r. 26.3(7A)**, does not therefore seem to hit the intended target. Secondly, it is possibly the case that **r. 26.3(10)** is contemplating the *use of the power to set aside* or vary under **r. 3.3(5)**. Again, this depends on the court having made an order on its own initiative (**r. 3.3(4)**). For similar reasons, the jurisdiction to set aside or vary under **r. 23.10** does not readily apply, partly because there is no prior interim application under **Part 23** when **r. 26.3(7A)** comes into operation, and partly because there is no order by a judge, just automatic striking out.

Where striking out occurs under **r. 26.3(7A)**, the more natural approach for the defaulting party is to apply for relief from sanctions under **r. 3.9**. As discussed in **chapter 48**, a defaulting party is unlikely to meet with a tolerant response from the court.

By the amended **r. 26.3(10)**, where an order has been made under **r. 26.3(7A)(b)**, a party who was in default will not normally be entitled to an order for the costs of any application to set aside or vary that order nor of attending any case management conference and will, unless the court thinks it unjust to do so, be ordered to pay the costs that the default caused to any other party.

Non-designated money claims: default in filing directions questionnaire

From 1 April 2013, **CPR, r. 26.3(8)**, provides that if a claim is not a designated money claim and a party does not comply with the notice served under **r. 26.3(1)** by the date specified, the court will make such order as it considers appropriate, including: **42.22**

(a) an order for directions;
(b) an order striking out the claim;
(c) an order striking out the defence and entering judgment; or
(d) listing the case for a case management conference.

As with designated money claims, where an order has been made under **r. 26.3(8)**, a party who was in default will not normally be entitled to an order for the costs of any application to set aside or vary that order nor of attending any case management conference and will, unless the court thinks it unjust to do so, be ordered to pay the costs that the default caused to any other party (**r. 26.3(10)**). The court will almost certainly order the costs of the hearing to be paid by the party in default on the indemnity basis, usually with a summary assessment of those costs and an order for them to be paid forthwith or within a stated period (**PD 26, para. 6.6(2)**).

Commentary

ALLOCATION HEARING

The court may hold an allocation hearing if it thinks it is necessary (**CPR, r. 26.5(4); PD 26, para. 6.1**). If the solicitors are not local, this is often organised as a telephone hearing. Alternatively, the court may treat any other interim hearing as an allocation hearing, the most likely candidates being applications for summary judgment and interim injunctions. At such a hearing the procedural judge will consider which track will be most suitable for the case, bearing in mind its financial value and the other factors set out at **42.26**, and give suitable case management directions. Consequently, the person attending for the parties should, if possible, be the person responsible for the case. In any event, the representative must be familiar with the case, be able to provide the court with the information it is likely to require, and have sufficient authority to deal with any issues that are likely to arise (**PD 26, para. 6.5**). **42.23**

If an allocation hearing was listed because one of the parties was in default of the requirement to file a directions questionnaire, and that party fails to attend the hearing, the court will usually make an order specifying the steps which that party is required to take, and providing that unless those steps are taken within stated periods of time that party's statement of case will be struck out (**PD 26, para. 6.6(3)**).

Allocation at case management conference

Alternatively, the court may convene a case management conference for the purpose of allocating the claim to a track and for making case management directions. Although it may **42.24** not be the intention in a particular case, often the need to hold an allocation hearing implies that one or more of the parties are in default in relation to directions questionnaires. Listing the case for a case management conference tends to avoid this implication.

Where a case is listed for a case management conference the parties will also need to comply with:

(a) the costs budgeting requirements in most multi-track claims (see **chapter 43**); and
(b) the requirement to serve and file disclosure reports in non-personal injuries multi-track claims (see **chapter 50**).

TRACK ALLOCATION DECISION

42.25 The usual position is that the procedural judge will decide which track to allocate a case to when all parties have filed their directions questionnaires, or when giving directions under **CPR, r. 26.3(8)** (**r. 26.5(1)**, and see **42.22**). There are some additional provisions dealing with track allocation in special cases, as follows:

(a) In cases where there is a stay for settlement (see **42.42**), allocation is dealt with at the end of the period of the stay (**r. 26.5(2)**).
(b) In cases which are automatically transferred, allocation decisions are taken after the transfer takes place and are made by a procedural judge of the destination court.
(c) In cases which could be allocated either to the fast track or to the multi-track, allocation decisions are usually taken in the court where the proceedings are commenced, but occasionally they will be transferred to the appropriate civil trial centre for allocation and directions.
(d) Where a claimant enters a default judgment for an amount of money to be decided by the court or for the value of goods or the amount of interest to be decided by the court, the case will not be 'defended' in that a defence will not have been filed. These cases therefore are not governed by the standard track allocation provisions. Instead, when judgment is entered the court will give any necessary directions and will, if appropriate, allocate the case to one of the three tracks (**r. 12.7(2)(b)**). These cases are considered further at **42.46**.
(e) When judgment is entered for damages to be decided on an admission by the defendant in a claim for money that has not been specified, then, as in (d), the court will give any necessary directions and, if appropriate, allocate the case to one of the three tracks (**r. 14.8**). These cases are also considered at **42.46**.
(f) Part 8 claims are treated as allocated to the multi-track (**r. 8.9(c)**). Nevertheless, the court can allocate a Part 8 claim to a different track when giving directions (see **rr. 8.1(3)** and **8.8(2)** and **PD 8A, para. 8.2**).
(g) Most types of specialist proceedings are treated as allocated to the multi-track. This includes claims in the Commercial Court (**CPR, r. 58.13(1)**), mercantile claims (**r. 59.11(1)**), claims allocated to the Technology and Construction Court (**r. 60.6(1)**), Admiralty Court claims (**r. 61.1(3)**, applying **Part 58**), arbitration claims (**r. 62.7(2)**), claims retained at the Royal Courts of Justice in the Queen's Bench Division (Queen's Bench Guide, para. 6.5.8), claims retained in the Chancery Division (Chancery Guide, para. 2.7), intellectual property claims under **CPR, Part 63** (**r. 63.1(3)**), directors disqualification proceedings (**PD Directors Disqualification Proceedings, para. 2.1**) and insolvency proceedings (Insolvency Rules 1986 (SI 1986/1925), **r. 7.51(2)**)). Proceedings under the Companies Acts are governed by **PD 49A**. This does not expressly refer to track allocation. However, most cases governed by **PD 49A** must be commenced by Part 8 claim form (**PD 49A, para. 5**), and so are allocated to the multi-track by **CPR, r. 8.9(c)**.

ALLOCATION RULES

The primary rules for track allocation are based on the financial value of the claim. Claims with a value up to £10,000 are usually allocated to the small claims track, claims between £10,000 and £25,000 are allocated to the fast track, and claims valued at over £25,000 are allocated to the multi-track. Monetary values for this purpose are calculated disregarding any amount not in dispute, any claim for interest or costs, and also disregarding any allegation of contributory negligence (**CPR, r. 26.8(2)**). It is for the court to assess the financial value of the claim, though it will take into account the way in which the claim is formulated in the particulars of claim and any information given in the directions questionnaire. Any sum for which the defendant does not admit liability is in dispute, but the court will not regard the following as in dispute (**PD 26, para. 7.4**): **42.26**

(a) sums for which summary judgment on a part of a claim has been entered;
(b) any distinct items in the claim for which the defendant has admitted liability; and
(c) any distinct items in the claim which have been agreed between the parties.

Generally claims are allocated in accordance with their financial value, but a claim may be allocated to a track which is not the one normally appropriate to its value if the procedural judge decides that it can be dealt with more justly on that other track, taking into account a number of factors set out in **CPR, r. 26.8** (see 42.31).

Until 1 April 2013 the court had no power to allocate a case to a track lower than that indicated by the claim's financial value unless all the parties consented. **Rule 26.7(3)**, which set this out, was removed from the CPR by the Civil Procedure (Amendment) Rules 2013, r. 7(g). This means that the court can insist on a claim being allocated to a lower track than indicated by its value regardless of the wishes of the parties. It may do so where the claim is a straightforward one and suitable for a lower track despite its financial value. **PD 26, para. 8.1(2)**, says the court will not normally allow more than one day for the hearing of a claim which is allocated to the small claims track even though it has a financial value above the small claims track limits set out in **r. 26.6(2)**. The implication is that if a claim needs more than a day for the hearing, normally it will not be allocated to the small claims track.

Small claims track

The small claims track is intended to provide a proportionate procedure for the most straightforward types of cases, such as consumer disputes, small accident claims, disputes about the ownership of goods, and landlord and tenant cases other than opposed claims under **CPR, Part 56**, disputed claims for possession under **Part 55**, and demotion claims (**PD 26, para. 8.1(1)(c)**). This is the normal track for defended claims with a value not exceeding £10,000 (**CPR, r. 26.6(3)**). **42.27**

Although most claims under £10,000 will end up in the small claims track, the following types of claim will not normally be allocated there even if they have a value under £10,000:

(a) personal injuries cases where the value of the claim for pain, suffering and loss of amenity exceeds £1,000 (**r. 26.6(1)(a)** and **(2)**);
(b) claims by tenants of residential premises seeking orders that their landlords should carry out repairs or other works to the premises where the value of the claim exceeds £1,000 (**r. 26.6(1)(b)**);
(c) claims by residential tenants seeking damages against their landlords for harassment or unlawful eviction (**r. 26.7(4)**); and
(d) claims involving a disputed allegation of dishonesty (**PD 26, para. 8.1(1)(d)**).

Even if the claim is worth less than £10,000 there may be other reasons why it should not be allocated to the small claims track. One relates to expert evidence, which is not allowed in small claims track cases, either by calling an expert at the hearing or simply relying on an expert's report, unless the court gives permission (**CPR, r. 27.5**). Although permission may be granted, there are also severe restrictions on the costs recoverable for expert evidence in small claims track cases, including a limit of £200 for each expert's fees (**PD 27, para. 7.3(2)** and see also **CPR, r. 35.4(3A)** and **(4)**), which may make it unjust for a small case which requires expert evidence to be allocated to the small claims track.

An explanatory note following **PD 26, para. 7.4**, is to the effect that if, in relation to a claim with a value above the small claims limit of £10,000, the defendant makes an admission before allocation reducing the amount in dispute below £10,000, the normal track for the claim will be the small claims track. Where such an admission is made, it may be in the interests of the claimant to apply for judgment on the admission under **CPR, Part 14**, in order to recover costs, although even in such an application recovery of costs will be discretionary (see **r. 44.4(3)**).

If the claim is worth more than £10,000, the parties may consent to it being allocated to the small claims track (**r. 26.7(3)**). However, the court retains control, and may refuse to allocate the case in accordance with the parties' wishes if it feels the case is not suitable for the small claims track (**PD 26, para. 8.1(2)(b)**). For example, it is unlikely to agree to a case being allocated to the small claims track if the hearing is likely to take more than a day (**PD 26, para. 8.1(2)(c)**). If the court agrees with the parties and allocates the case to the small claims track, the small claims track costs provisions apply unless the parties agree that the fast track costs provisions should apply (**CPR, r. 27.14(5)**). Where the parties agree that the fast track costs provisions are to apply, the claim and any appeal will be treated as if it were proceeding on the fast track, except that trial costs are in the discretion of the court (and cannot exceed the amounts set by **r. 45.38**, for which see 71.7) (**r. 27.14(6)**).

Fast track

42.28 The fast track is the normal track for cases broadly falling into the £10,000 to £25,000 bracket, and which can be disposed of by a trial which will not exceed a day. For proceedings issued before 6 April 2009, the upper limit of the fast-track bracket is £15,000 (**CPR, r. 26.6(4)(b)(ii)**), and for claims issued before 1 April 2013 the lower threshold is £5,000.

There are two factors for deciding whether the fast track is the normal track for defended cases that are not allocated to the small claims track. The first factor, financial value (**CPR, r. 26.6(1)** to **(4)**), is to the effect that the following cases will normally be allocated to the fast track:

(a) personal injuries cases with a financial value between £10,000 and £25,000;
(b) personal injuries cases with an overall value under £10,000, but where the damages for pain, suffering and loss of amenity are likely to exceed £1,000;
(c) claims by residential tenants for orders requiring their landlords to carry out repairs or other work to the premises where the financial value of the claim is between £1,000 and £25,000;
(d) claims by residential tenants for damages against their landlords for harassment or unlawful eviction where the financial value of the claim does not exceed £25,000; and
(e) other categories of cases where the financial value of the claim is between £10,000 and £25,000.

The second factor, disposal at trial (**r. 26.6(5)**), is to the effect that cases falling within the normal limits for allocation to the fast track must also be likely to be disposed of by a trial lasting no more than a day, and with oral expert evidence limited to experts in no more than two expert fields and to one expert per party per field of expertise. The possibility that the trial might last longer than a day (which in this context means five hours) is not necessarily a conclusive reason for allocating a case to the multi-track (**PD 26, para. 9.1(3)(c)**), though in practice such cases are almost always so allocated, because on the fast track there will be no costs allowed beyond the first day. The assessment of likely trial length and the nature of the expert evidence necessary usually has to be made in the early stages of the proceedings, although it can arise again on a subsequent application to reallocate the case.

Multi-track

The multi-track is the normal track for claims not falling within the rules in 42.27 and 42.28 for allocation to either the small claims or fast tracks (**CPR, r. 26.6(6)**). Typically these will be cases involving claims exceeding £25,000, and cases worth less than that sum where the trial is likely to exceed a day. Complex and important cases may be allocated to the multi-track even if they have a monetary value below £25,000, see the discretionary factors discussed at 42.31. **42.29**

Claims with no monetary value

Claims with no financial value will be allocated to the track which the procedural judge considers to be most suitable to enable it to be dealt with justly, taking into account the factors discussed at 42.31 (**CPR, r. 26.7(2)**). In these cases the importance of careful completion of the directions questionnaire cannot be overemphasised. **42.30**

Discretionary factors

In addition to the financial value of the claim (if it has one), when deciding which track to allocate it to the court is required to have regard to the following factors (**CPR, r. 26.8**): **42.31**

(a) the nature of the remedy sought;
(b) the likely complexity of the facts, law or evidence;
(c) the number of parties or likely parties;
(d) the value of any counterclaim or other additional claim and the complexity of any matters relating to those claims (the court will not aggregate the sums claimed in the claim, counterclaim and so on, but will generally simply look at the value of the largest of the cross-claims: **PD 26, para. 7.7**). Where a claim with a value under the small claims threshold is allocated to the multi-track because of the alleged value of a counterclaim, the defendant may be penalised in costs if the counterclaim is found to be inflated. See *Peakman v Linbrooke Services Ltd* [2008] EWCA Civ 1239, LTL 13/11/2008, where an order that the defendant should pay 50 per cent of the claimant's costs after allocation was substituted for no order as to costs for this reason;
(e) the amount of oral evidence which may be required;
(f) the importance of the claim to persons who are not parties to the proceedings;
(g) the views expressed by the parties, which will be regarded as important, though not binding on the court (**PD 26, para. 7.5**); and
(h) the circumstances of the parties.

These factors are not exclusive, and the court exercises its discretion taking into account all the circumstances including the nature of the case as disclosed by the statements of case and other relevant information provided by the parties. Complex claims are usually allocated to the multi-track, partly for case management reasons, and partly to ensure they are tried by a sufficiently senior judge. In practice, the following types of cases are allocated to the multi-track even if the amount at stake was within the normal financial value for allocation to the fast track:

(a) cases involving issues of public importance;
(b) test cases;
(c) medical negligence cases; and
(d) cases where there is a right to trial by jury, including deceit cases.

Other professional negligence cases and building cases that fall within the financial parameters of the fast track vary considerably in complexity, and should be allocated to the most suitable track depending on the complexity of each case.

Commentary

From time to time novel issues arise in otherwise fairly usual personal injuries claims which in practice involve considerable case handling complexities. Ultimately it is for the procedural judge to decide on the track allocation for these cases, but it would not be wrong for them to be allocated to the multi-track even if the value of an individual claim is considerably less than £25,000. An example is *Kearsley v Klarfeld* [2005] EWCA Civ 1510, [2006] 2 All ER 303, a low-impact road traffic accident, in which the defendant alleged that the claimant's alleged injuries could not possibly have been caused in a crash where the vehicles were travelling at less than 3 mph.

TRIAL IN THE ROYAL COURTS OF JUSTICE

42.32 In principle only the most important cases should be managed and tried in the Royal Courts of Justice as opposed to another civil trial centre, because only the most important cases justify use of the resources of the Royal Courts of Justice. Thus, in general cases with an estimated value of less than £50,000 will be transferred out of the Royal Courts of Justice to a county court (**PD 29, para. 2.2**). Exceptions are listed in **11.4**.

NOTICE OF ALLOCATION

42.33 After the court has decided on the track to which a case is allocated, it will send a notice of allocation to the parties, together with copies of all relevant directions questionnaires and further information provided by the other parties (**CPR, r. 26.9**). Several forms of notice of allocation have been devised for different circumstances. There are four different forms for cases allocated to the small claims track (N157 to N160), one for the fast track (N154) and one for the multi-track (N155). Each has a space for allocation directions and for the judge's reasons for the allocation decision.

ALLOCATION DIRECTIONS

42.34 The type of directions the court will make at the allocation stage depends on which track the case is allocated to, and the circumstances of the case. Typically the court will make standard directions in small claims track cases (see **chapter 45**). In fast track and multi-track cases it will consider making directions covering disclosure of documents, exchange of witness statements, disclosure of experts' reports and narrowing the expert evidence issues, and listing the claim for trial. There are standard directions for fast track claims in the appendix to **PD 28** and for multi-track claims on the Ministry of Justice website. In multi-track cases the court will also consider whether to convene a case management conference or a pre-trial review. These matters are considered in more detail in **chapters 46** and 47.

Directions and proportionality

42.35 When making directions the court will be astute to apply the overriding objective in all its aspects. It will seek to ensure that the case is prepared properly so that the claim can be determined justly, but it will also seek to avoid unnecessary expense. As discussed more fully in **chapter 43**, the court will have regard to any available costs budgets, and will take into account the costs involved in taking each procedural step, whenever it is making case management decisions (**CPR, r. 3.17(1)**). Information provided by the parties in their costs budgets will be extremely valuable in assessing what steps are required, and in what form, in order to progress the claim in a proportionate manner.

Directions timetables

Where appropriate it will impose timetables, seek to narrow the issues, or use its power under **CPR, r. 32.1**, to control the evidence that is prepared. A trial date or window is often set as part of allocation directions. It gives the parties a target date for the trial, enables witnesses (especially expert witnesses) to be warned at an early stage, and emphasises the fact that the court has control over the timetable. Any party unable to keep to the timetable has to explain to the court why the case may not be ready for the set trial date or window, and should understand that the court may refuse to vacate the date set for the trial unless there are exceptional circumstances (**PD 28, para. 5.4(1); PD 29, para. 7.4(1)**). **CPR, r. 32.1**, gives the court a wide-ranging power to give directions about the issues on which it requires evidence, the nature of the evidence which it requires to decide those issues, and the way in which the evidence is to be placed before the court. The power under the rule may be used to exclude evidence that would otherwise be admissible (**r. 32.1(2)**; *Grobbelaar v Sun Newspapers Ltd* (1999) *The Times*, 12 August 1999). However, it is primarily a case management power designed to enable the court to stop cases getting out of hand (*Post Office Counters Ltd v Mahida* [2003] EWCA Civ 1583, *The Times*, 31 October 2003). See also the more detailed discussion at **49.9**, and compare the power to extend time, discussed at **48.22** to **48.27**. **42.36**

For directions in possession claims by local authorities against Gypsies, see *Hillingdon London Borough Council v Collins* [2008] EWHC 3016 (Admin), LTL 16/12/2008.

DOCKETING

Docketing was defined in the *Jackson Report* as the system of assigning a case to one judge from issue up to and including trial. Under docketing, pre-trial case management deadlines and trial dates are crucial. Once set these dates should stay set (Lord Neuberger, 9th Implementation Lecture, para. 19). They should be moved only if there are exceptional circumstances beyond the control of the parties. This should mean that the parties concentrate on what is essential in preparing a case, with what is inessential not being pursued. The result should be that costs are reduced, and the early identification of the issues should promote early settlements. **42.37**

Having a system for implementing docketing is mainly a matter of court administration and resourcing, and so does not feature in the revisions to the CPR. However, legal representatives should also play a role in identifying cases suitable for docketing, and there may be directions dealing with docketing in individual cases. Normally, small claims and fast track cases will not be suitable for docketing (Lord Neuberger, 9th Implementation Lecture, para. 30). It is likely that in these cases having a single managing judge would increase costs. Docketing is not even right for every multi-track claim. Straightforward multi-track cases are unlikely to benefit from docketing. Generally, it will be the more complex and specialist claims which will be the most suitable for docketing. Complexity for this purpose may be based on the law or the facts. Suitable cases will include many Chancery claims, clinical negligence and complex personal injuries claims. There may be a need to review the position if, for example, a case that initially looked reasonably straightforward develops into something rather more complicated.

Practice in docketed claims

The Admiralty and Commercial Courts Guide contains the following provisions on the assignment of judges to specific cases in section D4, which were amended in the light of the *Jackson Report* to permit more frequent allocation of appropriate cases to designated judges. They may reasonably be regarded as a guide to the approach in other courts: **42.38**

D4.1 An application for the assignment of a designated judge to a case may be made in circumstances where any or all of the following factors [apply]:
i) the size of or complexity of the case,

ii) the fact that it has the potential to give rise to numerous pre-trial applications,
iii) there is a likelihood that specific assignment will give rise to a substantial saving in costs,
iv) the same or similar issues arise in other cases,
v) other case management considerations indicate that assignment to a specific judge at the start of the case, or at some subsequent date, is appropriate.

D4.2 An application for the appointment of a designated judge should be made in writing to the judge in charge of the list at the time of fixing the case management conference. In appropriate cases the court may assign a designated judge regardless of whether an application is made.

D4.3 If an order is made for allocation to a designated judge, the designated judge will preside at all subsequent pre-trial case management conferences and other hearings. Normally all applications in the case, other than applications for an interim payment, will be determined by the designated judge and he will be the trial judge.

D4.4 In all cases the Commercial Court listing office will endeavour to ensure a degree of judicial continuity. To assist in this, where a previous application in the case has been determined by a judge of the Commercial Court whether at a hearing or on paper, the parties should indicate clearly when lodging the papers, the identity of the judge who last considered the matter, so that so far as reasonably practicable, the papers can be placed before that judge.

DIRECT JUDICIAL CONTACT WITH THE PARTIES

42.39 Direct policing of case management directions has been enhanced by the insertion of **CPR, r. 3.1(8)**, with effect from 1 April 2013, which provides that the court may contact the parties from time to time in order to monitor compliance with directions. It also says that the parties must respond promptly to any such enquiries from the court. Perhaps it is not surprising that Sir Rupert Jackson found that experience in overseas jurisdictions suggests that a phone call or email from the court enquiring about progress on a case can have a dramatic effect (5th Implementation Lecture, para 3.3). As Sir Rupert went on to say, securing compliance with directions is far preferable than imposing sanctions for breach.

MAKING USE OF TECHNOLOGY

42.40 The courts are increasingly aware of the savings that can be made by the use of developing technology. In addition to judicial contact with solicitors by telephone or email under **CPR, r. 3.1(8)**, there is provision for holding interim hearings by telephone (see **32.24**). Some documents, particularly draft orders must be submitted to the court by email or on a digital storage device to facilitate production of the formal order. **PD 5C**, which operates in the Admiralty, Commercial and London Mercantile Courts, and the TCC and the Chancery Division of the High Court at the Royal Courts of Justice, provides for the electronic issuing of claim forms and electronic filing of responses, requests for default judgments and subsequent case management (but see **15.55**). On occasion, the court will go even further, such as by allowing evidence to be given by video conferencing (see **58.11**), or by ordering that substantial parts of the documentation be provided in electronic form, supported by hypertext or other links to enable the judge to move rapidly from one document to another. In *Morris v Bank of America National Trust* [2000] 1 All ER 954, the Court of Appeal stressed that use of technology is acceptable only if it will save time or money, and if it will not unfairly prejudice any of the parties.

CHANGING TRACKS

42.41 *After a claim has been allocated* to a track the court may make a subsequent order reallocating it to a different track (**CPR, r. 26.10**). Where a claim was initially allocated to the small claims track, and is later reallocated to another track, the small claims costs restrictions cease to apply from the date of reallocation (**r. 27.15**).

A party who is dissatisfied with an allocation decision may challenge the decision either by appealing up to the next higher court or by making an application back to the judge who made the initial decision (**PD 26, para. 11.1(1)**). Applications should be used where the decision was made without any hearing of which the party was given due notice or if there has been a material change of circumstances. If the party was present, represented or given due notice of the hearing where the decision was made, the only appropriate route is by way of appeal (**PD 26, paras 11.1** and **11.2**).

If an additional claim is issued, it may be necessary to redetermine the most suitable track for the proceedings. Mere issue of an additional claim will not have this effect, but where a defence to an additional claim has been filed the proceedings will be reconsidered by the procedural judge to determine whether the claim should remain on its existing track (particularly in cases on the small claims and fast tracks) and whether there needs to be any adjustment to the timetable. At the same time the procedural judge will consider whether the additional claim should be dealt with separately from the main claim.

When an amendment increases or reduces the amount of a claim, the court may consider reallocating the case to a different case management track. It will only do so if there is a good reason (*Maguire v Molin* [2002] EWCA Civ 1083, [2002] 4 All ER 325). In addition to the factors in **CPR, r. 26.8** (see **42.31**), the amount by which the claim now exceeds the normal limit for the allocated track is a highly relevant consideration. If the new value is substantially above the normal limit, the case will normally need to be reallocated. Another important factor is whether the trial date will be lost as a result of reallocating the claim (perhaps because of the limited trial jurisdiction of district judges, see **PD 2B, para. 11.1**), particularly if the amendment is sought after the trial has started (*Maguire v Molin*, where permission to amend was refused).

Commentary

STAY TO ALLOW FOR SETTLEMENT

One of the court's case management functions is to help the parties to settle the whole or part of the case (**CPR, r. 1.4(2)(f)**), and another is to encourage the parties to use alternative dispute resolution procedures if appropriate, and to facilitate the use of such procedures (**r. 1.4(2)(e)**). Although the court cannot force the parties to use mediation or any other form of ADR, it is part of its function to consider whether the parties should be encouraged to use ADR in an attempt to resolve the dispute. Since the implementation of the Jackson Reforms on 1 April 2013 the expectation of the judiciary is that some form of ADR should have been attempted in every case that goes to trial. Sir Rupert Jackson commented in the 11th implementation lecture that no rule changes were necessary because the courts already have all the powers they need in this area. What was required was a culture change. Recommendations 75 and 76 in the *Jackson Report* are to the effect that practitioners, parties and the judiciary need to be better informed about the range and effectiveness of ADR processes. To this end, as Lord Dyson, MR, explained in January 2013, *The Jackson ADR Handbook*, Blake, Brown and Sime (Oxford: OUP, 2013) was published in April 2013 under the auspices of the Judicial College, the Civil Justice Council and the Civil Mediation Council as a single authoritative handbook explaining ADR clearly, authoritatively and in an accessible way. **42.42**

The strength of the encouragement, if any, given by the judge may affect the decision on costs when the claim is finally determined (see *Halsey v Milton Keynes General NHS Trust* [2004] EWCA Civ 576, [2004] 1 WLR 3002). ADR is discussed in **chapter 73**. A simple ADR direction appears as direction 2 in the basic standard directions for multi-track claims on the Ministry of Justice website. Also useful is the somewhat more sophisticated Ungley order, which originated in clinical dispute claims. This provides:

The parties shall by [a date usually about three months before the trial window opens] consider whether the case is capable of resolution by ADR. If any party considers the case is unsuitable for resolution by ADR that party shall be prepared to justify that decision at the conclusion of the trial, should the trial judge consider that such means of resolution were appropriate, when he is considering the appropriate costs order to make. Such means of ADR as shall be adopted shall be concluded not less than 35 days prior to the trial.

The party considering the case unsuitable for ADR shall, not less than 28 days before the commencement of the trial, file with the court a witness statement, without prejudice save as to costs, giving the reasons upon which they rely for saying that the case is unsuitable. The witness statement shall not be disclosed to the trial judge until the conclusion of the case.

A note to the Ungley order says that 'ADR' includes a round-table conference at which the parties attempt to define and narrow the issues in the case, including those to which expert evidence is directed, early neutral evaluation, mediation and arbitration. The object is to try to reduce the number of cases settled at the door of the court, which are wasteful both of costs and judicial time. Despite the reference to arbitration, in practical terms unless a very contracted procedure is adopted, it will be impossible to arbitrate a dispute in what is effectively a period of less than two months. It is essential that parties use the time efficiently. Giving parties the opportunity to explore settlement of their case is not a good ground for adjourning a fixed date trial (*Fitzroy Robinson Ltd v Mentmore Towers Ltd* [2009] EWHC 3070 (TCC), [2010] CP Rep 15; *Elliott Group Ltd v GECC UK* [2010] EWHC 409 (TCC), LTL 10/3/2010).

The directions questionnaire allows a party to include a request for the proceedings to be stayed while the parties try to settle the case. If all the parties make such a request, the proceedings will be stayed for one month, and the court will notify the parties accordingly (**r. 26.4(2)**). The court may, of its own initiative, direct that the proceedings, either in whole or in part, be stayed for one month, or for such specified period as the court considers appropriate (**CPR, r. 26.4(2A)**). The court has power to extend the stay for such specified period as it thinks appropriate (**r. 26.4(3)**), which it will generally exercise on receipt of a letter from either party confirming that the extension is sought with the agreement of all the parties and giving a reasonable explanation of the steps being taken and the identity of the mediator or expert assisting with the process (**PD 26, para. 3.1(1)**). Extensions will not usually exceed four weeks at a time unless there are clear reasons to justify a longer time. During the period of such a stay the claimant is under a duty to inform the court if a settlement is reached (**CPR, r. 26.4(4)**). If, by the end of the defined period of the stay, the claimant has not told the court that the case has been settled, the court will often seek a report on progress, and will give such directions for the management of the case as it considers appropriate, including allocating it to an appropriate track (**rr. 26.4(5)** and **26.5(2)**).

The periods of stays under the above rules are carefully restricted so as to prevent the procedure being used to secure protracted 'authorised' delays after proceedings are commenced, under the guise of attempting to settle. A substantially longer stay of two years was ordered in *Phillips v Symes* [2006] EWHC 2595 (Ch), LTL 17/10/2006. This order was made pursuant to **r. 1.1** (the overriding objective) and **r. 3.1(2)(m)**, and was made in the context of an extremely expensive piece of litigation with the aim of containing costs and giving the parties time to resolve the dispute.

A complex commercial dispute which could be solved by means going outside the remedies available in a court or in commercial arbitration was particularly suitable for being stayed for the purpose of mediation (*C v RHL* [2005] EWHC 873 (Comm), LTL 12/5/2005).

LIMITING THE ISSUES TO BE TRIED

The court has power under **CPR, r. 32.1**, to give directions limiting the issues on which it wishes to be addressed, and on the evidence that may be adduced at trial on those issues, despite the fact that doing so may result in the exclusion of material that would otherwise be admissible under the law of evidence, and may take this into account when allocating (**PD 26, para. 9.1(3)(b)**). This power should only be exercised in accordance with the overriding objective. This requires that cases must be dealt with justly and fairly, so limiting evidence should not be so intrusive that it prevents either or both parties from proving their cases at trial. In a complex case, the parties should consider whether seeking a determination of the court on limiting the issues to be tried may turn out to be longer and more costly than allowing the case as pleaded to go to trial (*Korea National Insurance Corporation v Allianz Global Corporate and Specialty AG* [2008] EWCA Civ 1355, [2008] 2 CLC 837). In *McPhilemy v Times Newspapers Ltd* [1999] 3 All ER 775 Lord Woolf MR said that the courts' case management powers to restrain excess do not extend to preventing a party from putting forward allegations which are central to its case. That said, it is open to the court to attempt to control how those allegations are litigated with a view to limiting costs. This means that the procedural judge may cut out peripheral matters, or matters having little significant probative value (*Guerrero v Monterrico Metals plc* [2010] EWHC 3228 (QB), LTL 20/12/2010). In a libel claim this may mean that the judge can decide that a plea even of justification is either central or peripheral: it is essentially a matter within the discretion of the procedural judge (*Tancic v Times Newspapers Ltd* (1999) *The Times*, 12 January 2000). The parties should also keep the issues to be tried under review, and should not be unduly penalised (if at all) if they decide not to advance one of a number of points, even at a very late stage (*D. Pride and Partners v Institute for Animal Health* [2009] EWHC 1617 (QB), LTL 14/7/2009). An alternative approach is to separate certain issues for determination as preliminary issues (*GKR Karate UK Ltd v Yorkshire Post Newspapers Ltd* (2000) *The Times*, 9 February 2000). **42.43**

Commentary

CLINICAL CASE MANAGER

Clinical case managers are in some cases appointed to assist a severely injured person to deal with a dispute, typically involving litigation. The cost involved in having a clinical case manager is habitually included in any relevant damages claim. A clinical case manager must act in the best interests of his or her client, the injured person, and owes duties to that person, not to the court (*Wright v Sullivan* [2005] EWCA Civ 656, [2006] 1 WLR 172). This case held that where a clinical case manager attends a conference with legal advisers at which advice is being sought, the client can assert legal professional privilege, which can only be waived by the client. Conversely, where a clinical case manager enters into communications with an expert where obtaining legal advice is not the dominant purpose (see *Waugh v British Railways Board* [1980] AC 521), the occasion is not privileged, and the communications must be disclosed on standard disclosure. **42.44**

TIME APPLICATIONS, IRREGULARITY, THE SLIP RULE, ETC.

The courts possess a range of powers to assist with the just disposal of civil claims, and to deal with cases of procedural default. These powers are: **42.45**

(a) Time applications for extending time for complying with provisions in orders, directions, rules and practice directions under **CPR, r. 3.1(2)(a)**, see **15.40**, **48.23** to **48.28**.
(b) Time applications to abridge time for taking steps in litigation under **r. 3.1(2)(a)**, see **48.23**.

(c) Applications to extend the period of validity of a claim form under **r. 7.6**, see **15.30** to **15.34**.
(d) Miscellaneous case management powers are set out in **rr. 3.1(2)** and **25.1(1)**, see **32.33**.
(e) Applications to cure procedural irregularities under **r. 3.10**, see **15.23**, **15.32** and **48.29**.
(f) The slip rule enabling the correction of slips and errors in orders and judgments under **r. 40.12(1)**, see **37.64**, **63.42**.
(g) Relief from sanctions under **r. 3.9**, see **48.33** to **48.37**.
(h) The form of orders and judgments, see **63.7** to **63.16**.
(i) The requirement that orders and directions imposing time limits must include the time and date by which the step must be taken (**r. 2.9(1)**), see **63.8**.

ASSESSMENT OF DAMAGES CASES

42.46 Cases where judgment is entered for damages to be decided by the court do not fall into the usual pattern of 'defended' cases. In such a case the court will make what is called a 'relevant order', which is defined by **PD 26, para. 12.1(1)**, as meaning any order or judgment which requires the amount of money that has to be paid to be decided by the court. This includes orders that require:

(a) the assessment of damages;
(b) the assessment of interest;
(c) the taking of an account;
(d) the making of an inquiry as to any sum due, but does not include an order for the assessment of costs.

According to **PD 26, para. 12.1(2)**, relevant orders may be made on entry of judgment in default, on entry of judgment on an admission, on the striking out of a statement of case, on a summary judgment application, on the determination of a preliminary issue or on a split trial as to liability, or even by consent or at trial.

When making a relevant order, the court will give directions, which may (**PD 26, para. 12.2(1)**):

(a) list the claim for a disposal hearing (see **42.47**);
(b) allocate or reallocate the claim to a track;
(c) direct the parties to file directions questionnaires by a specified date;
(d) stay the claim while the parties try to settle by ADR or other means.

Stays for settlement are dealt with as described at **42.42**.

The directions given when making a relevant order in a claim which is not stayed for ADR depend, principally, on whether the financial value of the claim is such that the claim would, if defended, be allocated to the small claims track (**PD 26, para. 12.3**). Normally, if a relevant order is made in a claim which would otherwise be a small claim but has not previously been allocated to a track, the court will allocate it to the small claims track and list it for a disposal hearing at which the amount payable will be decided. If the claim is not a small claim and the amount payable appears to be genuinely disputed on substantial grounds, or if the dispute is not suitable to be dealt with at a disposal hearing, the court will allocate the claim to an appropriate track for further hearing (see **42.48**). As a result, most personal injuries claims above the fast-track threshold, where there are arguments about causation or quantum, are allocated to a track rather than being dealt with at a disposal hearing.

Disposal hearings

A disposal hearing of a relevant order is a hearing which will not normally last longer than 30 minutes, but at which the court will decide and give judgment for the amount payable under the relevant order, or will give directions for the future conduct of the proceedings (**PD 26, para. 12.4(1)** and **(2)**). If a claim in which a relevant order has been made is a small claim, the amount payable under the order will normally be decided at a disposal hearing and the court may treat the disposal hearing as a final hearing for the purposes of **CPR, Part 27** (**PD 26, para. 12.4(3)**). **42.47**

The court will not normally hear oral evidence at a disposal hearing (**PD 26, para. 12.4(1)(b)**). Evidence may, unless the court otherwise directs, be adduced under **CPR, r. 32.6** (see **PD 26, para. 12.4(4)**). This means that reliance may be placed on the matters set out in the particulars of claim (provided it is verified by a statement of truth) or by witness statement. The evidence relied upon must be served on the defendant at least three clear days before the disposal hearing.

Where the hearing is likely to exceed 30 minutes, or where the evidence is disputed, the court may allocate the case to a track and give assessment directions.

Assessment directions

If a relevant order is made by consent, the parties should file agreed directions with the draft consent order which they should invite the court to give (**PD 26, para. 12.2(3)**). For other relevant orders, other than those dealt with by stays for settlement or by way of a disposal hearing, the court will give directions, which may include allocating or reallocating the case to a case management track, directing that pre-trial checklists be filed within a stated period of time, and directing that the case be listed for a hearing or a further hearing (**para. 12.2(1)**). Allocating a case to the fast track or multi-track on making a relevant order should only happen if the amount payable is genuinely disputed on grounds that appear to be substantial, or if the dispute is not suitable to be dealt with at a disposal hearing (**para. 12.3**). If a claim has not been allocated to a track, and at the disposal hearing it becomes clear that its value is less than £10,000, in the ordinary case the small claims track costs regime should apply (*Voice and Script International v Alghafar* [2003] EWCA Civ 736, LTL 8/5/2003). **42.48**

Hearing to assess damages

A master or district judge may decide the amount payable under a relevant order irrespective of the financial value of the claim and of the track to which it has been allocated (**PD 26, para. 12.6**). But, when making a relevant order, the court may give directions specifying the level or type of judge who is to deal with the case (**para. 12.2(2)**). The designated circuit judge will from time to time set local guidelines for this purpose based on the value of the claim and the nature of any equitable relief sought. Hearings involving substantial damages or complex issues should usually be directed before a circuit judge or judge (*Sandry v Jones* (2000) *The Times*, 3 August 2000). **42.49**

On an assessment of damages the defendant can raise any point which goes to quantification of the damage, provided that it is not inconsistent with any issue settled by the judgment (*Lunnun v Singh* [1999] CPLR 587). Where judgment for damages to be assessed was entered after the court rejected a defence that the claimant was guilty of gross misconduct disentitling him to any damages, it was still open for the defence to raise mitigation of damages on the assessment (*Pugh v Cantor Fitzgerald International* [2001] CPLR 271).

SUBSEQUENT CASE MANAGEMENT

42.50 Chapters 45, 46 and 47 deal in more detail with the further progress of cases on each of the three case management tracks following allocation. **Figure 42.1** shows the routes which cases may take from either a defence being filed or a 'relevant order' being made, up to the decision to allocate the case to a case management track. **Figure 42.2** shows in broad terms what happens to cases on the three case management tracks from the time they are allocated to a track until trial.

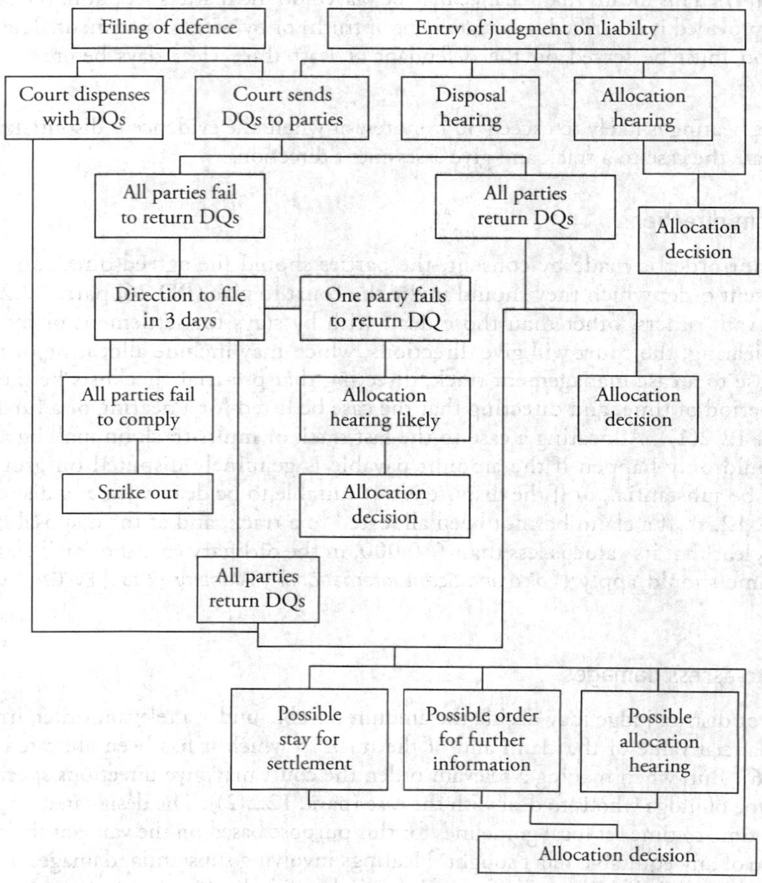

Figure 42.1 Routes to making track allocation decision
DQ = Directions questionnaire

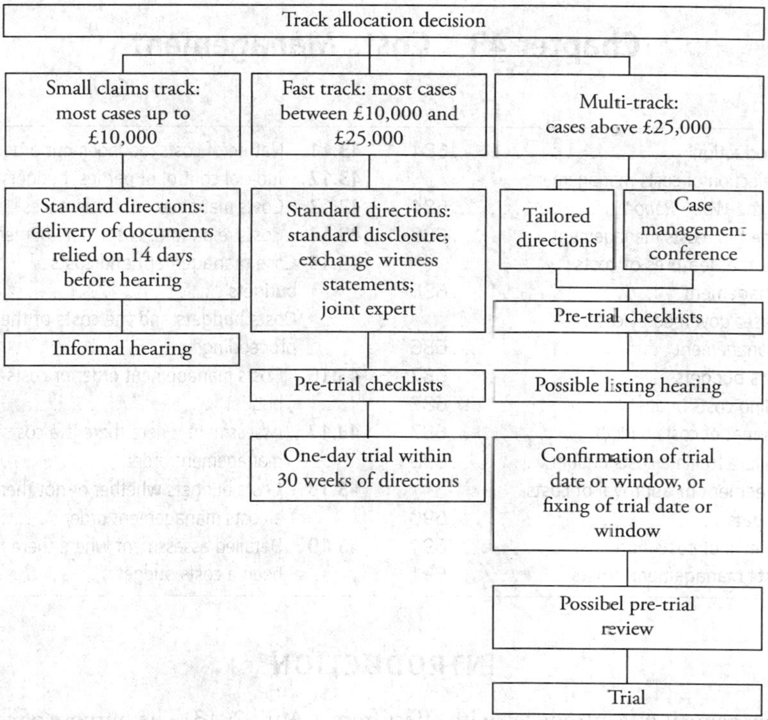

Figure 42.2 The case management tracks

Chapter 43 Costs Management

INTRODUCTION

43.1 Costs management was introduced with effect from 1 April 2013. The purpose of costs management is that the court should manage both the steps to be taken and the costs to be incurred by the parties to any proceedings so as to further the overriding objective (**CPR, r. 3.12(2)**). This is done on the basis of detailed costs budgets prepared by the parties, which are agreed between the parties or approved by the court, and which are used as the basis for making decisions on the proportionate steps needed for preparing the case for trial.

Costs management is the central theme tying together many of the detailed reforms introduced on 1 April 2013. Under the Jackson reforms the courts need to take on an important role in managing costs as a necessary part of case management. As Sir Vivian Ramsey said in the 16th Implementation Lecture: 'It is no longer acceptable for questions of costs to be left to the end of litigation when the costs have been spent. Some control on the expenditure of costs needs to be implemented as part of the case management of cases. That control will now be provided by costs management.'

Rejection of costs management in the *Woolf Report*

43.2 Costs budgeting was considered and rejected by Lord Woolf as part of his review of civil litigation in 1996. Lord Woolf referred to an issues paper by Adrian Zuckerman, which discussed a number of mechanisms for controlling costs in advance, such as budget setting, fixed fees related to value, fixed fees related to procedural activity or a mixture of the two. As stated in para. 17 of the *Woolf Report*:

> The paper occasioned a general outcry from the legal profession. Prospective budget-setting was seen as unworkable, unfair and likely to be abused by the creation of inflated budgets. The ability of judges to be involved in the hard detail of matters such as cost was generally doubted. The imposition of fixed fees, even relating only to *inter partes* costs, was seen as unrealistic and as interference with parties' rights to decide how to instruct their own lawyers. There was widespread concern that these suggestions heralded an attempt to control solicitor and own client costs. The restrictions were generally seen as 'artificial and unworkable'.

Lord Woolf's response was that if budgeting were unacceptable, then the problem of costs would be attacked by case management rather than by orders limiting the expenditure of recoverable costs (Sir Rupert Jackson *Preliminary Report*, ch. 48, para. 3.11).

Need for costs management

Sir Rupert Jackson in 2009 concluded that things had moved forward since 1996 with the development of costs capping and predictable costs (for which see **chapter 44**), and with judges becoming more familiar with the assessment of costs given their involvement in summary assessments and in other ways under the CPR. Introducing costs management is not without its risks. There are two significant negative factors which point against using costs management (*Jackson Report*, ch. 40, para. 7.1): **43.3**

(a) Costs management is an exercise that generates additional costs. It is only worth incurring these additional costs if there are net savings through the better management of the case as a result of the process.
(b) Costs management will impose additional demands on the limited resources of the court.

The counter-argument was first set out in the *Jackson Report* at ch. 40, paras 6.8 and 7.2 as follows:

(a) Litigation is in many instances a 'project', which both parties are pursuing for purely commercial ends.
(b) Any normal project costing thousands (or indeed millions) of pounds would be run on a budget. Litigation should be no different.
(c) The peculiarity of litigation is that at the time when costs are being run up, no one knows who will be paying the bill. There is sometimes the feeling that the more one spends, the more likely it is that the other side will end up paying the bill. This gives rise to a sort of 'arms race'.
(d) Under the present regime, neither party has any effective control over the (potentially recoverable) costs which the other side is running up.
(e) In truth both parties have an interest in controlling total costs within a sensible original budget, because at least one of them will be footing the bill.
(f) The parties' interests may, in truth, be best served if the court (i) controls the level of recoverable costs at each stage of the action, or alternatively (ii) makes less prescriptive orders (e.g. requiring notification when the budget for any stage is being overshot by, say, 20 per cent or more).

While in many cases litigation may be seen as a purely commercial project, it may be objected that in a great many it is not. The model fits well with the approach taken by many businesses, who weigh the expense and time commitment to litigation against its potential benefits. For many other litigants resort to the law is a matter of necessity or compulsion. An injured claimant does not enter litigation for purely commercial reasons, but to obtain the compensation they are entitled to as a matter of law. A business suing on unpaid invoices may do so for commercial purposes, but the main reason is to secure the assistance of the law in enforcing the payment obligations of customers who have not paid.

Point (b) in the list is, however, a compelling reason for having a budget of the anticipated costs of the contemplated litigation. The question remains as to how much time and effort should be devoted to developing and agreeing that budget. The force behind point (b) is that it is only fair to the client to ensure they have the information they need to make informed decisions about whether and how to pursue their legal remedies. Solicitors have professional responsibilities under the SRA Code of Conduct 2011, O 1.12 and O 1.13, and IB 1.14 to provide this form of information to their clients. Costs budgeting and costs management go further, because this information has to be shared with the other parties, and is subject to scrutiny and approval by the court.

Points (c) to (f) are well made. They do provide a justification for the further intervention of the courts, and are to be balanced against the negative factors mentioned above. There is not a great deal said about the second of those factors, the additional demands on court resources, but the *Jackson Report* at ch. 40, para. 7.15 says it is hoped that there will be a saving of judicial time through some cases settling earlier, given the parties' fuller understanding of their exposure on costs, and in more effective control of some of the present excesses of litigation. Research conducted in preparation for the *Jackson Report*, together with the experience gained from costs management pilot schemes in defamation claims (**PD 51D**) and in the Birmingham Mercantile Court and Technology and Construction Court (TCC), led to the conclusion that the benefits outweighed the risks.

The changes will demand new skills from litigators and judges. Costs budgeting involves the ability to assess and estimate the likely costs in a claim in advance, so is a very different discipline from assessing costs after they have been incurred at the end of a case or on a summary assessment at an interim hearing. It is not even purely an exercise in estimating what costs might be incurred in the future. Costs budgets also need to comply with the requirements of reasonableness and proportionality (in **CPR, r. 44.3**). Developing these skills needs to be a key component of continuing training for legal representatives and judges alike.

ESSENTIAL FEATURES OF COSTS MANAGEMENT

43.4 The essential elements of costs management are that:

(a) the parties prepare and exchange litigation budgets or, as the case proceeds, amended budgets;
(b) the court states the extent to which those budgets are approved;
(c) so far as possible, the court manages the case so that it proceeds within the approved budgets; and
(d) at the end of the litigation, the recoverable costs of the winning party are assessed in accordance with the approved budget.

Cases governed by costs management

43.5 Costs management applies by virtue of **CPR, r. 3.12(1)**, to all multi-track cases commenced on or after 1 April 2013 except:

(a) cases in the Admiralty and Commercial Courts;
(b) cases in the Chancery Division where the sum in dispute exceeds £2,000,000 excluding interest and costs; and
(c) cases in the Technology and Construction Court and the Mercantile Court where the sum in dispute exceeds £2,000,000 excluding interest and costs,

unless the proceedings are the subject of fixed costs or scale costs, or the court otherwise orders. **Rule 3.12(1)** continues by saying that costs management also applies to any other proceedings or interim applications where the court so orders.

Excluding the Admiralty and Commercial Courts cases reflects the conclusion in the *Jackson Report*, ch. 40, para. 7.4 that there is no case as yet for costs management in these cases. The exclusion of Chancery Division, the TCC and Mercantile Courts cases exceeding £2,000,000 is designed to prevent forum shopping between these courts and the Commercial Court, which share an element of concurrent jurisdiction. High-value Chancery Division, TCC and Mercantile Court claims are excluded from costs management except where the court so orders (pursuant to directions made under **r. 3.12(1)(b)** and (c) by the Chancellor of the High Court and by the *President of the Queen's Bench Division* on 18 February 2013). Fixed costs are laid down by **CPR, Part 45**, and scale costs apply to cases in a patents county court (**rr. 45.30 to 45.36**).

While the usual position is that costs management under **rr. 3.12** to **3.18** applies only to multi-track claims, the wording of **r. 3.12(1)** permits the court:

(a) to bring other claims, such as fast track claims and high-value Chancery Division, TCC and Mercantile Court claims, into the costs management regime. In fast track claims this is most likely where there are factors which give the court cause for concern, or where the likely costs mean that use of costs management is likely to be cost efficient. Fast track costs will frequently be below £25,000, so costs management in these cases will frequently be based on one-page costs budgets (see **43.7**); and
(b) to exclude costs management from multi-track claims that would normally be the subject of costs management.

COSTS BUDGETS

Filing costs budgets

Unless the court otherwise orders, all parties except litigants in person must file and exchange budgets as required by the rules or as the court otherwise directs (**CPR, r. 3.13**). Each party must do so within 28 days after service of any defence. A litigant in person, even though not required to prepare a budget, must nevertheless be provided with a copy of the budget of any other party (**PD 3E, para. 2.8**). **43.6**

Format of costs budgets

By **PD 3E, para. 1**, unless the court otherwise orders, a budget must be in the form of Precedent H annexed to **PD 3E**. It must be in landscape format with at least 12 point typeface. It requires each side to provide information on time costs and disbursements for the following phases in the litigation: **43.7**

(a) pre-action costs;
(b) issue and statements of case;
(c) case management conference;
(d) disclosure;
(e) witness statements;
(f) expert reports;
(g) pre-trial review;
(h) trial preparation;
(i) trial;
(j) ADR/settlement discussions; and
(k) contingencies, such as unlikely but possible interim applications.

Guidance on allocating costs to these phases is given in the guidance notes on Precedent H issued by the Ministry of Justice, which is reproduced in **figure 43.1**.

Allowance must be made in each phase for advising the client, taking instructions and corresponding with other parties and the court (Guidance Note, para. 2). It may be assumed that the costs to be included in the budget should include the time costs for attendance on the client, and general project and strategy management for each stage. A note to this effect was included in the documentation used on the defamation proceedings cost management scheme, **PD 51D**. The 'contingency' phases should be used for anticipated costs which do not fall into any of the main categories (Guidance Note, para. 3). They include the trial of preliminary issues, and the costs of mediation. In substantial cases, the court may direct that budgets be limited initially to part only of the proceedings and subsequently extended to cover the whole proceedings. In cases where a party's budgeted costs do not exceed £25,000, there is no obligation on that party to complete more than the first page of Precedent H (**PD 3E, para. 1**).

1. This is the form on which you should set out your budget of anticipated costs in accordance with CPR Part 3 and Practice Directions 3E and 3F.
2. This table identifies where within the budget form the various items of work, **in so far as they are required by the circumstances of your case**, should be included. Allowance must be made in each phase for advising the client, taking instructions and corresponding with the other party/parties and the court in respect of matters falling within that phase.

Phase	Includes	Does NOT include
Pre-action	• Pre-Action Protocol correspondence • Investigating the merits of the claim and advising client • Considering ADR, advising on settlement and Part 36 offers • All other steps taken and advice given pre-action	Any work already incurred in relation to any other phase of the budget
Statements of case	• Preparation of Claim Form • Issue and service of proceedings • Preparation of Particulars of Claim, Defence, Reply, including taking instructions, instructing counsel and any necessary investigation • Considering opposing statements of case and advising client • Part 18 requests (request and answer) • Any conferences with counsel primarily • relating to statements of case	Amendments to statements of case (see below)
CMC	• Completion of [Directions Questionnaires] • Arranging a CMC • Preparation of costs budget for first CMC and reviewing opponent's budget • Correspondence with opponents to agree directions and budgets, where possible • Preparation for, and attendance at, the CMC • Finalising the order	Subsequent CMCs
Disclosure	• Obtaining documents from client and advising on disclosure obligations • Reviewing documents for disclosure, preparing disclosure report or questionnaire response and list • Inspection • Reviewing opponent's list and documents, undertaking any appropriate investigations • Correspondence between parties about the scope of disclosure and queries arising • Consulting counsel, so far as appropriate, in relation to disclosure	• Applications for specific disclosure • Applications and requests for third party disclosure
Witness Statements	• Identifying witnesses • Obtaining statements • Preparing witness summaries • Consulting counsel, so far as appropriate, about witness statements • Reviewing opponent's statements and undertaking any appropriate investigations • *Applications for witness summaries*	Arranging for witnesses to attend trial (include in trial preparation)

Expert Reports	• Identifying and engaging suitable expert(s) • Reviewing draft and approving report(s) • Dealing with follow-up questions of experts • Considering opposing experts' reports • Meetings of experts (preparing agenda etc)	• Obtaining permission to adduce expert evidence (include in CMC or as separate application) • Arranging for experts to attend trial (include in trial preparation)
PTR	• [PTR] Bundle • Preparation of updated costs budgets and reviewing opponent's budget • Preparing and agreeing chronology, case summary and dramatis personae (if ordered and not already prepared earlier in case) • Completing and filing pre-trial checklists • Correspondence with opponents to agree directions and costs budgets, if possible • Attendance at the PTR	Assembling and/or copying the bundle (this is not fee earners' work)
Trial Preparation	• Trial bundles • Witness summonses, and arranging for witnesses to attend trial • Any final factual investigations • Supplemental disclosure and statements (if required) • Agreeing brief fee • Any pre trial conferences and advice from Counsel • Pre-trial liaison with witnesses	• Assembling and/or copying the trial bundle (this is not fee earners' work) • Counsel's brief fee and any refreshers
Trial	• Solicitors' attendance at trial • All conferences and other activity outside court hours during the trial • Attendance on witnesses during the trial • Counsel's brief fee and any refreshers • Dealing with draft judgment and related applications	• Preparation for trial • Agreeing brief fee
Settlement	• Settlement negotiations, including Part 36 and other offers and advising the client • Drafting settlement agreement or Tomlin order • Advice to the client on settlement (excluding advice included in the pre-action phase)	Mediation (should be included as a contingency)

3. The 'contingent cost' sections of this form should be used for **anticipated costs** which do not fall within the main categories set out in this form. Examples might be the trial of preliminary issues, a mediation, applications to amend, applications for disclosure against third parties or (in libel cases) applications re meaning. **Costs which are not anticipated** but which become necessary later are dealt with in paragraph 4.7 of the Practice Direction [in fact in **PD 3E, para 2.6**].
4. Any party may apply to the court if it considers that another party is behaving oppressively in seeking to cause the applicant to spend money disproportionately on costs and the court will grant such relief as may be appropriate.

Figure 43.1 Guidance Notes on Precedent H

A costs budget must be dated and verified by a statement of truth signed by a senior legal representative of the party (**PD 22, para. 2.2A**). The form of the statement of truth reflects the indemnity principle (see **71.30**), and is as follows:

The costs stated to have been incurred do not exceed the costs which my client is liable to pay in respect of such work. The future costs stated in this budget are a proper estimate of the reasonable and proportionate costs which my client will incur in this litigation.

Failure to file a costs budget

43.8 Unless the court otherwise orders, any party which fails to file a budget despite being required to do so will be treated as having filed a budget comprising only the applicable court fees (**CPR, r. 3.14**). Unfortunately, this automatic sanction is likely to give rise to a substantial body of satellite litigation. This topic is discussed further at **42.21** in relation to automatic striking out for failure to comply with a notice of proposed allocation under **r. 26.3(7A)(b)**.

A party who is in default of the requirement to file a costs budget will be able to apply under **r. 3.9** for relief from the sanction prescribed by **r. 3.14**. This is done by making an application in accordance with **Part 23** supported by evidence, see **32.12**.

Depriving a successful party of all its costs other than court fees is a draconian penalty for failing to comply with the requirement to file a costs budget. Probably this is intended to ensure that where there is a default an application for relief from the **r. 3.14** sanction is made promptly so that effective costs management can be achieved. If relief is granted it is also necessary to consider the terms to be imposed. In addition to paying the costs of and occasioned by the default, it is suggested that consideration should be given to disallowing all or part of the costs, apart from court fees, from the approved costs budget of the defaulting party for the period of the default. Where the default is persisted in until trial it becomes increasingly difficult to justify giving full relief.

AGREEMENT OR APPROVAL OF COSTS BUDGETS

43.9 The primary position is that costs budgets should be agreed by the parties. If the budgets or parts of the budgets are agreed between all parties, the court will record the extent of such agreement (**PD 3E, para. 2.3**). In so far as the budgets are not agreed, the court will review them and, after making any appropriate revisions, record its approval of the revised budgets (**para. 2.3**). Court approval is a forward-looking process, which deals with future costs yet to be incurred. Accordingly, the court may not approve costs incurred before the date of any budget as part of the costs management process. The court may, however, record its comments on those costs and should take those costs into account when considering the reasonableness and proportionality of all subsequent costs (**para. 2.4**).

Sir Vivian Ramsey has said a court considering disputed costs budgets will look at both the total costs and the overall costs of each stage of the proceedings (16th Implementation Lecture, para. 21). In doing so,

whilst the court will consider the underlying time estimate and applicable rate in reviewing the overall cost of a stage, the court is not embarking on a detailed assessment in advance. In this way there is discouragement of a detailed nit-picking approach which can lead, in itself, to increased costs and satellite issues. Rather, there is encouragement for a lighter approach which considers whether the total budgeted costs of each stage fall within the range of reasonable and proportionate costs for a given case.

The last point is important, because in approving a budget the court will apply the new proportionality test in **r. 44.3(5)** to the costs budget. The judge carrying out costs management will not only scrutinise the reasonableness of each party's budget, but will also stand back and consider whether the total sums on each side are proportionate in accordance with the new definition (*Jackson Report*, ch. 40, para. 7.23). If the total figures are not proportionate, the judge will only approve budget figures for each party which are proportionate. Thereafter both parties, if they choose to press on, will be litigating in part at their own expense, unless the conduct of the paying party results in a more generous assessment of costs.

The court's approval will relate only to the total figures for each phase of the proceedings, although in the course of its review the court may have regard to the constituent elements of each total figure. When reviewing budgets, the court will not undertake a detailed assessment in advance, but rather will consider whether the budgeted costs fall within the range of reasonable and proportionate costs.

After its budget has been approved, each party is required to re-file its budget in the form approved with recast figures, which shall be annexed to the order approving it (**PD 3E, para. 2.7**).

REVIEWS OF COSTS BUDGETS

Each party is required to revise its budget in respect of future costs upwards or downwards, if significant developments in the litigation warrant such revisions (**PD 3E, para. 2.6**). Such amended budgets must be submitted to the other parties for agreement. In default of agreement, the amended budgets have to be submitted to the court, together with a note of (a) the changes made and the reasons for those changes and (b) the objections of any other party. The court may approve, vary or disapprove the revisions, having regard to any significant developments which have occurred since the date when the previous budget was approved or agreed. **43.10**

The onus is on the parties to put forward revised budgets if significant developments in the litigation make this desirable (Sir Vivian Ramsey, 16th Implementation Lecture, para. 22). Solicitors may wish to diarise review dates for this purpose. As with the original budgets, a revised budget should initially be submitted to the other side for approval, and only referred to the court if this is not forthcoming. It may be necessary to hold a costs management conference for this purpose.

Anticipating possible events that will impact on costs estimates, such as unwanted interim applications by the other side, and including them in the original costs budget under 'contingencies', may avoid the need to return to court with revised costs budgets.

COSTS MANAGEMENT ORDERS

Nature of costs management orders

In addition to exercising its other powers, the court may manage the costs to be incurred by any party in any proceedings (**CPR, r. 3.15(1)**). It may do so by making a 'costs management order' (**r. 3.15(2)**). By such order the court will: **43.11**

(a) record the extent to which the budgets are agreed between the parties; or
(b) in respect of budgets or parts of budgets which are not agreed, record the court's approval after making appropriate revisions.

Sir Vivian Ramsey has said that there is a presumption in favour of making a costs management order (16th Implementation Lecture, para. 19). This applies also to cases outside the normal categories covered by **r. 3.12(1)**, because costs management is a necessary adjunct to proper case management and furthering the overriding objective. There will be circumstances, such as an impending mediation, that may justify postponing the decision to make a costs management order (16th Implementation Lecture, para. 18).

Judicial control of parties' budgets

43.12 If a costs management order has been made, the court will thereafter control the parties' budgets in respect of recoverable costs (**CPR, r. 3.15(3)**). The court may set a timetable or give other directions for future reviews of budgets (**PD 3E, para. 2.5**).

Costs management conferences

43.13 The court may convene a hearing which is solely for the purpose of costs management (for example, to approve a revised budget). Such a hearing is referred to as a 'costs management conference' (**CPR, r. 3.16(1)**). Where practicable, costs management conferences should be conducted by telephone or in writing (**r. 3.16(2)**).

Costs relating to costs management

43.14 Ensuring that the costs involved in the process do not themselves add to the problem of excessive litigation costs has always been a concern. Save in exceptional circumstances, **PD 3E, para. 2.2** says:

(a) the recoverable costs of initially completing Precedent H shall not exceed the higher of £1,000 or 1 per cent of the approved budget; and
(b) all other recoverable costs of the budgeting and costs management process shall not exceed 2 per cent of the approved budget.

In so far as such costs exceed these limits they will have to be borne by the client or be absorbed in the firm's overheads.

CASE MANAGEMENT AND COSTS BUDGETS

43.15 The primary purpose for the introduction of costs budgeting is to provide an effective case management tool for judges when considering the directions that are best suited to the case in hand. When making any case management decision, the court will have regard to any available budgets of the parties and will take into account the costs involved in each procedural step (**CPR, r. 3.17(1)**). This is so whether or not a costs budgeting order has been made (**r. 3.17(2)**). This means that in deciding what directions to make, the court will have to consider the costs impact of those steps (16th Implementation Lecture, para. 17).

Examples given by Sir Vivian Ramsey in the 16th Implementation Lecture included:

(a) whether full electronic disclosure will result in disproportionate costs;
(b) whether it is proportionate to have standard disclosure, or whether the costs of more limited disclosure would be more proportionate; and
(c) the impact on costs of expert evidence and witness statements.

COSTS BUDGETS AND THE COSTS OF THE PROCEEDINGS

Costs management order or costs budget

43.16 A two-speed approach is contemplated when assessing costs in claims that are subject to costs management. A distinction is drawn between:

(a) claims where there has been a costs management order. In these cases the court will not depart from the receiving party's costs budget unless there is a good reason to do so; and
(b) claims where there have been costs budgets, but no costs management order. In these cases, a 20 per cent difference between the costs claimed in a detailed assessment and those shown on the budget may result in the excess costs being disallowed.

Assessment where there is a costs management order

In cases where a costs management order has been made, **CPR, r. 3.18**, provides that when assessing costs on the standard basis, the court: **43.17**

(a) will have regard to the receiving party's last approved or agreed budget for each phase of the proceedings; and
(b) will not depart from such approved or agreed budget unless satisfied that there is good reason to do so.

In cases where there is a costs management order the parties will inevitably have filed costs budgets, so the provisions referred to at **43.18** and **43.19** also have to be complied with. Where there has been a costs management order, the need to show a good reason for departing from the budget should reduce the area of dispute on the assessment of costs. In these cases the paying party will have seen and considered the receiving party's budget from an early stage, so there are likely to be fewer disputes than before the Jackson reforms about the amount of costs payable at the end of the process (Sir Vivian Ramsey, 16th Implementation Lecture, para. 24). Where costs budgets have been approved by the court and revised at regular intervals, the receiving party is unlikely to persuade the court that costs incurred in excess of the budget are reasonable and proportionate (*Henry v News Group Newspapers Ltd* [2013] EWCA Civ 19, [2013] CP Rep 20 at [28]).

Costs budgets whether or not there is a costs management order

In cases where costs budgets have been used, but there has been no costs management order, one of the factors the court will have regard to when assessing costs is the receiving party's last approved budget (**CPR, r. 44.4(3)(h)**). This is mandatory. **PD 44, para. 3.4**, goes further, and says that the court has a discretion to have regard to any other budget previously filed by the receiving party. These provisions apply to all assessments, both on the standard basis and on the indemnity basis, and on summary and detailed assessments (**r. 44.4(1)**). Further provisions apply if the costs are being assessed on a detailed assessment (**PD 44, para. 3.2**, see **43.19**). While there is no presumption against departing from the budget (unlike the position where there has been a costs management order, see **43.16**), a 20 per cent discrepancy between the last costs budget and the billed costs may be taken as evidence the costs claimed were unreasonable or disproportionate (**PD 44, para. 3.7**). **43.18**

Detailed assessment where there has been a costs budget

On a detailed assessment (**PD 44, para. 3.2**), if there is a 20 per cent or more difference between the costs claimed by a receiving party and the costs shown in a costs budget filed by that party, the receiving party must provide a statement of the reasons for that difference. If a paying party claims to have reasonably relied on that budget, or if it wishes to rely on the budget to show the costs claimed are unreasonable or disproportionate, the paying party must serve a statement setting out its case in its points of dispute (**para. 3.3**). Where there is a 20 per cent difference and: **43.19**

(a) the court finds that the paying party reasonably relied on the budget, the court may restrict the recoverable costs to such sum as is reasonable for the paying party to pay in the light of that reliance (**para. 3.6**). This is so even if that sum is less than the amount of costs reasonably and proportionately incurred by the paying party; or
(b) the court finds the receiving party has not provided a satisfactory explanation for the difference, the court may regard the difference as evidence that the costs claimed are unreasonable or disproportionate (**para. 3.7**).

Commentary

Chapter 44 Costs capping and costs protection

INTRODUCTION

44.1 The Jackson reforms have moved the provisions on costs capping orders, which limit the amount of costs a party may be ordered to pay to its opponent, from the relative obscurity in CPR, Part 44, to the mainstream of costs management within **Part 3**. These orders will be considered in this chapter, together with a number of other costs protection orders, namely:

(a) *Beddoe* orders;
(b) protective costs orders;
(c) orders made in Aarhus Convention cases; and
(d) costs limitation orders.

Qualified one-way costs shifting is considered in **chapter 69**.

COSTS CAPPING

Nature of costs capping orders

44.2 A costs capping order is an order limiting the amount of future costs (including disbursements) which a party may recover pursuant to an order for costs subsequently made (**CPR, r. 3.19(1)**). For this purpose 'future costs' are those incurred in respect of work done after the date of the costs capping order, but excluding the amount of any additional liability (**r. 3.19(2)**).

PROCEDURE FOR APPLYING FOR A COSTS CAPPING ORDER

44.3 An application for a costs capping order may be made at any stage of the proceedings (**CPR, r. 3.19(5)**), although it should be made as soon as possible and preferably before the first case management hearing (**PD 3F, para. 1.2**). Where a costs capping order is sought in relation to trust funds, notice of the intention to apply for the order must be filed with the first statement of case or (in relation to Part 8 claims) with the evidence (**para. 5.5**). The application is made using the procedure in **CPR, Part 23** (**CPR, r. 3.20(1)**). The application notice must set out whether the order is sought in respect of the costs of the whole proceedings or on a particular issue which is ordered to be tried separately. It must be accompanied by a costs budget supported by a statement of truth setting out the costs incurred by the applicant to date and the likely future costs (**r. 3.20(2); PD 3F, para. 2**; and see **43.7** for costs budgets). Directions may be made for dealing with the application, which may include filing schedules of costs, time estimates and whether the judge should sit with an assessor (**r. 3.20(3)**).

Requirements for making costs capping orders

By **CPR, r. 3.19(5)**, a costs capping order can only be made if: **44.4**

(a) it is in the interests of justice to make the order;
(b) there is a substantial risk that without the order costs will be disproportionately incurred; and
(c) the risk of disproportionate costs cannot be adequately controlled by case management directions and orders or by the detailed assessment of costs.

If these conditions are made out, the court has a discretion whether to make the order, which it exercises taking into account all the circumstances of the case, but in particular (**r. 3.19(6)**):

(i) whether there is a substantial imbalance between the financial positions of the parties;
(ii) whether the costs of determining the amount of the cap are likely to be proportionate to the overall costs of the litigation;
(iii) the stage which the proceedings have reached; and
(iv) the costs which have been incurred to date and the future costs.

Discretion to make costs capping orders

The criteria for making costs capping orders set out in **44.4** demand a restrictive approach, and will be satisfied only in an exceptional case (**PD 3F, para. 1.1**; *Barr v Biffa Waste Services Ltd (No. 2)* [2009] EWHC 2444 (TCC), [2010] 3 Costs LR 317). This is in conflict with the statement in the *Jackson Report* at ch. 40, para. 7.18 that the intention was to remove the requirement for 'exceptional circumstances'. Delay weighs against making the order (**PD 3F, para. 1.2**). **44.5**

Pre-*Jackson* cases were not very consistent on when costs capping orders might be appropriate. In *Smart v East Cheshire NHS Trust* [2003] EWHC 2806 (QB), [2004] 1 Costs LR 124 at [22], Gage J said:

> The court should only consider making a costs cap order in cases where the applicant shows by evidence that there is a real and substantial risk that without such an order costs will be disproportionately or unreasonably incurred; and that this risk may not be managed by conventional case management and a detailed assessment of costs after a trial.

A different approach was adopted in *King v Telegraph Group Ltd* [2004] EWCA Civ 613, [2005] 1 WLR 2282 at [92] by Brooke LJ who said: '...it would be very much better for the court to exercise control over costs in advance, rather than to wait reactively until after the case is over and the costs are being assessed'. This is consistent with cases such as *Solutia UK Ltd v Griffiths* [2001] EWCA Civ 736, [2002] PIQR P16 and *Leigh v Michelin Tyre plc* [2003] EWCA Civ 1766, [2004] 1 WLR 846. The object of the order is to encourage the parties to plan the case in advance so as to ensure that costs are proportionate (*Jefferson v National Freight Carriers plc* [2001] EWCA Civ 2082, [2001] 2 Costs LR 313).

In *Henry v British Broadcasting Corporation* [2005] EWHC 2503 (QB), [2006] 1 All ER 154 a costs capping order was refused because the application was made at a very late stage, close to the trial. One of the reasons given in *Willis v Nicholson* [2007] EWCA Civ 199, [2007] PIQR P22 for refusing a cap beyond limiting the claimant to his latest estimate, rather than by a costs capping order, was a concern about the time and costs that would have been involved in having a costs judge decide what the costs cap should be.

Form of costs capping orders

Costs capping orders are usually drafted to avoid an inflexible cap, while enabling the court to retain control over the amount of costs at any time. Either party may apply to vary the order, which may be allowed only if there has been a material change of circumstances or if there is some other compelling reason why a variation should be allowed (**CPR, r. 3.19(7)**). An **44.6**

Commentary

application to vary is made in accordance with **CPR, Part 23 (r. 3.21)**, and should be supported by evidence and a revised costs budget. **Figure 44.1** is a typical costs capping order.

The future base costs of the [Claimant/Defendant] shall not without the permission of the court exceed the sum of £ (save that any costs awarded in favour of a party on any interim application shall not count towards the said £). Either party may apply without notice to increase the figure of £ and any such application shall be supported by a statement addressing the need for the increase and a revised costs budget calculated to trial.

Figure 44.1 Costs capping order

COSTS PROTECTION

Beddoe orders

44.7 By what is known as a *Beddoe* application, trustees and similar persons may apply to the court in the early stages of litigation for orders that they be indemnified against the costs of and incidental to the claim to be paid out of the trust or other fund. Such an application takes its name from *Re Beddoe* [1893] 1 Ch 547. Such a pre-emptive costs order, made well in advance of the trial, is, of course, of great benefit to trustees who have nothing to gain personally from proceedings, but are under a duty to preserve the funds under their care. Such orders have traditionally been made mainly in favour of trustees and executors, but the discretion is not necessarily restricted to those categories, and orders have been made in favour of a receiver in a company liquidation (*Re Wedstock Realizations Ltd* [1988] BCLC 354) and in favour of employees engaged in hostile litigation against their pension fund trustees (*McDonald v Horn* (1994) *The Times*, 10 August 1994).

A liquidator considering bringing proceedings for wrongful trading, preferences or in respect of transactions at an undervalue is not automatically entitled to the costs of those proceedings from the assets of the company (*Lewis v Commissioner of Inland Revenue* [2001] 3 All ER 499) and should consider making an application for a *Beddoe* order.

Where a derivative claim is made on behalf of a company, or other body capable of suing in its own name, that company or body may be ordered, under **CPR, r. 19.9E**, to indemnify the claimant against liability for costs. This was first established in *Wallersteiner v Moir (No. 2)* [1975] QB 373 and orders indemnifying claimants in derivative claims are sometimes called *Wallersteiner* orders.

Procedure for seeking a *Beddoe* order

44.8 The fact that a pre-emptive costs order is sought must be stated in the claim form (**PD 19C, para.** 2(2)). If an indemnity is also sought for the costs of the application for permission to continue the claim, that must be stated in the permission application (**PD 19C, para.** 2(2)).

Where trustees properly exercise a power vested in them to agree the costs of another party in relation to the administration of a trust there is no need for a court order, and the assessment of the costs can be dealt with under **CPR, r. 46.3**. Where the trustees have no such power, or decide against exercising it, an application will be necessary if a prospective costs order (PCO) is to be made, and Practice Statement (Trust Proceedings: Prospective Costs Orders) [2001] 1 WLR 1082 applies. This sets out a model form of PCO, and provides that in the absence of a dispute as to whether such an order is appropriate most such applications will be dealt with on the papers.

Where the application is made before proceedings are commenced, it is made by application notice in accordance with **CPR, r. 25.2**. Applications made during the course of existing proceedings are also made by application notice. In addition to asking for the indemnity as to costs mentioned above, the application normally also asks for directions whether the applicant should continue or defend the claim, and for any further or other relief. The application, in the usual case, is entirely domestic to the estate or trust concerned, so is often conducted in an informal manner, with material accepted on instructions without formal proof (see *Re Evans* [1986] 1 WLR 101). On the first return day the court may adjourn the application so that letters may be sent to the beneficiaries of the fund informing them of the nature of the application and of their right to file evidence and appear on any further hearing of the application.

Decision whether to make a *Beddoe* order

When the court is considering making a pre-emptive costs order in favour of a person making a derivative claim for the benefit of a company, it is not an inflexible rule that an order will be refused if the company is jointly owned by the claimant and defendant (*Mumbray v Lapper* [2005] EWHC 1152 (Ch), [2005] BCC 990). It is better to say that when considering whether to make such an order the court will take into consideration the effect the order would have on the defendant's interests in the company: it may be unfair that a successful defendant who is not required to pay the unsuccessful claimant's costs should nevertheless have to bear a substantial loss in the value of his shares when the company pays the costs (*Halle v Trax BW Ltd* [2000] BCC 1020). Despite obiter indications to the contrary in *Halle v Trax BW Ltd*, there is no rule that a successful derivative claimant has a lien, on assets recovered in the claim, for costs (*Qayoumi v Oakhouse Property Holdings plc* [2002] EWHC 2547 (Ch), [2003] 1 BCLC 352). **44.9**

A pre-emptive costs order was made in *Re Axa Equity and Life Assurance Society plc (No. 1)* (2000) *The Times*, 19 December 2000, in favour of an objector to a scheme of reorganisation of an insurance business which contained novel provisions and where the presence of the objector was necessary to test that the scheme was fair. Such orders will not be made where the litigation is really a hostile claim by one beneficiary against another (*Trustee Corporation Ltd v Nadir* [2001] BPIR 541). Nor will they be made where the litigation can be of no benefit to the trust (*Weth v Attorney-General* [2001] EWCA Civ 263, LTL 23/2/2001).

Each application depends on its own facts and is essentially a matter for the discretion of the master or judge who hears it. In exercising that discretion the court will take into account the following considerations:

(a) The importance of affording full and proper protection for the costs and expenses of trustees and personal representatives acting properly to protect the fund against adverse claims (*Re Turner* [1907] 2 Ch 126). Conversely, if after trial the court would be unlikely to make an order for payment of the trustee's costs out of the fund it would not be right to make a pre-emptive order (*Re Wedstock Realizations Ltd* [1988] BCLC 354), for example, as in the case of hostile litigation.

(b) The court has to form a view of the prospects of success or failure in the underlying action (*Re Dallaway* [1982] 1 WLR 756). In *National Anti-Vivisection Society Ltd v Duddington* (1989) *The Times*, 23 November 1989, Mummery J said that the fund in dispute should not be used to support contentions which were not made in good faith or on reasonable grounds. Obviously, the court should not be invited to conduct a mini-trial on the merits of the action. A weak claim against the fund would be a powerful reason for making an order in favour of the trustees (*Re Evans* [1986] 1 WLR 101 per Nourse LJ).

(c) A pre-emptive order should not be made if there is a real possibility of it operating unjustly. Where the beneficiaries are all adult, are not incapacitated and can make up their own minds whether the claim should be resisted or not, there must be countervailing considerations of some weight before it is right for the claim to be pursued or defended at the cost of the fund (*Re Evans* [1986] 1 WLR 101).

(d) Occasionally, there may be special factors to be weighed, for example where it is essential for a company administrator to obtain the court's decision because there is a large class of creditors who may be affected by the decision (*Re Exchange Securities and Commodities Ltd (No. 2)* [1985] BCLC 392).

PROTECTIVE COSTS ORDERS

44.10 A PCO is similar to a *Beddoe* order, but:

(a) Under a *Beddoe* order the applicant is given an indemnity for his costs by the company or out of the fund which he is seeking to protect.
(b) Under a PCO the applicant is given an immunity against paying the costs of the defendant. Typically, PCOs are made in judicial review proceedings where the claimant will gain no personal benefit from a successful result.

Procedure for seeking a PCO

44.11 The procedure for seeking a PCO, according to *R (Corner House Research) v Secretary of State for Trade and Industry* [2005] EWCA Civ 192, [2005] 1 WLR 2600, is that:

(a) the claim form should on its face include the claim for the PCO;
(b) if the defendant intends to resist the application, reasons should be set out in the acknowledgment of service under **CPR, r. 54.8**;
(c) a judge will consider the application on the papers (if the order is granted, the defendant has the right to apply to have the order set aside, but has to show compelling reasons to alter the order (*R (Compton) v Wiltshire Primary Care Trust* [2008] EWCA Civ 749, [2009] 1 WLR 1436));
(d) the same procedure applies to appeals to the Court of Appeal (*R (Compton) v Wiltshire Primary Care Trust*) except that any application for a PCO, costs capping order and permission to appeal should all be considered together and on paper (*R (Buglife — The Invertebrate Conservation Trust) v Thurrock Thames Gateway Development Corporation* [2008] EWCA Civ 1209, [2008] NPC 118);
(e) if the order is refused, the applicant can ask for a hearing, which should not exceed one hour;
(f) if a PCO is made, unless the applicant's lawyers are acting pro bono, it will be usual to impose a costs capping order (see **44.2**).

Decision whether to make a PCO

44.12 *R (Corner House Research) v Secretary of State for Trade and Industry* [2005] EWCA Civ 192, [2005] 1 WLR 2600 laid down the following requirements before a PCO can be made:

(a) The issues raised in the claim must be of general public importance. An issue may be of 'general public importance' if it affects a wide community, such as the closure of a unit at an NHS hospital. There is no requirement that the issue has to be of interest to all the public nationally (*R (Compton) v Wiltshire Primary Care Trust* [2008] EWCA Civ 749, [2009] 1 WLR 1436).
(b) The public interest must require the resolution of those issues. It does not necessarily follow that because an issue is of general importance that it is in the public interest to have it resolved (*Goodson v Her Majesty's Coroner for Bedfordshire and Luton* [2005] EWCA Civ 1172, *The Times*, 1 November 2005).
(c) The applicant must have no private interest in the outcome of the case. A disqualifying interest need not be financial. In *Goodson v Her Majesty's Coroner for Bedfordshire and Luton* the applicant was disqualified by her interest in seeking a fresh coroner's inquest into her father's death. *R (England) v Tower Hamlets London Borough Council* [2006] EWCA Civ 1742, LTL 20/12/2006, doubted the workability of requirement (c). The court suggested that to make requirement (c) work it may be necessary to distinguish between *the applicant's* private law interests, which if present would result in the application being refused, and interests which the applicant might share with other members of the public.

(d) Having regard to the financial resources of the applicant and respondent, and to the amount of costs likely to be involved, it must be fair and just to make the order. This is more likely to be satisfied where the applicant's lawyers are acting pro bono.

These requirements have to be adjusted when dealing with an application for a PCO by a respondent in an appeal, see *Weaver v London Quadrant Housing Trust* [2009] EWCA Civ 235, LTL 27/3/2009. Rather than considering the reasonableness of discontinuing, the question is whether the respondent would be acting reasonably in no longer taking part in the appeal.

In *R (Bullmore) v West Hertfordshire Hospitals NHS Trust* [2007] EWCA Civ 609, [2007] 6 Costs LR 844, a PCO was refused on the ground that the case was not sufficiently exceptional. If the PCO is not made, it was said in *R (Corner House Research) v Secretary of State for Trade and Industry* that the applicant may well decide to discontinue at that stage. If he does so, he will almost certainly be acting reasonably (and so should not be penalised in costs). In *R (Ministry of Defence) v Wiltshire and Swindon Coroner* [2005] EWHC 889 (Admin), [2006] 1 WLR 134, it was said that a PCO could in theory be ordered in favour of a defendant in judicial review proceedings. The fact that most such defendants are public bodies means that it is rare that they will need such protection. A reciprocal PCO in favour of the public body is reasonably readily granted once a PCO has been made in favour of the applicant (*R (Medical Justice) v Secretary of State for the Home Department* [2010] EWHC 1425 (Admin), [2010] ACD 70).

Commentary

ENVIRONMENTAL LAW: AARHUS CONVENTION CASES

R (Garner) v Elmbridge Borough Council [2010] EWCA Civ 1006, [2012] PTSR 250 held that where Council Directive 85/337/EEC on the assessment of the effects of certain public and private projects on the environment (the EIA Directive) applies, the established principles governing protected costs orders must be modified to comply with the requirement in art. 10a (implementing the Aarhus Convention) that procedures have to be fair, equitable, timely and not prohibitively expensive. (Following consolidation, Directive 85/337/EEC, art. 10a, is now Directive 2011/92/EU, art. 11). **44.13**

In respect of claims issued on or after 1 April 2013, the usual position in Aarhus Convention claims (as defined in **CPR, r. 45.41**) is that party and party costs orders are limited to the amounts specified by **PD 45, paras 5.1** and **5.2** (see **r. 45.43**). These limits are:

(a) £5,000 against a claimant where the claimant is claiming only as an individual and not as, or on behalf of, a business or other legal person;
(b) £10,000 against a claimant in all other cases; and
(c) £35,000 against a defendant.

To take advantage of these provisions the claimant is required to state in the claim form that the claim is an Aarhus Convention claim (**r. 45.44(1)**). A defendant may object by denying the claim is an Aarhus Convention claim in the acknowledgment of service, setting out the grounds for such denial, after which the court will determine whether the claim is an Aarhus Convention claim at the earliest opportunity (**r. 45.44(2)**). It is also open to the claimant to opt out of the protection given by the Aarhus Convention, such as by simply not stating in the claim form that it is an Aarhus Convention claim (**r. 45.42**).

COSTS LIMITATION ORDERS

There is jurisdiction to make a pre-emptive order limiting the costs an applicant might be ordered to pay the other side if the litigation is unsuccessful (*R v Lord Chancellor, ex parte Child Poverty Action Group* [1999] 1 WLR 347; *R v Hammersmith and Fulham London Borough Council, ex parte Council for the Protection of Rural England, London Branch (No. 2)* [2000] Env LR 544). A party seeking such an order should say so in the claim form (*R (Campaign for Nuclear Disarmament) v Prime Minister of the United* **44.14**

Kingdom [2002] EWHC 2712 (Admin), *The Times*, 27 December 2002). The discretion to make such an order should be exercised only in the most exceptional cases, and where the court is satisfied:

(a) that the issues raised are truly ones of general importance;
(b) that it has sufficient appreciation of the merits of the claim to conclude it is in the public interest to make an order; and
(c) that the respondent has a clearly superior capacity to bear the costs of the proceedings than the applicant.

Chapter 45 Small Claims

INTRODUCTION

The small claims track limit was raised from £5,000 to £10,000 on 1 April 2013. Detailed rules on allocating claims to the small claims track were considered at 42.27. Despite the adjective 'small', the track is of immense significance to the civil justice system. Every year over 55,000 judicial determinations are made of cases in the small claims track representing over 75 per cent of all cases disposed of by way of final hearing. 45.1

The term 'small claim' is unfortunate given that the upper limit of the financial jurisdiction represents a sum which many would consider a large claim. Cases within the small claims track can range from very modest consumer disputes or arguments over dry-cleaning through to technically complex disputes over credit hire and factually complicated disagreements over building extensions. Many small claims relate to road traffic accidents.

The small claims track provides an entirely different type of dispute determination from that offered by the other two tracks. The basic 'no costs' rule positively encourages parties to represent themselves. Pre-hearing preparation is less formal than on the other case management tracks. Standard and menu disclosures do not apply. Witness statements are exchanged on the small claims track only where the nature of the case makes this desirable. There are severe restrictions on the use of expert evidence. At the hearing the district judge may well adopt an interventionist approach designed to elicit the relevant information as quickly and as informally as possible.

For professional legal advisers the challenges are considerable. It is necessary to form a view of the merits of a case very quickly and often on the basis of a paucity of evidence. The client may not wish to incur the cost of legal representation at the hearing; in that case the role of the professional adviser is to advise on the merits of the case, to ensure that the client discloses copies of all the documents on which he intends to rely and to ensure that, if appropriate, the client's case is adequately set out in a witness statement. If necessary, the legal adviser may also assist in the preparation of an expert's report.

The European small claims procedure, which applies to cross-border civil and commercial cases which do not exceed €2,000, is considered at **45.33**.

SUMMARY JUDGMENT IN SMALL VALUE CLAIMS

45.2 It is open to a claimant or defendant to apply for summary judgment (see **chapter 34**). This should normally be done before track allocation (**PD 26, para. 5.3(1)**). If summary judgment is given before allocation in a claim which is otherwise suitable for the small claims track, subject to **CPR, r. 46.13(3)**, the successful party can apply for costs in the ordinary way and is not subject to the rule providing for only modest fixed costs on the small claims track (see **45.28** and **68.34**).

ALLOCATION TO THE SMALL CLAIMS TRACK

Allocation rules

45.3 The rules governing allocation to the small claims track are considered in **chapter 42**, especially at **42.26** and **42.27**.

Remedy claimed

45.4 There is no restriction on the nature of remedies which can be granted on the small claims track (**CPR, r. 27.3**). Thus injunctions, possession, restitution, specific performance and the like are available to the same extent as on the other tracks, though jurisdiction to grant freezing injunctions and search orders is restricted to the High Court (County Court Remedies Regulations 1991 (SI 1991/1222), regs 2 and 3).

DISTINCTIVE FEATURES OF THE SMALL CLAIMS TRACK

45.5 The important differences between small claims and the other tracks are:

(a) Some rules and procedures have no application on the small claims track (see **45.6**).
(b) The procedures after allocation are different (see **45.7** to **45.12**).
(c) Pre-trial checklists are not used on the small claims track.
(d) The procedure at the hearing is different (see **45.14** to **45.26**).
(e) The procedure on appeals (see **45.27**).
(f) Costs provisions are different (see **45.28** to **45.32**).

RESTRICTION ON APPLICATION OF THE CPR

45.6 **CPR, r. 27.2**, provides that on the small claims track the following parts of the CPR do not apply:

(a) **Part 25** (interim remedies) except as it relates to interim injunctions.
(b) **Part 31** (disclosure and inspection).

(c) **Part 32** (evidence) except **r. 32.1**, which gives the court a general power to control evidence.
(d) **Part 33** (miscellaneous rules about evidence).
(e) **Part 35** (experts and assessors) except **r. 35.1**, which restricts the use of expert evidence, **r. 35.3**, which sets out the expert's overriding duty to the court and **rr. 35.7** and **35.8** (use of a single joint expert). **Rules 35.4(3A)** (only one expert) and **35.5(2)** (expert not to attend the hearing unless necessary) have express references to the small claims track, and are intended to apply to these cases, despite a drafting defect in **r. 27.2**.
(f) **Part 18** (further information), but see **45.16**.
(g) **Part 36** (offers to settle), but see **45.29**.
(h) **Part 39** (hearings) except **r. 39.2**, which is the general rule that hearings are to be in public.

In principle the other parts of the CPR apply to small claims except to the extent that any rule limits such application.

SMALL CLAIMS TRACK PROCEDURE

Figure 45.1 is a flowchart of the small claims track procedure. 45.7

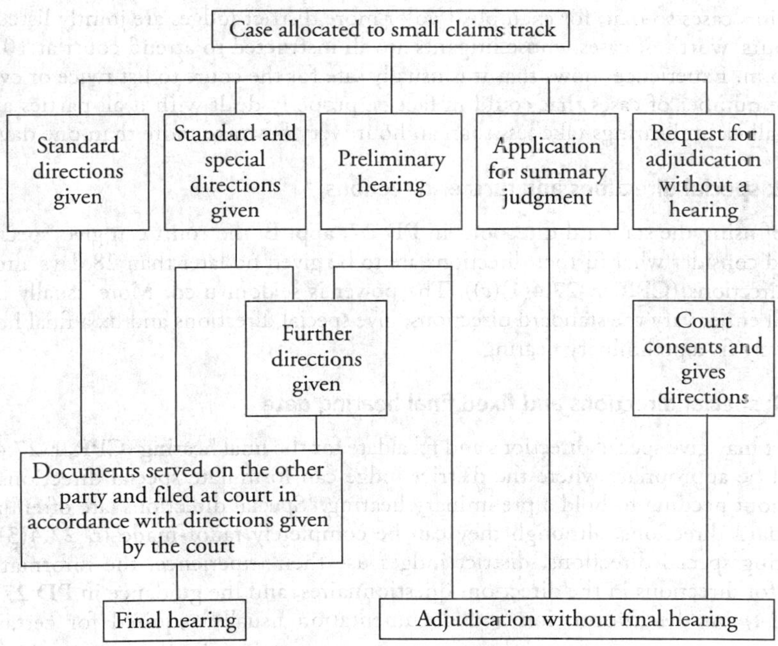

Figure 45.1 Small claims track procedure

Under **CPR, r. 27.4** once a case has been allocated to the small claims track the court has five options (described below) on how the case will be dealt with through to final disposal. Most small claims are given standard directions and a fixed hearing date (option 1). A party may ask the court to give particular directions (**PD 27, para. 2.4**), and should normally do so when returning the directions questionnaire. The court is given a general power under **CPR, r. 27.7**, to add to, vary or revoke directions.

Option 1: standard directions and fixed final hearing date

45.8 The court may give standard directions and fix a date for the final hearing (**CPR, r. 27.4(1)(a)**).

By **r. 27.4(3)(a)**, read together with **PD 27, para. 2.2**, and **app. B**, 'standard directions' means directions:

(a) that each party shall, at least 14 days before the date fixed for the final hearing, file and serve on every other party copies of all documents (including the letter before claim, any reply, and any expert's report) on which he intends to rely at the hearing;
(b) that the original documents must be brought to the hearing;
(c) fixing the hearing date and time allowed;
(d) encouraging the parties to contact each other with a view to trying to settle the claim or narrow the issues, and requiring the parties to notify the court immediately if the claim is settled; and
(e) informing the parties that they cannot rely on expert evidence at the hearing without a direction giving express permission to do so.

The relevant set of standard directions will be sent out by the court in the form of an order along with notification of the hearing date.

District judges' experience will usually enable them to give a reasonable estimate of the length of hearing for routine cases. Most courts adopt a 'back-to-back' system for listing small claims cases so that, for example, two or more district judges are jointly listed to hear many hours' worth of cases whose litigants are all instructed to attend court at 10.00 a.m. or 2.00 p.m. Experience shows that it is usually safe for the court to list twice or even three times the number of cases that could in fact be properly dealt with if all parties attended. Most small claim hearings take less than an hour; very few take more than one day.

Option 2: special directions and further directions

45.9 Instead of using the standard directions in **PD 27, app. B**, the court can give 'special directions' and consider what further directions are to be given no later than 28 days after giving special directions (**CPR, r. 27.4(1)(c)**). The power is seldom used. More usually a district judge will either vary the standard directions, give special directions and fix a final hearing or alternatively fix a preliminary hearing.

Option 3: special directions and fixed final hearing date

45.10 The court may give special directions and fix a date for the final hearing (**CPR, r. 27.4(1)(b)**). This will be appropriate where the district judge can formulate special directions for the case without needing to hold a preliminary hearing. 'Special directions' are often based on the standard directions, although they can be completely tailor-made (**r. 27.4(3)(b)**). In formulating special directions, district judges use their experience, the information and requests for directions in the directions questionnaires, and the guidance in **PD 27, app. A** (see **45.14**) on the information and documentation usually required for certain types of claim.

Option 4: preliminary hearing

45.11 The court may fix a date for a preliminary hearing (**CPR, r. 27.4(1)(d)**).

Consistent with the policy that the parties should attend court only when it is essential for them to do so, **r. 27.6** provides that the court may hold a preliminary hearing for the consideration of a small claim only in one of three situations:

(a) Where the court considers that special directions under **r. 27.4** are needed to ensure a fair hearing, and it appears necessary for a party to attend court to ensure that the party understands what must be done to comply with the special directions. This will be where the court considers (possibly from the content of the documents received) that it may be necessary to have the parties before the court to ensure that they understand what they must do in order that the case may be properly and efficiently progressed. Alternatively, it may be that special directions need to be considered, and that it would be inappropriate for the district judge to make them without hearing the parties.

(b) To enable the court to dispose of the claim on the basis that one of the parties has no real prospect of success. This may be obvious from the documents, for example, where the claim is based on a cause of action not known to English law. In less clear-cut cases, particularly where the only witnesses are the parties themselves, the better course would often be to have the case listed for a short final hearing. That would permit the party with no apparent prospect of success an opportunity to present his evidence before the judicial decision is reached.

(c) To enable the court to strike out the whole or part of a statement of case where it discloses no reasonable grounds for bringing or defending the claim. This provision follows on from the one before. Alternatively, if the failure to disclose a cause of action or defence is due to sloppy drafting, an opportunity should be given to amend.

By **r. 27.6(4)**, the court may treat a preliminary hearing as the final hearing of the claim if all parties agree. It is unlikely that this will commonly apply unless the point is a very short one, as it would otherwise mean that the preliminary appointment could take the same time as the substantive hearing.

After the preliminary hearing, the court will fix the date of the final hearing and inform the parties of the amount of time allowed, together with any other appropriate directions (**r. 27.6(5)**).

Option 5: proceeding without a hearing

The court may, if all parties agree, deal with a small claim without a hearing (**CPR, r. 27.10**). **Rule 27.10** is infrequently used. It appears to give the court a discretion to refuse to deal with a claim on paper even if that is what the parties want. Dealing with a small claim without a hearing might be appropriate where, for example, one party is living outside the jurisdiction and is either unable or unwilling to return for an oral hearing. In such a case the district judge would direct that copies of the relevant documents and witness statements be lodged; he would then give a written judgment. **45.12**

HEARING FEE

Within 14 days of the date of dispatch of the notice (or the date when oral notice is given if no written notice is given) of the hearing date (or window), the claimant must pay the hearing fee (**CPFO, fee 2.3**). This is: **45.13**

Value of claim	Hearing fee
Does not exceed £300	£25
£300.01 to £500	£55
£500.01 to £1,000	£80
£1,000.01 to £1,500	£110
£1,500.01 to £3,000	£165
Exceeds £3,000	£325

The hearing fee is payable by the defendant if the action is proceeding on the counterclaim alone. The fee for a case which exceeds the small claims track limit, but which is to be heard as a small claims track case, is £325 (rather than the fast track hearing fee of £545).

The hearing fee is refunded in full if the court receives notice in writing from the party who paid the fee, at least seven days before the date set for the hearing, that the case has been settled or discontinued.

SPECIAL DIRECTIONS

Information and documentation usually needed for particular types of claim

45.14 PD 27, app. A, sets out the type of information and documentation normally required for four types of claim frequently met on the small claims track. In the following lists, entries in square brackets have been added by the editors of this work.

(a) Road traffic accident claims:

- witness statements, including from the parties themselves;
- invoices and estimates for repairs;
- agreements and invoices for any car hire costs;
- the police accident report;
- sketch plan, which should be agreed if possible;
- photographs of the scene of the accident and the damage.

(b) Building disputes, repairs, sale of goods, and similar contract claims:

- any written contract [or correspondence evidencing the contract, including any specification for the contract works];
- photographs;
- any plans;
- a list of the works complained of;
- [written complaints by the customer and any responses];
- a list of any outstanding works;
- any relevant estimate, invoice or receipt including any relating to repairs to each of the defects;
- invoices for work done or goods supplied;
- estimates for work to be completed;
- a valuation of work done to date.

(c) Landlord and tenant claims:

- a calculation of the amount of rent alleged to be owing, showing amounts received;
- details of breaches of an agreement which are said to justify withholding any deposit itemised showing how the total is made up and with invoices and estimates to support them;
- [the tenancy agreement, or correspondence evidencing the agreement];
- [contemporaneous documentation proving rent received];
- [documents showing complaints by the tenant];
- [documents showing work done on behalf of the landlord].

(d) Breach of duty cases (negligence, deficient professional services, etc). Details of the following:

- what it is said by the claimant was done negligently by the defendant;
- *why it is said that the* negligence is the fault of the defendant;
- what damage is said to have been caused;

- what injury or losses have been suffered and how any (and each) sum claimed has been calculated;
- the response of the defendant to each of the above.

Format of special directions

To assist court users, PD 27, app. C, sets out model special directions dealing with: **45.15**

(a) further information to clarify a party's case;
(b) inspection of property;
(c) final hearing to take place at a location other than the court;
(d) requiring items to be brought to court;
(e) exchange of witness statements;
(f) warning that evidence will not be allowed if directions are not complied with;
(g) the form of an unless order;
(h) expert evidence;
(i) video evidence.

Requests for further information

The parties to a small claim are not permitted to make requests for further information under **CPR, Part 18**, see **r. 27.2(1)(f)**. This is subject to **r. 27.2(3)**, which says the court of its own initiative may order a party to provide further information if it considers it appropriate to do so. This is useful where the particulars of claim or defence are unclear and the court needs further information to clarify the case that the litigant intends to advance. **45.16**

Commentary

Documents

Parties to cases on the small claims track are not subject to the standard disclosure obligations of disclosing documents which adversely affect their case or support another party's case (**CPR, rr. 27.2(1)(b)** and **31.6**). Standard small claims directions do, however, require parties to file and serve, at least 14 days before the hearing, copies of the documents on which they intend to rely at the hearing (**r. 27.4(3)(a)**). When this is read together with the lists of documentation usually required in the types of cases considered in **PD 27, app. A**, it is clear that there is a fairly extensive obligation on the parties in small claims cases to provide documentation in support of their side of the dispute. **45.17**

Witness statements

In deciding whether to make an order for the exchange of witness statements in a small claim, **PD 27, para. 2.5**, provides that the court must have regard to: **45.18**

(a) whether either or both parties are represented;
(b) the amount in dispute;
(c) the nature of the matters in dispute. **PD 27, app. A**, says that witness statements will usually be required in road traffic accident claims. They may also be needed in more complex small claims, such as building disputes and holiday claims;
(d) whether the need for any party to clarify his case could better be dealt with by ordering him to provide further information under **PD 27, para. 2.3**;
(e) the need for the parties to have access to justice without undue formality, cost or delay.

By **CPR, r. 27.2(1)(c)**, the provisions of **rr. 32.2 to 32.19** (which include the provisions concerning the form and use of witness statements) do not apply to cases on the small claims track. Subject to the precise terms of the relevant direction, it is therefore permissible to use informal witness statements when these are ordered in small claims track cases.

Expert evidence

45.19 Most small claims can be resolved without expert evidence. The court is obliged to restrict expert evidence to that which is reasonably required to resolve the proceedings (**CPR, r. 35.1**), and normally only one expert may give evidence on a particular issue (**r. 35.4(3A)**). Where experts are required, permission must be expressly granted (**r. 27.5**). Usually the court will direct the evidence to be given through a written report of a jointly instructed expert (**PD 27, app. C; PD 35, annex (Protocol for the Instruction of Experts), para. 17.2; CPR, rr. 35.7** and **35.8**, on the power to direct evidence to be given by a single joint expert, and on instructions to a single joint expert, apply to cases on the small claims track, see **r. 27.2(1)(e)**). A direction for the expert to attend the hearing will be given only if necessary in the interests of justice (**r. 35.5(2)**). The court will normally also give directions allowing the parties to put written questions to the expert. If the court allows each side to instruct an expert, any discussions between the experts should be by telephone or letter (**PD 35, annex (Protocol for the Instruction of Experts), para. 18.4**). The costs which may be recovered by a successful party are limited to £750 for each expert (**PD 27, para. 7.3(2)**). While an expert on this track still owes an overriding duty to the court (**CPR, r. 35.3**), his or her report need not comply with all the requirements of **Part 35** (most of which is disapplied by **r. 27.2(1)(e)**). An informal letter from the expert will often suffice.

CONDUCT OF THE FINAL HEARING

45.20 The final hearing of a small claim will normally be before a district judge. The hearing may be assigned to a circuit judge (**PD 27, para. 1**), with that judge's consent (**PD 2B, para. 11.2**), but this rarely happens, not least because any appeal would have to be taken to the High Court.

Hearings are informal, the strict rules of evidence do not apply, and expert evidence (whether written or oral) may be given only with the court's permission (**CPR, rr. 27.5** and **27.8**). The district judge may well adopt an interventionist approach. In a small claim hearing the court will not always insist on the production of expert evidence, whereas it might be required for a similar case on one of the other tracks (*Bandegani v Norwich Union Fire Insurance Society Ltd* (1999) LTL 20/5/99, in which the claimant did not produce expert evidence for the value of a car which had been damaged in an accident).

Representation

45.21 By **PD 27, para. 3.2(1)**, at a hearing on the small claims track, a party's case may be presented:

(a) by the party personally;
(b) by a lawyer; or
(c) by a lay representative.

A 'lawyer' means a barrister, a solicitor or legal executive employed by a solicitor (**para. 3.1(1)**). A 'lay representative' means any other person (**para. 3.1(2)**).

By **para. 3.2(2)** and (3), the court's permission must be obtained for representation by a lay representative in the following circumstances:

(a) if the party being represented by the lay person is not present;
(b) if judgment has been given in the claim; or
(c) if the hearing is of an appeal against any decision made by the district judge in the proceedings.

The court may refuse to hear a lay representative in any proceedings if it is of the opinion that he or she is acting in an unruly manner in those proceedings (Courts and Legal Services Act 1990, s. 11(4)). The court must specify the conduct which warranted its refusal (s. 11(5)).

An individual may be prohibited by an order of a county court judge under s. 11(6) from acting as a lay representative. An order under s. 11(6) may be made where the judge has reason to believe that, in the present proceedings or any other proceedings, the individual has intentionally misled the court, or otherwise demonstrated unsuitability to exercise a right of audience. In *Paragon Finance plc v Noueiri* [2001] EWCA Civ 1402, [2001] 1 WLR 2357 (where a prohibition order was made by the Court of Appeal under its inherent jurisdiction), the representative's unsuitability was demonstrated by:

(a) his failure, or refusal, to understand crucial procedural rules;
(b) his bankruptcy, which meant that it would be futile to order him to pay wasted costs.

A corporate party is physically incapable of presenting its own case, but may be represented by a lawyer or a lay representative (*Avinue Ltd v Sunrule Ltd* [2003] EWCA Civ 1942, [2004] 1 WLR 634) or by any officer or employee (**PD 27, para. 3.2(4)**).

Public hearing

According to **PD 27, para. 4.1**, the hearing of a small claim will usually be in public, but the judge may decide to hold it in private if: **45.22**

(a) the parties agree, or
(b) a ground mentioned in **CPR, r. 39.2(3)**, applies.

PD 27 goes on to say at **para. 4.2** that a hearing that takes place at the court will generally be in the judge's room, but it may take place in a courtroom. It may involve a site visit if the time involved is proportionate, though judgment will be given in the judge's room rather than on site.

Method of proceeding

CPR, r. 27.8, allows the court to adopt any method of proceeding at a small claims hearing that it considers to be fair. The hearings are informal, evidence need not be taken on oath (and in practice rarely is) and the court may limit cross-examination. **PD 27, para. 4.3**, provides that the judge may in particular: **45.23**

(a) ask questions of any witness before allowing any other person to do so,
(b) ask questions of all or any of the witnesses before allowing any other person to ask questions of any witnesses,
(c) refuse to allow cross-examination of any witness until all the witnesses have given evidence-in-chief,
(d) limit cross-examination of a witness to a fixed time or to a particular subject or issue or both.

All the above is consistent with the interventionist approach. The district judge will have pre-read all the papers and is thus able to focus on areas of evidence materially in dispute. Such an approach is favoured by most unrepresented parties although it remains important to ensure that every party has a reasonable opportunity to say or ask all they want to.

If both parties are legally represented, matters may proceed more efficiently if the usual sequence of a court trial is observed, with short opening speeches if of assistance, formal evidence given in chief (although a direction for witness statements to stand as evidence-in-chief may be useful), cross-examination, re-examination and closing speeches. With unrepresented litigants, the district judge will assess the situation and the parties and decide what he or she needs to hear in order both to do justice and to ensure that the parties feel that within reason they have had their say. Although a district judge may control cross-examination by the parties, it would not be appropriate to forbid cross-examination entirely (*Chilton v Saga Holidays plc* [1986] 1 All ER 841).

Hearings without the parties

45.24 Under CPR, r. 27.9(1), a party to a small claim may request the court, by written notice given at least seven days before the hearing, to decide the claim without that party being present. A party who wishes to make use of this facility must serve every other party with copies of the documents filed at court at least seven days before the hearing (**r. 27.9(1)(b)**). If these steps are taken (and the party, as indicated, does not attend the hearing), the court will take into account the statement of case and any other documents filed by that party when deciding the claim (**r. 27.9(1)**).

If a *claimant* has not given notice under **r. 27.9(1)** but then does not attend the hearing, the court may, and usually will, strike out the claim (**r. 27.9(2)**).

The word 'may' in **r. 27.9(2)** gives the court a discretion and thus a party who has misunderstood the requirement to give seven days' notice and perhaps sends in a fax on the morning of the hearing, requesting the court to deal with the case on the basis of his written statements, will no doubt be given some indulgence. If the opposing party can demonstrate any prejudice caused by the lack of notice of the other party's non-appearance, an adjournment may be permitted. This may be, for example, because the party who is present needed to cross-examine the absent party about some feature of his case which would have demonstrated, e.g. the falseness of a particular piece of evidence, or that a certain document was not authentic. There may well also be a class of case where one party needs the other to attend in order to establish quantum, e.g. claims by former employees to commission payments based on sales. Generally speaking, a party who attends is likely to fare better than a party who does not attend.

If a *defendant* does not attend a hearing or give notice under **r. 27.9(1)**, and the claimant either does attend or has given the notice referred to, the court may, and usually will, decide the claim on the basis of the evidence of the claimant alone (**r. 27.9(3)**).

If *neither party* attends or gives notice, the court may strike out the claim and any defence and counterclaim (**r. 27.9(4)**).

Nothing in these provisions affects the general power of the court to adjourn a hearing for good reason, e.g. where a party who wishes to attend cannot do so because of illness.

Recording evidence and giving reasons

45.25 A court hearing of a small claim is tape-recorded by the court (**PD 27, para. 5.1**) and a party may thereafter obtain a transcript on payment of the proper charges. The fact that a party is exempt from paying court fees does not mean that he or she can obtain a transcript without charge, since such charges are not made by Her Majesty's Courts and Tribunals Service directly.

The court must give reasons for its decision (**CPR, r. 27.8(6)**) and will do so 'as briefly and simply as the nature of the case allows' (**PD 27, para. 5.3(1)**). Reasons are normally given orally at the hearing although they may be given later, either in writing or at a hearing fixed for that purpose (**para. 5.3(2)**).

Where the judge decides the case without a hearing under **CPR, r. 27.10**, or a party who has given notice under **r. 27.9(1)** does not attend the hearing, the judge will prepare a note of his or her reasons and the court will send a copy to each party (**PD 27, para. 5.4**).

One practical difficulty is that of an impecunious and unrepresented party who is unable to afford the cost of a transcript. In such circumstances a circuit judge, before hearing an appeal or when deciding whether to give permission to appeal, may be of the opinion that a note from the district judge setting out the main reasons for his decision would be of assistance;

such a note from the district judge to the circuit judge should be made available to all the parties.

Setting judgment aside and rehearing

A party to a small claim who was neither present nor represented at the hearing of the claim, and who did not give written notice to the court under **CPR, r. 27.9(1)**, may apply for an order that judgment shall be set aside and the claim reheard (**r. 27.11(1)**). **45.26**

To do this, application must be made not more than 14 days after the day on which notice of the judgment was served on that party (**r. 27.11(2)**). The court may then, by **r. 27.11(3)**, grant an application *only* if the applicant:

(a) had a good reason for not attending or being represented at the hearing or giving written notice to the court under **r. 27.9(1)**; and
(b) has a reasonable prospect of success at the hearing.

Compare **r. 39.3(5)**, discussed in **62.2**, which applies to setting aside a judgment given in the absence of a party on the fast track or multi-track, but does not (by **r. 27.2(1)(h)**) apply to the small claims track.

A party may not apply to set judgment aside under **r. 27.11** if the court dealt with the claim without a hearing under **r. 27.10** (i.e. by an order of the court with the consent of the parties dispensing with the hearing (**r. 27.11(5)**).

A party who was deliberately absent from court without a proper reason has no right to have a rehearing, however strong that party's case may be. If the court concludes that there is good reason for the absence, there is still an obligation on the party applying to show a reasonable prospect of success. This may go beyond consideration of whatever documents have been previously filed and may lead to the court asking for written evidence or further documentary evidence.

If judgment is set aside, the court must fix a new hearing (**r. 27.11(4)(a)**). The new hearing may take place immediately after the hearing of the application to set aside the judgment and may be dealt with by the judge who set aside the judgment (**r. 27.11(4)(b)**).

APPEALS

The procedure for appeals is considered in **chapters 74** and 75. An appeal against a court's order may be made only with the permission of that court or of the appeal court (**CPR, r. 52.3**). An appellant's notice in a small claim appeal must be in form N164 (**PD 27, para. 8A; PD 52B, para. 4.1**). A party to a case on the small claims track who wishes to appeal against an order made under **r. 27.10**, without a hearing, or in that party's absence in accordance with a request under **r. 27.9**, must apply to the appeal court for permission (**PD 27, para. 8.2**). When a decision has been made by a district judge (as is usual on the small claims track), the 'appeal court' for these purposes is the circuit judge at the same county court (**PD 52A, para. 3.5** and **Table 1**). If permission to appeal has not been given by the district judge, it must be requested in the appellant's notice (**CPR, r. 52.4(1)**). **45.27**

The documents to be filed with the appellant's notice are a sealed copy of the order under appeal, any order granting or refusing permission to appeal, and the grounds of appeal (**PD 52B, para. 4.2**). There is no requirement to file a transcript of the district judge's judgment in a small claims track appeal (**para. 6.2**). An appeal bundle must be filed within 35 days of filing the appellant's notice (**para. 6.3**), which must contain only those documents relevant to the appeal. Subject to any order by the appeal court, a list of documents that should be included in the appeal bundle is set out in **para. 6.4**.

If an appeal against an order made on the small claims track is allowed, the appeal court will, if possible, dispose of the case at the same time, rather than referring it back to the lower court or ordering a new hearing (**PD 27, para. 8.3**). The appeal court may dispose of the case without hearing further evidence (**para. 8.3**).

COSTS

Costs after allocation

45.28 After a claim has been allocated to the small claims track there are considerable restrictions on the costs that the successful party may recover. In principle (**CPR, r. 27.14(2)**) the court may not order a party to pay a sum to another party in respect of that other party's costs except:

(a) the fixed costs payable under **Part 45** (or which would be payable if **Part 45** applied) attributable to issuing the claim (**r. 27.14(2)(a)**);
(b) in proceedings which include a claim for an injunction or specific performance, an amount not exceeding £260 for legal advice and assistance relating to that claim (**r. 27.14(2)(b); PD 27, para. 7.2**);
(c) any court fees paid by the successful party (**r. 27.14(2)(c)**);
(d) expenses which a party or witness has reasonably incurred in travelling to or from a hearing or in staying away from home for the purposes of attending a hearing (**r. 27.14(2)(d)**);
(e) a sum not exceeding £90 a day for any loss of earnings or loss of leave by a party or witness due to attending a hearing or to staying away from home for the purpose of attending a hearing (**r. 27.14(2)(e); PD 27, para. 7.3**);
(f) a sum not exceeding £750 per expert for an expert's fees (**r. 27.14(2)(f); PD 27, para. 7.3**);
(g) such further costs as the court may assess by the summary procedure and order to be paid by a party who has behaved unreasonably;
(h) any unpaid Stage 1 and Stage 2 fixed costs under **CPR, r. 45.29**, pursuant to the RTA Protocol (see **8.30** to **8.60**) where the claimant reasonably believed the claim was valued at more than the small claims track limit and the defendant admitted liability; and
(i) in an appeal, the cost of any approved transcript reasonably incurred.

Unreasonable behaviour

45.29 Instead of the limited costs normally recoverable on the small claims track (see **45.28**), a successful party may seek to recover all of his costs from a party who has behaved unreasonably (**CPR, r. 27.14(2)(g)**). This inevitably involves the court exercising a wide discretion. The following may, it is suggested, be considered to be unreasonable:

(a) making a claim which the court has found to be wholly false;
(b) pursuing an untenable claim (*Memon v TNT UK Ltd* (2009) LTL 30/11/2009, claiming 30 days' loss of use of a car which was repaired in one day);
(c) failure to inform the court of the non-attendance of a witness;
(d) deliberate delay in dealing with an undeniable claim so as to force a party to issue proceedings;
(e) filing a spurious defence and then not attending the final hearing;
(f) paying the claim in full just before the final hearing;
(g) making unnecessary procedural applications;
(h) possibly, rejecting a Part 36 offer (see below).

A material factor may be that the rules in **Part 36** on offers to settle have no application in small claims proceedings (**r. 27.2(1)(g)**). **Rule 27.14(3)** provides that a party's rejection of an offer in settlement will not of itself constitute unreasonable behaviour under **r. 27.14(2)(g)**, but the court may take it into consideration when it is applying the unreasonableness test. A strong case should be required before the court holds that rejection of an offer is unreasonable behaviour.

When the court concludes that a party has behaved unreasonably, the court must conduct an immediate and summary assessment of the costs to be paid (**r. 27.14(2)(g)**). It will thus be important for a party who expects to be able successfully to press a claim for costs to have information available on the status of the fee earner, time claimed for attendances, correspondence, documents and so on, or even to have completed a formal statement of costs.

Costs after leaving the small claims track

If a case is reallocated from the small claims track to another track, the small claims costs provisions cease to apply after the claim has been reallocated and the fast track or multi-track rules will thereafter apply (**CPR, r. 27.15**). **45.30**

Costs before reallocation to the small claims track

If a claim has been on some other track before being reallocated to the small claims track, the rules applicable to the first track will apply up to the date of reallocation and the small claims track rules will apply after that date, unless the court orders otherwise (**CPR, r. 46.13(2)**). **45.31**

Allocation for assessment of damages

Claims may be allocated to the small claims track for determination of quantum after judgment has been entered for damages to be assessed. When this happens the limitation on costs in respect of the small claims hearing will apply, although costs of earlier stages will be based on the sums available on the track concerned. It is likely that if proceedings are to be transferred to the small claims track for the assessment of damages, the court will undertake a summary assessment of the costs incurred before the allocation to the small claims track. **45.32**

EUROPEAN SMALL CLAIMS PROCEDURE

Regulation (EC) No. 861/2007 of 11 July 2007 (the 'ESCP Regulation') establishes a European small claims procedure ('ESCP') with effect from 1 January 2009. The Regulation applies, in cross-border cases, to civil and commercial matters, whatever the nature of the court or tribunal, where the value of a claim does not exceed € 2,000 at the time when the claim form is received by the court or tribunal with jurisdiction, excluding all interest, expenses and disbursements (art. 2(1)). There are various excepted categories of claim in art. 2(1) and (2). The ESCP is intended to simplify and speed up litigation concerning small claims in cross-border cases, whilst reducing costs, by offering an optional tool in addition to the possibilities existing under the laws of the member States, which remain unaffected. The ESCP Regulation should also make it simpler to obtain recognition and to enforce a judgment given in the ESCP in another member State (recital 8). **45.33**

There is a special ESCP claim form, which is completed and filed in accordance with the ESCP Regulation, in particular art. 4(1), and which has a declaration which is treated in England and Wales in the same way as a statement of truth (**CPR, r. 78.13**). ESCP claims must be commenced in a county court (**High Court and County Courts Jurisdiction Order 1991**

(**SI 1991/724**), **art. 6B**). They are treated as if they are allocated to the small claims track (**CPR, r. 78.14(1)**), and the provisions of **Part 27** apply except for **r. 27.14** (costs in small claims track cases). There are also detailed procedural rules in the ESCP Regulation so these claims are primarily governed by the ESCP Regulation (**PD 78, para. 10**). Where the ESCP Regulation is silent, the CPR apply with necessary modifications. In particular, where the ESCP Regulation is silent on service, the Service Regulation and **CPR, Part 6**, apply as appropriate (**PD 78, para. 15**), and **CPR, Part 52**, applies to any appeals (**PD 78, para. 10**).

Although there are procedures in the ESCP Regulation for hearings, primarily this procedure is intended to provide a paper-based decision (art. 5(1)). An oral hearing will be convened only if the court considers this to be necessary or if a party so requests. The decision is ordinarily expected within 30 days of receipt of the response from the defendant (art. 7(1)), although it will be longer if there is an oral hearing. The unsuccessful party must bear the costs of the proceedings. However, the court or tribunal must not award costs to the successful party to the extent that they were unnecessarily incurred or are disproportionate to the claim (art. 16).

Chapter 46 Fast Track

Commentary

INTRODUCTION

The fast track is intended to cover the majority of defended claims within the £10,000 to £25,000 monetary band. For proceedings issued before 6 April 2009, the upper limit of the fast track bracket is £15,000 (**CPR, r. 26.6(4)(b)(ii)**), and for claims issued before 1 April 2013 the lower limit is £5,000. The fast track is also the track for non-monetary claims such as injunctions, declarations and claims for specific performance which are unsuitable for the small claims track and do not require the more complex treatment of the multi-track. The fast track provides a 'no-frills' procedure for medium-sized cases that do not justify the detailed and meticulous preparation appropriate for complex and important cases. Instead, a case allocated to this track will be progressed to trial within a short timescale after the filing of a defence. **CPR, r. 1.1(2)(c)**, provides that part of the overriding objective is that cases should be dealt with proportionately, and it is this idea that underlies the whole concept of having a fast track with limited costs. The intention is to increase access to justice by removing the uncertainty faced by many litigants over the cost of litigating, and to provide a means of obtaining justice speedily. **46.1**

When claims are allocated to the fast track, directions will be given setting out the timetable to be followed, with a fixed trial date or trial period no more than 30 weeks later. Such a timetable will be long enough for the parties to undertake the work necessary for preparing the case for trial, but sufficiently tight to discourage elaboration. The court will use its case management powers (see **chapter 42**) and its power to impose sanctions (**chapter 48**) to provide protection against oppressive or unreasonable behaviour, and in particular against a powerful opponent driving up the costs so as to overwhelm a weaker litigant.

In contrast to the small claims track, the full range of procedures under the CPR is available on fast track claims, together with traditional costs orders. There are adjustments to reflect the relatively modest value of many cases on the fast track. These include being released from the need to file a costs budget with the directions questionnaire (see **43.5**, unless the court orders otherwise), limitations on expert evidence (see **46.6**), and fixed (and reasonably modest) trial costs (see **71.6**) combined with summary assessment of the costs of the proceedings (see **46.23**).

Recommendations made by Sir Rupert Jackson's *Review of Civil Litigation Costs* (Ministry of Justice, December 2009) extending the fast track to certain specialist claims and for the implementation of a general fast track fixed costs regime were not implemented in the civil justice reforms of 2013.

ADVANCE PREPARATION

46.2 Once a case is allocated to the fast track and directions are given, there will be a limited period of no more than seven months in which to prepare the case for trial. Such is the importance of ensuring fast track claims are dealt with expeditiously that **PD 28, para. 3.12**, lays down a typical directions timetable providing for a trial 30 weeks after the notice of allocation. **Paragraph 3.13** envisages shortening this period in cases where some of the typical steps in the timetable are thought unnecessary. Claimants will therefore be well advised to ensure that their cases are in an advanced state of preparation before they issue proceedings, to make sure they do not fall behind schedule once the timetable starts running. They should ensure they have available for disclosure all disclosable documents, both on liability and the amount of damages. They should also have identified and if necessary traced all material witnesses, and preferably have reduced into writing at least draft statements for each witness. They should also have made some progress regarding obtaining any expert evidence that might be necessary. It is to be expected that in most fast track cases the court will direct that there should be joint instruction of experts. Prospective claimants will therefore be well advised to have identified possible experts to be instructed, and sought agreement with their prospective defendants for the joint instruction of agreed experts. Anything less than this will be storing up trouble for later on.

Defendants are in a similar, and sometimes more precarious, position. They too will easily find themselves in time difficulties later on unless they have completed at least some of the necessary preparation before the claim is issued. Full compliance with any relevant pre-action protocol will at least put them in a reasonably advanced state of preparedness. They should, at the very least, have available for disclosure their documentation on liability, and have draft statements from material witnesses. They should also be in the process of seeking agreement on the joint instruction of experts. Like claimants, failing to have these matters in hand will mean there will be little time to get the case ready before the trial arrives.

DIRECTIONS

46.3 When it allocates a case to the fast track, the court will at the same time give case management directions and set a timetable for the steps to be taken from that point through to trial (**CPR, r. 28.2(1)**). The directions given will be designed to ensure the issues are identified and the necessary evidence is prepared and disclosed (**PD 28, para. 3.3**). Usually the court will give directions of its own initiative without a hearing, and will take into account the respective statements of case, the directions questionnaires, and any further information provided by the parties. Occasionally it may hold a directions hearing, such as when it is proposing to make an unusual order, for example, to appoint an assessor (see **PD 28, para. 3.11**). It is the duty of the parties to ask for all directions that might be needed on any hearing that may be fixed (**para. 2.5**). If any direction or order is required that has not been provided for, it is the duty of the parties to make an application as soon as possible so as to avoid undue interference with the overall timetable (**para. 2.8**). If a directions hearing becomes necessary because of the default of any of the parties, the court will usually impose a sanction (**para. 2.3**).

Typically, by ***CPR, rr. 28.2(2)*** and **28.3**, the matters to be dealt with in directions given on allocation to the fast track will include:

(a) disclosure of documents;

(b) service of witness statements;
(c) expert evidence; and
(d) fixing a date for the trial, or a period (not exceeding three weeks) in which the trial is to take place.

Standard directions to be used in fast track cases are set out in the Appendix to **PD 28**. They include matters, such as orders for the provision of further information, which are not included in the basic list. This is because the directions given will be tailored by the procedural judge to the circumstances of each individual case. The time periods for taking the various steps will also be tailored to the requirements of each individual case, but a few indications of the probable times allowed for different steps will be given in the following paragraphs. Further directions may be given after consideration of pre-trial checklists (**CPR, r. 28.6(1)**, see **46.17** to **46.21**) or after failure to file or complete them (**r. 28.5(3)** to **(5)**, see **46.11**). The date for filing pre-trial checklists will be not more than eight weeks before the trial date or the beginning of the trial period (**r. 28.5(2)**). Further directions are usually given about four to six weeks before trial.

Disclosure

Disclosure is discussed fully in **chapter 50**. Disclosure in some form should have taken place before proceedings were issued in compliance with the pre-action protocols. Information about this should have been given with the directions questionnaire. Based on the respective statements of case and these questionnaires, the procedural judge may direct the parties to give standard disclosure as one of the directions made at this stage, or may direct that no disclosure need take place (where the parties confirm that disclosure has taken place and no further disclosure is required), or may specify the documents or classes of documents which the parties must disclose (**CPR, r. 28.3(2)**; **PD 28, para. 3**). The standard directions will provide for disclosure to be given by service of lists of documents, which must be delivered by a specified calendar date. It is also possible for disclosure to be given more informally without a list and with or without a disclosure statement. Disclosure is likely to be ordered for 28 days after service of the notice of allocation (**PD 28, para. 3.12**). **46.4**

Witness statements

The exchange of witness statements is considered further in **chapter 51**. Standard directions will usually provide for simultaneous exchange by a specified calendar date of statements from all the factual witnesses on whose evidence each party intends to rely. Exchange is likely to be required about 10 weeks from the order for directions (**PD 28, para. 3.12**). By **CPR, r. 32.9(1)**, witness summaries may be used in circumstances where witness statements cannot be obtained for practical reasons, but such instances should be exceptional. **Rule 32.5(4)** points firmly in the direction of full witness statements, as witnesses will only be allowed to amplify their statements if there is 'good reason' not to confine them to their disclosed witness statements. Trial judges usually take a strict view against allowing additional questions in-chief seeking to introduce new matters or to insulate a witness against cross-examination under the guise of 'amplifying' an exchanged statement. **46.5**

Expert evidence

For detailed consideration of directions about experts see **54.13** to **54.17**. Cases will not normally be on the fast track unless oral expert evidence at trial is limited to one expert per party in each expert field, and to two fields of expertise (**CPR, r. 26.6(5)**). It is difficult to see how any more experts could give evidence within the time limit for a fast track hearing. One of the powers available to the court is that of directing that the evidence on particular issues may be given by a single expert jointly instructed by the opposing parties (**r. 35.7**). Normally, **46.6** any permission will be for evidence from only one expert on any particular issue (**r. 35.4(3A)**). In order to keep down costs and to reduce the length of fast track trials, it will be usual for the court to make directions for the joint instruction of a single expert unless there is good reason for doing something else (**PD 28, para. 3.9(4)**). In addition, in fast track cases the court will not direct an expert to attend at trial unless it is necessary to do so in the interests of justice (**CPR, r. 35.5(2)**). It is expected that such directions will be rare.

If the parties are given permission to instruct their own experts, the court has a power under **r. 35.12** to direct a discussion between the experts with a view to producing an agreed statement of the issues on which they agree and the areas on which they are in disagreement. If the experts cannot reach agreement, the interests of justice are likely to be served only by allowing both parties to call their experts at the trial so the areas of disagreement can be adjudicated upon by the judge. In such cases it may not be possible to deal with the case in a single day, and the court may need to consider reallocating the case to the multi-track. This will be considered by the procedural judge on filing of pre-trial checklists by the parties.

Normally expert evidence should be prepared and/or exchanged about 14 weeks after the order giving directions (**PD 28, para. 3.12**). The standard fast track directions have several different options regarding expert evidence, as alternatives to the joint instruction of experts. Options provided within the standard directions are:

(a) Sequential service of experts' reports. Normally it will be the claimant who will serve first.
(b) Simultaneous exchange of reports on some issues, with sequential service on the others.
(c) Holding of a discussion between experts in cases where the other side's reports cannot be agreed within a short time (usually 14 days) after service. This form of direction provides for a specified calendar date by which the discussion must take place, and the filing of a joint statement of the agreed issues and those in dispute (with reasons for the lack of agreement) by another specified date (which will often be close to the date for filing pre-trial checklists).
(d) That expert evidence is not necessary and no party has permission to call or rely on expert-evidence at the trial without permission expressly given by the court following an application.
(e) That the parties may rely on experts' reports at trial, but cannot call oral expert evidence.
(f) That the parties may rely on experts' reports, and the court will reconsider whether there is any need for experts to be called on consideration of the filed pre-trial checklists.

Questions to experts

46.7 The standard directions also make provision pursuant to the power given by **CPR, r. 35.6**, for written questions to be put to the experts for the purpose of clarifying their reports.

Questions should be sent, if at all, no later than 28 days after receiving the report (**r. 35.6(2)(b)**). Questions can be sent direct to the expert, but copies should be sent to the other side's solicitors. No time is laid down for the answers (although this may be done by a specific court order), but 28 days would seem to be reasonable. Sensible questions can only be asked if the party (or more commonly its solicitor) is guided by its own expert. If its own expert knows the answers, there will be little point in asking the questions in the first place, so it must be sensible to clear the written questions with the party's own experts first. It will take a little time for a party to receive the other side's expert reports, consider them, *decide if it is a case where written questions should be put*, contact its own expert and take its expert's advice about the written questions to be put, formulate the questions, and then serve them. Experts are often busy consultants and professionals with many calls on their time, so a period of 28 days for questions and answers may seem rather tight, but is necessary if a fast track timetable is to be met. Solicitors must send copies of directions orders to experts so they are aware of the court's timetable (**PD 35, para. 8**) Solicitors should also ensure that experts are aware of their rights and duties under **CPR, Part 35**, particularly **r. 35.14**, which allows an expert to file written requests for directions.

Further statements of case

46.8 When giving directions, the procedural judge may also direct that a party must file a further statement of case, such as a reply or defence to counterclaim. The direction will specify a calendar date and time for doing so.

Requests for further information

46.9 Requests for further information are considered in more detail in **chapter 30**. Standard directions provide for two possible times for service of such requests (with either, both or neither being directed in any particular case):

(a) Within a short, specified, time after directions are given, where the request is based on the other side's statement of case. The direction will also specify the date by which the request must be dealt with. A response is usually required within 14 days.
(b) After disclosure or exchange of witness statements. The direction will lay down a limited time after disclosure or service of the statement within which the request must be served, and a limited time within which it must be dealt with.

PRE-TRIAL CHECKLISTS

46.10 Standard fast track directions provide for all parties to file completed pre-trial checklists, previously known as listing questionnaires, no later than specific dates set out in the directions, unless the court considers the claim can be listed for trial without them. They are used to ensure the case is on course for being ready for trial, and to enable the procedural judge to set a trial timetable. If a party wants additional directions, the form has to be accompanied by an application notice and draft directions. Explanations must be given for witness dates to avoid. Information about experts includes whether opposing experts have signed a joint statement. If the time estimate has changed, the parties must say whether they have agreed a new estimate. When they are used, pre-trial checklists must be returned within the time specified by the court, which will be no later than eight weeks before the trial date or the beginning of the trial period (**CPR, r. 28.5(2)**).

Failure to file or complete pre-trial checklists

46.11 If no party files the completed pre-trial checklist by the date specified, the court will order that unless a completed pre-trial checklist is filed within 7 days from service of that order, the claim, defence and any counterclaim will be struck out without further order of the court (**CPR, r. 28.5(3)**. If one party fails to file its pre-trial checklist, and if the court considers that a hearing is necessary to enable it to decide what directions to give in order to complete preparation of the case for trial, the court may give such directions as it considers appropriate (**CPR, r. 28.5(4)**). The court may require the parties to attend a hearing for this purpose, and if so will give at least three days' notice (unless abridged under **r. 3.1(2)(b)**) of the directions hearing using form N153 (**PD 28, para. 6.3**). Particularly where any of the parties are in default, the court may consider imposing sanctions and making 'unless' orders.

Notice of a pre-trial directions hearing will be in form N153.

LISTING AND HEARING FEES

46.12 When the claimant files his pre-trial checklist, two fees are payable. One is a listing fee of £110 (**CPFO, fee 2.2**), and the other is a hearing fee of £545 (**CPFO, fee 2.3**). Fee 2.3 is not payable in a case where the court fixed the hearing date on the issue of the claim. If the court fixes a trial date or trial week without requiring pre-trial checklists, fees 2.2 and 2.3 become payable within 14 days of the date of dispatch of the notice (or the date when oral notice is given if no written notice is given) of the trial date or week. The 'claimant' who has to pay the fees is the party making the relevant claim. Consequently, in *Penfold v Fuller* [2009] EWHC 1195 (Ch), LTL 8/6/2009, the original defendant had to pay the fees where the original claim had been compromised in a Tomlin order, and the hearing was to determine an application for specific performance of the Tomlin order brought by the original defendant. If the action is proceeding on a counterclaim alone, the fees are payable by the defendant. If either fee is not paid, the court will send a notice to pay in form N173, and failing payment within the time stated in the notice, the claim will be struck out (**CPR, r. 3.7**).

As an incentive to settle, the hearing fee of £545 will be refunded in whole or in part on a sliding scale if the court receives notice in writing from the party who paid the fee that the case has been settled or discontinued. The refunds are:

Court notified more than 28 days before the hearing	100 per cent
Court notified between 15 and 28 days before the hearing	75 per cent
Court notified between 7 and 14 days before the hearing	50 per cent

FIXING THE DATE FOR TRIAL

46.13 When giving directions the court will fix the trial date or a period, not exceeding three weeks, in which the trial is to take place, and which will be specified in the notice of allocation (**CPR, r. 28.2(2)** to (4)). A trial window will usually be given at the allocation stage and the trial directions will be given on consideration of pre-trial checklists. A trial date or window may be altered, but only as a last resort or where it is necessary to avoid injustice (see **46.16**). Whichever course is taken, the court must give the parties at least three weeks' notice of the date of the trial unless, in exceptional circumstances, the court directs that shorter notice will be given (**r. 28.6(2)**).

Rule 28.2(4) provides that the 'standard' period between the giving of directions and the trial will be not more than 30 weeks. It is therefore open for procedural judges to lay down even tighter timetables, which depends on the complexity of the case and whether any of the usual steps have already been taken (**PD 28, para. 3.13**). There is also scope, if the procedural judge can be persuaded that it is necessary, for the timetable to be longer than the standard period. Factors such as those mentioned at **46.16** may influence the court when considering a longer timetable in an individual case.

STANDARD FAST TRACK TIMETABLE

46.14 Table 46.1 charts the progress of a fast track case from issue, through allocation to the fast track, up to trial. The case illustrated takes 39 weeks, or about nine months, from issue to trial. The various stages will vary from case to case (such as where there is a stay for negotiation *or if the claimant effects* service rather than the court) and, as mentioned in **46.13**, even the 30-week period between directions and trial may be considerably reduced in some cases. It will be obvious that the parties will have to be in a high state of preparedness before

Table 46.1 Progress of fast track case to trial

Week after allocation	Step in the proceedings	Time limit
	Issue of proceedings. Service by court (takes effect on second business day after posting)	Usual limitation period 4 months from issue (6 months if outside the jurisdiction)
	Acknowledgment of service or filing of defence	14 days after deemed service of the particulars of claim
	Provisional track allocation notice	On filing defence
	Possible transfer to defendant's home court	On filing defence
	Return of directions questionnaires and other documents required by the notice of proposed allocation	Not less than 28 days after service of the notice of proposed allocation
0	Allocation decision and directions given by the procedural judge	After return of directions questionnaires
4	Disclosure of documents	Usually 4 weeks after allocation
10	Exchange of witness statements	Usually 10 weeks after allocation
10	Service of hearsay notices	With exchanged witness statements
14	Experts' reports	Usually 14 weeks after allocation
(Say) 17	Written questions to experts	Between reports and pre-trial checklists
(Say) 19	Answers from experts	Usually 2 weeks from written questions
20	Service of pre-trial checklists (may be dispensed with)	Usually 20 weeks after
22	Return of pre-trial checklists	Usually 22 weeks after allocation
(Say) 24	Any directions arising out of the pre-trial checklists	Optional
(24)	Hearing if pre-trial checklists not returned	Only if parties in default
27	Confirmation of trial date	3 weeks before trial
27	Service of notice to admit	3 weeks before trial
28/29	Lodge trial bundle	3 to 7 days before trial
29	Service and filing of statements of costs	Not less than 2 days before the hearing
30	Trial	30 weeks after allocation

proceedings are issued in all but the very simplest of cases if they are to have any real prospect of adhering to such tight timetables without being forced on the mercy of the courts.

AGREED DIRECTIONS

46.15 The parties are encouraged to seek to agree suitable directions to be submitted to the court with their directions questionnaires. If this is done, the court will at least take them into account when giving directions, and if they are suitable, will simply approve them. To be approved the directions should essentially follow the above rules (see **PD 28, para. 3**), which means they must deal with disclosure, witness statements and expert evidence, lay down a timetable by calendar dates, and provide for a trial or trial period no more than 30 weeks after the start of the timetable.

Commentary

VARYING THE DIRECTIONS TIMETABLE

46.16 A party that wishes to vary the date fixed by the court's directions for returning directions questionnaires, pre-trial checklists or for the trial must apply to the court (**CPR, rr. 26.3(6A)** and **28.4(1)**). Any other date set by the court also cannot be varied by the parties if the variation would make it necessary to vary the dates for either filing pre-trial checklists or trial (**r. 28.4(2)**). The effect of these rules is that it is quite permissible for the parties to agree to the variation of the other directions for service of lists of documents, witness statements and experts' reports without troubling the court, provided the two key dates (filing pre-trial checklists and trial) are not affected by slippage elsewhere. If the parties agree to a variation which does not impinge on any of the key dates, they can act on their agreement without having to file anything at court (**PD 28, para. 4.5(1)**).

The parties are required to help the court to further the overriding objective (**CPR, r. 1.3**), and the court must encourage the parties to cooperate with each other in the conduct of proceedings (**r. 1.4(2)(a)**). If a party falls a little behind on the timetable, one would expect the other side to assist by agreeing to a slight revision to the timetable, rather than insisting on strict compliance. Any significant departure from the timetable, however, is likely to be penalised in accordance with the need to enforce compliance with court orders as part of the overriding objective (**r. 1.1(2)(f)**). The court has a general power to extend and abridge the time for compliance with any rule, practice direction or court order, even if the application is made after the time for compliance has elapsed (**r. 3.1(2)(a)**).

A party who disagrees with the directions timetable laid down should either appeal or apply to the court for it to reconsider its directions (**PD 28, para. 4.3(1)**). Orders and directions made at hearings attended by a party or his representative or regarding which the party was given due notice, should be appealed (**para. 4.3(2)**), whereas an application is necessary in relation to directions made of the court's own initiative (**para. 4.3(3)**). Any appeal or application must be made as soon as possible (**para. 4.2(1)**). The court will assume for the purposes of any later application that a party who did not appeal, and who made no application to vary any directions given within 14 days, was content that they were correct in the circumstances then existing (**para. 4.2(2)**). Some courts expressly abridge this period to seven days after service, to be consistent with **CPR, r. 3.3(5)**. Obviously, parties should not feel forced into making speculative applications in relation to directions that are based on future events (such as requests for further information and questions to experts), and applications to extend these (and some of the other) time limits are dealt with realistically when the need arises.

It is made very clear by **PD 28, para. 5.4(6)**, that variations involving loss of the trial date will be considered matters of last resort. Examples include cases where there are significant problems with the evidence, where medical evidence requires re-tracking or further investigation, where there is a change of solicitor, where proceedings are issued at the very end of the limitation period, and in personal injuries cases where the prognosis is uncertain (*Woolf Report*, ch. 3, para. 19). If there is no option but to postpone the trial, the postponement will be for the shortest possible time, and the court will give directions for taking the necessary steps outstanding as rapidly as possible. In some of these cases the best course may be to have split trials of liability and quantum, or to proceed only on those issues that are ready (**PD 28, para. 5.4(4)**). Where this happens the court may disallow the costs of the remaining issues, or order them to be paid by the party in default in any event. If necessary the judge can decide issues while the case is allocated to the fast track, then reallocate the claim, if reallocating the claim immediately would cause substantial disruption to the litigation or unreasonable delay (*Maguire v Molin* [2002] EWCA Civ 1083, [2002] 4 All ER 325).

PRE-TRIAL DIRECTIONS

On receipt of the pre-trial checklists, under **CPR, r. 28.6(1)**, the court will: **46.17**

(a) Fix the date for the trial (or, if it has already done so, confirm the date).
(b) Give any further directions for the trial as may seem necessary, including setting a trial timetable. Standard directions for this stage are set out in the Appendix to **PD 28**.
(c) Specify any further steps that need to be taken before trial.

The parties should seek to agree directions, and they may submit a proposed order (**PD 28, para. 7.2(1)**). They should give reasons for any unusual directions. Usually directions will be made by the court without a hearing, but it may decide to hold a pre-trial directions hearing, giving the parties three clear days' notice (**PD 28, para. 6.3**).

Confirmation of expert directions

Pre-trial directions will confirm or make provision for the permission granted to the parties regarding reliance on written experts' reports and calling expert witnesses at trial. The direction will specify the experts by name, and say whether they can be called or whether it is only the expert's report that can be relied upon. Oral evidence from experts will only be allowed if the court believes it is necessary in the interests of justice (**PD 28, para. 7.2(4)**). **46.18**

Trial timetable

The court may, if it considers that it is appropriate to do so, set a timetable for the trial. Setting a timetable is discretionary (**CPR, r. 28.6(1)(b)**), and is easier if the managing judge will be the trial judge. If it decides to set a timetable, the court must consult with the parties (**r. 39.4**). A trial timetable defines how much time the court will allow at trial for the various stages of the trial itself. A simple direction may limit the time to be spent by each party in calling its evidence and in addressing the court in closing submissions. More sophisticated timetables will define how much time will be allowed for each witness, or even for cross-examination and re-examination. If a timetable is set, it will usually provide for a five-hour trial, to include all stages including judgment and the summary assessment of costs. **46.19**

Trial bundles

Standard pre-trial directions will provide that an indexed, paginated, bundle of documents contained in a ring binder must be lodged with the court not more than seven days or less than three days before the trial. Slightly inconsistently, the standard direction in the Appendix to **PD 28** provides that trial bundles must be lodged at least seven days before trial. The parties must seek to agree the contents of the trial bundle a reasonable time in advance, which in practical terms means no later than 14 days before the trial. For further details on the contents of the trial bundles, see **chapter 59**. The claimant is responsible for lodging the bundle. Lodgment at court is required so that the trial judge can read the case papers in advance of the trial. Judges are likely to take a very dim view if the bundle is not lodged in time. Identical bundles will be needed for each of the parties, with an additional bundle for the witness box. **46.20**

Case summary

Standard pre-trial directions give the procedural judge the option of directing that a case summary should be included in the trial bundle. This document is intended to be non-partisan, and to be agreed if possible. It should usually be no more than 250 words, and should outline the matters in issue, referring where appropriate to the relevant documents in the trial bundle. Again, responsibility for this rests with the claimant. **46.21**

FAST TRACK TRIALS

46.22 The trial of a fast track claim will usually take place in the county court where it is proceeding, but may take place in a civil trial centre or any other court if it is appropriate because of listing difficulties, the needs of the parties or for other reasons. The judge may be a district judge or a circuit judge. The trial judge will generally have read the trial bundle and will usually dispense with opening speeches. Unless the trial judge otherwise directs, the trial will be conducted in accordance with any order previously made (see **46.19**), although the judge is free to set a fresh trial timetable (**PD 28, para. 8.3**). Given the time constraints and the need for proportionality, the trial judge will almost invariably order witness statements to stand as the evidence-in-chief and otherwise control the evidence to be presented. If a trial is not concluded on the day it is listed, the judge will normally sit on the following day to complete it (**PD 28, para. 8.6**; though in many county courts this does not reflect reality). In such an event no further costs will be allowed to the parties.

COSTS IN FAST TRACK CASES

46.23 CPR, **r. 28.2(5)**, provides that the court's power to award trial costs is limited in accordance with **Part 46**, which sets fixed amounts for the costs of a fast track trial depending on the amount recovered, with a small uplift if counsel is attended by a solicitor (**r. 45.38**; see **71.6**).

The general rule is that at the end of a fast track trial the court will make a summary assessment of the costs of the whole claim immediately after giving judgment (**PD 44, para. 9.2**). To assist the judge in assessing costs, the parties are required to file and serve, not less than two days before the trial, signed statements of their costs for the interim hearing in form N260. A statement of costs must, by **PD 44, para. 9.5(2)**, set out:

(a) the number of hours claimed;
(b) the hourly rate claimed;
(c) the grade of fee earner;
(d) the amount and nature of disbursements;
(e) the legal representative's costs for attending or appearing at the hearing;
(f) counsel's fees; and
(g) VAT on the above.

Any failure to file or serve a statement of costs, without reasonable excuse, will be taken into account in deciding the costs order to be made regarding the claim, the trial, and/or any detailed assessment hearing that might become necessary as a result of that failure (**PD 44, para. 9.6**; see **32.31**). Summary assessment (see **71.3**) is not permitted of an assisted party's costs, nor of the costs of a person under disability, unless the solicitor representing the person under disability waives the right to further costs (**PD 44, paras 9.8** and **9.9**).

Parties should try to ensure that their costs statements are realistic. The fact that a party's costs statement is inflated may well be used against that party by the court and the other side if costs are awarded to the other side. Underpricing a party's costs may assist in attacking its opponent's costs if it loses, but will be counterproductive if it is awarded costs.

The judge retains responsibility for ensuring that the costs claimed are not disproportionate or unreasonable, even if they are not disputed by the paying party (**PD 44, para. 9.10**). The fact that the paying party does not dispute the amount claimed can be taken as some indication that the amount is proportionate and reasonable.

Chapter 47 Multi-track

INTRODUCTION

A vast range of cases are allocated to the multi-track from simple contractual disputes involving **47.1**
little more than £25,000, to complex commercial cases involving difficult issues of fact and law with values of several million pounds, to cases where perhaps no money is at stake but which raise points of real public importance. For proceedings issued before 6 April 2009, the upper limit of the fast track bracket is £15,000 (**CPR, r. 26.6(4)(b)(ii)**). Case management on the multi-track reflects the range of cases dealt with. Simpler cases are given standard directions without the need for hearings, and the parties are expected to comply with those directions without complicating or delaying matters. At the other end of the scale, the courts adopt a far more active approach, possibly with several directions hearings in the form of case management conferences and pre-trial reviews. The first case management conference is often an allocation and directions hearing. The courts adopt a flexible approach to ensure each case receives the right amount of case management input from the court (**PD 29, para. 3.2(2)**). Straightforward multi-track cases may be given tight timetables from defence to trial that are similar to those on the fast track. In such cases, the comments made in **46.1** apply with equal force about the need to be well prepared before commencing proceedings, the main difference being on costs. Even in complex multi-track cases it will be important for case preparation to be reasonably advanced before issue, because under the CPR there is a great deal 'front loading', and the procedural judge will want to be assisted by the parties in identifying the issues and the evidence required at the first case management conference.

Cases on the multi-track will generally be dealt with either in the Royal Courts of Justice or other civil trial centre (see **PD 29, paras 2** and **3.1**). The procedural judge may need to order a transfer on first consideration or at an allocation hearing, see **42.6**. Case management will generally be dealt with by masters and district judges (see **PD 2B**), unless the case has been selected for docketing (see **42.37**). It is the duty of the parties at all hearings to consider whether any directions should be made, as this can avoid the need for additional case management hearings later on (**PD 29, para. 3.5**).

Many of the civil justice reforms made in 2013 affect claims on the multi-track, and the case and costs management processes described in **chapters 42** and **43** need to be read together with this chapter.

CASE MANAGEMENT STAGES IN MULTI-TRACK CASES

47.2 Provisional track allocation takes place shortly after defences are filed (see **42.12**), but formal track allocation is decided by a procedural judge usually shortly after the return of directions questionnaires (see **42.25**) or at an allocation hearing (see **42.23**) or case management conference (see **42.24**). Once a case is allocated to the multi-track the court will give directions and hold such procedural hearings as may be appropriate in order to progress the case to trial or resolution by other means. **Figure 47.1** illustrates the main stages in the progress of a multi-track case to trial.

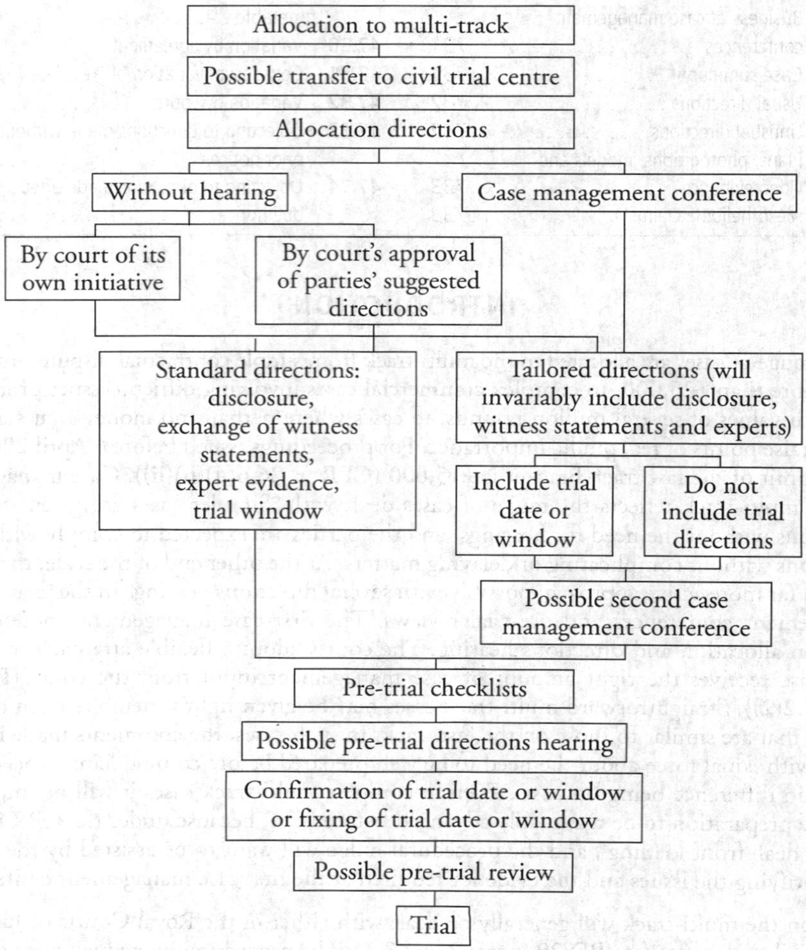

Figure 47.1 The multi-track

Directions on allocation

At the same time as a case is allocated to the multi-track the procedural judge will decide whether to give directions or to fix a case management conference or pre-trial review (or both a case management conference and a pre-trial review) and such other directions as are thought fit (**CPR, r. 29.2(1)**). The procedural judge will therefore take a view as to the complexity of the case, and the amount of work required to get it ready for trial, and decide whether or not it is necessary to call the parties in before the court for a procedural hearing. The judge will also consider whether the case should be stayed while ADR procedures are attempted, see **42.42**. **47.3**

The court will seek to tailor its directions to the needs of the case, and the steps the parties have already taken to prepare it for trial. It will also take into account the extent to which the parties have complied with any pre-action protocol (see **chapter 8**). The court's concern will be to ensure the issues between the parties are identified, and that the evidence required for the trial is prepared and disclosed (**PD 29, para. 4.3**).

Making an informed decision regarding directions

It is important that the court should be informed on the progress made by the parties in gathering the necessary evidence and in identifying the real issues in the case. It is in the interests of the parties to make sure that they provide all necessary information to the court. This will ensure the directions given are realistic and suitable for the case, and avoid the necessity for the court to ask for further information and perhaps impose sanctions. The information the court will act on may be gathered from: **47.4**

(a) the claim form;
(b) the particulars of claim (if provided separately from the claim form);
(c) the defence;
(d) any documents (such as witness statements and experts' reports) filed with the particulars of claim or defence;
(e) the completed directions questionnaires;
(f) costs budgets filed by the parties;
(g) disclosure reports, electronic documents questionnaires, and proposed disclosure directions;
(h) any further documents filed with the directions questionnaires, provided these are agreed between the parties, or have been served on the other parties, with a statement to that effect (**PD 26, para. 2.2(2)**);
(i) any further information that the parties may be required to produce on an order by the court to clarify the matters in dispute or to give additional information; and
(j) any proposed directions, particularly where they have been agreed between the parties (**PD 29, para. 4.6**).

Inadequate information

From time to time parties in cases allocated to the multi-track provide little or no information other than that contained in their statements of case. In such cases the court may call a case management conference, and it may order the parties to provide further information about their cases pursuant to **CPR, r. 26.5(3)**. An order for further information at the allocation stage will be made on form N156. The order will set out the nature of the information and documentation required, and provide that copies must be sent to the court and other parties by a specified time. A note on form N156 warns that if an allocation hearing becomes necessary through a failure to provide the information ordered, the defaulting party may be ordered to pay the costs of that hearing. **47.5**

However, it is perhaps more likely that the court will simply impose directions giving a tight timetable for trial (**PD 29, para. 4.10**). Doing so will put enormous pressure on the parties. They will either have to comply, or will find themselves in considerable difficulty unless they apply promptly for tailored directions. This is because the court will assume for the purposes of any later application (in the absence of any appeal or application within 14 days to vary)

Commentary

that the parties were content that the directions were correct in the circumstances then existing (**PD 29, para. 6.2(2)**).

The general approach in these cases where there is inadequate information is for directions along the following lines to be made by the court of its own initiative:

(a) filing and service of any further information required to clarify either party's case;
(b) standard disclosure between the parties (**para. 4.10(2)**, which is the source for this, has not been amended as part of the civil justice reforms of 2013, and may need to be reconsidered given the introduction of menu disclosure in multi-track claims. Standard disclosure is nevertheless a sensible fallback position. See **chapter 50**);
(c) simultaneous exchange of witness statements;
(d) for the appointment of a single expert unless there is good reason for not doing so;
(e) simultaneous exchange of experts' reports in cases or on issues where single expert directions have not been given (unless expert evidence is required on both liability and quantum, in which event the direction may be for simultaneous exchange on the liability issues, but sequential exchange on quantum issues);
(f) if experts' reports are not agreed, that there be a discussion between the experts for the purpose of identifying the expert evidence issues, and, if possible, reaching agreement between the experts, and the preparation of a statement setting out the issues on which they are agreed and a summary of their reasons on the issues where they disagree;
(g) listing a case management conference after the final date in the above directions;
(h) specifying a trial period; and
(i) if appropriate, directions for the parties to consider ADR.

An ADR direction may include provisions requiring the parties to file witness statements if they consider the case to be unsuitable for ADR giving their reasons for saying that the case is unsuitable (**PD 29, para. 4.10(9)**). This approach to ADR directions applies where the court does not hold a case management conference and where the court does not know what steps have been taken by the parties other than the exchange of statements of case, so is relatively unusual.

Avoiding the need for a directions hearing

47.6 If the parties in a multi-track case agree proposals for the management of the case and the court considers that the proposals are suitable, the court may simply approve them without the need for a directions hearing (**CPR, r. 29.4; PD 29, para. 4.6** and **4.7**). This is encouraged, as it obviously saves costs and court time. In order to obtain the court's approval the agreed directions should be based on the standard directions available on the Ministry of Justice website (**CPR, r. 29.1(2)**, and see **42.15**), and must:

(a) if appropriate, include a direction regarding the filing of a reply;
(b) if appropriate, provide for amending any statement of case;
(c) include provision about the disclosure of documents;
(d) include provision about both factual and expert evidence (the provision about expert evidence may be to the effect that no expert evidence is required);
(e) if appropriate, include dates for service of requests for further information and/or questions to experts, and when they should be answered;
(f) include a date or a period when it is proposed the trial will take place; and
(g) if appropriate, a date for a case management conference.

It will be seen that only items (c), (d) and (f) are obligatory in all cases, although the others will frequently arise in practice. Proposed agreed directions must lay down a timetable by reference to calendar dates. The court will scrutinise the timetable carefully, with particular attention to the proposals for the trial and case management conference, and will be astute to ensure these are no later than is reasonably necessary (**PD 29, para. 4.7(2)**). Ultimate responsibility for case management directions remains with the court, and it cannot be assumed that even agreed directions will always be approved.

By **PD 29, para.** 4.7(3) (which may need to be reconsidered given the introduction of menu disclosure in multi-track claims, see **chapter 50**), the provision in any agreed directions relating to disclosure may:

(a) limit disclosure to standard disclosure, or less than that; and/or
(b) direct that disclosure will take place by the supply of copy documents without a list of documents, but if so, it must say either that the parties must serve a disclosure statement with the copies, or that they have agreed to disclose in this way without a disclosure statement.

Under **PD 29, para.** 4.8(4), read together with **CPR, r.** 35.4(2), the provisions regarding factual and expert evidence should, if appropriate, deal with:

(a) whether the evidence should be disclosed simultaneously or sequentially;
(b) the use of a single expert;
(c) without prejudice discussions between the experts if a single expert is not going to be instructed;
(d) the field and issues which the expert evidence will address;
(e) if practicable, the name of the proposed expert; and
(f) the estimated costs of the proposed expert evidence.

The court is free to reject directions that have been agreed between the parties, but will take them into account when making its own directions (either without a hearing or on a case management conference). The ultimate responsibility for case management remains at all times with the court, and parties will be unwise to assume that agreed directions will be automatically approved.

Once directions have been made by consent, the court retains control, and can override them in the future if this is justified in the circumstances (*Re Debtors (Nos. 13-MISC-2000 and 14-MISC-2000)* (2000) *The Times*, 10 April 2000).

Commentary

CASE MANAGEMENT CONFERENCES

Case management conferences are an integral part of the new system of active case management by the courts. They are not simply directions hearings, but are intended to ensure that the real issues between the parties are identified. Side issues will be dispensed with either by agreement between the parties with due encouragement from the judge, or by means of summary judgment or striking-out determinations at an early stage. Case management conferences may be held immediately after a case is allocated to the multi-track or at any time thereafter through to the listing stage. They can be used as the vehicle for laying down directions at the allocation stage, or may be used later in order to assess how the case is progressing when the initial directions on allocation should have been completed. Normally the court has a discretion whether to call a case management conference. However, where it is contemplated that an order may be made either for the evidence on a particular issue to be given by a single expert, or that an assessor should be appointed, **PD 29, para. 4.13**, provides that a case management conference must be held unless the parties have consented to the order in writing. Some procedural judges use some case management conferences as mediation-style hearings to promote settlement. Judges adopting this practice will have extensive knowledge of the case, and will attempt to assist settlement so as to restrict and identify the issues to be tried. Whether this is a legitimate use of the judicial office, with the inherent pressure exerted by the presence of a judge and the lack of clear rules governing the roles of those present and how the hearing should be conducted, has yet to be decided. **47.7**

Where a case management conference is or may be dealt with by the trial judge, no reference should be made to any Part 36 offers whether in the case management bundle or at the hearing (see **66.3**). **CPR, r. 36.13**, does not prevent disclosure to procedural judges who will not be conducting the trial.

Case management conferences will also be called in cases where the court feels it cannot properly give directions on its own initiative, and where no agreed directions have been filed which it feels can be approved (**PD 29, para. 4.12**).

By encouraging the parties to settle their dispute or resolve it outside the court system, and by forcing the parties into identifying the real issues at an early stage, case management conferences are a means of using court time to save more time.

Procedure before a case management conference

47.8 There is a commitment towards having case management conferences listed as promptly as possible (**PD 29, para. 4.12(2)**). The minimum period of notice the court will give to the parties of the date for the case management conference is three clear days (**CPR, r. 3.3(3)**; **PD 29, para. 3.7**). In practice the parties need to anticipate the possibility of there being a case management conference some weeks in advance.

Matters to be addressed in advance of the first case management conference in multi-track claims include the following:

(a) Not less than 14 days before the first case management conference each party must file and serve a disclosure report complying with **r. 31.5(3)**, see **chapter 50**. Personal injuries claims are excepted from this requirement.
(b) The parties must seek to agree directions. This includes (in non-personal injuries claims) an obligation on the parties to meet or speak on the telephone at least seven days before the case management conference to seek to agree a proportionate proposal for disclosure of documents (**r 31.5(5)**). In all multi-track claims there is a more general obligation to endeavour to agree all the appropriate directions for the case (**r. 29.1(2)**).
(c) A costs budget (see **chapter 43**), unless the case is one of the specialist claims excluded from costs management (see **43.5**).
(d) Attempts to agree costs budgets if costs management applies.
(e) A case management bundle for use at the case management conference.
(f) Possibly, a case summary (see **47.11**).

Attendance at case management conferences

47.9 If a case management conference is to be attended by a legal representative on behalf of a party, the representative must be someone familiar with the case (**CPR, r. 29.3(2)**). It is unacceptable to send a trainee with a two-page briefing note on such a hearing. Instead it will have to be the fee earner concerned, or someone (possibly counsel) who is fully familiar with the file, the issues and the proposed evidence, who must attend. They must be able to field the questions that are likely to be covered at the hearing, and have the authority to agree and/or make representations on the matters reasonably to be expected to arise. Where the inadequacy of the person attending or his or her instructions leads to the adjournment of the hearing, it will be normal for a wasted costs order to be made (**PD 29, para. 5.2(3)**), or even an order for indemnity-basis costs and interest on damages at a higher rate than usual (see *Baron v Lovell* [1999] CPLR 630). Where a direction is made for the attendance of the parties and one of the parties is a company, the order should be that individuals with knowledge of the history of the case should attend (*Tarajan Overseas Ltd v Kaye* [2001] EWCA Civ 1859, *The Times*, 22 January 2002).

In the Chancery Division, whenever possible, the advocates instructed or expected to appear at trial should attend case management conferences and other case management hearings (Chancery Guide, para. 3.9). In the Admiralty and Commercial Courts, case management conferences should be attended on behalf of each party both by the fee earner with conduct of the case and by at least one of the advocates retained (Admiralty and Commercial Courts Guide, para. D8.2). Case management conferences in complex cases in the Admiralty and Commercial Courts are regarded as particularly significant stages in the litigation, and are conducted by a designated judge who will manage the case, and will usually subsequently be the trial judge (paras D4.1, D4.2, D4.3 and D8.3).

Business at case management conferences

At a case management conference the court will, as stated by **CPR, rr. 3.12(2)** and **3.17**, **PD 3E, para. 2.3**, and **PD 29, para. 5.1**: **47.10**

(a) make a thorough review of the steps the parties have taken to date in preparing the case for trial;
(b) consider the extent to which they have complied with any previous orders and directions;
(c) review any costs budgets that have not been agreed between all the parties, make appropriate revisions, and approve the revised budgets;
(d) decide on the directions needed to progress the action in accordance with the overriding objective and taking into account the costs budgets;
(e) ensure that reasonable agreements are made between the parties about the matters in issue and the future conduct of the claim; and
(f) record all such agreements.

To assist the court the legal representatives for all parties should ensure that all documents (and in particular witness statements and expert reports) the court is likely to ask to see are brought to court. The court may give directions for preparing a case management bundle. Legal representatives should consider whether the parties themselves should attend. If the witness statements and experts' reports have not been exchanged at the time of the case management conference, it should follow from *General Mediterranean Holdings SA v Patel* [2000] 1 WLR 272 that the only reports and statements that can legitimately be called for are those that have been disclosed or that may be voluntarily disclosed at the hearing.

It is not open to a judge to dismiss a claim at a hearing of an application for directions, particularly where dismissal of the claim is unprompted and without giving the parties advance notice so they can make representations (*Norbrook Laboratories Ltd v Carr* [2010] EWCA Civ 1108, LTL 14/10/2010).

Case summary

An additional matter the parties are required by **PD 29, para. 5.6**, to consider is whether the court may be assisted by a written case summary. This should be a short document not exceeding 500 words which is designed to assist the court in understanding and dealing with the issues raised in the case (**PD 29, para. 5.7**). It should give a brief chronology of the claim, and state the factual issues that are agreed and those in dispute, and the nature of the evidence needed to decide them. Responsibility for preparing the document rests with the claimant, and if possible it should be agreed by the other parties. **47.11**

In the Admiralty and Commercial Courts, the legal representatives for each party must liaise for the purpose of preparing a short case memorandum, which will be included in the case management bundle. They must also prepare an agreed list of important issues (with a separate section dealing with matters which are common ground between all or some of the parties), and the claimant's solicitors must prepare the case management bundle (Admiralty and Commercial Courts Guide, paras D5.1, D6.1 and D7.1). The case management bundle must contain these documents, together with the claim form and statements of case (if a case summary has been prepared, the bundles must contain the summary rather than the relevant statement of case), and any orders etc. made so far (see para. D7.2), being careful to avoid any reference to interim payments and Part 36 offers (as the case management judge could well be the trial judge, see paras D5.4 and D7.4). The case management bundle must be lodged with the Listing Office at least seven days before the first case management conference (para. D7.5).

In the Technology and Construction Court, the court will fix a case management conference within 14 days of filing of the acknowledgment of service or defence or any order transferring the claim to the TCC (**PD 60, para. 8.1**). The court will then notify the parties of the date for the case management conference, and send them a case management information sheet and a

Commentary

case management directions form (see **PD 60, para. 8.2**, app. A and app. B). These should be completed and exchanged, and then filed by 4 p.m. two days before the case management conference (**para. 8.3**). The parties are encouraged to agree directions.

Usual directions

47.12 In all cases the court will set a timetable at the case management conference for the steps it decides are necessary for preparing the case for trial (**PD 29, paras 5.3 and 5.4**). Typically the court will consider giving directions on the following matters:

(a) Whether the claimant has made clear the claim that is being made and the amount being claimed, and whether the defence is no more than a bare denial or is otherwise unclear. Orders for amendment and/or for further information may be appropriate if the statements of case are insufficiently clear for the other side to understand the case that has to be met.
(b) The scope of disclosure of documents required.
(c) The nature of the expert evidence required, and how and when it should be obtained. The court will not give permission for the use of expert evidence unless it can identify each expert by name or field of expertise, and say whether each expert's evidence should be given orally or by use of a report. Further matters that may be considered are whether the evidence on a particular issue should be given by a single expert, or that an assessor should be appointed, and whether there should be discussions between the experts.
(d) Disclosure of witness statements and summaries.
(e) Whether further information should be provided on matters other than statements of case, such as witness statements.
(f) Arrangements for questions that may be put to experts.
(g) Whether it would be just and save costs to have split trials on liability and quantum, or whether there should be the trial of one or more preliminary issues.
(h) Whether to make a costs management order (see **chapter 43**).
(i) Whether there should be another case management conference, a costs management conference, or a pre-trial review.
(j) Whether to assign the case to a particular judge for case management (docketing, see **42.37**).
(k) Whether it is possible to fix a date for the trial, or to give a trial 'window'. The court will be anxious to comply with the rule that the trial should be fixed as soon as practicable (**CPR, r. 29.2(2)**).
(l) Whether the trial should be dealt with by a High Court judge, or by a specialist judge. If so, the court will also consider transferring the case to the appropriate court (**PD 29, para. 5.9**).

At case management conferences in Admiralty or Commercial Court cases the judge will, if practicable, fix the entire pre-trial timetable, or as much of it as practicable (see Admiralty and Commercial Courts Guide, para. D8.7). A standard set of directions is set out in the Admiralty and Commercial Courts Guide, app. 8. The same practice is followed where possible in county courts, provided trial windows and the availability of judges are known. In a High Court district registry, trial dates are fixed by liaising with the presiding judge through the diary manager. On each circuit the district judges, designated civil judges and the presiding judge cooperate closely on timetabling issues.

Unusual directions

47.13 It is the duty of the parties to ensure that all interim matters are dealt with at the case management conference. If they want an order dealing with a matter that is not normally dealt with at a case management conference, such as an order for an interim payment or for specific disclosure, and they know the application is likely to be opposed, they should issue and serve an application notice (form N244) in time for it to be heard at the conference. If the time allowed for the conference is insufficient to deal also with the contested application, they must inform the court at once so that a fresh date can be fixed. Failure to take these steps may result in a costs sanction (**PD 29, para. 5.8**). **PD 23A, para. 2.10**, provides that where a party decides to make an application at a hearing that has already been fixed, but there is insufficient time to serve an application notice, it may be sufficient simply to give such written notice as is possible, and to make the application orally at the original hearing.

Other directions from those provided for by **CPR, r. 3.1(2)**, that may be considered in appropriate cases include:

(a) directing that part of the proceedings, such as a counterclaim, be dealt with as separate proceedings;
(b) staying the whole or part of the proceedings either generally or until a specified date or event;
(c) consolidating proceedings;
(d) trying two or more actions at the same time;
(e) deciding the order in which issues are to be tried; and
(f) excluding an issue from consideration.

Plans, photographs, models and video evidence

Generally a party intending to use photographs, plans, diagrams, models and similar items as evidence at trial must give notice to the other parties by the date for disclosing witness statements (**CPR, r. 33.6(4)**). The skeleton argument should refer to a document which must identify for the court all relevant features which appear in the maps, plans, diagrams or photographs to be used at the trial (*Hunte v E. Bottomley and Sons Ltd* [2007] EWCA Civ 1168, *The Times*, 21 November 2007). Video recordings fall into the wide definition of 'documents' for the purposes of **Part 31**, so the usual rules on disclosure and inspection apply (see **chapter 50**). Furthermore, there is an obligation to inform the court at the first opportunity that such evidence will be relied upon, as arrangements need to be made to ensure video equipment is available at trial, and extra time will be required for the trial for showing the evidence (*Rall v Hume* [2001] EWCA Civ 146, [2001] 3 All ER 248). **47.14**

Commentary

Mesothelioma claims

Mesothelioma claims are governed by **PD 3D**. In these cases the claim form and particulars of claim must be marked either 'Living Mesothelioma Claim' or 'Fatal Mesothelioma Claim' (**para. 3.1**). On filing and serving the claim form and particulars of claim, or as soon as possible thereafter, and in any event at least seven days before the case management conference, the claimant must file and serve any witness statements about liability (**para. 3.2**). At the first case management conference, unless there is a good reason not to do so, the defendant must be prepared to show cause why judgment should not be entered on liability and why the defendant should not make a standard interim payment (**para. 6.2**). If liability remains in issue, directions will usually be made at the first case management conference for the defendant to file and serve outline submissions showing cause, and for a show-cause hearing (**para. 6.4**). **47.15**

If the defendant fails to show cause, or admits liability, judgment will normally be entered for a sum to be determined (see **42.46** to **42.49**), and for a standard interim payment. Otherwise, the court will give directions including setting the trial date or window (**paras 6.5** to **6.8**). In living mesothelioma claims the trial will generally not be more than 16 weeks after service of the claim form (**para. 7.1**), and will often decide that strict compliance with the pre-action protocols was unnecessary (**para. 9**).

FIXING THE DATE FOR TRIAL

The court will fix the trial date or the period in which the trial is to take place as soon as practicable (**CPR, r. 29.2(2)**). This may be possible when it gives allocation directions, but in **47.16** complex cases (and also, perhaps, badly prepared cases and cases where the facts are developing, such as many personal injuries claims) this may have to be delayed, perhaps for a considerable period of time. Where fixing the trial date is postponed, it may be revisited either at a later case management conference, or on the application of the parties, or after further scrutiny by the court.

When the court fixes the date for trial (or lays down a trial period or 'window'), it will give written notice to the parties, and will also specify a date by which the parties must file pre-trial checklists (**r. 29.2(3)**). The court may alternatively make an order for an early trial on a fixed date and dispense with pre-trial checklists (**PD 29, para. 8.1(2)**), or may simply list the case for trial when it reconsiders the case at the time when pre-trial checklists would be sent out, dispensing with the need for checklists at that stage (**CPR, r. 29.6(1)**).

In Queen's Bench Division cases proceeding in the Royal Courts of Justice in London, other than cases in the Admiralty and Commercial Courts and the Technology and Construction Court, a direction will be given as early as possible (often the first case management conference) with a view to fixing the trial or trial window (see Queen's Bench Guide, para. 9.4.4). The court will often direct that the trial is not to begin before a specified date, or that it will be held within a specified period (para. 9.4.5). The claimant must then, within the next seven days, take out an appointment with the Listing Officer and give notice of the appointment to the other parties (para. 9.4.7). At the listing hearing the claimant must bring any case summary, the particulars of claim and any orders relevant to listing, and all parties must have details of the dates of availability of their witnesses, experts and counsel. The Listing Officer will try to provide the earliest firm trial date or trial window consistent with the case management directions (para. 9.4.8).

In most cases in the Admiralty and Commercial Courts, a fixed trial date will be given immediately after the pre-trial timetable has been set at the case management conference (Admiralty and Commercial Courts Guide, para. D16.1).

Fixed dates are given on the basis that if previous fixtures have been substantially underestimated, or urgent matters arise, the trial may be delayed for a few days. Where such a delay might cause particular inconvenience, the Clerk to the Commercial Court should be informed well in advance (para. D16.2).

In the Technology and Construction Court, the trial date is usually fixed at the first case management conference (**PD 60, para. 8.6**).

The power to adjourn the trial is considered at **61.9** to **61.14**, and listing and adjourning problems caused by the restricted availability of experts are discussed at **61.8**.

PRE-TRIAL CHECKLISTS

47.17 Pre-trial checklists, in form N170, will (unless dispensed with) be sent out to the parties by the court. These must be completed and returned by the date specified in the directions given when the court fixed the date or period for trial (**CPR, r. 29.6**). In multi-track claims directions for listing for trial are usually given on a case management conference at some stage after allocation. The forms should be served by the court at least 14 days before they must be returned. Each party is under an obligation to return a completed checklist before the specified date.

Purpose of checklists

47.18 Pre-trial checklists are used to check that earlier orders and directions have been complied with, and to provide up-to-date information to assist the court with deciding when to hold the trial and how long it will take, and in making trial timetable directions. Once all the checklists have been received, or the time limit has expired, the file will be placed before the procedural judge, who will make directions for trial along the same lines as those set out in **47.26**, or direct that there should be a pre-trial directions hearing or pre-trial review. A case management conference may be convened specifically to consider and limit issues.

Exchange of checklists

47.19 The CPR do not require the parties to exchange copies of their pre-trial checklists, but doing so may avoid the parties giving conflicting or incomplete information to the court (**PD 29, para. 8.1(5)**). Getting this right may avoid the need for a pre-trial directions hearing or pre-trial review.

Failure to file checklists

47.20 If no one returns a pre-trial checklist by the specified date, the court will order that unless a completed pre-trial checklist is filed within seven days from service of that order, the claim, defence and any counterclaim will be struck out without further order (**CPR, r. 29.6(3)**). Where only some of the parties file pre-trial checklists the court will fix a pre-trial directions hearing, under **r. 29.6(4)** (see **PD 29, para. 8.5**). It will also fix a directions hearing if any of the questionnaires do not provide the necessary information, or if the court considers that such a hearing is necessary to decide what further directions should be given to complete the preparations for trial (**CPR, r. 29.6(4)**).

LISTING AND HEARING FEES

47.21 When the claimant files his pre-trial checklist, two fees are payable. One is a listing fee of £110 (**CPFO, fee 2.2**), and the other is a hearing fee of £1,090 (**CPFO, fee 2.3**). Fee 2.3 is not payable if the court fixed the hearing date on the issue of the claim. If the court fixes a trial date or trial week without requiring pre-trial checklists, fees 2.2 and 2.3 become payable within 14 days of the date of dispatch of the notice (or the date when oral notice is given if no written notice is given) of the trial date or week. For discussion of who should pay these fees see **46.12**. If either fee is not paid, the court will send a notice to pay in form N173, and failing payment within the time stated in the notice, the claim will be struck out (**CPR, r. 3.7**).

As an incentive to settle, the hearing fee of £1,090 will be refunded in whole or in part on a sliding scale if the court receives notice in writing from the party who paid the fee that the case has been settled or discontinued. The refunds are:

Court notified more than 28 days before the hearing	100 per cent
Court notified between 15 and 28 days before the hearing	75 per cent
Court notified between 7 and 14 days before the hearing	50 per cent

PRE-TRIAL DIRECTIONS HEARINGS

47.22 Pre-trial directions hearings serve a similar purpose to pre-trial reviews, but concentrate on making the decisions relevant to fixing the date of the trial. They are fixed for dates as early as possible, and the parties are given at least three clear days' notice of the date. Even if a pre-trial directions hearing is fixed because some of the parties did not file their pre-trial checklists, the court will normally fix or confirm the trial date and make orders about the steps to prepare the case for trial (**PD 29, para. 8.3(2)**). The court is likely to make further directions similar to those set out in **47.28**.

PRE-TRIAL REVIEW

47.23 If a pre-trial review (rather than a pre-trial directions hearing, see 47.22) is listed, it is likely to take place about eight to 10 weeks before trial. The pre-trial review gives the court a further opportunity to check that the parties have complied with earlier orders and directions, and may help in promoting settlement. Pre-trial reviews are not held in all cases, but only in those that merit the additional hearing. An example is *JN Dairies Ltd v Johal Dairies Ltd* [2010] EWCA Civ 348, LTL 31/3/2010, where shortly before the trial both sides disclosed evidence in support of allegations of discreditable conduct by the other side. It was held that both sides should have applied to the court to list a pre-trial review to deal with amendments, further disclosure and other directions. The intention is that pre-trial reviews should be conducted by the eventual trial judge.

Before the pre-trial review

47.24 In some cases a pre-trial review may be required by directions made by the court at an earlier stage, such as on allocation or at a case management conference. In other cases the court may decide to hold a pre-trial review of its own initiative, such as when it considers the pre-trial checklists. In this event it will give the parties at least seven clear days' notice of the hearing of a pre-trial review (**CPR, r. 29.7**).

In the Chancery Division the claimant should, seven days before the pre-trial review, circulate a list of matters to be considered at the pre-trial review, including suggestions for how the case should be tried. Other parties must respond at least two days before the hearing (Chancery Guide, para. 3.23). The claimant should deliver to the Chancery Judges' Listing Office, by 10 a.m. on the day before the hearing of the pre-trial review, a bundle containing the lists of matters to be considered and proposals served by the parties on each other and the trial timetable, together with the results of the discussions between the parties on those matters, and any other useful documents (para. 3.24).

In the Commercial Court the parties should have completed Commercial Court pre-trial checklists (in the form set out in the Admiralty and Commercial Courts Guide, app. 13) in accordance with the pre-trial timetable directions. Before the pre-trial review, the parties must discuss and, if possible, agree a draft written timetable for the trial (**PD 58, para. 11.3**). The claimant's solicitor must ensure that the case management bundle is up to date (**PD 58, para. 10.9**).

Attendance

47.25 The same rules about a fully informed representative being present apply to pre-trial reviews as apply to case management conferences (see 47.9) and in the specialist courts in particular they should be attended by the trial advocates.

Pre-trial review directions

47.26 At a pre-trial review the court will not readily change earlier directions, and will apply the same principles as are applied generally when the parties fail to apply within 14 days for variation of case management directions (**PD 29, paras 6** and **9.3**; see 47.5).

Perhaps the most important task on a pre-trial review is to determine the timetable for the trial itself. This can lay down time limits for examination and cross-examination of witnesses, and for speeches. Doing this is intended to force advocates to focus their preparation, and to produce well-managed trials. Other matters to be dealt with are:

(a) Evidence, particularly expert evidence. At this stage there should have been full disclosure and perhaps also discussions between the experts. It may be possible to make more rigorous directions about which experts really do need to be called at the trial, and which experts (or which parts of the expert evidence) can be taken from the experts' reports.

(b) A time estimate for the trial.
(c) Preparation and organisation of trial bundles.
(d) Fixing a trial date or week.
(e) Fixing the place of trial. This will normally be at a civil trial centre but may be at another court depending on the convenience of the parties and the availability of court resources (**PD 29, para. 10.1**).

Agreed pre-trial review directions

The parties are required to seek to agree the directions to be made on the pre-trial review, and may file an agreed order (**PD 29, para. 9.2**). The court may then make an order in the terms agreed, or make some other order, or reject the proposals and continue with the pre-trial review. **47.27**

DIRECTIONS GIVEN AT OTHER HEARINGS

The court is not restricted to making case management directions on the occasions described above, but can do so on any occasion the case comes before the court (**PD 29, para. 3.4**). In fact, whenever there is a hearing it is the duty of the parties to consider whether any directions should be made, and to make any appropriate application on that occasion (**PD 29, para. 3.5**). Further, the court may hold a directions hearing on its own initiative on three clear days' notice whenever it appears necessary to do so. This can include situations where progress is delayed because one or other of the parties is in default of directions previously made (**PD 29, para. 3.6**). It can also occur because a party needs a direction not already in place, perhaps because a need to amend, or to ask for further information, has arisen since the last case management hearing. In such cases the application must be made as soon as possible so as to minimise the disruption to the original timetable (**PD 29, para. 3.8**). **47.28**

VARIATION OF CASE MANAGEMENT TIMETABLE

As mentioned in 47.5, the court will assume for the purposes of any later application that the parties were content that any case management directions given were correct in the circumstances existing when they were given, unless an appeal or application to vary is made within 14 days. It is also regarded as essential that any party wanting to vary the timetable should take steps to do so as soon as possible (**PD 29, para. 6.2**). A delay in making an essential application to vary the timetable may well have the effect of losing all the time used before the application is eventually heard, which is not going to be looked upon favourably given the objective of dealing with cases expeditiously (**CPR, r. 1.1(2)(d)**) and complying with court orders (**r. 1.1(2)(f)**). **47.29**

Variation by agreement

Case management directions fall into two categories: **47.30**

(a) Those that can be varied only by an order made by the court on an application by a party seeking a variation (**CPR, r. 29.5(1)**). These 'key dates' are:
  (i) dates fixed for holding a case management conference;
  (ii) dates fixed for holding a pre-trial review;
  (iii) dates specified for the return of pre-trial checklists; and
  (iv) dates fixed for trial (including a trial 'window').
(b) All other types of case management direction. These may be varied by the parties by consent, provided the variation does not affect any of the 'key dates' in category (a) above. There is no need to file anything with the court when a variation is agreed that does not affect any of the 'key dates' (**PD 29, para. 6.5(1)**).

Consensual variation of 'key dates'

47.31 If the parties agree to a variation of any of the key dates in the case management timetable as laid down by the court, they must apply for an order by consent, file a draft of the order sought, and also file an agreed statement of the reasons why the variation is sought (**PD 29, para. 6.5(2)**). If the procedural judge is satisfied with the stated reasons, an order will be made without a hearing, either in the terms agreed or as thought fit by the procedural judge. Otherwise, the application will be listed for hearing, at which the parties will need to justify their position.

Variation by court

47.32 The court has power to vary directions at any hearing of its own initiative (**PD 29, para. 3.4**). A court may vary previous directions without the need for an appeal where there has been a change of circumstances (**para. 6.4**). Courts act with considerable caution before making substantial variations in previous directions (such as cancelling previous directions for the trial of a preliminary issue), because doing so comes close to overruling the decision-making process of the earlier directions hearing. Whether a substantial variation should be allowed depends on the circumstances of the case, and an application of the overriding objective (*Umm Qarn Management Co. Ltd v Bunting* [2001] CPLR 21). If there has been a real change in circumstances there is usually no objection to the court reviewing previous directions. Where there are no changed circumstances, any review of directions made on notice has to be made by way of appeal (*Jameson v Lovis* [2001] EWCA Civ 1264, LTL 24/7/2001).

Objecting to directions made without prior notice

47.33 This paragraph deals with directions made in two circumstances:

(a) by the court of its own initiative; and
(b) where a party can establish it did not receive notice of the hearing where the directions were made.

A party who is dissatisfied with the directions given in such circumstances must apply for the court to reconsider its decision, and the application will normally be heard by the same judge as gave the original directions (**PD 29, para. 6.3**). The court will give the parties at least three clear days' notice of the hearing to reconsider the directions. At the hearing the court may confirm the original directions, or may make such different order as it thinks just.

Objecting to directions made after due notice

47.34 Directions made after due notice, where there has been no change of circumstances, can be varied only by mounting an appeal (**PD 29, para. 6.3(2)**). For reviewing interim decisions, see **32.41** to **32.44**. The procedure for appealing is considered in **chapter 74**.

Chapter 48 Non-compliance, Sanctions and Relief

Commentary

INTRODUCTION

So that the court can ensure that its case management directions and orders are complied with, and to retain control over the conduct of litigation, it needs to be armed with suitable coercive powers. Failure to enforce the rules of court will encourage parties to make tactical use of the legal process, which should not be allowed (*National Commercial Bank Jamaica Ltd v Olint Corporation Ltd* [2009] UKPC 16, [2009] 1 WLR 1405 at [15]). The most draconian sanction that may be imposed is striking out. **CPR, r, 3.4(2)(c)**, provides that the court may strike out the whole or part of a statement of case if it appears that there has been a failure to comply with a rule, practice direction or court order. Striking out the whole of a party's statement of case ought to be reserved for the most serious, or repeated, breaches or defaults (see *UCB Corporate Services Ltd v Halifax (SW) Ltd* [1999] CPLR 691). In less serious cases of default or breach the court may be prepared to impose a sanction which, to use a phrase used in some of the cases under the old rules, 'fits the crime'. **48.1**

It is to be expected that from time to time one or other of the parties to proceedings will be unable to keep to the directions timetable that will have been imposed by the court. This will not generally be a problem provided the parties cooperate and can still keep to the directions relating to the 'key dates' for filing directions questionnaires, case management conferences, pre-trial reviews, filing pre-trial checklists and trial (**rr. 26.3(6A), 28.4** and **29.5**). If the non-compliance is through events outside the control of the defaulting party or is otherwise not deliberate, normally it would be expected that the parties would cooperate in compliance with **r. 1.4(2)(a)** and resolve the difficulty by agreeing a new timetable that preserves the key dates. The time specified by any provision of the CPR or by the court for doing any act may be varied by the written agreement of the parties, unless there is an express prohibition on variation in the rules (**r. 2.11**). If non-compliance cannot be resolved without, say, impinging on one of the key dates, or if the other side insist on compliance, the matter is likely to come before the court.

In addition to situations where an innocent party applies for an order imposing a sanction for default, similar problems arise where a defaulting party seeks an extension of time for complying with directions, in that a failure to secure an extension may result in evidence being inadmissible. Where a sanction is applied, it is possible for the defaulting party to apply for relief from the sanction (**r. 3.9**). Among the recommendations made by Sir Rupert Jackson's *Review of Civil Litigation Costs* (Ministry of Justice, December 2009) is that a less tolerant attitude should be shown to procedural default, and that **r. 3.9** should be revised to make it more difficult to obtain relief (recommendation 86).

NON-COMPLIANCE WITH DIRECTIONS AND ORDERS

Non-compliance

48.2 Non-compliance may be obvious, for example, where nothing has been done by the deadline in a direction requiring a stated step to be taken by 4.00 p.m. on a stated day.

Cases of purported compliance can cause considerable difficulty. **PD 28, para. 4.2(2)**, and **PD 29, para. 6.2(2)**, are relevant to whether a sanction should be imposed for non-compliance with directions. They provide that the court will assume for the purposes of any later application that a party who did not appeal, and who made no application to vary within 14 days of service of any order containing directions, was content that the directions were correct in the circumstances then existing.

It is therefore important that a party's representatives are clear on what they have to do when directions or orders are made, and that they can comply within the time provided. Once an order or direction has been made, they must comply or appeal.

Purported compliance

48.3 It often happens that although documents are served by a deadline, the other side is far from content that they properly comply with the relevant order or direction. The first question is whether it is the order or the purported performance which is the problem. If the documents served technically comply with the terms of the order, the other side have either to accept the position or seek a more precise order from the court. There may be proportionality, delay or costs reasons against this. Where the view is that it is the performance which is defective, an application may be made for a sanction for breach.

The starting point is that directions and orders must be fully complied with. However, the overriding objective means that in considering purported performance a proportionate or balanced approach must be taken having regard to the practicalities of real life (*Sports Network Ltd v Calzaghe* [2008] EWHC 2566 (QB), LTL 3/11/2008, per Coulson J at [111]). Where an order requires the production of bank statements or other primary documents, there will be a breach where secondary evidence is provided (*Sports Network Ltd v Calzaghe*). In *E Group Ltd v Baker* [2008] EWHC 2349 (TCC), LTL 22/10/2008, an order which required a witness statement giving specific disclosure was breached when minor amendments were made to a document (which was not a witness statement) which had previously been rejected by the court as in almost total disregard of the original order.

The test on expiry of an unless order is whether there has been complete compliance with the terms of the order, subject only to *de minimis* exceptions (*Jani-King (GB) Ltd v Prodger* [2007] EWHC 712 (QB), LTL 10/4/2007; *Hytec Information Systems Ltd v Coventry City Council* [1997] 1 WLR 1666). A party may be regarded as in breach where there has been only 'nominal' or 'purported' compliance (*Top Layers Interior Ltd v Azure Maritime Holdings SA* [2007] EWHC 2844 (QB), LTL 10/12/2007).

RESPONDING TO THE OTHER SIDE'S DEFAULT

A party not in default faced with an opponent who has not complied with the court's directions is not entitled to try to make matters worse for the defaulting party by sitting back and waiting for the other side's default to get worse by the additional passage of time. Nor is the innocent party entitled to jump the gun by making an immediate application for an order with sanctions. In *Chilton v Surrey County Council* [1999] CPLR 525, which is discussed further at **48.7**, the Court of Appeal took against the defendant partly because it seemed the defendant was attempting to take tactical advantage of a mistake by the claimant's solicitors in overlooking to serve the revised statement of past and future loss and expense rather than cooperating with the claimant's solicitors to put matters right. **48.4**

Instead, the correct procedure is that laid down in **PD 28, paras 5.1** to **5.3** (for fast track cases) and **PD 29, paras 7.1** to **7.3** (which are in identical terms and apply in multi-track cases). The innocent party should first write to the defaulting party referring to the default, asking for it to be rectified within a short reasonable period (usually seven or 14 days), and giving warning of an intention to apply for an order if the default is not remedied. If there is continued default, the innocent party may apply for an order to enforce compliance or for a sanction to be imposed or both. Any application for such an order must be made without delay. If the innocent party does delay in making the application, the court may take the delay into account when it decides whether to make an order imposing a sanction or whether to grant relief from a sanction imposed by the rules or any practice direction.

Last-minute applications to strike out for breach of orders, particularly applications made without notice for hearing on the day of trial, were discouraged by the Court of Appeal in *Whittaker v Soper* [2001] EWCA Civ 1462, LTL 28/9/2001.

PRINCIPLES

Approach to non-compliance

In cases of simple non-compliance the court is usually primarily interested in the reasons for the non-compliance, whether the step has been taken before the application has been heard, the expected time for compliance if not, any prejudice caused to the other side, and the impact of the non-compliance on costs and the trial date. The court will seek to ensure compliance with its previous order or directions and will impose a proportionate sanction (if any) in accordance with the overriding objective. **48.5**

Commentary

A more serious view is taken if there is prejudice, if the default has an impact on the trial date, or if there is a history of non-compliance. This is particularly so where on the previous occasion the court expressed its order as being 'final'. How much more serious non-compliance is in either of these situations depends on the circumstances of the case. Based on its assessment of these factors, the court may view the default on any of four different levels of seriousness:

(a) Minor breaches are usually dealt with by allowing the defaulting party a limited period of time to comply, together with an adverse costs order in respect of any interim application needed to bring the matter before the court (*Colliers International Property Consultants v Colliers Jordan Lee Jafaar Sdn Bhd* [2008] EWHC 1524 (Comm), [2008] 2 Lloyd's Rep 368).
(b) If the matter is more serious the court will make it plain it requires compliance by stating that a revised deadline is 'final', usually combined with an adverse costs order. Proportionality has to be kept in mind (*TIP Communications LLC v Motorola Ltd* [2009] EWHC 212 (Pat), LTL 23/2/2009, where a hearing just to badge an order as 'final' was regarded as contrary to the overriding objective). Breach of a final order usually results in a sanction being imposed on a further application to the court (*Sports Network Ltd v Calzaghe* [2008] EWHC 2566 (QB), LTL 3/11/2008).
(c) More serious defaults will be met by enforcing compliance by making an 'unless' order with a stated sanction in default, again usually combined with an adverse costs order (see **48.30**). Imposition of an unless order is itself viewed as a sanction. Breach of an unless order results in the immediate imposition of the stated sanction (see **48.31**). Unless orders should only be made if the court is satisfied that in all the circumstances such a sanction is appropriate (*Marcan Shipping (London) Ltd v Kefalas* [2007] EWCA Civ 463, [2007] 1 WLR 1864). An unless order may be inappropriate where the volume of material covered by a disclosure order may make compliance difficult within a short time (*Imerman v Tchenguiz* [2009] EWHC 2902 (QB), LTL 20/11/2009).
(d) Very serious defaults result in the immediate imposition of a sanction, which may restrict the evidence that may be adduced, or restrict the value of the claim, or even consist of striking out part or the whole of a party's statement of case with judgment for the innocent party.

The Court of Appeal in *Biguzzi v Rank Leisure plc* [1999] 1 WLR 1926, in affirming a decision to strike out for wholesale disregard of the court's rules, commented that striking out would not always be the correct approach. Under the CPR the court has much wider powers than under the earlier rules for imposing proportionate sanctions. It is therefore possible to formulate suitable sanctions for breach of directions without resorting to draconian responses such as striking out. The CPR powers include making orders for indemnity costs, for paying money into court, and awarding interest at higher or lower rates. By a proper exercise of case management powers it should be possible for the courts to ensure that parties do not disregard timetables, whilst producing a just result.

However, *Biguzzi v Rank Leisure plc* must not be understood as promoting an unduly lenient approach to the imposition of sanctions. Each case has to be considered on its own facts, with the court seeking to do justice between the parties in the light of the overriding objective. There will, accordingly, be a number of cases where there has been serious default where immediate striking out is appropriate (*UCB Corporate Services Ltd v Halifax (SW) Ltd* [1999] CPLR 691; *Purdy v Cambran* [1999] CPLR 843).

When considering cases of delay, the court should be astute to apply the overriding objective to the facts of the case in hand, and should not be flooded with excessive citation of authorities, particularly short case summaries (*Hamblin v Field* (2000) *The Times*, 26 April 2000).

Preservation of trial date

48.6 The general approach that will be adopted where there has been a breach of case management directions that may impinge on the date or window fixed for the trial of a claim is set out in

PD 28, para. 5.4 (fast track), and **PD 29, para. 7.4** (multi-track). It is to be expected that a similar approach will be taken where the breach is of a practice direction or provision in the CPR. According to the relevant paragraphs of **PD 28** and **PD 29**:

(a) The court will not allow a failure to comply with directions to lead to the postponement of the trial unless the circumstances of the case are exceptional (see *AC Electrical Wholesale plc v IGW Services Ltd* (2000) LTL 10/10/2000).
(b) If practicable to do so, the court will exercise its powers in a manner that enables the case to come on for trial on the date or within the period previously set.
(c) In particular, the court will assess what steps each party should take to prepare the case for trial, direct that those steps are taken in the shortest possible time and impose a sanction for non-compliance. Such a sanction may, for example, deprive a party of the right to raise or contest an issue or to rely on evidence to which the direction relates.
(d) Where it appears that one or more issues are or can be made ready for trial at the time fixed while others cannot, the court may direct that the trial will proceed on the issues that are or will then be ready, and order that no costs will be allowed for any later trial of the remaining issues or that those costs will be paid by the party in default.
(e) Where the court has no option but to postpone the trial, it will do so for the shortest possible time and will give directions for the taking of the necessary steps in the meantime as rapidly as possible.
(f) Litigants and lawyers must be in no doubt that the court will regard the postponement of a trial as an order of last resort. The court may exercise its power to require a party, as well as the party's legal representative, to attend court at a hearing where such an order is to be sought.

In *Holmes v SGB Services plc* [2001] EWCA Civ 354, LTL 19/2/2001, a jointly instructed expert reported shortly before the trial date. The report did not support the claimant's pleaded case, but suggested an alternative explanation consistent with the claimant succeeding. The claimant therefore applied to amend, but this meant having to adjourn the trial. This created a tension between doing justice (**CPR, r. 1.1(1)**) and preserving the trial date (**PD 29, para. 7**), which was essentially a matter for the judge's discretion. On the facts permission to amend and an adjournment were granted.

Dealing with cases justly and at proportionate cost

The twin concepts set out in the overriding objective in **CPR, r. 1.1(1)**, are that the court should do justice between the parties, and that this should be achieved at proportionate cost. Shutting a litigant out through a technical breach of the rules will not often be consistent with this, because the civil courts are established primarily for deciding cases on their merits, not in rejecting them through procedural default. An example is *Jones v Telford and Wrekin Council* (1999) *The Times*, 29 July 1999, where service had been delayed beyond the period of validity because the claimant's solicitors had problems in obtaining psychiatric reports for service with the particulars of claim. The Court of Appeal upheld an extension of time largely because there were no previous authorities dealing with this situation, Lord Woolf MR commenting that the court must not lose sight of the fact that its primary concern was doing justice. Another example is *Chilton v Surrey County Council* [1999] CPLR 525, where the Court of Appeal indicated that dealing with a claim justly involves dealing with the real claim, and allowed the claimant to rely on a revised statement of past and future loss and expense served 12 days before trial quantifying the claim at about £400,000 rather than the original statement, which indicated a claim value of about £5,000. The fact that the real value of the claim was substantially greater than the figures stated in the original statement of past and future loss and expense was revealed many months previously when an employment expert's report was disclosed. The revised statement had not been served through a mistake by the claimant's solicitors, who believed it had already been served. The Court of Appeal disapproved of the defendant's tactics, but also commented that if the revised statement **48.7** was to be excluded it was for the defendant to point to details of any prejudice it might suffer because of late service.

See also the discussion on non-compliance with expert and witness statement directions at **48.26** and **48.28**, and seeking to rectify defective performance (**48.29**).

Allotting an appropriate share of the court's resources

48.8 An appeal was dismissed (with costs on the indemnity basis) in *Adoko v Jemal* (1999) *The Times*, 8 July 1999, on the ground that hearing it would be a waste of the court's resources. The appellant had failed to correct the notice of appeal despite a warning from the respondent that it was seriously defective, and had failed to comply with the directions relating to appeal bundles. The Court of Appeal spent over an hour trying to sort out the problem, and then decided it was inappropriate that any further court resources should be allocated to the appeal.

Client or solicitor at fault

48.9 Where protracted delay is the fault of the client rather than its solicitor, striking out may be justified (*Habib Bank Ltd v Jaffer* (2000) *The Times*, 5 April 2000), whereas if the fault is that of the solicitor combined with other circumstances, the claim may be allowed to continue (*Western Trust and Savings Ltd v Acland and Lensam* (2000) LTL 19/6/2000). Reduced weight was given to defects in complying with a court order in *Whittaker v Soper* [2001] EWCA Civ 1462, LTL 28/9/2001, because the defects were the fault of the solicitor rather than the party. An inconsistent decision is *Daryanani v Kumar and Co.* (2000) LTL 12/12/2000, where it was held that it is inappropriate to draw a distinction or to apportion responsibility between the litigant himself and his advisers on the issue of delay. Where a party failed to comply with a time limit because his solicitors in error amended the wrong document, it was held that striking out was too great a penalty (*Austin v Newcastle Chronicle and Journal Ltd* [2001] EWCA Civ 834, LTL 18/5/2001).

Both parties in default

48.10 Both parties have obligations regarding compliance with court directions and the provisions of the CPR, and are required to cooperate with each other (see **CPR, r. 1.4(2)(a)**). Where both sides are in breach of directions, it is difficult to justify imposing a sanction purely on the claimant, provided it is reasonably possible to have a fair trial notwithstanding the breach (*Western Trust and Savings Ltd v Acland and Lensam* (2000) LTL 19/6/2000). Some cases go further, pointing out that both sides have a duty to help the court to further the overriding objective (**r. 1.3**). Consequently it is inappropriate for defendants to sit back and let a claim go to sleep, and then complain about delay when the claimant resumes the claim (*Khalili v Bennett* [2000] EMLR 996; *Dainty v Reynolds* (2000) LTL 28/11/2000).

In *Hateley v Morris* [2004] EWHC 252 (Ch), [2004] 1 BCLC 582, there was an eight-month delay when neither side applied to relist a case management conference in an unfair prejudice petition. A striking-out order made by the registrar was overturned on appeal because:

(a) striking out was not fair or proportionate, given the delay was not that great;
(b) either side could have relisted the matter, and both sides have a duty to cooperate in progressing proceedings; and
(c) it was unlikely the quality of the evidence had been damaged due to the delay.

In *Artibell Shipping Co Ltd v Markel International Insurance Co. Ltd* [2008] EWHC 811 (Comm), LTL 2/5/2008, there was a two-year delay in fixing a case management conference, but, as it was open to the defendant to do this, striking out the claim was refused.

Unless orders

Applying the above principles, the court may take the view that the best way to ensure its directions are complied with by a defaulting party and that the trial date will be met, is to make an unless order. An unless order should be made only if the court is satisfied that in all the circumstances such a sanction is appropriate (*Marcan Shipping (London) Ltd v Kefalas* [2007] EWCA Civ 463, [2007] 1 WLR 1864; *Sports Network Ltd v Calzaghe* [2008] EWHC 2566 (QB), LTL 3/11/2008). Unless orders are hard to justify on the first occasion a step has to be taken in a case, where the automatic sanction is likely to be unduly harsh (*Kinsley v Commissioner of Police for the Metropolis* [2010] EWCA Civ 953, LTL 10/6/2010, where as a result relief from the sanction was granted under **CPR, r. 3.9**). It is likely to be appropriate to make an unless order where a party is in breach of an earlier order or direction, particularly where the earlier order was expressed to be 'final' (*Sports Network Ltd v Calzaghe* at [114]). Where the reason advanced for non-compliance with an earlier order is regarded as little more than an excuse, an unless order may be the only way to impress on the defaulting party the importance of complying with the relevant orders (*D. Morgan plc v Mace and Jones* [2010] EWHC 697 (TCC), LTL 4/5/2010, where reliance on the claimant's managing director's illness was regarded as an excuse, primarily because he had not been ill throughout the entire period). **48.11**

An unless order gives the defaulting party a final opportunity to comply, and imposes a sanction in default. Often a costs sanction will be imposed at the same time. The period to be allowed by an unless order depends on the circumstances. Often 14 to 28 days will be appropriate. A stricter approach is taken where the court feels there is blameworthy conduct than where a party is in default through events outside his control. A more generous period should be given for less contentious unless orders, such as for provision of security for costs (*Prince Radu of Hohenzollern v Houston* [2006] EWCA Civ 1575, *The Times*, 1 January 2007). The form of unless orders is considered at **48.30**.

Where an unless order is sought against a party for failure to comply with an earlier order, but the party provides written evidence that it has complied, the court may reject that evidence if it finds it is incredible. There is no higher standard, such as 'plainly incredible' (*Lexi Holdings plc v Luqman* [2007] EWCA Civ 1501, LTL 7/8/2007). If the evidence is rejected, it is almost inevitable that an unless order will be made. In *Forrester Ketley and Co. v Brent* [2005] EWCA Civ 270, LTL 2/3/2005 it was held that the court below had been fully entitled to make unless orders, with striking out in default, on both the following grounds, where the defendant:

(a) had failed to provide a single document which clearly stated his case; and
(b) had failed to pay earlier interim costs orders.

SANCTIONS

Sanctions available

The following is a non-exhaustive list of possible sanctions that may be imposed: **48.12**

(a) striking out the entire claim or defence (see **48.14**);
(b) striking out part of the defaulting party's statement of case (see **48.17**);
(c) debarring a party from amending or updating part of its statement of case or a schedule of future loss and expense (see **48.21**);
(d) debarring a party from calling one or more witnesses, including expert witnesses (see **48.26, 48.28**);
(e) depriving a claimant who is in default of all or some of the interest that would otherwise have been awarded (see **64.27**);
(f) increasing the rate of interest otherwise payable (if the default comprises non-compliance with a pre-action protocol) (see **8.4**);

(g) requiring a defaulting party to pay all or some of the other party's costs of the proceedings (see **48.18**);
(h) requiring the defaulting party to pay the costs of and occasioned by the application in which the default is considered;
(i) ordering adverse costs orders to be paid on the indemnity basis (see **48.18**);
(j) requiring adverse costs orders to be paid forthwith;
(k) requiring the defaulting party to provide security as a condition for being allowed to continue with the proceedings;
(l) ordering security for costs (see **48.20**).

The usual order on failing to comply with the CPR or practice directions is to allow the defaulting party a limited period of time to comply, together with an adverse costs order in respect of any interim application needed to bring the matter before the court (*Colliers International Property Consultants v Colliers Jordan Lee Jafaar Sdn Bhd* [2008] EWHC 1524 (Comm), [2008] 2 Lloyd's Rep 368, where there was a failure to verify a statement of case).

There are various provisions in the CPR and practice directions that impose various sanctions in default of due compliance. For example, **r. 35.13** provides that a party failing to disclose an expert's report may not use the report at the trial or call the expert to give evidence orally unless the court gives permission. A more severe sanction is imposed by **r. 3.7**, which provides for the striking out of claims for non-payment of allocation and listing fees after the time set by a notice of non-payment. An example from the practice directions is **PD 32, para. 25**, which provides that if an affidavit, witness statement or exhibit does not comply with the requirements of **CPR, Part 32**, or **PD 32**, the court may refuse to admit it as evidence and may refuse to allow the costs arising from its preparation. This last example differs from the previous two in that it provides for a sanction which the court may choose to impose, whereas the other two provide for sanctions which apply unless the court grants relief. The court will usually impose a sanction if it holds a hearing to give directions because of the default of a party or its legal representatives (**PD 29, para. 3.6**).

Non-compliance with applicable pre-action protocols

48.13 If, in the opinion of the court, there has been non-compliance with **PD Pre-action Conduct** or any relevant pre-action protocol, the court will consider the extent of the parties' compliance (**PD Pre-action Conduct, para. 4.1**) and the overall effect of the non-compliance on the other party when deciding whether to impose sanctions (**para. 4.5**). Minor or technical breaches are unlikely to result in sanctions (**para. 4.3(1)**). Orders the court may make include:

(a) imposing a stay of the proceedings until steps which ought to have been taken are taken (see **8.4**);
(b) an order that the party at fault pay the costs of the proceedings, or part of those costs, of the other party or parties;
(c) an order that the party at fault pay those costs on an indemnity basis;
(d) if the party at fault is a claimant in whose favour an order for the payment of damages or some specified sum is subsequently made, an order depriving that party of interest on such sum and in respect of such period as may be specified, and/or awarding interest at a lower rate than that at which interest would otherwise have been awarded;
(e) if the party at fault is a defendant and an order for the payment of damages or some specified sum is subsequently made in favour of the claimant, an order awarding interest on such sum and in respect of such period as may be specified at a higher rate, not exceeding 10 per cent above base rate, than the rate at which interest would otherwise have been awarded.

The **Pre-action Protocol for Personal Injury Claims, para. 1.5**, says that if the court has to consider the question of compliance, it will not be concerned with minor infringements, such as the failure by a short period to provide relevant information. A single minor breach will not exempt the 'innocent' party from complying with the protocol.

STRIKING OUT

Whether striking out is appropriate

An applicant seeking a straight striking-out order has the burden of proof, whereas on an application for relief from sanctions (under **CPR, r. 3.9**, see **48.36**) after non-compliance with an unless order (see **48.30, 48.31**) the onus is on the defaulting party (*Malekout v Medical Sickness Annuity and Life Assurance Society Ltd* [2003] EWHC 3302 (QB), LTL 30/10/2003). There are relatively few occasions where immediate striking out as opposed to some lesser sanction or the imposition of an unless order is appropriate. Striking out for failing to file a pre-trial checklist and being late for a case management hearing was regarded as disproportionate in *Lambeth London Borough Council v Onayomake* [2007] EWCA Civ 1426, *The Times*, 2 November 2007. **48.14**

In *UCB Corporate Services Ltd v Halifax (SW) Ltd* [1999] CPLR 691 the claimant had repeatedly failed to comply with court directions and provisions in the rules, and there was an unexplained delay of two years, at which point the defendant made an application to strike out. The claimant was regarded as being guilty of a total disregard of court orders, amounting to an abuse of process. Accordingly, the judge was held to have been entitled to strike out the claim rather than imposing a lesser penalty. Where there has been a history of delay, and several different orders have been breached, there will come a point when the court will say it is right to apply the ultimate sanction of striking out (*Necati v Metropolitan Police Commissioner* (2000) LTL 19/1/2001), or that 'enough is enough' (*Duggan v Wood* [2001] EWCA Civ 1942, LTL 22/11/2001).

Commentary

Protracted delay combined with a weak case on the merits may lead the court to conclude it is in accordance with the overriding objective to strike out the claim (*O'Donnell v Charly Holdings Inc.* (2000) LTL 14/3/2000). The court can take into account apparent weakness in the underlying claim even in a case which has survived an application to strike out on the merits or for summary judgment (*Cohort Construction Co. UK Ltd v Melchior* (2000) LTL 20/10/2000).

In *Circuit Systems Ltd v Zuken-Redac (UK) Ltd* [2001] BLR 253 a claim issued 11 years previously was struck out. An unless order had been made giving the claimant a final opportunity to plead the case in a form fit to be carried through to trial, after which a reamended statement of case had been served, which was still deficient. Although the claim was assumed to be meritorious, the claimant had failed without adequate explanation to put matters right after having been given a final chance to do so, and the failure meant that a six-week trial had to be adjourned. On the other hand, striking out for failure to give disclosure pursuant to an order not framed as an unless order would be inappropriate (*Johnson v Valks* (2000) LTL 15/3/2000).

In *Annodeus Entertainment Ltd v Gibson* (2000) *The Times*, 3 March 2000, Neuberger J stressed the windfall effect of striking out for delay. On striking out for fraud or other misconduct see **33.14**.

Prejudice

In *Axa Insurance Co. Ltd v Swire Fraser Ltd* [2000] CPLR 142, a case where the Court of Appeal held the judge had been wrong to strike out the claim despite a protracted failure to provide further information, it was said that proof of prejudice is not a requirement for an order for striking out under **CPR, r. 3.4(2)(c)**. That said, prejudice to the innocent party is clearly an important factor, and where it is present, such as in *Purdy v Cambran* [1999] CPLR 843, where the defendant's expert died in the period of delay, it may offset an argument that striking out would be a disproportionate sanction. **48.15**

In *Arogundade v Brent London Borough Council* (2000) LTL 16/10/2000 the judge was regarded as acting proportionately in striking out the claim where the claimant was in default of a number of orders to provide a properly pleaded reply and defence to counterclaim, and where the defendant was prejudiced by the default (because of mounting rent arrears). Where there is no prejudice it is correspondingly difficult to justify striking out (*Gaddafi v Telegraph Group Ltd* (2000) LTL 22/8/2000), and accordingly some lesser sanction will usually be imposed.

Fair trial

48.16 It has often been the approach of the courts under the CPR to say that it is unlikely to be consistent with the overriding objective or with the European Convention on Human Rights, **art. 6**, to strike out for delay where it is still possible to have a fair trial. In deciding whether it is still possible to have a fair trial the court should consider the effect of the delay on both the claim and any counterclaim which might extinguish the claim (*Habib Bank Ltd v Abbeypearl Ltd* (2001) LTL 26/1/2001). The right to a fair trial in **art. 6** is a right to have a fair hearing within a reasonable time. In this context it is therefore important to note that the defendant, as well as the claimant, has rights under the article (*Circuit Systems Ltd v Zuken-Redac (UK) Ltd* [2001] BLR 253).

Where striking out is based on delay, what is required is not considerable doubt, but a considerable risk or impossibility of a fair trial taking place (*Taylor v Anderson* [2002] EWCA Civ 1680, [2003] RTR 305). This test was approved by *Fay v Chief Constable of Bedfordshire Police* [2003] EWHC 673 (QB), *The Times*, 13 February 2003. However, Davies J said that the *Taylor v Anderson* test, although highly relevant, is not the only consideration. The *Taylor v Anderson* test does not apply in application for relief from sanctions (see **48.36**; *Hansom v E. Rex Makin* [2003] EWCA Civ 1801, LTL 18/12/2003). An order striking out a claim was overturned on appeal in *Asiansky Television plc v Bayer-Rosin* [2001] EWCA Civ 1792, [2002] CPLR 111. Breach of an order to set down for trial was not, in the context of the claim, so serious as to justify striking out, and the case could still be fairly tried. Where a claim has gone stale, with no sufficient explanation for the delay and a real risk that any trial will not be truly fair, it is appropriate to strike it out (*Rio Guadalete SA v Hopwood* [2001] EWCA Civ 445, LTL 27/3/2001).

In *Artibell Shipping Co. Ltd v Markel International Insurance Co. Ltd* [2008] EWHC 811 (Comm), LTL 2/5/2008, a fair trial was still possible despite full use of the six-year limitation period, then five years of litigation (including a two-year period in which no progress was made), and a further year to get to trial. Striking out was refused, but security for costs (see **48.20**) was ordered.

In *Beegum v Yousaf* [2002] EWCA Civ 60, LTL 23/1/2002, a claim for the rescission of a transfer of property, the outcome turned on the recollection of witnesses. This, combined with delays and the rejection of the claimant's explanation, meant that striking out the claim was not disproportionate. In *Al Chalabi v Kentucky Fried Chicken (Great Britain) Ltd* (2001) LTL 14/12/2001 Keith J said that it is possible to take the argument of the unreliability of witnesses too far. The passage of time always affects a person's memory. This was a claim alleging misstatement and/or breach of warranty concerning the profitability of a business, so most the evidence was documented. Consequently the claim was not dismissed despite delays. The death of the claimant during a period of delay was regarded as not affecting the fair trial of the claim so far as the defendant was concerned in *Anyiam-Osigwe v Gillam* (2001) LTL 13/7/2001. Any prejudice affected the claimant.

LESSER SANCTIONS

Striking out part of a statement of case

48.17 For example, a party may be in default of an order to provide further information on a single issue in a case where several issues are raised. A suitable sanction in such circumstances may be *striking out the part of the statement of case* dealing with that issue (see *QPS Consultants Ltd v Kruge Tissue (Manufacturing) Ltd* [1999] BLR 366).

Payment of costs

The normal costs order on a successful application to set aside a judgment entered in default of an unless order (see **48.28**) is that the claimant pay the defendant's costs, including the costs of and occasioned by the application to set aside. Orders requiring a defaulting party to pay the costs of the proceedings to date as a sanction involve a substantial risk of impairing that party's right of access to the courts. A reasonably lenient approach to this type of order should be adopted, at least in cases which have not reached the appeal stage (*Ford v Labrador* [2003] UKPC 41, [2003] 1 WLR 2082). Nevertheless, an order depriving the claimant of all her costs to date, and providing that the claimant would pay certain defence costs in any event, was made as an alternative to striking out in *Parnall v Hurst* [2003] EWHC 2164 (Ch), *The Times*, 10 July 2003. A mere failure to comply with an unless order is not enough to justify an order requiring the defaulting party to pay all the other side's costs (*Gore v Jones* (2000) *The Times*, 21 February 2001). Adverse costs orders covering all or part of the costs of the claim to date are not uncommon orders where the court allows a late amendment of a statement of case if the amendment makes a fundamental change to the nature of the case being advanced (*Beoco Ltd v Alfa Laval Co. Ltd* [1995] QB 137). However, the court will almost certainly impose a costs sanction, covering the costs of the application, on the defaulting party, even if it successfully opposes a striking-out application, because default is seen as bringing such applications on the defaulting party's own head (*Axa Insurance Co. Ltd v Swire Fraser Ltd* [2000] CPLR 142). 48.18

A sanction limited to indemnity costs was imposed despite protracted delay in *Royal Bank Invoice Finance Ltd v Bird* (2001) LTL 19/2/2001, because striking out or discharging a freezing injunction (the other options) were regarded as too draconian and unjust.

Paying security

In *Mealey Horgan plc v Horgan* (1999) *The Times*, 6 July 1999, the defendant served his witness statements two weeks late. The claimants sought an order requiring the defendant to pay a sum into court as a sanction for late service. Buckley J refused the order and said a sanction of that nature would be appropriate only in cases of repeated breach of timetables, or where the defaulting party's conduct gave rise to suspicion that it was not acting in good faith. 48.19

A striking-out order was set aside in *Grundy v Naqvi* (2001) LTL 1/2/2001 on the ground that this was a disproportionate response to a failure to comply with an order to disclose witness statements. The defaulting party had some reason for not having complied (in that she wanted to amend her statement of case, which would have impacted the content of the witness statements), albeit she was also guilty of delay in seeking permission to amend. An order was made requiring the defaulting party to pay £50,000 into court. The amount ordered must not be such that it will be impossible for the party to pay, because that would be the equivalent of striking out (see **20.21** and *Marstons plc v Charman* [2009] EWCA Civ 719, LTL 29/4/2009).

Ordering security for costs

There is a power in **CPR, r. 3.1(3)**, to make an order subject to conditions. This is wide enough to include making an order requiring the payment of money into court as security for the costs of the non-defaulting party (*Olatawura v Abiloye* [2002] EWCA Civ 998, [2003] 1 WLR 275). This power is not to be regarded as an easy way to obtain security for costs in situations where the conditions in **rr. 25.12** and **25.13** cannot be satisfied (*Huscroft v P and O Ferries Ltd* [2010] EWCA Civ 1483, [2011] 1 WLR 939). The purpose of **r. 3.1(3)** is to enable the court to grant relief on terms, and any condition imposed is only legitimate if it is a proportionate and effective means of achieving that purpose. In *Olatawura v Abiloye* factors to be taken into account when making an order tantamount to security for costs as a sanction were said to include: 48.20

(a) the ability of the respondent to pay;

(b) the respondent's conduct, including compliance with orders and pre-action protocols; and
(c) the apparent strength of the claim or defence (this is only to be taken into account where the defaulting party's case has no real prospect of success: *Ali v Hudson* [2003] EWCA Civ 1793, LTL 11/12/2003).

The court must be sensitive to the risk that it might be denying the respondent access to the court when making such an order (*Olatawura v Abiloye*). An order should not ordinarily be made unless the defaulting party can be shown to have regularly flouted court procedures or otherwise demonstrated a lack of good faith (*Ali v Hudson*). An order for security for costs was imposed as a sanction for defective performance of an unless order for disclosure of documents in *Carlco Ltd v Chief Constable of Dyfed-Powys Police* [2002] EWCA Civ 1754, LTL 18/11/2002. A distinction was drawn in *CIBC Mellon Trust Co. v Mora Hotel Corporation NV* [2002] EWCA Civ 1688, [2003] 1 All ER 564, between ordering security for costs incurred before the relevant default (which may be hard to justify if there is evidence that the defaulting party cannot afford to pay) and ordering security for the costs of the application, which may well be justifiable. In *Dardana Ltd v Yukos Oil Co.* [2002] EWCA Civ 543, [2002] 1 All ER (Comm) 819, it was held that an order for security for costs was wholly inappropriate when imposed on granting an adjournment at the request of the party obtaining the benefit of the security.

Depriving of interest and related sanctions

48.21 In *Walsh v Misseldine* [2000] CPLR 201 the claimant was guilty of inadequately justified delay of over four years. Liability was not in issue. If the claim had progressed normally it would have been tried in spring 1995. During the period of delay a revised schedule of special damages was prepared, substantially increasing the special damages claim. The Court of Appeal was able to substitute its own discretion for that of the judge below. It found that it was still possible, in 1999, to have a fair trial of the issues as they stood in 1995, but that it would not be fair to have a trial of the additional issues raised by the increased special damages claim. The Court of Appeal allowed the claim to proceed, but restricted to the issues as they stood in 1995. Stuart-Smith LJ made it clear that there is a real distinction between cases where liability is and is not in dispute. Where liability is admitted, depriving the claimant of interest or requiring the claimant to pay costs which can be set off against the damages award are effective sanctions for delay. They are not necessarily so if the claim turns out to be unsuccessful. A similar decision was reached in *Price v Price* [2003] EWCA Civ 888, [2003] 3 All ER 911, where the court allowed the claim to continue on condition that damages were restricted to the amount that might be substantiated by any medical report written before a stated date.

OBJECTING TO SANCTION IMPOSED

48.22 A defaulting party who thinks the sanction imposed, such as an unless order with striking out as a consequence of further default, is too onerous should appeal the order imposing the sanction rather than seeking relief from the sanction after further non-compliance (*Fred Perry (Holdings) Ltd v Brands Plaza Trading Ltd* [2012] EWCA Civ 224, [2012] FSR 28). By not appealing the original unless order the court dealing with any application for relief from sanctions has to focus on the reasons for, and effects of, the further non-compliance, and is not able to grant relief on the ground that the sanction, such as striking out, was not justified by the original default.

EXTENSIONS OF TIME

Applying to extend time

48.23 The court has a general power to extend and abridge time (CPR, r. 3.1(2)(a)). It can extend time on its own initiative under rr. 3.1(2)(a) and 3.3, even where the extension relates to an unless order (*Keen Phillips v Field* [2006] EWCA Civ 1524, [2007] 1 WLR 686). It also has a general power to impose conditions (**r. 3.1(3)**). It is generally expected that where the parties are in effective communication with each other and provided there is no substantial reason for refusing to agree, the parties should agree on extensions of time (*Vitol SA v Vaalco Gabon (Etame) Inc.* [2011] EWHC 3754 (Comm), LTL 5/5/2011). The 'key dates' in fast track (**46.16**) and multi-track (**47.30**) can only be varied by the court. A party who will be unable to comply with an order or direction in time (or who is already in breach), and who has not been able to agree an extension with the other side, may make an application asking the court to extend time for compliance. The discretion given to the court under **r. 3.1** is unfettered other than by the general requirement to further the overriding objective. Time may be extended even where the original order was made by consent. The fact a deadline was agreed is simply one of the circumstances to be taken into account (*Pannone LLP v Aardvark Digital Ltd* [2011] EWCA Civ 803, [2011] 1 WLR 2275). A party who is late in taking a particular step and who has not yet taken it may be treated differently from a party who has been late in taking a step but has rectified the position. The power to extend time may be exercised even where a rule says a step 'must' be taken within a stated period (*USF Ltd v Aqua Technology Hanson NV/SA* (2001) LTL 31/1/2001). The power to extend time in **r. 3.1(2)(a)** is wide enough to enable the court to extend the time for compliance with the provisions of an order previously made by the same court (*Omega Engineering Inc. v Omega SA* [2003] EWHC 1482 (Ch), *The Times*, 29 September 2003).

A two-day extension of time for serving a claim form issued under the Town and Country Planning Act, 1990, s. 287, and RSC, ord. 94 in CPR, sch. 1, was granted under **r. 3.1(2)(a)** in *Corus UK Ltd v Erewash Borough Council* [2005] EWHC 2821 (Admin), [2005] NPC 145. While delay was firmly discouraged, the court's function is to ensure public bodies acted lawfully, and the public were not to be artificially deprived of the opportunity of mounting a challenge to a public act. It is wrong to use the **r. 3.1(2)(a)** power to extend time for the purpose of nullifying the effect of a mandatory provision in the CPR (*Walker Residential Ltd v Davis* [2005] EWHC 3483 (Ch), LTL 9/12/2005, where the Court of Appeal overturned an extension of time for paying into court under old r. 36.10(3)(a), the effect of which had been to deprive the claimant of the mandatory costs order provided by old r. 36.13(1)).

Applying to extend time before time expires

There is a fundamental difference between applying for an extension of time before a time limit has expired, and seeking relief from a sanction after the event (*Robert v Momentum Services Ltd* [2003] EWCA Civ 299, [2003] 1 WLR 1577). In simple time applications under **CPR, r. 3.1**, the court applies the overriding objective, with the principal consideration being whether there is any prejudice caused to the other side through the delay in taking the step in question. **48.24**

An application made very close to the trial may be refused where its effect would be unfair on the other party (*Calenti v North Middlesex NHS Trust* (2001) LTL 10/4/2001).

An extension of time was allowed in *Glauser International SA v Khan* [2002] EWCA Civ 368, [2002] BLR 224, as there was no prejudice, and striking out was wholly disproportionate given the extension was very short and there had been no unless order. In *Becker v Baileys Shaw and Gillett* (1999) LTL 4/11/99 a decision to refuse to extend time for complying with an unless order to supply particulars of loss was described as 'plainly wrong'. Part of the reasoning was that the particulars were complex and required the evidence of a forensic accountant experienced in Lloyd's claims.

Extending time for compliance with an unless order

Before the civil justice reforms of 2013 it was held that the old list of factors governing applications for relief from sanctions in CPR, r. 3.9 (see **48.34**) was a convenient checklist to guide the court on an application to extend time (*Keith v CPM Field Marketing Ltd* (2000) *The Times*, **48.25**

Commentary

29 August 2000). The replacement of r. 3.9 (see 48.36) should mean that greater weight will be given to applying the overriding objective, and balancing the need to deal with the claim on its merits with the need to ensure court orders and directions are complied with. Important factors are likely to be:

(a) the seriousness of the default;
(b) the extent of the delays, both directly related to the present default, and generally in the history of the case;
(c) the reasons for the default;
(d) the extent of any prejudice, including whether it is still possible to have a fair trial; and
(e) ensuring court resources are not wasted, and that costs are kept proportionate.

Where the parties have agreed an unless order by consent, with a sanction to take effect in default, the court retains a power to extend the time for compliance (*Ropac Ltd v Inntrepreneur Pub Co.* [2001] CP Rep 31). However, where there is a clear agreement between the parties, the court will give great weight to the agreement, and would be slow, in the absence of special circumstances, to depart from the parties' agreement.

Non-compliance with expert directions

48.26 In *Newton v Dorset Travel Service Ltd* (1999) LTL 5/5/99 the judge refused the defendants a one-day extension for service of their psychiatric evidence in a personal injuries claim, saying the rules had to be obeyed. The Court of Appeal said that although the defendants' solicitors should have pushed their expert for the report, they had not deliberately flouted the order, the extension sought was minimal, and the need to enforce orders with vigour had to be tempered by proportionality. It was held that an extension should have been granted. *O'Hara v Rye* (1999) LTL 12/2/99 was a case under the old system, where the Court of Appeal stressed that when it becomes impossible to adhere to a directions timetable, it is important to disclose all material difficulties to the court so that the court can give directions that are realistic. In *Great Future International Ltd v Sealand Housing Corporation* [2002] EWCA Civ 1184, LTL 24/5/2002, the defendants failed to comply with the original timetable for disclosure of expert reports. As the trial was just over a month away, the Court of Appeal substituted orders that reports be served by dates within the following week, with orders refusing permission to rely on the experts in default.

On the other hand, if a party holds on to a report for some time, and then serves it at the last minute, permission to adduce the report may well be refused (*Baron v Lovell* [1999] CPLR 630, where there was a narrow difference between the two sides' medical evidence). Permission to call an additional expert two weeks before trial where the need to call that expert had been identified several months beforehand, and where there was no sufficient explanation for the delay, was refused in *Calenti v North Middlesex NHS Trust* (2001) LTL 10/4/2001. In *Hanley v Stage and Catwalk Ltd* [2001] EWCA Civ 1739, LTL 7/11/2001, it was held that the judge had been justified in granting the defendant permission two weeks before trial to call an expert in a new area of expertise. This was largely because at the same time the claimant was seeking permission to adduce evidence from an expert who had previously reported in the claim, but which was a substantial departure from the earlier report.

It will generally be just to allow a party in a personal injuries claim permission to adduce additional medical evidence to cover further evidence coming to light at a later stage, even after a notional trial date, but before the actual trial, as in *Snowdon v Thurstan Hoskins and Partners* (2002) LTL 19/11/2002.

Expert failing to answer written questions

48.27 *Where an expert fails* to answer written questions by the time stated in directions (see 54.32), the court may impose sanctions against the party instructing the expert. If there is continued non-compliance, the court may debar a party from relying on the report (**PD 35, annex (Protocol for the Instruction of Experts) para. 16.1**).

Non-compliance with directions on witness statements

If a witness statement or witness summary for use at trial is not served at the time specified in the court's directions, the witness may not be called to give oral evidence unless the court gives permission (**CPR, r. 32.10**; see **51.20**). This amounts to a sanction. Consequently, any application for permission under **r. 32.10** is an application for relief from sanctions, and **r. 3.9** applies, albeit within the context of considering all the circumstances and the overriding objective (*Papa Johns (GB) Ltd v Doyley* [2011] EWHC 2621 (QB), LTL 1/11/2011). Neither **r. 32.10** nor **r. 3.9** was referred to in *Nottingham and City of Nottingham Fire Authority v Gladman Commercial Properties Ltd* [2011] EWHC 1918 (Ch), [2011] 1 WLR 3235, where the judgment mainly considered the authorities on late amendments. While protesting about the use of the word at [33], the result in this case can only be described as relaxed, and is out of line with other authorities. **48.28**

On an application for permission to use a witness statement served out of time, the court will take into account that generally it is contrary to the overriding objective and contrary to the principle of ensuring a fair trial to make an order effectively depriving a party from being able to call any factual witness evidence. In most cases this is tantamount to deciding the case against the defaulting party. This principle is not absolute. There are cases of repeated or deliberate default where an order equivalent to striking out is appropriate (*UCB Corporate Services Ltd v Halifax (SW) Ltd* [1999] CPLR 691; *Mealey Horgan plc v Horgan* (1999) *The Times*, 6 July 1999).

The more important the evidence is, the more likely permission will be granted. Permission was refused in *Coore v Chief Constable of Leicestershire* (1999) LTL 10/5/99 where the evidence did not address the essential issue in the case.

If the additional evidence will significantly change the basis of the defaulting party's case, permission might be refused, particularly if permission is sought shortly before trial (*British Sugar plc v Cegelec Ltd* [2004] EWCA Civ 1450, LTL 7/10/2004). Whether the additional evidence comes from a witness who was available to both parties is a factor to be taken into consideration. There is no property in a witness (*Cowland v District Judges of the West London County Court* (1999) LTL 20/7/99), although there are practical and professional conduct problems in obtaining witness statements from employees of, and persons connected with, the other side.

In *Mealey Horgan plc v Horgan* witness statements were served two weeks late and six weeks before the trial. Buckley LJ said that making an order depriving the defaulting party of its evidence was out of proportion to the default. In *I. N. Newman Ltd v Adlem* [2004] EWCA Civ 1492, LTL 16/11/2004, permission was granted to serve witness statements five weeks before the trial, and the innocent party was ordered to pay the costs of the application for permission because it should have consented to the late service. In *Cowland v District Judges of the West London County Court* permission was granted for the use of a witness statement served on the morning of the trial where the witness was available to both sides and where the evidence plainly went to the heart of the issue between the parties. In *Hayes v Transco plc* [2003] EWCA Civ 1261, LTL 17/9/2003, an appeal was allowed partly on the ground that permission to adduce two supplementary witness statements had been wrongfully refused. The judge had refused permission to use the statements, but had granted the other side permission to use documents disclosed late, which was a failure to hold a fair balance between the parties.

Rectifying defective performance

On some occasions a default may arise through the defective performance of the requirements of a rule, practice direction or court order. For example, it may be that the wrong form was used, or that it was sent to the wrong address (but still came to the attention of **48.29** the other side), or that the document used was not completed correctly. These are errors of procedure. By **CPR, r. 3.10**, such errors do not invalidate the step purportedly taken, unless the court so orders. This rule is discussed in the context of extending the period of validity of a claim form at **15.32**. The court may make an order invalidating a step if it was so badly defective that the other side were misled, or where the defects are so great that it would not be right to regard the purported performance as performance at all. Further, by **r. 3.10(b)** the court may make an order to remedy any error of procedure. A defaulting party should consider seeking such an order where there is an objection made regarding defective performance.

A key factor in deciding whether to set aside or to rectify any irregularity is whether the other side have suffered any prejudice. In the absence of prejudice it is usual to allow the defaulting party to rectify the defect (*Colliers International Property Consultants v Colliers Jordan Lee Jafaar Sdn Bhd* [2008] EWHC 1524 (Comm), [2008] 2 Lloyd's Rep 368 (failure to serve complete copies of the exhibits with witness statements)). An obvious and technical defect in a Part 36 offer was ignored in *Hertsmere Primary Care Trust v Administrators of Balasubramanium's Estate* [2005] EWHC 320 (Ch), [2005] 3 All ER 274 (and it is submitted would have been cured under **r. 3.10**).

Where a party purports to serve a claim form within its period of validity, but by an incorrect method, or at an incorrect address, the court has a discretion whether to grant relief under **r. 3.10**, which is exercised in accordance with the overriding objective. On an application for an order remedying such an error in procedure, the court will consider whether the claimant has taken all reasonable steps to put the matter right once the problem was discovered (*Nanglegan v Royal Free Hampstead NHS Trust* [2001] EWCA Civ 127, [2002] 1 WLR 1043, where relief was refused). In *Phillips v Symes (No. 3)* [2008] UKHL 1, [2008] 1 WLR 180, it was thought that **r. 3.10** could be used to cure an irregularity in effecting service outside the jurisdiction.

An order rectifying an error in procedure was made in *Fawdry and Co. v Murfitt* [2002] EWCA Civ 643, [2003] QB 104, where a judge, without being aware she was not duly authorised, heard a case which had not been properly released to her for trial.

It is doubtful that **r. 3.10** can be used to validate a step (here withdrawing a Part 36 offer) which has not been taken if the result is to invalidate a procedural step (here the offeree's acceptance of the Part 36 offer) that actually has been taken (see *Re Kilopress Ltd* (2010) LTL 22/4/2010).

FORM OF ORDER WITH SANCTIONS

48.30 Like all other orders, orders with sanctions must specify the time within which the step under consideration must be taken by reference to a calendar date and a specific time (**CPR, r. 2.9**). The sanction part of the order may take the form of an unless provision. This is to the effect that if the terms of the order are breached, the other party may file a request for judgment to be entered and costs (**r. 3.5**). **PD 40B, para. 8.2**, lays down formulae for drafting unless orders. These are in the following forms (to be adapted as necessary):

(a) 'Unless the claimant serves his list of documents by 4.00 p.m. on Friday, 20 January 2014 his claim will be struck out and judgment entered for the defendant.' This is the preferred form.

(b) 'Unless the claimant serves his list of documents within 14 days of service of this order...' *This should be used where the defaulting party did not attend the hearing where the order was made.*

NON-COMPLIANCE WITH ORDER IMPOSING A SANCTION

An unless order takes effect on the day it is pronounced, except where the court specifies otherwise (**CPR, r. 40.7(1)**). An order must be complied with even if there is a delay in sealing it (*Rahamim v Reich* (2009) LTL 10/2/2009). The test on expiry of an unless order is whether there has been complete compliance with the terms of the order, subject only to *de minimis* exceptions (*Jani-King (GB) Ltd v Prodger* [2007] EWHC 712 (QB), LTL 10/4/2007). There is a reluctance, however, to be drawn into disputes over what may appear to be a poor attempt at performance at the interim stage rather than leaving the matter to trial, and it is not possible at the interim stage for adverse inferences to be drawn from, for example, the paucity of documents disclosed pursuant to an unless order for specific disclosure (*Rahamim v Reich*). **48.31**

If a party fails to comply with a rule, practice direction or court order imposing any sanction, the sanction will take effect unless the defaulting party applies for and obtains relief from the sanction (**CPR, r. 3.8**). **Rule 3.8(3)** provides that extensions cannot be agreed between the parties. Where a rule, practice direction or order uses the terms:

- 'shall be struck out or dismissed'; or
- 'will be struck out or dismissed',

the meaning is that the striking out or dismissal takes place automatically, and no further order from the court is necessary (**PD 3A, para. 1.9**).

The sanction embodied in an 'unless' order takes effect without the need for any further order if there is a material failure to comply (**CPR, r. 3.8**). In *Marcan Shipping (London) Ltd v Kefalas* [2007] EWCA Civ 463, [2007] 1 WLR 1864, it was held that if the innocent party applies for judgment under **r. 3.5**, the court's function is limited to deciding what order should properly be made to reflect the sanction which has already taken effect. The decision in *Langtree Group plc v Richardson* [2004] EWCA Civ 1447, LTL 14/10/2004, fails to give effect to **r. 3.8(1)**, and must be regarded as unsound. Failing to serve a schedule of special damages within the time stated by an unless order (which specified striking out of the special damages claim in default) resulted in the sanction taking effect automatically (*Tomer v Atlantic Cleaning Service Ltd* [2008] EWHC 1652 (QB), LTL 25/7/2008, applying *Marcan Shipping (London) Ltd v Kefalas*). Technical arguments to avoid this result, such as a purported voluntary withdrawal of the special damages claim, and the fact a schedule had never been served (so there never had been a special damages claim on which the unless order could bite), were rejected.

Procedure for entering judgment in default of an unless order

Where the court has made an order providing that a statement of case shall be struck out if a party does not comply with the order, **r. 3.5** sets out the procedure for obtaining judgment on non-compliance with the order. A number of different situations are dealt with: **48.32**

(a) Where the party in default is the claimant and the order provides for the striking out of the whole of the particulars of claim, the defendant may enter judgment with costs by filing a request (there is no prescribed form) stating that the right to enter judgment has arisen because the court's order has not been complied with (**r. 3.5(2)(a)** and **(3)**).
(b) Where the party in default is the defendant and the order provides for the striking out of the whole of the defence, and the claim is limited to one of the following forms of relief, namely, a specified sum of money, damages, and/or delivery of goods with the alternative of paying their value, the claimant may enter judgment with costs by filing a request (again there is no prescribed form) stating that the right to enter judgment has arisen because the court's order has not been complied with (**r. 3.5(2)(b)** and **(3)**).
(c) Where neither (a) nor (b) applies, such as where the order provided for striking out of only part of a statement of case, or where the defendant is in default and the claimant has claimed equitable relief, the party seeking to enter judgment for non-compliance with the

order must make an application in accordance with **Part 23** (**r. 3.5(4)**). This means that an application notice must be issued for a hearing on notice. As entering judgment for non-compliance with an order is not strictly an 'interim remedy', **r. 25.3(2)** does not apply and there is no specific requirement for evidence in support. However, particularly where equitable relief is sought, it will often be sensible to provide written evidence in support.

RELIEF FROM SANCTIONS

Procedure for seeking relief from sanctions

48.33 There are two mechanisms for seeking to retrieve the position once a sanction comes into effect:

(a) Where judgment has been entered under **CPR, r. 3.5** (see **48.32**), following the striking out of a statement of case for breach of an unless order, the defaulting party may apply to set aside the judgment under **r. 3.6**.
(b) A party in breach of any other rule, practice direction, or order imposing a sanction for non-compliance may apply for relief from the sanction (**r. 3.8(1)**).

In both types of application the court applies the principles governing relief from sanctions set out in **r. 3.9**, see **48.36**. Applications for relief from sanctions should be dealt with at a hearing rather than under **r. 23.8** without a hearing (*Collier v Williams* [2006] EWCA Civ 20, [2006] 1 WLR 1945; *Vernon v Spoudeas* [2010] EWCA Civ 666, LTL 6/5/2010).

The court has power to grant relief from a sanction without an application by the party in default by making an order on its own initiative extending time under **rr. 3.1(2)(a)** and **3.3** (*Keen Phillips v Field* [2006] EWCA Civ 1524, [2007] 1 WLR 686).

Pre-Jackson principles governing applications for relief

48.34 In its original form, CPR, r. 3.9(1), provided that on an application for relief from any sanction imposed for a failure to comply with any rule, practice direction or court order, the court had to consider all the circumstances including the following nine factors:

(a) the interests of the administration of justice;
(b) whether the application for relief has been made promptly;
(c) whether the failure to comply was intentional;
(d) whether there is a good explanation for the failure;
(e) the extent to which the party in default has complied with other rules, practice directions, court orders and any relevant pre-action protocol;
(f) whether the failure to comply was caused by the party or his legal representative;
(g) whether the trial date or the likely trial date can still be met if relief is granted;
(h) the effect which any failure to comply had on each party; and
(i) the effect which the granting of relief would have on each party.

Evidence from solicitors set out in the *Jackson Report* was to the effect that there were frequent failures to comply with directions, but very few meaningful penalties were imposed. That was not the original intention. However, early authorities on r. 3.9(1) held it was essential for the judge to consider each of the factors listed in r. 3.9(1) systematically, and then to weigh the various factors in deciding whether granting relief would accord with the overriding objective (*Woodhouse v Consignia plc* [2002] EWCA Civ 275, [2002] 1 WLR 2558; and *RC Residuals Ltd v Linton Fuel Oils Ltd* [2002] EWCA Civ 911, [2002] 1 WLR 2782). This formalistic approach was disapproved by *Khatib v Ramco International* [2011] EWCA Civ 605, [2011] CP Rep 35, where it was said the judge had to identify the factors from the r. 3.9(1) list that were relevant to the circumstances of the particular case, and conduct an appropriate review and balancing exercise.

Before the civil justice reforms of 1 April 2013 particular importance was given to the following factors on applications for relief from sanctions:

(a) Whether the breach was deliberate (*Bournemouth and Boscombe Athletic Football Club Ltd v Lloyds TSB Bank plc* [2003] EWHC 834 (Ch), LTL 24/4/2003). Deliberate permanent deletion of documents to avoid a party's disclosure obligations justified refusal of relief in *Rybak v Langbar International Ltd* [2010] EWHC 2015 (Ch), LTL 24/8/2010.
(b) The explanation for the delay (or absence of a good explanation) (*Shikari v Malik* (1999) *The Times*, 20 May 1999). More latitude was given to litigants in person (*Knowles v Knowles* [2008] EWCA Civ 788, LTL 13/6/2008).
(c) The effect the sanction had on the ability to have a fair trial (*Jones v Williams* [2002] EWCA Civ 897, LTL 27/2/2002, where barring a party from calling witnesses because witness statements were served two days late was held to be wrong; *Hansom v E. Rex Makin* [2003] EWCA Civ 1801, LTL 18/1/2003, and see **48.28**).
(d) Prejudice to other parties. Absence of serious prejudice, for example through complying with an order a short period after the deadline, meant relief would be readily granted (*Prince Radu of Hohenzollern v Houston* [2006] EWCA Civ 1575, *The Times*, 1 January 2007).

While individually each of these factors is unobjectionable, their cumulative effect and the way they were applied by the courts meant that it was comparatively rare for tough sanctions to be upheld on appeal. A particularly poor example of court control of litigation was provided by *Marine Rescue Technologies Ltd v Burchill* [2006] EWHC 3697 (Ch), LTL 17/5/2007; [2007] EWHC 1976 (Ch), LTL 21/8/2007. This case is important because trenchant criticism of the litigation by Professor Adrian Zuckerman was picked up by Sir Rupert Jackson in his *Final Report* at ch. 39. Professor Zuckerman analysed the history of the case and commented:

> By no stretch of the imagination can this be considered an efficient use of court resources, nor was it fair to other litigants waiting in the queue, nor did it provide effective protection to the defendant from being unnecessarily subjected to 6 years of futile litigation.... The main responsibility for this state of affairs must be accepted by the Court of Appeal. The Court of Appeal has steadfastly declined to develop a coherent policy for enforcing compliance with rules and case management directions. Its refusal to provide leadership in this regard is nowhere more apparent than in relation to its interpretation of r. 3.9.

Submissions from the Association of Her Majesty's District Judges to the Jackson review were to the effect that district judges who are prepared to make unpalatable decisions and impose robust but fair penalties should be supported by the appellate courts.

Article 6 and relief from sanctions

Woodhouse v Consignia plc [2002] EWCA Civ 275, [2002] 1 WLR 2558 was authority for saying that **48.35**
it had to be kept in mind that refusing relief deprives the defaulting party of access to the court, which has particular importance given **art. 6(1)** of the European Convention on Human Rights in the **Human Rights Act 1998, sch. 1**. It is submitted this remains the case after the reforms to **CPR, r. 3.9**, effected from 1 April 2013. In *Momson v Azeez* [2009] EWCA Civ 202, LTL 18/3/2009, the judge found that the defendant's breach of an unless order requiring disclosure had made a fair trial impossible. Given that finding, refusing relief from a sanction debarring the defendant from defending or counterclaiming did not infringe **art. 6(1)**, provided the sanction was proportionate and was for a legitimate purpose (which on the facts it was). Ideally, a judge dealing with an application for relief from sanctions under **CPR, r. 3.9**, should expressly state in his reasoning that he has considered the issues of legitimate aim and proportionality and the essence of the applicant's rights under **art. 6(1)** (*Al-Dawood Shipping Lines Ltd v Dynastic Maritime Inc.* [2010] EWCA Civ 104, LTL 19/2/2010). Where this is not done, an appeal court has to consider:

(a) whether the judge's decision constituted a legitimate aim, was proportionate in the circumstances, and did not destroy the essence of the applicant's **art. 6(1)** rights; and
(b) whether it is tolerably clear from the judge's reasoning that this is so.

Relief from sanctions from 1 April 2013

48.36 Given the criticism of the pre-1 April 2013 approach to CPR, r. 3.9, two changes have been made with effect from 1 April 2013:

(a) **Rule 1.1(2)** has been amended by adding sub-para. **(f)**, which says that dealing with cases justly and at proportionate cost includes enforcing compliance with rules, practice directions and orders; and

(b) **Rule 3.9(1)**, with its list of nine factors, has been replaced with a new **r. 3.9(1)** which simply provides:

> On an application for relief from any sanction imposed for a failure to comply with any rule, practice direction or court order, the court will consider all the circumstances of the case, so as to enable it to deal justly with the application, including the need—
> (a) for litigation to be conducted efficiently and at proportionate cost; and
> (b) to enforce compliance with rules, practice directions and orders.

Anticipating the change in approach, in a number of cases in 2012 the Court of Appeal emphasised that it is vital that it should support robust but fair case management decisions made by first instance judges. Examples are *Fred Perry (Holdings) Ltd v Brands Plaza Trading Ltd* [2012] EWCA Civ 224, [2012] FSR 28; *Deripaska v Cherney* [2012] EWCA Civ 1235, [2013] CP Rep 1 and *Stokors SA v IG Markets Ltd* [2012] EWCA Civ 1706, LTL 2/11/2012. Relief from sanctions is a discretionary remedy, and an appeal court should only intervene on an appeal if the first instance judge erred in principle or was plainly wrong.

Post-Jackson approach to relief from sanctions

48.37 Jackson LJ in *Fred Perry (Holdings) Ltd v Brands Plaza Trading Ltd* [2012] EWCA Civ 224, [2012] FSR 28 said the previous culture of non-compliance and delay was injurious to the civil justice system and to litigants generally. Lord Neuberger in the 9th Implementation Lecture at para. 19 said that the rigorous approach taken to compliance in the line of cases on extending claims forms culminating in *Hoddinott v Persimmon Homes (Wessex) Ltd* [2007] EWCA Civ 1203, [2008] 1 WLR 806 will become the standard approach under the revised **CPR, r. 3.9**. Consequently, under the present **r. 3.9** defaulting parties will receive considerably less indulgence than in the past.

In the discussion that follows, references in the cases to granting an extension to the period of validity of a claim form have been replaced by references (in square brackets) to granting relief from sanctions. A good starting point on the *Hoddinott v Persimmon Homes (Wessex) Ltd* line of cases is *Hashtroodi v Hancock* [2004] EWCA Civ 652, [2004] 1 WLR 3206. In this case the court said:

(a) the discretion to [grant relief from sanctions] should be exercised in accordance with the overriding objective; and

(b) the reason for the failure to [comply with the court's directions] within the specified period is a highly material factor. If there is a very good reason for the failure to [comply, relief] will usually be granted. If there is no more than a weak reason, the court is very unlikely to [grant relief from the sanction].

The application of this guidance was considered in *Collier v Williams* [2006] EWCA Civ 20, [2006] 1 WLR 1945.

Rix LJ in *Cecil v Bayat* [2011] EWCA Civ 135, [2011] 1 WLR 3086 at [109] adopted the following principles:

(a) [relief from sanctions] can only be granted if there is a good reason for granting [relief from sanctions]; and

(b) if there is a good reason, the court must consider the balance of hardship between the parties in either granting or refusing [relief from sanctions].

Good reasons are almost always based on difficulties outside the control of the party in default. Seeking [relief from sanctions] following the negligence or incompetence of the claimant's solicitors in failing to [comply with the court's orders] in time, perhaps because the legal representative simply overlooked the matter, will inevitably be regarded as a bad reason (*Hastroodi v Hancock* at [20]). The following are also regarded as inadequate reasons:

(a) deliberately not [complying] in order to avoid prejudicing ongoing negotiations. This was the result in *The Mouna* [1991] 2 Lloyd's Rep 221, and almost certainly remains the case under the CPR, given **r. 26.4**, which allows the court to grant a stay of the proceedings to allow for settlement of the case by ADR;
(b) awaiting an expert's report for the purposes of drafting the particulars of claim. This is a reason for obtaining an extension for service of the particulars of claim, not [an excuse for not complying with the requirements of the CPR] (*Collier v Williams*). A claimant in this situation should serve the claim form, and seek an extension of time for service of the particulars of claim from the court;
(c) seeking time to prepare the particulars of claim, schedule of loss and damage and medical evidence (*Mason v First Leisure Corporation plc* [2003] EWHC 1814 (QB), LTL 26/8/2003); and
(d) delays while arranging funding for the litigation. This situation should be addressed by seeking a stay of the claim while funding is arranged (*Cecil v Bayat*).

The position was summarised by Dyson LJ in *Hoddinott v Persimmon Homes (Wessex) Ltd* at [54]:

> A key element of the Woolf reforms was to entrust the court with far more control over proceedings than it had exercised under the previous regime. The rules must be applied so as to give effect to the overriding objective: this includes dealing with a case so as to ensure so far as is practicable that cases are dealt with expeditiously and fairly: r. 1.1(2)(d). That is why the court is unlikely to grant [relief from sanctions] if no good reason has been shown for the failure to [comply].

Relief may be granted on terms that the defaulting party fully complies with the terms of the relevant order (*Jani-King (GB) Ltd v Prodger* [2007] EWHC 712 (QB), LTL 10/4/2007).

Commentary

PROHIBITION FROM MAKING FURTHER APPLICATIONS

Where a litigant makes repeated applications of a similar nature, it is sometimes appropriate to make a civil restraint order to the effect that no further applications of a specified type can be made by the named litigant without the permission of a judge (see **14.51** to **14.60**). **48.38**

INORDINATE DELAY

Under the pre-CPR law, there were three bases on which claims could be struck out for delay: **48.39**

(a) On the ground of inordinate and inexcusable delay (also known as dismissal for want of prosecution, see *Birkett v James* [1978] AC 297). This was only available against a party in the position of a plaintiff; where there was inordinate and inexcusable delay; which had either given rise to a substantial risk that it would not be possible to have a fair trial, or which was likely to cause, or had caused, serious prejudice to the defendant; and, generally, the limitation period had to have expired.
(b) On the ground of non-compliance with a peremptory order. Guidelines for this type of case were laid down in *Hytec Information Systems Ltd v Coventry City Council* [1997] 1 WLR 1666 and other cases. These included the principle that unless orders were made as a last resort (which is no longer the case under the CPR) and a failure to comply would therefore usually result in the sanction being imposed; that late compliance would only be excused if there were compelling reasons, usually beyond the control of the defaulting party; that a party who deliberately flouted an order would not generally be absolved; that each case was considered on its own merits, with the key consideration being the interests of justice.
(c) On the ground that the delay amounted to an abuse of process (*Grovit v Doctor* [1997] 1 WLR 640; *Arbuthnot Latham Bank Ltd v Trafalgar Holdings Ltd* [1998] 1 WLR 1426). Where the

defaulting party's conduct, which could be prolonged inactivity, amounted to an abuse of the court's process the court would be justified in striking out the claim even where the limitation period had not expired and even where the defendant could not point to any prejudice arising from the delay.

Despite *Summers v Fairclough Homes Ltd* [2012] UKSC 26, [2012] 1 WLR 2004 at [35] and *Re Abermeadow Ltd* [2000] 2 BCLC 824 at pp. 829 and 830, it is clear that dismissal for inordinate and inexcusable delay has no application under the CPR. The principles survive in other Commonwealth jurisdictions. See, for example, *Icebird Ltd v Winegardner* [2009] UKPC 24, LTL 3/6/2009 (Bahamas).

Chapter 49 General Law of Evidence

Commentary

FACTS OPEN TO PROOF

49.1 The only facts which are open to proof, or disproof, are facts in issue, relevant facts and collateral facts.

Facts in issue

49.2 In a civil trial, the facts in issue are those which the claimant must prove in order to succeed in his claim together with those which the defendant must prove in order to succeed in his defence. The facts in issue in a case are therefore determined partly by reference to the substantive law and partly by reference to what the parties allege, admit, do not admit and deny. They should be identifiable by reference to the statements of case, which should set out the issues on which the parties agree and disagree so that it is known in advance what facts have to be proved or disproved at trial. Under **CPR, r. 16.4(1)**, particulars of claim must include a concise statement of the facts on which the claimant relies, and under **r. 16.5(1)** a defence must state which of the allegations in the particulars of claim are denied or not admitted, and which are admitted, by the defendant. See further, as to the circumstances in which a party shall be taken to require that an allegation be proved or shall be taken to admit an allegation, **r. 16.5(3) to (5)**. However, the CPR make it clear that the court also has a role to play in determining what the facts in issue are in any given case. **Rule 32.1** provides that 'the court may control the evidence by giving directions as to—

(a) the issues on which it requires evidence;
(b) the nature of the evidence which it requires to decide those issues; and
(c) the way in which the evidence is to be placed before the court'.

This provision invests the court with an extraordinarily wide power whereby it can override the views of the parties not only as to the nature of the evidence appropriate to decide the issues in the case, and as to the way in which the evidence should be given, for example, in documentary form rather than orally, but also as to the very issues that do or do not call for evidence. Thus if the court is of the opinion, for example, that the parties have misunderstood the substantive law in such a way as to lead them to believe, erroneously, that a certain matter does or does not have to be proved, then it may give appropriate corrective directions.

Relevant facts

Relevant facts are facts from which the existence or non-existence of a fact in issue may be inferred, and evidence of relevant facts is properly described as 'circumstantial evidence'. Some types of circumstantial evidence arise so often that they are referred to as presumptions of fact (see further, **49.22** to **49.24**). Typical examples of circumstantial evidence include evidence of motive to do a particular act, evidence of plans or other preparations for the performance of a particular act, evidence of opportunity, or lack of it, evidence of identity. Another example is evidence of lies told by a party, which may diminish credibility and make it harder for that party's case to be proved (see, for example, *MA (Somalia) v Secretary of State for the Home Department* [2010] UKSC 49, [2011] 2 All ER 65). Two final examples relate to the failure to give evidence or call witnesses, and standards of comparison. **49.3**

Where one party fails to give evidence or call witnesses, the court may be justified in drawing all reasonable inferences from the evidence given by an opponent of the facts which the first party chose to withhold (per Lord Diplock in *British Railways Board v Herrington* [1972] AC 877 at p. 930). Thus inferences have been drawn from the unexplained absence of witnesses who were apparently available and whose evidence was crucial to the case (see *Lewis v Eliades* [2005] EWHC 488 (Ch), LTL 6/4/2005, affirmed in *Karis v Lewis* [2005] EWCA Civ 1637, LTL 22/12/2005; and *Baigent v Random House Group Ltd* [2006] EWHC 719 (Ch), [2006] EMLR 16 at [213]–[215]). In *Wisniewski v Central Manchester Health Authority* [1992] Lloyd's Rep Med 223 Brooke LJ derived the following principles from the authorities on the point:

(1) In certain circumstances a court may be entitled to draw adverse inferences from the absence or silence of a witness who might be expected to have material evidence to give on an issue in an action.
(2) If a court is willing to draw such inferences they may go to strengthen the evidence adduced on that issue by the other party or to weaken the evidence, if any, adduced by the party who might reasonably have been expected to call the witness.
(3) There must, however, have been some evidence, however weak, adduced to the former on the matter in question before the court is entitled to draw the desired inference: in other words, there must be a case to answer on that issue.
(4) If the reason for the witness's absence or silence satisfies the court then no such adverse inference may be drawn. If, on the other hand, there is some credible explanation given, even if it is not wholly satisfactory, the potentially detrimental effect of his/her absence or silence may be reduced or nullified.

Similarly, it has been held that a defendant who has, in breach of statutory duty, made it difficult or impossible for a claimant to adduce relevant evidence runs the risk of adverse factual findings (*Keefe v Isle of Man Steam Packet Co. Ltd* [2010] EWCA Civ 683, LTL 17/6/2010)

Where it is necessary to decide whether a person's conduct meets some objective standard, evidence of what others would do in the same circumstances is admissible to show what that standard is. See, for example, *Chapman v Walton* (1833) 10 Bing 57, where for the purpose of deciding whether a broker had exercised a reasonable degree of care, skill and judgment in the performance of his duties, evidence was received from other brokers as to what they would have done in the same circumstances. See also *Noble v Kennoway* (1780) 2 Doug KB 510, which concerned the practice of delaying the discharge of a ship's cargo, and *Fleet v Murton* (1871) LR 7 QB126.

Collateral facts

Collateral facts are of three kinds. The first kind affects the credibility of witnesses, for example, the fact that a witness is biased towards one of the parties or has made a previous inconsistent statement. The second type of collateral fact, often referred to as a preliminary **49.4** fact, is a fact which must be proved as a condition precedent to the admissibility of an item of evidence. For example, under the Bankers' Books Evidence Act 1879, s. 4, a copy of an entry in a banker's book is only admissible under s. 3 of the Act if it is proved, *inter alia*, that the book was at the time of the making of the entry one of the ordinary books of the bank. See further at **49.80**. The third kind of collateral fact affects the competence of witnesses, for example, the fact that a potential expert witness is properly qualified in the subject calling for expertise.

RELEVANCE, ADMISSIBILITY AND THE DISCRETION TO EXCLUDE

49.5 The two governing principles underlying the English law of evidence are that:

(a) evidence must be sufficiently relevant in order to be admissible, but
(b) such evidence will only be admissible in so far as it is not excluded by the court either by virtue of a rule of law or in the exercise of its discretion.

However, there is no principle of law or practice which dictates that a judge cannot read or hear material that is actually or potentially inadmissible, especially if he or she is a judge of both law and fact (*Barings plc v Coopers and Lybrand* [2001] EWCA Civ 1163, [2001] CPLR 451). In that case, in which the judge, before the trial, was proposing to read background documentation by way of preparation for what was bound to be a long and complex case, it was held that there was no danger of his being so influenced by what he read that he would not decide the case only on the basis of the admissible evidence.

In general, disputes about the admissibility of evidence in civil proceedings are best resolved by the judge at the substantive hearing of an application or at the trial of a claim, rather than at a separate preliminary hearing, because the judge at a preliminary hearing will usually be less well informed about the case and preliminary hearings can cause unnecessary costs and delays (*Stroude v Beazer Homes Ltd* [2005] EWCA Civ 265, [2005] NPC 45).

The exclusionary rules of evidence, for example, the rules relating to opinion evidence and legal professional privilege, are covered elsewhere in this work. The following paragraphs consider relevance and discretionary exclusion.

Relevance

49.6 The word 'relevance' means that 'any two facts to which it is applied are so related to each other that according to the common course of events one either taken by itself or in connection with other facts proves or renders probable the past, present or future existence or non-existence of the other' (Stephen, *Digest of the Law of Evidence*, 12th edn., art. 1). Whether evidence is relevant is often a question of degree and determined not by strict logic but by common sense and experience.

Sometimes, evidence is plainly irrelevant. *Holcombe v Hewson* (1810) 2 Camp 391 concerned an alleged breach of covenant by the defendant, a publican, to buy his beer from the claimant, a brewer. The defence was that the claimant had previously supplied bad beer. Evidence purporting to rebut this, that the claimant had supplied other publicans with good beer, was held to be inadmissible because irrelevant: the issue was the quality of the beer supplied to the defendant, not the quality of different beer supplied to others. Similarly, in *Hollingham v Head* (1858) 27 LJ CP 241, where the defendant sought to establish that a contract was made on certain special terms, evidence that the claimant had entered into contracts with other customers on similar terms was held to be inadmissible because irrelevant: it afforded no reasonable inference as to the terms of the contract in question.

In other cases, relevance will be a question of degree. For example, evidence that after an accident the working practices of a defendant to a negligence action were altered and improved will not necessarily be relevant to the issue whether the accident was caused by negligence (see *Hart v Lancashire and Yorkshire Railway Co.* (1869) 21 LT 261). Conversely, in *Great Future International Ltd v Sealand Housing Corporation* [2002] EWCA Civ 1183, LTL 25/7/2002 evidence of an attempt by an employee (who was not called as a witness) of one of the claimants to persuade an expert retained for one of the defendants not to testify was held to be relevant to the question of mitigation of damage. In some cases evidence will be excluded because although it is undoubtedly of *some* relevance to the issues, it will give rise to a number of subsidiary issues which might well distract the court from the main issue. This may involve the court in a protracted investigation (see *Attorney-General v Hitchcock* (1847) 1 Ex 91 at p. 105) or a difficult controversy of the same kind as that which it has to decide (see *Metropolitan Asylum District Managers v Hill* (1882) 47 LT 29). A good illustration is *Agassiz v London Tramway Co.* (1872) 21 WR 199, in which a passenger in an omnibus claimed damages for personal injuries suffered as a result of a collision alleged to have been caused by the negligence of the driver. After the accident another passenger had suggested to the conductor that the driver's conduct hould be reported, to which the conductor had replied that the driver had been reported because he had been off the points five or six times that day. This evidence was held to have been properly excluded on the basis that it did not relate to the conduct of the driver at the relevant time and did not explain the cause of the collision, but gave rise to a multiplicity of side issues.

Commentary

Evidence obtained unlawfully, improperly or unfairly

Subject to three exceptions, at common law evidence obtained unlawfully, improperly or unfairly is admissible as a matter of law (see *Helliwell v Piggott-Sims* [1980] FSR 582; *Calcraft v Guest* [1898] 1 QB 759; and *Goddard v Nationwide Building Society* [1987] QB 670). The first exception relates to evidence obtained by torture. In *A v Secretary of State for the Home Department (No. 2)* [2005] UKHL 71, [2006] 2 AC 221, Lord Bingham of Cornhill held that, as a matter of constitutional principle, evidence obtained by torturing another may not lawfully be admitted against a party to proceedings in a British court, irrespective of where, or by whom, or on whose authority the torture was inflicted. The second exception is that evidence obtained by unjustifiable inhuman or degrading treatment contrary to the European Convention on Human Rights, art. 3, may also fall to be excluded (*Jalloh v Germany* (application 54810/00) (2006) 44 EHRR 32). The third exception relates to privileged documents. In civil proceedings, where a document protected by legal professional privilege, or secondary evidence of it, has been obtained by the wrongful act of the opponent of the party entitled to assert the privilege, that party may apply for an injunction to restrain the opponent from making any use of the confidential information (see 50.76 to 50.77). **49.7**

Discretion to exclude

Prior to the introduction of the CPR, a judge in a civil case had no discretion to exclude evidence admissible as a matter of law, and that principle applied even if the evidence in question had been obtained improperly or unlawfully (see per Lord Denning MR in *Helliwell v Piggott-Sims* [1980] FSR 582). On one view, there was an exception to this general rule whereby a judge could permit a witness, whether a party to the proceedings or not, to refuse to disclose information, typically information given and received under the seal of confidence, where disclosure would be a breach of some ethical or social value and non-disclosure would be unlikely to result in serious injustice in the case in which it was being claimed: see 16th Report of the Law Reform Committee, *Privilege in Civil Proceedings* (1967) Cmnd 3472, para. 1, and per Lords Hailsham of St Marylebone and Kilbrandon in *D v National Society for the Prevention of Cruelty to Children* [1978] AC 171. In that case, however, both Lord Simon of Glaisdale and Lord Edmund-Davies doubted the existence of such a wide discretionary power. **49.8**

CPR, r. 32.1(2), has introduced an exclusionary discretion of general application in civil cases, including claims allocated to the small claims track (see **CPR, r. 27.2(1)**). Under **r. 32.1(1)** the court may control the evidence by giving directions as to the issues on which it requires evidence, the nature of the evidence which it requires to decide those issues, and the way in which the evidence is to be placed before the court. **Rule 32.1(2)** provides that 'the court may use its power under this rule to exclude evidence that would otherwise be admissible' and **r. 32.1(3)** states that 'the court may limit cross-examination'. In exercising its powers under either **r. 32.1(2)** or **r. 32.1(3)**, the court must seek to give effect to the 'overriding objective' of the rules, to enable the court 'to deal with cases justly' (**r. 1.1**). The power conferred by **r. 32.1(2)** is extremely wide. Subject to **r. 1.1**, there are no express limitations as to the manner and extent of the exercise of the power (*Grobbelaar v Sun Newspapers Ltd* (1999) *The Times*, 12 August 1999). The court has always had the power to rule evidence inadmissible if it is of no more than marginal relevance (see **49.6**). **Rule 32.1(2)**, however, goes further: the court may exclude any type of otherwise admissible evidence, even if plainly relevant, although obviously the more relevant it is, the more reluctant the court is likely to be to exercise its power to exclude it. This was emphasised in *Great Future International Ltd v Sealand Housing Corporation* [2002] EWCA Civ 1183, LTL 25/7/2002, where it was said that the power under **r. 32.1(2)** has to be exercised with great circumspection. In *Post Office Counters Ltd v Mahida* [2003] EWCA Civ 1583, *The Times*, 31 October 2003, Hale LJ said, at [24], that the power to exclude admissible evidence under **r. 32.1(2)** is principally a case management power designed to allow the court to stop cases getting out of hand. This means the rule may be used by the court when managing cases with the aim of minimising the burden on litigants of slender means by excluding all peripheral material which is not essential to the just determination of the real issues between the parties and whose examination would be disproportionate to its importance to those issues (*McPhilemy v Times Newspapers Ltd* [1999] 3 All ER 775 per May LJ at p. 791). As to the exclusion of expert evidence by reason of non-compliance with **PD 35**, see *Stevens v Gullis* [2000] 1 All ER 527.

The court may also use **CPR, r. 32.1(2)**, to restrict the number of witnesses to be called, and to exclude any evidence thought to be superfluous.

In appropriate circumstances, the court may properly take the view that in order to give effect to the 'overriding objective' it should also exercise the discretion in **r. 32.1(2)** to exclude evidence that has been obtained illegally (for example, by a crime, tort or breach of contract or statute), improperly (for example, by trickery, deception, bribes, threats or inducements) or in breach of the right to respect for private and family life in the European Convention on Human Rights, **art. 8**, in the **Human Rights Act 1998, sch. 1** (for example, by covertly video-recording employees or claimants in personal injuries litigation). In *Jones v University of Warwick* [2003] EWCA Civ 151, [2003] 1 WLR 954, the defendant was allowed to use as evidence a video of the claimant obtained in breach of **art. 8** and by trespass, inquiry agents acting for the defendant's insurers having filmed the claimant without her knowledge after having gained access to her home by deception. Lord Woolf CJ held that the court had to consider two competing public interests: that in litigation the truth should be revealed and that the courts should not acquiesce in or encourage a party to use unlawful means to obtain evidence. Thus the judge's responsibility requires him, when exercising his discretion in accordance with the overriding objective, to consider not only the litigation before the court but also the effect of his decision on litigation generally. The weight to be attached to the two competing interests will vary according to the circumstances. The significance of the evidence will differ as will the gravity of the breach of **art. 8**. On the facts, it was held that it was not a case where the conduct of the insurers was so outrageous that the defence should be struck out and that it would be artificial and undesirable for the evidence to be excluded, which would have required the instruction of fresh medical experts. However, it was also stressed that the conduct of the insurers was improper and unjustified and that the trial judge should take it into account when deciding the appropriate order for costs. See also *Niemietz v Germany* (1992) 16 EHRR 97;

Halford v United Kingdom (1997) 24 EHRR 523; *Tchenguiz v Imerman* [2010] EWCA Civ 908, [2011] 1 All ER 555.

CPR, r. 32.1(3), may be used by the court to impose limits on the time permitted for cross-examination of witnesses at trial (see, for example, *Rall v Hume* [2001] 3 All ER 248). The question for the judge in deciding whether or not to limit cross-examination is how long is it necessary for the cross-examination to last in the interests of justice, for both parties and for the witness in question and, concerning the last, account may be taken of the witness's medical condition (see *Three Rivers District Council v Bank of England* [2005] EWCA Civ 889, LTL 23/8/2005).

Rule 32.1(3) supplements the pre-existing discretionary powers of the judge to prevent questions in cross-examination which, in his or her opinion, are unnecessary, improper or oppressive. At common law, cross-examination should be conducted with restraint and with a measure of courtesy and consideration to the witness (see per Sankey LC in *Mechanical and General Inventions Co. Ltd v Austin* [1935] AC 346 at p. 360; and the Code of Conduct of the Bar of England and Wales (2000), s. 1, para. 708 and s. 3, paras 5.10 and 5.11). Counsel should be restrained from embarking on lengthy cross-examination on matters that are not really in issue (*Mechanical and General Inventions Co. Ltd v Austin* at p. 359) or from framing questions in such a way as to invite argument rather than elicit evidence on the facts in issue (per Lord Hewart CJ in *R v Baldwin* (1925) 18 Cr App R 175).

In order to call into question a witness's credibility, the witness may be asked about his or her conviction for any offence, even if it is not one of dishonesty (see **49.68**), but the court may exercise its discretion under **CPR, r. 32.1(3)**, to limit such cross-examination to convictions for offences involving dishonesty. However, a judge sitting without a jury should be more hesitant to exclude otherwise relevant evidence and cross-examination, because a judge does not need to be protected from giving undue weight to evidence relating to a witness's credibility (*Watson v Chief Constable of Cleveland Police* [2001] EWCA Civ 1547, LTL 12/10/2001).

Circumstances vary infinitely, and for this reason it is submitted that it will normally be unnecessary and undesirable for the courts to provide general guidance, additional to that to be found in the inclusionary definition of 'dealing with a case justly' in **r. 1.1(2)**, on the way in which the discretionary powers under **r. 32.1(2)** and **(3)** should be exercised. For the same reason the exercise of these discretionary powers should only be open to appeal on the limited grounds discussed in **75.11**).

FORMAL ADMISSIONS

A fact which is formally admitted ceases to be in issue. Evidence of such a fact, being unnecessary, is inadmissible. Legal advisers owe a duty to their clients to consider whether any formal admissions can properly be made. Formal admissions should be made by a party in the case of facts as to which there is no serious dispute, thereby saving the other party to the case the unnecessary trouble and expense of proving them. A party may admit the truth of the whole or any part of another party's case (**CPR, r. 14.1(1)**), although once an admission has been made, the permission of the court is required to amend or withdraw it (**r. 14.1(5)**). A party who wishes to admit the truth of the whole or any part of another party's case before the commencement of proceedings may do so by giving notice in writing (see **r. 14.1A(1)**; see also **17.2** and **34.30**). A fact may be formally admitted in a variety of ways: by a defendant, in his or her defence, expressly (**r. 16.5(1)(c)**) or by default, i.e. by failing to deal with an allegation (**r. 16.5(5)**), and by either party in response to a notice to admit facts (**r. 32.18**) or in response to a written request, or court order, to give additional information (see **rr. 18.1** and **26.5(3)** and **PD 18**). Prior to the trial, a formal admission may also be made by a letter written by a legal adviser acting on behalf of a party (*Ellis v Allen* [1914] 1 Ch 904). According to **CPR, r. 14.1(2)**, a party may make an admission 'by giving notice in writing (such as in a **49.9**

Commentary

statement of case or by letter)'. However, it would seem that it remains possible for a formal admission to be made by a party or a party's legal adviser orally, either at the trial itself (see *Urquhart v Butterfield* (1887) 37 ChD 357) or in interim proceedings, in which case the admission may subsequently be withdrawn, provided that the other party has not acted on it so as to give rise to an estoppel (*H. Clark (Doncaster) Ltd v Wilkinson* [1965] Ch 694).

PRESUMPTIONS

Introduction

49.10 There are numerous common law, equitable and statutory presumptions. The following paragraphs deal with some of the most important of them. The presumption of legal origin and the equitable presumptions of undue influence and advancement are not considered.

Rebuttable presumptions of law

49.11 Where a rebuttable presumption of law operates, on the proof or admission of basic or primary facts, and in the absence of further evidence, another fact must be presumed. The party relying on the presumption bears the burden of establishing the basic facts, and his adversary bears either an evidential burden to adduce some evidence in rebuttal of the presumed fact or, as the case may be, a legal burden to disprove the presumed fact. A rebuttable presumption which operates to put an evidential burden on the party against whom it operates is referred to as an evidential presumption. If the party relying on an evidential presumption proves the basic facts, the presumed fact will be treated as having been established unless his opponent adduces some evidence in rebuttal, but where the opponent discharges the evidential burden in the usual way (see **49.36**) the effect will be as if the presumption had never come into play at all: the party relying on the presumption bears the legal burden to prove on a balance of probabilities the fact that otherwise could have been presumed. It follows from this, of course, that if at the end of the day, on all the evidence before the court, the probability of the existence of the presumed fact is equal to the probability of its non-existence, the opponent will succeed. A rebuttable presumption which operates to put a legal burden on the party against whom it operates is referred to as a 'persuasive' or 'compelling' presumption. If a party relying on a persuasive presumption proves the basic facts, a legal burden is placed on the opponent to disprove the presumed fact. The opponent will therefore lose on the issue not only by adducing no evidence to disprove the presumed fact, but also where on all the evidence before the court the probability of the existence of the presumed fact is equal to the probability of its non-existence.

Some rebuttable presumptions, such as the presumption of mental capacity, operate without the proof or admission of basic facts, and in truth, therefore, are nothing more than rules relating to the incidence of the burden of proof that have been cast in the language pertaining to presumptions.

49.12 **Presumption of marriage** There appear to be three types of presumption of marriage, a presumption of formal validity, a presumption of essential validity, and a presumption of marriage arising from cohabitation. They are considered here in outline only. (For a fuller treatment, see Keane, *The Modern Law of Evidence*, 8th edn. (2010) at pp. 654ff.)

The formal validity of a marriage depends upon the *lex loci celebrationis*. Under English law, for example, there are formal requirements, in the case of a Church of England marriage, to publish banns and to obtain a common licence, and in the case of other marriages to give due notice to the superintendent registrar. Under the presumption of the formal validity of a marriage, on the proof or admission of the basic facts that a marriage was celebrated between persons who intended to marry, the formal validity of the marriage will be presumed in the absence of sufficient evidence to the contrary. The presumption is a persuasive presumption.

The leading authority relating to an English marriage is *Piers v Piers* (1849) 2 HL Cas 331, where a marriage performed in a private house was held to be formally valid despite the absence of evidence that the bishop of the diocese had granted the necessary special licence. For an example of the application of the presumption to a foreign marriage, see *Mahadervan v Mahadervan* [1964] P 233. It has been said that the standard of proof to be met by the party with the legal burden of disproving formal validity is high (see *Piers v Piers*), but it is submitted that under the modern law there is little likelihood of the courts applying the decision in *Mahadervan v Mahadervan*, where Sir Jocelyn Simon P held that the presumption can only be rebutted by evidence which satisfies beyond reasonable doubt that there was no valid marriage (see further at **49.41** to **49.44**).

Under the presumption of the essential validity of a marriage, on proof or admission of the basic facts that a formally valid marriage was celebrated, in the absence of sufficient evidence to the contrary, the essential validity of the marriage will be presumed, i.e. it will be presumed that the parties had the capacity to marry, and therefore, under English law, for example, were not related within the prohibited degrees, were aged 16 or over and were not already married (see *Tweney v Tweney* [1946] P 180). The presumption is probably a persuasive presumption. Evidence of a valid prior marriage will suffice to rebut the presumption (*Gatty v Attorney-General* [1951] P 444; *Re Peete* [1952] 2 All ER 599), but not where the prior marriage is itself of doubtful validity (*Taylor v Taylor* [1967] P 25).

Under the persuasive presumption of marriage arising from cohabitation, on proof or admission of the basic fact that a man and woman have long cohabited as if man and wife, and have acquired the reputation of being husband and wife, it is presumed, in the absence of sufficient evidence to the contrary, that they were living together in consequence of a valid marriage (see *Sastry Velaider Aronegary v Sembecutty Vaigalie* (1881) 6 App Cas 364; *Al-Saedy v Musawi* [2010] EWHC 3293 (Fam), [2011] 2 FLR 287). The presumption applies even in the absence of evidence that a marriage ceremony has taken place (see *Re Taplin* [1937] 3 All ER 105 and *Re Taylor* [1961] 1 WLR 9). Evidence in rebuttal is required to meet a high standard (see *Re Taplin* and *Re Taylor*).

Presumption of legitimacy Under the persuasive presumption of legitimacy, on proof or admission of the basic fact that a child was born or conceived during lawful wedlock, it is presumed, in the absence of sufficient evidence to the contrary, that the child is legitimate. The presumption applies where there is a maintenance order in force against the husband, unless it contains a non-cohabitation clause (*Bowen v Norman* [1938] 1 KB 689), where proceedings for divorce or nullity have commenced (*Knowles v Knowles* [1962] P 161) and where the parties are living apart, whether or not under a separation agreement (*Ettenfield v Ettenfield* [1940] P 96). The presumption does not apply where a decree of judicial separation or a magistrate's separation order is in force (see *Hetherington v Hetherington* (1887) 12 PD 112). 49.13

The presumption applies both where a child is born so soon after a marriage ceremony that premarital conception is indicated (*Poulett Peerage Case* [1903] AC 395) and where a child is born so soon after the mother's termination of her marriage that conception during the marriage is indicated (*Maturin v Attorney-General* [1938] 2 All ER 214; *Re Heath* [1945] Ch 417). In *Re Overbury* [1955] Ch 122, six months after her first husband's death, a woman remarried, and two months later gave birth to a girl. It was held that the child was the legitimate daughter of the first husband, there being insufficient evidence to rebut the presumption.

The standard of proof to be met by the party seeking to rebut the presumption is governed by the Family Law Reform Act 1969, s. 26. It provides as follows:

> Any presumption of law as to the legitimacy or illegitimacy of any person may in any civil proceedings be rebutted by evidence which shows that it is more probable than not that the person is illegitimate or legitimate as the case may be and it shall not be necessary to prove that fact beyond reasonable doubt in order to rebut the presumption.

Thus even weak evidence against legitimacy must prevail if there is no other evidence to counterbalance it, but where the evidence is such that legitimacy is as probable as illegitimacy, the party seeking to rebut the presumption will fail (see *S v S* [1972] AC 24 at p. 41, applied in *T (HH) v T (E)* [1971] 1 WLR 429).

The presumption of legitimacy may be rebutted by evidence that the husband and wife did not have sexual intercourse as a result of which the child was conceived (*Banbury Peerage Case* (1811) 1 Sim & St 153), evidence of the husband's impotence (*Legge v Edmonds* (1855) 25 LJ Ch 125), an admission of paternity by another man (*R v King's Lynn Justices, ex parte M* [1988] 2 FLR 79), evidence of the wife's cohabitation with another man for an appropriate period of time before the birth of the child (*Re Jenion* [1952] Ch 454), evidence of a DNA test excluding the husband as the father, coupled with evidence of the putative father's refusal to comply with an order for a blood test (*F v Child Support Agency* [1999] 2 FLR 244) or evidence of the conduct of the wife and illicit partner towards the child (*Kanapathipillai v Parpathy* [1956] AC 580). The inference of paternity to be drawn from a refusal to undergo DNA testing outweighs the presumption of legitimacy (*Secretary of State for Work and Pensions v Jones* [2003] EWHC 2163 (Fam), [2004] 1 FLR 282). Evidence in rebuttal may also take the form of evidence of non-access or the use of reliable contraceptives. Evidence of adultery on the part of the mother will not rebut the presumption unless accompanied by evidence that at the time of conception sexual intercourse between the husband and wife did not take place (*Gordon v Gordon* [1903] P 141).

49.14 **Presumption of death** Under the presumption of death, if there is no acceptable affirmative evidence that a person was alive at some time during a continuous period of seven years or more, on the proof or admission of the basic facts that:

(a) there are persons who would be likely to have heard of him or her over that period,
(b) those persons have not heard of him or her, and
(c) all due enquiries have been made appropriate to the circumstances,

that person will be presumed to have died at some time within that period (per Sachs J in *Chard v Chard* [1956] P 259 at p. 272). The decision of the House of Lords in *Prudential Assurance Co. v Edmonds* (1877) 2 App Cas 487 suggests that this is an evidential presumption rebuttable by adducing sufficient evidence to raise the possibility of the existence of the absent person. As to the first of the basic facts, friends and relatives will not be treated as persons likely to have heard of the absent person where there are reasons which might have led the latter not to wish to be heard of by the former (see *Chard v Chard*) or where it is shown that the latter did not intend the former to hear of him or her (see *Watson v England* (1844) 14 Sim 28 and *Re Lidderdale* (1912) 57 SJ 3).

The authorities conflict on whether (c) above is among the basic facts to be proved or admitted before the presumption can arise (see *Willyams v Scottish Widows' Fund Life Assurance Society* (1888) 4 TLR 489; *Chipchase v Chipchase* [1939] P 391; and *Bradshaw v Bradshaw* [1956] P 274), the explanation for which is probably that in some cases the circumstances are such that it would not be appropriate to make any enquiries at all (see *Bullock v Bullock* [1960] 1 WLR 975).

Under the presumption of death, the court presumes only the fact of a person's death. Thus if it is sought to establish that the deceased died unmarried, childless or without next-of-kin, these additional facts require additional evidence (*Re Jackson* [1907] 2 Ch 354), although less evidence seems to be required than if the presumption had not applied (see *Dunn v Snowden* (1862) 32 LJ Ch 104; *Rawlinson v Miller* (1875) 1 ChD 52; *Greaves v Greenwood* (1877) 2 ExD 289). Additional evidence is also required to prove that the death took place at a particular period (per Giffard LJ in *Re Phené's Trusts* (1870) LR 5 Ch App 139 at p. 144). As to the date on which one may presume the fact of death, the authorities are in conflict. *Re Phené's Trusts* was taken by the Privy Council in *Lal Chand Marwari v Mahant Ramrup Gir* (1925) 42 TLR 159 at p. 160 to be an authority for the proposition that the fact of death is presumed at the date of the proceedings. However, the decisions in *Re Westbrook's Trusts* [1873] WN 167 (criticised in *Re Rhodes* (1887) 36 ChD 586) and

Chipchase v Chipchase [1939] P 391 are only consistent with the conflicting view that the fact of death may be presumed at the end of the continuous period of absence for seven years.

Presumption of regularity Under this evidential presumption, often expressed in the maxim *omnia praesumuntur rite esse acta* (all acts are presumed to have been duly done), on the proof or admission of the basic fact that a person has acted in a public or official capacity, it is presumed, in the absence of sufficient evidence to the contrary, that the person was regularly and properly appointed and that the act was regularly and properly performed. Those presumed to have been duly appointed have included a police officer (*R v Gordon* (1789) 1 Leach 515), an officer of the Post Office (*R v Borrett* (1833) 6 Car & P 124), a judge (*R v Roberts* (1878) 38 LT 690) and an inspector of the Health and Safety Executive (*Campbell v Wallsend Slipway and Engineering Co. Ltd* [1978] ICR 1015). In *R v Langton* (1876) 2 QBD 296 the presumption was used to establish the due incorporation of a company which had acted as such. In *R v Inland Revenue Commissioners, ex parte T. C. Coombs and Co.* [1991] 2 AC 283 a tax inspector, with the consent of a General Commissioner, had served notice under the Taxes Management Act 1970, s. 20, requiring stockbrokers to deliver documentary information relevant to the tax liability of one of their former employees. It was presumed, in the absence of evidence to the contrary, that both the inspector and the Commissioner had acted within the limits of their authority, with honesty and discretion. **49.15**

Presumption of mental capacity A party or witness is presumed to have mental capacity until the contrary is proved, the burden of proving the contrary resting on the party asserting incapacity (*Masterman-Lister v Brutton and Co. (Nos. 1 and 2)* [2002] EWCA Civ 1889, [2003] EWCA Civ 70, [2003] 1 WLR 1511). The court as a matter of practice should investigate the question of capacity whenever there is reason to suspect its absence, even if the matter is not in contention. The test is issue specific and depends on the nature and complexity of the transactions involved. The test is whether the person was capable of understanding the issues on which his or her consent or decision was necessary. However, although the decisions made are likely to be important indicators of the existence or lack of understanding, a person is not to be regarded as unable to make any rational decision merely because the decision made would not have been made by a person of ordinary prudence and, conversely, is not to be regarded as having mental capacity merely because his or her decision appears rational. The court must be astute not to accept a plea of incompetence when the evidence does not suggest a lack of competence (*Phillips v Symes* [2004] EWHC 1887 (Ch), LTL 18/8/2004). **49.16**

Presumptions in testamentary cases Under this evidential presumption, on the proof or admission of the basic fact that a rational will has been duly executed, it is presumed, in the absence of sufficient evidence to the contrary, that the testator was sane. Thus, in *Sutton v Sadler* (1857) 3 CB NS 87, in which the heir-at-law brought an action against the devisee alleging the insanity of the testator, it was held that the devisee bore the legal burden of proving that he was the devisee under a duly executed will; that proof of the due execution of a rational will gave rise to the presumption, placing an evidential burden on the heir-at-law; and that if the heir-at-law had raised sufficient evidence for the issue of sanity to go before the tribunal of fact, that tribunal should find against the devisee unless satisfied that he had discharged the legal burden of proving on a balance of probabilities that the testator was sane. **49.17**

There is a presumption of due execution on proof that a will contains the signatures of the deceased, two witnesses and an attestation clause. Although this is an evidential presumption, it can only be rebutted by the strongest evidence that the witness did not intend to attest the deceased's signature (*Sherrington v Sherrington* [2005] EWCA Civ 326, *The Times*, 24 March 2005). It is not rebutted merely because the attesting witnesses have no recollection of having signed (*Channon v Perkins* [2005] EWCA Civ 1808, LTL 1/12/2005).

Principle of *res ipsa loquitur* Under the principle of *res ipsa loquitur*, on proof or admission of the basic facts that some thing was under the management of the defendant or his or **49.18**

her employees and an accident occurred, being an accident which in the ordinary course of things does not occur if those who have the management of the thing use proper care, it may or must be presumed, in the absence of sufficient evidence to the contrary, that the accident was caused by the negligence of the defendant (see generally per Sir William Erle CJ in *Scott v London and St Katherine Docks Co.* (1865) 3 Hurl & C 596 at p. 601). This definition reflects the fact that in different cases the principle has been treated in different ways, as a persuasive presumption, as an evidential presumption (see **49.11**), and as a presumption of fact or provisional presumption (see **49.22**). In both *Woods v Duncan* [1946] AC 401 at pp. 419, 425 and 439 and *Barkway v South Wales Transport Co. Ltd* [1948] 2 All ER 460 at p. 471, it was treated as a persuasive presumption, shifting the onus of proof onto the defendant to show on the balance of probabilities that he was not negligent. See also per Lords Reid and Donovan in *Henderson v Henry E. Jenkins and Sons* [1970] AC 282 and also, it is submitted, *George v Eagle Air Services Ltd* [2009] UKPC 21, [2009] 1 WLR 2133 at [13]. In *The Kite* [1933] P 154, however, it was treated as an evidential presumption, so that if the defendant gives a reasonable explanation for the accident, which is equally consistent with the accident happening without his or her negligence as with it, then the burden of proof is on the claimant to show, as the claimant has to show from the beginning, that it was the negligence of the defendant that caused the accident. See also per Lord Pearson in *Henderson v Henry E. Jenkins and Sons*, per Lawton LJ in *Ward v Tesco Stores Ltd* [1976] 1 WLR 810, *Ng Chun Pui v Lee Chuen Tat* [1988] RTR 298 and *Dawkins v Carnival plc* [2011] EWCA Civ 1237; [2012] 1 Lloyd's Rep 1. Finally, there is authority that the principle of *res ipsa loquitur* is no more than a presumption of fact, so that proof of the basic facts gives rise to an inference of negligence which, in the absence of evidence to the contrary, may but need not be drawn (see per Greer LJ in *Langham v Wellingborough School Governors and Fryer* (1932) 101 LJ KB 513 at p. 518 and per Goddard LJ in *Easson v London and North Eastern Railway Co.* [1944] KB 421). There may be no anomaly in this diversity of approach. As it has been put elsewhere:

> Given that the facts calling for the application of the principle vary enormously from case to case so that in some the inference of negligence is slight, in others all but irresistible, efforts aimed at confining the principle to a single category seem ill-founded. At the risk of uncertainty, classification according to the facts of the case in question seems preferable. If the thing speaks for itself, it may do so with degrees of conviction. The hardship caused to the claimant may be remedied by placing the tactical, evidential or legal burden on the defendant depending on the strength of the basic facts in question. (Keane, *The Modern Law of Evidence*, 9th edn. (2012), at p. 668.)

49.19 **Presumption that a time clause is not of the essence of a contract** The Law of Property Act 1925, s. 41, contains a provision, first enacted in 1873, which fuses the common law and equitable rules on time in contracts. The effect is that, subject to three exceptions, a stipulation as to time in a contract (a time clause) is not deemed to be of the essence of the contract, and consequently it cannot be asserted that breach of such a stipulation repudiates the contract. The exceptions are:

(a) where the contract expressly states that time of performance is of the essence of the contract or must be strictly complied with;
(b) where the circumstances of the contract or its subject matter indicate that stipulations as to time must be strictly complied with; and
(c) where one party is guilty of undue delay and the innocent party gives notice that performance is required within a reasonable time.

There is a rebuttable presumption that stipulations as to time in rent review clauses are not of the essence of the contract (*United Scientific Holdings Ltd v Burnley Borough Council* [1978] AC 904). This presumption was rebutted in *Starmark Enterprises Ltd v CPL Distribution Ltd* [2001] EWCA Civ 1252, [2002] Ch 306, by a clause which stated that the tenant 'shall be deemed' to have agreed to an increased rent on failing to serve a counter-notice within one month of receipt of the rent notice. For a general discussion of when time is of the essence see *Re Gray* [2004] EWHC 1538 (Ch), [2005] 1 WLR 815.

Presumption that a fraudulent representation induced a contract On proof of a fraudulent representation of such a nature that it would be likely to have affected a reasonable person, it will be presumed that the representation induced the claimant to enter into the contract, unless the representor satisfies the court to the contrary. In *County NatWest Ltd v Barton* [2002] 4 All ER 494 it was held that the presumption alters the burden of proof, that the alteration remains unless and until the presumption is rebutted, and that the presumption continues to apply even if the representee gives evidence at the trial. **49.20**

Irrebuttable presumptions of law

On the operation of an irrebuttable or conclusive presumption of law, on the proof or admission of basic or primary facts, another fact must be presumed and the party against whom the presumption operates is barred from adducing any evidence in rebuttal. For examples, see the Civil Evidence Act 1968, s. 13(1) (considered at **49.97**), and the State Immunity Act 1978, s. 21(a), under which a certificate issued by the Secretary of State for the Foreign and Commonwealth Office is conclusive evidence of whether any country is a State for the purposes of part 1 of the Act or of the person or persons to be regarded for those purposes as the head of government of a State (see, for example, *R (HRH Sultan of Pahang) v Secretary of State for the Home Department* [2011] EWCA Civ 616, *The Times*, 13 June 2011). **49.21**

Presumptions of fact

On the operation of a presumption of fact, sometimes referred to as a provisional presumption, on the proof or admission of basic or primary facts, another fact may be presumed in the absence of sufficient evidence to the contrary, so that the party against whom the presumption operates bears a provisional or tactical burden in relation to the fact which may be presumed, not an evidential or legal burden. Presumptions of fact, therefore, are simply examples of circumstantial evidence, i.e. relevant facts, facts from which the existence or non-existence of a fact in issue may be inferred. In civil proceedings the only important examples of circumstantial evidence which have recurred so frequently as to be referred to as presumptions of fact are the presumption of continuance of life and the presumption of seaworthiness. **49.22**

Presumption of continuance of life On the operation of this presumption of fact, on the proof or admission of the basic or primary fact that a person was alive on a certain date, it may be presumed, in the absence of sufficient evidence to the contrary, that he or she was alive on a subsequent date (*McDarmaid v Attorney-General* [1950] P 218; *Re Peete* [1952] 2 All ER 599; *Chard v Chard* [1956] P 259). The strength of the presumption depends on the strength of the basic facts. If, for example, it were to be proved that a person was young and in good health on a certain date then, without more, the inference would be very strong that he or she was alive on the following day. If, on the other hand, it were to be proved that at a certain date a person was suffering from a terminal illness, then without more this would be unlikely to afford a reasonable inference that he or she was alive a year later (see *R v Lumley* (1869) LR 1 CCR 196 at p. 198). **49.23**

Presumption of seaworthiness On the operation of this presumption of fact, on the proof or admission of the basic fact that a ship sank or became unable to continue her voyage shortly after putting out to sea, it may be presumed, in the absence of sufficient evidence to the contrary, that she was unseaworthy on leaving port. It has been held that if, in the absence of evidence in rebuttal, the tribunal of fact were not to presume unseaworthiness, but were to find the contrary, then it would be such a finding against the reasonable inference to be drawn that it would amount to a verdict against the evidence (per Brett LJ in *Pickup v Thames and Mersey Marine Insurance Co. Ltd* (1873) 3 QBD 594 at p. 600; and see also *Ajum Goolam Hossen and Co. v Union Marine Insurance Co.* [1901] AC 362). **49.24**

Commentary

49.25 **Presumption of proper working order** There is a presumption, which comes into operation without the need for proof or admission of any basic or primary facts, that in the absence of sufficient evidence to the contrary, mechanical or other instruments of a kind that are usually in proper working order, were in proper working order at the time of their use. The party against whom the presumption operates bears an evidential burden to adduce some evidence to the contrary. The presumption has been applied, e.g. in the case of speedometers (*Nicholas v Penny* [1950] 2 KB 466) and traffic lights (*Tingle Jacobs and Co. v Kennedy* [1964] 1 WLR 638).

Conflicting presumptions

49.26 Where two evidential or two persuasive presumptions are relied upon in the same case, and as a result the court finds itself obliged to draw two conclusions, the one in conflict with the other, then the two presumptions can be treated as having cancelled each other out, with the effect that the case can be decided on the basis of the ordinary rules pertaining to the burden of proof. This solution was adopted in *Monckton v Tarr* (1930) 2 BWCC 504, where the presumption of essential validity of marriage applied to two different ceremonies, but when a similar conflict arose in *Taylor v Taylor* [1967] P 25, the court preferred to preserve the existing marriage, rather than avoid it by virtue of an earlier effectively moribund one, an approach which suggests that the court may reach its decision not only on the basis of the comparative likelihood of the two presumed facts, but also having regard to policy considerations.

It is submitted that where two conflicting presumptions are relied upon in the same case, but they are of unequal strength, as when a rebuttable presumption of law conflicts with a presumption of fact, the conflict is more apparent than real, because the determinative factor will be the incidence of the legal burden of proof: the party bearing the legal burden will lose on the issue in question if he fails to discharge it to the requisite standard of proof. The outcome in *R v Willshire* (1881) 6 QBD 366 is consistent with this view. See also *Re Peatling* [1969] VR 214 (Supreme Court of Victoria).

JUDICIAL NOTICE

49.27 The doctrine of judicial notice takes two distinct forms, which were defined and distinguished by Lord Sumner in *Commonwealth Shipping Representative v Peninsular and Oriental Branch Service* [1923] AC 191 at p. 212: 'Judicial notice refers to facts, which a judge can be called upon to receive and to act upon, either from his general knowledge of them, or from enquiries to be made by himself for his own information from sources to which it is proper for him to refer'. These two forms of judicial notice require separate consideration. Consideration is also given to the extent to which, if at all, a judge may make use of his or her personal knowledge of facts in issue or of facts relevant to the facts in issue.

Judicial notice without inquiry at common law

49.28 If a fact is so notorious or of such common knowledge that it requires no proof, the judge, without recourse to any extraneous sources of information, may take judicial notice of it and thereby treat it as proved, notwithstanding that it has not been established by evidence. The doctrine may be illustrated by the following examples: the duration of the normal period of human gestation is about nine months (*Preston-Jones v Preston-Jones* [1951] AC 391); cats are ordinarily kept for domestic purposes (*Nye v Niblett* [1918] 1 KB 23); the streets of London are full of traffic (*Dennis v A. J. White and Co.* [1916] 2 KB 1); and a postcard is the sort of document which might be read by anyone (*Huth v Huth* [1915] 3 KB 32). In all of these examples, the doctrine was expressly applied, but in the case of facts beyond all serious dispute, for example, that Tuesday follows Monday, or that there are seven days in the week, it is common for judicial notice to be taken tacitly.

At common law, judicial notice is also taken of public Acts passed before 1851, but in the absence of express provision to the contrary, a private Act passed before 1851 must be proved by evidence, for which purpose production of a Queen's Printer's copy or an HMSO copy suffices (Evidence Act 1845, s. 3, and Documentary Evidence Act 1882, s. 2). Statutory instruments also call for proof, for which purpose Queen's Printer's or Stationery Office copies also suffice (see *R v Ashley* (1967) 52 Cr App R 42 and Documentary Evidence Act 1868, s. 2), but some have acquired such notoriety that judicial notice may be taken of them (see *R v Jones* (1968) 54 Cr App R 63).

As a general rule, foreign law, being a question of fact normally calling for expert evidence, cannot be the subject of judicial notice (*Brenan and Galen's Case* (1847) 10 QB 492 at p. 498). The exceptions to this general rule include:

(a) the common law of Northern Ireland (*Re Nesbitt* (1844) 14 LJ MC 30 at p. 33);
(b) Scots law in civil cases, of which judicial notice may be taken by the House of Lords; and
(c) in civil cases only, notorious points of foreign law, e.g. that in Monte Carlo roulette is legal (see *Saxby v Fulton* [1909] 2 KB 208 and *R v Ofori (No. 2)* (1993) 99 Cr App R 223).

Judicial notice without inquiry pursuant to statute

Judicial notice of a fact, without inquiry, may be required by statute. Most of the statutory provisions require judicial notice to be taken of the fact that a judicial or other official document has been signed by the person by whom it purports to have been signed or has been sealed by the court by which it purports to have been sealed. This applies in the case of: 49.29

(a) a judicial or official document purporting to have been signed by a judge of the Supreme Court (Evidence Act 1845, s. 2);
(b) summonses and other documents issuing out of a county court and purporting to be sealed or stamped with the seal of the court (County Courts Act 1984, s. 134(2)).

At common law, judicial notice is taken of public Acts passed before 1851 (see 49.79). In the case of a UK statute (whether general, local and personal, or private) passed after 1850, the Interpretation Act 1978, s. 3, as supplemented by s. 22(1) and sch. 2, para. 2, requires judicial notice to be taken of it, unless the contrary is expressly provided by the Act. Evidence is therefore not required to prove either the contents of such an Act or that it has been duly passed by both Houses of Parliament. Judicial notice must also be taken of the European Community Treaties, the Official Journal of the Communities, and decisions of, or opinions by, the Court of Justice of the European Union (European Communities Act 1972, s. 3(2)).

Judicial notice after inquiry

If a fact is not sufficiently notorious to be the subject of judicial notice without inquiry, the judge may take judicial notice of it and thereby treat it as proved, notwithstanding that it has not been established by evidence, after referring to reliable extraneous sources of information, such as certificates from ministers, learned treatises, works of reference and expert witnesses. The inquiry is distinct from proof by evidence because the rules of evidence do not apply, the results of the inquiry are not open to evidence in rebuttal, and the result constitutes a precedent, except in the case of facts lacking constancy, such as the status of a foreign government. There is obvious scope for abuse of the doctrine, but this has to be balanced against the reality that some facts are readily demonstrable by reference to sources of virtually indisputable authority and are likely to be in issue again, in other cases, so that proof in the normal way is undesirable, having regard to considerations of cost and the need for uniformity of decision. This may go some way towards explaining *McQuaker v Goddard* [1940] 1 KB 687, where it was held that judicial notice after inquiry could be taken of the fact that a camel is a domestic animal. 49.30

Judicial notice after inquiry has usually been taken of three kinds of fact:

(a) facts which are readily demonstrable after reference to appropriate authoritative works of reference or learned treatises;
(b) customs and professional practices; and
(c) facts of a political nature.

49.31 **Readily demonstrable facts** Examples include the day of the week on which a certain date fell, after reference to a diary or almanac; the longitude and latitude of a place, after reference to an atlas; and the date and place of a well-known historical event, after reference to an authoritative historical work.

49.32 **Customs and professional practices** After consultation with suitably qualified expert witnesses, judicial notice may be taken of general customs and professional practices, such as the custom of the general lien of bankers on the securities of their customers (*Brandao v Barnett* (1846) 12 Cl & F 787; *George v Davies* [1911] 2 KB 445 at p. 448) and the practices of conveyancers (*Re Rosher* (1884) 26 ChD 801), ordnance surveyors (*Davey v Harrow Corporation* [1958] 1 QB 60) and accountants (*Heather v P-E Consulting Group Ltd* [1973] Ch 189).

49.33 **Political facts** Judicial notice after inquiry has been taken of facts of a political nature such as the status of foreign governments, the membership of diplomatic suites and the extent of territorial sovereignty. The inquiry will usually be made of a minister, whose certificate will be treated as accurate because as a matter of public policy it is desirable to avoid a conflict between the courts and the executive on such issues. Examples include the fact that a country exists as an independent sovereign state (*Duff Development Co. v Government of Kelantan* [1924] AC 797, and see also *Mighell v Sultan of Johore* [1894] 1 QB 149 and *Carl Zeiss Stiftung v Rayner and Keeler Ltd (No. 2)* [1967] 1 AC 853); the fact that this country is in a state of war with another (*R v Bottrill, ex parte Kuechenmeister* [1947] KB 41); the membership of the staff of an ambassador (*Engelke v Mussmann* [1928] AC 433); and the classification 'secret' appearing on a document originating in a government office, meaning that the document contains information and material the unauthorised disclosure of which would cause serious injury to the interests of the nation (*Secretary of State for Defence v Guardian Newspapers Ltd* [1985] AC 339 per Lord Diplock at p. 354).

Personal knowledge

49.34 When a judge takes judicial notice of a notorious fact, he or she makes use of his or her general knowledge. The extent to which, if at all, a judge may make use of his or her personal and particular knowledge of facts in issue or relevant to the facts in issue, is unclear. There is certainly authority that a judge may use personal knowledge of matters within the common knowledge of people in the locality, but that is a principle which derives from cases decided under the Workmen's Compensation Acts, under which county court judges sat as arbitrators and took into account, in assessing compensation, personal knowledge of the labour market (see *Keane v Mount Vernon Colliery Co. Ltd* [1933] AC 309 and *Reynolds v Llanelly Associated Tinplate Co. Ltd* [1948] 1 All ER 140). In *Mullen v Hackney London Borough Council* [1997] 1 WLR 1103 the Court of Appeal held that a county court judge, in deciding which penalty to impose on the council for its failure to carry out an undertaking to the court, was entitled to take judicial notice of his own knowledge of the council's conduct in relation to previous undertakings. As to judicial notice, the facts in this case were clearly not notorious or of the kind of which judicial notice has been held to have been properly taken after enquiry. The Court of Appeal appears to have treated the principle deriving from cases such as *Keane v Mount Vernon Colliery Co. Ltd* as one of general application in any county court case (see Allen, *International Journal of Evidence and Proof* (1998) vol. 2, No. 1, 37).

THE BURDEN AND STANDARD OF PROOF

Legal burden

In this chapter, the phrase 'the legal burden' will be used to denote what has been variously described as 'the burden of proof', the 'probative burden', 'the ultimate burden', 'the burden of proof on the pleadings', 'the risk of non-persuasion' and 'the persuasive burden'. The legal burden is the obligation imposed on a party by a rule of law to prove (in some cases to negative or disprove) a fact in issue: a party which fails to discharge the burden will lose on the issue in question. In civil proceedings the standard of proof required to discharge the burden is proof on the balance of probabilities (see **49.41**). Whether a party has discharged the burden is decided by the tribunal of fact, whether judge or jury, once only, after the parties to the litigation have called all of their evidence. **49.35**

In exceptional cases, a judge may find it impossible to make a finding, one way or the other, on a disputed issue of fact, and therefore may decide the issue by resort to the legal burden. The principles to be derived from the authorities, in this respect, were summarised in *Stephens v Cannon* [2005] EWCA Civ 222, *The Times*, 2 May 2005, at [46] as follows:

(a) The situation in which the court finds itself before it can dispatch a disputed issue by resort to the burden of proof has to be exceptional.
(b) Nevertheless the issue does not have to be of any particular type.... It may be more likely to arise following an enquiry into, for example, the identity of the aggressor in an unwitnessed fight; but it can arise even after an enquiry, aided by good experts, into, for example, the cause of the sinking of a ship.
(c) The exceptional situation which entitles the court to resort to the burden of proof is that, notwithstanding that it has striven to do so, it cannot reasonably make a finding in relation to a disputed issue.
(d) A court which resorts to the burden of proof must ensure that others can discern that it has striven to make a finding in relation to a disputed issue and can understand the reasons why it has concluded that it cannot do so. The parties must be able to discern the court's endeavour and to understand its reasons in order to be able to perceive why they have won and lost. An appellate court must also be able to do so because otherwise it will not be able to accept that the court below was in the exceptional situation of being entitled to resort to the burden of proof.
(e) In a few cases the fact of the endeavour and the reasons for the conclusion will readily be inferred from the circumstances and so there will be no need for the court to demonstrate the endeavour and to explain the reasons in any detail in its judgment. In most cases, however, a more detailed demonstration and explanation in [the] judgment will be necessary.

Judges sometimes refer to the 'shifting' of a burden from a party to that party's opponent. In the case of the legal burden, this can only happen at common law on the operation of a rebuttable presumption of law of the persuasive variety: once the party relying on the presumption has proved the primary or basic facts giving rise to the presumption, the legal burden can be said to have shifted, in that the opponent will then bear the legal burden to disprove the fact that will otherwise be presumed (see **49.11**). When reference is made to the shifting of the burden in other circumstances, it is merely to signify that at a given moment in the course of the trial the burden appears to have been satisfied by the party on whom it lies, but in so far as this places a burden on the opponent, it is a tactical burden, not a legal or evidential burden (see per Mustill LJ in *Brady v Group Lotus Car Companies plc* [1987] 3 All ER 1050 at p. 1059): as already noted, whether a legal burden has been discharged is determined only once, at the end of the trial.

Evidential burden and right to begin

The evidential burden, sometimes referred to as 'the burden of adducing evidence' and 'the duty of passing the judge', is the obligation to adduce sufficient evidence of a fact to allow **49.36** the issue in question to go before the tribunal of fact. The burden is discharged when there is sufficient evidence to justify, as a possibility, a favourable finding by the tribunal of fact. Whether a party has discharged the burden is decided only once in the course of the trial, and is decided by the judge, as opposed to the tribunal of fact. Thus a claimant who bears the evidential and legal burden on a particular issue, and fails to discharge the evidential burden, necessarily fails on the issue, since the judge will refuse to let the issue go before the tribunal of fact. However, discharge of the evidential burden will not necessarily result in discharge of the legal burden: the issue goes to the tribunal of fact, which may or may not find in favour of the claimant, although a defendant who adduces no evidence in rebuttal clearly runs the risk of losing on the issue.

As with the legal burden, judges sometimes refer to the 'shifting' of the evidential burden. However, this can only happen at common law on the operation of a rebuttable presumption of law of the evidential variety: where the party relying on such a presumption adduces sufficient evidence of the primary or basic facts, the adversary will bear an evidential burden to adduce some evidence in rebuttal of the presumed fact (see **49.11**). When reference is made to the shifting of the evidential burden in other circumstances, it is to signify that at a given moment during the course of the trial, the burden appears to have been discharged by the party on whom it lies, but this is to place no more than a provisional or tactical burden, as opposed to an evidential burden, on his opponent, because as has been said, an opponent who adduces no evidence in rebuttal clearly runs the risk of losing on the issue in question (see *Sutton v Sadler* (1857) 3 CB NS 87).

The right to be the first party to adduce evidence is determined by the incidence of the evidential burden. Usually the claimant will adduce his evidence first, but where the evidential burden on all the issues in the action lies on the defendant, or one of the defendants, the defendant or that defendant is entitled to begin (see *Pontifex v Jolly* (1839) 9 Car & P 202 and *Re Parry* [1977] 1 WLR 93). In *Mercer v Whall* (1845) 14 LJ QB 267 a clerk brought an action for unliquidated damages for wrongful dismissal. The defendant admitted the dismissal but claimed justification on the grounds of the clerk's misconduct. Although the defendant would have had the right to begin if the claim had been for a liquidated sum, because then the only issue would have been the issue of misconduct, on which the defendant bore the evidential burden, it was held that the clerk had the right to begin because he bore the evidential burden in relation to damages.

Incidence of the legal and evidential burden

49.37 Subject to cases in which reliance is placed upon evidential presumptions (see **49.11 to 49.25**), the evidential burden in relation to any given fact in issue will lie on the party bearing the legal burden on that fact in issue. As to the incidence of the legal burden, this may be fixed by agreement of the parties, but otherwise falls to be determined by rules of law to be found in statutes and at common law, where the general guiding principle to be derived from the precedents is that 'he who asserts must prove'.

49.38 **By agreement** The parties themselves may expressly agree upon the incidence of the legal burden (see, e.g. *Levy v Assicurazioni Generali* [1940] AC 791 and *Fred Chappell Ltd v National Car Parks Ltd* (1987) *The Times*, 22 May 1987), but where a written agreement such as an insurance policy contains no such express provision, the court may nonetheless have regard to the terms of the agreement and may treat the issue as a matter of construction. In *Munro, Brice and Co. v War Risks Association* [1918] 2 KB 78, a ship had disappeared for reasons unknown and a claim was made under a policy of insurance which covered the ship subject to an exemption in respect of loss by capture or in consequence of hostilities. The issue was whether the claimant had to prove that the ship was not lost by reason of enemy action. The court found for the claimant on the basis that it was for the defendant to prove that the facts fell within the exception, which they had failed to do. (Contrast, but question, *Hurst v Evans* [1917] 1 KB 352; and see also *Gorman v Hand-in-Hand Insurance Co.* (1877) IR 11 CL 224). However, where a claimant in such a case relies upon a proviso to an exemption clause, the court may conclude that the claimant must prove that the facts fall within the proviso. This was the outcome in *The Glendarroch* [1894] P 226. In that case, an action in negligence for non-delivery of goods, the goods having been lost when the boat carrying them sank, the bill of lading contained a clause exempting the defendants in respect loss or damage caused by perils of the sea, provided that they were not negligent. It was held that it was for the claimants to prove the contract and non-delivery; for the defendants, if they relied upon the exemption clause (loss caused by perils of the sea), to prove that the facts fell within it; and for the claimants, if they relied upon the proviso to the exemption clause (negligence on the part of the defendants), to prove that the facts fell within that proviso.

By statute The incidence of the legal burden may be determined by statute. For example, under the Consumer Credit Act 1974, s. 140B(9), if a debtor or a surety alleges that the relationship between the creditor and the debtor is unfair to the debtor, within the meaning of s. 140A of that Act, it is for the creditor to prove the contrary. A further example is to be found in the Employment Rights Act 1996, s. 98: in a claim of unfair dismissal, it is for the former employee to prove that he or she was dismissed, but it is for the employer to show the reason for the dismissal and that it amounts to one of the five grounds set out and for which a dismissal is capable of being fair, failing which the dismissal is treated as automatically unfair. **49.39**

At common law As to the incidence of the legal burden at common law, the general guiding principle to be derived from the precedents is that 'he who asserts must prove, not he who denies' (*Joseph Constantine Steamship Line Ltd v Imperial Smelting Corporation Ltd* [1942] AC 154, per Lord Maugham at p. 174). For example, in *Wakelin v London and South Western Railway Co.* (1886) 12 App Cas 41, an action in negligence, brought by a widow under the Fatal Accidents Act 1846, in which the only evidence was that the husband had been found dead near a level crossing at the side of a railway line, it was held that the claim must fail: the widow bore the burden of proving that the death had been caused by the defendants' negligence, but the evidence adduced was as capable of indicating negligence on the part of the husband as on the part of the defendants (cf. *Jones v Great Western Railway Co.* (1930) 144 LT 194). The principle is most useful, as in *Wakelin v London and South Western Railway*, when the issues are straightforward. Thus in an action for negligence, the claimant bears the legal burden of proving duty of care, breach of the duty and consequential loss, and the defendant bears the burden of proving contributory negligence, *volenti non fit injuria*, or any other defence which goes beyond a bare denial of the claimant's allegations. Similarly, in an action for breach of contract, the claimant bears the legal burden of proving the contract, its breach and consequential loss, and the defendant bears the burden of proving any defence which goes beyond a bare denial of the claimant's allegations, e.g. discharge by agreement or frustration. **49.40**

Commentary

The burden of proving a failure to mitigate rests on the defendant (*Geest plc v Lansiquot* [2002] UKPC 48, [2002] 1 WLR 3111, in which the Privy Council reviewed the authorities and agreed with both parties that the decision in *Selvanayagam v University of the West Indies* [1983] 1 WLR 585, that the burden lay on the claimant, cannot be relied upon).

In *BHP Billiton Petroleum Ltd v Dalmine SpA* [2003] EWCA Civ 170, [2003] BLR 271, it was held that in most cases the statements of case are likely to be a good guide to the incidence of the legal burden. The defendant manufactured and provided steel pipes used in the construction of a pipeline serving oil and gas fields in the Irish Sea. The pipeline failed after cracks developed in the welds which joined the pipes together. The defendant had fraudulently misrepresented that the pipes complied with the contractual specification, and the claimants, in reliance on this misrepresentation, had accepted and used the pipes which otherwise they would have rejected. On the question of causation, it was accepted by the claimants that they bore the burden of proving that the incorporation of non-compliant pipe caused the pipeline to fail and they succeeded in discharging this burden. However, the defendant in its defence averred that a pipeline made only of compliant pipe would have failed in any event. It was held that the defendant bore the burden of proving what it had averred.

It was accepted in *BHP Billiton Petroleum Ltd v Dalmine SpA* that although the statements of case are likely to be a good guide to the incidence of the legal burden, they cannot be definitive, because a party cannot, by poor pleading, take upon himself a burden which the law does not impose on him or free himself from a burden which the law does impose on him. Equally, a party cannot avoid a legal burden by an assertion cast in the form of a negative allegation, seeming to oblige his or her opponent to allege a positive. For example, in *Soward v Leggatt* (1836) 7 Car & P 613, the claimant landlord alleged that his tenant 'did not repair' a certain house, to which the defendant replied that he 'did well and sufficiently repair the house'. It was held that it was not the form of the issue which required consideration, but its substance and effect: the claimant, who might have pleaded instead that the defendant 'let the house become dilapidated', was alleging breach of covenant and therefore he had to prove it.

The limitations of the maxim 'he who asserts must prove' are highlighted by *Abrath v North Eastern Railway* (1883) 11 QBD 440 (affirmed on appeal, (1886) 11 App Cas 247, and applied in *Reynolds v Metropolitan Police Commissioner* (1984) 80 Cr App R 125). In that case, an action for malicious prosecution, the Court of Appeal held that the burden was on the claimant to prove not only that the defendant had instituted proceedings against him, but also that he had done so without reasonable and probable cause. Rejecting the submission that the burden of showing reasonable and probable cause fell on the defendant, Bowen LJ held that the assertion of a negative being an essential part of the claimant's case, the burden rested on him. The case illustrates the point that, in the absence of a precedent, if it is unclear whether an assertion is an essential part of the claim of the claimant or the defence of the defendant, the court must decide the matter. The authorities show that in these circumstances, the courts decide the matter having regard to matters of policy, such as the ease or otherwise that the respective parties would encounter in seeking to discharge the legal burden, and whether the objective of the rule of substantive law in question, whether a common law or statutory rule, would be likely to be achieved better by placing the burden on the one party or the other (see generally Stone (1944) 60 LQR 262).

An example, in the case of a statutory tort, is *Nimmo v Alexander Cowan and Sons Ltd* [1968] AC 107, a Scottish case brought by an injured workman under the Factories Act 1961, s. 29(1), which provided that 'every place at which any person has at any time to work... shall, so far as is reasonably practicable, be made and kept safe for any person working therein'. The workman alleged that his place of work was not kept safe, but did not aver that it was reasonably practicable to make it safe. By a majority, the House of Lords held that there was no burden on the workman to prove that it was reasonably practicable to keep the premises safe: it was for the defendant employers to prove that it was not reasonably practicable to keep the premises safe. The majority, in reaching this decision, were of the view that where, on the face of a statute, it is unclear on whom the burden should lie, a court, in order to determine Parliament's intention, may go beyond the mere form of the enactment and look to policy considerations such as the mischief at which the Act was aimed, and the ease or difficulty that the respective parties would encounter in discharging the burden. The defendant was clearly in a better position to discharge the burden. Furthermore the decision of the House, it is submitted, was the best way of achieving the object of the enactment, the provision of safe places of work.

A common law example is *Joseph Constantine Steamship Line Ltd v Imperial Smelting Corporation Ltd* [1942] AC 154. A ship on charter was destroyed by an explosion, the cause of which was unclear. The charterers claimed damages from the owners for failure to load. The defence was *frustration*. The charterers argued that the owners could not rely upon frustration unless they proved that the explosion was not caused by their fault. The House of Lords held that in order to defeat the defence, the burden was upon the charterers to prove fault on the part of the owners. The cause of the explosion being unclear, the appeal of the owners was allowed. The outcome may be justified on the basis that it is generally easier to prove fault than its absence, but there is no inflexible rule to that effect. Thus in bailment cases, the bailor having proved bailment, it is for the bailee to prove that the goods were lost or damaged without fault on his part (see *Coldman v Hill* [1919] 1 KB 443 and cf. *Levison v Patent Steam Carpet Cleaning Ltd* [1978] QB 69). In cases of conversion, the burden of proof is on the bailee to show that he dealt with the goods in good faith and without notice (*Marcq v Christie Manson and Woods Ltd* [2002] EWHC 2148 (QB), [2002] 4 All ER 1005, affirmed [2003] EWCA Civ 731, [2004] QB 286). Similarly, the burden of proof is on fiduciaries in relation to issues concerning the use of the assets in their trust (*Environmental Recycling Technologies plc v Daley* [2009] EWCA Civ 612, LTL 23/6/2009).

Standard of proof

In civil proceedings, the standard of proof generally required to be met by either party seeking to discharge a legal burden is proof on a balance of probabilities. This standard of proof is normally used at the end of the trial, after all the evidence has been called, but should also be used in reaching a decision on a submission of no case to answer when the defendant has elected not to adduce any evidence (*Miller v Cawley* [2002] EWCA Civ 1100, *The Times*, 6 September 2002). There are exceptions to this general rule. The standard in committal proceedings for civil contempt of court is proof beyond reasonable doubt (*Re Bramblevale Ltd* [1970] Ch 128; *Dean v Dean* [1987] 1 FLR 517). The standard of beyond reasonable doubt may also be required pursuant to statute (see *Judd v Minister of Pensions and National Insurance* [1966] 2 QB 580). An exacting civil standard of proof, which for all practical purposes is indistinguishable from the criminal standard, applies to applications for sex offender orders under the Crime and Disorder Act 1998, s. 2 (*B v Chief Constable of Avon and Somerset Constabulary* [2001] 1 WLR 340 at p. 354), for sexual offences prevention orders under the Sexual Offences Act 2003, s. 104 (*Chief Constable of Cleveland v H* [2009] EWHC 3231 (Admin), [2010] 3 All ER 506), and for football banning orders under the Football Spectators Act 1989, s. 14B (*Gough v Chief Constable of the Derbyshire Constabulary* [2002] EWCA Civ 351, [2002] QB 1213). The position is the same for anti-social behaviour orders, in relation to the Crime and Disorder Act 1998, s. 1(1), but pragmatism dictates that magistrates must in all such cases apply the *criminal* standard, which makes their task more straightforward (*R (McCann) v Crown Court at Manchester* [2002] UKHL 39, [2003] 1 AC 787 at [37], [83] and [114]–[117]). Classification of civil proceedings as criminal proceedings for the purposes of the European Convention on Human Rights, art. 6(3), in the **Human Rights Act 1998, sch. 1**, is a classification for the purposes of the Convention only and therefore will not alter the standard of proof from the civil standard to the criminal (*Commissioners of HM Revenue and Customs v Khawaja* [2008] EWHC 1687 (Ch), [2009] Bus LR 134, applying *Han v Commissioners of Customs and Excise* [2001] EWCA Civ 1040, [2001] 1 WLR 2253). However, in appropriate circumstances, and pursuant to the **Human Rights Act 1998, s. 3**, a statutory provision that requires the application of the civil standard of proof to the determination of a particular question may be read so as to apply the criminal standard of proof (see *R v Briggs-Price* [2009] UKHL 19, [2009] AC 1026). 49.41

Commentary

In *Miller v Minister of Pensions* [1947] 2 All ER 372 at p. 374, Denning J referred to the degree of cogency required to discharge the legal burden in a civil case in the following way: 'It must carry a reasonable degree of probability, but not so high as is required in a criminal case. If the evidence is such that the tribunal can say: "we think it more probable than not", the burden is discharged, but if the probabilities are equal it is not.'

The civil standard of proof always means more likely than not and the only higher degree of probability required by the law is the criminal standard (per Lord Hoffmann in *Secretary of State for the Home Department v Rehman* [2001] UKHL 47, [2003] 1 AC 153 at [55]). Thus there is no intermediate standard, nor is the civil standard to be broken down into subcategories designed to produce one or more intermediate standards (per Richards LJ, giving the judgment of the court, in *R (N) v Mental Health Review Tribunal (Northern Region)* [2005] EWCA Civ 1605, [2006] QB 468 at [60]). However, the single civil standard is flexible. There is authority to support the view that, in the case of a serious allegation, the flexibility of the standard lies in an upward adjustment of the degree of probability required for the allegation to be proved (see, e.g. per Denning LJ in *Bater v Bater* [1951] P 35 at p. 37 and in *Hornal v Neuberger Products Limited* [1957] 1 QB 247, considered at 49.42 and 49.43). That approach, however, has now been repudiated.

Although there is a single civil *standard* of proof on the balance of probabilities, it is flexible in its *application*. In particular, the more serious the allegation or the more serious the consequences if the allegation is proved, the stronger must be the evidence before a court will find the allegation proved on the balance of probabilities. Thus the flexibility of the standard lies not in any adjustment to the degree of probability required for an allegation to be proved (such that a more serious allegation has to be proved to a higher degree of probability), but in the strength or quality of the evidence that will in practice be required for an allegation to be proved on the balance of probabilities. (*R (N) v Mental Health Review Tribunal (Northern Region)* at [62], approved by the House of Lords in *Re D* [2008] UKHL 33, [2008] 1 WLR 1499.)

Another formulation of the flexibility of the civil standard in the case of serious allegations is furnished by the following dictum of Morris LJ in *Hornal v Neuberger Products Ltd* [1957] 1 QB 247 at p. 266, approved and adopted by the House of Lords in *Khera v Secretary of State for the Home Department* [1984] AC 74 at pp. 113–14:

Though no court and no jury would give less careful attention to issues lacking gravity than to those marked by it, the very elements of gravity become a part of the whole range of circumstances which have to be weighed in the scale when deciding as to the balance of probabilities.

A further formulation of the flexibility of the civil standard relies upon the probability or otherwise of what is being alleged. In *Re Dellow's Will Trusts* [1964] 1 WLR 451, Ungoed-Thomas J said: 'The more serious the allegation the more cogent is the evidence required to overcome the unlikelihood of what is alleged and thus to prove it'. Similarly, in *Re H (Minors) (Sexual Abuse: Standard of Proof)* [1996] AC 563, concerning the standard of proof in care proceedings, it was held that where a serious allegation is made, the inherent probability or improbability of an event is itself a matter to be taken into account when weighing the possibilities and deciding whether, on balance, the event occurred (per Lord Nicholls of Birkenhead at p. 586). This approach was followed in *Secretary of State for the Home Department v Rehman* [2001] UKHL 74, [2003] 1 AC 153, where Lord Hoffmann said, at [55]:

It would need more cogent evidence to satisfy one that the creature seen walking in Regent's Park was more likely than not to have been a lioness than to be satisfied to the same standard of probability that it was an Alsatian.

However, it does not follow from the foregoing that serious allegations *necessarily* call for more cogent evidence. In *Re D* [2008] UKHL 33, [2008] 1 WLR 1499, Lord Carswell, in a judgment with which the other members of the House of Lords were in agreement, said, at [28]:

The seriousness of the allegation requires no elaboration: a tribunal of fact will look closely into the facts grounding an allegation of fraud before accepting that it has been established. The seriousness of consequences is another facet of the same proposition: if it is alleged that a bank manager has committed a minor peculation, that could entail very serious consequences for his career, so making it the less likely that he would risk doing such a thing. These are all matters of ordinary experience, requiring the application of good sense on the part of those who have to decide such issues. They do not require a different standard of proof or a specially cogent standard of evidence, merely appropriately careful consideration by the tribunal before it is satisfied of the matter which has to be established.

In that case, on the issue whether a prisoner released on licence was the person who had committed serious sexual offences against his nieces, it was held to be sufficient that the tribunal deciding the issue had given the necessary critical attention to the evidence adduced in support of such serious charges.

In *Re B (Children) (Care Proceedings: Standard of Proof)* [2008] UKHL 35, [2009] 1 AC 11, the House of Lords went even further. On the question of the standard of proof, in care proceedings, in relation to facts on which the court can conclude that a child is suffering, or is likely to suffer, significant harm, it was held that there is no room for the nostrum 'the more serious the allegation, the more cogent the evidence needed to prove it'. Baroness Hale, in a speech with which the other members of the House agreed, said, at [70]–[72]:

> Neither the seriousness of the allegation nor the seriousness of the consequences should make any difference to the standard of proof to be applied in determining the facts. The inherent probabilities are simply something to be taken in account, where relevant, in deciding where the truth lies.
> As to the seriousness of the consequences, they are serious either way. A child may find her relationship with her family seriously disrupted; or she may find herself still at risk of suffering serious harm. A parent may find his relationship with his child seriously disrupted: or he may find himself still at liberty to maltreat this or other children in the future.
> As to the seriousness of the allegation, there is no logical or necessary connection between seriousness and probability. Some seriously harmful behaviour, such as murder, is sufficiently rare to be inherently improbable in most circumstances. Even then there are circumstances, such as a body with its throat cut and no weapon to hand, where it is not at all improbable. Other seriously harmful behaviour, such as alcohol or drug abuse, is regrettably all too common and not at all improbable. Nor are serious allegations made in a vacuum. Consider the famous example of the animal seen in Regent's Park. If it is seen outside the zoo on a stretch of greensward regularly used for walking dogs, then of course it is more likely to be a dog than a lion. If it is seen in the zoo next to the lions' enclosure when the door is open, then it may well be more likely to be a lion than a dog.

The reasoning in the final paragraph of this passage appears to be of general application, rather than confined to care proceedings, which suggests that there may be no room for the nostrum in question in the types of civil proceedings discussed in **49.42** to **49.44** below or indeed in any civil proceedings of any kind. However, it has since been held, albeit at first instance, that in the case of deceit, the court does not readily find that dishonest conduct is established and requires more convincing evidence to establish it than to establish negligence or other kinds of civil liability, because the law considers it less likely that people behave dishonestly (*Maple Leaf Macro Volatility Master Fund v Rouvroy* [2009] EWHC 257 (Comm), [2009] 2 All ER (Comm) 287 at [327], relying on *Hornal v Neuberger Products Ltd* [1957] 1 QB 247 at p. 258, considered at **49.42**).

Allegations of crime or fraud

In *Hornal v Neuberger Products Ltd* [1957] 1 QB 247 the claimant claimed damages for breach of warranty or alternatively for fraud. The company had sold a lathe to the claimant. The issue was whether, as the claimant alleged, one of the directors of the defendant company had represented that the lathe had been reconditioned. If such a representation was made, there had been a fraudulent misrepresentation, because the director knew that the lathe had not been reconditioned. The trial judge was satisfied on a balance of probabilities, but not beyond reasonable doubt, that the representation was made and awarded damages for fraud, but dismissed the claim for damages for breach of warranty on the basis that the parties did not intend the representation to have contractual effect. On appeal, the Court of Appeal held that on an allegation of crime in civil proceedings, the standard was not the criminal standard, but the ordinary, and flexible, civil standard of proof, on a balance of probabilities. Although Denning LJ was of the view that the court requires a degree of probability proportionate to the allegation, that view has now been repudiated in favour of the approach of Morris LJ, that the very elements of gravity have to be weighed in the scale when deciding as to the balance of probabilities (see **49.41**). **49.42**

Hornal v Neuberger Products Ltd was applied in *Re Dellow's Will Trusts* [1964] 1 WLR 451, where the issue was whether a woman had feloniously killed her husband, and also in *Post Office v Estuary Radio Ltd* [1967] 1 WLR 1396, which involved an allegation of a criminal offence under the

Wireless Telegraphy Act 1949. See also *Piermay Shipping Co. SA v Chester* [1979] 1 Lloyd's Rep 55 (an allegation of deliberately scuttling a ship), *Brazier v Bramwell Scaffolding (Dunedin) Ltd* [2001] UKPC 59, LTL 20/12/2001 (an allegation of conduct akin to fraud) and *Parks v Clout* [2003] EWCA Civ 1030, LTL 10/6/2003 (an allegation of obtaining letters of administration by fraud). Extreme and extraordinary allegations, such as asserting a conspiracy to pervert the course of justice, involving attempts to murder the appellant and fraud, will not be taken seriously without cogent supporting evidence (*R (Sivasubramaniam) v Wandsworth County Court* [2002] EWCA Civ 1738, [2003] 1 WLR 475).

Grounds of divorce

49.43 Prior to the Divorce Reform Act 1969, the old grounds for divorce were largely based on the concept of the matrimonial offence. For reasons of this kind, and because of the importance of divorce proceedings to both the parties and the state, the earlier authorities required the application of the criminal standard: see, in the case of allegations of cruelty, *Bater v Bater* [1951] P 35; in the case of al legations of adultery, *Ginesi v Ginesi* [1948] P 179, and also *Preston-Jones v Preston-Jones* [1951] AC 391 and *F v F* [1968] P 506, in both of which the finding of adultery would have rendered a child illegitimate; and see generally *Blyth v Blyth* [1966] AC 643. However, in *Bastable v Bastable* [1968] 1 WLR 1684, where adultery was in issue, Wilmer LJ and Winn LJ adopted as appropriate the dicta of Denning LJ in *Bater v Bater*, approved by the Court of Appeal in *Hornal v Neuberger Products Ltd* [1957] 1 QB 247, to the effect that the civil standard applies, but the court requires a degree of probability proportionate to the subject matter. Bearing in mind the present philosophy of divorce law, and the rejection of the view that in the case of serious allegations the degree of probability can be adjusted upwards, it is submitted that in all matrimonial causes the correct approach should be to consider the gravity of the allegation as part of the whole range of circumstances to be weighed in the scale when deciding on the balance of probabilities (see **49.41**).

Other cases

49.44 Other issues calling for flexibility in the application of the civil standard are set out below. In so far as some of the cases, on some of these issues, require, or seem to require, a standard at least as high as the criminal standard, it is submitted that they are unlikely to be followed, especially now that it is clear that the ordinary, flexible civil standard of proof is appropriate to allegations of crime in civil cases (see **49.42**).

(a) *Change of domicile*. A party seeking to prove an intention to change domicile must do so 'clearly and unequivocally' (*Moorhouse v Lord* (1863) 10 HL Cas 272 at p. 236; see also *Re Fuld (No. 3)* [1968] P 675 at p. 685).
(b) *Rebutting the presumption of the formal validity of a marriage*. The evidence in rebuttal of this strong common law presumption is required to be 'strong, distinct and satisfactory' (*Piers v Piers* (1849) 2 HL Cas 331 at p. 389) or 'evidence which satisfied beyond reasonable doubt that there was no valid marriage' (*Mahadervan v Mahadervan* [1964] P 233 at p. 246).
(c) *Rectification*. A party claiming rectification must prove his case by 'strong irrefragable evidence' (*Countess of Shelburne v Earl of Inchiquin* (1784) 1 Bro CC 338 at p. 341; and see also *Earl v Hector Whaling Ltd* [1961] 1 Lloyd's Rep 459).
(d) *Paternity*. The standard of proof required to make a finding of paternity is a heavy one, commensurate with the gravity of the issue, and although not the criminal standard, is more than the ordinary civil standard (*W v K* [1988] 1 FLR 86; and see also *Serio v Serio* (1983) 4 FLR 756).
(e) *Medical treatment for the mentally ill*. In order for a court to approve proposed medical treatment for an incompetent mentally ill patient without infringing the European Convention on Human Rights, **art. 3**, in the **Human Rights Act 1998, sch. 1**, it must be 'convincingly shown' that the treatment is medically necessary. This standard of proof

may be met notwithstanding the existence of a responsible body of opinion against the proposed treatment (*R (N) v Dr M* [2002] EWCA Civ 1789, [2003] 1 WLR 562).

(f) *Continuing detention of mentally ill patients.* Cogent evidence will in practice be required in order to satisfy a tribunal, on the balance of probabilities, that the conditions for continuing detention under the Mental Health Act 1983, ss. 72 and 73, have been met (*R (N) v Mental Health Review Tribunal (Northern Region)* [2005] EWCA Civ 1605, [2006] QB 468).

WITNESSES: COMPETENCE, COMPELLABILITY, OATHS AND PROCEDURE

Competence and compellability — the general rule

The general rule may be put in the form of two propositions: **49.45**

(a) any person is competent in any proceedings; and
(b) all competent witnesses are compellable.

The only remaining exceptions to these two propositions relate to children, persons with a disorder or disability of the mind, the Sovereign, heads of other sovereign states, diplomats and, in prescribed circumstances, bankers. Many former categories of exception to the first proposition — non-Christians and atheists, those with criminal convictions or a pecuniary and proprietary interest in the outcome of the proceedings, and the parties to civil proceedings and their spouses — have been removed, over the centuries, mostly by statutory reform. Concerning the parties to the proceedings, the consequence is that any party to civil proceedings may give evidence and may compel any other party to those proceedings to give evidence. As to the spouses of the parties to proceedings, in *Monroe v Twistleton* (1802) Peake Add Cas 219 (followed in *O'Connor v Marjoribanks* (1842) 4 Man & G 435) it was held that a former spouse is incompetent following the termination of his or her marriage in so far as his or her evidence relates to events which occurred during the marriage. Reversal of this decision is plainly long overdue, although it is arguable that it can be ignored on the basis that the words 'husbands' and 'wives' in the Evidence Amendment Act 1853, by which the spouses of parties were rendered competent and compellable, can be taken to cover former husbands and wives (but cf. *Shenton v Tyler* [1939] Ch 620).

Commentary

Children

The Children Act 1989, s. 96, provides as follows: **49.46**

(1) Subsection (2) applies where a child who is called as a witness in any civil proceedings does not, in the opinion of the court, understand the nature of an oath.
(2) The child's evidence may be heard by the court if, in its opinion —
    (a) he understands that it is his duty to speak the truth; and
    (b) he has sufficient understanding to justify his evidence being heard.

A child is a person under the age of 18 (s. 105). In deciding whether a child understands the nature of an oath, the courts are likely to be guided by the authorities which governed both civil and criminal cases before the law was changed, in criminal cases, by the Criminal Justice Act 1991, s. 52. Thus, in order to form an opinion on the issue, the judge will put preliminary questions to the child (see *R v Surgenor* (1940) 27 Cr App R 175), although whether the child warrants such an examination is a matter of judicial discretion. There is no fixed age at which a child should be treated as competent and below which he or she should be examined, but as a general working rule inquiry should be made of a child under the age of 14, although much depends on the type of child in question (*R v Khan* (1981) 73 Cr App R 190; and cf. *Bains v Director of Public Prosecutions* [1992] Crim LR 795). The watershed dividing children who are normally considered old enough to take the oath and those normally considered too young to do so probably falls between the ages of eight and 10 (see *R v Hayes* [1977] 1 WLR 234). The former practice was for judges to ask questions designed to discover whether the child was aware of the divine sanction of the oath, but in *R v Hayes* this practice was abandoned in favour of a secular approach. In that case, the Court of Appeal held that the important consideration is, 'whether the child has a sufficient appreciation of the solemnity of the occasion and the added responsibility to tell the truth, which is involved in taking an oath, over and above the duty to tell the truth which is an ordinary duty of social conduct'. If the child fails this secular test, then his or her evidence may be given unsworn if, in the opinion of the court, the conditions set out in the Children Act 1989, s. 96(2)(a) and (b), are met. It is submitted that 'the duty to speak the truth' to which s. 96(2)(a) refers, means the duty to tell the truth which is an ordinary duty of normal social conduct.

There is no presumption that a child should not give evidence in care proceedings. The court must weigh the possibility that the evidence will enable a better determination of the truth against the damage that may be done to the welfare of the child or any other child (*Re W (Children) (Family Proceedings: Evidence)* [2010] UKSC 12, [2010] 1 WLR 701).

Persons with a disorder or disability of the mind

49.47 In *R v Hill* (1851) 2 Den 254 it was established that if, in the opinion of the judge, a proposed witness, by reason of impaired intellect, does not understand the nature and sanction of an oath, he or she is incompetent to testify; and that a person of impaired intellect who does understand the oath may testify, in which case it will be for the tribunal of fact to attach such weight to his or her testimony as it sees fit, disregarding it altogether if it is so tainted with insanity as to be unworthy of credit. These propositions remain the law, except in one respect. The test to be applied should be the secular one adopted in *R v Hayes* [1977] 1 WLR 234 (see **49.46**): whether the proposed witness has a sufficient appreciation of the seriousness of the occasion and a realisation that taking the oath involves something more than the duty to tell the truth in ordinary day-to-day life (see *R v Bellamy* (1985) 82 Cr App R 222).

The Sovereign, heads of State and diplomats

49.48 The Sovereign and heads of foreign sovereign States are competent but not compellable. Diplomats, consular officials, and various officers of prescribed international organisations also enjoy varying degrees of immunity from compellability (see the Diplomatic Privileges Act 1964, the Consular Relations Act 1968, the International Organisations Act 1968, the Diplomatic and other Privileges Act 1971, and the State Immunity Act 1978).

Bankers

49.49 The Bankers' Books Evidence Act 1879 provides for the admissibility of copies of entries in bankers' books as evidence of their contents (see **49.80**). Section 6 of the Act provides as follows:

> A banker or officer of a bank shall not, in any legal proceeding to which the bank is not a party, be compellable to produce any banker's book the contents of which can be proved under this Act…, or to appear as a witness to prove the matters, transactions, and accounts therein recorded, unless by order of a judge made for special cause.

Oaths and affirmations

49.50 The general rule is that all witnesses must give sworn evidence, i.e. after having taken an oath or having made an affirmation. A judgment founded on unsworn evidence may be set aside as a nullity (*R v Marsham, ex parte Pethick Lawrence* [1912] 2 KB 362). In civil proceedings there are the following *four exceptions to the general rule*.

(a) In claims which have been allocated to the small claims track, the court need not take evidence on oath (**CPR, r. 27.8(4)**).

(b) Children under the age of 18 may be permitted to give their evidence unsworn (see **49.46**).
(c) A witness called only to produce a document may give unsworn evidence if the identity of the document is either not in dispute or is to be established by another witness (*Perry v Gibson* (1834) 1 Ad & El 48).
(d) Counsel may give unsworn evidence of the terms of a compromise reached by the parties (*Hickman v Berens* [1895] 2 Ch 638).

The form and manner of the administration of the oath in the case of Christians and Jews is governed by the Oaths Act 1978, s. 1(1). The officer administering the oath shall administer it in this form and manner without question unless the witness objects thereto, or is physically incapable of so taking the oath (s. 1(2)). For those of other religious belief, the oath shall be administered 'in any lawful manner' (s. 1(3)), upon such holy book as is appropriate. Whether an oath is administered in a lawful manner for these purposes depends on whether the oath appears to the court to be binding on the conscience of the witness and is one which the witness considers to be binding on his or her conscience, rather than on the intricacies of the witness's particular religion. Thus in *R v Kemble* [1990] 1 WLR 1111, an oath taken by a Muslim on the New Testament was held to have been administered in a lawful manner notwithstanding that under the strict tenets of Islam, an oath taken by a Muslim is only valid if taken on a copy of the Koran in Arabic. If the ground is properly laid for an expectation that a witness will take the oath on a particular holy book, but the witness affirms, the judge has a discretion to allow the reason why the witness did not take the oath on the holy book to be explored sensitively (*R v Mehrban* [2001] EWCA Crim 2627, [2002] 1 Cr App R 561). However, where a Muslim has affirmed, rather than having sworn on the Koran, cross-examining counsel should not be allowed to ask the witness whether he thinks that he is bound to tell the truth, except where there is good reason for such questioning and it has been approved by the judge (*R v Majid* [2009] EWCA Crim 2563, LTL 12/10/2009). Section 3 of the 1978 Act permits a person to be sworn with uplifted hand, in the form and manner in which an oath is usually administered in Scotland. Where an oath has been duly administered and taken, the fact that the person to whom it was administered had, at the time of taking it, no religious belief, shall not for any purpose affect its validity (s. 4(2)).

Any person who objects to being sworn shall be permitted to make his or her solemn affirmation instead (s. 5(1)), which shall be of the same force and effect as an oath (s. 5(4)). Where it is not reasonably practicable without inconvenience or delay to administer an oath in the manner appropriate to a person's religious belief, then he or she may be permitted, or required, to make his or her solemn affirmation instead (s. 5(2) and (3)).

Oral evidence, evidence by video link or other means and anonymous witnesses

Under **CPR, r. 32.2**, the general rule is that any fact which needs to be proved by the evidence of witnesses is to be proved: **49.51**
(a) at trial, by their oral evidence given in public; and
(b) at any other hearing, by their evidence in writing.

A court has no common law power to extend the use of the closed material procedure beyond the use thus far sanctioned by Parliament. In some circumstances, such a procedure is necessary in order to achieve real justice and a fair trial, for example, in cases involving children, and in intellectual property proceedings where disclosure of confidential material beyond 'confidentiality rings' would defeat the object of the proceedings brought to protect a commercial interest. Subject to these exceptions, the court should not sanction departure from the fundamental principles of open justice and natural justice. Under the closed material procedure a party is excluded from the closed part of the trial and therefore does not see the witnesses or see or read the closed documents, the submissions or the judgment. These flaws cannot be

Commentary

cured by a special advocate, who would be hampered by not being able to take instructions from his or her client (*Al-Rawi v Security Service* [2011] UKSC 34, [2012] 1 AC 531).

Under **r. 32.2(2)**, the general rule is subject:

(a) to any provision to the contrary contained in the CPR or elsewhere; or
(b) to any order of the court.

An example of the former is to be found in **r. 32.3**, which provides that the court may allow a witness to give evidence through a video link 'or by other means', e.g. by means of a telephone. No defined limit or set of circumstances should be placed upon this discretionary power, which is not restricted to cases in which the witness is seriously ill or cases of pressing need (*Rowland v Bock* [2002] 4 All ER 370). Lord Nicholls of Birkenhead in *Polanski v Condé Nast Publications Ltd* [2005] UKHL 10, [2005] 1 WLR 637, said that videoconferencing orders are readily available to all litigants in civil proceedings. This decision is discussed further at **58.11**. See also **PD 32, annex 3** and *Black v Pastouna* [2005] EWCA Civ 1389, *The Independent*, 2 December 2005, where Brooke LJ held that it is incumbent on those advising parties appearing before any court to take all the steps they can in accordance with **CPR, rr. 1.1** and **1.3**, to reduce the cost of the proceedings, including taking advantage of videoconferencing facilities whenever they are available and it is appropriate to use them. As to the use at trial of witness statements, see **chapter 51**. As to the power to direct that certain facts may not be proved by the oral evidence of proposed witnesses, see further at **49.52**, and generally at **49.8**.

The European Court of Human Rights has accepted, in the criminal context, that the Convention rights of witnesses include, where necessary, the preservation of their anonymity and has decided that such anonymity is not inconsistent with the right to a fair trial, provided that the need for anonymity is clearly established and, the ultimate test, the trial is fair. The jurisprudence of the European Court does not establish that a trial will inevitably be considered unfair simply because the evidence of an anonymous witness may be decisive to the outcome. However, a court should examine an application for anonymity with scrupulous care to ensure that it is necessary and that the witness is in genuine and justified fear of serious consequences if his true identify becomes known (*R v Davis* [2006] EWCA Crim 1155, [2006] 1 WLR 3130).

Directions in relation to witnesses

49.52 Before the CPR came into effect, the choice of witnesses to support a party's case, and the order in which they were to be called, were matters entirely for that party (*Briscoe v Briscoe* [1966] P 501). The judge had no right to call witnesses against the will of the parties (*Re Enoch and Zaretzky, Bock and Co.'s Arbitration* [1910] 1 KB 327), except in cases of civil contempt (*Yianni v Yianni* [1966] 1 WLR 120). Under **CPR, r. 32.1(1)**, the court may now control the evidence by giving directions as to not only the issues on which it requires evidence, but also as to the nature of the evidence which it requires to decide those issues and the way in which the evidence is to be placed before the court. Furthermore, under **r. 32.1(2)**, the court may use its power under the rule to exclude evidence that would otherwise be admissible. In exercising these powers, the judge must seek to give effect to the 'overriding objective'. **Rule 32.1(1)** does not empower the court to order a party to call a witness (*Society of Lloyd's v Jaffray* (2000) *The Times*, 3 August 2000). However, it is submitted that in appropriate circumstances a judge may take the view that in furtherance of the 'overriding objective' directions should be given under **r. 32.1(1)** as to the order in which witnesses should give their evidence, and as to which potential witnesses should not be called, on the basis either that the issue to which their evidence relates only requires evidence in written form or that their evidence, although admissible in law, should be excluded in the exercise of the judge's discretion. The judge also has the power to recall a witness called by a party (*Fallon v Calvert* [1960] 2 QB 201).

Judicial interventions

Interventions by a judge during the course of oral evidence inevitably carry the risk of depriving the judge of the advantage of calm and dispassionate observation. The greater the frequency of the interventions, the greater the risk, and where the interventions take the form of lengthy interrogation of the witnesses, the risk becomes a serious one. The risk does not depend on appearances or on what an objective observer of the process may think, but is that the judge may so hamper his ability properly to evaluate and weigh the evidence as to impair his judgement and, for that reason, render the trial unfair (*Southwark London Borough Council v Kofi-Adu* [2006] EWCA Civ 281, [2006] HLR 33). **49.53**

Time at which evidence should be adduced

As a general rule of practice, rather than law, a party should adduce all the evidence on which he intends to rely before the close of his case. The authorities in this regard, which are almost all criminal cases, indicate that there are two common law exceptions to the general rule and a 'wider discretion' to be exercised outside the two exceptions only very rarely. Under the first exception, evidence is allowed in rebuttal of matters arising *ex improviso*, which no ingenuity could have foreseen (*R v Frost* (1839) 4 St Tr NS 85). Under this exception, it is for the judge, in the exercise of his or her discretion, to decide whether the relevance of the evidence could reasonably have been anticipated (*R v Scott* (1984) 79 Cr App R 49; *R v Day* (1940) 27 Cr App R 168). A party may rely on the exception where the evidence in question was not at the outset clearly relevant, but only marginally, minimally or doubtfully relevant (*R v Levy* (1966) 50 Cr App R 198), or constituted fanciful and unreal statements, e.g. allegations which were obviously ridiculous and untrue (*R v Hutchinson* (1985) 82 Cr App R 51). Under the second exception, the judge has a discretion to admit evidence which has not been adduced by reason of inadvertence or oversight. The evidence is usually of a formal or uncontentious nature (see *v Waller* [1910] 1 KB 364; *Price v Humphries* [1958] 2 QB 353; and *Palastanga v Solman* [1962] Crim LR 334), but sometimes relates to a matter of substance (see *Piggott v Sims* [1973] RTR 15 and *Middleton v Rowlett* [1954] 1 WLR 831). It has been held that the judge's discretion to admit evidence after the close of a party's case is not confined to the two well-established exceptions, but the wider discretion should be exercised only on the rarest of occasions (*R v Francis* [1991] 1 WLR 1264), as when an important witness arrives late for reasons beyond his or her control (see, e.g. *James v South Glamorgan County Council* (1994) 99 Cr App R 321). **49.54**

Although the exceptions to the general rule of practice are well established, more recent authorities permit the court to take a generalised discretionary approach to admissibility, having regard to whether the defendant will be unfairly prejudiced (as when the defence would have been conducted differently had the evidence in question been adduced at an earlier stage). In *Jolly v Director of Public Prosecutions* [2000] Crim LR 471, applied in *Cook v Director of Public Prosecutions* [2001] Crim LR 321, it was said to be 'beyond argument' that there is a general discretion to permit the prosecution to call evidence after closing its case. Before exercising the discretion, the court would look carefully at the interests of justice overall and, in particular, the risk of any prejudice whatsoever to the defence. The result is that the discretion would be sparingly exercised, but it is doubtful whether it assists a court to speak in terms of 'exceptional circumstances'. Each case must be considered on its own facts. In civil cases, where obviously regard must be had to the overriding objective, a broadly similar approach has been adopted. In *Stocznia Gdanska SA v Latvian Shipping Co.* (2000) LTL 12/2/2001 the claimants, after the close of the trial but before judgment had been handed down, sought to adduce further relevant evidence, namely, a document which ought to have been disclosed by one of the defendants and which the claimants could not have obtained by other means. It was held that the claimants could rely on the document and that, in accordance with the overriding objective, it would not be just to ignore it.

Commentary

REFRESHING THE MEMORY

Refreshing memory in court

49.55 A witness who, in examination-in-chief, experiences difficulty in recollecting the events to which his or her evidence relates, may refer to a document such as a diary, log or other written statement, or, it seems, to a tape recording (see *R v Bailey* (2001) LTL 19/3/2001), in order to refresh his or her memory, provided that:

(a) it was made or verified by the witness at the time of the events to which it relates, or so shortly afterwards that the facts were still fresh in the witness's memory;
(b) it is produced for inspection by the court and opposite party; and
(c) it is, in prescribed cases, the original.

The principle operates not only where the witness does in fact refresh his or her memory, but also where the witness has no recollection of the events in question, but simply gives evidence as to the accuracy of the contents of the document. In both cases, however, it is the testimony of the witness, and not the document, which constitutes the evidence in the case. In *Maugham v Hubbard* (1828) 8 B & C 14 a witness called to prove that he had received a sum of money, looked at an unstamped acknowledgment that he had signed, and then gave evidence that he had no doubt that he had received the money, but had no recollection of having done so. It was held that his oral evidence sufficed to establish receipt of the money, the acknowledgment being incapable of being received in evidence because it was unstamped. In these circumstances, it is submitted that rather than preserve a fiction, it would be better to concede that the court is, in effect, admitting the written statement for the truth of its contents by way of exception to the hearsay rule. In fact the statement itself is admissible, with the permission of the court, as evidence of the truth of its contents, under the Civil Evidence Act 1995, s. 6(2)(a) (see **53.7**). Indeed, under the modern law, the scope for refreshing memory in court has been much reduced by reason of the existence of s. 6(2)(a) and the fact that in most cases it will be a witness's witness statement that stands as his or her evidence-in-chief (see **chapter 51**).

49.56 **Conditions** The document 'must have been written either at the time of the transaction or so shortly afterwards that the facts were fresh in [the witness's] memory' (*Phipson on Evidence*, 11th edn., 1970, at p. 634, para. 1528), a definition which provides a measure of elasticity and should not be taken to confine witnesses to an over-short period (*R v Richardson* [1971] 2 QB 484). The question is obviously one of fact and degree, and for this reason the precedents are of limited, if any, value. The entry in the document may have been made or verified by the witness. As to the former, the document may be used even if based on earlier notes or jottings, provided that when written up, the facts were still fresh in the memory (*Attorney-General's Reference (No. 3 of 1979)* (1979) 69 Cr App R 411). The witness may also refresh his or her memory from a copy of the original document, where the original has been destroyed, provided that the court is satisfied that the copy is accurate or substantially reproduces the original (*Topham v McGregor* (1844) 1 Car & K 320). See also *R v Mills* [1962] 1 WLR 1152 (notes written up by a witness with the assistance of a tape recording made by him but which was not itself admitted in evidence). The document may have been prepared by another, provided that the witness has verified it while the events were still fresh in his or her memory (*Burroughs v Martin* (1809) 2 Camp 112). Thus in *Anderson v Whalley* (1852) 3 Car & K 54, entries in a ship's log made by the mate and verified by the captain about a week later could be used by the latter to refresh his memory. A witness may also make use of a note dictated to another and then verified, whether by reading it personally or listening to it being read out, provided, in the latter case, that the other is called to prove that the note used in court is the note that was dictated and read back (*R v Kelsey (1981) 74 Cr App R 213*). In all cases, the document must be produced for inspection by the opposite party, who may wish to cross-examine the witness on its contents (*Beech v Jones* (1848) 5 CB 696). In cases, like *Maugham v Hubbard* (1828) 8 B & C 14, in which the witness has no recollection of the events in question but gives evidence as to the accuracy of what is recorded in the document, the original document must be produced (*Doe d Church and Phillips v Perkins* (1790) 3 TR 749), but where the original has been lost or destroyed, a verified or accurate copy will suffice (*Topham v McGregor* (1844) 1 Car & K 320).

Cross-examination on the document Cross-examining counsel may inspect the document without thereby making it evidence in the case. Counsel may also cross-examine on it without thereby making it evidence, but only if the cross-examination does not go beyond the parts used by the witness to refresh his or her memory. Cross-examination on other parts of the document entitles the party calling the witness to put the document in evidence and to let the tribunal of fact see the document on which the cross-examination has been based (*Gregory v Tavernor* (1833) 6 Car & P 280; *Senat v Senat* [1965] P 172 at p. 177). The document will then be admissible as evidence of the truth of its contents. The Civil Evidence Act 1995, s. 6, provides as follows: **49.57**

(4) Nothing in this Act affects any of the rules of law as to the circumstances in which, where a person called as a witness in civil proceedings is cross-examined on a document used by him to refresh his memory, that document may be made evidence in the proceedings.

(5) Nothing in this section shall be construed as preventing a statement of any description referred to above from being admissible by virtue of section 1 as evidence of the matters stated.

It seems reasonably clear that the intention underlying these two subsections, when taken together, was to perpetuate the rule formerly stated with clarity in the Civil Evidence Act 1968, s. 3(2), that where a memory-refreshing document is made evidence in the proceedings, any statement made in the document will be admissible as evidence of the matters stated. It is submitted that the subsections should be construed in this way notwithstanding that whereas subsection (5) refers to 'a statement of any description referred to above', subsection (4) refers not to 'a statement', but to 'a document'.

Refreshing memory out of court

It is a common practice for a witness, before giving testimony, to refresh his or her memory from statements or notes made by him or her at a time closer to the events in question, whether a private note or record, a proof of evidence, or a witness statement as such. Any rule to the contrary would be unenforceable, would make testimony more a test of memory than truthfulness, and would tend to create difficulties for honest witnesses, but be likely to do little to hamper dishonest witnesses (*R v Richardson* [1971] 2 QB 484). The conditions which apply in the case of a witness refreshing his memory while giving evidence do not apply to the witness who refreshes his or her memory outside the witness box (*R v Richardson*). However, as in the case of refreshing memory while giving evidence, cross-examining counsel is entitled to call for, inspect and cross-examine on a document which a witness has used to refresh his or her memory outside court but has not used while giving evidence, and if counsel cross-examines on material which has not been referred to by the witness, the party calling the witness may put the document in evidence, rendering it admissible as evidence of the matters it states (see *Owen v Edwards* (1983) 77 Cr App R 191 at p. 195, and the Civil Evidence Act 1995, s. 6(4) and (5), considered at **49.57**). **49.58**

It is open to the judge, in the exercise of his or her discretion and in the interests of justice, to permit a witness who has begun to give his or her evidence, to withdraw and refresh his or her memory from a statement made by him or her closer to the time of the events in question, even if not made at the time of the events or so soon thereafter that the facts were fresh in the memory, if the following conditions are met:

(a) the witness says that he or she cannot now recall the details of the events because of the lapse of time;

(b) the witness made a statement much nearer the time of the event, the contents of which represented his or her recollection at that time;

(c) the witness did not read the statement before giving evidence; and
(d) the witness wishes to read the statement before continuing to give evidence.

The witness may withdraw from the witness box to read the statement, in which case there must be no communication with the witness, or the statement may be read by the witness in the witness box, but either way, the statement must be removed from the witness when he or she continues to give evidence, and the witness should not be permitted to refer to it again (see *R v Da Silva* [1990] 1 WLR 31). An alternative solution to the problem, in appropriate circumstances, would be for the party calling the witness to seek leave to admit the previous statement for the truth of its contents under the Civil Evidence Act 1995, s. 6(2)(a) (see further at 53.7).

R v Da Silva has not created a rule of law that a witness, once in the witness box, can refer to a statement only if all four of the conditions specified in that case are met, because the court has a discretion whether to allow a witness to refresh his or her memory from a non-contemporaneous statement: see *R v South Ribble Magistrates, ex parte Cochrane* [1996] 2 Cr App R 544, where a witness who had read his statement before giving evidence, but had not taken it in properly, was allowed to refresh his memory. See also *R v Gordon* [2002] EWCA Crim 1, LTL 7/2/2002, where a witness, who was unable, because of dyslexia, to read his statement, adopted it after it was read out by counsel. It was held that there are no fixed and immutable rules to be followed before a witness can refresh memory by a document prepared when his or her memory was clearer, but there is a broad fact-sensitive judicial discretion to be exercised in the interests of fairness and justice.

PREVIOUS CONSISTENT STATEMENTS

The rule

49.59 At common law, as a general rule a previous consistent or self-serving statement of a witness is excluded as evidence of his or her consistency. Thus, a witness may not be asked in examination-in-chief about former oral or written statements made by him or her and consistent with the testimony which he or she is giving, and evidence about those statements should not be elicited from any other witness. The rule is usually justified on the basis that without it, a witness could manufacture evidence with ease (see, e.g. *R v Roberts* [1942] 1 All ER 187 at p. 191). In *Corke v Corke* [1958] P 93 a husband petitioned for divorce on the ground of adultery. One night he had accused his wife of having recently committed adultery with a lodger. The Court of Appeal held that the wife, who denied adultery, had been improperly permitted to give evidence that shortly after the husband's accusation, she had telephoned her doctor and asked him to examine herself and the lodger with a view to showing that there had been no recent sexual intercourse.

Exceptions

49.60 In civil proceedings, there are only three exceptions to the rule, under each of which the previous statement is admitted not only as evidence of consistency, but also as evidence of the facts it contains. They are:

(a) previous statements admissible, with the permission of the court, under the Civil Evidence Act 1995, s. 6(2);
(b) statements in documents used by a witness to refresh his or her memory, in cases in which cross-examination on the document has gone beyond the parts of it relied on by the witness, so that the document has become evidence in the case; and
(c) statements in rebuttal of allegations of recent fabrication.

The first two of these exceptions are considered at 53.7 and 49.57 respectively.

There is no general further exception to the effect that a witness who has been cross-examined to show inconsistencies, can be re-examined to show consistency by reference to a previous statement (*R v Beattie* (1989) 89 Cr App R 302 at p. 307). However, the court does have a residual discretion to permit such re-examination to ensure that the tribunal of fact is not positively misled by the cross-examination as to the existence of some fact or the terms of an earlier statement (*R v Ali* [2003] EWCA Crim 3214, [2004] 1 Cr App R 501).

Statements admissible to rebut allegations of recent fabrication

A previous consistent statement will not be admissible to bolster the credibility of a witness simply because his or her evidence was impeached in cross-examination, even if the impeachment took the form of showing a contradiction or inconsistency between his or her evidence and something he or she said on a previous occasion (see *R v Coll* (1889) 25 LR Ir 522 at p. 541 and *R v Beattie* (1989) 89 Cr App R 302 at pp. 306–7, and contrast, but question, *Ahmed v Brumfitt* (1967) 112 SJ 32). However, if in cross-examination it is suggested that a witness's version of events is a recent fabrication, evidence of his or her previous statements to the same effect will become admissible, and will normally be elicited in re-examination (*R v Oyesiku* (1971) 56 Cr App R 240; and see also *Flanagan v Fahy* [1918] 2 IR 361 and *Fox v General Medical Council* [1960] 1 WLR 1017). In *R v Oyesiku* the Court of Appeal adopted as a correct statement of the law the judgment of Dixon CJ in *Nominal Defendant v Clement* (1961) 104 CLR 476 (High Court of Australia), from which the following propositions derive: 49.61

(a) The exception requires a suggestion in cross-examination that the witness's account has been recently invented or reconstructed, even though not with conscious dishonesty.
(b) The previous statement is admissible if it was made contemporaneously with the event or at a time sufficiently early to be inconsistent with the suggestion of recent fabrication.
(c) The judge should exercise care to assure himself or herself that:
  (i) the account given is attacked on the ground of recent invention or reconstruction or a foundation for such an attack has been laid;
  (ii) the contents of the previous statement are to like effect as the account given in evidence; and
  (iii) the previous statement, having regard to the time and circumstances in which it was made, rationally tends to answer the attack.

The exception has no application where a cross-examination is on the basis that the witness's account was a fabrication from the outset, unless the effect of the cross-examination is in fact to create the impression of fabrication at a later stage (*R v Athwal* [2009] EWCA Crim 789, [2009] 1 WLR 2430).

In civil proceedings, a previous statement admissible under the exception is admissible not merely to confirm the witness's credit, but also as evidence of the facts contained in it. The Civil Evidence Act 1995, s. 6, provides as follows:

> (2) A party who has called or intends to call a person as a witness in civil proceedings may not in those proceedings adduce evidence of a previous statement made by that person, except—... (b) for the purpose of rebutting a suggestion that his evidence has been fabricated....
>
> (5) Nothing in this section shall be construed as preventing a statement of any description referred to above from being admissible by virtue of section 1 as evidence of the matters stated.

A cross-examiner who is pursuing a suggestion of recent fabrication should not ask whether the witness told his or her solicitor or counsel what he or she now says is the truth, because such a question would require the witness either to waive legal professional privilege or to suffer criticism for not doing so; the witness may elect to open up the communication with the lawyer, but this will amount to waiver of the privilege (see *R v Seaton* [2010] EWCA Crim 1980, [2011] 1 WLR 623 at [43]).

UNFAVOURABLE AND HOSTILE WITNESSES

Rule against attacking the credit of one's own witnesses

49.62 At common law, if a witness fails to come up to proof, or gives adverse evidence, such as evidence in support of the other party's version of the facts in issue, the general rule is that the party calling the witness is not thereby entitled to turn around and seek to impeach his or her credit or otherwise cross-examine the witness as if he or she were a witness for the opposite party: the party calling the witness will not be allowed, therefore, to question the witness about, or adduce evidence of, such matters as his or her bias or bad character, any previous convictions, or any previous inconsistent statements. The general rule, it seems, will not prevent the introduction of evidence of a witness's bad character so as to support some discrete part of the case of the party calling the witness, rather than to impeach the witness's credit in relation to his or her testimony (see *R v Ross* [2007] EWCA Crim 1457, [2008] Crim LR 306). The general rule has now been put on a statutory basis (see Criminal Procedure Act 1865, s. 3, at **49.64**). There are limited exceptions to this general rule in the case of hostile witnesses, but not in the case of witnesses who are merely unfavourable.

Unfavourable witnesses

49.63 An unfavourable witness is one who, displaying no hostility to the party calling him or her, fails to come up to proof or gives evidence unfavourable to that party. At common law, the party calling the witness is not permitted to impeach his or her credit, but may call other witnesses to give evidence of those matters as to which it was expected that the unfavourable witness would testify. In *Ewer v Ambrose* (1825) 3 B & C 746 a witness called by the defendant to prove a certain partnership, gave evidence to the contrary. It was held that the defendant, although not entitled to adduce general evidence to show that the witness was not to be believed on his oath, could contradict him by calling other witnesses. As Littledale J observed, were the rule otherwise, it would attach undue importance to the order in which witnesses are called: if a party with four witnesses to prove his case were to call first the one who happened to disprove it, he would be deprived of the evidence of the other three.

Hostile witnesses

49.64 A hostile witness is one who, in the opinion of the judge, shows no desire to tell the truth at the instance of the party calling him or her, to whom he or she displays a hostile animus (Stephen, *Digest of the Law of Evidence*, 12th edn., art. 147). In criminal cases, the prosecution may call a person as a witness even if that person has shown signs that he or she is likely to be a hostile witness, e.g. by retracting a statement or by making a second statement (see *R v Mann* (1972) 56 Cr App R 750 and *R v Dat* [1998] Crim LR 488). Similarly, in civil proceedings it seems that a party may call a witness who has indicated that he or she may be hostile, e.g. by refusing to make a statement or by refusing to testify having agreed to do so. (**CPR, r. 32.9**, under which a party unable to obtain a witness statement may seek permission to serve a witness summary instead, is discussed at **51.19**.)

At common law the judge has a discretion whether to treat a witness as hostile and allow the witness to be cross-examined by the party calling him or her, and the judge's decision will seldom be challenged successfully on appeal (*Rice v Howard* (1886) 16 QBD 681; *Price v Manning* (1889) 42 ChD 372). If a witness fails to give the evidence expected, or gives evidence contrary to an earlier statement, the judge should first consider inviting the witness to refresh his or her memory from material which can properly be used for that purpose, rather than simply proceeding to treat the witness as hostile, unless he or she displays such an excessive degree of hostility that that is the only appropriate course (*R v Maw* [1994] Crim LR 841). The judge will have regard to the attitude and demeanour of the witness, his or her willingness to cooperate, and any previous contradictory or inconsistent statements.

Under the Criminal Procedure Act 1865, s. 3, if a witness is treated as hostile, the party calling the witness may prove prior statements made by the witness and inconsistent with his or her evidence. Section 3 provides as follows:

A party producing a witness shall not be allowed to impeach his credit by general evidence of bad character, but he may, in case the witness shall, in the opinion of the judge, prove adverse, contradict him by other evidence, or, by leave of the judge, prove that he has made at other times a statement inconsistent with his present testimony; but before such last mentioned proof can be given the circumstances of the supposed statement, sufficient to designate the particular occasion, must be mentioned to the witness, and he must be asked whether or not he made such statement.

The word 'adverse', in s. 3, means hostile (*Greenough v Eccles* (1859) 5 CB NS 786, a decision under the Common Law Procedure (Amendment) Act 1856, s. 22, which was repealed but re-enacted by s. 3 of the 1865 Act). The first part of s. 3 applies to both unfavourable and hostile witnesses and is nothing more than a statutory re-statement of the common law rule against attacking the credit of one's own witnesses (see **49.62**). The next part of the section, which allows the party calling the witness to contradict him or her by other evidence, applies only to hostile witnesses, but has not affected the rule at common law that a party may contradict an *unfavourable* witness by calling other witnesses (*Greenough v Eccles*). The final part of the section, which permits proof of previous inconsistent statements, applies only in the case of hostile witnesses.

If a witness is treated as hostile, at common law the party calling the witness may ask him or her leading questions. Section 3 of the 1865 Act has not removed this right. Thus, where a witness has made a statement in favour of a party, but when called to testify, stands mute of malice and is treated as hostile, then although the case may not be governed by s. 3, because the witness has given no 'testimony', at common law he or she may be asked leading questions and the witness's previous statement may be put to him or her (*R v Thompson* (1976) 64 Cr App R 96, relying upon *Clarke v Saffery* (1824) Ry & M 126 and *Bastin v Carew* (1824) Ry & M 127). However, it is submitted that if, in these circumstances, the witness were to deny making the previous statement, it could not be proved at common law.

A hostile witness who is cross-examined on a previous inconsistent statement under s. 3 of the 1865 Act may or may not accept the truth of the contents of the statement. If its truth is accepted, the previous statement in effect becomes part of the witness's evidence and, subject to the assessment of his or her credibility, is capable of being accepted (*R v Maw* [1994] Crim LR 841; *R v Gibbons* [2008] EWCA Crim 1574, [2009] Crim LR 197). If its truth is not admitted by the witness, the previous statement is admissible as evidence of the matters stated by virtue of the Civil Evidence Act 1995, s. 6, which provides as follows:

(3) Where in the case of civil proceedings section 3 . . . of the Criminal Procedure Act 1865 applies, which [makes] provision as to—
  (a) how far a witness may be discredited by the party producing him, . . . this Act does not authorise the adducing of evidence of a previous inconsistent or contradictorystatement otherwise than in accordance with those sections. . . .

(5) Nothing in this section shall be construed as preventing a statement of any description referred to above from being admissible by virtue of section 1 as evidence of the matters stated.

It follows that if the witness does not admit the truth of the previous statement, the tribunal must decide whether to accept as true the contents of the previous statement or the evidence of the witness. The more recent criminal authorities suggest that there is no inflexible rule to the effect that a hostile witness's evidence should be regarded as unreliable where he or she is shown to have made previous inconsistent statements (see, e.g. *R v Pestano* [1981] Crim LR 397; *R v Governor of Pentonville Prison, ex parte Alves* [1993] AC 284 and *R v Goodway* [1993] 4 All ER 894 at p. 899; and contrast *R v Golder* [1960] 1 WLR 1169 at pp. 1172–3, approved in

Commentary

R v Oliva [1965] 1 WLR 1028). This more recent approach, it is submitted, has much to commend it, not least because in some cases the witness will be able to give a convincing explanation for the inconsistency. Whether the judge can give any credence to the witness, and if so, which parts of his or her evidence, if any, the judge should accept, are questions which fall to be resolved in the light of the particular circumstances of each case. Thus, where a hostile witness in the event proves not to be hostile and reverts to his original account, it may still be appropriate to approach his evidence with caution, in the light of the different accounts that he has given (*R v Greene* [2009] EWCA Crim 2282, *The Times*, 28 October 2009).

FAILURE TO CROSS-EXAMINE

49.65 A party who fails to cross-examine a witness on an issue in respect of which it is proposed to contradict his evidence-in-chief or impeach his credit by calling other witnesses, should not be permitted to invite the tribunal of fact to disbelieve the witness's evidence on the issue. The cross-examining party must lay a proper foundation by putting the matter to the witness so that he has an opportunity to give any explanation open to him (*Browne v Dunn* (1893) 6 R 67). It is not always necessary to put to the witness explicitly that he is lying, provided that the overall tenor of the cross-examination is designed to show that his account is not capable of belief (*R v Lovelock* [1997] Crim LR 821). However, there is a real danger in contradicting a young child witness that he will assent to what is being suggested simply to please or to bring the questioning to an end, or a speedier end, so that it can be very difficult to tell whether the child is truly changing his account or taking the line of least resistance (*R v W* [2010] EWCA Crim 1926, LTL 10/2/2011, at [28]–[31]).

FINALITY ON COLLATERAL ISSUES

The rule

49.66 The general rule at common law is that the answers given by a witness under cross-examination to questions on collateral issues, i.e. issues which are not directly relevant to the facts in issues in the case, must be treated as final, not in the sense that the tribunal of fact must accept the truth of the answers, but in the sense that the cross-examining party should not be allowed to call further evidence with a view to contradicting the witness. The rationale of the rule is to prevent the proliferation of issues of minimal or marginal relevance to the facts in issue, which would prolong the trial unnecessarily. Thus, it has been held that where a witness gives evidence through an interpreter and under cross-examination about his knowledge of English, denies that he is able to speak the language, the matter will normally be quite irrelevant to any matter directly in issue in the proceedings, and therefore evidence in rebuttal will normally be inadmissible (see *R v Burke* (1858) 8 Cox CC 44). In *Attorney-General v Hitchcock* (1847) 1 Ex 91, in which a prosecution witness, under cross-examination, denied that he had made an out-of-court statement to a certain Cook to the effect that Excise officers had offered to give him £20 to give false evidence, it was held that the defence were not allowed to call Cook to give evidence in rebuttal, on the basis that it was irrelevant to the matters in issue that someone had thought fit to offer a bribe, which was not accepted, to give an untrue account of a transaction. The decision is not easily reconciled with *R v M* [2004] EWCA Crim 2085, LTL 6/7/2004. In that case, the sexual offences which formed the basis of the charge came to light when a private investigator and enquiry agents, being used by a man, S, whose wife had been having an affair with the accused, interviewed the victims. The accused said that S had induced the victims to give evidence against him by offers of financial reward, but all the victims denied any such financial inducement. It was held that the accused should have been allowed to call a witness to give evidence that she had been approached by the private investigator, and that when she had refused to give adverse information, had been told that S had unlimited funds for the right information. The court was of the view that although the witness's evidence, viewed in isolation, was collateral and 'borderline', it was relevant as showing that the victims might have been offered money or been influenced by the offer of money.

According to Pollock CB in *Attorney-General v Hitchcock*, if the witness's answer is a matter on which the cross-examining party would be allowed to introduce evidence-in-chief, because of its connection with the issues in the case, then the matter is not collateral and may be rebutted. This test seems to be circular, and the cases show that it is not always easy to tell whether an issue is collateral. The explanation probably lies in the fact that relevance is a question of degree on which views may differ and the answer to which may turn on whether the matter which the cross-examining party seeks to prove is a single fact which is easy of proof or a broad issue involving a difficult and complex fact-finding task (see *R v S* [1992] Crim LR 307). Questions which go *merely* to the credit of the witness are clearly collateral, but it does not follow that questions on all other matters are not collateral. This is because in some cases the difference between questions going to credit and questions going to the issue will be barely discernible, if it can be said to exist at all. *R v Busby* (1981) 75 Cr App R 79 illustrates the point well. In that case, police officers under cross-examination denied two matters, that they had made up statements attributed to the accused and indicative of his guilt and that they had threatened W, a potential defence witness, to stop him from testifying. The Court of Appeal held that W should have been allowed to give evidence that he had been threatened by the officers, because it was evidence relevant to an issue in the case in that, if true, it showed that the police were prepared to go to improper lengths to secure a conviction, which would have supported the defence case that the statements attributed to him had been fabricated. Of this case, it has since been said that it has created a new exception to the general rule (see *R v Funderburk* [1990] 2 All ER 482 at p. 486), but it has also been said that the facts came within the exception of bias (see **49.69**) and that if the case cannot be explained on that basis, it is inconsistent with the general rule itself (*R v Edwards* [1991] 1 WLR 207 at p. 215).

Commentary

To the general rule there are exceptions in the case of the previous convictions of a witness, his or her bias, a physical or mental disability affecting his or her reliability, and his or her reputation for untruthfulness. It is also convenient and usual to treat as an exception to the general rule proof of a witness's previous inconsistent statement, although strictly speaking such proof is not covered by the general rule, because permitted only where the statement is 'relative to the subject matter of the . . . proceeding' (Criminal Procedure Act 1865, ss. 4 and 5, considered at **49.67**).

Previous inconsistent statements

The proof of previous oral or written statements in civil proceedings is governed by the Criminal Procedure Act 1865, ss. 4 and 5. Section 4 applies to both oral and written statements; s. 5 applies to written statements only (per Lord Taylor of Gosforth CJ in *R v Derby Magistrates' Court, ex parte B* [1996] AC 487 at pp. 498–9). They provide as follows: **49.67**

4. If a witness, upon cross-examination as to a former statement made by him relative to the subject matter of the indictment or proceeding, and inconsistent with his present testimony, does not distinctly admit that he has made such a statement, proof may be given that he did in fact make it; but before such proof can be given, the circumstances of the supposed statement, sufficient to designate the particular occasion, must be mentioned to the witness, and he must be asked whether or not he made such statement.
5. A witness may be cross-examined as to previous statements made by him in writing or reduced into writing relative to the subject matter of the indictment or proceeding, without such writing being shown to him; but if it is intended to contradict such witness by the writing, his attention must, before such contradictory proof can be given, be called to those parts of the writing which are to be used for the purpose of so contradicting him: provided always, that it shall be competent for the judge, at any time during the trial, to require the production of the writing for his inspection, and he may thereupon make such use of it for the purposes of the trial as he may think fit.

Both sections assume, correctly, the common law right to cross-examine a witness about previous inconsistent statements, and although they are not confined to previous statements made on oath (*R v Hart* (1957) 42 Cr App R 47; *R v O'Neill* [1969] Crim LR 260), they are confined to statements 'relative to the subject matter of the ... proceeding'. Under s. 4, proof may be given that the witness made a previous inconsistent statement if 'he does not distinctly admit that he has made such a statement', wording which covers not only the witness who denies that he or she made the statement, but also the witness who, when asked whether he or she made the statement, gives an equivocal answer, or states that he or she has no recollection of having done so, or declines to answer at all.

Under s. 5, a witness may be cross-examined about a previous inconsistent statement contained in a document, without the document being shown to the witness, but the cross-examining party must have the document with him or her, even if that party does not intend to contradict the witness with it, because under the section the judge may require production of the document for inspection and may make such use of it as he or she may think fit (*R v Anderson* (1929) 21 Cr App R 178). In the first instance, counsel may have the document handed to the witness, mentioning the circumstances 'sufficient to designate the particular occasion', draw the witness's attention to the relevant passage, ask the witness to read it to himself or herself, and then ask whether the witness adheres to the evidence already given. If the witness accepts the truth of the previous statement, it becomes part of his or her evidence which, to that extent, will have changed. If the witness adheres to the evidence he or she has already given, there is no obligation to prove the document, a course which counsel may wish to avoid if the discrepancy is minor or the statement taken as a whole tends to confirm rather than contradict the witness. This is because in civil proceedings, where a previous inconsistent statement is put in evidence, whether under s. 4 or s. 5 of the 1865 Act, it is admissible not only to impugn the credibility of the witness, but as evidence of the truth of its contents. The Civil Evidence Act 1995, s. 6 provides as follows:

(3) Where in the case of civil proceedings section ... 4 or 5 of the Criminal Procedure Act 1865 applies, which make provision as to — ...
(b) the proof of contradictory statements made by a witness, and
(c) cross-examination as to previous statements made in writing,
this Act does not authorise the adducing of evidence of a previous or contradictory statement otherwise than in accordance with those sections....

(5) Nothing in this section shall be construed as preventing a statement of any description referred to above from being admissible by virtue of section 1 as evidence of the matters stated.

In *Denton Hall Legal Services v Fifield* [2006] EWCA Civ 169, [2006] Lloyd's Rep Med 251 at [77], Buxton LJ suggested, obiter, that, in itself, proof of a previous inconsistent statement under the Criminal Procedure Act 1865, s. 4 or s. 5, goes only to the credibility of the witness and that s. 6(5) should be construed literally so that, in effect, the previous statement can only be treated as evidence of its contents in reliance on s. 1 of the 1995 Act. Where the previous statement is admitted as evidence of its contents, it does not follow that it has the same evidential weight as the testimony. The weight, if any, to be attached to the previous statement and the testimony is for the tribunal of fact, which, if it accepts the truth of the one, necessarily rejects the truth of the other (see *R v Billingham* [2009] EWCA Crim 19, [2009] 2 Cr App R 20 at [62]–[63]).

Previous convictions

49.68 The Criminal Procedure Act 1865, s. 6, provides as follows:

If, upon a witness being lawfully questioned as to whether he has been convicted of any felony or misdemeanour, he either denies or does not admit the fact, or refuses to answer, it shall be lawful for the cross-examining party to prove such conviction.

Although s. 6 appears to cover cross-examination and proof of any conviction of any witness, irrespective of relevance to either credibility or the issues in the case (see per Cairns J in *Clifford v Clifford* [1961] 1 WLR 1274 at p. 1276), it is submitted that the section operates subject to the general common law power of the judge to restrain unnecessary, irrelevant or unduly oppressive questions in cross-examination (see, e.g. per Lawton J in *R v Sweet-Escott* (1971) 55 Cr App R 316). *R v Sweet-Escott* applies equally to civil claims (*Watson v Chief Constable of Cleveland Police* [2001] EWCA Civ 1547, LTL 12/10/2001), so that convictions that are not relevant should not be put to witnesses. It is not only convictions for offences of dishonesty that reflect on the credibility of witnesses (*Clifford v Clifford*) and a number of offences can affect credibility. The operation of the section is also restricted by the Rehabilitation of Offenders Act 1974, whereby cross-examination of any witness about 'spent' convictions is prohibited (s. 4(1)), unless the judge is satisfied that it is not possible for justice to be done except by admitting the convictions (s. 7(3)). Evidence of the conviction may be admitted under s. 7(3) not only if relevant to an issue in the case, but also if relevant merely to credit, but the judge should weigh its relevance against its prejudicial effect and admit it only if satisfied that otherwise the parties would not have a fair trial or the witness's credit could not be fairly assessed (*Thomas v Commissioner of Police of the Metropolis* [1997] QB 813).

Bias

Evidence is admissible to rebut a witness's denial of bias or partiality towards one of the parties and to show that he or she is prejudiced in relation to the case in which he or she appears (see per Geoffrey Lane LJ in *R v Mendy* (1976) 64 Cr App R 4 at p. 6). Thus where a female employee of a party is called as his witness and under cross-examination denies that she is his kept mistress, the other party may call evidence to contradict her (*Thomas v David* (1836) 7 Car & P 350). Likewise evidence will be admissible to rebut the evidence of a witness who, under cross-examination, denies having threatened to be revenged on the cross-examining party following a quarrel with him or her (*R v Shaw* (1888) 16 Cox CC 503), or denies acceptance of a bribe to testify against the cross-examining party (*Attorney-General v Hitchcock* (1847) 1 Ex 91). 49.69

Evidence of disability affecting reliability

Expert medical evidence is admissible to show that a witness is suffering from some physical or mental disability that affects the reliability of his or her evidence. Such evidence is not confined to a general opinion of the unreliability of the witness, but may cover all the matters necessary to show not only the foundation of and reasons for the diagnosis, but also the extent to which the credibility of the witness is affected. Thus, if a witness says that he or she saw something from a distance of 50 yards, it is possible to adduce the evidence of an oculist to show that the witness cannot see beyond 20 yards, or the evidence of a surgeon who had removed a cataract from which the witness was suffering at the material time. Equally, it is permissible to call medical evidence of mental illness which makes a witness incapable of giving reliable evidence, whether through the existence of delusions or otherwise. 49.70

The principle only operates if the disability from which the witness suffers is a proper subject of expert evidence: partiality, prejudice, self-interest, imagination and inaccuracy are matters which, generally speaking, the tribunal of fact, helped by cross-examination and common sense, must assess without expert assistance (see per Lord Pearce in *Toohey v Metropolitan Police Commissioner* [1965] AC 595 at pp. 608–9. In *R v MacKenney* [2003] EWCA Crim 3643, [2004] 2 Cr App R 32, the accused were convicted of murder. At their trial, they alleged that the chief prosecution witness had fabricated his evidence and sought to call a psychologist by whom the witness had refused to be assessed. The psychologist watched the witness testify and formed the opinion that he was a psychopath who was likely to be lying and whose mental state meant that his demeanour and behaviour in giving evidence would not betray the usual indications to the jury that he was lying. The psychologist's evidence was ruled inadmissible and the convictions were upheld on appeal. On a subsequent referral to the Court of Appeal by the Criminal Cases Review Commission, there was fresh evidence from a psychiatrist, who also had not assessed the witness, whose opinion was very similar to that of the psychologist who had observed the witness at the trial. It was held that the evidence of the psychologist would today be admissible, and on that basis the conviction was quashed. It was held that the absence of a pre-trial assessment by the expert went to the weight to be attached to the opinion, not to its admissibility.

A party, A, cannot call a witness of fact, W, and then call a psychologist or psychiatrist to give reasons why the tribunal of fact should regard W as reliable. But if the other party, B, proposes to call an expert to say that W should be regarded as unreliable because of some mental abnormality calling for expert evidence, then A may call an expert in rebuttal or, anticipating B's evidence, as part of his own case. Where B does not call an expert, but puts a case in cross-examination that W is unreliable by reason of mental abnormality, this may also be open to rebuttal by expert evidence, although much may depend on the nature of the abnormality and of the cross-examination. If such expert evidence is admitted, it must be restricted to the specific challenge, and should not extend to 'oath-helping' (*R v Robinson* [1994] 3 All ER 346).

Evidence of reputation for untruthfulness

49.71 There is a long-established rule at common law that a party may call a witness to give evidence that in his or her opinion a witness called by the opposite party is not to be believed on his or her oath. The details of the rule, in its present form, are to be found in *R v Richardson* (1968) 52 Cr App R 317 at p. 323 and are not rehearsed here. The rule is rarely used, even in criminal proceedings, and it is submitted that in civil cases it would be better forgotten, because it encourages exactly that which the rule of finality was designed to prevent, namely the undue prolongation of trials from too close an examination of the credit of witnesses (see also per Lord Pearce in *Toohey v Metropolitan Police Commissioner* [1965] AC 595 at p. 606).

EVIDENCE OF CHARACTER AND DISPOSITION

Character as a fact in issue or relevant to a fact in issue

49.72 Evidence of the character of a party or non-party is clearly admissible if it is in issue or of direct relevance to the facts in issue in a case. The law of defamation provides a number of examples. Thus on the question of liability, in an action in which justification is pleaded, the claimant's character will clearly be in issue; the claimant, in order to rebut a defence of fair comment, may adduce evidence of his or her good reputation at the time of publication of the allegedly defamatory material; and the character of the claimant, if he or she succeeds, is of direct relevance to the quantum of recoverable damages (see *Cornwell v Myskow* [1987] 1 WLR 630).

Character relevant to credit

49.73 Anyone who testifies, whether or not a party to the proceedings, is open to cross-examination *on his or her character* in so far as it is relevant to his or her credibility as a witness, subject to the general discretion of the judge to prevent any questions in cross-examination which, in the judge's opinion, are unnecessary, improper or oppressive, and subject also to **CPR, r. 32.1(3)**, which baldly provides that 'The court may limit cross-examination'. In *Hobbs v Tinling* [1929] 2 KB 1 at p. 51, Sankey LJ held that the court, in the exercise of its discretion to disallow questions as to credit in cross-examination, should have regard to the following principles, which derive from the Indian Evidence Act (I of 1872), s. 148:

(1) Such questions are proper if they are of such a nature that the truth of the imputation conveyed by them would seriously affect the opinion of the court as to the credibility of the witness on the matter to which he testifies.
(2) Such questions are improper if the imputation which they convey relates to matters so remote in time, or of such a character, that the truth of the imputation would not affect, or would affect in a slight degree, the opinion of the court as to the credibility of the witness on the matter to which he testifies.
(3) Such questions are improper if there is a great disproportion between the importance of the imputation made against the witness's character and the importance of his evidence.

There are similar, but more detailed, provisions dealing with the character of witnesses in criminal cases in the Criminal Justice Act 2003, ss. 100 to 106 (see *Blackstone's Criminal Practice 2014*, F12–14). In *O'Brien v Chief Constable of South Wales Police* [2005] UKHL 26, [2005] 2 AC 534, the House of Lords said that while the Criminal Justice Act 2003 does not apply as such to civil claims, ss. 100 to 106 contain policy considerations which a civil judge will wish to keep in mind when exercising the discretion to exclude under **CPR, r. 32.1**.

In *R v Sweet-Escott* (1971) 55 Cr App R 316 at p. 320 Lawton J, in answer to the question, 'How far back is it permissible for advocates when cross-examining as to credit to delve into a man's past and to drag up such dirt as they can find there?', said 'Since the purpose of cross-examination as to credit is to show that the witness ought not to be believed on his oath, the matters about which he is questioned must relate to his likely standing after cross-examination with the tribunal which is trying him or listening to his evidence'.

As a general rule, the cross-examining party is not allowed to adduce evidence to contradict a witness's answer to a question going to his or her credit, but there are exceptions in the case of such matters as previous convictions and prejudice or bias on the part of the witness (see **49.66** to **49.71**).

Evidence of disposition

There is a dearth of modern authority on the question whether evidence of disposition towards good conduct on the part of the parties to civil litigation is admissible. It is submitted that such evidence should be admissible provided that it meets the ordinary requirement of relevance (but see *Attorney-General v Bowman* (1791) 2 Bos & P 532n). In *Hatton v Cooper* [2001] RTR 544, a case arising out of a collision between two cars in which there was an unusual dearth of relevant evidence, it was held that, on the question of liability, the trial judge had improperly relied on evidence from the claimant's employer that the claimant was an excellent driver, calm and assured, who never took risks. Jonathan Parker LJ said: 'In the context of a collision such as that which occurred in the instant case, the opinion of a third party as to the driving ability of either party is, in my judgment, completely worthless'. **49.74**

As to so-called 'similar fact evidence', i.e. evidence of the disposition of the defendant towards wrongdoing, or the commission of a particular kind of civil wrong, whereas in criminal cases the test for admissibility has properly reflected a concern to safeguard the accused from the admission of unduly prejudicial evidence, in civil cases tried by a judge alone, the test approximates to the ordinary test of relevance, the question being whether the evidence in question is of sufficient probative force in relation to the facts in issue. For example, in *Hales v Kerr* [1908] 2 KB 601, an action in negligence in which the claimant alleged that he had contracted ringworm from a dirty razor used by the defendant, a hairdresser, evidence was admitted that two other customers shaved by the defendant had contracted ringworm. In *Joy v Phillips, Mills and*

Co. Ltd [1916] 1 KB 849, a claim for workmen's compensation by the father of a deceased stable boy who had been kicked by a horse and had been found nearby holding a halter, evidence that the boy had previously teased horses with a halter was admitted in rebuttal of the allegation that the accident had occurred in the course of the boy's employment. In *Jones v Greater Manchester Police Authority* [2001] EWHC Admin 189, [2002] ACD 4, in proceedings for a sex offender order under the Crime and Disorder Act 1998, s. 2, it was held that evidence of propensity to commit sexual offences is relevant and admissible, because the court seeks to predict the extent to which past events give rise to reasonable cause for believing that an order is necessary to protect the public from serious harm, and that the admission of such evidence breaches neither art. 6 nor art. 8 of the European Convention on Human Rights. See also *Barrett v Long* (1851) 3 HL Cas 395, *Osborne v Chocqueel* [1896] 2 QB 109 and *Sattin v National Union Bank* (1978) 122 SJ 367.

In *Mood Music Publishing Co. Ltd v De Wolfe Publishing Ltd* [1976] Ch 119, an action for infringement of copyright in which the defendants admitted the similarity between the musical work in which the claimants owned the copyright and the work which they had produced, but alleged that the similarity was coincidental, evidence was admitted to show that on other occasions the defendants had produced musical works bearing a close resemblance to works which were the subject of copyright. It was held that the evidence had been properly admitted to rebut the allegation of coincidence. Lord Denning MR added a gloss to the ordinary test of relevance, although in so far as it relates to giving the other party fair notice of the intention to adduce the evidence, under the current cards-on-the-table approach to civil litigation it is of little significance. He said (at p. 127): 'In civil cases, the courts will admit evidence of similar facts if it is logically probative, that is, if it is logically relevant in determining the matter which is in issue: provided that it is not oppressive or unfair to the other side: and also that the other side has fair notice of it and is able to deal with it' (cf. *EG Music v SF (Film) Distributors Ltd* [1978] FSR 121 and *Berger v Raymond and Son Ltd* [1984] 1 WLR 625). This dictum, however, only applies to civil cases tried by a judge alone, who is trained to distinguish between what is probative and what is not: where there is a jury, the court must be more careful about admitting the evidence (per Dillon LJ in *Thorpe v Chief Constable of Greater Manchester Police* [1989] 1 WLR 665 at p. 670).

The leading authority is *O'Brien v Chief Constable of South Wales* [2005] UKHL 26, [2005] 2 AC 534. The claimant was convicted of murder. After serving 11 years in prison, his case was referred to the Criminal Cases Review Commission and his appeal was allowed. He then brought proceedings against the Chief Constable for misfeasance in public office and malicious prosecution, alleging that he had been 'framed' by a Detective Inspector L and a Detective Chief Superintendent C, who was alleged to have approved some aspects of the misconduct alleged against L. The House of Lords held that evidence had properly been admitted to show that L had behaved with similar impropriety on two other occasions and that C had done so on one other occasion. The House of Lords held that the test of admissibility in civil cases is different from that which applies in criminal cases. There is no warrant for the automatic application of the criminal test in a civil suit. To do so would be to introduce an inflexibility which is inappropriate and undesirable. Lord Phillips of Worth Matravers said (at [53] to [56]):

> [53] I would simply apply the test of relevance as the test of admissibility of similar fact evidence in a civil suit. Such evidence is admissible if it is potentially probative of an issue in the action.
>
> [54] That is not to say that the policy considerations that have given rise to the complex rules . . . in the Criminal Justice Act 2003, ss. 100 to 106 [see generally *Blackstone's Criminal Practice 2014*, F12] have no part to play in the conduct of civil litigation. They are policy considerations which the judge who has the management of the civil litigation will wish to keep well in mind. CPR, r. 1.2, requires the court to give effect to the overriding objective of dealing with cases justly. This includes dealing with the case in a way which is proportionate to what is involved in the case, and in a manner which is expeditious and fair. Rule 1.4 requires the court actively to manage the case in order to further the

overriding objective. Rule 32.1 gives the court the power to control the evidence. This power expressly enables the court to exclude evidence that would otherwise be admissible and to limit cross-examination.

[55] Similar fact evidence will not necessarily risk causing any unfair prejudice to the party against whom it is directed... It may, however, carry such a risk. Evidence of impropriety which reflects adversely on the character of a party may risk causing prejudice that is disproportionate to its relevance, particularly where the trial is taking place before a jury. In such a case the judge will be astute to see that the probative cogency of the evidence justifies this risk of prejudice in the interests of a fair trial.

[56] Equally, when considering whether to admit evidence, or permit cross-examination, on matters that are collateral to the central issues, the judge will have regard to the need for proportionality and expedition. He will consider whether the evidence in question is likely to be relatively uncontroversial, or whether its admission is likely to create side issues which will unbalance the trial and make it harder to see the wood from the trees.

For an example of the potential application of these principles, in a case where the similar fact evidence related to facts subsequent to the facts in issue, see *Desmond v Bower* [2009] EWCA Civ 667, [2010] EMLR 5.

DOCUMENTARY EVIDENCE

Proof of contents

Proof of the contents of a document on which a party seeks to rely is now largely, but not exclusively, governed by the Civil Evidence Act 1995, ss. 8 and 9, which are considered in detail at **53.15** to **53.17**. Under s. 8, where a statement contained in a document is admissible in evidence in civil proceedings, it may be proved by the production of that document, or, whether or not that document is still in existence, by the production of a copy of that document or the material part of it, authenticated in such manner as the court may approve (s. 8(1)); and it is immaterial for this purpose how many removes there are between a copy and the original (s. 8(2)). Under s. 9, a document which is certified as forming part of the records of a business or public authority may be received in evidence without further proof (s. 9(1) and (2)); and the absence of an entry in the records of a business or public authority may be proved by the affidavit of an officer of the business or authority. A document, for the purposes of both sections, means 'anything in which information of any description is recorded' (s. 13), a definition wide enough to cover maps, plans, graphs, drawings, discs, audiotapes, soundtracks, photographs, negatives, videotapes and films; and for the purposes of s. 8, a copy, in relation to a document, means, 'anything onto which information recorded in the document has been copied, by whatever means and whether directly or indirectly' (s. 13). **49.75**

Section 8 of the 1995 Act appears to be of general application, i.e. to apply to any statement contained in a document, and not merely statements admissible for the truth of their contents by virtue of the 1995 Act; and likewise s. 9 seems to apply to any document forming part of the records of a business or public authority. On this construction, these provisions have reversed the general common law rule (see **49.76**) that a party seeking to rely on the contents of a document must adduce primary evidence of those contents, i.e. usually the original. In any event, ss. 8 and 9 are permissive as to the means of proof. Section 14(2) of the Act provides that, 'Nothing in this Act affects the proof of documents by means other than those specified in section 8 or 9'. Sections 8 and 9, therefore, do not affect the operation of:

(a) the common law rule that where secondary evidence of the contents of a private document is admissible, it may take the form of oral evidence, which is not permitted under the 1995 Act;

(b) various statutory provisions, mostly relating to public and judicial documents, which provide for proof of their contents by copies which are required to take a particular form, such as an examined or certified copy (see **49.79**); or
(c) the Bankers' Books Evidence Act 1879, whereby copies of entries in bankers' books are admissible if certain conditions are met (see **49.80**).

Section 14(3) of the 1995 Act provides that nothing in the Act affects the operation of the following enactments:

(a) Documentary Evidence Act 1868, s. 2, which relates to the proof of certain official documents (see **49.79**);
(b) Documentary Evidence Act 1882, s. 2, which relates to documents printed under the superintendence of the Stationery Office (see **49.79**);
(c) Evidence (Colonial Statutes) Act 1907, which relates to proof of statutes of certain legislatures (see **49.101**);
(d) Evidence (Foreign, Dominion and Colonial Documents) Act 1933 (proof and effect of registers and official certificates of certain countries); and
(e) Oaths and Evidence (Overseas Authorities and Countries) Act 1963 (provision in respect of public registers of other countries).

Given the general saving in s. 14(2) of the 1995 Act, it is unclear why s. 14(3) refers to only some of the many pre-existing statutory provisions governing the proof of various specific types of document.

General rule at common law

49.76 The general rule at common law is that a party seeking to rely on the contents of a document must adduce primary evidence of the contents, that is:

(a) the original;
(b) an official copy, in the case of an enrolled document; or
(c) an informal admission.

As to originals, duplicates of a deed which have been executed by all parties are all originals (*Forbes v Samuel* [1913] 3 KB 706); a copy of a document which is signed or otherwise duly executed is an original; and a counterpart lease executed by the lessee alone is the original if tendered against him or her, and the other part is the original if tendered against the lessor (*Doe d West v Davis* (1806) 7 East 363). If a private document is required to be enrolled, i.e. officially filed in a court or other public office, the copy issued by the court or office is treated as the original. For example, where a grant of probate has been obtained, the probate copy of the will is treated as primary evidence of the contents of the will. Where a party to litigation makes an informal admission as to the contents of a document, it constitutes primary evidence of the contents and is admissible against him or her (*Slatterie v Pooley* (1840) 6 M & W 664; but see now the Civil Evidence Act 1995, s. 7(1), considered at **53.20** to **53.22**).

The general rule only applies where a party relies on the contents of the document. Thus whereas proof of the length of a tenancy or of the amount of rent due requires production of the lease, proof of the existence or fact of the tenancy, albeit created by a lease which defines its terms, may be proved by other means, such as parol evidence as to the payment of rent (see *Augustien v Challis* (1847) 1 Ex 279 (the amount of rent due) and *Twyman v Knowles* (1853) 13 CB 222 (the length of the tenancy); and cf. *R v Holy Trinity, Hull (Inhabitants)* (1827) 7 B & C 611 (the fact of a tenancy) and *Alderson v Clay* (1816) 1 Stark 405 (the fact of a partnership). Equally the rule does not apply where reference is made to a document merely for the purpose of establishing the bare fact of its existence (see *R v Elworthy* (1867) LR 1 CCR 103) or identifying it (see *Boyle v Wiseman* (1855) 11 Ex 360 at p. 367).

The general rule is well established, as are the common law exceptions to it, which are considered at **49.79** and **49.81** to **49.84**. However, the Court of Appeal in *Springsteen v Flute International Ltd* [2001] EMLR 654 appeared to reject the notion that, at common law, there is a general rule accompanied by a number of exceptions, in favour of a more generalised approach whereby the admissibility of secondary evidence of the contents of a document depends upon the weight to be attached to the secondary evidence. Observing 'with confidence' that the best evidence rule had finally expired, the court held that:

(a) Where the party seeking to adduce the secondary evidence could readily produce the document, it might be expected that, absent some special circumstances, the court would decline to admit the secondary evidence on the ground that it was worthless.
(b) At the other extreme, where that party genuinely could not produce the document, it might be expected that, absent some special circumstances, the court would admit the secondary evidence and attach such weight to it as it considered appropriate in the circumstances.
(c) In cases falling between these two extremes, it was for the court to make a judgment as to whether in all the circumstances any weight should be attached to the secondary evidence.
(d) Thus the admissibility of secondary evidence of the contents of documents is entirely dependent on whether or not any weight is to be attached to the evidence, which is a matter for the court to decide.

A similar approach was adopted in *Post Office Counters Ltd v Mahida* [2003] EWCA Civ 1583, *The Times*, 31 October 2003. The claimant had destroyed the primary documentary evidence proving the sums owed by the defendant, and relied on secondary evidence in the form of schedules drawn up by the claimant of the claims for payments and receipts submitted to it by the defendant. It was held to have been permissible to adduce this secondary evidence, but the judge had given it too much weight. The judge should have taken into account the claimant's delay in responding to the defendant's requests for the primary documents, and the claimant's failure to take proper care of that evidence.

Exceptions

Under the exceptions to the general rule, in the case of private documents, secondary evidence of the contents of a document may take the form of a copy, a copy of a copy (*Lafone v Griffin* (1909) 25 TLR 308), or oral evidence. Where a copy is produced, proof is required that it is a true copy of the original (see *R v Collins* (1960) 44 Cr App R 170). **49.77**

It has been said that 'there are no degrees of secondary evidence' (per Lord Abinger CB in *Doe d Gilbert v Ross* (1840) 7 M & W 102), which means that although less weight may attach to inferior forms of secondary evidence, there is no obligation to tender the best type of secondary evidence available. For example, oral evidence of the contents of a document is admissible even if a copy of the document is available. To this principle, however, there are numerous exceptions: many public documents may be proved by oral evidence only if examined, certified or other types of copy are unavailable (see **49.79**); bankers' books are generally proved by examined copies (see **49.80**); and the contents of a will admitted to probate may not be proved by oral evidence if the original or probate copy exists.

Hearsay statements Where the contents of a document, including a computer-produced document, are admissible by virtue of Civil Evidence Act 1995, they may be proved in accordance with ss. 8 and 9 of that Act (see **49.75** and generally at **53.15** to **53.17**). **49.78**

Public and judicial documents At common law, secondary evidence of the contents of public documents is admissible on the grounds that production of the originals would cause a high degree of inconvenience: see, e.g. *Mortimer v M'Callan* (1840) 6 M & W 58 (books of the **49.79**

Commentary

Bank of England). A number of statutes also provide for the proof of different types of public and judicial document by secondary evidence, which is usually required to take the form of:

(a) an examined copy, i.e. a copy proved by oral evidence to correspond with the original;
(b) a certified copy, i.e. a copy signed and certified to be accurate by an official who has custody of the original;
(c) an office copy, i.e. a copy prepared by a court officer who has custody of an original judicial document and the power to provide copies authenticated with the seal of the court; or
(d) a Queen's Printer's or Stationery Office copy.

There are two statutory provisions of general importance, the Evidence Act 1845, s. 1, and the Evidence Act 1851, s. 14. Under the former, where a statute provides for proof of a document by a certified, sealed, or stamped copy, the copy, provided that it purports to be signed, sealed or stamped, is admissible without any proof of the signature, seal or stamp, as the case may be. Under the Evidence Act 1851, s. 14, certified or examined copies may be used to prove the contents of any document provided that it is of such a public nature that it is admissible in evidence on production from proper custody and no other statute provides for proof of its contents by means of a copy.

Specific statutory provision is made for the proof by secondary evidence of the contents of the following types of public and judicial documents:

(a) Acts of Parliament and journals of either House of Parliament. Private Acts of Parliament and journals of either House may be proved by Queen's Printer's or Stationery Office copies (Evidence Act 1845, s. 3 and Documentary Evidence Act 1882, s. 2). As to public Acts, every Act passed after 1850 is a public Act to be judicially noticed as such unless the contrary is expressly provided by the Act (Interpretation Act 1978, s. 3). At common law, judicial notice is taken of earlier public Acts (see **49.29**).
(b) Royal proclamations and orders or regulations issued by the government. These documents may be proved by Queen's Printer's or Stationery Office copies, by a copy of the *Gazette* purporting to contain them, or by copies certified to be true by the appropriate official (Documentary Evidence Act 1868, ss. 2, 3, 5 and 6, and Documentary Evidence Act 1882, s. 2).
(c) By-laws. By-laws may be proved by certified printed copies (Local Government Act 1972, s. 238).
(d) Court proceedings. Every document purporting to be sealed or stamped with the seal or stamp of the Senior Courts shall be received in evidence without further proof (Senior Courts Act 1981, s. 132). Likewise, under **CPR, r. 2.6(3)**, a document purporting to bear the court's seal is to be admissible in evidence without further proof. Records of proceedings in the county courts and magistrates' courts may be proved by certified copies (County Courts Act 1984, s. 12; Magistrates' Courts Rules 1981, r. 68).
(e) Proclamations, treaties and other acts of state of foreign states or British colonies and judgments, decrees, orders, and other judicial proceedings of any court of justice in any foreign state or in any British colony, and affidavits, pleadings and other legal documents filed or deposited in any such court. These documents may be proved by examined copies or by copies authenticated with the seal of the foreign state, colony or court, as the case may be (Evidence Act 1851, s. 7).
(f) Foreign and colonial laws. Colonial statutes may be proved by certified copies (Colonial Laws Validity Act 1865, s. 6) or copies purporting to be printed by the Government printer of the possession in question (Evidence (Colonial Statutes) Act 1907, s. 1). Subject to these provisions, and excepting law ascertained by the British Law Ascertainment Act 1859, foreign and colonial law, including Scots law, cannot be proved merely by the production of documentary evidence, but generally requires proof by a

suitably qualified expert (see *Sussex Peerage Case* (1844) 11 Cl & F 85 and generally at **49.101**).

(g) Public records. Public records kept in the Public Record Office may be proved by examined, certified copies which have been sealed or stamped (Public Records Act 1958, s. 9).

(h) Births, deaths, marriages and civil partnerships. An entry in the register of births or deaths may be proved by a certified copy purporting to be sealed or stamped with the seal of the General Register Office and is admissible evidence of the birth or death to which it relates (Births and Deaths Registration Act 1953, s. 34; and see also the Adoption and Children Act 2002, s. 77(4)). Proof of the celebration of a marriage may be effected by the production of a certified copy of an entry kept at the General Register Office (Marriage Act 1949, s. 65(3)). Proof of a civil partnership may be effected by the production of a certified copy of an entry in the civil partnership register signed by a person authorised by the registration authority to issue the copy (Civil Partnership (Registration Provisions) Regulations 2005 (SI 2005/3176), reg. 14(4)). Births, deaths and marriages out of England may be proved by entries properly and regularly recorded in foreign registers kept under the sanction of public authority (*Lyell v Kennedy* (1889) 14 App Cas 437 at pp. 448–9). See also the Foreign Marriages Act 1892, s. 16 (ambassadors' or consular registers of marriages under British law by British subjects); the Registration of Births, Deaths and Marriages (Scotland) Act 1854 and the Registration of Births, Deaths and Marriages (Scotland) Amendment Act 1860; the Registration of Births, Deaths and Marriages (Army) Act 1879, s. 3; the Merchant Shipping Act 1995, s. 108 and the Merchant Shipping (Returns of Births and Deaths) Regulations 1979 (SI 1979/1577); and the Registration of Births, Deaths and Marriages (Special Provisions) Act 1957, s. 2 (births, deaths and marriages on Her Majesty's ships at sea and service aircraft).

(i) Minute-books of local authorities. The signed minutes of the proceedings of local authorities shall be received in evidence without further proof (Local Government Act 1972, sch. 12, para. 41); and a certified copy of the minutes shall be evidence of their terms (Local Government (Miscellaneous Provisions) Act 1976, s. 41(1)).

(j) Documents relating to insolvency. In this regard, any document purporting to be or to contain any order, direction or certificate issued by the Secretary of State shall be received in evidence and be deemed to be (or contain) that order or certificate or those directions without further proof, unless the contrary is shown (Insolvency Rules 1986 (SI 1986/1925), **r. 12.6**). As to use of copies of the *Gazette*, see also SI 1986/1925, r. 12.20.

Bankers' books The Bankers' Books Evidence Act 1879 provides for the admissibility of entries in bankers' books as evidence of the matters they record by way of exception to the common law rule against hearsay; and in order to avoid the inconvenience involved in the production of the originals of such books, permits the admission of copies. The Act provides as follows: **49.80**

3. Mode of proof of entries in bankers' books

Subject to the provisions of this Act, a copy of an entry in a banker's book shall in all legal proceedings be received as prima facie evidence of such entry, and of the matters, transactions, and accounts therein recorded.

4. Proof that book is a bankers' book

A copy of an entry in a banker's book shall not be received in evidence under this Act unless it be first proved that the book was at the time of the making of the entry one of the ordinary books of the bank, and that the entry was made in the usual and ordinary course of business, and that the book is in the custody or control of the bank.

Such proof may be given by a partner or officer of the bank, and may be given orally or by an affidavit sworn before any commissioner or person authorised to take affidavits. . . .

5. Verification of copy

A copy of an entry in a banker's book shall not be received in evidence under this Act unless it be further proved that the copy has been examined with the original entry and is correct.

Such proof shall be given by some person who has examined the copy with the original entry, and may be given either orally or by an affidavit sworn before any commissioner or person authorised to take affidavits. . . .

6. Case in which banker, etc., not compellable to produce book, etc.

A banker or officer of a bank shall not, in any legal proceeding to which the bank is not a party, be compellable to produce any banker's book the contents of which can be proved under this Act. . ., or to appear as a witness to prove the matters, transactions, and accounts therein recorded, unless by order of a judge made for special cause.

7. Court or judge may order inspection, etc.

On the application of any party to a legal proceeding a court or judge may order that such party be at liberty to inspect and take copies of any entries in a banker's book for any of the purposes of such proceedings. An order under this section may be made either with or without summoning the bank or any other party, and shall be served on the bank three clear days before the same is to be obeyed, unless the court or judge otherwise directs.

8. Costs

The costs of any application to a court or judge under or for the purposes of this Act, and the costs of anything done or to be done under an order of a court or judge made under or for the purposes of this Act shall be in the discretion of the court or judge, who may order the same or any part thereof to be paid to any party by the bank where the same have been occasioned by any default or delay on the part of the bank. Any such order against a bank may be enforced as if the bank was a party to the proceeding.

9. Interpretation of 'bank', 'banker', and 'bankers' books'

(1) In this Act the expression 'bank' and 'banker' mean—
  (a) a deposit-taker;
  (c) the National Savings Bank.

(1A) 'Deposit taker' means—
  (a) a person who has permission under Part 4A of the Financial Services and Markets Act 2000 to accept deposits; or
  (b) an EEA firm of the kind mentioned in paragraph 5(b) of Schedule 3 to that Act which has permission under paragraph 15 of that Schedule (as a result of qualifying for authorisation under paragraph 12(1) of that Schedule) to accept deposits or other repayable funds from the public.

(1B) But a person is not a deposit-taker if he has permission to accept deposits only for the purpose of carrying on another regulated activity in accordance with that permission.

(1C) Subsections (1A) and (1B) must be read with—
  (a) section 22 of the Financial Services and Markets Act 2000;
  (b) any relevant order under that section; and
  (c) Schedule 2 to that Act.

(2) Expressions in this Act relating to 'bankers' books' include ledgers, day books, cash books, account books and other records used in the ordinary business of the bank, whether those records are in written form or are kept on microfilm, magnetic tape or any other form of mechanical or electronic data retrieval mechanism.

10. Interpretation of 'legal proceeding', 'court', 'judge'

In this Act—

The expression 'legal proceeding' means any civil or criminal proceeding or inquiry in which evidence is or may be given, and includes—

(a) an arbitration;

(b) an application to, or an inquiry or other proceeding before, the Solicitors Disciplinary Tribunal or any body exercising functions in relation to solicitors in Scotland or Northern Ireland corresponding to the functions of that Tribunal; and

(c) an investigation, consideration or determination of a complaint by a member of the panel of ombudsmen for the purposes of the ombudsman scheme within the meaning of the Financial Services and Markets Act 2000;

The expression 'the court' means the court, judge, arbitrator, persons or person before whom a legal proceeding is held or taken;

The expression 'a judge' means with respect to England a judge of the High Court...

The judge of a county court may with respect to any action in such court exercise the powers of a judge under this Act.

In s. 9(2), the words 'other records used in the ordinary business of the bank' mean other records of the same type as ledgers, day books, cash books and account books, which are the means by which a bank records day-to-day financial transactions, and therefore records kept by the bank of conversations between its employees and customers or others or internal memoranda are not bankers' books (*Re Howglen Ltd* [2001] 1 All ER 376).

Paid cheques and paying-in slips retained by a bank after the conclusion of a banking transaction to which they relate are not bankers' books under the Act, because even if bundles of such documents can be treated as 'records used in the ordinary business of the bank', the addition of an individual cheque or paying-in slip cannot be regarded as making an 'entry' in those records (*Williams v Williams* [1987] 3 All ER 257). If such documents relate to the bank account of the other party to the action, an order for disclosure may be made and the bank, as agent holding the documents on that party's behalf, may then be required to disclose them. In other cases, the party seeking inspection may obtain a witness summons addressed to the appropriate officer of the bank and requiring him or her to attend at the hearing with all the relevant documents in the possession of the bank relating to the account in question.

An order under s. 7 of the Act is not a necessary precondition of producing evidence under s. 3 of the Act; the obtaining of an order under s. 7 enables bankers' books to be inspected and copied despite the duty of confidentiality owed by banker to customer and such an order is clearly unnecessary if, for instance, the customer waives his right to confidentiality and the bank agrees to inspection and copying of its books (*Wheatley v Commissioner of Police of the British Virgin Islands* [2006] UKPC 24, [2006] 1 WLR 1683, a decision relating to the equivalent British Virgin Islands statute).

Although s. 7 of the Act allows an application to be made without summoning the bank or any other party, there is much to be said for notice being given (per Widgery LJ in *R v Marlborough Street Magistrates' Court, ex parte Simpson* (1980) 70 Cr App R 291 at p. 294). An order may be made under s. 7 to inspect the account of a person who is not a party to the proceedings, even if that person is not compellable as a witness (*R v Andover Justices, ex parte Rhodes* [1980] Crim LR 644). However, an application under s. 7 in respect of the bank account of a third party will only be granted if:

(a) the court is satisfied that the account is in fact the account of the other party to the action or an account with which the other party is so much concerned that items in it would be admissible against him; and
(b) the applicant shows very strong grounds for suspicion, almost amounting to certainty, that there are items in the account which would be material evidence against the other party

(*South Staffordshire Tramways Co. v Ebbsmith* [1895] 2 QB 669 (a pre-trial application) and *D. B. Deniz Nakliyati TAS v Yugopetrol* [1992] 1 WLR 437 (an application against a judgment debtor)).

Save in exceptional circumstances, a foreign bank which is not a party to the proceedings should not be ordered to produce documents which are outside the jurisdiction and concern business transacted outside the jurisdiction, even if it carries on business within the jurisdiction, because an order under the 1879 Act is an exercise of sovereign authority to assist in the administration of justice and foreign banks owe their customers a duty of confidence

Commentary

regulated by their own laws (*MacKinnon v Donaldson Lufkin and Jenrette Securities Corporation* [1986] Ch 482). A party seeking to obtain documents from a foreign bank may apply to a master under **CPR, r. 34.13**, for the issue of letters of request to the courts of the country in question, or may apply directly to such a court under the relevant local law, having first obtained the permission of the English court on a hearing with notice.

The 1879 Act may not be used to compel disclosure of incriminating material (see *Waterhouse v Barker* [1924] 2 KB 759 and *R v Bono* (1913) 29 TLR 635).

49.81 **Failure to produce after notice** A party may produce the contents of a document by secondary evidence where the original is in the possession or control of another party to the proceedings who, having been served with a notice to produce it, has failed to do so (see *Dwyer v Collins* (1852) 21 LJ Ex 225). It is submitted that this rule subsists notwithstanding that the CPR make no provision for service of a formal notice to produce (see, formerly, RSC, ord. 24, r. 10). A notice to produce does not compel production of a document: a party who wishes to rely at the trial on the original of a document should serve a summons requiring a witness to produce the original to the court (see **CPR, r. 34.2**).

49.82 **Non-party's lawful refusal to produce** Secondary evidence of the contents of a document will be admissible where the original is in the possession of a stranger to the litigation who, having been served with a witness summons requiring production of the document to the court (see **CPR, r. 34.2**), lawfully refuses to do so, e.g. by reason of a valid claim to privilege (*Mills v Oddy* (1834) 6 Car & P 728), diplomatic immunity (*R v Nowaz* [1976] 3 All ER 5) or because he cannot be compelled to produce it, being outside the jurisdiction (*Kilgour v Owen* (1889) 88 LT Jo 7). If the stranger unlawfully refuses to produce the original, secondary evidence is inadmissible (see, but doubt, *R v Llanfaethly (Inhabitants)* (1853) 2 El & Bl 940).

49.83 **Lost documents** Secondary evidence of the contents of a document is admissible on proof that the original has been destroyed or cannot be found after due search, the quality of the proof required depending on the nature and value of the document in question (*Brewster v Sewell* (1820) 3 B & Ald 296).

49.84 **Production of original impossible** Secondary evidence is obviously admissible where production of the original is impossible, either physically, e.g. because it is an inscription on a tombstone (per Alderson B in *Mortimer v M'Callan* (1840) 6 M & W 58), or legally, e.g. because a notice required by statute to be constantly affixed at a factory (*Owner v Bee Hive Spinning Co. Ltd* [1914] 1 KB 105) or a document in the custody of a foreign court (*Alivon v Furnival* (1834) 1 Cr M & R 277).

Proof of due execution

49.85 The general rule at common law is that a document will only be admitted in evidence on proof of due execution. A major exception exists in the case of public and judicial documents, proof of the contents of which are governed by statute: most of the relevant statutory provisions also exempt from proof of due execution (see **49.79**). As to private documents, proof of due execution is frequently formally admitted, and in certain circumstances may be presumed, but otherwise usually involves proving handwriting, a signature, or attestation. Some documents are also required to be stamped for the purposes of stamp duty.

49.86 **Presumptions** It is provided in **CPR, r. 32.19(1)**, that a party to whom a document is disclosed under **Part 31** shall be deemed to admit its authenticity, unless he serves notice that he wishes the document to be proved at trial. Without such a notice, therefore, a party will be taken to admit that a document was printed, written, signed or executed as it purports to have been. Proof of due execution is also unnecessary where the document in question is in the possession of an opponent who has refused to comply with a notice to produce it (*Cooke v Tanswell* (1818) 8 Taunt 450). A document which is more than 20 years old and comes from proper custody is presumed to have been duly executed (see Evidence Act 1938, s. 4, whereby the period of 20 years was substituted for the 30-year period required at common law). Proper custody, for these purposes, does not require that the document comes from 'the best and most proper place of deposit', but if it is found elsewhere, the court must be satisfied that the other place was 'reasonable and natural' in the circumstances (*Meath (Bishop) v Marquis of Winchester* (1836) 3 Bing NC 183; cf. *Doe d Lord Arundel v Fowler* (1850) 14 QB 700).

There are three other common law presumptions relating to documents:

(a) that a document was made on the date which it bears (*Anderson v Weston* (1840) 6 Bing NC 296);
(b) that a deed was duly sealed (but see *Re Sandilands* (1871) LR 6 CP 411); and
(c) that an alteration or erasure in a deed was made before execution, but in a will was made after execution (per Lord Campbell CJ in *Doe d Tatum v Catomore* (1851) 16 QB 745).

Handwriting and signatures Proof that a document was written or signed by the person by whom it purports to have been written or signed may be effected by the following means: 49.87

(a) by the direct oral evidence of the author or signatory or by any witness to the execution of the document, or by admissible hearsay assertions to the same effect;
(b) by the opinion evidence of someone acquainted with the handwriting or signature (*Doe d Mudd v Suckermore* (1837) 5 Ad & El 703), although the weight to be attached to such evidence will obviously vary according to the circumstances; or
(c) by comparison of the disputed handwriting or signature with another document which is proved or admitted to have been written by the person in question, under Criminal Procedure Act 1865, s. 8, which provides as follows:

> Comparison of a disputed writing with any writing proved to the satisfaction of the judge to be genuine shall be permitted to be made by witnesses; and such writings, and the evidence of witnesses respecting the same, may be submitted to the court and jury as evidence of the genuineness or otherwise of the writing in dispute.

The court need only be satisfied as to the genuineness of the specimen handwriting on a balance of probabilities. The judge, in comparing the disputed and specimen writing, may be assisted by an expert in handwriting or by someone who, although not an expert, is familiar with the handwriting in question (*Fitzwalter Peerage Claim* (1844) 10 Cl & F 193). A witness who has not seen the original of the 'disputed writing', e.g. because it is lost, is entitled to use a photocopy of it to make the comparison (*Lockheed-Arabia Corporation v Owen* [1993] QB 806).

Any of the above-mentioned means of proving handwriting may be used in the case of documents which, although not required by law to be attested, were in fact attested: the Criminal Procedure Act 1865, s. 7 provides that such a document may be proved as if there had been no attesting witness thereto.

Attestation Except where probate is sought in common form, to prove the due execution of a will (or other testamentary document), one of the attesting witnesses, if available, must be called. Such witnesses are treated as the court's witnesses and may be cross-examined by the party seeking to prove due execution (*Oakes v Uzzell* [1932] P 19). Other evidence becomes admissible if the witness denies the execution (*Bowman v Hodgson* (1867) LR 1 P & D 362) or refuses to give evidence (*Re Ovens Goods* (1892) 29 LR Ir 451). If all the attesting witnesses are dead, insane, outside the jurisdiction or untraceable, proof is required of the handwriting of one of the attesting witnesses; and if, despite every effort to do so, it is impossible to prove such handwriting, other evidence of due execution becomes 49.88

admissible, such as the evidence of a non-attesting witness to the execution (*Clarke v Clarke* (1879) 5 LR Ir 451).

Under the Evidence Act 1938, s. 3, except in the case of a will or other testamentary document, any document required by law to be attested may, instead of being proved by an attesting witness, be proved in the manner in which it might be proved if no attesting witness were alive (e.g. by evidence of the handwriting of an attesting witness or by the evidence of a non-attesting witness to the execution).

49.89 **Stamped documents** A document requiring a stamp for the purposes of stamp duty shall not be given in evidence unless it is duly stamped in accordance with the law in force at the time when it was first executed or, the court having objected to the omission or insufficiency of the stamp, and the document being one which may be legally stamped after its execution, payment is made of the amount of unpaid duty, together with any penalty payable on stamping, and a further sum of one pound (Stamp Act 1891, s. 14). The parties cannot waive these rules (*Bowker v Williamson* (1889) 5 TLR 382). If a document requiring a stamp cannot be found or is in the possession of a party who refuses to comply with a notice to produce it, it is presumed to have been duly stamped; but if there is evidence to show that it was not duly stamped, then it is presumed, in the absence of sufficient evidence to the contrary, that this remained the case (*Closmadeuc v Carrel* (1856) 18 CB 36).

REAL EVIDENCE

Material objects and documents

49.90 Real evidence usually takes the form of a material object examined by the tribunal of fact as a means of proving its existence, condition or value; but subject to a formal admission by the party against whom it is tendered, and subject also to **CPR, r. 33.6** (which is considered at **49.94**), it needs to be accompanied by testimony to at least identify it or explain its provenance. A document may constitute real evidence, as when it is introduced not for the statements that it contains but as a material object, to show that it exists or the condition that it is in. There is no rule to the effect that oral evidence regarding a material object is inadmissible unless the object itself is produced, or its non-production excused (*Hocking v Ahlquist Brothers Ltd* [1944] 1 KB 120), but non-production of the object may affect the weight to be attached to the oral evidence and give rise to an inference adverse to the party failing to produce (see, e.g. *Armory v Delamirie* (1722) 1 Str 505).

Demeanour and appearance

49.91 The demeanour and attitude of a witness in the course of giving his or her evidence may be regarded as a form of real evidence which is relevant to the witness's credit and the weight to be attached to his or her evidence. Real evidence may also take the form of a person's physical appearance, as when injuries or scars are examined on a question of causation or quantum. The facial resemblance of a child to its alleged father and mother may be relevant on the question of legitimacy, although in many cases little weight should be attached to it (*C v C (Legitimacy: Photographic Evidence)* [1972] 1 WLR 1335; cf. *Slingsby v Attorney-General* (1916) 33 TLR 120 at pp. 122–3). The appearance of an animal may also constitute real evidence, as in *Line v Taylor* (1862) 3 F & F 731, where a dog alleged to be of a vicious disposition was examined in court.

Printouts, photographs, videotapes and films

49.92 A computer printout (or photograph, videotape or film) is a document for the purposes of the Civil Evidence Act 1995 (see **53.15**) and under that Act may be used to prove the matters stated therein. They are also documents for the purposes of disclosure and inspection (see **chapter 50**). At common law, where a computer or other device is used as a calculator, (i.e. as a tool which does not contribute its own knowledge, but merely performs a calculation, albeit sophisticated, which could have been performed manually), the resulting printout is not hearsay, but is treated as an item of real evidence. The actual proof and relevance of the printout depend on the evidence of the person using the computer, the computer programmer or other experts involved, who can testify as to such matters as the function and operation of the computer (see per Lord Lane CJ in *R v Wood* (1982) 76 Cr App R 23 at p. 26, in which a laborious mathematical process had been undertaken by a computer operated by chemists investigating the chemical composition of metal; and see also, in the case of a printout from a breathalyser, *Castle v Cross* [1984] 1 WLR 1372). The principle applies not only where the device in question processes information supplied to it, but also where it gathers information itself (*R v Spiby* (1990) 91 Cr App R 186, in which the printout came from a computerised machine used to monitor telephone calls and automatically record such information as the numbers to and from which calls were made, and the duration of the calls). In *R (O'Shea) v Coventry Magistrates' Court* [2004] EWHC 905 (Admin), [2004] Crim LR 948, automatically generated computer records of access and attempted access to web pages, including details matching O's credit card, email and home address, were admitted to show what had been recorded and not as evidence of the truth of what had been recorded. It was, therefore, real evidence and not hearsay. See also *R v Governor of Brixton Prison, ex parte Levin* [1997] AC 741.

In appropriate circumstances, the same principle applies in the case of photographs, video-tapes and films: see *R v Dodson* (1984) 79 Cr App R 220 (photographs taken by security cameras) and *Khan v Armaguard Ltd* [1994] 1 WLR 1204 (a videotape inconsistent with the claimant's claims about the nature of his injuries). It has been said that the photograph, together with the sketch and the photofit, are in a class of evidence of their own to which neither the rule against hearsay nor the rule against previous consistent statements applies (per Watkins LJ in *R v Cook* [1987] QB 417 at p. 425). In *The Statue of Liberty* [1968] 1 WLR 739, an action concerning a collision between two ships, a cinematograph film of radar echoes recorded by a shore radar station and produced mechanically and without human intervention was held to be admissible in evidence. Sir Jocelyn Simon P said (at p. 740):

> If tape recordings are admissible, it seems that a photograph of radar reception is equally admissible—or indeed, any other type of photograph. It would be an absurd distinction that a photograph should be admissible if the camera were operated manually by a photographer, but not if it were operated by a trip or clock mechanism. Similarly, if evidence of weather conditions were relevant, the law would affront common sense if it were to say that those could be proved by a person who looked at a barometer from time to time, but not by producing a barograph record. So, too, with other types of dial recordings.

Regarding video recordings, there is an obligation to inform the court at the first opportunity that such evidence will be relied upon, as arrangements need to be made to ensure video equipment is available at trial, and extra time will be required for the trial for showing the evidence (*Rall v Hume* [2001] 3 All ER 248). Use of videos at trial takes two forms. They can be used as part of a party's affirmative case. In this event the videotapes may need to be played in their entirety. Alternatively, a party may wish to use a videotape in cross-examination of the opposing party by playing certain parts of the video for comment by the witness being cross-examined in order to undermine the witness. Use of a tape in this way will usually be legitimate, even if an application for such use is made quite close to the trial date. However, a direction is likely to be made limiting the footage to be shown (in *Rall v Hume* the limit was 20 minutes). Some inquiry agents are not very discriminating when shooting covert videos, and the court will be astute to ensure that the footage used does not infringe the European Convention on Human Rights, art. 8(1) (the right to private life).

Views

49.93 A view is an inspection of a site or of an object that it is impossible or inconvenient to bring to court, e.g. an omnibus (see *London General Omnibus Co. Ltd v Lavell* [1901] 1 Ch 135). In some circumstances it will also be appropriate to conduct out-of-court demonstrations or reenactments, before which, it is submitted, the demonstrator should take the oath and thereby offer himself or herself for cross-examination (see *Buckingham v Daily News Ltd* [1956] 2 QB 534; and cf. *Goold v Evans and Co.* [1951] 2 TLR 1189 at pp. 1191–2). Each of the parties must be given the opportunity of being present at a view, and a failure to do so may result in a re-trial (*Goold v Evans and Co.*). However, it has been said that the judge may visit the *locus in quo* in order to see that which has previously been represented to him or her in court by plan and photograph on his or her own and without reference to the parties at all (per Widgery LJ in *Salsbury v Woodland* [1970] 1 QB 324 at pp. 343–4). See also per Lord Denning LJ in *Goold v Evans and Co.* [1951] 2 TLR 1189 at p. 1191. Such an exception was doubted by Leveson LJ in *M v Director of Public Prosecutions* [2009] EWHC 752 (Admin), [2009] 2 Cr App R 12, at [20], having regard to the importance attached to the principle that justice must both be done and be seen to be done by all those concerned. In that case it was further held (at [31]) that:

> What is critical before any court embarks upon any view is that there is absolute clarity about precisely what is to happen…, about who is to stand in what position, about what (if any) objects should be placed in a specific position and about who will do what. None of this should happen at the scene of a view, which should be conducted without discussion.

Notice and inspection of plans, photographs, models, etc.

49.94 CPR, r. 33.6, governs the admissibility of evidence (such as a plan, photograph or model) which is not—

(a) contained in a witness statement, affidavit or expert's report;
(b) to be given orally at trial; or
(c) evidence of which prior notice must be given under r. 33.2 (hearsay evidence; see 53.9).

Unless the court orders otherwise, the evidence shall not be receivable at a trial unless the party intending to put it in evidence has given notice to the other parties of his intention and given each of them an opportunity to inspect it and to agree to its admission without further proof. In *Orford v Rasmi Electronics Ltd* [2002] EWCA Civ 1672, [2003] CPLR 213, one of the reasons for ordering a retrial was that a plan was not shown to the claimant until the morning of the trial, though it had been in existence for over five months. The rule is wide enough to cover not only the illustrations given, i.e. plans, photographs and models, but also films and video films and other varieties of real evidence. The rule also covers documents which may be received in evidence without further proof under the Civil Evidence Act 1995, s. 9 (see 53.16). Where the evidence forms part of expert evidence, the notice must be given when the expert's report is served on the other party (CPR, r. 33.6(6)). Subject to this, where the intention is to use the evidence as evidence of any fact, then notice must be given not later than the latest date for serving witness statements. If there are not to be witness statements, or the intention is to put the evidence in solely in order to disprove an allegation made in a witness statement, notice must be given at least 21 days before the hearing (r. 33.6(5)). Where the evidence is being produced to the court for any reason other than as part of factual or expert evidence, notice must also be given at least 21 days before the hearing (r. 33.6(7)). The court needs to be able to understand any map, plan, diagram or photograph relied upon. A section in the skeleton argument should explain all the relevant features to be seen from such evidence (*Hunte v E. Bottomley and Sons Ltd* [2007] EWCA Civ 1168, *The Times*, 21 November 2007).

JUDGMENTS AS EVIDENCE

The decision of the Court of Appeal in *Hollington v F. Hewthorn and Co. Ltd* [1943] KB 587 tipped the balance in favour of the view supported by the bulk of authority by which it was preceded, that verdicts in criminal proceedings (or judgments in civil proceedings) are not admissible in subsequent proceedings as evidence of the facts on which they were based. Thus, in that case, an action in negligence against the driver of a car who had been convicted of careless driving at the time and place of the accident in question, it was held that the conviction was inadmissible as evidence of negligence, being inadmissible as evidence of the fact that the driver had committed the offence. The court was of the view that the civil court would know nothing of the evidence before the criminal court, and the arguments that were addressed to it, and that the opinion of the criminal court was irrelevant. The rule in *Hollington v F. Hewthorn and Co. Ltd* understandably attracted much criticism and, in so far as it applies not only to previous convictions, but also to findings of adultery and paternity in previous civil proceedings, it has been reversed by the Civil Evidence Act 1968, ss. 11 to 13. **49.95**

Previous convictions

Civil Evidence Act 1968, s. 11 Section 11 of the Civil Evidence Act 1968 reverses the decision in *Hollington v F. Hewthorn and Co. Ltd* [1943] KB 587, and creates a persuasive presumption that the person convicted shall be taken to have committed the offence in question unless the contrary is proved. A claimant who wishes to rely on evidence of a conviction under s. 11 must include in his or her particulars of claim a statement to that effect and give details of the type of conviction and its date, the court or court-martial which made it, and the issue in the claim to which it relates (**PD 16, para. 8.1**). Section 11 provides as follows: **49.96**

(1) In any civil proceedings the fact that a person has been convicted of an offence by or before any court in the United Kingdom or by a court-martial there or elsewhere shall (subject to subsection (3) below) be admissible in evidence for the purpose of proving, where to do so is relevant to any issue in those proceedings, that he committed that offence, whether he was so convicted upon a plea of guilty or otherwise and whether or not he is a party to the civil proceedings; but no conviction other than a subsisting one shall be admissible in evidence by virtue of this section.

(2) In any civil proceedings in which by virtue of this section a person is proved to have been convicted of an offence by or before any court in the United Kingdom or by a court-martial there or elsewhere—
   (a) he shall be taken to have committed that offence unless the contrary is proved; and
   (b) without prejudice to the reception of any other admissible evidence for the purpose of identifying the facts on which the conviction was based, the contents of any document which is admissible as evidence of the conviction, and the contents of the information, complaint, indictment or charge-sheet on which the person in question was convicted, shall be admissible in evidence for that purpose.

(3) Nothing in this section shall prejudice the operation of section 13 of this Act or any other enactment whereby a conviction or a finding of fact in any criminal proceedings is for the purposes of any other proceedings made conclusive evidence of any fact.

(4) Where in any civil proceedings the contents of any document are admissible in evidence by virtue of subsection (2) above, a copy of that document, or of the material part thereof, purporting to be certified or otherwise authenticated by or on behalf of the court or authority having custody of that document shall be admissible in evidence and shall be taken to be a true copy of that document or part unless the contrary is shown.

(5) Nothing in . . .
   (a) section 14 of the Powers of Criminal Courts (Sentencing) Act 2000 (under which a conviction leading to discharge is to be disregarded except as therein mentioned) . . . shall affect the operation of this section. . . .

(6) In this section 'court-martial' means a court-martial constituted under the Army Act 1955, the Air Force Act 1955 or the Naval Discipline Act 1957 or a disciplinary court constituted under section

52G of the said Act of 1957, and in relation to a court-martial 'conviction' means a finding of guilty which is, or falls to be treated as, the finding of the court, and 'convicted' shall be construed accordingly.

Section 18 provides that, for the purposes of s. 11, 'civil proceedings':

includes, in addition to civil proceedings in any of the ordinary courts of law—

(a) civil proceedings before any other tribunal, being proceedings in relation to which the strict rules of evidence apply; and

(b) an arbitration or reference, whether under an enactment or not,

but does not include civil proceedings in relation to which the strict rules of evidence do not apply.

A 'subsisting' conviction includes a conviction against which an appeal is pending, but not one which has been quashed on appeal; and therefore rather than finally dispose of civil proceedings in reliance on a conviction subsequently liable to be quashed, it is better to adjourn the civil proceedings pending the outcome of the appeal (see *Re Raphael* [1973] 1 WLR 998). Section 11 does not apply to foreign convictions (see *Union Carbide Corporation v Naturin Ltd* [1987] FSR 538). However, even if the rule in *Hollington v F. Hewthorn and Co. Ltd* covers foreign convictions, it will not apply where the issues in the criminal and civil proceedings are identical (*Director of the Assets Recovery Agency v Virtosu* [2008] EWHC 149 (QB), [2009] 1 WLR 2808 at [43], civil proceedings for a recovery order under the Proceeds of Crime Act 2002, s. 241). Foreign convictions may also be referred to in an affidavit in support of a freezing injunction where they are part of the narrative explanation of the case against the defendant and enable the claimant to comply with his or her duty to make full and frank disclosure to the court (*Arab Monetary Fund v Hashim (No. 2)* [1990] 1 All ER 673).

Section 11(2)(b) is 'without prejudice to the reception of any other admissible evidence for the purpose of identifying the facts on which the conviction was based'. Such other evidence could include a copy of the summing up, which would be admissible under the Civil Evidence Act 1995 (see *Brinks Ltd v Abu-Saleh (No. 2)* [1995] 1 WLR 1487, a decision under the Civil Evidence Act 1968), as would a transcript of the evidence given in the criminal case.

The authorities are in conflict as to when the pleadings of the subject of the criminal proceedings challenging the conviction can be struck out as an abuse of process. (On abuse of process generally, see **33.12 to 33.22**.) In *Brinks Ltd v Abu-Saleh* [1995] 1 WLR 1478 it was held, relying upon *Hunter v Chief Constable of West Midlands Police* [1982] AC 529, that such pleadings should be struck out in the absence of new evidence, not adduced at the criminal trial, that entirely changes the aspect of the case. In *J v Oyston* [1999] 1 WLR 694, on the other hand, Smedley J, although of the opinion that it may be unwise to say that there can never be an abuse where the subsequent civil proceedings are brought against the subject of the criminal proceedings, declined to follow *Brinks Ltd v Abu-Saleh*, pointing out that *Hunter v Chief Constable of West Midlands Police* was distinguishable, being a case where the subsequent civil proceedings were brought by the subject of the criminal proceedings. However, where a defendant in civil proceedings is entitled to challenge his conviction under s. 11(2), there may be an 'absence of realism' about his ability to prove that he did not commit the offence entitling the court to grant the claimant summary judgment: *CXX v DXX* [2012] EWHC 1535 (QB), 162 NLJ 806. (On summary judgment generally, see **chapter 34**.)

Section 11(2)(a) imposes on a party who wishes to 'go behind' a conviction the burden of proving, on the balance of probabilities, that the person convicted did not commit the offence, and therefore it is not sufficient to establish that the conviction is unsafe, that the judge in the criminal trial (or the Court of Appeal) made an error or that the prosecution was an abuse of process (*Raja v Van Hoogstraten* [2005] EWHC 1642 (Ch), LTL 22/8/2005).

There is a divergence of judicial opinion as to what weight should be attached to the conviction, in deciding whether a party has discharged the burden of proving 'the contrary' under s. 11(2)(a). In *Taylor v Taylor* [1970] 1 WLR 1148, Davies LJ was of the view that the standard to be met in order to upset the conviction was the balance of probabilities but that the verdict of the jury was entitled to very great weight (at p. 1152). Similar views were expressed by Lord Denning MR in *Stupple v Royal Insurance Co. Ltd* [1971] 1 QB 50. Lord Denning MR was of the opinion that the conviction does not merely shift the burden of proof, but is a weighty piece of evidence of itself (at p. 72). Buckley LJ, however, was of the view that the statutory presumption would give way to evidence establishing the contrary on the balance of probability without itself affording any evidential weight when deciding whether that onus had been discharged (at p. 76). See also, preferring the approach of Lord Denning, Moore-Bick J in *Phoenix Marine Inc. v China Ocean Shipping Co.* [1999] 1 All ER 138 at [143] and per Spencer J in *CXX v DXX* [2012] EWHC 1535 (QB), 162 NLJ 806 at [39]; and, preferring the view of Buckley LJ, per Stirling J in *Wright v Wright* (1971) 115 SJ 173. In *McIlkenny v Chief Constable of the West Midlands* [1980] QB 283 at p. 320 Lord Denning MR suggested, obiter, that a convicted man could only prove 'the contrary' under s. 11(2)(a) by proving that the conviction was obtained by fraud or collusion or by adducing fresh evidence which must be 'decisive' and 'conclusive'. On appeal, however, Lord Diplock disapproved the dictum, being of the opinion that the standard to be met, in proving 'the contrary' was proof on a balance of probabilities, but added that 'in the face of a conviction after a full hearing this is likely to be an uphill task' (*Hunter v Chief Constable of the West Midlands Police* [1982] AC 529 at p. 544).

Civil Evidence Act 1968, s. 13 Section 13 of the Civil Evidence Act 1968, which applies to defamation proceedings, reverses the decision in *Hollington v F. Hewthorn and Co. Ltd* [1943] KB 587 (**49.95**) and creates a conclusive presumption, that the person convicted shall be conclusively taken to have committed the offence in question. Thus a defamation claim based on the defendant's statement that the claimant committed an offence in respect of which he has been convicted, will be struck out as an abuse of the process of the court, unless the statement also contains some other legally defamatory matter (*Levene v Roxhan* [1970] 1 WLR 1322). Section 13 provides as follows: **49.97**

(1) In an action for libel or slander in which the question whether the plaintiff did or did not commit a criminal offence is relevant to an issue arising in the action, proof that at the time when that issue falls to be determined, he stands convicted of that offence shall be conclusive evidence that he committed that offence; and his conviction thereof shall be admissible in evidence accordingly.

(2) In any such action as aforesaid in which by virtue of this section the plaintiff is proved to have been convicted of an offence, the contents of any document which is admissible as evidence of the conviction, and the contents of the information, complaint, indictment or charge-sheet on which he was convicted, shall, without prejudice to the reception of any other admissible evidence for the purpose of identifying the facts on which the conviction was based, be admissible in evidence for the purpose of identifying those facts.

(2A) In the case of an action for libel or slander in which there is more than one plaintiff—
  (a) the references in subsections (1) and (2) above to the plaintiff shall be construed as references to any of the plaintiffs, and
  (b) proof that any of the plaintiffs stands convicted of an offence shall be conclusive evidence that he committed that offence so far as that fact is relevant to any issue arising in relation to his cause of action or that of any other plaintiff.

(3) For the purposes of this section a person shall be taken to stand convicted of an offence if but only if there subsists against him a conviction of that offence by or before a court in the United Kingdom or by a court-martial there or elsewhere.

(4) Subsections (4) to (6) of section 11 of this Act shall apply for the purposes of this section as they apply for the purposes of that section, but as if in the said subsection (4) the reference to subsection (2) were a reference to subsection (2) of this section.

Previous findings of adultery and paternity

49.98 The Civil Evidence Act 1968, s. 12, reverses the rule in *Hollington v F. Hewthorn and Co. Ltd* [1943] KB 587 (**49.95**), in so far as it applied to previous findings of adultery and paternity, and creates two persuasive presumptions, that the person found guilty of adultery shall be taken to have committed the adultery, and that the person found to be the father of a child shall be taken to be, or have been, the father of the child. A claimant who wishes to rely on evidence under s. 12 of a finding or adjudication of adultery or paternity must include in his or her particulars of claim a statement to that effect and give details of the finding or adjudication and its date, the court which made it, and the issue in the claim to which it relates (**PD 16, para. 8.1**). Section 12 provides as follows:

(1) In any civil proceedings—

(a) the fact that a person has been found guilty of adultery in any matrimonial proceedings; and

(b) the fact that a person has been found to be the father of a child in relevant proceedings before any court in England and Wales or Northern Ireland or has been adjudged to be the father of a child in affiliation proceedings before any court in the United Kingdom;

shall (subject to subsection (3) below) be admissible in evidence for the purpose of proving, where to do so is relevant to any issue in those civil proceedings, that he committed the adultery to which the finding relates or, as the case may be, is (or was) the father of that child, whether or not he offered any defence to the allegation of adultery or paternity and whether or not he is a party to the civil proceedings; but no finding or adjudication other than a subsisting one shall be admissible in evidence by virtue of this section.

(2) In any civil proceedings in which by virtue of this section a person is proved to have been found guilty of adultery as mentioned in subsection (1)(a) above or to have been found or adjudged to be the father of a child as mentioned in subsection (1)(b) above—

(a) he shall be taken to have committed the adultery to which the finding relates or, as the case may be, to be (or have been) the father of that child, unless the contrary is proved; and

(b) without prejudice to the reception of any other admissible evidence for the purpose of identifying the facts on which the finding or adjudication was based, the contents of any document which was before the court, or which contains any pronouncement of the court, in the other proceedings in question shall be admissible in evidence for that purpose.

(3) Nothing in this section shall prejudice the operation of any enactment whereby a finding of fact in any matrimonial or affiliation proceedings is for the purposes of any other proceedings made conclusive evidence of any fact.

(4) Subsection (4) of section 11 of this Act shall apply for the purposes of this section as if the reference to subsection (2) were a reference to subsection (2) of this section.

(5) In this section—

'matrimonial proceedings' means any matrimonial cause in the High Court or a county court in England and Wales or in the High Court in Northern Ireland, any consistorial action in Scotland, or any appeal arising out of any such cause or action; 'relevant proceedings' means—

(a) proceedings on a complaint under section 42 of the National Assistance Act 1948 or section 26 of the Social Security Act 1986;

(b) proceedings under the Children Act 1989;

(c) proceedings which would have been relevant proceedings for the purposes of this section in the form in which it was in force before the passing of the Children Act 1989;

(e) proceedings which are relevant proceedings as defined in section 8(5) of the Civil Evidence Act (Northern Ireland) 1971;

'affiliation proceedings' means, in relation to Scotland, any action of affiliation and aliment; and in this subsection 'consistorial action' does not include an action of aliment only between husband and wife raised in the Court of Session or an action of interim aliment raised in the sheriff court.

As to the meaning of 'civil proceedings', see s. 18(1), which is considered at **49.96**. Under s. 12(2) the party seeking to disprove the adultery or paternity bears the legal burden of doing so, and the standard of proof required to discharge the burden is the ordinary civil standard of proof on a balance of probabilities (*Sutton v Sutton* [1970] 1 WLR 183).

Previous acquittals

Parliament rejected the Law Reform Committee's recommendation that in defamation proceedings evidence of an acquittal should be conclusive evidence of innocence (see 15th Report (1967) Cmnd 3391, para. 26 et seq.) The question still remains, however, whether the principle of *Hollington v F. Hewthorn and Co. Ltd* [1943] KB 587 (**49.95**) should apply to previous acquittals so as to render them inadmissible as evidence of innocence in subsequent civil proceedings. It is submitted that, on balance, the question should be answered in the affirmative because although it is desirable that a person acquitted of an offence should be granted some measure of immunity from assertions to the contrary, an allegation which was not proved beyond reasonable doubt may still be susceptible to proof on a balance of probabilities, as it was in *Loughans v Odhams Press* [1963] 1 QB 299, a libel suit arising out of the publication of a statement suggesting that the claimant had committed a murder in respect of which he had been acquitted. However, in *Packer v Clayton* (1932) 97 JP 14, a decision pre-dating *Hollington v F. Hewthorn and Co. Ltd*, Avory J expressed the opinion that in affiliation proceedings, the respondent's acquittal of a sexual offence against the applicant would be admissible to show that the jury were not convinced by her evidence. **49.99**

Commentary

Other previous findings

The principle of *Hollington v F. Hewthorn and Co. Ltd* [1943] KB 587 would appear to apply, in civil proceedings, to all judicial findings in previous civil proceedings, except findings of adultery and paternity (see Civil Evidence Act 1968, s. 12, at **49.98**). In *Secretary of State for Trade and Industry v Bairstow* [2003] EWCA Civ 321, [2004] Ch 1, the Secretary of State began proceedings under the Company Directors Disqualification Act 1986, s. 8, seeking a disqualification order against B, the managing director of a company. By the time of the proceedings, B had been dismissed and his claim for damages for wrongful dismissal had been unsuccessful, both at first instance and on appeal. In the proceedings under the 1986 Act, the Court of Appeal held that the factual findings and conclusions of the judge at first instance in the wrongful dismissal proceedings were not admissible as evidence of the facts found in those proceedings. However, it was also held that the principle of abuse of process will prevent collateral attack on an earlier decision of a court of competent jurisdiction where relitigation of the same issues would be manifestly unfair or would bring the administration of justice into disrepute. See further at **33.12** to **33.21**. **49.100**

Parliament has established investigatory processes for providing the Secretary of State with reports, information or documents on which an opinion may be based that it is expedient in the public interest that a company should be wound up (Insolvency Act 1986, s. 124A(1)) or that a disqualification order should be made against a person (Company Directors Disqualification Act 1986, s. 8). It follows that the Secretary of State may use the relevant report etc. as evidence in support of a petition to wind up the company or an application for a disqualification order despite the rule in *Hollington v F. Hewthorn and Co. Ltd* (*Secretary of State for Business, Enterprise and Regulatory Reform v Aaron* [2008] EWCA Civ 1146, [2009] 1 BCLC 55).

In other proceedings, though, the principle in *Hollington v F. Hewthorn and Co. Ltd* does apply to previous findings of inspectors appointed under what is now the Companies Act 1985, part 14 (*Savings and Investment Bank Ltd v Gasco Investments (Netherlands) BV* [1984] 1 WLR 271), to an arbitration award, in later proceedings for the determination of a fair market rent (*Land Securities plc v Westminster City Council* [1993] 1 WLR 286) and to the findings of Lord Bingham of Cornhill in his extra-statutory report into the collapse of BCCI (*Three Rivers District Council v Bank of England (No. 3)* [2001] UKHL 16, [2003] 2 AC 1). In *Hill v Clifford* [1907] 2 Ch 236 the Court of Appeal held that a finding by the General Medical Council that a dentist had been guilty of professional misconduct was admissible as prima facie evidence of the misconduct in subsequent civil proceedings concerning the dissolution of his partnership; but in these circumstances the court is entitled to reach its own view of the facts as previously found (*Clifford v Timms* [1908] AC 12). Similarly, the principle of *Hollington v F. Hewthorn and Co. Ltd* has been held to apply to findings of the Solicitors Disciplinary Tribunal that a solicitor has been dishonest (*Conlon v Simms* [2006] EWCA Civ 1749, [2008] 1 WLR 484). See also the discussion of this case at **33.17** on the device of using striking out to achieve a result sidestepping *Hollington v F. Hewthorn and Co. Ltd.* See also *Faulder v Silk* (1811) 3 Camp 126 (inquisitions in lunacy as prima facie evidence of a person's unsoundness of mind). As to statements contained in public documents, which at common law are admissible for the truth of their contents, see **53.24** to **53.26**. Although a person who was not a party to the earlier proceedings cannot be bound by the result, they can be affected by it.

FINDINGS ON QUESTIONS OF FOREIGN LAW

49.101 Points of foreign law are questions of fact, and therefore fall to be decided on the evidence adduced, normally expert evidence, except in the case of:

(a) points of foreign law which are formally admitted (see **49.9**) or of which judicial notice may be taken (see **49.28**) and
(b) the construction of provisions of foreign legislation admitted under the Evidence (Colonial Statutes) Act 1907, whereby copies of Acts, ordinances and statutes passed by the legislature of any part of Her Majesty's dominions exclusive of the United Kingdom and of orders, regulations and other instruments issued or made under the authority of any such Act, ordinance or statute, if purporting to be printed by the Government printer of the possession, shall be received in evidence by all courts in the United Kingdom without proof that the copies were so printed (see the authorities cited in *Jasiewicz v Jasiewicz* [1962] 1 WLR 1426).

Under the British Law Ascertainment Act 1859, English courts may state a case on a point of foreign law for the opinion of a superior court in another part of Her Majesty's dominions, and the opinion pronounced is admissible in evidence on the point. See also the Foreign Law Ascertainment Act 1861.

Points of foreign law must always be decided by the judge. Under the Senior Courts Act 1981, s. 69(5), where, for the purposes of disposing of any action or other matter which is being tried by a judge with a jury, it is necessary to ascertain the law of any other country which is applicable to the facts of the case, any question as to the effect of the evidence given with respect to that law shall, instead of being submitted to the jury, be decided by the judge alone. To like effect, see also the County Courts Act 1984, s. 68.

Foreign law will usually be established by the opinion evidence of an expert, who may refer to foreign statutes, decisions and texts. If the evidence of the experts conflicts, the judge is bound to look at the sources of knowledge upon which they have relied in order to reach a decision (see per Lord Langdale MR in *Earl Nelson v Lord Bridport* (1845) 8 Beav 527 at p. 537; and per

Scarman J in *Re Fuld (No. 3)* [1968] P 675 at pp. 700–3), but should not conduct his or her own research into those sources and rely on material not adduced in evidence in order to reject the expert testimony (per Lord Chelmsford in *Duchess di Sora v Phillipps* (1863) 10 HL Cas 624 at p. 640; and per Purchas LJ in *Bumper Development Corporation Ltd v Metropolitan Police Commissioner* [1991] 1 WLR 1362 at pp. 1368–71).

Although points of foreign law are questions of fact, if a point has been decided, and the same point arises again in a subsequent case, it does not necessarily need to be decided afresh on new expert evidence. The Civil Evidence Act 1972, s. 4, provides as follows:

(2) Where any question as to the law of any country or territory outside the United Kingdom, or of any part of the United Kingdom other than England and Wales, with respect to any matter has been determined (whether before or after the passing of this Act) in any such proceedings as are mentioned in subsection (4) below, then in any civil proceedings (not being proceedings before a court which can take judicial notice of the law of that country, territory or part with respect to that matter)—
 (a) any finding made or decision given on that question in the first-mentioned proceedings shall, if reported or recorded in citable form, be admissible in evidence for the purpose of proving the law of that country, territory or part with respect to that matter; and
 (b) if that finding or decision, as so reported or recorded, is adduced for that purpose, the law of that country, territory or part with respect to that matter shall be taken to be in accordance with that finding or decision unless the contrary is proved:
 Provided that paragraph (b) above shall not apply in the case of a finding or decision which conflicts with another finding or decision on the same question adduced by virtue of this subsection in the same proceedings.
(3) Except with the leave of the court, a party to any civil proceedings shall not be permitted to adduce any such finding or decision as is mentioned in subsection (2) above by virtue of that subsection unless he has in accordance with rules of court given to every other party to the proceedings notice that he intends to do so.
(4) The proceedings referred to in subsection (2) above are the following, whether civil or criminal, namely—
 (a) proceedings at first instance in any of the following courts, namely the High Court, the Crown Court, a court of quarter sessions, the Court of Chancery of the county palatine of Lancaster and the Court of Chancery of the county palatine of Durham;
 (b) appeals arising out of any such proceedings as are mentioned in paragraph (a) above;
 (c) proceedings before the Judicial Committee of the Privy Council on appeal (whether to Her Majesty in Council or to the Judicial Committee as such) from any decision of any court outside the United Kingdom.
(5) For the purposes of this section a finding or decision on any such question as is mentioned in subsection (2) above shall be taken to be reported or recorded in citable form if, but only if, it is reported or recorded in writing in a report, transcript or other document which, if that question had been a question as to the law of England and Wales, could be cited as an authority in legal proceedings in England and Wales.

'Civil proceedings', for the purposes of s. 4(2) and (3), means civil proceedings before any tribunal, in relation to which the strict rules of evidence apply, whether as a matter of law or by agreement of the parties (s. 5). **CPR, r. 33.7**, sets out the procedure which must be followed by a party who intends to put in evidence a finding under the Civil Evidence Act 1972, s. 4(2). He or she must give notice of his or her intention:

(a) if there are to be witness statements, not later than the latest date for serving them, or
(b) otherwise, not less than 21 days before the hearing;

and the notice must specify the question on which the finding was made and enclose a copy of a document where it is reported or recorded.

Section 4(2)(b) effectively raises a presumption that the earlier decision is correct. The weight to be attached to the earlier decision, however, is a matter for the trial judge, and although it is obviously desirable to reach consistent conclusions, the section is not to be

Commentary

construed as if it laid down a general rule that the presumption can only be displaced by particularly cogent evidence (*Phoenix Marine Inc. v China Ocean Shipping Co.* [1999] 1 Lloyd's Rep 682).

EVIDENCE OF CONSENT OF TRUSTEE TO ACT

49.102 A document purporting to contain the written consent of a person to act as trustee and to bear his or her signature, verified by some other person, is evidence of such consent (CPR, r. 33.8).

Chapter 50 Disclosure

The following procedural checklists, which are at the front of the book, are relevant to this chapter:

Procedural checklist 25 Standard disclosure
Procedural checklist 26 Specific disclosure
Procedural checklist 27 Non-party disclosure

INTRODUCTION

50.1 Disclosure is the formal process by which parties to claims give each other copies of the documents in their control which are material to the issues in the claim. Formal disclosure under **CPR, Part 31**, applies to claims on the fast track and multi-track, but not to claims on the small claims track (see **45.17**). Disclosure should take place in accordance with directions made by the court. In most fast track and multi-track claims directions for disclosure are made when the claim is allocated to a track (**rr. 28.2(1), 28.3, 29.2(1)(a); PD 29, para. 4**). Otherwise, directions are given at a case management conference (**CPR, r. 29.2(1)(b)**). The usual direction in fast track claims is for standard disclosure (see **50.4**), which covers documents in the control of the party making disclosure which that party intends to rely on at the trial, and also documents which adversely affect that party or which support the other side. Multi-track claims (other than claims for personal injuries) are governed by menu option disclosure (see **50.10**). Disclosure takes place in two stages. First, the parties exchange lists of documents using form N265 or electronic documents questionnaires using the form on the schedule to **PD 31B**. A list of documents identifies all the documents which support or adversely affect any of the parties to the claim, and also asserts any privilege claimed against disclosure in respect of identified documents or categories of documents (see **50.50 to 50.83**). Secondly, the parties allow their opponents to inspect the non-privileged disclosed documents. Usually this happens by providing photocopies, but there is provision for physical inspection of the originals and for disclosure in electronic form.

The disclosure system includes the following features:

(a) The potential for incurring disproportionate costs on disclosure. Many disputes generate large quantities of documentary evidence that needs to be disclosed.
(b) Disclosure traditionally extends to all materials on which information is recorded (see **50.17**) and materials that are relied upon, and also those that support another party or which might be adverse to any party. There is always a fear that the other side might not fully comply with their disclosure obligations.
(c) Disclosure obligations extend to electronic documents and even metadata. Disclosure of electronic documents at proportionate cost can be very challenging.
(d) To meet these challenges parties and the court need to tailor the approach to giving disclosure in complex claims to the circumstances of the case.
(e) Application of the principle of proportionality to limit the extent of the searches required to find disclosable documents.
(f) A requirement to include a 'disclosure statement' in the list of documents to the effect that the party giving disclosure has complied with its duties under **CPR, Part 31**.
(g) A requirement that litigants, rather than their lawyers, must sign the disclosure statement. This obligation is intended to bring home to litigants that it is their personal responsibility to give full disclosure (*Arrow Trading and Investments Est 1920 v Edwardian Group Ltd* [2004] EWHC 1319 (Ch), [2005] 1 BCLC 696).

Where an opponent fails to give disclosure in accordance with directions, the innocent party should still usually comply with its own disclosure obligations, but may apply for a sanction (usually an 'unless' order, see **chapter 48**) or for specific disclosure (see **50.41**). Deliberate destruction of documents to avoid the obligation to give disclosure, particularly after an unless order, is likely to result in a severe sanction, such as striking out (*Rybak v Langbar International Ltd* [2010] EWHC 2015 (Ch), LTL 24/8/2010).

Documents disclosed under **Part 31** are deemed to be authentic (see **50.43**), and if this is disputed, the party receiving the copies should serve a notice to prove. Disclosed documents are provided for the purposes of the present litigation and must not be used for any collateral purpose (**50.45**), although this protection is usually lost once the documents are referred to in open court.

DOCUMENTATION ON THE SMALL CLAIMS TRACK

The rules on disclosure in **CPR, Part 31**, do not apply at all to the small claims track **50.2**
(**r. 27.2(1)(b)**). On the small claims track, parties are required to disclose only the documents on which they intend to rely at trial (see **r. 27.4(3)(a)** and **45.17**).

FAST TRACK AND MULTI-TRACK DISCLOSURE

To ensure disclosure takes place in a proportionate manner, disclosure in fast track claims and **50.3**
personal injuries cases on the multi-track is usually made in accordance with standard disclosure (see **50.4**), whereas in most other multi-track claims the courts adopt menu option disclosure (discussed at **50.10**). More technically:

(a) fast track claims, multi-track personal injuries claims, and other multi-track claims where the court makes a specific direction to this effect, are governed by **CPR, r. 31.5(1)**, which starts from the position that the parties must give standard disclosure; and
(b) all other multi-track claims are governed by **r. 31.5(3)–(8)**, which lays down the scheme for menu option disclosure.

STANDARD DISCLOSURE

50.4 The procedure for standard disclosure is summarised in **procedural checklist 25**, which is at the front of the book. In fast track and other claims in category (a) at **50.3** above, disclosure directions will usually expressly require standard disclosure, but a direction simply referring to disclosure in these cases means an order to give standard disclosure, unless the court directs otherwise (see **CPR, r. 31.5(1)(a)**). In these cases:

(i) the court may alternatively dispense with or limit standard disclosure (**r. 31.5(1)(b)**); or
(ii) the parties may agree in writing to dispense with or to limit standard disclosure (**r. 31.5(1)(c)**).

In the exercise of its case management powers in furtherance of the overriding objective, the court may decide to make orders limiting or dispensing with standard disclosure, and it should not be assumed that an order for standard disclosure will simply be rubber-stamped by the court (see **50.37**).

Documents covered by standard disclosure

50.5 By **CPR, r. 31.6**, standard disclosure requires a party to disclose only:

(a) the documents on which he relies; and
(b) the documents which—
  (i) adversely affect his own case;
  (ii) adversely affect another party's case; or
  (iii) support another party's case; and
(c) the documents which he is required to disclose by a relevant practice direction.

Although these categories do not include 'train of inquiry' documents (see **50.14**), they are nevertheless wide ranging, and many clients are surprised at the breadth of documentation that they are required to disclose. To ensure the system works fairly between the opposing parties, lawyers are under professional duties to advise their clients on their disclosure obligations (**50.31**), and clients must take personal responsibility by signing a disclosure statement (**50.22**).

While the categories set out in **r. 31.6** come close to the concept of relevance, that particular word is not used in **r. 31.6**, and is not the test (*Shah v HSBC Private Bank (UK) Ltd* [2011] EWCA Civ 1154, LTL13/10/2011). The category of documents upon which a party relies (**r. 31.6(a)**) is probably restricted to documents relied upon in support of that party's affirmative case or to rebut the case advanced by the other side. The fact a party does not intend to adduce a document as part of its evidence at trial is probably conclusive that the document does not fall into **r. 31.6(a)** (*Shah v HSBC Private Bank (UK) Ltd*). **Rule 31.6(a)** does not cover documents that may be referred to as a shield in cross-examination (*Favor Easy Management Ltd v Wu* [2010] EWCA Civ 1630, [2011] 1 WLR 1803 at [22]). **Rule 31.6(b)** is drafted in unqualified terms, and it is impermissible to read into it a qualification that it covers only documents that adversely affect another party's case 'as against another party' (*Serious Organised Crime Agency v Namli* [2011] EWCA Civ 1411, LTL 29/11/2011). The description 'documents which adversely affect [the disclosing party's] own case' (**r. 31.6(b)(i)**) is probably self-explanatory. **Rule 31.6(b)(ii)** is probably intended to cover documents in the control of party A in a multi-party claim which adversely affect the case of party B against party C (*Serious Organised Crime Agency v Namli* at [18]). If the other side does not have an affirmative case, there is nothing for **r. 31.6(b)(ii)** or **(iii)** to bite on (*Shah v HSBC Private Bank (UK) Ltd*). Whether a document falls into any of these categories is to be judged against the statements of case, and not by reference to matters raised elsewhere, even in exchanged witness statements (*Paddick v Associated Newspapers Ltd* [2003] EWHC 2991 (QB), LTL 12/12/2003). They do not cover documents which are relevant solely to credit (*Thorpe v Chief Constable of Greater Manchester Police* [1989] 1 WLR 665, confirmed by *Favor Easy Management Ltd v Wu*), on the ground this helps to keep disclosure within reasonable and sensible bounds (*Thorpe v Chief Constable of Greater Manchester Police* per Neill LJ at p. 673).

Standard disclosure in personal injury claims

Annex B to the **Pre-action Protocol for Personal Injury Claims** contains detailed lists of categories of documents that should be disclosed in various types of personal injury claims. For example, in tripping cases the highway authority should disclose its records for the 12 months prior to the accident dealing with inspections of the relevant stretch of highway; maintenance including records of independent contractors working in the relevant area; minutes of highway authority meetings where maintenance or repair policy was discussed or decided; complaints about the state of highways; and other accidents on the relevant stretch of highway. Annex B has even more detailed lists for accidents at work. Standard disclosure imposes similar obligations, but will include claims-handling documents and party-and-party correspondence, and (although, because privileged, inspection will not be required) documents relating to legal advice on the claim. **50.6**

The combined effect of **CPR, rr. 31.3, 31.6, 31.8** and **31.12(3)**, is to oblige a claimant in a personal injuries claim to disclose and give inspection of the claimant's GP and hospital records (*Bennett v Compass Group UK and Ireland Ltd* [2002] EWCA Civ 642, [2002] ICR 1177). This is so almost regardless of the nature of the dispute. The records will either confirm the claimant's injuries and their consequences, or will question those injuries or their extent, and will therefore support either the claimant's or the defendant's case (*OCS Group Ltd v Wells* [2008] EWHC 919 (QB), [2009] 1 WLR 1895). Where the claimant fails to cooperate in providing these records (which are under the claimant's control as defined by **r. 31.8(2)**), the court has the power to make an order that the claimant must provide the defendant with a signed authority for the release of the records, but such an order has to be carefully worded to ensure the claimant's rights are not infringed (*Bennett v Compass Group UK and Ireland Ltd*). This means that care should be taken to ensure the records to be disclosed are not wider (in terms of dates or nature of the document to be disclosed) than the nature of the case merits.

Standard disclosure in professional negligence claims

The solicitor's file under the original retainer is almost always, or always, covered by standard disclosure in a solicitors' professional negligence claim (*Martin v Triggs Turner Barton* [2008] EWHC 89 (Ch), *The Times*, 5 February 2008). Where particulars of claim in a property valuation negligence claim set out the loss by reference to the price paid for the property, and the defence pleaded that the purchase was structured to obtain an unlawful tax saving, standard disclosure by the claimant had to include its tax returns (*K/S Lincoln v CB Richard Ellis Hotels Ltd* [2009] EWHC 2344 (TCC), [2010] PNLR 5). **50.7**

Standard disclosure in commercial and contract claims

Contractual and commercial claims often generate considerable disclosable documentation. This will include the contractual documents, including the contract, tenders, offers, orders, shipping documents, delivery notes, invoices, documents recording or effecting payment, statements of account, and receipts; correspondence relating to forming the contract, its performance, and alleged breach; documents dealing with the effects of breach and any steps taken to mitigate damage; and often financial documentation, such as business accounts, tax records and financial records dealing with loss of profits or other heads of loss and damage. **50.8**

A standard disclosure order is appropriate even in complex patent claims where there is likely to be a vast amount of potentially disclosable documentation, rather than putting the burden on the opposite party to make an application for specific disclosure. In cases with large volumes of documents, the costs of disclosure can be kept under control by cooperation between the parties over the extent of the searches that each should make (*Hospira Inc. v Amgen Inc.* [2010] EWHC 176 (Pat), LTL 25/2/2010).

In *Marlton v Tektronix UK Holdings Ltd* [2003] EWHC 383 (Ch), LTL 10/2/2003 there was a dispute about whether a contractual document was sent by email, so disclosure was ordered of the relevant hard disks, back-ups and server. Diaries containing business and personal details, which were relevant to establishing how much time a director had spent in managing a business, were ordered to be disclosed in *Re Cawgate Ltd* [2004] EWHC 1773 (Ch), LTL 30/6/2004. In an unfair prejudice case (see **85.9**), where it was alleged the directors were receiving excessive remuneration, standard disclosure included financial documents such as accounts and budgets (*Arrow Trading and Investments Est 1920 v Edwardian Group Ltd* [2004] EWHC 1319 (Ch), [2005] 1 BCLC 696). In a patent infringement case there is no blanket immunity from standard disclosure concerning the obviousness of the patented invention, despite the objective nature of the question (*Nichia Corporation v Argos Ltd* [2007] EWCA Civ 741, [2007] Bus LR 1753). Seeking the names of employees who had made money laundering reports, whose names were redacted from the documents disclosed by a bank in a claim for breach of mandate, was held in *Shah v HSBC Private Bank (UK) Ltd* [2011] EWCA Civ 1154, LTL13/10/2011, to fall outside the categories in **r. 31.6** and to be a fishing expedition.

Standard disclosure in libel claims

50.9 A defendant who pleads justification is entitled to disclosure of all matters relating to the questions in issue as narrowed by the particulars (*Yorkshire Provident Life Assurance Co. v Gilbert and Rivington* [1895] 2 QB 148). The defendant was not entitled to disclosure of documents relating to unpleaded complaints by patients against the claimant doctor in *Taranissi v British Broadcasting Corporation* [2008] EWHC 2486 (QB), LTL 24/10/2008. A number of categories of documents were considered in the libel case of *Beckham v News Group Newspapers Ltd* [2005] EWHC 2252 (QB), LTL 25/10/2005:

(a) Disclosure of documents relating to the claimants' public relations strategies was refused, because there was no sufficient foundation to the defendant's case that the claimants had presented a false image to the public.
(b) Disclosure was also refused of documents relating to the claimants' move to Madrid, their commercial arrangements with a particular photographer, and the termination of an agency agreement with a public relations company.
(c) Disclosure of tapes of a television documentary about the claimants, including all unedited versions, was dealt with by an order that the claimants must use their best endeavours to find out from those involved in making the documentary about incidents relied on by the defendant and to communicate such information to the defendant.
(d) Disclosure of notes and tapes made by journalists when interviewing the claimants' former nanny was ordered. This was because the court needed to have regard to the totality of what the nanny said to the journalists, and because the items might be relevant to whether the nanny had appeared to be a credible source of information to the defendant's journalists.

MENU OPTION DISCLOSURE

50.10 In non-personal injuries multi-track claims, menu option disclosure applies unless the court *otherwise orders* (*CPR*, **r. 31.5(2)**). To the extent that the documents to be disclosed are electronic, the provisions of **PD 31B** (see **50.25**) apply in addition to the menu option provisions (**r. 31.5(9)**). Menu option disclosure takes place in three stages.

Stage 1: Disclosure report

Not less than 14 days before the first case management conference (CMC) each party must file and serve a disclosure report in form N263 (**CPR, r. 31.5(3)**). This must be served with their electronic documents questionnaire if this is required under **PD 31B** (**r. 31.5(4)**). A disclosure report must be verified by a statement of truth (**r. 31.5(3)**), and must: **50.11**

(a) describe briefly what documents exist or may exist that are or may be relevant to the matters in issue in the case;
(b) describe where and with whom those documents are or may be located;
(c) in the case of electronic documents, describe how those documents are stored;
(d) estimate the broad range of costs that could be involved in giving standard disclosure in the case, including the costs of searching for and disclosing any electronically stored documents. This should be consistent with the party's costs budget, see **chapter 43**; and
(e) state which of the directions under **r. 31.5(6)** or **(7)** are to be sought.

Stage 2: Agree proposal for disclosure

Not less than seven days before the first CMC the parties must, at a meeting or by telephone, discuss and seek to agree a proposal in relation to disclosure that meets the overriding objective (**CPR, r. 31.5(5)**). A similar discussion must also be held on any other occasion as the court may direct (**r. 31.5(5)**). Any agreed proposal should be filed at court. By **r. 31.5(6)**, if the parties agree proposals for the scope of disclosure which the court considers are appropriate in all the circumstances, the court may approve them without a hearing and give directions in the terms proposed. **50.12**

Stage 3: CMC menu disclosure

If disclosure directions have not been made without a hearing under **CPR, r. 31.5(6)**, at the first or any subsequent CMC the court will decide on the appropriate orders to make about disclosure. It will do so having regard to the overriding objective, the available costs budgets, and the need to limit disclosure to that which is necessary to deal with the case justly (**r. 31.5(7)**). The menu available under **r. 31.5(7)** comprises orders: **50.13**

(a) dispensing with disclosure;
(b) that a party disclose the documents on which it relies (this concept was discussed at **50.5**), and at the same time request any specific disclosure it requires from any other party;
(c) directing, where practicable, the disclosure to be given by each party on an issue-by-issue basis;
(d) that each party disclose any documents which it is reasonable to suppose may contain information which enables that party to advance its own case or to damage that of any other party, or which leads to an enquiry which has either of those consequences (see **50.14**);
(e) for standard disclosure (see **50.4**);
(f) in whatever form the court considers appropriate (see **50.15**).

Train of inquiry documents

Disclosure of train of inquiry documents is permitted by **CPR, r. 31.5(7)(d)**. These are documents which are not themselves relevant, but which could provide information that could lead to a train of inquiry resulting in finding relevant documents (*Compagnie Financiere et Commerciale du Pacifique v Peruvian Guano Co.* (1882) 11 QBD 55). In this case Brett LJ said, at p. 63: **50.14**

every document relates to the matters in question in the action, which not only would be evidence upon any issue, but also which, it is reasonable to suppose, contains information which *may*—not which *must*—either directly or indirectly enable the party [seeking discovery] either to advance his own case or to damage the case of his adversary... a document can properly be said to contain information which may enable the party [seeking discovery] either to advance his own case or to damage the case of his adversary, if it is a document which may fairly lead him to a train of inquiry, which may have either of these two consequences.

Under the Rules of the Supreme Court 1965, the obligation to disclose 'train of inquiry' documents was a major cause of unnecessary costs and was a principal source of complaint by practitioners and litigants alike. In *O Co. v M Co.* [1996] 2 Lloyd's Rep 347 Colman J, out of frustration with the position under the RSC, stated, at pp. 350–1:

The principle was never intended to justify demands for disclosure of documents at the far end of the spectrum of materiality which on the face of it were unrelated to the pleaded case of the plaintiff or defendant and which were required for purely speculative investigation... That formulation [Brett LJ's 'train of inquiry'] must not, in my judgment, be understood as justifying discovery demands which would involve parties to civil litigation being required to turn out the contents of their filing systems as if under criminal investigation merely on the off-chance that something might show up from which some relatively weak inference prejudicial to the case of the disclosing party might be drawn.

Train of inquiry documents are not covered by the definition of standard disclosure (see **50.4**), and are rarely required to be disclosed even in multi-track claims. A specific order to this effect must be obtained under the menu option if disclosure is to reach this far. Before making such an order the court will take into account all the circumstances of the case with particular regard to the overriding objective **(PD 31A, para. 5.4)**. An order was made in *Commissioners of Inland Revenue v Exeter City AFC Ltd* [2004] BCC 519 for the disclosure of communications between the Inland Revenue and 20 to 30 football clubs connected to proposed and actual entry into insolvency of those football clubs. These were train of inquiry documents which could have advanced the defendant football club's case that the Inland Revenue had not been unfairly treated by the club's voluntary arrangement.

Key of the warehouse order

50.15 **CPR, r. 31.5(7)(f)**, allows the court to make any other order in relation to disclosure that the court considers appropriate. It allows the court, for example, to make a 'key of the warehouse' order. Such an order requires each party to hand over all its documents after removing any privileged documents, and the other side can then choose which documents it wishes to use in the litigation.

Disclosure directions

50.16 By **CPR, r. 31.5(8)**, the court may at any point give directions as to how disclosure is to be given, and in particular may direct:

(a) what searches are to be undertaken, of where, for what, in respect of which time periods and by whom and the extent of any search for electronically stored documents;
(b) whether lists of documents are required;
(c) how and when the disclosure statement is to be given;
(d) in what format documents are to be disclosed (and whether any identification is required);
(e) what is required in relation to documents that once existed but no longer exist; and
(f) whether disclosure shall take place in stages.

MATERIALS TO BE DISCLOSED

Documents

50.17 *The regime for disclosure* and inspection in **CPR, Part 31**, is concerned only with documents, and not any other type of evidence. A 'document' is defined in **r. 31.4** as 'anything in which information of any description is recorded' and 'copy' in relation to a document, means anything onto which information recorded in the document has been copied, by whatever means and whether directly or indirectly'. Thus a 'document' is not confined to paper, but includes electronic documents, audio and video cassettes, and other similar material.

Electronic documents include emails, messages on mobile telephones, word-processed documents and databases. In addition, the definition covers documents that are stored on servers and back-up systems and electronic documents that have been 'deleted'. It also extends to additional information stored and associated with electronic documents known as metadata (**PD 31A, para. 2A.1**). Disclosure of the metadata behind a record of an important meeting which had been created long after the event was ordered in *Hellard v Money* [2008] EWHC 2275 (Ch), LTL 29/4/2008.

Control of documents

By **CPR, r. 31.8(1)**, a party's duty to disclose documents is limited to documents which are now or have been previously within the party's control. **Rule 31.8(3)** provides that a document is or was in a party's control if: **50.18**

(a) it is or was in the party's physical possession;
(b) the party has or has had a right to possession of it; or
(c) the party has or has had a right to inspect or take copies of it.

This does not seem any different from the 'possession, custody or power' criterion for giving discovery under the old rules. Therefore, it may be possible to require the controller of a company to disclose the company's documents in a claim to which the controller, but not the company, is a party (*B v B (Matrimonial Proceedings: Discovery)* [1978] Fam 181; *Lonrho Ltd v Shell Petroleum Co. Ltd* [1980] 1 WLR 627; *Re Tecnion Investments Ltd* [1985] BCLC 434).

Disclosure of copies

By **CPR, r. 31.9**, a copy of a document must be treated as a separate document, and therefore separately disclosed, if it contains a modification, obliteration or other marking or feature: **50.19**

(a) on which 'a party' (which clearly means the disclosing party) intends to rely; or
(b) which adversely affects the disclosing party's own case or supports another party's case.

So if, for example, several copies of a memorandum have been produced and some have been returned to the originator with other people's comments on them, and those comments are within (a) or (b) above, the copies must be disclosed. Otherwise it is not necessary to disclose the existence of copies of disclosed documents (**r. 31.9(1)**).

Reasonable search

CPR, r. 31.7 requires a party ordered to give standard disclosure to 'make a reasonable search for documents falling within r. 31.6(b) and (c)' (adverse material and documents specifically required by a practice direction). The effect of this, reinforced by **PD 31A, para. 2**, is to apply the principle of proportionality to searching for the purposes of standard disclosure. The searcher must search for the documents required by **CPR, r. 31.6(b)** and **(c)**, but may make a policy decision not to search in places where the cost of searching could not be justified by the small chance of finding anything disclosable. **50.20**

The duty to disclose under an order for standard disclosure is qualified by reasonableness. **CPR, r. 31.7(2)**, provides that the factors relevant in deciding the reasonableness of a search include the following:

(a) the number of documents involved;
(b) the nature and complexity of the proceedings;
(c) the ease and expense of retrieval of any particular document; and
(d) the significance of any document which is likely to be located during the search.

This list of factors is not intended to be exhaustive, and there may well be others which affect the reasonableness of disclosing documents. In applying these factors the court has to consider how central the documents are likely to be to the issues. It is particularly important to have contemporaneous documents where a case turns on the state of mind of a party (*Grace Shipping Inc. v C. F. Sharp and Co. (Malaya) Pte Ltd* [1987] 1 Lloyd's Rep 207), which may justify a wider search than might otherwise be the case (*Fiddes v Channel 4 Television Corporation* [2010] EWCA Civ 516, LTL 24/3/2010). If the documents could be described as secondary evidence (limited to being an aid in assessing the primary evidence), the extent of the search should be correspondingly limited (*Nichia Corporation v Argos Ltd* [2007] EWCA Civ 741, [2007] Bus LR 1753). In the first instance it is for the solicitor responsible for the disclosure process for each party to decide on what constitutes a reasonable search (**PD 31A, para. 2**). The rule does not demand that no stone be left unturned (*Abela v Hammonds Suddards* (2008) LTL 9/12/2008). A court asked to adjudicate on whether the search was sufficiently thorough might well be influenced by the diligence and conscientiousness displayed by the solicitor. Ultimately, it is for the court to decide whether the search was in fact reasonable (*Nichia Corporation v Argos Ltd*). This is not an exercise in reviewing the solicitor's decision (along the lines of judicial review), but of deciding what was reasonable.

A party who has not searched for a category or class of document on the grounds that to do so would be unreasonable, must state this in the disclosure statement (see **50.23**) and identify the category or class of document (**r. 31.7(3)**).

The extent of the search should be discussed by legal representative and client at all stages of litigation planning. Clients must provide their legal advisers with realistic information about the quantity of documents and the time and expense that may be involved in carrying out the search. It is the task of the lawyer to assess the legal significance and relevance of what might be disclosed if the search was extended, and all these factors must be taken into account and balanced against the value of the claim itself when deciding what kind of search would be reasonable.

LIST OF DOCUMENTS

50.21 When standard disclosure has been ordered, each party should make a list of the documents in its control which come within the categories set out in **CPR, r. 31.6** (see **50.5**). Lists of documents should be on form N265, and have to be served by the date stated in the court's directions on every other party (**r. 31.10(2); PD 31A, para. 3.1**). Although a party will usually give disclosure in a list of documents, the requirement in **CPR, r. 31.2**, to disclose a document 'by stating that the document exists or has existed' can be satisfied by referring to a document's existence in a witness statement or expert's report (*SmithKline Beecham plc v Generics (UK) Ltd* [2003] EWCA Civ 1109, [2004] 1 WLR 1479 at [29]). On form N265, as required by **rr. 31.10(4)** and **31.19(4)**, the list is in three parts:

(a) Documents presently in the disclosing party's control which the controlling party does not object to being inspected.

(b) Documents presently in the disclosing party's control which the controlling party objects to being inspected, giving the reason for the objection. According to **PD 31A, para. 4.5**, a right or duty to withhold a document, or part of a document, from inspection must be claimed in writing with a statement of the grounds on which it is claimed, and, according to **para. 4.6**, should normally be included in the disclosure statement (see **50.23**), although form N265 is not laid out in that way.

(c) Documents that have been, but are no longer, in the disclosing party's control. The *list must state* when each document was last in the party's control and where each is now.

PD 31A, para. 3.2, provides that compliance with **CPR, r. 31.10(3)**, will be achieved by listing documents in chronological order, numbering them consecutively, and giving each of them a concise description, for example, 'letter, claimant to defendant, 19 Jan 2012'. Where there is a large number of documents which all fall into a particular category, the disclosing party is permitted to list those documents as a category, rather than individually, thus, for example: '50 bank statements relating to account number 1234546 at Anywhere Bank, September 2009–November 2013'.

Disclosure statement

The disclosing party's list of documents (form N265) must include a disclosure statement (**CPR, r. 31.10(5)**). The form of the statement, which is set out in the annex to **PD 31A**, is included in form N265 with a signature box. A disclosure statement is the statement of the disclosing party, or that party's insurer or the Motor Insurers' Bureau, rather than a legal representative (**CPR, r. 31.10(6)**). A disclosure statement is not a mere technicality. Its purpose is to impose a positive duty on each party to give full standard disclosure. Making a false disclosure statement may be punished as a contempt of court (**rr. 81.17** and **81.18**, see **chapter 81**). If there are several defendants in a case, each should sign a disclosure statement. Providing a single composite list of documents does not satisfy **r. 31.10** (*Arrow Trading and Investments Est 1920 v Edwardian Group Ltd* [2004] EWHC 1319 (Ch), [2005] 1 BCLC 696). **50.22**

Where an insurer, or the Motor Insurers' Bureau, has a financial interest in the outcome of the proceedings, it may sign a disclosure statement on behalf of a party (**r. 31.10(9)**; **PD 31A, para. 4.7**).

If the disclosing party is an individual, the disclosure statement is either the party's own statement, signed by the party or the party's litigation friend, or is the statement of the party's insurer or the Motor Insurers' Bureau.

If the disclosing party is not an individual, the disclosure statement must identify the person who is making and signing it and explain why he or she is considered an appropriate person to make it (**CPR, r. 31.10(7)**). It must state that person's name and address and the office or position he or she holds in the disclosing party (**PD 31A, para. 4.3**). The same rules apply when a disclosure statement is signed by an insurer or the Motor Insurers' Bureau (**PD 31A, para. 4.7**).

If a disclosure order requires a particular person to make disclosure on behalf of a party, that person cannot delegate the duty (*Carlco Ltd v Chief Constable of Dyfed-Powys Police* [2002] EWCA Civ 1754, LTL 18/11/2002). In *Carlco Ltd v Chief Constable of Dyfed-Powys Police* a disclosure order required disclosure to be made by the claimant company's 'officer', which meant it could only be signed by an officer who was an individual, and it could not be signed by a corporate director.

Contents of disclosure statement

By **CPR, r. 31.10(6)**, a disclosure statement must: **50.23**

(a) set out the extent of the search that has been made to locate documents which are required to be disclosed;
(b) certify that the signatory understands the duty to disclose documents; and
(c) certify that to the best of his or her knowledge he or she has carried out that duty.

The disclosure statement certifies that a reasonable and proportionate search has been carried out to disclose all the documents required by the court's order.

PD 31A, para. 4.2, requires a disclosure statement expressly to state that the disclosing party believes the extent of the search to have been reasonable in all the circumstances; and

Commentary

CPR, r. 31.7(3), requires a party who has not searched for a category or class of document on the grounds that to do so would be unreasonable, to state this in the disclosure statement, and identify the category or class of document not searched for. In the prescribed form of disclosure statement in **PD 31A, annex**, and form N265 the statement required by **CPR, r. 31.7(3)**, is turned into a description of the boundaries of a search:

I did not search for documents —
pre-dating —
located elsewhere than —
in categories other than—
for electronic documents (if electronic documents were searched for, further details must be given of the limits of the search)

In the disclosure statement the disclosing party should draw attention to any particular limitations which were adopted for proportionality reasons and give the reasons why the limitations were adopted (**PD 31A, para. 4.2(2)**).

The searcher must search for the documents required by **CPR, r. 31.6(b)** and (c), but may make a policy decision not to search in places where the cost of searching could not be justified by the small chance of finding anything disclosable.

Rule 31.3(2) requires a party who considers that it would be disproportionate to the issues in the case (see **50.36**) to permit inspection of a category or class of documents to state that fact in the disclosure statement.

PD 31A, para. 4.4, requires the legal representative of a disclosing party to endeavour to ensure that the individual making the disclosure statement understands the duty of disclosure under **CPR, Part 31**.

Dispensing with list of documents

50.24 CPR, r. 31.10(8), provides that the parties may agree in writing to disclose documents without making a list, and to disclose documents without the disclosing party making a disclosure statement, but such agreement must be put into writing and lodged with the court (**PD 31A, para. 1.4**). Such agreements are comparatively uncommon, and form N265 is normally used.

ELECTRONIC DOCUMENTS

50.25 Disclosure of electronic documents is regulated by **PD 31B**, which was introduced on 1 October 2010. It applies to cases likely to be allocated to the multi-track (**PD 31A, para. 2A.2**), and provides a comprehensive and up-to-date set of rules governing the disclosure of electronic documents.

PD 31B, para. 6, sets out the following general principles:

(a) electronic documents should be managed efficiently in order to minimise the cost incurred;
(b) technology should be used in order to ensure that document management activities are undertaken efficiently and effectively;
(c) disclosure should be given in a manner which gives effect to the overriding objective;
(d) electronic documents should generally be made available for inspection in a form which allows the party receiving them the same ability to access, search, review and display the documents as the party giving disclosure; and
(e) disclosure of electronic documents which are of no relevance to the proceedings may place an excessive burden in time and cost on the party to whom disclosure is given.

In order to keep costs in proportion, the parties and their legal advisers are required to discuss the use of technology for the purposes of managing disclosure of electronic documents (**para. 8**). Particular topics to discuss are set out in **para. 9**, and include the tools to be used to reduce the burden and costs of disclosure, and the need to preserve electronic documents. In *Digicel (St Lucia) Ltd v Cable and Wireless plc* [2008] EWHC 2522 (Ch), [2009] 2 All ER 1094, the court ordered the parties' solicitors to meet to discuss the best way of restoring email accounts, in view of the possible cost of doing so.

Electronic documents questionnaire

An electronic documents questionnaire in the form in the schedule to **PD 31B** may be used to provide information relevant to the procedures for the disclosure of electronic documents. If used, the questionnaire has to be verified by a statement of truth (**PD 31B, para. 11**), and the questionnaire is treated as itself a disclosed document for the purpose of the collateral use rule in **CPR, r. 31.22**. **50.26**

Directions for disclosure of electronic documents

Emphasis is placed on the importance of obtaining appropriate directions for disclosure at the first case management conference, which in turn requires cooperation between the parties (**PD 31B, paras 14** to **19**). One of the main difficulties in keeping costs under control in relation to electronic documents is the extent of the searches required under **CPR, r. 31.7**. **PD 31B, paras 20** to **27**, give guidance which includes a list of factors to be taken into account in deciding on the ambit of the search under **CPR, r. 31.7**. These factors include the nature and complexity of the proceedings, the ease of retrieval, and the availability of the documents or their contents from other sources. In *Fiddes v Channel 4 Television Corporation* [2010] EWCA Civ 516, LTL 24/3/2010, the technical costs of doing a search of backup tapes for deleted emails was estimated at £10,000. Even in the context of a case where the costs were already estimated at £1 million, and where the relevant respondent had changed her story from saying she had deleted her emails because her email account was full to saying she had not sent any emails in the relevant period, a finding that the documents in the proposed search were unlikely to be significant or relevant meant that a refusal to order the search was not overturned on appeal. **PD 31B, paras 25** to **27** deal with keyword searches for electronic documents. A search based on targeted keyword electronic searches was held to be inadequate in *Digicel (St Lucia) Ltd v Cable and Wireless plc*, where email accounts of specified individuals were required. Limited searches for electronic documents were regarded as reasonable in *Abela v Hammonds Suddards* (2008) LTL 9/12/2008. **50.27**

Inspection of electronic documents

Lists of documents may be provided in electronic form in CSV (comma-separated values) or other agreed format (**para. 30(2)**). **Paragraph 30(7)** is a reminder that any supplementary list should run sequentially from the last numbered entry in the previous list. Inspection may be given in electronic form, and may take the form of the provision of disclosure data electronically, or electronic copies of disclosed documents (**paras 31** and **32**). Unless otherwise agreed or ordered, electronic documents should be disclosed in their native form (i.e. preserving any metadata) (**para. 33**). If electronic documents are best accessed using technology which is not readily available to the other side, there is a duty to cooperate in making the documents available (**para. 36**). **50.28**

ILLEGALLY OBTAINED DOCUMENTS

The Data Protection Act 1998, s. 55(1), provides that a person must not (and by s. 55(3) it is an offence to) knowingly or recklessly, without the consent of the data controller: **50.29**

(a) obtain or disclose personal data or the information contained in personal data; or
(b) procure the disclosure to another person of the information contained in personal data.

Section 55(2)(a) provides that s. 55(1) does not apply to a person who shows that the obtaining, disclosing or procuring of the personal data or information:

(a) was necessary for the purpose of preventing or detecting crime; or
(b) was required or authorised by or under any enactment, by any rule of law or by order of a court.

In *Hughes v Carratu International plc* [2006] EWHC 1791 (QB), LTL 26/7/2006, the applicant became aware that the respondent professional investigator had come into possession of details relating to his bank account, which had been sent to it by a sub-agent. This was regarded as a possibly serious breach of the criminal law. The evidence in the case indicated that it was possible that the sub-agent was under the impression that such material would not be unwelcome to the respondent, nor possibly its principal (a well-known firm of solicitors). This was supported in part by the fact that something similar had happened in another case referred to the respondent by the same firm of solicitors. An order was made requiring the respondent to disclose all documents presently or formerly in its possession or control relating to the applicant's personal affairs, and disclosing the identities of the parties on whose behalf the information was gathered, and the identities of the parties who gathered that information. Removing documents from refuse sacks on the street outside a party's offices, copying them for use in litigation, and then returning the originals to the refuse sacks, was regarded as not giving rise even to a prima facie case of unlawfulness in *Consolidated Contractors International Co. SAL v Masri* [2011] EWCA Civ 21, [2011] CP Rep 20. Use of documents obtained using spyware on the other side's computer was reflected in an adverse costs order in *Walsh v Singh* [2011] EWCA Civ 80, [2011] 2 FLR 599.

In *Guidance Note (Illegally Obtained Evidence in Civil and Family Proceedings)* issued by the General Council of the Bar (September 2003), the following principles were set out for the guidance of the profession (which it is submitted are of equal relevance for solicitors):

(a) Legal representatives must never advise that evidence be obtained illegally, including by methods infringing the Data Protection Act 1998. Updating or clarifying such evidence is just as illegal as obtaining it in the first place.
(b) There is an important distinction between obtaining such data in the first place, which is illegal, and disclosure of such material in civil proceedings. If disclosure is compulsory, it is likely to be lawful. Standard disclosure under **CPR, r. 31.6**, is a rule of law within the meaning of the Data Protection Act 1998, s. 55(2)(a)(ii), and so will be regarded as compulsory for the purposes of s. 55.
(c) A party who has obtained relevant documents illegally is not entitled to claim legal professional privilege over them (see **50.53** and *Dubai Aluminium Co. Ltd v Al Alawi* [1999] 1 WLR 1964). In addition to the illegally obtained evidence, the source of the evidence and the letters of instruction to the person who obtained it must also be disclosed.
(d) If a client refuses to comply with these disclosure obligations, the legal representatives will be obliged to withdraw.
(e) If disclosure is made, the data can be used in evidence in the claim in the usual way.
(f) If there is doubt about the use of data, or the need to disclose it, the Guidance Note suggests a without notice application should be made to the court. The need for tactical secrecy may justify the application being made without notice. Any order made by the court for disclosure or use will provide the necessary compulsion within the last five words of s. 55(2)(a)(ii).

Tugendhat J in *Hughes v Carratu International plc* felt that the guidance in the Note is of equal relevance to solicitors (at [34]), but decided against formally endorsing the advice it contains (at [36]). Solicitors will be concerned that they are not put into difficult positions by the conduct of enquiry agents they instruct. To reduce the dangers exposed by *Hughes v Carratu International plc* it is suggested that:

(a) Standard letters of instruction should be settled for use by fee earners. These should expressly say that personal data or information contained in personal data must not be obtained illegally, or communicated to the firm, and that sub-agents must be told to take as much care in complying with the Data Protection Act 1998 as the main agent.

(b) Care should be taken over which enquiry agents are instructed. Agents known to use illegal methods should be avoided.

(c) Where there has been an infringement of the Data Protection Act 1998, consideration should be given to reporting the matter to the Information Commissioner and/or the Serious Organised Crime Agency.

Illegal access to documents in ancillary relief proceedings has for some time been governed by what are commonly called the *Hildebrand* rules (*Hildebrand v Hildebrand* [1992] 1 FLR 244). These were summarised in *White v Withers LLP* [2009] EWCA Civ 1122, [2010] 1 FLR 859, by Drake LJ at [37] as follows:

> The family courts will not penalise the taking, copying and immediate return of documents but do not sanction the use of any force to obtain the documents, or the interception of documents or the retention of documents nor I would add, though it is not a feature of this case, the removal of any hard disk recording documents electronically. The evidence contained in the documents, even those wrongfully taken will be admitted in evidence because there is an overarching duty on the parties to give full and frank disclosure.

The '*Hildebrand* rules' were in fact a development from the original decision. *Hildebrand v Hildebrand*, as originally decided, was authority only as to the time when copies obtained unlawfully or clandestinely should be disclosed to a spouse.

In *Imerman v Tchenguiz* [2010] EWCA Civ 908, [2011] Fam 116, the wife's brothers accessed the husband's computer on nine occasions, downloaded electronic copies of his financial information and passed the electronic files to a forensic accountant for use in the wife's ancillary relief proceedings. The husband's computer had been password protected, with the files being stored on the wife's brothers' server. It was held that the wider *Hildebrand* rules are no longer good law, leaving just the narrow original decision in *Hildebrand v Hildebrand* as the surviving element of the rules. Instead, parties in ancillary relief proceedings who are concerned about spouses who may be attempting to salt away their assets should make use of freezing injunctions, search orders, preservation orders and the willingness of the courts to make adverse inferences against unforthcoming parties.

DUTIES ON PARTIES AND LAWYERS

Client's duty

The person responsible for making standard disclosure must certify, amongst other matters, that the duty to disclose is understood, and that to the best of his or her knowledge and belief, the duty has been discharged (**CPR, r. 31.10(6)(b)** and **(c)**). The certification is included in the disclosure statement required by **r. 31.10(5)** (see **50.19**) and has profound implications for the way in which a party should approach the whole disclosure process. **50.30**

Standard disclosure requires disclosure of *only* the documents listed in **r. 31.6**, and so it is not sufficient to conduct an indiscriminate trawl through all documentation in the control of the party, extracting every single item which may have some relevance to the litigation. Whilst this may attract criticism as being expensive, or for 'front-loading' the costs of the case, it is submitted that the resultant saving in time and expense amply redresses the balance.

Under **r. 31.10(6)** and **PD 31A, para. 4.4**, it is clear that the person signing the disclosure statement must have an understanding of the duty to search and all that it entails, and also knowledge of the documents and issues in the case. The responsible person should normally be present at case management conferences and any other hearings where the issue of disclosure is likely to arise. For large corporate parties, or organisations such as local authorities, that person will normally be an in-house lawyer with responsibility for the case, but this situation can occasionally present problems. It may well be that the person with first-hand knowledge of the dispute is a departmental head who does not occupy a senior position in the organisation and who may, therefore, not be the appropriate person to sign the disclosure statement.

Almost every business will have a document archiving and destruction policy. This is absolutely proper. As was stated in *Beckett Bemrose and Hagen Solicitors v Future Mortgages Ltd* [2010] EWHC 1997 (QB), LTL 12/7/2010, it is common practice for files to be destroyed once they are more than six years old (the usual limitation period for most causes of action) as they occupy valuable space, and the same is true of electronic records.

Administrative problems may arise when documents that have to be disclosed emanate from different departments within the organisation. Organisations need to have sound and efficient document management systems. It may well be that 'documents officers' will have to be appointed within organisations for this purpose, as it is clear from the format of the disclosure statement that it cannot be signed by a legal representative. Parties may be well advised to seek legal advice on compliance with the duty.

Legal representative's duties to advise

50.31 At an early stage in a claim, a solicitor should advise his or her client of the obligations of standard disclosure (**PD 31B, para.** 7; *Rockwell Machine Tool Co. Ltd v E. P. Barrus (Concessionaires) Ltd* [1968] 1 WLR 693). The documents to be preserved include electronic documents which would otherwise be deleted in accordance with a document retention policy or otherwise deleted in the ordinary course of business (**PD 31B, para.** 7). Solicitors owe a duty to the court to ensure their clients make full disclosure. As Salmon J said in *Woods v Martins Bank Ltd* [1959] 1 QB 55 at p. 60:

> It cannot be too clearly understood that solicitors owe a duty to the court, as officers of the court, carefully to go through the documents disclosed by their client to make sure, as far as possible, that no relevant documents have been omitted from their clients' affidavit [or list of documents].

It will often be sensible to give advice about keeping receipts and other documents commonly thrown away, and stopping routine destruction of documents. There may also be an obligation to advise a client to make an early and thorough search for documents which may need to be disclosed. It will often be sensible to explain the breadth of meaning of the word 'document' for this purpose (see **50.17**), emphasising that it includes emails and computer records. Solicitors (Law Society's Code for Advocacy, para. 5.1) and counsel (Code of Conduct of the Bar of England and Wales, para. 608(d)) must withdraw from a case if the client refuses to authorise the disclosure of documents which should be disclosed to the other side.

LIST GENERALLY CONCLUSIVE

50.32 There is a general rule that statements by a party about the status of documents in his control are conclusive at all stages up to the trial. In *Paddick v Associated Newspapers Ltd* [2003] EWHC 2991 (QB), LTL 12/12/2003, the claimant gave standard disclosure of extracts from two witness statements, and stated that the undisclosed parts were irrelevant. Disclosure of these parts was refused, the claimant's assertion as to relevance being conclusive. See also *Loutchansky v Times Newspapers* [2001] EWCA Civ 536, [2002] QB 321; *GE Capital Corporate Finance Group Ltd v Bankers Trust Co.* [1995] 1 WLR 172. Where a party credibly asserts that a category of documents is privileged, that assertion is also ordinarily a complete answer to an application for disclosure (*Beckham v News Group Newspapers Ltd* [2005] EWHC 2252 (QB), LTL 25/10/2005).

The purpose behind the general rule that statements on matters such as the privileged nature of documents withheld from disclosure are conclusive is the need to avoid mini trials at the interlocutory stage (*West London Pipeline and Storage Ltd v Total UK Ltd* [2008] EWHC 1729 (Comm), [2008] 2 CLC 258). While this is a very strong general rule, it is not absolute, because otherwise a party will be the judge in his own cause, and ultimately claims to privilege have to be proved. Beatson J referred to the following options where a claim to privilege is disputed:

(a) finding that the evidence before the court does not establish the privilege, and ordering inspection;
(b) ordering further evidence to be produced on oath on the claim to privilege;
(c) inspecting the documents under **CPR, r. 31.19** (for which see **50.35** and the principles laid down in *Atos Consulting Ltd v Avis Europe plc* [2007] EWHC 323 (TCC), [2008] Bus LR Digest D20); and
(d) ordering cross-examination of the witness making the claim to privilege under **r. 32.7**. This should be done only in an extreme case and where there is no alternative relief.

INSPECTION AND COPYING OF DOCUMENTS

The right of inspection of a disclosed document is contained in **CPR, r. 31.3**, which provides that a party to whom a document has been disclosed has a right to inspect it, except where: **50.33**

(a) the document is no longer in the control of the party who disclosed it;
(b) the party disclosing the document has a right or duty to withhold inspection of it (see **50.50** to **50.82**);
(c) the disclosing party considers that it would be disproportionate to the issues in the case to permit inspection of documents within a category or class of document disclosed under **r. 31.6(b)** (adverse documents) (see **50.36**); or
(d) disclosure and inspection arises out of cross-border mediations to which **r. 78.26** applies (see **73.14**).

Written notice of a wish to inspect a document must be given to the party who disclosed it (**r. 31.15 (a)**) and inspection must be permitted not more than seven days after the date of receipt of that notice (**r. 31.15(b)**). A party may, instead of physical inspection, request a copy of the document, and, provided there is also an undertaking to pay reasonable copying costs, the party who disclosed the document must supply a copy not later than seven days after the date of receipt of the request (**r. 31.15(c)**). This rule is unclear, but it is submitted that the seven-day period in respect of supplying copies should begin when the undertaking to pay for the copies is given.

The parties should cooperate at an early stage in an endeavour to agree the format in which electronic documents should be inspected (**PD 31A, para. 2A.3**). In case of difficulty or disagreement, the matter should be resolved by directions, preferably at the first case management conference.

There is in general no duty of confidence between opposing parties in litigation, so no restrictions (beyond the undertaking not to use documents for collateral purposes, see **50.45**, and any confidentiality undertakings a party is prepared to give) will be imposed as to which individuals will be allowed to inspect the documents on the inspecting party's side (*Virgin Media Communications Ltd v British Sky Broadcasting Group plc* [2008] EWCA Civ 612, [2008] 1 WLR 2854). Despite this, it seems that it is appropriate to require solicitors to give individual confidentiality undertakings where disclosed documents are commercially sensitive (*Interdigital Technology Corporation v Nokia Corporation* [2008] EWHC 969 (Pat), LTL 19/5/2008, where the undertakings were that the documents would remain in the solicitor's premises except to the extent necessary for making applications to the court and delivering papers to counsel, but no undertaking was required from counsel).

Under **r. 31.12** the court may make an order for specific inspection, which is an order that a party permit inspection of a document, named in the order, which the party sought to exclude from inspection under **r. 31.2(2)** (permission to inspect would be disproportionate to the issues in the case, see **50.36**). An application for an order under **r. 31.12** must be made by application notice (see **50.41**).

Inspection of documents mentioned in statements of case etc.

50.34 Apart from the general right to inspect documents disclosed either by standard or specific disclosure (see **50.33**), a party has, under **CPR, r. 31.14(1)**, the right to inspect a document mentioned in:

(a) a statement of case;
(b) a witness statement;
(c) a witness summary; or
(d) an affidavit.

This particular right arises as soon as the document concerned is mentioned, even prior to it being listed in form N265. It is submitted that the limitations on inspection listed in **r. 31.3** (see **50.33**), apply here too. The word 'mentioned' in **r. 31.14** is as general as is possible. A document does not have to be relied on, or referred to, in any particular way or for any particular purpose, in order for it to be mentioned. It is enough if there is a direct allusion to it (*Rubin v Expandable Ltd* [2008] EWCA Civ 59, [2008] 1 WLR 1099). In *Rubin v Expandable Ltd* a witness statement said 'he wrote to me', which was held to be a direct allusion to the letter. Inspection may be objected to using the procedure in **r. 31.19** (see **50.35**), for example, on the ground that the document referred to is protected by privilege (*Rubin v Expandable Ltd*, where the fact that **r. 31.14** applied to the letter did not waive any right or duty to object to inspection on the ground of privilege or public interest). Further reasons for refusing inspection include length, volume, confidentiality and public interest immunity (*Tweed v Parades Commission for Northern Ireland* [2006] UKHL 53, [2007] 1 AC 650). If a party makes reference to a document which is not in its control, the appropriate course will be to seek to obtain the document by means of an order under **r. 31.17** (orders for disclosure against a person not a party), **r. 34.2(4)** and (5) (witness summons), or **r. 34.8** (evidence by deposition).

In *Bennett v Compass Group UK and Ireland Ltd* [2002] EWCA Civ 642, [2002] ICR 1177, it was held that the defendants were entitled to inspect the claimant's GP and hospital notes under **CPR, r. 31.14**, because they had been referred to in the medical report attached to the particulars of claim. This case was decided under the rule before it was amended on 25 March 2002. The current version of **r. 31.14**, by sub-para. (2), requires a court order for inspection of documents referred to in experts' reports. An expert's report must state the substance of all material instructions on which the report is based (**r. 35.10(3)**). However, in relation to those instructions, the court will not order disclosure of any specific document or permit any questioning in court other than by the party who instructed the expert, unless it is satisfied that there are reasonable grounds to consider that the statement of material instructions is inaccurate or incomplete (**r. 35.10(4)**).

REFUSAL TO DISCLOSE OR PERMIT INSPECTION

50.35 A person holding a document may dispute aspects of disclosure or inspection on a number of bases, namely:

(a) there may be factual disputes about the disclosability or existence of the document;
(b) there may be factual disputes about whether the document is or has ever been under the party's control;
(c) there may be a claim by a person under **CPR, r. 31.3(2)**, that it would be 'disproportionate' to the issues in the case to permit inspection of documents (see **50.36**);

(d) there may be a claim to withhold inspection on the basis of private privilege, i.e. professional legal privilege, litigation privilege, or the privilege against self-incrimination (see **50.50** to **50.79**);
(e) there may be a claim to withhold disclosure on the basis of public interest immunity (see **50.80** to **50.82**);
(f) where the disclosure of the identities of persons named in documents would interfere with their private lives (European Convention on Human Rights, **art. 8**, in the **Human Rights Act 1998, sch. 1**; *Webster v Ridgeway Foundation School Governors* [2009] EWHC 1140 (QB), [2009] ELR 439);
(g) where the disclosure of personal data is contrary to the Data Protection Act 1998 (see **50.96**); and
(h) where there is a claim that the documents contain confidential information (which rarely succeeds, see **50.66**).

Under **CPR, r. 31.19(3)**, a person who claims to have a right or a duty to withhold inspection of a document or part of a document must assert the right or duty in writing and state the grounds on which it is claimed. That assertion must be in the list in which the document is disclosed, or, if there has been no list, in a notice to the person wishing to inspect the document (**r. 31.19(4)**). Any party may then apply to the court under **r. 31.19(5)** to decide whether a claim made under **r. 31.19(3)** should be upheld. Thus an application for the court's decision on whether a claim to withhold inspection is justified may be made either by the party seeking inspection or the party resisting it. It is suggested in **PD 31A, para. 6.1**, that a claim to withhold inspection of a document does not require an application to the court, so that, generally speaking, it is the party who wishes to challenge that claim who must apply to the court. Although this is applicable in the case of disputes about private privilege, in the case of public interest immunity **r. 31.19(1)** provides that a person may apply to the court, without notice to other parties, for an order permitting disclosure of a document to be withheld on the ground that disclosure would damage the public interest. To decide an application under **r. 31.19(1)** or (3), the court may require the person seeking to withhold inspection of a document to produce it to the court, and it may invite any person, whether or not a party, to make representations (**r. 31.19(6)**).

On a hearing under **r. 31.19**, *Atos Consulting Ltd v Avis Europe plc* [2007] EWHC 323 (TCC), [2008] Bus LR Digest D20, held that the correct procedure is:

(a) to consider the evidence produced on the application;
(b) to uphold the right to withhold inspection if this is established on the evidence and no sufficient grounds are put forward for challenging that right;
(c) to order inspection if the evidence does not establish a right to withhold the documents;
(d) to order further evidence to be produced if insufficient grounds have been shown for challenging the alleged right to withhold, or for the court to inspect the documents if there is no other means of deciding the matter; and
(e) to invite representations after any inspection.

On the facts, redacted parts of certain board minutes were irrelevant as they did not relate to the project in issue or related matters, so no inspection was ordered for these documents. Redacted parts of certain reports were alleged to contain privileged material, but the reports had been compiled by employees rather than lawyers, so there were sufficient grounds in the challenge to justify inspection. Disclosure of a redacted version of a document with the names of children removed did not amount to a concession that the whole of the document was relevant in *Webster v Ridgeway Foundation School Governors* [2009] EWHC 1140 (QB), [2009] ELR 439. In *Real Estate Opportunities Ltd v Aberdeen Asset Managers Jersey Ltd* [2006] EWHC 3249 (Ch), *The Times*, 23 January 2007, an order was made under **r. 31.19(5)** for inspection of interview transcripts supplied to one of the parties by the Financial Services Authority.

Commentary

For the practice in anti-competition cases involving the Commission of the European Communities, see *Akzo Nobel Chemicals Ltd v Commission of the European Communities* (cases T-125 and T-253/03) [2008] Bus LR 348.

Inspection disproportionate to the case

50.36 Under **CPR, r. 31.3(2)**, a party who considers that it would be disproportionate to the issues in the case to permit inspection of documents within a category or class of document, is not required to permit inspection of those documents, but must state in the disclosure statement that inspection of those documents will not be permitted on the ground that to do so would be disproportionate.

Inspection of a redacted version of a school's database recording the behaviour of pupils, with the names of the pupils removed, was a very substantial task and regarded as disproportionate within the meaning of **r. 31.3(2)** in *Webster v Ridgeway Foundation School Governors* [2009] EWHC 1140 (QB), [2009] ELR 439.

ORDERS OR AGREEMENTS LIMITING OR AFFECTING DISCLOSURE

50.37 Standard disclosure may be dispensed with or limited by the court or by agreement between the parties under **CPR, r. 31.5(1)(b)**, or (c), (standard disclosure), or under **r. 31.5(7)(a)** or **(f)** (menu option disclosure). Any written agreement between the parties, should be lodged with the court (**PD 31A, para. 1.4**). These powers can also be used at a later stage, with the effect of varying the initial disclosure order, provided there has been a change of circumstances (*Serious Organised Crime Agency v Namli* [2011] EWCA Civ 1411, LTL 29/11/2011). On the fast track the court may decide not to direct standard disclosure, but may direct that no disclosure takes place, or specify the documents or classes of documents which the parties must disclose (**CPR, r. 28.3(2)**). This is likely to occur if, for example, whether in pursuance of a pre-action protocol or otherwise, there has already been substantial or total disclosure at some early stage.

The fact that the ultimate responsibility for case management rests with the court precludes the parties from agreeing a form of disclosure without approval. It may well be that the court will not be prepared to accept an agreement between the parties, in which event it will supplant the agreement with its own orders under **r. 28.3** in fast track cases or **r. 29.2** in cases on the multi-track (**r. 31.5**). Often this may be because the court, having scrutinised the documents before it, decides that it would be appropriate to limit standard disclosure to what it perceives to be the relevant issues. For example, where the respective statements of case make it clear that the whole litigation turns on whether a written contract was or was not subsequently varied by agreement between the parties, the court might limit disclosure to 'documents relevant to the issue as to whether or not the contract dated 25 February 2013 was varied in the course of correspondence between the parties, between 15 April and 8 May 2013'.

Staged disclosure

50.38 Under **CPR, r. 31.13**, the court may direct, or the parties may agree in writing, that disclosure or inspection, or both, shall take place in stages. This may be appropriate, for example, in personal injuries claims if the court has ordered split trials of liability and quantum. It may also be appropriate in complex litigation, where to ensure the claim is managed efficiently the court may order the parties to disclose documents limited to selected issues, with a view to the case being reappraised at a later case management hearing. Although the rules are silent on the point, it is submitted that an agreement for staged disclosure should also be lodged with the court, in the same manner as an agreement for disclosure has to be lodged under **PD 31A, para. 1.4**.

Clarification of material

The court has the ability to order a party, under **CPR, Part 18**, to clarify any matter which is in dispute in the proceedings, or to give additional information in relation to any such matter, whether or not the matter is contained or referred to in a statement of case (see **chapter 30**). **50.39**

FAILURE TO DISCLOSE DOCUMENTS

Under **CPR, r. 31.21**, a party who has not disclosed, or not permitted inspection of, a document may not rely on it, unless the court gives permission. An application for permission is considered applying the overriding objective. Key issues will include the importance of the documents, the reasons why they were not disclosed, the extent of any notice given to the other party of their contents, and the extent of any prejudice to the other party. **50.40**

Failure to preserve documents covered by standard disclosure after the commencement of proceedings may result in adverse inferences being drawn (*Infabrics Ltd v Jaytex Ltd (No. 2)* [1985] FSR 75). Before the commencement of proceedings there is no duty on parties to preserve documents (*Douglas v Hello! Ltd (No. 2)* [2003] EWHC 55 (Ch), [2003] 1 All ER 1087). As a result, adverse inferences may be drawn in the case of destruction of documents before proceedings are commenced only if there is clear evidence that the destruction was deliberate and in anticipation of litigation (*Earles v Barclays Bank plc* [2009] EWHC 2500 (QB), *The Times*, 20 October 2009). Pre-action destruction of documents may be reflected in the order for costs even if adverse inferences cannot be drawn (*Earles v Barclays Bank plc*).

Commentary

SPECIFIC DISCLOSURE

Jurisdiction and procedure

A party who wishes to obtain copies of particular documents which are believed to be in the custody of another party may make an application for specific disclosure under **CPR, r. 31.12**, and **PD 31A, para. 5.1**. Applications for specific disclosure are most frequently made after standard disclosure has been given, and the disclosed documents have been inspected. There is no restriction in this respect, and the court also has jurisdiction to order specific disclosure before standard disclosure has taken place (*Dayman v Canyon Holdings Ltd* (2006) LTL 11/1/2006). An early application may not accord with the overriding objective, particularly if its effect is to increase costs. Until an issue is pleaded specific disclosure will not be ordered (*Taranissi v British Broadcasting Corporation* [2008] EWHC 2486 (QB), LTL 24/10/2008). The procedure is summarised in **procedural checklist 26**, which is at the front of the book. **50.41**

If the application is made and granted, the court may make an order under **CPR, r. 31.12**, ordering a party to do one or more of the following:

(a) disclose documents or classes of documents specified in the order;
(b) carry out a search to the extent stated in the order;
(c) disclose any documents located as a result of that search.

Any application for an order under **r. 31.12** must be made by application notice, specifying the order that the applicant intends to ask the court to make, and must be supported by evidence (**PD 31A, para. 5.2**). The rules do not provide what this evidence should contain, but it is suggested that it should briefly explain the nature of the dispute, the stage reached in the proceedings, and the facts which lead the applicant to conclude that the documents sought exist, are disclosable and are within the control of the opposing party. The documents sought from the other side are commonly described in a schedule to the draft order. They must be described with reasonable precision. An application for disclosure of 'all documents relating to [the other side's] financial and tax affairs which are necessary to prove the quantum of his counterclaim' was held to be too imprecise in *Morgans v Needham* (1999) *The Times*, 5 November 1999.

PD 31A, para. 5.3, provides that 'the grounds on which the order is sought' may be set out in the application notice itself or in the evidence filed in support. **CPR, r. 31.12**, does not specify the form in which compliance with an order for specific disclosure should be undertaken. Form N265 (which is expressed to be for standard rather than specific disclosure) could be adapted, but it is likely that the court will want more formality and would require the party against whom the order is made to file evidence, or certify in some form whether the documents exist, and the extent of any search made.

The court may make an order for costs on such an application, or, where appropriate, may reserve the costs to abide the determination of the issue as to whether or not the documents disclosed are relevant.

Discretion to order specific disclosure

50.42 **PD 31A, para. 5.4**, provides that in deciding whether or not to make an order for specific disclosure, the court will take into account all the circumstances of the case, and in particular, the overriding objective. The overriding objective requires the parties, so far as possible and so far as economically reasonable, to have access to documents which might help their case (*Commissioners of Inland Revenue v Exeter City AFC Ltd* [2004] BCC 519). In this case extensive disclosure was ordered of Inland Revenue documents relating to voluntary arrangement cases involving about 20 to 30 other football clubs. The issue raised had national importance, and the costs of the exercise were not disproportionate. In *Chantrey Vellacott v Convergence Group plc* (2006) LTL 6/2/2006 specific disclosure, in the form of an order to conduct a proper search for emails and draft documents, was ordered primarily because the claim was likely to turn on the documents. In *Harrods Ltd v Times Newspapers Ltd* [2006] EWCA Civ 294, LTL 22/2/2006, the Court of Appeal said that a party was not permitted to go on a roving exercise (also sometimes called a fishing expedition). The defendant had criticised the claimant's employment practices, and had named two individual executives in a published article. It was held that an order for disclosure against the claimant should be limited to documents relating to the two named executives. *Simba-Tola v Elizabeth Fry Hostel* [2001] EWCA Civ 1371, LTL 30/7/2001, concerned an allegation of racial discrimination against the claimant by other residents at the hostel. The hostel had disclosed its file on the claimant and its log book. None of the alleged incidents were recorded in these documents. The claimant sought disclosure of the hostel's files on other residents to see whether the incidents were recorded on those files. The Court of Appeal held it would not be proportionate to make an order for disclosure that would result in duplication. Further, as the court had seen the disclosed file and log book, it was possible to conclude that the further files would not have any relevant information. Further disclosure was therefore refused.

Paragraph 5.4 concludes by warning that:

> if the court concludes that the party from whom specific disclosure is sought has failed adequately to comply with the obligations imposed by an order for disclosure (whether by failing to make a sufficient search for documents or otherwise) the court will usually make such order as is necessary to ensure that those obligations are properly complied with.

This principle was applied in *Ovlas Trading SA v Strand (London) Ltd* [2009] EWHC 1025 (Ch), LTL 30/6/2009. Specific disclosure is not limited to documents covered by standard disclosure in **CPR, r. 31.6**, and it is possible, for example, to use **r. 31.12** to obtain disclosure of documents relevant solely to credit if sufficient grounds are shown (*Favor Easy Management Ltd v Wu* [2010] EWCA Civ 1630, [2011] 1 WLR 1803, at [20]).

Specific disclosure is often used to challenge the extent of the search made when giving standard disclosure (see **r. 31.12(2)(b)**; and see **50.20**). On such an application the court should take into account the factors in **r. 31.7(2)**, and (in relation to electronic documents) **PD 31B**,

para. 21, in considering the reasonableness of the proposed search (*Fiddes v Channel 4 Television Corporation* [2010] EWCA Civ 516, LTL 24/3/2010).

AUTHENTICITY OF DOCUMENTS DISCLOSED

The authenticity of documents disclosed to a party under **CPR, Part 31**, is deemed to be admitted, unless the party serves notice requiring the document to be proved at trial (**r. 32.19**). A notice to prove a document (form N268) must be served by the latest date for serving witness statements, or within seven days of disclosure of the document, whichever is later (**r. 32.19(2)**). **50.43**

CONTINUING DUTY TO DISCLOSE

The duty imposed by an order to give disclosure continues until the conclusion of the proceedings, that is, until the court gives its final judgment or order in the proceedings (which take effect when made: **CPR, r. 40.7**). If documents, to which a duty of disclosure extends, come to a party's notice at any time during the proceedings, every other party must be notified immediately (**r. 31.11(2)**). **PD 31A, para. 3.3**, provides that this should be done by a 'supplemental list', presumably in form N265. This further reinforces the suggestion made above that the duty of honest disclosure is precisely parallel to that under the previous rule. **50.44**

COLLATERAL USE OF DISCLOSED DOCUMENTS

Following previous law and practice, it is provided in **CPR, r. 31.22**, that a party to whom a document has been disclosed may use such document only for the purposes of the proceedings in which it is disclosed. A similar restriction on collateral use applies to electronic documents questionnaires (**r. 31.22(4)**). There is a similar implied obligation on parties to an English arbitration not to disclose or use documents prepared for and used in the arbitration for any purpose outside the arbitration (*Ali Shipping Corporation v Shipyard Trogir* [1999] 1 WLR 314). There are exceptions in **r. 31.22(1)** where: **50.45**

(a) the document has been read to or by the court, or referred to, at a hearing that has been held in public; or
(b) the court gives permission; or
(c) the party who disclosed the document and the person to whom the document belongs, agree.

The court may, however, make an order restricting or prohibiting the use of a document which has been disclosed, even though that document has been read to or by the court, or referred to at a public hearing (**r. 31.22(2)**). An application for such an order may be made by a party or by any person to whom the document belongs (**r. 31.22(3)**).

This preserves the principle that, as one is required to complete disclosure with absolute honesty and thus confidential documents may be disclosed, it is right that a party should have the protection of knowing that the documents are to be used only for the current litigation. The rule, which evolved from *Riddick v Thames Board Mills Ltd* [1977] QB 881, is that a document disclosed in proceedings may not be used, for example, for unrelated commercial purposes, or as the basis on which to found another claim. Indeed, misuse of such documents will constitute a serious contempt of court. The prohibition against using material for collateral purposes does not apply to documents referred to in affidavits and witness statements, as these are regarded as having been voluntarily disclosed (*Cassidy v Hawcroft* [2000] CPLR 624).

Confidentiality clubs

50.46 Occasionally a party to litigation establishes a 'confidentiality club' (also known as a 'confidentiality ring'), which restricts the persons who can have access to documents disclosed under **CPR, Part 31**. The purpose is to reduce the risk of the documents, or the information they contain, being used for a purpose outside the present proceedings. Confidentiality club orders are exceptional, and should be made only if there are grounds for deciding that the restrictions on collateral use set out in **r. 31.22** are insufficient and that the justice of the case demands greater protection (*Roussel-Uclaf v ICI (No. 2)* [1990] RPC 45; *Porton Capital Technology Funds v 3M UK Holdings Ltd* [2010] EWHC 114 (Comm), LTL 8/2/2010). Such orders are usually inappropriate for small businesses, because all the directors and key personnel are likely to be involved in providing proper instructions to the relevant lawyers (*Croft House Care Ltd v Durham County Council* [2010] EWHC 909 (TCC), LTL 7/7/2010).

After use in a public hearing

50.47 The prohibition against collateral use of disclosed documents disappears once the documents have been used in a public hearing (**CPR, r. 31.22(1)**, although the words 'or referred to' in **r. 31.22(1)(a)** may cause some difficulty). In *SmithKline Beecham Biologicals SA v Connaught Laboratories Inc.* [1999] 4 All ER 498, documents pre-read by the judge and 'economically' referred to in court were held to be in the public domain. The phrase 'read to or by the court' has been interpreted as including documents made available to the judge with the reading list before the trial starts (*Derby v Weldon (No. 2)* (1988) *The Times*, 20 October 1988).

Once documents have been used in open court, an order restricting or prohibiting subsequent use will only be made if there are very good reasons for departing from the usual rule of publicity (*Lilly Icos Ltd v Pfizer Ltd* [2002] EWCA Civ 2, [2002] 1 WLR 2253). Merely asserting a document is confidential is insufficient. Specific reasons why a party would be damaged by subsequent use are required. Permission to use disclosed material will be refused where there is a very strong risk of dishonest or malicious use of the material (*Eronat v Tabbah* [2002] EWCA Civ 950, LTL 10/7/2002).

Permission for collateral use

50.48 An order may, in any event, be made by the court permitting a party to use a document for other purposes, in its general discretion (**CPR, r. 31.22(1)(b)**). One example is *Apple Corps Ltd v Apple Computer Inc.* [1992] 1 CMLR 969, where documents, which had been disclosed in English proceedings, were required for the purposes of parallel proceedings before the European Commission, which constituted a cogent reason why the documents were permitted to be used outside the English proceedings. In relation to documents relating to an English arbitration, the High Court has jurisdiction to grant injunctions restraining and declarations that the confidentiality obligation does not apply (*Emmott v Michael Wilson and Partners Ltd* [2008] EWCA Civ 184, [2008] Bus LR 1361). Generally, arbitration documents should be kept confidential, unless disclosure is required in the interests of justice (*Ali Shipping Corporation v Shipyard Trogir* [1999] 1 WLR 314), such as where a court might be misled if it does not have access to the documents (*Emmott v Michael Wilson and Partners Ltd*). A material consideration in deciding whether to lift an order under **r. 31.22** is whether an order for non-party disclosure under **r. 31.17** (see **50.90**) could have been obtained (*SmithKline Beecham plc v Generics (UK) Ltd* [2003] EWCA Civ 1109, [2004] 1 WLR 1479 at [37]). There are cases where the discretion has to be exercised by balancing competing public interests (see *Marlwood Commercial Inc. v Kozeny* [2004] EWCA Civ 798, [2005] 1 WLR 104, where the competing interests were the due administration of justice of the civil claim and the investigation of an alleged serious fraud).

Family proceedings documents

The general rule is that hearings in family proceedings are in private (Family Procedure Rules 2010 (SI 2010/2955), r. 27.10). Part 12 of the Family Procedure Rules concerns proceedings relating to children (defined in rr. 12.1 and 12.2). Any information about proceedings relating to children held in private can be communicated only as permitted by rr. 12.72 to 12.75. The court may give permission for further disclosure (r. 12.73(1)(b)), but nothing in the rules permits communication to the public at large, or any section of the public (r. 12.73(2)). Other family proceedings are not automatically covered by secrecy even if heard in private. See *Clibbery v Allan* [2002] EWCA Civ 45, [2002] Fam 261, in which publication was allowed. **50.49**

PRIVILEGE

Introduction

A disclosed document may be withheld from inspection if the disclosing party has a right or duty to withhold it (**CPR, r. 31.3(1)(b)**). Such a right or duty is called a 'privilege'. A party asserting a privilege must do so in writing and state the grounds on which it is claimed (**r. 31.19(3)**). This must be done in the list in which the document is disclosed, if a list is given (**r. 31.19(4)**). Space is provided in the middle of the second page of form N265 for this purpose. **50.50**

There are three heads of privilege: the privilege against self-incrimination (**50.51** and **50.52**); legal professional privilege (**50.53** to **50.63**); and 'without prejudice' communications (**50.68**). The three heads of privilege confer a right to withhold disclosure. Public interest immunity (**50.80** to **50.82**) arises from a duty to withhold disclosure. The burden of proof in a disputed claim for privilege rests on the person asserting the privilege (*West London Pipeline and Storage Ltd v Total UK Ltd* [2008] EWHC 1729 (Comm), [2008] 2 CLC 258; *Akzo Nobel Chemicals Ltd v Commission of the European Communities* (cases T-125 and T-253/03) [2008] Bus LR 348). When considering these different heads of privilege, it is worth bearing in mind the comment made by Lord Edmund-Davies in *Waugh v British Railways Board* [1980] AC 521 at p. 543:

> we should start from the basis that the public interest is, on balance, best served by rigidly confining within narrow limits the cases where material relevant to litigation may be lawfully withheld. Justice is better served by candour than by suppression.

The court will not order disclosure and/or inspection where disclosing and/or allowing inspection would be an offence under English criminal law, but the court has a discretion whether to order disclosure and/or inspection which would be an offence under a foreign law to which the disclosing party is subject (*Morris v Banque Arabe et Internationale d'Investissement SA* (1999) *The Times*, 23 December 1999).

PRIVILEGE AGAINST SELF-INCRIMINATION

Common law rule

In *Blunt v Park Lane Hotel Ltd* [1942] 2 KB 253 Goddard LJ said, at p. 257: **50.51**

> the rule is that no one is bound to answer any question [or to produce any document] if the answer thereto would, in the opinion of the judge, have a tendency to expose [him] to any criminal charge, penalty, or forfeiture which the judge regards as reasonably likely to be preferred or sued for.

The claimant had objected to answering questions in a slander claim on the ground that her answers would tend to expose her to the risk of ecclesiastical penalties. It was held that it was purely fantastic to suppose that in 1942 she would be subject to any ecclesiastical penalty if she admitted adultery, and permission was granted to ask the questions. In civil proceedings

Commentary

the right applies only as regards criminal offences under the law of any part of the United Kingdom and penalties provided for by such law (Civil Evidence Act 1968, s. 14(1)). Exposure to the risk of a penalty under EU legislation forming part of the law of the UK by virtue of the European Communities Act 1972 is a penalty for these purposes (see *Rio Tinto Zinc Corporation v Westinghouse Electric Corporation* [1978] AC 547). A risk of exposure to a civil claim does not raise the privilege (Witnesses Act 1806). Statutory additional damages for breach of copyright are not penalties (*Rank Film Distributors Ltd v Video Information Centre* [1982] AC 380 at p. 425).

In *Rank Film Distributors Ltd v Video Information Centre* [1982] AC 380 it was held that where a criminal charge was more than a contrived, fanciful or remote possibility, the defendant could refuse to provide information by relying on the privilege. The privilege may arise, not only when answering might increase the risk of being prosecuted, but also where the prosecution may make use of the answer in deciding whether to prosecute, and where the prosecution may seek to rely on the answer in establishing guilt (*Den Norske Bank ASA v Antonatos* [1999] QB 271). Merely asserting there is a risk is not enough: the risk must be real and appreciable (*Rank Film Distributors Ltd v Video Information Centre*), and it is a matter for the court to determine the likelihood of a prosecution (*Rio Tinto Zinc Corporation v Westinghouse Electric Corporation* [1978] AC 547).

Subsequent committal proceedings for contempt of court are penal for this purpose (*Cobra Golf Inc. v Rata* [1998] Ch 109; *Memory Corporation plc v Sidhu* [2000] Ch 645), but disqualification proceedings under the Company Directors Disqualification Act 1986 are regulatory rather than penal (*Official Receiver v Stern* [2000] 1 WLR 2230). *Memory Corporation plc v Sidhu* discusses a possible exception to the privilege against incrimination where the risk of prosecution is for perjury arising out of the witness's conduct in the instant case. The cases on this exception are old and unsatisfactory, but the exception is probably good law. *Memory Corporation plc v Sidhu*, however, holds that even if the exception is good law relating to perjury, it does not extend to the risk of proceedings for contempt of court if the answers of a witness to an order requiring disclosure of assets are defective and hence a breach of the order.

The privilege extends to providing documents or answers that tend to expose the wife or husband of the person asserting the privilege to criminal proceedings or proceedings for the recovery of a penalty (Civil Evidence Act 1968, s. 14(1)). As a corporation has legal personality it can claim the privilege (*Triplex Safety Glass Co. Ltd v Lancegaye Safety (1934) Glass Ltd* [1939] 2 KB 395). It may be necessary to distinguish between the corporation and its officers and employees, and to consider whether all or only some of them may be at risk of criminal proceedings (*Sociedade Nacional de Combustiveis de Angola UEE v Lundqvist* [1991] 2 QB 310).

The precise scope of the privilege has been modified as a result of the incorporation into UK law of the European Convention on Human Rights by the **Human Rights Act 1998**. In criminal cases the privilege may be claimed only after the witness has been sworn and a question has been put. The pre-Human Rights Act position that the privilege applied to incriminating documents and articles (*Rank Film Distributors Ltd v Video Information Centre* [1982] AC 380) as well as answers to questions, is no longer followed. In *C plc v P* [2007] EWCA Civ 493, [2008] Ch 1, it was held that the privilege does not apply to material that has an existence independent of the relevant order. The result was that free-standing evidence (in this case images of children found on a computer which had been imaged under the terms of a search order) which had not been created in compliance with the terms of the search order could be passed to the police. The distinction is between 'real' or 'independent' evidence, which is not protected by the privilege, and 'compelled testimony', which is (per Longmore LJ at [38]).

The privilege against self-incrimination may be lost by the turn of events. Obviously, once the party has been tried, whether resulting in a conviction or an acquittal, there is usually no real possibility of a further trial in the criminal courts. The party may be given a pardon, which again eliminates the risk of prosecution (*R v Boyes* (1861) 1 B & S 311). If the Crown Prosecution Service indicate in writing that they will not make use of the information sought for the purposes of any criminal proceedings against the party or the party's spouse, and if a clause stating that no disclosure made in compliance with the order will be used in evidence in the prosecution of any offence committed by the party or spouse is included in the order, the court may conclude there is no realistic risk of use by the prosecution, and hold that the privilege does not apply (*AT and T Istel Ltd v Tully* [1993] AC 45).

Statutory limitations on the rule

One of the consequences of the privilege against self-incrimination is that the risk of documents being used against the party for the purposes of criminal proceedings is obviously greater in cases where the defendant is alleged to have been particularly dishonest, and the worse the conduct alleged the greater the prospect of a successful claim to the privilege. After *Rank Film Distributors Ltd v Video Information Centre* [1982] AC 380 there were fears that the privilege would operate to frustrate the use of search orders in intellectual property piracy claims, and Parliament intervened by enacting the Senior Courts Act 1981, s. 72, which has the effect of removing the privilege against self-incrimination in relation to claims involving the infringement of intellectual property rights and passing off, but also provides that the answers given shall not be used in any related criminal prosecution. Intellectual property has a wide meaning for this purpose (see s. 72(5)). Voicemail messages that contain both personal and commercially confidential material will come within the definition if the commercially confidential messages form a substantial proportion of the whole (*Phillips v News Group Newspapers Ltd* [2012] UKSC 28, [2013] 1 AC 1). **50.52**

Similarly, where the information sought for the purposes of civil proceedings may lead to a prosecution under the Theft Act 1968, the privilege against self-incrimination has been removed by the Theft Act 1968, s. 31(1). The Fraud Act 2006, s. 13, removes the privilege for fraud offences under the Act and for related offences. In *Kensington International Ltd v Republic of Congo* [2007] EWCA Civ 1128, [2008] 1 WLR 1144, the claimant was experiencing difficulty in enforcing a money judgment against the Republic of Congo. It obtained a *Norwich Pharmacal* order (see **50.97**) against a company and an individual who had been engaged in oil trading with the Republic requiring them to disclose information about certain payments said to have been bribes. It was held that the *Norwich Pharmacal* application was a form of 'proceedings relating to property' as required by s. 13, because it was ancillary to the ongoing attempts to enforce the judgment debt, and the word 'property' includes 'money' (s. 13(3)). The corruption offences identified by the respondents were not offences under the Fraud Act 2006, but they were 'related offences' for the purposes of s.13, as they involved 'fraudulent conduct or purpose'. In addition to conspiracy to defraud, offences are 'related' within the meaning of s. 13(4) if they involve any form of fraudulent conduct or purpose, so are not limited to offences involving fraudulent intent. This is judged by reference to the essential character of the offence rather than the means by which it was committed. On this basis, an offence under the Proceeds of Crime Act 2002, s. 328, is a related offence even if, for example, the underlying offence relates to drug trafficking (*JSC BTA Bank v Ablyazov* [2009] EWCA Civ 1124, [2010] 1 WLR 976). These various provisions do not, of course, completely remove the privilege from civil proceedings. It still has an effect, for example, in civil assault cases, cases involving sexual offences, and in motoring claims.

LEGAL PROFESSIONAL PRIVILEGE

There are two classes of legal professional privilege: one arises out of the relationship of legal adviser and client, even where no litigation is contemplated (legal advice privilege, see **50.55**); **50.53**

Commentary

and the other relates to communications connected with contemplated or pending litigation (see **50.60**). The privilege covers communications with a wide range of lawyers, including individuals who are not solicitors or barristers, but who are authorised persons for the purpose of providing advocacy, litigation, conveyancing or probate services (Legal Services Act 2007, s. 190). It covers in-house lawyers (*Alfred Crompton Amusement Machines Ltd v Commissioners of Customs and Excise (No. 2)* [1974] AC 405). It also extends to certain patent proceedings (Patents Act 1977, s. 103). It is, however, restricted to the legal profession and so does not apply to tax law advice provided by an accountant (*R (Prudential plc) v Special Commissioner of Income Tax* [2010] EWCA 1094, [2011] QB 669 or to doctors, priests or others entrusted with confidences (*Wheeler v Le Marchant* (1881) 17 Ch D 675). The privilege belongs to the client, not to the solicitor, though the solicitor is under a duty to the client to assert it unless it is waived by the client. A clinical case manager appointed to assist a severely disabled person who attends a conference or other occasion normally attracting legal professional privilege, is obliged to respect the claimant's privilege (*Wright v Sullivan* [2005] EWCA Civ 656, [2006] 1 WLR 172).

A number of cases in the House of Lords have described legal professional privilege as not merely a procedural right, but an important substantive right. Examples are *R (Morgan Grenfell and Co. Ltd) v Special Commissioner of Income Tax* [2002] UKHL 21, [2003] 1 AC 563 at [7]; *Three Rivers District Council v Bank of England (No. 6)* [2004] UKHL 48, [2005] 1 AC 610 at [25]; and *McE v Prison Service of Northern Ireland* [2009] UKHL 15, [2009] 1 AC 908 at [6]–[7]. Legal professional privilege is a fundamental human right long established in the common law (*R v Derby Magistrates' Court, ex parte B* [1996] AC 487). As Lord Taylor of Gosforth CJ said in this case, unless the privilege is waived by the client or abrogated it is absolute, so that:

> legal professional privilege is thus much more than an ordinary rule of evidence, limited to the facts of a particular case. It is a fundamental condition on which the administration of justice as a whole rests.

The policy behind litigation privilege was described by Sir George Jessel MR in *Anderson v Bank of British Columbia* (1876) 2 ChD 644 as follows, at p. 649:

> as, by reason of the complexity and difficulty of our law, litigation can only be properly conducted by professional men, it is absolutely necessary that a man, in order to prosecute his rights or to defend himself from an improper claim, should have recourse to the assistance of professional lawyers, and it being so absolutely necessary, it is equally necessary, to use a vulgar phrase, that he should be able to make a clean breast of it to the gentleman whom he consults with a view to the prosecution of his claim, or the substantiating his defence against the claim of others; that he should be able to place unrestricted and unbounded confidence in the professional agent, and that the communications he so makes to him should be kept secret, unless with his consent (for it is his privilege, and not the privilege of the confidential agent), that he should be enabled properly to conduct his litigation.

There is a slightly different policy justification for legal advice privilege, which is based on the sanctity of the rule of law. As Lord Scott of Foscote said in *Three Rivers District Council v Bank of England (No. 6)* [2004] UKHL 48, [2005] 1 AC 610 at [34]:

> it is necessary in our society, a society in which the restraining and controlling framework is built upon a belief in the rule of law, that communications between clients and lawyers, whereby the clients are hoping for the assistance of the lawyers' legal skills in the management of their (the clients') affairs, should be secure against the possibility of any scrutiny from others, whether the police, the executive, business competitors, inquisitive busybodies or anyone else.

In recent times legal professional privilege has been regarded as part of the right of privacy guaranteed by the European Convention on Human Rights, art. 8 (*Campbell v United Kingdom* (1992) 15 EHRR 137) and part of EU law (*AM and S Europe Ltd v Commission of the European Communities* (case 155/79) [1983] QB 878). This is subject to art. 8(2), which means the privilege can be overridden for example where this is necessary in the interests of the welfare or protection of children (*Essex County Council v R* [1994] Fam 167).

Statutory exclusion of legal professional privilege

A statute will not exclude legal professional privilege unless it does so expressly or by necessary implication (*R (Morgan Grenfell and Co. Ltd) v Special Commissioner of Income Tax* [2002] UKHL 21, [2003] 1 AC 563). Following *R (Morgan Grenfell and Co. Ltd) v Special Commissioner of Income Tax*, it was held in *B v Auckland District Law Society* [2003] UKPC 38, [2003] 2 AC 736, that the statute in question did not override legal professional privilege either expressly or by necessary implication. Unlike questions relating to confidential documents, protection of legally privileged documents does not depend on balancing competing private and public interests, nor will the privilege be excluded by any common law right to compel production. Circumstances in which a statute will be held to have excluded legal professional privilege by necessary implication will be rare. The presumption against the removal of legal professional privilege is even stronger where general words in a statute merely delegate a power to legislate (*General Mediterranean Holdings SA v Patel* [2000] 1 WLR 272). **50.54**

Legal advice privilege

Confidential communications between a legal representative and client made for the giving or receiving of legal advice are protected by legal professional privilege. This is so whether or not litigation is contemplated. The privilege applies to communications between a client and his legal advisers, to documents evidencing such communications, and to documents intended to be such communications even if they are not in fact communicated. However, these are the limits of the privilege, and it is not open to the court to extend them (*Three Rivers District Council v Bank of England (No. 5)* [2003] EWCA Civ 474, [2003] QB 1556). **50.55**

The principle is that a client should be able to get legal advice in confidence. This raises issues as to who is the client (see **50.56**), and what is legal advice (see **50.57**), for this purpose. Another issue is whether obtaining legal advice must be the dominant purpose of the communication (see **50.58**). Examples are given at **50.59**.

Client Where an individual seeks legal advice, it will usually be obvious that that individual is the client. The answer may not be so obvious where a litigation friend, trustee in bankruptcy, person acting under a power of attorney, or a personal representative is acting for someone else or an estate. In these cases the solicitor's retainer letter will or should make this clear. Where a solicitor is retained by a company or other corporation, it follows from *Three Rivers District Council v Bank of England (No. 5)* [2003] EWCA Civ 474, [2003] QB 1556, that the 'client' will be restricted to those personnel who have been authorised by the company or corporation to retain the services of the solicitor. On the facts the Bank had appointed three officials to deal with the Bank's communications with a private inquiry conducted by Lord Bingham of Cornhill as its 'Bingham Inquiry Unit', or 'BIU'. The BIU had sought legal assistance from a firm of solicitors. It was held that the BIU was the client for the purposes of legal advice privilege, so that communications between the solicitors and any other Bank official, even the Governor of the Bank, would not be protected. This decision may be too restrictive. There are hints in *Three Rivers District Council v Bank of England (No. 6)* [2004] UKHL 48, [2005] 1 AC 610, for example, at [118], that *Three Rivers District Council v Bank of England (No. 5)* might not survive if the matter were to be considered afresh by the House of Lords, but none of their lordships expressed a clear opinion on the issue. **50.56**

As a practical consequence, corporate clients would be well advised to nominate a defined group of suitable employees or officers who will be the client when retaining a solicitor. To ensure that all sensitive communications are covered by the privilege, solicitors should ensure the legal context of the retainer is set out in clear terms in the retainer letter, and should advise the client that only employees and officers in the defined 'client' group prepare documents for use in seeking advice under the retainer.

50.57 **Legal advice** 'Legal advice' covers telling a client the law, and also includes advice as to what should prudently and sensibly be done in the relevant legal context (Taylor LJ in *Balabel v Air India* [1988] Ch 317 at p. 330). Advice will not be protected unless it is for a legal purpose (*McE v Prison Service of Northern Ireland* [2009] UKHL 15, [2009] 1 AC 908). To be protected the advice must be sought or given in a relevant legal context. So, if a solicitor becomes a client's 'man of business' with responsibility for advising the client on all matters of business, such as investment policy and financial matters, the privilege does not apply because without more there is no legal context (*Three Rivers District Council v Bank of England (No. 6)* [2004] UKHL 48, [2005] 1 AC 610 at [38]). In doubtful cases, according to Lord Scott of Foscote, there are two questions. First, did the advice sought relate to the rights, liabilities, obligations or remedies of the client under private law or under public law? Secondly, if so, did the occasion on which the communication took place and its purpose make it reasonable to expect that the privilege would apply? Putting it a different way, according to Lord Rodger of Earlsferry, the important question is whether the lawyer is being asked in his capacity as a lawyer to provide legal advice (at [58]).

In *Balabel v Air India*, approved in *Three Rivers District Council v Bank of England (No. 6)* at [111], Taylor LJ said the privilege is not restricted to specific requests for advice from clients and documents containing legal advice from solicitors. Where information is passed by the solicitor or the client to the other as part of a continuum aimed at keeping both informed, so that advice may later be given, privilege will attach. Further, legal advice is not confined to telling the client the law. It includes advice on what should prudently be done in the relevant legal context.

A preparatory document drawn up by a client, even if created without the intention of sending it to the lawyer, may be protected by legal advice privilege, although such a claim has to be considered restrictively (*Akzo Nobel Chemicals Ltd v Commission of the European Communities* (cases T-125 and T-253/03) [2008] Bus LR 348).

Advice given by a solicitor who is known by the client to be struck off is not protected by legal professional privilege (*Dadourian Group International Inc. v Simms* [2008] EWHC 1784 (Ch), LTL 1/8/2008).

50.58 **Legal advice privilege and dominant purpose** In *Three Rivers District Council v Bank of England (No. 5)* [2003] EWCA Civ 474, [2003] QB 1556, and *Three Rivers District Council v Bank of England (No. 6)* [2004] EWCA Civ 218, [2004] QB 916, the Court of Appeal were of the view that seeking or giving legal advice must be the dominant purpose of the communication if the occasion was to be protected by legal advice privilege. One result was that each communication between the client and solicitor had to be looked at before deciding whether the privilege applied on each occasion (see *United States of America v Philip Morris Inc.* [2004] EWCA Civ 330, *The Times*, 16 April 2004). These Court of Appeal authorities must be considered as wrongly decided on this point given the decision of the House of Lords in *Three Rivers District Council v Bank of England (No. 6)* [2004] UKHL 48, [2005] 1 AC 610, and the approval of the continuum of advice approach in *Balabel v Air India* [1988] Ch 317. Establishing a dominant purpose of obtaining legal advice is, however, a requirement for litigation privilege, see **50.61**.

50.59 **Examples of legal advice privilege** Applying the above principles, legal advice privilege applies, for example, to the following:

(a) communications for the primary object of actual or contemplated civil or criminal proceedings (*Three Rivers District Council v Bank of England (No. 6)* [2004] UKHL 48, [2005] 1 AC 610 at [56]);

(b) conclusions reached by a solicitor from such communications (*Marsh v Sofaer* [2003] EWHC 3334, [2004] PNLR 24);

(c) advice from the solicitor on matters such as the conveyance of property or drawing up of a will (*Three Rivers District Council v Bank of England (No. 6)* [2004] EWCA Civ 218, [2004] QB 916 at [39]; [2004] UKHL 48, [2005] 1 AC 610 at [55]);
(d) confidential information given to a solicitor in the course of giving instructions relating to the drawing up of a will about matrimonial or financial difficulties, or about an anticipated inheritance (*Three Rivers District Council v Bank of England (No. 6)* [2004] UKHL 48, [2005] 1 AC 610 at [106]);
(e) confidential information given to a solicitor retained to give tax advice about family finances and family businesses (*Three Rivers District Council v Bank of England (No. 6)* [2004] UKHL 48, [2005] 1 AC 610 at [106]);
(f) advice or assistance from a lawyer to the promoter or opponent of a private Bill in Parliament (*Three Rivers District Council v Bank of England (No. 6)* [2004] UKHL 48, [2005] 1 AC 610 at [40]);
(g) advice from a solicitor on the best way to present evidence to a private, non-statutory inquiry, a coroner's inquest, a statutory inquiry or an ad hoc inquiry (*Three Rivers District Council v Bank of England (No. 6)* [2004] UKHL 48, [2005] 1 AC 610 at [44]);
(h) advice to a client about public law ramifications of a public inquiry (*Three Rivers District Council v Bank of England (No. 6)* [2004] UKHL 48, [2005] 1 AC 610);
(i) advice from in-house lawyers in the same circumstances as outside lawyers, provided the advice relates to legal as opposed to administrative matters (*Alfred Crompton Amusement Machines Ltd v Commissioners of Customs and Excise (No. 2)* [1974] AC 405); and
(j) instructions and briefs to counsel, and counsel's opinions, drafts and notes.

Legal advice privilege will not apply to the following:

(a) investment advice, or advice given by a solicitor as a patent or estate agent, because the advice is not given by the solicitor in his capacity as a solicitor;
(b) the actual conveyancing documents prepared by the solicitor (*R v Inner London Crown Court, ex parte Baines and Baines* [1988] QB 579, because they are not communications);
(c) a solicitor's client ledger accounts (*Nationwide Building Society v Various Solicitors* [1999] PNLR 53, because they are internal records, not communications dealing with advice);
(d) counsel's endorsement on a brief of the result of a hearing, because it is regarded as *publici juris* (*Nicholl v Jones* (1865) 2 Hem & M 588);
(e) documents prepared by the client's employees with the intention of sending them to the solicitors and in fact sent to the solicitors (*Three Rivers District Council v Bank of England (No. 5)* [2003] EWCA Civ 474, [2003] QB 1556);
(f) documents prepared by the client's employees with the dominant purpose of obtaining legal advice, but which are not sent to the solicitor (*Three Rivers District Council v Bank of England (No. 5)*); or
(g) communications with third parties, including documents obtained from third parties for the purpose of showing them to a solicitor for advice (*Wheeler v Le Marchant* (1881) 17 ChD 675).

Communications connected to litigation

Confidential communications between a solicitor or a client and a third party where the dominant purpose in creating the document is to use it or its contents in order to obtain legal advice or to help in the conduct of litigation which is at that time reasonably in prospect are privileged. This includes: **50.60**

(a) obtaining and collecting evidence to be used in litigation; and
(b) obtaining information which may lead to the obtaining of evidence to be used in litigation (*Anderson v Bank of British Columbia* (1876) 2 ChD 644; *Wheeler v Le Marchant* (1881) 17 ChD 675; *Southwark and Vauxhall Water Co. v Quick* (1878) 3 QBD 315).

This head of privilege is sometimes called litigation privilege. The rule is relatively straightforward in relation to solicitors' communications, and covers letters to and

Commentary

statements from witnesses, and letters to and reports from experts. In *Southwark and Vauxhall Water Co. v Quick* (1878) 3 QBD 315 the Court of Appeal held that, if litigation is reasonably in prospect, privilege attaches to documents brought into existence for the purpose of enabling lawyers to advise whether a claim should be made or resisted, whether or not a decision to instruct lawyers had been made at the time they were brought into being, as long as such purpose was the dominant purpose behind creating the documents. It is not a contempt of court for a client to show its lawyer a document connected to litigation, even where a court order prohibits disclosure of the document to anyone other than named individuals which did not include the lawyer (*Shadrokh-Cigari v Shadrokh-Cigari* [2010] EWCA Civ 21, [2010] 1 WLR 1311).

Documents which came into existence otherwise than for the purposes of the present litigation, but which have been obtained for a party's solicitor for the purpose of use in the present litigation, are not privileged and must be produced to the other for inspection (*Ventouris v Mountain* [1991] 1 WLR 607, CA). *Stax Claimants v Bank of Nova Scotia Channel Islands Ltd* [2007] EWHC 1153 (Ch), LTL 23/5/2007, dealt with meetings to discuss 'battle tactics' between lawyers on opposing sides who might have common interests (here the lawyers represented claimants and third parties). Discussions at such meetings will not be covered by without-prejudice privilege, but might well be protected by legal professional privilege. Views expressed on the strengths and weaknesses of the parties' claims and defences, and discussion of tactics in the litigation, are likely to be privileged. Discussions on disclosure were regarded as difficult, because the documents may or may not have been confidential. Discussion of case management issues and the administration of the litigation do not come within standard disclosure at all.

There is a general rule that 'once privileged, always privileged' (*Calcraft v Guest* [1898] 1 QB 759). Thus, the privilege applies in the existing or contemplated proceedings, and also in any other proceedings. However, the privilege can only be claimed by the person originally entitled to it, or by that person's successor in title to the document. There is no requirement that the person asserting the privilege should be a party to the subsequent proceedings, or that the subsequent claim should have any connection with the original claim (*The Aegis Blaze* [1986] 1 Lloyd's Rep 203).

This head of legal professional privilege does not, according to *Re L (A Minor) (Police Investigation: Privilege)* [1997] AC 16, apply to documents commissioned for the purposes of proceedings under part 4 of the Children Act 1989. This is because proceedings under part 4 are investigative and non-controversial, and are conducted with the welfare of the child as the primary consideration.

Litigation privilege: dominant purpose

50.61 In relation to clients' communications with persons other than their lawyers litigation privilege has a narrower scope than in relation to communications through their lawyers. In *Waugh v British Railways Board* [1980] AC 521 the claimant sought disclosure of an internal enquiry report prepared by two of the defendant's officers two days after the accident which was the subject of the claim. The report was headed 'For the information of the Board's solicitor', but the written evidence on the application for disclosure made it clear that there were in fact two purposes in preparing the report. One was to establish the cause of the accident so that safety measures could be introduced, and the second was to obtain legal advice in the event of any claim. The Board regarded both purposes as of equal importance. It was held that the report had to be disclosed. It would only have been protected by legal professional privilege if the legal advice aspect had been the dominant purpose. According to Lord Edmund-Davies, a dominant purpose is one with a 'clear paramountcy'. A solicitor's assertion that the dominant purpose of a particular communication was the obtaining of legal advice is not conclusive. This has to be determined by the court on the whole of the evidence (*United States of America* *v Philip Morris Inc.* [2003] EWHC 3028 (Comm), LTL 10/12/2003). In *Lask v Gloucester Health Authority* (1991) 2 Med LR 379 it was held that an accident report which was required by National Health circulars was not privileged, because the dominant purpose was the prevention of similar accidents, rather than seeking legal advice.

Just because a report is compiled shortly after the relevant event does not mean that it cannot be privileged. In *Re Highgrade Traders Ltd* [1984] BCLC 151 the Court of Appeal held that an insurer who instructed experts in fire investigation in a suspected insurance arson case was primarily interested in the question of liability, not the prevention of recurrence, so the report was privileged. This case is also authority for the proposition that the dominant purpose must be that of the person commissioning the report, not necessarily that of the author. The time at which the dominant purpose is to be judged is the time at which the document was created. The privileged status of the document will not be affected by any subsequent use to which it is put, or the subsequent intentions of the author or the person commissioning it. Thus, documents which were procured for the purpose of valuing goods for the purpose of purchase tax could not become privileged through some subsequent intention to use them for the purposes of litigation (*Alfred Crompton Amusement Machines Ltd v Commissioners of Customs and Excise (No. 2)* [1974] AC 405).

Copies of documents

Where a document is not privileged when a party receives it, a copy of that document made by the party and forwarded to its solicitor for the purpose of contemplated or pending proceedings does not become privileged (*Dubai Bank Ltd v Galadari* [1990] Ch 98; *Ventouris v Mountain* [1991] 1 WLR 607, CA). On the other hand, a selection of documents assembled or copied by a party's solicitor which would betray the trend of advice given to the party will be privileged (*Lyell v Kennedy (No. 3)* (1884) 27 ChD 1), provided the documents assembled were originally third-party, non-disclosable, documents. In principle, an assembly of translations of third-party documents will also be privileged if it will betray the trend of legal advice given. However, own-party documents (unprivileged documents disclosable by the party claiming privilege) are not protected by the *Lyell v Kennedy* principle (*Sumitomo Corporation v Credit Lyonnais Rouse Ltd* [2001] EWCA Civ 1152, [2002] 1 WLR 479). A lawyer's underlining or highlighting of documents (or the absence of such) does not give rise to legal professional privilege except in the unlikely event that the trend of advice may be revealed (*Imerman v Tchenguiz* [2009] EWHC 2902 (QB), LTL 20/11/2009). Counsel's annotations (which may separately be privileged) on documents may be redacted before the documents are disclosed. 50.62

Iniquity

Legal professional privilege does not apply where the purpose behind seeking legal advice is 'iniquitous', such as to devise a structure for a transaction to prejudice the interests of the client's creditors (see *Barclays Bank plc v Eustice* [1995] 1 WLR 1238). According to *Kuwait Airways Corporation v Iraqi Airways Co. (No. 6)* [2005] EWCA Civ 286, [2005] 1 WLR 2734: 50.63

(a) the fraud exception can apply both to litigation privilege and legal advice privilege;
(b) where the issue of fraud is one of the issues in the claim, there must be a very strong prima facie case of fraud;
(c) where fraud is not one of the issues in the claim, a prima facie case of fraud may be enough.

The privilege was lost on this ground in a case where a search order was obtained using information which had been gathered in breach of the Data Protection Act 1984 (*Dubai Aluminium Co. Ltd v Al Alawi* [1999] 1 WLR 1964). Communications in furtherance of a fraud or crime are not protected by privilege (*Finers v Miro* [1991] 1 WLR 35). It does not matter whether or not the solicitor was aware of the client's intent (*Gamlen Chemical Co. (UK) Ltd v Rochem Ltd* [1979] CA

Transcript 777). The principle applies whether or not the claim is founded on the particular fraud in question (*Dubai Bank Ltd v Galadari (No. 6)* (1991) *The Times*, 22 April 1991). Where fraud between the solicitor and client is established in relation to the litigation itself, legal professional privilege is removed from all the relevant advice obtained in the litigation (*Dadourian Group International Inc. v Simms* [2008] EWHC 1784 (Ch), LTL 1/8/2008). Communications which are criminal in themselves, or intended to further a criminal purpose, are not covered by legal professional privilege. An affidavit setting out the details of an abusive telephone call (which was an offence contrary to the Telecommunications Act 1984, s. 43(1)(a)) and a threat to rip someone's throat out (which was a threat to kill contrary to the Offences against the Person Act 1861, s. 16) was held not to be privileged in *C v C (Privilege: Criminal Communications)* [2001] EWCA Civ 469, [2002] Fam 42.

Common interest privilege

50.64 Common interest privilege is a form of legal professional privilege, see *Buttes Gas and Oil Co. v Hammer (No. 3)* [1981] QB 223. It is a privilege in aid of anticipated litigation in which several persons have a common interest, and applies to cases where some only of the persons who have sought legal advice are eventually made parties to the litigation. For example, owners of adjoining houses complain of a nuisance which affects them both. Both take legal advice, and both exchange relevant documents. However, only one becomes a claimant (for whatever reasons). The various documents shared between the persons who took the legal advice will be privileged provided they had a common interest in advancing or defending the anticipated proceedings (*R v Trutch* [2001] EWCA Crim 1750, LTL 27/7/2001).

Joint privilege

50.65 For joint privilege to apply there must be a joint interest at the time of the communication. In *BBGP Managing General Partner Ltd v Babcock and Brown Global Partners* [2010] EWHC 2176 (Ch), [2011] Ch 296 at [52] and [58], Norris J said:

> I consider that the authorities establish that where a solicitor accepts a joint retainer from parties with potentially conflicting interests one client cannot insist as against the other that legal professional privilege attaches to any of what passes between the solicitor and that client during the currency and in the course of the retainer: *Baugh v Cradocke* (1832) 1 Mood & R 182; *Perry v Smith* (1842) 9 M & W 681; *Shore v Bedford* (1843) 5 Man & G 271; *Ross v Gibbs* (1869) LR 8 Eq 522 and *Re Konigsberg* [1989] 1 WLR 1257....
>
> The right to confidentiality and privilege is a joint right of all the individual clients.... No one [client] can waive it.

The members of a partnership firm have joint privilege in legal advice about the firm's affairs, other than advice sought in their sectional interest by some only of the partners. As it is a joint privilege, none of the partners may disseminate or use the information contained in the advice in any legal proceedings without the joint waiver of the other partners. Joint privilege does not apply if advice is sought by one or more partners in respect of their sectional interest against other partners.

Other confidential situations

50.66 Confidentiality is only an element of the privilege, not its foundation. The fact that documents may contain confidential information is not in itself a reason for withholding inspection (*Croft House Care Ltd v Durham County Council* [2010] EWHC 909 (TCC), LTL 7/7/2010, where the documents were said to be commercially sensitive). Ultimately the question is whether inspection of the documents is necessary for disposing fairly of the proceedings, and in making that decision the court should consider whether any special measure, such as redaction of the documents, or holding hearings in private under **CPR, r. 39.2(3)**, should be adopted

(*Science Research Council v Nassé* [1980] AC 1028). Another approach is to preserve the confidentiality of the documents at the disclosure stage, subject to review later to decide whether in the light of the material then available the documents are required for disposing fairly of the proceedings (*Mears Ltd v Leeds City Council* [2011] EWHC 40 (QB), LTL 19/1/2011).

The fact that a settlement agreement contains a confidentiality clause does not mean it cannot be ordered to be disclosed in related litigation, as happened in *Cadogan Petroleum plc v Tolley* [2010] EWHC 1107 (Ch), LTL 19/5/2010, where certain terms in a settlement between the claimant and some of the defendants were relevant to the continuing litigation between the claimant and the remaining defendants. While interviews with medical advisers are not covered by legal professional privilege, they are often treated as being *in pari materia* with legal advice. This is partly because they may be covered by litigation privilege (see **50.60**), and partly because they are an aspect of the right to respect for private life which is protected by the European Convention on Human Rights, **art. 8**, in the **Human Rights Act 1998, sch. 1** (*McE v Prison Service of Northern Ireland* [2009] UKHL 15, [2009] 1 AC 908 at [72]). A third party, whether official or unofficial, who receives information in confidence with a view to conciliation between the parties will not be compelled by the courts to disclose what was said without the parties' agreement (*McTaggart v McTaggart* [1949] P 94; *D v National Society for the Prevention of Cruelty to Children* [1978] AC 171). This privilege, which is based on the sanctity of marriage, also extends to proceedings under the Children Act 1989 (*Re D (Minors) (Conciliation: Disclosure of Information)* [1993] Fam 231). A 'wish letter' written at the same time as a discretionary trust was set up is a confidential document, but the court may order it to be disclosed to the beneficiaries on an application for the court's sanction of a scheme of distribution where disclosure is in the best interests of the beneficiaries and the due administration of the trust (*Breakspear v Ackland* [2008] EWHC 220 (Ch), [2009] Ch 32).

Danger and confidentiality

A dilemma from time to time faced by professional people is whether they should alert the authorities to some danger when knowledge of the danger has come to them through a confidential relationship. In *Re B (Children: Patient Confidentiality)* [2003] EWCA Civ 786, [2003] 2 FLR 813, it was held to be proper for a psychiatrist to report to the local authority child protection services information giving rise to a concern of child abuse. The Court of Appeal stated that the psychiatrist should have limited herself to making a report, and should not have gone further and provided a witness statement on the matter. **50.67**

WITHOUT-PREJUDICE COMMUNICATIONS

Without-prejudice communications, whether oral or in writing, which are made with the intention of seeking a settlement of litigation, are privileged from disclosure, in both the present and subsequent proceedings (*Ofulue v Bossert* [2009] UKHL 16, [2009] AC 990). It applies to genuine attempts to negotiate a settlement of a dispute where the parties contemplate or might reasonably have contemplated litigation if they cannot agree. The question of proximity applies to the subject matter of the dispute, rather than the length of time before the threat or actual commencement of the contemplated litigation (*Barnetson v Framlington Group Ltd* [2007] EWCA Civ 502, [2007] 1 WLR 2443). The policy is to encourage litigants to settle their differences rather than litigate them to the finish (see Lord Griffiths in *Rush and Tompkins Ltd v Greater London Council* [1989] AC 1280). Privilege does this by removing the potential embarrassment of concessions made in the course of negotiations being used at trial against the party who made them. So, on an application for costs, it is not permissible to adduce without-prejudice communications, without the joint consent of the parties, to establish whether a party unreasonably refused a proposal for ADR. Further, it is impermissible to draw adverse inferences **50.68** from a party's reluctance to waive the joint privilege (*Reed Executive plc v Reed Business Information Ltd* [2004] EWCA Civ 887, [2004] 1 WLR 3026).

The privilege applies even if the words 'without prejudice' are not used, provided the purpose was to seek a settlement (*Chocoladefabriken Lindt & Sprungli AG v Nestlé Co. Ltd* [1978] RPC 287). It applies, for example, to joint settlement meetings, unless they are stated to be 'without prejudice save as to costs' (*Jackson v Ministry of Defence* [2006] EWCA Civ 46, LTL 12/1/2006). Without-prejudice privilege does not apply to apparently open correspondence which discusses repayment of an admitted liability, rather than negotiates the possible compromise of a disputed liability (*Bradford and Bingley plc v Rashid* [2006] UKHL 37, [2006] 1 WLR 2066). The question is whether the communication was genuinely intended to be a negotiating document (*Schering Corporation v Cipla Ltd* [2004] EWHC 2587 (Ch), *The Times*, 2 December 2004). In making this assessment the court must determine the author's intention, and must put itself in the position of a reasonable recipient to determine the message the communication conveyed (*South Shropshire District Council v Amos* [1986] 1 WLR 1271). Use of the words 'without prejudice' will not attach privilege to communications intended to prejudice the recipient or which are no more than an assertion of one party's rights (*Buckinghamshire County Council v Moran* [1990] Ch 623). A failure to use the words, coupled with a finding that the purpose of the communications was more administrative than with a view to settling a claim, meant that documents were not protected in *Prudential Assurance Co. Ltd v Prudential Insurance Co. of America* [2003] EWCA Civ 1154, [2004] ETMR 29. A letter marked 'without prejudice' proposing terms of a lease was not privileged, and the possibility of a dispute arising in the event the negotiations broke down was not sufficient to attract privilege (*Bath and North East Somerset District Council v Nicholson* (2002) LTL 22/2/2002).

Where the parties enter into 'without-prejudice' negotiations, continuing negotiations will be privileged until one party brings it home to the other party that the 'without-prejudice' basis of the negotiations is at an end. Thus, in *Cheddar Valley Engineering Ltd v Chaddlewood Homes Ltd* [1992] 1 WLR 820 it was held that prefacing one telephone offer with the word 'open' was insufficient to bring home the change in basis when further telephone negotiations and a letter did not repeat the word 'open'.

The public policy rationale of the privilege is, according to *Murrell v Healy* [2001] EWCA Civ 486, [2001] 4 All ER 345, directed solely to protecting admissions, and if documents are to be used for a different purpose, such as to show the amount of compensation paid for an earlier injury, they are admissible. This is not entirely consistent with *Unilever plc v Procter and Gamble Co.* [2000] 1 WLR 2436, and probably does not survive *Ofulue v Bossert* [2009] UKHL 16, [2009] AC 990, because it would create huge practical difficulties to dissect out identifiable admissions and withhold protection of the rest of without-prejudice communications. In *Re New Gadget Shop Ltd* [2005] EWHC 1606 (Ch), LTL 5/8/2005, the petitioner sought to dissect identifiable admissions out of without-prejudice communications, crafting its witness statements so as to include the alleged admissions but avoiding reference to any of the without-prejudice negotiations.

It was held that this approach was prohibited by *Unilever plc v Procter and Gamble Co.* [2000] 1 WLR 2436. The paragraphs seeking to achieve this were struck out.

A draft expert's report sent by the claimant 'without prejudice' in the early stages is inadmissible at trial on the question of deciding the amount of interest, even where the defendant is arguing that the award of interest should be reduced because of delays in formulating the value of the claim, and where the report dealt with quantifying the claim (*UYB Ltd v British Railways Board* (2000) *The Times*, 15 November 2000). This was not a legal professional privilege matter (in which event the claimant could have waived privilege), because the issue was when the defendant was first notified of the value of the claim.

In relation to mediated cross-border disputes governed by Directive 2008/52/EC, where a person seeks disclosure or inspection of mediation evidence in the control of a mediator or mediation administrator, an application must be made using the Part 23 procedure if there are pending proceedings, or using the Part 8 procedure if not (**CPR, r. 78.26(1)**). The mediator or mediation administrator must be made a respondent (**Part 23**) or party (**Part 8**). The evidence in support must include evidence that all parties to the mediation agree to the disclosure or inspection of the mediation evidence, or that disclosure is necessary for overriding considerations of public policy, or that disclosure is necessary to implement or enforce the mediation agreement (**r. 78.26(3)**).

Proof of settlement

Without-prejudice negotiations which result in a settlement are admissible to prove the terms of the settlement (*Walker v Wilsher* (1889) 23 QBD 335). A party to without-prejudice negotiations can also rely on anything said in the course of them to show that the settlement agreement should be rectified (*Oceanbulk Shipping and Trading SA v TMT Asia Ltd* [2010] UKSC 44, [2011] 1 AC 662 at [33]). Such negotiations can also be relied upon, where they are relevant under the normal rules governing the interpretation of contracts (usually as part of the factual matrix or surrounding circumstances to show the true construction of the agreement), where those facts have a bearing on the meaning to be given to the words of the settlement (*Oceanbulk Shipping and Trading SA v TMT Asia Ltd* at [36]–[48]). In *Jackson v Thakrar* [2007] EWHC 271 (TCC), 113 Con LR 58, a chain of letters came into being without an intention to create legal relations, and at best amounted to an agreement to agree on a single topic. No settlement had been reached. In *Brown v Rice* [2007] EWHC 625 (Ch), [2008] FSR 3, an offer made in mediation did not deal with how the litigation should be disposed of, and had not been made in writing as previously stipulated. It was therefore incomplete, and there was no final settlement. Where the terms of settlement reached in without-prejudice communications are relevant in determining the extent of the liability of another person who is then sued by one of the parties to the settlement for a contribution towards the original liability, the privilege will not prevent inspection of the without-prejudice communications (*Gnitrow Ltd v Cape plc* [2000] 1 WLR 2327). **50.69**

Abuse of without-prejudice rule

Unilever plc v Procter and Gamble Co. [2000] 1 WLR 2436 reiterated in a modern context the old rule that the without-prejudice rule will not protect statements made in circumstances where the rule is being unequivocally abused. Threats or other conduct which could be described as oppressive, dishonest or dishonourable could fall into this category. Thus, marking a letter 'without prejudice' will not protect the evidence of a threat of what will happen if an offer is not accepted (*Kitcat v Sharp* (1882) 48 LT 64). **50.70**

A mere inconsistency between an admission made on a without-prejudice occasion and the pleaded case or the facts stated in a witness statement of the party making the admission will not result in the privilege being lost (*Savings and Investment Bank Ltd v Fincken* [2003] EWCA Civ 1630, [2004] 1 WLR 667). This is so even if persistence in the inconsistent position might lead to perjury. The strength of the public policy protecting without-prejudice communications is such that it should be lost only in truly exceptional circumstances (*Savings and Investment Bank Ltd v Fincken*) or where there is a very clear case of abuse of a privileged occasion (*Berry Trade Ltd v Moussavi* [2003] EWCA Civ 715, *The Times*, 3 June 2003). In *Berry Trade Ltd v Moussavi* the privilege was not lost where the alleged admissions were made orally in a lengthy without-prejudice meeting which was not tape-recorded or made the subject of a detailed note, and where the alleged admissions were small, selected parts of the discussion.

Use in interim applications

Without-prejudice correspondence is often used in interim applications, particularly applications seeking sanctions for default, or relief from sanctions (*Family Housing Association (Manchester) Ltd v Michael Hyde and Partners* [1993] 1 WLR 354). While the duty of full and frank disclosure might mean that a without-prejudice document, or the fact it existed, must be disclosed, it was held that there was no breach of the duty in *Linsen International Ltd v Humpuss* **50.71**

Commentary

Sea Transport Pte Ltd [2010] EWHC 303 (Comm), LTL 1/3/2010. The defendant had deliberately chosen to withhold information about the without-prejudice negotiation, and neither the fact of the meeting nor what was discussed had any real bearing on the risk of dissipation of assets. Before using without-prejudice material the other side should be informed and given an opportunity to object, and before placing the material before the judge the court should be informed so it can react and rule on its use before the judge's knowledge is affected (*Berg v IML London Ltd* [2002] 1 WLR 3271). Use of without-prejudice material on an interim application by one party entitles the other party to use that material at trial, at least where the issues on the interim application included consideration of the underlying merits of the claim (*Somatra Ltd v Sinclair Roche and Temperley* [2000] 1 WLR 2453).

Use of without-prejudice material in subsequent proceedings

50.72 Once a document is protected by without-prejudice privilege, it will always (subject to the principles discussed in **50.68** to **50.70**) be privileged. Thus, an admission made in without-prejudice communications by one party will not be admissible in other proceedings against that party (*Rush and Tompkins Ltd v Greater London Council* [1989] AC 1280). If without-prejudice documents are used to found subsequent proceedings, those proceedings will be struck out as an abuse of process, unless the claimant in the subsequent proceedings can show that the statements relied upon were made improperly, or that there is some public interest favouring their subsequent use (*Unilever plc v Procter and Gamble Co.* [2000] 1 WLR 2436).

WAIVER OF PRIVILEGE

50.73 Legal professional privilege belongs to, and can be waived by, the client. The privilege against self-incrimination belongs to the witness, and can only be waived by him. The privilege in without-prejudice communications belongs to both sides jointly, and can only be waived if both sides consent (*Rush and Tompkins Ltd v Greater London Council* [1989] AC 1280). Adverse inferences will not be drawn from a refusal to waive privilege (*Sayers v Clarke Walker* [2002] EWCA Civ 910, LTL 26/6/2002; *Reed Executive plc v Reed Business Information Ltd* [2004] EWCA Civ 887, [2004] 1 WLR 3026).

Waiver of privilege may be given expressly, or implicitly such as by disclosing a privileged document to the other side. The public interest importance attached to legal advice privilege is such that something more than a reference to the effect of the advice is needed before any question of waiver can arise (*Brennan v Sunderland City Council* [2009] ICR 479). The underlying principle is that of fairness. There will be a waiver only if it would be unfair to allow the party making the disclosure not to reveal the whole of the relevant information because it may lead to the court or other parties having only a partial, and potentially misleading, impression of the material. In *R v Seaton* [2010] EWCA Crim 1980, [2011] 1 WLR 623, the defendant's evidence at trial differed in a significant way from the version of events in a statement presented to the police, through his solicitor, at interview. He explained the discrepancy by blaming his solicitor for getting the facts wrong. The solicitor was not called at trial. It was held that the defendant had waived his privilege, but only to the extent that was fair and necessary to avoid giving a misleading impression, and that the prosecution were entitled to comment in closing on the failure to call the defendant's solicitor to verify his explanation. From *Mac Hotels Ltd v Rider Levett Bucknall UK Ltd* [2010] EWHC 767 (TCC), LTL 28/4/2010, waiver of privilege through deployment of the privileged material in litigation has two elements:

(a) a clear reference to the existence of the privileged communications; and
(b) reliance on the privileged material for the purpose of making a particular point. If the reference to the privileged material is no more than mere narrative there is no waiver. If

the content of the privileged material is used to support a point which the party deploying the material wishes to make, there will be a waiver of the privilege.

Examples include disclosure by service of a hearsay notice; by inclusion as an exhibit to a witness statement; by using the document to refresh the memory of a witness while giving evidence; and use of documents in re-examination to rebut an allegation of recent fabrication. In *Compagnie Noga d'Importation et d'Exportation SA v Australia and New Zealand Banking Group Ltd* [2007] EWHC 85 (Comm), LTL 5/2/2007, the defendant had made five affidavits, with the assistance of solicitors, about his assets pursuant to clauses in a freezing injunction. As a result he had waived any claim to privilege on the issue of disclosure of his assets. In *Re D (A Child)* [2011] EWCA Civ 684, [2011] 4 All ER 434, the mother of the child in interim care proceedings explained a change in her story between two witness statements by referring to various meetings with her solicitor and barrister, and setting out parts of what was discussed in those meetings. It was held that she had waived privilege in all the meetings with her solicitor and barrister over a five-week period leading up to the second witness statement. The references to the meetings with her lawyers were more than 'glancing references', which would not have amounted to a waiver, but had gone further and disclosed the nature of the advice she had received. Privilege was waived by the mother despite the fact her witness statement was drafted by her solicitor, and despite the fact that neither she nor her solicitor realised that the material in her second witness statement amounted to a waiver of privilege.

Use by both parties of incidents (or the denial of incidents) which are alleged to have occurred during mediation amounts to mutual waiver of privilege as both parties have chosen to plead privileged matter in public documents (*Hall v Pertemps Group Ltd* (2005) *The Times*, 23 December 2005). A consent order in proceedings in Minnesota was held, on the wording of the order, not to be an implied waiver of privilege in *British American Tobacco (Investments) Ltd v United States of America* [2004] EWCA Civ 1064, LTL 30/7/2004. A party waives privilege for trial purposes by using materials in an interim application (*Derby and Co. Ltd v Weldon (No. 10)* [1991] 1 WLR 660).

In *Great Atlantic Insurance Co. v Home Insurance Co.* [1981] 1 WLR 529 the Court of Appeal held that where part of a document is used in counsel's opening, privilege in the whole of the document is waived unless it is a clearly separable document with different parts dealing with completely different subjects. A single letter can be a severable document if different parts of the letter are so distinct that they amount to different documents (*Pozzi v Eli Lilley and Co.* (1986) *The Times*, 3 December 1986). Where a document is severed, with privilege being asserted as to a part, the other parties must be informed that this has been done (*Nea Karteria Maritime Co. Ltd v Atlantic and Great Lakes Steamship Corporation (No. 2)* [1981] Com LR 138). If a document deals with a single subject matter, a party cannot waive privilege on a part, and assert privilege on the rest (*Great Atlantic Insurance Co. v Home Insurance Co.*). As Denning LJ said in *Burnell v British Transport Commission* [1956] 1 QB 187:

> It would be most unfair that cross-examining counsel should use part of the document which was to his advantage and not allow anyone else, not even the judge or the opposing counsel, a sight of the rest of the document, much of which might have been against him.

Once privilege on a subject has been waived, the waiver will be taken to extend to any associated material (*Derby and Co. Ltd v Weldon (No. 10)*), but the court will seek to define the subject matter of the waiver quite restrictively (*General Accident Fire and Life Assurance Corporation Ltd v Tanter* [1984] 1 WLR 100). There are two questions that need to be addressed. The first is to define the transaction in relation to which disclosure has been made, which has to be considered objectively. It is not open to the disclosing party to define the transaction as limited to what he has chosen to disclose (*Fulham Leisure Holdings Ltd v Nicholson Graham and Jones* [2006] EWHC 158 (Ch), [2006] 2 All ER 599). The second question is whether further disclosure is required going beyond the strict limits of the transaction in order to avoid unfairness or misunderstanding of what has been disclosed (*Fulham Leisure Holdings Ltd v Nicholson Graham and Jones*). In *United Building and Plumbing Contractors v Kajla* [2002] EWCA Civ 628, LTL 26/4/2002, a party who put in evidence of meetings between the parties for settlement negotiations was held to have waived the privilege in the without-prejudice negotiations at those meetings.

Where a party allows documents which were protected by legal professional privilege to be used by a third party for a limited purpose, there is a limited waiver restricted to that purpose. A limited waiver does not destroy the privilege for all purposes (*B v Auckland District Law Society* [2003] UKPC 38, [2003] 2 AC 736).

Implied waiver

50.74 In a claim against the claimant's former solicitor the claimant's privilege over all documents concerned with the claim is impliedly waived to the extent necessary to enable the court to adjudicate the dispute fully and fairly. In *Lillicrap v Nalder and Son* [1993] 1 WLR 94 property developers sued their solicitors for negligently failing to advise them about a right of way over some land they purchased. The claimants had retained the solicitors to advise on a number of other transactions, and the solicitors said their files on those other transactions showed the claimants habitually ignored their warnings, so would have bought the land even if they had been properly advised. The Court of Appeal held that the previous transactions were relevant to an issue in the present proceedings, so the implied waiver extended to them as well as to the transaction in question. However, there are limits on the implied waiver of privilege in solicitors' negligence claims. In *Paragon Finance plc v Freshfields* [1999] 1 WLR 1183 the first firm of solicitors had acted for the finance company in relation to a number of mortgage transactions. The finance company made a number of claims against insurance policies entered into in relation to the mortgages, which the insurer disputed. The finance company then retained a second firm of solicitors to pursue outstanding insurance claims, and later sued the first firm of solicitors for professional negligence. A question arose as to whether the finance company had, by suing the first firm of solicitors, impliedly waived its privilege in respect of the work done by the second firm in pursuing the insurance claims. It was held that by suing the first firm of solicitors the finance company had only put its relationship with that firm into the public domain, and had not done so in respect of the work done by the second firm, and so had not waived its privilege in respect of the work done by the second firm.

Apart from professional negligence claims against the client's former solicitor, there is no general rule that privilege is waived by placing in issue events evidenced by privileged communications (*Farm Assist Ltd v Secretary of State for the Environment, Food and Rural Affairs* [2008] EWHC 3079 (TCC), [2009] BLR 80). Thus, privilege over the claimant's solicitor's files is not impliedly waived even where the contents of those files is highly relevant to the claimant's date of knowledge on an application under the Limitation Act 1980, s. 14 or s. 14A (*Mac Hotels Ltd v Rider Levett Bucknall UK Ltd* [2010] EWHC 767 (TCC), LTL 28/4/2010).

Secondary evidence

50.75 It was held in *Calcraft v Guest* [1898] 1 QB 759 that secondary evidence, such as a copy, of otherwise privileged material is admissible at trial. In *Goddard v Nationwide Building Society* [1987] QB 670 Nourse LJ said that it makes no difference how the privileged material was obtained. Even if confidential documents have been obtained by theft, it is said that they will be admissible. However, the party who would otherwise be able to claim privilege may apply for an injunction to restrain use of such material if it has not yet been used in the litigation (*Goddard v Nationwide Building Society*). This was before the introduction of **CPR, r. 32.1(2)**, under which it is possible for the court to exercise its discretion to exclude stolen documents (see **49.8**). Alternatively, the court has always had a jurisdiction to grant an injunction to restrain use of privileged material which has fallen into the hands of another party, as long as the application is made before the material has been used in the litigation (*Goddard v Nationwide Building Society*).

Injunctions to restrain use of privileged material

In *ISTIL Group Inc. v Zahoor* [2003] EWHC 165 (Ch), [2003] 2 All ER 252, the claimant sought an injunction to restrain the defendant from using documents which the claimant had sent to a person who then gave them to the defendant. The claimant alleged that the documents were protected by legal professional privilege. The defendant said that he should be allowed to use the documents because they came into existence as part of a scheme by the claimant to present a false case to the court. Unlike the situation considered at **50.50** to **50.72** (where the question is whether a party can successfully assert privilege), in the present situation the allegedly privileged documents are already in the hands of the other side. Here the court will balance the public interest in supporting legal professional privilege against the public interest in the administration of justice. On the facts there had been forgery and an attempt to place a misleading case before the court, so the injunction was refused. **50.76**

The manner in which otherwise privileged materials came into the possession of the other party is important. If this happened illegally, the principles discussed at **50.29** apply. Alternatively, the circumstances may be taken as indicating that the party seeking to assert privilege has waived its privilege.

Waiver may arise inadvertently (*Great Atlantic Insurance Co. v Home Insurance Co.* [1981] 1 WLR 529). In *Guinness Peat Properties Ltd v Fitzroy Robinson Partnership* [1987] 1 WLR 1027 a privileged letter was inadvertently disclosed. The defendant allowed the claimant to inspect certain files before serving a list of documents. By accident, the letter was left in one of the files, and the claimant took a copy of it. The document later appeared in the defendant's list of documents, without a claim for privilege, and the claimant was again allowed to inspect it at the defendant's solicitors' office, but was not given a copy. Slade LJ said, at p. 1044:

> Care must be taken by parties to litigation in the preparation of their lists of documents and no less great care must be taken in offering inspection of the documents disclosed. Ordinarily, in my judgment, a party to litigation who sees a particular document referred to in the other side's list, without privilege being claimed, and is subsequently permitted inspection of that document, is fully entitled to assume that any privilege which might otherwise have been claimed for it has been waived.

As Slade LJ said, this is ordinarily the position. It is subject to two exceptions:

(a) where a party or its solicitor procures inspection of the relevant document by fraud; and
(b) where a party or its solicitor realises on inspection that the document has been disclosed as a result of an obvious mistake.

Where either of these exceptions applies, Slade LJ in *Guinness Peat Properties Ltd v Fitzroy Robinson Partnership* said the court should ordinarily intervene, unless there is some equitable reason for not doing so, such as delay.

Guinness Peat Properties Ltd v Fitzroy Robinson Partnership was an example of an obvious mistake, as, being a trained lawyer, the claimant's solicitor must have realised the privileged nature of the letter as soon as he read it. Another, more obvious, example is *English and American Insurance Co. Ltd v Herbert Smith* [1988] FSR 232, where counsel's clerk allowed counsel's instructions and papers (including witness statements and counsel's written opinion) to be sent to the other side's solicitors. An injunction was granted restraining use being made of any of the information in the papers.

Principles governing applications for injunctions In *Al Fayed v Commissioner of Police for the Metropolis* [2002] EWCA Civ 780, *The Times*, 17 June 2002, an injunction was refused because the recipient solicitors genuinely thought the other side's counsel's opinions had been disclosed on purpose. This case has a useful statement of the principles governing applications for injunctions to prevent use of privileged documents: **50.77**

(a) A party giving inspection of documents has to decide what privileged documents to disclose before doing so.

Commentary

(b) Although the privilege belongs to the client, the solicitor has ostensible authority to waive the privilege.
(c) A solicitor inspecting another party's documents owes no duty of care to the other party, and is generally entitled to assume that any privilege has been intentionally waived.
(d) Where privileged documents are given to the other side by mistake, it is generally too late thereafter to claim privilege by seeking an injunction to restrain use of those documents.
(e) Nevertheless, the court does have jurisdiction to grant such injunctions where justice requires.
(f) An injunction would be granted where documents were made available for inspection through an obvious mistake.
(g) A mistake was likely to be obvious where the receiving solicitor appreciated that a mistake had been made before making use of the documents or if it would have been obvious to a reasonable solicitor in the position of the receiving solicitor that a mistake had been made.
(h) In considering whether a mistake was obvious, it is relevant but not conclusive that a solicitor had considered the question and honestly concluded that the documents had not been made available by mistake.
(i) Even if there has been an obvious mistake, an injunction may be refused if it would be unjust or inequitable to grant an injunction.
(j) There are no rigid rules, because the court is exercising an equitable discretion.
(k) The same principles apply to the exercise of the discretion under **CPR, r. 31.20**.

The provisions of the CPR appear to reverse the common law position described above, with **r. 31.20** providing that where a party inadvertently allows a privileged document to be inspected, the party who has inspected the document may use it or its contents only with the permission of the court. Procedurally this means that there is no longer any need for the party making the inadvertent disclosure to apply for an injunction, and the onus must now be on the other party to seek an order giving permission to rely on the documents. However, in *Breeze v John Stacey and Sons Ltd* (1999) *The Times*, 8 July 1999, it was held that **r. 31.20** does no more than confirm the long-established principles set out above, and does not alter the law in any way.

Documents *publici juris*

50.78 Notes of proceedings in open court and counsel's endorsement on the brief of the order of the court are *publici juris* (in the public domain) and are not privileged (*Nicholl v Jones* (1865) 2 Hem & M 588). Likewise, public records and documents are also *publici juris*. However, a collection of extracts or copies from public documents may be protected from production by legal professional privilege where the collection is a product of the professional knowledge, research and skill of a party's legal advisers (*Lyell v Kennedy (No. 3)* (1884) 27 ChD 1).

Beneficiaries and shareholders

50.79 There is a general rule that a *cestui que trust* (for which see *Tugwell v Hooper* (1847) 10 Beav 348) and a shareholder (for which see *W. Dennis and Sons Ltd v West Norfolk Farmers' Manure and Chemical Co-operative Co. Ltd* [1943] Ch 220) are entitled to see opinions from counsel and advice from solicitors paid for out of the fund or the assets of the company (respectively) for the purpose of administering the fund or the company. The rule is subject to an exception where the legal advice is sought by the trustees or company in hostile litigation against the beneficiary or shareholder in question. It applies to a company whether it is public or private and however many shareholders it has (*CAS Nominees Ltd v Nottingham Forest plc* [2001] 1 All ER 954). But where a company is merely a necessary but nominal defendant in proceedings between its shareholders and directors there is no 'hostile' litigation for this purpose, and the general rule applies (*Re Hydrosan Ltd* [1991] BCLC 418).

PUBLIC INTEREST IMMUNITY

General principles

Certain documents must be withheld from disclosure and/or inspection on the ground that revealing the existence and/or contents of the documents would be injurious to the public interest. Claims to public interest immunity are of two types: (a) claims that all documents of certain classes must be protected; (b) claims that individual documents need to be protected because of their particular 'contents'. Contents immunity attaches, for example, to diplomatic dispatches and documents relating to national security. There is a wide variation in the 'classes' of documents protected, from Cabinet minutes to more routine documents such as local authority social work records (*Re M (A Minor)* (1989) 88 LGR 841). **50.80**

Ministerial certificates

The usual practice is that the responsible minister provides a certificate stating the grounds of the objection to disclosure and/or inspection, identifying the document in question. Such a certificate is not conclusive (*Conway v Rimmer* [1968] AC 910) and the court may require the document to be produced to it (**CPR, r. 31.19(6)**). It is, though, for the party seeking inspection to show that the claim to immunity should be rejected (*Air Canada v Secretary of State for Trade* [1983] 2 AC 394). A defective ministerial certificate may be amended (*R (Mohamed) v Secretary of State for Foreign and Commonwealth Affairs* [2008] EWHC 2100 (Admin), LTL 2/9/2008). If the party seeking disclosure establishes a counteracting interest to the claim for immunity, the court must balance the public interest in concealment against the public interest in the due administration of justice in favour of disclosure (see Lord Fraser of Tullybelton in the *Air Canada* case). **50.81**

Procedure

Under **CPR, r. 31.19(1)**, a person (who need not be a party) may apply, without notice, for an order permitting him to withhold disclosure of a document on the ground that disclosure would damage the public interest. Usually the applicant for such an order is the Secretary of State for the government department asserting public interest immunity in the document. By **r. 31.19(2)**, unless the court otherwise orders, any order made under this rule must not be served on any other person, and must not be open to inspection by any other person. Claims for protection may alternatively be made in the list of documents served by a party (**r. 31.19(4)**), or may be insisted upon by the court of its own initiative. **50.82**

It is questionable whether these procedures, particularly the procedure under **r. 31.19(1)**, comply with the European Convention on Human Rights, **art. 6(1)**, in the **Human Rights Act 1998, sch. 1**. In *Rowe v United Kingdom* (2000) 30 EHRR 1, the European Court of Human Rights considered the procedural aspects of withholding evidence in *criminal* trials on the grounds of public interest. It was held that to comply with **art. 6(1)** the accused had to be given information about the withheld information appropriate to the category of the evidence involved, and that it was for the trial judge (rather than a court on appeal) to decide whether the evidence should be withheld. **Rule 31.19** allows orders to be made without giving any information to the parties (or to just one side if one of the parties is the government department seeking to withhold disclosure), and for decisions to be made by judges other than the trial judge, which would seem to fall short of the safeguards contemplated by the European Court. In criminal trials there are the additional minimum rights given by **art. 6(3)**, which do not apply to civil cases, but this difference is unlikely to have a substantial effect on the implications of the decision in civil cases.

Commentary

Confidential documents

50.83 Confidentiality is not of itself a ground of privilege or public interest immunity, although it is an element in these concepts. Although there is a reluctance to order disclosure of confidential documents, if disclosure is necessary in the interests of the litigation, those interests override mere confidentiality (*Science Research Council v Nassé* [1980] AC 1028; *Three Rivers District Council v Bank of England (No. 5)* [2002] EWHC 2309 (Comm), LTL 8/11/2002, a point not dealt with on the appeal [2003] EWCA Civ 474, [2003] QB 1556). In such cases the court may consider whether confidentiality may be preserved while satisfying the needs of the litigation by ordering redactions, disclosure from other sources, and other appropriate means (*Science Research Council v Nassé*; *Wallace Smith Trust Co. Ltd v Deloitte Haskins and Sells* [1997] 1 WLR 257; *Three Rivers District Council v Bank of England*).

PRE-ACTION DISCLOSURE

50.84 The procedure for applying for disclosure of documents before proceedings have started is governed by **CPR, r. 31.16. Rule 31.17** deals with applications, after proceedings have started, for disclosure by a person who is not a party to the proceedings. These applications are made under the Senior Courts Act 1981, ss. 33(2) and 34, or the County Courts Act 1984, ss. 52(2) and 53. Until these sections were amended by the Civil Procedure (Modification of Enactments) Order 1998 (SI 1998/2940) such orders were available only in proceedings in respect of personal injury and wrongful death. Now they may be made in any type of case, except that pre-action disclosure does not apply where the underlying dispute is to be referred to arbitration (*Travelers Insurance Co. Ltd v Countryside Surveyors Ltd* [2010] EWHC 2455 (TCC), [2011] 1 All ER (Comm) 631). The court may not make an order under these provisions if it considers that complying with the order would be injurious to the public interest (Senior Courts Act 1981, s. 35(1); County Courts Act 1984, s. 54(1)).

Requirements for pre-action disclosure

50.85 The court has power to make an order for pre-action disclosure where the following conditions are satisfied:

(a) The respondent must be likely to be a party to subsequent proceedings (**CPR, r. 31.16(3)(a)**). 'Likely' means 'may well' as opposed to 'more probable than not' (*Black v Sumitomo Corporation* [2001] EWCA Civ 1819, [2002] 1 WLR 1562). The proceedings may be an additional claim as much as a Part 7 or 8 claim (*Moresfield Ltd v Banners* [2003] EWHC 1602 (Ch), LTL 3/7/2003), but not an arbitration (*EDO Corporation v Ultra Electronics Ltd* [2009] EWHC 682 (Ch), [2009] Bus LR 1306).

(b) The applicant must be likely to be a party to subsequent proceedings (**r. 31.16(3)(b)**).

(c) The applicant and respondent must be likely to be parties to 'subsequent proceedings' (Senior Courts Act 1981, s. 35(1); County Courts Act 1984, s. 54(1)).

(d) An order can be made only if, had proceedings been started, the respondent's duty by way of standard disclosure set out in **CPR, r. 31.6**, would extend to the documents or classes of documents of which the applicant seeks disclosure (**r. 31.16(3)(c)**). Thus, pre-action disclosure cannot be granted in respect of documents which would not be disclosable had proceedings actually been commenced. In the case of a class of documents (see **r. 31.16(3)(c)**), the applicant must show that the whole class would be covered by standard disclosure (*Hutchison 3G UK Ltd v O2 (UK) Ltd* [2008] EWHC 55 (Comm), LTL 22/1/2008). There is no obligation on the respondent to specify which of the documents potentially within the class might be covered by standard disclosure (*Wakefield v Outhwaite* [1990] 2 Lloyd's Rep 157).

(e) By **r. 31.16(3)(d)**, the court may only make an order if disclosure before the proceedings have started is desirable in order:

(i) to dispose fairly of the anticipated proceedings;

(ii) to assist the dispute to be resolved without proceedings; or
(iii) to save costs.

There is controversy about how the merits of the underlying cause of action should be established on an application for pre-action disclosure (requirement (c) above). It is submitted that the right approach is that laid down in *Black v Sumitomo Corporation* [2001] EWCA Civ 1819, [2002] 1 WLR 1562, namely that the applicant must have an arguable possible claim against the defendant. This is consistent with the use of the word 'likely' in **r. 31.16(3)(a)**, which was interpreted in *Black v Sumitomo Corporation* as meaning 'may well' as opposed to 'more probable than not'. An alternative test, based on *Rose v Lynx Express Ltd* [2004] EWCA Civ 447, [2004] 1 BCLC 455, is that it is necessary for the applicant to show a case with a real prospect of success. This difference in approach is causing difficulties in first-instance cases, with *Pineway Ltd v London Mining Co. Ltd* [2010] EWHC 1143 (Comm), LTL 24/5/2010, attempting to reconcile the two approaches, and *Kneale v Barclays Bank plc* [2010] EWHC 1900 (Comm), LTL 26/7/2010, preferring the *Black v Sumitomo Corporation* approach over that in *Rose v Lynx Express Ltd*.

Generally, the court should not embark on an investigation into issues such as justiciability or the elements of the alleged cause of action, on an application for pre-action disclosure (*Total E & P Soudan SA v Edmonds* [2007] EWCA Civ 50, LTL 31/1/2007). These matters can be left until after proceedings are issued. However, it follows from requirements (c) and (d) that the court has to be clear what the issues are likely to be in the anticipated proceedings, and must make sure that the documents being asked for are likely to adversely affect the case of one side or the other. Where there is no clear issue between the parties, the application should be refused (*Medisys plc v Arthur Andersen* [2002] PNLR 22; *Laurence v Commissioner of Police of the Metropolis* (2006) LTL 13/2/2006).

When considering requirement (e), the court has to undertake a balancing exercise to determine whether pre-action disclosure is 'desirable' in one of the three ways set out in **r. 31.16(3)(d)** (*Bermuda International Securities Ltd v KPMG* [2001] CPLR 252). Where the applicant has enough material to plead a claim, albeit not as perfectly as might be possible with further documentation from the respondent, it is unlikely to be 'desirable' to order pre-action disclosure (*First Gulf Bank v Wachovia Bank National Association* [2005] EWHC 2827 (Comm), LTL 15/12/2005). Pre-action disclosure of the medical records of a proposed claimant in a personal injuries claim was refused under **r. 31.16(3)(d)** in *OCS Group Ltd v Wells* [2008] EWHC 919 (QB), [2009] 1 WLR 1895, where the court preferred the approach on medical records expressed in *Bennett v Compass Group UK and Ireland Ltd* [2002] EWCA Civ 642, [2002] ICR 1177, to that in *Black v Sumitomo Corporation* [2001] EWCA Civ 1819, [2002] 1 WLR 1562. While medical records are relevant within the meaning of standard disclosure (**rr. 31.6** and **31.16(3)(c)**), as the issues between the parties will not have been precisely delineated at the time of most pre-action disclosure applications, such records may have little or no value in determining the claim, may increase the prospects of litigation, and may result in embarrassing information, unconnected to the claim, being disclosed to the defendant.

The test for granting an order for pre-action disclosure is strict, in that it requires not only that the document sought is disclosable, but that disclosing it at that stage will further one of the purposes set out in **r. 31.16(3)(d)**, for example, that its disclosure will indicate whether or not the claimant has a case (*Burrells Wharf Freeholds Ltd v Galliard Homes Ltd* [1999] 33 EG 82). Where a pre-action protocol applies, there should be little need for an application of this nature, as the protocols normally provide for the early exchange of documents and information before a claim is issued.

Discretion to order pre-action disclosure

All applications will obviously turn on their own facts, and the Court of Appeal has said that it is inappropriate to lay down guidelines (*Bermuda International Securities Ltd v KPMG* [2001] CPLR 252). Orders for pre-action disclosure are not exceptional, but they are unusual. The **50.86** discretion is likely to be exercised against an applicant who has enough material to plead a claim against the respondent, but is applying for pre-action disclosure to improve its case (*First Gulf Bank v Wachovia Bank National Association* [2005] EWHC 2827 (Comm), LTL 15/12/2005). Where the likely defendant had supplied a substantial proportion of the documents requested, an order for pre-action disclosure of the rest was refused, as the likely claimant had enough material to decide whether to bring proceedings (*Meretz Investments NV v First Penthouse Ltd* [2003] EWHC 2324 (Ch), LTL 16/10/2003). The court will not make an order for pre-action disclosure which would be oppressive, for example, where the proposed claim is speculative and there is real doubt that the documents sought would actually produce evidence to support the claim, rather than merely suggesting a possible line of inquiry (*Black v Sumitomo Corporation* [2001] EWCA Civ 1819, [2002] 1 WLR 1562).

It may be appropriate to make an order even if the substantive claim appears speculative, for example, where the likely defendant has refused to provide a clear answer to the alleged claim (*Jay v Wilder Coe* [2003] EWHC 1786 (QB) 1786, LTL 28/8/2003). In a complex claim, the desirability of having a focused pleading from the outset is a factor in favour of making the order (*Total E & P Soudan SA v Edmonds* [2007] EWCA Civ 50, LTL 31/1/2007). While the weakness of a case can be taken into account in deciding to refuse pre-action disclosure (*Snowstar Shipping Co. Ltd v Graig Shipping plc* [2003] EWHC 1367 (Comm), LTL 17/6/2003), usually the court should not embark on assessing the strength of the case, particularly where the issues are complex or the merits will be decided on evidence not available or tested at the pre-action stage (*Anglo Irish Bank Corporation plc v West LB AG* [2009] EWHC 207 (Comm), LTL 25/2/2009).

Pre-action provision of information

50.87 The court does not have the power under **CPR, r. 31.16**, to make an order to confirm or give information, as opposed to disclosure of documents (*Snowstar Shipping Co. Ltd v Graig Shipping plc* [2003] EWHC 1367 (Comm), LTL 17/6/2003). This might be possible under the *Norwich Pharmacal* jurisdiction, see **50.98**.

Procedure on applying for pre-action disclosure

50.88 An application for pre-action disclosure is brought by issuing an application notice in form N244, and must be supported by written evidence (**CPR, r. 31.16(2)**). The evidence must explain, for each document or class of documents sought from the likely defendant, how the requirements discussed in **50.85** are satisfied.

An order (and any draft order) for pre-action disclosure must specify the documents or classes of documents to be disclosed (**r. 31.16(4)(a)**). It is suggested, therefore, that a general application for 'standard disclosure' will fail. The order will further require the respondent to list any of the specified documents which are no longer in the respondent's control, or in respect of which the respondent claims a right or duty to withhold inspection (**r. 31.16(4)(b)**). It may require the respondent to indicate what has happened to any documents no longer in his control, and may specify the time and place for disclosure and inspection (**r. 31.16(5)**).

Costs of pre-action disclosure applications

50.89 Most applications for pre-action disclosure will be made on behalf of the potential claimant, although there may be exceptional cases where a potential defendant, having been notified of a possible claim, will seek to take the initiative in obtaining documents which are believed go to the heart of the action and which have not been voluntarily provided in advance by the claimant.

The rules on costs relating to special cases (**CPR, Part 46**) apply to pre-action disclosure, and applications for disclosure against non-parties. The general rule is that the person against whom an order for pre-action disclosure is sought will be awarded the costs of the application and of complying with any order made (**r. 46.1(2)**). Such costs will almost invariably be determined by summary assessment, although it may not be possible for the assessment to take place immediately after the application, simply because the respondent may not know what the cost of complying with the order will be.

The court may, however, by **r. 46.1(3)**, make a different costs order, having regard to all the circumstances, which include the extent to which it was reasonable for the person against whom the order was sought to oppose the application, and whether the parties to the application have complied with any relevant pre-action protocol. As the starting point is that the applicant must pay the respondent's costs (**r. 46.1(2)**), it is not usually unreasonable for a respondent to resist the application (*SES Contracting Ltd v UK Coal plc* [2007] EWCA Civ 791, *The Times*, 16 October 2007). It might be right to depart from the normal rule if the application were resisted in an unreasonable way, such as by using written evidence not backed up by contemporaneous documents (*SES Contracting Ltd v UK Coal plc*). It may be unreasonable where the respondent had an obligation to provide the documents in compliance with a pre-action protocol, or where the applicant has a contractual right to inspect the documents (*Moduleco Ltd v Carillion Construction Ltd* [2009] EWHC 250 (TCC), LTL 4/4/2009). Even where the respondent is regarded as acting unreasonably, costs against the respondent should be limited to the costs of the application, with the applicant still paying the costs of the exercise of disclosing the documents (*Bermuda International Securities Ltd v KPMG* [2001] CPLR 252).

Thus, as with all costs orders, the court will have regard to the general duty of cooperation between the parties and reasonableness of their conduct. In personal injury and clinical negligence cases, the protocols provide guidance as to reasonable pre-action behaviour, including the early exchange of information and documents. Any successful application for pre-action disclosure in such cases is almost certainly an indication that the pre-action protocols have not been complied with, and will therefore strongly suggest unreasonable behaviour on the part of the respondent, who should expect to be ordered to pay the applicant's costs.

Commentary

DISCLOSURE BY NON-PARTIES

The procedure for applying for a non-party disclosure order is summarised in **procedural checklist 27**, which is at the front of the book. Once proceedings have started, an application for an order for disclosure by a person who is not a party to the proceedings must be made in accordance with **CPR, Part 23** (see **chapter 32**), and must be supported by evidence (**r. 31.17(2)**). Notice of the application must be served on the respondent (**r. 23.4(1)**). The procedure enables the court to order a witness to produce relevant documents well before the trial, rather than having to wait until the trial and obtaining the documents from the witness under a witness summons. This can be extremely useful, as early disclosure can prevent the need to adjourn the trial. **50.90**

The ability of the court to make an order for non-party disclosure in all types of cases will diminish, but not totally extinguish, the need for practices of the kind used in *Khanna v Lovell White Durrant* [1995] 1 WLR 121, in which the court invented the concept of the 'production appointment' for witnesses to attend under subpoena to bring documents to a hearing before the trial, in order that they could be photocopied for use in the proceedings (see **50.95**).

Requirements for non-party disclosure orders

An order for the disclosure of documents may be made against a non-party if: **50.91**

(a) the documents sought are likely to support the case of the applicant or adversely affect the case of another party (**CPR, r. 31.17(3)**);

(b) the documents sought actually exist; and
(c) disclosure is necessary for the purpose of disposing of the claim fairly or saving costs (**r. 31.17(3)**).

'Likely' in this context means 'may well' support the applicant's case or adversely affect the case of another party (*Three Rivers District Council v Her Majesty's Treasury* [2002] EWCA Civ 1182, [2003] 1 WLR 210).

Disclosure against non-parties will only be granted where the documents sought are relevant (as opposed to disclosable under standard disclosure) (see *American Home Products Corporation v Novartis Pharmaceuticals UK Ltd* (2001) LTL 13/2/2001). The court should primarily consider relevance by a close analysis of the statements of case as they stand on the date of the application (*Flood v Times Newspapers Ltd* [2009] EWHC 411 (QB), [2009] EMLR 18). It should not embark on determining disputes of substance as to whether the documents are relevant (*Clark v Ardington Electrical Services* [2001] EWCA Civ 585, LTL 4/4/2001). There must be some evidential basis for the allegations in respect of which the documents are said to be relevant (*Re Skyward Builders plc* [2002] EWHC 1788 (Ch), [2002] 2 BCLC 750). The court is required to apply the test to each document sought, although the court is permitted to consider the documents on a sub-class by sub-class basis (*Three Rivers District Council v Her Majesty's Treasury* [2002] EWCA Civ 1182, [2003] 1 WLR 210).

Discretion to order non-party disclosure

50.92 Where the documents are relevant, it is then necessary to consider whether the court should refuse the order in its discretion, or impose some limit on disclosure, such as by ordering disclosure of documents only between stated dates. It will require a very exceptional case to justify ordering the disclosure of a non-party's confidential medical documents (*A v X* [2004] EWHC 447 (QB), LTL 6/4/2004). Further, the court will not make an order if it is not satisfied that the documents sought in fact exist. In *Re Howglen Ltd* [2001] 1 All ER 376 an application was made in general terms for documents against a non-party bank for bank records and interview notes. An order was made limited to the notes of three interviews identified in the evidence in support.

It will sometimes be possible to make an application under the Access to Health Records Act 1990, or the Bankers' Books Evidence Act 1879 (see **49.80**), as an alternative to making an application for non-party disclosure under the Senior Courts Act 1981, s. 34, or the County Courts Act 1984, s. 53.

An applicant for an order under **CPR, r. 31.17**, should consider carefully all alternative ways of obtaining the required documents. For example, it may be argued, in a particular case, that it is not necessary to see the document in advance of the trial, and that a witness summons or deposition will suffice. However, there will not be many cases in which the many documents sought will be sufficiently straightforward that they can be digested and properly dealt with by both parties on the morning of the trial, and without appearing in the trial bundle for pre-reading, and general principles of case management militate against last-minute surprises.

Form of order for non-party disclosure

50.93 An order for non-party disclosure must specify the documents or the classes of documents which the respondent must disclose, and require the respondent, when making disclosure, to specify any of these documents which are no longer in the respondent's control, or in respect of which the respondent claims a right or duty to withhold inspection (**CPR, r. 31.17(4)**). In addition, the court may order that the respondent be required to indicate what has happened to any documents now outside the respondent's control, and specify the time and place for disclosure and inspection (**r. 31.17(5)**).

The order may restrict access to the disclosed documents to the applicant's legal advisers and/or experts (Senior Courts Act 1981, s. 34(2); County Courts Act 1984, s. 52(2)). This may be appropriate where the documents include trade secrets (*Fremier Profiles Ltd v Tioxide Europe Ltd* (2002) LTL 25/9/2002).

The court may order the applicant to provide a sum of money to the respondent as a condition of compliance in advance of inspection (*Re Skyward Builders plc* [2002] EWHC 1788 (Ch), [2002] 2 BCLC 750, where the sum of £1,000 was ordered to be paid).

Costs of application for non-party disclosure

The rules on costs in **CPR, r. 46.1** (see **50.89**), apply equally to the costs of non-party disclosure as they do to the costs of pre-action disclosure. The presumption is that the court will award the non-party the costs of the application and of complying with the terms of any order made (**r. 46.1(2)**). However, the court has the power to make a different order to reflect what it may consider to be the reasonableness of the non-party's opposition to the application (**r. 46.1(3)**). **50.94**

Additional powers to order pre-action and non-party disclosure

CPR, r. 31.18, provides that **rr. 31.16** and **31.17** do not limit any other power which the court may have to order disclosure before proceedings have started, or to order disclosure against a person who is not a party to the proceedings. This allows continuation of the practice in *Khanna v Lovell White Durrant* [1995] 1 WLR 121 of production appointments (see **50.90**) if considered preferable to an order for non-party disclosure. **Rule 31.18** also preserves the jurisdiction to make a *Norwich Pharmacal* order (see **50.97**). Additionally, orders may be made under the Data Protection Act 1998 (see **50.96**) and pursuant to the decision in *Bankers Trust Co. v Shapira* [1980] 1 WLR 1274 (see **50.102**). **50.95**

Data protection

The Data Protection Act 1998, s. 7, applies where personal data about an individual are held by a data controller. On making a request in writing and paying a fee (if applicable), the individual is entitled to have communicated to him in an intelligible form any personal data relating to him and any information about the source of that data. For this purpose 'data' means information which is processed automatically (generally by computer), and also information recorded as part of a filing system, or which forms part of an accessible record (which, by s. 68, means health, education and accessible public records). The selection of data from various manual and electronic files is not 'processing' for this purpose (*Johnson v Medical Defence Union (No. 2)* [2007] EWCA Civ 262, [2008] Bus LR 503). A manual filing system will only be regarded as 'data' within the meaning of the Data Protection Act 1998 if it is of sufficient sophistication to provide the same or similar ready accessibility as a computerised filing system. This means the files must be referenced or indexed in a way that makes it possible to identify with reasonable certainty and speed whether they contain personal data without having to leaf through the files themselves (*Durant v Financial Services Authority* [2003] EWCA Civ 1746, [2004] FSR 28). 'Personal data' is defined as meaning data relating to a living individual who can be identified from that data (or other information in the possession of the data controller), and includes expressions of opinion about the individual (s. 1(1)). According to *Durant v Financial Services Authority* information will come within this definition if: **50.96**

(a) the information is biographical in a significant sense, going beyond mere involvement in the events described in the file; and
(b) the data subject (the applicant) is the focus of the information.

Thus, a file dealing with a complaint made to the Financial Services Authority by the applicant about a bank was not personal data because its focus was the complaint, not biographical information about the applicant.

There are various exemptions and further detailed provisions, such as a restriction on revealing information that would identify other individuals without their consent (s. 7(4)). When complying with a request for personal data which will also reveal details about other individuals, the data controller is required to balance the interests of the other individuals with the interests of the data subject. It may be permissible to redact the names of the other individuals if it is reasonable to do so.

The data controller is required to comply with a request promptly, and can be ordered to comply by the High Court or a county court (ss. 7(9) and 15(1)). For the purpose of determining whether the applicant is entitled to the information under s. 7, the court may require the information to be made available for inspection by the court (but not the applicant, who will not be allowed to inspect the information until after a determination in his favour (s. 15(2)). On an application for an order under ss. 7(9) and 15(1), the court has an untrammelled discretion whether to grant an order, but the main factor is that access under the Act is mainly for the purpose of correcting inaccuracy (*Durant v Financial Services Authority*). An individual who is refused an order under s. 7 on the ground that the information held is not personal data may subsequently be allowed access to the same information under any of the powers under **CPR, Part 31**, such as an application for specific disclosure (*Johnson v Medical Defence Union* [2004] EWHC 2509 (Ch), [2005] 1 WLR 750).

NORWICH PHARMACAL ORDERS

50.97 In *Norwich Pharmacal Co. v Commissioners of Customs and Excise* [1974] AC 133 it was held that a person who, albeit innocently, became 'mixed up in the tortious acts of others so as to facilitate their wrongdoing' was under a duty to assist the person who had been wronged by giving that person full information and disclosing the identity of the wrongdoers.

The jurisdiction is based on the ancient Chancery bill of discovery, and is useful where a party has a cause of action but does not have the names and addresses of persons who should be named as the defendants. Using Lord Reid's terminology from *Norwich Pharmacal Co. v Commissioners of Customs and Excise*, the court may make an order compelling a person to provide information identifying wrongdoers if:

(a) The respondent has become mixed up in the wrongdoing. There must be at least a good arguable case of wrongdoing by some person (in *R (Mohamed) v Secretary of State for Foreign and Commonwealth Affairs (No. 1)* [2008] EWHC 2048 (Admin), [2009] 1 WLR 2579, the word 'good' was dropped from this formulation at [67]). It has been held that an order can be made even if the underlying cause of action has not been clearly made out (*P v T Ltd* [1997] 1 WLR 1309). The respondent may be perfectly innocent, and may not even realise that there has been any wrongdoing (as in *Norwich Pharmacal Co. v Commissioners of Customs and Excise* itself). Where the respondent is a party to the wrongdoing it is usually named as defendant in the substantive claim, and is also under a duty to identify other wrongdoers (*British Steel Corporation v Granada Television Ltd* [1981] AC 1096). In cases of wilful evasion of court orders, it may be enough that the respondent has got mixed up in the affairs of the wrongdoer (*Mercantile Group (Europe) AG v Aiyela* [1994] QB 366).

(b) The respondent has facilitated the wrongdoing. Unwitting facilitation of the infringement of the claimants' patent by allowing infringing products into the country was sufficient in *Norwich Pharmacal Co. v Commissioners of Customs and Excise*. Providing information and questions to the security services of another country, which is then alleged to have used torture when questioning the claimant, was held to constitute the facilitation of arguable wrongdoing in *R (Mohamed) v Secretary of State for Foreign and Commonwealth Affairs (No. 1)* [2008] EWHC 2048 (Admin), [2009] 1 WLR 2579. However, a person who has done nothing to facilitate the wrongdoing, and is a mere witness, is under no obligation to disclose the identity of the wrongdoers (*Ricci v Chow* [1987] 1 WLR 1658). In *Harrington v Polytechnic of North London* [1984] 1 WLR 1293 the claimant was a student who claimed he was prevented from attending the polytechnic by student pickets. Photographs were taken of the pickets, and the claimant sought an order compelling the lecturers to identify the pickets. It was held that the lecturers were mere witnesses when acting in their private capacities, but the polytechnic was ordered to provide the information as it had become mixed up in and facilitated the wrongdoing.

(c) The applicant has a sufficient interest. Generally this is satisfied by showing a genuine intention to bring legal proceedings against the wrongdoers. The condition will also be satisfied if the applicant has no intention to sue, but does intend to discipline employee wrongdoers (*Ashworth Hospital Authority v MGN Ltd* [2002] UKHL 29, [2002] 1 WLR 2033). Disclosure of the names of customers of someone alleged to be infringing the claimant's patent will not usually be ordered unless there is some real grievance or some significant purpose in doing so (*Smith Kline and French Laboratories Ltd v Doncaster Pharmaceuticals Ltd* [1989] FSR 407).

(d) Provision of the documents or information is necessary (*Ashworth Hospital Authority v MGN Ltd* [2002] UKHL 29, [2002] 1 WLR 2033 at [57]). Authorities such as *Mitsui and Co Ltd v Nexen Petroleum UK Ltd* [2005] EWHC 625 (Ch), [2005] 3 All ER 511, which imposed a stringent test of necessity (requiring the evidence to be the final piece in the jigsaw, or *Norwich Pharmacal* orders to be a remedy of last resort), were deprecated in *R (Mohamed) v Secretary of State for Foreign and Commonwealth Affairs (No. 1)* [2008] EWHC 2048 (Admin), [2009] 1 WLR 2579. Rather, the court must consider all the circumstances, including the resources of the applicant, the urgency of the need for the information, and any public interest in satisfying the applicant's need for the information. The court will be very reluctant to order a bank to provide information under a *Norwich Pharmacal* order which involves a breach of confidence between a bank and its customer (*Koo Golden East Mongolia v Bank of Nova Scotia* [2007] EWCA Civ 1443, [2008] QB 717). In exercising its discretion the court will, where appropriate, take into account the principles in the Data Protection Act 1998 and the right to free speech in the European Convention on Human Rights, **art. 10**, in the **Human Rights Act 1998, sch. 1** (*Totalise plc v Motley Fool Ltd* (No. 2) [2001] EWCA Civ 187, [2002] 1 WLR 1233; *Smith v ADVFN plc* [2008] EWHC 577 (QB), LTL 8/5/2008).

(e) The court exercises its discretion to make the order (the relief being equitable). Relevant factors include proportionality, expense, time, intrusion, any public policy considerations, the needs of the case and its seriousness (*R (Mohamed) v Secretary of State for Foreign and Commonwealth Affairs (No. 1)* [2008] EWHC 2048 (Admin), [2009] 1 WLR 2579 at [133] and [140]).

(f) The information sought is not protected by privilege, public interest, or State immunity. In *Koo Golden East Mongolia v Bank of Nova Scotia* [2007] EWCA Civ 1443, [2008] QB 717, the respondent was a central bank and was held entitled to claim State immunity under the State Immunity Act 1978, so relief was refused. In cases of possible privilege the court may alternatively grant the order, with the respondent taking the privilege point by way of objection to inspection under **CPR, r. 31.19**.

Scope of *Norwich Pharmacal* jurisdiction

The *Norwich Pharmacal* jurisdiction is not restricted to claims in tort, but is of general application, and applies to claims in breach of confidence and breach of contract (*British Steel Corporation v Granada Television Ltd* [1981] AC 1096; *Ashworth Hospital Authority v MGN Ltd* [2001] 1 WLR 515 (CA); [2002] UKHL 29, [2002] 1 WLR 2033). The flexibility of the jurisdiction was emphasised in *R (Mohamed) v Secretary of State for Foreign and Commonwealth Affairs (No. 1)* [2008] EWHC 2048 (Admin), [2009] 1 WLR 2579 (disclosure of documents relevant to allegations of torture which were to be used to support an argument that confessions should be inadmissible in an overseas prosecution). In most cases where *Norwich Pharmacal* orders have been made it has been clear, or nearly so, that some tort or other civil wrong has been committed. *Re an Intended* **50.98**

Claim, Carlton Film Distributors Ltd v VDC Ltd [2003] EWHC 616 (Ch), LTL 21/3/2003 concerned an application for disclosure of information against an identified proposed defendant. The principle was extended in *Murphy v Murphy* [1999] 1 WLR 282, where an order was made against a settlor to disclose to a potential beneficiary the names and addresses of the trustees under a settlement, to enable the potential beneficiary to communicate with the trustees with a view to being considered for the distribution of trust property held on discretionary trusts. The trustees were obviously not wrongdoers for the purpose of the *Norwich Pharmacal* principle.

When it comes into force, the Justice and Security Act 2013, s. 17, will prevent *Norwich Pharmacal* orders being made in respect of 'sensitive information'. Broadly, sensitive information covers most material relating to the activities of the intelligence services (s. 17(3)).

Journalists' sources

50.99 The Contempt of Court Act 1981, s. 10 (which was enacted in response to *British Steel Corporation v Granada Television Ltd* [1981] AC 1096), provides:

> No court may require a person, nor is any person guilty of contempt of court for refusing to disclose, the source of information contained in a publication for which he is responsible, unless it be established to the satisfaction of the court that disclosure is necessary in the interests of justice or national security or for the prevention of disorder or crime.

The section provides a general protection to journalists' sources. It applies despite any proprietary claim for the delivery up of stolen documents if the documents could lead to the identification of the source (*Secretary of State for Defence v Guardian Newspapers Ltd* [1985] AC 339).

It also applies even if there has been no publication of the information, provided the information was supplied with a view to publication (*X Ltd v Morgan-Grampian (Publishers) Ltd* [1991] 1 AC 1). In *Totalise plc v Motley Fool Ltd* [2001] EMLR 750 a website operator was ordered to disclose the identity of a person who, it was alleged, had posted defamatory comments on the website. It was held that the Contempt of Court Act 1981, s. 10, had no application to the facts because the defendant took no responsibility for items posted on its website, since the section applied to information 'contained in a publication for which he is responsible'.

Disclosure of a journalist's source under one of the exceptions to s. 10 will only be ordered if 'necessary' for one of the exceptional reasons. The phrase 'interests of justice' is interpreted so 'that persons should be enabled to exercise important legal rights and to protect themselves from serious legal wrongs whether or not resort to legal proceedings in a court of law will be necessary to attain these objectives' (see Lord Bridge of Harwich in *X Ltd v Morgan-Grampian (Publishers) Ltd*). 'Prevention of crime' includes the detection and prosecution of crimes which are shown to have been committed and where detection and prosecution can sensibly be said to act as a practical deterrent to future criminal conduct of a similar type (see Lord Oliver of Aylmerton in *Re an Inquiry under the Company Securities (Insider Dealing) Act 1985* [1988] AC 660).

If one of the exceptions applies and is necessary, the court must then weigh the importance of disclosure for the exceptional reason against the importance of protecting the source of the information. Factors to be taken into account include the degree of confidentiality attaching to the information, the manner in which the information was obtained, the public interest in concealing journalists' sources, and whether the information brings to light iniquity on the part of the claimant. According to Lord Bridge in *X Ltd v Morgan-Grampian (Publishers) Ltd* disclosure should only be ordered if the balance is clearly on the side of disclosure, since otherwise the courts would be undermining the policy stated in the section. The interrelation between the Contempt of Court Act 1981, s. 10, the European Convention on Human Rights, **art. 10**, in the **Human Rights Act 1998, sch. 1** (freedom of expression), and *Norwich Pharmacal* orders was further considered in *Ashworth Hospital Authority v MGN Ltd* [2002] UKHL 29, [2002] 1 WLR 2033, and its sequel, *Mersey Care NHS Trust v Ackroyd* [2007] EWCA Civ 101, [2007] HRLR 19, decisions which almost certainly cannot be followed given the ruling in *Financial Times*

Ltd v United Kingdom (application 821/03) (2009) 50 EHRR 46. Given the chilling effects of journalists being seen to assist in identifying anonymous sources, merely seeking to eliminate the threat of damage through future leaks of confidential information was regarded as insufficient to outweigh the public interest encapsulated in art. 10.

Procedure for seeking *Norwich Pharmacal* orders

Norwich Pharmacal orders are usually sought by issuing a claim form against the facilitator, and then by issuing an application notice within that claim seeking the disclosure order. Applications have to be supported by witness statement evidence. It is possible in an urgent case to seek the order without giving notice (*Loose v Williamson* [1978] 1 WLR 639). The person from whom disclosure is sought may contact the person whose identity is sought and invite that person to submit reasons why disclosure should not be ordered; the court may require such contact to be made and may hear the person whose identity is sought (*Totalise plc v Motley Fool Ltd (No. 2)* [2001] EWCA Civ 187, [2002] 1 WLR 1233). **50.100**

The order

While the court can order the respondent to provide 'full information' (*Norwich Pharmacal Co. v Commissioners of Customs and Excise* [1974] AC 133), this does not provide a general right to disclosure or for gathering information (*Arab Monetary Fund v Hashim (No. 5)* [1992] 2 All ER 911 at p. 914). The material to be disclosed should be confined to necessary information and documents, but this does not mean that it is limited to disclosure of the identity of the wrong doer or the 'final piece of the jigsaw'. What is necessary depends on the circumstances of each case (*R (Mohamed) v Secretary of State for Foreign and Commonwealth Affairs (No. 1)* [2008] EWHC 2048 (Admin), [2009] 1 WLR 2579 at [133], [134]). **50.101**

Normally a successful applicant for a *Norwich Pharmacal* order should pay the costs of the party ordered to make disclosure, including the costs of making the disclosure (*Totalise plc v Motley Fool Ltd (No. 2)* [2001] EWCA Civ 1897, [2002] 1 WLR 1233). These costs may be recovered against the wrongdoer in the same or a subsequent claim (*Smith Kline and French Laboratories Ltd v R. D. Harbottle (Mercantile) Ltd* [1980] RPC 363).

BANKERS TRUST ORDERS

In *Bankers Trust Co. v Shapira* [1980] 1 WLR 1274 a bank, which was a defendant in proceedings, was ordered to disclose to the claimant certain confidential information, such as copies of correspondence, cheques, debit vouchers, transfer applications and internal memoranda, relating to two co-defendants, notwithstanding that those co-defendants had not yet been served with proceedings. The purpose of the order was to enable the applicant to trace the existence of and protect the assets claimed in the proceedings, in which, it was found, there was very strong evidence that the co-defendants had been guilty of fraud. Given the confidential nature of the documents to be disclosed, a party claiming an order of this kind must give an undertaking not to use the information obtained other than in the course of the proceedings. See also *Arab Monetary Fund v Hashim (No. 5)* [1992] 2 All ER 911 and *Omar v Omar* [1995] 1 WLR 1428. **50.102**

DISCLOSURE ORDERS IN AID OF ARBITRATION

Where a dispute is referred to arbitration, the Arbitration Act 1996, s. 43, provides that court procedures to procure documents or other material evidence may be used only with the permission of the arbitral tribunal or the agreement of the other parties. This provision does not prevent a court making a *Norwich Pharmacal* order (see 50.97) in the period before a dispute has **50.103** been referred to arbitration, where the power is used for preserving assets or remedies (*Glidepath Holding BV v Thompson* [2004] EWHC 2234 (Comm), [2005] 1 All ER (Comm) 434). Unless otherwise agreed by the parties, the court has under s. 44 five specified powers relating to the taking of evidence from witnesses, the preservation of evidence and making orders in relation to property (see **37.55**). These specified powers do not include orders for non-party disclosure under **CPR, r. 31.17** (see **50.90**). Where there is a risk that documents may cease to exist or become unavailable, it may be possible to obtain an order for their preservation, such as by copying, under s. 44(2)(b), see *Assimina Maritime Ltd v Pakistan National Shipping Corporation* [2004] EWHC 3005 (Comm), [2005] 1 All ER (Comm) 460).

Chapter 51 Witness Statements

Commentary

INTRODUCTION

It has always been the case that there is no property in a witness, and a party may interview and seek to call anyone who may be able to assist with relevant evidence. There are practical problems in seeking the assistance of witnesses who are employed or otherwise connected with the opposite party. A particular problem with employees of the other party is that they will owe duties of loyalty and confidentiality to their employer. In *Porton Capital Technology Funds v 3M UK Holdings Ltd* [2010] EWHC 114 (Comm), LTL 8/2/2010, it was held that an employee's duty of confidentiality is not altered by the employer being a party to litigation or disclosing confidential documents in the litigation. Such confidential documents may be shown to the receiving party's employees, but compliance with the duty of confidentiality owed by the disclosing party's employees may mean they cannot answer questions or provide information, even about the disclosed documents. **51.1**

A witness statement is a written statement signed by a person which contains the evidence which that person would be allowed to give orally (**CPR, r. 32.4(1)**). The text of the statement must, if practicable, be in the witness's own words, and should be expressed in the first person (**PD 32, para. 18.1**). They are used for two main purposes:

(a) for setting out the evidence in support of interim applications; and
(b) for setting out the evidence witnesses are expected to give at trial.

Witness statements take much the same form as traditional affidavits and affirmations (see **chapter 52**), except that they are not sworn or affirmed, and instead contain a simple statement of truth. Consequently most of the formalities required for affidavits, such as corner markings, and the rules on paragraphing, exhibits etc., have to be complied with. However, a witness statement will not have a commencement, and it will not have a jurat. Also, because it is not sworn there will be a saving of the fees payable for swearing an affidavit (see **52.3**).

An example of a witness statement for use in an interim application is shown in **figure 51.1**.

Figure 51.1 Witness statement seeking to set aside a judgment in default and transfer of claim

Made on behalf of the Defendant
Witness: B. Parkes
1st statement of witness
Exhibits: BP 1 to BP 3
Made: 19.11.2013

IN THE HIGH COURT OF JUSTICE — Claim No. HC13Q 98744

QUEEN'S BENCH DIVISION

BETWEEN

SHILTON MACHINE TOOLS LIMITED — Claimant

— and —

BANKS PLASTIC MOULDINGS LIMITED — Defendant

WITNESS STATEMENT OF BRIAN PARKES

1. I am Brian Parkes, of Unit 6, Elland Trading Estate, Leeds LS8 3AN. I am a director of the Defendant company. I have full knowledge of the facts of this case and I am duly authorised to make this statement on behalf of the Defendant in support of its application to set aside a default judgment entered on 8 October 2013. In so far as the contents of this statement are within my personal knowledge they are true, otherwise they are true to the best of my knowledge, information and belief.

2. The Defendant has a trading account with the Claimant, and it is true that it ordered 4 moulding machines from the Claimant on 15 June 2012 at a price of £60,000 plus VAT. Although the machines were delivered, they have been the subject of repeated breakdowns and have suffered a number of faults. The main problem with 2 of the machines is that despite a number of site attendances by the claimant's engineers they have proved incapable of producing mouldings to industry standards. I have been advised by Mr Edward Knight, a consulting engineer of 36 Harrogate Road, Leeds LS3 8DQ, that these two machines are so badly designed that it will be impossible to put them right.

pp. 41–65
pp. 66–94

3. As a result of the problems with all 4 machines the Defendant has suffered a substantial loss of business. In particular, it has lost a contract with United Plastic Containers plc, under which the Defendant was producing goods valued at between £10,000 and £20,000 per month. I refer to the bundle containing true copies of the Defendant's contractual documentation with United Plastic Containers plc, monthly invoices, and recent correspondence marked 'BP 1' in which the termination of the contract is explained. I have been advised by the Defendant's solicitors and believe that it has a substantial counterclaim with a value significantly above the value of the claim.

p. 95p. 96

4. As soon as I received the court papers in this action I raised the matter with Mrs Elaine Stepney, the finance director of the Claimant. I refer to the bundle of correspondence marked 'BP2', at page 1 of which is a true copy of my letter to her dated 17 September 2013. Her reply, at page 2, says she will look into the matter. Nevertheless, judgment was entered on 8 October 2013.

p. 98–102

5. For the reasons set out above, I ask that this judgment be set aside on the merits. I refer to the draft Defence and Counterclaim marked 'BP 3' which the Defendant intends to file if judgment is set aside, and I confirm the truth of the contents of the draft Defence and Counterclaim.

6. If judgment is set aside and the case allowed to continue, I respectfully ask that the claim be transferred to the Leeds County Court, the local court of the Defendant.

> **STATEMENT OF TRUTH**
> I believe the facts stated in this witness statement are true.
> Signed:
> Position: Director
> Dated: 19 November 2013.

PRINTING AND BINDING

Witness statements must be typed on one side only of durable A4 paper with a 35 mm margin (**PD 32, para. 19.1**(1) and (2)). The pages should be numbered consecutively (**para. 19.1**(4)). **51.2**

Wherever possible they should be securely bound in a manner that will not hamper filing (**para. 19.1**(3)). If they are not securely bound each page should bear the claim number and initials of the witness (**para. 19.1**(3)).

CORNER MARKINGS

At the top right-hand corner of the first page of the witness statement and of the backsheet there must appear the following details (**PD 32, para. 17.2**): **51.3**

(a) the party on whose behalf it is filed;
(b) the initials and surname of the maker of the statement;
(c) the number of the witness statement in relation to that deponent;
(d) the identifying initials and numbers of the exhibits referred to in the witness statement (if the statement is not the first one by this witness, the numbering of the exhibits must run consecutively from one statement to the next, and not start again with each statement: **para. 18.6**);
(e) the date it is signed.

HEADING

A witness statement should contain a formal heading with the title of the proceedings (**PD 32, para. 17.1**). It should be headed with the number of the claim, the court (and Division) where it is proceeding, the full names of the parties and their capacities (such as whether they are claimants or defendants). It is sufficient to identify the parties as being 'Between AB (and others) Claimants/Applicants and CD (and others) Defendants/Respondents' (**PD 32, para. 17.1**; **PD 7A, para.** 4). **51.4**

BODY OF WITNESS STATEMENT

A witness statement must, if practicable, be in the deponent's own words and should be expressed in the first person (**PD 32, para. 18.1**). A witness statement is not to be used as a vehicle for conveying legal argument (*Alex Lawrie Factors Ltd v Morgan* (1999) *The Times*, 18 August 1999). Nor should it contain lengthy quotations from documents (Admiralty and Commercial Courts Guide, para. H1.1(iii)). **51.5**

The opening paragraph should give details of the witness's occupation or description and his or her place of residence (**PD 32, para. 18.1**). If the statement is made in the witness's professional, business or other occupational capacity, the address given may be the address where the witness works, and the name of his or her firm or employer, and the position he or she holds, should be given. The statement should also state if the witness is a party in the proceedings, or employed by a party.

It is usually convenient to follow the chronological sequence of events. Each paragraph should be numbered, and, so far as possible, be confined to a distinct portion of the subject (**paras 19.1(5)** and **19.2**). All numbers, including dates, should be expressed in figures (**para. 19.1(6)**). Documents referred to in the statement should be formally exhibited.

Allegations of serious misconduct (whether or not they amount to fraud) must be set out clearly and with adequate particularity. Matters on which the witness can give direct evidence must be clearly distinguished in the witness statement from anything which is stated as a matter of inference (*Re Finelist Ltd* [2003] EWHC 1780 (Ch), [2004] BCC 877).

Hearsay in witness statements

51.6 Since the Civil Evidence Act 1995 has been in force it has been no objection that some of the evidence in a witness statement might be hearsay, but where it is, the witness should identify it as a matter based on information or belief, and give the source of that information or belief (**PD 32, para. 18.2**). This requirement is merely a procedural provision requiring the witness to identify, for the information of the other parties, the source of hearsay in the statement. If the source is a person, that person has to be identified with sufficient certainty to enable the other side to investigate the stated information or belief. The source should invariably be identified by name (*Consolidated Contractors International Co. SAL v Masri* [2011] EWCA Civ 21, [2011] CP Rep 20). There is no requirement that the source be identified using only admissible evidence, and the witness may use either recollection or opinion (*Clarke v Marlborough Fine Art (London) Ltd* [2002] 1 WLR 1731). Service of a witness statement containing hearsay evidence is sufficient notice of a party's proposal to adduce hearsay evidence for the purposes of the Civil Evidence Act 1995, s. 2 (**CPR, r. 33.2(1)**). If it is not proposed to call the witness to give oral evidence at trial, the party intending to rely on the hearsay evidence must, when serving the witness statement, inform the other parties that the witness is not being called to give oral evidence and give the reason for not calling the witness (**r. 33.2(2)**). There is no duty to give notice under the Civil Evidence Act 1995, s. 2, of an intention to adduce hearsay evidence at hearings other than trials (**CPR, r. 33.3(a)**).

EXHIBITS

51.7 When preparing witness statements, care should be taken to select appropriate documents and items of real evidence to be used as exhibits to each statement. Most exhibits are documents which are used to corroborate what the witness says in the body of the statement, or which are necessary items of evidence to establish the matters in dispute. Whether the witness statement is to be used at trial or on an interim application, the starting point is to identify the issues that need to be decided. It is then necessary to identify the evidence available, such as contractual documents, experts' reports, photographs and plans, official documents, bank statements, documents going to quantum, and relevant correspondence, and to organise the material into categories and chronological order. Then it is necessary to decide which witnesses are best placed to talk about each category of documents, and to include formal references to their exhibits at suitable points in the text of each statement.

Whenever documents are referred to in a witness statement, strictly those documents should be exhibited unless there is a sufficient reason for not doing so, such as length, volume, confidentiality or public interest immunity (*Tweed v Parades Commission for Northern Ireland* [2006] UKHL 53, [2007] 1 AC 650).

The requirements for exhibits to affidavits, which are set out in **PD 32, paras 11.3 to 15.5**, apply to exhibits to witness statements (**para. 18.5**). Numbering of exhibits has already been referred to (see **51.3**). In the body of the witness statement exhibits must be introduced with the words:

I refer to the [description of exhibit] marked '[witness's initials and exhibit number]'

followed by a description of the exhibit. Exhibits must be kept separate from the witness statement. They should have a frontsheet having the same markings in the top right corner and heading as the witness statement. Where an exhibit contains several documents the frontsheet should list them with their dates, and/or state the nature of the documents exhibited (such as so many original letters and so many copy letters). The frontsheet needs to bear the correct exhibit mark, and needs to be signed by the maker of the statement.

Documents of a similar nature, such as correspondence, should be gathered together into a single exhibit, and arranged chronologically with the earliest document on top, and with each page numbered consecutively at the bottom centre. A convenient alternative, which is widely adopted by City firms, is to use a single comprehensive exhibit for each witness. The approach is to organise the material into sections, with each section containing documents of a similar nature in chronological order with the earliest on top. In complex applications this can be helpful, because having numerous exhibits, each with its own pagination system, can be confusing. It is permissible to use copy documents in exhibits, provided the originals are available at the hearing should they be needed (**para. 13.1**). Illegible pages should be followed with a typed version with an 'a' number.

Exhibits other than documents should be clearly marked with the appropriate exhibit number in such a manner that the mark cannot become detached from the exhibit. Small items may be placed in a container, with the container being appropriately marked (**para. 14**).

A common mistake is to exhibit court documents. This is unnecessary as sealed copies of these documents prove themselves (**CPR, r. 2.6(3)**, a point specifically made by **PD 32, para. 13.2**).

Exhibits must not be stapled, but should be securely fastened in a way that does not hinder the reading of the documents they contain (**para. 15.1(1)**).

Bulky exhibits

Where, on account of their bulk, the service of exhibits on other parties would be difficult or impracticable, directions should be sought dealing with arrangements for bringing the exhibits to the attention of the other parties and their custody pending trial (**PD 32, para. 15.4**). **51.8**

Marginal references

A witness statement must 'give the reference to any document or documents mentioned either in the margin or in bold text in the body of the statement' (**PD 32, para. 19.1(7)**). It appears that this refers to the page references in the application or trial bundle, which will be added after the witness statement is signed. There is no objection to these references being added in manuscript (Admiralty and Commercial Courts Guide, app. 10, para. 3(i)). Time should be allowed for adding marginal references when preparing bundles. **51.9**

STATEMENT OF TRUTH

A witness statement must include a signed statement that the witness believes the facts it contains are true. False statements may be punished as contempt of court (**CPR, rr. 32.14, 81.17 and 81.18**; and see **23.15**). The form of statement of truth (see **PD 32, para. 20.2**) is: **51.10**

I believe that the facts stated in this witness statement are true.

In *Aquarius Financial Enterprises Inc. v Certain Underwriters at Lloyd's Subscribing to Contract KD 970212* (2001) LTL 20/5/2001 there was evidence that one of the witness statements had been obtained by bullying, threats and inducements. Toulson J said that where a witness statement is prepared by someone other than the witness, there should be a written declaration by the person who prepared the statement giving information about its preparation, and certifying compliance with any appropriate code of practice. Whether this will become the practice remains to be seen. It is improper to put pressure on a witness to give anything other than his own account of the matters in question, and it is also improper to serve a witness statement which is known to be false or which it is known the maker does not in all respects believe to be true (Admiralty and Commercial Courts Guide, para. H1.3).

Witness unable to read or sign

51.11 Where a witness statement is made by a person who is unable to read or sign the statement, it must contain a certificate made by an 'authorised person' (**PD 22, para. 3A.1**). An authorised person is someone able to administer oaths and take affidavits, but need not be independent of the parties or their representatives. The certificate must be in the form set out in annex 1 to PD 22. It says that the witness statement has been read to the witness, who appeared to understand it and approved its contents, that the statement of truth has been read to the witness, that the witness appeared to understand it and the consequences of making a false statement, and that the witness signed or made his or her mark in the presence of the authorised person.

ALTERATIONS

51.12 Alterations to a witness statement must be initialled by the person taking the statement or, if the witness is unable to read or sign, by the 'authorised person' (see **51.11**) (**PD 32, para. 22.1**). A witness statement which contains an alteration that has not been initialled may be used in evidence only with the permission of the court (**para. 22.2**).

FAILURE TO COMPLY WITH PD 32

51.13 If a witness statement or exhibit fails to comply with **PD 32**, the court may refuse to admit it as evidence and may refuse to allow the costs arising out of its preparation (**PD 32, para. 25.1**). Permission to use a defective witness statement may be obtained from a judge (meaning judge, master or district judge: **CPR, r. 2.3(1)**) of the court.

Striking out witness statements

51.14 There is no specific power in the CPR equivalent to the old RSC, ord. 41, r. 6, providing for the striking out of written evidence which is scandalous, irrelevant or oppressive. The general exclusionary discretion in **CPR, r. 32.1**, is probably the source for the continuing power to control evidence which it would be embarrassing for the court to have to keep on file, although **r. 32.2(2)(b)** seems to have been relied upon in *Stroude v Beazer Homes Ltd* [2004] EWHC 676 (Ch), LTL 15/3/2004. That there is such a power under the CPR was regarded as beyond doubt in *Sandhurst Holdings Ltd v Grosvenor Assets Ltd* (2001) LTL 25/10/2001. According to *Anglo Continental Educational Group (GB) Ltd v Capital Homes (Southern) Ltd* [2009] EWCA Civ 218, [2009] NPC 44, a party who is served with a witness statement which is thought to include inadmissible evidence has three courses of action:

(a) Write to the other side asking for the basis on which the evidence is said to be admissible. If dissatisfied with the answer, apply to exclude the evidence before replying to it.
(b) Issue an application, to be heard at the trial, to exclude the allegedly inadmissible evidence. The problem with this approach is that it potentially increases the costs

of the trial, and can lead to the detailed analysis of material which may be of minor importance.

(c) At a case management conference ask the court to direct the parties to identify in writing the precise point which they say the evidence establishes and why it is said that the evidence is admissible.

Sandhurst Holdings Ltd v Grosvenor Assets Ltd is authority for the proposition that the jurisdiction would be exercised sparingly, because the court's business would be seriously impeded if parties made striking-out applications as a matter of course whenever they perceived scandalous or irrelevant material was included in their opponents' evidence. A witness statement was ordered to be redacted to exclude inadmissible evidence of negotiations in *Stroude v Beazer Homes Ltd*. Likewise, in *Re New Gadget Shop Ltd* [2005] EWHC 1606 (Ch), LTL 5/8/2005, paragraphs in witness statements which used privileged material were struck out (see **50.68**).

FILING

If the court directs that a witness statement is to be filed, filing should be at the court (or Division of the court) where the case is or will be proceeding (**PD 32, para. 23.1**). **51.15**

FOREIGN LANGUAGE

Where the court directs that a witness statement in a foreign language is to be filed, the party relying on it must have the statement translated, and the translator must make an affidavit verifying the translation, exhibiting both the translation and a copy of the foreign language witness statement. Both the original statement and the translator's affidavit must be filed (**PD 32, para. 23.2**). The importance of the witness first making and signing a statement in his own language, followed by a translation into English, rather than a statement being made in English, and then translated into the witness's language prior to signing, was reiterated in *Re Phoneer Ltd* [2002] 2 BCLC 241. **51.16**

VOLUMINOUS WITNESS STATEMENTS AND EXHIBITS

The courts have for some time generally deprecated the use of voluminous written evidence. However, there are cases where it is inevitable, and then the witness statements and exhibits to be used should be put into separate bundles, with the pages numbered consecutively throughout (**PD 32, paras 15.3** and **18.5**). **51.17**

DIRECTIONS FOR THE EXCHANGE OF WITNESS STATEMENTS

Witness statements are sometimes required in cases allocated to the small claims track (see **45.18**). Directions dealing with witness statements tend to be made only in the slightly more complex small claims. The technical rules on witness statements (in **CPR, Part 32**) do not apply to claims on the small claims track (**r. 27.2(1)(c)**), so the following discussion is largely limited to claims on the fast and multi-tracks. For these cases, directions for the exchange of witness statements are mandatory. **51.18**

The court will order a party to serve on the other parties any witness statement of the oral evidence which the party serving the statement intends to rely on in relation to any issues of fact to be decided at the trial (**r. 32.4(2)**). Under **r. 32.2(3)**, directions for the exchange of witness statements may:

(a) identify or limit the issues to which factual evidence may be directed;
(b) identify the witnesses who may be called or whose evidence may be read; and
(c) limit the length or format of witness statements.

When directions are made on allocating a case to the fast track or multi-track, or at a case management conference, the court will make provision for the date by when witness statements must be exchanged. The court may give directions as to the order in which witness statements are to be served, and whether or not they should be filed (**r. 32.4(3)**). Normally mutual exchange is required, and it usually takes place a few weeks after disclosure and inspection of documents. Part of the reason why witness statements are exchanged after disclosure of documents is that the witnesses may need to comment on some of the documentation in their statements. If a witness statement is not served within the time specified in the directions, the witness may only be called with permission.

WITNESS SUMMARIES

51.19 A party who is unable to obtain signed witness statements before the time prescribed for exchange may apply, without notice, for permission to serve witness summaries instead of witness statements (**CPR, r. 32.9**). A witness summary is simply a summary of the evidence that would have been included in a witness statement. A witness summary could be an unsigned draft statement or even just an indication of the issues it is hoped the witness could deal with. Permission to serve a witness summary can only be granted if the party is unable to obtain the relevant witness statement. Unless the court orders otherwise, a witness summary must be served within the period in which a witness statement would have had to be served.

LATE SERVICE OF WITNESS STATEMENTS

51.20 If a witness statement or witness summary for use at trial is not served in respect of an intended witness within the time specified by the court, the witness may not be called to give oral evidence unless the court gives permission (**CPR, r. 32.10**). The case law dealing with non-compliance with directions for the exchange of witness statements is discussed at **48.28**.

USE OF WITNESS STATEMENTS AT TRIAL

51.21 A party who has served a witness statement, and wishes to rely at trial on the evidence of the witness who made the statement, must call the witness to give oral evidence, unless:

(a) an order has been made under **CPR, r. 32.2(3)(b)** that the witness statement is to be read; or
(b) the court orders otherwise under **r. 32.5(1)**; or
(c) the statement is put in as hearsay evidence pursuant to **r. 32.5(1)** and the Civil Evidence Act 1995, see **chapter 53**.

A party who has disclosed witness statements pursuant to directions cannot be ordered to call those witnesses at trial (*Society of Lloyd's v Jaffray* (2000) *The Times*, 3 August 2000), but should give prompt notice to the other parties that the witnesses will not be called. Despite the provisions of the Civil Evidence Act 1995, there are several reasons why judges tend to attach limited weight to statements relied upon as hearsay without calling the maker at trial. The fact that the witness is not present, in the absence of some good reason, tends to indicate that the witness does not have confidence in the statement. It will not have been tested by cross-examination. It may not have been possible to show weaknesses or limitations in the evidence, such as the distance from the scene of the witness, whether there were any obstructions, whether the witness saw what is dealt with in the statement rather than constructing it after the event, etc. Live witnesses are also thought to have great impact with the court (for better or for worse, depending on how they perform in the witness box). The result is that, wherever possible, witnesses are called to give evidence at trials.

Exchanged witness statements stand as the witnesses' evidence-in-chief unless the court otherwise orders (**CPR, r. 32.5(2)**). A witness may, however, and provided the court considers there is good reason not to confine the witness to the contents of the disclosed statement, amplify his or her witness statement and give evidence in relation to new matters that have arisen since the statement was served (**r. 32.5(3)** and **(4)**). These conditions are very restrictive, and the result is that generally witnesses should not be allowed to go outside their witness statements when they give evidence-in-chief. This also means that a witness statement should contain the whole of the evidence-in-chief that it is anticipated the witness will be able to give, as the judge may refuse permission to ask any supplementary questions. Consideration should be given to serving a supplementary statement if a witness needs to correct or materially add to an exchanged statement (see Admiralty and Commercial Courts Guide, para. H1.7(b)).

Consideration should have been given to making an order that witness statements were not to stand as the evidence-in-chief in *JN Dairies Ltd v Johal Dairies Ltd* [2010] EWCA Civ 348, LTL 31/3/2010. Shortly before the trial of a claim for breach of confidence the defendant disclosed an affidavit to the effect that the claimant had sought to bribe the former employee to commit perjury, which the claimant responded to by disclosing witness statements to the effect that the former employee had confessed to being paid £40,000 by the defendant to steal confidential documents from the claimant. It was not a case where it was merely alleged that witnesses were mistaken, but one where the allegation was that they were deliberately lying.

Commentary

Cross-examination

A witness who is called to give evidence at trial may be cross-examined on his or her witness **51.22**
statement, whether or not the statement or any part of it was referred to during the witness's evidence-in-chief (**CPR, r. 32.11**).

Use by other parties

CPR, r. 32.5(5), provides that where a witness statement is served, but the party on whose **51.23**
behalf it is served decides not to call the maker to give evidence at trial or to rely on the statement as hearsay evidence, any other party may introduce the witness statement as hearsay evidence. This rule effectively resolves the dispute under the old rules as to whether or not any vestiges of legal professional privilege continued to attach to a witness statement after it was exchanged, and it is now clear that service of witness statements waives the privilege (see *Society of Lloyd's v Jaffray* (2000) *The Times*, 3 August 2000).

Once it becomes clear that a party who has served a witness statement is not going to use it, and it is indicated that another party wishes to use the disclosed statement, the judge has a discretion whether to permit use of the statement (*McPhilemy v Times Newspapers Ltd (No. 2)* [2000] 1 WLR 1732). Generally the discretion will be exercised in accordance with the overriding objective. However, **r. 32.5(5)** cannot be used to override established rules of evidence. This means that permission will not be given for a witness statement to be put in evidence by a party if it substantially conflicts with the party's own case and the party will say that a substantial part of the statement must be disbelieved as untrue (*McPhilemy v Times Newspapers Ltd (No. 2)* [2000] 1 WLR 1732). This is because, with the exception of hostile witnesses, a party is not allowed under the rules of evidence to impeach his own witnesses (see *Ewer v Ambrose* (1825) 3 B & C 746 and **49.62**).

Availability of witness statements for inspection

51.24 Witness statements that stand as evidence-in-chief are open to inspection by the public during the course of the trial, unless the judge otherwise directs (**CPR, r. 32.13**). Normally witness statements used in this way have to be open to inspection, because proceedings are conducted in public and the public are entitled to know what evidence has been presented by a witness. The burden is accordingly on any person opposing an application for inspection. It is permissible for the court to allow inspection of a statement subject to editing out of details relating to issues which have been withdrawn before the witness testifies (*Cox v Jones* [2004] EWHC 1006 (Ch), LTL 18/5/2004). The right to inspect does not extend to exhibits or documents referred to in the statements used at trial (*GIO Personal Investment Services Ltd v Liverpool and London Steamship Protection and Indemnity Association Ltd* [1999] 1 WLR 984; *British Arab Commercial Bank v Algosaibi Trading Services Ltd* [2011] EWHC 1817 (Comm), LTL 9/8/2011). Anyone may ask the judge to make a direction that a witness statement should not be open to inspection, but such a direction will only be made in limited circumstances, such as where it is in the interests of justice or the public interest that it should not be made available to the public. The court also has a power to blank out certain passages from witness statements open to inspection by the public (**r. 32.13(4)**).

COLLATERAL USE

51.25 Once served, witness statements may be used only for the purposes of the proceedings in which they were served (**CPR, r. 32.12(1)**). This restriction does not apply if and to the extent either:

(a) the witness gives consent in writing to some other use of the statement;
(b) the court gives permission for some other use; or
(c) the witness statement has been put in evidence at a hearing held in public.

The prohibition against using material for collateral purposes does not apply to documents referred to in affidavits and witness statements, as these are regarded as having been voluntarily disclosed (*Cassidy v Hawcroft* [2000] CPLR 624).

WITNESS IMMUNITY

51.26 No one can be sued in defamation for anything said in court. The rule confers absolute immunity, and protects witnesses, lawyers and the judge (but see **54.11** for experts). The immunity extends to statements made out of court in the course of preparing evidence to be given in court (*Arthur J. S. Hall and Co. v Simons* [2002] 1 AC 615). Witness immunity extends to witness statements even if there is no trial (*Stanton v Callaghan* [2000] QB 75). It may also extend to exhibits to witness statements (*Autofocus Ltd v Accident Exchange Ltd* [2010] EWCA Civ 788, LTL 14/7/2010). It does not apply, however, to fabricated evidence (*Darker v Chief Constable of the West Midlands Police* [2001] 1 AC 435).

A statement made by a witness or prospective witness to a legal representative for the purposes of preparing a witness statement, proof of evidence or affidavit for use in court proceedings, or in contemplation of doing so, attracts absolute privilege for the purposes of possible defamation proceedings, unless it has no reference at all to the subject matter of the proceedings (*Smeaton v Butcher* (2000) *The Times*, 17 May 2000). The statement will also attract absolute privilege if used in other proceedings to which it relates (*Smeaton v Butcher*). In *Walsh v Sprecher Grier Halberstam* [2008] EWCA Civ 1324, [2009] CP Rep 16, these principles were applied to provide *immunity against proceedings* in misrepresentation and deceit in relation to contents of affidavits.

Chapter 52 Affidavits

Commentary

INTRODUCTION

Affidavits are sworn written statements. They take much the same form as modern witness statements (see **chapter** 51), but they have a few formal differences (principally the commencement and jurat). They were formerly the main means by which evidence was placed before the court on interim applications. That role has now largely been taken over by the use of witness statements, although there are a small number of situations where affidavits must still be used in interim applications. Their remaining main use is for putting evidence before the court at the final hearings of certain types of proceedings, particularly matrimonial and family proceedings, insolvency proceedings, director disqualification proceedings and proceedings brought using **CPR, Part 8**. 52.1

FORM OF AFFIDAVITS

CPR, r. 32.16, provides that affidavits must be in the form set out in the appropriate PD, which is **PD 32, paras 2 to 16**. The form of an affidavit is broadly similar to that of a witness statement, described in **chapter 51**: 52.2

(a) An affidavit must be typed on one side only of consecutively numbered sheets of durable A4 paper with a 35 mm margin (**PD 32, para.** 6.1(1), (2) and (4)).
(b) It must have the same corner markings as witness statements (**PD 32, para.** 3.2; see **51.3**).
(c) It must be headed in the same way as witness statements (see **51.4**).
(d) After the heading and before the body of the affidavit there should appear a commencement (**PD 32, para. 4.1**). This should read:

I [full name] of [address, which can be a business address if sworn in the deponent's professional, business or occupational capacity] state on oath:

(e) The comments about the body of the text in witness statements at **51.5** apply equally to affidavits (**PD 32, paras** 4.1 and 4.2).
(f) The same provisions apply to exhibits to affidavits as apply to exhibits to witness statements (see **51.7** and **51.8**).
(g) The comments about marginal references in witness statements at **51.9** apply equally to *affidavits* (*PD 32, para.* 6.1(7)).
(h) Alterations need to be initialled by both the deponent and the person taking the affidavit (**PD 32, para. 8.1**).
(i) Instead of a statement of truth (see **51.10**), an affidavit ends with a jurat. The jurat must follow on from the body of the affidavit, and must not appear on a separate page. After giving the oath the affidavit has to be signed by all deponents (exceptionally an affidavit may be sworn by more than one person) and be completed by the person taking the

affidavit. The person taking the affidavit must insert his or her full address, sign the jurat, and print his or her name and qualification under the signature (**PD 32, para. 5**).

QUALIFICATION OF PERSON TAKING AN AFFIDAVIT

52.3 A person who takes an affidavit must be duly qualified (solicitors, commissioners for oaths, magistrates, certain court officials and judges, British consuls and others authorised by statute, such as barristers), and independent of the parties and their representatives (**PD 32, para. 9**). For an affidavit taken by a court officer in the High Court or Court of Appeal, there is an £11 swearing fee, plus £2 per exhibit (**CPFO, fee 12**). But a commissioner for oaths may charge only £5 plus £2 per exhibit (Commissioners for Oaths (Fees) Order 1993 (SI 1993/2297)) and in a county court no fee is charged.

AFFIRMATIONS

52.4 Affirmations are similar to affidavits, but the deponent will affirm rather than swear when executing the document. They can be used whenever an affidavit may or must be used. All the provisions in **PD 32** relating to affidavits apply also to affirmations (**PD 32, para. 16**). For affirmations the commencement should read:

I [full name] of [address] do solemnly and sincerely affirm:

In an affirmation, the word 'sworn' in the jurat is replaced by the word 'affirmed'.

INABILITY OF DEPONENT TO READ OR SIGN AN AFFIDAVIT

52.5 Where an affidavit is sworn by a person who is unable to read or sign it, the person before whom it is sworn must certify in the jurat that he or she has read the affidavit to the deponent and that the deponent appeared to understand it (**PD 32, para. 7.1(1)** and **(2)**). The person who took the affidavit must also certify that, in his or her presence, the deponent signed it or made his or her mark (**para. 7.1(3)**). Two versions of the form of the certificate appear in annex 1 to **PD 32**. If such a certificate is not included in the jurat, the affidavit may not be used unless the court is satisfied that it was read to the deponent and he or she appeared to understand it (**para. 7.2**).

FILING AND MISCELLANEOUS TOPICS

52.6 Identical provisions apply to filing of affidavits and affirmations, in relation to foreign language affidavits, and the use of voluminous affidavits and exhibits, as apply to witness statements (see **51.15** to **51.17**, and **PD 32, paras 10** and **15.3**). Likewise as regards failing to comply with PD 32 (see **51.13** and **51.14**, and **PD 32, para. 25**).

SITUATIONS WHERE AFFIDAVITS MUST BE USED

52.7 Affidavits must be used whenever sworn evidence is required by an enactment, rule, order or practice directions (**PD 32, para. 1.4**). Examples include applications under the Protection from Harassment Act 1997, s. 3(5)(a), certain applications relating to confiscation and forfeiture in connection with criminal proceedings, and under the environmental control legislation. **PD 32** and **PD 25A** require affidavit evidence in support of applications for freezing injunctions and search orders and for orders to require an occupier to permit another to enter land.

Verification of a translation of a witness statement or affidavit must be on affidavit (**PD 32, paras 10.2** and **23.2**). Evidence in support of applications for judgment in default after service outside the jurisdiction without permission or against a State must be given on affidavit (**PD 12, para. 4.5**). Written evidence in support of or in opposition to a committal application or for permission to issue a writ of sequestration must be given by affidavit (**CPR, rr. 81.10, 81.11, 81.14** and **81.26**; **PD 81, para. 14.1**).

FALSE AFFIDAVITS

A witness swearing a false affidavit (or making a false affirmation) may be the subject of proceedings for contempt of court. **CPR, rr. 32.14, 81.17** and **81.18** (on false statements of truth, see **23.15**), has no application. The purpose behind **rr. 32.14, 81.17** and **81.18** is to provide jurisdiction to punish the makers of false statements used in proceedings in the absence of an oath. In respect of an affidavit or affirmation, there will be a contempt if the maker of the statement knew it was false, and that it was likely to interfere with the course of justice (*Malgar Ltd v R. E. Leach (Engineering) Ltd* [2000] FSR 393; *Hydropool Hot Tubs Ltd v Roberjot* [2011] EWHC 121 (Ch), LTL 11/2/2011). However, the maximum sentence that can be imposed for contempt of court is two years (Contempt of Court Act 1981, s. 14(1)), whereas courts have usually regarded a longer sentence as appropriate for giving false evidence in court proceedings. It is therefore usual for a giver of false evidence to be prosecuted either for perjury under the Perjury Act 1911, s. 1(1) (which, by s. 1(3), applies to statements in affidavits or affirmations made for the purposes of judicial proceedings as well as statements made in testimony during such proceedings), or for the common law offence of perverting the course of justice. The maximum sentence for perjury is seven years (Perjury Act 1911, s. 1(1)). The maximum sentence for a common law offence is life imprisonment. **52.8**

Chapter 53 Hearsay Evidence

INTRODUCTION

53.1 The Civil Evidence Act 1995 gives effect to the main recommendations of the Law Commission in its report, ***The Hearsay Rule in Civil Proceedings*** (Law Com. No. 216, Cm 2321, 1993). These were as follows:

(a) The hearsay rule should be abolished.
(b) A party calling a person as a witness should not adduce evidence of a previous statement made by that person without the permission of the court.
(c) A party intending to rely on hearsay evidence should be required to give notice of that fact, if it is reasonable and appropriate to do so, but failure to do so should not render the evidence inadmissible, although it may detract from its weight and result in the imposition of a costs sanction.
(d) A party should have the power to call a witness for cross-examination on his or her hearsay evidence.
(e) There should be guidelines to assist the court in assessing the weight of hearsay evidence.
(f) There should be no special conditions of admissibility or safeguards for business and other records, and the means of proving such records should be simplified.
(g) There should be no special conditions of admissibility or safeguards for statements contained in computer-produced documents: the potential for misuse of computers should be taken into account in considering the weight to be attached to such evidence.

The overall effect of the Civil Evidence Act 1995 has been to simplify the law and procedure relating to hearsay in civil cases and to render admissible much that would have been inadmissible under the regime of the Civil Evidence Act 1968 and its accompanying and unduly complex notice provisions.

ADMISSIBILITY OF HEARSAY UNDER THE 1995 ACT

The Civil Evidence Act 1995, s. 1, provides as follows: 53.2

(1) In civil proceedings evidence shall not be excluded on the ground that it is hearsay.
(2) In this Act—
  (a) 'hearsay' means a statement made otherwise than by a person while giving oral evidence in the proceedings which is tendered as evidence of the matters stated; and
  (b) references to hearsay include hearsay of whatever degree.

'Civil proceedings' means civil proceedings before any tribunal in relation to which the strict rules of evidence apply, whether as a matter of law or by agreement of the parties (s. 11). Thus the Act does apply in tribunals and arbitrations in which the strict rules of evidence are applied, but does not apply to the wardship jurisdiction of the High Court (see *Official Solicitor to the Supreme Court v K* [1965] AC 201) or to magistrates when considering, under the Local Government (Miscellaneous Provisions) Act 1976, whether there is reasonable cause to suspend a private hire vehicle licence (*Westminster City Council v Zestfair Ltd* (1989) 88 LGR 288; *Leeds City Council v Hussain* [2002] EWHC 1145 (Admin), *The Times*, 8 July 2002). Applications to commit for contempt, founded on breaches of orders made in civil proceedings, are themselves civil proceedings, despite the criminal standard of proof appropriate to such applications and their possible penal consequences (*Daltel Europe Ltd v Makki* [2006] EWCA Civ 94, [2006] 1 WLR 2704).

Under s. 1(1), 'evidence shall not be excluded on the ground that it is hearsay', wording which makes it clear that hearsay evidence will only be admissible if not open to exclusion on some other basis. The point is reinforced by s. 14(1) of the Act:

Nothing in this Act affects the exclusion of evidence on grounds other than that it is hearsay.
This applies whether the evidence falls to be excluded in pursuance of any enactment or rule of law, for failure to comply with rules of court or an order of the court, or otherwise.

The only 'hearsay' to which the safeguards and supplementary provisions of the Act apply is that defined in s. 1(2). The definition corresponds to the definition of hearsay at common law, and the Law Commission was of the view that there is likely to continue to be reference to the existing case law in cases in which the boundary of the definition is unclear (Law Com. No. 216, para. 4.6). 'Statement' means 'any representation of fact or opinion, however made' (s. 13). As to representations of opinion, these will only be admissible if admissible under the Civil Evidence Act 1972. The phrase 'however made' ensures that the Act covers statements made orally, in writing, whether manually or by any other means, and by conduct. A written statement in an affidavit, however, may perhaps not be covered (see per Harman J in *Rover International Ltd v Cannon Film Sales Ltd* [1987] 1 WLR 1597, at pp. 1603–4, doubting whether affidavits were documents under the Civil Evidence Act 1968). It is also unclear whether a 'representation' covers implied assertions, such as protests (e.g. 'Don't, Bill!'), greetings (e.g. 'Hello, Harriet') or other verbal utterances (e.g. 'Jack, please supply six tons of wheat'). It is debatable whether assertions of this kind should be treated as stating the facts which they imply (in the examples given, that Bill was doing something unwelcome to the person who protested, that Harriet was present at the place where she was greeted, and that Jack can supply wheat). It is equally unclear whether a 'representation' covers assertions which can be implied from conduct, as when customers who have ordered beer, taste it, do not finish it and then either leave it or throw it away (see per Farwell J in *Manchester Brewery Co. Ltd v Coombs* (1901) 82 LT 347 at p. 349, who was of the opinion, obiter, that such evidence would be admissible at common law). The Law Commission was content to duck the issue, being of the view that the question

Commentary

whether assertive or non-assertive conduct should come within the definition of hearsay was 'a matter for judicial consideration and development' (Law Com. No. 216, para. 4.35).

To come within the definition of hearsay in s. 1(2), the statement must have been made otherwise than by a person while giving 'oral evidence'. 'Oral evidence', for these purposes, includes evidence which, by reason of a defect of speech or hearing, a person called as a witness gives in writing or by signs (s. 13).

Hearsay and human rights

53.3 It is unnecessary and unwarranted to imply words into the Civil Evidence Act 1995 to give the court the power to exclude hearsay evidence. The admission of hearsay evidence under the 1995 Act is not incompatible with the **Human Rights Act 1998** and will not necessarily or automatically infringe a defendant's right to a fair trial under the European Convention on Human Rights, **art. 6(1)**, in the **Human Rights Act 1998, sch. 1** (*R (McCann) v Crown Court at Manchester* [2002] UKHL 39, [2003] 1 AC 787, at [35]). *McCann's* case concerned applications for anti-social behaviour orders. It was held (at [113], [116] and [117]) that, having regard to s. 4 of the 1995 Act, which lays down guidelines for assessing the weight of hearsay evidence (see **53.13**), a fair balance between the general interests of the community (represented by the weak and vulnerable who are the potential victims of anti-social behaviour) and protection of defendants' rights, requires the scales to come down in favour of the community and of the admission of hearsay evidence.

Defamation claims

53.4 The admissibility of hearsay evidence under the Civil Evidence Act 1995 has altered the common law rule in defamation claims that in establishing a defence of justification it was not permissible to rely upon hearsay (see *Shah v Standard Chartered Bank* [1999] QB 241 at p. 270C, which overlooked the 1995 Act). The present position is that hearsay evidence of whatever degree is admissible to prove the truth of the particulars of justification (*Chase v News Group Newspapers Ltd* [2002] EWCA Civ 1772, [2003] EMLR 11).

ADMISSIBILITY OF HEARSAY UNDER OTHER STATUTORY PROVISIONS

53.5 Apart from the Civil Evidence Act 1995, various statutory provisions and statutory instruments provide for the admissibility of particular types of hearsay evidence. These include, for example, the Bankers' Books Evidence Act 1879 (considered at **49.80**), the Marriage Act 1949, s. 65(3), the Births and Deaths Registration Act 1953, s. 34, the Solicitors Act 1974, s. 18, and the Children (Admissibility of Hearsay Evidence) Order 1993 (SI 1993/621). The purpose of s. 1(3) and (4) of the 1995 Act is to preserve the effect of all such provisions and to make it clear that evidence admissible under other statutory provisions is not subject to the requirements of competence and permission and the other safeguards set out in the 1995 Act. The subsections provide as follows:

(3) Nothing in this Act affects the admissibility of evidence admissible apart from this section.

(4) The provisions of sections 2 to 6 (safeguards and supplementary provisions relating to hearsay evidence) do not apply in relation to hearsay evidence admissible apart from this section, notwithstanding that it may also be admissible by virtue of this section.

COMPETENCE

53.6 Hearsay evidence may only be admitted under the Civil Evidence Act 1995 if the maker of the out-of-court statement would have been competent to give evidence at the time when he or she made the statement and, in cases in which the hearsay statement is to be proved by the statement of another (as when A's out-of-court oral statement is to be proved by B's written record of what was said), if that other person would have been competent to give evidence at the time when he or she made the statement. Section 5(1) provides as follows:

Hearsay evidence shall not be admitted in civil proceedings if or to the extent that it is shown to consist of, or to be proved by means of, a statement made by a person who at the time he made the statement was not competent as a witness.

For this purpose 'not competent as a witness' means suffering from such mental or physical infirmity, or lack of understanding, as would render a person incompetent as a witness in civil proceedings; but a child shall be treated as competent as a witness if he satisfies the requirements of section 96(2)(a) and (b) of the Children Act 1989 (conditions for reception of unsworn evidence of child).

The provisions of the Children Act 1989, s. 96(2)(a) and (b), are considered at **49.46**.

The burden of proof, under the Civil Evidence Act 1995, s. 5(1), is on the party seeking to exclude the hearsay evidence (*JC v CC* [2001] EWCA Civ 1625, LTL 25/10/2001).

PREVIOUS STATEMENTS

At common law, there is a general rule that a witness cannot be asked in examination-in-chief **53.7** about former oral or written statements made by that witness and consistent with his or her evidence in the proceedings. In civil cases, the rule was subject to only two common law exceptions: statements admissible to rebut allegations of recent fabrication and memory-refreshing documents rendered admissible as a result of cross-examination. The general effect of s. 6 of the Civil Evidence Act 1995 has been to relax the rule, by providing that previous statements may be admissible with permission, and to preserve the two exceptions to the rule. As to the rule, s. 6 reflects the view that a requirement for permission is necessary in the case of the previous consistent statements of a person called as a witness in order to prevent the pointless proliferation of superfluous evidence, which would needlessly prolong trials and increase costs (Law Com. No. 216, para. 4.30). In fact, s. 6 goes further and imposes a requirement of permission in the case of *any* previous statement, i.e. whether consistent or merely relating to matters other than those as to which the witness will give evidence. However, the concluding words of the section make it clear that it cannot be used to prevent a witness statement from standing as the witness's evidence-in-chief under **CPR, r. 32.5(2)** (see **51.21**). As to the common law exceptions to the rule against previous consistent statements, they have been preserved by s. 6(2)(b) (statements in rebuttal of allegations of recent fabrication, considered at **49.61**) and s. 6(4) (memory-refreshing documents, considered at **49.57**).

Section 6 of the Act provides as follows:

(1) Subject as follows, the provisions of this Act as to hearsay evidence in civil proceedings apply equally (but with any necessary modifications) in relation to a previous statement made by a person called as a witness in the proceedings.

(2) A party who has called or intends to call a person as a witness in civil proceedings may not in those proceedings adduce evidence of a previous statement made by that person, except—
   (a) with the leave of the court, or
   (b) for the purpose of rebutting a suggestion that his evidence has been fabricated.

This shall not be construed as preventing a witness statement (that is, a written statement of oral evidence which a party to the proceedings intends to lead) from being adopted by a witness in giving evidence or treated as his evidence.

The question naturally arises as to when permission should be granted. It is submitted that where the witness is incapable of giving direct evidence on the matter in question, then provided that his or her statement is sufficiently relevant to the facts in issue and its admission would not be unjust to the other parties to the proceedings, permission should normally be granted. Typically, the witness will be incapable of giving direct evidence where he or she has no recollection of the matter at all or where, although the witness is not incapable of giving direct evidence on the matter, his or her evidence is of questionable reliability, inconsistent or not wholly intelligible by reason of partial loss of memory, lapse of time, age or physical or mental infirmity. Such an approach would be in line with that taken in *Morris v Stratford-on-Avon Rural District Council* [1973] 1 WLR 1059, a decision under the equivalent leave requirement of the Civil Evidence Act 1968 (s. 2(2)). In that case, a claim for damages against the Council for the alleged negligence of one its employees, the trial only began some five years after the cause of action had arisen. The employee gave confused and inconsistent evidence. At the conclusion of his examination-in-chief, counsel for the defendant was granted leave to admit in chief a written statement made by the employee and given to the defendant's insurers about nine months after the events in question. The Court of Appeal held that the trial judge had not erred in allowing the evidence to be admitted.

Where permission is given to admit a previous statement under s. 6, there are no restrictions as to when it may be introduced in evidence. In some cases, therefore, it may be appropriate to give evidence of the statement before or during the examination-in-chief of the witness, as when this might render more intelligible the direct evidence to be given.

ADVANCE NOTICE

53.8 The principal objectives of the notice provisions under the Civil Evidence Act 1995 are the same as they were in the case of the notice provisions under the Civil Evidence Act 1968: to deal with all issues arising out of the adduction of hearsay evidence pre-trial and therefore to avoid surprise at trial. The current provisions, however, are simpler and more flexible. They are based on the following principles (see generally Law Com. No. 216, paras 4.9 and 4.10):

(a) The notice provision should require a party to give notice of the fact that he or she proposes to adduce hearsay, but should put the onus on the receiving party to demand such particulars as he or she requires in order to be able to make a proper assessment of the weight and cogency of the hearsay and to be in a position to respond to it adequately.
(b) Circumstances can arise in litigation rendering compliance with a notice requirement impracticable. For example, some hearings need to be arranged urgently. In other cases, albeit rarely, advance notification may carry a real risk of danger to the witness or someone else. For reasons of this kind, the new provisions make allowance for the possibility that in some circumstances it would be unreasonable and impracticable to give any notice at all.
(c) The notice provisions should be subject to rules of court to allow them to be disapplied in certain classes of proceedings if, as experience is gained, this is felt to be appropriate.
(d) The parties should be free to agree to exclude the notice provisions.

Section 2 of the 1995 Act provides as follows:

(1) A party proposing to adduce hearsay evidence in civil proceedings shall, subject to the following provisions of this section, give to the other party or parties to the proceedings—
  (a) such notice (if any) of that fact, and
  (b) on request, such particulars of or relating to the evidence, as is reasonable and practicable in the circumstances for the purpose of enabling him or them to deal with any matters arising from its being hearsay.
(2) Provision may be made by rules of court—
  (a) specifying classes of proceedings or evidence in relation to which subsection (1) does not apply, and
  (b) as to the manner in which (including the time within which) the duties imposed by that subsection are to be complied with in the cases where it does apply.

(3) Subsection (1) may also be excluded by the agreement of the parties; and compliance with the duty to give notice may in any case be waived by the person to whom notice is required to be given.

Concerning s. 2(2), see also **53.11**.

Notice of intention to rely on hearsay evidence

The relevant rules on notice of intention to rely on hearsay evidence are to be found in CPR, **Part 33**, which does not apply to claims which have been allocated to the small claims track. **53.9**

Under **r. 33.2(1)**, where a party intends to rely on hearsay evidence at trial and either that evidence is to be given by a witness giving oral evidence or is contained in a witness statement of a person who is not being called to give oral evidence, that party complies with s. 2(1)(a) of the Act by serving a witness statement on the other parties in accordance with the court's order. A party who intends to rely on a witness statement containing hearsay evidence without calling the maker of the statement, must, when serving the witness statement, inform the other parties that the witness is not being called to give oral evidence and give the reason why the witness will not be called (**r. 33.2(2)**). In all other cases where a party intends to rely on hearsay evidence at trial, for example where a party intends to rely on the contents of a letter or diary written by a person since deceased, or the contents of a computer printout, that party complies with s. 2(1)(a) of the Act by serving a notice on the other parties which:

(a) identifies the hearsay evidence;
(b) states that the party serving the notice proposes to rely on the evidence at trial; and
(c) gives the reason why the witness will not be called (**r. 33.2(3)**).

This notice must be served no later than the date for serving witness statements and, if the hearsay evidence is to be in a document, supply a copy to any party who requests him or her to do so (**r. 33.2(4)**). See further, in the case of documents which are shown to form part of the records of a business or public authority, **53.16**.

Consequences of failure to comply with the notice procedure

Section 2(4) of the 1995 Act provides as follows: **53.10**

(4) A failure to comply with subsection (1), or with rules under subsection (2)(b), does not affect the admissibility of the evidence but may be taken into account by the court—
  (a) in considering the exercise of its powers with respect to the course of proceedings and costs, and
  (b) as a matter adversely affecting the weight to be given to the evidence in accordance with section 4.

Thus where a party does not give notice, when in all the circumstances of the case it would have been reasonable and practicable for him or her to have done so, or fails to give proper notice, or gives late notice, although the court may not refuse to admit the evidence, there are a number of other potential consequences:

(a) under s. 2(4)(a), the court, in the exercise of its powers with respect to the course of proceedings, may grant an adjournment in order to compel a party to give notice, to perfect an inadequate notice, or to allow the other party time to deal with the effect of late notification;
(b) under s. 2(4)(a), the court may also impose a costs sanction; and
(c) under s. 2(4)(b), the court may reduce the weight to be given to the evidence.

Circumstances in which notice of intention is not required

It is provided in CPR, **r. 33.3** that the duty to give notice of intention to rely on hearsay evidence does not apply: **53.11**

(a) to evidence at hearings other than trials [i.e. on interim applications];
(aa) to an affidavit or witness statement which is to be used at trial but which does not contain hearsay evidence;

(b) to a statement which a party to a probate claim wishes to put in evidence and which is alleged to have been made by the person whose estate is the subject of the proceedings; or
(c) where the requirement is excluded by a practice direction.

Under **CPR, r. 33.3**, which is authorised by s. 2(2) of the 1995 Act (see **53.8**), the duty of notice to give intention to rely on hearsay evidence may be excluded by a practice direction. **PD 32, para. 27** (considered at **59.7**) would appear to be an example of such exclusion. In *Charnock v Rowan* [2012] EWCA Civ 2, [2012] CP Rep 18 at [22]–[23] it was held, obiter, that **PD 32, para. 27** reverses the notice requirement set out in s. 2(1) of the 1995 Act and that its effect is to treat the agreement of a bundle as the requisite notice, leaving it to the objecting party to serve a document-specific counter-notice.

POWER TO CALL WITNESSES FOR CROSS-EXAMINATION

53.12 Section 3 of the Civil Evidence Act 1995 provides as follows:

3. Rules of court may provide that where a party to civil proceedings adduces hearsay evidence of a statement made by a person and does not call that person as a witness, any other party to the proceedings may, with the leave of the court, call that person as a witness and cross-examine him on the statement as if he had been called by the first-mentioned party and as if the hearsay statement were his evidence-in-chief.

The relevant rule of court is **CPR, r. 33.4**, which provides that where a party proposes to rely on hearsay evidence and does not propose to call the person who made the original statement to give oral evidence, the court may, on the application of any other party, permit that party to call the maker of the statement to be cross-examined on the contents of the statement. An application for permission to cross-examine under this rule must be made not more than 14 days after the day on which a notice of intention to rely on the hearsay evidence was served on the applicant (**r. 33.4(2)**).

In the normal case, **r. 33.4** applies where a party has served a witness statement but does not propose to call its maker as a witness. It also applies where a party neither calls the maker of one of its witness statements nor puts the statement in as hearsay, and another party, under **r. 32.5(5)** (see **51.23**), puts the witness statement in as hearsay, so that the first party may then, with the permission of the court, call the witness and cross-examine him on the statement (*Douglas v Hello! Ltd* [2003] EWCA Civ 332, [2003] EMLR 633).

WEIGHT TO BE GIVEN TO HEARSAY EVIDENCE

53.13 Section 4 of the Civil Evidence Act 1995 sets out the various matters to which the court shall or may have regard in estimating the weight, if any, to be given to hearsay evidence. The provision was introduced for two reasons. First, since the 1995 Act all but abolishes the hearsay rule, the courts need to be particularly vigilant in testing the reliability of such evidence. Secondly, such a provision can operate to deter parties from abusing abolition of the rule, for example, by deliberately failing to give notice, by giving late or inadequate notice, by relying on hearsay rather than calling a dubious witness who can give direct evidence, or by amassing hearsay statements on a point in an attempt to conceal an essential witness (see Law Com. No. 216, para. 4.19). Section 4 provides as follows:

(1) In estimating the weight (if any) to be given to hearsay evidence in civil proceedings the court shall have regard to any circumstances from which any inference can reasonably be drawn as to the reliability or otherwise of the evidence.
(2) Regard may be had, in particular, to the following—
   (a) whether it would have been reasonable and practicable for the party by whom the evidence was adduced to have produced the maker of the original statement as a witness;

(b) whether the original statement was made contemporaneously with the occurrence or existence of the matters stated;
(c) whether the evidence involves multiple hearsay;
(d) whether any person involved had any motive to conceal or misrepresent matters;
(e) whether the original statement was an edited account, or was made in collaboration with another or for a particular purpose;
(f) whether the circumstances in which the evidence is adduced as hearsay are such as to suggest an attempt to prevent proper evaluation of its weight.

Section 13 provides that, in relation to hearsay evidence, 'the original statement':

means the underlying statement (if any) by:
(a) in the case of evidence of fact, a person having personal knowledge of that fact, or
(b) in the case of evidence of opinion, the person whose opinion it is.

Section 4(2) is of particular importance in cases in which hearsay carries inherent dangers, making it difficult for the judge to assess the truth in the absence of the original maker of the statement, as when a defendant to a claim for a possession or anti-social behaviour order is faced in court with serious complaints made by anonymous or absent witnesses about matters that took place, if at all, many months earlier (*Moat Housing Group-South Ltd v Harris* [2005] EWCA Civ 287, [2006] QB 606, applied in *R (Cleary) v Highbury Corner Magistrates' Court* [2006] EWHC 1869 (Admin), [2007] 1 WLR 1272).

As to s. 4(2)(a), it is submitted that an inference as to unreliability may be drawn even if, had the maker of the original statement been called as a witness, the court would have granted leave under s. 6(2) to adduce evidence of the statement (see further at 53.7). However, it is also submitted that such an inference is unlikely to be drawn under s. 4(2)(a) where the other party or parties have not applied for permission to call the maker of the original statement for cross-examination under s. 3 (see further at 53.12).

Concerning s. 4(2)(d), the phrase 'any person involved' will cover not only the maker (or, in cases of collaboration, makers) of 'the original statement', but also, in all cases in which the statement is proved at trial other than by the maker of the original statement, the person who claims to have heard the statement or to have recorded it in a document, and, in all cases of multiple hearsay, the intermediaries through whom the information contained in 'the original statement' was supplied.

In estimating the weight to be attached to hearsay evidence contained in computer-generated documents, the courts are likely to use s. 4 to have regard to a variety of circumstances, in addition to those set out in s. 4(2), from which inferences can be drawn as to the reliability or otherwise of the evidence, including in particular the following circumstances:
(a) the reliability or otherwise of the hardware and software;
(b) the accuracy or otherwise with which data was input; and
(c) the potential for misuse of the computer through the capacity to hack, corrupt and alter information.

IMPEACHING THE CREDIBILITY OF ABSENT WITNESSES

The general purpose of s. 5(2) of the Civil Evidence Act 1995 is to ensure that where the **53.14** maker of 'the original statement' (see further at 53.13), or the maker of any statement relied upon to prove 'the original statement', is not called as a witness, evidence relating to his or her credibility is as admissible as it would have been if he or she had been called as a witness. Section 5(2) provides as follows:

(2) Where in civil proceedings hearsay evidence is adduced and the maker of the original statement, or of any statement relied upon to prove another statement, is not called as a witness—
(a) evidence which if he had been so called would be admissible for the purpose of attacking his credibility as a witness is admissible for that purpose in the proceedings; and

(b) evidence tending to prove that, whether before or after he made the statement, he made any other statement inconsistent with it is admissible for the purpose of showing that he had contradicted himself.

Provided that evidence may not be given of any matter of which, if he had been called as a witness and had denied that matter in cross-examination, evidence could not have been adduced by the cross-examining party.

The meaning of the phrase 'the maker...of any statement relied upon to prove another statement' is unclear. It is submitted that the words 'another statement' should not be taken to mean a statement other than the original statement, but should be given a purposive construction so as to cover the statement of someone who has heard the original statement or recorded it in a document and, in the case of multiple hearsay, the statements of any intermediaries through whom the information contained in 'the original statement' was supplied. For example, if A makes an oral statement to B ('the original statement'), B tells C what A said, and C makes a written record of her conversation with B (by which means A's statement is to be proved), and if A, B and C are all unavailable to give evidence, it is submitted that for the purposes of s. 5(2), evidence relating to the credibility of A, B or C should be admissible.

The purpose of the proviso to s. 5(2) is to ensure that the rule on finality of answers to questions on collateral issues (see **49.66**) operates to restrict the evidence admissible under the subsection against the maker of the statement who is not called as a witness in the same way as it applies in relation to a person who is called as a witness. Evidence admissible for the purpose of attacking credibility under s. 5(2)(a) therefore includes the types of evidence admissible under exceptions to the rule on finality, namely evidence of bias, evidence of previous convictions, and evidence of mental or physical disability affecting reliability (see **49.68** to **49.70**). As to s. 5(2)(b), it seems that whereas a previous inconsistent statement of a person called as a witness is admissible not only to impugn his or her credibility but also as evidence of any matter stated (see s. 6(3) and (5) at **49.67**), a previous inconsistent statement of a maker of a statement not called as a witness and admissible under s. 5(2)(b) is admissible 'for the purpose of showing that he had contradicted himself', i.e. only for the purpose of impugning credibility.

By **CPR, r. 33.5**, a party who, in reliance on s. 5(2), wishes to call evidence to attack the credibility of 'the maker of the original statement', must give notice of intention to do so, to the party who proposes to give the hearsay statement in evidence, not more than 14 days after being served with the notice of intention to rely on the hearsay evidence. Somewhat curiously, there is no equivalent notice requirement where a party intends to attack the credibility of 'the maker...of any statement relied upon to prove another statement'.

PROOF OF STATEMENTS CONTAINED IN DOCUMENTS

53.15 Documents certified as forming part of the records of a business or public authority are capable of being received in evidence without further proof (see **53.16**). Notarial acts and instruments may also be received in evidence without further proof (see **53.18**). The proof of statements contained in other documents is governed by s. 8 of the Civil Evidence Act 1995, which provides as follows:

(1) Where a statement contained in a document is admissible as evidence in civil proceedings, it may be proved—

(a) by the production of that document, or

(b) whether or not that document is still in existence, by the production of a copy of that document or of the material part of it,

authenticated in such manner as the court may approve.

(2) It is immaterial for this purpose how many removes there are between a copy and the original.

A 'document', for the purposes of s. 8, means 'anything in which information of any description is recorded' (s. 13), a definition wide enough to embrace maps, plans, graphs, drawings, discs, CD-ROMs, computer-generated printouts, audiotapes, videotapes, negatives, photographs, films and microfilms. A 'copy', in relation to a document, means 'anything onto which information recorded in the document has been copied, by whatever means and whether directly or indirectly' (s. 13), a definition sufficiently wide to include transcripts of audiotapes. It is submitted that the requirement of 'authentication' at the end of s. 8(1) relates not to proof of the original of a document, but calls for authentication that a copy of a document is a true copy of the original (see *Ventouris v Mountain (No. 2)* [1992] 1 WLR 887, a decision under the Civil Evidence Act 1968). It is further submitted that, as under s. 6(1) of the 1968 Act, 'production' for the purposes of s. 8 of the 1995 Act refers not to counsel handing the document to the court, but to a witness who is qualified to do so in accordance with the rules producing the document and saying what it is (see per Staughton LJ in *Ventouris v Mountain (No. 2)* at p. 901). However, it seems that a statement contained in a document may also be proved by another hearsay statement. Thus, where it is sought to admit a statement which has been deliberately tape-recorded, but whose maker is unavailable to produce the tape and give direct evidence that it is the tape that he or she made, the tape may be proved by his or her out-of-court statements to the same effect (*Ventouris v Mountain (No. 2)*).

Commentary

DOCUMENTS FORMING PART OF THE RECORDS OF A BUSINESS OR PUBLIC AUTHORITY

Entries in the records of a business or public authority

Record keeping within many organisations has largely been taken over by technology and there is often no one witness who can give direct evidence of all aspects of the way in which the records were compiled. For reasons of this kind, provision has been made for documents certified as forming parts of the records of a business or public authority to be received in evidence without further proof (see Law Com. No. 216, paras 3.12 and 4.39). Section 9 of the Civil Evidence Act 1995 provides as follows: **53.16**

(1) A document which is shown to form part of the records of a business or public authority may be received in evidence in civil proceedings without further proof.

(2) A document shall be taken to form part of the records of a business or public authority if there is produced to the court a certificate to that effect signed by an officer of the business or authority to which the records belong.

For this purpose—

(a) a document purporting to be a certificate signed by an officer of a business or public authority shall be deemed to have been duly given by such an officer and signed by him; and

(b) a certificate shall be treated as signed by a person if it purports to bear a facsimile of his signature.

'Records' means 'records in whatever form' (s. 9(4)), a definition which gives the courts scope to abandon the narrow definition of the word under the Civil Evidence Act 1968, for the purposes of which it was taken to mean 'records which a historian would regard as original or primary sources, that is documents which either give effect to a transaction itself or which contain a contemporaneous register of information supplied by those with direct knowledge of the facts' (see *H v Schering Chemicals Ltd* [1983] 1 WLR 143). Section 9(4) provides that '"business" includes any activity regularly carried on over a period of time, whether for profit or not, by any body (whether corporate or not) or by an individual', and '"public authority" includes any public or statutory undertaking, any government department and any person holding office under Her Majesty'. Not all businesses, as defined, will have 'officers' in the strict sense of that word, and so in s. 9(4) 'officer' is defined to include 'any person occupying a responsible position in relation to the relevant activities of the business or public authority or in relation to its records'.

Although business and other records can often be regarded as likely to be reliable, there are bound to be exceptions, and for this reason the court has been given the discretionary power to disapply the certification provisions in s. 9. Section 9(5) provides that:

(5) The court may, having regard to the circumstances of the case, direct that all or any of the above provisions of this section do not apply in relation to a particular document or record, or description of documents or records.

Unless the court orders otherwise, a document which may be received in evidence under s. 9 shall not be receivable at trial unless the party intending to put it in evidence has given notice to the other parties (**CPR, r. 33.6(2)** and **(3)**). A party intending to use a s. 9 document as evidence of any fact must give notice not later than the latest date for serving witness statements (**r. 33.6(4)**), unless the evidence forms part of expert evidence, in which case notice must be given when the expert's report is served on the other party (**r. 33.6(6)**). A party who has given notice of intention to put in evidence under s. 9 must give every other party an opportunity to inspect it and to agree to its admission without further proof (**r. 33.6(8)**).

Absence of an entry in the records of a business or public authority

53.17 At common law it seems that the non-existence of a fact can be inferred, without offending the hearsay rule, by evidence of the absence of a recording of that fact in a record which, having regard to its compilation and custody, one would have expected that fact, had it existed, to have been recorded. Thus, it has been said that in order to prove that A is an illegal immigrant, an officer responsible for the compilation and custody of Home Office records of persons entitled to a certificate of registration in the UK, in which A's name does not appear, may give evidence that the method of compilation and custody of the records is such that if A's name is not there, he or she must be an illegal immigrant (per Bristow J in *R v Patel* [1981] 3 All ER 94 at p. 96, applied in *R v Shone* (1983) 76 Cr App R 72). Section 9(3) of the Civil Evidence Act 1995 facilitates the proof of the absence of an entry in the records of a business or public authority. It provides as follows:

(3) The absence of an entry in the records of a business or public authority may be proved in civil proceedings by affidavit of an officer of the business or authority to which the records belong.

In cases in which the court has any reason to suspect that the records are unlikely to be reliable, then it may direct that s. 9(3) does not apply by exercising its discretionary power under s. 9(5) (see **53.16**), in which case the absence of the entry will need to be proved either by calling the officer of the business or authority to give direct evidence or, if he or she cannot be called, by relying on a hearsay statement to the same effect.

NOTARIAL ACTS AND INSTRUMENTS

53.18 Notarial acts and instruments are bills of exchange which a notary has 'noted' or protested and documents which a notary has authenticated in private or public form (see *Halsbury's Laws of England*, 4th edn., reissue, vol. 33, paras 728 and 732). At common law, it was necessary to call the notary or his clerk to prove authentication etc. (*Sutton v Gregory* (1797) Peake Add Cas 150). However, **CPR, r. 32.20**, provides as follows:

A notarial act or instrument may be received in evidence without further proof as duly authenticated in accordance with the requirements of law unless the contrary is proved.

HEARSAY FORMERLY ADMISSIBLE AT COMMON LAW

General

53.19 Section 9 of the Civil Evidence Act 1968 preserved and gave statutory force to a number of common law exceptions to the rule against hearsay, without purporting to amend the law relating to those exceptions. The exceptions included informal admissions, works of reference, and public documents and records. The Civil Evidence Act 1995 perpetuates this state of affairs, except in the case of informal admissions, which are therefore now subject to the general provisions of the 1995 Act, including those relating to notice and weight. The other common law exceptions have been preserved for three reasons:

(a) statutory provisions such as the Evidence (Foreign, Dominion and Colonial Documents) Act 1933, s. 1, and the Oaths and Evidence (Overseas Authorities and Countries) Act 1963, s. 5, which are unaffected by the 1995 Act, presuppose the existence of the common law exceptions relating to public records;
(b) the procedural burden of the notice procedure should not be introduced where it has not been borne before; and
(c) the weight to be given to evidence admissible under the exceptions is rarely a matter for debate (see Law Com. No. 216, para. 4.33).

Informal admissions

Section 7(1) of the Civil Evidence Act 1995 provides that 'the common law rule effectively preserved by section 9(1) and (2)(a) of the Civil Evidence Act 1968 (admissibility of admissions adverse to a party) is superseded by the provisions of this Act'. 'Admissions adverse to a party' means informal admissions, i.e. statements by a party to the proceedings, or someone in privity with him or her, made other than while testifying in those proceedings, and adverse to his or her case. By virtue of s. 7(1), therefore, an informal admission shall not be excluded on the ground that it is hearsay (see s. 1(1) at **53.2**), but will be subject to the general provisions of the Act, including those relating to notice (s. 2) and weight (s. 4). The weight to be attached to an informal admission depends upon a variety of special considerations additional to those set out in s. 4 itself (see **53.13**). For example, regard should always be had to the whole statement, including any passages favourable to its maker which qualify, explain or even nullify those parts of the statement relied upon as an admission, because the favourable parts of the statement are as much evidence of the facts they state as the parts relied upon as constituting an admission. Equally, regard should be had to any contradictory evidence adduced by the maker of the statement at the trial. Regard should also be had to the circumstances in which the admission was made, including, for example, whether it was made as a result of some inducement or threat. There are two other important considerations: whether the admission contains facts of which its maker had personal knowledge, and whether the admission was vicarious, i.e. made by someone in privity with the party to the legal proceedings. **53.20**

Personal knowledge There is no requirement under the 1995 Act that the hearsay statement tendered, in order to be admissible, must have been made by someone with personal knowledge of the matters stated. However, the weight to be attached to a statement containing facts of which its maker has no personal knowledge will vary according to the circumstances. For example, an admission made by a party as to his or her age is obviously not based on personal knowledge, but it concerns a matter as to which it is reasonable to suppose that he or she has been accurately informed (see *R v Turner* [1910] KB 346 and *Lustre Hosiery Ltd v York* (1936) 54 CLR 134 (High Court of Australia)). However, an admission made as to the countries of origin of certain imported goods made solely in reliance on the fact that the goods bear marks and labels indicating that they came from those countries, is likely to be evidentially worthless (see per Lord Hodson in *Comptroller of Customs v Western Lectric Co. Ltd* [1966] AC 367 at p. 371). **53.21**

Vicarious admissions Prior to the 1995 Act, an informal admission could only be received in evidence if it had been made by a party to the proceedings personally, or vicariously, i.e. by someone in privity with him. Under the 1995 Act, an out-of-court statement adverse to the case of a party may be admitted whether made by that party or by any other person. However, the weight to be attached to an admission made by someone who, at common law, would have **53.22**

been in privity with a party, is likely to be greater than an adverse statement made by someone else. Those in privity included the following:

(a) a predecessor in title of a party to proceedings, provided that the admission concerned title to the property and was made at a time when he or she had an interest in it (*Woolway v Rowe* (1834) 1 Ad & El 114);
(b) a partner, provided that the admission concerned the partnership affairs and was made in the ordinary course of its business (see the Partnership Act 1890, s. 15);
(c) a referee (*Williams v Innes* (1808) 1 Camp 364); and
(d) agents, provided that:
 (i) the admission was made at a time when the agency existed (*Edwards v Brookes (Milk) Ltd* [1963] 1 WLR 795);
 (ii) the communication in which it was made was authorised, expressly or by implication, by the principal (*Wagstaff v Wilson* (1832) 4 B & Ad 339; *G (A) v G (T)* [1970] 2 QB 643); and
 (iii) the admission was made in the course of a communication with some third party, as opposed to the principal (*Re Devala Provident Gold Mining Co.* (1883) 22 ChD 593).

At common law there was no privity between:

(a) spouses, merely by virtue of the marital relationship;
(b) parent and child, merely by virtue of that relationship (*G(A) v G(T)*);
(c) co-claimants or co-defendants; or
(d) a witness and the party calling him or her (*British Thomson-Houston Co. Ltd v British Insulated and Helsby Cables Ltd* [1924] 2 Ch 160).

Works of reference

53.23 It is provided in the Civil Evidence Act 1995, s. 7(2)(a), that:

(2) The common law rules effectively preserved by section 9(1) and (2)(b) to (d) of the Civil Evidence Act 1968, that is, any rule of law whereby in civil proceedings—
 (a) published works dealing with matters of a public nature (for example, histories, scientific works, dictionaries and maps) are admissible as evidence of facts of a public nature stated in them…
shall continue to have effect.

The effect of s. 7(2)(a) is to preserve the common law rule that authoritative published works of reference dealing with matters of a public nature are admissible to prove, or to assist the court in deciding whether to take judicial notice of, facts of a public nature stated therein. Examples include:

(a) historical works concerning public facts (*Read v Bishop of Lincoln* [1892] AC 644);
(b) standard medical texts concerning the nature of a disease (*McCarthy v The Melita (Owners)* (1923) 16 BWCC 222);
(c) engineers' reports, within the common knowledge of engineers, on the nature of soil (*East London Railway Co. v Thames Conservators* (1904) 90 LT 347);
(d) Carlisle Tables, on average life expectancy (*Rowley v London and North Western Railway Co.* (1873) LR 8 Ex 221);
(e) dictionaries, on the meaning of English words (*Marchioness of Blandford v Dowager Duchess of Marlborough* (1743) 2 Atk 542; *R v Agricultural Land Tribunal, ex parte Benney* [1955] 2 QB 140); and
(f) published maps and plans concerning facts of geographical notoriety (*R v Orton* (1873) and *R v Jameson* (1896) *Stephen's Digest of the Law of Evidence*, 10th edn. at p. 48).

Public documents and records

53.24 It is provided in the Civil Evidence Act 1995, s. 7(2)(b) and (c), that:

(2) The common law rules effectively preserved by section 9(1) and (2)(b) to (d) of the Civil Evidence Act 1968, that is, any rule of law whereby in civil proceedings—
…

(b) public documents (for example, public registers, and returns made under public authority with respect to matters of public interest) are admissible as evidence of the facts stated in them, or
(c) records (for example, the records of certain courts, treaties, Crown grants, pardons and commissions) are admissible as evidence of facts stated in them, shall continue to have effect.

Examples This common law exception to the hearsay rule applies to a wide variety of documents made under public authority in relation to matters of public concern, and may be justified on the grounds of reliability and convenience. Examples include: 53.25

(a) recitals in public Acts of Parliament (*R v Sutton* (1816) 4 M & S 532);
(b) entries relating to acts of State and public matters in Parliamentary journals and governmental gazettes (*Attorney-General v Theakston* (1820) 8 Price 89);
(c) entries in parish registers (and foreign registers) of baptisms, marriages and burials (see per Lord Selborne in *Lyell v Kennedy* (1889) 14 App Cas 437 at pp. 448–9);
(d) entries in the public books of a corporation relating to matters of public interest (*Shrewsbury v Hart* (1823) 1 Car & P 113);
(e) the contents of a file from the Companies Register containing the statutory returns made by a company (*R v Halpin* [1975] QB 907);
(f) entries in university records relating to degrees conferred (*Collins v Carnegie* (1834) 1 Ad & El 695);
(g) records of assessment by commissioners of land tax (*Doe d Strode v Seaton* (1834) 2 Ad & El 171); and
(h) findings of professional misconduct by the General Medical Council (*Hill v Clifford* [1907] 2 Ch 236).

Conditions of admissibility The conditions of admissibility for statements in public documents vary to some extent according to the particular type of document in question. In general terms, however, a public document will only be admissible as evidence of the facts it contains if: 53.26

(a) it concerns a public matter;
(b) it was made by a public officer acting under a duty to inquire and record the results of his or her inquiry; and
(c) it was intended to be retained for public reference or inspection (see per Lord Blackburn in *Sturla v Freccia* (1880) 5 App Cas 623 at pp. 643–4).

As to the first of these conditions, 'public' must not be taken to mean the whole world: the matter in question may concern either the public at large or a section of the public (*Sturla v Freccia*; *Heath v Deane* [1905] 2 Ch 86). Under the second condition, the statement must have been made by a public officer, as opposed to a private individual, acting in discharge of a strict duty to inquire into, and satisfy himself or herself as to the truth of, the facts recorded (*Doe d France v Andrews* (1850) 15 QB 756; *White v Taylor* [1969] 1 Ch 150; *Wilton and Co. v Phillips* (1903) 19 TLR 390; *Brierly v Brierly* [1918] P 257; and cf. *Bird v Keep* [1918] 2 KB 692 at pp. 697–8 and 701 and *Re Stollery* [1926] Ch 284 at p. 322). In more recent times, however, it seems that strict compliance with the requirement of personal knowledge of the facts recorded is no longer required. Thus, where a duty is cast upon a company by statute to make accurate returns of company matters to the Registrar of Companies so that those returns can be filed and inspected by members of the public, all statements on the return are prima facie proof of the truth of their contents, notwithstanding that the relevant official at the Companies Register has no duty to inquire and satisfy himself or herself as to the truth of the recorded facts (*R v Halpin* [1975] QB 907).

The fact that the public official fails to record the matter in question promptly may affect the weight to be attached to the evidence, but does not affect its admissibility (*R v Halpin* at p. 916). The position is the same where the record in question was made by an interested party (*Irish Society v Bishop of Derry* (1846) 12 Cl & F 641, in which the Bishop's statements relating to advowsons in his diocese were admitted notwithstanding that some of them belonged to him).

Declarations as to pedigree or the existence of a marriage

53.27 At common law a declaration as to pedigree was admissible, after its maker's death, as evidence of the truth of its contents (see, e.g. *Johnson v Lawson* (1824) 2 Bing 86 and the *Berkeley Peerage Case* (1811) 4 Camp 401). Matters of pedigree concern the relationship by blood or marriage between persons, including the fact and date of births, marriages and deaths, legitimacy, celibacy, failure of issue and intestacy. This exception to the hearsay rule would cover, for example, oral declarations by deceased parents that one of their children, whose legitimacy was in issue, was born before their marriage, and written declarations such as entries in family Bibles or pedigrees hung up in the family home. There was no requirement, on the part of the declarant, of personal knowledge of the facts stated, which might amount to nothing more than reputation or family tradition handed down from one generation to another. Declarations as to pedigree are now admissible pursuant to the Civil Evidence Act 1995, and s. 7(3) of that Act provides as follows:

> (3) The common law rules effectively preserved by section 9(3) and (4) of the Civil Evidence Act 1968, that is, any rule whereby in civil proceedings—
>
> ...
>
> (b) evidence of reputation or family tradition is admissible—
>
> (i) for the purpose of proving or disproving pedigree or the existence of a marriage...
>
> shall continue to have effect in so far as they authorise the court to treat such evidence as proving or disproving that matter.
>
> Where any such rule applies, reputation or family tradition shall be treated for the purposes of this Act as a fact and not as a statement or multiplicity of statements about the matter in question.

In so far as s. 7(3) preserves the rule whereby evidence of reputation or family tradition is admissible for the purpose of proving or disproving the existence of a marriage, it is to be treated as applying in an equivalent way for the purpose of proving or disproving the existence of a civil partnership (Civil Partnership Act 2004, s. 84(5)).

Evidence of reputation or family tradition is usually made up of a multiplicity of hearsay statements, but if it were to be treated as such, strict application of the provisions of the 1995 Act relating to notice and weight would be impossible (see Law Com. No. 216, para. 4.34). For this reason, s. 7(3) requires such evidence to be treated as evidence of fact. The effect is that the party proposing to adduce such evidence, in complying with the notice requirement under s. 2 of the Act (see **53.8** and **53.9**), will not be expected to give to the other parties particulars of the person who had personal knowledge of the matters in question and of the intermediaries through whom the information was conveyed to him or her. A further effect is that the court, in assessing the weight of the evidence under s. 4 of the Act (see **53.13**), will not be expected to have regard to such matters as whether the person with personal knowledge of the matters stated made the 'original statement' contemporaneously with the occurrence or existence of the matters stated.

Declarations as to public and general rights

53.28 At common law, a declaration as to the reputed existence of a public or general right was admissible, after its maker's death, as evidence of the existence of the right in question. Public rights are those common to the public at large, such as rights to use paths (see *Radcliffe v Marsden Urban District Council* (1908) 72 JP 475) or landing places on the banks of a river (*Drinkwater v Porter* (1835) 7 Car & P 181). General rights are those common to a section of the public or a considerable class of persons, such as the inhabitants of a parish or the tenants of a manor (*Nicholas v Parker* (1805) 14 East 331n). Any person was competent to make a declaration as to the reputed existence of a public right, and the fact that the declarant had no knowledge of the subject went only to weight, not admissibility. A declaration as to general rights, however, was only admissible if it was made by a person with some connection with or knowledge of the matters in question (see *Rogers v Wood* (1931) 2 B & Ad 245 and *Crease v Barrett* (1835) 1 Cr M & R 919). Declarations as to public and general rights are now admissible pursuant to the Civil Evidence Act 1995, and s. 7(3) of that Act provides as follows:

(3) The common law rules effectively preserved by section 9(3) and (4) of the Civil Evidence Act 1968, that is, any rule whereby in civil proceedings—

...

(b) evidence of reputation or family tradition is admissible—...

(ii) for the purpose of proving or disproving the existence of any public or general right or of identifying any person or thing,

shall continue to have effect in so far as they authorise the court to treat such evidence as proving or disproving that matter.

Where any such rule applies, reputation or family tradition shall be treated for the purposes of this Act as a fact and not as a statement or multiplicity of statements about the matter in question.

As to the rationale of the concluding part of s. 7(3), see **53.27**.

Chapter 54 Experts and Assessors

INTRODUCTION

54.1 An 'expert' is a person who has been instructed to give or prepare expert evidence for the purposes of proceedings (**CPR, r. 35.2(1)**). While it is not every case that needs expert evidence, the rule of evidence is that if a matter is outside the ordinary experience of the trial judge, not only is expert evidence admissible, but it is necessary because the judge has to make a ruling based on evidence (see **54.2** to **54.9**). Practical issues about expert evidence include the fees that can be incurred, the need for other parties to know the expert evidence that is to be adduced (so they know the case they have to meet and can make informed decisions on seeking to compromise the dispute), and avoiding an unwarranted amount of court time being devoted to resolving apparent conflicts between opposing experts. The procedural rules described at **54.10** to **54.37** aim to address these issues and ensure cases are dealt with justly and at proportionate cost in accordance with **r. 1.1(1)**, while saving costs and promoting the principle of open trial preparation.

By **r. 35.1**, it is the duty of the court to restrict expert evidence to that which is reasonably required. The duty of the expert is expressed to be to help the court on matters within his or her expertise, a duty that overrides any obligation felt by the expert to whoever instructed him (**r. 35.3**). This is an overriding duty which liberates an expert from what may have been perceived previously as pressure to win the case for the party or parties from whom instructions are received. **PD 35, annex, para. 4.3**, expressly says that experts should not take it upon themselves to promote the point of view of the party instructing them or engage in the role of advocates.

Furthermore, **CPR, r. 35.4(1)**, provides that no party may rely upon expert evidence without first having received the court's permission to do so. This applies to both the presentation of a written report and the calling of the expert to give oral evidence at trial. **Rule 35.7** gives the court the power, where both parties wish to rely upon expert evidence relating to a particular issue, to direct that evidence on that issue be given by one expert only. A direction for a 'single joint expert' generally eliminates the problem of the overtly biased expert.

The court's powers of case management, particularly the setting of timetables, and sanctions for non-observance, are designed to prevent delay in the filing and serving of experts' reports, and answers to written questions. Non-compliance with directions on expert evidence is discussed at **48.26** and **48.27**.

Instruction of experts before proceedings are issued is governed primarily by any relevant pre-action protocol, or by **PD Pre-action Conduct** if the case is not governed by a specific protocol. Expert evidence obtained at this stage anticipates the directions that are likely to be made if the dispute results in a claim being issued. There is the risk that costs on expert evidence incurred before proceedings will be wasted if the court takes a different view on the nature of the expert evidence required, so there is a tendency towards caution at this stage. Key questions are:

(a) whether the case is likely to be allocated to the multi-track (where separate experts are more likely to be allowed) or the fast track (where joint selection or joint instruction are preferred methods);
(b) what expert evidence is required at this stage in order to ensure both sides are reasonably fully informed so they can make and consider proposals in settlement; and
(c) whether there is a need for the early instruction of an expert to preserve evidence.

PD 35, annex (the Protocol for the Instruction of Experts to give Evidence in Civil Claims), para. 2.2 (which will need to be amended following the replacement of PD Protocols by **PD Pre-action Conduct**), sets out the following objectives:

(a) to encourage the exchange of early and full information about the expert issues involved in the prospective legal claim;
(b) to enable the parties to avoid or reduce the scope of litigation by agreeing the whole or part of an expert issue before commencement of proceedings; and
(c) to support the efficient management of proceedings where litigation cannot be avoided.

CPR, Part 35, only applies where experts are instructed to give opinions which are relied upon for the purposes of court proceedings. It does not refer to advice given which the instructing party does not intend to adduce as evidence in the proceedings (see **PD 35, annex, para. 5.1**). **CPR, Part 35**, has to be supplemented, where applicable, by any relevant provisions from the various court guides and the rules and practice directions that apply in specialist proceedings (see **CPR, Parts 49** and **57 to 64**).

ADMISSIBILITY OF OPINION EVIDENCE

General rule

It is a general rule that opinion evidence is inadmissible. Under the general rule a witness may only attest to facts which are within his or her personal knowledge and is not permitted to draw inferences from those facts. There are two important exceptions to the rule: **54.2**

(a) A lay witness may express an opinion on matters which can only realistically be conveyed in that way, such as when describing a person's age, or the speed of a vehicle, or the state

Commentary

of the weather. This exception is confirmed by the Civil Evidence Act 1972, s. 3(2), which provides:

> It is hereby declared that where a person is called as a witness in any civil proceedings, a statement of opinion by him on any relevant matter on which he is not qualified to give expert evidence, if made as a way of conveying relevant facts personally perceived by him, is admissible as evidence of what he perceived.

(b) A properly qualified expert may state his or her opinion on matters falling within his or her particular area of expertise, if it is an expertise that the court does not possess (*Buckley v Thomas* (1554) Plowd 118 per Saunders J at p. 124; *Folkes v Chadd* (1782) 3 Doug KB 157).

Confirmation of this exception can be found in the Civil Evidence Act 1972, s. 3(1), which provides:

> (1) Subject to any rules of court…where a person is called as a witness in any civil proceedings, his opinion on any relevant matter on which he is qualified to give expert evidence, shall be admissible in evidence.

Parliament has established investigatory processes for providing the Secretary of State with reports, information or documents on which an opinion may be based that it is expedient in the public interest that a company should be wound up (Insolvency Act 1986, s. 124A(1)) or that a disqualification order should be made against a person (Company Directors Disqualification Act 1986, s. 8). It follows that the Secretary of State may use the relevant report etc. as evidence in support of a petition to wind up the company or an application for a disqualification order despite the rule against opinion evidence (*Secretary of State for Business, Enterprise and Regulatory Reform v Aaron* [2008] EWCA Civ 1146, [2009] 1 BCLC 55). A copy of any report of inspectors appointed under the Companies Act 1985, part 14, certified by the Secretary of State to be a true copy, is admissible in any legal proceedings as evidence of the opinion of the inspectors in relation to any matter contained in the report (Companies Act 1985, s. 441(1)).

Requirements for the admission of expert evidence

54.3 For expert evidence to be admissible in civil proceedings, the following requirements must be satisfied:

(a) there must be a matter which is outside the ordinary experience of the tribunal of fact (see 54.4);
(b) it must be a matter on which there is a recognised body of expertise governed by accepted rules and principles (see 54.5);
(c) the witness put forward by the party seeking to rely on expert evidence must be suitably qualified to give expert testimony on the subject (see 54.6 to 54.7); and
(d) the party seeking to rely on the expert's evidence must comply with the relevant rules of court under **CPR, Part 35**, including obtaining a direction granting permission to rely on the expert's evidence at trial under **r. 35.4(1)** (see 54.12 to 54.17).

Greater latitude is given in small claims track cases, where the strict rules of evidence do not apply. See 45.19 and 45.20.

Matter which is outside the ordinary experience of the judge

54.4 Typically, expert evidence will satisfy the first requirement if it addresses a matter of art or science beyond the experience of the tribunal of fact. Medical, engineering, valuation and accountancy issues are common examples. The rule is that if the matter is outside the ordinary experience of the tribunal of fact, expert evidence is admissible, and the converse is also true, that the tribunal of fact cannot reach a decision on that matter without the assistance of an expert because the court needs to act on evidence. In criminal law, the dividing line is illustrated by cases which have held that questions of intent (*R v Chard* (1971) 56 Cr App R 268) and provocation (*R v Turner* [1975] QB 834) are issues on which expert evidence is not admissible, because they are matters within the everyday experience of members of the jury. By way of contrast, the question of insanity or automatism (*R v Smith* [1979] 1 WLR 1445) are outside the normal experience of jurors, so expert evidence is required.

If the parties have used technical expressions in a contract, expert evidence is admissible to explain those technical expressions if they are outside the expertise of the judge (*Kingscroft Insurance Co. Ltd v Nissan Fire and Marine Insurance Co. Ltd* [2000] 1 All ER (Comm) 272). A case on the wrong side of this line was *J. P. Morgan Chase Bank v Springwell Navigation Corporation* [2006] EWHC 2755 (Comm), [2007] 1 All ER (Comm) 549, at [31]–[33].

Experts may not be called on matters which reasonably fall within the knowledge and experience of the tribunal of fact. Expert evidence is not usually admitted on questions of credibility of a witness, even where the witness under consideration is a child (*Re N (A Minor) (Sexual Abuse: Video Evidence)* [1997] 1 WLR 153, but contrast *Re M and R (Minors) (Sexual Abuse: Expert Evidence)* [1996] 4 All ER 239). Although an employment consultant may give expert evidence on the employment opportunities in an area, and the claimant's prospects of finding work, expert evidence is not admissible on a claimant's motivation for finding work (*Larby v Thurgood* [1993] ICR 66). In *esure Insurance Ltd v Direct Line Insurance plc* [2008] EWCA Civ 842, [2008] RPC 34, permission was refused to call an expert to give evidence about consumers' confusion over trademarks as the tribunal could form its own view. An accident reconstruction expert is permitted to give scientific evidence based on physical evidence of the road layout, vehicle positions, skid marks and the positions of debris, gouge and paint marks, and from that evidence to deduce minimum speeds and movements of the vehicles. However, such an expert is not permitted to analyse the witness statements and to draw conclusions as to what the drivers did, whether they should have seen each other, or taken avoiding action, as these are matters on which the trial judge does not need expert assistance (*Liddell v Middleton* [1996] PIQR P36).

In ordinary road traffic whiplash injuries there is no need for expert evidence on causation (*Casey v Cartwright* [2006] EWCA Civ 1280, [2007] 2 All ER 78, explaining *Kearsley v Klarfeld* [2005] EWCA Civ 1510, [2006] 2 All ER 303). It is only if the defendant contends that the nature of the collision, for example, at very low speed, makes it very unlikely that any injury was suffered in the accident, that medical evidence dealing with causation will be necessary. In such cases the defendant must satisfy the following formalities:

(a) within three months of receipt of the letter before claim, notify the other parties that the defendant contends this is a low impact case and that he intends to raise causation as an issue;
(b) the issue must be pleaded in the defence, and supported by a statement of truth; and
(c) within 21 days of serving the defence, the defendant must file and serve a witness statement clearly identifying the grounds on which the low impact issue is raised, making proper reference to the expert evidence on causation, including the circumstances of the impact and any resultant damage.

If the court is satisfied that the issue has been properly raised, it will generally give permission for the claimant to be medically examined on behalf of the defendant, and if the resultant report identifies a case on causation, it will generally give the defendant permission to rely on such evidence at trial.

Permission to adduce a report from a lawyer specialising in art law was refused in *Clarke v Marlborough Fine Art (London) Ltd* [2002] EWHC 11 (Ch), LTL 21/1/2002, because the report was unlikely to provide the court with material assistance on the issues (whether transactions were to the deceased's manifest disadvantage and whether the deceased had received independent legal advice). Experts may not be called on questions of English law, as this is within the expertise of the court (*Midland Bank Trust Co. Ltd v Hett, Stubbs and Kemp* [1979] Ch 384).

Commentary

A medical report which was no more than a history of events as recounted by an asylum seeker was regarded as inadequate for its intended task of corroborating the claimant's account in *SA (Somalia) v Secretary of State for the Home Department* [2006] EWCA Civ 1302, LTL 10/10/2006, although it may be objected that it was not admissible at all.

Recognised body of expertise

54.5 The court must be satisfied by the party seeking to call the evidence that there is a body of expertise governed by recognised standards or rules of conduct capable of influencing the court's decision on any of the issues which it has to decide, and that the witness has sufficient familiarity with and knowledge of the area of expertise to be of value to the court (see also *Liverpool Roman Catholic Archdiocesan Trustees Inc. v Goldberg (No. 3)* [2001] 1 WLR 2337).

Suitably qualified

54.6 In most situations the person tendered as an expert witness must possess suitable professional qualifications and experience. These must be stated by the expert in his or her report (**PD 35, para. 3.2**). The minimum level of qualification and experience required depends on the issue being addressed. General practitioners may be suitably qualified to give expert evidence in simple personal injuries claims. Medical experts in multi-track claims will typically be consultants in the relevant field of medicine with many years of experience. Where an injury involves a number of areas of medical science, different experts will be required for each of those areas. A similar approach is taken with accountancy, engineering and valuation experts. Experts with national or international reputations may be needed in complex commercial and intellectual property cases, and claims involving issues at the forefront of current science.

In simple cases there is no requirement that the expertise must have been acquired in a professional capacity or in the course of the expert's business. An expert is a competent expert witness if the court considers that he or she has the necessary expertise, however it was obtained (*R v Silverlock* [1894] 2 QB 766). A person suitably qualified by his or her knowledge or experience is competent to give expert evidence on the law of a foreign jurisdiction, whether or not he or she has practised law in that jurisdiction (Civil Evidence Act 1972, s. 4(1)). In practical terms, despite s. 4, if the foreign law issue, or the case as a whole, is of significant importance it will be unwise to use a pure academic, and a leading practitioner in the relevant jurisdiction is likely to be a better witness.

Independence

54.7 It is important that expert evidence should be, and should be seen to be, the independent product of the expert uninfluenced by the exigencies of the litigation (*Whitehouse v Jordan* [1981] 1 WLR 246 per Lord Wilberforce). A useful test for 'independence' is whether the expert would express the same opinion if given the same instructions by the opposite party (**PD 35, annex, para. 4.3**). Given that **CPR, r. 35.3**, provides that the expert has an overriding duty to the court rather than to the parties, an employee of a party involved in litigation can be an independent expert (*Field v Leeds City Council* [2000] 1 EGLR 54). A party proposing to use its employee's expert evidence should be given an opportunity to demonstrate that the employee has relevant experience and is aware of the primary duty to the court when giving expert evidence. It may help to demonstrate objectivity if training has been given to the employee on the special position of expert witnesses (*Field v Leeds City Council*). In *Liverpool Roman Catholic Archdiocesan Trustees Inc. v Goldberg (No. 3)* [2001] 1 WLR 2337 it was said that a professional relationship between a litigant and an expert prevented the expert from having the necessary independence to be called as an expert witness. This case was doubted, as being inconsistent with *Field v Leeds City Council* [2000] 1 EGLR 54, in *Admiral Management Services Ltd v Para-Protect Europe Ltd* [2002] EWHC 233 (Ch), [2002] 1 WLR 2722 at [33], and is probably wrong. It was also disapproved in *R (Factortame Ltd) v Secretary of State for Transport, Local Government and the Regions (No. 8)* [2002] EWCA Civ 932, [2003] QB 381, where Lord Phillips of Worth Matravers MR said at [70] the *Liverpool Roman Catholic Archdiocesan Trustees Inc.* case applied the wrong test (the test for apparent bias in a tribunal). In *DN v Greenwich London Borough Council* [2004] EWCA Civ 1659, [2005] LGR 597, an educational psychologist was held to be entitled to give expert evidence on his own behalf on why in his opinion his conduct did not fall below the relevant standard of care.

The mere fact that an expert has a conflict of interest does not prevent the expert being used as a witness (*Toth v Jarman* [2006] EWCA Civ 1028, [2006] 4 All ER 1276). Rather, the question is whether the conflict prevents the expert remaining independent. The presence of a conflict of interest may be a sufficient reason for the court refusing permission for the use of the expert. Where an expert has an interest in the proceedings, this should be disclosed to the court as soon as possible. Whether the expert's evidence should be allowed should be determined during the course of case management. In considering that question the judge will have to weigh the alternative choices available if the expert's evidence is excluded, having regard to the overriding objective (*R (Factortame Ltd) v Secretary of State for Transport, Local Government and the Regions (No. 8)* at [70]). In *Toth v Jarman* the court suggested that the protocol in **PD 35, annex**, should be amended to require an expert to state at the end of his or her report:

(a) that the expert has no conflict of interest of any kind, other than any disclosed in the report;
(b) that the expert did not consider that any interest which has been disclosed affects his or her suitability as an expert witness on any issue in the report; and
(c) that the expert will advise the instructing party if there is any change in these circumstances.

Commentary

Expert as factual witness

As a matter of practice, witnesses who are qualified to be experts are frequently called as witnesses of fact where they were personally involved in the matters relating to litigation. As factual witnesses, they are not subject to **CPR, Part 35**, and there is no requirement that permission be sought (see **54.12** to **54.15**). It is both inevitable and appropriate that a witness who happens to be a professional will give evidence of his actions based on his professional experience and expertise, because no professional person can explain or justify his actions and decisions save by reference to his training and experience (*ES v Chesterfield and North Derbyshire Royal Hospital NHS Trust* [2003] EWCA Civ 1284, [2004] Lloyd's Rep Med 90 at [31]). It would be intolerable if an architect suing for his fees had to adduce independent expert evidence as to what those fees should be (*Lusty Architects v Finsbury Securities Ltd* (1991) 58 BLR 66). A professional person is permitted to give evidence on his own conduct by reference to the professional literature reasonably available to him as a busy practitioner or by reference to his own professional experience. He may also rebut allegations made against him by the other side's expert as one professional person against another (*DN v Greenwich London Borough Council* [2004] EWCA Civ 1659, [2005] LGR 597 at [25]). The limit is that expressions of opinion from such a witness must be reasonably related to facts within his knowledge (*Multiplex Constructions (UK) Ltd v Cleveland Bridge UK Ltd* [2008] EWHC 2220 (TCC), LTL 2/10/2008). The lack of independence goes to weight rather than admissibility. **54.8**

Abolition of ultimate issue rule

The Civil Evidence Act 1972, s. 3(3), provides: **54.9**

(3) In this section 'relevant matter' includes an issue in the proceedings in question.

Section 3(1) is quoted at **54.2**. Section 3(3) abolishes what is often called the 'ultimate issue rule' in civil cases, which prohibited an expert from giving an opinion on 'the very issue which the court has to decide' (*Barings plc v Coopers and Lybrand* [2001] Lloyd's Rep (Bank) 85 at [54]).

However, it is not for experts to attempt to make findings of fact. Instead, they should express their opinions on the basis of assumed facts which should be clearly identified and stated in their reports (*J. P. Morgan Chase Bank v Springwell Navigation Corporation* [2006] EWHC 2755 (Comm), [2007] 1 All ER (Comm) 549 at [21]).

DUTIES OF EXPERTS

54.10 In order to achieve impartiality of experts, **CPR, r. 35.3**, provides that:

(a) it is the duty of an expert to help the court on the matters within his or her expertise; and

(b) this duty overrides any obligation to the person from whom the expert has received instructions or by whom the expert is paid.

Practitioners should advise their clients of the expert's overriding duty to the court, so that the client understands that the expert will consider the matter objectively and not with a view to advancing the interests of the client. It is sensible for solicitors to use standard letters for the instruction of experts, which should draw the expert's attention to the main duties imposed on experts by **Part 35**. Experts who may not be familiar with the requirements of the rules should be sent a copy of the protocol for the instruction of experts (**PD 35, annex**). Section 4 of the protocol sets out the duties of experts, and builds on Cresswell J's statement of principle in *National Justice Compania Naviera SA v Prudential Assurance Co. Ltd* [1993] 2 Lloyd's Rep 68. This states that:

(a) Experts always owe a duty to exercise reasonable skill and care to those instructing them (**PD 35, annex, para. 4.1**).

(b) Experts must comply with any relevant professional code of ethics (**annex, para. 4.1**).

(c) Experts have an overriding duty to help the court on matters within their expertise, and must not serve the exclusive interests of those instructing them (**annex, para. 4.2**).

(d) Experts are obliged to assist the court in accordance with the overriding objective, which includes dealing with cases proportionately, expeditiously and fairly (**annex, para. 4.2**). This includes an obligation to observe the court's directions and time limits, which is why **PD 35, para. 8**, requires the instructing party to provide copies of relevant orders for directions to the expert. An expert who is in any doubt may apply to the court for directions to assist him in carrying out his functions as an expert (**CPR, r. 35.14(1)**).

(e) Experts should provide independent opinions, and must not trespass into the role of the court in deciding facts or engaging in the role of advocates (**PD 35, annex, para. 4.3**).

(f) Experts should confine their opinions to matters which are material to the issues in the case, and must provide opinions only in relation to matters within their expertise. They should indicate without delay any questions or issues which are outside their expertise (**annex, para. 4.4**).

(g) Experts should take into account all material facts before them. They should set out those facts and any literature in their reports. They should indicate whether any opinion expressed is provisional or qualified, and whether any additional information is required (**annex, para. 4.5**).

(h) Experts should inform those instructing them without delay of any change in their opinions and the reasons for the change (**annex, para. 4.6**).

In relation to points (f) and (g) above, experts should exercise caution when expressing their opinions in areas where the underlying science is in the process of development. In *R v Cannings* [2004] EWCA Crim 1, [2004] 1 WLR 2607 at [29], Judge LJ said that this is especially so where scientific knowledge on a topic is limited or incomplete. Experts in many fields will acknowledge the possibility that future research will undermine the accepted wisdom of the day, but that does not of itself provide a basis for rejecting expert evidence, or for conjuring up fanciful doubts about the possible impact of future research (at [178]).

EXPERTS' IMMUNITY FROM SUIT

As a matter of public policy, lay witnesses have immunity from any civil proceedings brought in respect of the evidence they give in a court of law (see **51.26**). This immunity covers testimony in court, and also preparation for giving evidence in court, such as a proof, or Scottish precognition, or witness statement (*Watson v M'Ewan* [1905] AC 480). This immunity applies to a treating doctor, forensic scientist or other expert who is called to give factual evidence without having initially been retained by either party to the dispute, even if they are also asked for their professional opinion (*Jones v Kaney* [2011] UKSC 13, [2011] 2 AC 398 at [64]). All witnesses, including experts initially retained as experts in the case, are immune from suit in respect of claims in defamation (*Jones v Kaney* at [62]). Other than the above, the immunity from suit enjoyed by an expert witness, that is, someone who has been selected, instructed and paid for by a party, was abolished by *Jones v Kaney*. This means they may be sued in negligence or for breach of the implied term in the Supply of Goods and Services Act 1982, s. 13, to exercise reasonable skill and care, for example, if they are negligent in signing a joint statement without having read it. An expert's conduct may also justify a wasted costs order (*Phillips v Symes (No. 2)* [2004] EWHC 2330 (Ch), [2005] 1 WLR 2043; see **68.64**) or disciplinary proceedings by the expert's professional regulator (*Meadow v General Medical Council* [2006] EWCA Civ 1390, [2007] QB 462). **54.11**

COURT CONTROL OVER EXPERT EVIDENCE

An 'expert' for the purposes of **CPR, Part 35**, is a person who has been instructed to give or prepare expert evidence for the purpose of civil proceedings (**rr. 35.2(1)** and **2.1**). Expert evidence obtained for the purpose of other proceedings (for example, DNA evidence prepared for criminal proceedings) is still opinion evidence, and will be admissible in civil proceedings only if the requirements of **Part 35** are complied with (*Lavelle v Noble* [2011] EWCA Civ 441, LTL 18/4/2011). **54.12**

Rule 35.1 provides that expert evidence shall be restricted to that which is reasonably required to resolve the proceedings. In *J. P. Morgan Chase Bank v Springwell Navigation Corporation* [2006] EWHC 2755 (Comm), [2007] 1 All ER (Comm) 549, Aikens J warned against the natural tendency in complex litigation with voluminous documentation to resort to experts to assist in digesting the material, particularly in unusual areas of commercial practice. This can result in the judge being submerged by long and complicated reports which are expensive, time- consuming and possibly counter-productive. **Rule 35.1** can be used by the court to reject expert evidence if it is not reasonably required to resolve the proceedings.

Further protection is given by **r. 35.4(1)**, which provides that 'No party may call an expert or put in evidence an expert's report without the court's permission'. Practitioners should apply in good time for permission to call an expert or such permission will not be granted. In *Calenti v North Middlesex NHS Trust* (2001) LTL 10/4/2001, the defendant was refused permission to call a medical expert two weeks prior to trial because to do so would work a significant injustice on the claimant. A party applying for permission either to call an expert or to put in evidence an expert's report must identify (**r. 35.4(2)**):

(a) the field in which it is sought to rely on expert evidence; and
(b) where practicable, the name of the proposed expert.

If permission is granted under **r. 35.4**, it will be in relation only to the expert named or the field identified (**r. 35.4(3)**).

The court has power to limit the amount of an expert's fees and expenses that the party who wishes to rely on the expert may recover from any other party (**r. 35.4(4)**). This rule was amended, with effect from 1 October 2009, to make clear that the power to restrict fees and expenses applies to costs recoverable between the parties but does not interfere with the contractual fees agreed between any party and its expert. The court may also exercise its discretion to terminate the expert's appointment in appropriate circumstances (*Kranidiotes v Paschali* (2001) EWCA 357, LTL 8/5/2001). This power is in addition to the court's general powers to restrict experts' fees on a subsequent detailed assessment of costs under **Part 44**. An expert who has caused significant expense to be incurred through flagrant, reckless disregard of his duties to the court may be ordered to pay those costs (*Phillips v Symes (No. 2)* [2004] EWHC 2330 (Ch), [2005] 1 WLR 2043). Where an expert adopts a biased or irrational approach, it may be appropriate for the judge to refer the witness's conduct to the relevant professional body, after giving the witness a suitable period of time to make representations (*Pearce v Ove Arup Partnership Ltd* (2001) LTL 8/11/2001).

In the absence of a duty of confidence, it is contrary to public policy for an expert to agree not to act for another party (*Lilly Icos LLC v Pfizer Ltd* (2000) LTL 26/1/2001).

Permission to use expert evidence

54.13 On the fast and multi-tracks, no expert may give evidence, whether written or oral, at a hearing without the permission of the court (**CPR, r. 35.4(1)**). When the parties apply for permission they must provide an estimate of the costs of the proposed experts (**r. 35.4(2)**). Permission is generally only granted for named experts in named fields. Directions may specify the issues the expert evidence should address (**r. 35.4(3)**). Where possible, matters requiring expert evidence should be dealt with by only one expert (**PD 35, para. 1**).

The first stage at which the court may give directions in relation to experts is at the allocation stage. By this time the parties to proceedings will have completed their directions questionnaires in form N180 or N181. Question E asks whether the party completing the form wishes to use expert evidence at the hearing and whether any expert reports have yet been copied to the other parties. The party completing the form is required to list the experts whose evidence it may wish to use, their fields of expertise, the justification for using the expert, and the estimated cost. A party must also indicate whether it will use a single joint expert in any field. These answers will assist the court in deciding on track allocation as well as the form of directions to be made on allocation.

Although the court has power to limit the expert evidence the parties may call at trial, and to limit the costs recoverable for the use of expert evidence, it does not have power to limit the experts a party can instruct. The court cannot impose a condition that a party must obtain the court's permission before instructing an expert (*Vasiliou v Hajigeorgiou* [2005] EWCA Civ 236, [2005] 1 WLR 2195). Where directions require an act to be done by an expert, or otherwise affect an expert, the party instructing the expert must serve a copy of the order on the expert (**para. 8**).

Experts are comparatively rare on the small claims track, see **45.19**. On the small claims track, expert evidence, whether written or oral, requires permission (**CPR, r. 27.5**). On this track only **rr. 35.1** (duty to restrict expert evidence), **35.3** (overriding duty of experts to the court), **35.7** (power to direct single joint expert) and **35.8** (instructions to single joint expert) apply (**r. 27.2(1)(e)**). **Rules 35.4(3A)** (only one expert) and **35.5(2)** (expert not to attend the hearing unless necessary) have express references to the small claims track, and are intended to apply to these cases, despite a drafting defect in **r. 27.2**. Experts' reports on this track can therefore be somewhat informal.

Where a claim has been allocated to the small claims track or the fast track, if permission is given for expert evidence, it will normally be given for evidence from only one expert on a particular issue (**r. 35.4(3A)**). On these two tracks the court will not direct an expert to attend a hearing unless it is necessary to do so in the interests of justice (**r. 35.5(2)**).

Directions on the fast track

Where a case has been allocated to the fast track, **PD 28, para. 3.2**, provides: **54.14**

The court will seek to tailor its directions to the needs of the case and the steps of which it is aware that the parties have already taken to prepare the case. In particular it will have regard to the extent to which any PD pre-action Conduct or pre-action protocol has or (as the case may be) has not been complied with.

In most fast track claims the court will limit the expert evidence to one expert per party in relation to any field of expertise, and to expert evidence in no more than two expert fields (**CPR, r. 26.6(5)(b)**). Directions will be made for a single joint expert, unless there are good reasons for taking a different course (**PD 28, paras 3.7(4)** and **3.9(4)**). Fast track claims should ordinarily be capable of being tried within one day (**CPR, r. 26.6(5)(a)**). It is therefore important to be able to identify at an early stage whether there is likely to be a significant conflict in the expert evidence, so that a decision can be made whether to reallocate the claim to the multi-track. In a suitable case, such as *Baron v Lovell* [1999] CPLR 630, a judge is entitled at a pre-trial review to direct that the medical evidence needed to determine the issues relating to the claimant's personal injury claim could be provided by the claimant's medical expert only.

It is also possible for the parties to agree the directions sought and if this is the case, the proposed directions should where necessary contain a provision regarding the use of a single joint expert, or in cases where the use of a single expert has not been agreed, the exchange and agreement of expert reports (including whether exchange is to be simultaneous or sequential) and without-prejudice discussions of the experts (**PD 28, para. 3.7**). It is possible that the court will not approve the directions submitted by the parties and will instead substitute its own directions, having regard to the parties' suggested directions (**PD 28, para. 3.8**). Alternatively, the court may hold an allocation hearing at which directions will be given.

According to **PD 28, para. 3.9(5)**, where a direction for a single joint expert is not given, the court's general approach will be:

(a) to direct disclosure of experts' reports by way of simultaneous exchange; and
(b) if experts' reports are not agreed, to direct a discussion between the experts for the purpose set out in **CPR, r. 35.12(1)** (identification of and agreement of the issues in the case) and the preparation of a report under **r. 35.12(3)** (see **54.31**).

Where expert reports are to be exchanged, generally this should be done within 14 weeks of the directions order (**PD 28, para. 3.12**).

The court will not direct an expert to attend a hearing of a fast track claim, unless it is necessary to do so in the interests of justice (**CPR, r. 35.5(2)**).

Directions on the multi-track

Paragraphs 4.2, 4.6, 4.7, 4.9 and **4.10** of **PD 29** make virtually the same provision about directions on the multi-track concerning experts as those applicable on the fast track (see **54.14**). Proposed directions should take as their starting point the relevant model directions and standard directions available on the Ministry of Justice website (**CPR, r. 29.1(2)**). There is a greater willingness to allow the parties to instruct their own experts on the multi-track (*S (A Minor) v Birmingham Health Authority* (1999) LTL 23/11/99) and, as these claims are usually more complex than fast track claims, the time for exchanging experts' reports is likely to be longer than for fast track claims. There is also a greater willingness to allow experts to give oral evidence at trial in multi-track cases. The spirit and effect of the rules mean that even in multi-track claims great care will be taken before making expert directions. For example, in claims relating to the alleged infringement of registered designs, expert evidence may not be useful (see *Oren v Red Box Toy Factory Ltd* [1999] FSR 785) and may well not be allowed (see *Thermos Ltd v Aladdin Sales and Marketing Ltd* (1999) *The Independent*, 13 December 1999). **54.15**

Commentary

In *Mann v Chetty and Patel* (2000) LTL 26/10/2000 the Court of Appeal agreed that the judge had been right in a multi-track claim to refuse permission to call various experts, because the evidence would have been of minimal value, would not have been conclusive on the issues, and would have been disproportionate. In *Rawlinson v Cooper* [2002] EWCA Civ 392, LTL 11/3/2002, it was held that both an original report from a medical expert and a second report from the same witness, which included references to published papers on life expectancy and their application to the claimant's case, should be admitted in evidence. However, it is disproportionate to allow a party to call two experts in a single area (even if the expert was retained by the party in the matter in dispute, and so will be giving factual evidence as well) (*Carillion JM Ltd v Bath and North East Somerset Council* [2009] EWHC 166 (TCC), LTL 3/4/2009, architect in a construction case; *Beaumont v Ministry of Defence* [2009] EWHC 1258 (QB), LTL 18/6/2009, obstetrician in a clinical dispute). Calling two experts in such cases is permitted only if the circumstances are exceptional.

Directions for the exchange of scholarly information

54.16 In *Wardlaw v Farrar* [2003] EWCA Civ 1719, [2003] 4 All ER 1358, it was pointed out that there is a standard direction dealing with disclosure of scholarly information used by medical experts for use in clinical disputes, based on the direction used by Masters Ungley and Yoxall, which should be followed in all courts dealing with medical negligence claims. The direction, which is set out below, can also be used in other categories of claim.

> Any unpublished literature upon which any expert witness proposes to rely shall be served at the same time as service of his [report] together with a list of published literature and copies of any unpublished material. Any supplementary literature upon which any expert witness proposes to rely shall be notified to all other parties at least one month before trial. No expert witness shall rely upon any publications that have not been disclosed in accordance with this direction without [permission] of the trial judge on such terms as to costs as he deems fit.

Reports and privilege

54.17 Until an expert's report is disclosed to the other side, instructions to the expert and the expert's report will be protected by legal professional privilege (see **50.60**). While privilege applies, the court will not make an order compelling disclosure, as that would run counter to the privilege (*Worrall v Reich* [1955] 1 QB 296). By disclosing a report, whether voluntarily or pursuant to directions, a party waives privilege (see **50.73**). Disclosing the final version of an expert's report does not waive privilege in earlier drafts of the report (*Jackson v Marley Davenport Ltd* [2004] EWCA Civ 1225, [2004] 1 WLR 2926). For privilege in respect of jointly instructed and jointly selected experts, see **54.19**. For experts instructed only to advise see **8.23** and **54.22**.

The status of instructions to experts once a report is disclosed is considered at **54.30**.

JOINT AND SEPARATE EXPERTS

Single joint expert

54.18 Under CPR, r. 35.7, where two or more parties wish to submit expert evidence on a particular issue, the court has power to direct that evidence is to be given by a single joint expert only. A 'single joint expert' is an expert instructed to prepare a report for the court on behalf of two or more of the parties (including the claimant) (r. 35.2(2)). When considering whether to give permission for the parties to rely on expert evidence and whether that evidence should be from a single joint expert, **PD 35, para.** 7, provides that the court will take into account all the circumstances, and in particular whether:

(a) it is proportionate to have separate experts for each party on a particular issue with reference to:

(i) the amount in dispute;
(ii) the importance to the parties; and
(iii) the complexity of the issue;

(b) the instruction of a single joint expert is likely to assist the parties and the court to resolve the issue more speedily and in a more cost-effective way than separately instructed experts;
(c) expert evidence is to be given on the issue of liability, causation or quantum;
(d) the expert evidence falls within a substantially established area of knowledge which is unlikely to be in dispute or there is likely to be a range of expert opinion;
(e) a party has already instructed an expert on the issue in question and whether or not that was done in compliance with any practice direction or relevant pre-action protocol;
(f) questions put in accordance with **CPR, r. 35.6**, are likely to remove the need for the other party to instruct an expert if one party has already instructed an expert;
(g) questions put to a single joint expert may not conclusively deal with all issues that may require testing prior to trial;
(h) a conference may be required with the legal representatives, experts and other witnesses which may make instruction of a single joint expert impractical; and
(i) a claim to privilege makes the instruction of any expert as a single joint expert inappropriate.

The parties for whom that person is a joint expert are called the 'relevant parties'. It may be that the relevant parties cannot agree on who that expert should be, in which case the court may:

(a) select the expert from a list prepared or identified by the relevant parties, or
(b) direct that the expert be selected in such other manner as the court may direct.

The court may give directions about the payment of a single joint expert's fees and expenses and about any inspection, examination or experiments which the expert may wish to carry out (**r. 35.8(3)**). Before a single joint expert is instructed the court may limit the amount that can be paid by way of fees and expenses to the expert and direct that the relevant parties pay that amount into court (**r. 35.8(4)**). In any event, where a single joint expert is instructed, the relevant parties are jointly and severally liable for the payment of the expert's fees and expenses, unless the court directs otherwise (**r. 35.8(5); PD 35, annex, para. 17.8**). In this way, the parties will know in advance what their financial commitment is in the way of experts' fees.

The reasons for directing that a report be obtained from a single joint expert are that it saves time and costs and is usually proportionate to the issues in the case. It may be the case that in order to fulfil these objectives, it is simpler to use an employee of one of the parties, who is expert in the relevant discipline (see 54.7).

If a single joint expert's report is accepted by the parties, subject to receiving answers to written questions (see 54.32), it is inevitable that the report will be accepted at trial without needing to call the expert to give oral evidence. District judges frequently make this clear when giving directions at the allocation stage.

Joint selection of expert

Joint selection is to be contrasted with joint instruction of experts. A jointly instructed expert receives instructions from both sides, who both contribute to the expert's fees, and both are entitled to the expert's report. A jointly selected expert is one who is chosen (usually by one side providing a list of proposed experts, and the other side deciding whether to object to any of those named) by both sides, but who is instructed by one side only. That party is entirely responsible for the expert's fees, and is, at least initially, entitled to assert legal professional privilege over the report (*Carlson v Townsend* [2001] EWCA Civ 511, [2001] 1 WLR 2415). *Carlson v Townsend* was interpreted by *Edwards-Tubb v J. D. Wetherspoon plc* [2011] EWCA Civ 136, [2011] 1 54.19

Commentary

WLR 1373 at [14] as simply a decision that the expert in that case had been jointly selected and not jointly instructed. The court in *Edwards-Tubb v J. D. Wetherspoon plc* did not feel bound by the comments in *Carlson v Townsend* about the privileged nature of a jointly instructed expert's report, and felt that the need to prevent 'expert-shopping' overrides any absolute rule that a jointly selected expert's report is privileged unless privilege is waived. It accordingly held that where a party has obtained a report from a jointly selected expert, does not disclose that report, and then seeks to rely on the report of another expert, the court has a discretion, which it should usually exercise, to grant permission to rely on the new expert's evidence only on condition that the jointly selected expert's report is disclosed to the other side (at [31]). It is the same whether the joint instruction is pre-issue or post-issue. There are substantial practical and doctrinal problems with this decision, and there are questions over whether it will stand the test of time. Pre-action protocols often recommend joint selection of experts. Court directions tend to provide for joint instruction.

Joint expert or own experts

54.20 Whether a direction should be given for the instruction of a single joint expert depends on the nature of the issue being considered. Single joint experts are more appropriate where there is a settled and recognised body of expert knowledge. Separate experts are more suitable where it is known that there are different schools of thought in the area of expertise (*Oxley v Penwarden* [2001] CPLR 1), or where the opinions of the experts depend on issues of interpretation. Examples are issues as to appropriate surgical procedures, or disputes about outcomes in clinical dispute claims. In substantial claims where the central issues can only be resolved by expert evidence it is likely to be wrong for the court to insist on a single joint expert. In clinical disputes, it was suggested in *Peet v Mid-Kent Healthcare Trust* [2001] EWCA Civ 1703, [2002] 1 WLR 210, that the balance between proportionality and expense could be achieved by allowing the parties to call their own experts on the medical issues, but to direct the instruction of a joint expert on the non-medical issues. This is so even where the sums at stake are substantial.

Challenging joint report

54.21 Where a single joint expert has been agreed by the parties and the court has directed that expert to report, a party who is unhappy with that expert's conclusions will not be permitted to call further expert evidence by way of their own expert unless it would be unjust pursuant to the overriding objective not to allow that evidence (*Daniels v Walker* [2000] 1 WLR 1382). *Daniels v Walker* also held that refusing an additional expert after a direction for a single joint expert did not infringe the European Convention on Human Rights, **art. 6(1)**, in the **Human Rights Act 1998, sch. 1**. In considering whether it would be unjust not to allow an additional expert, *Peet v Mid-Kent Healthcare Trust* [2001] EWCA Civ 1703, [2002] 1 WLR 210, held that good, not fanciful, reasons are required. A preliminary requirement if further expert evidence is to be allowed is whether there is any rational criticism of the joint expert's report. A significant discrepancy between the valuation evidence of a single joint expert and a second expert instructed by one of the parties may be a sufficient basis for allowing the second expert's evidence (*Marston v Lewis* [2004] EWHC 2833 (Ch), LTL 4/11/2004). There are cases where a pivotal issue depends on expert evidence and the jointly instructed expert's view is not easily capable of challenge in the absence of other expert opinion. If so, justice may require permission to be granted to seek a second opinion (*W v Oldham Metropolitan Borough Council* [2005] EWCA Civ 1247, *The Times*, 7 November 2005, a family law case).

Factors bearing on the exercise of the discretion to allow additional expert evidence after a jointly instructed expert has reported include the reasons for seeking another report, the nature of the case and the amount at stake, the effect of allowing another expert to report and its impact on delay and the trial (*Cosgrove v Pattison* [2001] CPLR 177). See also **54.38** for cross-examination of a joint expert.

If there is no basis for rational criticism of a joint expert's report, and if the joint report totally undermines one side's case, the court may enter summary judgment. Thus, in *Smith v Peter North and Partners* [2001] EWCA Civ 1553, [2002] PNLR 12, a joint expert reported in a claim for damages against a surveyor that the value of the property was the same with and without the defects. Summary judgment was entered for the defendant because there was no prospect of the claimant persuading the court that the cost of repairs was the correct measure of damages. Contrast *Layland v Fairview New Homes plc* [2002] EWHC 1350 (Ch), LTL 10/7/2002, in which, after considering various criticisms of a single jointly instructed valuation expert's report (which concluded the claimants had suffered no loss), Neuberger J allowed the claim to go to trial as there was material which could fruitfully be exploited in cross-examination.

Experts instructed only to advise

Parties on occasion instruct an expert with no present intention of using the expert's opinions in court proceedings. This may arise: **54.22**

(a) in complex claims where a party to a dispute needs expert assistance as part of the investigative process; and

(b) where a litigant wants another expert to comment on a single joint expert's report.

In these circumstances, and while the report in question is not intended for use in the proceedings, neither **CPR, Part 35**, nor the Experts Protocol in **PD 35, annex** applies (**PD 35, annex, paras 5.1** and **5.2**). The expert's fees are unlikely to be recoverable as costs in the proceedings (**para. 17.5**). An expert who has advised in this way should only be proposed as a single joint expert if the other parties are given all relevant information about the previous involvement (**para. 17.4**).

Retaining an expert before directions are given

Retaining an expert without trying to agree a single joint expert with one's opponent carries the risk that the costs of the expert will not be allowed. Where it is necessary to instruct an expert before commencement of proceedings, the pre-action protocols encourage the joint selection of, and access to, experts (**Pre-action Protocol for Personal Injury Claims, para. 2.14**). If no specific protocol applies, the parties should, if possible, engage a single joint expert or an agreed expert (**PD Pre-action Conduct, annex C, para. 3**). **54.23**

Retaining one's own expert may lead to the following consequences:

(a) The court may not grant permission for the expert's report to be used, so that the party who wishes to rely on the report may not recover the costs of instructing the expert.

(b) The court may order that a different, jointly instructed expert be used, so that the costs of the first expert are wasted.

(c) The court may allow the report to be used, but disallow the costs, and allow the opponent to instruct and call its own expert.

(d) An attempt to persuade one's opponent to use one's expert's report as the only report in the case may involve disclosing it earlier than might have been ordered by the court and the opponent may still not agree to its use.

There are, however, circumstances in which it is important to obtain an expert's report for the claimant, for example:

(a) In many cases, it may not be until an expert's report has been obtained that a claimant can be sure of having a case at all.

(b) There may be such lengthy waiting lists to get a report from the chosen expert that the claimant needs to initiate these procedures as soon as solicitors are instructed.

(c) In straightforward cases and given that the letter of instructions will be disclosed, if the expert who is instructed is well known and accepted as reputable by the opponent, time may be saved and the report may be accepted, perhaps subject to further questions being put by the opponent under **CPR, r. 35.6**.

Commentary

It is nonetheless clear that the preferred approach is to communicate with one's opponent in an effort to agree on a mutually acceptable expert (*Carlson v Townsend* [2001] EWCA Civ 511, [2001] 1 WLR 2415).

INSTRUCTING EXPERTS

Appointment of experts

54.24 Before an expert is formally instructed, or the court's permission is sought, solicitors should establish (see **PD 35, annex, para. 7.1**):

(a) that the expert is suitably qualified;
(b) that the expert is familiar with his or her duties as an expert in court proceedings;
(c) that the expert can provide a report and answer written questions within a suitable time frame and at a cost proportionate to the issues;
(d) whether the expert will be available for the trial;
(e) that there is no potential conflict of interest.

In practical terms, saying that availability for trial should be established can be a counsel of perfection, because in some fields there is a shortage of experts, and a measure of double-booking has to be tolerated. In these cases, a view has to be taken on the risks, including prospects that some cases might settle, or for some latitude within the trial window or trial timetables to allow double-booked cases to go ahead. Courts are, however, very reluctant to adjourn on this ground.

Terms of appointment should be agreed at the outset (**para. 7.2**). These should include the services required from the expert, time for delivery of the report, the basis of the expert's charges (which may be daily or hourly rates with an estimate of the time likely to be required, or a total fee for the services) including cancellation fees and fees for attending court, and arrangements for answering written questions. Cancellation fees (if any) depend on the nature of the work done by the expert, the length of notice given of any adjournment, and whether it is feasible for the expert to book other work given those circumstances. Agreement to delay payment of fees until the end of the case is permissible, but fees contingent on the nature of the expert's advice, or dependent on the outcome of the case, are not (**paras 7.6** and **7.7**).

Instructions

54.25 Solicitors must give clear instructions to retained experts (**PD 35, annex, para. 8.1**). When instructing an expert it is important to state that the retainer is on terms that the expert will perform the functions specified in the CPR. By doing so the expert will agree with his client that he will perform the duties that he owes to the court, with the result that there should be no conflict between the duty that the expert owes to his client (see **54.11**) and the duty he owes to the court (*Jones v Kaney* [2011] UKSC 13, [2011] 2 AC 398 at [49]). Instructions to the expert should include:

(a) basic information, such as names, addresses, dates of birth, telephone numbers and dates of incidents;
(b) the nature and extent of the expertise called for;
(c) the purpose of the report, a description of what needs to be investigated and of the issues in the case;
(d) copies of the statements of case, witness statements and disclosed documents relevant to the report;
(e) where proceedings have not been commenced, whether that is the intention, and whether the expert is asked only for advice;
(f) an outline programme for all stages of the expert's work, consistent with good case management;

(g) where proceedings have started, the dates of any hearings and details of matters such as the case management track for the case, together with copies of relevant court directions and orders.

The expert should confirm, without delay, whether he or she accepts the instructions, and should inform the instructing party without delay of any problems or insufficiency in the instructions (**para. 9.1**). Once instructions are accepted, the expert must not withdraw without first discussing the reasons with those who gave the instructions (**para. 10.1**), and should consider whether it might be more appropriate to seek directions under **CPR, r. 35.14**.

It may be the case that one or other of the parties has access to information which is not reasonably available to another party and which may assist an expert in preparing his or her report. In these circumstances, the court may direct the party who has such access to prepare and file a document recording the information and to serve a copy of that document on the other party (**r. 35.9**). The document must include sufficient details of all the facts, tests, experiments and assumptions which underlie any part of the information to enable the party on whom it is served to make, or to obtain, a proper interpretation of the information and an assessment of its significance (**PD 35, para. 4**).

Instructions to a single joint expert

Where a direction has been given by the court, in accordance with **CPR, r. 35.7**, for a single joint expert to be used, the parties should try to agree joint instructions, and should try to agree what documents should be included with the instructions (**PD 35, annex, para. 17.6**). They should also attempt to agree what assumptions the expert should be allowed to make. In the event of disagreement, they should try to agree where the areas of disagreement lie and their instructions should make this clear (**para. 17.7**). Where they cannot agree, each instructing party may give instructions to the expert (**CPR, r. 35.8(1)**), but must send a copy, at the same time, to the other instructing parties (**r. 35.8(2)**). There is no rule, and in fact it is contrary to the express terms of **r. 35.8(1)**, that a party should be bound to the instructions to a single joint expert proposed by the other side. The court should not order one side to sign instructions they object to (*Yorke v Katra* [2003] EWCA Civ 867, LTL 9/6/2003). **54.26**

Single joint experts owe an equal duty to all parties, and must maintain independence, impartiality and transparency at all times (**PD 35, annex, para. 17.11**). They should keep all instructing parties informed of material steps they may take by copying correspondence to all parties (**para. 17.10**). A party will not be permitted to invite a jointly instructed expert to a conference without the written consent of the other parties or where the court has directed the meeting should take place (*Peet v Mid-Kent Healthcare Trust* [2001] EWCA Civ 1703, [2002] 1 WLR 210).

WRITTEN REPORTS

Oral or written evidence at trial

Expert evidence is to be given in a written report, unless the court directs otherwise (**CPR, r. 35.5(1)**). A decision on attendance at trial may be made in the initial case management directions, or upon filing the pre-trial checklists, or on an application under **Part 23**. The court has a wide discretionary power on what expert evidence is adduced and in what form (**rr. 35.4 and 35.5**). If a claim is on the fast track, the court will not direct an expert to attend a hearing, unless it is necessary to do so in the interests of justice (**r. 35.5(2)**). **54.27**

However, in the Commercial and Admiralty Courts a sole expert should be available to give oral evidence, unless his or her report is on discrete and substantially non-controversial matters collateral to the main issues (*Voaden v Champion* (2000) LTL 2/6/2000).

Commentary

If oral expert evidence is to be given it has been made clear that it is up to the party calling the witness to make sure that he or she will be available at the hearing and this is best achieved by planning well ahead and cooperating with the other side (*Matthews v Tarmac Bricks and Tiles Ltd* [1999] CPLR 463; *Rollinson v Kimberly Clark Ltd* [1999] CPLR 581).

An expert's report must be disclosed, otherwise it cannot be used at trial without the court's permission (**r. 35.13**). If an expert's report has not been disclosed, the expert cannot be called to give oral evidence without the court's permission (**r. 35.13**; and see **48.26** on sanctions, **54.13** on directions about experts, and **54.37** on disclosure of an abandoned expert's report).

If an expert who has been commissioned to prepare a report refuses to do so because of a reasonable fear that it will not be paid for, the court will not allow a witness summons to be issued requiring the expert to give evidence (*Brown v Bennett* (2000) *The Times*, 2 November 2000).

Use of other side's expert's report

54.28 Once an expert's report has been disclosed by the party which commissioned it, any other party may use it as evidence at the trial (**CPR, r. 35.11**). The parties have a right to rely on the experts' reports disclosed by other parties, unrestricted by any discretion in **rr. 35.1** and **35.7**, given the unqualified terms of **r. 35.11** (*Shepherd Neame Ltd v EDF Energy Networks (SPN) plc* [2008] EWHC 123 (TCC), [2008] Bus LR Digest D43). The right to do so in **r. 35.11** continues to apply after the instructing party drops out of the litigation. *Edwards-Tubb v J. D. Wetherspoon plc* [2011] EWCA Civ 136, [2011] 1 WLR 1373 at [32] said there may be some cases where this is a disproportionate consequence, and that there may be some cases where the opposing party should be allowed to rely on a disclosed report only on condition that the expert is called. Even if there is a discretion to refuse permission to rely on a written report disclosed by an opposing party, there are strong countervailing factors in favour of granting permission, particularly where the relevant expert has taken part in joint discussions with other experts.

Contents of expert's report

54.29 PD 35, **para. 3**, deals with the form and content of experts' reports. An expert's report should be addressed to the court and not to the party from whom instructions were received (**para. 3.1**). It must (**para. 3.2**):

(a) give details of the expert's qualifications;
(b) give details of any literature or other material which has been relied on in making the report;
(c) contain a statement setting out the substance of all facts and instructions which are material to the opinions expressed in the report or upon which those opinions are based;
(d) make clear which of the facts stated in the report are within the expert's own knowledge;
(e) say who carried out any examination, measurement, test or experiment which the expert has used for the report, give the qualifications of that person, and say whether or not the test or experiment has been carried out under the expert's supervision;
(f) where there is a range of opinion on the matters dealt with in the report:
 (i) summarise the range of opinions, and
 (ii) give reasons for the expert's own opinion;
(g) contain a summary of the conclusions reached;
(h) if the expert is not able to give an opinion without qualification, state the qualification; and
(i) contain a statement that the expert:
 (i) understands his or her duty to the court and has complied with that duty (this statement is required by **CPR, r. 35.10(2)**); and
 (ii) is aware of the requirements of **Part 35**, **PD 35**, and the protocol in **PD 35, annex**.

Extra detail is given in **PD 35, annex, paras 13.1** to **13.15**. An expert's report must be verified by a statement of truth (**PD 35, para. 3.3**; see **23.13** to **23.17**). The form of the statement of truth is:

I confirm that I have made clear which facts and matters referred to in this report are within my own knowledge and which are not. Those that are within my own knowledge I confirm to be true. The opinions I have expressed represent my true and complete professional opinions on the matters to which they refer.

Experts must not be asked to amend, expand or alter their reports in a manner which distorts their true opinion, and must refuse to do so if asked (**PD 35, annex, para. 15.2**). This prohibition does not prevent an expert being invited to amend or expand a report to ensure its accuracy, internal consistency, completeness, relevance to the issues and clarity (**para. 15.2**).

Where an expert's report fails to comply with the provisions of **PD 35, para. 3.2**, concerning contents it is a proper use of judicial discretion not to excuse that failure, and to debar the expert from giving evidence. It would not then be open to the parties to invite the court to make a consent order granting an extension of time for compliance (*Stevens v Gullis* [2000] 1 All ER 527).

Providing details of instructions

An expert's report must contain a statement setting out the substance of all material instructions (whether written or oral) on the basis of which the report was written (**CPR, r. 35.10(3)**). It should summarise the facts and instructions given to the expert which are material to the opinions expressed in the report or upon which those opinions are based. This can cause particular problems when expert's reports are disclosed before the disclosure of factual witness statements. If the expert was instructed with the provision of draft witness statements, those witness statements lose their privileged status because they form part of the expert's instructions (**r. 35.10(4)**, which is one of the reasons why most directions orders provide for the exchange of witness statements some time before service of experts' reports). **Rule 35.10(4)** goes on to say that the court will not order disclosure of the expert's instructions or disclosure of any specific document unless it is satisfied that there are reasonable grounds for believing the statement of instructions in the report is inaccurate or incomplete. The aim of these rules is to ensure that the factual basis on which an expert prepares a report is transparent. An expert's 'instructions' are not limited to any letters of instruction, but include materials, earlier experts' reports and witness statements supplied to the expert as part of the instructions (*Morris v Bank of India* (ChD, 15 January 2001); *Lucas v Barking, Havering and Redbridge Hospitals NHS Trust* [2003] EWCA Civ 1102, [2004] 1 WLR 220). A party who is served with an expert's report is not allowed, as a matter of course, to call for all the documents referred to in the report. Before being entitled to do so, there has to be some concrete fact giving rise to reasonable grounds for questioning the expert's statement of instructions (*Lucas v Barking, Havering and Redbridge Hospitals NHS Trust*). If the expert was asked to provide a report based on hypothetical facts posed by the solicitor providing the instructions, that should be made clear in the expert's report (*Morris v Bank of India* (2001) LTL 16/11/2001). 54.30

DISCUSSION BETWEEN EXPERTS

CPR, r. 35.12, provides that the court may, at any stage, direct a discussion between experts for the purpose of requiring them: 54.31

(a) to identify and discuss the expert issues in the proceedings; and
(b) where possible, to reach an agreed opinion on those issues.

Arrangements for such a discussion should be proportionate to the value of the case, and may take place by telephone or through correspondence as an alternative to a face-to-face meeting

(**PD 35, annex, para. 18.4**). Primary responsibility for producing an agenda for the meeting rests with the parties' solicitors (**para. 18.5**). The agenda should indicate the matters agreed between the parties and contain a concise summary of the matters still in issue. It is often helpful to include a list of the questions to be answered by the experts (**para. 18.6**). The court may specify the issues which the experts must discuss (**r. 35.12(2)**) and may also direct that following a discussion between them, the experts must prepare a statement for the court setting out the issues on which (**r. 35.12(3)**):

(a) they agree; and
(b) they disagree, with a summary of their reasons for disagreeing.

Unless directed by the court, discussions between experts are not mandatory (**PD 35, para. 9.1**). Parties must consider, with their experts, at an early stage, whether there is likely to be any useful purpose in holding an experts' discussion and if so when. The purpose of discussions between experts is not for experts to settle cases (**para. 9.2**), but to agree and narrow issues and in particular to identify (**para. 9.2**):

(a) the extent of the agreement between them;
(b) the points of and short reasons for any disagreement;
(c) action, if any, which may be taken to resolve any outstanding points of disagreement; and
(d) any further material issues not raised and the extent to which these issues are agreed.

Where the experts are to meet, the parties must discuss and if possible agree whether an agenda is necessary, and if so attempt to agree one that helps the experts to focus on the issues which need to be discussed (**para. 9.3**). The agenda must not be in the form of leading questions or hostile in tone. Unless ordered by the court, or agreed by all parties, and the experts, neither the parties nor their legal representatives may attend the discussion (**para. 9.4**; and see *Hubbard v Lambeth, Southwark and Lewisham Health Authority* [2001] EWCA Civ 1455, [2002] Lloyd's Rep Med 8).

After experts meet they must prepare a statement dealing with the points ((a) to (d) above) identified in **para. 9.2**. Individual copies of the statement must be signed by the experts at the conclusion of the discussion, or as soon thereafter as practicable, and in any event within seven days. Copies of the statement must be provided to the parties no later than 14 days after signing (**para. 9.6**). Experts must give their own opinions to assist the court and do not require the authority of the parties to sign a joint statement (**para. 9.7**). If an expert significantly alters his or her opinion, the joint statement must include a note or addendum by that expert explaining the change (**para. 9.8**).

A joint statement is produced for the court to assist in case management and is not a document for which a party can claim privilege (*Robin Ellis Ltd v Malwright Ltd* [1999] BLR 81).

However, the content of the experts' discussion is not to be referred to at the trial unless the parties agree (**r. 35.12(4)**). Where experts reach agreement on an issue during their discussions, that agreement will not bind the parties unless they expressly agree to be bound by it (**r. 35.12(5)**). In *Stallwood v David* [2006] EWHC 2600 (QB), [2007] 1 All ER 206, it was held that in exceptional cases permission may be granted allowing a party to adduce additional expert evidence following an agreement between opposing experts. The substantial nature of the claim or the mere fact that an expert has changed or modified an opinion following a discussion between the experts is not a sufficient reason for permitting a party to adduce evidence from a different expert. Adequate reasons might be that the original expert had stepped outside his expertise, or acted incompetently in reaching agreement, or if there is no proper basis for the expert's revised opinion. See also the cases discussed at **54.21** on challenging joint reports. In *Aird v Prime Meridian Ltd* [2006] EWCA Civ 1866, [2007] BLR 105, directions were given for mediation, with a joint statement to be prepared by the parties' experts. A draft joint statement was headed 'without prejudice', but the final version had these words removed. The mediation failed to settle the case. It was held that the joint statement was made pursuant to

r. 35.12, and did not acquire without-prejudice status by being used in the mediation, so was admissible in the proceedings.

Thus whether or not the parties request it, the court has power to direct that the experts have without prejudice discussions in an attempt to narrow the issues in the case upon which their expertise has been sought. Such discussions will normally be ordered in multi-track cases only where there are opposing experts. It is helpful that where the experts reach agreement on an issue in their without prejudice discussions, the parties are not bound by it (**r. 35.12(5)**). First, this permits the experts more freedom in their discussions, without fear of binding their respective instructing parties and secondly, if the parties were bound by the agreement then effectively there would be compulsory arbitration by a panel of experts.

WRITTEN QUESTIONS TO EXPERTS

CPR, r. 35.6, provides that a party may put written questions to an expert instructed by another party or to a single joint expert. This does not, of course, prevent a party putting written questions to his own expert (*Stallwood v David* [2006] EWHC 2600 (QB), [2007] 1 All ER 206 at [30]). **54.32**

Written questions must be proportionate (**r. 35.6(1)**), may only be put once, and must be put within 28 days of service of the expert's report (**r. 35.6(2)(a)** and **(b)**). They must be for the purpose only of clarification of the report, unless the court gives permission or the other party consents (**r. 35.6(2)(c)**). Questions must be purely for clarification if they are put to the expert without permission, but it is possible to ask about matters not in the expert's report (as long as they are within the expert's expertise) with the consent of the other side or the court's permission (*Mutch v Allen* [2001] EWCA Civ 76, [2001] CPLR 200). Where a party sends a written question direct to an expert, a copy of the question should, at the same time, be sent to the other party or parties (**PD 35, para. 6.1**). The party or parties who instructed the expert must pay his or her fees for answering questions put under **CPR, r. 35.6**, but this does not affect any decision by the court about who is ultimately to bear the expert's costs (**PD 35, para. 6.2**). The expert's answers to the questions put under **CPR, r. 35.6**, are treated as forming part of his or her report (**r. 35.6(3)**).

Where a party has put a written question to an expert instructed by another party in accordance with **r. 35.6** and the expert does not answer that question, the court may make an order that the party who instructed the expert may not rely on the evidence of that expert and/or that the party may not recover the fees and expenses of that expert from any other party (**r. 35.6(4)**). No sanction is specifically provided for failure by a jointly instructed expert to reply, but the failure may reduce the evidential value of the report.

The 28-day time limit in which questions are to be put to an expert requires that practitioners act speedily once an expert's report is served on them. It may be, in very complex cases, that a party would wish to instruct its own expert for the purpose of raising appropriate questions of the reporting expert and there may be some cases in which it will be necessary to have the questions themselves expertly drafted by counsel. It will be important to be able to justify increasing the costs of expert evidence in this way, or suffer disallowance of the extra costs on assessment.

If questioning reveals a fundamental disagreement with a single joint expert, it will be necessary to apply to the court for further directions.

Where there is an application that the court should, under **r. 35.6(4)**, disallow an expert's evidence on the ground of non-response to questions, the appropriateness of the questions may be examined and those which are clearly unreasonable or beyond the expert's area of expertise may themselves be disallowed and the application dismissed, which may result in costs sanctions.

EXPERT'S RIGHT TO ASK COURT FOR DIRECTIONS

54.33 It is clear from **CPR, r. 35.3**, that it is an expert's duty to assist the court rather than the parties from whom he or she has received instructions. Further, the court has control over an expert in respect of the issues on which he or she should report and has a power to give directions regarding any examination, inspection or experiment that an expert is to carry out. The court also has power to restrict the amount of fees and expenses to be paid to an expert. It would be wholly inappropriate, therefore, if an expert were to be unable to communicate with the court to clarify these matters from time to time. For example, an expert may find that it is necessary to carry out tests which had not been authorised by the court. Lines of communication between expert and court are opened by **r. 35.14**, and **PD 35, para. 8**. Under **CPR, r. 35.14**, an expert may file a written request for directions from the court, to assist the expert in carrying out his or her function as an expert. Under **PD 35, para. 8**, the instructing party is obliged to send copies of all the relevant orders to the expert. An expert who proposes to request directions under **CPR, r. 35.14**, must, unless the court orders otherwise, provide a copy of the proposed request to his or her instructing party at least seven days before filing it, and to all other parties at least four days before filing it (**r. 35.14(2)**). When the court gives directions to the expert, it may also order that a party be served with a copy of the directions (**r. 35.14(3)**). The wording of **r. 35.14(3)** is rather odd, stating that the court can order 'a party' to be served with a copy of the directions, but as the singular includes the plural, is to be interpreted as enabling the court to direct service on all the parties or such of the parties as may be specified in the directions.

INSPECTION, EXAMINATION AND TESTING OF PROPERTY

54.34 Invariably experts need to inspect, measure, examine and/or test the subject matter on which they are asked to report. The expert may delegate these tasks, but where this is done the report must identify and state the qualifications of the person who did the delegated tasks, and say whether they were done under the supervision of the expert (**PD 35, para. 3.2(5)**).

The subject matter could be goods, land, buildings or machinery relevant to the issues in the claim. Where the subject matter is under the control of the party instructing the expert there should be no problem. Where it is under the control of the other side or a non-party, it will be necessary to secure their consent to the expert having access for the purpose of conducting any necessary inspection, examination, etc. If consent is not given, it is usually possible to obtain an order (usually on a case management conference) giving access, a subject dealt with in detail in **chapter 41**.

In *SKB plc v Apotex* (2003) LTL 4/2/2003, a patent claim, the court held that a confidentiality agreement between the parties had the effect that **CPR, r. 31.22** (undertaking not to use information disclosed for collateral purposes, see **50.45**), applied to the test results on samples of the defendant's products. It is possible that an implied undertaking in similar terms would be imposed even without a confidentiality agreement, although it is better for collateral use to be expressly dealt with when permission to inspect property is sought.

MEDICAL EXAMINATION

54.35 In personal injuries claims the defendant is entitled to test the severity of the claimant's injuries by obtaining expert medical evidence on the claimant's history, present condition and prognosis. This is often done on a joint basis, particularly in claims suitable for the fast track, either in compliance with the **Pre-action Protocol for Personal Injury Claims** (see **8.23**) or as part of case management directions after proceedings are issued (see **46.6**

and 54.12 to 54.15). In these cases consent to the necessary medical examination is not usually an issue.

Where the parties intend to instruct competing experts, the defendant needs to request the claimant's consent to the medical examination by the defendant's experts. In practice, the defendant will usually provide a written consent form to be signed by the claimant for the release of the claimant's medical records at the same time. If the claimant fails to consent to the proposed medical examination, the court will not make a direct order requiring the claimant to comply. This is because any medical examination involves at least a technical assault on the patient, which is an infringement of the fundamental human right to liberty and security of person, and it is seen to be wrong to order a person to consent to an assault with the sanction of committal to prison in default. Instead, where a claimant refuses a reasonable request for a medical examination the court will make an order imposing a stay on the claim until the claimant submits to the examination (*Edmeades v Thames Board Mills Ltd* [1969] 2 QB 67). Where the medical examination relates to only part of a claim, it is likely that a limited stay will be imposed on the relevant issues only (*James v Baily Gibson and Co.* [2002] EWCA Civ 1690, LTL 30/10/2002).

In *Edmeades v Thames Board Mills Ltd* it was held that a stay will be imposed if it is just and reasonable in the circumstances. In *Starr v National Coal Board* [1977] 1 WLR 63 Scarman LJ said this has two elements:

(a) the defendant's request for the medical examination must be reasonable; and
(b) the claimant's refusal to consent to the examination, or consent subject to conditions, must be such as to prevent the just determination of the claim.

In complex claims it may be reasonable for the defendant to request the claimant to consent to examinations by experts in a number of different fields of medical science, and to consent to examinations for initial and updating reports.

A claimant is not allowed to consent to an examination by anyone other than certain experts (or even anyone other than a single named expert). The reason is that the claimant can go to anyone in the medical profession for a report, and the same freedom has to be allowed to the defendant (*Starr v National Coal Board* [1977] 1 WLR 63). Sometimes the claimant will refuse to consent because the proposed examination is particularly invasive, or even carries a risk of further injury. In these cases the court has to balance the need for the examination and proposed tests, for the proper preparation of the defendant's case, against the reasonableness of the claimant's objections based on the degree of pain, risk to health and inconvenience (*Prescott v Bulldog Tools Ltd* [1981] 3 All ER 869; see also *Aspinall v Sterling Mansell Ltd* [1981] 3 All ER 866).

Stays may also be imposed against defendants (*Cosgrove v Baker* (unreported) 14 December 1979); *Lacey v Harrison* (1992) *The Times*, 22 April 1992) and in non-personal injuries claims (*Jackson v Mirror Group Newspapers Ltd* (1994) *The Times*, 29 March 1994, a libel claim) if the relevant party's medical condition is relevant to an issue in the case.

Commentary

Conditions imposed by claimants

Claimants are entitled to require reasonable conditions to be met before consenting to a medical examination. Conditions usually regarded as reasonable include: **54.36**

(a) that the defendant pays any loss of earnings incurred by the claimant in attending;
(b) that the defendant pays any out-of-pocket expenses incurred in attending;
(c) that the expert will not discuss or question the claimant about the accident except so far as is necessary for the purpose of compiling the medical report;
(d) that a friend, relative or legal representative attends with the claimant for moral support, unless that person will interfere with the examination (such as may happen in psychiatric consultations: *Whitehead v Avon County Council* (1995) 29 BMLR 152).

Disclosure of defendant's report

54.37 It has been held that it is never reasonable to insist that the defendant must disclose the report compiled after the examination as a condition of consenting to an examination (*Megarity v D. J. Ryan and Sons Ltd* [1980] 1 WLR 1237). This is because the report is protected by legal professional privilege, and would give the claimant an advantage not enjoyed by the defendant. An exception was recognised in *Hookham v Wiggins Teape Fine Papers Ltd* [1995] PIQR P392 where past delay in the claim or the proximity of the trial may justify such a condition in the particular circumstances. In *Beck v Ministry of Defence* [2003] EWCA Civ 1043, [2005] 1 WLR 2206, the defendant was required to disclose a copy of the first report it had commissioned on the claimant's injuries as a condition for being given permission to instruct a second expert.

CROSS-EXAMINATION

54.38 The substance of the instructions sent to an expert must be stated in his or her report (**CPR, r. 35.10(3)**; see **54.29**) and are not privileged against disclosure, but the court will not either order disclosure of any specific document or permit any questioning in court, other than by the party who instructed the expert, unless it is satisfied that there are reasonable grounds to consider the statement of instructions to be inaccurate or incomplete (**r. 35.10(4)**). If the court is so satisfied, it will permit cross-examination of the expert on the contents of his or her instructions where it appears to the court that it is in the interests of justice to do so (**PD 35, para. 5**).

In the normal course of things, a jointly instructed expert's report should be the evidence in the case on the issues covered by that report. Normally there should be no need for such a report to be amplified or tested by cross-examination (*Peet v Mid-Kent Healthcare Trust* [2001] EWCA Civ 1703, [2002] 1 WLR 210). It might be appropriate to order attendance for cross-examination where a single joint expert delivers his report shortly before the trial, or where the expert has not considered all the written questions put to him (*Coopers Payen Ltd v Southampton Container Terminal Ltd* [2003] EWCA Civ 1223, [2004] 1 Lloyd's Rep 331 at [41]). If, exceptionally, the expert is called at trial, any cross-examination should be restricted as far as possible (*Peet v Mid-Kent Healthcare Trust*).

CONCURRENT EVIDENCE ('HOT-TUBBING')

54.39 Directions may be made that some or all of the experts from like disciplines must give their evidence concurrently (**PD 35, para. 11.1**). Concurrent evidence directions can be made at any time, but typically at the first case management conference. Under this procedure, instead of going into the witness box at the trial on their own and being examined in chief, cross-examined and re-examined like other witnesses, the experts in a discipline will all give evidence together from the witness box or witness table.

Where a direction for concurrent evidence has been made the court may direct that the parties agree an agenda of points to be discussed by the experts at trial (**para. 11.2**). This is usually based upon the areas of disagreement identified in the experts' joint statement made pursuant to **CPR, r. 35.12** (see **54.31**).

At the trial, when the time comes for the experts to give their evidence, each of the relevant experts will take the oath or affirm (**para. 11.3**). Typically, unless the court orders otherwise, the judge will initiate the discussion by asking the experts, in turn, for their views on the items on the agenda (**para. 11.4(1)**). Once an expert has expressed a view the judge may ask questions about it. At one or more appropriate stages when questioning a particular expert, the judge may invite the other experts to comment or to ask that expert's own questions of the first expert. The parties' representatives may then question the experts (**para. 11.4(2)**). While such questioning may be designed to test the correctness of an expert's view, or seek clarification of it, it should not cover ground which has been fully explored already. In general a full cross-examination or re-examination is neither necessary nor appropriate. After questioning by counsel, the judge may summarise the experts' different positions on the issue and ask them to confirm or correct that summary (**para. 11.4(3)**).

ASSESSORS

CPR, r. 35.15, applies where the court appoints one or more persons as assessors under the Senior Courts Act 1981, s. 70, or the County Courts Act 1984, s. 63. The jurisdiction to sit with assessors extends to judicial review proceedings (*T-Mobile (UK) Ltd v Office of Communications* [2008] EWCA Civ 1373, [2009] 1 WLR 1565 at [35]). An assessor is someone who assists the court in dealing with a matter within his or her skill and expertise and who generally sits with the judge. Factors to be taken into account when considering whether to appoint an assessor include the complexity of the arguments and the amount in issue (*Agrimex Ltd v Tradigrain SA* [2003] EWHC 1656 (Comm), [2003] 2 Lloyd's Rep 537). While it is appropriate to appoint assessors in technically complex or detailed cases, such as nautical collision claims, the Technology and Construction Court did not need the assistance of an assessor in a compulsory purchase quantum case involving consideration of the relevant government department's Compensation Code (*Balcombe Group plc v London Development Agency* [2008] EWHC 1392 (TCC), LTL 3/7/2008). **54.40**

Under **CPR, r. 35.15(3)**, an assessor shall take such part in the proceedings as the court may direct and, in particular, the court may direct the assessor to prepare a report for the court on any matter at issue in the proceedings and direct the assessor to attend the whole or any part of the trial to advise the court on any such matter. Where the assessor prepares the report for the court before the commencement of the trial, the court will send a copy to each of the parties enabling the parties to use the report at trial, although they are not permitted to question or cross-examine the assessor (**PD 35, para. 10.4**). To comply with the European Convention on Human Rights, **art. 6(1)**, in the **Human Rights Act 1998, sch. 1**, it is permissible for the judge to put questions to an assessor after discussion with counsel. The answers should then be disclosed to counsel, either orally or in writing, who are then permitted to make submissions to the judge on whether the advice of the assessor should be followed (*Bow Spring (Owners) v Manzanillo II (Owners)* [2004] EWCA Civ 1007, [2005] 1 WLR 144; *The Global Mariner* [2005] EWHC 380 (Admlty), [2005] 2 All ER (Comm) 389 at [14]).

Where it is intended to appoint an assessor to assist the court, at least 21 days before the appointment, the court will notify each party in writing of the name of the proposed assessor, of the matter in respect of which his or her assistance is sought and the qualifications of the assessor to give that assistance (**PD 35, para. 10.1**). An objection by a party to the appointment of an assessor, either on personal grounds or in relation to his or her qualifications, must be made in writing and filed with the court within seven days of receipt of the notification (**paras 10.2** and **10.3**). The court will consider any objections when deciding whether or not to make the appointment (**para. 10.3**).

Any consultation between assessors and the court must take place openly as part of the assembling of the evidence, and the parties are entitled to an opportunity to address the court on the assessor's advice (*Bow Spring (Owners) v Manzanillo II (Owners)*). The judge is not bound to accept the advice received from assessors (*Commissioners of the Admiralty v SS Ausonia (Owners)* (1920) 2 Ll L Rep 123 at p. 124).

The remuneration to be paid to the assessor for his or her services will be determined by the court and forms part of the costs of the proceedings (**CPR, r. 35.15(5)**). The court may order any party to deposit in the court office a specified sum in respect of the assessor's fees and, where it does so, the assessor will not be asked to act until the sum has been deposited (**r. 35.15(6)**), except in cases where the remuneration of the assessor is to be paid out of money provided by Parliament (**r. 35.15(7)**).

Chapter 55 Discontinuance

INTRODUCTION

From time to time a claimant may think better of having commenced proceedings, and will want to discontinue without incurring all the costs of litigating to trial. It may be, for example, that after seeing the evidence available to the defendant it will be clear that the claim has limited prospects of success. A claimant in this situation may be able to negotiate a compromise with the defendant, who may agree terms which are not too onerous on the claimant. Before the CPR, a claimant could simply allow the case to go to sleep. Under the CPR it is very much more difficult to allow a case simply to go to sleep, given the active case management regime now in place. In most situations, a claimant who decides not to proceed should therefore now either seek to come to an accommodation with the defendant, or should discontinue. Any other course will almost certainly result in increased costs liabilities, particularly if there is a contested hearing. 55.1

Commentary

A claimant who wishes to discontinue proceedings must file a notice of discontinuance. The general rule is that once a claim is discontinued, the claimant has to pay the defendant's costs of the claim.

DISTINCTION BETWEEN DISCONTINUING AND ABANDONING

Discontinuance as a concept is restricted to causes of action. If a single cause of action gives rise to more than one remedy (or more than one head of damages), some of the remedies or heads of damage may be abandoned without producing a formal discontinuance (**CPR, r. 38.1(2)**). A claimant abandoning some of the relief claimed simply has to comply with the rules on amendment (see **chapter 31**). The result is that if some of the relief claimed is abandoned, the claimant will almost certainly have to pay the costs of and arising from the amendments to the statements of case, but will incur no wider liability in relation to the costs of the claim. 55.2

WHAT MAY BE DISCONTINUED

A claimant may discontinue: 55.3

(a) the whole claim (**CPR, r. 38.1(1)**); or
(b) part of the claim (i.e. some of the causes of action pleaded: **r. 38.1(1)**); and
(c) against all of the defendants (**r. 38.2(3)**); or
(d) against some of the defendants (**r. 38.2(3)**).

Arbitration claims under **Part 62** (see **chapter** 72) are also subject to the rules on discontinuance in **Part 38** (*Sheltam Rail Co. (Pty) Ltd v Mirambo Holdings Ltd* [2008] EWHC 829 (Comm), [2009] Bus LR 302).

PERMISSION TO DISCONTINUE

55.4 Generally, a claimant has the right to discontinue without seeking permission first (**CPR, r. 38.2(1)**). However, in some circumstances permission is required. These are:

(a) If an interim injunction has been granted in relation to the claim being discontinued, permission has to be sought from the court (**r. 38.2(2)(a)**).

(b) If any party has given an undertaking to the court in relation to the claim being discontinued, permission has to be sought from the court (**r. 38.2(2)(a)**).

(c) If the claimant has received an interim payment (whether by agreement or pursuant to a court order) in relation to the claim being discontinued, permission must be sought from the court or consent must be given in writing by the defendant (**r. 38.2(2)(b)**).

(d) Where there is more than one claimant, the claimant wishing to discontinue must either obtain permission to discontinue from the court, or must obtain consent in writing from all the other claimants (**r. 38.2(2)(c)**). In group litigation, permission to discontinue is not required where the claim form of the claimant who is seeking to discontinue only has a single named claimant (*Sayers v Smithkline Beecham plc* [2004] EWHC 1899 (QB), [2005] PIQR P8).

(e) Where a claim is brought by a person under a disability, and the discontinuance of the claim amounts to a settlement or a compromise, approval of the court is required under **r. 21.10** (see **14.22** and *Sayers v Smithkline Beecham plc*).

If consent is required, the signed consent(s) must be obtained before the claimant files the notice of discontinuance. If the court's permission has to be sought, a separate application for permission must be issued, and the claimant is only allowed to file the notice of discontinuance after the order granting permission is made. There may be greater reluctance to give permission to discontinue in probate claims (*Green v Briscoe* (2005) LTL 9/5/2005).

PROCEDURE FOR DISCONTINUING

55.5 A claimant discontinues all or part of the claim by filing a notice of discontinuance (form N279) with the court, and serving a copy on all other parties. Regarding contents:

(a) The notice of discontinuance that is filed at court must state that copies have been served on all other parties (**CPR, r. 38.3(2)**).

(b) In cases where the consent of another party is required, all copies of the notice of discontinuance must have copies of the consent annexed (**r. 38.3(3)**).

(c) In cases where there is more than one defendant, the notice of discontinuance must identify the defendants against whom the claim is being discontinued (**r. 38.3(4)**).

SETTING ASIDE NOTICE OF DISCONTINUANCE

55.6 A defendant may apply for an order setting aside a notice of discontinuance served without consent or permission, provided the application is made within 28 days of the notice (**CPR, r. 38.4**). A notice of discontinuance was set aside in *Fakih Brothers v A. P. Moller (Copenhagen) Ltd [1994] 1 Lloyd's Rep 103*, where it was served to avoid the imposition of an onerous term in a consent order, and in *Ernst and Young v Butte Mining plc* [1996] 1 WLR 1605, where it was served in order to pre-empt the effective service of a counterclaim.

EFFECT OF DISCONTINUANCE

Notice of discontinuance takes effect, and brings the proceedings to an end as against each defendant, on the date it is served upon that defendant. This of course is subject to any right to apply to set aside the notice, and does not affect the court's power to deal with costs (**CPR, r. 38.5**). **55.7**

Costs after discontinuing

Unless the court orders otherwise, the claimant is liable for the defendant's costs up to the date of service of the notice of discontinuance (**CPR, r. 38.6(1)**). A costs liability taking effect by virtue of **r. 38.6(1)** is for costs on the standard basis. Alternatively, it is open to a defendant to seek an order for costs to be payable on the indemnity basis (*Jarvis plc v PricewaterhouseCoopers* (2000) *The Times*, 10 October 2000). The power to make some other order is exercised applying the factors set out in **r. 44.2** (see **68.5**) (*Longstaff International Ltd v Evans* [2005] EWHC 4 (Ch), LTL 26/1/2005). Unreasonably continuing a claim after it has become clear it is doomed to failure may justify an order for indemnity-basis costs from that date (*Wates Construction Ltd v HGP Greentree Allchurch Evans Ltd* [2005] EWHC 2174 (TCC), LTL 4/11/2005; and see **68.21**). **55.8**

It may be appropriate to depart from the usual rule in favour of the claimant where there has been a change of circumstances since proceedings were issued making it uneconomic to continue (*Re Walker Wingsail Systems plc* [2005] EWCA Civ 247, [2006] 1 WLR 2194). The court can reverse the usual costs rule on a discontinuance where the claimant has in effect obtained all the relief sought in the proceedings (*Amoco (UK) Exploration Co. v British American Offshore Ltd* (2000) LTL 13/12/2000). On the facts of *Dooley v Parker* [2002] EWCA Civ 1188, it was ordered, following a discontinuance by the claimant, that the justice of the matter was best served by making no order as to costs up to service of the notice of discontinuance, and to award the claimant costs thereafter. Where notice of discontinuance is served primarily to avoid the costs of trial, there is no material to justify departing from the usual costs rule in **r. 38.6** (*Messih v McMillan Williams* [2010] EWCA Civ 844, LTL 22/7/2010). The correct approach is to consider all the matters relied upon as justifying departing from **r. 38.6**, and then to decide whether they are sufficient for that purpose.

Where a claim becomes academic through some act on the part of the defendant or a non-party, the court should apply the general discretionary factors set out in **r. 44.2**, on the question of costs, rather than **r. 38.6** (*Dhillon v Siddiqui* [2010] EWHC 1400 (Ch), LTL 17/6/2010). The fall-back order where an appeal from an Immigration Appeal Tribunal is discontinued before the hearing with the Secretary of State consenting to a rehearing of the decision being appealed is to make no order as to costs (*Sengoz v Secretary of State for the Home Department* [2001] EWCA Civ 1135, *The Times*, 13 August 2001). Patent claims are governed by the usual principles in **r. 38.6**, and what used to be known as *Earth Closet* orders (from *Baird v Moule's Patent Earth Closet Co. Ltd* (1881) 17 ChD 139) should no longer be made (*Fresenius Kabi Deutschland GmbH v Carefusion 303 Inc.* [2011] EWCA Civ 1288, [2012] 1 All ER 794). There are no costs consequences regarding discontinued small claims track cases (**r. 38.6(3)**).

If only part of the claim is discontinued, the claimant's liability is limited to the costs of the part of the claim that has been discontinued. Usually the claimant does not have to pay the defendant's costs following a partial discontinuance until the conclusion of the action. However, the court may in its discretion order these costs to be paid immediately, either after they have been agreed between the parties or after they have been assessed by the court (**r. 38.6(2)**). Where the claimant is required to pay the costs of the discontinued part of the claim straight away, the liability to do so arises 14 days after the relevant costs are agreed or assessed by the court. Failure to pay gives grounds for the court imposing a stay on the remainder of the proceedings until the costs are paid (**r. 38.8**).

SUBSEQUENT PROCEEDINGS

55.9 A claimant who discontinues after a defence has been filed is not allowed to commence new proceedings against the same defendant arising out of the same or substantially the same facts as the original claim, unless the court first gives permission for the second claim to be issued (CPR, r. 38.7). If permission is granted, the court will normally give directions regarding issuing the substantive second claim (r. 25.2(3)).

Chapter 56 Stays

INTRODUCTION

By **CPR, r. 3.1(2)(f)**, the court has a general case management power to stay the whole or any part of any proceedings or judgment either generally or until a specified date or event. This rule derives from the Senior Courts Act 1981, s. 49(3), which provides that nothing in the Act affects the power of the High Court and Court of Appeal to stay proceedings where the court thinks fit to do so, either of its own motion or on the application of any person, whether or not a party to the proceedings. A stay may apply to only part of the proceedings, and where this applies obviously the remaining parts of the proceedings will continue. A stay may be lifted on proper grounds being shown (*Cooper v Williams* [1963] 2 QB 567). **56.1**

The glossary to the CPR says a 'stay' imposes a halt on proceedings, apart from taking any steps allowed by the CPR or the terms of the stay. Proceedings can be continued if the stay is lifted. This is quite important, because in times past (particularly in the late nineteenth century) the courts were in the habit of ordering stays when nowadays they would strike out or dismiss the proceedings. Old cases used to speak of absolute stays (meaning orders striking out proceedings) and conditional stays (having the modern meaning of stays). This old misuse of the word 'stay' should be a thing of the past.

Stays may be imposed in a great variety of different circumstances, and for widely varying reasons.

STAY ON SETTLEMENT

For the stay of a claim when a Part 36 offer is accepted see **66.33**. **56.2**

Ordinary consent orders following a compromise of a claim frequently provide for the stay of the proceedings (see *Rofa Sport Management AG v DHL International (UK) Ltd* [1989] 1 WLR 902). Similarly, a Tomlin order (see **63.16**) provides for the stay of the proceedings on the terms set out in a schedule to the order, with liberty to apply.

STAYS FOR LITIGATION REASONS

There may be reasons relating to the efficient progress of the proceedings which make granting a stay desirable. Examples are: **56.3**

(a) Where there is no issue on liability in a personal injury case, but a clear prognosis will not be possible for some time. This possibility is referred to in **PD 51A, para. 19(3)(b)**, where the machinery referred to is an adjournment to determine prognosis.

(b) Where a personal injuries claim is issued without complying with the pre-action protocol because the solicitor acting for the claimant is instructed shortly before the expiry of the limitation period. A stay may be granted in the early stages of the proceedings to enable the steps of the protocol to be completed (**Pre-action Protocol for Personal Injury Claims, para. 2.11**).

(c) Where a personal injuries claim is issued close to the expiry of limitation without sufficient medical evidence substantiating the claimant's injuries because of difficulties in obtaining the necessary evidence. This arose in *Knight v Sage Group plc* (1999) LTL 28/4/99, where the court gave the claimant three months to obtain and disclose the necessary evidence.

(d) Where a claim is commenced, and subsequent events show that there is a possibility that the proceedings will not serve a useful purpose. For example, a claim may be brought in professional negligence seeking an indemnity in respect of the claimant's potential liability to a stranger to the proceedings. If it transpires there is a possibility that the stranger to the litigation may never make a claim against the claimant, it may be appropriate to order a stay until the stranger's claim becomes time-barred. Similarly, a stay may be ordered under the court's inherent jurisdiction where the issues have been compromised between all but one of the parties, and the court may also make an order for costs involving the non-consenting party (although it is unlikely to be appropriate to make an order for costs against that party, see *Clark v Rice* (2000) LTL 29/6/2000). If costs are still in issue, usually the only way a determination can be made is if the issues are tried (*Markos v Goodfellow* (2000) LTL 7/6/2000).

(e) The court may order a stay at the allocation stage to allow for the possibility of settlement under **CPR, r. 26.4** (see **42.42**).

(f) The usual stay ordered as part of an order making a reference to the Court of Justice of the European Union (see **chapter 78**).

(g) Stays imposed pending the resolution of a test case (*Woods v Duncan* [1946] AC 401). If the other claim may take years to complete, a stay may be inappropriate (*Littlewoods Retail Ltd v Commissioners of HM Revenue and Customs* [2008] EWHC 2622 (QB), [2009] STC 22).

STAYS TO ENFORCE COMPLIANCE WITH ORDERS

56.4 Sometimes the court imposes stays as a means of enforcing compliance with its orders. This is only going to be effective against a claimant or a party in the position of a claimant, such as a defendant making a counterclaim. Examples are:

(a) Stays which are normally imposed pending the provision of security for costs (see **chapter 67**).

(b) A stay imposed where the claimant in a personal injuries claim refuses a reasonable request for a medical examination (see *Edmeades v Thames Board Mills Ltd* [1969] 2 QB 67; see **54.35**).

(c) A stay pending a satisfactory undertaking as to costs or otherwise connected with the way in which a claim is funded (*Grovewood Holdings plc v James Capel and Co. Ltd* [1995] Ch 80; *Abraham v Thompson* (1997) *The Times*, 15 May 1997).

(d) A second claim may be stayed pending payment of the costs of an earlier discontinued claim (see **55.9**) or the costs of an earlier claim that was struck out (**CPR, r. 3.4(4)**, confirming *Gardner v Southwark London Borough Council (No. 2)* [1996] 1 WLR 561). This is discussed in the context of abuse of process at **33.27**. A stay pending payment of the costs of an earlier claim does not conflict with the European Convention on Human Rights, art. 6(1). *Such a stay can be imposed* even where the parties were not entirely the same, provided the second claim arose out of substantially the same facts as the previous claim

(*Stevens v School of Oriental and African Studies* (2000) *The Times*, 2 February 2001). A stay can also be imposed where the claimant is the successor in title to the claimant in the previous claim (*Sinclair v British Telecommunications plc* [2001] 1 WLR 38).
(e) Where partners fail to supply a partnership membership statement of their names and addresses under **PD 7A, para. 5B.1**.

STAYS TO PROTECT CONCURRENT CLAIMS

There is a general public interest in avoiding a multiplicity of claims. Sometimes it is simply an abuse of process to bring duplicate sets of proceedings, with the result that the later proceedings will be struck out (see *Buckland v Palmer* [1984] 1 WLR 1109). The following examples stop a little way short of being suitable for striking out, but stays may be imposed instead: **56.5**

(a) Where the dispute should be dealt with by arbitration rather than by litigation (see **chapter 72**). The court has an inherent jurisdiction to stay court proceedings which have been brought in breach of an agreement that any dispute should be resolved in a particular way, such as where there is an adjudication clause under the Housing Grants, Construction and Regeneration Act 1996 (*DGT Steel and Cladding Ltd v Cubitt Building and Interiors Ltd* [2007] EWHC 1587 (TCC), [2008] Bus LR 132). In *Ardentia Ltd v British Telecommunications plc* [2008] EWHC 2111 (Ch), 119 Con LR 50, the contract between the parties contained a clause that they should refer disputes to dispute resolution rather than litigation, except for applications for interim injunctions. This meant that the court could only deal with interim injunction applications: making such an application did not open the door to the court having jurisdiction over the substantive dispute.
(b) Where the dispute should be dealt with in the administration of an insolvent person's estate (see **chapter 84**).
(c) Stays on the ground of *forum non conveniens* (see **chapter 16**).
(d) Stays under various provisions of **Regulation (EC) No. 44/2001** (see **arts 27** to **28** and **chapter 16**). The court may grant a stay to ensure that related proceedings in different jurisdictions are tried in a particular order if there are very strong grounds for doing so for case management reasons (*Reichhold Norway ASA v Goldman Sachs International* [2000] 1 WLR 173). The risk of irreconcilable judgments may be sufficient for this purpose (*Curtis v Lockheed Martin UK Holdings Ltd* [2008] EWHC 260 (Comm), [2008] 1 CLC 219, where the application was refused).
(e) Stays pending the resolution of connected criminal proceedings. There must be a pending criminal case, not merely the possibility of one (*Caledonian Contracting Partnership Ltd v Rodger* (2004) LTL 7/4/2004). Applications for such stays may be made by any party to the civil claim, or the prosecutor or any defendant to the criminal proceedings (**PD 23A, para. 11A.1**). The evidence in support of the application must contain an estimate of the expected duration of the stay, and must identify the respects in which continuing the civil claim may prejudice the criminal trial (**para. 11A.3**). The question is whether there is a real risk of prejudice to the defendant in the criminal proceedings, and this is unaffected by the enactment of the **Human Rights Act 1998** (*Mote v Secretary of State for Work and Pensions* [2007] EWCA Civ 1324, *The Times*, 28 December 2007).
(f) Stays of civil proceedings where there are parallel proceedings in the Competition Commission Appeal Tribunal (see *Synstar Computer Services (UK) Ltd v ICL (Sorbus) Ltd* (2001) *The Times*, 1 May 2001), the European Patent Office (*Glaxo Group Ltd v Genentech Inc.* [2008] EWCA Civ 23, [2008] Bus LR 888), or trade mark proceedings in the Office for Harmonisation in the Internal Market (*Kitfix Swallow Group Ltd v Great Gizmos Ltd* [2007] EWHC 2668 (Ch), [2008] Bus LR 465). In patent and trade mark cases there is no presumption either that a stay should be granted or that it should be refused (*Glaxo Group Ltd v Genentech Inc.*;

Kitfix Swallow Group Ltd v Great Gizmos Ltd). The length of time it is likely to take to obtain a decision is usually the most important factor (*Glaxo Group Ltd v Genentech Inc.*).

(g) A stay may be imposed to protect Parliamentary privilege and immunities (*R v Mote* [2007] EWCA Crim 3131, [2008] Crim LR 793, where the stay was lifted in respect of a prosecution of an MEP following a resolution by the European Parliament waiving the immunity).

EFFECT OF A STAY

56.6 While a stay is in place the proceedings remain alive, but no further steps may be taken to progress the claim other than applying to lift the stay. For some purposes time will continue to run during a stay, such as the limited period of validity for service of an originating process (*Aldridge v Edwards* [2000] CPLR 349). There is no need to apply to lift the stay imposed by a Tomlin order before making an application for a wasted costs order (*Wagstaff v Colls* [2003] EWCA Civ 469, [2003] PNLR 561). A stay on a judgment prevents any steps being taken to enforce it, until the stay is lifted.

Chapter 57 Witness Summonses

NATURE OF WITNESS SUMMONSES

A witness summons is a document issued by the court requiring a witness to attend court to give evidence or produce documents to the court (**CPR, r. 34.2(1)**). A witness summons must be in form N20 (**r. 34.2(2)**) and there must be a separate witness summons for each witness required to attend court (**r. 34.2(3)**). Two copies of the witness summons should be filed with the court for sealing, one of which will be retained on the court file (**PD 34A, para. 1.2**). A witness summons may, by **CPR, r. 34.2(4)**, require a witness to produce documents to the court either: 57.1

(a) on the date fixed for a hearing; or
(b) on such date as the court may direct.

The only documents that a summons under **Part 34** can require a person to produce before a hearing are documents which that person could be required to produce at the hearing (**r. 34.2(5)**). This means that they must be relevant to the issues and otherwise admissible in evidence at trial, and so is narrower than the scope of standard disclosure. **Rule 34.2(4)** may be considered as an alternative to non-party disclosure. It also incorporates the device used by the court in *Khanna v Lovell White Durrant* [1995] 1 WLR 121, in which the court invented the concept of the 'production appointment' for witnesses to attend under summons to bring documents to a hearing earlier than the trial, where, for example, the documents were required by one or other party to prepare the case properly for trial and production on the morning of the trial would have been insufficient.

ISSUE OF A WITNESS SUMMONS

A witness summons is issued on the date entered on the summons by the court (**CPR, r. 34.3(1)**). It must be issued by (**r. 34.3(3)**): 57.2

(a) the court where the case is proceeding; or
(b) the court where the hearing in question will be held.

The procedure is a simple one in which the party wishing to obtain a witness summons attends at court with the completed summons in form N20, which the court then seals for service. Where the witness summons is for the witness to attend at a trial, there is no requirement to obtain the court's permission, but permission must be obtained from the court under **r. 34.3(2)** where a party wishes:

(a) to have a summons issued less than seven days before the date of the trial;
(b) to have a summons issued for a witness to attend court to give evidence or to produce documents on any date except the date fixed for trial; or

Commentary

(c) to have a summons issued for a witness to attend court to give evidence or to produce documents at any hearing except the trial.

Thus the permission of the court is necessary where the witness summons is to be issued very close to the date of the trial, where a witness summons is required for attendance at an interim hearing or where a witness is required to attend to give oral evidence or produce documents at such a hearing. Applications for permission are made without notice to a district judge or master. There is no provision in **Part 34** for evidence in support of such applications and therefore it would seem sufficient to indicate orally, at the hearing of the application, the purpose for which the witness summons is sought.

Witness summons in aid of inferior court or tribunal

57.3 The High Court and the county courts have a discretion to issue a witness summons in aid of any court or tribunal that does not have power to issue a witness summons in relation to proceedings before it (**CPR, r. 34.4(1)**). For the applicable principles see *Inner West London Assistant Deputy Coroner v Channel 4 Television Corporation* [2007] EWHC 2513 (QB), [2008] 1 WLR 945. The court which issued a witness summons under this rule may set it aside (**r. 34.4(2)**). Such an application will be heard (**PD 34A, para. 2.3**):

(a) in the High Court by a master at the Royal Courts of Justice or by a district judge in a district registry, and
(b) in a county court by a district judge.

Unless the court directs otherwise, the applicant on the application to set aside must give no less than two days' notice of the application to the party that issued the witness summons. The application to set aside will normally be dealt with at a hearing (**PD 34A, para. 2.4**).

SERVICE OF WITNESS SUMMONS

Time for serving a witness summons

57.4 The general rule, as set out in **CPR, r. 34.5(1)**, is that a witness summons is binding if it is served at least seven days before the date on which the witness is required to attend before the court or tribunal. However, the court has a discretion to direct that the witness summons is binding even though it will be served less than seven days before that date (**r. 34.5(2)**). **Rule 34.5(3)** provides that a witness summons which is served in accordance with **r. 34.5**, and requires the witness to attend court to give evidence, is binding until the conclusion of the hearing at which the attendance of the witness is required.

Service by the court or the party

57.5 A witness summons is served by the court unless it is indicated in writing, at the time of asking the court to issue the summons, that the party on whose behalf it is issued will serve it.

The usual practice is for the court to serve a witness summons either by post or by county court bailiff. Practitioners who wish to ensure certainty and expeditious service are likely to prefer to undertake service themselves.

Witness expenses

57.6 At the time of service of a witness summons the witness must be offered or paid a sum reasonably sufficient to cover his or her expenses in travelling to and from the court and compensation for loss of time (**CPR, r. 34.7**). The amount to be paid as compensation for loss of time is to be based on the sums payable to witnesses in the Crown Court (**PD 34A, paras 3.1** to **3.3**). These are determined by the Lord Chancellor under the Costs in Criminal Cases (General) Regulations 1986 (SI 1986/1335), reg. 17.

A witness required to produce documents under a witness summons will only be paid conduct money, so will not be compensated for the expense of producing the documents, unlike the position on an application for non-party disclosure under **CPR, rr. 31.17** and **48.1(2)** (see *Re Howglen Ltd* [2001] 1 All ER 376 at p. 384 and **50.92**). However, in *Individual Homes Ltd v Macbream Investments Ltd* (2002) *The Times*, 14 November 2002, an order was made joining the witness as a party for the purpose of making a costs order in its favour for complying with a witness summons to produce documents.

If the witness summons is to be served by the court, the sum for expenses must be deposited in the court office (**CPR, r. 34.6(2)**). If the witness summons is to be served by the party issuing it, the sum must be offered to the witness when the summons is served (**PD 34A, para. 3.4**).

FAILURE TO OBEY A WITNESS SUMMONS

County courts

A person who refuses or neglects, without sufficient cause, to appear, or produce documents, as required by a witness summons issued by a county court may be fined up to £1,000 (County Courts Act 1984, s. 55(1) and (2)). A fine may also be imposed if a summoned witness attends court but refuses to be sworn or give evidence (s. 55(1)). A fine cannot be imposed unless witness expenses (see **57.6**) were paid or tendered at the time of serving the summons (s. 55(3)). A judge imposing a fine may, at his or her discretion, direct that all or part of it (after deducting costs) is to be applied to indemnifying the party injured by the refusal or neglect (s. 55(4)). These are statutory versions of the inherent powers of the High Court (see **57.8**), but a county court has no power to issue a bench warrant for the arrest of a witness. **57.7**

The power to impose a fine under s. 55 may be exercised by a circuit judge, district judge, assistant district judge or deputy district judge (s. 55(1) and (4A)).

Before or after imposing a fine under s. 55 for disobeying a witness summons or refusing to give evidence or to be sworn, the court may give notice to the witness under **CPR, r. 81.36**. That notice must state that if the witness can demonstrate any reason why the fine should not, or should not have been, imposed, that person may give evidence by witness statement, affidavit or otherwise on the date specified in the notice (**r. 81.36(2)**). Although the rule is expressed to confer a discretion on the judge, it is clear that, in the light of the European Convention on Human Rights, **art. 6**, in the **Human Rights Act 1998, sch. 1**, a fine should not be imposed without giving the offender an opportunity of submitting a defence. A witness who attends the trial but refuses to give evidence may give an explanation there and then. Otherwise the judge should direct the court officer to issue a notice naming a day on which cause is to be shown by witness statement, affidavit or otherwise. Repayment may be ordered of part or all of any fine already paid if, on considering the cause shown, the judge decides that the fine should have been of a lesser amount, not imposed at all or not enforced.

If a fine imposed for failure to obey a witness summons is not paid, the court must report the matter to the circuit judge, who may, under the County Courts Act 1984, s. 129, order the fine to be enforced by any method available for the enforcement of a county court judgment debt or a magistrates' court fine.

High Court

In the High Court failure to obey a witness summons is contempt of court (*Wyat v Wingford* (1729) 2 Ld Raym 1528), as is appearing in response to a summons but refusing to be sworn or to answer questions or to produce documents (*R v Daye* [1908] 2 KB 333). The procedure to be followed is laid down in **CPR, Part 81**, see **chapter 81**. No penalty may be imposed unless **57.8** witness expenses (see 57.6) were paid or tendered with the summons (*Fuller v Prentice* (1788) 1 H Bl 49; *Re Working Men's Mutual Society* (1882) 21 ChD 831). If disobedience was not wilful, no penalty will be imposed (*Horne v Smith* (1815) 6 Taunt 10; *Scholes v Hilton* (1842) 10 M & W 15) or enforcement of a penalty will be stayed (*R v Daye*). A person who has disobeyed a witness summons may be sued for damages by the party who obtained the summons, provided actual loss is proved (*Crewe v Field* (1896) 12 TLR 405; *Roberts v J. and F. Stone Lighting and Radio Ltd* (1945) 172 LT 240).

The High Court has an inherent power to issue a bench warrant for the arrest of a person required as a witness so as to secure his or her attendance in court (*Astrovlanis Compania Naviera SA v Linard (No. 2)* [1972] 2 Lloyd's Rep 187; *Zakharov v White* [2003] EWHC 2463 (Ch), *The Times*, 13 November 2003).

SETTING ASIDE OR VARYING A WITNESS SUMMONS

57.9 Under CPR, r. 34.3(4), the court may set aside or vary a witness summons. This may be on the application of any party or by the witness. The presumption is that the interests of justice are best served by the grant of a witness summons (*Tilbury Consulting Ltd v Gittins* [2004] STC (SCD) 1). A witness summons may be set aside if the witness has no connection with the claim, or where the witness summons is used for tactical purposes, as was the case in *Harrison v Bloom Camillin* (1999) *The Independent*, 28 June 1999, in which it was found that the defendants were attempting to conduct a fishing expedition. A witness summons to produce documents was set aside in *Tajik Aluminium Plant v Hydro Aluminium AS* [2005] EWCA Civ 1218, [2006] 1 WLR 767, on the ground that it did not identify the documents required with sufficient certainty. The documents must be sufficiently described so as to leave no doubt in the mind of the witness what he is required to produce. It is not necessary to describe documents individually. A compendious description will suffice provided it enables the witness to know specifically what is covered. In *Peters v Skylet Andrew* [2009] EWHC 1511 (QB), LTL 2/7/2009, the court refused to set aside a witness summons to produce certain telephone accounts which were relevant to the dispute, as there was no other obvious way of obtaining the information.

Chapter 58 Giving Evidence without Attending Court

INTRODUCTION

At both the allocation and pre-trial checklist stages, the court will timetable certain events in order to progress a case to trial, and at the pre-trial checklist stage in particular, the trial will be fixed for a date or period of time when it is thought that all the witnesses will be able to attend to give evidence. Prudent practitioners will have asked clients and witnesses to identify dates to avoid but it sometimes happens that, despite planning in advance, a witness is unable, physically, to attend court. On both the fast track and multi-track, the postponement of a trial is considered as an order of last resort (**PD 28, para. 5.4(6); PD 29, para. 7.4(6)**). Therefore, where a witness does have difficulties in attending court to give evidence in person, alternative means of giving evidence should be considered, in order that the trial is not postponed. **58.1**

It may also be the case that in the period leading up to the trial, a hearing is necessary in respect of an interim remedy, for which a crucial witness is unable or refuses to provide a witness statement, without which the party wishing to make the application is unable to proceed.

One way of overcoming these difficulties is to take the witness's evidence by deposition.

DEPOSITIONS

CPR, r. 34.8, provides that a party to a claim may apply for an order for a person to be examined before the trial of the claim or an interim hearing takes place. The person from whom evidence is to be obtained is referred to as a deponent and the evidence itself is referred to as a deposition. **58.2**

An order under **r. 34.8** is for the deponent to be examined on oath before either a judge, an examiner of the court or such other person as the court appoints (**r. 34.8(3)**). The order may also require the production of any document which the court considers is necessary for the purposes of the examination (**r. 34.8(4)**). Persons appointed by the Lord Chancellor as examiners of the court must be barristers or solicitor-advocates who have been practising for a period of at least three years (**r. 34.15**).

Witness expenses must be offered or paid when an order for examination is served (**r. 34.8(6)**) just as when a witness summons is served (see 57.6).

Commentary

An order for a deposition to be taken may also order the party who obtained the order to serve a witness statement or witness summary in relation to the evidence to be given by the person to be examined (**r. 34.8(7)**).

The party who obtains an order for the examination of a deponent before an examiner of the court must (**PD 34A, para. 4.2**):

(a) apply to the Foreign Process Section of the Masters' Secretary's Department at the Royal Courts of Justice for the allocation of an examiner; and
(b) provide the allocated examiner with copies of all documents in the proceedings necessary to inform the examiner of the issues.

Conduct of examination

58.3 CPR, **r. 34.9**, provides details of the procedure to be adopted in conducting the examination of a deponent. Subject to any directions contained in the order for examination, the examination must be conducted in the same way as if the witness were giving evidence at a trial (**r. 34.9(1)**). If all the parties are present, the examiner may conduct the examination of a person not named in the order for examination if the parties and the person to be examined consent (**r. 34.9(2)**). Therefore, as all parties are present, they effectively have the right to ask questions under the usual rules of evidence, albeit via the examiner. If the examiner considers it appropriate, he or she may conduct the examination in private (**r. 34.9(3)**).

In ensuring that the deponent's evidence is recorded in full, as required by **r. 34.9(4)**, the court or the examiner may permit it to be recorded on audiotape or videotape, but the deposition must always be recorded in writing by the examiner or by a competent shorthand writer or stenographer (**PD 34A, para. 4.3**). If the deposition is not recorded verbatim, it must contain, as nearly as may be, the statement of the deponent; the examiner may record word for word any particular questions and answers, which appear to him or her to have special importance (**PD 34A, para. 4.4**).

PD 34A, para. 4.12, provides that once an examination is completed the examiner must sign the deposition, both the examiner and the deponent must initial any amendments to it, and it must be endorsed by the examiner with:

(a) a statement of the time occupied by the examination, and
(b) a record of any refusal by the deponent to sign the deposition and of his or her reasons for not doing so.

The examiner must send a copy of the deposition to the person who obtained the order for the examination of the witness, and to the court where the case is proceeding, for filing on the court file (**CPR, r. 34.9(5); PD 34A, para. 4.12(4)**). The party who obtained the order must then send each of the other parties a copy of the deposition received from the examiner (**CPR, r. 34.9(6)**).

Enforcing attendance for examination

58.4 If a person served with an order to attend before an examiner fails to attend or refuses to be sworn for the purpose of the examination or to answer any lawful question or produce any document at the examination, a certificate of that failure or refusal, signed by the examiner, must be filed by the party requiring the deposition (**CPR, r. 34.10(1)**).

If a deponent objects to answering any question or where any objection is taken to any question, the examiner must (**PD 34A, para. 4.5**):

(a) record in the deposition or a document attached to it:
  (i) the question,
  (ii) the nature of and grounds of the objection, and
  (iii) any answer given; and

(b) give his or her opinion on the validity of the objection and any question of costs arising from it.

By **CPR, r. 34.10(2)**, on the certificate of failure or refusal being filed, the party requiring the deposition may apply, without notice, to the court for an order requiring the deponent to attend or to be sworn or to answer any question or produce any document, as the case may be. The court may order the person against whom an order is made under this rule to pay any costs resulting from the failure or refusal.

Fees and expenses of examiner

An examiner of the court may charge a fee for an examination (**CPR, r. 34.14(1)**) and is not required to send the deposition to the court unless the fee is paid (**r. 34.14(2)**). The examiner's fees and expenses must be paid by the party who obtained the order for examination (**r. 34.14(3)**) and if not paid within a reasonable time, the examiner may report that fact to the court (**r. 34.14(4)**). **58.5**

The court may order the party who obtained on order for examination to deposit in the court office a specified sum in respect of the examiner's fees, and the examiner will not be asked to act until that sum has been deposited (**r. 34.14(5)**).

Use of deposition at a hearing

A deposition ordered under **CPR, r. 34.8**, may be given in evidence at a hearing unless the court orders otherwise. A party intending to put a deposition in evidence at a hearing must serve notice of that intention on every other party at least 21 days before the day fixed for the hearing (**r. 34.11(1), (2)** and **(3)**). Under **r. 34.11(4)** the court may require a deponent to attend the hearing and give evidence orally. Where a deposition is given in evidence at trial, it shall be treated as if it were a witness statement for the purposes of **r. 32.13** (availability of witness statement for inspection) (see **51.24**). **58.6**

Restrictions on subsequent use of deposition taken for the purpose of any hearing except the trial

CPR, r. 34.12, provides that where the court orders a party to be examined about assets (whether the party's or any other person's) for the purpose of any hearing except the trial, the deposition may be used only for the purpose of the proceedings in which the order was made. It may, however, be used for some other purpose: **58.7**

(a) by the party who was examined;
(b) if the party who was examined agrees; or
(c) if the court gives permission.

Rule 34.12 is expressed to apply only to depositions relating to assets and will therefore be relevant to procedures concerning the enforcement of judgment, freezing orders, search orders and the like.

EXAMINATION OUT OF THE JURISDICTION

Requests to EU Regulation States

Regulation (EC) No. 1206/2001 on cooperation between the courts of Member States in the taking of evidence in civil and commercial matters (the 'Taking of Evidence Regulation') provides for taking evidence in one EU State for use in civil proceedings in another EU State. It does not apply to Denmark (art. 1). Each Regulation State has designated courts where evidence can be taken (in England and Wales these are the Royal Courts of Justice and the court **58.8** centres at Birmingham, Bristol, Cardiff, Manchester and Leeds, see **PD 34A, annex C**). Each Regulation State also has a central body (in England and Wales this is the Senior Master of the Queen's Bench Division, see **PD 34A, para. 9.2**) who is responsible for supplying information, seeking solutions to any difficulties that may arise, and, in exceptional cases, forwarding requests to the competent court.

A party to English civil proceedings seeking to obtain a deposition from a witness in a Regulation State must apply for an order for the issue of a request to a designated court in the Regulation State (**CPR, r. 34.23(2)**). The party seeking the order must undertake to be responsible for the costs sought by the requested court for fees for experts, interpreters and for the court's expenses (**r. 34.23(3)**). Requests for the taking of evidence under the Taking of Evidence Regulation need to be made in the official language of the requested court (art. 5), and must be in form A in the annex to the Taking of Evidence Regulation (art. 4). The request must include the questions to be put to the witness or a statement of the facts about which he is to be examined, and also include any request for the examination to be under oath or affirmation, and any special form to be used (such as recording the evidence in a deposition).

Within seven days of receipt of the request the requested court must send an acknowledgment to the requesting court (art. 7(1)). Where necessary, coercive measures (the local equivalent of a witness summons) may be applied by the requested court to secure the attendance of the witness (art. 13). A request should be executed within 90 days, failing which the requested court should inform the requesting court, stating the reasons for the delay (arts 10 and 15). Representatives of the requesting court should be able to be present when the evidence is taken if this is compatible with the law of the requesting court (art. 12), and representatives of the parties have the right to participate on such conditions as may be laid down by the requested court in accordance with local law (art. 11).

The requesting court can ask for use of communications technology, including videoconferencing and teleconferencing, for the purpose of taking the evidence (art. 10(4)). The party seeking the order must undertake to be responsible for the costs sought by the requested court for any communications technology used (**CPR, r. 34.23(3)**).

It is possible that Regulation (EC) No. 1206/2001 does not apply to applications for disclosure of assets orders against non-parties ancillary to freezing injunctions (see **38.25**). This is because there is no request for the taking of evidence in another member State (*Masri v Consolidated Contractors International (UK) Ltd (No. 4)* [2008] EWCA Civ 876, [2010] 1 AC 90; the decision in the House of Lords on the English law points meant this did not arise for decision on the appeal, [2009] UKHL 43, [2010] 1 AC 90).

Direct taking of evidence in Regulation States

58.9 A party can seek an order pursuant to **CPR, r. 34.23(5)**, for the submission of a request under art. 17 of the Taking of Evidence Regulation for the direct taking of evidence from a witness by the requested court. This involves the requesting court coming to this jurisdiction to take the witness's evidence itself. The party seeking the request must undertake to pay the court's expenses (**CPR, r. 34.23(6)(c)**). Direct taking of evidence is only permitted if it can be performed on a voluntary basis without the need for coercive measures (Taking of Evidence Regulation, art. 17(2)). The request must be in form I of the Taking of Evidence Regulation, and must be accompanied by a translation (**CPR, r. 34.23(6)(b)**). The central body of the requested court may only refuse the direct taking of evidence if the request does not fall within the scope of art. 1, or does not contain all the information required by art. 4, or if the direct taking of evidence is contrary to the fundamental principles of law of the requested State (art. 17(5)).

Non-EU countries: letters of request

CPR, r. 34.13, provides for a deposition to be taken from a witness in Denmark or a non-EU State for use in English proceedings. The High Court, not a county court, may order the issue of a letter of request to the judicial authorities of the country in which the proposed deponent is. All applications are dealt with at the RCJ. A letter of request is a request to a judicial authority to take the evidence of that person, or arrange for it to be taken (**r. 34.13(2)**). The High Court may make an order under this rule in relation to county court proceedings (**r. 34.13(3)**). **58.10**

An application for an order to issue a letter of request should be made by application notice in accordance with **Part 23** (**PD 34A, para. 5.2**). The documents listed in **CPR, r. 34.13(6)**, should be filed with the application notice, together with a draft order (**PD 34A, para. 5.3**). A draft letter of request should be in the form set out in **annex A** to **PD 34A**. The application will be dealt with by the Senior Master of the Queen's Bench Division of the High Court who will, if appropriate, sign the letter of request.

In exercising the discretion whether to order the issue of a letter of request the most important factor is the need to achieve justice. Thus, in *Banerji v Devi* (2005) LTL 29/6/2005 it was held to be wrong to refuse an order to take the evidence of a lawyer in India who had witnessed a signature which was alleged to have been forged, as the evidence was crucial on the forgery issue.

If the government of a country allows a person appointed by the High Court to examine a person in that country, the High Court may make an order appointing a special examiner (**CPR, r. 34.13(4)**), who may be the British consul or the consul-general or his or her deputy in the country where the evidence is to be taken (**PD 34A, para. 5.8**). If the country in question is not a party to a civil procedure convention providing for evidence to be taken, it will be necessary to obtain the Secretary of State's consent to the appointment of a consul.

Examination in a foreign country may be on oath or affirmation or in accordance with any procedure permitted in that country (**CPR, r. 34.13(5)**).

The procedural requirements set out in **PD 34A, paras 4.1** to **4.12**, relating to depositions taken in England and Wales for proceedings before courts in England and Wales apply to depositions to be taken abroad (**para. 5.9**).

The Criminal Justice (International Cooperation) Act 1990 empowers a judge in criminal proceedings to issue a letter of request to obtain evidence outside the United Kingdom. Section 3(7) provides that the evidence obtained shall not, without the consent of the appropriate authority, be used for any purpose other than that specified in the request. It was held in *BOC Ltd v Instrument Technology Ltd* [2001] EWCA Civ 854, [2002] QB 537, that, notwithstanding the apparently wide terms of s. 3(7), the provision is implicitly concerned only with the use of the evidence by the prosecuting authority or defendant in the criminal proceedings, and does not restrict use in civil proceedings.

Video links

A further means of presenting oral testimony from a witness who has difficulty in attending a hearing or trial is to have the witness's evidence given by video link, or other means which the court may allow under **CPR, r. 32.3**. If a party wishes to use this method, it is advisable to ascertain from the court whether the necessary technical facilities are available. **58.11**

Where the witness is in an EU State (other than Denmark), taking evidence by video link has to comply with the requirements of Regulation (EC) No. 1206/2001, which is discussed at **58.8**.

In *Polanski v Condé Nast Publications Ltd* [2005] UKHL 10, [2005] 1 WLR 637, the claimant brought libel proceedings in England, and sought permission to give evidence at the trial through a video link. In 1977 he had pleaded guilty in criminal proceedings in California, but had fled from the United States before sentence, and was living in France where he was safe from extradition. If he came to England to give evidence at his libel trial, there was a risk that he would be extradited to face the consequences of his United States conviction. Lord Nicholls of Birkenhead described videoconferencing facilities as being readily available to all litigants, and should not be denied to a party solely on the ground that he was a fugitive from justice. Indeed, the fact that he was a fugitive could be, and on the facts was, a sufficient reason for making a videoconferencing order. Videoconferencing directions were given in *Bank of Credit and Commerce International SA v Rahim* (2005) LTL 30/11/2005, where a witness in Pakistan was said to be in poor health (despite there being no medical evidence to this effect) and feared he might be arrested if he entered the UK. Other factors were the expense and inconvenience of bringing him from Pakistan, and the fact that as he was simply a witness, being outside the jurisdiction meant he could not be compelled to attend. Consideration should be given to allowing an expert to give evidence by video link where this is appropriate (**PD 35, annex, para. 19.2(c)**).

Detailed guidance on arranging and conducting videoconferencing is contained in **annex 3 to PD 32**. A list of the sites which are available for videoconferencing can be found at http://www.justice.gov.uk/guidance/courts-and-tribunals/courts/video-conferences/index.htm (**PD 32, para. 29.1**).

LETTERS OF REQUEST FROM FOREIGN COURTS

58.12 The statutory provisions on obtaining evidence for foreign courts are in the Evidence (Proceedings in Other Jurisdictions) Act 1975. The rules of court are in **CPR, rr. 34.16** to **34.21**, which should be read in conjunction with **PD 34A, paras 6.1** to **6.8**. To assist courts and practitioners there is an invaluable and very comprehensive *Treasury Solicitor's Guide to Letters of Request* produced by the Treasury Solicitor's Office.

Some letters of request from foreign courts are dealt with by officials and do not require action by legal representatives in England and Wales. Where a foreign court's letter of request cannot be dealt with in this way an application by an agent in England or Wales of a party to the foreign proceedings to give effect to the request should be made to the High Court by Part 8 claim form and should be supported by a witness statement or affidavit exhibiting the documents listed in **PD 34A, para. 6.3**. It may be made without notice being served on any other party (**CPR, r. 34.17(b)**).

A letter of request should be for the purpose of taking evidence on behalf of a foreign court. The High Court will not make an order for the examination of a witness where the letter of request is mainly of an investigatory nature. This is so even if the court is satisfied the witness can give some relevant and admissible evidence, unless it is possible to exclude the impermissible areas of the request without undue difficulty (*Re State of Norway's Application* [1987] QB 433; *United States of America v Philip Morris Inc.* [2003] EWHC 3028 (Comm), LTL 10/12/2003). It is very common for letters of request from the United States, where much wider discovery is permitted than in England and Wales, to be investigatory in nature, and sometimes oppressive. Such requests are often rejected, and have to be resubmitted in a truncated form, resulting in significant delays.

The order for the deponent to attend and be examined together with the evidence upon which the order was made must be served on the deponent (**PD 34A, para. 6.5**). Arrangements for the examination to take place at a specified time and place before an examiner of the court or such other person as the court may appoint shall be made by the applicant for the order and approved by the Senior Master (**CPR, r. 34.18**).

CPR, rr. 34.9 and **34.10**, and **PD 34A, paras 4.2** to **4.12**, apply to examinations requested by foreign courts, except that the examiner must send the deposition to the Senior Master (**PD 34A, para. 6.6**).

Requests from Regulation States

Requests for the taking of evidence in England and Wales from other Regulation States under the Taking of Evidence Regulation must be made to a designated court (the Royal Courts of Justice and the court centres at Birmingham, Bristol, Cardiff, Manchester and Leeds, see **CPR, r. 34.24(2)** and **PD 34A, Annex C**). The courts in England and Wales will act on requests in either English or French (**PD 34A, para 11.4**), but otherwise translations are required. Once a request is received it is sent to the Treasury Solicitor (**PD 34A, para 11.2**) who may apply on form N244 for an order for the evidence to be taken. The application is usually considered without notice (**CPR, r. 34.24(2)(c)**). The order and evidence in support must be served on the witness (**PD 34A, para. 11.5**). Arrangements for the taking of the evidence will be made by the Treasury Solicitor and approved by the court (**para. 11.6**), and the court will provide these details to the parties and the representatives of the foreign court (if they have indicated they wish to be present when the evidence is taken (**para. 11.7**). The evidence will be taken in accordance with **CPR, rr. 34.9, 34.10** and **34.18**, for which see **58.3** and **58.12** (**r. 34.24(3)**). **58.13**

The examiner will send the deposition to the requested court for transmission to the requesting court, and a copy of the deposition to the Treasury Solicitor (**r. 34.24(4)**).

Collateral use of depositions

A deposition obtained under **CPR, Part 34**, is obtained subject to an undertaking, implied at common law, not to use it for a collateral purpose without the consent of the witness or the permission of the requesting court. This includes depositions obtained under the Taking of Evidence Regulation. In exercising its discretion whether to grant permission for the collateral use of depositions, the court applies similar principles as apply in relation to the collateral use of disclosed documents (see **50.48**). The court also takes into account the purpose of the relevant power to take evidence on deposition. Thus, in *Dendron GmbH v Regents of the University of California* [2004] EWHC 589 (Pat), [2005] 1 WLR 200, permission was granted for the use of depositions obtained under the Taking of Evidence Regulation in related proceedings in other Regulation States, but not for use in the United States. **58.14**

Injunction restraining deposing witness

An injunction may be granted to restrain a party from deposing a witness for the purpose of foreign proceedings (*Benfield Holdings Ltd v Richardson* [2007] EWHC 171 (QB), LTL 1/3/2007). The basis of the jurisdiction to do so is unconscionable conduct. It may be unconscionable where the pursuit of foreign proceedings was vexatious or oppressive or interfered with the due process of the court. **58.15**

INJUNCTION TO RESTRAIN THREATS TO WITNESS OUTSIDE THE JURISDICTION

In *Masood v Zahoor* [2008] EWHC 328 (Ch), LTL 4/4/2008, an injunction was granted restraining the defendant for the duration of the proceedings from threatening a witness with disciplinary proceedings or taking any step in the witness's country which might inhibit or prohibit the witness from giving evidence in the English proceedings. **58.16**

Chapter 59 Trial Bundles

TIME FOR PREPARING TRIAL BUNDLES

59.1 All the documents likely to be referred to at trial should be placed into paginated trial bundles for use by the judge, witnesses and parties. Directions regarding the preparation and lodging of trial bundles will commonly be included with the directions made at the listing stage, but the rules in any event require the claimant to lodge the bundle not more than seven and not less than three days before the trial (**CPR, r. 39.5(2)**). If there is a trial 'window', presumably these periods are to be calculated from the start of the window. Although there is no duty to do so in the rules, defendants should, as a matter of practicality, notify the solicitor for the claimant about 14 days before the start of the trial of the documents the defendants want to be included in the trial bundles.

CONTENTS OF TRIAL BUNDLES

59.2 Detailed rules governing the format of trial bundles in non-specialist proceedings are to be found in **PD 39A, para. 3**. These are that:

(a) The bundles should contain copies of:
   (i) the claim form and all statements of case;
   (ii) a case summary and/or a chronology where appropriate;
   (iii) all requests for further information and responses to the requests;
   (iv) all witness statements and witness summaries to be relied upon;
   (v) any hearsay notices;
   (vi) any notices of intention to rely on plans, photographs, etc. under **CPR, r. 33.6**;
   (vii) all experts reports and responses to questions to those experts;
   (viii) any order giving trial directions; and
   (ix) any other necessary documents. This last category will include all the relevant contemporaneous documentation and documentary evidence, as well as relevant correspondence.

(b) The bundles should be continuously paginated throughout, and indexed with a description of each document with its page number.

(c) If any of the documents is illegible they should be followed by a typed transcript given an 'A' number and with a suitable cross-reference.

(d) Where the bundle exceeds 100 pages numbered dividers should be used between groups of documents.

(e) If the documentation is particularly voluminous, a separate core bundle should be compiled containing the most important documents with cross-references to where the documents it contains can be found in the main bundles.

(f) The bundles should normally be contained in ring or lever-arch files. Files should not be overfilled. 300 pages is a good guide to not overfilling files (*Leofelis SA v Lonsdale Sports Ltd* [2008] EWCA Civ 640, *The Times*, 23 July 2008). If more than one file is needed they should be in different colours or should be clearly marked by distinguishing letters, and obviously the same coding should be used for each set of the bundles. It is sometimes convenient to have a separate file containing the expert evidence.

The contents of the bundles should be agreed where possible (**PD 39A, para. 3.9**). The parties should also, if possible, agree which of the documents in the bundles are authentic, and which of the documents are to be treated as evidence of the facts they state even if hearsay notices have not been served. The last point seems to contain a misunderstanding of the Civil Evidence Act 1995, which provides in s. 1(1) that in civil proceedings evidence will not be excluded on the ground that it is hearsay, and by s. 2(4) any failure to serve a hearsay notice (even if required) does not affect admissibility, but only goes to the questions of costs and weight.

Where it is not possible to agree the contents of the bundles, a summary of the points on which the parties are unable to agree should be included.

There are cases where far too much paperwork is included in the trial bundles. There is often a considerable amount of material which might become relevant, but which is not, on its face, immediately relevant. Such material has to be available for inspection by the other side and one copy available for the court, but the parties need to use their discretion, and all such material does not have to be in the trial bundles (*R (London and South East Railway Ltd) v British Transport Police Authority* [2009] EWHC 1255 (Admin), LTL 1/7/2009).

PREPARING BUNDLES

The claimant will need to compile identical bundles for the court, for each of the parties, and one for use by the witnesses at the trial (**PD 39A, para. 3.10**). In jury trials sufficient copies must be provided for use by the jury (Queen's Bench Guide, para. 9.2.7). Under no circumstances should rival bundles be presented to the court (Chancery Guide, app. 6, para. 5). The originals of the documents in the bundle should be available for production at the hearing (**PD 39A, para. 3.3**). **59.3**

The CPR provide that it is for the claimant to file the trial bundles (**r. 39.5(1)**) unless the court orders otherwise. It was said in *Maltez v Lewis* (1999) *The Times*, 4 May 1999, by Neuberger J that where the defendant is in a better financial position than the claimant the court might order the bundles to be prepared by the defendant's solicitors in order to ensure a level playing field for the purposes of **r. 1.1(2)(a)**.

There is no provision in the rules relating to the preparation of trial bundles (unlike **r. 31.15(c)**, in relation to disclosure of documents) for payment for the copy sent to the defendant. The cost of preparing the bundles is therefore simply part of the general costs of the claimant.

TRANSLATIONS

Translations into English should be provided for all the important foreign-language documents in the trial bundles. Each should appear next to the original document in the bundle, suitably cross-referenced (by analogy with **PD 39A, para. 3.8**; Chancery Guide, app. 6, para. 13). The translation should be agreed or, if this is not possible, each party's proposed translation should be included. The overriding objective needs to be kept in mind, and it is not always necessary to translate everything if the cost of translation is disproportionately high (*Nichia Corporation v Argos Ltd* [2007] EWCA Civ 741, [2007] Bus LR 1753). **59.4**

PLANS, DRAWINGS, PHOTOGRAPHS

The rule is that the bundles available to the judge, advocates and witness box should be identical (**PD 39A, para. 3.10**; 'exactly the same', Chancery Guide, para. 7.12). This would mean that plans and drawings should be coloured in the same way in each bundle, and that all bundles should have prints of photographs rather than photocopies. This has to give way **59.5** to the overriding objective from time to time in the interests of proportionality and saving expense.

Large plans should be placed in an easily accessible file, which may have to be larger than the normal A4 format for trial bundles (Chancery Guide, app. 6, para. 16). The skeleton argument should refer to a document which must identify for the court all relevant features which appear in the maps, plans, diagrams or photographs to be used at the trial (*Hunte v E. Bottomley and Sons Ltd* [2007] EWCA Civ 1168, *The Times*, 21 November 2007).

OTHER PROVISIONS DEALING WITH BUNDLES

59.6 Different requirements apply to bundles used in the following situations:

(a) interim applications in non-specialist proceedings (**32.17**);
(b) Chancery Division hearings (see Chancery Guide, paras 7.9 to 7.17 and app. 6);
(c) Admiralty and Commercial Court applications (see Admiralty and Commercial Courts Guide, paras F6.4 to F6.8 and F11 to F13 and app. 10);
(d) Admiralty and Commercial Court case management bundles (see **PD 58, para. 10.8**; Admiralty and Commercial Courts Guide, para. D7 and app. 10);
(e) Admiralty and Commercial Court trials (see Admiralty and Commercial Courts Guide, para. J3 and app. 10);
(f) Patents Court (see Patents Court Guide, section 14 and standard direction 19);
(g) appeals (see **PD 52, paras 5.6, 5.6A, 15.2** to **15.4** and **15.11**); and
(h) judicial review (see **77.47**; **PD 52, para. 15.4**; and **PD 54A, paras 5.6** to **5.9**).

Under the electronic working scheme in the specialist courts of the High Court (see **15.55**), trial bundles are in paper copy only (**PD 5C, para. 14.1**).

USE OF BUNDLES AT THE HEARING

59.7 All the documents in an agreed bundle (see **59.2**) are admissible at the hearing unless the court orders otherwise or if a party gives a written notice objecting to the admissibility of particular documents (**PD 32, para. 27.2**).

In *Gough v Mummery* [2002] EWCA Civ 1573, LTL 4/10/2002, the trial bundle contained one version of a letter from an expert, but a different (and more favourable) version (with the same date) was in the papers of counsel for the side relying on the letter. It was held that the trial judge's decisions to refuse an adjournment to investigate the differences between the two versions of the letter, and to refuse permission to rely on the version in counsel's papers, were discretionary matters and were not plainly wrong.

READING LISTS AND TIME ESTIMATES

59.8 In all Queen's Bench Division and Chancery Division claims where bundles must be lodged, the claimant or applicant must at the same time lodge:

(a) a reading list for the judge who will conduct the hearing;
(b) an estimated length of reading time; and
(c) an estimated length for the hearing.

This must be signed by all the advocates who will appear at the hearing. Each advocate's name, business address and telephone number must appear below his or her signature. In the event of disagreement about any of these matters, separate reading lists and estimates must be signed by the appropriate advocates. See Practice Direction (Royal Courts of Justice: Reading Lists and Time Estimates) [2000] 1 WLR 208.

Chapter 60 Trial by Jury

INTRODUCTION

Almost all civil trials nowadays are tried before a judge sitting alone. The last vestiges of the former practice of conducting civil trials before juries are statutory rights in the County Courts Act 1984, s. 66, and the Senior Courts Act 1981, s. 69, for trial by jury in actions in deceit, libel, slander, malicious prosecution and false imprisonment. Libel and slander will be removed from this list when the Defamation Act 2013, s. 11, is brought into force. There are exceptions from the statutory rights to jury trial relating to cases involving prolonged examination of documents or accounts, or scientific or local investigations which cannot conveniently be made by a jury. Juries are not looked on favourably for a number of reasons. These include the fact they do not give reasons for their decisions, the experience that jury trials tend to take considerably longer than trials before a judge sitting alone, and the risk that a jury will fail to reach even a majority verdict. 60.1

STATUTORY RIGHTS TO TRIAL BY JURY

The Senior Courts Act 1981, s. 69(1), provides: 60.2

Where, on the application of any party to an action to be tried in the Queen's Bench Division, the court is satisfied that there is in issue—
(a) a charge of fraud against that party; or
(b) a claim in respect of libel, slander, malicious prosecution or false imprisonment; or
(c) any question or issue of a kind prescribed for the purposes of this paragraph,
the action shall be tried with a jury, unless the court is of opinion that the trial requires any prolonged examination of documents or accounts or any scientific or local investigation which cannot conveniently be made with a jury.

The County Courts Act 1984, s. 66(3), is in essentially the same terms for county court proceedings. The result is that the right to a jury only arises to claims proceeding in the Queen's Bench Division of the High Court and the county courts, and not while a claim is in the Chancery Division. Claims may be transferred to the Queen's Bench Division for the purpose of securing trial by jury, if appropriate. Note also that the right to trial by jury in fraud cases is only available to the defendant, but that either party has the right to a jury in claims for libel, slander, malicious prosecution and false imprisonment. 'Fraud' for this purpose is limited to claims in deceit (*Stafford Winfield Cook and Partners Ltd v Winfield* [1981] 1 WLR 458).

In considering whether the proviso to the Senior Courts Act 1981, s. 69(1), applies, according to *Phillips v Commissioner of Police of the Metropolis* [2003] EWCA Civ 382, *The Times*, 2 April 2003, three questions must be asked:

(a) Would there be a prolonged examination of documents or any scientific investigation?
(b) If so, could the examination be conveniently made with a jury?
(c) If not, should the court nevertheless exercise its discretion to order trial with a jury?

In *Oliver v Calderdale Metropolitan Borough Council* (1999) *The Times*, 7 July 1999, it was said as a secondary ground for refusing a jury that a substantial dispute between the experts dealing with the psychological effects of an alleged malicious prosecution rendered the case unsuitable for trial by a jury. 'Documents' for the purpose of the proviso to s. 69 includes video footage. Whether the examination of that material could be made conveniently with a jury depends on factors such as the quality of the recordings and the quantity of material (*MacIntyre v Chief Constable of Kent* (2002) LTL 6/2/2002). In *Beta Construction Ltd v Channel Four Television Co. Ltd* [1990] 1 WLR 1042 Stuart Smith LJ made the point that some cases are inconvenient for juries because of the physical problems of jurors trying to follow documentation being taken from several files simultaneously, or trying to grapple with large plans within the confined space of most jury boxes. Where a case involves prolonged examination of documents which cannot conveniently be made with a jury, it is within the judge's case management discretion to order trial by judge of those issues, with jury trial for the rest (*Phillips v Commissioner of Police of the Metropolis*). In exercising the discretion under s. 69(4) whether to order selected issues to be tried by judge or jury, the court must assess the relative advantages and disadvantages of the different modes of trial without any predisposition in favour of either option (*Armstrong v Times Newspapers Ltd (No. 2)* [2006] EWCA Civ 519, [2006] 1 WLR 2462). Being a matter of discretion, it is unlikely that a successful appeal could be mounted against such a decision (*Gregson v Channel Four Television Corporation* [2002] EWCA Civ 941, LTL 4/7/2002).

TIME TO APPLY FOR TRIAL BY JURY

60.3 The Senior Courts Act 1981, s. 69(2), provides that an application for trial by jury must be made not later than such time before trial as may be prescribed, which is within 28 days after service of the defence (**CPR, r. 26.11**). After this period the right to trial by jury is lost, with the judge having a discretion to order a jury trial on a late application which has to be exercised based on all the circumstances of the case (*Thornton v Telegraph Media Group Ltd* [2011] EWCA Civ 748, [2011] EMLR 29, where an order was made for trial by judge alone).

DISCRETION TO ORDER TRIAL BY JURY

60.4 In cases outside the categories where there is a right to a jury the court retains, in most cases, a discretion to make an order for jury trial. There is no power to grant a jury even on a discretionary basis in county court admiralty proceedings, and certain proceedings under the Rent (Agriculture) Act 1976, the Rent Act 1977, the Protection from Eviction Act 1977 and the Housing Act 1988 (see the County Courts Act 1984, s. 66(1)).

In other categories of case the court has a discretion, which must be exercised judicially and in accordance with the overriding objective, whether to make an order for trial by jury. However, the requirements of the **CPR, Part 1**, point strongly against the discretion being exercised, particularly the need for expedition and saving costs. Under the old rules it was in any event almost impossible to obtain a discretionary order for a jury, see *Ward v James* [1966] 1 QB 273, and *Williams v Beesley* [1973] 1 WLR 1295, and it was said in *Goldsmith v Pressdram Ltd* [1988] 1 WLR 64 that 'the emphasis now is against trial with juries, and the court should take this emphasis into account when exercising its discretion', per Lawton LJ.

JURY SELECTION

60.5 Juries must be selected randomly in accordance with the Juries Act 1974, ss. 2, 5 and 6 (see *R v Tarrant* (1997) *The Times*, 29 December 1997). The former practice of allowing peremptory challenges to prospective jurors has been abolished (Criminal Justice Act 1988, s. 118), but it is still possible to challenge for cause (Juries Act 1974, s. 12).

RELEASING JURORS

Releasing jurors part way through a trial is inconvenient, and can lead to the need to discharge the entire jury and for the trial to start again. In an effort to avoid this happening, particularly in lengthy trials, the trial judge should inquire of prospective jurors whether they will suffer inconvenience or hardship through having to serve for the estimated length of the trial, and excuse those who will be so affected (see Practice Direction (Juries: Length of Trial) [1981] 1 WLR 1129, which should be applied even under CPR). **60.6**

During the course of the trial the judge may discharge a juror on the ground of evident necessity. An example from criminal proceedings is *R v Richardson* [1979] 1 WLR 1316, where the judge discharged by telephone a juror whose husband had died during the night. It was held there was no material irregularity in the trial despite the fact the decision to discharge the juror had not been made in open court.

COMMUNICATIONS WITH THE JURY

All communications between the judge and jury should be conducted in open court and with the whole jury present (*R v Woods* (1987) 87 Cr App R 60). **60.7**

SUMMING UP

It is not the function of the judge to embark on a fact-finding exercise when sitting with a jury. The judge must sum up the case, with an agreed list of issues where there is a conflict (*Balchin v Chief Constable of Hampshire Constabulary* (2001) *The Times*, 4 May 2001). Where an expert in an assault claim against the police gave evidence which contradicted the account given by the claimant, the judge had to give adequate assistance to the jury on how to approach the conflicting evidence (*Masters v Chief Constable of Sussex* [2002] EWCA Civ 1482, LTL 3/10/2002). **60.8**

JURY VERDICTS

The jury should be told by the judge that they should deliberate on their verdict only when they are all together in the jury room (*R v Hastings* [2003] EWCA Crim 3730, *The Times*, 12 December 2003). A party who expressly asks for a question to be left to the jury cannot appeal against the jury's decision on the grounds that it is perverse (*McPhilemy v Times Newspapers Ltd (No. 3)* [2001] EMLR 832). **60.9**

If, after being discharged, the jury indicate that they have given the wrong verdict, the judge may invite them to retire again to reconsider their verdict and may accept a changed verdict if it is in the interests of justice to do so (*Igwemma v Chief Constable of Greater Manchester Police* [2001] EWCA Civ 953, [2002] QB 1012). In considering whether it is in the interests of justice, the judge should take into account: the time that has elapsed since the original verdict was returned; the reasons for seeking further assistance from the jury; and whether the jury may have been persuaded to change their view by anything said or done since they gave their original verdict.

Majority verdicts

High Court civil juries have 12 members. County court juries are eight strong. The jury must seek to reach a unanimous verdict, and the trial judge may only give a majority verdict direction where it appears that the jury has had such sufficient time for deliberation as the judge considers reasonable given the nature and complexity of the case (Juries Act 1974, s. 17(4)). **60.10**

Commentary

Permissible majority verdicts where there are not less than 11 jurors are 11:1, 10:2 and 10:1. Where there are only 10 jurors a 9:1 majority is permitted. In the county courts a majority of 7:1 is permissible. In addition, the court may accept a majority verdict with the consent of the parties (such as a simple majority verdict), and the parties may further agree to proceed with an incomplete jury (s. 17(5)).

Hung jury

60.11 Where the jury cannot reach a verdict, even a majority verdict, they should be discharged and the trial discontinued. The normal rule is that the costs of the inconclusive trial should be made to be in the case, so that whoever wins the subsequent trial recovers the costs of the first trial (*Camiller v Commissioner of Police of the Metropolis* (1999) *The Times*, 8 June 1999).

Chapter 61 Trial

The following procedural checklist, which is at the front of the book, is relevant to this chapter:

Procedural checklist 28 Trial preparation

INTRODUCTION

61.1 A key feature of the CPR is that the court must retain control of the progress of claims, and one of the ways in which this is achieved is by giving the parties trial dates or windows at an

Commentary

early stage. Trial directions are often given when a claim is allocated to a track, particularly in small claims and fast track claims. Small claims track cases are determined by district judges at informal hearings where the strict rules of evidence do not apply. They are usually conducted in the district judge's chambers. Hearings in small claims cases are discussed further in **chapter 45**. This chapter is principally concerned with trials in fast track and multi-track claims. The standard period between directions and the trial date or window in fast track claims is 30 weeks (**CPR, r. 28.2(4)**). Even in multi-track claims the court will fix a trial date or window as soon as practicable (**r. 29.2(2)**). Further ways in which the court maintains control, particularly over the trial process, include:

(a) holding pre-trial reviews in selected multi-track cases a few weeks before trial — these will usually be heard by the trial judge, and one of their main purposes is to decide how to conduct the trial in the most efficient manner;
(b) setting of trial timetables in advance, limiting the amount of time allowed for speeches and questioning of witnesses;
(c) an emphasis on written preparation;
(d) the use of Fridays as preparation days in long trials (although this is not set out anywhere in the CPR or practice directions, and is a matter for individual courts and judges).

PRE-TRIAL CHECKLISTS AND FIXING THE DATE OF TRIAL

61.2 These topics have already been considered in the context of the discussion of fast track cases (see **46.13** and **46.17**) and multi-track cases (see **47.16** and **47.17**). Essentially, directions made either on track allocation or at a case management conference or other directions hearing will fix a date for pre-trial checklists, and trial dates will be fixed as soon as possible. In fast track cases this means at the allocation stage. In multi-track cases, fixing the trial date as soon as possible may mean doing this at the allocation stage, but may mean doing so considerably later. If a trial date is given at an early stage it may be altered later, perhaps after the court considers the pre-trial checklists. Trial dates may either be fixtures, which obviously means that the trial will commence on a specific date, or may be given by means of a trial 'window' of up to three weeks.

Fast track listing

61.3 A trial date or a period in which the trial is to take place will usually be given in fast track cases as part of the standard directions at the track allocation stage. If a trial period is given, it should not exceed three weeks. The trial date or period should not be more than 30 weeks from the date of the directions. The trial date or period will be confirmed or altered at the listing stage, which is fixed as one of the standard fast track directions, and is usually about eight weeks before trial.

In his *Final Report*, ch. 3, para. 28, Lord Woolf said in relation to fast track listing, 'I attach great importance to trial dates being honoured and I know that the Court Service is already working towards developing an effective listing system to meet the needs of the fast track'. The report went on to explain the difficulties and delays that are likely if all cases are given fixed dates, which stem largely from the fact that most cases settle, and the probability that when this happens the courts will not be in use for a substantial part of the working week. It also identified a number of well-known problems. These include Her Majesty's Courts and Tribunals Service being unable to find a judge or court for some trials when they are listed; urgent applications being listed immediately before trials, resulting in trials being delayed or adjourned; the practice of the courts deliberately 'overbooking' in the hope that most of the cases booked for one particular day will settle; and 'block listing' a number of cases for the same time in circumstances where it is almost inevitable that the parties and witnesses in some of the cases blocked together will have to wait in court for a substantial time before their cases are reached. All these problems have a substantial impact on fast track cases. These cases are intended to be tried within a single day, and have restrictions on the costs recoverable, both of which may be rendered meaningless if listing shortcomings result in adjournments and part-heard trials.

As recognised by both the *Woolf Report* and the *Jackson Report*, ensuring fast track cases are tried as intended involves the cooperation of everyone involved. Practitioners are under an obligation to provide accurate information in their pre-trial checklists to enable hearing times to be calculated on a realistic basis. District judges need to make realistic assessments of hearing times based on the information on the court files. Listing officers need to make provision for hearing urgent matters in ways that do not interfere with fast track trials, and must provide specific staggered times for hearings rather than block lists.

Multi-track listing

The key obligation in the CPR regarding fixing multi-track cases for trial is in **r. 29.2(2)**, which provides that the court must fix the trial date or period in which the trial will take place as soon as practicable. The trial date or window will be confirmed as soon as practicable after the parties have filed their pre-trial checklists, or after any listing hearing or pre-trial review (**r. 29.8(c)(ii)**). Given the wide variety of cases on the multi-track this will vary considerably from case to case. For some cases the trial date or period may be given in the directions made at the track allocation stage. In other cases it may not be possible until a considerable time later, perhaps in a case management conference or pre-trial review. Like fast track cases, there is a pre-trial checklist procedure in multi-track cases (see **47.17**). Directions for filing these checklists will be made at some stage in the directions process, normally with a view to the checklists being filed about 10 weeks before the intended trial. The trial date will be confirmed or altered at that stage. **61.4**

As multi-track trials may sometimes stretch over several days or weeks, minor delays due to urgent applications being listed first are not so likely to have such an impact as in fast track cases, so the concerns noted in **61.3**, although still important, are not so fundamental.

It is interesting to note that if the court gives a trial window in a multi-track case instead of a fixture, the period should be just one week (**r. 29.8(c)(ii)**), rather than the possible three-week period for fast track cases.

Queen's Bench Division listing

In Admiralty, Commercial and Technology and Construction Court claims, trials are usually fixed at, or in consequence of, the first case management conference. **61.5**

In other Queen's Bench Division claims in the Royal Courts of Justice the Clerk of the Lists (Room WG3, Royal Courts of Justice) is in general responsible for listing. There are three lists, namely the jury list, the trial list, and the interim hearings list (Queen's Bench Guide, para. 9.2). The trial list is for non-jury trials, preliminary issues and proceedings for contempt of court (para. 9.4.1). Case management directions will be made with a view to fixing the date or week of the trial, or a trial window (**CPR, r. 29.2(2)**; Queen's Bench Guide, para. 9.4.4). For that purpose (see para. 9.4.5), the court may:

(a) direct that the trial is not to begin earlier than a specified date; and/or
(b) direct that the trial date be within a specified period; and/or
(c) specify the trial date or window.

If either option (a) or (b) is used, the court will also direct the parties to attend upon the listing officer to fix the trial date or window. The claimant (unless another party agrees to do it) must within the next seven days of a date directed by the court for the purpose take out an appointment with the listing officer and give notice of the appointment to the other parties (para. 9.4.7). At the listing hearing solicitors' representatives or counsel's clerks should attend with details of the availability of counsel, experts and witnesses, the trial estimate, and copies of any case summary prepared under **PD 29, paras. 5.6** and **5.7**, the particulars of claim and all orders relevant to fixing the trial (Queen's Bench Guide, para. 9.4.8). The Clerk of the Lists will try to ensure a speedy disposal of the trial by arranging a firm date as soon as possible within the time constraints imposed by the order for directions (para. 9.4.8). If exceptionally a trial date cannot be provided within the period set by the court's directions a date may be fixed for the first available date (para. 9.4.8).

Any party dissatisfied with a decision made by the Clerk of the Lists can, within seven days of the decision and on giving one day's notice to all other parties, apply to the judge in charge of the list. The application should be arranged through the Queen's Bench Listing Office in Room WG5 (Queen's Bench Guide, paras 9.1.1, 9.1.2 and 9.4.10).

The relevant listing office should be informed of any special needs of any witnesses prior to the hearing, so that suitable facilities, parking, access etc. can be dealt with (Queen's Bench Guide, para. 10.2.8; Chancery Guide, para. 8.13).

Most trials are assigned to a named judge when they appear in the daily cause list. Cases may be listed as 'unassigned cases', usually if the parties consent and there are no witnesses (Queen's Bench Guide, para. 9.6.1). These are heard, usually on the day listed, by judges whose assigned cases are ineffective. Parties in these cases should attend outside the court where the matter is listed, where they will be told which judge will hear the matter.

Chancery Division listing

61.6 There are three main Chancery Division lists called the trial list (for trials to be heard with witnesses), the interim hearings list (for interim applications and appeals from masters), and the general list (for all other matters) (Chancery Guide, paras 6.3 to 6.6). There is a warned list which is published on Fridays showing the cases liable to be heard in the following week. Chapter 6 of the Chancery Guide also deals with time estimates, appeals from masters, and listing of bankruptcy applications and appeals, companies applications and petitions, short applications and summary judgment, as well as revenue appeals and hearings in claims for the variation of trusts.

Expedited hearing

61.7 In cases of real urgency the court may order an expedited hearing, exercising its power under **CPR, r. 3.1(2)(b)**. An application for an expedited hearing, which of course involves leapfrogging over other litigants waiting to be heard, has to be supported by clear evidence of the need for a speedy trial (*Intervet (UK) Ltd v Merial* [2009] EWHC 1065 (Pat), LTL 21/5/2009). It can only be justified if there are very cogent reasons (*W. L. Gore and Associates GmbH v Geox SpA* [2008] EWHC 462 (Pat), LTL 7/4/2008). An argument that effective enforcement cannot be started until a final judgment has been obtained is not a convincing reason for expediting a trial (*Daltel Europe Ltd v Makki* [2004] EWHC 1631 (Ch), LTL 17/6/2004). Where the principal relief sought is money, or where declaratory relief is unlikely to resolve the dispute between the parties, it will be difficult to justify expediting the trial (*CPC Group Ltd v Qatari Diar Real Estate Investment Co.* [2009] EWHC 3204 (Ch), LTL 15/12/2009). A disputed claim for relief from forfeiture against a claim for delivery up of an aircraft may justify a speedy trial (*Celestial Aviation Trading 71 Ltd v Paramount Airways Private Ltd* [2009] EWHC 3142 (Comm), LTL 10/12/2009). Factors include any past delays, any prejudice to other parties, and the practicality of forcing parties to adhere to a tight timetable (*Law Debenture Trust Corporation plc v Elektrim SA* [2008] EWHC 2187 (Ch), LTL 1/10/2008). An example where an order was granted is *Wembley National Stadium Ltd v Wembley (London) Ltd* (2000) LTL 16/11/2000, where funding for a project which was dependent on the success of the proceedings was likely to be withdrawn within a limited time. The application should be made as early as possible (*Daltel Europe Ltd v Makki*). If the order is granted, the court will lay down a timetable with strict deadlines.

Availability of experts and listing

Two important concepts are that trials should be listed as soon as practicable, and once fixed should not be adjourned unless absolutely necessary. If a party wants to change experts in the run-up to trial, or to instruct an expert for the first time shortly before trial, they are obliged to instruct experts who will report in sufficient time and be available for the trial. In *Rollinson v Kimberly Clark Ltd* [1999] CPLR 581 an expert instructed about six months before trial was unable to attend trial. On an application made about three months before trial the judge refused to break the fixture, and her decision was upheld by the Court of Appeal. A decision of great practical importance is *Matthews v Tarmac Bricks and Tiles Ltd* [1999] CPLR 463. There had been some difficulty in fixing the trial, and the court convened a listing hearing which was attended by a young member of the Bar on behalf of the defendant. Counsel had been provided with a list of unavailable dates, which included 15 July. The judge asked why the defendant's two experts were unavailable on 15 July, to which counsel replied she had no instructions. The trial was then fixed for 15 July. The Master of the Rolls said it was not enough simply to tell the court which dates experts could not attend, but that reasons had to be given as well. Even if the actual reasons had been given, it did not follow that the court would not have still listed the case for 15 July. Experts have to be prepared to arrange their affairs to meet the commitments of the courts where that is practical. The case clearly underlines the importance of having someone familiar with the case and fully briefed attend at case management hearings (see **CPR, r. 29.3(2)**). However, it may be that the decision in this case turned on the history of difficulties in fixing the trial, and should not be seen as always applicable in other cases. **61.8**

ADJOURNMENT

Power to adjourn

CPR, r. 3.1(2)(b), gives the court a general power to adjourn. Adjournments may be necessary due to shortages of court resources. They may be sought by a party on the ground of some event outside their control which prevents them from presenting their full case at the hearing. They are also, regrettably, sometimes sought because a party or their lawyers have failed to prepare the case in time, and adjournments in these circumstances are often attended by breaches of case management directions previously made by the court. **61.9**

It is the duty of parties and their legal representatives to inform the court as soon as they become aware of any real prospect that a trial will not proceed so as to enable the court to reallocate its resources (*Albon v Naza Motor Trading Sdn Bhd (No. 5)* [2007] EWHC 2613 (Ch), [2008] 1 WLR 2380 at [12]).

In the Queen's Bench Division, a party seeking an adjournment must inform the Clerk of the Lists as soon as possible (Queen's Bench Guide, para. 9.8.2). If the application is by agreement, the parties should apply to the Clerk of the Lists in writing, who will consult the nominated judge who may grant the application and impose conditions, which usually include directions for a new trial date (para. 9.8.4). If the application is opposed, a hearing should be arranged through the Clerk of the Lists to be heard either by the nominated judge or the judge to whom the matter has been allocated. A short written summary of the reasons for the adjournment (formal evidence not being required) should be lodged with the Listing Office by 10.30 a.m. on the day before the application is heard (para. 9.8.5).

In the Chancery Division, a party seeking an adjournment must inform the Chancery Judges' Listing Officer as soon as possible (Chancery Guide, para. 7.39(1)). The procedure is similar to that in the Queen's Bench Division, except that the summary of the reasons for seeking the adjournment in an opposed application should be lodged at the Chancery Judges' Listing Office by 12 noon on the day before the application is heard (para. 7.39(5)).

In the county courts, agreed adjournments should be notified to the court office in writing as early as possible. Depending on the circumstances, the matter may be referred to the judge. If the adjournment is opposed, an application should be issued with the reasons for the adjournment being set out in the form N244.

There is greater reluctance to adjourn a fixed date trial than to put back a trial window (the effect of *Fitzroy Robinson Ltd v Mentmore Towers Ltd* [2009] EWHC 3070 (TCC), [2010] CP Rep 15; *Elliott Group Ltd v GECC UK* [2010] EWHC 409 (TCC), LTL 10/3/2010). Applications made immediately before the scheduled start of a trial should be avoided as they use up valuable court time, and often result in a waste of court resources and costs.

The power to grant an adjournment is discretionary, and should be exercised in accordance with the overriding objective (*Boyd and Hutchinson v Foenander* [2003] EWCA Civ 1516, [2004] BPIR 20). The court must ensure the parties are on an equal footing, that the case is dealt with proportionately, expeditiously and fairly, with an appropriate amount of the court's resources devoted to it taking into account the needs of other cases (*Fitzroy Robinson Ltd v Mentmore Towers Ltd* [2009] EWHC 3070 (TCC), [2010] CP Rep 15). Where an adjournment is sought for reasons outside the control of the party, it should usually be granted. Examples are where vital witnesses are unavoidably out of the country, or too ill to attend court. Adjourning to await the decision in an appeal in a different case on an issue raised in the present case is a pure case management matter, and the judge's decision is unlikely to be upset on appeal (*Corbett v South Yorkshire Strategic Health Authority* [2006] EWCA Civ 1797, LTL 6/12/2006). Adjournments are unlikely to be granted where a party is not ready for trial through their own fault, or where they have been given a previous adjournment and are still not ready, unless the circumstances are exceptional.

An adjournment was refused in *Powell v Pallisers of Hereford Ltd* [2002] EWCA Civ 959, LTL 1/7/2002, where the defendant wanted more time to enable a third party to take part in the trial, but where an early trial date, which would ensure that the claim was tried by the time of the 2002 harvest, had been set because the claimant was a farmer in financial difficulties. A judge has a wide discretion whether to adjourn, and it is not easy for an appeal court to interfere with that discretion (*Roshdi v Thames Trains Ltd* [2002] EWCA Civ 284, LTL 20/2/2002).

Problems obtaining representation

61.10 The availability of counsel of choice, particularly where replacement counsel will have to spend a substantial amount of time reading into the case, or where the client reposes a great deal of confidence in existing counsel, is a factor to be taken into account (*Collins v Gordon* [2008] EWCA Civ 110, LTL 21/1/2008). Where the problem is self-induced, such as through dismissing solicitors shortly before the hearing, a short adjournment may be all that the court should grant (*Property Investor's Courses Ltd v Secretary of State for Trade and Industry* [2008] EWCA Civ 872, LTL 14/7/2008, where the court granted a two-day adjournment in a straightforward case). In *Bates v Croydon London Borough Council* [2001], EWCA Civ 134, LTL 23/1/2001, an adjournment should have been given as the appellant was awaiting a determination of an application for legal aid, and she had been served with the respondents' witness statements and other documents very shortly before the hearing. The court should respect the right of a party to seek public funding by granting adjournments where appropriate (*Berry Trade Ltd v Moussavi* [2002] EWCA Civ 477, [2002] 1 WLR 1910). An adjournment should have been granted in *Henry Butcher International Ltd v KG Engineering* [2004] EWCA Civ 1597, LTL 22/10/2004, to enable a party to obtain legal representation where the case had a complex history and raised complex legal issues. Similarly, in *Ghadami v Harlow District Council* [2004] EWCA Civ 891, LTL 21/6/2004, an adjournment should have been given where the date listed conflicted with an earlier direction and would have deprived a party of his counsel of choice. In *Joyce v King* (1987) *The Times*, 13 July 1987, the claimant was unable to obtain expert evidence without legal aid, and there were problems in obtaining legal aid. It was held that the trial should have been adjourned because it was not possible for the claimant to obtain justice without being given further time. An adjournment was granted in *Islam v Meah* [2005] EWCA Civ 1485, LTL 11/11/2005, where the defendant had limited understanding of English, and the adjournment was needed so he could obtain legal funding and legal representation.

Breach of case management directions

The general approach that will be adopted where an adjournment is sought after there has been a breach of case management directions is set out in **PD 28, para.** 5.4 (fast track) and **PD 29, para.** 7.4 (multi-track). These provide that the court will not allow a failure to comply with directions to lead to the postponement of the trial unless the circumstances of the case are exceptional. Litigants and lawyers must be in no doubt that the court will regard the postponement of a trial as an order of last resort. If practicable to do so, the court will exercise its powers in a manner that enables the case to come on for trial on the date or within the period previously set, and it may set a new, but tight, timetable, with sanctions for non-compliance (*Elliott Group Ltd v GECC UK* [2010] EWHC 409 (TCC), LTL 10/3/2010). Where it appears that one or more issues are or can be made ready for trial at the time fixed while others cannot, the court may direct that the trial will proceed on the issues that are or will then be ready, and order that no costs will be allowed for any later trial of the remaining issues or that those costs will be paid by the party in default. Where the court has no option but to postpone the trial it will do so for the shortest possible time and will give directions for the taking of the necessary steps in the meantime as rapidly as possible. In these cases the court may disallow costs as between solicitor and client, or order the person responsible to pay costs, or make any other order including ordering costs on the indemnity basis (Queen's Bench Guide, para. 9.8.7; Chancery Guide, para. 7.39(7)). **PD 28, para.** 5.4 and **PD 29, para.** 7.4, apply only where there has been a breach of case management directions, and not where an adjournment is sought on the basis of unavailability of counsel or witnesses (*Collins v Gordon* [2008] EWCA Civ 110, LTL 21/1/2008). **61.11**

Commentary

In *Gilbart v Thomas Graham* [2008] EWCA Civ 897, LTL 24/6/2008, the Court of Appeal overturned a decision to refuse an adjournment of the trial date, in order to give effect to the overriding objective. The defendant had applied for the adjournment 21 days before the date for the trial, on realising that the claimant had not disclosed crucial documents. 21 days was an unrealistically short time for the defendant to obtain specific disclosure from the claimant and to instruct an expert on a loss of profits claim. In *Ratiopharm (UK) Ltd v Alza Corporation* [2008] EWHC 1182 (Ch), LTL 1/5/2008, six months was regarded as enough time to prepare a patent infringement claim for trial (the party seeking to avoid the trial date having received a letter with the allegations in the litigation 13 months before the trial date). An adjournment of a fast track claim based on an argument that the claimant had suffered psychiatric injuries (which were not mentioned in the disclosed medical evidence) and that the claim should be reallocated to the multi-track was refused in *Taylor v Graham* (2000) LTL 25/5/2000, largely because evidence was not adduced substantiating the more complex nature of the claim justifying reallocation. Failing to prepare for trial because there were ongoing negotiations for a settlement is unlikely to be regarded as a sufficient reason for an adjournment (*Assiouti v Hosseini* (1999) LTL 26/11/99). An application to adjourn in *AC Electrical Wholesale plc v IGW Services Ltd* (2000) LTL 10/10/2000 based on a need to include a claim for loss of profits in a counterclaim was refused as there were no exceptional *circumstances to explain* why this had not been pleaded earlier.

Late applications to adjourn

According to *Fitzroy Robinson Ltd v Mentmore Towers Ltd* [2009] EWHC 3070 (TCC), [2010] CP Rep 15, factors to be considered in eleventh-hour applications to adjourn include: **61.12**

(a) the parties' conduct and the reasons for any delays;
(b) the extent to which the consequences of delays can be overcome before trial;

(c) the extent to which a fair trial may be prejudiced by the delays;
(d) specific matters affecting the trial such as illness of a crucial witness; and
(e) the consequences of an adjournment for the parties and the court.

The fact that a party has not applied to adjourn until the day of the trial, despite knowing for many weeks that it is in difficulties, may be a sufficient reason to refuse an adjournment (*National Westminster Bank plc v Aaronson* [2004] EWHC 618 (QB), LTL 9/3/2004). Where both parties are to blame for the failure to instruct an expert and in not informing the court of the need to adjourn until the last minute, it is wrong to refuse to adjourn if only one party will suffer detriment from the lack of adjournment (*Thomson v O'Connor* [2005] EWCA Civ 1533, LTL 7/11/2005). In *Alderson v Stillorgan Sales Ltd* [2001] EWCA Civ 1060, LTL 13/6/2001, the claimants were refused permission to call their own expert, and the court directed that the parties jointly instruct an expert, who was to report just over two weeks before the trial. The expert was late, and delivered his report, which was favourable to the defendants, five days before trial. The day before trial the claimants sought an adjournment, which was refused, and a renewed application on the day of the trial was also refused. On appeal it was held that waiting to the day before trial was inappropriate. The appeal was dismissed partly because the claimants should have appealed the original order, or applied to adjourn when the expert missed the date for delivering his report, and partly because their case was weak in any event.

Witness availability and medical reasons

61.13 Adjournments on the basis of witnesses being unavailable are decided applying the overriding objective. Factors to be considered, based on *Albon v Naza Motor Trading Sdn Bhd (No. 5)* [2007] EWHC 2613 (Ch), [2008] 1 WLR 2380, include:

(a) court resources, particularly any court time lost through previous adjournments;
(b) the history of past compliance with or breach of directions and orders;
(c) whether there is medical evidence to the effect the witness cannot attend through ill-health;
(d) whether that witness's evidence is reasonably necessary to ensure the party's case is properly presented. Primary witnesses are more likely to be regarded as needed in person than witnesses regarded as secondary. The court will bear in mind that the witness's witness statement is admissible in evidence under the Civil Evidence Act 1995, with the lack of cross-examination going to weight rather than admissibility. Even that may be offset if the witness is able to be cross-examined by video link;
(e) the witness's availability at an adjourned hearing; and
(f) whether the respondent will suffer prejudice which cannot be compensated by an award of costs or otherwise.

In *Green v Northern General Transport* (1970) 115 SJ 59 a new trial was ordered after the judge refused to adjourn despite a material witness being unavailable. In *Re A (A Child)* [2005] EWCA Civ 862, LTL 14/7/2005, the judge was held entitled to conclude that the medical evidence about the father's post-operative condition did not justify an adjournment of more than about a week. Justice is a two-way street, and the other parties are as entitled to a fair and expeditious hearing as the party seeking the adjournment. In *Khudados v Hayden* [2007] EWCA Civ 1316, LTL 13/12/2007, a general practitioner's letter commenting that the claimant had been up in the night with vomiting and nausea justified adjournments on the Friday and Monday, but was not sufficient for a further adjournment on the Tuesday. Vague medical notes do not have to be accepted at face value (*R (Copyright Canary City Ltd) v Thames Magistrates' Court* [2010] EWHC 2185 (Admin), LTL 17/9/2010). An adjournment was refused in *Ahmed v Butt* [2005] EWCA Civ 1448, LTL 1/11/2005, where a litigant in person complained of having a sore throat. The judge said he would reassess the matter as the hearing progressed, but allowed the hearing to continue even though the litigant in person became inaudible. It was held that the judge was entitled to refuse the initial application on this provisional basis, but erred in not adjourning when it became apparent the party was not capable of making himself heard.

Cold feet and tactical reasons

In *Skipsey v O'Rourke* [2005] EWCA Civ 912, LTL 30/6/2005, medical evidence that the claimant was 'not in a fit frame of mind' to attend was rightly held to be insufficient to justify an adjournment. (It later transpired that the doctor had understated the claimant's condition, and an adjournment was allowed on that basis.) The court felt in *Law Debenture Trust Corporation plc v Elektrim Finance BV* [2005] EWCA Civ 1354, LTL 8/11/2005, that an adjournment was sought in order to leave the present proceedings unresolved, so as to secure a forensic advantage in related proceedings in Poland. On that basis the adjournment was refused. An adjournment of a mortgage possession hearing was refused in *Cheval Bridging Finance Ltd v Hastings* (2008) LTL 12/12/2008 where there was no prospect of the defendant discharging the mortgage debt in a reasonable period. 61.14

SETTLEMENT BEFORE TRIAL

If a claim is settled, whether by agreement or acceptance of a Part 36 offer, or is discontinued, in the period between the giving of a trial date or 'window' and the commencement of the trial, it is the duty of the parties to notify the listing officer for the trial court immediately (**PD 39A, para. 4.1**). The same applies if the trial is likely to be adjourned (see **61.9**). The court should be notified even if the settlement is reached at a late hour on the day before the hearing, and this certainly should be done where the case is being heard in the High Court. The High Court switchboard is open all night, and even a late notification may prevent a judge wasting time on pre-reading a case that has settled (see *Tasyurdu v Immigration Appeal Tribunal* [2003] EWCA Civ 447, [2003] CPLR 343, where the hearing was in the Court of Appeal). If an order giving effect to the settlement is drawn up, a copy should be filed with the listing officer (**PD 39A, para. 4.2**). Whether the hearing can be completely vacated depends on whether the terms agreed are suitable for a judgment or order by consent. If they are not, the court should still be informed because the time estimate will almost certainly be considerably reduced. Settlements of the substantive dispute reached in advance of trial are usually made between the parties' solicitors in correspondence (by letter or fax) or over the telephone. The agreed settlement is itself a contract, so is binding even if it is not made into a formal order of the court (*Thakrar v Ciro Citterio Menswear plc* [2002] EWHC 1975 (Ch), LTL 1/10/2002, where the court had refused to approve a draft Tomlin order). Giving written notice of the settlement or discontinuance at least seven days before the hearing will result in a refund of the hearing fee (see **45.13, 46.12, 47.21**). The percentage refund in fast track and multi-track claims is 100 per cent if the court is notified more than 28 days before the hearing; 75 per cent if notified between 15 and 28 days before the hearing; 50 per cent if notified between seven and 14 days before the hearing (**CPFO, notes following fee 2.3**). 61.15

The parties are under a duty to keep the Clerk of the Lists (in the Queen's Bench Division) or Chancery Judges' Listing Officer informed about negotiations for settlement and other matters having an impact on the likely length of the trial (Queen's Bench Guide, para. 9.8.1; Chancery Guide, paras 6.13 and 6.14). This duty continues through to the time judgment is delivered, see **63.3**.

PRE-TRIAL ARRANGEMENTS

Trial timetables

The court must, in consultation with the parties, set a timetable for the trial, unless it considers that it would be inappropriate to do so (**CPR, rr. 28.6 and 29.8**). In multi-track cases, if there is a pre-trial review, that is the occasion when the court should set the trial timetable. In other cases on the fast or multi-tracks, the court sets the timetable either at a listing hearing 61.16

(which should rarely be required) or when (or shortly after) it lists the case for trial (**rr. 28.6(1)** and **29.8(i)**). When the court sets a trial timetable it will do so in consultation with the parties (**r. 39.4**). If no trial timetable is laid down before trial, the trial judge may lay down a timetable at the start of the trial (**PD 28, para. 8.3**, for fast track cases; **PD 29, para. 10.3**, for cases on the multi-track).

Parties will need to make sure that any views they might have regarding the trial timetable are notified to the court at the same time as they file their pre-trial checklists. Among the matters to be considered are:

(a) whether an opening speech is required on behalf of the claimant, and if so, how long will be required for this;
(b) how much time will be required in chief to elucidate or expand upon the witness statements relied upon on behalf of the client;
(c) which of the other side's witnesses it will be necessary to cross-examine, and which of their witnesses' evidence can be agreed, whether in whole or in part (and if the latter, which parts);
(d) how much of the expert evidence can be agreed, and how many of the experts need to be called to give oral evidence at the trial;
(e) how long each of the closing speeches will require.

Other factors will include whether the trial should be limited to certain specified issues; the order in which witnesses should be called; and the length of time required for delivery of judgment and arguments about costs and any other outstanding matters. It is important that the trial timetable laid down is realistic because, unless the trial judge makes an order to the contrary, the trial will follow the pattern laid down in the timetable (**rr. 28.7** and **29.9**).

One of the objects in setting trial timetables is to limit the length of trials. The time given will therefore usually be restrictive. Advocates will consequently be forced to give even more careful consideration to the questions they want to put to the various witnesses, as time in court will be at a premium. The *Woolf Report* recognised that more time will be required for preparation, which is why recommendation 50 was that there would be no sittings on Fridays.

Statement of issues

61.17 One of the matters to be considered on a pre-trial review (if one is held) is the preparation of a statement of the issues to be tried. In complex cases this document will assist in focusing on the matters that need to be dealt with. In Admiralty and Commercial Court cases a list of issues must be compiled in accordance with the Admiralty and Commercial Courts Guide, para. D6, after the defence has been served. The court may decide to use some of its more far-reaching case management powers to ensure the trial is focused on what the court regards as the real issues in the case, rather than what the parties may want to keep in issue if they can. The court, for example, has power to:

(a) decide which issues need full investigation at trial, and to dispose of the others summarily (such as by fixing a summary judgment hearing of its own initiative: **CPR, r. 1.4(2)(c)**);
(b) direct that part of the proceedings be dealt with separately (**r. 3.1(2)(e)**);
(c) order the trial of preliminary issues, or the split trial of liability and quantum or other issues (**r. 3.1(2)(i)**, **(l)**, and see **61.43** to **61.60**;
(d) decide the order in which issues are to be resolved or tried (**rr. 1.4(2)(d)** and **3.1(2)(j)**);
(e) give directions on the issues on which it requires evidence (**r. 32.1(1)(a)**);
(f) give directions on the nature of the evidence it requires to decide the issues it identifies (**r. 32.1(1)(b)**); and
(g) direct how the evidence is to be placed before the court (**r. 32.1(1)(c)**).

In multi-track cases, **PD 29, paras 5.6** and **5.7**, provide that the parties are required to consider, before the court holds a case management conference, whether a case summary will be helpful.

This is not quite the same thing as a statement of issues, but is a document designed to assist the court in understanding the issues and questions in the case. The document should be no more than 500 words, should set out a brief chronology, must state the issues of fact which are agreed and in dispute, and should set out the evidence required to decide the disputed issues.

Reading guides and skeletons

Skeleton arguments are required for almost all High Court trials, and are often desirable for county court trials. Directions for the exchange of skeletons are often incorporated in ordinary case management directions. Normally skeletons are exchanged simultaneously. In the Queen's Bench Division, they should be filed in the Listing Office not less than two days before the trial (Queen's Bench Guide, para. 7.11.11). In the Chancery Division they should be filed with the trial bundles (Chancery Guide, para. 7.47). In complex claims sequential disclosure may be ordered, but the time between disclosure of the claimant's skeleton and that of the defendant should be short, giving the defendant time simply to refashion a draft rather than to formulate the entire argument (*Brown v Bennett* (2000) *The Times*, 13 June 2000). The discussion on skeleton arguments and authorities at **32.18** and **32.19** applies equally to trial skeletons. See Queen's Bench Guide, paras 7.11.11 and 7.11.12, and Chancery Guide, paras 7.49 to 7.52. For the practice in the Admiralty and Commercial Courts see the Admiralty and Commercial Courts Guide, paras J5 and J6 and app. 9. In the High Court, advocates must also provide reading lists for the trial judge, see **59.8**. **61.18**

In addition to the trial bundles the trial judge has a discretion about what other material to read by way of pre-trial preparation, and may read material containing inadmissible evidence (*Barings plc v Coopers and Lybrand* [2001] EWCA Civ 1163, [2001] CPLR 451).

Commentary

Disposal without an oral hearing

The *Final Report*, recommendation 49, was that suitable cases be determined on the statements of case without the need for an oral hearing, where this would save time and costs. **CPR, r. 1.4(2)(j)**, implements this by providing that active case management includes a power to deal with cases without the parties needing to attend at court. This power is used most often in cases raising straightforward points of construction or law, where the facts are agreed or not in dispute. However, the power cannot be exercised without the consent of the parties given the provisions of the European Convention on Human Rights, **art. 6(1)**, in the **Human Rights Act 1998, sch. 1**. **61.19**

Hearings in public and in private

The general rule in **CPR, r. 39.2(1)**, is that trials will be conducted in public. The general rule does not, however, impose an obligation to make special arrangements for accommodating members of the public. By way of exception to the general rule, **r. 39.2(3)** provides that hearings may be conducted in private if: **61.20**

(a) publicity would defeat the object of the hearing;
(b) it involves matters relating to national security;
(c) it involves confidential information (including information relating to personal financial matters) and publicity would damage that confidentiality; (see **37.44** and **37.45** for super-injunctions and anonymity orders);
(d) a private hearing is necessary to protect the interests of any child or patient;
(e) it is a hearing of an application made without notice and it would be unjust to any respondent for there to be a public hearing;
(f) it involves uncontentious matters arising in the administration of trusts or in the administration of a deceased's estate; or
(g) the court considers this to be necessary, in the interests of justice.

Further, the court may order that the identity of any party or witness must not be disclosed if it considers non-disclosure necessary in order to protect the interests of that party or witness (**CPR, r. 39.2(4)**).

This accords with the European Convention on Human Rights, **art. 6(1)**, in the **Human Rights Act 1998, sch. 1** which provides that everyone is entitled to a fair and public hearing, and goes on to say that:

> Judgment shall be pronounced publicly but the press and public may be excluded from all or part of the trial in the interests of morals, public order or national security in a democratic society, where the interests of juveniles or the protection of the private life of the parties so require, or to the extent strictly necessary in the opinion of the court in special circumstances where publicity would prejudice the interests of justice.

PD 39A, para. 1.4A, provides that in deciding whether to hold a hearing in public or private the judge must have regard to the European Convention on Human Rights, art. 6(1). Proceedings under the Prevention of Terrorism Act 2005 are often held in private (**CPR, r. 76.22**). As there will often be 'closed material' (see **r. 76.28**) in cases under this Act, the Attorney General may appoint a 'special advocate' to represent the interests of the relevant party (**r. 76.23**). *Secretary of State for the Home Department v AHK* [2009] EWCA Civ 287, [2009] 1 WLR 2049 deals with the discretion to appoint a special advocate in these cases. Similar, and extended, provisions dealing with closed material procedures will be made by the Justice and Security Act 2013 when ss. 6 to 14 are brought into force. These provisions will apply to all civil proceedings, and cover sensitive material, which means material which, if disclosed, would be injurious to the public interest (s. 6(11)).

It takes truly exceptional circumstances to justify anonymising the identity of a litigant given the potent public interest in justice being administered in public (*Commissioners of HM Revenue and Customs v Banerjee (No. 2)* [2009] EWHC 1229 (Ch), [2009] 3 All ER 930). See **63.35**.

A newspaper making an unsuccessful application for a hearing to be held in public may be ordered to pay costs if the application causes unnecessary disruption to the hearing (*A v Times Newspapers Ltd* [2002] EWHC 2444 (Fam), [2003] 1 All ER 587).

Guidance on live text messaging and the use of electronic devices in court is given in Practice Guidance (Court Proceedings: Live Text-based Communications) (No. 2) [2012] 1 WLR 12 (reproduced in **appendix 1**). An informal application to use a mobile phone, small laptop or similar piece of equipment to make live text-based communications about proceedings heard in public can be made through the court staff. Primarily this is to assist the media with the fair and accurate reporting of proceedings. Permission may be refused, for example, if it would cause a distraction, or interfere with the court's own recording equipment.

Hearings in private

61.21 Hearing all or part of a trial in private is exceptional, and should be ordered only where it is necessary, in the interests of justice, to do so (*Three Rivers District Council v Bank of England* [2005] EWCA Civ 933, LTL 18/8/2005) (or necessary and proportionate, *G v Wikimedia Foundation Inc.* [2009] EWHC 3148 (QB), LTL 7/12/2009). A number of specific types of proceedings which will, initially, be listed to be conducted in private are set out in **PD 39A, para. 1.5**, broadly as follows:

(a) mortgage possession claims against individuals;
(b) repossession claims for non-payment of rent in respect of dwelling houses;
(c) most hearings relating to the enforcement and execution of judgments, including applications to suspend warrants, applications to vary or suspend payment of judgment debts by instalments, applications for charging orders, third party debt orders, attachment of earnings, administration orders, the appointment of receivers, and obtaining information from judgment debtors;

(d) the determination of an assisted person's liability for costs under the Community Legal Service (Costs) Regulations 2000 (SI 2000/441), regs 9 and 10, and the Civil Legal Aid (General) Regulations 1989, reg. 127;
(e) applications for security for costs under **CPR, r. 25.13(2)(c)**;
(f) proceedings under the Consumer Credit Act 1974;
(g) proceedings under the Inheritance (Provision for Family and Dependants) Act 1975;
(h) proceedings under the Protection from Harassment Act 1997;
(i) hearings which involve the interests of a child or patient **CPR, r. 39.2(3)(d); PD 39A, para. 1.6**); and
(j) application by a trustee or personal representative for directions as to bringing or defending legal proceedings. It has been held in *Re Trusts of X Charity* [2003] EWHC 1462 (Ch), [2003] 1 WLR 2751, that applications by trustees for directions are essentially administrative, designed to provide guidance to the fiduciary, and therefore do not engage the European Convention on Human Rights, art. 6(1), at all, and so may be conducted entirely in private.

Whether a hearing that has taken place was in public or in private is a question of fact. **PD 39A, para. 1.5**, is not a deeming provision, so just because a hearing comes within one of the above categories does not make the hearing one held in private unless the public were in fact excluded (*North Shore Ventures Ltd v Anstead Holdings Inc. (No. 2)* [2011] EWHC 910 (Ch), [2011] 1 WLR 2265).

All arbitration claims (see **chapter 72**) other than hearings determining points of law under the Arbitration Act 1996, s. 45, and appeals under s. 69, are, subject to any order of the court, heard in private (**CPR, r. 62.10**). The presumption is that most arbitration claims will be heard in private (*Moscow City Council v Bankers Trust Co.* (2003) *The Times*, 1 September 2003).

By virtue of the **Human Rights Act 1998, s. 6**, read in conjunction with the Senior Courts Act 1981, s. 37, the court has the power to make an anonymity order restraining the publication of the name of a party to proceedings (*Re Guardian News and Media Ltd* [2010] UKSC 1, [2010] 2 AC 697). These orders are exceptional, because the usual rule is that judicial proceedings are held in public, parties are named in judgments, and full details may be reported in the media and law reports. Anonymity orders can be essential where the nature of the proceedings may impact on an individual's private and family life. The cases where this has been considered have raised issues related to possible international terrorism. In these cases there may also be a press interest in reporting full details. These cases potentially therefore raise competing claims which need to be weighed for:

(a) anonymity under the European Convention on Human Rights, **art. 8** in the **Human Rights Act 1998**; and
(b) the right to publish under **art. 10**.

Neither article has precedence over the other, so the weight to be attached on either side of the balance depends on the facts of the case.

In *Re Guardian News and Media Ltd* the interests of the media prevailed, in part because the whereabouts of two of the individuals was unknown, which limited the level of the **art. 8** interests, partly because some of the information was already in the public domain, and because of the legitimate public interest in the publication of a full account. In *Secretary of State for the Home Department v AP (No. 2)* [2010] UKSC 26, [2010] 1 WLR 1652, the balance favoured making an anonymity order. The press were not represented, and the individuals pointed to risks of violence and disruption to their family life.

Where a hearing is to proceed in private a sign will be place on the door to the court or room where a hearing is taking place to that effect. After a hearing in private the order drawn up will be clearly marked in the title 'Before [name of judge] sitting in private'.

Anyone other than a party will not be allowed to obtain a copy of the judgment or the order except with the permission of the judge who decided the matter (**PD 39A,**

para. 1.12). On the other hand, if the hearing was in public anyone can obtain copies of the judgment and order after paying the appropriate fee. Under the Administration of Justice Act 1960, the publication of information relating to proceedings before any court sitting in private is not of itself a contempt of court except in a number of specified cases. These include where the court sits in private for reasons of national security (s. 12(1)(c)), and where the court expressly prohibits the publication of all information relating to the proceedings (s. 12(1)(e)). An order for a hearing to take place in private under **CPR, r. 39.2(3)**, does not render all information in the proceedings secret (*A. F. Noonan (Architectural Practice) Ltd v Bournemouth and Boscombe Athletic Community Football Club Ltd* [2007] EWCA Civ 848, [2007] 1 WLR 2614). Giving an interview to the press about details in such a hearing will not be a contempt of court unless there is also an express order prohibiting publication of such information under the Administration of Justice Act 1960, s. 12(1)(e).

Privacy of family cases

61.22 No confidentiality attaches to witness statements, affidavits and the events in proceedings in the Family Division relating to money or property where no children are involved, even if the proceedings are heard in chambers (*Clibbery v Allan* [2002] EWCA Civ 45, [2002] Fam 261). Restricting publication of such material would be a restriction on the freedom of expression guaranteed by the European Convention on Human Rights, **art. 10**, in the **Human Rights Act 1998, sch. 1** and such a restriction could not be justified by reference to **arts 8** (right to respect for private and family life) and **6** (right to a fair trial). The denial of a hearing and pronouncement of judgment in public in child custody proceedings under what is now the Family Procedure Rules 2010 (SI 2010/2955), r. 27.10, is justifiable under **art. 6(1)** of the Convention (*B v United Kingdom* (2001) 34 EHRR 19).

Mortgage possession claims

61.23 Regarding claims by mortgagees against individuals for possession of land, where the hearing is listed to be held in private (as will be normal), **PD 39A, para. 1.15**, provides that any fact which needs to be proved by the evidence of witnesses may be proved by evidence in writing.

Term times and vacations

61.24 Sittings of the High Court and Court of Appeal, and the vacation arrangements for the High Court, are dealt with in **PD 39B**. The four sittings are:

Michaelmas: from 1 October to 21 December;
Hilary: from 11 January to the Wednesday before Easter Sunday;
Easter: from the second Tuesday after Easter Sunday to the Friday before the spring holiday at the end of May; and
Trinity: from the second Tuesday after the spring holiday to 31 July.

Where a claim proceeding in London needs to be heard immediately or promptly during a vacation, an application should be made for the claim to be heard in vacation (**PD 39B, para. 2.1(1)** and **(2)**) by the vacation judge. This provision was fully analysed in *Esso Petroleum Co. Ltd v Dawn Property Co. Ltd* [1973] 1 WLR 1450. No application which does not fall strictly within this category will be dealt with during vacation. For proceedings in the Queen's Bench Division, **para. 2.5** lists 10 types of application which may be listed for hearing before a master during August without first seeking permission. They include applications such as for extensions of time, setting aside judgment and approval of settlements. Likewise, Queen's Bench Division appeals to the judge during August will generally be limited to the 10 listed types of hearing. Applications to the judge in the Queen's Bench Division during August should be restricted to matters of real urgency (**para. 2.3(2)**). During September all types of applications and appeals may be made in the Queen's Bench Division, but a September hearing date may not be obtainable. Where it is important to have a Queen's Bench Division application or appeal heard in August or September it is wise to include a request with the papers to have the application marked 'fit for August' or 'fit for vacation' (see **para. 2.3(3)**).

In the Chancery Division masters deal with all types of application throughout the summer, with deputies dealing with much of the work during this period (**para. 2.4**). For High Court district registry cases circuit arrangements may be made for sittings in vacation (**para. 2.2**). When the vacation judge is not sitting in court, applications may be made if necessary, but only in cases of extreme urgency, to the judge personally. The address of the judge must first be obtained through the clerk to the judge on vacation duty, whose telephone number may be obtained from the listing office to the appropriate division, or, where the offices are closed, at the security office ((020) 7947 6260). Applications to the judge personally are not to be made except after reference to the judge's clerk or the office responsible for listing for the appropriate division.

Commentary

Trial location

Normally trials will take place at the court where the case has been proceeding, but it may be **61.25** transferred to another court for trial if this is appropriate having regard to the convenience of the parties and the availability of court resources (**PD 28, para. 8.1**, for the fast track; **PD 29, para. 10.1**, for cases on the multi-track). Multi-track cases will generally have been transferred to civil trial centres when allocated to the multi-track (if commenced in a feeder court), but they may be allowed to proceed elsewhere if that is appropriate given the needs of the parties and the availability of court resources.

Allocation to judiciary

While district judges in county courts have trial jurisdiction in claims allocated to the small **61.26** claims and fast tracks (**PD 2B, para. 11.1(a)**), the general rule is that claims on the multi-track are tried by county court and High Court judges (**paras 4.1 and 11.1(a)**). Small claims will be tried by a circuit judge only with his or her consent (**para. 11.2**).

There are slight differences between the rules on the trial jurisdiction of masters and district judges in the High Court and in county courts. In the High Court they have trial jurisdiction over Part 8 claims which are allocated to the multi-track by **r. 8.9(c)**, but they may try Part 7 claims only if the parties consent (**PD 2B, para. 4.1**). They can try assessments of damages with no monetary limit (**para. 4.2**).

County court district judges can try Part 8 claims allocated to the multi-track under **r. 8.9(c)** and also various other Part 8 claims as listed in **PD 8A, section B**, other than those listed in **PD 2B, para. 11.1(a)**. County court district judges can also try proceedings for the recovery of land and related landlord and tenant claims (**para. 11.1(b)**), assessments of damages (**para. 11.1(c)**) and any other proceedings with the permission of the designated civil judge (**para. 11.1(d)**).

In addition, there are restrictions on the jurisdiction of masters and district judges to grant or vary injunctions (**paras 2.2** and **2.3** for the High Court, **paras 8.1** to **8.3** for the county courts). These broadly allow county court district judges to grant these remedies in small claims and fast track cases, and district judges and masters in both courts to grant an injunction if its terms have been agreed or if it is ancillary to enforcement procedures. For the jurisdiction to make committal orders, see **81.8** and **88.11**.

Impartiality of judge

61.27 It has long been established that a judge must not sit in his or her own cause. The rule laid down in *Dimes v Proprietors of Grand Junction Canal* (1852) 3 HL Cas 759 by Lord Campbell is now interpreted as not being confined to a claim in which the judge is a party, but applies also to a claim in which the outcome could, realistically, affect an interest of the judge. In *R v Bow Street Metropolitan Stipendiary Magistrate, ex parte Pinochet Ugarte (No. 2)* [2000] 1 AC 119 the House of Lords held that the principle that a judge is automatically disqualified from hearing a matter in his or her own cause is not limited to cases where the judge has a pecuniary interest in the outcome, but applies also to cases where the judge's decision would lead to the promotion of a cause in which the judge was involved together with one of the parties. The automatic disqualification rule is subject to the *de minimis* principle, in that some supposed financial interests are so small they can be ignored (*Locabail (UK) Ltd v Bayfield Properties Ltd* [2000] QB 451). The same principles apply to arbitrators (*AT and T Corporation v Saudi Cable Co.* [2000] 2 Lloyd's Rep 127).

Under the European Convention on Human Rights, **art. 6(1)**, in the **Human Rights Act 1998, sch. 1**, litigants are entitled to a fair hearing before an impartial tribunal. ECHR jurisprudence has established that there will be a breach where the existence of a legitimate reason or fear of a lack of impartiality is objectively justified. Before the implementation of the Convention, the House of Lords had held that a judge should not sit if there is a real danger of bias (*R v Gough* [1993] AC 646). A synthesis of the two tests was accomplished by the Court of Appeal in *Re Medicaments and Related Classes of Goods (No. 2)* [2001] 1 WLR 700, where the court laid down a two-stage test. In *Porter v Magill* [2001] UKHL 67, [2002] 2 AC 357, Lord Bingham of Cornhill approved this two-stage test, but said that the reference to 'a real danger' of bias in the test should be deleted. The words no longer serve any useful purpose and have not been used in the jurisprudence of the European Court of Human Rights. Following *Porter v Magill*, the test for bias can, according to *Taylor v Lawrence* [2002] EWCA Civ 90, [2003] QB 528, and *Lawal v Northern Spirit Ltd* [2003] UKHL 35, [2003] ICR 856, be formulated as follows:

> The court must first ascertain all the circumstances which have a bearing on the suggestion that the judge was biased. It must then ask whether those circumstances would lead a fair-minded and informed observer to conclude that there was a real possibility that the tribunal was biased.

It was also said in *Taylor v Lawrence* that a judge should be circumspect about declaring the existence of a relationship where there is no real possibility of a fair-minded and informed observer regarding it as raising a possibility of bias. If it is clear that there is no possibility of bias being perceived, no purpose is served by mentioning the relationship. If it is clear that bias might be perceived, it is important that disclosure should be made. If the position is borderline, disclosure should be made so that the judge can consider, having heard the parties' submissions, whether to withdraw.

61.28 **Application of the informed observer test** An informed observer will be aware of the legal traditions and culture of this jurisdiction. In England and Wales judges are members of the legal profession and have regular contract with other members of the profession. The fact that a judge receives free legal services from the solicitors representing a party to a claim being heard by the judge would not, according to a five-judge Court of Appeal in *Taylor v Lawrence* [2002] EWCA Civ 90, [2003] QB 528, lead a fair-minded and informed observer to conclude that there was a real possibility that the judge was biased. Nor is there any apparent bias where the judge calls counsel into the judges' corridor to inform them that he thinks the case is weak and that the parties should consider a settlement (*Hart v Relentless Records Ltd* [2002] EWHC 1984 (Ch), *The Times*, 8 October 2002). There was no apparent bias in *Taylor v Williamsons* [2002] EWCA Civ 1380, [2003] CP Rep 20, where the judge forgot he had not heard final submissions, and had to withdraw his judgment when this was pointed out, and so could give judgment after considering final submissions.

Observing at the start of a trial that a party has no case gives the appearance of an inability to try the claim objectively (*Co-operative Group Ltd v International Computers Ltd* [2003] EWCA Civ 1955, *The Times*, 19 January 2004). It is unacceptable for a judge to form, or to give the impression of having formed, a firm view on the credibility of the evidence of one side before the other side has called any evidence (*Steadman-Byrne v Amjad* [2007] EWCA Civ 625, *The Times*, 30 July 2007). A judge should have recused himself in *Ealing London Borough Council v Jan* [2002] EWCA Civ 329, LTL 7/2/2002, having on a previous occasion twice stated in strong terms that he did not trust the defendant, even though the comments related to a different issue from the one to be determined in the subsequent hearing.

In *Re Medicaments and Related Classes of Goods (No. 2)* [2001] 1 WLR 700 one of the three members of the Restrictive Practices Court was an economist who had applied for a job during the course of the proceedings with a firm, one of whose members was providing expert evidence for one of the parties. When the member of the court realised the problem she immediately cancelled her job application and informed the parties, and the firm wrote stating that it had no jobs available in any event. It was held that a fair-minded observer would apprehend there was a real danger that the member of the court could not make an objective and impartial appraisal of the expert evidence. Before the start of a tribunal hearing in *Turner v Harada Ltd* [2001] EWCA Civ 599, LTL 6/4/2001, the chairman said: 'This is the seventh time that [Harada] have appeared here in the last six months....[They] turn up with excuses and arguments to avoid matters going to trial...it is not as though [they] come here with a slate which is exactly clean'. It was held that a fair-minded observer would have concluded there was a real danger of bias. A judge who has decided a case is not precluded from reconsidering the case after it is remitted following a successful appeal (*Secretary of State for the Home Department v AF (No. 2)* [2007] EWHC 2828 (Admin), [2008] 2 All ER 67). In *Lawal v Northern Spirit Ltd* [2003] UKHL 35, [2003] ICR 856, it was held that the practice of leading counsel who have appeared as advocates before the Employment Appeal Tribunal being appointed to sit as part-time judges in the same tribunal did not infringe the bias rule. However, it tended to undermine public confidence in the system and should be discontinued.

There will be an injustice if the judge was predisposed or prejudiced against one party's case for reasons unconnected with the merits of the case (see *R v Inner West London Coroner, ex parte Dallaglio* [1994] 4 All ER 139). Guidance on situations where there may be a real danger of bias was given by the Court of Appeal in *Locabail (UK) Ltd v Bayfield Properties Ltd* [2000] QB 451, which is of particular relevance to cases dealt with by solicitor and barrister deputy judges. The Court of Appeal could not conceive of circumstances in which an objection could be soundly based on the religion (see also *Seer Technologies Inc. v Abbas* (2000) *The Times*, 16 March 2000), ethnic or national origin, gender, age, class, means or sexual orientation of the judge. Membership of the International Association of Jewish Lawyers and Jurists did not give rise to a real possibility of bias in a judge dealing with an immigration appeal by a Palestinian seeking asylum (*Helow v Secretary of State for the Home Department* [2008] UKHL 62, [2008] 1 WLR 2416). Nor, at least ordinarily, could there be a valid objection based on the judge's social, educational, service or employment background, nor that of any member of his or her family. Nor could an objection be based on previous political associations, membership of social, sporting or charitable bodies, or Masonic associations; previous judicial decisions; extra-curial utterances, whether in textbooks, lectures, speeches, articles (but see *Hoekstra v HM Advocate (No. 2)* 2000 JC 391 discussed in **91.48**), interviews, reports or responses to consultation papers; previous receipt of instructions to act for or against any party, solicitor or advocate engaged in the current case; or membership of the same Inn, circuit, local Law Society or chambers. By contrast, there might be a real danger of bias if there was personal friendship or animosity between the judge and anyone other than the lawyers involved in the present case; or if the judge was closely acquainted with a witness whose credibility was in issue; or if the judge had ruled against the credibility of a witness in a previous case in outspoken terms such as to cast doubt on whether the judge could deal with the witness in the current case with an open mind

Commentary

(but not if the judge had commented adversely on a party or witness in a previous case in temperate terms); or if the judge had expressed views on a matter also in issue in the present case in such extreme terms as to throw into doubt his or her ability to try the case objectively. If there is any doubt, it should be exercised in favour of refusing to sit.

Impartiality may be thrown into doubt where a judge has had a direct involvement in the passage of legislation or of executive rules relevant to the case (*McGonnell v United Kingdom* (2000) 30 EHRR 289, in which the European Court of Human Rights held there was an infringement of art. 6(1) of the European Convention on Human Rights in Guernsey).

An appearance of bias where a witness is well known to the judge cannot be removed, even by the party intending to call the witness deciding not to call him, and substituting alternative witnesses (*Morrison v AWG Group Ltd* [2006] EWCA Civ 6, *The Independent*, 25 January 2006). In such a case the safe course is to remove all possibility of apparent bias by recusal of the judge.

61.29 **Bias and conflicting interests: procedure** Judges are obliged to mention any possible conflict when they become aware of its existence. Wherever possible this is done in advance of the commencement of the trial, so as to avoid the expense of an adjournment. If the matter becomes apparent at the commencement of a hearing (or during its course), the judge should mention it and the parties must consider whether they will waive the difficulty or ask the judge to decline to act or withdraw. Counsel should not seek to influence the decision of the client, whether by referring to the judge's integrity or (surprisingly) the costs that would be thrown away (in a case where the costs would be met by a trade union) (*Smith v Kvaerner Cementation Foundations Ltd* [2006] EWCA Civ 242, [2007] 1 WLR 370). Any challenge based on apparent bias must be made when it arises, rather than awaiting the result of the hearing (*Steadman-Byrne v Amjad* [2007] EWCA Civ 625, *The Times*, 30 July 2007). The judge will give great weight to the parties' wishes, particularly if the hearing has already commenced (or if there is no other available judge). A judge who doubts his or her ability to be impartial will withdraw, even if the parties do not require it. If the parties waive their right to object, they cannot later raise the matter by way of appeal. See *Locabail (UK) Ltd v Bayfield Properties Ltd* [2000] QB 451.

Where proceedings are abandoned because of the appearance of bias on the part of a member of the court, the Lord Chancellor is not liable for any of the costs incurred at the wasted hearing (*Re Medicaments and Related Classes of Goods (No. 4)* [2001] EWCA Civ 1217, [2002] 1 WLR 269).

Rights of audience

61.30 Rights of audience and the right to conduct litigation are reserved legal activities within the meaning of the Legal Services Act 2007 (s. 12 and sch. 2). The only persons entitled to carry on these activities are regulated persons authorised to do so by an approved regulator and persons who are exempt in relation to the relevant activity (ss. 13 and 176). Approved regulators include the Law Society, the General Council of the Bar, the Chartered Institute of Legal Executives, the Council for Licensed Conveyancers and the Association of Law Costs Draftsmen (sch. 4). As a result, the following persons have rights of audience:

(a) litigants in person (who are exempt, sch. 3, para. 1(6));
(b) counsel;
(c) solicitors;
(d) members of the Chartered Institute of Legal Executives;
(e) members of the Association of Law Costs Draftsmen;
(f) persons given express permission by the court in relation to the relevant proceedings (who are exempt, sch. 3, para. 1(2)); and
(g) persons given an express right of audience by statute (an example being the right given to local authority officers to present rent and possession claims on behalf of their employers under the County Courts Act 1984, s. 60).

A barrister who has not undertaken pupillage and who does not have a practising certificate (even if that person has appropriate professional indemnity insurance, provides details of his work to the Bar Council and makes his status clear to clients) is not authorised for the purpose of rights of audience in the courts (*R v K* [2008] EWCA Crim 1900, [2009] 1 WLR 694). Solicitors must comply with the Law Society advocacy qualifications before they can conduct High Court trials.

Members of the Association of Law Costs Draftsmen may be certified by the Association with rights of audience (Association of Law Costs Draftsmen Order 2006, SI 2006/3333). Unqualified costs negotiators are not properly instructed as agents of solicitors and therefore do not have rights of audience (*Ahmed v Powell* [2003] PNLR 22). A person with an enduring power of attorney does not have, in that capacity, a right of audience (*Gregory v Turner* [2003] EWCA Civ 183, [2003] 1 WLR 1149).

Practice Direction (Court Dress) (No. 4) [2008] 1 WLR 357 was made to ensure that solicitors and other authorised advocates are not precluded from wearing wigs when appearing in court.

Dress requirements for advocates appearing in the Senior Courts and in county courts are:

(a) Queen's Counsel wear a short wig and a silk (or stuff) gown over a court coat;
(b) junior counsel wear a short wig and stuff gown with bands;
(c) solicitors and other authorised advocates wear a black solicitor's gown with bands, and they may wear short wigs in circumstances where they would be worn by Queen's Counsel or junior counsel.

Under Practice Direction (Court Dress) (No. 5) [2008] 1 WLR 1700, a civil judge must wear a gown without wig or bands when sitting in court, whether in public or private. The relevant Head of Division or the Senior Presiding Judge may agree for good reason that a gown should not be worn.

Legal representative prejudicing administration of justice The court has a power to grant an injunction to restrain a legal representative from appearing at a hearing if continued participation would lead to any order made being set aside on appeal (*Geveran Trading Co. Ltd v Skjevesland* [2002] EWCA Civ 1567, [2003] 1 WLR 912). Such applications are not governed by the same principles as apply regarding the impartiality of judges (see **61.27** to **61.28**), and the court must not be too ready to remove an advocate from a case. Advocates have no obligation not to be partisan. An advocate who is aware of a personal factor making his or her continued participation likely to prejudice the administration of justice or cause a procedural irregularity should withdraw, and must disclose to the other side any personal factor which might reasonably be regarded as open to objection. **61.31**

McKenzie friends The phrase McKenzie Friend ('MF') comes from *McKenzie v McKenzie* [1971] P 33, and describes an unqualified person who assists a litigant who would otherwise be acting in person. The primary function of a MF is to provide moral support for a litigant at a hearing (a 'basic MF'). A MF is not permitted to conduct litigation or act as an advocate without the court's permission. Practice Note (McKenzie Friends: Civil and Family Courts) [2010] 1 WLR 1881 (the 'President's Guidance') sets out to provide guidance for all courts and is based on various decisions of the courts. The guidance provides that a MF may: **61.32**

(a) provide moral support for the litigant;
(b) take notes;
(c) help with case papers; and
(d) quietly give advice on points of law or procedure, issues the litigant may wish to raise in court, and questions the litigant may wish to ask witnesses. The litigant is permitted to communicate any information, including filed evidence, to the MF for these purposes.

The President's Guidance says a MF:

(a) has no right to act on behalf of a litigant. It is the right of the litigant who wishes to receive reasonable assistance from a MF;
(b) has no right to address the court, or examine witnesses. Any person doing these is an advocate, and requires the grant of a right of audience (see **61.34**); and
(c) may not act as the litigant's agent in relation to the proceedings, nor manage the litigant's case outside court, such as by signing court documents.

There are different rules for small claims track hearings, see **45.21**.

61.33 **Application to be a basic McKenzie friend** The President's Guidance says a litigant in person intending to make a request for the assistance of a MF should make the application as soon as possible, indicating who the MF will be. The proposed MF should:

(a) provide a short curriculum vitae or other statement setting out his or her relevant experience;
(b) confirm that he or she has no interest in the case;
(c) confirm that he or she understands the role of a MF, and the duty of confidentiality.

The MF is entitled to attend the application, and to assist the litigant in making the application.

A litigant has a right to reasonable assistance from a lay person, and should be permitted to have a basic MF except where fairness and the interests of justice indicate that the assistance of a MF is not required. It is for the court or the objecting party to provide sufficient reasons why the litigant should not receive such assistance. There is a strong presumption in favour of permitting a basic MF, and it is for the objecting party to rebut this presumption. It will not be rebutted merely because the proceedings relate to a child or are to be heard in private or are confidential or that the court papers contain sensitive information about a family's affairs. Nor is it rebutted where the litigant appears to be capable of conducting the case alone, that the litigant is acting in person through choice, that the objecting party is unrepresented, that the hearing is for case management purposes, or that the proposed MF belongs to an organisation promoting a particular cause.

Reasons for denying a litigant the assistance of a MF (President's Guidance, para. 13) include where the assistance is being provided for an improper purpose, the assistance is unreasonable in degree or nature, the MF is subject to a civil proceedings order, the MF is using the litigant as a puppet, the MF is directly or indirectly conducting the litigation, and where the MF does not understand the duty of confidentiality.

A decision on permission for the assistance of a MF can be appealed by either party (the fourth bullet point in the President's Guidance, which says decisions granting permission should be regarded as final, deals with revisiting permission at a later stage, not appeals).

61.34 **Rights of audience for McKenzie friends** An application that a MF be permitted a right of audience must be made at the start of the hearing (*Clarkson v Gilbert* [2000] 2 FLR 839). The question for the court is whether in all the circumstances of the case the court should exercise its discretion under the Legal Services Act 2007, ss. 12 to 19. The court will be very slow to grant a MF a right of audience (*Paragon Finance plc v Noueiri* [2001] EWCA Civ 1402, [2001] 1 WLR 2357 at [67]). The way it was put in *R (Koli) v Maidstone Crown Court* [2011] EWHC 2821 (Admin), LTL 10/5/2011, was that rights of audience would only be granted in exceptional circumstances. This is because a person exercising a right of audience must ordinarily be properly trained, be under professional discipline (including an obligation to have professional liability insurance), and be subject to the overriding duty to the court (President's Guidance, para. 19). Decisions between 2000 and 2008 laying down an 'exceptional circumstances' test are per incuriam (*Re N (A Child) (McKenzie Friend: Rights of Audience)* [2008] EWHC Civ 2042 (Fam), [2008] 1 WLR 2743 at [21]).

In applying these principles, the court seeks to do justice bearing in mind that there is a spectrum between the 'professional' (but unqualified) MF (where the order will be made only in exceptional circumstances) and, at the other end, the spouse or partner of the litigant. The court will bear in mind the limited availability of public funding. An important factor is whether a right of audience is required to ensure the litigant receives a fair hearing (*Re N (A Child) (McKenzie Friend: Rights of Audience)* at [42]).

Representation of companies at hearings **Paragraphs** 5.2 to 5.6 of **PD 39A** deal with the representation of companies and corporations at hearings by employees (which is of some importance following the abolition of the rule that companies have to act by solicitors in the High Court). **CPR, r. 39.6**, provides that a company or corporation may appear at a hearing through a duly authorised employee provided the court gives permission. **PD 39A, para. 5.3**, says that permission should usually be given unless there is some particular and sufficient reason why it should be withheld. Additional factors, according to *Tracto Teknik GmbH v LKL International Pty Ltd* [2003] EWHC 1563 (Ch), [2003] 2 BCLC 519, are: whether the company is able to afford legal representation, the ability of the proposed representative to do the work required in the litigation, and whether the representative is able to understand and discharge the obligations (such as disclosure of documents) involved in the litigation. **61.35**

Permission should generally be sought on an occasion prior to the hearing, but may be granted at the hearing itself. Permission may be sought informally. Like all representatives, the employee's status has to be included in the written statement of representatives pursuant to **PD 39A, para. 5.1**. In this case the statement must include the full name and registered number of the company or corporation, the employee's position within the company, and details of the board or other authorisation for the employee to act for the company.

In considering whether to grant permission for a company or other corporation to be represented by an employee, the matters to be taken into account include the complexity of the issues and the experience and position in the company or corporation of the proposed representative (**para. 5.3**). The trial judge in *Watson v Bluemoor Properties Ltd* [2002] EWCA Civ 1875, [2003] BCC 382, refused to permit a company to be represented by a former director who had been disqualified. The Court of Appeal said that the better course in such circumstances is to adjourn to give the company an opportunity to consider whether it wishes to continue, rather than entering judgment on the basis of non-attendance. Permission should not normally be granted in jury trials or contempt proceedings (**para. 5.6**). The Admiralty and Commercial Courts Guide, para. M3, says that, because of their complexity, in most Commercial Court cases it is not appropriate for a company litigant to be represented by an employee. See **45.21** for representation of companies in small claims track hearings.

CONDUCT OF THE TRIAL

Specific guidance for Chancery Division trials is given in the Chancery Guide, ch. 8, for the Queen's Bench Division in the Queen's Bench Guide, paras 10.2.1 to 10.2.8, and for Admiralty and Commercial Court trials by the Admiralty and Commercial Courts Guide, section J. The normal sequence of events in non-specialist cases is discussed in the following paragraphs and in **61.41** to **61.49**. **61.36**

Before the hearing the court should be provided with a written statement of the name and professional address of each advocate, his or her qualification as an advocate, and the party he or she acts for (**PD 39A, para. 5.1**). This is usually done by advocates completing a slip provided by the court on the day of the hearing.

The rules give the courts a great deal of flexibility regarding how they will deal with trials. As previously discussed, the court can lay down trial timetables prescribing how the time available for the trial will be used, and allocating specified, limited times, for examination-in-chief, cross-examination and so on. The trial will then follow the timetable previously laid down, or laid down by the trial judge at the start, or will follow the traditional sequence of events.

Generally it will be the claimant who begins. However, it will be the defendant if the defendant has admitted all the issues on which the burden of proof rests on the claimant, so that the only live issues have to be proved by the defendant.

Summary disposal of issues and striking out at trial

61.37 The court has the power to strike out a claim or a severable part of a claim at the start or at any stage of a trial (**CPR, rr. 1.4, 3.3 and 3.4; PD 3A, para. 1.2**). Striking out is decided applying the no realistic prospect of success test used in summary judgment applications (see **CPR, r. 24.2**), but keeping prominently in view the disruptive effect of such an order (particularly as it may be shown to be mistaken by further evidence or on an appeal) (*National Westminster Bank plc v Rabobank Nederland* [2006] EWHC 2959 (Comm), [2007] 1 All ER (Comm) 975). Under **r. 1.4(2)(c)**, a trial judge has a power to make an order excluding certain issues from the trial. This power is additional to those for striking out (**chapter 33**) and summary judgment (**chapter 34**), but should be used sparingly and by applying the test of whether the issues in question have a real prospect of success. In *Western Broadcasting Services v Seaga* [2007] UKPC 19, [2007] EMLR 18, these powers were assumed to be wide enough to encompass deciding in a summary fashion whether settlement negotiations had resulted in a binding agreement. However, given that a final decision was being made, doing so on the basis of written evidence alone was held to be unfair and outside the ambit of these powers, and the witnesses should have been called for cross-examination. In *Steenberg v Enterprise Inns plc* [2010] EWCA Civ 201, LTL 10/3/2010, on the second day of the trial, the judge proceeded to consider a preliminary issue based on the first day's evidence of the claimants' witnesses and the witness statements of the defendants' witnesses, and then struck out the claim. This procedure was regarded as so utterly flawed (involving accepting at face value disputed evidence from the defendants' witnesses) that the Court of Appeal commented that it should never be repeated. Similar criticism of summary disposal of claims at trial can be found in *Marson v Fattah* [2010] EWCA Civ 266, LTL 18/2/2010, and *Chasewood Park Residents Ltd v Kim* [2010] EWHC 579 (Ch), [2010] NPC 41. In most cases weak issues should be disposed of well before trial, and generally use of summary disposal at trial is deprecated as potentially time wasting and expensive (see *Royal Brompton Hospital NHS Trust v Hammond* [2001] BLR 297).

Rules 3.3 and **24.4(3)**, which require notice to be given to the parties of striking-out and summary judgment hearings listed by the court on its own initiative, only cover cases where the hearing is specifically set up for that purpose, and do not cover summary disposal at trial (*James v Evans* [2003] CPLR 163). However, a failure by the trial judge to give the claimant sufficient notice of an intention to give summary judgment against the claimant at trial justified setting aside the judgment in *Orford v Rasmi Electronics Ltd* [2002] EWCA Civ 1672, [2003] CPLR 213.

Concessions by advocates and abandonment of issues

61.38 In order to simplify the issues, or for tactical reasons, trial advocates may concede specified facts, issues, or legal arguments. In the absence of exceptional circumstances, failing to argue a point at a hearing which is raised in a party's statement of case or witness statements will result in the point being taken as abandoned (*Adams v Mason Bullock* [2004] EWHC 2910 (Ch), [2005] BPIR 241). The court has a discretion to allow a concession to be withdrawn. Where a party to an appeal seeks to withdraw a concession made in the court below, the appeal court has a discretion to permit this, but will be very cautious before granting permission (*Grobbelaar v News Group Newspapers Ltd* [2002] UKHL 40, [2002] 1 WLR 3024).

Permission to withdraw a concession was granted in *New Zealand Meat Board v Paramount Export Ltd* [2004] UKPC 45, [2005] 2 NZLR 447, where there was no possibility that the outcome would have been affected had the point been taken earlier.

Rulings by the judge

Trial judges frequently hear and determine all manner of procedural and evidential applications during the course of a trial. After ruling on such matters the judge is *functus officio.* Subject to the rules discussed at 74.54, advocates are not permitted to ask for such rulings to be reopened: if they wish to take the matter further they should seek permission to appeal (*R v Lashley* [2005] EWCA Crim 2016, *The Times*, 28 September 2005). **61.39**

Daily trial transcripts

Her Majesty's Courts and Tribunals Service does not provide daily transcripts of the evidence and submissions made at hearings. Instead, hearings are recorded, and may be transcribed after the event. Requests for transcripts should be made to the court transcribing service. They are quite expensive, and tend to be used for appeal purposes (see 74.27). **61.40**

Sometimes one of the parties, particularly in important cases, will arrange for daily transcripts to be produced. Often these are purely for the use of the lawyers acting for the party who has arranged for the transcripts. Where copies are provided to the judge, they must also be provided to the other parties (*Lloyds Bank plc v Cassidy* [2004] EWCA Civ 1767, *The Times*, 11 January 2005).

Commentary

Opening speech

The trial judge will generally have read the papers in the trial bundle before the trial. It will often be the case that in those circumstances there is no need for an opening speech, which may be dispensed with (**PD 28, para. 8.2**, for the fast track; **PD 29, para. 10.2**, for cases on the multi-track). In practice the claimant's advocate will normally begin the trial with a short opening speech, and the judge may allow the other parties to make short speeches (Queen's Bench Guide, para. 10.2.3; Chancery Guide, para. 8.4). In the Queen's Bench Division advocates should provide written summaries of their opening speeches if the points are not covered in their skeleton arguments. If an opening speech is allowed, counsel for the claimant will usually describe the nature of the claim, and will identify the issues to be tried by reference to the statements of case and/or the statement of issues. Some of the documentary evidence may be referred to. It sometimes happens that the judge will rise during the course of the opening to read some of the documents. The judge usually states at an early point in the trial how much pre-reading has been possible, and will deal with arrangements for additional reading. If there is a substantial amount of additional reading needed going beyond the filed reading lists, an additional list should be provided during the opening (Chancery Guide, para. 8.5). **61.41**

It is usually convenient to deal with any outstanding procedural matters in the course of, or immediately after, the opening speeches (Queen's Bench Guide, para. 10.2.4; Chancery Guide, para. 8.6).

Claimant's case

After the claimant's opening speech evidence will be called on behalf of the claimant. Broadly, evidence adduced at trial will be real evidence (i.e. physical items), contemporaneous documentary evidence, views of the site, and the evidence of witnesses (see **chapter 49**). **61.42**

Real evidence and documents admitted into evidence are made exhibits and are labelled with individual exhibits numbers. The judge has a discretion to inspect the *locus in quo* if there are compelling reasons to do so, outweighing the time and expense of a view. Inspections should generally be conducted in the presence of the parties.

There are occasions when evidence is adduced in a deposition, by affidavit or in the form of hearsay statements.

It is rather more usual for evidence from witnesses to be produced by calling the witnesses to give evidence from the witness box. Witnesses are sometimes asked to leave the court until they are called so they are not influenced by the evidence given by other witnesses, but they remain in court in the large majority of cases. Subject to any trial directions they may be called in any order. When called they are sworn or affirm in a manner they consider binding (Oaths Act 1978). A witness will be afforded anonymity, for example, by being allowed to give evidence behind a screen and without stating his or her name and address aloud, only in highly exceptional cases (*Re W (Children) (Care Proceedings: Witness Anonymity)* [2002] EWCA Civ 1626, *The Times*, 1 November 2002).

Exhibits which are handed in and proved during the course of the trial will be recorded in an exhibit list and kept in the custody of the court until the conclusion of the trial, unless the judge directs otherwise (**PD 39A, para.** 7). At the conclusion of the trial the parties have the responsibility for taking away and preserving the exhibits pending any possible appeal.

Examination-in-chief

61.43 Traditionally witnesses would give their evidence in answer to non-leading questions put to them by counsel for the party calling them. However, under the CPR witness statements of witnesses called at trial will stand as the evidence-in-chief unless the court otherwise orders (**r.** 32.5(2)). At least in the Chancery Division, witnesses are expected to have re-read their witness statements shortly before being called to give their evidence (Chancery Guide, para. 8.11). Technically, it is only possible to augment the evidence contained in the exchanged statements if, by virtue of **r.** 32.5(3) and (4), the court considers there is good reason not to confine the witness to the contents of his or her witness statement, and for the purpose of either:

(a) amplifying the witness statement; or
(b) giving evidence in relation to new matters which have arisen since the witness statement was served on the other parties.

What will be regarded as a sufficiently 'good reason' to allow supplementary questions remains to be seen. There is a fear that different judges will take different views. Witness statements drafted in a deliberately concise way in accordance with the ethos of the *Woolf Report* as contemplated at ch. 12, paras 54 to 59, of avoiding elaborate over-drafting therefore may fall into the trap (which was also mentioned in the *Woolf Report* at chapter 12, para. 55) of encountering a trial judge who refuses to allow the witness to depart from or amplify his or her witness statement.

The trial judge is entitled to rely on additional or revised evidence on an unresolved issue from an expert based on further experiments conducted by the expert after a pre-trial meeting of the experts and before or during the hearing (*Aintree Hospitals NHS Trust v Sutcliffe* [2008] EWCA Civ 179, [2008] LS Law Medical 230).

Cross-examination

61.44 After being examined in chief, each witness may be cross-examined by counsel for the defendant. Where there is more than one defendant, they cross-examine in the order they appear on the court record. Cross-examination may be conducted using leading questions (i.e. questions which suggest the required answer). Cross-examination is permitted on the witness's statement, whether or not the statements are referred to in chief (**CPR, r. 32.11**). Cross-examination provides the other side the opportunity to test and seek to undermine the evidence given in chief. One of the main obligations on an advocate cross-examining a witness is to put his or her client's case. This means that the witness must be challenged and given an *opportunity* to comment on the points of conflict between the evidence he or she has given and the case being advanced by the cross-examining party. If this is not done, the court may decide that the witness's account is accepted. Peter Smith J gave a reminder of the importance of putting one's case positively to the other side's witnesses in *EPI Environmental Technologies Inc. v Symphony Plastic Technologies plc* [2004] EWHC 2945 (Ch), [2005] 1 WLR 3456. A failure to do so usually means the point cannot be taken against the witness in the closing speech. This has become even more important with witness statements usually standing as the examination-in-chief, as it allows the judge to assess the witness's response by reference to his or her demeanour and the overall context of the case. It was held in *Re Share* [2002] BPIR 194 that the judge was wrong to reject the evidence of two witnesses which had not been tested in cross-examination (the petitioner having elected not to cross-examine in order to save costs), even though there was documentary evidence which was flatly inconsistent with the oral testimony of those witnesses. For further discussion see **chapter 49**, particularly **49.8**.

A witness who has been cross-examined may be re-examined by counsel for the claimant on matters covered in cross-examination. Leading questions are not allowed.

Witness called by the judge

A witness who is not relied upon by either side may be called by the judge, who may conduct **61.45**
the examination. As the witness is not called by another party, neither has a right to cross-examine, although the judge has a discretion to (and will usually) allow either or both parties to do so (*Fallon v Calvert* [1960] 2 QB 201).

Submissions of no case to answer

At the conclusion of the case for the claimant, the defendant may make a submission of no **61.46**
case to answer. This is made on the basis that on the evidence adduced by the claimant the claim cannot succeed. In *Benham Ltd v Kythira Investments Ltd* [2003] EWCA Civ 1794, LTL 15/12/2003, it was said that a submission of no case to answer should rarely, if ever, be entertained in a civil case tried without a jury. As the judge is the trier both of law and fact, it is embarrassing for the judge to be asked to rule on the merits of the claim while the evidence is still incomplete. Further, if the judge's ruling were to be reversed on appeal, there would be the added cost of having a retrial. It has therefore been the practice that a defendant seeking to make a submission of no case to answer had to elect to call no evidence before making the submission (*Alexander v Rayson* [1936] 1 KB 169; *Young v Rank* [1950] 2 KB 510).

Under the CPR it remains the case that, in general, the judge may require a defendant to elect to call no evidence before making a submission of no case to answer (*Blinkhorn v Hall* (2000) LTL 13/4/2000; *Miller v Cawley* [2002] EWCA Civ 1100, *The Times*, 6 September 2002). However, there may be circumstances where a submission may be entertained without putting the defendant to an election, as in *Mullan v Birmingham City Council* (1999) *The Times*, 29 July 1999. The power to dismiss on a submission of no case to answer without putting the defendants to their election whether to call evidence should be exercised with considerable caution (*Boyce v Wyatt Engineering* [2001] EWCA Civ 692, *The Times*, 14 June 2001).

Where the court allows a defendant to make a submission of no case to answer without being required to elect whether to call no evidence, the test by which the submission is determined is whether the claim has no real prospect of success (*Benham Ltd v Kythira Investments Ltd*). On the other hand, if the defendant is put to his election and decides to call no evidence, the submission of no case to answer is decided on the basis of whether the claimant has established the case on the balance of probabilities (*Miller v Cawley* [2002] EWCA Civ 1100, *The Times*, 6 September 2002). It is a serious procedural irregularity for a judge to fail to put the defendant to its election on calling evidence, and then to decide a submission of no case to answer applying the balance of probabilities as the standard of proof (*Graham v Chorley Borough Council* [2006] EWCA Civ 92, [2006] PIQR P24). It is the judge's duty to survey the expert evidence together with that of the defendant before deciding to accede to a submission of no case to answer (*Youssif v Jordan* [2003] EWCA Civ 1852, *The Times*, 22 January 2004).

Defence case

61.47 Where the defence decide to call evidence, they may be allowed to make an opening speech (though this is now rather unusual). They then call their evidence in the same way as the claimant. Where there is more than one defendant, they present their evidence in the order they appear on the record.

Closing speeches

61.48 Where the defence has called evidence, the defence closing speech is made before that of the claimant. Speeches usually deal with how the evidence that has been adduced and the inferences that can be drawn from that evidence support the case for the party in question on the factual issues involved. Counsel also argue any legal points that arise, sometimes making use of skeleton arguments. In lengthy and complex cases, counsel should provide written summaries of their closing submissions (Chancery Guide, para. 8.7). Where a case has overrun, the judge may adjourn, or may take other measures, such as ordering closing submissions to be made in writing, to be followed by a written judgment (*Sleeman v High Care Ltd* (1999) *The Times*, 3 November 1999).

A judge who, after the close of evidence, realises he may decide the case on a new footing not addressed earlier in the trial, should give the parties a specific warning that this course may be taken, and invite them to make submissions on the matter (*Maersk Co. Ltd v Wilson* [2004] EWCA Civ 313, LTL 25/3/2004).

Role of the judge

61.49 During the course of the trial the judge may put questions to the witnesses, particularly if matters remain obscure after counsel's questions. Depending on the circumstances, it may be the judge's duty to ask questions, including leading questions, to ensure an accurate picture of the events is adduced (*Currey v Currey* [2004] EWCA Civ 1799, *The Times*, 26 November 2004). Judges should be careful to avoid interrupting the flow of counsel's questions, particularly during cross-examination (*Jones v National Coal Board* [1957] 2 QB 55, although the principles stated in this case might need to be re-evaluated because attitudes to interventions by the judge have changed since 1957, see *Almeida v CVC/Opportunity Equity Partners Ltd* [2006] UKPC 44, 2006 CILR 430). Frequent or intemperate interventions may give grounds for an appeal (*Re R (Children)* [2001] EWCA Civ 1880, LTL 7/12/2001, where there were interventions on average every 50 seconds, but compare *Priestley v Harrogate Healthcare NHS Trust* [2002] EWCA Civ 183, LTL 7/2/20029 and *Cairnstores Ltd v AB Hässle* [2002] EWCA Civ 1504, [2003] FSR 23, where appeals based on excessive intervention by the judge were dismissed). There is a more tolerant attitude to extensive judicial questioning of experts (particularly where the judge is trying to understand technical evidence) than of lay witnesses (*Manning v King's College Hospital NHS Trust* [2009] EWCA Civ 832, 110 BMLR 175). The question is whether a fair-minded and informed observer, having considered the facts, would conclude that there was a real possibility that the judge was biased (*Almeida v CVC/Opportunity Equity Partners Ltd*).

There are occasions when the judge needs to issue warnings to litigants to keep to the relevant issues and not to use intemperate language. Doing so gives no basis for the judge needing to recuse himself (*R (Riseborough) v Lands Tribunal* [2010] EWHC 1436 (Admin), LTL 25/6/2010).

The judge will have to rule on any applications and any objections to the admissibility of evidence or questions during the course of the trial.

Deciding the case

61.50 After hearing the evidence the judge must decide where the truth lies, decide any points of law, and give judgment. As Baroness Hale of Richmond said in *Re B (Children) (Care*

Proceedings: Standard of Proof) [2008] UKHL 35, [2009] 1 AC 11 at [32], the judge is guided by any inherent probabilities, contemporaneous documentation or records, any circumstantial evidence tending to support one account or the other, and impressions made as to the character and motivations of the witnesses.

Generally, the judge is constrained by the pleadings, and has to make decisions on the pleaded issues, see **24.24**. There are limited exceptions. A judge should not be deterred from deciding a case on the correct basis where, through incompetent presentation, the underlying legal cause of action has not been identified by a party's representatives (*Watson v Durham University* [2008] EWCA Civ 1266, LTL 24/10/2008). The more usual course is to require the correct basis of the claim to be formulated through amended statements of case (see **chapter 31**), which can be done even at the end of closing speeches.The claimant has the burden of proof on a balance of probabilities. It is for the claimant to prove the case, and the judge should beware of too much speculative reconstruction (*Lynch v James Lynch and Sons (Transport) Ltd* (2000) LTL 8/3/2000). The law operates a binary system in which the only values are zero and one (*Re B (Children) (Care Proceedings: Standard of Proof)* per Lord Hoffmann at [2]). There is no halfway house for the judge who concludes there is a real possibility that a fact in issue took place (per Baroness Hale at [31], [32]). If the party with the burden of proof fails to discharge that burden, the fact is treated as not having happened. If the burden of proof is discharged, the court treats the fact as having happened.

Lord Hoffmann (at [3]) distinguished between:

(a) facts in issue. These are the facts which a legal rule requires to be proved in order to establish a legal right. These have to be proved on the balance of probabilities;

(b) facts used as a basis of making a prediction, which also have to be proved on the balance of probabilities (but compare *Secretary of State for the Home Department v Rehman* [2001] UKHL 47, [2003] 1 AC 153 at [56]); and

(c) facts which merely form part of the material from which a fact in issue may be inferred, which need not be proved to have happened.

Some facts are regarded as inherently improbable, so that strong evidence is required before the court can find them proved on the balance of probabilities. Examples are fraud, deliberate harm and child abuse. There is no necessary link between seriousness and probability. Instead, inherent probabilities have to be taken into account as a factor, 'to whatever extent is appropriate in the particular case' (*Re H (Minors) (Sexual Abuse: Standard of Proof)* [1996] AC 563 at p. 583; *Re B (Children) (Care Proceedings: Standard of Proof)* at [15], [72], [73]), but do not alter the balance of probabilities test.

In the absence of cross-examination (for example, where a witness statement is simply read to the court) the court cannot make findings against a party who denies what is alleged against him, unless the denial is self-evidently wrong, for example, because of other facts which are admitted or because the denial is plainly contradicted by reliable documents (*Re Hopes (Heathrow) Ltd* [2001] 1 BCLC 575). Some facts are so obvious they hardly require proof. An example is that closing windows in a house will reduce noise from outside (*Thornhill v Nationwide Metal Recycling Ltd* [2011] EWCA Civ 919, [2011] Env LR 33, and see judicial notice at 49.27).

Deciding between witnesses

Cases are decided by the quality of the evidence adduced at the trial, not by weight of numbers **61.51**
of witnesses on one side compared to the other (*Gurney Consulting Engineers v Gleeds Health and Safety Ltd* [2006] EWHC 43 (TCC) at [11]). In evaluating evidence given at trial, Peter Smith J in *EPI Environmental Technologies Inc. v Symphony Plastic Technologies plc* [2004] EWHC 2945 (Ch), [2005] 1 WLR 3456 at [74] gave the following guidance:

(a) It is essential to evaluate a witness's performance in the light of the entirety of his or her evidence. Witnesses can make mistakes, but those mistakes do not necessarily affect other parts of their evidence.

(b) Witnesses can regularly lie. However, lies themselves do not mean necessarily that the entirety of that witness's evidence is rejected. A witness may lie in a stupid attempt to bolster a case, but the actual case nevertheless remains good irrespective of the lie. Alternatively, a witness may lie because the case is a lie.
(c) It is essential that a witness is challenged with the other side's case. This involves putting the case positively. It is for the judge then to assess the witness's oral response and demeanour, and the likely veracity of the response in the overall context of the litigation.

In *Powell v Streatham Manor Nursing Home* [1935] AC 243, Lord Macmillan, referring to fraud cases, said, at p. 256, he found it essential to test the credibility of witnesses against objective facts proved independently, particularly the documents in the case. He also took into account their motives, and the overall probabilities of the case. In *Grace Shipping Inc. v C. F. Sharp and Co. (Malaya) Pte Ltd* [1987] 1 Lloyd's Rep 207 the Privy Council said witness evidence has to be assessed against the contemporaneous documents and the overall probabilities. A number of judges have said they find it almost impossible to tell whether a witness is telling the truth if they give evidence through an interpreter (Scrutton LJ in *Compañía Naviera Martiartu of Bilbao v Royal Exchange Assurance Corporation* (1922) 12 Ll L Rep 83 at p. 97; Lord Bingham of Cornhill in *The Business of Judging* (OUP, 2000) at p. 11; also *Pacific Inter-Link Sdn Bhd v EFKO Food Ingredients Ltd* [2011] EWHC 923 (Comm), LTL 12/5/2011). Adopting a two-stage approach of making preliminary findings on the evidence of lay witnesses, and then testing those findings against the expert evidence, is likely to be wrong. In *Hall v Jakto Transport Ltd* [2005] EWCA Civ 1327, *The Times*, 28 November 2005, an engineering expert's evidence was relevant to how an accident might have happened. It was held that the judge should have considered the expert's evidence when reaching his conclusions on the credibility of the other witnesses, rather than making preliminary findings based only on the lay witnesses, then reassessing those findings in the light of the expert's evidence.

When faced with competing property valuations, the judge does not necessarily have to decide that one rather than the other is correct. An alternative approach is to seek to find the probable value of the property in the light of the evidence of both valuers (*Stephens v Cannon* [2005] EWCA Civ 222, *The Times*, 2 May 2005).

Adjudicating on expert evidence

61.52 It is common for judges to have to decide between conflicting expert evidence. When this happens the duty of the judge is to make findings of fact and resolve the conflict (*Sewell v Electrolux Ltd* (1997), *The Times*, 7 November 1997). In *Roadrunner Properties Ltd v Dean* [2003] EWCA Civ 1816, LTL 21/11/2003, the claimant's expert gave evidence that cracks in a party wall were caused by the defendants' use of a jackhammer. The Court of Appeal held the judge had been wrong to prefer the evidence of the defendants' expert, who advanced a hypothesis that the damage was due to climate change, a theory otherwise unsupported by evidence. The court commented that the trial judge had given too much credence to a comment by the defendants' expert that coincidence (that the claimant's damage occurred after use of the jackhammer) was not a forensic tool.

Where there is a conflict between an expert and lay witnesses, generally the judge should refuse to accept the lay evidence in preference to uncontradicted expert evidence (*Re B (A Minor) (Split Hearings: Jurisdiction)* [2000] 1 WLR 790). However, the judge is not obliged to accept expert evidence if there are sufficient grounds for rejecting it, such as where it does not speak to a relevant issue (see *R v Lanfear* [1968] 2 QB 77), or where the judge does not believe the expert or is otherwise unconvinced by the expert's evidence (*Dover District Council v Sherred* (1997) *The Times*, 11 February 1997). In *Eckersley v Binnie* (1987) 18 Con LR 1, Henry LJ said: 'a coherent reasoned opinion by a suitably qualified expert should be the subject of a coherent reasoned rebuttal'. In *English v Emery Reimbold and Strick Ltd* [2002] EWCA Civ 605, [2002] 1 WLR 2409 at [20], Lord Phillips of Worth Matravers MR said this does not mean the judgment should contain a passage which suggests that the judge has applied the same, or even a superior, degree of expertise to that displayed by the expert. The judge simply has to provide an explanation as to why the evidence of one expert has been accepted over that of another. It may be that one expert's evidence accorded more satisfactorily with the facts found by the judge, or was more inherently credible than the other, or that one expert was better qualified or more objective. In *Coopers Payen Ltd v Southampton Container Terminal Ltd* [2003] EWCA Civ 1223, [2004] 1 Lloyd's Rep 331, Lightman J said at [67] that if there is no other direct evidence, the evidence given by a single joint expert is likely to be compelling. A judge may depart from it only in exceptional circumstances and after fully explaining the reasons. It is different if an expert, including a single joint expert, gives evidence on an issue of fact on which there is lay evidence. Where both the expert and the lay witness are credible, there is no rule of law or practice requiring the judge to prefer the evidence of the expert. The judge must consider whether the expert and lay evidence can be reconciled. If not, the judge must consider whether there is any explanation for the conflict or a possible error by a witness, and in the light of the circumstances, make a considered choice on which evidence to accept. The court in *Armstrong v First York Ltd* [2005] EWCA Civ 277, [2005] 1 WLR 2751, rejected the evidence of a jointly instructed expert who was called at the trial to give evidence in an emerging area of expertise (bio-mechanical accident reconstruction). Ultimately, litigation is conducted by trial by judge, not by experts (see Brooke LJ in *Armstrong v First York Ltd*).

The judge should not develop his own theory on a matter requiring expertise without recalling the experts for their guidance on the theory (*Deveron Joinery Co. Ltd v Perkins* [2003] EWCA Civ 1241, LTL 30/7/2003). In *Breeze v Ahmad* [2005] EWCA Civ 223, LTL 8/3/2005, the judge preferred the defendant's expert, who the judge said was 'compellingly supported' by the expert literature. None of the literature was introduced at the trial or shown to the claimant's expert. In fact it provided no support for the defendant's expert at all. The failure to adduce the literature was held to be a serious procedural irregularity, and a retrial was ordered. In *Re M (Child: Residence)* [2002] EWCA Civ 1052, [2002] 2 FLR 1059, it was held that it was not open to the judge to reject the uncontested evidence of three expert witnesses that the core personality of a father had been so damaged by childhood experiences as to make him unsuitable to be a child's primary carer simply on the basis of impressions while in the witness box. However, on issues such as future placement and parent-child attachment, a judge could depart from unanimous expert opinion. Also, there are cases where lay evidence may be preferred to expert evidence, such as where attesting witnesses are preferred to a handwriting expert over a contested will (*Fuller v Strum* (2000) *The Times*, 14 February 2001, reversed on other grounds [2001] EWCA Civ 1879, [2002] 1 WLR 1097).

Inadequate expert evidence

In *Woolley v Essex County Council* [2006] EWCA Civ 753, LTL 17/5/2006, a joint report by an employment consultant considered the claimant's loss of earnings. The expert referred to the fact the claimant was a highly skilled glazier, and was likely to earn in the top centile of earnings for glaziers. However, the figures in the conclusion of the report used average earnings for glaziers. Neither side called the expert, or put questions to him. On appeal it was held it was incumbent on the judge to analyse the expert's report and consider whether the expert had inadvertently made a mistake. It was wrong for the judge to assume the expert was correct. As all the figures were available, the Court of Appeal substituted the correct award. In *Chambers v Excel Logistics Ltd* [2006] EWCA Civ 1031, LTL 7/6/2006, the medical expert said in his report that an injury had accelerated the claimant's back condition by three years. The claimant was off work on full pay for almost three years, and then retired. It was therefore unclear whether the expert meant that the relevant three years were those immediately after the accident, or whether the date he would have to retire was three years earlier than if he had not been injured. The expert was not called and no written questions were put to him, although it was essential that the 61.53

point was clarified. The Court of Appeal had no material on which to resolve the issue, so the case was remitted back for reconsideration.

Resorting to the burden of proof

61.54 An appeal was allowed in *Cooper v Floor Cleaning Machines Ltd* [2003] EWCA Civ 1649, [2004] RTR 254, where the judge found that both drivers in a road traffic accident were not to be believed, and dismissed both the claim and counterclaim on the basis that neither side had proved its case on the balance of probabilities. Scott-Baker LJ said, at [3]:

> It is, on any view, a wholly exceptional situation for a judge to conclude, particularly in a case concerning a road traffic accident, that a claim and counterclaim both fail on the basis of failure to discharge the burden of proof.

In *Stephens v Cannon* [2005] EWCA Civ 222, *The Times*, 2 May 2005, Wilson J laid down the following principles:

(a) There have to be exceptional circumstances before the court can be justified in deciding a disputed issue by resorting to the burden of proof.
(b) The circumstances will be exceptional where, despite striving to make a finding on the evidence, the court finds it is not reasonable to do so.
(c) A judge resorting to the burden of proof must analyse the evidence and set out in the judgment the steps taken to make a finding on the evidence, and the reasons why the judge has concluded this is not possible, unless these can readily be inferred from the circumstances of the case.

There have been exceptional cases which have been validly decided on the burden of proof. *Ashraf v Akram* [1999] EWCA Civ 640, for example, was a case where there were conflicting stories producing 'an intractable evidential tangle' such that resort to the burden of proof was permissible. In other cases, like *Baker v Market Harborough Industrial Co-operative Society Ltd* [1953] 1 WLR 1472, where two vehicles collided head-on in the middle of the road leaving no survivors, the proper inference may be that both drivers were equally to blame.

Judgment

61.55 Judgment is often given immediately, but in complicated cases may be reserved. Particularly in the High Court, there are cases where the judge will reserve judgment and provide the legal representatives with a written draft judgment usually about one day before the date fixed for pronouncing judgment (see Admiralty and Commercial Court Guide, para. J12; Chancery Guide paras 9.1 to 9.3; Queen's Bench Guide, paras 10.3.5 to 10.3.7). Such a judgment is not delivered until it is formally pronounced in court. Retaining the word 'draft' after a judgment is pronounced does not render the judgment invalid (*Birmingham City Council v Yardley* [2004] EWCA Civ 1756, *The Times*, 13 December 2004). The draft usually contains a confidentiality notice to the effect that it must not be communicated to clients until an hour before the hearing. Advocates should familiarise themselves with the draft and be ready to deal with any points that arise when judgment is delivered, and should refer any typographical errors to the judge's clerk not later than 12 noon on the day before pronouncement.

If judgment is reserved, the court retains the power to entertain further evidence, but will consider factors similar to those laid down in *Ladd v Marshall* [1954] 1 WLR 1489 (see **75.15**) in deciding whether allowing further evidence will accord with the overriding objective (*Townsend v Achilleas* (2000) LTL 6/7/2000; and see the discussion of reconsideration of judgments etc at **63.43** to **63.47**). The whole of any hearing, whether in the High Court or a county court, will be recorded, unless the judge directs otherwise (**PD 39A, para. 6.1**). Unofficial tape-recording without permission (which will rarely be given) is a contempt of court. **Paragraphs 6.3** to **6.5** of **PD 39A** deal with obtaining transcripts of proceedings on payment of authorised charges.

Judges are required to give reasons for their judgments in order to comply with the European Convention on Human Rights, **art. 6(1)**, in the **Human Rights Act 1998, sch. 1** (*Torija v Spain* (application 18390/91) (1994) 19 EHRR 553 at [29]). Whether reasons are adequate depends on the nature of the case (*Flannery v Halifax Estate Agencies Ltd* [2000] 1 WLR 377). While it is desirable that a judgment should be comprehensible on first reading, that is not the test of whether reasons are adequate. This is tested in the context of understanding the pleadings, evidence and submissions at trial (*English v Emery Reimbold and Strick Ltd* [2002] EWCA Civ 605, [2002] 1 WLR 2409). There is no obligation to address every argument put forward by the parties, as long as they can see from the judgment the basis of the decision (*Eagil Trust Co. Ltd v Pigott-Brown* [1985] 3 All ER 119). Nor is it necessary to explain every factor the judge took into account in weighing the evidence. What the judge has to do is identify the issues which were vital to the decision, the manner in which the judge resolved them and record the matters which were critical to the decision (*English v Emery Reimbold and Strick Ltd* at [19]). Judgments need not be long. For example, it may be unnecessary to detail or even summarise items of evidence, provided the reasoning essential to the decision is clear to the parties.

It is counsel's duty to draw the judge's attention to any alleged deficiency in the judgment, and request clarification or a supplementary judgment on the issue, rather than raising the issue on an application for permission to appeal (*English v Emery Reimbold and Strick Ltd*; *Re S (Children)* [2007] EWCA Civ 694, *The Times*, 2 July 2007).

After judgment is given the court will deal with the question of costs, the form of the judgment, and any application for permission to appeal.

Further evidence after judgment and before order

The trial judge has a discretion to permit a party to adduce additional evidence after judgment **61.56** has been handed down and before the final order has been made (*Navitaire Inc. v Easyjet Airline Co. Ltd* [2005] EWHC 282, [2006] RPC 4; and see **49.54**).

A distinction may be drawn between:

(a) requests to reopen a hearing before the judge delivers judgment. In this situation the application should probably be dealt with in accordance with the overriding objective of dealing with the case justly and at proportionate cost; and
(b) requests to reopen a hearing after judgment has been delivered, but before the judgment is drawn up (see **63.37**). Here the court will have regard to the *Ladd v Marshall* [1954] 1 WLR 1489 principles (see **75.16**), but with more flexibility than in appeals (*Navitaire Inc. v Easyjet Airline Co. Ltd*).

Particular emphasis is placed on the first of the *Ladd v Marshall* principles, and an application was refused in *Fisher v Cadman* [2005] EWHC 2424 (Ch), *The Times*, 23 June 2005, principally because the evidence could have been made available at the right time if the applicant had exercised reasonable diligence.

PRELIMINARY ISSUES

As a general rule, it is in the interests of the parties and the administration of justice that all **61.57** issues arising in a dispute are tried at the same time. However, particularly in complex actions, costs and time can sometimes be saved if decisive, or potentially decisive, issues can be identified and ordered to be tried before or separately from the main trial. The court's decision on preliminary issues should be used by the parties as a basis for sensible discussions or negotiations. It should not be used as a platform from which the victor launches new, let alone unfounded, claims in order to transform its case on quantum (*Multiplex Constructions (UK) Ltd v Cleveland Bridge UK Ltd* [2008] EWHC 2220 (TCC), LTL 2/10/2008 at [1673]).

Commentary

There are three types of order that can be made:

(a) for the trial of a preliminary issue on a point of law;
(b) for the separate trial of preliminary issues or questions of fact;
(c) for separate trials of liability and quantum.

The jurisdiction to make these orders derives from **CPR, r. 3.1(2)**.

Factors to be taken into account when deciding whether to order the determination of a preliminary issue were laid down by Neuberger J in *Steele v Steele* (2001) *The Times*, 5 June 2001, as follows:

(a) Whether the determination of the preliminary issue will dispose of the whole case or at least one aspect of the case.
(b) Whether the determination of the preliminary issue will significantly cut down the cost and the time involved in pre-trial preparation and in connection with the trial itself.
(c) If the preliminary issue is an issue of law, the amount of effort involved in identifying the relevant facts for the purposes of the preliminary issue.
(d) If the preliminary issue is an issue of law, whether it can be determined on agreed facts. If there are substantial disputes of fact it is unlikely to be safe to determine the legal issue until the facts are found.
(e) Whether the determination of the preliminary issue will unreasonably fetter either of the parties or the court in achieving a just result.
(f) The risk that an order will increase the costs or delay the trial, and the prospects that such an order may assist in settling the dispute.
(g) The more likely it is that the issue will have to be determined by the court the more appropriate it is to have it determined as a preliminary issue.
(h) The risk that the determination may lose its effect by subsequent amendment of the statements of case.
(i) Whether it is just and right to order the determination of the preliminary issue.

Procedure for trial of preliminary issues

61.58 Orders for the trial of preliminary issues are made either on the application of a party or by the court of its own initiative. It is rare for the court to make such an order without the concurrence of at least one of the parties. It is not possible to make such an order by consent. Normally the application is made at the allocation or listing stage, or on a case management hearing, although it is not unknown for an application to be made to the trial judge at the beginning of a trial.

Where an order for the preliminary trial of an issue of law or fact is made, the court must formulate the issue to be tried. It is important that the issue is defined with precision so as to avoid future difficulties of interpretation (*Avraamides v Colwill* [2006] EWCA Civ 1533, [2006] NPC 120). A preliminary issue should be decided against a schedule of agreed or assumed facts (*McLoughlin v Jones* [2006] EWCA Civ 1167, LTL 5/7/2006). If it is impossible to define the issue, no order should be made (*Allen v Gulf Oil Refining Ltd* [1981] AC 1001). If the issue is one of law, the court must further order the issue to be tried either:

(a) on the statements of case;
(b) on a case stated; or
(c) on an agreed statement of facts.

In *Keays v Murdoch Magazines (UK) Ltd* [1991] 1 WLR 1184, an issue as to whether words were capable of a defamatory meaning was ordered to be tried on the pleadings in conjunction with the copy of the magazine in which the offending article appeared.

Preliminary issues of law or fact

In *Allen v Gulf Oil Refining Ltd* [1981] AC 1001, Lord Roskill said: **61.59**

The preliminary point procedure can in certain classes of case be invoked to achieve the desirable aim of economy and simplicity. But cases in which invocation is desirable are few.

Situations identified by Lord Roskill as being suitable for trial as preliminary issues include:

(a) where a single issue of law can be isolated from the other issues in a case, and its decision may be finally determinative of the case as a whole;
(b) where the facts are agreed and the sole issue is one of law.

Neuberger J in *Re Bank of Credit and Commerce International SA, Banque Arabe Internationale d'Investissement SA v Morris* [2001] 1 BCLC 263 said that preliminary issues of law would not be ordered unless:

(a) they are so formulated that they can be answered without making artificial findings of fact (i.e. findings of fact which are not agreed and are disputed);
(b) they would, if determined one way, enable the court to dismiss at least one of the claims made in the proceedings; and
(c) the point can be formulated into a reasonably arguable issue.

In *Ashmore v Corporation of Lloyd's* [1992] 1 WLR 446, preliminary points of law were ordered to decide:

(a) whether Lloyd's owed a duty of care to the claimants who were 'names' (underwriting members of Lloyd's organised in syndicates); and
(b) whether Lloyd's had immunity from suit under the Lloyd's Act 1982, s. 14.

Issues raised in personal injuries cases as to the claimant's 'date of knowledge' under the Limitation Act 1980, s. 14, may be suitable for trial as preliminary issues. In *Keays v Murdoch Magazines (UK) Ltd* [1991] 1 WLR 1184, the issue whether the words published were capable of bearing a defamatory meaning was determined as a preliminary issue. One of the key factors is whether the procedure is likely to achieve a saving in costs, or whether it is likely to increase expense and delay.

The House of Lords has on several occasions disapproved the practice of making orders to determine points of law on assumed facts. As Lord Scarman said in *Tilling v Whiteman* [1980] AC 1, they are 'too often treacherous short cuts. Their price can be delay, anxiety and expense.' If the court finds against the point of law, the case will be no further advanced than when the order was made. If the facts are found or agreed first, the hearing on the preliminary issue should finally determine the proceedings.

There appears to be a slightly increased willingness to order the trial of preliminary issues under the CPR. The way it is put in the Chancery Guide, for example, at para. 3.14, is that costs can sometimes be saved by identifying decisive issues, or potentially decisive issues, and ordering that they be tried first. The decision of one issue, which in itself may not be decisive, may still be appropriate, because it may enable the parties to settle the remainder of their dispute.

Separate trials of liability and damages

Such orders are regarded as exceptional, and are only made where a clear demarcation line **61.60** between the issues of liability and quantum can be drawn (*Marks v Chief Constable of Greater Manchester Police* (1992) *The Times*, 28 January 1992). Where certain items of evidence would need to be called at both trials, an order should not be made. In personal injuries cases where the long-term prognosis will only become clear some years after the event, unless quantum can be dealt with by provisional damages, it may be best for liability to be tried early while events are still relatively fresh, leaving quantum to be determined when the prognosis becomes clear (*Hawkins v New Mendip Engineering Ltd* [1966] 1 WLR 1341). If judgment is entered for damages to be assessed, it would be possible for the claimant to apply for an interim payment under **CPR, rr. 25.6** to **25.9** (see **chapter 36**). In these cases disclosure is normally initially limited to the issue of liability (*Baldock v Addison* [1995] 1 WLR 158).

Chapter 62 Non-attendance

NON-ATTENDANCE AT INTERIM HEARINGS

The court may proceed in the absence of any party to an application (**CPR, r. 23.11(1)**). **62.1**
When this happens the court has a general discretion to relist the application, which it may exercise of its own initiative or on application by the absent party (**r. 23.11(2)**). This gives the court power to rehear the application in full and make such order as may be appropriate (*Riverpath Properties Ltd v Brammall* (2000) *The Times*, 16 February 2000). Matters to be taken into account when exercising the discretion include the reasons for the absence, the interests of justice, any undue delay since the missed hearing, whether either party has acted on the order, and whether there is a real prospect of the court changing the original order (see *Shocked v Goldschmidt* [1998] 1 All ER 372, which is discussed in **62.2**, and *Riverpath Properties Ltd v Brammall*). An alternative procedure suggested in *Forcelux Ltd v Binnie* [2009] EWCA Civ 854, [2010] HLR 20, is to set aside the order under **r. 3.1(2)(m)** and (7). **Rule 3.1(7)** is considered at **32.43**.

NON-ATTENDANCE AT TRIAL

A trial may proceed despite the non-attendance of any of the parties, and the court may simply strike out the claim or defence, and any counterclaim or defence to counterclaim (**CPR, r. 39.3(1)**). A first hearing of a possession claim under **r. 55.8(1)** is not a 'trial' for this purpose (*Forcelux Ltd v Binnie* [2009] EWCA Civ 854, [2010] HLR 20; see **62.1**). If a party is not present but its legal representative is, the court should not exercise its power to strike out (*Rouse v Freeman* (2001) *The Times*, 8 January 2002). The court has a power to restore the proceedings (or any part of the proceedings) that may have been struck out due to non-attendance (**r. 39.3(2)**), and may set aside any judgment entered in such circumstances (**r. 39.3(3)**). An appeal court may treat an appeal as an application to set aside for non-attendance, applying the principles in **r. 39.3** (*Zambia v Meer Care and Desai* [2008] EWCA Civ 754, LTL 9/7/2008). Applications to set aside or restore must be supported by evidence (**r. 39.3(4)**). **Rule 39.3(5)** provides that orders to restore or set aside may only be granted if the applicant: **62.2**

(a) acted promptly on finding out about the order;
(b) had a good reason for not attending; and
(c) has a reasonable prospect of success at a reconvened trial.

These conditions are similar to those enunciated in *Shocked v Goldschmidt* [1998] 1 All ER 372, but under the CPR they are cumulative. If any of the conditions is not satisfied, there is no residual discretion to set aside (*Barclays Bank plc v Ellis* (2000) *The Times*, 24 October 2000). In this context, acting 'promptly' means acting with alacrity (*Regency Rolls Ltd v Carnall* (2000) LTL 16/10/2000). An application issued six weeks after trial in a complex claim was regarded as 'prompt' in *Watson v Bluemoor Properties Ltd* [2002] EWCA Civ 1875, [2003] BCC 382

The phrase 'good reason' in **r. 39.3(5)(b)** is sufficiently clear and does not need further definition (*Brazil v Brazil* [2002] EWCA Civ 1135, [2003] CP Rep 7, where judgment was set aside because the applicant, who was illiterate, did not receive notice of the trial date). It is undesirable to define the phrase 'good reason', although it must be applied so as to give effect

Commentary

to the overriding objective (*Estate Acquisition and Development Ltd v Wiltshire* [2006] EWCA Civ 533, *The Times*, 12 June 2006). An application to set aside in *Neufville v Papamichael* (1999) LTL 23/11/99) was refused, primarily because there was no adequate explanation for the claimant, who failed to attend trial, not having kept in contact with his solicitors. There may be 'good reason' for non-attendance where there was no letter before claim, several of the court documents were not translated into the defendant's language, and the defendant thought the documents required his involvement as a witness rather than as a party (*Zambia v Meer Care and Desai*).

A 'reasonable' prospect of success has the same meaning as 'real' prospect of success (*E. D. and F. Man Liquid Products Ltd v Patel* [2003] EWCA Civ 472, [2003] CPLR 384, and see **34.10** to **34.26**). The fact there is a pleaded defence does not mean it has a reasonable prospect of success (*Sinclair v Johnson* [2008] EWCA Civ 667, LTL 23/5/2008). *Barclays Bank plc v Ellis* shows that the court will take a rigorous approach to the question of whether the party who failed to attend has a reasonable prospect of success at a reconvened trial. See also *Stock v Stock* (2000) LTL 17/10/2000.

The requirements of **r. 39.3** were held to be satisfied in *Thakerar v Northwich Park and St Mark's NHS Trust* [2002] EWCA Civ 617, LTL 24/4/2002, where the claimant had been admitted to hospital with a heart condition and was discharged during the course of the first day of the trial. Once the conditions are satisfied, the discretion under **r. 39.3** should be exercised in favour of restoring the claim unless there is material justifying a refusal of the order.

Detailed guidance on the relationship between **r. 39.3** and permission to appeal under **Part 52** was given by Lord Neuberger MR in *Bank of Scotland plc v Pereira* [2011] EWCA Civ 241, [2011] 1 WLR 2391.

No notice of the trial date

62.3 In most classes of litigation there will be a great deal of correspondence and case management before trial to establish communication between the parties and the court. Mostly, the parties or their solicitors will know the trial date through attendance at directions hearings, being sent directions orders, and general correspondence. Occasionally, a litigant, who may be acting in person, does not receive the key document with the trial date, so misses the trial. Possession cases under **CPR, Part 55**, can be more of a problem, in that the claim form usually includes details for the final hearing of the matter. A defendant who does not receive this document may find that a final order has been made before becoming aware that there are court proceedings.

Assuming there is no reason to disbelieve a litigant who says he was not informed of the trial date, the first question is whether the party was nevertheless served with such notice. The rules in **Part 6**, apply. Provided the notice was sent by one of the methods prescribed by **r. 6.20** to the party's correct address for service as prescribed by **r. 6.23**, the notice will be deemed to have been served on the date calculated in accordance with **r. 6.26**. As discussed at **15.36** and **15.42**, this creates an irrebuttable presumption of due service (see *Godwin v Swindon Borough Council* [2001] EWCA Civ 1478, [2002] 1 WLR 997). Although the notice may have been lost in the post, or the party may have moved (without changing his address for service), technically the notice will have been properly served.

In *Akram v Adam* [2004] EWCA Civ 1601, [2005] 1 WLR 2762, where a possession claim form was sent to the correct address for service, the court refused to set aside a judgment entered in the absence of the defendant who was unaware of the proceedings. Another possession case, *Hackney London Borough Council v Driscoll* [2003] EWCA Civ 1037, [2003] 1 WLR 2602, was different in that the defendant had known of the proceedings and had attended two hearings where directions were given. The notice for the final hearing did not reach the defendant because it was sent to the address of the property which was the subject of the possession proceedings, the defendant having moved away and sublet that property. It was held that this case was *therefore different* from cases where the defendant had no notice of the proceedings, and the judgment could only be set aside applying the criteria in **r. 39.3(5)**. As the defendant failed to show a defence with a reasonable prospect of success, the judgment was not set aside. *Estate*

Acquisition and Development Ltd v Wiltshire [2006] EWCA Civ 533, *The Times*, 12 June 2006, was a possession claim in relation to a long lease. The claim form had been served correctly at the leased premises, but the defendant had no knowledge of the proceedings or the hearing because he had moved away. He acted promptly in applying to set aside the judgment obtained in his absence, and had a reasonable prospect of success on the merits. The lack of notice was a sufficiently good reason, and was not displaced by a supposed obligation on the tenant to keep the landlord informed of any changes of address.

A case where service failed to comply with **Part 6** was *Nelson v Clearsprings (Management) Ltd* [2006] EWCA Civ 1252, [2007] 1 WLR 962. The claim form was accidentally addressed to the defendant at 28 Brook Road, whereas the defendant lived at 26 Brook Road. As a result the defendant did not attend the hearing, and an order for possession was made. As this was a possession claim the judgment was not entered in default, but after a hearing under **Part 55**. This meant that the judgment could not be set aside under the default judgment provisions in **Part 13** (see **20.11** to **20.21**). Sir Anthony Clarke MR said that the intention cannot have been that a judgment entered when the defendant did not even know of the proceedings could only be set aside applying the criteria in **r. 39.3(5)**. Nor did it follow that such judgments would be set aside as of right. Instead:

(a) if the defendant can show he has not been served with the claim form at all, normally a judgment entered after a hearing would be set aside, with the claimant paying the costs;
(b) if the claimant could show there was no defence despite non-service, the claimant should cross-apply for summary judgment and an order dispensing with service of the claim form;
(c) if faced with such cross-applications, the court should make such order as is just; and
(d) if the defendant is guilty of inexcusable delay since learning of the judgment, that could of itself be a reason for refusing the application to set aside.

Both *Hackney London Borough Council v Driscoll* and *Nelson v Clearsprings (Management) Ltd* cite the pre-CPR case of *White v Weston* [1968] 2 QB 647, which held that an irregularly obtained judgment should be set aside as of right, with the claimant paying the costs. *White v Weston* was not cited in early editions of this book, because the wide, obligatory, rule it laid down has no place under the new code created by the CPR. It is no more than a non-binding illustration of what happened under the old system, and understood in that way it causes no harm.

Setting aside and appealing

In *Tennero Ltd v Arnold* [2006] EWHC 1530 (QB), [2007] 1 WLR 1025, the defendant was taken ill **62.4**
while abroad, and sent evidence to the court to the effect he was too ill to attend the trial. The first county court judge refused to adjourn the trial, and judgment was entered against him at the trial. On the advice of the Civil Appeals Office, the defendant made an application to set aside the judgment for non-attendance under **CPR, r. 39.3**. A second county court judge refused to set aside the judgment. The defendant then brought the present appeal against the first judge's order refusing the adjournment. Jack J held that, having applied to the second county court judge to set aside, it was thereafter no longer open to the defendant to appeal against the first county court judge's refusal of the application to adjourn.

Setting aside on terms

In most cases the party who did not attend will be at fault, so usually will be ordered to pay **62.5**
the costs thrown away. If the non-attendance arose without fault, it may be appropriate to make some other order, such as costs in the case. In addition to setting aside the judgment, the court will invariably need to make consequential directions for further steps in the proceedings and setting a new trial date or window.

A counterclaim was reinstated in *Watson v Bluemoor Properties Ltd* [2002] EWCA Civ 1875, [2003] BCC 382, on terms that the party applying to reinstate made an interim payment and provided security for future costs.

Chapter 63 Judgments and Orders

INTRODUCTION

63.1 Although there is likely to be a delay between judgment being pronounced and the judgment being sealed and served, CPR, r. 40.7(1), provides that judgment in fact takes effect from the day it was given. Where a written judgment is sent in draft to the legal representatives of the parties under Practice Statement (Supreme Court: Judgments) [1998] 1 WLR 825, it is not given or made for the purposes of r. 40.7(1) until it is pronounced in court (*Prudential Assurance Co. Ltd v McBains Cooper* [2000] 1 WLR 2000). After a judgment or order has been pronounced by the court, the next step is to have it drawn up. In *Holtby v Hodgson* (1889) 24 QBD 103 Lord Esher MR said, at p. 107, 'Pronouncing judgment is not entering judgment; something has to be done which will be a record'. Given r. 40.7, on the question of compliance it is irrelevant that the order is not sealed until after the time specified for compliance (*Rahamim v Reich* (2009) LTL 10/2/2009).

The distinction between judgments and orders is that a judgment is the final decision which disposes of a claim (subject to appeal), whereas an order is an interim decision. However, there is no practical difference between the two, and both are enforceable in the same way.

A party seeking to dispute an order or judgment is usually limited to applying for permission to appeal (see **chapters** 74 and 75). There are exceptions where an application to review an order can be made back to the same judge as made the original order (or to a judge at the same or equivalent level) without appealing. Orders made without notice can be reviewed by applying to set aside or vary within seven days of service of the order (**r. 23.10**). Default judgments can be set aside using the procedure in **Part 13**. If there is a change of circumstances it may be possible to vary case management directions (see **47.32**). If there is an accidental slip or error in an order, it may be corrected under the slip rule (see **63.42**). Orders and judgments can be reviewed by the judge in the period between pronouncement and drawing up (see **63.43**). It may be right to refuse an application to set aside or vary an order where an appeal from that order is pending (*Barrie v J. Barrie (Plant Hire) Ltd* [2001] EWCA Civ 614, LTL 14/2/2001).

SETTLEMENTS

An offer to settle which is stated to be 'subject to contract' will not create a binding contract until the parties have signed the contemplated agreement or award (*Morgan Walker Solicitors LLP v Zurich Professional and Financial Lines* [2010] EWHC 1352 (Ch), LTL 16/7/2010). Where the parties have agreed terms for settling the substantive issues in the claim, or on an interim application, they must also decide how those terms should be recorded. An important consideration in this regard is how the agreement can be enforced in the event of either party failing to abide by its terms. The simplest form of judgment provides for immediate payment of the sum agreed together with costs (often on the standard basis, to be the subject of a detailed assessment if not agreed). Enforcement proceedings can be taken on such a judgment on the same day as it is entered. Agreements are not always this simple. Five further ways of recording agreed terms were discussed by Slade J in *Green v Rozen* [1955] 1 WLR 741 (in the context of an agreement reached at the door of the court): **63.2**

(a) Where a claim is settled on terms as to the payment of money, judgment may be entered for the agreed sum, subject to a stay of execution pending payment of stated instalments. If the instalments fall into arrears, the stay will be lifted, and the judgment creditor can immediately take enforcement proceedings.
(b) A consent order may be drawn up embodying the undertakings of both parties in a series of numbered paragraphs. If any of the terms are not complied with, enforcement may be possible immediately or on application to the court depending on the nature of the term in question.
(c) The agreement may be recorded in a Tomlin order. A Tomlin order has the effect of staying the proceedings save for the purpose of carrying the terms set out in a schedule to the order into effect. See **63.16**.
(d) A consent order may be drawn up staying all further proceedings upon the agreed terms. If the agreement is reached immediately before the hearing its terms will usually be endorsed on counsel's briefs and the court will be asked to make a consent order in those terms. Unlike Tomlin orders, the courts are very unwilling to remove the stay imposed by such orders, so enforcement can usually only be effected by bringing fresh proceedings for breach of the contract embodied in the compromise (see *Rofa Sport Management AG v DHL International (UK) Ltd* [1989] 1 WLR 902).
(e) The court may be informed merely that the case has been settled upon terms endorsed on counsel's briefs. This is the most informal way of compromising a claim. Its effect is to supersede the existing claim with the compromise. Any breach can only be enforced by issuing fresh proceedings.

A sixth method was the subject of *Atkinson v Castan* (1991) *The Times*, 17 April 1991, where a consent order made 'no order' save as to costs, but set out the agreed terms in recitals. It was held that the claimants were entitled to enforce the terms stated in the recitals without the need to bring a fresh action.

Notifying court and effect of settling claim

63.3 Where terms are agreed in advance of a hearing, each party has a responsibility to inform the court so that the time set aside for the hearing can be reallocated to other litigants and the hearing fee may be refunded (**CPFO, fee 2.3**). However, as discussed above, it is usually desirable to incorporate the agreed terms in a judgment or order to facilitate enforcement in the event of breach. The options are largely as described above, except that entering the agreement on counsel's papers does not arise. Parties are under a continuing duty to keep the court informed if the prospects of settling the case may have an impact on listing for trial or on the pre-reading needed by the judge, see **61.15**. *Gurney Consulting Engineers v Gleeds Health and Safety Ltd (No. 2)* [2006] EWHC 536 (TCC), 108 Con LR 58, said that in the same way the court must be informed of settlement talks after the hearing and before judgment. This is to avoid the judge wasting time writing up a judgment which may not be needed.

Costs and terms of settlement

63.4 Settlements agreed after proceedings have been issued should deal with the costs of the parties and with the future status of the claim. Options on the latter include entering final judgment, dismissing the claim, granting a stay or discontinuing or withdrawing it. Care should be taken to ensure the wording used reflects the parties' intentions, especially as regards any previous interim costs orders. It should be kept in mind that if a claim is discontinued, the claimant is required to pay the defendant's costs unless specific provision is made to the contrary, and that the claimant is not necessarily barred from commencing fresh proceedings in respect of the same claim (see **chapter 55**). Care is also needed when drafting a consent order to ensure it reflects the parties' intentions on enforcement in the event of breach. For example, in landlord and tenant claims, a compromise may give the landlord a suspended possession order, which allows the landlord to proceed to enforcement by eviction if the tenant fails to comply. Alternatively, a compromise may reinstate the defendant as the lawful tenant, which merely allows the landlord to apply to the court to enforce compliance with any additional terms in the event of breach (*Gibb v Pubmaster Ltd* [2002] EWHC 2236 (Ch), LTL 9/10/2002).

ORDERS MADE AT HEARINGS

63.5 Counsel are under a duty to take notes of the court's judgment, and must endorse a note of the court's decision on the backsheet of their briefs. Instructing solicitors may use this as the basis for drawing up the court's order, so accuracy in noting is of great importance. If the orders are at all complex, counsel for both sides will often consult each other immediately after the hearing to ensure that both sides are clear on what the court has ordered. Counsel's endorsement of the order is not protected by legal professional privilege.

In addition, in interim applications the master, district judge or judge will either:

(a) initial the relevant paragraphs of the application notice or draft minutes of the order; or
(b) initial together with making amendments; or
(c) endorse the order on the affidavit, witness statement or application notice in abbreviated form or longhand.

Judgments in Queen's Bench Division trials are certified by the court associate.

The associate's function in this regard is to record what the judge said, and an order recording what the associate believed to be the judge's unexpressed intention was rectified in *Memminger-IRO GmbH v Triplite Ltd (No. 2)* (1992) *The Times*, 9 July 1992.

Remedies and findings beyond the statements of case

Remedies asked for by the claimant must be set out in the claim form (**CPR, r. 16.2(1)(b)**). **63.6**
Only exceptionally will relief be granted, without an amendment, where the relief claimed is based on implied allegations (*Kirin Amgen Inc. v Hoechst Marion Roussel Ltd* (2001) LTL 8/8/2001). Where the particulars of claim include a claim for 'further or other relief', unless the claimant obtains permission to amend, relief, according to *Kirin Amgen Inc. v Hoechst Marion Roussel Ltd*, will not normally be granted in respect of a claim which:

(a) is not pleaded; or
(b) is inconsistent with the relief specifically pleaded; or
(c) is not supported by the allegations in the pleaded case; or
(d) takes the defendant by surprise, unless there are exceptional circumstances.

The danger of a judge making findings of bad faith and giving false evidence when no bad faith had been pleaded is highlighted by *Co-operative Group Ltd v International Computers Ltd* [2003] EWCA Civ 1955, *The Times*, 19 January 2004, where an appeal was allowed partially on this ground.

Commentary

FORM OF JUDGMENTS AND ORDERS

The heading of a judgment or order is the same as that for the claim, except that the name of the judge, master or district judge, if any, is included above the names of the parties (**CPR, r. 40.2(1)**). There then follow any recitals. These are followed by the body of the order, which may be short or may be complex, and should include the court's pronouncement on costs. Undertakings tend to be set out in schedules to orders. The terms of the orders must accurately reflect the pronouncement made by the court. Often it is necessary to amplify the court's words, or to put them in imperative form. The operative parts of a decision must be recorded in the judgment or order, which should be limited to the formal disposal of the application, trial or appeal. It is impermissible for the judge to make a direction that costs should be assessed by reference to guidance set out in specified paragraphs of the judgment (*Richardson Roofing Co. Ltd v Ballast plc* [2009] EWCA Civ 839, LTL 13/2/2009). It is also impermissible to include comments, for example, on the repugnant nature of a letter, in the formal order (*D'Silva v University College Union* [2009] EWCA Civ 1269, LTL 30/11/2009). To simplify this task and to ensure consistency, in both the High Court and the county courts there are many prescribed forms for judgments and orders. There are also model form orders contained in some of the practice directions, such as those for freezing injunctions and search orders in **PD 25A**. These must be used where applicable, with such variations as the circumstances of the case may require. An order has to speak for itself, and extrinsic material, including earlier drafts, is not admissible as an aid to its proper construction (*Masri v Consolidated Contractors (Oil and Gas) Company SAL* [2009] EWCA Civ 36, [2009] 1 CLC 82, but contrast *Zipher Ltd v Markem Systems Ltd* [2009] EWCA Civ 44, [2009] FSR 14, discussed at **63.10**). **63.7**

Every judgment and order must bear the date on which it was given or made, and be sealed by the court (**r. 40.2(2)**).

Where an application or appeal is dismissed, and the judge considers that it was totally without merit, this fact must be recorded in the order (and the judge must consider whether to make a civil restraint order). See **rr. 3.3(7)**, **3.4(6)**, **23.12** and **52.10(6)**, and the discussion of civil restraint orders at **14.55** to **14.60**.

Appeals against almost all interim orders can only be made with permission (**r. 52.3**). Usually permission must initially be sought from the lower court, with a right to renew the application for permission to the appeal court. Where a party has sought permission to appeal from the lower court, that court's order must by **r. 40.2(4)** state:

(a) whether or not the judgment or order is final (for which, see **74.6**);
(b) whether an appeal lies from the judgment or order, and if so, to which appeal court (for which, see **74.4**);
(c) whether the lower court has given permission to appeal; and
(d) if not, the appeal court to which any further application for permission to appeal may be made (this requirement is to assist litigants in person who are often confused about which court deals with appeals).

Time limits

63.8 Where an order imposes a time limit for doing any act, the date for compliance must be expressed as a calendar date, and must include the time of day by which the act must be done (**CPR, r. 2.9(1)**). Orders may be made subject to conditions, and may, at the court's discretion, specify the consequences of failing to comply (**r. 3.1(3)**).

Orders requiring an act to be done ('unless orders')

63.9 Orders requiring an act to be done, other than the payment of money, must specify the time within which the act must be done. The consequences of failing to comply with the order must also be set out (**PD 40B, paras 8.1** and **8.2**). There are two suitable forms of wording, and the first form should be used wherever possible. The second form should be used where the defaulting party does not attend:

Unless the claimant serves his list of documents by 4.00 p.m. on Friday, 15 November 2013, his claim will be struck out and judgment entered for the defendant.

Unless the defendant serves his list of documents within 14 days of service of this order…

Injunction orders and penal notice

63.10 Injunction orders, whether prohibitory or mandatory, are intended to have penal consequences and can be punished as a contempt of court. These orders need to be endorsed with a penal notice in form N77 (**CPR, rr. 81.4** and **81.9; PD 4 Table 1**).

Undertakings in lieu of injunctions are also intended to have penal consequences, and can be punished as a contempt of court. While an undertaking can be enforced under **CPR, r. 81.4**, even if it does not contain a penal notice (**r. 81.9(2)**), it is the usual practice to reduce undertakings to writing using form N117, which must be served in accordance with **r. 81.7**. This includes a penal notice in the following terms:

If you do not comply with your promises to the court you may be held to be in contempt of court and imprisoned or fined, or your assets may be seized.

To ensure there is no doubt over the position, the court may refuse to accept an undertaking unless the person intending to give it personally signs the statement on the reverse of form N117 to the effect that they understand the undertaking they have given and the consequences of breach (**PD 81, para. 2.2**). This statement may alternatively be made in a separate letter which is filed at court (**para. 2.3**). If there is a dispute over whether an oral undertaking has been given (and in what terms), the Court of Appeal in *Zipher Ltd v Markem Systems Ltd* [2009] EWCA Civ 44, [2009] FSR 14, said:

(a) the relevant passages in the transcript of the hearing have to be read together and in their overall context;
(b) the court should avoid an overly semantic analysis of the words in the transcript;

(c) it is permissible to take into account what was said and done before and after the alleged undertaking to assist in resolving what was said and its effect; and
(d) if there is real doubt about the meaning or effect of what was said, it should be resolved in favour of the person who would be bound.

CONSENT ORDERS

Consent orders as contracts

Many orders are made 'by consent'. A true consent order is based on a contract between the parties. As such, the contract is arrived at by bargaining between the parties, perhaps in correspondence, and the consent order is simply evidence of that contract (*Wentworth v Bullen* (1840) 9 B & C 840). To be a true consent order there must be consideration passing from each side. If this is the case, then, unlike other orders, it will only be set aside on grounds, such as fraud or mistake, which would justify the setting aside of a contract (*Purcell v F. C. Trigell Ltd* [1971] 1 QB 358; *Centrehigh Ltd v Amen* (2001) LTL 18/7/2001). A common mistake of law can vitiate a consent order (applying the principles from *Kleinwort Benson Ltd v Lincoln City Council* [1999] 2 AC 349), but consent orders should not be set aside lightly. In *Brennan v Bolt Burdon* [2004] EWCA Civ 1017, [2005] QB 303, the claimant sought to set aside an agreement to discontinue a claim entered into on a mistaken view of the law before the law was clarified by *Anderton v Clwyd County Council (No. 2)* [2002] EWCA Civ 933, [2002] 1 WLR 3174. At the time of the agreement the law was in doubt, but the claimant entered into the agreement anyway, so there was no operative mistake. A consent order may be set aside on the ground that neither party intended to be bound by it (*Goodway v Zurich Insurance Co.* [2004] EWHC 137 (TCC), 96 Con LR 49). In theory a consent order may be void for uncertainty, but this applies only where it is legally or practically impossible to give the agreement any sensible content. This is likely to be extremely rare, because the court will lend its assistance in the working out of its orders or in their clarification (*Scammell v Dicker* [2005] EWCA Civ 405, [2005] 3 All ER 838). A consent order may have contractual effect, but leave the mechanics to be worked out by directions of the court, which may include giving one of the parties additional time to perform (*Chaggar v Chaggar* [2002] EWCA Civ 1637, LTL 30/10/2002). The court has jurisdiction to vary a consent order by discharging a term which is an unlawful restraint of trade while leaving the rest of the order in place (*Gerrard Ltd v Read* (2002) 152 NLJ 22). **63.11**

In *Green v Vickers Defence Systems* [2002] EWCA Civ 904, *The Times*, 1 July 2002, the deceased and the defendants entered into a consent order, settling a personal injuries claim arising out of the deceased having developed pleural plaques, under which the defendants paid a sum of money on a full-liability basis and on the assumption the deceased would not develop mesothelioma. It was held that the agreement meant that a subsequent claim based on the deceased developing mesothelioma would be paid on a full-liability basis. There is a common misapprehension that where a party fails to honour a term of a compromise agreement settling litigation the original claim is reopened. Although this can be the position where there are grounds for avoiding the contract, in most cases an agreement to compromise a claim brings proceedings on the claim to an end and replaces them with the contractual arrangements in the compromise. Breach of the compromise agreement gives rise to a new claim for breach of contract (*Lewis v Barnett* [2004] EWCA Civ 807, LTL 29/7/2004).

Tomlin orders made in commercial disputes are interpreted in the same way as other commercial agreements (*Sirius International Insurance Co. (Publ) v FAI General Insurance Ltd* [2004] UKHL 54, [2004] 1 WLR 3251). This means the court will seek to ascertain the contextual meaning of the language used. An objective approach is taken, with the court asking what a reasonable person would have understood the parties to have meant by the language used in the order.

See also **33.21**, on settlement acting as a bar to later proceedings.

Commentary

Submission to consent order

63.12 There is a long-established distinction between a true consent order, which has contractual effect and cannot be appealed, and a situation where an order is marked 'by consent', but in reality is one where one side did no more than not object to the order being made (*Ropac Ltd v Inntrepreneur Pub Co.* [2001] CP Rep 31, approved in *Pannone LLP v Aardvark Digital Ltd* [2011] EWCA Civ 803, [2011] 1 WLR 2275). In *Siebe Gorman and Co. Ltd v Pneupac Ltd* [1982] 1 WLR 185, Lord Denning MR said at p. 189:

> It should be clearly understood by the profession that, when an order is expressed to be made 'by consent', it is ambiguous...One meaning is this: the words 'by consent' may evidence a real contract between the parties. In such a case the court will only interfere with such an order on the same grounds as it would with any other contract. The other meaning is this: the words 'by consent' may mean 'the parties hereto not objecting'. In such a case there is no real contract between the parties. The order can be altered or varied by the court in the same circumstances as any other order that is made by the court without the consent of the parties.

In *Chanel Ltd v F. W. Woolworth and Co. Ltd* [1981] 1 WLR 485 a respondent was not permitted to reopen an interim order, previously disposed of by consent, on the ground that a subsequent authority had undermined the applicant's case. In *Di Placito v Slater* [2003] EWCA Civ 1863, [2004] 1 WLR 1605, the court refused permission to an applicant to be relieved from an undertaking previously given by consent. These cases were distinguished in *Kensington International Ltd v Republic of Congo* [2007] EWCA Civ 1128, [2008] 1 WLR 1144, where there was a clear difference between the matter previously disposed of by consent and the present application. The consent order had conceded that the respondent was under no obligation to disclose information about cargoes on a continuing basis from a stated date. The current application was for disclosure relating to two specific voyages, which was regarded as a different order made in different circumstances from the consent order.

Marking of consent orders

63.13 Consent judgments and orders must be expressed as being 'by consent' (**CPR, r. 40.6(7)(b)**) and must be signed by the legal representatives for each party (or by the litigants in person where this is allowed, see **63.38** and **63.39**). **PD 40B, para. 3.4**, provides that the signatures of the legal representatives may be those of the solicitors or counsel acting for the parties.

Consent orders in family proceedings

63.14 A further distinction relates to family proceedings. In these the legal effect of a consent order derives from the order, not the agreement of the parties. Consequently, there is no jurisdiction to vary a matrimonial consent order (*Thwaite v Thwaite* [1982] Fam 1). Where such an order was obtained by fraud, misrepresentation or mistake, the remedy is to appeal or bring fresh proceedings (*De Lasala v De Lasala* [1980] AC 546 per Lord Diplock).

Consent orders as estoppels

63.15 A consent order can act as an estoppel which can be raised if fresh proceedings are brought alleging matters encompassed by the compromise (*Keith v Walcott* [1929] AC 482). However, whether this is the effect depends on what was agreed in the consent order, and it may be that one party has reserved the right to bring proceedings on certain allegations although they were raised in the compromised action (*Rice v Reed* [1900] 1 QB 54 and contrast *Jameson v Central Electricity Generating Board* [2000] 1 AC 455, where the terms of the settlement extinguished a claim against a concurrent tortfeasor). Particular care must be taken when entering into a consent order to compromise a claim for specific performance. Such a consent order may be construed as replacing the agreement on which the proceedings were based, or it may be construed as simply replacing the terms of the original contract expressly dealt with in the consent order, with the rest of the original contract still subsisting (as in *Paige v Webb* [2001] EWCA Civ 1220, LTL 26/7/2001).

Tomlin orders

Tomlin orders are so named after Tomlin J who, in a Practice Note [1927] WN 290, said that where terms of compromise are agreed and it is intended to stay the claim with the terms scheduled to the order, the order should be worded: 63.16

> And, the [claimant] and the defendant having agreed to the terms set forth in the schedule hereto, it is ordered that all further proceedings in this claim be stayed, except for the purpose of carrying such terms into effect. Liberty to apply as to carrying such terms into effect.

Tomlin orders are used where complex terms are agreed, or where the terms of a compromise go beyond the boundaries of the claim (for example, *E. F. Phillips and Sons Ltd v Clarke* [1970] Ch 322), or where it is sought to avoid publicity of the agreement. In the event of the scheduled terms being breached, enforcement is a two-stage process. First, the claim must be restored under the 'liberty to apply' clause, and an order obtained to compel compliance with the term breached. Secondly, if that order is itself breached, enforcement can follow in the usual way. In *Community Care North East v Durham County Council* [2010] EWHC 959 (QB), [2012] 1 WLR 338, it was held that:

(a) the court has power under **CPR, rr. 1.1, 1.4 and 3.7**, to vary the terms in the body of a Tomlin order. This might be appropriate where there has been a material change in circumstances (the same approach as for any other court order); and
(b) the terms in the schedule are a contract, so the court has no power to vary them under the CPR. The only basis for varying or revoking provisions in the schedule are those which apply in relation to contracts (e.g. fraud, undue influence, misrepresentation, mistake).

By **PD 40B, para. 3.5**, where a consent order is in the form of a stay of proceedings on agreed terms recorded in a schedule (a Tomlin order), any direction for the payment of money out of court or for the payment and assessment of costs must be contained in the body of the order and not the schedule. The reason is that these two forms of direction require action on the part of the court, and must therefore be included in the public part of the order and not concealed in the schedule. If the amount of costs has been agreed this can be included in the schedule.

Commentary

JUDGMENTS

Money judgments and payment by instalments

A judgment for the payment of money (including costs) must be complied with within 14 days of the judgment, unless the court specifies some other date for compliance (**CPR, r. 40.11**). It may, for example, instead of requiring immediate payment, impose an order for payment by instalments. A judgment for payment by instalments must state the total amount of the judgment, the amount of each instalment, the number of instalments and the date on which each is to be paid, and to whom the instalments should be paid (**PD 40B, para. 12**). 63.17

Judgments in foreign currency

Since *Miliangos v George Frank (Textiles) Ltd* [1976] AC 443, the general rule has been that in cases with a foreign element it has been possible to enter judgment in a foreign currency, and the date of conversion into sterling for enforcement purposes is the date of payment. As Lord Fraser said at p. 502: 63.18

> Any conversion date earlier than the date of payment would, in my opinion, be open to the same objection as the breach date, *viz.* that it would necessarily leave a considerable interval of time between the conversion date and the date of payment. During that interval currency fluctuations might cause the sterling award to vary appreciably from the sum in foreign currency to which the creditor was entitled.... [Hence the date of conversion is] the date when the court authorises enforcement of the judgment.

Where judgment is given on a claim and a cross-claim in different currencies which are to be set off against each other (see **63.19**), the proper approach is to assess the principal amount payable on the claim and cross-claim, add interest to each, and then convert the smaller amount into the currency of the larger amount at the exchange rate prevailing at the date of the judgment (or agreement). The judgment should then set off the lesser from the greater, and provide for payment of the balance (*The Botany Triad* [1993] 2 Lloyd's Rep 259; *Fearns v Anglo-Dutch Paint and Chemical Co. Ltd* [2010] EWHC 2366 (Ch), [2011] 1 WLR 366).

For further discussion of the law on this subject, see *McGregor on Damages*.

Where a claimant intends to seek judgment in a foreign currency, the particulars of claim must specify the foreign currency, and must state why the claim is for payment in that currency, the sterling equivalent, and the source of the exchange rate relied upon (**PD 16, para. 9.1**). If the court orders a judgment to be entered in a foreign currency, by **PD 40B, para. 10**, the order must be in the following form:

> It is ordered that the defendant pay the claimant [*state the sum in the foreign currency*] or the sterling equivalent at the time of payment.

The CPR contain no express provisions on the *enforcement* of judgments in foreign currency. In *Carnegie v Giessen* [2005] EWCA Civ 191, [2005] 1 WLR 2510, the Court of Appeal held that the relevant pre-CPR practice direction, Queen's Bench Masters' Practice Direction (11), is to be treated as remaining in force. The text of this practice direction, updated to comply with CPR terminology, appears in **appendix 1**.

Counterclaims

63.19 Where a cross-claim amounts to a set-off (see **34.37**) it operates as a defence to the claim. If the set-off is successful, the amount assessed on the set-off must be deducted from the amount found due on the claim. If the set-off is less than the claim, judgment should be entered for the balance. If the set-off exceeds the claim, judgment should be entered for the defendant on the claim and, if the set-off has been pleaded as a counterclaim, judgment should be entered for the defendant on the counterclaim for the balance (*Hanak v Green* [1958] 2 QB 9). This should mean that the defendant is the successful party (subject to the discretion under the Senior Courts Act 1981, s. 51) on costs. The court has power to give separate judgments when dealing with cases where there are claims and counterclaims. It also has power to order a set-off between the two claims, and simply enter judgment for the balance (**CPR, r. 40.13(2)**). Where it does so, it retains power to make separate costs orders in respect of the claims and counterclaims (**r. 40.13(3)**).

According to *Fearns v Anglo-Dutch Paint and Chemical Co. Ltd* [2010] EWHC 2366 (Ch), [2011] 1 WLR 366, the courts also have inherent jurisdiction to allow cross-judgments in a single set of proceedings, or in different claims, to be set off against each other, even where the cross-judgment is not based on a cross-claim amounting to a set-off (*Edwards v Hope* (1885) 14 QBD 922; *Reid v Cupper* [1915] 2 KB 147; *Re a Debtor (No. 21 of 1950) (No. 2)* [1951] Ch 612). The survival of this inherent jurisdiction may be doubted given the terms of **r. 40.13**, see **1.2**. Set-off against judgments applies to judgments for damages and also to orders for costs (*Fearns v Anglo-Dutch Paint and Chemical Co. Ltd* at [37]). Ordering cross-judgments to be set off against each other is a matter of whether the court considers it just and equitable to exercise its discretion (*Fearns v Anglo-Dutch Paint and Chemical Co. Ltd* at [38]).

63.20 **Set-off of costs orders** Set-off of orders for costs was summarised by Scott LJ in five propositions in *Lockley v National Blood Transfusion Service* [1992] 1 WLR 492. Three of these related to public funding, but propositions 3 and 4 are of general application. The third proposition (although worded in the now discredited impeachment of title formula, see **34.37**), is to the effect that set-off is based on the principles of equitable set-off. In his fourth proposition Scott LJ said:

> Set-off of costs or damages to which one party is entitled against costs or damages to which another party is entitled depends upon the application of the equitable criterion [of equitable set-off]. . . . It is possible

to regard all questions regarding costs [set-off of costs against costs is permitted by **CPR, r. 44.12**] as being subject to the statutory discretion conferred upon the court by section 51 of the [Senior Courts] Act 1981. But I would not have thought that a set-off of damages against damages could properly be described as a discretionary matter, nor that a set-off of costs against damages could be so described.

This last proposition does not address set-off of damages against costs, which possibly is covered by s. 51 (*Fearns v Anglo-Dutch Paint and Chemical Co. Ltd* at [73]). There is in any event a wider discretion to order set-off between money judgments and costs orders based on the authorities discussed at **63.19** where this would be just and equitable.

It is the amounts agreed or assessed under cross-costs orders that should be set off against each other, not the percentages in cross-percentage-based costs orders, because each side's costs will almost always be in differing amounts (*Amin v Amin* [2010] EWHC 827 (Ch), LTL 20/4/2010).

State benefits recoupment

In personal injuries cases where some or all of the damages are subject to recovery under the Social Security (Recovery of Benefits) Act 1997, the judgment should include a preamble setting out the amounts awarded under each head of damage, and the amount by which it has been reduced in accordance with the Act (**PD 40B, para. 5.1**). The judgment should then provide for entry of judgment and payment of the balance. **63.21**

Interim payments

Detailed rules for the form of judgments given in cases where there have been interim payments are laid down in **PD 25B**. Further details are provided by **PD 40B, paras 5.1** and **5.1A**, for orders involving recoverable benefits or lump sum awards affected by the Social Security (Recovery of Benefits) Act 1997. In a preamble to the judgment in such a case there should be set out the total amount awarded and the amounts and dates of all interim payments. The total amount awarded should then be reduced by the total amount of the interim payments, with judgment being given for the balance. If the interim payments exceed the amount awarded at trial, by virtue of **CPR, r. 25.8(2)**, the judgment should set out any orders made for repayment, reimbursement, variation or discharge, and any award of interest on the overpaid interim payments. **63.22**

Provisional damages

At common law an award of damages had to be by way of a single lump sum. This did not always produce a just result in personal injuries cases involving a risk of the claimant suffering some future deterioration related to the original injury. Although the court would increase the damages awarded to take into account the risk of the future deterioration, the uplift would only be a fraction of the true loss if it occurred, and the claimant would be overcompensated if it did not occur. To remedy this shortcoming, the courts have been given power to award provisional damages by the Senior Courts Act 1981, s. 32A, and the County Courts Act 1984, s. 51. **63.23**

These sections provide that an award of provisional damages may be made in an:

action for damages for personal injuries in which there is proved or admitted to be a chance that at some *definite or indefinite time* in the future the injured person will, as a result of the act or omission which gave rise to the cause of action, develop some serious disease or suffer some serious deterioration in his physical or mental condition.

A provisional damages award has two elements:

(a) immediate damages in respect of the existing injuries, calculated on the assumption that the claimant will not develop the future disease or that the future deterioration will not be suffered; and

Commentary

(b) an entitlement to return to court to apply for further damages if the disease develops or the deterioration is suffered.

63.24 **Conditions for awarding provisional damages** There are four conditions:

(a) The particulars of claim must include a claim for provisional damages (**CPR, r. 41.2(1)(a)**).
(b) The future disease or deterioration must be to the claimant's physical or mental condition. A risk that the claimant may be discharged from long-term state-paid hospital care, with the result that he would then need a great deal of private medical care, is not a 'disease or deterioration' (*Adan v Securicor Custodial Services Ltd* [2004] EWHC 394 (QB), [2005] PIQR P79). An injury suffered in a second accident resulting from the injury suffered in the accident for which the defendant is responsible may be a 'deterioration' for these purposes (see *Hughes v Cheshire County Council* (unreported, 2 March 1989), mentioned in and doubted by *Willson v Ministry of Defence* [1991] 1 All ER 638).
(c) The future disease or deterioration must be 'serious'. According to Scott Baker J in *Willson v Ministry of Defence*, this connotes something beyond the ordinary or commonly experienced consequences of the injury in question. It is relevant to consider the effect on the particular claimant, for example, a hand injury will be more serious to a concert pianist than to most other claimants. One matter particularly considered in *Willson v Ministry of Defence* was whether possible future osteoarthritis could be the subject of a provisional damages award. An increased risk of the onset of osteoarthritis is a common factor where an accident victim has suffered fractured bones. As such, it is not beyond the ordinary, and Scott Baker J took the view that even if the future risk of osteoarthritis involved a possible need for surgery or a change in employment it would not be 'serious'.
(d) There must be a 'chance' that the future deterioration 'will' be suffered. If this is not admitted by the defendant, it must be proved on the balance of probabilities. The 'chance' that must be proved is one that is measurable as opposed to being fanciful. In *Patterson v Ministry of Defence* [1987] CLY 1194, Simon Brown J found that the claimant had about a 5 per cent risk of developing further pleural thickening, and decided there was a 'plain' chance of that happening for the purposes of making a provisional damages award.

63.25 **Discretion to award provisional damages** Once the above conditions have been established, the court has a discretion whether to make a provisional damages award as opposed to a conventional lump-sum award. The most important factor in the exercise of this discretion would appear to be one of balancing the desirability of putting an end to litigation against the possibility of doing better justice by reserving the claimant's right to return to court for further damages. Provisional damages are more appropriate where the risk of the future deterioration is high and the nature of the possible future deterioration is very serious (for example, a future risk of severe epilepsy). Provisional damages are also more likely to be awarded if the claimant can point to some clear-cut future event that will trigger the entitlement to return to court for further damages.

63.26 **Provisional damages orders** A provisional damages order:

(a) must specify the disease or type of deterioration in respect of which an application may be made for further damages as a future date;
(b) must specify the period within which that application may be made. The period for applying for further damages may be extended; and
(c) may be made in respect of more than one disease or type of deterioration, and may, in respect of each disease or type of deterioration, specify a different period for applying for further damages.

A model form of provisional damages judgment is set out in **PD 41A**. This includes the filing of a case file of documents to be preserved until the expiry of the period (or any extension) during which the claimant is entitled to apply for further damages if the specified disease develops or the specified deterioration is suffered. The documents that will usually be included in the case file are the judgment, the statements of case, a transcript of the judge's oral judgment, all medical reports relied upon, and a transcript of the claimant's own evidence in so far as the judge regards it as necessary (**PD 41A, para. 3.2**). The fact there may be a few 'loose ends' where the parties cannot agree does not prevent the court making a provisional damages award (*Hurditch v Sheffield Health Authority* [1989] QB 562).

Other matters dealt with in **PD 41A** are the entering of consent orders for provisional damages (**para.** 4) and default judgments (which can only be entered with the court's permission, with the master or district judge having to decide whether the case is an appropriate one for a provisional damages award, **para.** 5).

Applying for further damages If the deterioration occurs, an application for further damages should be made within the period specified in the order (as extended from time to time). Only one application for further damages can be made in respect of each disease or deterioration specified in the order. The claimant must give 28 days' notice of the intention to ask for further damages. Within 21 days of the expiry of the 28 days' notice the claimant has to apply to the court for directions. **63.27**

Structured settlements

By virtue of an agreement between the Inland Revenue and the Association of British Insurers in 1987, periodic payments made under certain settlements are deemed to be instalments of antecedent debts. The result is that the payments are capital and not income and therefore are not taxable. This tax advantage is obtained by using the whole or a part of the lump sum which would otherwise be available on settling a personal injury claim to purchase an annuity. There are four types of annuity which qualify under the scheme: **63.28**

(a) a basic term annuity, which runs for a fixed number of years;
(b) an index-linked (i.e. one which rises with inflation) fixed-term annuity;
(c) an annuity for life or for a minimum number of years (which survives for the claimant's beneficiaries);
(d) an index-linked life or minimum-term annuity.

Annuities are bought from life offices. A life office will quote a price of an annuity if given certain details about the claimant (age, sex, medical reports, level of income required, etc.). A quotation will normally only remain open for a limited time. The basic idea is that the tax advantage should be shared between the parties, so that the claimant obtains a more favourable settlement which will provide more income than that obtainable under a lump-sum award, and the defendant will pay less for the annuity than the conventional award. Both parties need to agree on a settlement being structured, and it is generally thought that structuring is only viable where damages run into six figures.

Periodical payments

In addition to the established structured settlements, the court can make an award in the form of periodical payments (Damages Act 1996, s. 2, as substituted by the Courts Act 2003, s. 100, from 1 April 2005). In deciding whether to make a periodical payment order, and in what form, the court's overall aim is to make whatever order objectively best meets the claimant's needs (*Thompstone v Tameside and Glossop Acute Services NHS Trust* [2008] EWCA Civ 5, [2008] 1 WLR 2207). An agreement between the parties to an award for periodical payments, even where they are of full age and capacity, does not bind the court, which has to make its own decision (**CPR, r. 41.7; PD 41B**; *Morton v Portal Ltd* [2010] EWHC 1804 (QB), LTL 30/7/2010). The court performs an inquisitorial role in doing this, in which there are no legal burdens of proof. An award in the form of periodical payments can be made where both parties agree, or may be ordered by the court where it awards damages for future pecuniary loss in respect of personal injuries. **63.29**

Such an award can only be made if the court is satisfied the continuity of payments under the order is reasonably secure (Damages Act 1996, s. 2(3)). Continuity problems involving the status of NHS foundation trusts were resolved in *YM (A Child) v Gloucestershire Hospitals NHS Foundation Trust* [2006] EWHC 820 (QB), [2006] PIQR P27, by arrangements being agreed and implemented between the National Health Service Litigation Authority and the Department of Health, which were, subject to conditions, agreed to by the Trust. Rules on continuity of payments are in s. 2(4), **CPR, r. 41.9**, and **PD 41B, para. 3**. The report in the PIQR includes a model form of Tomlin order for use in similar cases.

In *Thompstone v Tameside Hospital NHS Foundation Trust* [2008] EWHC 2948 (QB), [2009] PIQR P153, the court set out a model periodical payments order which needs to be adapted to meet the requirements of individual cases, but any departure in future cases will need to be justified before being approved by the court.

In a personal injuries claim, either side may state in its statement of case whether it considers periodical payments or a lump sum is the more appropriate form for all or part of any award of damages (**CPR, r. 41.5**). The Damages Act 1996, s. 2(8), provides that an order for periodical payments is to be treated as providing for the amount of the payments to vary by reference to the retail prices index at such times and in such manner as might be determined or in accordance with the CPR. This may be disapplied or modified by the court under s. 2(9). There are no restrictions on the types of modifications that may be made under s. 2(9)(b). They may include using a measure based on annual earnings and converted into an index in place of the retail prices index (*Thompstone v Tameside and Glossop Acute Services NHS Trust* [2008] EWCA Civ 5, [2008] 1 WLR 2207 at [4]–[43]). In deciding on a suitable index (see [52]–[58]), the court considers:

(a) the accuracy of the match of the particular data series to the loss and expenditure being compensated;
(b) the authority of the collector of the data;
(c) statistical reliability;
(d) accessibility;
(e) consistency over time;
(f) reproducibility in the future; and
(g) simplicity and consistency in application.

After judgment was entered for damages to be assessed, directions were made in *Flora v Wakom (Heathrow) Ltd* [2005] EWHC 2822 (QB), [2006] PIQR Q95, requiring the claimant to file a statement of case and expert financial evidence dealing with whether a periodical payments order should be made, and whether the court should depart from the usual retail price index under s. 2(9). The defendant was then required to file a statement of case in response and any expert evidence relied upon.The court is under a duty to consider and indicate to the parties its view on the matter as soon as practicable (**CPR, r. 41.6**). In considering whether periodical payments might be appropriate, and whether to make a periodical payments award, the court must have regard to all the circumstances of the case, and which form of award will best meet the claimant's needs (**r. 41.7**). Factors to take into account include, by **PD 41B, para. 1**:

(a) the scale of the annual payments taking into account any contributory negligence;
(b) the claimant's preference, including his reasons for that preference and the nature of any financial advice received; and
(c) the defendant's preference, and his reasons for that preference. In considering the defendant's preference, usually it is sufficient if this is indicated to the court on instructions, without the need to call expert evidence. There is no absolute bar on a defendant adducing the evidence of a financial advice expert (to oppose that of the claimant), but it would be rare for permission to be granted (*Thompstone v Tameside and Glossop Acute Services NHS Trust [2008] EWCA Civ 5, [2008] 1 WLR 2207* at [109]–[112]).

A periodical payments award must specify the annual amount of the award, how each payment is to be made and at what intervals, and the amounts of the main heads of loss (**CPR,**

r. 41.8(1)). There are further requirements where the court orders the award to continue after death for the benefit of the claimant's dependents, where the award is to increase or decrease, and where there is an award for substantial capital purchases (**r. 41.8(2)** to **(4)**, supplemented by **PD 41B, para. 2**). Variations may be permitted pursuant to the Damages (Variation of Periodical Payments) Order 2005 (SI 2005/841). Where the court is satisfied under the Damages Act 1996, s. 2(6)(a), that special circumstances make an assignment or charge of periodical payments necessary, it must also take into account whether the capitalised value of the assignment or charge represents value for money, whether the assignment or charge is in the claimant's best interests, and how the claimant will be financially supported thereafter (**CPR, r. 41.10** and **PD 41B, para. 4**).

As a result of the Damages Act 1996, s. 2, there are special rules on making Part 36 offers where a personal injuries claim includes damages for future pecuniary loss (**CPR, r. 36.5**, see **66.11**).

Where a claim which includes damages for future pecuniary loss is settled on behalf of a claimant under a disability, the usual rules in **Part 21** have to be complied with (see **14.22**), and also the rules in **PD 21, para. 6.3**. Where court approval is sought for a compromise, the court must be satisfied that the parties have considered whether there should be periodical payments (**para. 6.2**). Where the settlement includes periodical payments, the draft consent order must comply with **CPR, rr. 41.8** and **41.9** (see above). The court must be supplied with an opinion on the merits of the settlement or compromise given by counsel or the solicitor acting for the child or protected party (except in very clear cases), and a copy or record of any financial advice (**PD 21, para. 6.4**).

Commentary

Fatal accidents claims

With effect from 6 April 2007, **CPR, r. 41.3A**, applies where a claim includes claims under the **Fatal Accidents Act 1976** and the **Law Reform (Miscellaneous Provisions) Act 1934** and where a claim under the Fatal Accidents Act 1976 is made by or on behalf of more than one person. In such cases, if a single sum of money is ordered or agreed to be paid in satisfaction of the claim, the court must apportion the money between the different claims or between the persons entitled to the money. **63.30**

Part-owners in relation to claims for the detention of goods

In a claim by a person who is one of several people with interests in goods which are the subject of proceedings for wrongful interference and which is not based on a right to possession, any judgment can only be for damages unless every other part-owner gives written authority to the claimant to bring the claim on the part-owner's behalf as well as on the claimant's (**CPR, r. 40.14**). **63.31**

Miscellaneous technical requirements in orders

A number of technical provisions for different types of judgment are contained in **PD 40B**. **Paragraph 14** gives examples of forms that can be used for judgments, and lays down certain matters to be included in the preamble of a judgment, such as the questions put to a jury and their findings, any orders made during the trial regarding the use of evidence, and the findings of the judge in respect of each head of damage in a personal injury case. **63.32**

RESERVED JUDGMENTS

PD 40E applies to all reserved judgments in all courts (**para. 1.1**). Where judgment is reserved, a copy will normally be provided to the parties' legal representatives by 4 p.m. on the second **63.33**

working day before the day listed for handing down the judgment (**para. 2.3**). This is done to enable parties to spot typographical, spelling and minor factual errors, and to give them the opportunity to agree costs and consider an appeal. In *R (Edwards) v Environment Agency* [2008] UKHL 22, [2008] 1 WLR 1587, Lord Hoffmann said, at [66], that sending a 27-paragraph memorandum of submissions commenting on draft speeches was an abuse of process. The purpose of disclosing draft speeches is to obtain the help of counsel in correcting inadvertent errors and ambiguities. It is not to enable counsel to reargue the case. Any proposed corrections should be sent to the clerk of the judge, with a copy to the other parties (**para. 3.1**). Only in the most exceptional circumstances is it appropriate to ask the judge to reconsider a point of substance. Examples are where counsel feels the judge has not given adequate reasons, or has decided the case on a point not sufficiently argued, or has relied on an authority that was not considered. See *Egan v Motor Services (Bath) Ltd* [2007] EWCA Civ 1002, [2008] 1 WLR 1589. A further example given by Lord Judge CJ in *R (Mohamed) v Secretary of State for Foreign and Commonwealth Affairs (No. 2)* [2010] EWCA Civ 158, [2011] QB 218, is where a judgment contains detrimental observations about an individual or the lawyers which are not necessary to the judgment and which appear to be based on a misunderstanding of the evidence, or a concession, or a submission. In such cases the appropriate course is to reconvene the hearing, or for counsel to provide written submissions by 12 noon on the working day before handing down (**para. 4.4**).

The draft judgment must be kept confidential until the judgment is formally handed down. Premature publication of a handed down judgment is a contempt of court (*Re The Lawyer* [2006] EWHC 1131 (Ch), *The Times*, 24 May 2006). During the two-day period between circulation and handing down, the draft judgment can be shown, in confidence, to the parties (**para. 2.4**) and the legal team with immediate conduct of the case (*Director of Public Prosecutions v P (No. 2)* [2007] EWHC 1144 (Admin), [2008] 1 WLR 1024). Neither the judgment nor its substance may be disclosed to any other person, and no action may be taken on it other than internally (**para. 2.4**). This means that while it is appropriate for junior solicitors to consult with their immediate supervising solicitor (and vice versa), wider circulation within chambers or the firm is impermissible. It is just as much a breach of **para. 2.4** to circulate a letter or email from counsel making suggestions for alterations to a draft judgment as it is to circulate the judgment itself (*R (Mohamed) v Secretary of State for Foreign and Commonwealth Affairs (No. 2)* at [11]). If a solicitor is in doubt as to the propriety of a particular disclosure, a request should be made by email to the judge's clerk or the presiding judge for permission (*Director of Public Prosecutions v P (No. 2)* at [15]; **PD 40E, para. 2.7**). The court has the power to waive the confidentiality on a formal interim application to that effect (*R (Mohamed) v Secretary of State for Foreign and Commonwealth Affairs (No. 2)*).

The parties should consider whether they can agree a draft order based on the circulated draft judgment. If they can, they should fax or email a copy to the clerk to the judge or presiding judge, and file four copies (with completed backsheets) in the relevant court office by 12 noon on the working day before handing down (**para. 4.2**). If consequential orders are agreed, there is no need for advocates to attend when judgment is handed down, and costs may be disallowed if they do (**paras 5.1** and **5.2**). Where consequential orders cannot be agreed, the application must be made by filing written submissions with the clerk to the judge or presiding judge by 12 noon on the working day before handing down (**para. 4.4**). Unless the court orders otherwise, the application will be determined without a hearing if in an appeal court, or at a hearing if at first instance (**para. 4.5**).

REDACTED AND ANONYMISED JUDGMENTS

Redacted judgments

63.34 The fact that a judgment contains personal information not otherwise available is not in itself a reason for redacting the judgment (*Kazeminy v Siddiqi* [2010] EWHC 201 (Comm), LTL 2/3/2010).

Where a judgment includes passages that may be protected by public interest immunity (see **50.80** to **50.82**), the court may issue a redacted judgment after considering the strong public policy in favour of open justice and the material in support of immunity. Cogent reasons are required before the court will go behind a ministerial certificate seeking immunity (*R (Mohamed) v Secretary of State for Foreign and Commonwealth Affairs* [2010] EWCA Civ 65, *The Times*, 16 February 2010 at [130]). Genuinely secret material will be protected (see [56]), and in this case the Divisional Court protected a great deal of material relevant to the workings of the security service in a closed judgment, which was not the subject of the appeal (see [50]). However, the Court of Appeal refused to redact a number of paragraphs from an open judgment, and the judgments in the Court of Appeal give careful consideration to the range of factors that may be relevant. Lord Judge LCJ said a redaction order will be made only in extreme circumstances (at [40]).

Anonymised judgments

There is a broad power to order the non-disclosure of the identity of any party if this is necessary to protect the interests of that party (**CPR, r. 39.2(4)**). Courts have a duty to apply an intense focus on the particular circumstances (*Ivereigh v Associated Newspapers Ltd* [2008] EWHC 339 (QB)), and then to strike a balance between the interests of open justice and publicity for court proceedings, and the interests of a party or third person in protecting personal data (*Z v Finland* (application 22009/93) (1997) 25 EHRR 371; and see the European Convention on Human Rights, **arts 6(1)** and **8**, in the **Human Rights Act 1998, sch. 1**). The right to respect for private life under the European Convention on Human Rights, **art. 8**, is only engaged in this context if specific effects are identified by the applicant (*Karakó v Hungary* (application 39311/05) ECHR 28 April 2009). If they are, the court must consider whether there is sufficient general public interest in publishing a report of the proceedings which identifies the applicant to justify any resulting curtailment of his right, and his family's right, to respect for their private and family life (*Re Guardian News and Media Ltd* [2010] UKSC 1, [2010] 2 AC 697). It will only rarely be necessary for the identity of a child involved in proceedings to be revealed (*Ivereigh v Associated Newspapers Ltd*). Often the reasons for holding a hearing in private also justify anonymising any judgment, as do defamation claims of a sensitive nature (*Commissioners of HM Revenue and Customs v Banerjee (No. 2)* [2009] EWHC 1229 (Ch), [2009] 3 All ER 930 at [16], [28]). Otherwise, exceptional circumstances are required to justify anonymising a judgment (*Commissioners of HM Revenue and Customs v Banerjee (No. 2)* at [34]), and once material has been revealed in open court, it enters the public domain (*Commissioners of HM Revenue and Customs v Banerjee (No. 2)* at [38]). **63.35**

ACCOUNTS AND INQUIRIES

At any stage of proceedings, on application by a party or of its own initiative, the court may make an order directing accounts to be taken or inquiries to be made (**CPR, r. 25.1(1)(o)**). The practice on taking such accounts and conducting such inquiries is dealt with in **PD 40A**. When making such an order the court may also at the same time or later give directions as to how the account is to be taken or the inquiry conducted (**PD 40A, para. 1.1**). Among the directions that may be made are the following: **63.36**

(a) that the relevant books of account shall be evidence of their contents, subject to the parties having the right to make objections (**para. 1.2**);
(b) that an account must be made out and verified by an accounting party by exhibiting it to an affidavit or witness statement (**para. 2(1)**);
(c) that, if appropriate, and at any stage in the proceedings, the parties must serve points of claim and points of defence (**para. 5**);
(d) that the matter should be advertised (**para. 10**);
(e) (in an account of debts or other liabilities) that a party examine the claims of those alleging they are owed money, and to file written evidence on his findings and reasons (**para. 11.1(1)**); and

(f) (in an inquiry for next of kin or unascertained beneficiaries) that a party examine the claims made and file written evidence with his findings and reasons (**para. 11.1(3)**).

Unless the court orders otherwise, accounts and inquiries are conducted by masters or district judges (**para. 9**). The court may direct the inquiry to be investigated in any manner, and direct the person making the claim to give further details, file written evidence and attend court (**para. 12**).

A party alleging that an account drawn by an accounting party is inaccurate (or making similar allegations) must give written notice of the objections to the accounting party (**para. 3.1**). These objections must give full particulars, specify the grounds on which it is alleged the account is inaccurate, and be verified by a statement of truth (or exhibited to an affidavit or witness statement).

GENERAL RULES RELATING TO DRAWING UP ORDERS AND JUDGMENTS

63.37 **CPR, rr. 40.2(2), 40.3(1)** and **60.7**, provide that all judgments and orders have to be drawn up and sealed by the court, unless it dispenses with the need to do so. Normally the court will take responsibility for drawing up, but:

(a) unless otherwise ordered, every judgment or order in the Queen's Bench Division, including the Admiralty and Commercial Courts, and the Technology and Construction Court (but not the Administrative Court) must be drawn up by the parties;
(b) the court may order a party to draw up an order; or
(c) a party may, with the permission of the court, agree to draw up an order; or
(d) the court may direct a party to draw up the order subject to checking by the court before it is sealed; or
(e) the court may direct the parties to file an agreed statement of the terms of the order before the court itself draws up the order; or
(f) the order may be entered administratively by consent, in which event the parties will submit a drawn up version of their agreement for entry.

A party who is required to draw up a judgment is allowed seven days to file the relevant document, together with sufficient copies for all relevant parties, failing which any other party may draw it up and file it for sealing (**CPR, rr. 40.3(3)** and **40.4(1)**).

Every judgment or order (apart from judgments on admissions, default judgments, consent judgments and orders made by court officers under **rr. 70.5** and **71.2**) must state the name and judicial title of the judge who made it (**r. 40.2(1)**). Where a party has asked for permission to appeal, the lower court's order should, by **CPR, r. 40.2(3)** and **(4)** include:

(a) whether the judgment is final or not (see 74.6);
(b) whether an appeal lies, and if so, to which court (see 74.4);
(c) whether permission to appeal is granted; and
(d) if not, the appropriate court for making a renewed application for permission to appeal.

Once an order has been drawn up the court will serve sealed copies on the applicant and respondent, and also on any other person the court may order to be served (**r. 40.4(2)**). It will be the court that effects service unless one of the exceptions set out in **r. 6.21(2)** applies. The court is given a specific power by **r. 40.5** to order service on a litigant as well as the litigant's solicitor.

Entering administrative consent orders

63.38 In order to save time and costs, **CPR, r. 40.6**, allows certain types of consent orders to be entered by a purely administrative process without the need for obtaining the approval of a judge. However, this process may not be used if any of the parties is a litigant in person (**r. 40.6(2)(b)**). The types of orders covered are:

(a) judgments or orders for the payment of money;
(b) judgments or orders for the delivery up of goods (other than specific delivery);
(c) orders to dismiss the whole or part of the proceedings;
(d) orders for stays on agreed terms which dispose of the proceedings, including Tomlin orders;
(e) orders setting aside default judgments;
(f) orders for the payment out of money in court;
(g) orders for the discharge from liability of any party; and
(h) orders for the payment, waiver or assessment of costs.

The consent order has to be drawn up in the agreed terms, has to bear the words 'By Consent', and be signed by the solicitors or counsel acting for each of the parties. In cases where terms are annexed in a schedule, provisions dealing with the payment of money out of court and for the payment and assessment of costs should be contained in the body of the order rather than in the schedule (**PD 40B, para. 3.5**).

Consent orders approved by the court

If an order is agreed between the parties, but includes a provision going beyond the types of orders referred to in **63.38**, or if one of the parties is a litigant in person, it will have to be approved by a judge (often a district judge or master). It will be drawn up as above. The name of the judge will not be known, so the draft will have to include a space for the judge's details to be inserted (**PD 23A, para. 10.3**). If all the parties write to the court expressing their consent, the court will treat that as sufficient signing of the consent order (**PD 23A, para. 10.2**). The court will not necessarily make the order in accordance with the agreement between the parties, as the court retains ultimate control, particularly over case management matters. However, it will always take the terms agreed between the parties into account in whatever order it decides to make (see, for example, **PD 28, para. 3.8**). **63.39**

In cases where the court's approval must be sought, either party may make the application for approval, and the application may be dealt with without a hearing (**CPR, r. 40.6(5)** and **(6)**).

Chancery Division orders

Most Chancery Division orders are drawn up by the court (Chancery Guide, para. 9.9). This can usually be done more quickly if a draft order is handed in by the party for whom it is being made (para. 9.5). In all but the simplest cases a draft order should be prepared and brought to the hearing (para. 9.5) and it is helpful if the draft is provided by email or on a digital storage device (see para. 9.7 for details). **63.40**

REVIEW OF JUDGMENT

Appealing (see **chapters** 74 and 75) is the main way of impugning a decision. In limited circumstances a judgment or order may be corrected under the slip rule (**63.42**), or may be reconsidered (**63.43**) or recalled (**63.45**) before it is drawn up. There is also an exceptional power to reopen the whole proceedings where no appeal is possible (**63.46**). **63.41**

Slip rule

The court has power to correct any accidental slip or omission in any judgment (**CPR, r. 40.12(1)**). The slip rule can be used to amend an order to give effect to the intention of the court (*Swindale v Forder* [2007] EWCA Civ 29, [2007] 1 FLR 1905). It cannot be used to enable the **63.42** court to have second or additional thoughts (*Bristol-Myers Squibb Co. v Baker Norton Pharmaceuticals Inc. (No. 2)* [2001] RPC 913), or to correct a substantive issue (*Markos v Goodfellow* (2002) LTL 11/10/2002), or to correct provisions which have been deliberately included in an order (*Leo Pharma A/S v Sandoz Ltd* [2010] EWHC 1911 (Pat), [2010] FSR 41). It cannot be used to correct matters of substance, for which the appropriate avenue is to appeal (*R+V Versicherung AG v Risk Insurance and Reinsurance Solutions SA* [2007] EWHC 79 (Comm), *The Times*, 26 February 2007). An order in *Gesek v Nazdrowicz-Woodley* (1998) LTL 13/11/98 appointing a representative for a deceased claimant referred to 'proceedings to be instituted'. In fact the relevant proceedings had already been issued. It was held that the order should be corrected under the slip rule, even though the correction was sought at trial. **Paragraphs 4.1** to **4.5** of **PD 40B** deal with applications to correct errors in judgments and orders. If the error is obvious the court may deal with the application without notice. Opposed applications will normally be listed before the judge who gave the judgment or made the order.

Reconsideration before judgment is drawn up

63.43 The court may reconsider a judgment after it has been pronounced provided this is done before it is drawn up. During this period factual errors can be corrected (*Spice Girls Ltd v Aprilia World Service BV (No. 3)* (2000) *The Times*, 12 September 2000). The Court of Appeal may reconsider a judgment in the period between draft judgments being sent to the parties and formal delivery in court (*Royal Brompton Hospital NHS Trust v Hammond* [2001] BLR 317; see also the power to reopen an appeal under **CPR, r. 52.17**, discussed at **74.54**). The power to reconsider a judgment is not affected by **r. 40.7**, which provides that a judgment takes effect from the time of pronouncement (*Stewart v Engel* [2000] 1 WLR 2268). Reconsideration can be sought up to the time the judgment is sealed, a position that is not affected by **r. 52.4(2)(b)** (time for filing an appellant's notice runs from pronouncement) (*Paulin v Paulin* [2009] EWCA Civ 221, [2009] 3 All ER 88).

Reconsideration should be sought only in exceptional circumstances (*Re Barrell Enterprises* [1973] 1 WLR 19, as affirmed by *Stewart v Engel* and *Taylor v Lawrence* [2002] EWCA Civ 90, [2003] QB 528). The examples of exceptional circumstances justifying reconsideration of interim decisions, given by Neuberger J in *Re Blenheim Leisure (Restaurants) Ltd (No. 3)* (1999) *The Times*, 9 November 1999 (see **32.42**), would also justify reconsideration of a final judgment (*Stewart v Engel*). The fact that the party against whom judgment has been pronounced has a change of mind about not pursuing a particular cause of action is not an exceptional circumstance justifying reconsideration (*Stewart v Engel*). It would be a misuse of the jurisdiction to argue that a judge should reconsider an issue which was in dispute and already argued: that would be to subvert the appeal process (*Compagnie Noga d'Importation et d'Exportation SA v Abacha* [2001] 3 All ER 513). It is also an abuse of the procedure to advance points which were not argued before judgment was given (*Sheikh v Dogan* [2009] EWHC 2935 (Ch), LTL 24/11/2009).

Reconsideration of case management decisions

63.44 It may sometimes be appropriate for one judge to reconsider case management directions made on a previous occasion by another judge. Each case turns on its own facts, with the court seeking to give effect to the overriding objective, but if there has been a change of circumstances it may well be appropriate to interfere with the procedural regime previously laid down (*Umm Qarn Management Co. Ltd v Bunting* [2001] CPLR 21). It is only if there is a significant change in circumstances that a case management decision can be revisited on a later occasion (*Jameson v Personal Representatives of Smith* [2001] EWCA Civ 1264, [2001] CPLR 489). A change in a *party's appreciation* of the effect of an order is simply a change in perception, not a change of circumstances (*W. L. Gore and Associates GmbH v Geox SpA* [2008] EWHC 462 (Pat), LTL 7/4/2008). It is incumbent on a party to claim interim relief based on the same facts once and once only

(*Halifax plc v Chandler* [2001] EWCA Civ 1750, [2002] CPLR 41, where there were two applications to vary a freezing injunction). In *Leadmill Ltd v Omare* [2002] EWHC 1226 (Ch), LTL 23/4/2002, an interim injunction was granted restraining the defendant from calling his tapas bar 'The Treadmill', being sited close to the claimant's nightclub, 'The Leadmill'. The defendant applied to discharge the order on the basis he intended to change the colour and font of his signs. It was held that the defendant could have raised this at the initial hearing. As afterthoughts are not permitted, the application was refused. On the other hand, the production of extra evidence was regarded as a change of circumstances in *Bass Taverns Ltd v Carford Catering Equipment Ltd* [2002] EWCA Civ 671, LTL 23/4/2002.

Recalling judgment

A judge is under a positive obligation to recall a draft judgment sent to the legal representatives of the parties in advance of formal pronouncement (see **61.56**) if it becomes clear that the draft is wrong (*Robinson v Bird* [2003] EWCA Civ 1820, *The Times*, 20 January 2004). In *Taylor v Williamsons* [2002] EWCA Civ 1380, [2003] CP Rep 20, after hearing evidence on a preliminary issue, the case was adjourned with directions for the exchange and filing of written submissions. Before the deadline, and before receiving the claimant's submissions, the judge issued a written judgment dismissing the claim. When the mistake was discovered, the judge recalled his judgment, refused to recuse himself, and again gave judgment for the defendant. An appeal by the claimant was dismissed. It was held that a judge has a wide discretion to amend a judgment before it is perfected and to recall such a judgment, and there was no reason to think the judge in this case had not reconsidered the case fairly in the light of the further submissions. **63.45**

Commentary

Reopening proceedings

Like the Court of Appeal (*Taylor v Lawrence* [2002] EWCA Civ 90, [2003] QB 528, see **74.54**), the High Court has jurisdiction to reopen proceedings after they have been concluded to hear more evidence or further argument (*Seray-Wurie v Hackney London Borough Council* [2002] EWCA Civ 909, [2003] 1 WLR 257). The power should only be exercised where there has been a significant injustice and where there is no alternative remedy. There may be no alternative remedy where an appeal court has refused permission to appeal (see **74.16** and the **Access to Justice Act 1999, s. 54(4)**, which is a point made at **CPR, r. 52.17(7)**). Applications for permission to reopen should be made on paper (*Taylor v Lawrence*). **63.46**

The decisions referred to in the previous paragraph were both based on the court's inherent jurisdiction. This means they have no direct relevance to the question of whether there is jurisdiction for a county court circuit judge to reopen a decision (*Seray-Wurie v Hackney London Borough Council*, a point which appears to be confirmed by **r. 52.17(3)**).

Functus officio

A judgment may be reconsidered or recalled in the period between delivery and drawing up (**63.43 to 63.46**). Subject to the slip rule (**63.42**), once the judgment has been drawn up into an order the judge is *functus officio*, which operates as a bar to further alterations by the judge (*Earl of Malmesbury v Strutt and Parker* [2007] EWHC 2199 (QB), [2007] 42 EG 294 (CS)). **63.47**

PRESERVED PROVISIONS OF THE CCR RELATING TO JUDGMENTS AND ORDERS

The following provisions of the CCR have been preserved in **CPR, sch. 2**: **63.48**

(a) **CCR, ord. 22, r. 8**, on obtaining a certificate of judgment;

(b) **CCR, ord. 22, r. 10**, on applying to vary the date or rate of payment;
(c) **CCR, ord. 22, r. 11**, on setting off cross-judgments; and
(d) **CCR, ord. 22, r. 13**, on filing in the county court orders of the High Court and Court of Appeal after appeals have been determined.

REGISTER OF JUDGMENTS

63.49 Under the Courts Act 2003, s. 98, a register of money judgments from the High Court and the county courts, and also criminal fines, may be kept either by a body corporate in accordance with terms agreed with the Lord Chancellor, or it may be kept by the Lord Chancellor (Register of Judgments, Orders and Fines Regulations 2005, SI 2005/3595, regs 6 and 7). The relevant register is operated by Registry Trust Ltd. Appropriate officers in the High Court and county courts are required to provide the registrar with periodic returns of judgments and orders for the payment of money (reg. 8(1) and the definition of 'judgment' in reg. 3). The following are, by reg. 9, exempt from registration:

(a) judgments in family proceedings;
(b) judgments in the Administrative Court;
(c) judgments in the Technology and Construction Court;
(d) judgments under appeal, until the appeal has been determined;
(e) broadly, judgments in contested proceedings, until an order or application is made for payment by instalments, or the judgment creditor takes any step to enforce the judgment; and
(f) broadly, orders for the payment of money in claims for the recovery of land, until the judgment creditor takes any step to enforce the order.

Details given by the appropriate officer to the registrar include the debtor's full name, date of birth (which explains why this information is required in acknowledgments of service and defences), and the amount of the judgment debt (reg. 10). The amount may be increased, for example, after the assessment of costs (reg. 20). Registrations are removed after six years in any event (reg. 26). Registration may be cancelled if the judgment is satisfied within one month from the date of the judgment, or if it is set aside or reversed (reg. 11(2)). If the judgment is satisfied more than a month after judgment, the appropriate officer should notify the registrar who will endorse the entry with the fact the judgment has been satisfied (reg. 11(3)).

Records of judgments and orders

63.50 Official copies of court documents prove themselves (Senior Courts Act 1981, s. 132; **PD 32, para. 13.2**). This means, for example, that there is no need (and it is wrong) to exhibit a sealed judgment or order to a witness statement.

The district judge for every district must keep or cause to be kept records of proceedings in the county court (County Courts Act 1984, s. 12(1)). A certified copy of an entry in a book or other document kept for this purpose is admissible in evidence without further proof as evidence of the entry and of the proceeding referred to and the regularity of that proceeding (s. 12(2)). The position is similar in the High Court (Senior Courts Act 1981, s. 136). Where primary evidence of a court record has been destroyed or lost, secondary evidence is admissible to prove the existence of the originals (*Miller-Foulds v Secretary of State for Constitutional Affairs* (2008) LTL 20/11/2008).

Chapter 64 Interest

INTRODUCTION

Until *Sempra Metals Ltd v Commissioners of Inland Revenue* [2007] UKHL 34, [2008] 1 AC 561, the law on awarding interest was confused and based on the misapplication of principles (see [92]). The underlying problem was that the courts, following decisions in the eighteenth and nineteenth centuries, restricted the circumstances in which interest could be awarded, and generally restricted awards to simple as opposed to compound interest. This is contrary to economic reality. Money is not available commercially in return for simple interest only. This is true whether money is borrowed on overdraft or credit cards or mortgages, or when depositing money with banks or building societies (Lord Nicholls of Birkenhead at [52]). *Sempra Metals Ltd v Commissioners of Inland Revenue* reinterprets the leading authorities on awards of interest, and lays down a coherent set of principles which are consistent with the law on remoteness in contract and tort, and the modern law of restitution. **64.1**

Statutory interest

The most straightforward way of claiming interest in a claim for money is to seek interest pursuant to the County Courts Act 1984, s. 69, or the Senior Courts Act 1981, s. 35A. See **64.9** to **64.12**. Although such awards are technically discretionary, they are usually made as a matter of course, and can be made in the absence of evidence of actual loss through being kept out of the principal sum. Under these provisions the court is restricted to awarding simple interest. While the rate of interest is in the court's discretion, the starting point is 8 per cent per annum (the rate under the Judgments Act 1838). These provisions do not apply to debt claims which are paid before proceedings are commenced. Despite these restrictions, claiming interest under these statutory provisions will often be the most convenient and cost-effective method of seeking interest. **64.2**

There is a slightly more complicated statutory right to interest under the Late Payment of Commercial Debts (Interest) Act 1998 (see **64.15**). This again provides for simple interest only, but at a rate of 8 per cent over the Bank of England's official dealing rate. It does this by implying a term to pay interest, so it will be considered with contractual cases below. This Act applies only to claims for the contract price for the supply of goods or services where both the purchaser and supplier are acting in the course of a business. Where it applies this Act gives a right to interest, and at a better rate than under the County Courts Act 1984, s. 69, and the Senior Courts Act 1981, s. 35A.

Various other statutory powers to award interest are mentioned at **64.13**.

Contractual interest

64.3 Being contractual, such interest is payable as of right. It may provide for a high rate of interest, which may be either simple or compound as agreed by the parties. The main problems with contractual interest relate to proving the relevant term and interpreting it, although it is also possible for such a term to be struck down as extortionate. See **64.14**.

Special jurisdiction to award interest

64.4 Equity cases are considered at **64.16**.

Interest as part of the principal award

64.5 Interest can be awarded as part of the claimant's damages in claims in contract and tort, as part (or the whole) of the claimant's primary award in restitution, and in Admiralty cases. An award of interest as damages in contract or tort is subject to the usual rules on proof of loss, causation, remoteness and mitigation of damage. The award may include an element of compound interest. In restitution, the award is based on the benefit received by the defendant through the unjust use of the claimant's money. This is the main importance of *Sempra Metals Ltd v Commissioners of Inland Revenue* [2007] UKHL 34, [2008] 1 AC 561. While compound interest may be awarded, most of the key elements of the claim for interest have to be proved by the claimant (the exception is the rate of interest, where the burden of proof is on the defendant). Establishing interest as a head of damages or a restitutionary award is therefore likely to be complicated and costly. See **64.18** to **64.20**.

Statutory interest in addition to interest as damages or restitution

64.6 In *Sempra Metals Ltd v Commissioners of Inland Revenue* [2007] UKHL 34, [2008] 1 AC 561, the compound interest awarded as the main restitutionary remedy covered the period from when the claimant made certain mistaken payments until the dates when those mistaken payments were offset against tax legitimately payable. The court also awarded statutory interest under the Senior Courts Act 1981, s. 35A, on the restitutionary interest from the dates of the offsets to the date of the hearing.

Pleading interest

64.7 Any claim for interest must be pleaded in the particulars of claim (or counterclaim), see **64.21**.

Conflict of laws

64.8 For the purposes of the conflict of laws, the right to interest on damages for personal injuries under the Senior Courts Act 1981, s. 35A, is a remedy, not a substantive cause of action (*Maher v Groupama Grand Est* [2009] EWCA Civ 1191, LTL 12/11/2009).

STATUTORY INTEREST

Statutory interest on claims for damages

Statutory authority for adding interest to any sum recovered by way of damages is provided by the Senior Courts Act 1981, s. 35A(1), and by the County Courts Act 1984, s. 69(1), which are in identical terms (except for referring to the High Court and county courts respectively). The County Courts Act 1984, s. 69(1), provides: **64.9**

Subject to rules of court, in proceedings (whenever instituted) before a county court for the recovery of a debt or damages there may be included in any sum for which judgment is given simple interest, at such rate as the court thinks fit or as may be prescribed, on all or any part of the debt or damages in respect of which judgment is given, or payment is made before judgment, for all or any part of the period between the date when the cause of action arose and—

(a) in the case of any sum paid before judgment, the date of the payment; and
(b) in the case of the sum for which judgment is given, the date of the judgment.

Interest on damages is therefore discretionary, and may be awarded on all or part of the amount recovered, and for such period and at such rates as the court may think fit. However, it is a discretion which is usually exercised in favour of the party obtaining judgment. The way it was expressed by Gloster J in *Socimer International Bank Ltd v Standard Bank London Ltd* [2006] EWHC 2896 (Comm), LTL 8/12/2006, was that statutory interest should be awarded unless there is a good reason for departing from the usual rule. The principle on which the courts act is that interest should be paid to compensate the claimant for being kept out of the money which the judgment shows should have been paid at an earlier time (*Wentworth v Wiltshire County Council* [1993] QB 654). Since the time at which the money should have been paid, the claimant will have been forced either to borrow money, or to use funds which could have been employed profitably for other purposes, or have been deprived of the use of the money awarded by the judgment. An award of interest compensates for this loss. While statutory interest may be lost in an exceptional case where there is a delay in commencing proceedings (*Kuwait Airways Corporation v Kuwait Insurance Co. SAK* [2000] Lloyd's Rep IR 678), it is wrong to disallow interest to take into account conduct in relation to offers and negotiations (*Benedetti v Sawiris* [2010] EWCA Civ 1427, LTL 16/12/2010). The latter can be dealt with by the order as to costs.

The statutory provisions only allow the court to award simple interest. It is therefore wrong in principle to award damages for things such as bank interest if an award of statutory interest on the other heads of damage is made, as that would amount to double recovery (*Wentworth v Wiltshire County Council* [1993] QB 654).

In personal injuries claims it is even clearer that interest should ordinarily be awarded in addition to damages. The Senior Courts Act 1981, s. 35A(2), and the County Courts Act 1984, s. 69(2), both provide:

In relation to a judgment given for damages for personal injuries or death which exceed £200 subsection (1) shall have effect—

(a) with the substitution of 'shall be included' for 'may be included'; and
(b) with the addition of 'unless the court is satisfied that there are special reasons to the contrary' after 'given', where first occurring.

The Senior Courts Act 1981, s. 35A(7), and the County Courts Act 1984, s. 69(6), state that the term 'personal injuries' includes any disease or impairment of a person's physical or mental condition.

Statutory interest on debt claims

The main provisions in the Senior Courts Act 1981, s. 35A(1), and the County Courts Act 1984, s. 69(1) (see **64.9**), by their terms apply to debt claims as well as claims for damages. **64.10**

Accordingly, the court is given a general discretion to award simple interest on judgments for debts at such rates and for such periods as the court thinks fit. Restitution claims, and claims for sums of money subject to an obligation, no matter how they arise, are 'debt' claims within the meaning of the Senior Courts Act 1981, s. 35A, and the County Courts Act 1984, s. 69. They therefore attract discretionary simple interest (see *R (Kemp) v Denbighshire Local Health Board* [2006] EWHC 181 (Admin), [2007] 1 WLR 639).

In addition, s. 35A(3) of the 1981 Act and s. 69(3) of the 1984 Act (both of which are in the same terms apart from references to the High Court and county courts respectively) provide for the recovery of simple interest on debt claims which are paid after the commencement of proceedings even in the absence of a judgment. The County Courts Act 1984, s. 69(3), provides:

> Subject to rules of court, where—
> (a) there are proceedings (whenever instituted) before a county court for the recovery of a debt; and
> (b) the defendant pays the whole debt to the [claimant] (otherwise than in pursuance of a judgment in the proceedings),
>
> the defendant shall be liable to pay the [claimant] simple interest, at such rate as the court thinks fit or as may be prescribed, on all or any part of the debt for all or any part of the period between the date the cause of action arose and the date of payment.

These provisions do not apply if interest is payable on the debt for some other reason (see **64.13**), because s. 35A(4) of the 1981 Act and s. 69(4) of the 1984 Act provide:

> Interest in respect of a debt shall not be awarded under this section for a period during which, for whatever reason, interest on the debt already runs.

Payment before judgment

64.11 The reason why subsection (3) is in the Senior Courts Act 1981, s. 35A, and the County Courts Act 1984, s. 69, is that payment in full of a debt extinguishes the debt, and so subsection (3) is required to preserve a right to interest despite payment of the principal before judgment (see *Edmunds v Lloyds Italico & l'Ancora Compagnia di Assicurazione e Riassicurazione SpA* [1986] 1 WLR 492). On the other hand, payment of the sum claimed in a damages case does not extinguish the cause of action, and the court may still enter judgment for damages (even though full credit will be given so that no further damages will be paid) and interest. Consequently, there is no need for an equivalent provision to subsection (3) in relation to damages claims (*Edmunds v Lloyds Italico & l'Ancora Compagnia di Assicurazione e Riassicurazione SpA* [1986] 1 WLR 492).

Interest is not payable by virtue of s. 35A of the 1981 Act or s. 69 of the 1984 Act unless proceedings have been commenced (*President of India v La Pintada Compania Navigacion SA* [1985] AC 104; *Sempra Metals Ltd v Commissioners of Inland Revenue* [2007] UKHL 34, [2008] 1 AC 561 at [83]), though interest may be payable under other provisions (see **64.13** and **64.14**). In a damages claim there is nothing to stop the claimant insisting on an element representing interest to be included in any agreed settlement before proceedings are issued. In a debt claim where there is no defence, the debtor is well advised to pay the whole sum due before proceedings are commenced so as to avoid an order to pay interest as well. Once proceedings are commenced, interest may be claimed for the periods both before and after issue.

'Proceedings'

64.12 Statutory interest under the Senior Courts Act 1981, s. 35A, and the County Courts Act 1984, s. 69, applies 'in proceedings (whenever instituted)'. This normally means that a claim form has to be issued. In judicial review proceedings, the trigger point is when the judicial review claim form is submitted (*R (Kemp) v Denbighshire Local Health Board* [2006] EWHC 181 (Admin), [2007] 1 WLR 639).

Miscellaneous statutes

In addition to the general provisions in the Senior Courts Act 1981, s. 35A, and the County Courts Act 1984, s. 69, there are other statutes giving rights to interest. Examples are: 64.13

(a) The Bills of Exchange Act 1882, s. 57, which provides:

   Where a bill is dishonoured, the measure of damages, which shall be deemed to be liquidated damages, shall be as follows:

   (1) The holder may recover from any party liable on the bill and the drawer who has been compelled to pay the bill may recover from the acceptor, and an indorser who has been compelled to pay the bill may recover from the acceptor or from the drawer, or from a prior indorser:
      (a) The amount of the bill:
      (b) Interest thereon from the time of presentment for payment if the bill is payable on demand, and from the maturity of the bill in any other case:
      (c) The expenses of noting, or, when protest is necessary, and the protest has been extended, the expenses of protest.

   [(2) Repealed]

   (3) Where by this Act interest may be recovered as damages, such interest may, if justice require it, be withheld wholly or in part, and where a bill is expressed to be payable with interest at a given rate, interest as damages may or may not be given at the same rate as interest proper.

(b) In a claim against a carrier under the Convention on the Contract for the International Carriage of Goods by Road, the claimant is entitled to claim interest at 5 per cent per annum (Carriage of Goods by Road Act 1965, sch., art. 27).
(c) Under the Partnership Act 1890, s. 24(3), a partner who contributes more capital than the partnership agreement calls for is entitled to interest at 5 per cent per annum on the additional contribution from the date of payment, unless otherwise agreed.
(d) Under the Solicitors' (Non-contentious Business) Remuneration Order 1994 (SI 1994/2616), art. 14, a solicitor may charge interest at a rate not exceeding that payable on judgments on the amount of his or her unpaid costs in respect of non-contentious business or common form probate business, plus disbursements and VAT, subject to various conditions set out in the Order.
(e) Various revenue statutes provide for the payment of interest, such as the Taxes Management Act 1970, ss. 86 to 92.

CONTRACT CASES

Interest pursuant to contract

Interest may be payable under the express terms of a contract between the parties. Where this is the case, the interest is payable as of right, and is not a matter for the court's discretion. The only exception is where the rate of interest is extortionate within the meaning of the Consumer Credit Act 1974. Mortgage agreements and many other forms of credit agreement purport to give the lender an unfettered discretion to vary the rate of interest charged. Dyson LJ in *Paragon Finance plc v Nash* [2001] EWCA Civ 1466, [2002] 1 WLR 685, said that such a discretion is subject to an implied term that it is not to be exercised dishonestly, capriciously, arbitrarily or for an improper purpose. Express terms for the payment of interest often also provide that interest at the agreed rate shall be payable before and after proceedings, and even before and after judgment, until actual payment. The latter type of clause presents some difficulty over the form any judgment should take. One school of thought is to the effect that the judgment should only include contractual interest to the date of the judgment, leaving the creditor to bring a second action (if thought fit) to recover the post-judgment interest. The other school of thought would allow the court to make a judgment to include the interest to the date of judgment together with continuing interest at the contractual daily rate to payment. 64.14

Interest has also been awarded in cases where money has been lent on terms that it should be repaid on a set date with interest being payable until then. Where the loan is not repaid on the due date, the courts have awarded interest from the due date for repayment as damages (see *Cook v Fowler* (1874) LR 7 HL 27). As the award has been for damages, the courts have not always used the original interest rate as the measure of the damages for late payment.

Late payment of commercial debts

64.15 The Late Payment of Commercial Debts (Interest) Act 1998 was passed in compliance with Directive 2000/35/EC on combating late payment. Section 1(1) makes it an implied term in a contract to which the Act applies that any qualifying debt created by the contract carries simple interest subject to the terms of ss. 1 to 6 of the Act. The Act applies to contracts for the sale of goods and for the supply of services and related matters (s. 2), and a 'qualifying debt' is an obligation to pay the price under such a contract (s. 3(1)). With the exception of advance payments, interest runs from 30 days after the supplier performs its obligations under the contract, or 30 days after invoice or other notification of the price (s. 4(2), (4) and (5)). There is a maximum payment period of up to 30 days where the purchaser is a public authority, and in other cases a period of up to 60 days or longer as otherwise agreed (s. 4(3A) to (3C)). Where the payment period is longer than 60 days, the period must not be grossly unfair to the supplier (s. 4(3C)(b)). Where two invoices were used to bill the sum claimed, interest ran from the second invoice (*Ruttle Plant Hire Ltd v Secretary of State for the Environment, Food and Rural Affairs (No. 3)* [2008] EWHC 730 (TCC), [2009] 1 All ER (Comm) 73). The rate of interest is as prescribed by statutory instrument (s. 6); see the Late Payment of Commercial Debts (Rate of Interest) (No. 3) Order 2002 (SI 2002/1675), which sets the rate at 8 per cent over the Bank of England's official dealing rate. It is referred to as the 'UK clearing bank base lending rate' and is published every day (except on Sundays) in *The Financial Times*. Until August 2006 it was known as the 'Repo', since repos or sale and repurchase agreements are one type of monetary policy instrument used by the Bank of England. It is currently known as the Official Bank Rate. The relevant rates can be seen on the Bank of England website http://www.bankofengland.co.uk, click on 'statistics', then 'interest and exchange rates', and are shown in **64.1**.

Table 64.1 Bank of England Official Dealing Rates

Date	Interest (%)
	Repo Rate
8 October 1998	7.25
5 November 1998	6.75
10 December 1998	6.25
7 January 1999	6.00
4 February 1999	5.50
8 April 1999	5.25
10 June 1999	5.00
8 September 1999	5.25
4 November 1999	5.50
13 January 2000	5.75
10 February 2000	6.00
8 February 2001	5.75
5 April 2001	5.50
10 May 2001	5.25
2 August 2001	5.00
18 September 2001	4.75
4 October 2001	4.50
8 November 2001	4.00
6 February 2003	3.75

(*continued*)

Date	Interest (%)
	Repo Rate
10 July 2003	3.50
6 November 2003	3.75
5 February 2004	4.00
6 May 2004	4.25
10 June 2004	4.50
5 August 2004	4.75
4 August 2005	4.50
	Official Bank Rate
3 August 2006	4.75
9 November 2006	5.00
10 May 2007	5.50
5 July 2007	5.75
6 December 2007	5.50
7 February 2008	5.25
10 April 2008	5.00
8 October 2008	4.50
4 December 2008	2.00
8 January 2009	1.50
6 November 2008	3.00
5 February 2009	1.00
5 March 2009	0.50

The rate of interest may be reduced in the interests of justice on account of any misconduct by the supplier (s. 5).

The 1998 Act has been brought into effect as follows:

Phase	Applies to contracts from	Scope
1	1 November 1998	Small businesses can claim statutory interest for late payment from large businesses and most public-sector bodies.
2	1 November 2000	Small businesses can claim statutory interest from small businesses, large businesses and most public-sector bodies.
3	7 August 2002	All businesses and public-sector bodies can claim statutory interest.

A payment is deemed to be late when an agreed credit period has expired, or, if there is none, 30 days after the later of:

(a) delivery of the goods or performance of the services under the contract; and
(b) the date the purchaser was notified of the amount of the debt.

There are special rules for advance payments. Where the parties have a system of payment by the end of the month following the month in which the invoice is received, payment will be late for the purposes of the legislation at the end of the month following the month in which the invoice was received.

A seller making use of the legislation must notify the purchaser. Notification may be oral, but written notice is preferable in the event of a dispute. The notice should state the amount owed, what it is owed for, how the statutory interest is calculated, should quote the original invoice number, and state to whom and where payment should be made, by what date and by what method.

The Bank of England base rate on 31 December will be the 'reference rate' for the following 1 January to 30 June. Base rate on 30 June will be the reference rate for the period 1 July to

31 December. Statutory interest under the late payment legislation is 8 per cent above the appropriate reference rate. So, if the reference rate is 1.5 per cent p.a., the rate payable under the late payment legislation would be simple interest at 9.5 per cent p.a. (but fluctuating every six months with any variations in Bank of England base rate).

In addition, a seller is entitled to charge statutory compensation on late payments (s. 5A). The amount of compensation varies with the amount of the debt, as follows:

Size of unpaid debt	Amount of compensation
Up to £999.99	£40.00
£1,000 to £9,999.99	£70.00
Over £9,999.99	£100.00

If the reasonable costs of the supplier in recovering the debt are not met by the fixed compensation, the supplier is also entitled to a sum equivalent to the difference between the fixed sum and those costs (s. 5A(2A)).

Parties to a contract can contract out of the late-payment legislation, provided they make their own arrangements for contractual interest. To prevent abuse, contractual interest must be 'substantial', otherwise it will be void and the late-payment legislation will apply. In considering whether a contractual remedy is substantial, the court must consider all the circumstances, including the rate of interest applicable to late payments and the length of credit periods. If the credit period is considered excessive, the court can strike it down and replace it with a 30-day default period. 'Representative bodies' are given standing to challenge contractual terms which are grossly unfair on behalf of small and medium-sized enterprises (SMEs). SMEs are independent enterprises which have fewer than 250 employees and either a turnover of less than 40 million euro or an annual balance sheet total not exceeding 27 million euro.

EQUITY CASES

64.16 There is a long-established practice of awarding interest in the Chancery Division ancillary to equitable remedies such as the taking of an account or specific performance. Interest has been awarded in claims where defendants owing fiduciary duties have been found to have misapplied or withheld money, or been guilty of fraud (*Johnson v R* [1904] AC 817).

EXCEPTIONAL CASES WHERE INTEREST IS NOT AWARDED

64.17 Interest is not normally awarded on awards in libel cases, nor in claims for wrongful arrest or false imprisonment (*Holtham v Commissioner of Police for the Metropolis* (1987) *The Independent*, 26 November 1987). In *Saunders v Edwards* [1987] 1 WLR 1116 it was held that interest should not have been awarded on a sum for inconvenience and disappointment made in a misrepresentation claim.

INTEREST AS PART OF THE PRINCIPAL AWARD

Interest as damages

64.18 At common law, the rule was that a court had no power, in the absence of any agreement, to award interest as compensation for the late payment of a debt or damages (*London,*

Chatham and Dover Railway Co. v South Eastern Railway Co. [1893] AC 429). This decision was seen to be inconsistent with the general principles for the assessment of damages. It was interpreted by *President of India v La Pintada Compania Navigacion SA* [1985] AC 104 as applying to prevent claims to interest as damages where the loss fell within the first limb of *Hadley v Baxendale* (1854) 9 Exch 341, but not where it came within the second limb. The result was that where it was plain to everyone that interest loss would be suffered in the event of non-payment (the first limb), it could not be recovered. However, if the interest loss came about from circumstances known only to the contracting parties (the second limb), it was recoverable (*President of India v Lips Maritime Corporation* [1985] 2 Lloyd's Rep 180 at p. 185). This unsatisfactory position was swept away by *Sempra Metals Ltd v Commissioners of Inland Revenue* [2007] UKHL 34, [2008] 1 AC 561.

The present position is that, subject to the ordinary rules of remoteness, causation and mitigation of loss, any loss that is proved by the claimant arising as a result of the late payment of money is recoverable (*Sempra Metals Ltd v Commissioners of Inland Revenue* at [16], [92], [94]–[97], [165]). As Lord Hope of Craighead said, at [16]:

> The reality is that every creditor who is deprived of funds to which he is entitled and which he needs to run his business will have to incur an interest-bearing loan or employ other funds which could themselves have earned interest. It is a short step to say that interest losses will arise 'in the ordinary course of things' in such circumstances.

London, Chatham and Dover Railway Co. v South Eastern Railway Co. has not been overruled, but is confined to its own facts. It therefore applies only to claims at common law for unparticularised and unproven interest losses as damages for breach of a contract to pay a debt and claims for payment of a debt with interest (*Sempra Metals Ltd v Commissioners of Inland Revenue*, per Lord Nicholls of Birkenhead at [96]). In these cases, the claimant will usually be best advised to claim statutory interest under either the County Courts Act 1984, s. 69, or the Senior Courts Act 1981, s. 35A (see **64.9** to **64.12**). In fact, in any case where a party chooses not to prove his interest losses the remedy is to be found in the statutory interest provisions (*Sempra Metals Ltd v Commissioners of Inland Revenue* at [97]).

Commentary

Admiralty cases

In the Admiralty Court there is a long-established practice of awarding interest as damages in claims arising out of collisions at sea and in salvage awards (*The Aldora* [1975] QB 748; *The Rilland* [1979] 1 Lloyd's Rep 455). **64.19**

Restitution claims

The ancient position was that interest could not be awarded in a claim for money had and received (*Walker v Constable* (1798) 1 Bos & P 306). This was unprincipled, and stemmed from a misunderstanding of earlier authorities. Before *Sempra Metals Ltd v Commissioners of Inland Revenue* [2007] UKHL 34, [2008] 1 AC 561, it was recognised that awards in restitution were debts for the purposes of the Senior Courts Act 1981, s. 35A, and the County Courts Act 1984, s. 69 (see **64.10**). As a result, simple interest at the Judgments Act 1838 rate can be sought under the Senior Courts Act 1981, s. 35A, or the County Courts Act 1984, s. 69, on these awards without the claimant needing to prove his interest losses. **64.20**

In *Sempra Metals Ltd v Commissioners of Inland Revenue* the principal sum claimed was for the loss of use over time of sums the claimant had paid to the Revenue in the mistaken belief that it had to pay those sums in tax. Departing from the decision in *Westdeutsche Landesbank Girozentrale v Islington London Borough Council* [1996] AC 669, it was held that there is jurisdiction to award compound interest as substantive restitutionary relief. Different views were expressed on whether this was at common law (Lord Hope of Craighead, Lord Nicholls of Birkenhead and Lord Scott of Foscote) or in the exercise of the court's equitable jurisdiction (Lord Walker of Gestingthorpe and Lord Mance), although the result was the same under both routes.

PLEADING INTEREST

64.21 Under **CPR, r. 16.4(2)**, if the claimant is seeking interest, the particulars of claim must:

(a) state whether the claim is:
  (i) under the terms of a contract; or
  (ii) under an enactment, and if so which; or
  (iii) on some other basis, and if so which basis;

(b) if the principal claim is for a specified sum of money, the particulars of claim must:
  (i) state the percentage rate claimed for the interest and the date from which it is claimed;
  (ii) contain an interest calculation, giving a date (which should be no later than the date of issue of the claim form) to which past interest is calculated; and
  (iii) the daily rate at which future interest accrues.

If the claim is for an unspecified amount of money (as most damages claims are), it is sufficient, in addition to stating the basis on which interest is claimed, to say in the particulars of claim that interest is sought at such rates and for such periods on the sums found due to the claimant as the court may think fit, to be decided by the court. A claim to contractual interest requires the contractual term to be pleaded in the particulars of claim, together with an interest paragraph and a claim for the interest in the prayer. In claims for interest and statutory compensation under the Late Payment of Commercial Debts (Interest) Act 1998, the statutory implied term under s. 1(1) (and its extension to statutory compensation under s. 5A(3)) must be pleaded, together with an interest paragraph and a claim for the interest in the prayer. Where interest is sought as a primary remedy (see **64.18** to **64.20**), the claim to interest is set out in the loss and damage or remedies paragraphs in the particulars of claim, and also in the prayer.

RATE OF INTEREST

General rules

64.22 Interest pursuant to contract should be at the contract rate. Some statutes (such as the Partnership Act 1890) lay down specific rates for interest recoverable. Under the Late Payment of Commercial Debts (Interest) Act 1998, interest is at 8 per cent above Bank of England base rate. Otherwise, the rate of interest is in the discretion of the court. Where this is so, in practical terms the starting point in most classes of case is the Judgments Act 1838 rate, which has been 8 per cent a year since 1 April 1993 (see **table 64.2**). There are other methods of determining the rate of interest to be paid. The court may assess interest by reference to the rates provided by index-linked government stock, or by reference to the base rate of the Bank of England (see **table 64.1**), or one of the clearing banks (usually adding a number of percentage points to that rate).

Commercial claims

64.23 In commercial cases and claims on bills of exchange, traditionally interest has been awarded at 1 per cent above base rate. The same applies in Admiralty claims (*Polish Steam Ship Co. v Atlantic Maritime Co.* [1985] QB 41). However, this is no more than a practice, and may be displaced by evidence showing that the rate is unfair to either party (*Shearson Lehman Hutton Inc. v Maclaine Watson and Co. Ltd (No. 2)* [1990] 3 All ER 723). Interest at the actual rate paid by the successful party on loans to pay their legal costs was awarded in *F and C Alternative Investments (Holdings) Ltd v Barthelemy* [2011] EWHC 2807 (Ch), *The Times*, 1 December 2011, where the court also awarded indemnity-basis costs. Where an interest loss is awarded as damages for breach of contract, the loss (and hence the rate) depends on the circumstances of the case, and what the claimant can prove. The loss may be the cost to the claimant of borrowing money, or the claimant's loss of the opportunity to invest the promised money, or loss in some other form. It is a head of loss and damage, and has to be proved in the normal way (*Sempra Metals Ltd v Commissioners of Inland*

Table 64.2 Judgments Act 1838 and Special and Basic Account rates of interest

Date (from)	Judgments Act 1838 rate	Special Account rate	Basic Account rate
1.4.1984	12% (from 10.11.1982)	12%	8%
16.4.1985	15%	12%	8%
1.8.1986	15%	11.5%	7.5%
1.1.1987	15%	12.25%	8.5%
1.4.1987	15%	11.75%	8.5%
1.11.1987	15%	11.25%	8.5%
1.12.1987	15%	11%	8%
1.5.1988	15%	9.5%	7.5%
1.8.1988	15%	11%	9%
1.11.1988	15%	12.25%	10.25%
1.1.1989	15%	13%	10.75%
1.11.1989	15%	14.25%	11.25%
1.4.1991	15%	12%	9.5%
1.10.1991	15%	10.25%	8%
1.2.1993	15%	8%	6%
1.4.1993	8%	8%	6%
1.8.1999	8%	7%	5.25%
1.2.2002	8%	6%	4%
1.2.2009	8%	3%	2%
1.6.2009	8%	1.5%	1%
1.7.2009	8%	0.5%	0.3%

Revenue [2007] UKHL 34, [2008] 1 AC 561 at [95]). In *Jaura v Ahmed* [2002] EWCA Civ 210, *The Times*, 18 March 2002, the court recognised that borrowing costs for small businesses are higher than those available to first-class borrowers, and awarded interest at 3 per cent above base rate. A rate of 2 per cent above base rate was applied in *Adinstone Ltd v Gatt* (2008) LTL 18/6/2008, being the rate established by the evidence as being the rate on the claimant's overdraft facility, and the rate anyone dealing with the claimant might have expected it to pay. In *McGlinn v Waltham Contractors Ltd (No. 5)* [2007] EWHC 698 (TCC), [2008] Bus LR 278, interest at 1 per cent above base rate was awarded against a builder in respect of defective building work.

Personal injury claims

64.24 In personal injuries claims, interest on damages for pain, suffering and loss of amenity has in recent years been awarded at 2 per cent a year from the date proceedings are issued (*Wright v British Railways Board* [1983] 1 AC 352). Despite the decision in *Wells v Wells* [1999] 1 AC 345, the rate applied remains at 2 per cent (see *Lawrence v Chief Constable of Staffordshire* (2000) *The Times*, 25 July 2000). Past special damages (such as loss of earnings and out-of-pocket expenses) usually attract interest at half the appropriate rate of interest (to reflect the fact that the losses will usually be ongoing between the date of the accident and the trial, the court adopting a broad-brush approach to the precise dates when individual losses were incurred). The 'appropriate rate' for this purpose is the average rate allowed for money in the Special Account (formerly the short-term investment account) (see **table 64.2**). The Special Account rate is applied by the Court Funds Office to Court of Protection clients' accounts and children's funds accounts. There is also a Basic Account rate (see **table 64.2**), which is applied by the Court Funds Office to county court and Queen's Bench matters involving adults only. Where the bulk of the losses were incurred a long time before trial, it may be appropriate to award interest on special damages at a higher (and perhaps the full) rate (see *Dexter v Courtaulds Ltd* [1984] 1 WLR 372; *Prokop v Department of Health and Social Security* [1985] CLY 1037). Interest is recoverable in full on past loss of earnings despite the recoupment of State benefits under the Social Security (Recovery of Benefits) Act 1997 (see *Wisely v John Fulton (Plumbers) Ltd* [2000] 1 WLR 820). Obviously, no interest is allowed on future loss and expense or loss of earning capacity. A claim in professional negligence against a solicitor based on mishandling of a personal injuries claim will usually attract ordinary interest at the Judgments Act 1838 rate rather than under the rules discussed in this paragraph (*Pinnock v Wilkins and Sons* (1990) *The Times*, 29 January 1990).

Restitution claims

64.25 Where interest is awarded as a remedy in restitution (see **64.20**), it will be at conventional rates. This avoids the need for evidence on the matter of rates. The conventional rate is the reasonable cost the defendant would have incurred in borrowing the amount in question for the relevant period (*Sempra Metals Ltd v Commissioners of Inland Revenue* [2007] UKHL 34, [2008] 1 AC 561, at [103]). It is the cost to the defendant rather than the claimant because, unlike claims in contract and tort, restitutionary remedies are based on the gain made by the defendant (at [28]). The reasonable cost is the market value of the benefit the defendant acquired by having the use of the money. Different types of organisations can borrow money at different rates, so the conventional rate is the usual cost to organisations of the defendant's type (at [49] and [128]).

These usual rules can be displaced by evidence that there was no (or reduced) actual benefit to the defendant (at [48] and [118]), for example, where the money is placed by the defendant in a non-interest-bearing current account. There was a divergence of view on where the onus of proof lies, but the better view is that it rests on the defendant because it is a matter unlikely to be within the claimant's knowledge (see the cases at **49.40** and *Sempra Metals Ltd v Commissioners of Inland Revenue* at [47]).

Claimants' Part 36 offers and breach of protocols

64.26 Interest, including ordinary statutory interest under the Senior Courts Act 1981, s. 35A, or County Courts Act 1984, s. 69, at a rate up to 10 per cent above base rate (see **table 64.1**) may be awarded where the claimant has made a successful claimant's Part 36 offer (see **CPR, r. 36.14(3)**), or where the defendant has failed to comply with **PD Pre-action Conduct** or a relevant pre-action protocol (**PD Pre-action Conduct, para. 4.6(5)**). In deciding whether to award interest as high as 10 per cent above base rate under **CPR, r. 36.14(3)**, the court should evaluate whether doing so would itself work an injustice or result in a disproportionate advantage to the claimant, or a disproportionate disadvantage to the defendant (*Little v George Little Sebire and Co.* (1999) *The Times*, 17 November 1999).

COMPOUND INTEREST

64.27 Until *Sempra Metals Ltd v Commissioners of Inland Revenue* [2007] UKHL 34, [2008] 1 AC 561, the general rule has been that awards of interest are for simple interest. Simple interest is expressly provided for by the Senior Courts Act 1981, s. 35A, and the County Courts Act 1984, s. 69. As from 6 April 2008, interest on default sums payable under regulated agreements by the debtor or hirer is only payable if it is simple interest (Consumer Credit Act 1974, s. 86F, to be inserted by the Consumer Credit Act 2006, s. 13). However, to mark the court's disapproval in cases of breach of fiduciary duty the courts of equity would (and the Chancery Division will continue to) award compound interest with yearly (or such other as may seem appropriate) rests (*Wallersteiner v Moir (No. 2)* [1975] QB 373). Further it is the common practice of banks to charge their customers compound interest, and they are entitled to judgment at their usual compounded rates up to judgment or earlier payment (*National Bank of Greece SA v Pinios Shipping Co. (No. 1)* [1990] 1 AC 637). A deed of priority between two mortgagees giving priority to one mortgagee in the sum of £160,000 'together with interest thereon' was construed as meaning compound interest in *Whitbread plc v UCB Corporate Services Ltd* (2000) *The Times*, 22 June 2000. While the practice in most EU states is to award simple interest on awards of damages, compound interest is available in Germany, Poland and the Netherlands. Compound interest is the European Commission's method of choice in cases such as the infringement of EC competition rules and breach of obligations relating to state aid (see *Sempra Metals Ltd v Commissioners of Inland Revenue* [2007] UKHL 34, [2008] 1 AC 561 at [37] to [40]).

In *Sempra Metals Ltd v Commissioners of Inland Revenue* the House of Lords said that an element of compound interest is available where interest is claimed as damages for breach of contract or in tort (at [17], [95], [154]). It held that ordinarily compound interest would be awarded where an interest loss is the substantive relief in restitution (at [33], [34], [103] and [154]).

Commentary

PERIOD OF INTEREST

Interest normally runs from the date the cause of action accrued until judgment or earlier **64.28** payment. In the case of a claim on an unpaid invoice, the terms of the contract will determine when the invoice matured. In the absence of other evidence the practice is to take the date of maturity as being 30 days after the date of the invoice. In a contract for the sale of land, interest runs from the contractual date for completion notwithstanding the transfer has not been stamped or that the vendor was unable to comply with a request from the purchaser to register the transfer (*P and O Overseas Holdings Ltd v Rhys Braintree Ltd* [2002] EWCA Civ 296, *The Times*, 5 April 2002). Interest on property damaged by negligence is payable from the date of the repairs (or when a decision was made to write off the property damaged). See also *EP Exploration Co. (Libya) Ltd v Hunt (No. 2)* [1979] 1 WLR 783. In *McGlinn v Waltham Contractors Ltd (No. 5)* [2007] EWHC 698 (TCC), [2008] Bus LR 278, interest was awarded from the date of issue of proceedings against a builder in respect of defective building work.

Where either party is guilty of unjustifiable delay, the court may increase or reduce the rate of interest, or alter the period over which interest is payable, to reflect this fact (*Birkett v Hayes* [1982] 1 WLR 816; *Spittle v Bunney* [1988] 1 WLR 847). In *Beanan v Stoneham* (2001) LTL 16/5/2001 it was held that the judge had been wrong not to reduce the interest awarded on the claim for damages as the claimant had been guilty of delay. It is unnecessary for the defendant to establish prejudice. The starting point is to decide when the case could reasonably have been brought to trial. Interest for two years was disallowed. Reducing interest, even in the event of gross delay, may be unjust and give the defendant an unwarranted windfall if the defendant has been holding on to money that should have been paid to the claimant (*Adcock v Cooperative Insurance Society Ltd* (2000) *The Times*, 26 April 2000). In a case where there was unreasonable delay for two years, during which time there were high interest rates, the claimants were awarded interest at half the usual rate during the period of the delay (*Quorum AS v Schramm* [2002] CLC 77). Ultimately the decision is one within the discretion of the trial judge. The Senior Courts Act 1981, s. 35A(5), and the County Courts Act 1984, s. 69(5), provide that interest under the respective Acts may be calculated at different rates in respect of different periods.

INTEREST ON JUDGMENTS IN FOREIGN CURRENCY

Where judgment is given in a foreign currency, the rate of interest will be that appropriate for **64.29** the relevant country (usually the rate at which money could be borrowed in that country). Evidence of the rate contended for should be adduced. See *Miliangos v George Frank (Textiles) Ltd*

(No. 2) [1977] QB 489. In *Braspetro Oil Services Co. v FPSO Construction Inc.* [2007] EWHC 1359 (Comm), [2007] 2 All ER (Comm) 924, it was held that factors to be considered include:

(a) The place where the claimant is incorporated and carries on business.
(b) The financial markets available to a person in the position of the claimant for the purposes of borrowing the currency in question. The markets may be global or local.
(c) Where the claimant is a member of a group of companies, the relationship between the claimant and other companies in the group.
(d) The stability of the currency of account and the claimant's currency. If the currency of account is more stable than the claimant's currency, delay in payment by the defendant means the claimant has to borrow at higher rates pending payment (*Helmsing Schiffahrts GmbH & Co. KG v Malta Drydocks Corporation* [1977] 2 Lloyd's Rep 444).
(e) The claimant's standing as a borrower (good standing resulting in lower rates, see *Kuwait Airways Corporation v Kuwait Insurance Co. SAK (No. 2)* [2000] 1 All ER (Comm) 972).

INTEREST ON JUDGMENT DEBTS

64.30 The Judgments Act 1838, s. 17, and the County Courts Act 1984, s. 74, are general provisions which allow simple interest, currently at 8 per cent a year, on all High Court money judgments and on relevant county court money judgments (see below). An arbitration award registered as a judgment under the Arbitration Act 1996, s. 100, also attracts interest at the usual Judgments Act 1838, s. 17, rate (*Gater Assets Ltd v NAK Naftogaz Ukrainiy* [2008] EWHC 1108 (Comm), [2008] 2 Lloyd's Rep 295). Interest is payable from the date on which judgment is given unless the court orders otherwise under **CPR, r. 40.8(1)(b)**. The Judgments Act 1838, s. 17, provides:

(1) Every judgment debt shall carry interest at the rate of 8 per cent per annum from such time as shall be prescribed by rules of court, until the same shall be satisfied, and such interest may be levied under a writ of execution on such judgment.
(2) Rules of court may provide for the court to disallow all or part of any interest otherwise payable under subsection (1).

Interest on a judgment runs from the date it is pronounced, not the date it might be drawn up (*Erven Warnink BV v J. Townend and Son (Hull) Ltd (No. 2)* [1982] 3 All ER 312). It is inappropriate to seek to evade the 8 per cent a year rate of interest on judgment debts by adjusting the date from which interest is to run (*Schlumberger Holdings Ltd v Electromagnetic Geoservices AS* [2009] EWHC 773 (Pat), LTL 7/5/2009). In the case of a judgment for damages to be decided by the court, Judgments Act 1838 interest runs on the damages from the date the damages are finally decided. Until then, the claimant can only claim interest on damages under the ordinary principles (which, in a personal injuries case, will be at considerably lower rates). See *Hunt v R. M. Douglas (Roofing) Ltd* [1990] 1 AC 398.

The County Courts Act 1984, s. 74, on the other hand, is an enabling provision allowing the Lord Chancellor to make orders that county court judgments shall carry interest at such rates and for such periods as the rules may prescribe. The relevant rules are the County Courts (Interest on Judgment Debts) Order 1991 (SI 1991/1184), which provide that 'relevant judgments' are those for not less than £5,000 and those which are qualifying debts for the purposes of the Late Payment of Commercial Debts (Interest) Act 1998 (see **64.15**), and that interest at the Judgments Act 1838 rate (SI 1991/1184, art. 5) shall be payable from the date the judgment was given (art. 2(1)). However, there are exceptions. Interest is not payable:

(a) on claims based on regulated agreements under the Consumer Credit Act 1974 (SI 1991/1184, art. 2(3)(a));
(b) on judgments granting suspended orders for possession of dwelling houses, where the order is in favour of a landlord or mortgagee (art. 2(3)(b));
(c) in the case of a judgment deferring payment, until the date specified for payment (art. 3(a)); and

(d) in the case of a judgment payable by instalments, until instalments are in arrears, and then only on the arrears (art. 3(b)) (the same applies to High Court judgments, see *Caudery v Finnerty* (1892) 66 LT 684 and *Morse v Muir* [1939] 2 KB 106).

Where a judgment creditor takes enforcement proceedings on a relevant county court judgment, accrual of interest ceases from that point unless the enforcement proceedings fail (art. 4). For these purposes applying for a charging order is not regarded as proceeding for enforcement.

INTEREST ON COSTS

Under the **CPR, r. 40.8**, interest on costs runs from the date the judgment is given, unless a rule or practice direction provides otherwise, or the court orders otherwise. Interest on costs where judgment has been entered for damages to be assessed therefore generally runs from the date of the liability judgment, but the court has a discretion to award interest on costs from some other date. This discretion may be exercised to reflect the periods over which the costs in assessing damages were in fact incurred (**r. 44.2(6)(g)**; *Powell v Herefordshire Health Authority* [2002] EWCA Civ 1786, [2003] 3 All ER 253). As regards interest on costs after a claim is automatically struck out for non-payment of the fees payable at the allocation or listing stages, or after acceptance of an offer to settle, or after a claim is discontinued, by virtue of **r. 44.9** interest runs from the date of the event giving rise to the entitlement to costs (i.e. the date of striking out, acceptance, or the date of service of the notice of discontinuance). **64.31**

Conducting litigation for commercial reasons regardless of the rights and wrongs of the claim, with much of that party's evidence being rejected followed by a resounding defeat, was said in *Amoco (UK) Exploration Co. v British American Offshore Ltd* [2002] BLR 135 to give grounds for awarding interest on costs for the period before judgment from the time those costs were paid.

The conventional rate of interest on costs until the date of assessment before the costs judge is 1 per cent above base rate (*National Westminster Bank plc v Rabobank Nederland (No. 2)* [2007] EWHC 1742 (Comm), [2008] 1 All ER (Comm) 243). It is for the paying party to introduce evidence that some other rate should be applied. Expert evidence will be required if it is asserted that a body with the financial substance of the receiving party could borrow money below this rate. Second-hand expressions of understanding are not a safe basis for departing from the conventional rate (*National Westminster Bank plc v Rabobank Nederland (No. 2)*).

A rate of 1 per cent above base rate was applied to an order for the repayment of an interim payment in respect of costs in *Multiplex Construction Ltd v Cleveland Bridge Ltd* [2008] EWCA Civ 133, 118 Con LR 16. The power to award interest in this situation derives from **CPR, rr. 44.2(6)(g)** and **44.2(8)**.

Chapter 65 Solicitor and Own Client Costs

INTRODUCTION

65.1 The purpose of this chapter is to deal with some of the core issues which arise in relation to solicitor and own client billing. It is somewhat remarkable in this market-driven age that the legal profession is still regulated in how it charges for its services. The primary regulatory scheme governing the solicitor and client relationship is in the Solicitors Act 1974, which is supported by the Solicitors (Non-contentious Business) Remuneration Order 1994 (SI 1994/2616), the Non-contentious Probate Rules 1987 (SI 1987/2024) and **CPR, Parts** 44 to 48, in relation to contentious business. In this context the Solicitors Act 1974, supported by the SRA Code of Conduct 2011, regulates the arrangement between the solicitor and client, and provides machinery for finalising the amount of the solicitor's fees if they cannot be agreed. This chapter will concentrate on contentious business.

By tradition the profession, in observing the statutory framework, had generally grown used to basing charges for services upon an expense rate for the particular grade of fee-earner plus a mark-up for care and conduct, the latter being determined by reference to what used to be RSC, ord. 62, app. 1, part 1, generally known as the 'seven pillars of wisdom'. There was a growing resistance in the marketplace to the application of the variable percentage uplift on expense rates, particularly from those who were volume buyers of legal services. They preferred to agree that solicitors' charges would be based on a composite hourly rate or rates per grade of fee-earners. This also reflected the more general public mood that there should be more transparency and certainty in solicitors' charges. Solicitors are required to give detailed costs information to their clients (see **65.3** to **65.6**) to ensure a client is fully aware of how the solicitor will charge for the work done.

AGREEING SOLICITORS' CHARGES

65.2 The contract of retainer between the client and solicitor may be oral or written, but often will be partly oral and partly written or evidenced by writing. Client care letters, costs estimates and costs budgets tend to be the most important documents, particularly for consumer clients, although formal written contracts may be essential for clients providing bulk or high-cost work. Being a contract for the provision of services, the retainer will be subject to the Supply of Goods and Services Act 1982, which means that, by s. 15, the price of the solicitor's services will either be determined by the contract, left to be determined in a manner agreed by the contract or by the course of dealing between the parties, or be subject to an implied term that the client will pay a reasonable charge. What is a reasonable charge is a question of fact (s. 15(2)). Often charges will be based on hourly rates dependent on the status of the fee earner (see **71.47**), plus disbursements (see **71.53**), and will be subject to assessment under the provisions of the Solicitors Act 1974 (see **65.7**). Given the provisions of s. 15, it was held in *Mastercigars Direct Ltd v Withers LLP* [2007] EWHC 2733 (Ch), [2009] 1 WLR 881, to be unnecessary to imply a term into the retainer that the solicitors had to comply with the Solicitors' Costs Information and Client Care Code (now the SRA Code of Conduct 2011; see **65.3** to **65.6**). This case also held that while the solicitor had made a contractual promise to provide the client with updated costs estimates (see **65.6**), doing so was not a condition precedent to recovering charges which exceeded an earlier costs estimate.

It is of the utmost importance that the client responsible for giving instructions and incurring the liability for costs is clearly identified as being responsible for payment of those costs. This is of particular concern, for example, where acting for companies or a group of clients. A solicitor instructed to act for a company must make certain that the person giving instructions has proper authority to incur the costs which ultimately the company will be liable to pay. In *Lygoe v Ilsley* [2008] EWHC 831 (QB), LTL 28/4/2008, the court found the solicitor's case, that an individual was personally liable for the firm's fees for work done for various companies, was implausible in the absence of an agreement in writing. When acting for a group of clients it is necessary to determine how the costs are to be discharged and by whom.

Where solicitors are retained by executors to deal with non-contentious business, it is best practice for the solicitor to obtain prior agreement for the proposed charges not only from the executors, but also from any residuary beneficiary who is a statutory entitled party under the Solicitors' (Non-Contentious Business) Remuneration Order 1994 (SI 1994/2616) (*Jemma Trust Co. Ltd v Liptrott* [2003] EWCA Civ 1476, [2004] 1 WLR 646).

A written retainer from the client is always advisable and nearly always required by the SRA Code of Conduct 2011, O 1.13 and IB 1.13 to IB 1.20. These require clear explanations about fees, and the provision of information in a clear and accessible form that is appropriate for the client. Having a clear written agreement on charges should reduce the risk to the solicitor at a later stage when a bill of costs is rendered for the services provided. Indeed, with regard to contentious business, it is the duty of the solicitor to obtain a written authority from the client before a claim is commenced. Such authority must be signed by the party responsible for the solicitor's bill of costs and it must clearly identify the work to be carried out and extent of the retainer. This has long been the recognised position, see *Allen v Bone* (1841) 4 Beav 493.

CLIENT CARE

The SRA Code of Conduct 2011 provides that solicitors should: **65.3**

(a) discuss whether the potential outcomes of the client's matter are likely to justify the expense or risk involved, including any risk of having to pay someone else's legal fees (IB 1.13);
(b) agree an appropriate level of service with the client, for example the type and frequency of communications (IB 1.1);
(c) explain the solicitor's responsibilities and those of the client (IB 1.2); and
(d) ensure that the client is told, in writing, the name and status of the person(s) dealing with the matter and the name and status of the person responsible for its overall supervision (IB 1.3).

For example, the frequency of reports on progress to the client should be agreed, and options such as the use of ADR should be considered. Where the person dealing with the matter leaves the firm, the client should be informed of the changeover arrangements, preferably in advance.

If there are any limitations or conditions on the retainer resulting from the solicitor's relationship with a third-party funder or introducer, these should be explained to the client (IB 1.5). Some constraints are proper and do not require disclosure to the client. Examples are service standards relating to dealing with client enquiries within a specified period of time, the use of specified computer software, telecommunications systems, or particular training provisions. Constraints such as not issuing proceedings without the consent of the funder are proper provided they do not operate against the client's best interests, but must be disclosed to the client. Constraints which impair the solicitor's independence are improper and cannot be cured by disclosure to the client. If such a relationship involves sharing any client information with a third party, the solicitor must inform the client and obtain the client's consent. Failure to do so will be a breach of the client confidentiality rule (O 4.1), and may be a breach of the Data Protection Act 1998.

Clients must be informed in writing at the outset of their matter of their right to complain and how complaints can be made (O 1.9). Firms must have written complaints procedures, which are brought to the attention of clients at the commencement of a retainer (IB 1.22), which must be provided to a client on request (IB 1.23). In the event that a client makes a complaint, they must be provided with all necessary information concerning the handling of the complaint (IB 1.24). Clients must also be informed in writing, both at the time of engagement and at the conclusion of the firms' complaints procedure, of their right to complain to the Legal Ombudsman, the time frame for doing so and be given full details of how to contact the Legal Ombudsman (O 1.10). Clients must not be charged the costs of handling complaints (IB 1.22(f)).

Information about costs

65.4 The SRA Code of Conduct 2011, O 1.13, says that clients must receive the best possible information, both at the time of engagement and when appropriate as their matter progresses, about the likely overall cost of their matter. Such information is likely to include:

(a) advising the client of the basis and terms of the firm's charges;
(b) advising the client if the charges are to be increased;
(c) advising the client of likely payments which the client may need to make to others;
(d) discussing with the client how the client will pay, and in particular, whether they are eligible for public funding, whether the client's costs are covered by insurance, and whether they might be paid by someone else, such as an employer or trade union;
(e) advising the client that there are circumstances where the firm will be entitled to a lien;
(f) advising the client of their potential liability for the other side's costs;
(g) discussing with the client whether the liability for the other side's costs may be covered by existing or specially purchased insurance.

The purpose of O 1.13 is to ensure the client is given relevant costs information and that it is expressed clearly and in a way appropriate for the client. All costs information should be given in writing and regularly updated. The duty to advise means that the client must be informed of the implications involved in the various options available. It is often impossible to advise on the overall costs at the outset. In such cases the client should be given as much information as possible, told the reasons, and given either a ceiling or review dates. As the case progresses the client should be given updates on costs. Particular care is needed when advising a client on an offer to settle under **CPR, Part 36** (see **chapter 66**), to ensure the client understands the costs implications of the different options available (SRA Code of Conduct 2011, IB 1.13).

The actual terms of the retainer are a matter for negotiation between the firm and the client. There is no need for the client to be separately advised on the costs agreement unless the arrangement is unusual (such as the firm being paid by being issued with shares in a new company).

Additional duties in CFA and publicly funded cases

Where the firm is acting under a CFA (including a collective CFA), or any other method of funding governed by statute, there are additional duties under the SRA Code of Conduct 2011, IB 1.17, to give the client all relevant information relating to that arrangement. These are likely to include: **65.5**

(a) the circumstances in which the client may be liable for the firm's costs and whether the firm will seek these costs from the client if it is entitled to do so;
(b) the right to an assessment of the firm's costs (if there is an intention to seek payment of all or part of the firm's costs from the client);
(c) if applicable, any obligation on the firm under a fee-sharing agreement to pay to a charity any fees received.

Where the client is publicly funded, there are additional duties under IB 1.18 to explain how their publicly funded status affects the costs. The following points must usually be covered:

(a) the circumstances in which the client will be liable for the firm's costs;
(b) the effect of the statutory charge (see **7.19**);
(c) the client's duty to pay any fixed or periodic contribution assessed and the consequences of failing to do so;
(d) that even if the publicly funded client is successful, the other side may not be ordered to pay costs or may not be in a position to pay them.

Commentary

Client care letter and client estimates

The document generally referred to as a 'client care letter' has achieved a greater status in more recent times. In *Bailey v IBC Vehicles Ltd* [1998] 3 All ER 570 Judge LJ stated that 'in the ordinary case in which a "client care letter" has been provided the hourly rate claimed in the bill of costs should coincide with the terms of that letter' and further that 'in future, copies of the relevant documents (where they exist) or a short written explanation of the kind eventually provided in this case in September 1997, should normally be attached to the bill of costs'. In compliance with the SRA Code of Conduct 2011, O 1.13, in providing costs information for clients particular regard needs to be given to any estimates given. This is of vital importance, for example, where hourly rates are agreed with the client at the outset. Where the litigation is likely to span a number of years the solicitor should make provision for annual revision of those hourly rates. However, the client must be informed of any increase made on an annual review. **65.6**

This has been given effect by **PD 47, para. 13.2(i)**, which stipulates that where there is a dispute as to the receiving party's liability to pay costs to the solicitors who are acting for the receiving party, any letter or other written information provided by the solicitor to his or her client, explaining how the solicitor's charges are to be calculated, is to be lodged at court with the request for a detailed assessment hearing. The relevance of client care letters was further reinforced by *General of Berne Insurance Co. v Jardine Reinsurance Management Ltd* [1998] 1 WLR 1231 in the context of contentious business agreements.

It is advisable, but not an absolute requirement, that a solicitor acting for a client who may join in group litigation should say in the client care letter that some of the work done would be for the benefit of the group, and the individual client will be liable only for his share (*Brown v Russell Young and Co.* [2007] EWCA Civ 43, [2008] 1 WLR 525). Where several solicitors act for different parties in group litigation, the agreements between the solicitors should clearly define the arrangements for sharing the costs of generic work for the group. It is also sensible for careful records to be kept of the number of clients each solicitor is acting for at any specific time.

A breach of the former Solicitors' Practice Rules 1990 was a breach of subordinate legislation (*Swain v Law Society* [1983] 1 AC 598) which might have an effect on the solicitor's right to remuneration. Failing to send the client a client care letter does not prevent recovery, under a costs order, of the fees and disbursements incurred in fighting a claim (*Ghadami v Lyon Cole Insurance Group Ltd* [2010] EWCA Civ 767, LTL 13/7/2010). In *Garbutt v Edwards* [2005] EWCA Civ 1206, [2006] 1 WLR 2907, the solicitors representing the successful party failed to provide their client with any costs estimate in breach of the Solicitors' Costs, Information and Client Care Code (now the SRA Code of Conduct 2011, O 1.13). The Court of Appeal held this did not render the retainer unlawful or unenforceable, so was not a knock-out blow to the assessment of the successful party's costs. Although this did not arise on the facts, the court said the paying party may be able to obtain a reduction in the amount payable if the costs incurred would have been lower if the solicitor had complied with the Code of Conduct. In *Mastercigars Direct Ltd v Withers LLP* [2007] EWHC 2733 (Ch), [2009] 1 WLR 881, the court characterised the costs information given by the solicitors as an estimate rather than a quotation or a document fixing an upper limit on the costs the firm would charge. Applying *Garbutt v Edwards*, it was a factor in assessing reasonableness. Disapproving a passage in *Cook on Costs* (Butterworths, 2007), the court held that exceeding the estimate without informing the client did not mean the solicitors were unable to recover the excess.

A requirement for greater transparency is shown in *Ralph Hume Garry v Gwillim* [2002] EWCA Civ 1500, [2003] 1 WLR 510, in which the court considered what constituted a bill for assessment under the Solicitors Act 1974. A bill may be for a gross sum (see **65.13**), but it must contain sufficient narrative to identify what the client is being charged for and to enable the client to decide whether to ask for detailed assessment (*Haigh v Ousey* (1857) 7 El & Bl 578). Nowadays it is common for solicitors to record all work done in a computerised time costing system. Where this happens, the least that a client is entitled to is a printout of that record suitably redacted (*Ralph Hume Garry v Gwillim*). A bill can only charge for the services which the client contracted to pay for. Thus, where a client asked for a solicitor but was represented by a legal executive, the solicitors were not entitled to any fee as the client had not received the representation he contracted for (*Pilbrow v Peerless De Rougemont and Co.* [1999] 3 All ER 355; *Adrian Alan Ltd v Fuglers* [2002] EWCA Civ 1655, [2003] PNLR 305).

SOLICITORS ACT 1974

65.7 Sections 59 to 71 of the Solicitors Act 1974 regulate contentious business.

Section 59 permits solicitors to enter into written agreements, called 'contentious business agreements', concerning remuneration for contentious business (see **65.11**).

Sections 67 to 70 deal with the situation where there is no contentious business agreement with the client and the requirements for delivery of a bill of costs, proceedings to recover costs by the solicitor and applications by the client or the solicitor for the detailed assessment of the bill of costs.

Section 69 provides that no action shall be brought to recover any costs due before the expiration of one month from the date on which a bill of costs was delivered, subject to two exceptions. If the client is about to quit the jurisdiction, become bankrupt or compound with creditors, or is about to do any other act which would prevent or delay the solicitor obtaining payment, the High Court may, upon application, permit the solicitor to commence an action to recover his or her costs and may also order that those costs be referred to detailed assessment. A signed bill must have been delivered to the party to be charged.

Application for detailed assessment

65.8 Section 70 of the Solicitors Act 1974 provides for detailed assessment upon application of the party chargeable or the solicitor. If before the expiration of one month from delivery of a bill of costs, an application is made by the party chargeable, the court shall, without requiring any sum to be paid into court, order detailed assessment of the bill and that no claim be commenced until the assessment is completed. If no such application is made before expiration of the one-month period, the court may order detailed assessment on such terms, if any, as it thinks fit, but not terms as to costs of the assessment. Where an application is made by the party chargeable with the bill more than 12 months from its delivery, or after judgment has been obtained for recovery of the costs, or after the bill has been paid, no order for detailed assessment may be made except in special circumstances and, if an order is made, it may contain such terms as regards the costs of the detailed assessment as the court may think fit. The party chargeable with a bill is unable to obtain a detailed assessment under the Solicitors Act 1974 after 12 months from payment of the bill (s. 70(4)).

In *Connollys v Harrington* (2002) LTL 27/8/2002 it was held that the High Court has an inherent jurisdiction to order detailed assessment, even where the provisions of the Solicitors Act 1974 have not been complied with, and that the specific provisions in the Act do not oust that jurisdiction. Whether any such inherent jurisdiction exists in parallel with the Act is dubious and is inconsistent with *Harrison v Tew* [1990] 2 AC 523.

Two cases heard by the Court of Appeal have permitted detailed assessment more than 12 months after delivery of the bill (*Thomas Watts and Co. v Smith* (1998) 2 Costs LR 59 and *Turner and Co. v O. Palomo SA* [2000] 1 WLR 37). In each case the clients were entitled to challenge the solicitor's claim on the grounds that the fees claimed were unreasonably high even though the time for detailed assessment had expired. The statutory right to seek an order for detailed assessment was held not to exclude any other common law right to challenge the bills.

Section 71 provides that where a person other than the party chargeable with the bill has paid, or is or was liable to pay, a solicitor's bill, that person may apply for a detailed assessment of the bill as if that person were the party chargeable with it, and the court may make the same order as it might have made had the application been made by the party chargeable with the bill. However, where the court has no power to make an order, except in special circumstances, it may in considering whether there are special circumstances sufficient to justify the making of an order, take into account circumstances which affect the applicant but do not affect the party chargeable with the bill. The prohibition against a party chargeable with a bill seeking a detailed assessment more than 12 months after paying the bill in s. 70(4) does not apply in applications under s. 71, where the passing of time after payment is simply a factor to be taken into account in exercising the discretion in s. 71(3) whether to order the assessment of the bill (*McIlwraith v McIlwraith* [2002] EWHC 1757 (Ch), LTL 1/8/2002).

Conduct of detailed assessment

The procedure for seeking orders under the Solicitors Act 1974, part 3, leading up to the possible detailed assessment of the solicitor's charges, is laid down by **CPR, r. 46.10** and **Part 67**, and **PD 46, paras 6.4** to **6.19**; see **71.18**. The detailed assessment may deal with the profit costs or disbursements or both and the court may allow a claim to be commenced or to be continued for any costs not being challenged (s. 70(6)). The CPR apply in determining the amounts recoverable, see **65.18**. **65.9**

CONTENTIOUS AND NON-CONTENTIOUS BUSINESS

It is important to remember that contentious and non-contentious costs must not be intermingled and put in one bill (see *Re a Solicitor* [1955] 2 QB 252). Essentially, contentious and non-contentious business are each governed by different sections of the Solicitors Act 1974 and in the case of non-contentious business additionally by the Solicitors (Non-contentious Business) Remuneration Order 1994 (SI 1994/2616). A solicitor conducting non-contentious **65.10** business is entitled to charge both for the time spent on an hourly basis and a separate fee based on the value of the transaction or estate (*Jemma Trust Co. Ltd v Liptrott* [2003] EWCA Civ 1476, [2004] 1 WLR 646).

The definition of 'contentious business' in the Solicitors Act 1974, s. 87(1), uses the phrase 'in or for the purposes of proceedings'. This is to be construed as a composite whole (*Bilkus v Stockler Brunton* [2010] EWCA Civ 101, [2010] 1 WLR 2526). It covers pending proceedings and future proceedings. Enforcement proceedings are clearly proceedings. Other work done after the conclusion of proceedings is merely in consequence of those earlier proceedings. Nevertheless, work done by a firm for a client in valuing shares in a company which were ordered to be bought out by the respondents in an unfair prejudice petition under what is now the Companies Act 2006, s. 994, was carried out under a court order and pursuant to directions given by the court. It was therefore contentious business, and could not attract a value element.

CONTENTIOUS BUSINESS AGREEMENTS

65.11 A contentious business agreement made under the Solicitors Act 1974, s. 59, is not subject to a detailed assessment unless the agreement provides for the solicitor's remuneration to be by reference to an hourly rate (s. 60(1)). A contentious business agreement may provide that the solicitor be remunerated by a gross sum, an hourly rate or rates, salary or otherwise and at a higher or lower rate than the solicitor would ordinarily be entitled to (s. 59(1)). Sections 59 to 63 do not enable a solicitor to purchase an interest in the whole or part of the proceedings.

Any agreement pursuant to s. 59 must be in writing. An agreement will be a contentious business agreement if it satisfies the requirements of s. 59. There is no need for it to be expressly stated to be a 'contentious business agreement' (*Re Wilson Properties UK Ltd, Wilson v Specter Partnership* [2007] EWHC 133 (Ch), LTL 9/2/2007). The existence of a contentious business agreement does not affect the amount of, or any rights or remedies for recovery of, any costs payable by the client to, or to the client by, any person other than the solicitor, and that person may, unless bound by an agreement to the contrary, require the costs to be referred to detailed assessment (s. 60(2)). The client is not entitled to recover from any other person under an order for payment of any costs to which the contentious business agreement relates more than the amount payable by the client to the solicitor (s. 60(3); this is the indemnity principle — see **71.30**).

Since 2 June 2003 it has been possible for a solicitor to enter into a non-indemnity CFA under which the solicitor's costs are limited to those recoverable from the losing party. The paying party will no longer be able to use the indemnity principle to defeat such an agreement.

Enforcement of contentious business agreements

65.12 The Solicitors Act 1974, s. 61, provides that no action shall be brought to enforce a contentious business agreement, but on application a party to the agreement, or representative of a party, or a person who is liable to pay, or to be paid, the costs due, may apply to the court to enforce or set aside the agreement and determine its validity and effect. On any application, the court may enforce the agreement if it considers the same to be fair and reasonable or, if the contrary view is taken, may refer the agreement to detailed assessment.

If on a detailed assessment of any costs, a contentious business agreement is relied upon by the solicitor and the client objects, but does not allege that the agreement is unfair or unreasonable, the costs officer may review and consider the number of hours claimed by the solicitor and whether the number of hours claimed are excessive (s. 61(4B)).

Contentious business agreements have become more attractive in recent years particularly because they bring some certainty to the solicitor on the question of hourly rates and remove the entitlement to a detailed assessment, unless the court considers that the agreement is not fair and reasonable. The client also benefits from certainty on the question of hourly rates.

ASSESSMENT WHERE THERE IS NO CONTENTIOUS BUSINESS AGREEMENT

Section 64 of the Solicitors Act 1974 stipulates that a solicitor's bill of costs may, at the option of the solicitor, be either a bill containing detailed items or a gross sum bill. A client who receives a gross sum bill may, at any time before being served with proceedings for recovery of the costs included in the bill and before the expiration of three months from the date on which the bill was delivered, require the solicitor to replace it with a bill containing detailed items and upon making such request the gross sum bill will be of no effect (s. 64(2)). Where proceedings are commenced on a gross sum bill, the court will, if requested by the party chargeable with the bill before the expiration of one month from service, order that the bill be referred to detailed assessment and that the solicitor shall provide the court with such further details of the costs as the costs officer may require (s. 64(3) and (4)). **65.13**

PERIODIC BILLING

The modern trend is to bill clients on a more regular periodic basis. At the very least this helps the cash flow of the solicitor and keeps the client informed about the costs of the matter. **65.14**

However, there are pitfalls for the unwary. There must be an agreement with the client at the outset that interim or periodic bills will be delivered and become payable, otherwise there is no right to render an interim bill, unless it coincides with a natural break in the litigation. It is important also to distinguish between two classes of bills which can be rendered during the course of litigation:

(a) an interim bill which is final for the period of work covered by it; and
(b) an interim bill which is on account of a final bill which is yet to be delivered.

A bill of type (a) is covered by the Solicitors Act 1974 and can be referred to detailed assessment and sued upon by the solicitor for non-payment. A bill of type (b) cannot be referred to detailed assessment nor can the solicitor issue proceedings for recovery. This interpretation of the two classes of bill was dealt with in *Davidsons v Jones-Fenleigh* (1980) 124 SJ 204.

BILL OF COSTS

It has long been established that any bill to a client must be a complete bill containing sufficient information to enable the client to obtain advice about its detailed assessment (see *Haigh v Ousey* (1857) 7 El & Bl 578). The purpose of the Solicitors Act 1974, ss. 64 and 69, is to protect the innocent or ignorant client by providing adequate information to justify the amount charged. It is not to provide an unscrupulous client with an unmeritorious defence. The detail required in the narrative of a bill therefore varies from case to case, and deficiencies in the detail provided in a bill can be made good from the client's own knowledge and documents sent with the bill and other information already in the possession of the client (*Ralph Hume Garry v Gwillim* [2002] EWCA Civ 1 500, [2003] 1 WLR 510). To prevent disputes it may be sensible to provide clients with printouts of accounts department records, see 65.6. **65.15**

A bill of costs must include an adequate description of the work carried out coupled with the dates within which the services were rendered. Disbursements must relate to the period in question otherwise upon any detailed assessment there is a risk that any disbursements outside the scope of the period in question will be struck out and become irrecoverable.

There is a tendency not to pay much attention to the subject of billing and there is sometimes a remarkable lack of care and attention to detail, which is not lost on an astute client. Very often, the solicitor's bill of costs is the final professional service that the client receives on a particular matter and it represents the last opportunity that a firm has to promote itself positively. A sloppily composed bill of costs containing errors or incorrect information will leave the wrong impression with the client. There is also the temptation to add unnecessary narrative or explanation to the bill, in order, it would seem, to justify the fee. The majority of clients, and particularly commercial clients, can see through this. If there is an agreement to render interim bills, they should be delivered on the due dates.

DISBURSEMENTS

65.16 Only expenses which a solicitor incurs in order to provide his or her professional service are disbursements which can be so described in a bill of costs to the client (see **71.53**). Any other amounts paid on the client's behalf, such as payments into court, payments of damages and payment of other side's costs, should form part of the cash account which should accompany a bill of costs.

It is also important to ensure that any disbursements which are not paid as at the date of rendering the bill of costs, are described as 'not yet paid'. Otherwise, there is a real risk that these disbursements will not be recoverable.

INTEREST

65.17 Interest is recoverable for costs for non-contentious business, provided sufficient notice is given as required by the Solicitors (Non-contentious Business) Remuneration Order 1994 (SI 1994/2616). For contentious business, the opposite is the case. Ordinarily, a solicitor is not entitled to interest unless it is specified and agreed with the client at the inception of the retainer. Upon detailed assessment under the Solicitors Act 1974, if application is made to the costs officer, interest will be granted only upon disbursements already paid out by the solicitor.

As well as allowing interest to be charged on outstanding bills, the initial retainer may provide for the solicitor to receive a share of any interest to which the client may become entitled under the Judgments Act 1838, s. 17 (*Hunt v R. M. Douglas (Roofing) Ltd* [1990] 1 AC 398).

DETAILED ASSESSMENT

65.18 CPR, r. 46.9, sets out the basis of detailed assessment of solicitor and own client costs and applies to every assessment of a solicitor's bill to his or her client except a bill which is to be paid out of the Community Legal Service Fund. The Solicitors Act 1974, s. 74(3), applies unless the solicitor and client have entered into a written agreement which expressly permits payment of an amount of costs greater than that which could be recovered from another party to proceedings in the county court. Section 74(3) does not limit the costs between solicitor and client to the amount assessed between the parties (*Lynch v Paul Davidson Taylor* [2004] EWHC 89 (QB), [2004] 1 WLR 1753).

Pursuant to **CPR, r. 46.9(3)**, costs payable to a solicitor by his or her client are to be assessed on the indemnity basis. They are presumed to have been reasonably incurred if they were incurred with the expressed or implied approval of the client, to be reasonable in amount if the amount is expressly or impliedly approved by the client and to have been unreasonably incurred if they are of an unusual nature or amount and the solicitor did not tell the client that it might not be possible to recover all of them from the other parties. Questions of proportionality do not arise.

The assessment procedure is prescribed in **CPR, r. 46.10** (see **71.20**).

Chapter 66 Part 36 Offers

The following procedural checklist, which is at the front of the book, is relevant to this chapter:

Procedural checklist 29 Offer to settle

Commentary

INTRODUCTION

In order to encourage parties to settle their dispute, **CPR, Part 36,** lays down a system for making formal offers having costs consequences if they are unreasonably refused. It has long been recognised that there is a public interest in parties seeking to settle their disputes rather than allowing their claims to be litigated through to trial. Settlements bring disputes to a swift conclusion, avoid most of the costs involved in protracted litigation, save court time, and avoid a great deal of the antagonism that often underlies litigation. A party who receives a realistic formal offer will ordinarily accept that offer, thereby compromising the claim. If a formal offer is refused, the litigation will continue, but the principle is that the offeror will be awarded its costs from the date the offer expired if the offeree fails to do better than the terms of the offer when the claim is finally determined. **66.1**

The fundamental function of a **Part 36** offer is to put the offeree on risk as to costs if, as a result of the contingencies of litigation, it later transpires that the terms of the offer were at least as advantageous as the eventual outcome (*Matthews v Metal Improvements Co. Inc.* [2007] EWCA Civ 215, [2007] CP Rep 27).

This chapter describes the law as it applies to offers to settle made on or after 6 April 2007, which was when **Part 36** was completely replaced. **Part 36** is drafted as a self-contained code (*Gibbon v Manchester City Council* [2010] EWCA Civ 726, [2010] 1 WLR 2081, per Moore-Bick LJ at [5]). It contains a carefully constructed and highly prescriptive set of rules dealing with formal offers to settle which have specific consequences. It prescribes in some detail the manner in which a Part 36 offer is to be made, and in some respects, particularly **rr. 36.9(2)** and **36.14(3)**, departs quite markedly from the normal concepts governing the law of contract. While the basic concepts of offer and acceptance underpin **Part 36**, it does not follow that all the rules of law governing the formation of contracts are imported into **Part 36**. The way it was put by Moore-Bick LJ at [6] was that:

> Certainty is as much to be commended in procedural as in substantive law, especially, perhaps, in a procedural code which must be understood and followed by ordinary citizens who wish to conduct their own litigation. In my view, Part 36 was drafted with these considerations in mind and is to be read and understood according to its terms without importing other rules derived from the general law, save where that was clearly intended.

This approach is a recipe for disaster. **Part 36** is either a self-contained code or it is not. Saying the general rules of contract do not apply 'save where that was clearly intended' begs the question of where, within **Part 36**, these exceptions are clearly intended. If Moore-Bick LJ's principle was laid down to promote certainty, which is the stated objective, leaving a total lack of clarity over when contractual principles apply signally fails to achieve the objective. As will be seen from the following discussion at **66.6, 66.20** and **66.36**, the practical outcome of the decision in *Gibbon v Manchester City Council* leaves litigants in person, the group the principle is stated to be aimed at protecting, with no realistic hope of being able to understand the rules, and at the mercy of parties who are able to say things in correspondence that do not have the stated effect. The overall wisdom of having rules which are clearly based on offer and acceptance, but which do not follow the established rules of the law of contract (which are broadly understood by the general public) will almost inevitably lead to widespread confusion.

One particular problem is that the construction of **Part 36** adopted by *Gibbon v Manchester City Council* and subsequent cases gives rise to results that are not intended by the parties. Holding that a claim has (or has not) been settled contrary to the intentions of either or both parties is difficult to justify, and appears to be contrary to the overriding objective of dealing with cases justly. It places a premium on establishing that an offer is technically an offer to settle within **Part 36**, which (given there is no obligation to use form N242A when making a Part 36 offer) will inevitably lead to semantic arguments over whether differently worded offers come within **Part 36**. Another practical problem is that the decision in *Gibbon v Manchester City Council* that a Part 36 offer remains open for acceptance until formally withdrawn in accordance with **r. 36.3(7)** will be a potential trap in every case where there is a change in the person dealing with a claim on behalf of a client. Unless all the paperwork relating to the case is provided to the representative with current conduct of the case, there is a danger that the current representative will be unaware of a 'live' offer on the file of the former representative. This is a real problem when cases are transferred from insurers to solicitors, and when clients change solicitors where the former solicitor asserts a lien over the papers.

ADVISING ON PART 36 OFFERS

66.2 Advising on the terms to offer under **CPR, Part 36**, requires a great deal of professional judgment. Likewise, advising on whether an offer should be accepted requires a balancing of a number of factors, including risks on liability (including any contributory negligence and counterclaim or set-off) and risks on the amount of damages, as well as considering the likely level of interest that might be awarded. In claims where the prospects turn on whether evidence might be allowed in or disallowed, either in a future application or at trial, assessing the risks is even more difficult. Clients must be fully informed of the costs implications of the offer. This will include the amount that will be deducted by the adviser's firm in respect of costs, how that sum is calculated, and the client's right to the assessment of the firm's costs (SRA Code of Conduct 2011, O 1.13 and O 1.14). A legal adviser will be expected to give reasons for advice on whether offers should be accepted, and should concentrate on giving clear advice that can be readily understood by the client. Legal advisers are not required, particularly if advice is being given on the day of a trial, to engage in defensive advocacy by giving their clients a catalogue of every factor that might have a bearing on whether an offer should be accepted (*Moy v Pettman Smith* [2005] UKHL 7, [2005] 1 WLR 581).

NON-DISCLOSURE

Non-disclosure of Part 36 offers

66.3 There are restrictions on disclosure of Part 36 offers. **CPR, r. 36.13(1)**, provides that a Part 36 offer will be treated as 'without prejudice except as to costs'. The fact that a Part 36 offer has been made is not to be communicated to the trial judge until all questions of liability and quantum have been decided (**r. 36.13(2)**). Similar restrictions apply to appeals (see **r. 52.12(1)**). The restriction on disclosure in **r. 36.13(2)** applies to the trial judge, so does not prevent the offer being referred to the judge dealing with an application for summary judgment or striking out on the question of costs arising from that application, even if remedies have yet to be decided (*Experience Hendrix v Times Newspapers Ltd* [2008] EWHC 458 (Ch), LTL 14/3/2008). If this happens, other without-prejudice correspondence may be referred to in order to ensure the judge is not given a distorted picture (*Experience Hendrix v Times Newspapers Ltd*). In advance of trial a request should be made to the court office to remove all references to any offers to settle under **Part 36** (and interim payments) from the court file to avoid accidental disclosure to the trial judge. However, **r. 36.13(2)** will not apply where (**r. 36.13(3)**):

(a) the defence of tender before claim has been raised;
(b) the proceedings have been stayed under **r. 36.11** following acceptance of a Part 36 offer; or
(c) where the offeror and offeree agree in writing that it should not apply.

The embargo in **r. 36.13** on disclosing the existence of Part 36 offers to the judge until the case has been decided means that they are only relevant in deciding orders as to costs. They cannot be used on questions relating to the date for assessing damages or on the amount of interest to allow (*Johnson v Gore Wood and Co. (No. 2)* [2004] EWCA Civ 14, *The Times*, 17 February 2004).

If there is an inadvertent disclosure of a Part 36 offer, the judge has a discretion whether to order a new trial, but may continue if satisfied that no injustice will be done (*Millensted v Grosvenor House (Park Lane) Ltd* [1937] 1 KB 717). *Millensted v Grosvenor House (Park Lane) Ltd* was approved by *Garratt v Saxby* [2004] EWCA Civ 341, [2004] 1 WLR 2152. If, after inappropriate disclosure of a Part 36 offer, the judge thinks it proper or necessary for the due administration of justice, he may refuse to hear the trial any further and direct that it be tried by another judge. However, the judge should not be too ready to adopt this course, and if satisfied that no injustice will be done, may continue with the trial. Matters to consider include the overriding objective, saving expense and dealing with claims justly and proportionately. If a new trial is ordered, the court will almost certainly consider making a wasted costs order against the legal representative at fault.

Disclosure of a Part 36 offer outside the proceedings in a way which will not come to the judge's attention does not harm or infringe the integrity of the court's process and requires no action by the court (*Re a Company (No. 007466 of 2003)* [2004] EWHC 35 (Ch), [2004] 1 WLR 1357).

Applications and non-disclosure to the trial judge

Much of the activity relating to making and accepting Part 36 offers is done without needing court permission. Applications to the court are necessary for a number of purposes: **66.4**

(a) where a Part 36 offer is to be accepted by a child or a protected party, where court approval must be sought (see **66.31**);
(b) where there is an acceptance of an offer made by some of several defendants, or there are further deductible benefits, or an apportionment is required in a Fatal Accidents Act case (see **66.30** and **66.32**);
(c) where an acceptance is after the start of a trial (**CPR, r. 36.9(3)(d)**; **66.29**);
(d) where the offeree seeks to withdraw or reduce an offer during the offer period (see **66.17**); and
(e) where the offeree seeks an order clarifying a Part 36 offer (see **66.21**).

In situation (a) above, if proceedings have not been commenced, the application is made by issuing a Part 8 claim (see **PD 8A, para. 3.1**). All other types of application relating to Part 36 offers (including situation (a) after the substantive claim has been issued) are made under the usual interim procedure in **Part 23** or at the trial or other hearing (**PD 36A, paras 2.2** and **3.2**). In order to preserve the integrity of the offer in the event that the application is refused, such applications must be dealt with by a judge other than the judge (if any) allocated in advance to conduct the trial, unless the parties agree that such judge can hear the application (**PD 36A, paras 2.2** and **3.2**).

Split trials and Part 36 offers

66.5 *HSS Hire Services Group plc v BMB Builders Merchants Ltd* [2005] EWCA Civ 626, [2005] 1 WLR 3158, deals with cases where a claimant wins on liability at a split trial after the defendant has made a Part 36 offer. Other than in the most exceptional case, the question of costs should be reserved until determination of quantum. Costs should be reserved even in respect of costs which should be unaffected by any Part 36 offer by the defendant, because there could be a set-off of costs (*Tullett Prebon plc v BGC Brokers LP* [2010] EWHC 989 (QB), LTL 10/5/2010; see **63.20**). After the trial on liability the conditions for disclosing the amount of the offer in **CPR, r. 36.13(2)**, have not been met, and it will be only after the determination of quantum that the court can decide whether the Part 36 offer was effective for costs purposes. In *Shepherds Investments Ltd v Walters* [2007] EWCA Civ 292, LTL 3/4/2007, costs were reserved until the outcome of an account for profits in a case where there was a claimant's Part 36 offer. This case goes further than *HSS Hire Services Group plc v BMB Builders Merchants Ltd*, where the offer was made by the losing defendant, rather than the winning claimant.

OFFERS TO SETTLE UNDER PART 36

Offers to settle

66.6 An offer to settle within the meaning of **CPR, Part 36** (a 'Part 36 offer'), must be made in writing and comply with the formalities described at **66.7**. One basic set of formalities applies to all Part 36 offers, although there are additional requirements dealing with particular circumstances. There is no longer any requirement to pay money into court in money claims. The party making the offer is called the 'offeror', and the party to whom the offer is made is the 'offeree' (**r. 36.3(1)(a)** and **(b)**).

A Part 36 offer may be made at any time, including before the commencement of proceedings (**r. 36.3(2)(a)**) or in appeal proceedings (**r. 36.3(2)(b)**). A Part 36 offer only has the consequences set out in **r. 36.14** (see **66.36** to **66.48**) in relation to the costs of the proceedings in respect of which it is made, and not in relation to any appeal from the final decision in those proceedings (**r. 36.3(4)**). Parties are not obliged to use the Part 36 format when making an offer to settle, but if they do not, the consequences in **rr. 36.10, 36.11** and **36.14** do not apply (**r. 36.1(2)**). Instead, the fact that a party has made an admissible offer which does not comply with Part 36 is one of the matters that the court is obliged to take into account when having regard to all the circumstances in exercising its general discretion on costs in **r. 44.2(4)**.

A Part 36 offer remains open for acceptance until the offeror serves notice of withdrawal on the offeree (**r. 36.9(2)**; see **66.17** to **66.19**). According to *Gibbon v Manchester City Council* [2010] EWCA Civ 726, [2010] 1 WLR 2081, there is no objection to a party having more than one 'live' Part 36 offer at any one time (see Moore-Bick LJ at [32]–[33]). Strictly this is obiter as there was only one valid Part 36 offer in question in the case before his Lordship. On the basis of the reasoning in this judgment, multiple current Part 36 offers can arise:

(a) through the deliberate choice of the offeror. This might be done in a claim for non-monetary relief where differently formulated offers may be seen as a good way of protecting the costs position of the offeror. In a money claim it may be that, with the passage of time and increasing costs in the claim, the defendant might decide to keep on the table an earlier Part 36 offer of, say, £10,000, and make a later Part 36 offer for, say, £12,000 with its slightly different costs consequences; or
(b) through accident. This may occur where, for example, the defendant makes a Part 36 offer which is rejected, and, without formally withdrawing that offer, makes a later Part 36 offer. As the earlier Part 36 offer has not been withdrawn it is still 'live' even though it was rejected by the offeree (see **66.20**). Another example is where the offeror

intends to vary a Part 36 offer under **r. 36.3(6)**, with terms less advantageous to the offeree (without changing the effective date of the original offer), but fails to do so clearly enough so that the new terms are interpreted as a new offer rather than a variation (*Gibbon v Manchester City Council* at [32]).

If a Part 36 offer is withdrawn (see **66.17** to **66.19**) the offeror loses the costs and interest effects of a subsisting Part 36 offer (**r. 36.14(6)(a)**).

Formalities governing Part 36 offers: basic contents

A Part 36 offer intended to take effect in accordance with Part 36 must comply with the formalities set out in **CPR, r. 36.2**: **66.7**

(a) It must be in writing (**r. 36.2(2)(a)**). Although a Part 36 offer may be made in a letter, it is better to use form N242A (see **PD 36A, para. 1.1**).
(b) It must state on its face that it is intended to have the consequences of Part 36 (**r. 36.2(2)(b)**).
(c) If made at least 21 days before trial, it must specify a period of not less than 21 days within which the defendant will be liable for the claimant's costs in accordance with **r. 36.10** if the offer is accepted (**r. 36.2(2)(c)** and **(3)**).
(d) It must state whether it relates to the whole of the claim or part of it or to an issue that arises in the claim, and if so, which part or issue (**r. 36.2(2)(d)**).
(e) An offer may relate solely to liability (**r. 36.2(5)**). A defendant's offer to settle liability with a stated percentage deduction for contributory negligence is an offer on liability within **r. 36.2(5)** and is not an offer on part of a claim under either **r. 36.10(2)** or **r. 36.11(3)** (*Onay v Brown* [2009] EWCA Civ 775, LTL 10/8/2009).
(f) A Part 36 offer must state whether it takes into account any counterclaim (**r. 36.2(2)(e)**).

In addition, a Part 36 offer needs to state the terms of the proposed compromise, which should be sufficiently precise and certain for an effective contract to be formed if the offer is accepted. In cases involving the enjoyment of land and interests in land, often it is prudent to include a marked-up scale plan as an attachment to the offer. In all cases it is important to be clear whether the offer is in full and final settlement of all matters in dispute between the parties, or defined matters between the parties, and whether the offer takes into account matters such as any cross-claim or previous interim payment.

A developing question is the extent to which there must be strict compliance with these formalities and consistency with the other requirements of Part 36 for an offer to be a Part 36 offer to settle, a topic discussed at **66.16**.

Terms as to costs

There is a long-standing distinction, when it comes to costs, between disputes where proceedings have and have not been issued. If proceedings have been issued, the court has jurisdiction to award costs as the court seised of the proceedings. If there are no proceedings, costs can only be payable by agreement (see the Senior Courts Act 1981, s. 51(1), and **68.2**). In order to ensure that Part 36 offers have effective costs consequences, **CPR, r. 36.2(2)(c)**, provides that a Part 36 offer must specify a period of not less than 21 days within which the defendant will be liable for the claimant's costs in accordance with **r. 36.10** if the offer is accepted. Making express provision for costs in this way overturns the decision in *Mitchell v James* [2002] EWCA Civ 997, [2004] 1 WLR 158, which held under the old Part 36 that a post-issue Part 36 offer should not contain terms as to costs. **66.8**

A claimant making a Part 36 offer should not include or make any reference to uplift interest under **r. 36.14(3)(a)**, as this is a discretionary consequence of non-acceptance (*Ali Reza-Delta Transport Co. Ltd v United Arab Shipping Co. SAG (No. 2)* [2003] EWCA Civ 811, [2004] 1 WLR 168). The same should apply to the additional amount in (**r. 36.14(3)(d)**).

Commentary

Money claims: additional requirements

66.9 A Part 36 offer made by a defendant in a claim for money must offer to pay a single sum of money (**CPR, r. 36.4(1)**). This rule is subject to two exceptions, see **66.11** and **66.12**. An offer to pay all or part of a sum of money at a date later than 14 days following the date of any acceptance is not treated as a Part 36 offer unless the offeree accepts the offer (**r. 36.4(2)**).

The single sum required by **r. 36.4(1)** is by **r. 36.3(3)** treated as inclusive of all interest until:

(a) the end of the period stated in the offer during which the defendant will be liable to pay the claimant's costs if the offer is accepted, in cases where the Part 36 offer is made at least 21 days before the trial; or
(b) the date 21 days after the date the offer was made if it was made less than 21 days before the trial.

Under the new version of Part 36 there is no need for the detailed terms approved by *Crouch v King's Healthcare NHS Trust* [2004] EWCA Civ 1332, [2005] 1 WLR 2015, for Part 36 offers made by NHS trusts.

Personal injuries claims: deduction of benefits

66.10 When making a Part 36 offer in a claim for damages for personal injuries, the defendant should state (**CPR, r. 36.15(3)**) either:

(a) that the offer is made without regard to any liability for recoverable amounts; or
(b) that the offer is intended to include any deductible amounts.

A defendant who makes a compensation payment in a personal injuries claim is liable to pay the Secretary of State the amount of recoverable benefits paid to the claimant (see the Social Security (Recovery of Benefits) Act 1997, ss. 1, 8 and sch. 2) and also any recoverable lump sum payments as defined in the Social Security (Recovery of Benefits) (Lump Sum Payments) Regulations 2008 (SI 2008/1596), regs 4 and 12 (see the Social Security (Recovery of Benefits) Act 1997, s. 1A, the Pneumoconiosis etc. (Workers' Compensation) Act 1979, and the Mesothelioma Lump Sum Payments (Conditions and Amounts) Regulations 2008 (SI 2008/1963)). Recoverable State benefits arise in a great many personal injury claims, but only payments in pneumoconiosis and mesothelioma claims are recoverable lump sum payments (see the Social Security (Recovery of Benefits) Act 1997, s. 1A(2)). The term 'lump sum' in these provisions must not be confused with the same expression used in relation to periodical payments in **66.11**. As a result, most offers made by defendants are stated to include deductible amounts (see point (b) above). Before making such a Part 36 offer, the defendant must apply for a certificate which will provide details of recoverable benefits and recoverable lump sum payments (**CPR, r. 36.15(5)**). Once the certificate is received, the defendant will be able to comply with **r. 36.15(6)**, which requires the Part 36 offer to state:

(a) the amount of gross compensation;
(b) the name and amount of any deductible amount which will reduce the gross amount; and
(c) the net amount of compensation.

In a case where a defendant makes a Part 36 offer after a certificate has been applied for but before it is received, the defendant must within seven days of receipt of the certificate clarify the offer by stating the details required by **r. 36.15(6)** (**r. 36.15(7)**).

Permission is required to accept a Part 36 offer where further deductible benefits have accrued since the date of the offer, see **66.30**. The rules relating to success and liability for costs in personal injuries claims with recoverable benefits are discussed at **66.38**.

Personal injuries claims for future pecuniary loss

Claims for future pecuniary loss in personal injury claims are governed by the Damages Act 1996, s. 2(1), see **63.29**. **CPR, r. 36.5(3)**, provides that a Part 36 offer to settle a claim which is or includes a claim for future pecuniary loss (whether by the claimant or the defendant) may contain an offer to pay or accept: **66.11**

(a) the whole or part of the damages for future pecuniary loss in the form of either:
  (i) a lump sum (which must be a single sum of money: **rr. 36.5(5)** and **36.4**); or
  (ii) periodical payments; or
  (iii) both a lump sum and periodical payments;
(b) the whole or part of any other damages in the form of a lump sum.

Rule 36.5(4) lays down a number of compulsory and optional details to be included in a Part 36 offer to settle a personal injury claim involving damages for future pecuniary loss.

Compulsory elements are that the offer must:

(a) state the amount of any offer to pay the whole or part of any damages in the form of a lump sum (**r. 36.5(4)(a)**);
(b) state what part of the offer relates to damages for future pecuniary loss to be paid or accepted in the form of periodical payments (**r. 36.5(4)(c)**), and must specify:
  (i) the amount and duration of the periodical payment;
  (ii) the amount of any payments for substantial capital purchases and when they are to be made; and
  (iii) that each amount is to vary by reference to the retail prices index (or some other named index, or that it is not to vary by reference to any index); and
(c) state either that any damages in the form of periodical payment will be funded in a way that ensures that continuity of payment is reasonably secure, or how continuity of payment is to be secured (**r. 36.5(4)(d)**).

Optional elements are (**r. 36.5(4)(b)**) that the offer may:

(a) state what part of the lump sum, if any, relates to damages for future pecuniary loss; and
(b) state what part relates to other damages to be accepted in the form of a lump sum.

An offer comprising a lump sum and periodical payments can only be accepted as a whole (**r. 36.5(6)**). If the offeree accepts an offer which includes payment of any part of the damages through periodical payments, the claimant must within seven days of the acceptance apply to the court for an award of damages in accordance with **rr. 41.4** to **41.10** and **PD 41B** (see **CPR, r. 36.5(7)**).

Offers in provisional damages claims

Provisional damages are considered at **63.23** to **63.27**. A Part 36 offer made in a claim which includes a claim for provisional damages must specify whether the offer includes an award of provisional damages (**CPR, r. 36.6(2)**). A provisional damages offer must state a single sum in respect of the immediate damages element in respect of the claimant's existing injuries, calculated on the assumption that the claimant will not develop the disease or suffer the deterioration justifying a claim for further damages (**rr. 36.6(4)** and **36.4**). The offer must by **r. 36.6(3)** also state: **66.12**

(a) that the sum offered is in satisfaction of the claim for damages on the assumption that the claimant will not develop the disease or suffer the deterioration specified in the offer; and
(b) that the offer is subject to the condition that the claimant must make any claim for further damages within a specified period.

If the offeree accepts a Part 36 offer for provisional damages, the claimant must within seven days of the acceptance apply to the court for an award of provisional damages in accordance with **r. 41.2** and **PD 41A** (see **r. 36.6(5)**).

Defence of tender before claim

66.13 A defendant who wishes to rely on a defence of tender before claim must make a payment into court of the amount said to have been tendered (**CPR, r. 37.2**). The defence of tender before claim is not available until this has been done (**r. 37.2(2)**). The payment in should be paid at the time of filing the defence (*Greening v Williams* (1999) *The Times*, 10 December 1999). Usually the payment will be made by cheque, which must be made payable to the Accountant General of the Supreme Court (**PD 37, para. 1.1(1)(a)**). A litigant in person without a current account may, if the claim is proceeding in a county court or a district registry, lodge cash rather than using a cheque (**para. 1.2**). The payment must be accompanied by a copy of the defence and by Court Funds Office form 100. Notice of the payment in must be served on every other party, and a certificate of service (in form N215) must be filed in respect of each such notice (**CPR, r. 37.1**).

Money paid into court in support of a defence of tender before claim may not be paid out without the court's permission, except where a Part 36 offer is accepted without needing permission and the defendant agrees that the sum in court can be used to satisfy the offer (**r. 37.1**). If the claimant is willing to accept the sum in court, it usually means that the defendant has succeeded on his defence of tender before claim, in which event the claimant should pay the defendant's costs from the date of the pre-claim tender.

The rule that Part 36 offers must not be communicated to the trial judge does not apply to tenders before claim (**r. 36.13(3)(a)**).

Date a Part 36 offer is made

66.14 A Part 36 offer is made when it is served on the offeree (**CPR, r. 36.7(1)**). This wording removes the decision in *Charles v NTL Group Ltd* [2002] EWCA Civ 2004, LTL 13/12/2002, which held that the strict rules on service in Part 6 (see **chapter 15**), did not apply to Part 36 offers (although they did apply to Part 36 payments). The effect is that provided one of the prescribed methods of service in **r. 6.20** is used, there is no need for the offeree to prove receipt because of the irrebuttable presumption of service in **r. 6.26**. The intention appears to be that the provisions of Part 6 apply even to Part 36 offers made before proceedings are commenced.

Where the offeree is legally represented, the offer must be served on the legal representative (**PD 36A, para. 1.2**).

Relevant period for acceptance of a Part 36 offer

66.15 A Part 36 offer must specify a period of not less than 21 days within which the defendant will be liable for the claimant's costs in accordance with **CPR, r. 36.10**, if the offer is accepted (**r. 36.2(2)(c)**). There is no provision within Part 36 for suspension of the relevant period while the offeree investigates the offer (*Martin v Randall* [2007] EWCA Civ 1155, LTL 22/10/2007). If the offeree wants more time, a time application should be made (in the absence of consent) under **r. 3.1(2)(a)** (see **48.23**).

In the case of an offer made not less than 21 days before the trial, the period stated under **r. 36.2(2)(c)**, or such longer period as the parties may agree, is 'the relevant period' for the purposes of Part 36 (**r. 36.3(1)(c)**).

In the case of a Part 36 offer made less than 21 days before the trial, 'the relevant period' is the period up to the end of the trial or such other period as the court has determined (**r. 36.3(1)(c)**). In order for a Part 36 offer made less than 21 days before trial to have the full consequences in the event of non-acceptance set out in **r. 36.14**, it is necessary to obtain an order abridging the relevant period (see **rr. 3.1(2)(a)** and **36.14(6)(c)**).

Defects in a Part 36 offer

An offer which does not comply with the technical requirements of **CPR, r. 36.2**, does not have the consequences on acceptance or following judgment set out in **rr. 36.10**, **r. 36.11** and **r. 36.14** (see **r. 36.1(2)**). The requirements referred to in **r. 36.2** are the formal requirements which apply to all Part 36 offers (see **66.7**), and also the specific requirements which apply in personal injuries claims relating to damages for future pecuniary loss (**r. 36.5**; see **66.11**), provisional damages (**r. 36.6**; see **66.12**), and deduction of benefits (**r. 36.15**; see **66.10**). In considering whether a Part 36 offer is defective, and the extent of any defect, it was held before *Gibbon v Manchester City Council* [2010] EWCA Civ 726, [2010] 1 WLR 2081, that the offer should be interpreted as it would be read by a reasonable solicitor (*Onay v Brown* [2009] EWCA Civ 775, LTL 10/8/2009). **66.16**

In *C v D* [2011] EWCA Civ 646, [2012] 1 WLR 1962, it was held that a time-limited offer is inconsistent with **r. 36.9(2)**, which provides that a Part 36 offer can be accepted at any time unless it is withdrawn, and with **r. 36.14(3)** and **(6)**, which provide for costs and interest sanctions where judgment is at least as advantageous as a claimant's offer unless the claimant's offer is withdrawn. Time limiting the offer would circumvent **r. 36.14(6)** if such an offer took effect within Part 36. This is such an unattractive result that the Court of Appeal said that an offer should, wherever possible, be interpreted in a way that is consistent with Part 36. The offer in question was expressed to be 'open for 21 days from the date of this letter'. This was interpreted by the court below as a time-limited offer. The Court of Appeal interpreted the phrase as meaning the offer would not be withdrawn for 21 days, so was not time-limited, and was a Part 36 offer.

More serious departures from Part 36 will mean the offer is not a Part 36 offer. Thus an offer specifically excluding the claimant from recovering all or part of its costs, or only offering a fixed sum in respect of costs, does not comply with **rr. 36.2(2)(c)** and **36.10**, so will not be a Part 36 offer (*Howell v Lees-Millais* [2011] EWCA Civ 786, [2011] WTLR 1795). A letter offering an interim payment is not to be construed as a Part 36 offer (*Ali v Stagecoach* [2011] EWCA Civ 1494, LTL 28/10/2011).

The best way of avoiding making defective Part 36 offers is by using form N242A. A measure of protection may also be gained by including a request to the other side to notify the offeror of any defect as soon as possible (see *Seeff v Ho* [2011] EWCA Civ 401, [2011] 4 Costs LR 443).

It is arguable that an offer which complies with the technical requirements of Part 36, but is inconsistent with other provisions of Part 36 falls outside Part 36. In *C v D* at first instance ([2010] EWHC 2940 (Ch), [2011] 1 WLR 331) at [26] Warren J suggested that an offer to settle that said an acceptance would only be valid if hand-delivered would not stop the offer being a Part 36 offer. With respect, this ignores **rr. 36.7**, **36.9(1)** and **36.3(7)**, which provide that offers, acceptances and withdrawals of offers take effect on 'service'. Service is regulated by Part 6, and so these provisions must import all the means of service permitted by Part 6. Either Warren J's conclusion at [26] is wrong (in the interests of certainty within a self-contained code as explained by *Gibbon v Manchester City Council* [2010] EWCA Civ 726, [2010] 1 WLR 2081), or it is necessary to differentiate between material and non-material departures from the scheme in Part 36. If so, any material departure from the scheme in Part 36 will mean the offer is not governed by Part 36. For example, providing that the defendant will be liable for the claimant's indemnity-basis costs if the offer is accepted in the relevant period would presumably be a material departure from Part 36.

A question arises as to whether minor defects in any of these requirements can be put right using the power to cure errors of procedure in **r. 3.10**. This rule provides that errors of procedure do not invalidate steps taken in proceedings unless the court so orders. It is suggested that this means that **r. 3.10** does not apply to a defective offer, because **r. 36.1(2)** says that nothing in Part 36 prevents a party from making an offer to settle in whatever form he chooses. A defective offer is not therefore without validity in any event. It simply does not have the consequences set out in **rr. 36.10**, **36.11** and **36.14**. As the note to **r. 36.1** says, the court still has to take into account an offer that does not comply with **r. 36.2** when deciding the question of costs (**r. 44.2**). The implication is that this will not necessarily be in the same terms as if the offer had complied with **r. 36.2**, but it depends on the extent of the defect. In *Huntley v Simmonds* [2009] EWHC 406 (QB), LTL 6/3/2009, the Part 36 offer was defective in that it omitted the statement required in future pecuniary loss cases by **r. 36.5(4)(d)** (see **66.11**), that continuity of payments would be assured. It was held that while there would be cases where the court would not rectify formal defects, in this case there was no prejudice and the claimant understood the offer, so the court applied **r. 44.2(4)** and accorded the offer the same effect as one that complied with Part 36. This is discussed further at **66.47**.

A party who realises that an offer he has made does not fully comply with Part 36 should replace the offer, before acceptance, with an offer that does comply. The consequences set out in **rr. 36.10**, **36.11** and **36.14** will then apply from that time.

DEALING WITH THE OFFER

Withdrawing or changing a Part 36 offer before the expiry of the relevant period

66.17 Before the expiry of the relevant period (see **66.15**), a Part 36 offer may be withdrawn or its terms changed in a way less advantageous to the offeree only with the court's permission (**CPR, r. 36.3(5)**). This is a significant variation on the normal rules of offer and acceptance, and to this extent overturns the decision in *Scammell v Dicker* [2001] 1 WLR 631 (which held that the offeror is always free to withdraw a Part 36 offer before acceptance). There is no prescribed form for withdrawing a Part 36 offer. Any withdrawal must, however, comply strictly with the requirements of **r. 36.3(7)** if it is to be effective (*Gibbon v Manchester City Council* [2010] EWCA Civ 726, [2010] 1 WLR 2081 at [17]). It must be in writing, and should include an express reference to the date of the Part 36 offer and its terms, together with some words making it clear that the offer is being withdrawn (at [17]).

Permission to withdraw a Part 36 offer during the relevant period is sought by making an application in accordance with Part 23 (**PD 36A, para. 2.2(1)**).

The court probably has jurisdiction to allow a Part 36 offer to be withdrawn or changed in the 21-day period after service of the Part 36 offer even if the claimant serves a notice of acceptance during that 21-day period (*Flynn v Scougall* [2004] EWCA Civ 873, [2004] 1 WLR 3069, a case decided under old Part 36). In *Flynn v Scougall* May LJ said, at [30] and [34], that the court could entertain a defendant's application to withdraw or reduce a Part 36 payment which was made after the claimant had served notice of acceptance. It is submitted that this is pushing too far the old theory that payments in were not contractual (see [26], where May LJ quotes Goddard LJ saying this in *Cumper v Pothecary* [1941] 2 KB 58 at p. 67). The better view is that once a Part 36 offer has been accepted the case has been settled.

Whether to grant permission to withdraw or change a Part 36 offer will be considered applying the overriding objective. The following factors, if present, are likely, it is submitted, to render it just to allow a defendant to withdraw or change a Part 36 offer:

(a) the offer was induced by fraud; or
(b) a mistake affects the terms of the offer; or
(c) the discovery of further evidence puts a wholly different complexion on the case; or
(d) there has been a change in the legal outlook brought about by a judicial decision.

The fact the claimant has given notice of acceptance, if present, was said to be an important factor in *Flynn v Scougall*. Merely receiving an expert's report contradicting the evidence of the claimant's expert is unlikely to be a sufficient change of circumstances to warrant granting permission to the defendant (*Flynn v Scougall*).

Withdrawing or changing a Part 36 offer after the expiry of the relevant period

After expiry of the relevant period and provided the offeree has not previously served notice of acceptance, the offeror may withdraw the offer or change its terms to be less advantageous to the offeree without the permission of the court (**CPR, r. 36.3(6)**). The offeror withdraws or changes a Part 36 offer by serving written notice on the offeree (**r. 36.3(7)**); and see **66.17**. If a Part 36 offer is not withdrawn, it may be accepted even after the relevant period (**r. 36.9(2)**). **66.18**

A change in the terms of a Part 36 offer (whether it is an improved offer or one which is less advantageous to the offeree) takes effect when written notice of the change is served on the offeree (**rr. 36.2(2)(a)** and **36.7(2)**).

Effect of a withdrawn Part 36 offer

A withdrawn Part 36 offer does not have the effect on costs and interest (as laid down in **CPR, r. 36.14(2)** and **(3)**) of a subsisting Part 36 offer (**r. 36.14(6)(a)**). A note to **r. 36.14** points out that **r. 44.2(4)(c)** requires the court to consider any admissible offer to settle which does not have the costs consequences set out in Part 36 in deciding what order to make about costs. Without prejudice offers (see **50.68**) are not admissible, whereas open offers and offers made without prejudice save as to costs are admissible on the question of costs. This gives the court a wide scope on costs, to be exercised applying the overriding objective. In a suitable case the court can even treat the withdrawn Part 36 offer has having the same costs consequences as if it had not been withdrawn (see *Trustees of Stokes Pension Fund v Western Power Distribution (South West) plc* [2005] EWCA Civ 854, [2005] 1 WLR 3595, discussed at **66.47**). **66.19**

Commentary

Rejection of a Part 36 offer

There is no need for the offeree to give an express rejection of a Part 36 offer. In most cases the offeree will keep his options open by not responding to a Part 36 offer (see **66.26**). It was held in *Gibbon v Manchester City Council* [2010] EWCA Civ 726, [2010] 1 WLR 2081 at [16]–[17] that the rejection of a Part 36 offer by the offeree has no effect on its continuing validity. Likewise, there is no concept of an implied withdrawal of a Part 36 offer, such as where the offeror rejects a counter-offer from the offeree in terms similar to the terms of the offeror's offer. This is because the only way in which a Part 36 offer ceases to be live (in the absence of an acceptance or the final disposal of the claim) is by the offeror formally withdrawing its offer under **CPR, r. 36.3(7)**. This means that the rejected offer can be accepted as of right by the offeree (even after the relevant period has expired), which was the actual decision in the first appeal in *Gibbon v Manchester City Council*. **66.20**

Making a counter-offer does not operate as a rejection of a Part 36 offer. (**CPR, r. 36.9(2)** says a Part 36 offer may be accepted at any time 'whether or not the offeree has subsequently made a different offer', thereby reversing the effect of *Hawley v Luminar Leisure plc* [2006] EWCA Civ 30, *The Times*, 14 February 2006, a decision under the old Part 36.)

Clarification of a Part 36 offer

It may happen that a party makes a Part 36 offer, but that its terms are not clear to the offeree. This may occur where the claim raises more than one cause of action, or where there are joint claimants. It may also occur where the Part 36 offer fails to make clear what is included. In such cases, the offeree may request the offeror to clarify the offer, but the request must be made within seven days of the offer being made (**CPR, r. 36.8(1)**). The time when an offer or payment is made is defined as the date it is served (see **r. 36.7(1)**). If the offeror fails to give clarification as requested within seven days of receiving the request, the offeree may apply for an order that this be done, unless the trial has started (**r. 36.8(2)**). An application for an order requiring **66.21** clarification should be made in accordance with Part 23 and the application notice should state the respects in which the terms of the Part 36 offer are said to require clarification.

Where the Part 36 offer fails to make clear what it includes, an order to clarify will almost certainly be made, in accordance with the overriding objective. Cases where the claimant or claimants want a global offer broken down between the respective claimants are less clear cut. Under the RSC, the court could order a defendant to break down a global payment in on the ground that it was 'embarrassing'. **CPR, r. 36.8**, uses the term 'clarification', and is almost certainly intended to lay down a different test. It is arguable that the court only has jurisdiction under **r. 36.8** where the Part 36 offer is unclear. This would mean that, provided the offer gives the details required by Part 36, and states clearly whether it covers the whole claim, or which parts, and whether it includes interest and any counterclaim etc., no further breakdown can be ordered. The alternative argument that **r. 36.8** gives the court a wide discretion to order a more detailed breakdown, for example, into different heads of damages, or to give details of dates and rates applied, is unsustainable given the requirement in **r. 36.4(1)** that a Part 36 offer in a money claim must be for a single sum of money.

Where the court does order clarification to be given, the order must specify the date when the Part 36 offer is to be treated as having been made (**r. 36.8(3)**). Typically this will be from the date the offer is clarified (*Colour Quest Ltd v Total Downstream UK plc* [2009] EWHC 823 (Comm), LTL 23/4/2009). This allows the offeree more time in which to accept the offer without requiring the court's permission, and is therefore not necessarily in the interests of the offeror. It is suggested that offers should be suitably and succinctly drafted in order to avoid clarification applications.

ACCEPTANCE

Notice of acceptance of a Part 36 offer

66.22 A Part 36 offer is accepted by serving written notice of the acceptance on the offeror (**CPR, r. 36.9(1)**). It is also necessary to file the notice of acceptance with the court (**PD 36A, para. 3.1**).

The rules distinguish between the following situations on the timing of giving notice of acceptance:

(a) Normally, the offeror should aim to serve notice of acceptance during the relevant period. In this situation the claimant will be entitled to its costs from the defendant up to the date of notice of acceptance (see **66.23**).
(b) A notice of acceptance served after the relevant period is effective only if the offer has not been withdrawn before service of the notice of acceptance (the effect of **r. 36.9(2)**). Costs in this situation are as discussed at **66.26** below.
(c) If a notice of acceptance is served after the trial has started, the court's permission is required to accept it (**r. 36.9(3)(d)**).
(d) A notice of acceptance served after the end of the trial, but before judgment is handed down, is only effective if the parties agree (**r. 36.9(5)**).

In *Re Kilopress Ltd* (2010) LTL 22/4/2010 the respondent accepted the petitioner's Part 36 offer to sell his shares in the company to the respondent for a stated price with instalment payments over five years, with a requirement for a Tomlin order in the underlying unfair prejudice petition setting out the terms. The petitioner argued the Part 36 offer had been withdrawn and that the reference to the Tomlin order invalidated the offer. A declaration was made that the case had been settled. No written notice of withdrawal had been served under **r. 36.3(7)**. The settlement contract was in the Part 36 offer and the acceptance. The Tomlin order was merely the means of recording the bargain.

Costs consequences of accepting a Part 36 offer

Acceptance within the relevant period relating to the whole claim Subject to five exceptions (see below and **66.24** to **66.27**), where a Part 36 offer is accepted within the relevant period (see **66.15**) the claimant is entitled to the costs of the proceedings from the date on which notice of acceptance was served on the offeror (**CPR, r. 36.10(1)**). This applies whether the offer was made by the claimant or defendant. The claimant's costs include costs incurred both before and after proceedings are issued (*Thompson v Bruce* [2011] EWHC 2228 (QB), LTL 1/7/2011). The costs covered by **r. 36.10** also include any costs incurred in dealing with any counterclaim if the Part 36 offer states that it takes into account the counterclaim (**r. 36.10(6)**). In a defamation claim the defendant will usually be required to pay the claimant's costs of and relating to a statement in open court following acceptance of a Part 36 offer (*Phillipps v Associated Newspapers Ltd* [2004] EWHC 190 (QB), [2004] 1 WLR 2106). **66.23**

Costs recoverable under **r. 36.10** are assessed on the standard basis (see **71.36**) if the amount of costs is not agreed (**r. 36.10(3)**). There is no discretion to award indemnity-basis costs, even if the Part 36 offer is made by the defendant and is more advantageous to the claimant than a rejected Part 36 offer made by the claimant (*Dyson Appliances Ltd v Hoover Ltd (No. 3)* [2002] EWHC 2229 (Ch), [2003] FSR 21). Exceptionally, a claimant who accepts a pre-commencement Part 36 offer in a road traffic claim worth less than £10,000 is only entitled to fixed costs in Part 45 (*Solomon v Cromwell Group plc* [2011] EWCA Civ 1584, [2012] 1 WLR 1048).

Acceptance within the relevant period relating to part of the claim Where a defendant makes a Part 36 offer relating to only part of the claim, the claimant will be entitled to his standard-basis costs of the proceedings up to the date of the notice of acceptance if he accepts the offer within the relevant period and abandons the balance of the claim (**CPR, r. 36.10(2)**). This rule is stated to be subject to the court otherwise ordering. A claimant accepting a Part 36 offer is only entitled to the costs of the proceedings as of right where the acceptance brings the whole of the proceedings to an end (*Clark Goldring and Page Ltd v ANC Ltd* (2001) *The Times*, 27 March 2001). Where a Part 36 offer relates to part of the claim, and the rest is not abandoned, the effect of **rr. 36.10** and **36.11** is that the court has a discretion on the question of costs. **66.24**

Acceptance of Part 36 offers made less than 21 days before trial Where a Part 36 offer is made less than 21 days before the trial, and is accepted, the parties may agree the liability for costs, but if they do not, the court will make an order for costs (**CPR, r. 36.10(4)(a)**). **66.25**

Acceptance of Part 36 offers after the relevant period Where a Part 36 offer is accepted after the relevant period expires, the parties may agree the liability for costs, but if they do not, the court will make an order for costs (**CPR, r. 36.10(4)(b)**). Where the court makes an order for costs under **r. 36.10(4)(b)**, unless it orders otherwise, the order for costs will provide that: **66.26**

(a) the claimant is entitled to his costs of the proceedings up to the date when the relevant period expired; and
(b) the offeree will be liable for the offeror's costs for the period from the expiry of the relevant period to the date of acceptance (**r. 36.10(5)**).

Departing from the usual rule is exceptional, and should only be done where the usual costs consequences laid down by **r. 36.10(5)** would be unjust in the particular circumstances (*Lumb v Hampsey* [2011] EWHC 2808 (QB), LTL 11/10/2011). In *Matthews v Metal Improvements Co. Inc.* [2007] EWCA Civ 215, [2007] CP Rep 27, the Court of Appeal said it was a fundamental misunderstanding of the function of Part 36 offers to ask whether it had been reasonable for the claimant not to have accepted the offer based on the information available to the claimant at the time it was made. Part 36 offers are designed to put the claimant on risk as to costs if, as a result of the contingencies of litigation, it later transpires that the claimant is unable to beat the terms of the offer. A reduction in the value of the claim after the offer was made due to the

Commentary

onset of a non-accident-related medical condition provided no basis for departing from the position stated in **r. 36.10(5)**. Where it is a claimant's offer that is accepted after the relevant period, there is no presumption that the post-relevant period costs awarded to the claimant will be on the indemnity basis, and unless the claimant can demonstrate the necessary conduct under **r. 44.2**, those costs will be ordered on the standard basis (*Fitzpatrick Contractors Ltd v Tyco Fire and Integrated Solutions (UK) Ltd* [2009] EWHC 274 (TCC), [2009] BLR 144). It may, however, be appropriate to award enhanced interest on the post-relevant period costs (in *Fitzpatrick Contractors Ltd v Tyco Fire and Integrated Solutions (UK) Ltd* such interest was awarded at 1 per cent above base rate).

Acceptance in Warsaw/Montreal Convention cases

66.27 The Warsaw Convention 1929, art. 22(4) (as amended by The Hague Convention 1955), which is set out in the schedule to the Carriage by Air Act 1961, provides:

> The limits prescribed in this article shall not prevent the court from awarding, in accordance with its own law, in addition, the whole or part of the court costs and of the other expenses of the litigation incurred by the plaintiff. The foregoing provision shall not apply if the amount of damages awarded . . . does not exceed the sum which the carrier has offered in writing to the plaintiff within a period of six months from the date of the occurrence causing the damage, or before the commencement of the action, if that is later.

The equivalent provision in the Montreal Convention 2004 is art. 22(6).

In *GKN Westland Helicopters Ltd v Korean Air* [2003] EWHC 1120 (Comm), [2003] 2 All ER (Comm) 578, the defendant made an offer within six months of the issue of the claim, then made a Part 36 payment in a slightly larger amount. The Part 36 payment was accepted. It was held that because the Part 36 payment was higher than the Warsaw Convention offer, the normal rule in what is now **CPR, r. 36.10**, applied, and the defendant was liable to pay the claimant's costs of the claim. It was recognised that there is a latent conflict between **r. 36.10** and art. 22 of the Convention where a claimant accepts a Part 36 offer which is less than a previous Warsaw Convention offer. The better view is that in such circumstances the Warsaw Convention should prevail, and the defendant should be awarded its costs from the date of the Warsaw Convention offer.

Acceptance of offer of amends in defamation cases

66.28 Under the Defamation Act 1996, s. 2(1), a person who has published a statement alleged to be defamatory of another may offer to make amends, by making a suitable correction and a sufficient apology, which are to be published in a reasonable and practicable manner, and to pay such compensation and costs as may be agreed or determined (s. 2(4)). Such an offer must be in writing and comply with the requirements of s. 2(3). A party accepting such an offer may not bring or continue defamation proceedings (s. 3(2)), although the aggrieved party may apply to the court for an order that the other side fulfil his offer (s. 3(3)), and if compensation is not agreed, it shall be determined by the court (s. 3(5)). An offer of amends, if not accepted, may in certain circumstances act as a defence, and may be relied upon in mitigation of damages (s. 4).

In *Warren v Random House Group Ltd* [2008] EWCA Civ 834, [2009] QB 600, the defendant made an offer of amends which was accepted by the claimant. Before compensation had been decided under s. 3(5), the defendant sought to withdraw the offer and to plead justification. As in the case of accepted Part 36 offers, the court felt that an accepted offer of amends does not create a contract in the strict sense, because the agreement contains express provisions as to what should or should not happen next, and the court retains a role (Clarke MR at [17]). This means that the agreement can be set aside on the usual grounds on which a contract can be set aside, and also where there are special or exceptional circumstances, applying the same principles as apply on seeking to be released from an undertaking (see **37.64**).

Permission to accept

Acceptance after the start of the trial The court's permission is required for an acceptance of a Part 36 offer after the trial has started (**CPR, r. 36.9(3)(d)**). It is suggested that the principles enunciated in *Capital Bank plc v Stickland* [2004] EWCA Civ 1677, [2005] 1 WLR 3914, are a useful guide to how the discretion should be exercised under **r. 36.9(3)(d)**. This case concerned the late acceptance of a claimant's Part 36 offer under old Part 36. **66.29**

In the majority of cases permission will be granted, with the only question being as to costs (*Cumper v Pothecary* [1941] 2 KB 58 at p. 67, quoted with approval by Longmore LJ in *Capital Bank plc v Strickland* at [17]). However, the court has a wide discretion in the matter, and may refuse permission, for example, where the acceptance is made very late, where there is a doubt about the availability of the money, or where there has been a change of circumstances (at [16]).

If late acceptance is allowed by consent or with the court's permission, the usual rule is that the claimant recovers costs up to the end of the relevant period, and the defendant recovers costs thereafter. This is subject to the court's discretion, and there may be reasons for making some other costs order. For example, the claimant may have accepted the offer after late disclosure of evidence or late amendment by the defendant which has had a material effect on the claimant's prospects. If the change is just an excuse for late acceptance, the usual costs rule will be applied, but where the change has had a real impact the court may allow the claimant to recover costs of the claim up to some later point, even the date of acceptance (*Factortame Ltd v Secretary of State for the Environment, Transport and the Regions* [2002] EWCA Civ 22, [2002] 1 WLR 2438). In exercising its discretion on costs, the court is not restricted to considering the circumstances surrounding the offer, and should consider all the circumstances relevant under **r. 44.2**, including the parties' willingness to participate in proposed mediation (*Chaudry v Yap* [2004] EWHC 3380 (Ch), LTL 28/10/2004).

Other cases where permission to accept is required In addition to the situation where a Part 36 offer is accepted after the start of the trial (see **66.29**), permission to accept is required where: **66.30**

(a) The Part 36 offer is made by some, but not all, of a number of defendants and **CPR, r. 36.12(4)**, applies (**r. 36.9(3)(a)**, see **66.32**).
(b) The claim is for damages for personal injuries, the offer is intended to include any deductible amounts, and further deductible amounts have been paid to the claimant since the date of the offer (**r. 36.9(3)(b)**). In this situation the application must state the net amount offered in the Part 36 offer, the deductible amounts accrued at the date of the offer, and those that have subsequently accrued. The application must be accompanied by a copy of the current certificate of recoverable benefits and any recoverable lump sum (**PD 36A, para. 3.3**). If permission to accept is granted, the court may direct that the amount of the offer payable to the offeree shall be reduced by a sum equivalent to the deductible amounts paid to the claimant since the date of the offer (**CPR, r. 36.15(9)**).
(c) An apportionment is required under **r. 41.3A** (Fatal Accidents Act claims) (**r. 36.9(3)(c)**).
(d) Any of the parties is a child or protected party (**r. 21.10**, see **66.31**).

Acceptance by or on behalf of a child or protected party CPR, r. 21.10(1), provides that no settlement or compromise relating to a claim by or on behalf of, or against, a child or protected party shall be valid without the approval of the court. In such a case there is no binding agreement until the proposed settlement is approved by the court under **r. 21.10**. This means that until that time either party may repudiate the settlement (*Dietz v Lennig Chemicals Ltd* [1969] 1 AC 170; *Drinkall v Whitwood* [2003] EWCA Civ 1547, [2004] 1 WLR 462). **66.31**

66.32 **Acceptance of Part 36 offer made by some of the defendants** In cases where a claimant wishes to accept a Part 36 offer made by some of a number of defendants, there are three situations that need to be distinguished:

(a) If the defendants are sued jointly or in the alternative, the claimant may accept the Part 36 offer if he discontinues the claim against the other defendants and those other defendants give written consent to the acceptance of the offer (**CPR, r. 36.12(2)**).
(b) If the defendants are alleged to have a several liability, the claimant may accept the offer and continue his claims against the other defendants (**r. 36.12(3)**).
(c) In all other cases the claimant must apply to the court for an order permitting him to accept the Part 36 offer (**r. 36.12(4)**).

Other consequences of acceptance

66.33 **Stay on acceptance** If a Part 36 offer is accepted, the claim will be stayed (**CPR, r. 36.11(1)**). While an accepted Part 36 offer appears to form a contract, the better view is that it does not, because the court retains a role under the terms of Part 36. See *Flynn v Scourgall* [2004] EWCA Civ 873, [2004] 1 WLR 3069; *Scammell v Dicker* [2001] 1 WLR 631; *Orton v Collins* [2007] EWHC 803 (Ch), [2007] 1 WLR 2953; and *Warren v Random House Group Ltd* [2008] EWCA Civ 834, [2009] QB 600 at [21]. The stay will be on the terms of the offer where the Part 36 offer relates to the whole claim (**r. 36.11(2)**). Where the terms of the acceptance include the disposition of an interest in land, the court has the power to order the parties to sign a single document incorporating the terms of the settlement (*Orton v Collins* [2007] EWHC 803 (Ch), [2007] 1 WLR 2953). If the Part 36 offer only related to part of the claim:

(a) the claim is stayed as to that part on the terms of the offer; and
(b) unless the claimant abandons the balance of the claim (for which see **r. 36.10(2)**), unless the parties agree costs, the liability for costs shall be decided by the court (**r. 36.11(3)**).

66.34 **Time for payment** Unless the parties agree otherwise in writing, where a Part 36 offer to pay money is accepted, payment must be made within 14 days of the acceptance (**CPR, r. 36.11(6)(a)**). In the case of provisional damages awards and periodical payments awards, the 14 days run from the date of the court order, unless the court orders otherwise (**r. 36.11(6)(b)**). If the sum is not paid within these time limits, the offeree may enter judgment for the unpaid sum (**r. 36.11(7)**).

66.35 **Enforcement of agreed terms** A stay under **CPR, r. 36.11** (see **66.33**), does not affect the power of the court to enforce the terms of the Part 36 offer, nor to deal with any question of costs or interest on costs relating to the proceedings (**r. 36.11(5)**). Enforcement of a term for the payment of money is effected by entering judgment followed by use of the normal procedures for enforcing judgments (see **chapter 79**). Terms other than for the payment of money can be enforced by making an interim application to the court, there being no need to commence a new claim (**r. 36.11(8)**).

COSTS CONSEQUENCES OF NON-ACCEPTANCE

Failing to obtain a judgment more advantageous than a Part 36 offer

66.36 The main reason for making a Part 36 offer is to gain the costs and interest benefits set out in **CPR, r. 36.14**. These consequences apply (**r. 36.14(1)**), unless the court considers that their application would be unjust, where a Part 36 offer is not accepted and either:

(a) a claimant fails to obtain a judgment more advantageous than a Part 36 offer made by a defendant; or
(b) judgment is entered against a defendant which is at least as advantageous to the claimant as the proposals set out in a Part 36 offer made by the claimant.

Deciding whether a judgment is more advantageous than a Part 36 offer has proved controversial. For money claims, and for the money element of a claim, where the Part 36 offer is made on or after 1 October 2011, a judgment is 'more advantageous' where it is better than the Part 36 offer in money terms by any amount, however small (**r. 36.14(1A)**). Rule 36.14(1A) is intended to provide a clear-cut dividing line (*Fox v Foundation Piling Ltd* [2011] EWCA Civ 790, [2011] 6 Costs LR 961). If the judgment is even by the smallest margin better than a Part 36 offer then, subject to the discretion in **r. 44.2**, the claimant should be awarded its costs. This is so, particularly in personal injuries claims, even where the judgment is substantially lower than the amount claimed. In these cases the defendant should have protected itself by making a realistic, albeit modest, Part 36 offer (*Morgan v UPS* [2008] EWCA Civ 1476, [2009] 3 Costs LR 384). Like must be compared with like. Where a Part 36 offer includes interest, the court must recalculate its award of interest to the date of the Part 36 offer in order to determine whether the judgment exceeds the terms of the offer (*Blackham v Entrepose UK* [2004] EWCA Civ 1109, [2005] 1 Costs LR 68). A gloss on this was applied in *Gibbon v Manchester City Council* [2010] EWCA Civ 726, [2010] 1 WLR 2081 at [36], where the trial judge had awarded interest at 8 per cent per annum, but the Court of Appeal recalculated the award applying an interest rate of 4 per cent per annum. The stated reason was that no more than 4 per cent per annum 'could have been expected' when the Part 36 offer was made. An award of interest is just as much a part of a judgment as the principal sum, and it is, with respect, very difficult to understand why this additional element of uncertainty (guessing what is a reasonable rate of interest, as opposed to the actual rate of interest awarded by the judge) should be grafted on to the calculations that have to be made under Part 36.

Fox v Foundation Piling Ltd recognised in this context that there is a distinction between:

(a) cases where the reduction is as a result of surveillance or medical evidence, even if that shows the claimant's injuries have been exaggerated, where **r. 36.14(1A)** applies and the claimant should be awarded all standard-basis costs; and
(b) cases where the claimant has been dishonest, where different considerations apply.

Rule 36.14(1A) overrules the decision in *Carver v BAA plc* [2008] EWCA Civ 412, [2009] 1 WLR 113, which held that 'more advantageous' in **r. 36.14(1)** is a more open-textured concept than the pre-6 April 2007 phrase 'fails to better'. *Carver v BAA plc* appeared to hold that the court is entitled to decide that a judgment that exceeds a Part 36 offer by a small margin might not be more advantageous to a claimant given factors such as the costs of litigating a claim through to trial and the emotional stress of taking a case to trial. *Gibbon v Manchester City Council* [2010] EWCA Civ 726, [2010] 1 WLR 2081, said that *Carver v BAA plc* is binding on all courts up to the Court of Appeal, and, given the introduction of **r. 36.14(1A)**, this means for Part 36 offers made from 6 April 2007 until 30 September 2011. In *Carver v BAA plc* the costs were about £80,000, and judgment was entered for £4,686, which was just £51 more than the Part 36 offer. The court awarded the claimant her costs up to the end of the relevant period, and made no order as to costs thereafter. This approach was drastically curtailed even for money claim offers from 6 April 2007 until 30 September 2011 by *Gibbon v Manchester City Council*, where Moore-Bick LJ rightly said at [40] (and Carnwath LJ is to similar effect at [50]–[51]) that the courts should not be too ready to impose their own views of what is and what is not to the advantage of a litigant. This is particularly so in money claims, where achieving more than the sum offered is legitimately regarded as success. A party faced with a Part 36 offer should be entitled to take a rational view of whether further progress in the claim is likely to achieve a greater sum, bearing in mind any unrecoverable costs. In most cases obtaining judgment for an amount greater than the offer is likely to outweigh all other factors.

In a defamation claim, comparing the terms of an offer with the eventual judgment may, depending on the terms of the offer and the events at trial, involve considering the terms and

Commentary

value of any apology and any damage to the reputation of the claimant arising from the evidence given at the trial (*Jones v Associated Newspapers Ltd* [2007] EWHC 1489 (QB), [2008] 1 All ER 240).

Consistently with *Mitchell v James* [2002] EWCA Civ 997, [2004] 1 WLR 158, the court should ignore any terms in a claimant's Part 36 offer relating to indemnity-basis costs or enhanced interest (see **66.41**) in deciding whether the offer exceeds the judgment (*Ali Reza-Delta Transport Co. Ltd v United Arab Shipping Co. SAG (No. 2)* [2003] EWCA Civ 811, [2004] 1 WLR 168).

For non-money claims on and after 1 October 2011, it is submitted the approach suggested by Bingham MR in *Roache v News Group Newspapers Ltd* [1998] EMLR 161 at pp. 168–9 (cited with approval in *Carver v BAA plc*) has a continuing validity in deciding whether a judgment is more advantageous than a Part 36 offer:

> The judge must look closely at the facts of the particular case before him and ask: who, as a matter of substance and reality, has won? Has the [claimant] won anything of value which he could not have won without fighting the action through to the finish? Has the defendant substantially denied the [claimant] the prize which the [claimant] fought the action to win?

It is a fundamental error to make a costs order that penalises a party for failing to achieve a better result at trial than the terms of its own Part 36 offer (*Rolf v De Guerin* [2011] EWCA Civ 78, [2011] BLR 221).

Cases where rule 36.14 consequences do not apply

66.37 The consequences in **CPR, r. 36.14**, do not apply:

(a) where the court considers this would be unjust (**r. 36.14(2)–(4)**, see **66.43**);
(b) where the Part 36 offer has been withdrawn, or changed to terms less advantageous to the offeree than the judgment (**r. 36.14(6)(a)**, **(b)**, see **66.18**);
(c) if the Part 36 offer was made less than 21 days before the trial (unless the court abridges time) **r. 36.14(6)(c)**;
(d) where qualified one-way costs shifting applies (see **chapter 69**); or
(e) where an admissible offer does not comply with the technical requirements of Part 36.

It is wrong in principle to apply the intentionally draconian consequences set out in **r. 36.14** to offers that do not comply with Part 36. In these cases the offer is simply taken into account in deciding on the order for costs under **r. 44.2(4)(c)** (*F and C Alternative Investments (Holdings) Ltd v Barthelemy (No. 3)* [2012] EWCA Civ 843, [2013] 1 WLR 548).

Personal injuries claims: success and deductible amounts

66.38 The format of Part 36 offers in personal injuries claims with deductible State benefits and recoverable lump sum payments was discussed at **66.10**. **CPR, r. 36.14(1)(a)**, applies for the purpose of determining whether the claimant has failed to obtain a judgment more advantageous than such an offer (including a lump sum offered under **r. 36.5**, for which, see **66.11**). The question is whether the claimant has failed to recover, after taking away deductable amounts, a sum greater than the net amount stated in the Part 36 offer in compliance with **r. 36.15(6)(c)**. Comparison of the award with the net sum in the Part 36 offer is intended to be compliant with the Social Security (Recovery of Benefits) Act 1997, s. 8 and sch. 2. It solves the problem identified in *Williams v Devon County Council* [2003] EWCA Civ 365, [2003] PIQR Q68, where old Part 36 required the court to compare the judgment with the gross sum (old r. 36.23(4)).

In comparing the judgment with the net sum under **r. 36.15(8)**, care still needs to be taken to ensure compliance with the rules in the Social Security (Recovery of Benefits) Act 1997 on recouping benefits against appropriate heads of damages and, in relation to recoverable lump sums, between different dependants.

Successful defendant's Part 36 offer

Assuming the claimant has won on liability, but fails to obtain a judgment more advantageous than a Part 36 offer made by a defendant, unless the court considers it unjust to do so, the court will order: **66.39**

(a) the defendant to pay the claimant's costs up to the expiry of the relevant period applying the usual principle that costs follow the event (**CPR, r. 44.2(2)(a)**);
(b) the claimant to pay the defendant's costs from the expiry of the relevant period (**r. 36.14(2)(a)**); and
(c) the claimant to pay interest on the defendant's costs (**r. 36.14(2)(b)**). There is no power to award interest at an enhanced rate on a defendant's costs (*Excelsior Commercial and Industrial Holdings Ltd v Salisbury Hamer Aspden and Johnson* [2002] EWCA Civ 879, [2002] CP Rep 67; *J. Murphy and Sons Ltd v Johnston Precast Ltd* [2008] EWHC 3104 (TCC), LTL 22/12/2008).

Successful claimant's Part 36 offer

CPR, r. 36.14(3), provides that unless the court considers it unjust to do so, where judgment is entered against a defendant which is at least as advantageous to the claimant as the proposals set out in a claimant's Part 36 offer, the court will order that the claimant is entitled to: **66.40**

(a) Interest on the whole or part of the sum of money (excluding interest) awarded at a rate not exceeding 10 per cent above base rate for some or all of the period starting with the date on which the relevant period expired. Enhanced interest cannot be ordered in respect of heads of damages that do not attract awards of interest. This applies to defamation claims (*McPhilemy v Times Newspapers Ltd (No. 2)* [2001] EWCA Civ 933, [2002] 1 WLR 934, see **64.17**) and to awards for future loss in personal injuries claims (*Pankhurst v White* [2010] EWCA Civ 1445, [2011] 3 Costs LR 392). An order running from the date of the offer rather than the expiry of the relevant period will be corrected on appeal (*Martin v Randall* [2007] EWCA Civ 1155, LTL 22/10/2007). Where interest is also awarded on the same sum for the same period under any other power (such as the County Courts Act 1984, s. 69, or the Senior Courts Act 1981, s. 35A), the total rate of interest may not exceed 10 per cent above base rate (**CPR, r. 36.14(5)**).
(b) His costs on the indemnity basis (see **71.44**) from the date on which the relevant period expired and ending with the trial or other final disposal of the claim. It does not extend to post-judgment applications, such as an application for a non-party costs order (see **68.60** and *Chantrey Vellacott v Convergence Group plc* (2007) LTL 3/10/2007).
(c) Interest on those indemnity basis costs at a rate not exceeding 10 per cent above base rate. The purpose of an order for interest on indemnity costs is to compensate for the cost of money, or loss of the use of money, borne before trial in relation to payments made on account of costs (*KR v Bryn Alyn Community (Holdings) Ltd* [2003] EWCA Civ 383, [2003] CP Rep 49; *Chantrey Vellacott v Convergence Group plc* (2007) LTL 3/10/2007).
(d) An additional amount not exceeding £75,000 calculated in accordance with **r. 36.14(3)(d)** (see **66.42**).

Enhanced interest

The court should not start with the assumption that it should award the maximum enhanced interest under **CPR, r. 36.14(3)(a)**) but must stand back and ensure that the enhanced interest does not provide a disproportionate benefit (*Earl v Cantor Fitzgerald International (No. 2)* (2001) LTL 3/5/2001). Full 10 per cent above base rate interest was awarded in *Blue Sphere Global Ltd v Commissioners of HM Revenue and Customs* [2010] EWCA Civ 1448, LTL 16/12/2010. At first instance in *Pankhurst v White* [2010] EWHC 311 (QB), [2010] 3 Costs LR 402, enhanced interest on damages in a personal injuries claim was awarded at 10 per cent per annum on past losses (instead of **66.41**

Commentary

the then current 6 per cent special account rate), and at 4 per cent per annum (instead of 2 per cent) on damages for pain, suffering and loss of amenity.

Additional amount

66.42 Sir Rupert Jackson's *Review of Civil Litigation Costs* (Ministry of Justice, December 2009) felt that **CPR, r. 36.14(3)**, did not go far enough in rewarding a claimant making a successful Part 36 offer, and recommended that a claimant making a successful Part 36 offer should be awarded an extra 10 per cent on the damages award (recommendation 94). This was implemented through the enactment of the Legal Aid, Sentencing and Punishment of Offenders Act 2012, s. 55, the Offers to Settle in Civil Proceedings Order 2013 (SI 2013/93), and amendments to **CPR, r. 36.14(3)**, in force from 1 April 2013.

The additional amount is, in effect, a further head of damages, and is intended to provide a reward with real value to a claimant who makes a successful claimant's Part 36 offer. By the Offers to Settle in Civil Proceedings Order 2013, SI 2013/93, and **CPR, r. 36.14(3)(d)**, slightly different approaches are taken in money and non-money claims:

(a) in money claims the additional amount is 10 per cent on the first £500,000 of the damages or other money award, plus 5 per cent on any sum awarded above £500,000 and up to £1,000,000. Using these figures, the maximum additional amount is £75,000; and
(b) in non-money claims the additional amount is calculated at 10 per cent for the first £500,000 and 5 per cent on the next £500,000 of the costs awarded to the claimant.

The additional amount in **r. 36.14(3)(d)** was seen by Sir Rupert Jackson as being an integral part of the civil justice reforms of 2013, which included abolishing the recoverability of CFA success fees and other additional liabilities. As stated in the tenth implementation lecture, abolition of success fees, increasing damages by 10 per cent, and the ability of claimants to augment their damages by a further 10 per cent by making an effective Part 36 offer, are parts of a balanced package. The balance in the package of reforms will only be maintained if the courts are ready to impose awards of the additional amount where the claimant has made a successful claimant's Part 36 offer.

Unjust to make orders under rule 36.14

66.43 In considering whether it would be unjust to make an order under **CPR, r. 36.14(2)** or **(3)** (see **66.39** and **66.42**), the court will, by **r. 36.14(4)**), take into account all the circumstances of the case, including:

(a) the terms of any Part 36 offer;
(b) the stage in the proceedings when any Part 36 offer was made, and in particular the period between the offer and the start of the trial;
(c) the information available to the parties at the time when the Part 36 offer was made;
(d) the conduct of the parties with regard to giving or refusing to give information for the purposes of enabling the offer to be made or evaluated (conduct includes any failure by the claimant to give adequate disclosure to enable the defendant to assess the validity of the claim (*Mamidoil-Jetoil Greek Petroleum Co. SA v Okta Crude Oil Refinery AD* [2002] EWHC 2462 (Comm), [2003] 1 Lloyd's Rep 42));
(e) whether it would be unjust to make orders under **r. 36.14(3)** because the defendant had a good reason for rejecting the offer, such as a reasonable belief in its prospects of success based on the law as it then stood (*Mamidoil-Jetoil Greek Petroleum Co. SA v Okta Crude Oil Refinery AD*).

In *Hall v Stone* [2007] EWCA Civ 1354, [2008] CP Rep 263, Smith LJ at [82] said:

> In these days where both sides are expected to conduct themselves in a reasonable way and to seek agreement where possible, it may be right to penalise a party to some degree for failing to accept a reasonable offer or for failing to come back with a counter-offer.

The fact that the offeror is funded under a CFA is irrelevant when deciding whether to make an order under **r. 36.14(3)** (*CEL Group Ltd v Nedlloyd Lines (UK) Ltd* [2003] EWCA Civ 1871, [2004] 1 Lloyd's Rep 388).

Awarding indemnity-basis costs after a successful claimant's Part 36 offer implies no misconduct on the defendant (*McPhilemy v Times Newspapers Ltd (No. 2)* [2001] EWCA Civ 933, [2002] 1 WLR 934), its practical effect being to ensure that the claimant does not recover any less than the costs he has in fact incurred (*Petrotrade Inc. v Texaco Ltd* [2002] 1 WLR 947). Indemnity costs and enhanced interest on those costs can be awarded even where the claimant is publicly funded (*Earl v Cantor Fitzgerald International (No. 2)* (2001) LTL 3/5/2001). The enhanced rate of interest on indemnity-basis costs runs from the date upon which the work was done or liability for disbursements was incurred, and runs until judgment. Thereafter, interest on costs is payable under the Judgments Act 1838, s. 17, in the usual way (*McPhilemy v Times Newspapers Ltd (No. 2)*).

In *Huck v Robson* [2002] EWCA Civ 398, [2003] 1 WLR 1340, the claimant in a personal injuries claim made a Part 36 offer to settle a dispute on the basis that the defendant was 95 per cent liable. At trial the judge found for the claimant with no deduction for contributory negligence, and the claimant asked for indemnity-basis costs. It was held that while an offer based on marginally less than full liability might be illusory, that was not so in the present case, and the fact that no trial judge would make a finding of only 5 per cent contributory negligence was irrelevant. It was not unjust for the defendant to have to pay indemnity-basis costs and enhanced interest.

Commentary

Failing to exceed a withdrawn Part 36 offer

A withdrawn Part 36 offer does not have the costs consequences set out in **CPR, r. 36.14** (see **r. 36.14(6)(a)**). It may nevertheless have an effect on the orders the court makes on costs (**rr. 36.1(2)** and **44.2**). Where a withdrawn offer made by the defendant is more advantageous than the judgment, according to *Garner v Cleggs* [1983] 1 WLR 862 (approved by Longmore LJ in *Capital Bank plc v Stickland* [2004] EWCA Civ 1677, [2005] 1 WLR 3914 at [21]), the principled approach on costs is: **66.44**

(a) for the claimant to be awarded costs up to the end of the relevant period;
(b) for the defendant to be awarded costs from the end of the relevant period to the date of any relevant change of circumstances affecting the risks in the litigation; and
(c) for the claimant to be awarded costs thereafter.

It may well be that the new scheme introduced with effect from 6 April 2007 will mean this will no longer be followed. In particular, point (b) above was based on the old position that Part 36 payments could only be withdrawn with the court's permission, whereas under the new provisions there is a right to withdraw a Part 36 offer after the relevant period has expired (**r. 36.3(6)**).

Departing from the normal rule on costs

The normal rule on costs described at **66.39** and **66.40** has been departed from where: **66.45**

(a) a party was late in disclosing important evidence (*Ford v GKR Construction Ltd* [2000] 1 WLR 1397);
(b) a party has been unwilling to participate in proposed mediation (*Re Midland Linen Services Ltd* [2004] EWHC 3380 (Ch), LTL 28/10/2004);
(c) a claimant has deliberately exaggerated the claim (*Painting v University of Oxford* [2005] EWCA Civ 161, [2005] PIQR Q5).

Traditionally, the courts have taken a strict line that the normal rule should be followed even when the judge had been considering a slightly higher award (*Wagman v Vare Motors Ltd* [1959] 1 WLR 853). In *Jackson v Ministry of Defence* [2006] EWCA Civ 46, LTL 12/1/2006, the Court of Appeal approved a modest percentage reduction in the costs order to reflect the fact the claimant had only just beaten a Part 36 offer. Other factors may persuade a judge to depart from the normal rule, but there is great reluctance in countenancing such departures. Thus, in *Jones v Jones* (1999) *The Times*, 11 November 1999, there had been an offer of £120,000, and the claimant only recovered damages of £111,000. The amount of damages awarded was probably depressed by a third medical report served by the defendant some six months after the offer. These events occurred before the CPR came into force. The Court of Appeal held that the judge erred in principle in awarding the claimant costs up to the disclosure of the last medical report. Translated into CPR terms the Court of Appeal's substituted order would mean that the claimant would only recover her costs to the expiry of the relevant period. This decision may be at variance with the ethos of the CPR, and in particular with **r. 44.2**, which gives the court wide powers to take into account conduct on questions of costs. The case should be contrasted with *Ford v GKR Construction Ltd*, in which the Court of Appeal affirmed a decision to award the entire costs of the claim to the claimant who was awarded £85,000 despite an offer of £95,000. This was because her award was depressed below the level of the offer by virtue of video surveillance evidence introduced in the period of an adjournment between the first and second days of the trial, which was criticised as being late.

In *Painting v University of Oxford* the claimant pleaded loss and damage in excess of £400,000 on the basis that she suffered a long-term debilitating injury, and the defendant made an offer of £10,000. The judge found that the claimant had intentionally exaggerated her injuries, and awarded her £23,331. The Court of Appeal held that the essential question at trial was whether the claimant was exaggerating her injuries. The claimant's intentional exaggeration, combined with her failure to negotiate, justified making an order for the defendant to pay the claimant's costs to the expiry of the relevant period, and for the claimant to pay the defendant's costs thereafter, despite the judgment exceeding the amount in court.

An exaggeration of a claim was regarded in *Widlake v BAA Ltd* [2009] EWCA Civ 1256, [2010] PIQR P4, as an 'allegation' for the purposes of **r. 44.2(5)(b)** as well as being expressly part of **r. 44.2(5)(d)**, and so forms part of the conduct of the claimant in deciding what order to make on costs. Cases involving exaggeration are very fact-sensitive, as shown by *Allison v Brighton and Hove City Council* [2005] EWCA Civ 548, LTL 22/4/2005. Here the claim was for £45,000, but judgment was for £4,000. The claimant was awarded only 25 per cent of his costs in the period prior to an effective offer. Percentage costs orders of this type have been increasingly common since the introduction of the CPR.

In *Daniels v Commissioner of Police for the Metropolis* [2005] EWCA Civ 1312, *The Times*, 28 October 2005, the claimant was a serving police officer who was injured when thrown from her horse in a training session. She made a number of claimant's Part 36 offers, but the defendant refused to negotiate. At trial the claim was dismissed. The question on appeal was whether the refusal to negotiate was 'unreasonable' conduct in the *Halsey v Milton Keynes General NHS Trust* [2004] EWCA Civ 576, [2004] 1 WLR 3002, sense (see **68.19**). The Court of Appeal said it was difficult to imagine circumstances where rejecting a Part 36 offer could be characterised as unreasonable if the party who rejected the offer then won the case. That was particularly so on the facts, where the defendant routinely faced unmeritorious claims.

A decision illustrating the point that **r. 44.2** rarely overrides the usual rule where there has been a Part 36 offer exceeding the damages awarded is *Burgess v British Steel* (2000) *The Times*, 29 February 2000. In this case the Court of Appeal overturned a decision to award the claimant costs to the final date for accepting the offer (which was in the sum of £220,000), and to award no costs thereafter. Before making the offer the defendant had disclosed a medical report which asserted that the claimant was malingering and which implied the claimant was pursuing a bogus claim. At trial the claimant established that the claim was genuine, but only recovered £161,000. On appeal it was held this did not justify departing from the usual rule, and the second part of the costs order was altered so that the defendant recovered costs from the expiry of the relevant period.

Subject to the discussion at **66.36**, where the award at trial exceeds a Part 36 offer the court should not depart from the usual rule by examining whether the Part 36 offer was reasonable, nor by reason of the claimant having made a claimant's Part 36 offer which was higher than the award at trial (*Quorum AS v Schramm* [2002] CLC 77). In *Johnsey Estates (1990) Ltd v Secretary of State for the Environment* [2001] EWCA Civ 535, LTL 11/4/2001, the defendant made a first Part 36 offer of £200,000, followed by a second Part 36 offer of £250,000. At trial the judge awarded £200,000 plus interest of £36,000 to the date of the first Part 36 offer. The Court of Appeal overturned the judge's award of costs to the defendant from the date of the first Part 36 offer because this failed to take into account the award of interest, and substituted an award (apart from on one issue) to the claimant of its costs to the date of the second Part 36 offer, with the defendant recovering costs thereafter.

Awarding a defendant indemnity-basis costs

A defendant making a successful Part 36 offer will usually be awarded costs on the standard basis. An award of costs on the indemnity basis is normally reserved to cases where the court wishes to show its disapproval, but may extend to some cases where an offer has been made and rejected. Indemnity-basis costs may be appropriate where the claim is dismissed at trial, if the court also finds that the case was going to fail from the outset of the trial (*Reid Minty v Taylor* [2001] EWCA Civ 1723, [2002] 1 WLR 2800). In *Kiam v MGN Ltd (No. 2)* [2002] EWCA Civ 66, [2002] 1 WLR 2810, the Court of Appeal said that *Reid Minty v Taylor* decided no more than that conduct falling short of conduct deserving moral condemnation could still be so unreasonable as to justify an order of indemnity-basis costs. In *Kiam v MGN Ltd (No. 2)* it was held that such conduct needed to be unreasonable to a high degree, and the refusal of a settlement offer (not being a claimant's Part 36 offer) would rarely attract such an order. **66.46**

Commentary

Costs where the offer fails to comply with Part 36

By **CPR, r. 36.1(2)**, nothing in Part 36 prevents a party from making an offer to settle in whatever way he chooses, but if that offer is not made in accordance with Part 36, it will not have the consequences set out in Part 36. As mentioned at **66.16**, the note to **r. 36.1** says the court still has to take into account an offer that does not comply with **r. 36.2** when deciding the question of costs (**r. 44.2**). The implication is that this will not necessarily be in the same terms as if the offer had complied with **r. 36.2**. The following discussion is based on cases decided under old r. 36.1(2). This allowed the court to give full Part 36 effect to an offer that did not comply with old Part 36, so these cases probably disclose a rather over-indulgent approach to non-compliance. **66.47**

In *Amber v Stacey* [2001] 1 WLR 1225 the defendant made a written offer that did not comply with old Part 36, but which was more generous than the award eventually made by the court. It was held to be wrong in principle to treat the offer in the same way as if it had been a Part 36 offer for the purposes of costs. However, it was taken into account when considering costs, with the result that the defendant was awarded half his costs from the date of the offer, the court being influenced by the claimant's intemperate response to the written offer. In *Mitchell v James* [2002] EWCA Civ 997, [2004] 1 WLR 158, a claimant's Part 36 offer failed to comply with old r. 36.5(6)(b) in that it did not state that after 21 days the defendant could only accept it if costs liability was agreed or if the court gave permission. It was said that if this had been the only defect in the offer, the court would have waived it as a mere technicality (see **r. 3.10**).

In *Hardy v Sutherland* [2001] EWCA Civ 976, LTL 13/6/2001, the defendant made a Part 36 offer and, some time later, a Part 36 payment. The claim was for money, so the earlier Part 36 offer did not comply with old r. 36.3. It was held that proper recognition of the offer would be accorded by depriving the claimant of a percentage of his costs up to the date for acceptance of the Part 36 payment (after which the defendant recovered costs from the claimant).

Perhaps the most radical decision is *Trustees of Stokes Pension Fund v Western Power Distribution (South West) plc* [2005] EWCA Civ 854, [2005] 1 WLR 3595. This was a claim for damages of £780,000. The defendant made a written offer before proceedings of £35,000, but did not pay in after proceedings were started as required by old r. 36.10. The defendant later paid in £20,000 and informed the claimant that the earlier offer was withdrawn. At trial the claimant recovered £25,000. On appeal the £35,000 written offer was treated as a payment in because the following four conditions were satisfied:

(a) the written offer was expressed in clear terms, stating whether it took into account any counterclaim and interest, in line with old r. 36.5(2);
(b) it was expressed to be open for acceptance for at least 21 days and generally accorded with the form of Part 36 offers;
(c) it was a genuine offer, not a sham; and
(d) the defendant was clearly good for the money when the offer was made.

The fact the defendant withdrew the £35,000 offer was held to be irrelevant because there was no evidence the claimant would have accepted the offer at a later stage if it had remained open. The Court of Appeal substituted an order that the claimant had to pay the defendant's costs from 21 days after the written offer.

Cases such as *Trustees of Stokes Pension Fund v Western Power Distribution (South West) plc* are instances of the court using its discretion under old r. 36.1(2) to treat offers which do not comply with the strict requirements of old Part 36 as if they were Part 36 offers. Being discretionary, the court had a wide ambit in deciding on the appropriate consequences. It is an error of principle to treat an offer which does not comply with Part 36 as having either full or no effect, without considering intermediate positions (*Codent Ltd v Lyson Ltd* (2005) LTL 8/12/2005). In *Farag v Commissioner of Police of the Metropolis* [2005] EWCA Civ 1814, LTL 15/12/2005, the claim raised eight causes of action against the police. An offer to settle was refused, then withdrawn two years before the trial. All but one of the causes of action failed. The Court of Appeal took the offer into account in deciding to make no order as to costs. In *Codent Ltd v Lyson Ltd* an offer was made less than 21 days before trial and in the form of a Part 36 offer, whereas it should have been a Part 36 payment. The claimant was awarded 70 per cent of its costs up to the first day of the trial, and the defendant was awarded its costs thereafter.

Incomplete or unclear offers

66.48 An offer to settle made before the commencement of proceedings in *Phyllis Trading Ltd v 86 Lordship Road Ltd* [2001] EWCA Civ 350, [2001] 2 EGLR 85, did not refer to costs. Thorpe LJ said that an offeree takes a real risk in rejecting such an offer out of hand, and has an obligation to state what is acceptable and to seek clarification. It was held that the offeree had to pay the costs from the date of the offer.

What is required is a 'clear and concise' offer to settle (*Amber v Stacey* [2001] 1 WLR 1225), so the judge is entitled to disregard a letter which is only an offer to negotiate (*Press v Chipperfield* [2003] EWCA Civ 484, LTL 25/3/2003). There were complex proceedings in *Rio Properties Inc. v Gibson Dunn and Crutcher* [2005] EWCA Civ 534, LTL 22/4/2005. The claimant purported to make a *claimant's Part 36 offer* in respect of the costs of various interim applications. It was held that it was open to the judge to decide the offer was difficult to evaluate and therefore should be disregarded on the question of costs.

PART 36 OFFERS IN APPEALS

Part 36 and appeals

A Part 36 offer which is made before trial has effect in relation to the costs of the proceedings up to the final disposal of the proceedings at first instance (**CPR, r. 36.3(4)**). A party intending to obtain costs protection for appeal proceedings needs to make a separate Part 36 offer in the appeal proceedings (**rr. 36.3(2)(b)** and **36.3(4)**, confirming *East West Corporation v Dampskibsselskabet af 1912 A/S* [2003] EWCA Civ 174, [2003] 1 Lloyd's Rep 265; *Various Claimants v Bryn Alyn Community (Holdings) Ltd* [2003] EWCA Civ 383, LTL 24/3/2003). These provisions also apply to statutory appeals (*Blue Sphere Global Ltd v Commissioners of HM Revenue and Customs* [2010] EWCA Civ 1448, LTL 16/12/2010). **66.49**

A respondent in an appeal who makes an offer to accept all but a small fraction of the amount awarded by the court below will generally be regarded as having made a genuine offer to settle, and will usually be awarded indemnity costs (and possibly also enhanced interest) under **r. 36.14(3)**. As discussed in *CEL Group Ltd v Nedlloyd Lines (UK) Ltd* [2003] EWCA Civ 1871, [2004] 1 Lloyd's Rep 388, a respondent cannot reasonably be expected to give up a substantial part of the judgment under appeal, particularly where the appeal raises an all-or-nothing point.

PAYMENT UNDER COURT ORDER

CPR, r. 37.1, deals with payments into court under court orders. The party making the payment in must send the payment to the Court Funds Office. Usually the payment will be made by cheque, which must be made payable to the Accountant General of the Senior Courts (**PD 37, para. 1.1(1)(a)**). Lodgment of a cheque with the Court Funds Office is the effective date for making the payment (*ENE Kos 1 Ltd v Petróleo Brasileiro SA* [2009] EWCA Civ 1127, [2010] 1 WLR 1361). A litigant in person without a current account may, if the claim is proceeding in a county court or a district registry, lodge cash rather than using a cheque (**para. 1.2**). The payment must be accompanied by a sealed copy of the court order and by Court Funds Office form 100. Notice of the payment in must be served on every other party, and a certificate of service (in form N215) must be filed in respect of each such notice (**CPR, r. 37.1**). **66.50**

By **r. 37.3**, permission is in most cases required for the payment out of money paid into court under a court order. Permission is obtained by making an application in accordance with Part 23 (**PD 37, para. 3.2**). The application notice must state the grounds on which the order for payment out is sought, and it is often necessary to file a witness statement in support. Where the court gives permission, it will include a direction for the payment out of the money in court, including accrued interest (**para. 3.3**).

Permission for payment out is not required where:

(a) a Part 36 offer is accepted without needing the permission of the court (which is governed by **CPR, r. 36.9**, see **66.29** to **66.32**); and
(b) the defendant paid the sum in court and agrees that such sum should be used to satisfy the whole or part of the offer.

Where permission is not required for payment out of money in court, the requesting party should file a request in Court Funds Office form 201 with the Court Funds Office, which must state the details set out in **PD 37, para. 3.5**. The request must be accompanied by a statement that the defendant agrees to the money being used to satisfy a Part 36 offer, using Court Funds Office form 202 (**para. 3.4**). Interest on the money in court up to the date of acceptance is paid to the defendant (**para. 3.6**). The principal sum is in most cases paid by bank transfer to the legal representative of the party making the request (**para. 3.8(1)**). Exceptions are that payments in cases of unrepresented parties with public funding are made to the Legal Services Commission (**para. 3.8(2)**), and that parties can request payment out by cheque (**para. 3.7**).

PAYMENTS INTO COURT PURSUANT TO STATUTE

66.51 There are special provisions (made under **CPR, r. 37.4**) for payments into court pursuant to:

(a) the Life Assurance Companies (Payment into Court) Act 1896 (**PD 37, paras 4.1 to 5.2**);
(b) the Trustee Act 1925, s. 63 (**PD 37, paras 6.1 to 7.2**); and
(c) the Vehicular Access across Common and Other Land (England) Regulations 2002 (SI 2002/1711) (**PD 37, paras 8.1 to 8.5**).

RTA AND EL/PL PROTOCOL OFFERS TO SETTLE

66.52 Part 36 offers for RTA, employer's liability (EL) and public liability (PL) claims being dealt with under the RTA and EL/PL Protocols are governed by **CPR, rr. 36.16 to 36.22**, which came into effect on 30 April 2010 (RTA claims) and 31 July 2013 (EL and PL claims). An offer to settle in a relevant Protocol case must be set out in the court proceedings pack (part B) form (**r. 36.17(2)(a)**). It should contain the final total amount of the offers from both sides (in accordance with e.g. the **RTA Protocol, para. 7.55**). These amounts are treated as exclusive of all interest (**CPR, r. 36.19(a)**). A relevant Protocol offer is deemed to be made on the first business day after the court proceedings pack (parts A and B) is sent to the defendant. It must not be communicated to the court until the claim is determined, at which point the court will examine the relevant Protocol offer (**r. 36.20**). There is an absolute prohibition on any other form of offer being communicated to the court (**r. 36.20(b)**).

There are costs consequences for non-acceptance of relevant Protocol offers by virtue of **r. 36.21(1)** in three different situations:

(a) where the determination of the court is less than or equal to the amount of the defendant's relevant Protocol offer (**r. 36.21(1)(a)**), the court will order the claimant to pay the fixed costs under **r. 45.26** and interest on those fixed costs from the first business day after the deemed date of the relevant Protocol offer (**r. 36.21(2)**);
(b) where the determination of the court is more than a defendant's relevant Protocol offer, but less than the claimant's relevant Protocol offer (**r. 36.21(1)(b)**), the court will order the defendant to pay the fixed costs under **r. 45.20** (**r. 36.21(3)**);
(c) where the determination of the court is equal to or more than the claimant's relevant Protocol offer (**r. 36.21(1)(c)**), the court will order the defendant to pay interest on the whole of the damages at a rate not exceeding 10 per cent above base rate for all or part of the period from the deemed date of the relevant Protocol offer, fixed costs under **r. 45.20**, and interest on those costs at a rate not exceeding 10 per cent above base rate.

Rule 36.22 is similar to **r. 36.15(8)**, and provides that the amount of a judgment is less than a relevant Protocol offer where the judgment is less than the offer once deductible amounts identified in the judgment are deducted. Where a claim no longer continues under a relevant Protocol, costs are governed by **r. 36.14A**.

TRANSITIONAL PROVISIONS

66.53 Part 36 offers and Part 36 payments made before 6 April 2007 (together referred to in this section as 'old Part 36 offers') are governed by the transitional provisions in the Civil Procedure (Amendment No. 3) Rules 2006 (SI 2006/3435), r. 7, as explained by **PD 36B**. The basic principle is that old Part 36 offers will continue to have effect from 6 April 2007, and will continue to have costs and other Part 36 consequences (**PD 36B, para. 1.2**).

Acceptance of an old Part 36 offer from 6 April 2007

If permission to accept an old Part 36 offer would have been necessary under CPR, old Part 36, permission continues to be necessary from 6 April 2007 (SI 2006/3435, r. 7(3); **PD 36B, paras 2.1** to **2.2**). Situations where permission was required under CPR, old Part 36, to accept a Part 36 offer were: **66.54**

(a) Defendants' Part 36 offers and payment made less than 21 days before the trial where the parties did not agree the liability for costs (old r. 36.11(2)).
(b) Acceptances of defendants' Part 36 offers and payments given more than 21 days after the offer or notice of payment in where the parties did not agree the liability for costs (old r. 36.11(2)).
(c) Claimants' Part 36 offers made less than 21 days before the trial where the parties did not agree the liability for costs (old r. 36.11(2)).
(d) Acceptances of claimants' Part 36 offers given more than 21 days after the offer where the parties did not agree the liability for costs (old r. 36.12(2)).
(e) Some acceptances where Part 36 offers or payments were made by some but not all of the defendants in a claim (old r. 36.17).
(f) Acceptances by or on behalf of children and protected parties (**r. 21.10** and old r. 36.18(1)).

Stay, costs and interest consequences of old Part 36 offers from 6 April 2007

If an old Part 36 offer would have been effective under CPR, old Part 36, as from 6 April 2007 it will have the consequences set out in the new **CPR, rr. 36.10, 36.11** and **36.14** (SI 2006/3435, r. 7(2)). The relevant provisions under old Part 36 were: **66.55**

(a) the proceedings would be stayed if a Part 36 offer or payment relating to the whole claim was accepted (old r. 36.15(1));
(b) the defendant would be liable for the claimant's costs of the proceedings if a Part 36 offer or payment was accepted without the court's permission (old r. 36.13);
(c) the defendant would be liable for the claimant's costs of the proceedings if a claimant's Part 36 offer was accepted without needing the court's permission (old r. 36.14);
(d) unless it was unjust, the court would order the claimant to pay the defendant's costs from the last date for acceptance of a Part 36 offer or payment if the claimant failed to better the terms of the offer or payment (old r. 36.20); and
(e) the court had a discretion to award enhanced interest and indemnity basis costs (and enhanced interest on such costs) from the expiry of a claimant's Part 36 offer which was more advantageous for the defendant than the result at trial (old r. 36.21, which applied only to cases resolved at trial: *Petrotrade Inc. v Texaco Ltd* [2002] 1 WLR 947).

Payment out of court of old Part 36 payments

Payment out of court of old Part 36 payments is governed, from 6 April 2007, by the new **CPR, r. 37.3** (SI 2006/3435, r. 7(4)). This preserves in particular the requirement that permission is needed to withdraw such a payment (**PD 36B, para. 3.3**). **CPR, r. 37.3**, is discussed at **66.50**. **66.56**

Old Part 36 offers made less than 21 days before 6 April 2007

Where an old Part 36 offer is made less than 21 days before 6 April 2007, the rules in CPR, old Part 36, apply to that offer up to the expiry of the 21-day offer period, or the start of the trial, whichever is the sooner. Thereafter, the new regime, with the modifications on permission to accept, consequences and payment out, provided by the transitional provisions outlined in **66.54** to **66.56**, apply (SI 2006/3435, r. 7(5) and (6); **PD 36B, para. 4.4**). **66.57**

Old Part 36 offers made before proceedings and before 6 April 2007

66.58 An old Part 36 offer, complying with CPR, old r. 36.10, which was made at a time before proceedings were issued, will be taken into account on costs, and the court's permission is required to accept the offer once proceedings are commenced (SI 2006/3435, r. 7(7)). If proceedings are commenced after 6 April 2007, there is no need to fortify the pre-claim offer by paying money into court (**PD 36B, para. 5.4**).

To comply with CPR, old r. 36.10, an offer had to be expressed to be open for at least 21 days after the date it was made and, if it was made by a person who would be a defendant if proceedings were commenced, had to include an offer to pay the costs of the offeree incurred up to the date 21 days after the date it was made (old r. 36.10(2)). The offer was required to comply otherwise with old Part 36 (old r. 36.10(2)(c)). An offer under old r. 36.10 was 'made' when it was received by the offeree (old r. 36.10(5)).

If proceedings were started after a pre-commencement offer complying with old r. 36.10 had been made, the offer could not be accepted without the court's permission (old r. 36.10(4)) and, whether or not the offer was accepted, the court would take it into account when making any order as to costs (old r. 36.10(1)). If, however, proceedings were not started, the court had no jurisdiction to make any orders.

If a defendant to a money claim made a pre-commencement offer, and proceedings were then commenced, the defendant was required, in order to obtain the costs advantages provided by old Part 36, to make a Part 36 payment within 14 days of service of the claim form and the amount of the payment had to be not less than the sum offered before proceedings began (old r. 36.10(3)). This payment could not be accepted by the offeree without the court's permission (old r. 36.10(4)). A defendant who needed more time than the 14 days allowed by old r. 36.10(3) could apply for permission to extend time under **r. 3.1(2)(a)**, see *Walker Residential Ltd v Davis* [2005] EWHC 3483 (Ch), LTL 9/12/2005. The power to extend time under **r. 3.1(2)(a)** could not be used once money in court had been accepted without permission, because such an extension would overreach the mandatory costs order in favour of the claimant provided by old r. 36.13(1).

Chapter 67 Security for Costs

Commentary

INTRODUCTION

Generally, the question of who pays for the costs of a claim is not determined until the claim is finally disposed of, whether by consent, interim process or trial. This is because the usual rule is that the successful party recovers costs from the loser and the outcome on the merits is only known when judgment is obtained. It is for this reason that the parties are not generally allowed to anticipate the eventual costs order by asking for interim orders that their opponents provide funds as security to pay for the costs of the action. Despite this, it is accepted that there have to be exceptions for cases where there is a significant risk of defendants suffering the injustice of having to defend proceedings with no real prospect of being able to recover costs if they are ultimately successful. **67.1**

An order for security for costs can only be made: (a) before judgment (*Penny v Penny* [1996] 1 WLR 1204), or (b) for the costs of an appellant, or of a respondent to an appeal who also appeals (**CPR, r. 25.15**). Once security is given it may be retained, subject to the court's discretion, pending an appeal. An order for security for costs usually requires the claimant to pay money into court as security for the payment of any costs order that may eventually be made in favour of the defendant, and staying the claim until the security is provided. On the application three matters arise:

(a) whether there are grounds for ordering security for costs;
(b) if so, whether the court's discretion should be exercised in favour of making the order; and
(c) if so, how much security should be provided.

Each of these three matters will be considered after first looking at the procedure for making the application and the capacity of the respondent to the application.

PROCEDURE

67.2 A defendant may apply under **CPR, rr. 25.12** to **25.15**, for an order requiring the claimant to give security for costs. It is submitted that, like an application for an interim remedy, an application for security for costs may be made at any time after the defendant has filed an acknowledgment of service or a defence (see **r. 25.2(2)(c)**). The first application for security should normally be made at the first case management conference (see Admiralty and Commercial Courts Guide, app. 16, para. 1). It is made using the usual Part 23 procedure of issuing an application notice supported by written evidence (**r. 25.12(2)**). The written evidence should deal with the grounds on which security is sought, and with any factors relevant to the exercise of the court's discretion. These include the location of the claimant's assets, and any practical difficulties in enforcing any order for costs (see Admiralty and Commercial Courts Guide, app. 16, para. 3). It also needs to include an estimate of the defendant's likely costs of defending the claim, which should usually be given in the form of a costs budget in precedent H (see **chapter** 43).

Invariably the application should be made on notice to the claimant, and should be served on the claimant at least three clear days before the day appointed for hearing the application (**CPR, r. 23.7(1)(b)**). Applications against companies etc. under **r. 25.13(2)(c)** (see **67.12**), are in the first instance given hearings in private (**PD 39A, para. 1.5(8)**).

Applications for security for costs will be inappropriate in cases on the small claims track because of the restrictions on the recovery of costs in these claims. In fast track and multi-track claims it is the duty of the parties to make any application that may be appropriate at any hearing that has been fixed (**PD 28, para. 2.5** (fast track); **PD 29, para. 3.5** (multi-track)), so in many cases an application for security for costs should be made at the first case management hearing.

THE RESPONDENT

Claimants

67.3 Security for costs is generally available only against a claimant or a party in the position of being a claimant (**CPR, r. 25.12(1)**). An order for security for costs may be obtained against a person other than a claimant if that person assigned the claim under an arrangement designed to avoid the possibility of a costs order, or has contributed or agreed to contribute to the claimant's costs in return for a share of any property recovered in the proceedings (**r. 25.14**).

An order for security for costs should not be made against a claimant in proceedings to enforce a foreign award where the defendant objects to registration of the judgment on the ground of fraud. Enforcement of foreign awards (see **chapter 80**) is intended to be quasi-administrative. In substance it is the defendant who is attacking rather than defending, and it is wrong in principle to award security to such a defendant (*Gater Assets Ltd v NAK Naftogaz Ukrainiy* [2007] EWCA Civ 988, [2008] Bus LR 388).

By **r. 20.3**, the provisions on security for costs in **rr. 25.12** to **25.15** apply to an additional claim as if it were a claim. So a party bringing an additional claim may be ordered to give security for the costs of the additional claim in just the same way as an original claimant may be ordered to give security for the costs of the original claim. Under the old rules it was held that if a defendant makes an additional claim against a person other than the claimant, the defendant to that additional claim cannot obtain an order for security against the original claimant, unless, as a result of directions given in the additional claim (for which see **29.9**), the defendant to the additional claim is given permission to defend jointly with the original defendant (see *Taly NDC International NV v Terra Nova Insurance Co. Ltd* [1985] 1 WLR 1359 per Parker LJ). The question is one of capacity in the main claim. There is therefore no jurisdiction to order a defendant to provide security for the costs of any interim application it may make (*Taly NDC International NV v Terra Nova Insurance Co. Ltd*).

Where a counterclaim is an entirely separate cross-claim, with an independent validity of its own, it is treated as a separate claim and security for the costs of the counterclaim may be ordered (*Hutchison Telephone (UK) Ltd v Ultimate Response Ltd* [1993] BCLC 307; *Newman v Wenden Properties Ltd* [2007] EWHC 336 (TCC), 114 Con LR 95). This needs to be distinguished from set-offs, where it has been held that security will not usually be ordered (*Neck v Taylor* [1893] 1 QB 560). The reason for this distinction is that a set-off, if established, amounts to a defence to the claim, so a defendant raising a set-off is for this purpose regarded as simply defending and not as advancing a claim. The distinction between set-offs and other types of counterclaim was considered at **34.36** and **34.37**. Similarly, it will not be fair or just to order a defendant to provide security for costs of a counterclaim which sets out contentions which are in substance the mirror image of the allegations in the particulars of claim (*Samuel J. Cohl Co. v Eastern Mediterranean Maritime Ltd* [1980] 1 Lloyd's Rep 371; *Anglo Irish Asset Finance plc v Flood* [2011] EWCA Civ 799, LTL 11/7/2011). Where a defendant is counterclaiming, the question to be asked is whether, as a matter of substance, the position of the defendant can fairly be equated with that of a claimant, or whether, in truth, it does not go beyond that of a defendant (*Pimlott v Meregrove Holdings Ltd* [2003] EWHC 1766 (QB), [2003] All ER (D) 325 (Jun), in which it was held that the costs of pursuing the counterclaim would not add to the costs of defending the claim so there should be no security). Conversely, in *L/M International Construction Inc. v Circle Partnership Ltd* [1995] CLY 4010 the claimant sued for £1,000,000 and the defendant counterclaimed for £15,000,000. The court found that the defendant was in the position of a claimant and ordered it to give security.

If the issues raised on the counterclaim are wider than those raised by the claim, security for costs may be ordered against the defendant. The amount depends on the facts of the case. In *Petromin SA v Secnav Marine Ltd* [1995] 1 Lloyd's Rep 603 there was a significant claim and counterclaim based on identical facts. The court ordered the defendant to give security for the full amount of the claimant's costs on the counterclaim and not just the increase occasioned by defending the counterclaim. In *Kazakhstan Investment Fund Ltd v Aims Asset Management Sdn Bhd* (2002) LTL 23/5/2002 the court limited the costs to those of defending the counterclaim.

Parties other than claimants

Security for costs may be ordered against any party in the position of a claimant, even if they are not strictly 'claimants'. An example would be a petitioner on an unfair prejudice petition under the Companies Act 2006, s. 994 (*Re Unisoft Group Ltd (No. 1)* [1993] BCLC 1292). Another example is an appellant to an appeal (or a respondent who cross-appeals), see **CPR, r. 25.15**. By **r. 25.14**, an order for security for costs may also be made against someone other than a claimant if the court is satisfied that the person against whom the order is sought either: **67.4**

(a) assigned the claim to the claimant with a view to avoiding the possibility of a costs order being made against him; or
(b) has contributed or agreed to contribute to the claimant's costs in return for a share of any money or property which the claimant may recover in the proceedings.

Foreign governments

An order for security for costs may be made against a foreign government (*Government of Sierra Leone v Davenport* [2003] EWHC 1913 (Ch), LTL 4/4/2005). **67.5**

CONDITIONS FOR ORDERING SECURITY FOR COSTS

67.6 Security for costs can only be ordered if, having regard to all the circumstances of the case, it is just to make the order (**CPR, r. 25.13(1)(a)**), and if one or more of the conditions set out in **r. 25.13(2)**, is satisfied. The conditions are:

(a) the claimant is—
   (i) resident out of the jurisdiction; but
   (ii) not resident in a Brussels Contracting State, a Lugano Contracting State or a Regulation State, as defined in s 1(3) of the Civil Jurisdiction and Judgments Act 1982;

[(b) revoked]

(c) the claimant is a company or other body (whether incorporated inside or outside Great Britain) and there is reason to believe that it will be unable to pay the defendant's costs if ordered to do so;

(d) the claimant has changed his address since the claim was commenced with a view to evading the consequences of the litigation;

(e) the claimant failed to give his address in the claim form, or gave an incorrect address in that form;

(f) the claimant is acting as a nominal claimant, other than as a representative claimant under **Part 19**, and there is reason to believe that he will be unable to pay the defendant's costs if ordered to do so;

(g) the claimant has taken steps in relation to his assets that would make it difficult to enforce an order for costs against him.

There are some statutory restrictions on the availability of security for costs. For example, reg. 12 of the Civil Legal Aid (Costs) Regulations 2013 (SI 2013/611) provides that where a legally aided party is required to give security for costs, the amount of security must not exceed the amount, if any, which would be reasonable having regard to all the circumstances, including the legally aided party's financial resources and his or her conduct in the proceedings. Security for costs cannot be ordered against a national of a contracting State in proceedings arising out of the Convention on the Contract for the International Carriage of Goods by Road (Carriage of Goods by Road Act 1965, sch., art. 31(5)).

Security for costs as a sanction or condition

67.7 The conditions for ordering security for costs in the RSC were regarded as a complete and exhaustive code of circumstances in which security could be ordered (see *Condliffe v Hislop* [1996] 1 WLR 753). The court now has wider powers under the CPR.

Under **CPR, r. 3.1(5)**, the court may order a party to pay a sum into court where it has failed to comply with a rule, practice direction or pre-action protocol. Under this provision an order may be made which is tantamount to an order for security for costs (*Olatawura v Abiloye* [2002] EWCA Civ 998, [2003] 1 WLR 275).

Under **r. 3.1(3)(a)** any order of the court may be made subject to a condition to pay a sum of money into court, and there is a cross-reference to this provision after **r. 24.6** (court's powers when it determines an application for summary judgment). In *CIBC Mellon Trust Co. v Mora Hotel Corporation NV* [2002] EWCA Civ 1688, [2003] 1 All ER 564, an order for a stay of an application to set aside a default judgment was made subject to a condition that the stay would be lifted if security for the costs of the application was given, and this part of the order was upheld by the Court of Appeal. The *r. 3.1(3)(a) power cannot be used independently*: it can only be used to attach a condition to an order made in the exercise of another power of the court. However, a stay can be ordered under **r. 3.1(2)(f)** 'in any appropriate case' (*CIBC Mellon Trust Co. v Mora Hotel Corporation NV* at [20]) and a condition for security for costs can then be added (at [21]).

The court should exercise its power under r. 3.1(3)(a) or (5) to require a payment into court only in limited circumstances, and should only do so in the absence of good faith on the part of the party against whom the order is sought (*CIBC Mellon Trust Co. v Mora Hotel Corporation NV* at [38]). An order for payment in should not be made without first giving the unsuccessful party three days' notice and an opportunity to file evidence as to their means. Such notice can be informal in the form of a letter from one party to another (*Anglo-Eastern Trust Ltd v Kermanshahchi* [2002] EWCA Civ 198, [2002] CP Rep 36). An order for security for costs imposed when granting an adjournment at the request of the party obtaining the benefit of the security was set aside in *Dardana Ltd v Yukos Oil Co.* [2002] EWCA Civ 543, [2002] 1 All ER (Comm) 819. See **chapter 48**, especially **48.20**.

Resident outside the jurisdiction

Condition (a) in **CPR, r. 25.13(2)**, applies to a claimant, whether a natural or legal person, who is resident out of the jurisdiction and outside the States covered by the EU's **Brussels I Regulation** and the Brussels and Lugano Conventions (see **16.1**). In *Levene v Commissioners of Inland Revenue* [1928] AC 217 Viscount Cave LC quoted with approval the *Oxford English Dictionary* definition of 'reside' as 'To dwell permanently or for a considerable time, to have one's settled or usual abode, to live, in or at a particular place'. There is no general principle that a claimant outside the jurisdiction will be ordered to provide security if he fails to disclose where his assets are located (*Somerset-Leeke v Kay Trustees* [2003] EWHC 1243 (Ch), [2004] 3 All ER 406). **67.8**

Applications for security on the ground of residence outside the jurisdiction almost always turn on the exercise of the court's discretion. The general factors considered are discussed at **67.16** to **67.20**. Factors particularly relevant on this ground are discussed at **67.21** to **67.23**.

EU residents There has been some controversy over whether making an order for security for costs against a national of another EU country on the ground of residence outside the jurisdiction offends against the Treaty on the Functioning of the European Union, art. 18, which provides: 'Within the scope of application of the Treaties, and without prejudice to any special provisions contained therein, any discrimination on grounds of nationality shall be prohibited'. As nearly all EU nationals protected by art. 12 reside in Regulation or Convention States, this should no longer be a major issue. At one time it was held that there was a valid distinction between residence, which founds the jurisdiction to order security for costs, and nationality (see *Berkeley Administration Inc. v McClelland* [1990] 2 QB 407). This stance is now discredited, and the current approach, based on the CJEU decision of *Mund & Fester v Hatrex Internationaal Transport* (case C-398/92) [1994] ECR I-467, is that an English court should never exercise its discretion to order security for costs against an individual who is a national of and resident in another member State of the EU. **67.9**

Security for costs can be ordered where the claimant is resident in a State outside the scope of the **Brussels I Regulation** or the Conventions, even if the claimant has assets within such a State (*De Beer v Kanaar and Co.* [2001] EWCA Civ 1318, [2003] 1 WLR 38).

Companies resident outside Great Britain Although most companies reside in the country where they are incorporated, strictly they reside where their central control and management are. This is a question of fact. In *Re Little Olympian Each Ways Ltd* [1995] 1 WLR 560 Lindsay J identified the following as matters to be considered: the contents of the company's objects clause, its place of incorporation, where its real trade or business is carried on, where its books are kept, where its administrative work is done, where its directors meet or reside, where it 'keeps house', where its chief office is situated, and where its secretary resides. **67.10**

Commentary

Impecunious British companies can be ordered to provide security for costs under **CPR, r. 25.13(2)(c)** (see **67.12**), so ordering an impecunious company registered in another EU country to provide security for costs does not offend against the Treaty on the Functioning of the European Union, art. 18 (*Chequepoint SARL v McClelland* [1997] QB 51).

67.11 **Joint claimants** Security for costs may be ordered where there are joint claimants, some of whom are resident outside the jurisdiction. According to Lord Donaldson of Lymington MR in *Corfu Navigation Co. v Mobil Shipping Co. Ltd* [1991] 2 Lloyd's Rep 52 the basic principle underlying **CPR, r. 25.13(2)(a)**, is that it is prima facie unjust for a foreign claimant, who is in practical terms almost immune from the enforcement of any costs order that may be made, to be allowed to proceed with a claim without making funds available within the jurisdiction against which such an order can be enforced. Thus in *Okotcha v Voest Alpine Intertrading GmbH* [1993] BCLC 474 the court ordered security against a Nigerian company even though it was wholly owned by the co-claimant who would proceed with the claim in any event. It would, however, be appropriate to refuse to order security where it is probable that each of the joint claimants will be held to be liable for all the defendant's costs if the action is unsuccessful, provided the English claimants are likely to be able to pay those costs (see *Winthorp v Royal Exchange Assurance Co.* (1755) 1 Dick 282 as explained in *Slazengers Ltd v Seaspeed Ferries International Ltd* [1987] 1 WLR 1197 and in the light of *Corfu Navigation Co. v Mobil Shipping Co. Ltd*). Conversely, security may well be ordered where the English claimants are joined for the purpose of defeating an application for security (*Jones v Gurney* [1913] WN 72), or where it is impossible to predict the likely outcome on costs, or where each claimant is likely to be liable for only a portion of the defendant's costs (*Slazengers Ltd v Seaspeed Ferries International Ltd* [1987] 1 WLR 1197, [1988] 1 WLR 221).

Impecunious company or other body

67.12 Impecuniosity is no ground for ordering security for costs against an individual claimant, the principle being that individuals should not be prevented from seeking justice through want of means. Companies and other artificial persons need no such protection. With the repeal, as from 1 October 2009, of the Companies Act 1985, s. 726(1), by the Companies Act 2006, the jurisdiction to order security against impecunious corporations is now based solely on **CPR, r. 25.13(2)(c)**. This covers companies and also other bodies (whether incorporated inside or outside Great Britain). From this it is clear that the jurisdiction to order security for costs is available against unlimited companies, and also companies with a single member (*Jirehouse Capital v Beller* [2008] EWCA Civ 908, [2009] 1 WLR 751).

The question of whether there is 'reason to believe' a company would not be able to pay an order for costs is one of evaluating the risk, and does not have to be established on the balance of probabilities. No gloss (such as the phrase 'in significant danger' used in *Re Unisoft Group Ltd (No. 2)* [1993] BCLC 532) should be put on the words of the test in the rule (*Jirehouse Capital v Beller*). A company in liquidation will meet the test (*Hart Investments Ltd v Larchpark Ltd* [2007] EWHC 291 (TCC), [2008] 1 BCLC 589).

Applications based on **r. 25.13(2)(c)** usually require a comparison between the company's assets and the likely costs. The crucial question is whether the company will be able to meet the costs order at the time when the order has to be paid (*Re Unisoft Group Ltd (No. 2)* [1993] BCLC 532 at p. 534). A net asset balance is not therefore determinative of whether a company can pay a costs liability when it falls due: the court must consider the nature and liquidity of the company's assets (*Thistle Hotels Ltd v Gamma Four Ltd* [2004] EWHC 322 (Ch), [2004] 2 BCLC 174; *Longstaff International Ltd v Baker and McKenzie* [2004] EWHC 1852 (Ch), [2004] 1 WLR 2917). The judge is entitled to look behind the accounts at the reality of the situation, and to bear in mind the costs the company would have to pay for its own representation (*Autoweld Systems Ltd v Kito Enterprises LLC* [2010] EWCA Civ 1469, LTL 17/12/2010).

Inability to pay may be inferred from evidence that the claimant has declared unusually large dividends after the dispute arose (*Frost Capital Europe Ltd v Gathering of Developers Inc. Ltd* (2002) LTL 20/6/2002). Evidence of these matters should be included in the written evidence in support of the application. For example, in *Cheffick Ltd v JDM Associates* (1988) 43 BLR 52, the company's assets amounted to £1.2 million, and the defendant's costs were assessed at £800,000. Clearly, the claimant also had a large potential liability in costs to its own solicitors. It was held to be wrong in principle to order security against the company in view of its substantial assets. An offer undertaking to pay any costs ordered against the claimant by a related company was treated as a concession that the claimant was unable to pay the defendant's costs in *Longstaff International Ltd v Baker and McKenzie*. It may not be right to order security against a company which has no assets but which can meet the costs out of income (*Kim Barker Ltd v Aegon Insurance Co. (UK) Ltd* (1989) *The Times*, 9 October 1989).

An impecunious company ordinarily resident in Northern Ireland may be ordered to provide security under **r. 25.13(2)(c)** (*Re Dynaspan (UK) Ltd* [1995] 1 BCLC 536).

Nominal claimant

The court can order security against a nominal claimant (other than a representative appointed under **CPR, Part 19**) if there is reason to believe that he will be unable to pay the defendant's costs if ordered to do so (**r. 25.13(2)(f)**). The court is required to look at the reality of the situation. The fact that others will benefit from the claim does not render the claimant a nominal one. In *Farmer v Moseley (Holdings) Ltd* [2001] 2 BCLC 572 Neuberger J said that, in determining whether a claimant is a nominal claimant, assistance may be gained by looking 'with circumspection' at pre-CPR authorities (see **1.21** to **1.24**). In the 19th century the requirement for a nominal claimant to give security was primarily intended to deal with a claimant who assigned a cause of action to a person of no means, but in fact under the claimant's control, so as to avoid liability for costs (this situation is now specifically provided for in **r. 25.14**). In some cases under the old rules security was ordered when a claimant became insolvent, so that the claimant's creditors would be the recipients of the fruits of the claim (for example, *Lloyd v Hathern Station Brick Co. Ltd* (1901) 85 LT 158; *Semler v Murphy* [1968] Ch 183). In more recent cases it has been stressed that security will not be ordered unless there is something more than the mere existence of others who will benefit from the fruits of the claim but who will not be liable if the claim fails (*Envis v Thakkar* [1997] BPIR 189; *Farmer v Moseley (Holdings) Ltd*). In *Envis v Thakkar* Kennedy LJ said that in his view, 'before a person can be branded as a nominal [claimant] ... there must be some element of deliberate duplicity or window-dressing which operates and probably was intended to operate to the detriment of the defendant'. 67.13

Change of address

CPR, r. 25.13(2)(d), is aimed at the claimant who seeks to go to ground to avoid the possibility of having to pay the defendant's costs (*Aoun v Bahri* [2002] EWHC 29 (Comm), [2002] 3 All ER 182). **Rule 25.13(2)(d)** may be engaged where a claimant changes address more than once, so that the relevant change is not from the address stated on the claim form. In *Aoun v Bahri* the claimant was resident outside the jurisdiction when proceedings were issued, and subsequently moved to an address in England. Doing this to prevent an order for security for costs under **r. 25.13(2)(a)** would have given grounds for ordering security under **r. 25.13(2)(d)**. On the facts it was held that the move had been for personal reasons. 67.14

Taken steps to avoid enforcement

CPR, r. 25.13(2)(g), is not concerned with the claimant's motivation. It does not use the phrase 'with a view to' which can be found in **r. 25.13(2)(d)**, so it is simply a question of whether the effect of the steps taken by the claimant with his assets is to make it more difficult 67.15

to enforce an order for costs against him (*Aoun v Bahri* [2002] EWHC 29 (Comm), [2002] 3 All ER 182). On the facts, the sale of the claimant's home in Australia made it more difficult to enforce a costs order against him, and security was ordered. However, there has to be some connection between the steps alleged to have been taken to avoid enforcement and the proceedings. Examples are *Paragon Investments Inc. v Sharma* [2002] EWHC 2643 (Ch), LTL 22/11/2002, where the assets were moved several years before the proceedings, and *Somerset-Leeke v Kay Trustees* [2003] EWHC 1243 (Ch), [2004] 3 All ER 406, where the claimant had moved to Monaco many years before the events involved in the claim.

EXERCISE OF THE COURT'S DISCRETION

Factors to be taken into consideration

67.16 Once it has been established that the case comes within one of the conditions set out in **67.6**, the court has a general discretion whether to grant an order for security. In exercising this discretion the court will have regard to all the circumstances of the case and consider whether it would be just to make the order (see **CPR, rr. 25.13(1)(a)** and **25.14(1)(a)**). There is a conflict in the Court of Appeal authorities on whether it is appropriate to consider the pre-CPR cases on the exercise of the discretion to award security for costs. It is submitted that the better view, which is consistent with the CPR being a new procedural code, is that stated in *Nasser v United Bank of Kuwait* [2001] EWCA Civ 556, [2002] 1 WLR 1868, which is that the substantial body of pre-CPR case law on the subject is consigned to history. Instead, the discretion has to be exercised applying the overriding objective, and by affording a proportionate protection against the difficulty identified by the ground relied upon as justifying security for costs in the case in question. The contrary view is supported by *Vedatech Corporation v Seagate Software Information* [2001] EWCA Civ 1924, LTL 29/11/2001, where an appeal was allowed because the judge had failed to take into account the fact that a Part 36 offer had been made, with particular reliance being placed on pre-CPR cases such as *Sir Lindsay Parkinson and Co. Ltd v Triplan Ltd* [1973] QB 609.

Thus, where security is sought against a claimant outside the EU and Lugano Convention States, the order should reflect the obstacles in the way, or the costs of, enforcing an English judgment for costs against the particular claimant or in the particular country concerned. In the context of applications against impecunious limited liability companies, it is suggested that one of the key factors will be that it is generally unjust for a defendant to have to defend with no realistic prospect of recovering its costs even if successful, but that security should not be in an amount that would stifle an apparently genuine claim. It is further suggested that the following factors should be taken into account:

(a) The risk of not being able to enforce a costs order, and/or the difficulty or expense of being able to enforce a costs order, if the defendant is awarded costs.
(b) The merits of the claim, where this can be investigated without holding a mini-trial (*Porzelack KG v Porzelack (UK) Ltd* [1987] 1 WLR 420; *Swain v Hillman* [2001] 1 All ER 91). This has an impact on the risk of needing to enforce a costs order against the claimant.
(c) Whether the defendant may be able to recover costs from someone other than the claimant.
(d) The impact on the claimant of having to give security. In some cases a substantial order for security will effectively deprive the claimant of the ability to take the claim to trial. Where the claimant is sheltering in a tax haven the court is unlikely to be very sympathetic, but where the claimant's inability to pay has been caused by the defendant's conduct complained of in the claim, a substantial order may unjustly stifle the claim.
(e) Whether *the claimant's difficulty (if any)* in being able to provide security has been caused by the defendant's activities. If so, security may well be refused (*Interoil Trading SA v Watford Petroleum Ltd* [2003] EWHC 1806 (Ch), LTL 16/7/2003).

(f) Delay in making the application. Generally the application should be made shortly after proceedings are commenced, and delay may be reflected either in refusing the application or reducing the amount of security ordered.
(g) Suspicions about the claimant's financial position if the claim is lost are material (*Frost Capital Europe Ltd v Gathering of Developers Inc. Ltd* (2002) LTL 20/6/2002, where the person in control of the claimant company refused to provide a guarantee for the costs).

Human rights considerations

An order which requires a litigant to pay a sum which the litigant cannot afford may amount to a breach of the right of access to a court guaranteed by the European Convention on Human Rights, **art. 6(1)**, in the **Human Rights Act 1998, sch. 1**. For a full discussion see **91.45**. See also **67.19** on the court's reluctance to make an order for security which would stifle a genuine claim. **67.17**

See also the discussion in **67.22** of potential discrimination contrary to arts 6(1) and 14 of the Convention when making orders for security against persons not resident in Regulation or Convention States.

Prospects of success

There is no doubt that the prospect of success at trial is one of the matters that may sometimes be taken into account on the application (*Frost Capital Europe Ltd v Gathering of Developers Inc. Ltd* (2002) LTL 20/6/2002). If this is taken too far, an application for security may be blown up to an investigation similar to a trial. Robert Walker LJ in *Zappia Middle East Construction Co. Ltd v Clifford Chance* [2001] EWCA Civ 946 and also in *Antonelli v Allen* [2001] EWCA Civ 1563 said that evidence as to the merits of the claim or appeal is seldom helpful in an application for security for costs, and is rarely decisive unless it makes out an exceptionally strong case that a meritorious claim or appeal is likely to be stifled if security for costs is ordered. In a passage approved by the Court of Appeal in *Trident International Freight Services Ltd v Manchester Ship Canal Co.* [1990] BCLC 263, Browne-Wilkinson V-C in *Porzelack KG v Porzelack (UK) Ltd* [1987] 1 WLR 420 said at p. 423: **67.18**

> Undoubtedly, if it can clearly be demonstrated that the [claimant] is likely to succeed, in the sense that there is a very high probability of success, then that is a matter that can properly be weighed in the balance. Similarly, if it can be shown that there is a very high probability that the defendant will succeed, that is a matter that can be weighed. But for myself I deplore the attempt to go into the merits of the case, unless it can clearly be demonstrated one way or another that there is a high degree of probability of success or failure.

In the Commercial Court investigation of the merits is strongly discouraged (Admiralty and Commercial Courts Guide, app. 16, para. 4). Courts will keep control of applications in the interest of litigants in other actions by excluding evidence and making penal costs orders where the parties transgress the line and seek to delve into the merits in too much detail.

If there is no defence to the claim, it will almost certainly be unjust to order security. In such a case the defendant is highly unlikely to recover costs in any event, and ordering security often has the practical effect of preventing the claimant from proceeding with the claim. Lord Denning MR in *Sir Lindsay Parkinson and Co. Ltd v Triplan Ltd* [1973] QB 609 said at p. 627:

> I am quite clear that a payment into court, or an open offer, is a matter which the court can take into account. It goes to show that there is substance in the claim: and that it would not be right to deprive the company of it by insisting on security for costs.

In *Vedatech Corporation v Seagate Software Information* [2001] EWCA Civ 1924, LTL 29/11/2001, the Court of Appeal set aside an order for security, holding that the judge had been wrong in not taking into account the fact that the defendant had made a substantial Part 36 offer. The

Commentary

decision in *Simaan General Contracting Co. v Pilkington Glass Ltd* [1987] 1 WLR 516, where Judge Newey QC held that the public policy protecting without-prejudice negotiations prevented their use in security for costs applications in assessing the claimant's prospects of success, is inconsistent with *Vedatech Corporation v Seagate Software Information* and (from a different context) *Family Housing Association (Manchester) Ltd v Michael Hyde and Partners* [1993] 1 WLR 354, and it is submitted that Judge Newey's decision should not be followed.

Stifling a genuine claim

67.19 Where the claimant's claim has a good chance of success (there being no need for anything higher), the court will hesitate before making an order which will have the practical effect of preventing the claimant from proceeding. The claimant has the burden of satisfying the court that ordering security for costs will stifle a genuine claim. In *Kuenyehia v International Hospitals Group Ltd* [2007] EWCA Civ 274, LTL 27/2/2007, the claimant, who produced misleading documentation and made inconsistent statements about the assets available for funding the claim, was held to have failed to discharge this burden. The essential policy is that the need to protect the defendant has to yield to the claimant's right of access to the courts to litigate the dispute if it is a genuine claim (*Hamilton v Al Fayed (No. 2)* [2002] EWCA Civ 665, [2003] QB 1175, a case on costs orders against non-parties, where the importance of the European Convention on Human Rights, **art. 6(1)**, in the **Human Rights Act 1998, sch. 1** was stressed). If the case is one where the court feels that security should be ordered, it can fix the amount of the security at a level which will not stifle the claimant in proceeding further (*Innovare Displays plc v Corporate Broking Services Ltd* [1991] BCC 174). In deciding whether a claim is likely to be stifled by an order for security for costs, the court is entitled to take into account any ability the claimant might have of raising money from friends, relatives, or if it is a company, its directors, shareholders, or other backers or interested persons. As this information is likely to be entirely within the claimant's knowledge, it is generally for the claimant to satisfy the court how and why other sources of funding are not available to fund the claim (*Flender Werft AG v Aegean Maritime Ltd* [1990] 2 Lloyd's Rep 27; *Newman v Wenden Properties Ltd* [2007] EWHC 336 (TCC), 114 Con LR 95), though there are cases where the court will be prepared to infer that the company will be prevented from pursuing its claim if security is ordered (*Trident International Freight Services Ltd v Manchester Ship Canal Co.* [1990] BCLC 263 as interpreted in *Keary Developments Ltd v Tarmac Construction Ltd* [1995] 3 All ER 534).

Delay in applying

67.20 Applications for security for costs should be made at an early stage in the proceedings. Lateness may of itself be a reason for refusing an order (*PR Records Ltd v Vinyl 2000 Ltd* [2002] EWHC 2860 (Ch), LTL 9/12/2002). There have been cases where security has been refused because the application was made just a few days or even a few hours before the trial. In *Innovare Displays plc v Corporate Broking Services Ltd* [1991] BCC 174 the trial was fixed for 25 January 1991, the application seeking security was issued on 21 December 1990 and was heard on 17 and 24 January 1991. The claimants were in financial difficulties, and throughout had encountered problems in raising money to fight the action. The defendants sought to excuse their late application by saying that it was not until mid-December that the claimants confirmed that the action would proceed. They did not want to waste money making applications if there was a chance that the action would not proceed. Once they were told that it would, they acted with proper dispatch. However, their solicitors had written to the claimants' solicitors in November 1990 warning that if agreement to provide security for their costs was not forthcoming by 15 November 1990, an application for security would be made. It was held that they had not acted with all due expedition, but they were not so dilatory that they had to be deprived entirely of security. A reduced order was made.

Lateness is regarded even more seriously when the application for security is made in a pending appeal to the Court of Appeal. Thus, an application for security was dismissed solely because of its lateness in *A Co. v K Ltd* [1987] 1 WLR 1655 when it was made 14 days before the hearing. In that case Sir John Donaldson MR mentioned that 'proportionality' may have a bearing on the discretion whether to grant security. The claimants had obtained judgment for $US2.6 million, and it seemed the defendants' only asset in the jurisdiction was $US830,000 which was in court. The costs of the appeal were £20,000, which the Master of the Rolls regarded as quite a tiny sum in proportion to the other sums at stake.

An order for security for costs made shortly before trial may be made in an 'unless' form rather than in the usual form of staying the claim until security is provided (*Vedatech Corporation v Crystal Decisions (UK) Ltd* [2002] EWCA Civ 357, LTL 28/1/2002). Care must be taken that any such order does not act oppressively or disproportionately, and consequently it may not be right to order a large sum to be paid into court within a short period of time.

Claimant resident outside Regulation and Convention States

In *Porzelack KG v Porzelack (UK) Ltd* [1987] 1 WLR 420 Browne-Wilkinson V-C said: 67.21

> The purpose of ordering security for costs against a [claimant] ordinarily resident outside the jurisdiction is to ensure that a successful defendant will have a fund available within the jurisdiction of this court against which it can enforce the judgment for costs....
>
> [The court has] an entirely general discretion either to award or refuse security, having regard to all the circumstances of the case.... The question is what, in all the circumstances of the case, is the just answer.

In *De Bry v Fitzgerald* [1990] 1 WLR 552 Lord Donaldson of Lymington MR said that the rationale of **CPR, r. 25.13(2)(a)**, is that a defendant should be entitled to security if there is reason to believe that, in the event of succeeding and being awarded the costs of the claim, there will be real difficulty in enforcing the order. If the difficulty arises from where the claimant chooses to live and the location of the claimant's assets, so that an order for costs will be unenforceable or only enforceable with a significant expenditure of time or money, the defendant should be entitled to security. Despite the strength of the language used by Lord Donaldson, there is no presumption that an order for security should be made merely based on the fact the claimant resides in a non-Convention country (*Prince Radu of Hohenzollern v Houston* [2006] EWHC 231 (QB), LTL 15/3/2006, unaffected on this point by the appeal, [2006] EWCA Civ 1575, *The Times*, 1 January 2007). It is difficulty in enforcing in the place where the assets are likely to be, rather than enforcement in the country where the respondent happens to live, that has to be considered (*Aims Asset Management Sdn Bhd v Kazakhstan Investment Fund Ltd* [2002] EWHC 3225 (Ch), LTL 23/5/2002).

Country of residence Given that ease of enforcement is an important consideration, much turns on the actual country where the claimant's assets are situated. 67.22

'Outside the jurisdiction' (in **CPR, r. 25.13(2)(a)(i)**) means outside England and Wales. There is unchallenged authority that security for costs will not be ordered against a resident of another part of the United Kingdom (*Raeburn v Andrews* (1874) LR 9 QB 118), because English judgments can be enforced in Scotland and Northern Ireland by mere registration under the Judgments Extension Act 1868. It is for similar reasons, combined with the effect of the Treaty on the Functioning of the European Union, art. 18, that security for costs will not be granted against a person against whom an English judgment can be enforced under **Regulation (EC) No. 44/2001** or the Brussels or Lugano Conventions (**CPR, r. 25.13(2)(a)(ii)**; *Bunzl v Martin Bunzl International Ltd* (2000) *The Times*, 19 September 2000). Security for costs is therefore unavailable on the ground of residence against most claimants living in Europe.

The next category of countries is those with which there is a reciprocal enforcement convention, to which the Foreign Judgments (Reciprocal Enforcement) Act 1933 applies, see **chapter 80**. Denning J rejected an attempt to extend *Raeburn v Andrews* to such cases in *Kohn v Rinson and Stafford (Brod) Ltd* [1948] 1 KB 327. Nevertheless, a claimant can seek to defeat an application for security by adducing written evidence that any order for costs may be cheaply and easily enforced in the claimant's country of residence. The onus is on the claimant. Orders have been refused on account of the ease of enforcement in Monaco (*Somerset-Leeke v Kay Trustees* [2003] EWHC 1243 (Ch), [2004] 3 All ER 406) and the British Virgin Islands (*Longstaff International Ltd v Baker and McKenzie* [2004] EWHC 1852 (Ch), [2004] 1 WLR 2917). Ease of enforcement is not the sole or decisive factor, and may be outweighed by other matters (*Thune v London Properties Ltd* [1990] 1 WLR 562).

The final category comprises the rest of the world. In these cases the court will do what is just in the circumstances (*Leyvand v Barasch* (2000) *The Times*, 23 March 2000). Any order for security for costs must be objectively justified, and not be discriminatory (*Nasser v United Bank of Kuwait* [2001] EWCA Civ 556, [2002] 1 WLR 1868; *Zappia Middle East Construction Co. Ltd v Clifford Chance* [2001] EWCA Civ 946). **CPR, r. 25.13(2)(a)**, does not mean that a claimant can be ordered to provide security for costs merely because of not residing in a Regulation or Convention State: that would be discrimination in providing access to the courts, contrary to the European Convention on Human Rights, **arts 6(1)** and **14**, in the **Human Rights Act 1998, sch. 1**. An order for security for costs under **CPR, r. 25.13(2)(a)**, should reflect the obstacles in the way, or the costs of, enforcing an English judgment for costs against the particular claimant or in the particular country concerned (*Nasser v United Bank of Kuwait*). As Gross J said in *Texuna International Ltd v Cairn Energy Ltd* [2004] EWHC 1102 (Comm), [2005] 1 BCLC 579, the court has to decide whether the claimant's country is:

(a) one where the obstacles to enforcement are so great that the claimant should be required to give security for the whole costs of the claim; or
(b) one where enforcement is simply more expensive than in England and Wales. In these cases the security should reflect the likely additional expense.

Security may be ordered where it is obvious that enforcement will be difficult and costly, particularly where the claimant is a one-ship company resident in, say, Panama or Liberia (see the judgment of Parker LJ in *Berkeley Administration Inc. v McClelland* [1990] 2 QB 407; *Aims Asset Management Sdn Bhd v Kazakhstan Investment Fund Ltd* [2002] EWHC 3225 (Ch), LTL 23/5/2002). A finding that a costs order is likely to be unenforceable in another State (here Sudan) does not breach any principle of international comity (*Al-Koronky v Time-Life Entertainment Group Ltd* [2006] EWCA Civ 1123, [2007] 1 Costs LR 57).

67.23 **Factors where claimant resident outside Regulation and Convention States** Since the effectiveness of enforcement is the most important consideration, the following factors need to be taken into account if present:

(a) Whether the claimant has substantial assets within the jurisdiction. If it has this is a weighty factor against ordering security (*De Bry v Fitzgerald* [1990] 1 WLR 552). Assets within the jurisdiction include damages which the claimant hopes to recover in other proceedings (*Cripps v Heritage Distribution Corporation* (1999) *The Times*, 10 November 1999). The fact the claimant has ATE insurance covering the defendant's costs is important, but may be counterbalanced by insurance law restrictions. In *Al-Koronky v Time-Life Entertainment Group Ltd* [2006] EWCA Civ 1123, [2007] 1 Costs LR 57, security was ordered despite the presence of ATE insurance because the policy was voidable if the claimant lost, after not telling the truth. The court felt that if the claimant lost, it was likely to be for a reason enabling the insurer to avoid the policy.
(b) The degree of fixity or permanence of those assets, and whether the claimant has a substantial connection with this country (*Leyvand v Barasch* (2000) *The Times*, 23 March 2000).
(c) *Whether the claimant is* impecunious. In *Thune v London Properties Ltd* [1990] 1 WLR 562 the bankruptcy of the claimants outweighed the ease of enforcement in Norway, where the claimants were resident.

(d) The ability of the claimant to transfer assets around the world, as in *Berkeley Administration Inc. v McClelland* [1990] 2 QB 407.
(e) Any lack of information, or refusal to provide information, about the claimant's assets (*Paragon Investments Inc. v Sharma* (2002) LTL 22/11/2002; *Zappia Middle East Construction Co. Ltd v Clifford Chance* [2001] EWCA Civ 946).
(f) Any evidence of misapplication of the claimant's assets (*Paragon Investments Inc. v Sharma*).

Claimant an impecunious company or other body

As with foreign claimants, the rationale behind ordering security against an impecunious company is to safeguard the defendant against the prospect of encountering real difficulty in enforcing any order for the costs of the action. Describing the effects of what is now **CPR, r. 25.13(2)(c)**, Megarry V-C in *Pearson v Naydler* [1977] 1 WLR 899 said, at p. 906: **67.24**

It is inherent in the whole concept of the [rule] that the court is to have power to order the company to do what it is likely to find difficulty in doing, namely to provide security for the costs which *ex hypothesi* it is likely to be unable to pay. At the same time, the court must not allow the [rule] to be used as an instrument of oppression, as by shutting out a small company from making a genuine claim against a large company.

A start-up company bringing a large and complex claim can expect to be required to provide substantial security for the defendant's costs (*Automotive Latch Systems Ltd v Honeywell International Inc.* [2006] EWHC 2340 (Comm), LTL 27/9/2006). One factor mentioned by Lord Denning MR in *Sir Lindsay Parkinson and Co. Ltd v Triplan Ltd* [1973] QB 609 is whether the company's want of means has been brought about by any conduct by the defendant, such as, in an action for breach of contract, delay in payment or the defendant's delay in performing its part of the contract.

Commentary

AMOUNT

Procon (Great Britain) Ltd v Provincial Building Co. Ltd [1984] 1 WLR 557 establishes the principle that any security should be such as the court thinks fit in all the circumstances. The amount ordered should be neither illusory nor oppressive (*Hart Investments Ltd v Larchpark Ltd* [2007] EWHC 291 (TCC), [2008] 1 BCLC 589). The court needs assistance on the amount of costs the defendant is likely to incur in the claim, and for this reason it is usual to exhibit a summary statement of costs to the defendant's evidence in support. Security may be ordered for the entire costs of the proceedings, or up to a future point in the claim, and may include past as well as future costs. While security for costs can include pre-action costs, the court should be slow to exercise its discretion to include these as there is a risk that such an order could become penal in nature (*Lobster Group Ltd v Heidelberg Graphic Equipment Ltd* [2008] EWHC 413 (TCC), [2008] 2 All ER 1173). There is no rule of practice that the court will always reduce the defendant's estimate by a third (*Procon (Great Britain) Ltd v Provincial Building Co. Ltd*), but it is usual to make a deduction from the defendant's costs estimate to take into account any likely reduction on assessment of costs, and also to make an arbitrary discount in respect of future costs to take account of the chances of settling. In applications under **CPR, r. 25.13(2)(a)**, the amount is usually limited to the additional costs which would be incurred by reason of having to enforce any judgment for costs in the overseas jurisdiction (*Relational LLC v Hodges* [2011] EWCA Civ 774, [2012] ILPr 4). **67.25**

In suitable cases the court may sit with a costs officer as an informal assessor (see Admiralty and Commercial Courts Guide, app. 16, para. 7).

As was mentioned at **67.19** and **67.20**, relevant factors going to the court's discretion which are in the claimant's favour, but which are not strong enough to deprive the defendant of an order for security, may be taken into account when deciding the amount of security to order. Thus, in *Innovare Displays plc v Corporate Broking Services Ltd* [1991] BCC 174, which was discussed at **67.20**, the lateness of the application and the difficulty faced by the claimants in providing security were taken into account by ordering the claimants to provide security in the sum of £10,000 when the defendant's estimated costs were £147,000. In contrast, it is wrong in principle to order merely nominal security on the ground that the defendant has known all along that the claimant is a company of limited means (*Roburn Construction Ltd v Williams Irwin (South) and Co. Ltd* [1991] BCC 726, where the judge's order for security in the sum of £5,000 out of estimated costs of £150,000 was increased to £40,000).

Security may be ordered in respect of the 'defendant's costs'. This may, according to *Noterise Ltd v Haseltine Lake and Co.* [1992] BCC 497, if the circumstances merit it, include costs the defendant may incur as against a co-defendant in contribution or indemnity proceedings.

Cases dealing with calculating the costs occasioned by bringing a counterclaim are considered at **67.3**.

ORDER

67.26 Orders for security for costs should follow form PF 44 (**PD 4, table 2**). It is usual to require security to be given by payment into court, although bonds and guarantees are alternatives, as are solicitors' undertakings. Security for costs will not usually be allowed in the form of a charge on real property. If the property is valuable, there should be no difficulty in obtaining a bank guarantee or money to pay into court. If no bank would lend against the property, it follows that the security is inadequate (*AP (UK) Ltd v West Midlands Fire and Civil Defence Authority* [2001] EWCA Civ 1917, [2002] CPLR 57). ATE insurance is unlikely to provide a satisfactory alternative to the usual forms of security (*Belco Trading Co. v Kondo* [2008] EWCA Civ 205, LTL 4/6/2008). Until security is given the claim will be stayed. If the claimant fails to provide security in compliance with the order, the defendant can apply for the action to be struck out (*Speed Up Holdings Ltd v Gough and Co. (Handly) Ltd* [1986] FSR 330), or the order may provide that the claim will be struck out automatically if security for costs is not provided within the time stated in the order (*Zappia Middle East Construction Co. Ltd v Clifford Chance* [2001] EWCA Civ 946; *Antonelli v Allen* [2001] EWCA Civ 1563). The Court of Appeal in *Prince Radu of Hohenzollern v Houston* [2006] EWCA Civ 1575, *The Times*, 1 January 2007, questioned whether an unless order, having a similar effect to that in *Zappia Middle East Construction Co. Ltd v Clifford Chance*, was appropriate. A security for costs order is a special form of order which is intended to give the claimant a proper choice as to whether to put up the security and continue with the claim, or to withdraw the claim. It is not intended to be a weapon to be used by a defendant to obtain a speedy judgment without a trial. *Prince Radu of Hohenzollern v Houston* does not lay down an absolute rule, and there are cases where unless orders for security for costs are appropriate (*Allen v Bloomsbury Publishing plc* [2011] EWCA Civ 943, LTL 15/7/2011, where the claim was very weak). Nevertheless, in the light of *Prince Radu of Hohenzollern v Houston* it is doubtful that *Rajvel Construction Ltd v Bestville Properties Ltd* [2011] EWHC 2669 (TCC), LTL 8/9/2011, which decided the court has the power to grant a freezing injunction in support of an order for security for costs, is correct.

If security is provided, the claim continues. After trial, the defendant, if successful, will have a secured fund from which its costs can be paid.

In the Admiralty and Commercial Courts defendants are sometimes required to give undertakings in damages if security is ordered (Admiralty and Commercial Courts Guide, app. 16, para. 5), and instead of ordering a stay it is more usual to give a time for providing the security with liberty to apply for dismissal of the claim in the event of default (para. 6).

Applications to vary

An application to vary an order for security for costs may be made if there is a material change in circumstances since the order was made (*Gordano Building Contractors Ltd v Burgess* [1988] 1 WLR 890). An application to vary will be refused if it depends on evidence which was available at the time of the hearing at which the original order was made (*Gordano Building Contractors Ltd v Burgess*). **67.27**

An agreement on the amount of security is not in itself an agreement not to seek further security at a later stage, so an application to increase the amount of security will be considered on the usual material change of circumstances test (*Kazakhstan v Istil Group Inc.* [2005] EWCA Civ 1468, [2006] 1 WLR 596). An agreement may include a term that the agreed security for costs will not be increased even if there is a material change in circumstances. In such a case the court retains a residual discretion to allow an increase, but only if the circumstances are wholly exceptional (*Kazakhstan v Istil Group Inc.*).

It is common for the court to order security for costs up to a certain stage in the proceedings, for example, a pre-trial review, at which point a further order may be made. Otherwise a party applying for variation of an order must show a relevant change. The courts will be astute to avoid an appeal dressed up as a further application and there will be a heavy burden on a party seeking a further order.

SUCCESS BY THE CLAIMANT

In cases where the claimant is successful, the trial judge will normally accede to an application on the claimant's behalf for the security money in court to be repaid to the claimant, or for the release of any other security. If the defendant wishes to appeal, however, the court has a discretion whether to impose a stay on the release of the security so as to provide continued security for the costs up to trial in the event that the defendant's appeal succeeds (*Stabilad Ltd v Stephens and Carter Ltd* [1999] 1 WLR 1201). The stay is simply to preserve the security for the costs to trial. **67.28**

SECURITY FOR COSTS OF AN APPEAL

The respondent to an appeal may make an application under **CPR, r. 25.15**, for security for the costs of the appeal or for the retention of existing security policy pending determination of the appeal. This rule only applies where permission to appeal has been granted, and does not apply where there is a pending application for permission to appeal, even if the appeal is to follow immediately if the application is granted (*Kevythalli Design Ltd v Ice Associates Ltd* [2010] EWCA Civ 379, LTL 28/4/2010). In considering whether to make an order under **r. 25.15**, in *Stabilad Ltd v Stephens and Carter Ltd* [1999] 1 WLR 1201, Auld LJ said that the fact the claimant had succeeded at first instance was irrelevant. Factors to be considered were the risks of the claimant being unable to pay the costs to trial if the security was released, the claimant's need for the money provided as security for fighting the appeal, and the prospects of the appeal succeeding. The court should also consider whether ordering security might stifle a genuine appeal, but an appellant raising this question is under an obligation to put before the court full and frank evidence of its means (*Mahan Air v Blue Sky One Ltd* [2011] EWCA Civ 544, LTL 11/5/2011). A failure to disclose assets permits the court to infer that assets have been put out of the reach of creditors (*Dubai Islamic Bank PJSC v PSI Energy Holding Co BSC* [2011] EWCA Civ 761, LTL 4/7/2011). **67.29**

Normally, the amount of security ordered under **r. 25.15** should not exceed an approximate pre-estimate of the respondent's costs of the appeal (*Moore v Moore* [2009] EWCA Civ 433, [2009]

2 FLR 957). By a combination of the Senior Courts Act 1981, s. 15(3), and **CPR, rr. 25.12, 25.13** and **52.10**, it was held in *Dar International FEF Co. v Aon Ltd* [2003] EWCA Civ 1833, [2004] 1 WLR 1395, that the Court of Appeal has jurisdiction to order a claimant who was successful at first instance to provide security for the costs of the proceedings in the court below. It will be unusual for such an order to be made, not least because, if the claimant is based overseas, the order may be unenforceable.

Chapter 68 Costs Orders

Commentary

INTRODUCTION

68.1 Orders for costs are made both at the end of the trial or appeal and at the end of any interim hearings and enforcement proceedings made in the course of, or after judgment in, the proceedings. The costs of enforcement proceedings are often added to the judgment obtained in the action. The relationship between interim costs orders and the overall costs of the proceedings is considered at **68.26**.

The CPR set out a complete code on costs. Pre-CPR cases have no place in seeking to establish categories of claim where special rules on costs apply (*Cheltenham Borough Council v Laird* [2010] EWCA Civ 847, LTL 4/2/2010, where the Court of Appeal refuted the idea that there is any special rule on costs in fraud claims).

Legal costs will be incurred on behalf of a litigant from the time a solicitor is first consulted until the solicitor's retainer is terminated, perhaps after enforcement of any judgment that is obtained. The client (or the Legal Aid Agency (LAA) if the client is legally aided) bears the primary responsibility for paying its own solicitor's bill. The bill comprises the solicitor's remuneration for the work done on the case, together with counsel's and any experts' fees, court fees, and any other charges, expenses and disbursements.

Although each client is primarily responsible for its own solicitor's costs, it is usual for the successful party in proceedings to be awarded an order for costs against the unsuccessful party. This is sometimes known as 'costs shifting', a principle which is deeply embedded in the ethos of civil procedure and seems to have survived the root-and-branch review of costs conducted by Sir Rupert Jackson (*Review of Civil Litigation Costs* (Ministry of Justice, December 2009)). Recommendations of the *Review* included:

- Defining 'proportionality' (see **71.38**) by reference to the sum in issue (or value of the case), complexity, conduct, client reputation and public importance, and applying the concept globally (recommendation 1).
- Abrogating the indemnity principle (see **71.30**; recommendation 4), which has not been implemented.
- Repealing the Access to Justice Act 1999 provisions on the recoverability of ATE insurance premiums (recommendation 7) and repealing the Courts and Legal Services Act 1990, s. 58A(6) (costs orders to include fees payable under a CFA with a success fee) (recommendation 9). This was implemented with effect from 1 April 2013 (Legal Aid, Sentencing and Punishment of Offenders Act 2012, ss. 44 and 46–48).
- Referral fees in personal injuries claims should be banned (recommendation 20). This was implemented with effect from 1 April 2013 (Legal Aid, Sentencing and Punishment of Offenders Act 2012, ss. 56–60).
- There should be 'qualified one-way costs shifting' in favour of categories of litigants who merit protection against party-and-party costs orders (recommendations 8 and 19). This was implemented as part of the civil justice reforms of 2013, see **chapter 69**.
- Contingency fees should be allowed, but only after taking independent advice, and should not be recoverable from the other side (recommendations 14 and 15). These are called damages-based agreements (DBAs), and were implemented by the Legal Aid, Sentencing and Punishment of Offenders Act 2012, s. 45.
- Detailed recommendations for different categories of claims designed to reduce the cost of litigating (recommendations 22 to 69). Most of these have not been implemented.
- Detailed recommendations on aspects of general litigation, such as disclosure, experts, case management and appeals, again designed to reduce the cost of litigating (recommendations 70 to 94). These have been implemented by detailed amendments to the CPR that came into effect on 1 April 2013, and are discussed in the relevant chapters of this book.
- Recommendations on court administration and information technology (recommendations 95 to 103).

- More information to be provided on the N260 schedule of costs (see **71.4**) for trials and appeals to assist judges with summary assessments (recommendation 105). A more detailed form N260 was introduced with effect from 1 April 2013.
- New format for bills of costs (see **71.12**) to cut out boilerplate entries, and to produce a more informative document (recommendation 106), which was introduced on 1 April 2013.
- Development of software for time recording which will be able to produce the necessary information for summary assessments and detailed assessments (obviously this would be a complex and expensive project) (recommendation 107).
- A package of other proposals for detailed assessments (recommendation 108, chapter 45, section 5), which was implemented as part of the complete re-issue of **CPR, Parts** 44 to 48 and **PD 44** to **PD 48** on 1 April 2013.

The civil justice reforms broadly came into force on 1 April 2013. There are detailed transition arrangements set out in the Civil Procedure (Amendment) Rules 2013 (SI 2013/262), Updates 60 and 61, relevant commencement orders, and the other relevant statutory instruments implementing aspects of the civil justice reforms. These are discussed in *Blackstone's Guide to the Civil Justice Reforms 2013*, Sime and French (Oxford: OUP 2013), chapter 2. Slightly different transitional provisions apply to different aspects of the reforms. Among the most important are that the old law continues to apply to funding agreements entered into up to 31 March 2013, and the new law applies to funding agreements entered into on or after 1 April 2013. The new proportionality test in standard-basis assessments does not apply to claims commenced before 1 April 2013 (**CPR, r. 44.3(7)**). Most of the other amendments apply to existing claims as from 1 April 2013. This chapter sets out the law as it applies from 1 April 2013.

Commentary

CONTENTIOUS AND NON-CONTENTIOUS COSTS

Solicitors' costs are divided into contentious and non-contentious costs, the distinction being **68.2**
that contentious costs relate to cases where proceedings have been begun before a court (see the Solicitors Act 1974, s. 87(1)); but see **65.10**.

CPR, r. 46.14, applies where the parties have compromised the substantive dispute and agreed which party is 'to pay the costs', but they have failed to agree 'the amount of those costs' **PD 46, para. 9.4**, says that unless the court orders otherwise **Part 45, section II** (fixed costs) applies, the relevant costs in a **r. 46.14** application will be treated as being claimed on the standard basis. This implies that they are treated as contentious costs because standard-basis assessments do not apply to non-contentious costs.

Most litigators who negotiate a settlement of a civil dispute without proceedings being issued would regard it as obvious that if they have agreed that one side will pay 'the reasonable' costs of the other side, those costs will be quantified as though they were contentious costs and on the standard basis. Unless there is something very unusual in the circumstances this is likely to be held to be the common intention of both sides, and an implied term will be found to that effect. Cautious litigators may feel it appropriate to set this out expressly, such as by agreeing: '[ ] shall pay the reasonable costs of [ ], to be quantified as if they were contentious costs on the standard basis'.

This chapter is mainly concerned with the rules relating to contentious costs.

GENERAL PRINCIPLES

The two main principles when it comes to deciding which party should pay the costs of an **68.3**
application or of the whole proceedings are:

(a) the costs payable by one party to another are in the discretion of the court (Senior Courts Act 1981, s. 51; **CPR, r. 44.2(1)**); and

(b) the general rule, as now stated in **r. 44.2(2)**, is that the unsuccessful party will be ordered to pay the costs of the successful party ('costs follow the event' in the old terminology).

Costs shifting between the parties is achieved, if at all, through the party-and-party costs order. There is a general rule that a party cannot bring subsequent proceedings seeking the costs of earlier proceedings between the same parties by way of damages (*Carroll v Kynaston* [2010] EWCA Civ 1404, [2011] QB 959). The rule that costs usually follow the event is regarded as being reasonable for the purposes of the European Convention on Human Rights, **First Protocol, art. 1**, in the **Human Rights Act 1989, sch. 1**, because it may act as a disincentive to unnecessary litigation (*Antoniades v United Kingdom* (application 15434/89) (1990) 64 DR 232; *Hoare v United Kingdom* (application 16261/08) (2011) 53 EHRR SE1 at [57]).

Range of possible costs orders

68.4 Under **CPR, r. 44.2(6)**, there are seven possible variations from the main rule that the unsuccessful party should pay the whole of the successful party's costs. These variations are:

(a) that a party must pay only a proportion of another party's costs;
(b) that a party must pay a specified amount in respect of the other side's costs;
(c) that a party must pay costs from or until a certain date only;
(d) that a party must pay costs incurred before proceedings have begun;
(e) that a party must pay costs relating only to particular steps taken in the proceedings;
(f) that a party must pay costs relating only to a distinct part of the proceedings, although an order of this type can only be made if an order in either of the forms set out at (a) or (c) would not be practicable (**r. 44.2(7)**);
(g) that a party must pay interest on costs from or until a certain date, including a date before judgment.

All these variations restrict the amount of costs that a winning party may recover from the loser. They would seem appropriate, therefore, to mark the court's displeasure at some conduct on the part of the winning party, or to reflect a partial rather than a full win.

Waller LJ in *Drew v Whitbread plc* [2010] EWCA Civ 53, [2010] 1 WLR 1725 at [26]–[28], pointed out that the functions of **r. 44.2** and **r. 44.4** are different. **Rule 44.2** enables the court to make special orders as to costs when proceedings are finally disposed of. These include the various forms of order set out in **r. 44.2(6)**, with the decision being based on all the circumstances of the case, including factors such as conduct, any exaggeration of the value of the claim etc. set out in **r. 44.2(4)** and **(5)**. Once the trial judge has made the costs order, it is not open to the costs judge to vary or rescind it. On an assessment of costs (see **chapter 71**) the costs judge must have regard to all the circumstances and to the factors set out in **r. 44.4(3)**, which include conduct, the value of the claim etc.

Aaron v Shelton [2004] EWHC 1162 (QB), [2004] 3 All ER 561, on the extent to which a costs judge is bound by the costs decision at trial, was disapproved in *Drew v Whitbread plc*. On the face of it both the trial judge under **r. 44.2** and the costs judge under **r. 44.4** are required to consider many similar factors. If the trial judge makes an express ruling on any of those factors, that will bind the costs judge. For example, it may be appropriate for the trial judge to make a ruling that calling a particular witness was unnecessary, which will bind the costs judge (*Drew v Whitbread plc* at [36]). The trial judge may alternatively help the costs judge on a point by giving some indication of the trial judge's view, which will guide but not bind the costs judge. This may be useful where the trial judge is in a good position to comment on the point. A party seeking such an indication should expressly make a request to the trial judge (at [35], [37]). Failing to raise a point relevant to assessment of costs under **r. 44.4** with the trial judge does not preclude a party raising the point with the costs judge (at [35]).

Discretion on costs

The discretion granted by the Senior Courts Act 1981, s. 51(1), is very wide, and the courts are opposed to limitations being imposed on it by implication or rigid rules of practice (see *Aiden Shipping Co. Ltd v Interbulk Ltd* [1986] AC 965; *Bankamerica Finance Ltd v Nock* [1988] AC 1002). The court has full power to determine by whom and to what extent the costs of an action are to be paid (*Singh v Observer Ltd* [1989] 2 All ER 751). However, like any discretion, it must be exercised judicially and on reasons connected with the case (see *Donald Campbell and Co. Ltd v Pollock* [1927] AC 732, and the speech of Viscount Cave LC, which continues to represent the law after the introduction of the CPR, see *Groupama Insurance Co. Ltd v Aon Ltd* [2003] EWCA Civ 1846, [2004] 1 All ER (Comm) 893). **68.5**

In exercising its discretion on costs the court is required to have regard to all the circumstances, and in particular to the following matters (**CPR, r. 44.2(4)** and **(5)**):

(a) the conduct of all the parties, which means primarily, if not exclusively, their conduct in relation to the litigation (*Bontoft v East Lindsey District Council* [2008] EWHC 2923 (QB), LTL 18/12/2008). Conduct includes:
  (i) the extent to which the parties followed **PD Pre-action Conduct** or any relevant pre-action protocol;
  (ii) the extent to which it was reasonable for the parties to raise, pursue or contest each of the allegations or issues;
  (iii) the manner in which the parties pursued or defended the action or particular allegations or issues;
  (iv) whether the successful party exaggerated the value of the claim;

(b) whether a party was only partly successful; and

(c) any payment into court or admissible offer to settle.

Factor (a)(i) is one of the methods by which pre-action protocols will be enforced, albeit indirectly (others include a less tolerant attitude on applications by defaulting parties for more time and for relief from sanctions and the interest sanctions discussed in **chapter 48**). **PD Pre-action Conduct, para. 4.5**, provides that the court will look at the overall effect of any non-compliance with the protocols when deciding whether to impose sanctions. These may include ordering the defaulting party to pay all or part of those costs, or to pay those costs on an indemnity basis. In *Straker v Tudor Rose* [2007] EWCA Civ 368, [2008] Costs LR 205, the defendant solicitors acted for both sides in a proposed transaction to purchase two properties off-plan, conditional on obtaining finance by a particular date. The claimant sued the solicitors for failing to seek an extension to that date when the finance was not available in time. The solicitors made a Part 36 offer to the effect that the claimant would in any event only have obtained finance for one of the properties. At trial the claimant won in respect of only the one property, but recovered damages exceeding the amount offered by the solicitors. The judge awarded the claimant only limited pre-action costs, and no costs from issue, on the ground that the claimant had failed to negotiate, on the theory that if he had done so, the defendant would have improved the offer above the amount awarded at trial. This was held to be so seriously wrong that it was outside the generous ambit of the discretion on costs. Partial success on the claim justified a one-third or one-quarter reduction in the claimant's costs. Adding a proportionate further discount for non-compliance with the protocol (not negotiating), the Court of Appeal substituted an overall award of 60 per cent of the claimant's post-issue costs.

Factors (a)(ii) and (c) allow the court to take into account the extent to which the overall winner was in fact successful on the various issues, heads of claim etc. raised in the case, when dealing with costs. This is intended to support the aspects of the overriding objective relating to identifying the real issues in the case, and only pursuing those issues to trial (see **CPR, r. 1.4(2)(b)** and **(c)**). Factor (a)(iii), which covers unreasonable conduct, could also be used against parties

Commentary

who fail to conduct litigation in accordance with the overriding objective, such as those who are unreasonably uncooperative (see **r. 1.4(2)(a)**). Factors (a)(ii) and (a)(iii) seem to have been important in justifying reducing the costs ordered against the unsuccessful party in *Mansfield v Wright* (2000) LTL 17/7/2000, where both sides failed to act on an indication by the trial judge to attempt to negotiate a settlement when the trial was adjourned part heard.

Exaggeration of the value of a claim (factor (a)(iv)) will obviously be relevant where the claim is inflated for the purpose of bringing it in the High Court or to have the case allocated to a higher track than it deserves. Overestimating the value of a genuine claim does not amount to exaggeration within the meaning of **r. 44.2(4)(c)** (*Morton v Portal Ltd* [2010] EWHC 1804 (QB), LTL 30/7/2010). There will only be exaggeration where there is inflation of the claim meriting criticism (*Morton v Portal Ltd*). In *Midland Packaging Ltd v HW Chartered Accountants* [2010] EWHC B16 (Mercantile) (BAILII), LTL 10/8/2010, although the judge considered exaggeration in terms of money (recovery of only one-third of the amount of the claim), it is reasonably clear from the judgment that the real exaggeration that resulted in an adverse costs order took the form of exaggerated evidence. At [52] the problem identified was that the claimant had a tendency to exaggerate on very significant aspects of his case, and that this took up a considerable amount of time and costs at trial. It could also be used in cases where exaggeration of the claim makes it difficult for the defendant to assess its true value for the purposes of making an offer to settle. *Painting v University of Oxford* [2005] EWCA Civ 161, [2005] PIQR Q5, and *Allison v Brighton and Hove City Council* [2005] EWCA Civ 548, LTL 22/4/2005, cases involving exaggeration in relation to Part 36 offers, are discussed at **66.45**. In *Hooper v Biddle* [2006] EWHC 2995 (Ch), LTL 11/10/2006, the original claim was for £3.75 million, the proceedings claimed £350,000, but judgment was for £38,000. Given the degree of exaggeration, the court made no order as to costs. A failed accusation of exaggeration may warrant an indemnity costs order (*Clarke v Maltby* [2010] EWHC 1856 (QB), LTL 27/7/2010).

Shirley v Caswell [2001] Costs LR 1 is a decision on its facts, and does not lay down a principle that orders for payment of a proportion of the other side's costs should not be made in certain circumstances (such as after service of notice of discontinuance). See *Dooley v Parker* [2002] EWCA Civ 1188, LTL 5/7/2002.

Costs follow the event

68.6 The rule that costs follow the event generally means that the successful party will obtain a costs order against the loser. So the first question is which party has been successful. The judge must consider the underlying realities of the litigation (*Onay v Brown* [2009] EWCA Civ 775, LTL 10/8/2009). A claimant who establishes liability and recovers more than a Part 36 offer is successful for this purpose (*Jackson v Ministry of Defence* [2006] EWCA Civ 46, LTL 12/1/2006, see **66.45**; *Widlake v BAA Ltd* [2009] EWCA Civ 1256, [2010] PIQR P4). Likewise, a claimant who establishes liability subject to a 25 per cent reduction for contributory negligence is the successful party (*Onay v Brown*). Even where the claimant insists on 100 per cent liability, a finding of 20 per cent contributory negligence (which was less than the 25 per cent offered in the defendant's Part 36 offer) will not, of itself, amount to 'conduct' within **CPR, r. 44.2(5)**, to justify depriving the claimant of part of its costs (*Sonmez v Kebabery Wholesale Ltd* [2009] EWCA Civ 1386, LTL 22/10/2009).

While in general a claimant who establishes liability and the right to more than nominal damages will be the successful party, there are cases where the damages recovered are so minimal that the defendant is the victor for the purposes of costs. An example is *Marcus v Medway Primary Care Trust* [2011] EWCA Civ 750, [2011] PIQR Q4, where a claimant recovered £2,000 on a claim alleged to be worth £525,000, and was ordered to pay 75 per cent of the defendants' costs. In a case primarily about regulating the future relations between the parties as opposed to seeking damages for past events, there is a reduced significance in any money judgment forming part of the overall relief in deciding which party is successful (*L'Oréal SA v Bellure NV*

(2010) LTL 27/7/2010, where no order for costs was appropriate because in commercial terms the result was a draw).

Applying the general rule, in *Islam v Ali* [2003] EWCA Civ 612, LTL 26/3/2003, the court reversed the trial judge's costs order where he had failed to give due regard to the fact that the defendant had won in principle. See also *Adamson v Halifax plc* [2002] EWCA Civ 1134, [2003] 1 WLR 60. Having determined which party has won, the starting point is that the winner should recover its costs as against the unsuccessful party, although there are factors which may lead to a different order and they are discussed below. In *Scherer v Counting Instruments Ltd* [1986] 1 WLR 615 the Court of Appeal set out the following principles for the award of costs:

(a) The normal rule is that costs follow the event. The party who turns out to have unjustifiably either brought another party before the court, or given another party cause to have recourse to the court to obtain his rights, is required to recompense that other party in costs; but
(b) The judge has, under the Senior Courts Act 1981, s. 51, an unlimited discretion to make what order as to costs he considers that the justice of the case requires.
(c) Consequently a successful party has a reasonable expectation of obtaining an order for his costs to be paid by the opposing party, but has no right to such an order, for it depends upon the exercise of the court's discretion.
(d) This discretion is not one to be exercised arbitrarily; it must be exercised judicially, that is to say, in accordance with established principles and in relation to the facts of the case.
(e) The discretion cannot be well exercised unless there are relevant grounds for its exercise, for its exercise without grounds cannot be a proper exercise of the judge's function.
(f) The grounds must be connected with the case. This may extend to any matter relating to the litigation, but no further. In relation to an interim application, 'the case' is restricted to the application, and does not extend to the whole of the proceedings (see *Hall v Rover Financial Services (GB) Ltd* [2002] EWCA Civ 1514, *The Times*, 8 November 2002).
(g) If a party invokes the jurisdiction of the court to grant him some discretionary relief and establishes the basic grounds therefor, but the relief sought is denied in the exercise of discretion, as in *Dutton v Spink and Beeching (Sales) Ltd* [1977] 1 All ER 287 and *Ottway v Jones* [1955] 1 WLR 706, the opposing party may properly be ordered to pay his costs. But where the party who invokes the court's jurisdiction wholly fails to establish one or more of the ingredients necessary to entitle him to the relief claimed, whether discretionary or not, it is difficult to envisage a ground on which the opposing party could properly be ordered to pay his costs.

Under the CPR, in *Johnsey Estates (1990) Ltd v Secretary of State for the Environment* [2001] EWCA Civ 535, LTL 11/4/2001, the court repeated the above principles but added that:

(a) A judge may make different orders in relation to discrete issues in the case and should do so where a party has been successful in relation to some issues and unsuccessful on others.
(b) A party which has behaved unreasonably in relation to the litigation may be deprived of some or all of its costs.

It is incumbent on a judge to give reasons for departing from the usual rule that costs follow the event (*Brent London Borough Council v Aniedobe (No. 2)* (1999) LTL 23/11/99; *Aspin v Metric Group Ltd* [2007] EWCA Civ 922, LTL 25/9/2007). See also *Bellamy v Central Sheffield University NHS Trust* [2003] EWCA Civ 1124, LTL 2/7/2003. The approach, stated in *English v Emery Reimbold and Strick Ltd* [2002] EWCA Civ 605, [2002] 1 WLR 2409, to appeals against judgments with inadequate reasons (see **75.10**) applies also in this context (*Gould v Armstrong* [2002] EWCA Civ 1159, LTL 23/7/2002).

A court is not required to order costs. **CPR, r. 44.2(2)**, begins with the words 'If the court decides to make an order for costs'. Where a court feels that the appropriate exercise of the discretion leads to no order for costs, it may decline to make any order (*English v Emery Reimbold and Strick Ltd*). If there is no overall winner, an alternative achieving much the same result is to make an express order that there be no order for costs (*Cantor Gaming Ltd v Gameaccount Global Ltd* [2007] EWHC 2381 (Ch), LTL 25/9/2007).

Re Elgindata Ltd (No. 2) [1992] 1 WLR 1207 is authority for the proposition that a successful party is in normal circumstances entitled to have an order for costs against the loser, subject to limited exceptions such as where a successful party recovers no more than nominal damages or where the successful party has acted improperly or unreasonably. The Court of Appeal interfered with a costs order in *Alpha Chauffeurs Ltd v Citygate Dealership Ltd* [2002] EWCA Civ 207, LTL 21/2/2003, which placed the main burden of the costs on a party which had been broadly successful, and substituted an order complying with the principle that costs follow the event. It is different where a claimant wins on one issue, but the defendant is in reality the winner: in such a case it may be right to order the claimant to pay the defendant's costs (*HLB Kidsons v Lloyd's Underwriters Subscribing to Lloyd's Policy No. 621/PKID00101* [2007] EWHC 2699 (Comm), LTL 5/12/2007). Although *Re Elgindata Ltd (No. 2)* pre-dates the CPR it has been applied in a number of cases under the CPR (for example, *AEI Rediffusion Music Ltd v Phonographic Performance Ltd* [1999] 1 WLR 1507) and the starting point in most applications for costs is that the loser should pay the winner's costs. *Re Elgindata Ltd (No. 2)* provides a useful guide to the court's approach, but it cannot fetter the general discretion the court has under **r. 44.2**. As Lightman J put it in *Bank of Credit and Commerce International SA v Ali (No. 4)* (1999) 149 NLJ 1734, 'The straitjacket imposed on the court by *Re Elgindata Ltd (No. 2)*... is gone, and the search for justice is untrammelled by constraints beyond those laid down by the new code [i.e. the CPR] itself'.

Pre-CPR authorities must be treated with caution. The introduction of the CPR has encouraged parties to narrow issues and focus their attention on the points of dispute in a proportionate way. The courts have been encouraged to examine the degree of success and to tailor their orders to reflect that success and the justice of the case. Courts will also consider in detail the conduct of the parties. This has led to courts making issue-based orders and percentage orders (see *Johnsey Estates (1990) Ltd v Secretary of State for the Environment* and *Gwembe Valley Development Co. Ltd v Koshy (No. 2)* (2000) *The Times*, 30 March 2000, though some difficulties in making such orders were identified in *Shirley v Caswell* [2002] Lloyd's Rep PN 955; see **68.11** to **68.14**)

68.7 **Material change in successful party's case** When the basis of a party's case is changed, that party usually has to amend their statement of case, which usually results in an order that they pay the costs of and occasioned by the amendments (see **68.31** and **PD 19A**). Sometimes the court goes further and makes an order for costs covering all or part of the proceedings (*Beoco Ltd v Alfa Laval Co. Ltd* [1995] QB 137). It is a frequent occurrence that the case that emerges at trial is not exactly the same as that set out in the statements of case. It is a question of degree whether this will require the statements of case to be amended, and in practice it is only substantial changes which justify such a course. Likewise, it is a question of degree whether any difference between the pleaded case and the facts as they emerge at trial justify departing from the general rule that costs follow the event. It is wrong to depart from the general rule where any differences are small (*Alli v Luton and Dunstable NHS Trust* [2005] EWCA Civ 551, LTL 27/4/2005). Where the differences are material, and particularly where the losing party may have been misled, it would be appropriate to deprive the successful party of some or all of their costs.

68.8 **Where there is no 'event'** In *Dearling v Foregate Developments (Chester) Ltd* [2003] EWCA Civ 913, LTL 9/6/2003, at the invitation of the judge the parties had negotiated a commercial settlement with the defendant making a modest payment to the claimant. In the circumstances the settlement did not reflect the merits of the case, and it was impractical for the court to look into the facts. It was held that in the absence of any good reason for making some other order, the fall-back position was to make no order as to costs. Contrast *BCT Software Solutions Ltd v C. Brewer and Sons Ltd* [2003] EWCA Civ 939, LTL 11/7/2003, where an apportionment of costs by the trial judge after the claim was compromised, but with costs to be determined by the judge, was upheld on appeal. A judge limited to determine costs may legitimately decide there is no complete agreement to compromise a claim if the parties have not agreed the question of costs (see *BCT Software Solutions Ltd v C. Brewer and Sons Ltd*).

Success and State benefits

In *McCaffery v Datta* [1997] 1 WLR 870, the claimant was given judgment in a personal injuries case for £22,373. There had been a payment into court (which, under the CPR, would be a Part 36 offer to settle) of £2,500 (the maximum exempt sum under the former provisions of the Social Security Administration Act 1992) some time before trial. The amount of recoupable benefits under the Act was £25,419. The effect was that all the damages awarded had to be paid by the defendant to the compensation recovery unit of the Department of Social Security, leaving the claimant with nothing. In those circumstances the defendant contended that it should recover its costs from the date of the payment in. The Court of Appeal held that although the claimant had recovered nothing in the action, it could not be said that the defendant, who had to pay £22,373, was successful. The judge's costs order was therefore varied so as to award the claimant the costs of the action. **68.9**

The general costs rules where there has been a Part 36 offer to settle are considered at **66.36** to **66.48**. How those rules relate to benefits recoupment was considered in *Bajwa v British Airways plc* [1999] PIQR Q152. In this case the defendant paid into court the sum of £2,500 at a time when the CRU certificate was in the sum of £2,573.34. It was held that the effective payment in was these two sums added together, that is, £5,073.34. At trial the claimant recovered £4,874.43. An appeal against the CRU certificate resulted in the recoupable benefits being reduced to £142.80. The defendant therefore had to pay £142.80 to the Secretary of State and £4,731.63 to the claimant. However, the important figures for costs purposes were the judgment (£4,874.43), which was less than the effective payment in (£5,073.34). The correct order on costs was that the claimant should recover her costs to the last date for accepting the payment in, but had to pay the defendant's costs thereafter.

Commentary

Nominal damages

A claimant who has claimed substantial damages, but has only recovered nominal damages, will normally be ordered to pay the defendant's costs (*Texaco Ltd v Arco Technology Inc.* (1989) *The Times*, 13 October 1989; *Mappouras v Waldrons Solicitors* [2002] EWCA Civ 842, LTL 30/4/2002; for an exceptional case in which no order as to costs was made see *Bank of Credit and Commerce International SA v Ali (No. 4)* (1999) 149 NLJ 1734). Where a claimant recovers more than nominal damages, but only a small proportion of the amount claimed, costs should follow the event unless this conflicts with some other established principle (*Gupta v Klito* (1989) *The Times*, 23 November 1989), for example, that costs will be reduced if a claim has been exaggerated (see **68.15**). **68.10**

Partial success

Partial success to be taken into account The conduct that has to be taken into account in deciding orders as to costs includes whether the claimant has succeeded in whole or in part (**CPR, r. 44.2(4)(b)**), and also includes whether it was reasonable for a party to raise, pursue or contest a particular allegation or issue (**r. 44.2(5)(b)**). It may therefore be wrong in principle to allow a party all its costs where it has been unsuccessful on some issues, and hence such an order may in some circumstances be overturned on appeal (*Winter v Winter* (2000) LTL 10/11/2000; *Darougar v Belcher* [2002] EWCA Civ 1262, LTL 25/7/2002). **68.11**

Before the introduction of the CPR, an 'issue' for this purpose was a matter which in itself either gave a right to relief or constituted a defence. Thus, in running-down actions it was held that liability and quantum were separate issues (see *Wagstaffe v Bentley* [1902] 1 KB 124), but negligence and contributory negligence were not (see *Quirk v Thomas* [1916] 1 KB 516). There is no rule that costs must be awarded in the same percentages as the decision on contributory negligence (*Horth v Thompson* [2010] EWHC 1674 (QB), LTL 7/7/2010). The CPR avoid the word 'issue' and the phrase 'cause of action', and instead refer to a party being successful 'on part of its case' (**r. 44.2(4)(b)**). This is certainly a deliberate move away from the old technical cases (see, by analogy, *Stock v London Underground Ltd* (1999) *The Times*, 13 August 1999, a case dealing with what would now be Part 36 offers to settle). The question is whether a point on which the successful party lost is of such significance that it would be just for the court to make a separate costs order in respect of it (*D. Pride and Partners v Institute for Animal Health* [2009] EWHC 1617 (QB), LTL 14/7/2009). A slightly different formulation, based on *SmithKline Beecham plc v Apotex Europe Ltd (No. 2)* [2004] EWCA Civ 1703, [2005] Costs LR 293, is whether the successful party has lost on a discrete issue and whether the case is sufficiently exceptional to justify depriving the winner of some of its costs.

The result is that the court may reflect partial success in the order for costs whenever as a matter of reality the overall winner has not been totally successful, whether or not the partial failure was on a matter constituting of itself a right to relief or defence. Merely failing to recover as much as had been claimed does not give grounds for reducing the winner's costs (*Hall v Stone* [2007] EWCA Civ 1354, [2008] CP Rep 263). In general, a claimant who succeeds on primary liability is regarded as the overall winner, despite a finding of contributory negligence (*Krysia Maritime Inc. v Intership Ltd* [2008] EWHC 1880 (Admlty), [2008] 2 Lloyd's Rep 707, where it was also held the principle is the same in the Admiralty Court). There may be exceptions where the primary issue is the degree of contributory negligence, or where there is a finding of very substantial contributory negligence. A failure to mitigate may be reflected in a percentage reduction in the costs recovered (*Walsh v Singh* [2011] EWCA Civ 80, [2011] 2 FLR 599; *Abbott v Long* [2011] EWCA Civ 874, [2012] RTR 1).

The starting point on final costs orders is that the winner should be awarded the whole of its costs of the proceedings, even if there are issues on which he had been unsuccessful (*Actavis Ltd v Merck and Co. Inc.* [2007] EWHC 1625 (Pat), LTL 7/8/2007). However, depriving the winner of a percentage of his costs does not rest on a need to find unreasonable or improper conduct. Where the successful party had lost on a large number of issues the court was justified in making no order for costs (*Peer International Corporation v Editora Musical de Cuba* [2008] EWCA Civ 1260, LTL 26/11/2008).

Winter v Winter (2000) LTL 10/11/2000 made the point that the CPR have changed the position regarding awarding the whole costs to a party meeting with 'substantial success'. In *Stocznia Gdanska SA v Latvian Shipping Co.* (2001) *The Times*, 25 May 2001, Thomas J said that the reasonableness of raising an issue which was lost by the party who was the overall winner is not necessarily relevant to the question of depriving the successful party of part of its costs under **r. 44.2(4)(b)**. In *National Westminster Bank plc v Kotonou* [2007] EWCA Civ 223, LTL 26/2/2007, the defendant sought to have a guarantee set aside on five grounds, four of which were unsuccessful. The Court of Appeal held that the case called for a percentage costs order, and said it would have been a surprise if the judge had awarded the claimant the whole of its costs. Each side was ordered to pay 50 per cent of the other side's costs.

68.12 **Principles** It is suggested that the following principles emerge from the authorities:

(a) The courts are likely to concentrate on whether a party was successful on an issue not the reasonableness of raising the issue in the first place (*AEI Rediffusion Music Ltd v Phonographic Performance Ltd* [1999] 1 WLR 1507; *Stocznia Gdanska SA v Latvian Shipping Co. (No. 2)* [1999] 3 All ER 822).

(b) A party which abandons issues, either prior to, or during, a trial, may be taken to have lost on those issues, which may be reflected in the order as to costs (*English v Emery Reimbold and Strick Ltd* [2002] EWCA Civ 605, [2002] 1 WLR 2409; *Carver v Hammersmith and Queen Charlotte's Health Authority* (2000) LTL 7/3/2001).

(c) There will often be an overlap in the evidence relating to issues upon which a party is successful and those upon which it fails. This has to be taken into account. In such circumstances it may be appropriate to award the successful party a proportion of its costs taking into account the fact that the paying party will have to pay its lawyers for the entire costs of the proceedings (*Liverpool City Council v Rosemary Chavasse Ltd* (1999) LTL 19/8/99, in which the court discounted the successful party's costs to 75 per cent).

(d) The award of costs to the successful party may be tempered by the manner in which it took the points, hence late amendment may lead to the loss of some or all of the costs up to the point of amendment and, in extreme cases, the award of the costs of the claim up to amendment against the successful party (for example, *Antonelli v Allen* (2000) *The Times*, 8 December 2000).

(e) Whether the issues on which the successful party lost materially contributed to the costs of the proceedings. If they had a negligible impact on overall costs, it may be appropriate to award the successful party all its costs (*Fleming v Chief Constable of Sussex* [2004] EWCA Civ 643, LTL 5/5/2004).

(f) It is not an argument that the party with overall success had to take certain bad points in order to obtain ATE insurance (*Kew v Bettamix Ltd* [2006] EWCA Civ 1535, [2007] PIQR P210).

(g) Where it is clear there has been partial success, but (as happens sometimes when costs are reconsidered on appeal) there is inadequate material on which to decide on an apportionment, no order as to costs may be the appropriate order (*Hackney London Borough Council v Campbell* [2005] EWCA Civ 613, LTL 28/4/2005).

The above points can only represent a guide, and there is a danger that too much can be read into any single case. The courts are anxious to preserve a wide degree of flexibility and discretion in the award of costs. As Lightman J put it in *Bank of Credit and Commerce International SA v Ali (No. 4)* (1999) 149 NLJ 1734:

> My task is... to take an overview of the case as a whole... and reach a considered conclusion on two questions, first who succeeded in the action, and second (taking into account the answer to the first issue) what order for costs justice requires.

Percentage or issues-based costs orders Where both parties are successful on some, but not all, of the issues in a case, the court may, instead of awarding the whole costs of the action to the ultimately successful party, award the costs of proving some of the issues to the unsuccessful party. The usual approach in the event of partial success is to award the successful party a percentage of its costs rather than an 'issues-based' order (see **CPR, r. 44.2(7)**, which says that an issues-based order should only be made when other forms of order are impracticable). In *English v Emery Reimbold and Strick Ltd* [2002] EWCA Civ 605, [2002] 1 WLR 2409 at [115], Lord Phillips of Worth Matravers MR said that making issues-based orders create difficulties at the stage of assessing costs because the costs judge has to master the issues in detail before determining whether individual items are attributable to issues which have been allowed or disallowed. It is for this reason that percentage orders are generally to be preferred. **68.13**

It may be appropriate to make an issues-based costs order (rather than a percentage order) where there is a substantial imbalance between the amount of costs incurred by the different parties (*Research in Motion UK Ltd v Visto Corporation* [2008] EWHC 819 (Pat), LTL 22/4/2008). Such orders are unusual, though, because it is highly undesirable to make a costs order which results in the assessment of both sides' costs, and the disparity has to be substantial before this can be justified (*Abbott Laboratories Ltd v Evysio Medical Devices ULC* [2008] EWHC 1083 (Pat), LTL 21/5/2008). There is a well-established 'double deduction' rule when making a percentage costs order (e.g. *Earl of Malmesbury v Strutt and Parker* [2008] EWHC 424 (QB), 118 Con LR 68). Under this, if the claimant wins, but the defendant is successful on an issue representing 7.5 per cent of the claimant's costs, the claimant would be awarded 85 per cent of its costs (the 15 per cent deduction covering the 7.5 per cent of the claimant's costs on the issue he lost, and 7.5 per cent of the defendant's costs attributable to that issue which the claimant ought to pay). This rule is not applied mechanically. It is not a matter of simply calculating how many hours of the trial were taken up with the lost issue compared with the whole trial, or counting pages of the trial transcript (*Abbott Laboratories Ltd v Evysio Medical Devices ULC*). Often the judge needs to take into account work done before trial, the relative expense of the evidence required on the

Commentary

different issues, and the degree of overlap in investigating the successful and unsuccessful issues.

In most cases an essentially broad-brush approach is adopted in arriving at the figure for a percentage-based costs order (*HTC Corporation v Yozmot 33 Ltd* [2010] EWHC 1057 (Pat), LTL 8/6/2010). In a case where on cross-appeals the respondent succeeded on six out of the seven grounds of appeal, but where the appellant succeeded in reducing the judgment from £6 million to £3 million, as the greater proportion of the costs of the appeal was spent on the issues on which the respondent succeeded, the respondent was awarded 25 per cent of its costs, the discount reflecting the degree of financial success enjoyed by the appellant (*Cleveland Bridge UK Ltd v Multiplex Constructions (UK) Ltd* [2010] EWCA Civ 449, [2010] CILL 2863).

68.14 **Success on liability, refusal of relief** Related problems arise in cases where the claimant succeeds in proving the pleaded cause of action, but is not awarded any relief or remedy. Obviously, if damage is part of the cause of action, as in negligence, then the defendant succeeds and should get the costs of the action. Where, conversely, relief is refused on discretionary grounds, further investigation or analysis may be necessary before the question of costs can be decided. If it should have been clear to the claimant that no relief would be granted, costs should be awarded to the defendant. If the matter preventing the court from granting the remedy sought arose during the course of the litigation, such as the appointment of an administrator preventing the court granting relief under an unfair prejudice petition under the Companies Act 2006, s. 994, probably the best result would be for the claimant to be awarded costs up to the date of the event preventing relief being granted, and for the defendant to be awarded costs thereafter. See *Re a Company (No. 008126 of 1989)* [1992] BCC 542.

68.15 **Opponent's case unclear** In *Sengoz v Secretary of State for the Home Department* [2001] EWCA Civ 1135, *The Times*, 13 August 2001, an appeal from a tribunal was discontinued when the Secretary of State agreed to the matter being reheard before the tribunal. The court accepted that, until the grounds of appeal were fully considered, the Secretary of State was not in a position to decide on the appropriate course to take. In the circumstances there was no order as to costs.

Misconduct by the successful party

68.16 **Principles** Misconduct by the successful party may result in costs not following the event (**CPR, r. 44.2(4)(a)**). Misconduct for this purpose must relate to the proceedings, and exterior dishonest conduct is not a basis for depriving a successful party of its costs (*Hall v Rover Financial Services (GB) Ltd* [2002] EWCA Civ 1514, *The Times*, 8 November 2002, albeit a decision which was regarded as no more than a statement of practice in *Groupama Insurance Co. Ltd v Aon Ltd* [2003] EWCA Civ 1846, [2004] 1 All ER (Comm) 893). The court can take into account conduct before, as well as during, the proceedings, and in particular the extent to which the parties followed any relevant pre-action protocol. It can also take into account the manner in which a party pursued or defended the claim or a particular issue or allegation, and whether the claim was exaggerated by the claimant (**r. 44.2(5)(d)**). In *Hobbs v Marlowe* [1978] AC 16 the successful claimant was deprived of all of his costs apart from the issue fee because he had exaggerated his claim to avoid the action being referred to small arbitration.

68.17 **Misconduct and final costs orders** Much depends on the nature of the misconduct and its consequences. Misconduct which might justify depriving the successful party of its costs would not necessarily be sufficient to justify an order requiring the successful party to pay the unsuccessful party's costs (see *Scherer v Counting Instruments Ltd* [1986] 1 WLR 615 at p. 622). A successful defendant was deprived of half the costs of the hearing in *Cable v Dallaturca* (1977) 121 SJ 795 for failing to serve an expert's report in accordance with the rules of court. In *Liverpool City Council v Rosemary Chavasse Ltd* (1999) LTL 19/8/99 (discussed at **68.12**) the successful council had acted in flagrant disregard for the approach embodied in the CPR, and left matters to the last minute. This resulted in a costs order being reduced from 75 per cent to

50 per cent. In *Wright v HSBC Bank plc* [2006] EWHC 1473 (QB), LTL 30/6/2006, the unsuccessful claimant raised several arguments for disallowing all or part of the defendant's costs (21 months for the case to get to trial; failing to negotiate; and failing to inform the claimant of the true basis of her claim). None of these were meritorious points, but £5,000 was disallowed from the defendant's costs to reflect a failure to give full disclosure. In *Grupo Torras SA v Al-Sabah* [1999] CLC 1 a claim had been made against a number of defendants in conspiracy, dishonest assistance in breach of trust and related causes of action. The claims against the fourth, sixth and tenth defendants failed because the claimant failed to prove the essential element of dishonesty as against them. Mance LJ, who was the trial judge, held the fourth defendant would only recover 50 per cent of his costs because, although he did not realise there was a fraud, he was involved in deliberately backdating relevant documentation. The sixth defendant only recovered one-third of his costs. He was the finance director of one of the companies, and had deliberately deceived the auditors and gave untrue evidence at trial. The tenth defendant was a professional man who had created false documentation, misled the auditors and gave untruthful evidence at trial. He too only recovered one-third of his costs. Repeated lies by the successful defendant justified depriving her of two-thirds of her costs in *AXA Insurance plc v Sulaman* [2009] EWCA Civ 1331, *The Times*, 25 January 2010 (where it was emphasised that judges must be careful about relying on the facts of previous cases when deciding costs issues). In *Groupama Insurance Co. Ltd v Aon Ltd* [2003] EWCA Civ 1846, [2004] 1 All ER (Comm) 893, a second defendant which had to some extent brought the proceedings on itself by its conduct, but which succeeded at trial, recovered 90 per cent of its costs from the unsuccessful first defendant.

In *Smiths Ltd v Middleton (No. 2)* [1986] 1 WLR 598 the defendant had made a payment into court exceeding the amount recovered by the claimants, but the judge made no order as to costs after the payment in, because the defendant had brought the action on himself through keeping incomplete accounting records. A claimant who would have lost on the original statements of case, but who won on the basis of an amendment made at a very late stage was ordered to pay the defendant's costs of the action in *Anglo-Cyprian Trade Agencies Ltd v Paphos Wine Industries Ltd* [1951] 1 All ER 873.

Misconduct and interim costs orders A failure to make full and frank disclosure which was not sufficiently serious to justify discharging a without notice order was nevertheless used to justify depriving the successful party of 25 per cent of the costs of an interim application to discharge the order in *Re Industrial Services Group Ltd (No. 1)* [2003] BPIR 392. In *R (Teleos plc) v Commissioners of Customs and Excise* [2005] EWCA Civ 200, [2005] 1 WLR 3007, the claimant issued an interim payment application which came on for hearing seven days later. The defendant's evidence was largely an analysis of material supplied by the claimant and was served about the day before the hearing. Skeleton arguments were exchanged on the day before the hearing. The application was dismissed. In those circumstances the Court of Appeal held the judge had been wrong to make no order as to costs. There was insufficient time to negotiate (so as to avoid the need for a hearing), due to the short period secured by the claimant for the hearing. Although the defendant's evidence was technically late, there was no prejudice. An order for costs to follow the event under **CPR, r. 44.2(2)(a)**, was substituted. **68.18**

In *Jones v University of Warwick* [2003] EWCA Civ 151, [2003] 1 WLR 954, an enquiry agent tricked his way into the claimant's home posing as a market researcher and covertly filmed the claimant carrying out functions inconsistent with her claimed disability. The court allowed the video evidence but ordered the insurer to pay the costs of the admissibility hearing to mark the court's disapproval of the defendant's conduct.

Refusal to participate in ADR A successful party may be deprived of its costs for unreasonably refusing to participate in arbitration or mediation procedures. In *Dunnett v Railtrack plc* [2002] EWCA Civ 303, [2002] 1 WLR 2434, a successful appellant was deprived of its costs when it refused mediation because it was not prepared to pay the claimant any further sum and was confident that it would succeed in its appeal. In depriving the successful party of its costs the **68.19**

court stated that parties and their lawyers should ensure that they are aware that it is one of their duties fully to consider ADR, especially when the court has suggested it, and not merely to turn it down flatly. In *Leicester Circuits Ltd v Coates Industries plc* [2003] EWCA 333 Civ, LTL 5/3/2003, a successful appellant was deprived of costs when it withdrew from mediation shortly before the trial.

An order depriving a successful party of its costs is an exception to the rule that costs follow the event. The burden is on the unsuccessful party to establish that the rule should be departed from on the ground of an unreasonable refusal to agree to ADR (*Halsey v Milton Keynes General NHS Trust* [2004] EWCA Civ 576, [2004] 1 WLR 3002). The *Halsey* principle is not engaged through failing to initiate proposals for mediation (*Vale of Glamorgan Council v Roberts* [2008] EWHC 2911 (Ch), LTL 8/12/2008). Where a failure to mediate was caused by unreasonable attitudes taken by both sides, it is not open to the losing party to use the winner's failure as a basis for an adverse costs order (*Earl of Malmesbury v Strutt and Parker* [2008] EWHC 424 (QB), 118 Con LR 68). A party who agrees to mediation and takes an unreasonable stance in the mediation is in the same position as a party who unreasonably refuses to mediate at all (*Earl of Malmesbury v Strutt and Parker*).

Factors relevant to the question of whether a refusal to agree to ADR was unreasonable include, but according to Dyson LJ are not limited to:

(a) the nature of the dispute;
(b) the merits of the case (it may not be reasonable for a party with a weak case to insist on use of ADR);
(c) the extent to which other settlement methods had been attempted;
(d) whether the costs of the ADR procedure would be disproportionately high;
(e) whether any delay in setting up and attending the ADR procedure would be prejudicial; and
(f) whether it would be just to impose a costs sanction.

There is no presumption in favour of mediation or other forms of ADR. Each case depends on its own circumstances. A public authority is treated in the same way as any other category of party, and is under no additional responsibility to agree to the use of ADR.

Where a party reasonably declines mediation it will not be penalised in costs (*Société Internationale de Télécommunications Aéronautiques SC v Wyatt Co. (UK) Ltd* [2002] EWHC 2401 (Ch), LTL 15/11/2002). In *Hurst v Leeming* [2002] EWHC 1051 (Ch), [2003] 1 Lloyd's Rep 379, Lightman J held that a refusal to mediate was only justified if it would have no reasonable prospect of success. Refusing to negotiate after receiving Part 36 offers is unlikely to be unreasonable, see *Daniels v Commissioner of Police for the Metropolis* [2005] EWCA Civ 1312, *The Times*, 28 October 2005, discussed at **66.45**. Small building disputes are one kind of case for which mediation is suitable (*Burchell v Bullard* [2005] EWCA Civ 358, [2005] BLR 330).

See also **73.13**.

Other costs sanctions

68.20 As well as disallowing costs, the court has various other powers that may be exercised to reflect a finding of misconduct against either party. These powers include:

(a) Ordering costs to be paid on the indemnity basis rather than the standard basis. This is discussed in more detail at **68.21**.
(b) Ordering payment of interim costs forthwith, rather than requiring the party obtaining the costs order to wait until after trial for payment (**CPR, r. 44.2(1)(c)**). Note that an order stating the amount payable in respect of costs (such as a summary assessment) must be complied with within 14 days (**r. 44.7**).
(c) Ordering payment of interest on costs from or until a certain date, including a date before judgment (**r. 44.2(6)(g)**). The normal rule is that Judgments Act 1838 rate interest

(currently 8 per cent a year simple interest) is payable on costs arising from court orders and judgments from the date of the judgment on liability.

(d) Ordering interest on costs at a rate different from the Judgments Act 1838 rate (e.g. **PD Pre-action Conduct, para. 4.6(5)**, which allows the court to impose interest on costs at a rate up to 10 per cent above base rate in cases where there has been non-compliance with **PD Pre-action Conduct** or a relevant pre-action protocol).

Indemnity-basis costs to reflect misconduct

68.21 One of the circumstances in which the court may order one party to pay another party's costs on the indemnity basis (see **71.44**) is where the court wishes to penalise the paying party for its misconduct in relation to the proceedings. On an application for indemnity-basis costs of the proceedings, it is necessary to consider the criticised conduct in the context of the entire litigation. It is not the character of the misconduct which engages the court's discretion, but the justice of the circumstances in which the receiving party became involved in the proceedings. There is an important difference between mere errors of judgment in the conduct of a case and behaviour resulting in the overall unreasonable or unsatisfactory conduct of the litigation (*National Westminster Bank plc v Rabobank Nederland (No. 2)* [2007] EWHC 1742 (Comm), [2008] 1 All ER (Comm) 243). Where the losing party has acted consistently throughout, the absence of proportionality on an indemnity-basis assessment is a factor in favour of awarding costs on the standard basis (*Simms v Law Society* [2005] EWCA Civ 849, [2005] ACD 98).

The Court of Appeal has declined to set out principles on which the discretion to award indemnity-basis costs is to be exercised, beyond stating that an indemnity costs order will be appropriate where the facts of the case or the conduct of the parties removes it from the norm (*Excelsior Commercial and Industrial Holdings Ltd v Salisbury Hamer Aspden and Johnson* [2002] EWCA Civ 879, [2002] CP Rep 67). It follows that the following list can only be taken as indicative of situations where an indemnity costs order might be made:

(a) Where the claim is an abuse of the court's process. In *R (Taha) v Lambeth London Borough Council* (Administrative Court, 7 February 2002), the defendant council had failed to process a housing benefit application for eight months. It then sought possession on the basis of eight weeks' rent arrears. It was ordered to pay the tenant's costs on an indemnity basis. See also *Sodeca SA v NE Investments Inc.* [2002] EWHC 1700 (QB), LTL 27/8/2002.

(b) Where a party is involved in dishonesty, or has acted in such a way as deserves condemnation (*Sea Wanderer Ltd v Nigel Burgess Ltd* (CA, May 1990); *Wailes v Stapleton Construction and Commercial Services Ltd* [1997] 2 Lloyd's Rep 112). In *esure Services Ltd v Quarcoo* [2009] EWCA Civ 595, LTL 30/6/2009, it was held to be wrong not to award indemnity-basis costs against a party who dishonestly brought a claim.

(c) Where the party's conduct of the litigation has removed it from the usual and made it appropriate for an indemnity order to be made. In *Cooper v P and O Stena Line Ltd* [1999] 1 Lloyd's Rep 734 the court condemned an allegation of malingering as one of fraud which should be pleaded as such. In fact there was no evidence to support the allegation and indemnity costs were ordered. See also *Craig v Railtrack plc* [2002] EWHC 168 (QB), LTL 18/2/2002, and *Kiam v MGN Ltd (No. 2)* [2002] EWCA Civ 66, [2002] 1 WLR 2810, in which it was said that indemnity-basis costs would be justified if the conduct of the claim was unreasonable to a high degree. Unreasonable pre-action conduct combined with bringing the claim on a misguided basis justified an indemnity costs order in *Noorani v Calver (No. 2)* [2009] EWHC 592 (QB), LTL 27/3/2009.

(d) Flagrant breaches of court orders, including unless orders (*Baron v Lovell* [1999] CPLR 630).

(e) Unreasonable pursuit of a weak claim or defence. See, for example, *Amoco (UK) Exploration Co. v British American Offshore Ltd* [2002] BLR 135. There must be something to mark the case out as unusual (*Shaina Investment Corporation v Standard Bank London Ltd* [2002] CPLR 14). It was not unreasonable for two drivers to maintain their denials of liability through to trial in a claim brought by the passengers in one of the vehicles where the witness statements left open the possibility of blame resting with one or other of the drivers or being shared between them (*Burton v Kingsley* [2005] EWHC 1034 (QB), [2006] PIQR P2). Despite a resounding defeat in *Balmoral Group Ltd v Borealis (UK) Ltd* [2006] EWHC 2531 (Comm), LTL 24/10/2006, the claim did have a solid basis, so it was not a suitable case for an indemnity-basis costs order. A weak case does not justify an indemnity-basis costs order, but having a case doomed to failure may do so. In *Wates Construction Ltd v HGP Greentree Allchurch Evans Ltd* [2005] EWHC 2174 (TCC), LTL 4/11/2005, an indemnity-basis costs order was made from the point, after the exchange of witness statements, when the claimant knew or ought to have known the case would fail.

(f) Where a stay or anti-suit injunction is granted for breach of an arbitration or jurisdiction clause (*A v B (No. 2)* [2007] EWHC 54 (Comm), [2007] 1 All ER (Comm) 633). Other first-instance cases making indemnity-basis costs orders for breach of jurisdiction, anti-suit and arbitration clauses are *Kyrgyz Mobil Tel Ltd v Fellowes International Holdings Ltd* [2005] EWHC 1314 (Comm) and *National Westminster Bank plc v Rabobank Nederland (No. 3)* [2007] EWHC 1742 (Comm), [2008] 1 All ER (Comm) 266. A similar approach was adopted when a party took an unmeritorious point over jurisdiction in an adjudication case (*Harris Calnan Construction Co. Ltd v Ridgewood (Kensington) Ltd* [2007] EWHC 2738 (TCC), [2008] Bus LR 636). In *C v D* [2007] EWCA Civ 1282, [2008] Bus LR 843, Longmore LJ declined to come to a definitive conclusion on the proper approach on this question (at [32]), and made a standard-basis costs order on the facts of the case (which was based on the doctrine that agreement on the seat of an arbitration was analogous to an exclusive jurisdiction clause, as opposed to being an actual jurisdiction clause). In some cases the claimant will be able to formulate a claim for an anti-suit injunction as a separate claim for breach of a jurisdiction clause or anti-suit clause. In these cases the successful party may have a claim for damages representing the costs of defending any proceedings brought in breach of the clause, and may also be entitled to the costs of the English proceedings for the injunction. The costs as damages claim is assessed on the indemnity basis (*National Westminster Bank plc v Rabobank Nederland (No. 3)*).

(g) Failure to send a letter before claim (*Phoenix Finance Ltd v Fédération Internationale de l'Automobile* [2002] EWHC 1242 (Ch), *The Times*, 27 June 2002).

(h) Where litigation has been pursued for extraneous motives. In *Amoco (UK) Exploration Co. v British American Offshore Ltd* the claimant conducted itself on the basis that its commercial interests took precedence over all other considerations.

The above examples all suggest some degree of turpitude and condemnation from the court, but this is not a necessary prerequisite for an indemnity costs order (*Reid Minty v Taylor* [2001] EWCA Civ 1723, [2002] 1 WLR 2800). Indemnity-basis costs may be awarded where rejection of a Part 36 offer is held to have been highly unreasonable: see **66.46**. There are other special cases where indemnity-basis costs will be ordered because of the nature of the litigation (see **68.46** and **68.47**).

68.22 **Indemnity costs in favour of a publicly funded party** There has been debate about whether it is appropriate to make an indemnity costs order in favour of a party in receipt of public funding. The award of costs is compensatory and the litigant should not profit from any costs order made. In normal circumstances an indemnity costs order will ensure that the receiving party will receive more of their costs from the paying party (see **71.44**). However, a party in receipt of public funding has no obligation to pay costs. Thus the lawyer may receive a windfall, being the difference between a public funding assessment and an indemnity assessment. This reason for not awarding indemnity costs was rejected in *Brawley v Marczynski (No. 2)* [2002] EWCA Civ 1453, [2003] 1 WLR 813, in which it was held that an indemnity costs order can be made in favour of a publicly funded party where the court intends to mark its disapproval of the paying party's conduct.

Claims wrongly commenced in the High Court

Where a claim has been commenced in the High Court which should have been commenced in a county court in accordance with the **Courts and Legal Services Act 1990, s. 1**, or any other enactment, the court must take that error into account when quantifying costs (Senior Courts Act 1981, s. 51(8)). Usually this will result in a reduction in the costs which would otherwise be allowed, but such reduction must not be in excess of 25 per cent. **68.23**

Costs of unnecessary attendance

A party should not be ordered to pay the costs of another party who need not have attended a hearing (*Cullen v Paterson* [2002] EWCA Civ 339, LTL 8/3/2002). Respondents who file written submissions or attend on applications for permission to appeal are in particular danger of being deprived of their costs, even if permission to appeal is refused (*Jolly v Jay* [2002] EWCA Civ 277, *The Times*, 3 April 2002; **PD 52C, para. 20(1)**). **68.24**

INFORMING THE CLIENT

Where a costs order is made against a legally represented client who is not present in court when the order is made, the solicitor representing the client is under a duty to inform the client of the costs liability within seven days of the order being made (**CPR, r. 44.8**). The 'client' includes anyone, such as an insurer, trade union, the LSC or Lord Chancellor, which has instructed the solicitor or is liable for the solicitor's fees (**PD 44, para. 10.1**). At the same time as informing the client about the order, the solicitor should explain why it was made. The court has the power to order the solicitor to produce evidence that reasonable steps were taken to comply with the duty to notify the client (**PD 44, para. 10.3**). **68.25**

Commentary

INTERIM COSTS ORDERS

At the end of almost every interim application, and when almost any interim application is disposed of by consent, an order will be made or agreed declaring which party should pay the costs of that application. Costs of interim applications are in the discretion of the court, but the discretion is usually (but not always) exercised in favour of the party who was successful in the application. Success may be established either by winning a contested application, or by showing that the need to make the application arose through the default of the other party. In deciding on 'success' the court may take into account the correspondence, and in particular whether an adequate response was made to the letter before claim (if relevant) (*Fox Gregory Ltd v Hamptons Group Ltd* [2006] EWCA Civ 1544, LTL 4/10/2006). It is usual to order costs of the proceedings in favour of a successful applicant in a summary judgment or striking-out application, even if remedies are left over to be determined later (*Experience Hendrix v Times Newspapers Ltd* [2008] EWHC 458 (Ch), LTL 14/3/2008). If an application is merited, but is discontinued when the respondent takes steps (such as filing an amended statement of case) to meet the issue, the applicant is the successful party, and should be awarded its costs of the interim application (*Finning UK Ltd v Inveresk plc* [2006] EWHC 2031 (QB), LTL 18/9/2006). Likewise, a party who *consents* to an interim order at the last minute will almost certainly have to pay the costs of the application (see *Law Society v Hadcroft* [2009] EWHC 947 (Ch), LTL 28/5/2009). Other types of application are essentially of a case management nature, so there is no 'winner', and in these applications the costs are usually treated as part of the general costs of the claim. Conversely, if a case management matter is unreasonably opposed, the applicant should be awarded its interim costs (*Finning UK Ltd v Inveresk plc*). To cater for these various possibilities (and situations where neither party is entirely successful) the courts can resort to a wide selection of different interim costs orders. **68.26**

It is usual to reserve costs in applications for interim injunctions (*Picnic at Ascot Inc. v Derigs* [2001] FSR 2). This is not an invariable rule (*Albon v Naza Motor Trading Sdn Bhd (No. 4)* [2007] EWCA Civ 1124, [2008] 1 All ER (Comm) 351 at [21]), particularly where the interim injunction is granted on an issue which is unlikely to be determined at trial.

PD 44, para. 4.1, provides that the court may make an order about costs at any stage in a case, and in particular it may make interim costs orders when it deals with interim applications.

After proceedings have been dismissed the court still has jurisdiction to make an order concerning the costs of an application in the proceedings (*Re Ryan Developments Ltd* [2002] EWHC 1121 (Ch), [2002] 2 BCLC 792). Unless costs are reserved (see term 13 in **table 68.1** below) at the first hearing, the court on a second hearing (unless it is an appeal) in the same claim has no jurisdiction to make a costs order in respect of the first hearing. In *Griffiths v Commissioner of Police of the Metropolis* [2003] EWCA Civ 313, LTL 5/3/2003, there was an interim hearing at which the judge ordered that a wasted costs order (see **68.64**) in respect of the costs of the interim hearing against the claimant and his solicitor be considered at the trial. This order was defective because it made no provision for who should pay the costs of the interim hearing, which meant that each side had to bear its own costs (see term 18 in **table 68.1**), whereas the judge plainly intended the claimant to have to pay the defendant's costs. On appeal it was held that the trial judge had no jurisdiction to make an order as to the costs of the interim hearing.

Summary assessment of interim costs

68.27 The costs of an interim hearing which has lasted less than a day ought to be dealt with by way of summary assessment there and then (**PD 44, para. 9.2**). There are exceptions where there is good reason not to assess summarily (**para. 9.2**). These might include:

(a) where there are substantial grounds for disputing the sum claimed;
(b) where there is insufficient time to carry out the summary assessment;
(c) where there are complex legal arguments (*R v Cardiff City Council, ex parte Browne* (QBD, 11 August 1999));
(d) where the claim is a mortgage possession claim (**para. 9.3**);
(e) where the receiving party (as opposed to the paying party) is publicly funded (**para. 9.8**);
(f) where the receiving party (as opposed to the paying party) is under a disability (**para. 9.9**;
(g) where no statement of costs is served in time (see **32.30**, but see *MacDonald v Taree Holdings Ltd* [2000] CPLR 439, in which it was held that it may be permissible to conduct the summary assessment if time is given to the paying party to consider any schedule produced on short notice);
(h) in the early stages of continuing complex litigation (*Roundstone Nurseries Ltd v Stephenson Holdings Ltd* [2009] EWHC 1431 (TCC), [2009] 5 Costs LR 787 at [56]–[57]).

Where the court makes a summary assessment of interim costs, those costs will be stated in the order made by the court and will be payable in such period as the court decides (**CPR, r. 44.2(1)(c)**). Where the court does not specify a time for the payment of the costs, they are payable within 14 days (**r. 44.7**). Any application for an extension of time in which to pay such costs should be supported by evidence (*Pepin v Watts* [2001] CPLR 9).

Detailed assessment of interim costs

68.28 Orders for costs will be treated as requiring detailed assessment unless the order specifies the sum to be paid or states that fixed costs are to be paid (**PD 44, para. 8.2**). Detailed assessments generally take place after the proceedings are concluded (**CPR, r. 47.1**). The court may order, or the parties may agree in writing to treat the proceedings as concluded for this purpose (**PD 47, para. 1.2**), and the court may make an order allowing detailed assessment proceedings to commence where there is no realistic prospect of the claim proceeding (**para. 1.4**).

MEANINGS OF COSTS ORDERS

Various standard forms of wording are regularly used by the courts to express the decision on the incidence of costs. Usually it will be apparent from the whole of the document recording the order whether the costs provision covers the whole proceedings, or just some part of the claim (such as the costs of an interim application). Some of the forms used can apply to both final and interim costs, and some of the commonly occurring decisions can be expressed using more than one form of words, so some care is needed. **Table 68.1** sets out the meanings of the most commonly used forms of costs orders. More technical definitions for most of the terms can be found in **PD 44, para 4.2.** **68.29**

Table 68.1 Meanings of common costs orders

Term	Meaning
1. Claimant's costs	As a final order, the claimant is entitled to recover its costs of the proceedings from the defendant.
2. Defendant's costs	As a final order, the defendant is entitled to recover its costs of the proceedings from the claimant.
3. Claimant's costs	In an interim application, the claimant is entitled to recover its costs of the application from the defendant.
4. Defendant's costs	In an interim application, the defendant is entitled to recover its costs of the application from the claimant.
5. Claimant's costs in any event	Identical meaning to 1 and 3 above.
6. Defendant's costs in any event	Identical meaning to 2 and 4 above.
7. Costs in the case	This is an order made on interim applications and hearings, often where the court makes case management decisions or otherwise where there is no obvious winner of the interim application. The order means the interim costs form part of the general costs of the proceedings, so the party awarded its costs of the proceedings on the final disposal of the claim will be entitled to be paid its costs of the interim application.
8. Costs in the application	Identical meaning to 7 above.
9. Claimant's costs in case	This is an order half-way between 3 and 7 above. It is typically used where the claimant has met with partial success on an interim application. It means that if the claimant is awarded its costs of the proceedings on the final disposal of the claim, it will be entitled to be paid its costs of the interim application, but if the defendant is awarded costs on the final disposal of the claim, each party bears its own costs of the interim application.
10. Claimant's costs in application	Identical meaning to 9 above.
11. Defendant's costs in case	This is the reverse of 9 above. If the defendant is awarded its costs of the proceedings on the final disposal of the claim, it will be entitled to be paid its costs of the interim application, but if the claimant is awarded costs on the final disposal of the claim, each party bears its own costs of the interim application.
12. Defendant's costs in application	Identical meaning to 11 above.

Term	Meaning
13. Costs reserved	This is an interim costs order deferring the decision on costs to a later hearing, when the judge will usually make orders relating to both hearings. If the judge dealing with the second hearing does not make an order relating to the first hearing, the costs of that hearing are treated as being in the case (see 7 above). This form of order should not be used if nothing further can happen at the second hearing (which may be the trial) to affect the costs of the first hearing (*Elvee Ltd v Taylor* [2001] EWCA Civ 1943, [2002] FSR 48).
14. Costs thrown away	Broadly similar to 3 and 4 above. It is typically made when a judgment or order is set aside, such as on a successful application to set aside a default judgment. In such a case the order entitles the claimant to recover from the defendant the costs of: • preparing for and attending any hearing relating to making the original order or judgment that is now being set aside; • preparing for and attending any hearing to set aside the original order or judgment; • preparing for and attending any adjourned relevant hearing; and • any steps to enforce the original order or judgment.
15. Costs of and occasioned by	This is the usual order made when the court allows an application to amend a statement of case. See further **68.31**. This order requires the party making the amendment to pay the other party's costs of: • preparing for and attending any hearing seeking permission to amend; and • any consequential amendments to its own statement of case.
16. No order as to costs	Each party bears its own costs of the application or proceedings.
17. Each party to pay its own costs	Identical to 16 above.
18. Order silent on costs	The general rule is that neither side can recover costs (**CPR, r. 44.10(1)(a); PD 23A, para. 13.2**). Exceptions cover: • trustees and personal representatives who can always recover their costs out of the fund (**CPR, r. 44.10(1)(b)**); • parties entitled to recover costs pursuant to a lease, mortgage or other security, who continue to be entitled to recover their costs under a provision of the contract (**r. 44.10(1)(b)**); and • orders granting permission to appeal, orders granting permission to apply for judicial review, and orders and directions made on applications without notice. These are deemed to include an order for the applicant's costs in the case (**r. 44.10(2)**). Any party affected by such a deemed order for costs may apply at any time to vary the order (**r. 44.10(3)**).
19. Costs here and below	This is an order often made on disposal of appeals. The party who is successful on the appeal is by this order entitled to recover its costs both of the appeal and in the court below. See **68.36**.
20. Detailed assessment of the costs of the [Claimant] which are payable by the Lord Chancellor	Order authorising the court to assess the costs payable from public funds of a litigant (whether they are successful or not) with the benefit of public funding. This is the modern form of what used to be called a 'legal aid taxation' (Supreme Court Costs Office Guide 2006, para. 24.1(c) amended in consequence of the Legal Aid, Sentencing and Punishment of Offenders Act 2012, s. 2(4)).

Fit for counsel

68.30 **PD 44, para. 5.1**, allows the court when making a costs order for detailed assessment (including both interim costs orders and final costs orders made at trial) to state an opinion as to whether or not the hearing was fit for representation by one or more counsel. This will generally only be done where the paying party challenges the use of counsel, where the court wishes to record its opinion that the case was not fit for counsel, or where more than one counsel appeared for a party (**para. 5.1(2)**).

COSTS OF PARTICULAR TYPES OF PROCEEDINGS

Amendment

The costs of and arising from any amendment to a statements of case are, unless the court orders otherwise, borne by the party making the amendment (see notes to **PD 19A**). An order for payment of the costs of an amendment will also require payment of the costs of making consequential amendments to other documents. **68.31**

It is possible to ask for a less onerous costs order where, for example, the need to amend cannot be characterised as being the fault of the party seeking permission. Unreasonably refusing to consent to proposed amendments may result in the respondent being ordered to pay the applicant's costs of the application (although in principle, the applicant should remain responsible for the costs of and occasioned by the actual amendments). See *La Chemise Lacoste SA v Sketchers USA Ltd* (2006) LTL 24/5/2006. Another point is that if permission is sought at a very late stage to make amendments having a fundamental effect on the way the case is set out, particularly where the other side are prejudiced, such as by being unable to make an effective Part 36 offer to settle, the court may impose very stringent costs terms when granting permission to amend. Thus in *Beoco Ltd v Alfa Laval Co. Ltd* [1995] QB 137 permission to amend was granted on terms that the claimant paid the defendant's costs up to the date of the amendment, and 85 per cent of the defendant's costs thereafter. Such a penal approach is not always correct. In *Professional Information Technology Consultants Ltd v Jones* [2001] EWCA Civ 2103, *The Independent*, 28 January 2002, the claim succeeded on the basis of a late amendment, but this was reflected by simply reducing the costs of the claim recovered by the claimant by one-third.

Costs of pre-commencement disclosure and disclosure against non-parties

Applications for pre-commencement disclosure and for orders against persons who are not parties for disclosure of documents were considered in **chapter 50**. The general rule is that the court must award the costs of the application to the person against whom the order is sought (**CPR, r. 46.1**). The practice has been to add the costs of the application as a head of damages in the case of pre-commencement disclosure. This may no longer be necessary as under the CPR the pre-commencement application is made in the same action as the main claim, whereas under the old system the application formed a separate action commenced by its own originating process. In the case of disclosure against a non-party the costs will be part of the costs of the claim, and should be dealt with by a specific costs order between the parties. The court retains a discretion to make a different costs order in a particular case, having regard to all the circumstances, including the extent to which it may have been reasonable for the respondent to have opposed the disclosure application (**r. 46.1(3)**). This may be the case where the respondent has failed to honour its obligations under the Access to Health Records Act 1990 (which applies to most medical records compiled since 1 November 1991) or under any applicable pre-action protocol (which will potentially apply to many applications for pre-commencement disclosure against likely defendants). **68.32**

Costs after transfer

Subject to any order that may have been made by the original court, once a case is transferred, whether between the High Court and a county court, or between county courts, the new **68.33**

Commentary

court will deal with all questions as to costs, including the costs incurred before the transfer (County Courts Act 1984, s. 45; **CPR, r. 44.10(5)**).

Costs before track allocation or where the claim has never been allocated

68.34 The special rules relating to costs in cases on the small claims track and fast track do not apply until a claim is allocated to one of these tracks (**CPR, r. 46.11(1)** and **(2)**; **PD 46, para. 7.1(1)**). Once a claim is allocated to either of these tracks the special rules relating to that track will apply to work done before as well as after allocation, with the exception that any costs orders made before a claim is allocated to one of these two tracks are not affected by any subsequent allocation (**PD 46, para. 7.1(2)**). This means, for example, that where default judgment is entered on a small-value claim, the costs restrictions in **CPR, Part 27**, do not apply, although the fixed costs rules in **Part 45** would be applied instead.

Where a claim has not been allocated to a track the court retains a general discretion as to costs, but will attach considerable weight to the track that the matter would have been allocated to. In particular, the court may restrict the assessed costs to the costs that would have been allowed on the track to which the claim would have been allocated if allocation had taken place (**r. 46.13(3)**). Thus in *Voice and Script International v Alghafar* [2003] EWCA Civ 736, LTL 8/5/2003, a failure to allocate the case to the small claims track did not preclude the court from awarding the costs as if it had been. Conversely in *Woodings v British Telecommunications plc* (2003) LTL 17/3/2003 several related claims were settled, without issuing proceedings, for less than £1,000 per claimant. Although this would normally have indicated that the claims were small claims, the court was persuaded that, because of the extent of the technical and medical evidence required, they would have been allocated to the multi-track and accordingly costs could be awarded as for that track.

Reallocation from the small claims track

68.35 Before making an order to reallocate a claim from the small claims track to another track, the court must decide whether any party is to pay costs to any other party down to the date of the reallocation order (**PD 46, para. 8.1**). Such costs must be those payable under **CPR, Part 27**, which in effect means that they are limited to fixed costs and any further costs which may be ordered for unreasonable behaviour (**r. 27.14**). If a costs order is made on reallocation, the court should make an immediate summary assessment of those costs (**PD 46, para. 8.1**). Fast track or multi-track costs rules will apply from the date of reallocation (**CPR, r. 27.15**).

Costs after an appeal

68.36 A court dealing with a case on appeal can make orders relating to the costs of the proceedings giving rise to the appeal as well as the appeal itself (**CPR, r. 44.10(4)**). If an appeal is successful, the appeal court may order the losing party to pay the costs 'here and below', or may make different orders relating to the proceedings at the two levels, or may leave the costs order of the court below undisturbed while making whatever order may be appropriate for the costs of the appeal. It may be appropriate to deprive a party of its costs if the decision on the appeal turned on points not raised below, or on points not raised in the notice of appeal, or where the appeal is only partly successful or where the court's time has been wasted.

Wills cases

68.37 In a case involving a disputed will, costs normally follow the event. An alternative costs order may be made where the testator or those interested in the residue of the estate had been the *cause of the litigation* or if the circumstances led reasonably to an investigation. Applying these principles in *Re Good* [2002] EWHC 640 (Ch), *The Times*, 22 May 2002, Rimer J ordered the unsuccessful parties to pay only half the claimant's costs. In contentious probate cases, if the testator, or the person interested in the residue, is the real cause of the need for the litigation, costs usually come out of the estate (*Kostic v Chaplin* [2007] EWHC 2909 (Ch), *The Times*, 11 January 2008). If the circumstances led reasonably to an investigation of the matter, costs are usually borne by those who incur them (*Spiers v English* [1907] P 122; *Re Cutcliffe's Estate* [1959] P 6). In probate claims, a defendant requiring the will to be proved in solemn form (see **CPR, r. 57.7(5)**) will not be ordered to pay costs unless there is no reasonable ground for opposing the will (Supreme Court Costs Office Guide 2006, para. 2.8(e)).

Winding-up petitions

The 'usual compulsory order' on winding up a company includes provision for the payment of the petitioner's costs and one set of costs for the supporting creditors out of the assets of the company. It is therefore not the practice to ask for costs at the hearing. If there are opposing creditors and the petition succeeds, the costs of the opposing creditors are not paid out of the company's assets unless they are expressly allowed by the court (Supreme Court Costs Office Guide 2006, para. 2.13). **68.38**

Public law matters

Government departments are not exempt from costs orders (*R (Bahta) v Secretary of State for the Home Department* [2011] EWCA Civ 895, [2011] CP Rep 43). Costs in judicial review and other public law matters generally follow the event. However, an unsuccessful claimant in judicial review proceedings is not usually ordered to pay more than one set of costs where there are interested parties in addition to the defendant (*Bolton Metropolitan District Council v Secretary of State for the Environment* [1995] 1 WLR 1176). A second set of costs may be ordered where the interested party deals with a separate issue not dealt with by the defendant. An unsuccessful party is more likely to be ordered to pay a second set of costs at first instance than on an appeal (when the issues should have crystallised, and so there is less likelihood of a second party having a separate interest that needs to be represented), and paying a third set of costs will in any event be rarely justified (*Bolton Metropolitan District Council v Secretary of State for the Environment*). An order that the claimant pays the defendant's costs includes both the costs to the final hearing and the costs before the grant of permission(*R (Davey) v Aylesbury Vale District Council* [2007] EWCA Civ 1166, [2008] 1 WLR 878). **68.39**

Whether a coroner, inferior court or tribunal should be ordered to pay or recover its costs in proceedings to challenge its jurisdiction or decision largely depends on the stance it takes in the High Court. In *R (Davies) v HM Deputy Coroner for Birmingham* [2004] EWCA Civ 207, [2004] 1 WLR 2739, the Court of Appeal stated the following principles:

(a) The established practice is to make no order for costs where the inferior court or tribunal does not appear in the High Court (see also *Moore's (Wallisdown) Ltd v Pensions Ombudsman* [2002] 1 WLR 1649), unless there has been a flagrant instance of improper behaviour, or where the court or tribunal unreasonably refuses to sign a consent order.
(b) Where the inferior court or tribunal takes an active part, costs usually follow the event. Where the inferior court or tribunal loses, the costs it is usually ordered to pay are not limited to the amount by which the costs of other parties were increased by its participation (*Moore's (Wallisdown) Ltd v Pensions Ombudsman*).
(c) Where the inferior court or tribunal plays a neutral role, assisting the High Court on matters of jurisdiction or procedure, the established practice is to make no order for costs for or against it. This is subject to the court's overall discretion on costs, which may make it just for the applicant to be compensated in costs out of public funds through a costs order against the inferior court or tribunal.

The general principles governing costs when proceedings are discontinued, including *Sengoz v Secretary of State for the Home Department* [2001] EWCA Civ 1135, *The Times*, 13 August 2001, in relation to judicial review, are considered at **55.8**. If the court can with confidence conclude

Commentary

that an applicant would have won had the matter proceeded to a full hearing, the applicant can be awarded his costs (*R (G) v Worcestershire County Council* [2005] EWHC 2332 (Admin); *DB v Worcestershire County Council* [2006] EWHC 2613 (Admin), LTL 3/11/2006). Where the public body concedes and an application for judicial review is withdrawn by consent, it is wrong not to award the claimant its costs (*Mendes v Southwark London Borough Council* [2009] EWCA Civ 594, *The Times*, 7 April 2009). Likewise where the public body fails to provide reasons for a decision on having been invited to do so under the pre-action protocol, and provides reasons following a reference to the CJEU (*R (Mellor) v Secretary of State for Communities and Local Government* [2009] EWCA Civ 1201, LTL 18/11/2009).

Review proceedings concerning various environmental matters must not be prohibitively expensive (Directive 85/337/EEC, art. 10(a); Directive 96/61/EC, art. 15(a)). This is a matter that has to be addressed by the court as opposed to the costs judge (*R (Edwards) v Environment Agency (No. 2)* [2010] UKSC 57, [2011] 1 WLR 79). This should be done in the early stages of the proceedings. It may be addressed by making a protective costs order or a costs capping order (see **chapter 44**), and may need to be revisited at the end of the proceedings.

MISCELLANEOUS SITUATIONS IN WHICH COSTS DO NOT FOLLOW THE EVENT

68.40 The following are situations where costs orders usually do not follow the event:

(a) The costs of any application to extend time are borne by the party making the application.
(b) A party failing to make admissions of facts or in relation to documents after service of a notice to admit facts or documents, or after service of a list of documents, is usually responsible for paying the costs of proving those matters.
(c) In a claim for defamation concerning words which impute unchastity or adultery to a woman or girl, costs must not exceed the damages awarded, unless the court is satisfied there were reasonable grounds for bringing the claim (Slander of Women Act 1891, s. 1).
(d) If successive actions are brought against persons jointly or otherwise liable for the same damage, costs will be ordered in favour of the claimant in the first action only unless there were reasonable grounds for bringing the later actions (**Civil Liability (Contribution) Act 1978, s. 4**).

MULTIPLE PARTIES AND CLAIMS

Multiple defendants

68.41 Where a claimant succeeds against joint tortfeasors, costs will be ordered against each defendant, and the claimant can then recover costs against any one (or more) of the defendants (*Niru Battery Manufacturing Co. v Milestone Trading Ltd* [2003] EWHC 1032 (Comm)). Any defendant paying such costs can then seek a contribution from the others under the **Civil Liability (Contribution) Act 1978**. If successful defendants are separately represented, the claimant should be liable for any additional costs only if the separate representation was reasonable. An example of what can happen where joint defendants are successful is *Korner v H. Korner and Co. Ltd* [1951] Ch 10. Eight defendants were jointly represented, and seven of them were successful in the action. It was held that generally the defence costs should be regarded as incurred by each defendant equally, which would in this case have resulted in the claimant paying seven eighths of the total defence costs. However, as different defences had been delivered for each defendant, each successful defendant was awarded one eighth of the general costs of the proceedings, together with such costs and counsel's fees as were attributable to their own defence.

Bullock and *Sanderson* orders

Where a claimant claims against two defendants in the alternative, and succeeds against one only, the court may, in its discretion, make a special order that the unsuccessful defendant must pay the successful defendant's costs (*Irvine v Commissioner of Police for the Metropolis* [2005] EWCA Civ 129, LTL 3/2/2005). These orders cannot be made where the claim fails against both defendants (*McGlinn v Waltham Contractors Ltd (No. 5)* [2007] EWHC 698 (TCC), [2008] Bus LR 278) or where the defendants succeed in defending a large part of the claim (*Whitehead v Searle* [2007] EWHC 2046 (QB), LTL 11/9/2007). It is clear that in this area the court has a wide measure of discretion (*Goldsworthy v Brickell* [1987] Ch 378). That said, from *Besterman v British Motor Cab Co.* [1914] 3 KB 181, it is apparent that, in deciding whether to make a special order, the court must first look at all the facts the claimant knew or could reasonably have discovered as at the date the defendants were joined and consider whether the joinder was reasonable. Factors bearing on this, according to the Court of Appeal in *Irvine v Commissioner of Police for the Metropolis*, include: **68.42**

(a) whether the claims against the various defendants are made 'in the alternative';
(b) the nature of the evidence and allegations against the defendants who were eventually successful;
(c) whether the causes of action are connected with each other; and
(d) whether the unsuccessful defendant had blamed the other defendants.

If it was not reasonable to join the two defendants, costs should follow the event. In such a case the successful defendant will recover its costs from the claimant and the claimant will recover the costs of the claim against the unsuccessful defendant from the unsuccessful defendant. The unsuccessful defendant is not required to reimburse the claimant for the costs the claimant has to pay to the successful defendant.

If, on the other hand, it was reasonable to join the two defendants, the court has a choice of two special orders, the choice being in the court's discretion (per Lord Brandon of Oakbrook in *Bankamerica Finance Ltd v Nock* [1988] AC 1002). The special orders are known as *Bullock* orders, from *Bullock v London General Omnibus Co.* [1907] 1 KB 264, and *Sanderson* orders, from *Sanderson v Blyth Theatre Co.* [1903] 2 KB 533.

For the purposes of exposition, assume that the claim of the claimant ('C') against the first defendant ('D1') is dismissed, but that C obtains judgment against the second defendant ('D2'). In a *Bullock* order, C would be ordered to pay D1's costs, but would recover its own costs and would be reimbursed in respect of the costs it has had to pay to D1 from D2. The difference between a *Bullock* order and the usual rule that costs follow the event is that if costs followed the event C would not be reimbursed by D2 for the costs C had to pay D1. In a *Sanderson* order, D2 has to pay C's costs, and D2 also has to pay D1's costs direct. C has no liability to pay D1's costs. Provided all parties are solvent, the eventual effect of *Bullock* and *Sanderson* orders is the same. However, the *Bullock* form is more usual because it most closely follows the rule that costs follow the event. Traditionally, the *Sanderson* form has been said to be appropriate where C is either legally aided or insolvent, because in those circumstances only a *Sanderson* order adequately protects the successful D1. Despite the traditional view, a *Sanderson* order was upheld by the House of Lords in *Bankamerica Finance Ltd v Nock* [1988] AC 1002 where D2, not C, was insolvent, the judge having decided to make a *Sanderson* order because it tended to spread the hardship caused by irrecoverable costs most fairly between C and D1, the successful defendant.

Multiple claimants

Problems are not so likely to be caused through having different judgments in respect of different claimants because actions with joint claimants are only allowed to proceed if the claimants are jointly represented. It is implicit in this that there must be a large degree of identity of interest between the joint claimants, so split judgments must be very rare. **68.43**

Counterclaims

68.44 For set-off of costs orders see **63.20**. Where the claim and counterclaim are unrelated, it may be appropriate to award the winner on the claim the costs of the claim and the winner on the counterclaim the costs of the counterclaim. The effect of this form of order was considered in *Medway Oil and Storage Co. Ltd v Continental Contractors Ltd* [1929] AC 88, where the House of Lords decided that this form of judgment entitled the defendant to all its costs of the action save those costs exclusively referable to the counterclaim. Under this principle there is no apportionment of costs, but items of costs common to both the claim and counterclaim, such as counsel's brief fee, may be divided between the claim and counterclaim. The distinction between apportionment and division is rather technical. Different courts vary in their willingness to apply the *Medway Oil* principles. They were applied in *Hay v Szterbin* [2010] EWHC 1967 (Ch), LTL 2/8/2010, where a Tomlin order merely referred to costs that 'relate exclusively' to the claim against one of three defendants. Conversely, in *Bateman v Joyce* [2008] EWHC 90100 (Costs), LTL 26/6/2008, the court said it would apply the principles only if the order used words such as 'for the avoidance of doubt the principle in *Medway Oil* applies'.

The net effect of *Medway Oil and Storage Co. Ltd v Continental Contractors Ltd* is, if the issues on the claim and counterclaim are similar, that the party recovering costs of the claim obtains by far the largest share. Even before the introduction of the CPR it was recognised that this does not always produce a just result (per Denning LJ in *Chell Engineering Ltd v Unit Tool and Engineering Co. Ltd* [1950] 1 All ER 378). While the court continues to have the power to order a party to pay the costs relating to a distinct part of the proceedings (**CPR, r. 44.2(6)(f)**), it should only do so if it is not practicable to make an order for payment of a proportion of the other side's costs or costs from a certain date only (**r. 44.2(7)**). Where the claim and counterclaim are related to each other, the costs order should usually award a percentage of the total costs of claim and counterclaim to the party who has achieved overall success (*English v Emery Reimbold and Strick Ltd* [2002] EWCA Civ 605, [2002] 1 WLR 2409; *Burchell v Bullard* [2005] EWCA Civ 358, [2005] BLR 330).

Another refinement is typified by *Box v Midland Bank Ltd* [1981] 1 Lloyd's Rep 434. The claimant recovered £5,000, and the defendant established a £39,000 equitable set-off. The Court of Appeal held that the judge should have made no order for costs. The approach exemplified by *Medway Oil and Storage Co. Ltd v Continental Contractors Ltd* was recognised by the Court of Appeal in *Universal Cycles plc v Grangebriar Ltd* [2000] CPLR 42 as being the usual form of order where the claimant is successful on the claim and the defendant is successful on a counterclaim. Where there is a set-off, the Court of Appeal in *Universal Cycles plc v Grangebriar Ltd* approved the *Chell Engineering* approach of awarding the overall winner either the entire costs of the claim, or a proportion of those costs. In *Universal Cycles plc v Grangebriar Ltd* itself the claim was for the price of goods sold and delivered, and there was a counterclaim alleging the goods were not of satisfactory quality and not fit for their purpose, it being further alleged that the value of the counterclaim exceeded that of the claim. At trial judgment was given to the claimant for £109,000, and judgment for the defendant on the counterclaim for £25,000. Neither party wanted a costs order in the *Medway Oil* form. The judge awarded the claimant its costs to the date of the defence and counterclaim, and required the claimant to pay half the defendant's costs thereafter. The Court of Appeal held that the judge had erred in placing too much emphasis on the amount of time spent on the substantive issues on which the respective parties had succeeded, and too little emphasis on the fact that the claimant had been the overall winner and on the late service by the defendant of its schedule of loss. Further, the order made by the judge stepped over the well-known line that a successful party should not, in the absence of a Part 36 offer and save perhaps in very exceptional cases, be ordered to pay any of the losing party's costs. An order was substituted for the defendant to pay all the claimant's costs, apart from the costs of the trial itself. In *Williams Corporate Finance plc v Holland* [2001] EWCA Civ 1526, LTL 22/10/2001, the claim consisted of seven heads, totalling £40,000.

Most of the heads of claim were defeated, and the defendant succeeded on his counterclaim, but there was a net finding in favour of the claimant of about £2,500. The judge awarded the claimant its costs, but on appeal no order as to costs was substituted.

Additional claims under Part 20

Where a claimant succeeds in an action against a defendant, and the defendant successfully claims an indemnity from an additional party under **Part 20**, here referred to as a third party, the third party should be ordered to pay all the defendant's costs, including the costs the defendant will have been ordered to pay the claimant (*Jablochkoff Co. v McMurdo* [1884] WN 84). In such a case, if the defendant proves to be insolvent, the claimant will be unable to recover its costs from the third party, because it has no direct order against the third party. Therefore, it may, in a proper case, be appropriate to make an order akin to a *Sanderson* order requiring the third party to pay the claimant's costs directly (*Edginton v Clark* [1964] 1 QB 367). If a claimant succeeds against a defendant who succeeds against a third party, but the court considers that the defendant has defended the claim for reasons which provided no benefit to the third party, the third party will be ordered to pay the costs of the additional claim only (*Blore v Ashby* (1889) 42 ChD 682). **68.45**

It is wrong to order the defendant to pay the third party's costs where the original claim and additional claim are partially successful (*Burchell v Bullard* [2005] EWCA Civ 358, [2005] BLR 330). A percentage order is more appropriate.

When considering costs orders between a defendant and a third party where the main proceedings fail with the result that the additional claim also fails, the usual rule is that costs follow the event under **CPR, r. 44.2(2)(a)**. This means that the court should usually ignore the incidence of costs in the main proceedings. A successful third party should recover its costs from the defendant even if the claimant in the main proceedings is impecunious (*Arkin v Borchard Lines Ltd (Nos. 2 and 3)* [2005] EWCA Civ 655, [2005] 1 WLR 3055 at [77]). As between the claimant and defendant when both the claim and additional claim fail, it may be appropriate to order the claimant to pay the defendant's costs on the claim and to reimburse the defendant in respect of the costs of both sides on the additional claim. This may be appropriate where the nature of the claim made the additional claim both inevitable and reasonable (*Arkin v Borchard Lines Ltd (Nos. 2 and 3)*), or where the main and additional claims are based on interconnected facts with the additional claim being contingent on the result in the main proceedings (*Green v Sunset and Vine Productions Ltd* [2009] EWHC 1610 (QB), LTL 10/11/2009). In an appropriate case the court may make such order as to costs as between claimants, defendants and third parties as may be just in accordance with the overriding objective (see *Arkin v Borchard Lines Ltd (Nos. 2 and 3)* at [75] and [77]). In this case the defendants and third parties were alleged to have collective responsibility for alleged anti-competitive activities. Costs orders were therefore made to share the costs burden equally among them (at [78] and [79]). A claimant who discontinues will normally have to pay the costs both of the defendant and the third party, unless the parties agree that the costs in the additional claim should be considered by the court, and the court finds, for example, that the additional claim would have failed (*Young v J. R. Smart (Builders) Ltd (No. 2)* (2000) LTL 7/2/2000).

Additional claims and Part 36 offers to settle

In *Alpha Chauffeurs Ltd v Citygate Dealership Ltd* [2002] EWCA Civ 207, LTL 21/2/2003, judgment was given for the claimant in the sum of £47,862 against the first defendant. Judgment was given to the first defendant in the sum of £41,219 against the third party, and a counterclaim made by the first defendant against the claimant was dismissed. The third party was also joined as a second defendant, with the claimant recovering nominal damages of £2 against the third party (as a second defendant). The third party had made what would now be a Part 36 offer to settle **68.46** in respect of the sum claimed by the claimant, but no Part 36 offer to the defendant. Applying the rule that costs follow the event:

(a) The claimant should have been ordered to pay the third party's costs in its capacity as second defendant, applying the usual rule discussed at **68.10** where nominal damages are recovered.
(b) The first defendant was ordered to pay the claimant's costs of bringing its claim against the first defendant and in defending the first defendant's counterclaim.
(c) The third party was ordered to pay the first defendant's costs of the additional claim and the first defendant's costs of defending the main claim.
(d) The third party was ordered to reimburse the first defendant for the costs it was ordered to pay the claimant under point (b) for bringing the main claim against the first defendant, but not the costs of either the claimant or the first defendant in relation to the counterclaim.

SPECIAL CASES

Litigants under a disability

68.47 Generally, where money is ordered or agreed to be paid to, or is ordered to be paid by, a child or protected party, the court must order a detailed assessment of the costs payable by that party to his solicitor (**CPR, r. 46.4(1)** and **(2)**), including costs payable out of money belonging to the person under disability. On an assessment under **r. 46.4(2)**, the court must also assess any costs payable to the parties under disabilities (**r. 46.4(2)(b)**) unless:

(a) the court has issued a default costs certificate (see **71.15**) in relation to those costs; or
(b) the case is a road traffic accident claim where fixed costs are payable under **Part 45, Section II** (see **70.8** to **70.15**).

Exceptional cases where the court need not order the assessment of the costs payable by a party under a disability to his solicitor are set out in **PD 46, para. 2.1**. These cover cases where there is no need to protect the child or protected party by ordering an assessment. An example is where another party has agreed to pay a specified sum in respect of the child or protected party's costs and the solicitor waives the right to further costs (**para. 2.1(b)**).

An order for costs can be made against the litigation friend acting for a claimant who is a person under disability by virtue of the undertaking to pay the costs that may be ordered against the person under disability required by **CPR, r. 21.4(3)(c)**. A successful party seeking such an order must apply promptly after judgment. The litigant normally indemnifies the litigation friend, but will not be required to do so where the litigation friend has acted for his or her own personal benefit (*Huxley v Wooton* (1912) 29 TLR 132) or if the litigation friend is guilty of some misconduct in relation to the proceedings.

Trustees and personal representatives

68.48 Trustees and personal representatives are, in so far as costs are not recovered from another party, entitled to recover their costs out of the fund. The court may, however, order otherwise and may do so where the party otherwise entitled to the costs has acted unreasonably. A trustee or personal representative who has acted substantially for his or her own benefit is likely to be treated like any other party. This may be the case where the proceedings are adversarial in nature (see *Holding and Management Ltd v Property Holding and Investment Trust plc* [1989] 1 WLR 1313; *Shovelar v Lane* [2011] EWCA Civ 802, [2011] 4 All ER 669).

Mortgagees

68.49 It is an established principle that a mortgagee is entitled to add any properly incurred costs, charges or expenses to the secured debt. Many mortgages make express provision for this, but even if they do not such a term will be implied (*Cottrell v Stratton* (1872) LR 8 Ch App 295). A court may disallow any costs, charges or expenses which were not 'properly incurred', unless the mortgage makes express provision to alter this (although a mortgage deed that purported to entitle the mortgagee to add improperly incurred costs might be open to question on public policy grounds: *Gomba Holdings (UK) Ltd v Minories Finance Ltd (No. 2)* [1993] Ch 171).

As an exception to the established principle, a mortgagee will not be permitted to add its costs to the security where a stranger impugns the title to the mortgage, or the enforcement or exercise of some right or power accruing to the mortgagee under the mortgage, even if the costs have been reasonably and properly incurred by the mortgagee (*Parker-Tweedale v Dunbar Bank plc (No. 2)* [1991] Ch 26).

In *Gomba Holdings (UK) Ltd v Minories Finance Ltd (No. 2)* [1993] Ch 171, the Court of Appeal laid down the following principles:

(a) Where there is a contractual right to costs, the discretion in the Senior Courts Act 1981, s. 51, should ordinarily be exercised so as to reflect that right.
(b) The power to disallow a mortgagee from adding its costs to the security derives from the power of the courts of equity to fix the terms on which redemption will be allowed.
(c) A decision by the court to refuse costs, in whole or in part, to a mortgagee litigant may be a decision in the exercise of the discretion under the Senior Courts Act 1981, s. 51, or in the exercise of its power to fix the terms on which redemption will be allowed, or a decision on the extent of the mortgagee's contractual right to add its costs to the security or a combination of these.
(d) A mortgagee is not to be deprived of a contractual or equitable right to add costs to the security merely by reason of an order for payment of costs made without reference to the mortgagee's contractual or equitable rights and without any adjudication of whether or not the mortgagee should be deprived of those costs.
(e) The contractual basis of assessing costs under most mortgages will be the indemnity basis (see **71.39**).

The principles laid down in *Gomba Holdings (UK) Ltd v Minories Finance Ltd (No. 2)* are reflected by **PD 44, para.** 7.1 to 7.3, which are to the effect that generally the court will not assess a mortgagee's costs, because the mortgagee can simply add its indemnity-basis costs to the security. If the mortgagor wishes to object to the amount added to the security in this way, the mortgagor may apply for the taking of an account as to whether items added to the security were unreasonably incurred or were of an unreasonable amount. If the order is made, the account will be conducted before a costs officer.

Restrictive covenants

A claimant seeking a declaration of freedom from restrictive covenants under the Law of Property Act 1925, s. 84(2), is seeking for his own benefit the protection of a court order against the existence of possible adverse rights. For the declaration to be effective it is necessary for the claimant to join as defendants everyone who might have such an adverse right. The policy adopted by the courts is that defendants joined in this type of claim should be able to participate without risks as to costs until they can make an informed decision on whether to oppose the application. Guidelines laid down by *University of East London Higher Education Corporation v Barking and Dagenham London Borough Council (No. 2)* [2004] EWHC 2908 (Ch), [2005] Ch 354 (applying *Re Jeffkins' Indentures* [1965] 1 WLR 375 and *Re Wembley Park Estate Co. Ltd's Transfer* [1968] Ch 491) are: **68.50**

(a) the claimant must pay each defendant's costs on the indemnity basis up to the point when an informed decision could be made; and
(b) thereafter, any defendant opposing the application unsuccessfully must pay his own costs, but not those of the claimant.

GROUP LITIGATION

68.51 Where a claim is proceeding under a group litigation order (GLO), there will be 'individual costs' which are specific to that particular claim, and 'common costs', which will be those incurred on the GLO issues, the costs of a claim proceeding as a test claim, and the lead solicitor's costs in administering the group litigants (**CPR, r. 46.6(2)**). If the group loses, the general rule is that the common costs will be divided equally among group members, who will have several liability for them (**r. 46.6(3)**). The individual costs of a particular claim will be that claimant's liability. A group litigant who loses will usually be ordered to pay the winning side's costs, and will also be liable for the costs of his own claim and his share of the common costs (**r. 46.6(4)**). When making costs orders at hearings involving group and individual issues, the court will apportion the costs between the group and individual issues (**r. 46.6(5)**). Where a party joins the group register late, or leaves early, the court may make an order covering that party's responsibility for the common costs to date (**r. 46.6(6)** and **(7)**).

The appropriate costs orders to be made in group litigation in respect of the costs of individual claimants who settle or discontinue during the course of the proceedings were considered in *Sayers v Merck SmithKline Beecham plc* [2001] EWCA Civ 2027, [2002] 1 WLR 2274. It might be likely that the costs of common issues will be ordered to follow the determination of those issues rather than awaiting the individual fate of each claimant's claim, it would be wrong to say this is the presumptive position. Claimants who settle should deal with all aspects of costs, including common costs, as part of the settlement negotiations. In relation to discontinuing claimants, the costs of common issues should be determined following the trial of the common issues.

Care needs to be taken to control the costs in group litigation, with one particular concern being the considerable amount of administrative time often expended in these cases (*Solutia UK Ltd v Griffiths* [2001] EWCA Civ 736, [2001] CPLR 419).

Generic costs incurred in what was intended to be group litigation, but which was settled before proceedings were issued (and hence before a GLO was made), are recoverable in a detailed assessment following a Part 8 application under **r. 46.14** (*Brown v Russell Young and Co.* [2007] EWCA Civ 43, [2008] 1 WLR 525).

PUBLICLY FUNDED LITIGANTS

Successful publicly funded litigants

68.52 If a legally aided party or an LSC funded client (together referred to as 'publicly funded litigants') is successful, the court will make an order for costs on exactly the same principles as apply in unassisted claims. The publicly funded litigant has no beneficial interest in the costs, which must be paid to his or her solicitor to obtain a valid discharge. The recovered costs are used to pay the publicly funded costs. Any damages or property recovered or preserved in the proceedings will be subject to the Lord Chancellor's first charge under the Legal Aid, Sentencing and Punishment of Offenders Act 2012, s. 25, or the **Access to Justice Act 1999, s. 10(7)**, in respect of any shortfall between the solicitor's charges and the costs recovered from the paying party, and contributions from the publicly funded litigant.

Costs against a publicly funded litigant

68.53 **Cost protection** Many publicly funded litigants will be protected against adverse costs orders if they are unsuccessful. 'Cost protection' applies to assisted parties under the Legal Aid,

Sentencing and Punishment of Offenders Act 2012, by virtue of s. 26, and to LSC funded clients (see the Community Legal Service (Costs) Regulations 2000 (SI 2000/441)).

A litigant who obtains public funding by fraud does not obtain cost protection (*Jones v Congregational and General Insurance plc* [2003] EWHC 1027 (QB), [2003] 1 WLR 3001).

Determining costs payable by assisted party Where cost protection applies, the Legal Aid, Sentencing and Punishment of Offenders Act 2012, s. 26(1), and the **Access to Justice Act 1999, s. 11(1)**, both provide that, except in prescribed circumstances, any costs ordered to be paid by the publicly funded litigant shall not exceed the amount (if any) which is reasonable having regard to all the circumstances including: **68.54**

(a) the financial resources of all the parties to the proceedings; and
(b) their conduct in connection with the dispute to which the proceedings relate.

Exclusions from cost protection are provided for by the Civil Legal Aid (Costs) Regulations 2013, SI 2013/611, reg. 6, so that it does not apply to help at court, and in certain circumstances to legal help, help with family mediation and family help (lower). Unless they have competing interests in the proceedings, the publicly funded client's partner's resources are treated as the resources of the funded party (reg. 13(3)). However, the first £100,000 of the value of the publicly funded client's home is ignored (reg. 13(1)). Also ignored is the value of the publicly funded client's clothes and household furniture, unless the circumstances are exceptional (reg. 13(2)). The court can take into account any damages recovered by a funded party who fails to beat a Part 36 offer to settle, and any resulting costs liability under s. 26 has priority over the Lord Chancellor's first charge (*Cook v Swinfen* [1967] 1 WLR 457).

The court is required to consider whether, but for cost protection, it would have made a costs order against the publicly funded party, and, if so, whether it would have specified the amount payable (reg. 15(1)). If so (or if the court decides to make a reasonably modest order), and if the court considers it has enough information to do so, the court can immediately make an order under s. 26 specifying the amount the publicly funded party shall pay (reg. 15(2) and (3)). Usually, the 'reasonable' sum that a publicly funded litigant should pay will be relatively modest, or nothing. It may be a sum payable by instalments (*Williams v Walkett* [1994] CLY 3587) or a set-off against sums awarded in favour of the assisted party. Often the judge will be guided by the level of contribution payable by the publicly funded party under the Legal Aid, Sentencing and Punishment of Offenders Act 2012, s. 23 (*Mercantile Credit Co. Ltd v Cross* [1965] 2 QB 194), but must not do so blindly, because the test at this stage is not the same as the rules governing the level of contribution (*Gooday v Gooday* [1969] P 1).

If the court does not make an immediate order under s. 26, but decides it would have ordered costs against the publicly funded party but for the cost protection rule, the non-funded party has three months to request a hearing to determine the costs payable by the publicly funded party (reg. 16(2)). Regulation 16 lays down a detailed procedure for the determination of the amount, if any, payable.

Form of order The normal order where a party is publicly funded is for a detailed assessment of costs (*South Somerset District Council v Hughes* [2009] EWCA Civ 1245, LTL 15/7/2009). The court will be slow to depart from this position. An opposing party seeking a variation (with the effect that part of the costs of the publicly funded litigant will have to be paid by that party) should be on written notice supported by a short letter setting out the basis of the application and stating the source of the alleged jurisdiction for making the order and the rules relied upon. **68.55**

Under the Legal Aid Act 1988, it was common to make orders that were colloquially known as 'football pools orders', providing that the assisted party was to pay the other side's costs, not to be enforced without the permission of the court. These were intended to allow the non-assisted party to return to court in the event of the assisted party coming into money at a later date. Under the traditional wording, the non-assisted party could return to court during the six years following the order, but a more sophisticated wording was approved in *Parr v Smith* [1995] 2 All ER 1031, which allowed an indefinite time for the application. Under the Legal Aid, Sentencing and Punishment of Offenders Act 2012 once a s. 26 order has been made, the non-funded party should generally apply within the next three months. Any later application can be entertained only up to six years from the order, and only on the grounds of significant change in the funded party's circumstances, or material additional information coming to light about the funded party's resources, or other good reasons (Civil Legal Aid (Costs) Regulations 2013, SI 2013/611, reg. 19).

A court may make orders in favour of both parties on different issues, even where one party is publicly funded, which will be set off against each other without infringing the principle of cost protection (*Hill v Bailey* [2003] EWHC 2835 (Ch), [2004] 1 All ER 1210). In relation to interim costs orders against publicly funded litigants, the court may make an order that the costs shall be set off against any future award in the claim of damages or costs against the non-funded party (*Lockley v National Blood Transfusion Service* [1992] 1 WLR 492; *R (Burkett) v Hammersmith and Fulham London Borough Council (No. 2)* [2004] EWCA Civ 1342, *The Times*, 20 October 2004).

An unsuccessful party who has been publicly funded for only part of the time during which litigation has been pending obtains the benefit of cost protection (if applicable) only for the period during which public funding was in place (*Dugon v Williamson* [1964] Ch 59). The same result applies where, as in *Turner v Plasplugs Ltd* [1996] 2 All ER 939, proceedings continue beyond a limitation in a certificate without the certificate being amended to cover future stages of the litigation. Cost protection is lost where a certificate is discharged on the date of giving notice of acting in person or change of solicitor (*Burridge v Stafford* (1999) 149 NLJ 1474). The effect of revocation of a certificate is that the party is treated as never having cost protection. In *DEG-Deutsche Investitions- und Entwicklungsgesellschaft mbH v Koshy* [2001] EWCA Civ 79, [2001] 3 All ER 878 the Court of Appeal held that revocation of a certificate is arguably the most significant change that could happen to a person's circumstances, and justified the court varying earlier costs orders previously covered by cost protection.

Costs against the Lord Chancellor

68.56 Under the Legal Aid, Sentencing and Punishment of Offenders Act 2012, s. 26(6)(d), and the Civil Legal Aid (Costs) Regulations 2013, SI 2013/611, reg. 10, a court deciding a claim in favour of a non-publicly funded litigant as against one who is publicly funded may make an order requiring the Lord Chancellor to pay the non-publicly funded litigant's costs. Before such an order can be made, the following conditions must be satisfied:

(a) The proceedings must be finally decided in favour of the non-publicly funded litigant (reg. 10(1)). Where an appeal may be brought, any order against the Lord Chancellor will not take effect until the time limit for seeking permission to appeal has elapsed without permission being granted, or, if no permission is required, no appeal is brought within the time limit for bringing an appeal (reg. 10(5)). Where an appeal is brought by the publicly funded party, a fresh application may be brought in the appeal court.
(b) The non-publicly funded litigant must make the application for a costs order against the Lord Chancellor within three months of the making of a costs order (reg. 16(2)). A late application can be made where there is a good reason for the delay (reg. 10(3)(b)(ii)).
(c) The court must be satisfied that it is just and equitable in the circumstances that provision *for the costs should* be made out of public funds (reg. 10(3)(d)). It will normally be just and equitable that the Lord Chancellor should stand behind the client unless the costs

judge is aware of facts rendering that result unjust or inequitable (*R (Gunn) v Secretary of State for the Home Department* [2001] EWCA Civ 891, [2001] 1 WLR 1634).

Further, in respect of costs incurred in proceedings at first instance, the following additional conditions (in reg. 10(3)(c)) must be satisfied:
(i) The proceedings must have been instituted by the publicly funded litigant.
(ii) The applicant must be an individual.
(iii) It must be shown that the non-publicly funded litigant will suffer financial hardship if the order is not made.

The Divisional Court is not a court of first instance when reviewing the decision of a court or tribunal (*R v Leeds County Court, ex parte Morris* [1990] 1 QB 523), but is a court of first instance when reviewing the decision of a person or body other than a court or tribunal (*R v Greenwich London Borough Council, ex parte Lovelace (No. 2)* [1992] QB 155).

Claim finally decided in favour of the assisted person Proceedings are finally decided in favour of an unassisted person (condition (a) in **68.56**) when no appeal lies, or if the time for appealing has expired. In *Kelly v London Transport Executive* [1982] 1 WLR 1055 the unassisted defendant had made what would now be a Part 36 offer to settle exceeding the damages awarded to the claimant. The Court of Appeal held that the defendants had been substantially successful and that the action had been finally decided in its favour for these purposes. **68.57**

Financial hardship In *Hanning v Maitland (No. 2)* [1970] 1 QB 580, decided when the final condition required severe financial hardship, Lord Denning MR said the term should not be restrictively construed 'so as to exclude people of modest income or modest capital who would find it difficult to bear their own costs', but should exclude commercial concerns in a considerable way of business, insurance companies and 'wealthy folk' who would not feel the costs of the litigation. Public bodies, including government departments, could (under the pre-2001 Regulations) suffer severe financial hardship (*R (Gunn) v Secretary of State for the Home Department* [2001] EWCA Civ 891, [2001] 1 WLR 1634). In *Adams v Riley* [1988] QB 372 it was explained that the unassisted party's spouse's financial resources are not to be aggregated with those of the unassisted party in determining whether the unassisted party will suffer severe financial hardship if an order against the Lord Chancellor is refused, but are to be taken into account in that an unassisted party with a financially independent spouse is better placed than a party with a dependent spouse. In *Adams v Riley* the court determined the amount that the defendant could pay towards his costs without suffering financial hardship, and made an order that the rest should be paid from public funds. **68.58**

Commentary

Both parties publicly funded

An order cannot be made against the Lord Chancellor where both parties are publicly funded (see condition (a) at **68.56**). This can produce rather harsh results, as in *Almond v Miles* (1992) *The Times*, 4 February 1992. In this case a publicly funded defendant successfully resisted a claim by a publicly funded claimant to a share in the equity of the defendant's flat. Under what is now the Legal Aid, Sentencing and Punishment of Offenders Act 2012, s. 25, the defendant's costs of £18,000 were a first charge on her flat, which had been 'preserved' in the proceedings. The claimant had the benefit of cost protection, but was required to pay certain instalments towards the defendant's costs. Although the defendant had been financially prejudiced by the proceedings, the court could not make an order against public funds, because the defendant was herself publicly funded. **68.59**

NON-PARTY COSTS ORDERS

In *Aiden Shipping Co. Ltd v Interbulk Ltd* [1986] AC 965 the House of Lords decided that the Senior Courts Act 1981, s. 51, confers a sufficiently wide discretion on the court on the question of **68.60** costs to allow it to award costs against non-parties. In the case before the House of Lords two separate sets of proceedings were commenced. In the first, a shipowner made a claim against the charterers of the ship. In the second, essentially the same dispute was litigated between the charterers and their subcharterers. The actions were not consolidated. The House of Lords upheld the judge's order that the unsuccessful shipowner should pay the charterer's costs, such costs to include any costs the charterers had to pay the subcharterers in the second action.

The basic principle is that such an order will only be made where it is in accordance with the requirements of reason and justice. The essential policy is that the need to protect the successful party by granting an effective costs order has to yield to the right of access to the courts to litigate the dispute in the first place (*Hamilton v Al Fayed (No. 2)* [2002] EWCA Civ 665, [2003] QB 1175; European Convention on Human Rights, **art. 6(1)**, in the **Human Rights Act 1998, sch. 1**). It is in the public interest that funding for litigation should be available, provided the real motivation is to enable a party to litigate what the funders perceive to be a genuine case. In *Re Land and Property Trust Co. plc* [1991] 1 WLR 601, Nicholls LJ said 'the circumstances in which it will be just to make a costs order against a person who is not a party to the proceedings will be exceptional'. Consequently, a pure funder of litigation should not ordinarily be liable to a non-party costs order, and it is only if there is something exceptional in the circumstances that such an order can be justified (*Gulf Azov Shipping Co Ltd v Idisi* [2004] EWCA Civ 292, LTL 15/3/2004). 'Exceptional' means outside the ordinary run of cases where non-parties pursued or defended claims for their own benefit and at their own expense.

Non-parties who substantially control proceedings or who will benefit from them will ordinarily be ordered to pay the successful party's costs (*Dymocks Franchise Systems (NSW) Pty Ltd v Todd* [2004] UKPC 39, [2004] 1 WLR 2807). Substantial involvement by a non-party in a claim that was without merit and without justification was enough for a non-party costs order in *Systemcare (UK) Ltd v Services Design Technology Ltd* [2011] EWCA Civ 546, [2012] 1 BCLC 14). Personal satisfaction in defeating an opponent as a means of settling a score is a sufficient personal interest (*Latimer Management Consultants Ltd v Ellingham Investments Ltd* [2006] EWHC 3662 (Ch), [2007] 1 WLR 2569).

Even if there is some exceptional feature present, an order will be refused if there is no causation (*Hamilton v Al Fayed (No. 2)*). Nevertheless, such orders may possibly be made:

- against an outsider who was funding the litigation on behalf of the unsuccessful party (*Singh v Observer Ltd* [1989] 2 All ER 751), doubted in *Symphony Group plc v Hodgson* [1994] QB 179;
- against directors of a company who improperly cause the other side to incur costs in a winding-up petition (*Re a Company (No. 004055 of 1991)* [1991] 1 WLR 1003), although it is not necessary to find impropriety before making a non-party costs order (*BE Studios Ltd v Smith and Williamson Ltd* [2005] EWHC 2730 (Ch), [2006] 2 All ER 811; *Goodwood Recoveries Ltd v Breen* [2005] EWCA Civ 414, [2006] 1 WLR 2723);
- against a shareholder who was instrumental in commencing or defending proceedings for his own benefit (*CIBC Mellon Trust Co v Stolzenberg (No. 3)* [2005] EWCA Civ 628, *The Times*, 8 June 2005; and
- where the non-party has been found, under the law concerning maintenance and champerty, to have maintained the claim (*McFarlane v E. E. Caledonia Ltd (No. 2)* [1995] 1 WLR 366).

Personal costs orders were made in winding-up proceedings against a director who treated companies as extensions of himself (*Re North West Holdings plc* [2001] EWCA Civ 67, [2001] 1 BCLC 468), and where a director contested proceedings against the company for his personal reasons (*Re Aurum Marketing Ltd* [2000] 2 BCLC 645). Normally, however, if litigation is conducted in the name of a company in good faith, it is contrary to the principles of separate corporate personality and limited liability to make any person other than the company itself liable to pay another party's costs because the company loses (*Taylor v Pace Developments Ltd* [1991] BCC 406; *Floods of Queensferry Ltd v Shand Construction Ltd* [2002] EWCA Civ 918, in which the circumstances in which a director maintained a company's litigation were described by the trial judge as 'extraordinary').

The motivation of any outside funder will be a relevant consideration. In *Hamilton v Al Fayed (No. 2)* the court drew the distinction between 'pure funders' who fund litigation out of philanthropic or charitable motives and 'professional' funders who are normally contractually bound to fund litigation. The court held that it would be rare for pure funders to be exposed to a costs order where they acted out of altruistic motives and had reasonable grounds for believing that the party was acting properly. If pure funders were regularly exposed to costs orders, there was a real risk that the funds would dry up and that access to justice would be reduced. Regarding professional funders, *Arkin v Borchard Lines Ltd (Nos. 2 and 3)* [2005] EWCA Civ 655, [2005] 1 WLR 3055, said a balance has to be struck between the need not to discourage professional funding of claims brought by persons otherwise unable to afford litigation, and the fair application of the principle that costs follow the event. It was held that the professional funder should ordinarily (in the absence of champerty and unreasonable conduct) be liable up to the amount it contributed to the unsuccessful party's costs.

Non-party costs orders may be made in the case of wanton and officious intermeddling with litigation falling short of champerty in the strict sense (*Nordstern Allgemeine Versicherungs AG v Internav Ltd* [1999] 2 Lloyd's Rep 139). They can also be made against a solicitor where litigation was pursued entirely or substantially for the benefit of the solicitor (*Myatt v National Coal Board (No. 2)* [2007] EWCA Civ 307, [2007] 1 WLR 1559). Costs orders against non-parties can be made in cases where there is 'no order as to costs' between claimant and defendant (*Myatt v National Coal Board (No. 2)*). A costs order against a non-party may be made even where the non-party is domiciled outside the jurisdiction, and without the need to comply with the rules in (for example) **Regulation (EC) No. 44/2001, art. 2** (see **16.16**) (*National Justice Compania Naviera SA v Prudential Assurance Co. Ltd (No. 2)* [2000] 1 WLR 603). Costs orders against non-parties are, however, unlikely to be made against a liquidator funding litigation in the name of the company (*Eastglen Ltd v Grafton* [1996] 2 BCLC 279).

Procedure on non-party costs applications

An application for a costs order against a non-party follows a summary procedure. The fact that costs proceedings may take some time to determine does not stop them being summary (*Robertson Research International Ltd v ABG Exploration BV* (1999) *The Times*, 3 November 1999, Laddie J). This is a different approach to that adopted in wasted costs applications (see **68.64**). However, if the application is speculative or bound to fail the court should summarily dismiss it (*Bristol and West plc v Bhadresa (No. 2)* [1999] 2 CPLR 209). The person against whom the costs order is sought must be joined as a party for the purposes of costs only, and must be given a reasonable opportunity to attend the hearing to give reasons why the court should not make the order (**CPR, r. 46.2**). An application to join a non-party should ordinarily be acceded to (*PR Records Ltd v Vinyl 2000 Ltd* [2007] EWHC 1721 (Ch), LTL 25/7/2007). The court has a power under the Senior Courts Act 1981, s. 51(3), to determine by whom, and to what extent, costs are to be paid, and it therefore has an ancillary power to order a party to disclose who its funders were (*Raiffeisen Zentralbank Österreich AG v Crossseas Shipping Ltd* [2003] EWHC 1381 (Comm), LTL 13/6/2003, in which the successful claimant found that the defendant was impecunious and was granted an order to discover who was funding the defendant). **68.61**

The strict rules of evidence will not apply when the court considers whether to make the order. The court should limit the issues to be considered and, if necessary, the length of cross-examination and submissions. An order may accordingly be refused if the non-party against whom the application is made has not been provided with the basic safeguards required by natural justice, such as being informed in advance of the trial that the application will be made, and the issue against the non-party being accurately framed by statements of case (*Symphony Group plc v Hodgson* [1994] QB 179). In *Shah v Karanjia* [1993] 4 All ER 792 an application for costs against a brother of the claimant was refused principally because he had not been separately represented at the trial, the claim against him had not been formulated against him until after the trial, and he had been asked questions in cross-examination at trial with a view to obtaining information for the application for costs against him.

Costs orders against experts

68.62 In *Phillips v Symes (No. 2)* [2004] EWHC 2330 (Ch), [2005] 1 WLR 2043, it was held, by extension of the jurisdiction to order costs against non-parties, that the court has power to order costs to be paid by expert witnesses. Such an order may be made where an expert breaches his or her duties to the court and as a result significant costs are incurred, or where an expert produced a report without having examined the property in question (*Admiral Insurance Services Ltd v Daniels* (2007 Cambridge County Court) LTL 14/6/2007). A similar procedure to that discussed at 68.61 should be followed. The expert should be given a warning, and orders should follow the two-stage process of first considering whether there is a case to answer, followed by a hearing to allow the expert to appear and give reasons why an order should not be made.

Costs order in favour of non-party

68.63 In *J v Oyston* [2002] EWHC 819 (QB), [2002] CPLR 563, an order for costs was made in favour of the Solicitors' Indemnity Fund, a non-party which had taken over conduct of proceedings in the name of the claimant whom it had agreed to indemnify and in which it was successful. Such an order can be made under the Senior Courts Act 1981, s. 51, provided the court finds there are exceptional circumstances. The Fund would have been liable for the defendant's costs if he had won, and it would be unreasonable, unjust and extraordinary if the defendant were not to be ordered to pay the Fund's costs if he lost.

WASTED COSTS ORDERS

68.64 The court has a power under the Senior Courts Act 1981, s. 51(6), to make a legal representative liable for any wasted costs. This can take one of two forms:

(a) disallowing the costs of a party and ordering the legal representative to indemnify his or her client against the costs; and/or
(b) ordering the legal representative to pay the costs of another party.

The term 'wasted costs' is defined in the Senior Courts Act 1981, s. 51(7), to mean any costs incurred by a party:

(a) as a result of any improper, unreasonable or negligent act or omission on the part of any legal or other representative or any employee of such a representative; or
(b) which, in the light of any such act or omission occurring after they were incurred, the court considers it unreasonable to expect that party to pay.

The phrase 'improper, unreasonable or negligent' was considered by the Court of Appeal in *Ridehalgh v Horsefield* [1994] Ch 205, which is the leading authority in this field. Whether an act or omission is 'improper' is to be judged by the standards of the consensus of professional, including judicial, opinion and is not limited to breaches of the professional code. 'Unreasonable' includes behaviour that is:

> vexatious, designed to harass the other side rather than advance the resolution of the case, and it makes no difference that the conduct is the product of excessive zeal and not improper motive.... The acid test is whether the conduct admits of a reasonable explanation.

'Negligent':

> should be understood in an untechnical way to denote failure to act with the competence reasonably to be expected of ordinary members of the profession.

'Negligent' requires something more than mere negligence (*Persaud v Persaud* [2003] EWCA Civ 394, [2003] PNLR 519). Negligent handling of a client's case is not enough: the lawyer's conduct must also be a breach of duty to the court (*Radford and Co. v Charles* [2003] EWHC 3180 (Ch), [2004] PNLR 25). A wasted costs order will only be made if there is something akin to a legal representative being guilty of an abuse of process. A failure to address the Bar Council guidance on advising in publicly funded cases was regarded in *Persaud v Persaud* as a breach of duty to the legal aid authorities and not a breach of duty to the court, and was an insufficient basis for a wasted costs order.

The test to be applied to determine whether an act or omission justifies a wasted costs order is the same whether or not the party is publicly funded (*Filmlab Systems International Ltd v Pennington* [1995] 1 WLR 673). There must be a causal link between the legal representative's behaviour and the waste of costs (**PD 46, para. 5.5(b)**; *Ridehalgh v Horsefield*; *Brown v Bennett (No. 2)* [2002] 1 WLR 713).

It is appropriate for the court to make a wasted costs order only if it is just in all the circumstances to make a legal representative compensate a party for wasted costs (**PD 46, para. 5.5(c)**).

'Legal representative' includes solicitor and counsel. Acts or omissions by counsel which may lead to costs which may be the subject of a wasted costs order include both pre-trial paperwork and conduct during the trial (*Ridehalgh v Horsefield; Brown v Bennett (No. 2)*). Solicitors cannot avoid their responsibility to the parties and the court by slavishly following counsel's advice. It is incumbent on them to exercise an independent judgment (*Davy-Chiesman v Davy-Chiesman* [1984] Fam 48; *Locke v Camberwell Health Authority* (1991) 2 Med LR 249; *Ridehalgh v Horsefield*).

An application for a wasted costs order can be made against one's own legal representative and that of one's opponent (*Medcalf v Mardell* [2002] UKHL 27, [2003] 1 AC 120). An order will not be made against former solicitors who ceased to act before proceedings were issued (*Byrne v Sefton Health Authority* [2001] EWCA Civ 1904, [2002] 1 WLR 775). An application can be made against a non-party (*Lubrizol Ltd v Tyndallwoods Solicitors* (1998) LTL 10/4/98).

The courts must be astute to ensure that wasted costs applications do not become another form of satellite litigation. They will be reserved for exceptional cases where a party was injured by the unjustified behaviour of a legal representative (*Ridehalgh v Horsefield*). They should be confined to matters that are susceptible to summary disposal on agreed facts or after brief investigation. Complex, time-consuming enquiries are to be avoided. Compensation of a party who has suffered at the hand of a legal representative is only one of a number of competing interests to be considered (*Re Merc Property Ltd* [1999] 2 BCLC 286; *Wall v Lefever* [1998] 1 FCR 605; *Medcalf v Mardell*).

The legal representative against whom an application for a wasted costs order is made must be given an opportunity to respond before the court makes the order (**CPR, r. 46.8(2)**; *Re Wiseman Lee (Solicitors) (Wasted Costs Order) (No. 5 of 2000)* [2001] EWCA Crim 707, *The Times*, 5 April 2001). The court should not make an order against the legal representative of a party who is unable or unwilling to waive privilege, unless the court is satisfied that, if unconstrained, the legal representative could say nothing to resist the order and also that it is fair and just to make the order in the circumstances (*Medcalf v Mardell*).

Procedure on wasted costs applications

An application for a wasted costs order should be made to the judge who tried the matter (*Re P* [2002] 1 Cr App R 207). In certain limited circumstances it is possible for another court to have jurisdiction, such as where it is impracticable for the trial judge to deal with the matter, or where the parties agree to another judge dealing with it. Unless such an exception applies, a district judge has no jurisdiction to make a wasted costs order after a claim has been tried by a circuit judge (*Gray v Going Places Leisure Travel Ltd* [2005] EWCA Civ 189, LTL 7/2/2005). **68.65**

The fact that the trial judge has already criticised the conduct complained of will not necessarily mean that the judge is biased and should not hear the application (*Bahai v Rashidian* [1985] 1 WLR 1337).

Although an application can be made at any stage of proceedings, it should normally be made after trial (**PD 46, para. 5.2**; *Filmlab Systems International Ltd v Pennington* [1995] 1 WLR 673). An application can be made at any time up to and including the detailed assessment of costs (**PD 46, para. 5.2**; *Melchior v Vettivel* [2002] CP Rep 24). It can be made after the main proceedings have been stayed by consent following a Tomlin order (*Wagstaff v Colls* [2003] EWCA Civ 469, [2003] PNLR 561). The award of costs as between the parties and the making of a wasted costs order are two distinct functions (*Melchior v Vettivel*).

A party to proceedings may apply for a wasted costs order either orally or by filing an application notice under **CPR, Part 23** (**PD 46, para. 5.5**). The court can make an order of its own initiative (**PD 46, para. 5.3**). It should be slow to do so as the enquiry will necessarily involve a party in additional expense. Where application is made under **Part 23**, a copy of the application notice must be served, with a copy of the written evidence and a draft order, at least three days before the application is to be heard (**CPR, r. 23.7**). The application notice and evidence in support must (**PD 46, para. 5.9**) identify:

(a) what the legal representative is alleged to have done or failed to do; and
(b) the costs which the legal representative may be ordered to pay or which are sought to be paid.

Where the court initiates the enquiry it is incumbent on the judge to ensure that the order shows clearly the breach alleged so that the legal representative has sufficient information upon which to respond.

The application will generally be considered in two stages (**PD 46, para. 5.7**). In the first stage, the court must be satisfied:

(a) that it has before it evidence or other material which, if unanswered, would be likely to lead to a wasted costs order being made; and
(b) the wasted costs proceedings are justified notwithstanding the likely costs involved.

At the second stage (even if the court is satisfied at stage 1) the court will consider, after giving the legal representative an opportunity to give reasons why the court should not make a wasted costs order, whether it is appropriate to make a wasted costs order.

Elaborate proceedings, disclosure or requests for further information are not generally appropriate given the summary nature of the investigation (*Re Merc Property Ltd* [1999] 2 BCLC 286). The court has no power to direct that privileged documents must be disclosed (*General Mediterranean Holdings SA v Patel* [2000] 1 WLR 272; see *Medcalf v Mardell* [2002] UKHL 27, [2003] 1 AC 120, and *Brown v Bennett (No. 2)* [2002] 1 WLR 713 for the consequences of this).

The court will approach the application by considering the three points stated in **PD 46, para. 5.5**:

(a) Has the legal representative acted improperly, unreasonably or negligently?
(b) Has the legal representative's conduct caused a party to incur unnecessary costs (see *R v Secretary of State for the Home Department, ex parte Mach* [2001] EWCA Civ 645, LTL 27/4/2001)?
(c) Is it just in all the circumstances to order the legal representative to compensate that party for the whole or part of those costs?

It is submitted that there is no burden on the representative to exculpate him or herself.

The court can direct a costs judge or a district judge to decide the amount of costs to be disallowed or paid (**CPR, r. 46.8(3)(b)**).

Examples of wasted costs

The wasted costs powers against lawyers and other parties are compensatory in nature. **68.66**

Conduct justifying a wasted costs order may include failing to attend an appointment, failing to comply with the court's orders, negligent mispleading of the case, inefficient presentation of the case at trial through being ill-prepared, and pressing on with a claim after it has become hopeless (for example, through failing to read the materials disclosed by the other side on disclosure). Pleading an unjustified allegation of fraud in breach of the Bar Code of Conduct may be 'improper' conduct (*Medcalf v Mardell* [2002] UKHL 27, [2003] 1 AC 120, where an order was refused). A solicitor who swears an affidavit in support of a winding-up petition in circumstances where he knows that the petition, if fought on the merits, will fail, acts unreasonably and may be the subject of a wasted costs order (*Re a Company (No. 006798 of 1995)* [1996] 1 WLR 491). A solicitor is not entitled to abdicate all responsibility for a case by instructing counsel, but the more specialist the area the more reasonable it is to follow counsel's advice. Thus in *R v Horsham District Council, ex parte Wenman* [1995] 1 WLR 680 a solicitor was absolved from liability when acting on counsel's advice in judicial review proceedings. A finding that a claim had a less than 50 per cent chance of success is not enough. The requirements for wasted costs orders in weak cases are that the claim was hopeless and a breach of the solicitor's duty to the court (*Patel v Air India Ltd* [2010] EWCA Civ 443, LTL 14/5/2010). In *Ridehalgh v Horsefield* the Court of Appeal expressed the view that, largely because of the 'cab rank rule' whereby barristers (and to some extent solicitors) are not entitled to pick and choose their clients, it is not improper for a lawyer to represent a client who is bound to lose. However, pursuing a case which amounts to an abuse of process would be 'improper'. The distinction is largely one of degree. The Court of Appeal also made a point of deprecating the practice of making threats to apply for wasted costs orders as a means of unacceptable intimidation, although there is a distinction between that and giving proper notice that an application will be made in the case of persistent improper, unreasonable or negligent conduct.

Chapter 69 Qualified one-way costs shifting

INTRODUCTION

69.1 Unless a litigant has BTE insurance (such as in a motor insurance policy or household insurance), abolishing the recoverability of ATE insurance premiums means there is little incentive to insure the risk of having to pay the other side's costs if the claim is unsuccessful. There is nothing to stop a litigant taking out ATE cover, but premiums are often prohibitively expensive. Under the pre-Jackson system, a litigant reasonably confident of winning, but aware there is a risk of losing, was often prepared to pay a substantial ATE premium because, when the claim succeeded, the premium was repaid under the costs order by the losing party.

Sir Rupert Jackson recognised that removing CFA success fees, and abolishing the recoverability of ATE insurance premiums, brought the balance too far against claimants, and particularly individual claimants. This is addressed in the *Jackson Report* by recommendation 19 for the introduction of qualified one-way costs shifting ('QOCS'), together with recommendations 10 and 65 for an uplift of 10 per cent in awards of damages for pain and suffering, loss of amenity, physical inconvenience and discomfort, and social discredit as implemented by *Simmons v Castle* [2012] EWCA Civ 1039, [2012] EWCA Civ 1288, [2013] 1 WLR 1239.

NATURE OF QOCS

69.2 'Costs shifting' describes the usual rule that costs follow the event or that costs are otherwise paid by one side to the other (**CPR, r. 44.2(2)(a)**). The costs incurred by the successful party are 'shifted' to the losing party under the usual costs order. QOCS adjusts this traditional position by saying that the usual costs order should only be made in favour of one party, typically the claimant. This means that if the claimant wins, the defendant should be ordered to pay the claimant's costs in the usual way. However, if the claimant loses, QOCS means that while the claimant remains liable to pay its own lawyers' costs, the claimant will not also have to pay the successful defendant's costs under the usual order for costs to follow the event.

Under QOCS a claimant therefore has a valuable protection against paying the defendant's costs. As a result, there should be no need for a claimant who will have the benefit of QOCS to take out ATE insurance, because normally they will not be required to pay the defendant's costs even if they lose.

QOCS is 'qualified' one-way costs shifting, because this protection to the claimant is not absolute. It is recognised that if it was an invariable rule, it would be open to abuse, with some claimants indulging in costs-inflating practices secure in the knowledge they would never be brought to account. Accordingly, under the QOCS scheme that was introduced from 1 April 2013 there are exceptions for different types of misbehaviour, and no protection against the enforcement of adverse costs orders against damages and interest recovered in the proceedings.

CATEGORIES OF CASE COVERED BY QOCS

Transitional provisions governing QOCS

As from 1 April 2013, QOCS applies to personal injury and clinical negligence cases (**CPR, r. 44.13**). QOCS does not apply to proceedings in which the claimant has entered into a pre-commencement funding arrangement (as defined by **r. 48.2**, see **r. 44.17**). A pre-commencement funding arrangement is a funding arrangement as defined by **r. 43.2(1)(k)(i)**, as in force before 1 April 2013 (CFAs with success fees), where: **69.3**

(a) the agreement was entered into before 1 April 2013 specifically for the purposes of the provision to the person by whom the success fee is payable of advocacy or litigation services in relation to the matter that is the subject of the proceedings in which the costs order is to be made; or
(b) the agreement was entered into before 1 April 2013 and advocacy or litigation services were provided to that person under the agreement in connection with that matter before 1 April 2013 (**r. 48.2(1)(a)(i)**).

This means that if the claimant, for example, entered into a CFA with a success fee before 1 April 2013, QOCS will not apply.

Personal injuries claims governed by QOCS

Under **CPR, r. 44.13**, the provisions on QOCS in **rr. 44.14** to **44.16** apply to proceedings which include a claim for damages: **69.4**

(a) for personal injuries;
(b) under the Fatal Accidents Act 1976; or
(c) which arises out of death or personal injury and survives for the benefit of an estate by virtue of the **Law Reform (Miscellaneous Provisions) Act 1934, s. 1(1)**.

Applications for disclosure before proceedings start, pursuant to the Senior Courts Act 1981, s. 33, or the County Courts Act 1984, s. 52 (and see also **CPR, r. 31.16**), are excluded from the scope of QOCS (**r. 44.13(1)**, **proviso**).

There is an extended definition of 'claimant' for the purposes of the rules on QOCS in **r. 44.13(2)**, namely:

> In this Section, 'claimant' means a person bringing a claim to which this Section applies or an estate on behalf of which such a claim is brought, and includes a person making a counterclaim or an additional claim.

This is intended to mean that it does not matter whether the personal injuries claim is brought by an original claimant or in a defence and counterclaim or in an additional claim, such as a third-party claim, under **Part 20**. It probably achieves that aim by the use of the phrase 'person bringing a claim to which this Section applies' (**r. 44.13(2)**), being an implicit reference back to the personal injuries claims spelt out in **r. 44.13(1)**. The wording of **r. 44.13(2)** is perhaps not as clear as it could be, and it could be taken as meaning that a defendant to a claim for personal injuries (say the claimant's employer) who brings a third-party claim against another tortfeasor (say the occupier of the premises) is a 'claimant' for the purposes of QOCS because they have made an additional claim in proceedings in which a personal injuries claim has been brought. No doubt the courts will ensure such a strained interpretation of the provision is avoided.

Sir Rupert Jackson primarily recommended QOCS for personal injuries claims, but also said that it should be considered for other categories of claim, particularly those where traditionally there is an inequality of arms between claimants and defendants (*Jackson Report*, Executive Summary, para. 2.7), and proposed that QOCS should be applied to defamation claims (recommendation 65). Extending the categories of case covered by QOCS is a matter for the future.

No financial eligibility requirement

69.5 At one stage it was proposed that QOCS would not be available to the very wealthy (Reforming Civil Litigation Funding and Costs in England and Wales — Implementation of Lord Justice Jackson's Recommendations: The Government Response (Cm 8041, March 2011), para. 11). An obvious problem with that proposal was when and how the claimant's financial resources would be assessed for that purpose. As the financial means exception was only intended to apply to a very small number of 'very wealthy' claimants, the costs of making that assessment in all cases far outweighed its value. It has therefore been decided that QOCS will apply to all claimants whatever their means, so there is no financial test to determine eligibility.

EFFECT OF QOCS

69.6 One-way costs shifting is achieved by **CPR, r. 44.14(1)**, in a somewhat obscure fashion. This provides:

> Subject to rr. 44.15 and 44.16, orders for costs made against a claimant may be enforced without the permission of the court but only to the extent that the aggregate amount in money terms of such orders does not exceed the aggregate amount in money terms of any orders for damages and interest made in favour of the claimant.

Claimant loses the case

69.7 If the claimant loses the case with no award of damages, the effect is that no costs will be payable by the claimant, because the aggregate amount referred to in **CPR, r. 44.14(1)**, is nil. The rule does not prevent an adverse costs order being made against the unsuccessful claimant, but instead provides that any costs order that is made is not enforceable against the claimant. It is therefore rather like the costs protection granted to legally aided parties, and the familiar 'football pools' orders that have been made for many years (which provide that costs being ordered against an assisted party are not to be enforced without the court's permission). Although **r. 44.14(1)** is similar to a football pools order in effect, it is not the same. Under **r. 44.14(1)** all the court has to do is to make a normal adverse costs order against the unsuccessful claimant. The order may but need not say that it may not be enforced without the court's permission. **Rule 44.14(1)** then applies with the effect that (as nothing has been recovered in the litigation) nothing is payable by the claimant towards the defendant's costs. Procedures that apply in legal aid cases for seeking permission to enforce the costs order on the basis that the claimant's financial circumstances have improved do not apply, because under **r. 44.14(1)** the financial exposure of the claimant is limited to the money award in the actual proceedings.

Claimant partially successful

69.8 In cases where the claimant is partially successful, **CPR, r. 44.14(1)**, operates in a slightly different way. First, the court will have to decide what costs order to make given the respective degrees of success of the parties and the other factors set out in **r. 44.2**. If the court makes a full or partial costs award in favour of the claimant, **r. 44.14** has no application. However, if the court makes an adverse costs order against the claimant (whether a full costs order in favour of the defendant, or a percentage costs order in favour of the defendant), **r. 44.14(1)** applies to restrict the amount of costs that the defendant can recover from the claimant to the aggregate amount in money terms of any orders for damages and interest made in favour of the claimant. In such a case QOCS does not provide full costs protection for the claimant, because the money award may be eaten up by the costs order in favour of the defendant, but the claimant is protected in the sense that taking into account such sums as they were awarded in the case, the claimant will not have to pay anything beyond the total award to the defendant under the defendant's costs order.

QOCS and defendants' Part 36 offers

The main reason for the Byzantine wording of **CPR, r. 44.14(1)**, is to deal with split costs orders under **r. 36.14(2)** where the defendant has made a Part 36 offer and the claimant has failed to achieve a judgment more advantageous than that offer. Assuming the claimant with the benefit of QOCS has succeeded on liability and obtained a money award, **r. 36.14(2)** says that unless the court considers it unjust to do so, it will award costs to the claimant up to the end of the relevant period as defined by **r. 36.3(1)(c)** and award the defendant its costs thereafter. **69.9**

The two costs orders can be set off against each other (**r. 44.12**). The net effect, especially if the Part 36 offer was made in the early stages of the claim, is that there is often a net costs liability due from the claimant to the defendant under an order made under **r. 36.14(2)**. By virtue of **r. 44.14(1)**, that net costs liability can be enforced without permission against the awards in favour of the claimant for damages and interest, up to the extent of reducing those figures to zero.

QOCS and interim costs orders

Interim costs orders against a claimant with QOCS protection are dealt with in a similar way to Part 36 offers. Liability under such adverse interim costs orders can only be enforced against the claimant up to the amount the claimant eventually recovers by way of damages and interest (**CPR, r. 44.14(1)**). To ensure this happens, interim costs orders cannot be enforced against claimants with QOCS protection until the end of the case (**r. 44.14(2)**; see **69.11**). **69.10**

Time for enforcing costs orders against claimants

An order for costs made against a claimant may be enforced only after the proceedings have been concluded and the costs have been assessed or agreed (**CPR, r. 44.14(2)**). This is particularly relevant where there have been interim costs orders against a claimant with QOCS protection (see **69.10**). It allows the court to set off the main costs order in the proceedings against the adverse interim costs orders under **r. 44.12**, and to apply the QOCS protection rule in **r. 44.14(1)** to the balance to avoid any costs liability of the claimant exceeding the aggregate of the money award in damages and interest. **69.11**

Credit scoring

An order for costs which is enforced only to the extent permitted by **CPR, r. 44.14(1)**, shall not be treated as an unsatisfied or outstanding judgment for the purposes of any court record (**r. 44.14(3)**). **69.12**

MISBEHAVIOUR UNDER CPR, PART 44, SECTION II

69.13 CPR, r. 44.15, provides:

Orders for costs made against the claimant may be enforced to the full extent of such orders without the permission of the court where the proceedings have been struck out on the grounds that—
(a) the claimant has disclosed no reasonable grounds for bringing the proceedings;
(b) the proceedings are an abuse of the court's process; or
(c) the conduct of—
 (i) the claimant; or
 (ii) a person acting on the claimant's behalf and with the claimant's knowledge of such conduct,
 is likely to obstruct the just disposal of the proceedings.

With respect to the Civil Procedure Rule Committee, this comes nowhere near implementing the idea in the *Jackson Report*. Claimants who lose the protection granted by QOCS should be those who have forfeited the right to costs protection through either:
(a) advancing a fraudulent claim; or
(b) abusing the court system.
The expression used in point (b) above is deliberately not the same as the term 'abuse of process', which is used in **r. 3.4(2)(b)**. This is because claims are struck out regularly under **r. 3.4(2)** for all sorts of reasons that are not blameworthy, and do not amount to abusing the civil justice system. The genesis of the problem is no doubt the use of **r. 3.4(2)** phraseology in the Ministerial Statement of 17 July 2012 by the Parliamentary Under-Secretary of State, Ministry of Justice (Jonathan Djanogly) on the Implementation of Part 2 of the Legal Aid, Sentencing and Punishment of Offenders Act 2012: Civil Litigation Funding and Costs. What seems to have happened is that **r. 44.15** has faithfully reproduced the wording used in that statement, but has not necessarily enacted the intention behind it.

Claims that have been struck out

69.14 What **CPR, r. 44.15**, has done is largely to replicate the wording of **r. 3.4(2)**. Adopting the same words as are used in **r. 3.4(2)** means that the courts will inevitably apply the same principles in interpreting **r. 44.15** as they have done for many years in interpreting **r. 3.4(2)**. It means that costs protection will be lost under **r. 44.15** in, among others, the following situations:

(a) Where a claim is struck out due to drafting errors by the claimant's legal representatives or the claimant if acting in person. Striking out in such cases is on the ground the claim discloses no reasonable cause of action. It does not necessarily mean it is not a genuine claim.
(b) Where a claim is struck out on the basis that it is seeking to extend the situations where there is a duty of care, perhaps because the law is not yet ready to make the necessary extension. It would mean that many of the cases that have formulated the boundaries of the law of negligence are ones where costs protection under QOCS would not apply.
(c) Where a claim is time-barred. Time-barred claims are struck out on the basis that they are an abuse of process, because limitation is only a procedural defence, which does not determine whether there were reasonable grounds for bringing the claim. Many strike-out applications engaging the Limitation Act 1980, ss. 14 and 33, are very difficult to predict, and it seems bizarre that if they are successful then costs protection is lost. What is also strange is that costs protection under QOCS will not be lost under **r. 44.15** if, instead of the limitation point being taken on a striking-out application, it is taken as a preliminary issue, because **r. 44.15** only applies if the claim is struck out.
(d) A claim may be struck out as an abuse of process even if the strict rules of *res judicata* do not apply, but on the basis that the claim could and should have been brought in earlier proceedings (*Henderson v Henderson* (1843) 3 Hare 100; *Johnson v Gore Wood and Co.* [2002] 2 AC 1).

This may be a little more blameworthy than the other examples, but the cases in this area show that often incredibly tight distinctions are made in these applications (for example, *Jameson v Central Electricity Generating Board* [2000] 1 AC 455).

In all these cases costs protection will be lost. However, costs protection will not be lost if instead of taking a point on a striking-out application, judgment is obtained against the claimant, either on an application for summary judgment or on the trial of a preliminary issue. Where a claim has been struck out on any of the stated grounds, an order for costs against the claimant may be enforced to the full extent of the order without the permission of the court (**r. 44.15**). It seems from the wording that there is no discretion to reimpose QOCS costs protection in these cases.

There are plenty of other situations where claims are struck out under **r. 3.4(2)** where the claimant fully deserves to lose their costs protection under QOCS. Claims which are totally without merit, claims deliberately aimed at abusing the court's process, and fraudulent claims will fall into this category. A practical solution would be to adopt the first of these as being the test for automatic loss of QOCS protection under **r. 44.15**: that costs protection is lost if a claim is struck out under **r. 3.4(2)** with the court recording in the order that it considers that the claim was totally without merit under **r. 3.4(6)**. This could be extended to equivalent situations, such as refusing permission to appeal, striking out an appellant's notice, or dismissing an appeal that is totally without merit under **r. 52.10(5)**, **(6)**.

Commentary

Loss of QOCS costs protection: fraudulent claims

The second problem with **CPR, r. 44.15**, is that it only applies if the claim has actually been **69.15**
struck out. Many fraudulent claims will not come within **r. 44.15** because it is extremely difficult to strike out a claim on the basis it is fraudulent. The nature of such an allegation means it is rarely going to be a suitable issue to decide on an interim application, and so it will usually be left to be determined at trial. If the case proceeds through to trial, there are various reasons why it will not then be struck out even if fraud is found (*Summers v Fairclough Homes Ltd* [2012] UKSC 26, [2012] 1 WLR 2004, see **33.14**). In these cases the defendant may make an application for permission to remove the claimant's QOCS costs protection under **r. 44.16(1)**. For **r. 44.16(1)** to apply the court needs to find on the balance of probabilities that the claim was fundamentally dishonest.

While there are examples of actual striking-out orders being made in fraudulent claims (in which event costs protection under QOCS is lost automatically under **r. 44.15**), this is unusual. In most cases of alleged fraud the court will need to conduct a hearing to decide whether the required level of dishonesty can be established to the civil standard of proof. Usually this should be done at trial (**PD 44, para. 12.4(a)**), but it follows from *Summers v Fairclough Homes Ltd* that it will only rarely be appropriate to strike out the claim at that stage.

Allegations of fundamental dishonesty in settled and discontinued claims

Unless there are exceptional circumstances, the court will not enquire into whether the **69.16**
claim was fundamentally dishonest if the proceedings have been settled (**PD 44, para. 12.4(b)**). Under **CPR, r. 38.6(1)**, unless the court orders otherwise, a claimant who discontinues is liable for the costs of the defendant. Where a personal injuries claim has been discontinued, the effect of **CPR, r. 44.14(1)**, is that generally the claimant has costs protection under QOCS which overrides the usual costs position under **r. 38.6(1)**. However, the court may in such a case enquire into whether the claim was fundamentally dishonest under **r. 44.16(1)**, and can do so even if the notice of discontinuance has not been set aside (**PD 44, para. 12.4(c)**).

Proceedings for the financial benefit of another

69.17 The court may grant permission to enforce a costs order against a claimant who would otherwise have costs protection under QOCS if the proceedings include a claim which is made for the financial benefit of another person (**CPR, r. 44.16(2)**). Examples are subrogated claims and claims for credit hire (**PD 44, para. 12.2**), but do not include the provision of personal services rendered gratuitously for things like personal care, domestic assistance etc. (**PD 44, para. 12.3**). In such a case the court may also make a non-party costs order under the Senior Courts Act 1981, s. 51, and **CPR, r. 46.2**, against that other person (**r. 44.16(3)**), and in fact usually will do so (**PD 44, para. 12.5**).

Chapter 70 Fixed Costs etc.

INTRODUCTION

Fixed costs provide a means of ensuring certainty over how much litigation will cost a losing party under a party-and-party costs order, and a method by which the government can limit costs as a matter of policy. Certainty is obtained at the expense of flexibility, and while losing parties are protected by modestly calibrated fixed costs, successful parties have to meet any shortfall between the fixed amounts and their actual costs from their own resources. Part of the policy in using fixed costs is to put pressure on legal representatives to deliver the legal services covered by the fixed costs regime within the financial constraints laid down in the rules. 70.1

As part of the civil justice reforms of 2013 the whole of **CPR, Part 45**, on fixed costs was re-issued with substantial alterations with effect from 1 April 2013. This chapter deals with the post-1 April 2013 system. At present the fixed costs system is mainly focused on simple steps in the litigation process, low-value claims and trial costs in fast track claims (for which, see 71.7). There is also a scale costs system for patent claims in the county court, which covers substantial claims in a complex area of law, and a rule limiting costs in environmental law claims.

SOURCE OF THE FIXED COSTS REGIME

The term 'fixed costs' means costs the amounts of which are fixed by the CPR, whether or not the court has a discretion to allow some other or no amount, and includes the costs fixed by **CPR, rr. 45.1** to **45.8, 45.11, 45.18, 45.21, 45.37** and **45.38** (**r. 44.1(1)**). These fixed costs are adopted by **r. 27.14(2)(a)** for all claims decided on the small claims track. 70.2

SITUATIONS WHERE FIXED COSTS APPLY

CPR, Part 45, and various other provisions lay down the situations where fixed costs apply, broadly as follows: 70.3

(a) where the only claim is a claim for a specified sum of money which is more than £25 and judgment is given after the defendant admits all or part of the claim (**r. 45.1(2)(a)(ii)** and **(iii)**);

Commentary

(b) where the only claim is a claim for a specified sum of money which is more than £25 and judgment is entered by default (**r. 45.1(2)(a)(i)**);
(c) where the only claim is a claim for a specified sum of money which is more than £25 and summary judgment is entered (**r. 45.1(2)(a)(iv)**);
(d) where the only claim is a claim for a specified sum of money which is more than £25 and the claim succeeds after the defence is struck out as disclosing no reasonable grounds for defending the claim (**r. 45.1(2)(a)(v)**);
(e) where the only claim is for a specified sum of money and the defendant pays it together with the fixed commencement costs within 14 days of service of the particulars of claim (**rr. 45.1(2)(a)(vi)** and **45.3**; **r. 45.1(2)(a)(vi)** mistakenly refers to **r. 45.4** instead of **r. 45.3**);
(f) where judgment is given on a fixed date claim (see **r. 7.9** and **PD 7B**) for delivery of goods, worth more than £25 (**CPR, rr. 45.1(2)(b)** and **45.4**);
(g) in possession claims (with or without a money claim), including claims under **Part 55**, where the defendant gives up possession and pays the amount claimed with fixed commencement costs stated on the claim form (**rr. 45.1(2)(c)** and **45.5**);
(h) in possession claims based on non-payment of rent where the court gives a fixed date for the hearing when it issues the claim and judgment is given without the defendant denying liability (beyond making proposals for paying arrears of rent) (**rr. 45.1(2)(d)** and **45.5**);
(i) in accelerated possession claims of land let on assured shorthold tenancies under **Part 55, Section II**, where possession orders are made without the defendant denying liability (**rr. 45.1(2)(e)** and **45.5**);
(j) in successful demotion claims under **Part 65, Section III** (**rr. 45.1(2)(f)** and **45.5**);
(k) where a judgment creditor takes steps to enforce a judgment or order under **Parts 70** to **73** (**rr. 45.1(2)(g)** and **45.8**);
(l) on the issue of a default costs certificate (**PD 47, paras 10.7** and **10.8**); and
(m) on the determination of a small claims track claim (**CPR, r. 27.14(2)(a)**), and **PD 45, para. 1.2**.

The fixed costs regime in **Part 45, Section I** (**rr. 45.1** to **45.8**), applies unless the court orders otherwise (**r. 45.1(1)**). The fixed costs regime does not apply where the value of a claim for money or goods does not exceed £25 (**r. 45.1(3)**). Enforcement proceedings are not subject to a minimum value unless the enforcement is under **r. 70.5(4)** of awards made by tribunals other than the High Court and county courts (**r. 45.8**). In the small claims track, **r. 27.14(2)(g)** permits the court to order further costs to be paid by a party who has behaved unreasonably (see **45.29**).

The amounts fixed are intended to deliver a moderate and predictable scheme of costs where there are no unusual factors and no real contest. It follows that the court is likely to depart from this regime where it is clear that it will not deliver proper remuneration for cases outside the norm. It is suggested that the court will have in mind the factors listed in **r. 44.4** (factors to be taken into account in deciding the amount of costs) in deciding whether to depart from fixed costs. For example, the court is unlikely to confine a successful claimant to fixed costs on a contested application for summary judgment, but a court may restrict a claimant to fixed costs on a straightforward rent arrears possession claim.

SUMS INCLUDED IN FIXED COSTS

70.4 Where the fixed costs regime of **CPR, Part 45, Section I** (**rr. 45.1** to **45.8** covering tables 1 to 5), applies, the costs are incremental, with each increment corresponding to a step in the proceedings:

(a) commencement (table 1 or 3);

(b) entry of judgment (table 2);
(c) exceptional forms of service (table 4);
(d) enforcement (table 5).

In addition, the successful litigant is entitled to recover the relevant court fee, for example, the issue fee or (in the case of summary judgment) the application fee (r. 45.1(4)).

Because the scheme is incremental, the amount that can be entered or that will be awarded will be the aggregate of the applicable sums.

Amounts allowed

There are nine tables in **CPR, Part** 45, setting out the amounts allowed by way of fixed costs. These are: **70.5**

Table 1	Fixed costs on commencement of a claim for the recovery of money or goods (**r. 45.2**)
Table 2	Fixed costs on entry of judgment in a claim for the recovery of money or goods (**r. 45.4**)
Table 3	Fixed costs on commencement of a claim for the recovery of land or a demotion claim (**r. 45.5**, and see **rr. 65.11** to **65.20**)
Table 4	Miscellaneous fixed costs (**r. 45.7**)
Table 5	Fixed enforcement costs (**r. 45.8**)
Table 6	Fixed costs in relation to the RTA protocol (**r. 45.18**, and see **8.30** to **8.60**)
Table 7	Fixed costs on commencement of a county court claim conducted by an HMRC officer (**r. 45.34**)
Table 8	Fixed costs on entry of judgment in a county court claim conducted by an HMRC officer (**r. 45.35**)
Table 9	Fixed fast track trial costs (**r. 45.38**, see **71.6**)

Rule 45.6(1) provides for fixed costs under **r.** 45.1(2)(d) and (f) of £57.25 for entering judgment in possession claims and demotion claims. Where an order for possession is made in an accelerated possession claim, the fixed costs under **r.** 45.1(2)(e) for preparing and filing the claim form, the documents that accompany the claim form, and the request for possession, total £79.50 (**r.** 45.6(2)).

PD 47, para. 10.7, provides for fixed costs of £80 plus the appropriate court fee to be included in default costs certificates.

ENTERING FIXED COSTS ON THE CLAIM FORM

Where fixed costs are recoverable they should be inserted on the claim form or application (for example, simple claims for the recovery of money or possession of land, or where the party is seeking to enforce a tribunal award under **CPR, r.** 70.5) or the request for the enforcement process. At the bottom right-hand corner of the general claim form (N1) there is a box for entering a number of figures, including the issue fee and fixed costs for commencing the proceedings. *In claims where fixed costs do not apply* (i.e. most damages claims and claims for equitable relief), the relevant box on the claim form should be marked 'to be assessed' (**PD** 45, **para.** 1.3). **70.6**

SMALL CLAIMS TRACK FIXED COSTS

It is provided in **CPR, r.** 27.14(2)(a)(ii), that the fixed costs payable in small claims track cases are those which are payable under **Part** 45, or would be payable under **Part** 45 if that Part **70.7** applied to the case. This provision is necessary because the fixed costs rules in **Part 45** do not apply, for example, to unspecified money claims (most damages claims), and the plain intention behind **r. 27.14(2)(a)** is that the same fixed costs should be recoverable in all types of small claims track cases. This is confirmed by **PD 45, para. 1.2**, which says the fixed costs to be awarded in small claims track cases are the sum of the fixed commencement costs calculated in accordance with table 1 in **r. 45.2** and the appropriate court fees paid by the claimant.

PREDICTABLE COSTS IN ROAD TRAFFIC ACCIDENT CLAIMS

Disputes covered by the scheme

70.8 CPR, **Part 45, Section II (rr. 45.9 to 45.15)**, provides a scheme (which originally came into force on 6 October 2003) for predictable costs for certain road traffic claims that settle before the issue of proceedings and (from 1 April 2005), proceedings for the approval of a settlement or compromise under **r. 21.10(2)**. The rules are supplemented by **PD 45, paras 2.1** to **2.10**.

The provisions apply only to disputes arising out of road traffic accidents occurring on or after 6 October 2003. A road traffic accident is defined as 'an accident resulting in bodily injury to any person or damage to property caused by, or arising out of, the use of a motor vehicle on a road or other public place in England and Wales' (**CPR, r. 45.9(4)**). A motor vehicle is a mechanically propelled vehicle intended for use on roads (**r. 45.9(4)**) and a road is any highway and any other road to which the public has access, including bridges over which a road passes (**r. 45.9(4)**). Where a claim arises from a road traffic accident, such as where a passenger is injured when alighting from a coach, the predictable costs scheme in **rr. 45.9** to **45.15** applies and is not displaced by pleading the claim under the Occupiers' Liability Act 1957 or on any other legal basis (*Green v Kis Coaches and Taxis Ltd* (2008) LTL 13/5/2008 (Plymouth County Court)).

The provisions are confined to claims which settle before issue of proceedings (**PD 45, para. 2.1**) for agreed damages which do not exceed £10,000 (**CPR, r. 45.9(2)(c)**) and for which the small claims track would not have been appropriate (**r. 45.9(2)(d)**). The agreed damages must include damages in respect of personal injury and/or damage to property (**r. 45.9(2)(b)**). They must, by **PD 45, para. 2.3**, be calculated including:

(a) general and special damages and interest;
(b) interim payments;

but after deducting:

(c) an amount attributable to agreed contributory negligence;
(d) any amount which the compensating party is required by statute to pay directly to a third party (such as compensation recovery payments and National Health Service expenses).

Provided the above conditions are satisfied, there is no further requirement that the costs sought fall within the indemnity principle (see **71.30**). It is enough that the conditions are satisfied (*Nizami v Butt* [2006] EWHC 159 (QB), [2006] 1 WLR 3307).

Amount recoverable

70.9 The amount which can be allowed in costs-only proceedings relating to a dispute within **CPR, Part 45, Section II** (see **70.8**), is limited by **r. 45.10** to:

(a) fixed recoverable costs related to the amount of the agreed damages prescribed by **r. 45.11(1)** (see **70.10**);

(b) VAT on item (a) (**r. 45.11(3)**);
(c) disbursements (**r. 45.12(1)**), limited to the items listed in **r. 45.12(2)** (see **70.13**). Where there is more than one claimant in relation to a single accident, damages will be agreed in relation to them individually and costs will be calculated in relation to each of them accordingly (**PD 45, para. 2.7**).

Where the costs limit specified in **r. 45.10** is acceptable there is no need for costs-only proceedings. If it is considered that there are exceptional circumstances justifying a greater recovery, costs-only proceedings may be brought under **r. 45.13** (see **70.14**).

Fixed recoverable costs

The fixed recoverable costs which are to be allowed in relation to a dispute within **CPR, Part 45, Section II** (see 70.8), are, by **r. 45.11(1)** and **(2)**: **70.10**

(a) £800, plus
(b) 20 per cent of the damages agreed up to £5,000, plus
(c) 15 per cent of the damages agreed between £5,000 and £10,000, plus
(d) 12.5 per cent London weighting, where available (see **70.12**).

VAT can be added (**r. 45.11(3)**).

If the court considers that there are exceptional circumstances, it may entertain a claim for more than the fixed recoverable costs (**r. 45.13(1)**; see **70.14**).

Examples If agreed damages are £3,500 and no London weighting is available, the fixed recoverable costs are: **70.11**

£800 + 20% of £3,500 = £800 + £700 = £1,500

If a London weighting is available, the amount is increased by 12.5 per cent (12.5% of £1,500 is £187.50) to £1,687.50.

If agreed damages are £8,500 and no London weighting is available, the fixed recoverable costs are:

£800 + 20% of £5,000 + 15% of £3,500 = £800 + £1,000 + £525 = £2,325

The London weighting on £2,325 is 12.5% of £2,325, which is £290.62, giving a total of £2,615.62.

London weighting The 12.5 per cent London weighting is available under **CPR, r. 45.11(2)**, if the claimant lives or works in the area described by **PD 45, para. 2.6**, and instructs solicitors practising in that area. The designated area consists of the county court districts of: Barnet, Bow, Brentford, Bromley, Central London, Clerkenwell and Shoreditch, Croydon, Dartford, Edmonton, Gravesend, Ilford, Lambeth, Mayor's and City of London, Romford, Uxbridge, Wandsworth, West London, Willesden, and Woolwich. **70.12**

Disbursements

By **CPR, r. 45.12**, only the following disbursements can be recovered under the scheme: **70.13**

(a) the cost of obtaining medical records;
(b) the cost of obtaining a medical report;
(c) the cost of obtaining a police report;
(d) the cost of obtaining an engineer's report;
(e) the cost of a search of the records of the Driver and Vehicle Licensing Agency;
(f) where the claimant is a child or protected party, necessarily incurred counsels' and court fees for a court application for approval of the settlement;
(g) any other disbursement which has arisen due to a 'particular feature' of the dispute.

Claim for more than the fixed recoverable costs

70.14 If the court considers that there are exceptional circumstances, it may entertain a claim, in costs-only proceedings, for more than the fixed recoverable costs (**CPR, r. 45.13(1)**). If it considers the claim is appropriate, it may either assess the costs or make an order for them to be assessed (**r. 45.13(2)**). However, if the assessed figure is not 20 per cent or more above the fixed costs, the claimant will only be able to recover the fixed costs or, if they are less, the assessed costs (**r. 45.14**). If an application for an assessment is unsuccessful, or results in an assessment which is less than 20 per cent above the fixed costs, the claimant must pay the defendant's costs of defending the costs-only proceedings, and the court cannot make any order in respect of the claimant's costs of those proceedings (**r. 45.15**).

Practical implications

70.15 When a road traffic accident claim is within **CPR, Part 45, Section II**, a solicitor will simply be able to agree the costs set out in **rr. 45.10** to **45.12**, dispensing with any assessment of costs. It is hoped that this will enhance the cash flow for firms representing claimants and provide transparency and predictability for defendant insurers. It should also lead to a reduction in costs-only proceedings for relatively minor cases, as exemplified by the approach in *Nizami v Butt* [2006] EWHC 159 (QB), [2006] 1 WLR 3307 (see **70.8**).

Naturally there will be a temptation for the receiving party to bring costs-only proceedings in the hope of achieving a better level of remuneration from a detailed assessment. The scheme therefore places a considerable costs risk on a claimant who seeks to adopt this route (see 70.14). The provisions of **Part 36** and **r. 47.20** concerning offers to settle apply. In addition the assessment must beat the predictable costs by 20 per cent or more before anything extra is payable (**r. 45.15**). This creates something of an anomaly. The costs officer or costs judge will be able to work out from **r. 45.11** the predictable costs and will know when the critical 20 per cent is achieved. It might be suggested that **r. 45.14** is akin to an assessment hearing. Given the level of costs that can arise on costs-only proceedings, the receiving party will be at significant risk in commencing such proceedings.

RTA AND EL/PL PROTOCOL FIXED COSTS

70.16 CPR, rr. **45.16** to **45.28**, set out the code dealing with fixed costs recoverable in RTA Protocol claims (see **8.30** to **8.60**). The only costs allowed (**r. 45.17**) are:

(a) fixed costs under **r. 45.18**, which are set out in table 6 in **Part 45**;
(b) disbursements in accordance with **r. 45.19**;
(c) fixed costs for additional advice on quantum for claims over £10,000 in accordance with **r. 45.23B**;

The Stage 1 fixed costs for RTA claims up to £10,000 were reduced from £400 to £200, and the Stage 2 fixed costs were reduced from £800 to £300 with effect from 30 April 2013 (Civil Procedure (Amendment No. 3) Rules 2013, SI 2013/789). Stage 3 fixed costs are unchanged. For RTA claims over £10,000 and up to £25,000, with effect from 31 July 2013, Stage 2 fixed costs are £600. From 31 July 2013, fixed costs in EL and PL claims up to £25,000 are set out in table 6A in Part 45. Also from 31 July 2013, RTA and EL/PL Protocol claims that continue outside the relevant Protocol are governed by the fixed costs rules in rr. 45.29A to 45.29L.

SCALE COSTS IN THE PATENTS COUNTY COURT

70.17 CPR, rr. **45.30** to **45.32**, lay down rules for scale costs in proceedings in the Patents County Court. Scale costs do not apply where the court considers a party to have behaved in a manner that amounts to an abuse of the court's process, or where the claim concerns infringement or revocation of a patent or registered design the validity of which has been certified by a court in earlier proceedings (**r. 45.30(2)**).

The maximum amount of scale costs that the court will award for each stage of a Patents County Court claim are set out in **PD 45, para. 3.3**. This has two tables, table A for each stage up to determination of liability, and table B for each stage in an inquiry as to damages or an account of profits. Each entry in the tables is the maximum (to which VAT should be added, **r. 45.31(5)**) for that stage. For example, the maximum for particulars of claim is £6,125, and the maximum for making or defending an application is £2,500. Whatever the sums allowed under the various stages in tables A and B, **r. 45.31(1)** provides that in any event the total costs in Patents County Court claims cannot exceed:

(a) £50,000 on the final determination on liability; and
(b £25,000 on an inquiry as to damages or account of profits.

FIXED REVENUE AND CUSTOMS COSTS

CPR, rr. 45.33 to 45.36, set out fixed costs rules for commencing and entering judgment in county court debt claims brought by HMRC Officers under the Commissioners for Revenue and Customs Act 2005, s. 25(1A). **70.18**

ENVIRONMENTAL LAW CASES

CPR, rr. 45.41 to 45.44, provide rules to limit the costs of environmental law judicial review claims governed by the Aarhus Convention 1998. Claimants opt into the costs limitation rules in these cases by stating the claim is an Aarhus Convention claim in the claim form (**r. 45.44(1)**), although the defendant can object, in which case the court will determine whether the Convention applies. A claimant can opt out of the cost limitation rules by not stating that the claim is an Aarhus Convention claim in the claim form (**r. 45.42(a)**). Where it applies, the claimant's liability for costs is limited to £5,000 if they are an individual and not a business, and £10,000 in other cases (**PD 45, para. 5.1**). Costs liability of defendants is limited to £35,000 (**para. 5.2**). **70.19**

Chapter 71 Assessment of Costs

The following procedural checklist, which is at the front of the book, is relevant to this chapter:

Procedural checklist 30 Summary assessment of costs

INTRODUCTION

Once a costs order has been made, it is necessary to determine how much should be allowed in respect of those costs, that is, how much the paying party must pay to the receiving party. A similar determination must be made when a solicitor bills a client and when a solicitor is seeking to recover costs from the State in a publicly funded claim. The costs of and incidental to the proceedings are, by the Senior Courts Act 1981, s. 51(1), in the discretion of the court. It follows from this that once proceedings are started, a costs order will ordinarily cover pre-commencement costs as well as costs incurred from the date proceedings were issued. By **CPR, r. 44.1(1)**, 'costs' includes fees, charges, disbursements, expenses, remuneration, reimbursement allowed to a litigant in person under **r. 46.5**, and any fee or reward charged by a lay representative for acting on behalf of a party in proceedings allocated to the small claims track. Whether costs incurred in mediation are included is discussed at **8.6**. Generally, the costs incurred by a party in seeking funding for litigation do not form part of the costs of the claim (*National Westminster Bank plc v Kotonou* [2009] EWHC 3309 (Ch), LTL 17/12/2009, the exception being where the costs in seeking funding form the subject matter of the litigation). **71.1**

Commentary

There is no rule that the costs of one set of proceedings cannot be recovered as costs which are 'of and incidental to' another set of proceedings within the meaning of the Senior Courts Act 1981, s. 51(1) (*Roach v Home Office* [2009] EWHC 312 (QB), [2010] QB 256). It may therefore be possible to recover the costs of attending an inquest as incidental to subsequent civil proceedings. Relevant factors are:

(a) the purpose of the attendance at the inquest;
(b) the relevance of the attendance to the subsequent proceedings; and
(c) the reasonableness and proportionality of the costs incurred.

In **chapter 70** the system of fixed costs applicable to certain situations in litigation was considered. This chapter will deal with assessment of costs by the courts.

All references in this chapter, other than in **71.39** and **71.56** to **71.63**, are to the CPR and practice directions in force from 1 April 2013 following the civil justice reforms of 2013.

METHODS OF QUANTIFICATION OF COSTS

It is open to the parties to agree the amount of costs to be paid under a costs order Alternatively, costs may be assessed by the court. **CPR, r. 44.6**, provides that when the court makes a costs order it may either: **71.2**

(a) make a summary assessment of the costs; or
(b) order a detailed assessment by a costs officer.

A 'costs officer' is defined by **CPR, r. 44.1(1)**, to mean a costs judge (which in turn means a taxing master of the Senior Courts), a district judge or an authorised court officer (i.e. a civil servant, in a district registry, the Principal Registry of the Family Division, the Senior Courts Costs Office or a county court, who is authorised by the Lord Chancellor to assess costs).

AGREEING AMOUNT OF COSTS

71.3 Parties may agree the amount of costs to be paid when they settle a claim or when agreeing a consent order. If the agreement is to be drawn up in a consent order or judgment, the draft order should include a term that one party shall pay the agreed sum in costs to the other (**PD 47, para. 9.3**). If the agreement is reached after the order or judgment is made, either party may apply for a costs certificate in the amount agreed (**CPR, r. 47.10(1)**, and see **71.28**). Such an application is made under **r. 40.6**, and may be dealt with by a costs officer (**PD 47, para. 9.1**). The court will not give its approval to disproportionate or unreasonable costs. So, when the amount of costs has been agreed between the parties, any court order must state that the order is made by consent (**PD 44, para. 9.10**).

SUMMARY ASSESSMENT

71.4 Summary assessment involves a short assessment of a party's costs. Because it is a summary procedure it will not involve the lengthy consideration of items which is reserved for a detailed assessment. Thus in *Gould v Armstrong* [2002] EWCA Civ 1159, LTL 23/7/2002, the court approved a robust summary assessment as an effective and proportionate means of avoiding the cost and delay associated with a detailed assessment.

The procedure for summary assessment of costs is summarised in **procedural checklist 30**, which is at the front of the book.

Summary assessment of costs generally arises at the conclusion of a fast track trial or other hearings which do not last more than one day (**PD 44, para. 9.2**) (see **32.31**, **46.23** and **68.27**). There are situations where it will not be appropriate to conduct a summary assessment of costs even though the conditions of **para. 9.2** are met (for a list of these see **68.27**). Conversely there is nothing to prevent the court from summarily assessing the costs even where the conditions in **para. 9.2** are not met, for example, when the trial lasts for more than one day (*Q v Q (Family Proceedings: Costs Order)* [2002] 2 FLR 668). Summary assessment is not required where the parties have agreed the amount of the costs, in which event the order must state the order is by consent (**para. 9.10**).

Summary assessment is preceded by the service of a statement of costs on form N260 not less than 24 hours before the time fixed for the hearing (or two days before a fast track trial) (**para. 9.5(4)**). At first sight the wording of this provision suggests that the requirement to serve the costs statement is mandatory and that failure would lead to the loss of all costs or alternatively to a detailed assessment. This approach was rejected by the court in *MacDonald v Taree Holdings Ltd* [2000] CPLR 439, where the court made it clear that the loss of all costs was a disproportionate sanction unless the circumstances were exceptional and that the court should consider adjourning to give the paying party time to consider the receiving party's statement. However, any failure to serve the statement of costs without reasonable cause will be taken into account in the summary assessment (**para. 9.6**).

Statement of costs

71.5 A statement of costs must be in form N260 and must, by **PD 44, para. 9.5(2)**, address the following matters:

(a) The number of hours claimed, divided into detailed component parts of the work done as set out in the statement of costs form (N260).
(b) The hourly rate claimed. Practitioners may wish to consider **tables 71.2, 71.3** and **71.4**, *which set out* the guideline rate for each court in the country, based on figures from the Guide to the Summary Assessment of Costs published by the Senior Courts Costs Office (SCCO).

(c) The grade of fee earner. The name and grade of the fee earners working on the case must be entered on form N260, together with their hourly rates. It is important to refer to the four categories of fee earner found at the foot of the form N260 and to appreciate that they are experience based. Thus the term 'partner' has no place in the form N260, whereas a solicitor with over eight years' post-qualification experience in litigation is an acceptable description.
(d) The amount and nature of disbursements. Work which is outsourced should normally appear in the body of the bill as if carried out by the firm (*Smith Graham v Lord Chancellor's Department* (1999) 149 NLJ 1433). There is some concern as to whether a solicitor should be able to recover for work outsourced to agents. While there is no appellate authority on the issue, Judge Michael Cook found that such items could be allowed on an assessment, provided there is sufficient information to allow the judge to ascertain whether they were reasonably incurred and reasonable in amount (*Stringer v Copley* (2002) LTL 17/10/2002).
(e) The amount of the legal representative's costs for attending or appearing at the hearing.
(f) Counsel's fees.
(g) VAT on the above. Practitioners must be vigilant to ensure that VAT is included in the bill only if it is properly claimed. Costs are compensatory and thus VAT can only be charged if the receiving party will lose the VAT. Most VAT-registered parties will be able to reclaim VAT and thus it will not represent an overall loss. Hence VAT should not generally be claimed where the party is registered for VAT. (See **PD 44, paras 2.3** and **2.4** and **71.54**.)
(h) The statement of costs must be signed (**PD 44, para. 9.5(3)**). The signature is not an empty formality, it is a certificate given by an officer of the court that the statement is accurate and that there is no infringement of the indemnity principle. It affords a presumption of trust to the paying party (*Bailey v IBC Vehicles Ltd* [1998] 3 All ER 570). Where a solicitor failed to sign a statement of costs the court has been prepared to stay the issue of the costs order (*Wilson v Howard Pawnbrokers* [2002] EWHC 1489 (Ch), LTL 19/8/2002).

Commentary

Quantifying costs on a summary assessment

Courts sometimes develop conventional figures for summarily assessed costs for certain types **71.6**
of proceeding, such as the costs awarded for straightforward landlord and tenant possession proceedings. Although this may be acceptable in straightforward possession claims, it is contrary to principle in the majority of claims. On a summary assessment of costs the court must focus on the detailed breakdown of costs actually incurred by the party in question as shown on its statement of costs. The court is entitled to draw on its general experience of costs in comparable cases, and it may be helpful to draw on that experience when comparing the total from its assessment of the costs on the schedule to see whether those costs were reasonable and proportionate. What the court cannot do is to use a judicial tariff for different categories of claims (*1-800 Flowers Inc. v Phonenames Ltd* [2001] EWCA Civ 721, [2001] 2 Costs LR 286). For the same reasons it is an error for a court to fix a figure for costs at what the judge considers to be the upper reasonable limit for cases of that type without considering the actual costs on an item-by-item basis (*Morgan v Spirit Group Ltd* [2011] EWCA Civ 68, [2011] PIQR P9). The court can call for whatever evidence is available at the time in deciding on the figure to allow, such as looking at counsel's brief to see the brief fee, as well as looking at the costs statements and hearing the advocates on the work involved in the matter.

In *Edwards v Devon and Cornwall Constabulary* [2001] EWCA Civ 388, LTL 13/3/2001, on a summary assessment after a fast track trial, the judge reduced the claimant's costs schedule from £7,500 to £2,500 and did not allow counsel to address him on the reduction. After disbursements this gave the claimant's solicitors £620 in a non-straightforward personal injuries claim. The Court of Appeal substituted its own summary assessment of the claimant's costs. In *Contractreal Ltd v Davies* [2001] EWCA Civ 928, LTL 17/5/2001, the appellant's costs were reduced from £21,000 to

£1,750 on a summary assessment. On appeal it was held that the judge had placed too much weight upon the size of the bill in comparison with the amount in issue when considering proportionality, and had failed to distinguish between pre and post-CPR costs (proportionality only applies to the latter), and the court ordered a detailed assessment.

Where costs are assessed summarily they are payable within 14 days unless the court in its discretion thinks fit to order otherwise (**CPR, rr. 44.2** and **44.7**). A party seeking such a direction must apply for it and, where appropriate, must back up the application with evidence. The court can, of its own initiative, postpone the date of payment, where it considers there are appropriate reasons (*Pepin v Watts* [2001] CPLR 9 at [29]).

FAST TRACK TRIAL COSTS

Fixed trial costs

71.7 Part of the scheme of the Woolf proposals was that there should be restricted costs recoverable in fast track cases. This was partially brought into effect by a system of fixed trial costs in fast track claims. The amounts are set out in **CPR, r. 45.38**; see **table 71.1**.

For a successful claimant the value of the claim is the amount of the judgment excluding interest, costs and any reduction for contributory negligence, whereas for a successful defendant it is the amount the claimant specified on the claim form (or the maximum amount that could have been recovered on the pleaded case) (**r. 45.38(3)**). If there is a counterclaim and both parties succeed, the relevant amount is the difference between the value of the two claims (**r. 45.39(6)**). If there is a counterclaim with a greater value than the claim, and the claimant succeeds on the claim and defeats the counterclaim, the relevant amount is the value of the counterclaim (**r. 45.38(6)**). There are detailed rules dealing with cases where there are several claimants or several defendants, including whether more than one party can be awarded fast track trial costs, which are set out in **r. 45.40**. Claims for non-monetary remedies are deemed to have a value between £3,000 and £10,000, but the court has a discretion to make some other order, see **r. 45.38(4)**.

The court is not permitted to award more or less than the set figures for trial costs, unless it decides not to award any fast track trial costs or **r. 45.39** applies (**r. 45.38(2)**). Guidance given by the Senior Costs Judge to the Designated Civil Judges Conference on 24 November 2000 is to the effect that this means that unless a **r. 45.39** factor applies, the court must allow the standard trial costs even if the brief fee is lower than the standard amount. This is so notwithstanding the indemnity principle (see **71.30**).

The additional allowance for a solicitor attending with counsel is provided by **r. 45.39(2)**. This £345 fee will only be payable if the court awards fast track trial costs and if the court considers that it was necessary for a legal representative to attend to assist counsel (**r. 45.39(2)**).

Table 71.1 Fast track fixed trial costs for proceedings issued on or after 6 April 2009

Type of claim	Costs
Value up to £3,000	£485
Value £3,000.01 to £10,000	£690
Non-money remedies	£690
Value £10,000.01 to £15,000	£1,035
Value over £15,000	£1,650
Additional fee for solicitor attending trial with counsel	£345

Abortive preparation, split trials and misconduct

If a fast track claim settles before the start of the trial, costs may be allowed in respect of the advocate preparing for trial, but the amount allowed cannot be more than the above figures (**CPR, r. 46.12**). In deciding the amount to be allowed for the abortive preparation, the court will take into account when the claim settled and when the court was notified of that fact. **71.8**

If there are split trials, such as on liability and quantum, it is possible to be awarded a second tranche of fast track trial costs, but the second award should not exceed two thirds of the amount payable under the first award, subject to a minimum award of £485 (**r. 45.39(3)** and (**4**)).

A successful party may, by **r. 45.39(7)**, be awarded less than the above fixed fast track trial costs for unreasonable or improper behaviour during the trial, and the losing party may be ordered to pay an additional amount if it is guilty of behaving improperly during the trial (**r. 45.39(8)**).

INTERIM PAYMENT ON ACCOUNT OF COSTS

The court has a power to make an order for an amount to be paid on account of costs which will be assessed at some later stage (**CPR, r. 44.2(8)**). In the ordinary course, an order for an interim payment on account will be made if a final costs order has been made, subject to detailed assessment, provided there is no likelihood of an appeal and the paying party is not impecunious (*Soliman v Islington London Borough Council* (2001) LTL 16/10/2001). An important factor in exercising the discretion under **r. 44.2(8)** is that the receiving party should not be kept out of moneys that will almost certainly be found to be payable under the costs order (*Blakemore v Cummings* [2009] EWCA Civ 1276, [2010] 1 WLR 983). This factor may be outweighed by other circumstances, which will vary from case to case, such as the degree of uncertainty over the amount likely to be assessed, a relatively short time to the detailed assessment hearing, or delay. An order for an interim payment on account of costs may be made even where the receiving party is late in commencing detailed assessment proceedings (*Allason v Random House UK Ltd* (2002) LTL 28/2/2002, where a payment of £140,000 was ordered in respect of costs said to amount to at least £175,000). An interim payment on account of costs may be ordered even where there is no detailed breakdown of the costs (*Simms v Law Society* [2005] EWCA Civ 849, [2005] ACD 98). **71.9**

Where there has been a full trial, the successful party should normally be awarded an interim payment on account of costs under **r. 44.2(8)** in an amount up to the minimum sum which he will almost certainly be awarded on a detailed assessment (*Mars UK Ltd v Teknowledge Ltd* [1999] IP & T 26). Where there has been no full trial the judge is not constrained by any presumption one way or the other. It is for the successful party to justify the court making an order, and, bearing in mind **r. 47.16**, it may be inappropriate even to make an interim payment in the minimum sum the successful party will inevitably recover in a detailed assessment (*Dyson Ltd v Hoover Ltd (No. 4)* [2003] EWHC 624 (Ch), [2004] 1 WLR 1264).

If the paying party fails to pay an interim payment on account of costs, the court has jurisdiction to make an order debarring that party from taking part in the detailed assessment (*Days Healthcare UK Ltd v Pihsiang Machinery Manufacturing Co. Ltd* [2006] EWHC 1444 (QB), [2006] 4 All ER 233). Langley J said that the assessment hearing would still proceed, but simply without the paying party, as it would be wrong to rubber-stamp the bill without any adjudication by the costs judge.

A stay on payment of an interim payment on account of costs may be ordered where immediate payment runs the risk that justice will not be done, for example, where there is an appeal (*Renewable Power and Light plc v Renewable Power and Light Services Inc.* (2008) LTL 7/4/2008).

Commentary

DETAILED ASSESSMENT

71.10 Unlike summary assessment, a detailed assessment is not generally conducted until the conclusion of the proceedings (**CPR, r. 47.1**). Proceedings are concluded when the court has finally determined the matters in issue in the claim, whether or not there is an appeal (**PD 47, para. 1.1**). However, the court retains a power to order an assessment at an earlier stage. An order may be made allowing detailed assessment proceedings to be commenced if there is no realistic prospect of the claim continuing (**PD 47, para. 1.5**).

Appropriate office

71.11 All applications and requests in detailed assessment proceedings must be made to or filed at the 'appropriate office' (**CPR, r. 47.4**). In High Court cases this is usually the Senior Courts Costs Office (SCCO). If the court dealing with the case when the judgment or order was made or when the event occurred which gave rise to the right to assessment, or to which the case has subsequently been transferred, is the Principal Registry of the Family Division or a district registry or a county court then that registry or court is the appropriate office (**PD 47, para. 4.1**). County courts normally deal with detailed assessments from tribunals and similar bodies (**para. 4.1(b)**). County courts can specify another county court as the appropriate office for the assessment of costs (**CPR, r. 47.4(3)**). Any court can direct that the SCCO is to be the appropriate office (**CPR, r. 47.4(2)**), but should only do so having regard to the size of the bill of costs, its difficulty, length of hearing and costs to the parties (**PD 47, para. 4.3(2)**). An order transferring a bill to another court or to the SCCO can be made on the application of a party or on the court's own initiative.

Detailed assessments in London county courts (Barnet, Bow, Brentford, Central London, Clerkenwell and Shoreditch, Croydon, Edmonton, Ilford, Lambeth, Mayor's and City of London, Romford, Wandsworth, West London, Willesden and Woolwich) will take place in the SCCO unless the court orders otherwise (**PD 47, para. 4.2**). However, default costs certificates and applications to set aside default costs certificates should be issued and heard in the relevant county court (**para. 4.2(2)(b)**), and appeals are lodged at the Central London Civil Justice Centre (**para. 4.2(2)(c)**).

Commencement of detailed assessment proceedings

71.12 Detailed assessment proceedings must be commenced within three months of the judgment, order, award or other determination giving rise to the right to costs (**CPR, r. 47.7**). The period may be extended or shortened by agreement between the parties (**PD 47, para. 6.1**). A similar three-month period is laid down in respect of cases terminated by discontinuance, dismissal or acceptance of Part 36 offers (**CPR, r. 47.7**). Detailed assessment proceedings are commenced by serving on the paying party a notice of commencement (form N252) together with a copy of the bill of costs (**r. 47.6(1)**). The receiving party is also required to serve copies of counsel's fee notes and experts' fee invoices, written evidence for all disbursements exceeding £500, and a statement giving the name and address for service of any person upon whom the receiving party intends to serve the notice of commencement (**PD 47, para. 5.2**). The persons referred to in the previous sentence are known as 'relevant persons', who are defined by **PD 47, para. 5.5**, as persons who took part in the proceedings and who are directly liable to pay the costs under a costs order, and also persons who have given notice that they have a financial interest in the outcome of the assessment and any other person the court may direct to be treated as a relevant person. Relevant persons must also be served with the notice of commencement and with the bill of costs (**CPR, r. 47.6(2)**). These additional persons are thereafter regarded as being parties to the assessment proceedings.

In cases where the costs to be assessed are payable out of the legal aid fund, the assessment is commenced by filing a request for a detailed assessment (form N258A), which must be served on the assisted person (**r. 47.18(3)**). Again, this must be done within three months from the date when the right to detailed assessment arose (**r. 47.18(2)**). In assessments of publicly funded costs, in addition to the documents referred to in the previous paragraph. the request for a detailed assessment must, by **PD 47, para. 17.2**, be accompanied by the legal aid certificates, LSC certificates, certificates recording the determinations of the Director of Legal Aid Casework, any relevant amendments and authorities, and any certificate of discharge, revocation or withdrawal.

The relevant papers in support of the bill described in **PD 47, para. 13.12**, have to be lodged only if requested by the costs officer (**para. 17.2(2)**). Names and addresses of any person with financial interests in the assessment, and of the assisted person, if he or she wishes to attend, must be provided.

The effect of failing to commence proceedings for the detailed assessment of costs within the prescribed time limit is considered at 71.25.

Bill of costs

There are four model forms of bill of costs set out in the schedule to PD 47, precedents A to D. See also the guidance in the Supreme Court Costs Office Guide 2006, sect. 3. **PD 47, paras 5.7** and **5.12** provide that a bill of costs may consist of such of the following sections as may be appropriate: **71.13**

(a) a title page;
(b) background information;
(c) items of costs claimed under the following headings:
  (i) attendances on the court and on counsel up to the date of the notice of commencement;
  (ii) attendances on and communications with the receiving party;
  (iii) attendances on and communications with witnesses including expert witnesses;
  (iv) attendances to inspect any property or place for the purposes of the proceedings;
  (v) attendances on and communications with other persons, including offices of public records;
  (vi) communications with the court and with counsel;
  (vii) work done on documents;
  (viii) attendances on and communications with London and other agents and work done by them;
  (ix) other other work done which was of or incidental to the proceedings and which is not already covered in the heads listed above.
(d) a summary showing the total costs claimed on each page of the bill;
(e) schedules of time spent on non-routine attendances; and
(f) appropriate certificates as set out in precedent F in the schedule to **PD 47**.

The bill may be divided into two or more parts to distinguish between times when the receiving party was acting in person and by different firms of solicitors, and between times before and during the continuance of legal aid (**PD 47, para. 5.8**).

Where the receiving party was represented by different legal representatives during the course of proceedings, the bill should be divided into different parts so as to distinguish between the costs payable in respect of each legal representative (**PD 47, para. 5.8(3)**). If the receiving party fails to do this, and the costs judge completes the assessment and issues a final certificate, the receiving party cannot claim a further assessment of the omitted costs (*Moat Housing Group-South Ltd v Harris (No. 2)* [2007] EWHC 3092 (QB), [2008] 1 WLR 1578). If one of the firms' costs are omitted from the bill, and the parties agree the costs in the bill, whether the bill can be amended depends on the construction of the agreement, and whether the receiving party has communicated an intention to make a later claim for the costs incurred by the other solicitors.

Each item in the bill must be consecutively numbered (**PD 47, para. 5.15**). The bill may be organised into five columns, headed 'Item', 'Amount claimed', 'VAT', with the last two left blank, but headed 'Amount allowed' and 'VAT' (**PD 47, para. 5.17** and precedents A to C).

Points of dispute

71.14 In a detailed assessment of costs the paying party and others served with the notice of commencement may dispute any item in the bill by serving all the other parties with points of dispute. Points of dispute should be short and to the point, and should follow as closely as possible precedent G in the schedule to **PD 47** (**PD 47, para. 8.2**; Supreme Court Costs Office Guide 2006, para. 5.2). They must:

(a) identify any general points or matters of principle which require decision before the individual items in the bill are addressed; and
(b) identify specific points, stating concisely the nature and grounds of the dispute.

Once a point has been made it should not be repeated, but the item numbers where the point arises should be inserted in the left hand box as shown in precedent G (**para. 8.2**). Copies of the points of dispute should also be served on other persons appearing on the statement of persons whom the receiving party intended to serve with the notice of commencement. These must be served within 21 days after service of the notice of commencement (see **CPR, r. 47.9(2)**).

Default costs certificate

71.15 If the paying party fails to serve points of dispute within the permitted time, the receiving party may, on filing a request (form N254), obtain a default costs certificate (**CPR, rr. 47.9(4)** and **47.11**; Supreme Court Costs Office Guide 2006, sect. 6), which means that all the costs in the bill are allowed. A default certificate includes an order to pay the relevant costs (**r. 47.11(2)**; see forms N255 and N255HC). The right to a default certificate is lost if the receiving party delays making the request until after the paying party serves points of dispute, albeit late. A party who serves points of dispute late will not be heard on the assessment hearing, unless the court so permits (**r. 47.9(3)**). There is a power to set aside a default costs certificate on the ground of there being good reason to do so. The court will also be concerned to see a draft of the proposed points of dispute and will take into account whether the application to set aside was made promptly (**r. 47.12; PD 47, paras 11.1** to **11.3**).

Reply

71.16 The receiving party has the right, but is not obliged, to serve a reply to any points of dispute. Any reply should be served on the party who served the points of dispute within 21 days after service (**CPR, r. 47.13**). A reply may take the form of an annotation of the points of dispute, or may be set out in a separate document (Supreme Court Costs Office Guide 2006, para 5.3(c)). Filing a reply does not avoid the receiving party's obligation under **PD 47, para 13.2(d)**, when requesting a detailed assessment hearing, to file a copy of the points of dispute annotated to show which items have been agreed and their value and to show the items still in dispute and their value.

Applications within assessment proceedings

71.17 Applications within detailed assessment proceedings, such as for time for commencing the proceedings, for extensions of time for service of points of dispute or replies, or for case management directions, are made under **CPR, Part 23** (Supreme Court Costs Office Guide 2006, sect. 17). They therefore require an application notice in form N244 and written evidence. This can be avoided if there has been a previous order made in the assessment giving 'liberty to apply', in which case it is enough to write to the court requesting the restoration of the previous application.

Provisional assessment

Provisional assessment applies to any detailed assessment proceedings commenced in the High Court or a county court on or after 1 April 2013 in which the costs claimed do not exceed £75,000 (**CPR, r. 47.15(1)** and **PD 47, para. 14.1**). **Part 47** is modified as set out in **PD 47, para.** 14.2. In these cases, when the receiving party files its request for a detailed assessment in form N258 it must also file the documents listed at **paras 8.3** and **13.2**, an additional copy of the bill, including a statement of the costs claimed in respect of the detailed assessment drawn on the assumption there will not be a hearing (which is not to exceed £1,500, **CPR, r.** 47.15(5)), and the offers made in the assessment. Part 36 offers and without prejudice offers must be in a sealed envelope marked 'Part 36 offers'. **71.18**

On receipt of these papers the court will undertake a provisional assessment of the bill (**r.** 47.15(3)), normally within six weeks. No party is permitted to attend the provisional assessment (**PD 47, para. 14.4(1)**). Once the provisional assessment has been carried out the court will return Precedent G (the points of dispute and any reply) with the court's decisions noted upon it (**para.** 14.4(2)), together with a notice stating that any party who wishes to challenge any aspect of the provisional assessment must, within 21 days of the receipt of the notice, file and serve on all other parties a written request for an oral hearing. If no such request is filed and served within that period, the provisional assessment shall be binding upon the parties, save in exceptional circumstances (**CPR, r.** 47.15(7)).

Within 14 days of receipt of Precedent G the parties must agree the total sum due to the receiving party on the basis of the court's decisions. If the parties are unable to agree the figures, they must refer the dispute back to the court for a decision on the basis of written submissions (**PD 47, para.** 14.4(2)). If a party requests an oral hearing under **CPR, r.** 45.15(7), its written request must identify the items it wishes to be reviewed, and it must provide a time estimate for the hearing (**r.** 47.15(8)). A party who requests an oral hearing will pay the costs of and incidental to the hearing unless either the costs are adjusted by at least 20 per cent in its favour or the court otherwise orders (**r.** 47.15(10)).

Assessment hearing

Once points of dispute have been served the receiving party must, within three months of the expiry of the period for commencing the detailed assessment proceedings, file a request for an assessment hearing (**CPR, r.** 47.14). If the receiving party fails to do so, the paying party may apply under **r.** 47.14(2) for an order that the receiving party must file the request within a specified period, and the court may direct that if there is a breach of that direction, the receiving party will lose all or part of the costs that would otherwise have been recoverable (**r.** 47.14(3)). There will be cases where the receiving party fails to request an assessment hearing within the three-month period, the paying party makes no application requiring a request, and the receiving party then makes a late request for the assessment hearing. In these cases, if the court is minded to impose a sanction to mark the delay in making the request, it will normally be restricted to disallowing interest (**r.** 47.14(4)). **71.19**

In publicly funded cases, unless the assisted party wishes to attend, the court will provisionally assess the costs without a hearing unless it considers a hearing is necessary (**r.** 47.18(5)). If a bill is provisionally assessed, the solicitor has 14 days after it is returned to request an assessment hearing. In cases where the assisted party wants to attend, the solicitor will certify to this effect, and the court will fix the assessment hearing (**r.** 47.18(7)).

Rights of audience at assessment hearings are considered in the Supreme Court Costs Office Guide 2006, para. 1.2. Costs draftsmen are treated as if they are in the employ of

Commentary

the firm of solicitors instructing them. Members of the Association of Law Costs Draftsmen may be certified by the Association with rights of audience (Association of Law Costs Draftsmen Order 2006 (SI 2006/3333)). The usual reluctance to allow McKenzie friends applies also to assessment hearings (para. 1.2(g)). Hearings are in public, although admitting members of the public is often impracticable as hearings are often in district judges' or costs judges' private rooms (para. 9.1(a)). Hearings are as informal as is consistent with the need to see that justice is done to all parties (para. 9.1(d)). Hearings are usually recorded (para. 9.2(a)). The court will usually consider the matters raised by the points of dispute item by item, considering the evidence and argument on an item and giving an oral decision on that item before moving on to the next item (para. 9.2(b)). Unless the court otherwise permits, only matters raised in the points of dispute may be raised at the hearing (**CPR, r. 47.14(6)**).

Assessment under the Solicitors Act 1974, part 3

71.20 The statutory provisions regulating the remuneration of solicitors in the Solicitors Act 1974, part 3, including the right to apply for a detailed assessment, are discussed at **65.7** to **65.9**. The principles on which such costs are assessed are considered at **65.18**. A claim for an order under the Solicitors Act 1974, part 3, can in all cases be issued in the SCCO (**PD 67, para. 2.1** (2)). Alternatively, a claim under part 3 can be made to the relevant county court where the costs relate to contentious business done in a county court or are within the financial limit of the county court's jurisdiction specified in the Solicitors Act 1974, s. 69(3) (**CPR, r. 67.3(1)(a)**). In every other case, proceedings under the Solicitors Act 1974, part 3, must be brought in the High Court (**CPR, r. 67.3(1)(b)**), and, if in London, in the SCCO (**PD 67, para. 2.1(1)**). A claim for an assessment must be brought under **CPR, Part 8**, by issuing a form N208, unless the application is made in existing proceedings, when the Part 23 procedure is used (**r. 67.3(2)**). In Part 8 claims under the Solicitors Act 1974, ss. 70 and 71, the court will fix a date for the hearing of the claim when the claim form is issued (**PD 67, para. 2.2A**). **Rule 8.5** on filing written evidence does not apply in uncontested cases (**PD 67, para. 4**). By **CPR, r. 67.3(3)**, a claim in the High Court may be determined by:

(a) a High Court judge (though direct application to a judge will be justified only in exceptional circumstances: **PD 67, para. 3.2**), a master, costs judge, or district judge of the Principal Registry of the Family Division, or
(b) a district judge, if the costs are for contentious business in a district registry, contentious business in a county court in the district of a district registry, or non-contentious business (**CPR, r. 67.3(3)**).

Within 28 days of an order made under the Solicitors Act 1974, part 3, for the assessment of costs payable to a solicitor by his or her client, the solicitor must serve the client with a breakdown of the costs (**CPR, r. 46.10(2)**). The client must serve points of dispute within 14 days of service of the breakdown, and the solicitor may serve a reply within 14 days thereafter (**r. 46.10(3)** and **(4)**). When points of dispute have been served, and in any event no later than three months from the date of the original order, either party may file a request for a hearing date. The provisions relating to default costs certificates do not apply to Solicitors Act 1974 assessments (**PD 46, para. 6.8**). Further detailed provisions for these cases can be found in **PD 46, paras 6.6** to **6.19**.

The costs of the detailed assessment are paid in accordance with the event (Solicitors Act 1974, s. 70(9)). If the bill is reduced by one-fifth, the solicitor must pay the costs, but otherwise the party chargeable must pay the costs of the detailed assessment, unless the order for the detailed assessment was made on the application of the solicitor and the party chargeable does not attend the assessment hearing, or the order for the detailed assessment provides otherwise (s. 70(9)).

Assessment of legal aid costs

A publicly funded party will need an order for the 'detailed assessment of [its] costs which are payable out of the [Community Legal Service Fund]' (Supreme Court Costs Office Guide 2006, para. 24.1(c); **CPR, r. 47.18(1)**). **71.21**

Where costs are payable by another person as well as out of public funds, the normal rules concerning commencing detailed assessment, points of dispute and replies apply (para. 24.2(a)). There are special forms of bills (**PD 47, Schedule of Costs Precedents, precedents C** and **D**). The request for a detailed assessment hearing must be accompanied by the relevant public funding certificates and authorities (**PD 47, para. 17.2(1)(f)**; Supreme Court Costs Office Guide 2006, para. 24.2(b)). The publicly funded party's solicitor prepares a legal aid/ LSC schedule in advance of the hearing. The assessment hearing is conducted in two parts: the first deals with the costs payable between the parties, and the second considers the public funding sections of the bill. The paying party is not normally entitled to remain in attendance for the second part (para. 24.3).

Where costs are payable only out of public funds, the publicly funded party's solicitor may request a detailed assessment within three months after the date on which the right to a detailed assessment arose. The request must be in form N258A, and must be filed with a copy of the bill of costs and the other documents listed in **PD 47, para. 17.2**. There was an unjustifiable delay of four years in lodging a bill for assessment in *Official Receiver v Dobson* (2001) LTL 30/11/2001, which the costs judge penalised under the Civil Legal Aid (General) Regulations 1989 (SI 1989/339), reg. 109, by disallowing 100 per cent of the solicitors' profit costs. On appeal this was held to be disproportionate to the default, and the order was varied by substituting a 30 per cent disallowance.

Costs of assessment

Generally, by virtue of **CPR, r. 47.20(1)**, the paying party must also pay the receiving party's costs of the assessment proceedings. This creates a rebuttable presumption that the receiving party should recover the costs of the assessment (*Bufton v Hill* [2002] EWHC 977 (QB), LTL 7/5/2002). The normal expectation is that the receiving party will be awarded its costs of the assessment (*Chrulew v Borm-Reid and Co.* [1992] 1 WLR 176, approved in *Horsford v Bird* [2006] UKPC 55, LTL 4/12/2006). Launching a successful appeal against a decision not to transfer the assessment to the Senior Courts Costs Office is not a sufficient (or any) ground for depriving the receiving party of some of the costs of an assessment (*Bufton v Hill* [2002] EWHC 977 (QB), LTL 7/5/2002). The fact that the amount allowed on the bill is substantially less than the amount claimed, without an offer to settle costs, is not in itself a sufficient reason for departing from the general rule in **r. 47.20(1)** (*Horsford v Bird*). The court will usually summarily assess the costs of detailed assessment proceedings at the conclusion of those proceedings (**r. 47.20(5)**). It is not necessary to provide details of the costs of the assessment in advance unless the court orders this to be done (Supreme Court Costs Office Guide 2006, para. 11.1). However, by **CPR, r. 47.20(3)**, the court may make some other order as to the costs of the assessment having regard to all the circumstances, including: **71.22**

(a) the conduct of all the parties;
(b) the amount, if any, by which the bill of costs is reduced; and
(c) whether it was reasonable for particular items to appear in the bill, or for particular objections to have been taken.

Part 36 offers to settle costs

The paying party may make a Part 36 offer to settle the costs in dispute in detailed assessment proceedings (**CPR, r. 47.20(4)**. For this purpose the detailed assessment proceedings are treated as an independent claim (**r. 47.20(7)**). The general provisions in **Part 36** (see **71.23**

chapter 66) apply to Part 36 offers made under **r. 47.20**, but with minor adjustments as set out in **r. 47.20(4)**. Where an offer to settle is made, whether under **Part 36** or otherwise, it should specify whether or not it is intended to be inclusive of the cost of preparing the bill, interest and VAT (**PD 47, para. 19**). Unless the offer states otherwise it will be treated as being inclusive of these items. In *Crosbie v Munroe* [2003] EWCA Civ 350, [2003] 1 WLR 2033, the claimant issued a costs-only Part 8 claim under **CPR, r. 46.14** (see **71.68**). The defendant then made an offer to settle costs, which was accepted by the claimant. It was held that the settlement related only to the costs of the substantive claim, which meant the costs of the Part 8 claim were still to be resolved.

Interest on costs

71.24 Interest on the costs of the claim normally runs from the date of the judgment or order disposing of the claim (**CPR, rr. 40.8** and **44.2(6)(g)**). Final costs certificates do not record this interest (except where enforcement is to be taken abroad). However, an application using form N244 can be made seeking a certificate of the interest that has accrued and the daily rate of future interest (Supreme Court Costs Office Guide 2006, para. 15.2). Written evidence has to justify the rate and calculation of the interest, explaining the effect of any payments on account.

Simcoe v Jacuzzi UK Group plc [2012] EWCA Civ 137, [2012] 1 WLR 2393, held that **CPR, r. 40.8(1)** is ineffective in county court proceedings because it was made without the concurrence of the Treasury, which was required by the County Courts Act 1984, s. 74. In the event it made no real difference in *Simcoe v Jacuzzi UK Group plc*, because the fallback provisions in the County Courts (Interest on Judgment Debts) Order 1991, SI 1991/1184, art. 2 produce the same answer.

Simcoe v Jacuzzi UK Group plc also holds that in both the High Court and county courts interest on orders for costs to be assessed runs from the date of the costs order (the 'incipitur date') rather than the date on which the costs are assessed or agreed (the 'allocatur date'). This is the normal rule (see at [35]), and as **CPR, r. 40.8(1)**, expressly says, can be departed from if the court otherwise orders.

Failure to adhere to time limits

71.25 There are strict time limits for commencing detailed assessment (see **71.12**). Failure to adhere to the time limits may incur sanctions. These come in two forms. Stage 1 is **CPR, r. 47.8(3)**, which provides that the receiving party's failure to commence the detailed assessment in time may lead to the loss of interest but no other sanction. Stage 2 comes into operation if the paying party seeks an order (on giving seven days' notice) requiring the receiving party to commence the detailed assessment (**PD 47, para. 7**). Here the sanction is that a failure to commence the proceedings will lead to the loss of some or all of the costs (**CPR, r. 47.8(2)**). The court must adopt a proportionate approach when exercising the power under this provision. Thus in *Q v J* [2003] EWHC 251 (Fam), LTL 14/5/2003, the receiving party failed to commence a detailed assessment but was paid £60,000 on account. After two years the paying party sought and obtained an order that unless the assessment was commenced within seven days, no further sums would be payable to the receiving party. The assessment was not commenced in time. Sumner J overturned the district judge's refusal to allow the receiving party any further costs as being too draconian, and substituted an order that the claimant receive 80 per cent of her assessed costs. (See also *Tanfern Ltd v Cameron-MacDonald* [2000] 1 WLR 1311 and **71.25**.)

Misconduct

71.26 **CPR, r. 44.11**, deals with cases where there has been a failure to conduct detailed assessment proceedings in accordance with the rules, and where the court finds that the conduct of a party or a legal representative before or during the proceedings was unreasonable or improper. The word 'unreasonable' in **r. 44.11(1)(b)** has to be construed narrowly (*Haji-Ioannou v Frangos (No. 2)* [2006] EWCA Civ 1663, [2008] 1 WLR 144; *Lahey v Pirelli Tyres Ltd* [2007] EWCA Civ 91, [2007] 1 WLR 998). Improper conduct includes steps likely to prevent or inhibit the court from furthering the overriding objective (**PD 44, para. 11.2**). In any of these cases the court has a power to disallow all or part of the costs being assessed, or to order the party or legal representative in default to pay any other party's costs incurred because of the misconduct. Before making such an order the court must give the party or legal representative a reasonable opportunity to attend a hearing and give reasons why the proposed order should not be made (**PD 44, para. 11.1**). The court's approach can be seen from three cases, *Q v J* [2003] EWHC 251 (Fam), LTL 14/5/2003, *Tanfern Ltd v Cameron-MacDonald* [2000] 1 WLR 1311 and *MacDonald v Taree Holdings Ltd* [2000] CPLR 439. In each case the court was being asked to take action that would have resulted in the successful party being deprived of all or a substantial portion of its costs. Although such an approach may have been within the ambit of the CPR, it was felt that the court had to act proportionately. Dressing up an application complaining of late commencement (see **71.25**) as an application based on misconduct, even after eight years' delay, is unlikely to be successful (*Botham v Niazi* [2004] EWHC 2602 (QB), LTL 18/11/2004). In *Haji-Ioannou v Frangos (No. 2)* [2006] EWCA Civ 1663, [2008] 1 WLR 144, it was held that the key to the apparent tension between **rr. 44.11** and **47.8** lies in the word 'misconduct'. While non-compliance with a rule, practice direction or court order is the only jurisdictional requirement before **r. 44.11** is engaged, it will usually be necessary to consider the extent of the misconduct as a matter of discretion before costs (as opposed to interest) are disallowed under **r. 44.11**. A bad breach, for example, inordinate and inexcusable delay combined with prejudice, might come into that category, whereas inordinate delay without prejudice might not. On the facts there was a five-year delay, but no prejudice, so the court only disallowed interest.

Commentary

Interim costs certificate

Although the court has a general power to order costs on account (see **CPR, rr. 44.2(8)** and **71.9**), there is also a power to issue an interim costs certificate under **r. 47.16**. This power only arises once the receiving party has lodged a request for a detailed assessment. Generally the order will require that the payment under the interim certificate will be made to the receiving party within 14 days, although there is a power to order the sum to be paid into court. Application is made on notice in the usual way in accordance with **Part 23**. The court has a general discretion and there does not have to be any agreement on the amount to be paid. In practice the court takes into account the matters revealed by the points of dispute and it is good practice to be able to tell the judge the amount that is undisputed. **71.27**

Final costs certificate

Within 14 days after the end of the detailed assessment hearing the receiving party must complete the bill and return it to the court (**CPR, r. 47.17(2)**) together with receipted fee notes and accounts (**PD 47, para. 16.4**). Once the completed bill is filed at the court, a final costs certificate, which includes an order to pay the costs to which it relates, will be served by the court on all the parties to the assessment proceedings (**CPR, r. 47.17(3)** and **(5)**). **71.28**

Appeals against assessment decisions

There are special rules dealing with appeals from decisions made by authorised court officers in detailed assessment proceedings (see **CPR, rr. 47.21** to **47.24**, and **PD 47, paras 20.1** to **20.6**). Appeals from assessment decisions by district judges, masters, costs judges, circuit judges etc. follow the usual rules for appeals described in **chapters 74** and **75**. This paragraph deals with appeals from authorised officers. These appeals are made to a costs judge or a district judge of the High Court (**CPR, r. 47.22**). There is no requirement to seek permission or **71.29** for written reasons (**PD 47, para. 20.2**). The appellant must file an appellant's notice in form N161 within 21 days after the decision appealed against (**CPR, r. 47.23(1)**). The appellant's notice should be accompanied by a suitable record of the decision appealed against (**PD 47, para. 20.5**), which may be the official transcript, or the officer's comments written on the bill, or the advocates' notes of the reasons given. On receipt of the appeal notice the court will serve copies on the parties together with notice of the appeal hearing (**CPR, r. 47.23(2)**). The appeal takes the form of a rehearing of the assessment proceedings (**r. 47.24**).

INDEMNITY PRINCIPLE

71.30 The 'indemnity principle' is that a party cannot be liable to pay more to the other side in costs than the winner is liable to pay its own lawyers. Once it is established that solicitors were acting for a receiving party there is a presumption that the client is liable to pay the solicitor, and the onus is on the paying party to rebut that presumption. In order to rebut the presumption it has to be shown there are no circumstances in which the solicitor would look to the client for payment (*Meretz Investments NV v ACP Ltd* [2007] EWHC 2635 (Ch), LTL 21/11/2007). Thus, if the lawyers representing the successful party have intimated that their client need 'not worry' about paying their fees, there is a prospect that the court will hold the loser has no liability in costs (*British Waterways Board v Norman* (1993) 26 HLR 232). However, this decision has to be compared with *Times Newspapers Ltd v Burstein* [2002] EWCA Civ 139, 28/11/2002. The receiving party's lawyers produced evidence of a valid retainer to pay their fees. In reply the paying party produced evidence to show that the receiving party was impecunious and did not have the wherewithal to pay his solicitors. The receiving party thus argued that the retainer was, in truth, an illegal CFA, that there was no valid retainer and that there was no liability on the paying party to pay his lawyers. The Court of Appeal relied on the fact that there was a retainer in rejecting the receiving party's argument.

For a short time it was thought that the indemnity principle had passed into history after the decision in *Thai Trading Co. v Taylor* [1998] QB 781. However, subsequent developments such as *Hughes v Kingston upon Hull City Council* [1999] QB 1193, *Awwad v Geraghty and Co.* [2001] QB 570, amendments made to the Solicitors' Practice Rules 1990, r. 8(1) (made pursuant to the Solicitors Act 1974, s. 31), and the Solicitors Act 1974, s. 60(3) (which provides that a client of a solicitor is not entitled to recover from any other person under an order for the payment of any costs to which a contentious business agreement relates more than the amount payable to the solicitor in respect of those costs under the agreement), have made it clear that the indemnity principle is still adhered to. The **Access to Justice Act 1999, s. 31**, amended the Senior Courts Act 1981, s 51(2), by adding that rules of court may provide that the amount awarded to a party in respect of costs need not be limited to the amount that would have been payable by the party if costs had not been awarded. This is primarily aimed at enabling the CPR to provide for a losing party to pay all the costs where the successful party has entered into a conditional fee arrangement (which was implemented by the now revoked CPR, r. 44.3A), but also permits removal of part or even the entire operation of the indemnity principle. The *Jackson Report* recommended the abolition of the indemnity principle (recommendation 4), but this has not been implemented.

A CFA in the prescribed form 'shall not be unenforceable' as being champertous (see **Courts and Legal Services Act 1990, s. 58**, as amended by the Legal Aid, Sentencing and Punishment of Offenders Act 2012). This means that CFAs that do not comply with the requirements of **s. 58** (see **6.6** to **6.9**) are unenforceable (*Times Newspapers Ltd v Burstein* [2002] EWCA Civ 1739, LTL 28/11/2002). Where a solicitor acts for an impecunious client without a CFA, if it is alleged there has been an infringement of the indemnity principle, it is necessary for the court to determine the true nature of the retainer.

Between 2 June 2003 and 31 October 2005, the Conditional Fee Agreements Regulations 2000 (SI 2000/692), reg. 3A, allowed a client to enter into a CFA with a legal representative which provided that the client would be liable to pay the lawyer's fees and expenses only if and to the extent that costs were recovered in the proceedings. This in effect abrogated the indemnity principle for this type of CFA. Predictable costs under **rr. 45.9** to **45.15** (see **70.8** to **70.15**) are not affected by the indemnity principle (*Nizami v Butt* [2006] EWHC 159 (QB), [2006] 1 WLR 3307).

If the arrangement between the solicitor and the client amounts to an unlawful agreement to conduct litigation on a contingency basis (without complying with the requirements for damages-based agreements in the Legal Aid, Sentencing and Punishment of Offenders Act 2012, s. 45, and the Damages-Based Agreements Regulations 2013, SI 2013/609), the client will not be entitled to seek an order for costs even if successful (*Hughes v Kingston upon Hull City Council* [1999] QB 1193). In *General of Berne Insurance Co. v Jardine Reinsurance Management Ltd* [1998] 1 WLR 1231 it was held that the indemnity principle has to be applied on an item-by-item basis rather than on a global basis. This means that if the client would not have been liable to pay an individual item in the solicitor's bill, it will be disallowed between the parties simply on the indemnity principle, even if the client is liable to pay the rest of the bill. In *Nederlandse Reassurantie Groep Holding NV v Bacon and Woodrow* (1998) LTL 9/6/98 it was held that the item-by-item approach applies whether or not the receiving party and its solicitor have entered into a contentious business agreement.

In *Bailey v IBC Vehicles Ltd* [1998] 3 All ER 570 it was held that the court has the power to order disclosure of documents and the provision of information to check whether the indemnity principle has been infringed, but went on to say that the jurisdiction to do so should not be over-enthusiastically deployed.

For older cases, the principle derived from *R v Miller* [1983] 1 WLR 1056 is that there is a presumption that a solicitor's client is personally liable for the costs incurred by the solicitor. The presumption can be rebutted if it is established that there is a clear express or implied agreement that the client would not have to pay the solicitor's costs in any event. Further, statements of costs and bills of costs have to be signed by the solicitor acting for the receiving party. The signature is no empty formality. It operates as a certificate by an officer of the court that the receiving party's solicitors are not seeking to recover in relation to each item more than they have agreed to charge their client (see per Henry LJ in *Bailey v IBC Vehicles Ltd* [1998] 3 All ER 570 at p. 575). The indemnity principle is not infringed where the firm invoices the client in euros, even where the costs order is in sterling (*Schlumberger Holdings Ltd v Electromagnetic Geoservices AS* [2009] EWHC 775 (Pat), LTL 16/4/2009).

Since September 1999 there has been a professional requirement that solicitors must provide a client care letter for every case setting out the charging arrangements between them and their client (see **5.3**). That letter, or any other written arrangement affecting the costs payable between solicitor and client, must be filed with the court as part of any detailed assessment if liability to pay the receiving party's solicitor is disputed by the receiving party (**PD 47, para. 13.2(i)**). For the effect of breach of these requirements see **65.6**. Further, the bill of costs used in any detailed assessment must set out a short but adequate explanation of any agreement or arrangement between the solicitor and client which affects the costs claimed against the paying party. Underlining the continuing importance of the indemnity principle, a costs budget must contain a statement of truth which must be signed by a senior legal representative of the party in the form set out in **PD 22, para. 2.2A**, which includes a statement to the effect that the costs incurred do not exceed the costs the client is liable to pay.

Proving infringement of the indemnity principle

If the issue of whether the indemnity principle has been infringed is raised, the receiving party can ask the costs judge to rule on whether there is a genuine issue. If not, that is the end of the **71.31** matter. If a genuine issue is raised (or the receiving party accepts that a genuine issue is raised without asking for a ruling on this preliminary point), the costs judge will have to rule on whether the indemnity principle has in fact been infringed. This will almost certainly require the receiving party to adduce documents such as the client care letter, the terms of any retainer contract, and any bills sent to the client. **PD 47, para. 13.13**, and the Supreme Court Costs Office Guide 2006, s. 10, provide that the court may direct the receiving party to produce any document which, in the opinion of the court, is necessary to enable it to reach its decision. These documents will in the first instance be produced to the court, but the court may ask the receiving party to elect whether to disclose the particular document to the paying party in order to rely on the contents of the document, or whether to decline disclosure and instead rely on other evidence.

Where there is a substantial dispute about whether the indemnity principle has been infringed and/or whether confidential documents should be produced, it may be appropriate to seek directions for split hearing dates or times (Supreme Court Costs Office Guide, para. 10.5).

Costs of pro bono representation

71.32 Under the Legal Services Act 2007, s. 194(3), the court may order any person to make a payment to the prescribed charity in respect of pro bono representation of a party. The prescribed charity is the Access to Justice Foundation (s. 194(8); Legal Services Act 2007 (Prescribed Charity) Order 2008 (SI 2008/2680)). In considering whether to order a payment to the prescribed charity, and the terms of such an order, the court must have regard to whether it would, apart from s. 194, have made an order in favour of the party with the pro bono representation and the terms of the order it would have made (s. 194(4)). Such an order cannot be made in respect of representation before 1 October 2008 (s. 194(11)). Nor can it be made against another person with pro bono representation, or a person with public funding (s. 194(6)).

An order under s. 194(3) must be for fixed costs where **CPR, Part 45**, would otherwise apply (**r. 46.7(1)(a)**). Where **Part 45** does not apply, the court may by **r. 46.7(1)(b)** determine the amount of the payment (other than a sum equivalent to fixed costs) to be made by the paying party to the prescribed charity by:

(a) making a summary assessment; or
(b) making an order for detailed assessment,

of a sum equivalent to all or part of the costs the paying party would have been ordered to pay to the party with pro bono representation in respect of that representation had it not been provided free of charge.

Under **PD 44, para. 9.2** and **PD 46, para. 4.1**, the general rule is that the court will make a summary assessment of costs in the circumstances unless there is good reason not to do so. To assist the court in making a summary assessment of the amount payable to the prescribed charity, the party who has pro bono representation must prepare, file and serve, in accordance with **PD 44, para. 9.5(2)**, a written statement of costs of the sum equivalent to the costs that party would have claimed for that legal representation had it not been provided free of charge (**PD 46, para. 4.1**).

Where there is an order for detailed assessment and the receiving party had pro bono representation for part only of the proceedings, the bill of costs must be divided into different parts to differentiate between the different periods of funding (**PD 47, para. 5.8**). The bill of costs must not include a claim for VAT in respect of the pro bono costs (**PD 44, para. 2.14**).

An order under the Legal Services Act 2007, s. 194(3), must specify that the payment by the paying party must be made to the prescribed charity (**r. 46.7**). The receiving party is required to keep the prescribed charity informed by sending it copies of relevant orders and certificates (**r. 46.7(3)**, order under s. 194(3); **r. 47.11(4)**, default costs certificate; **r. 47.12(3)**, order setting aside or varying default costs certificate; **r. 47.17(6)**, final costs certificate).

Documents and information relating to funding

In *Dickinson v Rushmer* (2002) 152 NLJ 58 it was held that if confidential documents are shown to the costs judge, they should also be disclosed to the paying party. Alternatively, the receiving party can maintain legal professional privilege in these documents, and rely on secondary evidence of the retainer (although this might be difficult or impossible if the assessment hearing is being dealt with by a costs draftsman). In *South Coast Shipping Co. Ltd v Havant Borough Council* [2002] 3 All ER 779 Pumfrey J said that in the great majority of cases the paying party would be content to agree that the costs judge alone should see privileged documents, and it is only where it is necessary and proportionate that the receiving party should be put to an election whether to allow privileged documents to be disclosed to the paying party. In *Giambrone v JMC Holidays Ltd* [2002] EWHC 495 (QB), LTL 25/3/2002, it was held the costs judge had been wrong not to follow **PD 47, para. 13.13**, the costs judge having ordered the receiving party's solicitor to serve a witness statement on the paying party exhibiting the relevant documents on whether the indemnity principle had been infringed, as this deprived the receiving party of the right to claim privilege in the documents. **71.33**

In *Hutchings v British Transport Police Authority* [2006] EWHC 90064 (Costs) (BAILII), LTL 4/12/2006, there was no evidence the receiving party had BTE insurance. There was a complete statement of prior advice which said there was none, which was repeated in the correspondence. The paying party raised a request for further information under **CPR, Part 18**, containing 13 questions aimed at discovering whether, despite the signature on the bill, there was in fact BTE cover available to the receiving party. The district judge regarded the whole exercise as a fishing expedition. On appeal it was held:

(a) The starting point is the overriding objective and deprecating satellite litigation over costs issues.
(b) A paying party is entitled to know the case against it and to challenge items felt unreasonable or disproportionate.
(c) It was permissible to ask by way of a request for further information:
  (i) Do you have insurance?
  (ii) With whom?
  (iii) Do you have any legal expenses insurance?

Any other points that the paying party may want to raise should be by way of points of dispute, not a request for further information.

Similarly, in *Arroyo v BP Exploration Co. (Colombia) Ltd* (2010) LTL 4/6/2010, a request for further information for the disclosure of the claimant's ATE cover was refused, and disclosure of the ATE policy was held to fall outside both standard disclosure and 'train of inquiry' disclosure, and was in any event privileged.

CFAs and the indemnity principle

Even after the abolition of recoverability of success fees and additional liabilities connected with CFAs with effect from 1 April 2013, it is still open to a paying party to argue that infringements of the requirements as to form of CFAs (discussed in **chapter 6**) render the retainer illegal with the result that there was no payment obligation on the CFA-funded client, and hence no costs liability on the unsuccessful party by reason of the indemnity principle (see **71.30**). A number of related issues were brought together in *Hollins v Russell* [2003] EWCA Civ 718, [2003] 1 WLR 2487. The Court of Appeal came to the following conclusions: **71.34**

(a) The presumption that the bill is accurate afforded by the solicitor's signature on the bill does not apply where the point of substance relates to compliance with the legal requirements for an effective CFA.

Commentary

(b) The funding agreement is a privileged document and its production cannot be compelled. However, on a standard-basis assessment, the receiving party will have to show compliance. Thus in practice the CFA will normally be produced, suitably redacted if it contains sensitive commercial information. Other memoranda and documents should not generally be produced. Partial disclosure in accordance with *Hollins v Russell* is difficult to justify, unless it is regarded as a limited waiver (see **50.73**).
(c) Not every breach of the Regulations will lead to a breach of the indemnity principle. The costs judge should ask the following question:

Has the particular departure from a regulation or requirement in the Courts and Legal Services Act 1990, s. 58, either on its own or in conjunction with any other such departure in this case, had a materially adverse effect either upon the protection afforded to the client or upon the proper administration of justice?

(d) Even where the indemnity principle does work in favour of the paying party, disbursements and any insurance premium will still be payable.
(e) Costs officers must be astute to ensure that issues over the indemnity principle do not develop into time-consuming and expensive satellite litigation (*Times Newspapers Ltd v Burstein* [2002] EWCA Civ 139, LTL 28/11/2002).

BASIS OF QUANTIFICATION

The two bases

71.35 Costs may be quantified either on the standard or the indemnity basis. Under the old system there was a twofold test to be applied when deciding whether to allow costs on either basis. Costs would only be recoverable if, first, they were reasonably incurred and secondly, to the extent that they were reasonable in amount. These concepts were approached from opposite directions under the two different bases, with doubts resolved in favour of the paying party on the standard basis, and in favour of the receiving party under the indemnity basis. Under the CPR it still is necessary to consider both whether individual items of costs should have been incurred, and whether they should be allowed in full or reduced. However, to tie in with the overriding objective, on an assessment on the standard basis the court is required to consider not only concepts of reasonableness, but also of proportionality.

Standard basis

71.36 On an assessment on the standard basis, **CPR, r. 44.3(2)**, provides that the court will:
(a) only allow costs which are proportionate to the matters in issue. Costs which are disproportionate in amount may be disallowed or reduced even if they were reasonably or necessarily incurred; and
(b) resolve any doubt which it may have about whether costs were reasonably and proportionately incurred or were reasonable and proportionate in amount in favour of the paying party.

Principles for determining reasonableness

71.37 In deciding whether costs were reasonably incurred or were reasonable and proportionate in amount, the court is to have regard to all the circumstances. Under the old system the court was assisted in this task by what were called the 'seven pillars', which included the complexity of the item or the action, and the difficulty or novelty of the questions involved. The 'seven pillars' were set out in RSC, ord. 62, appendix 2, para. 1. In the **CPR, r. 44.4(3)** provides for eight matters to be taken into account. They echo the former position, but have been expanded to include the conduct of the parties before as well as during the proceedings (and thus take into account compliance, or otherwise, with any applicable pre-action protocol) and their efforts to resolve the dispute. The matters to be taken into account omit the old third pillar, which required the court to have regard to the number and importance of the documents prepared or perused. However, time spent on documentation can still be charged for as is plain from **PD 47, para. 5.12(7)**, which includes work on documents. Any costs budgets will be taken into account under **CPR, r. 44.4(3)(h)**, as more fully explained at **43.16** to **43.19**.

A costs judge has the power to disallow entire sections of costs if they are held to be 'unreasonably incurred', or to reduce items to reasonable amounts, which is a sufficient safeguard against excess in most circumstances. Where there has been unreasonable or improper conduct, the costs judge also has the powers described at **71.26**. However, a costs judge does not have jurisdiction to vary a costs order, even one deemed to be made after acceptance of an offer to settle under **CPR, Part 36**, by making a percentage reduction in the costs payable before starting a detailed assessment (*Lahey v Pirelli Tyres Ltd* [2007] EWCA Civ 91, [2007] 1 WLR 998).

Proportionality

One of the main aims of the CPR is to provide a system of civil justice which is affordable and proportionate to the importance of the claim. The overriding objective requires the court to deal with claims justly and at proportionate cost. This includes ensuring claims are conducted in ways that will save expense and which are proportionate to the nature of the case (**CPR, r. 1.1(2)**). The parties are required to cooperate in achieving this aim, which means they must conduct themselves in ways that do not involve unnecessary costs, or costs which are not really justified by the nature or importance of the claim. The court will not give its approval to disproportionate or unreasonable costs (see **PD 44, para. 9.10**). **71.38**

Former guidance on the practice to be adopted when deciding whether costs are proportionate on standard basis assessments given in *Lownds v Home Office* [2002] EWCA Civ 365, [2002] 1 WLR 2450 (see **71.39**) has been swept away by the amendments to what are now **CPR, rr. 44.3** and **44.4** made with effect from 1 April 2013. The new proportionality test applies to claims commenced on or after 1 April 2013 (see **71.35** and **71.40**). For cases governed by the new rule, cases like *Hoare v United Kingdom* (application 16261/08) (2011) 53 EHRR SE1, which said at [60] that costs of £770,000 in a personal injury claim arising out of criminal conduct were described as substantial but not unreasonable, can no longer be relied upon.

Pre-1 April 2013 proportionality test

The discussion in **71.39** applies to claims commenced before 1 April 2013, and references here are to the provisions of the CPR and practice directions in force immediately before that day. In a case where proportionality is an issue, a preliminary judgment on the proportionality of the costs as a whole should be made at the outset. This is done having particular regard to the factors in CPR, r. 44.5(3). If the judge concludes that the costs are not disproportionate, the various items of costs are then considered one by one, applying the reasonableness tests in r. 44.4(2). If the judge concludes that the costs as a whole may be disproportionate, each item will be scrutinised applying both the reasonableness and necessity tests (for the latter, see below). A failure to follow the two-stage process laid down in *Lownds v Home Office* resulted in the assessment being set aside in *Morgan v Spirit Group Ltd* [2011] EWCA Civ 68, [2011] PIQR P9. **71.39**

In applying the test of proportionality on a standard-basis assessment under **r. 44.4(2)**, it is said in PD 43–48, para. 11.1, that the relationship between the total costs incurred and the financial value of the claim is not always a reliable guide. Still less can the court simply apply a fixed percentage to the value of the claim and say that any costs above that percentage are disproportionate (para. 11.1).

The key to proportionality, according to the Court of Appeal in *Lownds v Home Office* [2002] EWCA Civ 365, [2002] 1 WLR 2450 at [26] to [28], was to be found in PD 43–48, para 11.2, which stated that: 'In any proceedings there will be costs which will inevitably be incurred and which are *necessary* for the successful conduct of the case' (emphasis added). If the appropriate conduct of the proceedings made costs necessary then the requirement of proportionality did not prevent recovery of those costs. The threshold required to meet necessity was higher than that of reasonableness, but Lord Woolf CJ in *Lownds v Home Office* at [37] said it was still a standard which a competent solicitor should be able to achieve without undue difficulty, and the courts should be careful not to impose too high a standard with the benefit of hindsight. Solicitors were not obliged to conduct litigation at uneconomic rates, which meant that in modest claims the proportion of costs was likely to be higher than in larger claims (PD 43–48, para. 11.2). The time spent on an issue at trial may not be an accurate guide to the amount of time properly spent in preparing that issue for trial (para. 11.3). The court would have regard to whether the appropriate level of fee earner and counsel were employed, whether offers to settle had been made, whether unnecessary experts had been instructed, and the other matters set out in CPR, r. 44.5(3). Regard should also be had to the amount which it was reasonable for the receiving party to believe might be recovered. For a claimant this was the sum it was reasonable for him to believe he might recover at the time the claim was made (*Lownds v Home Office* at [39]). For a defendant this was likely to be the sum claimed. In deciding what was necessary, the paying party's conduct was highly relevant, because cooperation can reduce costs, and being uncooperative can increase costs.

Counsel spending 12 days preparing for a striking-out application was regarded as being disproportionate in *Orwin v British Coal Corporation* [2003] EWHC 757 (Ch), LTL 24/4/2003, and the fee was reduced by two-thirds. Costs of £770,000 in a personal injury claim arising out of criminal conduct were described as substantial but not unreasonable in *Hoare v United Kingdom* (application 16261/08) (2011) 53 EHRR SE1 at [60].

Proportionality from 1 April 2013

71.40 For claims commenced from 1 April 2013 proportionality is defined in CPR, r. 44.3(5), as follows:

Costs incurred are proportionate if they bear a reasonable relationship to—
(a) the sums in issue in the proceedings;
(b) the value of any non-monetary relief in issue in the proceedings;
(c) the complexity of the litigation;
(d) any additional work generated by the conduct of the paying party; and
(e) any wider factors involved in the proceedings, such as reputation or public importance.

On a standard basis assessment the court will not allow costs which have been unreasonably incurred or are unreasonable in amount (r. 44.3(1)). A key amendment made with effect from 1 April 2013 to r. 44.3(2)(a) (see 71.35), is that costs which are disproportionate in amount may be disallowed or reduced even if they were reasonably or necessarily incurred. Also new is the reference to proportionality in resolving doubts in r. 44.3(2)(b). 'Proportionality' under the new r. 44.3(2) is intended to come into play on those occasions when an assessment of 'reasonable' costs will result in an excessive figure. As stated in the *Jackson Report* at ch. 40, para. 7.22, in essence proportionality trumps reasonableness.

A deliberate decision has been made not to elaborate on the new proportionality test by including detailed guidance in the relevant practice direction. As stated in the third implementation lecture at para. 2.1, the rule as drafted is sufficiently clear. Simplicity is felt to promote certainty and the avoidance of technical satellite litigation (para. 2.3, and which is part of the purpose behind recommendation 2 of the *Jackson Report*).

Operation of the new proportionality test

This was discussed in the third implementation lecture at para. 2.2. What Sir Rupert Jackson envisaged was that the proportionality test would be applied in different ways in different situations. They may be categorised as follows: 71.41

(a) Cases where it is obvious at the outset that the costs claimed are proportionate. In these cases the only issue to consider under **CPR, r. 44.3** is the reasonableness of the individual items on the bill of costs.
(b) Cases where it is obvious from the outset that the costs claimed are disproportionate. In these cases the costs judge will have to consider the reasonableness of each item on the bill. The judge will also have to consider how to reduce the bill to a proportionate level. This may be achieved by reducing particular items, or by reducing the overall total to reach a proportionate figure.
(c) Borderline cases where it is unclear whether the bill is disproportionate until after the costs judge has dealt with the reasonableness of the individual items in the bill. In these cases the costs judge should not be constrained, whether by a practice direction or anything else, on how to approach the task of ensuring the costs allowed are both reasonable and proportionate.

Commentary

Case planning

Increasingly the courts are expecting to see evidence of case planning. The aspiration was set out in *Jefferson v National Freight Carriers plc* [2001] EWCA Civ 2082, LTL 4/10/2001, when Lord Woolf CJ cited with approval the following extract of the trial judge's comments: 71.42

> In modern litigation, with the emphasis on proportionality, it is necessary for parties to make an assessment at the outset of the likely value of the claim and its importance and complexity, and then to plan in advance the necessary work, the appropriate level of person to carry out the work, the overall time that would be necessary and [the] appropriate spend on various stages in bringing the action to trial, and the likely overall cost. While it was not unusual for costs to exceed the amount in issue, it was, in the context of modern litigation such as the present case, one reason for seeking to curb the amount of work done, and the cost by reference to the need for proportionality.

It follows that the courts are increasingly expecting to see evidence that the issue of costs and proportionality was addressed at the outset of the case rather than the amount of costs simply developing as the case progressed. Consideration of the costs budgets and reference to a case plan will assist the judge in deciding on how the case should be managed (see **CPR, r. 3.17**) and whether the costs are proportionate for the purposes of **r. 44.3**.

Costs based on track appropriate for trial result

A costs judge is not permitted to reopen the costs order made by the trial judge or recorded in an interim or consent order (*O'Beirne v Hudson* [2010] EWCA Civ 52, [2010] 1 WLR 1717 at [16]; *Drew v Whitbread plc* [2010] EWCA Civ 53, [2010] 1 WLR 1725, and see the discussion at **68.4**). If the costs order provides for assessment on the standard basis, it is therefore not open to the costs judge to conduct the assessment of costs on the small claims track basis (*O'Beirne v Hudson*), or on the fast track basis (with fixed fast track trial costs) if the claim has been allocated to the multi-track (*Drew v Whitbread plc*). 71.43

While the costs judge is not permitted to rewrite the costs order in the manner described in the previous paragraph, the costs judge is entitled to take into account all the circumstances of the case (**CPR, r. 44.4(1)**), which may include the fact that the claim 'would almost certainly have been allocated to the small claims track if it had been allocated' (**r. 46.13(3)**; *O'Beirne v Hudson* per Waller LJ at [16]). At that stage the costs judge may consider whether it was reasonable for the paying party to pay the costs of a lawyer. The costs judge would not be bound to disallow the costs of retaining a lawyer, but the fact the claim would have been allocated to the small claims track is a highly material circumstance in deciding what to allow on the assessment (*O'Beirne v Hudson* per Waller LJ at [17]). In making that decision the costs judge should give the items on the bill very anxious scrutiny to see whether the costs of each item were necessarily or reasonably incurred, and thus whether it is reasonable for the paying party to pay more than would be recoverable in a case that was allocated to the small claims track (*O'Beirne v Hudson* per Waller LJ at [19] and [22]).

An apparently similar approach was taken in *Drew v Whitbread plc* in relation to a case which had been allocated to the multi-track, but where the damages awarded at trial were less than the multi-track threshold. It is not permissible to assess costs on the fast track basis in such a case, because that would be rescinding an order that provided for the assessment of standard-basis costs. However, if the claim 'was in reality a fast track case' (see *Drew v Whitbread plc* at [39]), it may be reasonable to allow only fast track fixed trial costs. The difficulty with the application of this principle in *Drew v Whitbread plc* is that, unlike *O'Beirne v Hudson*, in this case there was an order allocating the case to the multi-track. While the approach of the Court of Appeal may avoid rescinding the trial judge's order for costs, it is hard to see how it is not rescinding the procedural judge's allocation order. This would only be permissible if there had been a material change of circumstances, pursuant to **r. 3.1(7)**.

A similar case of quasi-revisiting of the track allocation decision is *Morgan v Spirit Group Ltd* [2011] EWCA Civ 68, [2011] PIQR P9, see **71.6**, where judgment was given for £14,000 in a claim valued at £40,000. These cases may be seen as a welcome discipline for claimants who may be tempted to overvalue their claims for costs reasons. It is submitted that the cases are in fact unprincipled (because they directly or indirectly overturn allocation decisions in the absence of an appeal), and are likely to give rise to further satellite litigation. Values given to claims at the allocation stage are given before disclosure and the exchange of witness and expert evidence. Allocation decisions should stand or fall based on the evidence available at that time, rather than on the fuller evidence available at trial. Deciding that an allocation decision can be circumvented because 'it almost certainly' would or should have been made differently invites a contest between the parties, possibly with the need to adduce evidence of the state of knowledge of the value of the claim of at least the claimant's solicitors at the date of allocation. Instead, inflation of a claim for track allocation purposes should be dealt with under **r. 44.2(5)(d)**, which covers exaggeration, or, if the costs are out of proportion to the value of the claim, by applying the proportionality rules discussed at **71.40**.

Indemnity basis

71.44 On an assessment on the indemnity basis there is no reference to proportionality, and any doubts on whether costs were reasonably incurred or were reasonable in amount is resolved in favour of the receiving party (**CPR, r. 44.3(3)**).

Choice of basis

71.45 Costs orders should identify the intended basis of quantification. Unless the phrase 'indemnity basis' is used, quantification will be on the standard basis (**CPR, r. 44.3(4)**). Inclusion of the word 'reasonable' in an order that provides for payment of the claimant's 'reasonable costs and disbursements on the standard basis' adds nothing, and the assessment is simply on the standard basis (*O'Beirne v Hudson* [2010] EWCA Civ 52, [2010] 1 WLR 1717). The usual rule in contentious litigation is that costs are payable on the standard basis. Indemnity basis costs are normally used only where there is some misconduct deserving such a course (*Reid Minty v Taylor* [2001] EWCA Civ 1723, [2002] 1 WLR 2800). Parties who act in the capacity of trustee, personal representative or mortgagee are in general entitled to costs on the indemnity basis, but the court may order otherwise if the party has acted otherwise than for the benefit of the fund (**r. 46.3**).

Assessments between solicitor and own client (other than in publicly funded cases and where there is a conditional fee agreement) are by virtue of r. 46.9 dealt with on the indemnity basis, but subject to the following presumptions:

(a) that costs were reasonably incurred if they were incurred with the express or implied approval of the client;
(b) that costs were reasonable in amount if the amount was expressly or impliedly approved by the client; and
(c) that costs were unreasonably incurred if they are unusual in nature or amount and the solicitor did not tell the client that for that reason they might not be recoverable from the other side.

AMOUNT TO BE ALLOWED

Hourly rates

71.46 Before the Woolf reforms, one of the most common methods for computing the cost of a solicitor's time in conducting litigation was to apply the direct cost to the firm of the fee earner engaged in the matter to the amount of time spent, and then to add a 'mark-up' to reflect imponderable factors, such as general supervision, skill, responsibility and commercial profit. Most county courts developed conventional hourly rates for their courts, which were sometimes refined by applying different hourly rates to different grades of fee earners. It was extremely difficult to persuade a district judge to depart from the conventional figures for his or her court. However, in theory different rates could be applied if an individual firm could show the direct cost for its fee earners was different from the conventional rate. The mark-up percentage could vary for different items on the bill. In *Johnson v Reed Corrugated Cases Ltd* [1992] 1 All ER 169 it was suggested that an uplift starting at 50 per cent was appropriate for ordinary cases, and in *Brush v Bower Cotton and Bower* [1993] 1 WLR 1328 it was suggested that 35 per cent was the appropriate uplift for interim applications where the solicitor sat behind counsel. For more complex cases higher levels of mark-up were appropriate, up to 100 or even 120 per cent for complex commercial or clinical dispute claims. Non-straightforward interim applications dealt with by a solicitor without the assistance of counsel might justify a mark-up of 60 per cent or more.

The modern approach is to apply a single hourly rate to the work done by the solicitor. Clients find this less confusing, and, by applying a suitable rate, it is not difficult to find a figure which provides the same rate of remuneration as the old system of direct cost plus mark-up. It is also the modern approach to provide different rates for different grades of fee earner.

Category of fee earner

71.47 Her Majesty's Courts and Tribunals Service has published guideline hourly rates for the summary assessment of costs. They are commonly used in detailed assessments as well. The rates have a built-in 50 per cent uplift (*Various Ledward Claimants v Kent and Medway Health Authority* [2003] EWHC 2551 (QB), LTL 4/11/2003). Various locations in England and Wales have been divided into three bands (see **table 71.2**), and different hourly rates have been laid down (from January 2003, and with inflation-related revisions from January 2005, January 2007 and January 2009) for four grades of fee-earner (see **table 71.3**). There is a separate table of guideline rates for London-based firms (see **table 71.4**). The figures given in **tables 71.3** and **71.4** are guidelines, and it is open to the designated civil judge to lay down more exact guidelines for rates in his area. It is also open for a firm to seek to establish a different rate (either generally or for individual claims where the notional 50 per cent uplift is inappropriate), and for this purpose the costs estimate for the paying party may be relevant evidence (see further at **71.48**).

Table 71.2 Solicitors' hourly rates: areas covered by the three provincial bands

Band one (January 2003)

Aldershot, Farnham, Bournemouth; Birmingham Inner; Cambridge City Centre; Canterbury, Maidstone, Medway and Tunbridge Wells; Cardiff (Inner); Kingston, Guildford, Reigate, Epsom; Leeds Inner (within 1 km of the City Art Gallery); Lewes; Liverpool, Birkenhead; Manchester Central; Newcastle City Centre (within 2 miles of St Nicholas Cathedral); Norwich; Nottingham City; Southampton, Portsmouth; Swindon, Basingstoke.

Band two (January 2003)

Bath, Cheltenham and Gloucester; Bristol; Bury; Chelmsford North, Cambridge County, Peterborough, Bury St Edmunds, Norfolk; Essex and East Suffolk; Lowestoft; Chelmsford South; Hampshire, Dorset, Wiltshire, Isle of Wight; Hull (City); Leeds Outer, Wakefield and Pontefract; Leigh; Luton, Bedford, St Albans, Hitchin and Hertford; Manchester Outer, Oldham, Bolton, Tameside; Milton Keynes and Aylesbury; Oxford (Inner/Outer), Reading, Slough; Sheffield and South Yorkshire; Southport; St Helens; Stockport, Altrincham, Salford; Swansea, Newport, Cardiff (Outer); Watford; Wigan; York, Harrogate.

Band three (January 2003)

Accrington, Burnley, Blackburn, Rawtenstall and Nelson; Birmingham Outer; Bradford (Dewsbury, Halifax, Huddersfield, Keighley and Skipton); Chester and North Wales; Coventry, Rugby, Nuneaton, Stratford and Warwick; Cumbria; Devon, Cornwall, Exeter, Taunton and Yeovil; Grimsby; Hull Outer; Kidderminster; Lincoln; Newcastle (other than City Centre); Northampton and Leicester; Nottingham and Derbyshire; Plymouth; Preston, Lancaster, Blackpool, Chorley; Scarborough and Ripon; South and West Wales; Stafford, Stoke, Tamworth; Teesside; Trowbridge; Weston-super-Mare; Wolverhampton, Walsall, Dudley and Stourbridge; Worcester, Hereford, Evesham and Redditch; Shrewsbury, Telford, Ludlow, Oswestry.

Band one (January 2005 and January 2007)

Aldershot, Farnham, Bournemouth (including Poole); Birmingham Inner; Bristol; Cambridge City, Harlow; Canterbury, Maidstone, Medway and Tunbridge Wells; Cardiff (Inner); Chelmsford South, Essex and East Suffolk; Fareham, Winchester; Hampshire, Dorset, Wiltshire, Isle of Wight; Kingston, Guildford, Reigate, Epsom; Leeds Inner (within 2 km of the City Art Gallery); Lewes; Liverpool, Birkenhead; Manchester Central; Newcastle City Centre (within 2 miles of St Nicholas Cathedral); Norwich City; Nottingham City; Oxford, Thames Valley; Southampton, Portsmouth; Swindon, Basingstoke; Watford.

Band two (January 2005 and January 2007)

Bath, Cheltenham and Gloucester, Taunton, Yeovil; Bury; Chelmsford North, Cambridge County, Peterborough, Bury St Edmunds, Norfolk, Lowestoft; Chester and North Wales; Coventry, Rugby, Nuneaton, Stratford and Warwick; Exeter, Plymouth; Hull (City); Leeds Outer, Wakefield and Pontefract; Leigh; Lincoln; Luton, Bedford, St Albans, Hitchin, Hertford; Manchester Outer, Oldham, Bolton, Tameside; Newcastle (other than City Centre); Nottingham and Derbyshire; Sheffield, Doncaster and South Yorkshire; Southport; St Helens; Stockport, Altrincham, Salford; Swansea, Newport, Cardiff (Outer); Wigan; Wolverhampton, Walsall, Dudley and Stourbridge; York, Harrogate.

Band three (January 2005 and January 2007)

Birmingham Outer; Bradford (Dewsbury, Halifax, Huddersfield, Keighley and Skipton); Cumbria; Devon, Cornwall; Grimsby, Skegness; Hull Outer; Kidderminster; Northampton and Leicester; Preston, Lancaster, Blackpool, Chorley, Accrington, Burnley, Blackburn, Rawtenstall and Nelson; Scarborough and Ripon; Stafford, Stoke, Tamworth; Teesside; Worcester, Hereford, Evesham and Redditch; Shrewsbury, Telford, Ludlow, Oswestry; South and West Wales.

Band one (January 2008)

Aldershot, Farnham, Bournemouth (including Poole); Birmingham Inner; Bristol; Cambridge City, Harlow; Canterbury, Maidstone, Medway and Tunbridge Wells; Cardiff (Inner); Chelmsford South, Essex, East Suffolk; Chester; Fareham, Winchester; Hampshire, Dorset, Wiltshire, Isle of Wight; Kingston, Guildford, Reigate, Epsom; Leeds Inner (within 2 km of the City Art Gallery); Lewes; Liverpool, Birkenhead; Manchester Central; Newcastle — City Centre (within 2 miles of St Nicholas Cathedral); Norwich City; Nottingham City; Oxford, Thames Valley; Southampton, Portsmouth; Swindon, Basingstoke; Watford

Band two (January 2008)

Bath, Cheltenham and Gloucester, Taunton, Yeovil; Bury; Chelmsford North, Cambridge County, Peterborough, Bury St Edmunds, Norfolk, Lowestoft; Cheshire and North Wales; Coventry, Rugby, Nuneaton, Stratford and Warwick; Exeter, Plymouth; Hull (City); Leeds Outer, Wakefield and Pontefract; Leigh; Lincoln; Luton, Bedford, St Albans, Hitchin, Hertford; Manchester Outer, Oldham, Bolton, Tameside; Newcastle (other than City Centre); Nottingham and Derbyshire; Sheffield, Doncaster and South Yorkshire; Southport; St Helens; Stockport, Altrincham, Salford; Swansea, Newport, Cardiff (Outer); Wigan; Wolverhampton, Walsall, Dudley and Stourbridge; York, Harrogate

Band three (January 2008)

Birmingham Outer; Bradford (Dewsbury, Halifax, Huddersfield, Keighley and Skipton); Cumbria; Devon, Cornwall; Grimsby, Skegness; Hull Outer; Kidderminster; Northampton and Leicester; Preston, Lancaster, Blackpool, Chorley, Accrington, Burnley, Blackburn, Rawtenstall and Nelson; Scarborough and Ripon; Stafford, Stoke, Tamworth; Teesside; Worcester, Hereford, Evesham and Redditch; Shrewsbury, Telford, Ludlow, Oswestry; South and West Wales

Table 71.3 Guideline hourly charging rates

	Grade			
	A	B	C	D
Band one				
January 2003	175	155	130	95
January 2005	184	163	137	100
January 2007	195	173	145	106
January 2008	203	180	151	110
January 2009	213	189	158	116
1 April 2010	217*	192	161	118
Band two				
January 2003	165	145	120	90
January 2005	173	152	126	95
January 2007	183	161	133	101
January 2008	191	168	139	105
January 2009	198	174	144	109
1 April 2010	201*	177	146	111
Band three				
January 2003	150	135	115	85
January 2005	158	142	121	90
January 2007	167	150	128	95
January 2008	174	156	133	99
January 2009	198	174	144	109
1 April 2010	201*	177	146	111

* An hourly rate in excess of the guideline figures may be appropriate for Grade A fee earners in substantial and complex litigation where other factors, including the value of the litigation, the level of complexity, the urgency or importance of the matter as well as any international element would justify a significantly higher rate to reflect higher average costs.

Table 71.4 London hourly rates

	Grade A	B	C	D
London 1				
City of London Jan 2003	342*	247	189	116
City of London Jan 2005 EC1, EC2, EC3, EC4	359	259	198	122
City of London Jan 2007 EC1, EC2, EC3, EC4	380	274	210	129
City of London Jan 2008 EC1, EC2, EC3, EC4	396	285	219	134
City of London Jan 2009	402	291	222	136
City of London 1 April 2010 EC1, EC2, EC3, EC4	409*	296	226	138
London 2				
Central London Jan 2003	263	200	163	105
Central London Jan 2005 W1, WC1, WC2, SW1	276	210	171	110
Central London Jan 2007 W1, WC1, WC2, SW1	292	222	181	116
Central London Jan 2008 W1, WC1, WC2, SW1	304	231	189	121
Central London Jan 2009	312	238	193	124
Central London 1 April 2010 W1, WC1, WC2, SW1	317*	242	196	126
Outer London Jan 2003 (including Bromley, Croydon, Dartford, Gravesend, Uxbridge)	189–221	142–189	137	100
Outer London Jan 2005 (All other London postcodes: W, NW, N, E, SE, SW and Bromley, Croydon, Dartford, Gravesend and Uxbridge)	198–232	149–198	144	105
Outer London Jan 2008 (All other London postcodes: W, NW, N, E, SE, SW and Bromley, Croydon, Dartford, Gravesend and Uxbridge)	219–256	165–219	158	116
Outer London Jan 2009	225–263	169–255	162	119
Outer London 1 April 2010 (All other London postcodes: W, NW, N, E, SE, SW and Bromley, Croydon, Dartford Gravesend and Uxbridge)	229–267*	172–229	165	121

* An hourly rate in excess of the guideline figures may be appropriate for Grade A fee earners in substantial and complex litigation where other factors, including the value of the litigation, the level of complexity, the urgency or importance of the matter as well as any international element would justify a significantly higher rate to reflect higher average costs.

The four grades of fee earner are:

A Solicitors with over eight years' post-qualification experience including at least eight years' litigation experience.

B Solicitors and legal executives (i.e. fellows of the Chartered Institute of Legal Executives) with over four years' post-qualification experience including at least four years' litigation experience.

C Other solicitors and legal executives and fee earners of equivalent experience.

D Trainee solicitors, paralegals and fee earners of equivalent experience.

Fee earners who are not fellows of the Chartered Institute of Legal Executives are not entitled to call themselves legal executives. Unqualified clerks may fall into grades B, C or D depending on their experience. Legal executives generally spend two years in a solicitor's office before passing their Part 1 general examinations, then take a further two years before passing their Part 2 specialist examinations, then complete a further two years in practice before being able to become fellows. Unqualified fee earners need to have equivalent experience if they are to be regarded as coming into grades B or C.

Many High Court cases justify category A fee earners, but specific tasks within the proceedings, such as sitting behind counsel at interim hearings, may only justify a fee earner in a lower category. A complex, high-value clinical negligence claim in *Higgs v Camden and Islington Health Authority* [2003] EWHC 15 (QB), LTL 22/1/2003, justified the employment of a senior partner (a category A fee earner), and the client was entitled to expect no less. In the county courts, the nature and complexity of the various items of work will dictate the level of fee earner that will be reasonable. In *Bensusan v Freedman* (2001) LTL 6/11/2001 the work was of a type typically dealt with by grade B fee earners, so the hourly rate was reduced from the amount claimed to the appropriate grade B rate. It is recognised that it is often more economical to brief counsel than for a solicitor to act as the advocate. Where having a solicitor advocate leads to an increase in costs the court will consider whether the increase can be justified.

Exceeding a guideline rate

The rates in **tables 71.3** and **71.4** are no more than a guide and can be exceeded where the nature of the case warrants it. When considering whether the guideline rate provides proper remuneration, the court will take into account the factors set out in **CPR, r. 44.4(3)**, which include the conduct of the parties, the amount involved, any complexity or novelty, the skill, effort and specialist knowledge required, the time spent on the case, any international element and the place where and the circumstances in which the work was done. Thus in *Higgs v Camden and Islington Health Authority* [2003] EWHC 15 (QB), LTL 22/1/2003, the appellate court upheld a rate of £300 per hour where the case involved a child who was brain-damaged from birth. The court indicated that the SCCO guideline figures were not intended to replace the experience and knowledge of those familiar with the local area and with the field generally. **71.48**

London solicitors

Whether it is reasonable to instruct expensive London solicitors rather than more economical provincial solicitors involves an objective element of reasonableness which nevertheless has to be considered in the context of the particular circumstances of the particular clients (*Wraith v Sheffield Forgemasters Ltd* [1998] 1 WLR 132; *Truscott v Truscott* [1998] FLR 265). The list of factors in *Wraith v Sheffield Forgemasters Ltd* was a list prepared for that case, and, although useful, other factors are likely to be relevant in other cases (*Higgins v Ministry of Defence* [2010] EWHC 654 (QB), [2010] 6 Costs LR 867). In *A v Chief Constable of South Yorkshire* [2008] EWHC 1658 (QB), [2008] 6 Costs LR 935, it was held that it was unreasonable for a claimant in Sheffield to instruct specialist London solicitors for a complex personal injuries claim against the police. In *Solutia UK Ltd v Griffiths* [2001] EWCA Civ 736, [2001] CPLR 419, it was held to be reasonable to have instructed London solicitors in litigation which could have been handled far more cheaply by provincial solicitors where the London solicitors had previously conducted related, and more complex litigation, arising out of the same facts. Likewise in *Higgins v Ministry of Defence* [2010] EWHC 654 (QB), [2010] 6 Costs LR 867, it was held to have been reasonable for an 82-year-old claimant living in Broadstairs, Kent, to instruct a central London firm on an asbestosis claim. In *Ryan v Tretol Group Ltd* (2002) Supreme Court Costs Office Case Summaries No. 10 of 2002 it was held to have been reasonable to change from provincial to London solicitors in an asbestosis claim after the fee earner dealing with the claim (who was an asbestosis expert) left the provincial firm. The London firm had been recommended by an asbestosis support organisation, and it was not apparent that there were any firms with experience of asbestosis claims in the local area. In *Gazley v Wade* [2004] EWHC 2675 (QB), LTL 25/11/2004, it was held to have been unreasonable to instruct specialist London solicitors for a libel claim. Although it was not a 'Norfolk **71.49** case', the claimant was living in Norwich, there was evidence that local non-specialist firms had the necessary competence, and any technical advice could have been sought from specialist members of the Bar.

Retaining two firms simultaneously

71.50 A party will not recover costs which are duplicated by instructing two firms of solicitors, even if the second firm is based overseas in a claim with an international dimension (*Bühler AG v FP Spomax SA* [2008] EWHC 1109 (Pat), LTL 7/7/2008).

Correspondence and attendances

71.51 Routine letters out and emails out (those which by reason of their simplicity should not be regarded as items of substance) and routine telephone calls (which cannot properly amount to an attendance) will in general be allowed on a unit basis of six minutes each, the charge being calculated by reference to the appropriate hourly rate. The unit charge for letters and emails out will include perusing and considering the relevant letters or emails in, and no separate charge should be made for incoming letters and emails. The court may, in its discretion, allow an actual time charge for preparation of electronic communications other than emails sent by solicitors, which properly amount to attendances, provided that the time taken has been recorded (**PD 47, para. 5.22(2)**). Local travelling expenses incurred by solicitors (normally within 10 miles of the court) will not be allowed. Travelling and waiting time is usually allowed at the rate agreed between solicitor and client. The cost of postage, couriers, outgoing telephone calls, fax and telex messages will in general not be allowed unless unusually heavy. Nor will the cost of making copies normally be allowed, unless the documents to be copied were unusually numerous. Agency charges as between a principal solicitor and his or her agent will be dealt with normally on the basis that the charges form part of the principal solicitor's charges (**PD 47, para. 5.22(6)**).

Counsel's fees

71.52 Counsel's fees are based on a judgment taking into account all the relevant circumstances, including:

(a) the seniority of counsel;
(b) the amount of time reasonably spent on the work;
(c) the number of documents perused and their importance and technicality (even if brief);
(d) the specialist knowledge and skill of counsel;
(e) the complexity of the work undertaken;
(f) the difficulty or novelty of the questions involved;
(g) the value of the claim and its importance;
(h) the responsibility involved;
(i) the place and circumstances where the work is performed; and
(j) whether there is any overlap with other work performed by counsel which reduces the work that would otherwise have been necessary.

Matthews v Dorkin (2000) LTL 10/11/2000 is an interesting example of an appeal dealing with several different fees of counsel of nine years' call in a substantial personal injuries claim. For example, a fee of £875 was allowed for a written advice and schedule of loss and damage reasonably taking seven hours. A fee of £335 was allowed for a 24-minute telephone conference which required two hours and 15 minutes preparation. A fee of £750 was allowed for a 4½ hour conference with experts at the solicitor's office which required three hours' preparation.

In *Matthews v Dorkin* brief fees were allowed of £350 on an application to break a fixture on account of the unavailability of experts, £525 on a 30-minute hearing requiring two and a half hours' preparation, and trial brief fees (at 50 per cent of those of leading counsel) of £4,000 with refreshers of £600 per day. The general approach is that junior counsel are allowed between 50 and 67 per cent of the leader's brief fees. Where there are several counsel on one side, their respective fees should reflect their seniority and responsibility in the conduct of the case (*Loveday v Renton (No. 2)* [1992] 3 All ER 184 at p. 194).

In *Hornsby v Clark Kenneth Leventhal* [2000] 4 All ER 567 it was held, in relation to counsel's fees for an appeal to the Court of Appeal, that the first stage is to assess the fee for the skeleton argument. This is assessed largely by reference to the time reasonably spent in reading the documents, researching the law and drafting the skeleton. Next the brief fee should be assessed applying the guidance in *Loveday v Renton (No. 2)* at p. 194 (which essentially identified the factors set out in points (a) to (j) above). In so far as preparation for the skeleton argument reduced the amount of preparation required for the hearing, that should not be included in the brief fee. The third stage is to aggregate the fees for the skeleton and the brief, to cross-check that the total is not too large or too small, and to adjust accordingly.

The Senior Courts Costs Office has also published figures for counsel's fees based on run-of-the-mill cases in the Queen's Bench and Chancery Divisions. These are set out in **table 71.5**. They are regarded as a useful starting point when assessing counsel's fees. The appropriate figure does not depend wholly on counsel's seniority, but also the level of counsel merited by the application and the circumstances of the individual case.

Table 71.5 Guidelines for counsel's fees

	Jan 2003, hearings of		Jan 2005, hearings of		Jan 2007, hearings of	
	1 hour	½ day	1 hour	½ day	1 hour	½ day
Queen's Bench Division						
Junior up to 5 years call	220	385	245	425	259	450
Junior 5–10 years call	330	655	365	725	386	767
Junior 10+ years call	500	1,000	550	1,100	582	1,164
Chancery Division						
Junior up to 5 years call	250	475	275	525	291	556
Junior 5–10 years call	425	800	470	880	497	931
Junior 10+ years call	650	1,200	715	1,320	757	1,397
Administrative Court						
Junior up to 5 years call	325	500	360	550	381	582
Junior 5–10 years call	600	1,000	660	1,100	698	1,164
Junior 10+ years call	850	1,500	935	1,650	989	1,746

Disbursements

Disbursements are payments made by a solicitor for goods or services other than items which **71.53**
enable the solicitor to render its service to the client. Office overheads therefore are not disbursements. It was held in *Crane v Canons Leisure Centre* [2007] EWCA Civ 1352, [2008] 1 WLR 2549, that the distinction is between charges by the solicitors for work that they do themselves or are directly responsible for (which are base costs), and expenses they incur for the client and which they pass to the client at cost (which are disbursements). The distinction does not depend on whether the solicitors do the work themselves or delegate it, but rather whether the solicitors remain in control and responsible for the work. Work delegated to another solicitor or to a costs draftsman or costs consultant is therefore part of the solicitor's base costs, not a disbursement.

Expenses legitimately claimed as disbursements are shown and charged separately on the solicitor's bill, and the client is not charged with VAT on these items. *The VAT Guide* (February 2011) (HMRC Notice 700) at para. 25.1 sets out eight conditions that must be satisfied if an item is to be treated as a disbursement:

(a) the solicitor must have acted as the agent for the client when paying the third party;
(b) the client must have actually received and used the goods or services provided by the third party (this condition usually prevents the solicitor's travelling and subsistence expenses, telephone bills and postage being treated as disbursements);
(c) the client must be responsible for paying the third party;
(d) the client must have authorised the solicitor to make the payment on the client's behalf;
(e) the client must have known the goods or services would be provided by a third party;
(f) the solicitor's outlay must be separately itemised in the bill (or invoice);
(g) the solicitor can only recover the exact amount paid to the third party; and
(h) the goods or services must be clearly additional to the supplies which the solicitor has made to the client on his own account.

Further guidance is given in **PD 44, para. 2.11**. Examples of valid disbursements are court fees, fees on affidavits, estate duty and stamp duty payable by clients, fees for experts' reports and services such as reproducing photographs. A referral fee (see now the Legal Aid, Sentencing and Punishment of Offenders Act 2012, ss. 56 to 60) paid by a claims handling company to its subsidiary was held not to be a disbursement in *Sharratt v London Central Bus Co. Ltd (No. 2)* [2004] EWCA Civ 575, [2004] 3 All ER 325, because it related to work done before the solicitor's retainer came into existence. Generally, it is only advantageous to treat a payment as a disbursement for VAT purposes where no VAT is chargeable on the supply by the third party, or where the client is not entitled to reclaim the VAT as input tax.

Counsel's fees are not technically disbursements because they are part of the services provided by the solicitor. They should therefore be included in the solicitor's services part of the bill and charged with VAT. This is so even if the barrister is not VAT registered. However, there is a long-standing HMRC concession which allows solicitors to readdress non-VAT-registered barristers' fee notes to the client, who pays counsel directly or provides a separate cheque for the barrister's fees. When this is done, the fees payable to counsel do not appear in the solicitor's bill at all (and are not included in the solicitor's quarterly VAT return).

VALUE ADDED TAX

71.54 Every statement, bill of costs, fee sheet, account or voucher on which VAT is included must state the VAT registration number of the provider (**PD 44, para. 2.2** and **PD 47, para 5.10(3)**). VAT should not be included in a claim for costs if the receiving party is able to recover the VAT as input tax (**PD 44, para. 2.3**) or if the receiving party is a government department in respect of the costs of services rendered by its legal staff (**para. 2.13**). Where there is a dispute about whether the receiving party is VAT registered, the receiving party's solicitors or auditors must provide a certificate in the form of precedent F in the schedule to **PD 47** (**PD 44, para. 2.5**).

Whenever there is a dispute about whether a service is zero rated, reference should be made to HM Revenue and Customs so that the official view can be made known at the assessment (**PD 44, para. 2.6**). Medical reports prepared for the purposes of litigation are liable to VAT if the expert is VAT registered (Directive 77/388/EEC; *d'Ambrumenil v Commissioners of Customs and Excise* (case C-307/01) [2003] ECR I-13989). Petty or general disbursements, such as postage, fares, telephone charges and costs of telegraphic transfers are normally treated as part of the solicitor's overheads, included in the firm's profit costs, and charged to VAT (**PD 44, para. 2.11**).

The summary in a bill of costs must show the total profit costs and disbursements separately from the total VAT claimed (**PD 47, para. 5.20**). Where there is a change to the rate of VAT during the course of proceedings, the bill should be divided into separate parts to distinguish work done at the different rates (**para. 5.8**, but see also **PD 44, paras 2.7** and **2.8** on electing to charge the lower rate, and **para. 2.9** on apportionment where there is a lump-sum charge for work spanning both periods).

APPORTIONMENT BETWEEN JOINT PARTIES

In the absence of express agreement, the general rule is that costs incurred by joint parties are to be divided equally between them (*Meretz Investments NV v ACP Ltd* [2007] EWHC 2635 (Ch), LTL 21/11/2007). This will be displaced where specific costs are shown to be attributable to a particular party. **71.55**

CONDITIONAL FEE AGREEMENTS

The discussion in **71.56** to **71.63** concerns CFAs entered into before 1 April 2013 and CFAs entered into after that date in relation to insolvency-related proceedings, publication and privacy proceedings or mesothelioma claims. For these CFAs, the provisions of CPR, Parts 43 to 48, relating to funding arrangements, and the attendant provisions of the old PD 43–48, as in force immediately before 1 April 2013, continue to apply (see the current **CPR, Part 48**, and **PD 48**). All references to the CPR and practice directions in the following paragraphs of **71.56** to **71.63** are to rules and directions in force immediately before 1 April 2013. **71.56**

Where a party is funded under a CFA (a funding arrangement as defined in CPR, r. 43.2), there will be two elements to that party's costs: the 'base costs' and the 'additional liability'. 'Costs' recoverable under a party and party costs order include any additional liability incurred under a funding arrangement (r. 43.2(1)(a)). The base costs are those that are charged in the usual way to reflect the solicitor's basic remuneration and are defined as costs other than the amount of any additional liability (PD 43–48, para. 2.1). The 'additional liability' means the percentage increase that a lawyer may charge to reflect his or her involvement in the case, any insurance premium charged or any amount in respect of provision made by a membership organisation (CPR, r. 43.2(1)(o)). This reflects the three most common forms of funding conditional fee litigation. In some cases the solicitor may charge an uplift expressed as a percentage of the base costs. Either additionally or alternatively the client may insure to cover its own costs, or both sides' costs, or indeed any one of a number of permutations of costs orders that may be made. Subject to the points below, this premium can be charged to the paying party. A litigant may enter into an agreement with one of a number of approved membership organisations (such as trade unions) to meet his legal costs. An amount to secure this benefit may be recovered from the paying party.

In *MGN Ltd v United Kingdom* (application 39401/04) (2011) 53 EHRR 5 a newspaper publisher applied to the European Court of Human Rights complaining that the 95 per cent and 100 per cent success fees payable for a hearing in the House of Lords were an interference with the newspaper's right to freedom of expression under the European Convention on Human Rights, art. 10. It was held that paying success fees at this level was plainly an interference with the newspaper's right to freedom of expression (at [192]). Given the statutory scheme underpinning CFAs, they were clearly prescribed by law (at [194]), and they performed a legitimate aim in that they promoted the widest public access to legal services for civil litigation funded by the private sector, and thus the protection of the rights of others within the meaning of art. 10(2) (at [197]). Nevertheless, the court decided the requirement that the applicant pay success fees to the claimant was a violation of art. 10 because paying the success fees was not necessary in a democratic society, was disproportionate having regard to the legitimate aims sought to be achieved and exceeded even the broad margin of appreciation accorded to the government in such matters.

While the court may summarily assess base costs at various stages during the case, there will be no assessment of the additional liability until the conclusion of the case or the part of the case to which a funding arrangement relates (r. 44.3A(1)). The parties can by agreement provide for an earlier assessment if they so wish.

Procedure for assessing an additional liability

71.57 Assessment of an additional liability is commenced in the same way as any other detailed assessment, save that the receiving party has to serve on the paying party and any other relevant persons relevant details of the additional liability (PD 43–48, para. 32.4). What constitutes 'relevant details' is set out fully at para. 32.5. Otherwise the assessment proceeds in the usual way to assess both base costs and any additional liability. The consideration of each of the two elements must be separate (para. 11.5).

Recovering additional liabilities from the paying party

71.58 CPR, r. 44.3B(1), provided that, unless the court otherwise orders, additional liabilities are not recoverable under a party-and-party costs order in favour of a CFA litigant:

(a) in respect of the percentage increase relating to the cost to the legal representative of the postponement of payment;
(b) in respect of the cost of a membership organisation exceeding the likely premium for an equivalent insurance policy;
(c) during a period when the receiving party has failed to provide information about the funding arrangement;
(d) in respect of a percentage increase where there has been a failure to state the reasons for setting the percentage increase at the level stated in the CFA; and
(e) in respect of an insurance premium where the receiving party has failed to provide information about the insurance policy in question by the time required by a rule, practice direction or court order.

In relation to the last three matters a party who has entered into a funding arrangement is obliged to give notice to its opponents of the fact at the earliest opportunity. This is done by serving a notice in form N251 (CPR, r. 44.15; PD 43–48, paras 19.1 to 19.5; PD Pre-action Conduct, para. 9.3). A party which has failed to serve the form N251 or has otherwise transgressed CPR, r. 44.3B(1), is precluded (unless the court orders otherwise) from claiming the additional liability for the period when the notice was not served or there was any other default. It is submitted that, as with any other sanction, the court should address the factors set out in r. 3.9 before ordering otherwise.

In *Crane v Canons Leisure Centre* [2007] EWCA Civ 1352, [2008] 1 WLR 2549, a collective CFA defined base costs as 'charges for work done by or on behalf of the Solicitors which would have been payable if this agreement did not provide for a success fee, calculated on the basis of the fees allowable for that work in the court in which the [claim] in question is conducted or would be conducted if proceedings were to be issued'. The costs of the detailed assessment, which was actually conducted by costs consultants engaged by the solicitors, were held to be part of the solicitors' base costs, and to attract the success fee on the same footing as the base costs on the substantive claim.

Assessing the percentage uplift

71.59 Guidance on the court's approach to assessing an additional liability was given in PD 43–48, section 11. In respect of any additional liability, the court will view matters as they reasonably appeared to the practitioner at the time that he entered into the agreement (para. 11.7). If the success fee was reasonable at that time, the court cannot substitute different rates for different periods of the proceedings as the risks change when more information becomes available (*U v Liverpool City Council* [2005] EWCA Civ 475, [2005] 1 WLR 2657).

In deciding whether a percentage increase is reasonable, relevant factors to be taken into account include (para. 11.8):

(a) the risk that the circumstances in which the costs, fees or expenses would be payable might or might not occur;
(b) the legal representative's liability for any disbursements;
(c) what other methods of financing the costs were available to the receiving party.

The costs officer has a power to allow different percentages to cover different items of costs or different periods. So different percentages may be applied for any protocol period, up to the issue of proceedings and for the trial. It is also acceptable to have a particular percentage applicable to one possible outcome (for example, settling within the protocol period) and another to cover a different eventuality (the case being contested to trial). See *Callery v Gray* [2001] EWCA Civ 1117, [2001] 1 WLR 2112.

A percentage increase will not be disallowed on the basis that the total of the additional liability and the base costs seems disproportionate (PD 43–48, para. 11.9). Doing so might run the risk of penalising a solicitor for entering into a funding arrangement, by allowing a lesser sum than might be permitted to a non-funded party.

Amounts allowed

The appellate courts have been reluctant to give guidance on the amount that a court will grant by way of uplift for the good reason that each case will turn on its own facts. The predictable costs rules for road traffic claims in accidents from 6 October 2003 (**CPR, Part 45, Sections II and III**), and for employers' liability claims in accidents from 1 October 2004 (**Part 45, Section IV**), lay down fixed success fees for these types of claim. See the discussion at **70.8** to **70.20**. These provide for two-stage success fees. Broadly, 100 per cent uplifts are applied to claims which are taken to trial, but 12.5 per cent (road traffic) and 25 per cent (employers' liability) uplifts apply where the claim is disposed of before trial. These figures should be seen as some guidance for other types of claim. Two-stage success fees are encouraged for all types of case (*Atack v Lee* [2004] EWCA Civ 1712, [2005] 1 WLR 2643). Other categories of case may involve substantially greater risks, and may justify significantly higher success fees for cases which do not go to trial. **71.60**

Before the introduction of **Part 45, Sections II to IV**, there were a number of decisions on rates for success fees, mainly dealing with straightforward road traffic claims. In *Callery v Gray* [2001] EWCA Civ 1117, [2001] 1 WLR 2112, Lord Woolf CJ said that every case has some risk. Experience suggests that at least 90 per cent of straightforward road traffic claims settle without the need to issue proceedings. For this type of claim an uplift of 20 per cent is the maximum that could reasonably be agreed. Naturally if there are other factors then this limit might be exceeded. The court was also of the view that it is permissible to set a success fee on the basis that the matter fought to trial (say 100 per cent) but to rebate that down to 20 per cent if the case settled in the protocol period. The court stressed that this was an indication given on the basis of the present evidence and that it might be appropriate to refine the figures later.

In *Halloran v Delaney* [2002] EWCA Civ 1258, [2003] 1 WLR 28, the court felt that an increase of 5 per cent was appropriate for cases that settled before the issue of proceedings, and that the 5 per cent would be appropriate for any Part 8 costs-only proceedings. In *Re Claims Direct Test Cases* [2003] EWCA Civ 136, [2003] 4 All ER 508, the court said that *Halloran v Delaney* was not a case intended to give general guidance, that it was only intended to refer to the most straightforward of cases where the prospect of success is virtually 100 per cent, and that solicitors would be well advised to adopt the two-tier approach to the success fee advocated in *Callery v Gray*.

Faced with these difficult authorities there is still a regrettable lack of certainty about percentage uplifts, even in the most straightforward cases. It is suggested that a case which settles in the protocol period (or before the issue of proceedings) may still attract a 5 per cent success fee or even the 12.5 per cent success fee allowed under the predictable costs regime (see **70.9**), provided there is no suggestion to the solicitor that there is anything unusual about the case. To cater for such dangers lurking under the limpid pools of otherwise tranquil litigation a solicitor would be well advised to adopt the two-stage approach outlined in *Callery v Gray*.

It is suggested that it would be wrong in principle to extrapolate from the above cases any general propositions applicable to other areas of litigation. It has to be understood that the cases are predicated on very straightforward litigation where statistics suggest there is a 90 per cent settlement rate. To take this conclusion into another area of litigation, for example, clinical negligence, is to ignore this aspect of the above cases. It is sometimes suggested that *Bensusan v Freedman* (2001) LTL 6/11/2001 is an authority for the contrary proposition. In that case an uplift of 20 per cent was permitted for a case that settled after the defendant had denied liability and asserted contributory negligence. This is a first-instance decision which fails to give due weight to the risks in contested litigation and it is suggested that it may well not be followed.

Assessing an insurance premium

71.61 The **Access to Justice Act 1999, s. 29**, enabled a successful client to claim the premium from the unsuccessful opponent. It provided:

> Where in any proceedings a costs order is made in favour of any party who has taken out an insurance policy against the risk of incurring a liability in those proceedings, the costs payable to him may, subject in the case of court proceedings to rules of court, include costs in respect of the premium of the policy.

In general the same considerations apply to insurance premiums as apply to percentage uplifts. A 'premium' for this purpose is the sum paid by the client to the insurer (*Re Claims Direct Test Cases* [2003] EWCA Civ 136, [2003] 4 All ER 508). A fee charged by a claims handling company for a basket of services is not converted into a 'premium' simply by describing it as such (*Sharratt v London Central Bus Co. Ltd (No. 2)* [2004] EWCA Civ 575, [2004] 3 All ER 325). In this case the Court of Appeal upheld the costs judge's approach of finding how much the company had paid to its underwriters, and making adjustments to that figure to find the premium recoverable under the **Access to Justice Act 1999, s. 29**. The specific considerations relating to insurance cover are in PD 43–48, para. 11.10:

> In deciding whether the cost of insurance cover is reasonable, relevant factors to be taken into account include:
> (1) where the insurance cover is not purchased in support of a CFA with a success fee, how its cost compares with the likely cost of funding the case with a CFA with a success fee and supporting insurance cover;
> (2) the level and extent of the cover provided;
> (3) the availability of any pre-existing insurance cover;
> (4) whether any part of the premium would be rebated in the event of early settlement;
> (5) the amount of commission payable to the receiving party or his legal representatives or other agents.

Where there is a dispute about the insurance premium in a staged policy (within the meaning of PD 43–48, para. 19.4(3A)), it will normally be sufficient for the receiving party to set out in any reply (see **71.16**) the reasons for choosing the particular insurance policy and the basis on which the insurance premium is rated, whether block rated or individually rated *(PD 43–48, para. 39.2)*. There is an evidential burden on the paying party to adduce at least some material to support the argument that the premium is unreasonably high (*Rogers v Merthyr Tydfil County Borough Council* [2006] EWCA Civ 1134, [2007] 1 WLR 808). An objection can only be sustained on the basis of evidence and analysis, not by assertion (*Kris Motor Spares Ltd v Fox Williams LLP* [2010] EWHC 1008 (QB), LTL 13/5/2010).

In *Callery v Gray* [2001] EWCA Civ 1117, [2001] 1 WLR 2112, and *Callery v Gray (No. 2)* [2001] EWCA Civ 1246, [2001] 1 WLR 2142, the Court of Appeal considered whether an ATE insurance premium is recoverable in a case that settles prior to the issue of proceedings. The court held that it could be recovered as 'insurance...against the risk of incurring a liability' within the **Access to Justice Act 1999, s. 29**. Provided the premium is reasonable, it will usually be recoverable against an unsuccessful defendant even though it is taken out soon after the solicitor is retained, and before the defendant's response is known. On the facts of that decision the premium of £350 was recoverable.

The decisions in *Callery v Gray* and *Callery v Gray (No. 2)* were affirmed by the House of Lords in *Callery v Gray (Nos. 1 and 2)* [2002] UKHL 28, [2002] 1 WLR 2000, in which it was held that it is for the Court of Appeal to lay down principles in this area.

The question of when an ATE insurance policy should be taken out was considered further by the Senior Costs Judge, Chief Master Hurst, in *Re Claims Direct Test Cases* (2002) LTL 29/7/2002. He found that where an incident occurred, particularly a minor road traffic accident causing slight injury, and where liability was accepted at the outset, it would be generally disproportionate and unreasonable to take out an ATE policy. That is likely to have a substantial impact upon the insurance market. Bulk providers generally insist that all cases from panel solicitors are insured, even if liability is, or is very likely to be, accepted. This allows a fixed premium to be set, with the stronger cases subsidising the weaker ones. If the stronger cases are filtered out because the premium is not recoverable, premiums are likely to rise. The Chief Master held that only the insurance element of the package of products included in the Claims Direct contract was recoverable, and allowed £621.13 (against the £1,525 claimed). The claimant's appeal was dismissed (*Re Claims Direct Test Cases* [2003] EWCA Civ 136, [2003] 4 All ER 508).

Some ATE insurers have sought to set their premium by reference to the amount of damages actually awarded. In *Pirie v Ayling* (2003) LTL 5/3/2003 the premium was stated to be 20 per cent of the damages awarded. Chief Master Hurst held that the agreement was not champertous, as there was no real danger that the purity of justice might be offended: the insurance company makes its profit from the insurance not from the litigation, the litigation simply provides the means of satisfying the insured's liability for the premium. However, the effect of the agreement was that the premium was £2,600. That was held not to be reasonable or proportionate in a road traffic accident case worth £13,000. In line with *Callery v Gray (No. 2)* [2001] EWCA Civ 1246, [2001] 1 WLR 2142, the premium allowed was £350.

PD 43–48, para. 11.10, requires the court to consider whether there was an existing policy of insurance (before-the-event or BTE insurance) and whether it would be reasonable for the successful party to have used that policy rather than obtaining fresh ATE insurance. This was considered in *Sarwar v Alam* [2001] EWCA Civ 1401, [2002] 1 WLR 125. The court held that a solicitor is under a duty to make reasonable enquiries to ascertain whether there is a BTE policy. Often such policies are linked to housing or motor insurance. Where there is such a policy, it is unlikely to be reasonable to incur a fresh premium for ATE insurance. However, there may be circumstances where it is inappropriate for the BTE insurance policy to be used. Where, for example, a passenger is covered by the driver's BTE policy, but wants to sue the driver. This might be particularly the case where the policy allows the driver's BTE insurer full control over the claim.

In more complex litigation the courts seem to be taking a more generous stance. In *Ashworth v Peterborough United Football Club Ltd* (2002) LTL 4/7/2002 the SCCO considered the reasonableness of an ATE insurance premium taken out in a multi-track commercial dispute. By consent the defendant was ordered to pay Mr Ashworth £66,000 in damages plus his costs on the standard basis. The bill of costs came to £104,858, of which £45,937.50 was the

ATE premium. The defendant contended that the premium was unreasonable because the insurance could have been taken earlier, that it was disproportionate and excessive and that the claimant did not disclose the amount of the expected premium before it was taken out. The master held that on the evidence available, insurance was probably not available at the outset, and that the defendant could not show that it was disproportionate to the matter in issue (not just as against the sum insured). Further it was not reasonable to have expected the claimant to obtain cover elsewhere given the restrictive market conditions at the time. It was not unlawful for the claimant to obtain retrospective own-cost cover, and the claimant gave as much information to the defendant as he was obliged to give.

In *Inline Logistics Ltd v UCI Logistics Ltd* [2002] EWHC 519 (Ch), *The Times*, 2 May 2002, the amount paid as an ATE premium (£40,000 plus £2,000 tax) was not disputed, though there was an unsuccessful argument that the premium was not recoverable (see **5.13**). Unfortunately the report does not record the level of cover purchased for that sum.

In *Sarwar v Alam* (2003) LTL 23/3/2003 the claimant appealed an important test case to the Court of Appeal having lost before both the district judge and the circuit judge. The claimant took out an ATE policy with a limit of indemnity of £125,000. The premium was £62,500 subject to a 50 per cent no-claims bonus. The full amount was paid in advance. The discount only applied if the paying party made no challenge to the amount of the premium, to the frustration of the defendant. However, Master Rogers allowed the premium in full, saying:

> I have come to the conclusion that although the premium was high, it was unlikely that the claimant's advisers could have obtained an alternative quotation at a lower rate. They tried but were unsuccessful. Law and practice were in a state of flux and insurers were understandably reluctant to commit themselves on a large potential liability.

Assessing a fee to a membership organisation

71.62 A court assessing the reasonableness of a fee to a membership organisation has to consider how this form of funding compares with the alternatives. PD 43–48, para. 11.11, requires:

> Where the court is considering a provision made by a membership organisation, CPR, r. 44.3B(1)(b), provides that any such provision which exceeds the likely cost to the receiving party of the premium of an insurance policy against the risk of incurring a liability to pay the costs of other parties to the proceedings is not recoverable. In such circumstances the court will, when assessing the additional liability, have regard to the factors set out in para. 11.10 [see **71.61**], in addition to the factors set out in r. 44.5.

This will require the court to construe each document as different CFAs may differ in their wording. In *Arkin v Borchard Lines Ltd* (2001) LTL 19/6/2001, interim costs orders had been made in favour of the claimant and the defendant respectively on different interim applications. The claimant had entered into a CFA, and wished to set off the two sets of interim costs. Colman J held that the terms of the CFA in question, which said the lawyers were successful if they 'recover[ed] costs…or interim awards during the litigation', meant that the costs award in favour of the claimant did not infringe the indemnity principle (see **71.30** to **71.34**). It was held to be unarguable that the word 'recover' in the CFA meant that actual receipt was necessary. The two costs orders could therefore be set off against each other. Further, where one costs order is summarily assessed, and the competing costs order is directed to be subject to a detailed assessment, the court could legitimately preserve the set-off by varying the time for payment of the summarily assessed costs.

Application to assess

71.63 A client who retains a solicitor under a CFA may apply to the court for it to assess the base costs (i.e. the costs other than the percentage increase) or the percentage increase (i.e. the percentage increase pursuant to the CFA either between the solicitor and client or between the solicitor and counsel, and otherwise sometimes known as the success fee) or both (Solicitors

Act 1974, part 3; **CPR, rr. 48.8** and **48.10**; Supreme Court Costs Office Guide 2006, sect. 20). Base costs are assessed on the indemnity basis as if there was no CFA. The percentage increase may be reduced if the court considers it disproportionate having regard to all the relevant factors as they appeared to the solicitor or counsel when the CFA was entered into. This is discussed in detail at **6.12** to **6.16** and **6.18** to **6.21**.

LITIGANTS IN PERSON

A litigant in person may be awarded costs (Litigants in Person (Costs and Expenses) Act 1975), which may be quantified either by summary or detailed assessment in the court's discretion. When quantifying these costs, **CPR, r. 46.5(2)**, provides that the litigant will not recover more than two thirds of the costs and all the disbursements which would have been allowed if the litigant had been represented by a legal representative. In quantifying the costs for time spent on the litigation, the litigant in person will be allowed his or her financial loss for doing the work on the case. A copy of the evidence proving the financial loss must be served on the paying party at least 24 hours before the assessment hearing (**PD 46, para. 3.2**). A litigant who cannot establish any such loss will be allowed an amount in respect of time spent reasonably doing the work at a rate of £9.25 per hour until 30 September 2011, and £18 per hour from 1 October 2011 (**PD 46, para. 3.4**). A litigant in person is not entitled to a witness allowance for his or her own attendance at court. **71.64**

By **CPR, r. 46.5(6)**, a company acting without a legal representative is regarded as a litigant in person, as is a barrister, solicitor, solicitor's employee or authorised litigator who is acting for him or herself (*Khan v Lord Chancellor* [2003] EWHC 12 (QB), [2003] 1 WLR 2385; *Boyd and Hutchinson v Joseph* [2003] EWHC 413 (Ch), *The Times*, 28 April 2003). Similarly a qualified barrister as a litigant will have to show good reason for employing another barrister (*Jackson v Lord Chancellor* [2003] EWHC 626 (QB), LTL 31/3/2003). A solicitor who, instead of acting personally, is represented by his or her firm or by him or herself in his or her firm name, is not regarded as a litigant in person (*Malkinson v Trim* [2002] EWCA Civ 1273, [2003] 1 WLR 463).

In a complex case a litigant in person may need to spend an extremely long time researching matters. In *R (Wulfsohn) v Legal Services Commission* [2002] EWCA Civ 250, LTL 8/2/2002, the Court of Appeal accepted that a litigant in person had spent 1,200 hours in preparation for five hearings, and took into account that a firm of solicitors had estimated the costs if they had been retained at £15,000 to £20,000. Applying the cap of two-thirds of the amount which would have been allowed if the client had been represented by lawyers (**CPR, r. 46.5(2)**), the court allowed £10,460. See also the Supreme Court Costs Office Guide 2006, sect. 22.

Litigation work done by litigant's employees

The general rule is that work done by a litigant personally in the course of instructing his solicitor is not recoverable as costs (*Re Nossen's Letter Patent* [1969] 1 WLR 638). Nor, in general, are costs recoverable for work done by a litigant who happens to be an insolvency office-holder, such as a liquidator or administrator (*Sisu Capital Fund Ltd v Tucker* [2005] EWHC 2321 (Ch), [2006] 1 All ER 167). The original rule (for which, see *London Scottish Benefit Society v Chorley* (1884) 13 QBD 872) extended to all costs incurred by litigants in person, other than a solicitor acting for himself. As discussed at **71.64**, the old rule has been removed for litigants in person by the Litigants in Person (Costs and Expenses) Act 1975, and for companies acting without legal representatives by **CPR, r. 46.5(6)**. The general rule continues to apply to prevent work done by a litigant in instructing his lawyers from being recoverable as costs (*Admiral Management Services Ltd v Para-Protect Europe Ltd* [2002] EWHC 233 (Ch), [2002] 1 WLR 2722). **71.65**

Commentary

By way of exception to the general rule, work done by specialists employed by a litigant may be recoverable as costs, provided:

(a) the staff have a sufficient level of expertise to qualify as experts (*Admiral Management Services Ltd v Para-Protect Europe Ltd*);
(b) the work done was of an expert nature, not merely factual (*Richards and Wallington (Plant Hire) Ltd v Monk and Co. Ltd* (1984) Costs LR (Core Vol) 79); and
(c) the amount recovered is limited to a reasonable sum for the actual and direct costs of the work done by the specialists, and does not include any element for the general overheads of the business (*Re Nossen's Letter Patent*).

Litigation work done by unauthorised persons

71.66 There is no jurisdiction to allow a party to recover the fees of a person who is not legally qualified who has assisted in the preparation and presentation of a claim (*United Building and Plumbing Contractors v Kajla* [2002] EWCA Civ 628, LTL 26/4/2002). Rights to conduct litigation are governed by the Legal Services Act 2007, see **61.30**. Where a client retains an unauthorised person to act on his behalf in litigation, the client is regarded for costs purposes as acting as a litigant in person (*Agassi v Robinson (No. 2)* [2005] EWCA Civ 1507, [2006] 1 WLR 2126). A successful party represented by an unauthorised person cannot recover the cost of work which it was not lawful for the unauthorised person to perform. If the unauthorised person is a specialist with expertise in the area, it may be that the expense of some of the work done can be recovered as disbursements under **CPR, r. 46.5(3)(a)(ii)** (*Agassi v Robinson (No. 2)*).

COSTS-ONLY PROCEEDINGS

Settling before proceedings are issued

71.67 It frequently happens that disputes are resolved before proceedings are issued on the basis that one side shall do or abstain from doing something (often it is simply the payment of compensation) and shall also pay the other side's reasonable costs. Ideally, the parties will at the same time, or soon afterwards, agree the amount of those costs. If they cannot agree the amount of the costs payable, several problems may arise. One analysis of the situation is that there is no complete agreement between the parties. This may be so because a term such as 'reasonable costs' used between the parties may not be sufficiently precise to constitute a contract of compromise. It is submitted that the term 'reasonable costs' has been in use for several decades, and is understood by almost the entire profession as meaning 'standard basis costs, to be agreed between the parties, failing which such amount as would be assessed by the court on a detailed assessment'. However, there are problems. One is that as proceedings have not been issued, the costs of the receiving party are arguably non-contentious costs (Solicitors Act 1974, s. 87(1)). In *Bilkus v Stockler Brunton* [2010] EWCA Civ 101, [2010] 1 WLR 2526, it was held that work 'for the purposes of proceedings' in s. 87(1) includes costs for the purpose of future proceedings. This may assume the future proceedings have to be issued for such costs to (become) contentious, but if not, the problem identified here disappears. Standard basis assessments only arise in the context of contentious costs, so there is a technical problem in the accepted meaning of the term 'reasonable costs' in settlements reached before proceedings are issued. Further, there is scope for disagreement as to what should happen if the parties cannot agree the amount of the receiving party's costs.

Assuming the terms of the settlement are held to be sufficiently precise to amount to a contract, the next problem is how to get an adjudication of the amount of costs payable if the parties cannot agree the amount that should be paid. The traditional method, which can still be used (**PD 46, para. 9.12**), is for the receiving party to issue proceedings using a Part 7 claim form for breach of the compromise agreement seeking damages in the amount of their reasonable costs. Assuming liability was not disputed, the court would enter judgment for damages to be assessed, or for a specified sum in respect of costs. If judgment was entered for damages to be assessed, the court would then convene a hearing to assess damages (rather than a hearing for a detailed assessment), at which hearing the court would assess the amount of costs that was reasonable in accordance with the compromise agreement. This in turn would (potentially) raise difficulties as to the intention of the parties on the question of the basis on which the reasonableness of the receiving party's costs should be judged.

Part 8 claim for an order for costs

In an attempt to avoid most of the difficulties identified in 71.67, **CPR, r. 46.14**, provides that where parties to a dispute have a written agreement on all matters in dispute, except the amount of costs to be paid, either party to the compromise agreement may start Part 8 proceedings seeking an order for costs. If such an order is made, there will then be a court order for costs (**CPR, r. 46.14(5)**) which can form the basis of assessment proceedings. A claim form issued under **CPR, r. 46.14** must identify the claim or dispute giving rise to the compromise, state the date and terms of the compromise, state the amount of costs claimed and whether they are claimed on the standard or indemnity basis, and a draft order (**PD 46, para. 9.3**). The written evidence in support has to include copies of documents relied upon to prove the defendant's agreement to pay costs (**para. 9.5** and **CPR, r. 46.14(4)**). The former rule that the court had to dismiss the claim if it was opposed has been removed as has the former restriction that only a detailed assessment could be ordered. Instead, when the time for acknowledging service has expired, unless the defendant indicates an intention to defend the claimant can make a request in writing for an order for a detailed or summary assessment of the its costs (**PD 46, para. 9.7**). The general rule is that an order will be made for a detailed assessment, but if the court is in a position to make a summary assessment it should generally do so (**para. 9.9**). The claim may be dealt with without being allocated to a track (**para. 9.11**). A defendant may oppose the claim by filing a witness statement in accordance with **CPR, r. 8.5(3)** (**PD 46, para. 9.10**). The court will then give directions, which may include a direction that the claim proceeds as a Part 7 claim. If a defendant acts unreasonably in forcing a claimant into using the Part 7 procedure rather than the procedure under **r. 46.14**, the court can award costs of the Part 7 claim on the indemnity basis (*Bensusan v Freedman*) (2001) LTL 6/11/2000. **71.68**

Commentary

Chapter 72 Arbitration Claims

The following procedural checklist, which is at the front of the book, is relevant to this chapter:

Procedural checklist 31 Arbitration claim

INTRODUCTION

72.1 Arbitration claims are governed by **CPR, Part 62, and PD 62.**

CPR, Part 62, is part of 'a new procedural code with the overriding objective of enabling the court to deal with cases justly' (**r. 1.1(1)**). However, when dealing with applications under the Arbitration Act 1996, the court must observe the general principles in s. 1 of that Act. These are:

(a) the object of arbitration is to obtain the fair resolution of disputes by an impartial tribunal without unnecessary delay or expense;
(b) the parties should be free to agree how their disputes are resolved, subject only to such safeguards as are necessary in the public interest;
(c) in matters governed by part 1 of the Act the court should not intervene except as provided by that part.

In *Kalmneft JSC v Glencore International AG* [2002] 1 All ER 76the Commercial Court heard an application under **CPR, r. 3.1(2)(a)**, to extend the 28-day time limit specified in the Arbitration Act 1996, s. 70(3), for making applications under ss. 67 and 68. Colman J held that, in exercising its discretion under **CPR, r. 3.1(2)(a)**, the court must take into consideration both the general principles of the 1996 Act and the overriding objective of the CPR, and held that the most significant factor is the need, stated in s. 1(a) of the 1996 Act, to avoid unnecessary delay. The application in this case was made before **CPR, Part 62,** came into force, but it is submitted that the replacement of PD 49G by **CPR, Part 62,** should make no difference to the approach taken by Colman J, given the fundamental importance of the principles in the Arbitration Act 1996, s. 1, to arbitrations in England and Wales. This approach was endorsed in *Gold Coast Ltd v Naval Gijon SA* [2006] EWHC 1044 (Comm), [2006] 2 Lloyd's Rep 400.

CPR, Part 62, is very similar to the old PD 49G. Accordingly, it is likely that case law under PD 49G and its predecessor, RSC, ord. 73, would be considered relevant in determining cases arising out of it. In deciding *Vale do Rio Doce Navegação SA v Shanghai Bao Steel Ocean Shipping Co. Ltd* [2000] 2 Lloyd's Rep 1 Thomas J stated, at p. 8:

It seems to me clear that the principles applicable to the approach to the former RSC, ord. 73, and PD 49G are the same, as the principles are premised on the nature of an arbitration.

Although the judge said that it should generally be unnecessary to consider cases under the old law, he considered previous law extensively when deciding how best to interpret the provisions of what is now **CPR, r. 62.5(1)**. His reason for doing so was that: 'the underlying rationale in those cases remains applicable' (at p. 7).

Part 62 is divided into three sections. Section I deals with claims under the Arbitration Act 1996, Section II deals with claims under the old law and Section III applies to all enforcement proceedings other than by an action or claim on the award.

CLAIMS UNDER THE ARBITRATION ACT 1996

Starting the claim

An arbitration claim must be brought using the arbitration claim form, form N8. It should be issued using the standard **CPR, Part 8**, procedure (see **chapter 13; CPR, r. 62.3(1); PD 62, para. 2.2**). An application for an interim remedy under the Arbitration Act 1996, s. 44, must be made using an arbitration claim form (**PD 62, para. 8.1**). However, an application to the court to stay legal proceedings in favour of arbitration should be made by application notice to the court dealing with those proceedings, using form N244 (or in the Commercial Court N244(CC)) (**CPR, r. 62.3(2)**). **72.2**

Commentary

An arbitration claim form may be issued in one of the following (**PD 62, para. 2.3(1)**):

(a) The Admiralty and Commercial Registry at the Royal Courts of Justice, London. The arbitration claim will be entered into the Commercial List.
(b) The Technology and Construction Court Registry at St Dunstan's House, London. The arbitration claim will be entered into the TCC List.
(c) A district registry of the High Court where a Mercantile Court has been established (see **2.19**). The arbitration claim will be entered into the list of the Mercantile Court.
(d) A district registry of the High Court with the arbitration claim form marked 'Technology and Construction Court' in the top right-hand corner. The arbitration claim will be entered into the TCC List.

However, if the arbitration claim relates to a landlord and tenant or partnership dispute, it must be issued in the Chancery Division of the High Court (**PD 62, para. 2.3(2)**).

A claimant should have regard to the principles set out in the High Court and County Courts (Allocation of Arbitration Proceedings) Order 1996 (SI 1996/3215) in determining where an arbitration claim is to be issued (**PD 62, para. 2.1**). Pursuant to SI 1996/3215, art. 5(4), the following criteria should be taken into account:

(a) the financial substance of the dispute, including the value of any claim or counterclaim;
(b) the nature of the dispute, for example, whether it arises out of a commercial or business transaction or relates to engineering, building or other construction work;
(c) whether the proceedings are otherwise important and, in particular, whether they raise questions of importance to persons who are not parties; and
(d) whether the balance of convenience points to having the proceedings taken in the Central London Civil Justice Centre Mercantile List.

Where the financial substance of the dispute exceeds £200,000, the proceedings are to be taken in the High Court unless they do not raise questions of general importance to persons who are not parties.

The principles contained in **CPR, r. 30.5(3)**, relating to transfer between Divisions and to and from a specialist list apply with the effect that the High Court, or a judge of the Technology and Construction Court, may order arbitration claims to be transferred to another Division or specialist list (**CPR, r. 62.3(4)**).

The Admiralty and Commercial Courts Guide, paras O19.1 and O19.2, state that an arbitration claim which raises no significant point of arbitration law or practice will normally be transferred from the Commercial Court:

(a) to the Chancery Division, if it is a rent-review arbitration;
(b) to the Technology and Construction Court, if it is a construction or engineering arbitration;
(c) to the Central London County Court Mercantile List (now the London Mercantile Court), if it is an employment arbitration; or
(d) to the Admiralty Court, if it is a salvage arbitration.

Contents of arbitration claim form

72.3 An arbitration claim form must include a concise statement of the remedy claimed and (where appropriate) the questions on which the claimant seeks the decision of the court (**CPR, r. 62.4(1)(a)**). A reference in the arbitration claim form to a witness statement or affidavit filed in support of the claim is not sufficient to comply with the requirements of **r. 62.4(1)(a)** (Admiralty and Commercial Courts Guide, para. O3.2).

Where the claimant is challenging an arbitration award, the part or parts of the award being challenged must be identified and the grounds of the challenge must be shown. The claimant must identify the defendants against whom any claim for costs is made. The claimant must also specify the section of the Arbitration Act 1996 under which the application is brought and show that any statutory requirements laid down by the Act for the application being brought have been satisfied (**CPR, r. 62.4(1)(b)** to **(e)**).

An arbitration claim form must give the names and addresses of the persons on whom it is to be served. It must state their role in the arbitration and whether they are defendants. If the arbitration claim is being made without notice in an urgent application pursuant to the Arbitration Act 1996, s. 44(3) (order for the preservation of evidence or assets), that fact must be stated and the grounds relied upon should be specified (**CPR, r. 62.4(1)(f)**).

Service of arbitration claim form

72.4 Unless the court orders otherwise, the claimant must serve an arbitration claim form within one month from the date of issue (**CPR, r. 62.4(2)**). A claimant may apply to extend the time for service in accordance with the provisions of **r. 7.6** (see **15.30** to **15.33**).

A certificate of service (**r. 6.17**) must be filed within seven days of service of an arbitration claim form by the claimant (**PD 62, para. 3.2**). The court may exercise its powers under **CPR, r. 6.15**, to permit service of an arbitration claim form at the address of a party's solicitor or representative acting for that party in the arbitration (**PD 62, para. 3.1**).

Service of arbitration claim form out of the jurisdiction

72.5 The court may give permission to serve an arbitration claim form out of the jurisdiction in the following circumstances (**CPR, r. 62.5(1)**):

(a) When the claimant seeks to challenge an arbitration award or to appeal to the court on a question of law arising out of an award. For the court to be able to give permission in these circumstances the award must have been made in England and Wales.
(b) *If the claim is for an order under the* Arbitration Act 1996, s. 44 (court powers exercisable in support of arbitral proceedings; see **37.55**). The court may give permission for service out of the jurisdiction notwithstanding that the only remedy sought is in respect of arbitral proceedings which are taking (or will take) place outside of England and Wales.

(c) Any other situation where the claimant seeks a remedy or requires a question to be determined by the court which affects an arbitration (whether pending or anticipated), an arbitration agreement or an arbitration award. However, for this general provision to apply, the seat of the arbitration must be in England and Wales. If this is not the case the court may give permission nonetheless as long as the seat has not been designated or if, by reason of a connection with England and Wales or Northern Ireland, the court is satisfied that it is appropriate to do so in line with the Arbitration Act 1996, s. 2(4)(b). *Steamship Mutual Underwriting Association (Bermuda) Ltd v Sulpicio Lines Inc.* [2008] EWHC 914 (Comm), [2008] 2 Lloyd's Rep 269, is an example of where the existence of extraterritorial jurisdiction has been confirmed in the context of **CPR, r. 62.5(1)(c)**. In *Enercon GmbH v Enercon (India) Ltd* [2012] EWHC 689 (Comm), [2012] 1 Lloyd's Rep 519, Eder J held that, because the claimant had participated in parallel proceedings in the Indian courts, it was for an Indian court to determine the proper seat of the arbitration and it would therefore be inappropriate for the English court to grant permission to serve the claim form out of the jurisdiction, even though he would have held that the seat was England and Wales.

In *Vale do Rio Doce Navegação SA v Shanghai Bao Steel Ocean Shipping Co. Ltd* [2000] 2 Lloyd's Rep 1 Thomas J decided that these provisions as set out in the former PD 49G only apply to claims brought by and against parties to an arbitration. The court did not consider an application by or against a non-party (e.g. a witness) to be something 'affecting an arbitration'. Accordingly, service of an arbitration claim form outside the jurisdiction would not be permitted in such a case. This decision was followed in *Starlight Shipping Co. v Tai Ping Insurance Co. Ltd, Hubei Branch* [2007] EWHC 1893 (Comm), [2008] 1 All ER (Comm) 593, where Cooke J held that a person who is not a party to an arbitration agreement cannot take advantage of the rule.

An application for the grant of permission must be supported by written evidence stating the grounds on which the application is made. The evidence must also show in what place or country the person to be served is or probably may be found (**r. 62.5(2)**). In *Bitumex (HK) Company Ltd v IRPC Public Co. Ltd* [2012] EWHC 1065 (Comm), [2012] 2 All ER (Comm) 1131, HHJ Mackie QC granted an application for a retrospective order for alternative service out of the jurisdiction on the basis that the case was exceptional because it concerned the service of an arbitration claim form.

The provisions of **rr. 6.40 to 6.46**, which regulate the service of claim forms abroad, apply to the service of arbitration claim forms out of the jurisdiction (**r. 62.5(3)**).

Notice

Some provisions of the Arbitration Act 1996 require an application to be made on notice. On an application to remove an arbitrator (Arbitration Act 1996, s. 24), to consider and adjust the amount of fees and expenses for which the parties are liable (s. 28), or to determine the fees and expenses payable to the arbitrators where the arbitrators have withheld the award pending payment (s. 56), the arbitrators concerned must be made defendants to the application (**CPR, r. 62.6(1)**). In this way the statutory requirement for notice is fulfilled by serving the arbitration claim form on them together with any written evidence in support (**r. 62.6(2)**). Where the Arbitration Act 1996 requires an application to the court to be made on notice to any other party to the arbitration, that notice must be given by making that party a defendant (**CPR, r. 62.6(3)**). **72.6**

Supply of documents from court records

An arbitration claim form may only be inspected with the permission of the court (**PD 62, para. 5.1** which overrides **CPR, r. 5.4**). In *Glidepath BV v Thompson* [2005] EWHC 818 (Comm), [2005] 2 Lloyd's Rep 549, a third party made an application under **r. 5.4(5)** requesting copies of certain documents on the court file following a successful application for a stay under the Arbitration Act 1996, s. 9. The applicant, to assist him in presenting an employment tribunal case, sought access to the particulars of claim, notices of application in respect of a freezing **72.7** injunction and a *Norwich Pharmacal* application made before the proceedings were stayed. The Commercial Court refused to order production of the documents requested as neither the specific interest of the applicant in establishing his alleged rights before the employment tribunal, nor the interests of justice generally, could justify the granting of access to the documents. The court stated that it must be clearly established that the document sought will play an essential part in establishing the right of defence in question. 'To set the reasonable necessity threshold no higher than a requirement of evidential relevance would represent a most undesirable invasion by the courts of the confidentiality of arbitration in this country' (at [27]).

Acknowledgment of service

72.8 A defendant to an arbitration application may acknowledge service by completing form N15 or, as an alternative in the Commercial Court, form N210(CC) (Admiralty and Commercial Courts Guide, para. O5.1(b)). The general rule is that the defendant must acknowledge service within 14 days after service of the arbitration claim form (**CPR, r. 10.3(1)(b)**). If the court authorises service of the arbitration claim form out of the jurisdiction in accordance with **r. 62.5(1)** (see 72.5), it will set a time limit for acknowledgment of service (**r. 62.5(4)**).

An arbitrator (or ACAS) who is sent a copy of an arbitration claim form for his information may apply to be made a defendant. Such an application must be served on the claimant but need not be served on any other party. Alternatively an arbitrator (or ACAS), without becoming a party to the arbitration claim, may make representations by filing written evidence or in writing to the court (**PD 62, paras 4.1 to 4.3**).

Case management

72.9 All arbitration claims are allocated to the multi-track (although **CPR, Part 29**, does not apply). There is no requirement to file a directions questionnaire (**CPR, r. 62.7(1) to (3)**).

The following directions apply automatically unless the court orders otherwise (**CPR, r. 62.7(4); PD 62, para. 6.1**):

(a) A defendant who wishes to rely on evidence before the court must file and serve his written evidence within 21 days after the date by which he was required to acknowledge service or, if an acknowledgment of service is not required, within 21 days after service of the arbitration claim form (**PD 62, para. 6.2**).
(b) A claimant who wishes to put evidence before the court in reply to written evidence filed under (a) above must file or serve his written evidence within seven days after service of the defendant's evidence (**PD 62, para. 6.3**).
(c) Agreed indexed and paginated bundles of all the evidence and other documents to be used at the hearing must be prepared by the claimant (**PD 62, para. 6.4**).
(d) Not later than five days before the hearing date, estimates for the length of the hearing must be filed together with a complete set of the documents to be used (**PD 62, para. 6.5**).
(e) Not later than two days before the hearing date the claimant must file and serve:
    (i) a chronology of the relevant events cross-referenced to the bundle of documents;
    (ii) where necessary, a list of persons involved; and
    (iii) a skeleton argument which lists succinctly:
        (1) the issues which arise for decision;
        (2) the grounds for relief (or opposing relief) to be relied upon;
        (3) the submissions of fact to be made with references to the evidence; and
        (4) the submissions of law with references to the relevant authorities (**PD 62, para. 6.6**).
(f) Not later than the day before the hearing date the defendant shall file and serve a skeleton argument which lists succinctly:
    (i) the issues which arise for decision;

(ii) the grounds for relief (or opposing relief) to be relied upon;
(iii) the submissions of fact to be made with the references to the evidence; and
(iv) the submissions of law with references to the relevant authorities (**PD 62, para. 6.7**).

The Admiralty and Commercial Courts Guide, para. O6.2, states that claimants should apply for a hearing date as soon as possible after issuing an arbitration claim form or, in the case of an appeal, obtaining permission to appeal.

In the Commercial Court an application for directions in a pending arbitration claim should be made by application notice under **CPR, Part 23** (Admiralty and Commercial Courts Guide, para. O6.5).

Where an arbitration application involves recognition and/or enforcement of an agreement to arbitrate and that application is challenged on the grounds that the parties to the application were not bound by an agreement to arbitrate, it will usually be necessary for the court to resolve that issue in order to determine the application. For this purpose it may be necessary for there to be disclosure of documents and/or factual and/or expert evidence. In that event, it is the responsibility of those advising the applicant to liaise with the other party and to arrange with the Listing Office for a case management conference to be listed as early as possible to enable the court to give directions as to the steps to be taken before the hearing of the application (Admiralty and Commercial Courts Guide, para. O6.5).

Commentary

Application for stay of legal proceedings

An application for a stay of legal proceedings under the Arbitration Act 1996, s. 9, is governed **72.10** by **CPR, Part 62**; there is no indication that **Part 11** applies in relation to such proceedings (*Bilta (UK) Ltd v Nazir* [2010] EWHC 1086 (Ch), [2010] Bus LR 1634). An application notice seeking a stay of legal proceedings under the Arbitration Act 1996, s. 9, must be served on all parties to the relevant proceedings who have given an address for service (**CPR, r. 62.8(1)**). It should also be served on any party to those legal proceedings who has not given an address for service by sending a copy of the application notice to his last known address or at a place where it is likely to come to his attention. This can be done whether or not the party is within the jurisdiction (**r. 62.8(2)**).

On an application for a stay where a question arises as to whether an arbitration agreement has been concluded or as to whether the particular dispute which is the subject matter of the proceedings falls within the terms of an arbitration agreement, the court may determine that question. See, for example, *City of London v Sancheti* [2008] EWCA Civ 1283, [2008] 2 CLC 730, in which the Court of Appeal upheld a county court's refusal to grant a stay where the applicant was not a party to the relevant arbitration agreement. Alternatively it may give directions for its determination. The court may order proceedings to be stayed pending its decision (**r. 62.8(3)**).

Securing the attendance of witnesses

The Arbitration Act 1996, s. 43, allows a party to an arbitration to use court proceedings to **72.11** secure the attendance of witnesses at an arbitration. A party wishing to invoke this procedure may apply for a witness summons in accordance with **CPR, Part 34** (see **chapter 57**) (**PD 62, para. 7.1**). The application should be made to the Admiralty and Commercial Registry, or, if the attendance of the witness is required within the district of a district registry, to that registry (**PD 62, para. 7.2**). This power is only available if the witness is in the United Kingdom and if the arbitral proceedings are being conducted in England and Wales or Northern Ireland (Arbitration Act 1996, s. 43(3)). The courts may also, under s. 44, issue an order in support of arbitral proceedings with a seat outside England and Wales. Section 2(3) gives a discretion to use it in relation to other arbitrations (see *Commerce and Industry Insurance Co. of Canada v Certain Underwriters at Lloyd's of London* [2002] 1 WLR 1323). The s. 44 powers are available only to the extent that the arbitral tribunal does not possess these powers or is unable to act (s. 44(5)) (see *ASM Shipping Ltd v TTMI Ltd (No. 2)* [2007] EWHC 927 (Comm), [2007] 2 Lloyd's Rep 155).

The applicant must file an affidavit or witness statement showing that the application is made with the permission of the tribunal or the agreement of the other parties **(PD 62, para. 7.3)**.

This process was used in *Tajik Aluminium Plant v Hydro Aluminium AS* [2005] EWCA Civ 1218, [2006] 1 WLR 767. To ensure the attendance of witnesses at an arbitration, the claimants had obtained the consent of the tribunal to make an application to court under the Arbitration Act 1996, s. 43, to obtain a witness summons to compel third parties to attend the official hearing and to produce documents. The Court of Appeal held that documents so requested had to be specifically identified or at least described in some compendious manner that enabled the individual documents falling within the scope of the witness summons to be clearly identified. The Court of Appeal upheld the order to set aside the witness summonses on the ground that the schedules contained broad descriptions of documents but failed to identify them in a sufficiently certain manner.

Time limit for challenges to or appeals from awards

72.12 The Arbitration Act 1996, s. 70(3), provides that any challenge to or appeal from an award brought under ss. 67 to 69 must be brought within 28 days of the date of the award. However, as long as the time limit has not expired, a claimant may apply without notice on a Part 23 application notice for an order extending that time limit **(CPR, r. 62.9(1)** and **(2); PD 62, para. 11.1(1))**. The Admiralty and Commercial Courts Guide, para. O9.2, states that any challenge to an award should be made without delay and the court will require cogent reasons for extending time. The court will generally make its decision without a hearing **(PD 62, para. 10.2)**. Where the court makes an order extending the time limit, the defendant must file his written evidence within 21 days from service of the order **(PD 62, para. 10.2)**.

If the time limit has already expired, a claimant is not precluded from applying retrospectively for an extension of time. In such circumstances the claimant must set out in a separately identified part in the arbitration claim form the grounds why an order extending time should be made **(CPR, r. 62.9(3)(a); PD 62, para. 11.1(2))**. Any defendant who wishes to oppose the extension of time application may file written evidence in opposition within seven days after service of the arbitration claim form **(CPR, r. 62.9(3)(b))**. If the court makes an order extending the time limit, each defendant's time for acknowledging service and serving evidence shall start to run as if the arbitration claim form had been served on the date when the court's order is served on that defendant **(r. 62.9(3)(c))**.

In *Kalmneft JSC v Glencore International AG* [2002] 1 All ER 76 Colman J held that applications both for an extension of the 28-day time limit provided by the Arbitration Act 1996, s. 70(3), and for challenging an award under ss. 67 to 69 are governed by s. 80(5). This provides that such applications are governed by the provisions of the CPR for extending periods of time. Colman J stated that in exercising any discretion available under **CPR, r. 3.1**, the court should have in mind the general principles set out in the Arbitration Act 1996, s. 1. These differ from the overriding objective of the CPR, because they emphasise the principles of party autonomy and finality of awards and restrict the supervisory role of the courts. Accordingly much weight must be accorded to the avoidance of delay at all stages of an arbitration, both before and after an interim or final award. This was stated to be a distinct public policy factor to be given due weight in the discretionary balance. Other factors emphasised by Colman J were:

(a) whether the claimant had acted reasonably in all the circumstances;
(b) whether the defendant or the arbitrator had caused or contributed to the delay;
(c) whether the defendant would suffer irremediable prejudice;

(d) whether the arbitration had proceeded during the period of delay and, if so, what impact on the progress of the arbitration or the costs incurred in respect of it the determination of the application by the court might now have;
(e) the strength of the application; and
(f) whether in the broadest sense it would be unfair to the claimant for him to be denied the opportunity of having the application determined.

The principles laid down in *Kalmneft JSC v Glencore International AG* [2002] 1 All ER 76 were applied by the Court of Appeal in *Nagusina Naviera v Allied Maritime Inc.* [2002] EWCA Civ 1147, LTL 10/7/2002. Mance LJ identified the 'primary factors' in considering an application as being delay, reasonableness and causation. In his Lordship's view factor (c) was not 'an essential pre-condition' and factor (d) was a relatively minor consideration.This approach was endorsed in *Surefire Systems Ltd v Guardian ECL Ltd* [2005] EWHC 1860 (TCC), LTL 9/11/2005. Jackson J accepted the seven relevant considerations in relation to applications for extension of time cited by Colman J in *Kalmneft JSC v Glencore International AG*. The principles were also applied in *Peoples' Insurance Company of China, Hebei Branch v Vysanthi Shipping Co. Ltd* [2003] EWHC 1655 (Comm), LTL 18/7/2003, with the important gloss that the Arbitration Act 1996, s. 67, expressly draws attention to the fact that parties might lose the right to object if they fail to make a challenge within the requisite time. *Dulwich Estate v Baptiste* [2007] EWHC 410 (Ch), *The Times*, 22 February 2007, also applied the criteria set out in *Kalmneft* and clarified (in relation to a 21 or 31-day delay) that the total period of delay is not in itself going to be determinative of the application. However, in *Nestor Maritime SA v Sea Anchor Shipping Co. Ltd* [2012] EWHC 996 (Comm), [2012] 2 Lloyd's Rep 144, the claimant's delay of six months after the expiry of the 28-day deadline in making an application to extend time for a challenge under s. 68 weighed heavily in the court's decision to refuse the application. The judge, referring to the principles laid down in *Kalmneft JSC v Glencore International AG*, was also swayed by the weakness of the underlying challenge and the fact that it was 'doomed to fail' under s. 73 due to the claimant's continued participation in the arbitral proceedings.

In *DDT Trucks of North America Ltd v DDT Holdings Ltd* [2007] EWHC 1542 (Comm), [2007] 2 Lloyd's Rep 213, the court stated that the *Kalmneft* principles should be applied more strictly in relation to s. 67 applications where the jurisdiction of the arbitrator is challenged. Notable in this case also was the court's willingness to take into account the fact that the defendants' conduct of the proceedings depended upon the existence of a conditional fee agreement (CFA). Cooke J concluded that the grant of an extension of time would inevitably result in the protraction of proceedings, and the need to conclude further CFAs. This amounted to relevant prejudice to the defendants for these purposes.

Permission to appeal against the decision of a court under the Arbitration Act 1996, ss. 67 to 69, can only be granted by the trial judge (s. 67(4); *Athletic Union of Constantinople v National Basketball Association (No. 2)* [2002] EWCA Civ 830, [2002] 1 WLR 2863). However, the Court of Appeal retains a residual jurisdiction to ensure that a fair hearing of the application for permission to appeal has been afforded. Such applications are 'only very rarely going to succeed' (*Republic of Kazakhstan v Istil Group Inc.* [2007] EWCA Civ 471, [2007] 2 Lloyd's Rep 548).

Challenging the substantive jurisdiction of the tribunal

A challenge to substantive jurisdiction can be brought to the court under the Arbitration Act 1996, s. 32, 67 or 72. **72.13**

Section 32(1) gives the parties to the dispute the right to apply to the courts to rule on a preliminary question as to the substantive jurisdiction of the arbitral tribunal prior to the handing down of the award. The application should be made upon notice to the other parties (s. 32(1)). The application also requires either the written agreement of all the parties to the proceedings (s. 32(2)(a)) or the permission of the tribunal and the court's satisfaction that (i) the determination will result in substantial cost savings, (ii) the application has been made without delay, and (iii) there is a good reason for the matter to be decided by the court (s. 32(2)(b)(i) to (iii)).

A party may, under s. 67, challenge an award made by an arbitral tribunal on the ground that the tribunal did not have substantive jurisdiction. A challenge to the substantive jurisdiction of an arbitral tribunal under s. 67(1) requires the permission of the High Court (s. 67(4)). For the limited jurisdiction of the Court of Appeal to review a refusal of permission, see the cases discussed at **72.15**. A court hearing such an arbitration claim may examine the arguments already addressed to the tribunal in a far wider manner than a court hearing a challenge to an award under the Arbitration Act 1996, ss. 68 and 69, and where a party alleges that he has not submitted to the arbitrator's jurisdiction, he is entitled to a full judicial determination on evidence of an issue of jurisdiction before the English court under s. 67, or under s. 72 if he has taken no part in the arbitration (see *Dallah Real Estate and Tourism Holding Co. v Ministry of Religious Affairs of the Government of Pakistan* [2010] UKSC 46, [2011] 1 AC 763).

In *Dallah* the jurisdiction of the tribunal was challenged as part of resisting enforcement of an award made in France, pursuant to s. 103 rather than by way of a challenge to the award under s. 67. The Supreme Court, however, held that the standard of review of a tribunal's finding on jurisdiction should not differ depending on whether the review is carried out by the courts of the seat or the courts where enforcement of the award is sought. As to the review, the tribunal's own view of its jurisdiction has no legal or evidential value. The starting point for a challenge must be an independent investigation, and a full rehearing by the court is appropriate because the court should not be placed in a worse position than the arbitrator in determining the issue which in a given case might turn on contested issues of fact. Whilst the court may have regard to the reasoning and findings of the tribunal if they are helpful, the court is neither bound nor restricted by those findings. The parties will be allowed to introduce additional evidence which was not before the arbitrator. The grounds of objection to jurisdiction taken in an arbitration are not to be examined as closely as in a statement of case, so a party may, taking a broad view, be permitted to adduce new evidence in support of a new or different argument, coming within the existing 'grounds of objection', on an appeal under s. 67 (*Primetrade AG v Ythan Ltd* [2005] EWHC 2399 (Comm), [2006] 1 All ER 376).

Section 72 gives a person alleged to be a party to the dispute, but who has no wish to take part in the proceedings, the right to apply to the court for a declaration or injunction or other appropriate relief to determine the question of whether: (a) there is a valid arbitration agreement, (b) whether the tribunal is properly constituted or (c) what matters have been submitted in accordance with the arbitration agreement (s. 72(1)(a) to (c)). In *Broda Agro Trade (Cyprus) Ltd v Alfred C. Toepfer International GmbH* [2010] EWCA Civ 1100, [2011] 1 Lloyd's Rep 243, the applicant applied for a ruling under s. 72 that there was no valid arbitration agreement and that the original award on jurisdiction was not binding on it. The applicant argued that although it had participated in the arbitration proceedings, it had done so only on the merits whilst it continued to deny the arbitral tribunal's jurisdiction, and had not participated in the separate arbitral proceedings on jurisdiction. The Court of Appeal, however, saw no basis for an implied restriction of the statute's words 'takes no part in the proceedings' to the proceedings relating to determining the arbitral tribunal's jurisdiction. Accordingly, where a party participates in any part of the arbitral proceedings, that party no longer has recourse to an application under s. 72.

The Court of Appeal in *Broda Agro Trade (Cyprus) Ltd v Alfred C. Toepfer International GmbH* also stated that the restrictions in ss. 67 and 72 on challenges to the jurisdiction of an arbitral tribunal cannot be circumvented by making a claim at common law. The jurisdiction of the court to make a declaration regarding an arbitration agreement is subject to the restrictions in the *Arbitration Act 1996*. Accordingly, Broda's request for a common law declaration as to the effect of the arbitration agreement added nothing. This statement from the Court of Appeal casts doubt on the possibility of requesting the court to make a declaration concerning an arbitration agreement using its inherent jurisdiction. Accordingly, the analysis in *British Telecommunications plc v SAE Group Inc.* [2009] EWHC 252 (TCC), [2009] BLR 231, should be treated with caution. In *British Telecommunications plc v SAE Group Inc.* (which was not cited in *Broda*) an application was made for a declaration that there was no valid and binding arbitration agreement. The application sought a declaration using the court's inherent jurisdiction, or, in the alternative, pursuant to ss. 32 or 72 of the Act. Ramsey J found on the facts that there was no valid arbitration agreement, and applied an analysis which resulted in the relief being granted pursuant to the court's inherent jurisdiction, rather than by the powers granted by the Arbitration Act 1996.

Challenging an award for serious irregularity

There are directions relating to challenging an award for serious irregularity under the Arbitration Act 1996, s. 68, in the Admiralty and Commercial Courts Guide, paras O8.6 to O8.10. Such applications are only appropriate where there are grounds for thinking both: **72.14**

(a) that an irregularity has occurred; and
(b) that that irregularity has caused or will cause *substantial* injustice to the party making the challenge (para. O8.6(a), emphasis in original).

An application challenging an award on the grounds of serious irregularity should not therefore be regarded as an alternative to, or as a means of supporting, an application for permission to appeal (para. O8.6(b)).

A challenge to an award must be supported by evidence of the circumstances on which the claimant relies as giving rise to the irregularity complained of and the nature of the injustice which has been or will be caused to him (para. O8.7). If the nature of the challenge itself or the evidence filed in support of it leads the court to consider that the claim has no real prospect of success, the court may exercise its powers under **CPR**, **r. 3.3(4)**, to dismiss the application summarily. In such a case the claimant will have the right under **r. 3.3(5)** to apply to the court to set aside the order and to seek directions for the hearing of the claim (Admiralty and Commercial Courts Guide, para. O8.8).

If the arbitration claim form includes both a challenge to an award by way of an appeal and a challenge on the grounds of serious irregularity, the applications should be set out in separate sections of the arbitration claim form and the grounds on which they are made should be separately identified (para. O8.9). The papers will be placed before a judge to consider how the applications may most appropriately be disposed of. It will usually be more appropriate to dispose of the application to set aside or remit the award before considering the application for permission to appeal (para. O8.10).

Failing to ensure that experienced counsel understood a point taken by the other side is not a serious irregularity, unless the arbitrator was aware of the misunderstanding (*Bandwidth Shipping Corporation v Intaari* [2007] EWCA Civ 998, [2008] Bus LR 702). Likewise, it is not a serious irregularity within the Arbitration Act 1996, s. 68(2), for an arbitrator to fail to point out arguments that one or other side may have missed in support of their case. An arbitrator has no duty to do so (under s. 33) (*E. D. and F. Man Sugar Ltd v Belmont Shipping Ltd* [2011] EWHC 2992 (Comm), LTL 1/12/2011). An arbitrator's decision not to hold an oral hearing, which might have caused the arbitrator to reach a different conclusion, did not amount to serious irregularity but rather the exercise of the arbitrator's discretion pursuant to s. 34(2)(h) (*O'Donoghue v Enterprise Inns plc* [2008] EWHC 2273 (Ch), [2008] NPC 103). There is no obligation to address a dissenting arbitrator's concerns, and a failure to do so would not amount to a serious irregularity within s. 68(2) where there is no reason to suppose that the majority would have reached a different view had they specifically addressed the arbitrator's concerns (*Ispat Industries Ltd v Western Bulk Pte Ltd* [2011] EWHC 93 (Comm), LTL 4/2/2011). A further issue raised in *Bandwidth Shipping Corporation v Intaari* also appeared in *Compañía Sud-Americana de Vapores SA v Nippon Yusen Kaisha* [2009] EWHC 1606 (Comm), [2010] 1 Lloyd's Rep 1. Where a challenge is made on the grounds of serious irregularity, the reasoning to be applied requires that the court ask whether, but for the irregularity which caused the tribunal to reach its decision, the tribunal would have reached the same conclusion. This reasoning appears to run contrary to that which appears in *Van der Giessen-de Noord Shipbuilding Division BV v Imtech Marine & Offshore BV* [2008] EWHC 2904 (Comm), [2009] 1 Lloyd's Rep 273, where it was held, *inter alia*, that in determining whether there had been a substantial injustice, it was not for the court to decide what would have happened in the arbitration had there been no irregularity. The case gave further guidance in relation to challenges for serious irregularity. First, the power to set aside an award in whole or in part was not available simply because the tribunal had made a mistake, whether of fact or law. Furthermore, this power was not available merely because the arbitrators did not deal with all the points made or arguments advanced, or because they did not set out each step by which they reached their conclusion. Second, a failure to deal with an issue was not deemed to be the same as a failure to set out the reasoning for rejecting a particular argument.

This approach was applied in *Petrochemical Industries Co. (KSC) v Dow Chemical Co.* [2012] EWHC 2739 (Comm), [2012] 2 Lloyd's Rep 691, where Andrew Smith J gave useful guidance on whether a particular question was an 'issue' within the meaning of s. 68(2)(d), whether that issue was 'put to' the tribunal, and whether the tribunal failed to 'deal with' it. The judge rejected a number of previous tests for determining what an 'issue' is and preferred instead to give that phrase its ordinary meaning. He did, however, distinguish between 'issues' on the one hand and 'arguments', 'points', 'lines of reasoning' or 'steps' in an argument on the other. As to whether the tribunal 'dealt with' an issue, Andrew Smith J confirmed that this depends on a consideration of the award but a tribunal does not have to set out every step by which it reaches its conclusion or deal with each point made by the parties.

As noted above, it is not sufficient that there has been a serious irregularity of the kinds listed in s. 68. The irregularity must also be of a kind the court considers has caused or will cause substantial injustice to the applicant. This was highlighted in *CNH Global NV v PGN Logistics Ltd* [2009] EWHC 977 (Comm), [2009] 1 CLC 807, a case that arose out of what Burton J referred to as a 'howler' by the arbitral tribunal (a failure to award interest) which the tribunal had corrected by a subsequent addendum to the award issued pursuant to what is now the ICC Arbitration Rules (2012) art. 35. Article 35 covers the correction of a 'clerical, computational, or typographical error, or any errors of similar nature'. The claimant challenged the addendum on the basis that the error it corrected was not of that nature and that by issuing the addendum the tribunal had exceeded its powers (one of the categories of serious irregularity listed in the Arbitration Act 1996, s. 68(2)(b)). Burton J agreed that the error corrected was not a clerical or computation error, and that the tribunal did not have any power to correct it at all. The addendum was therefore beyond its powers and an irregularity falling within s. 68(2)(b). However, as the addendum was simply correcting 'the original howler' which had in turn caused substantial injustice to the defendant, and its effect on the claimant was only to remove a wholly undeserved windfall, Burton J concluded it could not possibly be argued that the addendum caused substantial injustice to the applicant and therefore dismissed the s. 68 application.

Applications for permission to appeal

72.15 The Arbitration Act 1996, s. 69, provides that in certain circumstances, unless otherwise agreed by the parties, a party to arbitral proceedings may appeal to the court on a question of law arising out of an award. Exclusion of s. 69 can be achieved only by sufficiently clear wording: the phrase 'final, conclusive and binding' in an arbitration agreement is not sufficient (*Shell Egypt West Manzala GmbH v Dana Gas Egypt Ltd* [2009] EWHC 2097 (Comm), [2010] 1 Lloyd's Rep 109). An appeal under s. 69 cannot be entertained where the law applied by the arbitrators was not the law of England and Wales (Arbitration Act 1996, s. 82(1)(a); *Schwebel v Schwebel* [2010] EWHC 3280 (TCC), 161 NLJ 29).

The question must be a question of law, not fact. The classic examination of what amounts to a question of law is that of Mustill J in *Finelvet AG v Vinava Shipping Co. Ltd* [1983] 1 WLR 1469:

(1) The arbitrator ascertains the facts. This process includes the making of findings on any facts which are in dispute.
(2) The arbitrator ascertains the law. This process comprises not only the identification of all material rules of statute and common law, but also the identification and interpretation of the relevant parts of the contract, and the identification of those facts which must be taken into account when the decision is reached.
(3) In the light of the facts and the law so ascertained, the arbitrator reaches his decision.

An appeal on a point of law is possible only in relation to matters falling within (2). The question of law must arise out of an award made in arbitral proceedings to which the appellant was party. A party cannot appeal on a new point of law which was not raised before the tribunal (see, for example, *STX Pan Ocean Co. Ltd v Ugland Bulk Transport AS* [2007] EWHC 1317 (Comm), [2008] 1 Lloyd's Rep 210).

Unless the claimant can obtain the agreement of all the other parties to the proceedings, an appeal cannot be brought without the permission of the court (s. 69(2)).

PD 62, para. 12.6(2), does not say whether the reasons relied on by the respondent in opposing the grant of permission to appeal under the Arbitration Act 1996, s. 69, need to be points of law. This was considered in *CTI Group Inc. v Transclear SA (No. 2)* [2007] EWHC 2340 (Comm), [2008] 1 All ER (Comm) 203, by Field J. He concluded that s. 69 grounds 'must be based on a point or points of law' and that deciding a question of mixed fact and law would go against the clear policy of the Arbitration Act 1996 to restrict grounds on which arbitral awards may be challenged. Further, even if an agreement between the parties exists which would allow an appeal on questions of fact, such an agreement cannot expand the jurisdiction of the court to entertain such an appeal under s. 69, and it is very doubtful whether the courts have any inherent jurisdiction to entertain such an appeal (*Guangzhou Dockyards Co Ltd v ENE Aegiali I* [2010] EWHC 2826 (Comm), [2011] 1 Lloyd's Rep 30).

According to criteria set out in the Arbitration Act 1996, s. 69(3), permission to bring an appeal will only be granted if:

(a) the determination of the question will substantially affect the rights of one or more of the parties;
(b) the question is one which the tribunal was asked to determine;
(c) on the basis of the findings of fact in the award:
    (i) the decision of the tribunal on the question is obviously wrong; or
    (ii) the question is one of general public importance and the decision of the tribunal is at least open to serious doubt; and
(d) despite the agreement of the parties to resolve the matter by arbitration, it is just and proper in all the circumstances for the court to determine the question.

On an application for permission, the arbitration claim form must identify the question of law, state the grounds (but not the argument) on which the claimant alleges that permission should be granted be accompanied by a skeleton argument and append the award (**PD 62, para. 12.1**). The claimant should file written evidence in support of the application only if it is necessary to show (insofar as it is not apparent from the award itself) that the matters set out in s. 69(3) have been satisfied and to satisfy the court that permission should be granted (**para. 12.4**). Unless there is a dispute as to whether the question raised in the appeal is one which the tribunal was asked to determine, no documents adduced in or produced for the purposes of the arbitration may be put before the court other than the award and any document referred to in the award which the court needs in order to determine the point of law (**para. 12.5**).

If the defendant wishes to oppose the grant of permission, it must file a respondent's notice setting out the grounds (but not the argument) on which the defendant opposes the application (**para. 12.6(1)**).

Commentary

The respondent's notice should also specify whether the defendant wishes to contend that the award should be upheld for reasons not expressed (or not fully expressed) in it. The reasons for any such contentions should be stated (**para. 12.6(2)**). The respondent's notice should be accompanied by a skeleton argument (**para. 12.7**) and evidence that complies with the requirements of **PD 62, para. 12.4** (**para. 12.8**). The claimant may file and serve evidence or argument in reply only if it is necessary to do so and any such evidence must be as brief as possible (**para. 12.9**). In *CMA CGM SA v Beteiligungs-Kommanditgesellschaft MS 'Northern Pioneer' Schiffahrtsgesellschaft mbH & Co.* [2002] EWCA Civ 1878, [2003] 1 WLR 1015, the Court of Appeal emphasised that the written material should be capable of being read and digested by the judge within 30 minutes. A failure to comply with **PD 62, paras 12.1** to **12.9** may carry costs consequences (**para. 12.11**). An oral hearing is not normally required to decide such an application for leave to appeal and it can be determined entirely on paper (**para. 12.12**; see *BLCT (13096) Ltd v J Sainsbury plc* [2003] EWCA Civ 884, [2004] 1 CLC 24 and *HMV UK Ltd v Propinvest Friar LP* [2011] EWCA Civ 1708, [2012] 1 Lloyd's Rep 416).

The judge should give brief reasons on refusing permission to appeal, which need to be sufficient to identify which of the statutory tests has not been met (**PD 62, para. 12.14**; *North Range Shipping Ltd v Seatrans Shipping Corporation* [2002] EWCA Civ 405, [2002] 1 WLR 2397). It is sufficient to say 'for the reasons given by the arbitrators' if that is the judge's reason. In some cases it is necessary to go further, but reasons should still be brief. The Court of Appeal has confirmed that it has a residuary discretion to review decisions of the first instance court to refuse leave to appeal where there was clear unfairness in the process. However, in *CGU International Insurance plc v AstraZeneca Insurance Co. Ltd* [2006] EWCA Civ 1340, [2007] Bus LR 162, the Court of Appeal found no reason to believe that the judge's refusal was perverse or arbitrary. The Court also confirmed that *North Range Shipping Ltd v Seatrans Shipping Corporation* had not been decided per incuriam. The same residuary discretion applies to applications for leave to appeal under the Arbitration Act 1996, s. 68(4) (see *ASM Shipping Ltd v TTMI Ltd* [2006] EWCA Civ 1341, [2006] 2 CLC 471).

The residuary discretion recognised by *CGU International Insurance plc v AstraZeneca Insurance Co. Ltd*, to review a judge's decision to refuse permission, is strictly limited. It may be used where there has been procedural unfairness in the judge's decision, or if there has been a failure to engage with the arguments on the limited question of an appeal (*Kazakhstan v Istil Group Ltd (No. 2)* [2007] EWCA Civ 471, [2008] Bus LR 878). The refusal of a first-instance judge to grant permission to appeal under s. 69 does not affect the jurisdiction of the Court of Appeal to hear an appeal on whether there was an exclusion agreement in relation to the right to appeal, and s. 69(6) does not apply so the court's permission is not required (*Sumukan Ltd v Commonwealth Secretariat* [2007] EWCA Civ 243, [2007] Bus LR 1075). These limited rights of access to the courts to challenge an award are compliant with the European Convention on Human Rights, **art. 6(1)**, in the **Human Rights Act 1998, sch. 1**. The High Court judge in effect operates as a second-tier appeal court, because, under the Arbitration Act 1996, an objection to jurisdiction is normally made first to the arbitrators. It is therefore a proportionate and legitimate restriction to provide in most cases that the High Court judge, rather than the Court of Appeal, is the final appeal court (*Kazakhstan v Istil Group Ltd (No. 2)*). An objection to an arbitral tribunal's jurisdiction should be raised before the tribunal itself. Failure to do so may result in loss of any right to object (*UR Power GmbH v Kuok Oils and Grains Pte Ltd* [2009] EWHC 1940 (Comm), [2009] 2 Lloyd's Rep 495, where the comment was obiter).

Hearings

72.16 The general rule in **CPR, r. 39.2(1)**, providing for all hearings to be held in public, is displaced in the case of arbitration claims (**r. 62.10(1)** and **(2)**). Although the court has a discretion to order that an arbitration claim be heard either in public or in private, the presumption is that all arbitration claims are to be heard in private. However, arbitration claims concerning the determination of a preliminary point of law under the Arbitration Act 1996, s. 45, or an appeal under s. 69 on a question of law arising out of an award will be heard in public unless the court orders otherwise (**CPR, r. 62.10(3)**). This exception does not apply to hearings to determine the preliminary question of whether the court, on an application to determine a preliminary point of law, is satisfied that the determination of the question is likely to produce substantial savings on costs and was made without delay. It also does not apply to applications for permission to appeal on a point of law (**r. 62.10(4)(a)** and **(b)**).

Rule 62.10 was considered in *Department of Economics, Policy and Development of the City of Moscow v Bankers Trust Co.* [2004] EWCA Civ 314, [2005] QB 207. The Court of Appeal noted that **r. 62.10** introduced a starting point of privacy for arbitration claims which differs from the usual position prevailing under the CPR. However, this is not a blanket rule and in every case, while it is appropriate to start the hearing in private, the court should be ready to hear representations from one or other party that the hearing should continue in public, and should, if appropriate, raise the possibility with the parties. The Court of Appeal also held that in applying **r. 62.10(3)**, the starting point is to treat the parties' wish for confidentiality and privacy as outweighing the public interest in a public hearing (applied in *Emmott v Michael Wilson and Partners Ltd* [2008] EWCA Civ 184, [2008] Bus LR 1361). In *Glidepath BV v Thompson* [2005] EWHC 818 (Comm), [2005] 2 Lloyd's Rep 549, the Commercial Court referred to *Bankers Trust* and confirmed, at [17], that the 'character of confidentiality is further reflected in CPR, r. 62.10'.

Judgments on arbitration applications are usually made public. Any application for privacy or anonymity should be supported by written evidence at the time the application is made (*C v D* [2007] EWCA Civ 1282, [2008] Bus LR 843).

APPLICATIONS UNDER THE OLD LAW

CPR, rr. 62.11 to 62.16, deal with the procedure to be adopted on applications to the court to which the 'old law', as specified in the Arbitration Act 1996, s. 107, applies. These applications are becoming increasingly rare, and will not be considered further. **72.17**

ENFORCEMENT OF AWARDS

Action on the award

CPR, Part 62, does not apply to enforcement of awards by bringing a claim on the award (**r. 62.17**). A party enforcing an award in such a manner, rather than using the simpler statutory methods of enforcement, should commence the claim under **Part 8**. Such proceedings would not be an arbitration claim and the usual provisions of the CPR would apply. **72.18**

Statutory enforcement

Applications for permission to enforce awards under the statutory regime (Arbitration Act 1996, ss. 66 and 101; Arbitration Act 1950, s. 26; or Arbitration Act 1975, s. 3(1)(a)) may be made without notice as an arbitration claim using form N8 (see 72.2; **CPR, r. 62.18(1)**). **72.19**

On an application for permission to enforce, the court may direct that the arbitration claim form be served on such parties to the arbitration as it may specify (**r. 62.18(2)**). With the permission of the court, the arbitration claim form may be served out of the jurisdiction irrespective of where the award was, or is treated as having been, made (**r. 62.18(4)**). If the court directs that the arbitration form be served on the parties to the arbitration, the parties on whom it is served must acknowledge service and the enforcement proceedings will continue as if they were an arbitration claim governed by all applicable rules of **Part 62** (**r. 62.18(3)**).

On an application for permission to enforce an agreed award (Arbitration Act 1996, s. 51(2)), the arbitration claim form must state that the award is an agreed award. Any order made by the court must also contain such a statement (**CPR, r. 62.18(5)**).

An application for permission to enforce an award must be supported by written evidence exhibiting the arbitration agreement and the original award (or copies thereof). If the application is to enforce a New York Convention award under the Arbitration Act 1996, s. 101, or the Arbitration Act 1975, s. 3(1)(a), the duly authenticated original award and the original arbitration agreement (or duly certified copies) must be exhibited (**CPR, r. 62.18(6)(a)**). If the New York Convention award or agreement is in a foreign language, a translation certified by an official or sworn translator or by a diplomat or consular agent must be provided.

The written evidence must state the name and the usual or last-known place of residence or business of the claimant and of the person against whom it is sought to enforce the award (**r. 62.18(6)(b)**). It must also state that the award has not been complied with or, alternatively, the extent to which it has not been complied with at the date of the application (**r. 62.18(6)(c)**).

The Admiralty and Commercial Courts Guide, para. O18.4, states that two copies of the draft order must accompany the application. If the claimant wishes to enter judgment, the form of the judgment must correspond to the form of the award.

The claimant must draw up the order giving permission. It must be served by delivering a copy to the defendant personally or by sending a copy to the defendant's usual or last-known place of residence or business (**CPR, r. 62.18(7)**). The court's permission is not required for the order to be served out of the jurisdiction and any order to be served outside the jurisdiction should be served in accordance with **rr. 6.40** to **6.46** as if the order were an arbitration claim form (**r. 62.18(8)**).

Any application to set aside the order must be brought within 14 days after service and the award cannot be enforced until this period has expired. If the defendant applies within this period, the award cannot be enforced until after the application is finally disposed of. If the order is to be served out of the jurisdiction, the court may fix some other time limit within which the defendant must apply to have it set aside (**r. 62.18(9)**).

In *Colliers International Property Consultants v Colliers Jordan Lee Jafaar Sdn Bhd* [2008] EWHC 1524 (Comm), [2008] 2 Lloyd's Rep 368, a draft order for a claim served in Malaysia had led the judge to give a deadline of 14 days for an application to set it aside rather than 24 days, which was the appropriate time limit for that jurisdiction. However, since no steps had been taken to enforce the judgment, no prejudice had been suffered by the applicant and the application was therefore dismissed.

The order served on the defendant must contain a statement of the right to make an application to set it aside. It must also state the fact that the award cannot be enforced until after the time limit has expired or until after the application is finally disposed of, should the defendant make an application to set aside the award (**r. 62.18(10)**).

If the defendant is a body corporate, the arbitration claim form and any order giving permission to enforce should be served at its registered or principal address (**r. 62.18(11)**).

In *Svenska Petroleum Exploration AB v Lithuania (No. 2)* [2006] EWCA Civ 1529, [2007] QB 886, the claimant had applied to strike out the respondent's application to set aside an order giving permission to enforce an ICC interim award in England under the Arbitration Act 1996, s. 103(1). On appeal to the Court of Appeal, one of the grounds upon which the respondent continued to object was that the award was not final and conclusive. The determination of whether an award is final and binding depends on its status in the country where it was made. The interim award was issued in Denmark and, under Danish law, an arbitral award on jurisdiction is reviewable by the Danish courts. Initially, the learned deputy judge held that the award was not final and binding since the right to challenge the award under Danish law had not been lost irretrievably. Following a hearing on this point, however, Gloster J concluded that the award was in fact final, because any right to challenge the award had most likely been lost through delay. This decision was upheld by the Court of Appeal although it was confirmed that the finality of an award depends upon the laws of the country in which it was rendered. However, in *Yukos Capital S v OJSC Rosneft Oil Co.* [2012] EWCA Civ 855, [2013] 1 All ER 223, the Court of Appeal held that the English courts were not barred by the act of State doctrine from investigating and potentially refusing recognition of decisions by the Russian courts setting aside two ICC awards handed down in Russia, on the basis that those decisions were alleged to be 'partial and dependent'. Moreover, an earlier decision to this effect by the Dutch courts did not raise an issue estoppel in the English proceedings because the Dutch decision was based on Dutch public policy while the English decision would be based on English public policy, and the two might be different. In *Gater Assets Ltd v NAK Naftogaz Ukrainiy* [2007] EWCA Civ 988, [2008] Bus LR 388, the Court of Appeal considered whether an order for security for costs could be made against a claimant seeking to enforce a New York Convention arbitration award. The three Lord Justices each arrived at a different conclusion as to whether, and in what circumstances, the court had jurisdiction to award security against an award creditor. However, the majority concluded that as a matter of principle the court should be reluctant, save in an exceptional case, to order security for costs against an award creditor, even if the power to do so should be technically available.

In *IPCO (Nigeria) Ltd v Nigerian National Petroleum Corporation* [2008] EWCA Civ 1157, [2009] 1 Lloyd's Rep 89, the court confirmed, in relation to a New York Convention award, that it can order partial enforcement of arbitral awards. The Court of Appeal has also confirmed that the court has the power to enter judgment in terms of a declaratory award under s. 66 (*West Tankers Inc. v Allianz SpA* [2012] EWCA Civ 27, [2012] Bus LR 1701).

Commentary

As discussed at **72.13**, the Supreme Court in *Dallah Real Estate and Tourism Holding Co. v Ministry of Religious Affairs of the Government of Pakistan* [2010] UKSC 46, [2011] 1 AC 763, held that where a court is asked to enforce an award, and an application is made to resist enforcement under the Arbitration Act 1996, s. 103, on the basis that the tribunal did not have jurisdiction, a party is entitled to a full determination on evidence of the issue of jurisdiction. The standard of review does not differ depending on whether the review is carried out at the courts of the seat of the arbitration (domestic and pursuant to s. 67) or the courts where enforcement is sought. See **72.13** for further discussion of the appropriate standard of review.

Interest on award

An applicant seeking to enforce an award of interest where the whole or any part of the interest relates to a period after the date of the award must file a statement giving the following particulars (**CPR, r. 62.19(1)**): **72.20**

(a) whether simple or compound interest was awarded;
(b) the date from which interest was awarded;
(c) whether rests were provided for, in which case they should be specified;
(d) the rate of interest awarded; and
(e) a calculation showing the total amount claimed up to the date of the certificate. Any sums which will become due thereafter should be shown on a daily-rate basis.

Such a statement must be filed whenever the amount of interest has to be quantified for the purpose of obtaining a judgment or order for the enforcement of an award (Arbitration Act 1996, s. 66) or enforcing such a judgment or order (**CPR, r. 62.19(2)**).

Chapter 73 Alternative Dispute Resolution

INTRODUCTION

73.1 The introduction of the CPR began a process designed to reform court procedures to make them more effective and more affordable. However, whatever changes are introduced, a fair trial of complex issues will always be expensive. By its nature, adversarial litigation may not be able to provide a resolution to the parties' dispute which is truly in their best interests. Accordingly, recognising the limits of litigation, Lord Woolf noted in his *Interim Report* (ch. 18, paras 1 and 2) that:

> In recent years there has been, both in this country and overseas, a growth in alternative dispute resolution (ADR) and an increasing recognition of its contribution to the fair, appropriate and effective resolution of civil disputes. The fact that litigation is not the only means of achieving this aim, and may not in all cases be the best, is my main reason for including ADR in an Inquiry whose essential focus is on improving access to justice through the courts. My second reason is to increase awareness still further among the legal professional and the general public, of what ADR has to offer.... From the point of view of the Court Service, ADR has the obvious advantage of saving scarce judicial and other resources. More significantly, in my view, it offers a variety of benefits to litigants or potential litigants.

While the courts were not to become involved in administering ADR, Lord Woolf recommended that the two systems worked together:

> Where there is a satisfactory alternative which offers a prospect of resolving a dispute in a way which is to the advantage of the litigants, then the court should encourage the use of this alternative. This is a responsibility which the courts should accept. It is in their interest that they should do so. (*Interim Report*, ch. 18, para. 31.)

Since the CPR were introduced the courts have been balancing their support for ADR with the right of access to the courts. The leading case is now the Court of Appeal decision in *Halsey v Milton Keynes General NHS Trust* [2004] EWCA Civ 576, [2004] 1 WLR 3002. The central message of this case (at [11]) is that:

> Parties sometimes need to be encouraged by the court to embark on an ADR. The need for such encouragement should diminish in time if the virtue of ADR in suitable cases is demonstrated even more convincingly than it has been thus far. The value and importance of ADR have been established within a remarkably short time. All members of the legal profession who conduct litigation should

now routinely consider with their clients whether their disputes are suitable for ADR. But we reiterate that the court's role is to encourage, not to compel. The form of encouragement may be robust.

For an example of robust encouragement, see *Egan v Motor Services (Bath) Ltd* [2007] EWCA Civ 1002, [2008] 1 WLR 1589. Here the Court of Appeal expressed its dismay ('completely cuckoo') at seeing legal costs of more than £100,000 being spent on a dispute over £6,000.

Judicial support for alternative dispute resolution

In *R (Cowl) v Plymouth City Council* [2001] EWCA Civ 1935, [2002] 1 WLR 803, Lord Woolf restated his support for ADR judicially. He spoke of 'the paramount importance of avoiding litigation whenever this is possible' and how both sides must 'be acutely conscious of the contribution alternative dispute resolution can make to resolving disputes in a manner which both meets the needs of the parties and the public and saves time, expense and stress'. 73.2

Judicial support for alternative dispute resolution was extended to holding that agreements to mediate, entered into before a dispute has arisen, are enforceable. This contrasts with the usual English law position that agreements to negotiate are unenforceable. In *Cable and Wireless plc v IBM United Kingdom Ltd* [2002] EWHC 2059 (Comm), [2002] 2 All ER (Comm) 1041, Colman J stated that 'for the courts now to decline to enforce contractual references to ADR on the grounds of intrinsic uncertainty would be to fly in the face of public policy as expressed in the CPR'. However, the Court of Appeal declined to follow this decision in *Sulamerica Cia Nacional de Seguros SA v Enesa Engenharia SA* [2012] EWCA Civ 638, [2013] 1 WLR 102 where the court held that a relatively detailed mediation provision was incapable of giving rise to a binding obligation because it failed to define a mediation process. *Sulamerica* was applied in *Tang Chung Wah v Grant Thornton International Ltd* [2012] EWHC 3198 (Ch), [2013] 1 Lloyd's Rep 11. This case arose out of a dispute within an international accountancy network. Before commencing arbitration proceedings the relevant agreement called for disputes to be referred to the Chief Executive and thereafter to a Panel of Board Members for resolution. The court relied on *Sulamerica* in finding that the process was too nebulous and equivocal to be enforceable. It also laid down a test whereby the court should assess (1) whether there is a sufficiently clear and unequivocal commitment to commence a process, (2) whether the steps a party should take to commence the process can be discerned and (3) whether the process itself is sufficiently clearly defined to allow the court to determine the minimum required of the parties in terms of participation in a process and when or how the process can be terminable without breach.

In appropriate circumstances, the courts will impose costs sanctions on parties they perceive to have insufficiently explored the possibilities of alternative dispute resolution (see 73.23).

There is no official framework or rules for ADR in the CPR. However, the CPR are framed so that ADR is always to be considered as an alternative to pursuing a claim through the courts. There are a number of provisions whereby court proceedings intersect with ADR. These are described at 73.9 to 73.23.

WHAT IS ADR?

ADR is understood to mean any alternative process to litigation through the courts. The various types of ADR broadly fall into two main categories. The first category involves processes that are, similar to litigation, adjudicatory. These result in a final and binding determination on the parties. The second category includes procedures that facilitate a negotiated settlement between the disputing parties within a structured framework. These, the non-adjudicative processes, usually involve some kind of third-party involvement. 73.3

ADJUDICATIVE ADR

The adjudicative procedures include such processes as arbitration and expert determination where a final and binding determination is made on the dispute. These types of ADR are widely used in 73.4

commercial contracts. For example, arbitration is often used for the resolution of rent review disputes under commercial leases while expert determination is included in energy contracts for disputes that relate to specific technical accounting matters. In such cases, an expert accountant will be nominated by the parties to make a determination on the matters in dispute.

Adjudication under the Housing Grants, Construction and Regeneration Act 1996

73.5 In common with certain other jurisdictions, the various United Kingdom jurisdictions have imposed by statute a quasi-judicial process for certain construction disputes. The Housing Grants, Construction and Regeneration Act 1996 created a right to refer to adjudication a dispute arising under any agreement which is a construction contract, entered into after that date. The Act applies to England, Wales and Scotland, and there is equivalent legislation for Northern Ireland. To be covered by the Act, a construction contract must comply with certain statutory requirements. Contracts with residential occupiers are not included (s. 106). Certain matters which would normally be called construction work (including most oil and gas, process plant and utility construction work) are outside the scope of statutory adjudication as a result of the detailed definition of 'construction operations' in the Act (s. 105). Other types of contract (including leases, contracts relating to shares and guarantees) are exempted by regulations made by the Secretary of State (the Construction Contracts (England and Wales) Exclusion Order 1998 (SI 1998/648) and its Scottish and Northern Irish counterparts).

In the absence of a compliant adjudication provision in a construction contract a statutory scheme applies as a term of the contract implied by statute. The scheme is set out in sch. 1 to the Scheme for Construction Contracts (England and Wales) Regulations 1998 (SI 1998/ 649) made under the Act. Under para. 12 of the scheme an adjudicator is obliged to act impartially, reach his decision in accordance with the relevant contract terms and the law applicable to the contract and 'avoid incurring unnecessary expense'. Absent any agreement between the parties on the appointment of an adjudicator, a nominating body, for example, the Royal Institute of Chartered Surveyors (RICS), may make an appointment at the request of one of the parties.

The Act lays down a framework for the conduct of adjudication: for example, the adjudicator must reach a decision within 28 days of the dispute having been referred to him or such longer period as the parties may agree (s. 108(2)). Within this broad outline, the parties are free to agree more detailed express terms, and often do so by reference to published sets of rules.

Adjudication is a fast and often effective mechanism for resolving construction disputes. The adjudicator's decision is binding until 'the dispute is finally determined by legal proceedings, by arbitration…or by agreement' (s. 108(3)). The parties can agree that the adjudicator's decision will be final and binding. Enforcement is by way of an application to court for sums owing under the contract. Speed is the critical factor in adjudication proceedings as most parties want to have a determination of the dispute as quickly as possible without having to resort to litigation or arbitration.

Expert determination

73.6 Expert determination is where the parties choose to refer a particular type of dispute to an independent third party to decide the matter applying his own expertise. The third party is chosen by the parties and usually possesses expertise and technical knowledge relevant to the subject of the dispute, but need not be a lawyer. It is important that the contract sets out a default appointment process to be used if the parties are unable to agree who is to act as expert. It is usual to provide that an industry body such as the Institute of Chartered Accountants in England and Wales (ICAEW) or the Law Society is to make the appointment. This type of process is most suitable for determining technical aspects of a complex dispute. Provisions for expert determination, to resolve financial or technical issues, are also common in long-term contracts or where there is an ongoing commercial relationship between the parties. An expert is only vested with the powers prescribed in the relevant contract. It is therefore advisable to set out clearly the manner in which the expert determination should proceed to avoid any delay at the time the dispute arises. There are no procedural restrictions on the parties, although if a speedy outcome is sought a simpler process is preferable. It is useful to include a provision in the contract allowing the parties to agree the procedure for the expert determination. If the parties cannot so agree, a default arrangement should provide for the expert himself to determine the process. This can prevent time being wasted on agreeing a procedure once a dispute has arisen and is referred to expert determination. An expert does not, unless there is a provision to the contrary, have to receive formal submissions from the parties, oral or written. He may reach his final decision based on his own investigations and expertise. However, in practice, it is generally accepted that each party will make at least written submissions on the matters in dispute. The parties and the expert agree terms of reference, setting out the procedure to be followed and the expert's terms of engagement.

Expert determination is particularly useful for resolving technical issues, for example, accounting disputes, valuation of corporate shareholdings and the calculation of sums paid under oil and gas joint operation agreements. The decision of an expert is final and the parties can and usually do expressly agree in the contract to be bound by the decision of the expert. The exceptions to such finality are fraud and manifest error. An expert's determination cannot be enforced in the same way as an arbitration award. The Arbitration Act 1996 does not apply to expert determination so enforcement is a matter of implementing the contract provisions. The English courts will recognise the expert's determination as final and binding save in cases of fraud or if the expert has exceeded his mandate.

An expert differs from an arbitrator in that an expert can be sued for negligence by the parties, though experts usually seek to limit such liability in their terms of reference. An arbitrator is immune under the Arbitration Act 1996, s. 29, unless the alleged act or omission was shown to be committed in bad faith. A clause in a contract may not always be clear as to which type of dispute resolution is being used, expert determination or arbitration. The dispute resolution provision in a contract does not need to refer to an arbitrator or arbitration for it to fall into that category. Accordingly, parties need to be careful when drafting their dispute resolution clause to ensure that their intention is clear. In *David Wilson Homes Ltd v Survey Services Ltd* [2001] EWCA Civ 34, [2001] 1 All ER (Comm) 449, the Court of Appeal confirmed that in interpreting the dispute clause 'the important thing is that there should be an agreement to refer disputes to a person other than the court who is to resolve the dispute in a manner binding on the parties to the agreement' (at [11]). Despite the lack of any reference to arbitration, the Court of Appeal confirmed it was in fact an arbitration clause and not expert determination. Many expert determination clauses clearly state that the expert is acting as an expert and not as an arbitrator to avoid any such confusion. Usually the scope and remit of the expert is narrower than that of an arbitral tribunal and does not involve determinations on questions of law.

Arbitration

Arbitration is a private, usually contractual, dispute resolution option where an impartial tribunal issues a final and binding award on the matters in dispute. It is consensual in nature and it must be clear from the parties' agreement that they intended to arbitrate. All signatory states to the Convention on the Recognition and Enforcement of Foreign Arbitral Awards 1958 (the New York Convention) will recognise an agreement to arbitrate and stay litigation proceedings. Prima facie evidence of an agreement to arbitrate is required unless the national court finds that the arbitration agreement is 'null and void, inoperative, or incapable of being performed' (art. II(3)). In general, the courts in England and Wales will order a stay of litigation proceedings under the Arbitration Act 1996, s. 9, in the face of an arbitration agreement even if it is unclear and badly drafted (*McNicholas plc v AEI Cables Ltd* (TCC 25 May 1999); *Sonatrach Petroleum Corporation v Ferrell International Ltd* [2002] 1 All ER (Comm) 627). 73.7

The cornerstone of arbitration is party autonomy. The parties are free to agree exactly how any disputes should be resolved in arbitral proceedings. The Arbitration Act 1996 gives effect to this principle by reducing the intervention of the courts to a minimum. They have a purely supportive and supervisory role in arbitration proceedings. The courts can assist the arbitration process, for example, by ordering witnesses to attend hearings, but cannot review the merits of an award. There are limited grounds of appeal should an aggrieved party wish to challenge the tribunal's award.

There are two main options available to commercial entities considering incorporating an arbitration clause into a contract: ad hoc arbitration or institutional arbitration.

In ad hoc arbitration, there is no administering body so the parties are free to agree the type of arbitration procedure that best suits their needs. Should they be unable to do so, the tribunal will determine the process. The parties in ad hoc arbitration only have to pay for the tribunal's costs as there are no additional administrative fees. In reality, it is not unusual for the chairman of an ad hoc tribunal to nominate a secretary to the tribunal to assist in the smooth running of the case. Parties in ad hoc arbitration often apply the UNCITRAL Arbitration Rules which provide some guidance for the tribunal on procedure.

The second option, institutional or administered arbitration, is where the parties incorporate into the contract the rules of a designated international arbitration institution, for example, the LCIA or ICC. Each of the international institutions has its own set of rules and they have varying degrees of regulation. The ICC, for example, has a very supportive secretariat with a high level of regulation throughout the process. This includes scrutiny of an award by the ICC Court before it is issued by the tribunal. In contrast other institutions rely more heavily on the calibre of tribunals to work efficiently and produce well crafted and enforceable awards. Parties often prefer to choose institutional arbitration in their contracts given the level of support and to a certain extent assistance on enforcement.

There are certain types of international disputes that are referred to particular institutions. Investment disputes, for example, between an investor and a host State, are often referred to the International Centre for Settlement of Investment Disputes (ICSID) at the World Bank in Washington. The ICC also has about 10 per cent of its cases each year that involve a State or State entity. Some of these investment disputes arise under concession contracts that have specific arbitration clauses. In other cases, the investor will base its claim on a relevant investment treaty, bilateral or multilateral. These types of international arbitrations are not contractual but rely on the State's standing offer to arbitrate certain types of disputes set out in the relevant treaty.

Domestically, the best-known arbitration institute is the Chartered Institute of Arbitrators. It plays a leading role in training arbitrators and promoting the process generally. It also promulgates arbitration rules and administers more than 100 bespoke arbitration schemes for consumer and commercial markets.

The parties to an arbitration agreement can choose the number of tribunal members, usually three. Although a sole arbitrator is the default position under the Arbitration Act 1996, s. 15(3), parties often prefer to be able to nominate one member each of a three-member tribunal. The parties can also agree the procedure for the arbitration including limiting document production to clear and specific categories. In international arbitration there is usually only limited document disclosure. The IBA Rules on the Taking of Evidence are often referred to by arbitrators to ensure that full common law style discovery is avoided. Parties can if they so wish expressly include these IBA Rules into their contract, in whole or in part, as a means of reducing uncertainty in the procedure to be applied by the tribunal should a dispute arise in the future.

The flexibility and private nature of arbitration makes it a popular option in commercial contracts. In addition, the finality of the award provides commercial certainty. **CPR, r. 62.18(1)**, requires that an application must be made to the court for permission to enforce an award. Once this permission has been granted, an arbitral award is enforceable in England and Wales under the Arbitration Act 1996, s. 66, as if it was a court judgment. If necessary, it can also be enforced abroad in all of the contracting States to the New York Convention on the Recognition and Enforcement of Foreign Arbitral Awards 1958.

Arbitration is used in a huge range of commercial transactions from sport to construction. Certain types of transactions have given rise to their own specialised arbitration procedures. A good example of this is 'baseball arbitration', or last offer arbitration. This type of arbitration was first used in the United States by sports clubs in negotiations over professional athletes' salaries. It is now more widely used, for example, in reinsurance contracts, and where parties have an ongoing relationship. The arbitrator's ability to determine quantum in the case is restricted. After making their submissions to the tribunal both parties must recommend a figure that they believe would settle the dispute. The arbitrator can only choose the figure which he finds is closest to what he would have awarded. There are therefore only two possible outcomes in a baseball arbitration. Clearly both sides will try to be reasonable in their proposed figure as they would not wish to alienate the tribunal forcing it to choose the other party's suggestion. This type of arbitration is only appropriate where the parties agree sums are due and payable under a contract, but the actual amount is disputed. There are clear risks in this type of arbitration, but as the parties are forced to make reasonable quotes it often encourages settlement.

Trade arbitration

London is an international centre for commodity disputes, from maritime to metals. Each commodity association has its own distinct set of arbitration rules, many of which contain an appellate body system. Examples include GAFTA (Grain and Feed Trade Association) and FOSFA (Federation of Oils Seeds and Fats Association). The London Metal Exchange is the world's leading market for base metals. Any disputes arising under a metal contract must be referred to arbitration under the LME Arbitration Rules. The same is true for the Refined Sugar Association (RSA), originally founded in 1891. Although each association has its own rules these arbitrations do add to the jurisprudence under the Arbitration Act 1996. In *Rustal Trading Ltd v Gill & Duffus SA* [2000] 1 Lloyd's Rep 14, for example, the High Court had to decide whether one of the arbitrators in an RSA arbitration was biased as he had been involved in an earlier dispute involving one of the parties. This argument was dismissed as the previous dispute was two years earlier and in any event the court did not find it out of the ordinary that the parties in such trade arbitrations may have had previous experience with each other. 73.8

Commodity trade arbitration is a specialist form of arbitration. Nevertheless, maritime arbitration under the LMAA (London Maritime Arbitrators Association) has generated a large number of cases before the English courts. The fundamental principles that govern these arbitrations are the same for general commercial matters, and the Arbitration Act 1996 applies when the seat of the arbitration is in England.

NON-ADJUDICATIVE ADR

A wide range of processes fall into the category of non-adjudicative ADR. These procedures are often used to assist parties to ongoing litigation to reach a settlement away from the courts. They are widely used in England in labour relations and family law disputes, and throughout the commercial sector. They can cut short a dispute and save time and money if an amicable settlement can be agreed. This type of ADR involves the intervention of an independent, neutral third party. The flexibility of procedure and informality allowed lends itself to a positive outcome. Parties can control exactly how the process will take place and can be more forthright in their discussions as non-adjudicative ADR is a confidential process and the result is non-binding and usually unenforceable. 73.9

Conciliation/negotiation

Negotiation is often a useful form of ADR in commercial disputes where the relationship between the parties is ongoing. The parties can use the time of negotiation as a cooling-off period to try to resolve their dispute quickly and cheaply. In many contracts, negotiation 73.10

is a precondition to arbitration or litigation. Many commercial contracts have a multi-tiered dispute resolution clause that will impose an obligation to try to reach an amicable settlement through negotiation. Usually a certain time period is designated for this purpose, for example, seven or 15 days. There are not the same negative costs implications in failure to engage in pre-agreed forms of ADR followed by arbitration as exist for litigation (see 73.23).

Negotiation can take place with just the parties present or an independent third party can be involved. The role of the negotiator is purely to facilitate the parties in reaching a resolution. He does not take sides although he can have separate caucus meetings with each side to see if he can bring them any closer to reaching an amicable settlement. A conciliation process takes place in a similar way. A neutral conciliator will also try to assist the parties in finding a mutually satisfactory resolution to the dispute. The procedure in the negotiation or conciliation is driven by the parties and flexibility is essential. It is unlikely there will be any formal written or oral submissions, but it can be a very useful mechanism through which each party gets a better understanding of the subject matter of the dispute.

Negotiation is also used during an ongoing arbitration or litigation. The parties may, having commenced formal proceedings, be more willing to reach a compromise solution. Many cases are settled successfully in this way. A party should take care in using arbitration as a tool to force a respondent to negotiate a settlement. Once an arbitration is commenced it cannot be unilaterally withdrawn. The consent of both parties is required. If no negotiated settlement is reached, the arbitration will continue, whether the party chooses to participate or not. It is therefore worth making a genuine attempt to reach a negotiated settlement prior to any formal proceedings being commenced.

Mediation

73.11 **What kind of cases are suitable for mediation?** Virtually all civil disputes can be resolved by mediation. The remedies available in mediation are potentially far wider than those which can be obtained through litigation as the parties to a mediation can agree, or be guided to, any resolution of their dispute which they wish. However, mediation may be less suitable in cases where:

(a) a party is contemplating or facing a large number of similar claims for which it seeks to set some kind of legal precedent;
(b) a party is confident it can swiftly vindicate its legal rights and obtain full relief by proceeding to summary judgment; or
(c) a party requires speedy injunctive relief.

The fact that a dispute raises complicated issues of fact or law, involves more than two parties or has given rise to an acrimonious relationship between the litigants, should be no barrier to mediation. In all these cases mediation may ultimately provide the parties with a more satisfactory resolution to their dispute than the courts can provide.

73.12 **What happens at the mediation?** The venue for a mediation will generally consist of one large room where the parties and the mediator can meet together and private rooms for the parties either to meet separately with the mediator or to discuss the matter alone when the mediator is with the other party or parties.

At the start of the mediation, the parties will usually meet in the presence of the mediator and briefly explain their case. In some mediations the parties will have had the opportunity, before the mediation meeting begins, to provide the mediator with a written submission outlining their positions and with copies of documents they believe to be relevant.

Having made their opening presentations the parties will retire to their private rooms and the mediator will move between them trying to help them reach an agreement. The mediator will be able to influence the parties during this stage by controlling the flow of information, deciding on how to present a party's evidence to the other side and ultimately by suggesting or influencing the architecture of any settlement.

The mediation can end at any time as the parties and the mediator are under no obligation to remain. If a settlement is reached, it will normally be recorded in writing at the mediation.

The mediation process is confidential and without prejudice. If the mediation does not lead to settlement, a party will not generally be able to make use of information it obtained during the mediation in the continuing court proceedings. The nature of confidentiality, privilege and the without-prejudice principle in relation to mediation was considered in *Farm Assist Ltd v Secretary of State for the Environment, Food and Rural Affairs (No. 2)* [2009] EWHC 1102 (TCC), [2009] BLR 399. The claimant had served a witness summons on a mediator to procure her attendance to give evidence in relation to a claim that the agreement reached at mediation had been procured through duress. The mediator applied to set aside the witness summons. The court concluded that mediation proceedings are confidential both as between the parties and as between the parties and the mediator. However, where necessary in the interests of justice for evidence to be given of confidential matters, the court could order evidence to be given. Further, the proceedings are covered by without-prejudice privilege. This privilege exists between the parties and does not belong to the mediator. Accordingly, the parties can waive this privilege. There is also a further 'privilege', which arises other than the mediator's right to confidentiality in relation to the mediation proceedings. Nonetheless, in the interests of justice, the court ordered the mediator to give evidence of what was said and done in the mediation.

Usually, the mediator's and mediation institution's fees will be divided equally, and each party bears its own costs of attending the mediation. Mediation costs were considered by the SCCO in *National Westminster Bank plc v Feeney* [2006] EWHC 90066 (Costs). The parties had engaged in mediation using standard CEDR terms. These provided for the costs of the mediation to be shared equally. In contrast, the wording of the Tomlin order settling the claim provided for the claimant to pay the defendant's costs. The court held that the parties' costs of attending the mediation did not fall within the Tomlin order and thus would not be payable by the claimant to the defendant. However, the costs of the mediator should be included in the Tomlin order undertaking to pay the other party's costs. It is submitted that the logic of this distinction is not apparent.

Costs of mediation were again considered in *Lobster Group Ltd v Heidelberg Graphic Equipment Ltd* [2008] EWHC 413 (TCC), [2008] 2 All ER 1173. The court held that costs incurred in a pre-action mediation would not form part of an order for security for costs for the main proceedings. This was because mediation costs which failed to prevent the commencement of proceedings over two years later could not be described as 'costs of and incidental to the proceedings' within the Senior Courts Act 1981, s. 51(1). Additionally, in any event, the parties had agreed in the mediation agreement to bear their own costs, and it would be a breach of that agreement to allow a party to recover its share of the mediation costs by way of an order for security. In *Roundstone Nurseries Ltd v Stephenson Holdings Ltd* [2009] EWHC 1431 (TCC), [2009] 5 Costs LR 787, the court made an order in respect of costs incurred during a mediation on the basis that the mediation took place as part of the pre-action protocol process.

Does mediation work? There is much speculation as to whether mediation does, as its supporters claim, lead to settlements in most cases in which it is used. A report by Professor Hazel Genn, published by the Lord Chancellor's Department in 2002, assessed the impact of ADR orders made in the Commercial Court (*Court-based ADR Initiatives for Non-family Civil Disputes* (Research Paper 1/2002)). The paper is based upon data collected from court files and interviews with solicitors relating to 233 ADR orders made between July 1996 and June 2000. **73.13**

Professor Genn found that ADR was undertaken in just over half of the cases in which an ADR order was made. However, the figures showed an increasing use of ADR towards the end of her review period. Of the cases in which ADR was attempted, 52 per cent settled through ADR and a further 20 per cent settled some time after the conclusion of the ADR procedure. Only 5 per cent continued to trial. Where ADR was not attempted, 15 per cent went to trial and 63 per cent settled, with about one-fifth of the cases that settled attributing the settlement to the making of an ADR order.

73.14 **How will the European Mediation Directive change the mediation landscape?** Directive 2008/52/EC (the Mediation Directive) aims to promote and regulate the development of mediation throughout the EU. The Mediation Directive applies to cross-border disputes in civil and commercial matters, save for rights and obligations which are not at the parties' disposal under the relevant applicable law (for example, in the context of family law or employment law matters).

The Mediation Directive is implemented in England and Wales by **CPR, Part 78, Section III.**

Section III only applies to mediated cross-border disputes that are within the scope of the Mediation Directive. Perhaps the most pertinent aspect of **Section III** is that it provides for the enforcement of a mediation settlement agreement. To enforce a mediation settlement, the parties, or one party with the explicit consent of the others, may make an application in accordance with **Part 23** (where there are existing proceedings in England and Wales) or in accordance with **Part 8** (where there are no existing proceedings in England and Wales). The mediation settlement agreement must be annexed to the application notice or claim form when it is filed. Where only one party makes the application, evidence of the explicit consent of the other parties must also be included with the application. The court will make an order making the mediation settlement enforceable, without the need for a hearing (unless the court directs otherwise).

The other aspects of **Section III** relate to the disclosure or inspection of mediation evidence that is within the control of the mediator or the mediation administration, and where a party wishes to obtain mediation evidence from a mediator or mediation administration. In support of such an application, the party seeking disclosure or inspection, or evidence of a witness, must include evidence that all parties to the mediation agree to the application, or that the mediation evidence is necessary for overriding considerations of public policy, or that the mediation evidence is necessary to implement or enforce the mediation settlement agreement.

The mediation of cross-border disputes, to which the Mediation Directive (and **CPR, Part 78, Section III**) apply, probably represents only a small percentage of the UK mediation workload. It remains to be seen how much impact the Mediation Directive will have in practice.

Early neutral evaluation

73.15 Early neutral evaluation aims to provide parties with an early and frank evaluation by an independent party of the merits of their claim. It usually takes place at a much earlier stage than arbitration, although, like negotiation and conciliation, it can be used at any time during a dispute. The concept of early neutral evaluation was conceived in the United States as a mechanism to reduce the costs of litigation. The English courts have encouraged the use of all forms of ADR since the introduction of the CPR in 1999. The Commercial Court offers an early evaluation scheme, where a judge can give an assessment of the merits of the claims (Admiralty and Commercial Courts Guide, para. G2). Although this is non-binding it has not been widely used.

The assessment of the judge or third-party evaluator is non-binding on the parties but often works to ensure that the parties reach a settlement before expending time and resources on litigation or arbitration proceedings. The assessment will focus on the central issues involved in the dispute and the relevant law. The evaluation is usually issued in written form to the parties. The costs involved in the process are a lot less than arbitration or litigation and the entire procedure takes place quite quickly. Several ADR centres offer advice on appointing an appropriate evaluator, for example CEDR Solve (http://www.cedr.co.uk).

Mini-trial or executive trial

The mini or executive trial is not in reality a trial. It is a structured settlement process where the parties make summary submissions on the particular dispute. The executives of the parties attend the meeting with an independent adviser, often nominated by an appropriate dispute resolution institution. The executives having heard the summary submissions try to reach an agreement. If this is not possible the neutral adviser issues an advisory opinion. This is not binding on the parties, but usually a further meeting between the executives is held after the opinion has been given in a final attempt to reach an amicable settlement. The mini-trial was introduced to meet a business need. It is a fast and efficient means of resolving a dispute where the control rests exclusively with the business executives. 73.16

Med-arb

A hybrid form of dispute resolution is mediation-arbitration or 'med-arb'. Originally conceived in the 1970s med-arb was thought to provide disputing parties with the best of both options. Each stage of the process is kept separate. The mediation process takes place first and if that fails to produce a solution to the dispute, arbitration proceedings will commence with the mediator sitting as arbitrator. One of the main disadvantages of med-arb is that parties may be less open during the mediation process as they know that if the mediation is unsuccessful they will have the same independent third party acting as an arbitrator with the power to issue a final and binding award. This drawback has given rise to debate on whether the process itself is fundamentally flawed at law. Can a person who has already acted as a mediator and been privy to certain confidential information from the parties in private caucus meetings really be an independent unbiased arbitrator? The Arbitration Act 1996, s. 24(1), requires the tribunal to be impartial and a legitimate concern may be raised as to whether a person who has acted as a mediator first necessarily complies with this obligation. A similar obligation of impartiality and independence exists under the European Convention on Human Rights. In any event, med-arb is used quite extensively throughout Asia, for example in CIETAC and SIAC arbitrations, without any such issues being a problem. Parties seem to be happy that the independent third party is familiar with the dispute from the outset and, if an agreed settlement cannot be reached after the initial mediation, for him to continue to act as arbitrator. 73.17

Commentary

CONTRACT TERMS

The type of dispute resolution clause in any particular contract will depend on the type of transaction, the parties to the contract, the forum and the applicable law. Choice of any form of adjudicative ADR will determine an issue definitively whereas non-adjudicative ADR provides a forum within which the parties can reach an agreed settlement. 73.18

When drafting a contract particular care and attention should be given to the dispute resolution clause. A decision must be made about which type of ADR should be chosen or whether a range of options is required under the contract. Unfortunately, at the time of drafting a contract most parties do not envisage anything going wrong so it can be difficult to discuss in any detail the significance of the type of ADR chosen. It is always essential to consider the preferred dispute resolution option of each client. It is best to explain the implications of each option so that there are no unrealistic expectations should a dispute arise under the contract in the future.

Contract terms should be drafted clearly to avoid any controversy or disagreement as to the scope and extent of the dispute resolution clause. This is particularly true if the contract provides or hybrid or bifurcated dispute resolution provisions, under which different procedures apply to particular types of dispute. For example, technical issues may be referred to an expert accountant, with all other disputes under the contract being referred to arbitration.

It has become quite common to include several different forms of dispute resolution provisions in a multi-tiered clause. In this way, parties seek to minimise their time and costs spent on any future dispute. The options provided in these clauses usually start with mandatory negotiations, move to mediation and then on to arbitration or litigation depending on the will of the parties. The most important consideration for such a multi-tiered clause is to include time limits for each of the non-binding dispute resolution options. Otherwise one party could use them as a mere dilatory tactic rather than a genuine attempt at resolution. Such time limits can range from 15 days to 90 days depending on the type of contract. Clearly the final option of arbitration or litigation cannot be so prescribed. Arbitration can have rigorous time limits imposed in a contract, often referred to as fast-track arbitration. It must, however, be left open to the parties to agree an extension if necessary, otherwise the tribunal's jurisdiction may expire.

The decisions in *Sulamerica Cía Nacional de Seguros SA v Enesa Engenharia SA* [2012] EWCA Civ 638, [2013] 1 WLR 102 and *Tang Chun Wah v Grant Thornton International Ltd* [2012] EWHC 3198 (Ch), [2013] 1 Lloyd's Rep 11 mentioned at **73.2** give guidance to contract drafters seeking to craft enforceable ADR provisions as a precursor to litigation or arbitration. It seems that the safest course will be to adopt model clauses promulgated by the mediation institutions (a list of the most active UK institutions appears at **73.24** below), but anyone wanting to draft an enforceable ADR provision should start with the guidance offered by the court in *Tang Chun Wah*.

RELATIONSHIP BETWEEN THE COURTS AND ADR

73.19 In his ***Final Report*** (ch. 1, para. 7(d)) Lord Woolf stated how ADR should be among the tools used by the court to resolve disputes at an early stage:

> Two other significant aims of my recommendations need to be borne in mind: that of encouraging the resolution of disputes before they come to litigation, for example by greater use of pre-litigation disclosure and of ADR, and that of encouraging settlement, for example by introducing plaintiffs' offers to settle, and by the disposing of issues so as to narrow the dispute. All these are intended to divert cases from the court system or to ensure that those cases which do go through the court system are disposed of as rapidly as possible. I share the view, expressed in the Commercial Court Practice Statement of 10 December 1993, that although the primary role of the court is as a forum for deciding cases it is right that the court should encourage the parties to consider the use of ADR as a means to resolve their dispute. I believe that the same is true of helping the parties to settle a case.

The courts' encouragement of mediation forces litigation practitioners to familiarise themselves with ADR processes. This familiarity leads to an increased demand for mediation. The courts' attitude also goes some way to removing the concern that by suggesting ADR a party could be taken to lack confidence in the strength of its case.

ADR and active case management

73.20 Encouraging ADR is part of the court's active case management role, which in turn is how the court furthers the overriding objective. **CPR, r. 1.4**, includes 'encouraging the parties to use an alternative dispute resolution procedure if the court considers that appropriate and facilitating the use of such procedure' among the matters expressly included within active case management.

CPR, r. 1.3, which requires the parties to help the court to further the overriding objective, places the parties under a duty in relation to ADR. Practically, this will require the parties to be aware of ADR and to consider seriously the possibility of using it to resolve their dispute.

The extent of a party's obligation to consider ADR was considered in detail by the Court of Appeal in *Halsey v Milton Keynes General NHS Trust* [2004] EWCA Civ 576, [2004] 1 WLR 3002. The court made reference to the judgment of Brooke LJ in *Dunnett v Railtrack plc* [2002] EWCA Civ 303, [2002] 1 WLR 2434, who had emphasised how 'skilled mediators are now able to achieve results satisfactory to both parties in many cases which are quite beyond the power of lawyers and courts to achieve'. However, the court rejected the submission that there should be a presumption in favour of mediation. It also emphasised that any compulsion of ADR would be an unacceptable constraint on the right of access to the court and therefore a violation of the European Convention on Human Rights, **art. 6**, in the **Human Rights Act 1998, sch. 1**.

In the Glossary to the CPR, 'alternative dispute resolution' is broadly defined as a:

collective description of methods of resolving disputes otherwise than through the normal trial process.

The well-advised litigant will consider the possibility of resorting to ADR at the earliest possible stage, even before proceedings are initiated. **PD Pre-action Conduct, para. 8.1**, requires all parties, in accordance with the overriding objective, to try to avoid the necessity for starting proceedings and to consider whether some form of alternative dispute resolution procedure would be more suitable than litigation. This may include conducting genuine and reasonable negotiations with a view to settling the claim economically.

In certain circumstances the court will use its powers under other provisions of the CPR to assist the parties to mediate. For example, in *Arrow Trading and Investments Est 1920 v Edwardian Group Ltd* [2004] EWHC 1319 (Ch), [2005] 1 BCLC 696, the court granted advance disclosure of documents relating to quantum to put the claimant in a position whereby it could meaningfully mediate the dispute.

The court's encouragement of mediation has even extended to proceedings which the parties have agreed to conduct outside of the usual court processes. In *C v RHL* [2005] EWHC 873 (Comm), LTL 12/5/2005, the court was only asked to issue an anti-suit injunction preventing a party from continuing court proceedings in Russia in breach of an agreement to arbitrate. Instead of issuing the injunction, the court directed the parties to mediate and issued a standard ADR order.

Commentary

ADR and the directions questionnaire

CPR, r. 26.4(1), provides that a party filing a directions questionnaire may request the proceedings be stayed while the parties try to settle the case by ADR or other means. Where all parties request a stay, the court will direct that the proceedings be stayed for one month (**r. 26.4(2)**). If the court otherwise considers that such a stay would be appropriate, it will direct that the proceedings, either in whole or in part, be stayed for one month, or for such other period as it considers appropriate (**r. 26.4(2A)**). **73.21**
If only one party requests a stay, the court is likely to try to ascertain why the other party is refusing (this may be a matter addressed at a case management conference).

ADR and case management conferences

The subject of ADR may be raised at the case management conference, especially if the judge believes that the parties have not previously considered it themselves. The judge may 'invite' the parties to try ADR (see, for example, the Admiralty and Commercial Courts Guide, paras G1.3 and G1.6 to G1.8 and appendix 7 for a draft ADR order; Chancery Guide, para. 17.3). **73.22**

The draft ADR order set out in app. 7 to the Admiralty and Commercial Courts Guide provides for the parties to inform the court of the steps they have taken towards ADR, should ADR not be successful. Without prejudice to matters of privilege, they have to inform the court why such steps have failed. Accordingly, while the court cannot ask the parties to provide details of their attempts to settle (questions such as 'How much is between you now?' would be off-limits), the parties can expect to be asked whether they agreed to attend a mediation. If they refused, this may have to be justified. Similarly, a party who did something to frustrate the mediation, such as sending a representative without authority to settle, may have to justify its actions.

Consequences of refusing to consider ADR

73.23 A party which does not take its duty to consider ADR seriously is likely to be penalised when the court looks to the question of costs. In exercising its discretion as to the award of costs, the court is obliged to have regard to the conduct of the parties (**CPR, r. 44.2(4)**). This includes considering:

The manner in which a party pursued or defended his case or a particular allegation or issue (**CPR, r. 44.2(5)(c)**).

Accordingly a winning party may find its recovery of costs reduced by reason of a failure to cooperate in relation to ADR. An unsuccessful defendant who refused to consider ADR to try to settle the case before trial could be liable for interest on costs (perhaps running from a date before judgment) (**CPR, r. 44.2(6)(g)**) or indemnity costs.

The Court of Appeal in *Halsey v Milton Keynes General NHS Trust* [2004] EWCA Civ 576, [2004] 1 WLR 3002, stated that a party who refuses even to consider ADR is always at risk of an adverse costs order. The court set out a number of factors which may be relevant in considering whether a party has acted unreasonably in refusing ADR. These include, but are not limited to:

(a) the nature of the dispute;
(b) the merits of the case (it may not be reasonable for a party with a weak case to insist on the use of ADR);
(c) the extent to which other settlement methods have been attempted;
(d) whether the costs of ADR would be disproportionately high;
(e) whether any delay in setting up and attending the ADR would have been prejudicial; and
(f) whether the ADR had a reasonable prospect of success.

The Court of Appeal also stated that the unsuccessful party should have the burden of showing that mediation would have had a reasonable prospect of success.

The Court of Appeal has subsequently applied the *Halsey* principles both to uphold a party's refusal to mediate (*Reed Executive plc v Reed Business Information Ltd* [2004] EWCA Civ 887, [2004] 1 WLR 3026) and to characterise a refusal as unreasonable (*Burchell v Bullard* [2005] EWCA Civ 358, [2005] BLR 330). In *Reed Executive plc v Reed Business Information Ltd* the court was guided by the fact that the offer to mediate came late and the successful party reasonably believed itself to have a good case. In *Burchell v Bullard* the court favoured mediation in a case where the amounts in dispute were dwarfed by the legal costs. It also stated that a party cannot rely on its own obstinacy to assert that mediation had no reasonable prospect of success. In *Earl of Malmesbury v Strutt and Parker* [2008] EWHC 424 (QB), 118 Con LR 68, the court was critical of a claimant who attended a mediation but adopted a position that 'was plainly unrealistic and unreasonable'. Such an approach was characterised as being not dissimilar in effect to an unreasonable refusal to engage in mediation. This was stated to be something the court should take account of when applying the principles considered in *Halsey*.

Halsey was applied by the Court of Appeal in *Swain-Mason v Mills and Reeve LLP* [2012] EWCA Civ 498, [2012] STC 1760. The defendant solicitors' firm had prevailed in a claim brought against it by a former client. The trial judge had penalised the defendant for refusing to mediate in the belief, which proved to be correct, that the claim against it was without merit. The Court of Appeal reversed this decision. A reasonable refusal to mediate did not become unreasonable just because it was maintained over a long period. Further, if a party with a reasonable belief in the strength of its case was to be compelled to mediate it could not be said that mediation was a voluntary process. To punish a defendant in such a position would be making mediation compulsory for all.

A further significant holding in *Reed Executive plc v Reed Business Information Ltd* was that the court cannot compel production of without-prejudice material in order to assess whether a failure to mediate was unreasonable. The court would have to base any assessment on material that was either open or marked 'without prejudice subject to costs'.

USEFUL ADDRESSES

ADR Group 73.24
Grove House
Grove Road
Redland
Bristol
BS6 6UN
Tel: 44 (0) 117 946 7180
Fax: +44 (0) 117 946 7181
Email: info@adrgroup.co.uk
Web: www.adrgroup.co.uk

Centre for Effective Dispute Resolution
International Dispute Resolution Centre
70 Fleet Street
London EC4Y 1EU
United Kingdom
Tel: +44 (0)20 7536 6000
Fax: +44 (0)20 7536 6001
Email: info@cedr.com
Web: www.cedr.com/CEDR_Solve/

The Chartered Institute of Arbitrators
International Arbitration and Mediation Centre
12 Bloomsbury Square
London WC1A 2LP
Ph: (0) 20 7421 7444
Fax: (0) 20 7404 4023
Email: info@arbitrators.org
Web: www.arbitrators.org

ICC International Chamber of Commerce
38 cours Albert I[er]
75008 Paris
France
Tel: +33 (0)1 49 53 29 05
Fax: +33 (0)1 49 53 29 33
E-mail: arb@iccwbo.org
Web: www.iccwbo.org/index_court.asp

LCIA
International Dispute Resolution Centre
70 Fleet Street
London
EC4Y 1EU
Great Britain

Commentary

Tel: +44 (0)20 7936 6200
Fax: +44 (0)20 7936 6211
Email: lcia@lcia.org
Web: www.lcia.org

National Mediation Helpline
Clerksroom Mediation
Equity House
Blackbrook Park Avenue
Taunton
TA1 2PX
Tel: +44 (0)845 033 3000
Email: mail@clerksroom.com
Web: www.clerksroom.com

RICS Dispute Resolution Service
Surveyor Court
Westwood Way
Coventry
CV4 8JE
UK
Tel: +44 (0)20 7334 3806
Email: drs@rics.org
Web: www.rics.org/disputeresolution

ICAEW/ADR Group — Resolving commercial disputes
Chartered Accountants' Hall
PO Box 433
Moorgate Place
London
EC2R 6EA
UK
Tel: +44 (0)20 7920 8100
Fax: +44 (0)20 7920 0547
Email: info@resolvingcommercialdisputes.com
Web: www.icaew.com/en/members/business-services/resolving-disputes

Chapter 74 The Appeals System

The following procedural checklists, which are at the front of the book, are relevant to this chapter:

Procedural checklist 32 Appeals within the county courts and High Court
Procedural checklist 33 Appeals to the Court of Appeal

INTRODUCTION

74.1 From time to time decisions are made in error, and the system of appeals is designed to ensure that these are corrected. There is a strong public interest in regarding judicial decisions as final and binding, and an open-ended appeals system would undermine this by encouraging unsuccessful litigants to have 'another bite at the cherry'. Striking a balance between encouraging finality and correcting mistakes is not easy, and explains some of the complications that arise in the area of appeals.

Careful thought must be given before embarking on an appeal. In his annual review of 1989–90, in considering appeals to the Court of Appeal, Lord Donaldson of Lymington MR said:

> The question which the adviser may ask himself is whether, looking at the matter objectively, there are sufficient grounds for believing not only that the case should have been decided differently, but that in all the circumstances it can be demonstrated to the satisfaction of the Court of Appeal that there are grounds for reversing the judge's findings. In considering this question the adviser must never forget the financial risk which an appellant undertakes of having not only to pay his own costs of the appeal, but those of his opponent and, for this purpose, the adviser has two clients if the litigant is [publicly funded]. Nor must he underrate the effect upon his client of the emotional and other consequences of a continued state of uncertainty pending an appeal. In a word, one of the most important duties of a professional legal adviser is to save his clients from themselves and always to remember that, whilst it may well be reasonable to institute or to defend particular proceedings at first instance, a wholly new and different situation arises once the claim has been fully investigated by the court and a decision given.

DECISIONS SUSCEPTIBLE TO APPEAL

74.2 The Court of Appeal has jurisdiction to hear appeals from High Court 'judgments' and 'orders' (Senior Courts Act 1981, s. 16(1)) and county court 'determinations' (County Courts Act 1984, s. 77(1)). This means that a party is not entitled to appeal against the reasons for a decision given in his favour (*Compagnie Noga d'Importation et d'Exportation SA v Australia and New Zealand Banking Group Ltd* [2002] EWCA Civ 1142, [2003] 1 WLR 307) and a witness who is criticised in findings of fact cannot appeal against those findings (*Re B and H (Children)* [2009] EWCA Civ 228, LTL 8/4/2009). The practice and procedure to be followed in appeals within the county courts and the High Court are governed by the CPR (Civil Procedure Act 1997, s. 1(1)). Although the County Courts Act 1984, s. 77(1A), says that such rules may provide for who is to hear any appeal 'from the exercise by a district judge, assistant district judge or deputy district judge of any power' given by any enactment, it is submitted that these appeals are restricted in the same way as appeals to the Court of Appeal.

APPELLANT

74.3 A person who was not a party to the proceedings in the lower court can be an 'appellant' for the purposes of **CPR, r. 52.1(3)(d)** (*George Wimpey UK Ltd v Tewkesbury Borough Council* [2008] EWCA Civ 12, [2008] 1 WLR 1649). In deciding whether to grant permission to appeal to such a person the court will take into account whether any application was made to add the person in the lower court, and whether the person has a real interest in the appeal.

ROUTES OF APPEAL

The basic civil appeals structure is, by the **Access to Justice Act 1999 (Destination of Appeals) Order 2000** (SI 2000/1071) (the Destination of Appeals Order), **PD 52A**, and the Constitutional Reform Act 2005, as follows: **74.4**

(a) Decisions of county court district judges may be appealed to the county court circuit judge.
(b) Decisions of High Court masters, district judges and registrars may be appealed to a High Court judge.
(c) Decisions of county court circuit judges may be appealed to a High Court judge.
(d) Decisions of High Court judges may be appealed to the Court of Appeal.
(e) Court of Appeal decisions may be appealed to the Supreme Court.

Tables on appeal routes are set out in **PD 52A, para. 3.5**, and are summarised in **table 74.1** below. These basic routes of appeal also apply in relation to deputy judges and their equivalents, such as recorders sitting as county court circuit judges (for which, see **PD 52A, para. 4.4(b)**). Appeals from county court district judges (category (a) above) are the simplest administratively, with the claim remaining within the same court for the appeal, and simply being listed

Table 74.1 Structure of the civil appeals system

Decision appealed from	Appeal to	Period for commencing appeal	Whether permission is required
Magistrates' court licensing matters	Crown Court	21 days from decision (liquor) or notification (others)	No
Magistrates' court Children Act 1989 cases	Family Division single judge	14 days from determination	No
Magistrates' court interim maintenance	Family Division Divisional Court	6 weeks from order	No
Inferior court on point of law or jurisdiction	QBD Divisional Court	21 days after decision	No
Inferior court by way of judicial review	QBD Divisional Court	3 months from ground arising	Yes, from Divisional Court
Statutory appeals	High Court	28 days	Depends on statute
County court district judge interim decisions; and district judge small claims and fast track final decisions	County court circuit judge	21 days from decision	Yes
County court final decision in multi-track or specialist claims from district judge or circuit judge	Court of Appeal	21 days from decision	Yes
County court circuit judge interim decisions and small claims and fast track final decisions	High Court judge	21 days from decision	Yes
High Court master, district judge or registrar	High Court judge	21 days from decision	Yes
High Court master, district judge or registrar final decision in multi-track or specialist claim	Court of Appeal	21 days from decision	Yes

Decision appealed from	Appeal to	Period for commencing appeal	Whether permission is required
Part 8 claims (interim or final) from county court district judge	County court circuit judge	21 days from decision	Yes
Part 8 claims (interim or final) from county court circuit judge or High Court master	High Court judge	21 days from decision	Yes
High Court judge	Court of Appeal	21 days from decision	Yes
Court of Appeal	Supreme Court	28 days from decision (14 days in contempt appeals)	Yes
Leapfrog appeal from High Court	Supreme Court	14 days from decision	Yes, from both High Court judge and Supreme Court

for the appeal before the judge. Appeals in small claims cases are considered at **45.27**. Appeals to High Court judges (categories (b) and (c)) may involve the appeal being heard in a new court, see **74.9**. The Court of Appeal is located at the Royal Courts of Justice, and its administrative office is known as the Civil Appeals Office. The Civil Appeals Office staff include a number of lawyers who, among other tasks, ensure that the Court of Appeal has jurisdiction to consider prospective appeals and that permission to appeal is sought where necessary. By way of exception to the basic routes of appeal, appeals are made to the Court of Appeal rather than to a High Court judge (categories (b) and (c) above) if the hearing in the lower court was either:

(a) a final decision (see **74.6**) made in any of the proceedings described in **74.5** (multi-track claims and specialist proceedings) (**Destination of Appeals Order, art. 4**); or
(b) itself an appeal from a county court district judge (in other words, the current appeal is a second appeal, see **Destination of Appeals Order, art. 5**; **74.8**).

Final decisions in specialist and multi-track claims

74.5 **Final appeals are to the Court of Appeal** An appeal under the **Destination of Appeals Order, art. 4**, is an exception to the usual rule that an appeal is to the next level of judge in the court hierarchy (*Tanfern Ltd v Cameron-MacDonald* [2000] 1 WLR 1311). By **art. 4**, and **PD 52A, paras. 3.4** and **3.5**, an appeal against a final decision (see **74.6**) of a High Court master, district judge or registrar, or a district judge or circuit judge in a county court, is to the Court of Appeal instead of the circuit judge or the High Court if it was made in:

(a) a Part 7 claim allocated to the multi-track under the CPR (but not a Part 8 claim, which must be appealed to the circuit judge (if the first instance decision was that of a county court district judge) or to a High Court judge (if the first instance decision was that of a master): **PD 52A Table 1** and *Massie v H* [2011] EWCA Civ 115, LTL 14/2/2011); or
(b) proceedings under the Companies Act 1985 or 1989, or the provisions of the Companies Act 2006 corresponding to a repealed provision of those Acts (Companies Act 2006, s. 1297(5)); or
(c) proceedings to which any of the following Parts of the CPR apply (and which are all allocated to the multi-track by those Parts):
    (i) **CPR, Part 57, Section I** (probate);

(ii) **Parts 58** to **63** (Commercial Court, Mercantile Courts, Technology and Construction Court, Admiralty claims, intellectual property claims, arbitration claims (even though they follow the Part 8 procedure));

(d) proceedings to which either **section II** (rectification of wills) or **section III** (substitution or removal of personal representatives) of **Part 57** applies.

If a non-specialist claim has never been allocated to a track, an appeal will not be to the Court of Appeal even if the judge would have allocated the claim to the multi-track had track allocation been considered (*Clark v Perks* [2000] 4 All ER 1). This can arise, for example, if the claim is dealt with as an assessment of damages.

Final decision By the **Destination of Appeals Order, art. 1(2)(c)**, and **PD 52A, para. 3.6**, a decision is final, so that an appeal is to the Court of Appeal instead of the next level of judge, if it would finally determine (subject to any possible appeal or detailed assessment of costs) the entire proceedings whichever way the court decided the issues before it. According to *Dooley v Parker* [2002] EWCA Civ 96, [2002] CPLR 251, para. 17 of the judgment in *Tanfern Ltd v Cameron-MacDonald* [2000] 1 WLR 1311 should be taken as saying that a final decision 'does not include a decision only on the detailed assessment of costs'. Consequently, a decision on liability for the costs of a claim is a final decision, which should be appealed to the Court of Appeal if the claim has been allocated to the multi-track. On the other hand, orders on summary and detailed assessments of costs, and on applications to enforce final decisions, are not themselves 'final' (**PD 52A, para. 3.8(2)**). **74.6**

A decision is treated as final where it is made at the conclusion of part of a hearing or trial which has been split into parts, and would, if made at the conclusion of that hearing or trial, be a final decision because it determines the entirety of that part of the claim (**Destination of Appeals Order, art. 1(3)**); **PD 52A, para. 3.8(1)**. This means that if a judge makes a final decision on any aspect of a claim, such as limitation, or on part of a claim which has been directed to be tried separately, this is a final decision within the meaning of the provision (*Tanfern Ltd v Cameron-MacDonald*). In *Roerig v Valiant Trawlers Ltd* [2002] EWCA Civ 21, [2002] 1 WLR 2304, the decision under appeal was made on the trial of a preliminary issue as to whether the Fatal Accidents Act 1976, s. 4, applied to the claim or whether the claimant had to give credit for benefits received if the damages were assessed under Dutch law. It was held that a broad common-sense test should be applied when deciding whether the issue would have formed part of the final trial. On the facts it was, so the decision was final, and the appeal was to the Court of Appeal. On the other hand, orders giving summary judgment (*Scribes West Ltd v Relsa Anstalt* [2004] EWCA Civ 965, [2005] 1 WLR 1839) and orders striking out the proceedings or a statement of case are not final decisions, because they are not decisions that would finally determine the entire proceedings whichever way the court decided the issues before it (**PD 52A, para. 3.8(2)**; *Tanfern Ltd v Cameron-MacDonald*).

The question whether an order is final or not has to be determined by considering the language of the order of the court below. Where a party has asked for permission to appeal, the lower court's order should by **CPR, r. 40.2(3)** and **(4)**, include a number of details, including whether the judgment is final or not. Judges and court staff in the appeal court have to determine whether their court has jurisdiction simply by looking at the face of the order being appealed, and are not required to consider the background of the case or application before deciding whether the decision is final. A party who believes an order has not been drawn up correctly can apply for it to be corrected under the slip rule (see **63.42**). Any refusal to correct the order can itself be a ground of appeal, but does not change the court having jurisdiction to hear the appeal (*Scribes West Ltd v Relsa Anstalt*).

Appeals in Part 8 claims

Although Part 8 claims are automatically allocated to the multi-track by **CPR, r. 8.9(c)**, the exception laid down in the **Destination of Appeals Order, art. 4**, does not apply to this **74.7**

Commentary

category of claim (**PD 52A, Table 1** and *Massie v H* [2011] EWCA Civ 115, LTL 14/2/2011). Therefore appeals in these claims, even from final orders, follow the general routes of appeal. Where the normal appeal court is not the Court of Appeal, a court granting permission to appeal in such a case from a final order should consider whether to order the appeal to be transferred to the Court of Appeal under **CPR, r. 52.14** (see **74.10**).

Second-tier appeals

74.8 The second exception referred to at **74.4** is where the appeal is a second appeal. These appeals are taken to the Court of Appeal, even though the decision being appealed was that made by a circuit judge (**Destination of Appeals Order, art. 5**). Typically this will cover interim applications dealt with by a county court district judge, which are appealed to the circuit judge. If a second appeal is taken, under this exception it must be taken to the Court of Appeal.

In *Southern and District Finance plc v Turner* [2003] EWCA Civ 1574, LTL 7/11/2003, a county court district judge dismissed an application to set aside a possession order. Eight months later the defendant brought an appeal against that decision, but omitted to seek permission to appeal out of time (see **74.21**). The circuit judge dismissed the appeal on the ground that no permission to extend time for appealing had been included in the appellant's notice. An appeal from the circuit judge's refusal to consider extending time (whether this was on the basis of the judge deciding he had no jurisdiction to extend time, or a decision not to extend time) was held to be a first appeal, not a second appeal coming within **art. 5**, so should have been taken to a High Court judge under **art. 3(1)**. In *Convergence Group plc v Chantrey Vellacott* [2005] EWCA Civ 290, *The Times*, 25 April 2005, there was an application to amend a statement of case. The master refused permission for certain amendments, but did not deal with others through lack of time. The matter was taken to the judge, who refused all the proposed amendments. It was held that an appeal to the Court of Appeal was a first appeal, because the appeal in relation to the amendments which had not been considered by the master was a first appeal, and the others could be regarded as raising common issues. This case must be treated with caution. Its logic could be reversed, producing the opposite result. It also misapplies *Uphill v BRB (Residuary) Ltd* [2005] EWCA Civ 60, [2005] 1 WLR 2070, a case discussed at **74.15**.

An appeal to the Court of Appeal from the Patents Court under the Patents Act 1977, s. 97(3), is a specific procedure for patent appeals, and is not governed by the restrictions on second-tier appeals in the **Access to Justice Act 1999, s. 55**. See *Smith International Inc. v Specialised Petroleum Services Group Ltd* [2005] EWCA Civ 1357, [2006] 1 WLR 252.

The principles governing obtaining permission to appeal in second-tier appeals are considered at 74.15.

Appeal centres

74.9 Appeals within a county court, appeals from a county court, and appeals within the High Court to a judge of the High Court must be brought in the appropriate appeal centre (**PD 52B, para. 2.1**). There are two lists of appeal centres for each of the six circuits and district registry appeals in **PD 52B**. The venue for an appeal within a county court is determined by the Designated Civil Judge, and may be different from the appeal centre (**para. 2.1**).

Leapfrog appeals to the Court of Appeal

74.10 If the normal route for a first appeal from a decision of a district judge or master would be to a circuit judge or to a High Court judge, either the lower court or the appeal court may order the appeal to be transferred to the Court of Appeal. This may be done if it is considered that the appeal will raise an important point of principle or practice or there is some other compelling reason for the Court of Appeal to hear it (**CPR, r. 52.14(1)**). There may be a compelling reason where the case was not allocated to the multi-track because of an administrative error

(*Ollivierre v Chief Constable of Thames Valley* [2011] EWCA Civ 1733, LTL 1/12/2011). Where the judge in the lower court refuses permission to appeal, he cannot make an order under **r. 52.14**, because, until permission to appeal is granted, there is no appeal to be transferred (*7E Communications Ltd v Vertex Antennentechnik GmbH* [2007] EWCA Civ 140, [2007] 1 WLR 2175). The Master of the Rolls has a similar power to divert appeals to the Court of Appeal (**Access to Justice Act 1999, s. 57(1)**).

Judicial review of county court decisions

There are only very limited circumstances in which a claim may be made for judicial review of a county court's decision, as an appeal court, on an application for permission to appeal. The **Access to Justice Act 1999, s. 54(4)** (see **74.16**), which prevents appeals against decisions on permission to appeal, does not impliedly remove the High Court's jurisdiction of judicial review of county court decisions (*R (Sivasubramaniam) v Wandsworth County Court* [2002] EWCA Civ 1738, [2003] 1 WLR 475). Permission to claim judicial review will, however, normally be refused where there is a suitable alternative procedure, such as a statutory appeal procedure (*R (Sivasubramaniam) v Wandsworth County Court*). Judicial review is confined to very rare cases where the county court has acted without jurisdiction or failed to afford the appellant a fair hearing (*R (Mahon) v Taunton County Court* [2001] EWHC 1078 (Admin), [2002] ACD 192; *Gregory v Turner* [2003] EWCA Civ 183, [2003] 1 WLR 1149). Cases where the county court judge had simply got it wrong, even extremely wrong, on the law or facts are not sufficiently exceptional to justify judicial review. Suitable cases include those where the county court embarked on an inquiry where it lacked power, or failed to adjudicate on a matter which it had an unequivocal duty to address, and cases where there has been a clear frustration or corruption of the judicial process (*Strickson v Preston County Court* [2007] EWCA Civ 1132, LTL 9/11/2007). **74.11**

Commentary

PERMISSION TO APPEAL

When permission is required

There is a general requirement in **CPR, r. 52.3**, for permission to appeal from any decision of a judge in a county court or the High Court except for appeals against: **74.12**

(a) orders, listed in **r. 52.3(1)(a)**, which affect individuals' liberty; and
(b) decisions of authorised court officers in detailed assessment proceedings (**rr. 47.21, 47.22** and **52.1(2)**).

Rule 52.3(1)(a) provides that permission is not required for an appeal:

(a) by a contemnor against an order for committal to prison, whether immediate or suspended (**r. 52.3(1)(a)(i)**). Appeals against fines and sequestration orders require permission (*Masri v Consolidated Contractors International Co. SAL* [2011] EWCA Civ 898, [2012] 1 WLR 223). An appeal against a committal order where the contemnor is the respondent requires permission (*Poole Borough Council v Hambridge* [2007] EWCA Civ 990, [2008] CP Rep 1);
(b) against refusal to grant habeas corpus (**r. 52.3(1)(a)(ii)**);
(c) against a secure accommodation order made under the Children Act 1989, s. 25 (**CPR, r. 52.3(1)(a)(iii)**).

Permission to appeal is not required for a first appeal from a committal order made by a circuit judge. 'Committal orders' are orders which commit a person to prison. Permission is required for any other order or decision of a circuit judge made in the exercise of the jurisdiction to punish for contempt (*Barnet London Borough Council v Hurst* [2002] EWCA Civ 1009, [2002] 4 All ER 457). Permission is required on appeals by claimants asserting that the lower court was wrong to find that a defendant had purged his contempt, or that the lower court imposed an unduly light penalty for contempt of court (*Government of Sierra Leone v Davenport* [2002] EWCA Civ 230, [2002] CPLR 236). Second appeals in contempt proceedings apparently always require permission, see **r. 52.13** and *Barnet London Borough Council v Hurst*. The guidance given in *Barnet London Borough Council v Hurst* about appeals in contempt proceedings from decisions of district judges is probably wrong as it appears to overlook the fact that the word 'judge' in **r. 52.3** is defined in **r. 2.3(1)** as meaning, unless the context requires otherwise, a judge, master or district judge or a person authorised as such, and is not restricted to circuit judges.

Seeking permission

74.13 Generally, permission to appeal may be sought either from the lower court at the hearing at which the decision to be appealed was made or from the appeal court (**CPR, r. 52.3(2)**). Permission from the appeal court must be sought within 21 days after the decision of the lower court (**r. 52.4(2)(b)**). This period may be extended either by the lower court or appeal court, see 74.20. However, **r. 52.13(1)** provides that permission is required from the Court of Appeal for all appeals to that court from a decision of a county court or the High Court which was itself made on appeal. Where the lower court refuses an application for permission to appeal, a further application for permission to appeal may be made to the appeal court (**r. 52.3(3)**).

Applications for permission to appeal sought from the lower court are made orally at the end of the hearing, usually as the last item of business after costs have been determined. A party who needs more time to decide whether to appeal can ask the lower court to adjourn, in which event the application for permission can be made to the lower court at the relevant hearing, albeit at a later date. If permission is not sought at the hearing in the lower court (perhaps because of a change of mind), the only option, given the wording of **r. 52.3(2)**, is to seek permission from the appeal court (*Balmoral Group Ltd v Borealis (UK) Ltd* [2006] EWHC 2228 (Comm), LTL 6/9/2006). Permission that is sought from the appeal court is asked for initially by seeking permission in writing in the appellant's notice (**r. 52.3(2)(b)**); **PD 52A, para. 4.2**) and is normally considered without a hearing, although a hearing may be convened (**PD 52B, para. 7.1**); **PD 52C, para. 15**). If permission is granted the parties are notified in writing (**para. 4.12**). If permission is refused, the appellant can request the matter to be reconsidered at an oral hearing (see 74.17). Short reasons are usually all that is given on a refusal of permission. Just because they are short does not mean they infringe the requirement for a reasoned decision in the European Convention on Human Rights, **art. 6**, in the **Human Rights Act 1998, sch.1** (*Hyams v Plender* [2001] 1 WLR 32 at [17]).

An appellant is under a duty to inform the Civil Appeals Office in writing of any facts affecting the giving or refusing of permission to appeal (*Walbrook Trustees (Jersey) Ltd v Fattal* [2008] EWCA Civ 427, LTL 11/3/2008). If such facts arise after permission is granted, the appellant should write to the Civil Appeals Office and seek directions.

Test for granting permission

74.14 CPR, r. 52.3(6), provides that permission to appeal may be given only where either:

(a) the court considers that the appeal would have a real prospect of success; or
(b) there is some other compelling reason why the appeal should be heard.

Lord Woolf MR said in *Swain v Hillman* [2001] 1 All ER 91 that a 'real' prospect of success means that the prospect of success must be realistic rather than fanciful. The court considering a request for permission is not required to analyse whether the grounds of the proposed appeal will succeed, but merely whether there is a real prospect of success (*Hunt v Peasegood* (2000) *The Times*, 20 October 2000). Its function is limited to a review of the decision of the court below (see 75.5) to see whether a prospective appellant has an arguable case, fit to present to the full court on appeal, that the decision below was plainly wrong or unjust through a serious irregularity (see 75.6 and *Re W (Children) (Permission to Appeal)* [2007] EWCA Civ 786, [2007] Fam Law 897). Even hopeless appeals may be allowed to proceed where the area of law in question is the subject of considerable controversy (*Beedell v West Ferry Printers Ltd* [2001] EWCA Civ 400, [2001] ICR 962).

A failure by a judge to address an issue may be a compelling reason within **r. 52.3(6)** (*Sofola v Lloyds TSB Bank* [2005] EWHC 1335 (QB), LTL 5/7/2005). There may be a compelling reason for the appeal where the lower court's decision has been overtaken by a subsequent authority, but there is unlikely to be a compelling reason if the lower court was not informed of a binding authority due to a failure by the appellant's advocate (*Sofola v Lloyds TSB Bank*). Apparently, the court should take into account an appellant's strong feelings of injustice when considering whether to grant permission, at least where those feelings are arguably objectively justified (*Malcolm v MacKenzie* [2004] EWCA Civ 584, LTL 18/5/2004).

There is some reluctance in giving permission to appeal against case management decisions, such as disclosure orders and orders dealing with the timetable of the claim. In these cases the court will also consider whether the issue is of sufficient significance to justify the costs of an appeal; the procedural consequences of an appeal (such as losing a trial date); and whether it would be more convenient to determine the point at or after trial (**PD 52A, para. 4.6**).

Second appeals to the Court of Appeal

As discussed at 74.13, generally permission to appeal may be sought from either the lower court or from the appeal court. Second appeals are in a different category. The **Access to Justice Act 1999, s. 55(1)**, and the **CPR, r. 52.13(1)**, provide that permission is required from the Court of Appeal (and cannot be given by the lower court) for any appeal to that court from a decision of a county court or the High Court which was itself made on appeal. The question of what amounts to a second-tier appeal is considered at 74.8. By **r. 52.13(2)**, the Court of Appeal will not give permission unless it considers that either: **74.15**

(a) the appeal would raise an important point of principle or practice; or
(b) there is some other compelling reason for the Court of Appeal to hear it.

Under **r. 52.13(2)(a)**, the point must be an important one. It is not enough that the grounds of appeal may have a real prospect of success. An issue can fall within **r. 52.13(2)(a)** only when it has not yet been determined by previous authority. An appeal based on whether an established point has been correctly applied does not come within the rule (*Uphill v BRB (Residuary) Ltd* [2005] EWCA Civ 60, [2005] 1 WLR 2070). The decision on the first appeal will therefore often be the final decision, with second appeals being something of a rarity (see *Tanfern Ltd v Cameron-MacDonald* [2000] 1 WLR 1311).

The *Uphill v BRB (Residuary) Ltd* approach means that even if the lower court's decision is plainly wrong there is no compelling reason for granting permission for a second appeal (*GB v RJB* [2009] EWCA Civ 545, [2009] 2 FLR 632). The same principle applies even if the would-be appellant won at first instance, but lost on a first appeal. It is increasingly felt that this may be unjust, as there is a real difference between an appellant who has lost twice but wants a third chance to win, and one who, having won at first instance, loses a first appeal on grounds which the single judge in the Court of Appeal feels are arguably wrong (*Farmer v Wilkinson* [2009] EWCA Civ 1143, LTL 16/11/2009). Future reform on this point is merited.

Veitch v Avery (2002) LTL 26/7/2002 was an appeal for which permission was granted under **r. 52.13(2)(b)**. No point of practice or principle was raised in the second appeal, but the judge dealing with the first appeal had allowed an appeal from a district judge and struck out the claim based on the original particulars of claim despite there being amended particulars which raised an arguable claim. Conversely, permission was refused in *Uphill v BRB (Residuary) Ltd* where it was emphasised that 'compelling' is a very strong word. Dyson LJ said that even if the prospects of success on the appeal are very high there may not be a compelling reason. However, where there has been a procedural irregularity rendering the first appeal unfair, there may be a compelling reason even if the overall prospects are not very high. Embarking on a mini-trial in an appeal from a summary judgment decision was not a compelling reason in *Miller v Garton Shires* [2006] EWCA Civ 1386, LTL 31/10/2006.

Refusal of permission to appeal

74.16 There is no appeal from a decision of the appeal court, made at an oral hearing or on the papers, to allow or refuse permission to appeal to that court (**Access to Justice Act 1999, s. 54(4)**). The ban in **s. 54(4)** prevents the Court of Appeal from reviewing a High Court judge's refusal of permission to appeal from the decision of a costs judge, and there is no residual inherent jurisdiction to hear such an appeal (*Riniker v University College London* [2001] 1 WLR 13).

A judge faced with an application for permission to appeal made out of time may come to the conclusion that the appeal is both weak on the merits and that time should not be extended. By reason of the **Access to Justice Act 1999, s. 54(4)**, refusing permission to appeal will result in an end to the appeal process. Taking the easier course of refusing permission to extend time will not, as the appellant can apply for permission to appeal the refusal of the extension, which can be renewed to the Court of Appeal. This difference should be kept in mind when deciding which course to take (*Foenander v Bond Lewis and Co.* [2001] EWCA Civ 759, [2002] 1 WLR 525).

Reconsideration of whether to grant permission

74.17 Where the appeal court, without a hearing, refuses permission to appeal, the person seeking permission may ask for the decision to be reconsidered at a hearing (**CPR, r. 52.3(4)**; *Cassie v Ministry of Defence* [2002] EWCA Civ 838, LTL 17/4/2002). Reconsideration of a refusal is not an appeal against refusal, which is not permitted (see **74.16**). In publicly funded cases, the Court of Appeal requires confirmation that the Legal Aid Agency has been sent a copy of the court's reasons for refusing permission on the papers (**PD 52C, para.** 17). Where a judge of the Court of Appeal or the High Court, or a Designated Judge or a Specialist Circuit Judge, refuses permission without a hearing and considers the application is totally without merit, an order can be made to the effect that the application cannot be reconsidered at a hearing (**r. 52.3(4A)**, as amended with effect from 1 October 2012).

A request for reconsideration of whether to grant permission to appeal must be filed within seven days after service of the notice that permission has been refused (**r. 52.3(5)**). In appeals to the Court of Appeal, within 14 days of filing the appellant's notice the appellant must lodge a bundle containing only those documents which are necessary for the court to determine the application (**PD 52C, para. 14**). If the appellant is represented, the appellant's advocate must file and serve on the respondent at least four days before the hearing a brief written statement (**para. 16**). This must:

(a) set out the points which are to be raise at the hearing; and
(b) set out the reasons why permission should be granted.

There is a recognised principle in the Court of Appeal that permission hearings will not be adjourned for the convenience of counsel, the view being that these can be readily dealt with by junior counsel (*Bracknell Forest Borough Council v N* [2006] EWCA Civ 1562, [2007] Fam Law 121).

Notice of permission hearing to respondent

74.18 A copy of an appellant's request for reconsideration of the question of permission at an oral hearing must be served on the respondent at the same time as it is filed (**PD 52B, para. 7.4(a)**). The respondent will also have been served with the appellant's notice and skeleton argument shortly after they were filed (see **74.23** and **74.28**). The court will give notice of the permission hearing to the respondent, but the respondent is not required to attend unless the court orders or requests him to do so (**para. 8.1(a)**). Proceeding to determine the substantive appeal on this hearing, in the absence of the respondent, is a serious procedural irregularity for the purposes of **CPR, r. 52.11(3)(b)** (*Howard v Stanton* [2011] EWCA Civ 1481, LTL 16/11/2011, and see 75.14).

The purpose of requiring these documents to be served on the respondent is to ensure he is informed of the landmarks in the appeal process. Respondents should not file submissions at the permission stage or attend the permission hearing unless the court so directs (**PD 52C, paras 16(2), 19** and **20**). An exception is where the respondent files submissions addressed to the point that the appeal does not meet the threshold test for permission, or if there is some material inaccuracy in the papers placed before the court (*Jolly v Jay* [2002] EWCA Civ 277, *The Times*, 3 April 2002).

If the court requests the respondent's attendance at the permission hearing, the appellant must supply the respondent with a copy of the skeleton argument and any documents to which the appellant intends to refer (**PD 52C, para. 16(3)**).

Where the court does not order or request submissions or attendance by the respondent, costs will not normally be allowed to a respondent (**PD 52B, para. 8.1(a)**. Where the court requests submissions or attendance, normally the respondent will be awarded costs if permission is refused (**PD 52C, para. 20(2)**).

Limiting the issues on granting permission

By **CPR, r. 52.3(7)**, an order giving permission to appeal may limit the issues to be heard and **74.19**
be made subject to conditions. If a court confines its permission to some issues only, it should expressly refuse permission on any remaining issues, or adjourn the question of permission on any remaining issues to the appeal court (**PD 52C, para. 18(1)**). If the question of permission on an issue is adjourned to the appeal court, the appellant must, within 14 days after service of the court's order, inform the appeal court and the respondent in writing whether the reserved issue is to be pursued (**para. 18(2)**). An appellant can make a request, following the procedure in 74.17, for the reconsideration at an oral hearing of permission on any issues for which permission is refused if the refusal was on the papers (**para. 18(3)**), but not if the refusal was at a hearing (**Access to Justice Act 1999, s. 54(4)**). In **PD 52C, para. 18(1)**, the expression the 'court' is the lower court, so the power to revisit is restricted to situations where the lower court limits the issues on granting permission to appeal. Where the issues are limited by the appeal court on an application for permission, the appeal court cannot revisit the issues to be considered at the final hearing of the appeal (*Fieldman v Markovitch* (2001) *The Times*, 31 July 2001). Where a party is given a choice between proceeding with an appeal on a limited basis, or starting a fresh claim, choosing to proceed with the appeal does not amount to an election, but does mean that starting a fresh claim will be an abuse of process (*Koshy v DEG-Deutsche Investitions- und Entwicklungsgesellschaft mbH* [2008] EWCA Civ 27, LTL 5/2/2008).

TIME FOR APPEALING

Time limits

An appellant must normally initiate an appeal (by filing an appellant's notice in form N161) no **74.20**
later than 21 days from the date of the decision of the lower court (**CPR, r. 52.4(2)(b)**). The appellant's notice may be filed online in the Court of Appeal by following the guidance at http://www.justice.gov.uk/courts/rcj-rolls-building/court-of-appeal/civil-division/filing.

The lower court may direct some other period for filing a notice of appeal (which may be longer or shorter than 21 days) (**CPR, r. 52.4(2)(a)**). An extension should be granted by the lower court only in exceptional circumstances (*Aujla v Sanghera* [2004] EWCA Civ 122, LTL 23/1/2004). The reason for this restrictive approach is that the appeal court exercises the main jurisdiction on granting extensions of time in appeals (see **74.21** and **74.22**). This means that stronger grounds are required to justify an enlargement of the usual 21 days than mere pressure on a prospective appellant's solicitors caused by the 21-day time limit (*City Television v Conference and Training Office Ltd* [2001] EWCA Civ 1770, LTL 16/11/2001). Judgments and orders take effect from the date they are given or made, or such other date as the court may specify (**CPR, r. 40.7(1)**). Delays in formally drawing up the order do not, therefore, delay time running for the purposes of appeals. During the course of a detailed assessment of a bill of costs in *Kasir v Darlington and Simpson Rolling Mills Ltd* (2001) LTL 1/5/2001 the costs judge made a number of decisions, which the appellant wished to appeal. He did not appeal until the detailed assessment process was completed five months later. It was held that time started running in respect of each decision when it was made, and permission to appeal was refused.

Where the lower court judge announces a decision and reserves the reasons for the judgment until a later date, it may be appropriate for the judge to exercise the power under **r. 52.4(2)(a)** in fixing the period for filing a notice of appeal to take account of the delay in giving reasons. A lower court judge can exercise the power under **CPR, r. 52.4(2)(a)**, even after the 21-day appeal period has expired, but should not do so after an appellant's notice has been lodged with the appeal court (*Aujla v Sanghera*).

Extending time for appealing

74.21 The court may extend or shorten the time for compliance with any rule, practice direction or court order, even if an application for extension is made after the time for compliance has expired (**CPR, r. 3.1(2)(a)**). The time for bringing an appeal may be extended under this power. By **r. 52.6(1)**, an application to vary the time limit for filing an appellant's notice must be made to the appeal court. The parties may not (by **r. 52.6(2)**) agree between themselves to extend any date or time limit for the purposes of appealing.

Permission to extend time for appealing is sought by including an application for more time in the appellant's notice (**PD 52B, para. 3.2**). The notice should state the reason for the delay and the steps taken prior to the application being made. Bringing an appeal out of time without seeking permission in the appellant's notice to extend time is an irregularity, which the court has jurisdiction to cure under **CPR, r. 3.10** (*Southern and District Finance plc v Turner* [2003] EWCA Civ 1574, LTL 7/11/2003).

Where an extension is sought and permission to appeal is given (usually the respondent is not given an opportunity to make representations on whether permission to appeal should be granted, see **74.18**), the respondent has the right to be heard on whether an extension of time should be allowed. However, a respondent who unreasonably opposes an extension of time runs the risk of being ordered to pay the appellant's costs of the application to extend time (**PD 52C, para. 4.3(b)**).

Principles for granting extensions of time

74.22 The principles laid down in pre-CPR cases on extending time for appealing are no longer good law (*Sayers v Clarke Walker* [2002] EWCA Civ 645, [2002] 1 WLR 3095). Typically, the court will consider the reason for the delay and the steps taken prior to the application to extend time being made, the need for litigation to be conducted efficiently and at proportionate cost, and the need to comply with procedural rules (**CPR, r. 3.9(1)**, and see **48.36**). It is necessary to avoid judge-made checklists of matters to consider (*Sayers v Clarke Walker*). Each application must be viewed by reference to the criterion of justice, and it is important to bear in mind that time limits are there to be observed, and that justice may be seriously defeated if there is any laxity in this regard. *Southern and District Finance plc v Turner* [2003] EWCA Civ 1574, LTL 7/11/2003, which said the court should give particular weight to the prospects of success, and *Hyams v Plender* [2001] 1 WLR 32, which said at [15] that a failure to state reasons for the delay in the appellant's notice, (see 74.21) may not in itself be a reason for refusing an extension, may need to be reappraised given the Jackson reforms of 1 April 2013.

APPELLANT'S NOTICE

An appellant must file an appellant's notice at the appeal court within such period as may be directed by the lower court or, where the court makes no such direction, 21 days after the date of the decision of the lower court that the appellant wishes to appeal (**CPR, r. 52.4(2)**). An appellant's notice must be in form N161 (N164 for small claims appeals). It must set out the grounds of the appeal, which must identify as concisely as possible the respects in which the decision of the lower court is either wrong or unjust through serious procedural or other irregularity (**PD 52B, para. 4.2(d)**; **PD 52C, para. 5(1)**). The reasons why the lower court's decision is wrong or unjust must be confined to the skeleton argument (**para. 5(2)**). Grounds of appeal must identify specific incidents, directions or findings made by the court below which are alleged to be wrong or unjust. Each ground should be stated as an appeal on a point of law or against a finding of fact. Drafting of grounds of appeal is therefore of great importance, because they define the complaints being made against the decision of the court below. **74.23**

In a second appeal, **PD 52C, para. 5A** provides that the grounds of appeal must state the important point of principle or practice, or the compelling reason, which is said to justify the grant of permission to appeal.

By **CPR, r. 52.11(5)**, an appellant may not rely at the hearing of the appeal on a matter not contained in the appeal notice unless the appeal court gives permission. Similarly, the Court of Appeal may refuse to hear argument on a point not included in the skeleton argument (**PD 52C, para. 31(3)**). Failing to make clear the real basis for challenging the decision below is unfair on the appeal court (whose pre-reading is wasted) and unfair on respondents, who will not know the case they have to meet (*IS Innovative Software Ltd v Howes* [2004] EWCA Civ 275, *The Times*, 10 March 2004). Normally, an appellant seeking to change the basis of its case should apply for permission amend the grounds of appeal (**CPR, r. 52.8**) and to file a supplementary skeleton argument. Procedure for amending the appellant's notice is set out in **PD 52C, para. 30**, and for filing supplementary skeleton arguments in **para. 32**.

The requirement to state whether grounds are on points of law or findings of fact is important when the jurisdiction of the appeal court is limited to appeals on points of law (*Scribes West Ltd v Relsa Anstalt (No. 1)* [2004] EWCA Civ 835, *The Times*, 8 July 2004 at [3]). The distinction is also important because of the reluctance to interfere with decisions on the facts, because it is the trial judge who sees the witnesses (see 75.9).

Points of law include errors concerning the elements of causes of action and defences; errors concerning the standard and burden of proof; evidential errors concerning questions such as the admissibility and relevance of evidence and the effect of presumptions.

Points of law can include a failure to deal with an issue in the judgment, and wrongfully withdrawing issues from determination at trial.

Appeals on questions of fact include misstating the facts given in evidence; treating the evidence given by one side unfairly; where there is a jury, summing up the evidence unclearly or illogically or with inappropriate comments (although the judge has a fairly wide area of discretion on the comments that can fairly be made).

Unless permission to appeal is not needed, or has been given by the lower courts an application for permission to appeal must be included in the appellant's notice (**PD 52A, para. 4.2**) with, if necessary, an application for permission to appeal out of time stating the reason for the delay and the steps taken prior to the application being made (**PD 52B, para. 3.2**). An appellant's notice may include applications for interim remedies in the course of the appeal (**para. 4.3**). An appellant seeking, for the first time, to rely on any issue or to seek any remedy under the **Human Rights Act 1998** must include information complying with **PD 16, para. 15.1**, in the appellant's notice.

LODGING DOCUMENTS

74.24 An appellant must lodge the following documents at the appeal court with the appellant's notice (see **PD 52B, para. 4.2**):

(a) three copies of the appellant's notice and one additional copy for each respondent;
(b) a sealed copy of the order of the lower court;
(c) any order giving or refusing permission to appeal (including such an order from the lower court) together with a copy of the reasons for that decision; and
(d) grounds of appeal, which must be set out on a separate sheet attached to the appellant's notice.

There is a longer list of documents to be filed in appeals to the Court of Appeal (**PD 52C, para. 3(3)**), which include:

(i) any written evidence in support of any interim application included in the appellant's notice;
(ii) in second appeals, the first order and the reasons given by the judge;
(iii) a copy of the order allocating the case to a track (if any).
(iv) the appellant's skeleton argument in support of the appeal; and
(v) the approved transcript of the judgment.

Where it is not possible to file all the above documents, the appellant must complete the appeal notice on the basis of the available documents (**PD 52C, para 6**).

Appeal bundles: contents

74.25 As soon as practicable, but in any event within 35 days of filing the appellant's notice, the appellant must file an appeal bundle (**PD 52B, para. 6.3**). In appeals to the Court of Appeal, the appellant must serve a proposed bundle index on every respondent within seven days after the date of the listing window notification. The appeal bundles need to be agreed within 21 days after the date of the listing window notification, and must be lodged no later than 42 days before the appeal hearing (**PD 52C, para. 21, Timetables 1 and 2**).

An appeal bundle must contain only those documents relevant to the appeal (**PD 52B, para. 6.3; PD 52C, para. 27(1)**). It must be paginated and in chronological order, and must contain an index. Subject to any order made by the court, the appeal bundle must contain the documents listed in **PD 52B, para. 6.4(1)** or **PD 52C, para. 27(2)** and may include such of the documents listed in **PD 52B, para. 6.4(2)** or **PD 52C, para. 27(3)** if they are relevant to the appeal. Compulsory documents include a copy of the appellant's notice, a copy of any skeleton arguments, and a copy of the order under appeal. Documents to be included if relevant include statements of case, application notices, witness statements and other documents which the appellant or respondent consider to be relevant to the appeal.

The key to deciding what to include in the appeal bundle is having a clear grasp of the real issues raised by the appeal. What the appeal court does not want is an appeal bundle put together in an unthinking manner, including the whole trial bundle and miscellaneous superfluous documents, such as solicitors' correspondence, unless these materials go to the issues raised by the appeal (*Scribes West Ltd v Relsa Anstalt (No. 1)* [2004] EWCA Civ 835, *The Times*, 8 July 2004 at [11]). No more than a single copy of each document should be included unless there is a good reason for doing so.

In complex appeals, particularly where several related appeals are to proceed together, bundles may need to be put together in chronological files (with the documents usually identifying their original file numbers) even though this may not comply with the terms of **PD 52B or 52C**. Agreement should be attempted between the parties, and, if achieved, a consent order should be sought from the deputy master or supervising Lord Justice, on paper (*Leofelis SA v Lonsdale Sports Ltd* [2008] EWCA Civ 640, *The Times*, 23 July 2008).

A respondent who has been served with an appeal bundle and who considers that relevant documents have been omitted may file and serve on all other parties a respondent's supplementary appeal bundle (**PD 52B, para 8.2**). This bundle must be filed and served as soon as practicable after service of the appeal bundle, but in any event not less than seven days before the hearing.

Appeal bundles are primarily for use by the judges in the appeal court, particularly to assist them with pre-reading. The ban on thoughtlessly copying trial bundles into appeal bundles does not prevent a party producing a trial bundle at the hearing of the appeal in case it transpires it contains an important document, but the appeal bundle must be limited as required by **PD 52B** and **PD 52C** (*Scribes West Ltd v Relsa Anstalt (No. 1)* at [11]).

Appeal bundles: format

Appeal bundles must be copied single-sided, and in exactly the same form with no extra markings other than pagination as those given to the judge at the hearing below (Civil Appeals Form 204, paras 5.5 and 5.6). All staples, clips etc. must be removed. Every page in the appeal bundle must be paginated consecutively, in bold figures at the bottom of the page, but differently from the form of pagination used in the hearing below. Statements of case must appear in 'chapter' form, with the claim followed by particulars of claim, and further information following the relevant statement of case. Statements of case overtaken by amendments should be excluded. Documents within categories should appear chronologically. The pages, other than transcripts, must be placed in lever arch files, ring binders or robust plastic folders, filled sensibly (not too many or few pages for the binder), with the Court of Appeal reference and case name appearing clearly on the spine and front of each file. 300 pages is a good guide to not overfilling files (*Leofelis SA v Lonsdale Sports Ltd* [2008] EWCA Civ 640, *The Times*, 23 July 2008). An index must be included at the front of the bundle **(PD 52B, para. 6.3)**; **PD 52C, para.** 27(1). Where several files are needed, experience dictates that colour-coded files help at the hearing (*Scribes West Ltd v Relsa Anstalt (No. 1)* at [16]). **74.26**

Pages sent to the court to be added to the appeal bundle must be sent already punched and paginated for immediate inclusion in the existing binders. They should be filed as soon as practicable, and in any event no less than seven days before the hearing (**PD 52B, para. 6.6**).

Core bundles

Core bundles are often used where there is a great deal of documentation. A core bundle should contain the documents which are central to the appeal, and ought not normally to exceed 150 pages. Pagination should usually be the same as the main appeal bundle. **74.27**

Skeleton argument: procedural requirements

In appeals to the county court and High Court, subject to any order of the court, **PD 52B, para. 8.3** says the parties to an appeal should file and serve skeleton arguments only where: **74.28**

(a) the complexity of the issues of fact or law in the appeal justify them; or
(b) skeleton arguments would assist the court in respects not readily apparent from the papers in the appeal.

In appeals to the Court of Appeal the appellant must file a skeleton argument at the same time as filing the appellant's notice (**PD 52 C, para. 3(3)(g)**). A respondent who files a respondent's notice must file and serve its skeleton argument at the same time (**PD 52C, para. 21, Timetable 1**). Replacement skeleton arguments with cross-references to the appeal bundle must be filed by the appellant no later than 14 days before the hearing, and by the respondent no later than seven days before the hearing (**PD 52C, paras 1 and 21, Timetable 2**).

Skeleton arguments: contents

74.29 Form N163 should be used (or used as a cover sheet) for the skeleton arguments. The purpose of a skeleton argument is to assist the court by setting out as concisely as practicable the arguments upon which a party intends to rely (**PD 52B, para. 5.1(1)**). By **para. 5.1(2)** a skeleton argument must:

(a) be concise;
(b) both define and confine the areas of controversy;
(c) be set out in numbered paragraphs;
(d) be cross-referenced to any relevant document in the bundle;
(e) be self-contained and not incorporate by reference material from previous skeleton arguments; and
(f) not include extensive quotations from documents or authorities.

Documents to be relied on must be identified (**para. 5.1(3)**). Where it is necessary to refer to an authority, a skeleton argument must state the proposition of law the authority demonstrates, and identify the parts of the authority that support the proposition (**para. 5.1(4)**). If more than one authority is cited in support of a given proposition, the skeleton argument must briefly state why. In the case of questions of fact, the skeleton should state briefly the basis on which it is contended that the Court of Appeal can interfere with the finding of fact concerned, with cross-references to the passages in the transcript or notes of evidence which bear on the point (see Practice Direction (Court of Appeal: Procedure) [1995] 1 WLR 1191).

For appeals to the Court of Appeal, skeleton arguments must not normally exceed 25 pages and must be printed on A4 paper in not less than 12 point font and 1.5 line spacing (**PD 52C, para. 31(1)**). In the past it has been said that for a one-day appeal on a point of law 10 pages should be enough. Skeleton arguments should not be prepared as verbatim scripts or as footnoted theses. They are aids to oral advocacy, not substitutes. A skeleton argument in *D. Pride and Partners v Institute for Animal Health* [2009] EWHC 1617 (QB), LTL 14/7/2009, was criticised for resembling the style of a textbook. Any statement of costs must show the amount claimed for the skeleton argument separately (**PD 52B, para. 5.3**). The court may disallow the cost of preparing a skeleton argument that does not comply with the requirements of **PD 52B** and **PD 52C (PD 52C, para. 31(4))**.

Detailed guidance was given by the Court of Appeal in *Raja v Van Hoogstraten (No. 9)* [2008] EWCA Civ 1444, [2009] 1 WLR 1143 at [126]–[128]:

> 126. We remind practitioners that skeleton arguments should not be prepared as verbatim scripts to be read out in public or as footnoted theses to be read in private. Good skeleton arguments are tools with practical uses: an agenda for the hearing, a summary of the main points, propositions and arguments to be developed orally, a useful way of noting citations and references, a convenient place for making cross-references, a time-saving means of avoiding unnecessary dictation to the court and laborious and pointless note-taking by the court.
>
> 127. Skeleton arguments are aids to oral advocacy. They are not written briefs which are used in some jurisdictions as substitutes for oral advocacy. An unintended and unfortunate side effect of the growth in written advocacy (written opening and closing submissions and 'speaking notes', as well as skeleton arguments) has been that too many practitioners, at increased cost to their clients and diminishing assistance to the court, burden their opponents and the court with written briefs. They are anything but brief. The result is that there is no real saving of legal costs, or of precious hearing, reading and writing time....

128. The skeletal nature of written advocacy is in danger of being overlooked. In some cases we are weighed down by the skeleton arguments and when we dare to complain about the time they take up, we are sometimes told that we can read them 'in our own time' after the hearing. In our judgment, this is not what appellate advocacy is about, or ought to be about, in this court.

Record of the judgment of the lower court

If the judgment of the lower court was recorded, an application for an approved transcript should be made as soon as possible, and in any event within seven days after filing the appellant's notice (**PD 52B, para. 6.2**). Photocopies are not acceptable. If there is no official transcript, the next best is the lower court judge's written judgment signed by the judge. If the lower court's judgment was oral and not recorded, the advocates should confer and submit, if possible, an agreed note of the judgment to the judge for signature. If the note cannot be agreed, both versions should be submitted with a covering letter explaining the situation. These points are important, because appeals, even from district judges and masters, can only succeed by attacking the decision-making process in some way, and injustice may result if no reliable record is available of what was said in the lower court. **74.30**

A request may be made for the provision of transcripts at the public expense on the ground of poor financial circumstances, and this should wherever possible be made to the lower court when asking for permission to appeal. Applications can be made in the Court of Appeal to a deputy master, with a right of review to a judge of the Court of Appeal (see *Hyams v Plender* [2001] 1 WLR 32 at [28], where comments are made by Brooke LJ suggesting that similar arrangements should be made for appeals to the High Court). An order for provision of transcripts at public expense was refused in *Perotti v Westminster City Council* [2005] EWCA Civ 581, *The Times*, 30 May 2005. In this case the litigant said the transcript was needed for formulating his grounds of appeal, but he had tape recorded the judgment, and could have asked for the note of judgment made by the respondent's advocate.

Transcripts or notes of the evidence (as opposed to the judgment) are not generally needed on applications for permission to appeal, but may become necessary if permission is granted for the purposes of the substantive appeal.

SERVICE ON THE RESPONDENT

By **CPR, r. 52.4(3)**, unless the appeal court orders otherwise, an appellant's notice must be served on each respondent as soon as practicable, and in any event not later than seven days, after it is filed. A certificate of service must be filed (**PD 52B, para. 6.1**). **74.31**

If permission to appeal is not required, or was given by the lower court, a copy of the appeal bundle must be served on each respondent at the same time as the appeal bundle is filed (**para. 6.5(a)**).

If the appellant is asking the appeal court for permission to appeal, the appeal bundle generally has to be served as soon as practicable after notification, and in any event within 14 days of permission being granted (**para. 6.5(b)**). Where the appeal court directs that the application for permission be heard on the same occasion as the appeal, the appeal bundle must be served as soon as practicable, and in any event within 14 days after notification of the hearing date (**para. 6.5(c)**).

AFTER PERMISSION TO APPEAL IS GIVEN

Notification

In cases where permission to appeal has to be obtained from the appeal court, the appeal court will send the parties copies of the order granting permission and any other directions given by the court. **74.32**

Commentary

If permission to appeal is granted, and if the appeal court is not the Court of Appeal, the appeal court will send the parties notification of the hearing or the period during which the appeal is likely to be heard ('the listing window'). Appeals in the Court of Appeal are given a listing window notification. The hear-by date is the last day of the listing window (**PD 52C, para. 22**). Listing in the Court of Appeal is considered at **74.35**.

Service of appeal papers

74.33 The normal rule is that service must be effected by the parties (**PD 52B, para. 6.1; PD 52C, para. 7.1**).

Appeal questionnaires

74.34 For Court of Appeal cases, at the same time as giving the parties a listing window notification, the Civil Appeals Office will send the appellant an appeal questionnaire. This must be returned within 14 days, and must include the appellant's advocate's time estimate for the hearing, confirmation that the transcript of evidence given at the lower court's hearing has been requested, confirmation that appeal bundles are being prepared (though this should be unnecessary, as appeal bundles should have been filed with the appellant's notice before permission was granted), and confirmation that copies of the questionnaire and appeal bundle have been served on the respondents (**PD 52C, para. 23**). A respondent who disagrees with the time estimate must inform the court within seven days of receipt of the questionnaire (**para. 24**). Where the appeal court is the High Court, use of appeal questionnaires is optional.

Court of Appeal listing

74.35 Appeals to the Court of Appeal are divided into seven categories, or lists.

These are:

(a) The applications list. This includes all applications for permission to appeal, as well as applications for interim remedies in pending appeals.
(b) The appeals list. These are cases where permission to appeal has been given and cases where an appeal lies without needing permission.
(c) The expedited list. This includes applications and appeals where the Court of Appeal has directed an expedited hearing in accordance with the practice laid down in *Unilever plc v Chefaro Proprietaries Ltd* [1995] 1 WLR 243. Asylum appeals, appeals where rights might be irrevocably conferred on third parties, and cases where unlawful material is about to be published, may typically be allocated to this list.
(d) The stand-out list. This is for appeals and applications which are not ready for hearing and which have, for good reasons, been stood out by judicial direction.
(e) The special fixtures list, which is a subdivision of the appeals list, where there is a need to list cases before particular judges, or in a particular order, or at a particular location or time.
(f) The second fixtures list. Appeals designated as 'second fixtures' are given hearing dates on the express basis that the list is fully booked for the period in question, and therefore they will only be heard if a suitable gap occurs in the list.
(g) The short warned list. This is for appeals which the court considers may be prepared for hearing by an advocate other than the one originally instructed on either a half day's notice, or, if the court so directs, 48 hours' notice. An appeal or application on this list may be called on at any time with the appropriate short notice. Further details are given in Practice Note (Court of Appeal: Listing) [2001] 1 WLR 479. An objection to being included in this list may be made to a Lord Justice or the master of the Court of Appeal,

but will be granted only for the most compelling reasons. An example would be where the appeal cannot be mastered by a substitute advocate within the contemplated time. If the original advocate cannot deal with the hearing because of prior commitments, he or she is under a professional duty to take all practicable measures to ensure the lay client is represented at the hearing by an advocate who is fully instructed and able to argue the appeal. A failure in this duty may be visited by a wasted costs order. There has been a short warned list for many years, and surprisingly few complaints have been made about it despite the fact there are occasions when appeals are handed over to an advocate who has had no prior involvement with the case on very short notice.

In addition, the Court of Appeal sits at various times at a number of provincial trial centres. Partly this is for the convenience of parties, but it also serves a number of wider public interest purposes relating to access to justice and informing the public and senior judiciary (purposes which can be traced back to Magna Carta 1215, ss. 17 and 18). There is great reluctance in breaking fixtures for hearings in provincial centres, even where counsel of choice is unavailable for such a hearing through being pre-booked (*Newport City Council v Charles* [2008] EWCA Civ 893, *The Times*, 29 July 2008).

Hear-by dates for various categories of appeals to the Court of Appeal are set out in Practice Note (Court of Appeal: Listing Windows) [2003] 1 WLR 838. The longest hear-by date is nine months, and many periods are six months. Arrangements for dealing with applications for expedition and for a hearing beyond a hear-by date are described in Practice Note (Court of Appeal: Listing Windows) [2001] 1 WLR 1517.

SHORT HEARINGS BY VIDEOCONFERENCING

Where appropriate and available, parties should use technology, such as videoconferencing, to reduce costs. In *Black v Pastouna* [2005] EWCA Civ 1389, *The Independent*, 2 December 2005, it was said that the additional costs of travelling a long distance to court may be disallowed on short (up to 30-minute) appeals if videoconferencing facilities are available. **74.36**

RESPONDENT'S NOTICE AND OTHER DOCUMENTS

Respondent's notice

In any appeal a respondent may file and serve a respondent's notice (**CPR, r. 52.5(1)**). The respondent's notice may be filed online in the Court of Appeal by using the online form. By **CPR, r. 52.5(2)**, a respondent's notice must be filed by a respondent who: **74.37**

(a) is seeking permission to appeal from the appeal court; or
(b) wishes to ask the appeal court to uphold the order of the lower court for reasons different from or additional to those given by the lower court.

Respondents accordingly fall into three broad categories:

(a) Respondents who simply wish to uphold the decision of the court below for the same reasons as given by the judge below. Such a respondent need not serve a respondent's notice.
(b) Respondents who wish to uphold the decision of the court below for reasons different from or additional to those given by the lower court. Such a respondent is not appealing as such, so there is no question of seeking permission to cross-appeal. However, a respondent's notice is required for the purpose of setting out the different or additional reasons (**PD 52C, para. 8(3)**). A respondent who does not file a respondent's notice is not entitled to address the appeal court on any reason not relied on in the judgment of the lower court, unless the appeal court gives permission. It is not a legitimate exercise of the lower court

judge's discretion to make a declaration in terms of factual findings in order to convert what would otherwise be reasons for the primary decision into 'judgments' or 'orders' or 'determinations' within the meaning of the Senior Courts Act 1981, s. 16(1), or the County Courts Act 1984, s. 77(1), if the only purpose is to force the respondent to seek permission under **CPR, r. 52.3(1)**, for what would otherwise be a purely defensive respondent's notice. See *Compagnie Noga d'Importation et d'Exportation SA v Australia and New Zealand Banking Group Ltd* [2002] EWCA Civ 1142, [2003] 1 WLR 307.

(c) Respondents who wish to ask the appeal court to vary the order of the lower court are cross-appealing, and permission to appeal must be sought on the same basis as for an appellant (**PD 52C, para.** 8(3)). A respondent's notice is required for setting out the grounds on which it is to be argued that the order of the court below should be varied.

Form of respondent's notice

74.38 A respondent's notice is similar to an appellant's notice (see 74.23) and must be in form N162. Together with appellants' notices they are called 'appeal notices' in the **CPR** (**r.** 52.1(3)(f)). A respondent who seeks permission to cross-appeal from the appeal court must do so in the respondent's notice (**r.** 52.5(3)).

Filing and serving a respondent's notice

74.39 Generally, a respondent's notice must be filed within such period as may be directed by the lower court. Where the court makes no such direction, the notice must be filed within 14 days after the date laid down by **CPR, r.** 52.5(5), relevant to the circumstances of the appeal. This date will be either:

(a) the date the respondent was served with the appellant's notice in cases where permission to appeal was given by the lower court, or permission to appeal was not required; or
(b) the date the respondent was served with notification that the appeal court gave the appellant permission to appeal; or
(c) the date the respondent was served with notification that the application for permission to appeal and the appeal itself are to be heard together.

Unless the appeal court orders otherwise, a respondent's notice must be served on the appellant and any other respondent as soon as practicable, and in any event not later than seven days after it is filed (**r.** 52.5(6)). An extension of time for service of a respondent's notice was readily granted in *Bell Electric Ltd v Aweco Appliance Systems GmbH & Co.* [2002] EWCA Civ 1501, [2003] 1 All ER 344.

Respondent's skeleton argument

74.40 A respondent who files a respondent's notice in an appeal to the Court of Appeal must lodge and serve a skeleton argument (**PD 52C, para.** 9). It should conform to the principles applicable to appellants' skeletons (see 74.29), but should also seek to answer the arguments in the appellant's skeleton. A respondent in an appeal to the Court of Appeal who does not file a respondent's notice (see 74.37) must lodge and serve his skeleton argument no later than 42 days after the date of the listing window notification (**para.** 21, **Timetable** 1). An unrepresented respondent need not file a skeleton argument (**para.** 13(1)).

Respondent's documents

74.41 A respondent's notice must, by **PD 52C, para.** 10, be lodged with:

(a) two additional copies of the respondent's notice for the appeal court; and
(b) one copy of the respondent's notice for each appellant and any other respondents.

Supplementary skeleton argument

PD 52C, para. 32, lays down a timetable for supplementary skeleton arguments in the Court of Appeal. Supplementary skeleton arguments may become necessary sometimes when new advocates are appointed, or when the law has moved on, or where there is a need to respond to a point raised in an opponent's skeleton argument. An appellant in this situation must file and serve its supplementary skeleton argument as soon as practicable. Only exceptionally will the court allow the use of a supplementary skeleton argument if lodged less than seven days before the hearing. **74.42**

FINAL DEADLINE

For appeals to the Court of Appeal, all the papers needed for the appeal must be filed at least seven days before the hearing (**PD 52C, para. 21, Timetable 2**). If the seven-day deadline cannot be met, both the court and the other parties must be informed. Permission to file out of time may be granted if there are exceptional circumstances or an understandable reason for the delay (*Mlauzi v Secretary of State for the Home Department* [2005] EWCA Civ 128, *The Times*, 15 February 2005). Any party who fails to comply may be required to attend before the presiding Lord Justice to explain what is or is not being done, and seek permission to proceed with or to oppose the appeal (*Jeyapragash v Secretary of State for the Home Department* [2004] EWCA Civ 1260, [2005] 1 All ER 412). The Court of Appeal expects strict compliance with this final deadline, because it is essential for effective pre-reading by the judges. Any party summoned is advised to ensure that all documents have been filed before attending before the presiding Lord Justice (*Scribes West Ltd v Relsa Anstalt (No. 1)* [2004] EWCA Civ 835, *The Times*, 8 July 2004 at [31]). See also 74.48 to 74.49 for the more general jurisdiction of appeal courts to impose sanctions and to dismiss appeals for non-compliance. **74.43**

Commentary

APPLICATIONS WITHIN APPEALS

Notice of an application made to the appeal court for a remedy incidental to the appeal (such as an application for security for costs) should be included in the appellant's notice (**PD 52B, para. 4.3**), or may be made by an ordinary application notice under **CPR, Part 23**. **74.44**

The applicant must file the following documents with the application (see **PD 52, para. 11.2**):

(a) one additional copy of the application notice for the appeal court and one copy for each of the respondents;
(b) where applicable, a sealed copy of the order which is the subject of the main appeal; and
(c) a bundle of documents, which should include the application notice and any written evidence in support of the application.

An application notice may be filed online in the Court of Appeal. In the Court of Appeal, interim applications within appeals are often determined by a single Lord Justice. Short, half-hour, applications to the Court of Appeal may be suitable for hearing through video link. Details can be obtained through the Civil Appeals Office. Costs may be disallowed where counsel travel unnecessary distances instead of using this facility (*Babbings v Kirklees Metropolitan Borough Council* [2004] EWCA Civ 1431, *The Times*, 4 November 2004).

The Master of the Rolls may designate an eligible officer to be the Court of Appeal master to exercise judicial authority under **CPR, r. 52.16**, to deal with matters incidental to appeals, matters where there is no substantial dispute, and dismissal of appeals and applications for procedural default. There are also deputy masters. However, masters and deputies cannot give permission to appeal, grant stays (other than temporary stays of the decision of the lower court over a period when the Court of Appeal is not sitting or cannot conveniently be convened) or grant injunctions (**CPR, r. 52.16(3)**). A party is entitled, within seven days of being served with notice of the decision, to request that any decision by a court officer be reviewed by the Court of Appeal (**r. 52.16(5), (6)** and **(6A)**). A single judge may refer any matter for a decision by a court consisting of two or more judges (**r. 52.16(7)**).

AMENDMENT OF AN APPEAL NOTICE

74.45 An appeal notice (appellant's or respondent's) may be amended with permission (**CPR, r. 52.8**). An application for permission to amend will normally be dealt with at the hearing of the appeal, unless that course would cause unnecessary expense or delay, in which case a request should be made for the application to amend to be heard in advance (**PD 52C, para. 30(3)**).

STAY OF EXECUTION

74.46 Initiating an appeal does not have the automatic effect of staying execution on any judgment obtained in the lower court. By **CPR, r. 52.7**, an appeal will operate as a stay of any order or decision of the lower court only if:

(a) the appeal court or the lower court so orders; or
(b) the appeal is from the Asylum and Immigration Tribunal.

The basic rule is that a litigant is entitled to enjoy the fruits of its success (*BMW AG v Commissioners of HM Revenue and Customs* [2008] EWCA Civ 1028, LTL 7/10/2008). This means that enforcement should be allowed to proceed unless in all the circumstances of the case and having regard to the risk of injustice to the parties a stay ought to be imposed (*Gater Assets Ltd v NAK Naftogaz Ukrainiy* [2008] EWCA Civ 1051, LTL 8/10/2008). The court has an unfettered discretion to impose a stay of execution if the justice of the case so demands (*BMW AG v Commissioners of HM Revenue and Customs*). Relevant questions are (*Hammond Suddard Solicitors v Agrichem International Holdings Ltd* [2001] EWCA Civ 1915, LTL 18/12/2001):

(a) If a stay is refused, what are the risks of the appeal being stifled?
(b) If a stay is granted and the appeal fails, what are the risks that the respondent will be unable to enforce the judgment?
(c) If a stay is refused and the appeal succeeds, and the judgment is enforced in the meantime, what are the risks of the appellant being able to recover what has been paid to the respondent?

The appeal court also has a discretion to suspend an order for possession pending the appeal (*Admiral Taverns (Cygnet) Ltd v Daniel* [2008] EWHC 1688 (QB), [2008] NPC 86).

Evidence in support of an application for a stay must be full, frank and clear (*Hammond Suddard Solicitors v Agrichem International Holdings Ltd*).

REVOKING PERMISSION, STRIKING OUT, IMPOSING CONDITIONS

74.47 By **CPR, r. 52.9(1)**, an appeal court has the following powers: it may strike out the whole or part of an appeal notice; it may set aside permission to appeal in whole or in part; or it may impose or vary conditions upon which an appeal may be brought. These powers may be exercised only where there is a compelling reason (**r. 52.9(2)**). In *Angel Airlines SA v Dean and Dean* [2006] EWCA Civ 1505, [2007] 3 Costs LR 355, permission to appeal to the Court of Appeal had been granted by Gloster J in the High Court. Rix LJ, at [29], said that in the circumstances the power to revoke the permission granted by Gloster J under **r. 52.9** was vested in the High

Court. This misunderstands the phrase 'the appeal court' as it appears in **r. 52.9(1)**, which is defined in **r. 52.1(3)(b)** to mean the court to which an appeal is made. In any event *Angel Airlines SA v Dean and Dean* held that the Court of Appeal has power to revoke permission to appeal, either under **r. 52.10** (which says the appeal court has all the powers of the lower court, see **75.19**) or in the court's inherent jurisdiction. In addition to its powers under **r. 52.9**, an appeal court may impose conditions under its general case management powers in **rr. 2.1** and **3.1**, which can be exercised even after an application to impose conditions has been refused by the judge in the court below (*Contract Facilities Ltd v Rees's Estate* [2003] EWCA Civ 1105, LTL 24/7/2003). Applications to set aside or impose conditions on the grant of permission to appeal should be made within 14 days of service of the order granting permission (*Mamidoil-Jetoil Greek Petroleum Company SA v Okta Crude Oil Refinery AD* [2003] EWCA Civ 808, *The Times*, 19 June 2003).

It is recognised that the power to strike out an appeal notice 'is one that is just as capable of abuse as is the power to put in hopeless notices of appeal' (*Burgess v Stafford Hotel Ltd* [1990] 1 WLR 1215 per Glidewell LJ). Requiring a 'compelling reason' for the exercise of the powers under **r. 52.9(1)** deliberately sets a high standard, in part in order to comply with the requirement in the European Convention on Human Rights, **art. 6(1)**, in the **Human Rights Act 1998, sch. 1**, of ensuring appellants have a fair trial of their appeals (*Dadourian Group International Inc. v Simms* [2009] EWCA Civ 169, [2009] 1 Lloyd's Rep 601). There may be a compelling reason where the appeal is being brought to secure some collateral advantage, or where the application will achieve a substantial saving of time. This may be so where there are cogent grounds demonstrating the appeal had no prospects of success. Otherwise, in all ordinary circumstances the granting of permission to appeal is conclusive (*Hunt v Peasegood* (2000) *The Times*, 20 October 2000). A party who was present at the hearing at which permission was given may not subsequently apply for an order that the court exercise its powers to set aside permission or to impose conditions (**r. 52.9(3)**).

Commentary

Sanctions and conditions in appeals

Bell Electric Ltd v Aweco Appliance Systems GmbH & Co. KG [2002] EWCA Civ 1501, [2003] 1 All ER 344, **74.48**
which said there is a wholly unfettered discretion under **CPR, r. 52.9(1)(c)**, to impose and vary conditions upon which appeals may be brought, should be understood as referring to the width of the conditions that may be imposed, rather than the circumstances in which conditions may be imposed, which require a compelling reason (**r. 52.9(2)**). In this case the appellant was found to have disregarded the orders of the court below in a deliberate and cynical manner, and ordered that unless the appellant complied with the terms of the order below within the next 14 days the appeal would be stayed. A condition requiring an appellant to pay the costs whether he won or lost was held to be excessive in *King v Daltray* [2003] EWCA Civ 808, LTL 4/6/2003. An order that there be no order as to costs on the appeal was substituted. In *Masri v Consolidated Contractors International (UK) Ltd* [2007] EWCA Civ 702, LTL 31/7/2007, a condition was imposed requiring payment of an interim payment and costs ordered in the court below, with a sanction of striking out the appeal in the event of default. A condition requiring a payment into court may be varied on the ground that the appellant cannot afford to make the payment, but evidence will be required that the amount is such as to prevent the appellant funding the appeal (*Branch Empire Ltd v Coote* [2003] EWHC 1674, LTL 16/6/2003). In *R (Medical Justice) v Secretary of State for the Home Department* [2011] EWCA Civ 269, [2011] 1 WLR 2852, the Secretary of State was granted permission to appeal by Silber J on condition that, whatever the outcome of the appeal, the Secretary of State would pay the costs of the hearing in the lower court and the respondent's costs of the appeal. An appeal by the Secretary of State against these conditions was dismissed on the ground there was no jurisdiction by virtue of the **Access to Justice Act 1999, s. 54(4)** (see **74.16**). Permission to appeal is a composite decision. An appellant who objects to conditions set by the lower court can abandon the prospective appeal,

accept the conditions, or make a fresh application for permission from the appeal court under **r. 52.3(3)** (see 74.13).

DISMISSAL FOR NON-COMPLIANCE

74.49 Where the rules on lodging documents, skeleton arguments etc. are broken, an appeal may be considered for dismissal. In the Court of Appeal such cases may be considered by the Head of the Civil Appeals Office or by a deputy master. The court sees it as its duty to protect the interests of respondents, who already have a decision of a competent authority in their favour, by insisting on all reasonable expedition and strict compliance with the timetable laid down. See *Hyams v Plender* [2001] 1 WLR 32.

DISPOSAL OF APPEALS BY CONSENT

74.50 Where the parties to an appeal have reached a settlement disposing of the appeal, they may make a joint request asking for the appeal to be dismissed by consent (**PD 52A, para. 6.3**). An appellant who does not wish to pursue an appeal may make a request to the appeal court for the appeal to be dismissed. If granted, this will usually be on terms that the appellant pays the costs (**para. 6.1**), but may be on the basis of no order as to costs if the respondent's representative signs a consent to that effect (**para. 6.2**). An appeal may be allowed by consent, but the appeal court must first be satisfied that the lower court's decision was wrong (**para. 6.4**). Appeals and applications settled where one of the parties is under a disability require the court's approval (**para. 6.5**). In these cases the proposed consent order should be supported by an opinion from the advocate acting for the child advising on whether the terms are for the benefit of the child or protected party.

Solicitors and counsel have a duty to inform the court, by letter if possible, as soon as it is known that an appeal which has been listed for hearing will not proceed (*Red River UK Ltd v Sheikh* [2009] EWCA Civ 643, *The Times*, 6 May 2009). Even if a case settles very late in the day steps must taken through the Royal Courts of Justice switchboard to notify the appeal court judges' clerks, to prevent unnecessary preparation (*Tasyurdu v Immigration Appeal Tribunal* [2003] EWCA Civ 447, [2003] CPLR 343; *Yell Ltd v Garton* [2004] EWCA Civ 87, *The Times*, 26 February 2004).

AUTHORITIES

Cases

74.51 In the High Court lists of authorities should be provided to the Head Usher by 5.30 p.m. on the working day before the appeal hearing. In the county courts it is usually necessary to have photocopies of reports available at the hearing.

For Court of Appeal hearings (only), bundles of authorities containing photocopies of the principal authorities each side will be relying upon must be lodged no later than seven days before the hearing (**PD 52C, para. 21, Timeline 2; para. 29**). Obviously, this can only be done after conferring with the advocate for the respondent. There is no need to provide authorities for propositions not in dispute. Normally, the bundle should contain no more than 10 authorities with the relevant passages marked for pre-reading. **Paragraph 29(4)(b)** recognises that the scale of the appeal may warrant more extensive citation. The bundle must *include a certificate signed* by the advocates that the requirements of **para. 29** on citing and marking up authorities has been complied with.

The *Law Reports* published by the Incorporated Council of Law Reporting for England and Wales should be cited in preference to other reports, as they contain counsel's arguments and are readily available (**Practice Direction: Citation of Authorities** (2012)). Next best are the *Weekly Law Reports* and *All England Law Reports* if a case is not, or not yet, reported in the official *Law Reports*. Other reports, even obscure reports, may be used for sufficient reason, but advocates should provide photocopies (of the title page and relevant pages only). Occasionally it is useful to refer to more than one source if there are discrepancies between reports. There are restrictions on using certain authorities, discussed in Practice Direction (Citation of Authorities) [2001] 1 WLR 1001, see **32.19**. If unreported decisions are relied upon, the official transcript should be produced rather than the handed-down text of the judgment (**Practice Direction: Citation of Authorities** (2012), para. 10), and they should only be used if they contain statements of principle not found in reported authorities (**Practice Direction: Citation of Authorities** (2012), para. 10). Excessive citation of authorities, and reliance on summaries of cases not prepared by a professional lawyer, will not be tolerated (*Hamblin v Field* (2000) *The Times*, 26 April 2000).

Use of *Hansard* extracts

It was decided in *Pepper v Hart* [1993] AC 593 that Parliamentary material may be used as an aid **74.52**
to determining the true intention of the legislature where:

(a) the legislation is ambiguous or obscure or the literal meaning leads to an absurdity;
(b) the material relied upon consists of statements by a minister or promoter of the Bill and such other material as is necessary to understand those statements; and
(c) the statements relied on are clear.

It is permissible to have recourse to ministerial statements and explanatory notes prepared by the relevant government department while the Bill was proceeding through Parliament, where doing so complies with the principles in *Pepper v Hart*. However, reference to debates in Parliament is contrary to the Bill of Rights (1688), art. 9, so cannot be justified as an aid to interpretation in court (see *Wilson v First County Trust Ltd (No. 2)* [2003] UKHL 40, [2004] 1 AC 816). Even where use of ministerial statements and explanatory notes is permissible, the court must be careful not to give these documents determinative effect, as Members of Parliament may not have generally agreed with the stated reasons or conclusions (*Wilson v First County Trust Ltd (No. 2)*). In *McDonnell v Congregation of Christian Brothers Trustees* [2003] UKHL 63, [2003] 1 AC 1101, Lord Bingham of Cornhill said he would need much persuasion, save possibly in exceptional circumstances, that it is proper to depart from a previous decision of the House of Lords on the basis that the previous decision is inconsistent with the will of Parliament as discovered from *Hansard*. Lord Steyn in the same case said there is a view that *Pepper v Hart* allows the court to treat the intentions of government revealed in debates in Parliament as reflecting the will of Parliament. That view raises serious conceptual and constitutional difficulties. The better view is that it has been decided by *Wilson v First County Trust Ltd (No. 2)* that use of debates from *Hansard* is not permissible.

Any party intending to refer to extracts from *Hansard* in accordance with the principles laid down in *Pepper v Hart* must give reasonable advance notice to the court and other parties. In the Court of Appeal the extracts should be included in the bundle of authorities (see 74.51).

FORM OF APPEAL ORDERS

The general rules relating to drawing up orders (see **chapter 63**) apply to orders made after **74.53**
appeal hearings. However, to assist the Civil Appeals Office in sifting applications for permission to bring a second appeal (see 74.15 for the restrictions on such appeals), orders made on first appeals must (see *Tanfern Ltd v Cameron-MacDonald* [2000] 1 WLR 1311):

(a) state the name and status of the judge in the lower court; and

Commentary

(b) if it is a final order, state which track (if any) the claim was allocated to, and whether it was a Part 8 claim.

REOPENING APPEALS

74.54 Confirming the decision in *Taylor v Lawrence* [2002] EWCA Civ 90, [2003] QB 528, it is now provided in **CPR, r. 52.17**, that the Court of Appeal and High Court may reopen an appeal (or application for permission to appeal: **PD 52A, para. 7.1** and *Barclays Bank plc v Guy (No. 2)* [2010] EWCA Civ 1396, [2011] 1 WLR 681) in exceptional circumstances. This power derives from the court's inherent jurisdiction, and so is not available to a circuit judge in the county court (**CPR, r. 52.17(3)**). An appeal may be reopened (see **r. 52.17(1)**) if all of the following three conditions are satisfied:

(a) It is necessary to do so to avoid real injustice (such as where new facts come to light after the court makes its decision, as in *Taylor v Lawrence*, or where the appeal court was misled by false evidence into an erroneous conclusion, as in *Feakins v Department for Environment Food and Rural Affairs* [2006] EWCA Civ 699, [2006] NPC 66).

(b) The circumstances are exceptional and make it appropriate to reopen the appeal. A case is exceptional if it is possible a significant injustice will occur and there is no effective alternative remedy (*Re Uddin (A Child)* [2005] EWCA Civ 52, [2005] 1 WLR 2398). This might be found where the integrity of the earlier process has been critically undermined. The admission of fresh evidence (see **75.16**), or establishing that the decision was wrong, will not be enough. It is necessary to show the decision was arrived at by a corrupted process, such as fraud or bias (*Guy v Barclays Bank plc* [2010] EWCA Civ 1396, [2011] 1 WLR 681). Appeal decisions alleged to have been obtained through fraud should, save in the most exceptional circumstances, be brought by way of fresh proceedings (*Jaffray v Society of Lloyd's* [2007] EWCA Civ 586, [2008] 1 WLR 75; see **75.18**). Exceptional cases are those where there is incontestable, admissible, evidence of the fraud.

(c) There is no alternative effective remedy (so if the injustice could be remedied by a readily available further appeal, the court will not reopen the present appeal).

Procedure for reopening appeals

74.55 Permission is required to reopen an appeal, even if permission was not required for the initial appeal (**CPR, r. 52.17(4)**). An application for permission is made by application notice (in form N244) supported by written evidence (**PD 52A, para. 7.2**), and is made to the court whose decision the applicant wishes to reopen (**para. 7.1**). There is no right to an oral hearing unless the judge so directs (**CPR, r. 52.17(5)**), and the application must not be served on any other party, again unless the court otherwise directs (**PD 52A, para. 7.2**). An application cannot be granted unless the judge makes a direction for service on the other party and gives them an opportunity to make representations (**CPR, r. 52.17(6)**). The respondent has 14 days from being served to file and serve written evidence in reply (**PD 52A, para. 7.3**). There is no right of appeal or review from a decision on an application for permission to reopen, which is final (**CPR, r. 52.17**; *Meghani v Nessfield Ltd* [2008] EWHC 2827 (Ch), LTL 19/12/2008).

APPEALS BY WAY OF CASE STATED

74.56 A number of statutes provide that appeals may be brought to the High Court by way of case stated. Among the most well known are the Magistrates' Courts Act 1980, s. 111, and the Senior Courts Act 1981, s. 28. These provide for appeals by case stated from decisions made by magistrates' courts and the Crown Court on the ground they are wrong in law or in excess of jurisdiction. See *Blackstone's Criminal Practice 2014*, paras D29.17 to D29.24 and D29.37 to D29.39. A decision of the High Court on an appeal by case stated under either of these provisions is final, subject to the right of appeal in criminal cases to the Supreme Court under the Administration of Justice Act 1960 (see Senior Courts Act 1981, s. 28A(4), where, at least in the text at www.legislation.gov.uk, the description of the effect of the 1960 Act mistakenly refers to appeals to the Senior Courts instead of the Supreme Court because of the unintended effect of blanket amendments made by the Constitutional Reform Act 2005, s. 59(6), and sch. 11, para. 26).

Consequently, in a civil case the Court of Appeal has no jurisdiction to entertain a further appeal from the High Court's decision (*Westminster City Council v O'Reilly* [2003] EWCA Civ 1007, [2004] 1 WLR 195).

PD 52E applies to cases where enactments provide for appeals to be by way of case stated and to cases where a question of law may be referred to the court by way of case stated. In these cases the general provisions of **CPR, Part 52**, apply, subject to certain amendments. **PD 52E, paras 2.1** to **2.4**, apply to appeals by way of case stated from the Crown Court or magistrates' courts. In these appeals the appellant's notice must be filed in the High Court within 10 days after receipt of the stated case (**para. 2.2**). **Paragraphs 3.1** to **3.14** apply to appeals from ministers, government departments, tribunals and other persons by way of case stated. In these cases the appellant's notice and the stated case must be filed and served within 14 days after stating the case (**para. 3.6**). The minister or government department is entitled to attend the appeal hearing and to make representations (**para. 3.10**).

STATUTORY APPEALS

PD 52D applies to all statutory appeals, and to other appeals which are subject to special provision, but not to appeals by way of case stated (for which see 74.56). These appeals are governed by the main provisions of **CPR, Part 52**, but with certain refinements. **74.57**

Where any statute prescribes a period within which an appeal must be filed, unless the statute provides otherwise, the appeal court may not extend that period (**PD 52D, para. 3.5**). Where the appellant wishes to appeal against a decision of the Administrative Appeals Chamber of the Upper Tribunal, the appellant's notice must be filed within 21 days of the date on which the Upper Tribunal's decision on permission to appeal to the Court of Appeal is given (**para. 3.3(1)**). Where the appellant wishes to appeal against a decision of any other Chamber of the Upper Tribunal, the appellant's notice must be filed within 28 days of the date on which the Upper Tribunal's decision on permission to appeal to the Court of Appeal is given (**para. 3.3(2)**).

The appellant is required to serve the appellant's notice on the chairman of the tribunal, minister of State, government department or other person from whose decision the appeal is brought, in addition to the respondents (**para. 3.4(1)**). In a statutory appeal any person may apply for permission to file evidence or make representations in the appeal (**CPR, r. 52.12A**). Such an application must be made promptly (**r. 52.12A(2)**). An application for permission must be made by letter to the relevant court office, identifying the appeal, explaining who the applicant is and indicating why and in what form the applicant wants to participate in the hearing (**PD 52D, para. 3.7**).

A clear distinction must be made between the provisions which provide the court with jurisdiction in a statutory appeal, and the provisions in **CPR, Part 52**, and **PD 52D** which govern the conduct of the appeal thereafter. **CPR, Part 52**, and **PD 52D** do not impose a requirement for seeking permission to appeal for statutory appeals where otherwise the right of appeal is unrestricted (*Colley v Council for Licensed Conveyancers* (2001) *The Times*, 6 August 2001). Once seised of an appeal, **CPR, Part 52**, applies, which means, for example, that an appellant's notice is required even in appeals by way of case stated (*Woodpecker v Commissioners of HM*

Revenue and Customs [2009] EWHC 3442 (Ch), LTL 21/10/2009). Conditions upon which a statutory appeal may be brought may be imposed under **r. 52.9**, which applies both to appeals requiring permission and those which can be brought as of right (*Calltel Telecom Ltd v Commissioners of HM Revenue and Customs* [2008] EWHC 2107 (Ch), [2009] Bus LR 513).

Costs in statutory appeals etc

74.58 For costs against inferior courts, coroners, etc. see **68.39**.

For orders limiting appeal costs in appeals from non-costs jurisdictions, see **75.22**.

Special appeal provisions

74.59 **Section 4 of PD 52D** contains a large number of special rules applicable to various categories of specialist appeals. These include appeals from various tribunals to the Court of Appeal (such as appeals from the Immigration and Asylum Chamber of the Upper Tribunal), and appeals to the High Court under various statutory provisions, most of which are highly specialised. For appeals under the Trade Marks Act 1938, s. 18, see *E. I. Dupont de Nemours and Co. v S. T. Dupont* [2003] EWCA Civ 1368, [2006] 1 WLR 2793. Appeals under the Party Wall etc. Act 1996 were considered in *Zissis v Lukomski* [2006] EWCA Civ 341, [2006] 1 WLR 2778, which also considered how technical errors in bringing a statutory appeal could be cured by amendment or by invoking the overriding objective.

CPR powers, for example, to dispense with service, do not apply to time limits laid down in primary legislation for bringing statutory appeals (*Mucelli v Government of Albania* [2009] UKHL 2, [2009] 1 WLR 276, see **15.24**). *Mucelli v Government of Albania* was a decision under the Extradition Act 2003, but the same principle applies to a range of other statutory appeals (*Massan v Secretary of State for the Home Department* [2011] EWCA Civ 686, LTL 30/6/2011, an application to extend time for filing the appellant's notice in an appeal under the Asylum and Nationality Act 2006; *R (Harrison) v General Medical Council* [2011] EWHC 1741 (Admin), LTL 8/6/2011, an appeal under the Medical Act 1983; *R (Modaresi) v Secretary of State for Health* [2011] EWCA Civ 1359, LTL 23/11/2011, an appeal under the Mental Health Act 1983).

74.60 **Extradition Act 2003** Appeal procedures under **CPR, Part 52**, in appeals under the Extradition Act 2003 are modified by **PD 52D, para. 21.1**. Appeals must be brought in the Administrative Court (**para. 21.1(2)**). Different appeal provisions in the Extradition Act 2003 lay down different periods for filing and serving the appellant's notice. It is seven days from the order in appeals under ss. 26 and 28, and 14 days from being informed of the Secretary of State's order for appeals under s. 103. It is the filed appellant's notice that must be served within these time limits, not a pre-filing draft, although a copy of the filed but not yet stamped document may be permitted (*Regional Court in Konin, Poland v Walerianczyk* [2010] EWHC 2149 (Admin), [2011] 3 All ER 944). While it is highly desirable that an appellant's notice in form N161 be used for this purpose, there is no mandatory requirement to this effect, but the document used has to set out at least the identity of the appellant and the decision under appeal, and the gist of the basis of the appeal (*Pomiechowski v Poland* [2011] EWHC 2060 (Admin), [2012] ACD 9).

74.61 **Housing Act 1996, ss. 204 and 204A** Appeals under both ss. 204 and 204A of the Housing Act 1996 should be included in one appellant's notice, unless this is not possible because of urgency (**PD 52D, para. 28.1(2)**). An appeal under s. 204 was held in *Van Aken v Camden London Borough Council* [2002] EWCA Civ 1724, [2003] 1 WLR 684, to have been brought within the 21-day time limit laid down by s. 204(2) where the documents were put through the court's letter box after the court had closed on the 21st day.

74.62 **Law of Property Act 1922** Appeals against decisions of the Secretary of State under the Law of Property Act 1922, sch. 15, para. 16, lie to the High Court (**CPR, r. 52.18**).

Osteopaths Act 1993 Substantive appeals under the Osteopaths Act 1993 lie to the High Court under **CPR, Part 52**, and so do appeals against interim suspension orders pending resolution of substantive appeals. Unless the High Court forms the view that the substantive appeal is bound to succeed, it should be slow to allow an appeal against an interim suspension order because it will not be in a position to assess whether the decision was wrong within the meaning of **r. 52.11(3)(a)** (*Moody v General Osteopathic Council* [2007] EWHC 2518 (Admin), [2008] 2 All ER 532). **74.63**

Planning legislation An appeal, on a point of law, against the Secretary of State's decision on an appeal against an enforcement notice, a notice under the Town and Country Planning Act 1990, s. 207, or a listed building enforcement notice, lies to the High Court (**CPR, r. 52.20**). **74.64**

Transport Tribunal An appeal to the Court of Appeal from the Transport Tribunal does not require permission, but can be made only on a point of law (*Banga v Secretary of State for Transport* [2008] EWCA Civ 188, *The Times*, 29 January 2008). **74.65**

Tribunals and Inquiries Act 1992 Decisions of a limited list of tribunals can be challenged on points of law either by appealing to the High Court or by requesting the tribunal to state and sign a special case for the opinion of the High Court. See the Tribunals and Inquiries Act 1992, s. 11(1), and **CPR, r. 52.19**. **74.66**

Chapter 75 Hearing of Appeals

INTRODUCTION

75.1 This chapter will discuss the nature of appeal hearings, and the grounds on which an appeal court may overturn the decision of the court below.

COMPOSITION OF THE COURT

75.2 An appeal from a county court district judge will be to a county court circuit judge. An appeal from a High Court master or district judge will be to a High Court judge. The same is true with appeals from county court circuit judges (other than appeals from final decisions in multi-track and specialist jurisdiction proceedings, where the appeal is to the Court of Appeal).

The Senior Courts Act 1981, s. 54(2), provides that the Court of Appeal shall be duly constituted for the purposes of exercising any of its jurisdiction if it consists of one or more judges. Section 54(3) provides that the Master of the Rolls may give directions about the minimum number of judges required for different descriptions of proceedings and, by s. 54(4) the Master of the Rolls or any designated Lord Justice can determine the number of judges who will sit in any particular proceedings. In the absence of special circumstances, there is nothing wrong with a judge who refused permission to appeal on the papers being one of the judges hearing the substantive appeal after permission is granted on a renewed application (*Sengupta v Holmes* [2002] EWCA Civ 1104, 99 (39) LSG 39). Normally, two Lords Justices sit on interim appeals, and three sit on final appeals. Where a two-judge court is equally divided, either party may apply for a rehearing before a three-judge court.

Occasionally an appeal court will sit with assessors, as in some appeals on costs issues.

THE HEARING

75.3 Normally it is unnecessary for the advocate for the appellant to open the appeal, as the judges usually do fairly extensive pre-reading. In most cases the judges will have pre-read the appeal bundle and skeleton arguments, and usually will have read the core authorities bundle (if there is one). The judge (or presiding judge in a multi-member court) usually indicates the extent of the pre-reading that has been done. In appeals to the Court of Appeal, if it is felt that it would be helpful for the appellant's advocate to open the appeal, the presiding judge will notify the advocates in advance. The intention is that court time is spent dealing with the substance of the arguments and that time should not be wasted in extensive reading from documents.

PART 36 OFFERS

The fact that a Part 36 offer has been made must not be disclosed to the court on any application for permission to appeal or on any appeal until all questions (other than costs) have been determined (**CPR, r. 52.12(1)**). This is for the same reason (the risk of unfairly influencing the court) as applies at trial (see **r. 36.13**). However, the embargo does not apply if the Part 36 offer is relevant to the substance of the appeal, or if the fact that a Part 36 offer has been made is properly relevant to the matter to be decided (**r. 52.12(2)** and **(3)**). **75.4**

REVIEW OF THE DECISION BELOW

Review not rehearing

By **CPR, r. 52.11(1)**, every appeal will be limited to a review of the decision of the lower court unless: **75.5**

(a) a practice direction makes different provision for a particular category of appeal; or
(b) the court considers that in the circumstances of an individual appeal it would be in the interests of justice to hold a rehearing.

There are very few exceptions. The power to conduct an appeal by way of rehearing is to be exercised in rare cases where necessary in order for justice to be done. The fair trial requirements of the European Convention on Human Rights, **art. 6**, in the **Human Rights Act 1998, sch. 1** do not compel the court to conduct rehearings in appeals from without-notice decisions (*Dyson Ltd v Registrar of Trademarks* [2003] EWHC 1062 (Ch), [2003] 1 WLR 2406). The exceptional nature of holding a rehearing rather than a review on an appeal was stressed in *Lewis v Secretary of State for Trade and Industry* [2001] 2 BCLC 597. It had been submitted that a rehearing was appropriate because the lower court had not stated reasons for its decision. Neuberger J said that even in such cases the appeal should be by way of review unless the court below had been asked to give its reasons and had refused to do so, or there was some good reason for not asking the lower court to give its reasons. The limited circumstances in which an appeal should take the form of a rehearing rather than a review, particularly where the decision appealed against is one based on discretion, were stressed in *Audergon v La Baguette Ltd* [2002] EWCA Civ 10, [2002] CPLR 192. In *Richardson v Ealing London Borough Council* [2005] EWCA Civ 1798, *The Times*, 14 December 2005, the Court of Appeal reiterated the practice requiring an exceptional case before conducting an appeal as a rehearing. In *McFaddens Solicitors v Chandrasekaran* [2007] EWCA Civ 220, LTL 26/2/2007, the appeal court could only have fulfilled its task in an appeal against a summary judgment decision by reference to all the material put before the master. While this looks like a rehearing, it was to be regarded as a review within the meaning of **CPR, r. 52.11**. *Bank of Ireland v Robertson* (2003) LTL 21/2/2003 was an exceptional case where an appeal was conducted by way of rehearing. The appellant was a litigant in person, had been unable to attend the hearing, and this was the first occasion on which he had been able to present his case.

Grounds for allowing appeals

The restriction of an appeal court's function to a review of the lower court's decision means that for almost all appeals, the appeal court will allow an appeal only where (**CPR, r. 52.11(3)**) the decision of the lower court was: **75.6**

(a) wrong; or
(b) unjust because of a serious procedural or other irregularity in the proceedings in the lower court.

In addition, a decision will only be wrong or unjust if the matter of complaint would have made a difference to the decision of the lower court (*Ebden v Richardson* [2008] EWCA Civ 1589, LTL 10/11/2008).

Duty to take point in lower court

75.7 An appellant is not allowed to present a totally new argument that is not stated in the grounds of appeal and was not taken in the court below (*Gover v Propertycare Ltd* [2006] EWCA Civ 286, [2006] ICR 1073). This obligation was infringed in *City and General (Holborn) Ltd v Royal and Sun Alliance Insurance plc* [2010] EWCA Civ 911, [2010] BLR 639, where in the court below both parties argued for an all-or-nothing approach on whether the claim was time-barred under the Limitation Act 1980, but on appeal the claimant sought to argue that there were three causes of action, each with a different date of accrual. There is a discretion to permit a new point to be taken on an appeal if there is a sufficient reason. This may arise where there has been a recent legal development, although in *Thorne v Lass Salt Garvin* [2009] EWHC 100 (QB), LTL 5/2/2009, the court refused permission where the 'recent' authority forming the basis of the new point had been reported several months before the hearing in the lower court, but the legal representatives of the appellant had not appreciated its relevance to the case in hand.

It is counsel's duty in the lower court to draw the judge's attention to any alleged deficiency in a judgment, and request clarification or a supplementary judgment on the issue. It is not open to counsel to keep quiet and then raise the issue on an application for permission to appeal (*Re S (Children)* [2007] EWCA Civ 694, *The Times*, 2 July 2007). See also the discussion on handed-down judgments at **63.33** and **75.20**.

Wrong decisions

75.8 'Wrong' in **CPR, r. 52.11(3)(a)**, means unsustainable (*Abrahams v Lenton* [2003] EWHC 1104 (QB), LTL 20/5/2003). An insubstantial point, even if a technical error, does not render a decision wrong (*Orford v Rasmi Electronics Ltd* [2004] EWCA Civ 809, LTL 4/8/2004). An arithmetical error in computing damages may be sufficient (*Pope v Energem Mining (IOM) Ltd* [2011] EWCA Civ 1043, LTL 6/9/2011).The strength of the other evidence at trial may mean that, despite an error, the decision below was not wrong (*Daly v Sheikh* [2004] EWCA Civ 119, LTL 13/2/2004). In *DEG-Deutsche Investitions- und Entwicklungsgesellschaft mbH v Koshy* [2001] EWCA Civ 79, [2001] 3 All ER 878, Robert Walker LJ at [24] rejected a submission that there is no power to allow an appeal where the lower court's decision was correct on the law and evidence as it stood before the lower court, even though a change in the law, or fresh evidence, or supervening events, show it (with hindsight) to have been wrong. The Court of Appeal seems to have gone even further in *Law v St Margarets Insurance Ltd* [2001] EWCA Civ 30, LTL 18/1/2001, where the appeal was allowed on the basis of furthering the overriding objective rather than holding that the lower court's discretion fell outside the generous ambit given to discretionary decisions. Similarly, in *Ayonrinde v Oyemomilara* [2001] EWCA Civ 1296, LTL 17/7/2001, it was difficult to say that the lower court's decision was wrong on the material before the judge below. However, the decision in the lower court caused injustice to the appellant, and the case was treated as an exceptional case which justified setting aside the decision below.

Questions of fact

75.9 The trial judge sees the demeanour of witnesses, and can assess their intelligence and credibility in a way that an appeal court cannot, even with the benefit of a transcript. It is accordingly very difficult to succeed on an appeal based on arguments that findings of fact by the court below were wrong (*Orford v Rasmi Electronics Ltd* [2004] EWCA Civ 809, LTL 4/8/2004). Appeal courts are more likely to interfere with inferences that may be drawn from the evidence (see 75.12).

The appeal court's function is to review the decision of the court below. It is not to embark on making original findings of fact (*Designer Guild Ltd v Russell Williams (Textiles) Ltd* [2000] 1 WLR 2416). An appeal court has to accept the findings of fact of the court below on an interim appeal, and is not entitled to take a different view of the facts on which the decision below was founded (*Momson v Azeez* [2009] EWCA Civ 202, LTL 18/3/2009).

A trial finding of fact can be upset on appeal if there was no evidence to support that finding, or if the finding was against the weight of the evidence as a whole (*Bank of Credit and Commerce International (Overseas) Ltd v Akindele* [2001] Ch 437). An appeal on a question of fact was allowed in *George Ralph Architects v Lazarowicz* (2000) LTL 27/10/2000, where the judge found an agreement by preferring one side's witnesses, but where the agreement was not referred to in the contemporaneous documents.

Failure to give reasons

The definition of issues, marshalling of evidence and giving reasons are the building blocks of the reasoned judicial process. See **61.55**. An analysis of the judgment in *Glicksman v Redbridge Healthcare NHS Trust* [2001] EWCA Civ 1097, LTL 12/7/2001, showed that the judge below had made findings expressed as conclusions without giving reasons for the implicit rejection of testimony going the other way. Further, there were no findings on the secondary issues on which counsel had relied. The judgment was set aside with an order for a retrial. A case just on the other side of the line was *Harris v CDMR Purfleet Ltd* (2008) LTL 20/11/2008), where although there were doubts as to the judge's reasons, it was reasonably clear why the judge had reached his decision, and his conclusions were clear. A judge must address the main evidential conflicts, and identify why (for example) certain witnesses have been found to be truthful and others to be untruthful or inaccurate (*Baird v Thurrock Borough Council* [2005] EWCA Civ 1499, *The Times*, 15 November 2005). Making findings in a column in a Scott schedule is no substitute for a reasoned judgment on the issues (*Habib Bank Ltd v Liverpool Freeport (Electronics) Ltd* [2004] EWCA Civ 1062, LTL 29/7/2004). In *Clifford v Grimley* [2001] EWCA Civ 1658, LTL 23/10/2001, the judge failed to weigh up many of the issues, which were dealt with in a robust manner which was cursory and superficial. Nevertheless, the short analysis did not sufficiently undermine the findings of fact to justify interference on appeal. Further, in a well-known area an experienced judge is not expected to spell out every nuance of the principles that are being applied in coming to the decision (*Novus Aviation Ltd v Onur Air Tas, ımacılık AS* [2009] EWCA Civ 122, [2009] 1 Lloyd's Rep 576). **75.10**

Commentary

An unsuccessful party should not seek to upset a judgment on the ground of inadequate reasons unless, despite considering the judgment in the light of the evidence and submissions at trial, they are unable to understand why the judge had decided against them (*English v Emery Reimbold and Strick Ltd* [2002] EWCA Civ 605, [2002] 1 WLR 2409). It is the advocate's duty to draw the judge's attention to any ambiguity or alleged deficiency in the judge's reasoning (*Re A and L (Children)* [2011] EWCA Civ 1205, [2012] 1 FLR 134).When an application for permission to appeal is made to the trial judge on the ground of inadequate reasons, the trial judge should consider whether his judgment was defective. If so, the judge should seek to remedy this by giving additional reasons, and refuse permission to appeal as the problem is thereby remedied. Where an appeal court finds a renewed application for permission on this ground to be well founded, it should consider adjourning the application and remitting the case to the trial judge with an invitation to provide additional reasons for the decision. If the application proceeds to an appeal hearing, the appeal will only succeed if the reasons cannot be discerned even in the context of the evidence and submissions at the trial (*English v Emery Reimbold and Strick Ltd*). A failure to address an issue was not sufficient to justify interference on appeal where the judgment was otherwise a careful one in *Powell v Pallisers of Hereford Ltd* [2002] EWCA Civ 959, LTL 1/7/2002. The practice of giving no reasons for decisions on costs could only comply with the European Convention on Human Rights, **art. 6(1)**, in the **Human rights Act**

1998, sch. 1, if the reason for the decision is implicit from the circumstances (*English v Emery Reimbold and Strick Ltd*).

Discretion

75.11 The most important statement on the role of an appellate court in a discretionary matter is that of Lord Diplock in *Hadmor Productions Ltd v Hamilton* [1983] 1 AC 191. This was a case dealing with an appeal in respect of an interim injunction, but his lordship's comments are equally applicable in other types of interim appeals. His lordship said, at p. 220:

> Upon an appeal from the judge's grant or refusal of an [interim] injunction the function of an appellate court, whether it be the Court of Appeal or your lordships' House, is not to exercise an independent discretion of its own. It must defer to the judge's exercise of his discretion and must not interfere with it merely upon the ground that the members of the appellate court would have exercised the discretion differently. The function of the appellate court is initially one of review only. It may set aside the judge's exercise of his discretion on the ground that it was based upon a misunderstanding of the law or of the evidence before him or upon an inference that particular facts existed or did not exist, which, although it was one that might legitimately have been drawn upon the evidence that was before the judge, can be demonstrated to be wrong by further evidence that has become available by the time of the appeal; or upon the ground that there has been a change of circumstances after the judge made his order that would have justified his acceding to an application to vary it. Since reasons given by judges for granting or refusing [interim] injunctions may sometimes be sketchy, there may also be occasional cases where even though no erroneous assumption of law or fact can be identified the judge's decision to grant or refuse the injunction is so aberrant that it must be set aside upon the ground that no reasonable judge regardful of his duty to act judicially could have reached it. It is only if and after the appellate court has reached the conclusion that the judge's exercise of his discretion must be set aside for one or other of these reasons, that it becomes entitled to exercise an original discretion of its own.

Thus, discretionary decisions may be reversed on appeal where the judge below erred in principle in his approach, or left out of account or took into account some feature he should not have considered, or that his decision was wholly wrong because he failed to balance the various factors fairly in the scale (*Adamson v Halifax plc* [2002] EWCA Civ 1134, [2003] 1 WLR 60). The way it was put by Lord Fraser of Tullybelton in *G v G (Minors: Custody Appeal)* [1985] 1 WLR 647 is that the appeal court 'should only interfere when it considers that the judge of first instance has not merely preferred an imperfect solution which is different from an alternative imperfect solution which the Court of Appeal might or would have adopted, but has exceeded the generous ambit within which a reasonable disagreement is possible'.

Any conclusion reached at a case management conference is made at the judge's discretion, and, unless the judge has clearly erred by failing to fulfil the overriding objective, there is a distinct reluctance to interfere on an appeal (*Powell v Pallisers of Hereford Ltd* [2002] EWCA Civ 959, LTL 1/7/2002). There may be an even greater reluctance to interfere with a discretion exercised by a trial judge (*Swain-Mason v Mills and Reeve LLP* [2011] EWCA Civ 14, [2011] 1 WLR 2735 at [78]). In *Raja v Van Hoogstraten (No. 9)* [2008] EWCA Civ 1444, [2009] 1 WLR 1143 at [119], Mummery LJ said that an appeal court will not interfere with the wide discretion of the judge on costs unless there was some error of principle or some other reason why the judge's decision was plainly wrong. In *Straker v Tudor Rose* [2007] EWCA Civ 368, [2008] 2 Costs LR 205, Waller LJ at [2], [10], pointed out that appeal courts are loath to interfere with the discretion exercised by a judge in any area, and particularly so in the area of costs. A number of Court of Appeal authorities had been cited to the court, and Waller LJ commented:

> I do not gain much assistance from them. In the area of costs, where all cases are different and fact specific, I would suggest that authorities apart from those that lay down clear principles are of little assistance. It is to the Rules that one should go, and it is by reference to the Rules that one should test whether the judge has gone wrong in any particular case.

Inferences

It takes a strong case before an appeal court will decide that a decision was wrong on the basis of inferences drawn by the trial judge from eyewitness evidence; the question being whether the inferences could fairly be drawn from the evidence (*Silverlink Trains Ltd v Collins-Williamson* [2009] EWCA Civ 850, LTL 31/7/2009). An appeal court may draw its own inferences of fact which it considers justified on the evidence (**CPR, r. 52.11(4)**). This includes inferences to be drawn from the facts found by the judge in the lower court and inferences to be drawn from the documents (*The Mouna* [1991] 2 Lloyd's Rep 221). **75.12**

New point of law

On an appeal it is possible to raise a new point of law that was not presented to the court below. There is some reluctance to allow this, and normally permission will be granted only if there is no possibility of any injustice occurring, such as through the failure to raise the point of law at first instance affecting the conduct of the trial, the evidence, or the evaluation of the evidence. There is even greater reluctance to allow a point of mixed law and fact to be raised for the first time on an appeal. A mixed point will almost certainly require an amendment to the appellant's statement of case, which will not be granted where permission to amend would have been refused if the point had been raised at trial (*Jones v Environcom Ltd* [2011] EWCA Civ 1152, [2012] PNLR 5, and see **31.6** and **31.13**). **75.13**

Serious procedural irregularities

Procedural irregularities include misdirections to the jury (in jury trials) and the improper admission or non-admission of evidence. By **CPR, r. 52.11(3)**, a procedural irregularity is a valid ground for appeal only if it was a serious one and it caused an unjust decision in the lower court (*Tanfern Ltd v Cameron-MacDonald* [2000] 1 WLR 1311). An appeal on this ground is an onerous one, and the procedural irregularity must have caused an injustice to the appellant (*Keith Davy (Crantock) Ltd v Ibatex Ltd* [2001] EWCA Civ 740, LTL 2/5/2001). While not providing the opposite party with a letter sent to the judge, and thereby failing to give the other side an opportunity to respond to it, was held to be a serious procedural irregularity in *National Westminster Bank plc v Rushmer* [2010] EWHC 554 (Ch), [2010] 2 FLR 362, it only affected an alternative case, and so did not render the entire decision unjust. **75.14**

Examples of serious procedural irregularity

Allowing one party to adduce additional evidence but not the other, and restricting the cross-examination of a key witness, amounted to a serious procedural irregularity in *Hayes v Transco plc* [2003] EWCA Civ 1261, LTL 17/9/2003). Refusing permission to call a witness who would have made no difference was insufficient in *Wade v Varney* [2003] EWCA Civ 1279, LTL 22/9/2003. In *Aberavon and Port Talbot Rugby Football Club v Welsh Rugby Union Ltd* [2003] EWCA Civ 584, LTL 9/4/2003, it was held that the appellant had been given sufficient opportunity in the court to make representations by being given the opportunity to make written representations. **75.15**

Arguments that the judge in the lower court was predisposed against the appellant, often because of previous decisions, are frequently made but there is rarely any material to support such an allegation (*Hicks v Russell Jones and Walker* [2008] EWCA Civ 340, LTL 3/3/2008). In *Taylor v Williamsons* [2002] EWCA Civ 1380, [2003] CP Rep 20, discussed at **63.45**, an appeal was dismissed despite the judge issuing a written judgment before receiving the submissions from one of the parties. The judge had recalled the judgment, and given a new judgment after hearing submissions. An appeal may be based on excessive delay in delivering judgment where this impedes the judge's recollection of the evidence (*Manning v King's College Hospital NHS Trust* [2009] EWCA Civ 832, (2009) 110 BMLR 175, where eight months' delay in a complex case was forgiven;

Cobham v Frett [2001] 1 WLR 1775 where a 12-month delay was regarded as excessive; *Bond v Dunster Properties Ltd* [2011] EWCA Civ 455, LTL 21/4/2011, where a 22-month delay did not make the decision unsafe). A delay of three months calls for some explanation (*Habib Bank Ltd v Liverpool Freeport (Electronics) Ltd* [2004] EWCA Civ 1062, LTL 29/7/2004). In appeals based on delay, the appellate court should consider the quality of the judge's notes, and carefully scrutinise the findings of fact and the reasons given by the judge. It is only if there are errors possibly attributable to the delay that an appeal should be allowed on this ground (*Cobham v Frett*).

Fresh evidence

75.16 By **CPR, r. 52.11(2)**, unless it orders otherwise, the appeal court will not receive oral evidence or any evidence which was not before the lower court. Under the old rules a restrictive approach was taken to the introduction of fresh evidence on appeals, the guiding principles being laid down in *Ladd v Marshall* [1954] 1 WLR 1489 (see 75.17). The rule in *Ladd v Marshall* applied to appeals from trials and final determinations, and reflected the policy of requiring parties to advance their entire case at trial, and not deliberately leaving over points for the purpose of appeals (and thereby obtaining a 'second bite at the cherry'). With the introduction of the CPR, the discretion to admit fresh evidence on an appeal has to be exercised in accordance with the overriding objective (*Evans v Tiger Investments Ltd* [2002] EWCA Civ 161, [2002] 2 BCLC 185). However, the *Ladd v Marshall* principles remain relevant as matters which must necessarily be considered, although not as strict rules (*Banks v Cox* (2000) LTL 17/7/2000). Strong grounds have to be shown before fresh evidence will be admitted, and the *Ladd v Marshall* principles will be looked at with considerable care (*Hertfordshire Investments Ltd v Bubb* [2000] 1 WLR 2318). The Court of Appeal has to be particularly cautious where the appellant seeks to put further questions to witnesses (whether lay or expert) where the witness has been cross-examined at trial (*Riyad Bank SAL v Ahli United Bank (UK) plc* [2005] EWCA Civ 1419, *The Times*, 16 December 2005). It will be a rare case where the *Ladd v Marshall* conditions are not satisfied but the court nevertheless admits fresh evidence on an appeal (*Shaker v Al-Bedrawi* [2002] EWCA Civ 1452, [2003] 1 BCLC 157 at [88]). An example is where the appeal court receives an undertaking from a party (*Sharab v Prince Al-Waleed bin Talal bin Abdal-Aziz-Al-Saud* [2009] EWCA Civ 353, [2009] 2 Lloyd's Rep 160). On the facts the undertaking was declined by the appeal court because it effectively would have created a different situation, so would have required the appeal court to exercise its own discretion rather than reviewing that of the judge below.

Ladd v Marshall concerns applications to adduce fresh evidence after trial. A more flexible approach is adopted in appeals against procedural decisions (*Anglo Irish Asset Finance plc v Flood* [2011] EWCA Civ 799, LTL 11/7/2011). On an interim appeal fresh evidence might be admitted if there has been a material change of circumstances (*R (Iran) v Secretary of State for the Home Department* [2005] EWCA Civ 982, [2005] Imm AR 535).

Applications for permission to adduce fresh evidence can be made to the master of the Court of Appeal, but they are often directed to be listed for hearing at the same time as the appeal (Practice Direction (Court of Appeal: Procedure) [1995] 1 WLR 1191). A separate bundle should be prepared for the further evidence application, so that it can be kept separate from the main appeal bundles.

Ladd v Marshall principles

75.17 Under *Ladd v Marshall* [1954] 1 WLR 1489 fresh evidence would be allowed on an appeal against a final decision only if the evidence:

(a) could not have been obtained with reasonable diligence for use at the hearing in the lower court;
(b) would probably have an important influence on the result; and
(c) was apparently credible.

In considering whether evidence could have been obtained with reasonable diligence, no distinction is to be made between the knowledge of the lay client and that of the solicitor (*Evans v Tiger Investments Ltd* [2002] EWCA Civ 161, [2002] 2 BCLC 185). Evidence from a witness who was not called at trial will not satisfy condition (a) if the witness (although uncooperative) had given enough information for a draft witness statement to be prepared, as the draft statement could have been adduced as hearsay (see **chapter 53**) and the witness could have been compelled to attend the trial (see **chapter 57**) (see *Transview Properties Ltd v City Site Properties Ltd* [2009] EWCA Civ 1255, LTL 24/11/2009). The *Ladd v Marshall* test will rarely be satisfied where the fresh evidence goes merely to credit (*Hamilton v Al Fayed (No. 1)* [2001] EMLR 394). Where the new evidence is credible and there has been a clear attempt to deceive the court, the requirements of justice would point strongly towards admitting the evidence (*Daly v Sheikh* [2002] EWCA Civ 1630, LTL 24/ 10/2002). A relaxation of the strict *Ladd v Marshall* principles may be appropriate where it is in the public interest that fraudulent road traffic claims are exposed (*Singh v Habib* [2011] EWCA Civ 599, LTL 12/4/2011). In *Singh v Habib* once certain items of credible fresh evidence were identified, other, less convincing, evidence which formed part of the whole picture of the case, was also admitted. Evidence obtained after trial in *Arundel Corporation v Khokher* [2003] EWCA Civ 491, LTL 9/4/2003, from the respondent's solicitor's former employees contradicted evidence given at trial by the respondent and his solicitor. Permission to adduce the evidence was granted, because the evidence was credible and raised a prima facie case that the finding at trial should be reversed. There may be other reasons for refusing permission to adduce new evidence. In *Sadrolashrafi v Marvel International Food Logistics Ltd* [2004] EWHC 777 (Ch), [2004] BPIR 729, permission was refused because the new evidence was entirely contrary to the evidence given by the appellant at the hearing below and which the appellant knew was untrue. Evidence produced at a very late stage (Thursday for an appeal heard the following Monday) was disallowed in *Rakusens Ltd v Baser Ambalaj Plastik Sanayi Ticaret AS* [2001] EWCA Civ 1820, [2002] 1 BCLC 104, on the ground that it was completely unreasonable to expect the other side to deal with the evidence on such short notice.

Judgment obtained by fraud

Where the judge has been wilfully deceived by fraudulent evidence, justice requires a retrial (*Prentice v Hereward Housing Association* [2001] 2 All ER (Comm) 900). Likewise where there is a risk that a fraud has been perpetrated on the court below (*Couwenbergh v Valkova* [2004] EWCA Civ 676, LTL 27/5/2004). There are two lines of authority on how a judgment obtained by fraud should be dealt with: **75.18**

(a) remit for retrial: *Hamilton v Al-Fayed (No. 4)* [2001] EMLR 15; or
(b) bring fresh proceedings: *Kuwait Airways Corporation v Iraqi Airways Co.* [2001] 1 WLR 429.

The difference between them is that remitting for retrial is appropriate in cases where the fraud is admitted or incontrovertible, but fresh proceedings are appropriate where the allegation of fraud is contested (*Owens v Noble* [2010] EWCA Civ 224, [2010] 1 WLR 2491). It is permissible, and may be more efficient, in cases which are to be remitted for the case to be remitted to the trial judge (*Owens v Noble* [2010] EWCA Civ 284, LTL 18/3/2010).

GENERAL POWERS VESTED IN THE APPEAL COURT

By **CPR, r. 52.10(1)**, in relation to an appeal the appeal court has all the powers of the lower court. In particular, by **r. 52.10(2)**, the appeal court has power to do any of the following things: **75.19**

(a) Affirm set aside or vary any order or judgment made or given by the lower court. The power to vary does not extend to making a different type of order from the order the court below had been asked to make (*King v Telegraph Group Ltd* [2004] EWCA Civ 613, [2005] 1 WLR 2282). Where the appeal court allows an appeal against the exercise of a discretion and substitutes its own discretionary decision, it should do so on the basis of the material that was before the court below and normally nothing else. Otherwise, a successful appellant will often find that having complied with the now overturned earlier decision will make it difficult for the appeal court to exercise the discretion in his favour (*Swain-Mason v Mills and Reeve LLP* [2011] EWCA Civ 14, [2011] 1 WLR 2735, at [102]).

(b) Refer any claim or issue for determination by the lower court (**r. 52.10(2)(b)**). This power is stated in general terms, and allows the court to refer back a point to the trial judge which is only contingently relevant in the present appeal (*Hicks v Russell Jones and Walker* [2007] EWCA Civ 844, [2009] 1 WLR 487). The judge in the lower court may give directions for written submissions or further evidence to assist with this. Where the appeal court refers such a question to the lower court for a supplementary judgment, permission to appeal may be set aside where the supplementary judgment results in the appeal having no real prospect of success (*Hicks v Russell Jones and Walker* [2008] EWCA Civ 340, LTL 3/3/2008).

(c) Order a new trial or hearing, which is a last resort (*White v White* [2001] EWCA Civ 955, LTL 21/6/2001). If an appeal court orders a rehearing, it should make it clear on the face of its order whether the rehearing should be at appeal court level, or whether the case should be remitted back to the lower court for the rehearing (*Fowler de Pledge v Smith* [2003] EWCA Civ 703, *The Times*, 27 May 2003).

(d) Make orders for the payment of interest.

(e) Make a costs order.

In rare cases, the Court of Appeal has jurisdiction to take a point of general importance of its own motion which was not raised in the court below (*Bulale v Secretary of State for the Home Department* [2008] EWCA Civ 806, [2009] QB 536).

By **r. 52.10(3)**, in an appeal from a claim tried with a jury, the Court of Appeal may, instead of ordering a new trial, make an order for damages or the award made by the jury. If the appeal court refuses permission to appeal, strikes out an appellant's notice, or dismisses an appeal, and it considers the matter was totally without merit, that fact must be recorded in the court's order, and the court must consider whether to make a civil restraint order (**r. 52.10(5)**; see **14.55**).

HANDED-DOWN JUDGMENTS

75.20 Below the Court of Appeal, it is usual for the court to give judgment immediately after the arguments, although occasionally judgment will be reserved. This is rather more common in the Court of Appeal. The procedure for handing down reserved judgments in writing is set out in **PD 40E** (see **63.33**). On an appeal, an application for a consequential order is determined without a hearing (**PD 40E, para. 4.5(a)**).

COSTS

75.21 Under **CPR, r. 52.10(2)(e)**, the appeal court has power to make costs orders in relation to the appeal hearing and for the proceedings in the lower court.

Costs of appeals are likely to be summarily assessed if the hearing lasts not more than one day (see **PD 44, para. 9.2(b)**.

Appeal costs in appeals from no-costs jurisdictions

75.22 An appeal from a tribunal decision will involve moving from a no-costs jurisdiction to a costs-shifting jurisdiction in the appeal court. Protective costs orders (for which, see **44.10**) are available only in limited circumstances, and will not be available if the claim is not made in public law litigation (*Eweida v British Airways plc* [2009] EWCA Civ 1025, [2010] CP Rep 6). In that case an alternative application for a costs capping order (for which, see 44.2) was refused largely on the ground that, even if there was a risk of costs being disproportionately incurred by the other side, that could be controlled by the costs judge on assessment. *Eweida v British Airways plc* seems to have been accepted by *Unison v Kelly* [2012] EWCA Civ 1148, [2012] IRLR 951, where an alternative route to providing costs protection was found by granting permission to appeal on condition that no costs were sought from the respondent. The unsatisfactory result in these cases has been addressed with effect from 1 April 2013 by **CPR, r. 52.9A**, which provides that in any proceedings in which costs recovery is normally limited or excluded at first instance, an appeal court may make an order that the recoverable costs of an appeal will be limited to the extent which the court specifies. In making such an order the court will have regard to:

(a) the means of both parties;
(b) all the circumstances of the case; and
(c) the need to facilitate access to justice.

An application for such an order must be made as soon as practicable and will be determined without a hearing unless the court orders otherwise (**r. 52.9A(4)**).

Chapter 76 Appeals to the Supreme Court

INTRODUCTION

76.1 By the Constitutional Reform Act 2005, ss. 23–60, the newly constituted Supreme Court of the United Kingdom has replaced the Appellate Committee of the House of Lords as the highest court in the land. The main provisions dealing with the Supreme Court were brought into effect from 1 October 2009 (see the Constitutional Reform Act 2005 (Commencement No. 11) Order 2009 (SI 2009/1604)), which is the date the Supreme Court came into operation. One of the reasons for the change is to provide greater clarity in the country's constitutional arrangements by continuing the process of separating the judiciary from the legislature.

The Supreme Court is a superior court of record (Constitutional Reform Act 2005, s. 40(1)) and is intended to:

- be the final court of appeal for all United Kingdom civil cases, and criminal cases from England, Wales and Northern Ireland;
- hear appeals on arguable points of law of general public importance;
- concentrate on cases of the greatest public and constitutional importance; and
- maintain and develop the role of the highest court in the United Kingdom as a leader in the common law world.

The Supreme Court Rules 2009 (SI 2009/1603) ('SCR') have been made under the Constitutional Reform Act 2005, s. 45, and govern the procedure of the Supreme Court. The overriding objective of the SCR is to secure that the Supreme Court is accessible, fair and efficient (r. 2(2)). The SCR came into force on 1 October 2009, together with 14 practice directions:

General Note and the Jurisdiction of the Supreme Court (PD 1 Supreme Court)
The Registry of the Supreme Court (PD 2 Supreme Court)
Applications for Permission to Appeal (PD 3 Supreme Court)
Notice of Appeal (PD 4 Supreme Court)
Papers for the Appeal Hearing (PD 5 Supreme Court)

The Appeal Hearing (PD 6 Supreme Court)
Applications, Documents, Forms and Orders (PD 7 Supreme Court)
Miscellaneous Matters (bankruptcy, grouping or linking appeals, cross-appeals, death of a party, dispute between parties being settled, exhibits, fees and security for costs, interveners, new submissions, opposed procedural applications, patents, public funding and legal aid, specialist advisers and advocates to the Court, stay of execution, transcription, withdrawal of appeals and applications, broadcasting, and enforcement of orders made by the Supreme Court) (PD 8 Supreme Court)
The Human Rights Act 1998 (PD 9 Supreme Court)
Devolution Jurisdiction (PD 10 Supreme Court)
The European Court of Justice (PD 11 Supreme Court)
Criminal Proceedings (PD 12 Supreme Court)
Costs (PD 13 Supreme Court)
Filing Documents in the Registry of the Supreme Court by Electronic Means (PD 14 Supreme Court)

The SCR and Practice Directions can be accessed at the Supreme Court website, http://www.supremecourt.gov.uk.

TRANSITIONAL PROVISIONS

Transitional provisions in the Constitutional Reform Act 2005, sch. 10, define 'transferred jurisdiction' as any jurisdiction of: 76.2

(a) the House of Lords, or
(b) the Judicial Committee of the Privy Council,

that is transferred to the Supreme Court by virtue of the Constitutional Reform Act 2005 (sch. 10, para. 1). As from the transfer day (1 October 2009), transferred proceedings may be continued in the Supreme Court as if they had been begun in that court (para. 3(1)). Anything done in accordance with the rules of the original court in relation to transferred proceedings is, after the transfer day, to be treated as if it had been done in accordance with any Supreme Court Rules applicable to corresponding proceedings in the Supreme Court (para. 4(2)).

Unless the Court or the Registrar directs otherwise, the SCR, r. 55(1), provides that the SCR shall apply, with any necessary modifications, to appeals which were proceeding, and petitions for leave which were lodged, in the House of Lords before 1 October 2009. The Court or the Registrar may give special directions, as and when necessary, in relation to appeals in pre-1 October 2009 House of Lords proceedings notwithstanding anything that was done in accordance with the Practice Directions and Standing Orders of the House of Lords (r. 55(2)).

JURISDICTION

The jurisdiction of the Supreme Court is defined by the Constitutional Reform Act 2005, s. 40. Its jurisdiction corresponds to that of the House of Lords in its judicial capacity under the Appellate Jurisdiction Acts 1876 and 1888 (which are repealed) together with devolution matters under the Scotland Act 1998, the Northern Ireland Act 1998 and the Government of Wales Act 2006, which are transferred to the Supreme Court from the Judicial Committee of the Privy Council. It is specifically provided that an appeal lies to the Supreme Court from any order or judgment of the Court of Appeal in England and Wales in civil proceedings (Constitutional Reform Act 2005, s. 40(2)), and the Supreme Court assumes the jurisdiction previously exercised by the House of Lords under various statutes set out in sch. 9 (see s. 40(4)). This chapter will concentrate on the civil jurisdiction of the Supreme Court. 76.3

LEAPFROG APPEALS

76.4 Very exceptionally, a direct appeal from the decision of a High Court judge to the Supreme Court is possible under the Administration of Justice Act 1969, ss. 12 to 15. There are five conditions:

(a) the appeal must involve a point of law of general public importance;
(b) the point of law must either relate to the construction of an Act of Parliament or statutory instrument, or else be a point on which the judge at first instance is bound by a decision of the Court of Appeal or of the House of Lords or the Supreme Court;
(c) all parties must consent;
(d) the trial judge must certify, either immediately at the end of the trial or within the next 14 days, that the case is a suitable one for a direct appeal to the Supreme Court;
(e) the Supreme Court must grant permission to bring the appeal direct on an application made by any of the parties within one month of the date of the judge's certificate.

Detailed procedural requirements are in PD 3 Supreme Court, paras 3.6.1 to 3.6.16.

In *R (Jones) v Ceredigion County Council* [2007] UKHL 24, [2007] 1 WLR 1400, an appellant with two grounds of appeal was given permission to use the leapfrog procedure on only one ground. The permission to use the leapfrog procedure is couched in terms of a proposal. If taken up, the appellant is limited to the terms of the proposal, and so in this case would have had to abandon the other ground. As it had refused the proposal, it was able (with the appropriate permission) to take both grounds to the Court of Appeal. What is to be avoided is allowing a party to bring appeals in parallel to both the Court of Appeal and Supreme Court on different issues arising from the same order.

APPEALS FROM THE COURT OF APPEAL

Permission to appeal

76.5 An appeal from the Court of Appeal can only be made with permission from the Court of Appeal or the Supreme Court (Constitutional Reform Act 2005, s. 40(6)), but this is subject to any restriction on such an appeal in any enactment. The most important general restriction on rights of appeal is the **Access to Justice Act 1999, s. 54(4)** (see **74.16**). The effect of this provision is that the Supreme Court may not entertain any appeal against an order of the Court of Appeal refusing permission for an appeal to the Court of Appeal from a lower court.

This means, for example (as explained by PD 1 Supreme Court, para. 1.2.21, in relation to appeals in judicial review cases), that if the Court of Appeal refuses permission to appeal to it against the Administrative Court's refusal of permission to apply for judicial review, there is no appeal to the Supreme Court. The Supreme Court has no jurisdiction to entertain such an appeal (*R v Secretary of State for Trade and Industry, ex parte Eastaway* [2000] 1 WLR 2222, applying *Lane v Esdaile* [1891] AC 210). However, if the Court of Appeal grants permission to appeal to it against the Administrative Court's refusal of permission to apply for judicial review, but then itself refuses permission to apply for judicial review, the Supreme Court does have jurisdiction to hear an appeal against the Court of Appeal's refusal of permission to apply for judicial review (*R (Burkett) v Hammersmith and Fulham London Borough Council* [2002] 1 WLR 1593).

Permission from the Court of Appeal

76.6 The initial application for permission to appeal should be made to the Court of Appeal immediately after judgment has been pronounced (SCR, r. 10(2)). Procedures dealing with seeking permission in the Court of Appeal were formerly contained in PD 52, paras 15.13 to 15.21 (now deleted). Those paragraphs are referred to here as they may continue to provide some guidance.

They provided that the Court of Appeal can deal with an application for permission to appeal by written submissions (PD 52, para. 15.19). The parties will usually receive the Court of Appeal judgment in draft two working days in advance (para. 15.13). A party seeking to appeal must fax a copy of the written submissions to the clerk to the presiding Lord Justice and file four copies at the Civil Appeals Office no later than 12 noon on the working day before the judgment is handed down (para. 15.20). A lower court considering whether to give permission to appeal should apply the same criteria as those applied by the Supreme Court (*Henry Boot Construction Ltd v Alstom Combined Cycles Ltd* [2005] EWCA Civ 814, [2005] 1 WLR 3850, at [84], and see **76.11**).

Permission from the Supreme Court

If permission is refused by the Court of Appeal, an application for permission to appeal may be made to the Supreme Court on form SC001, which is a combined notice of appeal and application for permission to appeal (SCR, r. 10(1); PD Supreme Court 3, para. 3.1.2). The application must be served (see **76.14**) on every respondent and any intervener in the court below before it is filed (SCR, r. 12). Filing in the Registry of the Supreme Court must be in accordance with r. 7 (see **76.15**), and effected within 28 days of the date of the order of the court below (r. 11(1)). This period runs from the date of the substantive order appealed from, not from the date on which the order is sealed or the date of any subsequent procedural order (e.g. an order refusing permission to appeal) (see PD 2 Supreme Court, para. 2.1.12(a)). There is an exception for applications for permission to appeal involving civil contempt (where the time limit is 14 days, see Administration of Justice Act 1960, s. 2). On filing the original of the application the appellant must also: **76.7**

(a) File three copies of the application (PD 3 Supreme Court, para. 3.1.7).
(b) File a certificate of service (SCR, r. 12).
(c) File a copy of the order appealed from (r. 14(1)(a)). If the order is not immediately available, the application for permission must still be served and filed keeping to the above time limits, with the order being filed as soon as it is available (r. 14(1)).
(d) If separate, file a copy of the order of the court below refusing permission to appeal (r. 14(1)(b)).
(e) Pay fee 1.1 in the Supreme Court Fees Order 2009 (SI 2009/2131) (£800).

Where a party to a proposed appeal has applied for public funding and the Registrar is informed of the application, the time limits for serving and filing the application for permission to appeal are extended until 28 days after the final determination of the application for public funding (SCR, r. 5(5)).

Extending time to appeal

The Supreme Court may extend the time for bringing an application for permission to appeal or a notice of appeal (SCR, r. 5(1)), and may exercise the power to do so after the time limit has expired (r. 5(4)). The application for permission or notice of appeal must set out the reasons why it was not filed on time (PD 2 Supreme Court, para. 2.1.13). **76.8**

Notice of objection

Within 14 days after being served, every respondent wishing to object to the application for permission to appeal must serve and then file a notice of objection in form SC003 (with three additional copies, PD 3 Supreme Court, para. 3.1.8), together with a certificate of service (SCR, r. 13) and the prescribed fee of £160 (Supreme Court Fees Order 2009, fee 1.2). Respondents may submit written objections giving their reasons why permission to appeal should be refused when they file notice of objection in accordance with SCR, r. 13 (PD 3 Supreme Court, para. 3.3.6). **76.9**

A respondent who does not file notice of objection is not permitted to participate in the application, will not be informed of its progress (SCR, r. 13(3)), and will not be awarded costs (PD 3 Supreme Court, para. 3.1.10).

Further documents to be filed

76.10 Within seven days after filing the application for permission to appeal, SCR, r. 14(2), requires the following additional documents, as specified by PD 3 Supreme Court, para. 3.2.1, to be filed by the appellant for use by the Appeal Panel:

(a) four copies of the application;
(b) four copies of the order appealed against;
(c) if separate from the order at (b) above, four copies of the order of the court below refusing permission to appeal to the Supreme Court;
(d) four copies of the official transcript of the judgment of the court below;
(e) four copies of the final order(s) of all other courts below;
(f) four copies of the official transcript of the final judgment(s) of all other courts below;
(g) four copies of any unreported judgment(s) cited in the application or judgment of a court below;
(h) four copies of a document which sets out the history of the proceedings.

These documents must be presented in a form which is robust, manageable and not excessively heavy, presented in bound form, properly labelled and indexed (PD 3 Supreme Court, para. 5.2.1). No other papers are required (PD 3 Supreme Court, para. 3.2.1).

Deciding whether to grant permission to appeal

76.11 Applications for permission to appeal are considered on paper without a hearing by a panel of Justices (SCR, r. 16(1)). The panel may grant or refuse permission, but may alternatively invite the parties to file written submissions (which will be considered without a hearing), or direct an oral hearing, before deciding on whether to grant permission. Permission may be granted on terms (PD 3 Supreme Court, para. 3.3.11).

Permission to appeal is granted for applications that, in the opinion of the Appeal Panel, raise an arguable point of law of general public importance which ought to be considered by the Supreme Court at that time, bearing in mind that the matter will already have been the subject of judicial decision and may have already been reviewed on appeal (PD 3 Supreme Court, para. 3.3.3). An application which in the opinion of the Appeal Panel does not raise such a point of law is refused on that ground. The Appeal Panel gives brief reasons for refusing permission to appeal.

The formulation in PD 3 Supreme Court, para. 3.3.3, is in almost exactly the same terms as the House of Lords Direction 4.7, which laid down a test of whether the appeal raised 'an arguable point of law of general public importance which ought to be considered by the House at this time, bearing in mind that the matter will already have been the subject of judicial decision and reviewed on appeal'. There are relatively few appeals 'which ought to be considered by the Supreme Court'.

Questions on the law of procedure and practice are traditionally regarded as within the province of the Court of Appeal rather than the Supreme Court. Interventions in this area by the highest appellate tribunal have not always received universal approbation (see Lord Walker of Gestingthorpe JSC in *Roberts v Gill and Co.* [2010] UKSC 22, [2011] 1 AC 240 at [94], referring to Sir Henry Brooke's chapter in *The Civil Procedure Rules Ten Years On* (ed. Dwyer) (OUP, 2009), pp. 453–9).

Costs on permission application

76.12 Costs of successful applications for permission to appeal become costs in the appeal (PD 3 Supreme Court, para. 3.5.4). If permission is refused, guidance on costs can be found at paras 3.5.1 to 3.5.3 and 3.5.5 to 3.5.7.

CROSS-APPEALS

A respondent who wishes to argue that the order appealed from should be upheld on grounds different from those relied on by the court below, must state that clearly in the respondent's written case (but need not cross-appeal, see SCR, r. 25(1)). Other than for appeals as of right, a respondent who wishes to argue that the order appealed from should be varied must obtain permission to cross-appeal (r. 25(2)). This is sought from the Supreme Court and can be filed only after permission to appeal has been granted to the original appellant (PD 8 Supreme Court, para. 8.3.2). A similar procedure is followed to that on seeking permission to appeal, with such modifications as are appropriate. **76.13**

SERVICE AND FILING

Service

Documents in Supreme Court appeals are served (SCR, r. 6(1)) by any of the following methods: **76.14**

(a) personal service;
(b) first class post (or an alternative service which provides for delivery on the next working day);
(c) (with the consent of the party to be served) through a document exchange;
(d) (with the consent of the party to be served or at the direction of the Registrar) by electronic means in accordance with the relevant practice direction.

A document served by first class post or through a document exchange will be taken to have been served on the second day after it was posted or left at the document exchange, as the case may be (not including days which are not business days) (r. 6(3)). Where the address of the person on whom a document is to be served is unknown, the Registrar may direct that service is to be effected by an alternative method (r. 6(2)).

Filing

SCR, r. 7(1), permits a document to be filed by any of the following methods: **76.15**

(a) personal delivery;
(b) first class post (or an alternative service which provides for delivery on the next working day);
(c) through a document exchange;
(d) (with the consent of the Registrar) by electronic means in accordance with PD 14 Supreme Court.

Except with the consent of the Registrar, SCR, r. 7(3), provides that the contents of documents:

(a) filed in hard copy must also be provided to the Registry by electronic means, and
(b) filed by electronic means must also be provided to the Registry in hard copy.

PROCEDURAL APPLICATIONS

Any procedural application must be made in form SC002 (SCR, r. 30(2); PD 7 Supreme Court, para. 7.1.2) and must (SCR, r. 30(2); PD 7 Supreme Court, para. 7.1.3): **76.16**

(a) state the order the applicant is seeking;
(b) set out the reasons for making the application; and
(c) where necessary, be supported by written evidence.

There is a prescribed fee of £350 on filing an application (Supreme Court Fees Order 2009, fee 3.3). A copy of the application must be served on every other party before it is filed (SCR, r. 30(3)). The original must be filed together with three copies and a certificate of service.

A party who wishes to oppose an application must, within seven days after service, file notice of objection in form SC003 together with three copies, and must (before filing) serve a copy on the applicant and any other parties (r. 30(4)). There is a prescribed fee of £150 (Supreme Court Fees Order 2009, fee 3.4).

Applications are dealt with without a hearing wherever possible. Unless the Registrar directs otherwise, opposed procedural applications are referred to a panel of Justices and may be decided with or without an oral hearing (PD 7 Supreme Court, para. 7.1.6).

NOTICE OF APPEAL

76.17 Where permission to appeal is granted by the Supreme Court, the application for permission to appeal will stand as the notice of appeal and the grounds of appeal are limited to those on which permission has been granted (SCR, r. 18(1)). The appellant must, within 14 days of the grant of permission to appeal, file notice under r. 18(1)(c) that he intends to proceed with the appeal. When the notice is filed, the application for permission to appeal will be resealed and the appellant must then serve a copy on each respondent, on any intervener whose submissions have been taken into account under r. 15, and on any intervener in the court below. After service, the appellant must file the original notice of appeal and three copies (r. 18(2); PD 4 Supreme Court, para. 4.1.1) together with a certificate of service.

In any other case an appellant must serve and then file a notice of appeal in form SC001 (with three copies) together with a certificate of service (SCR, rr. 18(3), 19(1) and 20). Filing must take place within 42 days of the date of the order or decision of the court below (r. 19(2)). There is a further prescribed fee at this stage, which is £800 (Supreme Court Fees Order 2009, fee 2.1) in cases where notice to proceed is filed, and £1,600 in cases where there is notice of appeal (fee 2.2).

ACKNOWLEDGMENT BY RESPONDENT

76.18 Each respondent who intends to participate in the appeal must, within 14 days after service of the notice of appeal under SCR, rr. 18(2)(a) or 20, serve and then file notice of objection/acknowledgment in form SC003, together with a certificate of service (r. 21). A respondent who does not file notice will not be permitted to participate in the appeal, will not be given notice of its progress (r. 21(3)), and will not obtain an order for costs (PD 4 Supreme Court, para. 4.6.4).

There is a prescribed fee of £320 (Supreme Court Fees Order 2009, fee 2.4).

DOCUMENTS

76.19 Multiple copies of the documents required on appeals to the Supreme Court must be produced, partly to inform the other parties, partly for use of the Justices dealing with the appeal, and partly for records purposes. The minimum numbers laid down in the practice directions do *not include the copies required for the party's own use*, and may need to be increased where there are multiple parties in the appeal. The basic requirements are summarised in **table 76.1**.

Table 76.1 Copies of documents to be filed in the Registry and served on other parties

Document	Copies for Registry	Copies for other parties
By the appellant		
Notice of appeal	Original and 3 copies	1
Statement of facts and issues	Original and 7 copies	As arranged
Appendix Part 1	8	1
Appendix Part 2 and any subsequent Parts	10	1
Appellant's case	Original and 7 copies	As arranged
Core volumes	10	As arranged
Authorities volumes	10	As arranged
By the respondent and interveners		
Respondent's acknowledgment	Original and 3 copies	1
Respondent's (intervener's) case	Original and 7 copies	As arranged. 10 for core volumes
Respondent's authorities	Nil	10 for joint set of authorities
Respondent's additional documents	10	As arranged
Applications		
Application in form SC002	Original and 3 copies	1
Notice of objection	Original and 3 copies	1
Oral hearing: affidavits, witness statements and other documents	8	1

Statement of facts and issues

A statement of facts and issues is a single document, which is drafted initially by the appellant but must be submitted to, and agreed with, every respondent before being filed (SCR, r. 22(2)). The statement must set out the relevant facts and, if the parties cannot agree on any matter, the statement should make clear what items are disputed. The statement should contain references to every law report of the proceedings below, and should state the duration of the proceedings below. It should be signed by counsel for all parties (PD 5 Supreme Court, para. 5.1.2). It must be filed within 112 days after filing the notice of appeal (SCR, r. 22(1)). 76.20

Appendix

The documents to be included in the appendix are, by PD 5 Supreme Court, para. 5.1.5: 76.21

(a) the order appealed against;
(b) if separate from the order at (a) above, the order refusing permission to appeal to the Supreme Court;
(c) the official transcript of the judgment of the court below;
(d) the final order(s) of all other courts below;
(e) the official transcript of the final judgment(s) of all other courts below;
(f) (where they are necessary for understanding the legal issues and the argument) the relevant documents filed in the courts below; and
(g) (where they are necessary for understanding the legal issues and the argument) the relevant documents and correspondence relating to the appeal.

The appendix should contain only such material as is necessary for understanding the legal issues and the argument to be presented to the Supreme Court (SCR, r. 22(2)). It should not contain documents which were not in evidence below, nor should it contain transcripts of the proceedings or evidence below unless they are essential to the legal argument (PD 5 Supreme Court, para. 5.1.4). If necessary, the appendix should be prepared in several parts, with only the most essential documents being included in part 1. It is only part 1 that will be included in the core volumes (see **76.23**). The appendix must be submitted to, and agreed with, every respondent before being filed (SCR, r. 22(2)), with the deadline for filing being 112 days after filing the notice of appeal (r. 22(1)).

Appellants' and respondents' cases

76.22 After the Registrar has informed the parties of the date fixed for the hearing (see **76.26**), the appellant and every respondent (and any intervener and advocate to the court) must sequentially exchange their respective written cases and file them (SCR, r. 22(4)). A 'case' is the statement of a party's argument in the appeal (PD 6 Supreme Court, para. 6.3.1). There is no prescribed maximum length, but the Supreme Court favours brevity, and a case should be a concise summary of the submissions to be developed. The case should be confined to the heads of argument that counsel propose to submit at the hearing, and omit material contained in the statement of facts and issues (para. 6.3.2). It must conclude with a numbered summary of the reasons upon which the argument is founded, and must be signed by counsel. Its purpose is to enable counsel to concentrate their arguments on the real issues in the appeal (*M. V. Yorke Motors v Edwards* [1982] 1 WLR 444). Unreported cases should be cited only if they are binding on the Court of Appeal and if the substance of the decision is not to be found in any fully reported case (*Roberts Petroleum Ltd v Bernard Kenny Ltd* [1983] 2 AC 192). Any intention to invite the Supreme Court to depart from one of its (or the House of Lords') earlier decisions must be clearly stated in a separate paragraph in the case.

There is further guidance in PD 6 Supreme Court, paras 6.3.3 to 6.3.13. The appellant must file seven copies of its case at least five weeks before the hearing, and the respondent must file seven copies of its case at least three weeks before the hearing (paras 6.3.9 and 6.3.10).

Core volumes

76.23 As soon as the parties' cases have been exchanged and in any event not later than 14 days before the date fixed for the hearing, the appellant must file ten copies of the core volumes and, if necessary, additional volumes containing further parts of the appendix (SCR, r. 23; PD 6 Supreme Court, para. 6.4.3). The core volumes contain:

(a) the notice of appeal or the resealed application for permission to appeal;
(b) notice of cross-appeal (if any);
(c) statement of facts and issues;
(d) appellants' and respondents' cases, with cross-references to the appendix and authorities volume(s);
(e) case of the advocate to the court or intervener, if any;
(f) part 1 of the appendix; and
(g) index to the authorities volume(s).

Authorities

76.24 The volumes of authorities that may be referred to during the hearing must be prepared in accordance with PD 6 Supreme Court, paras 6.5.1 to 6.5.8, and ten copies of the volumes of authorities must be filed by the appellant at the same time as the core volumes (SCR, r. 24; PD 6 Supreme Court, para. 6.5.1). These should be a joint set of authorities, which should appear in alphabetical order and be divided into domestic, Strasbourg (ECHR), foreign and academic material. The appellants have the initial responsibility for producing the authorities volumes and for filing them at the Registry but, to enable the appellants to file the volumes, the respondents must provide the appellants with ten copies of any authorities which the respondents require but which the appellants do not, or arrange with the appellants for their photocopying.

Exhibits

Parties who require exhibits to be available for inspection at the hearing must apply to the Registrar for permission in advance of the hearing (PD 8 Supreme Court, para. 8.6.1). **76.25**

FIXING THE HEARING

A prescribed fee of £4,820 is payable when the appellant files the statement of relevant facts and issues and appendix (Supreme Court Fees Order 2009, fee 2.5). Within seven days thereafter, every party must notify the Registrar that the appeal is ready for listing, and provide a time estimate from counsel (SCR, r. 22(3)). The Registrar will then inform the parties of the date fixed for the hearing, which takes the form of a provisional date agreed with the parties (see PD 6 Supreme Court, para. 6.6.1). Any request for an expedited hearing should be made to the Registrar (SCR, r. 31(1)). Wherever possible the views of all parties should be obtained before a request is made (r. 31(2); PD 4 Supreme Court, para. 4.8.1). **76.26**

THE HEARING

The Supreme Court has a President, Deputy President, and 10 Justices of the Supreme Court. **76.27**
At the request of the President of the Supreme Court, the Constitutional Reform Act 2005, s. 38, allows the following to be appointed as acting judges of the Court:

(a) a person who holds office as a senior territorial judge (as defined in s. 38(8), including Court of Appeal judges);
(b) a member of the supplementary panel under s. 39 (recently retired Supreme Court Justices).

The Supreme Court sits with an uneven number of judges, being at least three in number with a majority being permanent Justices (s. 42(1)). The Justices should be addressed as 'My Lord' or 'My Lady' (PD 6 Supreme Court, para. 6.6.8). Hearings are conducted in accordance with PD 6 Supreme Court and any directions given by the Court (SCR, r. 27(4)). These may limit oral submissions to a specified duration. Counsel must assume the Justices have read the printed cases and judgment under appeal, but not all the papers that have been filed (para. 6.6.7).

No more than two counsel will be heard on behalf of a party, or a single counsel for an intervener (para. 6.6.5). Counsel briefed to appear in the Supreme Court are expected to be present at and throughout the hearing. Hearings in the Supreme Court take precedence over hearings in lower courts, and counsel should not ordinarily accept instructions to appear in the Supreme Court on a hearing for a fixed date if they already have a conflicting engagement. If through unforeseen circumstances counsel will find it difficult or embarrassing to appear in the Supreme Court, they should write to the presiding Justice and seek leave to be absent. This will ordinarily be given if sufficient reason is shown. See Practice Statement (House of Lords: Appearance of Counsel) [2008] 1 WLR 1143.

Supreme Court proceedings are exempted from the prohibitions on broadcasting and photography (Constitutional Reform Act 2005, s. 47), but visitors to the Supreme Court are prohibited from taking photographs or filming its proceedings. Legal representatives and members of the public are, however, permitted to use text-based communications from the court provided these are silent and avoid disruption (Practice Guidance (Court Proceedings: Live Text-based Communications) (No. 2) [2012] 1 WLR 12 (reproduced in **appendix** 1)). Exceptions relate to cases with reporting restrictions, cases involving children, and where there is an order against reporting to avoid influencing a lower court.

JUDGMENT AND COSTS

76.28 Judgment is usually delivered in open court, but may be promulgated by the Registrar (SCR, r. 28). One junior counsel may attend when judgment is delivered in open court (PD 6 Supreme Court, para. 6.8.2). The Supreme Court has all the powers of the court below (SCR, r. 29(1)) and may:

(a) affirm, set aside or vary any order or judgment made or given by that court;
(b) remit any issue for determination by that court;
(c) order a new trial or hearing;
(d) make orders for the payment of interest;
(e) make a costs order (for which see rr. 46 to 53; PD 6 Supreme Court, paras. 6.3.7, 6.7.1, 6.7.2 and 6.9.5; and PD 13 Supreme Court). The fees of two counsel only are allowed on assessment unless the court orders otherwise on application on the hearing of the appeal (PD 6 Supreme Court, para. 6.3.7).

In an appropriate case the Supreme Court can overrule the order below and substitute its own order (*Manchester City Council v Pinnock (Nos. 1 and 2)* [2011] UKSC 6, [2011] 2 AC 104).

An order of the Supreme Court may be enforced in the same way as an order of the court below (SCR, r. 29(2); see **79.2**).

Chapter 77 Judicial Review

Commentary

The following procedural checklist, which is at the front of the book, is relevant to this chapter:

Procedural checklist 34 Claim for judicial review

INTRODUCTION

77.1 Judicial review is the means by which the courts control administrative action by public bodies (including inferior courts and tribunals). It is a supervisory jurisdiction which reviews administrative action rather than being an appellate jurisdiction.

The primary legislation dealing with judicial review is the Senior Courts Act 1981.

The principal rules of court governing claims for judicial review are in **CPR, Part 54**, supplemented by **PD 54A. CPR, r. 54.1** (2)(a), defines a claim for judicial review as:

a claim to review the lawfulness of—
(i) an enactment; or
(ii) a decision, action or failure to act in relation to the exercise of a public function.

Although other remedies may be asked for, the characteristic remedies in judicial review claims are the prerogative mandatory, prohibiting and quashing orders (see **77.53** to **77.60**), which county courts do not have power to grant (County Courts Act 1984, s. 38(3)(a)). Judicial review claims are assigned to the Queen's Bench Division in the High Court by the Senior Courts Act 1981, sch. 1, para. 2(b), and are dealt with in the Administrative Court.

A judicial review claim may be transferred to the Upper Tribunal if the conditions in the Senior Courts Act 1981, s. 31A, are met. Lord Judge LCJ has ordered that from 17 October 2012 challenges to a decision of the Secretary of State for the Home Department not to entertain an asylum or human rights claim are to be transferred to the Upper Tribunal for determination under the Tribunals, Courts and Enforcement Act 2007, ss. 15 and 18.

There are two conditions necessary to determine whether a decision by a body is judicially reviewable:

(a) the decision or action must be made by a public body (see **77.3** and **77.4**); and
(b) the public body must make a public law decision or take a public law action (see **77.5**).

BODIES OPEN TO JUDICIAL REVIEW

77.2 Any body performing public law duties or powers is susceptible to judicial review. Historically, the most important factor considered by the courts in identifying activities subject to judicial review was the source of the power being exercised by the decision-maker whose decision was sought to be challenged. However, the courts have recognised that such an approach is too restrictive and they are now influenced by the type of function performed by the decision-maker (*R v Panel on Take-overs and Mergers, ex parte Datafin plc* [1987] QB 815).

The essential elements which comprise a public law body are (1) a 'public element' (which can take many different forms); and (2) the exclusion of bodies whose sole source of power is consensual submission to their jurisdiction (per Sir John Donaldson MR in *R v Panel on Take-overs and Mergers, ex parte Datafin plc*). Thus, the test of what is a public body is not solely an examination of the source of the regulator's power but also a consideration of the regulator's functions.

Central government and statutory bodies

77.3 Central government and bodies which derive authority from statute are susceptible to judicial review. Central government's powers derive from the prerogative (as to which see below) or statute. The range of statutory bodies which have been held to be reviewable also includes inferior courts, local authorities, tribunals and inquiries and regulators with a statutory basis. Ministers acting on behalf of the Crown are also subject to judicial review (*Re M* [1994] 1 AC 377). The Parliamentary Commissioner for Standards has been held not to be reviewable because he or she is one of the means by which the Select Committee on Standards and Privileges carries out its functions, and those functions form part of the proceedings of Parliament (*R v Parliamentary Commissioner for Standards, ex parte Al Fayed* [1998] 1 WLR 669) and the courts will not intervene in the affairs of Parliament.

Other courts and tribunals susceptible to judicial review include magistrates' courts, coroners' courts, local election courts (*R v Cripps, ex parte Muldoon* [1984] QB 68 (DC), [1984] QB 686 (CA)), patents appeal tribunals (*Baldwin and Francis Ltd v Patents Appeal Tribunal* [1959] AC 663), county courts (save where they perform the functions of a superior court) and statutory tribunals in certain circumstances (where a High Court judge does not sit, and dependent upon their powers and relationship with the High Court according to its enabling statute) (see *R v Cripps, ex parte Muldoon* [1984] QB 686). Judicial review does not lie against the High Court or the Court of Appeal, but only against the decisions of inferior courts. The decision of a district judge under the Extradition Act 2003 is deemed to be a decision of the High Court for these purposes and therefore not amenable to judicial review (*R (Okandeji) v Bow Street Magistrates' Court* [2005] EWHC 2925 (Admin), [2006] 1 WLR 674). The High Court did have jurisdiction to judicially review the decision of a county court refusing permission to appeal (*R (Sivasubramaniam) v Wandsworth County Court* [2002] EWCA Civ 1738, [2003] 1 WLR 475). However, where the claimant had sought judicial review of the original decision, and had not sought permission to appeal it, judicial review was not available since the proper remedy was to seek permission to appeal the decision of the county court in the first instance. It would only be in rare cases that judicial review would be permitted against the decision of a county court to refuse permission to appeal (*Sivasubramaniam*). Examples of such rare cases would include where the lower court had fundamentally departed from the correct procedures, where it could be said that the judicial process itself had been frustrated or corrupted or where the lower court had acted in complete disregard of its duties (*Strickson v Preston County Court* [2007] EWCA Civ 1132, LTL 9/11/2007).

Following the creation of a single tribunal structure by the Tribunals, Courts and Enforcement Act 2007, it has been held by the Supreme Court that a decision of the Upper Tribunal is subject to judicial review only if there is an important point of practice or principle or some other compelling reason for the case to be reviewed (*R (Cart) v Upper Tribunal* [2011] UKSC 28, [2012] 1 AC 663). See also *R (NB (Algeria)) v Secretary of State for the Home Department* [2012] EWCA Civ 1050, [2013] 1 WLR 31. Any historical exceptions relating to judicial review of immigration and asylum decisions identified in *R (Sivasubramaniam) v Wandsworth County Court* [2002] EWCA Civ 1738, [2003] 1 WLR 475, cannot now apply to the centralised tribunal system (*R (Rana) v Upper Tribunal (Immigration and Asylum Chamber)* [2010] EWHC 3558 (Admin), LTL 20/1/2011).

The Senior Courts Act 1981, s. 29(3), enables the High Court to make prerogative orders against the Crown Court to the same extent as it may against an inferior court other than in relation to the Crown Court's jurisdiction in trial on indictment matters. Trial on indictment includes decisions as to sentence, such as confiscation and compensation orders, as they are an integral part of the trial process and therefore outside the scope of judicial review (*R (Faithfull) v Crown Court at Ipswich* [2007] EWHC 2763 (Admin), [2008] 1 WLR 1636).

Nationalised industries are also subject to judicial review. For example, the British Coal Corporation has been held to be reviewable in respect of its decision to close coal pits (*R v British Coal Corporation, ex parte Vardy* [1993] ICR 720).

A person or body exercising prerogative powers (i.e. non-statutory acts of executive government) may be amenable to judicial review (*R v Criminal Injuries Compensation Board, ex parte Lain*

Commentary

[1967] 2 QB 864). In *Council of Civil Service Unions v Minister for the Civil Service* [1985] AC 374 the House of Lords held that prerogative powers were reviewable, but Lord Roskill listed six examples of prerogative powers which he thought would not be reviewable, i.e. treaty making, defence of the realm, prerogative of mercy, grant of honours, dissolution of Parliament and the appointment of ministers. The prerogative of mercy has subsequently been held to be judicially reviewable (*R v Secretary of State for the Home Department, ex parte Bentley* [1994] QB 349). The prerogative power of colonial governance does not enjoy immunity from judicial review (*R (Bancoult) v Secretary of State for Foreign and Commonwealth Affairs (No. 2)* [2008] UKHL 61, [2009] 1 AC 453). The exclusion of existing treaties from the scope of judicial review has been confirmed given their non-binding status in domestic law which means they are unable to form the basis of a judicial review challenge (*R (Corner House Research) v Director of the Serious Fraud Office* [2008] UKHL 60, [2009] 1 AC 756). However, in *R (Wheeler) v Office of the Prime Minister* [2008] EWHC 1409 (Admin), [2008] ACD 70, the issue of political promises made in relation to the government entering into a treaty was within the scope of judicial review, although it was found that in the specific circumstances there had been no breach of legitimate expectation by the government's decision not to hold a referendum before entering into the Lisbon Treaty.

The High Court has reviewed the exercise of prerogative powers by the Crown in certain instances, including a decision of the Foreign Secretary to refuse to issue an applicant with a passport (*R v Secretary of State for Foreign and Commonwealth Affairs, ex parte Everett* [1989] QB 811) and the residual power of the Home Secretary to depart from immigration rules (*R v Secretary of State for the Home Department, ex parte Beedassee* [1989] COD 525).

Judicial review would lie against a refusal of the Foreign Office to render diplomatic assistance to a British national in a foreign State but the expectation which an individual could legitimately hold of a response to a request for assistance would be limited (*R (Abbasi) v Secretary of State for Foreign and Commonwealth Affairs* [2002] EWCA Civ 1598, [2003] UKHRR 76).

It is possible for a statute to confer on a private body public functions and therefore, at least in relation to the performance of those functions, a body could be subject to judicial review. Therefore professional bodies incorporated by royal charter or under the Companies Act 2006 may have statutory powers and duties conferred upon them.

Non-statutory bodies

77.4 Non-statutory bodies which carry out public law functions will also be susceptible to judicial review. Bodies concerned with the regulation of commercial and professional activities to ensure compliance with proper standards, e.g. the Law Society and the Institute of Chartered Accountants, may be susceptible to judicial review whether or not their powers derive from statute or royal charter. Other self-regulating organisations and other private institutions may also perform some types of public function.

The Panel on Takeovers and Mergers was held in *R v Panel on Take-overs and Mergers, ex parte Datafin plc* [1987] QB 815 to be judicially reviewable despite the fact that it had no direct statutory authority. The Court of Appeal was influenced by the fact that the Panel 'oversees and regulates a very important part of the United Kingdom financial market' without any legal support. It considered that if the body in question exercised public law functions or the exercise of its functions had public law consequences, this would be sufficient to make it reviewable. The Panel clearly exercised public functions.

Following *R v Panel on Take-overs and Mergers, ex parte Datafin plc* the Advertising Standards Authority was found to be a public body upon the basis that, in the absence of a self-regulatory body such as the Authority, its function would be exercised by the Director General of Fair Trading (*R v Advertising Standards Authority, ex parte Insurance Service plc* (1990) 2 Admin LR 77). Similarly, although financial services self-regulating organisations lack statutory underpinning (but were contemplated by the Financial Services Act 1986), they have been found to be reviewable (*R v Life Assurance Unit Trust Regulatory Organisation Ltd, ex parte Ross* [1993] QB 17), as has the London Metal Exchange, which is a recognised investment exchange (*R v London Metal Exchange, ex parte Albatros Warehousing BV* (2000) LTL 31/3/2000). However, the decisions of bodies set up by self-regulating organisations pursuant to regulatory powers are not also automatically reviewable. The Insurance Ombudsman Bureau (a body recognised by LAUTRO as performing a complaints investigation function for the purposes of the Financial Services Act 1986 and with voluntary membership) has been held to possess power over its members which was solely derived from contract and was not therefore regarded as a public body (*R v Insurance Ombudsman Bureau, ex parte Aegon Life Assurance Ltd* [1994] COD 426).

Lloyd's, which has powers derived from a private Act (initially the Lloyd's Act 1871) and which does not extend to any persons other than those who wish to operate in the section of the market governed by Lloyd's and who have to commit themselves by entering into Lloyd's uniform contract, has been held not to be a public body for the purposes of judicial review (*R v Lloyd's of London, ex parte Johnson* (unreported, 16 August 1996)). However, certain of Lloyd's functions have been held to be public law functions and amenable to judicial review, although relations between Lloyd's and its names not involving the exercise of regulatory or disciplinary functions are governed by private law (*Doll-Steinberg v Society of Lloyd's* [2002] EWCA Civ 996). Bodies will not be reviewable where their source of authority is contractual or consensual, or if they do not exercise governmental powers (e.g. *R v Association of British Travel Agents, ex parte Sunspell Ltd* [2001] ACD 16) and this can be the case even though in relation to a particular industry or activity the person concerned effectively has no choice other than to sign up to a contract to be bound by a body's rules or regulations, e.g. *R v Panel of the Federation of Communication Services Ltd, ex parte Kubis* (1999) 11 Admin LR 43 concerning dealers in the mobile telephone industry.

The Court of Appeal has held it arguable that the Press Complaints Commission is a body subject to judicial review (*R v Press Complaints Commission, ex parte Stewart-Brady* (1997) 9 Admin LR 274).

Bodies exercising monopolistic powers may be reviewable. Reviewability was accepted by the Privy Council in the case of a bulk electricity supplier in New Zealand (*Mercury Energy Ltd v Electricity Corporation of New Zealand Ltd* [1994] 1 WLR 521).

A housing association, as a registered provider of social housing, is amenable to judicial review in respect of its functions in managing and allocating its housing stock (*R (Weaver) v London and Quadrant Housing Trust* [2009] EWCA Civ 587, [2010] 1 WLR 363 at [83]).

However, *R v Panel on Take-overs and Mergers, ex parte Datafin plc* has been interpreted narrowly in some subsequent cases. In *R v Chief Rabbi, ex parte Wachmann* [1992] 1 WLR 1036, Simon Brown J stated that, '[t]o attract the court's supervisory jurisdiction there must be not merely a public but potentially a governmental interest in the decision making power in question'. Sports bodies not backed by statute are generally outside the scope of judicial review. In *R v Disciplinary Committee of the Jockey Club, ex parte Aga Khan* [1993] 1 WLR 909 the Court of Appeal also took a slightly different approach and required the existence of governmental and not simply 'public' functions and possibly actual (as opposed to potential) governmental intervention. Therefore the Jockey Club was held to fall outside the scope of the court's supervisory jurisdiction because it did not form part of a system of governmental control. The court was also influenced by the fact that the Club's source of power was contractual and that a private law remedy was available to the claimant (see 77.5; see also *R (Mullins) v Appeal Board of the Jockey Club* [2005] EWHC 2197 (Admin), [2006] ACD 2; and *R v Football Association Ltd, ex parte Football League Ltd* [1993] 2 All ER 833).

In some instances both public law and private law rights may be protected. For example, the Court of Appeal has accepted that for certain functions the Institute of Chartered Accountants

Commentary

is a public body and that its members might also have contractual rights against it (*Andreou v Institute of Chartered Accountants in England and Wales* [1998] 1 All ER 14).

Decisions of leaders of particular faiths on disciplinary issues have consistently been held not to be judicially reviewable (*R v Chief Rabbi, ex parte Wachmann*; *R v Imam of Bury Park Jame Masjid Luton, ex parte Sulaiman Ali* [1994] COD 142; *R v London Beth Din, ex parte Bloom* [1998] COD 131; *R v Provincial Court of the Church in Wales, ex parte Williams* [1999] COD 163). However, the consistory courts of the Church of England have been deemed to be within the jurisdiction of the High Court because of their regulation by measures which have the effect of Acts of Parliament and therefore form part of the fabric of the state (*R v Chancellor of the Chichester Consistory Court, ex parte News Group Newspapers* [1992] COD 48). The position with the Provincial Court of the Church of Wales was held to be different in that, following its disestablishment under the Welsh Church Act 1914, its legal authority arises solely from consensual submission to its jurisdiction and it is therefore analogous to other religious bodies not established as part of the State (*R v Provincial Court of the Church in Wales, ex parte Williams*).

The university visitor, whose authority is based upon common law, is subject only to limited review. The House of Lords has held that the jurisdiction of a university visitor is reviewable only in circumstances where the university visitor acts outside his or her jurisdiction or if the university visitor abuses his or her power in a manner wholly incompatible with his or her judicial role or in breach of the rules of natural justice (*Page v Hull University Visitor* [1993] AC 682). Therefore only certain of the visitor's decisions are reviewable on the basis that he or she is in a unique position where it is highly desirable that there should be finality of decisions. This decision has been followed upon the same limited basis (*R v Visitors to the Inns of Court, ex parte Calder* [1994] QB 1). (See also *R (Varma) v Visitor to Cranfield University* [2004] EWHC 1705 (Admin), [2004] ELR 616.)

Decisions concerning pupils made by a non-maintained school for children with special educational needs were not amenable to judicial review even though the school received most of its funding from a local education authority (*R v Muntham House School, ex parte R* [2000] LGR 255).

On the other hand, a decision by managers of a private psychiatric hospital to change the focus of one of its wards is an act of a public nature susceptible to judicial review (*R (A) v Partnerships in Care Ltd* [2002] EWHC 529 (Admin), [2002] 1 WLR 2610).

A defendant private limited company, set up by a local authority to manage local farmers' markets, and having as directors stallholders of those markets, was a public body amenable to judicial review. The defendant owed its existence to the authority, which had set it up using its statutory powers, the defendant had effectively stepped into the authority's shoes and the authority had assisted the defendant in many respects (*R (Beer) v Hampshire Farmers Market Ltd* [2003] EWCA Civ 1056, [2004] 1 WLR 233).

A private company limited by guarantee, operating on a mutual basis, whose members were healthcare professionals who were afforded the right to request certain discretionary benefits, such as professional indemnity or insurance cover, in exchange for an annual fee, was not amenable to judicial review. Its relevant functions were not governmental, but rather those of an insurance company. The company was not woven into the fabric of public regulation just because it operated in the healthcare sphere or because there was a public interest in patients being indemnified against negligent treatment (*R (Moreton) v Medical Defence Union Ltd* [2006] EWHC 1948 (Admin), [2007] LS Law Medical 180).

DECISIONS OPEN TO JUDICIAL REVIEW

77.5 Primary legislation may be reviewed to determine its compatibility with European Union (EU) law. Where national law conflicts with any directly effective provision of EU law, the rule of national law must be set aside and EU law applied (*R v Secretary of State for Transport, ex parte Factortame Ltd (No. 2)* [1991] 1 AC 603). As to the reviewability of primary legislation for compatibility with the European Convention on Human Rights in the **Human Rights Act 1998, sch. 1**, see **chapter 91**.

Subordinate legislation which has been debated in and approved by affirmative resolution of both Houses of Parliament is susceptible to judicial review (*R (Asif Javed) v Secretary of State for the Home Department* [2001] EWCA Civ 789, [2002] QB 129).

Only decisions or actions which are made in a public law context are subject to judicial review. Even if a body may in some circumstances be susceptible to judicial review, not every decision will be reviewable. There must be a decision with a public law element sufficient to justify judicial review (*R v British Broadcasting Corporation, ex parte Lavelle* [1983] 1 WLR 23).

However, even where there is a private law cause of action, judicial review may still be appropriate where there is a sufficiently public issue. For example, judicial review was appropriate where the question was whether the Secretary of State had exceeded his powers in granting consent to a market authority to grant leases (*R (Corporation of London) v Secretary of State for Environment, Food and Rural Affairs* [2004] EWCA Civ 1765, [2005] 1 WLR 1286, reversed on another point [2006] UKHL 30, [2006] 1 WLR 1721). Similarly, even though declarations can be granted in private law proceedings on the construction of private law contracts without the affected party being a party to the proceedings, where the dispute concerned the construction of a planning agreement under the Town and Country Planning Act 1990, s. 106, in reality the document was about the planning objectives of a planning authority, which were therefore public law matters which ought to be dealt with in judicial review proceedings with the local planning authority as a party (*Milebush Properties Ltd v Tameside Metropolitan Borough Council* [2011] EWCA Civ 270, [2011] PTSR 1654).

The existence of a contractual relationship or a decision based upon the consent of the parties will always make it difficult to establish that the decision is amenable to judicial review (*R v Criminal Injuries Compensation Board, ex parte Lain* [1967] 2 QB 864; *R v National Joint Council for the Craft of Dental Technicians (Dispute Committee), ex parte Neate* [1953] 1 QB 704).

Thus ordinary employment cases are generally deemed to be governed by private law. Clearly cases relating purely to the construction of contractual terms and conditions of employment are not reviewable (*McClaren v Home Office* [1990] ICR 808). A disciplinary tribunal set up by the BBC in relation to the dismissal of an employee depended solely upon the contract of employment between the claimant and the BBC and was therefore a procedure of a merely private or domestic character and so not judicially reviewable (*R v British Broadcasting Corporation, ex parte Lavelle* [1983] 1 WLR 23). The terms of a senior nursing officer's employment have been regarded as a matter of private law notwithstanding that they incorporated the NHS Whitley Council agreement on conditions of service, a form of statutory negotiation between employers' and employees' representatives (*R v East Berkshire Health Authority, ex parte Walsh* [1985] QB 152). (See also *R (Tucker) v Director-General of the National Crime Squad* [2003] EWCA Civ 2, [2003] ICR 599; *Skidmore v Dartford and Gravesham NHS Trust* [2003] UKHL 27, [2003] ICR 721.)

However, public law issues may arise where an employer exercises a power which is not wholly contract-based. A decision to suspend a claimant in breach of a code of discipline which had statutory force was reviewable (*R v Secretary of State for the Home Department, ex parte Attard* (1990) 2 Admin LR 641). The employment conditions of police constables are underpinned by statute and accordingly reviewable (*Chief Constable of North Wales Police v Evans* [1982] 1 WLR 1155). A decision is reviewable if it involves a constitutional or public law principle such as the appointment of Crown prosecutors (*R v Crown Prosecution Service, ex parte Hogg* (1994) 6 Admin LR 778). Public law issues arise where the question is whether the public body had authority to enter into the contract, but not where the only issue is whether or not there is a breach by a public authority of its own internal procedures or standing orders (as was the case in

Commentary

R v Lambeth London Borough Council, ex parte Thompson [1996] COD 217). The Court of Appeal has left open the question whether a decision of the Civil Service Board that a claimant had not been unfairly dismissed from his position as a civil servant was reviewable on the basis that he had no contract of employment and there was a sufficient public law element involved (*R v Civil Service Appeal Board, ex parte Bruce* [1989] 2 All ER 907).

A body exercising a public function which makes a promise that it would behave in a certain way in the future is making a representation which has the character of a contract, but a breach of that promise may still be amenable to judicial review if the breach amounts to an abuse of power (*R v North and East Devon Health Authority, ex parte Coughlan* [2001] QB 213).

The current position in considering the availability of judicial review in cases involving public procurement appears to be as follows:

(a) if it is shown that the tendering process is subject to mandatory statutory provisions then judicial review will be available;
(b) in order to establish whether the process is subject to statutory requirements, it is necessary to look at the wording, scheme and purpose of the relevant statute;
(c) in order to allege breach of the principles of natural justice in the tendering process, the claimant must be able to spell out the procedural requirements from the statute by express wording or necessary implication; and
(d) even if the tendering process is not carried out under a mandatory statutory provision, if there is a sufficient public law element to the decision it may still be reviewable (see *R v Bridgend County Borough Council, ex parte Jones* [2002] 2 LGLR 361 and *Cookson and Clegg Ltd v Ministry of Defence* [2005] EWCA Civ 811, [2006] Eu LR 1092).

A number of cases establish that public procurement procedures by public authorities can be the subject of judicial review proceedings, e.g. where a local authority boycotted products in order to pressurise companies to withdraw their interests in South Africa (*R v Lewisham London Borough Council, ex parte Shell UK Ltd* [1988] 1 All ER 938; and note *R v Derbyshire County Council, ex parte The Times Supplements Ltd* (1991) 3 Admin LR 241). A more restrictive approach was adopted in relation to tendering for shorthand writers' contracts (*R v Lord Chancellor's Department, ex parte Hibbit and Saunders* [1993] COD 326) and concerning tenders under part 2 of the Environmental Protection Act 1990 (*Mass Energy Ltd v Birmingham City Council* [1994] Env LR 298).

However, in *R v Legal Aid Board, ex parte Donn and Co.* [1996] 3 All ER 1 the court held that the decision of a Legal Aid Committee, in awarding a contract to solicitors for the conduct of a multi-party action, was justiciable in public law, first, because the nature and purpose of the selection process and its consequences were one indivisible whole and, secondly, in view of the function exercised by the Committee, the purpose for which the Committee was empowered to act, and the consequences of the decision-making process. Similarly, in *R (Bevan and Clarke LLP) v Neath Port Talbot County Borough Council* [2012] EWHC 236 (Admin), [2012] BLGR 728, a local authority decision on rates paid to private-sector operators of residential care homes was in principle amenable to judicial review, although the court should be cautious of providers wishing to improve their contractual negotiating position by recourse to public law principles and bear in mind the alternative remedial structure in competitive tendering for contracts with public authorities.

It has been held that breach of the Public Contracts Regulations 2006 (SI 2006/5) in relation to public procurement can give rise to public law as well as private law remedies where the claimant is affected by the departure in some way or where the departure is of such gravity that it justifies the public law remedy in any event (*R (Chandler) v Secretary of State for Children, Schools and Families* [2009] EWCA Civ 1011, [2010] PTSR 749). See also *R. (Unison) v NHS Wiltshire Primary Care Trust* [2012] EWHC 624 (Admin), [2012] ACD 84.

Procedural exclusivity

Where the invalidity of a decision arises as a collateral issue in a claim for infringement of a private law right of the claimant, the issue should be resolved as a private law matter (per Lord Diplock in *O'Reilly v Mackman* [1983] 2 AC 237). Consequently, an action for damages against a local planning authority for negligence comprises a private law action (*Davy v Spelthorne Borough Council* [1984] AC 262); a reduction in a general practitioner's practice allowance by a family practitioner committee was a private law issue (*Roy v Kensington and Chelsea and Westminster Family Practitioner Committee* [1992] 1 AC 624); a claim in respect of inordinate delay in paying compensation for handguns surrendered under the Firearms (Amendment) Act 1997 was a private law matter (*Steed v Secretary of State for the Home Department* [2000] 1 WLR 1169); but an action against a local authority in respect of an alleged breach of its duties under the Housing (Homeless Persons) Act 1977 was a public law matter which should have proceeded by way of judicial review (*Cocks v Thanet District Council* [1983] 2 AC 286); a defendant was unable to challenge the validity of an enforcement notice under s. 87 of the Town and Country Planning Act 1971 on the basis that such matters should have been raised by way of judicial review and were not suitable for decision by a criminal court (*R v Wicks* [1998] AC 92); but, subject to clear Parliamentary intention to the contrary, the legality of a decision made pursuant to a by-law could be raised as a defence to a criminal charge (*Boddington v British Transport Police* [1999] 2 AC 143); and an ordinary action was held to be the more appropriate procedure to deal with an action against a local authority to recover sums due under improvement grants (*Trustees of the Dennis Rye Pension Fund v Sheffield City Council* [1998] 1 WLR 840). A defendant may raise a public law defence to private law proceedings where there has been an infringement of a pre-existing private law right (*Wandsworth London Borough Council v Winder* [1985] AC 461; *Wandsworth London Borough Council v A* [2000] 1 WLR 1246). **77.6**

Although the courts will not strike out a private law claim simply on the grounds that it would have been more appropriate to use judicial review, they will do so if it amounts to an abuse of process. It is therefore important for a claimant to select the correct route of challenge. In deciding whether using a private law claim for a public law issue amounts to an abuse of process the court will consider whether the private law route has been used to take advantage of a longer limitation period, in view of the short time limits for judicial review claims (see **77.36**), or whether other judicial review rules have been flouted (*Clark v University of Lincolnshire and Humberside* [2000] 1 WLR 1988). It has been held that where a litigant has a claim which could be brought either by judicial review or by an ordinary action the choice of either might amount to an abuse of process. The exercise of the jurisdiction to strike out the claim on this ground would depend on a consideration of all the relevant circumstances, including any matters occurring before the proceedings were instituted and which remedy would be more appropriate (*Phonographic Performance Ltd v Department of Trade and Industry* [2004] EWHC 1795 (Ch), [2004] 1 WLR 2893; see also *Jones v Powys Local Health Board* [2008] EWHC 2562 (Admin), [2009] 12 CCL Rep 68). For example, proceedings commenced by a landowner seeking declarations in respect of a breach of condition notice in the planning context should have been brought by judicial review since service of a breach of condition notice was a purely public law act, and therefore could not be challenged by private law proceedings (*Trim v North Dorset District Council* [2010] EWCA Civ 1446, [2011] 1 WLR 1901).

The practical consequences of the choice made between public and private law should be considered rather than merely technical questions concerning the distinction between public and private rights (*Trustees of the Dennis Rye Pension Fund v Sheffield City Council*). A similar approach has been taken where the factual circumstances of cases are such that they may fall into both public law and private law (*Andreou v Institute of Chartered Accountants in England and Wales* [1998] 1 All ER 14 — a finding of the Disciplinary Committee of the Institute of Chartered Accountants).

GROUNDS OF JUDICIAL REVIEW

77.7 Judicial review is not an appeal mechanism, but a review of public law functions (*R v Richmond upon Thames London Borough Council, ex parte JC* (2000) *The Times*, 26 April 2000 (QBD); [2001] LGR 146 (CA)). There are a number of classifications of the grounds upon which a decision by a public authority may be found to be invalid. A commonly used classification is the tripartite distinction in *Council of Civil Service Unions v Minister for the Civil Service* [1985] AC 374 between:

(a) illegality,
(b) irrationality, and
(c) procedural impropriety.

This classification is not set in stone. Within each of the three heads are a number of grounds which are capable of being characterised in more than one way. In addition, many factual situations can be analysed in more than one way. For example, where a statute lays down a procedure with which a public authority needs to comply, a failure to follow the wording of the statute could fall under both the illegality head (see **77.8** to **77.11**) and the procedural impropriety head (see **77.22** to **77.29**).

Illegality

77.8 Illegality arises where a decision-maker who must understand correctly the law that regulates his or her decision-making power and must give effect to it fails to do so (Lord Diplock in *Council of Civil Service Unions v Minister for the Civil Service* [1985] AC 374). Illegality also includes acts done beyond the powers of the person or body performing or authorising the act ('*ultra vires*'). It also includes an act performed or authorised in error as to what the law authorising the person or body permits that person or body to do. An error in relation to a precedent (jurisdictional) fact is also often placed under the illegality heading. An action or decision is said to be tainted by illegality if:

(a) it was purportedly taken under legislation which does not contain the requisite power; or
(b) it was purportedly taken under legislation which contains precise limits on the circumstances in which a power or duty can be used, and the action or decision in question either exceeds these limits or fails to perform the power or duty in a proper way.

'Illegal' could also be used to describe a statutory instrument which conflicts with primary legislation, or an Act of Parliament which is incompatible with European Union law. One particular aspect of illegality is an allegation of a breach of Convention rights under the **Human Rights Act 1998** (see **chapter 91**). For example, where a public body fails to comply with the public sector equality duty imposed by the Equalities Act 2010, s. 149, its decision will be susceptible to review. However, this duty is not to be treated as a tick box exercise; the court should ask whether as a matter of substance there has been compliance (*R (Greenwich Community Law Centre) v Greenwich London Borough Council* [2012] EWCA Civ 496, [2012] Eq LR 572).

77.9 ***Ultra vires* acts** Whether or not a decision is *ultra vires* depends upon the relevant primary or secondary legislation and its interpretation on the particular facts and circumstances of each case. Therefore few general rules can be laid down. The permitting legislation should be considered in order to establish what the body exercising the public function is entitled to do and what limits there are on the steps that may be taken in performance of the function. Where the relevant body either exceeds the stipulated function or purports to perform the function in a manner not permitted by the legislation, its powers will have been exceeded and the decision will therefore be open to review.

77.10 **Errors of law** An alternative way of analysing illegality is as an error of law. This is where a public body makes a decision based upon an incorrect interpretation of the law. For example, the House of Lords has held that the defendant borough council misinterpreted s. 4(2)(b) of the Housing (Homeless Persons) Act 1977 in holding that the immigrant claimant became 'intentionally homeless' by bringing his homeless family to the United Kingdom to live with him (*Re Islam (Tafazzul)* [1983] 1 AC 688).

Precedent (jurisdictional) fact/error of fact Although error of fact has not historically been regarded as a ground for judicial review (*R v Hillingdon London Borough Council, ex parte Puhlhofer* [1986] AC 484), the courts will review instances where the public body has failed to establish a vital fact which triggers its power and makes the exercise of its powers lawful, e.g. the requirement to establish that a person is an 'illegal entrant' before the power of deportation can lawfully arise under the Immigration Act 1971 (*Khera v Secretary of State for the Home Department* [1984] AC 74). Factual aspects of a decision may be reviewed in some limited circumstances (see per Lords Slynn of Hadley, Nolan and Clyde in *R (Alconbury Developments Ltd) v Secretary of State for the Environment, Transport and the Regions* [2001] UKHL 23, [2003] 2 AC 295). **77.11**

For there to be a sufficient mistake of fact giving rise to unfairness the following criteria need to be fulfilled:

(a) there must be a mistake as to an existing fact, including mistake as to the availability of evidence;
(b) the fact or evidence must now be uncontentious and objectively verifiable;
(c) the claimant or his advisers must not have been responsible for the mistake of fact; and
(d) the mistake must have played a material (but not necessarily decisive) part in the Tribunal's reasoning (*E v Secretary of State for the Home Department* [2004] EWCA Civ 49, [2004] QB 1044). (See also *R (Ross) v West Sussex Primary Care Trust* [2008] EWHC 2252 (Admin), [2008] 11 CCL Rep 787; *Connolly v Secretary of State for Communities and Local Government* [2009] EWCA Civ 1059, [2009] NPC 114; and *R (March) v Secretary of State for Health* [2010] EWHC 765 (Admin), [2010] Med LR 271.)

There is a distinction to be made between cases where an appeal court is satisfied, on new evidence, that a minister or inferior body or tribunal took a decision on the basis of a belief as to the existence of a material fact that has now been demonstrated to be plainly wrong, and cases where it took its decision in the mistaken belief that there was in fact no apparently cogent evidence to refute a material finding it had made (see *Shabana Shaheen v Secretary of State for the Home Department* [2005] EWCA Civ 1294, [2006] Imm AR 57, where, on the facts, the Court of Appeal held that the Immigration Appeal Tribunal had not made an error of law).

Irrationality

A decision may be tainted by irrationality where the decision-making body allegedly: **77.12**

(a) acted for an improper purpose;
(b) acted with bad faith;
(c) fettered its discretion;
(d) improperly delegated its functions;
(e) reached a conclusion that no body properly directing itself on the relevant law and acting reasonably could have reached;
(f) failed to take into account relevant matters or took into account irrelevant matters;
(g) abused its powers or infringed a legitimate expectation; or, possibly,
(h) acted in a disproportionate manner; or
(i) did not act consistently.

The **Human Rights Act 1998** may also provide a backdrop to claims based upon the ground of irrationality. When scrutinising an executive decision which interferes with human rights, the court will ask, applying an objective test, whether the decision-maker could reasonably have concluded that the interference was necessary to achieve one or more of the legitimate aims recognised by the Convention (*R (Mahmood) v Secretary of State for the Home Department* [2001] 1 WLR 840). The proportionality of any interference will now be an issue in any review by the courts of the decision of a public authority (*R 'Daly) v Secretary of State for the Home Department* [2001] 2 AC 532) in a case raising the **Human Rights Act 1998**.

77.13 **Improper purpose** In cases where a power granted to a public body for one purpose is exercised by it for a different purpose, that power is deemed not to have been validly exercised, e.g. where a local authority decided to avoid the products of a company in order to put pressure upon its parent companies to withdraw their interests from South Africa (*R v Lewisham London Borough Council, ex parte Shell UK Ltd* [1988] 1 All ER 938); where a transaction by a local council was for the improper purpose of circumventing its restrictions on borrowing and spending (*Crédit Suisse v Allerdale Borough Council* [1997] QB 306).

Generally the interpretation by the courts of the purpose of a statutory provision involves a search for the 'natural and ordinary meaning' of the word or term. Although reference may be made to Parliamentary records to aid the construction of legislation which is ambiguous or obscure (*Pepper v Hart* [1993] AC 593) this principle is not applicable in relation to the determination of the general purpose of a statutory scheme, but only to resolve ambiguity in a statutory provision.

77.14 **Bad faith** A decision is made in bad faith if it has been affected by motives such as fraud, malice, or personal self-interest. A power is deemed to have been exercised fraudulently where the decision-maker had an intention to achieve an object other than that which it claimed to be seeking, e.g. the promotion of another public or private interest. A power is regarded as exercised maliciously if an action or decision is motivated by a personal animosity towards those who are directly affected by its exercise, e.g. the decision by a county council to cease advertising in journals controlled by Times Newspapers (which had written an article criticising a councillor) was explicitly held to be motivated by bad faith and declared invalid (*R v Derbyshire County Council, ex parte The Times Supplements Ltd* (1991) 3 Admin LR 241).

77.15 **Fettering of discretion** Where a public body maintains a rigid policy with no exceptions it thereby fetters its discretion. Although a public authority can have a policy, it must consider particular cases rather than fetter its discretion by always following its stated policy blindly. Thus, for example, a rule of the Board of Trade which excluded grants for items costing less than £25 each was only permissible provided that the Board was always willing to listen to anyone with something new to say (*British Oxygen Co. Ltd v Board of Trade* [1971] AC 610); a policy formulated on the premises that amusement arcades would be harmful to young persons was unlawful (*Sagnata Investments Ltd v Norwich Corporation* [1971] 2 QB 614); a policy to restrict access to a solicitor by a person remanded in custody was unlawful (*R v Chief Constable of South Wales, ex parte Merrick* [1994] 1 WLR 663); the policy of a licensing committee which provided that an applicant for a betting office licence must have a legal interest in the premises was unlawful (*R v Forest Betting Licensing Committee, ex parte Noquet* (1988) *The Times*, 21 June 1988).

The courts may be prepared to scrutinise closely the conduct of a decision-maker in assessing whether or not he or she has unlawfully fettered his or her discretion, e.g. a course of conduct involving the consistent rejection of applications belonging to a particular class may justify an inference that the public body has adopted a policy to refuse them all. However, it is unlikely that the courts will deem a decision-maker to have fettered his or her discretion in circumstances where he or she afforded those individuals affected the ability to make representations, e.g. decisions of local authorities in relation to the disposition of planning appeals or proposals for the compulsory acquisition of land have been upheld in circumstances where the decision was made after a public inquiry (*Franklin v Minister of Town and Country Planning* [1948] AC 87; *Stringer v Minister of Housing and Local Government* [1970] 1 WLR 1281).

77.16 **Improper delegation** In general a public law function must be exercised only by the body to whom it has been given. When a power is provided to a person in circumstances indicating that trust is being placed in his or her individual judgment and discretion, that person must *exercise that power* personally unless he or she has been expressly empowered to delegate it to another. Public bodies which exercise functions analogous to the judiciary are precluded from delegating their powers of decision unless there is express authority to that effect (*General*

Council of Medical Education and Registration of the United Kingdom v Dental Board of the United Kingdom [1936] Ch 41).

Where an authority vested with discretionary powers affecting private rights then empowers one of its committees, members or officers to exercise those powers independently without any supervisory control, the exercise of those powers is likely to be held invalid. Thus, for example, a delegation by the Director of Public Prosecutions to non-qualified lawyers of the power to review prosecutions in order to decide whether there was sufficient evidence to proceed was held to be unlawful because the statute giving the power to the Director clearly contemplated that it would only be delegated to a member of the Crown Prosecution Service who was a lawyer (*R v Director of Public Prosecutions, ex parte Association of First Division Civil Servants* (1988) *The Times*, 24 May 1988).

However, in the case of local authorities, s. 101 of the Local Government Act 1972 expressly permits some delegation. The degree of control maintained by the delegating authority is an important factor in determining the validity of the delegation. The control must be close enough for the decision to be identified as that of the delegating authority (*Hall v Manchester Corporation* (1915) 84 LJ Ch 732). Clearly it is improper for an authority to delegate wide discretionary powers to another authority over which it is incapable of exercising direct control, unless it is expressly permitted so to delegate. Also relevant to the proper delegation of powers are the nature of the power and the impact of its exercise upon individual interests.

The courts have recognised that duties imposed upon and powers granted to government ministers are normally exercised under the authority of ministers by responsible officials of the department (*Carltona Ltd v Commissioners of Works* [1943] 2 All ER 560). Thus, decisions taken in this manner will not have involved an impermissible delegation. This principle has been applied to the Benefits Agency, which was held to be part of the Department of Social Security, and the Agency staff therefore were regarded as part of the Civil Service (*R v Secretary of State for the Home Department, ex parte Sherwin* (1996) 32 BMLR 1). There may, however, be matters of such importance that the minister is legally required to address them personally. The presumption in relation to ministers may be expressly excluded by legislation (e.g. as in the Immigration Act 1971).

***Wednesbury* unreasonableness** Lord Greene MR stated in *Associated Provincial Picture Houses Ltd v Wednesbury Corporation* [1948] 1 KB 223: **77.17**

> it may be still possible to say that, although the local authority have kept within the four corners of the matters which they ought to consider, they have nevertheless come to a conclusion so unreasonable that no reasonable authority could ever have come to it.

In order to prove '*Wednesbury* unreasonableness' something overwhelming must be proved but this test has been fulfilled in a number of cases, e.g. a local authority resolution to ban a rugby club from its property for not putting pressure upon three of its players not to participate in a tour of South Africa (*Wheeler v Leicester City Council* [1985] AC 1054); a justices' clerk's refusal to supply duplicate legal aid orders (*R v Liverpool Justices, ex parte R. M. Broudie and Co.* (1994) 7 Admin LR 242); and the Lottery Commission's refusal to allow a bidder one month to allay its concerns about the bid (*R v National Lottery Commission, ex parte Camelot Group plc* [2001] EMLR 3).

Failure to take account of relevant considerations A further limb of the ground of irrationality comprises failure to take account of relevant considerations or the taking into account of an irrelevant consideration. For example, the court held that a borough council took into account irrelevant (philanthropic) considerations in deciding to overpay its staff, and also failed to take into account relevant considerations of comparable wages and the costs of living (*Roberts v Hopwood* [1925] AC 578). **77.18**

Commentary

Guidance or circulars may also be material considerations that should be taken into account when making decisions on how to implement legislation, although they cannot override legislation. Failure to take such guidance contained in circulars into account was an error of law amenable to judicial review and also breached the claimant's legitimate expectation that such guidance would be taken into account (*R (Jeeves) v Gravesham Borough Council* [2006] EWHC 1249 (Admin), [2007] 1 P & CR 15).

A statute may expressly or impliedly make clear considerations to which regard must or must not be had. There may also be considerations to which the decision-maker may have regard in the exercise of his discretion subject to normal public law principles (see *CREEDNZ Inc. v Governor-General* [1981] 1 NZLR 172).

A failure to assess the evidence properly, resulting in a decision which appears to be unsupported by the evidence, can also be characterised as a failure to take account of relevant considerations. This may arise where the court is unable to identify the evidence to support a decision, in which event the decision will be flawed in law (*AJ (Liberia) v Secretary of State for the Home Department* [2006] EWCA Civ 1736, LTL 15/12/2006).

It is not necessary to prove that the influence of irrelevant factors was the chief or main influence upon the decision made or action taken. As a general rule it is enough to prove that the influence was material or substantial (*R v Inner London Education Authority, ex parte Westminster City Council* [1986] 1 WLR 28). Where a decision-maker leaves out of account some relevant matter, the legal test is whether that factor might realistically have caused the decision-maker to reach a different conclusion (*W v Special Educational Needs Tribunal* (2000) *The Times*, 12 December 2000).

If the challenge is based upon a claim that relevant considerations were not taken into account, the courts will normally try to assess the actual or potential importance of the factor that was overlooked, even though this may involve a degree of speculation. Examples of decisions challenged under this ground include the unlawful expenditure of public funds by a board of guardians in cancelling a series of loans to miners without taking into account the ability of the debtors to repay their loans (*Attorney-General v Tynemouth Poor Law Union Guardians* [1930] 1 Ch 616) and the decision of a university to refuse to permit a controversial meeting on its premises which had been influenced by an irrelevant consideration, namely, the likelihood of violence outside the premises (*R v University of Liverpool, ex parte Caesar-Gordon* [1991] 1 QB 124).

A number of cases have reviewed the situation where local authorities have sought to use lack of resources as justification for reducing the level of provision of services they are under a statutory duty to provide. For example, a local authority could take into account its resources in assessing 'needs' under s. 2 of the Chronically Sick and Disabled Persons Act 1970 (*R v Gloucestershire County Council, ex parte Barry* [1997] AC 584). However, although a local authority was entitled to have regard to its resources in determining whether claimants were 'in need of care and attention' under s. 21(1) of the National Assistance Act 1948, once a need was established the authority was not then able to take account of its lack of resources in deferring the carrying out of these duties (*R v Sefton Metropolitan Borough Council, ex parte Help the Aged* [1997] 4 All ER 532).

When a local education authority performed its statutory duty under s. 298 of the Education Act 1993 to provide suitable education for children of compulsory school age, it was not entitled to take into account the availability of financial resources when deciding what sort of education was suitable (*R v East Sussex County Council, ex parte Tandy* [1998] AC 714). Similar reasoning has been applied to local authorities in determining whether or not to approve an application for a disabled facilities grant for purposes under s. 23(1) of the Housing Grants, Construction and Regeneration Act 1996 (*R v Birmingham City Council, ex parte Mohammed* [1999] 1 WLR 33) and in determining whether to make a mandatory order under the Housing Act 1996, s. 193, in respect of the provision of suitable accommodation (*R v Newham London*

Borough Council, ex parte Khan (2000) 33 HLR 269). Where the parole board was required, in the exercise of its functions, to consider whether a prisoner's state of mind meant that it should expedite either a recall hearing or a parole hearing, administrative inconvenience and problems with resources could not justify a delay of over three months before such a hearing took place (*R (Cooper) v Parole Board* [2007] EWHC 1292, [2007] ACD 101). However, a Chief Constable's decision to provide policing only two days a week to protect the transport of livestock for shipment to France from animal rights protesters was lawful having regard to the Chief Constable's lack of resources, whether viewed from a domestic or European law perspective (*R v Chief Constable of Sussex, ex parte International Trader's Ferry Ltd* [1999] 2 AC 418). See also *R (Pfizer Ltd) v Secretary of State for Health* [2002] EWCA Civ 1566, *The Times*, 11 November 2002; *R (Spink) v Wandsworth London Borough Council* [2005] EWCA Civ 302, [2005] 1 WLR 2884.

Abuse of power/substantive legitimate expectation There is authority that an undertaking or promise by a public authority may lead to a legitimate expectation which must not be thwarted (*R v Liverpool Corporation, ex parte Liverpool Taxi Fleet Operators' Association* [1972] 2 QB 299). The fulfilment of substantive expectations has been upheld, e.g. an expectation contained in the terms of a Home Office circular setting out the conditions for the adoption of children from abroad (*R v Secretary of State for the Home Department, ex parte Asif Mohammed Khan* [1984] 1 WLR 1337) and an expectation that foreign doctors given particular immigration status would be able to seek and obtain employment in the UK in their field (which subsequent guidance then sought to restrict) (*R (Bapio Action Ltd) v Secretary of State for the Home Department* [2008] UKHL 27, [2008] 1 AC 1003). In considering a claim based on a substantive legitimate expectation, the court is required to apply a rigorous standard, bearing in mind the duty of public authorities to exercise powers in the public interest (*R (Godfrey) v Southwark London Borough Council* [2012] EWCA Civ 500, [2012] BLGR 683). A suggestion that the concept of substantive legitimate expectation is nothing more than a challenge based upon *Wednesbury* unreasonableness grounds (*R v Secretary of State for the Home Department, ex parte Hargreaves* [1997] 1 WLR 906) was effectively circumvented in *R v North and East Devon Health Authority, ex parte Coughlan* [2001] QB 213. **77.19**

The House of Lords has regarded a case of substantive unfairness, involving failure by the Inland Revenue to comply with a written assurance, as an abuse of power requiring either an improper motive or conduct equivalent to breach of contract or representation (*Re Preston* [1985] AC 835). However, it was not an abuse of power for the Inland Revenue to seek to extract a tax contrary to an advance clearing given by it where there had not been full disclosure by the taxpayer (*R v Inland Revenue Commissioners, ex parte Matrix Securities Ltd* [1994] 1 WLR 334). Nor was it an abuse of power for the Inland Revenue to withdraw tax relief in circumstances where its published documents were not sufficiently clear, unambiguous and devoid of qualification to give rise to a legitimate expectation which a court would protect (*Fletcher v Thompson* [2002] EWHC 1448 (Admin), [2002] STC 1149). There need not be an explicit representation by the public authority. It may be based on a practice established over a number of years, e.g. *R v Inland Revenue Commissioners, ex parte Unilever plc* (1996) 86 TC 205.

The general principles derived from these cases suggest that, in order to qualify for protection under the head of substantive legitimate expectation, the following qualities are necessary:

(a) the representation or expectation sought to be relied upon must be clear, unambiguous and unqualified, with the relevant question being how, on a fair reading of the representation, it would have been reasonably understood by those to whom it was made (*Paponette v Attorney General of Trinidad and Tobago* [2010] UKPC 32, [2012] 1 AC 1);
(b) the claimant must be within the class of persons entitled to rely upon the representation or alternatively it must be reasonable for the claimant to rely upon it;
(c) there must usually be reliance upon the representation to the detriment of the claimant, although the claimant need not always demonstrate detriment (*R (Bibi) v Newham London Borough Council* [2001] EWCA Civ 607, [2002] 1 WLR 237); and

(d) there must be no overriding public interest which would entitle the defendant to renege from its representation.

There can be a legitimate expectation that a policy will be applied even where the claimant was unaware of the policy (*R (Rashid) v Secretary of State for the Home Department* [2005] EWCA Civ 744, [2005] Imm AR 608).

Where a public authority issues a practice or promise, the law requires that practice or promise to be honoured unless there is a good reason not to do so, i.e. where it would be the public body's legal duty or otherwise a proportionate response to a legitimate aim pursued by the public body in the public interest. This is part of the principle of fairness and good administration by public bodies in the way they deal with the public (*R (Nadarajah) v Secretary of State for the Home Department* [2005] EWCA Civ 1363, *The Times*, 14 December 2005).

Where there is a substantial public interest in a public body behaving in a particular way, then, absent a marked degree of unfairness to the claimant or disproportionality, judicial review is likely to be refused. Some unfairness will not be sufficient. Where, for example, the Revenue and Customs Commissioners had allowed for years an agreement out of accord with their general practice in the industry and where substantial amounts of tax properly payable would be unrecovered if that agreement were allowed to stand, there was a substantial public interest in allowing them to resile from the agreement which outweighed any private interest in keeping the agreement (*R (Bamber) v Commissioners of HM Revenue and Customs* [2005] EWHC 3221 (Admin), [2006] STC 1035).

Although the concept of conspicuous unfairness amounting to abuse of power appears to have become a stand-alone ground linked to legitimate expectations in recent cases, in particular after the decision in *R (Rashid) v Secretary of State for the Home Department* [2005] EWCA Civ 744, [2005] Imm AR 608, there has been some doubt cast on the development of the law in this area. Abuse of power should not be seen as a magic ingredient able to achieve remedial results which other forms of illegality cannot match. It is not a special and more extreme category of illegality, but rather a general concept underlying other particular forms. However, in extreme cases it is accepted that a court could hold that unfairness is so obvious and the remedy so plain that there is only one way in which the Secretary of State could reasonably exercise his discretion (*R (S) v Secretary of State for the Home Department* [2007] EWCA Civ 546, [2007] ACD 94).

The public law concepts of legitimate expectation and abuse of power, rather than the private law concept of estoppel, have been held to be relevant to planning law. Situations could therefore arise in the planning field where it would be a breach of legitimate expectation and therefore an abuse of power for a public body to act in a particular way (*R (Reprotech (Pebsham) Ltd) v East Sussex County Council* [2002] UKHL 8, [2003] 1 WLR 348) but such situations will be rare (*Henry Boot Homes Ltd v Bassetlaw District Council* [2002] EWCA Civ 983, [2003] 1 P & CR 23).

The doctrine of estoppel can offer no more protection than the principle of legitimate expectation (*R (Capital Care Services (UK) Ltd) v Secretary of State for the Home Department* [2012] EWCA Civ 1151, LTL 24/7/2012). However, cause of action estoppel, rather than the public law concept of legitimate expectation, will still be relevant in the context of enforcement notice appeals (*R (East Hertfordshire District Council) v First Secretary of State* [2007] EWHC 834 (Admin), [2007] JPL 1304).

77.20 **Proportionality** Proportionality is a concept central both to EU law and to the European Convention on Human Rights and means that remedies or measures should be proportionate to the legitimate aim that is sought to be achieved or the state of affairs they are intended to redress, and thus the administrative process should be in proportion to the outcome of the process (see **91.13**). The conventional view is that proportionality is simply a facet of irrationality/*Wednesbury* unreasonableness (see above) and there is no separate ground of proportionality within the domestic context (*R v Secretary of State for the Home Department, ex parte Brind* [1991] 1 AC 696). However, it is clear that the tests of proportionality and *Wednesbury* unreasonableness do not always yield the same results but are moving closer together (*R (Association of British Civilian Internees: Far East Region) v Secretary of State for Defence* [2003] EWCA Civ 473, [2003] QB 1397). Although there is an overlap between the traditional grounds of judicial review and the approach of proportionality, the intensity of review is greater under the proportionality approach (*R (Daly) v Secretary of State for the Home Department* [2001] UKHL 26, [2001] 2 AC 532). Proportionality has been raised in the context of personal liberty (*R v Secretary of State for the Home Department, ex parte Pegg* [1995] COD 84) and has also been applied where a sentencing decision is susceptible to judicial review (*R v Highbury Corner Justices, ex parte Uchendu* (1994) 158 JP 409).

The failure of a decision-maker expressly to refer to proportionality in a decision does not necessarily render the decision liable to be quashed. Where a decision-maker has taken account of all material considerations, there is no 'straitjacket' imposed requiring the presence of the word in the final decision (*Lough v First Secretary of State* [2004] EWCA Civ 905, [2004] 1 WLR 2557).

Administrative consistency There is a general principle, as one aspect of irrationality as a ground for review, that like cases should be treated alike (but clearly where cases are not alike this may justify differential treatment). **77.21**

Where the Agricultural Wages Board established a new category of worker whose minimum wage was lower than that of a standard worker, but excluded mushroom harvesters from those who could be paid this rate, this exclusion was found to infringe the principle of public administration that all persons in a similar situation should be treated similarly (*R (Middlebrook Mushrooms Ltd) v Agricultural Wages Board of England and Wales* [2004] EWHC 1447 (Admin), *The Times*, 15 July 2004).

Similarly, where a policy which applied to Iraqi Kurds was not applied to a claimant who could show a direct comparison with two other Iraqi Kurds who were in precisely the same position as the claimant, and who had both been granted refugee status under this policy, the court found that the application of unequal treatment to refugees in a like position was so unfair as to amount to a misuse of governmental power (*R (Rashid) v Secretary of State for the Home Department* [2005] EWCA Civ 744, [2005] Imm AR 608). The principle of consistency also required that categorisation of prisoners should not depend on subjective differing professional judgments of various prison governors in different prisons, but should be dealt with on a consistent basis (*R (Lowe) v Governor of Liverpool Prison* [2008] EWHC 2167 (Admin), [2009] Prison LR 197). However, where one party's subsidy was lower than competitors' because it was based on information that was more up to date and accurate than the older figures used to calculated competitors' subsidies, it was simply 'bad luck' for the particular company because to have allowed that company to benefit from an increased subsidy based on out-of-date information would have resulted in an unjustified windfall and would not have been in the public interest (*Tate and Lyle Sugars Ltd v Secretary of State for Energy and Climate Change* [2011] EWCA Civ 664, [2011] ACD 92).

Procedural impropriety

Procedural impropriety is concerned with the procedure by which a decision is reached, not the ultimate outcome. In order to prove procedural impropriety the claimant must show that the decision was reached in an unfair manner. If there is no statutory framework which expressly stipulates the relevant procedural requirements, there are two applicable common law rules under this head, namely: **77.22**

(a) the rule against bias, which requires the public body to be impartial and to be seen to be so; and

(b) the right to a fair hearing whereby those affected by a decision of a public body are entitled to know what the case is against them and to have a proper opportunity to put their case forward.

Infringement of express procedural rules

77.23 A decision made or action taken by a public body should not infringe express procedural rules outlined in primary or secondary legislation, e.g. a notice of school closure was quashed where there was a failure to consult under s. 184 of the Education Act 1993 and a government circular (*R v Lambeth London Borough Council, ex parte N* [1996] ELR 299); procedural codes are laid out in the town and country planning legislation which set out the procedure for an appeal or a full structured inquiry. Courts may be called upon to adjudicate upon the extent to which the statutory procedure is fulfilled. There have also been cases where the courts have supplemented a statutory scheme over and above that which is expressly specified (e.g. *Fairmount Investments Ltd v Secretary of State for the Environment* [1976] 1 WLR 1255). However, it is generally recognised that such supplementation should be exercised only in extreme circumstances where considered necessary to promote the purpose of the legislation (*Wiseman v Borneman* [1971] AC 297).

Implied procedural rules

77.24 The requirement to comply with express procedural rules is supported by the common law obligation to provide a fair hearing. The rules of natural justice embody a duty to act fairly. Whenever a public function is performed there is an inference, in the absence of an express requirement to the contrary, that the function is required to be performed fairly. This is more compelling in the case of any decision which may adversely affect a person's rights or interests (e.g. *R v Liverpool Corporation, ex parte Liverpool Taxi Fleet Operators' Association* [1972] 2 QB 299) but will not apply to situations which are too remote to qualify for a fair hearing.

The two fundamental common law rules set out in **77.22** also apply where there is no statutory procedural code.

Bias

77.25 In cases where the decision-maker has a direct personal or proprietary interest in the outcome of a matter, he or she should always be disqualified from adjudicating upon the issue. However, when the interest is indirect, the courts generally apply the following test. First, the court should ascertain all the circumstances which have a bearing on the suggestion that the tribunal is biased. Secondly, it should ask whether those circumstances would lead a fair-minded and informed observer to conclude that there is a real possibility that the tribunal is biased (*Porter v Magill* [2001] UKHL 67, [2002] 2 AC 357; see also **91.48**). See also *Bolkiah v Brunei Darussalam* [2007] UKPC 62, LTL 9/11/2007.

The House of Lords has held a judge in the House of Lords involved with Amnesty International to be automatically disqualified because his participation in a case where Amnesty was an intervener offended the fundamental principle that a man may not be a judge in his own cause. Although this principle normally applies only in cases where the judge has a pecuniary interest, the court confirmed that it could and did extend to cases where the judge has a non-pecuniary interest (sufficient to amount to an interest in the outcome of the proceedings) in one of the parties thereto (*R v Bow Street Metropolitan Stipendiary Magistrate, ex parte Pinochet Ugarte (No. 2)* [2000] 1 AC 119, subsequently applied in *Locabail (UK) Ltd v Bayfield Properties Ltd* [2000] QB 451).

In considering the question of apparent bias it is necessary to look beyond pecuniary or personal interests and to consider in addition whether, from the point of view of the fair-minded and informed observer, there is a real possibility that the decision-maker is biased in the sense of approaching the decision with a closed mind and without impartial consideration of all relevant issues (*Georgiou v Enfield London Borough Council* [2004] EWHC 779 (Admin), [2004] LGR 497). The two concepts of automatic disqualification and apparent bias can also be analysed as two strands of a single overarching requirement that judges or tribunal members should not sit or should face disqualification where there is a real possibility, assessed by a fair-minded and informed observer, that the tribunal objectively appears to be or could be biased. Taking this approach it could be said that the automatic disqualification test deals with cases where the personal interests of the judge concerned can be deemed to constitute apparent bias. It is not always necessary therefore to choose between the two doctrines in the analysis of the case (*R (Darsho Kaur) v Institute of Legal Executives Appeal Tribunal* [2011] EWCA Civ 1168, [2012] 1 All ER 1435).

In relation to the apparent bias of advisers to decision-making bodies, the correct question is whether the observer, knowing the composition and remit of both the advisory body and the deciding body, would perceive a real possibility both of bias in the advice and of its infecting the decision (*R (Royal Brompton and Harefield NHS Foundation Trust) v Joint Committee of Primary Care Trusts* [2012] EWCA Civ 472, 126 BMLR 134).

The question of independence should be tested by reference to the fair-minded and informed observer's knowledge of all the information which could have been ascertained by a fair-minded outside observer (*Re P (A Barrister)* [2005] 1 WLR 3019). The fair-minded observer would not reach a conclusion without seeking to obtain the full facts (*Virdi v Law Society* [2010] EWCA Civ 100, [2010] 1 WLR 2840). However, the information to be attributed to the fair-minded and informed observer includes that which would be apparent to the court upon investigation and is not restricted to that available to a hypothetical observer at an original hearing (*National Assembly for Wales v Condron* [2006] EWCA Civ 1573, [2006] NPC 127). The attributes of the fair-minded and informed observer include reserving judgment until she has seen and fully understood both sides of an argument, taking the trouble to inform herself on all relevant matters, taking a balanced approach to any information she is given, being able to put material into social, political or geographical context, knowing that judges like anyone else have their weaknesses but knowing that fairness requires judges to be, and be seen to be, unbiased (*Helow v Secretary of State for the Home Department* [2008] UKHL 62, [2008] 1 WLR 2416, subsequently applied in *Competition Commission v BAA Ltd* [2010] EWCA Civ 1097, [2011] UKCLR 1).

A public body should not allow decisions to be made by people who have a financial interest in the decision or a family/business connection with any party. However, it has been held that no bias arose in the case of a grant of planning permission to develop a rugby club's land where it was subsequently discovered that the club had an interest in acquiring land belonging to the chairman of the planning authority (*R v Secretary of State for the Environment, ex parte Kirkstall Valley Campaign Ltd* [1996] 3 All ER 304), nor where a planning officer had to consider various development proposals, including one put forward by her husband's company, since her decision was actually adverse to that company (*R (Persimmon Homes Ltd) v Vale of Glamorgan Council* [2010] EWHC 535 (Admin), LTL 22/3/2010). Bias may also arise because of a personal business relationship between the adjudicator and one of the parties, or because of partisanship by the adjudicator in relation to the issues to be resolved. Where a decision-maker takes part in the determination of an appeal against one of his or her own decisions (unless he or she is expressly authorised to do so by statute) it will be tainted by apparent bias, e.g. a clerk to a statutory tribunal could not act as clerk to the appeal tribunal hearing the appeal against that decision (*R v Salford Assessment Committee, ex parte Ogden* [1937] 2 KB 1). See also *R (Al-Hasan) v Secretary of State for the Home Department* [2005] UKHL 13, [2005] 1 WLR 688.

However, membership of the freemasons should not prevent a member of local government from making decisions whenever another freemason had an interest in the outcome of the decision, based on the true nature of freemasonry whereby freemasons were required to obey the law and were not required to be partial to any other freemason. A fair-minded observer

Commentary

informed of the facts in connection with freemasonry which had been placed before the court would not have concluded that there was a real possibility of bias in these circumstances (*R (Port Regis School Ltd) v North Dorset District Council* [2006] EWHC 742 (Admin), [2006] LGR 696). In appointing members to the Northern Ireland Parades Commission it was important to ensure that the Commission would be accepted as independent, objective and impartial in its approach. Therefore the appointment of two loyalists who were prominent and outspoken in their views was unlawful (*Re Duffy* [2008] UKHL 4, [2008] NI 152).

It is acceptable for decision-makers not acting in a judicial or quasi-judicial capacity to come to a decision with their own views, as long as there is no predetermination, they are open to new arguments right up to the moment of the decision, and make that decision based on the merits of the particular situation. In the planning context, therefore, a planning permission was not rendered unlawful simply because the planning committee members were all of a single political group and had previously expressed views on planning issues, as there was little evidence to suggest that they were any more politically motivated than would normally be expected from elected policy makers (*R (Lewis) v Redcar and Cleveland Borough Council* [2008] EWCA Civ 746, [2009] 1 WLR 83).

Local authority councillors were entitled to have regard to and apply policies that they had voiced support for in local elections and which had formed part of their manifesto, such as planning or land disposal policies. The court could not interfere in the political process in this way. Evidence of proper observations or apparent favouring of a particular decision was not enough for the court to quash a decision: there would need to be positive evidence that the local authority had approached the decision with a closed mind (*R (Island Farm Development Ltd) v Bridgend County Borough Council* [2006] EWHC 2189 (Admin), [2006] NPC 100).

It is important to distinguish between the concepts of predetermination, i.e. approaching a matter with a closed mind, and appearance of bias. Bias is concerned with appearances whereas predetermination concerns what in fact happened. The test of apparent bias relating to predetermination is a difficult one to satisfy (*R (Persimmon Homes Ltd) v Vale of Glamorgan Council* [2010] EWHC 535 (Admin), LTL 22/3/2010).

There is no absolute rule that knowledge of prejudicial publicity (such as knowledge of previous convictions) is fatal to the fairness and impartiality of the proceedings (*R (Mahfouz) v Professional Conduct Committee of the General Medical Council* [2004] EWCA Civ 233, [2004] Lloyd's Rep Med 389). Bias or apparent bias is not to be equated with knowledge of inadmissible and potentially prejudicial information. However, the effect of this knowledge has to be considered in the context of the proceedings as a whole, including the likely impact of the oral evidence and the legal advice available. Where the tribunal was made up of experienced and sophisticated members it could be assumed they would understand the proper approach and the need to disregard irrelevant material. Similarly, where members of an administrative decision-making board looking into alleged financial irregularities were appointed by a government minister who had made public comments about the irregularities, there was no reason to think that the appointees, as professional men who had sworn an oath to perform their functions conscientiously, would not do so. There was therefore no appearance of bias (*Belize Bank Ltd v Attorney General of Belize* [2011] UKPC 36, LTL 20/10/2011).

A party may waive its objections to a decision-maker who may otherwise have been disqualified on the ground of bias (*R (Giant's Causeway etc. Tramway Co.) v Antrim Justices* [1895] 2 IR 603). Any objection may be deemed to have been waived if the party or its legal representative knew of the disqualification and agreed to take part in the proceedings by failing to raise an objection at the earliest opportunity. For example, a claimant waived his right to complain that a decision not to grant him British citizenship was, or appeared to have been, prejudged following a newspaper article reporting that the decision-maker would not grant the application, because he had not objected to that decision-maker continuing to deal with the application and making the decision (*R v Secretary of State for the Home Department, ex parte Al Fayed* [2001] Imm AR 134). Clearly there is no presumption of waiver if there is no complete disclosure of an interest or if the party was not aware of the interest. Statutes may also provide an express exemption in certain instances.

In the absence of bias in respect of an earlier decision which had been remitted, or an expressed view from which it was impossible to depart, a decision-maker could rehear a remitted matter rather than recuse himself and have the matter determined by a different decision-maker (*Jones v Department of Transport Welsh Traffic Office* [2005] EWCA Civ 58, 102 (11) LSG 31). (See also *Secretary of State for the Home Department v AF (No. 2)* [2007] EWHC 2828 (Admin), [2008] 2 All ER 67, reversed on another point in *Secretary of State for the Home Department v AF (No. 2)* [2008] EWCA Civ 117, [2008] 1 WLR 2528.)

The common law rules on bias are now applied in the context of the requirement in art. 6(1) of the European Convention on Human Rights that civil rights and obligations (and criminal charges) must be determined by 'an independent and impartial tribunal' (see **91.48**).

Right to a fair hearing

The right to a fair hearing embodies the idea of even-handedness between the parties in relation to obtaining information which is made available, and the provision of an opportunity to make representations. The concept of a fair hearing varies from case to case. For example, there may be an entitlement to an oral hearing in cases where the livelihood or liberty of the claimant is at stake, whereas such an entitlement will not be deemed necessary in relation to more minor matters with less potentially adverse consequences. The two main elements of procedural fairness are: **77.26**

(a) the right to know the opposing case; and
(b) a fair opportunity to answer that case.

The overall test is what a reasonable man would consider to be fair in the particular circumstances (*Ridge v Baldwin* [1964] AC 40). (For the right to fairness and information in relation to consultation see 77.29.)

The right to information on the case against an individual includes entitlement to notice of the allegations made against him or her so that the individual has an adequate opportunity to prepare his or her own case, arrange for representation (if necessary) and appear at any hearing. The right to notice includes, by implication, provision of sufficient detail of the opposing case to provide a fair opportunity to prepare one's own case, e.g. a rating assessment which was determined upon a valuer's report which had not been disclosed to the other party was quashed (*R v Westminster Assessment Committee, ex parte Grosvenor House (Park Lane) Ltd* [1941] 1 KB 53). However, the use of anonymous witness statements by a governing body considering whether to exclude a pupil from school was considered to be fair in the particular circumstances of that case (*R (T) v Elliott School Head Teacher* [2002] EWCA Civ 1349, [2003] ELR 160; *R (A) v North Westminster Community School Head Teacher* [2002] EWHC 2351, [2003] ELR 378).

The procedure required to satisfy the requirements of a fair hearing will depend to a large extent on the nature of the decision-making body in question. The necessity for an oral hearing will depend upon the seriousness of the circumstances of the case and the subject matter being dealt with. In many instances an opportunity to make written representations will be sufficient, provided that the demands of fairness are met, e.g. the Army Board of the Defence Council could deal with a complaint of racial discrimination by way of written representations (*R v Army Board of the Defence Council, ex parte Anderson* [1992] QB 169). By contrast, in some situations express procedural rules may provide a right to an oral hearing, by way of oral representations. For example, in the homelessness context a right to make oral representations (although not the right to a full hearing with third-party witnesses and

Commentary

cross-examination) is provided by express regulations in advance of decisions to terminate tenancies and obtain possession, whereas the same requirement is not expressly set out in advance of administrative decisions concerning the provision of new accommodation. The difference in effect of the decisions makes the difference in process entirely understandable (*Makisi v Birmingham City Council* [2011] EWCA Civ 355, [2011] PTSR 1545). This illustrates that the exact requirements of a fair hearing will depend on the context. For example, in *R (Smith) v Parole Board (No. 2)* [2005] UKHL 1, [2005] 1 WLR 350, the House of Lords held that, while the common law duty of procedural fairness did not require the Parole Board to hold an oral hearing in every case, the Parole Board's duty was not as constricted as previously assumed. The prisoner should have the benefit of a procedure which fairly reflected, on the facts of his particular case, the importance of what was at stake for him and for society. The Parole Board might be assisted in its task of assessing risk by having some exposure to the prisoner. See also *R (Hammond) v Secretary of State for the Home Department* [2005] UKHL 69, [2006] 1 AC 603.

On the other hand, where on the facts of the case it is thought that an oral hearing would be a mere formality, there is no absolute right to a public and oral hearing at every stage in proceedings where the prisoner has had a fair and public hearing at his original trial. To provide for oral hearings in every case would cause delay and it has not been shown that any good purpose would be served by adopting such a procedure generally (*R (Dudson) v Secretary of State for the Home Department* [2005] UKHL 52, [2006] AC 245). It may be sufficient for the prisoner to be given the opportunity to make written representations (*R v Secretary of State for the Home Department ex parte Doody* [1994] 1 AC 531). See also *R (Thompson) v Law Society* [2004] EWCA Civ 167, [2004] 1 WLR 2522; *Naraynsingh v Commissioner of Police* [2004] UKPC 20, 64 WIR 392; *R (Osborn) v Parole Board* [2010] EWCA Civ 1409, [2011] UKHRR 35.

There is no clear entitlement to legal representation. Again, this will depend upon the seriousness or complexity of the charges made. The courts have held that prisoners charged with serious disciplinary offences have no general right to legal representation under the rules of natural justice, but the Boards of prison visitors have a discretion whether to allow it in the individual circumstances of each case (*R v Secretary of State for the Home Department, ex parte Tarrant* [1985] QB 251; *R v Board of Visitors of HM Prison, the Maze, ex parte Hone* [1988] AC 379). See also *R (S) v Knowlsey NHS Primary Care Trust* [2006] EWHC 26 (Admin), [2006] Lloyd's Rep Med 123; and *Kulkarni v Milton Keynes Hospital NHS Foundation Trust* [2009] EWCA Civ 789, [2010] ICR 101.

As long as the claimant is given an opportunity to set out his case at some stage during the proceedings, it does not appear to be contrary to the right to a fair hearing for a decision to be made without the claimant or his legal representative being present (e.g. *Auburn Court Ltd v Kingston and Saint Andrew Corporation, Building Surveyor* [2004] UKPC 11, 64 WIR 210).

In addition to the right to legal representation, in some circumstances a fair hearing may require that a party be allowed to adduce expert evidence. Where expert evidence is not permitted, a party may be deprived of an adequate opportunity to present its case (*Cummings v Weymouth and Portland Borough Council* [2007] EWHC 1601 (Admin), [2007] 2 P & CR 25).

Practical limitations may be placed upon the right to a fair process. For example, although the presence of an interpreter and/or representative in an interview in respect of an asylum claim provides a practical safeguard against faulty record-keeping and protects the claimant's interests to ensure the requisite standard of fairness, where such a safeguard is no longer practically available due to changes in public funding, a tape recording of the interview would be the only sensible method of redressing the imbalance of the Secretary of State being able to rely on a document without an adequate opportunity for the claimant to refute it (*R (Dirshe) v Secretary of State for the Home Department* [2005] EWCA Civ 421, [2005] 1 WLR 2685).

Reasons

77.27 There is no general duty under English law upon a decision-maker to give reasons for his or her decisions although statute does provide for such a duty in certain instances (e.g. Housing Act 1985, s. 64). However, in *R v Civil Service Appeal Board, ex parte Cunningham* [1992] ICR 816 Lord Donaldson MR stated that:

I do not accept that, just because Parliament has ruled that some tribunals should be required to give reasons for their decisions, it follows that the common law is unable to impose a similar requirement upon other tribunals, if justice so requires.

In *R v Ministry of Defence, ex parte Murray* [1998] COD 134, the Divisional Court confirmed that although the law did not at present recognise a general duty to give reasons, there was a perceptible trend towards an insistence on greater transparency in decision-making. Where a statute conferred a power to make decisions affecting individuals, the court would readily apply necessary additional procedural safeguards so as to ensure the attainment of fairness. The Court of Appeal has acknowledged that it might be the trend for requirements to give reasons to become the norm rather than the exception, but despite this there remains no general duty at common law to give reasons for an administrative decision. Indeed the Court of Appeal considered that the Freedom of Information Act 2000 was Parliament's considered statutory framework for the disclosure of information held by public authorities, and its enactment therefore militated against the incremental imposition by the judiciary of a common law general duty to give reasons (*Hasan v Secretary of State for Trade and Industry* [2008] EWCA Civ 1312, [2009] 3 All ER 539).

Reasons should therefore be given where either:

(a) a decision without reasons was insufficient to achieve justice; or
(b) the decision appeared aberrant.

In determining whether reasons should be given, relevant considerations include the absence of any right of appeal, the importance of an effective means of detecting the kind of error which would entitle the court to intervene, and whether the body in question exercises a judicial function. Factors which militate against such a duty include the placing of an undue burden on decision-makers, considerations of public interest, or inexpressible value judgments. Therefore the requirement of fairness may require the giving of reasons in circumstances where there is no express statutory authority stipulating this. The position is influenced by the fact that there is an obligation at common law, and also in accordance with the European Convention on Human Rights, **art. 6**, in the **Human Rights Act 1998, sch. 1**, at least to give a short statement of the reasons for a decision when determining civil rights and obligations or criminal charges.

Cases suggest that a duty to give reasons arises in cases where the body departs from its usual policy or practice (*R v Islington London Borough Council, ex parte Rixon* [1997] ELR 66), and where a failure to give reasons or the giving of inadequate reasons would lead to the quashing of the decision in question (*R v Westminster City Council, ex parte Ermakov* [1996] 2 All ER 302).

Circumstances may require reasons to be given even if there is no specific requirement. Although neither the Medical Act 1983 nor its rules of procedure expressly or impliedly imposed on the Council a duty to state reasons for its decisions, this did not exclude an obligation to give reasons where the common law would require reasons to be given (*Stefan v General Medical Council* [1999] 1 WLR 1293; *Selvanathan v General Medical Council* [2001] Lloyd's Rep Med 1). Although there is no general obligation upon the Director of Public Prosecutions to give reasons for a decision not to prosecute, it has been held that he would, in the absence of compelling reasons to the contrary, be expected to do so where his refusal concerned a death in custody, in respect of which a properly directed jury had returned a verdict of unlawful killing (*R v Director of Public Prosecutions, ex parte Manning* [2001] QB 330). Similarly, where an immigrant had her application for indefinite leave to remain on the grounds of domestic violence refused, fairness required that the tribunal should have given proper reasons for its rejection of the evidence on domestic violence (*AG (India) v Secretary of State for the Home Department* [2007] EWCA Civ 1534, LTL 5/12/2007) and proper reasons should also be given for an immigration judge's findings on the credibility of a particular witness (*MO (Iraq) v Secretary of State for the Home Department* [2008] EWCA Civ 995, LTL 24/7/2008).

However, reasons are less important when a decision is essentially a matter of judgment. Upon the challenge of a planning decision, a local authority was entitled to repeat its statement of a pure value judgment when an inspector disagreed with that judgment (*Welsh Development Agency v Carmarthenshire County Council* (1999) 80 P & CR 192). When deciding against an application for a capital grant, the Millennium Commission had only to say that another application was preferred and did not have to elucidate further (*R (Asha Foundation) v Millennium Commission* [2002] EWHC 916 (Admin), [2002] ACD 79; [2003] EWCA Civ 88, [2003] ACD 50).

Where reasons are required, such as reasons for a decision to grant planning permission, they need only be intelligible and adequate, and need only refer to the main issues in the dispute and not to every material consideration (*South Bucks District Council v Porter (No. 2)* [2004] UKHL 33, [2004] 1 WLR 1953). Although reasons need only be brief, they must be sufficient to explain the decision. They must be clear and adequate and deal with the substantial issues in the case but what are good reasons in any particular case depends on the circumstances of the case (*R v Immigration Appeal Tribunal, ex parte Jebunisha Kharvaleb Patel* [1996] Imm AR 161). An adjudicator refusing permission to appeal against a refusal to grant asylum was not required to address every point raised at length. Rather, sufficient reasons should be given to enable an appellant or other relevant person to see why a claimant had lost on any particular issue. If this test is satisfied, usually a more schematic approach would not be necessary (*R (Bahrami) v Immigration Appeal Tribunal* [2003] EWHC 1453 (Admin), LTL 4/6/2003 and *R (Macrae) v County of Herefordshire District Council* [2012] EWCA Civ 457, [2012] JPL 1356). See also **91.49**.

A trial judge must address evidential conflicts and assess that evidence to explain the judgment he reached. A failure to do so renders the decision inadequate and the finding of the trial judge should be quashed (*Baird v Thurrock Borough Council* [2005] EWCA Civ 1499, *The Times*, 15 November 2005).

Reasons must include the findings of fact in relation to each aspect of the decision and why they lead to the particular conclusion. Where insufficient reasons were given by the Conduct and Competence Committee of the Health Professions Council the decision was quashed and remitted to a freshly constituted committee (*Ryell v Health Professions Council* [2005] EWHC 2797 (Admin), [2007] Imm AR 81).

Where a fact-finding tribunal notes discrepancies in evidence its job is to evaluate them in making its decision. Usually it will need to do no more than describe them and state the conclusion reached. However, in some cases the inconsistencies would be such that the conclusion reached would require an explanation, for example, where the decision-maker decided the inconsistencies were insignificant. A failure to do this would amount to inadequate reasoning for the decision (*AK v Secretary of State for the Home Department* [2006] EWCA Civ 1117, [2007] Imm AR 81).

Where a number of reasons were given for the rejection of evidence, the fact that some of the reasons did not bear analysis was not enough to justify setting aside the decision. However, in an exceptional case where little of the reasoning could survive the scrutiny of the appellate court, the reasoning was sufficiently defective overall to justify the conclusion that the decision could not be upheld on that basis and the decision should therefore be remitted for fresh determination (*HK v Secretary of State for the Home Department* [2006] EWCA Civ 1037, *The Independent*, 27 July 2006).

The Court of Appeal does not have the power to invite a decision-maker to give supplementary reasons for its decision. Rather, in the rare cases where the appellant could not understand why the particular finding had been made and where the decision-maker appeared to have taken an erroneous approach to the evidence, the case should be remitted for reconsideration (*Hatungimana v Secretary of State for the Home Department* [2006] EWCA Civ 231, *The Times*, 2 March 2006).

Where there is a statutory duty to give reasons as part of the notification of the decision, the court will only accept subsequent evidence of the reasons in exceptional circumstances. In other cases, the court will be cautious about accepting late reasons. Relevant considerations which the court will take into account include: whether the new reasons are consistent with the original reasons, whether the new reasons are the original reasons of the whole tribunal, whether there is a real risk that the later reasons were composed subsequently in order to support the tribunal's decision, and the circumstances in which the later reasons are put forward. The degree of scrutiny and caution to be applied by the court to subsequent reasons is dependent on the subject matter of the administrative decision in question. Furthermore, the court will bear in mind the qualifications and experience of the persons on the tribunal (*R (Nash) v Chelsea College of Art and Design* [2001] EWHC 538 (Admin), *The Times*, 25 July 2001).

Commentary

Procedural legitimate expectation

A procedural legitimate expectation arises in circumstances where a decision deprived the claimant of: 77.28

> some benefit or advantage which either (i) he had in the past been permitted by the decision-maker to enjoy and which he can legitimately expect to be permitted to continue to do until there has been communicated to him some rational grounds for withdrawing it on which he has been given an opportunity to comment; or (ii) he has received assurance from the decision-maker that it will not be withdrawn without giving him first an opportunity of advancing reasons for contending that they should not be withdrawn. (Lord Diplock in *Council of Civil Service Unions v Minister for the Civil Service* [1985] AC 374).

The concept of procedural legitimate expectation has been applied to ensure that no adverse decision will be taken without first giving the affected party an opportunity of making representations.

An expectation will be derived from an express promise or representation or an implied representation based upon past actions. In order for a promise to have this effect it must be clear and unambiguous and the claimant must have made full relevant disclosure prior to obtaining it (*R v Inland Revenue Commissioners, ex parte MFK Underwriting Agencies Ltd* [1990] 1 WLR 1545) (see 77.19). The court has acknowledged that the concept of legitimate expectation will only be protected where there is no contrary public interest (*R v North and East Devon Health Authority, ex parte Coughlan* [2001] QB 213).

Examples of legitimate expectations are that taxi drivers had a legitimate expectation of consultation prior to the issue of licences in circumstances where such consultation had been expressly promised (*R v Liverpool Corporation, ex parte Liverpool Taxi Fleet Operators' Association* [1972] 2 QB 299); civil servants had a legitimate expectation of consultation prior to the removal of trade union rights, subject to considerations of national security (*Council of Civil Service Unions v Minister for the Civil Service* [1985] AC 374); coal miners' unions had a legitimate expectation of consultation on pit closures (*R v British Coal Corporation, ex parte Vardy* [1993] ICR 720); illegal immigrants had a legitimate expectation of an opportunity to state their case prior to deportation (*R v Attorney-General of Hong Kong, ex parte Ng Yuen Shiu* [1983] 2 AC 629); residents had a legitimate expectation of being consulted about all the options in respect of a traffic order (*R (Montpeliers and Trevors Association) v City of Westminster* [2005] EWHC 16 (Admin), [2006] LGR 304).

Consultation

77.29 A public authority may be under an express or implied obligation to consult. An obligation to consult also arises where a failure to do so would be so unfair as to amount to an abuse of power (*R (Dudley Metropolitan Borough Council) v Secretary of State for Communities and Local Government* [2012] EWHC 1729 (Admin), [2013] BLGR 68).

In many areas consultation is playing an increasingly important role. For example, in the context of environmental decisions, consultation is particularly significant given the Government's obligations under the Convention on Access to Information, Public Participation in Decision-Making and Access to Justice in Environmental Matters 1998 (the Aarhus Convention). There are four basic requirements of an adequate consultation:

(a) It must be at a time when proposals are still at a formative stage.
(b) The proposer must give sufficient reasons for any proposal to allow intelligent consideration and response.
(c) Adequate time must be given for consideration and response.
(d) The product of consultation must be conscientiously taken into account in finalising any proposals.

See *R v North and East Devon Health Authority, ex parte Coughlan* [2001] QB 213, adopting the formulation of Stephen Sedley QC in *R v Brent London Borough Council, ex parte Gunning* (1985) 84 LGR 168. Where it is alleged that a consultation process is unfair, it must be shown that there is a clear error precluding proper consultation, although it is sufficient to show that the unfairness affects only a group of the persons affected by the consultation (*R (Royal Brompton and Harefield NHS Foundation Trust) v Joint Committee of Primary Care Trusts* [2012] EWCA Civ 472, 126 BMLR 134).

On the issue of new-build nuclear power plants, the court found that the government's consultation paper had been inadequate in that it contained no proposals as such, the information given was insufficient, there was no discussion of the public considerations that would apply to the issue, the period given for consultation was inadequate and it could not be said that the decision eventually made would have been reasonably foreseeable by those consultees who took the consultation document at face value and relied upon it (*R (Greenpeace Ltd) v Secretary of State for Trade and Industry* [2007] EWHC 311 (Admin), [2007] Env LR 29). In the context of a statutory duty to consult on proposals to establish a unitary local authority, the Boundary Committee had a degree of flexibility as to the way in which the consultation should be carried out. However, this was subject to the need to comply with the general requirements set out in *R v North and East Devon Health Authority, ex parte Coughlan* (see above) and in particular to publish sufficient material in a form which members of the public could understand, in order to enable all those interested to respond intelligently (see *R (Breckland District Council) v Boundary Committee* [2009] EWCA Civ 239, [2009] BLGR 589). In circumstances where a decision-maker was discharging an important public function which engaged a strong public interest, fairness and the right to information meant that the consultation process should have involved a high degree of transparency and disclosure. Failure to disclose the fully executable version of an economic model that was central to the decision-making process was therefore unfair, as without it consultees could not properly review and test the model and therefore they were unable to make properly informed representations on it. The additional cost and time involved in releasing the fully executable version of the model should not weigh heavily in the balance in deciding whether fairness required disclosure (*R (Eisai Ltd) v National Institute for Health and Clinical Excellence* [2008] EWCA Civ 438, 101 BMLR 26). However, consultation with each affected individual would not be practicable where an urgent and difficult decision is required (*R (Legal Remedy UK) v Secretary of State for Health* [2007] EWHC 1252 (Admin), 96 BMLR 191).

Although there is a duty to re-consult if the final proposal is significantly different from what has been consulted upon, this duty does not arise if the differences are very slight and clearly not such as to impose a duty of fairness on the body to re-consult, or where the final proposal itself has emerged from the consultation exercise (*R v East Kent Hospital NHS Trust, ex parte Smith* [2002] EWHC 2640 (Admin), LTL 9/12/2002). Neither does the duty to consult while proposals are still at a formative stage mean that there must be a first round of consultation on whether the possible options should be reduced to one and then a second round of consultation on that last option. A limited consultation may be considered fair in circumstances where a full and formal consultation has recently been carried out (*R (Milton Keynes Council) v Secretary of State for Communities and Local Government* [2011] EWCA Civ 1575, [2012] JPL 728). Whether there can be said to have been a legitimate expectation as to the extent of the consultation will depend on the context and evidence in each particular case (*R (Tinns) v Secretary of State for Transport* [2006] EWHC 193 (Admin), LTL 11/1/2006).

There will still be circumstances where fairness does not require consultation, for example, where legislation has prescribed a particular procedure for a rule-making process which is subject to other control mechanisms and which does not include an express duty to consult (*R (Bapio Action Ltd) v Secretary of State for the Home Department* [2008] UKHL 27, [2008] 1 AC 1003). Alternatively there may be situations where the statutory scheme is such that a court is bound to follow a particular process even in the face of a failure to consult, contrary to a procedural legitimate expectation. This is an extension of the general principle that a legitimate expectation cannot override the law (see **77.19**). Where a licensing application was made and relevant representations, within the meaning of the statutory scheme, were not received within the required timescale, the applicant had a public law right to the grant of the application even though the authority had failed to carry out a proper notification and consultation process (*Corporation of the Hall of Arts and Sciences v Albert Court Residents' Association* [2011] EWCA Civ 430, [2011] BLGR 616).

Commentary

ALTERNATIVE REMEDIES TO JUDICIAL REVIEW

Generally, any alternative remedies should be exhausted before resorting to judicial review in cases where the alternative remedy is adequate to resolve the complaint (*R v Sandwell Metropolitan Borough Council, ex parte Wilkinson* (1998) 31 HLR 22). Although the jurisdiction of the court to grant relief by way of judicial review is not ousted by the existence of an alternative remedy, it may exercise its discretion to refuse relief, refuse to grant permission or adjourn the case until after the alternative remedy has been used. **77.30**

There should not in commercial disputes be two sets of parallel proceedings based on the same facts and seeking the same remedies, with two sets of costs and duplication of the time, effort and resources of both the parties and the court (see *Cookson and Clegg Ltd v Ministry of Defence* [2005] EWCA Civ 811, [2006] Eu LR 1092, where the judicial review claim was dismissed).

Where there is an alternative remedy available that is more suitable, a judicial review will not be permitted to continue in the Administrative Court. For example, where a matter concerning the lawfulness of the arrest and detention of various individuals could have instead been brought in private law as false imprisonment, and where there were complex factual issues and disputes of fact involved which were wholly inappropriate for judicial review proceedings, the matter should have been addressed in an ordinary Queen's Bench claim (*Sher v Chief Constable of Greater Manchester* [2010] EWHC 1859 (Admin), [2011] 2 All ER 364).

A number of cases have indicated that judicial review is to be regarded as a remedy of last resort. For example, permission to apply for judicial review of a decision of the Law Society was set aside because of the existence of an alternative remedy in the form of an appeal to the Master of the Rolls (*R v Law Society, ex parte Kingsley* [1996] COD 59); permission to apply for judicial review was set aside where a claimant had a statutory right of appeal to the Secretary of State under the Town and Country Planning Act 1990, s. 78, against a grant of planning permission subject to conditions (*R v Secretary of State for the Home Department, ex parte Watts* [1997] COD 152); judicial review of a decision of the Customs and Excise Commissioners was refused because the claimant should have invoked a statutory right of recourse to a value added tax and duties tribunal (*R v Commissioners of Customs and Excise, ex parte Bosworth Beverages Ltd* (2000) *The Times*, 24 April 2000); judicial review of a decision of the Secretary of State for the Home Department to issue a notice of liability to a civil penalty under the Immigration and Asylum Act 1999, s. 35, was refused on the basis that the claimant's remedy was to defend civil proceedings brought by the Home Secretary after the expiry of the time prescribed for payment of the penalty (*R (Balbo B & C Auto Transporti Internazionali) v Secretary of State for the Home Department* [2001] EWHC 195 (Admin), [2001] 1 WLR 1556); a challenge to the service of prohibition notices by the FSA should have been by way of appeal to the Financial Services and Markets Tribunal rather than by way of judicial review (*R (Davies) v Financial Services Authority* [2003] EWCA Civ 1128, [2004] 1 WLR 185).

Even in a case where there was a public law element, because it was a dispute under a tenancy agreement with a registered social landlord, it was held that the matter could have been brought either as a claim for breach of contract or under the housing legislation since it was essentially a contractual relationship that happened to possess a public law dimension. Judicial review is a remedy of last resort and should not be used where other remedies, including private law remedies, are available and have not been used (*R (McIntyre) v Gentoo Group Ltd* [2010] EWHC 5 (Admin), 154(2) SJLB 829).

It is possible to depart from this principle in exceptional circumstances, e.g. an urgent case where interim relief is required which would not be available in the appeal or complaint. Factors which the courts have taken into account in order to decide whether the circumstances are exceptional include: the speed of the appeal, whether it is convenient, whether the matter demands a particular or technical knowledge, and whether the alternative remedy is one which the claimant could first be expected to use, e.g. the delay in instituting disciplinary charges against police officers was such a serious breach of police regulations that the officers need not first exercise a right of appeal to the Secretary of State (*R v Chief Constable of Merseyside Police, ex parte Calveley* [1986] QB 424). Gross procedural unfairness in an appeal may be regarded as an exceptional case, so that it would be permissible to allow judicial review of an interim decision by an immigration judge, despite there being an alternative remedy available under the relevant legislation (*R (AM (Cameroon)) v Asylum and Immigration Tribunal* [2007] EWCA Civ 131, *The Times*, 11 April 2007). However, truly exceptional reasons must be given in order to bypass any statutory appeal procedure in favour of judicial review. Despite the apparent bias of a governing body which decided to exclude two pupils from school, any resulting unfairness could be remedied by the Independent Appeals Panel and any unfairness at an earlier stage in the proceedings was not so serious as to have contaminated an appeal (*R (A) v Kingsmead School Governors* [2002] EWCA Civ 1822, [2003] ELR 104.

Where there is an avenue for an appeal from an inferior court or tribunal to the Court of Appeal or High Court the claimant should appeal rather than seek a judicial review of the inferior court's decision in the Administrative Court. Where that avenue has been followed by the claimant and the appeal has been dismissed or the claimant has been refused permission to appeal, the claimant will not normally be permitted to re-litigate the same matter by way of judicial review, because that would be an abuse of the process of the court (see *R (Sivasubramaniam) v Wandsworth County Court* [2002] EWCA Civ 1738, [2003] 1 WLR 475). However, in exceptional cases, such as where the judicial process itself has been frustrated or corrupted and there has been a substantial denial of the right to a fair trial, judicial review may be permitted despite permission to appeal the decision of the lower court being refused (*Strickson v Preston County Court* [2007] EWCA Civ 1132, LTL 9/11/2007; see also 77.3). This may also be the case where the tribunal has acted outside its jurisdiction (*R (Rana) v Upper Tribunal (Immigration and Asylum Chamber)* [2010] EWHC 3558 (Admin), LTL 20/1/2011). However, only in the case of the clearest provision will a court conclude that judicial review is excluded (*Leech v Deputy Governor of Parkhurst Prison* [1988] AC 533).

PERMISSION TO PROCEED WITH A CLAIM FOR JUDICIAL REVIEW

Pre-action protocol

The **Pre-action Protocol for Judicial Review** sets out a code of good practice and contains the steps which the parties should generally follow before making a claim for judicial review. Litigants should also note the general **PD Pre-Action Conduct**, which applies to judicial review. 77.31

All claimants must consider whether they should follow the protocol, depending upon the circumstances of their case. Where the protocol applies, the court will normally expect all parties to comply with it and will take into account compliance or non-compliance when giving directions for case management proceedings or when making orders for costs (e.g. *Aegis Group plc v Commissioners of Inland Revenue* [2005] EWHC 1468 (Ch), [2006] STC 23; see also **PD Pre-action Conduct**). In planning or procurement cases where a shorter time limit applies (see 77.36), the parties should still attempt to comply with the protocol, but normal costs sanctions will not be applied where the court is satisfied that it has not been possible to comply because of the shorter time limits.

The protocol requires that, before making a claim, the claimant should send a letter to the defendant. The purpose of the letter is to identify the issues in dispute and establish whether litigation can be avoided. The letter should normally contain the details of any interested parties known to the claimant. A copy of the letter before claim should be sent to all interested parties for information. The defendant should normally respond within 14 days to the letter before claim. Failure to do so will be taken into account by the court and sanctions may be imposed unless there are good reasons. Public body defendants, including government departments with limited resources, are not exempt from the general rules on costs, and if a claimant sends an adequate letter of claim, it is unacceptable for a defendant not to give an adequate response. In particular, if the claimant then issues proceedings and seeks relief, there would be an expectation that the claimant would be entitled to costs (*R (Bahta) v Secretary of State for the Home Department* [2011] EWCA Civ 895, [2011] CP Rep 43).The response should be sent to all interested parties identified by the claimant and contain details of any other parties whom the defendant considers also have an interest.

One of the purposes of the protocol is to identify the extent to which the exchange of information can lead to the avoidance of litigation. The protocol includes consideration of alternative dispute resolution. This links with the recent approach of the Court of Appeal, which has stipulated that courts should ask parties to judicial review proceedings to explain what steps they have taken to resolve the dispute, and why a complaints procedure or some other form of alternative dispute resolution has not been used to resolve or reduce the issues in dispute (*R (Cowl) v Plymouth City Council* [2001] EWCA Civ 1935, [2002] 1 WLR 803; Practice Statement (Administrative Court: Administration of Justice) [2002] 1 WLR 810).

Test for permission

Permission to proceed with a claim for judicial review must be obtained from a High Court judge (usually one of the Queen's Bench Division who has been assigned to hear matters listed in the Administrative Court Office List) (**CPR, r. 54.4**; Senior Courts Act 1981, s. 31(3)). To grant permission the court has to be satisfied that: 77.32

(a) there is an arguable case for review;
(b) the claimant has a 'sufficient interest' (see 77.35); and
(c) there has not been 'undue delay' (see 77.36).

Traditionally the test for the grant of permission has been that a claimant must demonstrate to the court upon 'a quick perusal of the papers' that there is an arguable case for granting relief (*R v Inland Revenue Commissioners, ex parte National Federation of Self-Employed and Small Businesses Ltd* [1982] AC 617).

Permission should be granted if on the material available the court considers, without going into the matter in depth, that there is an arguable case for granting the relief claimed by the claimant. The Court of Appeal has held that the test to be applied in deciding whether to grant permission is whether the judge is satisfied that there is a case fit for further investigation at a full with-notice hearing of a substantive claim for judicial review (*R v Secretary of State for the Home Department, ex parte Begum* [1990] COD 107). However, some judges seem to apply more stringent criteria and require a claimant to demonstrate something approaching a reasonable prospect of success or a strong prima facie case.

The court will generally, in the first instance, consider the question of permission without a hearing (**PD 54A, para. 8.4**). In the event of a hearing, neither the defendant nor any other interested party need attend, unless the court directs otherwise (**PD 54A, para. 8.5**). If, for example, on considering the papers, the judge cannot decide whether there is an arguable case, he or she may invite the proposed defendant to attend the hearing of the permission application and make representations as to whether permission should be granted.

Permission will be refused where an application is frivolous, vexatious or hopeless; or a claim is made by 'busybodies with misguided or trivial complaints of administrative error' (*R v Inland Revenue Commissioners, ex parte National Federation of Self-Employed and Small Businesses Ltd* [1982] AC 617); or a claim is misconceived, unarguable or groundless. Rigorous examination by the judge is required at the permission stage of a judicial review claim so as to restrict the exploitation of judicial review as a commercial weapon by rival property developers (*R (Noble Organisation Ltd) v Thanet District Council* [2005] EWCA Civ 782, [2006] Env LR 8). Permission will also be refused if there is a more appropriate alternative procedure (see **77.30**); or a claim for judicial review is an inappropriate procedure, e.g. because the matter relates to private law and should therefore be commenced by way of a claim form under **CPR, Part 7**.

Procedure on an application for permission

77.33 A claim for judicial review may be commenced either at the Administrative Court Office at the Royal Courts of Justice in London or at one of the Regional Offices in Birmingham, Cardiff, Leeds and Manchester. Where the claim is in an excepted class as set out in **PD 54D, para. 3**, however, proceedings must be started in London. The excepted classes of claim are:

(1) proceedings to which **Part 76** or **Part 79** applies:
  (a) proceedings relating to control orders under **Part 76**;
  (b) financial restriction proceedings under **Part 79**;
  (c) proceedings relating to terrorism or allegations of terrorism; and
  (d) proceedings in which a special advocate is, or is to be, instructed;
(2) proceedings to which RSC, ord. 115 in **CPR, sch. 1**, applies;
(3) proceedings under the Proceeds of Crime Act 2002;
(4) appeals to the Administrative Court under the Extradition Act 2003;
(5) proceedings which must be heard by a Divisional Court; and
(6) proceedings relating to the discipline of solicitors.

The following documents must be filed when seeking permission to proceed with a claim for judicial review:

(a) a claim form (form N461);
(b) *written evidence in support* of the claim;
(c) a copy of any order that the claimant seeks to have quashed;
(d) where the claim for judicial review relates to a decision of a court or tribunal, an approved copy of the reasons for reaching that decision;

(e) copies of any documents on which the claimant proposes to rely;
(f) copies of any relevant statutory material; and
(g) a list of essential documents for advance reading by the court.

Where it is not possible to file all of these documents, the claimant must indicate which documents have not been filed and the reasons why they are not currently available (**PD 54A, para. 5.8**). The claim form should set out a detailed statement of the claimant's grounds for bringing the claim and the facts which the claimant will seek to rely on (**PD 54A, para. 5.6**). It should state the claimant's name and description, the relief sought and the grounds on which it is sought, the name and address of the claimant's solicitor (if any) and the claimant's address for service. The claim form must also include or be accompanied by any application to extend the time limit for filing the claim form and any application for directions (**PD 54A, para. 5.6**). The claim form must also state the name and address of any person the claimant considers to be an interested party, that the claimant is requesting permission to proceed with a claim for judicial review, and any remedy (including any interim remedy) sought (**CPR, r. 54.6(1)**). Where the claimant seeks to raise any issue under the **Human Rights Act 1998**, or seeks any remedy available under that Act, the claim form must include the information required by **PD 16, para. 15** (**PD 54A, para. 5.3**). Where the claimant intends to raise a devolution issue, the claim form must specify that the claimant wishes to raise a devolution issue and identify the relevant provisions of the Government of Wales Act 2006, the Northern Ireland Act 1998 or the Scotland Act 1998, and contain a summary of the facts, circumstances and points of law on the basis of which it is alleged that a devolution issue arises (**PD 54A, para. 5.4**).

The written evidence to be filed with the claim form will generally be in witness-statement form. The evidence in support must verify the facts relied upon in support of the application, establish a sufficient interest by the claimant in the subject matter of the claim, exhibit a copy of the decision challenged and make full and frank disclosure of all relevant facts, even those not in the claimant's favour. The witness statement should ideally be signed by someone having first-hand personal knowledge of the facts. If permission is obtained upon the basis of false statements or the suppression of material facts, the court may set aside permission or refuse the relief sought at the substantive hearing (*R v Kensington Income Tax Commissioners, ex parte Princess Edmond de Polignac* [1917] 1 KB 486; *R v Jockey Club Licensing Committee, ex parte Wright* [1991] COD 306). On filing a claim form for judicial review, the claimant's solicitor must also lodge two copies of a paginated indexed bundle containing all the documents referred to above (**PD 54A, para. 5.9**) and a further bundle of the relevant legislative provisions and statutory instruments required for the proper consideration of the application (Practice Direction (Crown Office List: Legislation Bundle) [1997] 1 WLR 52).

Urgent cases procedure

The Administrative Court has issued guidance on the procedure to be followed for cases which are urgent or which include applications for interim injunctions in Practice Statement (Administrative Court: Listing and Urgent Cases) [2002] 1 WLR 810. **77.34**

A claimant seeking urgent consideration must complete form N463 stating the reasons for urgency, the proposed timescale for consideration of the permission application, and the date by which the full hearing of the merits should take place if permission is granted. A claimant who applies for an interim injunction must also provide a draft order and a statement of the grounds on which the injunction is sought. The application must be served by fax and post, along with the claim form, on the defendant and interested parties. The defendant and interested parties must be advised that they may make representations on the application.

Each day a judge will act as the 'urgent judge' to hear urgent applications on that day. A judge will consider the application within the time requested, and may order that an oral hearing should take place. The judge will then make such order as is appropriate.

Standing of the claimant

77.35 Section 31(3) of the Senior Courts Act 1981 provides that the court will not grant permission to proceed with a claim for judicial review 'unless it considers that the [claimant] has a sufficient interest in the matter to which the [claim] relates'.

The phrase 'sufficient interest' has been given a wide interpretation by the courts. They will assess the extent of the claimant's interest against the factual and legal circumstances of the claim. The test for deciding whether a claimant has sufficient interest was considered by the House of Lords in *R v Inland Revenue Commissioners, ex parte National Federation of Self-Employed and Small Businesses Ltd* [1982] AC 617. The court held that not only was standing a ground in itself upon which permission could be refused, it should also be considered at the substantive hearing after the relevant law and facts were examined in full. The court added that there are different tests for standing at the permission and the substantive stages. At the former stage it is merely a 'threshold' question for the court, designed to weed out frivolous or vexatious cases. However, at the substantive hearing the claimant must be able to show a strong case on the merits, judged in relation to the claimant's own concern with the subject matter of the claim (*R v Monopolies and Mergers Commission, ex parte Argyll Group plc* [1986] 1 WLR 763).

Since *R v Inland Revenue Commissioners, ex parte National Federation of Self-Employed and Small Businesses Ltd*, the courts have adopted a broad and flexible approach to this test. The more important the issue and the stronger the merits of the claim, the more ready will the courts be to grant permission, notwithstanding the limited personal involvement of the claimant. Standing will normally extend to individuals affected by the decision or action in question, e.g. a person threatened with deportation, or an individual with a direct financial or legal interest. For example, an elector and taxpayer was deemed to have sufficient standing to claim that a government undertaking to pay a contribution to the European Community was *ultra vires* (*R v Her Majesty's Treasury, ex parte Smedley* [1985] QB 657). Similarly a taxpayer was permitted to challenge a decision of the Inland Revenue on its method of valuation of a rival company's profits (*R v Attorney-General, ex parte Imperial Chemical Industries plc* [1987] 1 CMLR 72). An owner of land within the green belt in the vicinity of a proposed development had sufficient standing, even though not directly affected by the development (*R v Selby District Council, ex parte Samuel Smith Old Breweries* [2001] PLCR 6). Similarly, an inhabitant of Rugby (although temporarily homeless at the time) had standing to challenge the grant of a permit to a cement company with a plant near Rugby town centre because as an inhabitant he would be affected by any adverse impact on the environment (*R (Edwards) v Environment Agency* [2004] EWHC 736 (Admin), [2004] 3 All ER 21). It was not necessary for him to have been active in a campaign on the issue to have an interest. A Palestinian living in the Occupied Territories had sufficient interest to bring judicial review proceedings in relation to the Secretary of State's decision to grant licences for the export of military items to Israel (*Hasan v Secretary of State for Trade and Industry* [2007] EWHC 2630 (Admin), [2008] ACD 10).

Even where a claimant had been active in a matter, appearing as an objector at a public inquiry, where the compulsory purchase orders in question raised no issue as to any right or interest of the claimant, and where the orders did not deprive the claimant of anything, his application could not succeed as the court's role was to decide disputes between parties and not to pronounce on hypothetical questions, however interesting, where there was no dispute to be resolved (*R (Murley) v Secretary of State for Transport* [2005] EWHC 2324 (Admin), LTL 10/1/2006).

The members of a victim's family had no standing to bring a challenge to a decision by the Lord Chief Justice on the appropriate tariff of a juvenile detainee (*R (Bulger) v Secretary of State for the Home Department* [2001] EWHC 119 (Admin), [2001] 3 All ER 449).

Standing also extends to representative groups. For example, the Child Poverty Action Group was held to have standing sufficient to commence proceedings relating to the interpretation of social security legislation (*R v Secretary of State for Social Services, ex parte Child Poverty Action Group* [1990] 2 QB 540); the Law Society in a challenge to the Lord Chancellor's cuts to legal aid eligibility (*R v Lord Chancellor, ex parte Law Society (No. 2)* (1994) 6 Admin LR 833); the Royal College of Nursing in a challenge to a government circular advising on abortion-related work for nurses (*Royal College of Nursing of the United Kingdom v Department of Health and Social Security* [1981] AC 800); and the National Union of Mineworkers in relation to the reduction of supplementary benefits to striking workers (*R v Chief Adjudication Officer, ex parte Bland* (1985) *The Times*, 6 February 1985).

Pressure groups acting in the public interest have also been granted standing. For example, Greenpeace were held to have sufficient interest to seek judicial review of the Inspectorate of Pollution's decision to vary authorisations for the discharge of radioactive waste from Sellafield (*R v Inspectorate of Pollution, ex parte Greenpeace Ltd* [1994] 1 WLR 570). The judge was influenced by the fact that, if the claim failed on its merits, the persons whom Greenpeace represented might not have an effective way to bring these issues before the court. He held that the issue of whether an interest group or other representative body had sufficient standing should be decided on the facts of each individual case as a matter of discretion. The World Development Movement was held to have standing to challenge a decision of the Foreign Secretary to use overseas aid money to fund the Pergau Dam project in Malaysia (*R v Secretary of State for Foreign and Commonwealth Affairs, ex parte World Development Movement Ltd* [1995] 1 WLR 386). The Divisional Court took into account factors such as the importance of the issue raised, the likely absence of any other responsible challenger, and the prominent role of the claimants in giving advice on overseas aid. However, a company set up specifically to save a theatre did not have sufficient standing to challenge the Secretary of State's refusal to list the theatre site as an ancient monument (*R v Secretary of State for the Environment, ex parte Rose Theatre Trust Co.* [1990] 1 QB 504).

It would be misconceived at the permission stage to elevate the question of standing 'above the elementary level of excluding busybodies and troublemakers and to demand something akin to a special private interest in the subject matter' (*R v Somerset County Council, ex parte Dixon* [1997] COD 323). There is no authority for the proposition that a court is compelled to refuse permission where the interest of the claimant is shared with the generality of the public.

The 'sufficient interest' standing test differs from the test under the **Human Rights Act 1998**, which provides that the claimant must be a 'victim' of the alleged violation of the Convention: that is, the claimant must have a personal interest in the claim (**Human Rights Act 1998, s. 7(1)**). **Section 7(3)** of the Act makes clear that it is the victim test which must prevail in human rights judicial review proceedings. This excludes judicial review challenges by representative bodies or pressure groups on human rights issues which are of general, rather than individual, importance.

Requirement for prompt commencement

In a claim for judicial review the claim form must normally be filed promptly, and in any event not later than three months after the grounds to make the claim first arose (**CPR, r. 54.5(1)**). However, the deadline is shortened to six weeks from the date on which the grounds arose in judicial reviews relating to a decision under the Town and Country Planning Act 1990, the Planning (Listed Buildings and Conservation Areas) Act 1990, the Planning (Hazardous Substances) Act 1990 and the Planning (Consequential Provisions) Act 1990, and to 30 days from the date on which the claimant first knew or ought to have known that grounds had arisen in relation to a decision governed by the Public Contracts Regulations 2006 (SI 2006/5) (**CPR, r. 54.5(5)** and **(6)**). These shorter deadlines are intended to bring judicial review into line with the timescales for bringing statutory challenges to planning and procurement decisions. See also below for the different position in relation to EU claims. **77.36**

The time limit may not be extended by agreement between the parties (**r. 54.5(2)**). Where the High Court considers that there has been undue delay in making a claim for judicial review, the court may refuse to grant permission or any relief sought in the claim if it considers that the grant of the relief sought would be 'likely to cause substantial hardship to, or substantially prejudice the rights of, any person or would be detrimental to good administration' (Senior Courts Act 1981, s. 31(6)). Time taken to comply with the **Pre-action Protocol for Judicial Review** is not a good excuse for failing to issue judicial review proceedings promptly (see Introduction to the protocol and footnote 1).

The wide discretion granted to the courts in relation to the grant or refusal of relief is restricted by the Senior Courts Act 1981, s. 31(7), and by **CPR, r. 54.5(3)**, which provide that s. 31(6) and **r. 54.5(1)** are without prejudice to any other statutory provisions which have the effect of limiting the time within which a claim for judicial review must be made.

Section 7(5) of the **Human Rights Act 1998** introduces a general time limit of one year for proceedings based upon a Convention right. However, this time limit is expressly stated to be without prejudice to stricter time limits, such as those that usually apply in judicial review proceedings.

A claim form filed after the time limit set by **CPR, r. 54.5(1)**, must be accompanied by an application to extend the limit (**PD 54A, para. 5.6**).

A claimant seeking judicial review must file the claim form promptly and is not necessarily entitled to wait up to three months before commencing proceedings. In certain situations the utmost promptitude is expected, particularly where third parties may be adversely affected by the overturning of a decision, e.g. *R v Independent Television Commission, ex parte TVNi* [1996] JR 60. It has also been held that the importance of acting promptly applies with particular force in cases where it is sought to challenge a planning permission, and this is not affected by the sending of a pre-action protocol letter. Therefore where there was no explanation for why proceedings had not been issued until the end of the three-month period the claim was not brought promptly (*Finn-Kelcey v Milton Keynes Borough Council* [2008] EWCA Civ 1067, [2009] Env LR 17). Grounds for a judicial review application in respect of a planning permission first arise for the purposes of **CPR, r. 54.5(1)**, from the date of the grant of permission, not from the earlier date when the planning committee passed a resolution authorising one of the authority's officers to grant outline permission on fulfilment of conditions precedent (*R (Burkett) v Hammersmith and Fulham London Borough Council* [2002] UKHL 23, [2002] 1 WLR 1593). Permission may be granted where a challenged decision was made in circumstances where the claimant for judicial review did not know of its susceptibility to challenge until long after the interveners had incurred most or all of the expense and effort upon which they relied to establish the prejudice in opposition to the grant of permission (*R v Licensing Authority, ex parte Novartis Pharmaceuticals Ltd* [2000] COD 232).

A claimant who has failed to bring proceedings within the time limit may apply to the court for an extension (under **CPR, r. 3.1(2)(a)**) of the time limit for filing the claim form. The onus is on the claimant to show that there is a good reason for extending time for applying for judicial review (*R v Warwickshire County Council, ex parte Collymore* [1995] ELR 217). Examples of 'good reasons' which have been accepted include:

(a) the claimant's lack of knowledge (it has been held that delay is no bar to relief when material matters were not known to the claimant until a later point in time, e.g. *R v Department of Transport, ex parte Presvac Engineering Ltd* (1992) 4 Admin LR 121);
(b) sensible and reasonable behaviour by the claimant which has caused no prejudice (*R v Commissioner for Local Administration, ex parte Croydon London Borough Council* [1989] 1 All ER 1033);
(c) exhaustion of all alternative remedies by the claimant prior to commencing proceedings (e.g. *R v Rochdale Metropolitan Borough Council, ex parte Cromer Ring Mill Ltd* [1982] 3 All ER 761);
(d) delay by the claimant in securing legal aid — provided that the application for legal aid has been expeditiously pursued on the part of the claimant (e.g. *R v Stratford-on-Avon District Council, ex parte Jackson* [1985] 1 WLR 1319);

(e) issues in the public interest (*R v Secretary of State for the Home Department, ex parte Ruddock* [1987] 1 WLR 1482, which concerned the challenge by a member of CND of the defendant's decision to tap her telephone; *R v Secretary of State for Trade and Industry, ex parte Greenpeace Ltd* [2000] 2 CMLR 94, which related to the incomplete and unlawful implementation by the United Kingdom of an EC Directive and the defendant's legally erroneous approach to the Directive);
(f) ongoing negotiations between the parties (*R v Greenwich London Borough Council, ex parte Patterson* (1994) 26 HLR 159);
(g) poor legal advice — courts have in particular sought to protect the interests of individual claimants in housing and immigration cases where it may not be possible to compensate the claimant by way of a damages award (e.g. *R v Secretary of State for the Home Department, ex parte Oyeleye* [1994] Imm AR 268);
(h) in certain circumstances, awaiting the decision of the Secretary of State on whether to call in a grant of planning permission (*R (Burkett) v Hammersmith and Fulham London Borough Council* [2002] UKHL 23, [2002] 1 WLR 1593).

An extension of time has been granted in circumstances where the claim was in substance the same as an earlier discontinued claim that had been brought for the benefit of a wider group (*R (SDR) v Bristol City Council* [2012] EWHC 859 (Admin), LTL 5/4/2012). However, the grant of an extension of time involves an exercise of discretion on the part of the court and there is no guarantee that an extension will be given in any particular case.

The courts have not been persuaded by arguments for an extension of time in circumstances where: there is a risk of prejudice to third parties (e.g. *R v Independent Television Commission, ex parte TVNi* [1996] JR 60); an extension of time would adversely affect market dealings which have been undertaken in good faith (*R v Independent Television, ex parte TVNi*); an intention had been expressed by the claimant to bring proceedings but a significant period of time elapsed before anything was done (*R v Independent Television Commission, ex parte White Rose Television Ltd* (unreported, 24 January 1992)).

Where an issue of EU law is involved, only the three-month limit applies and the additional requirement for promptness does not apply, because it does not meet the criteria of certainty and effectiveness which must be met when transposing EU Directives (*R (Buglife) v Medway Council* [2011] EWHC 746 (Admin), [2011] Env LR 27, applying *Uniplex (UK) Ltd v NHS Business Services Authority* (case C-406/08) [2010] PTSR 1377; see also *R (U and Partners (East Anglia) Ltd) v Broads Authority* [2011] EWHC 1824 (Admin), [2011] JPL 1583 and *R (Berky) v Newport City Council* [2012] EWCA Civ 378, [2012] 2 CMLR 44).

As to compatibility of the judicial review time limit with the Human Rights Act 1998 see **91.42**. The claim form must be served on the defendant and any person the claimant considers to be an interested party (unless the court directs otherwise) within seven days after the date of issue (**CPR, r. 54.7**). Where the claim for judicial review relates to proceedings in a court or tribunal, any other parties to those proceedings must be named in the claim form as interested parties and therefore served with the claim form (**PD 54A, para. 5.1**).

Acknowledgment of service

Any person who has been served with a claim form commencing proceedings for judicial review and who wishes to take part in the proceedings must file an acknowledgment of service (form N462) (**CPR, r. 54.8(1)**). The acknowledgment of service must be filed not more than 21 days after service of the claim form and must be served on the claimant and any other person named in the claim form as soon as practicable and, in any event, not later than seven days after it is filed (**r. 54.8(2)**). These time limits may not be extended by agreement between the parties (**r. 54.8(3)**). **77.37**

If the intention is to contest the claim, the acknowledgment of service must set out a summary of the grounds for doing so, and must also state the name and address of any person whom the person filing the acknowledgment considers to be an interested party (**r. 54.8(4)**). The acknowledgment of service may also include or be accompanied by an application for directions. A defendant who succeeds at the substantive hearing is in principle entitled to recover the costs of submitting an acknowledgment of service (*R (Leach) v Local Commissioner for Administration* [2001] EWHC 455 (Admin), [2001] CP Rep 97).

A person served with a judicial review claim form who does not acknowledge service in accordance with **r. 54.8** may not, without the court's permission, take part in the hearing to decide whether permission to proceed should be given (**r. 54.9(1)(a)**). However, if the person complies with **r. 54.14** (filing and service of a response by the defendant or any other person served with the claim form) or any other direction of the court regarding filing and service of detailed grounds for contesting the claim or supporting it on additional grounds, and any written evidence, he may take part in the judicial review hearing (**r. 54.9(1)(b)**).

Where a person takes part in the judicial review hearing, the court may take his failure to file an acknowledgment of service into account when deciding what order to make about costs (**r. 54.9(2)**).

Under the rules on non-party access to documents in **Part 5**, a non-party to judicial review has a right to have sight of the claim form, acknowledgment of service and detailed grounds, the latter falling within the CPR definition of defence (*R (Corner House Research) v Director of the Serious Fraud Office* [2008] EWHC 246 (Admin), [2008] ACD 63).

Relevant considerations in deciding whether or not to grant permission

77.38 If the court considers that there has been undue delay in claiming judicial review, permission to proceed with the claim, or relief at the substantive hearing, may be refused if it would be likely to lead to substantial hardship or prejudice or detriment to good administration (Senior Courts Act 1981, s. 31(6)). For example, in *R v Secretary of State for Health, ex parte Furneaux* [1994] 2 All ER 652 relief was refused because of prejudice to a rival pharmacy, but in other cases with serious consequences for a party or third party, relief has not been refused, e.g. in *R v Port Talbot Borough Council, ex parte Jones* [1988] 2 All ER 207 the grant of relief required the defendant to leave her home, and in *R v Secretary of State for the Environment, ex parte Chichester District Council* [1993] 2 PLR 1 relief caused a third party to face criminal proceedings.

In *R v Dairy Produce Quota Tribunal, ex parte Caswell* [1990] 2 AC 738 the House of Lords held that matters of particular importance in determining whether or not there is detriment to good administration, apart from the length of time itself, will be the extent of the effect of the relevant decision, and the impact which would be felt if it were to be reopened. Section 31(6) of the Senior Courts Act 1981 requires affirmative evidence of detriment, i.e. the foreseen consequences of granting the relief sought must be positive harm to good administration, or at least evidence from which it can properly be inferred, and in considering detriment the court can take into account the effect on other potential claimants and the consequences if their claims were successful.

The effect of *R v Criminal Injuries Compensation Board, ex parte A* [1998] QB 659 (CA), [1999] 2 AC 330 (HL), is that permission to proceed and the substantive hearing should be regarded as two distinct stages. Permission should not be granted if:

(a) the claim form for judicial review was not filed promptly and in any event within three months and there is no good reason to extend time (**CPR, rr. 3.1(2)(a) and 54.5(1)**); or
(b) relief would be likely to cause substantial hardship, substantial prejudice or detriment to good administration (Senior Courts Act 1981, s. 31(6)).

At the substantive hearing delay may again be considered but the defendant will be permitted to recanvass an issue of promptness which was decided at the permission stage in the claimant's favour only if any of the following conditions are satisfied:

(a) if the judge hearing the original application expressly so indicated;
(b) if new and relevant material was introduced at the substantive hearing;

(c) if, exceptionally, the issues as they had developed at the full hearing put a different aspect on the question of promptness; or
(d) if the first judge had plainly overlooked some relevant matter or otherwise reached a decision per incuriam.

See *R (Lichfield Securities Ltd) v Lichfield District Council* [2001] EWCA Civ 304, 3 LGLR 35.

It has been held that there is nothing in EU law which prevents the court from applying the Senior Courts Act 1981, s. 31(6), even in the case of an alleged breach of EU law by the defendant (*R v North West Leicestershire District Council, ex parte Moses* [2000] Env LR 443). Only in exceptional circumstances will the court entertain a judicial review claim that has become purely academic by the withdrawal of the original decision by the public body. Such circumstances may arise where there are allegations of bad faith (*R (K) v Entry Clearance Officer, Tashkent* [2012] EWHC 2875 (Admin), LTL 5/10/2012).

Amendment of application for permission

A judicial review claim form may be amended in accordance with the general principles of CPR, Part 17, discussed in **chapter 31**. In general, amendments will be allowed for the purpose of putting the claimant's case fully before the court, provided that the defendant is not unfairly prejudiced as a result. **77.39**

Commentary

DETERMINATION OF THE APPLICATION FOR PERMISSION

Once a judicial review claim form and supporting evidence have been filed, the general rule is that, in the first instance, the court will consider the question of permission to proceed with the claim without a hearing (**PD 54A, para. 8.4**). Where this rule applies, the papers are passed to a judge to read and to make a decision without hearing oral arguments. **77.40**

If permission to proceed is given, the court may also give directions (**CPR, r. 54.10(1)**), which may include a stay of proceedings to which the claim relates (**r. 54.10(2)**).

The court may give permission to proceed subject to conditions, or on certain grounds only (**r. 54.12(1)**). This was not possible before the CPR (*R v Criminal Injuries Compensation Board, ex parte A* [1998] QB 659).

The court will serve its order giving or refusing permission to proceed with a claim for judicial review, and any directions, on the parties and any other person who filed an acknowledgment of service (**r. 54.11**). The order will be accompanied by the court's reasons if it refuses permission or gives permission to proceed either subject to conditions or on certain grounds only (**r. 54.12(2)**).

The claimant may not appeal against a refusal of permission to proceed, or against permission given subject to conditions or on certain grounds only, but may normally request that the decision be reconsidered at a hearing (**r. 54.12(3)**). However, where the court considers the application to be 'totally without merit' on the papers, a request for oral reconsideration will not be entertained (**r. 54.12(7)**). A request for reconsideration of a decision must be filed within seven days after service of the court's reasons for the decision (**r. 54.12(4)**). The parties and any other person who has filed an acknowledgment of service will be given at least two days' notice of the hearing date (**r. 54.12(5)**).

Neither the defendant nor any other person served with the claim form may apply to set aside an order giving permission to proceed with a claim for judicial review (**r. 54.13**).

If, contrary to the general rule, the court, in its discretion, decides that there should be an oral hearing of an application for permission to proceed with a claim for judicial review, the Administrative Court Office will fix a hearing date without any intervening consideration of the papers. The application is made to a judge in open court unless the court directs that it should be made in private or to a Divisional Court. The defendant and other interested parties are not required to attend, unless the court directs otherwise (**PD 54A, para. 8.5**). If the defendant or any other party does attend, the court will not generally order the claimant to pay their costs of doing so (**para. 8.6**) (*R (Mount Cook Land Ltd) v Westminster City Council* [2003] EWCA Civ 1346, [2004] CP Rep 12; *Payne v Caerphilly County Borough Council* [2004] EWCA Civ 433, LTL 17/3/2004). In Practice Statement (Judicial Review: Costs) [2004] 2 All ER 994 it was confirmed that a grant of permission to pursue a claim for judicial review would be deemed to contain an order that costs of that application be costs in the case. A different costs order can be specifically made by the judge granting permission.

Normally no witnesses attend a permission hearing and the claimant is not required to be there in person. An application for permission to proceed with a claim for judicial review is listed on the basis that the application will take no more than 20 minutes, and any reply by a defendant who attends will take no more than 10 minutes (Practice Direction (Crown Office List) (No. 2) [1991] 1 WLR 280). If permission is granted, any applications for interim relief or special directions are considered. If permission is refused, the decision can be appealed to the Court of Appeal with that court's permission (**CPR, r. 52.15(1)**).

An appeal to the Court of Appeal after permission is refused in an oral application will be heard by a full Court of Appeal (rather than a single Lord Justice). An application for permission to appeal against the High Court's refusal to permit a claim for judicial review to proceed must be made within seven days of the High Court's decision (**r. 52.15(2)**). The appellant's notice must be accompanied by the documents specified in **PD 52C, para.** 3(3). A copy of it must be served on all respondents to the appeal in accordance with **CPR, r.** 52.4(3) (**PD 52C, paras** 3(1) and 7.2). Instead of granting permission to appeal, the Court of Appeal may proceed directly to give the permission to proceed with the claim which was initially sought (**CPR, r. 52.15(3)**) and the case will be returned to the High Court, unless the Court of Appeal orders otherwise (**r. 52.15(4)**; see *R (Werner) v Commissioners of Inland Revenue* [2002] EWCA Civ 979, [2002] STC 1213 at [30] to [33]). The Court of Appeal should be cautious about retaining the substantive proceedings (see *R (AA) v Secretary of State for the Home Department* [2012] EWCA Civ 23, *The Times*, 5 March 2012), but this would be appropriate where, for example, the High Court is bound by authority or, for some other reason, a further appeal to the Court of Appeal would be inevitable (**PD 52, para. 15.3**). If permission has been refused by the Court of Appeal, the court of first instance may, nevertheless, subsequently grant permission if there have been developments of which the Court of Appeal was unaware (*R v Radio Authority, ex parte Wildman* [1999] COD 255). If the Court of Appeal refuses permission there is generally no appeal or possibility of renewing the application to the Supreme Court (*Re Poh* [1983] 1 WLR 2; *R v Secretary of State for Trade and Industry, ex parte Eastaway* [2000] 1 WLR 2222). Where, however, the Court of Appeal grants permission to appeal but then refuses permission for judicial review (for example, on the grounds of delay), the Supreme Court has jurisdiction to grant permission to appeal against this decision (*R (Burkett) v Hammersmith and Fulham London Borough Council* [2002] UKHL 23, [2002] 1 WLR 1593).

A claimant who no longer requires any substantive relief but wishes the claim to go forward to test the lawfulness of the defendant's procedures in general must inform the defendant that he wishes the court to scrutinise the defendant's practices and procedures (*R (Tshikangu) v Newham London Borough Council* [2001] EWHC 92 (Admin), [2001] NPC 33). The parties should consider whether a test case is appropriate, and if so what that case should be. If they are not agreed, application should be made to the court for it to consider the matter before the costs of a substantive hearing are incurred.

PROCEDURE ONCE PERMISSION HAS BEEN GRANTED

Defendant's evidence and evidence in reply

77.41 If permission is given to proceed with a claim for judicial review, the order granting permission will be served on the defendant and any other person who filed an acknowledgment of service (**CPR, r. 54.11**). Any of those persons who wish to contest the claim, or to support it on additional grounds, must, within 35 days after service of the permission order, file and serve the detailed grounds for contesting or supporting and their written evidence (**r. 54.14(1)**). If it is intended to rely on documents not already filed, a paginated bundle of the new documents must be filed with the detailed grounds (**PD 54A, para. 10.1**). In judicial review proceedings, **CPR, r. 54.14(1)**, applies instead of **r. 8.5(3)** to **(6)** (**r. 54.14(2)**). The 35-day time limit can be extended or shortened on application to a master of the Administrative Court Office or a High Court judge (**r. 3.1(2)(a)**). The 35-day time limit applies both to written evidence and to detailed grounds for contesting the claim or supporting it on additional grounds (*R (J) v Newham London Borough Council* [2001] EWHC 992 (Admin), *The Independent*, 10 December 2001). Failure to serve within the time limit may be dealt with by the general discretion of the court to extend time, subject to the overriding objective. Any evidence in reply should include details of the facts which the defendant intends to rely upon, its answers to issues raised by the claimant, a response to the claimant's evidence, and should exhibit all documents relevant to the decision challenged which have not been exhibited with the claimant's evidence and which the defendant wishes to rely upon at the substantive hearing. The written evidence should also make clear if there is any factual conflict between the claimant and the defendant. The written evidence should be filed in the Administrative Court Office.

Permission to proceed with a judicial review claim is permission to proceed on specified grounds only. The claimant will not be able to rely on other grounds without further permission from the court (**r. 54.15**). Notice of intention to rely on additional grounds must be given to the court, and to any other person served with the claim form, no later than seven clear days before the hearing (or the warned date if one has been given) (**PD 54A, para. 11.1**). Where there is good reason to allow argument on an additional ground, permission should be granted. Each case should be considered on its facts. In exercising discretion, a judge should bear in mind that if permission to rely on a ground is refused, the Court of Appeal on an appeal from the hearing at first instance would not be able to consider it (*R (Smith) v Parole Board* [2003] EWCA Civ 1014, [2003] 1 WLR 2548). Cf. the approach in *Opoku v Principal of Southwark School* [2002] EWHC 2092 (Admin), [2003] 1 WLR 234).

The service of written evidence in reply by the claimant may be considered necessary where there is a factual dispute, where new circumstances have arisen since applying for permission to proceed, or in order to comment upon documents disclosed by the defendant.

Interim remedies

Although most forms of interim remedies are available in judicial review proceedings, obtaining interim remedies is more restricted than in private law actions. Generally the most appropriate time to apply for interim remedies is at the stage of applying for permission but a court may grant interim remedies to any of the parties during the course of judicial review proceedings. (If interim remedies are sought after the substantive application has been dismissed, pending appeal, it will be necessary to show that the appeal has a good prospect of success.) **77.42**

A claim form for judicial review must state any interim remedy which is claimed. In particular, it may ask for the court, when giving permission for the claim to proceed to direct (under **CPR, r. 54.10(2)**) a stay of proceedings to which the claim relates. A stay under **r. 54.10(2)** has the effect that the public body's decision or procedure which is the subject of challenge should not continue or take effect until the judicial review challenge is determined. In considering whether to grant a stay, the court will take into account the effect on third parties and may refuse a stay notwithstanding a grant of permission to proceed with the claim for judicial review, applying balance of convenience considerations. A stay is available as a remedy against all public bodies against whom permission has been granted, including the Crown in the form

Commentary

of a government department or minister (*R v Secretary of State for Education, ex parte Avon County Council* [1991] 1 QB 558). A cross-undertaking for damages to a party to the action may be made a condition of a stay (*R v Inspectorate of Pollution, ex parte Greenpeace Ltd* [1994] 1 WLR 570).

The court may also at any time grant in the proceedings interim remedies in accordance with **CPR, Part 25**. The general principles governing the grant of interim remedies apply also in relation to judicial review proceedings (*R v Ministry of Agriculture, Fisheries and Food, ex parte Monsanto plc* [1999] QB 1161). However, these have to be applied in the context of the public law questions raised in such proceedings (see **77.58**). **Rule 25.1** lists the interim remedies which include an interim injunction (**r. 25.1(1)(a)**), interim declaration (**r. 25.1(1)(b)**), freezing injunction (**r. 25.1(1)(f)**), search order (**r. 25.1(1)(h)**), and an order for the detention and inspection of relevant property (**r. 25.1(1)(c)**). Generally, notice of an application for an interim remedy should be given to all parties (**r. 25.3(1)**).

Injunctions are the main type of interim relief ordered in judicial review proceedings. To obtain an interim injunction in a civil case, it must be established that the claimant has a serious issue to be tried on the merits and that the 'balance of convenience' favours the making of an interim order (*American Cyanamid Co. v Ethicon Ltd* [1975] AC 396; see **chapter 37**). The balance of convenience test involves the court considering whether there is an adequate alternative remedy in damages, the interests of the general public to whom the duties are owed, the importance of upholding the law of the land, and the duty upon certain authorities to enforce the law in the public interest. There is a presumption in favour of a cross-undertaking in damages (**PD 25A, para. 5.1(1)**). The approach to applications for interim injunctions in judicial review proceedings is similar to that adopted in applications for interim injunctions in private law claims (*R v Kensington and Chelsea Royal London Borough Council, ex parte Hammell* [1989] QB 518). However, where public bodies are concerned the balance of convenience may be more difficult to make out — i.e. ordinary financial considerations may be qualified by recognition of the interests of the general public (*Smith v Inner London Education Authority* [1978] 1 All ER 411). Usually an application is for a prohibitory injunction to prevent a public body from doing something. Where a mandatory injunction is sought, the order will not be granted unless the court has a high degree of assurance of the merits of the case.

An interim injunction is available against a government minister but will only be granted in limited circumstances, i.e. where it is necessary for the court to have power to prevent irreparable harm to the citizen by unauthorised governmental action (*Re M* [1994] 1 AC 377). An interim injunction has been granted against a minister of the Crown to restrain him from implementing a new regime authorised by an Act of Parliament where there was a strong prima facie case that the Act was in breach of European Union law (*R v Secretary of State for Transport, ex parte Factortame Ltd (No. 2)* [1991] 1 AC 603). The Court of Justice of the European Union ruled that where a national court was seised of a case involving EU law issues and it was necessary to grant interim relief in order to ensure the full effectiveness of the rights claimed under directly applicable EU law, any rule of national law preventing the grant of such interim relief must be set aside. A reference to the Court of Justice of the European Union is required to establish whether domestic or EU law is applicable when a domestic court is asked to grant an injunction to restrain the government from making regulations during the implementation period pursuant to an EC Directive (*R v Secretary of State for Health, ex parte Imperial Tobacco Ltd* [2001] 1 WLR 127). EU law permits applications for an injunction in the domestic courts in support of an application to the domestic court challenging the validity of an EC Directive. In order to grant an injunction, serious doubts are required as to the validity of the EU measure and the need to avoid serious and irreparable damage (which is not purely financial) to the party seeking the injunction.

CPR, r. 25.1(1)(b), provides for the grant of an interim declaration. Prior to the introduction of the CPR the existence of such a remedy was uncertain. Interim declarations are granted on a similar basis to interim injunctions. The decision whether or not to grant an interim injunction or declaration is a matter of discretion for the court of first instance, with which the Court of Appeal will not interfere unless there is an error of law or plain error of fact or assessment. In deciding whether to grant an interim remedy, the court should have regard to the 'threshold condition' that legislation ought to be fulfilled in all but exceptional cases. Thereafter, considering the balance of convenience, the concurrent elements are the strength of the case and the parties' respective losses if the declaration were granted or refused (*R v Secretary of State for Trade and Industry, ex parte Trades Union Congress* [2000] IRLR 565). An interim declaration of unlawfulness has been granted in respect of arrangements for the control of pesticides made under regulations which were made by statutory instrument, pending determination by the Court of Justice of the European Union of a reference made in another case concerning interpretation of the Directive which the regulations were made to implement (*R v Ministry of Agriculture, Fisheries and Food, ex parte British Agrochemicals Association Ltd (No. 2)* [2000] 1 CMLR 826). However, the grant of an interim declaration to render national legislation inoperative pending the decision of the Court of Justice of the European Union will be rare, as there is a presumption in favour of the national law being applicable (*R v Secretary of State for Trade and Industry, ex parte Trades Union Congress* [2001] 1 CMLR 8).

Commentary

Interim applications

An interim application may be made to any judge or to a master of the Queen's Bench Division. However, a master or district judge outside of London may not grant most types of interim relief other than orders by consent (see **PD 2B, paras 2** and **3**) although he or she may deal with applications for interim procedural relief by case management. Where the application for judicial review is to be heard by a Divisional Court, any appeal from a decision of a master will lie to the Divisional Court itself. Contested interim applications are normally heard by a judge nominated to hear Administrative Court Office List cases. Uncontested interim applications are dealt with by the Administrative Court without the need for attendance (Practice Direction (Administrative Court: Uncontested Proceedings) [2008] 1 WLR 1377). **77.43**

CPR, Part 23, and **PD 23A** apply to interim applications in judicial review proceedings. **Part 23** requires that all applications are to be made by filing and serving an application notice (**r. 23.3(1)**). An application will not necessarily result in a hearing even if one is requested (**r. 23.8**).

Interim applications may have to be made seeking the exercise of the court's general powers of management under **r. 3.1(2)**, e.g. to extend or shorten the time for compliance with any rule, practice direction or court order (**r. 3.1(2)(a)**), consolidation in order that two or more matters be tried at the same time (**r. 3.1(2)(h)**), or to adjourn or expedite a hearing (**r. 3.1(2)(b)**).

Disclosure

The court has jurisdiction to order cross-examination of witnesses and disclosure in judicial review proceedings but the assumption is that disclosure is not required unless the court orders otherwise (**PD 54A, para. 12.1**). **77.44**

There is no automatic right to disclosure of documents in judicial review proceedings, but this is a context where there is already a separate duty of candour on the part of defendants who must set out fully what they did and why, so far as is necessary, fully and fairly to meet the challenge (*R v Lancashire County Council, ex parte Huddleston* [1986] 2 All ER 941). Disclosure will only be ordered where it is required to ensure the justice of the case and to dispose fairly of the matter (*R v Inland Revenue Commissioners, ex parte J. Rothschild Holdings plc* [1987] STC 163). The courts have held (Lord Scarman in *R v Inland Revenue Commissioners, ex parte National Federation of Self-Employed and Small Businesses Ltd* [1982] AC 617):

> Upon general principles, discovery should not be ordered unless or until the court is satisfied that the evidence reveals reasonable grounds for believing that there has been a breach of public

duty; and it should be limited strictly to documents relevant to the issue which emerges from the affidavits.

Where an application for judicial review involves a consideration of the proportionality of the defendant's actions, the disclosure of documents will be ordered more readily than in an application where no issues of proportionality arise. However, whether disclosure should be ordered will depend on the balancing of several factors, of which proportionality is only one, albeit a significant one. In cases where disclosure is ordered, it should always be carefully limited to the issues which require it in the interests of justice (*Tweed v Parades Commission* [2006] UKHL 53, [2007] 1 AC 650).

The courts will not permit the claimant to obtain disclosure to go behind an assertion in the defendant's written evidence and check its accuracy unless the claimant has some evidence that the contents are false or not accurate (*R v Secretary of State for the Environment, ex parte Islington London Borough Council* [1992] COD 67). Disclosure and inspection may also be withheld on the grounds of public interest immunity. However, the courts may come under particular pressure to order disclosure in **Human Rights Act 1998** cases, which may involve a factual examination of the merits of a case (see **chapter 91**). In *R (Al-Sweady) v Secretary of State for Defence* [2009] EWHC 2387 (Admin), [2010] HRLR 2, the High Court held that where the outcome of a judicial review application might depend upon the determination of a factual dispute, the court should give urgent consideration to ordering disclosure and cross-examination. It envisaged that such orders might occur with increasing regularity in cases involving crucial factual disputes relating to human rights issues.

The duty of candour should not be taken to impose an obligation of disclosure on a public body, particularly where no exercise of discretion is involved. The duty, and a requirement to produce information, applies to cases where it is not possible for the court to assess the merits of an issue unless the public authority provides the court with information which it alone can provide. It should not be used to transfer to the public authority the onus of proving matters which the claimant is under a duty and in a position to prove, such as the reasonableness or otherwise of the decision (*Marshall v Deputy Governor of Bermuda* [2010] UKPC 9, *The Times*, 7 June 2010).

There seems to be no reason in principle why the provisions for pre-action and non-party disclosure (see **50.84** to **50.96**) would not apply to judicial review proceedings but, in practice, it will be very difficult to obtain an order under those provisions in judicial review proceedings. Further, in the case of pre-action disclosure there is the practical issue for a potential claimant of needing to apply for permission to seek judicial review promptly and the timescale may make it impractical to seek pre-action disclosure first.

It is extremely difficult to obtain an order to provide clarification or further information in judicial review proceedings. Claimants who wish defendants to answer a request for further information should first serve them informally, requesting a response within a reasonable time, prior to making an application to the court (**PD 18, para. 1.1**).

Interested parties and interveners

77.45 A claimant seeking judicial review is under a duty to serve a copy of the claim form upon any person the claimant considers to be an interested party, unless the court directs otherwise (**CPR, r. 54.7**). 'Interested party' is defined as any person (other than the claimant and the defendant) who is directly affected by the claim (**r. 54.1(2)(f)**). The meaning of persons 'directly affected' was considered by the House of Lords in *R v Rent Officer Service, ex parte Muldoon* [1996] 1 WLR 1103. It was suggested (per Lord Keith of Kinkel at p. 1105), 'That a *person is directly affected by* something connotes that he is affected without the intervention of any intermediate agency'. The Secretary of State for Social Security was held to be only indirectly affected by a judicial review claim which challenged a failure to determine claims for housing benefit, as it was the local authority which would have to pay the claimants if the claim were successful. Similarly, the courts have refused to regard tobacco companies as 'directly affected' by a claim for judicial review of a refusal by the Legal Aid Board to grant the claimants legal aid to bring proceedings against the tobacco company (*R v Legal Aid Board, ex parte Megarry* [1994] COD 468).

The role of an interested party is restricted to making submissions in relation to the main claim and therefore there is jurisdiction for them to be heard only where they are directly affected by that main claim. There is no provision allowing an interested party to advance a different claim against the defendant, and a person who is not seeking the same relief as the claimant will not be directly affected by the claim and therefore cannot be heard as an interested party (*R (McVey) v Secretary of State for Health* [2010] EWHC 1225 (Admin), [2010] ACD 95).

Any person served with the claim form who wishes to take part in the judicial review must file an acknowledgment of service in accordance with **r. 54.8**. Failure to file an acknowledgment of service means that the permission of the court will be required to take part in a hearing to decide permission to proceed with the claim (**r. 54.9(1)(a)**).

An interested party who has not acknowledged service cannot take part in the substantive hearing without filing and serving detailed grounds for contesting the claim or supporting it on additional grounds, and any written evidence (**r. 54.9(1)(b)**).

Filing an acknowledgment of service entitles an interested party to be served with the court's order giving or refusing permission to proceed and any directions (**r. 54.11**). If the claimant requests that a refusal of permission be reconsidered at a hearing, any person who has filed an acknowledgment of service will be given at least two days' notice of the hearing (**r. 54.12(5)**). Any person served with the claim form may not apply to set aside an order giving permission to proceed (**r. 54.13**).

No interested party need attend a hearing on the question of permission to proceed unless the court directs otherwise (**PD 54A, para. 8.5**). Where the defendant or any other party does attend a hearing, the court will not generally make an order for costs against the claimant (**PD 54A, para. 8.6**).

Any person served with the claim form who wishes to contest the claim or support it on additional grounds must file and serve detailed grounds for contesting or supporting the claim and any written evidence within 35 days after service of the order giving permission to proceed (**CPR, r. 54.14(1)**).

Any person may apply for permission to file evidence or to make representations at the substantive judicial review hearing (**r. 54.17(1)**). Such an application must be made promptly (**r. 54.17(2)**) since it will usually be essential not to delay the hearing (**PD 54A, para. 13.5**). An application for permission to file evidence or make representations at the hearing of the judicial review claim should be made by letter to the Administrative Court Office, identifying the claim, explaining who the applicant is and indicating why and in what form the applicant wants to participate in the hearing (**PD 54A, para. 13.3**). If the applicant is seeking a prospective order as to costs, the letter should say what kind of order and on what grounds (**PD 54A, para. 13.4**). Where all the parties consent, the court may deal with such an application without a hearing (**PD 54A, para. 13.1**). Where the court gives permission for a person to file evidence or make representations at the substantive hearing, it may do so on conditions and may give case management directions (**PD 54A, para. 13.2**).

There is no general right for a third party to be heard on appeal, although the Court of Appeal may exercise its discretion to permit this.

The court will rarely grant two sets of costs in judicial review proceedings to two parties who appear in the same interest (*R v Industrial Disputes Tribunal, ex parte American Express Co. Inc.* [1954]

Commentary

1 WLR 1118; *Bolton Metropolitan District Council v Secretary of State for the Environment* [1995] 1 WLR 1176). However, in exceptional circumstances the court may grant two sets of costs, e.g. where the issues are complex or important or the interests of the two parties concerned are divergent (*R v Registrar of Companies, ex parte Central Bank of India* [1986] QB 1114).

SUBSTANTIVE HEARING

Listing the hearing

77.46 The court may decide a claim for judicial review without a hearing if all the parties agree (**CPR, r. 54.18**). The effect of this rule is that once permission has been granted for judicial review the claim can only be substantively disposed of by an oral hearing, unless all parties agree. It is not possible to deal with the matter in any other way (*R (Parsipoor) v Secretary of State for the Home Department* [2011] EWCA Civ 276, [2011] 1 WLR 3187). If the parties agree about the final order to be made in a claim for judicial review, the claimant must file at the court two copies of a document signed by all the parties setting out the terms of the proposed agreed order, together with a short statement of the matters relied upon as justifying the proposal and copies of any authorities or statutory provisions relied on (**PD 54A, para. 17.1**). The court will consider the documents and will make the order if satisfied that the order should be made (**para. 17.2**). If the court is not satisfied that the order should be made, a hearing date will be set (**para. 17.3**). Where the agreement relates to an order for costs only, the parties need only file a document signed by all the parties setting out the terms of the proposed order (**para. 17.4**). Where a claim is entered for hearing it must be entered in the Administrative Court Office List in accordance with Practice Direction (Crown Office List) [1987] 1 WLR 232. All applications for judicial review are included within the Administrative Court Office List which is divided into five parts. These are:

Part A: cases not ready to be heard, i.e. permission has not yet been obtained or the time limits for the filing of evidence have not yet expired.

Part B: cases ready to be heard, i.e. the warned list. All applications are entered in Part B once all relevant time limits have expired, i.e. usually after the 35-day period for service of the defendant's written evidence has ended. When a case enters Part B the claimant or the claimant's solicitors will be informed of this by letter and must duly inform their counsel, the defendant and any other interested parties of the likelihood of the case being listed at short notice. Applications for adjournments will be granted only in exceptional circumstances (Practice Direction (Crown Office List: Preparation for Hearings) [2000] 2 All ER 896).

Part C: cases stood out, i.e. where a case appears in Part B or Part E and any party is not ready to be heard, the case may be stood out of the list into Part C upon application to the master of the court office, and may be appealed to a judge or the Divisional Court by a court application.

Part D: the expedited list, i.e. cases listed to be heard as soon as practicable. An application to be entered in Part D should initially be made to the master of the Administrative Court Office, and may be appealed to a Divisional Court or judge by a court application.

Part E: cases listed for hearing, i.e. cases where a date for the substantive hearing has been fixed. When a case is about to be listed under Part E, the Administrative Court Office will send a letter to the claimant's solicitors asking them to confirm that the case is still active and informing them that it will be listed shortly. If the claimant does not confirm within two weeks that the case is still active, the case may be put before the court and struck out for want of prosecution. The listing policy of the Administrative Court in fixing substantive hearings, the operation of the short warned list and vacating fixtures is set out in Practice Statement (Administrative Court: Listing and Urgent Cases) [2002] 1 WLR 810.

Documentation

Skeleton arguments are mandatory in all cases in the Administrative Court Office List. The claimant's counsel is required to file a skeleton argument with the Administrative Court Office and serve a copy on counsel for the defendant at least 21 working days before the date of the hearing or warned date (**PD 54A, para. 15.1**). The defendant and any other party wishing to make representations at the substantive hearing must file and serve a skeleton argument not less than 14 working days before the date of the hearing or the warned date (**para. 15.2**). If the application is to be heard by a Divisional Court, two copies of the skeleton argument must be lodged. The skeleton arguments may be supplemented up to one working day before the hearing (Practice Direction (Crown Office List: Preparation for Hearings) [1994] 1 WLR 1551). The skeleton arguments must quote the Administrative Court Office reference number and the warned/fixed date, provide a time estimate for the complete hearing (including delivery of judgment), and must also contain a list of issues, a list of the legal points to be taken (together with any relevant authorities with page references to the passages relied on), a chronology of events (with page references to the bundle of documents to be filed), a list of essential documents for the advance reading of the court (with page references to the passages relied on) (if different to that filed with the claim form), a time estimate for that reading, and a list of persons referred to (**PD 54A, para. 15.3**). Time estimates will be required from each party once the application is entered in Part B of the List. Great care must be taken by counsel to provide a well-judged and realistic time estimate for the hearing (Practice Direction (Crown Office List: Estimated Length of Hearing) [1987] 1 All ER 1184). The obligations upon counsel in the practice directions apply equally to a solicitor advocate. **77.47**

For the use of extracts from *Hansard* under the rule in *Pepper v Hart* [1993] AC 593 see the guidance at 74.52. Where this is permitted, the party must serve upon all other parties and the Administrative Court Office the relevant extract together with a brief summary of the argument based on the extract at least five working days before the hearing (Practice Direction (*Hansard*: Citation) [1995] 1 WLR 192).

The claimant's solicitor is responsible for preparing a paginated and indexed bundle of documents which must be lodged in the Administrative Court Office at the same time as the skeleton argument is filed (**PD 54A, para. 16.1**). The bundle must also include documents required by the defendant and any other party who is to make representations at the hearing (**para. 16.2**). If the claim is to be heard by a Divisional Court, two copies of each bundle must be lodged. The bundles must contain copies of the claim form, the decision complained of (if not separately exhibited), any relevant correspondence between the parties and any orders made in the course of the proceedings, and the written evidence filed by both parties. Where possible, the parties' solicitors should agree the contents of the bundles.

If the obligation to lodge a proper bundle is not complied with, the application for judicial review may be struck out and the costs imposed upon the claimant or the claimant's solicitor (*R v Home Secretary, ex parte Meyer-Wulff* [1986] Imm AR 253).

Oral evidence

In judicial review proceedings the Administrative Court may, either under **CPR, r. 32.1**, or its inherent jurisdiction, hear oral evidence and order the cross-examination of witnesses (*R (G) v Ealing London Borough Council* [2002] EWHC 250 (Admin), [2002] ACD 48). In practice, the courts very rarely allow cross-examination in judicial review cases on the basis that it is not usually required in the interests of justice (*Khera v Secretary of State for the Home Department* [1984] AC 74; *George v Secretary of State for the Environment* (1979) 77 LGR 689). Generally, applications to cross-examine will be successful only where they are necessary in relation to disputes over the factual circumstances, in particular, applications based upon procedural impropriety where there is a material conflict of evidence about the procedure followed by the defendant, or **77.48**

Commentary

where bad faith and/or bias is alleged against the defendant. In *R (Bancoult) v Secretary of State for Foreign and Commonwealth Affairs* [2012] EWHC 2115 (Admin), LTL 27/7/2012, cross-examination of two witnesses of the defendant in relation to confidential documents sent between Washington and London was exceptionally permitted, as the proceedings could not be fairly determined without resolving the claimant's allegation based on those documents. In the absence of cross-examination the defendant's evidence of the facts must be assumed to be correct, unless there are documents which show that this evidence cannot be correct. Therefore, the proper course of action for a claimant who wishes to challenge the defendant's evidence is to apply for cross-examination of the relevant witness, despite the general practice of not permitting cross-examination (*R (McVey) v Secretary of State for Health* [2010] EWHC 1225 (Admin), [2010] ACD 95).

A court considering making an order for compulsory treatment of a detained person under the Mental Health Act 1983 which might involve breaches of his rights under the European Convention on Human Rights should fully review the merits of the proposed treatment and, for that purpose, allow cross-examination of the specialists instructed on both sides (*R (Wilkinson) v Responsible Medical Officer Broadmoor Hospital* [2001] EWCA Civ 1545, [2002] 1 WLR 419). However, this approach should not be used as a charter for routine applications to the court for oral evidence in human rights cases generally. The decision whether to allow cross-examination will depend largely on the nature of the right that has allegedly been breached and the nature of the alleged breach. It should not be overlooked that the court's role is essentially one of review (*R (N) v Dr M* [2002] EWCA Civ 1789, [2003] 1 WLR 562; see also *R (Al-Sweady) v Secretary of State for Defence* [2009] EWHC 2387 (Admin), [2010] HRLR 2).

Expert evidence

77.49 The general approach to evidence in judicial review proceedings is that fresh evidence can only be adduced in very limited circumstances (*R v Secretary of State for the Environment, ex parte Powis* [1981] 1 WLR 584). However, in some cases fairness may require that new expert evidence is used, although such cases will be very rare. Expert evidence will be allowed only to explain technical processes, and not to give an opinion on the reasonableness of the expert tribunal's decision, which would amount to an attempt to challenge the technical judgment of the tribunal on the merits of the case (*R (Lynch) v General Dental Council* [2003] EWHC 2987 (Admin), [2004] 1 All ER 1159).

Constitution of the court

77.50 A claim for judicial review in a civil matter should be made to a judge sitting in open court, unless the court directs that it should be made to a judge in private or to a Divisional Court of the Queen's Bench Division.

Substantive judicial review applications in civil matters are therefore generally heard by a single judge sitting in open court. There may be cases involving regulatory issues in which a private hearing may be ordered in the light of **CPR, r. 39.2(3)(a)** or (c), in circumstances involving confidential information of significance or where there is a special reason to fear that reporting of the case may be unbalanced (*R (Amvac Chemical UK Ltd) v Secretary State for the Environment, Food and Rural Affairs* [2001] EWHC 1011 (Admin), [2002] ACD 219). A substantive application in a civil case is heard by the Divisional Court only in exceptional circumstances, such as where the application raises questions of difficulty, complexity or importance. Occasionally, the hearing may be before a judge in chambers. In exceptional cases the Court of Appeal may, where it deals with an appeal against refusal to give permission to proceed with a claim for judicial review (see **77.40**), hear the substantive application (e.g. as in *British Airways Board v Laker Airways Ltd* [1984] QB 142). However, usually the substantive hearing is heard by a different judge or court from that which granted permission.

Transfer of proceedings

CPR, Part 30, applies to transfers to and from the Administrative Court (r. 54.20). The court may order a claim to continue as if it had not been started under Part 54, and where it does so it may give directions about the future management of the claim. PD 54A, para. 14.1 draws attention to CPR, r. 30.5, which provides that the High Court may order proceedings in any Division of the High Court to be transferred to another Division and to or from a specialist list. An application for the transfer of proceedings to or from a specialist list must be made to a judge dealing with claims in that list (r. 30.5(3)). 77.51

In deciding whether a claim is suitable for transfer to the Administrative Court, the court will consider whether it raises issues of public law to which Part 54 should apply (PD 54A, para. 14.2).

The court may, if it thinks appropriate where a claim for damages is included in an application for judicial review, determine the public law issues and then order issues relating to private law liability to proceed as if commenced under CPR, Part 7. Alternatively, the court may award damages at the judicial review hearing and leave quantum to be assessed by the court subsequently. However, it is likely that where the only remedies sought are public law remedies the court will not allow the matter to proceed as if commenced under Part 7. In order to permit the transfer of a case under r. 54.20 it is likely that the court would require that the issues be sufficiently clearly defined, and at least some of the claims that are sought to be pursued in a Part 7 claim must already be in existence (*R v East Berkshire Health Authority, ex parte Walsh* [1985] QB 152).

A claim in contract will not be struck out because it could more appropriately be made under Part 54, unless there is an abuse of process, for example, delay in starting proceedings (*Clark v University of Lincolnshire and Humberside* [2000] 1 WLR 1988).

Settlement, withdrawal or discontinuance

Settlement, withdrawal or discontinuance of proceedings is dealt with by Practice Direction (Administrative Court: Uncontested Proceedings) [2008] 1 WLR 1377. This provides that draft orders and statements signed by all parties should be presented to the court for consideration in the case of settlement. Where matters are to be withdrawn or discontinued and there is a need for the leave of the court or an order as to costs, again a statement and draft order signed by all parties should be put before the court. The order will then be made without the need for parties to attend court. Where no leave or costs order is required the claimant should simply notify the court and all other parties of the discontinuance using the procedure in CPR, Part 38 (see chapter 55). 77.52

REMEDIES

All the remedies available in judicial review proceedings are subject to the discretion of the court, so that even if a case is proved the court may refuse any or all of the remedies sought by the claimant. The High Court may exercise its discretion under the Senior Courts Act 1981, s. 31, to make the prerogative mandatory, prohibiting and quashing orders and provide the private law remedies of injunction, declaration, damages, restitution or the recovery of any sum due. The Administrative Court may make a declaration of incompatibility under the Human Rights Act 1998, s. 4. These remedies may be sought individually (except that a judicial review claim may not seek a money remedy alone: CPR, r. 54.3(2)), alternatively or in combination. Declaratory and injunctive relief are obtainable in proceedings for judicial review even when one of the prerogative orders is capable of being granted (*R v Secretary of State for Employment, ex parte Equal Opportunities Commission* [1995] 1 AC 1). 77.53

The **CPR, Part 54**, procedure must be used for a judicial review claim seeking a prerogative order or an injunction under the Senior Courts Act 1981, s. 30, restraining a person from acting in an office in which he or she is not entitled to act (**CPR, r. 54.2**). It may be used for a judicial review claim seeking a declaration or an injunction, but must be used if a declaration or injunction is sought in addition to a prerogative order or an injunction under the Senior Courts Act 1981, s. 30 (**CPR, r. 54.3(1)**).

The discretionary nature of remedies

77.54 All public law remedies are discretionary, i.e. even though the claimant has standing to commence judicial review proceedings, the decision or action in question is reviewable, and the grounds for review are proved, the court may yet decide not to award the claimant all or part of the remedies requested. The court has withheld remedies on a number of grounds.

The court may refuse to grant the relief requested if suitable alternative remedies have not been pursued (e.g. *R v Secretary of State for the Home Department, ex parte Swati* [1986] 1 WLR 477) (see **77.30**).

A court may refuse relief because of the claimant's conduct or motives, for example, where the claimant suppressed or misrepresented material facts in presenting the claim (*R v Kensington Income Tax Commissioners, ex parte Princess Edmond de Polignac* [1917] 1 KB 486), or delayed in commencing proceedings. The time limits set out in **CPR, r. 54.5(1)** and the Senior Courts Act 1981, s. 31, must be adhered to strictly and therefore undue delay may result in the refusal of any relief (see **77.36**). The court may also refuse to grant relief if it believes the likely effect of a remedy will serve no practical purpose, e.g. in cases where the public body has already remedied its position to meet the claimant's demands (*R v Gloucestershire County Council, ex parte P* [1994] ELR 334) or where a public body shows that it is doing all it can to comply with its statutory duty. Similarly, where the defendant had already conceded that it had broken its obligations under EU law, the concession spoke for itself and declaratory relief was unnecessary (*R (Clientearth) v Secretary of State for the Environment, Food and Rural Affairs* [2011] EWHC 3623 (Admin), [2012] 1 CMLR 47). The quashing of a challenged planning permission may be withheld where it is impossible to sever the part to which the claimant's challenge relates from the rest of the planning permission, which was lawfully granted. In those circumstances relief would simply take the form of a declaration that the local authority had failed to consult properly before granting planning permission (*R (Guiney) v Greenwich London Borough Council* [2008] EWHC 2012 (Admin), [2009] JPL 211). Breach of a statutory provision may have such an insignificant effect that the court may refuse relief (as in *R v Dairy Produce Quota Tribunal, ex parte Davies* [1987] 2 CMLR 399). In exercising its discretion, the court will take into account whether others will be directly or indirectly affected by its decision — e.g. a decision which has the potential to affect a large number of individuals such as an inquiry into a new motorway. Therefore reliance upon a decision by third parties may also induce the court not to grant the remedy claimed.

If an issue is theoretical, then in ordinary civil proceedings this may be a compelling factor against the grant of relief. However, the court may occasionally grant an advisory opinion, e.g. in the form of a declaration, where it is desirable that it should do so (*R v Secretary of State for Employment, ex parte Equal Opportunities Commission* [1995] 1 AC 1).

Quashing order

77.55 A quashing order deprives the decision which is being reviewed of all legal effect and the decision challenged is therefore effectively set aside. Until a decision is quashed, it is deemed to possess a *'presumption of validity'* and is disobeyed at the claimant's risk pending the substantive judicial review hearing (*F. Hoffmann-La Roche & Co. AG v Secretary of State for Trade and Industry* [1975] AC 295).

A quashing order is available to quash the decisions of inferior courts or tribunals and any other public body 'having legal authority to determine questions affecting the rights of subjects, and having the duty to act judicially' (per Lord Atkin in *R v Electricity Commissioners, ex parte London Electricity Joint Committee Co. (1920) Ltd* [1924] 1 KB 171). The courts have subsequently accepted that a quashing order is not confined to the review of decisions of a judicial nature (*R v Hillingdon London Borough Council, ex parte Royco Homes Ltd* [1974] QB 720). The court will consider the nature of the power exercised in order to determine whether this test has been satisfied. A quashing order may be claimed against a broad range of administrative decision-makers, e.g. local authorities, legal committees and ministers of the Crown and may relate to administrative decisions and delegated legislation.

Where a quashing order is sought and the court is satisfied that there are grounds for quashing the decision it may in addition remit the matter to the decision-maker and 'direct it to reconsider the matter and reach a decision in accordance with the judgment of the court' (**CPR, r. 54.19(2)(a)**). This power may be used to ensure that a decision is reconsidered and a new decision made. However, there is no guarantee that a different result will be reached: the decision-maker is justified in reaching the same result again provided that the matter is reconsidered in accordance with the law. Where the court considers that there is no purpose to be served in remitting the matter to the decision-maker, it may, subject to any statutory provision, take the decision itself (**r. 54.19(2)(b)**). (However, where a power is given by statute to a tribunal, person or other body, it may be the case that the court cannot take the decision itself.)

Commentary

Prohibiting order

A prohibiting order prevents the decision-maker from acting or continuing to act in excess of jurisdiction. Therefore, if a public body threatens to make an unlawful decision which could be quashed had it been made, the court may make a prohibiting order to prevent the decision being made. For example, a local council was prohibited from increasing the number of taxi licences in breach of an undertaking to consult the local professional association (*R v Liverpool Corporation, ex parte Liverpool Taxi Fleet Operators' Association* [1972] 2 QB 299). **77.56**

If a want of jurisdiction is apparent, a prohibiting order may be claimed immediately. If it is not apparent, the claimant must wait until the tribunal has stepped outside its jurisdiction or is undoubtedly about to do so (*Zohrab v Smith* (1848) 17 LJ QB 174). Doubts have been expressed about the power to claim a prohibiting order for an anticipatory excess of jurisdiction (*Re Ashby* [1934] OR 421). A prohibiting order is not granted lightly (*Governors of Queen Anne's Bounty v Pitt-Rivers* [1936] 2 KB 419). A prohibiting order is not available against a public body which has already completed the acts complained of (*Yates v Palmer* (1849) 6 Dowl & L 283). A prohibiting order is also not available to review a finding of fact made by an inferior court for the purpose of assuming jurisdiction (*Joseph v Henry* (1850) 19 LJ QB 369). It may be refused in a case of laches (see **10.40**) or misconduct by the applicant (*Parochial Church Council of St Magnus-the-Martyr v Chancellor of London* [1923] P 38).

Mandatory order

A mandatory order requires an inferior court or tribunal or a person or body of persons charged with a public duty to carry out its judicial or other public duty. A mandatory order may compel a court or tribunal to state its case (*R v Watson, ex parte Bretherton* [1945] KB 96) and to give reasons for its decision where it was required to do so by statute (*Brayhead (Ascot) Ltd v Berkshire County Council* [1964] 2 QB 303). This includes the provision of adequately intelligible reasons (*Earl Iveagh v Minister of Housing and Local Government* [1964] 1 QB 395). A mandatory order can compel a public body to exercise its discretion in accordance with the law, though the court is reluctant to use the remedy in this way (e.g. *R v Barnet London Borough Council, ex parte Nilish Shah* [1983] 2 AC 309). **77.57**

It is preferable that the claimant is able to say that performance of the duty has been demanded and that the performance has been refused by the authority obliged to discharge it (*State (Modern Homes (Ireland) Ltd) v Dublin Corporation* [1953] IR 202). Therefore, before applying for judicial review, a claimant should make a specific demand or request to the authority to perform the duty imposed upon it. This corresponds with the requirement upon a claimant to write an appropriate 'letter before action' prior to claiming judicial review (see **77.31**).

The court has a wide discretion to refuse to make a mandatory order. One will not be granted unless the defendant has an absolute duty, or has already decided in the claimant's favour all factors necessary to render it subject to a duty, to do that which the claimant seeks. A mandatory order cannot be made against the Crown (Crown Proceedings Act 1947, s. 40) but can be made against ministers.

Injunctions

77.58 Under the Senior Courts Act 1981, s. 31(2), in judicial review proceedings the court may make a declaration or grant an injunction if it considers that it would be just and convenient having regard to:

(a) the nature of the matters in respect of which a remedy may be granted by way of a mandatory, prohibiting or quashing order;
(b) the nature of the persons and bodies against whom a remedy may be granted by way of such an order; and
(c) all the circumstances of the case.

In a claim for judicial review a final injunction can be granted in order to restrain a public body from acting unlawfully, restrain the implementation of an unlawful decision or compel a public authority to comply with its statutory duties. Injunctive relief does not lie against the Crown itself (Crown Proceedings Act 1947, ss. 21 and 38) but injunctions can be granted against ministers and other officers of the Crown in their official as well as their private capacities (*Re M* [1994] 1 AC 377) and, in particular, an injunction may be granted against a minister of the Crown in order to give a remedy in favour of a party invoking rights derived from directly applicable EU law (*R v Secretary of State for Transport, ex parte Factortame Ltd (No. 2)* [1991] 1 AC 603).

The discretion conferred upon the court under the conditions stipulated in the Senior Courts Act 1981, s. 31(2), is broad but must be exercised in accordance with recognised principles. An injunction will be refused if the injury complained of is very trivial or if it has ceased and there is no likelihood of its recurrence. Further, a court will not order an injunction to do something which is impossible, or where the grant of an injunction would be oppressive.

A final injunction, although granted at the conclusion of the proceedings, need not be expressed to have perpetual effect, i.e. it may be awarded for a fixed period. However, a mandatory injunction will not be granted to ensure the performance of a continuing series of acts which the court cannot supervise although the court may award a prohibitory injunction to restrain the discontinuance of a public service.

Declarations

77.59 A declaration may be granted in judicial review proceedings in the circumstances set out in the Senior Courts Act 1981, s. 31(2) (see **77.58**).

Declaratory relief and any other private law remedy may be granted by a court even if none of the prerogative remedies is available, provided the case is within the realm of public law.

The court has a broad discretion to grant declaratory relief (*Barnard v National Dock Labour Board* [1953] 2 QB 18). Declarations may be sought in order to challenge the legality of decisions taken or policies adopted by a public body, to challenge delegated legislation, to determine the ambit of public law obligations, to pronounce upon questions of law and the compatibility of primary legislation with EU law (*R v Secretary of State for Employment, ex parte Equal Opportunities Commission* [1995] 1 AC 1).

The court may consider granting relief because of any public interest element involved (*R v Her Majesty's Treasury, ex parte Smedley* [1985] QB 657) or as a means of securing a private law entitlement (*Roy v Kensington and Chelsea and Westminster Family Practitioner Committee* [1992] 1 AC 624). The court may grant a declaration in relation to future rights (*R v Her Majesty's Treasury, ex parte Smedley*). However the circumstances must be appropriate for the grant, e.g. not too complex or uncertain. The courts are also willing to grant a negative declaration, e.g. a declaration of no right or no liability.

There are some limitations upon the scope of declaratory relief. Declaratory relief does not lie in respect of claims which are legally unenforceable (*Mutasa v Attorney-General* [1980] QB 114); *intra vires* errors of law appearing on the face of the record (*Punton v Minister of Pensions and National Insurance (No. 2)* [1964] 1 WLR 226); and matters which are academic or hypothetical. Courts should not make general declarations which are unnecessary and irrelevant for the particular claimant in the case, especially in circumstances where a claimant has been persuaded to bring a claim for judicial review by those who wish to challenge an issue generally (*R (Burke) v General Medical Council* [2005] EWCA Civ 1003, [2006] QB 273). The civil courts are also reluctant to grant declaratory relief if a declaration could interfere with criminal proceedings (*R v Medicines Control Agency, ex parte Pharma Nord Ltd* (1997) 10 Admin LR 646).

Commentary

Damages

Damages arising from any matter to which a judicial review claim relates may be awarded if the court is satisfied that they would have been awarded in an ordinary claim started at the same time as the judicial review claim (Senior Courts Act 1981, s. 31(4)). **77.60**

A person who has suffered loss as a result of unlawful administrative conduct has to claim and establish liability under a recognised cause of action to claim damages. This will usually be a tort claim, e.g. negligence, negligent misstatement, breach of statutory duty (including breach of Convention rights under the **Human Rights Act 1998**), misfeasance in public office.

There are circumstances in which a public law breach of European Union law gives rise to a claim for damages in judicial review proceedings. The Court of Justice of the European Union has held that member States must pay compensation for harm caused to an individual for failure to implement an EU Directive (*Francovich v Italy* (cases C-6 and 9/90) [1995] ICR 722). The CJEU has subsequently held that a right to compensation from member States is a universal principle and exists where three conditions are met:

(a) the rule of law infringed must be intended to confer rights on individuals;
(b) the breach must be sufficiently serious; and
(c) there must be a direct causal link between the breach and the damage sustained (*Brasserie du Pêcheur SA v Germany* (cases C-46 & 48/93) [1996] QB 404).

Subsequent cases have applied these principles (e.g. *R v Her Majesty's Treasury, ex parte British Telecommunications plc* (case C-392/93) [1996] QB 615; *R v Ministry of Agriculture, Fisheries and Food, ex parte Hedley Lomas (Ireland) Ltd* (case C-5/94) [1997] QB 139; *R v Secretary of State for Transport, ex parte Factortame Ltd (No. 5)* [2000] 1 AC 524).

However, damages are not available simply because an application for judicial review is successful (*R v Metropolitan Borough of Knowsley, ex parte Maguire* [1992] COD 499).

CPR, Part 16, applies to making a claim for damages in a judicial review claim, i.e. the normal rules as to statements of case apply and the loss or damage suffered must be fully particularised.

Suspension of the effect of orders

77.61 The Supreme Court has held that it should not lend itself to procedures designed to obfuscate the effect of its judgments. In *Her Majesty's Treasury v Ahmed* [2010] UKSC 5, [2010] 2 AC 534, the court declined to temporarily suspend the effect of its judgment declaring certain freezing orders aimed at terrorists *ultra vires* in order to allow the Treasury to address the effects of the order. Despite the substantial public policy reasons in favour of such a suspension, to do so would have required the court to enforce regulations that it had found to be unlawful.

APPEALS

77.62 An appeal against the decision of the High Court in a substantive hearing of a judicial review claim lies to the Court of Appeal and thereafter to the Supreme Court in the normal way. The procedure for substantive appeals is discussed in **chapters 75** and **76**. Appeals from decisions to refuse permission to apply for judicial review were considered at **77.40**.

When considering whether to grant permission to appeal from a substantive hearing for judicial review, the court will consider whether there is a prima facie case that an error has been made; whether there is an issue of legal principle involved (*R v Secretary of State for the Environment, ex parte Kirkstall Valley Campaign Ltd* [1996] 3 All ER 304); whether the issue is one which should be examined by the Court of Appeal in the public interest; and whether the appeal raises an issue where the law requires clarification (*Smith v Cosworth Casting Processes Ltd* [1997] 1 WLR 1538). The task of the Court of Appeal in a judicial review appeal is to resolve genuine questions of law: it does not reconsider the original decision-maker's findings of fact where the original tribunal disbelieved the claimant (*R (Nine Nepalese Asylum Seekers) v Immigration Appeal Tribunal* [2003] EWCA Civ 1892, *The Independent*, 21 January 2004). A further appeal to the Supreme Court may be entertained in a public law matter (provided it is otherwise a suitable case for an appeal to the Court) even in cases where there is no longer any *lis* between the parties (*R v Secretary of State for the Home Department, ex parte Salem* [1999] 1 AC 450), although academic appeals will only be heard if there are good reasons in the public interest for doing so.

Chapter 78 References to the Court of Justice of the European Union

INTRODUCTION

An English court faced with a question of European Union law may sometimes decide it itself, or may refer it to the Court of Justice of the European Union (CJEU) in Luxembourg for a preliminary ruling. If a reference is made, the English proceedings will be stayed pending the ruling of the CJEU. Once it is made, the ruling is binding on the English court, but it is only a preliminary ruling, in that the English court is left to apply the ruling to the facts of the case and to give judgment. The general policy is that EU law should be applied consistently in all member States. 78.1

QUESTIONS WHICH MAY BE REFERRED

References may be made: 78.2

(a) under art. 267 of the Treaty on the Functioning of the European Union (TFEU); or
(b) on the interpretation of any of the instruments referred to in the Civil Jurisdiction and Judgments Act 1982, s. 1(1), or the Contracts (Applicable Law) Act 1990, s. 1.

Until the Treaty Establishing the European Coal and Steel Community expired in July 2002, it was also possible to make a reference under art. 41 of that treaty.

Article 267 TFEU is representative of the various treaties and enactments mentioned above. It provides in its first paragraph:

> The Court of Justice of the European Union shall have jurisdiction to give preliminary rulings concerning:
> (a) the interpretation of the Treaties;
> (b) the validity and interpretation of acts of the institutions, bodies, offices or agencies of the Union.

'The Treaties' are the TFEU and the Treaty on European Union (art. 1(2) TFEU). Under para. (b) of art. 267 the CJEU can rule on the validity or interpretation of Regulations, Directives and Decisions of the Council or Commission. Although the CJEU can give rulings on the interpretation of the Brussels Convention and **Regulation (EC) No. 44/2001** (see **chapter 16**), it cannot do so on the modified versions of those documents governing allocation of jurisdiction within the UK (*Kleinwort Benson Ltd v Glasgow City Council* (case C-346/93) [1996] QB 57).

Questions referred for preliminary rulings must concern only the interpretation or validity of a provision of EU law, since the CJEU does not have jurisdiction to interpret national law or to assess its validity. It is for the referring court to apply the relevant provision of EU law to the case (**CJEU Information Note, para.** 7). (All references in this chapter to the CJEU Information Note are to the 2011 version of the note, which is annexed to **PD 68 in appendix 1**.)

The Charter of Fundamental Rights of the EU was given direct effect by the coming into force of the Lisbon Treaty in December 2009 and binds member States when implementing EU law. Some claimants are now relying on the rights in the Charter instead of the European Convention on Human Rights (e.g. *Rugby Football Union v Consolidated Information Services Ltd* [2012] UKSC 55, [2012] 1 WLR 3333). The relationship between the Charter and the Convention is likely to continue to draw attention and has been the subject of a reference to the CJEU in the context of the rights of asylum seekers (*NS v Secretary of State for the Home Department* (case C-411/10) [2012] All ER (EC) 1011).

REFERRING COURT OR TRIBUNAL

78.3 It is a matter for the CJEU to decide whether a body is a court or tribunal for the purposes of art. 267 TFEU, and the categorisation of that body under national law is not conclusive (*Politi v Italy* (case 43/71) [1971] ECR 1039; *Corbiau v Administration des Contributions* (case C-24/92) [1993] ECR I-1277). The CJEU will take a number of factors into account when making this determination, including: whether the body is established by law, whether it is permanent, whether its jurisdiction is compulsory, whether its procedure is *inter partes*, whether it applies rules of law, and whether it is independent (*Dorsch Consult Ingenieurgesellschaft mbH v Bundesbaugesellschaft Berlin mbH* (case C-54/96) [1997] ECR I-4961; *Denuit v Transorient—Mosaïque Voyages et Culture SA* (case C-125/04) [2005] ECR I-923). For example, a Dutch body, called the Appeals Committee for General Medicine, which operated with the consent of the public authorities and with their cooperation, and which, after an adversarial procedure, delivered decisions, which were recognised as final, was considered as a court or tribunal within the meaning of art. 267 (*Broekmeulen v Huisarts Registratie Commissie* (case 246/80) [1981] ECR 2311). Also, the court or tribunal making the reference must be in a member State. Whether an arbitral court or tribunal can be regarded as an emanation of a member State will depend on the nature of the arbitration in question. The fact that the arbitral body gives a judgment according to law, and that the award is binding between the parties, will not, however, be sufficient. There must be a closer link between the arbitration procedure and the ordinary court system in a member State for the body to be considered as a court or tribunal of a member State (*Nordsee Deutsche Hochseefischerei GmbH v Reederei Mond Hochseefischerei Nordstern AG & Co. KG* (case 102/81) [1982] ECR 1095).

MANDATORY REFERENCES

78.4 Article 267 TFEU provides:

> Where any such question is raised in a case pending before a court or tribunal of a member State against whose decisions there is no judicial remedy under national law, that court or tribunal shall bring the matter before the Court.

Accordingly, references are mandatory in courts of last instance. In England, from October 2009 this is generally the Supreme Court, unless by statute or rule some lower court is the final court of appeal. However, even in the Supreme Court there must be a 'question' that needs to be referred. If a point is covered by considerable and consistent authority from the CJEU such that its answer is obvious, there is no 'question' within the meaning of art. 267

(per Lord Diplock in *Garland v British Rail Engineering Ltd* [1983] 2 AC 751 at p. 771; *Srl Cilfit v Ministry of Health* (case 283/81) [1982] ECR 3415). If it is not necessary to decide either whether EU law applies or the scope of its application to the present case, the reference procedure is not available even in the Supreme Court (*R v Secretary of State for Health, ex parte Imperial Tobacco Ltd* [2001] 1 WLR 127).

DISCRETIONARY REFERENCES

For courts below the Supreme Court, art. 267 TFEU provides: 78.5

> Where such a question is raised before any court or tribunal of a member State, that court or tribunal may, if it considers that a decision on the question is necessary to enable it to give judgment, request the Court to give a ruling thereon.

Two questions arise in such cases:

(a) whether a decision on the question of EU law is necessary to enable the court to give judgment; and
(b) if so, whether the court should in the exercise of its discretion order that a reference be made.

Guidelines on both questions were given by the Court of Appeal in *H. P. Bulmer Ltd v J. Bollinger SA* [1974] Ch 401 by Lord Denning MR at pp. 422–5. Whether to make a discretionary reference, and the extent of the questions to be posed to the CJEU, are essentially case management matters which are unlikely to be overturned on appeal (*Evans v Secretary of State for the Environment, Transport and the Regions* [2001] EWCA Civ 32, [2001] 2 CMLR 10).

Guidelines for discretionary references

In *H. P. Bulmer Ltd v J. Bollinger SA* [1974] Ch 401 Lord Denning MR laid down four guidelines as to whether a decision from the European Court is necessary. They are no more than guidelines, and cannot be considered as binding (*Lord Bethell v SABENA* [1983] 3 CMLR 1). 78.6

Whether the point will be conclusive Article 267 TFEU provides that the court must consider whether 'a decision on the question is necessary to enable it to give judgment'. Lord Denning's view was that the point must be such that, whichever way it is decided, it will be conclusive of the case. This is probably too onerous. Ormrod LJ in *Polydor Ltd v Harlequin Record Shops Ltd* [1982] CMLR 413 said it was sufficient if the point was 'reasonably necessary', and Bingham J in *Customs and Excise Commissioners v ApS Samex* [1983] 1 All ER 1042 said that the question must be substantially, if not quite totally, determinative of the litigation. 78.7

Previous ruling As Lord Denning said in *H. P. Bulmer Ltd v J. Bollinger SA* [1974] Ch 401: 78.8

> In some cases . . . it may be found that the same point—or substantially the same point—has already been decided by the European Court in a previous case. In that event it is not necessary for the English court to decide it. It can follow the previous decision without troubling the European Court.

This is subject to the proviso that, with changing social and economic factors, the CJEU is not bound by its earlier decisions.

Acte claire Lord Denning MR went on to say: 78.9

> In other cases the English court may consider the point is reasonably clear and free from doubt. In that event there is no need to interpret the Treaty but only to apply it.

This should be read in the light of Lord Diplock's comment in *R v Henn* [1981] AC 850 at p. 906 that the court should not be 'too ready to hold that because the meaning of the English text (which is one of [nine] of equal authority) seems plain no question of interpretation can be involved'. A point may be *acte claire* after considering the text, together with decisions of the CJEU and relevant *travaux préparatoires* (*Lucasfilm Ltd v Ainsworth* [2009] EWCA Civ 1328, [2010] Ch 503 at [114], [129]; reversed in part on another point [2011] UKSC 39, [2012] 1 AC 208).

78.10 **Deciding the facts first** In general, it is best to decide the facts before making a reference, because it should then be clear if the question of EU law is necessary, and it enables the CJEU to take into account all the relevant facts when making its ruling. In any event, it is usually best not to make the reference at least until it is possible to define, if only hypothetically, the factual and legal context of the question (**CJEU Information Note, para. 19**). It is also usually best not to make a reference until both sides have been heard (*Simmenthal SpA v Amministrazione delle Finanze dello Stato* (case 70/77) [1978] ECR 1453).

78.11 **Amending questions** An English court may amend the questions set out in an order for reference to the CJEU by exercising its power under **CPR, r. 3.1**(7). However, the court may refuse an application to amend the wording of questions which have been referred to the CJEU, particularly in circumstances where there is (a) no finding that the court has made the order on a false basis, and (b) no material change of circumstances since the order (*SAS Institute Inc. v World Programming Ltd* [2010] EWHC 3012 (Ch), [2011] FSR 12).

Factors relevant to the discretion

78.12 General guidance has been provided by the CJEU on when it is appropriate to refer matters. The following factors were identified by Lord Denning MR in *H. P. Bulmer Ltd v J. Bollinger SA* [1974] Ch 401 as being relevant in the exercise of the court's discretion:

(a) delay in obtaining a ruling from the CJEU (delays have been reduced in recent years);
(b) the importance of not overloading the CJEU;
(c) expense to the parties;
(d) the wishes of the parties. Although clearly relevant, the court can nevertheless make a reference even if both parties object, and, also, there is no such thing as a reference by consent. Ultimately the decision is that of the judge;
(e) difficulty and importance, for example, where a case raised a vital question as to the limit of EC competences conferred by the Treaties and a tension between fundamental principles of national security and basic procedural fairness which was not straightforward (*ZZ v Secretary of State for the Home Department* [2011] EWCA Civ 440, LTL 19/4/2011). Simple points should be decided by the English court;
(f) questions involving the comparison of texts in the different languages of the member States are best decided by the CJEU (*Customs and Excise Commissioners v ApS Samex* [1983] 1 All ER 1042);
(g) questions requiring a panoramic view of the EU and its institutions, the functioning of the Internal Market or a broad view of the orderly development of the EU should be decided by the CJEU (*Customs and Excise Commissioners v ApS Samex*);
(h) whether the application for a reference is made in bad faith so as to delay judgment being given (*Customs and Excise Commissioners v ApS Samex*).

Additionally, where the arguments of the parties and the material facts are not sufficiently clear for the court to confidently frame clear and precise questions, the court may decline to make a reference (*Dr Reddy's Laboratories (UK) Ltd v Warner-Lambert Co LLC* [2012] EWHC 1791 (Pat), [2012] Eu LR 747).

Questioning the validity of institutional acts

78.13 Where a national court intends to question the validity of an act of an institution, body, office or agency of the EU or where the validity of an institutional act is brought into issue by the parties, it must refer the question to the CJEU (*Foto-Frost v Hauptzollamt Lübeck-Ost* (case

314/85) [1987] ECR 4199; *R (International Air Transport Association) v Department for Transport* (case C-344/04) [2006] ECR I-403). Where the national court has serious doubts about the validity of an institutional act on which a national measure is based, the national court may, in an exceptional case, suspend or grant interim relief in respect of the national measure, but it must refer the question of validity to the CJEU (*Zuckerfabrik Süderdithmarschen AG v Hauptzollamt Itzehoe* (cases C-143/88 and C-92/89) [1991] ECR I-415) (**CJEU Information Note, para. 17**). The right to question the validity of institutional acts does not extend to the preparatory acts of European institutions (*Conex Banninger Ltd v European Commission* [2010] EWHC 1978 (Ch), [2011] Eu LR 100).

PROCEDURE IN ENGLAND

An order referring a question to the CJEU may be made at any stage of the proceedings, and may be made by the court of its own initiative or on an application made by a party in accordance with **CPR, Part 23** (see **r. 68.2(1)**). An order for a reference (a request to the CJEU for a preliminary ruling: **r. 68.1(d)**) must be made by a judge, the Court of Appeal or the Supreme Court. It cannot be made by consent, or by a master or district judge (**r. 68.2(2)**). Although it can be made at any stage, it is usual for a reference to be made at trial after the facts have been found (see **78.10**). However, once the English court has given final judgment in a claim it is *functus officio* and has no power at that stage to order a reference (*Chiron Corporation v Murex Diagnostics Ltd (No. 8)* [1995] FSR 309). **78.14**

Commentary

Where the English court decides to make a reference, the request for the preliminary ruling of the CJEU has to be set out in a schedule to the court's order (**r. 68.2(3)**). Often the applicant will prepare a draft, or the court may direct one of the parties to do so, but the order will be settled finally by the court (**PD 68, para. 1.1**). As it will need to be translated into the other official languages, the question on which a ruling is sought must be expressed as clearly and precisely as possible (**PD 68, para. 1.2**), avoiding superfluous detail (**CJEU Information Note, para. 21**). A precedent reference based on *Garland v British Rail Engineering Ltd* [1983] 2 AC 751 is illustrated at **figure 78.1**. The question should be stated in a general form, and not in a specific form tied to the facts of the case in hand. The reference must not exceed 20 pages and must (**PD 68, para. 1.3**):

(a) give the full name of the referring court;
(b) identify the parties;
(c) summarise the nature and history of the proceedings, including the salient facts, indicating whether these have been proved, admitted or assumed;
(d) set out the relevant rules of national law;
(e) summarise the relevant contentions of the parties;
(f) explain why a ruling of the CJEU is being sought;
(g) identify the provisions of EU law which the CJEU is being requested to interpret;
(h) state the question on which a ruling of the CJEU is sought; and
(i) state any opinion on the answer to the question that may have been expressed by the court in the course of delivering judgment.

The reference must be set out in a schedule to the order and the court may give directions on the preparation of the schedule (**CPR, r. 68.2(3)**). It may direct the parties to produce a draft of the reference, but responsibility for the terms of the reference nevertheless lies with the court making the reference, and not with the parties (**PD 68, para. 1.1**).

Unless the court orders otherwise, the English proceedings will be stayed pending the ruling of the CJEU (**CPR, r. 68.4**). There is jurisdiction under **r. 19.2(2)(a)** to add parties to the English proceedings as claimants solely for the purpose of enabling them to take part in the reference to the CJEU (*Football Association Premier League Ltd v QC Leisure* [2008] EWHC 2897 (Ch), [2009] 1 WLR 1603). As the additional claimants had no other interest in the proceedings, conditions were imposed requiring them to provide the defendants 28 days' advance notice of any written observations they intended to make, and to limit their oral submissions in the CJEU to 15 minutes each (see [21]).

The senior master sends a copy of the order making the reference to the CJEU (**r. 68.3(1)**) at the Registry of Court of Justice of the European Communities, L-2925 Luxembourg. County court references are sent to the senior master by a court officer for onward transmission to the CJEU (**r. 68.3(2)**) together with the court file (**PD 68, para. 2.2**). Unless the court orders otherwise, the senior master will not send a copy of the order to the CJEU until the time for appealing has expired, any application for permission to appeal has been refused, or any appeal has been determined (**CPR, r. 68.3(3)**). The order for reference must be succinct, but sufficiently complete, and must set out the matters listed in **CJEU Information Note, para. 22**.

The domestic court making the reference to the CJEU can request the President of the CJEU to consider whether there are special circumstances which would justify a case being given priority under art. 55 of the Rules of Procedure of the CJEU and whether the case raises matters of exceptional urgency under art. 104a of those Rules. In *R (International Air Transport Association) v Department for Transport* [2004] EWHC 1721 (Admin), [2004] 3 CMLR 20, such a request was made when the Administrative Court found that there was evidence to show a significant risk that low-cost airline operators would suffer serious damage and be liable to criminal proceeding if they became liable to the provisions of a Regulation due to come into force in the next year.

Figure 78.1 Order for reference to the CJEU

IN THE SUPREME COURT
ON APPEAL FROM HER MAJESTY'S COURT OF APPEAL (ENGLAND)
BETWEEN

EILEEN MARY GARLAND *Petitioner*

— and —

BRITISH RAIL ENGINEERING LIMITED *Respondents*

It is ordered that the questions set out in the schedule hereto concerning the interpretation of (a) article 157 of the Treaty on the Functioning of the European Union ('TFEU'), (b) article 1 of Council Directive 75/117/EEC, and (c) article 1 of Council Directive 76/207/EEC be referred to the Court of Justice of the European Union for a preliminary ruling in accordance with article 267 of the TFEU.

And it is ordered that all further proceedings in the above-named cause be stayed until the said Court of Justice has given its ruling on the said questions or until further order.

SCHEDULE
REQUEST FOR PRELIMINARY RULING OF THE COURT OF JUSTICE OF THE EUROPEAN COMMUNITIES

1 The appellant in this appeal is Mrs Eileen Mary Garland of [address] and the respondents are British Rail Engineering Ltd, whose registered office is at [address].

2 Mrs Eileen Mary Garland is a married woman employed by the respondents, British Rail Engineering Limited ('B.R.E.L.'). The whole of the shareholding in B.R.E.L. is held by the British Railways Board which is a public authority charged by statute with the duty of providing railway services in Great Britain.

3 All employees of B.R.E.L. enjoy certain valuable concessionary travel facilities during the period of their employment. These facilities entitle each employee, regardless of sex, to travel free or at a reduced rate on British Rail and certain foreign railways. Such facilities are extended not only to the employee, but to his or her spouse and dependent children.

4 After employees of B.R.E.L. retire from their employment on reaching retiring age (which is earlier for women than for men) there is a difference in their treatment depending on their sex. In the case of former male employees, they continue to be granted (though on a reduced scale) travel facilities for themselves, their wives and dependent children. In the case of former female employees, they receive (on a similarly reduced scale) travel facilities for themselves, but no such facilities are granted in respect of their husbands or dependent children. These facilities are not enjoyed by former employees as a matter of contractual right, but employees have a legitimate expectation that they will enjoy them after retirement and it would be difficult in practice for B.R.E.L. to withdraw them unilaterally without the agreement of the trade unions of which their employees are members.

5 On 25 November 1976, Mrs Garland complained to an industrial tribunal that B.R.E.L. were discriminating against her contrary to the provisions of a United Kingdom Act of Parliament, the Sex Discrimination Act 1975. Her complaint after consideration also by two intermediate appellate courts, the Employment Appeal Tribunal [1978] ICR 495 and the Court of Appeal sub nom. *Roberts v Cleveland Area Health Authority*, [1979] 1 WLR 754 has now reached the Supreme Court which is a court against whose decision there is no judicial remedy under United Kingdom law.

The preliminary ruling of the Court of Justice of the European Union is accordingly requested on the following questions:

1 Where an employer provides (though not bound to do so by contract) special travel facilities for former employees to enjoy after retirement which discriminate against former female employees in the manner described above, is it contrary to:

(a) Article 157 of the TEFU?
(b) Article 1 of Council Directive 75/117/EEC?
(c) Article 1 of Council Directive 76/207/EEC?

2 If the answer to questions 1(a), 1(b) or 1(c) is affirmative, is article 157 or either of the Directives directly applicable in member States so as to confer enforceable Community rights upon individuals in the above circumstances?

Dated the 17th day of October 2013.

Urgent preliminary rulings

The CJEU has an urgent preliminary ruling procedure (see Protocol (No 3) on the Statute of the Court of Justice of the European Union, art. 23a; Rules of Procedure of the CJEU, art. 104b; **CJEU Information Note, paras 33** to 43). This applies only to a reference for a preliminary ruling relating to the area of freedom, security and justice (Protocol (No 3) on the Statute of the Court of Justice of the European Union, art. 23a). **78.15**

Any request by an English court, which makes a reference to the CJEU, for it to be dealt with under the urgent preliminary ruling procedure must be made in a document separate from the order for the reference or in a covering letter (**CPR, r. 68.2A**). The request to the CJEU to apply its urgent preliminary ruling procedure must, by **PD 68, para. 1A.1**, set out:

(a) the matters of fact and law which establish the urgency;

(b) the reasons why the urgent preliminary ruling procedure applies; and
(c) as far as possible, the court's view on the answer to the question referred to the CJEU for a preliminary ruling.

PROCEDURE IN THE CJEU

78.16 The registrar of the CJEU notifies the parties, member States and the Commission of any reference filed, and each have two months to submit written observations. A notice is published in the *Official Journal* indicating the names of the parties involved and a summary of the questions on which a preliminary ruling is being sought. The court can make orders for discovery. There may then be a hearing, where interested parties can present oral argument.

The case is then adjourned, during which the advocate general delivers an opinion, followed by the judgment of the court. The CJEU Registry stays in contact with the national court until judgment is given, and sends various documents to the national court, including written observations, report of the hearing, opinion of the advocate general, and the judgment of the CJEU. The ruling binds the domestic court on the interpretation of the provision of EU law in question, but the domestic court has to apply the ruling to the facts of the case in which it arose. It is for the domestic court alone to find the facts, and the domestic court is entitled to disregard any conclusion reached by the CJEU in so far as it is based on a factual background inconsistent with the findings of the domestic court (*Arsenal Football Club plc v Reed (No. 2)* [2003] EWCA Civ 696, [2003] 3 All ER 865). Where the CJEU makes a finding of fact which is not inconsistent with the findings of the domestic court, and which is inevitable in the circumstances, the domestic court should follow the ruling of the CJEU (*Arsenal Football Club plc v Reed (No. 2)*).

Individual concern

78.17 Article 263 TFEU provides that the CJEU may review the legality of acts adopted by the EU. Such proceedings may be brought by a member State, the European Parliament, the Council or the Commission. Proceedings may also be brought by a natural or legal person to whom the regulation or decision under review is addressed or is of direct and individual concern. This is usually interpreted as meaning that the applicant, if not a State or the Council or Commission, must be affected by the measure by reason of certain attributes peculiar to the applicant or a factual situation which differentiated the applicant from all other persons and distinguished it individually (*Plaumann & Co. v Commission* (case 25/62) [1963] ECR 95).

Individuals are therefore not permitted to challenge decisions which are not addressed to them personally (*Unión de Pequeños Agricultores v Council of the European Union* (case C-50/00P) [2003] QB 893, where it was held that the CJEU did not have jurisdiction to examine in an individual case whether national procedural rules permitted a challenge to the legality of EU measures).

However, art. 263 now provides that a natural or legal person may also institute proceedings against any regulatory act which is of direct concern to them and does not entail implementing measures. This appears to have extended the scope of individual action.

COSTS

The costs of the parties in seeking a ruling from the CJEU are always reserved to the domestic court (**CJEU Information Note, para. 28**). No order for costs is made in respect of the involvement of member States or the Commission. **78.18**

Chapter 79 Enforcement

INTRODUCTION

79.1 Entering judgment does not provide a litigant with the remedy sought in the proceedings. Parties may well refuse to comply with the judgments and orders of the court. Public confidence in the legal system would be eroded if the courts were without powers to enforce compliance. In fact, a range of enforcement procedures are available, each being designed to deal with different situations. Where a number of procedures are available, a judgment creditor can choose whichever one seems likely to be the most effective. Largely, the procedures are similar in both the High Court and the county courts. The major exception is that attachment of earnings orders (**79.19**) are generally only available in the county courts. One practical difference is that High Court enforcement is carried out by enforcement officers, who are independent of the courts, whereas county court enforcement is carried out by bailiffs, who are employed by Her Majesty's Courts and Tribunals Service. It is often suggested that enforcement officers, who are remunerated by fees and poundage on money they recover, have a greater incentive than bailiffs and hence have a reputation for being more successful.

The enforcement system is in the process of transition. Some of the rules on enforcement are in **CPR, Parts 69** to **73**, with the rest being preserved provisions of the old rules to be found in the schedules to the CPR. Further assimilation into the CPR is expected. The legal sources governing the various enforcement procedures are:

(a) General provisions on enforcement: **CPR, Part 70**, and certain surviving provisions of **RSC, ord. 45** in CPR, sch. 1, and **CCR, ord. 25** in CPR, sch. 2.
(b) General provisions on writs of execution: **RSC, ord. 46** in CPR, sch. 1 (High Court).
(c) Execution by writ of fieri facias: **RSC, ord. 47** in CPR, sch. 1 (High Court).
(d) Warrants of execution, delivery and possession: **CCR, ord. 26** in CPR, sch. 2 (county court).
(e) Obtaining information from judgment debtors: **CPR, Part 71**.
(f) Attachment of earnings is governed by the Attachment of Earnings Act 1971, with procedural rules in **CCR, ord. 27** in CPR, sch. 2 (county court).
(g) Judgment summonses: **CCR, ord. 28** in CPR, sch. 2.
(h) Committal (see **chapter 81**): **CPR, Part 81**;
(i) Third party debt orders: **CPR, Part 72**.
(j) Charging orders are governed by the Charging Orders Act 1979. The rules also include stop orders and stop notices. The procedural rules are in **CPR, Part 73**.
(k) Receivers: **CPR, Part 69**.
(l) Administration orders: **CCR, ord. 39** in CPR, sch. 2 (county court).

Enforcement of final foreign judgments is dealt with in **chapter 80**. Interim enforcement in the High Court in support of foreign proceedings is also possible using the powers conferred by the **Civil Jurisdiction and Judgments Act 1982, s. 25** (see **37.16**).

The Tribunals, Courts and Enforcement Act 2007 makes a number of far-reaching revisions to the law relating to enforcement of money judgments. The changes concern:

(a) information requests and orders (see **79.6**) (Tribunals, Courts and Enforcement Act 2007, ss. 95 to 105);
(b) enforcement by taking control of goods (see **79.7** to **79.11**) (ss. 62 to 70 and sch. 12);
(c) administration orders (see **79.12**) (s. 106), and new enforcement restriction orders (s. 107);
(d) attachment of earnings (see **79.19** to **79.22**) (ss. 91 to 92 and sch. 15);
(e) charging orders (see **79.23** to **79.28**) (ss. 93 to 94 in force from 1 October 2012);
(f) debt relief orders, which are new, and should be considered alongside insolvency and individual voluntary arrangements (see **83.40**) (s. 108, sch. 18 and sch. 19, which came into force on 6 April 2009) and debt management schemes (ss. 109 to 123).

The 2007 Act is being brought into force in stages, and at the time of writing only the provisions concerning debt relief orders and charging orders have been brought into force. It is expected that many of the provisions now found in the schedules to the CPR relating to enforcement will be revoked and replaced by new provisions in the main body of the CPR when the relevant provisions of the 2007 Act are brought into effect.

TRANSFER OF PROCEEDINGS

A case may need to be transferred before enforcement proceedings are taken: **79.2**

(a) A county court claim (other than one under the Consumer Credit Act 1974) will have to be transferred to the High Court if execution against goods is sought of a judgment exceeding £5,000 (**High Court and County Courts Jurisdiction Order 1991 (SI 1991/724), art. 8(1)(a)**). While the county courts have unlimited jurisdiction to make charging orders, enforcement of a charging order by sale (see **79.27**) must take place in the High Court if the amount owing exceeds £30,000 (County Courts Act 1984, s. 23(c)).

Commentary

(b) A High Court claim will have to be transferred to a county court if:
 (i) execution against goods is sought of a judgment under £600 (**High Court and County Courts Jurisdiction Order 1991, art. 8(1)(b)**);
 (ii) a charging order is sought where the judgment debt is under £5,000 (Charging Orders Act 1979, s. 1(2)); or
 (iii) an attachment of earnings order is sought (Attachment of Earnings Act 1971, s. 1).

(c) A county court claim will have to be transferred:
 (i) where the judgment creditor applies for an attachment of earnings order, to the county court serving the district where the judgment debtor resides (**CCR, ord. 27, r. 3** in CPR, sch. 2; **CPR, r. 70.3(2)**, and **PD 70, paras 2.1** to **2.4**); and
 (ii) where the judgment creditor applies for a judgment summons, to the county court serving the district where the judgment debtor resides or carries on business (**CCR, ord. 28, r. 1** in CPR, sch. 2; **CPR, r. 70.3(2)**, and **PD 70, paras 2.1** to **2.4**); and
 (iii) where the claim is a designated money claim which has not been transferred to another court, any application to obtain further information from the judgment debtor and any other form of enforcement must be made to the court where the defendant resides or carries on business (**CPR, rr. 71.2(2)(b)(ii)**; **72.3(b)(ii)**; **73.3(2)(e)**; **CCR ord. 27, r. 3(4)** in CPR, sch. 2; **PD 70, paras 8.1** to **11.1**).

(d) A possession claim against trespassers (see **CPR, Part 55**, and **chapter 35**) may be enforced either in the High Court or a county court (**High Court and County Courts Jurisdiction Order 1991, art. 8B**).

A judgment creditor seeking to enforce a county court judgment or order in the High Court should issue an application to transfer the claim to the High Court under the County Courts Act 1984, s. 42, and should then apply for a certificate of judgment under **CCR, ord. 22, r. 8** in CPR, sch. 2. The request for the certificate is made in writing, must state it is needed for the purpose of enforcement against goods (if this is the case) and confirm that the application to transfer has been made, attaching a copy of the application. Granting the certificate operates as an order to transfer the proceedings to the High Court (**CCR, ord. 25, r. 13** in CPR, sch. 2).

A judgment creditor wishing to enforce a High Court judgment or order in a county court must apply to the High Court for an order transferring the proceedings in accordance with **CPR, r. 70.3**. Once a transfer order has been obtained, **PD 70, para. 3**, requires the judgment creditor to file at the county court:

(a) a copy of the judgment or order which is being enforced;
(b) a copy of the order transferring the proceedings;
(c) a certificate verifying the amount due under the judgment or order being enforced;
(d) a copy of any enforcement officer's return if a writ of execution has been issued; and
(e) an application notice or request for enforcement in the county court.

A judgment creditor needing to transfer proceedings from one county court to another for enforcement must make a request in writing to the court where the claim is presently proceeding for the transfer (**PD 70, para. 2.1**). A court officer will then transfer the proceedings unless a judge orders otherwise (**para. 2.2**), and give notice of the transfer to all parties (**para. 2.3**).

ENFORCEMENT OF AWARDS BY TRIBUNALS ETC.

79.3 Statutes provide that certain decisions of courts (other than the High Court and county courts), tribunals and other bodies, and certain compromises, are enforceable as though they were court orders, or that the amount payable under such a decision or compromise is recoverable as if payable under a court order. In these cases, the decision or compromise can be enforced using the procedures in **CPR, Parts** 71 to 73 (information against debtors, third party debt orders and charging orders), or by enforcement against goods or land, attachment of earnings, judgment summons or committal (**CPR, r. 70.5**(1) and (2A)). Where the enactment provides that a sum of money is recoverable as if it were payable under a county court order:

(a) it must be enforced in a county court if it is for less than £600;
(b) it may be enforced in either a county court or the High Court if it is for £600 or more but less than £5,000; and
(c) it must be enforced in the High Court if it is for £5,000 or more (**High Court and County Courts Jurisdiction Order 1991 (SI 1991/724), art. 8**(2), which was inserted by the High Court and County Courts Jurisdiction (Amendment) Order 2009 (SI 2009/577), art. 4). There are exceptions in **SI 1991/724, art. 8**(3), relating to enforcement under the Employment Tribunals Act 1996, ss. 15(1) and 19A(3). **CPR, r. 70.5**, does not apply to arbitration awards, confiscation and forfeiture proceedings, or traffic enforcement (all of which have their own special rules relating to enforcement, see **r. 70.5**(2)).

Enforcement of a 'conditional compromise', which is one where the person to whom money is payable under a compromise agreement has to do something in addition to discontinuing or not starting proceedings, must be commenced by making an application on notice (**r. 70.5**(4A)). Applications to enforce other awards under **r. 70.5** are made without notice, with the application being filed in the court for the district where the judgment debtor resides or carries on business, unless the court orders otherwise (**r. 70.5**(4)). The application is made on form N332B (**PD 70, para. 4.1**) and must include the information set out at **para. 4.3**. If the enactment provides that decisions or compromises are enforceable only if a court so orders, the application is made using form N332A, and a copy of the decision or compromise must be filed with the application notice (**CPR, r. 70.5**(6)). If the enactment requires registration in the High Court, an application to the head clerk of the Action Department at the RCJ must be made in accordance with **r. 70.5**(8) and **PD 70, paras 5.1** and **5.2**.

An order of the Supreme Court (**chapter 76**) may be enforced by applying to make it an order of the High Court using the procedure in **PD 40B, paras 13.1** to **13.3**. An application needs to be issued using the Part 23 procedure in the High Court supported by the evidence set out in **PD 40B, para. 13.2**. The application is usually heard without notice by the procedural judge.

CRIMINAL CONFISCATION ORDERS

Confiscation orders made by the criminal courts are discussed in *Blackstone's Criminal Practice* **79.4**
2014 at E19. The result of an all assets confiscation order will be that there will be nothing available for a civil judgment creditor. If there is a single loser in the criminal proceedings who has also obtained a civil judgment, it may be appropriate for the criminal court to quash a confiscation order under the Criminal Justice Act 1988 to allow the judgment creditor to enforce its civil judgment (*R v Silvester* [2009] EWCA Crim 2182, LTL 9/11/2009).

STAY OF EXECUTION

A judgment debtor who is unable to pay or who alleges that it is otherwise inexpedient to **79.5**
enforce an order may apply for a stay of execution (**RSC, ord. 47, r. 1** in CPR, sch. 1; **CCR, ord. 25, r. 8** in CPR, sch. 2). Such an application must be made in accordance with **CPR, Part 23**, and must be supported by a witness statement or affidavit substantiating the grounds relied on, and usually has to include a full statement of the debtor's means. Often the result of a successful application will be a stay of execution pending payment of the judgment by instalments.

ORDERS TO OBTAIN INFORMATION FROM JUDGMENT DEBTORS

79.6 Where little is known about a judgment debtor's finances, application may be made without notice for an order to obtain information from the judgment debtor. Where the judgment debtor is a company or other corporation, an officer of that body may be required to attend court to provide information about the judgment debtor's means or any other matter to assist with enforcement (**CPR, r. 71.2(1)(b)**). 'An officer of that body' includes a director of the judgment debtor, but not a director of a corporate director of the judgment debtor (*Masri v Consolidated Contractors International (UK) Ltd (No. 4)* [2008] EWCA Civ 876, [2010] 1 AC 90; a point not overturned on the appeal, [2009] UKHL 43, [2010] 1 AC 90) or a former officer (*Vitol SA v Capri Marine Ltd* [2008] EWHC 378 (Comm), [2009] Bus LR 271). The House of Lords in *Masri v Consolidated Contractors International (UK) Ltd (No. 4)* held that, where a company is a judgment debtor, **r. 71.2** does not permit an order to be made for the examination of an officer of the company who is domiciled outside the jurisdiction. It is different if the judgment debtor is an individual, against whom an order may be made under **r. 71.2** together with permission to serve abroad under **Part 6**.

An application for an order to obtain information under **Part 71** must be made using the prescribed application notice (form N316). This must state the debtor's name and address, identify the judgment and state the amount presently owing under the judgment (**PD 71, para. 1.2**). If the creditor wishes the debtor to be questioned before a judge (which will only be allowed if there are compelling reasons: **para. 2.2**) or to produce specific documents (such as bank statements and other financial material), these matters must be stated in the application notice (**para. 1.2**). If the application complies with these requirements, it will be dealt with by a court officer without a hearing (**CPR, r. 71.2**), and the officer will make an order requiring the debtor to attend court, produce documents and answer questions. That order must be served personally on the judgment debtor not less than 14 days before the hearing (**r. 71.3**), with service usually being effected by the creditor rather than the court (**PD 71, para. 3**). Once served, the debtor has seven days to ask the judgment creditor for a reasonable sum to cover the debtor's travelling expenses to court, which must be paid (**CPR, r. 71.4**). The judgment creditor must swear an affidavit (a witness statement being insufficient) giving details of service of the order, any request for and payment of travelling expenses, and how much of the judgment remains unpaid. This affidavit must be filed two days before the hearing or produced at the hearing (**r. 71.5**).

At the hearing the court officer will ask a set of standard questions which are set out in form EX140 for the examination of individuals, and EX141 for officers of companies or corporations. The judgment creditor may ask questions, or may request the court officer to ask additional, written questions (**PD 71, para. 4.2**). If the hearing takes place before a judge, the judgment creditor must attend (**CPR, r. 71.6**) and the questioning is conducted by the creditor or the creditor's legal representative (**PD 71, para. 5.1**). 'The examination is not only intended to be an examination, but to be a cross-examination, and that of the severest kind' (per James LJ in *Republic of Costa Rica v Stronsberg* (1880) 16 ChD 8). The basic policy is to prevent a judgment debtor defeating a judgment by dissipating or concealing assets. Accordingly, the debtor is required to answer all questions fairly directed to establishing the debtor's financial circumstances, including amounts, names, account and policy numbers. The evidence is recorded and signed by the debtor.

If the debtor fails to attend or otherwise fails to comply, the court usually makes a suspended committal order, which gives the debtor a second chance to comply (**PD 71, para. 7.1**). If the debtor again fails to comply, a committal order can be made by the judge (**CPR, r. 71.8**).

EXECUTION AGAINST GOODS

Introduction

Execution against goods is the most common method of enforcement. The word 'execution' in **RSC, ord. 46, r. 8** in CPR, sch. 1, is limited to the act of seizing goods or taking possession of land, and does not refer to the whole process of enforcement (*H v N* [2009] EWHC 640 (Fam), [2009] 1 WLR 2335). In the High Court it is effected through the writ of fieri facias, often abbreviated to 'fi. fa.', and in the county courts by warrants of execution. **79.7**

Issue of writ or warrant of execution

Issue is usually purely a matter of producing the correct documents and paying a fee. In the High Court the judgment creditor produces a draft writ of fieri facias, a praecipe and the judgment. The writ is issued by being sealed (**RSC, ord. 46, r. 6** in CPR, sch. 1). It is then served on an enforcement officer under the Courts Act 2003. In the county court the judgment creditor simply sends a request for the issue of a warrant of execution to the court, and the court informs its bailiffs. **79.8**

Enforcement after six years

Where six years have elapsed since the date of the judgment or order, permission to enforce is required (**RSC, ord. 46, r. 2** in CPR, sch. 1; **CCR, ord. 26, r. 5** in CPR, sch. 2). The six-year period is regarded as a hurdle rather than a limit (*Society of Lloyd's v Longtin* [2005] EWHC 2491 (Comm), [2005] 2 CLC 774). While the exercise of the court's discretion is directed at doing justice between the parties in all the circumstances of the case (*Good Challenger Navegante SA v Metalexportimport SA* [2003] EWCA Civ 1668, [2004] 1 Lloyd's Rep 67), the court will only extend the six-year period where it is demonstrably just to do so. The burden of proof is on the judgment creditor to establish that it is just (*Duer v Frazer* [2001] 1 WLR 919). **79.9**

Seizing goods

Since the Courts Act 2003, s. 99 and sch. 7, came into force (on 15 March 2004), enforcement officers executing a warrant of execution are limited to enforcement at a specified address (*Huntress Search Ltd v Canapeum Ltd* [2010] EWHC 1270 (QB), LTL 1/6/2010). The enforcement officer or bailiffs (together referred to in this chapter as 'bailiffs') must first gain lawful entry to the debtor's premises. Outer doors must not be broken open, nor is it lawful to place a foot in an open door and push it open against the debtor's attempts to close it. The use of force to gain entry is under review. Once inside, sufficient goods will be seized to satisfy the judgment and the costs of enforcement. 'Goods' includes motor vehicles, money, promissory notes and securities, furniture etc., but excludes, by the County Courts Act 1984, s. 89(1), and the Senior Courts Act 1981, s. 138(3A): **79.10**

(i) such tools, books, vehicles and other items of equipment as are necessary to [the debtor] for use personally by him in his employment, business or vocation;
(ii) such clothing, bedding, furniture, household equipment and provisions as are necessary for satisfying the basic domestic needs of [the debtor] and his family.

The dividing line is whether such goods are 'necessary'. A debtor claiming the protection of this provision must give notice to the bailiff within five days of the seizure identifying the goods and the grounds for the claim in respect of each item. Further, the goods seized must belong to the debtor. Goods belonging to other members of the debtor's family, a limited company (even if itself owned by the debtor) or a hire-purchase company must not be seized. If there is doubt about the ownership of goods seized, the bailiff can gain protection by interpleading, see **14.75** to **14.82**.

Commentary

Under **RSC, ord.** 17, **r.** 2(4) in **CPR, sch.** 1, an enforcement officer may apply for an order restraining the bringing of a claim against him in respect of his having taken possession of goods where the execution creditor admits the goods taken do not belong to the judgment debtor. An order under **r.** 2(4) may be refused if there is a real and substantial grievance (*Smith v Critchfield* (1885) 14 QBD 873). This may arise where there has been a sale at an undervalue or where the enforcement officer was heavy-handed in executing the warrant (*Huntress Search Ltd v Canapeum Ltd* [2010] EWHC 1270 (QB), LTL 1/6/2010).

Once goods have been seized, it is usual for the bailiff to enter into an agreement with some responsible person in the house to take 'walking possession' of the goods. The goods can then remain where they are until payment or sale, the responsible person promising not to remove or damage them without the bailiff's permission, and authorising the bailiff to re-enter the premises at any time to complete the process of enforcement (*National Commercial Bank of Scotland v Arcam Demolition and Construction Ltd* [1966] 2 QB 593). Once walking possession has been taken, the bailiff can use force to retake possession (*McLeod v Butterwick* [1996] 1 WLR 995).

REMOVAL AND SALE

79.11 Often, the threat of sale is sufficient incentive to persuade the debtor to pay. On payment the execution is superseded and the goods are released, see, e.g. the County Courts Act 1984, s. 87(2). Otherwise, the goods will be removed and sold. Usually this is by public auction, but an application may be made for an order under the Courts Act 2003, sch. 7, para. 10, permitting sale otherwise than through auction (see **RSC, ord.** 47, **r.** 6 in CPR, sch. 1). On removal the debtor must be provided with an inventory, and must be given advance notice of the auction. The auction must be publicly advertised and must be conducted by an appointed broker or appraiser. After the sale the debtor is given a detailed account in writing of the sale and the application of the proceeds. Purchasers of goods sold after execution acquire good title (see, e.g. County Courts Act 1984, s. 98(1)).

ADMINISTRATION ORDERS

79.12 By virtue of the County Courts Act 1984, s. 112, and **CCR, ord.** 39 in CPR, sch. 2, a county court may make an administration order in respect of an individual debtor's debts listed in a schedule to the order if the debtor is unable to pay forthwith the amount of a judgment debt and the debtor's whole indebtedness (including the judgment) is no more than £5,000. An administration order may be made of the court's own initiative, on consideration of information provided under **CPR, Part** 71, or on the application of the debtor. The order has the immediate effect of restricting creditors named in the order from joining in bankruptcy petitions against the debtor. The order will usually provide for the debtor to make specified payments by instalments, with periodic dividends being paid to the named creditors.

The Tribunals, Courts and Enforcement Act 2007, s. 106, provides for a substantially revised administration order scheme, but it has not been brought into force.

THIRD PARTY DEBT ORDERS

79.13 Third party debt orders (formerly called garnishee proceedings) have the effect of transforming a debt payable by a third party (the garnishee under the old terminology) to the judgment debtor into an obligation to pay the debt to the judgment creditor. Third party debt orders are a particularly effective method of enforcement where the debt to be attached is owed by a responsible body, such as a bank or building society. They are not restricted to such bodies.

Third party debt orders can be made where there is a 'debt due or accruing due to the judgment debtor from a third party' (**CPR, r. 72.2(1)(a)**). This rule applies in a simple and mechanistic way only to debts owed to the judgment debtor, and not to debts owed to other persons even if connected to the judgment debtor (*Continental Transfert Technique Ltd v Federal Government of Nigeria* [2009] EWHC 2898 (Comm), LTL 18/11/2009). Contingent liabilities are not debts for this purpose (*Kier Regional Ltd v City and General (Holborn) Ltd* [2008] EWHC 2454 (TCC), [2008] CILL 2639), nor is money in a joint bank account (*Hirschon v Evans* [1938] 2 KB 801). A court could and should, in the absence of contrary indications, accept as sufficient for this purpose evidence that the judgment debtor previously held an account at a bank which appears to have been in credit at that time (*Alawiye v Mahmood* [2006] EWHC 277 (Ch), [2007] 1 WLR 79). Lindsay J also said that evidence that in the past a bank account was overdrawn might be enough if there is nothing to indicate that overall the bank is owed money by the judgment debtor (see [8]). A third party debt order was made against a bank account in the name of an unincorporated association in *Huntingdon Life Sciences Group plc v Stop Huntingdon Animal Cruelty* [2005] EWHC 2233 (QB), [2005] 4 All ER 899. A third party debt order can be made against a third party who owes a judgment debt to the judgment debtor in unrelated proceedings. This is so even where the earlier judgment debt is covered by a public funding statutory charge, but the third party debt order in such a case has to provide for payment to the judgment debtor's provider in the earlier proceedings, in accordance with what is now the Civil Legal Aid (Statutory Charge) Regulations 2013 (SI 2013/503), reg. 13 (*Beechwood Construction Ltd v Afza* [2008] EWHC 2671 (Ch), LTL 6/11/2008). It is essential that there is a relationship of creditor and debtor between the judgment debtor and the third party. If the evidence goes no further than showing that the judgment debtor might ultimately have a beneficial interest in money in a bank account held by a trustee there is no such relationship. In such a case a third party debt order will be refused (*AIG Capital Partners Inc. v Republic of Kazakhstan* [2005] EWHC 2239 (Comm), [2006] 1 WLR 1420).

Commentary

Application for an interim order

Third party debt orders follow a two-stage process. The first stage is commenced by a without notice application (**CPR, r. 72.3**) verified by a statement of truth in form N349 containing the information prescribed by **PD 72, para. 1.2**. The required information includes details of the judgment debtor, the judgment, and details of the third party debt. Speculative applications will be rejected, and orders will only be made if there is evidence substantiating a belief that the debtor has (say) an account with a specific bank or building society (**PD 72, para. 1.3**). The application is considered by a judge without a hearing (**CPR, r. 72.4(1)**), with most applications being dealt with by masters and district judges. *Thakerar v Lynch Hall and Hornby (No. 2)* [2005] EWHC 2752 (Ch), [2006] 1 WLR 1513, held that a bankruptcy registrar has jurisdiction to deal with an application made in insolvency proceedings. **79.14**

If satisfied there is a debt due or accruing due to the judgment debtor, the judge may make an interim third party debt order directing the third party not to make any payment which reduces the amount he owes the judgment debtor to less than the amount specified in the order. The judge will also fix a hearing to consider making the order final. The amount specified will be the total outstanding on the judgment or order being enforced, together with fixed costs (**r. 72.4(3)**).

Service of the interim order

An interim order must be served on the third party who owes money to the judgment debtor not less than 21 days before the date fixed for the hearing to consider making the order final (**CPR, r. 72.5(1)(a)**), and is binding on the third party when it is served on the third party (**r. 72.4(4)**). If the third party is a bank or building society it must carry out a search to identify all accounts held by the judgment debtor, and must disclose to the court and the judgment creditor the account numbers, whether they are in credit, and, if so, whether the balance is sufficient to cover the amount specified in the interim order, or the amount in the account **79.15** if insufficient (r. 72.6(1) and (2)). It must also state if it asserts any right to the money in the account, for example, by set-off, giving details of the ground for that assertion (r. 72.6(2)(c)(iii)). A third party which is not a bank or building society has seven days after service to notify the court and the judgment creditor in writing if nothing is owed to the judgment debtor or the amount owed is less than the amount specified in the interim order (r. 72.6(4)).

The interim order must also be served on the judgment debtor. This needs to be done not less than seven days after service on the third party, and not less than seven days before the date fixed for the hearing (r. 72.5(1)(b)). Where service is effected by the judgment creditor, a certificate of service must be filed not less than two days before the hearing, or must be produced at the hearing (r. 72.5(2)). A judgment debtor who is an individual and who is suffering hardship in meeting ordinary living expenses as a result of the interim order may apply for a hardship payment order permitting one or more payments out of the account (r. 72.7; PD 72, paras 5.1 to 5.6).

Application for final third party debt order

79.16 The second stage is when the court considers whether to make a final third party debt order on the date fixed when the interim order was made. A judgment debtor or third party objecting to the final order, or who knows or believes someone else has a claim to the money, must file and serve written evidence stating the grounds of any objection or details of the other claim not less than three days before the hearing (CPR, r. 72.8). If the court is notified that another person has a claim to the money it will serve notice of the application and the hearing on that person (r. 72.8(5)). At the hearing the court may make a final third party debt order, discharge the interim order, decide any issues or direct a trial of any issues (r. 72.8(6)). A final third party debt order is enforceable as an order to pay money. By r. 72.9(2), to the extent of the amount paid under the final order, the third party's debt to the judgment debtor is discharged.

Attachable money

79.17 It is possible to obtain a third party debt order only over debts due to the judgment debtor. Examples are money in a bank account, trade debts, judgment debts, and rent due to a landlord. Conversely, claims for damages, matrimonial maintenance orders, and salary not presently payable are not attachable. Most conditions imposed by banks and building societies restricting the right to withdraw money from the judgment debtor's account are disregarded once a third party debt order is made (Senior Courts Act 1981, s. 40; County Courts Act 1984, s. 108; CPR, r. 72.2(3)).

Discretion to make third party debt orders

79.18 A third party debt order may be refused if it would be inequitable to grant it. The onus of proof is on the judgment debtor to show why an interim third party debt order should not be made final (*Westacre Investments Inc. v Yugoimport SDPR* [2008] EWHC 801 (Comm), [2009] 1 All ER (Comm) 780). It is a fundamental feature of a third party debt order that the third party must be discharged from its liability to the judgment debtor in the amount that the third party pays to the judgment creditor. If the third party is located in a jurisdiction which will not recognise such a discharge, a court in England or Wales should not make a third party debt order (*Société Eram Shipping Co. Ltd v Compagnie Internationale de Navigation* [2003] UKHL 30, [2004] 1 AC 260; *Kuwait Oil Tanker Co. SAK v Qabazard* [2003] UKHL 31, [2004] 1 AC 300). The insolvency of the judgment debtor is a sufficient reason for refusing to make an order, because its effect may be to prefer the judgment creditor over the general body of creditors (*Roberts Petroleum Ltd v Bernard Kenny Ltd* [1983] 2 AC 192). Conversely, if a judgment creditor secured a charging order or third party debt order in competition with other creditors who had not been so quick off the mark, that should not affect the court's discretion to make the order final (*Reed v Oury* (2000) LTL 12/2/2001). The burden of proof remains on the judgment debtor in cases where the third party debt order is sought more than six years after the judgment, the lapse of time being no more than one of the factors to be considered in making the decision. Arguments that the judgment creditor could have discovered the third party debt sooner, or that a few months beyond six years have elapsed, are unlikely to be significant factors (*Westacre Investments Inc. v Yugoimport SDPR* [2008] EWHC 801 (Comm), [2009] 1 All ER (Comm) 780).

ATTACHMENT OF EARNINGS

Where a judgment debtor is employed, but has no other substantial assets, the most effective method of enforcement is by obtaining an attachment of earnings order. Such an order can only be made, unless the application is by the debtor, if the debtor has failed to make one or more payments as required by the relevant adjudication (Attachment of Earnings Act 1971, s. 3(3)). The Attachment of Earnings Act 1971, s. 6(1), provides: **79.19**

An attachment of earnings order shall be an order directed to a person who appears to the court to have the debtor in his employment and shall operate as an instruction to that person—

(a) to make periodical deductions from the debtor's earnings . . . and
(b) at such times as the order may require, or as the court may allow, to pay the amounts deducted to the collecting officer of the court, as specified in the order.

The High Court has no jurisdiction to make attachment of earnings orders, and High Court actions need to be transferred to a county court for enforcement in this manner. Magistrates' courts have some jurisdiction to make these orders, such as to enforce payment of arrears of council tax.

Earnings attachable

An attachment of earnings order may be made in respect of wages, salaries, fees, bonuses, commission and overtime payable under a contract of service, including occupational pensions and statutory sick pay. An order cannot be made in respect of self-employed income, nor State pensions, benefits or allowances (Attachment of Earnings Act 1971, s. 24). **79.20**

Procedure for applying for an attachment of earnings order

An application for an attachment of earnings order is made by filing a request in a standard form certifying the amount of money remaining due under the judgment, and paying the fee. The court then notifies the debtor of a hearing date at least 21 days in advance, enclosing a questionnaire concerning the debtor's means. The questionnaire should be completed by the debtor and filed at court within eight days after service. A copy of the questionnaire is sent to the judgment creditor. The questionnaire is considered by an administrative officer of the court, who may make an attachment of earnings order if there is sufficient information to do so (**CCR, ord. 27, r.** 7(1) in CPR, sch. 1). If either party objects, or if the court officer decides not to make an order, the application is referred to the district judge. **79.21**

At the hearing the district judge confirms that the debtor is not unemployed or self-employed. Provided the debtor is employed, the district judge will consider the debtor's income and regular outgoings, and will fix:

(a) The debtor's protected earnings rate. This is the amount the debtor is considered to need to maintain his or her family, each week or month, and any deductions made under the order will not reduce the debtor's income below this level.
(b) The debtor's normal deduction rate. This is the amount, subject to the protected earnings rate, which is deducted from the debtor's earnings each week or month.

Normally, the order will then be served on the debtor's employer, who will make the deductions specified and pay the money deducted to the court. Alternatively, the court may make a suspended attachment of earnings order, which will only be served on the employer if the debtor fails to pay agreed instalments promptly. A debtor with several creditors may be ordered to file a list of creditors with a view to making an administration order (**79.12**) or a consolidated attachment of earnings order.

Supplementary points

79.22 While an attachment of earnings order is in force, permission of the court is required before a warrant of execution will be issued for the judgment debt (Attachment of Earnings Act 1971, s. 8(2)(b)). Also, during the currency of the order the debtor is under a duty (enforceable by imprisonment or a fine: s. 23) to notify the court of any change in his or her employment (s. 15).

CHARGING ORDERS

79.23 A charging order is defined by the Charging Orders Act 1979, s. 1(1), as an order 'imposing on any such property of the debtor as may be specified in the order a charge for securing the payment of any money due or to become due under [a] judgment or order'. In addition to money judgments, a charging order can be made in respect of assessed costs, but not unassessed costs (*Monte Developments Ltd v Court Management Consultants Ltd* [2010] EWHC 3071 (Ch), [2011] 1 WLR 1579). A charging order secures a judgment debt: it does not of itself produce any money. By s. 3(4) a charge imposed by a charging order has the same effect, and is enforceable in the same way, 'as an equitable charge created by the debtor by writing under his hand'. It may therefore be enforced either by sale (see **79.27**) or through the appointment of a receiver (see **79.35**) (*Midland Bank plc v Pike* [1988] 2 All ER 434). It is possible to obtain a charging order in respect of a judgment payable by instalments even where the instalments are not in arrears (s. 1(6), (7)). The Lord Chancellor may impose a minimum threshold below which a charging order cannot be made (**s. 3A**). A charging order of course takes effect subject to any prior charges or mortgages. Once obtained and registered at the Land Registry, a charging order can give a measure of long-term security, which is necessary if there is no immediate prospect of recovery by other methods. It was held in *Ezekiel v Orakpo* [1997] 1 WLR 340, that a charging order extends to cover the judgment debt, interest and costs even if it does not expressly say so. As a charging order is simply security for payment, it is possible to make an order for payment by instalments as well as a charging order, provided the interim charging order is made before the instalment order (*Robaigealach v Allied Irish Bank plc* (2001) LTL 12/11/2001).

Exceptionally, it may be possible to enforce the charge by bringing sale proceedings (see **79.27**), or the charge may result in the judgment being paid if the charged property is sold by the judgment debtor and the purchaser wishes (as is usual) to purchase it clear of encumbrances. Neither LA 1980, s. 20 (mortgages), nor s. 24 (judgments) applies to enforcement of a charging order, with the result there is no limitation period (*Ezekiel v Orakpo*; *Yorkshire Bank Finance Ltd v Mulhall* [2008] EWCA Civ 1156, [2009] 2 All ER (Comm) 164).

Chargeable property

79.24 A charge may be imposed by the Charging Orders Act 1979 only on the types of property listed in s. 2 of the Act. These are the judgment debtor's interest in land, securities and partnership property. Section 2(1) allows a charging order to be made on the interest of a beneficiary under a trust for sale. If land is held by the judgment debtor alone, any charging order should be expressed to attach to his legal and beneficial interest in the land. Likewise, if there are joint debtors who own the entire beneficial interest, the charging order should cover their whole legal and beneficial interests (*Clark v Chief Land Registrar* [1994] Ch 370). Where there is one judgment debtor who is a co-owner of land, the charging order should secure his beneficial interest in the land (*National Westminster Bank Ltd v Stockman* [1981] 1 WLR 67). It may be possible to obtain a charging order against a company which is an organ of a State which is a judgment debtor (*Kensington International Ltd v Republic of Congo* [2005] EWHC 2684 (Comm), [2006] 2 BCLC 296; *Walker International Holdings Ltd v Republic of Congo* [2005] EWHC 2813 (Comm), LTL 16/12/2005; *Continental Transfert Technique Ltd v Federal Government of Nigeria* [2009] EWHC 2898 (Comm), LTL 18/11/2009), although the law on this is evolving. In *Habib Bank Ltd v Ahmed* [2004] EWCA Civ 805, *The Independent*, 30 June 2004, the debtor sought to put real property out of the reach of a charging order by transferring title to members of his family. The transfers were set aside under the Insolvency Act 1986, s. 423, as transactions at an undervalue, and the charging order was made absolute. Likewise, transfers of industrial units from the judgment debtor to related companies, between judgment and the assessment of costs, were set aside under s. 423 so that charging orders could be made in *Beckenham MC Ltd v Centralex Ltd* [2004] EWHC 1287 (Ch), [2004] 2 BCLC 764. In *Walker International Holdings Ltd v Congo* [2005] EWHC 2813 (Comm), LTL 16/12/2005, it was held that shares nominally owned by one company were in reality owned through a second company by the judgment debtor, with the result that an interim charging order was properly made in respect of the shares.

An application for a charging order under the Solicitors Act 1974, s. 73, is not precluded by the standard restriction in precedent L (**PD 46, para. 6.5**) or the Solicitors Act 1974, s. 70(2)(b), precluding proceedings to enforce a solicitor's bill until detailed assessment proceedings are concluded (*Mastercigars Direct Ltd v Withers LLP* [2007] EWHC 2733 (Ch), [2009] 1 WLR 881).

Procedure on applying for a charging order

There is a two-stage process for obtaining charging orders. The first stage is to apply for an interim charging order by issuing an application notice in form N379 verified by a statement of truth (**CPR, r. 73.3(4)**) containing the information prescribed by **PD 73, para. 1.2**. The required information includes details of the judgment debtor, the judgment, and the property which it is intended to charge. Evidence of the property where it is sought to charge the debtor's interest in land is usually provided by an office copy entry obtained from the Land Registry under the Land Registration Act 1988. The application is considered, without a hearing, by a judge who will consider making an interim order and fixing a hearing to consider making a final charging order (**CPR, r. 73.4**). If the interim order relates to registered land, it is usual, as a precaution, to protect it by entering a unilateral or agreed notice under the Land Registration Act 2002, ss. 32 and 34. Applications for charging orders are expressly stated to be writs or orders affecting land by the Charging Orders Act 1979, s. 3(2). Protection by notice is not available in cases excluded by the Land Registration Act 2002, s. 33, which include interests under a trust of land and settlements under the Settled Land Act 1925. In these cases the judgment creditor's interest should be protected by a restriction (ss. 40 to 47, and in particular, s. 42(1)(c) and (4); see *Ruoff and Roper on the Law and Practice of Registered Conveyancing* (Sweet & Maxwell), ch. 44). At least 21 days before the final hearing (which is the second stage) the judgment debtor, such other creditors as the court may direct, and certain other specified persons must be served with the interim charging order, application notice and any supporting documents (**CPR, r. 73.5(1)**). Service of an interim charging order effectively prevents dealings with the assets charged pending the final hearing (**r. 73.6**). **79.25**

The second stage is the hearing to consider making the order final. If service of the interim order was effected by the judgment creditor, a certificate of service must be filed at least two days before the final hearing, or produced at the hearing (**r. 73.5(2)**). Any person objecting to the order being made final must file and serve written evidence setting out the grounds of the objection not less than seven days before the hearing (**r. 73.8**). At the hearing the court may make a final charging order, discharge the interim order, decide any issues or direct a trial of any issues (r. 73.8(2)).

Once a final charging order has been made, consideration should be given to registering it under the Land Registration Act 2002. In practice this is usually done in order to be safe. It is arguable that registration of the final order is unnecessary if the interim charging order was itself protected by a notice, because **CPR, r. 73.8(2)**(a), says the court may 'make a final charging order confirming that the charge imposed by the interim charging order shall continue, with or without modification'. Consequently, there is only the one charging order which is merely continued by the final order, so a second notice is unnecessary. See *Ruoff and Roper on the Law and Practice of Registered Conveyancing* (Sweet & Maxwell), paras 42.023, 42.023.01 and 42.023.04.

In the case of unregistered land, the charging order should be registered in the register of writs and orders under the Land Charges Act 1972, s. 6 (see *Ruoff and Roper on the Law and Practice of Registered Conveyancing* (Sweet & Maxwell), para. 42.023.03).

Discretion to make a charging order

79.26 Particular matters laid down in the Charging Orders Act 1979, s. 1(5), that the court must consider in deciding whether to make a charging order are:

(a) the personal circumstances of the debtor; and
(b) whether any other creditor of the debtor would be likely to be unduly prejudiced by the making of the order.

Where a charging order is sought to secure a judgment payable by instalments, the fact (if it be the case) that there has been no default has to be taken into account in deciding whether to make the order (s. 1(8)).The court exercises its discretion equitably, having regard to the interests of the persons set out in s. 1(5). It is for the judgment debtor to discharge the burden of showing grounds for not making an interim order final (*Roberts Petroleum Ltd v Bernard Kenny Ltd* [1982] 1 WLR 301). This may arise where the judgment debt is small but the property to be charged has a substantial value (*Robinson v Bailey* [1942] Ch 268). A final order will be refused if the judgment debtor has entered into an insolvency procedure, because in such a case the debtor's assets should be dealt with in accordance with the insolvency legislation (*Roberts Petroleum Ltd v Bernard Kenny Ltd* [1983] 2 AC 192). Once a final order has been made, the judgment creditor can retain the benefit of that order despite the subsequent commencement of an insolvency procedure relating to the judgment debtor (Insolvency Act 1986, ss. 183 and 346). Where the judgment debtor is not subject to the English insolvency regime, the general rule is 'first past the post', and the creditor who is first to obtain a charging order takes priority (*FG Hemisphere Associates LLC v Democratic Republic of Congo* [2005] EWHC 3103 (QB), *The Times*, 27 February 2006). This is subject to exceptional cases where a particular creditor is unduly prejudiced (Charging Orders Act 1979, s. 1(5)(b)). Prejudice to other creditors can only be 'undue' if there is something about the creditor's conduct that would cause undue prejudice if the order is made final, or if there are exceptional circumstances producing prejudice over and above the prejudice that inevitably follows if a final order is made (*Burston Finance Ltd v Godfrey* [1976] 1 WLR 719). The fact that other creditors are likely to recover nothing is not an exceptional circumstance (*British Arab Commercial Bank plc v Algosaibi* [2011] EWHC 2444 (Comm), [2011] BPIR 1568).

Sale proceedings

79.27 Proceedings for the sale of charged property owned by the judgment debtor alone are governed *by* ***CPR, r. 73.10****. Such* proceedings are commenced by issuing separate proceedings using a **CPR, Part 8**, claim form, supported by evidence by witness statement or affidavit. The written evidence gives details of the charging order, the property charged, verifies the debtor's title to the property charged, identifies prior encumbrances and persons in possession, certifies the amount outstanding on the judgment, and estimates the price which would be obtained on sale. It is usual to apply for an order that the debtor vacate the premises as well, so that a sale can be made with vacant possession. Such an order can be enforced by writ or warrant of possession, see **79.33**.

The power to enforce a charging order under the Trusts of Land and Appointment of Trustees Act 1996, s. 14, is compatible with the European Convention on Human Rights in the **Human Rights Act 1998, sch. 1**, but in exercising its discretion under s. 15 of the 1996 Act, the court must bring into the balance the rights of the creditor under **Protocol 1, art. 1**, and the rights of those affected by the sale under **art. 8** (*National Westminster Bank plc v Rushmer* [2010] EWHC 554 (Ch), [2010] 2 FLR 362). Enforcement of a charge to secure a judgment payable by instalments is permitted only if there is a continuing default in payment of an instalment (Charging Orders Act 1979, s. 3(4C), (4E)).

In identifying a minimum sale price in a sale order the court should take a relatively conservative approach, finding a realistic figure which protects the owner from the risk that a fire sale would not recoup the true value of the property (*Packman Lucas Ltd v Mentmore Towers Ltd* [2010] EWHC 1037 (TCC), [2010] BLR 465). A sale order may be refused where the judgment debt is too small in comparison with the value of the property. In *Packman Lucas Ltd v Mentmore Towers Ltd* a judgment debtor owed £34,000. The creditor had a charging order on property worth possibly £15 million, which the debtor hoped to sell imminently. In these circumstances it was held that it was appropriate to refuse the order for sale and give the judgment debtor a final opportunity to pay the debt.

Commentary

Sale where more than one person has an interest in the land

Where the charged property is owned by more than one person, instead of using **CPR, r. 73.10**, any application for an order for sale has to be made under the Trusts of Land and Appointment of Trustees Act 1996, s. 14 (**PD 73, para. 4.5**). The judgment debtor and all other proprietors should be joined as defendants and served with proceedings and notice of the return day. The hearing takes place before a master or district judge. From 1 January 1997 jointly held property (including property previously held on trust for sale) has been held on the trusts of land introduced by the Trusts of Land and Appointment of Trustees Act 1996. By s. 14 any person having an interest in property subject to a trust of land may apply to court for an order relating to the exercise by the trustees of any of their functions. By s. 15, in determining such an application the court must have regard to the intentions of the persons who created the trust, the purposes for which the property is held, the welfare of any child occupying the land as his or her home, and the interests of any secured creditor of any beneficiary. Section 15 does not apply to applications made by trustees in bankruptcy (s. 15(4)). It is clear that these sections have made a fundamental change to the court's function in considering an application for an order for sale by a creditor with the benefit of a charging order. On the question of the exercise of the court's discretion see *Mortgage Corporation v Shaire* [2001] Ch 743, where it is said that the interests of the chargee are just one of the factors to be taken into account, and there is no suggestion in s. 15 that it is to be given more importance than the interests of the family residing in the property. However, in *Bank of Ireland Home Mortgages Ltd v Bell* [2001] 2 All ER (Comm) 920 the Court of Appeal said that a powerful consideration under s. 15 is that a creditor should not be kept out of his money. The fact that the debtor's spouse has children just short of their majority living in the property is a very slight consideration to be weighed against making an order for sale (*Bank of Ireland Home Mortgages Ltd v Bell*). 79.28

Standard forms of order for sale following a charging order are in **appendix A** of **PD 73**.

INSOLVENCY

79.29 Often a failure to pay a judgment debt is evidence that the judgment debtor is insolvent. Consequently, it may be more apt to bring bankruptcy or winding-up proceedings than to apply for enforcement. For further details, see **chapters 82** and **83**.

It is a fundamental principle of insolvency procedures that all unsecured creditors must recover their debts only through the insolvency procedure, in which they will all be treated equally. Once an insolvency procedure has commenced, all legal proceedings against the insolvent person, including execution of existing judgments, are controlled by the rules discussed at **84.16** to **84.37**.

In winding up (of companies) and bankruptcy (of individuals), there are specific rules concerning execution in progress when the procedure commences. If a creditor of a company issues execution against the company's goods or land, or attaches any debt due to the company, and the company is subsequently wound up (whether by the court or voluntarily), the creditor is not entitled to retain the benefit of the execution or attachment against the liquidator, unless the court orders otherwise, if the execution or attachment was not completed before the commencement of the winding up (Insolvency Act 1986, s. 183). A voluntary winding up initiated by adopting a resolution for voluntary winding up commences at the time the resolution is adopted (s. 86). When a winding-up order is made on a winding-up petition, the commencement of the winding up is backdated to the time when the petition was presented (s. 129(2)), unless the company was in voluntary winding up at that time, in which case it is further backdated to the commencement of the voluntary winding up (s. 129(1)). Similarly, if a creditor of an individual issues execution against the individual's goods or land, or attaches any debt due to the individual, and the individual is subsequently adjudged bankrupt, the creditor is not entitled to retain the benefit of the execution or attachment against the official receiver or the bankrupt's trustee, unless the court orders otherwise, if the execution or attachment was not completed before the commencement of the bankruptcy (s. 346(1) and (6)). A bankruptcy commences with the day on which the bankruptcy order is made (s. 278). Sections 183(3) and 346(5) define when an execution or attachment is complete. Execution against goods is completed by seizure and sale or by making a charging order under the Charging Orders Act 1979, s. 1. Attachment of a debt is completed by receipt of the debt. Execution against land is completed by seizure, or by the appointment of a receiver or by the making of a charging order under the Charging Orders Act 1979, s 1. In order to constitute completion of execution against land, the appointment of a receiver must be by a final order: an interim appointment on an application without notice will not suffice (*Roberts Petroleum Ltd v Bernard Kenny Ltd* [1983] 2 AC 192; *Coutts and Co. v Clarke* [2002] EWCA Civ 943, LTL 17/6/2002).

An officer carrying out execution against a person (individual or company) must hand over any property seized or the proceeds of any sale to a provisional liquidator, liquidator, official receiver or trustee if notified that the person's winding up, provisional liquidation or bankruptcy has commenced (ss. 184(1) and (2) and 346(3)). If execution is levied against any person for more than £500, the proceeds of sale, or money paid in order to avoid sale, must be kept for 14 days, during which notice can be given that a winding-up or bankruptcy petition against the person has been presented, or a meeting has been convened to consider a resolution for the person's voluntary winding up. The money must then be paid to the liquidator, official receiver or trustee if the winding-up or bankruptcy order is made or the resolution for voluntary winding up is adopted (ss. 184(3) and (4) and 346(4)).

If a court makes an interim charging order against property of a person or an interim third party debt order in respect of a debt owed to a person, and, before the court determines whether to make the order final, a petition is presented for the compulsory winding up or bankruptcy of the person, an order can be obtained under s. 126 (winding up) or s. 285(1) (bankruptcy) staying or restraining the charging or attachment proceedings. In general, such an order will be made, except in very special circumstances (*Bowkett v Fullers United Electric Works Ltd* [1923] 1 KB 160). Even if an order under s. 126 or s. 285(1) is not obtained, a court considering whether to make a final charging or third party debt order should refuse to do so if presentation of the petition shows that the person is likely to be insolvent and that the execution creditor should not be given an advantage over other unsecured creditors (*Rainbow v Moorgate Properties Ltd* [1975] 1 WLR 788 (winding up); *Industrial Diseases Compensation Ltd v Marrons* [2001] BPIR 600 (bankruptcy)). The general principle is that the court will not make a final order which would or could have the effect of circumventing a statutory regime which operates on insolvency (*FG Hemisphere Associates LLC v Republic of Congo* [2005] EWHC 3103 (Comm), *The Times*, 27 February 2006). However, if the court makes a final charging or third party debt order against an individual when it is unaware that a bankruptcy petition has been presented, the order will be effective despite the subsequent making of a bankruptcy order, because the commencement of bankruptcy is not backdated, and the court ought not to discharge the charging or third party debt order (*Nationwide Building Society v Wright* [2009] EWCA Civ 811, [2010] Ch 318). It is clearly unsatisfactory that one creditor should be able to gain an advantage over other creditors in this way. It is to be hoped that courts will be able to insist that an applicant for a final charging or third party debt order against an individual must search for any pending bankruptcy petition against the individual and report the result of the search to the court.

Commentary

JUDGMENT SUMMONSES

A judgment summons is a procedure for punishing a defaulting judgment debtor who could pay, but has chosen not to, with a period of up to six weeks in prison (Debtors Act 1869, s. 5). The punitive nature of the provision was stressed by the Court of Appeal in *Woodley v Woodley* (1993) *The Times*, 15 March 1993. Since the Administration of Justice Act 1970, s. 11, came into force, judgment summonses have only been available for enforcing maintenance orders (defined in the Administration of Justice Act 1970, s. 28(1) and sch. 8) and arrears of some taxes (listed in sch. 4). The procedure in the county courts is in **CCR, ord. 28** in CPR, sch. 2. There are prescribed forms for the request for a judgment summons (form N342) and request for a warrant of committal (form N344). An application under the Debtors Act 1869, s. 5, should be treated in the same way as an application for committal for contempt of court (see **chapter 81**) (*Murbarak v Murbarik* [2001] 1 FLR 698). **79.30**

ENFORCEMENT OF JUDGMENTS FOR THE DELIVERY OF GOODS

Enforcement of judgments for the delivery of goods is by means of warrants (or, in the High Court, writs) of delivery. There are two types, corresponding with the forms of relief stated in the Torts (Interference with Goods) Act 1977, s. 3. The first is known as a warrant (or writ) of specific delivery. It requires the bailiff (or enforcement officer) to seize the goods specified in the judgment, with no alternative of seizing other goods up to the assessed value of the goods forming the subject matter of the judgment. The second is known as a warrant (or writ) of delivery. It requires the bailiff (or enforcement officer) to seize either the goods specified in the judgment, or other goods up to the value (specified in the judgment) of the goods forming the subject matter of the judgment. **79.31**

As with execution against goods (**79.8** and **79.9**), issue is simply a matter of the creditor filing a request (county court) or praecipe, draft writ of delivery and judgment (High Court), and paying the court fee.

ENFORCEMENT OF JUDGMENTS FOR THE POSSESSION OF LAND

Common law

79.32 At common law, a claimant who has obtained judgment for the possession of land may enter the land after the judgment has been obtained and take it back, provided no force is used. This right does not apply to land within the scope of the Rent Act 1977, Housing Act 1988, Landlord and Tenant Act 1954, part 1, etc., and see the Protection from Eviction Act 1977. The invariable practice in present times is for enforcement to be effected under warrants (county court) or writs (High Court) of possession.

Procedure on writ or warrant of possession

79.33 Like execution against goods (**79.8** and **79.9**), issue is simply a matter of filing a request (county court) or a praecipe, draft writ of possession and judgment (High Court) and paying a fee. It is of the utmost importance that the land is adequately described. The police are often informed of the time when possession will be enforced, as entry may be gained by force if necessary. The claimant will also usually need to attend to change the locks and make the premises secure after possession is obtained.

When enforcing the warrant or writ, the bailiff or enforcement officer is required to turn out everyone on the premises, even if they are not parties (*R v Wandsworth County Court, ex parte Wandsworth London Borough Council* [1975] 1 WLR 1314). However, there is a divergence of practice regarding goods in the premises. In the High Court, these too must be removed by the enforcement officer, but in the county courts this is unnecessary (County Courts Act 1984, s. 111(1)).

For the practice on enforcement in mortgage possession cases see **87.49** to **87.58**.

Warrants and writs of restitution

79.34 It sometimes happens that persons ejected when a warrant or writ of possession is enforced regain entry at some later date. Such persons may be removed a second time under a warrant (county court) or writ (High Court) of restitution. These are a species of warrant (or writ) in aid of a primary warrant (or writ). Permission is required for the issue of such warrants or writs (**RSC, ord. 46, r. 3** in CPR, sch. 1; **CCR, ord. 26, r. 17(4)** in CPR, sch. 2). The application is made using the **CPR, Part 23**, procedure, but the application notice need not be served on the respondent unless the court otherwise directs. The application must be supported by evidence by witness statement or affidavit giving evidence of wrongful re-entry. The court looks for a plain and sufficient nexus between the original recovery of possession and the need to effect further recovery of the same land (*Wiltshire County Council v Frazer (No. 2)* [1986] 1 WLR 109).

RECEIVERS BY WAY OF EQUITABLE EXECUTION

Nature of receivership

79.35 Courts are empowered to appoint receivers by the Senior Courts Act 1981, s. 37 (powers of the High Court regarding receivers), and the County Courts Act 1984, ss. 38 (remedies available in the county courts) and 107 (receivers by way of equitable execution) where this is just and convenient. *Masri v Consolidated Contractors International (UK) Ltd (No. 2)* [2008] EWCA Civ 303, [2009] QB 450, established that the jurisdiction under s. 37 is not limited to the circumstances where a receiver could have been appointed in 1873 (the date of the Supreme Court of Judicature Act 1873), and that a receiver by way of equitable execution may be appointed over an asset whether or not the asset is at that time amenable to execution at law. The law governing the jurisdiction is capable of being developed incrementally to new situations. It extends to enable the appointment of a receiver by way of equitable execution over a power to revoke a discretionary trust vested in the judgment debtor where the objects of the trust include the judgment debtor (*Tasarruf Mevduatı Sigorta Fonu v Merrill Lynch Bank and Trust Company (Cayman) Ltd* [2011] UKPC 17, [2011] 4 All ER 704). A receivership order has the effect of appointing some responsible person to receive rents, profits and moneys receivable in respect of the judgment debtor's interest in certain property, and to apply that income in specified ways, including payment of a judgment debt. According to *Maclaine Watson and Co. Ltd v International Tin Council* [1988] Ch 1, such an order can only be made where:

(a) it is impossible to enforce using any of the other methods of enforcement; and
(b) the appointment of a receiver will be effective.

These conditions are not always applied rigidly (*Manchester and Liverpool District Banking Co. Ltd v Parkinson* (1889) 22 QBD 173). Enforcement of a judgment outside the EU may be sufficiently difficult in practical terms as to justify the appointment of a receiver (*Masri v Consolidated Contractors International Co. SAL* [2008] EWHC 2492 (Comm), LTL 28/10/2008). An appointment of a receiver by way of equitable execution operates *in personam*, so the extraterritorial restrictions relating to applications for third party debt orders (for which see **79.18**) do not apply (*Masri v Consolidated Contractors International (UK) Ltd (No. 2)* [2008] EWCA Civ 303, [2009] QB 450).

On the question whether the appointment of a receiver will be effective, the Senior Courts Act 1981, s. 37(1), provides that an appointment can only be made if it is just and convenient. Under **PD 69, para. 5**, when considering an application for the appointment of a receiver as a method of enforcing a judgment, the court must have regard to the amount claimed by the judgment creditor, the amount likely to be obtained by the receiver, and the probable costs of the appointment.

A receiver might be appointed where the judgment debtor has some valuable right not in the nature of a debt (and hence not amenable to a third party debt order). A receiver might also be appointed to receive rents from a number of tenants who are suing their landlord for failing to maintain the premises, and to apply the money in effecting necessary repairs (*Hart v Emelkirk Ltd* [1983] 1 WLR 1289).

Procedure for seeking the appointment of a receiver

An application for the appointment of a receiver in existing proceedings is made using the **CPR, Part 23**, procedure, and must be supported by two witness statements or affidavits. The first explains the reasons why the appointment is required, gives details of the property which it is proposed that the receiver should get in or manage, estimates the value of the property and amount of income likely to be produced, gives details of the judgment or order being enforced and the extent to which the judgment debtor has failed to comply with it and why judgment cannot be enforced in any other way (**PD 69, para. 4.1**). It should also give the name, address and position of the proposed receiver ('the nominee', **para. 4.2(1)**). The second witness statement should be by a person who knows the nominee, and needs to state a belief that the nominee is a suitable person to be appointed, and the basis of that belief (**para. 4.2(2)**). The written evidence must be accompanied by a signed consent from the nominee (**para. 4.2(3)**). **79.36**

Order appointing a receiver

The order appointing a receiver may: **79.37**

(a) require the receiver to provide security, usually by bond (in the case of insolvency practitioners) or guarantee (**CPR, r. 69.5; PD 69, para. 7.2**) — the security is usually fixed at twice the annual income from the property;

(b) allow the receiver proper remuneration (**CPR, r. 69.7; PD 69, paras 9.1 to 9.6**);
(c) require the receiver to submit periodic accounts (**CPR, r. 69.8; PD 69, paras 10.1 to 10.3**);
(d) require moneys received to be paid into court (**PD 69, para. 6.3(3)**);
(e) authorise the receiver to carry on an activity or incur an expense (**PD 69, para. 6.3(4)**).

ENFORCEMENT AGAINST PARTICULAR TYPES OF PARTY

Partnerships

79.38 With effect from 2 October 2006, a judgment or order made against a partnership may be enforced without permission against:

(a) any property of the partnership within the jurisdiction (**PD 70, para. 6A. 1**);
(b) any person who was within the jurisdiction when the claim form was issued and who is not a limited partner, if that person acknowledged service of the claim form as a partner, or having been served as a partner with the claim form, failed to acknowledge service of it, or admitted in his statement of case that he is or was a partner at the material time, or was found by the court to have been a partner at the relevant time (**PD 70, para. 6A.2**); or
(c) any person who was ordinarily resident outside the jurisdiction when the claim form was issued and who is not a limited partner, if that person acknowledged service of the claim form as a partner, or was served within the jurisdiction as a partner, or who was served outside the jurisdiction as a partner with permission under **CPR, Part 6, Section III** (**PD 70, para. 6A.3**).

A judgment or order may be enforced against a person not falling into the categories set out in points (a) to (c) above only with the court's permission (**PD 70, para. 6A.4**). This will include limited partners, and other partners who do not come within **PD 70, paras 6A.2** or **6A.3**.

There are special provisions dealing with service and appearance at court by a partnership in relation to enforcement by:

(a) attaching debts due or accruing due to a judgment creditor by a partnership (see **PD 72, paras 3A.1** to **3A.3**); and
(b) charging order or interim charging order against property within the jurisdiction belonging to a judgment debtor that is a partnership (see **PD 73, paras 4A.1** to **4A.3**).

Representative parties

79.39 If a claim is brought or ordered to be continued against a representative party under **CPR, r. 19.6(1)**, any judgment or order given in the claim is binding on all persons represented, unless the court orders otherwise (**r. 19.6(4)**). However, the judgment or order cannot be enforced against a person who is not a party to the claim unless the court gives permission (**r. 19.6(4)**). The same applies to a claim in which the court has, under **r. 19.7(2)**, appointed a representative of persons who cannot be ascertained (**r. 19.7(7)**).

The Crown

79.40 A successful claimant may not enforce a judgment against the Crown by process of execution (Crown Proceedings Act 1947, s. 25(4)). None of the provisions of **CPR, Parts 69** to **73**, **RSC, ords 45** to **47** and **52** in CPR, sch. 1, or **CCR, ords 25** to **29** in CPR, sch. 2, apply to the Crown (**CPR, r. 66.6**). The Crown, on the other hand, may enforce a judgment in its favour against a private litigant in the normal way (Crown Proceedings Act 1947, s. 26(1)).

In order to obtain satisfaction of orders against the Crown, a successful claimant must follow the procedure set out in the Crown Proceedings Act 1947, s. 25. It is as follows:

(a) The claimant should apply to the court, at least 21 days after the date of the order, for a certificate in form No. 95 or No. 96 in the High Court, or form N293A in a county court.
(b) The certificate must set out full particulars of the order made, including, where appropriate, the amount payable by the Crown.
(c) Once obtained, the certificate should be served on the solicitors acting for the Crown.
(d) The Crown will then make payment.

The Crown Proceedings Act 1947 gives no deadline for payment of the amount due by the Crown. The court may order that payment be suspended pending appeal (s. 25(3)).

Attaching Crown debts

A person who has obtained judgment against a defendant who is owed money by the Crown **79.41** may obtain an order under the Crown Proceedings Act 1947, s. 27(1), directing payment of the money to the judgment creditor instead of the judgment debtor. The application is made by application notice using the Part 23 procedure, supported by written evidence setting out the facts giving rise to the application, stating the name and last known address of the person to be restrained, identifying the order to be enforced and the amount outstanding under it, and identifying the debt owed by the Crown in respect of which the application is made (CPR, r. 66.7).

Chapter 80 Enforcement of Foreign Judgments

INTRODUCTION

80.1 English law provides for enforcement of foreign judgments under common law and under four different statutory schemes based upon international instruments (Administration of Justice Act 1920, Foreign Judgments (Reciprocal Enforcement) Act 1933, Brussels and Lugano Conventions, **Brussels I Regulation**). The choice of the appropriate mechanism will depend on the country of origin of the judgment.

The common law and the statutory schemes are not mutually exclusive. However, where a statutory scheme is available, it should be preferred because its regime is generally more favourable to the party seeking enforcement.

COMMON LAW

80.2 At common law, a foreign judgment creates an implied contract to pay, which can be enforced in England subject to certain defences (*Grant v Easton* (1883) 13 QBD 302). The party seeking to enforce the foreign judgment must commence proceedings in the appropriate English court based on this implied contract to pay. This party will usually seek to obtain summary judgment on the basis that the defendant has no reasonable prospect of defending the claim.

Foreign court must have had jurisdiction over the defendant

80.3 *The foreign court must have* had jurisdiction over the defendant according to English conflict of laws rules (*Sirdar Gurdyal Singh v Rajah of Faridkote* [1894] AC 670). Thus, the defendant, at the date of the commencement of the proceedings, must have been present in the foreign country (*Adams v Cape Industries plc* [1990] Ch 433). Alternatively, the defendant must have submitted, or agreed to submit, to the jurisdiction of the foreign court. Actual submission includes voluntary appearance in the foreign court other than for disputing jurisdiction. Agreement to submit includes contractual non-exclusive and exclusive jurisdiction clauses as well as clauses relating to acceptance of service of process. The court will not permit enforcement of a foreign judgment against a person who has played no part in the foreign proceedings (*Rubin v Eurofinance SA* [2012] UKSC 46, [2013] 1 AC 236).

Conditions relating to the foreign judgment

To be enforceable at common law, the judgment of the foreign court must be conclusive on its merits. In particular, the foreign court must have ruled it had jurisdiction and accordingly decided on the cause of action, without the possibility of its decision being varied, reopened or set aside by that court (*The Sennar (No. 2)* [1985] 1 WLR 490). A right to appeal the foreign judgment to a higher court does not prevent it from being conclusive. However, if a stay of execution has been granted, the judgment may not be enforced (*Colt Industries Inc. v Sarlie (No. 2)* [1966] 1 WLR 1287). The claim must be for a definite sum or for a sum ascertainable by a simple calculation (*Beatty v Beatty* [1924] 1 KB 807). Foreign judgments for the enforcement of penal (*United States of America v Inkley* [1989] QB 255) or revenue (*Re State of Norway's Application (Nos. 1 and 2)* [1990] 1 AC 723) laws may not be enforced in the English courts. Revenue debts due in other EU States may be recovered under the Finance Act 2011, s. 87 and sch. 25. A judgment will not be registered in England and Wales if the nature of the judgment is unclear (*La Caisse Régionale du Crédit Agricole Nord de France v Ashdown* [2007] EWCA Civ 574, LTL 15/5/2007). **80.4**

Commentary

Defences to an enforcement claim

In addition to the conditions set out at **80.3** and **80.4**, a defendant can resist the claim by raising a number of defences. The defendant may argue that the foreign judgment was obtained by fraud (*Jet Holdings Inc. v Patel* [1990] 1 QB 335) whether on the part of the foreign court or the successful party. The defendant may claim that the judgment is contrary to public policy (*Soleimany v Soleimany* [1999] QB 785). The defendant may contend that the proceedings leading to the foreign judgment were contrary to natural or substantive justice (*Adams v Cape Industries plc* [1990] Ch 433). In deciding whether to recognise a foreign judgment, an English court would have regard to its obligation to act in a manner consistent with the right to a fair trial guaranteed by the European Convention on Human Rights, **art. 6**, in the **Human Rights Act 1998, sch. 1** (*Al-Bassam v Al-Bassam* [2004] EWCA Civ 857, [2004] WTLR 757). A default judgment for enforcement of a foreign judgment will not be set aside on the ground that the judgment sought to be enforced has been set aside if the English court finds that setting aside the foreign judgment breached the European Convention on Human Rights, **art. 6** (*Merchant International Co. Ltd v Natsionalna Aktsionerna Kompaniia Naftogaz Ukrainy* [2012] EWCA Civ 196, [2012] 1 WLR 3036). For multiple damages see **80.6**. **80.5**

COMMONWEALTH JUDGMENTS

Under the Administration of Justice Act 1920 (the '1920 Act') a without-notice application can be made for the registration of a judgment of a superior court of a Commonwealth country in the High Court within 12 months of the date of the judgment in question. The court has a discretion whether to register the judgment, and the defendant can make use of most of the defences available at common law. **80.6**

A foreign judgment for multiple damages will not be registered under either the Administration of Justice Act 1920 or the Foreign Judgments (Reciprocal Enforcement) Act 1933, and it is a defence to proceedings at common law for the recovery of any sum payable under such a judgment (Protection of Trading Interests Act 1980, s. 5(1)). A judgment arrived at by multiplying the amount assessed as compensation is a judgment for multiple damages (s. 5(3)). Where a foreign judgment consists of identifiable compensatory damages and multiple damages, it is only the multiple damages part of the judgment which is not enforceable (*Lewis v Eliades* [2003] EWCA Civ 1758, [2004] 1 WLR 692).

RECIPROCAL ENFORCEMENT ARRANGEMENTS

80.7 Under the Foreign Judgments (Reciprocal Enforcement) Act 1933 (the '1933 Act') an application can be made for the registration of judgments of recognised courts and tribunals of States with which this country has entered into reciprocal enforcement arrangements, provided the application is made within six years of the judgment. The 1933 Act considerably increased the circumstances in which foreign judgments can be registered, but enforcement is subject to a wide range of defences similar to those available at common law. For multiple damages see **80.6**.

BRUSSELS CONVENTION JUDGMENTS

80.8 Under the Civil Jurisdiction and Judgments Act 1982, s. 4, a judgment of a court of another contracting State to the Brussels Convention (i.e. Aruba and the French overseas departments) may be registered in the courts of this country. The same applies to a judgment of a Gibraltar court (Civil Jurisdiction and Judgments Act 1982 (Gibraltar) Order 1997 (SI 1997/2602)). When registered, such a judgment has the same force and effect as if the judgment had been given in this country. Articles 27 and 28 of the Convention set out a number of defences to registration, such as recognition being contrary to public policy, the defendant not having been duly served with the document instituting the foreign proceedings, and the judgment being irreconcilable with another judgment. However, art. 29 provides that there cannot, under any circumstances, be a review of the substance of such a judgment.

Third-party debt orders are a means of enforcement of a judgment in rem against the debt. Accordingly, exclusive jurisdiction for enforcement by this method is given to the courts where the debt is situated by the Lugano Convention 1988, art. 16(5) (which is identical with art. 16(5) of the Brussels Convention) (*Kuwait Oil Tanker Co. SAK v Qabazard* [2003] UKHL 31, [2004] 1 AC 300).

Recognition of a Dutch judgment which had been obtained in manifest contravention of art. 6(1) of the European Convention on Human Rights was refused as being contrary to public policy under art. 27(1) of the Brussels Convention in *Maronier v Larmer* [2002] EWCA Civ 774, [2003] QB 620. *TSN Kunststoffrecycling GmbH v Jurgens* [2002] EWCA Civ 11, [2002] 1 WLR 2459 involved a judgment entered in default in Germany which was registered for enforcement in England. The judgment debtor alleged that the 14-day period for responding to the claim provided by the German rules of procedure was insufficient, and argued that under art. 27(2) the judgment should not be recognised because he had not been served in sufficient time to be able to arrange for his defence. It was held that to do justice both to the judgment debtor's right to a fair trial and to ensure the free movements of judgments, the exception provided by art. 27(2) should not be expanded further than was reasonably necessary to protect the judgment debtor's right to a fair trial. It was found that five weeks had elapsed between service and entry of the default judgment, so registration was not set aside.

A default judgment, or a judgment entered after striking out for breach of an unless order, can be registered under the Brussels Convention. Recognition of such a judgment may be refused on public policy grounds under art. 27 of the Convention if such recognition is contrary to public policy in the member State in which recognition is sought. Recourse to the public policy defence is available only where recognition or enforcement of the judgment would be at variance to an unacceptable degree with the legal order of the member State in which enforcement is sought. The infringement would have to constitute a manifest breach of a rule of law regarded as essential in the legal order of the member State in which enforcement is sought or of a right recognised as being fundamental within that legal order (*Gambazzi v DaimlerChrysler Canada Inc.* (case C-394/07) [2009] 1 Lloyd's Rep 647).

BRUSSELS I REGULATION AND LUGANO CONVENTION 2007

Since 1 March 2002 (1 July 2007 in the case of Denmark), **Regulation (EC) No. 44/2001**, the '**Brussels I Regulation**', has replaced the provisions on enforcement under the Brussels Convention in all EU countries. The Lugano Convention 2007 (which applies to Iceland, Norway and Switzerland) is in the same terms. The principles are almost identical to those applicable under the Brussels and the previous Lugano 1988 Conventions. For legal proceedings instituted on or after 10 January 2015, **Regulation (EC) No. 44/2001** is replaced by Regulation (EU) No. 1215/2012, the 'recast Brussels I Regulation', which will be discussed in the next edition of *Blackstone's Civil Practice*. **80.9**

Conditions for application of the Brussels I Regulation or the Lugano Convention 2007

To obtain registration, the claimant must show that three conditions are fulfilled: **80.10**

(a) the foreign judgment must fall within the scope of the Regulation, that is, the subject matter of the dispute must be commercial or civil (**Brussels I Regulation, art. 1(1)** and **(2)**).
(b) The proceedings must have been instituted on or after 1 March 2002. Earlier proceedings will be enforced under the Regulation if instituted after the entry into force of the Brussels and Lugano Conventions in the State of origin and the State of enforcement and if judgment is given on or after the date of entry into force of the Regulation in both the member State of origin and the member State addressed (**art. 66**; *Wolf Naturprodukte GmbH v SEWAR spol sro* (case C-514/10) CJEU judgment 21 June 2012). The Regulation will also apply if the jurisdiction of the court of origin of the foreign judgment was founded upon rules which accorded with those provided for in Chapter II of the Regulation or in a convention concluded between the member State of origin and the member State addressed which was in force when the proceedings were instituted. A judgment of a court of the Republic of Cyprus should be recognised and enforced in other member States even where it relates to land in Northern Cyprus. Recognition and enforcement is not precluded by the fact that the application of EU law is suspended in those areas of Cyprus in which the government of the Republic of Cyprus does not exercise effective control (*Apostolides v Orams* (case C-420/07) [2009] ECR I-3571; *Orams v Apostolides* [2010] EWCA Civ 9, [2011] QB 519).
(c) The ruling for which enforcement is sought must be a judgment given by a court or tribunal of a member State, whatever the judgment may be called, including a decree, order, decision or writ of execution, as well as the determination of costs or expenses by an officer of the court (**art. 32**).

Authentic instruments and court settlements are also enforceable. A document formally drawn up or registered as an authentic instrument and which is enforceable in one Regulation State must be registered as a foreign judgment (**arts 57 and 58**).

The conditions to be fulfilled under the Lugano Convention 2007 are the same (Lugano Convention 2007, **arts 1(1) and (2), 32, 57, 58 and 63**).

Grounds of defence

A defendant may raise one of four grounds of defence set out in the **Brussels I Regulation, art. 34**. **80.11**
Recognition of a foreign judgment may be refused because it is manifestly contrary to public policy

of the member State in which recognition is sought (**art. 34(1)**). The judgment will not be recognised where it was given in default of appearance, if the defendant has not been served with the document instituting proceedings in sufficient time and in such a way as to enable him to arrange his defence, unless the defendant failed to commence proceedings to challenge the judgment when it was possible for him to do so (**art. 34(2)**). 'Service' in **art. 34(2)** has the same meaning as in **art. 30** (see **16.37**) and Regulation (EC) No. 1348/2000 (see **16.58**) (*Tavoulareas v Tsavliris (No. 2)* [2006] EWCA Civ 1772, [2007] 1 WLR 1573). Mere notification of proceedings is not service. 'Default of appearance' encompasses failing to comply with procedures involving returning a formal document to the court and actual physical attendance at court (*Tavoulareas v Tsavliris (No. 2)*). A defendant will only have been able to challenge the judgment for the purposes of the proviso to the **Brussels I Regulation, art. 34(2)**, if the judgment was served on him in sufficient time to enable him to arrange his defence in the courts of the State in which the judgment was given (*ASML Netherlands BV v Semiconductor Industry Services GmbH* (case C-283/05) [2007] 1 All ER (Comm) 949). A judgment will also not be recognised where it is irreconcilable with a judgment given in a dispute between the same parties in the State in which recognition is sought (**art. 34(3)**). The same applies to a judgment that is irreconcilable with an earlier judgment given in another Regulation State or in a third State involving the same cause of action and between the same parties (**art. 34(4)**).

Where an ordinary appeal has been lodged, the court of the country in which recognition is sought may stay the enforcement proceedings (**art. 37**).

NORTHERN IRISH AND SCOTTISH JUDGMENTS

80.12 Under the Civil Jurisdiction and Judgments Act 1982 (the '1982 Act'), s. 18, judgments of the courts of Northern Ireland and Scotland can be enforced in England and Wales by a simple process of registration of a certificate of the judgment in question. The only defences are that the procedure has not been complied with or that there has been an earlier judgment dealing with the same matter. The procedure is set out in **CPR, rr. 74.14 to 74.18**.

REGISTRATION IN ENGLAND AND WALES OF FOREIGN JUDGMENTS

80.13 **CPR, rr. 74.2 to 74.11**, set out the procedure for registering judgments under:

(a) the Administration of Justice Act 1920 (the '1920 Act'; see **80.6**);
(b) the Foreign Judgments (Reciprocal Enforcement) Act 1933 (the '1933 Act'; see **80.7**);
(c) the Civil Jurisdiction and Judgments Act 1982 (the '1982 Act'; see **80.8**); and
(d) the **Brussels I Regulation** or the Lugano Convention 2007 (see **80.9**).

For this purpose, a 'judgment' means any judgment of a foreign court or tribunal, whatever it may be called, and includes decrees, orders, decisions, writs of execution and costs determinations (**CPR, r.** 74.2(1)(c)).

Applications for registration must be made to the Queen's Bench Division of the High Court (r. 74.3(2); **PD 74A, para. 4.1**). Applications may be made without notice (**CPR, r. 74.3(2)**) in accordance with Part 23 (**PD 74A, para. 4.4**) and must be supported by written evidence complying with **CPR, r.** 74.4 (see **80.14 to 80.18**).

Common requirements for evidence under the 1920, 1933 and 1982 Acts

80.14 Applications for registration under the 1920, 1933 and 1982 Acts (but not the **Brussels I Regulation** *or the Lugano Convention* 2007, for which see **80.18**) must, by **CPR, r. 74.4(1)** and (2), be supported by written evidence which:

(a) states the name of the judgment creditor and an address for service within the jurisdiction;

(b) states the name and address of the judgment debtor;
(c) states the grounds on which the judgment creditor is entitled to enforce the judgment;
(d) states the amount outstanding (if a money judgment);
(e) states details of any interest recoverable on the judgment, including the rate, dates and amounts;
(f) exhibits the judgment or a verified or certified or otherwise authenticated copy of the judgment;
(g) exhibits a translation of the judgment (if not in English) into English certified by a notary public or other qualified person, or which is confirmed to be accurate.

Evidence under the 1920 Act

In addition to the matters set out at 77.14, the evidence in support of an application for registration under the 1920 Act must, by **CPR, r. 74.4(3)**: **80.15**

(a) state that the judgment is not a judgment which under the 1920 Act, s. 9, cannot be registered (r. 74.4(3)(a));
(b) state that the judgment is not one to which the Protection of Trading Interests Act 1980, s. 5, applies (r. 74.4(3)(b)).

Evidence under the 1933 Act

In addition to the matters set out at **80.14**, the evidence in support of an application for registration under the 1933 Act must, by **CPR, r. 74.4(4)**, state that it is a money judgment, confirm that it can be enforced by execution in the State of origin, and deal with various other matters, including providing any further evidence required by the relevant Order in Council. **80.16**

Evidence under the 1982 Act

In addition to the matters set out at **80.14**, the evidence in support of an application for registration under the 1982 Act must, by **CPR, r. 74.4(5)**, exhibit documents showing that the judgment is enforceable against the judgment debtor in the State of origin, and, where appropriate, documents proving service of the originating process (if judgment was entered in default) and any legal aid certificate from the State of origin. **80.17**

Evidence under the Brussels I Regulation or the Lugano Convention 2007

Written evidence in support of applications for registration in the High Court of judgments given in EU or Lugano Convention 2007 States must comply with **CPR, r. 74.4(6)**; **PD 74A, paras 6.1** to **6.5** or **6A.1** to **6A.5**, and the **Brussels I Regulation, arts 40, 53, 54** and **55**, or the same articles of the Lugano Convention 2007. The evidence must, in particular: **80.18**

(a) state an address for service within the jurisdiction (**Brussels I Regulation, art.** 40(2); Lugano Convention 2007, art. 40(2));
(b) state details of any interest recoverable on the judgment, including the rate, dates and amounts (**CPR, r.** 74.4(2)(e));
(c) exhibit a copy of the judgment in a form establishing its authenticity (**Brussels I Regulation, art.** 53(1); Lugano Convention 2007, art. 53(1));
(d) exhibit a certificate in the form set out in Annex V to the Regulation or the Convention (**Brussels I Regulation, art.** 53(2); Lugano Convention 2007, art. 53(2));
(e) exhibit a certified translation of the certificate (**Brussels I Regulation, art.** 55(2); Lugano Convention 2007, art. 55(2)); and
(f) exhibit a translation of the judgment (if not in English) into English certified by a notary public or other qualified person, or which is confirmed to be accurate (**CPR, r.** 74.4(6)).

REGISTRATION ORDERS

80.19 An order granting permission to register a judgment must be drawn up by the judgment creditor and served on the judgment debtor (**CPR, r. 74.6(1)**). The order must give full particulars of the original judgment, and the name and address for service within the jurisdiction of the judgment creditor. It must also set out the rights to apply to set aside (under the 1920 and 1933 Acts) or to appeal against the registration (under the 1982 Act, the **Brussels I Regulation** or the Lugano Convention 2007), the time for making such application or appeal, and that no enforcement measures will be taken until the end of that period (**CPR, r. 74.6(3)** and see **r. 74.9**). Registration serves as a decision that the judgment is recognised for the purposes of the 1982 Act, and the **Brussels I Regulation** or the Lugano Convention 2007 (**CPR, r. 74.10**). The Central Office keeps registers of foreign judgments ordered to be enforced under the 1920,1933 and 1982 Acts, the **Brussels I Regulation** and the Lugano Convention 2007 (**PD 74A, para. 3(1)**).

Service of registration orders

80.20 Service must be effected by the judgment creditor on the judgment debtor by delivering the order personally, or by serving a company in accordance with the Companies Act 2006 or as directed by the court (**CPR, r. 74.6(1)**). Permission is not required for service outside the jurisdiction (**r. 74.6(2)**). A party seeking to enforce after registration must file evidence of service of the registration order and any other relevant court order (**r. 74.9(2)**).

Applications to set aside under the 1920 and 1933 Acts

80.21 Applications to set aside under the 1920 and 1933 Acts must be made within the time allowed in the registration order (**CPR, r. 74.7(1)**). This time limit can be extended by a court, but an application for an extension must be made before the end of the period as originally fixed or extended (**r. 74.7(2)**). The court hearing an application may order any issue between the parties to be tried (**r. 74.7(3)**).

Appeals under the 1982 Act, the Brussels I Regulation and the Lugano Convention 2007

80.22 Appeals against the granting or refusal of registration under the 1982 Act, the **Brussels I Regulation** or the Lugano Convention 2007 are made in accordance with **CPR, Part 52**, but no permission to appeal is required (**r. 74.8(1)** and **(2)**). The appellant's notice must be filed within the period specified in the registration order (**rr. 52.4(2)(a)** and **74.6(3)(d)**) or, in the case of an appeal against the refusal of registration, within 21 days of the relevant order (**r. 52.4(2)(b)**). The appellant's notice must be served on the respondent within one month of the order (two months in the case of an appeal against the granting of registration where service is to be effected on a party outside the jurisdiction) (**r. 74.8(4)**).

ENFORCEMENT IN ENGLAND AND WALES OF EUROPEAN COMMUNITY JUDGMENTS

80.23 'Community judgments' are defined by **CPR, r. 74.19**, as judgments, decisions and orders enforceable under:

(a) the Treaty establishing the European Community, arts 244 or 256 (now the Treaty on the Functioning of the European Union, arts 280 and 299);
(b) *the Euratom Treaty, arts 18, 159 or 164;*
(c) the Treaty establishing the European Coal and Steel Community, arts 44 or 92 (this treaty expired in July 2002);

(d) Regulation (EC) No. 40/94 (on the Community trade mark), art. 82; or
(e) Regulation (EC) No. 6/2002 (on Community designs), art. 71.

Enforcement of Community judgments requires an application (which can be made without notice) to the Queen's Bench Division of the High Court (**CPR, r. 74.20; PD 74A, para. 4.1**). Written evidence in support must comply with **CPR, r. 74.21**. Any order granting permission to register a Community judgment must be served on every person against whom the judgment was given (**r. 74.22**).

ENFORCEMENT IN ENGLAND AND WALES OF EUROPEAN ENFORCEMENT ORDERS

'European enforcement order' (EEO) is defined, by **CPR, r. 74.27**, as having the meaning given in Regulation (EC) No. 805/2004 creating a European enforcement order for uncontested claims (the EEO Regulation). For a judgment on an uncontested claim (for payment of a sum of money) to be certified as an EEO, the conditions in art. 6 of the EEO Regulation must be fulfilled: **80.24**

(a) the judgment must be enforceable in the member State of origin of the foreign judgment; and
(b) the judgment must not conflict with the rules on jurisdiction in sections 3 and 6 of Chapter II of the **Brussels I Regulation**.

In addition to the above, where the claim is uncontested as a result of the debtor having never objected to the claim, or where the debtor did not appear or was not represented at the original court hearing:

(a) the court proceedings in the member State of origin must have met minimum procedural standards (laid down in Chapter III of the EEO Regulation); and
(b) where the judgment relates to a contract concluded by a consumer (being the debtor) for a purpose outside his trade or profession, the judgment must have been given in the member State of the debtor's domicile.

To enforce an EEO it is necessary, by **CPR, r. 74.31**, to lodge at the court in which enforcement proceedings are to be brought the following documents:

(a) a copy of the judgment;
(b) a copy of the EEO certificate;
(c) where necessary, a transcription or translation of the EEO certificate.

To enforce an EEO expressed in a foreign currency, the application must contain a certificate of the sterling equivalent of the judgment sum at the close of business on the date nearest preceding the date of the application (**r. 74.31(2)**).

An application by the judgment debtor that the court should either refuse to enforce an EEO under the EEO Regulation, art. 21 (**CPR, r. 74.32**) or stay or limit the enforcement proceedings under the EEO Regulation, art. 23 (**CPR, r. 74.33**) must be made in accordance with **Part 23** to the court in which the EEO is being enforced. Any such order made must be served on all other parties to the proceedings and any other person affected by the order and on any court in which enforcement proceedings are pending in England and Wales. Upon service of any order made under the EEO Regulation, art. 21, all enforcement proceedings under the EEO will cease (**CPR, r. 74.32(3)**).

Commentary

Chapter 81 Committal and Sequestration

INTRODUCTION

81.1 A person who disobeys a court order, whether interim or final, obtained in civil proceedings is said to commit a civil contempt of court and is described as a 'contemnor'. The person who obtained the order may apply to the court for the contemnor to be committed to prison (see **81.4**) or for the contemnor's assets to be sequestrated (see **81.27** to **81.29**). Sequestration is most commonly used where committal is not possible because the contemnor is a non-natural person, such as a company or a trade union.

Breach of an undertaking is treated in the same way as breach of an order (see **81.25**).

Punishment for a civil contempt of court is not in itself a remedy: it is a means of enforcing a remedy. A civil contempt of court is prosecuted as a matter between parties to proceedings and is punishable primarily in order to enforce compliance with an order of the court, for the benefit of the party who obtained the order. There is also a penal element in the punishment, which serves the public purpose of enforcing respect for court orders and for the rule of law, which is an essential element of our civil society (*Re S (A Child) (Contact Dispute: Committal)* [2004] EWCA Civ 1790, [2005] 1 FLR 812).

It is usually expected that imposition of the punishment will persuade the contemnor to comply with the court's order so that the committal order can be discharged, because its coercive purpose will have been achieved and the need for penalty mitigated (see **81.22**).

The procedure for enforcement of judgments, orders and undertakings by committal and sequestration is now dealt with in **CPR, Part 81** and **PD 81**, which apply to all applications in relation to contempt of court made on or after 1 October 2012.

A criminal contempt of court is conduct which frustrates or impedes the due administration of justice and is punishable in the public interest (*Attorney-General v Times Newspapers Ltd* [1992] 1 AC 191). The following particular types of criminal contempt of court are considered elsewhere in this edition of *Blackstone's Civil Practice*:

(a) For contempt of court by making a false statement in a document verified by a statement of truth see **23.15**.
(b) For false affidavits see **52.8**.
(c) For contempt of court by failure to obey a High Court witness summons see 57.8.

Criminal contempt of court is considered generally in *Blackstone's Criminal Practice 2014*, paras B14.79 to B14.129.

Vicarious liability

An employer who is subject to a court order is vicariously liable for any employee's breach of the order and it is no defence to say that all reasonable steps were taken to prevent employees breaching the order (*Director General of Fair Trading v Pioneer Concrete (UK) Ltd* [1995] 1 AC 456). It is not right to qualify an injunction against an employer so as to state that it does not apply where the employer has exercised due diligence to prevent it being breached by employees: the extent to which steps have been taken to prevent breach by employees may, however, mitigate the penalty for any contempt which does occur (*British Telecommunications plc v Nextcall Telecom plc* [2000] FSR 679). **81.2**

Judicial review proceedings

If there is a failure to comply with an injunction granted against a government minister or other Crown officer in a judicial review claim, the court may make a finding of civil contempt, but normally no penalty should be imposed and it is to be expected that the finding will be enough to bring about compliance with the injunction (*Re M* [1994] 1 AC 377). It follows that normally a declaration is sufficient and an injunction is unnecessary. **81.3**

COMMITTAL FOR DISOBEYING AN ORDER OR JUDGMENT OTHER THAN FOR THE PAYMENT OF MONEY

Judgments and orders which may be enforced by committal

CPR, r. 81.4(1) and (2), provide for enforcement of a judgment or order by committal of a person refusing or neglecting to do what the judgment or order requires. The paragraphs apply where: **81.4**

(a) a person required by a judgment or order to do an act (a mandatory order) does not do it within the time fixed by the judgment order (or which is subsequently extended by the court);
(b) a person disobeys a judgment or order requiring the person not to do an act (a prohibitory order).

If the person is a company or other corporation, a committal order may be made against any director or other officer of the body (**r. 81.4(3)**). If a company is subject to a prohibitory order, a director of the company who is aware of the order is under a duty to take reasonable steps to ensure that it is obeyed. If the director wilfully fails to take those steps, and the order is breached, the director is guilty of contempt (*Attorney-General for Tuvalu v Philatelic Distribution Corporation Ltd* [1990] 1 WLR 926).

These rules are expressed to be subject to the Debtors Act 1869, the Debtors Act 1878 and the provisions of the CPR. The Debtors Act 1869 prescribes the only circumstances in which an individual can be arrested or imprisoned for making default in payment of a sum of money. They are:

(a) under s. 4, default in payment of a non-contractual penalty, default in payment of a sum recoverable summarily before justices of the peace, default by a trustee or fiduciary in paying money in their hands when ordered by a court, default by a solicitor in paying either costs ordered for misconduct or moneys payable as an officer of court, and default by a bankrupt in complying with an income payments order; and
(b) under s. 5, failure, when capable of paying, to pay maintenance or taxes (see **79.30**).

An order for committal under s. 4 must state which category of default has been found (*Re Wilde* [1910] WN 128). The Debtors Act 1870 gives the court discretion in relation to the orders it may make on applications for committal of trustees, fiduciaries or solicitors. Judgments for the recovery of money cannot, therefore, generally be enforced by committal and this position cannot be changed by making a supplementary order fixing a certain date for payment (see *Hulbert v Cathcart* [1894] 1 QB 244 and *Re Oddy* [1906] 1 Ch 93). Money judgments are accordingly usually enforced by the methods described in **chapter 79**.

A judgment or order requiring a person to deliver goods or pay their value may not be enforced by committal (**CPR, r. 81.4(5)(a)**). Instead, the order should be enforced by the means specified in **CPR, sch. 1, ord. 45, r. 4(2)**. An order requiring that the goods be delivered within a specified time is an order that may be enforced by committal (**r. 81.4(5)(b)** and **(c)**).

A county court possession order in relation to land should be enforced by executing a warrant of possession (see **79.32** and **79.33**). If opposition by the person against whom the possession order was made prevents successful execution of a warrant, the order may be reissued with a penal notice. This may lead, as a last resort, to committal so that recovery of the land may be effected (see, for example, *De Grey v Ford* [2005] EWCA Civ 1223, LTL 30/9/2005; *De Grey v Ford* [2005] EWCA Civ 1791, LTL 22/12/2005).

Need for service of order

81.5 A judgment or order may not be enforced by committal unless a copy of the order has been served personally on the person required to do or not do the act in question (**CPR, rr. 81.5(1)** and **81.6**). In the case of a mandatory order requiring a person to do an act, the copy must be served personally before the end of the time fixed for doing the act (**r. 81.5(1)(a)**). A copy of any subsequent order or agreement varying the time for doing the act must also have been served (**r. 81.5(1)(b)**). Where a mandatory judgment or order is made pursuant to an earlier judgment or order, for example, one requiring delivery of goods or payment of their value, the earlier order must also have been served (**r. 81.5(1)(c)**).

An order or judgment requiring a company or other corporation to do or not do an act may not be enforced by committal of a director or other officer unless (**r. 81.5(2)**):

(a) a copy of the order has also been served personally on the officer against whom an order of committal is sought, and
(b) in the case of a mandatory order, the copy has been so served before the end of the time fixed for doing the act.

Methods of personal service are specified in **r. 6.5**, which applies by **r. 6.22(3)**. The court may make an order for service by an alternative method or at an alternative place (**r. 81.8(2)(b)**).

The court may dispense with service of a prohibitory order on a person if satisfied that the person had notice of it, either by being present when it was made or by being notified of its terms by telephone, email, or otherwise (**r. 81.8(1)**).

The court has a general power to dispense with service of an order (mandatory or prohibitory) if it thinks it just to do so (**r. 81.8(2)(a)**). This may be done after a contempt has been committed where it is clear that the contemnor was aware of the order and its consequences at the time of the contempt (*Davy International Ltd v Tazzyman* [1997] 1 WLR 1256; *Jolly v Circuit Judge of Staines County Court* [2000] 2 FLR 69; *Benson v Richards* [2002] EWCA Civ 1402, LTL 11/10/2002).

Penal notices

A judgment or order may not be enforced by committal unless a penal notice is prominently displayed on the front of the copy served on the person sought to be committed (**CPR, r. 81.9(1)**). The notice must warn that disobedience to the order would be a contempt of court punishable by imprisonment, a fine, or sequestration of assets (**r. 81.9**). The notice must be in the following terms (or in words to substantially the same effect) (**PD 81, para. 1**): **81.6**

If you the within-named [ ] do not comply with this order you may be held to be in contempt of court and imprisoned or fined, or your assets may be seized.

This notice is not part of the court's order and does not require the judge's sanction: it may be added by the person who makes the copy which is to be served (*Anglo-Eastern Trust Ltd v Kermanshahchi* (2002) *The Times*, 8 November 2002).

Omission of the penal notice is not fatal to enforcement by committal provided that the person sought to be committed was well aware of the consequences of disobedience (*Sofroniou v Szgetti* [1991] FCR 332). The court may dispense with a penal notice under the power to dispense with service (**CPR, r. 81.8(2)(a)**; *Jolly v Circuit Judge of Staines County Court* [2000] 2 FLR 69). The onus is on the applicant to show that no injustice would be done by waiving any defect in the presentation of the penal notice (*Leicester City Council v Saracen Dyers Ltd* [2002] EWHC 2068 (QB), [2003] Env LR 18, in which the court decided that service of an order was not sufficient for the purposes of a committal application because the penal notice was on the last page rather than the front of the order).

An order made by the Administrative Court against a public body does not require a penal notice (*R (JM) v Croydon London Borough Council* [2009] EWHC 2474 (Admin), [2010] 1 WLR 1658).

Order must be unambiguous

It is an elementary principle of justice and fairness that no order will be enforced by committal unless it is expressed in clear, certain and unambiguous language (*Harris v Harris* [2001] 2 FLR 895 at [288]). An order should not require the person to whom it is addressed to cross-refer to other documents to discover what obligation it is imposing (*Ellerman Lines Ltd v Read* [1928] 2 KB 144 at p. 157). Contempt will not be established where the alleged breach is of an order which is ambiguous or which does not require or forbid the performance of a particular act within a specified time frame (*Shadrokh-Cigari v Shadrokh-Cigari* [2010] EWCA Civ 21, [2010] 1 WLR 1311 at [17]). But an order to give up possession of land by a particular date is breached by re-entering the land after that date, and there is no need to issue a new order (*De Grey v Ford* [2005] EWCA Civ 1791, LTL 22/12/2005). If an ambiguous order has two possible meanings, the court will not order committal for breach of one only of those meanings (*Commission for Equality and Human Rights v Griffin* [2010] EWHC 3343 (Admin), [2011] ACD 22). **81.7**

APPLICATION FOR A COMMITTAL ORDER

Judge

A master or district judge may not make an order relating to the liberty of a subject (**PD 2B, para. 3.1(1)**), unless (in the case of a district judge) authorised to do so by an enactment (**para. 8.3**). District judges are authorised to commit for breach of court orders in the case of **81.8** a person arrested for breach of an injunction under the Housing Act 1996, s. 153C or s. 153D, to which a power of arrest has been attached (**CPR, r. 65.6(6)**; see **88.11**). Except in these cases, a committal order can only be made by a High Court judge or circuit judge or a person authorised to act as a High Court or circuit judge (**PD 81, para. 10.2**). In insolvency proceedings, applications for committal for contempt must be made direct to the judge (**PD Insolvency Proceedings, para. 3.2(1)**).

Application notice and supporting affidavit

81.9 An application to enforce a judgment or order by committal is made by an application notice (**CPR, Part 23**) in the proceedings in which the judgment or order was made (**r. 81.10(1)**). The application notice must identify the proceedings in which the application is made and bear the same title and reference number (**PD 81, para. 13.1**). **CPR, Part 23**, applies, subject to the provisions of **Part 81** and **PD 81** (**PD 81, para. 13.2(1)**).

The application notice must contain a prominent notice stating the possible consequences if the court makes a committal order or the respondent does not attend the hearing (**para. 13.2(2)**). A form of notice is in **PD 81, annex 3**.

An application notice applying for a committal order must set out in full the grounds on which the committal application is made and should identify, separately and numerically, each alleged act of contempt including, if known, the date of each of the alleged acts (**CPR, r. 81.10(3)(a)**; *Dorrell v Dorrell* [1985] FLR 1089). It must be supported by an affidavit or affidavits containing all the evidence relied on (**r. 81.10(3)(b)**).

The court should not hesitate to strike out a committal application which does not identify each alleged act of contempt as required by **r. 81.10(3)(a)** (*Masri v Consolidated Contractors International Co. SAL* [2010] EWHC 2458 (Comm), [2011] Bus LR D55 at [29]). But the evidence supporting each allegation does not have to be set out in the application notice. 'The essential point is that the alleged contemnor should be told, with sufficient particularity to enable him to defend himself, what exactly he is said to have done or omitted to do which constitutes contempt of court' (*Attorney-General for Tuvalu v Philatelic Distribution Corporation Ltd* [1990] 1 WLR 926 at pp. 934–5). If the applicant did not personally witness the acts complained of, the application notice 'must make clear the thrust of the case' that will be presented to the court, so that the alleged contemnor can prepare to meet that case (*Attorney-General for Tuvalu v Philatelic Distribution Corporation Ltd* at p. 935). If the application is for committal of a director or officer of a company for the company's contempt, the application notice must disclose a case for establishing the responsibility of the director for the impugned acts of the company (*Attorney-General for Tuvalu v Philatelic Distribution Corporation Ltd*; *Sectorguard plc v Dienne plc* [2009] EWHC 2693 (Ch), LTL 10/11/2009; *Masri v Consolidated Contractors International Co. SAL*).

An application notice applying for a committal order may be amended only with the permission of the court (**PD 81, para. 13.2(4)**).

Hearing date

81.10 When filing an application notice applying for a committal order, the applicant must obtain a date for the hearing of the application (**PD 81, para. 15.1**). The hearing date must be specified in the application notice or in a notice of hearing attached to and served with it (**para. 15.2**).

Service

81.11 *An application notice applying* for a committal order, the evidence in support and, if necessary, a notice of hearing must be served personally on the person sought to be committed (**CPR, r. 81.10(4)**). The court may dispense with service, if it thinks it just to do so (**r. 81.10(5)(a)**). It may be appropriate to dispense with service in cases of urgency, or where there have been persistent breaches of court orders, or the respondent is evading service.

There must be at least 14 clear days between the service of the claim form and the date of the hearing, unless the court orders otherwise (**PD 81, para. 15.2**).

Methods of personal service are specified in **CPR, r. 6.5**, which applies by **r. 6.22(3)**. The court may make an order for service by an alternative method or at an alternative place (**r. 81.10(5)(b)**).

Arrest

The High Court has an inherent power to issue a bench warrant for the arrest of an alleged contemnor to secure his or her attendance in court (*Zakharov v White* [2003] EWHC 2463 (Ch), *The Times*, 13 November 2003). There are also statutory provisions under which a power of arrest can be attached to an injunction, for example, under the Housing Act 1996, s. 153C (see **88.5**) and s. 153D (see **88.6**), the Police and Justice Act 2006, s. 27 (see **88.12**), and the Policing and Crime Act 2009, s. 36 (see **88.47**). For arrest for breach of an anti-harassment injunction see **88.38**. **81.12**

It is in the interests of justice that an individual charged with contempt should be given every opportunity to appear in court to respond to the charge, and the court will normally adjourn a hearing which the respondent does not attend. The issue of an arrest warrant to secure attendance may be necessary to prevent the respondent exploiting this principle to frustrate consideration of a committal application (*Law Society v McPhail* (2011) *The Times*, 15 April 2011).

Case management

On the hearing date, the court may give case management directions with a view to a hearing of the committal application on a future date or if the committal application is ready to be heard, the court may proceed to hear it (**PD 81, para. 15.4**). **81.13**

The court must have regard to the need for the respondent to have details of the alleged contempt and an opportunity to respond to the application and prepare a defence (**PD 81, paras 15.5 and 15.6(1)**). The court should ensure that the respondent is aware that assistance may be available from the Legal Aid Agency (**para. 15.6(2)**) and, if the respondent is unrepresented, should give him or her an opportunity to obtain legal advice (**para. 15.6(3)**; *Berry Trade Ltd v Moussavi* [2002] EWCA Civ 477, [2002] 1 WLR 1910). If the respondent is unable to understand English, the court should assist, if necessary, in finding an interpreter to attend the hearing (**para. 15.6(4)**).

Whether an allegation of contempt in respect of an interim order should be heard before, during or after the trial of the claim itself is a case management decision to be taken having regard to the circumstances of the particular case (*JSC BTA Bank v Ablyazov (No. 7)* [2011] EWCA Civ 1386, [2012] 1 WLR 1988 at [41]). The fact that issues will be common to both hearings is a factor to be taken into account but does not inevitably mean that the contempt hearing should be after the main trial (*JSC BTA Bank v Ablyazov (No. 7)* at [42]). In order to be able to hear before the main trial allegations of extensive failure to comply with interim orders, the court may select some allegations for hearing, leaving others to be pursued on another occasion (*JSC BTA Bank v Ablyazov (No. 7)*). Although it is desirable that all extant allegations are considered on a single occasion, particularly because the maximum term of committal on any one occasion is two years (Contempt of Court Act 1981, s. 14(1)), there is no fixed rule (*JSC BTA Bank v Ablyazov (No. 7)* at [29]).

A committal application may not be discontinued without the permission of the court (**PD 81, para. 16.3**). The court may not dispose of a committal application without a hearing (**para. 13.3**).

Striking out

81.14 PD 81, para. 16.1, states that the court may, either on the application of the respondent or of its own initiative, strike out a committal application on the following grounds:

(a) The committal application and the evidence served in support of it disclose no reasonable ground for alleging that the respondent is guilty of contempt of court.
(b) The committal application is an abuse of the court's process or, if made in existing proceedings, is otherwise likely to obstruct the just disposal of those proceedings.
(c) There has been a failure to comply with a rule, practice direction or court order.

This is equivalent to **CPR, r. 3.4(2)**, which is discussed in **chapter 33**. Disputes about facts or law will not be determined on an application to strike out. If there are such disputes which ought to be determined at a substantive hearing, the committal application will not be struck out (*Masri v Consolidated Contractors International Co. SAL* [2010] EWHC 2458 (Comm), [2011] Bus LR D55).

A committal application is an abuse of process if it is not made for a proper purpose (*Sectorguard plc v Dienne plc* [2009] EWHC 2693 (Ch), LTL 10/11/2009). Committal proceedings are appropriate, albeit as a last resort, for seeking to obtain compliance with a court order or an undertaking to the court, or for bringing to the court's attention serious, but not technical and certainly not involuntary, breaches of an order or undertaking (*Sectorguard plc v Dienne plc* at [47]). Proceedings relating to purely technical breaches, or not directed at obtaining compliance, will be struck out (*Sectorguard plc v Dienne plc* at [47]).

An applicant's failure to comply with a rule or practice direction may not be fatal to the application. **PD 81, para. 16.2**, provides that any procedural defect in the commencement or conduct by the applicant of a committal application may be waived by the court if the court is satisfied that no injustice has been caused to the respondent by the defect.

HEARING A COMMITTAL APPLICATION

General

81.15 Although they are civil proceedings (*Daltel Europe Ltd v Makki* [2006] EWCA Civ 94, [2006] 1 WLR 2704), committal proceedings are treated as criminal proceedings for the purposes of the European Convention on Human Rights, **art. 6** in the **Human Rights Act 1998, sch. 1**, so that **art. 6(3)** applies (*Berry Trade Ltd v Moussavi* [2002] EWCA Civ 477, [2002] 1 WLR 1910 at [31]; *Raja v Van Hoogstraten* [2004] EWCA Civ 968, [2004] 4 All ER 793). An allegation of civil contempt of court must be proved beyond reasonable doubt (**PD 81, para. 9**).

A committal application should be heard separately from any other application in the proceedings (*Lexi Holdings plc v Luqman* [2007] EWHC 1508 (Ch), LTL 9/7/2007 at [4]).

It is a fundamental principle of the administration of justice in England and Wales that applications for committal for contempt should be heard and decided in public, that is, in open court (Practice Guidance (Committal Proceedings: Open Court) [2013] 1 WLR 1316, para. 1). Any discretion to hear a committal application in private should be exercised only in exceptional cases where it is necessary in the interests of justice (para. 2). The fact that the committal application is being made in proceedings relating to a child does not of itself justify the application being heard in private (para. 2). The fact that the hearing may involve disclosure of material which ought not to be published does not of itself justify hearing the application in private if such publication can be restrained by an appropriate order (para. 2). *Every committal application* should at the outset be listed and heard in public (para. 5). Whenever the court decides to exercise its discretion to sit in private the judge should, before continuing the hearing in private, give a judgment in public setting out the reasons for doing so (para. 5). Prescribed information about a committal order made in private must be given (see **81.17**).

To show that a person is in contempt, it must be established that his or her conduct was intentional and that he or she knew of all the facts which made that conduct a breach of the order, but it is not necessary to prove that he or she appreciated that the conduct did breach the order (*Heaton's Transport (St Helens) Ltd v Transport and General Workers' Union* [1973] AC 15; *Spectravest Inc. v Aperknit Ltd* [1988] FSR 161 per Millett J at pp. 173–4; see also *Adam Phones Ltd v Goldschmidt* [1999] 4 All ER 486 on the view that it should be necessary to prove intention to breach the order). If it is impossible to comply with an order, failure to comply with it may be breach of the order but is not contempt (*Sectorguard plc v Dienne plc* [2009] EWHC 2693 (Ch), LTL 10/11/2009 at [33]). If the respondent alleges impossibility, the onus is on the applicant to make the judge sure that the respondent could comply (*Re A (A Child) (Removal from Jurisdiction: Contempt of Court)* [2008] EWCA Civ 1138, [2009] 1 WLR 1482).

Where more than one breach is alleged, the court must consider whether each of them has been proved beyond reasonable doubt, but in deciding whether the breaches justify committal, the court must consider the whole picture to see whether it portrays a respondent seeking to comply with the orders of the court or one bent on flouting them (*Gulf Azov Shipping Co. Ltd v Idisi* [2001] EWCA Civ 21, LTL 16/1/2001 at [18]).

At the end of the applicant's case, the respondent may make a submission of no case to answer (*Shadrokh-Cigari v Shadrokh-Cigari* [2010] EWCA Civ 21, [2010] 1 WLR 1311 at [24]). However, as the judge is tribunal of both fact and law, a submission of no case to answer should be entertained only on the basis that the respondent has elected not to put forward any evidence (*Lawrie v Raglan* [1942] 1 KB 152; *Benham Ltd v Kythira Investments Ltd* [2003] EWCA Civ 1794, LTL 15/12/2003; *Jobsearch Ltd v Relational Designers Ltd* [2004] EWHC 661 (Ch), [2004] FSR 36 at [11]).

For appeals in contempt proceedings see **74.12**.

Evidence

Written evidence in support of or in opposition to a committal application must be given by affidavit (**PD 81, para. 14.1**) and, unless the court directs otherwise, must be filed (**para. 14.2**). The court may give directions requiring the attendance for cross-examination of a witness who has given written evidence (**CPR, r. 81.28(4)**). **81.16**

The following rules do not apply to committal applications (**PD 81, para. 14.3**):

(a) **CPR, r. 35.7** (court's power to direct that evidence is to be given by a single joint expert);
(b) **r. 35.8** (instructions to single joint expert); and
(c) **r. 35.9** (power of court to direct a party to provide information).

Unless the court hearing a committal application otherwise permits, the applicant may not rely on (**r. 81.28(1)**):

(a) any grounds other than those set out in the application notice; or
(b) any evidence unless it has been served in accordance with **r. 81.10** and **PD 81**.

A respondent is not a compellable witness (*Re B (A Minor) (Contempt of Court: Affidavit Evidence)* [1996] 1 WLR 627), but may give oral evidence at the hearing, despite not filing or serving any written evidence (**r. 81.28(2)(a)**). A respondent who gives oral evidence may be cross-examined (**r. 81.28(2)(a)**). The respondent may call a witness to give evidence at the hearing even though that witness has not made an affidavit or witness statement, provided the court gives permission (**r. 81.28(2)(b)**). Orders for further information under **r. 18.1** may not be made against a respondent to a committal application (**PD 81, para. 14.4**). Additional information

Commentary

should not be necessary in committal applications where the breaches are listed in the application notice and it is a matter for the court to determine whether those breaches are made out. For appropriate orders and undertakings to prevent prejudicial use of information obtained by a receiver appointed to enforce the respondent's compliance see *Milsom v Ablyazov* [2011] EWHC 1846 (Ch), LTL 22/7/2011.

The court may require or permit any party or other person (other than the respondent) to give oral evidence at the hearing (**CPR, r. 81.28(3)**).

The admission of hearsay evidence is governed by the Civil Evidence Act 1995, because committal proceedings are civil proceedings despite being treated as criminal proceedings for the purposes of the European Convention on Human Rights, **art. 6** in the **Human Rights Act 1998, sch. 1** (*Daltel Europe Ltd v Makki* [2006] EWCA Civ 94, [2006] 1 WLR 2704).

ORDERS THE COURT MAY MAKE

Committal

81.17 A court may commit a contemnor to prison for up to two years (Contempt of Court Act 1981, s. 14(1)).

A committal order must adequately particularise the breaches which have been proved and for which the sentence has been imposed (*Nicholls v Nicholls* [1997] 1 WLR 314). It should expressly state what the breaches were rather than refer to an application notice or claim form (*Nicholls v Nicholls*). A judge signing a committal order has a duty to ensure that it is properly drawn (*Nicholls v Nicholls*).

Any court which decides to make an order of committal (including a suspended order) must state in public (**CPR, r. 81.28(5)**; Practice Guidance (Committal Proceedings: Open Court) [2013] 1 WLR 1316, para. 4):

(a) the name of the respondent;
(b) in general terms the nature of the contempt of court in respect of which the committal order is being made; and
(c) the length of the period of the committal order.

There are never any circumstances in which anyone may be committed to custody without these matters being publicly stated (Practice Guidance (Committal Proceedings: Open Court), para. 4). The judge should ensure that, as soon as reasonably practicable, a transcript is prepared of the judgment (including any reasons for a hearing in private and the statement of the points listed in **CPR, r. 81.28(5)**) and published on the BAILII website (Practice Guidance (Committal Proceedings: Open Court), para. 6).

There is no jurisdiction to remand a contemnor in custody to await sentencing (*Delaney v Delaney* [1996] QB 387), except in the case of an injunction to which a power of arrest has been attached under the Housing Act 1996, s. 153C or s. 153D (see **88.11**), or the Police and Justice Act 2007, s. 27 (see **88.12**), or the Policing and Crime Act 2009, s. 36 (see **88.47**), or in respect of which a warrant for arrest has been issued under the Housing Act 1996, s. 155(3) (see **88.11**) or the Policing and Crime Act 2009, s. 36 (see **88.47**).

A committal order is an order for the issue of a warrant of committal (**CPR, r. 81.30(1)**). A copy of the committal order must be served on the respondent either before or at the time of executing the warrant (**r. 81.30(2)(a)**). Alternatively, if the warrant has been signed by the judge, the order may be served at any time within 36 hours after the warrant is executed (**r. 81.30(2)(b)**). A warrant of committal cannot be executed more than two years after it is issued without a further order of the court (**r. 81.30(3)**).

If a committal order has been made in the respondent's absence, the court may, on its own initiative, fix a date and time when the respondent is to be brought before the court (**r. 81.28(6)**). It may order the respondent's solicitor to disclose contact details given in confidence so that the respondent may be apprehended to serve the sentence (*JSC BTA Bank v Solodchenko (No. 3)* [2011] EWHC 2163 (Ch), [2013] Ch 1). But such an order will not be made if it is foreseeable that it would deprive the respondent of access to legal advice (*JSC BTA Bank v Ablyazov* [2012] EWHC 1252 (Comm), LTL 17/5/2012). If a committal order is made in the respondent's absence for failure to comply with an interim order, the court may bar the respondent from taking any further part in the proceedings unless he or she surrenders to custody (*JSC BTA Bank v Ablyazov* [2012] EWCA Civ 1411, [2013] 2 All ER 515). But an appeal against the committal order itself should not be subject to such a condition (*JSC BTA Bank v Ablyazov* [2012] EWCA Civ 639, LTL 16/5/2012). Such a condition is a means of persuading a contemnor to comply rather than a further punishment for the contempt (*JSC BTA Bank v Ablyazov* [2012] EWCA Civ 1411 per Maurice Kay LJ at [201]–[202]).

A person aged under 21 may not be committed to prison (Powers of Criminal Courts (Sentencing) Act 2000, s. 89(1)(b)). A contemnor who is at least 18 but under 21 may be committed to be detained under s. 108 of the 2000 Act and the Secretary of State will direct where the person is to be detained (s. 108(5)). Committal for detention under s. 108 may not be ordered unless the court is of the opinion that no other method of dealing with the person is appropriate (s. 108(3), which lists matters which the court must take into consideration). The minimum age for imprisonment will be lowered to 18 when the Criminal Justice and Court Services Act 2000, s. 61, is brought into force, and then the provision for committal for detention of persons aged 18 to 20 will be repealed. An injunction should not be made against a person aged under 18, as it cannot be enforced by committal, and the person is unlikely to have assets which could be used to pay a fine or which could be sequestrated (*Wookey v Wookey* [1991] Fam 121; *Harrow London Borough Council v G* [2004] EWHC 17 (Q3), LTL 23/1/2004).

Commentary

Other punishments

In addition to, or instead of, committing to prison, the court may impose a fine (Contempt of Court Act 1981, s. 14), take security (a recognisance) for good behaviour, make a summary award of damages (*Midland Marts Ltd v Hobday* [1989] 1 WLR 1148), make a sequestration order or deliver a reprimand. Nothing in **CPR, Part 81** detracts from the court's power to fine a person or require security (a recognisance) for good behaviour (**r. 81.2(2)**). **81.18**

Sentencing decision

A sentence of imprisonment for contempt of court must be for a fixed term of not more than two years (Contempt of Court Act 1981, s. 14(1)), but the court has a power to discharge a committed contemnor (see **81.22**), which will be done on acceptance by the court that the contemnor's contempt has been purged. In any case, a person who is committed to a term of imprisonment for contempt of court must be released unconditionally after serving half of the term (Criminal Justice Act 2003, s. 258). The court may order suspension of a committal order (see **81.20**). **81.19**

Committal for any period is always a sanction of last resort (*Ansah v Ansah* [1977] Fam 138 per Ormrod LJ at p. 144; *Belgolaise SA v Purchandani* [1999] Lloyd's Rep Bank 116; *Gulf Azov Shipping Co. Ltd v Idisi* [2001] EWCA Civ 21, LTL 16/1/2001, at [70]). It is only appropriate where there has been 'some extra obstinate or obstructive dimension' to the contemnor's breach of the court's order (*Broomleigh Housing Association Ltd v Okonkwo* [2010] EWCA Civ 1113, [2011] HLR 5, at [22]). This extra dimension is often described as 'contumacy'.

In every case the court must consider whether committal is necessary, what is the shortest period of imprisonment necessary, and whether a sentence of imprisonment can be suspended or dispensed with altogether (*Templeton Insurance Ltd v Thomas* [2013] EWCA Civ 35, LTL 5/2/2013, at [42]).

Breach of a freezing order is such an attack on the administration of justice that it usually merits an immediate term of imprisonment of some not insubstantial amount (*Templeton Insurance Ltd v Thomas*, at [42]).

The two-year maximum should not be exceeded on any single occasion, even if the judge is dealing with the activation of a suspended sentence as well as a more recent contempt (*Villiers v Villiers* [1994] 1 WLR 493). Nevertheless, if a contemnor has served a maximum sentence for not complying with a court order and still refuses to comply, the court may make a new order in the same terms and impose a further maximum sentence for not complying with the new order. It is for the court to decide whether this course is both necessary and proportionate (*Wilkinson v Anjum* [2011] EWCA Civ 1196, [2012] 1 WLR 1036).

Suspension

81.20 A court making an order of committal may also order that its execution will be suspended for such period, or on such terms or conditions, as the court may specify (**CPR, r. 81.29(1)**). A court imposing a sentence of imprisonment for contempt should always expressly consider whether the sentence might properly be suspended (*Slade v Slade* [2009] EWCA Civ 748, [2010] 1 WLR 1262, at [25]). If, as is usual, committal is suspended so as to give the contemnor a chance to comply with the court's order, the court must specify the period of suspension and the terms or conditions of the suspension (*Bluffield v Curtis* [1998] 1 FLR 170 at p. 173). Where the execution of a committal order is suspended, the applicant for the committal order must, unless the court directs otherwise, serve a copy of the suspension order on the respondent (**r. 81.29(2)**). In the county court form N79 must be used (**PD 4, Table 3**) and failure to use it is a fundamental defect which will invalidate the order so that it cannot be activated (*Couzens v Couzens* [2001] 2 FLR 701). The standard of proof for breach of a suspension condition is the civil standard of balance of probabilities (*Alfa Laval Tumba AB v Pacy* [2010] EWHC 674 (Ch), LTL 30/3/2010). Care must be taken to distinguish between an allegation that a condition for suspension of committal has been breached and an allegation that there has been a further act of contempt (*Phillips v Symes* [2003] EWCA Civ 1769, LTL 5/12/2003).

Criminal proceedings for the same act

81.21 An act which contravenes a court order in civil proceedings may be both a civil contempt of court and a criminal offence. There is no abuse of process in bringing both criminal proceedings and proceedings for civil contempt in respect of the same act (*Director of Public Prosecutions v Tweddell* [2001] EWHC 188 (Admin), [2002] 2 FLR 400), though the court hearing the second proceedings should take into account any punishment already imposed (*Lomas v Parle* [2003] EWCA Civ 1804, [2004] 1 WLR 1642) and the contemnor must not be sentenced twice for the same conduct. This means that even if the second court considers that the first court's sentence for that conduct was inadequate, it cannot impose a further punishment (*Slade v Slade* [2009] EWCA Civ 748, [2010] 1 WLR 1262). If the second court is sentencing for contempt, it must confine itself to sentencing for:

(a) other aspects of the contemnor's conduct that breached the court's order; and
(b) the fact, irrelevant to the criminal proceedings, that particular conduct which had been punished in the criminal court was also a civil contempt (*Slade v Slade* at [22]).

In relation to point (b), the civil court's task is to sentence only for the fact of the contempt and not for its content, though it may take into consideration the seriousness of the contempt (*Slade v Slade* at [23]). Putting this into practice may be very difficult indeed.

Use of both civil contempt and criminal proceedings is forbidden by statute in the case of *non-molestation orders* (Family Law Act 1996, s. 42A(3) and (4)) and anti-harassment injunctions (Protection from Harassment Act 1997, s. 3(7) and (8); see **88.37**).

Discharge

81.22 A person committed to prison for contempt of court may apply to the court to be discharged (**CPR, r. 81.31**). The application is made in writing attested by the governor of the prison (or any other officer of the prison not below the rank of principal officer) showing that the applicant has purged or wishes to purge his or her contempt. Not less than one day before the application is made, notice must be served on the party, if any, at whose instance the warrant of committal was issued (**r. 81.31(2)**). These requirements do not apply to an application made by the Official Solicitor acting for the contemnor, or where the committal was in connection with an attachment of earnings order to secure payments under a maintenance order or a judgment summons (**r. 81.31(3)**). The Official Solicitor has a duty to review all committals to prison for contempt of court and to take such action as he considers necessary (see *R v Official Solicitor to the Supreme Court, ex parte Harris* [2001] EWHC 798 (Admin), LTL 26/10/2001). The Official Solicitor normally informs a committed person of the possibility of applying for discharge, and may make the application if it appears that the committed person is incapable of managing his or her affairs and there is no one else who will act.

In a county court, unless the committal order directs that any application for discharge must be made to a judge, the application for discharge may be made to a district judge (**r. 81.31(4)**). In the High Court, the application for discharge may be made to a single judge of the Division in which the committal order was made (**r. 81.31(5)**).

Usually, contempt is purged by apologising to the court for failing to comply with its order in the past and expressing a willingness to comply in the future. The court may require undertakings of compliance to be given. On any application for discharge from committal, the contemnor must advance a reason why it is now unnecessary for the original sentence to be served in full (*CJ v Flintshire County Council* [2010] EWCA Civ 393, [2010] 2 FLR 1224 at [37]). That must be a reason known to the law. The court must first consider whether the contemnor has been punished enough for the contempt. The court will examine, at the least, whether the contemnor now not only accepts that he or she was guilty of contempt, but also that the contemnor is genuinely sorry for his or her misdeeds and repents them (*CJ v Flintshire County Council* at [28]). Discharge will probably not be ordered if there has been insufficient punishment (*Enfield London Borough Council v Mahoney* [1983] 1 WLR 749) unless there are extenuating circumstances (*CJ v Flintshire County Council* at [28]). The court must also consider whether discharge now would prejudice the public interest in upholding the rule of law. Discharge will not be ordered if there would be significant prejudice to the public interest (*CJ v Flintshire County Council* at [22]).

If the order that has been breached is a mandatory order requiring the contemnor to do something, the court must next consider whether a further period of imprisonment is required to coerce the contemnor to comply. It may have to be recognised that imprisonment will not have any coercive effect (*Enfield London Borough Council v Mahoney* [1983] 1 WLR 749).

If the order that has been breached is a prohibitory order, the court must consider whether further imprisonment is necessary in the interests of the persons whom the order is intended to protect. In *CJ v Flintshire County Council* Wilson LJ at [21], said that there are eight, somewhat overlapping, questions to be asked (the first two are considered above as they apply to mandatory orders as well):

(i) Can the court conclude, in all the circumstances as they now are, that the contemnor has suffered punishment proportionate to his contempt?
(ii) Would the interest of the State in upholding the rule of law be significantly prejudiced by early discharge?
(iii) How genuine is the contemnor's expression of contrition?

Commentary

(iv) Has he done all that he reasonably can to demonstrate a resolve and an ability not to commit a further breach if discharged early?

(v) In particular has he done all that he reasonably can (bearing in mind the difficulties of his so doing while in prison) in order to construct for himself proposed living and other practical arrangements in the event of early discharge in such a way as to minimise the risk of his committing a further breach?

(vi) Does he make any specific proposal to augment the protection against any further breach of those whom the order which he breached was designed to protect?

(vii) What is the length of time which he has served in prison, including its relation to (a) the full term imposed upon him and (b) the term which he will otherwise be required to serve prior to release pursuant to the Criminal Justice Act 2003, s. 258(2)?

(viii) Are there any special factors which impinge upon the exercise of the discretion in one way or the other?

On hearing an application to be discharged from custody, the court's options are to allow the application to discharge immediately, dismiss it, or adjourn it to be heard on a future date: there is no jurisdiction to suspend the remainder of the sentence (*Harris v Harris* [2001] EWCA Civ 1645, [2002] Fam 253).

Rule 81.32 provides for the discharge of a contemnor who has been committed for failing to comply with a judgment or order requiring him or her to deliver up property, or to deposit it in court or elsewhere, in cases where sequestrators take possession of the item under a writ of sequestration. In these cases the court may give such directions for dealing with the thing taken by the sequestrators as it thinks fit.

Effect of technical defects

81.23 A committal order will not be set aside on appeal, because of a defect in the application or the order itself, unless it is in the interests of justice to set it aside, for example, if there was prejudice to the person committed, or the hearing was unfair (*Nicholls v Nicholls* [1997] 1 WLR 314). There is a particular need to observe formalities when the person against whom an order is made is unrepresented, especially if English is not the person's first language (*Shadrokh-Cigari v Shadrokh-Cigari* [2010] EWCA Civ 21, [2010] 1 WLR 1311 at [16]).

Procedural sanctions

81.24 It is not appropriate to prevent a party to proceedings from taking further part in them as a punishment for not obeying an order made in the course of the proceedings (*Re Swaptronics Ltd* (1998) *The Times*, 17 August 1998), though if a party's disobedience to an order seriously interferes with the fair conduct of the trial, it may be necessary to stay the proceedings or strike out that party's claim or defence (*Arrow Nominees Inc. v Blackledge* [2000] 2 BCLC 167). The court may find that failure by a party to comply with an interim order should debar the party from taking any further part in the proceedings and may make an unless order to that effect (*JSC BTA Bank v Ablyazov* [2012] EWCA Civ 1411, [2013] 2 All ER 515). A party who has been found to be in contempt by failing to comply with an order made in proceedings, and who has made no attempt to purge that contempt, may be prevented from pursuing an appeal in those proceedings: the appellate court should ask whether, in the circumstances of the case, the interests of justice are best served by hearing or by refusing to hear a party in contempt, bearing in mind the paramount importance to be attached to the prompt and unquestioning observance of court orders (*Arab Monetary Fund v Hashim* (1997) LTL 9/6/99; *Raja v Van Hoogstraten* [2004] EWCA Civ 968, [2004] 4 All ER 793 at [82]). This principle has been extended to an application for correction of a judgment under **CPR, r. 40.12** (*Riva Bella SA v Tamsen Yachts GmbH (Costs)* [2011] EWHC 2338 (Comm), LTL 15/9/2011).

BREACH OF AN UNDERTAKING

An undertaking to the court is equivalent to an injunction and may be enforced in the same way (*London and Birmingham Railway Co. v Grand Junction Canal Co.* (1835) 1 Ry & Can Cas 224; *Roberts v Roberts* [1990] 2 FLR 111 at p. 113). **81.25**

There is a distinction to be drawn between an undertaking to the court, which is given voluntarily, even if unwillingly, by the person concerned, and an order which is imposed by the court. Although an undertaking is often recorded in an order of the court, it is the undertaking, and not the order, which requires the giver of the undertaking to act in accordance with its terms. A failure so to act is a breach of the undertaking, but cannot be called a refusal or neglect to act in accordance with the order which happens to record the undertaking or disobedience of that order (*Hussain v Hussain* [1986] Fam 134). The distinction between an order and an undertaking is, however, of little practical effect, except where there is a statutory power to attach a power of arrest to an order, as such a power cannot be attached to an undertaking.

An ambiguity in an undertaking should be construed in favour of the person sought to be committed (*Haddonstone Ltd v Sharp* [1996] FSR 767 per Rose and Stuart-Smith LJJ; *Jobsearch Ltd v Relational Designers Ltd* [2004] EWHC 661 (Ch), [2004] FSR 36).

The court may decline to accept an undertaking unless the party giving it has made a signed statement to the effect that the party understands the terms of the undertaking and the consequences of failure to comply with it (**PD 81, para. 2.2**). That statement may be endorsed on the order containing the undertaking or may be filed in a separate document such as a letter (**para. 2.3**). In county court proceedings, form N117 may be used (**para. 2.4**). The court may decline to consider proceedings for contempt of court for disobeying an undertaking which was not accompanied by such a statement (**para. 2.2**).

The procedure for committing for breach of an undertaking is the same as that relating to breach of court orders and judgments (see **81.4** to **81.24**) with such modifications as are necessary (**CPR, r. 81.4(4)**, applying **rr. 81.4** to **81.11** so far as applicable).

Rules 81.5 and **81.6** do not apply to undertakings. Instead, **r. 81.7(1)** provides that when a court accepts an undertaking it will deliver, to the person who gave the undertaking, a copy of a document recording it:

(a) by handing a copy to that person before he or she leaves the court building; or
(b) where that person's place of residence or business is known, by posting a copy to that address; or
(c) by posting a copy to that person's solicitor.

Where delivery cannot be effected in this way, the court officer must deliver a copy of the document to the party for whose benefit the undertaking is given, and that party must serve it personally as soon as is practicable (**r. 81.7(2)**).

If an undertaking has been given by a company or other corporation, it cannot be enforced against a director or other officer unless he or she has been served with 'a copy of the judgment or order' (**r. 81.7(3)**), meaning, presumably, a judgment or order which refers to or incorporates the undertaking.

There are occasions when a solicitor is required to give an undertaking to the court, for example, when an application is made as a matter of urgency and there has not been time to issue the proceedings in which the application is made. An application for committal for breach of a solicitor's undertaking cannot be made without the court's permission (**r. 81.11(1)**). Application for permission must be made by application notice under **Part 23** (**r. 81.11(2)**). It must be supported by an affidavit setting out the grounds on which committal is sought (**r. 81.11(3)**).

It may be made without notice (**r. 81.11(4)**) and **r. 23.9** (service after disposal of without-notice application) and **r. 23.10** (setting aside or variation) do not apply (**r. 81.11(5)**). If permission is given, it must be acted on within 14 days (**r. 81.11(6)**). See further **21.18** and **21.19**.

COURT'S POWER TO ORDER COMMITTAL OF ITS OWN INITIATIVE

81.26 Nothing in **CPR, Part 81** affects the power of the High Court or the Court of Appeal to make an order of committal of its own initiative against a person guilty of contempt of court (**r. 81.2(3)**). A judge has power to initiate committal proceedings personally for breach of an order of the court, in the absence of an application. However, in these circumstances another judge should try the matter (*Re M (A Minor) (Contempt of Court: Committal of Court's Own Motion)* [1999] Fam 263).

SEQUESTRATION

Nature of sequestration

81.27 A writ of sequestration appoints sequestrators who are empowered to enter the contemnor's land and to seize the contemnor's personal property, which they will hold until the contempt is purged and their remuneration and expenses are paid. A writ of sequestration must be in form No. 67 (**CPR, r. 81.27**). The court may order the sale of sequestrated assets (*Richardson v Richardson* [1989] Fam 95).

A county court may order sequestration of assets to enforce compliance with an order it has made (*Rose v Laskington Ltd* [1990] 1 QB 562), but the rules on applying for writs of sequestration are expressed to apply only to applications to the High Court (**r. 81.19**). This suggests that proceedings should be transferred to the High Court for enforcement by sequestration, as contemplated by **r. 81.26(1)(a)**.

Rules

81.28 For the purposes of **RSC, ord. 46**, a writ of sequestration is a writ of execution (**RSC, ord. 46, r. 1**) and is subject to the rules in **RSC, ord. 46** (see **79.7** to **79.9**).

Generally, the rules in **Part 81, Section 7** make the same provision for sequestration as the rules in **Part 81, Section 2** concerning committal.

Rule 81.20 on the circumstances in which a judgment, order or undertaking may be enforced by a writ of sequestration against a person's property is in the same terms as **r. 81.4** (see **81.4**), except that the Debtors Acts 1869 and 1878 are not relevant and there is no exception for an order for delivery of goods or payment of their value, because sequestration is one of the permitted means of enforcing such an order (**CPR, sch. 1, RSC, ord. 45, r. 2**).

Rules 81.21, **81.22** and **81.24** on service of judgments and orders are in the same terms as **rr. 81.5**, **81.6** and **81.8** (see **81.5**). **Rule 81.23** on service of undertakings is in the same terms as **r. 81.7** (see **81.25**).

Rule 81.25 (penal notice) is in the same terms as **r. 81.9**, and **PD 81, para. 1** is applied by **para. 6** (see **81.6**).

Application for permission to issue writ of sequestration

81.29 A *writ of sequestration can be issued only* with the court's permission (**CPR, r. 81.20(1)**). An application for permission must be made by filing an application notice under **Part 23** (**r. 81.26(2)**). It must be made (**r. 81.26(1)**):

(a) to a single judge of the Division of the High Court in which the proceedings were commenced or to which they have subsequently been transferred; or
(b) in any other case, to a single judge of the Queen's Bench Division.

Rule 81.26(3) (contents of application notice) is in the same terms as **r. 81.10(3)**, and **PD 81, paras 13.1** and **13.2** apply (see **81.9**). **PD 81, paras 15.1** and **15.2** (hearing date), apply (see **81.10**). **Rule 81.26(4)** and (5) (service) are in the same terms as **r. 81.10(4)** and (5) (see **81.11**). All the provisions of **CPR, Part 81** and **PD 81** discussed at **81.13** to **81.16** apply.

Dies non

A writ of sequestration may not be executed on a Sunday, Good Friday or Christmas Day (**PD 81, para. 7.1**) unless: **81.30**

(a) the court orders otherwise (**para. 7.1**); or
(b) it enforces a judgment, order or undertaking in an Admiralty claim *in rem* (**para. 7.2**).

Renewal after 12 months

For the purposes of **CPR, sch. 1, RSC, ord. 46, r. 8**, which requires renewal of a writ of execution if it has not been wholly executed within 12 months, a writ of sequestration is wholly executed either when the sequestrators have effectively seized all the contemnor's assets or when there is compliance with the court's order. If those objectives have been achieved within 12 months, the sequestrators may deal with consequential matters without renewal of the writ (*H v N* [2009] EWHC 640 (Fam), [2009] 1 WLR 2335). **81.31**

ACTS IN OTHER PROCEEDINGS TREATED AS CONTEMPT

Various statutes provide that if a person fails to cooperate with various tribunals and investigative processes, that fact may be certified to the High Court which may punish the person as for contempt of court. **PD 81, para. 3** identifies some provisions to that effect. There is a much longer list in appendix F to the Law Commission's consultation paper on Contempt of Court (Consultation Paper 209). The procedure for certifying or applying is set out in **CPR, r. 81.15**, and the general rules for committal and sequestration proceedings considered in this chapter apply. **81.32**

Commentary

Chapter 82 Winding Up and Administration of Registered Companies

The following procedural checklist, which is at the front of the book, is relevant to this chapter:

Procedural checklist 35 Application by a creditor whose debt is presently payable to wind up a company incorporated in England and Wales

NATURE OF WINDING UP AND ADMINISTRATION

Winding up

The Insolvency Act 1986 confers on the High Court and county courts a jurisdiction to order **82.1**
the winding up of virtually any kind of business, other than one conducted by a sole trader.

Sole traders are excluded from the winding-up jurisdiction because they are subject to bankruptcy law (see **chapter 83**). The making of a winding-up order is discretionary.

In practice the great majority of applications for winding up are to wind up companies which have been incorporated by registration with the Registrar of Companies in England and Wales under the Companies Act 2006 or its predecessors. These include private limited companies and plcs. They are often referred to as 'registered companies', though in the legislation they are simply called 'companies'.

The winding-up provisions of the Insolvency Act 1986 are primarily drafted to apply to registered companies, which are the subject of part 4 of the Act (ss. 73 to 219). Part 4 is applied in various ways to other business entities, for example, to societies registered, or deemed to be registered, under the Industrial and Provident Societies Act 1965 (s. 55 of that Act), building societies (Building Societies Act 1986, ss. 86 to 103 and sch. 15), incorporated friendly societies (Friendly Societies Act 1992, ss. 22 and 23 and sch. 10), insolvent partnerships (Insolvent Partnerships Order 1994 (SI 1994/2421)) and limited liability partnerships (Limited Liability Partnerships Regulations 2001 (SI 2001/1090), reg. 5). Part 4 of the Insolvency Act 1986 is also extended by part 5 of the Act to the winding up of what it calls 'unregistered companies', which include companies formed outside the United Kingdom. The present chapter concentrates on the winding up of registered companies.

The winding up of a company by order of the court is known as a 'compulsory' winding up to contrast it with a winding up effected without a court order, which is called a 'voluntary' winding up (as in the Insolvency Act 1986, s. 84(2)).

The procedure for compulsory winding up serves three principal purposes:

(a) It enables unsecured creditors of an insolvent company to have it liquidated for their benefit (and in this respect compulsory liquidation has some affinity with bankruptcy, which is discussed in **chapter 83**).
(b) It enables members of a solvent company to have it liquidated for their benefit. (The Insolvency Act 1986 is misleadingly titled: it applies to the winding up of solvent as well as insolvent companies. In the special jargon of insolvency, the members of a company are referred to as 'contributories', see **82.63**.)
(c) It enables the Secretary of State and other public officials to have a company liquidated in the public interest.

The winding up or liquidation (the terms are used interchangeably) of a company is carried out by its liquidator. The provisions of the Insolvency Act 1986, ss. 136 to 140, ensure that a company has a liquidator as from the time that a court makes an order for it to be wound up. Initially the liquidator is the official receiver (see **82.16**), but if the assets are sufficient, an insolvency practitioner, who must be qualified to act in relation to the company (see **82.15**), may be appointed.

The liquidator of a company being wound up by the court entirely displaces the company's directors and performs his or her duties as an officer of the court subject to its control. The task of the liquidator of a company is to remove the company from all its legal relationships. Its contracts must be completed, transferred or otherwise brought to an end; it must cease carrying on its business except so far as may be necessary for its beneficial winding up; its liabilities (including post-liquidation interest) must be paid, as far as possible; and its legal disputes must be settled.

The members are entitled to benefit from any property remaining unless the company's constitution provides otherwise. Surplus non-cash assets may be sold and the proceeds distributed to the members or, if the company's constitution provides, the property may be distributed in kind.

In the compulsory winding up of an insolvent company the official receiver is required to report to the Secretary of State if it appears to the official receiver that the conduct of any person who has been a director of the company makes that person unfit to be concerned in the management of a company, and an application may then be made for a disqualification order (Company Directors Disqualification Act 1986, ss. 6 and 7) (see **chapter 86**).

The liquidation of a registered company is completed by dissolving it, which means removing its name from the Register of Companies so that it ceases to exist as a juristic person.

Winding up is a process undertaken for the collective benefit of a company's creditors and members. A winding-up order is said to operate 'in favour of all the creditors and of all contributories of the company' (Insolvency Act 1986, s. 130(4)).

Administration

For an insolvent registered company, administration is an alternative to both winding up and the appointment of an administrative receiver. An administrator of a company manages its affairs, business and property in accordance with a proposal approved by creditors and usually does so in the interests of all the company's creditors (Insolvency Act 1986, sch. B1, paras 1(1) and 3(2)). The statute law on administration is in the Insolvency Act 1986, part 2 (s. 8) and sch. B1. **82.2**

A company enters administration when the appointment of an administrator takes effect (Insolvency Act 1986, sch. B1, para. 1(2)). Until 14 September 2003, only the court could appoint an administrator. Now an administrator of a company may be appointed out of court by the company itself or its directors or by the holder of a qualifying floating charge in respect of the company's property (sch. B1, paras 14 and 22), though such an appointment does not take effect until notice of appointment is filed in court (sch. B1, paras 18,19, 29 and 31). Persons who are entitled to appoint an administrator out of court may alternatively apply to the court to make an appointment, by means of an administration order under sch. B1, para. 10 (see **82.102** to **82.117**), and in certain circumstances (see **82.103**) must do so. An application for an administration order may also be made by certain persons, such as creditors who do not hold qualifying floating charges, who are not entitled to make an appointment out of court (see **82.103**). The making of an administration order is discretionary.

An administrator of a company is asked to formulate, if possible, proposals for achieving the purpose of administration (see **82.105**). The proposals must be submitted, within 10 weeks of the administrator's appointment, to the company's unsecured creditors for approval (sch. B1, para. 51). If the proposals are approved, the administrator must manage the affairs, business and property of the company in accordance with them (sch. B1, para. 68).

The administrator of a company is required to report to the Secretary of State if it appears to the administrator that the conduct of any person who has been a director of the company makes that person unfit to be concerned in the management of a company, and an application may then be made for a disqualification order (Company Directors Disqualification Act 1986, ss. 6 and 7) (see **chapter 86**).

PROCEDURAL RULES

Insolvency Rules 1986

Applications for winding-up and administration orders are proceedings under the Insolvency Act 1986 and are therefore 'insolvency proceedings' for the purpose of the Insolvency Rules 1986 (SI 1986/1925) (IR 1986), by r. 13.7 of these rules. IR 1986, r. 7.51A(2), provides that all provisions of the CPR (including related practice directions) which are not either specifically applied or expressly excluded apply to proceedings under the Insolvency Act 1986 or IR 1986 with any necessary modifications, except so far as inconsistent with IR 1986. **82.3**

The IR 1986 also govern bankruptcy proceedings, which are considered in **chapter 83**. Applications and appeals in relation to insolvency proceedings are considered in **chapter 84**. The CPR and IR 1986 are supplemented by **PD Insolvency Proceedings**, which is printed in **appendix 1**.

As the requirement that an application for a winding-up order or bankruptcy order must be made by petition is imposed by statute, the court has no power under the CPR to waive a failure to comply with it (*Re Osea Road Camp Sites Ltd* [2004] EWHC 2437 (Ch), [2005] 1 WLR 760).

Track allocation

82.4 All insolvency proceedings, including winding-up and bankruptcy petitions and administration applications, are allocated to the multi-track by IR 1986, r. 7.51A(3), and so the provisions of the CPR concerning directions questionnaires and track allocation do not apply.

Forms

82.5 The forms contained in sch. 4 to the IR 1986 must be used in and in connection with insolvency proceedings, whether in the High Court or a county court (IR 1986, r. 12A.30(1)). The forms must be used with such variations, if any, as the circumstances may require (r. 12.A.30(2)).

Forms can be downloaded from the Insolvency Service website: http://www.insolvency.gov.uk.

Time limits

82.6 Where by any provision of the Insolvency Act 1986 or the IR 1986 about winding up, the time for doing anything is limited, the court may extend the time, either before or after it has expired, on such terms, if any, as it thinks fit (IR 1986, r. 4.3). (The same provision is made in relation to bankruptcy proceedings by the Insolvency Act 1986, s. 376.) The court may also, under **CPR, r. 3.1(2)(a)**, as applied by IR 1986, r. 12A.55(2), extend or shorten the time for compliance with anything required or authorised to be done by the IR 1986, even if an application for extension is made after the time for compliance has expired. An application to extend or abridge time in winding-up proceedings is made to the member of court staff in charge of the winding-up list in the RCJ or a district judge in a district registry or a county court (**PD Insolvency Proceedings, paras 12.1** and **12.2**).

IR 1986, r. 12A.55(1), provides that the provisions of **CPR, r. 2.8** (see **chapter 3**), apply, as regards computation of time, to anything required or authorised to be done by IR 1986.

Meaning of 'business day'

82.7 In IR 1986, 'business day' means (by r. 13.13(1)) any day other than a Saturday, a Sunday, Christmas Day, Good Friday or a day which is a bank holiday in any part of England and Wales under or by virtue of the Banking and Financial Dealings Act 1971.

WHICH COURT?

82.8 Subject to Regulation (EC) No. 1346/2000, art. 3 (see **82.9**), the High Court has jurisdiction to wind up any company incorporated by registration in England and Wales (Insolvency Act 1986, s. 117(1) and (7)).

High Court proceedings under the enactments relating to companies are assigned to the *Chancery Division by the* Senior Courts Act 1981, sch. 1, para. 1. Specific Chancery Division judges are designated to deal with company matters and there is a separate registry for such matters. This administrative arrangement is known as the Companies Court.

Subject to Regulation (EC) No. 1346/2000, art. 3 (see **82.9**), if the amount of a registered company's share capital paid up or credited as paid up does not exceed £120,000, the county court which has insolvency jurisdiction for the district in which the company's registered office is situated has concurrent jurisdiction with the High Court to wind up the company (Insolvency Act 1986, s. 117(2) and (7)). If, in the six months immediately preceding presentation of a petition to wind up a company, it has had different addresses for its registered office then it is the place which has longest been its registered office in that period which determines which county court has jurisdiction (s. 117(6)). Under s. 117(4) and the Civil Courts Order 1983 (SI 1983/713), art. 9 and sch. 3, about half of the county courts do not have insolvency jurisdiction: the districts of those courts are attached either to other county courts or, in the London area, to the High Court for the purposes of winding-up jurisdiction. This means that in the London area, only the High Court has winding-up jurisdiction.

A court in England and Wales does not have jurisdiction to wind up a company registered in Scotland (*Re Scottish Joint Stock Trust* [1900] WN 114; *Re Helene plc* [2000] 2 BCLC 249). A petition to wind up a Scottish registered company must be presented to the Court of Session or a sheriff court.

The government has dropped its proposal that unopposed orders for compulsory winding up on the ground of insolvency should be made without any court proceedings (Insolvency Service, Consultation: Reform of the Process to Apply for Bankruptcy and Compulsory Winding Up, November 2011).

Commentary

Regulation (EC) No. 1346/2000

The jurisdiction of English courts in relation to winding up companies is, by the Insolvency Act 1986, s. 117(7), subject to Regulation (EC) No. 1346/2000, art. 3. The same applies to jurisdiction in relation to the bankruptcy of individuals (Insolvency Act 1986, s. 265(3)). The Regulation applies to the winding up of a company only if the winding up is on the ground of insolvency. **82.9**

The scheme of the Regulation is that the main insolvency proceedings in the EU (apart from Denmark which has opted out of applying the Regulation) in relation to a debtor should be opened in the EU State where the 'centre of the debtor's main interests' (see **82.10**) is located. Those main insolvency proceedings should be universal, that is, they should deal with all the debtor's assets wherever they are located.

If a debtor with a centre of main interests in one EU State has an establishment (see **82.11**) in another EU State, insolvency proceedings may be opened in that State, but must be limited to dealing with the assets in that State, and are known as 'territorial proceedings' if main proceedings have not been opened or 'secondary proceedings' if main proceedings have been opened.

According to recital 14 in the preamble, the Regulation does not apply to insolvency proceedings relating to a debtor whose centre of main interests is in Denmark or outside the EU. For an example of a case where the Regulation did not apply because the debtor's centre of main interests was outside the EU see *Skjevesland v Geveran Trading Co. Ltd* [2002] EWHC 2898 (Ch), [2003] BCC 391. The Regulation applies to a company whose centre of main interests is in an EU State, even if the company is incorporated outside the EU (*Re BRAC Rent-A-Car International Inc.* [2003] EWHC 128 (Ch), [2003] 1 WLR 1421).

Centre of main interests

Recital 13 in the preamble to Regulation (EC) No. 1346/2000 states that the 'centre of main interests' (COMI) of a debtor should correspond to the place where the debtor conducts the administration of his interests on a regular basis, and asserts that this should be ascertainable by third parties, but the term is left undefined in the body of the Regulation. A debtor **82.10** can have only one COMI (*Re BRAC Rent-A-Car International Inc.* [2003] EWHC 128 (Ch), [2003] 1 WLR 1421 at [23]), but may move it at will (*Shierson v Vlieland-Boddy* [2005] EWCA Civ 974, [2005] 1 WLR 3966). A court must not take any account of movement of a debtor's COMI to another jurisdiction after a request to open insolvency proceedings in respect of the debtor has been filed (*Staubitz-Schreiber* (case C-1/04) [2006] ECR I-701, overruling on this point *Shierson v Vlieland-Boddy*).

The COMI of a company is presumed to be where its registered office is, in the absence of proof to the contrary (art. 3(1)). The registered office of a company registered in England and Wales must be in England and Wales (Companies Act 2006, s. 9(6)(a)).

Recital 13 and art. 3(1), reflect an intention 'to attach greater importance to' the place where a company has its central administration as the criterion for jurisdiction (*Interedil Srl v Fallimento Interedil Srl* (case C-396/09) [2012] Bus LR 1582 at [48]). It is also of great importance that the COMI can be ascertained by third parties. The presumption that the COMI is at the company's registered office (art. 3(1)) reflects the fact that this normally corresponds to the head office and is also readily ascertainable by third parties, as every company must state the location of its registered office in letters and order forms, whether in paper form or in any other medium, and on its websites (Directive 2009/101/EC, art. 5, implemented in the UK by the Companies (Trading Disclosures) Regulations 2008 (SI 2008/495), regs 6 and 7).

The location of a debtor's COMI is a question of fact to which the usual civil standard of proof on balance of probabilities applies (*Shierson v Vlieland-Boddy*). In the case of a company, this is subject to the presumption that the COMI is at its registered office. That presumption can be displaced only if 'factors which are both objective and ascertainable by third parties enable it to be established that an actual situation exists which is different from' that presumption (*Re Eurofood IFSC Ltd* (case C-341/04) at [34]; *Re Stanford International Bank Ltd* [2010] EWCA Civ 137, [2010] Bus LR 1270 at [56]). Those factors must be assessed in a comprehensive manner, taking account of the particular circumstances of each case (*Rastelli Davide e C Snc v Hidoux* (case C-191/10) (CJEU 1st Chamber 15 December 2011) at [36]). What is ascertainable by third parties is what is in the public domain and what they would learn in the ordinary course of business with the company, not what can be ascertained only on enquiry (*Re Stanford International Bank Ltd* at [56]; *Interedil Srl v Fallimento Interedil Srl* at [49]). The factors to be taken into account include, in particular, all the places in which the company pursues economic activities or holds assets, so far as they can be ascertained by third parties (*Interedil Srl v Fallimento Interedil Srl* at [52]).

82.11 **Establishment** The term 'establishment' is defined in Regulation (EC) No. 1346/2000, art. 2(h), to mean 'any place of operations where the debtor carries out a non-transitory economic activity with human means and goods'. 'With human means and goods' is a literal translation of the French 'avec des moyens humains et des biens', which might be better rendered as 'using human and physical resources'.

The existence of an establishment must be determined on the basis of objective factors which are ascertainable by third parties (*Interedil Srl v Fallimento Interedil Srl* (case C-396/09) [2012] Bus LR 1582 at [63]). The concept of an establishment requires a minimum level of organisation and a degree of stability necessary for the purpose of pursuing economic activity. The presence of goods or a bank account does not by itself meet that requirement (*Interedil Srl v Fallimento Interedil Srl* at [64]).

82.12 **Types of enterprise to which the Regulation does not apply** By art. 1(2), Regulation (EC) No. 1346/2000 does not apply to insolvency proceedings concerning insurance undertakings, credit institutions, investment undertakings which provide services involving the holding of funds or securities for third parties, or collective investment undertakings. These types of enterprise are being dealt with by special rules made under Directives which ensure that such enterprises are wound up in the State where they are primarily regulated. Insurance undertakings are covered by the Insurers (Reorganisation and Winding up) Regulations 2003

(SI 2003/1102); credit institutions are covered by the Credit Institutions (Reorganisation and Winding up) Regulations 2004 (SI 2004/1045).

Effect on winding up of companies registered in England and Wales Article 3 of Council Regulation (EC) No. 1346/2000 affects a company incorporated by registration in England and Wales only if the company's COMI is in another EU State (apart from Denmark). If that is the case, a winding-up order may be made in England and Wales only if the company possesses an establishment here (art. 3(2)) and there are restrictions on who may apply for the order (art. 3(4); see **82.17**). The winding up will be limited to dealing with the company's assets in the United Kingdom. **82.13**

Effect of proceeding in the wrong court

By the Insolvency Act 1986, s. 118(1), nothing in s. 117 invalidates a proceeding by reason of its being taken in the wrong court (see, for example, *Re Pleatfine Ltd* [1983] BCLC 102). The winding up of a company by the court, or any proceedings in the winding up, may be retained in the court in which the proceedings were commenced, although it may not be the court in which they ought to have been commenced (s. 118(2); IR 1986, r. 7.12(b)). However, under IR 1986, r. 7.12(a) and (c), where winding-up proceedings are commenced in the wrong court, that court may order the transfer of the proceedings to the court in which they ought to have been commenced or order the proceedings to be struck out. **82.14**

QUALIFIED INSOLVENCY PRACTITIONERS

Any person who acts as, among other things, a liquidator or provisional liquidator of a company (known as 'acting as an insolvency practitioner in relation to the company') without being qualified to do so commits an offence punishable by imprisonment for up to two years and/or a fine (IA 1986, s. 389(1) and sch. 10). This does not apply to official receivers (see **82.16**) (s. 389(2)). A person can be appointed administrator of a company only if qualified to act as an insolvency practitioner in relation to the company (sch. B1, para. 6). **82.15**

There are two aspects to being qualified to act as an insolvency practitioner in relation to a company:

(a) qualification to act as an insolvency practitioner generally;
(b) qualification to act in relation to the particular company concerned.

Qualification to act as an insolvency practitioner generally is obtained by being authorised to do so, either by a recognised professional body or by the Secretary of State (s. 390(2)). The recognised professional bodies are specified in the Insolvency Practitioners (Recognised Professional Bodies) Order 1986 (SI 1986/1764).

Qualification to act in relation to a specific company is obtained by posting a bond under which a surety accepts liability for the proper performance of the practitioner's duties in relation to that company (Insolvency Act 1986, s. 390(3); Insolvency Practitioners Regulations 2005 (SI 2005/524), reg 12 and sch. 2).

Only an individual can act as an insolvency practitioner (Insolvency Act 1986, s. 390(1)): companies and partnerships are not eligible. An individual cannot act as an insolvency practitioner while an undischarged bankrupt, while subject to a director disqualification order, or while lacking capacity under the mental health legislation (s. 390(4)).

OFFICIAL RECEIVERS

Each court in England and Wales with insolvency jurisdiction has attached to it one or more official receivers who are appointed by, and act under the general authority and directions of, **82.16**

Commentary

the Secretary of State (Insolvency Act 1986, s. 399(2), (3), (5) and (6) and s. 400(2)). The same official receiver may be attached to two or more different courts (s. 399(5)).

The main tasks of an official receiver are to investigate the causes of insolvencies and to act as trustee in bankruptcy and as liquidator or provisional liquidator in compulsory liquidations of companies. Although the creditors of an insolvent person can put their own appointee (who must be a qualified insolvency practitioner) in place of the official receiver as trustee or liquidator, most insolvent estates are not sufficiently valuable to remunerate an insolvency practitioner.

For the purposes of the Insolvency Act 1986, 'the official receiver', in relation to any winding up, is the person who is authorised under s. 399(4) or (6) to act as the official receiver in relation to that winding up (s. 399(1)).

An official receiver exercises the functions of his or her office as an officer of the court in relation to which those functions are exercised (s. 400(2)).

WHO CAN PETITION FOR WINDING UP?

82.17 A person may petition for the compulsory liquidation of a company only if given standing to do so by the legislation that applies to the company (*Mann v Goldstein* [1968] 1 WLR 1091 at p. 1094). The persons who may petition are:

(a) any creditor or creditors of the company (including any contingent or prospective creditor or creditors) (Insolvency Act 1986, s. 124(1));
(b) any contributory or contributories of the company (s. 124(1));
(c) the company itself (s. 124(1));
(d) the directors of the company (s. 124(1));
(e) a supervisor of a voluntary arrangement of the company (s. 7(4)(b));
(f) the designated officer for a magistrates' court (if the company has failed to pay a fine) (s. 124(1); Criminal Justice Act 1988, s. 62(2));
(g) a liquidator (within the meaning of Regulation (EC) No. 1346/2000, art. 2(b)) appointed in proceedings in another EU State (apart from Denmark) by virtue of art. 3(1) of the Regulation, or a temporary administrator (within the meaning of art. 38 of the Regulation) (Insolvency Act 1986, s. 124(1));
(h) all or any of the parties listed in (a) to (g) together or separately (s. 124(1));
(i) the Secretary of State (s. 124(4));
(j) an official receiver (though only if the company is already in voluntary liquidation) (s. 124(5));
(k) an administrator of the company (sch. B1, para. 60; sch. 1, para. 21)—an administrator of a company is deemed to act as the company's agent (sch. B1, para. 69);
(l) an administrative receiver of the company (s. 42(1) and (2); sch. 1, para. 21)—an administrative receiver of a company is deemed to act as the company's agent (s.44(1));
(m) a receiver (other than an administrative receiver) appointed under a charge on property of the company, if the charge was created as a floating charge and s. 176A (share of assets for unsecured creditors) applies (IR 1986, rr. 3.39 and 3.40);
(n) a foreign representative appointed in a foreign main proceeding or a foreign non-main proceeding in Denmark or a State outside the EU (Cross-Border Insolvency Regulations 2006 (SI 2006/1030), sch. 1, art. 11).

In addition, various public officials and bodies have statutory powers to petition for the winding up of particular types of company. For example, the Financial Services Authority may petition for the winding up of a company which provides financial services (Financial Services *and Markets Act 2000, s. 367*).

The Secretary of State may petition for the winding up of a company under the Insolvency Act 1986, s. 124(4)(b), if the case falls within s. 124A. A case falls within s. 124A if the company is not already being wound up by the court (s. 124A(2)) and it appears to the Secretary of State that it is expedient in the public interest that the company should be wound up, this being apparent from a report made or information obtained using various powers of inspection and investigation listed in s. 124A(1). Petitions in cases falling within s. 124A are known as 'public-interest petitions'.

Regulation (EC) No. 1346/2000 governs who may apply for a winding-up order in England and Wales in relation to an English company whose COMI is in another EU State (apart from Denmark) (see **82.9** to **82.13**). An application for such a company to be wound up may be made only if the company possesses an establishment in the United Kingdom (art. 3(2)). If insolvency proceedings (main proceedings) have been opened in the State where the company's COMI is located, then, by arts 27 and 29 and the Insolvency Act 1986, s. 124(1), provided the main proceedings are of a type listed in annex A to the Regulation, an application may be made (in secondary proceedings) in England and Wales for a winding-up order by:

(a) the liquidator in the main proceedings (called a 'member State liquidator' in IR 1986: see r. 13.13(11)), or
(b) a temporary administrator appointed in the main proceedings, or
(c) any other person authorised by s. 124.

If insolvency proceedings have not yet been opened in the State where the company's COMI is located, an application for a winding-up order may be made (in territorial proceedings) in England and Wales only by a creditor who is domiciled or habitually resident in the United Kingdom or has its registered office in the United Kingdom, or a creditor whose claim arises from the operation of the company's establishment in the United Kingdom (Regulation, art. 4(b)). This restriction does not apply if insolvency proceedings cannot be opened in the State where the company's COMI is located, because of the conditions laid down by the law of that State (art. 4(a)). The exception in art. 4(a) is limited to a situation in which the law of the COMI State prevents insolvency proceedings being opened at all and does not cover a situation in which insolvency proceedings cannot be opened because of the specific circumstances in which the opening is requested. In particular, the fact that the COMI State's law does not give the proposed petitioner standing to request the opening of main proceedings, but does give other persons standing, does not mean that main proceedings cannot be opened (*Procureur-generaal bij het hof van beroep te Antwerpen v Zaza Retail BV* (case C-112/10) (CJEU 1st Chamber, 17 November 2011)).

In practice, the most important classes of petitions are those by creditors and those by contributories (and about 95 per cent of petitions are by creditors). The noticeable difference between these two classes of petitions is that, in general, creditors petition to wind up insolvent companies, whereas contributories petition to wind up solvent companies. The procedure for contributories' petitions is not the same as the procedure on other types of petition and is considered separately in **82.66** to **82.73**. For procedural purposes a petition to wind up a company presented at the instance of the company's administrator or by the supervisor of a voluntary arrangement in force for the company is treated as a contributory's petition.

Effect of voluntary arrangement and administration moratoriums

A petition for a company to be wound up by the court cannot be presented while a morato- **82.18**
rium under the Insolvency Act 1986, s. 1A (moratorium when directors propose a voluntary arrangement), is in force in relation to the company (sch. A1, para. 12(1)(a)).

While a company is in administration, and while an interim moratorium is in force when an administration application has been presented or notice of intention to appoint an administrator out of court has been filed, the court may not make a winding-up order, except on a public-interest petition presented by the Secretary of State or the Financial Services Authority (sch. B1, paras 42 and 44). When the court makes an administration order it must dismiss any outstanding winding-up petition (para. 40(1)(a)).

A petition for the winding up of a company must be 'suspended' while the company is in administration following an appointment out of court by the holder of a floating charge (sch. B1, para. 40(1)(b)), unless it is a public-interest petition (para. 40(2)). During the suspension, s. 127(1) (avoidance of property dispositions) does not apply to anything done by the administrator (s. 127(2)). It is clear that the suspension automatically comes to an end when the administration comes to an end.

FORM AND CONTENTS OF WINDING-UP PETITION

Prescribed form

82.19 Under r. 4.7 of the IR 1986 the prescribed form of petition for the winding up of a company, if the petitioner is not a contributory, is form 4.2 in sch. 4 to the Rules. (Rule 4.7 does not apply to contributories' petitions, by r. 4.2(2).)

Heading

82.20 A winding-up petition must be entitled, 'In the matter of [the company sought to be wound up] and in the matter of the Insolvency Act 1986'.

A petition can refer to only one company because a winding-up order can refer to only one company (*Re Shields Marine Insurance Co., Lee and Moor's Case* (1867) 17 LT 308). In order to wind up a group of companies it is necessary to present a separate petition for each company in the group (*Re a Company* [1984] BCLC 307). However, the rules permit the petitioner to provide one statement of truth verifying several petitions (IR 1986, r. 4.12(7); see **82.25**).

Prescribed paragraphs

82.21 The prescribed paragraphs of a petition (form 4.2) to wind up a registered company state:

(1) The name and date of incorporation of the company, and which Companies Act it was registered under.

(2) The address of its registered office.

(3) Its nominal capital (otherwise known as authorised share capital) and how that is divided into shares, and its paid-up capital.

(4) The principal objects of the company.

(5) The 'grounds on which a winding-up order is sought'. In the case of a creditor's petition, this paragraph must state that the company is unable to pay its debts, which is shown by the fact that it has not paid the petitioner's debt. Details should then be given of how that debt arose, including the nature of the transaction, order number and date, invoice number and date, and interest claimed.

(6) A statement of whether the company is or is not one of the types of company to which Regulation (EC) No. 1346/2000 does not apply (see **82.12**).

(7) A statement of whether the proceedings will be main, secondary or territorial proceedings (see **82.9**). When petitioning for the winding up of a company registered in England and Wales, we recommend that this paragraph should be completed as follows. If it has been identified in para. (6) that the Regulation does not apply, or if the COMI of the company is in Denmark or is outside the EU, or if the petition is on a ground other than insolvency, state that the Regulation does not apply. Otherwise, state that the Regulation does apply and identify the proceedings as 'main proceedings', unless the

centre of the company's main interests is in another EU State apart from Denmark. If the centre of the company's main interests is in another EU State (apart from Denmark) and main proceedings have not been opened there, identify the petition proceedings as 'territorial proceedings'. If main proceedings have been opened in the State where the COMI is located, identify the petition proceedings as 'secondary proceedings'.

(7A) A statement, if applicable, that the reasons why more than four months have elapsed since a statutory demand was served on the company are set out in the statement of truth filed in support of the petition.

(8) A statement that: 'In the circumstances it is just and equitable that the company should be wound up'.

There is then a prayer that the company named may be wound up by the court under the provisions of the Insolvency Act 1986 or that such other order may be made as the court thinks fit.

It is very important that items (1) to (3) correspond exactly with the data on the company's file at Companies House.

The prescribed form of petition ends with a section headed 'endorsement'. This has spaces to be filled in by a court official with the venue for hearing the petition (see **82.26**) and spaces to be filled in with the name, address and telephone number of the petitioner's solicitors and their reference number and equivalent details of their London agents. The information about the petitioner's solicitors must be completed before the petition is filed.

Commentary

Grounds on which a winding-up order is sought

A petition for a winding-up order must allege the existence of one or more of the circumstances in which the court may make a winding-up order and state the facts from which it may be concluded that the alleged circumstance or circumstances exist. **82.22**

The circumstances in which a registered company may be wound up by the court are listed in the Insolvency Act 1986, s. 122(1):

A company may be wound up by the court if—
(a) the company has by special resolution resolved that the company be wound up by the court,
(b) being a public company which was registered as such on its original incorporation, the company has not been issued with a trading certificate under section 761 of the Companies Act 2006 (requirement as to minimum share capital) and more than a year has expired since it was so registered,
(c) it is an old public company, within the meaning of Schedule 3 to the Companies Act 2006 (Consequential Amendments, Transitional Provisions and Savings) Order 2009 [SI 2009/1941],
(d) the company does not commence its business within a year from its incorporation or suspends its business for a whole year,
(e) *[repealed]*
(f) the company is unable to pay its debts,
(fa) at the time at which a moratorium for the company under section 1A comes to an end, no voluntary arrangement approved under Part 1 has effect in relation to the company,
(g) the court is of the opinion that it is just and equitable that the company should be wound up.

A petition is bound to fail if it does not allege any facts from which it may be concluded that at least one of the prescribed circumstances exists (*Re Wear Engine Works Co.* (1875) LR 10 Ch App 188; *Securum Finance Ltd v Camswell Ltd* [1994] BCC 434, in which it was said that such a petition would be an abuse of process).

Evidence that company is unable to pay its debts

By far the most common type of petition is a creditor's petition alleging that the company is unable to pay its debts and the Insolvency Act 1986, s. 123, provides several means of proving that circumstance in the case of a registered company: **82.23**

(1) A company is deemed unable to pay its debts—
   (a) if a creditor (by assignment or otherwise) to whom the company is indebted in a sum exceeding £750 then due has served on the company, by leaving it at the company's registered office, a written demand (in the prescribed form) requiring the company to pay the sum so due and the company has for three weeks thereafter neglected to pay the sum or to secure or compound for it to the reasonable satisfaction of the creditor, or
   (b) if, in England and Wales, execution or other process issued on a judgment, decree or order of any court in favour of a creditor of the company is returned unsatisfied in whole or in part, or
   (c) if, in Scotland, the induciae of a charge for payment on an extract decree, or an extract registered bond, or an extract registered protest, have expired without payment being made, or
   (d) if, in Northern Ireland, a certificate of unenforceability has been granted in respect of a judgment against the company, or
   (e) if it is proved to the satisfaction of the court that the company is unable to pay its debts as they fall due.
(2) A company is also deemed unable to pay its debts if it is proved to the satisfaction of the court that the value of the company's assets is less than the amount of its liabilities, taking into account its contingent and prospective liabilities.

Unlike the position in bankruptcy proceedings, it is not necessary for a creditor of a company to present a statutory demand or issue execution before presenting a winding-up petition. In practice, it is common for a creditor petitioner to rely on the fact that the company has not paid a debt owed to the petitioner as proof (under s. 123(1)(e)) of the company's inability to pay its debts (see *Taylors Industrial Flooring Ltd v M and H Plant Hire (Manchester) Ltd* [1990] BCLC 216 at p. 219; *Re a Company (No. 003079 of 1990)* [1991] BCLC 235 at pp. 235–6).

If a statutory demand is used, it must be in the prescribed form, which is form 4.1 in sch. 4 to the IR 1986. A statutory demand can be served only for an amount due for payment at the time of service: it cannot, for example, be served for a contingent debt where the contingency has not occurred (*JSF Finance and Currency Exchange Co. Ltd v Akma Solutions Inc.* [2001] 2 BCLC 307). Unlike bankruptcy, there is no procedure for obtaining a court order setting aside a statutory demand served on a company.

Only an undisputed creditor of a company has standing to petition for it to be wound up: if there is a dispute on substantial grounds about the existence of the petitioner's debt, the petition will be dismissed (see **82.30**).

Need to establish case in petition

82.24 In winding-up proceedings the petitioner's case must be stated in the petition: the petitioner cannot leave it to the hearing to establish the ground for the petition. At the hearing the petitioner will be limited to the grounds stated in the petition (*Re Spence's Patent Non-conducting Composition and Cement Co.* (1869) LR 9 Eq 9; *Re Fildes Bros Ltd* [1970] 1 WLR 592; *Re Armvent Ltd* [1975] 1 WLR 1679 at p. 1683).

A petitioner cannot rely on disclosure and inspection of documents (*Re a Company, ex parte Burr* [1992] BCLC 724 per Vinelott J at p. 736 and on appeal sub nom. *Re Saul D. Harrison and Sons plc* [1995] 1 BCLC 14 per Hoffmann LJ at p. 22) or cross-examination of the company's witnesses (*Re a Company* (1917) 34 DLR 396) to reveal facts to support the petition.

The grounds on which a winding up is sought must be stated in the petition itself: it is not sufficient to state them in an accompanying affidavit or witness statement. In *Re a Company (No. 007936 of 1994)* [1995] BCC 705 a statement in a petition that, 'The petitioners will rely on *the substantial correspondence exhibited* to the affidavit verifying this petition, as the particulars are too numerous to be conveniently set out here' was described by the judge as 'completely unacceptable' (at p. 716).

Verification of the petition

A petition must be verified by a statement of truth (IR 1986, rr. 4.7(1) and 4.12(1)) in accordance with **CPR, Part 22** (IR 1986, r. 13.13(17)). IR 1986, r. 4.12(3), requires the statement of truth to state: **82.25**

(a) whether, in the opinion of 'the person making the application', Regulation (EC) No. 1346/2000 will apply; and
(b) if so, whether the proceedings will be main proceedings or territorial proceedings.

For advice on these statements see the commentary in **82.21** on para. 7 of the prescribed form of petition. That paragraph of the prescribed form of petition states that the supporting statement of truth states the reasons for these opinions, but r. 4.12(8), which came into force on 1 April 2005, requires only the opinions to be stated.

Rule 4.12(4) provides that the statement of truth must be authenticated by:

(a) the petitioner (or if there are two or more petitioners, any one of them); or
(b) some person such as a director, company secretary or similar company officer, or a solicitor, who has been concerned in the matters giving rise to the presentation of the petition; or
(c) some responsible person who is duly authorised to make the affidavit or witness statement and has the requisite knowledge of those matters.

In cases (b) and (c) the person verifying the petition must state the capacity in which, and the authority by which, he or she does so, and the means of knowing the matters contained in the written evidence (IR 1986, r. 4.12(5)). In r. 4.12(4)(b) 'solicitor' does not include a body recognised by the Law Society under the Administration of Justice Act 1985, s. 9, as suitable to carry on legal services (Solicitors' Recognised Bodies Order 1991 (SI 1991/ 2684), arts 2(1) and 4(a) and sch. 1).

The court has a discretion to accept verification from a person not mentioned in r. 4.12(4) (*Re African Farms Ltd* [1906] 1 Ch 640).

If there are simultaneous petitions to wind up several companies (e.g. all companies in a group), it is permissible to make one statement of truth referring to all the companies and submit a photocopy with each petition (IR 1986, r. 4.12(7)). There must be a photocopy for each petition and the statement of truth must refer to all the companies by name.

FILING OF PETITION AND FIXING OF VENUE

A petition for the winding up of a company must be filed in court together with copies to be served on the company and sent to other persons. A court officer seals all copies of the petition and fixes a venue for hearing the petition which is endorsed on all copies of the petition (IR 1986, r. 4.7). **82.26**

Unless the petition is presented by the company itself, it must be accompanied by a copy for service on the company (r. 4.7(3)). (If the company is the petitioner, service on the company is not required.)

Rule 4.7(4) requires additional copies of the petition in the following circumstances:

(a) if the company is in course of being wound up voluntarily, and a liquidator has been appointed, one copy of the petition to be sent to the voluntary liquidator;
(b) if the company is in administration, one copy to be sent to the administrator;
(c) if an administrative receiver has been appointed in relation to the company, one copy to be sent to that administrative receiver;

(d) if there is in force for the company a voluntary arrangement under part 1 (ss. 1 to 7) of the Insolvency Act 1986, one copy for the supervisor of the arrangement.

There are also special provisions when the company sought to be wound up is a bank (r. 4.7(4)(e)), an insurance company (Financial Services and Markets Act 2000, s. 369(1)) or an open-ended investment company (Open-Ended Investment Companies Regulations 2001 (SI 2001/1228), reg. 31(3)).

FEE AND DEPOSIT

82.27 On filing a winding-up petition, a court fee of £220 must be paid (**CPFO, fee 3.3**). The petitioner must deposit £1,165 as security for the administration fee which will become payable to the official receiver if a winding-up order is made and transmitted to the official receiver (Insolvency Act 1986, s. 414(4); Insolvency Proceedings (Fees) Order 2004 (SI 2004/593), art. 6(1)). A petition cannot be filed unless the receipt for the deposit is produced (IR 1986, r. 4.7(2)). The deposit is security for the official receiver's administration fee and must be used to discharge that fee to the extent that the company's assets are insufficient (SI 2004/593, art. 6(2)); the administration fee is £2,235 (SI 2004/593, sch. 2, fee W1). The court must transmit the deposit to its official receiver (SI 2004/593, art. 6(3)). If a winding-up order is made, any part of the deposit which is not required to pay the administration fee must be returned (art. 6(5)). If the petition is dismissed or withdrawn, the whole of the deposit must be repaid (art. 6(4)). The court fee is not repayable.

STOPPING PRESENTATION OF, OR PROCEEDING WITH, PETITION

Introduction

82.28 Presentation of a petition for the winding up of a company may cause it considerable disruption. The provisions of the Insolvency Act 1986, s. 127, for the control of transactions while a petition is pending mean that the company's bank account will be frozen. Advertisement of the petition is taken up by credit reference agencies and may damage the company's business and reputation. Despite the great inconvenience that can be caused by the presentation of an unsuccessful winding-up petition, a petitioner is never required to give an undertaking in damages unless there is an application for the appointment of a provisional liquidator (*Re Highfield Commodities Ltd* [1985] 1 WLR 149).

If the court considers that a petition to wind up a company is an abuse of process, it will:

(a) if the petition has not already been presented, restrain presentation of the petition;

(b) if the petition has been presented, either restrain notification of the petition and the taking of further steps to prosecute it, or strike out the petition or restrain notification of the petition and strike it out; the usual order is to dismiss the petition.

An application to restrain presentation of a petition to wind up a company must be made to a court having jurisdiction to wind up the company (IR 1986, r. 4.6A(a)). It must be listed before a judge (**PD Insolvency Proceedings, para. 3.2(3)**). Applications to stop proceedings on a petition that has already been presented are made by application in those proceedings. The procedure on applications is described in **84.1 to 84.5**.

An order made by the court on an application to restrain presentation of a petition is not made in the exercise of its jurisdiction to wind up companies, and therefore cannot be reviewed, rescinded or varied by it under IR 1986, r. 7.47 (*Re Portedge Ltd* [1997] BCC 23 at p. 27).

In any proceedings to prevent the prosecution of a petition for the compulsory winding up of a company, the company must prove that the petition or proposed petition would constitute an abuse of process by showing, for example:

(a) That it is bound to fail because it is a disputed debt or cross-claim petition (see **82.30** and **82.31**).
(b) That it is an abuse of process because it is oppressive or unfair (*Cadiz Waterworks Co v Barnett* (1874) LR 19 Eq 182 at pp. 194–7).
(c) That it is an abuse of process because it has been presented for a collateral purpose and not for the benefit of creditors generally (or the benefit of contributories if it is a contributory's petition) (*Cadiz Waterworks Co v Barnett* (1874) LR 19 Eq 182 at pp. 195–6).
(d) That it is an abuse of process or is bound to fail, because the petitioner is seeking to wind up the company instead of pursuing an alternative and more appropriate remedy (*Charles Forte Investments Ltd v Amanda* [1964] Ch 240). This reason is most often found in relation to contributories' petitions, where the suitable alternative remedy may be an unfair prejudice petition under the Companies Act 2006, s. 994, or a fair offer to purchase the petitioner's shares. When a creditor's petition is based on an undisputed, unpaid debt, it cannot be objected that there is a suitable alternative remedy (*Cornhill Insurance plc v Improvement Services Ltd* [1986] 1 WLR 114 at p. 118). In particular, if there are no substantial grounds for disputing the petitioner's debt, the petitioner is not required to obtain judgment for it before presenting a winding-up petition (*Cornhill Insurance plc v Improvement Services Ltd* [1986] 1 WLR 114; *Re a Company (No. 003079 of 1990)* [1991] BCLC 235 at pp. 235–6).
(e) In the case of a petition that has already been presented, that it is bound to fail as a matter of law or because of lack of evidence (*Charles Forte Investments Ltd v Amanda* [1964] Ch 240).

A contractual obligation of a creditor not to apply for winding up (or administration) will be enforced by the court, if necessary by striking out, and is not contrary to public policy (*Re a Company (No. 00928 of 1991)* [1991] BCLC 514; *Re COLT Telecom Group plc* [2002] EWHC 2815 (Ch), LTL 20/12/2002). But a company's articles of association cannot remove its members' statutory right to apply as contributories for it to be wound up (*Re Peveril Gold Mines Ltd* [1898] 1 Ch 122).

Improper purpose

A winding-up order operates in favour of all creditors and contributories of the company (Insolvency Act 1986, s. 130(4)). It is an abuse of process for a person to petition for a company's compulsory liquidation otherwise than for the purpose of providing for all its creditors and contributories the benefits that the liquidation will produce (though no doubt self-interest will be the petitioner's primary concern) (*Re Wheal Lovell Mining Co.* (1849) 1 Mac & G 1 at p. 22; *Re a Company (No. 001573 of 1983)* [1983] BCLC 492). In *Re Southbourne Sheet Metal Co. Ltd* [1992] BCLC 361 Harman J said, at p. 364: **82.29**

> a winding-up petition is not a *lis inter partes* [lawsuit between parties] for the benefit of A as against B. It is the invoking by A of a class remedy for the benefit of himself and other members of the class. Nonetheless, it is (a) based upon a commercial interest of the person invoking the remedy, and (b) it is for the benefit of himself, amongst other members of the class.

If other members of the petitioner's class take the view that it is not expedient to pursue the petition, the court will consider their views when deciding whether to exercise its discretion to make a winding-up order. The idea of a petitioner as a representative of a class applies primarily to creditors' petitions.

Disputed debts

82.30 If there is a dispute about the existence of a petitioner's debt then, as a matter of practice, it is usual, on the company's application, to strike out the petition (*Re Gold Hill Mines* (1883) 23 ChD 210; *Re a Company (No. 0013734 of 1991)* [1993] BCLC 59). A disputed debt petition is prevented from proceeding even if the company sought to be wound up is insolvent (*Mann v Goldstein* [1968] 1 WLR 1091; *Re Record Tennis Centres Ltd* [1991] BCC 509 at p. 514; *Re a Company (No. 00212 of 1995)* (1995) *The Times*, 7 April 1995). However, the petition may be adjourned on the assumption that another creditor will apply to be substituted as petitioner (*Re R. A. Foulds Ltd* (1986) 2 BCC 99,269; *Vertex Trading Sàrl v Infinity Holdings Ltd* [2009] EWHC 461 (Ch), LTL 30/10/2009).

A disputed debt petition is prevented from proceeding because proceedings on a creditor's winding-up petition are not suited to determining a dispute about the debt on which the petition is based. A dispute about a debt should be tried as an ordinary claim. A disputed debt petition will not be prevented from proceeding if the court decides that it would be proper for the dispute to be determined in the winding-up proceedings (*Re Claybridge Shipping Co. SA* [1997] 1 BCLC 572).

If the fact that a company is indebted to a creditor is not disputed, but the amount to be paid, and/or the time at which it is to be paid, is disputed (in particular, if only part of the petitioner's debt is disputed) then the petitioner's standing is not in question and the petition will not be struck out (*Re Tweeds Garages Ltd* [1962] Ch 406; *Re Claybridge Shipping Co. SA* [1997] 1 BCLC 572 per Lord Denning MR at pp. 574–5; *Re Pendigo Ltd* [1996] 2 BCLC 64; *Corbern v Whatmusic Holdings Ltd* [2003] EWHC 2134 (Ch), LTL 1/10/2003).

If it is found that only part of the debt is disputed and there is no evidence of the company's ability to pay the undisputed part, the petition may be adjourned for a short time to allow the company to pay the undisputed debt if it can (*Re Javelin Promotions Ltd* [2003] EWHC 1932 (Ch), LTL 30/9/2003).

In practice it may be difficult to distinguish between a dispute about existence and a dispute about quantum (see *Re a Company (No. 003729 of 1982)* [1984] 1 WLR 1090; *Re R. A. Foulds Ltd* (1986) 2 BCC 99,269).

It is irrelevant that the company has not paid money to the person who is petitioning or threatening to petition in response to a statutory demand for the disputed amount claimed: the fact that the claim is disputed means that the company has a reasonable excuse for not complying with the statutory demand and so has not 'neglected' to comply with it, and so is not deemed to be unable to pay its debts (*Re London and Paris Banking Corporation* (1874) LR 19 Eq 444; *Re a Company (No. 003729 of 1982)* [1984] 1 WLR 1090).

The court will not prevent a disputed debt petition proceeding unless it is satisfied that 'the debt is disputed on some substantial ground (and not just on some ground which is frivolous or without substance and which the court should, therefore, ignore)' (*Mann v Goldstein* [1968] 1 WLR 1091 per Ungoed-Thomas J at p. 1096). In *Stonegate Securities Ltd v Gregory* [1980] Ch 576 Goff LJ, at p. 589, expressed the court's task as distinguishing 'whether there is a bona fide dispute or whether it is insubstantial or trumped up'.

A bona fide belief that there is a dispute is not enough in itself because it does not prove that there is substance in the dispute (*Re a Company (No. 001946 of 1991)* [1991] BCLC 737, in which Harman J said (at p. 740) that: '"Bona fides", in the sense of good faith, has nothing to do with the matter').

It is for the court hearing the petition to decide whether the dispute is substantial enough to justify dismissing the petition: the question is not decided by the continuance of other proceedings brought by the petitioner to recover the debt, even if an application by the petitioner for summary judgment in those proceedings has failed (*Re Welsh Erick Industries Ltd* [1946] 2 All ER 197). If the court hearing the petition decides there is not a substantial dispute then the petition must continue even if other proceedings are also continuing (*James Dolman and Co. Ltd v Pedley* [2003] EWCA Civ 1686, LTL 25/9/2003).

Cross-claim against petitioner

If a creditor of a company presents a petition for the compulsory winding up of the company, but the company claims from the petitioner a sum which is greater than or equal to the petitioner's debt, or falls short of it by £750 or less, the practice is to treat the petition in the same way as a disputed debt petition (*Re Portman Provincial Cinemas Ltd* [1999] 1 WLR 157; *Re LHF Wools Ltd* [1970] Ch 27; *Re Bayoil SA* [1999] 1 WLR 147). Unless there are special circumstances, the petition will be prevented from proceeding. **82.31**

If the company's cross-claim against the petitioner is less than the petitioner's debt and it is shown that the company is unable to pay its debts, a winding-up order will be made (*Blue Star Security Services (Scotland) Ltd* 1992 SLT (Sh Ct) 80).

According to Nourse LJ in *Re Bayoil SA* [1999] 1 WLR 147 at p. 155, the company has the burden of proving:

(a) that its cross-claim is larger than the admitted debt of the petitioner or falls short of it by £750 or less (*Greenacre Publishing Group v The Manson Group* [2000] BCC 11);
(b) that its cross-claim has substance (per Lord Denning MR in *Re Portman Provincial Cinemas Ltd* [1999] 1 WLR 157), or is 'genuine and serious' (*Re Bayoil SA* [1999] 1 WLR 147 per Nourse LJ at p. 155 and Ward LJ at p. 156) or is 'genuine, serious and of substance' (*Orion Media Marketing Ltd v Media Brook Ltd* [2002] 1 BCLC 184 at p. 191); provided the cross-claim meets this standard, it does not matter that it is disputed.

The fact that there has been delay in taking steps to establish a cross-claim by arbitration or litigation may show that the cross-claim is not based on substantial grounds (*Re a Debtor (No. 544/SD/98)* [2000] 1 BCLC 103 per Robert Walker LJ at p. 114; *Guardi Shoes Ltd v Datum Contracts* [2002] CILL 1934). But it is wrong to require a company to prove that it has been unable to litigate a cross-claim as a condition for preventing presentation of, or proceeding with, a creditor's winding-up petition (*Bolsover District Council v Dennis Rye Ltd* [2009] EWCA Civ 372, [2009] 4 All ER 1140 at [23]; *Accessory People Ltd v Rouass* [2010] EWCA Civ 302, LTL 13/4/2010).

Costs of proceedings to stop a petition

Orders as to costs of proceedings for preventing a petition are at the discretion of the court but will normally follow the event (*Cannon Screen Entertainment Ltd v Handmade Films (Distributors) Ltd* (1988) 5 BCC 207). Abuse of process by presenting a petition to put pressure on a solvent company to pay a disputed debt is 'a high risk strategy', and the petitioner may be ordered to pay the company's costs on an indemnity basis (*Re a Company (No. 0012209 of 1991)* [1992] 1 WLR 351). **82.32**

COMMENCEMENT OF WINDING UP, GOING INTO LIQUIDATION, ETC.

The Insolvency Act 1986, s. 129(2), provides that if an order for the winding up of a company is made on a petition presented when the company was not in voluntary liquidation, the winding up by the court is deemed to have commenced at the time when the petition was presented. This is not at the beginning of the day on which the petition was presented but at the moment of presentation, because s. 129(2) refers to the time rather than the date of presentation of the petition (*Re London and Devon Biscuit Co.* (1871) LR 12 Eq 190; *Re Blackburn Industries Pty Ltd* [1980] **82.33**

QdR 211 per D. M. Campbell J at p. 217 and Dunn J at p. 224; see also the latter case on appeal sub nom. *Wilde v Australian Trade Equipment Co. Pty Ltd* (1981) 145 CLR 590).

If a winding-up order is made on an administration application (see **82.116**), the winding up commences on the making of the order (s. 129(1A)).

If an order for the winding up of a registered company is made on a petition presented after a resolution for voluntary winding up has been adopted, the winding up is deemed to have commenced at the time when that resolution was adopted (s. 129(1)).

The Insolvency Act 1986 also uses the phrase, 'to go into liquidation'. By s. 247(2), a company goes into liquidation when it adopts a resolution for voluntary winding up or when an order for its winding up is made (unless it had already passed a resolution for voluntary winding up, in which case the date of that resolution is the date of going into liquidation).

SERVICE OF PETITION

General rule

82.34 Unless a petition to wind up a company is presented by the company itself, a copy of the petition must be served on the company (IR 1986, r. 4.8(1)). It must be served at least seven business days *before* it is advertised in the *London Gazette* (see **82.41**), and the advertisement must appear at least seven business days before the hearing date (IR 1986, r. 4.11(4)(b)). 'Business day' is defined in r. 13.13(1) (see **82.7**). Service is the responsibility of the petitioner and will not be undertaken by the court (**PD Insolvency Proceedings, para. 6.2**).

Service on solicitors

82.35 If solicitors are properly instructed, they can accept service on behalf of the company (IR 1986, r. 13.4; *Re Regent United Service Stores* (1878) 8 ChD 75; *Re Fletcher Hunt (Bristol) Ltd* [1989] BCLC 108 per Knox J at p. 113).

Service at the registered office

82.36 If service of a petition to wind up a registered company is not to be on the company's solicitors, the petition must be served at the company's registered office, if it has one (IR 1986, r. 4.8(2)).

A petition may be served at the company's registered office in any of the following ways (IR 1986, r. 4.8(3)):

(a) it may be handed to a person who there and then acknowledges him or herself to be — or to the best of the server's knowledge, information and belief is — a director or other officer, or employee, of the company; or
(b) it may be handed to a person who there and then acknowledges him or herself to be authorised to accept service of documents on the company's behalf; or
(c) in the absence of any such person as is mentioned in (a) or (b), it may be deposited at or about the registered office in such a way that it is likely to come to the notice of a person attending at the office.

It is clear from r. 4.8(6) that service at the registered office may not be effected in any other way (for example, by post) without the court's approval or direction.

Service at principal place of business or on officer of company

82.37 Rule 4.8(4) of the IR 1986 specifies methods for serving a winding-up petition on the company sought to be wound up if:

(a) service at its registered office is not practicable, or
(b) the company has no registered office.

In either of those cases the petition may be served by:

(a) leaving it at the company's last known principal place of business in such a way that it is likely to come to the attention of a person attending there; or
(b) delivering it to the secretary or some director, manager or principal officer of the company, wherever that person may be found.

Option (a) only authorises service at a place of business within the jurisdiction (*Re Tea Trading Co. K. and C. Popoff Brothers* [1933] Ch 647 at p. 651).

Order for alternative service

If for any reason it is impracticable to effect service as provided by IR 1986, r. 4.8(2) to (4) (see **82.36** and **82.37**), the petition may be served in such other manner as the court may approve or direct (r. 4.8(6)). An application for the court's approval or direction under r. 4.8(6) may be made without notice to other parties (r. 4.8(7)). An application must be accompanied by a witness statement setting out what steps have been taken to comply with r. 4.8(2) to (5) and the reasons why it is impracticable to effect service as provided in those paragraphs (r. 4.8(7)). **82.38**

Certificate of service

Service of a winding-up petition must be proved by a certificate of service (IR 1986, r. 4.9A(1)). This must be sufficient to identify the petition served and must specify the matters set out in r. 4.9A(2). If substituted service has been ordered, the certificate of service must have attached to it a sealed copy of the order (r. 4.9A(3)). A certificate of service must be verified by a statement of truth (r. 13.13(16)) in accordance with **CPR, Part 22** (IR 1986, r. 13.13(17)). The certificate of service must be filed in court as soon as reasonably practicable after service, and in any event not less than five business days (see **82.7**) before the hearing of the petition (r. 4.9A(4)). **82.39**

Commentary

Copies for other persons

If a petition is presented to wind up a company which has a voluntary liquidator, an administrator, a supervisor of a voluntary arrangement and/or an administrative receiver, a copy of the petition must be sent to that officer on the next business day after the petition is served on the company (IR 1986, r. 4.10(1), (2), (3) and (5)). 'Business day' is defined in r. 13.13(1) (see **82.7**). There are special rules for banks (r. 4.10(4) and (5)), insurance companies (Financial Services and Markets Act 2000, s. 369(1)) and open-ended investment companies (Open-Ended Investment Companies Regulations 2001 (SI 2001/1228), reg. 31 (3)). There are rules requiring notice to be given to regulatory authorities when a petition is presented to wind up railway companies (Railways Act 1993, s. 61(1)(a)), PPP companies (Greater London Authority Act 1999, s. 222(1)(a); Railways and Transport Safety Act 2003, s. 114(5)(c)), air traffic services licence companies (Transport Act 2000, s. 26(4), notice must be given before presenting petition), protected energy companies (Energy Act 2004, s. 160(1) and (2)(a)) and registered providers of social housing (Housing and Regeneration Act 2008, s. 144). **82.40**

If a winding-up petition asks for the opening of secondary proceedings against a company which is already the subject of main insolvency proceedings in another EU State (see **82.9**), a copy of the petition must be served on a member State liquidator appointed in the main proceedings (see **82.17**) unless that liquidator is the petitioner (IR 1986, r. 4.10(3A)).

PUBLICISATION OF PETITION

Need for and timing of notice

A winding-up order is a collective remedy and the order operates in favour of all creditors and contributories (Insolvency Act 1986, s. 130(4)), who can all appear at the hearing of the **82.41** petition to support or oppose it. Therefore, unless the court otherwise directs, notice of a winding-up petition must be given by the petitioner (IR 1986, r. 4.11(1)). The notice must be given by 'gazetting' (r. 4.11(2)), that is, by one advertisement in the *London Gazette* (r. 13.13(4) and (4A)). If gazetting is not reasonably practicable, notice must be given in such other manner as the court thinks fit (r. 4.11(3)). The notice serves to invite creditors and contributories to appear on the hearing of the petition and submit their views to the court: the notice is a substitute for, and renders unnecessary, service of the petition on them (*Re National Credit and Exchange Co. Ltd* (1862) 7 LT 817; *Re Marlborough Club Co.* (1865) LR 1 Eq 216; *Re New Gas Co.* (1877) 5 ChD 703). The contents of the advertisement of a winding-up petition in the *London Gazette* are specified in IR 1986, rr. 4.11(5), 12A.33, 12A.34 and 12A.36 (see r. 13.13(4B)(a)). The prescribed form of an advertisement is form 4.6 in sch. 4 to the IR 1986.

Notice of a petition must appear at least seven business days *before* the date appointed for the hearing, and, unless the company itself is the petitioner, must not appear until at least seven business days *after* service of the petition on the company (IR 1986, r. 4.11(4)). 'Business day' is defined in r. 13.13(1) (see **82.7**).

If notice of a winding-up petition is not given in accordance with r. 4.11, the petition may be dismissed (r. 4.11(6)). Rule 4.11(6) applies where no notice at all is given and it applies to notice that is given for the purpose of complying with r. 4.11, but is given at the wrong time or is wrongly worded. It does not apply to any notification of the petition that is not made for the purpose of complying with r. 4.11 (see **82.43**).

The period of seven days between service of the petition on the company and notification of the petition is required so that the company may, depending on the circumstances:

(a) apply for the petition to be struck out;
(b) pay the debt on a creditor's petition;
(c) consider its position generally with regard to the petition;
(d) if necessary, make an application under the Insolvency Act 1986, s. 127, for an anticipatory validation order (*Re Signland Ltd* [1982] 2 All ER 609 at p. 609; *Re a Company (No. 0013925 of 1991)* [1992] BCLC 562 at p. 564).

The power to dismiss a prematurely advertised petition to wind up a company is a discretionary disciplinary power and might not be exercised on the company's application if the company does not show that it has been prejudiced, e.g. by showing on a creditor's petition that it could have paid the debt (*Re Roselmar Properties Ltd* (1986) 2 BCC 99,156; *Re Corbenstoke Ltd* [1989] BCLC 496; *Re Garton (Western) Ltd* [1989] BCLC 304).

Equally, the timely advertisement of a creditor's petition is important to ensure that the class remedy of winding up by the court is available to all creditors, and is not used as a means of putting pressure on the company to pay the petitioner's debt or costs (**PD Insolvency Proceedings, para. 11.5.1**). The court may, under r. 4.11(6), dismiss a petition if there has been a failure to advertise it without good reason accepted by the court (**PD Insolvency Proceedings, para. 11.5.1**).

A company may apply for a direction that a petition for it to be wound up should not be advertised. It is for the company to show sufficient reason for departure from the normal practice of advertising petitions other than contributories' petitions (*Re a Company (No. 007946 of 1993)* [1994] Ch 198; *Re a Company (No. 007923 of 1994)* [1995] 1 WLR 953), but it is not necessary for the company to show that the petition is bound to fail (*Re a Company (No. 007923 of 1994)* [1995] 1 WLR 953). If the company has not obtained an order under the Insolvency Act 1986, s. 127, validating dispositions in the ordinary course of the company's business, the court will not direct that the petition should not be advertised, other than in exceptional circumstances (*Applied Data Base Ltd v Secretary of State for Trade and Industry* [1995] 1 BCLC 272 at pp. 274–5).

Provision of copies of the petition

When a petition has been presented for the winding up of a company, the petitioner (or the petitioner's solicitor, if there is one) must, on request, supply to any director, contributory or creditor of the company a copy of the petition. A copy must be supplied within two days of being applied for and a fee of 15p per A4 or A5 page (30p per A3 page) may be charged (IR 1986, rr. 4.13 and 13.11(b)). **82.42**

Other publicisation of the petition

Publicity for a winding-up petition, given otherwise than for the purpose of complying with IR 1986, r. 4.11, is not 'notice' for the purposes of that rule and, in particular, r. 4.11(6) (which provides a power to dismiss a petition for failure to comply with r. 4.11) does not apply (*Re a Company (No. 0013925 of 1991)* [1992] BCLC 562; *SN Group plc v Barclays Bank plc* [1993] BCC 506; *Secretary of State for Trade and Industry v North West Holdings plc* [1999] 1 BCLC 425, overruling *Re a Company (No. 001127 of 1992)* [1992] BCC 477). However, in *Re FSA Business Software Ltd* [1990] BCLC 465 Warner J said, at p. 829: 'It is at least a breach of the spirit of the rules of this court for publicity to be given to a winding-up petition before it has been advertised'. **82.43**

The court may dismiss a petition if its existence is notified before the expiry of seven business days from service on the company and the notification was designed to put pressure on the company: such conduct is an abuse of process (*Re a Company (No. 0013925 of 1991)* [1992] BCLC 562; *Re a Company (No. 001127 of 1992)* [1992] BCC 477). In *SN Group plc v Barclays Bank plc* [1993] BCC 506 it was found that the publicisation of the petition was not designed to put pressure on the company (which was found to be insolvent) and the company's application to have the petition dismissed was rejected.

Publicisation of an intention to present a petition may be an abuse of process which may be punished by striking out the petition when it is presented (*Re Doreen Boards Ltd* [1996] 1 BCLC 501).

Errors in notice

If there is an error or inaccuracy in notice of a winding-up petition then, unless the court waives it, the person who was responsible for giving the notice must, as soon as reasonably practicable, give fresh notice for the purpose of correcting the error or inaccuracy (IR 1986, r. 12A.37(3)). The court has a discretion to waive an error (*Re Worthing Royal Sea House Hotel Co.* [1872] WN 74). **82.44**

In *Re Vidiofusion Ltd* [1974] 1 WLR 1548 the advertisement incorrectly gave the company's name as 'Videofusion Ltd' ('e' instead of 'i'). Megarry J waived the mistake and said that, normally, an error would be waived if four conditions are satisfied:

(a) There must be no other company on the register with a similar name.
(b) The true name and the misspelt name should have substantially the same pronunciation.
(c) There should be no marked visual difference between the true name and the misspelt name (so that 'Jaxen' for 'Jackson' would not be waived despite the similarity of pronunciation).
(d) The error must not materially affect the alphabetical order of the names.

It is submitted that it is no longer appropriate to waive errors in spelling, now that there are over 2 million British registered companies and now that banks and other persons checking whether they deal with companies which are the subject of winding-up petitions use computer searches which are usually not capable of recognising such errors.

CONTROL OF TRANSACTIONS AND LITIGATION WHILE PETITION IS PENDING

82.45 If a winding-up order is made against a company, the winding up is deemed to have commenced at the time when the petition was presented, or the time the company went into voluntary liquidation, if earlier (Insolvency Act 1986, s. 129). The general principle of winding up is that all non-preferential unsecured creditors are treated equally. So the Act makes provision to prevent specific unsecured creditors recovering payment of debts at the expense of the other unsecured creditors. (The winding up of a company does not, in general, affect security interests in the company's property.) Provision is made for the stay of other proceedings against the company while the petition is pending (Insolvency Act 1986, s. 126, see 84.17), for all dispositions of the company's property to be invalid unless sanctioned by the court (s. 127), and for avoidance of attachments, sequestrations, distresses and executions against the company's property (s. 128). The company itself and its directors may not appoint an administrator out of court (sch. B1, para. 25(a)), though a holder of a qualifying floating charge may do so unless a provisional liquidator has been appointed (para. 17(a)). The Act also prevents alterations in the status of the company's members without the approval of the court (s. 127).

APPOINTMENT OF A PROVISIONAL LIQUIDATOR

Function of a provisional liquidator

82.46 A provisional liquidator of a company may be appointed by the court under the Insolvency Act 1986, s. 135. An appointment may be made at any time in the period between presentation of a petition for the compulsory winding up of the company and the court's disposal of the petition (by making a winding-up order, dismissing the petition or striking it out) (Insolvency Act 1986, s. 135(1) and (2); *Re a Company (No. 00315 of 1973)* [1973] 1 WLR 1566).

The usual object of the appointment is that an independent person will take charge of the company's affairs, maintain the status quo and prevent prejudice either to those supporting the winding-up petition or to those against it, pending the court's decision on the petition (per Lord President Clyde in *Levy v Napier* 1962 SC 468 at p. 477; per Street J in *Re Carapark Industries Pty Ltd* (1966) 86 WN (Pt 1) (NSW) 165 at p. 171). Provisional liquidators are independent persons operating under the direction of the court for a purpose that is entirely one of preservation during an interim period: a provisional liquidator does not represent any one group of creditors (*Re Bank of Credit and Commerce International SA (No. 2)* [1992] BCLC 579). The name 'provisional liquidator' is misleading because the one thing that a provisional liquidator of a company does not do is carry out the liquidation of the company.

The appointment of a provisional liquidator of a company terminates the powers of the directors as effectively as does the making of a winding-up order (*Re Mawcon Ltd* [1969] 1 WLR 78). The directors do, however, have standing to apply for the provisional liquidator's appointment to be discharged (*Re Union Accident Insurance Co. Ltd* [1972] 1 WLR 640) or apply for an administration order to be made in relation to the company (*Re Gosscott (Groundworks) Ltd* [1988] BCLC 363 per Mervyn Davies J at p. 366).

Who may apply for a provisional liquidator to be appointed

82.47 When a petition has been presented for the compulsory liquidation of a company, an application to appoint a provisional liquidator may be made by (IR 1986, 4. 25(1)):

(a) the petitioner,
(b) a creditor of the company,

(c) a contributory of the company,
(d) the company itself,
(e) the Secretary of State,
(f) a temporary administrator (see **82.17**),
(g) a member State liquidator appointed in main proceedings (see **82.17**),
(h) any person who would, under any enactment, be entitled to present a petition to wind up the company.

Application procedure

82.48 An application to the court for the appointment of a provisional liquidator of a company must be supported by a witness statement stating (IR 1986, r. 4.25(2)):

(a) The grounds for the appointment.
(b) If the proposed provisional liquidator is not the official receiver, that the person proposed has consented to act and that he or she is, to the best of the applicant's knowledge, a qualified insolvency practitioner.
(c) Whether or not the official receiver has been informed of the application and, if so, whether a copy of the application has been sent to the official receiver. Whether or not it is proposed that the official receiver should be the provisional liquidator, a copy of the application and supporting affidavit must be sent to the official receiver, who may attend the hearing and make representations (r. 4.25(3)). If it is not possible to send these copies, the official receiver must at least be informed of the application in time to attend the hearing (r. 4.25(3)).
(d) Whether, to the applicant's knowledge:
    (i) there has been proposed, or is in force, for the company a voluntary arrangement;
    (ii) an administrator or administrative receiver is acting in relation to the company;
    (iii) a voluntary liquidator has been appointed.
(e) The applicant's estimate of the value of the assets in respect of which the provisional liquidator is to be appointed.

In *Re W. F. Fearman Ltd* (1987) 4 BCC 139, in view of the urgency of the case, Harman J heard, and acceded to, an application to appoint a provisional liquidator which had not been made in writing and did not conform to any of the relevant procedural requirements.

The court may make the appointment applied for, on such terms as it thinks fit, if satisfied that sufficient grounds are shown for the appointment (r. 4.25(4)).

In the High Court, an application for the appointment of a provisional liquidator must be listed before a judge (**PD Insolvency Proceedings, para. 3.2(4)**).

An application may be heard in private if it is necessary, in order to protect the company, its creditors and its shareholders, to prevent the appointment of a provisional liquidator becoming known (*Re London and Norwich Investment Services Ltd* [1988] BCLC 226).

The court may make other orders instead of appointing a provisional liquidator (*Re a Company (No. 00596 of 1986)* [1987] BCLC 133, in which a receiver was appointed; *Re Senator Hanseatische Verwaltungsgesellschaft mbH* [1996] 2 BCLC 562, in which injunctions were issued to prevent a foreign company which administered a pyramid investment scheme recruiting new members or remitting cash abroad).

Application without notice to other parties

82.49 As it is not inevitable that a winding-up order will be made after the appointment of a provisional liquidator, if an application for such an appointment is made without notice to the company and the court has no opportunity to hear the company's views, the court will not make the appointment unless the applicant gives an undertaking in damages (i.e. undertakes that if winding up is not ordered the applicant will compensate the company for any loss it suffers as a result of the appointment: the company would not be able to sue for damages because the damage would have been caused by court order). However, if an application is made in those circumstances by the Crown in connection with a public-interest winding-up petition, an undertaking in damages will not be required (*Re Highfield Commodities Ltd* [1985] 1 WLR 149). An undertaking in damages is not usually required if the company had an opportunity to give the court its views on the application (*Re Highfield Commodities Ltd* at p.155).

According to Hoffmann J in *Re First Express Ltd* [1991] BCC 782 at p. 785 and *Re Secure and Provide plc* [1992] BCC 405, an order should not be made without notice to other parties unless:

(a) giving the company an opportunity to be heard appears likely to cause injustice to the applicant, because of:
  (i) the delay involved, or
  (ii) action which it is likely will be taken before the order can be made; and
(b) the court is satisfied that any damage which the company may suffer from the appointment of the provisional liquidator may be compensated through the applicant's undertaking in damages or that the risk of incompensable loss is clearly outweighed by the risk of injustice to the applicant if the order is not made.

Form of order

82.50 The order appointing a provisional liquidator of a company should be in form 4.15 in sch. 4 to the IR 1986 and it must specify the functions to be carried out by the provisional liquidator in relation to the company's affairs (IR 1986, r. 4.26(1)). The appointment of a provisional liquidator may be made on such terms as the court thinks fit (r. 4.25(4)).

Transmission of order

82.51 Having made an order appointing a provisional liquidator of a company, the court will send a sealed copy of the order to the person appointed as provisional liquidator, and (if the person appointed is not the official receiver) to the official receiver, and to the company's administrative receiver, if there is one (IR 1986, r. 4.26(2) and (3)). Further copies are provided to the provisional liquidator to be sent to the company (or to its voluntary liquidator, if there is one) and to Companies House (r. 4.26(2) and (3)).

Public notification

82.52 A provisional liquidator must notify Companies House of his or her appointment (IR 1986, r. 4.26(2) and (3)) and, unless the court orders otherwise, gazette it (r. 4.25A(3)).

Joint provisional liquidators

82.53 If two or more persons are appointed joint provisional liquidators of a company, the order of appointment must state whether any act required or authorised under any enactment to be done by the provisional liquidator is to be done by all or any one or more of the persons for the time being holding the office (Insolvency Act 1986, s. 231).

Deposit for the official receiver's remuneration and expenses

82.54 On applying for the official receiver to be appointed provisional liquidator of a company, the applicant must deposit with the official receiver such sum as the court directs to cover remuneration and expenses (IR 1986, r. 4.27(1)). Alternatively, security for the amount may be given if the official receiver agrees (r. 4.27(1)).

From time to time the official receiver may apply to the court to order a further amount to be deposited or secured, and if the order is not complied with within two days of service, the court may discharge the official receiver's appointment as provisional liquidator (r. 4.27(2)).

Control of litigation after provisional liquidator appointed

Section 130(2) of the Insolvency Act 1986 provides that when a provisional liquidator has been appointed, no action or proceeding shall be proceeded with or commenced against the company or its property, except by permission of the court and subject to such terms as the court may impose. See **84.18.** No one may appoint an administrator out of court (sch. B1, paras 17(a) and 25(a)). **82.55**

CERTIFICATE OF COMPLIANCE

Before the date appointed for the hearing of a winding-up petition, the petitioner or the petitioner's solicitor must file in court a certificate of compliance with the rules relating to service and advertisement (IR 1986, r. 4.14(1)). The prescribed form of certificate is form 4.7 in IR 1986, sch. 4. A certificate must (r. 4.14(2)): **82.56**

(a) state the date of presentation of the petition;
(b) state the date fixed for hearing it;
(c) state the date or dates on which the petition was served and notice of it was given in compliance with the rules;
(d) be accompanied by a copy of the notice. If filing a copy of the notice is not reasonably practicable, a description of the form and content of any notice given is to be filed.

Rule 4.14(1) requires the certificate of compliance to be filed at least five business days (see **82.7**) before the hearing of the petition.

Failure to file a certificate of compliance is a ground on which the court may, if it thinks fit, dismiss the petition (r. 4.14(3)). In *Re J. Lang and Co. Ltd* (1892) 36 SJ 271 North J thought that a petition should not be dismissed for failure to file a certificate of compliance unless the failure had caused substantial injustice which could not be remedied by an order of the court.

A copy or description of the notice must be filed with the certificate even if it was defective in some way, for example, because it was published at the wrong time or omitted or misprinted important words (**PD Insolvency Proceedings, para. 11.5.2**). If the petition has not been notified because of an order forbidding notification, the prescribed form of certificate should be adapted to state that the petition was served but that notification has been forbidden by the court (see *Re a Company (No. 002791 of 1986)* (1986) 2 BCC 99,281). Failure to notify a petition in pursuance of such an order is not in itself a ground for dismissing the petition (*Re Five Oaks Construction Ltd* (1968) 112 SJ 86).

A petitioner who has given notice of the petition but has decided not to pursue it should nevertheless file a copy or description of the notice (**PD Insolvency Proceedings, para. 11.5.2**) and a certificate of compliance so as to be entitled to costs.

PERMISSION TO WITHDRAW A PETITION

Under IR 1986, r. 4.15, a person petitioning for a company to be wound up may apply to the court without notice to other parties for permission to withdraw the petition. The following conditions must be satisfied: **82.57**

(a) The petition must not have been advertised and no notices with reference to the petition (whether in support of or in opposition to it) must have been received by the petitioner, either under r. 4.16 (see **82.82**) or otherwise (*Re Wavern Engineering Co. Ltd* (1986) 3 BCC 3).
(b) The company must consent to the court giving permission to withdraw the petition.

(c) The parties must have agreed who is to pay costs. If there has been no agreement, the petition must be heard so that the court can make an order, but then the petition must be advertised (*Re Shusella Ltd* [1983] BCLC 505).
(d) The application must be made at least five business days (see **82.7**) before the day fixed for hearing the petition.

An application for permission to withdraw a petition is heard by the member of court staff in charge of the winding-up list in the RCJ or a district judge in a district registry or a county court (**PD Insolvency Proceedings, paras 12.1** and **12.2**). The prescribed form of order for permission to withdraw a petition is form 4.8 in sch. 4 to the IR 1986.

The procedure of r. 4.15 is used when a creditor who has petitioned for winding up is paid the debt before the petition is advertised.

COMPANY'S EVIDENCE IN OPPOSITION

82.58 If a petition to wind up a company has been presented and it is to be opposed by the company, the company's witness statement in opposition must be filed in court not less than five business days (see **82.7**) before the day fixed for hearing the petition (IR 1986, r. 4.18(1)). A copy of the written evidence must be sent to the petitioner forthwith after filing (r. 4.18(2)). Written evidence in response to the company's evidence filed under r. 4.18 cannot be filed unless the court directs the filing of further evidence or otherwise gives permission (*Re Multicultural Media Centre for the Millennium Ltd* [2001] EWCA Civ 1687, *The Times*, 16 November 2001).

SUBSTITUTION OF PETITIONER

Circumstances in which a substitution may be made

82.59 When a winding-up petition is pending, r. 4.19 of IR 1986 permits the substitution of a new petitioner if the original petitioner:

(a) is subsequently found not entitled to petition;
(b) fails to advertise the petition, within the time prescribed by IR 1986 (see **82.41**) or such extended time as the court may allow;
(c) consents to withdraw the petition;
(d) consents to allow the petition to be dismissed;
(e) consents to an adjournment of the petition;
(f) fails to appear in support of the petition when it is called on in court on the day originally fixed for the hearing or on a day to which it is adjourned; or
(g) appears when the petition is called on in court but does not apply for an order in the terms of the prayer of the petition.

In circumstances (b) and (c), substitution may be ordered at any time (r. 4.19(3)). An application in the High Court for the substitution of a petitioner is heard by the member of court staff in charge of the winding-up list in the RCJ or a district judge in a district registry or a county court (**PD Insolvency Proceedings, paras 12.1** and **12.2**), or may be dealt with at the hearing of the petition.

Who may be substituted?

82.60 Any creditor or contributory who, in the court's opinion, would have a right to present a petition, and who is desirous of prosecuting it, may be substituted (IR 1986, r. 4.19(2)). The rule permits the substitution as petitioner of any creditor or contributory with a right to present *a* petition, not *the* petition that is being abandoned by its petitioner. Thus the substituted petitioner may have different grounds for petitioning and need not be from the original petitioner's class.

A creditor who is substituted need not have been a creditor at the time the petition was originally presented (*Perak Pioneer Ltd v Petroliam Nasional Bhd* [1986] AC 849; *Re Richbell Strategic Holdings Ltd* [1997] 2 BCLC 429 at p. 455).

If a petitioning creditor's debt is assigned after the petition is presented, the assignee will normally be substituted as petitioner (*Perak Pioneer Ltd v Petroliam Nasional Bhd* [1986] AC 849).

On a petition for the opening of secondary proceedings (see **82.9**) the member State liquidator (see **82.17**) appointed in the main proceedings may be substituted (IR 1986, r. 4.19(2A)).

Effect of substitution

If a substitution is ordered, the hearing will be adjourned, the petition will have to be amended and re-verified, and it may need to be re-served and re-advertised. A petition is a single proceeding from presentation to order notwithstanding that there may have been one or more substitutions (*Re Bostels Ltd* [1968] Ch 346 at p. 351). Substitution of petitioner and amendment of the petition does not mean that a new petition is presented (*Re Western Welsh International System Buildings Ltd* (1984) 1 BCC 99,296). This means that if a winding-up order is made, the date of commencement of the winding up is the date the petition was presented by its original petitioner. **82.61**

FURTHER INFORMATION AND DISCLOSURE

Any party to insolvency proceedings may apply to the court under IR 1986, r. 7.60, for further information to be given by another party under **CPR, Part 18**, or to obtain disclosure and inspection of documents under **CPR, Part 31**. **82.62**

Such an application (see **84.1 to 84.5**) may be made without notice being served on any other party (IR 1986, r. 7.60(2)). But, on a petition for the winding up of a company the court is very unlikely to order the company to give disclosure to the petitioner (*Re COLT Telecom Group plc* [2002] EWHC 2503 (Ch), [2003] 1 BCLC 290). This is because a petition should not be presented unless it can be supported by evidence which, if accepted at the hearing, would found a claim for relief: it is improper to present a petition in the hope that evidence to support it may be found by disclosure (*Re a Company, ex parte Burr* [1992] BCLC 724 per Vinelott J at p. 736 and on appeal sub nom. *Re Saul D. Harrison and Sons plc* [1995] 1 BCLC 14 per Hoffmann LJ at p. 22).

PROCEEDINGS ON CONTRIBUTORY'S PETITION

Contributories

Definition The Insolvency Act 1986 does not mention members or shareholders of a company as persons entitled to petition for it to be wound up. Instead the legislation uses the term 'contributories', who are the persons who are liable to contribute to the assets of a company in the event of its being wound up (Insolvency Act 1986, s. 79(1)). Section 74(1) provides that 'every present and past member' of a company is liable to contribute to its assets when it is wound up, so every past and present member is a contributory of the company. However, this is subject to the extensive limitations set out in the rest of s. 74, the most significant of which is s. 74(2)(d): **82.63**

> in the case of a company limited by shares, no contribution is required from any member exceeding the amount (if any) unpaid on the shares in respect of which he is liable as a present or past member.

The emphasis on members as persons contributing to the assets of a company being wound up was very important in the early days of registered companies when shares were usually partly paid. When companies moved to having only fully paid shares the courts took the pragmatic step of deciding that members with fully paid shares are nevertheless contributories for the purposes of the legislation, and have the same rights and duties as other contributories, except that they are not required to contribute anything (*Re National Savings Bank Association* (1866) LR 1 Ch App 547; *Re Anglesea Colliery Co.* (1866) LR 1 Ch App 555; *Re Phoenix Oil and Transport Co. Ltd* [1958] Ch 560).

82.64 **Qualifying period of membership** Standing of a contributory to petition is restricted by the Insolvency Act 1986, s. 124(2), which provides that, unless the number of members of a company has been reduced below two (s. 124(2)(a)), a contributory may petition for its winding up only if:

(a) shares which give the petitioner the status of contributory were originally allotted to the petitioner; or
(b) such shares have been registered in the petitioner's name for at least six of the 18 months preceding presentation of the petition; or
(c) they have devolved on the petitioner through the death of a former holder (s. 124(2)(b)).

Condition (b) is satisfied only if there has been actual registration for six months — an entitlement to be registered is not enough (*Re Gattopardo Ltd* [1969] 1 WLR 619). Registration is sufficient to satisfy condition (b): provided the contributory has been registered as holder of the shares for the requisite period it does not matter that the contributory was not the beneficial owner of them throughout the period (*Re Wala Wynaad Indian Gold Mining Co.* (1882) 21 ChD 849).

82.65 **Tangible interest** A winding-up order will not be made on a contributory's petition unless the petitioner has a sufficient interest (usually described as a 'tangible interest') in having the company wound up (*Re Rica Gold Washing Co.* (1879) 11 ChD 36; *O'Connor v Atlantis Fisheries Ltd* 1998 SCLR 401).

A contributory's tangible interest may be an interest in receiving something or an interest in limiting a liability.

It seems that the only tangible interest in receiving something which can be claimed by a contributory of a registered company is the probability of receiving a dividend in the winding up, and it must be shown that more than a negligible amount will be received (*Bryanston Finance Ltd v De Vries (No. 2)* [1976] Ch 63 per Buckley LJ at p. 75).

According to Oliver J in *Re Chesterfield Catering Co. Ltd* [1977] Ch 373 at p. 380, preventing an increase in a contributory petitioner's liability (for example, on partly paid shares) may be enough to satisfy the court that the petitioner has a tangible interest in having the company wound up.

The burden of proving a tangible interest is on the petitioner (*Re Lancashire Brick and Tile Co. Ltd* (1865) 34 LJ Ch 331), and a sufficient interest must be alleged in the petition (*Re W. R. Willcocks and Co. Ltd* [1974] Ch 163).

Procedure on a contributory's petition

82.66 **Introduction** Most of the procedures described in **82.19** to **82.61** do not apply to contributories' petitions. This is because, by IR 1986, r. 4.2(4), the rules in ch. 3 of part 4 of IR 1986 (rr. 4.7 to 4.21A) do not apply to contributories' petitions but instead ch. 4 (rr. 4.22 to 4.24) applies. No certificate of compliance is required for a contributory's petition and there is no provision for substitution of petitioner.

In terms of procedure, a petition to wind up a company presented at the instance of the supervisor of a voluntary arrangement in force for the company or by the company's administrator is treated as a contributories' petition (r. 4.7(9)).

Presentation of a petition A contributory's petition for the compulsory liquidation of a company must be in form 4.14 in IR 1986, sch. 4: it must specify the grounds on which it is presented and must be filed in court with one copy for service on the company (IR 1986, r. 4.22(1)). **82.67**

A contributory's petition is required by **PD 49B, paras 2** to 7, to state the petitioner's attitude to validation, under the Insolvency Act 1986, s. 127, of the company's transactions pending hearing of the petition.

Although IR 1986, r. 4.12, requiring verification of a winding-up petition by a statement of truth does not apply to a contributory's petition (r. 4.2(4)), para. 7 of the prescribed form of contributory's petition (form 4.14) requires 'the statement of truth . . . filed in support hereof' to give the same evidence of the application of Regulation (EC) No. 1430/2000 (the EC Regulation) as is required by the prescribed form for petitions other than by contributories (see **82.25**).

Fee and deposit A court fee and deposit (IR 1986, r. 4.22(1A)) must be paid as for any other petition — see **82.27**. **82.68**

Fixing a return day The court will fix a hearing for a day (called the 'return day') on which, unless the court otherwise directs, the petitioner and the company must attend for directions to be given in relation to the procedure on the petition (IR 1986, r. 4.22(2)). **82.69**

Service of the petition The petitioner must, at least 14 days before the return day, serve a sealed copy of the petition on the company (IR 1986, r. 4.22(4)). Service must be effected in accordance with **CPR, Part 6**. A petition is a claim form for the purposes of that Part (r. 6.2(c)). **82.70**

Directions Rule 4.23(1) of the IR 1986 requires the court, on the return day, or at any time after it, to give such directions as it thinks appropriate with respect to the following matters: **82.71**

(a) service of the petition, whether in connection with the venue for a further hearing, or for any other purpose (the court must, by r. 4.23(2), consider whether any of the persons specified in r. 4.10 — see **82.40** — should be served with a copy of the petition);
(b) whether particulars of claim and defence are to be delivered;
(c) whether, and if so by what means, the petition is to be advertised;
(d) the manner in which any evidence is to be adduced at any hearing before the judge, including the matters to be dealt with in evidence;
(e) any other matter affecting the procedure on the petition or in connection with the hearing and disposal of the petition.

The directions may order the petition to stand as particulars of claim (*Re a Company (No. 007936 of 1994)* [1995] BCC 705 at p. 708).

In r. 4.23(1)(c), 'advertised' includes any form of notification: if it is ordered that there is to be no advertisement, mentioning the petition in a letter contravenes the order (*Re a Company (No. 00687 of 1991)* [1992] BCLC 133).

Notice of petition Notice of a contributory's petition is given only if the court directs (IR 1986, r. 4.23(1)(c)). A contributory's petition usually relates to a solvent company whose creditors would be uninterested in appearing at the hearing of the petition but who could be unnecessarily alarmed by the announcement of a petition which they would assume was a creditor's petition on the ground of inability to pay debts. **82.72**

No publicity may be given to a contributory's petition unless directions for it to be advertised have been given under the IR 1986, r. 4.23(1) (*Re a Company (No. 00687 of 1991)* [1992] BCLC 133; *Re Doreen Boards Ltd* [1996] 1 BCLC 501, in which the petition was struck out after the

Commentary

petitioner had telephoned the company's bank, invoice factors and local Inland Revenue office to inform them of the petition).

82.73 **Appearances** The rules on notices and lists of appearances (see **82.82**) apply to contributories' petition as they do to other petitions (IR 1986, r. 4.24).

Costs of defending a contributory's petition

82.74 Where a petition for the compulsory winding up of a company arises from a personal dispute between members of the company, it is a misapplication of the company's money for it to pay any costs of the proceedings (other than as ordered by the court) except for costs necessarily incurred in representing the company as a separate person (*Re A and BC Chewing Gum Ltd* [1975] 1 WLR 579 at p. 592; *Re Kenyon Swansea Ltd* [1987] BCLC 514; *Re Elgindata Ltd* [1991] BCLC 959).

HEARING A WINDING-UP PETITION AND MAKING THE ORDER

Judge

82.75 A winding-up petition is heard by the registrar or district judge, who may give any necessary directions and may, in the exercise of his or her discretion, either hear and determine it or refer it to the judge (**PD Insolvency Proceedings, para. 3.1**). The registrar exercises the jurisdiction of the High Court, but not as a deputy judge of that court (*Re Calahurst Ltd* [1989] BCLC 140 per Harman J).

Who may be heard?

82.76 **Company as a litigant in person** For representation of a company by an employee see **61.35**.

82.77 **Directors** As part of their general management powers conferred, for example, by art. 3 of each set of model articles of association in the Companies (Model Articles) Regulations 2008 (SI 2008/3229) the directors of a company sought to be wound up have power to instruct solicitors and counsel to appear for the company, even if the company is in administrative receivership (*Re Reprographic Exports (Euromat) Ltd* (1978) 122 SJ 400, but see **82.79**) or a provisional liquidator has been appointed (*Re Union Accident Insurance Co. Ltd* [1972] 1 WLR 640). However, the managing director of a company does not have implied authority to make crucial decisions following the presentation of a petition to wind up the company, and, in particular, does not have implied authority to instruct solicitors to oppose the petition (*Re Qintex Ltd (No. 2)* (1990) 2 ACSR 479; *Nece Pty Ltd v Ritek Incorporation* (1997) 24 ACSR 38).

82.78 **Contributories** A person wishing to appear as a contributory must admit to being a contributory (*Re Eastern Counties Junction and Southend Railway Co.* (1850) 14 LT OS 369) and must have a tangible interest (see **82.65**) in the company (*Re Rodencroft Ltd* [2004] EWHC 862 (Ch), [2004] 1 WLR 1566).

82.79 **Administrative receiver** By the Insolvency Act 1986, s. 42 and sch. 1, para. 21, an administrative receiver of a company has a power to defend a petition to wind up the company. It may be questioned whether this power is given so that the receiver can represent the company's interests or the interests of the creditor who appointed the receiver. In *Bank of New Zealand v Essington Developments Pty Ltd* (1991) 5 ACSR 86 a similar provision of Australian law was interpreted to mean that the receiver could assume the carriage of the proceedings on the company's behalf but could not actively resist the petition. If the receiver exercised the power then this would supersede the directors' power to defend the petition. Accordingly the receiver should only choose to exercise the power if the purposes of the receivership would be best served by the company going into compulsory liquidation. It is submitted that if an administrative receiver is opposed to a winding-up petition then the creditor who appointed the receiver should appear to state that opposition, not the receiver. In *Re Thames Freightlines Ltd* (1981) 1 NZCLC 98,112 Greig J observed that a receiver appearing to oppose a petition (in that case without statutory power to do so) could either be regarded as representing the creditor by whom he or she was appointed or as a creditor for the costs and expenses of the receivership.

Voluntary liquidator If a petition is presented to wind up a company in voluntary liquidation, the voluntary liquidator should instruct counsel to appear for the company: there should not be separate appearances for the liquidator and the company (*Re A. W. Hall and Co. Ltd* (1885) 53 LT 633; *Re Mont de Piété of England* [1892] WN 166; *Re William Adler and Co. Ltd* [1935] Ch 138). The appearance should be for the purpose of providing information and arguing the company's case: the liquidator should not take sides in an argument among creditors or between contributories and creditors (*Re Roselmar Properties Ltd (No. 2)* (1986) 2 BCC 99,157; *Re Arthur Rathbone Kitchens Ltd* [1997] 2 BCLC 280). If the petition criticises the liquidator's conduct of the voluntary winding up, the liquidator should answer the criticisms fully (*Re Arthur Rathbone Kitchens Ltd*; *Re Leading Guides International Ltd* [1998] 1 BCLC 620). **82.80**

Provisional liquidator If a provisional liquidator has been appointed then he or she does not, it seems, have a right to appear at the hearing of the winding-up petition (*Re General International Agency Co. Ltd* (1865) 36 Beav 1; *Re Laverton Nickel NL* (1979) 3 ACLR 945 at p. 947) but, if heard as advocate to the court, will be awarded the costs of appearing out of the company's assets (*Re Times Life Assurance and Guarantee Co.* (1869) LR 9 Eq 382; *Re Laverton Nickel NL*). **82.81**

Notice of appearance

By IR 1986, r. 4.16, any person wishing to appear on the hearing of a winding-up petition must send notice to the petitioner or the petitioner's solicitor to arrive not later than 4 p.m. on the business day before the date appointed for the hearing (or the date of an adjournment). 'Business day' is defined in r. 13.13(1) (see **82.7**). **82.82**

A notice of appearance must be in form 4.9 in IR 1986, sch. 4, and must state whether the appearance will be to support or oppose the petition (r. 4.16(2)(b)). The notice must also state the name and address of the person giving it, and any telephone number and reference which may be required for communication with that person or with any other person (to be also specified in the notice) authorised to speak or act on behalf of the person giving the notice (r. 4.16(2)(a)). The notice must also state the amount and nature of the debt claimed by the person giving the notice (r. 4.16(2)(c)) — clearly this applies only if the person is a creditor.

The petitioner must prepare for the court a list of persons who have given notice of intention to appear, stating whether they support or oppose the petition, and must hand a copy of the list to the court before the hearing commences (IR 1986, r. 4.17: prescribed form is 4.10 in sch. 4).

A person who has not given notice in accordance with r. 4.16 may appear on the hearing of the petition only with the permission of the court (r. 4.16(5)).

The petitioner must add to the list required by the IR 1986, r. 4.17, the name of anyone given permission by the court to appear without having given proper notice (r. 4.17(4)).

ORDERS THAT THE COURT MAY MAKE

82.83 On hearing a winding-up petition the court has, by virtue of the Insolvency Act 1986, s. 125(1), the following options:

(a) make the winding-up order applied for;
(b) dismiss the petition;
(c) adjourn the hearing conditionally;
(d) adjourn the hearing unconditionally;
(e) make an interim order;
(f) make any other order that it thinks fit.

Form of order

82.84 The prescribed form of winding-up order (the usual compulsory order) is form 4.11 in sch. 4 to the IR 1986.

The court cannot add to a winding-up order any conditions about how the winding up is to be conducted: 'The court has a discretion in relation to the making of an order, but none as to its operation when made' (per Roxburgh J in *Re Banque des Marchands de Moscou (Koupetschesky)* [1958] Ch 182 at p. 193).

Court's discretion

82.85 The fact that one or more of the circumstances in which a company may be compulsorily wound up exists does not mean that a winding-up order will be made as a matter of course (*Re Metropolitan Railway Warehousing Co. Ltd* (1867) 36 LJ Ch 827 per Lord Cairns LJ at p. 829). The court's power to order the winding up of a company is discretionary—the Insolvency Act 1986, s. 122(1), says that a registered company '*may* be wound up by the court' in the circumstances specified in the subsection. In relation to a creditor's petition, even if the creditor's debt is undisputed and unpaid, the court nevertheless has a discretion whether or not to make a winding-up order (*Re P. and J. Macrae Ltd* [1961] 1 WLR 229; *Re Southard and Co. Ltd* [1979] 1 WLR 1198).

The basic rule is that where the debt is undisputed and not satisfied and there are no exceptional circumstances, the creditor is entitled to expect the court to exercise its jurisdiction in the way of making a winding-up order (per Buckley LJ in *Re Southard and Co. Ltd* [1979] 1 WLR 1198 at p. 1203). But, as a winding-up order on a creditor's petition should be for the benefit of creditors generally, the court will consider the views of creditors other than the petitioner. In *Re Crigglestone Coal Co. Ltd* [1906] 2 Ch 327 the elder Buckley J said, at pp. 331–2, in relation to a creditor's petition:

> the order which the petitioner seeks is not an order for his benefit, but an order for the benefit of a class of which he is a member. The right *ex debito justitiae* [by an obligation of justice] is not his individual right, but his representative right. If a majority of the class are opposed to his view, and consider that they have a better chance of getting payment by abstaining from seizing the assets, then, upon general grounds and upon [the Insolvency Act 1986, s. 195], the court gives effect to such right as the majority of the class desire to exercise.

So it may be said that, as between the company and an unpaid admitted creditor, the creditor is entitled to a winding-up order as a matter of course, but, as between the petitioning creditor and the other creditors, the majority's opposition to compulsory liquidation may prevail (see *Re Great Western (Forest of Dean) Coal Consumers' Co.* (1882) 21 ChD 769 at p. 773; *Re Chapel House Colliery Co.* (1883) 24 ChD 259 at pp. 265–6). Those who oppose the petition of an unpaid admitted creditor must produce reasons to persuade the court to vary its normal practice of making a winding-up order on such a petition; the court does not simply abide by a majority decision that there should not be a compulsory liquidation. In *Re J. D. Swain Ltd* [1965] 1 WLR 909 Diplock LJ said, at p. 915:

> if the only circumstances which are available are that the petitioner seeks a compulsory winding up and the majority of the creditors seek that there should be no winding up at all, then prima facie the petitioning creditor is entitled to a winding up unless there are some additional reasons for deciding to the contrary.

The court will not pay so much regard to the views of creditors who are connected with the company — for example, as directors, shareholders or subsidiaries — as to genuine outside creditors, even if the outsiders' debts are smaller (*Re ABC Coupler and Engineering Co. Ltd* [1961] 1 WLR 243 at p. 245; *Re Holiday Stamps Ltd* (1985) 82 LS Gaz 2817; *Re Lowerstoft Traffic Services Ltd* [1986] BCLC 81 at p. 84; *Re Lummus Agricultural Services Ltd* [2001] 1 BCLC 137).

The court will not, unless there are special circumstances, make a winding-up order on a creditor's petition if the amount owed to the creditor is less than the minimum amount for which a statutory demand may be served, currently £750 (*Re Herbert Standring and Co.* [1895] WN 99; *Re Fancy Dress Balls Co.* [1899] WN 109).

Interim or other order; alternative remedies

The power given to the court by the Insolvency Act 1986, s. 125(1), to make an interim or other order is limited to making ancillary orders in furtherance of or otherwise in connection with a present or prospective winding-up order: the subsection does not empower the court to order some remedy other than winding up. The power to make any other order the court thinks fit is at the end of a list of powers in s. 125(1) and is subject to the *eiusdem generis* rule (*Re Bank of Credit and Commerce International SA (No. 10)* [1997] Ch 213 at p. 239). It does not, for example, empower the court to direct that the company's claim for damages for petitioning maliciously be heard in the winding-up proceedings (*Partizan Ltd v O. J. Kilkenny and Co. Ltd* [1998] 1 BCLC 157). It does not empower the court to direct how the liquidation is to be conducted (*Re Bank of Credit and Commerce International SA (No. 10)* [1997] Ch 213 at p. 239). 82.86

COSTS

General

In relation to a winding-up petition, as with any court proceedings, the question of costs is always at the discretion of the court (Senior Courts Act 1981, s. 51(1); **CPR, r. 44.2(1)**). The general rule is that the unsuccessful party will be ordered to pay the costs of the successful party, but the court may make a different order (**CPR, r. 44.2(2)**). The following paragraphs state how the costs of various parties to winding-up proceedings would normally be dealt with by the court. 82.87

The petitioner

Successful petition The petitioner's costs of a successful petition are normally ordered to be paid as an expense of the liquidation (*Re Humber Ironworks Co.* (1866) LR 2 Eq 15; *Re Bostels Ltd* [1968] Ch 346 at p. 350). These are included in the usual compulsory order, so there is no need to ask for them separately at the hearing. The petitioner is also entitled to the costs of any interim applications, unless there is good reason to the contrary (*Re Ryan Developments Ltd* [2002] EWHC 1121 (Ch), [2002] 2 BCLC 792). 82.88

If a petition succeeds after substitution of the petitioner, the original petitioner's costs of presenting and advertising the petition will be ordered to be paid as an expense of the liquidation (*Re Bostels Ltd* [1968] Ch 346), even if the original petitioner does not appear at the hearing as a supporter (*Re Castle Coulson and MacDonald Ltd* [1973] Ch 382).

If the effective opposition to a successful petition came from a party other than the company itself, that party may be ordered to pay the petitioner's costs (*Re Worldhams Park Golf Course Ltd* [1998] 1 BCLC 554 (contributory's petition opposed by another contributory)).

82.89 **Unsuccessful petition** Normally, if a petition is unsuccessful, the petitioner must pay the company's costs (see **82.92**), one set of costs to opposing creditors and one set to opposing contributories (see **82.96**).

If the petition of an unpaid creditor whose debt is undisputed is refused only because the court accepts the view of opposing creditors that there should not be a compulsory liquidation, no order as to costs will be made unless the petitioner was acting unreasonably, for example, where the petitioner ought to have known that the petition would fail (*Re Chapel House Colliery Co.* (1883) 24 ChD 259; *Re East Kent Colliery Co. Ltd* (1914) 30 TLR 659; *Re R. W. Sharman Ltd* [1957] 1 WLR 1008; *Re A. E. Hayter and Sons (Porchester) Ltd* [1961] 1 WLR 1008; *Re Sklan Ltd* [1961] 1 WLR 1013; *Re Riviera Pearls Ltd* [1962] 1 WLR 722). In *Re Arrow Leeds Ltd* [1986] BCLC 538 the company was ordered to pay the petitioner's costs because it did not become clear that the majority of creditors opposed winding up until the petition had been adjourned twice.

In some cases, a costs penalty has been imposed on a company for not giving timely information to a petitioner about the circumstances which would lead to dismissal of the petition (*Re M. McCarthy and Co. (Builders) Ltd (No. 2)* [1976] 2 All ER 339; *Re Lanaghan Bros Ltd* [1977] 1 All ER 265).

82.90 **Creditor's petition achieving payment of the petitioner's debt** If a creditor petitioner's debt is paid before the hearing and no winding-up order is asked for at the hearing then, provided the petition has been advertised, the company will be ordered to pay the petitioner's costs (*Re Alliance Contract Co.* [1867] WN 218) even if the company does not appear (*Re Shusella Ltd* [1983] BCLC 505). The petitioner is regarded as having effectively succeeded (*Re Nowmost Co. Ltd* [1996] 2 BCLC 492). However, the court may make no order as to part or all of the petitioner's costs as a penalty for unreasonable pre-action behaviour (**CPR, r. 44.2(4)(a)** and **(5)(a)**).

The company

82.91 **Successful petition** The company's costs of preparing for and appearing at the hearing of a successful winding-up petition are normally ordered to be paid as an expense of the liquidation (*Re Humber Ironworks Co.* (1866) LR 2 Eq 15; *Re Bostels Ltd* [1968] Ch 346 at p. 350). However, the company's assets available for distribution to its creditors should not be expended unjustifiably. If the company has unjustifiably opposed the petition or tried to prevent it proceeding, the court may order the person who instigated the company's opposition to pay its costs (*Re a Company (No. 004055 of 1991)* [1991] 1 WLR 1003). There must be an opportunity for the person against whom such a costs order is sought to submit a defence and, if necessary, put in evidence, before the order is made (*Re a Company (No. 004055 of 1991)*).

In *Re Gosscott (Groundworks) Ltd* [1988] BCLC 363, after a petition for the winding up of the company was presented by a creditor, the directors of the company presented a petition for an administration order to be made in respect of the company, in good faith and on the advice of competent professionals. The administration petition was abandoned and a winding-up order was made. The company's costs in relation to the administration petition were allowed as costs of the winding up.

Unsuccessful petition The company's costs of opposing an unsuccessful winding-up petition must be paid by the petitioner unless there are exceptional circumstances (*Re Humber Ironworks Co.* (1866) LR 2 Eq 15; *Re Fernforest Ltd* [1990] BCLC 693). The company will be awarded its costs against the petitioner if the petition is dismissed for failure to file a certificate of compliance (*Re Royal Mutual Benefit Building Society* [1960] 1 WLR 1143). **82.92**

Supporting creditors and contributories

Successful petition When a winding-up order is made, creditors who appeared to support the petition will be awarded one set of costs between them to be paid as an expense of the liquidation, and a second set of costs will be awarded on the same basis to supporting contributories (*Re European Banking Co.* (1866) LR 2 Eq 521; *Re Peckham etc. Tramways Co.* (1888) 57 LJ Ch 462 per Chitty J at p. 463; *Re Bostels Ltd* [1968] Ch 346 at p. 350). It is an invariable rule that only one set of costs is awarded to successful supporting creditors even if several persons legitimately appear to present separate views (*Re Esal (Commodities) Ltd* [1985] BCLC 450). The creditors and contributories must arrange among themselves how to divide up the costs. **82.93**

Costs ordered to be paid to supporting creditors and contributories rank equally with the petitioner's costs in the order of priority of payments set out in r. 4.218 of the IR 1986 (where they are item (h)).

Supporters who instruct the same solicitors as the petitioner are not allowed separate costs and solicitors instructed in such circumstances should not instruct counsel to represent the supporters in addition to counsel instructed to represent the petitioner (*Re Military and General Tailoring Co. Ltd* (1877) 47 LJ Ch 141; *Re Brighton Marine Palace and Pier Co. Ltd (1897)* 13 TLR 202).

Unsuccessful petition Supporters of an unsuccessful petition are not entitled to costs (*Re Humber Ironworks Co.* (1866) LR 2 Eq 15). **82.94**

Opposing creditors and contributories

Successful petition Creditors or contributories appearing to oppose a successful petition are not entitled to costs (*Re Humber Ironworks Co.* (1866) LR 2 Eq 15 at p. 18; *Re Criterion Gold Mining Co.* (1889) 41 ChD 146 at p. 149; *Re Bathampton Properties Ltd* [1976] 1 WLR 168 at p. 171). **82.95**

Unsuccessful petition Creditors who appear to oppose an unsuccessful petition may be given one set of costs between them from the petitioner and so may opposing contributories if their interests are distinct from the company's (*Re European Banking Co.* (1866) LR 2 Eq 521; *Re Anglo-Egyptian Navigation Co.* (1869) LR 8 Eq 660; *Re Heaton's Steel and Iron Co.* [1870] WN 85; *Re Carnarvonshire Slate Co. Ltd* (1879) 40 LT 35; *Re Peckham etc. Tramways Co.* (1888) 57 LJ Ch 462 per Chitty J at p. 463; not following *Re Humber Ironworks Co.* (1866) LR 2 Eq 15). A contributory whose interests are not distinct from the company's will not be awarded costs (*Re Times Life Assurance and Guarantee Co., ex parte Nunneley* (1870) LR 5 Ch App 381). **82.96**

Opposers who instruct the same solicitors as the company are not allowed separate costs (*Re Brighton Marine Palace and Pier Co. Ltd* (1897) 13 TLR 202).

Assessment

The court may order costs of proceedings on a winding-up petition to be decided by detailed assessment (IR 1986, r. 7.34A(5)). If costs of a successful petition to wind up a company are payable as an expense out of the insolvent estate, they must be decided by detailed assessment unless agreed between the liquidator and the person entitled to payment (r. 7.34A(1)). In the **82.97**

Commentary

absence of agreement, the liquidator may serve notice requiring detailed assessment proceedings to be commenced by the person entitled to payment (r. 7.34A(2)(a)). Such a notice must be served if required by the liquidation committee (r. 7.34A(2)(b)). Detailed assessment proceedings must be commenced in the court to which the winding-up proceedings are allocated (r. 7.34A(3)).

NOTICE TO OFFICIAL RECEIVER AND PERFECTION OF THE ORDER

82.98 When a winding-up order is made the court gives notice to its official receiver forthwith (IR 1986, r. 4.20(1)).

The petitioner, and every person who appeared on the hearing of the petition, must, not later than the business day after the order is made, leave at the court all documents necessary to enable the order to be completed (r. 4.20(2)). 'Business day' is defined in r. 13.13(1) (see **82.7**). It is not normally necessary to appoint a time for settlement of the order (r. 4.20(3)). The court will draw up the order (**PD Insolvency Proceedings, para. 8.1**).

When a winding-up order has been made, the court sends three sealed copies to the official receiver (IR 1986, r. 4.21(1)). The official receiver sends one of those copies by post to the company at its registered office (r. 4.21(2)). (If there is no registered office the company's copy may be sent to the company's principal, or last known principal, place of business, or be served on such person or persons as the court directs: r. 4.21(2).) A second copy is forwarded to the registrar of companies (r. 4.21(3)) who must enter it in his records relating to the company (Insolvency Act 1986, s. 130(1)) and officially notify receipt of it in the *London Gazette* (Companies Act 2006, ss. 1077 and 1078(1) and (2)).

If a winding-up order made against a registered company has been erroneously made against the wrong company, it may be rescinded and the registrar of companies may be ordered to correct the records at Companies House (*Re Calmex Ltd* [1989] 1 All ER 485).

Having received copies of a winding-up order the official receiver must forthwith cause the order to be gazetted and may also advertise notice of the order in such other manner as he or she thinks fit (IR 1986, r. 4.21(4)).

A copy of the *Gazette* containing the notice of the order may, in any proceedings, be produced as conclusive evidence that the order was made on the date specified in the notice (IR 1986, r. 12A.37(2)).

If a winding-up order that has been gazetted is varied by the court, the official receiver must cause the variation of the order to be gazetted (r. 12A.37(3)). If an order has been erroneously or inaccurately gazetted, the official receiver must cause a further entry to be made in the *Gazette* for the purpose of correcting the error or inaccuracy (r. 12A.37(3)).

PERMISSION FOR LITIGATION AGAINST COMPANY IN LIQUIDATION

82.99 Section 130(2) of the Insolvency Act 1986 provides that when a winding-up order has been made, no action or proceeding shall be proceeded with or commenced against the company or its property, except by permission of the court and subject to such terms as the court may impose. See **84.19**.

CORRECTION OF ERRORS

The court may at any time correct an accidental slip or omission in a judgment or order (**CPR, r. 40.12**). **82.100**

An application for permission to amend an error in a petition discovered after the winding-up order has been made should be made to the member of court staff in charge of the winding-up list in the RCJ or a district judge in a district registry or a county court (**PD Insolvency Proceedings, para. 11.6.1**). Details are given in **PD Insolvency Proceedings, paras 11.6.2** and **11.6.3**.

RESCISSION AND APPEAL

A winding-up order may be rescinded by the court which made it on the application of an interested party (IR 1986, r. 7.47(1)). See **84.10**. **82.101**

An appeal against an order made by a court on hearing a winding-up petition is subject to the same rules as any other appeal in insolvency proceedings, for which see **84.11** to **84.15**.

ADMINISTRATION APPLICATIONS

Which court?

An application for an administration order to be made in respect of a company may be presented to a court which has jurisdiction to order the company to be wound up (see 82.8). An application must be made by means of an administration application (Insolvency Act 1986, sch. B1, para. 12(1); IR 1986, r. 2.2(1)). **82.102**

Standing to apply

An application for an administration order to be made in relation to a company may be made by: **82.103**

(a) the company itself (Insolvency Act 1986, sch. B1, para. 12(1)(a));
(b) the directors of the company (para. 12(1)(b));
(c) one or more creditors of the company (para. 12(1)(c)) — 'creditor' includes a contingent creditor and a prospective creditor (para. 12(4));
(d) the designated officer for a magistrates' court (if the company has failed to pay a fine) (para. 12(1)(d); Magistrates' Courts Act 1980, s. 87A);
(e) a supervisor of a voluntary arrangement of the company (Insolvency Act 1986, s. 7(4)(b) and sch. B1, para. 12(5));
(f) a combination of persons listed in (a) to (e) (sch. B1, para. 12(1)(e));
(g) a foreign representative appointed in a foreign main proceeding or a foreign non-main proceeding (Cross-Border Insolvency Regulations 2006 (SI 2006/1030), sch. 1, art. 11).

In *Hammonds v Pro-Fit USA Ltd* [2007] EWHC 1998 (Ch), [2008] 2 BCLC 159, it was held that a person with a claim against a company is a creditor with standing to apply for an administration order even if the company has a genuine and substantial cross-claim, and that an administration order can be made on such a person's application without resolving the cross-claim. However, the court decided not to make an order provided the company reversed a transaction which the applicant claimed had been at an undervalue.

The company, the directors of the company, or a creditor who holds what the legislation calls a 'qualifying floating charge in respect of the company's property', may alternatively appoint an administrator without court proceedings (Insolvency Act 1986, sch. B1, paras 14 and 22), though such an appointment does not take effect until notice of appointment is filed in court (sch. B1, paras 18, 19, 29 and 31). The wide-ranging definition of 'qualifying floating charge in respect of a company's property' in sch. B1, para. 14, will, in practice, include any floating charge which, alone or in conjunction with other charges, covers the whole or substantially the whole of the company's property.

In the following circumstances persons with the power to appoint an administrator out of court cannot do so and must instead apply to the court for an appointment, if the right to apply is available:

(a) If the company is being wound up voluntarily or by the court, an administrator cannot be appointed out of court and an administration application may be made only by the liquidator (sch. B1, paras 8 and 38) or (if it is a winding up by the court) by the holder of a qualifying floating charge (paras 8 and 37).
(b) If an administrative receiver of the company has been appointed, an administrator cannot be appointed out of court and the court will make an appointment only if the chargee who appointed the receiver consents or the court is satisfied that if an order were made the floating charge under which the receiver was appointed would be discharged or avoided or declared invalid by the court under ss. 238 to 240 (transactions at an undervalue and preferences) or s. 245 (avoidance of floating charges given to secure existing debts) (sch. B1, paras 17(b), 25(c) and 39). The administrative receiver must vacate office if an administrator is appointed (para. 41(1)).
(c) If a petition has been presented asking for the company to be wound up by the court and has not been disposed of, the company itself and its directors may not appoint an administrator out of court (para. 25(a)), though a holder of a qualifying floating charge may do so unless a provisional liquidator has been appointed (para. 17(a)).
(d) If an administration application has been made and has not been disposed of, the company itself and its directors may not appoint an administrator out of court (para. 25(b)), though a holder of a qualifying floating charge may do so.
(e) An appointment may not be made out of court by the company or its directors within 12 months of the ending of a previous administration initiated by it or them (para. 23) or within 12 months of a moratorium under sch. A1 (moratorium to enable preparation of a voluntary arrangement) which failed to produce a workable voluntary arrangement (sch. B1, para. 24).
(f) While a moratorium under sch. A1 is in force, an administrator cannot be appointed out of court, and an administration application cannot be made to the court (sch. A1, para. 12(1)(d)).

Need for insolvency

82.104 Unless the administration application is made by the holder of a qualifying floating charge, the court cannot make an administration order in relation to a company unless it is satisfied that the company is, or is likely to become, unable to pay its debts (Insolvency Act 1986, sch. B1, para. 11(a)). To show that a company is likely to become unable to pay its debts it must be shown that it is more probable than not that it will be unable to pay its debts (*Re COLT Telecom Group plc* [2002] EWHC 2815 (Ch), LTL 20/12/2002).

If an administration application by the holder of a qualifying floating charge states that it is made in reliance on sch. B1, para. 35, the court may make an administration order without proof of the company's insolvency, but only if satisfied that the conditions for appointing an administrator out of court, under para. 14, are satisfied. The most important of these conditions are that the floating charge must presently be enforceable (para. 16), and the holder of any prior qualifying floating charge must either give written consent or be given at least two business days' notice (para. 15).

Statutory purpose

The court may not make an administration order in relation to a company unless it considers that the order is reasonably likely to achieve the purpose of administration (Insolvency Act 1986, sch. B1, para. 11(b)). The purpose of administration is the objective with which the administrator must perform his or her functions, defined in sch. B1, para. 3(1), as: **82.105**

(a) rescuing the company as a going concern; or
(b) achieving a better result for the company's creditors as a whole than would be likely if the company were wound up (without first being in administration); or
(c) realising property in order to make a distribution to one or more secured or preferential creditors.

Objective (a) must be given priority unless the administrator believes it is not reasonably practicable or that objective (b) would achieve a better result for the company's creditors as a whole (para. 3(3)). Objective (c) may be pursued only if the administrator believes (i) it is not reasonably practicable to achieve either objective (a) or objective (b) and (ii) the interests of the creditors of the company as a whole will not be harmed unnecessarily (para. 3(4)).

In order to show that an administration order is 'reasonably likely to achieve the purpose of administration' it is necessary to show that there is a real prospect that the purpose of administration will be achieved (*Hammonds v Pro-Fit USA Ltd* [2007] EWHC 1998 (Ch), [2008] 2 BCLC 159 at [24]).

Contents of application

The prescribed form of administration application is form 2.1B in sch. 4 to IR 1986. The applicant's address for service must be given in accordance with IR 1986, rr. 2.2(4) and 2.3(1) to (4), the provisions of which are summarised in **table 82.1**. **82.106**

The application must specify the name and address of the person it is proposed should be appointed as administrator (form 2.1B, para. 9), and the nominee's written consent (form 2.2B), stating his or her opinion that the purpose of administration is likely to be achieved, must be attached (r. 2.3(5)).

Table 82.1 Address for service of applicant for administration order

Applicant	Address for service
The company, or supervisor of the company's voluntary arrangement	The company's registered office, unless there are special reasons to the contrary.
The company's directors	The company's registered office, unless there are special reasons to the contrary.
One creditor	That creditor's address for service.
Two or more creditors	The address for service of one of the creditors, named in the application as applying on his, her or its behalf and on behalf of the other creditors (who must all be named in the application).

Commentary

The application must state:

(a) whether or not the company is one of the types of company to which Regulation (EC) No. 1346/2000 does not apply (see **82.12**) (form 2.1B, para. 6);
(b) whether the Regulation does apply; and, if it does apply, whether the proceedings will be main, secondary or territorial proceedings (form 2.1B, para. 7).

The advice on answering these questions given in relation to winding-up petitions (**82.21**) applies to administration applications.

Supporting witness statement

82.107 An administration application must be supported by a witness statement (IR 1986, rr. 2.2 and 2.4). If the application is presented by the company, its directors or the supervisor of a voluntary arrangement, the supporting witness statement must be made by a director or secretary of the company (r. 2.2(2) and (4)); if presented by creditors, it must be made by a person acting under their authority and must state the nature of that authority and the means of his or her knowledge of the matters stated (r. 2.2(3)). The supporting witness statement must state (r. 2.4):

(a) the company's financial position, specifying (to the best of the applicant's knowledge and belief) its assets and liabilities, including contingent and prospective liabilities (r. 2.4(2)(a));
(b) either the reasons for the applicant's belief that the company is, or is likely to become, unable to pay its debts (form 2.1B, para. 8) or, if the application is by the holder of a qualifying floating charge in reliance on the Insolvency Act 1986, sch. B1, para. 35 (see **82.104**) or para. 37 (where the company is in liquidation), sufficient details to satisfy the court that the applicant is entitled to appoint an administrator under sch. B1, para. 14 (IR 1986, rr. 2.4(4) and 2.11(2));
(c) details of any securities known or believed to be held by creditors of the company, whether any creditor is entitled to appoint an administrative receiver or administrator and whether an administrative receiver has been appointed (r. 2.4(2)(b));
(d) details of any insolvency proceeding in relation to the company including any winding-up petition that has been presented (r. 2.4(2)(c));
(e) whether, in the opinion of the applicant, Regulation (EC) No. 1346/2000 will apply, and the reasons for that opinion, and, if the Regulation will apply, whether the proceedings will be main, secondary or territorial proceedings (r. 2.4(4); form 2.1B, para. 7);
(f) if two or more persons are to be appointed administrators, (i) which functions (if any) are to be exercised by the persons appointed acting jointly, (ii) which functions (if any) are to be exercised by any or all of the persons appointed (r. 2.4(2)(d); Insolvency Act 1986, sch. B1, para. 100(2));
(g) any other information that would assist the court (IR 1986, r. 2.4(2)(e)).

If the company is already in liquidation, the supporting witness statement must also, by r. 2.11, contain (i) full details of the proceedings, (ii) the name and address of the liquidator, the date he or she was appointed and by whom, (iii) the reasons why it has subsequently been considered appropriate that an administration application should be made, (iv) all other matters that would, in the opinion of the applicant, assist the court in considering the need to make provisions in respect of matters arising in connection with the liquidation.

Filing of application

82.108 Enough copies of the application must be made for service (see **82.109**).

The application and supporting witness statement, and the copies for service, must be filed in court for sealing and endorsement with the date and time of filing and with the venue for the hearing (IR 1986, r. 2.5(1) to (3)).

A fee of £175 must be paid (**CPFO, fee 3.2**).

Service of application

As soon as is reasonably practicable, and not less than five business days (see **82.7**) before the date fixed for the hearing, a copy of the application sealed by the court, together with a copy of the supporting affidavit or witness statement and the documents attached to the application, must be served on the following persons (Insolvency Act 1986, sch. B1, para. 12(2); IR 1986, rr. 2.6 and 2.8(1)): **82.109**

(a) any person who has appointed an administrative receiver of the company;
(b) any person who is or may be entitled to appoint an administrative receiver of the company;
(c) any holder of a floating charge who is or may be entitled to appoint an administrator of the company out of court under the Insolvency Act 1986, sch. B1, para. 14;
(d) an administrative receiver of the company, if there is one;
(e) if a petition for the compulsory winding up of the company is pending, the petitioner;
(f) a provisional liquidator of the company, if there is one;
(g) a member State liquidator appointed in main proceedings in relation to the company, if there is one;
(h) the person proposed as administrator;
(i) the company, unless it, or a supervisor of its voluntary arrangement, is the applicant.

Service must be effected by the applicant, or the applicant's solicitor, or a person instructed by either of them (r. 2.8(1)).

Service on the company is by delivering the documents to its registered office or, if that is not practicable, to its last known principal place of business in England and Wales (r. 2.8(2)(a) and (3)). Service on a person other than the company is by delivering the documents to the person's 'proper address' (r. 2.8(2)(b)). General rules on service are in rr. 12A.16 to 12A.20, which apply **CPR, Part 6.**

The proper address of an authorised deposit-taker, which is to be served as a person which has appointed an administrative receiver, or is, or may be, entitled to appoint, an administrative receiver or administrator, is the address of the branch where the company's account is kept, if that is known to the applicant, or the deposit-taker's registered office or usual or last known address (r. 2.8(5)). The proper address of any other person is an address the person has previously notified as an address for service or, if there has been no notification, the person's usual or last known address (r. 2.8(4)).

Alternatively the court may direct the manner of service (r. 2.8(2)(c)).

Certificate of service

Service of an administration application must be verified by a certificate of service (IR 1986, r. 2.9(1)). This must be sufficient to identify the petition served and must specify the matters set out in r. 2.9(1A). A certificate of service must be verified by a statement of truth (r. 13.13(16)) in accordance with **CPR, Part 22** (IR 1986, r. 13.13(17)). The certificate of service must be filed with the court as soon as reasonably practicable after service, and in any event not less than one business day (see **82.7**) before the hearing of the petition (r. 2.9(2)). **82.110**

Commentary

Notice to enforcement officer and distrainors

82.111 Rule 2.7 of IR 1986 requires the applicant, as soon as reasonably practicable after filing the application, to give notice of its presentation to:

(a) any enforcement officer or other officer who, to the applicant's knowledge, is charged with an execution or other legal process against the company or its property; and
(b) any person who, to the applicant's knowledge, has distrained against the company or its property.

Notification of other insolvency proceedings

82.112 A person who has filed an administration application in court has a duty to notify the court in writing immediately on becoming aware of the existence of any proceedings under the Insolvency Act 1986, IR 1986 or Regulation (EC) No. 1346/2000 (IR 1986, r. 2.5(4)).

Withdrawal

82.113 An administration application may not be withdrawn without the permission of the court (Insolvency Act 1986, sch. B1, para. 12(3)).

Nomination of administrator by holder of qualifying floating charge

82.114 If an administration application is made by a person who does not hold a qualifying floating charge in respect of the company's property (defined in the Insolvency Act 1986, sch. B1, para. 14), the holder of such a charge may apply to have a specified person appointed administrator instead of the person nominated in the application (sch. B1, para. 36). The application must, by IR 1986, r. 2.10, be supported by:

(a) the written consent of every holder of a prior qualifying floating charge (defined in the Insolvency Act 1986, sch. B1, para. 15(2));
(b) the consent of the applicant's proposed administrator in form 2.2B;
(c) sufficient evidence to satisfy the court that the applicant is entitled to appoint an administrator under sch. B1, para. 14.

The court must grant the application unless it thinks it right not to do so because of the particular circumstances of the case (sch. B1, para. 36(2)).

Appearance at hearing of the application

82.115 By IR 1986, r. 2.12(1), at the hearing of an application to make an administration order in relation to a company, the following may appear or be represented:

(a) the applicant;
(b) the company;
(c) one or more of the company's directors;
(d) the company's administrative receiver, if one has been appointed;
(e) any person who has presented a petition for the winding up of the company;
(f) the person proposed for appointment as administrator;
(g) a member State liquidator appointed in main proceedings in relation to the company, if there is one;
(h) any holder of a qualifying floating charge;
(i) a supervisor of a voluntary arrangement, if there is one; and
(j) with the permission of the court, any other person who appears to have an interest justifying appearance.

Court's powers on hearing an application

On hearing an application for an administration order to be made in relation to a company the court may, by the Insolvency Act 1986, sch. B1, para. 13(1), make the order, or dismiss the application, or adjourn the hearing conditionally or unconditionally, or make an interim order, or treat the application as a winding-up petition and make any order which it could make under s. 125 (see **82.83**), or make any other order that it thinks fit. If a winding-up order is made, the winding up commences on the making of the order (s. 129(1A)). **82.116**

If an administration order is made, the costs of the applicant, and of any other person whose costs are allowed by the court, are payable as an expense of the administration (IR 1986, r. 2.12(3)).

An administration order must be in form 2.4B in IR 1986, sch. 4 (r. 2.12(2)). If the company was in liquidation, the order must provide for the transition from liquidation to administration, as specified in the Insolvency Act 1986, sch. B1, paras 37 and 38, and IR 1986, r. 2.13. If a winding-up petition was pending, it must be dismissed (Insolvency Act 1986, sch. B1, para. 40(1)(a)).

An interim order may restrict the exercise of a power of the company or of its directors (sch. B1, para. 13(3)(a)). An interim order may make provision conferring a discretion on the court, or on a qualified insolvency practitioner, in relation to the company (para. 13(3)(b)). The appointment of an insolvency practitioner to supervise under para. 13(3)(b) is analogous to the appointment by the court of a receiver of disputed property that is in jeopardy; such a person is not an administrator, because the appointment is not by an administration order, and so the rights of the holder of a floating charge to intervene (para. 36) or veto the appointment (para. 39) do not arise (*Re a Company (No. 00175 of 1987)* (1987) 3 BCC 124).

If an administrative receiver of the company has been appointed, and the chargee who made the appointment has not consented to the making of an administration order, and the court is not satisfied that the charge would be discharged or avoided or declared invalid under ss. 238 to 240 or s. 245, the court can only dismiss the application (sch. B1, para. 39; *Re a Company (No. 00175 of 1987)* (1987) 3 BCC 124). This applies whether the administrative receiver was appointed before or after the administration application was made (sch. B1, para. 39(2)).

Notice of court's order

If an administration order is made, the appointment of the administrator takes effect when the order is made, unless some other time is specified in the order (Insolvency Act 1986, sch. B1, para. 13(2)). The court must, as soon as reasonably practicable, send two sealed copies of the order to the applicant (IR 1986, r. 2.14(1)), who must, as soon as reasonably practicable, send one of them to the person appointed as administrator (r. 2.14(2)). **82.117**

If the court makes an interim order under the Insolvency Act 1986, sch. B1, para. 13(1)(d), or an order under para. 13(1)(f) (power to make any other order which the court thinks appropriate), the court must give directions as to the persons to whom, and how, notice of that order is to be given (IR 1986, r. 2.14(3)).

Costs where there is both a winding-up petition and an administration application

Where a company has been subject to both a winding-up petition and an administration application, and either winding up or administration is ordered, the court has a discretion to order that the costs of applying for the insolvency process that has not been put in place are **82.118** to be paid as expenses of the process that has been put into effect (*Re Gosscott (Groundworks) Ltd* [1988] BCLC 363; *Irish Reel Productions Ltd v Capitol Films Ltd* [2010] EWHC 180 (Ch), [2010] Bus LR 854). The person applying for the order must make out a case for it (see *Unadkat and Co. (Accountants) Ltd v Bhardwaj* [2006] EWHC 2785 (Ch), [2007] BCC 452 at [17]). When a winding-up order has been made there have been sharply differing views on how the discretion should be exercised in respect of the costs of an administration application. On one side it has been said that such costs should be allowed if the application was made in good faith, reasonably and on professional advice (*Re Gosscott (Groundworks) Ltd*). On the other side it has been said that the fact that an application has been made in good faith, reasonably and on professional advice is not a reason for making the creditors pay for it (*Re W. F. Fearman Ltd (No 2)* (1987) 4 BCC 141; *EPIS Services Ltd v Commissioners of HM Revenue and Customs* [2007] EWHC 3534 (Ch), LTL 30/4/2010).

Chapter 83 Bankruptcy

The following procedural checklist, which is at the front of the book, is relevant to this chapter:

Procedural checklist 36 Application by a creditor whose debt is presently payable for a bankruptcy order

INTRODUCTION

Bankruptcy is a procedure by which an insolvent individual surrenders virtually all of his or her assets to a trustee in bankruptcy for distribution among creditors in return for cancellation of debts. For a period of usually one year, until the discharge of the bankruptcy, all assets acquired by the bankrupt also go to the trustee. Bankruptcy may be achieved only by court order and is an entirely statutory process, governed now by the Insolvency Act 1986. Following amendments made by the Enterprise Act 2002 (including reducing the duration of bankruptcy: s. 256 and sch. 19), the punitive aspects of bankruptcy (such as disqualification 83.1

Commentary

from Parliament or the magistracy), which used to apply to all bankrupts, now apply only to those subject to a bankruptcy restrictions order or undertaking (Insolvency Act 1986, s. 281A and sch. 4A). However, it is likely that many bankrupts will still find that the procedure is remarkably costly and often unexpectedly unpleasant for the bankrupt and his or her family. Some of the disadvantages of bankruptcy may be avoided by obtaining the agreement of creditors to an individual voluntary arrangement (IVA), by which an insolvent individual's assets are distributed among creditors outside of bankruptcy (see **83.36** to **83.38**). In practice creditors will not agree to an IVA unless it obliges the debtor to pay an agreed proportion of debts in instalments from earnings over a substantial period (typically five years) and/or an immediate contribution from (usually) a member of the debtor's family. For alternatives to bankruptcy where debts are small, see **83.40**.

PROCEDURAL RULES

83.2 An application for an order adjudging an individual bankrupt must be made by petition (a 'bankruptcy petition') presented to the court under the Insolvency Act 1986, s. 264. An individual subject to bankruptcy proceedings is usually referred to as a 'debtor'. As a bankruptcy petition is a proceeding under the Insolvency Act 1986 it is an insolvency proceeding for the purposes of the Insolvency Rules 1986 (SI 1986/1925) (IR 1986), by r. 13.7 of those rules. The scope of the IR 1986 and general rules on track allocation, forms, time limits and the meaning of 'business day' are described in **82.3** to **82.7**.

JURISDICTION

Scope of English bankruptcy law

83.3 Only debtors with a sufficient connection with England and Wales can be made bankrupt under English law. The required connection is specified in the Insolvency Act 1986, s. 265. The debtor must:

(a) be domiciled in England and Wales;
(b) be personally present in England and Wales on the day on which the petition is presented; or
(c) at any time within the three years ending with the day the petition was presented:
    (i) have been ordinarily resident, or have had a place of business, in England and Wales; or
    (ii) have carried on business in England and Wales.

It is sufficient, for the purposes of condition (c)(ii), that the debtor was a member of a firm or partnership carrying on business, or that an agent or manager carried on the business for the debtor or for a firm or partnership of which the debtor was a member (s. 265(2)).

Where domicile is in dispute, the onus is on the petitioner to establish that the debtor is domiciled in England and Wales, but if the petitioner establishes that England and Wales is the debtor's domicile of origin, the onus is on the debtor to prove a change of domicile (*Henwood v Barlow Clowes International Ltd* [2007] EWHC 1579 (Ch), [2007] BPIR 1329).

The scope of English bankruptcy law is, by s. 265(3), subject to Regulation (EC) No. 1346/2000, art. 3 (see **82.9**). The effect of art. 3 on bankruptcy jurisdiction is that if the centre of main interests of an individual who would otherwise be covered by the Insolvency Act 1986, s. 265, is in another EU State (apart from Denmark), a bankruptcy order may be made in England and Wales only if the individual possesses an establishment in the United Kingdom (art. 3(2)), and there are restrictions on who may apply for a bankruptcy order here (art. 3(4); see **83.5**). An individual's centre of main interests ought to be the place where he or she can be contacted by creditors (*Skjevesland v Geveran Trading Co. Ltd* [2002] EWHC 2898 (Ch), [2003] BCC 391 at [60]).

Appropriate court

Both the High Court and some county courts have bankruptcy jurisdiction. Under the Insolvency Act 1986, s. 374, and the Civil Courts Order 1983 (SI 1983/713), art. 9 and sch. 3, about half of county courts do not have bankruptcy jurisdiction: the districts of those courts are attached to other county courts to form larger insolvency districts. In order to determine which court is the appropriate one for presentation of a bankruptcy petition, it is necessary to establish: **83.4**

(a) whether the proceedings are allocated by IR 1986, r. 7.10ZA, to the London insolvency district;
(b) whether the debtor is resident in England and Wales. If the petitioner is unable to ascertain the place where the debtor resides or, if the debtor carries on business in England and Wales, both where the debtor resides and where the debtor carries on business, the petition is allocated to the London insolvency district (r. 7.10ZA(c)(i)) and must be presented to the High Court (r. 6.9A(2)).

The London insolvency district consists of the districts of the following county courts: Barnet, Bow, Brentford, Central London, Clerkenwell and Shoreditch, Edmonton, Lambeth, Mayor's and City of London, Wandsworth, West London, and Willesden (London Insolvency District (Central London County Court) Order 2011 (SI 2011/761), art. 2).

A bankruptcy petition in respect of a debtor who is resident in England and Wales is allocated by IR 1986, r. 7.10ZA, to the London insolvency district if, within the six months immediately preceding the presentation of the petition:

(a) the debtor carried on business within the area of the London insolvency district:
   (i) for the greater part of those six months; or
   (ii) for a longer period in those six months than in any other insolvency district (r. 7.10ZA(a)(i)); or
(b) the debtor did not carry on business in England and Wales but resided within the area of the London insolvency district for:
   (i) the greater part of those six months; or
   (ii) a longer period in those six months than in any other insolvency district (r. 7.10ZA(a)(ii)).

Such a petition must be presented to the High Court if the petition debt is £50,000 or more, or to the Central London County Court if it is less than £50,000 (r. 6.9A(1) (creditor's petition); r. 6.40A(1) (debtor's petition)). The district judges assigned to bankruptcy work in the Central London County Court sit in the Thomas More Building of the Royal Courts of Justice.

A bankruptcy petition in respect of a debtor who is not resident in England and Wales is allocated to the London insolvency district if, within the six months immediately preceding the presentation of the petition:

(a) the debtor carried on business within the area of the London insolvency district (r. 7.10ZA(a)(iii)); or
(b) the debtor did not carry on business in England and Wales but resided within the area of the London insolvency district (r. 7.10ZA(a)(iv)); or
(c) the debtor neither carried on business nor resided in England and Wales (r. 7.10ZA(a)(v)).

In circumstances (a) and (b) the petition must be presented to the High Court if the petition debt is £50,000 or more, or to the Central London County Court if it is less than £50,000

(r. 6.9A(1) (creditor's petition); r. 6.40A(1) (debtor's petition)). In circumstance (c) the petition must be presented to the High Court (r. 6.9A(2) (creditor's petition); r. 6.40A(2) (debtor's petition)).

If proceedings are not allocated to the London insolvency district, the petition must be presented to 'the debtor's own county court' if the debtor is resident in England and Wales (IR 1986, r. 6.9A(3) (creditor's petition); r. 6.40A(3) (debtor's petition)).

For a debtor who has carried on business in England and Wales within the six months immediately preceding the presentation of the petition, the debtor's own county court is the county court for the insolvency district where for the longest period during those six months:

(a) the debtor carried on business, or
(b) the principal place of business was located, if business was carried on in more than one insolvency district (r. 6.9A(4)(a)).

For a debtor who has not carried on business in England and Wales within the six months immediately preceding the presentation of the petition, the debtor's own county court is the county court for the insolvency district where the debtor resided for the longest period during those six months (r. 6.9A(4)(b)).

If a debtor is not resident in England and Wales, but was resident or carried on business here within the six months before presentation of the petition, unless proceedings are allocated to the London insolvency district, the petition may be presented either to the debtor's own county court or to the High Court (r. 6.9A(5) (creditor's petition); r. 6.40A(4) (debtor's petition)).

There are special rules for a petition presented by a minister of the Crown or a government department (rr. 6.9A(1) and 7.10ZA(b)) and for members of partnerships which are subject to winding-up proceedings (rr. 6.9A(2) and 7.10ZA(c)(ii)).

If the above rules would require a debtor's petition to be presented at a county court with only limited facilities for dealing with insolvency matters, the petition may be presented instead to the nearest full-time court specified in IR 1986, sch. 2 (IR 1986, r. 6.40A(6)). Also, where the debtor's residence and business are in different insolvency districts, the debtor may present his or her own petition in the residential district if doing so would expedite the petition (r. 6.40A(6)(a)(i)).

A bankruptcy petition which is presented at a time when an IVA is in force for the debtor must be presented to the court in which proceedings relating to the IVA have been taken (r. 6.9A(6) (creditor's petition); r. 6.40A(7) (debtor's petition)).

A bankruptcy petition must contain sufficient information to establish that it is presented in the appropriate court (r. 6.9A(7) (creditor's petition); r. 6.40A(8) (debtor's petition)). See para. 2 of the prescribed forms of petition (forms 6.7, 6.8, 6.9, 6.10 and 6.27).

WHO MAY PRESENT A BANKRUPTCY PETITION?

83.5 By the Insolvency Act 1986, s. 264(1), a petition for an order adjudging an individual bankrupt may be presented by:

(a) one of the individual's unsecured creditors, or by two or more unsecured creditors jointly (see **83.6 to 83.27**);
(b) the individual personally (see **83.28 to 83.35**);
(c) the supervisor of, or any person (other than the individual) who is for the time being bound by, an approved IVA (see **83.39**).

The Financial Services Authority may petition for an individual's bankruptcy under the Financial Services and Markets Act 2000, s. 372, alleging the individual's inability to pay debts incurred in the course of activities regulated by the 2000 Act. The procedure on such a petition is governed by the Bankruptcy (Financial Services and Markets Act 2000) Rules 2001 (SI 2001/3634).

Regulation (EC) No. 1346/2000 governs who may apply for a bankruptcy order in England and Wales in relation to a debtor whose centre of main interests is in another EU State (apart from Denmark) (see **82.9** to **82.12**). An application for a bankruptcy order in respect of such a debtor may be made only if the debtor possesses an establishment in the United Kingdom (art. 3(2)). If insolvency proceedings (main proceedings) have been opened in the State where the debtor's centre of main interests is located, then, by arts 27 and 29 and the Insolvency Act 1986, s. 264(1), provided the main proceedings are of a type listed in annex A to the Regulation, an application may be made (in secondary proceedings) in England and Wales for a bankruptcy order by:

(a) the liquidator in the main proceedings (called a 'member State liquidator' in IR 1986: see r. 13.13(11)), or
(b) a temporary administrator (corresponding to an English interim receiver, see **83.16**) appointed in the main proceedings, or
(c) any other person authorised by s. 264.

If insolvency proceedings have not yet been opened in the State where the debtor's centre of main interests is located, an application for a bankruptcy order may be made (in territorial proceedings) in England and Wales only by a creditor who is domiciled or habitually resident in the United Kingdom or has its registered office in the United Kingdom, or a creditor whose claim arises from the operation of the debtor's establishment in the United Kingdom (Regulation, art. 4(b)). This restriction does not apply if insolvency proceedings cannot be opened in the State where the debtor's centre of main interests is located, because of the conditions laid down by the law of that State (art. 4(a)). The exception in art. 4(a) is limited to a situation in which the law of the COMI State prevents insolvency proceedings being opened at all and does not cover a situation in which insolvency proceedings cannot be opened because of the specific circumstances in which the opening is requested. In particular, the fact that the COMI State's law does not give the proposed petitioner standing to request the opening of main proceedings, but does give other persons standing, does not mean that main proceedings cannot be opened (*Procureur-generaal bij het hof van beroep te Antwerpen v Zaza Retail BV* (case C-112/10) (CJEU 1st Chamber 17 November 2011)).

If a debtor is already subject to a foreign insolvency proceeding in Denmark or a State outside the EU, a foreign representative appointed in that proceeding has standing to petition for the debtor's bankruptcy in England and Wales (Cross-Border Insolvency Regulations 2006 (SI 2006/1030), sch. 1, art. 11).

In *R v Lord Chancellor, ex parte Lightfoot* [2000] QB 597 Simon Brown LJ (with whom Rattee J agreed) held that proceedings on a debtor's petition are not subject to art. 6(1) (fair trial) of the European Convention on Human Rights, because, in his Lordship's view, a debtor's petition does not involve a dispute with anyone. It is submitted with respect that it is questionable whether this is the correct test for the application of art. 6(1). The article is concerned with the determination of civil rights and obligations, which is what a court does when making a bankruptcy order (see *R v Davison* (1954) 90 CLR 353, in which the High Court of Australia held that proceedings on a debtor's petition are judicial rather than administrative in character).

CREDITOR'S PETITION

Who may petition as a creditor?

A creditor can present a petition only in respect of a liquidated debt payable immediately or at some certain, future time (Insolvency Act 1986, s. 267(2)(b)) and the debt must be at least £750 **83.6**

(s. 267(2)(a) and (4)). A secured creditor cannot petition (s. 267(2)(b)) unless the petition states that if a bankruptcy order is made, the creditor will surrender the security for the benefit of all creditors (s. 269(1)(a)). A partially secured creditor may divide the debt into a secured and an unsecured part and petition in respect of the unsecured part (s. 269(1)(b) and (2)).

For the purposes of the law of bankruptcy, the term 'creditor' is given a very wide definition in the Insolvency Act 1986, s. 383 (which must be read with s. 382). However, a bankruptcy petition can be filed only in respect of a debt for a liquidated sum payable to the petitioning creditor (or one or more of joint petitioners) immediately or at some certain, future time (s. 267(2)(b)) and the debt must be at least £750 (s. 267(2)(a) and (4)).

The term 'liquidated sum' is not defined in the legislation. A debt for a liquidated sum 'must be a pre-ascertained liability under the agreement which gives rise to it' (*McGuinness v Norwich and Peterborough Building Society* [2011] EWCA Civ 1286, [2012] BPIR 145 at [36]). A contractual liability is for a liquidated sum if the amount due is to be ascertained in accordance with a contractual formula or machinery which will produce a figure (*McGuinness v Norwich and Peterborough Building Society* at [36]). A claim in tort is invariably unliquidated, because a judicial process is required to ascertain the damages due (*McGuinness v Norwich and Peterborough Building Society* at [36]). A claim for liquidated damages is a debt for a liquidated sum (*McGuinness v Norwich and Peterborough Building Society* at [37]–[41]). Whether a claim under a guarantee of another person's debt is a debt for a liquidated sum depends on the wording of the guarantee, as discussed in detail in *McGuinness v Norwich and Peterborough Building Society*. A judgment debt is a debt for a liquidated sum.

For this purpose, a solicitor's bill is for an unliquidated sum, unless the amount of the bill is liquidated by judicial assessment or determination or by the client's agreement (*Truex v Toll* [2009] EWHC 396 (Ch), [2009] 1 WLR 2121; see *Phillips and Co. v Bath Housing Cooperative Ltd* [2012] EWCA Civ 1591, [2013] BPIR 102). The fact that the period of 12 months for applying for assessment of the bill has passed without an application being made is irrelevant. A mere acknowledgment by the client is not an agreement sufficient to make the debt liquidated: there must be an agreement from which the client is bound not to resile.

For restrictions on who may petition as a creditor when the debtor's centre of main interests is in another EU State (other than Denmark) and main insolvency proceedings have not been opened in that State, see **83.5**.

A claim which, though it could be enforced against the debtor in proceedings outside bankruptcy, is not provable in bankruptcy is theoretically sufficient to entitle the claimant to petition for bankruptcy, but in practice the court would not make an order on the petition, because the petitioner would have no interest in the proceedings (*Levy v Legal Services Commission* [2001] 1 All ER 895). Whether or not a claim is provable in bankruptcy is determined by IR 1986, r. 12.3. Any obligation arising under an order made in family proceedings is not provable (r. 12.3(2)(a)) and this leads to difficult problems in relation to orders made in foreign matrimonial proceedings, see *Cartwright v Cartwright* [2002] EWCA Civ 931, [2002] 2 FLR 610. It is submitted that a person with a claim against an individual which is wholly unenforceable (for example, because it is statute-barred) is not a creditor and has no standing to petition for bankruptcy.

In order to obtain an adjudication of bankruptcy, a creditor petitioner must be able to show, if the petition debt is payable immediately, that the debtor appears to be unable to pay it, or, if the debt is payable in the future, that the debtor appears to have no reasonable prospect of being able to pay it (Insolvency Act 1986, s. 267(2)(c)). This is usually shown by the debtor's failure to comply with a statutory demand for the debt (see **83.7**).

Service of a statutory demand

83.7 The effect of the Insolvency Act 1986, ss. 267 and 268, is that a creditor who presents a petition in respect of a debt which is payable immediately must prove that the debtor appears to be unable to pay it, and this may be proved only by showing either that a statutory demand for the debt was served on the debtor and not complied with or (if the debt is a judgment debt) that execution issued in respect of it was returned wholly or partly unsatisfied. (Proof of apparent inability to pay a judgment debt may be either by unsatisfied judgment or by failure to comply with a statutory demand.) The demand must be in the prescribed form, which is form 6.1 in IR 1986, sch. 4 (or form 6.2 if the debt is a judgment debt). Similarly, a creditor who presents a petition in respect of a debt which is payable at some certain, future time must prove that the debtor appears to have no reasonable prospect of being able to pay the debt, and this may be proved only by showing that a statutory demand for the creditor to establish a reasonable prospect of paying was not complied with. The prescribed form for a statutory demand for a future debt is form 6.3.

Where a debt is owed to joint creditors, one of them alone may make a statutory demand for it, provided payment to that one creditor would discharge the debt (*Mahmood v Penrose* [2004] EWHC 1500 (Ch), [2005] BPIR 170).

A statutory demand may be for a sum in a foreign currency: tendering the sterling equivalent of the amount demanded in a foreign currency would be regarded as compounding the debt in a manner which the creditor could not reasonably refuse (*Re a Debtor (No. 51-SD-1991)* [1992] 1 WLR 1294).

Service of a statutory demand is not an insolvency proceeding (*Re a Debtor (No. 190 of 1987)* (1988) *The Times*, 21 May 1988) and it is not possible to apply to the court for directions on service, which is governed entirely by IR 1986 and **PD Insolvency Proceedings**. The creditor is under an obligation to do all that is reasonable in the circumstances to bring the statutory demand to the debtor's attention (IR 1986, r. 6.3(2)). If practicable in the particular circumstances, there must be personal service of the demand in accordance with **CPR, rr. 6.5(3)** and **6.22(3)**, and **PD Insolvency Proceedings, para. 13.3.4(1)** (IR 1986, r. 6.3(2)). If the procedure in **PD Insolvency Proceedings, para. 13.3.4(1)** fails to effect service, the steps specified in **para. 13.3.4(2)**, (3) and (4), which may involve substituted service by first-class post or insertion through a letter box, must be followed (**para. 13.3.3**). If the debt is a judgment debt, service of the statutory demand may be by newspaper advertisement if the debtor has absconded or is avoiding service and there is no real prospect of recovering the debt by execution (IR 1986, r. 6.3(3); **PD Insolvency Proceedings, para. 13.3.2**). Information on service abroad (for which court permission is not required) is given in **PD Insolvency Proceedings, para. 13.2**.

When the petition is filed in court it must be accompanied by a certificate of service in accordance with IR 1986, r. 6.11. The prescribed forms of evidence of service are form 6.11 and, for substituted service, 6.12, in IR 1986, sch. 4. Care must be taken to provide all the required information in the certificate of service, which is an essential item of evidence that the conditions for making a bankruptcy order have been fulfilled.

A debtor is allowed three weeks to comply with a statutory demand and normally a petition based on failure to comply with a statutory demand cannot be presented until the three weeks have elapsed, though it can be presented immediately after the three weeks have elapsed. However, the Insolvency Act 1986, s. 270, permits presentation before the three weeks have elapsed if there is a serious possibility that the debtor's property or the value of any of the debtor's property will be significantly diminished during the three weeks, and the petition contains a statement to that effect. Within 18 days of service of a statutory demand, the person on whom it is served may apply to the court for the demand to be set aside (see **83.8**) and the creditor cannot present a petition while such an application is pending (s. 267(2)(d)).

Application to set aside a statutory demand

An individual on whom a statutory demand has been served may apply under IR 1986, r. 6.4, to the appropriate court for an order setting the statutory demand aside. Rule 6.4(2) provides **83.8** that the appropriate court is normally the court to which the debtor may present his or her own petition in accordance with r. 6.40A (see **83.4**), but it is the High Court where the creditor is a minister of the Crown or a government department intending to petition in the High Court, which intention must be stated in the statutory demand (r. 6.4(2A)). An application to set aside a statutory demand must be made within 18 days of service of the demand (r. 6.4(1)). It is made using form 6.4 in IR 1986, sch. 4, which must be accompanied by written evidence in form 6.5. No court fee is charged (**CPFO, note following fee 3.12**). For further details see **PD Insolvency Proceedings, para. 13.4**, and IR 1986, r. 6.5.

The court may, of its own initiative, dismiss an application to set aside a statutory demand without a hearing if satisfied that no sufficient cause is shown for it (r. 6.5(1)). Reasons must be given for the dismissal (*Vaidya v Wijayawardhana* [2010] EWHC 716 (Ch), [2010] BPIR 1016).

The circumstances in which the court may grant an application to set aside a statutory demand are listed in r. 6.5(4) as follows:

(a) the debtor appears to have a counterclaim, set-off or cross-demand which equals or exceeds the amount of the debt or debts specified in the statutory demand; or
(b) the debt is disputed on grounds which appear to the court to be substantial; or
(c) it appears that the creditor holds some security in respect of the debt claimed by the demand, and either rule 6.1(5) [which requires that the statutory demand must be only for the net amount of the debt after deducting the value of the security] is not complied with in respect of it, or the court is satisfied that the value of the security equals or exceeds the full amount of the debt; or
(d) the court is satisfied, on other grounds, that the demand ought to be set aside.

In r. 6.5(4)(a) the terms 'counterclaim' and 'cross-demand' comprehend counterclaims and cross-demands that are not legal or equitable set-offs, and a statutory demand based on dishonour of a cheque or other bill of exchange may be set aside if the debtor has a counterclaim or cross-demand, even if it would not be a defence to the claim on the bill or cheque (*Hofer v Strawson* [1999] 2 BCLC 336). If a court has already dismissed proceedings brought by the debtor advancing the counterclaim etc. which is said to equal or exceed the debt claimed in a statutory demand, the bankruptcy court may nevertheless set aside the statutory demand if persuaded that an appeal against the first decision has a realistic, as opposed to fanciful, prospect of success (*Society of Lloyd's v Bowman* [2003] EWCA Civ 1886, [2004] BPIR 324).

The test for setting aside a bankruptcy statutory demand when the debtor claims to have a counterclaim, set-off or cross-demand, or disputes the debt, is whether, in the court's opinion, the debtor has raised a 'genuine triable issue' (**PD Insolvency Proceedings, para 13.4.4**; *Kellar v BBR Graphic Engineers (Yorks) Ltd* [2002] BPIR 544; *Crossley-Cooke v Europanel (UK) Ltd* [2010] EWHC 124 (Ch), [2010] BPIR 561). The court cannot find that a triable issue is 'genuine', or that the grounds of a dispute appear to be 'substantial' (IR 1986, r 6.5(4)(b)), simply by finding that the debtor's case is arguable. There has to be something to suggest that the debtor's assertion is sustainable, and this may mean that the 'genuine triable issue' criterion is the same as having a real prospect of success (*Collier v P. and M. J. Wright (Holdings) Ltd* [2007] EWCA Civ 1329, [2008] 1 WLR 643 per Arden LJ at [21]).

Under r. 6.5(4)(d) a statutory demand will be set aside if no bankruptcy order would be made on a petition based on not complying with it, for example, because it is for an unprovable debt (*Levy v Legal Services Commission* [2001] 1 All ER 895).

If the amount of the debt is overstated in the demand, the debtor will be deemed to have complied with it if the correct amount is paid within the time allowed (IR 1986, r. 6.25(3)).

A creditor's petition in respect of a debt or debts cannot be presented at a time when there is an outstanding application to set aside a statutory demand served in respect of the debt or any of the debts (Insolvency Act 1986, s. 267(2)(d)). An application made out of time, and for which the court has not extended time, does not count for the purposes of s. 267(2)(d) (*Re Chohan* (2000) LTL 7/11/2000), nor does an appeal against a dismissed application (*Hurst v Bennett* (2001) *The Independent*, 9 April 2001).

Usually, a court's decision to set aside a statutory demand does not determine any substantive dispute about the existence or size of the debt demanded. It follows that on an appeal against a decision to set aside, further evidence concerning that dispute may be admitted even if it does not satisfy the tests established in *Ladd v Marshall* [1954] 1 WLR 1489 (see **75.16** and **75.17**) (*Heavy Duty Parts Ltd v Anelay* [2004] EWHC 960 (Ch), LTL 5/4/2004). The court should consider: (a) the importance of the evidence to the party seeking to adduce it, (b) the reasons for not adducing it in the court below, (c) the extent of any prejudice which its admission would cause the opposing party, and (d) the overriding objective (*Sadrolashrafi v Marvel International Food Logistics Ltd* [2004] EWHC 777 (Ch), [2004] BPIR 729 at [16]).

If the person who served the statutory demand ought to have known of the circumstances which would lead to it being set aside, the costs of applying under r. 6.4 may be awarded on an indemnity basis (*Re Kirkman-Moeller* [2005] EWHC 205 (Ch), LTL 19/1/2005 (sub nom. *Re Moller*)).

On an application to set aside a statutory demand, the court may make a consent order dismissing the application, setting aside the demand, or giving permission to withdraw the application, without the attendance of the parties (**PD Insolvency Proceedings, para. 16.3(1)**). Such orders may be made with or without an order for costs as may be agreed. A consent order dismissing an application to set aside a statutory demand will give permission to present a petition on or after the seventh day after the date of the order, unless a different date is agreed.

Commentary

Form and contents of creditor's petition

There are three prescribed forms for a creditor's petition (forms 6.7, 6.8 and 6.9 in IR 1986, sch. 4). Form 6.7 is used when the petition is based on failure to comply with a statutory demand for a liquidated sum payable immediately. Form 6.8 is used when the petition is based on failure to comply with a statutory demand for a liquidated sum payable at a future date. Form 6.9 is used for a petition based on partially or wholly unsatisfied execution. **83.9**

If the petition is based on failure to comply with a statutory demand and more than four months have elapsed since the demand was served, the petition must include a statement explaining the reasons for the delay (r. 6.12(7)).

There is detailed advice on creditors' bankruptcy petitions in **PD Insolvency Proceedings, paras 14.1** to **14.7**.

Verification of creditor's petition

A creditor's petition must be verified by a statement of truth (IR 1986, rr. 6.10(1) and 6.12(1)) using form 6.13A in IR 1986, sch. 4. The statement of truth must repeat the reasons given in the petition for waiting more than four months to rely on a statutory demand and must add an explanation of the circumstances which have contributed to late presentation of the petition. **83.10**

Rule 6.12(4) provides that the statement of truth must be authenticated by:

(a) the petitioner (or if there are two or more petitioners, any one of them); or
(b) some person such as a director, company secretary or similar company officer, or a solicitor, who has been concerned in the matters giving rise to the presentation of the petition; or
(c) some responsible person who is duly authorised to make the affidavit or witness statement and has the requisite knowledge of those matters.

In cases (b) and (c) the person authenticating the statement of truth must state the capacity in which, and the authority by which, he or she does so, and the means of knowing the matters verified (r. 6.12(5)).

Filing of creditor's petition and fixing of venue

83.11 A creditor's bankruptcy petition must be filed in court together with one copy for service on the debtor (IR 1986, r. 6.10(1) and (3)). A court officer seals all copies of the petition and fixes a venue for hearing it, which is endorsed on all copies (r. 6.10(3) and (5)).

The court must forthwith send notice of the petition to the Chief Land Registrar to be noted in the register of pending actions (r. 6.13). If the petition is dismissed, or withdrawn with the court's permission, the court must order the registration of the petition as a pending action to be vacated (r. 6.27). Damages cannot be recovered for breach of the duty imposed by r. 6.13 (or, it is submitted, r. 6.27) (*Poulton's Trustee v Ministry of Justice* [2010] EWCA Civ 392, [2011] Ch 1).

A debtor is allowed three weeks to comply with a statutory demand and normally a petition based on failure to comply with a statutory demand cannot be presented until the three weeks have elapsed. However, the Insolvency Act 1986, s. 270, permits presentation before the three weeks have elapsed if there is a serious possibility that the debtor's property or the value of any of the debtor's property will be significantly diminished during the three weeks, and the petition contains a statement to that effect.

Fee and deposit

83.12 On filing a creditor's bankruptcy petition, a court fee of £220 must be paid (**CPFO, fee 3.1(b)**). The petitioner must deposit £700 as security for the administration fee which will become payable to the official receiver if a bankruptcy order is made and transmitted to the official receiver (Insolvency Act 1986, s. 415(3); Insolvency Proceedings (Fees) Order 2004 (SI 2004/593), art. 6(1)). A petition cannot be filed unless the receipt for the deposit is produced (IR 1986, r. 6.10(2)). For details of the payment procedure see **PD Insolvency Proceedings, para. 14.4**. The deposit is security for the official receiver's administration fee and must be used to discharge that fee to the extent that the assets in the bankrupt's estate are insufficient (SI 2004/593, art. 6(2)); the administration fee is £1,715 (SI 2004/593, sch. 2, fee B1). The court must transmit the deposit to its official receiver (SI 2004/593, art. 6(3)). If a bankruptcy order is made, any part of the deposit which is not required to pay the administration fee must be returned (art. 6(5)). If the petition is dismissed or withdrawn, the whole of the deposit must be repaid (art. 6(4)). The court fee is not repayable.

Service of creditor's petition

83.13 The debtor must be served personally with a sealed copy of a creditor's petition (IR 1986, r. 6.14(1)). If the court is satisfied by written evidence that prompt personal service cannot be effected because the debtor is avoiding service, or for any other cause, it may make an order for substituted service to be effected in such manner as it thinks fit (r. 6.14(2)). **PD Insolvency Proceedings, para. 13.3.4** sets out what must normally be done to justify an order for substituted service. If the debtor dies before service of the petition, the court may order it to be served on the deceased's personal representatives, or on such other persons as it thinks fit (IR 1986, r. 6.16).

If a bankruptcy petition asks for the opening of secondary proceedings against a debtor who is already the subject of main insolvency proceedings in another EU State (see **83.5**), a copy of the petition must be sent to a member State liquidator appointed in the main proceedings *(IR 1986, r. 6.14(5))*. Rule 6.14(5) does not make allowance for the member State liquidator being the petitioner.

Proof of service

Service of a creditor's bankruptcy petition must be proved by a certificate of service (IR 1986, r. 6.15A(1)) using form 6.17A (personal service) or form 6.18A (substituted service) in IR 1986, sch. 4. The certificate of service must be filed in court as soon as reasonably practicable after service, and in any event not less than five business days (see **82.7**) before the hearing of the petition (r. 6.15A(4)). **83.14**

Control of transactions and litigation while petition is pending

If a bankruptcy order is made, all dispositions of the debtor's property since the bankruptcy petition was presented are void unless made with the consent of the court or subsequently ratified by the court (Insolvency Act 1986, s. 284). For control of litigation while a bankruptcy petition is pending see **84.24**. **83.15**

Appointment of interim receiver

At any time after the presentation of a bankruptcy petition, but before a bankruptcy order is made, the court may, under the Insolvency Act 1986, s. 286, appoint the official receiver as interim receiver of the debtor's property. It must be shown that the appointment is necessary for the protection of the debtor's property (s. 286(1)). **83.16**

An application for the appointment of an interim receiver may be made by the debtor or any creditor, or, if the proceedings are secondary proceedings (see **83.5**), a temporary administrator or member State liquidator appointed in the main proceedings (IR 1986, r. 6.51(1)). The application (see **84.1** to **84.5**) must be supported by a witness statement showing (r. 6.51(2)):

(a) the grounds for the appointment;
(b) whether or not the official receiver has been informed of the application and has been provided with a copy of it;
(c) whether, to the applicant's knowledge, an IVA has been proposed or is in force;
(d) the applicant's estimate of the value of the property or business in respect of which the interim receiver is to be appointed.

The applicant must send copies of the application and evidence to the official receiver (r. 6.51(4)), who may attend the hearing of the application and make representations (r. 6.51(5)). If it is not possible to send these copies, the official receiver must at least be informed of the application in time to attend the hearing (r. 6.51(4)).

The court may make the appointment applied for, on such terms as it thinks fit, if satisfied that sufficient grounds are shown for the appointment (r. 6.51(6)).

Before an order appointing the official receiver as interim receiver of a debtor may be issued, the applicant must deposit with the official receiver such sum as the court directs to cover remuneration and expenses (r. 6.53(1)). Alternatively, security for the amount may be given if the official receiver agrees (r. 6.53(1)).

From time to time the official receiver may apply to the court to order a further amount to be deposited or secured, and if the order is not complied with within two days of service, the court may discharge the official receiver's appointment as interim receiver (r. 6.53(2)).

The court's order of appointment must state the nature of and describe the property to which the appointment relates and state what duties are to be performed in relation to the debtor's affairs (r. 6.52(1)). For control of litigation against a debtor when an interim receiver has been appointed see **84.25**.

Commentary

Permission to withdraw a petition

83.17 A bankruptcy petition cannot be withdrawn without the court's permission (Insolvency Act 1986, s. 266(2)). Permission to withdraw a creditor's petition will not be given until the petition is heard (IR 1986, r. 6.32(3)). If a creditor has given notice of intention to appear at the hearing, or if the court so orders, a witness statement must be filed specifying the grounds of the application and the circumstances in which it is made (r. 6.32(1)). If any payment has been made to the petitioner since the petition was filed, the witness statement must include the information set out in r. 6.32(2), which will reveal whether the payment might be avoided under the Insolvency Act 1986, s. 284, if another creditor were to be substituted as petitioner (see **83.20**) and a bankruptcy order made.

If the petition has not been served and either form 6.21 (see **83.19**) or a statement that no notices have been received from supporting or opposing creditors is given by or on behalf of the petitioning creditor, the court may make a consent order, giving permission to withdraw the petition (with no order for costs), without the attendance of the parties (**PD Insolvency Proceedings, para. 16.3(2)**).

Opposition by debtor

83.18 If the debtor intends to oppose a creditor's bankruptcy petition, a notice specifying the grounds of objection must be filed in court at least five business days (see **82.7**) before the day fixed for the hearing (IR 1986, r. 6.21). A copy must be sent to the petitioner or the petitioner's solicitor (r. 6.21).

Notice of appearance

83.19 By IR 1986, r. 6.23, any creditor wishing to appear on the hearing of a creditor's bankruptcy petition must send notice to the petitioner to arrive not later than 4 p.m. on the business day (see **82.7**) before the date appointed for the hearing (or the date of an adjournment).

A notice of appearance must be in form 6.20 in IR 1986, sch. 4, and must state whether the appearance will be to support or oppose the petition (r. 6.23(2)(b)). The notice must also state the name and address of the person giving it, and any telephone number and reference which may be required for communication with that person or with any other person (to be also specified in the notice) authorised to speak or act on behalf of the person giving the notice (r. 6.23(2)(a)). The notice must also state the amount and nature of the debt claimed by the person giving the notice (r. 6.23(2)(c)).

The petitioner must prepare for the court a list of persons who have given notice of intention to appear, stating whether they support or oppose the petition, and must hand a copy of the list to the court before the commencement of the hearing (IR 1986, r. 6.24; prescribed form is form 6.21 in sch. 4).

A person who has not given notice in accordance with r. 6.23 may appear on the hearing of the petition only with the permission of the court (r. 6.23(4)).

The petitioner must add to the list required by r. 6.24 the name of anyone given leave by the court to appear without having given proper notice (r. 6.24(4)).

Substitution of petitioner

83.20 When a bankruptcy petition is pending, r. 6.30 of IR 1986 permits the substitution of a new petitioner if the original petitioner:

(a) *is subsequently found not entitled* to petition;
(b) consents to withdraw the petition;
(c) consents to allow the petition to be dismissed;

(d) consents to an adjournment of the petition;
(e) fails to appear in support of the petition when it is called on in court on the day originally fixed for the hearing or on a day to which it is adjourned; or
(f) appears when the petition is called on in court but does not apply for an order in the terms of the prayer of the petition.

Any creditor who has (a) given notice of intention to appear on the hearing, (b) is desirous of prosecuting the petition, and (c) would have been in a position to petition for the debtor's bankruptcy on the date on which the present petition was presented, may be substituted as petitioner (IR 1986, r. 6.30(2)).

If a bankruptcy petition asks for the opening of secondary proceedings (see **83.5**), and the member State liquidator appointed in the main proceedings is not the petitioner, that member State liquidator may be substituted as petitioner if he or she is desirous of prosecuting the petition (r. 6.239).

It is also possible to make a change of carriage order at the hearing of the petition (see **83.26**).

Change of venue

Extension of time for hearing If a creditor's bankruptcy petition has not been served, the petitioner may apply under IR 1986, r. 6.28, for the court to appoint another venue for the hearing. The application (see **84.1** to **84.5**) must state the reasons why the petition has not been served (r. 6.28(2)). If another date is appointed, the petitioner must forthwith notify any creditor who has given notice of intention to appear on the hearing. **83.21**

Adjournment If the court adjourns the hearing of a creditor's bankruptcy petition, the petitioner must (unless the court otherwise directs) notify the debtor and any creditor who has given notice of intention to appear on the hearing (IR 1986, r. 6.29). **83.22**

Expedited hearing Normally the hearing of a creditor's bankruptcy petition cannot take place until 14 days after it was served on the debtor (IR 1986, r. 6.18(1)). However, the court may, under r. 6.18(2), hear the petition at an earlier date if: **83.23**

(a) it appears that the debtor has absconded;
(b) the court is satisfied that it is a proper case for an expedited hearing; or
(c) the debtor consents.

HEARING A CREDITOR'S PETITION AND MAKING THE ORDER

Orders that the court may make

On the hearing of a creditor's bankruptcy petition, the court may make a bankruptcy order if satisfied that the statements in the petition are true, and that the debt on which it is founded has not been paid, or secured or compounded for (or, if it is a future debt, that the debtor has no reasonable prospect of being able to pay when it falls due) (Insolvency Act 1986, s. 271(1); IR 1986, r. 6.25(1)). The payment referred to in the Insolvency Act 1986, s. 271(1), is a payment which is unconditional in the sense that it is not liable to be avoided under s. 284(1) if a bankruptcy order is made (*Smith v Ian Simpson and Co.* [2001] Ch 239). The court will normally be satisfied that a debt has not been paid, or secured or compounded for if a certificate (known as a certificate of continuing debt) is provided in the form set out in **PD Insolvency Proceedings, para. 14.5**. **83.24**

If the petition is in respect of a judgment debt, or a sum ordered to be paid by a court, the court may stay or dismiss the petition if an appeal is pending from the judgment or order, or if execution of the judgment has been stayed (IR 1986, r. 6.25(2)). On a petition in respect of a judgment debt, if there is no appeal against or application to stay judgment, the only grounds on which the correctness of the judgment may be challenged are that: (a) it was obtained fraudulently, (b) it was obtained by collusion between the debtor and the claimant, or (c) there was a miscarriage of justice (*Dawodu v American Express Bank* [2001] BPIR 983).

A petition will not be dismissed on the ground that the amount of the debt was overstated in a statutory demand, unless the debtor notified the creditor, within the three weeks allowed for complying with the demand, that he or she disputed its validity (r. 6.25(3)).

Ordinarily, a debtor will not be permitted to re-argue, on the hearing of a petition, a contention that the statutory demand was invalid if that contention has already been rejected on a substantive hearing of an application to set aside the statutory demand (*Turner v Royal Bank of Scotland plc* [2000] BPIR 683). The same applies if a contention advanced in preparation for an application to set aside was abandoned (*Adams v Mason Bullock* [2004] EWHC 2910 (Ch), [2005] BPIR 241). The question may be reopened if there has been a change of circumstances (*Turner v Royal Bank of Scotland* at p. 294). The principle does not apply if there has been no reasoned determination at all at the earlier stage (*Commissioners of Inland Revenue v Lee-Phipps* [2003] BPIR 803; *Vaidya v Wijayawardhana* [2010] EWHC 716 (Ch), [2010] BPIR 1016). If no reasons were given for dismissing the application to set aside the statutory demand without a hearing, the court cannot infer that a particular contention of the debtor had been considered and rejected (*Vaidya v Wijayawardhana*).

If either form 6.21 (see **83.19**) or a statement that no notices have been received from supporting or opposing creditors is given by or on behalf of the petitioning creditor, the court may make a consent order, dismissing the petition, with or without an order for costs as may be agreed, without the attendance of the parties (**PD Insolvency Proceedings, para. 16.3(2)**).

Non-appearance of creditor

83.25 If the petitioning creditor fails to appear on the hearing of the petition, no subsequent petition against the same debtor may be presented by the same creditor in respect of the same debt, unless the court to which the first petition was presented gives permission (IR 1986, r. 6.26). There is detailed consideration of r. 6.26 in *Omgate Ltd v Gordon* [2001] BPIR 909.

Change of carriage of creditor's petition

83.26 At the hearing of a creditor's petition, the court may, under IR 1986, r. 6.31, give another creditor carriage of the petition if it appears that the petitioning creditor:

(a) intends by any means to secure the postponement, adjournment or withdrawal of the petition; or
(b) does not intend to prosecute the petition, either diligently or at all.

After a change of carriage order the petition is still based on the original petitioner's debt, unlike the position where there is a substitution of petitioner.

Settlement and transmission of bankruptcy order

83.27 If a bankruptcy order is made on a creditor's petition, the court will settle it (IR 1986, r. 6.33(1)). Two sealed copies will be sent to the official receiver, who will forthwith send one to the bankrupt (r. 6.34(1)).

The official receiver will send a notice to the Chief Land Registrar for registration in the register of writs and orders affecting land, cause the order to be gazetted, cause prescribed information to be entered in the individual insolvency register, and may also advertise notice of the order in such other manner as he or she thinks fit (rr. 6.34(2) and 6A.4). However, the bankrupt or a creditor may apply to the court for an order requiring the official receiver not to do these things pending a further order by the court (r. 6.34(3)). An application for such an order (see **84.1** to **84.5**) must be supported by a witness statement stating the grounds for applying (r. 6.34(3)). If the order is made, the applicant must deliver it forthwith to the official receiver (r. 6.34(4)).

For control of litigation against a bankrupt see **84.26**.

DEBTOR'S PETITION

New procedure

83.28 The Enterprise and Regulatory Reform Act 2013, s. 71, sch. 18 and sch. 19, make amendments to the Insolvency Act 1986 to provide a new procedure for an individual's application to be made bankrupt. The application will be made to an adjudicator appointed by the Secretary of State and not to a court. These provisions had not been brought into force when this edition went to press. The following paragraphs briefly describe the current procedure.

Form and contents of debtor's petition

83.29 The only ground on which a debtor may petition for his or her own bankruptcy is inability to pay his or her debts (Insolvency Act 1986, s. 272(1)) and that fact must be admitted in the petition (IR 1986, r. 6.39(1)). The prescribed form of petition is form 6.27 in IR 1986, sch. 4. The petition must be accompanied by a statement of the petitioner's affairs (Insolvency Act 1986, s. 272(2)), which must be in form 6.28 in IR 1986, sch. 4, and must be verified by a statement of truth (IR 1986, rr. 6.41(1) and 6.68). The petition itself does not have to be verified.

If a debtor's centre of main interests is in another EU State (apart from Denmark) and insolvency proceedings have not yet been opened in that State, the debtor is not entitled to apply for a bankruptcy order to be made here, unless insolvency proceedings cannot be opened in the State where the debtor's centre of main interests is located, because of the conditions laid down by the law of that State (Regulation (EC) No. 1346/2000, art. 4).

Filing of petition and fixing of venue

83.30 A debtor's petition and statement of affairs must be filed with three copies of the petition and two copies of the statement (IR 1986, r. 6.42(1)). The court may hear the petition forthwith or fix a venue for the hearing (r. 6.42(2)). If there is an IVA in force for the debtor, the court must fix a venue and give at least 14 days' notice of it to the IVA supervisor, who may appear and be heard on the petition (r. 6.42(2A)). If a venue is fixed, it is endorsed on the copies of the petition. One copy of the petition and of the statement of affairs is sent to the official receiver by the court, unless the court directs the petitioner to deliver it (r. 6.42(3), (4) and (6)). The court will forthwith send notice of the petition to the Chief Land Registrar to be noted in the register of pending actions (IR 1986, r. 6.43).

Fee and deposit

83.31 A court fee and deposit must be paid, as for a creditor's petition (see **83.12**), except that the fee is £175 (**CPFO, fee 3.1(a)**) and the deposit is £525 (Insolvency Proceedings (Fees) Order 2004 (SI 2004/593), art. 6(1)). A petition cannot be filed unless the receipt for the deposit is produced (IR 1986, r. 6.42(1)). Though the court fee may be remitted because of the petitioner's poverty (**CPFO, art. 5** and **sch. 2**) the deposit will not (*R v Lord Chancellor, ex parte Lightfoot* [2000] QB 597).

Control of transactions and litigation while petition is pending

83.32 The rules on control of transactions and litigation while a petition is pending (see 83.15) apply to a debtor's petition as well as to a creditor's petition.

Appointment of interim receiver

83.33 During the period when a debtor's petition is pending an interim receiver may be appointed, following the procedure set out in 83.16.

Investigation of possibility of voluntary arrangement

83.34 Section 273 of the Insolvency Act 1986 provides for special treatment of a debtor's petition where the aggregate amount of the debtor's unsecured debts is less than £40,000 and the debtor has not, within the five years preceding presentation of the present petition:
(a) been adjudged bankrupt; or
(b) made a composition with his or her creditors; or
(c) made a scheme of arrangement of his or her affairs.

If, in such a case, it appears that the debtor's assets are worth at least £4,000, the court may appoint a qualified insolvency practitioner to investigate, under s. 274, whether an IVA can be made. The court will send the appointed practitioner a sealed copy of the order of appointment and copies of the petition and statement of affairs (IR 1986, r. 6.44(1)(a)). It will also fix a venue for the practitioner's report to be considered and send notice of the venue to the practitioner and the debtor (r. 6.44(1)(b) and (c)). The court may also appoint the practitioner interim receiver of the debtor's property (Insolvency Act 1986, s. 286(2)). On receipt of the report, the court will pay the practitioner a fee of £450 out of the petitioner's deposit (see 83.31) (Insolvency Proceedings (Fees) Order 2004 (SI 2004/593), art. 5). On consideration of the insolvency practitioner's report the court may either make an interim order imposing a moratorium while a proposed IVA is considered (see 83.37) or, if it seems that an IVA would not succeed, make a bankruptcy order (Insolvency Act 1986, s. 274(3)).

Settlement and transmission of order

83.35 The procedures for settlement and transmission of a bankruptcy order made on a debtor's petition are set out in IR 1986, rr. 6.45 and 6.46, and are the same as for an order made on a creditor's petition (see 83.27).

INDIVIDUAL VOLUNTARY ARRANGEMENTS

Nature of voluntary arrangements

83.36 An individual who is either an undischarged bankrupt or is able to petition for his or her own bankruptcy may, under part 8 (ss. 252 to 263G) of the Insolvency Act 1986, propose to his or her creditors a composition in satisfaction of their debts or a scheme of arrangement of his or her affairs. A composition or scheme under part 8 is referred to in that part as a 'voluntary arrangement' and in IR 1986 as an individual voluntary arrangement, which is usually abbreviated as IVA.

If the procedures of part 8 are followed, a debtor's composition or scheme of arrangement becomes binding on all creditors when it is approved by three quarters of the creditors (by value of their unsecured debts) who vote (Insolvency Act 1986, ss. 260(2) and 263D(2); IR *1986, rr. 5.23 and 5.43*). A 'supervisor', who must be a qualified insolvency practitioner or the official receiver, must act in relation to an IVA either as trustee or otherwise for the purpose of supervising its implementation (s. 253(2)).

Undischarged bankrupts may use the procedure for fast-track voluntary arrangement in ss. 263A to 263G (see **83.37**).

As explained in **83.29**, a debtor whose centre of main interests is in another EU State (apart from Denmark) is not usually able to petition for his or her own bankruptcy here if main insolvency proceedings have not been opened in that State (Regulation (EC) No. 1346/2000, art. 4). It follows that such a person cannot propose an IVA. If main insolvency proceedings have been opened in the State where the centre of the debtor's main interests is located, the only form of secondary proceedings which may be opened here is bankruptcy and an IVA cannot be proposed (arts 2(c) and 3(3)).

Proposal and interim order

The following procedures do not apply where the court has appointed an insolvency practitioner under the Insolvency Act 1986, s. 273, to investigate the possibility of an IVA in a small bankruptcy (see **83.34**). **83.37**

The first stage in creating an IVA is to prepare a proposal for a composition or scheme and persuade someone to be the debtor's nominee for supervisor if the IVA is approved. The official receiver may be nominated if the debtor is an undischarged bankrupt (Insolvency Act 1986, s. 389B). Otherwise, at present, the nominee must be a qualified insolvency practitioner, who will usually have advised on the preparation of the proposal.

If the official receiver is the nominee, it is likely that the fast-track procedure will be used (s. 263A). In the fast-track procedure the debtor's proposal, conforming with IR 1986, r. 5.37, is submitted to the official receiver with a statement of affairs (Insolvency Act 1986, s. 263B(1)). The official receiver will invite creditors to approve the proposal if he or she considers that it has a reasonable prospect of being approved and implemented (s. 263B(2)).

If the fast-track procedure is not being used, the proposal must conform with IR 1986, r. 5.3, and must be sent to the intended nominee with a notice conforming with r. 5.4 and a statement of affairs conforming with r. 5.5.

An application may be made to the court under the Insolvency Act 1986, s. 253, for an interim order under s. 252. In the fast-track procedure, the application cannot be made until the official receiver has decided whether or not to invite creditors to approve the proposal (s. 263B(5)). While it is in force, the effect of an interim order is, by s. 252(2), that:

(a) no bankruptcy petition relating to the debtor may be presented or proceeded with;
(b) no other proceedings, and no execution or other legal process, may be commenced or continued against the debtor or his or her property except with the permission of the court.

If the debtor is an undischarged bankrupt, the application for an interim order may be by the debtor, his or her trustee in bankruptcy or the official receiver; in any other case only the debtor may apply (s. 253(3)). If the debtor is an undischarged bankrupt, the application must be made to the court having the conduct of the bankruptcy and is made by application (see **84.1** to **84.5**) in those bankruptcy proceedings (IR 1986, r. 5.8(3)). Otherwise the application is to a court in which the debtor would be entitled to present his or her own bankruptcy petition (see **83.4**) (r. 5.8(1)). The application must contain sufficient information to establish that it is brought in the appropriate court (r. 5.8(2)). The application must be accompanied by a witness statement of the matters listed in r. 5.7(1), a copy of the r. 5.4 notice to the intended nominee endorsed with his or her agreement to act, and a copy of the debtor's proposal (r. 5.7(2)).

On receiving an application for an interim order, the court will fix a venue for hearing it (IR 1986, r. 5.7(3)). If the debtor is an undischarged bankrupt, the applicant must give at least two business days' notice of the hearing to the nominee (r. 5.7(4)(c)) and to whichever of the following is not the applicant: the bankrupt, the official receiver, the trustee in bankruptcy

(r. 5.7(4)(a)). Otherwise the applicant must give notice to the nominee and to any creditor who has, to the applicant's knowledge, presented a bankruptcy petition against him or her (r. 5.7(4)(b) and (c)). Any of the persons given notice under r. 5.7(4) may appear or be represented at the hearing of the application (r. 5.9(1)) and the court must take account of their representations (r. 5.9(2)).

For control of litigation against the debtor while an application for an interim order is pending see **84.23**.

If the court makes an interim order, it will normally last for only 14 days (Insolvency Act 1986, s. 255(6)). At least two business days before the order expires, the nominee must submit a report to the court stating whether, in his or her opinion, a meeting of creditors should be summoned to consider the proposed IVA, and, if so, when (s. 256(1); IR 1986, r. 5.11(1)). On making an interim order the court must fix a venue for consideration of that report (r. 5.9(3)). Any of the persons given notice under r. 5.5(4) may appear or be represented at the hearing to consider the report (r. 5.13(1)).

If the nominee's report under the Insolvency Act 1986, s. 256 (interim order) or s. 256A (no interim order), opines that a creditors' meeting should be held, the nominee will summon one unless (where there is an interim order) the court otherwise directs (s. 257(1)). If an interim order has been made, the court will direct that it shall continue in force to enable the proposal to be considered (s. 256(5)).

If, as is usual, the nominee prepared the proposal, the report under s. 256 that a creditors' meeting should be held can be filed with the first application for an interim order. The court can then make what is known as a 'concertina order' combining the 14-day initial order and an order enabling consideration of the proposal.

If the debtor is not an undischarged bankrupt and there is no bankruptcy petition pending, the court may make standard interim orders without the attendance of the parties (**PD Insolvency Proceedings, para. 16.1**).

If there is a proposal prepared in good faith by respected insolvency practitioners and a reputable nominee, the court will usually make an interim order, leaving it to the creditors to decide whether to approve the proposal. However, the court has a discretion to refuse to make an interim order and will refuse one if it is clear that bankruptcy will be preferable to an IVA (*Hurst v Kroll Buchler Phillips Ltd* [2002] EWHC 2855 (Ch), [2003] BPIR 872).

If there is no application for an interim order, and the fast-track procedure is not being used, the nominee reports to the debtor's creditors in accordance with the Insolvency Act 1986, s. 256A, and IR 1986, r. 5.14A.

In the fast-track procedure, if the official receiver agrees to act as nominee, the proposal is not reported to the court. Instead the official receiver invites creditors to vote by post on the proposal (IR 1986, rr. 5.39 to 5.43).

Approval of voluntary arrangement

83.38 If a meeting of creditors is held, its chairman must report the result to the court (Insolvency Act 1986, s. 259(1); IR 1986, r. 5.27).

If the result is that the creditors have declined to approve the proposal, the court may discharge any interim order (Insolvency Act 1986, s. 259(2)).

If the creditors accept the proposal, the IVA will take effect as if made at the meeting (s. 260(1) and (2)) and any interim order will cease to have effect 28 days after the chairman's report is made to the court (s. 260(4)). The chairman must report the approval of the IVA to the Secretary of State for entry in the register of IVAs (IR 1986, rr. 5.28 and 5.29). If a bankruptcy petition is pending against the debtor, it is deemed to have been dismissed when the interim order ceases to have effect, unless the court orders otherwise (Insolvency Act 1986, s. 260(5)). If the debtor is an undischarged bankrupt, the court must annul the bankruptcy order on an application made by the bankrupt or by the official receiver (s. 261; IR 1986, rr. 5.51 to 5.56, 5.60 and 5.61).

It is unnecessary to obtain the court's approval of an IVA which has been approved by a creditors' meeting, but a dissentient creditor may apply to the court under s. 262 to revoke or suspend the approval because the creditor's interests are prejudiced by the IVA and/or the meeting was vitiated by a material irregularity. Such an application must be made within 28 days after the chairman's report is made to the court. For the procedure if a revocation or suspension order is made see IR 1986, r. 5.30. An application under the Insolvency Act 1986, s. 262, may also be made by the nominee, the official receiver or the debtor. If the meeting declined to approve the proposal, those persons can also apply under s. 262 for an order directing a further meeting to reconsider the proposal on the ground that there was a material irregularity in the first meeting.

In the fast-track procedure, the official receiver must notify the Secretary of State whether the proposal has been approved or rejected by the creditors (s. 263C). If the official receiver reports approval, the IVA takes effect (s. 263D(1) and (2)) and the court must annul the bankruptcy order on the application of the official receiver (s. 263D(3); IR 1986, rr. 5.57 to 5.61). Section 263F provides for revocation of a fast-track IVA by the court on an application made within 28 days of notification under s. 263C. The procedure if a revocation order is made is in IR 1986, r. 5.46.

Commentary

BANKRUPTCY PETITION ALLEGING DEFAULT IN CONNECTION WITH VOLUNTARY ARRANGEMENT

A bankruptcy petition may be presented against a debtor who has entered into an approved IVA, but the court will not make a bankruptcy order unless it is satisfied that one of the circumstances listed in the Insolvency Act 1986, s. 276(1), exists. Those circumstances are failure by the debtor to comply with his or her obligations under the IVA, provision of false or misleading information to procure approval of the IVA, and failure of the debtor to cooperate with the IVA supervisor. It is possible to make a bankruptcy order even though a default has been remedied (*Carter-Knight v Peat* [2000] BPIR 968). A petition may be presented by the supervisor of, or any person (other than the debtor) who is for the time being bound by, the IVA (s. 264(1)(c)) and is subject to the same rules as a creditor's petition (IR 1986, r. 6.6). If the petitioner is not the supervisor of the IVA, an extra copy of the petition must be filed for service on the supervisor (IR 1986, rr. 6.10(3) and 6.14(4)). **83.39**

DEBT RELIEF ORDERS AND ADMINISTRATION ORDERS

A debtor may obtain an order dealing with specified debts within fairly low financial limits. The two forms of order are: **83.40**

(a) debt relief orders (DROs) (Insolvency Act 1986, ss. 251A to 251X);
(b) administration orders (AOs) (County Courts Act 1984, ss. 112 to 117).

A DRO is made by an official receiver and normally there is no court involvement. An application must be made through an approved intermediary designated by the Secretary of State. A DRO has the same effect on debts as a bankruptcy order but applies only to the debts listed in the DRO, which can only be unsecured debts for liquidated sums payable either immediately or at a certain future time (Insolvency Act 1986, s 251A). A DRO is available only to a debtor whose finances are within the following limits: maximum total debts for liquidated sums £15,000, maximum surplus income £50 a month, maximum total value of property £300 (Insolvency Act 1986, sch. 4ZA, paras 6 to 8; Insolvency Proceedings (Monetary Limits) Order 1986 (SI 1986/1996), sch., part 2).

An AO is a court-administered debt management scheme for an individual with total debts of no more than £5,000, one of which must be a judgment debt. The order is made by a county court and requires periodic instalments to pay all, or a realistic proportion, of specified debts. An AO may be made on the debtor's application, or by the court on consideration of information provided under **CPR, Part 71**. See 79.12.

Chapter 84 Insolvency Applications and Appeals

Commentary

APPLICATIONS IN INSOLVENCY PROCEEDINGS

Procedural rules

Applications in insolvency proceedings are governed by rr. 7.1 to 7.10 of the Insolvency Rules 1986 (SI 1986/1925) (IR 1986). Rules 7.1 to 7.10 apply, according to r. 7.1, to any application made to the court under the Insolvency Act 1986 or IR 1986, apart from a petition for a winding-up order or an administration application (see **chapter 82**) and a bankruptcy petition (see **chapter 83**). However, the Insolvency Rules 1986 were not made for the purposes of all provisions of the Insolvency Act 1986: by ss. 411(1) and 412(1), they could have been made only for the purposes of parts 1 to 11 (ss. 1 to 385) of the Act. Accordingly IR 1986, rr. 7.1 to 7.10, do not apply, for example, to the provisions in the Insolvency Act 1986, **84.1** part 16, for reversing transactions defrauding creditors (*Re Banco Nacional de Cuba* [2001] 1 WLR 2039 at p. 2048). This chapter outlines the general procedural rules relating to applications in insolvency proceedings and discusses in some detail applications to stay, commence or continue litigation against persons who are the subject of insolvency proceedings.

Form and content

84.2 The prescribed form for an application in insolvency proceedings is form 7.1A (application notice) in IR 1986, sch. 4. It is necessary to state on this form whether or not the application is in insolvency proceedings which are already before the court. Applications that are not in proceedings already before the court include an application for an order forbidding the presentation of a winding-up petition (see **82.28**), an application under the Insolvency Act 1986, s. 252, for an interim order, if the applicant is not an undischarged bankrupt (see **83.37**), an application under s. 35 by a receiver or manager of a company's property, appointed out of court, for directions, and any application in a voluntary winding up (*Re Continental Assurance Co. of London plc (No. 2)* [1998] 1 BCLC 583).

Applications that are made in insolvency proceedings which are already before the court include any interim application while a petition for a winding-up, administration or bankruptcy order is pending.

Where there are two joined matters between the same parties, one of which is an insolvency application and the other requires a different form of originating process, both may be commenced by the insolvency application (**CPR, r. 7.3**; *Re Prestige Grindings Ltd* [2005] EWHC 3076 (Ch), [2006] 1 BCLC 440).

An application must state the matters set out in IR 1986, r. 7.3(1). It must be signed by the applicant, if acting in person, or by, or on behalf of, the applicant's solicitor (r. 7.3(3)).

Filing and fee

84.3 An insolvency application must be filed with the court, accompanied by one copy in any event, plus enough copies for service on every person who is to be served (IR 1986, r. 7.4(1)).

If an application is not in insolvency proceedings which are already before the court, the court fee is £155 (**CPFO, fee 3.5**). The court fee for an application in proceedings which are before the court is £35 if the application is by consent or without notice (**fee 3.11**), or £70 if it is with notice (**fee 3.12**).

Venue, directions, track allocation

84.4 When an application is filed, the court must fix a venue for it to be heard unless (IR 1986, r. 7.4(2)):

(a) it considers it not appropriate to do so — the court may, for example, direct that no venue is to be fixed before service and may set a time limit for service (*Re Continental Assurance Co. of London plc (No. 2)* [1998] 1 BCLC 583);
(b) the rule under which the application is brought provides otherwise; or
(c) the relevant provisions of IA 1986 or IR 1986 do not require service of the application on, or notice of it to be given to, any person, in which case the court may either fix a venue or hear the application as soon as reasonably practicable without fixing a venue (r. 7.5A).

Any application should be made, in the High Court, to the registrar, and in the county court, to the district judge, unless (r. 7.6A(2) and (3)):

(a) a direction to the contrary has been given; or
(b) the registrar or district judge does not have power to make the order required (see **PD 2B**).

In the RCJ a general direction has been given that applications relating to the matters listed in **PD Insolvency Proceedings, para. 12.1** are to be heard by the member of court staff in charge of the winding-up list. If the registrar or district judge thinks that the matter should properly be decided by the judge, it may be referred up (IR 1986, r. 7.6A(4)).

The court may at any time give such directions as it thinks fit concerning service or notice of the application, the procedure on the application, and evidence (rr. 7.4(4) and 7.10(2) and (3)).

All insolvency proceedings are allocated to the multi-track by IR 1986, r. 7.51A(3), and so the provisions of the CPR concerning directions questionnaires and track allocation do not apply.

The hearing of an application is in open court, unless the court orders otherwise (IR 1986, r. 7.6A(1)). For the circumstances in which a hearing may be in private see **CPR, r. 39.2** and **PD 39A, paras 1.1** to **1.15**.

Service

A sealed copy of an insolvency application must be served on the respondent named in it (IR 1986, r. 7.4(3)) at least 14 days before the date fixed for the hearing, unless (r. 7.4(5)): **84.5**

(a) the provision of IA 1986 or IR 1986 under which the application is made specifies a different period; or
(b) the application is urgent, in which case the court may hear it immediately, even without notice to, or attendance by, other parties, or may authorise a period of service shorter than 14 days (r. 7.4(6)).

CPR, Part 6 (service of documents), apart from **rr. 6.30** to **6.47** (service of the claim form and other documents out of the jurisdiction) and **rr. 6.48** to **6.51** (service of documents from foreign courts or tribunals), applies to service in England and Wales with such modifications as the court may direct (IR 1986, rr. 7.51A(1), 12A.16(1) and 12A.17), treating an application against a respondent as a claim form (r. 12A.16(3)).

If it is necessary to serve an application outside England and Wales, the court must be asked to direct how **CPR, Part 6**, excluding **rr. 6.30** to **6.47** (service of the claim form and other documents out of the jurisdiction), is to apply (IR 1986, rr. 7.51A(1), 12A.16 and 12A.20), treating an application against a respondent as a claim form (r. 12A.16(3)). Before the CPR came into force, the insolvency court's discretion in this respect was held to be more extensive than under RSC, ord. 11, and the practice of the courts in dealing with applications under RSC, ord. 11, was irrelevant to applications in insolvency proceedings (*Re Busytoday Ltd* [1992] 1 WLR 683). In particular, it was not necessary for service in a foreign jurisdiction to be effected in accordance with the law of that jurisdiction (*Re Busytoday Ltd*; see now **CPR, r. 6.40(3)(c)** and **(4)**, and *Habib Bank Ltd v Central Bank of Sudan* [2006] EWHC 1767 (Comm), [2007] 1 WLR 470).

Where there are joint office-holders in insolvency proceedings service on one of them is to be treated as service on all of them (IR 1986, r. 12A.19).

REVIEW, RESCISSION AND VARIATION OF AN ORDER MADE IN INSOLVENCY PROCEEDINGS

Statutory provision

Rule 7.47(1) of IR 1986 provides: **84.6**

> Every court having jurisdiction for the purposes of Parts 1 to 4 of the [Insolvency Act 1986] and Parts 1 to 4 of the [IR 1986] may review, rescind or vary any order made by it in the exercise of that jurisdiction.

An equivalent provision in relation to bankruptcy jurisdiction is made by the Insolvency Act 1986, s. 375(1).

Commentary

Jurisdiction

84.7 Any Chancery Division judge may review, rescind or vary an order made by another Chancery Division judge, because the legislation provides that 'the court' may review etc. its decisions (*Re W. and A. Glaser Ltd* [1994] BCC 199 at p. 206), but there has been doubt about who can review etc. a decision of a bankruptcy registrar. Formerly it had been held that the registrars in bankruptcy did not form a separate court within the Chancery Division (*Re Rolls Razor Ltd (No. 2)* [1970] Ch 576 at pp. 590–1). However, the creation by the 1986 legislation of a procedure for appealing from a registrar to a judge (see **84.13**) appeared to constitute the registrars as a separate court, and it was held in *Re SN Group plc* [1994] 1 BCLC 319 that a decision made by a registrar could be reviewed etc. only by the registrar, though the registrar could adjourn the matter to be heard by the judge (as in *Re Dollar Land (Feltham) Ltd* [1995] 2 BCLC 370). In *Re Piccadilly Property Management Ltd* [1999] 2 BCLC 145, though, Judge Colyer QC, sitting as a High Court judge, held that the registrars are not a separate court and that a decision of a registrar may be reviewed etc. by the registrar or by a judge. This means that when an order has been made by a registrar it is possible both to apply to the judge to rescind or review the order and to appeal against it, though this should be rare (*Re Piccadilly Property Management Ltd*).

In *Re a Debtor (No. 32 of 1991) (No. 2)* [1994] BCC 524 at p. 528 Vinelott J said that the procedure for review etc.:

> should not be resorted to in place of the ordinary process of appeal, save in cases where the court is satisfied that there has been something amounting to a miscarriage of justice which cannot be corrected by the ordinary process of appeal.

Nature of process

84.8 The power to review, rescind or vary is unfettered but must be exercised judicially (*Mond v Hammond Suddards* [2000] Ch 40 per Chadwick LJ at p. 49). It is not to be used in order to hear an appeal against a decision of a judge of coordinate jurisdiction, save in the most exceptional circumstances (*Mond v Hammond Suddards* [2000] Ch 40 at p. 49). Such an exceptional circumstance might be where the court is satisfied that there has been something amounting to a miscarriage of justice which cannot be corrected by the ordinary process of appeal (*Re a Debtor (No. 32 of 1991) (No. 2)* [1994] BCC 524 per Vinelott J at p. 528).

The distinction between an appeal and an application to review, rescind or vary is that the question on an appeal against a decision is whether the decision was right or wrong or was otherwise unjust through a serious procedural or other irregularity, whereas the question on an application to review, rescind or vary is whether the original order ought to remain in force in the light either of changed circumstances or further evidence (per Millett J in *Re a Debtor (No. 32-SD-1991)* [1993] 1 WLR 314 at p. 319; *Mond v Hammond Suddards* [2000] Ch 40 per Chadwick LJ at p. 49; **CPR, r. 52.11(3)**). It is submitted that further evidence should be admitted on an application to review, rescind or vary a decision on the same basis as it would be admitted on an appeal against the decision (see **75.16** and **75.17**).

An application to review, rescind or vary a decision must not be used merely to obtain a rehearing (*Egleton v Commissioners of Inland Revenue* [2003] EWHC 3226, [2004] BPIR 476) or merely to restate the applicant's case in what is hoped to be a more persuasive way (*RWH Enterprises Ltd v Portedge Ltd* [1998] BCC 556; *Re Thirty-Eight Building Ltd (No. 2)* [2000] 1 BCLC 201; *Papanicola v Humphreys* [2005] EWHC 335 (Ch), [2005] 2 All ER 418 at [26]).

The court's approach

84.9 In *Papanicola v Humphreys* [2005] EWHC 335 (Ch), [2005] 2 All ER 418 at [25], Laddie J summarised the principles on which the court will exercise its wide discretion to review, rescind or vary orders in insolvency proceedings. Among the points made by his Lordship are:

(2) The onus is on the applicant to demonstrate the existence of circumstances which justify exercise of the discretion [to review, rescind or vary] in his favour.
(3) Those circumstances must be exceptional.
(4) The circumstances relied on must involve a material difference to what was before the court which made the original order. In other words there must be something new to justify the overturning of the original order.
(5) There is no limit to the factors which may be taken into account. They can include, for example, changes which have occurred since the making of the original order and significant facts which, although in existence at the time of the original order, were not brought to the court's attention at that time.
(6) Where the new circumstances relied on consist of or include new evidence which could have been made available at the original hearing, that, and any explanation... the applicant gives for the failure to produce it then or any lack of such explanation, are factors which can be taken into account in the exercise of the discretion.

In relation to point (4), there is a material difference if the party seeking review etc. of an order was not present or represented when the order was made, but is now (*Holtham v Kelmanson* [2006] EWHC 2588 (Ch), [2006] BPIR 1422).

RESCISSION OF A WINDING-UP ORDER

An application under IR 1986, r. 7.47(1), for a winding-up order to be rescinded must be made within five business days of the date on which the order was made (r. 7.47(4)) though this time limit may be extended by the court under r. 4.3 as in *Re Calmex Ltd* [1989] 1 All ER 485 and *Re Virgo Systems Ltd* [1990] BCLC 34. An extension of time is unlikely to be granted if liquidators have incurred expense in investigating the company's insolvency (*Re Mid East Trading Ltd* [1997] 3 All ER 481 at p. 489, in which the application was about 14 months late). **84.10**

Applications for rescission of winding-up orders are regulated by **PD Insolvency Proceedings, para. 11.7**. An application must be accompanied by written evidence of assets and liabilities to demonstrate solvency. An application may be made only by a creditor or a contributory (though the company may join in the application) (*Re Mid East Trading Ltd* [1997] 3 All ER 481) and the costs of an unsuccessful application will be paid by the creditor or contributory applicant even when the company has been joined.

The hearing of an application to rescind a winding-up order is a rehearing of the petition on which the order was made and that petition is restored to the court. Accordingly, any person who might have been heard on the hearing of the petition may appear on the hearing of the application to rescind, and IR 1986, r. 4.16 (which requires notice of intention to appear or the permission of the court — see **82.82**), applies (*Re Dollar Land (Feltham) Ltd* [1995] 2 BCLC 370).

An applicant for rescission of a winding-up order must adduce new material which tends to show that the original order ought not to have been made, and which was not before the court on the making of the order (*Re Mid East Trading Ltd* [1997] 3 All ER 481 at p. 490).

APPEALS IN INSOLVENCY PROCEEDINGS

Procedural rules

PD Insolvency Proceedings, para. 19.9.1 (which has not been updated to refer to the new practice directions supplementing **CPR, Part 52**) specifies that the procedural rules and practice which apply to appeals in insolvency proceedings are **CPR, Part 52** (IR 1986, r. 7.49A(3); see **chapters** 74 and 75), and relevant provisions in the old PD 52. These are **84.11**

Section I (general provisions about appeals, now **PD 52A, PD 52B and PD 52C**) and Section IV (provisions about reopening appeals, now **PD 52A, Section VII**), except for (**PD Insolvency Proceedings, para. 19.9.2**):

(a) PD 52, paras 8.2 to 8.8 (venue for appeals and filing of notices, now **PD 52B, Section II**; see **PD Insolvency Proceedings, paras 19.5** and **19.6**);
(b) the last sentence of PD 52, para. 8.9 (consent for transfer to an appeal centre on a different circuit, not carried forward into current practice directions); and
(c) paras 8.13, 8.14 and 8A.1 (judges hearing appeals, now **PD 52A, paras 4.3, 4.4** and **4.5**; see **PD Insolvency Proceedings, paras 19.7** and **19.8**).

Tribunal and permission to appeal

84.12 **From a first-instance decision by a High Court judge** An appeal from an order made by a High Court judge is to the Court of Appeal in the normal way (IR 1986, r. 7.47(2)(b)). Permission to appeal must be obtained from the judge or the Court of Appeal (IR 1986, r. 7.49A(1)). The appellant must file an appellant's notice within 21 days after the date of the decision being appealed (IR 1986, r. 7.49A(2)).

84.13 **From a first-instance decision by a High Court registrar or a county court** An appeal from an order made by a county court or a registrar of the High Court lies to a single judge of the High Court (IR 1986, r. 7.47(2)(a) (winding up); Insolvency Act 1986, s. 375(2) (bankruptcy); **PD Insolvency Proceedings, para. 19.1**). Permission to appeal must be obtained from the judge or registrar who made the decision being appealed or from the High Court (IR 1986, r. 7.49A(1)).

An order made by a district judge sitting in a county court is an order made by the county court and so the only appeal is under IR 1986, r. 7.47(2), or the Insolvency Act 1986, s. 375(2), and IR 1986, r. 7.48(2), to a single judge of the High Court, not to the judge of the county court or to the Court of Appeal under the **Access to Justice Act 1999 (Destination of Appeals) Order 2000** (SI 2000/1071), arts 3(2) and 4(b) (Insolvency Act 1986, s. 375(3); *Re Langley Marketing Services Ltd* [1992] BCC 585).

A decision by a High Court judge on a first appeal may be appealed to the Court of Appeal, but only with the permission of that court (**Access to Justice Act 1999, s. 55; CPR, r. 52.13**).

Appeal against a winding-up order: security for costs

84.14 On the petitioner's application, the Court of Appeal will order a person other than the company to give security for the costs of an appeal against a winding-up order. The security should be in the nature of an indemnity. This is because, normally, the costs of an unsuccessful appeal should not be borne by the creditors or contributories of the company but by the person instigating the appeal (*Re Photographic Artists' Co-operative Supply Association* (1883) 23 ChD 370 (creditor's petition); *Re Consolidated South Rand Mines Deep Ltd* [1909] WN 66 (contributory's petition); *Re E. K. Wilson and Sons Ltd* [1972] 1 WLR 791 (contributory's petition)).

Stay of proceedings in a winding up pending appeal

84.15 It has been said that it is not the practice of the court to stay proceedings in the winding up of a company pending determination of an appeal against the winding-up order (*Re A and BC Chewing Gum Ltd* [1975] 1 WLR 579 at pp. 592–3; *Re Calahurst Ltd* [1989] BCLC 140 at p. 141). However, there are several reported cases on appeals which incidentally mention that the winding up was stayed, so the practice is not invariable (see, for example, *Re Westbourne Galleries Ltd* [1971] Ch 799 at p. 813 (contributory's petition); *Re Industrial and Commercial Securities plc* (1988) 5 BCC 320 (where the petitioner's debt had been paid after the winding-up order was made and it may be that this payment would, in itself, have justified a stay of proceedings); *Re Dollar Land (Feltham) Ltd* [1995] 2 BCLC 370 at p. 378).

LITIGATION AGAINST PERSONS SUBJECT TO INSOLVENCY PROCEEDINGS

Introduction

One of the objectives of winding up a company or administering a debtor's estate in bankruptcy is to distribute the insolvent person's free assets to unsecured creditors equally. The amount of each creditor's claim is to be settled by the liquidator or trustee in bankruptcy, subject to appeal to the court. Accordingly legal proceedings against the estate, including proceedings to execute judgments, must not be taken without the court's permission (see **84.19** and **84.26**), which will always be refused if the proceedings will upset the orderly administration and distribution of the estate (see **84.30**). Similarly the administration of a company is intended to manage the company in accordance with a plan agreed by the majority of unsecured creditors, and so legal proceedings against a company in administration can only be taken with the court's permission or the administrator's consent, so that particular creditors cannot gain any advantage over others (see **84.22**). **84.16**

Litigation against companies and individuals is also controlled while preparations are made for winding up, administration, bankruptcy, and company and individual voluntary arrangements. The different insolvency procedures are subject to two types of control:

(a) An optional power given to an insolvent person and, in the case of companies, to creditors to ask for proceedings to be stayed, either by the court in which the proceedings are pending or by the court controlling the insolvency proceedings. This power is available when:
   (i) a winding-up petition is pending (see **84.17**);
   (ii) a bankruptcy petition is pending (see **84.24**);
   (iii) an application for an interim order allowing for preparation of an individual voluntary arrangement is pending (see **84.23**);
   (iv) a bankruptcy order is in force (see **84.26**), except in relation to creditors (see (b)(vi)).
(b) A prohibition on proceedings being brought or continued without the permission of the court which is controlling the insolvency procedure. This applies when:
   (i) a provisional liquidator has been appointed (see **84.18**);
   (ii) a winding-up order has been made (see **84.19**);
   (iii) a moratorium is in force allowing preparation of a company voluntary arrangement (see **84.21**);
   (iv) an administration application is pending or notice has been filed of the appointment of an administrator out of court, or a company is in administration (see **84.22**);
   (v) an interim order is in force allowing preparation of an individual voluntary arrangement (see **84.23**);
   (vi) a bankruptcy order is in force or an interim receiver has been appointed, in relation to a creditor only (see **84.26**).

An optional power to ask the court which controls the winding up to stay proceedings is available in the voluntary liquidation of a company (see **84.20**).

Although the CPR treat a claim against a partnership as being against the firm as a single defendant, permission should be sought if any member of the partnership is subject to an insolvency proceeding (*Bank of Scotland v Breytenbach* [2012] BPIR 1 at [7]–[8]).

There are no provisions for the control of litigation against a company when an administrative receiver is appointed.

While a winding-up petition is pending

84.17 After a petition has been presented asking for the compulsory winding up of a company, but before the final hearing of the petition, an application may be made, by the company, or any creditor or contributory, for any claim or proceeding against the company to be stayed (Insolvency Act 1986, s. 126).

Applications under s. 126 to stay or restrain a pending action or proceeding against the company are made as follows:

(a) Where the action or proceeding is pending in the High Court, the application is for a stay and is made using form N244. It must be made to the master or district judge in the division or district registry (or specialist court) in which the matter is proceeding (*Re People's Garden Co.* (1875) 1 ChD 44; *Garbutt v Fawcus* (1875) 1 ChD 155; *Re Morriston Patent Fuel and Brick Co.* [1877] WN 20; *Re Artistic Colour Printing Co.* (1880) 14 ChD 502; *Re General Service Co-operative Stores* [1891] 1 Ch 496).

(b) Where the pending proceeding is an appeal to the Court of Appeal, the application is for a stay and is made to the Court of Appeal, Civil (or Criminal) Division (Insolvency Act 1986, s. 126(1)(a)). In the Civil Division the application is made using form N244 and is made to the single judge (**CPR, r. 52.16(3)(d)**).

(c) Where the pending action or proceeding is in any other tribunal (including the county courts and magistrates' courts), the application is for an order to restrain further proceedings in the action or proceeding (Insolvency Act 1986, s. 126(1)(b)). The application is made to the court having jurisdiction to wind up the company. As it is an application for an injunction it must be listed before a judge (**PD Insolvency Proceedings, para. 3.2(3)**).

An order under the Insolvency Act 1986, s. 126, will be made on an application made without notice to other parties if the applicant gives an undertaking in damages (see **37.24** to **37.26**) (*Re London and Suburban Bank Ltd* (1871) 25 LT 23; *Masbach v James Anderson and Co. Ltd* (1877) 37 LT 440).

In *Bowkett v Fullers United Electric Works Ltd* [1923] 1 KB 160 Bankes LJ said, at pp. 163–4:

> The general policy of the court in exercising this jurisdiction, when a petition has been presented which may result in a winding-up order or a scheme, is to secure that no creditor shall thenceforward gain priority over others of his class, and when an application is made to stay proceedings under [s. 126] very exceptional circumstances must exist to justify the court in refusing to accede to the application, because if the plaintiff's action is not stayed he will get payment in full while if his action is stayed he will take his place properly among other creditors of his class.... No doubt the court has a discretion whether it will stay a plaintiff's action, but it is against the policy of the court to exercise that discretion by allowing a plaintiff to proceed except in very special circumstances.

When a provisional liquidator is appointed

84.18 If, while a winding-up petition is pending against a company, a provisional liquidator is appointed, the effect on claims or proceedings against the company is the same as when a winding-up order is made, that is, they cannot proceed without the permission of the winding-up court (Insolvency Act 1986, s. 130(2); see **84.19**).

When a winding-up order has been made

84.19 When a winding-up order has been made against a company no claim or proceeding may be proceeded with or commenced against the company except by permission of the court, and subject to such terms as the court may impose (Insolvency Act 1986, s. 130(2)).

The court by which permission must be given under s. 130(2) is the court which made the winding-up order (*Wilson v Natal Investment Co.* (1867) 36 LJ Ch 312; *Thames Plate Glass Co. v Land and Sea Telegraph Construction Co.* (1871) LR 6 Ch App 643). That court will issue an injunction to prevent the continuance of any proceedings which it will not sanction (*Re Waterloo Life etc. Insurance Co. (No. 2)* (1862) 31 Beav 589; *Re International Pulp and Paper Co.* (1876) 3 ChD 594). Any judge of the High Court may exercise its jurisdiction in this respect (*Fabric Sales Ltd v Eratex Ltd* [1984] 1 WLR 863).

Permission will not be given on an application made without notice to the company (*Western and Brazilian Telegraph Co. v Bibby* (1880) 42 LT 821) other than in exceptional cases where permission is urgently required (*Fabric Sales Ltd v Eratex Ltd* [1984] 1 WLR 863 at p. 866).

When a company is in voluntary liquidation

In the voluntary liquidation of a company, an application may be made under the Insolvency Act 1986, s. 112, for the court to exercise its power to restrain or stay proceedings against the company (*Re Keynsham Co.* (1863) 33 Beav 123; *Re Life Association of England Ltd* (1864) 34 LJ Ch 64; *Re Peninsular etc. Banking Co.* (1866) 35 Beav 278; *Re East Kent Shipping Co. Ltd* (1868) 18 LT 748; *Re Paraguassu Steam Tramroad Co., Black and Co.'s Case* (1872) LR 8 Ch App 254 at p. 263). An application may be made by the liquidator or any creditor or contributory (s. 112(1)). If satisfied that it will be just and beneficial to restrain or stay the proceedings, the court may accede wholly or partially to the application on such terms and conditions as it thinks fit, or may make such other order on the application as it thinks just (s. 112(2)). An application under s. 112 concerning the voluntary winding up of a company should be made to a court having jurisdiction to wind up the company. However, it is not entirely clear whether the statutory power of the court which is invoked by an application to restrain proceedings is the s. 126 or the s. 130 power. Older cases support the view that where a claim is proceeding in the Court of Appeal or the High Court against a company in voluntary liquidation, an application under s. 126, using the CPR, Part 23, procedure may be made to the Court of Appeal or the High Court Division in which the claim is proceeding (*Walker v Banagher Distillery Co. Ltd* (1875) 1 QBD 129; *Needham v Rivers Protection and Manure Co.* (1875) 1 ChD 253). **84.20**

Commentary

Moratorium in force in relation to a company

While a moratorium under the Insolvency Act 1986, s. 1A (moratorium when directors propose a voluntary arrangement), is in force in relation to a company, no proceedings and no execution or other legal process may be commenced or continued against the company or its property, except with the permission of the court (sch. A1, para. 12(1)(h)). **84.21**

While a moratorium is in force in relation to a company no petition for the company to be wound up by the court may be presented, other than by the Secretary of State or the Financial Services Authority (sch. A1, para. 12(1)(a), (4) and (5)), and no administration application may be made (sch. A1, para. 12(1)(d)).

Administration and preparation for administration

While a company is in administration, no legal process (including legal proceedings, execution and distress) may be instituted against the company or its property except with the consent of the administrator or the permission of the court (Insolvency Act 1986, sch. B1, para. 43(1) and (6)). This protection is known as a moratorium. The same protection applies (except that only the court can give permission) during the following periods of preparation for administration (para. 44): **84.22**

(a) from when an application is made to the court for an administration order until the court's administration order takes effect or the application is dismissed;

(b) from when the holder of a floating charge files with the court a notice of intention to appoint an administrator until the appointment takes effect, provided this is within five business days;
(c) from when a notice of intention to appoint an administrator is filed with the court by the company or its directors until the appointment takes effect, provided this is within 10 business days.

Protection under para. 44 is known as an interim moratorium. It does not prevent or require the court's permission for (para. 44(7)):

(a) the presentation of a public-interest winding-up petition by the Secretary of State or the Financial Services Authority;
(b) the appointment of an administrator by the holder of a floating charge;
(c) the appointment of an administrative receiver;
(d) the carrying out by an administrative receiver of his or her functions.

Interim order in respect of an individual voluntary arrangement

84.23 While an interim order is in force, under the Insolvency Act 1986, s. 252, in respect of an individual, a moratorium is imposed so that a voluntary arrangement may be prepared for approval by creditors. The effect is that no bankruptcy petition, other proceedings, execution or other legal process may be commenced or continued against the individual, or his or her property, except with the permission of the court (s. 252(2)). Application for permission is by application in the voluntary arrangement proceedings.

While an application for an interim order in respect of an individual is pending, the court to which the application has been made may stay any action, execution or other legal process against the property or person of the individual (s. 254(1)). An application for a stay should be made by application in the voluntary arrangement proceedings. Alternatively a court in which other proceedings are pending may stay them, or allow them to continue on such terms as it thinks fit, on proof that an application for an interim order has been made by the defendant (s. 254(2)). An application under s. 254(2) should use the CPR, Part 23 procedure.

While a bankruptcy petition is pending

84.24 After a bankruptcy petition has been presented against an individual, but before the final hearing of the petition, the court in which the petition is pending may stay any action, execution or other legal process against the property or person of the individual (Insolvency Act 1986, s. 285(1)). Application for a stay under s. 285(1) is by application in the bankruptcy proceedings. Alternatively a court in which other proceedings are pending may stay them, or allow them to continue on such terms as it thinks fit, on proof that a bankruptcy petition has been presented against the defendant (s. 285(2)). An application under s. 285(2) should use the CPR, Part 23 procedure.

When an interim receiver has been appointed

84.25 When an interim receiver of an individual's property has been appointed under the Insolvency Act 1986, s. 286, the effect on other proceedings against the individual is the same as if a bankruptcy order had been made against the individual (s. 286(6); see **84.26**).

When a bankruptcy order has been made

84.26 The Insolvency Act 1986, s. 285(3), provides that, once an individual has been adjudicated bankrupt, a person who is a creditor in respect of a debt provable in the bankruptcy:

(a) does not have any remedy against the property or person of the bankrupt in respect of the debt;

(b) until the individual's discharge from bankruptcy, may not commence any claim or other legal proceedings against the bankrupt, except with the permission of the court and on such terms as the court may impose.

In addition, the provisions of s. 285(1) and (2) (see **84.24**) continue to apply after a bankruptcy order has been made. A claim for possession of property let to the bankrupt, on the ground that rent is in arrears, is not a remedy in respect of the arrears, and so is not taken away by s. 285(3) (*Sharples v Places for People Homes Ltd* [2011] EWCA Civ 813, [2012] 1 All ER 582). The debts that are provable in bankruptcy are defined in IR 1986, r. 12.3.

General principles governing the exercise of discretion to grant permission

The following paragraphs discuss the general principles which apply when permission is sought to commence or continue proceedings against a defendant who is subject to insolvency proceedings. **84.27**

Existence of discretion Whether or not a claimant is given permission to proceed is a matter for the discretion of the court (*Thames Plate Glass Co. v Land and Sea Telegraph Construction Co.* (1871) LR 6 Ch App 643; *Re Atlantic Computer Systems plc* [1992] Ch 505 at p. 523), which is free to make such order as is 'right and fair in the circumstances' (*Re Aro Co. Ltd* [1980] Ch 196 at p. 209; *Re Exchange Securities and Commodities Ltd* [1983] BCLC 186). **84.28**

Onus The onus is on the applicant to show a case for giving permission (*Re Lancashire Cotton Spinning Co., ex parte Carnelley* (1887) 35 ChD 656; *Re Higginshaw Mills and Spinning Co.* [1896] 2 Ch 544). However, on an application to restrain or stay proceedings against a company in voluntary liquidation the onus is on the applicant to show why the order should be made (*Currie v Consolidated Kent Collieries Corporation Ltd* [1906] 1 KB 134). **84.29**

Purpose of the provisions In *Re David Lloyd and Co.* (1877) 6 ChD 339 James LJ said, at p. 344, that the provisions in winding-up and bankruptcy legislation enabling the court to interfere with claims: **84.30**

> were intended, not for the purpose of harassing, or impeding, or injuring third persons, but for the purpose of preserving the limited assets of the company or bankrupt in the best way for distribution among all the persons who have claims upon them. There being only a small fund or a limited fund to be divided among a great number of persons, it would be monstrous that one or more of them should be harassing the company with actions and incurring costs which would increase the claims against the company and diminish the assets which ought to be divided among all the creditors.

See also *Langley Constructions (Brixham) Ltd v Wells* [1969] 1 WLR 503 at p. 508; *Re J. Burrows (Leeds) Ltd* [1982] 1 WLR 1177 at p. 1181.

Substantiality of claim The court should not be asked to order a liquidator or trustee in bankruptcy to waste the assets he or she is administering on defending insubstantial claims (*Re Hartlebury Printers Ltd* [1992] ICR 559). Permission will not be given to commence proceedings if there is no prospect that the court would grant the relief claimed (*Re Polly Peck International plc (No. 2)* [1998] 3 All ER 812). The test is the same as on an application for summary judgment (see **34.10**) (*Enron Metals and Commodity Ltd v HIH Casualty and General Insurance Ltd* [2005] EWHC 485 (Ch), *The Times*, 6 April 2005). The old practice was to require an affidavit from an applicant seeking permission to commence or continue proceedings verifying the claim made in the proceedings (*Re St Cuthbert's Lead Smelting Co. (No. 2)* [1866] WN 154). This practice would seem to be unnecessary now that **CPR, r. 22.1** requires every statement of case to be verified by a statement of truth. The court does not examine the merits of the applicant's case, provided it is satisfied that the claim is not clearly unsustainable (*Bristol and West Building Society v Trustee of the Property of Back* [1998] 1 BCLC 485). The question of the substantiality of the applicant's case is decided on the material presented by the applicant: the company or debtor or trustee in bankruptcy will not be granted an order for disclosure of documents to test the applicant's case (*Re Bank of Credit and Commerce International* **84.31**

Commentary

SA (No. 4) [1994] 1 BCLC 419). It is open to the court to limit permission initially to issue of the claim form and particulars of claim and service of defence, after which it can assess the nature of the claim (as in *Thames Plate Glass Co. v Land and Sea Telegraph Co.* (1870) LR 11 Eq 248).

84.32 **Appropriateness of forum** The procedure for making a claim against an insolvent person in liquidation or bankruptcy is by submitting a proof to the liquidator or trustee and, if necessary, appealing to the court in charge of the insolvency against the liquidator or trustee's decision. The advantages of this procedure to those interested in the insolvency are that claims are generally dealt with quickly and at a low cost. Usually, the essential question on an application to commence or proceed with an action or proceeding is whether the action or proceeding is a better way of dealing with the matter. Permission will not be given to bring or continue proceedings if the question at issue can just as well be resolved in the winding-up or bankruptcy proceedings (*Re St Cuthbert Lead Smelting Co.* (1866) 35 Beav 384; *Re Exchange Securities and Commodities Ltd* [1983] BCLC 186). Determining the appropriate method of dealing with the applicant's claim is the essential question on an application for permission to commence or continue proceedings against an insolvent person (*Re Bank of Credit and Commerce International SA (No. 4)* [1994] 1 BCLC 419).

Proceedings in respect of a claim for which the claimant has already put in a proof in the winding up or bankruptcy will not be allowed to continue because the claimant has elected to have the matter dealt with in the insolvency (*Craven v Blackpool Greyhound Stadium and Racecourse Ltd* [1936] 3 All ER 513).

84.33 **Insolvent person necessary party to proceedings against others or where claim is insured** Permission will normally be given for a claim or proceeding against an insolvent person if that person is a necessary defendant to a claim against another person, or the claim is insured, and the claimant undertakes not to enforce any order obtained in the claim against the insolvent person, without the insolvency court's permission (*McEwen v London Bombay and Mediterranean Bank Ltd* (1866) 15 LT 495; *Re Breech Loading Armoury Co.* [1867] WN 75; *Bristol and West Building Society v Trustee of the Property of Back* [1998] 1 BCLC 485).

Retrospective permission

84.34 The courts of England and Wales have oscillated between answering yes and no to the question: Can retrospective permission be given to commence a claim against a company after a provisional liquidator has been appointed or a winding-up order made, or against an undischarged bankrupt? In 19th-century cases the answer was yes (*Re Marine Investment Co. Ltd* (1868) 17 LT 535; *Re Wanzer Ltd* [1891] 1 Ch 305). Those cases were temporarily forgotten when retrospective permission was said to be beyond the court's powers in *Wilson v Banner Scaffolding Ltd* (1982) *The Times*, 22 June 1982, and *Re National Employers Mutual General Insurance Association Ltd* [1995] 1 BCLC 232. In the 1990s the courts returned to granting retrospective permission (*Re Saunders* [1997] Ch 60; *Bristol and West Building Society v Trustee of the Property of Back* [1998] 1 BCLC 485; *Re Linkrealm Ltd* [1998] BCC 478, in which retrospective permission was given to continue a claim which could not have been started again because of the expiry of the limitation period). However, in *Re Taylor* [2006] EWHC 3029 (Ch), [2007] Ch 150, Judge Kershaw QC held that proceedings commenced without permission are void and cannot be revived by the court giving permission retrospectively. Since then, English judges have expressed a clear preference for the view that *Re Saunders* is correct and retrospective permission can be given. Retrospective permission would have been given, if necessary, in *Godfrey v Torpy* [2007] EWHC 919 (Ch), [2007] Bus LR 1203 (a bankruptcy case), and *Gaardsoe v Optimal Wealth Management Ltd* [2012] EWHC 3266 (Ch), [2013] 2 WLR 550 (administration). In two recent cases, retrospective permission has been granted (*Bank of Scotland v Breytenbach* [2012] BPIR 1 (bankruptcy); *Bank of Ireland v Colliers International UK plc* [2012] EWHC 2942 (Ch), [2013] 2 WLR 895 (winding up)) and the judges have stated that their judgments are intended to resolve uncertainties and to establish the principle that retrospective permission may be given and so may be cited despite being given on applications which only one party attended. In both *Seal v Chief Constable of South Wales Police* [2007] UKHL 31, [2007] 1 WLR 1910 and *Adorian v Commissioner of Police of the Metropolis* [2009] EWCA Civ 18, [2009] 1 WLR 1859, it was assumed that *Re Saunders* is correct and should not be overruled, but *Re Taylor* was not cited in either case.

Defending claim by the insolvent person

If a person who has issued a claim pursues it while subject to insolvency proceedings, permission is not required for a counterclaim to the extent that the counterclaim is a defence (*Dominion Trust Co. v Brydges* (1920) 28 BCR 451; *Standard Trust Co. v Turner Crossing Inc.* (1992) 15 CBR (3d) 75), but if judgment is sought on the counterclaim for an amount exceeding the insolvent's claim then permission is required (*Langley Constructions (Brixham) Ltd v Wells* [1969] 1 WLR 503). These rules are derived from *Mersey Steel and Iron Co. v Naylor Benzon and Co.* (1882) 9 QBD 648, (1884) 9 App Cas 434, though the provisions which are now the Insolvency Act 1986, ss. 130(2) and 285(3), were not in issue in that case, and the rules remain questionable. **84.35**

Permission is not required to pursue an appeal against a judgment in favour of an insolvent person in a claim which that person has proceeded with since a winding-up or bankruptcy order (*Humber and Co. v John Griffiths Cycle Co.* (1901) 85 LT 141).

How does a party 'proceed with' a claim?

In Australia it has been held that 'not everything that happens in litigation involves a person who proceeds with litigation' (*FAI Workers Compensation (NSW) Ltd v Philkor Builders Pty Ltd* (1996) 20 ACSR 592 at p. 595): the test is whether what is done moves the litigation 'from an incipient stage to consummation' (*FAI Workers Compensation (NSW) Ltd v Philkor Builders Pty Ltd* at p. 596). So a person who has commenced proceedings against an insolvent person does not proceed with them by applying to have them dismissed (*FAI Workers Compensation (NSW) Ltd v Philkor Builders Pty Ltd* at p. 596; *Re DIM Furniture Wholesale (NSW) Pty Ltd* (1998) 28 ACSR 407), even though the application may result in the defendant being ordered to pay costs (*FAI Workers Compensation (NSW) Ltd v Philkor Builders Pty Ltd*). An application for permission to proceed with a claim is not itself a 'fresh proceeding' in the claim, because it does not, if successful, advance the claim towards completion: it merely removes a bar against taking further steps (*Re M and M Outdoor Centre Pty Ltd* (1996) 135 FLR 179). **84.36**

Costs

The costs of a successful application to proceed with a claim should be added to the costs of the claim (*Re Aro Co. Ltd* [1980] Ch 196 at p. 211). However, the costs of an application for retrospective permission must normally be paid by the applicant who failed to obtain permission at the proper time (*Re Wanzer Ltd* [1891] 1 Ch 305). **84.37**

If proceedings against a company in liquidation are necessary in order to establish and/or quantify a claim against the company, any costs which the company is ordered to pay must be proved for dividend in the winding up (*Re Poole Firebrick and Blue Clay Co.* (1873) LR 17 Eq 268; *Re Thurso New Gas Co.* (1889) 42 ChD 486; *Re British Gold Fields of West Africa* [1899] 2 Ch 7). But if the company is ordered to pay the costs of proceedings which the liquidator has chosen to carry on in the hope of benefiting the company then the costs are payable in full as an expense of the liquidation (*Re Trent and Humber Ship-building Co., Bailey and Leetham's Case* (1869) LR 8 Eq 94; *Re Wenborn and Co.* [1905] 1 Ch 413). The principles are the same whether the winding up is voluntary or by the court (*Re Pacific Coast Syndicate Ltd* [1913] 2 Ch 26). The costs that are recoverable in full include costs incurred before the commencement of the winding up (*Re London Drapery Stores* [1898] 2 Ch 684; *Norglen Ltd v Reeds Rains Prudential Ltd* [1999] 2 AC 1 at p. 21).

Commentary

When proceedings by a creditor are halted by the Insolvency Act 1986, s. 130(2), the creditor is entitled to prove for the costs of the proceedings up to the time that s. 130(2) took effect (*Re Welsh Potosi Mining Co., ex parte Tobin* (1858) 28 LJ Ch 44).

LITIGATION IN WINDING UP

84.38 As far as possible, litigation by or against a company being wound up is to be conducted within the winding-up proceedings. A claim against the company must be submitted to the liquidator, who will decide whether to accept it in whole or part, subject to appeal to the court. The Insolvency Act 1986, ss. 212 (see **84.39**), 213 and 214 (see **84.40**), and sch. B1, para. 75 (see **84.39**), allow some claims of a company in liquidation to be brought by application in the winding-up proceedings, with a consequent saving in court fees, and authorise the company's liquidator and other persons to make such an application.

Misfeasance proceedings

84.39 The Insolvency Act 1986, s. 212 and sch. B1, para. 75, provide that some claims by a company which is being wound up may be pursued by an application in the winding-up proceedings. Applications under these provisions are known as 'misfeasance proceedings' and they are an optional alternative to an ordinary claim. There are limits on which defendants and which causes of action may be pursued in misfeasance proceedings.

By s. 212(1), the only persons against whom misfeasance proceedings may be taken under s. 212 are persons who:

(a) are, or have been, officers of the company;
(b) have acted as liquidator or administrative receiver of the company; or
(c) are, or have been, concerned, or have taken part, in the promotion, formation or management of the company.

The only causes of action which may be pursued in s. 212 misfeasance proceedings are those which allege that the defendant has misapplied or retained, or become accountable for, any money or other property of the company, or has been guilty of any misfeasance or breach of any fiduciary or other duty in relation to the company (s. 212(1)). Where the defendant has acted as liquidator of the company, this includes any misfeasance or breach of duty in connection with the carrying on of his or her functions as liquidator (s. 212(2)).

Schedule B1, para. 75, makes the same provision in relation to proceedings against a person who:

(a) is, or purports to be, the administrator of the company; or
(b) has been, or has purported to be, its administrator (sch. B1, para. 75(1)).

An application under s. 212 may be made by the official receiver, the company's liquidator or any creditor or contributory of the company (s. 212(3)). An application under sch. B1, para. 75, may be made by any of those persons or by the company's administrator (sch. B1, para. 75(2)), and may be made if the company is in administration without being wound up.

The permission of the court must be obtained for an application:

(a) by a contributory under s. 212 (but not under sch. B1, para. 75) (s. 212(5));
(b) against a liquidator or administrator who has been released or discharged from liability (s. 212(4); sch. B1, para. 75(6)).

If a claim in the name of a company in liquidation is brought against an officer etc. of the company, the court may convert it into misfeasance proceedings by substituting the liquidator (or other authorised applicant) for the company as claimant, under **CPR, r. 19.2(4)**, and allowing consequential amendments (*Parkinson Engineering Services plc v Swan* [2009] EWCA Civ 1366, [2010] Bus LR 857). In *Parkinson Engineering Services plc v Swan* the claim was against a former administrator and the court made the substitution after the expiry of the limitation period, as the claim could not properly be continued because it was barred by the previous discharge of the administrator under what is now the Insolvency Act 1986, sch. B1, para. 98, and that bar could be disapplied only in misfeasance proceedings (sch. B1, para. 75(6)). It was crucial to the exercise of the power under **CPR, r. 19.5(3)(b)** that the switch from Part 7 claim to misfeasance proceedings involved no change in the cause of action or the facts to be asserted.

Fraudulent and wrongful trading

The Insolvency Act 1986, ss. 213 and 214, provide causes of action which can be asserted only **84.40**
in the course of the winding up of a company, and only by an application by the liquidator. An application under s. 213 may be made against any persons who were knowingly parties to the carrying on of any business of the company with intent to defraud creditors (of the company or any other person), or for any fraudulent purpose. An application under s. 214 may be made against a person if (s. 214(2)):

(a) the company has gone into insolvent liquidation (defined in s. 214(6));
(b) at some time before the commencement of the winding up of the company that person knew or ought to have concluded that there was no reasonable prospect that the company would avoid going into insolvent liquidation; and
(c) that person was a director of the company at that time.

Chapter 85 Applications under the Companies Acts and Related Legislation

INTRODUCTION

Jurisdiction to hear applications under the Companies Acts

85.1 The Companies Act 2006, like its predecessors going back to the Joint Stock Companies Act 1856, enables the incorporation of companies by registration with the Registrar of Companies in England and Wales.

In the Companies Act 2006, s. 2, the term 'the Companies Acts' is defined to mean:

(a) parts 1 to 39 of the 2006 Act;
(b) the provisions of part 45 to 47 of the Act (which are mainly formal) in so far as they apply for the purposes of parts 1 to 39;
(c) the Companies (Audit, Investigations and Community Enterprise) Act 2004, part 2 (community interest companies);
(d) the provisions of the Companies Act 1985 that remain in force (from 1 October 2009, this is just parts 14 and 15, which deal with investigation of companies and their affairs, the short title and some provisions relating to Scotland);
(e) the provisions of the Companies Consolidation (Consequential Provisions) Act 1985 that remain in force (the Consequential Provisions Act was completely repealed on 1 October 2009).

The Companies Acts have numerous provisions for applications to be made to 'the court' to deal with various types of question relating to the internal affairs of companies. In England and Wales, 'the court' means the High Court or a county court to which jurisdiction under the Companies Acts has been allocated by the Lord Chancellor (Companies Act 2006, s. 1156). High Court proceedings under the enactments relating to companies are assigned to the Chancery Division by the Senior Courts Act 1981, sch. 1, para. 1. The county courts with jurisdiction in companies matters are the same as those with insolvency jurisdiction (see **82.8**).

Unlike the insolvency jurisdiction, there is no limit to the size of company for which an application under the Companies Acts or related legislation may be made to a county court.

Purpose of applications under the Companies Acts

Some of the Companies Acts provisions for applications to the court are for the resolution of particular kinds of internal dispute, for example, the Companies Act 2006, s. 125, on the rectification of a register of members and ss. 994 to 999, on the relief of unfairly prejudicial conduct of a company's affairs. Others enable a company to obtain court orders to assist in the administration of its affairs, for example, ss. 895 to 901 on court-sanctioned arrangements and reconstructions and s. 794 on freezing orders to enable a public company to discover who has interests in its shares. Some provisions give the court a supervisory power, for example, the requirement that a public company cannot reduce its capital without court permission (s. 641(1)). Others enable the court to support BIS's supervisory and investigatory powers, for example, the Companies Act 1985, s. 436, on punishment, for contempt of court, of persons failing to assist investigations. **85.2**

Procedural rules on litigation concerning the affairs of companies

All proceedings under the Companies Acts 1985 and 2006 are governed by **PD 49A**, apart from derivative claims under the Companies Act 2006, part 11, chapter 1 (see **14.27** and **14.28**), and petitions for protection of members against unfair prejudice (ss. 994 to 999; see **85.9** to **85.20**) (see **PD 49A, para. 2**). There are further rules of practice in the Chancery Guide, ch. 20. **85.3**

PD 49A also applies (by **paras 2** and **3**) to:

(a) Any proceedings under the Companies Act 1985 or the Companies Act 2006 as they apply to limited liability partnerships by virtue of the Limited Liability Partnerships Regulations 2001 (SI 2001/1090) or the Limited Liability Partnerships (Application of Companies Act 2006) Regulations 2009 (SI 2009/1804).

(b) Any proceedings under the Financial Services and Markets Act 2000, part 7 (transfers of banking and insurance businesses). These proceedings must be started in the High Court (Financial Services and Markets Act 2000, s. 107(4)).

(c) Any proceedings under Regulation (EC) No. 2157/2001, arts 22, 25 or 26 (appointment of independent expert or scrutiny of legality of merger of companies to form an SE). These proceedings are the subject of **PD 49A, paras 19, 20** and **21**.

(d) Any proceedings under the Companies (Cross-Border Mergers) Regulations 2007 (SI 2007/2974). These proceedings are the subject of **PD 49A, paras 22** to **25**.

(e) Any proceedings under the Criminal Justice and Police Act 2001, s. 59, for return of property seized in the exercise of the power conferred by the Companies Act 1985, s. 448(3) (warrant to seize documents requisitioned under part 14 of the 1985 Act), either on its own or as extended by s. 50 of the 2001 Act (power to seize material so as to assess whether it is what is sought or which is inseparable from material which is sought). These proceedings are the subject of **PD 49A, para. 26**.

Proceedings in relation to companies' affairs are brought not only under the Companies Acts, but also under the Insolvency Act 1986 under a completely separate set of rules, which have their own forms of originating process (see **chapters 82** and **84**). The court's jurisdiction to deal with a company's affairs on an application under the Companies Acts or the Insolvency Act 1986 arises only by virtue of the statutes and is limited to the matters mentioned in the various provisions authorising applications to be made. Any claim by or against a company which is not within those provisions must be pursued by some other form of litigation, such as a claim in equity, contract or tort. Where an application is brought under the Companies Acts and in a related case in the Chancery Division at the same time, special arrangements can be made, on request to the Chancery Judges' Listing Officer, for the applications to be heard by the same judge (Chancery Guide, para. 20.22).

PROCEEDINGS UNDER THE COMPANIES ACTS

Commencement under Part 7 or Part 8

85.4 All proceedings to which **PD 49A** applies must be commenced by Part 8 claim form (**PD 49A, para.** 5(1)), except for the following, which must be commenced by Part 7 claim form:

(a) an application under the Companies Act 2006, s. 370 (claim by members of a company in its name for a remedy for breach of the provisions requiring members' approval of political donations and expenditure) (**PD 49A, para. 11**);

(b) an application under the Companies Act 2006, s. 955 (for an order to secure compliance with the City Code or with a requirement under s. 947 to disclose documents or information to the Panel on Takeovers and Mergers) (**PD 49A, para. 16**);

(c) an application under the Companies Act 2006, s. 968(6) (for compensation for breach of an agreement which has been invalidated by a takeover bid because the company is opted into the provisions overriding takeover barriers) (**PD 49A, para. 17**).

In the High Court the claim form must be issued out of the office of the Companies Court Registrar or a Chancery district registry; in the county court it will be issued out of a county court office (**para.** 5(2)).

For proceedings started by Part 8 claim form, the provisions of **CPR, Part 8** apply, except where modified by **PD 49A** or any other practice direction (**PD 49A, para. 5(1)(b)**).

Title of proceedings

85.5 Every claim form starting proceedings to which **PD 49A** applies (except proceedings under the Criminal Justice and Police Act 2001) must be entitled in the matter of the company in question and in the matter of the relevant Act (**PD 49A, para.** 4(1)). The same applies to all affidavits, witness statements, notices and other documents in the proceedings.

Where a company changes its name in the course of proceedings, the title must be altered by substituting the new name for the old, and inserting the old name in brackets at the end of the title (**PD 49A, para.** 4(2)).

Parties

85.6 If the company concerned is not the claimant in a claim under the Companies Act 2006, it should be made a defendant to the claim, unless the court orders otherwise (**PD 49A, para.** 7(1)). Where an application is made in proceedings to which the company concerned is, or is required to be, a defendant, the company must be made a respondent to the application unless the court orders otherwise (**para.** 7(2)). **Paragraph** 7 does not apply where different provision is made by any other enactment, the CPR or another practice direction.

A claim commenced by the company concerned need not have a defendant if it is under:

(a) the Companies Act 2006, part 26 (arrangements and reconstructions) or part 27 (mergers and divisions of public companies) (**PD 49A, para.** 15);

(b) Regulation (EC) No. 2157/2001, art. 25 or art. 26 (**PD 49A, paras 19(4)** and **21(2)**);

(c) the Companies (Cross-Border Mergers) Regulations 2007 (SI 2007/2974), reg. 6 or reg. 16 (**PD 49A, paras** 23(2) and 25(3)).

Service

85.7 The parties are responsible for service of documents in proceedings to which **PD 49A** applies (*PD 49A, para. 28*).

For some types of claim, **PD 49A** requires notification of the claim to specific persons. This means that, unless the court orders otherwise, the person must be sent a copy of the claim form as soon as reasonably practicable after the claim form has been issued (**PD 49A, para.** 5(3)). The proceedings concerned are:

(a) an application for an order under the Companies Act 2006, s. 169(5) (**PD 49A, para. 8**);
(b) an application for an order under the Companies Act 2006, s. 295 or 317 (**PD 49A, para. 10**);
(c) an application for a declaration under the Companies Act 2006, s. 456(1) (**PD 49A, para. 12**);
(d) an application for an order under the Companies Act 2006, s. 511(6), 514(7), 515(7) or 518(9) (**PD 49A, para. 13**);
(e) an application for an order under the Companies Act 2006, s. 527(5) (**PD 49A, para. 14**).

An application under the Companies Act 2006, s. 1132 (production and inspection of books where offence suspected), may be made without notice to any person against whom an order is sought (**PD 49A, para. 18**).

Other rules for specific types of claim

There are specific rules relating to: **85.8**

(a) an application for an order under the Companies Act 2006, part 26 or part 27, to sanction a compromise or arrangement (**PD 49A, para. 15**);
(b) an application to confirm a reduction in capital (**PD 49A, para. 27**).

UNFAIR PREJUDICE

Statutory provision

Section 994 of the Companies Act 2006 entitles a member of a company to apply to the court **85.9** by petition for an order giving relief in respect of conduct of the company's affairs which is unfairly prejudicial to the interests of its members generally or of some part of its members (including at least the petitioner), or any actual or proposed act which is or would be so prejudicial.

Procedural rules

The Companies (Unfair Prejudice Applications) Proceedings Rules 2009 (SI 2009/2469) **85.10** apply to all proceedings under the Companies Act 2006, s. 994. The CPR apply to proceedings on an unfair prejudice petition, with any necessary modifications, except so far as they are inconsistent with the Companies Act 2006 or SI 2009/2469 (SI 2009/2469, r. 2(2)). The procedure provided by SI 2009/2469 follows the procedure for contributories' winding-up petitions (see **82.66** to **82.74**). An unfair prejudice petition may seek a winding up by the court as an alternative remedy, though **PD 49B, para. 1** says that it is undesirable to do that as a matter of course: 'The petition should not ask for a winding-up order unless that is the relief which the petitioner prefers or it is thought that it may be the only relief to which the petitioner is entitled'.

The requirement that an application under the Companies Act 2006, s. 994, must be made by petition is imposed by statute and so the court has no power under the CPR to waive a failure to comply with it (*Re Osea Road Camp Sites Ltd* [2004] EWHC 2437 (Ch), [2005] 1 WLR 760).

Form and contents of petition

The prescribed form for a petition under the Companies Act 2006, s. 994, is set out in the **85.11** schedule to SI 2009/2469 and is to be used with such variations, if any, as the circumstances may require (SI 2009/2469, r. 3(1)). The petition must specify the grounds on which it is presented and the nature of the relief which is sought by the petitioner (SI 2009/2469, r. 3(2)).

The extensive powers of the court to make orders on an unfair prejudice petition are set out in the Companies Act 2006, s. 996. The relief sought must be appropriate to the conduct of which the petition complains (*Re J. E. Cade and Son Ltd* [1992] BCLC 213 at p. 223), though it need not be directed solely towards remedying the particular things that have happened (*Re Hailey Group Ltd* [1993] BCLC 459 at p. 472). The court is required to make the order that is appropriate at the time of the hearing (*Re Hailey Group Ltd* at p. 472).

If a winding-up order is asked for, the petition must comply with **PD 49B** on orders under the Insolvency Act 1986, s. 127, sanctioning transactions by the company while the petition is pending.

The petition must state the names of persons on whom it is intended to serve the petition (known as the 'respondents'), one of whom will be the company itself.

There is no provision for verification of an unfair prejudice petition by affidavit or statement of truth.

Filing the petition and fixing a return day

85.12 An unfair prejudice petition must be delivered to the court for filing with copies for service on all the respondents (including the company itself) named in the petition (SI 2009/2469, r. 3(2)). The court will fix a hearing for a day (called the 'return day') on which, unless the court otherwise directs, the petitioner and any respondent (including the company) must attend for directions to be given in relation to the procedure on the petition (SI 2009/2469, r. 3(3)).

A fee of £220 must be paid on filing a petition (**CPFO, fee 3.3**).

Service of the petition

85.13 The petitioner must, at least 14 days before the return day, serve a sealed copy of the petition on all respondents named in the petition (including the company itself) (SI 2009/2469, r. 4). The applicable rules on service are those of **CPR, Part 6**. If the petition also prays for a winding up, there must be personal service in accordance with **CPR, rr. 6.5(3)** and **6.22(3)** (see **82.70**).

Directions

85.14 SI 2009/2469, r. 5, requires the court, on the return day, or at any time after it, to give such directions as it thinks appropriate with respect to the following matters:

(a) service of the petition, whether in connection with the venue for a further hearing, or for any other purpose;
(b) whether particulars of claim and defence are to be delivered;
(c) whether, and if so by what means, the petition is to be advertised;
(d) the manner in which any evidence is to be adduced at any hearing before the judge and in particular:
  (i) the taking of evidence wholly or in part by affidavit or witness statements or orally;
  (ii) the cross-examination of any deponents to affidavits or witness statements;
  (iii) the matters to be dealt with in evidence;
(e) any other matter affecting the procedure on the petition or in connection with the hearing and disposal of the petition;
(f) such orders, if any, including a stay for any period, as the court thinks fit, with a view to mediation or other form of alternative dispute resolution.

The registrar should consider directing the parties and/or their advisers to meet with a view to *narrowing the issues*, identifying what issues are really important, what issues are really in dispute, how those issues are to be resolved or proved, and resolving and narrowing any other matters which in the context of the particular petition could reasonably be expected to be narrowed (*Re Rotadata Ltd* [2000] 1 BCLC 122 at p. 127).

Interim orders

The court will grant interim injunctions to preserve the status quo if, but only if, departure from the status quo might affect the remedy sought in an unfair prejudice petition (*Callard v Pringle* [2007] EWCA Civ 1075, [2008] 2 BCLC 505). See, for example, *Re a Company (No. 002612 of 1984)* [1985] BCLC 80; *Re Sticky Fingers Restaurant Ltd* [1992] BCLC 84; *Re a Company (No. 003061 of 1993)* [1994] BCC 883; *Incasep Ltd v Jones* [2002] EWCA Civ 961, [2003] BCC 226. An interim injunction will not be granted unless the court considers that the petition has a real prospect of success (*Re X Ltd* (2001) *The Times*, 5 June 2001). 85.15

In proceedings on an unfair prejudice petition the court does not have jurisdiction to order an interim payment under **CPR, Part 25** (*Re a Company (No. 004175 of 1986)* [1987] 1 WLR 585; *Re a Company (No. 004502 of 1988)* [1991] BCC 234). The court will not make a freezing order against any party to an unfair prejudice petition, unless it alleges what amounts to a cause of action against that party (*Re Premier Electronics (GB) Ltd* [2002] 2 BCLC 634). An interim injunction prohibiting the company from paying a director remuneration which has not been authorised may be made without joining the director as a party (*Riener v Gershinson* [2004] EWHC 76 (Ch), [2004] 2 BCLC 376).

A minority member of a company who is petitioning under the Companies Act 2006, s. 994, may also be frustrating the holding of general meetings, by refusing to attend so that any meeting will be inquorate, so as to prevent prejudicial resolutions being adopted. The majority may apply under s. 306 for an order convening a meeting with the usual quorum rules suspended. The court hearing the s. 306 application will take into account the existence of s. 994 proceedings when deciding whether to make an order under s. 306 (*Re Sticky Fingers Restaurant Ltd*; *Re Whitchurch Insurance Consultants Ltd* [1993] BCLC 1359; *Re Woven Rugs Ltd* [2002] 1 BCLC 324).

Unlike a winding-up petition, it is not necessary to strike out an unfair prejudice petition where there is a dispute about the petitioner's standing: an unfair prejudice petition may be stayed to enable the petitioner to establish standing (*Re Starlight Developers Ltd* [2007] EWHC 1660 (Ch), [2007] BCC 929).

Stay in favour of arbitration

The Court of Appeal has now upheld the effectiveness of an arbitration agreement which covers the disputes giving rise to an unfair prejudice petition (*Fulham Football Club (1987) Ltd v Richards* [2011] EWCA Civ 855, [2012] Ch 833, overruling *Exeter City Association Football Club Ltd v Football Conference Ltd* [2004] EWHC 2304 (Ch), [2004] 1 WLR 2910, and disagreeing with the Northern Ireland Court of Appeal in *Re Wine Inns Ltd* [2000] NIJB 343). This means a party to the arbitration agreement who is made a party to the proceedings on the petition can apply to the court under the Arbitration Act 1996, s. 9, for proceedings on the petition to be stayed so that the matter can be dealt with by arbitration instead of by the court. The Court of Appeal held that an arbitrator is capable of deciding whether there has been unfair prejudice (at [77]). However, it is possible that in some cases an arbitrator will not be able to order suitable remedies, particularly if they involve persons who are not party to the arbitration agreement. In such a case it would be necessary to make an application to the court to make suitable orders in the light of the arbitrator's findings. 85.16

In the light of the decision in *Fulham Football Club (1987) Ltd v Richards*, it is likely that many private companies will want to include arbitration agreements in their constitutions so that future disputes will be settled by arbitration rather than by petitioning the court under the Companies Act 2006, s. 994.

Commentary

Amendment

85.17 An unfair prejudice petition may be amended to add an instance of alleged prejudicial conduct which has occurred since the petition was presented (*Cobden Investments Ltd v RWM Langport Ltd* [2007] EWHC 3048 (Ch), LTL 4/1/2008).

Costs

85.18 It is a misapplication of the company's money to pay any costs of proceedings on an unfair prejudice petition (other than as ordered by the court), except for those necessarily incurred in representing the company as a separate person (*Re Kenyon Swansea Ltd* [1987] BCLC 514; *Re Elgindata Ltd* [1991] BCLC 959). The court may order the company to indemnify the petitioner for the costs of obtaining an order in favour of the company as a separate person (*Clark v Cutland* [2003] EWCA Civ 810, [2004] 1 WLR 783). The company may provide a qualifying third party indemnity, as permitted by the Companies Act 2006, s. 234, to a director who successfully defends an allegation of negligence, default, breach of duty or breach of trust contained in an unfair prejudice petition (*Branch v Bagley* [2004] EWHC 426 (Ch), LTL 10/3/2004).

The court will issue an interim injunction to prevent misapplication of the company's assets on funding a defence to a petition. It may also restrain expenditure on other proceedings started against the petitioner which concern the same issues, if they were started in response to the petition (*Pollard v Pollard* (2007) LTL 26/9/2007).

Court's order

85.19 If the court is satisfied that the applicant's petition is well founded it is empowered by the Companies Act 2006, s. 996(1), to make such order as it thinks fit for giving relief in respect of the matters complained of. More particularly, under s. 996(2), the court may:

(a) regulate the conduct of the company's affairs in the future; this could include ordering an alteration of the company's memorandum or articles or preventing the company from making any, or any specified, alteration to the memorandum or articles without the court's permission;

(b) require the company to refrain from doing or continuing an act complained of by the petitioner or to do an act which the petitioner has complained it has omitted to do;

(c) authorise civil proceedings to be brought in the name and on behalf of the company by such person or persons and on such terms as the court may direct;

(d) require the company not to make any, or any specified, alterations in its articles without the leave of the court;

(e) provide for the purchase of the shares of any members of the company by other members or by the company itself and, in the case of a purchase by the company itself, the reduction of the company's capital accordingly.

The court has jurisdiction to make orders against persons who are not members of the company or who are not involved in the conduct complained of (provided they have been made parties to the proceedings), but it is inconceivable that the court would order a person who was not a member of the company to buy the petitioner's shares (*Re Little Olympian Each-ways Ltd* [1994] 2 BCLC 420).

The court has a power under s. 996(1) to make such orders as it considers will enable the company, for the future, to be properly run, and for its affairs to be under the conduct of somebody who the shareholders generally can be confident will conduct the affairs of the company properly (*Re a Company (No. 00789 of 1987)* [1990] BCLC 384 per Harman J at p. 395, followed in *Re Hailey Group Ltd* [1993] BCLC 459).

The rule that he who comes to equity must come with clean hands does not apply to unfair prejudice petitions. In other words, a petitioner's own misconduct is not in itself a reason for rejecting the petition, though it may show that the petitioner was not unfairly prejudiced or may affect the remedy given by the court (*Re London School of Electronics Ltd* [1986] Ch 211; *Richardson v Blackmore* [2005] EWCA Civ 1356, [2006] BCC 276).

The most common order is that the majority shareholders must buy the petitioner's shares. Exceptionally, in *Re Brenfield Squash Racquets Club Ltd* [1996] 2 BCLC 184 the majority shareholder was ordered to sell its shares to the petitioner.

If it is plain that the appropriate solution to the situation which the petitioner is complaining about is sale of the petitioner's shares, if other members of the company are willing to buy them, and if the articles provide a procedure for determining the price to be paid on a sale from one member to another, that procedure should be adopted, instead of petitioning under s. 994. A petition is appropriate, for the purpose of obtaining the court's valuation of the shares, if there is any risk that the procedure provided by the articles will undervalue them (*Re a Company (No. 00330 of 1991)* [1991] BCLC 597). However, if an offer is made which proposes a genuinely independent valuation, the court will strike out the petition as an abuse of process: the petitioner is not entitled to insist on the court carrying out a valuation which can be performed more cheaply by an accountant (*Re a Company (No. 00836 of 1995)* [1996] 2 BCLC 192).

There is a helpful discussion of what counts as a reasonable offer to purchase a petitioner's shares in *O'Neill v Phillips* [1999] 1 WLR 1092 at pp. 1107–8. An offer is not reasonable if the offeror cannot finance it (*West v Blanchet* [2000] 1 BCLC 795). In many cases the petitioner contends that the value of the shares has been diminished by the conduct complained of in the petition and some way has to be found for a valuer to take this into account. If the value of the shares depends on the answer to a question of law, the question should be left for the court to decide (*North Holdings Ltd v Southern Tropics Ltd* [1999] 2 BCLC 625).

A Tomlin order (see **63.16**) should not be made if the petition asked alternatively for the winding up of the company (*Re a Company (No. 003324 of 1979)* [1981] 1 WLR 1059).

Notification of the court's order

If the court considers that an order it has made in unfair prejudice proceedings should be advertised, it must give directions as to the manner and time of advertisement (SI 2009/2469, r. 6). **85.20**

Chapter 86 Director Disqualification

STATUTORY PROVISIONS

Nature of a disqualification order

86.1 The Company Directors Disqualification Act 1986 (CDDA 1986) enables the civil and criminal courts to protect the public by making disqualification orders which ban persons from acting as company directors when it is shown that they are unfit to do so.

By CDDA 1986, s. 1(1), the main practical effect of a disqualification order is that the person against whom the order is made must not, without leave of a court (see **86.38**), be a director of a company or in any way, whether directly or indirectly, be concerned or take part in the management of a company, for the duration of the order. The person is also banned from being concerned or taking part, in any way, whether directly or indirectly, in the promotion or formation of a company, from acting as receiver of a company's property or from acting as an insolvency practitioner.

A disqualification undertaking (see **86.4**) has the same effect as a disqualification order but is made without court proceedings.

The acts which a disqualified person is prohibited from doing are listed in two paragraphs in s. 1(1), but the only form of disqualification order which may be made is one disqualifying a person from doing all the things listed: it is not possible to disqualify from only a selection of them (*Official Receiver v Hannan* [1997] 2 BCLC 473; *R v Cole* [1998] 1 BCLC 234; *Re Adbury Park Estates Ltd* [2003] BCC 696). It is not possible to make a disqualification order limited to a particular class of companies, such as public companies (*R v Ward* (2001) *The Times*, 10 August 2001). Disqualification orders are not confined to individuals: companies may also be disqualified from being directors (*Official Receiver v Brady* [1999] BCC 258).

Acting in contravention of a disqualification order is an offence triable either way (CDDA 1986, s. 13). In addition a person who contravenes a disqualification order by being a director of a company, or being concerned, whether directly or indirectly, or taking part, in the management of a company, may be made personally liable for all debts and liabilities of the company incurred while so acting (CDDA 1986, s. 15(1)(a), (3)(a) and (4)). A person liable under s. 15 is jointly and severally liable with the company itself and with any other person who is also jointly and severally liable for the debts (whether under s. 15 or some other provision) (CDDA 1986, s. 15(2)).

In CDDA 1986, 'company' means not only registered companies, but all unregistered companies capable of being wound up under part 5 of the Insolvency Act 1986 (see **82.1**) (CDDA 1986, s. 22(2) and (9)). This includes partnerships (Insolvent Partnerships Order 1994 (SI 1994/2421)) and it is submitted that it was wrong for Rattee J to suggest in *Secretary of State for Trade and Industry v Barnett* [1998] 2 BCLC 64 at p. 70 that a disqualified person could run a business in partnership with his wife. CDDA 1986 is applied, with modifications, to limited liability partnerships by the Limited Liability Partnerships Regulations 2001 (SI 2001/1090), reg. 4(2).

Grounds for disqualification

The circumstances in which a disqualification order may be made are summarised in table 86.1. **86.2**

The vast majority of disqualification orders are made under CDDA 1986, s. 6, and this chapter will concentrate on applications under s. 7 for orders under s. 6 and applications under s. 8 (which have many similarities to those under s. 7).

In ss. 6 to 9A, 'director' includes a shadow director (ss. 9E(5) and 22(4)) and 'shadow director' is defined in s. 22(5) in the same way as it is defined in the Companies Act 2006, s. 251. The definition of shadow director is discussed in *Secretary of State for Trade and Industry v Deverell* [2001] Ch 340.

CDDA 1986 also extends to directors and officers of building societies (s. 22A) and incorporated friendly societies (s. 22B), to officers of insolvent partnerships (Insolvent Partnerships Order 1994, art. 16 and sch. 8), and to members of limited liability partnerships (Limited Liability Partnerships Regulations 2001 (SI 2001/1090), reg. 4(2)(g)).

Purpose of disqualification under sections 6 and 8

In *Re Sevenoaks Stationers (Retail) Ltd* [1991] Ch 164 Dillon LJ said, at p. 176: **86.3**

> It is beyond dispute that the purpose of CDDA 1986, s. 6, is to protect the public, and in particular potential creditors of companies, from losing money through companies becoming insolvent when the directors of those companies are people unfit to be concerned in the management of a company.

See also *Re Lo-Line Electric Motors Ltd* [1988] Ch 477; *Re Westmid Packing Services Ltd* [1998] 2 All ER 124 at p. 131. Protection is not necessarily limited to the British public (*Re Westminster Property Management Ltd (No. 2)* [2001] BCC 305 at p. 358).

A further, related purpose is to raise standards of responsibility among those who make use of limited liability (per Nicholls V-C in *Secretary of State for Trade and Industry v Ettinger* [1993] BCLC 896 at p. 899). This was described by Scott V-C in *Re Barings plc* [1998] BCC 583 at p. 590 as subsidiary to the main purpose of protection of the public.

Table 86.1 Circumstances in which a disqualification order may be made

Section of CDDA 1986	Circumstance	Court which may make order	Who may apply for order	Period of disqualification
s. 2	Conviction of an indictable offence in connection with the promotion, formation, management, liquidation or striking off of a company, with the receivership of a company's property or with being an administrative receiver of a company.	(a) Convicting court, or (b) court with jurisdiction to wind up any company in relation to which offence was committed.	(a) Court's own motion. (b) See note 1.	Up to 15 years (five if made by magistrates' court).
s. 3	Persistent default in filing returns, accounts or other documents	Court with jurisdiction to wind up any company in relation to which default committed.	See note 1.	Up to five years.
s. 4	Fraud or fraudulent trading revealed in winding up.	Court with jurisdiction to wind up any company in relation to which fraud was committed.	See note 1.	Up to 15 years.
s. 5	Three convictions for failure to file documents with registrar.	Convicting court.	Court's own motion.	Up to five years.
s. 6	Conduct while director of a company which has become insolvent shows unfitness.	See 86.6.	Secretary of State, see note 2.	Two to 15 years.
s. 8	After investigation of company.	High Court.	Secretary of State.	Up to 15 years.
s. 9A	Competition disqualification order.	High Court.	OFT or a specified regulator.	Up to 15 years.
s. 10	Participation in wrongful trading.	Court which finds wrongful trading.	Court's own motion.	Up to 15 years.

Note 1. The persons who may apply for an order under s. 2, 3 or 4 are (by s. 16(2)) the Secretary of State or the official receiver, or the liquidator or any past or present member or creditor of any company in relation to which the offence or other default was committed or is alleged to have been committed. An applicant must have a legitimate interest in having the defendant disqualified (Re Adbury Park Estates Ltd [2003] BCC 696).

Note 2. The application is made under s. 7. If the company which became insolvent is being or has been wound up by the court, the Secretary of State may direct the official receiver to apply (s. 7(1)).

In *Re Blackspur Group plc* [1998] 1 WLR 422 the Court of Appeal said, at p. 426:

The purpose of [CDDA 1986] is the protection of the public, by means of prohibitory remedial action, by anticipated deterrent effect on further misconduct and by encouragement of higher standards of honesty and diligence in corporate management, from those who are unfit to be concerned in the management of a company.

See also per Sir Andrew Park in *Re Morija plc* [2007] EWHC 3055 (Ch), [2008] 2 BCLC 313, at [33]. Other judges at first instance have taken raising standards to be the primary purpose of disqualification: see Lawrence Collins J in *Re Bradcrown Ltd* [2001] 1 BCLC 547 at p. 550 (apparently misreading the mention of it in *Re Westmid Packing Services Ltd* at p. 129 as a statement by the court of the law whereas in fact it was only a summary of counsel's argument) and Peter Smith J in *Re J. A. Chapman and Co. Ltd* [2003] EWHC 532 (Ch), [2003] 2 BCLC 206 at [9]. That this is the primary purpose may be indicated by the rule that, if unfitness is proved, a disqualification order must be made under s. 6 (which requires a disqualification period of at least two years), whether or not the court thinks that the defendant is a danger to the public (*Re Grayan Building Services Ltd* [1995] Ch 241).

The purpose of a disqualification order is not to mete out retribution for aggrieved creditors (*Re Cubelock Ltd* [2001] BCC 523 at p. 536).

DISQUALIFICATION UNDERTAKINGS

Instead of applying to the court under CDDA 1986, s. 7 or s. 8, for an order disqualifying a person from being a director, since 2 April 2001 it has been possible for the Secretary of State to accept from the person a disqualification undertaking, if expedient in the public interest (ss. 7(2A) and 8(2A)). Instead of applying under s. 9A for a competition disqualification order the OFT or a specified regulator may, under s. 9B, accept a disqualification undertaking. A disqualification undertaking is an undertaking by a person not to do any of the things which are prohibited by a disqualification order, for a specified period of time. (ss. 1A and 9B). Sections 13 and 15 apply to disqualification undertakings as well as disqualification orders, so that the penalties for breaching an undertaking are the same as for acting contrary to a disqualification order. **86.4**

Giving a disqualification undertaking because of inability to fund a trial is not the result of a violation of the European Convention on Human Rights, **art. 6(1)**, in the **Human Rights Act 1998, sch. 1**, and is not a ground for setting aside the undertaking (*Secretary of State for Trade and Industry v Davies* [2006] EWHC 299 (Ch), [2006] 2 BCLC 489).

The Secretary of State refuses to accept a disqualification undertaking unless it is accompanied by an agreed statement of the facts which showed the person's unfitness to be a director, and the Secretary of State is entitled to insist on such a statement (*Re Blackspur Group plc (No. 3)* [2001] EWCA Civ 1595, [2002] 2 BCLC 263).

PROCEDURAL RULES

All applications under s. 7, s. 8 or s. 9A of the CDDA 1986 are governed by the Insolvent Companies (Disqualification of Unfit Directors) Proceedings Rules 1987 (SI 1987/2023) as amended by the Insolvent Companies (Disqualification of Unfit Directors) Proceedings (Amendment) Rules 1999 (SI 1999/1023). SI 1987/2023, r. 2(1), provides that the CPR and any relevant practice direction apply in respect of any application under CDDA 1986, s. 7, s. 8 or s. 9A, except where SI 1987/2023 makes provision to inconsistent effect. **86.5**

The relevant practice direction is **PD Directors Disqualification Proceedings**, which, by para. 1.3, applies to applications for disqualification orders under any section of the CDDA 1986, applications to act as a director despite being disqualified and any application under **CPR, Part 23**, in connection with such proceedings.

Disqualification proceedings are not insolvency proceedings and the Insolvency Rules 1986 (SI 1986/1925) do not apply to them (*Dobson v Hastings* [1992] Ch 394) except in relation to appeals (see **86.36** and **86.38**).

MAKING THE APPLICATION

Court to which application is to be made

86.6 An application under CDDA 1986, s. 7, for a disqualification order under s. 6, alleges:

(a) that the defendant is, or has been, a director or shadow director of a company (known as the 'lead company') which has at any time become insolvent (whether while the defendant was a director or subsequently), and
(b) that the defendant's conduct as a director or shadow director of the lead company (either taken alone or taken together with conduct as a director or shadow director of any other company — known as a 'collateral company') makes the defendant unfit to be concerned in the management of a company.

For these purposes a company 'becomes insolvent' if (s. 6(2)):

(a) the company goes into liquidation (see **82.33**) at a time when its assets are insufficient for the payment of its debts and other liabilities and the expenses of the winding up (s.6(2)(a)); or
(b) the company enters administration (s. 6(2)(b)); or
(c) an administrative receiver of the company is appointed (s. 6(2)(c)).

For the purposes of s. 6(2)(a), post-liquidation interest, either payable or receivable, cannot be taken into account, but the liquidator's remuneration, if properly approved, must be (*Official Receiver v Moore* [1995] BCC 293).

The court to which a s. 7 application for a disqualification order must be made depends on the type of insolvency procedure to which the lead company is subject when the proceedings commence, or has been subject to in the past.

If the lead company is being, or has been, wound up compulsorily, the disqualification application must be made to the court which is carrying out, or has carried out, the winding up (s. 6(3)(a)).

If the lead company is being, or has been, wound up voluntarily, the application must be made to a court which has (or had) jurisdiction to wind it up (s. 6(3)(b)). The rules on jurisdiction in winding up are set out in **82.8**. The rules which determine which county court has jurisdiction (where paid-up capital is £120,000 or less) are to be read with references to presentation of the petition for winding up replaced by references to the passing of the resolution for voluntary winding up (s. 6(3A)(a)). It is submitted that when s. 6(3)(b) refers to a company which 'has been wound up voluntarily' it means a completed voluntary liquidation, so that where a voluntary liquidation is succeeded by a compulsory liquidation, s. 6(3)(a) applies.

If the lead company has never been in liquidation but has at any time been in administration or administrative receivership, the disqualification application must be made to a court which has jurisdiction to wind it up (s. 6(3)(c)). In the rules which determine which county court has jurisdiction, references to presentation of the petition for winding up are to be read as references to the appointment of the administrator or (as the case may be) the appointment of the administrative receiver (s. 6(3A)(b)).

By s. 6(3B), nothing in s. 6(3) invalidates disqualification proceedings by reason of their being taken in the wrong court.

An application under s. 8 alleges that the defendant's conduct in relation to one or more companies makes the defendant unfit to be concerned in the management of a company. An application under s. 9A alleges that the defendant is a director or shadow director of a company which commits a breach of competition law and that the defendant's conduct as a director or shadow director makes him unfit to be concerned in the management of a company. The application must be made to the High Court or to the Court of Session in Scotland, whichever has jurisdiction to wind up the company or companies concerned (ss. 8(3) and 9E(3); *Re Helene plc* [2000] 2 BCLC 249).

An application may be made in respect of two or more lead companies (*Re Surrey Leisure Ltd* [1999] 2 BCLC 457). *Re Surrey Leisure Ltd* concerned s. 7 applications, but it was conceded in *Re Helene plc* that the decision applies to s. 8 applications as well and it seems that it must also apply to s. 9A applications.

Proper claimant

An application under CDDA 1986, s. 7 or s. 8, must be made by the Secretary of State, who must consider that it is expedient in the public interest that a disqualification order should be made. Decisions on when to apply for disqualification orders are taken in the Disqualification Unit of the Insolvency Service, which is an executive agency of the Department for Business, Innovation and Skills (http://www.insolvency.gov.uk). **86.7**

If the lead company in an application under s. 7 is being or has been wound up by the court, the Secretary of State may direct the official receiver to make the application (s. 7(1)). If the lead company has never been in compulsory liquidation (for example, if it is in administration), the official receiver does not have standing to make an application, which can only be made by the Secretary of State. The court may order a substitution of claimant if proceedings are started by the wrong claimant (*Re NP Engineering and Security Products Ltd* [1993] 1 BCLC 208).

Leave of the court after two years

An application under CDDA 1986, s. 7, may be made without the leave of the court if it is made within two years of the date on which the lead company became insolvent (s. 7(2)). This is the date when one of the events mentioned in s. 6(2) occurred. If more than one of them occurred, it is the date when the first of them occurred (*Re Tasbian Ltd (No. 1)* [1991] BCLC 54). An application is made when the claim form is received by the court (**PD 7A, para. 5.1**; *Secretary of State for Trade and Industry v Normand* [1995] 2 BCLC 297; *Secretary of State for Trade and Industry v Vohora* [2007] EWHC 2656 (Ch), [2008] Bus LR 161). If the court office is closed on the last day of the two-year period, the period is extended to the next day on which the office is open (*Re Philipp and Lion Ltd* [1994] 1 BCLC 739). **86.8**

When the two-year period has expired an application may be made only with the leave of the court (s. 7(2)). Leave is applied for by application notice under **CPR, Part 23**, as amplified by **PD Directors Disqualification Proceedings, paras 17 and 19**.

The two-year period is not properly described as a limitation period after which a person is immune from a claim: the need to obtain the leave of the court should be seen as an additional condition which applies after two years (*Secretary of State for Trade and Industry v Davies* [1996] 4 All ER 289 per Millett LJ at pp. 298–9).

An applicant for leave after the two-year period must satisfy the court that leave should be granted (*Secretary of State for Trade and Industry v Davies* at p. 298). According to Scott LJ in *Re Probe Data Systems Ltd (No. 3)* [1992] BCLC 405 at p. 416, Hoffmann LJ in *Secretary of State for Trade and Industry v McTighe* [1994] 2 BCLC 284 at p. 287 and Millett LJ in *Secretary of State for*

Trade and Industry v Davies at pp. 296–7, in considering whether to give leave to make an application after two years the court should take account of all relevant circumstances, including, but not limited to:

(a) the length of the delay,
(b) the reasons for the delay,
(c) the gravity of the charges against the defendant, and
(d) the degree of prejudice caused to the defendant by the delay.

An important factor in favour of granting leave is that disqualification proceedings are brought, not to vindicate a private right, but to protect the public from the actions of a person alleged to be unfit to be a director of a company (*Secretary of State for Trade and Industry v Davies* per Millett LJ at pp. 296–7).

The applicant must explain why the application for leave is necessary, which necessarily involves giving reasons for the delay (*Secretary of State for Trade and Industry v Davies* at p. 299). However, there is no rule that an application for leave will not be considered unless the applicant gives a satisfactory reason for the delay: the satisfactoriness of the reason is just one of the factors to be taken into account by the court when exercising its discretion (*Secretary of State for Trade and Industry v Davies*).

Warning notice

86.9 By CDDA 1986, s. 16(1), any person intending to apply to a county court or the High Court for the making of a disqualification order must give not less than 10 days' notice of that intention to the person against whom the order is sought. An application made without giving the correct period of notice is not a nullity (*Secretary of State for Trade and Industry v Langridge* [1991] Ch 402), but may be an abuse of process, for which one possible sanction would be to strike out the claim (*Re Finelist Ltd* [2003] EWHC 1780 (Ch), [2004] BCC 877 at [93]).

Use of Part 8 procedure, track allocation, form of application

86.10 An application under s. 7, s. 8 or s. 9A of the CDDA 1986 for a disqualification order must be made using the procedure in **CPR, Part 8** (see **chapter 13**) (SI 1987/2023, r. 2(2)), and must use form N500 (by **PD Directors Disqualification Proceedings, para. 4.2**).

In the High Court the claim form must be issued out of the office of the Companies Court Registrar or a Chancery district registry; in the county court it will be issued out of a county court office (**PD Directors Disqualification Proceedings, para. 4.1A**).

All disqualification proceedings are allocated to the multi-track by **PD Directors Disqualification Proceedings, para. 2.1**, and so the provisions of the CPR relating to track allocation and directions questionnaires do not apply.

When the claim form is issued, the court will fix a date for the first hearing of the claim, which must not be less than eight weeks from the date of issue of the claim form (SI 1987/2023, r. 7(1)).

In disqualification proceedings the court's power to allow a Part 8 claim to continue as a Part 7 claim (**CPR, r. 8.1(3)**) is disapplied and Part 20 claims are not permitted (SI 1987/2023, r. 2(3)).

The title for the claim form and all affidavits, notices and other documents in the proceedings is, 'In the matter of [the company or companies in question] and in the matter of the Company Directors Disqualification Act 1986' (**PD Directors Disqualification Proceedings, para. 5.1**). *In an application* under CDDA 1986, s. 7, only the lead company or companies should be named in the heading (**PD Directors Disqualification Proceedings, para. 5.1**).

CPR, r. 8.2 (contents of Part 8 claim form), does not apply (**SI 1987/2023, r. 2(3)**). Instead **PD Directors Disqualification Proceedings, para. 6.1**, requires the claim form to include the information required by SI 1987/2023, r. 4, augmented with information relevant to applications under CDDA 1986, ss. 2 to 5. Form N500 has been designed to comply with these requirements. An important feature is that the claim form must identify the section of the Act under which the application is made and an endorsement on the form spells out the maximum periods of disqualification under each section.

The claim form must be verified by a statement of truth.

Case against the defendant

When the claim form is issued, evidence in support of the application must be filed in court (SI 1987/2023, r. 3(1)). It must be in the form of one or more affidavits and must include a statement of the matters by reference to which the defendant is alleged to be unfit to be concerned in the management of a company (r. 3(2) and (3)). These matters are commonly referred to as 'charges' (see **86.22**). If the official receiver is making the application, the evidence can be in the form of an official receiver's report (with or without affidavits from other persons), which shall be treated as if it had been verified by affidavit by the official receiver and shall be prima facie evidence of any matter contained in it (SI 1987/2023, r. 3(2)). Exhibits must be lodged with the court, where they will be retained until the conclusion of the proceedings (**PD Directors Disqualification Proceedings, para. 9.3(2)**). **86.11**

The applicant may subsequently file further evidence, provided the defendant has an adequate opportunity to deal with it (*Secretary of State for Trade and Industry v Andrews* [2005] EWHC 3513 (Ch), LTL 27/1/2005).

In *Re Pinemoor Ltd* [1997] BCC 708 Chadwick J asked persons preparing affidavits in support of disqualification applications to be careful to distinguish between the facts which they are able to establish by direct evidence, the inferences which they invite the court to draw from those facts, and the matters which are said to amount to unfitness on the part of the defendant. This would help defendants to concentrate on the factual matters which they need to address in their own affidavits.

In practice a relatively short affidavit is prepared by an official in the Disqualification Unit of the Insolvency Service referring to charges which are specified in a detailed report prepared by the insolvency practitioner who has investigated the company. In *Secretary of State for Trade and Industry v Hickling* [1996] BCC 678 Judge Weeks QC said, at p. 690, that the investigative report should not omit significant available evidence in favour of a defendant. It should attempt to deal with any explanation the defendant has already offered. Where there are several defendants, it should endeavour to apportion responsibility. It should avoid sweeping statements for which there is no evidence.

The applicant has a duty to present the case against the defendant fairly (*Secretary of State for Trade and Industry v Hickling* [1996] BCC 678 at p. 690; *Re Finelist Ltd* [2003] EWHC 1780 (Ch), [2004] BCC 877). The defendant should have been invited to comment on the proposed charges before the claim was issued (*Secretary of State for Trade and Industry v Blake* [1997] 1 BCLC 728; *Re Finelist Ltd*).

An allegation of dishonesty must be made 'fairly and squarely' in the affidavit (*Secretary of State for Trade and Industry v Goldberg* [2003] EWHC 2843 (Ch), [2004] 1 BCLC 597, at [53]).

Service

The claim form and a copy of the case against the defendant must be served on the defendant (SI 1987/2023, rr. 3(1) and 5(1)). Service may be by first-class post to the defendant's last known address, in which case the date of service will, unless the contrary is shown, be deemed **86.12** to be the seventh day next following that on which the claim form was posted (r. 5(1)). Service may be effected in some other way (*Official Receiver v Hodgkinson* (2000) LTL 13/10/2000). Apart from the deemed date of service by post, **CPR, Part 6, Sections I, II and III,** apply (**PD Directors Disqualification Proceedings, para.** 7.2). The court will not serve the claim form (para. 7.1). Provision for service out of the jurisdiction is made by SI 1987/2023, r. 5(2), and **PD Directors Disqualification Proceedings, para. 7.3. CPR, r. 10.3(2)** (period for acknowledgment of service of claim form served out of the jurisdiction), is disapplied by **PD Directors Disqualification Proceedings, para. 8.1.**

Acknowledgment of service

86.13 The claim form must be accompanied by form N502, acknowledgment of service (SI 1987/2023, r. 5(3), which disapplies **CPR, r. 8.3(2)** (contents of **Part 8** acknowledgment of service); **PD Directors Disqualification Proceedings, para. 8.1**). This form complies with SI 1987/2023, r. 5(4), by asking the defendant to indicate the grounds on which it is intended to dispute the claim.

The defendant must file the acknowledgment of service not more than 14 days after service of the claim form and serve it on the claimant and any other party (**PD Directors Disqualification Proceedings, para. 8.3**). A defendant who fails to file an acknowledgment in time may attend the hearing of the application but may not take part unless the court gives permission (**para. 8.4**).

Exchange of evidence

86.14 Any affidavit evidence which the defendant wishes the court to take into consideration in opposition to the application must be filed within 28 days of service of the claim form (SI 1987/2023, r. 6(1)). Copies must be served on the claimant and any other defendant (r. 6(1); **PD Directors Disqualification Proceedings, paras 9.4 and 9.5**). Rule 6(1) of SI 1987/2023 means that all the evidence which the defendant wishes the court to take into consideration must ordinarily be by affidavit: oral evidence-in-chief at the trial of the application will be allowed only in exceptional circumstances (*Re Rex Williams Leisure plc* [1994] Ch 350). Since disqualification proceedings are penal in nature, the defendant cannot be required to give evidence, but a defendant who chooses to file his or her own affidavit may be ordered to attend for cross-examination on it (*Re Dominion International Group plc* [1995] 1 WLR 649). If the defendant is not cross-examined, the court cannot find a charge proved if the defendant's affidavit denies it, unless the denial is self-evidently wrong, for example, because of other facts which are admitted or because it is plainly contradicted by reliable documents (*Re Hopes (Heathrow) Ltd* [2001] 1 BCLC 575).

Defendants have been criticised for filing evidence, for example, from accountants, which goes way beyond what is permissible in expert evidence (*Re Oakfame Construction Ltd* [1996] BCC 67; *Re Dominion International Group plc (No. 2)* [1996] 1 BCLC 572 at p. 600).

Once the defendant has filed evidence, the claimant then has 14 days in which to file further evidence (SI 1987/2023, r. 6(2); **PD Directors Disqualification Proceedings, para. 9.6**). Before the first hearing the parties may vary these time limits by written agreement, but after the first hearing extension of time for filing evidence is governed by **CPR, rr. 2.11 and 29.5 (PD Directors Disqualification Proceedings, para. 9.7). PD Directors Disqualification Proceedings, para. 9.8,** asks for all evidence to be filed before the first hearing, so far as is possible.

In *Secretary of State for Trade and Industry v Davies* [1996] 4 All ER 289 Millett LJ said, at p. 299, that an application for extension of the time for filing evidence should be considered in the same way as an application for leave to commence proceedings after the two-year time limit (see **86.8**). His lordship went on to say:

> But it must be more difficult to justify a failure even to issue the originating process within the time limit than to justify the failure to serve adequate supporting evidence at the same time; and the fact that the

process has been issued within time must be a relevant factor to be taken into account, particularly if it is accompanied, as it was in the present case, with a statement of the grounds upon which the Secretary of State alleges that the [defendant] is unfit to be a director of a company.

Disclosure

Any material which would be of assistance to the defendant's case in disqualification proceedings should be disclosed, as in criminal proceedings (*Secretary of State for Trade and Industry v Baker* [1998] Ch 356; *Re Astra Holdings plc* [1998] 2 BCLC 44). A report made to the Secretary of State under CDDA 1986, s. 7(3) or (4), by an official receiver, liquidator, administrator or administrative receiver is not privileged (*Secretary of State for Trade and Industry v Baker*). **86.15**

Delay, effect of other proceedings

A claim for the making of a disqualification order may be struck out if there is delay in proceeding to trial and the delay has substantially damaged the possibility of a fair trial or has otherwise prejudiced the defendant, as long as striking out would not be contrary to the public interest (*Re Noble Trees Ltd* [1993] BCLC 1185; *Official Receiver v B Ltd* [1994] 2 BCLC 1; *Re Manlon Trading Ltd* [1996] Ch 136). The type of delay which justifies striking out is usually described as inordinate and inexcusable, but in *Re Abermeadow Ltd* [2000] 2 BCLC 824 the court continued to consider whether to strike out a claim even after finding that the delay was excusable. **86.16**

A disqualification claim against a person need not be adjourned to await the outcome of civil proceedings against the person in relation to matters relied on as evidence of unfitness (*Re Rex Williams Leisure plc* [1994] Ch 350). Formerly it was usual to adjourn a disqualification claim to await the conclusion of criminal proceedings against the same defendant, if the same facts would be in issue in the two proceedings, so as to avoid prejudicing the criminal trial. However, such adjournments are less necessary now that CDDA 1986, s. 20, has been amended to provide that a statement made by a person in pursuance of a requirement imposed by or under ss. 6 to 10 cannot be used by the prosecution in criminal proceedings against that person (except for proceedings for perjury in making the statement itself). This provision covers statements made in the defendant's affidavits in opposition to a disqualification claim and statements made in cross-examination at the hearing of the claim (*Secretary of State for Trade and Industry v Crane* [2001] 2 BCLC 222).

In *Davies v United Kingdom* (application 42007/98) [2006] 2 BCLC 351, director disqualification proceedings continued for five years and six months until the defendant agreed to the use of the *Carecraft* procedure (see **86.20**). Both applicant and defendant failed to meet deadlines for filing evidence, and proceedings were delayed until the conclusion of a criminal case against other directors of the defendant's company. The European Court of Human Rights held that, 'in all the circumstances', the proceedings were not pursued with the diligence required by art. 6(1) of the European Convention on Human Rights, and awarded 4500 euro for inferred distress, anxiety and frustration. It is to be hoped that nowadays, active case management and relaxation of the practice of waiting for the outcome of criminal proceedings would prevent many of the delays which occurred in Mr Davies's case. See also *Eastaway v United Kingdom* (application 74976/01) [2006] 2 BCLC 361, which concerned another defendant in the same case. A breach of art. 6(1) by delay does not mean that proceedings must be dismissed, unless there can no longer be a fair hearing or it would otherwise be unfair for proceedings to continue (*Secretary of State for Trade and Industry v Davies* [2006] EWHC 299 (Ch), [2006] 2 BCLC 489).

If a criminal court has convicted a person of an offence, but did not consider making a disqualification order, it is not an abuse of process for an application to be made in civil proceedings for a disqualification order based on the conduct for which the person was convicted in the criminal court (*Re Denis Hilton Ltd* [2002] 1 BCLC 302).

If a criminal court disqualifies a person under CDDA 1986, s. 2, after conviction for an offence in relation to a company, it is not necessarily an abuse of process to apply for a further disqualification order to be made against the same person under s. 6 or s. 8 based on conduct while a director of the same company (*Secretary of State for Trade and Industry v Rayna* [2001] 2 BCLC 48 (ChD); [2001] EWCA Civ 1083, [2004] BCC 65).

It is not necessarily an abuse of process to pursue director disqualification proceedings against a defendant who has already been subject to disciplinary proceedings before a professional or industry regulator arising from the same conduct. This is because the director disqualification proceedings will be concerned with preventing the person from acting as a director etc. of any company whereas regulatory proceedings will be concerned only with a particular profession or industry (*Secretary of State for Trade and Industry v Baker (No. 2)* [1999] 1 WLR 1985; *Re Migration Services International Ltd* [2000] 1 BCLC 666).

HEARING THE APPLICATION

First hearing

86.17 The first hearing of a disqualification application is in public (SI 1987/2023, r. 7(2)). In the High Court in London it is before a registrar in bankruptcy; in a district registry it is before the district judge; in a county court it is before a district judge (r. 7(2); **PD Directors Disqualification Proceedings, para. 27.1**). The registrar or district judge shall either determine the case or adjourn it (SI 1987/2023, r. 7(3)) and must adjourn it if (r. 7(3)):

(a) he or she forms the provisional opinion that a disqualification order ought to be made and that a disqualification period longer than five years is appropriate; or
(b) he or she is of the opinion that questions of law or fact arise which are not suitable for summary determination.

If the case is adjourned at the first hearing, the registrar or district judge must state the reasons for the adjournment and give directions on various matters set out in SI 1987/2023, r. 7(5), and **PD Directors Disqualification Proceedings, paras 10.6** and **11.1**. One of the matters on which directions must be given by the registrar under SI 1987/2023, r. 7(5), is whether the case is to be heard by a registrar or by the judge. In *Lewis v Secretary of State for Trade and Industry* [2001] 2 BCLC 597 Neuberger J said that the factors which would favour a hearing by the judge are:

(a) the likely length of the hearing,
(b) complexity,
(c) high profile,
(d) special factors such as likely hearing date and choice of tribunal desired by the parties.

Trial

86.18 The court may direct a pre-trial review, a case management conference or pre-trial checklists (form N504) and will fix a trial date or trial period in accordance with **CPR, Part 29** (**PD Directors Disqualification Proceedings, para. 11.4**).

Paragraph 12 of PD Directors Disqualification Proceedings sets out requirements for the provision of trial bundles and documents.

Official receivers' right of audience

86.19 Official receivers and deputy official receivers have a right of audience in any disqualification proceedings, including those where the Secretary of State is applying for a disqualification order (SI 1987/2023, para. 10; **PD Directors Disqualification Proceedings, para. 3.1**).

Summary *'Carecraft'* procedure

The applicant for a disqualification order under CDDA 1986, s. 6 or s. 8, must prove the case against the director—there is no procedure analogous to pleading guilty to a criminal charge (*Re New Generation Engineers Ltd* [1993] BCLC 435 at p. 436). However, **PD Directors Disqualification Proceedings** provides for the use of what has come to be known as the *Carecraft* procedure (it was first used in *Re Carecraft Construction Co. Ltd* [1994] 1 WLR 172). This was described by Scott V-C in *Secretary of State for Trade and Industry v Rogers* [1996] 1 WLR 1569 at pp. 1571–2 as follows: **86.20**

> an agreed statement of facts is placed before the court, no oral evidence is given (so no cross- examination takes place), the court is informed of the bracket into which the parties agree the disqualification should fall and the parties' counsel address the judge on that basis. The procedure enables the case to be disposed of expeditiously and with a substantial saving of costs that would be incurred in a full-blown trial.

Use of this procedure does not mean that the judge must make the disqualification order for the agreed period or within the agreed bracket. It is for the judge to decide what the appropriate order is in the light of the evidence presented. The judge must not speculate what might have been shown by other evidence which the parties have agreed not to present (*Re SIG Security Services Ltd* [1998] BCC 978). A judge who thinks, having seen other evidence which is no longer relied on, that it is a more serious case than is revealed by the agreed statement of facts may adjourn the case for a short period and invite the Secretary of State to reconsider, but otherwise must deal with the case on the basis of the evidence put before the court by the parties (*Secretary of State for Trade and Industry v Rogers* at pp. 1573–4). A judge who decides to impose a disqualification period materially different from that agreed by the parties should give notice to them of that intention, so that they may reconsider their positions (*Re BPR Ltd* [1998] BCC 259 per Rimer J at p. 260).

If the parties decide to invite the court to use the *Carecraft* procedure, they should inform the court immediately and obtain a date for the hearing (**PD Directors Disqualification Proceedings, para. 13.1**). The claim form (form N500) draws attention to the possibility of using the *Carecraft* procedure, but not in terms intelligible to the lay defendant.

If the *Carecraft* procedure is to be used, the claimant must, unless the court directs otherwise, submit a written statement of the agreed or unopposed facts, and specify the period of disqualification which the parties agree those facts justify (**PD Directors Disqualification Proceedings, para. 13.2**). A range of years may be specified (**para. 13.2(2)**). The statement should spell out the facts clearly, leaving no room, or need, for filling in or interpretation by way of inference of secondary facts (*Secretary of State for Trade and Industry v Banarse* [1997] 1 BCLC 653).

It is usual for the statement to be preceded by a statement of the basis on which it is made, in particular, that it is made only for the purposes of a summary disposal of the application and cannot be relied on if the court orders a full trial instead. The usual form of words is set out in *Secretary of State for Trade and Industry v Rogers* at p. 1575 and was approved in *Official Receiver v Cooper* [1999] BCC 115.

Unless the court otherwise orders, a hearing under the *Carecraft* procedure will be in private (**PD Directors Disqualification Proceedings, para. 13.4**), but judgment will be given in public and the statement of agreed or unopposed facts will be annexed to the disqualification order, if one is made (**para. 13.5**).

If the court refuses to make a disqualification order under the *Carecraft* procedure, it will give directions for the hearing of the application (**para. 13.6**).

Commentary

FACTORS WHICH THE COURT CONSIDERS IN AN APPLICATION UNDER SECTION 6 OR 8

Unfitness must be proved

86.21 The court cannot disqualify a person under CDDA 1986, s. 6, unless it is satisfied that the person's conduct as a director or shadow director of a particular company — either taken alone or taken in conjunction with conduct as director or shadow director of any other company — makes that person unfit to be concerned in the management of a company. This means unfit to be concerned in the management of companies generally, though not necessarily every company in the country (*Re Polly Peck International plc (No. 2)* [1994] 1 BCLC 574; *Re Barings plc (No. 5)* [2000] 1 BCLC 523 at p. 535): it is possible to give permission for a disqualified person to manage a particular company (see **86.38**). If the court does find that the defendant's past conduct renders the defendant unfit, it must make a disqualification order for at least two years, regardless of subsequent reform of character (*Re Grayan Building Services Ltd* [1995] Ch 241; *Re Migration Services International Ltd* [2000] 1 BCLC 666 at p. 673). Subsequent reform of character may be taken into account when fixing the length of the disqualification period (see **86.32**).

The court's approach should not be that it will make a disqualification order if unfitness is proved, unless there are exceptional circumstances. The court should instead consider whether all the evidence, including evidence of extenuating circumstances, proves unfitness (*Cathie v Secretary of State for Business, Innovation and Skills* [2012] EWCA Civ 739, LTL 1/6/2012).

On an application under s. 8, the court may, at its discretion, disqualify a defendant whose conduct in relation to a particular company demonstrates unfitness to be concerned in the management of a company. There is no minimum period of disqualification under s. 8, but otherwise the principles which the court applies in deciding cases are the same as for s. 6 (*Secretary of State for Trade and Industry v Hollier* [2006] EWHC 1804 (Ch), [2007] Bus LR 352 at [50] and [59]). The two sections are compared and contrasted in *Re J. A. Chapman and Co. Ltd* [2003] EWHC 532 (Ch), [2003] 2 BCLC 206, at [2] to [9].

In *Re Sevenoaks Stationers (Retail) Ltd* [1991] Ch 164 Dillon LJ said, at p. 176:

> The test laid down in s. 6—apart from the requirement that the person concerned is or has been a director of a company which has become insolvent—is whether the person's conduct as a director of the company or companies in question 'makes him unfit to be concerned in the management of a company'. These are ordinary words of the English language and they should be simple to apply in most cases. It is important to hold to those words in each case.

Evidence

86.22 The matters by reference to which the defendant is alleged to be unfit (commonly known as the 'charges') must be specified by the claimant in a statement filed with the claim form (SI 1987/2023, r. 3(3)). Whatever other evidence is before the court, its reasons for making a disqualification order must be limited to proved charges: this ensures the defendant knows what case has to be answered (*Re Deaduck Ltd* [2000] 1 BCLC 148 at pp. 159 and 164–5; *Re Cubelock Ltd* [2001] BCC 523). Only proved charges may be taken into account when setting the period of disqualification (*Re Sevenoaks Stationers (Retail) Ltd* [1991] Ch 164 at p. 177). But other evidence may show the context in which the proved misconduct occurred and may influence the court's assessment of its gravity, either when deciding whether the proved charges demonstrate unfitness (*Re Deaduck Ltd* at pp. 159 and 164–5) or (at least in so far as it provides mitigation) when determining the period of disqualification (*Re Sevenoaks Stationers (Retail) Ltd* at p. 177).

The r. 3(3) statement need not be treated like an indictment in a criminal trial. The court has a discretion whether to allow the claimant to add to or alter the charges made in the r. 3(3) statement, the paramount requirement being that the defendant must know the charges that have to be met (*Re Sevenoaks Stationers (Retail) Ltd* at p. 177; *Re Stephenson Cobbold Ltd* [2000] 2 BCLC 614; *Kappler v Secretary of State for Trade and Industry* [2006] BCC 845).

Whether a defendant is unfit is a question of fact (*Re Sevenoaks Stationers (Retail) Ltd* at p. 176). Determining that question:

> involves the evaluation of the seriousness of the charges which have been proved and a judgment of the trial judge as to whether, taking all the circumstances into account, including all matters of mitigation and extenuation, the director is or is not unfit. (*Re Hitco 2000 Ltd* [1995] 2 BCLC 63 at p. 65.)

Charges must be viewed cumulatively, so that it is no defence to say that no individual instance of misconduct merits disqualification (*Re Barings plc (No. 5)* [2000] 1 BCLC 523 at p. 535). Circumstances which may be taken into account include the defendant's health at the time of the alleged misconduct (*Re CEM Connections Ltd* [2000] BCC 917; *Secretary of State for Trade and Industry v Mitchell* 2002 SLT 658). It is irrelevant that some other remedy has been or might be obtained for the misconduct (*Re Grayan Building Services Ltd* [1995] Ch 241). General evidence of character is irrelevant (*Re Dawes and Henderson (Agencies) Ltd* [1997] 1 BCLC 329) though it may be relevant in determining the period of disqualification (*Re Barings plc* [1998] BCC 583 at p. 590; *Re Westmid Packing Services Ltd* [1998] 2 All ER 124 at p. 133).

Parliament has established investigatory processes for providing the Secretary of State with reports, information or documents on which an opinion may be based that it is expedient in the public interest that a disqualification order should be made against a person (CDDA 1986, s. 8). It follows that the Secretary of State may use the relevant report etc. as evidence in support of an application for a disqualification order despite the rules against evidence of opinion and findings of fact (*Re Barings plc (No. 2)* [1998] 1 BCLC 590; *Re Barings plc (No. 5)* [1999] 1 BCLC 433; *Secretary of State for Business, Enterprise and Regulatory Reform v Aaron* [2008] EWCA Civ 1146, [2009] 1 BCLC 55). This is so whether the application is for disqualification under s. 6 or s. 8 (*Secretary of State for Trade and Industry v Ashcroft* [1998] Ch 71). A copy of any report of inspectors appointed under the Companies Act 1985, part 14, certified by the Secretary of State to be a true copy, is admissible in any legal proceedings as evidence of the opinion of the inspectors in relation to any matter contained in the report (Companies Act 1985, s. 441(1)). However, the rules against evidence of opinion and findings of fact apply to other material, including other court proceedings (*Secretary of State for Trade and Industry v Bairstow* [2003] EWCA Civ 321, [2004] Ch 1). In *Secretary of State for Trade and Industry v Bairstow* the conduct of Mr Bairstow which was in issue in disqualification proceedings had also been in issue in a claim by Mr Bairstow for wrongful dismissal which he had lost. It was held (following *Hollington v F. Hewthorn and Co. Ltd* [1943] KB 587) that the judgments given in the wrongful dismissal claim were not admissible evidence of the facts found in that claim. It was also held that it was not an abuse of process for Mr Bairstow to require the Secretary of State to prove those facts by admissible evidence. The test is whether the relitigation (a) would be manifestly unfair to a party to the disqualification proceedings or (b) would bring the administration of justice into disrepute. In this case it was clearly not unfair to any party and it was necessary in the interests of justice for the Secretary of State's serious charges to be proved to the satisfaction of the court by legally admissible evidence. On the other hand, in *Secretary of State for Business, Innovation and Skills v Potiwal* [2012] EWHC 3723 (Ch), LTL 8/1/2013, it was unfair to require the Secretary of State to spend a large quantity of public money (£400,000) on proving again aspects of the defendant's character which had already been ruled on by a tribunal in proceedings between the defendant's company and HMRC. It was held that there was privity between the defendant and the company of which he was sole director and 40 per cent shareholder, but there was no privity between HMRC and the Secretary of State.

For the purposes of the European Convention on Human Rights, **art. 6**, in the **Human Rights Act 1998, sch. 1**, directors disqualification proceedings in civil courts under CDDA

Commentary

1986, ss. 6 to 10, are civil rather than criminal proceedings (*DC v United Kingdom* (application 39031/97) [2000] BCC 710). The safeguards required to protect the defendant are therefore less than in criminal proceedings. In particular, it may be allowable to use in evidence the defendant's own admissions of wrongdoing made under threat of punishment for not providing information to, for example, an insolvency office holder under the Insolvency Act 1986, s. 235 (*DC v United Kingdom*; *Official Receiver v Stern* [2000] 1 WLR 2230). The European Court of Human Rights has so far accepted that it is fair to use compulsorily obtained evidence in directors disqualification proceedings only where the evidence is not contested and is not a significant part of the case (*DC v United Kingdom*). The Court of Appeal has said that it is generally best for the trial judge to decide questions of fairness, either at a pre-trial review or in the course of the trial, having regard to all relevant factors (*Official Receiver v Stern* [2000] 1 WLR 2230). So far, the court has not accepted that hearing a claim for a disqualification order when the defendant is unable to pay for professional representation, even in a complex case, is a breach of art. 6 (*Secretary of State for Trade and Industry v Davies* [2006] EWHC 299 (Ch), [2006] 2 BCLC 489; *Re City Truck Group Ltd* [2007] EWHC 350 (Ch), [2007] 2 BCLC 649).

The standard of proof is the civil standard of balance of probabilities. It is not an abuse of process to allege, in director disqualification proceedings, misconduct that would constitute a criminal offence, even though the criminal standard of proof is not required (*Re Mea Corporation Ltd* [2006] EWHC 1846 (Ch), [2007] 1 BCLC 618).

A court hearing a director disqualification claim must consider:
(a) what the defendant did (see **86.23**);
(b) whether the defendant's actions were due to the defendant's lack of probity or incompetence or both (see **86.24**);
(c) whether the case against the defendant is serious enough to warrant disqualification (see **86.24**).

What the defendant did

86.23 The limitations on the conduct from which charges may be formulated are considered at **86.25** to **86.28**.

The court must have regard to matters specified in CDDA 1986, sch. 1 (see **86.29**). It may take into account matters not listed in sch. 1 (*Re Bath Glass Ltd* [1988] BCLC 329 at p. 332; *Re Sykes (Butchers) Ltd* [1998] 1 BCLC 110 at p. 125) and the fact that they are not in the schedule does not mean that they are less significant than the matters that are in the schedule. Any allegation of unfitness must be considered on its merits irrespective of whether it is in the schedule (*Re Amaron Ltd* [2001] 1 BCLC 562 at p. 568). The contrary view accepted in *Secretary of State for Trade and Industry v Goldberg* [2003] EWHC 2843 (Ch), [2004] 1 BCLC 597 at [11], without reference to *Re Amaron Ltd*, must be wrong. In practice there are recurring themes in cases, notably the way in which defendants have financed trading while insolvent by using money owed to unsecured trade creditors and involuntary creditors such as HM Revenue and Customs (see **86.30**). In *Re Firedart Ltd* [1994] 2 BCLC 340 Arden J said, at p. 351:

> there are a number of matters which if proved would generally lead me to the conclusion that a director was unfit to be concerned in the management of a company. They include: trading while insolvent; taking personal benefits over and above any proper remuneration; failing to keep proper accounting records.

For trading while insolvent see **86.30**. Arden J's reference to taking personal benefits is echoed by Lindsay J in *Re Polly Peck International plc (No. 2)* [1994] 1 BCLC 574, who said that any breach of duty designed to benefit the defendant who owed the duty is likely to be regarded as serious enough to warrant disqualification, but a breach of duty which was not intended to benefit the defendant might not warrant disqualification (see also *Re Deaduck Ltd* [2000] 1 BCLC 148 at p. 160). On failure to keep proper accounting records see per Nicholls V-C in *Secretary of State for Trade and Industry v Ettinger* [1993] BCLC 896 at p. 900.

In *Secretary of State for Trade and Industry v McTighe (No. 2)* [1996] 2 BCLC 477 Morritt LJ said that persistent failure to cooperate with the liquidator and the official receiver would demonstrate unfitness.

Seriousness of case

86.24 In *Re Grayan Building Services Ltd* [1995] Ch 241 Hoffmann LJ said, at p. 253, that the court must decide whether the defendant's conduct,

> viewed cumulatively and taking into account any extenuating circumstances, has fallen below the standards of probity and competence appropriate for persons fit to be directors of companies.

As the minimum period of disqualification under CDDA 1986, s. 6, is two years, a disqualification order should not be made at all if the defendant's misconduct is not serious enough to merit two years' disqualification (*Re Polly Peck International plc (No. 2)* [1994] 1 BCLC 574).

Although the mere fact that a defendant's misconduct is neither dishonest nor contrary to the law does not mean that it cannot render the director unfit (*Re Deaduck Ltd* [2000] 1 BCLC 148 at p. 167), the courts have generally been more ready to disqualify for lack of probity than for incompetence. In *Re Lo-Line Electric Motors Ltd* [1988] Ch 477 Browne-Wilkinson V-C said, at p. 486:

> Ordinary commercial misjudgment is in itself not sufficient to justify disqualification. In the normal case, the conduct complained of must display a lack of commercial probity, although I have no doubt that in an extreme case of gross negligence or total incompetence disqualification could be appropriate.

In *Re McNulty's Interchange Ltd* (1988) 4 BCC 533 Browne-Wilkinson V-C repeated that commercial misjudgment does not demonstrate unfitness and went on to say that an application for a disqualification order should not be made where all that is alleged is mere mismanagement. In *Re Sevenoaks Stationers (Retail) Ltd* [1991] Ch 164 Dillon LJ said, at p. 184, that he did not think it was necessary for incompetence to be 'total', as suggested by Browne-Wilkinson V-C in *Re Lo-Line Electric Motors Ltd*, to render a director unfit: incompetence or negligence 'in a very marked degree' was sufficient in the case before him. In *Re Barings plc (No. 5)* [1999] 1 BCLC 433 Jonathan Parker J, at pp. 483–4, reconciled the two approaches by saying:

> Where... [the claimant's] case is based solely on allegations of incompetence... the burden is on [the claimant] to satisfy the court that the conduct complained of demonstrates incompetence of a high degree.

On appeal in *Re Barings plc (No. 5)* [2000] 1 BCLC 523 the Court of Appeal, at p. 535, said that it wished to emphasise what Jonathan Parker J had said. The Court of Appeal went on to suggest that it is unnecessary to require an exaggerated degree of incompetence to justify the penalty of disqualification, given that the court can give leave to act during a period of disqualification (see **86.38**). But it is surely better to adopt the view of Lindsay J in *Re Polly Peck International plc (No. 2)* that the court's power to give leave is not something to be taken into account when deciding whether to disqualify. It is not right to deal with misconduct that is not serious enough to warrant the minimum period of two years' disqualification by disqualifying and then giving leave to act despite being disqualified: the right course is not to disqualify at all. In *Re Cubelock Ltd* [2001] BCC 523 Park J said, at p. 536, that 'the Court of Appeal [in *Re Barings plc (No. 5)*] did not to any appreciable extent diminish the level of incompetence which would be required to justify a disqualification'. Jonathan Parker J's formulation has been followed in *Re Bradcrown Ltd* [2001] 1 BCLC 547 and *Secretary of State for Trade and Industry v Walker* [2003] EWHC 175 (Ch), [2003] 1 BCLC 363. For examples of incompetence of such seriousness as to amount to unfitness see *Re Barings plc* [1998] BCC 583 and *Re Barings plc (No. 5)*.

De facto directorships included

86.25 The past conduct that the court considers is conduct as a director whether properly appointed as such or not (*Re Eurostem Maritime Ltd* [1987] PCC 190; *Re Lo-Line Electric Motors Ltd* [1988] Ch 477; *Re Moorgate Metals Ltd* [1995] 1 BCLC 503). In *Re Lo-Line Electric Motors Ltd* Browne-Wilkinson V-C said that Parliament's plain intention was to have regard to the conduct of a person acting as a director, whether validly appointed, invalidly appointed or just assuming to act as a director without any appointment at all. (A person who acts as a director without being properly appointed is known as a de facto director.) It may be very difficult to decide whether what a person has done amounts to acting as a director so as to make the individual liable to disqualification, though in practice the question may be inextricably linked with whether what he or she has done in itself merits disqualification — see *Secretary of State for Trade and Industry v Tjolle* [1998] 1 BCLC 333. In *Re Kaytech International plc* [1999] 2 BCLC 351 the Court of Appeal refused to lay down a definition of de facto director, but found that in the case before it an individual had acted as a director. *Re Sykes (Butchers) Ltd* [1998] 1 BCLC 110 is another case in which a defendant was found to have been a de facto director. There is a full review of the authorities in *Secretary of State for Trade and Industry v Becker* [2002] EWHC 2200 (Ch), [2003] 1 BCLC 555 and in *Secretary of State for Trade and Industry v Hollier* [2006] EWHC 1804 (Ch), [2007] Bus LR 352.

Geographical coverage

86.26 The court may consider conduct that occurred outside England and Wales, and persons who are not British subjects or are not domiciled in England and Wales may be disqualified under CDDA 1986, s. 6 (*Re Seagull Manufacturing Co. Ltd (No. 2)* [1994] Ch 91; *Re Kaytech International plc* [1999] 2 BCLC 351; *Official Receiver v Vass* [1999] BCC 516).

Lead and collateral companies

86.27 An application to disqualify a person under CDDA 1986, s. 6, arises because the person has been a director of a company which has become insolvent (s. 6(1)(a)), but, under s. 6(1)(b), the court may consider the person's conduct as director both of that company (the 'lead company') and any other company or companies ('collateral companies'). Any conduct in relation to collateral companies which tends to show that the director is unfit may be considered: the court is not restricted to considering conduct which arises from or is in some way connected with the affairs of the lead company (*Secretary of State for Trade and Industry v Ivens* [1997] 2 BCLC 334). Conduct in relation to a collateral company may be considered even though it became insolvent more than two years before proceedings commenced (*Secretary of State for Trade and Industry v Ivens*). But if there is in fact nothing in the director's conduct in relation to the lead company which shows that the director is unfit, the court cannot consider anything done in relation to collateral companies (*Secretary of State for Trade and Industry v Ivens*).

Conduct in relation to other companies can only be considered for the purpose of proving unfitness. A finding that a defendant's conduct in relation to the lead company demonstrates unfitness cannot be negatived by consideration of his or her conduct in relation to other companies (*Re Bath Glass Ltd* [1988] BCLC 329 at pp. 331–2).

It is possible to apply in respect of two or more lead companies (*Re Surrey Leisure Ltd* [1999] 2 BCLC 457).

Conduct in relation to the insolvency

86.28 For the purposes of CDDA 1986, s. 6, conduct as a director of a company includes, where the company has become insolvent, conduct in relation to any matter connected with or arising out of the insolvency of that company (s. 6(2)). This includes conduct in relation to the director disqualification claim itself (*Secretary of State for Trade and Industry v Reynard* [2002] EWCA Civ 497, [2002] 2 BCLC 625).

Statutory list of matters to be considered

When considering whether a person's conduct in relation to a company makes the person unfit to be a director, the court is required by CDDA 1986, s. 9, to have regard in particular to the matters mentioned in part 1 of sch. 1 to the Act. These matters include: **86.29**

(a) Any misfeasance or breach of any fiduciary or other duty by the director in relation to the company (sch. 1, para. 1). A finding of breach of duty is neither necessary nor sufficient for a finding of unfitness: a defendant may be found to be unfit though no breach of duty has been proved; a defendant may be found not to be unfit even though a breach of duty is proved (*Re Barings plc (No. 5)* [2000] 1 BCLC 523 at p. 535).
(b) Any misapplication or retention by the director of, or any conduct by the director giving rise to an obligation to account for, any money or other property of the company (sch. 1, para. 2).
(c) The extent of the director's responsibility for any failure by the company to comply with various accounting and publicity requirements of the Companies Act 2006 (CDDA 1986, sch. 1, paras 4 and 5).

Where the company has become insolvent, the court is to have regard in particular to the matters mentioned in part 2 of sch. 1. These include:

(a) The extent of the director's responsibility for the causes of the company becoming insolvent (sch. 1, para. 6). Responsibility is to be assessed broadly and not by reference to legal concepts of causation (*Re Barings plc (No. 5)* [2000] 1 BCLC 523 at p. 535).
(b) The extent of the director's responsibility for any failure by the company to supply any goods or services which have been paid for (in whole or in part) (sch. 1, para. 7).

The fact that particular matters are listed in sch. 1 does not mean that the court may not have regard to other matters (see **86.23**).

Taking unwarranted risks with creditors' money

In *Secretary of State for Trade and Industry v Creegan* [2002] 1 BCLC 99 it was held that unfitness is not demonstrated merely by allowing a company to trade while knowing it to be insolvent: it must also be shown that the defendant knew or ought to have known that there was no reasonable prospect of meeting creditors' claims. The phrase 'taking unwarranted risks with creditors' money' is used in some of the cases to describe this kind of misconduct (see *Re Living Images Ltd* [1996] 1 BCLC 348; *Re City Pram and Toy Co. Ltd* [1998] BCC 537). **86.30**

A policy of not paying on time creditors who do not press for payment may demonstrate unfitness, especially where the money is used to finance trading while insolvent (*Re Sevenoaks Stationers (Retail) Ltd* [1991] Ch 164). A non-payment policy may demonstrate unfitness even if it is not shown that the defendant intended that the creditors would never be paid (*Secretary of State for Trade and Industry v McTighe (No. 2)* [1996] 2 BCLC 477; *Re Structural Concrete Ltd* [2001] BCC 578), but the mere fact that debts are routinely paid late may not show unfitness (*Re Funtime Ltd* [2000] 1 BCLC 247). A non-payment policy may demonstrate unfitness if adopted while the company is solvent (*Re Hopes (Heathrow) Ltd* [2001] 1 BCLC 575). Although it is often so-called Crown debts (especially value added tax and employees' national insurance and tax contributions) that are the subject of a non-payment policy, the identity of the creditor is not the crucial factor demonstrating unfitness, and the court must consider the significance of the non-payment policy and whether the defendant was taking unfair advantage of the creditor's forbearance (*Re Sevenoaks Stationers (Retail) Ltd* at p. 183; *Re Amaron Ltd* [2001] 1 BCLC 562 at pp. 571–3).

Commentary

MAKING THE ORDER

Absence of defendant

86.31 On hearing an application for a disqualification order, the court may make the order even if (SI 1987/2023, r. 8(1)):

(a) the defendant has not acknowledged service of the claim form;
(b) the defendant has not filed evidence;
(c) the defendant has not appeared at the hearing.

However, a disqualification order made in the absence of the defendant may be set aside or varied by the court on such terms as it thinks just (r. 8(2)).

Period of disqualification

86.32 In *Re Sevenoaks Stationers (Retail) Ltd* [1991] Ch 164 Dillon LJ accepted, at p. 179, the following guidelines for disqualification under s. 6:

> (i) the top bracket of disqualification for periods over 10 years should be reserved for particularly serious cases. These may include cases where a director who has already had one period of disqualification imposed on him falls to be disqualified yet again. (ii) The minimum bracket of two to five years' disqualification should be applied where, though disqualification is mandatory, the case is, relatively, not very serious. (iii) The middle bracket of disqualification for from six to 10 years should apply for serious cases which do not merit the top bracket.

In a case under s. 2, the Court of Appeal decided that fraudulent trading for four years resulting in losses of about £0.75 million was a middle-bracket offence meriting eight years' disqualification (*R v Millard* (1993) 15 Cr App R (S) 445). In *Secretary of State for Trade and Industry v McTighe (No. 2)* [1996] 2 BCLC 477, a case under s. 6, the Court of Appeal imposed disqualification for 12 years in a 'particularly serious case' in which a man had caused three companies successively to trade at the risk of their creditors, ultimately leaving unpaid debts of well over £1 million. Over £½ million had been misappropriated in a way that was 'tantamount to theft' and the director had failed to cooperate with the liquidator or official receiver.

In *Re Westmid Packing Services Ltd* [1998] 2 All ER 124 there is an extensive review by the Court of Appeal of the approach to be taken when determining the period of disqualification. The Court of Appeal wanted the process to be kept simple and disapproved of extensive citation from previous cases. The trial court should exercise its jurisdiction 'in a summary manner' (p. 135). The Court of Appeal emphasised, at p. 132, that determining the length of a period of disqualification is little different from determining the sentence in a criminal case:

> The period of disqualification must reflect the gravity of the offence. It must contain deterrent elements. That is what sentencing is all about, and that is what fixing the appropriate period of the disqualification is all about.

The fact that the court has already decided to grant leave to act as a director during the period of disqualification (see **86.38**) should not affect the length of the period. The period of disqualification is a matter for the judge's discretion, which, like any exercise of judicial discretion, must be decided in the light of all relevant circumstances, which can include mitigating factors such as: 'the former director's age and state of health, the length of time he has been in jeopardy, whether he has admitted the offence, his general conduct before and after the offence, and the periods of disqualification of his co-directors that may have been ordered by other courts' (at p. 134).

Whatever other evidence is before the court, only proved charges (see **86.22**) may be taken into account when setting the period of disqualification (*Re Sevenoaks Stationers (Retail) Ltd* [1991] Ch 164), though other evidence may show the context in which the seriousness of the proved charges is to be evaluated (*Re Deaduck Ltd* [2000] 1 BCLC 148).

Costs

Although disqualification applications are brought in the public interest, costs are awarded on the usual principle that the unsuccessful party will be ordered to pay the costs of the successful party (**CPR, r. 44.2(2)**). There is no principle that a defendant will be ordered to pay the costs of an unsuccessful claimant if there were good reasons for bringing the claim (*Re Southbourne Sheet Metal Co. Ltd* [1993] 1 WLR 244). There is also no rule that a successful claimant should be awarded costs on the indemnity basis: costs are awarded on the standard basis except in special circumstances (*Re Dicetrade Ltd* [1994] BCC 371). Indemnity costs were ordered in *Secretary of State for Trade and Industry v Blake* [1997] 1 BCLC 728. **86.33**

An official receiver who exercises his or her right of audience (see **86.19**) is a litigant in person for the purposes of the Litigants in Person (Costs and Expenses) Act 1975 (*Re Minotaur Data Systems Ltd* [1999] 1 WLR 1129).

If an application under CDDA 1986, s. 7 or s. 8, is discontinued because the Secretary of State accepts a disqualification undertaking, the defendant will usually be ordered to pay the applicant's costs, unless the circumstances are such that the court should make another order (**PD Directors Disqualification Proceedings, para. 28**).

Commencement of disqualification

Unless the court orders otherwise, the period of disqualification imposed by a disqualification order starts at the end of the period of 21 days beginning with the date of the order (CDDA 1986, s. 1(2)). The delay is to enable the disqualified person to resign directorships and so on (*Secretary of State for Trade and Industry v Edwards* [1997] BCC 222; *Re Cannonquest Ltd* [1997] BCC 644 at pp. 648–9). **86.34**

Service and registration

It is the responsibility of the claimant to serve a disqualification order (**PD Directors Disqualification Proceedings, para. 15.1**). **86.35**

Within 14 days after a disqualification order is made by the court, it must be notified by a prescribed court officer to the Secretary of State (Companies (Disqualification Orders) Regulations 2009 (SI 2009/2471)) for inclusion in the register maintained under CDDA 1986, s. 18. Disqualification undertakings are also recorded in this register. Variations of orders and undertakings, and grants of leave to act in spite of an order or undertaking, must also be reported.

APPEAL

Procedure

Appeals in disqualification proceedings are governed by the Insolvency Rules 1986 (SI 1986/1925), rr. 7.47 and 7.49 (*Re Tasbian Ltd (No. 2)* [1991] BCLC 59; *Re Probe Data Systems Ltd (No. 3)* [1992] BCLC 405; *Secretary of State for Trade and Industry v Jones* [1999] BCC 336). This procedure is described in **84.11 to 84.13**. **86.36**

Stay pending appeal

The High Court and the Court of Appeal have inherent jurisdiction to stay a disqualification order pending an appeal (*Secretary of State for Trade and Industry v Bannister* [1996] 1 WLR 271, in which a stay was refused and which left open the question whether a county court could grant a stay). **86.37**

LEAVE TO ACT DURING A PERIOD OF DISQUALIFICATION

86.38 A person subject to a disqualification order or undertaking may apply for permission to do any of the things which it prohibits, apart from acting as an insolvency practitioner (CDDA 1986, ss. 1(1) and 1A(1)).

Leave may be given at the same time as a disqualification order is made under s. 6, s. 8 or s. 9A. A person facing disqualification proceedings who envisages applying for leave if disqualified should do so in those proceedings so that the application can be heard by the judge who makes the disqualification order (*Secretary of State for Trade and Industry v Collins* [2000] 2 BCLC 223) and the application should be made by application notice under **CPR, Part 23** (**PD Directors Disqualification Proceedings, para. 20.2**). After a disqualification order has been made under CDDA 1986, s. 6, s. 8 or s. 9A, an application to do any of the things prohibited by the order must be made to the court which made the order (s. 17(1)) and the application should be made by claim form under **CPR, Part 8** (form N208). If there are two or more orders, the application should be made to the court which made the last of them (s. 17(4)).

An application to do anything prohibited by a disqualification undertaking accepted under s. 7(2A) or s. 8(2A) may be made to any court to which, if the undertaking had not been accepted, the Secretary of State could have applied for a disqualification order (CDDA 1986, s. 17(3)). An application for leave to act despite an undertaking accepted under s. 9B must be made to the High Court or, in Scotland, to the Court of Session.

The title for the application notice or claim form and all affidavits, notices and other documents in the proceedings is 'In the matter of [the company or companies in question] and in the matter of the Company Directors Disqualification Act 1986' (**PD Directors Disqualification Proceedings, para. 21.1**).

Evidence in support of an application must be by affidavit (**PD Directors Disqualification Proceedings, para. 22.1**). Clear evidence is required of the precise role the applicant is to play in the company in question together with up-to-date and adequate information about the company (*Secretary of State for Trade and Industry v Collins* [2000] 2 BCLC 223). If the applicant's disqualification was made under the summary *Carecraft* procedure, the applicant should not be permitted to offer evidence about his or her past behaviour in addition to that contained in the agreed *Carecraft* statement, unless asked to do so by the court (*Secretary of State for Trade and Industry v Collins* [2000] 2 BCLC 223). The same applies to the agreed statement of facts in a disqualification undertaking (*Re Morija plc* [2007] EWHC 3055 (Ch), [2008] 2 BCLC 313).

The application notice or claim form and supporting evidence must be served on the Secretary of State (**para. 23.1**). Service of an application notice will not be undertaken by the court (**PD Directors Disqualification Proceedings, para. 26.1**). The Secretary of State must appear on a hearing of an application for leave, in order to call the court's attention to any relevant matters, and may give evidence or call witnesses (CDDA 1986, s. 17(5)). The matters which the Secretary of State may raise on the application for leave are not limited to those which were considered when making the disqualification order, though the disqualified person must be given adequate notice of new matters, which will not be possible if the application for leave is heard immediately after the disqualification order is made (*Re Westminster Property Management Ltd (No. 2)* [2001] BCC 305 at 355). The Secretary of State's appearance is required only because of the disqualified person's wish to act as a director etc. despite disqualification, and so the disqualified person should be ordered to pay the Secretary of State's costs (*Secretary of State for Trade and Industry v Collins* [2000] 2 BCLC 223). If the application is for leave to act despite an order under s. 9A or an undertaking under s. 9B, it is the OFT or the regulator who applied for the order or accepted the undertaking who must appear instead of the Secretary of State (s. 17(6) and (7)).

Applications for leave are allocated to the multi-track by **PD Directors Disqualification Proceedings, para. 2.1**, and so the provisions of the CPR relating to track allocation and directions questionnaires do not apply.

In *Re Westminster Property Management Ltd (No. 2)* [2001] BCC 305 at 355 Lloyd J said, at p. 361, that the applicant's burden of showing justification for being allowed to act as a director or be concerned in the management of a company:

> is likely only to be satisfied if it can be shown that the corporate body in question has a need for the services of the person in question, that there is no risk to the public from the person in question acting as a director, and further that to allow the person in question to act as a director would not subvert or reduce the effect of the disqualification order, even if only in its deterrent effect.

Leave will be given only if there is a need for it (*Re Cargo Agency Ltd* [1992] BCLC 686) and that must be the company's need for the disqualified person's services, not that person's desire to manage companies (*Re Gibson Davies Ltd* [1995] BCC 11). When the person who is applying for leave to manage a company is substantially the only person interested in the company's equity capital, it is difficult to find any company need that is separate from the applicant's. In those circumstances the question is, according to Rattee J in *Secretary of State for Trade and Industry v Barnett* [1998] 2 BCLC 64 at p. 72:

> whether it is necessary for [the applicant] to be a director of a company in order to protect some legitimate interest of [the applicant] himself, or of any third party, which it is in all the circumstances of the case reasonable that the court should seek to protect. If it is so necessary, then the next question is whether that need can be met without infringing the protection of the public secured by the disqualification order.

Saving tax may be a legitimate interest for this purpose (*Re Dawes and Henderson (Agencies) Ltd (No. 2)* [1999] 2 BCLC 317).

The principles to be applied when deciding whether to grant leave were reviewed by Scott V-C in *Re Barings plc (No. 3)* [2000] 1 WLR 634. His lordship said that leave should never be granted without serious consideration (at p. 641). If leave is granted, the reasons for doing so must be consistent with the reasons for making the disqualification order (at p. 640). In particular the court should ask whether the situation in which the disqualified person would be given leave to act would risk recurrence of the particular faults for which he or she had been disqualified (at p. 641).

Adequate protection of the public must be provided. For example, an independent chartered accountant or solicitor must act as co-director (*Re Majestic Recording Studios Ltd* [1989] BCLC 1; *Secretary of State for Trade and Industry v Palfreman* [1995] 2 BCLC 301). In *Re Gibson Davies Ltd* 10 protective undertakings were given. The court does not tolerate imperfect compliance with such undertakings (*Re Brian Sheridan Cars Ltd* [1996] 1 BCLC 327), but this raises the question of who is to check that the undertakings are being observed. In *Re Hennelly's Utilities Ltd* [2004] EWHC 34 (Ch), [2005] BCC 542, the court required the finance director, of the company which the disqualified person was applying to manage, to provide quarterly reports to the Department of Trade and Industry on the disqualified person's compliance with undertakings he had given. The learned deputy judge said, at [63]:

> the court has to balance any need for the director to act against the protection of the public from the conduct that led to the disqualification order. But the protection of the public (i.e. creditors, employees, lenders, investors and all those with whom the company will do business) is . . . paramount.

See further, D Milman, 'Partial disqualification orders' (1991) 12 Co Law 224; Robert Goddard, 'Leave to act and the disqualified director: *Re Hennelly's Utilities Ltd*' (2004) 25 Co Law 222. The practice of granting leave subject to conditions was criticised in *Re TLL Realisations Ltd* [2000] BCC 998 by Ferris J, who said that 'If it is felt that leave should not be unconditional this may suggest that the better view is that it should not be granted at all'.

Commentary

The court must bear in mind that the purpose of a disqualification order or undertaking is to protect the public (a) from misconduct by the disqualified person, (b) by deterring others from doing what the disqualified person did and (c) by maintaining and improving standards of integrity of directors (*Re Morija plc* [2007] EWHC 3055 (Ch), [2008] 2 BCLC 313 at [33]). The more serious the misconduct which led to the disqualification order or undertaking, the greater the risk of future misconduct and the greater the need to maintain disqualification as a deterrent to others (*Re Morija plc* at [35]).

It is not the policy of the Act to prevent a disqualified director from earning his or her living, only from doing so with the insulation from liability available to company directors. Being a member of an unlimited company imposes unlimited liability when the company is wound up and so an application to be a director of an unlimited company of which the applicant will be substantially the only interested member may be looked on favourably by the court, provided there are undertakings to maintain the company's unlimited status (*Re Dawes and Henderson (Agencies) Ltd (No. 2)*).

Appeals against decisions on applications for leave are governed by the Insolvency Rules 1986 (SI 1986/1925), rr. 7.47 and 7.49 (*Re Britannia Homes Centres Ltd* [2001] 2 BCLC 63). This procedure is described in **84.11** to **84.13**.

VARIATION OF DISQUALIFICATION UNDERTAKING

86.39 A person who has given a disqualification undertaking may apply under CDDA 1986, s. 8A, for an order reducing or ending the period for which the undertaking is to be in force. The application may be made to any court to which, if the undertaking had not been accepted, the Secretary of State could have applied for a disqualification order (s. 8A(3)). The application must be made under **CPR, Part 8**, using form N501 (**PD Directors Disqualification Proceedings, para. 30.2**). The Secretary of State must be made the defendant to the application (**para. 30.5**), which must be served by the applicant, by first-class post, on the Treasury Solicitor (**para. 30.6**). On the hearing of the application, the Secretary of State must appear, in order to call the court's attention to any relevant matters, and may give evidence or call witnesses (CDDA 1986, s. 8A(2)). **Paragraphs 29 to 34 of PD Directors Disqualification Proceedings** give full details of the procedure to be followed, which has much in common with the procedure for applying for a disqualification order.

Disqualification undertakings were created in order to avoid court proceedings, so variation of an undertaking should be ordered only where circumstances have arisen since the undertaking was given which could not have been foreseen or which were not intended to be covered by the undertaking (*Re INS Realisations Ltd* [2006] EWHC 135 (Ch), [2006] 1 WLR 3433, at [39]–[40]). An application for variation should not normally be made just because the undertaking was given without legal advice or because other directors of the company were given shorter disqualification periods by the court (*Re INS Realisations Ltd* at [43]).

Chapter 87 Mortgage Possession Claims

The following procedural checklists, which are at the front of the book, are relevant to this chapter:

Procedural checklist 37 Residential mortgage possession claims
Procedural checklist 38 Enforcement of possession orders

NATURE OF MORTGAGES

Rights to possession

87.1 A legal mortgage of a freehold or leasehold is a charge created by deed to secure financial liabilities owed to the mortgagee (Law of Property Act 1925, ss. 85 and 86). Part 3 of the 1925 Act sets out a framework of rights, powers and obligations of parties to a mortgage. These are subject to the terms of the mortgage deed itself. The mortgagee has a legal estate in the charged property and has an immediate right to possession of the property (*Four-Maids Ltd v Dudley Marshall (Properties) Ltd* [1957] Ch 317 at p. 320), but mortgage deeds usually make exercise of this right depend on default by the mortgagor. In practice, a mortgagee who wishes to realise the security will normally require possession so as to sell the mortgaged property (see ss. 101 to 103). In order to be able to take possession of mortgaged property against the wishes of the mortgagor or anyone else occupying the property, a mortgagee must obtain a court order for delivery of possession, which can be enforced by a warrant of possession.

Types of mortgage

87.2 Most mortgages granted by major financial institutions are instalment mortgages, under which the mortgagor agrees to repay capital, and accrued interest, over a set term of years by regular instalments. Usually, both rate of interest and monthly payment may be varied by the mortgagee, but in some mortgages the interest rate is fixed for an initial period after which it rises, usually to a higher than market rate. Either way, if the mortgagor pays all the instalments, the mortgage debt will be discharged.

Under an endowment mortgage the regular instalments are of interest only. The borrower maintains a life assurance policy which ultimately matures so as to repay the capital. The increasingly popular genuine interest-only mortgage offers maximum borrowing at minimum cost. The borrower is left to raise the capital to redeem the mortgage, by sale or otherwise, within the term.

In contrast are 'all money' charges. Usually granted to a bank to secure a business overdraft, they require the whole sum outstanding to be repaid following demand. The distinction between these and instalment (or term) mortgages is crucial when considering the powers of the court to postpone possession.

A distinct regime covers secured (usually smaller) loans by regulated financial institutions under the Consumer Credit Act 1974, over which the county court has exclusive jurisdiction.

COMMENCEMENT OF PROCEEDINGS

Pre-action protocol

87.3 The **Pre-action Protocol for Possession Claims Based on Mortgage or Home Purchase Plan Arrears in Respect of Residential Property** (the **Mortgage Protocol**) initially came into force on 19 November 2008 and has since been refined. The aim was to encourage initial communication between the parties and out-of-court resolution of disputes. That notwithstanding, there will be cases where a possession order is necessary. The **Mortgage Protocol** contains no specific sanctions for non-compliance. However, non-compliance may be indicative of unreasonable conduct, which may entitle the court to disallow certain costs (see 87.45) or adjourn or stay the proceedings (see 87.36). This is consistent with **PD Pre-action Conduct, Section II**, which governs the approach of the court where there is a relevant pre-action protocol.

Practitioners should refer to the specific requirements of the **Mortgage Protocol**. In essence when a borrower falls into arrears there are obligations on mortgage lenders to provide full financial statements, to attempt discussion with the borrower as to the causes of the problem, consider changes to the monthly payment date, respond promptly to borrowers' proposals, and give borrowers adequate time to respond to their own requirements. If an agreement is breached, 15 business days' notice must be given of the intention to go to court (**para.** 5).

Mortgage lenders should, before starting a claim, allow the borrower an opportunity to make a claim under the Mortgage Rescue Scheme or under a mortgage protection policy if it would (together with any other payments the borrower can make) cover the arrears or claim through the Department for Work and Pensions ('DWP') for support for mortgage interest (**para. 6.1**). If the borrower can demonstrate reasonable steps have been or can be taken to sell the property at an 'appropriate' price in accordance with professional advice, the mortgage lender should consider not issuing a claim. But the borrower must reciprocate, by actively marketing the property and keeping the mortgage lender informed (**paras 6.2** and **6.3**). If the lender decides against postponing issuing (perhaps because of negative equity, or an errant co-owner) it must give five business days' notice before starting proceedings (**para. 6.4**).

Starting a possession claim is a last resort which normally must not be used unless all reasonable attempts to resolve the position have failed. Claims must not normally be started when settlement is being actively explored. Lenders are encouraged to consider a wide range of options, including extending the term, changing the type of mortgage, deferring interest or capitalising arrears (**para.** 7). Further restrictions operate if an apparently genuine complaint has been made to the Financial Ombudsman (**para.** 8). However there is no compulsion on lenders to adopt any particular solution. Compliance with the **Mortgage Protocol** is evidenced at the hearing by production of a standard-form checklist (see 87.23).

Commentary

Procedural framework

A possession claim brought by a mortgagee must follow the procedure set out in **CPR, Part 55**, and **PD 55A**. However, a judgment creditor seeking to enforce a charging order by sale, even if also seeking possession, uses the procedure in **CPR, Part 73** (**r. 73.10**; see 79.27). **87.4**

Other pre-issue considerations

A mortgagee should check all relevant terms of the mortgage contract when contemplating possession proceedings. The mortgage deed rarely reflects the entire arrangement negotiated between lender and borrower. A mortgage deed is usually in short form, incorporating the lender's then current printed standard conditions. Further terms, such as the amount of the loan and the initial interest rate, may appear in an offer letter. Conditions may prevent proceedings being brought until two months' default. **87.5**

Care should be taken, particularly with flats, or new properties where the estate conveyancing may have used plot numbers, to identify the correct postal address of the property, including postcode. Specific enquiry should be made by solicitors of their lender client as to what its records show as the last known address of the proposed defendants. When joint mortgagors separate, the deserted partner may supply the mortgagee with the other's new address.

Office copy Land Registry entries should be obtained, a matrimonial homes search made, and instructions taken on them for the material to be included in the claim form and particulars of claim.

If a possession order has been suspended provided defined payments were made, even if all the arrears the subject of that order have been paid up, there is no need to start fresh proceedings (see *Bank of Scotland plc v Zinda* [2011] EWCA Civ 706, [2012] 1 WLR 728). This means that unless leave to issue a warrant is sought, independent verification of whether indeed further arrears have accrued, and the protection for other persons with an interest in the property, provided in new claims by **CPR, Part 55**, depend on any specific directions of the district judge on any warrant suspension application.

Status of those with registered interests

87.6 The Land Registry search and entries may identify others with relevant rights in the property, and their status must be considered. Although all mortgagors and any surety should be parties to the action, it is unwise to add unnecessary parties. Those with registered matrimonial homes rights are entitled to be joined, and must be notified (**PD 55A, para.** 2.5(1)), ideally by sending copies of the proceedings.

If the mortgagor is already subject to insolvency proceedings, it may be necessary to obtain permission to commence or continue a claim (see **84.16** to **84.37**). The rights of a mortgagee are generally unaffected by the bankruptcy (or winding up) of the mortgagor. A bankrupt mortgagor is a proper defendant. He or she is entitled to be heard on the question of possession of the property, even though it is part of the estate vested in the trustee, who should be served with a copy of the proceedings.

CPR, r. 55.10(2), requires the claimant to give notice of the hearing to other mortgagees (see **87.17**). This may forestall proceedings by another mortgagee, or facilitate case management by the court of existing claims affecting the same property (see **r. 1.4**).

Tenancies pose particular problems: see **87.26**.

Venue

87.7 Possession claims are normally commenced in the county court for the district in which the charged property is located. Claim form N5 must be used and separate particulars of claim must be filed and served with it. A claim may be commenced in the High Court only if a certificate is filed with the claim form stating the reasons for bringing the claim in that court (**CPR, r.** 55.3(2); **PD 55A, para.** 1.3). Factual or legal complexity, or points of law of general importance may indicate a High Court case: value alone does not (**PD 55A, paras 1.3** and **1.4**). If foreclosure or sale of residential property outside Greater London is also claimed, the High Court has exclusive jurisdiction (County Courts Act 1984, s. 21(4)). This chapter deals only with proceedings in county courts.

Alternatively, claims may be issued under the electronic web-based PCOL (Possession Claims Online) system, covered by **PD 55B** (see **87.11 to 87.14**).

PARTICULARS OF CLAIM

Content of particulars of claim

87.8 The content of the particulars of claim in a possession claim generally (including possession claims against tenants and trespassers) is prescribed by **PD 55A, para. 2.1**. Form N120 should be used. **CPR, r.** 55.4, reminds the claimant to comply with the often ignored Part 16, the mortgage being a contract in writing (see **PD 16, para.** 7.3). This is reinforced by the specific provisions of **PD 55A, para. 2.1**. In all possession claims the particulars must:

(a) identify the land in question;
(b) indicate whether the claim includes residential property;
(c) state the *ground for possession*, e.g. arrears;
(d) state full details of the relationship between the parties — to be noted if any original party to the deed has transferred their interest;

(e) identify all persons who, to the best of the claimant's knowledge and belief, are in possession. Care should be taken with buy-to-let mortgages.

Form N120 requires the claimant to identify the relief sought. In practice the choice is whether also to seek a money judgment for the outstanding balance. The claim form must be verified by statement of truth.

Extra information for mortgage claims

There are additional requirements for particulars of claim in mortgage possession cases (**PD 55A, paras 2.5** and **2.5A**): **87.9**

(a) Matrimonial homes rights must be identified (**para. 2.5(1)**).
(b) The state of the mortgage account must be set out, showing the amount of the advance (and further advances), periodic repayments and regular payments of interest due (**para. 2.5(2)(a)**).
(c) There must be a statement of the amount necessary to redeem the mortgage on a projected date less than 14 days after issue, separately showing costs and administration fees (**para. 2.5(2)(b)**).
(d) If the secured loan is a regulated consumer credit agreement, that fact must be stated (**para. 2.5(2)(c)**) together with the dates of any default or termination notices under the Consumer Credit Act 1974, ss. 76 or 87, and, if appropriate, whether the loan is affected by s. 141 (**PD 55A, para. 2.5(4)** and **(5)**).
(e) If the claim is made for non-payment of instalments, there must be a schedule giving details of dates and amounts of payments due and made under the mortgage for the preceding two years, or since the first date of default if later (thus demonstrating how the arrears have accumulated since the account was last up to date). It is imperative that the schedule carries a running total of the arrears, and is intelligible to both average borrower and judge. The temptation to attach a spreadsheet produced for other purposes should be resisted, unless clearly charting the arrears pattern. Also the schedule must show other payments due under the mortgage, and whether they fall within the contractual payments and are in arrears (**para. 2.5(3)**).
(f) If relying on over two years' arrears, a full schedule must be exhibited to a witness statement (**para. 2.5A**).
(g) Relevant information about the defendant's circumstances must be provided, in particular, about social security benefits payable, to the defendant or to the mortgage lender (**para. 2.5(6)**). Relevant information includes details of bankruptcy, or the belief that the defendant receives rents sufficient, say, to pay the mortgage.
(h) Previous steps taken to recover the debt secured by the mortgage must be stated. Past proceedings must be disclosed, quoting their outcome. Their existence may be relevant to how the court exercises any discretion to adjourn, or to suspend any order (**para. 2.5(8)**).

Service

After issue, the court will serve the proceedings, in accordance with **CPR, Part 6**. The norm is postal service at the last known address of the defendant, which may not be the property address. For service outside England and Wales see **chapter 16**. **87.10**

POSSESSION CLAIMS ONLINE (PCOL)

Mortgage possession claims can now be brought online, with a reduced issue fee. Their progress can be monitored at any time. The procedure is regulated by **CPR, r. 55.10A**, and **PD 55B**. **87.11**

Commentary

Availability of PCOL

87.12 PCOL is available for mortgage possession claims brought, by claimants with United Kingdom addresses, solely on the grounds of arrears. The conventional procedure must be adopted if another breach of covenant is alleged or if the relief sought is other than possession and a money judgment for the balance, interest and costs. If any defendant has an address for service outside England and Wales, or the claimant cannot provide a postcode for the mortgaged property, PCOL is not available (**PD 55B, para. 5.1**). PCOL is not to be used if the defendant is known to be a child or protected party (**para. 5.2**).

Access to PCOL

87.13 Claimants request the issue of a claim electronically by accessing the PCOL website at https://www.possessionclaim.gov.uk/pcol/. It is important to access the website for further information generally and in particular to identify how to monitor and progress the claim. PCOL users access the site by complying with a customary security system of username and password, and make fee payments for PCOL applications by debit or credit card or, for frequent users, by an account system. The website is clearly claimant orientated, and whilst in theory defendants can use the site, there are practical difficulties, not least for defendants who wish to make applications requiring fees remission (**PD 55B, para. 4.2**).

Procedure

87.14 The claimant requests issue of the claim form by completing an online form and paying the fee through the website, or in another approved way (**PD 55B, para. 6.1**). PCOL differs from the conventional procedure principally in that the particulars of claim must be included in the online form and not filed separately (**para. 6.2**). There is no need to file a copy mortgage deed (**para. 6.2**). If the claimant has already provided the defendant with a full schedule of arrears, the particulars can be abbreviated (**PD 55B, paras 6.3A and 6.3B**).

If there is only an arrears summary in the particulars, the claimant must serve within seven days of issue the full arrears history containing the information required under **para. 6.3**. The claimant must also either make a confirmatory witness statement dealing with the full arrears history, or verify by way of oral evidence compliance and produce the arrears history.

Acknowledgment of receipt by the court of the claim form is not confirmation of either issue or service (**para. 6.5**). An online claim is 'brought' for limitation purposes when the online claim form is received by the court's computer system (**para. 6.6**).

Upon issue, the court serves a printed version of the claim form, and a defence form for completion by the defendant, and sends notice of issue to the claimant (**para. 6.7**). The claim is deemed to be served on the fifth day after issue, whether a business day or not (**para. 6.8**).

PCOL issues the proceedings in the designated court, based on the postcode of the mortgaged property, as provided by the claimant (**para. 6.11**). That court then has jurisdiction to hear the claim and enforce the judgment (**para. 6.11**). If an error caused by mistyping the postcode or computer glitches is spotted, that court may transfer to the correct local court. Non-local cases are likely to be transferred, both for the convenience of the defendant and to aid enforcement of any possession order.

Each claim form carries a unique customer identification number or password enabling the defendant to access it on the PCOL website (**para. 6.10**).

A defendant may file an electronic defence to a PCOL claim. A hard copy must not also be filed at the local court (**para. 7**). The requirement for statements of case (and application notices) to be verified by statement of truth and the method of online signature (by entry of the name) are addressed in **PD 55B, paras 8** and **9**. A form which is required to be signed by a person is deemed to be signed if that person's name is entered in the form online. Sanctions for abuse are in **CPR, r. 32.14**.

PRE-HEARING STEPS

Date of hearing

When issuing a claim form in a mortgage possession case, the court will fix a hearing date not less than 28 days distant (**CPR, r. 55.5**). The standard period between issue and hearing is from eight to 10 weeks. If the computer system in PCOL cases allocates a hearing date within the minimum period provided by **CPR, r. 55.5(3)**, it is good practice to request a fresh date immediately. The defendant must be served with the claim form and particulars of claim not less than 21 days before the hearing (**r. 55.5(3)**). If service is to take place outside the jurisdiction, the standard time may be exceeded. The court may, under **r. 3.1(2)(a)**, vary the time for compliance with any rule. **87.15**

Defence

When the court effects service, it sends, with the claim form and particulars, a pack including notes for guidance (N7) and a defence form (N11M). That seeks, in questionnaire style, details of the defendant's financial position, as well as providing space for specific reasons to oppose the making of a possession order. **87.16**

No acknowledgment of service is required (**CPR, r. 55.7(1)**) nor is there any real sanction if the defendant fails to file a defence within the time specified in **r. 15.4**. Defendants ideally should include in their statement of case (the defence) all the evidence relied upon, including, if applicable, details of housing benefit claims.

Notice to tenants and others

To comply with **CPR, r. 55.10**, not less than five days after receiving notification of the hearing date, the claimant must send a notice: (a) to the property, addressed to 'the tenant or occupier', (b) to the housing department of the local authority in whose area the property is situated, and (c) to the proprietor of any other registered charge. The notice must state that the claim has been commenced in respect of the property, quoting its full address, the name and address of claimant and defendant, and the court issuing the claim form, plus date, time and place of hearing. 'Send' means dispatch, not serve. Customarily the notice is given in a standard-form letter. Care should be taken to ensure the accuracy of the property address. If the court is not satisfied with compliance, the hearing will be adjourned. **87.17**

Claimant's evidence

CPR, r. 55.8(4), provides that all witness statements must be filed and served at least two days before the hearing. Any fact to be proved at the hearing may be proved by witness statement, unless there is a genuine dispute of fact (**PD 55A, para. 5.4**). Usually, the only evidence before the court is a claim form, verified by statement of truth, and an updating claimant's witness statement. Despite the requirements of **PD 55A, para. 5.1**, to the effect that the claimant should, wherever possible, include in its statement of case all its evidence, in practice this rarely happens because of the need to comply with **CPR, r. 55.10** (see 87.17). The statement of the claimant should be made by a person with knowledge of the mortgage account, and of suitable seniority and delegated authority. Its timing is delicate: if too close to the hearing, a defendant may seek an adjournment to take advice. The ideal is about 14 days before hearing. **87.18**

Contents of the claimant's witness statement

87.19 The claimant's evidence should deal specifically with the following:

(a) matters not dealt with in the particulars of claim and changes to any facts stated therein;
(b) in PCOL cases, and if not earlier produced, a copy of the mortgage deed, terms and conditions and any default notices under Consumer Credit Act 1974;
(c) the term of the mortgage;
(d) the amount of the arrears, both at the statement date and those potentially existing at the hearing date, assuming no further payments — if there is more than one mortgage account, the figures for the accounts should be separately stated, and totalled;
(e) the outstanding balance(s) on the mortgage account(s);
(f) the date the next instalment is due;
(g) the date of the last payment;
(h) compliance with **CPR, r. 55.10**, if not dealt with by filing a separate certificate;
(i) up-to-date evidence of title; and
(j) a Land Registry search in form HRR to discover the existence of any registered family law rights. A spouse, cohabitant or civil partner, present or past, not a party, may apply to be joined to the proceedings.

Evidence of compliance with the **Mortgage Protocol** is covered at the hearing by form N123 (see 87.23), which has its own statement of truth. Guidance notes in the form may assist in completing it.

Land Registry entries

87.20 Evidence of title involves the production of office or electronic Land Registry copies ideally not more than a month old. These reveal any changes to registered entries, such as further charges, transfers of the legal estate, or notes of bankruptcy orders. The Land Registration Act 2002, s. 67(1), provides that an official copy ('the office copy') of the register, part thereof or any filed document, is admissible to the same extent as the original. In the exceedingly rare case of unregistered title, the original mortgage must be produced, together with a Land Charges search.

Change of mortgagee

87.21 It is increasingly common for financial institutions to refinance their 'mortgage books', which may mean that a claimant mortgagee has assigned its interest before the hearing. As most mortgage possession hearings are undertaken by agent solicitors, the mortgagee's advocate may be unaware of such a change. If there is a change of title between issue and hearing, formalities can be resolved at the hearing by directing that the case continue with the new claimant. Formal evidence is needed, and the official copies may prove the change in title. The current state of the mortgage account needs to be proved, and this requires both a notice of assignment, to redirect future payments, and a witness statement from the new claimant. The advocate appearing at the hearing for the mortgagee must be instructed by the new claimant. Unless a cooperative borrower appears at court, it may be difficult for the court to proceed that day.

Pre-hearing adjournments

87.22 In the spirit of the **Mortgage Protocol**, a mortgagee may seek adjournment of a possession claim where arrears have been reduced to less than two months, even if the mortgage contract does not require two months' arrears as a precondition for exercising the right to possession. *If, whatever the arrears,* the mortgagee's policy is to hold off only with the protection of a suspended possession order, the hearing must proceed. If a satisfactory payment plan can be agreed, the mortgagee may simply wish to adjourn. Because there is no prejudice to the mortgagor, most courts adjourn on the written application of the mortgagee only. Because of lack of time, a consent application for an adjournment signed by both sides in advance of the hearing is rarely lodged. The usual order is for the case to be adjourned generally on the basis that if not restored by a certain date it will be struck out. This does not preclude the mortgagee later instituting proceedings for fresh arrears. Following such an order, the mortgagee should monitor the situation and take action if necessary to restore before the strike-out date.

Most mortgagees write seeking an adjournment and pay the application fee. This fee can be added to the borrower's account and is less than the cost of attending a hearing. No fee is payable if the application to adjourn is by consent and is received by the court at least 14 days before the date set for the hearing (CPFO, **notes to fee 2.7**). Others ask for the letter to be put before the district judge at the hearing for him then to make the order. The latter approach may save the fee, but does not vacate the hearing in advance. As an adjournment order may not issue from the court in sufficient time to reach the mortgagor, the mortgagee should confirm with the mortgagor what it has done, to save the mortgagor wasting time attending an aborted hearing. Letters to the court should emphasise in the heading the hearing date and time.

An adjourned case can be restored by complying with any provisions of the order granting the earlier adjournment. Even if not ordered, an updating witness statement will be required dealing with the current arrears.

Commentary

FIRST HEARING

Matters to be considered

All court hearings dealing with mortgage possession cases are in private (**PD 39A, para. 1.5**). **87.23**
The hearing normally takes place before a district judge. Customarily only a few minutes are allocated. Within this time, the court must be satisfied that all formalities have been complied with, and will receive from the claimant's solicitor, up-to-date Land Registry entries, fresh search in form HRR, and (if not filed) copy mortgage documents. Form N123 must be handed in, with a copy for the defendant. There is a certain tension as to when the N123 is prepared. If completed prior to starting the claim, it will not offer the court at the hearing up-to-date information on recent attempts by the borrower to forestall proceedings. Lenders' advocates should be in a position to assist the court on such matters. An oral update on the crucial figures (last payment, existing arrears and balance outstanding) is given. These figures should have been checked with the lender that day and be at the advocate's fingertips. Advocates should tell the court the length of the term and type of mortgage, and indicate any unusual features of the case. They must be succinct.

Usually the facts and figures are not disputed. If a defendant attends, it is usually to propose a payment plan, or seek time to make a proposal, and oppose an outright possession order. It is rare for a defence to be filed beforehand. The court must identify any issues in the case. The court will usually have insufficient time then to resolve any but the most straightforward problems, because there will be many other cases waiting to be heard. The court will adjourn to a longer hearing, and may give interim directions, such as to file a defence, or clearer defence, to encapsulate what is raised for the first time at the hearing.

ISSUES AND POSSIBLE DEFENCES

Nature of a possession order

The claimant seeks a possession order. This is enforceable by bailiff's warrant. A warrant for **87.24**
possession operates against the land, and does not distinguish between individual occupiers.

Therefore, if the claimant would not be entitled to execute a warrant for possession, it would be premature to make any possession order. So, if there are two borrowers and one of them has not been served, or claims to have a defence, it is inappropriate to make an order at this stage. In *Albany Homes Ltd v Massey* [1997] 2 All ER 609 it was held that possession proceedings should be adjourned until the outstanding issues with one of the defendants, involving undue influence, had been determined.

Overriding interests

87.25 Although form N120 (particulars of claim) requires the claimant in a mortgage possession claim to have enquired of those in occupation of the property before issue, occupants' rights must be considered, and the notice required by **CPR, r. 55.10**, is intended to give them an opportunity to attend the hearing of the claim. The equitable interest of one partner, as a result often of capital contributions to the property, may have priority over the mortgagee.

For a discussion of these issues see *Lloyds Bank plc v Rosset* [1991] 1 AC 107 and *Abbey National Building Society v Cann* [1991] 1 AC 56. The actions of mortgagees in postponing these rights when granting advances, and the ever-increasing trend to owning properties in joint names, has reduced the need for such issues to be raised.

Tenants

87.26 Tenants are at real risk in a mortgage possession claim. Frequently, if the borrower does not attend there is no evidence before the court of the existence, let alone status, of a tenant. The claimant's solicitor should be prepared to assist the court in this regard, if only to forestall future applications. As well as the **CPR, r. 55.10**, notice (see **87.17**), good practice suggests writing to any known tenant informing them of the proceedings, the nature of any order sought and inviting them to seek advice and attend the hearing.

If tenants have paid their rent, their landlord, the mortgagor, may have assuaged their concerns by promises of clearing the arrears. If the tenancy pre-dates the mortgage, unless the tenant's rights have been postponed in writing to those of the mortgagee at the granting of the mortgage, the tenant should be joined and served. If the tenancy is binding on the mortgagee, the tenant will be entitled to resist a possession order. The tenant will have an overriding interest, in priority to the mortgagee (*Woolwich Building Society v Dickman* [1996] 3 All ER 204). If the mortgagee has expressly consented in writing to any letting, a possession order should not be made if the tenant remains lawfully in occupation, as a possession order operates against the land, and serves to deprive any occupier of the right to remain. The arguments raised in *Albany Homes Ltd v Massey* [1997] 2 All ER 609, by analogy, preclude the making of a possession order. If the tenancy was created by the mortgagor after the mortgage, without the consent of the mortgagee, the tenancy is unauthorised, and is no bar to a possession order (*Brittania Building Society v Earl* [1990] 1 WLR 422), even though the tenant may have a claim against the mortgagor. Although the mortgagee may be entitled to possession against unauthorised tenants let in by the mortgagor, with 'buy-to-let' mortgages the borrower is encouraged to let. Whether that encouragement amounts to permission to let to a particular tenant is a matter for each case and the terms of the mortgage offer and agreement. The issue of implied permission remains unclear, and mortgagees submit that they are not bound by tenancies to which they did not actually consent, and of which they may be unaware. However, the mortgagee must act in good faith in seeking possession, and the court will look at the actual, rather than the formal relationship of the parties (see *Quennell v Maltby* [1979] 1 WLR 318). A mortgagor may, nonetheless, adopt a tenancy, or be estopped from denying being bound by it.

Before considering joining a tenant to the proceedings under **CPR, Part 19**, the court must identify whether that tenancy can potentially operate as a defence to the claim. Joinder gives a right to disclosure of all the documents in the action and may have costs implications.

Since 1 October 2010, the Mortgage Repossessions (Protection of Tenants etc.) Act 2010 and the Dwelling Houses (Execution of Possession Orders by Mortgagees) Regulations 2010 (SI 2010/1809) have given some limited protection to unauthorised tenants, defined as persons occupying under assured, protected, or statutory tenancies, whose tenancies do not bind the mortgagee. **CPR, r. 55.10** (4A), enables applications to be made to the court by such tenants, although not parties to the action. By virtue of s. 1(2) of the 2010 Act, when making a possession order the court may, on the application of the tenant, postpone the date for delivery of possession for a period not exceeding two months. The court would presumably act in this way if the tenant turned up at the hearing pursuant to the **CPR, r. 55.10**, notice. Under the 2010 Act the court will take account of the tenant's circumstances and any breach of the tenancy. So a tenant already in breach of his obligations might not be granted such an extension, unless his non-payment of rent was due to housing benefit delays. There is a power to direct rental payments to the mortgagee without thereby creating any fresh tenancy (see also 87.53).

Appointment of a receiver

If there is a lawful tenant in the property, the mortgage lender should not seek a possession order, but should instead appoint a receiver of the rents and profits of the property under the Law of Property Act 1925, s. 103. That receiver can, if appropriate, seek to terminate the tenancy. If terminating the tenancy gives the receiver vacant possession, the mortgage lender can sell without further order, as in *Horsham Properties Group Ltd v Clark* [2008] EWHC 2327 (Ch), [2009] 1 P & CR 8. **87.27**

Undue influence

Sometimes the reason for the inability to sustain the contractual payments is family breakdown. One party, often the wife or female partner, wishes to challenge the mortgage, or a further advance. Perhaps one of two joint owners used the security of the property to raise business funds. The other may raise the defence of undue influence, contending that the charge, or further advance, be set aside. **87.28**

The leading case is *Barclays Bank plc v O'Brien* [1994] 1 AC 180. If there is nothing to put the mortgage lender on notice, undue influence cannot operate as a defence to possession, no matter what other remedies the disadvantaged homeowner may have against his or her former partner.

Since the *O'Brien* case, banks have developed practices to prevent undue influence defences succeeding. They now regularly obtain a letter from the joint mortgagor's solicitor confirming that the effect of the transaction has been explained to him or her. In *Royal Bank of Scotland plc v Etridge (No. 2)* [2001] UKHL 44, [2002] 2 AC 773, the House of Lords explained *O'Brien* and added detailed guidance. As a result of banks following this guidance, the flow of like cases has substantially diminished.

Forgery

If the signature of one of two joint mortgagors on the mortgage deed has been forged, the aggrieved party has the right to set aside the mortgage so as not to be bound by it. Forgery may take place when one borrower wishes to raise additional funds without the knowledge of his or her co-owner. **87.29**

Misrepresentation

Misrepresentations given by or on behalf of the mortgagee, inducing a mortgagor to enter into the transaction, may afford a potential defence. If the misrepresentation was by an agent of the mortgagee, the mortgagor must prove that it was made in the course of the agency so as to make the mortgagee vicariously liable. **87.30**

Commentary

Unfair terms

87.31 Unfair terms in non-individually negotiated mortgage contracts do not bind consumer mortgagors. See the Unfair Terms in Consumer Contracts Regulations 1999 (SI 1999/ 2083) and **chapter 90**. However, main terms concerning the price paid and the value of the mortgage product are exempt from control (SI 1999/2083, reg. 6(2)) if set out in plain intelligible language. If a mortgage can continue without the offending term, that term can be severed and the mortgage can still be enforced.

Technical defences

87.32 A mortgage contract made by a person in the course of carrying on a regulated activity in contravention of the general prohibition in the Financial Services and Markets Act 2000, s. 19 (prohibition against carrying on a regulated activity in the United Kingdom except by authorised and exempt persons) is unenforceable against the mortgagor (ss. 26 and 27), unless the court considers it is just and equitable in the circumstances of the case for it to be enforced (s. 28). Breaches of the technical requirements of the Consumer Credit Act 1974 on default notices or otherwise may offer defences. Occupation by the mortgagor for 12 years since the last mortgage payment offers a potential defence under the Limitation Act 1980 (*Ashe v National Westminster Bank plc* [2008] EWCA Civ 55, [2008] 1 WLR 710).

Challenging arrears

87.33 Even if the mortgage is admitted, there may be a dispute over the figures contended for by the mortgagee. Payments may go astray, sometimes into the holding accounts of the mortgagee, awaiting tracing and allocating, or take longer in clearance than expected. The court should not treat as a dispute of substance (and consequent track allocation) every case where the arrears statement is not agreed. The mortgagee claimant will not want this, because of the delay: the mortgagor defendant may gain time, but end up paying for the litigation. The preferable course is to adjourn a few weeks to enable the parties to try to narrow the issues. This may result in the need to try only a discrete issue, such as whether the arrears are £2,000 or £3,000, or the making of an order based on a minimum agreed arrears figure.

It is important to distinguish between arrears and other payments due under the mortgage. These should have been separately identified in the statement annexed to the particulars (**PD 55A, para. 2.5(3)**). A mortgagee may make payments to protect its security, for example, debiting the mortgage account with the property insurance premium. With leasehold properties the mortgagee may pay ground rent or service charges to avoid forfeiture of the lease. Such payments may correctly have been debited to the mortgage account, meaning that the mortgage cannot be redeemed without the mortgagor repaying them with accrued interest. But they would not necessarily be arrears upon which a possession claim can be founded. Examination of the terms and conditions of the mortgage should reveal if the mortgagee is entitled to capitalise these, and adjust the monthly payment accordingly, or to claim these as an addition to the monthly instalment.

There may be challenges to how the mortgagee has calculated the monthly instalment, or whether payments made by the mortgagor in reduction of capital have been correctly attributed.

Track allocation

87.34 If disputed matters remain unresolved, and a defence has been filed, case management directions given under **CPR, r. 55.8(1)(b)**, will include track allocation. Allocation principles are dealt with in **r. 55.9**. The court has to consider all the normal factors set out in **r. 26.8**, as applicable to a case of this nature: the amount of the arrears, the importance to the defendant of retaining possession of the land and the importance to the claimant of vacant possession.

The level of arrears alone may be under the small claims limit, but the value of the property, and usually the balance outstanding under the mortgage (often claimed in the action) will substantially exceed the fast track limit. The perceived advantages of the fast track are speed and limitation of trial costs. Given the usual costs covenant in mortgage deeds, the latter consideration is less relevant. Allocation to the multi-track is usually appropriate, and, save in the most complex of cases, speedy trial can be achieved by fixing a trial window near to, or sooner than, the 27 weeks for a fast track case. Once allocated to the fast track or multi-track, unless the court otherwise directs, all the evidence will be orally tested, in accordance with **Part 32**.

UNDEFENDED CASES: DELAYING POSSESSION

The court's approach

If the court is satisfied on all the formalities, and there are no substantial areas of dispute, it will proceed to deal with the case. The inherent powers of the court to adjourn at the request of the mortgagor are very limited. In practice, a degree of pragmatism exists. If a defendant writes indicating a hospital appointment on the hearing date, there is little point in the claimant urging upon the court the making of a possession order. It begs an application to set aside the order under **CPR, r. 3.1(2)(m)**, causing added delay and costs. Likewise if the claimant has failed to comply with an aspect of procedure, application of the overriding objective leads the court usually to adjourn rather than dismiss. So, short purposive adjournments exist in practice. Otherwise, unless mortgagees consent, inherently the only purpose of an adjournment is to afford the borrower a brief opportunity to redeem the entire mortgage (*Birmingham Citizens Permanent Building Society v Caunt* [1962] Ch 883). **87.35**

Suspended orders under the Administration of Justice Act 1970, s. 36

The draconian regime described in 87.35 is tempered for mortgages of residential property by the Administration of Justice Act 1970, s. 36. This gives the court power to adjourn the proceedings, or make a possession order but stay, suspend or postpone the date for possession, if satisfied the sums due can be made good within a reasonable period of time. In the case of an instalment mortgage, the requirement is for the arrears of instalments to be made good. Section 36 provides that: **87.36**

(1) Where the mortgagee under a mortgage of land which consists of or includes a dwelling-house brings an action in which he claims possession of the mortgaged property,... the court may exercise any of the powers conferred on it by subsection (2) below if it appears to the court that in the event of it exercising the power the mortgagor is likely to be able within a reasonable period to pay any sums due under the mortgage or to remedy a default consisting of a breach of any other obligation arising under or by virtue of the mortgage.
(2) The court—
   (a) may adjourn the proceedings, or
   (b) on giving judgment, or making any order, for delivery of possession of the mortgaged property, or at any time before the execution of such judgment or order, may—
      (i) stay or suspend execution of the judgment or order, or
      (ii) postpone the date for delivery of possession,
   for such period or periods as the court thinks reasonable.

In exercising these powers, the court may impose conditions of payment by the mortgagor of sums secured by the mortgage (or remedying other default) (s. 36(3)).

The Administration of Justice Act 1973, s. 8, extended and modified these provisions to deal with cases where failure to pay an instalment triggers an obligation to pay the entire mortgage balance.

These provisions apply only if the security includes a dwelling-house. By the Administration of Justice Act 1970, s. 39(1), this includes any building or part of a building which is used as a dwelling (see *Royal Bank of Scotland plc v Miller* [2001] EWCA Civ 344, [2002] QB 255). The provisions do not apply to regulated agreements (see **87.46** to **87.48**) under the Consumer Credit Act 1974 (Administration of Justice Act 1970, s. 38A).

There are two issues for the court:
(a) whether there is sufficient evidence to support the borrower's proposals; and
(b) whether the timescale proposed for discharge of the arrears is reasonable.

The options for the court making a possession order are an outright order, which is usually made effective after 28 days, or a suspended order. If the court exercises its powers under s. 36, the period of suspension must be defined (*Royal Trust Co. of Canada v Markham* [1975] 1 WLR 1416). With a suspended order, possession will be ordered in (usually) 28 days, suspended on payment by the mortgagor of current instalments as they fall due, plus defined regular sums off the then arrears. A first payment date, normally when the next contractual instalment is due, should be specified. Absent a specific order for review, the court may, on application, at any time reconsider the matter and vary the order (s. 36(4)).

The s. 36 jurisdiction is not engaged if possession is obtained without court proceedings (see *Horsham Properties Group Ltd v Clark* [2008] EWHC 2327 (Ch), [2008] NPC 127).

The section 36 discretion: evidence needed to satisfy the court

87.37 In *Cheltenham and Gloucester Building Society v Grant* (1994) 26 HLR 703 a practical approach was adopted. The Court of Appeal declined to lay down rigid rules for busy first-instance judges. They must be allowed to act without hearing evidence. It is for the judge to decide whether to act on the basis of informal material, thereby allowing a first-instance court to accept evidence that does not comply with **CPR, Part 32**. The effect of the *Grant* case is that if the mortgagee submits the court should not accept what it is told by the borrower, the consequence may be an adjournment.

A common-sense approach is favoured. The mortgagor may be present: he could be put on oath if required; much of the information tendered, as to future earnings and expenses, will be incapable of ready challenge. If applying at a warrant stage, information may be in the application notice, verified by a statement of truth, as required by **Part 22**. If a mortgagor attends court and explains reasons for past default and hopes for future improvement, it is rare for the representative of the mortgagee to seek to ask questions. With an offer of remortgage, it can be more effective for submissions to be made on that offer letter, pointing out its deficiencies, than directly to challenge the mortgagor, or require the author of the letter to attend court.

It is helpful for a mortgagor to produce to the court a full financial statement to show that there genuinely is the scope to make payments. Citizens Advice Bureaux, and other debt-counselling agencies, produce good examples, which, typed and totalled, offer the hard-pressed judge easy-to-digest evidence of ability, or inability, to pay.

The section 36 discretion: a reasonable period to pay the arrears

87.38 The Court of Appeal in *Cheltenham and Gloucester Building Society v Norgan* [1996] 1 WLR 343 held that it is reasonable to take account of the whole of the remaining part of the original term of the mortgage. Although the *Norgan* case was on a warrant, the same principles apply to the initial decision whether and on what basis to suspend any order. Having identified the amount of the arrears, the following are potentially relevant to the exercise of discretion:
(a) the amount the mortgagor could reasonably afford to pay, now and in the future;
(b) the duration of any temporary financial crisis;

(c) the reason for the accumulation of arrears;
(d) the nature of the security;
(e) the length of the remaining term;
(f) the type of mortgage and relevant contractual provisions, for example, date of repayment of the principal;
(g) whether it is a case under the Administration of Justice Act 1973, s. 8; and
(h) the period over which it is reasonable to expect the mortgagee to recoup arrears of interest, or whether it is reasonable to capitalise them.

Consideration of these factors lies at the heart of the argument on terms for suspension. If the outstanding balance is close to the current value of the property, a much shorter repayment period may be indicated. The disadvantage to the mortgagor of extending arrears payments throughout the term is the lack of margin for future default. The means of the mortgagor may dictate a modest monthly payment can be made off the arrears. If the court has sufficient available material to indicate a potential improvement to finances (for example, if the partner will be going back to work part-time when the youngest child goes to school), it can either make a stepped order increasing the instalments off arrears at fixed future dates, or bring the case back for review. The existence of a future review date does not preclude enforcement if the order is breached in the interim.

The problem faced by many mortgagors is convincing the court to exercise discretion in their favour. If someone has failed to make instalment payments in the past, how can they persuade the court that they are now likely to be able to pay both monthly instalments and something off the arrears? If the mortgagor can point to a period of limited earnings during ill-health, or a period of redundancy, it will help. A chequered payment history must be explained to show why matters will improve.

Commentary

Intended sale

A common plea by those who have exhausted every other avenue of keeping their home is for time to sell. Better they should sell the house, as owner-occupier, than the mortgagee take possession, when with the windows boarded up and garden unkempt, purchasers seek a knock-down price. Mortgagees must take reasonable care to ensure they obtain the best price they reasonably can (*Michael v Miller* [2004] EWCA Civ 282, *The Times*, 30 March 2004), but few householders trust the mortgagee to sell for as much as they believe they can obtain. The concerns are not one-sided. The mortgagee fears a deliberate delay, the mortgagor wanting to link sale to obtaining fresh accommodation, or trying to achieve an unreasonably high price. Whether the mortgagee should itself sell or adopt the mortgagor's proposed sale is an argument explored in a number of cases. All these cases should now be considered in the light of the **Mortgage Protocol, para. 6.** 87.39

In *Target Home Loans v Clothier* [1994] 1 All ER 439 it was decided that if there is a prospect of an early sale, the court must ask if it is better for all parties that it is conducted by the mortgagor or the mortgagee. If the view is that the prospects of an early sale for the mortgagee as well as for the mortgagor are best served by deferring an order for possession, that is a solid reason for making a suspended order. But deferment should be short. In the *Clothier* case it was for three months. *National and Provincial Building Society v Lloyd* [1996] 1 All ER 530 suggested that on clear evidence of completion of the sale 'in six or nine months, or even a year', that was a reasonable period. This was rejected as a general proposition in *Bristol and West Building Society v Ellis* (1997) 29 HLR 282. In the *Ellis* case a proposal to discharge arrears of £11,000 at £10 per month until sale in three to five years' time met no favour. There were doubts that the proceeds would cover the mortgage debt and arrears, and insufficient evidence that the mortgagor would really sell. What is a reasonable period depends on the facts of each case. The arrears level and extent of the security are factors. Letters from estate agents giving likely sale prices should be treated with reserve.

The position where there is negative equity was considered in *Cheltenham and Gloucester Building Society v Krausz* [1997] 1 WLR 1558. The Administration of Justice Act 1970, s. 36, cannot be used to delay possession simply to enable mortgagors to sell, if they will not give good title at completion, because of inability to discharge the mortgage.

Comprehensive proposals

87.40 The court may be able to look favourably on a mixed package of proposals by the mortgagor. Perhaps the mortgagor can, in the short term, by calling in favours and delaying payment to less pressing creditors, afford the current instalments plus a small amount off the arrears monthly for, say, three months. In principle, that proposal, plus an as yet loosely formulated plan to sell, may be a basis for a suspended order with review.

Firm evidence of particular sale

87.41 The historic stance of many lenders that, without firm evidence, they should not be prevented from gaining possession to exercise their power of sale, must now be viewed in the light of the **Mortgage Protocol, para. 6**, and pre-2008 cases should be treated with caution. Whenever potential sale is advanced, can it be reasonable for the mortgage lender to reject the proposal without full inquiry? An adjournment to investigate may be required.

That aside, the court will assist if there is an exchange of contracts with an arm's-length purchaser, and will postpone possession, if necessary staying a warrant, to enable completion of the sale. The court will suspend if comprehensive proposals (see **87.40**) are approved. Beyond that, the more compelling the evidence of likely sale and the larger the equity, the longer will be the likely postponement. In practice, any order giving 56 days or less is unlikely to be worth appealing. Any initial suspension period is, in reality, a window for the mortgagor to exchange contracts unconditionally.

Interrelationship with orders for sale

87.42 The Law of Property Act 1925, s. 91, gives the court power to order the sale of property subject to a mortgage. Sale may be the practical conclusion of a possession claim, and what the mortgagor seeks time to effect. Section 91 orders historically have rarely featured in domestic mortgage litigation as the amount of the mortgage balance usually offended the upper limit of county court equity jurisdiction and necessitated an application to the High Court.

In *Cheltenham and Gloucester Building Society v Krausz* [1997] 1 WLR 1558 the Court of Appeal held there was no discretion to suspend a warrant of possession to facilitate an s. 91 application. Parliament did not intend the Administration of Justice Act 1970, s. 36, to curtail the rights of mortgagees to possession unless the sale proceeds are sufficient to clear the mortgage debt.

Two cases under the Law of Property Act 1925, s. 91, turned on their peculiar facts. In *Palk v Mortgage Services Funding plc* [1993] Ch 330 a sale was ordered against the wishes of a mortgagee proposing to let the property at a rent insufficient to meet the instalments. Despite negative equity, a sale would limit the exposure of the mortgagors. In *Cheltenham and Gloucester plc v Booker* (1997) 29 HLR 634 the Administration of Justice Act 1970, s. 36, was not available as the arrears could not be cleared within a reasonable period. But, satisfied that the mortgagors being in occupation would enhance a sale, and of their total cooperation, the court deferred possession to enable the mortgagee to sell the property. There are potential risks to a mortgagee, as contractual seller, if mortgagors do not vacate on completion.

Money judgment

Opinion differs on whether to claim a money judgment at all, and if so, to seek its adjournment at trial. Much depends on the likelihood of satisfaction of the mortgage debt from the sale proceeds. *Cheltenham and Gloucester Building Society v Grattidge* (1993) 25 HLR 454 decided that the mortgage lender was entitled to a money judgment for the outstanding balance due at the hearing date. Courts may require clear, verified, up-to-date evidence of the outstanding balance and often direct that money judgments will not be enforceable whilst the possession order remains suspended, continuing the stay whilst any warrant is suspended. As the financial goalposts will change before enforcement of the money claim, an argument exists for an account to be drawn before the mortgagee can enforce the money judgment. **87.43**

Costs: general approach

Mortgagees can reimburse themselves out of the mortgaged property for all costs, charges and expenses reasonably and properly incurred in enforcing or preserving their security (*Parker-Tweedale v Dunbar Bank plc (No. 2)* [1991] Ch 26). Conventionally mortgages contain clauses that the mortgagor will pay the costs of the mortgagee, both of proceedings under the mortgage, and those properly incurred in preserving the security. **87.44**

Mortgagees generally should not seek costs within possession proceedings. Conflict is created between contractual solicitor-and-client costs under the deed and assessment under the court order. The range of options available is set out in **PD 44, paras** 7.1 to 7.3.

Costs orders

Suppose the mortgagee makes a mistake, causing additional hearings? Its costs have been unreasonably incurred. But if a mortgagor needs time to assemble cogent evidence of a payment plan or proposed sale, an adjournment of perhaps six weeks to the next available date is helpful, and justice is done if the order remains silent on costs. **87.45**

Gomba Holdings (UK) Ltd v Minories Finance Ltd (No. 2) [1993] Ch 171 established certain principles (see **68.49**). Although costs orders are discretionary, the discretion should normally be exercised to reflect any contractual right to costs. The power of the court to disallow a mortgagee's costs sought to be added to the security derives from the court's equitable jurisdiction to fix the terms of redemption of a mortgage and not from the Senior Courts Act 1981, s. 51. A mortgagee is not to be deprived of the right to add costs to the security merely because of a costs order made without reference to the contractual provisions.

A mortgagor succeeding on an issue may be entitled to costs against the mortgagee. The court can make such an order, and one depriving the mortgagee of the right to add both costs it has to pay the borrower, and its own costs, to the security. Also, the court may decide that it should limit the contractual entitlement to costs as to part because the mortgagee has acted unreasonably.

Any *Gomba Holdings* order should specify precisely what costs are involved, e.g. 'the costs of preparing the witness statement of AB shall not be added to the security'.

REGULATED AGREEMENTS

If a mortgage is a regulated agreement under the Consumer Credit Act 1974, the additional details required by **PD 55A, para.** 2.5(4) and (5) (see **87.9**) must be stated in the particulars **87.46** of claim. For a mortgagor seeking to resist a claim for possession, the provisions for suspension under the Administration of Justice Act 1970 do not apply (s. 38A). Instead the court can make a 'time order' pursuant to the Consumer Credit Act 1974, s. 129. A time order, coupled with its attendant order under s. 135, changes the contractually agreed terms.

Many second mortgages, particularly loans for double-glazing and home improvements, are regulated agreements, and subject to the regime of time orders.

Time orders

87.47 A time order under the Consumer Credit Act 1974, s. 129, may deal with one or both of the following, as the court considers just:

(a) payment by the debtor, or any surety, of any sum owed under a regulated agreement, or a security, by such instalments, payable at such times, as the court, having regard to the means of the debtor and any surety, considers reasonable; and/or
(b) remedy by the debtor of any breach of the regulated agreement (other than the non payment of money) within such period as the court may specify.

The approach is more beneficial to the mortgagor than under the Administration of Justice Act 1970, s. 36 (see **87.38**).

In *Southern and District Finance plc v Barnes* (1995) 27 HLR 691 time orders were reviewed generally and a number of principles set out. Where an application for a time order is made, the court must consider whether it is just to make it. That consideration involves looking at all aspects of the case, the position of lender as much as borrower. A time order should usually be made for a stipulated period on account of temporary financial difficulty. If the borrower is unlikely to be able to resume payment of the whole indebtedness by at least the amount of the contractual instalments, no order should be made. In such circumstances it is more equitable for the regulated agreement to be enforced (*First National Bank plc v Syed* [1991] 2 All ER 250).

When a time order is made after financial default, the court must look at 'the sum owed'. In possession proceedings that will usually mean the entire mortgage indebtedness. If a time order is made in relation to the entire mortgage balance, this will affect either the interest rate or the duration of the loan, or both.

The court must consider what instalments are reasonable, their amount and timing, having regard to the borrower's means. The court has a power to vary the interest rate.

If justice requires the making of a time order, the possession order should be suspended for so long as the terms of the time order are complied with.

Procedure for time orders

87.48 An application for a time order should be made in accordance with **PD 7B**. It is potentially independent, and can be made in advance, of possession proceedings. In practice, time order applications on secured loans usually arise in the possession proceedings. **PD 55A, para. 7.1**, provides that an application by a defendant for an order under the Consumer Credit Act 1974, s. 129, may be made either in the defence or by application notice within those possession proceedings. The mortgagor will either complete the defence form with appropriate details of means, or his or her financial position will be before the court in a statement of means perhaps prepared by the local Citizens Advice Bureau. The court may address the matter in much the same way as it would an application to suspend a conventional instalment mortgage, albeit applying different criteria, and deal with the matter at the first hearing. However, an adjournment for formal evidence, with more time for argument, is likely.

ENFORCEMENT OF COUNTY COURT POSSESSION ORDERS

Warrants of possession

If a mortgagor breaches a suspended order, or fails to vacate to comply with an outright order, enforcement is by paper application for a bailiff's warrant (form N325) (see 87.53). No permission is needed within six years of the order. The warrant is initially valid for one year, but may be extended. When the warrant is executed the bailiff must evict everyone in the property (*R v Wandsworth County Court, ex parte Wandsworth London Borough Council* [1975] 1 WLR 1314). The bailiff usually visits the property prior to the actual eviction appointment and will report to the court anything that requires its attention. It may be necessary to invoke the assistance of others to execute the warrant, for example, the police if a breach of the peace is feared. The mortgagee is given adequate notice, so it can secure the premises once the bailiff has obtained possession. **87.49**

Further postponement of possession

Until completion of execution of a warrant of possession, the court retains its powers under the Administration of Justice Act 1970, s. 36, or the Consumer Credit Act 1974, ss. 129 and 135(1). Any change in the circumstances of the mortgagor affecting ability to pay the mortgage arrears may found a further application, usually for suspension of the warrant. A stay normally connotes a brief delay in the enforcement procedure, whether or not terms are also imposed, whereas a suspension will be granted for a longer term. **87.50**

There is no theoretical limit to the number of successive applications for suspension. The facts behind a failed application should not found a further one, but be the subject of appeal. In practice the line is blurred. Slight changes to the factual matrix found fresh applications. It is often speedier to allow the court to adjudicate on a further application than to appeal. If there is a mix of rehearing and new facts, the appellate court may direct a rehearing. It may not disturb the original exercise of discretion. Accordingly mortgagees may decide against challenging the jurisdiction to hear what appears to be a 'similar facts' application. If the target is speedy possession, taking some technical points may be self-defeating.

Available orders

It is common for mortgagors to wait until the last minute before applying to suspend a warrant of possession, delaying the application in the hope of a change in their circumstances. Often the evidence produced is less than convincing. What is contended to have happened is still in the future. The mortgagor may fail to bring a crucial document. Dismissal of the application may only beg an appeal or fresh application. The court can, using its general case-management and listing powers, adjourn for a short period. Time given may test the promises or aspirations of the mortgagor. An applicant saying that his purchaser will exchange tomorrow may not later persuade a court to suspend, if that promise has been broken. The dangers of failing properly to formulate proposals to pay until the appeal stage, and the need then to satisfy the court that in the light of past failures there is a *realistic prospect* of payment, were highlighted in *Jameer v Paratus AMC* [2012] EWCA Civ 1924, [2013] HLR 18, applying *Bank of Scotland plc v Zinda* [2011] EWCA Civ 706, [2012] 1 WLR 728. **87.51**

If satisfied on the mortgagor's application, the warrant will be suspended on payment of the arrears at a determined rate, identifying the date of next payment. If further information is required, the court may adjourn for a short period, staying the warrant during the adjournment and directing that certain payments be made in the interim. In a borderline case there appears no reason in principle why the court cannot direct that, notwithstanding the stay, the mortgagee can immediately obtain a new date for the warrant to be executed, provided it is after the return date.

Discouraging repeated applications

87.52 A mortgagee at the 'warrant suspension' stage, wishing to inhibit unmeritorious applications, each causing successive warrant execution appointments to be vacated, may consider various pragmatic solutions:

(a) On dismissal of the borrower's application, it may ask for an order that no further application be made without the permission of the court. This does not preclude the borrower from applying for permission, and the court suspending the warrant, without notice, pending the hearing for permission.
(b) In preference to a short adjournment or stay, the court may dismiss the application, having there and then refixed the warrant execution date sufficiently distant to meet the borrower's minimum requirements. This solution is useful when the mortgagor raises compassionate grounds of questionable legal merit.
(c) Reserving the case to the same judge may signal that the court will view with scepticism an identical argument being revisited.
(d) Although the application is dismissed, the warrant is ordered to lie in the court and not actually be executed, for a few days.
(e) Cases of misuse of the court's procedures may be met by a civil restraint order (see **14.55** to **14.60**).

Non-party applicants

87.53 Since 1 October 2010 a mortgagee of a dwelling-house must give written notice to tenants and occupiers that it intends to apply for a warrant for possession (Mortgage Repossessions (Protection of Tenants etc.) Act 2010; Dwelling Houses (Execution of Possession Orders by Mortgagees) Regulations 2010 (SI 2010/1809); **CCR, ord. 26, r. 17(2A)** in CPR, sch. 2). A warrant cannot be executed before the end of the prescribed period of 14 days beginning with the day of service of that notice (2010 Act, s. 2(2); SI 2010/1809, reg. 3). The notice must be in the form set out in the schedule to SI 2010/1809 (reg. 4). It may be given (reg. 5):

(a) by first class or registered post, addressed to a tenant by name, or otherwise to 'the tenant or occupier';
(b) by leaving it at or affixed to the property; or
(c) by personal service on an apparent resident.

Giving this notice may spark a last-minute reaction by the tenant.

Section 1(4) of the 2010 Act provides that the court may, on the application of any unauthorised tenant, stay or suspend execution of a possession order for a period not exceeding two months if:

(a) the court did not exercise its powers under s. 1(2) when making the order or, if it did, the applicant was not the tenant when it exercised those powers;
(b) the applicant has asked the mortgagee to give an undertaking in writing not to enforce the order for two months beginning with the date the undertaking is given; and
(c) the mortgagee has not given such an undertaking.

In considering the exercise of its powers the court must take into account the circumstances of the tenant and the nature of any breach of the tenancy agreement, and can (s. 1(5), (6) and (7)) impose terms (see also **87.26**).

For such a short enactment the 2010 Act is not without its interpretation problems, but it is suggested that sub-paragraphs (a) and (b) of s. 1(4) are to be construed disjunctively. This would accord with Parliament's intention to give an innocent tenant a two-month stay, which would be time to find another home while, incidentally, continuing to occupy premises for which he may have paid advance rent.

Whilst a court can, under **CPR, r. 23.8**, deal on paper with applications by occupiers, whether specifically under the 2010 Act, or otherwise for joinder and suspension, it is unwise to dismiss these without a hearing. Until an applicant appears before the court, it is difficult to ascertain his or her true standing. The applicant may be a licensee, an unauthorised tenant, or even a tenant whose interest would have defeated the claim to possession and who would be entitled to joinder (see **87.26**). Frustrating as it is for mortgagees, the result may be the cancellation of a warrant appointment, as the court will almost inevitably, upon receipt of the application, stay the warrant pending an oral hearing on the application.

Party unaware of proceedings

Sometimes in family breakdown situations one partner hides from the other both non-payment of the mortgage, and the possession proceedings themselves. Although the original service of proceedings may have been good (service to last known address), the unsuspecting partner has a right to apply to set aside the possession order or warrant. A **Part 55** hearing is not a trial (*Forcelux Ltd v Binnie* [2009] EWCA Civ 854, [2010] HLR 20) and any application is under **CPR, r. 3.1(2)(m)**. The court must consider all the circumstances under **r. 3.9**, giving precedence to the requirements of **r. 39.3(5)** (*Hackney London Borough Council v Findlay* [2011] EWCA Civ 8, [2011] HLR 15). If the applicant shows the potential for a different order, if only a suspension on less onerous terms, that may suffice, provided the application has been made promptly. **87.54**

Paying the arrears

If after a warrant issues, a sufficient payment (of arrears accruing since the possession order or otherwise) is made so that the mortgagee allows the mortgagor to remain in occupation on the basis of the former suspended possession order, the warrant can be withdrawn by letter. If the mortgagor again defaults, and the warrant has neither expired nor been formally discharged, a fresh eviction date can be sought by letter. If the basis of agreement is that, despite an outright order, there is now to be a suspended arrangement, a variation order is important. If the entire arrears are paid, so that the mortgage account is brought fully up to date, it should be remembered that the original suspended order remains in full force, if only as an obligation to pay the contractual mortgage instalments, and a fresh warrant can thereafter issue for subsequent arrears (see *Bank of Scotland plc v Zinda* [2011] EWCA Civ 706, [2012] 1 WLR 728). **87.55**

Completion of execution

It is unnecessary to remove all the furniture and belongings of the mortgagor to complete execution under a county court warrant (County Courts Act 1984, s. 111(1)). In practice, mortgagees allow mortgagors an opportunity within a fortnight to make arrangements to collect their effects. Standard mortgage terms may cover the situation and protect the mortgagee from liability. **87.56**

Once execution is complete, the court has no further powers to stay or suspend, unless the possession order can be set aside, or the warrant was obtained by fraud, or there has been abuse of process, such as oppressive conduct. An example of oppressive conduct is if a mortgagee states that it will agree to suspend only if all arrears are paid immediately, and if impossible, not to bother making an application to suspend (see *Cheltenham and Gloucester Building Society v Obi* (1996) 28 HLR 22, applying *Hammersmith and Fulham London Borough Council v Hill* (1995) 27 HLR 368 to mortgage cases).

Forcible re-entry

87.57 If a borrower ousted lawfully by execution of a bailiff's warrant forcibly re-enters, the remedy is a warrant of restitution (**CCR, ord. 26, r. 17(4)** in CPR, sch. 2; see **79.34**). Permission to apply for the warrant is needed. The application is without notice, under **CPR, Part 23**, supported by a witness statement, establishing the wrongful re-entry was undertaken by or on behalf of a party to the proceedings. The court staff should be invited to refer the file immediately to the district judge for the warrant to issue.

Redemption of the mortgage

87.58 Execution of a warrant of possession does not of itself extinguish the proprietary rights of a mortgagor. A mortgagor who redeems the mortgage, even when out of occupation, can re-enter.

Chapter 88 Anti-social Behaviour and Harassment

INTRODUCTION

This chapter deals with the powers of the civil courts to make orders controlling behaviour which causes distress, nuisance or annoyance. The powers considered in this chapter arise under: **88.1**

(a) the Housing Act 1996, part 5, chapter 3 (anti-social behaviour injunctions and injunctions against unlawful use of premises) (**88.2** to **88.11**);

(b) the Police and Justice Act 2006, s. 27 (power of arrest added to local authority's injunction) (**88.12**);

Commentary

(c) the Crime and Disorder Act 1998, ss. 1B and 1D (anti-social behaviour orders, ASBOs) (**88.13** to **88.22**);
(d) the Anti-social Behaviour Act 2003, ss. 26A, 26B and 26C (parenting orders) (**88.23** to **88.26**);
(e) the Violent Crime Reduction Act 2006, ss. 1 to 14 (drinking banning orders) (**88.27** to **88.32**);
(f) the Protection from Harassment Act 1997, ss. 3 and 3A (**88.33** to **88.39**);
(g) the Policing and Crime Act 2009, part 4 (injunctions to prevent gang-related violence) (**88.42** to **88.52**).

Powers (a) to (e) and (g) are exercised in the public interest on the application of bodies exercising public functions. Power (f) is a private law remedy, though it can be used to protect large groups of people.

The legal devices employed are injunctions (powers (a) and (g)), injunctions enhanced by a power of arrest (powers (a) and (b)) and orders of the civil courts which it is a criminal offence to disobey (powers (c) to (f)). Compliance with an injunction may be enforced by committal (see **chapter 81**). Powers of arrest are used to bring to court people who have breached injunctions so that applications to commit them may be heard. If a power of arrest is not attached to an injunction, it may be possible to obtain a warrant for arrest (powers (a) and (f)).

HOUSING ACT 1996 INJUNCTIONS

Types of injunction

88.2 The Housing Act 1996, part 5, chapter 3 (ss. 153A to 158), enables landlords of low-cost housing to protect their residents and staff by obtaining injunctions restraining certain behaviour. The following types of injunction are available:

(a) an anti-social behaviour injunction (s. 153A);
(b) an injunction against unlawful use of premises (s. 153B).

These injunctions may also, if the behaviour complained of meets certain criteria of seriousness, exclude the injuncted person from specified premises or a specified area, even from his or her own home (s. 153C(1) and (2); see **88.5**).

These injunctions can only be obtained on the application of a 'relevant landlord' (ss. 153A(2) and 153B(2)). This means (by s. 153E(7)):

(a) a housing action trust (HAT);
(b) a local authority;
(c) a registered social landlord (RSL);
(d) a non-profit registered provider of social housing.

An injunction under s. 153A or s. 153B may be obtained or varied against a person on an application made without notice to that person (s. 153E(4); see **88.7**).

Any injunction may be enforced by committal (see **chapter 81**). In addition, if the behaviour complained of meets the seriousness criteria, the court may add to an injunction under s. 153A or s. 153B a power of arrest (s. 153C(1) and (3); see **88.5** and **88.9**).

Under s. 153D an exclusion provision and a power of arrest may also be attached to an injunction against breach of a tenancy agreement with a relevant landlord, provided seriousness criteria are met (see **88.6**).

Sections 153A to 153E were inserted by the Anti-social Behaviour Act 2003. They replaced *similar* provisions in ss. 151 and 152 of the 1996 Act, and it was hoped that the wording of the new provisions would avoid some problems encountered with the former provisions. For an extended discussion of these problems see Jonathan Manning, Claire-Louise Manning and Victoria Osler, *Blackstone's Guide to the Anti-social Behaviour Act 2003* (Oxford University Press, 2004). The new provisions came into force on 30 June 2004 in England and 30 September 2004 in Wales.

As from 6 April 2007, a new s. 153A has been substituted by the Police and Justice Act 2006, s. 26.

Anti-social behaviour injunction

An anti-social behaviour injunction is an injunction that prohibits a person from engaging in housing-related anti-social conduct of a kind specified in the injunction (Housing Act 1996, s. 153A(1)). 'Anti-social conduct' means conduct capable of causing nuisance or annoyance to some person (who need not be a particular identified person) (s. 153A(1)). 'Housing-related' means directly or indirectly relating to or affecting the housing management functions of a relevant landlord (s. 153A(1); 'relevant landlord' is defined in s. 153E(7) — see **88.2**). 'Conduct' means conduct anywhere (s. 153A(1)). **88.3**

Conduct prohibited by an anti-social behaviour injunction may be described by reference to a person or persons (s. 153A(4)). If it is, it may be described by reference:

(a) to persons generally;
(b) to persons of a description specified in the injunction; or
(c) to persons, or a person, specified in the injunction.

On the application of a relevant landlord (see **88.2**), the court may grant an anti-social behaviour injunction (s. 153A(2)) if the condition in s. 153A(3) is satisfied. That condition is that the person against whom the injunction is sought is engaging, has engaged or threatens to engage in housing-related conduct capable of causing a nuisance or annoyance to:

(a) a person with a right (of whatever description) to reside in or occupy housing accommodation owned or managed by a relevant landlord;
(b) a person with a right (of whatever description) to reside in or occupy other housing accommodation in the neighbourhood of housing accommodation mentioned in paragraph (a);
(c) a person engaged in lawful activity in, or in the neighbourhood of, housing accommodation mentioned in paragraph (a); or
(d) a person employed (whether or not by a relevant landlord) in connection with the exercise of a relevant landlord's housing management functions.

'Housing management functions' include functions conferred by or under any enactment, and the powers and duties of the landlord as the holder of an estate or interest in housing accommodation (s. 153E(11)). 'Housing accommodation' includes flats, lodging-houses and hostels (s. 153E(9)(a)); and the yards, gardens, outhouses and appurtenances belonging to the accommodation or usually enjoyed with it (s. 153E(9)(b)). The 'neighbourhood' of housing accommodation owned or managed by a relevant landlord is said, somewhat circularly, by s. 153E(9)(c), to include the neighbourhood of the whole of the housing accommodation owned or managed by the relevant landlord in the neighbourhood and any common areas used in connection with the accommodation.

The jurisdiction under s. 153A is to be regarded as a broad rather than a narrow one. Provided the respondent's conduct taken as a whole is 'housing-related' in that it directly or indirectly relates to or affects the local authority's housing management functions, an injunction can be granted. In particular, there is no requirement that a respondent has to be a tenant or an occupier of property owned by the local authority before an injunction can be granted under s. 153A (*Swindon Borough Council v Redpath* [2009] EWCA Civ 943, [2010] BLGR 28).

Injunction against unlawful use of premises

88.4 Under the Housing Act 1996, s. 153B, the court may grant an injunction prohibiting a person from engaging in conduct which consists of or involves using or threatening to use housing accommodation owned or managed by a relevant landlord for an unlawful purpose. The concept of ownership of housing accommodation is explained in s. 153E(10).

Exclusion conditions and power of arrest

88.5 Under the Housing Act 1996, s. 153C, the court may add to an anti-social behaviour injunction or an injunction against unlawful use of premises:

(a) a provision prohibiting the person in respect of whom it is granted from entering or being in:
   (i) any premises specified in the injunction;
   (ii) any area specified in the injunction;
(b) a power of arrest.

An exclusion provision may have the effect of excluding a person from his or her normal place of residence (s. 153E(2)(b)).

These provisions may be added to an anti-social behaviour injunction or an injunction against unlawful use of premises only if the court thinks that:

(a) the conduct consists of or includes the use or threatened use of violence; or
(b) there is a significant risk of harm to a person mentioned in s. 153A(3)(a) to (d) (see **88.3**).

'Harm' includes serious ill-treatment or abuse, whether physical or not (s. 153E(12)).

As summary arrest and detention are a serious interference with a person's liberty, the provisions of an order to which a power of arrest is attached should be carefully and precisely drafted. The court should not attach a power of arrest to any provisions of an order unless it is satisfied that the defendant has used or threatened violence to one or more of the persons who are to be protected by the order, or that, without the deterrence of a power of arrest, there would be a significant risk of harm to them. When considering whether to attach a power of arrest to an injunction which it intends to grant on a without-notice basis, the court must additionally consider the matters set out in s. 154.

Injunction against breach of a tenancy agreement

88.6 Under the Housing Act 1996, s. 153D, exclusion provisions and a power of arrest (see **88.5**) can be attached to any injunction granted to a relevant landlord against a tenant in respect of the breach or anticipated breach of a tenancy agreement on the grounds that the tenant:

(a) is engaging or threatening to engage in conduct that is capable of causing nuisance or annoyance to any person, or
(b) is allowing, inciting or encouraging any other person to engage or threaten to engage in such conduct.

'Tenancy agreement' includes any agreement for the occupation of residential accommodation owned or managed by a relevant landlord (s. 153D(5)). 'Tenancy' includes a licence (s. 158(1)). For the purposes of s. 153D, 'relevant landlord' is extended by s. 153E(8) to include a charitable housing trust (defined in s. 158(1)) which is neither a non-profit registered provider of social housing nor a registered social landlord.

Exclusion and arrest provisions may be attached under s. 153D if the court is satisfied:

(a) that the conduct includes the use or threatened use of violence, or
(b) that there is a significant risk of harm to any person.

When considering whether to attach a power of arrest to an injunction which it intends to grant on a without-notice basis, the court must additionally consider the matters set out in s. 154.

Application procedure

An application under the Housing Act 1996, ss. 153A to 153E, for an injunction must be commenced in the court for the district in which the defendant resides or the conduct complained of occurred (**CPR, r. 65.3(2)(b)**). An injunction may be granted by the High Court or a county court (Housing Act 1996, s. 153E(6)). An application for an injunction must be made as a **CPR, Part 8**, claim (see **chapter 13**), but using form N16A, which is treated as the Part 8 claim form (**r. 65.3(1); PD 65, para. 1**). Form N16A must state the terms of the injunction applied for (**CPR, r. 65.3(3)**). Each provision of the injunction to which a power of arrest is attached (see **88.5**) must be set out in a separate paragraph (**r. 65.4(1) and (2)(a)**). An application for an injunction must be supported by a witness statement, which, as in all Part 8 claims, must be filed with the claim form (**r. 65.3(2)(c)**). **88.7**

An application for an injunction may be made without notice (Housing Act 1996, s. 153E(4)), but the witness statement in support must state the reasons why notice has not been given (**CPR, r. 65.3(4)(a)**). If an application is made without notice, the rules on acknowledgment of service (**rr. 8.3** and **8.4**) and exchange of evidence (**r. 8.5(2)** to **(6)**) do not apply, and it is not possible to make an additional claim or for the defendant to object, under **r. 8.8**, to the use of the Part 8 procedure (**r. 65.3(4)(b)**).

In *Moat Housing Group-South Ltd v Harris* [2005] EWCA Civ 287, [2006] QB 606 at [72], the Court of Appeal stated the following principles governing the making of orders without notice. An order may be made without notice only if there are exceptional circumstances. An example of an exceptional circumstance is that there is a risk of significant harm to some person or persons attributable to the conduct of the defendant if the order is not made immediately. The order must not be wider than is necessary and must be proportionate as a means of avoiding the apprehended harm. At [80] the Court of Appeal said that a power of arrest should be attached to a provision of an order made without notice only if the court is satisfied:

(a) that the defendant has used or threatened violence against some person or persons mentioned in what is now the Housing Act 1996, s. 153A(3) (see **88.3**); and
(b) that there is a risk of significant harm to one or more of those persons, attributable to the conduct of the defendant, if the power of arrest is not attached immediately.

In *KY v DD (Without-Notice Applications)* [2011] EWHC 1277 (Fam), [2011] Fam Law 797, the court set out additional guidance which should be followed when making without-notice applications. Such applications should only be made in cases of genuine urgency. The information put before the court to substantiate a without-notice order should be closely scrutinised. If the applicant is not present to verify it in person, it should be substantiated by the production of a contemporaneous note of the instructions. If additional information is put before the court orally, there should be a direction for the filing of evidence to confirm that information within a very short period of time. It is incumbent on those considering the making of a without-notice application to consider carefully whether it is justified and to be clear about the evidential basis for it.

If an application is made on notice, the claim form and supporting evidence must be served on the defendant personally (**CPR, r. 65.3(5)**). If an application on notice is listed for hearing before the normal time for acknowledging service would expire, the claim form and evidence must be served on the defendant not less than two days before the hearing, and the defendant may take part in the hearing despite not filing an acknowledgment of service (**r. 65.3(6)**).

An injunction under the Housing Act 1996, ss. 153A, 153B or 153D, may be granted by a district judge (**PD 2B, para. 8.1(d)**).

Duration and variation of injunctions

88.8 An injunction granted under the Housing Act 1996, ss. 153A to 153D, may be made for a specified period or until varied or discharged (s. 153E(2)(a)). It may be varied or discharge on the application of the injuncted person or the relevant landlord (s. 153E(3)).

Power of arrest

88.9 If the court grants an injunction with a power of arrest, the claimant must deliver a copy of provisions to which the power is attached (each of those provisions must be in a separate paragraph) to any police station for the area where the conduct occurred (**CPR, r. 65.4(1)** and **(2)**). If the injunction was granted without notice, delivery to a police station cannot be done until the injunction has been served on the defendant (**r. 65.4(3)**).

If a provision of an injunction to which a power of arrest is attached is varied or discharged, the claimant must immediately inform the police station to which it delivered the copy of the provision and deliver a copy of the order which varies or discharges it (**r. 65.4(4)**).

If a constable has reasonable cause for suspecting that a person is in breach of provision of an injunction provision to which a power of arrest has been attached, the constable may arrest that person without warrant (Housing Act 1996, s. 155(1)). The person who obtained the injunction must be informed of the arrest forthwith (s. 155(1)) and the arrestee must be brought before a judge within 24 hours, excluding a Sunday, Christmas Day and Good Friday (s. 155(2)). The judge before whom the arrestee must be brought is a judge of the High Court, if that court granted the injunction, or otherwise a judge or district judge of a county court (s. 158(1)).

Warrant for arrest

88.10 If an injunction was granted which could have had a power of arrest attached under the Housing Act 1996, s. 153C(3) or 153D(4) (see **88.5** and **88.6**), but does not contain one, and the authority which applied for the injunction considers that there is a failure to comply with it, that authority may apply under s. 155(3) for a warrant to be issued for the arrest of the injuncted person. An application may also be made under s. 155(3) where a power of arrest has not been attached to all provisions of an injunction and there is an apparent failure to comply with provisions to which a power of arrest has not been attached.

An application under s. 155(3) must be made under **CPR, Part 23**, and may be made without notice (**r. 65.5(1)**). It must be substantiated on oath (Housing Act 1996, s. 155(4)(a)), by either affidavit or oral evidence (**CPR, r. 65.5.(2)**) and the judge may not issue a warrant unless there are reasonable grounds for believing there has been a failure to comply with the injunction (Housing Act 1996, s. 155(4)(b); **PD 65, para. 2.1**).

Dealing with arrestee

88.11 Normally the purpose of a hearing to deal with a person who has failed to comply with an injunction is to consider an application for the person to be committed (see **chapter 81**). **CPR Part 81, ss. 2** and **8** apply where an application is made in a county court to commit a person for breach of an injunction as if references in those sections to the judge included references to a district judge (**CPR, r. 65.6(6)**). Where the person has been arrested under a power of arrest attached to an injunction under the Housing Act 1996, s. 153C or s. 153D, or a warrant issued under s. 155(3) (see **88.5, 88.6, 88.9** and **88.10**), a district judge has power to make a committal order (**CPR, r. 65.6(6)**). The judge before whom such a person is first brought may deal with the matter or adjourn proceedings (**r. 65.6(2)**). If the matter is not dealt with forthwith, the judge may remand the arrestee (Housing Act 1996, s. 155(2)(b) and (5)), either in custody or on bail, in accordance with sch. 15. The procedure for applying for bail is in **CPR, r. 65.7** and **PD 65, paras 3.1** to **3.3**. There is also a power under the Housing

Act 1996, s. 156, to remand for a medical report or a report on mental condition (see **PD 65, para. 4.1**). Time spent on remand, ordinarily, should be set off against the period of imprisonment that is imposed for contempt of court (*Kirklees Council v Davis* [2008] EWCA Civ 632, [2009] HLR 3). This set-off must be incorporated in the court's sentence, because there is no automatic deduction under the Criminal Justice Act 1967, s. 67(1) (see s. 104(1)). The Sentencing Council's guidelines in relation to breaches of anti-social behaviour orders are relevant to committal proceedings in civil courts (*Amicus Horizon Ltd v Thorley* [2012] EWCA Civ 817, [2012] HLR 43. See also *Doey v Islington London Borough Council* [2012] EWCA Civ 1825, [2013] HLR 13).

A party who obtains an order can waive a breach of it. As to conduct which may amount to a waiver, see *Accent Foundation Ltd v Lee* [2007] EWCA Civ 665, [2008] HLR 3.

An arrestee who is released when proceedings are adjourned must be dealt with (whether by the same or another judge) within 28 days of the first court appearance (**CPR, r. 65.6(4)(a)**) and must be given at least two days' notice of the hearing (**r. 65.6(4)(b)**). 'Must' in **r. 65.6(4)(a)** is directory rather than mandatory, as it is provided in **r. 65.6(5)** that failure to meet the 28-day deadline does not invalidate any application notice seeking committal for contempt.

Commentary

POWER OF ARREST ADDED TO LOCAL AUTHORITY'S INJUNCTION

The Local Government Act 1972, s. 222, enables a local authority to bring, defend or appear in proceedings for the promotion or protection of the interests of inhabitants of its area. However, s. 222 should not be used to obtain, in effect, an anti-social behaviour order under the court's general discretion to grant injunctions under the Senior Courts Act 1981, s. 37. The authority should instead seek an anti-social behaviour order under the relevant statutes so that the detailed checks and balances developed by Parliament and in the decided cases will apply (*Birmingham City Council v Shafi* [2008] EWCA Civ 1186, [2009] 1 WLR 1916). In *A Local Authority v DL* [2010] EWHC 2675 (Fam), [2011] Fam Law 26, it was held that the High Court has an inherent jurisdiction to make a non-molestation order against the son of elderly vulnerable parents, on the application of a local authority, despite the fact that the parents did not lack capacity to bring their own proceedings. An order could be made under the court's jurisdiction even if an ASBO or injunction order could not be obtained under the Crime and Disorder Act 1998 or the Housing Act 1996, s. 153A. If the facts warrant an injunction order under the court's inherent jurisdiction, they also warrant an order under the Local Government Act 1972, s. 222. The two stand or fall together. **88.12**

Where an injunction is obtained by a local authority by virtue of the Local Government Act 1972, s. 222, which prohibits conduct capable of causing nuisance or annoyance to a person (the potential victim), the court may attach a power of arrest to any provision of the injunction (Police and Justice Act 2006, s. 27(2)). By the Police and Justice Act 2006, s. 27(2) and (3), the court may attach a power of arrest if it thinks that either:

(a) the conduct being prohibited consists of or includes the use or threatened use of violence, or
(b) there is a significant risk of harm to the potential victim — harm being defined in s. 27(12) as including serious ill-treatment or abuse (whether physical or not).

An application for a power of arrest to be attached to an injunction must be made in the proceedings seeking the injunction. It may be made in the claim form, the acknowledgment of service, the defence or counterclaim in a Part 7 claim, or an application under **CPR, Part 23** (**r. 65.9(1)**). It must be supported by written evidence (**r. 65.9(2)**). If the application is made on notice, the local authority must serve it, with a copy of the evidence, personally on the person against whom the injunction is sought, not less than two days before the hearing (**r. 65.9(3)**). **Rule 65.4** (notification of police, see **88.9**) applies to a power of arrest added under the Police and Justice Act 2006, s. 27 (**CPR, r. 65.10(1A)(a)**).

Where a power of arrest is added, under the Police and Justice Act 2006, s. 27, to any provision of an injunction obtained by a local authority, a constable may arrest, without warrant, a person whom he has reasonable cause for suspecting to be in breach of that provision (s. 27(4)). After making an arrest, the constable must, as soon as is reasonably practicable, inform the local authority (s. 27(5)). The arrestee must be brought before the court within 24 hours of arrest, excluding Christmas Day, Good Friday or any Sunday (s. 27(6)(a) and (7)). When the arrestee is first brought before a judge, that judge may deal with the matter or adjourn proceedings (**CPR, r. 65.6(2)** applied by **r. 65.10(1A)(b)**). If the matter is not disposed of forthwith, the arrestee may be remanded (Police and Justice Act 2006, s. 27(6)(b)), either in custody or on bail, in accordance with sch. 10. The procedure for applying for bail is in **CPR, r. 65.7**, and **PD 65, paras 3.1** to **3.3**, as applied by **para. 4A.1**.

There is also a power under the Police and Justice Act 2006, s. 27(9), (10) and (11), to remand for a medical report or a report on mental condition (see **PD 65, paras 4.1** and **4A.2**).

Paragraphs (4) and (5) of **CPR, r. 65.6** (time limit on dealing with an arrestee who is released, see **88.11**) apply (**r. 65.10(1A)(b)**).

ANTI-SOCIAL BEHAVIOUR ORDERS

ASBOs

88.13 Provisions for courts to make anti-social behaviour orders (ASBOs) are in the Crime and Disorder Act 1998. Under s. 1(1) the conditions for making an ASBO against a person aged 10 or over are that:

(a) the person has acted in an anti-social manner, that is, 'in a manner that has caused or was likely to cause harassment, alarm or distress to one or more persons not of the same household as himself' (s. 1(1)(a)); and

(b) it is necessary to protect relevant persons (defined in s. 1(1B)) from further anti-social acts by the person (s. 1(1)(b)).

Condition (a) must be proved to the criminal standard, but condition (b) is a matter of judgment and evaluation rather than proof (*R (McCann) v Crown Court at Manchester* [2002] UKHL 39, [2003] 1 AC 787; *Chief Constable of Lancashire v Potter* [2003] EWHC 2272 (Admin), *The Times*, 10 November 2003). This remains the position notwithstanding recent decisions in *Re D* [2008] UKHL 33, [2008] 1 WLR 1499, and *Re B (Children) (Care Proceedings: Standard of Proof)* [2008] UKHL 35, [2009] 1 AC 11, which make it clear that, except in a few exceptional cases, the standard of proof in civil proceedings is proof on the balance of probabilities (see *Birmingham City Council v Shafi* [2008] EWCA Civ 1186, [2009] 1 WLR 1916). 'Likely' in s. 1(1)(a) means more probable than not (*Chief Constable of Lancashire v Potter*). Likelihood of causing harassment etc. is to be judged only in relation to persons not of the same household actually present. An action is not within s. 1(1)(a) if the claimant does not establish, to the criminal standard of proof, that the defendant's behaviour had actually caused or was likely to cause harassment, distress or alarm to one or more persons not of the same household as himself (*R (Gosport Borough Council) v Fareham Magistrates' Court* [2006] EWHC 3047 (Admin), [2007] 1 WLR 634).

The order must meet the test of necessity set out in s. 1(1)(b). Other orders to which a person is subject must be taken into account before considering the imposition of an ASBO (*R (McGarrett) v Kingston Crown Court* [2009] EWHC 1776 (Admin), LTL 27/7/2009; see also *R v Gilbertson* [2009] EWCA Crim 1715, LTL 19/8/2009).

Where an anti-social behaviour order is based on conduct which engages the individual's **art. 10** rights, the court must work through the **art. 10** considerations in order to ensure that any interference with those rights is necessary and proportionate when balanced against the behaviour complained of (*Perry v Chief Constable of Humberside* [2012] EWHC 3226 (Admin), LTL 24/10/2012).

Behaviour that occurs after the making of an application but before the court hearing can be taken into account by the court in deciding whether an ASBO is necessary (*Birmingham City Council v Dixon* [2009] EWHC 761 (Admin), [2010] 1 WLR 32).

ASBOs are civil, not criminal, orders. It follows that hearsay evidence can be relied on in support of the application (*R (McCann) v Crown Court at Manchester*).

Contravention of an ASBO is a criminal offence (s. 1(10)). As breach of an ASBO exposes the defendant to criminal penalties, it is important that the basis on which the order is granted should be clearly stated and the terms of the order should be precise and unambiguous (see *C v Sunderland Youth Court* [2003] EWHC 2385 (Admin), [2004] 1 Cr App R (S) 76). The terms of the order should be clear and not drafted so widely that they are incapable of being understood by the defendant or incapable of being effectively enforced. The terms of the order should also be proportionate and commensurate with the anti-social behaviour which it is sought to prevent (*R v Boness* [2005] EWCA Crim 2395, [2006] 1 Cr App R (S) 120; see also *Director of Public Prosecutions v T* [2006] EWHC 728 (Admin), [2007] 1 WLR 209).

ASBOs are made principally by magistrates' courts, but provisions which were inserted into the 1998 Act by the Police Reform Act 2002 (which generally revised the ASBO system) enable ASBOs to be made against parties to county court proceedings (see **88.14**). An application to a county court for an ASBO may be made only by a 'relevant authority' (see **88.14**).

Commentary

ASBOs incidental to county court proceedings

A county court may make an ASBO against a party to proceedings before it, under the Crime and Disorder Act 1998, s. 1B(4). An order may not be made unless it is proved that the conditions mentioned in s. 1(1) (see **88.13**) are satisfied (s. 1B(4)). An ASBO under s. 1B(4) prohibits a person from doing anything described in the order. The prohibitions which may be imposed are those necessary for the purpose of protecting persons from further anti-social acts by the person against whom the order is made (s. 1(6) applied by s. 1B(7)). The persons to be protected may be the relevant persons (defined in s. 1(1B)) in the local area or persons elsewhere in England and Wales (s. 1(6)). **88.14**

An ASBO must be for a specified period of at least two years or until further order (s. 1(7) applied by s. 1B(7)). Although an ASBO must run for a minimum of two years, it is not necessary for each and every provision within the order to run for that period (*R (Lonergan) v Crown Court at Lewes* [2005] EWHC 457 (Admin), [2005] 1 WLR2570).

Contravention of an ASBO made by a county court is a criminal offence (s. 1(10) applied by s. 1B(7)).

An ASBO under s. 1B(4) may only be made if applied for by a 'relevant authority', which is party to the proceedings: a relevant authority may apply to be joined to enable it to apply for an ASBO (s. 1B(2) and (3)). The relevant authorities are local authorities, chief officers of police (including the Transport Police), any non-profit registered provider of social housing which provides or manages any houses or hostel in a local government area, registered social landlords, housing action trusts (HATs), the Environment Agency and Transport for London (s. 1(1A); Crime and Disorder Act 1998 (Relevant Authorities and Relevant Persons) Order 2006 (SI 2006/2137)). Any person or employee of a person who exercises a local housing authority's management functions pursuant to an agreement under the Housing Act 1985, s. 27, may discharge the authority's functions under the Crime and Disorder Act 1998, ss. 1 to 1E (Local Authorities (Contracting Out of Anti-Social Behaviour Order Functions) (England) Order 2007 (SI 2007/1441)).

A relevant authority may apply for an ASBO to be made against a party to county court proceedings (or apply to be joined to proceedings so as to apply for an ASBO) only if it considers that it would be reasonable for it to make an application against that person in the magistrates' court (s. 1B(2) and (3)).

If a relevant authority is already a party to county court proceedings, it may apply for a person to be joined to those proceedings to enable an ASBO to be made against him or her (s. 1B(3A) and (3B)). It must consider that the person has acted in an anti-social manner (s. 1B(3A)(a)), as defined in s. 1(1)(a) (see **88.13**). A person may not be joined to proceedings under s. 1B(3B) unless his or her anti-social acts are material in relation to those proceedings (s. 1B(3C)). No person under 18 may be joined (Anti-social Behaviour Act 2003 (Commencement No. 2) Order 2004 (SI 2004/690), art. 2(b)(ii); **PD 65, para. 13.2**).

Before making an application for an anti-social behaviour order under the Crime and Disorder Act 1998, s. 1 or s. 1B, consultation must take place between the chief officer of police for the local area and the council for a local government area (s. 1E(2) and (3)). If the application is being made by a relevant authority other than a council for a local government area or the chief officer of police for the area, the applicant should consult both the council and the chief officer of police for that area (s. 1E(4)).

Individual support orders

88.15 The Criminal Justice and Immigration Act 2008, s. 124(6), provided for amendments to be made to the Crime and Disorder Act 1998, ss. 1AA and 1AB, and for those sections to apply in relation to orders made under s. 1B, with any necessary modifications, as they apply in relation to anti-social behaviour orders (s. 1B(8) and (9)).

By s. 1AA, where the court makes an anti-social behaviour order in respect of a child or young person, it must consider whether the individual support conditions set out in s. 1AA(3) are fulfilled, and if so it must make an individual support order under s. 1AA(2). Failure to comply with an individual support order is a criminal offence (s. 1AB(3)).

The individual support conditions (s. 1AA(3)) are:

(a) that an individual support order would be desirable in the interests of preventing any repetition of the kind of behaviour which led to the making of the anti-social behaviour order, or an order varying that order (in a case where the variation is made as a result of further anti-social behaviour by the defendant);
(b) that the defendant is not already subject to an individual support order; and
(c) that the court has been notified by the Secretary of State that arrangements for implementing individual support orders are available in the area in which it appears to it that the defendant resides or will reside and the notice has not been withdrawn.

An individual support order is an order (s. 1AA(2)) that:

(a) requires the defendant to comply, for a period not exceeding six months, with such requirements specified in the order (which can include a requirement to participate in activities, or present himself to a person or persons at a place and time specified, or comply with any arrangements for his education, although not for more than two days in any week (s. 1AA(6) and (7)); and
(b) requires the defendant to comply with any directions given by the responsible officer with a view to the implementation of the requirements under paragraph (a).

The responsible officer will be a social worker of a local authority, a person nominated by a person appointed as chief education officer under the Education Act 1996, s. 532, or a member of the *youth offending team* (Crime and Disorder Act 1998, s. 1AA(10)).

If the court is not satisfied that the individual support conditions are fulfilled, it must state in open court that it is not so satisfied and why it is not (s. 1AA(4)).

Before making an individual support order, the court must obtain from a social worker of a local authority, or a member of a youth offending team, any information which it considers necessary in order to determine whether the individual support conditions are fulfilled, or to determine what requirements should be imposed by an individual support order (s. 1AA(9)).

Before making an individual support order, the court should explain to the defendant the effect of the order, and the consequences which may follow if he fails to comply with any of the requirements included in it, and that the court has power to review the order on the application of the defendant or the responsible officer (s.1AB(1)).

Review of anti-social behaviour orders

The Criminal Justice and Immigration Act 2008, s. 123, has added new ss. 1J and 1K to the Crime and Disorder Act 1998. These provide that the relevant authority that applied for an order made under s. 1 or s. 1B must review the operation of the order made if it was made in respect of a person under the age of 17. The review of the operation of the order must be carried out at the times specified in s. 1J(2) and (3). The review should include consideration of the following matters (s. 1J(6)): **88.16**

(a) the extent to which the person subject to the order has complied with it;
(b) the adequacy of any support available to the person to help him comply with it;
(c) any matters relevant to the question whether an application should be made for the order to be varied or discharged.

In carrying out the review, the relevant authority that applied for the order must cooperate with the appropriate chief officer of police. If the relevant authority was not a local authority, there must also be cooperation with the appropriate local authority (s. 1K(3), (4) and (5)). Any other relevant person may be invited to participate in the review (s. 1K(6)).

Parenting orders ancillary to ASBOs

The Crime and Disorder Act 1998, s. 9(1B), requires a court making an ASBO in respect of a person under the age of 16 to make a parenting order in respect of that person's parent or guardian if it is satisfied that the relevant condition (in s. 8(6)) is fulfilled. If it is not satisfied that the relevant condition is fulfilled, it must state in open court that it is not and why it is not. The relevant condition is that a parenting order would be desirable in the interests of preventing any repetition of the kind of behaviour which led to the anti-social behaviour order being made (s. 8(6)). **88.17**

A parenting order (s. 8(4)) is an order which requires the parent:

(a) to comply, for a period not exceeding 12 months, with such requirements as are specified in the order, and
(b) subject to s. 8(5), to attend, for a concurrent period not exceeding three months, such counselling or guidance programme, which may include a residential course (see s. 8(7A)), as may be specified in directions given by the responsible officer.

Responsible officer is defined in s. 8(8) as an officer of a local probation board, an officer of a provider of probation services, a social worker of a local authority, a person nominated by the chief education officer under the Education Act 1996, s. 532, or a member of a youth offending team.

The court must obtain and consider information about the person's family circumstances and the likely effect of the parenting order on those circumstances (s. 9(2)).

Breach of a parenting order is a criminal offence (s. 9(7)).

Before making a parenting order, the court should (s. 9(3)) explain to the parent, in ordinary language:

(a) the effect of the order and of the requirements proposed to be included in it;
(b) the consequences which may follow if he fails to comply with any of those requirements;
(c) that the court has power (under s. 9(5)) to review the order (by discharging or varying it) on the application of the parent or the responsible officer.

Intervention orders ancillary to ASBOs

88.18 A relevant authority which applies for an ASBO under the Crime and Disorder Act 1998, s. 1B, may also seek an intervention order (see s. 1G and s. 1H) if the conditions in s. 1G(1) and (4) are satisfied. An intervention order is an order which requires the defendant to comply, for a period not exceeding six months, with such requirements as are specified in the order (s. 1G(5)). It is aimed at preventing a repetition of the behaviour (the trigger behaviour), for example, misuse of drugs, which led to the anti-social behaviour order being granted.

Procedure

88.19 Any application for an ASBO to be made under the Crime and Disorder Act 1998, s. 1B(4), must be accompanied by written evidence, which must include evidence that s. 1E (consultation among relevant authorities) has been complied with (**CPR, r. 65.25**). The court is obliged to consider whether the local authority has complied with the consultation requirements in s. 1E (*Manchester City Council v M* [2006] EWCA Civ 423, LTL 20/3/2006). An application for an ASBO should be made as soon as possible after the relevant authority becomes aware of the circumstances which lead it to apply (**rr. 65.22(2), 65.23(1)(c)** and **65.24(2)(a)**). The application must normally be on notice to the person against whom the ASBO is sought (**rr. 65.22(3), 65.23(3)** and **65.24(2)(b)**).

If a relevant authority wishes to apply as a party to county court proceedings for an ASBO to be made under the Crime and Disorder Act 1998, s. 1B(4), against another party, it should make the application in its claim form or, if it is a defendant, in an application notice filed with the defence (**CPR, r. 65.22(1)**). If the relevant authority only becomes aware at a later stage of the need for an ASBO, it must apply for one as soon as possible by application notice (**r. 65.22(2)**).

An application to join a person to county court proceedings so that an ASBO may be made under the Crime and Disorder Act 1998, s. 1B(4), is an application for addition of a party and must be made under **CPR, Part 19, Section I** (see **14.83** to **14.89**) (**r. 65.23(1)(a)**). It should be made in the same application notice as the application for the ASBO (**r. 65.23(1)(b)**). It must contain the authority's reasons for claiming the anti-social acts are material in relation to the proceedings, and details of the anti-social acts alleged (**r. 65.23(2)**).

An application to be joined to county court proceedings so as to apply for an ASBO to be made against one of the existing parties is also an application for addition of a party and so must be made under **CPR, Part 19, Section I** (see **14.83** to **14.89**) (**r.65.24(1)(a)**). It should be made in the same application notice as the application for the ASBO(**r. 65.24(1)(b)**).

Interim orders

88.20 On an application for an ASBO to be made under the Crime and Disorder Act 1998, s. 1B(4) (see **88.19**), the court may, if it considers it just to do so, make an interim ASBO under s. 1D before determining the main application. An interim order must be for a fixed period (which may be extended) and will automatically cease to have effect on the determination of the main application (s. 1D(4)).

Contravention of an interim order is a criminal offence (s. 1(10) applied by s. 1D(5)).

An application for an interim ASBO is an application for an interim remedy, which must be made in accordance with **CPR, Part 25** (see **chapter 32**) (**r. 65.26(1)**). An application for an interim ASBO should normally be made in the claim form or application notice seeking the final ASBO, and on notice to the person against whom the order is sought (**r. 65.26(2)**).

Service

An ASBO made under the Crime and Disorder Act 1998, s. 1B(4), or an interim order made under s. 1D, must be served personally on the person subject to the order (**PD 65, para. 13.1**). **88.21**

Variation and discharge

A person against whom an ASBO has been made under the Crime and Disorder Act 1998, s. 1B(4), and the authority which applied for the order, may apply to the county court which made the order for it to be varied or discharged (s. 1B(5)). However, unless both those persons consent, an ASBO cannot be discharged less than two years after it is served (s. 1B(6)). **88.22**

A person against whom an interim order has been made under s. 1D, and the authority which applied for the order, may apply to the court which made the order for it to be varied or discharged (s. 1(8) applied by s. 1D(5)). Section 1(8) (which is drafted to apply to magistrates' courts) specifies that such an application is to be by complaint.

It is not necessary to establish a fresh act of anti-social behaviour in order to obtain a variation of the terms of the order. The key question that the court has to consider is whether the variation is necessary to protect the public (*James v Birmingham City Council* [2010] EWHC 282 (Admin), 174 JP 250).

PARENTING ORDERS

The Anti-social Behaviour Act 2003, ss. 26A, 26B and 26C, enable local authorities and relevant housing providers to seek parenting orders from the court. 'Relevant housing provider' means a non-profit registered provider of social housing or a registered social landlord (ss. 25B(1A) and 29(1)). **88.23**

A magistrates' court or, where s. 26C applies, a county court may make a parenting order, under s. 26A (on the application of a local authority) or s. 26B (on the application of a relevant housing provider), in respect of a parent of a child or young person, if it is satisfied:

(a) that the child or young person has engaged in anti-social behaviour; and
(b) that making the order would be desirable in the interests of preventing the child or young person from engaging in further anti-social behaviour.

An individual is a child if aged under 14, a young person if aged 14 or over but under 18 (Crime and Disorder Act 1998, s. 117(1), applied by the Anti-social Behaviour Act 2003, s.29(1)).

A parenting order is an order which requires the parent:

(a) to comply, for a period not exceeding 12 months, with such requirements as are specified in the order (ss. 26A(3)(a) and 26B(3)(a)); and
(b) to attend, for a concurrent period not exceeding three months, such counselling or guidance programme as may be specified in directions given by the responsible officer (defined in s. 26A(8) and s. 26B(9) and (10)).

Requirement (b) may, but need not, be included if another parenting order has been obtained under s. 26A, s. 26B or any other enactment in respect of the same parent on a previous occasion (s. 26A(3)(b) and (4); s. 26B(3)(b) and (4)). A counselling or guidance programme may be, or include, a residential course (ss. 26A(5) and 26B(5)), but only if the court is satisfied

Commentary

that the attendance of the parent at a residential course is likely to be more effective than attendance at a non-residential course in preventing the child or young person from engaging in further anti-social behaviour (ss. 26A(6) and 26B(6)). Also the court must be satisfied that any interference with family life which is likely to result from the attendance of the parent at a residential course is proportionate in all the circumstances (ss. 26A(7) and 26B(7)).

A relevant housing provider must not make an application for a parenting order without first consulting the local authority in whose area the child or young person in question resides or appears to reside (s. 26B(8)). If the child or young person resides or appears to reside in a place which is within the area of a county council and a district council, then each local authority must be consulted (s. 26B(8A)).

Parenting orders incidental to county court proceedings

88.24 The Anti-social Behaviour Act 2003, s. 26C, provides for parenting orders under s. 26A or s. 26B to be made in county court proceedings. The provisions are similar to those under which ASBOs may be made.

A 'relevant authority' may apply for a parenting order to be made, in county court proceedings to which it is a party (s. 26C(1)). A relevant authority may apply to be joined to proceedings for the purpose of making an application (s. 26C(2)). If it is a party to county court proceedings, it may apply for an individual to be joined in those proceedings so that it may apply for a parenting order, provided it considers that a child or young person of which that person is a parent has engaged in anti-social behaviour that is material to those proceedings (s. 26C(3)). No person under 18 may be joined (**PD 65, para. 16.3**).

For parenting orders the relevant authorities are local authorities and relevant housing providers (Anti-social Behaviour Act 2003, s. 26C(1)).

Procedure

88.25 Any application for a parenting order to be made under the Anti-social Behaviour Act 2003, s. 26A or s. 26B, must be accompanied by written evidence (**CPR, r. 65.41**). If the application is by a relevant housing provider, there must be evidence that it has consulted the relevant local authority in accordance with the Anti-social Behaviour Act 2003, s. 26B(8) (**PD 65, para. 16.1**). An application should be made as soon as possible after the relevant authority becomes aware of the circumstances which lead it to apply for a parenting order (**CPR, rr. 65.38(2), 65.39(2)(a)** and **65.40(1)(b)**). The application must normally be on notice to the person against whom the parenting order is sought (**rr. 65.38(3), 65.39(2)(b)** and **65.40(4)**).

If a relevant authority wishes to apply as a party to county court proceedings for a parenting order to be made against another party, it should make the application in its claim form or, if it is a defendant, in an application notice filed with the defence (**r. 65.38(1)**). If the relevant authority only becomes aware at a later stage of the need for a parenting order, it must apply for one as soon as possible by application notice (**r. 65.38(2)**).

An application to be joined to county court proceedings so as to apply for a parenting order to be made against one of the existing parties is an application for addition of a party and so must be made under **Part 19, Section I** (**r. 65.39(1)(a)**). It should be made in the same application notice as the application for the parenting order (**r. 65.39(1)(b)**).

An application to join a person to county court proceedings so that a parenting order may be made is an application for addition of a party and must be made under **Part 19, Section I,** but **r. 19.2** does not apply (**r. 65.40(2)**). It should be made in the same application notice as the application for the parenting order (**r. 65.40(1)(a)**). It must contain the authority's reasons for claiming the anti-social behaviour of the child or young person is material in relation to the proceedings, and details of the behaviour alleged (**r. 65.40(3)**).

Service

A parenting order made under the Anti-social Behaviour Act 2003, s. 26A or s. 26B, must be served personally on the defendant (**PD 65, para. 16.2**). **88.26**

DRINKING BANNING ORDERS

The Violent Crime Reduction Act 2006, ss. 1 to 14, provide for drinking banning orders (DBOs) to be made in magistrates' or county courts. A DBO is an order that imposes prohibitions on an individual ('the subject') which are necessary for the purpose of protecting other persons from criminal or disorderly conduct by the subject while under the influence of alcohol. A DBO must prohibit, as far as the court considers necessary, the subject from entering premises licensed to retail alcohol or supply it to club members or guests (s. 1(3)). It must not prohibit the subject from having access to his or her residence, attending at a place of work, education, training or medical treatment, or attending at any place he or she is required to attend by or under any enactment or by an order of a court or tribunal (s. 1(4)). A DBO must be for a specified period of not less than two months or more than two years (s. 2(1)). Different provisions may be made for different periods, provided that, in each case, the period is not less than two months or more than two years (s. 2(2)). **88.27**

A DBO can provide for termination on satisfactory completion of an approved course (s. 2(3)), but only if a place on the course is available for the subject and the subject agrees (s. 2(6)). The court must inform the subject, 'in ordinary language', about the effect of a requirement to attend an approved course, including the attendance commitments, and how much it will cost (s. 2(7)). If no provision is made in a DBO for attendance at an approved course, the court must give its reasons in open court for not including the provision (s. 2(8)).

Contravention of a DBO is a criminal offence (s. 1(11)).

DBOs incidental to county court proceedings

The Violent Crime Reduction Act 2006, s. 4, provides for DBOs to be made in county court proceedings. The provisions are similar to those under which ASBOs may be made. **88.28**

A 'relevant' authority may apply for a DBO to be made in county court proceedings to which it is a party (s. 4(2)). A relevant authority may apply to be joined to proceedings for the purpose of making an application (s. 4(3)). If it is a party to county court proceedings, it may apply for an individual to be joined in those proceedings so that it may apply for a DBO, provided it considers that the individual has engaged in criminal or disorderly conduct while under the influence of alcohol and that conduct is relevant to the proceedings (s. 4(4) and (5)). No person under 18 may be joined (**PD 65, para. 15.2**).

For DBOs, the relevant authorities are local authorities, chief police officers and the Chief Constable of the British Transport Police (Violent Crime Reduction Act 2006, s. 14(1)). Before applying for a DBO or for joinder to proceedings for the purpose of applying for a DBO, a relevant authority must (s. 4(6)) consult other relevant authorities ('the appropriate persons') as defined in s. 14(1).

Under s. 4(7), the court may make a DBO against an individual if it is proved:

(a) that the conditions in s. 3(2) are satisfied in relation to the individual (namely that the individual has, after the commencement of that section (namely, 31 August 2009), engaged in criminal or disorderly conduct while under the influence of alcohol and that such order is necessary to protect other persons from further similar conduct by him whilst he is under the influence of alcohol); and

(b) the individual's criminal or disorderly conduct whilst under the influence of alcohol is material in relation to the proceedings.

Procedure

88.29 If a relevant authority wishes to apply as a party to county court proceedings for a DBO to be made against another party, it should make the application in its claim form or, if it is a defendant, in an application notice filed with the defence (**CPR, r. 65.32(1)**). If the relevant authority becomes aware only at a later stage of the need for a DBO, it must apply for one as soon as possible by application notice (**r. 65.32(2)**).

An application to be joined to county court proceedings so as to apply for a DBO to be made against one of the existing parties is an application for the addition of a party and so must be made under **Part 19, Section I** (**r. 65.33(1)(a)**). It should be made in the same application notice as the application for the DBO (**r. 65.33(1)(b)**). The application must be made as soon as possible after the relevant authority becomes aware of the principal proceedings and should normally be made on notice to the person against whom the order is sought (**r. 65.33(2)**).

An application to join a person to county court proceedings so that a DBO may be made is an application for the addition of a party and must be made under **Part 19, Section I** (**r. 65.34(1)(a)**). It should be made in the same application notice as the application for a DBO (**r. 65.34(1)(b)**) and as soon as possible after the relevant authority considers that the criteria for a DBO are met (**r. 65.34(1)(c)**). It must contain the authority's reasons for claiming the person's conduct is material in relation to the proceedings, and details of the conduct alleged (**r. 65.34(2)**).

Any application for a DBO to be made under the Violent Crime Reduction Act 2006, s. 4, must be accompanied by written evidence, which must include evidence that s. 4(6) (consultation among relevant authorities) has been complied with (**CPR, r. 65.35**). The application must normally be on notice to the person against whom a DBO is sought (**rr. 65.32(3), 65.33(2)(b)** and **65.34(3)**).

Interim DBOs

88.30 On an application for a DBO to be made under the Violent Crime Reduction Act 2006, s. 4, the court may, if it considers it just to do so, make an interim DBO under s. 9 before determining the main application. An interim order must be for a fixed period (which may be extended) of not more than four weeks and will automatically cease to have effect on determination of the main application (s. 9(6) and (7)).

Contravention of an interim order is a criminal offence (s. 11(1)).

An application for an interim DBO is an application for an interim remedy, which must be made in accordance with **CPR, Part 25** (**r. 65.36(1)**). An application for an interim DBO should normally be made in the claim form or application notice seeking a final DBO, and on notice to the person against whom the order is sought (**r. 65.36(2)**). If the court gives permission, an application for an interim DBO can be made without notice to, and in the absence of, the individual against whom the order is sought (Violent Crime Reduction Act 2006, s. 9(3), (4) and (5); **CPR, r. 65.36(3)**). Permission may be given only if the court is satisfied that it is necessary for the application to be made without notice to the individual in question and that it is not necessary for the application to be heard in his or her presence.

Service

88.31 A DBO made under the Violent Crime Reduction Act 2006, s. 4, or an interim order made under s. 9 must be served personally on the person subject to the order (**PD 65, para. 15.1**).

Variation and discharge

A person against whom a DBO has been made under the Violent Crime Reduction Act 2006, s. 4, or the authority which applied for the order, may apply to the county court which made the order for it to be varied or discharged (s. 5). However, unless the authority consents, a DBO cannot be discharged unless half of the original period has expired (s. 5(6)). The order may not be varied so as to extend the specified period to more than 2 years (s. 5(5)). Section 5 (with the omission of s. 5(5) and (6)) is applied to interim DBOs by s. 9(8). **88.32**

PROTECTION FROM HARASSMENT ACT 1997

The Protection from Harassment Act 1997 prohibits a person knowingly pursuing a course of conduct which amounts to harassment of another (s. 1(1)) or, in certain circumstances, a course of conduct which involves harassment of two or more persons (s. 1(1A)). The definition of harassment is considered in more detail in **88.34** to **88.36**. The Act provides both criminal (ss. 2, 2A, 4, 4A and 5) and civil (ss. 3 and 3A) sanctions. Civil proceedings are considered in **88.37** to **88.39**. **88.33**

Conduct amounting to harassment

The Protection from Harassment Act 1997, s. 1(1), provides that a person must not pursue a course of conduct which amounts to harassment of another and which he or she knows or ought to know amounts to harassment of the other. By s. 1(1A) a person must not pursue a course of conduct which involves harassment of two or more persons and which he or she knows, or ought to know, involves harassment of those persons and by which he or she intends to persuade any person not to do something which that person is entitled to do or to do something which that person is not under any obligation to do. Section 1(1A) will be particularly useful in cases where a campaign of harassment is carried out by pressure groups in respect of a business or property, and there is no 'course of conduct' against any one victim for the purposes of s. 1(1), because no individual is affected twice (see **88.35**). **88.34**

By s. 1(2), a person ought to know that conduct amounts to or involves harassment if a reasonable person in possession of the same information would think that the course of conduct amounted to or involved harassment. Whether or not an individual has contravened this prohibition is determined objectively by considering whether a reasonable person would think that what the individual did amounted to harassment (*R v Colohan* [2001] EWCA Crim 1251, [2001] 2 FLR 757). In civil proceedings the standard of proof of contravention of s. 1(1) is the civil standard on the balance of probabilities (*Hipgrave v Jones* [2004] EWHC 2901 (QB), [2005] 2 FLR 174).

It appears that the definition of harassment has been left deliberately imprecise. The interpretation section (s. 7(2)) defines harassing a person as including 'alarming the person or causing the person distress', but Lord Phillips of Worth Matravers MR said in *Thomas v News Group Newspapers Ltd* [2001] EWCA Civ 1233, [2002] EMLR 4 at [29]–[30]:

> There are many actions that foreseeably alarm or cause a person distress that could not possibly be described as harassment. It seems to me that s. 7 is dealing with that element of the offence which is constituted by the effect of the conduct rather than with the types of conduct that produce that effect. . . . 'Harassment' is a word which has a meaning which is generally understood. It describes conduct targeted at an individual which is calculated to produce the consequences described in s. 7 and which is oppressive and unreasonable.

It is not necessary to prove an intention to alarm or distress: it is sufficient that the conduct is liable to produce those consequences (*Banks v Ablex Ltd* [2005] EWCA Civ 173, [2005] IRLR 357).

Newspaper articles likely to incite racial hatred of an individual may be harassment of that individual (*Thomas v News Group Newspapers Ltd* [2001] EWCA Civ 1233, [2002] EMLR 4). Damage

Commentary

to the claimants' shop windows, obstructing their customers and sending offensive letters and materials constituted harassment in *Silverton v Gravett* (2001) LTL 31/10/2001.

By s. 7(4) 'conduct' includes speech, which seems common sense given the nature of the distress which the 1997 Act is intended to relieve.

Course of conduct

88.35 The Protection from Harassment Act 1997, s. 1, prohibits a 'course of conduct'. By s. 7(3), in the case of conduct in relation to a single individual, this must involve conduct on at least two occasions in relation to that individual (*Banks v Ablex Ltd* [2005] EWCA Civ 173, [2005] IRLR 357). In the case of conduct in relation to two or more persons (see s. 1(1A)), a course of conduct must involve conduct on at least one occasion in relation to each of those persons (s. 7(3)(b)). The two or more incidents of harassment do not therefore need to be against the same person in a case which is brought under s. 1(1A).

'The requirement of a course of conduct shows that Parliament was conscious that it might not be in the public interest to allow the law to be set in motion for one boorish incident' (Lord Hoffmann in *Wainwright v Home Office* [2003] UKHL 53, [2004] 2 AC 406, at [46]).

Two separate incidents may amount to a course of conduct, if they are shown to be motivated by a common purpose of harassment (compare *Baron v Crown Prosecution Service* (2000) LTL 13/6/2000, in which two letters, clearly intended as harassment, amounted to a course of conduct, with *Lau v Director of Public Prosecutions* [2000] 1 FLR 799, in which no connection was proved between two incidents six months apart). Even if there are two or more incidents, they may not all be sufficiently serious to amount to harassment within the meaning of the 1997 Act. The gravity of the misconduct has to be sufficiently serious to sustain criminal liability under s. 2 (*Sunderland City Council v Conn* [2007] EWCA Civ 1492, [2008] IRLR 324; *Lipscombe v Forestry Commission* [2008] EWHC 3342 (QB), LTL 4/2/2009). In *Pratt v Director of Public Prosecutions* (2001) *The Times*, 22 August 2001, the Administrative Court emphasised that the fewer and wider spread the incidents put in evidence, the less likely they would be found to constitute a course of conduct (see also *R v Nitin Patel* [2004] EWCA Crim 3284, [2005] 1 Cr App R 27; *James v Crown Prosecution Service* [2009] EWHC 2925 (Admin), [2010] Crim LR 580). A gift of a plant, sending a letter and redirecting a misdirected package could not themselves amount to harassment, but when combined with secretly filming the victim and going through her rubbish, they could (*King v Director of Public Prosecutions* (2000) *The Independent*, 31 July 2000). Computer-generated bills and communications from a company may amount to a course of harassment (*Ferguson v British Gas Trading Ltd* [2009] EWCA Civ 46, [2009] 3 All ER 304).

An alleged act of harassment which occurred around 18 months after the previous acts of harassment, and in a different place under different circumstances, did not form part of a course of conduct when considered with the previous incidents (*Marinello v Edinburgh City Council* [2010] CSOH 17, 2010 SLT 349).

An act which occurred during the course of proceedings and after the issue of the claim form can be relied upon to establish a course of conduct (*Iqbal v Dean Manson Solicitors* [2011] EWCA Civ 123, [2011] CP Rep 26). The commencement and service of civil proceedings may amount to harassment as they may be a form of conduct that might well cause anxiety, alarm and distress. The prevention of harassment is a legitimate social objective that may justify a restriction on the respondent's rights under the European Convention on Human Rights, **art. 6**, in the **Human Rights Act 1998, sch. 1** (*R (on the application of Waxman) v Crown Prosecution Service* [2012] EWHC 133 (Admin), 176 JP 121.

Posting threatening communications on the internet and by email can amount to a 'course of conduct' (*XY v Facebook Ireland Ltd* [2012] NIQB 96, LTL 24/12/2012). See also *WXY v Gewanter* [2012] EWHC 496 (QB), LTL 15/3/2012, [2013] EWHC 589 (QB), LTL 21/3/2013, and *AMP v Persons*

Unknown [2011] EWHC 3454 (TCC), [2011] Info TLR 25). An allegation of harassment by publication is likely to engage the defendant's rights under the European Convention on Human Rights, art. 10. Accordingly, the test in the **Human Rights Act 1998, s. 12(3)**, as explained in *Cream Holdings Ltd v Banerjee* [2004] UKHL 44, [2005] 1 AC 253, should be applied. An applicant for an interim injunction must establish that they are 'likely' to succeed at trial in obtaining permanent relief in respect of the harassment, and the court should grant an interim in unction only if that test is satisfied (*Neocleous v Jones* [2011] EWHC 3459 (QB), LTL 5/1/2012). See also *Law Society v Kordowski* [2011] EWHC 3185 (QB), LTL 14/12/2011, and *ZAM v CFW* [2011] EWHC 476 (QB), LTL 9/3/2011.

False allegations made to neighbours and to the police about a claimant which led to many police visits to the claimant's house were held to be a course of conduct amounting to harassment in *Mitton v Benefield* [2011] EWHC 2098 (QB), LTL 4/8/2011. On the other hand, six incidents over a nine-month period, all of which included an element of violence, during a close and affectionate relationship were held not to amount to a course of conduct or harassment in *R v Widdows* [2011] EWCA Crim 1500, [2011] 2 FLR 869.

A course of conduct which amounts to stalking is an offence under s. 2A or, where it involves a fear of violence or serious alarm or distress, s. 4A (inserted by the Protection of Freedoms Act 2012, s. 111, with effect from 25 November 2012).

Commentary

Excluded situations

88.36 The Protection from Harassment Act 1997, s. 1, does not apply if the person who pursued what would otherwise have been a course of conduct amounting to harassment, shows that it was pursued for the purpose of preventing or detecting crime (s.1(3)(a)), or under any enactment or rule of law, or duty imposed by an enactment(s.1(3)(b)), or that in the particular circumstances the pursuit of the course of conduct was reasonable (s. 1(3)(c)). A person's explanation of the purpose of their conduct is part of the evidence of all of the circumstances which the court must assess in ascertaining whether that conduct came within s. 1(3) (*Hayes v Willoughby* [2011] EWCA Civ 1541, *The Times*, 13 January 2012). Section 1(3)(a) is confined to a course of conduct designed to prevent or detect crime and it has to be read in the context of s. 1(3)(c) (*Hayes v Willoughby*). The mere fact that the alleged conduct occurred in the context of police work is not enough (*Dowson v Chief Constable of Northumbria* [2009] EWHC 907 (QB), LTL 7/5/2009). If a course of conduct was pursued partly to prevent or detect crime and partly for other reasons, a person might claim the protection of s. 1(3)(c) and show that their conduct was reasonable in the circumstances. If a person invokes both s. 1(3)(a) and (c), the court should first determine whether the sole purpose of the conduct was to prevent or detect crime. If the detection or prevention of crime was not the only purpose of the conduct, then the court should consider whether the conduct was in any event reasonable under s. 1(3)(c) (*Hayes v Willoughby*).

Section 1 also does not apply to any act, by a specified person, which is certified by the Secretary of State to have been related to national security, the economic well-being of the United Kingdom, or the prevention or detection of serious crime (s. 12).

Civil proceedings

88.37 Section 3(1) of the Protection from Harassment Act 1997 provides that an actual or apprehended breach of s. 1(1) may be the subject of a claim in civil proceedings by the victim or potential victim. On such a claim, damages may be awarded for (among other things) any anxiety and/or any financial loss caused by the harassment (s. 3(2)).

The claimant does not need to establish that any injury or loss sustained by the harassment was foreseeable. Section 1 is concerned with deliberate conduct of a kind which the defendant knew or ought to have known would amount to harassment of the claimant. Once that is proved, the defendant is responsible (by s. 3) for damages for the injury and loss which flowed from that conduct. There is nothing in the language of the statute to import an additional requirement of forseeability (*Jones v Ruth* [2011] EWCA Civ 804, [2012] 1 All ER 490).

A corporation cannot make a claim under s. 3 (*Daiichi Pharmaceuticals UK Ltd v Stop Huntingdon Animal Cruelty* [2003] EWHC 2337 (QB), [2004] 1 WLR 1503). If a campaign against a company involves harassment under s. 1(1) of individuals who are employees, directors or shareholders of the company, each of those individuals may take action under s. 3. In *Emerson Developments Ltd v Avery* [2004] EWHC 194 (QB), LTL 26/1/2004, one individual, who was a director and employee of a company, sued as a representative of all employees of the company under **CPR, r. 19.6**, and this is now usual in such cases.

An employer may be held vicariously liable under the Protection from Harassment Act 1997, s. 3, for harassment by one of its employees acting in the course of his or her employment (*Majrowski v Guy's and St Thomas's NHS Trust* [2006] UKHL 34, [2007] 1 AC 224; *Green v DB Group Services (UK) Ltd* [2006] EWHC 1898 (QB), [2006] IRLR 764). Vicarious liability for harassment may be established either by proving that one employee, on at least two occasions, pursued a course of conduct which amounted to harassment, or that there have been acts of harassment by more than one employee, each acting on different occasions in furtherance of some joint design (*Daniels v Commissioner of Police of the Metropolis* [2006] EWHC 1622 (QB), LTL 12/7/2006).

A claim under s. 3 must use the **CPR, Part 8**, procedure (see **chapter 13**) (**r. 65.28(a)**). In the High Court it must be commenced in the Queen's Bench Division; otherwise it must be commenced in the county court for the district in which the defendant resides or carries on business, or the court for the district in which the claimant resides or carries on business (**r. 65.28(b)**).

A civil claim for breach or apprehended breach of the Protection from Harassment Act 1997, s. 1, may ask for an injunction to restrain future breach. In a county court an injunction may be granted by a district judge (**PD 2B, para. 8.1(d)**). Contravention of such an injunction without reasonable excuse is a criminal offence (Protection from Harassment Act 1997, s. 3(6) and (9)). Alternatively, breach of an injunction can be punished by committal (see **chapter 81**) and s. 3 provides for a warrant for arrest to be issued to bring a person who breaches such an injunction to court to consider an application for committal (see **88.38**). Committal for contempt and criminal proceedings are mutually exclusive alternatives (s. 3(7) and (8)).

An injunction may create an exclusion zone if that is reasonably necessary for the protection of the claimant's legitimate interests (*Burris v Azadani* [1995] 1 WLR 1372; *Church of Jesus Christ of Latter-Day Saints v Price* [2004] EWHC 3245 (QB)). See also *Slade v Slade* [2009] EWCA Civ 748, [2010] 1 WLR 1262.

If claimant and defendant are within the jurisdiction, an injunction may be granted to restrain harassment of the claimant when abroad (*Potter v Price* [2004] EWHC 781 (QB), LTL 28/7/2004).

Under s. 3A, where there is an actual or apprehended breach of s. 1(1A) (course of conduct involving harassment of two or more persons), an injunction may be granted restraining the relevant person from pursuing any conduct which amounts to harassment in relation to any person or persons mentioned or described in the injunction. An application for an injunction under s. 3A may be made to the High Court or a county court by any person who is or may be the victim of the course of conduct in question, or any person who is or may be a person falling within s. 1(1A)(c) (a person whom the wrongdoer intends to persuade not to do something he is entitled to do or to do something which he is not under any obligation to do). A company may apply for an injunction under s. 3A in circumstances where the company falls within s. 1(1A)(c). 'Person' in s. 1(1A)(c) is not limited to individuals and may be a body corporate (*SmithKline Beecham plc v Avery* [2009] EWHC 1488 (QB), LTL 1/7/2009). Section 3A(3) applies s. 3(3) to (9) (sanctions for breach of an injunction order) to an order granted under s. 3A.

Although s. 3A has widened the scope of the Act to encompass victims who are not parties, where a representative defendant has been appointed under **CPR, r. 19.6**, the provisions of **r. 19.6(4)(b)** cannot be circumvented (*AGC Chemicals Europe Ltd v Stop Huntington Animal Cruelty* [2010] EWHC 3674 (QB), LTL 11/6/2010). **Rule 19.6(4)(b)** requires the court's permission for enforcement of an order against a person who is not a party (see *Astellas Pharma v Stop Huntingdon Animal Cruelty* [2011] EWCA Civ 752, *The Times*, 11 July 2011). Permission to enforce an order against unidentified non-parties may not be granted in the order itself (*SmithKline Beecham plc v Avery* [2007] EWHC 948 (QB), LTL 9/5/2007; *Huntingdon Life Sciences Group plc v Stop Huntingdon Animal Cruelty (SHAC)* [2007] EWHC 522 (QB), LTL 19/4/2007). Therefore, it is not possible to declare in the order that any represented person not named in the order is a 'defendant' for the purposes of the Protection against Harassment Act 1997, s. 3(3) (warrant for arrest) or s. 3(6) (contravention of order is an offence) (*AGC Chemicals Europe Ltd v Stop Huntington Animal Cruelty* [2010] EWHC 3674 (QB), LTL 11/6/2010).

Warrant for arrest

Where the court grants an injunction for the purpose of restraining the defendant from pursuing any conduct which amounts to harassment, and the claimant considers that the defendant is in breach, the claimant may apply for a warrant for the defendant's arrest (Protection from Harassment Act 1997, s. 3(3) and s. 3A(3)). Such application may be to a High Court judge if the injunction was granted by that court (s. 3(4)(a)), or to a judge or district judge of the issuing, or any other, county court (s. 3(4)(b)). Such a warrant can only be issued if the application is substantiated on oath (i.e. it must be supported by an affidavit or sworn testimony), and the judge or district judge has reasonable grounds for believing that there may have been a breach of the injunction (s. 3(5)(a) and (b)). The evidence must set out the grounds of the application, state whether the claimant has informed the police of the conduct of the defendant as described in the affidavit, and state whether, to the claimant's knowledge, criminal proceedings are being pursued (**CPR, r. 65.29(2)**). **88.38**

Dealing with arrestee

Where a person is arrested in execution of a warrant issued under the Protection from Harassment Act 1997, s. 3(3), the judge before whom the person is first brought may deal with the matter or adjourn proceedings (**CPR, r. 65.30(1)**). An arrestee who is released when proceedings are adjourned must be dealt with (whether by the same or another judge) within 28 days of the first court appearance (**r. 65.30(2)(a)**) and must be given at least two days' notice of the hearing (**r. 65.30(2)(b)**). Unlike the position in proceedings on a warrant issued under the Housing Act 1996, s. 155(3) (see **88.11**), there is no provision that failure to meet the 28-day deadline does not invalidate any application notice seeking committal for contempt, there is no provision for remand, and a district judge does not have power to commit. **88.39**

Conviction for the offence of doing something prohibited by an anti-harassment injunction precludes punishment of the same act as a civil contempt of court (Protection from Harassment Act 1997, s. 3(7)). Conversely, a person cannot be criminally convicted for conduct which has been punished as contempt of court (s. 3(8)).

BEHAVIOUR CONTROL AND HUMAN RIGHTS

Relevant Convention rights

Orders granted under the Police and Justice Act 2006, s. 27(2) (**88.12**), the Crime and Disorder Act 1998 (**88.13** to **88.22**), or the Protection from Harassment Act 1997 (**88.33** to **88.39**) may potentially infringe an individual's rights under the European Convention on **88.40**

Human Rights in the **Human Rights Act 1998, sch. 1**. This is particularly so in cases of harassment arising from the acts of protest groups. An order which seeks to ban an individual from particular premises or a particular area may infringe his **art. 8** right to a private or family life. An order preventing an individual speaking or publishing specified words may contravene his **art. 10** right to freedom of expression. An order that prevents an individual from associating with other named individuals or specified groups or organisations, or prevents him from demonstrating, for example, against an animal testing laboratory, could infringe his **art. 11** right to freedom of assembly and to freedom of association with others.

An individual's rights under each of these articles are limited and restrictions can be placed on them which are prescribed by law and are necessary in a democratic society for the prevention of disorder or crime, for the protection of health or morals, or for the protection of the rights of others (**arts 8(2)**, **10(2)** and **11(2)**). **Article 11** also does not prevent the imposition of lawful restrictions on the exercise of the rights of freedom of assembly and association by members of the armed forces, the police or the administration of the State (**art. 11(2)**).

Impact of Convention rights in harassment and anti-social behaviour cases

88.41 The courts have shown no reluctance in granting orders discussed in this chapter if the individual has acted in a way which causes harassment, alarm or distress to others. However, the orders granted must be proportionate in the sense of being commensurate with the risk to be guarded against, particularly where the order will interfere with a right protected by the **Human Rights Act 1998** (*R v Boness* [2005] EWCA Crim 2395, [2006] 1 Cr App R (S) 120; *Percy v Director of Public Prosecutions* [2001] EWHC 1125 (Admin), [2002] Crim LR 835). A parenting order (see **88.23** to **88.26**) with a residential course for counselling or guidance may be made only if any interference with family life (**art. 8**) is proportionate in all the circumstances (Anti-social Behaviour Act 2003, ss. 26A(7) and 26B(7)).

While most restrictions on freedom of expression or assembly will be granted only if there is a risk or threat of violence, an injunction to prevent harassment is not limited to acts which place the victim in fear of violence but can be granted when rights of protest and expression amount to harassment (*EDO MBM Technology Ltd v Campaign to Smash EDO* [2005] EWHC 837; *SmithKline Beecham plc v Avery* [2009] EWHC 1488 (QB), LTL 1/7/2009; *Law Society v Kordowski* [2011] EWHC 3185 (QB), LTL 14/12/2011).

The common law of nuisance and the Protection from Harassment Act 1997 can limit an individual's right to freedom of expression and manifestation of his religious belief under the European Convention on Human Rights, **art. 9**, in the **Human Rights Act 1998, sch. 1**, in the interests of public order and for the protection of others, and an exclusion order can be granted even if it interferes with the defendant's lawful actions and right to move freely along the highway (*Church of Jesus Christ of Latter-Day Saints v Price* [2004] EWHC 3245 (QB)).

A fair balance should be struck between the rights of the defendant and the proper protection of the claimants. Such a balance was struck by the court in *Hall v Save Newchurch Guinea Pigs (Campaign)* [2005] EWHC 372 (QB), *The Times*, 7 April 2005, where the claimants sought and obtained injunctive relief under the Protection from Harassment Act 1997 against animal rights activists, even though the defendants' conduct was not of itself tortious or unlawful in that it amounted to a peaceful demonstration, as an injunction was reasonably necessary for the protection of the claimant's legitimate interests. The court also imposed an exclusion zone around the premises. To strike a balance between the rights of the claimants and the rights of the demonstrators, the court provided that the defendants would be entitled to protest once per week between certain hours, although it limited the number of protesters who could be present at each demonstration.

A similar balance was struck in the order made against animal rights protesters in *Huntingdon Life Sciences Group plc v Stop Huntingdon Animal Cruelty (SHAC)* [2007] EWHC 522 (QB), LTL 19/4/2007, where an injunction was granted in favour of the claimants although the terms of the order specified the maximum number of protesters, the requirement to give notice to the police prior to a demonstration, provision for parking and delivery of protesters to and from a designated protest area, a ban on the use of megaphones and restriction of protest processions to one every three months. See also *RWE npower plc v Carrol* [2007] EWHC 947 (QB), LTL 9/5/2007; *SmithKline Beecham plc v Avery* [2007] EWHC 948 (QB), LTL 9/5/2007; *Bayer Cropscience Ltd v Stop Huntingdon Cruelty (SHAC)* [2009] EWHC 3289 (QB), LTL 8/3/2010. In *Novartis Pharmaceuticals UK Ltd v Stop Huntington Animal Cruelty* [2009] EWHC 2716 (QB), LTL 6/11/2009, the court had to balance the rights, of freedom of assembly and association and freedom of expression, of animal rights activists against the right to respect for private and family life of the pharmaceutical company's employees. The court held that any restrictions on the freedom of expression or freedom of assembly or both had to be: convincingly established, justified by compelling reasons, subject to careful scrutiny, proportionate and no more than necessary. The giving of notice to the police in relation to demonstrations and compliance with police conditions were reasonable and acceptable, but the balance of convenience was strongly against making an order prohibiting protesters from wearing blood-splattered clothing or costumes as it was likely to be practically unenforceable and was not proportionate. It was not so easy to decide where the balance lay in relation to the prohibition sought in relation to the wearing of balaclavas, face coverings and masks. Although ghoulish masks had the potential to cause anxiety and distress and could be used to disguise the identity of someone intent on harassing conduct, given the late application for such a provision, the practical difficulties it would cause for the police, the risk of it raising tensions and the interference it would cause to those who wished to wear inoffensive masks, such an order was not made in the circumstances of that case. A permanent injunction was granted preventing demonstrations by animal rights groups at the applicant's medical laboratory together with an order banning photography, balaclavas and masks. A balance was achieved between the applicant's **art. 8** rights and the protesters' **art. 10** and **11** rights by allowing the protesters to demonstrate opposite the premises once a week for three hours, although the number of protesters was limited to 25 and they were required to give 24 hours' advance notice of a demonstration to the police and the applicant, and by giving them the right to a larger demonstration of up to 100 people once a year (*Harlan Laboratories UK Ltd v Stop Huntingdon Animal Cruelty (SHAC)* [2012] EWHC 3408 (QB), LTL 11/12/2012).

The court is also, in appropriate circumstances, prepared to look at the human rights of an individual protester separately from those of a larger group. In *Mayor of London v Hall* [2010] EWCA Civ 817, [2011] 1 WLR 504, the Court of Appeal remitted for reconsideration to the High Court the question whether it was proportionate to grant an order for possession and an injunction against a protester in respect of his protest and camping on Parliament Square Gardens as his human rights had not been considered separately from the group of protesters. The individual was in a different position from the other protestors. He had been demonstrating for far longer, his demonstration pitch was in a different part of Parliament Square Gardens and his demonstration had not put off visitors or damaged the flora. The judge should consider his individual rights under the European Convention on Human Rights, arts 10 and 11. The High Court held that the orders were proportionate and the interference with rights under arts 10 and 11 was justified (*Mayor of London v Haw* [2011] EWHC 585 (QB), LTL 24/3/2011).

The court granted an order for possession of land occupied by protesters who set up camps next to St Paul's Cathedral and other injunctive relief as the protesters were occupying the land to the exclusion of the landowners and the extent and duration of the obstruction was causing a public nuisance and interfering with the **art. 9** rights of worshippers and visitors to the Cathedral. Any interference the orders caused to the rights of the protesters under **arts. 10** and **11** were lawful, necessary and proportionate to safeguard the rights of the landowners and the rights and freedoms of others, the interests of public health and safety, the prevention of disorder and crime and to protect the environment within the City of London. Determining

Commentary

the limits to the **art. 10** and **11** rights of lawful assembly on the highway is fact-sensitive and relevant factors include the extent to which the continuation of the protest breaches domestic law, the importance of the precise location of the protesters, the duration of the protest, the degree to which the protesters occupy the land and the extent to which the protest interferes with the rights of others, including the owners of the land and members of the public (*City of London Corporation v Samede* [2012] EWCA Civ 160, [2012] PTSR 1624). See also *Islington London Borough Council v Jones* [2012] EWHC 1537 (QB), LTL 1/6/2012).

The rights of freedom of expression and assembly are qualified rights and must give way, where it is necessary and proportionate, to the rights of others. An order preventing protesters from entering or remaining without consent on land intended for the 2012 London Olympic Games was granted where the protest was obstructing the rights of the person with exclusive rights of possession to the site (*Olympic Delivery Authority v Persons Unknown* [2012] EWHC 1012 (Ch), LTL 3/5/2012).

The provisions in the Police Reform and Social Responsibility Act 2011, part 3, which conferred powers on the police and authorised officers of the local authority to stop protesters from erecting and using tents for the purposes of sleeping or staying in Parliament Square did not infringe the protesters' rights of freedom of expression and assembly. The provisions are of limited effect and relate only to sleeping and do not impede or prevent any other form of protest or demonstration in Parliament Square at any time of the day or night (*R (Gallastegui) v Westminster City Council* [2013] EWCA Civ 28, [2013] 2 All ER 579).

In relation to relief which might interfere with the Convention right to freedom of expression, the **Human Rights Act 1988, s. 12(3)**, provides that no relief is to be granted so as to restrain publication before trial unless the court is satisfied that the applicant is likely to establish that publication should not be allowed. 'Likely' means 'more likely than not' (*Cream Holdings Ltd v Banerjee* [2004] UKHL 44, [2005] 1 AC 253). See also *Neocleous v Jones* [2011] EWHC 3459 (QB), LTL 5/1/2012, and EWQ v GDF [2012] EWHC 2182 (QB), LTL 3/8/2012.

On an application for an injunction to prevent harassment by publication of newspaper articles and photographs, an individual's **art. 8** rights did not prevail over a newspaper's **art. 10** rights of freedom of expression where, because of the applicant's association with a public figure, she had no reasonable expectation of privacy (*Trimingham v Associated Newspapers Ltd* [2012] EWHC 1296 (QB), [2012] 4 All ER 717). On the other hand, in *SKA v CRH* [2012] EWHC 2236 (QB), LTL 3/8/2012, an injunction was granted preventing the respondent from disclosing private information about the applicants and harassing them because their **art. 8** rights substantially outweighed the respondent's rights under **art. 10**.

Many of the remedies for anti-social behaviour and harassment arise in a criminal context, such as orders under the Public Order Act 1986 or orders to disperse groups under the Antisocial Behaviour Act 2003, s. 30. Protests are not excluded from those powers, and no fundamental Convention rights will be overridden, provided the use of the powers is proportionate. The question to ask is whether the making of a dispersal order for the protection of the public from harassment, alarm or distress was disproportionate having regard to the defendant's rights under the **Human Rights Act 1998** (*R (Singh) v Chief Constable of the West Midlands* [2005] EWHC 2840 (Admin), [2006] Crim LR 442).

INJUNCTIONS UNDER THE POLICING AND CRIME ACT 2009

Injunctions to prevent gang-related violence

88.42 *Either the High Court* or a county court can grant an injunction to prevent gang-related violence under the provisions of part 4 (ss. 34 to 50) of the Policing and Crime Act 2009. 'Gang-related violence' means violence or a threat of violence which occurs in the course of, or is otherwise related to, the activities of a group that consists of at least three people, uses a name, emblem or colour or has any other characteristic that enables its members to be identified by others as a group, and is associated with a particular area (s. 34(5)). An injunction cannot be made against a person aged under 14 (s. 34(1)).

The application

An application for an injunction under the Policing and Crime Act 2009, s. 34, can be made by (s. 37): **88.43**

(a) the chief officer of police for a police area; or
(b) the chief constable of the British Transport Police Force; or
(c) the local authority (meaning a district council, a county council, a London borough council, the Common Council of the City of London, the Council of the Isles of Scilly, or in Wales, a county council or a county borough council).

Before applying for an injunction, the applicant must consult any local authority, any chief police officer or any other body or individual that the applicant thinks it is appropriate to consult (s. 38).

If the respondent is under the age of 18, the applicant must also consult the youth offending team in the area in which the respondent resides and if it appears that the respondent resides in the area of two or more youth offending teams, the applicant must consult the teams that he thinks appropriate (s. 38(2)(aa) and (3)).

The application must be made by form N16A (**PD 65, para. 1.1**) and must be commenced in the court for the district in which the defendant resides or the conduct complained of occurred (**CPR, r. 65.43(2)(a)** and **(b)**). Unless the court otherwise orders, an application on notice under **r. 65.43** or any other hearing requiring the respondent's attendance must be heard at one of the designated county courts set out in **PD 65, para. 1.2**. Form N16A must state the matters required by **CPR, r. 8.2**, and the terms of the injunction applied for (**r. 65.43(3)**; **PD 65, para. 1.1**). The application must be supported by a witness statement which is filed with the claim form (**CPR, r. 65.43(2)(c)**). The application must be served, together with a copy of the witness statement, by the claimant on the defendant personally (**r. 65.43(5)**). An application made on notice can be listed for hearing before the expiry of the time for the defendant to file an acknowledgment of service under **r. 8.3**. In such a case, the claimant must serve the application notice and witness statement on the defendant not less than two days before the hearing and the defendant may take part in the hearing whether or not he has filed an acknowledgment of service (**r. 65.43(6)**).

Without-notice application

An application for an injunction under the Policing and Crime Act 2009, s. 34, can be made without giving notice to the respondent (s. 39). If a without-notice application is made, the applicant need not comply with the consultation requirements in s. 38. Where a without-notice application is made, the witness statement in support of the application must state the reasons why notice has not been given (**CPR, r. 65.43(4)**). **88.44**

The court cannot make an order immediately on a without-notice application. It must either dismiss the application or adjourn it (Policing and Crime Act 2009, s. 39(4)). If the court adjourns the proceedings, the applicant must comply with the consultation requirements before the date of the full hearing on notice (s. 39(5)).

Applications for an injunction which includes a power of arrest

If an application for an injunction under the Policing and Crime Act 2009, s. 34, made with or without notice, includes an application for a power of arrest to be attached to any provision **88.45**

Commentary

of the injunction, it must be made in the proceedings seeking the injunction by claim form or an application under **CPR, Part 23**, and every application must be supported by evidence (**r. 65.49(1)**). Every application made on notice must be served personally by the applicant on the respondent, together with a copy of the written evidence, not less than two days before the hearing (**r. 65.49(3)**).

The injunction order

88.46 The court can grant an injunction under the Policing and Crime Act 2009, s. 34, if two conditions are met (s. 34(2) and (3)):

(a) the court must be satisfied on the balance of probabilities that the respondent has engaged in, or has encouraged or assisted, gang-related violence; and
(b) the court must think that it is necessary to grant the injunction for either or both of the following purposes:
  (i) to prevent the respondent from engaging in, or encouraging or assisting, gang-related violence;
  (ii) to protect the respondent from gang-related violence.

The prohibitions that can be included in the injunction (see s. 35(2)) may, in particular, have the effect of prohibiting the respondent from:

(a) being in a particular place (place includes an area: s. 35(7));
(b) being with particular persons in a particular place;
(c) being in charge of a particular species of animal in a particular place;
(d) wearing particular descriptions of articles of clothing in a particular place;
(e) using the internet to facilitate or encourage violence.

The requirements that can be included in the injunction (see s. 35(3)) may, in particular, have the effect of requiring the respondent to:

(a) notify the person who applied for the injunction of the respondent's address and of any change of that address;
(b) be at a particular place between particular times on particular days, although this cannot require the respondent to be at a particular place for more than eight hours in any day (s. 35(4));
(c) present himself or herself to a particular person at a place where he or she is required to be between particular times on particular days;
(d) participate in particular activities between particular times on particular days.

The prohibitions and requirements included in the injunction must, so far as is practicable, be such as to avoid any conflict with the respondent's religious beliefs, and any interference with the times at which the respondent works or attends any educational establishment (s. 35(5)).

The court cannot include a prohibition or requirement that has effect after the end of the period of two years beginning with the day the injunction is granted (s. 36(2)).

Power of arrest

88.47 When making an injunction under the Policing and Crime Act 2009, s. 34, the court can attach a power of arrest to any prohibition or requirement in the injunction, other than one which has the effect of requiring the respondent to participate in particular activities (s. 36(6)). If the court attaches a power of arrest, it may specify that the power is to have effect for a shorter period than the prohibition or requirement to which it relates (s. 36(7)). If an injunction contains one or more provisions to which a power of arrest is attached ('the relevant provisions'), each relevant provision must be set out in a separate paragraph of the injunction and the claimant must deliver a copy of the relevant provisions to any police station for the area where the conduct occurred (**CPR, r. 65.44(1)** and **(2)**). If the injunction has been granted without notice, the claimant must not deliver a copy of the relevant provisions to any police station before the defendant has been served with the injunction containing the relevant provisions (**r. 65.44(3)**).

If a power of arrest is attached to a provision of an injunction, a constable can arrest without warrant a person whom he has reasonable cause to suspect to be in breach of the injunction (s. 43(2)). If an arrest is made, the constable must inform the person who applied for the injunction (s. 43(3)).

The person who applied for an injunction can also apply to a relevant judge for a warrant for the arrest of the respondent if the respondent is in breach of the terms of the injunction (s. 44(2)). The relevant judge can issue a warrant on such an application only if there are reasonable grounds for believing that the respondent is in breach of any provision of the injunction (s. 44(3); **PD 65, para. 2.1(2)**). If a person is brought before the court under a warrant issued under s. 44(3), but the matter is not disposed of, the court may remand the person (s. 44(4)).

An application for a warrant of arrest must be made in accordance with **CPR, Part 23**, and may be made without notice. An application for a warrant of arrest must be supported by an affidavit (which must be filed with the application notice) setting out the grounds for the application or the applicant must give oral evidence of the grounds for the application at the hearing (**r. 65.46(2)**; **PD 65, para. 2.1**). If oral evidence is given at the hearing, the applicant must produce a written record of that evidence, which must be served on the person arrested at the time of the arrest (**CPR, r. 65.46(3)**).

A person arrested must be brought before a relevant judge within the period of 24 hours beginning with the time of the arrest (Policing and Crime Act 2009, s. 43(4)). In calculating the period of 24 hours, Christmas Day, Good Friday and any Sunday are to be disregarded (see s. 43(6)). Where the injunction was granted by the High Court, the relevant judge is a judge of that court, and where the injunction was granted by a county court, the relevant judge is a judge or district judge of that or any other county court (s. 43(7)).

If a person is arrested pursuant to a power of arrest attached to a provision of an injunction or a warrant of arrest, the judge before whom a person is brought following his arrest can either deal with the matter or adjourn the proceedings (**CPR, r. 65.47(1)** and **(2)**). If the matter is not disposed of when the person is brought before the court, the judge may remand the person (Policing and Crime Act 2009, s. 43(5)). If the proceedings are adjourned and the arrested person is released, the matter must be dealt with (whether by the same or another judge) within 28 days of the date on which the arrested person appears in court and the arrested person must be given not less than two days' notice of the hearing (**CPR, r. 65.47(3)**). An application notice seeking the committal for contempt of court of the arrested person may be issued even if the arrested person is not dealt with within the 28-day period (**r. 65.47(4)**). The person arrested can apply for bail either orally or by an application notice (**PD 65, para. 3.1**). An application notice seeking bail must comply with the requirements in **PD 65, para. 3.2**.

Remand

The provisions of the Policing and Crime Act 2009, sch. 5, apply to the remand of a person. **88.48**
Only a person aged 18 or over can be remanded in custody. If, in accordance with sch. 5, para. 2(2)(b), the court fixes the amount of any recognisance with a view to it being taken subsequently, the recognisance may be taken by any of the persons set out in **CPR, r. 65.48(1)**, with the same consequences as if it had been entered into before the court. The person having custody of an applicant for bail must release that person if satisfied that the required recognisances have been taken (**r. 65.48(2)**).

The court also has power to remand a person who has been brought before the court under the Policing and Crime Act 2009, s. 43 or s. 44, for the purposes of enabling a medical examination to take place and a report to be made (s. 45(2)). If a person is remanded in custody for that purpose, the adjournment may not be for more than three weeks at a time (s. 45(3)). If the person is remanded on bail for that purpose, the adjournment may not be for more than four weeks at a time (s. 45(4)).

Section 36(4A) provides that where the respondent is under the age of 18 on the injunction date, and any prohibition or requirement in the injunction is to have effect after the respondent reaches that age and for at least the period of four weeks beginning with the respondent's 18th birthday, the court must order the applicant and the respondent to attend a review hearing on a specified date within that period. This does not apply if a variation is made within or at any time after the period of four weeks ending with the respondent's 18th birthday (s. 42(4A)).

Breach of an order by a person under the age of 18

88.49 The Policing and Crime Act 2009, s. 46A and sch. 5A, contain detailed provisions about the power of the court in relation to breach of an injunction by a respondent under the age of 18. Schedule 5A provides that the court may make supervision (if necessary, with electronic monitoring requirements) or detention orders in such cases.

Review of the injunction order

88.50 A court which has made an injunction under the Policing and Crime Act 2009, s. 34, has power to order the applicant and the respondent to attend one or more review hearings on a specified date or dates to review whether the injunction should be varied or discharged (s. 36(3) and (5)).

If any prohibition or requirement in the injunction is to have effect after the end of the period of one year beginning with the injunction date, the court must order the applicant and the respondent to attend a review hearing on a specified date within the last four weeks of the one-year period (s. 36(4)).

Variation or discharge of the injunction order

88.51 The court can vary or discharge an injunction made under the Policing and Crime Act 2009, s. 34, if a review hearing is held, or an application to vary or discharge the injunction can be made by the applicant or the respondent (s. 42(1) and (2)). Before making such an application, the applicant or respondent must first consult with any local authority, chief police officer or any other body or individual that the applicant or respondent thinks it appropriate to consult (s. 42(5)).

An application to vary or discharge an injunction must be made in accordance with **CPR, Part 23** (**r. 65.45(1)**). The application should normally be made on notice, but if the application is made without giving notice, the application notice must state why notice has not been given (**r. 65.45(2)** and (3)).

The power to vary an injunction includes (Policing and Crime Act 2009, s. 42(3)) power to:

(a) include an additional prohibition or requirement in the injunction;
(b) extend the period for which a prohibition or requirement in the injunction has effect, provided this does not extend beyond the period of two days beginning with the day on which the injunction is granted;
(c) attach a power of arrest or extend the period for which a power of arrest attached to the injunction has effect.

If an application to vary or discharge an injunction is dismissed, no further application to vary or discharge it may be made by any person without the consent of the court (s. 42(6)).

If an order is made varying or discharging any provision which contains a power of arrest, the claimant must immediately inform the police station to which the relevant provision was delivered and deliver a copy of the order varying or discharging that provision to that police station (CPR, r. 65.44(4)).

Interim injunction orders

If an application for an injunction under the Policing and Crime Act 2009, s. 34, has been made on notice to the respondent and the court adjourns the hearing of the application, the court may grant an interim injunction if it considers that it is just and convenient to do so (s. 40(1) and (2)). If an interim injunction is granted, the court has power to attach any of the provisions to the injunction which it has power to include in an injunction granted under s. 34, including a power of arrest (s. 40(3)). **88.52**

However, if an application is made without notice and the proceedings are adjourned, the court can make an interim injunction only if it is necessary to do so (s. 41(2)). This is intended to be a more onerous test to satisfy in order to provide an additional safeguard for interim injunctions granted without notice. In such cases, the court can only grant an injunction if it is necessary rather than it being merely just and convenient to do so. The provisions that can be attached to an interim injunction granted without notice to the respondent are more limited than those that can be attached to an interim injunction which has been made after notice as an interim injunction granted without notice cannot require the respondent to participate in particular activities (s. 41(3)).

Chapter 89 Sale of Goods

INTRODUCTION

89.1 Most United Kingdom contracts for the sale of goods are governed by the **Sale of Goods Act 1979** (**SoGA 1979**). A sale of goods contract is one by which the seller transfers or agrees to transfer the property in goods to the buyer for a money consideration called the price (**SoGA 1979, s. 2(1)**). This covers the usual situation where goods are sold and where ownership of the goods is simultaneously transferred to the buyer. The related situation where the transfer of the property in the goods is to take place at a future date, or subject to some condition (such as payment of the price at some time in the future), is called an agreement to sell (**SoGA 1979, s. 2(4)**). Transactions which do not transfer property are not sales of goods.

If a contract is categorised as a sale of goods contract, it will be governed by the general law of contract as modified by the provisions of **SoGA 1979**. The modifications made by the Act are in fact wide ranging, covering most aspects of the transaction. The Act lays down general rules governing matters such as the obligations to deliver the goods and pay for them, when property and risk passes from the seller to the buyer, implied terms about quality and fitness for purpose, and remedies for breach. Many of the general rules set out in the Act are subject to the express or implied intention of the parties, although there are restrictions on contracting out of some provisions.

Major changes have taken place in relation to consumer sales. The **SoGA 1979** has been amended as from 31 March 2003 to give wide new rights to consumers. New provisions about consumer guarantees have been brought into force. Various provisions of the Enterprise Act 2002 came into force on 20 June 2003 giving wide powers to enforce consumer rights, particularly a new category of 'super-complaint' which permits designated bodies to give notice to the Office of Fair Trading (OFT) of an area of concern and allows the OFT only 90 days in which to publish a response on how the problem will be addressed. There have already been a number of super-complaints. The power under the Stop Now (EC Directive) Orders Regulations 2001 (SI 2001/1422) has been repealed and replaced by similar powers under the Enterprise Act 2002, part 8. The Law Commission and the Scottish Law Commission have proposed the replacement of the **Unfair Contract Terms Act 1977** and the Unfair Terms in Consumer Contracts Regulations 1999 (SI 1999/2083) with a single Act written in plain English (*Unfair Terms in Contracts* (Consultation Paper No. 166) (London: TSO, 2002)).

GENERAL RULES AND DEFINITIONS

Sale of goods or supply of services

In some cases it is difficult to decide whether what is being provided is goods or a service. The distinction is essentially that in a contract for the sale of goods the principal consideration provided by the seller is the transfer of ownership of the goods, whereas in a contract for the supply of services, which could include supplying goods, the principal consideration provided by the supplier is the work done in providing the service, rather than the value of any goods supplied in the course of providing the service. For example, in a building contract the main consideration provided by the builder is usually the value of the work done, rather than the value of the bricks, cement, plaster, wood, nails and other materials supplied. Such a contract is therefore one for the supply of services, but with the incidental supply of goods. It is not a contract for the sale of goods within the meaning of **SoGA 1979**. The supply of services aspect of the building contract would, however, be subject to the provisions of the Supply of Goods and Services Act 1982 (SoGSA 1982), part 2, and the materials supplied under the contract would be subject to the provisions of the SoGSA 1982, part 1. **89.2**

In deciding whether the contract is for the sale of goods or for services, the main tests to be applied can be summarised as follows:

(a) if there is a sale of goods which are later to be fixed to chattels or land as a subsidiary obligation, the contract will be for the sale of goods;
(b) if there is an agreement to fix goods to land or to another chattel to which the sale of the goods is a subsidiary obligation, the contract will be for supply of services;
(c) if the principal obligation is the supply of goods with any work to them being incidental, then the contract will be for sale of goods; and
(d) if the customer supplies materials which are to be worked on (with or without other materials) by the supplier, the contract will be for the supply of services.

The distinction is no longer as important as it once was, as the statutory implied terms about the quality of goods are very similar to those for the quality of services. There are some differences. For example, the property in goods sold under **SoGA 1979** generally passes, in the absence of a term dealing with the matter, in accordance with the rules in **SoGA 1979, s. 18** (see **89.13**). Property often passes in accordance with these rules when the contract for the sale of goods is made. Different considerations apply in contracts for the supply of goods and services, and property in goods supplied may not pass until they are fixed (such as to the land of the customer) or even until the completion of the work of installation (see *Seath v Moore* (1886) 1 App Cas 350 per Lord Watson at p. 381). Another example is the effect of the buyer defaulting at some time after having paid a sum on account. In a contract for the sale of goods, such a sum will usually be recoverable by the defaulting buyer, subject to a set-off by the seller for damages for the buyer's default. In a contract for the supply of goods and services, such an advance may not be recoverable at all by the defaulting buyer (see *Hyundai Heavy Industries Co. Ltd v Papadopolos* [1980] 1 WLR 1129).

Sales distinguished from other contracts

89.3 The concept of 'bailment' covers a number of situations. It includes situations where the owner of goods (the 'bailor') delivers them to another who looks after them for the bailor; where the bailor loans goods to the bailee, either gratuitously or for hire; where the bailor pledges goods by delivering them to another as security for money borrowed by the bailor; where the bailor delivers goods to a carrier for the purpose of having the goods transported somewhere; and where the bailor delivers goods to a tradesman for something to be done to the goods (often repairs or improvements). Bailments are obviously not sales of goods. Even bailments with an option to purchase (such as hire purchase agreements) are not sales of goods (*Helby v Matthews* [1895] AC 471). This is because the hirer under such an agreement has not 'bought or agreed to buy' the goods within the meaning of **SoGA 1979, s. 25(1)**.

If the contract is intended to operate by way of mortgage, charge, pledge or other security it is not a sale of goods (**SoGA 1979, s. 62(4)**). A pledge can exist at common law and under the Consumer Credit Act 1974, and is an actual or constructive delivery and bailment of the goods by the debtor to the creditor to be kept until the debt has been discharged. Property in the goods does not pass, but the pledgee has a right to sell the goods.

A common form of transaction is a 'sale and lease back' where the owner sells the goods to a finance company and then leases those same goods back. A genuine transaction will be upheld as a sale of the goods rather than a charge over them, the test being the true intention of the parties rather than the legal form (*North Central Wagon Finance Co. v Brailsford* [1962] 1 WLR 1288).

Definition of 'goods'

89.4 The definition of 'goods' appears in **SoGA 1979, s. 61(1)**, and includes all personal chattels other than things in action and money. Things in action are rights to procure the payment of money through court proceedings, such as rights on bills of exchange or on insurance policies. The main definition means that although computer disks, being physical objects, are 'goods', a software programme is not (*St Albans City and District Council v International Computers Ltd* [1996] 4 All ER 481). This was considered in *Southwark London Borough Council v IBM UK Ltd* [2011] EWHC 549 (TCC), 135 Con LR 136, where Akenhead J at [96], [97], said it depends on what is being sold. If it is software under licence, there are no goods. Conversely, if it is a compact disc on which software is impressed that is sold, the sale is of goods.

Goods may be classified as existing goods or future goods (**SoGA 1979, s. 5(1)**). 'Existing goods' are those already owned or possessed by the seller. 'Future goods' are goods to be manufactured or acquired by the seller after making the contract.

SoGA 1979 also divides goods into specific goods and unascertained goods. 'Specific goods' are defined as goods identified and agreed on at the time a contract of sale is made and includes an undivided share of goods identified and agreed on (**SoGA 1979, s. 61(1)**). Most everyday sale of goods contracts involve specific existing goods as the buyer selects the product on display which he or she wishes to buy. The definition of specific goods is wide enough to also include identified goods not owned by the seller at the time of the contract but which the seller intends to acquire in order to transfer them to the buyer, and even to a contract for the sale of potatoes to be grown in a particular field (see *Howell v Coupland* (1876) 1 QBD 258). The term 'unascertained goods' is not defined, but means all goods which are not specific goods.

Money consideration

There must be a money consideration for a contract for the sale of goods. A gift is not provided for money consideration. Promotional gifts are unlikely to give rise to a sale of goods as the consideration is usually the purchase of other goods and not money (*Esso Petroleum Co. Ltd v Customs and Excise Commissioners* [1976] 1 WLR 1). A simple exchange of goods or barter is not a sale of goods. A common difficulty exists when goods (usually motor vehicles) are part exchanged. The court has to decide whether there is an exchange of goods (with or without some balancing payment) or whether there are there two separate, back-to-back, sale of goods transactions with only any credit balance being paid in money. The test is: what is the contractual intention? Each case will turn on its own facts: compare *G. J. Dawson (Clapham) Ltd v H. and G. Dutfield* [1936] 2 All ER 232 and *Forthright Finance Ltd v Ingate* [1997] 4 All ER 99. **89.5**

Formation of the contract

There must be a binding consensual contract between the buyer and the seller. That is determined applying the usual rules of contract law. Since the abolition in 1954 of the requirement for writing in contracts for the sale of goods over £10, there have been no formalities for a sale of goods contract (see now **SoGA 1979, s. 4**). Capacity to enter into the contract is governed by the general law. A reasonable price must be paid for necessaries sold and delivered to children, or to persons who are incompetent by reason of mental incapacity or drunkenness (**SoGA 1979, s. 3(2)**). **89.6**

Between parties of full capacity, there will be no contract unless the essential terms are agreed (*May and Butcher v R* [1934] 2 KB 17n). This does not preclude there being a valid and binding contract for the sale of goods where no price is agreed for the goods. The price may be fixed in a manner agreed between the parties or may be determined by a course of dealing between the parties (**SoGA 1979, s. 8(1)**). Alternatively, the price may be left unstated and not capable of being determined in accordance with **s. 8(1)**, in which event a reasonable price is payable (**s. 8(2)**). Finally, **s. 9** provides for the unusual cases where the price for the goods is to be fixed by a third party identified in the contract. If the third party does not make the valuation, the contract is avoided, but if any of the goods have been delivered the buyer must pay a reasonable price for them.

MAIN OBLIGATIONS IN A CONTRACT FOR THE SALE OF GOODS

Under a contract for the sale of goods, the seller agrees to transfer ownership in goods to the buyer, and the buyer agrees to accept them and pay the agreed price. The buyer will want to be able to make use of the goods (either personally or by way of resale), and an important question is that of the contractual responsibility for delivering the goods. A related question is the determination of when risk passes to the buyer, which is important if the goods are lost in transit or otherwise before they are received by the buyer. These various matters are discussed at **89.8** to **89.16**. **89.7**

Delivery

The seller's primary obligation is to deliver the goods to the buyer in accordance with the terms of the contract (**SoGA 1979, s. 27(1)**). The contract should define (expressly or by implication) the place where the goods should be delivered. This may be the seller's place of business, or those of the buyer, or some other place (such as a construction site where the goods are to be used, or the place of business of a carrier or a ship to be used to transport the goods to the buyer). **SoGA 1979, s. 61(1)** defines 'delivery' as the voluntary transfer of possession from one person to another. Often this is done by the seller handing the goods to the **89.8** buyer, or the buyer selecting them from the stock of the seller, and paying for them. There are more difficult situations. 'Possession', which is a key concept in the definition of delivery, is not defined in **SoGA 1979**, and is notoriously difficult to define. A seller may transfer possession, for example, by giving the buyer the means of access to goods, such as by handing over the keys to the warehouse where they are stored (see *Hilton v Tucker* (1888) 39 ChD 669). There are four further common situations that should be noted:

(a) Where the goods are in the possession of a third person (such as a warehouseman), delivery takes place when that third person acknowledges to the buyer that the goods are held on behalf of the buyer (**SoGA 1979, s. 29(4)**). This is known as 'attorning'.

(b) A seller can deliver goods for the purposes of a contract for the sale of goods by delivering to the buyer a document of title to the goods. Delivery takes place on delivery of a document of title even if the goods are in the possession of a third person and even if the third person has not attorned to the buyer. This method of delivery is very common in international sales. Documents of title are defined in the Factors Act 1889, s. 1(4), as being any bill of lading, dock warrant, warehouse keeper's certificate, a warrant or order for the delivery of goods, and any other document used in the ordinary course of business as proof of possession or control of goods. Delivery orders, warehouse keepers' receipts and warrants for goods are not, or not always, regarded as documents of title.

(c) Delivery of goods to a carrier for transmission to the buyer is prima facie deemed to be delivery to the buyer (**SoGA 1979, s. 32(1)**).

(d) In a sale and lease-back transaction, the seller makes constructive delivery of the goods to the buyer, which then leases the goods back to the seller, even though the goods never leave the seller's possession (*Michael Gerson (Leasing) Ltd v Wilkinson* [2001] QB 514).

The definition of 'delivery' was extended as from 18 September 1995 by amendments made by the Sale of Goods (Amendment) Act 1995, s. 2, so that delivery, in relation to sales from a bulk under **SoGA 1979, ss. 20A and 20B**, includes such appropriation of goods to the contract as results in property in the goods being transferred to the buyer. **Sections 20A and 20B** are considered at **89.14**.

Delivery is to be distinguished from passing title in the goods, as title can pass before delivery, at the time of delivery or after delivery. The obligation to deliver the goods may be separate from the obligation to pay for them, but in the absence of agreement they are concurrent conditions (**SoGA 1979, s. 28**). **SoGA 1979, s. 29**, sets out the rules for delivery; **s. 30** deals with the quantity to be delivered; **s. 31** deals with instalments; and **s. 33** deals with deliveries to the buyer at a distant place.

What must be delivered

89.9 The delivery must be of the goods contracted for. This means:

(a) in the case of specific goods, delivery must be of the actual goods agreed upon;
(b) in the case of ascertained goods, delivery must be of the goods ascertained;
(c) in the case of unascertained goods, delivery must be of goods corresponding to the description, since the sale will be by description;
(d) in the case of a sale of goods by sample, delivery must be of goods which correspond to the sample; and
(e) in the case of goods where property passes before delivery, delivery must be of the goods the buyer then owns.

Acceptance

89.10 *The buyer's duty is to accept* the goods and pay for them in accordance with the terms of the contract (**SoGA 1979, s. 27**). Acceptance is deemed to have occurred when it is intimated by the buyer to the seller, or when the goods have been delivered and the buyer does any act in relation to them which is inconsistent with the seller's ownership (s. 35(1)). Once goods are delivered, if the buyer has not previously examined them, acceptance is not deemed to have occurred until the buyer has had a reasonable opportunity of examining them for the purpose of ascertaining whether they are in conformity with the contract (s. 35(2)(a)). Acceptance is also deemed to have occurred when after a lapse of a reasonable time the buyer retains the goods without intimating to the seller that they have been rejected (s. 35(4)). In determining whether the buyer has had the goods for a reasonable time, the court will take into account whether the buyer has had a reasonable opportunity of examining the goods for the purpose of ascertaining whether they conform with the contract (s. 35(5)).

By, s. 35(6), a buyer is not deemed to have accepted the goods merely because:

(a) the buyer asks for, or agrees to, their repair by or under an arrangement with the seller; or
(b) the goods are delivered to another under a sub-sale or other disposition.

A buyer does not have to act reasonably in deciding whether to reject goods which are in breach of the implied condition as to quality. The question is whether the buyer has lost the right to reject by acceptance. The notorious decision in *Bernstein v Pamson Motors (Golders Green) Ltd* [1987] 2 All ER 220 (right to reject new car lost after 140 miles' use, and less than four weeks' ownership) has now been expressly stated not to survive the 1995 amendments to **SoGA 1979** (*Clegg v Olle Andersson* [2003] EWCA Civ 320, [2003] 1 All ER (Comm) 721).

Payment

The obligation upon the buyer is to make payment in accordance with the terms of the contract between the parties (**SoGA 1979, s. 27**). The price will usually be fixed by the contract, but may be ascertained in a manner agreed by the contract or by a course of dealing between the parties (s. 8(1)). Otherwise the buyer must pay a reasonable price, which is a question of fact depending on all the circumstances of the particular case (s. 8(2) and (3)). **Section 28** of the **SoGA 1979** provides that unless otherwise agreed, delivery of the goods and payment of the price are concurrent conditions, and the seller must be ready and willing to give possession of the goods to the buyer in exchange for the price and the buyer must be ready and willing to pay the price in exchange for possession of the goods. **89.11**

Place and method of payment

The place of payment may be specified in the contract in which case the payment must be made at that place. Where there is no express provision in the terms of the contract, the intention of the parties may be determined from the surrounding circumstances, or from the method of payment provided for. If the intention of the parties cannot be ascertained then, by **SoGA 1979, ss. 28** and **29(2)**, the obligation seems to be to make payment at the seller's place of business or residence. **89.12**

In default of agreement between the parties, the manner of payment is cash. Payment by post will be at the seller's risk of loss or delay only if payment by that method is expressly or impliedly authorised by the contract. The defence of tender before claim, which is available to the buyer in an action by the seller for the price, depends upon tender having taken place in cash unless the contract otherwise provides or unless the seller has waived the right to demand cash payment. Tender before claim is a CPR glossary term, and now applies to claims for specified amounts and unspecified amounts. The defence of tender before claim must be included in the statement of case (usually the defence), and the defence is only available if the money is paid into court (**CPR, r. 37.3**).

Passing of property

When goods are sold, three things pass to the buyer: property, possession, and risk. Although they are connected, they are distinct concepts. 'Property' is used in the sense of title or **89.13** ownership, or a proprietary right in the goods. It may be transferred before delivery, at delivery or after delivery (e.g. on payment). If the contract is clear on this aspect, then property passes in accordance with the terms of the contract (**SoGA 1979, s. 17(2)**). If the intention of the parties is not clear then **s. 18** contains five rules to be applied to determine when property is to pass.

The five rules in **SoGA 1979, s. 18** are as follows (**r. 5** is subdivided into four sub-rules, set out at (e) to (h)):

(a) Where there is an unconditional contract for the sale of specific goods in a deliverable state, the property in the goods passes to the buyer when the contract is made, and it is immaterial whether the time of payment or the time of delivery or both be postponed (**SoGA 1979, s. 18, r. 1**). An 'unconditional' contract is not defined in **SoGA 1979**, but means that there are no later conditions which must be fulfilled (e.g. payment of the price) before property passes. Goods will be in a 'deliverable state' if they are in such a condition that the buyer would under the contract be bound to take delivery of them (**s. 61(5)**). Contracts falling within r. 1 are not common as the courts are very ready to infer that property only passes upon payment (*R. V. Ward Ltd v Bignall* [1967] 1 QB 534).

(b) Where there is a contract for the sale of specific goods and the seller is bound to do something to the goods for the purpose of putting them into a deliverable state, the property does not pass until the thing is done and the buyer has had notice that it has been done (**s. 18, r. 2**). The key event is that the seller has given notice that the goods are now in a deliverable state.

(c) Where there is a contract for the sale of specific goods in a deliverable state, but the seller is bound to weigh, measure, test, or do some other act or thing with reference to the goods for the purpose of ascertaining the price, the property does not pass until the act or thing is done and the buyer has had notice that it has been done (**s. 18, r. 3**). The obligation to weigh, measure, test or do some other act must be on the seller, and the act must be for the purpose of ascertaining the price of goods already in the deliverable state. As with **r. 2**, the key event is that notice must be given to the buyer that the step has been taken.

(d) When goods are delivered to the buyer on approval or on sale or return or other similar terms, the property in the goods passes to the buyer:
   (i) when the buyer signifies approval or acceptance to the seller or does any other act adopting the transaction;
   (ii) if the buyer does not signify approval or acceptance to the seller but retains the goods without giving notice of rejection, then, if a time has been fixed for the return of the goods, on the expiration of that time, and, if no time has been fixed, on the expiration of a reasonable time (**s. 18, r. 4**). Sales on approval and transactions involving sale or return are common, and this rule will govern the passing of title if the parties have not reached some other agreement.

(e) Where there is a contract for the sale of unascertained or future goods by description, and goods of that description and in a deliverable state are unconditionally appropriated to the contract, either by the seller with the assent of the buyer or by the buyer with the assent of the seller, the property in the goods passes to the buyer; and the assent may be express or implied, and may be given either before or after the appropriation is made (**s. 18, r. 5(1)**).

(f) Where, in pursuance of the contract, the seller delivers the goods to the buyer or to a carrier or other bailee or custodier (whether named by the buyer or not) for the purpose of transmission to the buyer, and does not reserve the right of disposal, the seller is to be taken to have unconditionally appropriated the goods to the contract for the purposes of **r. 5(1)** so that property passes at that time (**s. 18, r. 5(2)**).

(g) Where there is a contract for the sale of a specified quantity of unascertained goods in a deliverable state forming part of a bulk which is identified either in the contract or by subsequent agreement between the parties, and the bulk is reduced to (or to less than) that

quantity, then, if the buyer under that contract is the only buyer to whom the goods are then due out of the bulk:
(i) the remaining goods are to be taken as appropriated to that contract at the time when the bulk is so reduced; and
(ii) the property in those goods then passes to the buyer (**s. 18, r. 5(3)**).

(h) **Rule** 5(3) also applies where the bulk is reduced to (or to less than) the aggregate of the quantities due to a single buyer under separate contracts relating to that bulk and that buyer is the only buyer to whom goods are then due out of that bulk (**s. 18, r. 5(4)**).

Rules 5(1) to 5(4) deal with the unconditional appropriation of deliverable goods to the contract by express or implied agreement. 'Appropriation' is not defined in **SoGA** 1979, but means an intention to attach the contract irrevocably to those goods so that those goods and no others are the subject of the sale and become the property of the buyer. Sales of goods forming part of a bulk are now governed by **ss. 20A** and **20B** (**89.14**).

Commentary

Sales of goods held in bulk

A contract may provide for the sale of (say) 100 tonnes of wheat from a cargo of 2,000 tonnes presently on board a named ship. This would be a sale of a specified quantity of unascertained goods forming part of a bulk which is identified in the agreement between the parties. Once the buyer pays the price for some or all of the 100 tonnes subject to the contract, **SoGA** 1979, **s. 20A**, applies (see **s. 20A(1)**). If the section applies, by **s. 20A(2)**: **89.14**

(a) property in an undivided share in the bulk is transferred to the buyer; and
(b) the buyer becomes an owner in common of the bulk.

The rest of s. 20A deals with calculating the size of the undivided share of the buyer, particularly where the bulk is insufficient for all the purchasers, and with the situation where a buyer has paid only part of the price. When s. 20A applies, the buyer is deemed to consent to other purchasers taking delivery of their shares out of the bulk, and the section does not impose an obligation on a buyer from the bulk to compensate any other buyer for any shortfall in the goods delivered (**s. 20B**).

Passing of possession

The concept of possession, and some of the situations encountered in sale contracts, were considered at **89.8**. Normally, possession passes on physically handing over the goods to the buyer. **89.15**

Passing of risk

Risk is important in cases where goods are damaged or lost and in deciding who has an insurable interest in goods. Unless otherwise agreed, risk is presumed to pass with property (**SoGA** 1979, **s. 20(1)**). Risk may be transferred to the buyer before delivery if, for example, property passes before delivery. **89.16**

Risk in transit is primarily governed by the contract between the parties. In international sales this is usually provided for expressly, or by reference to well-known forms of international sale agreement — such as cif ('carriage, insurance, freight') and fob ('free on board'), etc. terms. Some aspects of risk in transit are dealt with by **ss. 32** and **33**. If the seller fails to make a reasonable contract with a carrier having regard to the nature of the goods and the other circumstances of the case, the buyer may decline to treat delivery to the carrier as a delivery to the buyer (**s. 32(2)**). The result would be that goods damaged in transit would be treated as not delivered to the buyer, so the seller would retain ownership of the goods (presumably lost or damaged), and would be liable to the buyer for non-delivery. Unless otherwise agreed, where goods are sent by the seller by sea transport in circumstances where it is usual to insure, the seller must give the buyer sufficient notice to enable the buyer to insure the goods during transit. If the seller fails to give such notice, the goods remain at the risk of the seller during the transit by sea (**s. 32(3)**).

In relation to consumer contracts important amendments have been made to **s. 20** from 31 March 2003. The goods now remain at the seller's risk until they are delivered (**s. 20(4)**). Where a carrier is used in a consumer contract, delivery to the carrier is not delivery to the consumer (**s. 32(4)**).

DETAILED CONTRACTUAL TERMS

89.17 As discussed at **89.6**, there are no legal formalities required for a contract for the sale of goods. A great many contracts for the sale of goods are simply entered into orally, or even without any words being exchanged, such as where uncommunicative customers present goods for payment at a cash till, and the sales assistant simply processes the transaction without saying anything. Usually such a contract will be evidenced by writing in the form of the sales receipt produced by the cash till and handed to the customer. In such contracts the main obligations will take place there and then, with the goods having been selected by the customer, and with delivery, acceptance and payment all taking place on the spot. Where the customer pays in cash, the transaction will be a simple sale of goods governed by **SoGA 1979**. Beyond the main obligations just mentioned, the Act will also imply such of the statutory terms discussed at **89.29** to **89.35** as are appropriate into the contract. If the transaction is paid for by credit card and the customer is an individual, the shop in fact looks to the credit card company for payment and the transaction has Consumer Credit Act 1974 ramifications. Where the customer pays by cheque, the contract will be a simple sale of goods, but with a secondary contract based on the cheque. If the cheque is dishonoured, the shop can take advantage of the simple method of obtaining summary judgment on the cheque discussed at **34.40**.

Although it is possible for detailed contractual terms to be agreed orally, it is far more common for people agreeing oral terms to restrict themselves to matters such as the description of the goods, price, and time and place for delivery. There are plenty of other issues that could be included as terms in a contract of sale. These include insurance of the goods until they are delivered; which party bears the loss if the goods are stolen, damaged or destroyed before delivery; the consequences of minor or major defects in the goods; the arrangements for effecting repairs to rectify defects present when the goods are delivered, including where the repairs should take place; liabilities to third parties arising out of the performance of the contract; limitations in the liability of the parties for consequential losses (particularly loss of profits) in the event of breach and other exclusions of liability; the effect of events outside the control of either party; and choice of law and jurisdiction in the event of litigation. These (and other detailed terms) can often be found in contractual documents. Occasionally, detailed terms will be negotiated between the parties, and reduced to writing in a contract specifically drawn up for the purpose. Far more commonly, detailed terms are found in the small print on the reverse of order forms, confirmation of order forms, invoices, delivery documents and other documents used by the parties. Sometimes such standard terms are simply referred to, such as the quotation form which says it is made on 'our standard terms of trading which are available on request'.

The law relating to the incorporation of express terms into contracts is discussed at **89.18** to **89.20**. The consequences of the classification of different types of terms are discussed at **89.21** *to* **89.28**. *The statutory implied* terms in sale of goods contracts are discussed at **89.29** to **89.35**. Breach of the main provisions in sale of goods contracts is discussed at **89.36** to **89.44**.

INCORPORATION OF EXPRESS TERMS INTO CONTRACTS

Signed contracts

If the contract is in writing and has been signed by a party, that party will be bound by those written terms even if he or she has not read them (*L'Estrange v F. Graucob Ltd* [1934] 2 KB 394), or was unable to understand them (*The Luna* [1920] P 22; *Barclays Bank plc v Schwertz* (1995) *The Times*, 3 August 1995). This clear rule is qualified by the following requirements and exceptions: 89.18

(a) The party signing must be aware that the document being signed contains or refers to some written terms.
(b) The terms referred to must actually be present or available so that, for example, where documents sent by facsimile refer to terms stated on the back which are not stated or otherwise communicated that gives rise to a cogent inference that the terms were not intended to apply (*Poseidon Freight Forwarding Co. Ltd v Davies Turner Southern Ltd* [1996] CLC 1264).
(c) The party signing must be given reasonably sufficient notice of the exact terms relied upon by the other side — a concept which the courts apply particularly to unusual or onerous terms (see **89.20**).
(d) Where a complete contract already existed rather than mere negotiations between the parties, subsequent signing of a document including new terms will not bind either party unless there is a variation (for which consideration will be required) or a novation.
(e) Terms cannot be relied upon where the contract is void or unenforceable as a result of a mistake.
(f) An exception exists under the doctrine of *non est factum*, which is a rare and special category of mistake which applies only where a party to the contract has been misled into signing a contract without being negligent (*Saunders v Anglia Building Society* [1971] AC 1004).
(g) Terms cannot be relied on where there has been a misrepresentation of the terms or effect of a clause (*Curtis v Chemical Cleaning and Dyeing Co. Ltd* [1951] 1 KB 805).
(h) Terms cannot be relied on where the contract is voidable as a result of duress (*Atlas Express Ltd v Kafco (Importers and Distributors) Ltd* [1989] QB 833). However, not every form of pressure will amount to duress (*CTN Cash and Carry Ltd v Gallagher Ltd* [1994] 4 All ER 714 and *Alf Vaughan and Co. Ltd v Royscot Trust plc* [1999] 1 All ER (Comm) 856).

The fact that a signed written contract exists will not normally prevent there being other express terms of that contract which have not been put into the signed document, provided they are not inconsistent with the written terms. However, many written contracts contain an 'entire agreement' clause which seeks to exclude the existence of other terms. Such clauses are not always wholly effective, see, for example, *Thomas Witter Ltd v TBP Industries Ltd* [1996] 2 All ER 573, where the claimant was allowed to recover damages for misrepresentation in relation to pre-contract negotiations despite an 'entire agreement' clause partly because a term purporting to confine the parties to the written terms of the contract was insufficiently clear to achieve this end, and partly because the clause was ineffective under the **Misrepresentation Act 1967, s. 1**, if the representation had become a warranty of the contract. See also *Deepak Fertilisers and Petrochemicals Ltd v Davy McKee (London) Ltd* [1999] 1 All ER (Comm) 69. There could be a collateral contract between the same parties. If the 'entire agreement' clause excludes misrepresentations or implied terms then it will be subject to the statutory rules limiting the effectiveness of such clauses.

Standard terms of trading

In commercial transactions there is often a dispute as to which set of standard terms applies to the contract. This is usually resolved by examining the events chronologically looking for 89.19

the offer or counter-offer which has actually been accepted (often by performing the contract) which means that the party firing the last shot in the negotiations will usually succeed in showing that the last terms are the basis for the contract (*British Road Services Ltd v Arthur V. Crutchley and Co. Ltd* [1968] 1 WLR 811). However, sometimes the last shot is construed as an acceptance of the previous terms sent by the other side, with the effect that the other side's standard terms apply to the contract (see *Butler Machine Tool Co. Ltd v Ex-Cell-O Corporation (England) Ltd* [1979] 1 WLR 401). It is also noteworthy that a clause purporting to provide that those standard terms shall prevail over the terms of the other party, is ineffective if the other side then respond by sending their standard terms in the usual situation where this is regarded as the making of a counter-offer (see *Butler Machine Tool Co. Ltd v Ex-Cell-O Corporation (England) Ltd*).

Onerous or unusual terms

89.20 If a contract contains some particularly onerous or unusual terms the court will look with great care to see whether the onerous term has been incorporated into the contract at all. This approach is at variance with the general approach that a party is bound by the terms which that party is aware are in a written agreement, despite not reading them (see **89.18**). This exception is limited to unusual or onerous terms. The most striking description of this rule is to be found in the judgment of Denning LJ in *J. Spurling Ltd v Bradshaw* [1956] 1 WLR 461 at p. 466, where he said, 'Some clauses I have seen would need to be printed in red ink on the face of the document with a red hand pointing to it before the notice could be held to be sufficient'. The importance of this rule has been slightly reduced by the statutory control of exemption clauses. Nevertheless it remains an important way of challenging onerous or unusual express terms of a written contract. It is still being applied today with important consequences for the parties: see, for example, the decisions of the Court of Appeal in *Interfoto Picture Library Ltd v Stiletto Visual Programmes Ltd* [1989] QB 433 and *AEG (UK) Ltd v Logic Resource Ltd* [1996] CLC 265.

CONSEQUENCES OF CLASSIFICATION OF TERMS

Classification of terms

89.21 Contract terms are usually divided into conditions or warranties. Breach of a condition discharges the innocent party from further performance of the contract and damages may be claimed for loss caused by the breach. Breach of a warranty gives the innocent party only a right to claim damages, the measure of damages being defined in the **SoGA 1979, s. 53**.

A term is a condition if it is expressly made such by statute. What is less clear is the effect of a label given to the obligation in the contract itself. It seems that a term need not be a condition merely because it is so described in the contract (*Wickman Machine Tool Sales Ltd v L. Schuler AG* [1974] AC 235, although contrast *Lombard North Central plc v Butterworth* [1987] QB 527, where the clause provided that terms in the contract had 'the property that any breach of them is treated as going to the root of the contract'). Whether a term is a condition (breach of which may give rise to a right to treat the contract as repudiated), or a warranty (breach of which may give rise to a claim for damages but not to a right to reject the goods and treat the contract as repudiated) depends in each case on the construction of the contract and a clause may be a condition, even though called a warranty in the contract (**SoGA 1979, s. 11(3)**).

There is also a further category of terms known as intermediate terms, where the nature and seriousness of the breach will determine whether the innocent party is discharged from further performance or merely entitled to damages.

Construing written contracts

The object of the rules of construction of written terms is always to discover the intention of the parties from the words used in the contract. There are no special rules for construction of mercantile contracts or business documents. The main rules of construction are: **89.22**

(a) the ordinary meaning should be given to the words used unless:
   (i) there is some well-known trade custom or trade practice which means that a special meaning is to be given to words (probably the best known example being a 'baker's dozen' meaning 13), or
   (ii) there is some local custom which means words have a particular meaning in that locality, or
   (iii) the words are technical words, in which case the normal accepted technical meaning should be applied;
(b) words should be construed so as to avoid absurd or inconsistent provisions as the parties cannot have intended that the contract should be absurd or inconsistent;
(c) the whole contract will be considered so that individual words or phrases are considered in their context, and any recitals may be used as a guide to the interpretation of the operative parts of a contract;
(d) in written contracts, as in statutes, general words which follow several specific words are to be construed in a similar manner — the *eiusdem generis* rule; and
(e) a written contract is construed more strongly against its grantor or maker — the *contra proferentem* rule. This only arises where there remains an ambiguity which has not been resolved by the application of the earlier rules.

The function of the court is to decide the objective intention of the parties. The question is not what the parties understood the words or document to mean but the meaning which the document would convey to a reasonable person having all the background knowledge which would reasonably have been available to the parties in the situation in which they were at the time of the contract (*Investors Compensation Scheme Ltd v West Bromwich Building Society* [1998] 1 WLR 896).

A common problem is the poorly drafted written contract. There are no special rules of construction, but in applying the rules set out above, in *Antaios Compania Naviera SA v Salen Rederierna AB* [1984] AC 676, Lord Diplock said: 'if a detailed semantic syntactical analysis of words in a commercial contract is going to lead to a conclusion that flouts business common sense, it must yield to business common sense'. This is an important reflection of the purpose of all rules of construction, namely to ascertain the intention of the parties.

When construing a written contract it is important to remember the effect of the parol evidence rule under which oral evidence cannot be admitted to contradict, vary, add to or subtract from the terms of a written contract. Parol evidence will not even be admitted to establish a mutual but unexpressed intention of both parties to the contract (*New Hampshire Insurance Co. v MGN Ltd* (1995) *The Times*, 25 July 1995). The parol evidence rule applies in most situations, but will not apply if the contract is partly oral and partly in writing, or only evidenced in writing. Evidence of earlier drafts of the contract or negotiations cannot be admitted (save where the court is being asked to rectify the text of the agreement). However, this will not prevent evidence being admitted of the customary meaning of words in a particular trade or of a special technical meaning of words (see **49.30**).

The limits of the role of the court in trying to apply business common sense to a poorly drafted written clause are demonstrated by *Royal and Sun Alliance Insurance plc v Dornoch Ltd* [2005] EWCA Civ 238, [2005] 1 All ER (Comm) 590. The Court of Appeal highlighted the problem

Commentary

for the court where the parties had used a standard term which turned out to be unsuitable and, at [18], held (in construing an exemptions clause) that it is:

> not . . . any part of the court's function to go out of its way to give a purposive or business commonsense construction to one part of a clause in favour of one party and thus enable that party to seek to take advantage of another part of the clause which has draconian consequences for the other party.

Exemption and indemnity clauses

89.23 The ordinary rules of construction apply to exemption clauses which exempt one party from the consequences of some breach of contract and to indemnity clauses which require the innocent party to indemnify the party in breach against claims from third parties. The burden of proof is upon the party claiming that some liability is excluded to show that the particular liability falls within the ambit of the particular clause. The party making this claim should therefore set it out in the statement of case (**CPR, r. 16.5(2)(b)**). When ascertaining the intention of the parties:

(a) an exemption clause must be clear so that a clause which effectively absolves one party from any performance at all may be held to be meaningless as it could not have been the intention of the parties that there were no mutual obligations (*Tor Line AB v Alltrans Group of Canada Ltd* [1984] 1 WLR 48); and

(b) when considering exemption clauses excluding liability for negligence the three tests in *Canada Steamship Lines Ltd v The King* [1952] AC 192 are applied, namely:
   (i) if the clause plainly excludes such liability then (subject to statutory control) effect will be given to it;
   (ii) if the clause is unclear it will be construed *contra proferentem*; and
   (iii) if the clause covers liabilities other than negligence (e.g. damage by lightning) then it will be held not to cover negligence.

Force majeure clauses

89.24 *Force majeure* clauses are intended to deal with the consequences of one or other of the parties being unable to perform the contract through the intervention of government action or other circumstances outside the party's control. There is no general concept of *force majeure* in English law, and the courts have often seemed reluctant to accept the concept at all. Sale of goods contracts often contain express *force majeure* clauses which limit the seller's liability in circumstances anticipated by the clause with or without provision for notice to be given to the buyer. The true effect of a *force majeure* clause is to limit the seller's obligation to perform and it is not therefore an exemption clause which excludes liability for breach of contract as no breach will have occurred. An important consequence is that such terms may not be required to satisfy the test of reasonableness under the **Unfair Contract Terms Act 1977**. The burden of proving that the clause applies is upon the party seeking to rely upon it, usually the seller. A party making this claim should therefore set it out in its statement of case (**CPR, rr. 16.4 and 16.5**).

Liquidated damages and penalty clauses

89.25 A sum of money which is payable, under a provision of a contract by a party who is in default of contractual obligations in some stated way or ways, may be either liquidated damages or a penalty. Incentives for early performance or payment will not be classified as a penalty. Thus a clause, properly incorporated into the contract, which provides for a 10 per cent discount on the agreed price if it is paid within 28 days will be upheld. Even an acceleration clause, saying that the whole of a sum outstanding shall become due and payable forthwith on default of any payment, is not a penalty (*Wallingford v Mutual Society* (1880) 5 App Cas 685). On the other hand, a clause which provides for a 10 per cent increase in the contract price if the payment is received after 28 days, will be unenforceable as a penalty as it is not (or at least is highly unlikely to be) a genuine pre-estimate of the loss suffered by payment being late. A clause providing for acceleration of payment combined with payment of interest was regarded as a penalty in *The Angelic Star* [1988] 1 Lloyd's Rep 122.

A common problem is 'default interest' payable under a contract. Default interest in regulated agreements is controlled by CCA 1974, s. 93. Default interest is also controlled at common law as a possible penalty. In *Patel v Zubowski* [1996] GCCR 2173 interest of 80 per cent which was payable if money owed to a solicitors' firm was not paid on the due date was held to be a penalty and wholly irrecoverable. A provision for 'default interest' in a consumer contract will not necessarily be an unfair contract term, particularly if it is expressed fully, clearly and legibly, and contains no concealed pitfalls or traps (*Director General of Fair Trading v First National Bank plc* [2001] UKHL 52, [2002] 1 AC 481).

A clause which provides for the payment of a sum of money on the happening of a certain event which is not itself a breach of contract by either party will not be a liquidated damages or penalty clause (*Export Credits Guarantee Department v Universal Oil Products Co.* [1983] 1 WLR 399).

There are no special rules of construction for liquidated damages or penalty clauses in contracts, and thus the onerous clauses rule and the *contra proferentem* rule are often of practical importance. If the sum stipulated in the contract is a penalty, the clause will not be enforced. If the sum is a genuine pre-estimate of damage, looked at when the contract was made, it will be a liquidated damages clause and enforceable. The label given by the parties to the clause is a guide, but is not determinative, of whether it is a penalty or a liquidated damages clause (*Dunlop Pneumatic Tyre Co. Ltd v New Garage and Motor Co. Ltd* [1915] AC 79).

Commentary

Forfeiture clauses

Confusion exists over the effect of forfeiture clauses where a sum, usually the deposit, is forfeited on breach of contract by the buyer. *Workers Trust and Merchant Bank Ltd v Dojap Investments Ltd* [1993] AC 573 suggested that the court can consider the reasonableness of such clauses: contrast *BICC plc v Burndy Corporation* [1985] Ch 232 and *Sport International Bussum BV v InterFootwear Ltd* [1984] 1 WLR 776. **89.26**

Timing of delivery

A common issue is whether the stipulation as to time for delivery is a condition or warranty or intermediate term (see **89.21**). The **SoGA 1979, s. 10(2)**, provides that whether time is of the essence (i.e. is a condition) depends upon the terms of the contract. It is open to the parties to make time of the essence. **89.27**

Time of payment

A further common problem relates to the classification of terms about the payment of the price. **SoGA 1979, s. 10(1)**, provides that unless a different intention appears from the terms of the contract, stipulations as to time of payment are not of the essence of the contract (i.e. are not conditions). In effect this creates a statutory presumption for the timing of payment. **Section 10(2)**, mentioned at **89.27**, provides that whether any other stipulation as to time is or is not of the essence of the contract depends on the terms of the contract, the different wording making it plain that the statute is not creating a presumption either way. **89.28**

Where goods are perishable or notice is given of an intention to resell, **SoGA 1979, s. 48(3)**, provides that if the buyer does not pay or tender the price within a reasonable time, the unpaid seller may resell the goods and recover from the original buyer damages representing any loss occasioned by the buyer's breach.

If the contract does not otherwise provide, the result of these provisions is as follows:
(a) if time for delivery is of the essence then so is the time for payment as they are concurrent obligations;
(b) conversely, if time for delivery is not of the essence then neither is the time of payment; and
(c) if the goods are perishable or if notice of intention to resell has been given by the seller, then payment must be made within a reasonable time and is of the essence.

If the seller has waived or is estopped from relying upon the original date of payment, the buyer may argue that no new date for payment has been agreed and that no reasonable notice has been given (*Charles Rickards Ltd v Oppenheim* [1950] 1 KB 616 and *State Trading Corporation of India Ltd v Compagnie Française d'Importation et de Distribution* [1983] 2 Lloyd's Rep 679).

IMPLIED TERMS

The implied terms of the contract

89.29 Terms may be implied into a contract in three main ways:
(a) to reflect the actual intention of the parties — the unexpressed terms (*Shirlaw v Southern Foundries (1926) Ltd* [1939] 2 KB 206, affirmed [1940] AC 701);
(b) to give business efficacy to the agreement — the terms which the court presumes the parties would have expressed if they had considered the position (*Luxor (Eastbourne) Ltd v Cooper* [1941] AC 108); and
(c) by law — not as a result of the actual or presumed intention of the parties, but as a result of general considerations of policy (in this context, the statutory implied terms in **SoGA 1979, ss. 12 to 15**, see **89.30** to **89.35**).

The implication of a term as being the actual intention of the parties can be based on:
(a) custom within the trade or locality, but only if the custom is notorious, certain, legal and reasonable (e.g. *British Crane Hire Corporation Ltd v Ipswich Plant Hire Ltd* [1975] QB 303); or
(b) a previous course of dealing between the parties; or
(c) the circumstances and express obligations of the contract.

There is often an overlap between terms implied because they reflect the intentions of the parties and those which are necessary to give business efficacy to the contract. Terms are implied to give business efficacy when they are required in order to enable the contract to work satisfactorily on the assumption that the parties would have agreed such terms if they had thought about the position. No term will be implied under the first two tests if the suggested term is unreasonable, but the mere fact that the term is reasonable will not mean that it is to be implied into the contract.

The main implied terms imposed by **SoGA 1979** are:
(a) implied terms about title (**s. 12**);
(b) implied terms where there has been a sale by description (**s. 13**);
(c) implied terms about quality or fitness (**s. 14**); and,
(d) implied terms where there is a sale by sample (**s. 15**).

Those implied terms can be varied or excluded by express agreement between the parties, by course of dealings between the parties or by such usage as binds both parties to the contract (**SoGA 1979, s. 55(1)**). These statutory implied terms are considered further at **89.30** to **89.35**.

Liability for breach of the implied terms is strict (*Slater v Finning Ltd* [1997] AC 473 per Lord Steyn), so there is no scope for any finding of contributory negligence (*Hi-Lite Electrical Ltd v Wolseley UK Ltd* [2011] EWHC 2153 (TCC), [2011] BLR 629).

Implied terms about title

Section 12(1) of **SoGA 1979** creates an implied condition on the part of the seller that in the case of a sale the seller has the right to sell the goods, and in the case of an agreement to sell the seller will have that right at the time when the property is to pass. By the **Unfair Contract Terms Act 1977, s. 6(1)(a)**, this condition cannot be excluded or restricted by reference to any contract term in either consumer or non-consumer sales. The right to sell involves two concepts. First, the buyer must be able to pass good title. Secondly, the sale must not be unlawful (e.g. an infringement of a trade mark). **SoGA 1979, s. 12(2)**, creates an implied warranty on the part of the seller that: **89.30**

(a) the goods are free, and will remain free until the time when property is to pass, from any charge or encumbrance not disclosed or known to the buyer before the contract is made; and
(b) the buyer will enjoy quiet possession of the goods except in so far as it may be disturbed by the owner or other person entitled to the benefit of any charge or encumbrance so disclosed or known.

Implied terms in sales by description

Where there is a contract for sale by description there is an implied term, which is a condition, that the goods will correspond to the description (**SoGA 1979, s. 13(1)**). If the sale is by sample and description, the goods must correspond to the description as well as to the sample (**s. 13(2)**). A sale is not prevented from being by description merely because being exposed for sale or hire the goods are selected by the buyer (**s. 13(3)**). In consumer sales the obligations imposed by **s. 13** cannot be excluded or restricted by reference to any contract term (**Unfair Contract Terms Act 1977, s. 6(2)(a)**). In non-consumer sales liability can be restricted or excluded only in so far as the term satisfies the test of reasonableness (**Unfair Contract Terms Act 1977, s. 6(3)**). **89.31**

Sales by description are a common type of contract for the sale of goods. All sales of unascertained goods will be by description, as will all sales of goods which the buyer has not seen at all, and many sales by sample. This implied condition can be extremely important in practice. If the seller is not acting in the course of a business, such as in private sales of second-hand cars, the statutory terms about quality and fitness will not be implied. The only remedy for the buyer may be to rely upon a breach of this condition.

Implied terms about quality and fitness

SoGA 1979, s. 14, implies terms that goods sold should be of satisfactory quality and reasonably fit for their purpose. These are the implied terms which arise in most sale of goods litigation. These implied terms are conditions (**s. 14(6)**). The old standard of merchantable quality has been replaced (with effect from 3 January 1995) by the concept of satisfactory quality (see **89.33**). The implied terms apply where the seller sells the goods in the course of a business (**s. 14(2)**). In consumer sales the obligations imposed by **s. 14** cannot be excluded or restricted by reference to any contract term (**Unfair Contract Terms Act 1977, s. 6(2)(a)**). In non-consumer sales liability can be restricted or excluded only in so far as the term satisfies the test of reasonableness (**Unfair Contract Terms Act 1977, s. 6(3)**). **89.32**

Satisfactory quality

'Satisfactory quality' means the standard that a reasonable person would regard as satisfactory, taking account of any description of the goods, the price (if relevant) and all other relevant **89.33** circumstances (**SoGA 1979, s. 14(2A)**). Quality of goods includes their state and condition and the following (among others) are in appropriate cases aspects of the quality of goods:

(a) fitness for the purpose for which goods of the kind in question are commonly supplied;
(b) appearance and finish;
(c) freedom from minor defects;
(d) safety; and
(e) durability (**s. 14(2B)**).

In consumer contracts made after 31 March 2003, the relevant circumstances also specifically include any public statements on the specific characteristics of the goods made by the seller, the producer or his representative, particularly in advertising or labelling (**s. 14(2D)**) unless one of the limited exceptions applies (**s. 14(2E)**).

The implied term of satisfactory quality does not, by **s. 14(2C)**, extend to any matter making the goods unsatisfactory:

(a) which is specifically drawn to the buyer's attention before the contract is made;
(b) where the buyer examines the goods before the contract is made, which that examination ought to reveal; or
(c) in the case of a contract for sale by sample, which would have been apparent on a reasonable examination of the sample.

Pre-1995 cases need to be read with the slight change in the test from 'merchantable quality' to 'satisfactory quality' in mind. Nevertheless, it has been held that Coalite delivered with an explosive substance accidentally included in the delivery (and which blew up in the claimant's fireplace) was not of merchantable quality (*Wilson v Rickett Cockrell and Co. Ltd* [1954] 1 QB 598). Nor was a bun which contained a stone (*Chaproniere v Mason* (1905) 21 TLR 633). In *Mash and Murrell Ltd v Joseph I. Emmanuel Ltd* [1961] 1 WLR 862 (at first instance, reversed on other grounds) Diplock J held that potatoes were not of merchantable quality as they were not loaded on board a ship for transportation to the buyer in a state that they would endure the normal sea voyage and arrive in a merchantable condition. All of these decisions would be decided the same way under the new test.

There will be a breach of the condition of satisfactory quality when a new car is sold with a number of minor defects (as in a case under the merchantable test, *Rogers v Parish (Scarborough) Ltd* [1987] QB 933, where the car had minor bodywork defects and also minor mechanical problems that resulted in it misfiring and being excessively noisy). More tolerance is given to sellers of second-hand cars, having regard to the fact they are described as second-hand, and also the fact that prices will be considerably lower than for new vehicles of the same kind. In *Business Appliances Specialists Ltd v Nationwide Credit Corporation Ltd* [1988] RTR 332 it was stressed that merchantability in relation to second-hand goods is not restricted to safety (or in the case of cars, roadworthiness). A second-hand car may of course be sold for ordinary motoring purposes, or for scrap, or as a source for spare parts. More will be expected if the car is bought and sold with the intention that it is still roadworthy. Further, more will be expected of a car that is not very old and with a relatively low mileage, than from a car sold at a lower price near the end of its useful life. The fact that a vehicle breaks down soon after being sold may be evidence that it was defective at the time of purchase (*Crowther v Shannon Motor Co.* [1975] 1 WLR 30).

In *Business Appliances Specialists Ltd v Nationwide Credit Corporation Ltd* the buyer purchased a second-hand Mercedes for £14,850 with 37,000 miles recorded on the clock. After a further 800 miles it broke down with excessive wear evident in its valves (well beyond that expected in a car of that age). It was held there was no breach of the merchantability test, second-hand cars being expected to have ordinary wear and tear. If the valve defect really was ordinary wear and tear, no doubt this decision would be the same today, but the expert evidence in the case indicated it was worse than that, and it is submitted that the case would be decided differently under the present satisfactory quality test. A second-hand vehicle that was in fact a rebuilt insurance write-off would be sold in breach of the merchantability test, even in the absence of any specific defects, if the fact it had been rebuilt was not disclosed (see *Shine v General Guarantee Corporation Ltd* [1988] 1 All ER 911). The description used when the item is sold is of considerable importance. In *Bartlett v Sydney Marcus Ltd* [1965] 1 WLR 1013, a second-hand car was sold with a defective clutch. Before the sale there was a discussion between the buyer and seller, and the seller indicated that if the buyer wanted the seller to repair the clutch the price would be £25 more. The buyer decided to have it repaired elsewhere, and it cost £84. It was held there was no breach of the merchantability test, the case really being one where the repairs turned out to be more expensive than anticipated.

The current statutory test of satisfactory quality was considered by the Court of Appeal in *Clegg v Olle Andersson* [2003] EWCA Civ 320, [2003] 1 All ER (Comm) 721. The test is not whether a reasonable person would find the goods acceptable but is an objective comparison of the state of the goods with the standard which a reasonable person would find acceptable. Thus, for a high-priced quality product, the customer may be entitled to expect that it is free from even minor defects, in other words perfect or very nearly so. In consumer contracts made after 31 March 2003, public statements such as advertising can be taken into account in applying this test. In *Egan v Motor Services (Bath) Ltd* [2007] EWCA Civ 1002, [2008] 1 WLR 1589, the Court of Appeal put the test for satisfactory quality slightly differently. The case involved what Ward LJ labelled as 'a very expensive motor car'. The statutory test is an objective test and is a matter of judgment for the judge on the individual facts of each case. However, it seemed to the court unlikely that a buyer would be entitled to reject goods simply because he can point to a minor defect. The claimant must also persuade the judge that a reasonable person would think that the minor defect is of sufficient consequence to make the goods unsatisfactory.

Commentary

Fitness for purpose

A term of fitness for a particular purpose is implied where the seller sells in the course of a business and the buyer makes known any particular purpose for which the goods are being bought, except where the circumstances show that the buyer does not rely or that it is unreasonable for the buyer to rely on the skill or judgment of the seller (**SoGA 1979, s. 14(3)**). The particular purpose for which the goods are bought may be made known to the seller either expressly or by implication (*Jewson Ltd v Boyhan* [2003] EWCA Civ 1030, [2004] 1 Lloyd's Rep 505). Where a seller knew the buyer had already bought plumbing components of a particular type for a building project, it was held in *BSS Group plc v Makers (UK) Ltd* [2011] EWCA Civ 809, [2011] TCLR 7, to be an inescapable inference that the seller knew that valves it later sold to the buyer had to be compatible with the previously purchased components. A seller's only obligation under **s. 14(3)** is to ensure the goods are fit for the purpose they will ordinarily be used for, unless the buyer makes known to the seller any abnormal feature or idiosyncrasy which will put additional demands on the goods (*Slater v Finning Ltd* [1997] AC 473). The particular purpose for which goods may have been bought may in fact be the only usual purpose for those goods (see *Priest v Last* [1903] 2 KB 148, where the goods were a hot-water bottle). If a buyer of goods for installation in a house relies on the seller's skill and judgment, the goods will be in breach of **s. 14(3)** if they breach building or other regulations, even if they are supplied in strict conformity to the contract (*Lowe v W. Machell Joinery Ltd* [2011] EWCA Civ 794, [2012] 1 All ER (Comm) 153). **89.34**

The wording of **s. 14(3)** shows that the burden of proving that the section does not apply on the ground that the buyer has not, or that it was unreasonable for him to rely, on the seller's skill or judgment rests on the seller (*Slater v Finning Ltd* per Lord Steyn). Normally, it will be taken to be the case that a buyer, simply by going to a retailer to buy something, relies on that retailer to exercise skill and judgment in selecting suitable stock (see *Grant v Australian Knitting Mills Ltd* [1936] AC 85). Where the seller is also the manufacturer, it is nigh on impossible to rebut the presumption of reliance (*Kendall v Lillico* [1969] AC 31). The presumption also applies where both parties are traders, but of course it is easier to rebut it. In cases where a buyer intends to use the goods in another country, it will usually be the case that the presumption will be rebutted in so far as the issue may be whether the goods are reasonably fit for use in that other country, because usually it will be the buyer who will be best placed to know this (see *Teheran-Europe Co. Ltd v S. T. Belton Ltd* [1968] 2 QB 545).

If the buyer has some unusual susceptibility to contaminants found in the goods sold, it is a question of fact and degree whether the goods breach the condition. *Griffiths v Peter Conway Ltd* [1939] 1 All ER 685 has been described as a highly special case (in *Ashington Piggeries Ltd v Christopher Hill Ltd* [1972] AC 441), but in this case it was held that there was no breach of the condition where a buyer contracted dermatitis from a coat sold by the seller, the buyer having an unusually sensitive skin, and the coat not being such as to harm any normal purchaser. On the other hand, in *Ashington Piggeries Ltd v Christopher Hill Ltd* animal meal was contaminated with a trace of a toxic substance that was harmful to many animals, but which was peculiarly harmful to the buyer's mink. It was held there was a breach of the condition.

Sale by sample

89.35 The implied conditions in a contract of sale by sample are:

(a) that the bulk will correspond to the sample in quality (**SoGA 1979, s. 15(2)(a)**); and
(b) that the goods will be free from any defect making their quality unsatisfactory which would not be apparent on reasonable examination of the sample (**s. 15(2)(c)**).

In consumer sales the obligations imposed by **SoGA 1979, s. 15**, cannot be excluded or restricted by reference to any contract term (**Unfair Contract Terms Act 1977, s. 6(2)(a)**). In non-consumer sales liability can be restricted or excluded only in so far as the term satisfies the test of reasonableness (**Unfair Contract Terms Act 1977, s. 6(3)**).

BREACH OF THE MAIN PROVISIONS

Breach by the seller

89.36 **Consumer contracts** In consumer contracts made after 31 March 2003, wide additional remedies for the buyer are contained in **SOGA 1979, ss. 48A to 48F**. If the goods do not conform to the contract at any time within six months after delivery, they must be taken not to have conformed at the date of delivery (**s. 48A(3)**) unless:

(a) it is established that they did so conform and the burden of proof must be on the seller, although that is not specified (**s. 48A(4)(a)**) or;
(b) the rule is incompatible with the nature of the goods or the nature of the lack of conformity, which will cover goods such as perishables (**s. 48A(4)(b)**).

Goods do not confirm if there is a breach of an express term of the contract or of s. 13, 14 or 15. There is a right to require the seller to repair or replace the goods (**s. 48B**) save where that would be impossible, disproportionate to other remedies or disproportionate in comparison to a reduction in purchase price or rescission. The remedy of repair may be important where, for example, the product cannot be repaired by others, because that would breach a warranty, or essential equipment or access codes are required for the repair. The repair or replacement must be within a reasonable time and without significant inconvenience to the buyer and at the cost of the seller.

There is a separate right to a reduction in the purchase price or rescission of the contract (**s. 48C**). This right can be exercised where the buyer cannot require repair or replacement, or where *repair or replacement* cannot be done within a reasonable time and without significant inconvenience to the buyer. The reduction in price is 'by an appropriate amount' which is not defined. It is, presumably, a reduction to the price which would have been paid for the goods in their actual state. This new right to rescind is quite separate from the right to reject goods. There is express power for the reimbursement of the purchase price to be reduced to reflect the use the buyer has had of the goods since delivery.

The court has express power in these consumer cases (in addition to all existing remedies) to make an order for specific performance or reimbursement unconditionally or on such terms and conditions as to damages, payment of the price and otherwise as it thinks fit (s. 48E).

Non-delivery Where the seller fails to deliver in accordance with the contract the recoverable sums are: **89.37**

(a) damages for non-delivery (s. 51); and
(b) any special damages and interest (s. 54).

Alternatively, the buyer may sue for specific performance if the goods were specific or ascertained goods (s. 52). The damage recoverable under s. 51 is the estimated loss directly and naturally resulting, in the ordinary course of events, from the seller's breach of contract (s. 51(2)). Where there is an available market for the goods the measure of damages is usually the difference between the contract price and the market or current price of the goods at the time or times when they ought to have been delivered (s. 51(3)).

An outright refusal by the seller to perform his or her obligations will amount to a repudiatory breach of contract unless the seller's obligations under the contract were limited, or the contract has become frustrated. The ordinary contract law concepts of repudiatory breach, the need for acceptance of that breach, and of anticipatory breach, will apply. If a repudiatory breach exists and is accepted by the buyer, the buyer will have the following remedies:

(a) a claim in restitution for the money paid, on a total failure of consideration; or
(b) a claim for damages for non-delivery; or
(c) a claim for specific performance if the goods are specific goods or are ascertained goods.

Wrongful resale by the seller If the buyer has the right to possession of the goods, a second sale by the seller will amount to a wrongful interference with the buyer's goods. The right to possession is not dependent upon property having passed. A right to possession can only exist where the goods are specific, or have become ascertained goods by the time of the second sale. If the buyer has a right to possession and the seller has sold the goods to someone else, the buyer will have remedies against the seller and may have remedies against the subsequent buyer. The remedies against the seller will be: **89.38**

(a) a claim in restitution for the money paid, on a total failure of consideration; or
(b) a claim in restitution for the money received by the seller on the subsequent sale; or
(c) a claim for damages for non-delivery; or
(d) a claim for wrongful interference with goods.

If the buyer has no right to possession of the goods, the buyer's remedies will be only against the seller and will be:

(a) a claim in restitution for the money paid, on a total failure of consideration; or
(b) a claim for damages for non-delivery.

Loss of the goods Goods may be lost before the contract is made, partially lost before the contract is made, or may be lost between contract and delivery. If all the goods the seller intended to supply to the buyer are lost before the contract is made, and the contract is for unascertained generic goods, then the goods cannot easily be said to be lost as another source should be available. If the seller does not deliver the buyer will have the following remedies: **89.39**

(a) a claim in restitution for the money paid, on a total failure of consideration; or
(b) a claim for damages for non-delivery.

Commentary

If all the goods are lost before the contract is made and the contract is for goods from a specific source, or there is only one source, then the contract may be void for mistake (*Bell v Lever Brothers Ltd* [1932] AC 161) or under **SoGA 1979, s. 6**. The buyer will then be entitled to recover any money paid. Damages will only be awarded to the buyer if the seller has warranted that the goods exist. Similarly, if by the contract the buyer has accepted the risk that the goods may not exist, the contract will not be void for mistake and the buyer will have to pay the contract price notwithstanding the non-existence of the goods.

If there has been only a partial loss of goods before the contract is made the position is that it is a question of construction whether the parties intended that the contract be wholly discharged or not, and if it is not to be wholly discharged the seller must deliver and the buyer must pay for the goods which have not been lost (*H. R. and S. Sainsbury Ltd v Street* [1972] 1 WLR 834). If the seller has warranted the existence of the goods he or she must make delivery of the quantity which is not lost and the ordinary rules applying to delivery of a wrong quantity will apply. If the risk of loss is on the buyer, the seller must deliver the goods which have not been lost and the buyer must pay for them.

If goods are lost after the contract is made a distinction must be drawn between specific and unascertained goods.

Where specific goods perish and:

(a) property and risk have not vested in the purchaser, and
(b) there is no fault by either party,

the contract will be avoided (**SoGA 1979, s. 7**). Where **s. 7** applies, the Law Reform (Frustrated Contracts) Act 1943 does not apply and the common law rules must be used. This means that if there has been a total failure of consideration any money paid can be recovered and no allowance is made for the seller's expenses. Where **s. 7** applies but only part of the specific goods perish, it seems that the seller is not obliged to tender what remains (*Barrow, Lane and Ballard Ltd v Phillip Phillips and Co. Ltd* [1929] 1 KB 574, but contrast *H. R. and S. Sainsbury Ltd v Street* [1972] 1 WLR 834). Where there is a partial failure of consideration on a non-severable contract the common law rules apply: the seller cannot compel payment but the buyer cannot compel the return of money already paid. If the seller has undertaken absolutely to deliver the goods **s. 7** will not apply and on a failure to deliver the buyer will have the following remedies:

(a) a claim in restitution for the money paid, on a total failure of consideration; or
(b) a claim for damages for non-delivery.

Where the goods are unascertained goods the seller will only be able to argue that the contract has been frustrated if all sources of supply have been destroyed. In most situations the seller will have to obtain the goods from another source and failure to do so will give the buyer the following remedies:

(a) a claim in restitution for the money paid, on a total failure of consideration; or
(b) a claim for damages for non-delivery.

89.40 **Delay in delivery** If the time for delivery is of the essence, or more than a reasonable time for the delivery has passed and the seller has not delivered the goods, the seller will be in repudiatory breach of contract (*Hartley v Hymans* [1920] 3 KB 475). The buyer will then be able:

(a) to accept the repudiatory breach and claim damages for non-delivery; or
(b) rarely, to seek specific performance of the contract.

Breach by the buyer

89.41 The buyer's duty is to accept the goods and pay for them in accordance with the terms of the contract (see **89.10**). Where the parties have a number of separate contracts it is important to note that (in the absence of express terms in each contract) a claim arising under one contract will not give rise to a defence in another (*B. Hargreaves Ltd v Action 2000 Ltd* [1993] BCLC 1111).

Late payment Many written contracts provide for interest to be charged on late payments. In litigation interest can be claimed under the Senior Courts Act 1981, s. 35A, or the County Courts Act 1981, s. 69. In contracts covered by the Late Payment of Commercial Debts (Interest) Act 1998 a statutory implied term is inserted into the contract that the debt carries simple interest at the prescribed statutory rate. **89.42**

Failure to accept goods If the buyer does not accept the goods, the seller can maintain an action for the price if property in the goods has passed to the buyer or where the price is payable irrespective of delivery (**SOGA 1979, s. 49**). The more usual course is to sue for damages occasioned by the refusal of delivery and a reasonable charge for care of the goods under **s. 37**. Damages for non-acceptance are governed by **s. 50**. The measure of damages is the estimated loss directly and naturally resulting from the buyer's breach of contract. If there is an available market for the goods, the seller must resell the goods and the damages will be: **89.43**

(a) the difference in price; and
(b) the reasonable costs of sale.

If there is no available market for the goods, the seller should resell in order to mitigate the loss and can still claim the costs incurred. An action for the price has obvious advantages where it may be difficult to prove any loss has been suffered, or where arguments over mitigation of loss may arise.

Seller's rights in the goods The seller's rights in the goods can be of particular importance if the buyer is insolvent. Retention of title clauses until payment are now common. Where there are no contract terms, if property has passed, the unpaid seller (defined in **SoGA 1979, s. 38**) usually has, by virtue of **s. 39**: **89.44**

(a) a statutory lien on the goods;
(b) a right of stoppage in transit in case of insolvency; and
(c) a right of resale.

The statutory right of resale arises under s. 48. If property has not passed, the seller may have a claim for delivery up of the goods and damages for wrongful interference with the goods against the buyer and any other person in possession.

Commentary

SALES BY NON-OWNERS

The traditional rule remains that no one can pass better title than that person possesses: *nemo dat quod non habet*. There are nine main exceptions to this rule: **89.45**

(a) Estoppel — where the owner is precluded by conduct from denying the seller's authority to sell (**SoGA 1979, s. 21(1)**).
(b) Sales under the Factors Act 1889 — sales by mercantile agents who are in possession of the goods or documents of title to the goods with the consent of the true owner who sell in the ordinary course of their business to a person acting in good faith without notice will, pass title (**SoGA 1979, s. 21(2)(a)**; Factors Act 1889).
(c) Sales under special powers — this exception covers a large group of sales such as sales of goods distrained upon, sales by mortgagors, receivers and under bills of sale and sale of uncollected goods under the Torts (Interference with Goods) Act 1977, ss. 12 and 13 (**SoGA 1979, s. 21(2)(b)**).
(d) Sales under voidable title — where a sale of goods contract is voidable (e.g. by misrepresentation, undue influence, mistake or duress), the buyer's title will be voidable and a sale on of the goods to someone in good faith without notice of the defect in title can pass title (**SoGA 1979, s. 23**).
(e) Sales by seller in possession — this is a very similar situation to sales under the Factors Act 1889, s. 8, so that a seller who remains in possession of goods or the documents of title, can sell goods a second time to someone else acting in good faith and without notice of

the first sale and will pass title (**SoGA 1979, s. 24**; *Michael Gerson (Leasing) Ltd v Wilkinson* [2001] QB 514).

(f) Sales by buyer in possession — this is similar to the Factors Act 1889, s. 9, and renders valid a sale by the buyer who has possession of the goods or the documents of title and sells on the goods which he or she does not yet own to any person acting in good faith and without notice of a lien or other right of the original seller (**SoGA 1979, s. 25**).

(g) Sales of motor vehicles within part 3 of the Hire Purchase Act 1964 — motor vehicles which are hired under hire purchase agreements or agreed to be sold under conditional sale agreements and are sold by the hirer to a private purchaser in good faith without notice of the hire purchase or conditional sale agreement will pass title in the motor vehicle. Where a fraudster obtains a vehicle from a dealer by purporting to enter into a hire purchase agreement, the hire purchase company (which obtains title by buying the vehicle from the dealer) remains the legal owner of the vehicle, and is not defeated by s. 27, if the fraudster then sells the car to an innocent purchaser. This is because the fraudster is not a 'debtor' under the hire purchase agreement within the meaning of **s. 29(4)** (*Shogun Finance Ltd v Hudson* [2003] UKHL 62, [2004] 1 AC 919).

(h) Sales by agents can also pass title under the ordinary rules of agency if the agent has actual or apparent authority to bind his or her principal as the ordinary rules of agency apply (**SoGA 1979, s. 62(2)**).

(i) Under the Torts (Interference with Goods) Act 1977 payment of damages under s. 5 will extinguish the title of the original owner enabling the person paying damages to pass title in those goods.

Chapter 90 Unfair Contracts

INTRODUCTION

Statutory control limiting the normal freedom to contract upon any terms which the parties agree is not new. Even many centuries ago there was legislation, such as the Statute of Frauds (1677) and the usury laws, regulating the formation of binding contracts (e.g. certain contracts had to be in writing or be evidenced in writing) and the content or effectiveness of contract terms (e.g. limits on recoverable interest). Statutory control of contract terms is now of considerable importance. Much of the control which implements European Directives exists in favour of consumers only. Other legislation, notably the **Unfair Contract Terms Act 1977** (UCTA 1977), contains provisions some of which apply to consumers and some of which are of general application. 90.1

The main policy behind the modern legislation is to provide essential safeguards against the worst excesses of the principle of freedom of contract. The law is particularly concerned to protect consumers as they are often in a weak bargaining position compared to large retailers and other large businesses, and cannot realistically enter into contracts other than on the terms insisted upon by the businesses they are dealing with. The law is also concerned to curb the worst excesses of the use of standard terms of trading. However, the approach is somewhat limited. The legislation is reasonably effective in limiting exclusions of liability (particularly in relation to breaches causing personal injuries or death, and in relation to the statutory implied terms in contracts for the sale of goods and the supply of services), and limiting terms allowing a party to render no performance or a performance substantially different from that reasonably expected. However, there is no general requirement that terms must be fair. Nor does the legislation do anything to protect customers who feel they have been charged an unfair price.

The main statutory provisions are:

(a) **UCTA 1977**, which introduced important controls on exclusion clauses and standard terms in contracts, and which limits the right to contract out of the main obligations under the **Sale of Goods Act 1979** (**SoGA 1979**) (see **chapter 89**) and the Supply of Goods (Implied Terms) Act 1973. It also controls certain other unfair terms.

(b) The Cancellation of Contracts Made in a Consumer's Home or Place of Work etc. Regulations 2008 (SI 2008/1816) (referred to in this chapter as 'the 2008 Regulations'), which provide consumers with the right to cancel a contract for goods or services made during a visit by a trader, whether unsolicited or solicited, to the consumer's home, place of work, the home of another person, or on an excursion organised by the trader away from his business premises. The 2008 Regulations implement Directive 85/577/EEC, but also provide considerably wider consumer protection in the United Kingdom.

(c) The Unfair Terms in Consumer Contracts Regulations 1999 (SI 1999/2083) (in this chapter referred to as 'the 1999 Regulations'), which make consumer contracts subject to a concept of good faith, require written terms to be in plain and intelligible language and give powers of investigation and enforcement to consumer groups and the Office of Fair Trading (OFT). The 1999 Regulations implement Directive 93/13/EEC.

(d) The Consumer Protection (Distance Selling) Regulations 2000 (SI 2000/2334) came into force on 31 October 2000 to implement Directive 97/7/EC. Distance selling is any sale where the supplier and consumer are not face to face and covers telephone sales, mail order and e-commerce. A cooling-off period is provided for in the same way as in the 2008 Regulations.

Directive 85/577/EEC and Directive 97/7/EC have been repealed and replaced by Directive 2011/83/EU (the Consumer Rights Directive), which is designed to simplify and update the applicable rules, remove inconsistencies and close unwanted gaps (recital 2). Legislation transposing the new Directive must come into force on 13 June 2014 (art. 28). **UCTA 1977** and the 1999 Regulations contain inconsistent and overlapping provisions, using different language and concepts to produce similar but not identical effects. The Law Commission and the Scottish Law Commission have drafted a Bill which rewrites both pieces of legislation in a way that is much clearer and easier to follow and also plugs some gaps in protection (*Unfair Terms in Contracts* (Law Com. No. 292, Cm 6464, 2005)). The government has consulted on an extensive programme of reforms to implement the Consumer Rights Directive and the Law Commissions' proposals in a consumer bill of rights. A draft Consumer Rights Bill was announced in the Queen's Speech 2013. One provision of the Directive has been brought into force on 6 April 2013 in a restricted form (see **90.31**).

MEANING OF 'CONSUMER'

90.2 In the legislation on unfair contracts there are two different definitions of 'consumer'. In the European Directives which are implemented by the 1999, 2000 and 2008 Regulations, 'consumer' is defined as a natural person who has entered into the contract in question for purposes which are outside his or her trade, business or profession (Directive 85/577/EEC, art. 2; Directive 93/13/EEC, art. 2(b); Directive 97/7/EC, art. 2(2)). Directive 2011/83/EU, art. 2(1), is in the same terms except that the purposes must be outside the person's trade, business, craft or profession. For the purposes of these Directives, the term 'consumer' must be given an autonomous European meaning which does not depend on national laws (*Turner and Co. (GB) Ltd v Abi* [2010] EWHC 2078 (QB), [2011] 1 CMLR 17). An individual who enters into a contract appointing an agent to sell shares in a company, where the individual is a full-time working director of the company, does so for the purposes of his or her trade, business or profession and is not a consumer (*Turner and Co. (GB) Ltd v Abi*).

A much wider definition of consumer is used in **UCTA 1977**, in which there is no requirement that a consumer must be an individual (*R and B Customs Brokers Co. Ltd v United Dominions Trust Ltd* [1988] 1 WLR 321).

For the purposes of **UCTA 1977**, the concept of dealing as consumer is defined by **s. 12(1)**, which was amended with effect from 31 March 2003. A person deals as consumer if he neither makes the contract in the course of a business nor holds himself out as doing so, and the other party makes the contract in the course of a business. Further, save where the buyer is an individual, in the case of sales of goods, the goods passing under or in pursuance of the contract must be of a type ordinarily supplied for private use or consumption. A person operating a business may deal as consumer if the transaction is not entered into as an integral part of the business carried on, and is not a transaction carried on with some regularity (*R and B Customs Brokers Co. Ltd v United Dominions Trust Ltd* [1988] 1 WLR 321). Sales at public auction which can be attended in person, where the buyer is an individual and the goods are second-hand goods, are excluded, as are any auction or sale by competitive tender where the buyer is not an individual (**s. 12(2)**). There is a statutory presumption that a party claiming to do so was dealing as consumer, so the burden of proof is on the other side to show that this was not the case (**s. 12(3)**).

UNFAIR CONTRACT TERMS ACT 1977

Application of the Act

UCTA 1977 came into force on 1 February 1978. It does not apply to contracts made before that date, but does apply to any loss or damage which is suffered on or after that date (**s. 31**). The provisions relating to sale and hire-purchase contracts apply to any contract and not only to business contracts. The other provisions apply only to business liability. 'Business' includes a profession and the activities of any government department or local or public authority (**s. 14**). 'Business liability' is liability for breach of an obligation or duty arising from things done or to be done by a person in the course of a business (whether that person's own or another's) (**s. 1(3)**). It does not matter whether any breach of duty or obligation is inadvertent or intentional, or whether liability arises directly or vicariously. 'Person' is not defined and so includes a body of persons corporate or unincorporate (Interpretation Act 1978, sch. 1). **90.3**

Negligence liability

By **UCTA 1977, s. 1(1)**, 'negligence' means the breach of: **90.4**

(a) any obligation arising from the express or implied terms of a contract to take reasonable care or exercise reasonable skill in the performance of the contract;

(b) any common law duty to take reasonable care or exercise reasonable skill (but not any stricter duty); and

(c) the duty of care imposed by the Occupiers' Liability Act 1957.

UCTA 1977 prevents contract terms or notices which exclude or restrict liability for personal injury or death from being effective at all (**s. 2(1)**). Loss or damage (other than for personal injury or death) can only be excluded or restricted in so far as a clause satisfies the test of reasonableness (**s. 2(2)**). Knowledge of or agreement to a contract term or notice which excludes or restricts liability is not of itself to be taken as indicating acceptance of any risk (**s. 2(3)**).

Contract terms

Before considering whether a purported term may fall foul of **UCTA 1977**, it is first necessary to determine whether it was in fact a term of the contract (see **89.23**: this is a point specifically mentioned also in **UCTA 1977, s. 11(2)**), and secondly whether the term purports to apply on the facts of the case. If the term appears to apply, it will also be necessary to consider whether it may be cut down by **UCTA 1977**. **90.5**

Where one party deals as a consumer or on another's written standard terms of business, there can be no exclusion or restriction of liability in respect of a breach by that other person save where the term satisfies the test of reasonableness (**UCTA 1977, s. 3(2)(a)**). Similarly, a person dealing with a consumer or on standard terms cannot claim to be contractually entitled to render a contractual performance substantially different from that reasonably expected, or no performance at all, unless the contract terms satisfies the test of reasonableness (**s. 3(2)(b)**).

A person dealing as a consumer cannot by reference to a contract term be made to indemnify another person in respect of liability that may be incurred for negligence or breach of contract, except in so far as the contract term satisfies the test of reasonableness (**s. 4(1)**).

Statutory implied terms

90.6 Prohibitions on excluding liability for breach of the statutory implied terms under **SoGA 1979** and the Supply of Goods (Implied Terms) Act 1973 (SoGITA 1973) are contained in **UCTA 1977, s. 6**. The restrictions may be summarised as follows:

(a) an absolute prohibition on excluding or restricting the implied terms about title in **SoGA 1979, s. 12**, and SoGITA 1973, s. 8;
(b) an absolute prohibition in consumer cases on excluding or restricting the implied terms in **SoGA 1979, ss. 13–15**, about sale by description, quality or fitness, and sale by sample; and in relation to the equivalent provisions in the SoGITA 1973, ss. 9–11; and
(c) a qualified prohibition in non-consumer cases on excluding or restricting the implied terms in **SoGA 1979, ss. 13–15**, and the SoGITA 1973, ss. 9–11, so that to be effective an exclusion or restriction must satisfy the test of reasonableness (which is provided for by **UCTA 1977, s. 11** and **sch. 2**).

Misrepresentations

90.7 Similar protection to that provided under **UCTA 1977** is provided under the **Misrepresentation Act 1967, s. 3**, in relation to the exclusion of liability in respect of misrepresentations. A term purporting to exclude or restrict liability for any misrepresentation made before contract, or to exclude or restrict any remedies available by reason of such misrepresentations, is of no effect except in so far as the term satisfies the test of reasonableness set out in **UCTA 1977, s. 11**.

Reasonableness

90.8 The test of reasonableness is set out in **UCTA 1977, s. 11**. By **s. 11(1)**, the requirement of reasonableness for the purposes of **UCTA 1977** and the **Misrepresentation Act 1967, s. 3**, is that the term must have been a fair and reasonable one to be included having regard to the circumstances which were, or ought reasonably to have been, known to or in the contemplation of the parties when the contract was made. It is for those claiming that a contract term or notice satisfies the test of reasonableness to show that it does (**UCTA 1977, s. 11(5)**). In *Sheffield v Pickfords Ltd* [1997] CLC 648 the Court of Appeal held that any claim concerning standard terms of business implicitly raises the question whether those terms are reasonable, and it is not essential for the party seeking to enforce the terms to assert in a statement of case that they are reasonable. It was also held that particulars of any specific fact or matter relied upon could be given before any issue is raised.

Particular situations are governed by the following additional provisions:

(a) In determining for the purposes of non-consumer contracts governed by **UCTA 1977, s. 6** (sale of goods and hire-purchase) and **s. 7** (miscellaneous contracts, other than sale and hire-purchase, under which ownership or possession of goods passes), whether a contract term satisfies the test of reasonableness, the court must have regard to the matters set out in **sch. 2** to the Act (see **90.9**) (**s. 11(2)**).
(b) In relation to a notice (not being a notice which has contractual effect, such as a notice purporting to restrict or exclude liability in respect of theft), the requirement of reasonableness

is that it should be fair and reasonable to allow reliance on it, having regard to all the circumstances obtaining when the liability arose or (but for the notice) would have arisen (**s. 11(3)**).

(c) Where the question arises whether a term or notice seeking to restrict a person's liability to a specified sum or money satisfies the requirement of reasonableness, regard shall be had (in the case of contract terms) to the matters mentioned in (a) above, and in all cases to:
   (i) the resources which that person could expect to have available for the purpose of meeting the liability should it arise; and
   (ii) how far it was open to that person to obtain insurance cover for the liability (**s. 11(4)**).

Reasonableness guidelines for non-consumer sales etc.

The guidelines set out in **UCTA 1977, sch. 2**, need to be considered only in relation to an attempt to exclude or restrict liability for breach of the implied terms about conformity with description or sample or about quality or fitness in a sale of goods, hire-purchase or similar transaction with a person who is not acting as a consumer (**UCTA 1977, ss. 6(3), 7(3)** and **(4)**). In deciding whether the exclusion or restriction is reasonable in these non-consumer cases, **sch. 2** requires regard to be had to: **90.9**

(a) the strength of the bargaining position of the parties relative to each other, taking into account (amongst other things) alternative means by which the customer's requirements could have been met;
(b) whether the customer received an inducement to agree to the term, or in accepting it had an opportunity of entering into a similar contract with other persons, but without having to accept such a term;
(c) whether the customer knew or ought reasonably to have known of the existence of the term (having regard, amongst other things, to any custom of the trade and any previous course of dealings between the parties);
(d) where the term excludes or restricts any relevant liability if some condition is not complied with, whether it was reasonable at the time of the contract to expect that compliance with that condition would be practicable;
(e) whether the goods were manufactured, processed or adapted to the special order of the customer.

In *St Albans City and District Council v International Computers Ltd* [1995] FSR 686, the council suffered a £1.3 million loss due to an error made by the computer company. The company sought to rely on a clause in its contract restricting its liability to £100,000. Scott Baker J took into account the following factors: (a) the parties were of unequal bargaining power; (b) the defendant had not justified the figure of £100,000, which was small in relation to the potential risk; (c) the defendant was insured in an aggregate figure of £50 million worldwide; (d) whether it was better for the risk to fall on a council or an international computer company. Despite the facts that both parties were free to make their own bargains, that the council entered into the contract with its eyes open, that such restrictions were commonplace in the computer industry, and that the software involved was a developing technology, it was held that the defendant had failed to discharge its burden of proof. The term was therefore unreasonable and unenforceable.

The fact that a contract is the result of negotiations between substantial companies is likely to indicate that the court should not find that its terms are unreasonable. In *Watford Electronics Ltd v Sanderson CFL Ltd* [2001] 1 All ER (Comm) 696 Peter Gibson LJ quoted with approval the following remarks of Judge Thayne Forbes in *Salvage Association v CAP Financial Services Ltd* [1995] FSR 654:

Generally speaking, where a party well able to look after itself enters into a commercial contract and, with full knowledge of all relevant circumstances, willingly accepts the terms of the contract which

Commentary

provides for apportionment of the financial risks of that transaction, I think it is very likely that those terms will be held to be fair and reasonable.

In *Watford Electronics Ltd v Sanderson CFL Ltd* Chadwick LJ said, at [55]:

Where experienced businessmen representing substantial companies of equal bargaining power negotiate an agreement, they may be taken to have had regard to the matters known to them. They should in my view be taken to be the best judge of the commercial fairness of the agreement which they have made; including the fairness of each of the terms in that agreement.

Terms in a standard-form contract are more likely to be held to be reasonable if they were negotiated between trade associations (as opposed to standard terms simply imposed by one party), as in such cases there is no substantial difference in bargaining power (see *R. W. Green Ltd v Cade Bros Farms Ltd* [1978] 1 Lloyd's Rep 602, and compare *George Mitchell (Chesterhall) Ltd v Finney Lock Seeds Ltd* [1983] 2 AC 803, where standard conditions were used by seed merchants without objection from farmers). The guidelines in **sch. 2** are not exhaustive of the circumstances that may be considered. So, in *R and B Customs Brokers Co. Ltd v United Dominions Trust Ltd* [1988] 1 WLR 321 it was said that the court could take into account the question whether the party seeking to rely on an exclusion or restriction had an opportunity to discover the defect covered by the term.

Reasonableness in other contracts

90.10 In cases where terms are subject to the test of reasonableness under **UCTA 1977**, but the guidelines in **sch. 2** (see **90.9**) do not apply (for example, if the term does not purport to restrict the statutory implied terms, or if the dispute concerns the exclusion of liability for misrepresentations, or the contract is not one involving the sale etc. of goods), the court must apply the general test of reasonableness set out at **90.8**. However, the court can apply the sch. 2 guidelines by analogy (see *Singer Co. (UK) Ltd v Tees and Hartlepool Port Authority* [1988] 2 Lloyd's Rep 164).

As regards insurance (**UCTA 1977, s. 11(4)(b)**), the court will consider the availability of insurance rather than the actual insurance cover of the defendant (*Singer Co. (UK) Ltd v Tees and Hartlepool Port Authority*). Limitation of liability may well be reasonable for a person who stores or carries another's goods without being informed of their value, particularly if the goods could be more cheaply insured by the owner (*Singer Co. (UK) Ltd v Tees and Hartlepool Port Authority*).

In *Smith v Eric S. Bush* [1990] 1 AC 831 the question arose as to whether it was reasonable for surveyors instructed by the mortgagee to exclude or restrict liability in relation to their survey reports prepared in connection with the sale of ordinary houses. The House of Lords held, having regard to the relative expense to the purchaser of buying a house, and the high rates of interest charged to borrowers, that it was not reasonable to throw the risk of loss flowing from the incompetence or carelessness of the surveyor on to the purchaser, and exclusion clauses were held to be unenforceable. On the other hand, in relation to very expensive houses, and industrial property, it was said that prudent purchasers would obtain their own survey reports, and it may well be reasonable for surveyors to exclude their liability, or at least to restrict it to the amount of their insurance cover.

Excluded contracts

90.11 Certain contracts are excluded either in whole or in part from the provisions of **UCTA 1977** by **sch. 1**. The provisions on negligence liability (**s. 2**), liability in contract (**s. 3**) and unreasonable indemnity clauses (**s. 4**) do not apply to the types of contract listed in **sch. 1, para. 1**. These exclusions may be summarised as contracts relating to insurance, creation or transfer of an interest in land, intellectual property, formation or dissolution of a company or its constitution, and the creation or transfer of securities. Special provisions exist in relation to certain marine and hovercraft contracts (**paras 2** and **3**). The exclusions of negligence liability in **s. 2(1)** and **(2)** only apply to employment contracts in favour of the employee (**sch. 1, para. 4**).

In *Commerzbank AG v Keen* [2006] EWCA Civ 1536, [2007] IRLR 132, the Court of Appeal rejected as unarguable that general provisions of **UCTA 1977** applied to contracts of employment. Moses LJ observed that:

> It is all too easy in analysing authority and discussion of the application of the 1977 Act to contracts of employment to overlook the impact of the words 'consumer' and 'business' used in ss. 3 and 12 of the Act. An employee does not deal with an employer as a consumer. A bank's business is not entering into contracts of employment with its employees.

Practice

In *Sheffield v Pickfords Ltd* [1997] CLC 648 the Court of Appeal held that it was not essential for a party relying on contract terms or standard terms to assert that those terms are reasonable. That allegation is implicit if a party relies in a statement of case on terms which have to satisfy the test of reasonableness. However, the better practice is to make at least a general assertion of reasonableness of such contract or standard terms in the statement of case. Further information can then be sought or ordered of the facts and matter relied on as showing reasonableness, if necessary. **90.12**

Commentary

CANCELLATION OF CONTRACTS MADE IN A CONSUMER'S HOME OR PLACE OF WORK ETC. REGULATIONS 2008

Scope of the Regulations

The Cancellation of Contracts Made in a Consumer's Home or Place of Work etc. Regulations 2008 (SI 2008/1816) (the 2008 Regulations) apply to contracts made by consumers on or after 1 October 2008. The 2008 Regulations provide a statutory cooling-off period during which a consumer has the right to cancel a contract which is within the scope of the Regulations (reg. 7(1)). A trader entering into a cancellable contract with a consumer must give the consumer written information about the consumer's cancellation rights (reg. 7(2)). Breach of that obligation is a criminal offence (reg. 17) and it makes the contract unenforceable by the trader (reg. 7(6)). There is no provision in the Regulations which prevents enforcement of a contract by the consumer against the trader. **90.13**

The 2008 Regulations apply (reg. 5) to a contract for the supply of goods or services by a trader to a consumer, which is made between the consumer and the trader:

(a) during a visit, whether solicited or unsolicited, by the trader to the consumer's home or to the home of another person, or to the consumer's place of work — this covers traditional doorstep selling and sales calls or consultations made by appointment;
(b) on an 'excursion' organised by the trader away from the trader's business premises, which includes, for example, a sales presentation at a hotel to which consumers have been invited (*Re TAG World Services Ltd* [2008] EWHC 1866 (Ch), LTL 6/8/2008 at [24]); and
(c) after an offer to contract made by the consumer to the trader in the circumstances mentioned in (a) or (b) above — this avoids there being any distinction between the situation where the contract is agreed and where the consumer merely offers to make a contract and the contract is formed when that offer is accepted later.

'Consumer' has the standard European definition (reg. 2(1); see **90.2**). 'Trader' means a person who, in making a contract to which the Regulations apply, is acting in his commercial or professional capacity and anyone acting in the name or on behalf of a trader (reg. 2(1)).

It is not possible to contract out of any provision in the 2008 Regulations for the protection of the consumer (reg. 15).

Some contracts are exempt — see **90.14**.

The 2008 Regulations replace the Consumer Protection (Cancellation of Contracts Concluded away from Business Premises) Regulations 1987 (SI 1987/2117), which did not generally apply to contracts made during solicited visits. The 1987 Regulations continue to apply to contracts made before 1 October 2008.

Exempt contracts

90.14 Contracts which the 2008 Regulations do not apply to are listed in reg. 6 and sch. 3. They include contracts for the sale of food, drink or other goods by regular roundsmen (sch. 3, para. 2); insurance contracts (sch. 3, para. 4); contracts concerning investment in shares and similar securities which are regulated under the Financial Services and Markets Act 2000 (2008 Regulations, sch. 3, para. 8); any contract under which credit within the meaning of the Consumer Credit Act 1974 does not exceed £35 (other than a hire-purchase or conditional sale agreement) (2008 Regulations, sch. 3, para. 5) and any other type of contract under which the total payments to be made by the consumer do not exceed £35 (sch. 3, para. 6). Catalogue sales are exempt (sch. 3, para. 3) if they fulfil the following three conditions:

(a) the contract is concluded on the basis of a trader's catalogue which the consumer has a proper opportunity of reading in the absence of the trader's representative;
(b) there is intended to be continuity of contact between the trader's representative and the consumer in relation to that or any subsequent transaction; and
(c) both the catalogue and the contract contain a prominent notice informing the consumer of his rights to return goods to the supplier within a period of not less than seven days of receipt or otherwise to cancel the contract within that period without obligation of any kind other than to take reasonable care of the goods.

Contracts relating to the construction, sale or rental of immovable property, or concerning other rights relating to immovable property are generally exempt (sch. 3, para. 1), but the following are not exempt:

(a) a contract for the construction of extensions, patios, conservatories or driveways;
(b) a contract for the supply of goods and their incorporation in immovable property; and
(c) a contract for the repair, refurbishment or improvement of immovable property.

A consumer credit agreement which is regulated under the Consumer Credit Act 1974 is exempt from the 2008 Regulations if:

(a) it is a cancellable agreement (reg. 6(1)(b)), or offers similar rights (reg. 6(1)(c)) or is subject to a right of withdrawal (reg. 6(1)(ca)); or
(b) it is made during a solicited visit, or is made after an offer made during a solicited visit (reg. 6(1)(d)(iii); the term 'solicited visit' is defined in reg. 6(3)).

The exemption for credit agreements made during a solicited visit also extends to:

(a) a regulated mortgage, home purchase plan or home reversion plan if the making or performance of such a contract constitutes a regulated activity for the purposes of the Financial Services and Markets Act 2000 (2008 Regulations, reg. 6(1)(d)(i));
(b) a consumer credit agreement secured on land which is regulated or exempt under the Consumer Credit Act 1974.

Notice of cancellation rights

If the 2008 Regulations apply to a contract, it will not be enforceable against the consumer unless the trader has delivered to the consumer a notice in writing indicating the right to cancel the contract within seven days (reg. 7(2), (3)(b) and (6)). The notice setting out the right to cancel must be served on the consumer at the time of making the contract or at the time the consumer makes an offer to the trader (reg. 7(2)). If the contract is wholly or partly in writing, the notice must be incorporated in the same document (reg. 7(4)). It must be set out in a separate box with the heading 'Notice of the Right to Cancel' (reg. 7(5)(a)). It must be easily legible (reg. 7(3)(c)) and have as much prominence as any other information in the contract or document apart from the heading and the names of the parties to the contract and any information inserted in handwriting (reg. 7(5)(b)). It must contain the information set out in sch. 4, part 1 (reg. 7(3)(d)(i)), and, if applicable, the warnings in reg. 7(3)(e). A cancellation form, in the form set out in sch. 4, part 2, must be provided as a detachable slip (reg. 7(3)(d)(ii)). **90.15**

The seven-day cancellation period begins when the consumer receives the notice of the right to cancel (reg. 2(1)).

There is no saving provision permitting the court to waive any breach of these requirements (even if the breach has caused no prejudice), or to grant leave to enforce, or to permit partial enforcement of the contract.

Commentary

Cancelling the contract

A consumer wishing to cancel an agreement falling within the 2008 Regulations must serve a notice, which may be informally expressed and need not be on the cancellation form, on the trader (or on another person specified in the trader's notice of the right to cancel) within the cancellation period (reg. 8). If the consumer sends the cancellation notice by post, it is deemed to have been served at the time of posting whether or not it is actually received (reg. 8(5)). A cancellation notice sent by email is taken to have been served on the day on which it is sent (reg. 8(6)). **90.16**

If the consumer serves a cancellation notice within the cancellation period, the contract is cancelled and must be treated as if it had never been entered into by the consumer (reg. 8(1) and (2)). The 2008 Regulations make detailed provision for return of money paid (reg. 10), cancellation of a related credit agreement (reg. 11), repayment of credit and payment of interest (reg. 12); return of the goods (reg. 13, which makes it plain that the duty to return the goods is limited to returning them to the trader at the consumer's own premises); and return or payment for goods part-exchanged (reg. 14).

Practice

By analogy with the approach to **UCTA 1977** adopted in *Sheffield v Pickfords Ltd* [1997] CLC 648 (see **90.12**), it is submitted that any claim concerning a contract to which the 2008 Regulations apply implicitly raises the question whether the contract complies with the Regulations, and it is not essential for the party seeking to enforce the contract to assert in a statement of case that it does comply. **90.17**

If a consumer wishes to allege any breach of the 2008 Regulations, the breach ought to be specifically asserted by the consumer in his or her statement of case. However, a court should refuse to enforce a contract if it becomes aware of a breach of the 2008 Regulations, even if the breach has not been set out in a statement of case because the Regulations absolutely prohibit enforcement. If it is asserted that the contract or offer has been cancelled by giving notice, that fact should be specifically asserted by the consumer, who should also specifically seek any consequential remedies (such as return of money paid or goods).

A consumer who is party to a claim concerning a contract to which the 2008 Regulations apply should consider an application for summary judgment under **CPR, r. 24.2**, and/or to strike out under **r. 3.4** to prevent any enforcement of the contract. In most cases the court can decide without hearing oral evidence whether or not the 2008 Regulations apply and whether or not they have been complied with. If the consumer alleges that he or she returned the cancellation notice by post, it is possible to rely on the deeming provision that it was served when posted whether or not it was actually received (reg. 8(5)).

UNFAIR TERMS IN CONSUMER CONTRACTS REGULATIONS 1999

Scope of the Regulations

90.18 The Unfair Terms in Consumer Contracts Regulations 1999 (SI 1999/2083, the 1999 Regulations) came into force on 1 October 1999, replacing the Unfair Terms in Consumer Contracts Regulations 1994 (SI 1994/3159), which applied to contracts made on or after 1 July 1995. The 1999 Regulations differ from UCTA 1977 in that they apply only to consumer contracts. The Arbitration Act 1996 extends the 1999 Regulations to arbitration agreements within s. 89(1) of that Act and, in relation to those agreements only, a consumer does not have to be a natural person.

The 1999 Regulations apply to contracts concluded between a seller or a supplier and a consumer (reg. 4(1)). 'Consumer' has the standard European definition (reg. 3(1); see **90.2**). A 'seller or supplier' is any natural or legal person who, in the contract, is acting for purposes relating to his trade, business or profession, whether publicly owned or privately owned (reg. 3(1)). It follows that the Regulations do not apply to non-business transactions and do not apply to transactions between businesses.

Plain and intelligible language

90.19 A seller or supplier must ensure that any written term of a contract covered by the 1999 Regulations is expressed in plain, intelligible language (reg. 7(1)). The main sanction for breach of this requirement is that, in legal proceedings between the seller or supplier and the consumer, if there is doubt about the meaning of a written term, the interpretation which is most favourable to the consumer shall prevail (reg. 7(2)). In addition, being in plain and intelligible language is a condition for the exemption of terms defining the subject matter or price from the fairness requirement.

Unfair contract terms

90.20 A term in a contract covered by the 1999 Regulations is unfair if (reg. 5(1)):

(a) it has not been individually negotiated;

(b) it causes a significant imbalance in the parties' rights and obligations arising under the contract, to the detriment of the consumer, in a manner or to an extent which is contrary to the requirement of good faith.

Schedule 2 to the Regulations provides an indicative and non-exhaustive list of terms which may be regarded as unfair. In *Director General of Fair Trading v First National Bank plc* [2001] UKHL 52, [2002] 1 AC 481, Lord Bingham of Cornhill said, at [17]:

> The requirement of significant imbalance is met if a term is so weighted in favour of the supplier as to tilt the parties' rights and obligations under the contract significantly in his favour. This may

be by the granting to the supplier of a beneficial option or discretion or power, or by the imposing on the consumer of a disadvantageous burden or risk or duty. The illustrative terms set out in sch. 3 to the regulations provide very good examples of terms which may be regarded as unfair; whether a given term is or is not to be so regarded depends on whether it causes a significant imbalance in the parties' rights and obligations under the contract. This involves looking at the contract as a whole. But the imbalance must be to the detriment of the consumer; a significant imbalance to the detriment of the supplier, assumed to be the stronger party, is not a mischief which the regulations seek to address. The requirement of good faith in this context is one of fair and open dealing. Openness requires that the terms should be expressed fully, clearly and legibly, containing no concealed pitfalls or traps. Appropriate prominence should be given to terms which might operate disadvantageously to the customer. Fair dealing requires that a supplier should not, whether deliberately or unconsciously, take advantage of the consumer's necessity, indigence, lack of experience, unfamiliarity with the subject matter of the contract, weak bargaining position or any other factor listed in or analogous to those listed in sch. 2 of the regulations. Good faith in this context is not an artificial or technical concept; nor, since Lord Mansfield was its champion, is it a concept wholly unfamiliar to British lawyers. It looks to good standards of commercial morality and practice. Regulation 4(1) lays down a composite test, covering both the making and the substance of the contract, and must be applied bearing clearly in mind the objective which the Regulations are designed to promote.

The factors which must be taken into account in assessing the unfairness of a contractual term are (reg. 6(1)):

(a) the nature of the goods or services for which the contract was concluded;
(b) all the circumstances attending the conclusion of the contract; and
(c) all the other terms of the contract or of another contract on which it is dependent.

But in so far as a term is in plain and intelligible language, the assessment of its fairness must not relate (reg. 6(2)):

(a) to the definition of the main subject matter of the contract; or
(b) to the adequacy of the price or remuneration, as against the goods or services supplied in exchange.

Terms concerned with the matters specified in reg. 6(2) are usually called 'core terms'. Payments to be made if the consumer defaults are not part of the price or remuneration for this purpose (*Director General of Fair Trading v First National Bank plc*). But bank charges levied on personal current account customers in respect of unauthorised overdrafts are part of the price or remuneration for the banking services provided (*Office of Fair Trading v Abbey National plc* [2009] UKSC 6, [2010] 1 AC 696).

Individually negotiated

The general test of fairness in the 1999 Regulations applies only to terms which have not been individually negotiated. There is no definition of individual negotiation. But it is provided that any term shall be regarded as not having been individually negotiated (i.e., will be covered by the 1999 Regulations) if it is drafted in advance and the consumer has not been able to influence the substance of the term (reg. 5(2)). If certain terms or certain aspects of a contract have been individually negotiated, the 1999 Regulations apply to the rest of the contract if an overall assessment of the contract indicates that it is a pre-formulated standard contract (reg. 5(3)). The burden of showing that a term was individually negotiated is upon the seller or supplier (reg. 5(4)). 90.21

Consequence of unfairness

An unfair term in a contract concluded with a consumer by a seller or supplier is not binding on the consumer (1999 Regulations, reg. 8(1)). The contract will continue to bind the parties if it is capable of continuing in existence without the unfair term (reg. 8(2)). Nothing in the 90.22

1999 Regulations prevents enforcement of any term (even an unfair term) by the consumer against the trader.

Action by the OFT

90.23 The OFT may apply for an injunction (including an interim injunction) against any person appearing to be using, or recommending use of, an unfair term drawn up for general use in contracts concluded with consumers (1999 Regulations, reg. 12(1)). Other 'qualifying bodies' listed in sch. 1 (including industry regulators, weights and measures (trading standards) authorities and the Consumers' Association) may apply for an injunction provided they notify the OFT (reg. 12(2)). The OFT has a duty to consider complaints about allegedly unfair terms (reg. 10) and may refer such a complaint to an appropriate qualifying body (reg. 11). The OFT and qualifying bodies have a power to require disclosure of documents and information (reg. 13). They can accept undertakings concerning the use of terms. An injunction may prevent enforcement of an unfair term in existing contracts as well as preventing its use in future contracts (*Office of Fair Trading v Foxtons Ltd* [2009] EWCA Civ 288, [2010] 1 WLR 663).

Practice

90.24 The burden of proof is on the seller or supplier if alleging that a term was individually negotiated (1999 Regulations, reg. 5(4)). Whether or not a term is in plain intelligible language is a matter of law for the court.

By analogy with the approach to **UCTA 1977** adopted in *Sheffield v Pickfords Ltd* [1997] CLC 648 (see **90.12**), it is submitted that any claim concerning a contract to which the 1999 Regulations apply implicitly raises the question whether the contract complies with the Regulations, and it is not essential for the party seeking to enforce the contract to assert in a statement of case that it does comply.

If a consumer wishes to allege that a term is not in plain intelligible language, that fact ought to be specifically asserted in the consumer's statement of case, particularly if there is to be a challenge to a core term (which can only be challenged if it is not in plain intelligible language). An allegation by a consumer that a term is unfair ought to appear in the consumer's statement of case. However, a mere failure to assert unfairness should not prevent the court refusing to enforce the term, as an unfair term is not binding on the consumer.

If it appears to the court that the 1999 Regulations apply and a term is not in plain intelligible language or a term which is not individually negotiated is unfair, the court should adjudicate on those points whether or not they appear in the statement of case.

CONSUMER PROTECTION (DISTANCE SELLING) REGULATIONS 2000

Scope of the Regulations

90.25 The Consumer Protection (Distance Selling) Regulations 2000 (SI 2000/2334) came into force on 31 October 2000. They apply to any distance contract which is defined as 'any contract concerning goods or services concluded between a supplier and a consumer under an organised distance sales or service provision scheme run by the supplier who, for the purposes of the contract, makes exclusive use of one or more means of distance communication up to and including the moment which the contract is concluded'. Distance communication is defined as any means which, without the simultaneous physical presence of the supplier and the consumer, may be used for the conclusion of a contract between those parties, and an indicative list of such means is contained in sch. 1 to the Regulations.

If the contract is a distance contract then, subject to three qualifications, the regulations will apply:

(a) The first qualification is that certain distance contracts are wholly exempt. Regulation 5 lists the six categories of 'excepted contracts': sale or disposition of land (other than a rental contract); construction of a building where the contract also provides for the sale or other disposition of an interest in land; financial services (a non-exhaustive list of which is contained in sch. 2 to the regulations); automatic vending machines or automated commercial premises; contracts concluded with a telecommunications operator through a public payphone; and auctions.
(b) The second qualification is that certain contracts are partially exempt. Regulation 6 lists the four categories of contract which are partially exempt: timeshare agreements (within the meaning of the Timeshare Act 1992); food, beverages or other goods intended for everyday consumption supplied to the consumer's house or workplace by regular roundsmen; contracts for accommodation, transport, catering or leisure services where the supplier undertakes, when the contract is concluded, to provide the services on a specific date or within a specific period; and package holidays (within the meaning of the Package Travel, Package Holidays and Package Tours Regulations 1992 (SI 1992/3288)) which are sold or offered for sale within a member State.
(c) The third qualification is that the right to cancel will not exist in respect of six categories of contract. Regulation 13 lists these categories: contracts for the supply of services where the supply has started before the end of the cancellation period; contracts for the supply of goods where the price fluctuates in the financial market which cannot be controlled by the supplier; contracts for the supply of goods which are personalised or are liable to deteriorate or expire rapidly; contracts for the supply of audio or video recordings or computer software if they are unsealed by the consumer; contracts for the supply of newspapers, magazines or periodicals; and contracts for the supply of gaming, betting or lottery services.

The Court of Justice of the European Union has ruled (on a reference by the Chancery Division) that the exemption relating to 'transport' is to be interpreted as meaning contracts for the provision of transport services and therefore includes car-hire services (*easyCar (UK) Ltd v Office of Fair Trading* (case C-336/03) [2005] ECR I-1947).

Effect of the Regulations

The Regulations require information to be provided to the consumer in good time prior to the conclusion of the contract (reg. 7). Further information is required not later than during performance (in the case of services) and at the time of delivery (in the case of goods, other than goods to be delivered to third parties) (reg. 8). There is then a seven-day cooling-off period in which there is a right to cancel. Detailed provisions about notice of this right and the calculation of the start and end of the seven-day period are in regs 10–12. **90.26**

If a distance contract is cancelled, any related credit agreement is automatically cancelled (reg. 15). Detailed provisions are made for the return of money and goods (including goods part-exchanged) in regs 16–18.

If the contract is not cancelled, then (unless there is agreement to the contrary) it must be performed by the supplier within 30 days (reg. 19).

New provision is made to regulate inertia selling (reg. 24). Unsurprisingly, there is a prohibition on contracting out of the Regulations (reg. 25).

Weights and measures authorities and the OFT are charged with enforcing the Regulations. They may apply for injunctions to restrain breaches of the Regulations (reg. 27).

UNFAIR RELATIONSHIPS

90.27 The Consumer Credit Act 1974, ss. 140A to 140D, which were inserted by the Consumer Credit Act 2006 and came into force on 6 April 2007, introduced the concept of 'unfair relationships' between creditors and debtors arising out of credit agreements. For the purposes of these sections, a credit agreement is any agreement between an individual (the 'debtor') and any other person (the 'creditor') by which the creditor provides the debtor with credit of any amount (s. 140C(1)). The sections apply to agreements whether or not they are otherwise regulated by the Act. They replace earlier provisions for reopening extortionate credit bargains.

Concept of unfair relationship

90.28 The Consumer Credit Act 1974, s. 140A(1), provides that the court may exercise its powers under s. 140B (see **90.29**) if it determines that the relationship between the creditor and debtor, arising out of a credit agreement, is unfair to the debtor because of one or more of the following:

(a) any terms of the agreement or any related agreement;
(b) the way in which the creditor has exercised or enforced any of his rights;
(c) any other thing done (or not done) by or on behalf of the creditor either before or after the making of the agreement or any related agreement.

The court is to have regard to all matters it thinks relevant. Very little guidance exists concerning the extremely wide concept of an unfair relationship. There is some OFT guidance (OFT 854), and the courts are now beginning to rule on what amounts to an unfair relationship. In *Patel v Patel* [2009] EWHC 3264 (QB), LTL 16/12/2009, the court found that a consolidating loan was part of an unfair relationship and reduced the amount payable under s. 140B. The fact that payment protection insurance, provided by an associated company, is sold by the creditor to the debtor at a high price when it is readily available more cheaply elsewhere does not indicate unfairness in the relationship, nor does non-disclosure of a startling level of commission earned by the creditor on such sales (*Harrison v Black Horse Ltd* [2011] EWCA Civ 1128, [2012] Lloyd's Rep IR 521).

Where an allegation is made that an unfair relationship exists, it is for the creditor to prove the contrary (s. 140B(9)).

Powers available

90.29 If the court decides that there is or was an unfair relationship, arising out of a credit agreement, it can exercise the following powers under the Consumer Credit Act 1974, s. 140B:

(a) require the creditor to repay any sum;
(b) require the creditor to do or not to do anything specified in the order;
(c) reduce or vary any sum payable;
(d) direct the return to any surety of any property provided by him as security;
(e) set aside in whole or in part any duty imposed on the debtor or surety;
(f) alter the terms of the agreement;
(g) direct accounts to be taken.

These powers can be exercised:

(a) on an application by the debtor or surety (s. 140B(2)(a)), which must be made to a county court (s. 140B(4)(a)); or
(b) at the instance of the debtor or surety in enforcement proceedings (s. 140B(2)(b)) or any other proceedings where the amount paid or payable is relevant (s. 140B(2)(c)).

The procedure to be adopted is set out in **PD 7B, para. 10**.

Transitional provisions

There are transitional provisions in the Consumer Credit Act 2006, sch. 3, paras 14 to 16. The court has power to make an order under the Consumer Credit Act 1974, s. 140B, in connection with an agreement made before 6 April 2007, but only: **90.30**

(a) on an application by the debtor or surety, under s. 140B(2)(a), made after 6 April 2008, or, under s. 140B(2)(b) or (c), in proceedings commenced before that date to enforce the agreement or any related agreement or in which the amount payable or paid is relevant; and
(b) if the agreement did not become a completed agreement before that date.

In determining whether or not an agreement is a related agreement, it is immaterial when the agreement was made.

CONSUMER RIGHTS (PAYMENT SURCHARGES) REGULATIONS 2012

The Consumer Rights (Payment Surcharges) Regulations 2012 (SI 2012/3110) prohibit surcharges imposed by traders on consumers in respect of the use of a given means of payment, where the surcharges exceed the cost to the trader of using that means of payment (reg. 4). The effect of this prohibition on contract terms is that any provision of a contract requiring a consumer to pay a prohibited fee is unenforceable to the extent of the excess charged, and the contract is to be treated as providing for the excess to be repaid to the consumer. Supplies of gas, electricity and water (except in limited quantities) and digital content are excluded (reg. 5(1)). There is a remarkably long list of exempted contracts (reg. 5(2)). **90.31**

These regulations came into force on 6 April 2013 and have given early implementation to one provision of the Consumer Rights Directive, which comes into force generally on 13 June 2014. Until the general implementation date, micro-businesses (fewer than 10 employees) are exempt (SI 2012/3110, reg. 6 and sch.).

Chapter 91 Human Rights and Civil Procedure

INTRODUCTION

On 2 October 2000 most provisions of the **Human Rights Act 1998** came into force in England and Wales and much of the European Convention on Human Rights was incorporated into English law. As a consequence, public authorities are required to comply with Convention rights such as the right to a fair hearing and freedom of expression. Individuals and companies are able to rely on the Convention directly in cases against the government and other public authorities. Also, courts and tribunals fall within the Act's definition of public authorities and so must comply with the Act. **91.1**

In 1951, the United Kingdom was amongst the first countries to ratify the European Convention on Human Rights. However, it was not until 2 October 2000 that the Convention could be directly relied upon in the English and Welsh courts. An individual who alleges an infringement of the Convention can still apply to the European Court of Human Rights in Strasbourg notwithstanding the right to rely on the Convention in the domestic courts. However, an application to Strasbourg may only be brought once all domestic remedies, including court and appeal hearings, have been exhausted. Proceedings may then be brought against the United Kingdom government, alleging a failure to ensure that national law is in accordance with the Convention (e.g. *Pretty v United Kingdom* (2002) 35 EHRR 1).

Until the **Human Rights Act 1998** came into force the role of the Convention in the English courts was restricted to, for example, being used to resolve an ambiguity (*R v Secretary of State for the Home Department, ex parte Brind* [1991] 1 AC 696) and being relied upon where the rules of common law or equity were uncertain (*R v Secretary of State for the Environment, ex parte NALGO* (1993) 5 Admin LR 785). Breaches of Convention rights occurring before the coming into force of the 1998 Act will not be entertained by the courts (*R v Lyons (No. 3)* [2002] UKHL 44, [2003] 1 AC 976), though earlier legislation must be interpreted in accordance with the Convention (see **91.3**).

In *Locabail (UK) Ltd v Waldorf Investment Corporation (No. 4)* [2000] UKHRR 592, the applicant applied in the High Court for a stay of execution of a warrant of possession while the European Court of Human Rights considered her complaint that she had been denied her right to a fair trial. The argument that success in Strasbourg would render the initial possession order unlawful did not succeed: the European Court of Human Rights is not a further court of appeal from the domestic courts.

Since the European Court of Human Rights is not an appellate court in the English jurisdiction, the English courts, in deciding whether to enforce their own judgments, do not have to take into account any ruling which the European Court might in the future give on an application regarding the circumstances of liability (*Westminster City Council v Porter* [2002] EWHC 1589 (Ch), [2003] Ch 436).

In relation to overseas territories, the Convention will only apply to nationals of that territory if the governing State has notified the Council of Europe of such intention under art. 56(1). The same principle will apply to protocols enacted under the Convention. Unless there is a specific extension to another territory for whose international relations a contracting State is responsible, actions affecting individuals in that territory will not be subject to the Convention (*R (Quark Fishing Ltd) v Secretary of State for Foreign and Commonwealth Affairs* [2005] UKHL 57, [2006] 1 AC 529). Furthermore, a national of a contracting State who is outside of the jurisdiction of that State cannot rely on the Convention or the Act if his rights are breached in a non-contracting State (see *R (Abbasi) v Secretary of State for Foreign and Commonwealth Affairs* [2002] EWCA Civ 1598, [2003] UKHRR 76, concerning a British national captured by United States forces in Afghanistan and detained in Guantánamo Bay in Cuba and note also *R (Al Rawi) v Secretary of State for Foreign and Commonwealth Affairs* [2006] EWCA Civ 1279, [2008] QB 289).

Where the US government sought to have a confiscation order made in the United States registered in the UK so that it could be enforced against the appellant's UK assets, it was accepted that the order would have constituted a breach of **art. 6** if it had taken place in a Convention State. However, given the territorial limitation on the reach of the Convention the House of Lords found that it was difficult to see how registration of the enforcement order in the UK could constitute a breach of the Convention. **Article 6** was therefore not engaged. Only a case of extreme unfairness (which this was not) would justify using the exception to the principle of territoriality so as to give indirect effect to the Convention (*Barnette v United States of America* [2004] UKHL 37, [2004] 1 WLR 2241). See also *United States of America v Montgomery (No. 2)* [2004] UKHL 37, [2004] 1 WLR 2241.

However, actions taken abroad by UK diplomatic or consular officials who exercise the authority of the State will be governed by domestic human rights law and therefore could be the subject of a claim under the **Human Rights Act 1998** (*R (B) v Secretary of State for Foreign and Commonwealth Affairs* [2004] EWCA Civ 1344, [2005] QB 643). This exception also extends to UK vessels, aircraft and even a British military prison operating in Iraq where the victim was within the jurisdiction of the UK for the purposes of **art. 1** of the Convention (*R (Al-Skeini) v Secretary of State for Defence* [2007] UKHL 26, [2008] 1 AC 153; confirmed by *Al-Skeini v United Kingdom* (application 55721/07) (2011) 53 EHRR 18). United Kingdom troops on active service overseas are within UK jurisdiction for the purposes of **art. 1** only when they are on a UK military base (*R (Smith) v Secretary of State for Defence* [2010] UKSC 29, [2011] 1 AC 1). Where British forces exercised complete control, both by force and in law, over premises in Iraq, prisoners detained by them were under the UK's jurisdiction for the purposes of **art. 1**; see European Court of Human Rights decision on admissibility, *Al-Saadoon v United Kingdom* (application 61498/08) (2009) 51 EHRR 9 and *Al-Skeini v United Kingdom*). There is a further exception to the principle of territoriality where the State party has 'effective control' of an area (either lawfully or unlawfully), but this does not apply in territories outside the regional sphere of the party States of the Convention.

Even where an act is carried out under authority of international law, that will not necessarily displace obligations under the **Human Rights Act 1998** since UN Resolutions, for example, should be interpreted with a presumption that they would not conflict with member States' obligations under human rights law. Where a UN Resolution authorised British forces to take any measures necessary for stability and security in Iraq this did not justify a breach of **art. 5** since it did not specifically authorise internment (*Al-Jedda v United Kingdom* (application 27021/08) (2011) 53 EHRR 23).

MAIN PROVISIONS OF THE HUMAN RIGHTS ACT 1998

Sources of European human rights law

91.2 By virtue of the **Human Rights Act 1998, s. 2(1)**, a court or tribunal determining a question which has arisen in connection with a Convention right must take into account any judgment, decision, declaration or advisory opinion of the European Court of Human Rights. The court or tribunal must also take into account any opinion or decision of the Commission or decision of the Committee of Ministers, whenever made or given, so far as, in the opinion of the court or tribunal, it is relevant to the proceedings in which that question has arisen. The words 'take into account' were chosen deliberately to make it clear that these decisions are to be used as guidance and are not intended to operate as binding precedent.

The House of Lords has explained that:

Under the Convention, the United Kingdom is bound to accept a judgment of the Strasbourg court as binding. But a court adjudicating in litigation in the United Kingdom about a domestic 'Convention right' is not bound by a decision of the Strasbourg court. It must take it into account. (*Re McKerr* [2004] UKHL 12, [2004] 1 WLR 807, per Lord Hoffmann at [66].)

However, Lord Rodger of Earlsferry, also in the House of Lords, has said:

while the decisions of the European Court of Human Rights on the interpretation of the Convention are not binding, they provide authoritative guidance which courts have to take into account when interpreting the rights in domestic law. (*R (S) v Chief Constable of the South Yorkshire Police* [2004] UKHL 39, [2004] 1 WLR 2196, at [66].)

Where there is a clear and consistent line of Strasbourg authority it would require some special reason to depart from that line of authority. Lord Bingham of Cornhill has commented that:

This reflects the fact that the Convention is an international instrument, the correct interpretation of which can be authoritatively expounded only by the Strasbourg court. From this it follows that a national court subject to a duty such as that imposed by s. 2 should not without strong reason dilute or weaken the effect of the Strasbourg case law. (*R (Ullah) v Secretary of State for the Home Department* [2004] UKHL 26, [2004] 2 AC 323, at [20].)

Although the non-binding status of Strasbourg authority is accepted, the correct approach seems to be that a clear line of authority is to be treated as so persuasive that only special reasons would justify departure from it. However, national courts are given a margin of appreciation in some areas, for example, where the Strasbourg court had decided previously that national courts could in general determine the rules for extinction of title and adverse possession and that the UK legislative provisions were Convention compliant in this area. Once such a margin of appreciation has been granted it applies to all cases and it is not open to the domestic court not to follow it because a case is distinguishable on the facts (*Ofulue v Bossert* [2008] EWCA Civ 7, [2009] Ch 1, affirmed on other grounds [2009] UKHL 16 [2009] 1 AC 990). Where the extent of the margin of appreciation has not been tested, domestic courts should not be inhibited from going further than the current state of authority of the Strasbourg court given the general margin of appreciation member States have in matters of delicate social policy. Therefore domestic courts are free to give what they consider to be a principled and rational interpretation in deciding that discrimination on the grounds of marital status would be likely to violate **art. 14**, notwithstanding that the matter has not yet been decided upon by the Strasbourg court (*Re G (Adoption: Unmarried Couple)* [2008] UKHL 38, [2009] 1 AC 173).

There may be cases where the Strasbourg jurisprudence is not entirely clear and the domestic courts may have difficulty in identifying clear principles from it. In *N v Secretary of State for the Home Department* [2005] UKHL 31, [2005] 2 AC 296, Lord Hope of Craighead expressed the view, at [25], that:

It is not for us to search for a solution…which is not to be found in the Strasbourg case law. It is for the Strasbourg court, not for us, to decide whether its case law is out of touch with modern conditions and to determine what further extensions, if any, are needed to the rights guaranteed by the Convention. We must take the case law as we find it, not as we would like it to be.

The duty to take into account decisions of the Strasbourg court does not displace the doctrine of precedent in domestic law, even where domestic authority appears to be inconsistent with Strasbourg case law. There is a clear duty to give practical recognition to the principles laid down by the Strasbourg court as governing the Convention rights. However, a court faced with an apparent inconsistency between a domestic decision of a higher court and a Strasbourg decision should still follow the domestic decision, under the normal rules of precedent, and should deal with the inconsistency by expressing a view on this and giving leave to appeal. By doing so the domestic court will have discharged its duty under the **Human Rights Act 1998** (*Kay v Lambeth London Borough Council* [2006] UKHL 10, [2006] 2 AC 465).

Interpretation of legislation

91.3 The interpretation of legislation is dealt with in the **Human Rights Act 1998, s. 3(1)**, which provides that so far as it is possible to do so, primary and subordinate legislation must be read and given effect in a way which is compatible with the Convention rights. **Section 3** applies to primary and subordinate legislation whenever enacted but does not affect the validity, continuing operation or enforcement of any incompatible primary legislation, or of any incompatible subordinate legislation if primary legislation prevents removal of the incompatibility (**s. 3(2)**). The courts are free to give a new meaning to legislation which they have interpreted previously where the earlier interpretation was in conflict with a Convention right. However, they will be reluctant to do so if the new interpretation of that legislation would affect transactions that have created rights and obligations on which the parties intend to rely. If interpreting legislation in line with **s. 3** would mean that the rights and obligations of the parties to an agreement entered into before 2 October 2000 would be different now to what they were at the time the agreement was entered into then this would result in unfairness to one or another of the parties (*Wilson v First County Trust Ltd (No. 2)* [2003] UKHL 40, [2004] 1 AC 816; *Law v Society of Lloyd's* [2003] EWCA Civ 1887, *The Times*, 23 January 2004).

Section 3 will sometimes require the adoption of an interpretation which linguistically may appear strained. The techniques to be used will not only involve the reading down of express language in a statute, but also the implications of provisions (*R v A (No. 2)* [2001] UKHL 25, [2002] 1 AC 45). However, a reading of legislation which 'departs substantially from a fundamental feature of an Act of Parliament is likely to have crossed the boundary between interpretation and amendment' (*Re S (Minors) (Care Order: Implementation of Care Plan)* [2002] UKHL 10, [2002] 2 AC 291, per Lord Nicholls of Birkenhead at [40]). The courts will not interpret legislation in a way which would effectively amend it. It must be possible to give the provision as it stands the Convention-compatible interpretation required by **s. 3** (*R (Wilkinson) v Commissioners of Inland Revenue* [2005] UKHL 30, [2005] 1 WLR 1718).

However, the House of Lords has held that the courts have in the past concentrated excessively on the linguistic features of the particular statute. Their lordships rejected a literal approach and instead emphasised a broad approach, which concentrated in a purposive way on the importance of the fundamental right involved (*Ghaidan v Godin-Mendoza* [2004] UKHL 30, [2004] 2 AC 557).

Declaration of incompatibility

91.4 Under the **Human Rights Act 1998, s. 4**, where the court is satisfied that a provision in primary legislation is incompatible with a Convention right, it may make a declaration of incompatibility. Such a declaration may also be made in proceedings in which a court considers that a provision of subordinate legislation, made in the exercise of a power conferred by primary legislation, is incompatible. Declarations of incompatibility may only be made in respect of subordinate legislation where the court is satisfied that (disregarding any possibility of revocation) the primary legislation concerned prevents removal of the incompatibility. A person cannot apply for a declaration of incompatibility unless he is adversely affected by the legislation in question (*Taylor v Lancashire County Council* [2005] EWCA Civ 284, [2005] 1 WLR 2668).

A declaration of incompatibility may be made only by the High Court, Court of Appeal or Supreme Court (**s. 4(5)**). Such a declaration is not binding on the parties to the proceedings *in which it is made* and does not affect the validity, continuing operation or enforcement of the provision in respect of which it is given (**s. 4(6)**). A declaration of incompatibility does, however, enable Parliament to amend the relevant legislation through a fast-track procedure.

The court may not make a declaration of incompatibility unless 21 days' notice, or such other period of notice as the court directs, has been given to the Crown. Where notice has been given to the Crown, a minister or other person permitted by the Act shall be joined as a party on giving notice to the court (**CPR, r. 19.4A**). The Crown should be joined to the proceedings in advance of any appeal hearing in which an issue is raised which might lead the Supreme Court to consider making a declaration of incompatibility (*R v A* [2001] 1 WLR 789).

A number of declarations of incompatibility have been made by the courts, including declarations in respect of:

(a) the Mental Health Act 1983, s. 73, which placed the burden of proof on a restricted patient to show that he was no longer suffering from a mental disorder warranting detention in order to satisfy the mental health review tribunal that he was entitled to discharge, contrary to **art. 5** of the Convention (*R (H) v Mental Health Review Tribunal, North and East Region* [2001] EWCA Civ 415, [2002] QB 1);

(b) part 2 of the Immigration and Asylum Act 1999, which penalised carriers of illegal immigrants into the United Kingdom, in breach of **art. 6** of the Convention (*International Transport Roth GmbH v Secretary of State for the Home Department* [2002] EWCA Civ 158, [2003] QB 728);

(c) the Social Security Contributions and Benefits Act 1992, ss. 36 to 38, which applied a different treatment of benefits as between widows and widowers, contrary to **art. 8** of the Convention (*R (Hooper) v Secretary of State for Work and Pensions* [2005] UKHL 29, [2005] 1 WLR 1681);

(d) the Matrimonial Causes Act 1973, s. 11(c), which requires a marriage to be between a man and a woman in order for it to be valid, contrary to **arts 8** and **12** of the Convention (in the context of post-operative transsexuals applying for a marriage declaration) (*Bellinger v Bellinger* [2003] UKHL 21, [2003] 2 AC 467);

(e) the Housing Act 1996, s. 185(4), which had the effect that a person who had been subject to immigration control was not afforded the same priority need for accommodation as a comparable person who had not been subject to immigration control, thus infringing **art. 14** in conjunction with **art. 8** (*R (Morris) v Westminster City Council* [2005] EWCA Civ 1184, [2006] 1 WLR 505);

(f) the Care Standards Act 2000, s. 82(4)(b), pursuant to which care workers could be provisionally listed as unsuited to working with vulnerable adults, without giving them an opportunity to answer the allegations, contrary to **arts 6(1)** and **8(1)** (*R (Wright) v Secretary of State for Health* [2009] UKHL 3, [2009] 1 AC 739).

It appears that the declaration of incompatibility procedure cannot extend to breaches of positive rights. That is, the absence of a provision guaranteeing a particular Convention right in statute does not in itself mean that the statute is incompatible with **art. 6(1)** of the Convention, but rather signifies at most the existence of a lacuna in the statute (see Lord Nicholls of Birkenhead in *Re S (Minors) (Care Order: Implementation of Care Plan)* [2002] UKHL 10, [2002] 2 AC 291 at p. 322).

Statement of compatibility

Since 24 November 1998, under the **Human Rights Act 1998, s. 19**, a minister of the Crown **91.5**
in charge of a Bill in either House of Parliament has been required before the second reading of the Bill:

(a) to make a statement to the effect that in his or her view the provisions of the Bill are compatible with Convention rights ('a statement of compatibility'); or

(b) to make a statement to the effect that although he or she is unable to make a statement of compatibility the government nevertheless wishes the House to proceed with the Bill.

This statement must be in writing and be published in such manner as the minister making it considers appropriate. The statement of compatibility is designed to minimise the number of domestic statutes that are incompatible with Convention rights.

Obligations of public authorities

91.6 The **Human Rights Act 1998, s. 6**, requires public authorities to act in a way which is compatible with Convention rights. **Section 6(1)** provides that: 'It is unlawful for a public authority to act in a way which is incompatible with a Convention right'. An 'act' includes a failure to act but, by **s. 6(6)**, does not include a failure: (a) to introduce in, or lay before, Parliament a proposal for legislation; or (b) to make any primary legislation or remedial order.

The Act provides no exhaustive definition of a public authority. Bodies such as government departments, local authorities, the police and health authorities will clearly be considered public authorities. In addition to these traditional public authorities, the definition of a public authority also includes bodies 'certain of whose functions are functions of a public nature' (**s. 6(3)**) and these are known as quasi-public authorities. Traditional public organisations must act in accordance with the Convention in respect of all their functions — whether under public or private law — but quasi-public authorities are only required to conform to the Convention in relation to public functions and not private law matters. For example, doctors in general practice will be considered as public authorities in relation to their National Health Service functions, but not in relation to their private patients.

A housing association generally is not a public authority for the purposes of **s. 6** (*R (Heather) v Leonard Cheshire Foundation* [2001] EWHC Admin 429, [2002] 2 All ER 936) nor is a private-sector service provider which has a contractual relationship with a local authority to supply residential accommodation (*R (Servite Houses) v Goldsmith* (2001) 33 HLR 35). However, a housing association may be deemed to be a public authority if it was created by a local authority which controls it and has an integrated relationship with it (*Poplar Housing and Regeneration Community Association Ltd v Donoghue* [2001] EWCA Civ 595, [2002] QB 48). Similarly, a private limited company set up by a local authority to manage local farmers' markets and having as directors, stallholders in those markets, was a public authority since the company owed its existence to the authority and initially worked alongside it (*R (Beer) v Hampshire Farmers Market Ltd* [2003] EWCA Civ 1056, [2004] 1 WLR 233).

In all cases it is necessary to look at the context and the basis on which a private law body acted, with the ultimate focus on the nature of the functions undertaken. The State can in some circumstances remain responsible for the conduct of a private body to which it has delegated State powers, but the mere possession of special powers conferred by Parliament does not of itself mean that the body has functions of a public nature. Equally there could be bodies without special statutory powers that fall within the definition of public authority. Where a body acted as a private, profit-making company, that motivation would point against treating it as a body with functions of a public nature (see *YL v Birmingham City Council* [2007] UKHL 27, [2008] 1 AC 95, where it was decided that a private care home, when providing care to a resident pursuant to agreements made with a local authority under the relevant legislation, was not performing functions of a public nature within the meaning of **s. 6(3)(b)**). On the other hand, in *R (Weaver) v London and Quadrant Housing Trust* [2009] EWCA Civ 587, [2010] 1 WLR 363, it was held that a registered social landlord was performing a public function for the purposes of **s. 6(3)(b)** when it terminated a tenancy. The Court of Appeal found that the function of allocating and managing subsidised housing was a governmental function and that the act of termination was so inextricably linked to that function that it was also a public act. It was found that it would severely limit the significance of identifying certain bodies as hybrid or quasi-public authorities if the fact that the relevant act was contractual meant that it was necessarily a private act falling within **s. 6(5)**.

Bodies which have been held not to be a public authority for the purposes of s. 6 include: a parochial church council in the context of its service of notices on lay rectors, living in church property, requiring them to fund necessary repairs to the chancel (*Aston Cantlow and Wilmcote with Billesley Parochial Church Council v Wallbank* [2003] UKHL 37, [2004] 1 AC 546); the RSPCA in the context of its intention to adopt a policy to exclude from membership persons whose application was for the real or predominant purpose of bringing about a change in RSPCA policy in respect of field sports (*Royal Society for the Prevention of Cruelty to Animals v Attorney-General* [2002] 1 WLR 448); an adjudicator exercising functions under the Housing Grants, Construction and Regeneration Act 1996 (*Austin Hall Building Ltd v Buckland Securities Ltd* [2001] BLR 272); the Jockey Club (*R (Mullins) v Appeal Board of the Jockey Club* [2005] EWHC 2197 (Admin), [2006] ACD 2) and Railtrack (*Cameron v Network Rail Infrastructure Ltd* [2006] EWHC 1133 (QB), [2007] 1 WLR 163).

Section 6(2) may provide a defence to an allegation of a breach of the Convention under **s. 6(1)** either if the public authority could not have acted differently under the relevant statute (**s. 6(2)(a)**) or if the public authority was acting so as to give effect to the relevant legislation (**s. 6(2)(b)**) (e.g. *R (Hooper) v Secretary of State for Work and Pensions* [2005] UKHL 29, [2005] 1 WLR 1681).

Section 6(3) expressly includes courts and tribunals as public authorities. Courts and tribunals therefore will be bound to act in a manner that is compatible with the Convention. Unless legislation explicitly states otherwise, judges need to be mindful of the Convention in all proceedings, even those involving only private parties. The Act is therefore developing a degree of ***horizontal effect*** between private individuals and companies as well as the intended ***vertical effect*** between public authorities and individuals, both because of s. 6 and because of the Convention's influence on the common law, as in *Douglas v Hello! Ltd* [2001] QB 967.

Both Houses of Parliament are outside the definition of public authority (**s. 6(3)**).

Victims

Proceedings alleging a breach of Convention rights may only be brought by a 'victim' (**Human Rights Act 1998, s.** 7). The term 'victim' in this context has a more restrictive definition than that used to establish standing in judicial review. Companies and individuals are able to invoke the Convention. Although the point has not been fully argued, it seems that parents of a minor whose human rights have been breached do have standing to complain as victims under **s.** 7 (*R (Holub) v Secretary of State for the Home Department* [2001] 1 WLR 1359). However, public-interest and pressure groups are unable to bring claims based on the **Human Rights Act 1998** unless a 'victim' is found to act as a figurehead applicant (e.g. *Greenpeace Schweiz v Switzerland* (1997) 23 EHRR CD 116). A trade association is not a victim for this purpose (*Re Medicaments and Related Classes of Goods (No. 4)* [2001] EWCA Civ 1217, [2002] 1 WLR 269). A local authority cannot be a victim for the purposes of **s.** 7 (*R (Westminster City Council) v Mayor of London* [2002] EWHC 2440 (Admin), [2003] LGR 611), nor can an NHS trust (*Grampian University Hospitals NHS Trust v Napier* 2004 JC 117). The expected recipient of a pending decision is not a victim for the purposes of **s. 7** because no act or decision capable of being the subject of judicial review has taken place (*R (Hirst) v Secretary of State for the Home Department* [2002] EWHC 1592 (Admin)). 91.7

Time limits

Cases against public bodies alleging a breach of the Convention must be brought within one year of the date on which the relevant act took place (**Human Rights Act 1998, s.** 7(5)). This time limit may be extended where the court considers it equitable to do so, for instance where the cause of the delay is out of the claimant's hands and the balance of potential prejudice lies in the claimant's favour in the context of a well-founded claim alleging serious 91.8

shortcomings that need to be properly explored (*D v Commissioner of Police of the Metropolis* [2012] EWHC 309 (QB), LTL 23/2/2012). However, where another rule imposes a shorter time limit (e.g. the judicial review time limit) the shorter time limit prevails (s. 7(5)).

Remedies

91.9 The **Human Rights Act 1998, s. 8**, provides that in relation to any act (or proposed act) of a public authority which the court finds is (or would be) unlawful, it may grant such relief or remedy or make such order within its powers as it considers just and appropriate. A court may grant any remedy which it deems appropriate provided that it has jurisdiction to grant that remedy (**s. 8(11)**).

Damages may be awarded only by a court which has power to make such an award, or to order the payment of compensation, in civil proceedings **s. 8(2)**. No award may be made unless the court is satisfied that such an award is necessary to 'afford just satisfaction to the person in whose favour it is made' **s. 8(3)** and in considering an award, a court must take into account all the circumstances of the case including:

(a) any other relief or remedy granted, or order made, in relation to the act in question (by that or any other court); and
(b) the consequences of any decision (of that or any other court) in respect of that act.

In determining whether to award damages or the amount of an award, the court must take into account the principles applied by the European Court of Human Rights in relation to the award of compensation under art. 41 of the Convention. Article 41 also proceeds on the basis of affording 'just satisfaction'. There is no automatic entitlement to an award of damages and the Strasbourg court's decision is guided by the particular circumstances of each case having regard to equitable considerations. The European Court of Human Rights often holds that no award of damages should be made since a finding of violation may itself constitute sufficient 'just satisfaction' (e.g. *R (Greenfield) v Secretary of State for the Home Department* [2005] UKHL 14, [2005] 1 WLR 673). Otherwise, the court's awards of damages are usually modest although in some cases, particularly relating to an infringement of property rights, such as expropriation, substantial damages may be awarded.

Where an individual was detained under powers conferred by the Mental Health Act 1983, and then later applied for the Mental Health Review Tribunal to review the detention, delays occurring in the hearings of those applications were held to constitute an infringement of **art.** 5(4) and an award for damages under **art.** 5(5) would be made 'where necessary' if on the facts the distress and frustration that occurred justified such an award. By contrast, when awarding damages for custodial detention for a prolonged period due to delay by State authorities, in breach of **art.** 5(4), it was not appropriate to award damages for distress and anxiety separately from the damages awarded for loss of liberty (*R (Faulkner) v Secretary of State for Justice* [2011] EWCA Civ 349, [2011] HRLR 23). See also *R (Hester) v Secretary of State for Justice* [2011] EWHC 3926 (Admin), LTL 20/12/2011. There may, however, be occasions where aggravated damages under **art.** 5 will be appropriate. In *R (M) v Secretary of State for the Home Department* [2011] EWHC 3667 (Admin), [2012] ACD 34, the Secretary of State's behaviour in removing the claimant family on an erroneous ground, failing to notify them in advance of their removal and her subsequent delay in admitting the unlawful nature of the detention and removal justified such a remedy.

In assessing quantum an English court should derive assistance from similar Strasbourg cases rather than from English decisions in analogous cases (*van Colle v Chief Constable of the Hertfordshire Police* [2007] EWCA Civ 325, [2007] 1 WLR 1821; reversed on another point [2008] UKHL 50, [2009] 1 AC 225). See also *Anufrijeva v Southwark London Borough Council* [2003] EWCA Civ 1406, [2004] QB 1124.

Damages may be awarded for future infringement of rights under the **Human Rights Act 1998** (*Marcic v Thames Water Utilities Ltd (No. 2)* [2001] EWHC Technology 394, [2002] QB 1003; although on the facts there was no infringement: *Marcic v Thames Water Utilities Ltd* [2003] UKHL 66, [2004] 2 AC 42).

An individual applicant in judicial review proceedings is not entitled to claim damages under the **Human Rights Act 1998** in respect of a local authority's conduct in breach of the European Convention on Human Rights, on the basis that proceedings for judicial review are not brought 'by or at the instigation of a public authority' under the **Human Rights Act 1998, s. 22(4)** (*R (Ben-Abdelaziz) v Haringey London Borough Council* [2001] EWCA Civ 303, [2001] 1 WLR 1485).

The Strasbourg court also has the power to make a costs order.

Judicial acts

Courts and tribunals are public authorities for the purposes of the **Human Rights Act 1998** (by **s. 6(3)**) but **s. 9** provides that proceedings in respect of a judicial act may be brought only: **91.10**

(a) by exercising a right of appeal;
(b) on an application for judicial review; or
(c) in such other forum as may be prescribed by rules.

Any rule of law which prevents a court from being the subject of judicial review is not affected (**s. 9(2)**). Where proceedings are brought in respect of a judicial act done in good faith, damages may be awarded to compensate the victim only to the extent required by **art. 5(5)** of the Convention (which provides that everyone who has been the victim of arrest or detention in contravention of the provisions of **art. 5** shall have an enforceable right to compensation). A claim in respect of a judicial act maybe brought only in the High Court (**CPR, r. 7.11(1)**). Where a claim is in respect of a judicial act which is alleged to have infringed the claimant's **art. 5** rights and which is based on a finding by a court or tribunal that the claimant's Convention rights have been infringed, the court hearing the claim (a) may proceed on the basis of the finding of that other court or tribunal that there has been an infringement but it is not required to do so, and (b) may reach its own conclusion in the light of that finding and of the evidence heard by that other court or tribunal (**CPR, r. 33.9**).

Where a claim is made under the **Human Rights Act 1998** for damages in respect of a judicial act that claim must be set out in the statement of case or the appeal notice; and notice must be given to the Crown. Where the appropriate person has not applied to be joined as a party within 21 days, or such other period as the court directs, after the notice is served, the court may join the appropriate person as a party (**CPR, r. 19.4A**).

Proceedings affecting the right to freedom of expression

The **Human Rights Act 1998, s. 12**, applies where a court (or tribunal) is considering granting relief in civil proceedings which might affect the exercise of the right to freedom of expression (**s. 12(1)** and **(5)**). The court must not grant such relief if the person against whom the application is made (the respondent) is not present, unless the court is satisfied that the applicant has taken all practicable steps to notify the respondent or there are compelling reasons why the respondent should not be notified (**s. 12(2)**). No relief is to be granted so as to restrain publication before trial, unless the court is satisfied that the applicant is likely to establish that publication should not be allowed (**s. 12(3)**). This means that an applicant's prospects of success at trial must be sufficiently favourable to justify an order being made in the particular circumstances of the case and a court will be 'very slow' to make an interim restraint order unless satisfied that the applicant is more likely than not to succeed at trial, but there will be cases where a lesser **91.11** degree of likelihood will suffice (*Cream Holdings Ltd v Banerjee* [2004] UKHL 44, [2005] 1 AC 253 and see, e.g. *E v Channel Four* [2005] EWHC 1144 (Fam), [2005] 2 FLR 913). The court must have 'particular regard' to the importance of the right of freedom of expression (**s. 12(4)**). If the proceedings relate to journalistic, literary or artistic material the court is required by **s. 12(4)** to have particular regard to two conflicting factors:

(a) the extent to which the material has, or is about to, become available to the public, or it is, or would be, in the public interest for the material to be published; and
(b) any relevant privacy code.

CONVENTION RIGHTS

Derogation from Convention rights

91.12 The Convention rights which are incorporated into domestic law are set out in the **Human Rights Act 1998, sch. 1**. The articles detailing the Convention rights fall into three broad groups: those which are absolute, those which may be derogated from and those which are qualified. Those that are absolute must never be infringed by any of the Convention States. An example is **art. 3**, which prohibits torture or inhuman or degrading treatment. Some rights may be derogated from, for example, in times of war or other emergency which threatens a State. The United Kingdom entered a derogation, which was set out in **sch. 3** to the Act, from **art. 5** of the Convention (right to liberty and security) so that foreign nationals who were suspected international terrorists thought to be a risk to national security could be detained indefinitely to await deportation but this was held by the House of Lords to be disproportionate and discriminatory (*A (FC) v Secretary of State for the Home Department* [2004] UKHL 56, [2005] 2 AC 68) and has been withdrawn.

Certain rights are qualified in order to balance the competing interests of individuals as against the public interest or, indeed, the interests of other individuals. Qualified rights are, therefore, rights with which a State may legitimately interfere in the interests of the protection of others or of the State itself. Qualified rights are set out in **arts 8 to 11**, all of which provide that interference with the rights must be in accordance with the law, pursuant to a legitimate aim and necessary in a democratic society.

Any interference with a qualified Convention right must be necessary in a democratic society and consequently 'correspond to a pressing social need' (*Dudgeon v United Kingdom* (1981) 4 EHRR 149) and 'be proportionate to the legitimate aim pursued' (*Silver v United Kingdom* (1983) 5 EHRR 347). State intervention in the lives of individuals should be minimal, and the duty of the State to protect legitimate aims does not permit it to restrict disproportionately the rights of individuals. When considering whether or not a measure is proportionate the court is to conduct a balancing exercise 'between the demands of the general interests of the community and the requirement of the protection of the individual's fundamental rights' (*Soering v United Kingdom* (1989) 11 EHRR 439).

Proportionality

91.13 When considering whether Convention rights have been breached, the European Court of Human Rights has employed the principle of 'proportionality'. A restriction on a freedom guaranteed by the Convention must be 'proportionate to the legitimate aim pursued' (*Handyside v United Kingdom* (1976) 1 EHRR 737). Proportionality is established if the legislative objective is sufficiently important to justify limiting a fundamental right, the measures designed to meet the legislative objective are rationally connected to that objective, and the means used to impair the right are no more than necessary to accomplish the legitimate objective (*De Freitas v Permanent Secretary of Ministry of Agriculture, Fisheries, Lands and Housing* [1999] 1 AC 69; and see, e.g. *R (Countryside Alliance) v Attorney-General* [2005] EWHC 1677 (Admin), [2005] NPC 107; [2006] EWCA Civ 817, [2007] QB 305; [2007] UKHL 52, [2008] 1 AC 719).

The proportionality of any interference may now be an issue in any consideration by the courts of certain articles of the Convention. Proportionality has to be considered in two distinct stages, first to ask whether the objective of the measure could be achieved by means involving less interference with an individual's rights, and secondly, to ask whether the measure has an excessive or disproportionate effect on the interests of affected persons. In deciding this last question, the Strasbourg Court assesses whether a fair balance has been struck between the individual's rights and those of the State (*R (Samaroo) v Secretary of State for the Home Department* [2001] UKHRR 1150). The question of whether a fair balance has been struck between the rights of the individual and the rights of the community as a whole is an important one which should never be overlooked in assessing proportionality (*Huang v Secretary of State for the Home Department* [2007] UKHL 11, [2007] 2 AC 167, citing *R (Razgar) v Secretary of State for the Home Department* [2004] UKHL 27, [2004] 2 AC 368). See also **77.20**.

Where Convention rights are in question as part of a judicial review, therefore, the court must not simply exercise a review function but should instead consider for itself whether the relevant Convention rights have been violated (*Secretary of State for the Home Department v Nasseri* [2009] UKHL 23, [2010] 1 AC 1).

Margin of appreciation

When considering whether Convention rights, particularly qualified rights, have been breached, the European Court of Human Rights has employed the concept of the 'margin of appreciation', which permits a State latitude in the manner in which it takes and enforces public policy decisions. This makes allowances for each country's cultural and political identities as it adopts and adapts to this international treaty. For example, what might constitute free speech in one country could be interpreted as an invasion of privacy in another. However, the doctrine cannot directly be applied to cases where United Kingdom courts interpret Convention rights under the **Human Rights Act 1998** because domestic courts can be expected to have a better understanding of domestic UK issues than the Strasbourg court. The domestic application of this doctrine was examined by Lord Hope of Craighead in *R v Director of Public Prosecutions, ex parte Kebilene* [2000] 2 AC 326. He recognised that in certain areas (e.g. economic and social policy) the executive will be given an area of judgment within which the judiciary will defer to the decision in question. **91.14**

ARTICLES OF THE CONVENTION INCORPORATED INTO THE HUMAN RIGHTS ACT 1998

Article 2: right to life

Article 2 establishes a country's positive duty to take steps to safeguard the lives of its citizens, and sets out the limited exceptions to the right to life. These centre on the maintenance of law and order and focus on curbing violence and controlling criminals and prisoners. The overriding objective is to limit the level of permissible force to that which is 'absolutely necessary'. **91.15**

Article 3: prohibition of torture

Article 3 prohibits torture and inhuman or degrading treatment or punishment. This article cannot be derogated from even in times of war and public emergency. Article 3, together with the common law position and other international conventions, requires that evidence obtained by torture should be inadmissible as unreliable, unfair and offensive to ordinary standards of humanity and decency. Whether and in what circumstances this rule could be overridden must be left to the legislature, and would require nothing short of an express legislative provision. Evidence should not be admitted where it is concluded on a balance of probabilities that **91.16**

Commentary

it was obtained by torture. If there is doubt as to whether the evidence was obtained by torture or not, then it should be admitted but the doubt should be borne in mind when evaluating the evidence (*A v Secretary of State for the Home Department (No. 2)* [2005] UKHL 71, [2006] 2 AC 221).

Article 4: prohibition of slavery and forced labour

91.17 There can be no derogation from this article under any circumstances.

Article 5: right to liberty and security of person

91.18 Article 5 aims to ensure that no one is deprived of liberty in an arbitrary fashion. It provides that a person can be deprived of liberty only in limited cases.

Article 6: right to a fair trial

91.19 Article 6(1) provides:

> In the determination of his civil rights and obligations or of any criminal charge against him, everyone is entitled to a fair and public hearing within a reasonable time by an independent and impartial tribunal established by law. Judgment shall be pronounced publicly but the press and public may be excluded from all or part of the trial in the interest of morals, public order or national security in a democratic society, where the interests of juveniles or the protection of the private life of the parties so require, or to the extent strictly necessary in the opinion of the court in special circumstances where publicity would prejudice the interests of justice.

91.20 **Scope of article 6(1)** In addition to court and arbitration hearings, **art. 6(1)** will cover other proceedings which determine rights or obligations. For example, **art. 6(1)** applies to disciplinary proceedings which determine the right of someone to practise a profession (*Le Compte v Belgium* (1981) 4 EHRR 1). On the other hand, for example, a reprimand or the imposition of a fine following a disciplinary hearing held in private by a domestic tribunal of the Law Society does not involve a determination of civil rights and obligations and therefore **art. 6** is not engaged (*R (Thompson) v Law Society* [2004] EWCA Civ 167, [2004] 1 WLR 2522). **Article 6(1)** has no relevance to an investigation under the Companies Act 1985, part 14, which makes a critical report, as this does not determine the criticised person's rights (*Fayed v United Kingdom* (1994) 18 EHRR 393). An assessment of refugee status does not amount to civil proceedings for the purposes of **art. 6** (*HH (Iran) v Secretary of State for the Home Department* [2008] EWCA Civ 504, LTL 14/4/2008). The right to accommodation given by the Children Act 1989, s. 20, is (probably) not a civil right for the purposes of **art. 6** (*R (A) v Croydon London Borough Council* [2008] EWCA Civ 1445, [2009] 1 FLR 1325; [2009] UKSC 8, [2009] 1 WLR 2557 at [45] and [65]). Indeed, any situations where the award of services or benefits depends on a series of evaluative judgments by the provider, rather than being rights of which the applicant could consider himself the holder, would not give rise to 'civil rights' and therefore would not engage **art. 6(1)**. Rights to accommodation under the Housing Act 1993 fall within this category (*Ali v Birmingham City Council* [2010] UKSC 8, [2010] 2 AC 39). If there is no exercisable right in domestic law then there will be no right to a determination under **art. 6** (*R (Kehoe) v Secretary of State for Work and Pensions* [2005] UKHL 48, [2006] 1 AC 42).

'Civil rights and obligations' are given an autonomous meaning. For example, the right to practise medicine was held to be a civil right despite its domestic categorisation as public (*König v Germany* (1978) 2 EHRR 170).

The classification of proceedings as 'civil' will not conclusively determine whether a matter should be regarded as civil. When considering whether a matter is civil or criminal (with the additional safeguards which attach to the latter) the European Court of Human Rights looks at three factors: (a) how the proceedings are classified in domestic law; (b) the nature of the offence; and (c) the possible sanctions (*Engel v Netherlands* (1976) 1 EHRR 647). For example, proceedings to obtain an anti-social behaviour order are civil (*Clingham v Kensington and Chelsea Royal London Borough Council* [2002] UKHL 39, [2003] 1 AC 787) as were proceedings before the disciplinary and appeals tribunals of the Securities and Futures Authority (*R (Fleurose) v Securities and Futures Authority* [2001] EWCA Civ 2015, [2002] IRLR 297).

The European Court of Human Rights has held that substantive tax matters are outside the scope of **art. 6** (*Ferrazzini v Italy* [2001] STC 1314). Although the imposition of tax surcharges does not determine any civil rights or obligations within **art. 6** (*Bancroft v Crutchfield* [2002] STC 347), a VAT assessment has been held to determine a civil right, but not a criminal charge, on the basis that it is civil in nature and there is no penal or deterrent element (*Ali v Commissioners of Customs and Excise* (2002) LTL 15/7/2002). Proceedings brought in a magistrates' court for condemnation of goods seized by customs officers are civil not criminal (*R (Mudie) v Dover Magistrates' Court* [2003] EWCA Civ 237, [2003] QB 1238) and the same classification applies to an application for restoration of goods seized by customs officers (*Gora v Commissioners of Customs and Excise* [2003] EWCA Civ 525, [2004] QB 93). Determinations of penalties by Inland Revenue commissioners (*King v Walden* [2001] STC 822) and the imposition of penalties by Customs and Excise for dishonest evasion of VAT (*Han v Commissioners of Customs and Excise* [2001] EWCA Civ 1040, [2001] 1 WLR 2253) have been held to be criminal but the imposition of a fixed penalty of £50 for a failure to supply documents and information pursuant to a notice was held to be civil (*Sharkey v Commissioners of HM Revenue and Customs* [2006] EWHC 300 (Ch), [2006] STC 2026).

It is possible for a party to expressly or impliedly waive rights under **art. 6**. Where criminal proceedings were found to be incompatible with the offenders' rights under **art. 6** but the offenders had delayed by more than two years in objecting to those proceedings, this was held to be acquiescence to the resulting convictions and sentences (*Ruddy v Procurator Fiscal* [2006] HRLR 16). Parties who enter into arbitration agreements are contracting into the restricted supervisory regime of the Arbitration Act 1996. These restricted provisions are not inconsistent with the Convention. Equally if they mutually agreed to exclude a right of appeal altogether, that would not be contrary to **art. 6** as they had preferred the 1996 process and could not therefore be permitted to rely on **art. 6** (*Sumukan Ltd v Commonwealth Secretariat* [2007] EWCA Civ 243, [2007] Bus LR 1075). A party could be taken to have waived his right to go to court under **art. 6** in favour of the arbitral process (*Stretford v Football Association Ltd* [2007] EWCA Civ 238, [2007] Bus LR 1052). However, if there was duress or undue influence which invalidated the arbitration agreement, there would be no waiver of relevant rights under **art. 6** (*El Nasharty v J. Sainsbury plc* [2007] EWHC 2618 (Comm), [2008] 1 Lloyd's Rep 360).

Rights protected by article 6 The **art. 6(1)** requirement to provide a fair hearing breaks down into various rights: **91.21**

(a) The right of access to a court, which is an integral part of **art. 6(1)** despite not being expressly set out there (*Jones v Ministry of the Interior of Saudi Arabia* [2004] EWCA Civ 1394, [2005] UKHRR 57 reversed in part, although not on this point, [2006] UKHL 26, [2007] 1 AC 270). The **Fatal Accidents Act 1976, s. 2(3)** (which provides that not more than one action should lie for and in respect of the same subject matter of complaint), has been construed in such a way as to safeguard the right of access to a court (*Cachia v Faluyi* [2001] EWCA Civ 998, [2001] 1 WLR 1966).

(b) A hearing in one's own presence. There is a right to an oral hearing although in a civil trial a party has the right to be present only if the tribunal is required to carry out an appraisal of his or her personal character (*Muyldermans v Belgium* (1991) 15 EHRR 204).

(c) Equality of arms. In putting its case, a party must not be put at a substantial disadvantage as regards the opposing party. Thus, for example, each party must have the same opportunity to summon witnesses and each party must have an opportunity to oppose the arguments advanced by the other side. Both the common law and the Convention regard fairness as including the need for the court to know, before it reaches its conclusion, what the parties have to say about the issues and the evidence that the court has before it.

Where the judge in an Admiralty claim has sought advice from nautical assessors, for example, that advice should be disclosed to the parties for them to make their own representations as to whether the judge should accept the advice (*Bow Spring (Owners) v Manzanillo II (Owners)* [2004] EWCA Civ 1007, [2005] 1 WLR 144).

(d) Prejudicial publicity. There should be no commentary which prejudges the accused in a criminal trial.

(e) Reasoned judgment. Judgments must be supported by reasoning. The extent and substance of the reasons depend upon the circumstances. They need not be elaborate or lengthy, but they should be such as to tell the parties in broad terms why the decision was reached (*Stefan v General Medical Council* [1999] 1 WLR 1293).

(f) A public hearing. An oral public hearing must be available unless exceptional circumstances dictate otherwise (*Werner v Austria* (1997) 26 EHRR 310). This is not absolute but can be limited only to the extent that is 'strictly necessary…in special circumstances'.

(g) A hearing within a reasonable time. Numerous factors will have a bearing on what constitutes a reasonable time from the commencement of proceedings to the final determin-ation of the case, for instance, the importance of the subject matter, the difficulties of the case, whether they be legal or factual, and the behaviour of the individual and the public body (e.g. *EDC v United Kingdom* [1998] BCC 370 concerning the length of time taken to deal with directors disqualification proceedings).

(h) An independent and impartial tribunal. To assess independence, it is necessary to have regard to the manner of appointment of a tribunal's members, their term of office, the existence of guarantees against outside pressures and whether the body presents an appearance of independence (*Bryan v United Kingdom* (1995) 21 EHRR 342). The appearance of independence of any tribunal is to be assessed on an objective basis. 'Impartial' means lack of prejudice or bias (*Piersack v Belgium* (1982) 5 EHRR 169). A tribunal and its members are to be presumed impartial unless proved otherwise (*Le Compte v Belgium* (1981) 4 EHRR 1). The court will examine the actual prejudices, if any, the tribunal holds and also whether undertakings given by the tribunal are sufficient to exclude doubts over impartiality (see further **61.27** and 77.25).

(i) A tribunal established by law. The de facto doctrine validates the acts as well as the office of a judge, where he mistakenly presides over a court without proper authority, when the world at large believes that he has proper authority (*Coppard v Commissioners of Customs and Excise* [2003] EWCA Civ 511, [2003] QB 1428).

91.22 **Specific guarantees in criminal cases** Article 6(2) preserves the principle that the accused is innocent until proved guilty. It does not, however, prevent a burden being placed on the accused to prove a defence. Nor does it prohibit presumptions of law or fact. Strict liability offences are acceptable under art. 6(2) so long as they still require the prosecution to establish the elements of the offence (Salabiaku v France (1988) 13 EHRR 379).

Article 6(3) guarantees five further rights in criminal cases. These lay down the minimum requirements for procedural fairness in a criminal trial. They are not exhaustive. Indeed, **art.** 6(1) may require further protection to be given than is provided for by **art.** 6(3). The **art.** 6(3) rights are the right to be informed of a charge, adequate time and facilities for the preparation of a defence, legal representation including legal aid, attendance and examination of witnesses and free translation. In *Kulkarni v Milton Keynes Hospital NHS Foundation Trust* [2009] EWCA Civ 789, [2010] ICR 101, the Court of Appeal suggested that the right to legal representation may extend to internal disciplinary proceedings where the consequence of such proceedings would be the end of an individual's professional career.

Article 7: no punishment without lawful authority

Article 7 protects citizens against retrospective criminal laws. A defendant may not be convicted in a criminal case when the relevant action was not illegal at the time it was carried out.

Article 8: right to respect for private and family life

Article 8(1) provides that 'Everyone has the right to respect for his private and family life, his home and his correspondence'. This article imposes primarily negative obligations on the State not to disclose or delve into personal matters confidential to an individual. **91.24**

Private life has been held to have a broad definition including the protection of corporeal rights, personal identity, private space, and respect for sexual orientation (*Dudgeon v United Kingdom* (1981) 4 EHRR 149). As a result, for instance, compulsory blood (*X v Austria* (1979) 18 DR 154) and urine (*Peters v Netherlands* (1994) 77-A DR 75) tests and severe corporal punishment (*B v United Kingdom* (1998) 5 BHRC 137) have been found to violate **art. 8**. Not only does respect for the home include a residence but it can also include an office and business premises (*Niemietz v Germany* (1992) 16 EHRR 97). However, it is unclear whether or not a company can have a right to a private life. In *R v Broadcasting Standards Commission, ex parte British Broadcasting Corporation* [2001] QB 885 it was held that the BBC's actions in surreptitiously filming on a company's premises constituted an unwarranted infringement of the company's privacy under the Broadcasting Act 1996. However, Lord Woolf MR emphasised that the meaning of privacy in this context was not the same as under **art. 8** of the Convention. Lord Mustill, whilst concurring on the facts, regarded privacy as an 'essentially human and personal concept' and could not see how it could apply to a company, 'which has no sensitivities to wound and no selfhood to protect'. However, the decision of the European Court of Human Rights in *Société Colas Est v France* (application 37971/97) (2002) 39 EHRR 17 suggests that a company may have **art. 8** rights. Although the case concerned the question of whether the protection offered by **art. 8** covered the right to respect for a company's registered office, branches or other business premises, building on the *Niemietz* case, the Court also noted that:

> Building on its dynamic interpretation of the Convention, the Court considers that the time has come to hold that in certain circumstances the rights guaranteed by art. 8 of the Convention may be construed as including the right to respect for a company's registered office, branches or other business premises.

This is supported by *R (Amro International SA) v Financial Services Authority* [2010] EWCA Civ 123, [2010] Bus LR 1541, in which the court commented that **art. 8** 'is or may be engaged' in respect of documents being obtained in a corporate context and therefore proportionality must be considered.

A definitive ruling on whether a company can claim under **art. 8** is, however, still awaited.

The definition of family life is broad including family relationships between husband and wife and parent and child (*Johansen v Norway* (1996) 23 EHRR 33). Ties between unmarried couples (*Kroon v Netherlands* (1994) 19 EHRR 263), parents and their illegitimate children (*Johnston v Ireland* (1986) 9 EHRR 203) and grandparents and grandchildren (*Marckx v Belgium* (1979) 2 EHRR 330) have also fallen into this category.

Unauthorised settlement on one's own land (in a caravan occupied without planning permission) falls within the concept of 'home' under art. 8 (*Buckley v United Kingdom* (1996) 23 EHRR 101).

Article 8(1) is qualified by **art. 8(2)**. Any interference by a public authority with the exercise of the rights guaranteed by **art. 8(1)** must both be in accordance with the law and also be necessary in a democratic society in the interests of national security, public safety or the economic well-being of the country, for the prevention of disorder or crime, for the protection of health or morals, or the protection of the rights and freedoms of others. No interference with the right under **art. 8(1)** may be greater than is necessary to achieve its intended objective.

Rights under **art. 8** may be violated when the State obtains personal and private details about an individual without his or her consent and without statutory authority. In *Halford v United Kingdom* (1997) 24 EHRR 523 it was established that interference with private telephone calls made at work in a private office on a personal line was a breach of **art. 8**. See also *Khan v United Kingdom* (2000) 31 EHRR 45, where **art. 8** was held to be infringed by the police obtaining evidence using a covertly installed listening device at the applicant's home, and *Armstrong v United Kingdom* (2002) 36 EHHR 30. A statutory framework for the interception of communications and covert surveillance by security, law enforcement and other public authorities is now provided by the Regulation of Investigatory Powers Act 2000. The government believes that action taken in accordance with that Act will be 'in accordance with the law' for the purposes of **art. 8(2)**.

It appears that **art. 8(1)** has effectively given rise to a limited cause of action generating rights to equitable remedies and damages for breach of confidence, albeit there is no freestanding cause of action for breach of privacy (see *Wainwright v Home Office* [2003] UKHL 53, [2004] 2 AC 406; but cf. *Wainwright v United Kingdom* (application 12350/04) (2006) 44 EHRR 40; see also **91.55**). **Article 8** is capable of being infringed by noise resulting from schemes implemented by public authorities if it seriously affects an individual's private life. The absence of any possibility of a grant to help protect against the noise, or any compensation, is capable of negativing any justification for interference with the **art. 8** right (*Andrews v Reading Borough Council* [2004] EWHC 970 (Admin), [2004] UKHRR 599).

Article 9: freedom of thought, conscience and religion

91.25 **Article 9** establishes the right to manifest religion and beliefs, rather than simply to hold particular views. For example, a parent's religious convictions are a relevant consideration for a local education authority when considering the admission of a child to a particular school (*R (K) v Newham London Borough Council* [2002] EWHC 405 (Admin), [2002] ELR 390). **Article 9(2)** provides that this freedom may be limited by law where necessary in a democratic society in the interests of public safety, for the protection of public order, health or morals or for the protection of the rights and freedoms of others (see, for example, *R (Shabina Begum) v Denbigh High School* [2006] UKHL 15, [2007] 1 AC 100).

Article 10: freedom of expression

91.26 **Article 10(1)** provides that:

> Everyone has the right to freedom of expression. This right shall include freedom to hold opinions and to receive and impart information and ideas without interference by public authority and regardless of frontiers. This Article shall not prevent States from requiring the licensing of broadcasting, television or cinema enterprises.

The term 'expression' has been given a broad definition and includes words, works of art (*Müller v Switzerland* (1988) 13 EHRR 212), images (*Chorherr v Austria* (1993) 17 EHRR 358) and dress (*Stevens v United Kingdom* (1986) 46 DR 245). The types of expression covered include political, journalistic, artistic and commercial expression. All legal entities including companies are protected by **art. 10** (*Autronic AG v Switzerland* (1990) 12 EHRR 485). The right to freedom of expression also includes the right to be provided with information (*Open Door Counselling and Dublin Well Woman v Ireland* (1992) 15 EHRR 244).

Generally, **art. 10(1)** is qualified by **art. 10(2)** in that it:

> may be subject to such formalities, conditions, restrictions or penalties as are prescribed by law and are necessary in a democratic society, in the interests of national security, territorial integrity or public safety, for the prevention of disorder or crime, for the protection of health or morals, for the protection of the reputation or rights of others, for preventing the disclosure of information received in confidence, or for maintaining the authority and impartiality of the judiciary.

In practice, commercial and artistic expression have tended to receive less protection from the Strasbourg court than political or journalistic expression, although the court requires a strong justification for interfering with the right to freedom of expression and will need to be satisfied that the restriction is 'prescribed by law' and that a pressing 'social need' is 'convincingly established' (*Handyside v United Kingdom* (1976) 1 EHRR 737). The right to freedom of expression carries with it certain responsibilities which include avoiding expression which does not contribute to public debate and which is gratuitously offensive to others (*Otto-Preminger Institute v Austria* (1994) 19 EHRR 34). Additionally, when an individual agrees or contracts to limit his or her freedom of expression, generally actions by the State will not be interpreted as an interference (*Vereniging Rechtswinkels Utrecht v Netherlands* (1986) 46 DR 200).

Article 11: freedom of assembly and association

Article 11 provides not only the freedom of peaceful assembly but also guarantees the right to public processions and meetings both in private and in public and includes the right to form and join trade unions. The right in **art. 11** can be limited by restrictions prescribed by law which are necessary in a democratic society in the interests of national security or public safety, for the prevention of disorder or crime, for the protection of health or morals or for the protection of the rights and freedoms of others. **91.27**

Article 12: right to marry

Article 12 provides the right to marry and found a family. **Article 12** rights apply to those already married and those intending to marry. The legislation concerning adoption of children falls within **art. 12**. **91.28**

Article 14: prohibition of discrimination in enjoyment of Convention rights

Article 14 establishes the principle of equality of application of the Convention. The rights and freedoms protected by the Convention must be available to everyone regardless of sex, race, colour, language, religion, political or other opinion, national or social origin, association with a national minority, property, birth or other status. **91.29**

The following test is guidance for the application of **art. 14**:

(a) Do the facts of the case fall within the ambit of one or more of the substantive Convention provisions?
(b) Is there different treatment as respects the Convention right between the complainant on the one hand and other persons put forward by comparison ('the chosen comparators') on the other?
(c) Are the chosen comparators in an analogous situation to the complainant's situation?
(d) If so, does the difference have an objective and reasonable justification, or, otherwise stated, does it pursue a legitimate aim, and does the differential treatment bear a reasonable relationship of proportionality to the aim sought to be achieved?
(e) Is the difference in treatment based on one or more of the grounds prescribed, expressly or by inference, in **art. 14**?

(See also *Ghaidan v Godin-Mendoza* [2004] UKHL 30, [2004] 2 AC 557; *A v Secretary of State for the Home Department* [2004] UKHL 56, [2005] 2 AC 68.)

However, it is not always necessary to follow the sequential analysis set out in *Michalak v Wandsworth London Borough Council* (see *R (Carson) v Secretary of State for Work and Pensions* [2005] UKHL 37, [2006] 1 AC 173, where the House of Lords recognised that the *Michalak* questions did not suit every case and context, although they may be useful in some cases; and note *Carson v United Kingdom* (application 42184/05) (2008) 48 EHRR 41).

In deciding whether a comparator enjoying preferential treatment is in an analogous or relevantly similar situation it is pertinent to have regard to the purpose of the measure in question. The ground for differential treatment must amount to status in the sense of a personal characteristic, rather than historical fact (*R (S) v Chief Constable of the South Yorkshire Police* [2004]

UKHL 39, [2004] 1 WLR 2196). A personal characteristic cannot be defined by the differential treatment of which a person complains. The length of sentence to be served by a prisoner was not found to fall within the 'other status' ground of **art. 14**, as it depended not on a personal characteristic but on what the prisoner had done (*R (Clift) v Secretary of State for the Home Department* [2006] UKHL 54, [2007] 1 AC 484). Overall a generous meaning should be given to the term 'other status' and the term 'personal characteristic' simply requires concentration on what somebody is, rather than what he is doing or what is done to him. Therefore homelessness is a personal characteristic and an 'other status' for the purposes of **art. 14**, despite being a voluntary choice, not being a legal status and not having previously been recognised as a status by the European Court of Human Rights (the issue never having been raised before that court) (*R (RJM) v Secretary of State for Work and Pensions* [2008] UKHL 63, [2009] 1 AC 311). Being a prisoner is also accepted as an 'other status' (*Shelley v United Kingdom* (application 23800/06) (2008) 46 EHRR SE16). However, whereas discrimination on any of the core or primary grounds listed in **art. 14**, such as sex or race, is regarded as 'suspect' and therefore requires intense scrutiny, discrimination on other grounds merely requires some rational justification (*Stewart v Secretary of State for Work and Pensions* [2011] EWCA Civ 907, [2011] UKHRR 1048).

Discrimination on the grounds of disability, which is not among the core grounds listed in **art. 14**, has received special treatment in this regard. The court has accepted that disability discrimination may fall into the 'suspect' group of grounds because of its recognition in domestic law and numerous international instruments (*AM (Somalia) v Entry Clearance Officer* [2009] EWCA Civ 634, (2009) UKHRR 1073). However, the court has found that in cases of indirect discrimination or where the discrimination lies in a failure to make an exception from a policy of general application, particularly where there are social issues at stake, the proportionality review must be conducted by way of the usual rather than enhanced standard (*Burnip v Birmingham City Council* [2012] EWCA Civ 629, [2013] PTSR 117).

Administrative convenience cannot be a sufficient justification for discrimination without some other justification as to why those in analogous or relevantly similar situations are being excluded (*Francis v Secretary of State for Work and Pensions* [2005] EWCA Civ 1303, [2006] 1 WLR 3202). It is accepted, however, that seeking to clear a backlog of cases to allow subsequent cases to be dealt with more efficiently is a legitimate aim for any administrative system. With that overall aim in mind it was acceptable to apply different treatment to young adults with parents (whose right to family life was engaged) and young adults who were without parents (where the only right engaged was the private life of the young adults in question), given that there was not differential treatment in relation to exactly the same Convention right (*AL (Serbia) v Secretary of State for the Home Department* [2008] UKHL 42, [2008] 1 WLR 1434). The trigger for the application of **art. 14** is whether the facts in issue 'fall within the ambit' of one or more of the other Convention provisions (see *Secretary of State for Work and Pensions v M* [2006] UKHL 11, [2006] 2 AC 91), but the finding of a violation under **art. 14** is not dependent on first establishing a violation of some other Convention right (*Michalak v Wandsworth London Borough Council* [2002] EWCA Civ 271, [2003] 1 WLR 617).

Article 16: restrictions on political activity of aliens

91.30 **Article 16** establishes that nothing in **arts 10** (freedom of expression), **11** (freedom of assembly and association) and **14** (prohibition against discrimination) shall prevent governments from imposing restrictions on the political activities of aliens (a term which includes stateless persons).

Article 17: prohibition of abuse of rights

91.31 *Article 17 states that the* Convention may not be interpreted as allowing any State, group or person any right to participate in any activities aimed at the destruction of any of the rights and freedoms set out in the Convention.

Article 18: limitation on use of restrictions of rights

Article 18 states that restrictions on rights under the Convention cannot be applied for any purposes other than those for which those restrictions have been prescribed. **Article 18** (like **art.** 14) may not be used individually but only in conjunction with a claim for a breach of some other article of the Convention. 91.32

Article 1 of the First Protocol: protection of property

Article 1 of the First Protocol provides that: 91.33

> Every natural or legal person is entitled to the peaceful enjoyment of his possessions. No one shall be deprived of his possessions except in the public interest and subject to the conditions provided for by law and by the general principles of international law.

However, this provision does not in any way impair the right of a State to enforce such laws as it deems necessary to control the use of property in accordance with the general interest or to secure the payment of taxes or other contributions or penalties.

A diverse number of economic interests are included within this article, including not only tangible interests such as a house, but shares, patents, the entitlement to a pension, the right to exercise a profession and even a legal claim, so long as it is concrete and adequately specified.

According to the European Court of Human Rights in *Sporrong v Sweden* (1982) 5 EHRR 35, in order to show that **art.** 1 of the First Protocol has been violated, it must be demonstrated that:

(a) the peaceful enjoyment of the applicant's possessions has been interfered with by the State; or
(b) the applicant has been deprived of possessions by the State; or
(c) the applicant's possessions have been subjected to control by the State.

These rights are to be balanced against the State's rights to interfere with the peaceful enjoyment of property in the public interest or to control use of property in accordance with the general interest. There is a wide margin of appreciation although an interference with property, including raising taxes, must be proportionate.

Any deprivation under **art.** 1 of the First Protocol must be necessary and proportionate. In the context, necessary means reasonably necessary, rather than strictly or absolutely necessary. The test of what is necessary is driven by a balancing exercise, rather than by a requirement to use the approach which is least intrusive of Convention rights (*R (Clays Lane Housing Co-operative Ltd) v Housing Corporation* [2004] EWCA Civ 1658, [2005] 1 WLR 2229).

Failure by a sewerage undertaker to carry out works to bring an end to repeated flooding to the claimant's property did not constitute an unjustifiable interference with the claimant's rights under **art.** 1 of the First Protocol and **art.** 8 of the Convention (*Marcic v Thames Water Utilities Ltd* [2003] UKHL 66, [2004] 2 AC 42). The imposition of financial penalties upon lorry drivers and haulage companies under the Immigration and Asylum Act 1999, as persons responsible for clandestine entrants into the United Kingdom, was incompatible with both **art.** 6 of the Convention and **art.** 1 of the First Protocol (*International Transport Roth GmbH v Secretary of State for the Home Department* [2002] EWCA Civ 158, [2003] QB 728).

Article 2 of the First Protocol: right to education

Article 2 of the First Protocol establishes that no one shall be denied the right to education and that the State shall respect the right of parents to ensure such education and teaching is in conformity with their own religious and philosophical convictions. Education has been defined to include primary and secondary education, and the European Commission of 91.34

Human Rights has accepted that access to university education may be limited. The United Kingdom has made a reservation adopting this Article only 'so far as it is compatible with the provision of efficient instruction and training, and the avoidance of unreasonable public expenditure'.

Article 3 of the First Protocol: right to free elections

91.35 **Article 3** of the First Protocol provides that States must hold elections at regular intervals which will allow the free expression of the opinion of the people in choosing the legislature.

Thirteenth Protocol: abolition of the death penalty

91.36 **Article 1** of the Thirteenth Protocol abolishes the death penalty and provides that no one shall be condemned to such penalty or executed.

IMPACT OF THE HUMAN RIGHTS ACT 1998 ON CIVIL LITIGATION

91.37 Although **Human Rights Act 1998** points may be raised in civil litigation, they need to be raised carefully and only in appropriate circumstances. There have been a number of cases where bad arguments have been raised and there has been judicial comment about taking a responsible attitude to when it is right to raise a **Human Rights Act 1998** point. For example, Lord Woolf MR was critical of such points being raised in a case management context (*Daniels v Walker* [2000] 1 WLR 1382) and Mummery LJ has also said that the temptation to turn a court hearing into an international human rights seminar should be resisted (*Williams v Cowell* [2000] 1 WLR 187). In instances where the European Convention on Human Rights has been cited in domestic law, judges have been reluctant to accept 'the deployment of generalised propositions from the Convention' (*R v North West Lancashire Health Authority, ex parte A* [2000] 1 WLR 977) and simply referring to the Convention without specific case law is regarded as unhelpful to the court in doing justice to an argument (*Barclays Bank plc v Ellis* (2000) *The Times*, 24 October 2000). However, the Court of Appeal has accepted that the **Human Rights Act 1998** provides the courts with an extra tool for interpreting the language of a rule of court so as to produce a just result and avoid any question of the violation of a litigant's right to a fair trial under **art. 6** of the Convention (*Goode v Martin* [2001] EWCA Civ 1899, [2002] 1 WLR 1828).

The manner and formalities by which evidence is provided to the court to permit it to take account of European Court of Human Rights (ECHR) judgments, decisions, declarations or opinions are set out in rules which specify the law reports or other versions of cases which may be used and require that parties give the court and other parties three days' notice of the authorities they intend to cite (**PD 39A, para. 8**).

RIGHT TO A FAIR AND PUBLIC HEARING AND CIVIL LITIGATION

Presence of litigant

91.38 In order to comply with the requirements of **art. 6** of the Convention, an adjournment will usually have to be granted for a litigant whose presence is needed for the fair trial of a case but who is unable to attend through no fault of his own, although the applicant for the adjournment must be able to demonstrate that the inability to attend is genuine (*Teinaz v Wandsworth London Borough Council* [2002] EWCA Civ 1040, [2002] ICR 1471).

The right to attend a civil trial and give evidence is not an absolute right. The question in every individual case is whether, viewed as a whole, the trial process is fair. It is unlikely that any party has an absolute right to be present throughout proceedings; this would need to be balanced against the interests of other parties (*Zambia v Meer Care and Desai* [2006] EWCA Civ 390,

[2006] 1 CLC 436). See also *Dhillon v Asiedu* [2011] EWCA Civ 1020, [2012] CP Rep 44; *Three Mile Inn Ltd v Daley* [2012] EWCA Civ 970, LTL 27/8/2012.

Equality of arms

Courts are bound to give effect to the overriding objective set out in **CPR, r. 1.1(1)**, 'to deal with cases justly' and are given guidelines in **r. 1.1(2)** as to how this might be achieved. Article 6 of the European Convention on Human Rights introduces the principle of equality of arms. It has been held that notwithstanding these principles, the court has no power to veto a party's choice of legal representative. In *Maltez v Lewis* (1999) *The Times*, 4 May 1999, a party who could only afford less experienced representation than her opponent, who had instructed leading counsel, argued that this was against the 'level playing field envisaged by the CPR. As a consequence, it was argued that her opponent should be debarred from instructing such experienced counsel. It was held that the court could not interfere with a party's choice of legal representative, but that any imbalance could be dealt with in other ways, for example, by allowing a smaller firm of solicitors more time to carry out work or requiring a larger firm to prepare bundles for the court. The principle of equality of arms should not affect the approach adopted in *Maltez v Lewis*. In *R v Bow County Court, ex parte Pelling* [1999] 1 WLR 1807 the refusal to allow the claimant to act as a McKenzie friend was held not to contravene **art. 6(1)**. **91.39**

Equality of arms was considered in *R v Secretary of State for the Home Department, ex parte Quaquah* [2000] HRLR 325, in which the Secretary of State was not allowed to remove the claimant from the UK while he was pursuing an outstanding claim for damages for malicious prosecution against the Home Office. The claimant was entitled to have adequate time and facilities to pursue his tort claim.

Commentary

Limitation periods

Limitation periods must be considered in the light of the right of access to a court. Although the effect of a limitation period is to prevent a claimant having a hearing, this does not infringe **art. 6(1)** of the European Convention on Human Rights, provided the limitation period is proportionate (*Pérez de Rada Cavanilles v Spain* (1998) 29 EHRR 109). Limitation periods fulfil legitimate aims, including certainty and conclusiveness and prevent courts being forced to consider claims where evidence is either no longer available or not reliable. Where the time limit reflects a proportionate pursuit of these aims, it will be acceptable. However, a particularly strict application of a three-day time limit for requesting a judgment to be set aside was held to be contrary to **art. 6** (*Pérez de Rada Cavanilles v Spain* (1998) 29 EHRR 109). Conversely in *Stubbings v United Kingdom* (applications 22083/93 and 22095/93) (1996) 23 EHRR 213 the ECHR endorsed the application of a six-year limitation period so as to bar a claim arising out of alleged sexual abuse (but see now *A v Hoare* [2008] UKHL 6, [2008] 1 AC 844). A 14-day time limit to challenge the valuation of livestock was held to be compatible with **art. 6** (*J. and P. M. Dockeray v Secretary of State for the Environment, Food and Rural Affairs* [2002] EWHC 420 (Admin), [2002] HRLR 27) and a two-month time limit under **CPR, r. 74.8**, for filing a notice of appeal was held to be compliant with **art. 6**, notwithstanding that the court had jurisdiction under **r. 3.1(2)(a)** to extend time (*Citibank NA v Rafidian Bank* [2003] EWHC 1950 (QB), [2003] 2 All ER (Comm) 1054). In circumstances where the time limit cannot be extended for good reason or where the ability to extend is extremely limited, issues may arise. **91.40**

There is doubt about whether the obligation to apply 'promptly' in judicial review is sufficiently certain to comply with **art. 6** (*R (Burkett) v Hammersmith and Fulham London Borough Council* [2002] UKHL 23, [2002] 1 WLR 1593). However, the ECHR has dismissed a complaint that the judicial review time limit of 'promptly and in any event within three months' is misleading and contrary to the principles of legal certainty because of the inconsistent and discretionary views taken by the domestic courts of the applicable time limits. The ECHR regarded the time limit as a strict procedural requirement which served a public-interest purpose, namely, the need to avoid prejudice being caused to third parties who may have altered their situation on the strength of administrative decisions. The time limit is not contrary to **art. 6** (*Lam v United Kingdom* (application 41671/98) decision 5 July 2001).

Substitution of parties to a claim so that a new party is being sued may be allowed even after a limitation period has expired. Where the claimant sought to substitute an individual named solicitor for a firm of solicitors as defendant, it was clear that she had always intended to sue this solicitor, indeed he was mentioned by name in her particulars of claim. There was no cause of action against the firm but only against the individual solicitor. The approach to be taken in light of **art. 6** was to interpret rules of court so as to produce a just result and avoid unjustifiable infringement of a litigant's right of access to court. Substitution should be allowed even though the limitation period had expired (*Kesslar v Moore and Tibbits* [2004] EWCA Civ 1551, [2005] PNLR 17).

CPR, r. 17.4 (which prohibits amendment of a statement of case to include a new claim for which the limitation period has expired if the new claim does not arise out of the same facts as the original claim), has been interpreted broadly in the light of the right of access to a court (*Goode v Martin* [2001] EWCA Civ 1899, [2002] 1 WLR 1828; see **31.25**).

Strike-out applications and default and summary judgment

91.41 The court has a duty actively to manage cases (**CPR, r. 1.4** and **Part 26**). This includes deciding promptly which issues need full investigation and trial and accordingly disposing summarily of the others (**r. 1.4(2)(c)**). The power to make orders for summary disposal of issues includes the power to strike out a statement of case in whole or in part under **r. 3.4**, in addition to the power to give summary judgment under **Part 24**, where a claimant or defendant has no reasonable prospect of success. These powers may be exercised on the court's own initiative, without hearing the parties or giving them an opportunity to make representations (**r. 3.3(4)**).

One issue is whether striking out for failure to comply with procedural rules or orders is a denial of the right of access to a court. In *Canada Trust Co. v Stolzenberg* (unreported, 14 October 1998) a party who failed to comply with an unless order unsuccessfully claimed he had been deprived of the right to a fair trial contrary to **art. 6** of the European Convention on Human Rights. The court held that he had deprived himself of that right by his own non-compliance. However, in *Re Swaptronics Ltd* (1998) *The Times*, 17 August 1998, and *Arrow Nominees Inc. v Blackledge* [2000] 1 BCLC 709 (point not considered on appeal) it was held that striking out as a penalty for contempt of court could only be consistent with **art. 6** if the contempt led to a 'real risk' that a fair trial could not happen.

A defendant's right to a fair trial was not violated by the operation of **CPR, rr. 6.5(6)** and **6.7**, as they were worded before 1 October 2008, which deemed that the claim form and particulars of claim had been served even though he had not received them (*Akram v Adam* [2004] EWCA Civ 1601, [2005] 1 WLR 2762). The judge had found that the defendant had no defence, and there was therefore no need to set aside the judgment in default and make the claimant apply for summary judgment, with all the time and expense that would involve. **Article 6** does not, as of right, entitle the defendant to a trial or oblige the claimant to show on some other occasion that the defendant has no arguable defence.

Refusal to set aside a judgment entered in default of compliance of an unless order raises an **art. 6** issue as the losing party would be deprived of a trial of his defence on the merits, but the State can impose restrictions on the right of access to a court provided they serve a legitimate aim, are proportionate and do not destroy the very essence of the right. The legitimate aim of imposing the sanction of judgment in default of compliance is to secure compliance with court orders (*CIBC Mellon Trust Co. v Stolzenberg* [2004] EWCA Civ 827, *The Independent*, 2 July 2004).

The summary judgment procedure has been held to be compliant with **art. 6(1)** (*Monsanto plc v Tilly* [2000] Env LR 313; *S v Gloucestershire County Council* [2001] Fam 313). Care must be taken where the grant of summary judgment would interfere with the right of a journalist to freedom of expression (*Al Misnad v Azzaman Ltd* [2003] EWHC 1783, LTL 22/7/2003).

Convention rights may also be relevant where claims are struck out on the ground that there is no cause of action. This question has arisen in the context of claims against public authorities in negligence. In *Osman v United Kingdom* (1998) 29 EHRR 245 the ECHR held that it was a breach of the applicant's **art. 6(1)** right of access to a court to strike out a negligence claim on the basis that the imposition of a duty of care would not be fair, just or reasonable. However, in its more recent judgments in *TP v United Kingdom* [2001] 2 FLR 549 and *Z v United Kingdom* [2001] 2 FLR 612 the Court effectively overruled *Osman* and held that there was no violation of the right of access to a court in such cases. The Court did, however, hold that in striking out negligence claims arising from local authorities' exercise of their child protection functions, the English courts had denied the claimants an effective remedy for violations of certain substantive Convention rights, contrary to **art. 13** of the Convention (which has not been incorporated into United Kingdom law). These decisions might suggest that the courts should not strike out negligence claims which affect substantive Convention rights, but since an apparently effective remedy is now available under the **Human Rights Act 1998**, the right of access under **art. 6** is likely to have a very limited application to the striking out of negligence claims or other civil claims.

Although *Osman* can no longer be regarded as correct, the effect of English decisions since *Osman* is that some cases which might previously have been the subject of a strike-out application will instead have to proceed to trial (see *Barrett v Enfield London Borough Council* [2001] 2 AC 550). Although Lord Woolf MR held in *Kent v Griffiths* [2001] QB 36 at p. 51, that cases should still be struck out when the position is clear, many English judges now seem to regard questions about the existence of a duty of care in negligence as difficult matters which should generally be decided only after careful consideration of the evidence at trial (e.g. Lord Browne-Wilkinson in *Barrett*; Otton LJ in *L (A Child) v Reading Borough Council* [2001] 1 WLR 1575; and see *D v East Berkshire Community Health NHS Trust* [2005] UKHL 23, [2005] 2 AC 373; note also *Matthews v Ministry of Defence* [2003] UKHL 4, [2003] 1 AC 1163).

Time limits and delay

The CPR aim at dispensing justice without delay and provide sanctions where parties have failed to comply with time limits imposed for carrying out steps in litigation (see **r. 3.4(2)** and **chapter 48**). **Article 6(1)** of the European Convention on Human Rights requires the hearing of the merits of a claim to take place within a reasonable time. It is possible to invoke **art. 6(1)** when opposing applications for time extensions, although delay in proceedings will not of itself violate **art. 6(1)**, unless the delay is found to be unreasonable (*Darnell v United Kingdom* (1993) 18 EHRR 205; *Re Swaptronics Ltd* (1998) *The Times*, 17 August 1998). Civil proceedings will only be struck out as an abuse of process by reason of the claimant's delay where it would no longer be possible for the defendant to receive a fair trial (*Re McHugh Southern Ltd* [2002] EWHC 3069 (Ch), *The Times*, 30 January 2003). **91.42**

Where criminal proceedings, from the time of the initial arrest to the time when the applicant was finally refused leave to appeal to the House of Lords, lasted eight years and five months, of which there were four years and three months of almost total inactivity, that amounted to breach of **art. 6(1)**, particularly considering that the applicant's liberty was involved. The relevant factors to have regard to are the complexity of the case, the conduct of the applicant and the relevant authorities and the importance of what was at stake for the applicant (*Crowther v United Kingdom* (application 53741/00) (2005) *The Times*, 11 February 2005). See also *Minshall v United Kingdom* (application 7350/063) (2012) 55 EHRR 36.

Where it took four years to deal with costs questions there was a violation of **art. 6(1)** (*Robins v United Kingdom* (1997) 26 EHRR 527). The principle that it is not possible to rebut, by evidence of the actual date of receipt, the presumption that service of a claim form occurred on the day deemed by **CPR, r. 6.7**, as it was worded before 1 October 2008 is compatible with **art. 6** (*Anderton v Clwyd County Council (No. 2)* [2002] EWCA Civ 933, [2002] 1 WLR 3174).

When considering whether to stay proceedings (for example, until the determination of parallel disciplinary proceedings), the court must consider the significance of taking any step which impinges on a litigant's right to have issues determined by a court within a reasonable time under **art. 6(1)**. The burden is on the applicant seeking a stay to demonstrate through cogent evidence that there are sound reasons for granting a stay (*Wakefield v Channel Four Television Corporation* [2005] EWHC 2410 (QB), LTL 4/11/2005).

A breach of the right in **art. 6** to a hearing within a reasonable time might ground a claim to a just and appropriate remedy but would not entitle a defendant to a stay or dismissal of the proceedings against him unless there could no longer be a fair hearing or it would otherwise be unfair to continue with the proceedings against him (*Secretary of State for Trade and Industry v Davies* [2006] EWHC 299 (Ch), [2006] 2 BCLC 489; see also *Eastaway v Secretary of State for Trade and Industry* [2007] EWCA Civ 425, [2008] 1 BCLC 153).

Directions and evidence

91.43 As part of its case management powers, the court has power to exclude an issue from consideration (**CPR, r. 3.1(2)(k)**) and power to control evidence by giving directions about the issues on which it requires evidence, the nature of the evidence which it requires to decide those issues and the way in which the evidence is to be placed before the court, as well as the power to limit cross-examination (**r. 32.1**).

Receipt of hearsay evidence, consisting of statements made by someone who cannot be cross-examined, does not inevitably prevent a fair trial under **art. 6** (*Clingham v Kensington and Chelsea Royal London Borough Council* [2002] UKHL 39, [2003] 1 AC 787). However, failure by the prosecution to lay evidence before the trial judge and thus permit him to rule on the question of disclosure is contrary to **art. 6** (*Atlan v United Kingdom* (2001) 34 EHRR 33). The court's refusal to permit a party to give evidence by way of video link in order to avoid the risk of being arrested on warrant should he return to the United Kingdom was held not to pay sufficient regard to **art. 6** and the need to ensure that the parties were on an equal footing (*Rowland v Bock* [2002] EWHC 692 (QB), [2002] 4 All ER 370). Taking a child's evidence by video link in a criminal case did not contravene the defendant's right to a fair trial under **art. 6** (*R (D) v Camberwell Green Youth Court* [2005] UKHL 4, [2005] 1 WLR 393).

The rules on the use of experts encourage the use of a single joint expert and permit the court to control the manner in which the expert investigates the issues as well as limiting the amount which the expert may be paid for his or her services (**CPR, r. 35.8(3)(b)** and **(4)(a)**).

These rules must be seen in the context of the right to a fair trial in **art. 6(1)** of the European Convention on Human Rights. **Article 6(1)** does not guarantee the right to call expert evidence, save where it is necessary to ensure the fairness of the proceedings. **CPR, r. 35.1**, requires the court to restrict expert evidence, and **r. 35.7** allows it to direct that evidence shall be given by a single joint expert instructed by both parties. The appointment of a single joint expert will not be contrary to **art. 6(1)**, although the right to a fair trial may demand that the parties participate equally in the preparation of the expert's report, including attending interviews and examining the documents on which the report is based (*Mantovanelli v France* (1997) 24 EHRR 370). In *Daniels v Walker* [2000] 1 WLR 1382 the judge refused to allow a defendant, who was dissatisfied with the instructions to a joint expert and the resulting report, to instruct another expert of his own. Lord Woolf MR accepted that additional questions could be put to the expert, but rejected the defendant's argument that the procedure conflicted with

art. 6(1). The overriding objective of the CPR, which requires the court to deal with cases 'justly', enables it to ensure that all CPR procedures operate in accordance with **art. 6**.

The power of a court to regulate its own procedures is subject to limitations. There is no power in the CPR, nor any common law power, to adopt a procedure in ordinary civil litigation whereby one party would not be allowed access to evidence and would be excluded from part of the trial (a closed material procedure). Where a trial involves evidence that is sensitive, for example, on national security grounds, the public interest immunity test exists, which is consistent with the right to a fair trial since it does not exclude one party and there is therefore no unfairness or inequality of arms. Any departure from the ordinary principles of open and natural justice, which a closed material procedure would be, must be explicitly authorised by Parliament (*Al-Rawi v Security Service* [2011] UKSC 34, [2012] 1 AC 531).

Injunctions

It is arguable that there are ample safeguards by virtue of the undertakings to be provided by the applicant as set out in the draft orders in the annex to **PD 25A** and the normally short return date given by the court to enable the case for the respondent to be put (*Chappell v United Kingdom* (1989) 12 EHRR 1). However, before granting an injunction without notice, the court will have regard to all the circumstances of the case and take account of **art. 6(1)** of the European Convention on Human Rights. In particular, there may be an issue under **art. 6** where an order requires answers to questions. Further, the court has discharged freezing and search orders on the basis of material non-disclosure, namely, failure by the applicant to disclose the fact that evidence relied upon in a without notice application was obtained in breach of **art. 8(1)** of the Convention (*St Merryn Meat Ltd v Hawkins* [2001] CP Rep 116). **91.44**

It was found to be inconsistent with **art. 6(3)** rights for a judge to proceed to a hearing on an application to commit for contempt of court for breach of a freezing and disclosure order without giving the breaching party an opportunity to be heard where the judge knew that the absent party wished to be heard in person, but was prevented from being present by matters over which he had no control (*Raja v Van Hoogstraten* [2004] EWCA Civ 968, [2004] 4 All ER 793).

Financial constraints on access to justice

Financial burdens placed on parties to litigation, such as security for costs orders or court fees must be considered in the light of the right of access to a court. **91.45**

The Convention is intended to guarantee practical and effective rights, particularly with regard to the right of access to a court. It is central to the concept of a fair trial, in civil as in criminal proceedings, that a litigant is not denied the opportunity to present his case effectively before the court and that he is able to enjoy equality of arms with the opposing side. However, **art. 6(1)** leaves the State with a free choice as to the means to be used to guarantee litigants these rights. The right of access to a court is not absolute and may be subject to restrictions, provided that they pursue a legitimate aim and are proportionate. Moreover, it is not incumbent on the State to ensure total equality of arms between the assisted party and the opposing side, as long as each side is given a reasonable opportunity to present his case under conditions that do not place him at a substantial disadvantage.

Under **CPR, r. 3.1(5)**, the court may order a party to pay a sum of money into court if that party has, without good reason, failed to comply with a rule, practice direction or a relevant pre-action protocol. Such an order may be made against a claimant or a defendant and the sum of money will be security for any sum payable by that party to any other party in the proceedings (**r. 3.1(6A)**). Before making such an order, the court must have regard to the amount in dispute, the costs incurred and the costs to be incurred (**r. 3.1(6)**).

In deciding whether to require security, the court may anticipate the arguments likely to be put forward on an application under **r. 3.9** for relief from sanctions, including the effect which the granting of relief would have on each party.

The court must, under **art. 6(1)** of the European Convention on Human Rights, take into account inability to pay where that would result in a party being unable to proceed with a claim. In *Tolstoy Miloslavsky v United Kingdom* (1995) 20 EHRR 442, the ECHR found that an order for security for costs in relation to appellate proceedings would not infringe **art. 6(1)**, but there could be a violation if an order for security denies access to a court of first instance (*Aït-Mouhoub v France* (1998) 30 EHRR 382). In *Federal Bank of the Middle East Ltd v Hadkinson* [2000] 1 WLR 1695 the Court of Appeal found no contravention of **art. 6 (1)** by an order requiring security for the costs of an appeal from a summary judgment. An order for security for costs against a claimant was not upheld where the claimant was not represented at the hearing of the application (*Nasser v United Bank of Kuwait* [2001] EWCA Civ 556, [2002] 1 WLR 1868).

The right to a fair trial pursuant to **art. 6** also requires that a conditional order as to costs, imposed as a condition of defending a claim, should be reasonable on the basis that, in circumstances where a party cannot comply with such an order, the effect of the order extends beyond limiting his right of access to the court and impairs the very essence of the right (*Anglo-Eastern Trust Ltd v Kermanshahchi* [2002] EWCA Civ 198, [2002] CP Rep 36).

A litigant who wishes to instruct counsel and solicitors to defend an application in committal proceedings but has insufficient means to do so has a right to apply for public funding which should be respected by the courts (*Berry Trade Ltd v Moussavi* [2002] EWCA Civ 477, [2002] 1 WLR 1910).

It may be possible to argue that there is a breach of **art. 6(1)** if public funding is not available (*Airey v Ireland* (1979) 2 EHRR 305; and see *Perotti v Collyer-Bristow* [2003] EWCA Civ 1521, [2004] 2 All ER 189). The question of whether legal aid is necessary to guarantee a fair hearing must be determined on the particular facts of each case and will depend on the importance of what is at stake for the applicant in the proceedings, the complexity of the relevant law and procedure and the applicant's capacity to represent himself effectively. In unusually lengthy and complicated defamation proceedings, where the applicants were of very limited means and were represented pro bono whereas their opponents were one of the most wealthy companies in the world and employed substantial experienced legal teams, it was found that the denial of legal aid deprived the applicants of the opportunity to present their case effectively and contributed to an unacceptable inequality of arms (*Steel v United Kingdom* (application 68416/01) (2005) 41 EHRR 22). Where legal aid was refused for an appeal on the grounds that there was no reasonable prospect of success and where the costs of the claim would have been disproportionate to the sum at stake, the refusal of legal aid was not contrary to **art. 6** (*Stewart-Brady v United Kingdom* (1997) 24 EHRR CD38). However, the withdrawal of a claimant's public funding soon before trial on the basis that it appeared that neither of the defendants had sufficient assets to satisfy any judgment against them was a breach of **art. 6(1)** (*R (Alliss) v Legal Services Commission* [2002] EWHC 2079 (Admin), [2003] ACD 16). **Article 6** does not require the Criminal Injuries Compensation Authority to pay a claimant's costs of representation (*C v Secretary of State for the Home Department* [2003] EWHC 1295 (QB), LTL 22/5/2003). Funding for the representation of the family of a deceased person must be provided where an inquiry into the cause of death is required by **art. 2** if there is a sufficient degree of State responsibility for the death (*R (Khan) v Secretary of State for Health* [2003] EWCA Civ 1129, [2004] 1 WLR 971; *R (Amin) v Secretary of State for the Home Department* [2003] UKHL 51, [2004] 1 AC 653). However, where the primary cause of death was not State involvement, such as a rail accident caused by a private individual, but the State was still responsible for a framework of rail safety, there would not necessarily be a requirement for relatives of the deceased to be funded to enable them to have full legal representation at the inquest, particularly where the court found that the coroner could carry out a full investigation into the deaths without the benefit of full legal representation from the family (*R (Main) v Minister for Legal Aid* [2007] EWCA Civ 1147, [2008] HRLR 8).

The scheme chosen by Parliament to allow success fees in CFAs to be recoverable from the losing party in an action for defamation is compatible with **art. 10** and therefore the threat of liability to pay such a sum does not infringe the defendant's right to freedom of expression. It is a proportionate measure chosen by Parliament to provide other litigants access to justice (*Campbell v MGN Ltd (No. 2)* [2005] UKHL 61, [2005] 1 WLR 3394).

Vexatious litigants

The Senior Courts Act 1981, s. 42, which restricts vexatious proceedings, does not infringe the European Convention on Human Rights or the **Human Rights Act 1998** (*Ebert v Official Receiver* [2001] EWCA Civ 340, [2002] 1 WLR 320). Further, a fair and reasonable opportunity to put one's case before the court does not involve an unlimited and uncontrolled opportunity to address the court (*Attorney-General v Covey* [2001] EWCA Civ 254, *The Times*, 2 March 2001). **91.46**

This is on the basis that there is inherent in the Convention the need to balance the interests of the individual against the interests of the community, and if litigants were given unlimited time to make oral submissions, this would prejudice other litigants waiting to have their cases heard, and result in unnecessary expense to the justice system. See also *Attorney-General v D'Souza* (2004) 148 SJLB 1061.

Oral public hearing

CPR, r. 39.2(1), provides that, as a general rule, hearings are to be in public. This includes the trial. **Article 6(1)** of the European Convention on Human Rights provides that every person is entitled to a public hearing, although there are some very limited exceptions. The cases where hearings must be heard in private should be covered by the exceptions in **art. 6(1)**. **91.47**

Witnesses may only rely on **art. 2** to avoid giving evidence in public where they can demonstrate that to do so would pose an objectively verifiable real and immediate risk to their lives (*Deripaska v Cherney* [2012] EWCA Civ 1235, [2013] CP Rep 1).

Article 6(1) states that judgment should be pronounced publicly, even where the hearing has been in private, and this may cause more difficulty. However, where a hearing in private is strictly necessary because publicity would prejudice the interests of justice, judgment need not be pronounced publicly (*Re Trusts of X Charity* [2003] EWHC 1462 (Ch), [2003] 1 WLR 2751). **PD 39A, para. 1.11**, provides that when a hearing takes place in public, members of the public may obtain a transcript of any judgment given or a copy of any order made, upon payment of the appropriate fee. However, where the judgment is given or an order made in private, anyone who seeks a transcript of the judgment or copy order must seek the judge's permission (**PD 39A, para. 1.12**).

Although in some cases, particularly sentencing cases, fairness might not require an oral hearing, there must still be the possibility of an oral hearing where it is considered necessary for fairness. Where a prisoner faced the prospect of lengthy imprisonment and fairness required an oral hearing, this was not an entitlement of which he should be lightly deprived. A rule which denied a sentencing judge any possibility of holding a fair hearing is therefore incompatible with **art. 6** (*R (Hammond) v Secretary of State for the Home Department* [2005] UKHL 69, [2006] 1 AC 603).

It is not a requirement of **art. 6** that there should be an oral hearing of an application for permission to appeal under the Arbitration Act 1996, s. 69, unless the circumstances are exceptional (*BLCT (13096) Ltd v J. Sainsbury plc* [2003] EWCA Civ 884, [2004] 1 CLC 24).

Independent and impartial tribunal

The guarantee of a fair hearing in **art. 6(1)** of the European Convention on Human Rights includes the right to an independent and impartial tribunal. **91.48**

Commentary

The requirement of an independent and impartial tribunal cast doubt on the position of temporary sheriffs in Scotland trying criminal cases, where they did not have sufficient security of tenure (*Starrs v Ruxton* 2000 JC 208) but note the position of a temporary judge (*Kearney v HM Advocate* [2006] HRLR 15). Lack of security of tenure need not be a problem when trying a case to which the State is not a party (*Clancy v Caird* 2000 SC 441).

In *Hoekstra v HM Advocate (No. 2)* 2000 JC 391 it was held that the test of impartiality is both subjective and objective. A judge, who had, with two other judges, just heard an appeal in which issues relating to the application of the Convention were raised, wrote an article for a national newspaper that was highly critical of the Convention and its incorporation into national law. It was held that this did not pass the objective test of impartiality. The judgment in the appeal in question had to be set aside as it had been given by a court which was not properly constituted by three impartial judges.

In the same way the objective test of impartiality may not be fulfilled where a judge is called upon to rule judicially on the effect of legislation that he or she has drafted or promoted during the parliamentary process. The fair-minded and informed observer might conclude that there was a real possibility that the judge would subconsciously strive to avoid reaching a conclusion which would undermine the very clear assurances he had given to Parliament as to the effect of the legislation (*Davidson v Scottish Ministers* [2004] UKHL 34, [2009] 2 All ER 501).

In some circumstances the requirement of an independent and impartial tribunal can be satisfied by the possibility of a judicial review of a decision of the Secretary of State even when the Secretary of State is not impartial and independent, having formulated the policy which related to the decision under challenge (*R (Alconbury Developments Ltd) v Secretary of State for the Environment, Transport and the Regions* [2001] UKHL 23, [2003] 2 AC 295).

In some cases 'full jurisdiction' would necessitate jurisdiction over findings of primary fact and in others it would not. A local authority's administrative decision that accommodation offered to the homeless claimant was suitable, combined with judicial review, guaranteed compliance with **art. 6(1)** (*Runa Begum v Tower Hamlets London Borough Council* [2003] UKHL 5, [2003] 2 AC 430; see also *Ali v Birmingham City Council* [2008] EWCA Civ 1228, [2009] 2 All ER 501, affirmed [2010] UKSC 8, [2010] 2 AC 39). However, the right for asylum seekers to apply for judicial review did not remedy the procedural unfairness of the system operated by the Secretary of State in deciding whether asylum seekers had made their claims as soon as reasonably practicable after arrival in the United Kingdom. Judicial review did not allow sufficiently close review of determinations of fact to satisfy **art. 6**. However, the Court of Appeal held that if the Secretary of State were to remedy the deficiencies in procedure the combination of his decision-making process and judicial review of that process would then satisfy the requirements of **art. 6(1)** (*R (Q) v Secretary of State for the Home Department* [2003] EWCA Civ 364, [2004] QB 36). This was also the approach taken in *Tsfayo v United Kingdom* (application 60860/00) (2006) 48 EHRR 18, where the ECHR held that, where a first-instance tribunal decision is essentially a finding of fact, judicial review is not sufficient to protect **art. 6** rights as the court does not have the power to make fresh findings of fact. See also *R (Bono) v Harlow District Council* [2002] EWHC 423 (Admin), [2002] 1 WLR 2475; *Adan v Newham London Borough Council* [2001] EWCA Civ 1916, [2002] 1 WLR 2120; *R (S) v Brent London Borough Council* [2002] EWCA Civ 693, [2002] ACD 90; *Secretary of State for Health v Personal Representative of Christopher Beeson* [2002] EWCA Civ 1812, [2003] UKHRR 353; *Feld v Barnet London Borough Council* [2004] EWCA Civ 1307, [2005] HLR 9.

The courts have reconciled the domestic law on apparent bias (see 77.25) with the jurisprudence of the ECHR by applying the following test. First, the court should ascertain all the circumstances which have a bearing on the suggestion that the judge is biased. Second, it should ask whether those circumstances would lead a fair-minded and informed observer to conclude that there is a real possibility that the tribunal is biased (*Porter v Magill* [2001] UKHL 67, [2002] 2 AC 357). The use by a judge of a firm of solicitors for personal services does not give rise to the expectation that the judge would, in his judicial capacity, favour another client of the same firm of solicitors (*Taylor v Lawrence* [2002] EWCA Civ 90, [2003] QB 528). An adjudicator was no longer impartial as a result of his involvement in settlement negotiations (*Glencot Development and Design Co. Ltd v Ben Barrett and Son (Contractors) Ltd* [2001] BLR 207)

There is a real possibility of bias where the adjudicator has had a number of private conversations with one party and thus appears to have taken into account submissions from that party which were not made available to the other party (*Discain Project Services Ltd v Opecprime Development Ltd* [2001] BLR 285); where the judge's brother was chairman of a company with whom the defendant had been in (an unrelated) dispute (*Perot Systems Europe Ltd v Johnson* [2003] EWHC 1635 (QB), LTL 4/6/2003); where a potential witness was well known to the judge, even where that witness did not give evidence at the trial, as he was still involved in the case and replacement witnesses may have given the evidence that he would have given (*AWG Group Ltd v Morrison* [2006] EWCA Civ 6, [2006] 1 WLR 1163); where a part-time judge of the Employment Appeal Tribunal appeared as an advocate before that Tribunal, chaired by another judge sitting with two lay members, one or both of whom had previously sat with that part-time judge (*Lawal v Northern Spirit Ltd* [2003] UKHL 35, [2003] ICR 856); where the chairman of an employment tribunal had commented before any evidence was called that the appellant faced an uphill struggle with the case, indicating that the tribunal had prejudged the matter before hearing the relevant evidence (*Project v Hutt* (2006) 150 SJLB 702); where a judge had had previous dealings with a partner in a firm of solicitors, in relation to him joining the firm, which had ended acrimoniously, and the judge was then due to hear an application in which another partner in the same firm was involved (*Howell v Millais* [2007] EWCA Civ 720, [2007] NPC 88); and where a judge had commented to counsel in chambers before hearing all the evidence that he believed one party's evidence and could not see how the other party could win, because it indicated that he had prematurely closed his mind to the possibility that the other party's evidence might change his mind (*Amjad v Steadman-Byrne* [2007] EWCA Civ 625, [2007] 1 WLR 2484).

There has been held to be no real possibility of bias in the following circumstances: if a judge sits on a substantive appeal after refusing permission to appeal on paper (*Sengupta v Holmes* [2002] EWCA Civ 1104, (2002) 99 (39) LSG 39); where a memory lapse caused a judge to write and circulate his judgment before having the opportunity of considering the closing submissions of the parties' legal advisers, but said he would subsequently consider the judgment in the light of the submissions (*Taylor v Williamsons* [2002] EWCA Civ 1380, [2003] CP Rep 20); where an employment tribunal indicated to the parties before the evidence was completed that the respondent's treatment of the applicant had been 'appalling', because the views expressed were only preliminary (*Southwark London Borough Council v Jiminez* [2003] EWCA Civ 502, [2003] ICR 1176); where a judge had acted as a legal member of a mental health review tribunal after sentencing the patient to the sentence that was being reviewed, as a fair-minded and informed observer would take account of various factors including the fact that the tribunal had no power to question the validity of the original sentence and that a judge would not be reluctant to change his mind if and when there was a rational basis for doing so — the decision facing the tribunal was different from the one the judge had made earlier (*R (M) v Mental Health Review Team* [2005] EWHC 2791 (Admin), 90 BMLR 65); and where the judge had intervened and asked numerous questions throughout the hearing, including during examination of witnesses, in particular of one party against whom he had become increasingly hostile, since it was found that despite the judge's conduct it was inevitable that any judge would have reached the same conclusion — even if the trial had been fair, the result would have been the same (*Mortgage Credit Ltd v Kalli* [2007] EWCA Civ 1156, LTL 15/10/2007).

Courts should be careful not to accede to applications by people who do not want a case to be heard by a particular judge unless there are sufficient grounds for such recusal (*Phillips v Symes* [2004] EWHC 490 (Ch), LTL 21/3/2005; see also *Dobbs v Triodos Bank NV* [2005] EWCA Civ 468, [2006]

CP Rep 1). Mere complaint about the conduct of a chairman of an employment tribunal does not give rise to an automatic decision to recuse. The substance of the allegations should be addressed and analysed (*Ansar v Lloyds TSB Bank plc* [2006] EWCA Civ 1462, [2007] IRLR 211). For example, where a judge had been sent a letter making serious allegations about the other party, to say that the judge might have been biased was an artificial way of putting the complaint. The true complaint was that the party had not received a fair trial because she had not been given the opportunity to defend herself against damaging allegations going to her credit (*Diedrichs-Shurland v Talanga-Stiftung* [2006] UKPC 58, LTL 7/12/2006).

A judge has to be free from any actual or apparent bias, but counsel has no such duty. The court should prevent an advocate from acting only where there is a risk of disclosure of relevant confidential information or in very exceptional circumstances (*Geveran Trading Co. Ltd v Skjevesland* [2002] EWCA Civ 1567, [2003] 1 WLR 912). Similarly **art. 6** does not impose any requirement as to the independence or impartiality of the prosecutor in and of itself, although if a lack of such independence and impartiality results in unfairness to a defendant that might be a violation of **art. 6(1)** (*R (Haase) v Independent Adjudicator* [2008] EWCA Civ 1089, [2009] QB 550).

Further the test of apparent bias is not relevant to whether or not an expert witness should be permitted to give evidence, although the duties of an expert witness are to give an objective and unbiased opinion (*Saunder v Birmingham City Council* (EAT 21 May 2008) LTL 12/6/2008).

Where an allegation of bias had been dealt with at a public and impartial hearing and the decision reached that although there had been apparent bias the irregularity had been waived by the party failing to make a timely application to remove the umpire, there was no apparent contravention of **art. 6. Article 6** does not contain an overarching principle that an award tainted by apparent bias must be set aside. It is for national courts to decide whether to set the decision aside or not, the critical question being whether the decision of the court on the bias question discloses any violation of **art. 6**. Where the judge had then refused permission to appeal under the Arbitration Act 1996, the Court of Appeal would only have a residual jurisdiction to grant permission to appeal if there was unfairness in the decision-making process or a contravention of **art. 6**, which in this case there was not (*ASM Shipping Ltd v TTMI Ltd* [2006] EWCA Civ 1341, [2006] 2 CLC 471).

There was nothing untoward in an arbitrator considering the question of his own jurisdiction. It is not uncommon for arbitrators to consider the issue of whether they are competent to act by reason of bias. There was therefore no reason to restrain an arbitrator from holding a hearing to consider his own jurisdiction where the parties, each receiving independent legal advice, had expressly agreed that their dispute should be resolved by the arbitrator, according to the principles of the law of international arbitration. It would require exceptional circumstances before an English court would interfere with that agreement and infringe those principles (*Weissfisch v Julius* [2006] EWCA Civ 218, [2006] 1 Lloyd's Rep 716). If one arbitrator has withdrawn on the grounds of apparent bias, there is no invariable rule, nor is it necessarily the case, that the other two arbitrators would be affected second hand by apparent bias and therefore should recuse themselves or be excluded from the proceedings (*ASM Shipping Ltd v Bruce-Harris* [2007] EWHC 1513 (Comm), [2008] 1 Lloyd's Rep 61).

Reasoned judgment

91.49 **Article 6** of the European Convention on Human Rights requires reasons to be given for any decision on the merits and where permission to appeal is not given in order that the parties are aware of the grounds on which the decision was reached. The extent of reasoning required by the ECHR does not go any further than that which is required under domestic law (*English v Emery Reimbold and Strick Ltd* [2002] EWCA Civ 605, [2002] 1 WLR 2409). Where there are legitimate restraints on a right of appeal, such as the need for a matter to be of general importance, it is sufficient for the court to refer to those limitations. **Article 6** does not require reasons to be given for refusing permission to appeal against arbitral awards (*Mousaka Inc. v Golden Seagull Maritime Inc.* [2002] 1 WLR 395). In refusing leave to appeal under the Arbitration Act 1969, s. 69, adequate reasons would in almost all cases be given by identifying the threshold test or tests which the applicant has failed, without explaining why the relevant test had been failed (*North Range Shipping Ltd v Seatrans Shipping Corporation* [2002] EWCA Civ 405, [2002] 1 WLR 2397). Where the tribunal's decision is not obviously wrong or open to serious doubt, it might not always be enough simply to refer to the statutory test but it would be enough for the judge to uphold the arbitrator's reasons. Otherwise it might be necessary to go further, but any further reasons need only be brief so as to show the losing party why he had lost (see also 77.27).

Inattentive tribunal

There may not be a fair trial, as required by the European Convention on Human Rights, **art. 6**, if the tribunal does not give full attention to the case. In *Stansby v Datapulse plc* [2003] EWCA Civ 1951, [2004] ICR 523, a hearing by an employment tribunal was unfair because a lay member fell asleep having consumed alcohol. Conversely in *R v Betson* [2004] EWCA Crim 254, [2004] 2 Cr App R 52, a criminal trial by jury was not unfair, even though the judge fell asleep during counsel's speeches to the jury, because the judge's summing up could not be criticised and the jury were apparently not influenced by his lapse. **91.50**

Enforcement of foreign judgments and restraining foreign proceedings

Where a party has not received a fair trial in another jurisdiction contrary to **art.** 6(1) of the Convention, it would be contrary to public policy for the United Kingdom to enforce the judgment (*Maronier v Larmer* [2002] EWCA Civ 774, [2003] QB 620). **91.51**

However, the domestic courts will not refuse to register or enforce a foreign judgment or order just because some aspect constituted a breach of **art. 6** where it is not contrary to the overall interests of justice to register the order (*Barnette v United States of America* [2004] UKHL 37, [2004] 1 WLR 2241). Only a flagrant denial of the right to a fair trial would make it contrary to the interests of justice to enforce the foreign order (*United States of America v Montgomery (No. 2)* [2004] UKHL 37, [2004] 1 WLR 2241). While there is a strong presumption that courts in Convention States will be in compliance with their obligations under the Convention, the domestic court is still entitled to consider whether this is the case on the particular facts. In *Merchant International Co. Ltd v Natsionalna Aktsionerna Kompanii Naftogaz Ukrainy* [2012] EWCA Civ 196, [2012] 1 WLR 3036, a judgment of the Ukrainian court was a flagrant breach of the principle of legal certainty and the English court was entitled to refuse to recognise it.

Although a foreign judgment given in proceedings which in the view of an English court do not meet the requirements of a fair trial will not be recognised in England, it is not for the English court to restrain a party in proceedings before it from suing in another jurisdiction where that country is not itself bound by the Convention (*Al-Bassam v Al-Bassam* [2004] EWCA Civ 857, [2004] WTLR 757). The fear as to the fairness of the foreign proceedings and the enforceability of the foreign judgment in England should not be considered until the foreign judgment has been given. Limited interim restraint of the right to sue in another jurisdiction may, however, be necessary to protect the process of the English court from misuse.

RIGHT TO PRIVACY AND CONFIDENTIALITY AND CIVIL LITIGATION

Article 8 of the European Convention on Human Rights provides a right to confidentiality in communications passing between a lawyer and his or her client. In *General Mediterranean* **91.52**

Commentary

Holdings SA v Patel [2000] 1 WLR 272 it was contended that the former CPR, r. 48.7(3), was *ultra vires* the Civil Procedure Rule Committee. This provided that for the purposes of determining an application for a wasted costs order, the court could direct the disclosure of privileged documents to the court and, if the court so directed, to the other party to the application. It was held that the general words, 'may modify the rules of evidence' in the Civil Procedure Act 1997, sch. 1, para. 4, did not give the rule-makers power to abrogate or limit a person's right to legal confidentiality. To the extent that r. 48.7(3) diminished the substantive right to legal confidentiality it was *ultra vires*.

Toulson J also addressed the human rights issue and said that, as a matter of discretion, the court would not have ordered disclosure under r. 48.7(3) because the defendants had a right of confidentiality under **art. 8** of the European Convention in respect of their communications with their solicitors unless there was justification for the court to interfere with that right under **art. 8**(2). Adjudicating an application for a wasted costs order did not justify such interference.

Legal professional privilege is not impliedly overridden by the Inland Revenue's power under the Taxes Management Act 1970, s. 20(1), to require delivery of documents in a person's possession or power (*R (Morgan Grenfell and Co. Ltd) v Special Commissioner of Income Tax* [2002] UKHL 21, [2003] 1 AC 563). This decision highlighted the importance of legal professional privilege as 'a fundamental human right long established in the common law' as well as part of the right to privacy guaranteed by **art. 8** of the Convention, but note *McE v Prison Service of Northern Ireland* [2009] UKHL 15, [2009] 1 AC 908.

CPR, r. 35.10, requires an expert's report to state the substance of his or her instructions and effectively removes any privilege which would have attached to those instructions. It is arguable (though not likely) that this requirement might infringe a party's right to privacy under **art. 8**, although in a case concerning communications with experts who were instructed solely for the purpose of related criminal proceedings, the High Court has held that a witness should neither volunteer, nor be compelled to disclose, such privileged communications unless the privilege has been waived (*S County Council v B* [2000] Fam 76). The without-prejudice rule should be applied with restraint and only in cases in which the public interest plainly justifies its use (*Prudential Assurance Co. Ltd v Prudential Insurance Co. of America* [2003] EWCA Civ 1154, [2004] ETMR 29).

When considering a search order, the court ought to have regard to the **art. 8** right to respect for home life and this can extend to an individual's office (*Niemietz v Germany* (1992) 16 EHRR 97).

The refusal of the defendant local authority to supply the claimant with confidential information, in order to assist her decision whether to apply to remove the defendant as guardian of a child in care, constituted a breach of the claimant's rights under **arts 6** and **8** on the basis that a balance was required to be struck between the public and private interest in maintaining the confidentiality of the information and the public and private interest in permitting its disclosure for certain purposes (*R (Stevens) v Plymouth City Council* [2002] EWCA Civ 388, [2002] 1 WLR 2583).

Other areas where **art. 8** might be infringed are:

(a) in applications seeking disclosure of medical records; and
(b) surveillance evidence particularly in personal injury claims and covert videos of employees at work (see *Halford v United Kingdom* (1997) 24 EHRR 523).

However, the actions of the defendant insurers in *Jones v University of Warwick* [2003] EWCA Civ 151, [2003] 1 WLR 954 in filming the claimant covertly at home in order to vitiate her personal injury claim did not necessarily render the evidence inadmissible. The Convention does not decide what is to be the consequence of evidence being obtained in breach of **art. 8**(1), but rather it is for the domestic court to decide whether or not admitting the evidence would be in keeping with **art. 8(2)**. Such evidence is admissible under **art. 8(2)**, provided that the inquiries made and the surveillance carried out were reasonable and proportionate in the circumstances and necessary in a democratic society (see also *Martin v McGuiness* 2003 SLT 1424).

Admitting as evidence a covert video recording made by a childcare employee, depicting the unwanted sexual advances made towards her by her employer in front of his child, engaged the child's **art. 8** rights to respect to his private life. However, where that interference is necessary to protect a claimant's right to a fair trial under **art. 6**, the court will allow such evidence to be produced. The employment tribunal was directed to view the video in private to protect the child's rights as much as possible (*XXX v YYY* [2004] EWCA Civ 231, [2004] IRLR 471). In contrast where the police covertly filmed a person in a custody suite for identification purposes and used the videotape in the prosecution against him, such interference was not in accordance with the law, because the police had failed to comply with the procedures set out in relevant Codes of Practice under the Police and Criminal Evidence Act 1984, s. 66 (*Perry v United Kingdom* (2003) 39 EHRR 3).

RIGHT TO FREEDOM OF EXPRESSION AND CIVIL LITIGATION

One particular issue concerning the right to freedom of expression is the extent to which it sometimes has to be balanced against conflicting rights, such as whether the right of an individual to a fair trial will be prejudiced by the publication of information about the proceedings (*Observer v United Kingdom* (1991) 14 EHRR 153) and the effect on the right to privacy of others (e.g. *Lingens v Austria* (1986) 8 EHRR 103). Racist material does not enjoy the protection of **art. 10** because it breaches the rights of others (*Thomas v News Group Newspapers Ltd* [2001] EWCA Civ 1233, [2002] EMLR 4). **91.53**

Article 10 of the European Convention on Human Rights was cited successfully in reducing excessive damages awarded by a jury in a defamation case (*Tolstoy Miloslavsky v United Kingdom* (1995) 20 EHRR 442), but the article does not affect the principles underlying the defence of justification in the law on defamation (*Chase v News Group Newspapers Ltd* [2002] EWCA Civ 1772, [2003] EMLR 11).

The principle of strict liability for unintentional defamation is an interference with freedom of expression under **art. 10** (*O'Shea v MGN Ltd* [2001] EMLR 943). So too is a ban on the defendant in libel proceedings relying at all on leaked confidential documents crucial to its defence of justification and *Reynolds* public interest (*Commissioner of Police of the Metropolis v Times Newspapers Ltd* [2011] EWHC 2705, (QB) LTL 28/10/2011). The repetition and conduct rules in defamation (which deny a defence of justification to a publisher who repeats a libel and require that an allegation of reasonable suspicion be defended by relying on the claimant's conduct) are not incompatible with **arts. 6** and **10** (*Berezovsky v Forbes Inc.* [2001] EWCA Civ 1251, [2001] EMLR 45). In *Times Newspapers Ltd (Nos. 1 and 2) v United Kingdom* (applications 3002/03 and 23676/03) [2009] EMLR 14, the ECHR held that there had been no violation of **art. 10** by the 'internet publication rule', whereby each internet publication of a defamatory statement gave rise to a separate cause of action. For corporate claimants, the principle that libel is actionable without proof of special damage does not infringe **art. 10** (*Jameel v Wall Street Journal Europe Sprl* [2005] EWCA Civ 74, [2005] QB 904, reversed on another point [2006] UKHL 44, [2007] 1 AC 359). The **Human Rights Act 1998** has rendered the courts more likely to entertain a submission that pursuit of a libel action is an abuse of process, particularly where the publications that took place in England did not amount to a real and substantial tort and the costs of the proceedings would be disproportionate to the damage and vindication that would result from a judgment in the claimant's favour (*Jameel v Dow Jones and Co. Inc.* [2005] EWCA Civ 75, [2005] QB 946).

The High Court has the power to impose a cost-capping regime in appropriate cases, such as defamation cases where extravagant claimant's costs might inhibit the defendant's exercise of his right to freedom of expression (*King v Telegraph Group Ltd* [2004] EWCA Civ 613, [2005] 1 WLR 2282). The usual costs rules may also be altered in privacy and defamation cases where the right to freedom of expression might otherwise be violated, so that where the defendant's case was not entirely without merit, the costs had far exceeded the damages awarded and the claimant was a wealthy celebrity, a requirement on an unsuccessful defendant to pay a substantial success fee was disproportionate (*MGN Ltd v United Kingdom* (application 39401/04) (2011) 53 EHRR 5).

The 'public interest' exception to press freedom has been raised in a number of cases concerning protection of a journalist's source. For example, in *Goodwin v United Kingdom* (1996) 22 EHRR 123 the ECHR considered that on the facts the case for disclosing a source neither outweighed the need to protect democratic freedoms nor satisfied the requirement of proportionality. In the later case of *Camelot Group plc v Centaur Communications Ltd* [1999] QB 124 the Court of Appeal considered that where there was a continuing threat of leaks the 'interests of justice' as specified in s. 10 of the Contempt of Court Act 1981 outweighed the need to protect press freedoms. The court justified its approach by impliedly equating the 'interests of justice' with the public interest exception in **art. 10(2)** (see also *John v Express Newspapers* [2000] 1 WLR 1931, *Ashworth Hospital Authority v MGN Ltd* [2002] UKHL 29, [2002] 1 WLR 2033; cf. *Mersey Care NHS Trust v Ackroyd* [2003] EWCA Civ 663, [2003] Lloyd's Rep Med 379; *Mersey Care NHS Trust v Ackroyd* [2007] EWCA Civ 101, [2007] HRLR 19; *Malik v Crown Court at Manchester* [2008] EWHC 1362 (Admin), [2008] 4 All ER 403). On the other hand, in *Financial Times Ltd v United Kingdom* (application 821/03) (2009) 50 EHRR 46), emphasising the chilling effect of journalists being seen to assist in the identification of anonymous sources, the ECHR found that there had been a violation of **art. 10** by virtue of a disclosure order made against newspapers in relation to the source of leaked information. The public interest in the protection of journalists' sources was sufficient to outweigh any threat of damage through the future dissemination of a company's confidential information or any possibility of obtaining damages for past breaches of confidence. The Supreme Court has noted the parallels between the *Reynolds* public interest defence to defamation and the balancing exercise between **arts. 8** and **10**, and has reiterated the importance of **art. 10** in ensuring press freedom to publish matters of genuine public interest (*Flood v Times Newspapers Ltd* [2012] UKSC 11, [2012] 2 AC 273).

The Code of Practice of the Advertising Standards Authority is compliant with the European Convention on Human Rights, **art. 10(2)** (*R v Advertising Standards Authority Ltd, ex parte Matthias Rath BV* [2001] EMLR 22).

PRIVACY, FREEDOM OF EXPRESSION AND INJUNCTIONS

91.54 The key provisions in relation to privacy, freedom of expression and injunctions are **arts 8** and **10** of the European Convention on Human Rights and s. 12 of the **Human Rights Act 1998** (see **91.11**).

Article 8

91.55 **Article 8** informs the right of personal privacy under the equitable doctrine of breach of confidence (*Douglas v Hello! Ltd* [2001] QB 967). It may, for example, be relied upon in order to prevent publication of photographs of the interior of a party's home for security reasons (*Beckham v MGN Ltd* (2001) LTL 30/7/2001; see also *A v B plc* [2002] EWCA Civ 337, [2003] QB 195). *However, there is no separate* cause of action in England for invasion of privacy (*Wainwright v Home Office* [2003] UKHL 53, [2004] 2 AC 406; cf. *Wainwright v United Kingdom* (application 12350/04) (2006) 44 EHRR 40). **Article 8** may be engaged in the sense that information could relate to family life without it necessarily following that there was a reasonable expectation of privacy (which would be required for a breach of **art. 8** in this context) (*Hutcheson v News Group Newspapers Ltd* [2011] EWCA Civ 808, [2012] EMLR 2).

Article 8 has also been relied upon to prevent the publication of photographs of the claimant, a children's television presenter, visiting a brothel on the basis that freedom of expression was outweighed by the 'peculiar degree of intrusion into the integrity of the claimant's personality' by their publication (*Theakston v MGN Ltd* [2002] EWHC 137 (QB), [2002] EMLR 22). The broad test has been said to be 'whether disclosure of the information about the individual would give substantial offence to a person of ordinary sensibilities assuming that person was placed in similar circumstances' (*Campbell v Mirror Group Newspapers Ltd* [2004] UKHL 22, [2004] 2 AC 457 per Lord Hope of Craighead at [92]). Pictures of the claimant's attendance at Narcotics Anonymous and the details of her treatment were private information and imported a duty of confidence as the claimant had a reasonable expectation that this information would be kept confidential, although it was justifiable to publish the fact that she was misleading the public when she said she did not take drugs. There was also a reasonable expectation of privacy in relation to sexual activities carried on between consenting adults on private property, and serious reasons would need to exist before interference with this expectation could be justified. In the circumstances, exposure could not be justified in the public interest and amounted to a breach of confidence and a breach of **art. 8** rights (*Mosley v News Group Newspapers Ltd* [2008] EWHC 1777 (QB), [2008] EMLR 20). See also *Lady Archer v Williams* [2003] EWHC 1670 (QB), [2003] EMLR 38 and *McKennitt v Ash* [2006] EWCA Civ 1714, [2008] QB 73.

Commentary

Once it has been decided that the information is confidential and of a private nature, the test to be applied when considering whether it is necessary to restrict freedom of expression in order to prevent disclosure is not simply whether the information is a matter of public interest but whether in all the circumstances it is in the public interest that the duty of confidence should be breached. In applying the test of proportionality the nature of the relationship that gave rise to the duty of confidentiality might be important. Where an employee of the Prince of Wales had disclosed his journals, it was relevant that there was an important public interest in employees respecting the obligations of confidence they had assumed. The public interest in disclosure of the journals' contents did not outweigh the confidential nature of the information and the relationship of confidence under which it had been received (*Prince of Wales v Associated Newspapers Ltd* [2006] EWCA Civ 1776, [2008] Ch 57). However, the mere fact that information was imparted in the course of a relationship of confidence does not create an expectation of privacy. It is a question to be decided on a case-by-case basis following a detailed examination of the circumstances, including the nature of the information and the circumstances in which it had been imparted or obtained (*Lord Browne of Madingley v Associated Newspapers Ltd* [2007] EWCA Civ 295, [2008] QB 103). Private correspondence attracts the protection of **art. 8** not only when in the hands of the writer or during transmission, but also once received by the recipient or in someone else's hands (*Warner v Verfides* [2008] EWHC 2609 (Ch), [2009] Bus LR 500). Even where material has already been sent to a media organisation in such a way that private information could easily be accessed (such as in circumstances where redaction carried out was ineffective), the redacted material still attracts the protection of **art. 8** and an injunction to restrain publication would still be appropriate as the only way to stop the people who had received the material from reading and publishing it (*Ambrosiadou v Coward* [2011] EWCA Civ 409, [2011] 2 FLR 617).

A photograph taken of an infant child on the street in a public place could arguably breach the reasonable expectation of privacy. The fact that the subject is a child is of great significance as the law should protect the children of parents who are in the public eye from intrusive media attention. Whether or not there is a breach will depend on the circumstances. It is not possible to draw a general distinction between activities that are part of a person's private recreation time (which are protected from intrusion) and other activities such as walking down the street or a trip to the shop to buy milk. It is not necessarily the case that such routine activities should not attract a reasonable expectation of privacy. It will depend on the circumstances (*Murray v Express Newspapers plc* [2008] EWCA Civ 446, [2009] Ch 481).

Generally, when a court is deciding where the balance lies between **art. 8** and **art. 10** rights, it should accord particular weight to the rights of children likely to be affected by any publication, but the interests of those children cannot be treated as overriding and the public interest in disclosure must still be weighed against the likely harm done through the interference with privacy rights (*ETK v News Group Newspapers Ltd* [2011] EWCA Civ 439, [2011] 1 WLR 1827).

One of the essential features of the protection of private law under **art. 8** is that it enables people to live freely according to their own choices. However, the courts have stated that while the freedom to live as one chooses is a valuable freedom, so also is the freedom to criticise (within the limits of the law) the conduct of other members of society as being harmful or wrong. Where the substance of an application to restrict publication of details about a personal relationship was essentially aimed at protecting the applicant's business relationship, it was likely that newspapers would publish the story in a way that was capable of being defended in accordance with the law of defamation. Therefore the applicant was not likely to succeed in a claim for breach of confidence or misuse of private information, and as such no injunction could be granted (*LNS v Persons Unknown* [2010] EWHC 119 (QB), [2010] 2 FLR 1306).

Similarly, the courts are reluctant to allow individuals to hide behind **art. 8** to avoid a complainant's attempt to seek redress. While sexual activity would normally lead to a reasonable expectation of privacy therefore, this could not be the case where the activity amounted to sexual harassment (*BUQ v HRE* [2012] EWHC 774 (QB), [2012] IRLR 653).

Where the identity of the applicant has already been revealed in local and national media in an unjustified manner, contrary to **art. 8**, the actions of the applicant in attracting further publicity as the victim of such interference do not nullify his claim. The disclosure by a local authority of closed circuit television footage and photographs of a person during a suicide bid to local and national media without taking adequate steps to ensure that his identity was masked was held to be a disproportionate and therefore unjustified interference with his private life (*Peck v United Kingdom* (application 44647/98) [2003] EMLR 15).

A third party, who knows or ought to be aware that an individual has information which is private or personal to which he can properly deny access to third parties and from which he intends to profit commercially, will be in breach of duty if he uses or publishes the material without authority to the detriment of the owner. However, such material is only protected by the law of confidence and is not treated as property that can be owned or transferred. The publisher who has the right to publish the material has no right of confidence in unauthorised publication of that material by a third party and has no cause of action in that respect (*Douglas v Hello! Ltd (No. 3)* [2005] EWCA Civ 595, [2006] QB 125).

Article 8 does not impose a positive requirement on the press to notify individuals in advance of an intention to publish potentially private information so as to give them the opportunity to seek an injunction. The imposition of such a requirement might give rise to a chilling effect on freedom of expression, and would be difficult to give effect to in practice where, for example, a public interest exception would probably be required (*Mosley v United Kingdom* (application 48009/08) (2011) 53 EHRR 30).

Article 10

91.56 Injunctions to protect information which might lead to the identification of the claimants have been granted on the basis that the claim fell within the exceptions to the **art. 10(1)** right *of freedom of expression* on a narrow interpretation of all the criteria within **art. 10(2)** of the Convention. Those criteria were, first, the grant of an injunction had to be in accordance with the law. Second, there had to be a strong and pressing need for confidentiality to be protected.

If the relevant information has become generally accessible and in the public domain such that it has ceased to be confidential information then no injunction will be granted (*BBC v HarperCollins Publishers Ltd* [2010] EWHC 2424 (Ch), [2011] EMLR 6). Third, the remedy sought had to be proportionate to the legitimate aim pursued (*Venables v News Group Newspapers Ltd* [2001] Fam 430, where **art. 10** was overridden by **arts. 2** and **3**, and see also *X, a Woman Formerly Known as Mary Bell v S* [2003] EWHC 1101 (QB), [2003] FSR 850). However, in criminal proceedings, given the weight traditionally given to the importance of open reporting of criminal proceedings in particular, it is appropriate in carrying out the balancing exercise to begin by acknowledging the force of the argument under **art. 10** before considering whether the right under **art. 8** is sufficient to outweigh it. Where an injunction was sought to protect the identity of a child who was not itself directly involved in proceedings, but whose mother was the defendant, the **art. 8** right was held not to outweigh the strong rule in favour of unrestricted publicity of any proceedings in a criminal trial (*Re S (A Child) (Identification: Restrictions on Publication)* [2004] UKHL 47, [2005] 1 AC 593).

However, a local authority was entitled to an injunction restraining the publication of the identity of a defendant and victim in a criminal trial and their HIV status, to protect the privacy of their children who were not involved in the trial but were the subject of care proceedings. In the circumstances knowledge of the identity was not essential in order to give the public an adequate understanding of the issues for the purposes of open justice or general discussion. The naming of the parents was likely to inflict substantial damage on the children's **art. 8** rights (*A Local Authority v W* [2005] EWHC 1564 (Fam), [2006] 1 FLR 1).

The right to reputation is protected by **art. 8** and may in certain circumstances, where allegations are particularly serious given the position of the individual and where he has clearly been caused severe distress, mean that it is necessary for the identity of parties to litigation to be withheld to avoid an unjustifiable interference with his private life. However, cogent reasons would be needed before the principle of open justice is derogated from, and media speculation is not sufficient (*Gray v UVW* [2010] EWHC 2367 (QB), LTL 25/10/2010). See also **61.21**.

In the majority of cases the public interest in favour of publication and freedom of expression can be satisfied without any need to identify the vulnerable individuals in question. Where the BBC had produced a television programme about adoption which would have constituted a massive intrusion into the privacy of the subject of the programme, to the extent that it would undermine her dignity as a human being and mean there was a risk that she would be greeted with a hostile and abusive reaction from viewers who might recognise her following the broadcast, the value of the broadcaster's expression under **art. 10** could not be proportionate to the violation of her privacy. The programme could still be broadcast but without identifying the subject or her child (*T v British Broadcasting Corporation* [2007] EWHC 1683 (QB), [2008] 1 FLR 281).

However, in some cases, even reporting restrictions in child care proceedings should not be too wide where the parents of the child in question wish there to be publicity. The **art. 10** rights of the parents should not be disproportionately interfered with, particularly in light of the fundamental principle that justice should be administered in public, and particularly in relation to alleged miscarriages of justice where it is essential that there be open and public debate in the media in order to promote public confidence in the judicial process and to deter abuses of power (*Re Webster* [2006] EWHC 2733 (Fam), [2007] EMLR 7). See also *Re British Broadcasting Corporation* [2009] UKHL 34, [2010] 1 AC 145.

Similarly where it was in the public interest for there to be open debate concerning the use of freezing orders on suspected terrorists, that public interest justified the interference with the applicant's private life by revealing his identity, particularly where the evidence as to the effect on his private life had been general and therefore not compelling. Without identifying a relevant individual, stories in the media are less compelling and given less importance by editors, and therefore public debate and information would in fact suffer by not identifying him,

Commentary

meaning that in this case there was a powerful public interest in allowing the suspect to be identified (*Re Guardian News and Media Ltd* [2010] UKSC 1, [2010] 2 AC 697) (but note *Secretary of State for the Home Department v AP (No. 2)* [2010] UKSC 26, [2010] 1 WLR 1652, where there was no evidence of the strong public interest in open media reporting before the court and therefore anonymity was granted in proceedings relating to a control order).

It is important to recognise that in applications for anonymity orders each case is likely to turn on its own facts and much will depend on the evidence before the court as to the extent of the damage to private life as compared to the evidence of the public interest in disclosure (see, for example, *AMM v HXW* [2010] EWHC 2457 (QB), 160 NLJ 1425, and *KJH v HGF* [2010] EWHC 3064 (QB), LTL 26/11/2010). Generally, however, it is likely that if an individual is identified, significant other information about the proceedings would have to be withheld from disclosure, whereas if the party were to remain anonymous, greater details of the matter could be published, which may better serve the public interest (*H v News Group Newspapers Ltd* [2011] EWCA Civ 42, [2011] 1 WLR 1645). Another alternative is an order under the Children and Young Persons Act 1933, s. 39, prohibiting the identification of a child in newspaper reports, since this would protect the rights of a vulnerable child but interfere less with the principle of open justice and freedom of expression and be less restrictive than a full anonymity order (*A (A Child) v Cambridge University Hospitals NHS Foundation Trust* [2011] EWHC 454 (QB), [2011] EMLR 18). Note *R(Y) v Aylesbury Crown Court* [2012] EWHC 1140 (Admin), [2012] EMLR 26.

Article 10 requires the provision of full and public reasons for decisions of the court, which are also required under **art. 6**. There is no reason to prevent publication of a judge's full reasons in circumstances where the relevant information has already been published so that it is no longer confidential in any event (*Long Beach Ltd v Global Witness Ltd* [2007] EWHC 1816 (QB), LTL 2/8/2007).

A defendant protester's right to freedom of expression under **art. 10** would be interfered with in granting an injunction to make him cease his protest and remove placards which encroached on to the public highway but did not interfere with the public's right to pass and repass on the highway (*Westminster City Council v Haw* [2002] EWHC 2073).

The provisions of the Copyright, Designs and Patents Act 1988 fulfil the requirements of **art. 10(2)** of the Convention in that the needs of a democratic society include the recognition and protection of private property including intellectual property. Rare circumstances could arise where the right to freedom of expression under **art. 10** conflicts with the protection afforded by the 1988 Act, notwithstanding the express exceptions in the Act (*Ashdown v Telegraph Group Ltd* [2001] EWCA Civ 1142, [2002] Ch 149). In those circumstances the court is bound to apply the 1988 Act in a manner which accommodates the right of freedom of expression, which requires the court to look closely at the facts of individual cases. Usually this can be achieved by declining the discretionary relief of an injunction.

Interim injunctions

91.57 The **Human Rights Act 1998** has not substantially altered the test for the grant of interim injunctions in *American Cyanamid Co. v Ethicon Ltd* [1975] AC 396. Although the requirement in the **Human Rights Act 1998, s. 12(3)**, that the applicant 'is likely to establish' at trial that publication should not be allowed is slightly higher in the scale of probability than 'a real prospect' of success, the difference between the two is so small that there would not be many, if any, cases that would proceed under *American Cyanamid* but fail under **s. 12(3)** (*Imutran Ltd v Uncaged Campaigns Ltd* [2001] 2 All ER 385).

The right of an author and publisher to freedom of expression under **art. 10** is secondary to the countervailing public interest within **art. 10(2)**, namely, the public policy exemplified in the law of contract whereby the courts regularly enforce provisions for the restriction of competition provided they are reasonable and proportionate. Accordingly, an interim injunction was granted to restrain publication until trial of a claim that the defendant publisher had induced or procured a breach of contract between another publisher and the claimant (*Psychology Press Ltd v Flanagan* [2002] EWHC 1205 (QB), LTL 24/6/2002).

Where the potential consequences of not granting injunctive relief may be grave this will be a factor in the court's decision as to whether to grant relief. Where the claimant sought an interim injunction restraining the defendants from pursuing conduct that amounted to harassment of the claimant's employees, the court found that there was a serious likelihood that in the absence of injunctive relief the employees would suffer unlawful harassment of a serious nature and therefore it was just and convenient to afford protection to them when the claimant had established a real prospect of success at trial (*Emerson Developments Ltd v Avery* [2004] EWHC 194 (QB), LTL 26/01/2004).

Where the public interest justifies the publication of information, it is less likely that an injunction will be granted. The public interest justified the disclosure of undercover filming in a food production company that supplied the NHS by an investigative journalist posing as an employee. The public interest in disclosure was not qualified by the need to give the owner of the information a right to respond. Furthermore, the court was not convinced that this was in fact confidential information at all. Mann J stated that there had to be something more than an employee filming the workplace to have the quality of confidential information, and it was not made confidential simply because of the confidentiality provisions in the employee's contract (*Tillery Valley Foods Ltd v Channel Four Television Corporation* [2004] EWHC 1075 (Ch), [2004] 101 (22) LSG 31).

The body of case law building up under the **Human Rights Act 1998** regarding the need to balance the competing interests in **art. 8** and **art. 10** relates to breach of confidence, and is not equally applicable to interim injunction applications in the law of defamation. Where a claimant sought an interim injunction in libel proceedings and relied on the **Human Rights Act 1998, s. 12(3)**, as interpreted in *Cream Holdings Ltd v Banerjee* [2004] UKHL 44, [2005] 1 AC 253, to argue that the test for restraint of publication should be whether the claimant was able to demonstrate at this stage that she would be more likely than not to establish at trial that publication should not be allowed, the court held that the test to be applied in defamation proceedings is that the claimant must demonstrate that it is clear that the alleged libel is untrue and that the plea of justification is bound to fail (*Bonnard v Perryman* [1891] 2 Ch 269). This test is still good law. The authorities put forward by the claimant dealt with protection of confidential information, and had not changed the law of defamation (*Greene v Associated Newspapers Ltd* [2004] EWCA Civ 1462, [2005] QB 972). However, in trade mark infringement actions involving comparative advertising it has been held that the general rule is that in *Cream Holdings Ltd v Banerjee*, so an interim injunction will not be granted unless it is shown that the claimant will probably succeed at trial (*Boehringer Ingelheim Ltd v Vetplus Ltd* [2007] EWCA Civ 583, [2007] Bus LR 1456).

Commentary

Chapter 92 Changes in Terminology Made by the CPR

92.1 The reforms of civil procedure begun by the CPR in 1998 have introduced new terminology. Sometimes this is a straightforward change of name, for example, from plaintiff to claimant. Often the change of terminology reflects a change of procedure, for example, discovery has been replaced by disclosure of documents. Very little legislation dating from before the CPR has been amended to use the new terminology. For example, there are still several references in the County Courts Act 1984 to 'plaintiffs' and none to 'claimants'. Table 92.1 is a brief guide to the changes in terminology, which will aid in translating older legislation, cases and textbooks.

Table 92.1 New terminology

Old term	New term
action	claim
affidavit of service	certificate of service
amicus curiae	advocate to the court
Anton Piller order	search order
assessment (of costs)	summary assessment
Calderbank letter (or offer)	Part 36 offer or offer to settle
certiorari, order of	quashing order
close of pleadings	(no equivalent)
conditional leave to defend	conditional order
costs in the cause	costs in the case
counterclaim	a counterclaim is an additional claim but the term 'counterclaim' is also still in use
Crown Office	Administrative Court Office
discovery	disclosure
entering an appearance	acknowledgment of service
ex parte	without notice (to other parties)
garnishee order	third party debt order
Grepe v Loam order	civil restraint order
guardian *ad litem*	litigation friend
in camera	in private
in open court	in public
inter partes hearing	hearing with notice (or hearing on notice) (to other parties)
interlocutory	interim
interlocutory judgment for damages to be assessed	judgment for an amount to be decided by the court
interrogatory	request for further information
leave	permission
legal aid taxation	detailed assessment of costs payable out of the Community Legal Service Fund or by the Lord Chancellor under Part 1 of the Legal Aid, Sentencing and Punishment of Offenders Act 2012
mandamus, order of	mandatory order
Mareva injunction (or order)	freezing injunction
minor	child
motion (in Chancery)	judge's application
motions day (in Chancery)	applications day
next friend	litigation friend
not admitted	required to prove
oral examination	obtaining information from judgment debtor
originating application	Part 8 claim form (application notice in insolvency proceedings)

Old term	New term
originating summons	Part 8 claim form
patient	protected person
plaintiff	claimant
pleading	statement of case
preliminary act (Admiralty proceedings)	collision statement of case
prohibition, order of	prohibiting order
rebutter	(no equivalent)
rejoinder	(no equivalent)
request for further and better particulars	request for further information
schedule of special damages	schedule of past and future loss and expense
setting down (for trial)	listing (for trial)
small claims arbitration	small claims track
specific discovery	specific disclosure
statement of claim	particulars of claim
subpoena	witness summons
substituted service	alternative service
summons for directions	case management conference
summons (for interim application)	application notice
summons (to commence proceedings in a county court)	claim form
Supreme Court Taxing Office	Senior Courts Costs Office
surrebutter	(no equivalent)
surrejoinder	(no equivalent)
taxation (of costs)	detailed assessment
taxing master	costs judge
third-party proceedings	additional claim
triable issue	real prospect of success
writ (to commence proceedings)	claim form (writs are still used in execution of judgments)

Appendix 1 Civil Procedure Rules 1998 and Practice Directions

CPR 1–25 & PDs

CPR 1–25 & PDs

CPR 1–25 & PDs

CPR 1–25 & PDs

Introduction

What is in Appendix 1

This appendix contains the text of the Civil Procedure Rules 1998 (SI 1998/3132) as amended, with the text of all supplementing practice directions. Each practice direction has been placed after the Part of the CPR which it supplements. Practice Direction — Protocols is in **appendix 2**. The text of the rules and practice directions incorporates all amendments in force on 1 July 2013, except those made by SI 2013/1571 (which inserted CPR, Part 82, and made consequential amendments).

To clarify the headings, we have inserted 'CPR' at the beginning of the heading of each Part of the CPR, and 'PD' and the relevant Part number at the beginning of the heading of each practice direction.

In SI 1998/3132 there is a contents list at the beginning of each Part of the CPR (except Parts 4, 49, 50 and 51). We have updated those contents lists to reflect subsequent amendments to the CPR.

In this appendix, unless otherwise stated, a reference to a Part or rule is a reference to a Part or rule of the CPR. A footnote in square brackets is editorial.

The places where a Part of the CPR is referred to in **chapters 1** to **92** of *Blackstone's Civil Practice* are listed under the title of the Part. The places where a rule is referred to are listed under the title of the rule. And similarly for practice directions and their paragraphs.

There is a list of amendments to the CPR, the dates they came into force and transitional provisions in Notes on text of the CPR after CPR, sch. 2.

Civil Procedure Rules 1998 Preamble

The Civil Procedure Rule Committee, having power under section 2 of the Civil Procedure Act 1997 to make rules of court under section 1 of that Act, make the following rules which may be cited as the Civil Procedure Rules 1998.

Introduction to the Practice Directions

1 The practice directions to the Civil Procedure Rules apply to civil litigation in the Queen's Bench Division and the Chancery Division of the High Court and to litigation in the county courts other than family proceedings. Where relevant they also apply to appeals to the Civil Division of the Court of Appeal.

2 Since the coming into force of the Constitutional Reform Act 2005 in April 2006, the power to make practice directions for the civil courts falls to the Lord Chief Justice (with the approval of the Lord Chancellor in most instances). This power is governed by the Civil Procedure Act 1997, s. 5 (as amended).

3 The Lord Chief Justice has power under the Constitutional Reform Act 2005, sch. 2, part 1, to nominate a judicial office holder to perform his functions with regards making designated directions. He has therefore nominated the Master of the Rolls to make practice directions for the civil courts.

Historical making powers

4 Until the inception of the Constitutional Reform Act 2005, practice directions were made:
(1) for the Queen's Bench Division by the Lord Chief Justice as president of that Division;
(2) for the Civil Division of the Court of Appeal by the Master of the Rolls as president of that Division;
(3) for the Chancery Division by the Vice-Chancellor as vice-president of that Division; and
(4) for the county courts by the Lord Chancellor or a person authorised to act on his behalf under the County Courts Act 1984, s. 74A.

CPR 1–25 & PDs

5 From April 1999 to July 2000 the Lord Chancellor authorised the Vice-Chancellor, Sir Richard Scott (as he then was) under s. 74A of the 1984 Act. The Vice-Chancellor made all practice directions for county courts during that time.

6 From July 2000 to September 2003 the Lord Chancellor authorised Lord Justice May to make these practice directions. Lord Justice May made all practice directions for county courts during that time.

7 From September 2003 until April 2006 the Lord Chancellor authorised Lord Justice Dyson to make practice directions for the county courts.

CPR Part 1 Overriding Objective

Part 1 **24.24, 30.2, 33.1, 60.4, 92.1** [For commentary on a specific rule, please refer to the cross-references after the title of the rule.]

1.1 The Overriding Objective

r.1.1 **1.11, 1.12, 1.13, 1.21, 1.27, 12.2, 49.8, 49.51, 54.1, 63.16**
r.1.1(1) **1.2, 1.11, 1.29, 48.6, 48.7, 72.1, 91.39**
r.1.1(2) **1.28, 15.32, 15.40, 42.3, 49.8, 71.38, 91.39**
r.1.1(2)(a) **59.3**
r.1.1(2)(b) **1.15, 37.10**
r.1.1(2)(c) **1.32, 46.1**
r.1.1(2)(c)(i)–(iii) **1.28**
r.1.1(2)(d) **1.32, 32.6, 47.29, 48.37**
r.1.1(2)(e) **1.28, 37.10**
r.1.1(2)(f) **42.3, 46.16**

(1) These Rules are a new procedural code with the overriding objective of enabling the court to deal with cases justly and at proportionate cost.
(2) Dealing with a case justly and at proportionate cost includes, so far as is practicable—
  (a) ensuring that the parties are on an equal footing;
  (b) saving expense;
  (c) dealing with the case in ways which are proportionate—
    (i) to the amount of money involved;
    (ii) to the importance of the case;
    (iii) to the complexity of the issues; and
    (iv) to the financial position of each party;
  (d) ensuring that it is dealt with expeditiously and fairly;
  (e) allotting to it an appropriate share of the court's resources, while taking into account the need to allot resources to other cases; and
  (f) enforcing compliance with rules, practice directions and orders.

1.2 Application by the Court of the Overriding Objective

r.1.2 **1.12, 1.13, 49.74**

The court must seek to give effect to the overriding objective when it—
  (a) exercises any power given to it by the Rules; or
  (b) interprets any rule,
subject to rules 76.2, 79.2 and 80.2.

1.3 Duty of the Parties

r.1.3 **1.12, 1.38, 21.2, 41.2, 42.3, 46.16, 48.10, 49.51, 73.20**

The parties are required to help the court to further the overriding objective.

1.4 Court's Duty to Manage Cases

r.1.4 **49.74, 61.37, 63.16, 73.20, 87.6, 91.41**
r.1.4(1) **42.3**
r.1.4(2)(a) **46.16, 48.1, 48.10, 68.5**
r.1.4(2)(b) **33.6, 68.5**
r.1.4(2)(c) **33.1, 33.6, 34.5, 61.17, 61.37, 68.5, 91.41**
r.1.4(2)(d) **61.17**
r.1.4(2)(e) **42.42**
r.1.4(2)(f) **42.42**
r.1.4(2)(h) **32.1**
r.1.4(2)(i) **PC 20, 32.1, 37.10**
r.1.4(2)(j) **13.15, 32.24, 61.19**
r.1.4(2)(k) **32.24**

(1) The court must further the overriding objective by actively managing cases.
(2) Active case management includes—
  (a) encouraging the parties to co-operate with each other in the conduct of the proceedings;

CPR 1–25 & PDs

(b) identifying the issues at an early stage;
(c) deciding promptly which issues need full investigation and trial and accordingly disposing summarily of the others;
(d) deciding the order in which issues are to be resolved;
(e) encouraging the parties to use an alternative dispute resolution(GL) procedure if the court considers that appropriate and facilitating the use of such procedure;
(f) helping the parties to settle the whole or part of the case;
(g) fixing timetables or otherwise controlling the progress of the case;
(h) considering whether the likely benefits of taking a particular step justify the cost of taking it;
(i) dealing with as many aspects of the case as it can on the same occasion;
(j) dealing with the case without the parties needing to attend at court;
(k) making use of technology; and
(l) giving directions to ensure that the trial of a case proceeds quickly and efficiently.

CPR Part 2 Application and Interpretation of the Rules

Part 2 [For commentary on a specific rule, please refer to the cross-references after the title of the rule.]

2.1 Application of the Rules

r.2.1 49.74, 54.12, 74.47
r.2.1(1) 1.11, 40.2
r.2.1(2) 1.11, 85.10

(1) Subject to paragraph (2), these Rules apply to all proceedings in—
  (a) county courts;
  (b) the High Court; and
  (c) the Civil Division of the Court of Appeal.

(2) These Rules do not apply to proceedings of the kinds specified in the first column of the following table (proceedings for which rules may be made under the enactments specified in the second column) except to the extent that they are applied to those proceedings by another enactment—

	Proceedings	Enactments
1.	Insolvency proceedings	Insolvency Act 1986, ss. 411 and 412
2.	Non-contentious or common form probate proceedings	Senior Courts Act 1981, s. 127
3.	Proceedings in the High Court when acting as a Prize Court	Prize Courts Act 1894, s. 3
4.	Proceedings before the Court of Protection	Mental Capacity Act 2005, s. 51
5.	Family proceedings	Matrimonial and Family Proceedings Act 1984, s. 40
6.	Adoption proceedings	Adoption Act 1976, s. 66 or Adoption and Children Act 2002, s. 141
7.	Election petitions in the High Court	Representation of the People Act 1983, s. 182

2.2 The Glossary

(1) The glossary at the end of these Rules is a guide to the meaning of certain legal expressions used in the Rules, but is not to be taken as giving those expressions any meaning in the Rules which they do not have in the law generally.

(2) Subject to paragraph (3), words in these Rules which are included in the glossary are followed by '(GL)'.

(3) The words 'counterclaim', 'damages', 'practice form' and 'service', which appear frequently in the Rules, are included in the glossary but are not followed by '(GL)'.

2.3 Interpretation

r.2.3 5.20, 6.9, 23.2, 23.13, 42.8
r.2.3(1) 14.1, 14.51, 14.55, 15.54, 15.56, 17.9, 17.10, 20.6, 20.20, 23.2, 23.5, 23.12, 32.2, 42.6, 42.7, 42.8, 51.13, 74.12
r.2.3(2) 11.4

(1) In these Rules—

'child' has the meaning given by rule 21.1(2);

'civil restraint order' means an order restraining a party—

(a) from making any further applications in current proceedings (a limited civil restraint order);

(b) from issuing certain claims or making certain applications in specified courts (an extended civil restraint order); or

(c) from issuing any claim or making any application in specified courts (a general civil restraint order).

'claim for personal injuries' means proceedings in which there is a claim for damages in respect of personal injuries to the claimant or any other person or in respect of a person's death, and 'personal injuries' includes any disease and any impairment of a person's physical or mental condition;

'claimant' means a person who makes a claim;

'CCR' is to be interpreted in accordance with Part 50;

'court officer' means a member of the court staff,

'defendant' means a person against whom a claim is made;

'defendant's home court' means—

(a) if the claim is proceeding in a county court, the county court for the district in which the defendant resides or carries on business; and

(b) if the claim is proceeding in the High Court, the district registry for the district in which the defendant resides or carries on business or, where there is no such district registry, the Royal Courts of Justice;

(Rule 6.23 provides for a party to give an address for service)

'designated money claim' means any claim which—

(a) is started in a county court under Part 7;

(b) is only a claim for either or both a specified amount of money or an unspecified amount of money; and

(c) is not a claim for which special procedures are provided in these rules;

'filing', in relation to a document, means delivering it, by post or otherwise, to the court office;

'judge' means, unless the context otherwise requires, a judge, Master or district judge or a person authorised to act as such;

'jurisdiction' means, unless the context requires otherwise, England and Wales and any part of the territorial waters of the United Kingdom adjoining England and Wales;

'legal representative' means a—

(a) barrister;

(b) solicitor;

(c) solicitor's employee;

(d) manager of a body recognised under section 9 of the Administration of Justice Act 1985; or

(e) person who, for the purposes of the Legal Services Act 2007, is an authorised person in relation to an activity which constitutes the conduct of litigation (within the meaning of that Act),

who has been instructed to act for a party in relation to proceedings;

'litigation friend' has the meaning given by Part 21;

'preferred court' means, if the claim is proceeding in a county court, the county court the claimant has specified in practice form N1 as the court to which the proceedings should be transferred if necessary;

'protected party' has the meaning given by rule 21.1(2);

'RSC' is to be interpreted in accordance with Part 50;

'statement of case'—

(a) means a claim form, particulars of claim where these are not included in a claim form, defence, Part 20 claim, or reply to defence; and

(b) includes any further information given in relation to them voluntarily or by court order under rule 18.1;

'statement of value' is to be interpreted in accordance with rule 16.3; 'summary judgment' is to be interpreted in accordance with Part 24.

(2) A reference to a 'specialist list' is a reference to a list(GL) that has been designated as such by a rule or practice direction.
(3) Where the context requires, a reference to 'the court' means a reference to a particular county court, a district registry, or the Royal Courts of Justice.

2.4 Power of Judge, Master or District Judge to Perform Functions of the Court

r.2.4 32.3, 40.3, 42.5

Where these Rules provide for the court to perform any act then, except where an enactment, rule or practice direction provides otherwise, that act may be performed—

(a) in relation to proceedings in the High Court, by any judge, Master or district judge of that Court; and
(b) in relation to proceedings in a county court, by any judge or district judge.

2.5 Court Staff

(1) Where these Rules require or permit the court to perform an act of a formal or administrative character, that act may be performed by a court officer.
(2) A requirement that a court officer carry out any act at the request of a party is subject to the payment of any fee required by a fees order for the carrying out of that act.

(Rule 3.2 allows a court officer to refer to a judge before taking any step)

2.6 Court Documents to Be Sealed

r.2.6(1)–(2) 12.3
r.2.6(3) 49.79, 51.7

(1) The court must seal(GL) the following documents on issue—
    (a) the claim form; and
    (b) any other document which a rule or practice direction requires it to seal.
(2) The court may place the seal(GL) on the document—
    (a) by hand; or
    (b) by printing a facsimile of the seal on the document whether electronically or otherwise.
(3) A document purporting to bear the court's seal(GL) shall be admissible in evidence without further proof.

2.7 Court's Discretion as to Where It Deals With Cases

r.2.7 32.2

The court may deal with a case at any place that it considers appropriate.

2.8 Time

r.2.8 3.1, 3.3, 15.36, 15.42, 32.22, 82.6
r.2.8(1) 3.3
r.2.8(2) PC 28, 3.2, 36.6
r.2.8(3) PC 26, PC 27, 3.2
r.2.8(3)(b) PC 15
r.2.8(4) 3.3
r.2.8(4)(b) 3.3
r.2.8(5) 3.5

(1) This rule shows how to calculate any period of time for doing any act which is specified—
    (a) by these Rules;
    (b) by a practice direction; or
    (c) by a judgment or order of the court.
(2) A period of time expressed as a number of days shall be computed as clear days.
(3) In this rule 'clear days' means that in computing the number of days—
    (a) the day on which the period begins; and
    (b) if the end of the period is defined by reference to an event, the day on which that event occurs are not included.

Examples

(i) Notice of an application must be served at least 3 days before the hearing.
An application is to be heard on Friday 20 October.
The last date for service is Monday 16 October.

(ii) The court is to fix a date for a hearing.
The hearing must be at least 28 days after the date of notice.
If the court gives notice of the date of the hearing on 1 October, the earliest date for the hearing is 30 October.

(iii) Particulars of claim must be served within 14 days of service of the claim form.
The claim form is served on 2 October.
The last day for service of the particulars of claim is 16 October.

(4) Where the specified period—
(a) is 5 days or less; and
(b) includes—
(i) a Saturday or Sunday; or
(ii) a Bank Holiday, Christmas Day or Good Friday, that day does not count.

Examples

Notice of an application must be served at least 3 days before the hearing.
An application is to be heard on Monday 20 October.
The last date for service is Tuesday 14 October.

(5) Subject to the provisions of Practice Direction 5C, when the period specified—
(a) by these Rules or a practice direction; or
(b) by any judgment or court order,
for doing any act at the court office ends on a day on which the office is closed, that act shall be in time if done on the next day on which the court office is open.

2.9 Dates for Compliance to Be Calendar Dates and to Include Time of Day

r.2.9 3.1, 48.30
r.2.9(1) 3.6, 32.33, 42.45, 63.8
r.2.9(2) 3.6

(1) Where the court gives a judgment, order or direction which imposes a time limit for doing any act, the last date for compliance must, wherever practicable—
(a) be expressed as a calendar date; and
(b) include the time of day by which the act must be done.

(2) Where the date by which an act must be done is inserted in any document, the date must, wherever practicable, be expressed as a calendar date.

2.10 Meaning of 'Month' in Judgments, etc.

r.2.10 3.1, 3.4

Where 'month' occurs in any judgment, order, direction or other document, it means a calendar month.

2.11 Time Limits May Be Varied by Parties

r.2.11 3.1, 3.7, 15.35, 48.1, 86.14

Unless these Rules or a practice direction provide otherwise or the court orders otherwise, the time specified by a rule or by the court for a person to do any act may be varied by the written agreement of the parties.

(Rules 3.8 (sanctions have effect unless defaulting party obtains relief), 28.4 (variation of case management timetable — fast track) and 29.5 (variation of case management timetable — multi-track) provide for time limits that cannot be varied by agreement between the parties)

PD 2A Practice Direction 2A — Court Offices

This practice direction supplements CPR, Part 2.

[For commentary on a specific paragraph, please refer to the cross-references after the title of the paragraph.]

Central Office of the High Court at the Royal Courts of Justice

1 The Central Office shall be divided into such departments, and the business performed in the Central Office shall be distributed among the departments in such manner, as is set out in the Queen's Bench Division Guide.

Business in the Offices of the Senior Courts

para.2.1 2.7, 3.5

2.1 (1) The offices of the Senior Courts will be open on every day of the year except—
- (a) Saturdays and Sundays;
- (b) Good Friday;
- (c) Christmas Day;
- (d) a further day over the Christmas period determined in accordance with the table annexed to this practice direction;
- (e) Bank Holidays in England and Wales under the Banking and Financial Dealings Act 1971; and
- (f) such other days as the Lord Chancellor, with the concurrence of the Lord Chief Justice, the Master of the Rolls, the President of the Queen's Bench Division, the President of the Family Division, and the Chancellor of the High Court ('the Heads of Division') may direct.

(2) The hours during which the offices of the Senior Courts at the Royal Courts of Justice and at the Principal Registry of the Family Division at First Avenue House, 42–49 High Holborn, London WC1V 6NP will be open to the public are as follows—
- (a) from 10 am to 4.30 pm;
- (b) such other hours as the Lord Chancellor, with the concurrence of the Heads of Division, may from time to time direct.

(3) Every District Registry shall be open on the days and during the hours that the Lord Chancellor from time to time directs and, in the absence of any such directions, shall be open on the same days and during the same hours as the county court offices of which it forms part are open.

2.2 One of the masters of the Queen's Bench Division (the 'Practice Master') shall be present at the Central Office on every day on which the office is open for the purpose of superintending the business performed there and giving any directions which may be required on questions of practice and procedure.

County Courts

para.3.2 2.2, 3.5 para.3.3 3.5

3.1 Every county court shall have an office or, if the Lord Chancellor so directs, two or more offices, situated at such place or places as he may direct, for the transaction of the business of the court.

3.2 Every county court office, or if a court has two or more offices at least one of those offices, will be open on every day of the year except—
- (a) Saturdays and Sundays;
- (b) Good Friday;
- (c) Christmas Day;
- (d) a further day over the Christmas period determined in accordance with the table annexed to this practice direction;
- (e) Bank Holidays in England and Wales under the Banking and Financial Dealings Act 1971; and
- (f) such other days as the Lord Chancellor may direct.

CPR 1–25 & PDs

3.3 The hours during which any county court office is open to the public will be those published from time to time by, and available to the public on, the website of Her Majesty's Courts and Tribunals Service,[1] or such other hours as the Lord Chancellor may from time to time direct.

ANNEX COURT OFFICE CLOSURES AT CHRISTMAS AND NEW YEAR

Christmas Day	Bank Holiday	Further day	New Year Bank Holiday
Sunday 25 December	Monday 26 and Tuesday 27 December	Wednesday 28 December	Monday 2 January
Monday 25 December	Tuesday 26 December	Wednesday 27 December	Monday 1 January
Tuesday 25 December	Wednesday 26 December	Monday 24 December	Tuesday 1 January
Wednesday 25 December	Thursday 26 December	Friday 27 December	Wednesday 1 January
Thursday 25 December	Friday 26 December	Wednesday 24 December	Thursday 1 January
Friday 25 December	Monday 28 December	Thursday 24 December	Friday 1 January
Saturday 25 December	Monday 27 and Tuesday 28 December	Friday 24 December	Monday 3 January

[1] The court office opening hours are published for each court in the 'Court Finder' section of Her Majesty's Courts and Tribunals Service website. [<http://hmctsformfinder.justice.gov.uk>.]

PD 2B Practice Direction 2B — Allocation of Cases to Levels of Judiciary

PD 2B 2.8, 37.2, 40.3, 45.5, 47.1, 84.4 [For commentary on a specific paragraph, please refer to the cross-references after the title of the paragraph.]

para.1.1 42.5

1.1 Rule 2.4 provides that judges, masters and district judges may exercise any function of the court except where an enactment, rule or practice direction provides otherwise. This practice direction sets out the matters over which masters and district judges do not have jurisdiction or which they may deal with only on certain conditions. It does not affect jurisdiction conferred by other enactments. Reference should also be made to other relevant practice directions (e.g. PD 24, para. 3, and PD 26, paras 12.1–10). References to circuit judges include recorders and assistant recorders and references to masters and district judges include deputies.

1.2 Wherever a master or district judge has jurisdiction, he may refer the matter to a judge instead of dealing with it himself.

THE HIGH COURT

Injunctions

para.2 2.8, 32.3, 77.33
para.2.1 2.10, 40.3
para.2.4 38.31
para.2.2 2.10, 20.17, 61 26
para.2.3 2.10, 41.5, 61.26

2.1 Search orders (r. 25.1(1)(h)), freezing orders (r. 25.1(1)(f)), an ancillary order under r. 25.1(1)(g) and orders authorising a person to enter land to recover, inspect or sample property (r. 25.1(1)(d)) may only be made by a judge.

2.2 Except where paras 2.3 and 2.4 apply, injunctions and orders relating to injunctions, including orders for specific performance where these involve an injunction, must be made by a judge.

2.3 A master or a district judge may only make an injunction:

(a) in terms agreed by the parties;

(b) in connection with or ancillary to a charging order;

(c) in connection with or ancillary to an order appointing a receiver by way of equitable execution; or

(d) in proceedings under r. 66.7 (order restraining person from receiving sum due from the Crown).

2.4 A master or district judge may make an order varying or discharging an injunction or undertaking given to the court if all parties to the proceedings have consented to the variation or discharge.

Other Pre-trial Orders and Interim Remedies

para.3 2.8, 77.33
para.3.1 2.10, 42.5
para.3.1(1) 81.8
para.3.1A 2.10
para.3.2 2.8

3.1 A master or district judge may not make orders or grant interim remedies:

(a) relating to the liberty of the subject;

(b) relating to criminal proceedings or matters except procedural applications in appeals to the High Court (including appeals by case stated) under any enactment;

(c) relating to a claim for judicial review, except that interim applications in claims for judicial review may be made to masters of the Queen's Bench Division;

(d) relating to appeals from masters or district judges;

(e) in appeals against costs assessment under Parts 43 to 48, except on an appeal under r. 47.20 against the decision of an authorised court officer;

(f) in applications under s. 42 of the Senior Courts Act 1981 by a person subject to a civil or a criminal or an all proceedings order (vexatious litigant) for permission to start or continue proceedings;

(g) in applications under the Mental Health Act 1983, s. 139, for permission to bring proceedings against a person.

3.1A Notwithstanding the provisions of para. 3.1 a master of the Crown Office or a master of the Administrative Court may—

(a) make orders and grant interim remedies relating to claims for judicial review (including claims for judicial review relating to criminal causes, appeals under the Extradition Act 2003 and applications to vary bail conditions, provided the prosecutor does not oppose the variation);

(b) determine liability for costs and make summary assessments of costs in relation to claims for judicial review; and

(c) make orders and grant interim remedies relating to applications under the Senior Courts Act 1981, s. 42, for permission to start or continue claims for judicial review.

3.2 This practice direction is not concerned with family proceedings. It is also not concerned with proceedings in the Family Division except to the extent that such proceedings can be dealt with in the Chancery Division or the Family Division e.g. proceedings under the Inheritance (Provision for Family and Dependants) Act 1975 or under s. 14 of the Trusts of Land and Appointment of Trustees Act 1996. District judges (including district judges of the Principal Registry of the Family Division) have jurisdiction to hear such proceedings, subject to any direction given by the President of the Family Division.

Trials and Assessments of Damages

para.4 **2.8** paras.4.1–4.2 **2.9, 61.26**

4.1 A master or district judge may, subject to any practice direction, try a case which is treated as being allocated to the multi-track because it is proceeding under Part 8 (see r. 8.9(c)). He may try a case which has been allocated to the multi-track under Part 26 only with the consent of the parties. Restrictions on the trial jurisdiction of masters and district judges do not prevent them from hearing applications for summary judgment or, if the parties consent, for the determination of a preliminary issue.

4.2 A master or a district judge may assess the damages or sum due to a party under a judgment without limit as to the amount.

Chancery Proceedings

para.5 **2.8**
para.5.1 **2.11, 42.5**
para.5.1(a) **PC 6, 14.22**
para.5.1(d) **2.9**
para.5.1(k) **2.11**

5.1 In proceedings in the Chancery Division, a master or a district judge may not deal with the following without the consent of the Chancellor of the High Court—

(a) approving compromises (other than applications under the Inheritance (Provision for Family and Dependants) Act 1975) (i) on behalf of a person under disability where that person's interest in a fund, or if there is no fund, the maximum amount of the claim, exceeds £100,000 and (ii) on behalf of absent, unborn and unascertained persons;

(b) making declarations, except in plain cases;

(c) making final orders under s. 1(1) of the Variation of Trusts Act 1958, except for the removal of protective trusts where the interest of the principal beneficiary has not failed or determined;

(d) where the proceedings are brought by a Part 8 claim form, seeking determination of any question of law or as to the construction of a document which is raised by the claim form;

(e) giving permission to executors, administrators and trustees to bring or defend proceedings or to continue the prosecution or defence of proceedings, and granting an indemnity for costs out of the trust estate, except in plain cases;

(f) granting an indemnity for costs out of the assets of a company on the application of minority shareholders bringing a derivative [claim], except in plain cases;

(g) making an order for rectification, except for:

(i) rectification of the register under the Land Registration Act 1925; or

(ii) alteration or rectification of the register under the Land Registration Act 2002, in plain cases;

(h) *making orders to vacate entries* in the register under the Land Charges Act 1972, except in plain cases;

(i) making final orders on applications under s. 19 of the Leasehold Reform Act 1967, s. 48 of the Administration of Justice Act 1985 and ss. 21 and 25 of the Law of Property Act 1969;

(j) making final orders under the Landlord and Tenant Acts 1927 and 1954, except (i) by consent, and (ii) orders for interim rents under ss. 24A to 24D of the 1954 Act;
(k) making orders in proceedings in the Patents Court except—
(i) orders by way of settlement, except settlement of procedural disputes;
(ii) applications for extension of time;
(iii) applications for permission to serve out of the jurisdiction;
(iv) applications for security for costs;
(v) other matters as directed by a judge of the court; and
(vi) enforcement of money judgments.

5.2 A master or district judge may only give directions for early trial after consulting the judge in charge of the relevant list.

5.3 Where a winding-up order has been made against a company, any proceedings against the company by or on behalf of debenture holders may be dealt with, at the Royal Courts of Justice, by a registrar and, in a district registry with insolvency jurisdiction, by a district judge.

Assignment of Claims to Masters and Transfer between Masters

para.6 2.8, 2.12
para.6.1 42.5
para.6.2 32.3

6.1 The Senior Master and the Chief Master will make arrangements for proceedings to be assigned to individual masters. They may vary such arrangements generally or in particular cases, for example, by transferring a case from a master to whom it had been assigned to another master.

6.2 The fact that a case has been assigned to a particular master does not prevent another master from dealing with that case if circumstances require, whether at the request of the assigned master or otherwise.

Freezing Orders: Cross-examination of Deponents about Assets

para.7 2.8, 2.10, 38.27

7 Where the court has made a freezing order under r. 25.1(1)(f) and has ordered a person to make a witness statement or affidavit about his assets and to be cross-examined on its contents, unless the judge directs otherwise, the cross-examination will take place before a master or a district judge, or if the master or district judge directs, before an examiner of the court.

Human Rights

para.7A 2.8, 2.9

7A A deputy High Court judge, a master or district judge may not try:
(1) a case in a claim made in respect of a judicial act under the Human Rights Act 1998; or
(2) a claim for a declaration of incompatibility in accordance with s. 4 of the Human Rights Act 1998.

COUNTY COURTS

Injunctions, Anti-social Behaviour Orders and Committal

para.8 42.5
para.8.1 2.4, 42.5, 61.26
para.8.1(a)–(c) 2.4
para.8.1(d) 2.4, 88.7, 88.37
para.8.1A 2.4, 88.25
para.8.2 61.26
para.8.3 2.4, 61.26, 81.8

8.1 Injunctions which a county court has jurisdiction to make may only be made by a circuit judge, except:
(a) where the injunction is to be made in proceedings which a district judge otherwise has jurisdiction to hear (see para. 11.1 below);
(b) where the injunction is sought in a money claim which has not yet been allocated to a track and the amount claimed does not exceed the fast track financial limit;
(c) in the circumstances provided by para. 2.3;
(d) where the injunction is to be made under any of the following provisions:
(i) the Housing Act 1996, s. 153A, 153B or 153D;
(ii) the Protection from Harassment Act 1997, s. 3; or
(iii) the Policing and Crime Act 2009, ss. 34, 40 or 41.

CPR 1–25 & PDs

8.1A A district judge has jurisdiction to make an order under:
(1) the Crime and Disorder Act 1998, s. 1B or 1D (anti-social behaviour);
(2) the Anti-social Behaviour Act 2003, s. 26A, 26B or 26C (parenting orders); and
(3) the Violent Crime Reduction Act 2006, s. 4 or 9 (drinking banning orders).

8.2 A district judge may make orders varying or discharging injunctions in the circumstances provided by para. 2.4.

8.3 A district judge may only make an order committing a person to prison or attach a power of arrest to an injunction or remand a person where an enactment authorises this: see the Attachment of Earnings Act 1971, s. 23; the County Courts Act 1984, ss. 14 and 118; the Housing Act 1996, ss. 153C, 153D and 154 to 158; the Policing and Crime Act 2009, ss. 36, 40 to 45 and 48 and sch. 5; and the relevant rules.

Homelessness Appeals

para.9 42.5

9 A district judge may not hear appeals under s. 204 or s. 204A of the Housing Act 1996.

Other Pre-trial Orders and Interim Remedies

10.1 In addition to the restrictions on jurisdiction mentioned at paras 8.1–3, para. 3.1(d) and (e) above applies.

Trials and Assessments of Damages

para.11.1 2.3, 2.4, 32.3, 42.5, 42.41
para.11.1(a) 2.3, 31.19, 61.26
para.11.1(b) 61.26
para.11.1(c) 61.26
para.11.1(d) 2.3, 31.19, 61.26
para.11.2 2.3, 45.20, 61.26

11.1 A district judge has jurisdiction to hear the following:
(a) any claim which has been allocated to the small claims track or fast track or which is treated as being allocated to the multi-track under r. 8.9(c) and the table at section B of PD 8A, except claims:
(i) under the Landlord and Tenant Act 1927, part I;
(ii) for a new tenancy under the Landlord and Tenant Act 1954, s. 24, or for the termination of a tenancy under s. 29(2);
(iii) for an order under the Landlord and Tenant Act 1987, s. 38 or 40;
(iv) under the Agricultural Holdings Act 1986, s. 27, or sch. 11, para. 26 or 27;
(v) under the Matrimonial Causes Act 1973, s. 45(2), for a declaration of legitimation by virtue of the Legitimacy Act 1976;
(vi) under the Fair Trading Act 1973, s. 35,38 or 40;
(vii) under the Mental Health Act 1983, part II;
(b) proceedings for the recovery of land, proceedings under the Housing Act 1985, s. 82A(2), or the Housing Act 1988, s. 6A(2) (demotion claims), or proceedings in a county court under the Housing Act 1996, part 5, chapter 1A (demoted tenancies);
(c) the assessment of damages or other sum due to a party under a judgment without any financial limit;
(d) with the permission of the designated civil judge in respect of that case, any other proceedings.

11.2 A case allocated to the small claims track may only be assigned to a circuit judge to hear with his consent.

Freezing Orders: Cross-examination of Deponents about Assets

12 To the extent that a county court has power to make a freezing order, para. 7 applies as appropriate.

Distribution of Business between Circuit Judge and District Judge

para.13 2.5
para.14 2.5

13 Where both the circuit judge and the district judge have jurisdiction in respect of any proceedings, the exercise of jurisdiction by the district judge is subject to any arrangements made by the designated civil judge for the proper distribution of business between circuit judges and district judges.

14.1 In district registries of the High Court and in the county court, the designated civil judge may make arrangements for proceedings to be assigned to individual district judges. He may vary such arrangements generally or in particular cases.

14.2 The fact that a case has been assigned to a particular district judge does not prevent another district judge from dealing with the case if the circumstances require.

Human Rights

para.15 2.3

15 A district judge may not try a case in which an allegation of indirect discrimination is made against a public authority that would, if the court finds that it occurred, be unlawful under the Race Relations Act 1976, s. 19B.

CPR Part 3 The Court's Case and Costs Management Powers

Part 3 [For commentary on a specific rule, please refer to the cross-references after the title of the rule.]

I CASE MANAGEMENT

3.1 The Court's General Powers of Management

r.3.1 **8.4, 15.34, 32.33, 48.23, 48.24, 72.12, 74.47**
r.3.1(2) **14.2, 20.3, 32.33, 42.45, 47.13, 61.57, 77.43**
r.3.1(2)(a) **PC 14, PC 37, 1.24, 3.8, 15.40, 18.7, 19.3, 26.5, 32.7, 35.7, 42.45, 46.16, 48.23, 48.33, 66.15, 66.58, 72.1, 74.21, 77.36, 77.38, 77.41, 77.43, 82.6, 87.15, 91.40**
r.3.1(2)(b) **PC 28, PC 37, 32.28, 32.44, 35.7, 46.11, 61.7, 61.9, 77.43**
r.3.1(2)(d) **32.24**
r.3.1(2)(e) **28.1, 29.7, 61.17**
r.3.1(2)(f) **56.1, 67.7**
r.3.1(2)(g) **14.61**
r.3.1(2)(h) **14.61, 77.43**
r.3.1(2)(i) **1.27, 61.17**
r.3.1.2(j) **28.1, 61.17**
r.3.1(2)(k) **91.43**
r.3.1(2)(l) **61.17**
r.3.1(2)(m) **15.23, 20.12, 32.25, 42.42, 62.1, 87.35, 87.54**
r.3.1(3) **20.11, 20.21, 32.33, 34.9, 48.20, 48.23, 63.8**
r.3.1(3)(a) **15.38, 67.7**
r.3.1(4) **1.8, 8.3**
r.3.1(5) **1.8, 8.3, 8.4, 34.9, 67.7, 91.45**
r.3.1(6) **34.9, 91.45**
r. 3.1(6A) **91.45**
r. 3.1(7) **14.22, 17.4, 32.43, 37.72, 62.1, 71.43, 78.11**
r. 3.1(8) **42.39, 42.40**

(1) The list of powers in this rule is in addition to any powers given to the court by any other rule or practice direction or by any other enactment or any powers it may otherwise have.

(2) Except where these Rules provide otherwise, the court may—
   - (a) extend or shorten the time for compliance with any rule, practice direction or court order (even if an application for extension is made after the time for compliance has expired);
   - (b) adjourn or bring forward a hearing;
   - (c) require a party or a party's legal representative to attend the court;
   - (d) hold a hearing and receive evidence by telephone or by using any other method of direct oral communication;
   - (e) direct that part of any proceedings (such as a counterclaim) be dealt with as separate proceedings;
   - (f) stay(GL) the whole or part of any proceedings or judgment either generally or until a specified date or event;

(g) consolidate proceedings;
(h) try two or more claims on the same occasion;
(i) direct a separate trial of any issue;
(j) decide the order in which issues are to be tried;
(k) exclude an issue from consideration;
(l) dismiss or give judgment on a claim after a decision on a preliminary issue;
(ll) order any party to file and serve an estimate of costs;
(m) take any other step or make any other order for the purpose of managing the case and furthering the overriding objective.

(3) When the court makes an order, it may—
(a) make it subject to conditions, including a condition to pay a sum of money into court; and
(b) specify the consequence of failure to comply with the order or a condition.

(4) Where the court gives directions it will take into account whether or not a party has complied with the Practice Direction (Pre-action Conduct) and any relevant pre-action protocol(GL).

(5) The court may order a party to pay a sum of money into court if that party has, without good reason, failed to comply with a rule, practice direction or a relevant pre-action protocol.

(6) When exercising its power under paragraph (5) the court must have regard to—
(a) the amount in dispute; and
(b) the costs which the parties have incurred or which they may incur.

(6A) Where a party pays money into court following an order under paragraph (3) or (5), the money shall be security for any sum payable by that party to any other party in the proceedings.

(7) A power of the court under these Rules to make an order includes a power to vary or revoke the order.

(8) The court may contact the parties from time to time in order to monitor compliance with directions. The parties must respond promptly to any such enquiries from the court.

3.2 Court Officer's Power to Refer to a Judge

r.3.2 33.5

Where a step is to be taken by a court officer—
(a) the court officer may consult a judge before taking that step;
(b) the step may be taken by a judge instead of the court officer.

3.3 Court's Power to Make Order of Its Own Initiative

r.3.3 14.55, 48.23, 48.33, 61.37
r.3.3(1) 32.25
r.3.3(2) 32.25
r.3.3(3) 32.26, 47.8
r.3.3(4) 32.44, 42.21, 72.14, 91.41
r.3.3(5) 32.44, 42.21, 46.16, 72.14
r.3.3(5)(a) 32.23
r.3.3(5)(b) 32.23, 32.25
r.3.3(6) 32.23, 32.25
r.3.3(7) 14.51, 14.55, 32.25, 63.7

(1) Except where a rule or some other enactment provides otherwise, the court may exercise its powers on an application or of its own initiative.
(Part 23 sets out the procedure for making an application)

(2) Where the court proposes to make an order of its own initiative—
(a) it may give any person likely to be affected by the order an opportunity to make representations; and
(b) where it does so it must specify the time by and the manner in which the representations must be made.

(3) Where the court proposes—
(a) to make an order of its own initiative; and
(b) to hold a hearing to decide whether to make the order,
it must give each party likely to be affected by the order at least 3 days' notice of the hearing.

(4) The court may make an order of its own initiative, without hearing the parties or giving them an opportunity to make representations.

(5) Where the court has made an order under paragraph (4)—
(a) a party affected by the order may apply to have it set aside varied or stayed(GL); and
(b) the order must contain a statement of the right to make such an application.

(6) An application under paragraph (5)(a) must be made—
  (a) within such period as may be specified by the court; or
  (b) if the court does not specify a period, not more than 7 days after the date on which the order was served on the party making the application.
(7) If the court of its own initiative strikes out a statement of case or dismisses an application (including an application for permission to appeal or for permission to apply for judicial review), and it considers that the claim or application is totally without merit—
  (a) the court's order must record that fact; and
  (b) the court must at the same time consider whether it is appropriate to make a civil restraint order.

3.4 Power to Strike Out a Statement of Case

r.3.4 PC 21, PC 22, 23.2, 26.3, 31.24, 33.1, 33.5, 33.6, 61.37, 90.17, 91.41
r. 3.4(1) 33.2
r.3.4(2) 17.4, 33.2, 69.13, 69.14, 81.14, 91.42
r. 3.4(2)(a) 33.7, 33.8, 34.1
r.3.4(2)(b) 17.4, 33.2, 33.12, 33.23, 34.31, 69.13
r.3.4(2)(c) 42.3, 48.1, 48.15
r.3.4(3) 33.25
r.3.4(4) 33.27, 56.4
r.3.4(5) PC 21, 33.2
r.3.4(6) 14.55, 33.25, 63.7, 69.14

(1) In this rule and rule 3.5, reference to a statement of case includes reference to part of a statement of case.
(2) The court may strike out(GL) a statement of case if it appears to the court—
  (a) that the statement of case discloses no reasonable grounds for bringing or defending the claim;
  (b) that the statement of case is an abuse of the court's process or is otherwise likely to obstruct the just disposal of the proceedings; or
  (c) that there has been a failure to comply with a rule, practice direction or court order.
(3) When the court strikes out a statement of case it may make any consequential order it considers appropriate.
(4) Where—
  (a) the court has struck out a claimant's statement of case;
  (b) the claimant has been ordered to pay costs to the defendant; and
  (c) before the claimant pays those costs, he starts another claim against the same defendant, arising out of facts which are the same or substantially the same as those relating to the claim in which the statement of case was struck out,

  the court may, on the application of the defendant, stay(GL) that other claim until the costs of the first claim have been paid.
(5) Paragraph (2) does not limit any other power of the court to strike out(GL) a statement of case.
(6) If the court strikes out a claimant's statement of case and it considers that the claim is totally without merit—
  (a) the court's order must record that fact; and
  (b) the court must at the same time consider whether it is appropriate to make a civil restraint order.

3.5 Judgment without Trial after Striking Out

r.3.5 42.8, 48.30, 48.31, 48.32, 48.33
r.3.5(2)(a) 48.32
r.3.5(2)(b) 48.32
r.3.5(3) 48.32
r.3.5(4) 48.32

(1) This rule applies where—
  (a) the court makes an order which includes a term that the statement of case of a party shall be struck out if the party does not comply with the order; and
  (b) the party against whom the order was made does not comply with it.
(2) A party may obtain judgment with costs by filing a request for judgment if—
  (a) the order referred to in paragraph (1)(a) relates to the whole of a statement of case; and
  (b) where the party wishing to obtain judgment is the claimant, the claim is for—
    (i) a specified amount of money;
    (ii) an amount of money to be decided by the court;
    (iii) delivery of goods where the claim form gives the defendant the alternative of paying their value; or
    (iv) any combination of these remedies.

(3) Where judgment is obtained under this rule in a case to which paragraph (2)(b)(iii) applies, it will be judgment requiring the defendant to deliver the goods, or (if he does not do so) pay the value of the goods as decided by the court (less any payments made).
(4) The request must state that the right to enter judgment has arisen because the court's order has not been complied with.
(5) A party must make an application in accordance with Part 23 if he wishes to obtain judgment under this rule in a case to which paragraph (2) does not apply.

3.5A Automatic Transfer

r.3.5A 42.8

If—

(a) a claimant files a request for judgment which includes an amount of money to be decided by the court in accordance with rule 3.5; and
(b) the claim is a designated money claim,

the court will transfer the claim to the preferred court upon receipt of the request for judgment.

3.6 Setting Aside Judgment Entered after Striking Out

r.3.6 48.33

(1) A party against whom the court has entered judgment under rule 3.5 may apply to the court to set the judgment aside.
(2) An application under paragraph (1) must be made not more than 14 days after the judgment has been served on the party making the application.
(3) If the right to enter judgment had not arisen at the time when judgment was entered, the court must set aside(GL) the judgment.
(4) If the application to set aside(GL) is made for any other reason, rule 3.9 (relief from sanctions) shall apply.

3.7 Sanctions for Non-payment of Certain Fees

r.3.7 14.55, 42.18, 46.12, 47.21, 48.12, 63.16 r.3.7(8) 42.18
r.3.7(7) 42.18

(1) This rule applies where—
 (a) a directions questionnaire or a pre-trial checklist (listing questionnaire) is filed without payment of the fee specified by the relevant Fees Order;
 (b) the court dispenses with the need for an allocation questionnaire or a pre-trial checklist or both;
 (c) these Rules do not require an allocation questionnaire or a pre-trial checklist to be filed in relation to the claim in question;
 (d) the court has made an order giving permission to proceed with a claim for judicial review; or
 (e) the fee payable for a hearing specified by the relevant Fees Order is not paid.

(Rule 26.3 provides for the court to dispense with the need for a directions questionnaire and rules 28.5 and 29.6 provide for the court to dispense with the need for a pre-trial checklist)
(Rule 54.12 provides for the service of the order giving permission to proceed with a claim for judicial review)

(2) The court will serve a notice on the claimant requiring payment of the fee specified in the relevant Fees Order if, at the time the fee is due, the claimant has not paid it or made an application for full or part remission.
(3) The notice will specify the date by which the claimant must pay the fee.
(4) If the claimant does not—
 (a) pay the fee; or
 (b) make an application for full or part remission of the fee, by the date specified in the notice—
  (i) the claim will automatically be struck out without further order of the court; and
  (ii) the claimant will be liable for the costs which the defendant has incurred unless the court orders otherwise.

(Rule 44.12 provides for the basis of assessment where a right to costs arises under this rule and contains provisions about when a costs order is deemed to have been made and applying for an order under section 194(3) of the Legal Services Act 2007)

CPR 1–25 & PDs

(5) Where an application for—
(a) full or part remission of a fee is refused, the court will serve notice on the claimant requiring payment of the full fee by the date specified in the notice; or
(b) part remission of a fee is granted, the court will serve notice on the claimant requiringpayment of the balance of the fee by the date specified in the notice.
(6) If the claimant does not pay the fee by the date specified in the notice—
(a) the claim will automatically be struck out without further order of the court; and
(b) the claimant will be liable for the costs which the defendant has incurred unless the court orders otherwise.
(7) If—
(a) a claimant applies to have the claim reinstated; and
(b) the court grants relief,
the relief will be conditional on the claimant either paying the fee or filing evidence of full or part remission of the fee within the period specified in paragraph (8).
(8) The period referred to in paragraph (7) is—
(a) if the order granting relief is made at a hearing at which a claimant is present or represented, 2 days from the date of the order;
(b) in any other case, 7 days from the date of service of the order on the claimant.

3.7A

r.3.7A 28.3, 42.18

(1) This rule applies where—
(a) a defendant files a counterclaim without—
(i) payment of the fee specified by the relevant Fees Order; or
(ii) making an application for full or part remission of the fee; or
(b) the proceedings continue on the counterclaim alone and—
(i) a directions questionnaire or a pre-trial check list (listing questionnaire) is filed without payment of the fee specified by the relevant Fees Order;
(ii) the court dispenses with the need for a directions questionnaire or a pre-trial check list or both;
(iii) these Rules do not require a directions questionnaire or a pre-trial checklist to be filed in relation to the claim in question; or
(iv) the fee payable for a hearing specified by the relevant Fees Order is not paid.
(2) The court will serve a notice on the defendant requiring payment of the fee specified in the relevant Fees Order if, at the time the fee is due, the defendant has not paid it or made an application for full or part remission.
(3) The notice will specify the date by which the defendant must pay the fee.
(4) If the defendant does not —
(a) pay the fee; or
(b) make an application for full or part remission of the fee,
by the date specified in the notice, the counterclaim will automatically be struck out without further order of the court.
(5) Where an application for —
(a) full or part remission of a fee is refused, the court will serve notice on the defendant requiring payment of the full fee by the date specified in the notice; or
(b) part remission of a fee is granted, the court will serve notice on the defendant requiring payment of the balance of the fee by the date specified in the notice.
(6) If the defendant does not pay the fee by the date specified in the notice, the counterclaim will automatically be struck out without further order of the court.
(7) If —
(a) the defendant applies to have the counterclaim reinstated; and
(b) the court grants relief,
the relief will be conditional on the defendant either paying the fee or filing evidence of full or part remission of the fee within the period specified in paragraph (8).

(8) The period referred to in paragraph (7) is—
(a) if the order granting relief is made at a hearing at which the defendant is present or represented, 2 days from the date of the order;
(b) in any other case, 7 days from the date of service of the order on the defendant.

3.7B Sanctions for Dishonouring Cheque

r.3.7B **42.18**

(1) This rule applies where any fee is paid by cheque and that cheque is subsequently dishonoured.
(2) The court will serve a notice on the paying party requiring payment of the fee which will specify the date by which the fee must be paid.
(3) If the fee is not paid by the date specified in the notice —
(a) where the fee is payable by the claimant, the claim will automatically be struck out without further order of the court;
(b) where the fee is payable by the defendant, the defence will automatically be struck out without further order of the court, and the paying party shall be liable for the costs which any other party has incurred unless the court orders otherwise.

(Rule 44.12 provides for the basis of assessment where a right to costs arises under this rule)

(4) If —
(a) the paying party applies to have the claim or defence reinstated; and
(b) the court grants relief,

the relief shall be conditional on that party paying the fee within the period specified in paragraph (5).

(5) The period referred to in paragraph (4) is —
(a) if the order granting relief is made at a hearing at which the paying party is present or represented, 2 days from the date of the order;
(b) in any other case, 7 days from the date of service of the order on the paying party.
(6) For the purposes of this rule, 'claimant' includes a Part 20 claimant and 'claim form' includes a Part 20 claim.

3.8 Sanctions Have Effect Unless Defaulting Party Obtains Relief

r.3.8 **8.3, 48.31**
r.3.8(1) **48.31, 48.33**
r.3.8(3) **3.7, 48.31**

(1) Where a party has failed to comply with a rule, practice direction or court order, any sanction for failure to comply imposed by the rule, practice direction or court order has effect unless the party in default applies for and obtains relief from the sanction.

(Rule 3.9 sets out the circumstances which the court will consider on an application to grant relief from a sanction)

(2) Where the sanction is the payment of costs, the party in default may only obtain relief by appealing against the order for costs.
(3) Where a rule, practice direction or court order—
(a) requires a party to do something within a specified time, and
(b) specifies the consequence of failure to comply,

the time for doing the act in question may not be extended by agreement between the parties.

3.9 Relief from Sanctions

r.3.9 **6.15, 8.4, 13.10, 15.34, 15.40, 42.18, 42.21, 42.45, 43.8, 48.1, 48.11, 48.14, 48.25, 48.28, 48.33, 48.35, 48.36, 48.37, 71.58, 74.21, 87.54, 91.45**
r.3.9(1) **20.14, 20.15, 48.34, 48.35, 74.22**
r.3.9(1)(e) **1.8**
r.3.9(1)(f) **20.15**

(1) On an application for relief from any sanction imposed for a failure to comply with any rule, practice direction or court order, the court will consider all the circumstances of the case, so as to enable it to deal justly with the application, including the need—
(a) for litigation to be conducted efficiently and at proportionate cost; and
(b) to enforce compliance with rules, practice directions and orders.
(2) An application for relief must be supported by evidence.

3.10 General Power of the Court to Rectify Matters Where There Has Been an Error of Procedure

r.3.10 2.2, 12.2, 15.23, 15.32, 15.34, 16.37, 20.17, 23.14, 29.9, 35.7, 37.18, 42.45, 48.29, 66.16, 66.47, 74.21
r.3.10(b) 48.29

Where there has been an error of procedure such as a failure to comply with a rule or practice direction —

(a) the error does not invalidate any step taken in the proceedings unless the court so orders; and
(b) the court may make an order to remedy the error.

3.11 Power of the Court to Make Civil Restraint Orders

r.3.11 14.55, 14.59

A practice direction may set out —

(a) the circumstances in which the court has the power to make a civil restraint order against a party to proceedings;
(b) the procedure where a party applies for a civil restraint order against another party; and
(c) the consequences of the court making a civil restraint order.

II COSTS MANAGEMENT

3.12 Application of this Section and the Purpose of Costs Management

rr.3.12–3.18 43.5
r.3.12(1) 43.5, 43.11
r.3.12(1)(b) 43.5
r.3.12(1)(c) 43.5
r.3.12(2) 43.1, 49.10

(1) This Section and Practice Direction 3E apply to all multi-track cases commenced on or after 1st April 2013, except—
  (a) cases in the Admiralty and Commercial Courts;
  (b) such cases in the Chancery Division as the Chancellor of the High Court may direct; and
  (c) such cases in the Technology and Construction Court and the Mercantile Court as the President of the Queen's Bench Division may direct,

  unless the proceedings are the subject of fixed costs or scale costs or the court otherwise orders. This Section and Practice Direction 3E will apply to any other proceedings (including applications) where the court so orders.
(2) The purpose of costs management is that the court should manage both the steps to be taken and the costs to be incurred by the parties to any proceedings so as to further the overriding objective.

3.13 Filing and Exchanging Budgets

r.3.13 42.14, 43.6

Unless the court otherwise orders, all parties except litigants in person must file and exchange budgets as required by the rules or as the court otherwise directs. Each party must do so by the date specified in the notice served under rule 26.3(1) or, if no such date is specified, seven days before the first case management conference.

3.14 Failure to File a Budget

r.3.14 43.8

Unless the court otherwise orders, any party which fails to file a budget despite being required to do so will be treated as having filed a budget comprising only the applicable court fees.

3.15 Costs Management Orders

r.3.15(1) 43.11
r.3.15(2) 43.11
r.3.15(3) 43.12

(1) In addition to exercising its other powers, the court may manage the costs to be incurred by any party in any proceedings.

(2) The court may at any time make a 'costs management order'. By such order the court will—
(a) record the extent to which the budgets are agreed between the parties;
(b) in respect of budgets or parts of budgets which are not agreed, record the court's approval after making appropriate revisions.
(3) If a costs management order has been made, the court will thereafter control the parties' budgets in respect of recoverable costs.

3.16 Costs Management Conferences

r.3.16(1) **43.13** r.3.16(2) **43.13**

(1) Any hearing which is convened solely for the purpose of costs management (for example, to approve a revised budget) is referred to as a 'costs management conference'.
(2) Where practicable, costs management conferences should be conducted by telephone or in writing.

3.17 Court to Have Regard to Budgets and to Take Account of Costs

r.3.17 **49.10, 71.42** r.3.17(2) **43.15**
r.3.17(1) **42.35, 43.15**

(1) When making any case management decision, the court will have regard to any available budgets of the parties and will take into account the costs involved in each procedural step.
(2) Paragraph (1) applies whether or not the court has made a costs management order.

3.18 Assessing Costs on the Standard Basis where a Costs Management Order has been Made

r.3.18 **43.17**

In any case where a costs management order has been made, when assessing costs on the standard basis, the court will—
(a) have regard to the receiving party's last approved or agreed budget for each phase of the proceedings; and
(b) not depart from such approved or agreed budget unless satisfied that there is good reason to do so.
(Attention is drawn to rule 44.3(2)(a) and rule 44.3(5), which concern proportionality of costs.)

III COSTS CAPPING

3.19 Costs Capping Orders — General

r.3.19(1) **44.2** r.3.19(6) **44.4**
r.3.19(2) **44.2** r.3.19(7) **44.6**
r.3.19(5) **44.3, 44.4**

(1) A costs capping order is an order limiting the amount of future costs (including disbursements) which a party may recover pursuant to an order for costs subsequently made.
(2) In this rule, 'future costs' means costs incurred in respect of work done after the date of the costs capping order but excluding the amount of any additional liability.
(3) This rule does not apply to protective costs orders.
(4) A costs capping order may be in respect of—
(a) the whole litigation; or
(b) any issues which are ordered to be tried separately.
(5) The court may at any stage of proceedings make a costs capping order against all or any of the parties, if—
(a) it is in the interests of justice to do so;
(b) there is a substantial risk that without such an order costs will be disproportionately incurred; and
(c) it is not satisfied that the risk in subparagraph (b) can be adequately controlled by—
(i) case management directions or orders made under this Part; and
(ii) detailed assessment of costs.

(6) In considering whether to exercise its discretion under this rule, the court will consider all the circumstances of the case, including—
(a) whether there is a substantial imbalance between the financial position of the parties;
(b) whether the costs of determining the amount of the cap are likely to be proportionate to the overall costs of the litigation;
(c) the stage which the proceedings have reached; and
(d) the costs which have been incurred to date and the future costs.

(7) A costs capping order, once made, will limit the costs recoverable by the party subject to the order unless a party successfully applies to vary the order. No such variation will be made unless—
(a) there has been a material and substantial change of circumstances since the date when the order was made; or
(b) there is some other compelling reason why a variation should be made.

3.20 Application for a Costs Capping Order

r.3.20(1) 44.3 r.3.20(3) 44.3
r.3.20(2) 44.3

(1) An application for a costs capping order must be made on notice in accordance with Part 23.

(2) The application notice must—
(a) set out—
(i) whether the costs capping order is in respect of the whole of the litigation or a particular issue which is ordered to be tried separately; and
(ii) why a costs capping order should be made; and
(b) be accompanied by a budget setting out—
(i) the costs (and disbursements) incurred by the applicant to date; and
(ii) the costs (and disbursements) which the applicant is likely to incur in the future conduct of the proceedings.

(3) The court may give directions for the determination of the application and such directions may—
(a) direct any party to the proceedings—
(i) to file a schedule of costs in the form set out in paragraph 3 of Practice Direction 3F — Costs capping;
(ii) to file written submissions on all or any part of the issues arising;
(b) fix the date and time estimate of the hearing of the application;
(c) indicate whether the judge hearing the application will sit with an assessor at the hearing of the application; and
(d) include any further directions as the court sees fit.

3.21 Application to Vary a Costs Capping Order

r.3.21 44.6

An application to vary a costs capping order must be made by application notice pursuant to Part 23.

PD 3A Practice Direction 3A — Striking Out a Statement of Case

This practice direction supplements CPR, r. 3.4.

[For commentary on a specific paragraph, please refer to the cross-references after the title of the paragraph.]
para.3A 33.7

Introductory

para.1.2 33.1, 61.37
para.1.5 33.2, 33.23
para.1.7 33.1, 33.3, 34.1
para.1.9 48.31

1.1 Rule 1.4(2)(c) includes as an example of active case management the summary disposal of issues which do not need full investigation at trial.

1.2 The rules give the court two distinct powers which may be used to achieve this. Rule 3.4 enables the court to strike out the whole or part of a statement of case which discloses no reasonable grounds for bringing or defending a claim (r. 3.4(2)(a)), or which is an abuse of the process of the court or otherwise likely to obstruct the just disposal of the proceedings (r. 3.4(2)(b)). Rule 24.2 enables the court to give summary judgment against a claimant or defendant where that party has no real prospect of succeeding on his claim or defence. Both those powers may be exercised on an application by a party or on the court's own initiative.

1.3 This practice direction sets out the procedure a party should follow if he wishes to make an application for an order under r. 3.4.

1.4 The following are examples of cases where the court may conclude that particulars of claim (whether contained in a claim form or filed separately) fall within r. 3.4(2)(a):
(1) those which set out no facts indicating what the claim is about, for example 'Money owed £5000',
(2) those which are incoherent and make no sense,
(3) those which contain a coherent set of facts but those facts, even if true, do not disclose any legally recognisable claim against the defendant.

1.5 A claim may fall within r. 3.4(2)(b) where it is vexatious, scurrilous or obviously ill-founded.

1.6 A defence may fall within r. 3.4(2)(a) where:
(1) it consists of a bare denial or otherwise sets out no coherent statement of facts, or
(2) the facts it sets out, while coherent, would not even if true amount in law to a defence to the claim.

1.7 A party may believe he can show without a trial that an opponent's case has no real prospect of success on the facts, or that the case is bound to succeed or fail, as the case may be, because of a point of law (including the construction of a document). In such a case the party concerned maymake an application under r. 3.4 or Part 24 (or both) as he thinks appropriate.

1.8 The examples set out above are intended only as illustrations.

1.9 Where a rule, practice direction or order states 'shall be struck out or dismissed' or 'will be struck out or dismissed' this means that the striking out or dismissal will be automatic and that no further order of the court is required.

Claims Which Appear to Fall within Rule 3.4(2)(a) or (b)

para.2.1 33.5
paras.2.3–2.6 33.5

2.1 If a court officer is asked to issue a claim form which he believes may fall within r. 3.4(2)(a) or (b) he should issue it, but may then consult a judge (under r. 3.2) before returning the claim form to the claimant or taking any other step to serve the defendant. The judge may on his own initiative make an immediate order designed to ensure that the claim is disposed of or (as the case may be) proceeds in a way that accords with the rules.

2.3 The judge may allow the claimant a hearing before deciding whether to make such an order.

2.4 Orders the judge may make include:
(1) an order that the claim be stayed until further order,

CPR 1–25 & PDs

(2) an order that the claim form be retained by the court and not served until the stay is lifted,

(3) an order that no application by the claimant to lift the stay be heard unless he files such further documents (for example a witness statement or an amended claim form or particulars of claim) as may be specified in the order.

2.5 Where the judge makes any such order or, subsequently, an order lifting the stay he may give directions about the service on the defendant of the order and any other documents on the court file.

2.6 The fact that a judge allows a claim referred to him by a court officer to proceed does not prejudice the right of any party to apply for any order against the claimant.

Defences Which Appear to Fall within Rule 3.4(2)(a) or (b)

para.3 33.5

3.1 A court officer may similarly consult a judge about any document filed which purports to be a defence and which he believes may fall within r. 3.4(2)(a) or (b).

3.2 If the judge decides that the document falls within r. 3.4(2)(a) or (b) he may on his own initiative make an order striking it out. Where he does so he may extend the time for the defendant to file a proper defence.

3.3 The judge may allow the defendant a hearing before deciding whether to make such an order.

3.4 Alternatively the judge may make an order under r. 18.1 requiring the defendant within a stated time to clarify his defence or to give additional information about it. The order may provide that the defence will be struck out if the defendant does not comply.

3.5 The fact that a judge does not strike out a defence on his own initiative does not prejudice the right of the claimant to apply for any order against the defendant.

General Provisions

para.4.2 33.25

4.1 The court may exercise its powers under r. 3.4(2)(a) or (b) on application or on its own initiative at any time.

4.2 Where a judge at a hearing strikes out all or part of a party's statement of case he may enter such judgment for the other party as that party appears entitled to.

Applications for Orders under Rule 3.4(2)

para.5.1 33.3
para.5.2 33.3, 33.7

5.1 Attention is drawn to Part 23 (General Rules about Applications) and to PD 23A. The practice direction requires all applications to be made as soon as possible and before allocation if possible.

5.2 While many applications under r. 3.4(2) can be made without evidence in support, the applicant should consider whether facts need to be proved and, if so, whether evidence in support should be filed and served.

Applications for Summary Judgment

para.6.1 33.1

6.1 Applications for summary judgment may be made under Part 24. Attention is drawn to that Part and to PD 24.

Vexatious Litigants

para.7 14.54 para.7.9 14.54

7.1 This practice direction applies where a 'civil proceedings order' or an 'all proceedings order' (as respectively defined under the Senior Courts Act 1981, s. 42(1A)) is in force against a person ('the litigant').

7.2 An application by the litigant for permission to begin or continue, or to make any applicationin, any civil proceedings shall be made by application notice issued in the High Court and signed by the litigant.

7.3 The application notice must state:

(1) the title and reference number of the proceedings in which the civil proceedings order or the all proceedings order, as the case may be, was made,

(2) the full name of the litigant and his address,
(3) the order the applicant is seeking, and
(4) briefly, why the applicant is seeking the order.

7.4 The application notice must be filed together with any written evidence on which the litigant relies in support of his application.

7.5 Either in the application notice or in written evidence filed in support of the application, the previous occasions on which the litigant made an application for permission under s. 42(1A) of the said Act must be listed.

7.6 The application notice, together with any written evidence, will be placed before a High Court judge who may:
(1) without the attendance of the applicant make an order giving the permission sought;
(2) give directions for further written evidence to be supplied by the litigant before an order is made on the application;
(3) make an order dismissing the application without a hearing; or
(4) give directions for the hearing of the application.

7.7 Directions given under para. 7.6(4) may include an order that the application notice be served on the Attorney-General and on any person against whom the litigant desires to bring the proceedings for which permission is being sought.

7.8 Any order made under paras 7.6 or 7.7 will be served on the litigant at the address given in the application notice. Part 6 will apply.

7.9 A person may apply to set aside the grant of permission if:
(1) the permission allowed the litigant to bring or continue proceedings against that person or to make any application against him, and
(2) the permission was granted other than at a hearing of which that person was given notice under para. 7.7.

7.10 Any application under para. 7.9 must be made in accordance with Part 23.

PD 3B Practice Direction 3B — Sanctions for Non-payment of Fees

This practice direction supplements CPR, r. 3.7.

PD 3B 42.18

1 If a claim is struck out under r. 3.7, the court will send notice that it has been struck out to the defendant.

2 The notice will also explain the effect of r. 25.11. This provides that any interim injunction will cease to have effect 14 days after the date the claim is struck out under r. 3.7. Paragraph (2) provides that if the claimant applies to reinstate the claim before the interim injunction ceases to have effect, the injunction will continue until the hearing of the application unless the court orders otherwise. If the claimant makes such an application, the defendant will be given notice in the ordinary way under r. 23.4.

PD 3C Practice Direction 3C — Civil Restraint Orders

This practice direction supplements CPR

PD 3C 14.55

Introduction

1 This practice direction applies where the court is considering whether to make:
(a) a limited civil restraint order;
(b) an extended civil restraint order; or
(c) a general civil restraint order,
against a party who has issued claims or made applications which are totally without merit.

(Rules 3.3(7), 3.4(6) and 23.12 provide that where a statement of case or application is struck out or dismissed and is totally without merit, the court order must specify that fact and the court must consider whether to make a civil restraint order. Rule 52.10(6) makes similar provision where the appeal court refuses an application for permission to appeal, strikes out an appellant's notice or dismisses an appeal.)

Limited Civil Restraint Orders

para.2.1 14.56
para.2.2(1)–(3) 14.56
para.2.3(1)–(2) 14.56
paras.2.6–2.9 14.56

2.1 A limited civil restraint order may be made by a judge of any court where a party has made two or more applications which are totally without merit.

2.2 Where the court makes a limited civil restraint order, the party against whom the order is made:
(1) will be restrained from making any further applications in the proceedings in which the order is made without first obtaining the permission of a judge identified in the order;
(2) may apply for amendment or discharge of the order provided he has first obtained the permission of a judge identified in the order; and
(3) may apply for permission to appeal the order and if permission is granted, may appeal the order.

2.3 Where a party who is subject to a limited civil restraint order:
(1) makes a further application in the proceedings in which the order is made without first obtaining the permission of a judge identified in the order, such application will automatically be dismissed:
(a) without the judge having to make any further order; and
(b) without the need for the other party to respond to it;
(2) repeatedly makes applications for permission pursuant to that order which are totally without merit, the court may direct that if the party makes any further application for permission which is totally without merit, the decision to dismiss the application will be final and there will be no right of appeal, unless the judge who refused permission grants permission to appeal.

2.4 A party who is subject to a limited civil restraint order may not make an application forpermission under para. 2.2(1) or (2) without first serving notice of the application on the other party in accordance with para. 2.5.

2.5 A notice under para. 2.4 must:
(1) set out the nature and grounds of the application; and
(2) provide the other party with at least seven days within which to respond.

2.6 An application for permission under para. 2.2(1) or (2):
(1) must be made in writing;
(2) must include the other party's written response, if any, to the notice served under para. 2.4; and
(3) will be determined without a hearing.

2.7 An order under para. 2.3(2) may only be made by:
(1) a Court of Appeal judge;
(2) a High Court judge or master; or
(3) a designated civil judge or his appointed deputy.

2.8 Where a party makes an application for permission under para. 2.2(1) or (2) and permission is refused, any application for permission to appeal:
(1) must be made in writing; and
(2) will be determined without a hearing.

2.9 A limited civil restraint order:
(1) is limited to the particular proceedings in which it is made;
(2) will remain in effect for the duration of the proceedings in which it is made, unless the court otherwise orders; and
(3) must identify the judge or judges to whom an application for permission under paras 2.2(1), 2.2(2) or 2.8 should be made.

Extended Civil Restraint Orders

para.3.1 14.57
para.3.2(1) 14.57
para.3.2(2)–(3) 14.58
para.3.3(1)–(2) 14.58
paras.3.6–3.8 14.58
paras.3.9–3.11 14.57

3.1 An extended civil restraint order may be made by:
(1) a judge of the Court of Appeal;
(2) a judge of the High Court; or
(3) a designated civil judge or his appointed deputy in the county court,
where a party has persistently issued claims or made applications which are totally without merit.

3.2 Unless the court otherwise orders, where the court makes an extended civil restraint order, the party against whom the order is made:
(1) will be restrained from issuing claims or making applications in:
(a) any court if the order has been made by a judge of the Court of Appeal;
(b) the High Court or any county court if the order has been made by a judge of the High Court; or
(c) any county court identified in the order if the order has been made by a designated civil judge or his appointed deputy,
concerning any matter involving or relating to or touching upon or leading to the proceedings in which the order is made without first obtaining the permission of a judge identified in the order;
(2) may apply for amendment or discharge of the order provided he has first obtained the permission of a judge identified in the order; and
(3) may apply for permission to appeal the order and if permission is granted, may appeal the order.

3.3 Where a party who is subject to an extended civil restraint order:
(1) issues a claim or makes an application in a court identified in the order concerning any matter involving or relating to or touching upon or leading to the proceedings in which the order is made without first obtaining the permission of a judge identified in the order, the claim or application will automatically be struck out or dismissed:
(a) without the judge having to make any further order; and
(b) without the need for the other party to respond to it;
(2) repeatedly makes applications for permission pursuant to that order which are totally without merit, the court may direct that if the party makes any further application for permission which is totally without merit, the decision to dismiss the application will be final and there will be no right of appeal, unless the judge who refused permission grants permission to appeal.

3.4 A party who is subject to an extended civil restraint order may not make an application for permission under para. 3.2(1) or (2) without first serving notice of the application on the other party in accordance with para. 3.5.

3.5 A notice under para. 3.4 must:
(1) set out the nature and grounds of the application; and
(2) provide the other party with at least seven days within which to respond.

3.6 An application for permission under para. 3.2(1) or (2):
(1) must be made in writing;

(2) must include the other party's written response, if any, to the notice served under para. 3.4; and
(3) will be determined without a hearing.

3.7 An order under para. 3.3(2) may only be made by:
(1) a Court of Appeal judge;
(2) a High Court judge; or
(3) a designated civil judge or his appointed deputy.

3.8 Where a party makes an application for permission under para. 3.2(1) or (2) and permission is refused, any application for permission to appeal:
(1) must be made in writing; and
(2) will be determined without a hearing.

3.9 An extended civil restraint order:
(1) will be made for a specified period not exceeding two years;
(2) must identify the courts in which the party against whom the order is made is restrained from issuing claims or making applications; and
(3) must identify the judge or judges to whom an application for permission under paras 3.2(1), 3.2(2) or 3.8 should be made.

3.10 The court may extend the duration of an extended civil restraint order, if it considers it appropriate to do so, but it must not be extended for a period greater than two years on any given occasion.

3.11 If he considers that it would be appropriate to make an extended civil restraint order:
(1) a master or a district judge in a district registry of the High Court must transfer the proceedings to a High Court judge; and
(2) a circuit judge or a district judge in a county court must transfer the proceedings to the designated civil judge.

General Civil Restraint Orders

para.4.1 14.51, 14.59
para.4.2(1) 14.59, 14.60
para.4.2(2)–(3) 14.60
para.4.3(1)–(2) 14.60
paras.4.6–4.7 14.60
para.4.9–4.10 14.59

4.1 A general civil restraint order may be made by:
(1) a judge of the Court of Appeal;
(2) a judge of the High Court; or
(3) a designated civil judge or his appointed deputy in a county court,
where the party against whom the order is made persists in issuing claims or making applications which are totally without merit, in circumstances where an extended civil restraint order would not be sufficient or appropriate.

4.2 Unless the court otherwise orders, where the court makes a general civil restraint order, the party against whom the order is made:
(1) will be restrained from issuing any claim or making any application in:
(a) any court if the order has been made by a judge of the Court of Appeal;
(b) the High Court or any county court if the order has been made by a judge of the High Court; or
(c) any county court identified in the order if the order has been made by a designated civil judge or his appointed deputy,
without first obtaining the permission of a judge identified in the order;
(2) may apply for amendment or discharge of the order provided he has first obtained the permission of a judge identified in the order; and
(3) may apply for permission to appeal the order and if permission is granted, may appeal the order.

4.3 Where a party who is subject to a general civil restraint order:
(1) issues a claim or makes an application in a court identified in the order without first obtaining the permission of a judge identified in the order, the claim or application will automatically be struck out or dismissed:
(a) without the judge having to make any further order; and
(b) without the need for the other party to respond to it;

(2) repeatedly makes applications for permission pursuant to that order which are totally without merit, the court may direct that if the party makes any further application for permission which is totally without merit, the decision to dismiss that application will be final and there will be no right of appeal, unless the judge who refused permission grants permission to appeal.

4.4 A party who is subject to a general civil restraint order may not make an application for permission under para. 4.2(1) or (2) without first serving notice of the application on the other party in accordance with para. 4.5.

4.5 A notice under para. 4.4 must:
(1) set out the nature and grounds of the application; and
(2) provide the other party with at least seven days within which to respond.

4.6 An application for permission under para. 4.2(1) or (2):
(1) must be made in writing;
(2) must include the other party's written response, if any, to the notice served under paragraph 4.4; and
(3) will be determined without a hearing.

4.7 An order under para. 4.3(2) may only be made by:
(1) a Court of Appeal judge;
(2) a High Court judge; or
(3) a designated civil judge or his appointed deputy.

4.8 Where a party makes an application for permission under para. 4.2(1) or (2) and permission is refused, any application for permission to appeal:
(1) must be made in writing; and
(2) will be determined without a hearing.

4.9 A general civil restraint order:
(1) will be made for a specified period not exceeding two years;
(2) must identify the courts in which the party against whom the order is made is restrained from issuing claims or making applications; and
(3) must identify the judge or judges to whom an application for permission under paras 4.2(1), 4.2(2) or 4.8 should be made.

4.10 The court may extend the duration of a general civil restraint order, if it considers it appropriate to do so, but it must not be extended for a period greater than two years on any given occasion.

4.11 If he considers that it would be appropriate to make a general civil restraint order:
(1) a master or a district judge in a district registry of the High Court must transfer the proceedings to a High Court judge; and
(2) a circuit judge or a district judge in a county court must transfer the proceedings to the designated civil judge.

General

paras.5.1–5.2 14.55

5.1 The other party or parties to the proceedings may apply for any civil restraint order.

5.2 An application under para. 5.1 must be made using the Part 23 procedure unless the court otherwise directs and the application must specify which type of civil restraint order is sought.

5.3 Examples of a limited civil restraint order, an extended civil restraint order and a general civil restraint order are annexed to this practice direction. These examples may be modified as appropriate in any particular case.

[The forms annexed to PD 3C are online at <http://hmctsformfinder.justice.gov.uk>.

Form N19 Limited civil restraint order

Form N19A Extended civil restraint order

Form N19B General civil restraint order]

PD 3D Practice Direction 3D — Mesothelioma Claims

This practice direction supplements CPR, r. 3.1.

PD 3D 47.15

Scope

1 This practice direction applies to claims for compensation for mesothelioma.

Definitions

2 In this practice direction:

'show cause procedure' means (without prejudice to the court's general case management powers in Part 3 of the CPR) the procedure set out in para. 6;

'outline submissions showing cause' means an outline or skeleton argument of the defendant's case within the show cause procedure; and

'standard interim payment' means the standard payment in respect of interim damages, and (if appropriate) interim costs and disbursements as determined from time to time by the Head of Civil Justice. The amount of this payment is currently £50,000.

Starting Proceedings

para.3.1 47.15 para.3.2 47.15

3.1 The claim form and every statement of case must be marked with the title 'Living Mesothelioma Claim' or 'Fatal Mesothelioma Claim' as appropriate.

3.2 In order for the court to adopt the show cause procedure in the first case management conference, the claimant must file and serve any witness statements about liability (as are available):

(1) either:

(a) at the same time as filing and serving the claim form and (where appropriate) the particulars of claim; or

(b) as soon as possible after filing and serving the claim form and (where appropriate) the particulars of claim; and

(2) in any event not less than seven days before the case management conference.

3.3 Any witness statement about liability must identify as far as is possible:

(1) the alleged victim's employment history and history of exposure to asbestos;

(2) the identity of any employer where exposure to asbestos of the alleged victim is alleged;

(3) details of any self-employment in which the alleged victim may have been exposed; and

(4) details of all claims made and payments received under the Pneumoconiosis etc. (Workers' Compensation) Act 1979.

3.4 The claimant must also attach to the claim form:

(1) a work history from HM Revenue and Customs (where available); and

(2) any pre-action letter of claim.

Claimants with Severely Limited Life Expectancy

4.1 Where the claimant believes that the claim is particularly urgent then on issue of the claim form, the claimant:

(1) may request in writing that the court file is placed immediately before a judge nominated to manage such cases in order to fix a case management conference; and

(2) must explain in writing to the court why the claim is urgent.

4.2 Where the court decides that the claim is urgent (and notwithstanding that a claim has not yet been served or a defence has not yet been filed) it will:

(1) fix the date for the case management conference to take place within a short period of time; and

(2) give directions as to the date by which the claimant must serve the claim form if it has not been served already.

CPR 1–25 & PDs

Fixing the Case Management Conference for Other Claims

5.1 Where para. 4 does not apply and:
(1) a defence is filed by the defendant or one of the defendants (where there is more than one); or
(2) the claimant has obtained a default judgment,
the court file will be referred to a judge nominated to manage such cases and the judge will give directions for the date of the case management conference.

5.2 Claims marked 'Living Mesothelioma Claim' will be given priority when fixing a case management conference.

The Show Cause Procedure

para.6.2 47.15 paras.6.4–6.8 47.15

6.1 The show cause procedure is a requirement by the court, of its own initiative and usually on a 'costs in the case' basis, for the defendant to identify the evidence and legal arguments that give the defendant a real prospect of success on any or all issues of liability. The court will use this procedure for the resolution of mesothelioma claims.

6.2 At the first case management conference, unless there is good reason not to do so, the defendant should be prepared to show cause why:
(1) a judgment on liability should not be entered against the defendant; and
(2) a standard interim payment on account of damages and (if appropriate) costs and disbursements should not be made by the defendant by a specified date.

6.3 At the first case management conference if liability remains in issue the court will normally order that the defendant show cause within a further given period.

6.4 The order requiring the defendant to show cause within a further given period will direct:
(1) that the defendant file and serve on the claimant by a specified date outline submissions showing cause and:
(a) if the outline submissions are not filed and served by a specified date, judgment, for a sum to be determined by the court, will be entered against the defendant without the need for any further order and the defendant will be ordered to make a standard interim payment by a specified date; or
(b) if the outline submissions are filed and served by the specified date, the claim will be listed for a show cause hearing; or
(2) that the defendant show cause at a hearing on a date fixed by the court.

6.5 At the first case management conference the court will:
(1) fix the date or trial window for the determination of damages and give any other case management directions as appropriate where the defendant admits liability or judgment is entered;
(2) fix the date or trial window for the determination of damages and give any other case management directions as appropriate where an order to show cause under para. 6.3 has been made (if the defendant subsequently shows cause then the determination date or trial window may be utilised for the trial of any issue); or
(3) in cases in which there is to be a trial on liability, give directions including the date or window for the trial.

6.6 Where the defendant fails to show cause on some issues, the court will normally enter judgment on those issues.

6.7 Where the defendant fails to show cause on all issues, the court will enter judgment for a sum to be determined and will normally order that a standard interim payment be made.

6.8 Where the defendant succeeds in showing cause on some or all issues, the court will order a trial of those issues. The court may also require the issue of quantum or apportionment (as appropriate) to be dealt with at the trial provided that it does not delay the date for the fixing of the trial.

Setting the Trial Date

para.7.1 47.15

7.1 In Living Mesothelioma Claims the date of the determination of damages or the trial will generally not be more than 16 weeks following service of the claim form.

7.2 In Fatal Mesothelioma Claims the hearing date may be more than 16 weeks following service of the claim form.

Taking Evidence by Deposition

8 Any party who for good reason wishes evidence to be taken by deposition may apply to the court at any time for such an order. However, the court will normally expect that such a request is made at a case management conference. The order will include a direction for the recording of such evidence on DVD and for the provision of a transcript. The parties must also be prepared to arrange for the provision of equipment to view the DVD by the court.

(Part 34 contains provisions for evidence to be taken by deposition.)

Compliance with Pre-action Protocols

para 9 8.2, 47.15

9 In Living Mesothelioma Claims the court may decide not to require strict adherence to Practice Direction (Pre-action Conduct) and any relevant pre-action protocol.

PD 3E Practice Direction 3E — Costs Management

This practice direction supplements Section II of CPR, Part 3.

Budget Format

para.1 43.7

1 Unless the court otherwise orders, a budget must be in the form of Precedent H annexed to this practice direction. It must be in landscape format with an easily legible typeface. In substantial cases, the court may direct that budgets be limited initially to part only of the proceedings and subsequently extended to cover the whole proceedings. A budget must be dated and verified by a statement of truth signed by a senior legal representative of the party. In cases where a party's budgeted costs do not exceed £25,000, there is no obligation on that party to complete more than the first page of Precedent H.

(The wording for a statement of truth verifying a budget is set out in PD 22.)

Costs Management Orders

para.2.2 43.14
para.2.3 43.9, 47.10
para.2.4 43.9
para.2.5 43.12
para.2.6 43.10
para.2.7 43.9
para.2.8 43.6

2.1 If the court makes a costs management order under rule 3.15, the following paragraphs apply.

2.2 Save in exceptional circumstances—

(1) the recoverable costs of initially completing Precedent H shall not exceed the higher of £1,000 or 1 per cent of the approved budget;

(2) All other recoverable costs of the budgeting and costs management process shall not exceed 2 per cent of the approved budget.

2.3 If the budgets or parts of the budgets are agreed between all parties, the court will record the extent of such agreement. In so far as the budgets are not agreed, the court will review them and, after making any appropriate revisions, record its approval of those budgets. The court's approval will relate only to the total figures for each phase of the proceedings, although in the course of its review the court may have regard to the constituent elements of each total figure. When reviewing budgets, the court will not undertake a detailed assessment in advance, but rather will consider whether the budgeted costs fall within the range of reasonable and proportionate costs.

2.4 As part of the costs management process the court may not approve costs incurred before the date of any budget. The court may, however, record its comments on those costs and should take those costs into account when considering the reasonableness and proportionality of all subsequent costs.

2.5 The court may set a timetable or give other directions for future reviews of budgets.

2.6 Each party shall revise its budget in respect of future costs upwards or downwards, if significant developments in the litigation warrant such revisions. Such amended budgets shall be submitted to the other parties for agreement. In default of agreement, the amended budgets shall be submitted to the court, together with a note of (a) the changes made and the reasons for those changes and (b) the objections of any other party. The court may approve, vary or disapprove the revisions, having regard to any significant developments which have occurred since the date when the previous budget was approved or agreed.

2.7 After its budget has been approved, each party shall re-file and re-serve the budget in the form approved with recast figures, annexed to the order approving it.

2.8 A litigant in person, even though not required to prepare a budget, shall nevertheless be provided with a copy of the budget of any other party.

2.9 *If interim applications are made* which, reasonably, were not included in a budget, then the costs of such interim applications shall be treated as additional to the approved budgets.

ANNEX

Precedent H 43.7

[The following forms are annexed to PD 3E:

Precedent H
Guidance Notes for Precedent H
These forms are online at <http://hmctsformfinder.justice.gov.uk>.]

PD 3F Practice Direction 3F — Costs Capping

This practice direction supplements Section III of CPR, Part 3.

SECTION I — GENERAL RULES ABOUT COSTS CAPPING

When to Make an Application

para.1.1 44.5 para.1.2 44.3, 44.5

1.1 The court will make a costs capping order only in exceptional circumstances.

1.2 An application for a costs capping order must be made as soon as possible, preferably before or at the first case management hearing or shortly afterwards. The stage which the proceedings have reached at the time of the application will be one of the factors the court will consider when deciding whether to make a costs capping order.

Costs Budget

para.2 44.3

2. The budget required by rule 3.20 must be in the form of Precedent H annexed to PD 3E.

Schedule of Costs

3. The schedule of costs referred to in rule 3.20(3)—
   (a) must set out—
      (i) each subheading as it appears in the applicant's budget (column 1);
      (ii) alongside each subheading, the amount claimed by the applicant in the applicant's budget (column 2); and
      (iii) alongside the figures referred to in subparagraph (ii) the amount that the respondent proposes should be allowed under each subheading (column 3); and
   (b) must be supported by a statement of truth.

Assessing the Quantum of the Costs Cap

4.1 When assessing the quantum of a costs cap, the court will take into account the factors detailed in rule 44.5 and the relevant provisions supporting that rule in PD 44. When considering a party's budget of the costs they are likely to incur in the future conduct of the proceedings, the court may also take into account a reasonable allowance on costs for contingencies.

SECTION II — COSTS CAPPING IN RELATION TO TRUST FUNDS

Costs Capping Orders in relation to Trust Funds

para.5.5 44.3

5.1 In this Section, 'trust fund' means property which is the subject of a trust, and includes the estate of a deceased person.

5.2 This Section contains additional provisions to enable—
   (a) the parties to consider whether to apply for; and
   (b) the court to consider whether to make of its own initiative,
   a costs capping order in proceedings relating to trust funds.

5.3 This Section supplements rules 3.19 to 3.21 and Section I of this practice direction.

5.4 Any party to such proceedings who intends to apply for an order for the payment of costs out of the trust fund must file and serve on all other parties written notice of that intention together with a budget of the costs likely to be incurred by that party.

5.5 The documents mentioned in paragraph 5.4 must be filed and served—
   (a) in a Part 7 claim, with the first statement of case; and
   (b) in a Part 8 claim, with the evidence (or, if a defendant does not intendto serve and file evidence, with the acknowledgment of service).

5.6 When proceedings first come before the court for directions the court may make a costs capping order of its own initiative whether or not any party has applied for such an order.

CPR Part 4 Forms

4

(1) The forms set out in a practice direction shall be used in the cases to which they apply.

(2) A form may be varied by the court or a party if the variation is required by the circumstances of a particular case.

(3) A form must not be varied so as to leave out any information or guidance which the form gives to the recipient.

(4) Where these Rules require a form to be sent by the court or by a party for another party to use, it must be sent without any variation except such as is required by the circumstances of the particular case.

(5) Where the court or a party produces a form shown in a practice direction with the words 'Royal Arms', the form must include a replica of the Royal Arms at the head of the first page.

PD 4 Practice Direction 4 — Forms

This practice direction supplements CPR, Part 4.

[For commentary on a specific paragraph, please refer to the cross-references after the title of the paragraph.]

Scope of This Practice Direction

1.1 This practice direction lists the forms to be used in civil proceedings on or after 26 April 1999,when the Civil Procedure Rules (CPR) came into force.

1.2 The forms may be modified as the circumstances require, provided that all essential information, especially information or guidance which the form gives to the recipient, is included.

1.3 This practice direction contains 3 tables —

- Table 1 lists forms required by CPR, Parts 1 to 81
- Table 2 lists High Court forms in use before 26 April 1999 which have remained in use on or after that date (see para. 4 below)
- Table 3 lists county court forms in use before 26 April 1999 that will remain in use on or after that date (see para. 5 below)

1.4 Former prescribed forms are shown as 'No. 00'. The former practice forms where they are appropriate for use in either the Chancery or Queen's Bench Division (or where no specific form is available for use in the county court, in that court also) are prefixed 'PF' followed by the number. Where the form is used mainly in the Chancery or Queen's Bench Division, the suffix CH or QB follows the form number.

Other Forms

2.1 Other forms may be authorised by practice directions. For example the forms relating to Part 61 Admiralty claims are authorised by, and annexed to, PD 61.

Table 1 'N' Forms

table 1 **63.10**

Contents

3.1 This table lists the forms that are referred to and required to be used by rules or practice directions supplementing particular Parts of the CPR. For ease of reference, forms required for claims in the Commercial Court, Technology and Construction Court and for Admiralty claims and arbitration claims, are separately listed.

3.2 There are Court Funds Office forms referred to in Part 37. These are not listed below. They are form 100 (request for lodgment (general)), form 201 (request for payment out of money in court to satisfy a Part 36 offer) and form 202 (notice of defendant's consent to payment out of money in court to satisfy a Part 36 offer). It should also be noted that use of form N242A (offer to settle – Part 36), referred to in PD 36A, para. 1.1, and in the table below, is not mandatory.

No.	Title
N1	Part 7 (general) claim form (PD 7, para. 3.1)
N1CPC	Claim Production Centre ('CPC') claim form (r. 7.10)
N1A	Notes for claimant
N1C	Notes for defendant
N1(FD)	Notes for defendant (Consumer Credit Act cases)
N2	Claim form (probate claim) (PD 57, para. 2.1)
N2A	Claimant's notes for guidance (probate claim)
N2B	Defendant's notes for guidance (probate claim)
N3	*Acknowledgment of service (probate claim) (r. 57.4(1))*
N5	Claim form for possession of property (PD 55, para. 1.5)
N5A	Claim form for relief against forfeiture (PD 55, para. 1.5)

No.	Title
N5B	Claim form for possession of property (accelerated procedure) (assured shorthold tenancy) (PD 55, para. 1.5)
N5C	Notes for the claimant (accelerated possession procedure)
N6	Claim form for demotion of tenancy (PD 65, para. 5.2)
N7	Notes for defendant (mortgaged residential premises)
N7A	Notes for defendant (rented residential premises)
N7B	Notes for defendant — forfeiture of the lease (residential premises)
N7D	Notes for defendant — demotion/suspension claim
N8	Claim form (arbitration)
N8A	Arbitration claim (notes for claimant)
N8B	Arbitration claim (notes for defendant)
N9	Acknowledgment of service/response pack (PD 10, para. 2)
N9A	Admission and statement of means (specified amount) (PD 14, para. 2.1)
N9B	Defence and counterclaim (specified amount) (PD 15, para. 1.3)
N9C	Admission and statement of means (unspecified amount and non money claims) (PD 14, para. 2.1)
N9D	Defence and counterclaim (unspecified amount and non money claims) (PD 15, para. 1.3)
N10	Notice that acknowledgment of service has been filed (r. 10.4)
N11	Defence form (PD 55, para. 1.5)
N11B	Defence form (accelerated possession procedure) (assured shorthold tenancy) (PD 55, para. 1.5)
N11D	Defence form (demotion of tenancy) (PD 65, para. 5.2)
N11M	Defence form (mortgaged residential premises) (PD 55, para. 1.5)
N11R	Defence form (rented residential premises) (PD 55, para. 1.5)
N15	Acknowledgment of service (arbitration)
N16	General form of injunction
N16(1)	General form of injunction (formal parts only)
N16A	General form of application for injunction
N17	Judgment for claimant (amount to be decided by court)
N19	Limited civil restraint order
N19A	Extended civil restraint order
N19B	General civil restraint order
N20	Witness summons (PD 34, para. 1.2)
N21	Order for examination of deponent before the hearing (PD 34, para. 4.1)
N24	Blank form of order or judgment
N26	Order for possession
N26A	Order for possession (accelerated possession procedure) (assured shorthold tenancy)
N27	Order for possession on forfeiture (for rent arrears)
N27(2)	Order for possession on forfeiture (for rent arrears) (suspended)
N28	Order for possession (rented premises) (suspended)
N28A	Order for possession (rented premises) (postponed)
N30	Judgment for claimant (default HC)
N30	Judgment for claimant (default CC)
N30(1)	Judgment for claimant (acceptance HC)
N30(1)	Judgment for claimant (acceptance CC)
N30(2)	Judgment for claimant (after determination HC)
N30(2)	Judgment for claimant (after determination CC)
N30(3)	Judgment for claimant (after redetermination HC)
N30(3)	Judgment for claimant (after redetermination CC)
N31	Order for possession (mortgaged premises) (suspended)

CPR 1–25 & PDs

No.	Title
N32	Judgment for return of goods
N32(1) HP/CCA	Judgment for delivery of goods
N32(2) HP/CCA	Judgment for delivery of goods (suspended)
N32(3) HP/CCA	Judgment for delivery of goods
N32(4)	Variation order (return of goods)
N32(5) HP/CCA	Order for balance of purchase price
N33	Judgment for delivery of goods
N34	Judgment for claimant (after amount decided by court HC)
N34	Judgment for claimant (after amount decided by court CC)
N37	Hardship payment order
N39	Order to attend court for questioning
N40A(CC)	Warrant of arrest
N40A(HC)	Warrant of arrest
N40B(CC)	Warrant of committal
N40B(HC)	Warrant of committal
N54	Notice of eviction
N77	Penal notice
N78	Notice to show good reason why an order for your committal to prison should not be made
N79	Committal or other order upon proof of disobedience of a court order or breach of an undertaking
N79A	Suspended committal order (for disobedience)
N80	Warrant of committal to prison
N81	Notice to solicitor to show cause why an undertaking should not be enforced by committal to prison
N82	Order for committal for failure of solicitor to carry out undertaking
N84	Interim third party debt order
N85	Final third party debt order
N86	Interim charging order
N87	Final charging order
N110A	Power of arrest
N113	Anti-social behaviour order under the Crime and Disorder Act 1998, s. 1B(4)
N117	General form of undertaking
N119	Particulars of claim for possession (rented residential premises) (PD 55, para. 2.1)
N119A	Notes for guidance on completing particulars of claim form (rented residential premises)
N120	Particulars of claim for possession (mortgaged residential premises) (PD 55, para. 2.1)
N121	Particulars of claim for possession (trespassers) (PD 55, para. 2.1)
N122	Particulars of claim for demotion of tenancy (PD 65, para. 5.2)
N123	Mortgage pre-action protocol checklist
N130	Application for an interim possession order
N133	Witness statement of the defendant to oppose the making of an interim possession order
N134	Interim possession order
N136	Order for possession
N138	Injunction order (Protection from Harassment Act 1997)
N139	Application for warrant of arrest
N140	Warrant of arrest
N142	*Guardianship* order
N143	(Interim) Hospital order
N144	Recognisance of defendant

No.	Title
N145	Recognisance of surety
N147	Remand order (bail granted)
N148	Remand order (bail not granted)
N149A	Notice of proposed allocation to small claims track
N149B	Notice of proposed allocation to fast track
N149C	Notice of proposed allocation to multi-track
N150A	Master/DJ's directions on allocation
N151A	Master/DJ's directions on allocation
N152	Notice that [defence] [counterclaim] has been filed (PD 26, para. 2.5)
N153	Notice of allocation or listing hearing (PD 26, para. 6.2)
N154	Notice of allocation to fast track (PD 26, paras 4.2 and 9)
N155	Notice of allocation to multi-track (PD 26, paras 4.2 and 10)
N156	Order for further information (for allocation) (PD 26, para. 4.22))
N157	Notice of allocation to small claims track (PD 26, paras 4.2 and 8)
N158	Notice of allocation to small claims track (preliminary hearing) (PD 26, paras 4.2 and 8)
N159	Notice of allocation to small claims track (no hearing) (PD 26, paras 4.2 and 8)
N160	Notice of allocation to small claims track (with parties' consent) (PD 26, paras 4.2 and 8)
N161	Appellant's notice (PD 52, para. 5.1)
N161A	Guidance notes on completing the appellant's notice
N161B	Important notes for respondent
N162	Respondent's notice (PD 52, para. 7.3)
N162A	Guidance notes on completing the respondent's notice
N163	Skeleton argument (PD 52, paras 5.9 and 7.10)
N164	Appellant's notice (small claims track only) (PD 52, para. 5.8(1A))
N165	Certificate of notification/non-notification (appeals from the Court of Protection to the Court of Appeal) (PD 52, para. 21.12(6) to (8))
N170	Listing questionnaire (pre-trial checklist) (PD 28, para. 6.1)
N171	Notice of date for return of listing questionnaire (PD 26, para. 6.1 and PD 28, para. 8.1)
N172	Notice of trial date
N173	Notice of non-payment of fee (r. 3.7)
N180	Directions questionnaire (small claims track)
N181	Directions questionnaire (fast track and multi-track)
N205A	Notice of issue (specified amount)
N205B	Notice of issue (unspecified amount)
N205C	Notice of issue (non-money claim)
N205D	Notice of issue (probate claim)
N206A	Notice of issue (accelerated possession procedure) (assured shorthold tenancy)
N206B	Notice of issue (possession claim)
N206D	Notice of issue (demotion claim)
N208	Part 8 claim form (PD 8A, para. 2.2)
N208A	Part 8 notes for claimant
N208C	Part 8 notes for defendant
N209	Part 8 notice of issue
N210	Part 8 acknowledgment of service (PD 8A, para. 3.2)
N210A	Part 8 acknowledgment of service (costs-only claim) (PD 43–48, para. 17.9)
N210B	Part 8 acknowledgment of service (PD 8B)
N210C	Acknowledgement of service (Part 81, Section 4 — Certification or application under the Charities Act 2011, s. 336, in relation to conduct alleged to constitute contempt of court (CPR, Part 81, Section 4))

No.	Title
N211	Part 20 claim form (r. 20.7)
N211A	Part 20 notes for claimant
N211C	Part 20 notes for defendant
N212	Part 20 notice of issue
N213	Part 20 acknowledgment of service (r. 20.12)
N215	Certificate of service (r. 6.10)
N216	Notice of returned document (r. 6.11)
N217	Order for substituted service (r. 6.8)
N218	Notice of service on a partner (PD 6, para. 4.2)
N225	Request for judgment and reply to admission (specified amount) (PD 12, para. 3)
N225A	Notice of part admission (specified amount) (r. 14.5)
N226	Notice of admission (unspecified amount) (r. 14.7)
N227	Request for judgment by default (amount to be decided by the court) (r. 12.5)
N228	Notice of admission (return of goods) (PD 7B, para. 8.5)
N235	Certificate of suitability of litigation friend (PD 21, para. 2.3)
N236	Notice of defence that amount claimed has been paid (r. 15.10)
N242A	Notice of offer to settle — Part 36
N244	Application notice (PD 23, para. 2.1)
N244A	Notice of hearing of application (PD 23, para. 2.2)
N251	Notice of funding of case or claim
N252	Notice of commencement of assessment (PD 43–48, para. 2.3)
N253	Notice of amount allowed on provisional assessment (PD 43–48, para. 6.5)
N254	Request for default costs certificate (PD 43–48, para. 3.1)
N255	Default costs certificate HC (PD 43–48, para. 3.3)
N255	Default costs certificate CC (PD 43–48, para. 3.3)
N256	Final costs certificate HC (PD 43–48, para. 5.11)
N256	Final costs certificate CC (PD 4–48, para. 5.11)
N257	Interim costs certificate (PD 43–48, para. 5.11)
N258	Request for detailed assessment hearing (non-legal aid) (PD 43–48, para. 4.3)
N258A	Request for detailed assessment hearing (legal aid only)
N258B	Request for detailed assessment (costs payable out of a fund other than the Community Legal Service Fund)
N258C	Request for detailed assessment hearing pursuant to an order under part III of the Solicitors Act 1974
N259	Notice of appeal (PD 43–48, para. 48.1)
N260	Statement of costs (summary assessment) (PD 43–48, para. 3.2)
N265	List of documents (PD 31, para. 3.1)
N266	Notice to admit facts/admission of facts (r. 32.18)
N268	Notice to prove documents at trial (r. 32.19)
N271	Notice of transfer of proceedings (r. 30)
N279	Notice of discontinuance (r. 38.3)
N292	Order on settlement on behalf of child or protected party (PD 21, para. 10.3)
N294	Claimant's application for a variation order
N316	Application for order that debtor attend court for questioning (PD 71, para. 1.1)
N316A	Application that an officer of a company attend court for questioning (PD 71, para. 1.1)
N322	*Order for recovery of an award*
N322A	Application to enforce an award (PD 70, para. 4.1)
N322H	Request to register a High Court judgment or order for enforcement
N349	Application for third party debt order (PD 72, para. 1.1)

No.	Title
N367	Notice of hearing to consider why fine should not be imposed (r. 34.10)
N368	Order for fining a witness for non-attendance
N370	Order for commitment or imposing a fine for insult or misbehaviour
N379	Application for charging order on land or property (PD 73, para. 1.1)
N380	Application for charging order on securities (PD 73, para. 1.1)
N434	Notice of change of solicitor (rule 42.2)
N446	Request for reissue of enforcement or an order to obtain information from a judgment debtor (not warrant)
N460	Reasons for allowing or refusing permission to appeal
N461	Judicial review claim form (PD 54)
N461 (notes)	Guidance notes on completing the judicial review claim form
N462	Judicial review acknowledgment of service (PD 54)
N463	Judicial review — application for urgent consideration
No. 32	Order for examination within jurisdiction of witness before trial (r. 34.8)
No. 33	Application for issue of letter of request to judicial authority out of jurisdiction (r. 34.13)
No. 34	Order for issue of letter of request to judicial authority out of jurisdiction (r. 34.13)
No. 35	Letter of request for examination of witness out of jurisdiction (r. 34.13)
No. 37	Order for appointment of examiner to take evidence of witness out of jurisdiction (r. 34.13(4))
No. 41	Default judgment in claim relating to detention of goods (r. 12.4(1)(c))
No. 44	Part 24 judgment for claimant
No. 44A	Part 24 judgment for defendant
No. 45	Judgment after trial before judge without jury (PD 40B, para. 14)
No. 46	Judgment after trial before judge with jury (PD 40B, para. 14)
No. 47	Judgment after trial before a judge of the Technology and Construction Court or a master or district judge (PD 40B, para. 14)
No. 48	Order after trial of issue directed to be tried under r. 3.1(2)(i)
No. 49	Judgment against personal representatives (PD 40B, para. 14.3)
No. 52	Notice of claim (r. 19.8A(4)(a))
No. 52A	Notice of judgment or order to an interested party
No. 82	Application for appointment of a receiver
No. 83	Order directing application for appointment of receiver and granting injunction meanwhile
No. 84	Order for appointment of receiver by way of equitable execution (Senior Courts Act 1981, s. 37)
No. 93	Order under the Evidence (Proceedings in Other Jurisdictions) Act 1975
No. 94	Order for production of documents in marine insurance action [r. 58.14*]
No. 109	Order for reference to the European Court
No. 111	Certificate of money provisions contained in a judgment for registration in another part of the United Kingdom (Civil Jurisdiction and Judgments Act 1982, sch. 6)
No. 112	Certificate issued under the Civil Jurisdiction and Judgments Act 1982, sch. 7, in respect of non-money provisions for registration in another part of the United Kingdom
PF 1	Application for time (r. 3.1(2)(a))
PF 2	Order for time (r. 3.1(2)(a))
PF 3	Application for an extension of time for serving a claim form (r. 7.6)
PF 4	Order for an extension of time for serving a claim form (r. 7.6)
PF 6(A)	Application for permission to serve claim form out of jurisdiction (r. 6.21)
PF 6(B)	Order for service out of the jurisdiction (r. 6.21(4))

[* The reference in the text issued by the Ministry of Justice is to a superseded practice direction.]

CPR 1–25 & PDs

No.	Title
PF 7QB	Request for service of document abroad (rr. 6.26(2)(a) and 6.27(2)(a))
PF 8	Standard 'unless' order (r. 26.5(5, PD 26, para. 2.5 and N150A)
PF 11	Application for Part 24 judgment (whole claim) (r. 24.2)
PF 12	Application for Part 24 judgment (one or some of several claims) (r. 24.2)
PF 13	Order under Part 24 (No. 1)
PF 14	Order under Part 24 (No. 2)
PF 15	Order under Part 24 for amount found due upon detailed assessment of solicitor's bill of costs
PF 16	Notice of court's intention to make an order of its own initiative (r. 3.3(2) and (3))
PF 17	Order made on court's own initiative without a hearing (r. 3.3(4) and (5))
PF 19	Group Litigation Order (r. 19.1)
PF 20	Application for Part 20 directions
PF 21	Order for Part 20 directions
PF 21A	Order to add person as defendant to counterclaim (r. 20.5)
PF 22	Notice claiming contribution or indemnity against another defendant (r. 20.6)
PF 43	Application for security for costs (r. 25.12, also Companies Act 1985, s. 726)
PF 44	Order for security for costs (r. 25.12, also Companies Act 1985, s. 726)
PF 48	Court record available for use before and at hearing
PF 49	Request to parties to state convenient dates for hearing of 1st CMC
PF 50	Application for directions (Part 29)
PF 52	Order for case management directions in the multi-track (Part 29)
PF 53	Order for separate trial of an issue (r. 3.1(2)(i))
PF 56	Request for further information or clarification with provision for response (PD 18, para. 1.6(2))
PF 57	Application for further information or clarification (PD 18, para. 5)
PF 58	Order for further information or clarification (r. 18.1)
PF 63	Interim order for receiver in pending claim
PF 67	Evidence in support of application to make an order of the Supreme Court an order of the High Court (PD 40B, para. 13.2)
PF 68	Order making an order of the Supreme Court an order of the High Court (PD 40B, para. 13.3)
PF 72	List of exhibits handed in at trial (PD 39, para. 7)
PF 74	Order for trial of whole claim or of an issue by master or district judge (PD 2B, para. 4.1)
PF 78 QB	Solicitor's undertaking as to expenses (re letter of request) (r. 34.13(6)(b) and PD 34, para. 5.3(5))
PF 83	Judgment (non-attendance of party) (r. 39.3)
PF 84A	Order on application arising from a failure to comply with an order or condition (r. 3.13)
PF 84B	Judgment on application arising from a failure to comply with an order (r. 3.5(1) and (4))
PF 85A	Request for judgment (r. 3.5(2))
PF 85B	Judgment on request arising from a failure to comply with an order (r. 3.52)
PF 113	Evidence in support of application for service by an alternative method (PD 6, para. 9.1)
PF 130	Form of advertisement (r. 6.8)
PF 147	Application for order declaring solicitor ceased to act (death etc.)
PF 148	Order declaring solicitor has ceased to act
PF 149	Application by solicitor that he has ceased to act
PF 150	Order that solicitor has ceased to act
PF 152 QB	Evidence in support of application for examination of witness under the Evidence (Proceedings in Other Jurisdictions) Act 1975
PF 153 QB	Certificate witness under the Evidence (Proceedings in Other Jurisdictions) Act 1975
PF 154 QB	Order for registration of foreign judgment under the Foreign Judgments (Reciprocal Enforcement) Act 1933
PF 155	Certificates under s. 10 of the Foreign Judgments (Reciprocal Enforcement) Act 1933

No.	Title
PF 156 QB	Evidence in support of application for registration of a Community judgment
PF 157 QB	Order for registration of a Community judgment
PF 158 QB	Notice of registration of a Community judgment
PF 159 QB	Evidence in support of application for registration of a judgment of another Contracting State or Regulation State
PF 160 QB	Order for registration of a judgment of another Contracting State or Regulation State under the Civil Jurisdiction and Judgments Act 1982, s. 4
PF 161 QB	Notice of registration of a judgment of another Contracting State or Regulation State
PF 163 QB	Evidence in support of application for certified copy of a judgment for enforcement in another Contracting State or Regulation State
PF 164	Evidence in support of application for certificate as to money provisions of a judgment of the High Court for registration elsewhere in the United Kingdom
PF 165	Evidence in support of application for registration of a judgment of a court in another part of the United Kingdom containing non-money provisions
PF 166 QB	Certificate as to finality etc. of arbitration award for enforcement abroad (Arbitration Act 1996, s. 58)
PF 167 QB	Order to stay proceedings under the Arbitration Act 1996, s. 9 [r. 62.8*]
PF 168	Order to transfer claim from the High Court to county court (County Courts Act 1984, s. 40; High Court and County Courts Jurisdiction Order 1991; r. 30.3)
PF 170A	Application for child or patient's settlement in personal injury or Fatal Accidents Act claims before proceedings begun (r. 21.10(2); PD 21, paras 6 and 7)
PF 170B	Application for child or patient's settlement in personal injury or fatal accident claims in existing proceedings (r. 21.10(2); PD 21, paras 6 and 7)
PF 172 QB	Request for directions in respect of funds in court or to be brought into court (r. 21.11)
PF 197	Application for order for transfer from the Royal Courts of Justice to a district registry or vice versa or from one district registry to another (r. 30.2(4))
PF 198	Order under PF 197
PF 205	Evidence in support of application for permission to execute for earlier costs of enforcement under the Courts and Legal Services Act 1990, s. 15(3) and (4)
PF 244 RCJ	Application notice
PF 12 CH	Advertisement for creditors (PD 40, para 10)
PF 13 CH	Advertisement for claimants other than creditors
PF 14 CH	[Witness statement] [Affidavit] verifying list of creditors' claims
PF 15 CH	List of claims by persons claiming to be creditors following advertisement (Exhibit A referred to in [witness statement] [affidavit] in PF 14 CH)
PF 16 CH	List of claims by persons claiming to be creditors other than those sent in following advertisement (Exhibit B referred to in [witness statement] [affidavit] in PF 14 CH)
PF 17 CH	List of sums of money which may be due in respect of which no claim has been received (Exhibit C referred to in [witness statement] [affidavit] in PF 14 CH)
PF 18 CH	Notice to creditor to prove claim
PF 19 CH	Notice to creditor or other claimant to produce documents or particulars in support of claim
PF 20 CH	Notice to creditor of allowance of claim
PF 21CH	Notice to creditor of disallowance of claim in whole or in part
PF 22 CH	Order for administration: beneficiaries' action reconstituted as creditors' claim (Van Oppen order)
PF 23 CH	[Witness statement] [Affidavit] verifying list of claims other than creditors' claims
PF 24 CH	List of claims not being creditors' claims sent following advertisement (Exhibit D referred to in [witness statement] [affidavit] in PF 23 CH)
PF 25 CH	List of claims not being creditors' claims other than those sent in following advertisement (Exhibit E referred to in [witness statement] [affidavit] in PF 23 CH)
PF 26 CH	Notice to claimant other than a creditor to prove claim

[* The reference in the text issued by the Ministry of Justice is to a superseded practice direction.]

No.	Title
PF 27 CH	[Witness statement] [Affidavit] verifying accounts and answering usual enquiries in administration claim (rr. 32.8 and 32.16)
PF 28 CH	Executors' [or administrators'] account (account A in PF 27 CH)
PF 29 CH	Master's order stating the results of proceedings before him on the usual accounts and inquiries in an administration claim
PF 30 CH	Security of receiver or administrator pending determination of a probate claim (PD 57*)
PF 31 CH	Consent to act as trustee (r. 33.8)
PF 32 CH	[Witness statement] [Affidavit] in support of application for appointment of new litigation friend of child claimant
PF 33 CH	Order for distribution of a Lloyd's estate
PF 34 CH	Order in inquiry as to title in proceedings to enforce charging order where the defendant's title is not disclosed
PF 36 CH	Order appointing administrator pending determination of probate claim (PD 57*)
PF 38 CH	Order in probate claim approving compromise (PD 57*)
Commercial Court forms (Part 58)	
N1(CC)	Claim form (PD 58, para. 2.4)
N1C(CC)	Notes for the defendant
N9(CC)	Acknowledgment of service (PD 58, para. 5.1)
N208(CC)	Claim form (Part 8) (PD 58, para. 2.4)
N208C(CC)	Notes for the defendant
N210(CC)	Acknowledgment of service (Part 8) (PD 58, para. 5.2)
N211(CC)	Claim form (Part 20) (PD 58, para. 12)
N211C(CC)	Notes for defendant (Part 20)
N213(CC)	Acknowledgment of service (Part 20)
N244(CC)	Application notice (PD 58, para. 10.7(2))
N265(CC)	List of documents
Technology and Construction forms (Part 60)	
TCC/CM1	Case management information sheet (PD 60, para. 8.2)
TCC/PTR1	Pre-trial review questionnaire (PD 60, para. 9.1)
Admiralty forms (Part 61)	
ADM1	Claim form (Admiralty claim *in rem*) (PD 61, para. 3.1)
ADM1A	Claim form (Admiralty claim) (PD 61, para. 12.3)
ADM1C	Notes for the defendant on replying to an *in rem* claim form
ADM2	Acknowledgment of service for Admiralty claims *in rem* (PD 61, para. 3.4)
ADM3	Collision statement of case (PD 61, para. 4.1)
ADM4	Application and undertaking for arrest and custody (PD 61, para. 5.1(1))
ADM5	Declaration in support of an application for warrant of arrest (PD 61, para. 5.1(2))
ADM6	Notice to consular officer of intention to apply for warrant of arrest (PD 61, para. 5.4)
ADM7	Request for caution against arrest (PD 61, para. 6.2)
ADM9	Warrant of arrest (PD 61, para. 5.5(1))
ADM10	Standard directions to Admiralty Marshal (PD 61, para. 5.6)
ADM11	Request for caution against release (PD 61, para. 7.1)
ADM12	Request for undertaking for release (PD 61, para. 7.4)
ADM12A	Request for withdrawal and caution against release (PD 61, para. 7.5)
ADM13	Application for judgment in default (PD 61, para. 8.1)
ADM14	Order for sale of a ship (PD 61, para. 9.2)
ADM15	Claim form (Admiralty limitation claim) (PD 61, para. 10.1(1))

[* The text issued by the Ministry of Justice mistakenly refers to PD 44.]

No.	Title
ADM15B	Notes for defendant on replying to an Admiralty limitation claim
ADM16	Notice of admission of right of claimant to limit liability (PD 61, para. 10.3)
ADM16A	Defence to Admiralty limitation claim (PD 61, para. 10.2)
ADM16B	Acknowledgment of service (Admiralty limitation claim) (PD 61, para. 10.4)
ADM17	Application for restricted limitation decree (PD 61, para. 10.5)
ADM17A	Application for general limitation decree (PD 61, para. 10.6)
ADM18	Restricted limitation decree (PD 61, para. 10.5)
ADM19	General limitation decree
ADM20	Defendant's claim in limitation (PD 61, para. 10.14)
ADM21	Declaration as to liability of a defendant to file and serve statement of case under a decree of limitation (PD 61, para. 10.16)
Arbitration forms (Part 62)	
N8	Claim form (arbitration) (PD 62, para. 2.1)
N8A	Notes for claimant (arbitration)
N8B	Notes for defendant (arbitration)
N15	Acknowledgment of service (arbitration claim)

Table 2 Practice Forms

table 2 67.26

Contents

4.1 This table lists the practice forms that may be used under this practice direction. It contains forms that were previously:

- Prescribed forms contained in Appendix A to the Rules of the Supreme Court 1965
- Queen's Bench masters' practice forms
- Chancery masters' practice forms

4.2 Where a rule permits, a party intending to use a witness statement as an alternative to an affidavit should amend any form in this Table to be used in connection with that rule so that 'witness statement' replaces 'affidavit' wherever it appears in the form.

4.3 The forms in this list are reproduced in [*Practice Forms for Use in Proceedings in the High Court* (London: Royal Courts of Justice, 2000)], in practitioners' textbooks, and on Her Majesty's Courts and Tribunals Service website.*

No.	Title
No. 53	Writ of fieri facias (sch. 1, RSC, ord. 45, r. 12)
No. 54	Writ of fieri facias on order for costs (sch. 1, RSC, ord. 45, r. 12)
No. 55	Notice of seizure (sch. 1, RSC, ord. 45, r. 2)
No. 56	Writ of fieri facias after levy of part (sch. 1, RSC, ord. 45, r. 12)
No. 57	Writ of fieri facias against personal representatives (sch. 1, RSC, ord. 45, r. 12)
No. 58	Writ of fieri facias de bonis ecclesiasticis (sch. 1, RSC, ord. 45, r. 12)
No. 59	Writ of sequestrari de bonis ecclesiasticis (sch. 1, RSC, ord. 45, r. 12)
No. 62	Writ of fieri facias to enforce Northern Irish or Scottish judgment (sch. 1, RSC, ord. 45, r. 12)
No. 63	Writ of fieri facias to enforce foreign registered judgment (sch. 1, RSC, ord. 45, r. 12)
No. 64	Writ of delivery: delivery of goods, damages and costs (sch. 1, RSC, ord. 45, r. 4)
No. 65	Writ of delivery: delivery of goods or value, damages and costs (sch. 1, RSC, ord. 45, r. 12(2))
No. 66	Writ of possession (sch. 1, RSC, ord. 45, r. 12(3))
No. 66A	Writ of possession (sch. 1, RSC, ord. 113, r. 7)
No. 67	Writ of sequestration (rr. 81.26 to 81.28)

[* The Court Form Finder is at <http://hmctsformfinder.justice.gov.uk>.]

CPR 1–25 & PDs

No.	Title
No. 68	Writ of restitution (sch. 1, RSC, ord. 46, rr. 1 and 3)
No. 69	Writ of assistance (sch. 1, RSC, ord. 46, rr. 1 and 3)
No. 71	Notice of renewal of writ of execution (sch. 1, RSC, ord. 46, r. 8)
No. 85	Order of committal or other penalty upon finding of contempt of court (Part 81)
No. 87	Claim form for writ of habeas corpus ad subjiciendum
No. 88	Notice of adjourned application for writ of habeas corpus
No. 89	Writ of habeas corpus ad subjiciendum
No. 90	Notice to be served with writ of habeas corpus ad subjiciendum
No. 91	Writ of habeas corpus ad testificandum
No. 92	Writ of habeas corpus ad respondendum
No. 95	Certificate of order against the Crown (sch. 1, RSC, ord. 77, r. 15, and Crown Proceedings Act 1947, s. 25)
No. 96	Certificate of order against the Crown (sch. 1, RSC, ord. 77, r. 15, and Crown Proceedings Act 1947, s. 25)
No. 97	Claim form to grant bail (criminal proceedings) (sch. 1, RSC, ord. 79, r. 9(1)))
No. 97A	Claim form to vary arrangements for bail (criminal proceedings) (sch. 1, RSC, ord. 79, r. 9(1)))
No. 98	Order to release prisoner on bail (sch. 1, RSC, ord. 79, r. 9(6), (6A) and (6B))
No. 98A	Order varying arrangements for bail (sch. 1, RSC, ord. 79, r. 9(10)
No. 99	Order of Court of Appeal to admit prisoner to bail
No. 100	Notice of bail (sch. 1, RSC, ord. 79, r. 9(7)
No. 101	Witness summons — Crown Court
No. 103	Witness summons — Crown Court
No. 104	Attachment of earnings order (Attachment of Earnings Act 1971)
No. 105	Notice under the Attachment of Earnings Act 1971, s. 10(2)
No. 110	Certificate under s. 12 of the Civil Jurisdiction and Judgments Act 1982
PF 23 QB	Notice by sheriff of claim to goods taken in execution (sch. 1, RSC, ord. 17, r. 22)
PF 24 QB	Notice by execution creditor of admission or dispute of title of interpleader claimant
PF 25 QB	Interpleader application (sch. 1, RSC, ord. 17, r. 3)
PF 26 QB	Interpleader application by an enforcement officer
PF 27 QB	Evidence in support of interpleader application (sch. 1, RSC, ord. 17, r. 34)
PF 28 QB	Interpleader order (1) claim barred where an enforcement officer interpleads
PF 29 QB	Interpleader order (1a) enforcement officer to withdraw
PF 30 QB	Interpleader order (2) interpleader claimant substituted as defendant (sch. 1, RSC, ord. 17)
PF 31QB	Interpleader order (3) trial of issue
PF 32 QB	Interpleader order (4) conditional order for an enforcement officer to withdraw and trial of issue
PF 34 QB	Interpleader order (6) summary disposal
PF 86	Praecipe for writ of fieri facias (sch. 1, RSC, ord. 45, r. 12(1) and ord. 46, r. 6)
PF 87	Praecipe for writ of sequestration (r. 81.27 and sch. 1, RSC, ord. 46, r. 6)
PF 88	Praecipe for writ of possession (sch. 1, RSC, ord. 45, r. 12(3), ord. 46, r. 6 and ord. 113, r. 7)
PF 89	Praecipe for writ of possession and fieri facias combined (sch. 1, RSC, ord. 45, r. 12 and ord. 46, r. 6)
PF 90	Praecipe for writ of delivery (sch. 1, RSC, ord. 45, r. 12(2) and ord. 46, r. 6)
PF 97 QB	Order for sale by an enforcement officer by private contract
PF 102	Bench warrant (sch. 1, RSC, ord. 52)
PF 103	Warrant of committal (general) (Part 81) (not for orders to obtain information — use forms N40A and N40B)
PF 104	Warrant of committal (contempt in face of court) (Part 81)
PF 105	Warrant of committal (failure of witness to attend) (Part 81)

No.	Title
PF 106	Warrant of committal (of prisoner) (Part 81)
PF 141	Witness statement/affidavit of personal service of judgment or order (sch. 1, RSC, ord. 45, r. 7)
PF 177	Order for written statement as to partners in firm (PD 7, para. 5B)
PF 179 QB	Evidence on registration of a bill of sale (Bills of Sale Act 1878; sch. 1, RSC, ord. 95)
PF 180 QB	Evidence on registration of an absolute bill of sale, settlement and deed of gift (sch. 1, RSC, ord. 95)
PF 181 QB	Evidence in support of an application for re-registration of a bill of sale (Bills of Sale Act 1878, s. 11; sch. 1, RSC, ord. 95)
PF 182 QB	Order for extension of time to register or re-register a bill of sale (Bills of Sale Act 1878, s. 14; sch. 1, RSC, ord. 95)
PF 183 QB	Evidence for permission to enter a memorandum of satisfaction on a bill of sale (Bills of Sale Act 1878, s. 15; sch. 1, RSC, ord. 95; PD RSC Ord. 95, para. 1)
PF 184 QB	Claim form for entry of satisfaction on a registered bill of sale (Bills of Sale Act 1878, s. 15; sch. 1, RSC, ord. 95, r. 2; PD RSC Ord. 95, para. 3)
PF 185 QB	Order for entry of satisfaction on a registered bill of sale (Bills of Sale Act 1878, s. 14; sch. 1, RSC, ord. 95, r. 2)
PF 186 QB	Evidence on registration of assignment of book debts (Insolvency Act 1986, s. 344; sch. 1, RSC, ord. 95, r. 62)
PF 187	Claim form for solicitor's charging order (Solicitors Act 1974, s. 73; sch. 1, RSC, ord. 106, r. 2)
PF 188	Charging order: solicitor's costs (Solicitors Act 1974, s. 73; sch. 1, RSC, ord. 106, r. 2) PF 6 CH Certificate on application for permission to issue execution on suspended order for possession where defendant in default of acknowledgment of service (sch. 1, RSC, ord. 46, rr. 2 and 4 and CPR, Part 23)
PF 7 CH	Inquiry for persons entitled to the property of an intestate (sch. 1, RSC, ord. 85)
PF 8 CH	Application notice after master's findings on kin enquiry (*Re Benjamin* order) giving permission to distribute estate upon footing (sch. 1, RSC, ord. 85)
PF 9 CH	Order giving leave to distribute estate upon footing (*Re Benjamin*) (sch. 1, RSC, ord. 85)
PF 10 CH	Judgment in beneficiaries' administration claim (sch. 1, RSC, ord. 85)
PF 11 CH	Judgment in creditors' administration claim (sch. 1, RSC, ord. 85)

Table 3

table 3 81.20

Contents

5.1 This table lists county court forms in use before 26 April 1999 that have continued to be used on or after that date.

5.2 Where a rule permits, a party intending to use a witness statement as an alternative to an affidavit should amend any form in this Table to be used in connection with that rule so that 'witness statement' replaces 'affidavit' wherever it appears in the form.

No.	Title
N16	General form of injunction
N16(1)	General form of injunction (formal parts only)
N16A	General form of application for injunction
N27	Judgment for claimant in action of forfeiture for non-payment of rent
N35	Variation order
N35A	Variation order (determination)
N41	Order suspending judgment or order, and/or warrant of execution/committal

CPR 1–25 & PDs

No.	Title
N41A	Order suspending warrant (determination)
N42	Warrant of execution
N46	Warrant of delivery and execution for damages and costs
N48	Warrant of delivery, where, if goods are not returned, levy is to be made for their value
N49	Warrant for possession of land
N50	Warrant of restitution (CCR, ord. 26, r. 17)
N51	Warrant of restitution (CCR, ord. 24, r. 6(1))
N52	Warrant of possession under CCR, ord. 24
N53	Warrant of execution or committal to district judge of foreign court
N55	Notice of application for attachment of earnings order
N55A	Notice of application for attachment of earnings order (maintenance)
N56	Form for replying to an attachment of earnings application (statement of means)
N58	Order for defendant's attendance at an adjourned hearing of an attachment of earnings application (maintenance)
N59	Warrant of committal under the (Attachment of Earnings Act 1971, s. 231)
N60	Attachment of earnings order (judgment debt)
N61	Order for production of statement of means
N61A	Order to employer for production of statement of earnings
N62	Summons for offence under Attachment of Earnings Act 1971
N63	Notice to show cause (Attachment of Earnings Act 1971, s. 23)
N64	Suspended attachment of earnings order
N64A	Suspended attachment of earnings order (maintenance)
N65	Attachment of earnings order (priority maintenance)
N65A	Attachment of earnings arrears order
N66	Consolidated attachment of earnings order
N66A	Notice of application for consolidated attachment of earnings order
N67	Judgment summons under the Debtors Act 1869
N68	Certificate of service (judgment summons)
N69	Order for debtor's attendance at an adjourned hearing of judgment summons
N70	Order of commitment under the County Courts Act 1984, s. 110
N71	Order revoking an order of commitment under the County Courts Act 1984, s. 110
N72	Notice to defendant where a committal order made but directed to be suspended under Debtors Act 1869
N73	New order on judgment summons
N74	Warrant of committal on a judgment summons under the Debtors Act 1869
N75	Endorsement on a warrant of committal sent to a foreign court
N76	Certificate to be endorsed on duplicate warrant of committal issued for rearrest of debtor
N83	Order for discharge from custody under warrant of committal
N88	Interpleader summons to execution creditor
N88(1)	Interpleader summons to claimant claiming goods or rent under an execution
N89	Interpleader summons to persons making adverse claims to debt
N90	Summons for assaulting an officer of the court or rescuing goods
N91	Order of commitment and/or imposing a fine for assaulting an officer of the court or rescuing goods
N92	Request for administration order
N93	*List of creditors furnished* under the Attachment of Earnings Act 1971
N94	Administration order

No.	Title
N95	Order revoking an administration order
N95A	Order suspending or varying an administration order
N110	Power of arrest attached to injunction under the Domestic Violence and Matrimonial Proceedings Act 1976, s. 2
N110A	Antisocial behaviour injunction — power of arrest Housing Act 1996, s. 152/153
N112	Order for Arrest under the County Courts Act 1984, s. 110
N112A	Power of arrest, Attachment of Earnings Act 1971, s. 23
N118	Notice to defendant where committal order made but directed to be suspended
N130	Application for possession including application for interim possession order
N133	Affidavit to occupier to oppose the making of an interim possession order
N136	Order for possession
N200	Petition — Note old number was N208
N201	Request for entry of appeal — Note old number was N209
N202	Order for party to sue or defend on behalf of others having the same interest — Note old number was N210
N203	Notice to persons on whose behalf party has obtained leave to sue or defend — Note old number was N211
N204	Notice to person against whom party has obtained leave to sue or defend on behalf of others — Note old number was N212
N206	Notice of issue of fixed date claim
N207	Plaint note (adoption freeing for adoption)
N224	Request for service out of England and Wales through the court
N245	Application for suspension of a warrant and/or variation of an instalment order
N246	Claimant's reply to defendant's application to vary instalment order
N246A	Claimant's reply to defendant's application to suspend warrant of execution
N270	Notes for guidance (application for administration order)
N276	Notice of hearing of interpleader proceedings transferred from High Court
N277	Notice of pre-trial review of interpleader proceedings transferred from the High Court
N280	Order of reference of proceedings or questions for inquiry and report
N285	General form of affidavit
N288	Order to produce prisoner
N289	Judgment for defendant
N293	Certificate of judgment or order
N293A	Combined certificate of judgment and request for writ of fieri facias
N295	Order for sale of land
N296	Notice of judgment or order to party directed to be served with notice
N297	Order for accounts and inquiries in creditors' administration action
N298	Order for administration
N299	Order for foreclosure nisi of legal mortgage of land
N300	Order for sale in action by equitable mortgagee
N302	Judgment in action for specific performance (vendor's action, title accepted)
N303	Order for dissolution of partnership
N304	Notice to parties to attend upon taking accounts
N305	Notice to creditor to prove his claim
N306	Notice to creditor of determination of claim
N307	District judge's order (accounts and inquiries)
N309	Order for foreclosure absolute

CPR 1–25 & PDs

No.	Title
N310	Partnership order on further consideration
N311	Administrative action order on further consideration
N313	Endorsement on certificate of judgment (transfer)
N317	Bailiff's report
N317A	Bailiff's report to the claimant
N319	Notice of execution of warrant of committal
N320	Request for return of, or to, warrant
N322	Order for recovery of money awarded by tribunal
N323	Request for warrant of execution
N324	Request for warrant of goods
N325	Request for warrant for possession of land
N326	Notice of issue of warrant of execution
N327	Notice of issue of warrant of execution to enforce a judgment or order
N328	Notice of transfer of proceedings to the High Court
N329	Notes for guidance on completion of N79
N330	Notice of sale or payment under execution in respect of a judgment for a sum exceeding £500
N331	Notice of withdrawal from possession or payment of moneys on notice of receiving or winding-up order
N332	Inventory of goods removed
N333	Notice of time when and where goods will be sold
N334	Request to hold walking possession and authority to re-enter
N336	Request and result of search in the attachment of earnings index
N337	Request for attachment of earnings order
N338	Request for statement of earnings
N339	Discharge of attachment of earnings order
N340	Notice as to payment under attachment of earnings order made by the High Court
N341	Notice of intention to vary attachment of earnings order under the Attachment of Earnings Act 1971, s. 10(2)
N342	Request for judgment summons
N343	Notice of result of hearing of a judgment summons issued on a judgment or order of the High Court
N344	Request for warrant of committal on judgment summons
N345	Certificate of payment under the Debtors Act 1869
N353	Order appointing receiver of real and personal property
N354	Order appointing receiver of partnership
N355	Interim order for appointment of receiver
N356	Order for appointment of receiver by way of equitable execution
N358	Notice of claim to goods taken in execution
N359	Notice to claimant to goods taken in execution to make deposit or give security
N360	Affidavit in support of interpleader summons other than an execution
N361	Notice of application for relief in pending action
N362	Order on interpleader summons under an execution where the claim is not established
N363	Order on interpleader summons under an execution where the claim is established
N364	Order on interpleader summons (other than execution) where there is an action
N365	Order on interpleader summons (other than execution) where there is no action
N366	Summons for neglect to levy execution

No.	Title
N372	Order for rehearing
N373	Notice of application for an administration order
N374	Notice of intention to review an administration order
N374A	Notice of intention to revoke an administration order
N375	Notice of further creditors' claim
N376	Notice of hearing administration order (by direction of the court)
N377	Notice of dividend
N388	Notice to probate registry to produce documents
N390	Notice that a claim has been entered against the Crown
N391	Crown Proceedings Act 1947 affidavit in support of application directing payment by Crown to judgment creditor
N392	Crown Proceedings Act 1947 notice of application for order directing payment by the Crown to the judgment creditor
N432	Affidavit on payment into court under the Trustee Act 1925, s. 63
N436	Order for sale of land under charging order
N437	District judge's report
N438	Notice to charge holder under Matrimonial Homes Act 1983
N440	Notice of application for time order by debtor or hirer — Consumer Credit Act 1974
N441	Notification of request for certificate of satisfaction or cancellation
N441A	Certificate of satisfaction or cancellation of judgment debt
N444	Details of sale under a warrant of execution
N445	Request for reissue of warrant
N447	Notice to claimant of date fixed for adjourned hearing
N448	Request to defendant for employment details, attachment of earnings
N449	Notice to employer, failure to make deductions under attachment of earnings order

CPR Part 5 Court Documents

[For commentary on a specific rule, please refer to the cross-references after the title of the rule.]
Part 5 **15.58, 77.37**

5.1 Scope of this Part

This part contains general provisions about—

(a) documents used in court proceedings; and
(b) the obligations of a court officer in relation to those documents.

5.2 Preparation of Documents

(1) Where under these Rules, a document is to be prepared by the court, the document may be prepared by the party whose document it is, unless—
  (a) a court officer otherwise directs; or
  (b) it is a document to which—
    (ii) CCR Order 25, rule 8(9) (reissue of warrant where condition upon which warrant was suspended has not been complied with); or
    (iii) CCR Order 28, rule 11(1) (issue of warrant of committal), applies.
(2) Nothing in this rule shall require a court officer to accept a document which is illegible, has not been duly authorised, or is unsatisfactory for some other similar reason.

5.3 Signature of Documents by Mechanical Means

r.5.3 **23.14**

Where any of these Rules or any practice direction requires a document to be signed, that requirement shall be satisfied if the signature is printed by computer or other mechanical means.

5.4 Register of Claims

r.5.4 **15.54, 72.7**
r.5.4(1) **12.3, 15.56**
r.5.4(2) **15.56**

(1) A court or court office may keep a publicly accessible register of claims which have been issued out of that court or court office.
(2) Any person who pays the prescribed fee may, during office hours, search any available register of claims.

(Practice Direction 5A contains details of available registers)

5.4A Supply of Documents to Attorney-General from Court Records

r.5.4A(1) **15.56**
r.5.4A(2) **15.56**

(1) The Attorney-General may search for, inspect and take a copy of any documents within a court file for the purpose of preparing an application or considering whether to make an application under section 42 of the Senior Courts Act 1981 or section 33 of the Employment Tribunals Act 1996 (restriction of vexatious proceedings).
(2) The Attorney-General must, when exercising the right under paragraph (1)—
  (a) pay any prescribed fee; and

(b) file a written request, which must—
  (i) confirm that the request is for the purpose of preparing an application or considering whether to make an application mentioned in paragraph (1); and
  (ii) name the person who would be the subject of the application.

5.4B Supply of Documents to a Party from Court Records

r.5.4B 15.56
r.5.4B(1) 15.57
r.5.4B(2) 15.57, 15.58

(1) A party to proceedings may, unless the court orders otherwise, obtain from the records of the court a copy of any document listed in paragraph 4.2A of Practice Direction 5A.
(2) A party to proceedings may, if the court gives permission, obtain from the records of the court a copy of any other document filed by a party or communication between the court and a party or another person.

5.4C Supply of Documents to a Non-party from Court Records

r.5.4C 15.56, 15.58, 37.43
r.5.4C(1)(a) 15.56
r.5.4C(1)(b) 15.56
r.5.4C(1B) 15.56
r.5.4C(2)–(3) 15.56
r.5.4C(4) 15.58
r.5.4C(6) 15.58

(1) The general rule is that a person who is not a party to proceedings may obtain from the court records a copy of—
  (a) a statement of case, but not any documents filed with or attached to the statement of case, or intended by the party whose statement it is to be served with it;
  (b) a judgment or order given or made in public (whether made at a hearing or without a hearing), subject to paragraph (1B).
(1A) Where a non-party seeks to obtain a copy of a statement of case filed before 2nd October 2006—
  (a) this rule does not apply; and
  (b) the rules of court relating to access by a non-party to statements of case in force immediately before 2nd October 2006 apply as if they had not been revoked.

(The rules relating to access by a non-party to statements of case in force immediately before 2nd October 2006 were contained in the former rule 5.4(5) to 5.4(9). Practice Direction 5A sets out the relevant provisions as they applied to statements of case.)

(1B) No document—
  (a) relating to an application under rule 78.24(1) for a mediation settlement enforcement order;
  (b) annexed to a mediation settlement enforcement order made under rule 78.24(5);
  (c) relating to an application under rule 78.26(1) or otherwise for disclosure or inspection of mediation evidence; or
  (d) annexed to an order for disclosure or inspection made under rule 78.26 or otherwise, may be inspected without the court's permission.
(2) A non-party may, if the court gives permission, obtain from the records of the court a copy of any other document filed by a party, or communication between the court and a party or another person.
(3) A non-party may obtain a copy of a statement of case or judgment or order under paragraph (1) only if—
  (a) where there is one defendant, the defendant has filed an acknowledgment of service or a defence;
  (b) where there is more than one defendant, either—
    (i) all the defendants have filed an acknowledgment of service or a defence;
    (ii) at least one defendant has filed an acknowledgment of service or a defence, and the court gives permission;
  (c) the claim has been listed for a hearing; or
  (d) judgment has been entered in the claim.
(4) The court may, on the application of a party or of any person identified in a statement of case—
  (a) order that a non-party may not obtain a copy of a statement of case under paragraph (1)
  (b) restrict the persons or classes of persons who may obtain a copy of a statement of case;

(c) order that persons or classes of persons may only obtain a copy of a statement of case if it is edited in accordance with the directions of the court; or
(d) make such other order as it thinks fit.

(5) A person wishing to apply for an order under paragraph (4) must file an application notice in accordance with Part 2

(6) Where the court makes an order under paragraph (4), a non-party who wishes to obtain a copy of the statement of case, or to obtain an unedited copy of the statement of case, may apply on notice to the party or person identified in the statement of case who requested the order, for permission.

5.4D Supply of Documents from Court Records — General

r.5.4D(1) 15.58

(1) A person wishing to obtain a copy of a document under rule 5.4B or rule 5.4C must pay any prescribed fee and—
(a) if the court's permission is required, file an application notice in accordance with Part 23; or
(b) if permission is not required, file a written request for the document.

(2) An application for an order under rule 5.4C(4) or for permission to obtain a copy of a document under rule 5.4B or rule 5.4C (except an application for permission under rule 5.4C(6)) may be made without notice, but the court may direct notice to be given to any person who would be affected by its decision.

(3) Rules 5.4, 5.4B and 5.4C do not apply in relation to any proceedings in respect of which a rule or practice direction makes different provision.

5.5 Filing and Sending Documents

r.5.5 15.55

(1) A practice direction may make provision for documents to be filed or sent to the court by—
(a) facsimile; or
(b) other electronic means.

(2) Any such practice direction may—
(a) provide that only particular categories of documents may be filed or sent to the court by such means;
(b) provide that particular provisions only apply in specific courts; and
(c) specify the requirements that must be fulfilled for any document filed or sent to the court by such means.

PD 5A Practice Direction 5A — Court Documents

This practice direction supplements CPR, Part 5.

[For commentary on a specific paragraph, please refer to the cross-references after the title of the paragraph.]

Signature of Documents by Mechanical Means

1 Where, under rule 5.3, a replica signature is printed electronically or by other mechanical means on any document, the name of the person whose signature is printed must also be printed so that the person may be identified. This paragraph does not apply to claim forms issued through the Claims Production Centre.

Form of Documents

para.2.1 24.4

2.1 Statements of case and other documents drafted by a legal representative should bear his/her signature and if they are drafted by a legal representative as a member or employee of a firm theyshould be signed in the name of the firm.

2.2 Every document prepared by a party for filing or use at the court must:

(1) Unless the nature of the document renders it impracticable, be on A4 paper of durable quality having a margin, not less than 3.5 centimetres wide,

(2) be fully legible and should normally be typed,

(3) where possible be bound securely in a manner which would not hamper filing or otherwise each page should be endorsed with the case number,

(4) have the pages numbered consecutively,

(5) be divided into numbered paragraphs,

(6) have all numbers, including dates, expressed as figures, and

(7) give in the margin the reference of every document mentioned that has already been filed.

2.3 A document which is a copy produced by a colour photostat machine or other similar device may be filed at the court office provided that the coloured date seal of the court is not reproduced on the copy.

Supply of Documents to New Parties

3.1 Where a party is joined to existing proceedings, the party joined shall be entitled to require the party joining him to supply, without charge, copies of all statements of case, written evidence and any documents appended or exhibited to them which have been served in the proceedings by or upon the joining party which relate to any issues between the joining party and the party joined, and copies of all orders made in those proceedings. The documents must be supplied within 48 hours after a written request for them is received.

3.2 If the party joined is not supplied with copies of the documents requested under paragraph 3.1 within 48 hours, he may apply under Part 23 for an order that they be supplied.

3.3 The party by whom a copy is supplied under paragraph 3.1 or, if he is acting by a solicitor, his solicitor, shall be responsible for it being a true copy.

Supply of Documents from Court Records

para.4.1 15.56
para.4.2 15.56
para.4.2A 15.57

4.1 Registers of claims which have been issued are available for inspection at the following offices of the High Court at the Royal Courts of Justice:

(1) the Central Office of the Queen's Bench Division;

(2) Chancery Chambers;

(3) the Admiralty and Commercial Court Registry.

4.2 No registers of claims are at present available for inspection in county courts or in district registries or other offices of the High Court.

4.2A A party to proceedings may, unless the court orders otherwise, obtain from the records of the court a copy of:
(a) a certificate of suitability of a litigation friend;
(b) a notice of funding;
(c) a claim form or other statement of case together with any documents filed with or attached to or intended by the claimant to be served with such claim form;
(d) an acknowledgment of service together with any documents filed with or attached to or intended by the party acknowledging service to be served with such acknowledgment of service;
(e) a certificate of service, other than a certificate of service of an application notice or order in relation to a type of application mentioned in sub-paragraph (h)(i) or (ii);
(f) a notice of non-service;
(g) a directions questionnaire;
(h) an application notice, other than in relation to:
(i) an application by a solicitor for an order declaring that he has ceased to be the solicitor acting for a party; or
(ii) an application for an order that the identity of a party or witness should not be disclosed;
(i) any written evidence filed in relation to an application, other than a type of application mentioned in sub-paragraph (h)(i) or (ii);
(j) a judgment or order given or made in public (whether made at a hearing or without a hearing);
(k) a statement of costs;
(l) a list of documents;
(m) a notice of payment into court;
(n) a notice of discontinuance;
(o) a notice of change; or
(p) an appellant's or respondent's notice of appeal.

4.3 An application under r. 5.4B(2), r. 5.4C(1B), r. 5.4C(2) or r. 5.4C(3)(b)(ii) for permission to obtain a copy of a document, even if made without notice, must be made under Part 23 and the application notice must identify the document or class of document in respect of which permission is sought and the grounds relied upon.

4.4 An application under r. 5.4C(4) by a party or a person identified in a claim form must be made:
(1) under Part 23; and
(2) to a master or district judge, unless the court directs otherwise.

4.5 Rule 5.4B allows a person who is a party to proceedings to obtain copies of documents from court records. A person is a party to proceedings who has been named as a party on a statement of case irrespective of whether they have been served with that statement of case.

Supply of Documents from Court Records — Statements of Case Filed before 2 October 2006

paras.4A.1–4A.9 15.56 paras.4A.2 42.8

4A.1 Rule 5.4C(1A) provides that the rules of court relating to access by a non-party to statements of case in force immediately before 2 October 2006 apply to statements of case filed before that date as if they had not been revoked. For ease of reference, those rules are set out in the following paragraphs as they applied to statements of case, along with the relevant supplementary provisions previously contained in this practice direction.

4A.2 A person who is not a party to proceedings may:
(1) unless the court orders otherwise, obtain from the records of the court a copy of a claim form, but not any documents filed with or attached to or intended by the claimant to be served with such claim form, subject to para. 4A.3 and to any order of the court under para. 4A.4; and
(2) if the court gives permission, obtain from the records of the court a copy of any other statement of case.

4A.3 A person may obtain a copy of a claim form under para. 4A.2(1) only if:
(1) where there is one defendant, the defendant has filed an acknowledgment of service or a defence;

(2) where there is more than one defendant, either:
(a) all the defendants have filed an acknowledgment of service or a defence;
(b) at least one defendant has filed an acknowledgment of service or a defence, and the court gives permission;
(3) the claim has been listed for a hearing; or
(4) judgment has been entered in the claim.

4A.4 The court may, on the application of a party or any person identified in the claim form:
(1) restrict the persons or classes of persons who may obtain a copy of the claim form;
(2) order that persons or classes of persons may only obtain a copy of the claim form if it is edited in accordance with the directions of the court; or
(3) make such other order as it thinks fit.

4A.5 A person wishing to obtain a copy of a document under para. 4A.2 must pay any prescribed fee and:
(a) if the court's permission is required, file an application notice in accordance with Part 23; or
(b) if permission is not required, file a written request for the document.

4A.6 An application for permission to obtain a copy of a statement of case, or for an order under para. 4A.4, may be made without notice, but the court may direct notice to be given to any person who would be affected by its decision.

4A.7 An application under para. 4A.3(2)(b) for permission to obtain a copy of a claim form must be made under Part 23.

4A.8 An application notice under para. 4A.2(2) or para. 4A.3(2)(b) must identify the document or class of document in respect of which permission is sought and the grounds relied upon.

4A.9 An application under para. 4A.4 by a party or a person identified in a claim form must be made:
(a) under Part 23; and
(b) to a master or district judge, unless the court directs otherwise.

Documents for Filing at Court

para.5.1 15.54
para.5.2 15.54
para.5.3 15.55
para.5.3(6) 3.5

5.1 The date on which a document was filed at court must be recorded on the document. This may be done by a seal or a receipt stamp.

5.2 Particulars of the date of delivery at a court office of any document for filing and the title of the proceedings in which the document is filed shall be entered in court records, on the court file or on a computer kept in the court office for the purpose. Except where a document has been delivered at the court office through the post, the time of delivery should also be recorded.

5.3 Filing by Facsimile
(1) Subject to paragraph (6) below, a party may file a document at court by sending it by facsimile ('fax').
(2) Where a party files a document by fax, he must not send a hard copy in addition.
(3) A party filing a document by fax should be aware that the document is not filed at court until it is delivered by the court's fax machine, whatever time it is shown to have been transmitted from the party's machine.
(4) The time of delivery of the faxed document will be recorded on it in accordance with paragraph 5.2.
(5) It remains the responsibility of the party to ensure that the document is delivered to the court in time.
(6) If a fax is delivered after 4 p.m. it will be treated as filed on the next day the court office is open.
(7) If a fax relates to a hearing, the date and time of the hearing should be prominently displayed.
(8) Fax should not be used to send letters or documents of a routine or non-urgent nature.
(9) Fax should not be used, except in an unavoidable emergency, to deliver:
(a) a document which attracts a fee;
(b) [*deleted*]
(c) a document relating to a hearing less than two hours ahead;
(d) trial bundles or skeleton arguments.

(10) Where (9)(a) or (b) applies, the fax should give an explanation for the emergency and include an undertaking that the fee or money has been dispatched that day by post or will be paid at the court office counter the following business day.

(11) Where courts have several fax machines, each allocated to an individual section, fax messages should only be sent to the machine of the section for which the message is intended.

5.4 Where the court orders any document to be lodged in court, the document must, unless otherwise directed, be deposited in the office of that court.

5.5 A document filed, lodged or held in any court office shall not be taken out of that office without the permission of the court unless the document is to be sent to the office of another court (for example, under CPR Part 30 (transfer)), except in accordance with CPR rule 39.7 (impounded documents) or in accordance with paragraph 5.6 below.

5.6 (1) Where a document filed, lodged or held in a court office is required to be produced to any court, tribunal or arbitrator, the document may be produced by sending it by registered post (together with a certificate as in paragraph 5.6(8)(b)) to the court, tribunal or arbitrator in accordance with the provisions of this paragraph.

(2) Any court, tribunal or arbitrator or any party requiring any document filed, lodged or held in any court office to be produced must apply to that court office by sending a complete drequest (as in paragraph 5.6(8)(a)), stamped with the prescribed fee.

(3) On receipt of the request the court officer will submit the same to a master in the Royal Courts of Justice or to a district judge elsewhere, who may direct that the request be complied with. Before giving a direction the master or district judge may require to be satisfied that the request is made in good faith and that the document is required to be produced for the reasons stated. The master or district judge giving the direction may also direct that, before the document is sent, an official copy of it is made and filed in the court office at the expense of the party requiring the document to be produced.

(4) On the direction of the master or district judge the court officer shall send the document by registered post addressed to the court, tribunal or arbitrator, with:

(a) an envelope stamped and addressed for use in returning the document to the court office from which it was sent;

(b) a certificate as in paragraph 5.6(8)(b);

(c) a covering letter describing the document, stating at whose request and for what purpose it is sent, referring to this paragraph of the practice direction and containing a request that the document be returned to the court office from which it was sent in the enclosed envelope as soon as the court or tribunal no longer requires it.

(5) It shall be the duty of the court, tribunal or arbitrator to whom the document was sent to keep it in safe custody, and to return it by registered post to the court office from which it was sent, as soon as the court, tribunal or arbitrator no longer requires it.

(6) In each court office a record shall be kept of each document sent and the date on which it was sent and the court, tribunal or arbitrator to whom it was sent and the date of its return. It shall be the duty of the court officer who has signed the certificate referred to in para. 5.6(8)(b) below to ensure that the document is returned within a reasonable time and to make inquiries and report to the master or district judge who has given the direction under paragraph (3) above if the document is not returned, so that steps may be taken to secure its return.

(7) Notwithstanding the preceding paragraphs, the master or district judge may direct a court officer to attend the court, tribunal or arbitrator for the purpose of producing the document.

(8) (a) I, of , an officer of the Court/Tribunal at /an arbitrator of /the Claimant/Defendant/Solicitor for the Claimant/Defendant [*describing the Applicant so as to show that he is a proper person to make the request*] in the case of v. [19 No.]
REQUEST that the following document [or documents] be produced to the Court/Tribunal/arbitrator on the day of 19 [and following days] and I request that the said document [or documents] be sent by registered post to the proper officer of the Court/Tribunal/arbitrator for production to that Court/Tribunal/arbitrator on that day.
(Signed).
Dated the day of 1999/2

(b) I, A. B., an officer of the Court of certify that the document sent here with for production to the Court/Tribunal/arbitrator on the day of 1999/2 in the case of v. and marked 'A.B.' is the document requested on the day of 1999/2 and I FURTHER CERTIFY that the said document has been filed in and is produced from the custody of the Court.
(Signed)
Dated the day of 1999/2

Enrolment of Deeds and Other Documents

6.1 (1) Any deed or document which by virtue of any enactment is required or authorised to be enrolled in the Senior Courts may be enrolled in the Central Office of the High Court.
(2) Attention is drawn to the Enrolment of Deeds (Change of Name) Regulations 1994 which are reproduced in the appendix to this practice direction.

6.2 The following paragraph of the practice direction describes the practice to be followed in any case in which a child's name is to be changed and to which the 1994 Regulations apply.

6.3 (1) Where a person has by any order of the High Court, county court or Family Proceedings Court been given parental responsibility for a child and applies to the Central Office, Filing Department, for the enrolment of a deed poll to change the surname (family name) of a child who is under the age of 18 years (unless a child who is or has been married or has formed a civil partnership), the application must be supported by the production of the consent in writing of every other person having parental responsibility.
(2) In the absence of that consent, the application will be adjourned generally unless and until permission is given in the proceedings, in which the said order was made, to change the surname of the child and the permission is produced to the Central Office.
(3) Where an application is made to the Central Office by a person who has not been given parental responsibility for a child by any order of the High Court, county court or Family Proceedings Court for the enrolment of a deed poll to change the surname of the child who is under the age of 18 years (unless the child is or has been married or has formed a civil partnership), permission of the court to enrol the deed will be granted if the consent in writing of every person having parental responsibility is produced or if the person (or, if more than one, persons) having parental responsibility is dead or overseas or despite the exercise of reasonable diligence it has not been possible to find him or her for other good reason.
(4) In cases of doubt the Senior Master or, in his absence, the practice master will refer the matter to the Master of the Rolls.
(5) In the absence of any of the conditions specified above the Senior Master or the Master of the Rolls, as the case may be, may refer the matter to the Official Solicitor for investigation and report.

APPENDIX

Regulations made by the Master of the Rolls, Sir Thomas Bingham MR, on 3 March 1994 (SI 1994/604) under the Senior Courts Act 1981, s. 133(1).

1 (1) These regulations may be cited as the Enrolment of Deeds (Change of Name) Regulations 1994 and shall come into force on 1 April 1994.
(2) These Regulations shall govern the enrolment in the Central Office of the Supreme Court of deeds evidencing change of name (referred to in these Regulations as 'deeds poll').

2 (1) A person seeking to enrol a deed poll ('the applicant') must be a Commonwealth citizen as defined by section 37(1) of the British Nationality Act 1981.
(2) If the applicant is a British citizen, a British Dependent Territories citizen or a British Overseas citizen, he must be described as such in the deed poll, which must also specify the section of the British Nationality Act under which the relevant citizenship was acquired.
(3) In any other case, the applicant must be described as a Commonwealth citizen.

CPR 1–25 & PDs

(4) The applicant must be described in the deed poll as single, married, widowed, divorced, a civil partner or former civil partner and, if a former civil partner, whether the civil partnership ended on death or dissolution.

3 (1) As proof of the citizenship named in the deed poll, the applicant must produce
(a) a certificate of birth; or
(b) a certificate of citizenship by registration or naturalisation or otherwise; or
(c) some other document evidencing such citizenship.

(2) In addition to the documents set out in paragraph (1), an applicant who is married or a civil partner must—
(a) produce his certificate of marriage or a civil partnership certificate; and
(b) show that the notice of his intention to apply for the enrolment of the deed poll has been given to his spouse or civil partner by delivery or by post to his spouse's or civil partner's last known address; and
(c) show that he has obtained the consent of his spouse or civil partner to the proposed change of name or that there is good reason why such consent should be dispensed with.

4 (1) The deed poll and the documents referred to in regulation 3 must be exhibited to a statutory declaration by a Commonwealth citizen who is a householder in the United Kingdom and who must declare that he is such in the statutory declaration.

(2) The statutory declaration must state the period, which should ordinarily not be less than 10 years, during which the householder has known the applicant and must identify the applicant as the person referred to in the documents exhibited to the statutory declaration.

(3) Where the period mentioned in paragraph (2) is stated to be less than 10 years, the Master of the Rolls, may, in his absolute discretion decide whether to permit the deed poll to be enrolled and may require the applicant to provide more information before so deciding.

5 If the applicant is resident outside the United Kingdom, he must provide evidence that such residence is not intended to be permanent and the applicant may be required to produce a certificate by a solicitor or as to the nature and probable duration of such residence.

6 The applicant must sign the deed poll in both his old and new names.

7 Upon enrolment the deed poll shall be advertised in the London Gazette by the clerk in charge for the time being of the Filing and Record Department at the Central Office of the Supreme Court.

8 (1) Subject to the following provisions of this regulation, these Regulations shall apply in relation to a deed poll evidencing the change of name of a child as if the child were the applicant.

(2) Paragraphs (3) to (8) shall not apply to a child who has attained the age of 16 and is or has been married or a civil partner.

(3) If the child is under the age of 16, the deed poll must be executed by a person having parental responsibility for him.

(4) If the child has attained the age of 16, the deed poll must, except in the case of a person mentioned in paragraph (2), be executed by a person having parental responsibility for the child and be endorsed with the child's consent signed in both his old and new names and duly witnessed.

(5) The application for enrolment must be supported—
(a) by a witness statement showing that the change of name is for the benefit of the child, and
(i) that the application is submitted by all persons having parental responsibility for the child; or
(ii) that it is submitted by one person having parental responsibility for the child with the consent of every other person; or
(iii) that it is submitted by one person having parental responsibility for the child without the consent of every other such person, or by some other person whose name and capacity are given, for reasons set out in the affidavit;
and
(b) by such other evidence, if any, as the Master of the Rolls may require in the particular circumstances of the case.

(6) Regulation 4(2) shall not apply but the statutory declaration mentioned in regulation 4(1) shall state how long the householder has known the deponent under paragraph (5) (a) and the child respectively.
(7) Regulation 6 shall not apply to a child who has not attained the age of 16.
(8) In this regulation 'parental responsibility' has the meaning given in section 3 of the Children Act 1989.

9 The Enrolment of Deeds (Change of Name) Regulations 1983 and the Enrolment of Deeds (Change of Name) (Amendment) Regulations 1990 are hereby revoked.

[The text of the appendix incorporates amendments made by the Enrolment of Deeds (Change of Name) (Amendment) Regulations 2005 (SI 2005/2056).]

PD 5B Practice Direction 5B — Electronic Communication and Filing of Documents

This practice direction supplements CPR, r. 5.5.

PD 5B 15.55

General

1.1 Section I of this practice direction provides for parties to claims in specified courts to:
(1) communicate with the court by email; and
(2) file specified documents by email.

1.2 Section II of this practice direction provides for parties to claims in specified courts to file specified documents electronically via an online forms service.*

1.3 Section III of this practice direction contains general provisions which apply to both Section I and Section II.

1.4 This practice direction does not allow:
(1) communication with the court or the filing of documents by email; or
(2) use of the online forms service,
in proceedings to which the Civil Procedure Rules do not apply.

I COMMUNICATION AND FILING OF DOCUMENTS BY EMAIL

Interpretation

Para 2.1 15.55

2.1 For the purposes of this Section:
(1) a specified court is a court or court office which has published an email address for the filing of documents on Her Majesty's Courts and Tribunals Service website; and
(2) a specified document is a document listed on Her Majesty's Courts and Tribunals Service website as a document that may be sent to or filed in that court by email.

Communications and Documents Which May Be Sent by Email

para.3.2A 15.55 para.3.3A 15.55

3.1 Subject to para. 3.2, a party to a claim in a specified court may send a specified document to the court by email.

3.2 Subject to para. 3.2A, a party must not use email to take any step in a claim for which a fee is payable.

3.2A A party may make an application using email in the Preston Combined Court, where he is permitted to do so by PREMA (Preston Email Application Service) User Guide and Protocols.

3.3 Subject to para. 3.3A, if:
(a) a fee is payable on the filing of a particular document; and
(b) a party purports to file that document by email,
the court shall treat the document as not having been filed.

3.3A A party may file by email an application notice in the Preston Combined Court where permitted to do so by PREMA (Preston Email Application Service) User Guide and Protocols.

(Rules 6.3(1)(d) and 6.20(1)(d) permit service by email in accordance with the relevant practice direction. Rule 6.23(6) and PD 6A, para. 4, set out the circumstances in which a party may serve a document by email.)

Technical Specifications of Email

4.1 The email message must contain the name, telephone number and email address of the sender and should be in plain text or rich text format rather than HTML.

[* This was a pilot scheme which has now closed.]

4.2 Correspondence and documents may be sent as either text in the body of the email, or as attachments, except as mentioned in para. 4.3.
4.3 Documents required to be in a practice form must be sent in that form as attachments.
4.4 Court forms may be downloaded from Her Majesty's Courts and Tribunals Service website.
4.5 Attachments must be sent in a format supported by the software used by the specified court to which it is sent. The format or formats which may be used in sending attachments to a particular specified court are listed on Her Majesty's Courts and Tribunals Service website.
4.6 An attachment which is sent to a specified court in a format not listed on Her Majesty's Courts and Tribunals Service website as appropriate for that court will be treated as not having been received by the court.
4.7 The length of attachments and total size of email must not exceed the maximum which a particular specified court has indicated that it can accept. This information is listed on Her Majesty's Courts and Tribunals Service website.
4.8 Where proceedings have been commenced, the subject line of the email must contain the following information:
(1) the case number;
(2) the parties' names (abbreviated if necessary); and
(3) the date and time of any hearing to which the email relates.

II ONLINE FORMS SERVICE*

Scope and Interpretation

5.1 Reference to an online forms service is reference to a service available on Her Majesty's Courts and Tribunals Service website. The website contains certain documents which a user may complete online and then submit electronically to a specified court.
5.2 For the purposes of this Section:
(1) a specified court is a court or court office listed on Her Majesty's Courts and Tribunals Service website as able to receive documents filed electronically via the online forms service; and
(2) a specified document is a document which is available for completion on the website.

(PD 52, para. 15.1B, provides for certain notices to be filed electronically at the Court of Appeal, Civil Division using the online forms service on the Court of Appeal, Civil Division website.)

Filing of Documents Online

6.1 A party to a claim in a specified court may send a specified document to the court using the online forms service.
6.2 A party may use the online forms service to take a step in a claim for which a fee is payable. The fee must be paid, using the facilities available at the online forms service, before the application, or other document attracting a fee, is forwarded to the specified court.
6.3 The online forms service will assist the user in completing a document accurately but the user is responsible for ensuring that the rules and practice directions relating to the document have been complied with. Transmission by the service does not guarantee that the document will be accepted by the specified court.

III GENERAL PROVISIONS

Interpretation

7 In this Section:
(1) filing or sending a document 'electronically', means filing or sending it in accordance with *Section I or Section II*; and
(2) a reference to 'transmission' means, unless the context otherwise requires:
(a) in relation to Section I, the email sent by the party to the court; and
(b) in relation to Section II, the electronic transmission of the form by the online forms service to the court.

[* This service has now closed.]

Provisions Relating to the Filing of Documents Electronically

para.8 3.5 para.8.9 15.55

8.1 Where a party files a document electronically, he must not send a hard copy of that document to the court.

8.2 A document is not filed until the transmission is received by the court, whatever time it is shown to have been sent.

8.3 The time of receipt of a transmission will be recorded electronically on the transmission as it is received.

8.4 If a transmission is received after 4 p.m.:
(1) the transmission will be treated as received; and
(2) any document attached to the transmission will be treated as filed,on the next day the court office is open.

8.5 A party:
(1) sending an email in accordance with Section I; or
(2) using the online forms service in accordance with Section II,
is responsible for ensuring that the transmission or any document attached to it is filed within any relevant time limits.

8.6 The court will normally reply by email where:
(1) the response is to a message transmitted electronically; and
(2) the sender has provided an email address.

8.7 Parties are advised not to transmit electronically any correspondence or documents of a confidential or sensitive nature, as security cannot be guaranteed.

8.8 If a document transmitted electronically requires urgent attention, the sender should contact the court by telephone.

8.9 A document that is required by a rule or practice direction to be filed at court is not filed when it is sent to the judge by email.

Statement of Truth in Documents Filed Electronically

9 Where a party wishes to file a document containing a statement of truth electronically, that party should retain the document containing the original signature and file with the court a version of the document satisfying one of the following requirements:
(1) the name of the person who has signed the statement of truth is typed underneath the statement;
(2) the person who has signed the statement of truth has applied a facsimile of his signature to the statement in the document by mechanical means; or
(3) the document that is filed is a scanned version of the document containing the original signature to the statement of truth.

PD 5C Practice Direction 5C — Electronic Working Scheme

This practice direction supplements CPR, rr. 5.5 and 7.12.

PD 5C 3.5, 12.7, 15.55, 42.40

General

Para 1.2 3.5 Para 1.2(1)(b) 15.53

1.1 (1) This practice direction is made under rr. 5.5 and 7.12. It provides for a scheme ('Electronic Working') to—

(a) operate from 1 April 2010;

(b) operate in the Admiralty, Commercial and London Mercantile Courts, the Technology and Construction Court, and the Chancery Division of the High Court at the Royal Courts of Justice, including in the case of the Chancery Division the Patents Court and the Bankruptcy and Companies courts. It is intended that this practice direction should continue to apply to those jurisdictions when they transfer to the Rolls Building, and to the bankruptcy jurisdiction of the Central London County Court (the Rolls Building jurisdictions); and

(c) (i) apply to claims started on or after 1 April 2010; and

(ii) apply to claims started or continued electronically under the Electronic Working Pilot Scheme between 1 April 2009 and 31 March 2010.

(2) Where the provisions of this practice direction conflict with the provisions of PD 5B this practice direction shall take precedence.

(3) In this practice direction 'document key' means the unique alphanumeric identifier set out on the court form to obtain the relevant document where there is no electronic link.

1.2 (1) This practice direction provides for a scheme of electronic working by which—

(a) proceedings may be started and all subsequent steps may be taken electronically; and

(b) proceedings which have not been started electronically, may be continued electronically after documents in paper format in those proceedings have been converted to an electronic format by means of a scanning procedure by the court and the proceedings shall then continue under the scheme as if they had been started electronically.

(2) As an electronic system, the Electronic Working scheme will operate 24 hours a day all year round, including weekends and bank holidays. This will enable claim forms to be issued and documents to be filed in electronic format out of normal court office opening hours. However, there will be two exceptions to this—

(a) planned 'downtime': as with all electronic systems, there will be some planned periods for system maintenance and upgrades when Electronic Working will not be available; and

(b) unplanned 'downtime': in the event of unplanned periods during which Electronic Working will not be available due, for example, to a system failure or power outage.

1.3 The Electronic Working scheme will be subject to the following provisions of the CPR, unless specifically excluded or revised by this practice direction:

Part 57 (probate actions)
Part 58 (Commercial Court claims)
Part 59 (Mercantile Court claims)
Part 60 (Technology and Construction Court claims)
Part 61 (Admiralty claims)
Part 62 (arbitration claims)
Part 63 (patent claims)

(Litigants will need to give careful consideration to: the Chancery Guide, the Queen's Bench Division Guide, the Admiralty and Commercial Courts Guide, the Technology and Construction Court Guide and the Patents Court Guide.)

1.4 (1) This practice direction enables claimants to start or continue electronically claims in the Rolls Building jurisdictions.

(2) Where a claim has been started or is continuing electronically any party may file electronically all forms and documents, using where necessary, the multi-purpose form.

1.5 Any form or document which is filed electronically—

(a) must not be filed in paper format unless this is required by a court order, rule, or practice direction;

(b) must consist of one copy only with no further copies unless required by a court order, rule or practice direction; and

(c) will receive an automated response to acknowledge receipt.

1.6 (1) Persons wishing to use the Electronic Working scheme are required, wherever possible, to communicate with the court by means of email. For the purposes of email communications a person using the Electronic Working scheme must—

(a) provide the court with at least one and not more than three email address(es) at which that person can be contacted;

(b) use the email address provided by the court to file documents at the court; and

(c) use the document keys where provided by the court, to populate the subject line of the email or use the electronic link to obtain the relevant document.

(2) Where persons using the Electronic Working scheme include their email address on any court form, document or statement of case this is not confirmation or agreement that they are prepared to accept service by email of documents between the parties to the proceedings unless they expressly agree to do so. Paragraph 4.1(2)(c) of PD 6A does not apply.

1.7 (1) A claim filed electronically under the Electronic Working scheme will be issued by the Admiralty Court, the Commercial Court, the London Mercantile Court, the Technology and Construction Court, or the Chancery Division of the High Court as appropriate and the claim will proceed in that court unless it is transferred to another court.

(2) If the claim is transferred to another court which is not operating the Electronic Working scheme it will come out of the scheme and this practice direction shall not apply to the proceedings in relation to any step taken after the date of transfer.

(Paragraph 15 contains further provisions about the transfer of proceedings.)

1.8 Unless the court orders otherwise, any form, statement of case, document or order issued or filed by any party under the Rolls Building jurisdiction whether in electronic or paper format, which is required to be served shall be served by the party who requested it.

Security

2.1 Her Majesty's Courts and Tribunals Service will take such measures as it thinks fit to ensure the security of steps taken or information communicated or stored electronically. These may include requiring persons using Electronic Working to—

(1) enter a customer identification and/or password;

(2) provide personal information for identification purposes; and

(3) comply with any other security measures, as may from time to time be required before taking any of the steps mentioned in para. 1.4 or 1.5.

2.2 Her Majesty's Courts and Tribunals Service may provide such method of encryption to promote security of email communications as may be deemed appropriate.

(PD 5B, para. 8.7 (electronic communications and filing of documents) contains provisions concerning the transmission of documents or correspondence electronically.)

Fees

3.1 Where this practice direction provides for a fee to be paid, it may be paid by any method which Her Majesty's Courts and Tribunals Service may permit including any online or offline payment facility.

3.2 In certain circumstances, a party may be entitled to a remission or part remission of fees. Her *Majesty's Courts and Tribunals Service* website contains guidance as to when this entitlement might arise. A party, who wishes to apply for remission or part remission of fees, must do so prior to taking any step which requires a fee to be paid.

3.3 (1) On issuing or filing electronically any form or document which requires the payment of a fee, the person issuing or filing that document shall—
(a) pay the appropriate fee; or
(b) apply for fee remission in accordance with para. 3.2.
(2) The form or document will be subject to an initial automated validation to ensure all mandatory fields have been completed.
(3) Once validated the form or document will be issued, sealed where appropriate, and returned to the person filing or requesting the issue of the same.

(Paragraph 7 contains provisions about the filing of counterclaims and other Part 20 claims.)

Forms

Para 4 15.53

4.1 Persons using the Electronic Working scheme must ensure that all forms, documents, schedules and other attachments filed at court are in PDF format.

4.2 Persons using the Electronic Working scheme must, where they are available, use the PDF forms which have been created by Her Majesty's Courts and Tribunals Service specifically for Electronic Working.

4.3 Persons using the Electronic Working scheme and wishing to file any document which has not been created specifically for Electronic Working must before filing that document—
(1) convert the document to PDF format if it is already in an electronic form or if it is only available in paper copy scan the document into PDF format; and
(2) attach the document to the multi-purpose form for that case which has been created specifically for Electronic Working.

Scope of Electronic Working

Para 5 15.53

5 The Electronic Working scheme may be used to start claims pursuant to Part 7, Part 8 and Part 20 and also arbitration claims and Admiralty proceedings as appropriate in the Admiralty and Commercial Court, the London Mercantile Court, the Technology and Construction Court, and in the Chancery Division of the High Court.

Starting a Claim

Para 6.4 15.53 Para 6.4(1) 3.5

6.1 A claimant may request the issue of a claim form by—
(a) obtaining the electronic claim form from Her Majesty's Courts and Tribunals Service in the following manner:
(i) typing in the form number the claimant requires in the subject line of an email; and
(ii) sending the email to getform@justice.gsi.gov.uk;
(b) completing and sending the electronic claim form and such other forms or documents as may be required to start the claim by email to submit@justice.gsi.gov.uk; and
(c) paying the appropriate issue fee.
(The annex to this practice direction lists and contains relevant forms.)

6.2 The particulars of claim may be included in or attached to the electronic claim form, or may be filed separately in accordance with rr. 58.5, 59.4, 61.3 or 7.4, where applicable, by attaching the particulars of claim to the electronic multi-purpose form.

6.3 When a claim form is received electronically at the address provided by the court—
(1) subject to the automated validation referred to in para. 3.3, the claim form will be issued, sealed and returned to the claimant for service; but
(2) if the form fails the automated validation it will be returned to the claimant together with notice of the reasons for failure.

6.4 (1) The court will accept receipt of claim forms filed through Electronic Working out of normal court office opening hours. Claim forms received by the court up to midnight will bear the date they are received as the issue date.
(2) When the court issues a claim form through Electronic Working following a validated request under paras 6.1 and 6.3—
(a) the court will seal the claim form with the date on which the claim form was received by the court through Electronic Working and this shall be the issue date; and

(b) the court will keep a record of when claim forms filed through Electronic Working are received.

(Paragraph 1.2(2) contains provisions about system 'downtime' which may prevent immediate issue of claim forms.)

6.5 (1) When the court issues a claim form through Electronic Working the court will—

(a) return an electronic sealed version in PDF format for service by the claimant; and

(b) return a further electronic version in PDF format which must be retained by the claimant in case the form needs to be amended.

(2) It is a party's responsibility to print and serve any form requiring service by that party unless the party or parties to be served have agreed to accept service by email or other electronic means.

(Paragraph 1.6(2) contains provisions for service by email and para. 1.8 contains provisions about the service of forms and documents.)

6.6 A document key or electronic link will be printed on the sealed claim form and this will allow the party by whom it is served to obtain and file the acknowledgment of service through Electronic Working, together with other document keys or electronic links which will then allow the parties to obtain other forms required for the purposes of the proceedings.

Electronic Working Response

Para 7.2(a) 15.53 Para 7.3 15.53

7.1 A party wishing to file—

(a) an acknowledgment of service under Part 10;

(b) an admission or part admission;

(c) a defence or defence and counterclaim under Part 15;

(d) a Part 20 claim; or

(e) any other document,

may obtain the Electronic Working version of the following documents or forms—

(i) requests for judgment on acceptance of an admission of the whole of the amount claimed;

(ii) statements of case and any amended statements of case;

(iii) requests for further information and any replies;

(iv) applications for an order, whether before or after the start of proceedings;

(v) witness statements or affidavits and exhibits;

(vi) draft orders and orders for sealing;

(vii) case summaries, lists of issues, chronologies, skeleton arguments, case management information sheets, progress monitoring information sheets, directions questionnaires where appropriate and pre-trial checklists;

(viii) statements of costs;

by using the document keys referred to in para. 6.6 and file the same electronically.

7.2 Where a party files a form or document through Electronic Working—

(a) the form or document is not filed until it is acknowledged as received by the court, notwithstanding when it may have been sent;

(b) the defendant may file forms and documents electronically through Electronic Working out of normal court office opening hours; and

(c) a form acknowledged as received electronically out of normal court office opening hours but before midnight will be treated as having been filed the same day.

7.3 When a document is issued or filed electronically by a party an automated response will be sent to acknowledge receipt.

7.4 (1) The electronic copy must—

(a) be filed electronically by email;

(b) be formatted as one PDF document with bookmarks for each document and where appropriate with section headings within the document;

(c) not exceed such size in megabytes as Her Majesty's Courts and Tribunals Service may from time to time specify.

(2) In the event that the bundle exceeds the maximum limit in sub-para. 1(c) it shall be filed on CD-ROM, DVD, or such other removable storage media as may be acceptable to Her Majesty's Courts and Tribunals Service.

Statement of Truth

8.1 Part 22 and PD 22 which requires certain documents and forms to be verified by a statement of truth shall apply to any Electronic Working forms filed electronically.

8.2 The statement of truth for documents and forms in Electronic Working must be in the form—

'[I believe][The claimant believes] that the facts stated in this claim form (or as the case may be) are true.'; or

'[I believe][The defendant believes] that the facts stated in this defence (or as the case may be) are true.', as appropriate.

8.3 Rule 32.14, which sets out the consequences of making, or causing to be made, a false statement in a document verified by a statement of truth without an honest belief in its truth, applies to any false statement in a statement of truth in a document filed electronically.

Signature

Para 9 15.53

9 Any provision of the CPR which requires a document (other than an affidavit) to be signed by any person is satisfied by that person or an authorised person typing his or her name on an electronic version of the form.

Request for Judgment or Issue of Warrant

10.1 If, in proceedings under the Electronic Working scheme—

(1) the claimant wishes to apply for judgment in default in accordance with Part 12; or

(2) the defendant has filed or served an admission of the whole of the claim in accordance with r. 14.4,

the claimant may request judgment to be entered in default or on the admission (as the case may be) by completing and sending the electronic version of the appropriate form to the email address which will be provided to the parties.

10.2 When judgment has been entered following a request under para. 10.1 and the claimant is entitled to the issue of a warrant of execution without requiring the permission of the court, the claimant may request the issue of a warrant of execution by—

(1) completing and sending an Electronic Working request form to the email address which will be provided by the court to the parties; and

(2) paying the appropriate fee in accordance with para. 3.1.

10.3 A request under para. 10.1 or 10.2 will be treated as being filed—

(1) on the day the court acknowledges receipt of the request, if it receives it before 10 a.m. on a working day (which is any day on which the court office is open);

(2) otherwise, on the next working day after the court receives the request.

Inspecting the Case Record

11.1 The parties shall be entitled to inspect an electronic record of the proceedings and obtain documents in the electronic court file.

(Rule 5.4B contains provisions about the supply to a party to the proceedings of documents from the court record.)

11.2 The record of proceedings will be automatically updated.

11.3 Information concerning the availability of this facility under the Electronic Working scheme will be communicated by Her Majesty's Courts and Tribunals Service in such manner as is deemed appropriate including Her Majesty's Courts and Tribunals Service website.

Applications in Proceedings

12 (1) Where prior to the commencement of, or in the course of proceedings under, the Electronic Working scheme a party to those proceedings issues an application for an order electronically,

CPR 1–25 & PDs

whether a hearing is required or not, the party issuing the application shall lodge an application bundle with the court.

(2) The application bundle must—
(a) be filed in both paper copy and electronic format;
(b) contain the application notice and the evidence in support, including exhibits together with such other documents as may be required by any rule, practice direction, order of the court or court guide; and
(c) be filed in accordance with the time limits required by any applicable rule, practice direction, or order of the court.

(3) The electronic copy must:
(a) be filed electronically by email using the multi-purpose form available to the parties;
(b) be formatted as one PDF document with bookmarks as appropriate for each document and with section headings within the document;
(c) not exceed such size in megabytes as Her Majesty's Courts and Tribunals Service may from time to time specify; and
(d) be updated as required and filed in compliance with sub-sub-paras (a) to (c).

(4) In the event that the bundle exceeds the maximum limit in sub-para. (3)(c) it shall be filed on CD-ROM, DVD, or such other removable storage media as may be acceptable to Her Majesty's Courts and Tribunals Service.

(5) The copy in paper format should be indexed and should correspond exactly to the electronic version of the bundle including sequential pagination.

(6) Unless the judge otherwise directs the paper copy shall be returned to the parties at the conclusion of the hearing.

Allocation and Case Management

Para 13.1 15.53 Para 13.2 15.53

13.1 Where a rule, practice direction or order of the court requires a directions questionnaire be filed with the court and a party wishes to file the directions questionnaire electronically—
(1) the directions questionnaire together with any other forms required by a rule, practice, or order of the court must be filed in both paper and electronic format; and
(2) the paper copy of the directions questionnaire should be accompanied by other relevant documents including all statements of case, draft directions or case summaries and costs schedules in paper format.

13.2 (1) Where—
(a) a rule, practice direction, or order of the court requires:
(i) the court to give case management or other directions; or
(ii) a bundle to be filed with the court in connection with case management or other directions; and
(b) a party wishes to file the bundle electronically, the bundle must contain:
(i) such documents as are required; and
(ii) in all Part 8 claims, the statements of case and evidence in support.

(2) The bundle must be filed in both paper copy and electronic format.

(3) The electronic copy must—
(a) be filed electronically by email, using the multi-purpose form available to the parties;
(b) be formatted as one PDF document with bookmarks for each document and where appropriate with section headings within the document;
(c) not exceed such size in megabytes as Her Majesty's Courts and Tribunals Service may from time to time specify; and
(d) be updated as required and filed in compliance with sub-sub-paras (a) to (c).

(4) In the event that the bundle exceeds the maximum limit in sub-para. (3)(c) the electronic copy must be filed on CD-ROM, DVD, or such other removable storage media as may be acceptable to Her Majesty's Courts and Tribunals Service.

(5) The paper copy should be indexed and should correspond exactly with the electronic version of the bundle with sequential pagination.

(6) Unless the judge otherwise directs, the paper copy shall be returned to the parties at the conclusion of the hearing.

Trial Bundles

Para 14.1 15.53

14.1 The trial bundle must be filed with the court in paper format.
14.2 An electronic version of the trial bundle must also be filed if the court so orders, in which case it must comply with the requirements of para. 13.2(3) and the paper copy must comply with para. 13.2(5).
14.3 The court will retain any electronic copy of the trial bundle for a period of two months after judgment has been delivered, after which it may be deleted.
14.4 The time in para. 14.3 may be extended by order of the court at the request of a party or on the court's own initiative.

Transfer of Proceedings

15.1 If proceedings under the Electronic Working scheme are subsequently transferred to a court not operating under the scheme the parties must ensure that a version of the court file in paper format is made available to that court.
15.2 If proceedings which have not been started under the Electronic Working scheme are transferred to a court operating under the scheme all subsequent steps may be taken electronically after documents in paper format in those proceedings have been converted to an electronic format pursuant to para. 1.2(1)(b).

Public Kiosk Service

16.1 A version of the electronic court file allowing access only to those documents which are available to non-parties pursuant to r. 5.4C(1) or 5.4C(1A) and subject to r. 5.4C(4) will be made available through a public kiosk service.
(Part 5 contains provisions about access to court documents by non-parties.)
16.2 Persons wishing to obtain copies of documents available to non-parties—
(1) may select the documents they require using the computer facilities provided by the public kiosk service; and
(2) must pay the appropriate fee.
16.3 Electronic copies of the documents will be sent by email to an address supplied by the person applying for copies.

Scanning Documents Filed in Paper Format

17.1 Proceedings issued after 1 April 2010 in the Admiralty and Commercial Court, the London Mercantile Court, the Technology and Construction Court, and the Chancery Division of the High Court will be stored by the court in electronic format. Any claims which are not started by issuing a claim form electronically will be converted to an electronic format by means of a scanning procedure by the court and the provisions of para. 1.2(1)(b) shall apply to those proceedings.
17.2 Documents which the parties wish to file with the court may be lodged either by using the Electronic Working scheme or by lodging copies in paper format.
17.3 In the event that a party lodges a document in paper format the court will—
(1) where appropriate seal the paper copy of the document;
(2) obtain payment of any fee due;
(3) enter the relevant information for the document on to an electronic equivalent to create or update an electronic working case file;
(4) convert the document to an electronic format and automatically attach this scanned copy to the electronic working case file;
(5) where the party filing has given an email address, send by email to that address:
(a) a scanned image of the original document; and
(b) an electronic version of the document submitted on paper as entered on to the system by the court; and
(6) return the sealed copy of the document originally lodged.

ANNEX

ELECTRONIC WORKING SCHEME FORMS

All the electronic forms available for use under the scheme can be obtained from Her Majesty's Courts and Tribunals Service by:

(1) Typing in the form number required in the subject line of an email; and
(2) Sending the email to <getform@justice.gsi.gov.uk>.

Once the form has been completed it should be emailed to <submit@justice.gsi.gov.uk>.

[The following claim forms and multi-purpose form, which are attached to PD 5C for information, may be viewed at <http://www.justice.gov.uk/courts/procedure-rules/civil>:

Claim form (Chancery)
Claim form (Admiralty and Commercial)
Claim form (Technology and Construction)
Non-monetary claim
Multi-purpose form]

The claim forms have references to the other relevant forms which are not listed here and these can also be obtained electronically.

CPR Part 6 Service of Documents

CPR 1–25 & PDs

Part 6 PC 5, PC 17, PC 18, 1.11, 13.6, 15.1, 15.2, 15.9, 15.10, 15.17, 15.36, 15.47, 15.48, 15.51, 16.1, 16.45, 16.63, 22.2, 45.33, 62.3, 66.14, 66.16, 79.6, 79.38, 82.70, 82.109, 84.5, 85.13, 87.10

I SCOPE OF THIS PART AND INTERPRETATION

r.6.1(a) 1.11

6.1 Part 6 Rules about Service Apply Generally

This Part applies to the service of documents, except where—

(a) another Part, any other enactment or a practice direction makes different provision; or
(b) the court orders otherwise.

(Other Parts, for example, Part 54 (Judicial Review) and Part 55 (Possession Claims) contain specific provisions about service.)

6.2 Interpretation

r.6.2(a) 15.36, 15.42
r.6.2(b) 1.18, 15.36, 15.42
r.6.2(c) 15.3, 15.38, 15.39, 15.45, 15.52, 32.5, 32.12, 37.5, 82.70
r.6.2(d) 15.9
r.6.2(e) 15.9

In this Part—

(a) 'bank holiday' means a bank holiday under the Banking and Financial Dealings Act 1971 in the part of the United Kingdom where service is to take place;
(b) 'business day' means any day except Saturday, Sunday, a bank holiday, Good Friday or Christmas Day;
(c) 'claim' includes petition and any application made before action or to commence proceedings and 'claim form', 'claimant' and 'defendant' are to be construed accordingly;
(d) 'solicitor' includes any other person who, for the purposes of the Legal Services Act 2007, is an authorised person in relation to an activity which constitutes the conduct of litigation (within the meaning of that Act); and
(e) 'European Lawyer' has the meaning set out in article 2 of the European Communities (Services of Lawyers) Order 1978 (S. I. 1978/1910).

(The European Communities (Services of Lawyers) Order 1978 is annexed to Practice Direction 6A.)

II SERVICE OF THE CLAIM FORM IN THE JURISDICTION OR IN SPECIFIED CIRCUMSTANCES WITHIN THE EEA

6.3 Methods of Service

r.6.3 PC 4, PC 15, 15.10, 15.22
r.6.3(1) 15.49, 15.50
r.6.3(1)(b) 15.12, 15.47
r.6.3(1)(c) 15.13
r.6.3(2) 15.47, 15.48
r.6.3(2)(a)–(b) 15.47
r.6.3(3) 15.47, 15.51

(1) A claim form may (subject to Section IV of this Part and the rules in this Section relating to service out of the jurisdiction on solicitors, European Lawyers and parties) be served by any of the following methods—
  (a) personal service in accordance with rule 6.5;
  (b) first class post, document exchange or other service which provides for delivery on the next business day, in accordance with Practice Direction 6A;
  (c) leaving it at a place specified in rule 6.7, 6.8, 6.9 or 6.10;
  (d) fax or other means of electronic communication in accordance with Practice Direction 6A; or
  (e) any method authorised by the court under rule 6.15.
(2) A company may be served—
  (a) by any method permitted under this Part; or
  (b) by any of the methods of service permitted under the Companies Act 2006.
(3) A limited liability partnership may be served—
  (a) by any method permitted under this Part; or
  (b) by any of the methods of service permitted under the Companies Act 2006 as applied with modification by regulations made under the Limited Liability Partnerships Act 2000.

6.4 Who Is to Serve the Claim Form

r.6.4 PC 3
r.6.4(1) 15.5
r.6.4(1)(b) 15.7
r.6.4(2) PC 3, 15.6
r.6.4(3) 12.4, 15.6

(1) Subject to Section IV of this Part and the rules in this Section relating to service out of the jurisdiction on solicitors, European Lawyers and parties, the court will serve the claim form except where—
  (a) a rule or practice direction provides that the claimant must serve it;
  (b) the claimant notifies the court that the claimant wishes to serve it; or
  (c) the court orders or directs otherwise.
(2) Where the court is to serve the claim form, it is for the court to decide which method of service is to be used.
(3) Where the court is to serve the claim form, the claimant must, in addition to filing a copy for the court, provide a copy for each defendant to be served.
(4) Where the court has sent—
  (a) a notification of outcome of postal service to the claimant in accordance with rule 6.18; or
  (b) a notification of non-service by a bailiff in accordance with rule 6.19, the court will not try to serve the claim form again.

6.5 Personal Service

r.6.5 15.9, 15.10, 15.28, 81.5, 81.11
r.6.5(1) 15.11
r.6.5(2)(b) 15.52
r.6.5(3) PC 36, 15.28, 15.36, 83.7, 85.13
r.6.5(3)(a) 15.11
r.6.5(3)(b) 15.47, 15.48, 15.49
r.6.5(3)(c) 15.50

(1) Where required by another Part, any other enactment, a practice direction or a court order, a claim form must be served personally.
(2) In other cases, a claim form may be served personally except—
  (a) where rule 6.7 applies; or
  (b) in any proceedings against the Crown.

(Part 54 contains provisions about judicial review claims and Part 66 contains provisions about Crown proceedings.)

(3) A claim form is served personally on—
  (a) an individual by leaving it with that individual;
  (b) a company or other corporation by leaving it with a person holding a senior position within the company or corporation; or
  (c) a partnership (where partners are being sued in the name of their firm) by leaving it with—
    (i) a partner; or
    (ii) a person who, at the time of service, has the control or management of the partnership business at its principal place of business.

(Practice Direction 6A sets out the meaning of 'senior position'.)

6.6 Where to Serve the Claim Form — General Provisions

r.6.6(1) 15.5
r.6.6(2) 23.5

(1) The claim form must be served within the jurisdiction except where rule 6.7(2), 6.7(3) or 6.11 applies or as provided by Section IV of this Part.
(2) The claimant must include in the claim form an address at which the defendant may be served. That address must include a full postcode or its equivalent in any EEA state (if applicable), unless the court orders otherwise.

(Paragraph 2.4 of Practice Direction 16 contains provisions about postcodes.)

(3) Paragraph (2) does not apply where an order made by the court under rule 6.15 (service by an alternative method or at an alternative place) specifies the place or method of service of the claim form.

CPR 1–25 & PDs

6.7 Service on a Solicitor or European Lawyer within the United Kingdom or in Any Other EEA State

rr.6.7–6.10 15.6
r.6.7 15.6, 15.9, 15.10, 15.11, 15.12, 15.14, 15.15, 15.47, 15.49, 15.50, 15.51, 22.2
r.6.7(1) 15.9, 15.15
r.6.7(2) 15.9, 22.2
r.6.7(3) 15.9

(1) **Solicitor within the jurisdiction:** Subject to rule 6.5(1), where—
(a) the defendant has given in writing the business address within the jurisdiction of a solicitor as an address at which the defendant may be served with the claim form; or
(b) a solicitor acting for the defendant has notified the claimant in writing that the solicitor is instructed by the defendant to accept service of the claim form on behalf of the defendant at a business address within the jurisdiction,
the claim form must be served at the business address of that solicitor.
('Solicitor' has the extended meaning set out in rule 6.2(d).)

(2) **Solicitor in Scotland or Northern Ireland or EEA state other than the United Kingdom:** Subject to rule 6.5(1) and the provisions of Section IV of this Part, and except where any other rule or practice direction makes different provision, where—
(a) the defendant has given in writing the business address in Scotland or Northern Ireland of a solicitor as an address at which the defendant may be served with the claim form;
(aa) a solicitor acting for the defendant has notified the claimant in writing that the solicitor is instructed by the defendant to accept service of the claim form on behalf of the defendant at a business address within Scotland or Northern Ireland;
(b) the defendant has given in writing the business address within any other EEA state of a solicitor as an address at which the defendant may be served with the claim form; or
(c) a solicitor acting for the defendant has notified the claimant in writing that the solicitor is instructed by the defendant to accept service of the claim form on behalf of the defendant at a business address within any other EEA state,
the claim form must be served at the business address of that solicitor.

(3) **European Lawyer in any EEA state:** Subject to rule 6.5(1) and the provisions of Section IV of this Part, and except where any other rule or practice direction makes different provision, where—
(a) the defendant has given in writing the business address of a European Lawyer in any EEA state as an address at which the defendant may be served with the claim form; or
(b) a European Lawyer in any EEA state has notified the claimant in writing that the European Lawyer is instructed by the defendant to accept service of the claim form on behalf of the defendant at a business address of the European Lawyer,
the claim form must be served at the business address of that European Lawyer.
('European Lawyer' has the meaning set out in rule 6.2(e).)
(For Production Centre Claims see paragraph 2.3(7A) of Practice Direction 7C; for Money Claims Online see paragraph 4(6) of Practice Direction 7E; and for Possession Claims Online see paragraph 5.1(4) of Practice Direction 55B.)

6.8 Service of the Claim Form Where before Service the Defendant Gives an Address at Which the Defendant May Be Served

r.6.8 15.6, 15.8, 15.10, 15.12, 15.15, 15.20, 15.47, 15.49, 15.50, 15.51, 22.2 r.6.8(a) 15.14

Subject to rules 6.5(1) and 6.7 and the provisions of Section IV of this Part, and except where any other rule or practice direction makes different provision—
(a) the defendant may be served with the claim form at an address at which the defendant resides or carries on business within the UK or any other EEA state and which the defendant has given for the purpose of being served with the proceedings; or
(b) in any claim by a tenant against a landlord, the claim form may be served at an address given by the landlord under section 48 of the Landlord and Tenant Act 1987.
(For Production Centre Claims see paragraph 2.3(7A) of Practice Direction 7C; for Money Claims Online see paragraph 4(6) of Practice Direction 7E; and for Possession Claims Online see paragraph 5.1(4) of Practice Direction 55B.)
(For service out of the jurisdiction see **rules 6.40** to 6.47.)

6.9 Service of the Claim Form Where the Defendant Does Not Give an Address at Which the Defendant May Be Served

r.6.9 15.6, 15.10, 15.15, 15.24
r.6.9(2) 15.12, 15.13, 15.14, 15.47, 15.48, 15.49, 15.50, 15.51, 22.2
r.6.9(3) 15.14, 15.32
r.6.9(4)(a) 15.14

(1) This rule applies where—
  (a) rule 6.5(1) (personal service);
  (b) rule 6.7 (service of claim form on solicitor or European Lawyer); and
  (c) rule 6.8 (defendant gives address at which the defendant may be served),
  do not apply and the claimant does not wish to effect personal service under rule 6.5(2).

(2) Subject to paragraphs (3) to (6), the claim form must be served on the defendant at the place shown in the following table.

Nature of defendant to be served	Place of service
1. Individual	Usual or last known residence.
2. Individual being sued in the name of a business	Usual or last known residence of the individual; or principal or last known place of business.
3. Individual being sued in the business name of a partnership	Usual or last known residence of the individual; or principal or last known place of business of the partnership.
4. Limited liability partnership	Principal office of the partnership; or any place of business of the partnership within the jurisdiction which has a real connection with the claim.
5. Corporation (other than a company) incorporated in England and Wales	Principal office of the corporation; or any place within the jurisdiction where the corporation carries on its activities and which has a real connection with the claim.
6. Company registered in England and Wales	Principal office of the company; or any place of business of the company within the jurisdiction which has a real connection with the claim.
7. Any other company or corporation	Any place within the jurisdiction where the corporation carries on its activities; or any place of business of the company within the jurisdiction.

(3) Where a claimant has reason to believe that the address of the defendant referred to in entries 1, 2 or 3 in the table in paragraph (2) is an address at which the defendant no longer resides or carries on business, the claimant must take reasonable steps to ascertain the address of the defendant's current residence or place of business ('current address').

(4) Where, having taken the reasonable steps required by paragraph (3), the claimant—
  (a) ascertains the defendant's current address, the claim form must be served at that address; or
  (b) is unable to ascertain the defendant's current address, the claimant must consider whether there is—
    (i) an alternative place where; or
    (ii) an alternative method by which,
  service may be effected.

(5) If, under paragraph (4)(b), there is such a place where or a method by which service may be effected, the claimant must make an application under rule 6.15.

(6) Where paragraph (3) applies, the claimant may serve on the defendant's usual or last known address in accordance with the table in paragraph (2) where the claimant—
  (a) cannot ascertain the defendant's current residence or place of business; and
  (b) cannot ascertain an alternative place or an alternative method under paragraph (4)(b).

(For service out of the jurisdiction see **rules 6.40** to **6.47**.)

6.10 Service of the Claim Form in Proceedings against the Crown

r.6.10 15.6, 15.10, 15.52, 20.7

In proceedings against the Crown—
(a) service on the Attorney General must be effected on the Treasury Solicitor; and
(b) service on a government department must be effected on the solicitor acting for that department.

(Practice Direction 66 gives the list published under section 17 of the Crown Proceedings Act 1947 of the solicitors acting in civil proceedings (as defined in that Act) for the different government departments on whom service is to be effected, and of their addresses.)

6.11 Service of the Claim Form by Contractually Agreed Method

r.6.11(1) 15.16 r.6.11(2) 15.16

(1) Where—
  (a) a contract contains a term providing that, in the event of a claim being started in relation to the contract, the claim form may be served by a method or at a place specified in the contract; and
  (b) a claim solely in respect of that contract is started, the claim form may, subject to paragraph (2), be served on the defendant by the method or at the place specified in the contract.

(2) Where in accordance with the contract the claim form is to be served out of the jurisdiction, it may be served—
  (a) if permission to serve it out of the jurisdiction has been granted under rule 6.36; or
  (b) without permission under rule 6.32 or 6.33.

6.12 Service of the Claim Form Relating to a Contract on an Agent of a Principal Who Is Out of the Jurisdiction

r.6.12 15.53, 18.2 r.6.12(3) 15.53, 17.6, 18.2, 18.5, 26.3
r.6.12(2) 15.53 r.6.12(4) 15.53
r.6.12(2)(a) 15.53 r.6.12(5) 15.53

(1) The court may, on application, permit a claim form relating to a contract to be served on the defendant's agent where—
  (a) the defendant is out of the jurisdiction;
  (b) the contract to which the claim relates was entered into within the jurisdiction with or through the defendant's agent; and
  (c) at the time of the application either the agent's authority has not been terminated or the agent is still in business relations with the defendant.

(2) An application under this rule—
  (a) must be supported by evidence setting out—
    (i) details of the contract and that it was entered into within the jurisdiction or through an agent who is within the jurisdiction;
    (ii) that the principal for whom the agent is acting was, at the time the contract was entered into and is at the time of the application, out of the jurisdiction; and
    (iii) why service out of the jurisdiction cannot be effected; and
  (b) may be made without notice.

(3) An order under this rule must state the period within which the defendant must respond to the particulars of claim.

(4) Where the court makes an order under this rule—
  (a) a copy of the application notice and the order must be served with the claim form on the agent; and
  (b) unless the court orders otherwise, the claimant must send to the defendant a copy of the application notice, the order and the claim form.

(5) This rule does not exclude the court's power under rule 6.15 (service by an alternative method or at an alternative place).

6.13 Service of the Claim Form on Children and Protected Parties

r.6.13 14.19, 15.45 r.6.13(4) 15.45
r.6.13(1) 15.45 r.6.13(7) 15.45
r.6.13(2) 15.45

(1) Where the defendant is a child who is not also a protected party, the claim form must be served on—
  (a) one of the child's parents or guardians; or
  (b) if there is no parent or guardian, an adult with whom the child resides or in whose care the child is.

(2) Where the defendant is a protected party, the claim form must be served on—
 (a) one of the following persons with authority in relation to the protected party as—
  (i) the attorney under a registered enduring power of attorney;
  (ii) the donee of a lasting power of attorney; or
  (iii) the deputy appointed by the Court of Protection; or
 (b) if there is no such person, an adult with whom the protected party resides or in whose care the protected party is.

(3) Any reference in this Section to a defendant or a party to be served includes the person to be served with the claim form on behalf of a child or protected party under paragraph (1) or (2).

(4) The court may make an order permitting a claim form to be served on a child or protected party, or on a person other than the person specified in paragraph (1) or (2).

(5) An application for an order under paragraph (4) may be made without notice.

(6) The court may order that, although a claim form has been sent or given to someone other than the person specified in paragraph (1) or (2), it is to be treated as if it had been properly served.

(7) This rule does not apply where the court has made an order under rule 21.2(3) allowing a child to conduct proceedings without a litigation friend.

(Part 21 contains rules about the appointment of a litigation friend and 'child' and 'protected party' have the same meaning as in rule 21.1.)

6.14 Deemed Service

r.6.14 PC 3, PC 15, PC 18, 3.3, 15.3, 15.26, 15.36, 20.14, 20.18, 20.22

A claim form served within the United Kingdom in accordance with this Part is deemed to be served on the second business day after completion of the relevant step under rule 7.5(1).

6.15 Service of the Claim Form by an Alternative Method or at an Alternative Place

r.6.15 15.10, 15.14, 15.15, 15.17, 15.18, 15.19, 15.20, 15.24, 15.43, 15.53, 72.4
r.6.15(1) 15.17, 15.20, 16.56
r.6.15(2) 15.18, 15.20, 15.34, 16.56
r.6.15(3) 15.43
r.6.15(3)(a)–(b) 15.21
r.6.15(4)(c) 15.21

(1) Where it appears to the court that there is a good reason to authorise service by a method or at a place not otherwise permitted by this Part, the court may make an order permitting service by an alternative method or at an alternative place.

(2) On an application under this rule, the court may order that steps already taken to bring the claim form to the attention of the defendant by an alternative method or at an alternative place is good service.

(3) An application for an order under this rule—
 (a) must be supported by evidence; and
 (b) may be made without notice.

(4) An order under this rule must specify—
 (a) the method or place of service;
 (b) the date on which the claim form is deemed served; and
 (c) the period for—
  (i) filing an acknowledgment of service;
  (ii) filing an admission; or
  (iii) filing a defence.

6.16 Power of Court to Dispense with Service of the Claim Form

r.6.16 15.15, 15.17, 15.24, 15.34, 16.37
r.6.16(1) 15.24
r.6.16(2)(a)–(b) 15.24

(1) The court may dispense with service of a claim form in exceptional circumstances.

(2) An application for an order to dispense with service may be made at any time and—
 (a) must be supported by evidence; and
 (b) may be made without notice.

6.17 Notice and Certificate of Service Relating to the Claim Form

r.6.17 PC 4, 20.3, 72.4
r.6.17(1) PC 3, 15.6
r.6.17(2) 20.17
r.6.17(2)(a) PC 15, 15.7
r.6.17(2)(b) 15.7
r.6.17(3) PC 4, 15.7

(1) Where the court serves a claim form, the court will send to the claimant a notice which will include the date on which the claim form is deemed served under rule 6.14.
(2) Where the claimant serves the claim form, the claimant—
  (a) must file a certificate of service within 21 days of service of the particulars of claim, unless all the defendants to the proceedings have filed acknowledgments of service within that time; and
  (b) may not obtain judgment in default under Part 12 unless a certificate of service has been filed.
(3) The certificate of service must state—
  (a) where rule 6.7, 6.8, 6.9 or 6.10 applies, the category of address at which the claimant believes the claim form has been served; and
  (b) the details set out in the following table.

Method of service	Details to be certified
1. Personal service	Date of personal service.
2. First class post, document exchange or other service which provides for delivery on the next business day	Date of posting, or leaving with, delivering to or collection by the relevant service provider.
3. Delivery of document to or leaving it at a permitted place	Date when the document was delivered to or left at the permitted place.
4. Fax	Date of completion of the transmission.
5. Other electronic method	Date of sending the e-mail or other electronic transmission.
6. Alternative method or place	As required by the court.

6.18 Notification of Outcome of Postal Service by the Court

r.6.18 15.6
r.6.18(1) PC 3
r.6.18(2) PC 3, 15.6

(1) Where—
  (a) the court serves the claim form by post; and
  (b) the claim form is returned to the court, the court will send notification to the claimant that the claim form has been returned.
(2) The claim form will be deemed to be served unless the address for the defendant on the claim form is not the relevant address for the purpose of rules 6.7 to 6.10.

6.19 Notice of Non-service by Bailiff

r.6.19 PC 3, 15.6

Where—
(a) the court bailiff is to serve a claim form; and
(b) the bailiff is unable to serve it on the defendant,
the court will send notification to the claimant.

III SERVICE OF DOCUMENTS OTHER THAN THE CLAIM FORM IN THE UNITED KINGDOM OR IN SPECIFIED CIRCUMSTANCES WITHIN THE EEA

6.20 Methods of Service

r.6.20 15.41, 32.12, 37.10, 62.3, 66.14

(1) Subject to Section IV of this Part and the rules in this Section relating to service out of the jurisdiction on solicitors, European Lawyers and parties, a document may be served by any of the following methods—
  (a) personal service, in accordance with rule 6.22;
  (b) first class post, document exchange or other service which provides for delivery on the next business day, in accordance with Practice Direction 6A;

(c) leaving it at a place specified in rule 6.23;
(d) fax or other means of electronic communication in accordance with Practice Direction 6A; or
(e) any method authorised by the court under rule 6.27.

(2) A company may be served—
(a) by any method permitted under this Part; or
(b) by any of the methods of service permitted under the Companies Act 2006.

(3) A limited liability partnership may be served—
(a) by any method permitted under this Part; or
(b) by any of the methods of service permitted under the Companies Act 2006 as applied with modification by regulations made under the Limited Liability Partnerships Act 2000.

6.21 Who Is to Serve

r.6.21 PC 15, 32.12, 37.10
r.6.21(1) 15.5, 15.39, 18.4, 32.1, 32.22
r.6.21(2) 15.38, 32.22, 32.40, 61.37
r.6.21(3) 15.38, 32.22
r.6.21(4) 15.38

(1) Subject to Section IV of this Part and the rules in this Section relating to service out of the jurisdiction on solicitors, European Lawyers and parties, a party to proceedings will serve a document which that party has prepared except where—
(a) a rule or practice direction provides that the court will serve the document; or
(b) the court orders otherwise.

(2) The court will serve a document which it has prepared except where—
(a) a rule or practice direction provides that a party must serve the document;
(b) the party on whose behalf the document is to be served notifies the court that the party wishes to serve it; or
(c) the court orders otherwise.

(3) Where the court is to serve a document, it is for the court to decide which method of service is to be used.

(4) Where the court is to serve a document prepared by a party, that party must provide a copy for the court and for each party to be served.

6.22 Personal Service

r.6.22 32.12, 37.10
r.6.22(1) 15.41
r.6.22(2)(a) 15.41
r.6.22(3) 81.5, 81.11, 83.7, 85.13

(1) Where required by another Part, any other enactment, a practice direction or a court order, a document must be served personally.

(2) In other cases, a document may be served personally except—
(a) where the party to be served has given an address for service under rule 6.23; or
(b) in any proceedings by or against the Crown.

(3) A document may be served personally as if the document were a claim form in accordance with rule 6.5(3).

(For service out of the jurisdiction see **rules 6.40 to 6.47**.)

6.23 Address for Service to Be given after Proceedings are Started

r.6.23 15.41, 16.65, 22.2, 26.12, 29.11, 32.12, 37.10, 62.3
r.6.23(1) 15.15, 15.41
r.6.23(2) 15.41, 21.3, 22.2, 22.4
r.6.23(2)(a) 16.65, 21.3
r.6.23(2)(c) 22.2
r.6.23(5) 15.15, 15.41
r.6.23(6) 15.41
r.6.23(7) 15.52

(1) A party to proceedings must give an address at which that party may be served with documents relating to those proceedings. The address must include a full postcode or its equivalent in any EEA state (if applicable) unless the court orders otherwise.

(Paragraph 2.4 of Practice Direction 16 contains provisions about postcodes.)

(2) Except where any other rule or practice direction makes different provision, a party's address for service must be—
(a) the business address either within the United Kingdom or any other EEA state of a solicitor acting for the party to be served; or
(b) the business address in any EEA state of a European Lawyer nominated to accept service of documents; or

(c) where there is no solicitor acting for the party or no European Lawyer nominated to accept service of documents—
  (i) an address within the United Kingdom at which the party resides or carries on business; or
  (ii) an address within any other EEA state at which the party resides or carries on business.

(For Production Centre Claims see paragraph 2.3(7A) of Practice Direction 7C; for Money Claims Online see paragraph 4(3A) and (6) of Practice Direction 7E; and for Possession Claims Online see paragraph 5.1(3A) and (4) of Practice Direction 55B.)

(3) Where none of subparagraphs (2)(a), (b) or (c) applies, the party must give an address for service within the United Kingdom.

(Part 42 contains provisions about change of solicitor. Rule 42.1 provides that where a party gives the business address of a solicitor as that party's address for service, that solicitor will be considered to be acting for the party until the provisions of Part 42 are complied with.)

(4) Subject to the provisions of Section IV of this Part (where applicable), any document to be served in proceedings must be sent or transmitted to, or left at, the party's address for service under paragraph (2) or (3) unless it is to be served personally or the court orders otherwise.

(5) Where, in accordance with Practice Direction 6A, a party indicates or is deemed to have indicated that they will accept service by fax, the fax number given by that party must be at the address for service.

(6) Where a party indicates in accordance with Practice Direction 6A that they will accept service by electronic means other than fax, the e-mail address or electronic identification given by that party will be deemed to be at the address for service.

(7) In proceedings by or against the Crown, service of any document in the proceedings on the Crown must be effected in the same manner prescribed in rule 6.10 as if the document were a claim form.

(8) This rule does not apply where an order made by the court under rule 6.27 (service by an alternative method or at an alternative place) specifies where a document may be served.

(For service out of the jurisdiction see rules 6.40 to 6.47.)

6.24 Change of Address for Service

r.6.24 15.41, 22.2, 32.12, 37.10

Where the address for service of a party changes, that party must give notice in writing of the change as soon as it has taken place to the court and every other party.

6.25 Service on Children and Protected Parties

r.6.25 18.5, 32.12, 37.10
r.6.25(2) 15.46
r.6.25(3) 15.46
r.6.25(4) 15.46
r.6.25(5) 15.46
r.6.25(6) 15.46

(1) An application for an order appointing a litigation friend where a child or protected party has no litigation friend must be served in accordance with rule 21.8(1) and (2).

(2) Any other document which would otherwise be served on a child or a protected party must be served on the litigation friend conducting the proceedings on behalf of the child or protected party.

(3) The court may make an order permitting a document to be served on the child or protected party or on some person other than the person specified in rule 21.8 or paragraph (2).

(4) An application for an order under paragraph (3) may be made without notice.

(5) The court may order that, although a document has been sent or given to someone other than the person specified in rule 21.8 or paragraph (2), the document is to be treated as if it had been properly served.

(6) This rule does not apply where the court has made an order under rule 21.2(3) allowing a child to conduct proceedings without a litigation friend.

6.26 Deemed Service

r.6.26 PC 15, PC 28, 1.18, 3.3, 15.36, 15.40, 15.42, 20.22, 32.12, 32.22, 37.10, 62.3, 66.14

A document, other than a claim form, served within the United Kingdom in accordance with these *Rules or any relevant practice direction* is deemed to be served on the day shown in the following table—

Method of service	Deemed date of service
1. First class post (or other service which provides for delivery on the next business day)	The second day after it was posted, left with, delivered to or collected by the relevant service provider provided that day is a business day; or if not, the next business day after that day.
2. Document exchange	The second day after it was left with, delivered to or collected by the relevant service provider provided that day is a business day; or if not, the next business day after that day.
3. Delivering the document to or leaving it at a permitted address	If it is delivered to or left at the permitted address on a business day before 4.30 p.m., on that day; or in any other case, on the next business day after that day
4. Fax	If the transmission of the fax is completed on a business day before 4.30 p.m., on that day; or in any other case, on the next business day after the day on which it was transmitted.
5. Other electronic method	If the e-mail or other electronic transmission is sent on a business day before 4.30 p.m., on that day; or in any other case, on the next business day after the day on which it was sent.
6. Personal service	If the document is served personally before 4.30 p.m. on a business day, on that day; or in any other case, on the next business day after that day.

(Paragraphs 10.1 to 10.7 of Practice Direction 6A contain examples of how the date of deemed service is calculated.)

6.27 Service by an Alternative Method or at an Alternative Place

r.6.27 15.17, 15.43, 32.12, 32.22, 37.10 r.6.27(2) 15.41

Rule 6.15 applies to any document in the proceedings as it applies to a claim form and reference to the defendant in that rule is modified accordingly.

6.28 Power to Dispense with Service

r.6.28 15.43, 32.12, 37.10 r.6.28(2) 15.43

(1) The court may dispense with service of any document which is to be served in the proceedings.
(2) An application for an order to dispense with service must be supported by evidence and may be made without notice.

6.29 Certificate of Service

r.6.29 15.44, 32.12, 37.10 r.6.31(1)(i) 16.47

Where a rule, practice direction or court order requires a certificate of service, the certificate must state the details required by the following table—

Method of Service	Details to be certified
1. Personal service	Date and time of personal service.
2. First class post, document exchange or other service which provides for delivery on the next business day	Date of posting, or leaving with, delivering to or collection by the relevant service provider.
3. Delivery of document to or leaving it at a permitted place	Date and time of when the document was delivered to or left at the permitted place.
4. Fax	Date and time of completion of the transmission.
5. Other electronic method	Date and time of sending the e-mail or other electronic transmission.
6. Alternative method or place permitted by	As required by the court.

IV SERVICE OF THE CLAIM FORM AND OTHER DOCUMENTS OUT OF THE JURISDICTION

rr.6.30–6.47 84.5

6.30 Scope of This Section

This Section contains rules about—
(a) service of the claim form and other documents out of the jurisdiction;
(b) when the permission of the court is required and how to obtain that permission; and
(c) the procedure for service.
('Jurisdiction' is defined in rule 2.3(1).)

6.31 Interpretation

r.6.31(1)(i) 16.45

For the purposes of this Section—
(a) 'the Hague Convention' means the Convention on the service abroad of judicial and extra-judical documents in civil or commercial matters signed at the Hague on 15 November 1965;
(b) 'the 1982 Act' means the Civil Jurisdiction and Judgments Act 1982;
(c) 'Civil Procedure Convention' means the Brussels and Lugano Conventions (as defined in section 1(1) of the 1982 Act) and any other Convention (including the Hague Convention) entered into by the United Kingdom regarding service out of the jurisdiction;
(d) 'the Judgments Regulation' means Council Regulation (EC) No. 44/2001 of 22 December 2000 on jurisdiction and the recognition and enforcement of judgments in civil and commercial matters, as amended from time to time and as applied by the Agreement made on 19 October 2005 between the European Community and the Kingdom of Denmark on jurisdiction and the recognition and enforcement of judgments in civil and commercial matters;
(e) 'the Service Regulation' means Regulation (EC) No. 1393/2007 of the European Parliament and of the Council of 13 November 2007 on the service in the Member States of judicial and extra-judicial documents in civil or commercial matters (service of documents), and repealing Council Regulation (EC) No. 1348/2000, as amended from time to time and as applied by the Agreement made on 19 October 2005 between the European Community and the Kingdom of Denmark on the service of judicial and extrajudicial documents on civil and commercial matters;
(f) 'Commonwealth State' means a state listed in Schedule 3 to the British Nationality Act 1981;
(g) 'Contracting State' has the meaning given by section 1 (3) of the 1982 Act;
(h) 'Convention territory' means the territory or territories of any Contracting State to which the Brussels or Lugano Conventions (as defined in section 1(1) of the 1982 Act) apply; and
(i) 'domicile' is to be determined—
  (i) in relation to a Convention territory, in accordance with sections 41 to 46 of the 1982 Act; and
  (ii) in relation to a Member State, in accordance with the Judgments Regulation and paragraphs 9 to 12 of Schedule 1 to the Civil Jurisdiction and Judgments Order 2001.
(j) 'the Lugano Convention' means the Convention on jurisdiction and the recognition and enforcement of judgments in civil and commercial matters, between the European Community and the Republic of Iceland, the Kingdom of Norway, the Swiss Confederation and the Kingdom of Denmark and signed by the European Community on 30th October 2007.

6.32 Service of the Claim Form Where the Permission of the Court Is Not Required — Scotland and Northern Ireland

r.6.32 PC 13, PC 16, 15.2, 15.16, 16.40, 16.67, 18.2, 18.5, 20.8, 20.9

(1) The claimant may serve the claim form on a defendant in Scotland or Northern Ireland where each claim made against the defendant to be served and included in the claim form is a claim which the court has power to determine under the 1982 Act and—
  (a) no proceedings between the parties concerning the same claim are pending in the courts of any other part of the United Kingdom; and

(b) (i) the defendant is domiciled in the United Kingdom;
(ii) the proceedings are within paragraph 11 of Schedule 4 to the 1982 Act; or
(iii) the defendant is a party to an agreement conferring jurisdiction, within paragraph 12 of Schedule 4 to the 1982 Act.

(2) The claimant may serve the claim form on a defendant in Scotland or Northern Ireland where each claim made against the defendant to be served and included in the claim form is a claim which the court has power to determine under any enactment other than the 1982 Act not with standing that—
(a) the person against whom the claim is made is not within the jurisdiction; or
(b) the facts giving rise to the claim did not occur within the jurisdiction.

6.33 Service of the Claim Form Where the Permission of the Court Is Not Required — Out of the United Kingdom

r.6.33 PC 13, PC 14, PC 16, 15.16, 16.40, 16.44, 16.67, 18.2, 18.5, 20.8, 20.9
r.6.33(1)–(2) 16.17, 16.40
r.6.33(3) 16.40

(1) The claimant may serve the claim form on the defendant out of the United Kingdom where each claim against the defendant to be served and included in the claim form is a claim which the court has power to determine under the 1982 Act or the Lugano Convention and—
(a) no proceedings between the parties concerning the same claim are pending in the courts of any other part of the United Kingdom or any other Convention territory; and
(b) (i) the defendant is domiciled in the United Kingdom or in any Convention territory;
(ii) the proceedings are within article 16 of Schedule 1 to the 1982 Act or article 22 of the Lugano Convention; or
(iii) the defendant is a party to an agreement conferring jurisdiction, within article 17 of Schedule 1 to the 1982 Act or article 23 of the Lugano Convention.

(2) The claimant may serve the claim form on a defendant out of the United Kingdom where each claim made against the defendant to be served and included in the claim form is a claim which the court has power to determine under the Judgments Regulation and—
(a) no proceedings between the parties concerning the same claim are pending in the courts of any other part of the United Kingdom or any other Member State; and
(b) (i) the defendant is domiciled in the United Kingdom or in any Member State;
(ii) the proceedings are within article 22 of the Judgments Regulation; or
(iii) the defendant is a party to an agreement conferring jurisdiction, within article 23 of the Judgments Regulation.

(3) The claimant may serve the claim form on a defendant out of the United Kingdom where each claim made against the defendant to be served and included in the claim form is a claim which the court has power to determine other than under the 1982 Act or the Lugano Convention or the Judgments Regulation, notwithstanding that—
(a) the person against whom the claim is made is not within the jurisdiction; or
(b) the facts giving rise to the claim did not occur within the jurisdiction.

6.34 Notice of Statement of Grounds Where the Permission of the Court Is Not Required for Service

r.6.34 23.19
r.6 34(1)–(2) 16.40

(1) Where the claimant intends to serve a claim form on a defendant under rule 6.32 or 6.33, the claimant must—
(a) file with the claim form a notice containing a statement of the grounds on which the claimant is entitled to serve the claim form out of the jurisdiction; and
(b) serve a copy of that notice with the claim form.

(2) Where the claimant fails to file with the claim form a copy of the notice referred to in paragraph (1)(a), the claim form may only be served—
(a) once the claimant files the notice; or
(b) if the court gives permission.

6.35 Period for Responding to the Claim Form Where Permission Was Not Required for Service

r.6.35 17.6, 18.2, 19.2
r.6.35(2) PC 13, 16.64
r.6.35(3) PC 13, 16.64
r.6.35(4) PC 13, 16.64

(1) This rule sets out the period for—
(a) filing an acknowledgment of service;
(b) filing an admission; or
(c) filing a defence,
where a claim form has been served out of the jurisdiction under rule 6.32 or 6.33.
(Part 10 contains rules about acknowledgments of service, Part 14 contains rules about admissions and Part 15 contains rules about defences.)

Service of the claim form on a defendant in Scotland or Northern Ireland

(2) Where the claimant serves on a defendant in Scotland or Northern Ireland under rule 6.32, the period—
(a) for filing an acknowledgment of service or admission is 21 days after service of the particulars of claim; or
(b) for filing a defence is—
(i) 21 days after service of the particulars of claim; or
(ii) where the defendant files an acknowledgment of service, 35 days after service of the particulars of claim.

(Part 7 provides that particulars of claim must be contained in or served with the claim form or served separately on the defendant within 14 days after service of the claim form.)

Service of the claim form on a defendant in a Convention territory within Europe or a Member State

(3) Where the claimant serves the claim form on a defendant in a Convention territory within Europe or a Member State under rule 6.33, the period—
(a) for filing an acknowledgment of service or admission, is 21 days after service of the particulars of claim; or
(b) for filing a defence is—
(i) 21 days after service of the particulars of claim; or
(ii) where the defendant files an acknowledgment of service, 35 days after service of the particulars of claim.

Service of the claim form on a defendant in a Convention territory outside Europe

(4) Where the claimant serves the claim form on a defendant in a Convention territory outside Europe under rule 6.33, the period—
(a) for filing an acknowledgment of service or admission, is 31 days after service of the particulars of claim; or
(b) for filing a defence is—
(i) 31 days after service of the particulars of claim; or
(ii) where the defendant files an acknowledgment of service, 45 days after service of the particulars of claim.

Service on a defendant elsewhere

(5) Where the claimant serves the claim form under rule 6.33 in a country not referred to in paragraph (3) or (4), the period for responding to the claim form is set out in Practice Direction 6B.

6.36 Service of the Claim Form Where the Permission of the Court Is Required

r.6.36 PC 11, PC 13, PC 14, 15.16, 16.1, 16.68, 38.5

In any proceedings to which rule 6.32 or 6.33 does not apply, the claimant may serve a claim form out of the jurisdiction with the permission of the court if any of the grounds set out in paragraph 3.1 of Practice Direction 6B apply.

6.37 Application for Permission to Serve the Claim Form Out of the Jurisdiction

r.6.37 PC 11, 16.43, 16.63, 32.29
r.6.37(3) PC 13, 16.53
r.6.37(5) PC 13
r.6.37(5)(b)(i) 15.18, 16.56

(1) An application for permission under rule 6.36 must set out—
(a) which ground in paragraph 3.1 of Practice Direction 6B is relied on;
(b) that the claimant believes that the claim has a reasonable prospect of success; and
(c) the defendant's address or, if not known, in what place the defendant is, or is likely, to be found.
(2) Where the application is made in respect of a claim referred to in paragraph 3.1(3) of Practice Direction 6B, the application must also state the grounds on which the claimant believes that there is between the claimant and the defendant a real issue which it is reasonable for the court to try.
(3) The court will not give permission unless satisfied that England and Wales is the proper place in which to bring the claim.
(4) In particular, where—
(a) the application is for permission to serve a claim form in Scotland or Northern Ireland; and
(b) it appears to the court that the claimant may also be entitled to a remedy in Scotland or Northern Ireland, the court, in deciding whether to give permission, will—
(i) compare the cost and convenience of proceeding there or in the jurisdiction; and
(ii) (where relevant) have regard to the powers and jurisdiction of the Sheriff court in Scotland or the county courts or courts of summary jurisdiction in Northern Ireland.
(5) Where the court gives permission to serve a claim form out of the jurisdiction—
(a) it will specify the periods within which the defendant may—
(i) file an acknowledgment of service;
(ii) file or serve an admission;
(iii) file a defence; or
(iv) file any other response or document required by a rule in another Part, any other enactment or a practice direction; and
(b) it may—
(i) give directions about the method of service; and
(ii) give permission for other documents in the proceedings to be served out of the jurisdiction.

(The periods referred to in paragraphs (5)(a)(i), (ii) and (iii) are those specified in the Table in Practice Direction 6B.)

6.38 Service of Documents Other Than the Claim Form — Permission

r.6.38(1) 16.65
r.6.38(2) 16.65
r.6.38(3) 15.2, 16.65

(1) Unless paragraph (2) or (3) applies, where the permission of the court is required for the claimant to serve the claim form out of the jurisdiction, the claimant must obtain permission to serve any other document in the proceedings out of the jurisdiction.
(2) Where—
(a) the court gives permission for a claim form to be served on a defendant out of the jurisdiction; and
(b) the claim form states that particulars of claim are to follow, the permission of the court is not required to serve the particulars of claim.
(3) The permission of the court is not required if a party has given an address for service in Scotland or Northern Ireland.

6.39 Service of Application Notice on a Non-party to the Proceedings

r.6.39(2) 19.3

(1) Where an application notice is to be served out of the jurisdiction on a person who is not a party to the proceedings rules 6.35 and 6.37(5)(a)(i), (ii) and (iii) do not apply.
(2) Where an application is served out of the jurisdiction on a person who is not a party to the proceedings, that person may make an application to the court under Part 11 as if that person were a defendant, but rule 11(2) does not apply.

(Part 11 contains provisions about disputing the court's jurisdiction.)

6.40 Methods of Service — General Provisions

r.6.40 PC 31, 16.55
r.6.40(2) 16.57
r.6.40(3) 15.15
r.6.40(3)(a) 16.55
r.6.40(3)(a)(i)–(ii) 16.55
r.6.40(3)(b) 16.55
r.6.40(3)(c) 16.55, 84.5
r.6.40(4) 16.55, 84.5

(1) This rule contains general provisions about the method of service of a claim form or other document on a party out of the jurisdiction.

Where service is to be effected on a party in Scotland or Northern Ireland

(2) Where a party serves a claim form or other document on a party in Scotland or Northern Ireland, it must be served by a method permitted by Section II (and references to 'jurisdiction' in that Section are modified accordingly) or Section III of this Part and rule 6.23(4) applies.

Where service is to be effected on a party out of the United Kingdom

(3) Where a party wishes to serve a claim form or other document on a party out of the United Kingdom, it may be served—
- (a) by any method provided for by—
  - (i) rule 6.41 (service in accordance with the Service Regulation);
  - (ii) rule 6.42 (service through foreign governments, judicial authorities and British Consular authorities); or
  - (iii) rule 6.44 (service of claim form or other document on a State);
- (b) by any method permitted by a Civil Procedure Convention or Treaty; or
- (c) by any other method permitted by the law of the country in which it is to be served.

(4) Nothing in paragraph (3) or in any court order authorises or requires any person to do anything which is contrary to the law of the country where the claim form or other document is to be served.

(The texts of the Civil Procedure Treaties which the United Kingdom has entered into may be found on the Foreign and Commonwealth Office website at—
<http://www.fco.gov.uk/en/about-the-fco/publications/treaties/lists-treaties/bilateral-civilprocedure>)*.

6.41 Service in Accordance with the Service Regulation

r.6.41 PC 31
r.6.41(2) 16.59
r.6.41(3) 16.59
r.6.41(4) 16.67

(1) This rule applies where a party wishes to serve the claim form or other document in accordance with the Service Regulation.

(2) The party must file—
- (a) the claim form or other document;
- (b) any translation; and
- (c) any other documents required by the Service Regulation.

(3) When a party files the documents referred to in paragraph (2), the court officer will forward the documents to the Senior Master.

(4) Rule 6.47 does not apply to this rule.

(The Service Regulation is annexed to Practice Direction 6B.)

(Article 20(1) of the Service Regulation provides that the Regulation prevails over other provisions contained in any other agreement or arrangement concluded by Member States. The Regulation does not apply to service in EEA states that are not member states of the EU.)

6.42 Service through Foreign Governments, Judicial Authorities and British Consular Authorities

r.6.42 PC 31
r.6.42(1)(a) 16.60
r.6.42(1)(b) 16.61
r.6.42(2) 16.62
r.6.42(3) 16.62
r.6.42(3)(a) 16.62

(1) Where a party wishes to serve a claim form or any other document in any country which is a party to a Civil Procedure Convention or Treaty providing for service in that country, it may be served—
- (a) through the authority designated under the Hague Convention or any other Civil Procedure Convention or Treaty (where relevant) in respect of that country; or

[* Now <http://www.fco.gov.uk/en/publications-and-documents/treaties/lists-treaties/bilateral-civil-procedure>.]

(b) if the law of that country permits—
 (i) through the judicial authorities of that country, or
 (ii) through a British Consular authority in that country (subject to any provisions of the applicable convention about the nationality of persons who may be served by such a method).

(2) Where a party wishes to serve a claim form or any other document in any country with respect to which there is no Civil Procedure Convention or Treaty providing for service in that country, the claim form or other document may be served, if the law of that country so permits—
 (a) through the government of that country, where that government is willing to serve it; or
 (b) through a British Consular authority in that country.

(3) Where a party wishes to serve the claim form or other document in—
 (a) any Commonwealth State which is not a party to the Hague Convention or is such a party but HM Government has not declared acceptance of its accession to the Convention;
 (b) the Isle of Man or the Channel Islands; or
 (c) any British overseas territory, the methods of service permitted by paragraphs (1)(b) and (2) are not available and the party or the party's agent must effect service direct, unless Practice Direction 6B provides otherwise.

(A list of British overseas territories is reproduced in paragraph 5.2 of Practice Direction 6B.)

6.43 Procedure Where Service Is to Be through Foreign Governments, Judicial Authorities and British Consular Authorities

r.6.43 PC 31, 16.60 r.6.43(5) 16.66
r.6.43(1) 16.62

(1) This rule applies where a party wishes to serve a claim form or any other document under rule 6.42(1) or 6.42(2).

(2) Where this rule applies, that party must file—
 (a) a request for service of the claim form or other document specifying one or more of the methods in rule 6.42(1) or 6.42(2);
 (b) a copy of the claim form or other document;
 (c) any other documents or copies of documents required by Practice Direction 6B; and
 (d) any translation required under rule 6.45.

(3) Where a party files the documents specified in paragraph (2), the court officer will—
 (a) seal(GL) the copy of the claim form or other document; and
 (b) forward the documents to the Senior Master.

(4) The Senior Master will send documents forwarded under this rule—
 (a) where the claim form or other document is being served through the authority designated under the Hague Convention or any other Civil Procedure Convention or Treaty, to that authority; or
 (b) in any other case, to the Foreign and Commonwealth Office with a request that it arranges for the claim form or other document to be served.

(5) An official certificate which—
 (a) states that the method requested under paragraph (2)(a) has been performed and the date of such performance;
 (b) states, where more than one method is requested under paragraph (2)(a), which method was used; and
 (c) is made by—
  (i) a British Consular authority in the country where the method requested under paragraph (2)(a) was performed;
  (ii) the government or judicial authorities in that country; or
  (iii) the authority designated in respect of that country under a Civil Procedure Convention or Treaty,

is evidence of the facts stated in the certificate.

(6) A document purporting to be an official certificate under paragraph (5) is to be treated as such a certificate, unless it is proved not to be.

CPR 1–25 & PDs

6.44 Service of Claim Form or Other Document on a State

r.6.44 PC 31, 16.58 r.6.44(7) 16.58

(1) This rule applies where a party wishes to serve the claim form or other document on a State.
(2) In this rule, 'State' has the meaning given by section 14 of the State Immunity Act 1978.
(3) The party must file in the Central Office of the Royal Courts of Justice—
(a) a request for service to be arranged by the Foreign and Commonwealth Office;
(b) a copy of the claim form or other document; and
(c) any translation required under rule 6.45.
(4) The Senior Master will send the documents filed under this rule to the Foreign and Commonwealth Office with a request that it arranges for them to be served.
(5) An official certificate by the Foreign and Commonwealth Office stating that a claim form or other document has been duly served on a specified date in accordance with a request made under this rule is evidence of that fact.
(6) A document purporting to be such a certificate is to be treated as such a certificate, unless it is proved not to be.
(7) Where—
(a) section 12(6) of the State Immunity Act 1978 applies; and
(b) the State has agreed to a method of service other than through the Foreign and Commonwealth Office,

the claim form or other document may be served either by the method agreed or in accordance with this rule.

(Section 12(6) of the State Immunity Act 1978 provides that section 12(1) enables the service of a claim form or other document in a manner to which the State has agreed.)

6.45 Translation of Claim Form or Other Document

r.6.45 PC 31, 16.58, 16.60

(1) Except where paragraph (4) or (5) applies, every copy of the claim form or other document filed under rule 6.43 (service through foreign governments, judicial authorities etc.) or 6.44 (service of claim form or other document on a State) must be accompanied by a translation of the claim form or other document.
(2) The translation must be—
(a) in the official language of the country in which it is to be served; or
(b) if there is more than one official language of that country, in any official language which is appropriate to the place in the country where the claim form or other document is to be served.
(3) Every translation filed under this rule must be accompanied by a statement by the person making it that it is a correct translation, and the statement must include that person's name, address and qualifications for making the translation.
(4) A party is not required to file a translation of a claim form or other document filed under rule 6.43 (service through foreign governments, judicial authorities etc.) where the claim form or other document is to be served—
(a) in a country of which English is an official language; or
(b) on a British citizen (within the meaning of the British Nationality Act 1981), unless a Civil Procedure Convention or Treaty requires a translation.
(5) A party is not required to file a translation of a claim form or other document filed under rule 6.44 (service of claim form or other document on a State) where English is an official language of the State in which the claim form or other document is to be served.

(The Service Regulation contains provisions about the translation of documents.)

6.46 Undertaking to Be Responsible for Expenses

r.6.46 PC 31, 16.60

Every request for service filed under rule 6.43 (service through foreign governments, judicial authorities etc.) or rule 6.44 (service of claim form or other document on a State) must contain an undertaking by the person making the request—

(a) to be responsible for all expenses incurred by the Foreign and Commonwealth Office or foreign judicial authority; and

(b) to pay those expenses to the Foreign and Commonwealth Office or foreign judicial authority on being informed of the amount.

6.47 Proof of Service before Obtaining Judgment

r.6.47 16.67

Where—
(a) a hearing is fixed when the claim form is issued;
(b) the claim form is served on a defendant out of the jurisdiction; and
(c) that defendant does not appear at the hearing,
the claimant may not obtain judgment against the defendant until the claimant files written evidence that the claim form has been duly served in accordance with this Part.

V SERVICE OF DOCUMENTS FROM FOREIGN COURTS OR TRIBUNALS

6.48 Scope of This Section

rr.6.48–6.51 84.5

This Section—
(a) applies to the service in England and Wales of any document in connection with civil or commercial proceedings in a foreign court or tribunal; but
(b) does not apply where the Service Regulation (which has the same meaning as in rule 6.31(e)) applies.

6.49 Interpretation

In this Section—
(a) 'convention country' means a country in relation to which there is a Civil Procedure Convention (which has the same meaning as in rule 6.31(c));
(b) 'foreign court or tribunal' means a court or tribunal in a country outside of the United Kingdom; and
(c) 'process server' means—
  (i) a process server appointed by the Lord Chancellor to serve documents to which this Section applies, or
  (ii) the process server's agent.

6.50 Request for Service

The Senior Master will serve a document to which this Section applies upon receipt of—
(a) a written request for service—
  (i) where the foreign court or tribunal is in a convention country, from a consular or other authority of that country; or
  (ii) from the Secretary of State for Foreign and Commonwealth Affairs, with a recommendation that service should be effected;
(b) a translation of that request into English;
(c) two copies of the document to be served; and
(d) unless the foreign court or tribunal certifies that the person to be served understands the language of the document, two copies of a translation of it into English.

6.51 Method of Service

The Senior Master will determine the method of service.

6.52 After Service

(1) Where service of a document has been effected by a process server, the process server must—
  (a) send to the Senior Master a copy of the document, and
    (i) proof of service; or
    (ii) a statement why the document could not be served; and
  (b) if the Senior Master directs, specify the costs incurred in serving or attempting to serve the document.

(2) The Senior Master will send to the person who requested service—
  (a) a certificate, sealed with the seal of the Senior Courts for use out of the jurisdiction, stating—
    (i) when and how the document was served or the reason why it has not been served; and
    (ii) where appropriate, an amount certified by a costs judge to be the costs of serving or attempting to serve the document; and
  (b) a copy of the document.

PD 6A Practice Direction 6A — Service within the United Kingdom

This practice direction supplements CPR, Part 6.

PD 6A 15.1, 15.10, 16.2, 18.5, 32.22

Scope of This Practice Direction

1.1 This Practice Direction supplements:
(1) Section II (service of the claim form in the jurisdiction) of Part 6;
(2) Section III (service of documents other than the claim form in the United Kingdom) of Part 6; and
(3) r. 6.40 in relation to the method of service on a party in Scotland or Northern Ireland.
(PD 6B contains provisions relevant to service on a party in Scotland or Northern Ireland, including provisions about service out of the jurisdiction where permission is and is not required and the period for responding to an application notice.)

When Service May Be by Document Exchange

para.2.1 15.12

2.1 Service by document exchange (DX) may take place only where:
(1) the address at which the party is to be served includes a numbered box at a DX, or
(2) the writing paper of the party who is to be served or of the solicitor acting for that party sets out a DX box number, and
(3) the party or the solicitor acting for that party has not indicated in writing that they are unwilling to accept service by DX.

How Service Is Effected by Post, an Alternative Service Provider or DX

para.3.1 15.12 para.3.1(3) 16.47

3.1 Service by post, DX or other service which provides for delivery on the next business day is effected by:
(1) placing the document in a post box;
(2) leaving the document with or delivering the document to the relevant service provider; or
(3) having the document collected by the relevant service provider.

Service by Fax or Other Electronic Means

para.4.1 15.15, 15.17, 16.63 para.4.2 15.15
para.4.1(2)(a) 15.15 para.4.2(a) 15.15
para.4.3 15.15

4.1 Subject to the provisions of r. 6.23(5) and (6), where a document is to be served by fax or other electronic means:
(1) party who is to be served or the solicitor acting for that party must previously have indicated in writing to the party serving:
  (a) that the party to be served or the solicitor is willing to accept service by fax or other electronic means; and
  (b) the fax number, email address or other electronic identification to which it must be sent; and
(2) the following are to be taken as sufficient written indications for the purposes of para. 4.1(1):
  (a) a fax number set out on the writing paper of the solicitor acting for the party to be served;
  (b) an email address set out on the writing paper of the solicitor acting for the party to be served but only where it is stated that the email address may be used for service; or
  (c) a fax number, email address or electronic identification set out on a statement of case or a response to a claim filed with the court.

4.2 Where a party intends to serve a document by electronic means (other than by fax) that party must first ask the party who is to be served whether there are any limitations to the recipient's

CPR 1–25 & PDs

agreement to accept service by such means (for example, the format in which documents are to be sent and the maximum size of attachments that may be received).

4.3 Where a document is served by electronic means, the party serving the document need not in addition send or deliver a hard copy.

Service on Members of the Regular Forces and United States Air Force

5.1 The provisions that apply to service on members of the regular forces (within the meaning of the Armed Forces Act 2006) and members of the United States Air Force are annexed to this practice direction.

Personal Service on a Company or Other Corporation

para.6.1 15.49
para.6.2 15.49, 23.13
para.6.2(1) 15.47

6.1 Personal service on a registered company or corporation in accordance with r. 6.5(3) is effected by leaving a document with a person holding a senior position.

6.2 Each of the following persons is a person holding a senior position:

(1) in respect of a registered company or corporation, a director, the treasurer, the secretary of the company or corporation, the chief executive, a manager or other officer of the company or corporation; and

(2) in respect of a corporation which is not a registered company, in addition to any of the persons set out in sub-para. (1), the mayor, the chairman, the president, a town clerk or similar officer of the corporation.

Certificate of Service Where Claimant Serves the Claim Form

7.1 Where, pursuant to r. 6.17(2), the claimant files a certificate of service, the claimant is not required to and should not file:

(1) a further copy of the claim form with the certificate of service; and

(2) a further copy of:

(a) the particulars of claim (where not included in the claim form); or

(b) any document attached to the particulars of claim,

with the certificate of service where that document has already been filed with the court.

(Rule 7.4 requires the claimant to file a copy of the particulars of claim (where served separately from the claim form) within seven days of service on the defendant.)

Service by the Court

para.8.1 PC 3, 15.6, 15.38
para.8.2 15.6, 15.38

8.1 Where the court serves a document in accordance with r. 6.4 or 6.21(2), the method will normally be first-class post.

8.2 Where the court serves a claim form, delivers a defence to a claimant or notifies a claimant that the defendant has filed an acknowledgment of service, the court will also serve or deliver a copy of any notice of funding that has been filed, if:

(1) it was filed at the same time as the claim form, defence or acknowledgment of service, and

(2) copies of it were provided for service.

(Rule 44.15 deals with the provision of information about funding arrangements.)

Application for an Order for Service by an Alternative Method or at an Alternative Place

para.9.1 15.17, 15.21
para.9.2 15.17, 15.20
para.9.3 15.19

9.1 Where an application for an order under r. 6.15 is made before the document is served, the application must be supported by evidence stating:

(1) the reason why an order is sought;

(2) *what alternative method* or place is proposed, and

(3) why the applicant believes that the document is likely to reach the person to be served by the method or at the place proposed.

9.2 Where the application for an order is made after the applicant has taken steps to bring the document to the attention of the person to be served by an alternative method or at an alternative place, the application must be supported by evidence stating:
(1) the reason why the order is sought;
(2) what alternative method or alternative place was used;
(3) when the alternative method or place was used; and
(4) why the applicant believes that the document is likely to have reached the person to be served by the alternative method or at the alternative place.
9.3 Examples:
(1) an application to serve by posting or delivering to an address of a person who knows the other party must be supported by evidence that if posted or delivered to that address, the document is likely to be brought to the attention of the other party;
(2) an application to serve by sending a SMS text message or leaving a voicemail message at a particular telephone number saying where the document is must be accompanied by evidence that the person serving the document has taken, or will take, appropriate steps to ensure that the party being served is using that telephone number and is likely to receive the message; and
(3) an application to serve by email to a company (where para. 4.1 does not apply) must be supported by evidence that the email address to which the document will be sent is one which is likely to come to the attention of a person holding a senior position in that company.

Deemed Service of a Document Other Than a Claim Form

para.10 15.42

10.1 Rule 6.26 contains provisions about deemed service of a document other than a claim form. Examples of how deemed service is calculated are set out below.

Example 1
10.2 Where the document is posted (by first-class post) on a Monday (a business day), the day of deemed service is the following Wednesday (a business day).

Example 2
10.3 Where the document is left in a numbered box at the DX on a Friday (a business day), the day of deemed service is the following Monday (a business day).

Example 3
10.4 Where the document is sent by fax on a Saturday and the transmission of that fax is completed by 4.30 p.m. on that day, the day of deemed service is the following Monday (a business day).

Example 4
10.5 Where the document is served personally before 4.30 p.m. on a Sunday, the day of deemed service is the next day (Monday, a business day).

Example 5
10.6 Where the document is delivered to a permitted address after 4.30 p.m. on the Thursday (a business day) before Good Friday, the day of deemed service is the following Tuesday (a business day) as the Monday is a bank holiday.

Example 6
10.7 Where the document is posted (by first-class post) on a bank holiday Monday, the day of deemed service is the following Wednesday (a business day).

ANNEX

SERVICE ON MEMBERS OF THE REGULAR FORCES

annex 15.10

1. The following information is for litigants and legal representatives who wish to serve legal documents in civil proceedings in the courts of England and Wales on parties to the proceedings who are (or who, at the material time, were) members of the regular forces (as defined in the Armed Forces Act 2006).

2. The proceedings may take place in the county court or the High Court, and the documents to be served may be claim forms, interim application notices and pre-action application notices. Proceedings for divorce or maintenance and proceedings in the Family Courts generally are subject to special rules

as to service which are explained in a practice direction issued by the Senior District Judge of the Principal Registry on 26 June 1979.

3. In this Annex, the person wishing to effect service is referred to as the 'claimant' and the member of the regular forces to be served is referred to as 'the member'; the expression 'overseas' means outside the United Kingdom.

Enquiries as to address

4. As a first step, the claimant's legal representative will need to find out where the member is serving, if this is not already known. For this purpose the claimant's legal representative should write to the appropriate officer of the Ministry of Defence as specified in para. 10 below.

5. The letter of enquiry should in every case show that the writer is a legal representative and that the enquiry is made solely with a view to the service of legal documents in civil proceedings.

6. In all cases the letter must give the full name, service number, rank or rate, and Ship, Arm or Trade, Regiment or Corps and Unit or as much of this information as is available. Failure to quote the service number and the rank or rate may result either in failure to identify the member or in considerable delay.

7. The letter must contain an undertaking by the legal representative that, if the address is given, it will be used solely for the purpose of issuing and serving documents in the proceedings and that so far as is possible the legal representative will disclose the address only to the court and not to the claimant or to any other person or body. A legal representative in the service of a public authority or private company must undertake that the address will be used solely for the purpose of issuing and serving documents in the proceedings and that the address will not be disclosed so far as is possible to any other part of the legal representative's employing organisation or to any other person but only to the court. Normally on receipt of the required information and undertaking the appropriate office will give the service address.

8. If the legal representative does not give the undertaking, the only information that will be given is whether the member is at that time serving in England or Wales, Scotland, Northern Ireland or overseas.

9. It should be noted that a member's address which ends with a British Forces Post Office address and reference (BFPO) will nearly always indicate that the member is serving overseas.

10. The letter of enquiry should be addressed as follows:

(a) *Royal Navy and Royal Marine Officers, Ratings and Other Ranks*

Director Naval Personnel
Fleet Headquarters
MP 3.1
Leach Building
Whale Island
Portsmouth
Hampshire
PO2 8BY

(b) *Army Officers and Other Ranks*

Army Personnel Centre
Disclosures 1
MP520
Kentigern House
65 Brown Street
Glasgow G2 8EX

(c) *Royal Air Force Officers and Other Ranks*

Manning 22E
RAF Disclosures
Room 221B
Trenchard Hall
RAF Cranwell
Sleaford
Lincolnshire
NG34 8HB

Assistance in serving documents on members

11. Once the claimant's legal representative has ascertained the member's address, the legal representative may use that address as the address for service by post, in cases where this method of service is allowed by the Civil Procedure Rules. There are, however, some situations in which service of the proceedings, whether in the High Court or in the county court, must be effected personally; in these cases an appointment will have to be sought, through the Commanding Officer of the Unit, Establishment or Ship concerned, for the purpose of effecting service. The procedure for obtaining an appointment is described below, and it applies whether personal service is to be effected by the claimant's legal representative or the legal representative's agent or by a court bailiff, or, in the case of proceedings served overseas (with the leave of the court) through the British Consul or the foreign judicial authority.

12. The procedure for obtaining an appointment to effect personal service is by application to the Commanding Officer of the Unit, Establishment or Ship in which the member is serving. The Commanding Officer may grant permission for the document server to enter the Unit, Establishment or Ship but if this is not appropriate the Commanding Officer may offer arrangements for the member to attend at a place in the vicinity of the Unit, Establishment or Ship in order that the member may be served. If suitable arrangements cannot be made the legal representative will have evidence that personal service is impracticable, which may be useful in an application for service by an alternative method or at an alternative place.

General

13. Subject to the procedure outlined in paras 11 and 12, there are no special arrangements to assist in the service of legal documents when a member is outside the United Kingdom. The appropriate office will, however, give an approximate date when the member is likely to return to the United Kingdom.

14. It sometimes happens that a member has left the regular forces by the time an enquiry as to address is made. If the claimant's legal representative confirms that the proceedings result from an occurrence when the member was in the regular forces and the legal representative gives the undertaking referred to in para. 7, the last known private address after discharge will normally be provided. In no other case, however, will the Ministry of Defence disclose the private address of a member of the regular forces.

Service on Members of United States Air Force

15. In addition to the information contained in the memorandum of 26 July 1979, and after some doubts having been expressed as to the correct procedure to be followed by persons having civil claims against members of the United States Air Force in England and Wales, the Lord Chancellor's Office (as it was then) issued the following notes for guidance with the approval of the appropriate United States authorities.

16. Instructions have been issued by the United States authorities to the commanding officers of all their units in England and Wales that every facility is to be given for the service of documents in civil proceedings on members of the United States Air Force. The proper course to be followed by a creditor or other person having a claim against a member of the United States Air Force is for that person to communicate with the commanding officer or, where the unit concerned has a legal officer, with the legal officer of the defendant's unit requesting the provision of facilities for the service of documents on the defendant. It is not possible for the United States authorities to act as arbitrators when a civil claim is made against a member of their forces. It is, therefore, essential that the claim should either be admitted by the defendant or judgment should be obtained on it, whether in the High Court or a county court. If a claim has been admitted or judgment has been obtained and the claimant has failed to obtain satisfaction within a reasonable period, the claimant's proper course is then to write to: Office of the Staff Judge Advocate, Headquarters, Third Air Force, RAF Mildenhall, Suffolk, enclosing a copy of the defendant's written admission of the claim or, as the case may be, a copy of the judgment. Steps will then be taken by the Staff Judge Advocate to ensure that the matter is brought to the defendant's attention with a view to prompt satisfaction of the claim.

ANNEX
EUROPEAN COMMUNITIES (SERVICES OF LAWYERS) ORDER 1978 (SI 1978/1910)

[Only the definition of 'European lawyer', which is referred to in CPR, r. 6.2(e), is reproduced here. The definition was substituted by the European Communities (Services of Lawyers) (Amendment) Order 2004 (SI 2004/1117), art. 3, and amended by the European Communities (Lawyer's Practice and Services of Lawyers) (Amendment) Regulations 2008 (SI 2008/81), reg. 2, and 2013 (SI 2013/1605), reg. 2. The complete statutory instrument may be seen at <http://www.legislation.gov.uk>.]

Interpretation

2. In this Order, unless the context otherwise requires—

... 'European lawyer' means a person entitled to pursue his professional activities in a state in column 1 under the designation referred to in column 2—

State	Designation(s)
Austria	Rechtsanwalt
Belgium	Avocat/Advocaat
Bulgaria	Адвокат
Croatia	Odvjetnik/Odvjetnica
Cyprus	Δικηγόρος
Czech Republic	Advokát
Denmark	Advokat
Estonia	Vandeadvokaat
Finland	Asianajaja/Advokat
France	Avocat
Germany	Rechtsanwalt
Hellenic Republic	Dikegoros
Hungary	Ügyvéd
Iceland	Lögmaður
Republic of Ireland	Barrister/solicitor
Italy	Avvocato
Latvia	Zvērināts advokāts
Liechtenstein	Rechtsanwalt
Lithuania	Advokatas
Luxembourg	Avocat-avoué
Malta	Avukat/Prokuratur Legali
Netherlands	Advocaat
Norway	Advokat
Poland	Adwokat/Radca prawny
Portugal	Advogado
Romania	Avocat
Slovakia	Advokát/Komerčný právnik
Slovenia	Odvetnik/Odvetnica
Spain	Abogado/Advocat/Avogado/Abokatu
Sweden	Advokat
Switzerland	Avocat/Advokat/Rechtsanwalt/Anwalt/Fürsprecher/Fürsprech/Avvocato

PD 6B Practice Direction 6B — Service out of the Jurisdiction

This practice direction supplements Section IV of CPR, Part 6.

PD 6B PC 13, 15.1, 16.2, 16.64, 16.67

Scope of This Practice Direction

1.1 This Practice Direction supplements Section IV (service of the claim form and other documents out of the jurisdiction) of Part 6.

(PD 6A contains relevant provisions supplementing r. 6.40 in relation to the method of service on a party in Scotland or Northern Ireland.)

Service out of the Jurisdiction Where Permission of the Court Is Not Required

para.2.1 **16.40, 23.19**

2.1 Where r. 6.34 applies, the claimant must file form N510 when filing the claim form.

Service out of the Jurisdiction Where Permission Is Required

para.3 **16.44**
para.3.1 **PC 11, 16.42, 16.43**
para.3.1(1) **16.45**
para.3.1(1)(i) **16.45**
para.3.1(2) **16.46**
para.3.1(3) **PC 11, 16.43, 16.47, 16.53**
para.3.1(4) **16.47**
para.3.1(5) **16.46**
para.3.1(6) **16.48**
para.3.1(6)(a)–(d) **16.48**
para.3.1(7)–(8) **16.48**
para.3.1(8)(a) **16.48**
para.3.1(9) **16.49**
para.3.1(10) **16.50**
para.3.1(11) **16.51**
para.3.1(12) **16.52**
para.3.1(15) **16.52**

3.1 The claimant may serve a claim form out of the jurisdiction with the permission of the court under r. 6.36 where:

General grounds

(1) A claim is made for a remedy against a person domiciled within the jurisdiction.

(2) A claim is made for an injunction(GL) ordering the defendant to do or refrain from doing an act within the jurisdiction.

(3) A claim is made against a person ('the defendant') on whom the claim form has been or will be served (otherwise than in reliance on this paragraph) and:

(a) there is between the claimant and the defendant a real issue which it is reasonable for the court to try; and

(b) the claimant wishes to serve the claim form on another person who is a necessary or proper party to that claim.

(4) A claim is an additional claim under Part 20 and the person to be served is a necessary or proper party to the claim or additional claim.

Claims for interim remedies

(5) A claim is made for an interim remedy under section 25(1) of the Civil Jurisdiction and Judgments Act 1982.

Claims in relation to contracts

(6) A claim is made in respect of a contract where the contract:

(a) was made within the jurisdiction;

(b) was made by or through an agent trading or residing within the jurisdiction;

(c) is governed by English law; or

(d) contains a term to the effect that the court shall have jurisdiction to determine any claim in respect of the contract.

(7) A claim is made in respect of a breach of contract committed within the jurisdiction.

(8) A claim is made for a declaration that no contract exists where, if the contract was found to exist, it would comply with the conditions set out in sub-para. (6).

Claims in tort

(9) A claim is made in tort where:

(a) damage was sustained within the jurisdiction; or

(b) the damage sustained resulted from an act committed within the jurisdiction.

Enforcement

(10) A claim is made to enforce any judgment or arbitral award.

Claims about property within the jurisdiction

(11) The whole subject matter of a claim relates to property located within the jurisdiction.

Claims about trusts etc.

(12) A claim is made for any remedy which might be obtained in proceedings to execute the trusts of a written instrument where:

(a) the trusts ought to be executed according to English law; and

(b) the person on whom the claim form is to be served is a trustee of the trusts.

(13) A claim is made for any remedy which might be obtained in proceedings for the administration of the estate of a person who died domiciled within the jurisdiction.

(14) A probate claim or a claim for the rectification of a will.

(15) A claim is made for a remedy against the defendant as constructive trustee where the defendant's alleged liability arises out of acts committed within the jurisdiction.

(16) A claim is made for restitution where the defendant's alleged liability arises out of acts committed within the jurisdiction.

Claims by HM Revenue and Customs

(17) A claim is made by the Commissioners for HM Revenue and Customs relating to duties or taxes against a defendant not domiciled in Scotland or Northern Ireland.

Claim for costs order in favour of or against third parties

(18) A claim is made by a party to proceedings for an order that the court exercise its power under the Senior Courts Act 1981, s. 51, to make a costs order in favour of or against a person who is not a party to those proceedings.

(Rule 48.2 sets out the procedure where the court is considering whether to exercise its discretion to make a costs order in favour of or against a non-party.)

Admiralty claims

(19) A claim is:

(a) in the nature of salvage and any part of the services took place within the jurisdiction; or

(b) to enforce a claim under the Merchant Shipping Act 1995, s. 153, 154, 175 or 176A.

Claims under various enactments

(20) A claim is made:

(a) under an enactment which allows proceedings to be brought and those proceedings are not covered by any of the other grounds referred to in this paragraph; or

(b) under the Directive of the Council of the European Communities dated 15 March 1976 No. 76/308/EEC, where service is to be effected in a member State of the European Union.

Documents to Be Filed under r. 6.43(2)(c)

para.4.1 **16.60** para.4.2 **16.60**

4.1 A party must provide the following documents for each party to be served out of the jurisdiction—

(1) a copy of the particulars of claim if not already contained in or served with the claim form and any other relevant documents;

(2) a duplicate of the claim form, a duplicate of the particulars of claim (if not already contained in or served with the claim form), copies of any documents accompanying the claim form and copies of any other relevant documents;

(3) forms for responding to the claim; and

(4) any translation required under r. 6.45 in duplicate.

4.2 Some countries require legalisation of the document to be served and some require a formal letter of request which must be signed by the Senior Master. Any queries on this should be addressed to the Foreign Process Section (Room E02) at the Royal Courts of Justice.

Service in a Commonwealth State or British Overseas Territory

para.5.1 **16.62** para.5.2 **16.62**

5.1 The judicial authorities of certain Commonwealth States which are not a party to the Hague Convention require service to be in accordance with r. 6.42(1)(b)(i) and not r. 6.42(3). A list of such countries can be obtained from the Foreign Process Section (Room E02) at the Royal Courts of Justice.

5.2 The list of British overseas territories is contained in the British Nationality Act 1981, sch. 6. For ease of reference, these are:

(a) Anguilla;
(b) Bermuda;
(c) British Antarctic Territory;
(d) British Indian Ocean Territory;
(e) British Virgin Islands;
(f) Cayman Islands;
(g) Falkland Islands;
(h) Gibraltar;
(i) Montserrat;
(j) Pitcairn, Henderson, Ducie and Oeno;
(k) St Helena and Dependencies;
(l) South Georgia and the South Sandwich Islands;
(m) Sovereign Base Areas of Akrotiri and Dhekelia; and
(n) Turks and Caicos Islands.

Period for Responding to a Claim Form

para.6.2 **PC 13, 17.6, 18.2, 18.5, 19.2** para.6.6 **16.64**
para.6.4(2) **16.64**

6.1 Where r. 6.35(5) applies, the periods within which the defendant must:
(1) file an acknowledgment of service;
(2) file or serve an admission; or
(3) file a defence,
will be calculated in accordance with para. 6.3, 6.4 or 6.5.

6.2 Where the court grants permission to serve a claim form out of the jurisdiction the court will determine in accordance with para. 6.3, 6.4 or 6.5 the periods within which the defendant must:
(1) file an acknowledgment of service;
(2) file or serve an admission; or
(3) file a defence.
(Rule 6.37(5)(a) provides that when giving permission to serve a claim form out of the jurisdiction the court will specify the period within which the defendant may respond to the claim form.)

6.3 The period for filing an acknowledgment of service under Part 10 or for filing or serving an admission under Part 14 is the number of days listed in the Table after service of the particulars of claim.

6.4 The period for filing a defence under Part 15 is:
(1) the number of days listed in the Table after service of the particulars of claim; or
(2) where the defendant has filed an acknowledgment of service, the number of days listed in the Table plus an additional 14 days after the service of the particulars of claim.

6.5 Under the State Immunity Act 1978, where a State is served, the period permitted under paras 6.3 and 6.4 for filing an acknowledgment of service or defence or for filing or serving an admission does not begin to run until two months after the date on which the State is served.

6.6 Where particulars of claim are served out of the jurisdiction any statement as to the period for responding to the claim contained in any of the forms required by r. 7.8 to accompany the particulars of claim must specify the period prescribed under r. 6.35 or by the order permitting service out of the jurisdiction under r. 6.37(5).

Period for Responding to an Application Notice

para.7.1 **16.65**

7.1 Where an application notice is served out of the jurisdiction, the period for responding is seven days less than the number of days listed in the Table.

Further information

7.2 Further information concerning service out of the jurisdiction can be obtained from the Foreign Process Section, Room E02, Royal Courts of Justice, Strand, London WC2A 2LL (telephone (020) 7947 6691).

Table

table **16.63, 17.6, 18.2, 18.5**

Place or country	Number of days
Afghanistan	23
Albania	25
Algeria	22
Andorra	21
Angola	22
Anguilla	31
Antigua and Barbuda	23
Antilles (Netherlands)	31
Argentina	22
Armenia	21
Ascension Island	31
Australia	25
Austria	21
Azerbaijan	22
Azores	23
Bahamas	22
Bahrain	22
Balearic Islands	21
Bangladesh	23
Barbados	23
Belarus	21
Belgium	21
Belize	23
Benin	25
Bermuda	31
Bhutan	28
Bolivia	23
Bosnia and Herzegovina	21
Botswana	23
Brazil	22
British Virgin Islands	31
Brunei	25
Bulgaria	23
Burkina Faso	23
Burma	23
Burundi	22
Cambodia	28
Cameroon	22
Canada	22
Canary Islands	22
Cape Verde	25
Caroline Islands*	31

[* There are separate entries in the table for Micronesia and Palau.]

Place or country	Number of days
Cayman Islands	31
Central African Republic	25
Chad	25
Chile	22
China	24
China (Hong Kong)	31
China (Macau)	31
China (Taiwan)	23
China (Tibet)	34
Christmas Island	27
Cocos (Keeling) Islands	41
Colombia	22
Comoros	23
Congo (formerly Congo Brazzaville or French Congo)	25
Congo (Democratic Republic)	25
Corsica	21
Costa Rica	23
Croatia	21
Cuba	24
Cyprus	31
Czech Republic	21
Denmark	21
Djibouti	22
Dominica	23
Dominican Republic	23
East Timor	25
Ecuador	22
Egypt	22
El Salvador	25
Equatorial Guinea	23
Eritrea	22
Estonia	21
7Ethiopia	22
Falkland Islands and Dependencies	31
Faroe Islands	31
Fiji	23
Finland	24
France	21
French Guyana	31
French Polynesia	31
French West Indies	31
Gabon	25
Gambia	22

Place or country	Number of days
Georgia	21
Germany	21
Ghana	22
Gibraltar	31
Greece	21
Greenland	31
Grenada	24
Guatemala	24
Guernsey	21
Guinea	22
Guinea-Bissau	22
Guyana	22
Haiti	23
Holland (Netherlands)	21
Honduras	24
Hungary	22
Iceland	22
India	23
Indonesia	22
Iran	22
Iraq	22
Ireland (Republic of)	21
Ireland (Northern)	21
Isle of Man	21
Israel	22
Italy	21
Ivory Coast	22
Jamaica	22
Japan	23
Jersey	21
Jordan	23
Kazakhstan	21
Kenya	22
Kiribati	23
Korea (North)	28
Korea (South)	24
Kosovo	21
Kuwait	22
Kyrgyzstan	21
Laos	30
Latvia	21
Lebanon	22
Lesotho	23
Liberia	22
Libya	21
Liechtenstein	21
Lithuania	21
Luxembourg	21
Macedonia	21
Madagascar	23
Madeira	31

Place or country	Number of days
Malawi	23
Malaysia	24
Maldives	26
Mali	25
Malta	21
Mariana Islands	26
Marshall Islands	32
Mauritania	23
Mauritius	22
Mexico	23
Micronesia	23
Moldova	21
Monaco	21
Mongolia	24
Montenegro	21
Montserrat	31
Morocco	22
Mozambique	23
Namibia	23
Nauru	36
Nepal	23
Netherlands	21
Nevis	24
New Caledonia	31
New Zealand	26
New Zealand Island Territories	50
Nicaragua	24
Niger (Republic of)	25
Nigeria	22
Norfolk Island	31
Norway	21
Oman (Sultanate of)	22
Pakistan	23
Palau	23
Panama	26
Papua New Guinea	26
Paraguay	22
Peru	22
Philippines	23
Pitcairn, Henderson, Ducie and Oeno Islands	31
Poland	21
Portugal	21
Portuguese Timor*	31
Puerto Rico	23
Qatar	23
Reunion	31
Romania	22

[* Now East Timor, for which there is a separate entry in the Table.]
[** Now American Samoa.]

Place or country	Number of days
Russia	21
Rwanda	23
Sabah	23
St Helena	31
St Kitts and Nevis	24
St Lucia	24
St Pierre and Miquelon	31
St Vincent and the Grenadines	24
Samoa (USA Territory)** (See also Western Samoa)	30
San Marino	21
Sao Tome and Principe	25
Sarawak	28
Saudi Arabia	24
Scotland	21
Senegal	22
Serbia	21
Seychelles	22
Sierra Leone	22
Singapore	22
Slovakia	21
Slovenia	21
Society Islands (French Polynesia)	31
Solomon Islands	29
Somalia	22
South Africa	22
South Georgia (Falkland Island Dependencies)	31
South Orkneys	21
South Shetlands	21
Spain	21
Spanish Territories of North Afririca	31
Sri Lanka	23
Sudan	22
Surinam	22

Place or country	Number of days
Swaziland	22
Sweden	21
Switzerland	21
Syria	23
Tajikistan	21
Tanzania	22
Thailand	23
Togo	22
Tonga	30
Trinidad and Tobago	23
Tristan da Cunha	31
Tunisia	22
Turkey	21
Turkmenistan	21
Turks & Caicos Islands	31
Tuvalu	23
Uganda	22
Ukraine	21
United Arab Emirates	22
United States of America	22
Uruguay	22
Uzbekistan	21
Vanuatu	29
Vatican City State	21
Venezuela	22
Vietnam	28
Virgin Islands – USA	24
Wake Island	25
Western Samoa*	34
Yemen (Republic of)	30
Zaire**	25
Zambia	23
Zimbabwe	22

[* Now Samoa.]
[** Now Democratic Republic of the Congo.]

ANNEX
SERVICE REGULATION (R. 6.41)

[The text of Regulation (EC) No. 1393/2007 (the Service Regulation) may be downloaded from the EUR-Lex site: <http://eur-lex.europa.eu>.]

CPR Part 7 How to Start Proceedings — The Claim Form

Part 7 **8.2, 8.50, 11.9, 13.2, 13.4, 13.5, 13.6, 15.53, 17.9, 17.10, 20.6, 20.20, 23.4, 23.5, 42.6, 42.8, 50.85, 61.26, 71.67, 71.68, 74.5, 77.32, 77.51, 85.4**

[For commentary on a specific rule, please refer to the cross-references after the title of the rule.]

7.1 Where to Start Proceedings

Restrictions on where proceedings may be started are set out in the relevant practice directions supplementing this Part.

7.2 How to Start Proceedings

r.7.2 **12.5, 15.26**
r.7.2(1) **12.3, 12.5**
r.7.2(2) **PC 18, 12.5**

(1) Proceedings are started when the court issues a claim form at the request of the claimant.
(2) A claim form is issued on the date entered on the form by the court.

(A person who seeks a remedy from the court before proceedings are started or in relation to proceedings which are taking place, or will take place, in another jurisdiction must make an application under Part 23)

(Part 16 sets out what the claim form must include)

(The Costs Practice Direction [PD 43–48] sets out the information about a funding arrangement to be provided with the claim form where the claimant intends to seek to recover an additional liability)

('Funding arrangement' and 'additional liability' are defined in rule 43.2)

7.2A

Practice Direction 7A makes provision for procedures to be followed when claims are brought by or against a partnership within the jurisdiction.

7.3 Right to Use One Claim Form to Start Two or More Claims

r.7.3 **14.2, 16.34, 84.2**

A claimant may use a single claim form to start all claims which can be conveniently disposed of in the same proceedings.

7.4 Particulars of Claim

r.7.4 **14.2, 18.5, 24.1**
r.7.4(1) **PC 15, 14.2, 15.40, 24.1**
r.7.4(2) **PC 15, 14.2, 15.40**
r.7.4(3) **PC 15, 15.40**

(1) Particulars of claim must—
  (a) be contained in or served with the claim form; or
  (b) subject to paragraph (2) be served on the defendant by the claimant within 14 days after service of the claim form.
(2) Particulars of claim must be served on the defendant no later than the latest time for serving a claim form.

(Rule 7.5 sets out the latest time for serving a claim form)

CPR 1–25 & PDs

(3) Where the claimant serves particulars of claim separately from the claim form in accordance with paragraph (1)(b), the claimant must, within 7 days of service on the defendant, file a copy of the particulars except where—
   (a) paragraph 5.2(4) of Practice Direction 7C applies; or
   (b) paragraph 6.4 of Practice Direction 7E applies.

(Part 16 sets out what the particulars of claim must include)
(Part 22 requires particulars of claim to be verified by a statement of truth)

7.5 Service of a Claim Form

r.7.5 PC 5, PC 18, 13.6, 15.26, 15.27, 15.28, 15.29, 15.30, 15.32, 15.33, 15.34, 15.35, 15.36, 15.40, 16.2, 16.37
r.7.5(1) 15.36

(1) Where the claim form is served within the jurisdiction, the claimant must complete the step required by the following table in relation to the particular method of service chosen, before 12.00 midnight on the calendar day four months after the date of issue of the claim form.

Method of service	**Step required**
First class post, document exchange or other service which provides for delivery on the next business day	Posting, leaving with, delivering to or collection by the relevant service provider
Delivery of the document to or leaving it at the relevant place	Delivering to or leaving the document at the relevant place
Personal service under rule 6.5	Completing the relevant step required by rule 6.5(3)
Fax	Completing the transmission of the fax
Other electronic method	Sending the e-mail or other electronic transmission

(2) Where the claim form is to be served out of the jurisdiction, the claim form must be served in accordance with Section IV of Part 6 within 6 months of the date of issue.

7.6 Extension of Time for Serving a Claim Form

r.7.6 PC 10, 13.6, 14.2, 15.30, 15.32, 15.34, 15.35, 42.45, 72.4
r.7.6(2) 15.32, 15.33
r.7.6(3) 15.28, 15.32, 15.33, 15.34, 15.40, 16.44
r.7.6(3)(a) 15.6, 15.33
r.7.6(3)(b) 15.33
r.7.6(4) 15.33, 32.7
r.7.6(4)(a) 15.30
r.7.6(4)(b) PC 10, 15.30

(1) The claimant may apply for an order extending the period for compliance with rule 7.5.
(2) The general rule is that an application to extend the time for compliance with rule 7.5 must be made—
   (a) within the period specified by rule 7.5; or
   (b) where an order has been made under this rule, within the period for service specified by that order.
(3) If the claimant applies for an order to extend the time for compliance after the end of the period specified by rule 7.5 or by an order made under this rule, the court may make such an order only if—
   (a) the court has failed to serve the claim form; or
   (b) the claimant has taken all reasonable steps to comply with rule 7.5 but has been unable to do so; and
   (c) in either case, the claimant has acted promptly in making the application.
(4) An application for an order extending the time for compliance with rule 7.5—
   (a) must be supported by evidence; and
   (b) may be made without notice.

7.7 Application by Defendant for Service of Claim Form

r.7.7 14.64, 15.25

(1) Where a claim form has been issued against a defendant, but has not yet been served on him, the defendant may serve a notice on the claimant requiring him to serve the claim form or discontinue the claim within a period specified in the notice.

(2) The period specified in a notice served under paragraph (1) must be at least 14 days after service of the notice.

(3) If the claimant fails to comply with the notice, the court may, on the application of the defendant—
  (a) dismiss the claim; or
  (b) make any other order it thinks just.

7.8 Form for Defence etc. Must Be Served with Particulars of Claim

r.7.8 20.17
r.7.8(1) PC 3, PC 4, 15.4, 15.40, 17.6, 18.1
r.7.8(2) PC 5, 13.6, 15.4
r.7.8(2)(b) 18.1

(1) When particulars of claim are served on a defendant, whether they are contained in the claim form, served with it or served subsequently, they must be accompanied by—
  (a) a form for defending the claim;
  (b) a form for admitting the claim; and
  (c) a form for acknowledging service.

(2) Where the claimant is using the procedure set out in Part 8 (alternative procedure for claims)—
  (a) paragraph (1) does not apply; and
  (b) a form for acknowledging service must accompany the claim form.

7.9 Fixed Date and Other Claims

r.7.9 12.9, 70.3

A practice direction—

(a) may set out the circumstances in which the court may give a fixed date for a hearing when it issues a claim;

(b) may list claims in respect of which there is a specific claim form for use and set out the claim form in question; and

(c) may disapply or modify these Rules as appropriate in relation to the claims referred to in paragraphs (a) and (b).

7.10 Production Centre for Claims

r.7.10 42.6

(1) There shall be a Production Centre for the issue of claim forms and other related matters.

(2) Practice Direction 7C makes provision for—
  (a) which claimants may use the Production Centre;
  (b) the type of claims which the Production Centre may issue;
  (c) the functions which are to be discharged by the Production Centre;
  (d) the place where the Production Centre is to be located; and
  (e) other related matters.

(3) Practice Direction 7C may disapply or modify these Rules as appropriate in relation to claims issued by the Production Centre.

7.11 Human Rights

r.7.11 11.2
r.7.11(1) 91.10

(1) A claim under section 7(1)(a) of the Human Rights Act 1998 in respect of a judicial act may be brought only in the High Court.

(2) Any other claim under section 7(1)(a) of that Act may be brought in any court.

7.12 Electronic Issue of Claims

r.7.12 12.10

(1) A practice direction may make provision for a claimant to start a claim by requesting the issue of a claim form electronically.

(2) The practice direction may, in particular—
  (a) specify—
    (i) the types of claim which may be issued electronically; and
    (ii) the conditions which a claim must meet before it may be issued electronically;

(b) specify—
  (i) the court where the claim will be issued; and
  (ii) the circumstances in which the claim will be transferred to another court;
(c) provide for the filing of other documents electronically where a claim has been started electronically;
(d) specify the requirements that must be fulfilled for any document filed electronically; and
(e) provide how a fee payable on the filing of any document is to be paid where that document is filed electronically.

(3) The practice direction may disapply or modify these Rules as appropriate in relation to claims started electronically.

(Practice Direction 5C deals with electronic issue of claims started or continued under the Electronic Working scheme.)

PD 7A Practice Direction 7A — How to Start Proceedings — The Claim Form

This practice direction supplements CPR, Part 7.

[For commentary on a specific paragraph, please refer to the cross-references after the title of the paragraph.]

General

1 Subject to the following provisions of this practice direction, proceedings which both the High Court and the county courts have jurisdiction to deal with may be started in the High Court or in a county court.

Where to Start Proceedings

paras.2.1–2.4 11.4
para.2.5 11.6
para.2.6 11.2, 11.5
para.2.8 11.5
para.2.9 11.2

2.1 Proceedings (whether for damages or for a specified sum) may not be started in the High Court unless the value of the claim is more than £25,000.

2.2 Proceedings which include a claim for damages in respect of personal injuries must not be started in the High Court unless the value of the claim is £50,000 or more (art. 9 of the High Court and County Courts Jurisdiction Order 1991 (SI 1991/724 as amended) describes how the value of a claim is to be determined).

2.3 A claim must be issued in the High Court or a county court if an enactment so requires.

2.4 Subject to paras 2.1 and 2.2 above, a claim should be started in the High Court if by reason of:
(1) the financial value of the claim and the amount in dispute, and/or
(2) the complexity of the facts, legal issues, remedies or procedures involved, and/or
(3) the importance of the outcome of the claim to the public in general,
the claimant believes that the claim ought to be dealt with by a High Court judge.
(CPR, Part 30, and PD 30 contain provisions relating to the transfer to the county court of proceedings started in the High Court and vice versa.)

2.5 A claim relating to Chancery business (which includes any of the matters specified in the Senior Courts Act 1981, sch. 1, para. 1) may, subject to any enactment, rule or practice direction, be dealt with in the High Court or in a county court. The claim form should, if issued in the High Court, be marked in the top right-hand corner 'Chancery Division' and, if issued in the county court, be marked 'Chancery Business'. (For the equity jurisdiction of county courts, see the County Courts Act 1984, s. 23.)

2.6 A claim relating to any of the matters specified in the Senior Courts Act 1981, sch. 1, para. 2(a) and (b), must be dealt with in the High Court and will be assigned to the Queen's Bench Division.

2.7 Practice directions applying to particular types of proceedings, or to proceedings in particular courts, will contain provisions relating to the commencement and conduct of those proceedings.

2.8 A claim in the High Court for which a jury trial is directed will, if not already being dealt with in the Queen's Bench Division, be transferred to that Division.

2.9 The following proceedings may not be started in a county court unless the parties have agreed otherwise in writing:
(1) a claim for damages or other remedy for libel or slander, and
(2) a claim in which the title to any toll, fair, market or franchise is in question.

2.10 (1) The normal rules apply in deciding in which court and specialist list a claim that includes issues under the Human Rights Act 1998 should be started. They also apply in deciding which procedure to use to start the claim: Part 7, Part 8 or Part 54 (judicial review).
(2) The exception is a claim for damages in respect of a judicial act, which should be commenced in the High Court, If the claim is made in a notice of appeal then it will be dealt with according to the normal rules governing where that appeal is heard.
(A county court cannot make a declaration of incompatibility in accordance with s. 4 of the Human Rights Act 1998. Legislation may direct that such a claim is to be brought before a specified tribunal.)

CPR 1–25 & PDs

The Claim Form

para.3 **23.8**
para.3.5 **1.16, 23.19**
paras.3.8–3.9 **23.8**

3.1 A claimant must use form N1 or form N208 (the Part 8 claim form) to start a claim (but see paras 3.2 and 3.4 below).

3.2 Rule 7.9 deals with fixed date claims and r. 7.10 deals with the Production Centre for the issue of claims; there are separate practice directions supplementing rr. 7.9 and 7.10.

3.3 If a claimant wishes the claim to proceed under Part 8, or if the claim is required to proceed under Part 8, the claim form should so state. Otherwise the claim will proceed under Part 7. But note that in respect of claims in specialist proceedings (listed in Part 49) and claims brought under the RSC or CCR set out in the schedules to the CPR (see Part 50) the CPR will apply only to the extent that they are not inconsistent with the rules and practice directions that expressly apply to those claims.

3.4 Other practice directions may require special forms to be used to commence particular types of proceedings, or proceedings in particular courts.

3.5 Where a claim form to be served out of the jurisdiction is one which the court has power to deal with:
(a) under the Civil Jurisdiction and Judgments Act 1982; and
(b) the Judgments Regulation (which has the same meaning as in r. 6.31(d)),
the claim form must, pursuant to r. 6.34, be filed and served with the notice referred to in that rule and PD 6B, para. 2.1.

3.6 If a claim for damages or for an unspecified sum is started in the High Court, the claim form must:
(1) state that the claimant expects to recover more than £25,000 (or £50,000 or more if the claim is for personal injuries) or
(2) state that some enactment provides that the claim may only be commenced in the High Court and specify that enactment or
(3) state that the claim is to be in one of the specialist High Court lists (see CPR Parts 49 and 58 to 62) and specify that list.

3.7 If the contents of a claim form commencing specialist proceedings comply with the requirements of the specialist list in question the claim form will also satisfy para. 3.6 above.

3.8 If a claim for damages for personal injuries is started in the county court, the claim form must state whether or not the claimant expects to recover more than £1000 in respect of pain, suffering and loss of amenity.

3.9 If a claim for housing disrepair which includes a claim for an order requiring repairs or other work to be carried out by the landlord is started in the county court, the claim form must state:
(1) whether or not the cost of the repairs or other work is estimated to be more than £1000, and
(2) whether or not the claimant expects to recover more than £1000 in respect of any claim for damages.[1]

If either of the amounts mentioned in (1) and (2) is more than £1000, the small claims track will not be the normal track for that claim.

(PD 43–48, Section 19, contains details of the information required to be filed with a claim form to comply with r. 44.15 (providing information about funding arrangements).)

Title of Proceedings

para.4 **51.4**
para.4.1 **14.3, 24.9, 37.18**
para.4.1(3) **1.17**
para.4.2 **24.9**

4.1 The claim form and every other statement of case, must be headed with the title of the proceedings. The title should state:
(1) the number of proceedings,
(2) the court or division in which they are proceeding,
(3) the full name of each party,
(4) each party's status in the proceedings (i.e. claimant/defendant).

(PD 16, para. 2.6, sets out what is meant by a full name in respect of each type of claimant.)

[1] See rr. 16.3(4) and 26.6.

4.2 Where there is more than one claimant and/or more than one defendant, the parties should be described in the title as follows:

(1) AB
(2) CD
(3) EF *Claimants*

and

(1) GH
(2) IJ
(3) KL *Defendants*

Starting a Designated Money Claim

para.4A.1 **11.9, 23.5, 42.3**
para.4A.2 **11.9, 17.9, 17.10, 20.6, 20.20, 23 5**

4A.1 In all designated money claims, practice form N1 must be sent to: County Court Money Claims Centre, PO Box 527, M5 0BY. The claims will then be issued in Northampton County Court.

4A.2 In proceedings referred to in para. 4A.1, the claimant must specify the preferred court on practice form N1.

Start of Proceedings

para.5.1 **10.6, 12.5, 86.8**
para.5.2 **10.6, 12.5**
para.5.3 **10.6**
para.5.4 **10.6, 12.5**
para.5.5 **14.12**

5.1 Proceedings are started when the court issues a claim form at the request of the claimant (see rule 7.2) but where the claim form as issued was received in the court office on a date earlier than the date on which it was issued by the court, the claim is 'brought' for the purposes of the Limitation Act 1980 and any other relevant statute on that earlier date.

5.2 The date on which the claim form was received by the court will be recorded by a date stamp either on the claim form held on the court file or on the letter that accompanied the claim form when it was received by the court.

5.3 An enquiry as to the date on which the claim form was received by the court should be directed to a court officer.

5.4 Parties proposing to start a claim which is approaching the expiry of the limitation period should recognise the potential importance of establishing the date the claim form was received by the court and should themselves make arrangements to record the date.

5.5 Where it is sought to start proceedings against the estate of a deceased defendant where probate or letters of administration have not been granted, the claimant should issue the claim against 'the personal representatives of A.B. deceased'. The claimant should then, before the expiry of the period for service of the claim form, apply to the court for the appointment of a person to represent the estate of the deceased.

Claims by and against Partnerships within the Jurisdiction

para. 5A.1 **14.31, 15.50**
para. 5A.2 **14.31**
para.5A.3 **14.31, 15.50**

5A.1 Paragraphs 5A and 5B apply to claims that are brought by or against two or more persons who:

(1) were partners; and
(2) carried on that partnership business within the jurisdiction, at the time when the cause of action accrued.

5A.2 For the purposes of this paragraph, 'partners' includes persons claiming to be entitled as partners and persons alleged to be partners.

5A.3 Where that partnership has a name, unless it is inappropriate to do so, claims must be brought in or against the name under which that partnership carried on business at the time the cause of action accrued.

Partnership Membership Statements

para.5B **14.32**
para.5B.1 **15.50, 56.4**
para.5B.2 **14.32, 15.50**

5B.1 In this paragraph a 'partnership membership statement' is a written statement of the names and last known places of residence of all the persons who were partners in the partnership at the time when the cause of action accrued, being the date specified for this purpose in accordance with para. 5B.3.

5B.2 If the partners are requested to provide a copy of a partnership membership statement by any party to a claim, the partners must do so within 14 days of receipt of the request.

5B.3 In that request the party seeking a copy of a partnership membership statement must specify the date when the relevant cause of action accrued.

(Signing of the acknowledgment of service in the case of a partnership is dealt with in PD 10, para. 4.4.)

Persons Carrying on Business in Another Name

para.5C 14.34

5C.1 This paragraph applies where:
(1) a claim is brought against an individual;
(2) that individual carries on a business within the jurisdiction (even if not personally within the jurisdiction); and
(3) that business is carried on in a name other than that individual's own name ('the business name').

5C.2 The claim may be brought against the business name as if it were the name of a partnership.

Particulars of Claim

para.6.2 15.4

6.1 Where the claimant does not include the particulars of claim in the claim form, they may be served separately:
(1) either at the same time as the claim form, or
(2) within 14 days after service of the claim form[2] provided that the service of the particulars of claim is within four months after the date of issue of the claim form[3] (or six months where the claim form is to be served out of the jurisdiction).[4]

6.2 If the particulars of claim are not included in or have not been served with the claim form, the claim form must contain a statement that particulars of claim will follow.[5]

(These paragraphs do not apply where the Part 8 procedure is being used. For information on matters to be included in the claim form or the particulars of claim, see Part 16 (statements of case) and PD 16.)

Statement of Truth

7.1 Part 22 requires the claim form and, where they are not included in the claim form, the particulars of claim, to be verified by a statement of truth.

7.2 The form of the statement of truth is as follows:
'[I believe] [the claimant believes] that the facts stated in [this claim form] [these particulars of claim] are true.'

7.3 Attention is drawn to r. 32.14 which sets out the consequences of verifying a statement of case containing a false statement without an honest belief in its truth.

Extension of Time

para.8.2 PC 10, 15.30

8.1 An application under r. 7.6 (for an extension of time for serving a claim form under r. 7.6(1)) must be made in accordance with Part 23 and supported by evidence.

8.2 The evidence should state:
(1) all the circumstances relied on,
(2) the date of issue of the claim,
(3) the expiry date of any r. 7.6 extension, and
(4) a full explanation as to why the claim has not been served.

(For information regarding (1) written evidence see Part 32 and PD 32 and (2) service of the claim form see Part 6 and PD 6A and 6B.)

[2] See rr. 7.4(2) and 7.5(1).
[3] See rr. 7.4(2) and 7.5(2).
[4] See r. 7.5(2).
[5] See r. 16.2(2).

PD 7B Practice Direction 7B — Consumer Credit Act — Unfair Relationships

This practice direction supplements CPR, r. 7.9.

PD 7B 12.9, 24.1, 24.6, 70.3, 87.48 [For commentary on a specific paragraph, please refer to the cross-references after the title of the paragraph.]

1.1 In this practice direction 'the Act' means the Consumer Credit Act 1974, a section referred to by number means the section with that number in the Act, and expressions which are defined in the Act have the same meaning in this practice direction as they have in the Act.

1.2 'Consumer Credit Act procedure' means the procedure set out in this practice direction.

When to Use the Consumer Credit Act Procedure

2.1 A claimant must use the Consumer Credit Act procedure where he makes a claim under a provision of the Act to which paragraph 3 of this practice direction applies.

2.2 Where a claimant is using the Consumer Credit Act procedure the CPR are modified to the extent that they are inconsistent with the procedure set out in this practice direction.

2.3 The court may at any stage order the claim to continue as if the claimant had not used the Consumer Credit Act procedure, and if it does so the court may give any directions it considers appropriate.

2.4 This practice direction also sets out matters which must be included in the particulars of claim incertain types of claim, and restrictions on where certain types of claim may be started.

The Provisions of the Act

para.3 12.9

3.1 Subject to paragraph 3.2 and 3.3 this practice direction applies to claims made under the following provisions of the Act:
(1) section 141 (claim by the creditor to enforce regulated agreement relating to goods etc.),
(2) section 129 (claim by debtor or hirer for a time order),
(3) section 90 (creditor's claim for an order for recovery of protected goods),
(4) section 92(1) (creditor's or owner's claim to enter premises to take possession of goods),
(5) section 140B(2)(a) (debtor's or surety's application for an order relating to an unfair relationship);
(6) creditor's or owner's claim for a court order to enforce a regulated agreement relating to goods or money where the court order is required by—
(a) section 65(1) (improperly-executed agreement),
(b) section 86(2) (death of debtor or hirer where agreement is partly secured or unsecured),
(c) section 111(2) (default notice etc. not served on surety),
(d) section 124(1) or (2) (taking of a negotiable instrument in breach of terms of section 123), or
(e) section 105(7)(a) or (b) (security not expressed in writing, or improperly executed).

3.2 This practice direction does not apply to any claim made under the provisions listed in paragraph 3.1 above if that claim relates to the recovery of land.

3.3 This practice direction also does not apply to a claim made by the creditor under section 141 of the Act to enforce a regulated agreement where the agreement relates only to money. Such a claim must be started by the issue of a Part 7 claim form.

Restrictions on Where to Start Some Consumer Credit Act Claims

para.4 11.3

4.1 Where the claim includes a claim to recover goods to which a regulated hire purchase agreement or conditional sale agreements relates, it may only be started in the county court for the district in which the debtor, or one of the debtors:
(1) resides or carries on business, or

CPR 1–25 & PDs

(2) resided or carried on business at the date when the defendant last made a payment under the agreement.

4.2 In any other claim to recover goods, the claim may only be started in the court for the district:
(1) in which the defendant, or one of the defendants, resides or carries on business, or
(2) in which the goods are situated.

4.3 A claim of a debtor or hirer for an order under s. 129(1)(b) or (ba) of the Act (a time order) may only be started in the court where the claimant resides or carries on business.

(Rule 45.1(2)(b) allows the claimant to recover fixed costs in certain circumstances where such a claim is made.)

(Paragraph 7 sets out the matters the claimant must include in his particulars of claim where he is using the Consumer Credit Act procedure.)

The Consumer Credit Act Procedure

para. 5 **12.9** para.5.2 **24.1**

5.1 In the types of claim to which paragraph 3 applies the court will fix a hearing date on the issue of the claim form.

5.2 The particulars of claim must be served with the claim form.

5.3 Where a claimant is using the Consumer Credit Act procedure, the defendant to the claim is not required to:
(1) serve an acknowledgment of service, or
(2) file a defence, although he may choose to do so.

5.4 Where a defendant intends to defend a claim, his defence should be filed within 14 days of service of the particulars of claim. If the defendant fails to file a defence within this period, but later relies on it, the court may take such a failure into account as a factor when deciding what order to make about costs.

5.5 Part 12 (default judgment) does not apply where the claimant is using the Consumer Credit Act procedure.

5.6 Each party must be given at least 28 days' notice of the hearing date.

5.7 Where the claimant serves the claim form, he must serve notice of the hearing date at the same time, unless the hearing date is specified in the claim form.

Powers of the Court at the Hearing

6.1 On the hearing date the court may dispose of the claim.

6.2 If the court does not dispose of the claim on the hearing date:
(1) if the defendant has filed a defence, the court will:
(a) allocate the claim to a track and give directions about the management of the case, or
(b) give directions to enable it to allocate the claim to a track,
(2) if the defendant has not filed a defence, the court may make any order or give any direction it considers appropriate.

6.3 Rule 26.5(3) to (5) and rules 26.6 to 26.10 apply to the allocation of a claim under paragraph 6.2.

Matters Which Must Be Included in the Particulars of Claim

para.7 **24.6**

7.1 Where the Consumer Credit Act procedure is used, the claimant must state in his particulars of claim that the claim is a Consumer Credit Act claim.

7.2 A claimant making a claim for the delivery of goods to enforce a hire purchase agreement or conditional sale agreement which is:
(1) a regulated agreement for the recovery of goods, and
(2) let to a person other than a company or other corporation, must also state (in this order) in his particulars of claim:
(a) the date of the agreement,
(b) the parties to the agreement,
(c) the number or other identification of the agreement (with enough information to allow the debtor to identify the agreement),
(d) where the claimant was not one of the original parties to the agreement, the means by which the rights and duties of the creditor passed to him,

(e) the place where the agreement was signed by the defendant (if known),
(f) the goods claimed,
(g) the total price of the goods,
(h) the paid up sum,
(i) the unpaid balance of the total price,
(j) whether a default notice or a notice under section 76(1) or section 88(1) of the Act has been served on the defendant, and, if it has, the date and the method of service,
(k) the date on which the right to demand delivery of the goods accrued,
(l) the amount (if any) claimed as an alternative to the delivery of goods, and
(m) the amount (if any) claimed in addition to:
 (i) the delivery of the goods, or
 (ii) any claim under sub paragraph (l) above with the grounds of each such claim.

7.3 A claimant who is a debtor or hirer making a claim for an order under s. 129(1)(b) or (ba) of the Act (a time order) must state (in the following order) in the particulars of claim:
(1) the date of the agreement,
(2) the parties to the agreement,
(3) the number or other means of identifying the agreement,
(4) details of any sureties,
(5) if the defendant is not one of the original parties to the agreement then the name of the original party to the agreement,
(6) the names and addresses of the persons intended to be served with the claim form,
(7) the place where the claimant signed the agreement,
(8) details of the notice served by the creditor or owner giving rise to the claim for the time order,
(9) the total unpaid balance the claimant admits is due under the agreement, and:
 (a) the amount of any arrears (if known), and
 (b) the amount and frequency of the payments specified in the agreement,
(10) the claimant's proposals for payments of any arrears and of future instalments together with details of his means,
(11) where the claim relates to a breach of the agreement other than for the payment of money the claimant's proposals for remedying it.

7.3A A claimant who is a debtor or hirer making a claim for an order under s. 129(1)(ba) of the Act must attach to the particulars of claim a copy of the notice served on the creditor or owner under s. 129A(1)(a) of the Act.

7.4 (1) This paragraph applies where a claimant is required to obtain a court order to enforce a regulated agreement by:
(a) section 65(1) (improperly-executed agreement),
(b) section 105(7)(a) or (b) (security not expressed in writing, or improperly executed),
(c) section 111(2) (default notice etc. not served on surety),
(d) section 124(1) or (2) (taking of a negotiable instrument in breach of terms of section123), or
(e) section 86(2) of the Act (death of debtor or hirer where agreement is partly secured or unsecured).

(2) The claimant must state in his particulars of claim what the circumstances are that require him to obtain a court order for enforcement.

Admission of Certain Claims for Recovery of Goods under Regulated Agreements

8.1 In a claim to recover goods to which section 90(1)[1] applies:
(1) the defendant may admit the claim, and
(2) offer terms on which a return order should be suspended under section 135(1)(b).

[1] Section 90(1) provides that:
'At any time when—
(a) the debtor is in breach of a regulated hire-purchase or a regulated conditional sale agreement relating to goods, and
(b) the debtor has paid to the creditor one-third or more of the total price of the goods, and
(c) property in the goods remains in the creditor, the creditor is not entitled to recover possession of the goods from the debtor except on an order of the court.'

8.2 He may do so by filing a request in form N9C.

8.3 He should do so within the period for making an admission specified in rule 14.2(b). If the defendant fails to file his request within this period, and later makes such a request, the court may take the failure into account as a factor when deciding what order to make about costs.

8.4 On receipt of the admission, the court will serve a copy on the claimant.

8.5 The claimant may obtain judgment by filing a request in form **N228**.

8.6 On receipt of the request for judgment, the court will enter judgment in the terms of the defendant's admission and offer and for costs.

8.7 If:

(1) the claimant does not accept the defendant's admission and offer, and

(2) the defendant does not appear on the hearing date fixed when the claim form was issued,

the court may treat the defendant's admission and offer as evidence of the facts stated in it for the purposes of sections 129(2)(a)[2] and 135(2).[3]

Additional Requirements about Parties to the Proceedings

9.1 The court may dispense with the requirement in section 141(5) (all parties to a regulated and any surety to be parties to any proceedings) in any claim relating to the regulated agreement agreement, if:

(1) the claim form has not been served on the debtor or the surety, and

(2) the claimant either before or at the hearing makes an application (which may be made without notice) for the court to make such an order.

9.2 In a claim relating to a regulated agreement where:

(1) the claimant was not one of the original parties to the agreement, and

(2) the former creditor's rights and duties under the agreement have passed to him by:

(a) operation of law, or

(b) assignment,

the requirement of section 141(5) (all parties to a regulated agreement and any surety to be parties to any proceedings) does not apply to the former creditor, unless the court otherwise orders.

9.3 Where a claimant who is a creditor or owner makes a claim for a court order under section 86(2) (death of debtor or hirer where agreement is partly secured or unsecured) the personal representatives of the deceased debtor or hirer must be parties to the proceedings in which the order is sought, unless no grant of representation has been made to the estate.

9.4 Where no grant of representation has been made to the estate of the deceased debtor or hirer, the claimant must make an application in accordance with Part 23 for directions about which persons (if any) are to be made parties to the claim as being affected or likely to be affected by the enforcement of the agreement.

9.5 The claimant's application under paragraph 9.4:

(a) may be made without notice, and

(b) should be made before the claim form is issued.

Notice to Be Given to Reopen a Consumer Credit Agreement

para.10 **90.29**

10.1 Paragraph 10.2 applies where:

(1) a debtor or any surety intends to seek an order relating to an unfair relationship between a creditor and that debtor, arising out of a credit agreement (taken together with any related agreement);

---

[2] Section 129(2) provides that:

'A time order shall provide for one or both of the following, as the court considers just—

(a) payment by the debtor or hirer or any surety of any sum owed under a regulated agreement or a security by such instalments, payable at such times, as the court, having regard to the means of the debtor or hirer and any surety, considers reasonable;

(b) remedying by the debtor or hirer of any breach of a regulated agreement (other than non-payment of money) within *such period as the court may specify.*'

[3] Section 135(2) provides that:

'The court shall not suspend the operation of a term [in an order relating to a regulated agreement] requiring the delivery up of goods by any person unless satisfied that the goods are in his possession or control.'

(2) a claim relating to that agreement or any related agreement has already begun; and
(3) section 140B(2)(b) or section 140B(2)(c) applies.

10.2 The debtor or surety must serve written notice of intention on the court and every other party to the claim within 14 days of service of the claim form.

10.3 A debtor or surety (as the case may be) who serves a notice under para. 10.2 will be treated as having filed a defence for the purposes of the Consumer Credit Act procedure.

PD 7C Practice Direction 7C — Production Centre

This practice direction supplements CPR, r. 7.10.

PD 7C **12.8**, **42.6**, **42.13** [For commentary on a specific paragraph, please refer to the cross-references after the title of the paragraph.]

General

para.1.3(2)(e)–(f) **12.8**
para.1.4(1)**12.8**
para.1.4(3A) **12.8**, **24.3**

1.1 In this Practice Direction—
'the Centre' means the Production Centre;
'Centre user' means a person who is for the time being permitted to start a claim through the Centre, and includes a legal representative acting for such a person;
'officer' means the court officer in charge of the Centre or another officer of the Centre acting on the former's behalf;
'national creditor code' means the number or reference allotted to a Centre user by the officer;
'Code of Practice' means any code of practice which may at any time be issued by Her Majesty's Courts and Tribunals Service relating to the discharge by the Centre of its functions and the way in which a Centre user is to conduct business with the Centre; and
'data' means any information which is required to be given to the court or which is to be contained in any document to be sent to the court or to any party.

1.2 For any purpose connected with the exercise of its functions, the Centre will be treated as part of the office of the court whose name appears on the claim form to which the functions relate, or in whose name the claim form is requested to be issued, and the officer will be treated as an officer of that court.

1.3 (1) The functions of the Centre include the provision of a facility which, through the use of information technology, enables a Centre user to have claim forms issued and served, whether or not those claim forms are to be treated as issued in the Northampton County Court or in another county court.

(2) If a Centre user files claim forms in the name of Northampton County Court, the functions of the Centre also include—
(a) the handling of defences and admissions;
(b) the entry of judgment in default, on admission, on acceptance, or on determination;
(c) the registration of judgments;
(d) the issue of warrants of execution;
(e) where the defendant is an individual, the transfer to the defendant's home court of any case that is to continue following the filing of a defence or where a hearing is required before judgment; or, where the defendant is not an individual, the transfer to the court for the area of the claimant's, or where legally represented, the claimant's legal representative's address; and
(f) the transfer to the defendant's home court of any case for the questioning of the defendant pursuant to an order for information under Part 71 or where enforcement of a judgment (other than by warrant of execution, charging order or third party debt order) is to follow.

1.4 (1) Where the officer is to take any step, any rule or practice direction which requires a document to be filed before such step is taken will be treated as complied with if the data which that document would contain are delivered to the Centre in computer readable form in accordance with the Code of Practice.

(2) Data relating to more than one case may be included in a single document or delivery of data.

(3) Rules 6.4(3) and 6.21(4) (copies of documents to be served by the court) do not apply to any document which is to be produced by electronic means from data supplied by a Centre user.

(3A) The requirement in PD 16, para. 7.3 (statements of case), for documents to be attached to the particulars of contract claims does not apply to claims to be issued by the Centre, unless the particulars of claim are served separately in accordance with para. 5.2 of this practice direction.
(4) PD 22 (statements of truth) is modified as follows—
(a) a single statement of truth may accompany each batch of requests to issue claim forms and may be in electronic form;
(b) the form of such a statement must be: 'I believe that the facts stated in the attached claim forms are true.'; and
(c) the signature of the appropriate person (as to which see PD 22, para. 3) may be in electronic form.

Claims Which May Not Be Issued through the Centre

2.1 The Centre will not issue any claim form which is to be issued in the High Court.
2.2 The Centre will only issue a claim form if the claim is for a specified sum of money less than £100,000.
2.3 The Centre will not issue any of the following types of claim—
(1) a claim against more than two defendants;
(2) a claim against two defendants where a different sum is claimed against each of them;
(3) a claim against the Crown;
(4) a claim for an amount in a foreign currency;
(5) a claim where either party is known to be a child or protected party within Part 21;
(6) a claim where the claimant is a legally assisted person within the meaning of the Legal Aid Act 1988;
(7) a claim where the claimant's address for service as it appears on the claim form is not in the United Kingdom;
(7A) a claim where the defendant's address for service as it appears on the claim form is not in England and Wales;
(8) a claim which is to be issued under Part 8.

Centre Users

3.1 Only a Centre user may start or conduct claims through the Centre.
3.2 The officer may permit any person to be a Centre user.
3.3 The officer may withdraw the permission for any person to be a Centre user.
3.4 A Centre user must comply with the provisions of the Code of Practice in dealing with the Centre.
3.5 The officer will allot a national creditor code to each Centre user.

The Code of Practice

4.1 The Code of Practice will contain provisions designed to ensure that the Centre can discharge its functions efficiently, and it may in particular provide for—
(1) the forms of magnetic media that may be used;
(2) the circumstances in which data may or must be supplied in magnetic form;
(3) the circumstances in which data may or must be supplied in a document and the form that such a document must take;
(4) how often data may be supplied;
(5) the numbering of cases and data relating to cases;
(6) data to be given to the Centre by the Centre user about cases which have been settled or paid or are otherwise not proceeding; and
(7) accounting arrangements and the method of payment of fees.
4.2 Her Majesty's Courts and Tribunals Service may change the Code of Practice from time to time.

Other Modifications to the Civil Procedure Rules

para.5.2 12.8, 24.3
para.5.2(1) 23.6, 24.1
para.5.3 12.8

Powers of the officer to make orders

5.1 The officer may make the following orders—

(1) an order to set aside a default judgment where, after that judgment has been entered, the claim form is returned by the Post Office as undelivered;

(2) an order to set aside a judgment on application by a Centre user;

(3) an order to transfer a case to another county court for enforcement or for a judgment debtor to attend court for questioning pursuant to an order for information under Part 71.

Filing separate particulars of claim

5.2 (1) Subject to the sub-paragraphs below, the claimant may serve and file particulars of claim separately from the claim form but the claimant must in the claim form—

(a) state that the particulars of claim will follow; and

(b) include a brief summary of the claim.

(2) Where the claimant serves the particulars of claim separately from the claim form pursuant to sub-para. (1), the claimant must—

(a) serve the particulars of claim in accordance with r. 7.4(1)(b); and

(b) file a certificate of service in form N215 at the Centre within 14 days of service of the particulars of claim on the defendant.

(3) The claimant must file the particulars of claim at the court to which the proceedings are transferred under para. 1.3(2)(e) within seven days of service of the notice of transfer.

(4) Where the proceedings are not transferred under para. 1.3(2)(e) and remain at the Centre, the claimant is not required to file the particulars of claim unless ordered to do so.

Procedure on the filing of a defence

5.3 (1) This paragraph applies where a Centre user has started a claim in the Northampton County Court and the defendant has filed a defence to the claim or to part of the claim.

(2) On the filing of the defence the officer will serve a notice on the Centre user requiring the Centre user to state within 28 days whether the claim is to proceed.

(3) If the Centre user does not notify the officer within the time specified in the notice that the claim is to proceed, the claim will be stayed, and the officer will notify the parties accordingly.

(4) The proceedings will not be transferred as provided by para. 1.3(2)(e) until the Centre user notifies the officer that the claim is to continue.

PD 7D Practice Direction 7D — Claims for the Recovery of Taxes and Duties

This practice direction supplements CPR, r. 7.9.

Scope

1.1 This practice direction applies to claims by HM Revenue and Customs for the recovery of:
- (a) income tax,
- (b) corporation tax,
- (c) capital gains tax,
- (d) interest, penalties and surcharges on income tax, corporation tax or capital gains tax which by virtue of the Taxes Management Act 1970, s. 69, are to be treated as if they are taxes due and payable,
- (e) national insurance contributions and interest, penalties and surcharges thereon,
- (f) student loan repayments deducted by and recoverable from an employer under the Education (Student Loans) (Repayment) Regulations 2000 (SI 2000/944), part 4,
- (g) value added tax and interest and surcharges thereon,
- (h) insurance premium tax and interest and penalties thereon,
- (i) stamp duty land tax and interest and penalties thereon,
- (j) the following environmental taxes—
  - (i) landfill tax and interest and penalties thereon,
  - (ii) aggregates levy and interest and penalties thereon, and
  - (iii) climate change levy and interest and penalties thereon,
- (k) the following duties of customs and excise—
  - (i) amusement machine licence duty and penalties thereon,
  - (ii) air passenger duty and interest and penalties thereon,
  - (iii) beer duty and penalties thereon,
  - (iv) bingo duty and penalties thereon,
  - (v) cider and perry duty,
  - (vi) excise and spirits duty,
  - (vii) excise wine duty,
  - (viii) gaming duty and penalties thereon,
  - (ix) general betting duty,
  - (x) lottery duty and penalties thereon,
  - (xi) REDS (registered excise dealers and shippers) duty,
  - (xii) road fuel duty and penalties thereon,
  - (xiii) tobacco duty, and
  - (xiv) wine and made-wine duty.

Procedure

2.1 If a defence is filed, the court will fix a date for the hearing.

2.2 Part 26 (case management — preliminary stage) with the exception of rr. 26.2 and 26.2A does not apply to claims to which this practice direction applies.

At the Hearing

3.1 On the hearing date the court may dispose of the claim.
(The Commissioners for Revenue and Customs Act 2005 ('the 2005 Act'), provides that a certificate of an officer of Revenue and Customs that, to the best of that officer's knowledge and belief, a sum payable to the Commissioners under or by virtue of an enactment or by virtue of a contract settlement (within the meaning of s. 25(6) of the 2005 Act) has not been paid is sufficient evidence that the sum mentioned in the certificate is unpaid.)

3.2 But exceptionally, if the court does not dispose of the claim on the hearing date it may give case management directions, which may, if the defendant has filed a defence, include allocating the case.

CPR 1–25 & PDs

PD 7E Practice Direction 7E — Money Claim Online

This practice direction supplements CPR, Part 7.

PD 7E 15.55 [For commentary on a specific paragraph, please refer to the cross-references after the title of the paragraph.]

General

para.1.2(1)–(2) **12.10** para.1.4 **12.10**

1.1 This practice direction provides for a scheme in which, in the circumstances set out in this practice direction, a request for a claim form to be issued and other specified documents may be filed electronically ('Money Claim Online').

1.2 This practice direction enables claimants—
- (1) to start certain types of county court claims by requesting the issue of a claim form electronically via Her Majesty's Courts and Tribunals Service website; and
- (2) where a claim has been started electronically—
  - (a) to file electronically a request for—
    - (i) judgment in default;
    - (ii) judgment on acceptance of an admission of the whole of the amount claimed; or
    - (iii) the issue of a warrant of execution; and
  - (b) to view an electronic record of the progress of the claim.

1.3 This practice direction also enables defendants—
- (1) to file electronically—
  - (a) an acknowledgment of service;
  - (b) a part admission;
  - (c) a defence; or
  - (d) a counterclaim (if filed together with a defence); and
- (2) to view an electronic record of the progress of the claim.

1.4 Claims started using Money Claim Online will be issued by Northampton County Court and will proceed in that court unless they are transferred to another court. The address for filing any document, application or request (other than one which is filed electronically in accordance with this practice direction) is Northampton County Court, St Katharine's House, 21–27 St Katharine's Street, Northampton NN1 2LH, DX 702885 Northampton 7, fax 0845 6015889.

Security

2. Her Majesty's Courts and Tribunals Service will take such measures as it thinks fit to ensure the security of steps taken or information stored electronically. These may include requiring users of Money Claim Online—
- (1) to enter a customer identification and password;
- (2) to provide personal information for identification purposes; and
- (3) to comply with any other security measures,

before taking any of the steps mentioned in para. 1.2 or 1.3.

Fees

3.1 Where this practice direction provides for a fee to be paid electronically, it may be paid by—
- (1) credit card;
- (2) debit card; or
- (3) any other method which Her Majesty's Courts and Tribunals Service may permit.

3.2 A step may only be taken using Money Claim Online on payment of the prescribed fee. The Civil Proceedings Fees Order 2008 (SI 2008/1053) provides that a party may, in certain circumstances, be entitled to a remission or part remission of a fee prescribed by that Order. Her Majesty's Courts and Tribunals Service website contains guidance as to when this entitlement might arise.

3.3 A claimant who wishes to apply for a remission or part remission of fees must not use Money Claim Online and must file the claim form at a court office.

Types of Claims Which May Be Started Using Money Claim Online

para.4 12.10

4. A claim may be started using Money Claim Online if it meets all the following conditions—
(1) the only remedy claimed is a specified amount of money—
(a) less than £100,000 (excluding any interest or costs claimed); and
(b) in sterling;
(2) the procedure under Part 7 is used;
(3) the claimant is not—
(a) a child or protected party; or
(b) funded by the Legal Services Commission;
(3A) the claimant's address for service is within the United Kingdom;
(4) the claim is against—
(a) a single defendant; or
(b) two defendants, if the claim is for a single amount against each of them;
(5) the defendant is not—
(a) the Crown; or
(b) a person known to be a child or protected party; and
(6) the defendant's address for service is within England and Wales.
('Protected party' has the same meaning as in r. 21.1(2).)

Starting a Claim

para.5.1 12.10
para.5.2 12.10
para.5.2(1) 24.1
para.5.2(2) 23.6, 24.1, 24.3
paras.5.4–5.5 12.10
para.5.7 12.10

5.1 A claimant may request the issue of a claim form by—
(1) completing and sending an online claim form; and
(2) electronically paying the appropriate issue fee,
via Her Majesty's Courts and Tribunals Service website.

5.2 Detailed particulars of claim must either be—
(1) included in the online claim form but must be limited in size to not more than 1080 characters (including spaces); or
(2) served and filed by the claimant separately from the claim form in accordance with para. 6 but the claimant must—
(a) state that detailed particulars of claim will follow; and
(b) include a brief summary of the claim,
in the online claim form in the section headed 'particulars of claim'.

5.2A The requirement in PD 16, para. 7.3 (statements of case), for documents to be attached to particulars of contract claims does not apply to the claims started using an online claim form, unless the particulars of claim are served separately in accordance with para. 5.2 of this practice direction.

5.3 When an online claim form is received by the Money Claim Online website, an acknowledgment of receipt will automatically be sent to the claimant. The acknowledgment of receipt does not constitute a notice that the claim form has been issued.

5.4 When the court issues a claim form following the submission of an online claim form, the claim is 'brought' for the purposes of the Limitation Act 1980 and any other enactment on the date on which the online claim form is received by the court's computer system. The court will keep a record, by electronic or other means, of when online claim forms are received.

5.5 When the court issues a claim form, it will—
(1) serve a printed version of the claim form on the defendant; and
(2) send the claimant notice of issue.

5.6 The claim form will have printed on it a unique customer identification number or a password by which the defendant may access details of the claim on Her Majesty's Courts and Tribunals Service website.

5.7 The claim form will be deemed to be served on the fifth day after the claim was issued irrespective of whether that day is a business day or not. 'Business day' has the same meaning as in r. 6.2(b).

Particulars of Claim and Certificate of Service

para.6.1 **12.10**

6.1. Where the particulars of claim are served by the claimant separately from the claim form pursuant to para. 5.2(2), the claimant must—
(1) serve the particulars of claim in accordance with r. 7.4(1)(b); and
(2) file a certificate of service in form N215 at Northampton County Court within 14 days of service of the particulars of claim on the defendant.

6.2 The certificate of service may be filed at the court by sending form N215 by email to mcolaos@hmcourts-service.gsi.gov.uk. However, the subject line to the email must contain the claim number.

6.3 The claimant must file the particulars of claim at the court to which the proceedings are transferred under para. 12.1 or 12.2 within seven days of service of the notice of transfer by the court.

6.4 Where the proceedings are not transferred under para. 12.1 or 12.2 and remain at Northampton County Court, the claimant is not required to file the particulars of claim at that court unless ordered to do so.

Online Response

7.1 A defendant wishing to file—
(1) an acknowledgment of service of the claim form under Part 10;
(2) a part admission under r. 14.5;
(3) a defence under Part 15; or
(4) a counterclaim (to be filed together with a defence),
may, instead of filing a written form, do so by completing and sending the relevant online form at <www.hmcourts-service.gov.uk/onlineservices/mcol>.

7.2 Where a defendant files an online form—
(1) a hard copy must not be sent in addition;
(2) the form is not filed until it is received by the court, whatever time it is shown to have been sent;
(3) an online form received after 4 p.m. will be treated as filed on the next day the court office is open; and
(4) where a time limit applies, it remains the responsibility of the defendant to ensure that the online form is filed in time.

Counterclaim

8 Where a counterclaim is filed using an online form, any fee payable must be paid to the court to which the claim is transferred under para. 12.1 or 12.2.

Statement of Truth

9.1 Part 22 requires any statement of case to be verified by a statement of truth. This applies to all online forms.

9.2 The statement of truth in an online statement of case must be in the form—
'[I believe][The claimant believes] that the facts stated in this claim form are true.'; or
'[I believe][The defendant believes] that the facts stated in this defence are true.', as appropriate.

9.3 Attention is drawn to—
(1) PD 22, para. 3, which provides who may sign a statement of truth; and
(2) r. 32.14, which sets out the consequences of making, or causing to be made, a false statement in a document verified by a statement of truth, without an honest belief in its truth.

Signature

10 Any provision of the CPR which requires a document to be signed by any person is satisfied by that person entering their name on an online form.

Request for Judgment or Issue of Warrant

11.1 If, in a claim started using Money Claim Online—
(1) the claimant wishes to apply for judgment in default in accordance with Part 12; or

(2) the defendant has filed or served an admission of the whole of the claim in accordance with r. 14.4,

the claimant may request judgment to be entered in default or on the admission (as the case may be) by completing and sending an online request form at <www.hmcourts-service.gov.uk/onlineservices/mcol>.

11.2 Where—

(1) judgment has been entered following a request under para. 11.1; and

(2) the claimant is entitled to the issue of a warrant of execution without requiring the permission of the court, the claimant may request the issue of a warrant of execution by—

(a) completing and sending an online request form; and

(b) electronically paying the appropriate fee,

at <www.hmcourts-service.gov.uk/onlineservices/mcol>.

(CCR, ord. 26 in CPR, sch. 1, contains rules about warrants of execution. Among other matters, CCR, ord. 26, r. 1, contains restrictions on when a warrant of execution may be issued if the court has made an order for payment of a sum of money by instalments, and CCR, ord. 26, r. 5, sets out certain circumstances in which a warrant of execution may not be issued without the permission of the court.)

11.3 A request under para. 11.1 or 11.2 will be treated as being filed—

(1) on the day the court receives the request, if it receives it before 9 a.m. on a working day (which is any day on which the court is open); and

(2) otherwise, on the next working day after the court receives the request.

Transfer of Claim

para.12 12.10

12.1 Where the defendant is an individual and Northampton County Court is not their home court, the court will transfer the claim to the defendant's home court—

(1) under r. 13.4, if the defendant applies to set aside or vary judgment;

(2) under r. 14.12, if there is to be a hearing for a judge to determine the time and rate of payment;

(3) under r. 26.2, if a defence is filed to all or part of the claim; or

(4) if either party makes an application which cannot be dealt with without a hearing.

12.2 Where the defendant is not an individual, if—

(1) the claimant's address for service on the claim form is not within the district of Northampton County Court; and

(2) one of the events mentioned in para. 12.1 arises,

the court will transfer the claim to the county court for the district in which the claimant's address for service on the claim form is situated.

Viewing the Case Record

para.13 2.10

13.1 A facility will be provided for parties or their legal representatives to view an electronic record of the status of claims started using Money Claim Online.

13.2 The record of each claim will be reviewed and, if necessary, updated at least once each day until the claim is transferred from Northampton County Court.

CPR Part 8 Alternative Procedure for Claims

Part 8 **1.32, 8.48, 11.7, 12.1, 13.1, 13.2, 13.4, 13.5, 13.6, 13.10, 13.14, 14.22, 15.4, 15.30, 15.58, 18.3, 23.4, 34.20, 42.11, 42.17, 42.20, 42.25, 44.3, 50.68, 50.85, 61.26, 68.51, 71.20, 71.23, 71.68, 72.2, 72.18, 73.14, 74.4, 79.27, 85.4, 86.10, 86.13, 86.38, 86.39, 88.37**

[For commentary on a specific rule, please refer to the cross-references after the title of the rule.]

8.1 Types of Claim in Which Part 8 Procedure May Be Followed

r.8.1(2) **13.1**
r.8.1(2)(a) **13.2**
r.8.1(3) **13.2, 13.12, 42.25, 86.10**
r.8.1(5) **PC 5, 13.9**
r.8.1(6) **13.1**

(1) The Part 8 procedure is the procedure set out in this Part.
(2) A claimant may use the Part 8 procedure where—
   (a) he seeks the court's decision on a question which is unlikely to involve a substantial dispute of fact; or
   (b) paragraph (6) applies.
(3) The court may at any stage order the claim to continue as if the claimant had not used the Part 8 procedure and, if it does so, the court may give any directions it considers appropriate.
(4) Paragraph (2) does not apply if a practice direction provides that the Part 8 procedure may not be used in relation to the type of claim in question.
(5) Where the claimant uses the Part 8 procedure he may not obtain default judgment under Part 12.
(6) A rule or practice direction may, in relation to a specified type of proceedings—
   (a) require or permit the use of the Part 8 procedure; and
   (b) disapply or modify any of the rules set out in this Part as they apply to those proceedings.

(Rule 8.9 provides for other modifications to the general rules where the Part 8 procedure is being used)

(Part 78 provides procedures for European orders for payment and for the European small claims procedure. It also provides procedures for applications for mediation settlement enforcement orders in relation to certain cross-border disputes.)

8.2 Contents of the Claim Form

r.8.2 **8.48, 13.7, 86.10, 88.43**

Where the claimant uses the Part 8 procedure the claim form must state—
(a) that this Part applies;
(b) (i) the question which the claimant wants the court to decide; or
   (ii) the remedy which the claimant is seeking and the legal basis for the claim to that remedy;
(c) if the claim is being made under an enactment, what that enactment is;
(d) if the claimant is claiming in a representative capacity, what that capacity is; and
(e) if the defendant is sued in a representative capacity, what that capacity is.

(Part 22 provides for the claim form to be verified by a statement of truth)
(Rule 7.5 provides for service of the claim form)
(The Costs Practice Direction [PD 43–48] sets out the information about a funding arrangement to be provided with the claim form where the claimant intends to seek to recover an additional liability)
('Funding arrangement' and 'additional liability' are defined in rule 43.2)

8.2A Issue of Claim Form without Naming Defendants

r.8.2A 13.7

(1) A practice direction may set out the circumstances in which a claim form may be issued under this Part without naming a defendant.
(2) The practice direction may set out those cases in which an application for permission must be made by application notice before the claim form is issued.
(3) The application notice for permission–
  (a) need not be served on any other person; and
  (b) must be accompanied by a copy of the claim form that the applicant proposes to issue.
(4) Where the court gives permission it will give directions about the future management of the claim.

8.3 Acknowledgment of Service

r.8.3 13.8, 18.1, 88.7, 88.43
r.8.3(1) PC 5, 13.8
r.8.3(2) 86.13
r.8.3(2)(a)–(b) 13.8

(1) The defendant must–
  (a) file an acknowledgment of service in the relevant practice form not more than 14 days after service of the claim form; and
  (b) serve the acknowledgment of service on the claimant and any other party.
(2) The acknowledgment of service must state—
  (a) whether the defendant contests the claim; and
  (b) if the defendant seeks a different remedy from that set out in the claim form, what that remedy is.
(3) The following rules of Part 10 (acknowledgment of service) apply—
  (a) rule 10.3(2) (exceptions to the period for filing an acknowledgment of service); and
  (b) rule 10.5 (contents of acknowledgment of service).

(The Costs Practice Direction [PD 43–48] sets out the information about a funding arrangement to be provided with the acknowledgment of service where the defendant intends to seek to recover an additional liability)
('Funding arrangement' and 'additional liability' are defined in rule 43.2)

8.4 Consequence of Not Filing an Acknowledgment of Service

r.8.4 PC 5, 8.48, 13.9, 88.7

(1) This rule applies where—
  (a) the defendant has failed to file an acknowledgment of service; and
  (b) the time period for doing so has expired.
(2) The defendant may attend the hearing of the claim but may not take part in the hearing unless the court gives permission.

8.5 Filing and Serving Written Evidence

r.8.5 13.10, 13.15, 71.20
r.8.5(1) PC 5, 13.7, 15.4
r.8.5(2) 13.7, 15.4, 88.7
r.8.5(3) PC 5, 13.10, 71.68
r.8.5(4) PC 5, 13.10
r.8.5(5) PC 5, 13.13
r.8.5(6) PC 5, 13.13

(1) The claimant must file any written evidence on which he intends to rely when he files his claim form.
(2) The claimant's evidence must be served on the defendant with the claim form.
(3) A defendant who wishes to rely on written evidence must file it when he files his acknowledgment of service.
(4) If he does so, he must also, at the same time, serve a copy of his evidence on the other parties.
(5) The claimant may, within 14 days of service of the defendant's evidence on him, file further written evidence in reply.
(6) If he does so, he must also, within the same time limit, serve a copy of his evidence on the other parties.
(7) The claimant may rely on the matters set out in his claim form as evidence under this rule if the claim form is verified by a statement of truth.

8.6 Evidence — General

r.8.6(1) 13.13
r.8.6(1)(b) 13.10, 13.13, 13.15
r.8.6(2) 13.15
r.8.6(3) 13.15

(1) No written evidence may be relied on at the hearing of the claim unless—
  (a) it has been served in accordance with rule 8.5; or
  (b) the court gives permission.
(2) The court may require or permit a party to give oral evidence at the hearing.
(3) The court may give directions requiring the attendance for cross-examination[(GL)] of a witness who has given written evidence.

(Rule 32.1 contains a general power for the court to control evidence)

8.7 Part 20 Claims

r.8.7 13.16

Where the Part 8 procedure is used, Part 20 (counterclaims and other additional claims) applies except that a party may not make a Part 20 claim (as defined by rule 20.2) without the court's permission.

8.8 Procedure Where Defendant Objects to Use of the Part 8 Procedure

r.8.8 88.7
r.8.8(1) PC 5, 13.12
r.8.8(2) 13.12, 42.25

(1) Where the defendant contends that the Part 8 procedure should not be used because—
  (a) there is a substantial dispute of fact; and
  (b) the use of the Part 8 procedure is not required or permitted by a rule or practice direction,

he must state his reasons when he files his acknowledgment of service.

(Rule 8.5 requires a defendant who wishes to rely on written evidence to file it when he files his acknowledgment of service)

(2) When the court receives the acknowledgment of service and any written evidence it will give directions as to the future management of the case.

(Rule 8.1 (3) allows the court to make an order that the claim continue as if the claimant had not used the Part 8 procedure)

8.9 Modifications to the General Rules

r.8.9(a) 8.48
r.8.9(a)(i) 13.1, 13.7, 24.1
r.8.9(a)(ii) 13.1, 13.8
r.8.9(a)(iv) 13.6
r.8.9(b) 8.48
r.8.9(b)(i) 13.8
r.8.9(b)(ii) PC 5, 13.6
r.8.9(c) PC 5, 13.1, 13.14, 42.25, 61.26, 74.7

Where the Part 8 procedure is followed—
(a) provision is made in this Part for the matters which must be stated in the claim form and the defendant is not required to file a defence and therefore—
  (i) Part 16 (statements of case) does not apply;
  (ii) Part 15 (defence and reply) does not apply;
  (iii) any time limit in these Rules which prevents the parties from taking a step before a defence is filed does not apply;
  (iv) the requirement under rule 7.8 to serve on the defendant a form for defending the claim does not apply;
(b) the claimant may not obtain judgment by request on an admission and therefore—
  (i) rules 14.4 to 14.7 do not apply; and
  (ii) the requirement under rule 7.8 to serve on the defendant a form for admitting the claim does not apply; and
(c) the claim shall be treated as allocated to the multi-track and therefore Part 26 does not apply.

PD 8A Practice Direction 8A — Alternative Procedure for Claims

This practice direction supplements CPR, Part 8 and sch. 1 and sch. 2.

[For commentary on a specific paragraph, please refer to the cross-references after the title of the paragraph]

Terminology

1.1 In this Practice Direction, 'schedule rules' means provisions contained in the schedules to the CPR, which were previously contained in the Rules of the Supreme Court (1965) or the County Court Rules (1981).

Application of This Practice Direction

para.2.2 PC 5

2.1 Section A contains general provisions about claims and applications to which Part 8 applies. Section B comprises a table listing claims, petitions and applications under various enactments which must be made under Part 8. Section C contains certain additions and modifications to the Part 8 procedure that apply to the particular claims and applications identified.

2.2 Some of the claims and applications listed in the table in Section B are dealt with in the schedule rules in the CPR. The table in Section B contains cross-reference to the relevant schedule rules.

SECTION A
GENERAL PROVISIONS APPLICABLE TO PART 8 CLAIMS

Types of Claim in Which the Part 8 Procedure May Be Used

para.3.1 13.1, 13.2, 14.22, 66.4
para.3.2 13.1, 13.2, 13.8
para.3.3 13.1, 13.2
para.3.4 13.2

3.1 The types of claim for which the Part 8 procedure may be used include:

(1) a claim by or against a child or protected party, as defined in r. 21.1(2), which has been settled before the commencement of proceedings and the sole purpose of the claim is to obtain the approval of the court to the settlement; or

(2) a claim for provisional damages which has been settled before the commencement of proceedings and the sole purpose of the claim is to obtain a consent judgment.

3.2 (1) The Part 8 procedure must be used for those claims, petitions and applications listed in the table in Section B.

(2) Where a claim is listed in the table in Section B and is identified as a claim to which particular provisions of Section C apply, the Part 8 procedure shall apply subject to the additions and modifications set out in the relevant paragraphs in Section C.

3.3 The Part 8 procedure must also be used for any claim or application in relation to which an Act, rule or practice direction provides that the claim or application is brought by originating summons, originating motion or originating application.

3.4 Where it appears to a court officer that a claimant is using the Part 8 procedure inappropriately, he may refer the claim to a judge for the judge to consider the point.

3.5 The court may at any stage order the claim to continue as if the claimant had not used the Part 8 procedure and, if it does so, the court will allocate the claim to a track and give such directions as it considers appropriate.

Issuing the Claim

para.4.2 PC 5

4.1 Part 7 and PD 7A contain a number of rules and directions applicable to all claims, including those to which Part 8 applies. Those rules and directions should be applied where appropriate.

4.2 Where a claimant uses the Part 8 procedure, the claim form (form N208) should be used and must state the matters set out in r. 8.2 and, if r. 8.1(6) applies, must comply with the requirements of the rule or practice direction in question. In particular, the claim form must state that Part 8 applies; a Part 8 claim form means a claim form which so states.

(PD 43–48 contain details of the information required to be filed with a claim form to comply with r. 44.15 (providing information about funding arrangements).)

Responding to the Claim

para.5.2 **13.7** para.5.3 **PC 5**

5.1 The provisions of Part 15 (defence and reply) do not apply where the claim form is a Part 8 claim form.

5.2 Where a defendant who wishes to respond to a Part 8 claim form is required to file an acknowledgment of service, that acknowledgment of service should be in form N210.

5.3 Where a defendant objects to the use of the Part 8 procedure, and his statement of reasons includes matters of evidence, the acknowledgment of service must be verified by a statement of truth.

Managing the Claim

para.6 **PC 5** para.6.1–6.2 **13.14**

6.1 The court may give directions immediately a Part 8 claim form is issued either on the application of a party or on its own initiative. The directions may include fixing a hearing date where:
(1) there is no dispute, such as in child and protected-party settlements; or
(2) where there may be a dispute, but a hearing date could conveniently be given.

6.2 Where the court does not fix a hearing date when the claim form is issued, it will give directions for the disposal of the claim as soon as practicable after the defendant has acknowledged service of the claim form or, as the case may be, after the period for acknowledging service has expired.

6.3 Certain applications may not require a hearing.

6.4 The court may convene a directions hearing before giving directions.

Evidence

para.7.1 **PC 5**
para.7.2 **PC 5, 13.10**
para.7.4 **PC 5 13.10, 13.13**
para.7.5 **13.13**
para.7.5(1) **13.10, 13.13**
para.7.5(2) **13.10**
para.7.5(2)(a) **PC 5**
para.7.5(3) **13.13**

7.1 A claimant must file the written evidence on which he relies when his Part 8 claim form is issued (unless the evidence is contained in the claim form itself).

7.2 Evidence will normally be in the form of a witness statement or an affidavit but a claimant may rely on the matters set out in his claim form provided that it has been verified by a statement of truth.

(For information about (1) statements of truth see Part 22 and PD 22, and (2) written evidence see Part 32 and PD 32.)

7.3 A defendant wishing to rely on written evidence, must file it with his acknowledgment of service.

7.4 A party may apply to the court for an extension of time to serve and file evidence under r. 8.5 or for permission to serve and file additional evidence under r. 8.6(1).

(For information about applications see Part 23 and PD 23A.)

7.5 (1) The parties may, subject to the following provisions, agree in writing on an extension of time for serving and filing evidence under r. 8.5(3) or r. 8.5(5).
(2) An agreement extending time for a defendant to file evidence under r. 8.5(3):
(a) must be filed by the defendant at the same time as he files his acknowledgment of service; and
(b) must not extend time by more than 14 days after the defendant files his acknowledgment of service.
(3) An agreement extending time for a claimant to file evidence in reply under r. 8.5(5) must not extend time to more than 28 days after service of the defendant's evidence on the claimant.

Hearing

para.8.1 **13.15** para.8.2 **13.14, 42.25**

8.1 The court may on the hearing date:
(1) proceed to hear the case and dispose of the claim;
(2) *give case management directions.*

8.2 Case management directions may include the specific allocation of a case to a track.

8.3 Rules 26.5(3) to (5) and 26.6 to 26.10 apply to the allocation of a claim under para 8.2.

SECTION B
CLAIMS AND APPLICATIONS THAT MUST BE MADE UNDER PART 8

Section B 13.2, 13.3, 13.14, 14.78, 61.26

9.1 The claimant must use the Part 8 procedure if the claim is listed in the table below.

9.2 Section C of this Practice Direction contains special provisions modifying the Part 8 procedure, and where it does so, those provisions should be followed. The table below refers to the relevant paragraph of Section C where it applies.

9.3 Some of the claims and applications listed in the table below are dealt with in the schedule rules, and those rules modify the Part 8 procedure. A cross-reference to the relevant schedule rule is contained in the table below.

9.4 For applications that may or must be brought in the High Court, where no other rule or practice direction assigns the application to a Division of the court, the table specifies the Division to which the application is assigned.

Type of claim or application	Paragraph of Section C	Division	Schedule rule
Application under the Bills of Sale Act 1878, s. 14 (rectification of register)	10A	Queen's Bench Central Office	
Application under the Bills of Sale Act 1878, s. 15 (entry of satisfaction)	11	Queen's Bench Central Office	
Application under the Bills of Sale Act 1878, s. 16 (search of the bills of sale register)	11A	Queen's Bench Central Office	
Application under the proviso to the Bills of Sale Act (1878) Amendment Act 1882, s. 7 (restraining removal or sale of goods seized)		Queen's Bench Central Office	
Application under the Public Trustee Act 1906 (free-standing proceedings)	12	Chancery	
Application under the Deeds of Arrangement Act 1914, s. 7 (rectification of register)	12A	Queen's Bench Central Office	
Proceedings under the Trustee Act 1925		Chancery	
Applications under the Public Order Act 1936, s. 2(3)	13	Chancery	
Proceedings under jurisdiction conferred by the Railway and Canal Commission (Abolition) Act 1949, s. 1	14	Chancery	
Administration of Justice Act 1960 (applications under the Act)		Divisional Court	RSC, ord. 109, r. 1(3)
Administration of Justice Act 1960 (appeals under s. 13 of the Act)		Divisional Court	RSC, ord. 109, r. 2(4)
Proceedings under the Commons Registration Act 1965, s. 14		Chancery	
Application under the Mines (Working Facilities and Support) Act 1966	15	Chancery	
Proceedings under the Law of Property Act 1969, s. 21 or 25		Chancery	
Local Government Act 1972 (claims under s. 92 — *proceedings for disqualification*)		Queen's Bench Central Office	
Application under the Mortgaging of Aircraft Order 1972 (SI 1972/1268), art. 10 (rectification of register)	15A	Chancery	
Application to register an assignment of book debts (Insolvency Act 1986, s. 344)	15B	Queen's Bench Central Office	
Proceedings under the Control of Misleading Advertisements Regulations 1988 (SI 1988/915)		Chancery	

Type of claim or application	Paragraph of Section C	Division	Schedule rule
Application under the Senior Courts Act 1981, s. 42	16	Administrative Court	
Proceedings in the High Court under the Representation of the Peoples Act	17A	Queen's Bench Central Office	
Applications under the Mental Health Act 1983, part II	18	Administrative Court	
Applications under the Coroners Act 1988, s. 13	19	Administrative Court	
Application for an injunction to prevent environmental harm under the Town and Country Planning Act 1990, s. 187B or 214A; the Planning (Listed Buildings and Conservation Areas) Act 1990, s. 44A; or the Planning (Hazardous Substances) Act 1990, s. 26AA	20	Queen's Bench	
Confiscation and forfeiture in connection with criminal proceedings (Drug Trafficking Act 1994 and Criminal Justice (International Co-operation) Act 1990 — application for a confiscation order)		Queen's Bench	RSC, ord. 115, r. 2B(1)
Confiscation and forfeiture in connection with criminal proceedings (Drug Trafficking Act 1994 and Criminal Justice (International Co-operation) Act 1990 — application for a restraint order or charging order)		Queen's Bench	RSC, ord. 115, r. 3(1)
Confiscation and forfeiture in connection with criminal proceedings (Drug Trafficking Act 1994 and Criminal Justice (International Co-operation) Act 1990 — realisation of property)		Queen's Bench	RSC, ord. 115, r. 7(1)
Criminal Procedure and Investigations Act 1996 (application under s. 54(3))		Administrative Court	
Confiscation and forfeiture in connection with criminal proceedings (Terrorism Act 2000 — application for a restraint order)		Queen's Bench	RSC, ord. 115, r. 26(1)
Proceedings under the Financial Services and Markets Act 2000	21	Chancery	
Application for an injunction under the Energy Act 2008, s. 12 or 26	20	Queen's Bench	
Interpleader (mode of application)		Chancery or Queen's Bench	RSC, ord. 17, r. 3(1)
Criminal proceedings (estreat of recognisances)		Queen's Bench	RSC, ord. 79, r. 8(2)
Criminal proceedings (bail)		Queen's Bench	RSC, ord. 79, r. 9(2)
Application under an enactment giving the High Court jurisdiction to quash or prohibit any order, scheme, certificate or plan, any amendment or approval of a plan, any decision of a Minister or government department or any action on the part of a Minister or government department	22	Administrative Court	

SECTION C
SPECIAL PROVISIONS

Section C 13.3

10.1 The following special provisions apply to the applications indicated.

Applications under Section 14 of the Bills of Sale Act 1878

10A.1 This paragraph applies to an application under the Bills of Sale Act 1878, s. 14, for an order to rectify an omission or misstatement in relation to the registration, or renewal of the registration, of a bill of sale:
(1) by inserting in the register the true name, residence or occupation of a person; or
(2) by extending the time for registration of the bill of sale or an affidavit of its renewal.

10A.2 The application must be made:
(1) by claim form under Part 8 or
(2) by witness statement.

10A.3 Where the application is made by witness statement:
(1) Part 23 will apply to the application;
(2) the witness statement constitutes the application notice under that Part;
(3) the witness statement does not need to be served on any other person; and
(4) the application will normally be dealt with without a hearing.

10A.4 The application must set out:
(1) the particulars of the bill of sale and of the omission or misstatement; and
(2) the grounds on which the application is made.

10A.5 The application must be made to a master of the Queen's Bench Division and accompanied by payment of the prescribed fee.

Applications under Section 15 of the Bills of Sale Act 1878

11.1 This paragraph applies where an application is made under the Bills of Sale Act 1878, s. 15, for an order that a memorandum of satisfaction be written on a registered copy of a bill of sale.

11.2 If the person entitled to the benefit of the bill of sale has not consented to the satisfaction, the claim form:
(1) must be served on that person; and
(2) must be supported by evidence that the debt (if any) for which the bill of sale was made has been satisfied or discharged.

11.3 If the person entitled to the benefit of the bill of sale has consented to the satisfaction, the application may be made by:
(1) claim form under Part 8; or
(2) witness statement.

11.4 Where para. 11.3 applies and the application is made by Part 8 claim form, the claim form:
(1) must contain details of the consent;
(2) must be supported by a witness statement by a person who witnessed the consent verifying the signature on it; and
(3) must not be served on any person other than the person entitled to the benefit of the bill of sale.

11.5 Where para. 11.3 applies and the application is made by witness statement:
(1) Part 23 will apply to the application;
(2) the witness statement will constitute the application notice under that Part;
(3) the witness statement does not need to be served on any other person; and
(4) the application will normally be dealt with without a hearing.

Applications under Section 16 of the Bills of Sale Act 1878

11A.1 This paragraph applies to an application under the Bills of Sale Act 1878, s. 16, for a search of the bills of sale register and for a certificate of the results of the search.

11A.2 The application must be made:
(1) by claim form under Part 8; or
(2) by written request.

11A.3 The application must give sufficient information to enable the relevant bill of sale to be identified.

11A.4 The application must be made to a master of the Queen's Bench Division and accompanied by payment of the prescribed fee.

Application under the Public Trustee Act 1906

12.1 An application under the Public Trustee Act 1906 must be made:
(1) where no proceedings have been issued, by a Part 8 claim;
(2) in existing proceedings, by a Part 23 application.

12.2 Without prejudice to the Public Trustee Act 1906, ss. 10(2) and 13(7), the jurisdiction of the High Court under the Act is exercised by a single judge of the Chancery Division sitting in private.

Applications under Section 7 of the Deeds of Arrangement Act 1914

para.12A **12.1**

12A.1 This paragraph applies to an application under the Deeds of Arrangement Act 1914, s. 7, for an order to rectify an omission or misstatement in relation to the registration of a deed of arrangement:
(1) by inserting in the register the true name, residence or description of a person; or
(2) by extending the time for registration.

12A.2 The application must be made:
(1) by claim form under Part 8; or
(2) by witness statement.

12A.3 Where the application is made by witness statement:
(1) Part 23 applies to the application;
(2) the witness statement constitutes the application notice under that Part;
(3) the witness statement does not need to be served on any other person; and
(4) the application will normally be dealt with without a hearing.

12A.4 The application must set out:
(1) the particulars of the deed of arrangement and of the omission or misstatement; and
(2) the grounds on which the application is made.

12A.5 The application must be made to a master of the Queen's Bench Division and accompanied by payment of the prescribed fee.

Application under Section 2(3) of the Public Order Act 1936

13.1 The Attorney-General may determine the persons who should be made defendants to an application under the Public Order Act 1936, s. 2(3).

13.2 If the court directs an inquiry under s. 2(3), it may appoint the Official Solicitor to represent any interests it considers are not sufficiently represented and ought to be represented.

Proceedings under Section 1 of the Railway and Canal Commission (Abolition) Act 1949

14.1 Paragraphs 15.3 to 15.14 apply, with appropriate modifications, to proceedings in which has been conferred on the High Court by the Railway and Canal Commission (Abolition) Act 1949, s. 1, except to the extent that:
(1) an Act;
(2) a rule;
(3) a practice direction, provides otherwise.

Application under the Mines (Working Facilities and Support) Act 1966

15.1 In this paragraph:
(1) 'the Act' means the Mines (Working Facilities and Support) Act 1966;
(2) 'the applicant' means the person who has applied for the grant of a right under the Act.

15.2 This paragraph applies where the Secretary of State refers an application to the High Court under any provision of the Act.

15.3 The Secretary of State must:
(1) file a reference signed by him or a person authorised to sign on his behalf in the Chancery Division of the High Court;

(2) file, along with the reference, any documents and plans deposited with him by the applicant in support of his application; and
(3) within 3 days of filing the reference, give notice to the applicant that the reference has been filed.

15.4 Within 10 days of receiving the notice referred to in para. 15.3(3), the applicant must issue a claim form.

15.5 The claim form:
(1) must identify the application under the Act and the remedy sought; and
(2) need not be served on any other party.

15.6 Within seven days of the claim form being issued, the applicant must:
(1) apply for the claim to be listed for a hearing before a master; and
(2) give notice of the hearing date to the Secretary of State.

15.7 The applicant must, not less than two days before the date fixed for a hearing, file at court:
(1) a witness statement in support of the claim, giving details of all persons known to the applicant to be interested in, or affected by, the application; and
(2) a draft of any proposed advertisement or notice of the application.

15.8 At the hearing, the master will:
(1) fix a date by which any notice of objection under para. 15.9 must be filed;
(2) fix a date for a further hearing of the claim; and
(3) give directions about:
(a) any advertisement that is to be inserted or notice of the application and hearing date that is to be given; and
(b) what persons are to be served with a copy of the application or any other document in the proceedings.

15.9 Any person who wishes to oppose the application must, within the time fixed by the court under para. 15.8, serve notice of objection on the applicant, stating:
(a) his name and address;
(b) the name and address of his solicitor, if any;
(c) the grounds of his objection;
(d) any alternative method for effecting the objects of the application that he alleges may be used; and
(e) the facts on which he relies.

15.10 Any document that is required to be served on the person who has given notice of objection ('the objector') may be served by posting it to the following address:
(1) where the notice of objection gives the name and address of a solicitor, to the solicitor;
(2) in any other case, to the objector at the address stated in the notice of objection.

15.11 The objector may appear, or be represented at any further hearing, and may take such part in the proceedings as the court allows.

15.12 The applicant must, not less than two days before the date set for the further hearing, file at court:
(1) any notices of objection served on him;
(2) a list of objectors, together with:
(a) their names and addresses;
(b) the names and addresses of their solicitors, if any; and
(c) a summary of their respective grounds of objection.

15.13 If the objector does not appear, or is not represented, at the further hearing:
(1) his notice of objection will have no effect; and
(2) he will not be entitled to take any further part in the proceedings unless the court orders otherwise.

15.14 At the further hearing, the court will:
(1) give directions about the future conduct of the claim, including:
(a) any further information the applicant is required to give in relation to any of the grounds or facts relied on in support of the application;
(b) any further information the objector is required to give in relation to any of the grounds or facts relied on in opposition to the application;
(c) whether the applicant may serve a reply to any notice of objection;
(d) whether any particular fact should be proved by a witness statement;

(e) whether any statements of case or points of claim or defence are to be served; and

(2) adjourn the claim for hearing before a judge.

Applications under Article 10 of the Mortgaging of Aircraft Order 1972

15A.1 This paragraph applies to an application under the Mortgaging of Aircraft Order 1972 (SI 1972/1268), art. 10, for an order to amend the Register of Aircraft Mortgages.

15A.2 The application must be made by claim form under Part 8.

15A.3 Every person (other than the claimant) who appears in the register as mortgagor or mortgagee of the aircraft concerned must be made a defendant to the claim.

15A.4 A copy of the claim form must be sent to the Civil Aviation Authority.

15A.5 The application will be assigned to the Chancery Division.

15A.6 The Civil Aviation Authority is entitled to be heard in the proceedings.

Applications under Section 344 of the Insolvency Act 1986 for Registration of Assignments of Book Debts

15B.1 This paragraph applies to an application under the Insolvency Act 1986, s. 344, to register an assignment of book debts.

15B.2 The application must be made:

(1) by claim form under Part 8; or

(2) by witness statement.

15B.3 The application must be made to a master of the Queen's Bench Division and accompanied by payment of the prescribed fee.

15B.4 Where the application is made by witness statement:

(1) Part 23 applies to the application;

(2) the witness statement constitutes the application notice under that Part;

(3) the witness statement does not need to be served on any other person; and

(4) the application will normally be dealt with without a hearing.

15B.5 The application:

(1) must have exhibited to it a true copy of the assignment and of every schedule to it;

(2) must set out the particulars of the assignment and the parties to it; and

(3) must verify the date and time of the execution of the assignment, and its execution in the presence of a witness.

15B.6 Upon the court being satisfied, the documents so exhibited will be filed and the particulars of the assignment and of the parties to it entered in the register.

Application under Section 42 of the Senior Courts Act 1981

para.16 14.53

16.1 An application under the Senior Courts Act 1981, s. 42, is heard and determined by a Divisional Court.

16.2 The claim form must be filed at the Administrative Court and:

(1) be accompanied by a witness statement in support; and

(2) be served on the person against whom the order is sought.

Application for Detailed Assessment of a Returning Officer's Account

17.1 An application by the Secretary of State under the Representation of the People Act 1983, s. 30, for the detailed assessment of a returning officer's account must be made by claim form.

17.2 When it issues the claim form, the court will fix a date for the hearing of the detailed assessment to be dealt with if the application is granted.

17.3 The returning officer may, on the application, apply to the court to examine any claim made against him in respect of matters charged in the account.

17.4 To make an application under para. 17.3, the returning officer must file an application within seven days of being served with a copy of the application for detailed assessment.

17.5 When an application is filed under para. 17.3, the court will:

(a) fix a date for the hearing;

(b) give notice of the hearing date to the returning officer; and

(c) serve a copy of the application and notice of hearing on the claimant.

17.6 The examination and detailed assessment may take place on the same day, provided that the examination is determined before the detailed assessment is concluded.

17.7 The district judge may hear and determine:
(a) an application for detailed assessment;
(b) any application under para. 17.3.

17.8 The court will serve a copy of the order made in the application on:
(a) the Secretary of State;
(b) the returning officer; and
(c) in an application under para. 17.3, the claimant.

Other Proceedings under the Representation of the People Acts

17A.1 (1) This paragraph applies to proceedings under the Representation of the People Acts (other than proceedings under the Representation of the People Act 1983, s. 30).
(2) The jurisdiction of the High Court under those Acts in matters relating to Parliamentary and local government elections will be exercised by a Divisional Court except that:
(a) any jurisdiction, under a provision of any of those Acts, exercisable by a single judge will be exercised by a single judge;
(b) any jurisdiction, under any such provision, exercisable by a master will be exercised by a master; and
(c) where the court's jurisdiction in matters relating to Parliamentary elections is exercisable by a single judge, that jurisdiction in matters relating to local government elections is also exercisable by a single judge.

Application under Mental Health Act 1983

18.1 In this paragraph:
(1) a section referred to by a number refers to the section so numbered in the Mental Health Act 1983 and 'part II' means part II of that Act;
(2) 'hospital manager' means the manager of a hospital as defined in s. 145(1) of the Act; and
(3) 'place of residence' means, in relation to a patient who is receiving treatment as an in-patient in a hospital or other institution, that hospital or institution.

18.2 The claim form must be filed:
(1) in the court for the district in which the patient's place of residence is situated; or
(2) in the case of an application under s. 30, in the court that made the order under s. 29 which the application seeks to discharge or vary.

18.3 Where an application is made under s. 29 for an order that the functions of the nearest relative of the patient are to be exercisable by some other person:
(1) the nearest relative must be made a respondent, unless
(a) the application is made on the grounds that the patient has no nearest relative or that it is not reasonably practicable to ascertain whether he has a nearest relative; or
(b) the court orders otherwise; and
(2) the court may order that any other person shall be made a respondent.

18.4 Subject to paragraph 18.5, the court may accept as evidence of the facts relied upon in support of the application, any report made:
(1) by a medical practitioner; or
(2) by any of the following acting in the course of their official duties:
(a) a probation officer;
(b) an officer of a local authority;
(c) an officer of a voluntary body exercising statutory functions on behalf of a local authority; or
(d) an officer of a hospital manager.

18.5 The respondent must be informed of the substance of any part of the report dealing with his fitness or conduct that the court considers to be material to the determination of the claim.

18.6 An application under part II shall be heard in private unless the court orders otherwise.

18.7 The judge may, for the purpose of determining the application, interview the patient. The interview may take place in the presence of, or separately from, the parties. The interview may be conducted elsewhere than at the court. Alternatively, the judge may direct the district judge to interview the patient and report to the judge in writing.

Applications under Section 13 of the Coroners Act 1988

19.1 An application under the Coroners Act 1988, s. 13, is heard and determined by a Divisional Court.

19.2 The application must, unless made by the Attorney-General, be accompanied by the Attorney-General's fiat.

19.3 The claim form must:
(1) state the grounds for the application;
(2) be filed at the Administrative Court; and
(3) be served upon all persons directly affected by the application within six weeks of the grant of the Attorney-General's fiat.

Application for Injunction to Prevent Environmental Harm or Unlicensed Activities

20.1 This paragraph relates to applications under:
(1) the Town and Country Planning Act 1990, s. 187B or 214A;
(2) the Planning (Listed Buildings and Conservation Areas) Act 1990, s. 44A;
(3) the Planning (Hazardous Substances) Act 1990, s. 26AA; or
(4) the Energy Act 2008, s. 12 or 26.

20.2 An injunction may be granted under those sections against a person whose identity is unknown to the applicant.

20.3 In this paragraph, an injunction refers to an injunction under one of those sections and 'the defendant' is the person against whom the injunction is sought.

20.4 In the claim form, the applicant must describe the defendant by reference to:
(1) a photograph;
(2) a thing belonging to or in the possession of the defendant; or
(3) any other evidence.

20.5 The description of the defendant under para. 20.4 must be sufficiently clear to enable the defendant to be served with the proceedings.

(The court has power under Part 6 to dispense with service or make an order permitting service by an alternative method or at an alternative place.)

20.6 The application must be accompanied by a witness statement. The witness statement must state:
(1) that the applicant was unable to ascertain the defendant's identity within the time reasonably available to him;
(2) the steps taken by him to ascertain the defendant's identity;
(3) the means by which the defendant has been described in the claim form; and
(4) that the description is the best the applicant is able to provide.

20.7 When the court issues the claim form it will:
(1) fix a date for the hearing; and
(2) prepare a notice of the hearing date for each party.

20.8 The claim form must be served not less than 21 days before the hearing date.

20.9 Where the claimant serves the claim form, he must serve notice of the hearing date at the same time, unless the hearing date is specified in the claim form.

(Rules 3.1(2)(a) and (b) provide for the court to extend or shorten the time for compliance with any rule or practice direction, and to adjourn or bring forward a hearing.)

20.10 The court may on the hearing date:
(1) proceed to hear the case and dispose of the claim; or
(2) give case management directions.

Proceedings under the Financial Services and Markets Act 2000

21.1 This paragraph applies to proceedings in the High Court under the Financial Services and Markets Act 2000.

21.2 Proceedings in the High Court under the Act (other than applications for a mandatory order) and actions for damages for breach of a statutory duty imposed by the Act shall be assigned to *the Chancery Division*.

21.3 Such proceedings and actions must be begun by claim form (except for applications by petition by the Financial Services Authority under s. 367 of the Act).

21.4 The Financial Services Authority may make representations to the court where there is a question about the meaning of any rule or other instrument made by, or with the approval or consent of, the Financial Services Authority.

Application to Quash Certain Orders, Schemes, etc.

para.22 13.9

22.1 This paragraph applies where the High Court has jurisdiction under any enactment, on the application of any person to quash or prohibit any:
(1) order, scheme, certificate or plan of;
(2) amendment or approval of a plan of;
(3) decision of;
(4) action on the part of,
a Minister or government department.

22.2 The jurisdiction shall be exercisable by a single judge of the Queen's Bench Division.

22.3 The claim form must be filed at the Administrative Court and served within the time limited by the relevant enactment for making the application. PD 54D applies to applications under this paragraph.)

22.4 Subject to para. 22.6, the claim form must be served on the appropriate Minister or government department and on the person indicated in the following table.

If the application relates to: (i) a compulsory purchase order made by an authority other than the appropriate Minister or government department; or (ii) a clearance order under the Housing Act 1985.	The authority that made the order.
If the application relates to a scheme or order: (i) to which the Highways Act 1980, s. 2, applies; and (ii) which was made by an authority other than the Secretary of State.	The authority that made the scheme or order.
If the application relates to a structure plan, local plan or other development plan within the meaning of the Town and Country Planning Act 1990.	The local planning authority who prepared the plan.
If the application relates to any decision or order, or any action on the part of a Minister of the Crown to which: (i) the Land Compensation Act 1961, s. 21; or (ii) the Town and Country Planning Act 1990, s. 288, applies.	(a) The authority directly concerned with such decision, order or action; or (b) if that auhtority is the applicant, on every person who would, if he were aggrieved by the decision, order or action, be entitled to apply to the High Court under the Land Compensation Act 1961, s. 21, or the Town and Country Planning Act 1990, s. 288, as the case may be.
If the application relates to a scheme to which the Local Government, Planning and Land Act 1980, sch. 32, applies.	The body which adopted the scheme.

22.5 In para. 22.4, 'the appropriate Minister or government department' means the Minister of the Crown or government department:
(1) by whom the order, scheme, certificate, plan, amendment, approval or decision in question was or may be made, authorised, confirmed, approved or given;
(2) on whose part the action in question was or may be taken.

22.6 Where the application relates to an order made under the Road Traffic Regulation Act 1984, the claim form must be served:
(1) if the order was made by a Minister of the Crown, on that Minister;

(2) if the order was made by a local authority with the consent, or following a direction, of a Minister of the Crown, on that authority and also on that Minister;
(3) in any other case, on the local authority by whom the order was made.

22.7 Evidence at the hearing of an application under this paragraph is by witness statement.

22.8 The applicant must:
(1) file a witness statement in support of the application in the Administrative Court within 14 days after service of the claim form; and
(2) serve a copy of the witness statement and of any exhibit on the respondent at the time of filing.

22.9 The respondent must:
(1) file any witness statement in opposition to the application in the Administrative Court within 21 days after service on him of the applicant's witness statement; and
(2) serve a copy of his witness statement and of any exhibit on the applicant at the time of filing.

22.10 A party must, when filing a witness statement, file a further copy of the witness statement, including exhibits, for the use of the court.

22.11 Unless the court otherwise orders, the application will not be heard earlier than 14 days after the time for filing a witness statement by the respondent has expired.

PD 8B Practice Direction 8B — Pre-Action Protocol for Low Value Personal Injury Claims in Road Traffic Accidents — Stage 3 Procedure

This practice direction supplements r. 8.1(6).

PD 8B 2.4, 8.38, 8.48, 8.51, 8.52, 8.54, 8.55, 11.3, 13.1, 13.4

General

para.1.1(2) 8.54 para.1.2 2.4, 11.3

1.1 This practice direction sets out the procedure ('the Stage 3 Procedure') for a claim where—

(1) the parties—

(a) have followed the Pre-Action Protocol for Low Value Personal Injury Claims in Road Traffic Accidents ('the RTA Protocol'); but

(b) are unable to agree the amount of damages payable at the end of Stage 2 of the RTA Protocol;

(2)

(a) the claimant is a child;

(b) a settlement has been agreed by the parties at the end of Stage 2 of the RTA Protocol; and

(c) the approval of the court is required in relation to the settlement in accordance with r. 21.10(2); or

(3) compliance with the RTA Protocol is not possible before the expiry of a limitation period and proceedings are started in accordance with para. 16 of this practice direction.

1.2 A claim under this practice direction must be started in a county court and will normally be heard by a district judge.

Modification of Part 8

2.1 The claim is made under the Part 8 procedure as modified by this practice direction and subject to para. 2.2.

2.2 The claim will be determined by the court on the contents of the Court Proceedings Pack. The following rules do not apply to a claim under this practice direction—

(1) r. 8.2A (issue of claim form without naming defendants);

(2) r. 8.3 (acknowledgment of service);

(3) r. 8.5 (filing and serving written evidence);

(4) r. 8.6 (evidence — general);

(5) r. 8.7 (Part 20 claims);

(6) r. 8.8 (procedure where defendant objects to use of the Part 8 procedure); and

(7) r. 8.9(c).

Definitions

3.1 References to 'the Court Proceedings Pack (Part A) Form', 'the Court Proceedings Pack (Part B) Form' and 'the CNF Response Form' are references to the forms used in the RTA Protocol.

3.2 'RTA Protocol offer' has the meaning given by r. 36.17.

3.3 'Settlement hearing' means a hearing where the court considers a settlement agreed between the parties (whether before or after proceedings have started) and the claimant is a child.

3.4 'Stage 3 hearing' means a final hearing to determine the amount of damages that remain in dispute between the parties.

Types of Claim in Which This Modified Part 8 Procedure May Be Followed

para.4.1 8.51

4.1 The court may at any stage order a claim that has been started under Part 7 to continue under the Part 8 procedure as modified by this practice direction.

An Application to the Court to Determine the Amount of Damages

5.1 An application to the court to determine the amount of damages must be started by a claim form.

5.2 The claim form must state—

(1) that the claimant has followed the procedure set out in the RTA Protocol;

(2) the date when the Court Proceedings Pack (Part A and Part B) Form was sent to the defendant. (This provision does not apply where the claimant is a child and the application is for a settlement hearing);

(3) whether the claimant wants the claim to be determined by the court on the papers (except where a party is a child) or at a Stage 3 hearing;

(4) where the claimant seeks a settlement hearing or a Stage 3 hearing, the dates which the claimant requests should be avoided; and

(5) the value of the claim.

Filing and Serving Written Evidence

para.6.1 **8.49** para.6.5 **8.54**

6.1 The claimant must file with the claim form—

(1) the Court Proceedings Pack (Part A) Form;

(2) the Court Proceedings Pack (Part B) Form (the claimant and defendant's final offers) in a sealed envelope. (This provision does not apply where the claimant is a child and the application is for a settlement hearing);

(3) copies of medical reports;

(4) evidence of special damages;

(5) evidence of disbursements (for example the cost of any medical report) in accordance with r. 45.30(2); and

(6) any notice of funding.

6.2 The filing of the claim form and documents set out in para. 6.1 represent the start of Stage 3 for the purposes of fixed costs.

6.3 Subject to para. 6.5 the claimant must only file those documents in para. 6.1 where they have already been sent to the defendant under the RTA Protocol.

6.4 The claimant's evidence as set out in para. 6.1 must be served on the defendant with the claim form.

6.5 Where the claimant is a child the claimant must also provide to the court the following in relation to a settlement made before or after the start of proceedings—

(1) the draft consent order;

(2) the advice by counsel, solicitor or other legal representative on the amount of damages; and

(3) a statement verified by a statement of truth signed by the litigation friend which confirms whether the child has recovered in accordance with the prognosis and whether there are any continuing symptoms. This statement will enable the court to decide whether to order the child to attend the settlement hearing.

6.6 Where the defendant is uninsured and the Motor Insurers' Bureau ('MIB') or its agents have consented in the CNF Response Form to the MIB being joined as a defendant, the claimant must name the MIB as the second defendant and must also provide to the court a copy of the CNF Response Form completed by or on behalf of the MIB.

6.7 Where this practice direction requires a step to be taken by the defendant, it will be sufficient for this step to be taken by the MIB.

Evidence — General

para.7.2(1) **8.53** para.7.2(2) **8.51**

7.1 The parties may not rely upon evidence unless—

(1) it has been served in accordance with para. 6.4;

(2) it has been filed in accordance with para. 8.2 and 11.3: or

(3) (where the court considers that it cannot properly determine the claim without it), the court orders otherwise and gives directions.

7.2 Where the court considers that—

(1) further evidence must be provided by any party; and

(2) the claim is not suitable to continue under the Stage 3 Procedure,

the court will order that the claim will continue under Part 7, allocate the claim to a track and give directions.

7.3 Where para. 7.2 applies the court will not allow the Stage 3 fixed costs.

Acknowledgment of Service

para.8.1 8.50 para.8.2 8.50

8.1 The defendant must file and serve an acknowledgment of service in Form N210B not more than 14 days after service of the claim form.

8.2 The defendant must file and serve—

(1) with the acknowledgment of service, any notice of funding; and

(2) with the acknowledgment of service, or as soon as possible thereafter, a certificate that is in force.

('Certificate' is defined in r. 36.15(1)(e)(i).)

8.3 The acknowledgment of service must state whether the defendant—

(1)

(a) contests the amount of damages claimed;

(b) contests the making of an order for damages;

(c) disputes the court's jurisdiction; or

(d) objects to the use of the Stage 3 Procedure;

(2) wants the claim to be determined by the court on the papers or at a Stage 3 hearing.

8.4 Where the defendant objects to the use of the Stage 3 Procedure reasons must be given in the acknowledgment of service.

8.5 The acknowledgment of service may be signed and filed by the defendant's insurer who may give their address as the address for service.

Dismissal of the Claim

para.9.1 8.50

9.1 Where the defendant opposes the claim because the claimant has—

(1) not followed the procedure set out in the RTA Protocol; or

(2) filed and served additional or new evidence with the claim form that had not been provided under the RTA Protocol,

the court will dismiss the claim and the claimant may start proceedings under Part 7.

(Rule 45.36 sets out the costs consequences of failing to comply with the RTA Protocol.)

Withdrawal of the RTA Protocol Offer

para.10.1 8.52

10.1 A party may only withdraw an RTA Protocol offer after proceedings have started with the court's permission. Where the court gives permission the claim will no longer continue under the Stage 3 Procedure and the court will give directions. The court will only give permission where there is good reason for the claim not to continue under the Stage 3 Procedure.

Consideration of the Claim

para.11.1 8.53

11.1 The court will order that damages are to be assessed—

(1) on the papers; or

(2) at a Stage 3 hearing where—

(a) the claimant so requests on the claim form;

(b) the defendant so requests in the acknowledgment of service (Form N210B); or

(c) the court so orders,

and on a date determined by the court.

11.2 The court will give the parties at least 21 days notice of the date of the determination on the papers or the date of the Stage 3 hearing.

11.3 Where further deductible amounts have accrued since the final offer was made by both parties in the Court Proceedings Pack (Part B) Form, the defendant must file an up to date certificate at least 5 days before the date of a determination on the papers.

11.4 Where the claim is determined on the papers the court will give reasons for its decision in the judgment.

('Deductible amount' is defined in r. 36.15(1)(d).)

Settlement at Stage 2 Where the Claimant is a Child

para.12.5 8.54

12.1 Paragraphs 12.2 to 12.5 apply where—
(1) the claimant is a child;
(2) there is a settlement at Stage 2 of the RTA Protocol; and
(3) an application is made to the court to approve the settlement.

12.2 Where the settlement is approved at the settlement hearing the court will order the costs to be paid in accordance with r. 45.33(2).

12.3 Where the settlement is not approved at the first settlement hearing and the court orders a second settlement hearing at which the settlement is approved, the court will order the costs to be paid in accordance with r. 45.33(4) to (6).

12.4 Where the settlement is not approved at the first settlement hearing and the court orders that the claim is not suitable to be determined under the Stage 3 Procedure, the court will order costs to be paid in accordance with r. 45.35 and will give directions.

12.5 Where the settlement is not approved at the second settlement hearing the claim will no longer continue under the Stage 3 Procedure and the court will give directions.

Settlement at Stage 3 Where the Claimant is a Child

13.1 Paragraphs 13.2 and 13.3 apply where—
(1) the claimant is a child;
(2) there is a settlement after proceedings have started under the Stage 3 Procedure; and
(3) an application is made to the court to approve the settlement.

13.2 Where the settlement is approved at the settlement hearing the court will order the costs to be paid in accordance with r. 45.34(2).

13.3 Where the settlement is not approved at the settlement hearing the court will order the claim to proceed to a Stage 3 hearing.

Adjournment

14.1 Where the court adjourns a settlement hearing or a Stage 3 hearing it may, in its discretion, order the costs to be paid in accordance with r. 45.39.

Appeals — Determination on the Papers

15.1 The court will not consider an application to set aside a judgment made after a determination on the papers. The judgment will state the appeal court to which an appeal lies.

Limitation

para.16.2 13.4 para.16.5 13.4

16.1 Where compliance with the RTA Protocol is not possible before the expiry of a limitation period the claimant may start proceedings in accordance with para. 16.2.

16.2 The claimant must—
(1) start proceedings under this practice direction; and
(2) state on the claim form that—
(a) the claim is for damages; and
(b) a stay of proceedings is sought in order to comply with the RTA Protocol.

16.3 The claimant must send to the defendant the claim form together with the order imposing the stay.

16.4 Where a claim is made under para. 16.1 the provisions in this practice direction, except paras 1.2, 2.1, 2.2 and 16.1 to 16.6, are disapplied.

16.5 Where—
(1) a stay is granted by the court;
(2) the parties have complied with the RTA Protocol; and

(3) the claimant wishes to start the Stage 3 Procedure,

the claimant must make an application to the court to lift the stay and request directions.

16.6 Where the court orders that the stay be lifted—

(1) the provisions of this practice direction will apply; and

(2) the claimant must—

(a) amend the claim form in accordance with para. 5.2; and

(b) file the documents in para. 6.1.

16.7 Where, during Stage 1 or Stage 2 of the RTA Protocol—

(1) the claim no longer continues under that Protocol; and

(2) the claimant wishes to start proceedings under Part 7,

the claimant must make an application to the court to lift the stay and request directions.

Modification to the General Rules

para.17.1 8.53

17.1 The claim will not be allocated to a track. Parts 26 to 29 do not apply.

CPR Part 9 Responding to Particulars of Claim — General

Part 9 17.1

9.1 Scope of This Part

(1) This Part sets out how a defendant may respond to particulars of claim.
(2) Where the defendant receives a claim form which states that particulars of claim are to follow, he need not respond to the claim until the particulars of claim have been served on him.

9.2 Defence, Admission or Acknowledgment of Service

para.9.2 PC 18

When particulars of claim are served on a defendant, the defendant may—
(a) file or serve an admission in accordance with Part 14;
(b) file a defence in accordance with Part 15, (or do both, if he admits only part of the claim); or
(c) file an acknowledgment of service in accordance with Part 10.

CPR Part 10 Acknowledgment of Service

Part 10 **PC 17, 18.5** [For commentary on a specific rule, please refer to the cross-references after the title of the rule.]

10.1 Acknowledgment of Service

r.10.1(3) **18.1**

(1) This Part deals with the procedure for filing an acknowledgment of service.
(2) Where the claimant uses the procedure set out in Part 8 (alternative procedure for claims) this Part applies subject to the modifications set out in rule 8.3.
(3) A defendant may file an acknowledgment of service if—
 (a) he is unable to file a defence within the period specified in rule 15.4; or
 (b) he wishes to dispute the court's jurisdiction.

(Part 11 sets out the procedure for disputing the court's jurisdiction)

10.2 Consequence of Not Filing an Acknowledgment of Service

If—

(a) a defendant fails to file an acknowledgment of service within the period specified in rule 10.3; and
(b) does not within that period file a defence in accordance with Part 15 or serve or file an admission in accordance with Part 14,

the claimant may obtain default judgment if Part 12 allows it.

10.3 The Period for Filing an Acknowledgment of Service

r.10.3 **PC 15, PC 16, PC 18**
r.10.3(1) **PC 13, 18.2**
r.10.3(1)(a) **20.17**
r.10.3(1)(b) **PC 31, 72.8**
r.10.3(2) **13.8, 86.12**
r.10.3(2)(a)–(b) **18.2**

(1) The general rule is that the period for filing an acknowledgment of service is—
 (a) where the defendant is served with a claim form which states that particulars of claim are to follow, 14 days after service of the particulars of claim; and
 (b) in any other case, 14 days after service of the claim form.
(2) The general rule is subject to the following rules—
 (a) Rule 6.35 (which specifies how the period for filing an acknowledgment of service is calculated where the claim form is served out of the jurisdiction under rule 6.32 or 6.33);
 (b) rule 6.12(3) (which requires the court to specify the period for responding to the particulars of claim when it makes an order under that rule); and
 (c) rule 6.37(5) (which requires the court to specify the period within which the defendant may file an acknowledgment of service calculated by reference to Practice Direction 6B when it makes an order giving permission to serve a claim form out of the jurisdiction).

10.4 Notice to Claimant That Defendant Has Filed an Acknowledgment of Service

r.10.4 **18.2**

On receipt of an acknowledgment of service, the court must notify the claimant in writing.

10.5 Contents of Acknowledgment of Service

r.10.5 **13.8** r.10.5(a)–(b) **18.3**

An acknowledgment of service must—

(a) be signed by the defendant or the defendant's legal representative; and

(b) include the defendant's address for service.

(Rule 6.23 makes provision in relation to addresses for service.)

(Rule 19.8A modifies this Part where a notice of claim is served under that rule to bind a person not a party to the claim.)

PD 10 Practice Direction 10 — Acknowledgment of Service

This practice direction supplements CPR, Part 10.

[For commentary on a specific paragraph, please refer to the cross-references after the title of the paragraph.]

Responding to the Claim

1.1 Part 9 sets out how a defendant may respond to a claim.

1.2 Part 10 sets out the provisions for acknowledging service (but see rule 8.3 for information about acknowledging service of a claim under the Part 8 procedure).

The Form of Acknowledgment of Service

2 A defendant who wishes to acknowledge service of a claim should do so by using form N9.

Address for Service

para.3.2 **18.3**

3.1 The defendant must include in his acknowledgment of service an address for the service of documents.[1]

3.2 Where the defendant is represented by a legal representative[2] and the legal representative has signed the acknowledgment of service form, the address must be the legal representative's business address; otherwise the address for service that is given should be as set out in rule 6.5 and the practice direction which supplements Part 6.

Signing the Acknowledgment of Service

para.4.2 **13.8**
para.4.3 **13.8, 18.3**
para.4.4 **13.8, 15.50, 18.3**
para.4.4(2) **15.50**
para.4.5 **18.3**

4.1 An acknowledgment of service must be signed by the defendant or by his legal representative.

4.2 Where the defendant is a company or other corporation, a person holding a senior position in the company or corporation may sign the acknowledgment of service on the defendant's behalf, but must state the position he holds.

4.3 Each of the following persons is a person holding a senior position:
(1) in respect of a registered company or corporation, a director, the treasurer, secretary, chief executive, manager or other officer of the company or corporation, and
(2) in respect of a corporation which is not a registered company, in addition to those persons set out in (1), the mayor, chairman, president, town clerk or similar officer of the corporation.

4.4 Where a claim is brought against a partnership
(1) service must be acknowledged in the name of the partnership on behalf of all persons who were partners at the time when the cause of action accrued; and
(2) the acknowledgment of service may be signed by any of those partners, or by any person authorised by any of those partners to sign it.

4.5 Children and protected parties may acknowledge service only by their litigation friend or his legal representative unless the court otherwise orders.[3]

General

para.5.3 **18.3, 22.2**
para.5.4 **18.3**

5.1 The defendant's name should be set out in full on the acknowledgment of service.

5.2 Where the defendant's name has been incorrectly set out in the claim form, it should be correctly set out on the acknowledgment of service followed by the words 'described as' and the incorrect name.

5.3 If two or more defendants to a claim acknowledge service of a claim through the same legal representative at the same time, only one acknowledgment of service need be used.

---

1 See rule 6.5.
2 See rule 2.3 for the definition of legal representative.
3 See Part 21.

5.4 An acknowledgment of service may be amended or withdrawn only with the permission of the court.

5.5 An application for permission under paragraph 5.4 must be made in accordance with Part 23 and supported by evidence.

(PD 6A, para. 8.2, makes provision for the service on the claimant of any notice of funding filed with an acknowledgment of service.)

CPR Part 11 Disputing the Court's Jurisdiction

Part 11 13.11, 14.50, 16.3, 19.1, 19.2, 19.3, 19.4, 26.3, 72.10 [For commentary on a specific rule, please refer to the cross-references after the title of the rule.]

11 Procedure for Disputing the Court's Jurisdiction

r.11(2) PC 14, 19.2
r.11(3) 18.1, 19.4
r.11(4) PC 14, 19.3, 19.4
r.11(4)(a) 13.11, 19.3
r.11(4)(b) 19.3
r.11(5)(b) 19.3
r.11(6) 19.6
r.11(7) 19.7
r.11(7)(c) PC 14, 19.7
r.11(8) 19.7
r.11(9) 18.5, 19.3, 26.3
r.11(9)(a) PC 14, 19.5
r.11(9)(b) 19.5

(1) A defendant who wishes to—
  (a) dispute the court's jurisdiction to try the claim; or
  (b) argue that the court should not exercise its jurisdiction,

  may apply to the court for an order declaring that it has no such jurisdiction or should not exercise any jurisdiction which it may have.

(2) A defendant who wishes to make such an application must first file an acknowledgment of service in accordance with Part 10.

(3) A defendant who files an acknowledgment of service does not, by doing so, lose any right that he may have to dispute the court's jurisdiction.

(4) An application under this rule must—
  (a) be made within 14 days after filing an acknowledgment of service; and
  (b) be supported by evidence.

(5) If the defendant—
  (a) files an acknowledgment of service; and
  (b) does not make such an application within the period specified in paragraph (4), he is to be treated as having accepted that the court has jurisdiction to try the claim.

(6) An order containing a declaration that the court has no jurisdiction or will not exercise its jurisdiction may also make further provision including—
  (a) setting aside the claim form;
  (b) setting aside service of the claim form;
  (c) discharging any order made before the claim was commenced or before the claim form was served; and
  (d) staying(GL) the proceedings.

(7) If on an application under this rule the court does not make a declaration—
  (a) the acknowledgment of service shall cease to have effect;
  (b) the defendant may file a further acknowledgment of service within 14 days or such other period as the court may direct; and
  (c) the court shall give directions as to the filing and service of the defence in a claim under Part 7 or the filing of evidence in a claim under Part 8 in the event that a further acknowledgment of service is filed.

(8) If the defendant files a further acknowledgment of service in accordance with paragraph (7)(b) he shall be treated as having accepted that the court has jurisdiction to try the claim.

(9) If a defendant makes an application under this rule, he must file and serve his written evidence in support with the application notice, but he need not before the hearing of the application file—
  (a) in a Part 7 claim, a defence; or
  (b) in a Part 8 claim, any other written evidence.

CPR Part 12 Default Judgment

Part 12 **12.9, 13.9, 15.7, 16.67, 18.6, 20.1, 20.13, 26.2, 26.5, 28.5, 29.9, 29.10** [For commentary on a specific rule, please refer to the cross-references after the title of the rule.]

12.1 Meaning of 'Default Judgment'

r.12.1 **18.6**

In these Rules, 'default judgment' means judgment without trial where a defendant—
(a) has failed to file an acknowledgment of service; or
(b) has failed to file a defence.
(Part 10 contains provisions about filing an acknowledgment of service and Part 15 contains provisions about filing a defence)

12.2 Claims in Which Default Judgment May Not Be Obtained

r.12.2 **20.2**
r.12.2(h) **13.1**

A claimant may not obtain a default judgment—
(a) on a claim for delivery of goods subject to an agreement regulated by the Consumer Credit Act 1974;
(b) where he uses the procedure set out in Part 8 (alternative procedure for claims); or
(c) in any other case where a practice direction provides that the claimant may not obtain default judgment.

12.3 Conditions to Be Satisfied

r.12.3 **PC 14, 20.3, 20.17**
r.12.3(2) **PC 17**
r.12.3(3) **33.4**
r.12.3(3)(a) **26.3, 34.6**
r.12.3(3)(a)(ii) **PC 22**

(1) The claimant may obtain judgment in default of an acknowledgment of service only if—
  (a) the defendant has not filed an acknowledgment of service or a defence to the claim (or any part of the claim); and
  (b) the relevant time for doing so has expired.
(2) Judgment in default of defence may be obtained only—
  (a) where an acknowledgment of service has been filed but a defence has not been filed;
  (b) in a counterclaim made under rule 20.4, where a defence has not been filed,
  and, in either case, the relevant time limit for doing so has expired.
(Rules 10.3 and 15.4 deal respectively with the period for filing an acknowledgment of service and the period for filing a defence)
(Rule 20.4 makes general provision for a defendant's counterclaim against a claimant, and rule 20.4(3) provides that Part 10 (acknowledgment of service) does not apply to a counterclaim made under that rule)
(3) The claimant may not obtain a default judgment if—
  (a) the defendant has applied—
    (i) to have the claimant's statement of case struck out under rule 3.4; or

(ii) for summary judgment under Part 24,
and, in either case, that application has not been disposed of;
(b) the defendant has satisfied the whole claim (including any claim for costs) on which the claimant is seeking judgment; or
(c) (i) the claimant is seeking judgment on a claim for money; and
(ii) the defendant has filed or served on the claimant an admission under rule 14.4 or 14.7 (admission of liability to pay all of the money claimed) together with a request for time to pay.

(Part 14 sets out the procedure where a defendant admits a money claim and asks for time to pay)

(Rule 6.17 provides that, where the claim form is served by the claimant, the claimant may not obtain default judgment unless a certificate of service has been filed)

(Article 19(1) of the Service Regulation (which has the same meaning as in rule 6.31(e)) applies in relation to judgment in default where the claim form is served in accordance with that Regulation)

12.4 Procedure for Obtaining Default Judgment

r.12.4 **11.9, 20.4, 20.6, 42.8**
r.12.4(1) **20.1**
r.12.4(1)(a)–(b) **PC 15**
r.12.4(2) **20.8, 20.9**
r.12.4(3) **20.4**
r.12.4(4) **14.47, 20.7**

(1) Subject to paragraph (2), a claimant may obtain a default judgment by filing a request in the relevant practice form where the claim is for—
(a) a specified amount of money;
(b) an amount of money to be decided by the court;
(c) delivery of goods where the claim form gives the defendant the alternative of paying their value; or
(d) any combination of these remedies.

(2) The claimant must make an application in accordance with Part 23 if he wishes to obtain a default judgment—
(a) on a claim which consists of or includes a claim for any other remedy; or
(b) where rule 12.9 or rule 12.10 so provides,
and where the defendant is an individual, the claimant must provide the defendant's date of birth (if known) in Part C of the application notice.

(3) Where a claimant—
(a) claims any other remedy in his claim form in addition to those specified in paragraph (1); but
(b) abandons that claim in his request for judgment,
he may still obtain a default judgment by filing a request under paragraph (1).

(4) In civil proceedings against the Crown, as defined in rule 66.1(2), a request for a default judgment must be considered by a Master or district judge, who must in particular be satisfied that the claim form and particulars of claim have been properly served on the Crown in accordance with section 18 of the Crown Proceedings Act 1947 and rule 6.10.

12.5 Nature of Judgment Where Default Judgment Obtained by Filing a Request

r.12.5 **11.9, 20.5, 20.6, 42.8**
r.12.5(3) **20.6**

(1) Where the claim is for a specified sum of money, the claimant may specify in a request filed under rule 12.4(1)—
(a) the date by which the whole of the judgment debt is to be paid; or
(b) the times and rate at which it is to be paid by instalments.

(2) Except where paragraph (4) applies, a default judgment on a claim for a specified amount of money obtained on the filing of a request, will be judgment for the amount of the claim (less any payments made) and costs—
(a) to be paid by the date or at the rate specified in the request for judgment; or
(b) if none is specified, immediately.

(Interest may be included in a default judgment obtained by filing a request if the conditions set out in Rule 12.6 are satisfied)

(Rule 45.4 provides for fixed costs on the entry of a default judgment)

(3) Where the claim is for an unspecified amount of money a default judgment obtained on the filing of a request will be for an amount to be decided by the court and costs.

(4) Where the claim is for delivery of goods and the claim form gives the defendant the alternative of paying their value, a default judgment obtained on the filing of a request will be judgment requiring the defendant to—
(a) deliver the goods or (if he does not do so) pay the value of the goods as decided by the court (less any payments made); and
(b) pay costs.
(Rule 12.7 sets out the procedure for deciding the amount of a judgment or the value of the goods)
(5) The claimant's right to enter judgment requiring the defendant to deliver goods is subject to rule 40.14 (judgment in favour of certain part owners relating to the detention of goods).

12.5A Automatic Transfer

r.12.5A 11.9, 20.6, 42.8

If—

(a) a claimant files a request for judgment which includes an amount of money to be decided by the court in accordance with rules 12.4 and 12.5; and
(b) the claim is a designated money claim,
the court will transfer the claim to the preferred court upon receipt of the request for judgment.

12.6 Interest

r.12.6 20.5 r.12.6(2) 20.5

(1) A default judgment on a claim for a specified amount of money obtained on the filing of a request may include the amount of interest claimed to the date of judgment if—
(a) the particulars of claim include the details required by rule 16.4;
(b) where interest is claimed under section 35A of the Senior Courts Act 1981 or section 69 of the County Courts Act 1984, the rate is no higher than the rate of interest payable on judgment debts at the date when the claim form was issued; and
(c) the claimant's request for judgment includes a calculation of the interest claimed for the period from the date up to which interest was stated to be calculated in the claim form to the date of the request for judgment.
(2) In any case where paragraph (1) does not apply, judgment will be for an amount of interest to be decided by the court.
(Rule 12.7 sets out the procedure for deciding the amount of interest)

12.7 Procedure for Deciding an Amount or Value

r.12.7 20.6 r.12.7(2)(b) 42.25

(1) This rule applies where the claimant obtains a default judgment on the filing of a request under rule 12.4(1) and judgment is for—
(a) an amount of money to be decided by the court;
(b) the value of goods to be decided by the court; or
(c) an amount of interest to be decided by the court.
(2) Where the court enters judgment it will—
(a) give any directions it considers appropriate; and
(b) if it considers it appropriate, allocate the case.

12.8 Claim against More Than One Defendant

r.12.8 20.10 r.12.8(2)(b) 20.10
r.12.8(1) 20.10 r.12.8(3) 20.10

(1) A claimant may obtain a default judgment on request under this Part on a claim for money or a claim for delivery of goods against one of two or more defendants, and proceed with his claim against the other defendants.
(2) Where a claimant applies for a default judgment against one of two or more defendants—
(a) if the claim can be dealt with separately from the claim against the other defendants—
(i) the court may enter a default judgment against that defendant; and
(ii) the claimant may continue the proceedings against the other defendants;

(b) if the claim cannot be dealt with separately from the claim against the other defendants—
(i) the court will not enter default judgment against that defendant; and
(ii) the court must deal with the application at the same time as it disposes of the claim against the other defendants.

(3) A claimant may not enforce against one of two or more defendants any judgment obtained under this Part for possession of land or for delivery of goods unless—
(a) he has obtained a judgment for possession or delivery (whether or not obtained under this Part) against all the defendants to the claim; or
(b) the court gives permission.

12.9 Procedure for Obtaining a Default Judgment for Costs Only

r.12.9(1)(b) **20.8**

(1) Where a claimant wishes to obtain a default judgment for costs only—
(a) if the claim is for fixed costs, he may obtain it by filing a request in the relevant practice form;
(b) if the claim is for any other type of costs, he must make an application in accordance with Part 23.

(2) Where an application is made under this rule for costs only, judgment shall be for an amount to be decided by the court.

(Part 45 sets out when a claimant is entitled to fixed costs)

12.10 Default Judgment Obtained by Making an Application

r. 12.10 **20.1, 20.8**
r.12.10(a)(i) **14.17, 20.4**
r.12.10(b)(i)–(ii) **16.67**

The claimant must make an application in accordance with Part 23 where—
(a) the claim is—
(i) a claim against a child or protected party; or
(ii) a claim in tort by one spouse or civil partner against the other.
(b) the claimant wishes to obtain a default judgment where the defendant has failed to file an acknowledgment of service—
(i) against a defendant who has been served with the claim out of the jurisdiction under rule 6.32(1), 6.33(1) or 6.33(2) (service where permission of the court is not required);
(ii) against a defendant domiciled in Scotland or Northern Ireland or in any other Convention territory or Regulation State;
(iii) against a State;
(iv) against a diplomatic agent who enjoys immunity from civil jurisdiction by virtue of the Diplomatic Privileges Act 1964; or
(v) against persons or organisations who enjoy immunity from civil jurisdiction pursuant to the provisions of the International Organisations Acts 1968 and 1981.

12.11 Supplementary Provisions Where Applications for Default Judgment Are Made

r.12.11(1) **20.1, 20.9**
r.12.11(2) **PC 16**
r.12.11(3) **PC 16, 20.9**
r.12.11(4) **PC 16, 20.9**
r.12.11(4)(a) **PC 16**
r.12.11(5) **PC 16**

(1) Where the claimant makes an application for a default judgment, judgment shall be such judgment as it appears to the court that the claimant is entitled to on his statement of case.

(2) Any evidence relied on by the claimant in support of his application need not be served on a party who has failed to file an acknowledgment of service.

(3) An application for a default judgment on a claim against a child or protected party or a claim in tort between spouses or civil partners must be supported by evidence.

(4) An application for a default judgment may be made without notice if—
(a) the claim under the Civil Jurisdiction and Judgments Act 1982 or the Lugano Convention or the Judgments Regulation, was served in accordance with rules 6.19(1) or 6.19(1A) as appropriate;
(b) the defendant has failed to file an acknowledgment of service; and
(c) notice does not need to be given under any other provision of these Rules.

(5) Where an application is made against a State for a default judgment where the defendant has failed to file an acknowledgment of service—
  (a) the application may be made without notice, but the court hearing the application may direct that a copy of the application notice be served on the State;
  (b) if the court—
    (i) grants the application; or
    (ii) directs that a copy of the application notice be served on the State,
  the judgment or application notice (and the evidence in support) may be served out of the jurisdiction without any further order;
  (c) where paragraph (5)(b) permits a judgment or an application notice to be served out of the jurisdiction, the procedure for serving the judgment or the application notice is the same as for serving a claim form under Section III of Part 6 except where an alternative method of service has been agreed under section 12(6) of the State Immunity Act 1978.

(Rule 23.1 defines 'application notice')

(6) For the purposes of this rule and rule 12.10—
  (a) 'domicile' is to be determined—
    (i) in relation to a Convention territory, in accordance with sections 41 to 46 of the Civil Jurisdiction and Judgments Act 1982;
    (ii) in relation to a Member State, in accordance with the Judgments Regulation and paragraphs 9 to 12 of Schedule 1 to the Civil Jurisdiction and Judgments Order 2001;
  (b) 'Convention territory' means the territory or territories of any Contracting State, as defined by section 1(3) of the Civil Jurisdiction and Judgments Act 1982, to which the Brussels Conventions or Lugano Convention apply;
  (c) 'State' has the meaning given by section 14 of the State Immunity Act 1978; and
  (d) 'Diplomatic agent' has the meaning given by Article 1(e) of Schedule 1 to the Diplomatic Privileges Act 1964; and
  (e) 'the Judgments Regulation' means Council Regulation (EC) No. 44/2001 of 22nd December 2000 on jurisdiction and the recognition and enforcement of judgments in civil and commercial matters, as amended from time to time and as applied by the Agreement made on 19th October 2005 between the European Community and the Kingdom of Denmark on jurisdiction and the recognition and enforcement of judgments in civil and commercial matters.
  (f) 'the Lugano Convention' means the Convention on jurisdiction and the recognition and enforcement of judgments in civil and commercial matters, between the European Community and the Republic of Iceland, the Kingdom of Norway, the Swiss Confederation and the Kingdom of Denmark and signed by the European Community on 30th October 2007.

PD 12 Practice Direction 12 — Default Judgment

This practice direction supplements CPR, Part 12.

[For commentary on a specific paragraph, please refer to the cross-references after the title of the paragraph.]

Default Judgment

para.1.1 20.3 para.1.2 20.2

1.1 A default judgment is judgment without a trial where a defendant has failed to file either:
(1) an acknowledgment of service, or
(2) a defence.
For this purpose a defence includes any document purporting to be a defence.
(See Part 10 and PD 10 for information about the acknowledgment of service, and Parts 15 and 16, PD 15 and PD 16 for information about the defence and what it should contain.)

1.2 A claimant may not obtain a default judgment under Part 12 (notwithstanding that no acknowledgment of service or defence has been filed) if:
(1) the procedure set out in Part 8 (alternative procedure for claims) is being used, or
(2) the claim is for delivery of goods subject to an agreement regulated by the Consumer Credit Act 1974.

1.3 Other rules and practice directions provide that default judgment under Part 12 cannot be obtained in particular types of proceedings. Examples are:
(1) admiralty proceedings;
(2) arbitration proceedings;
(3) contentious probate proceedings;
(4) claims for provisional damages;
(5) possession claims.

Obtaining Default Judgment

para.2.3 20.8

2.1 Rules 12.4(1) and 12.9(1) describe the claims in respect of which a default judgment may be obtained by filing a request in the appropriate practice form.

2.2 A default judgment on:
(1) the claims referred to in rules 12.9(1)(b) and 12.10, and
(2) claims other than those described in rule 12.4(1), can only be obtained if an application for default judgment is made and cannot be obtained by filing a request.

2.3 The following are some of the types of claim which require an application for a default judgment::
(1) against children and patients,[1]
(2) for costs (other than fixed costs) only,[2]
(3) by one spouse against the other[3] on a claim in tort,[4]
(4) for delivery up of goods where the defendant will not be allowed the alternative of paying their value,
(5) [*deleted*], and
(6) against persons or organisations who enjoy immunity from civil jurisdiction under the provisions of the International Organisations Acts 1968 and 1981.

---

1 See rule 12.10(a)(i).

2 See rule 12.9(b).

3 See rule 12.10(a)(ii).

4 Tort may be defined as an act or a failure to do an act which causes harm or damage to another person and which gives the other person a right to claim compensation without having to rely on a contract with the person who caused the harm or damage.

Default Judgment by Request

para.3 PC 15
para.3.2 20.4

3.1 Requests for default judgment:

(1) in respect of a claim for a specified amount of money or for the delivery of goods where the defendant will be given the alternative of paying a specified sum representing their value, or for fixed costs only, must be in form N205A or N225, and

(2) in respect of a claim where an amount of money (including an amount representing the value of goods) is to be decided by the court, must be in form N205B or N227.

3.2 The forms require the claimant to provide the date of birth (if known) of the defendant where the defendant is an individual.

Evidence

para.4 PC 16
para.4.1 20.3
para.4.2 20.9
para.4.2(1) 14.17, 20.8
para.4.3 20.9
para.4.4 20.9
para.4.5 20.9, 52.7

4.1 Both on a request and on an application for default judgment the court must be satisfied that:

(1) the particulars of claim have been served on the defendant (a certificate of service on the court file will be sufficient evidence),

(2) either the defendant has not filed an acknowledgment of service or has not filed a defence and that in either case the relevant period for doing so has expired,

(3) the defendant has not satisfied the claim, and

(4) the defendant has not returned an admission to the claimant under rule 14.4 or filed an admission with the court under rule 14.6.

4.2 On an application against a child or patient:[5]

(1) a litigation friend[6] to act on behalf of the child or patient must be appointed by the court before judgment can be obtained, and

(2) the claimant must satisfy the court by evidence that he is entitled to the judgment claimed.

4.3 On an application where the defendant was served with the claim either:

(1) outside the jurisdiction[7] without leave under the Civil Jurisdiction and Judgments Act 1982 or the Lugano Convention, or

(2) within the jurisdiction but when domiciled[8] in Scotland or Northern Ireland or in any other Convention territory[9] or member State,

and the defendant has not acknowledged service, the evidence must establish that:

(a) the claim is one that the court has power to hear and decide,

(b) no other court has exclusive jurisdiction under the Act or the Sugano Convention or Jurisdiction and Judgments Regulation to hear and decide the claim, and

(c) the claim has been properly served in accordance with art. 20 of sch. 1 to the Act, art. 26 of the Lugano Convention, para. 15 of sch. 4 to the Act, or art. 26 of the Jurisdiction and Judgments Regulation.

4.4 On an application against a State[10] the evidence must:

(1) set out the grounds of the application,

(2) establish the facts proving that the State is excepted from the immunity conferred by s. 1 of the State Immunity Act 1978,

(3) establish that the claim was sent through the Foreign and Commonwealth Office to the Ministry of Foreign Affairs of the State or, where the State has agreed to another form of service, that the claim was served in the manner agreed, and

[5] As defined in rule 21.1(2).
[6] As defined in PD 21.
[7] *As defined in rule 2.3.*
[8] As determined in accordance with the provisions of ss. 41 to 46 of the Civil Jurisdiction and Judgments Act 1982.
[9] Means the territory of a Contracting State as defined in s. 1(3) of the Civil Jurisdiction and Judgments Act 1982.
[10] As defined in s. 14 of the State Immunity Act 1978.

(4) establish that the time for acknowledging service (which is extended to two months by s. 12(2) of the Act when the claim is sent through the Foreign and Commonwealth Office to the Ministry of Foreign Affairs of the State) has expired.

(See rule [40.10*] for when default judgment against a State takes effect.)

4.5 Evidence in support of an application referred to in paragraphs 4.3 and 4.4 above must be by affidavit.

4.6 On an application for judgment for delivery up of goods where the defendant will not be given the alternative of paying their value, the evidence must identify the goods and state where the claimant believes the goods to be situated and why their specific delivery up is sought.

General

para.5.1 **20.9**

5.1 On all applications to which this practice direction applies, other than those referred to in paragraphs 4.3 and 4.4 above,[11] notice should be given in accordance with Part 23.

5.2 Where default judgment is given on a claim for a sum of money expressed in a foreign currency, the judgment should be for the amount of the foreign currency with the addition of 'or the sterling equivalent at the time of payment'.

[* The text issued by the Ministry of Justice mistakenly refers to r. 40.8.]

[11] See rule 12.11(4) and (5).

CPR Part 13 Setting Aside or Varying Default Judgment

Part 13 **1.16, 18.6, 20.11, 20.22, 62.3, 63.1** [For commentary on a specific rule, please refer to the cross-references after the title of the rule.]

13.1 Scope of this Part

r.13.1 **20.15**

The rules in this Part set out the procedure for setting aside or varying judgment entered under Part 12 (default judgment).

(CCR Order 22, r. 10 sets out the procedure for varying the rate at which a judgment debt must be paid)

13.2 Cases Where the Court Must Set Aside Judgment Entered under Part 12

r.13.2 **1.16, 20.1, 20.12**
r.13.2(a)–(c) **20.12**

The court must set aside a judgment entered under Part 12 if judgment was wrongly entered because—

(a) in the case of a judgment in default of an acknowledgment of service, any of the conditions in rule 12.3(1) and 12.3(3) was not satisfied;

(b) in the case of a judgment in default of a defence, any of the conditions in rule 12.3(2) and 12.3(3) was not satisfied; or

(c) the whole of the claim was satisfied before judgment was entered.

13.3 Cases Where the Court May Set Aside or Vary Judgment Entered under Part 12

r.13.3 **1.16, 20.14, 20.17, 62.2**
r. 13.3(1) **20.13, 20.18**
r.13.3(1)(a) **20.16, 20.17, 32.29**
r.13.3(1)(b) **15.4, 15.7, 15.40, 20.15, 20.17, 20.18**
r.13.3(2) **20.15**

(1) In any other case, the court may set aside(GL) or vary a judgment entered under Part 12 if—

  (a) the defendant has a real prospect of successfully defending the claim; or

  (b) it appears to the court that there is some other good reason why—

    (i) the judgment should be set aside or varied; or

    (ii) the defendant should be allowed to defend the claim.

(2) In considering whether to set aside(GL) or vary a judgment entered under Part 12, the matters to which the court must have regard include whether the person seeking to set aside the judgment made an application to do so promptly.

(Rule 3.1(3) provides that the court may attach conditions when it makes an order)

(Article 19(4) of the Service Regulation (which has the same meaning as in rule 6.31(e)) applies to applications to appeal a judgment in default when the time limit for appealing has expired)

13.4 Application to Set Aside or Vary Judgment — Procedure

r.13.4 **11.19, 12.10**
r.13.4(1) **20.20, 42.7**
r.13.4(1A) **42.8**
r.13.4(1B) **11.9, 20.20**
r. 13.4(3) **20.20, 32.15**

(1) Where—

  (a) the claim is for a specified amount of money;

  (b) *the judgment* was obtained in a court which is not the defendant's home court;

  (c) the claim has not been transferred to another defendant's home court; and

  (d) the defendant is an individual

the court will transfer an application by a defendant under this Part to set aside[GL] or vary judgment to the defendant's home court.

(1B) Where—

(a) the claim is for a specified amount of money;

(b) the claim is a designated money claim;

(c) the claim has not been transferred to another court; and

(d) the defendant is not an individual,

the court will transfer an application by a defendant under this Part to set aside or vary the judgment to the preferred court.

(2) Paragraph (1) does not apply where the claim was commenced in a specialist list.

(3) An application under rule 13.3 (cases where the court may set aside[GL] or vary judgment) must be supported by evidence.

13.5 [*Revoked*]

r.13.5 20.22

13.6 Abandoned Claim Restored Where Default Judgment Set Aside

r.13.6 20.4

Where—

(a) the claimant claimed a remedy in addition to one specified in rule 12.4(1) (claims in respect of which the claimant may obtain default judgment by filing a request);

(b) the claimant abandoned his claim for that remedy in order to obtain default judgment on request in accordance with rule 12.4(3); and

(c) that default judgment is set aside[GL] under this Part,

the abandoned claim is restored when the default judgment is set aside.

CPR Part 14 Admissions

Part 14 **17.2, 17.4, 20.2, 26.6, 29.9, 42.27** [For commentary on a specific rule, please refer to the cross-references after the title of the rule.]

14.1 Admissions Made after Commencement of Proceedings

r.14.1 **17.4**
r.14.1(1)–(2) **17.3, 29.9, 49.9**
r.14.1(4) **17.6**
r.14.1(4)(a)–(b) **14.22**
r.14.1(5) **17.4, 17.6, 34.30, 34.31, 49.9**

(1) A party may admit the truth of the whole or any part of another party's case.
(2) He may do this by giving notice in writing (such as in a statement of case or by letter).
(3) Where the only remedy which the claimant is seeking is the payment of money, the defendant may also make an admission in accordance with—
  (a) rule 14.4 (admission of whole claim for specified amount of money);
  (b) rule 14.5 (admission of part of claim for specified amount of money);
  (c) rule 14.6 (admission of liability to pay whole of claim for unspecified amount of money); or
  (d) rule 14.7 (admission of liability to pay claim for unspecified amount of money where defendant offers a sum in satisfaction of the claim).
(4) Where the defendant makes an admission as mentioned in paragraph (3), the claimant has a right to enter judgment except where—
  (a) the defendant is a child or protected party; or
  (b) the claimant is a child or protected party and the admission is made under rule 14.5 or 14.7.

(Rule 21.10 provides that, where a claim is made by or on behalf of a child or protected party or against a child or protected party, no settlement, compromise or payment shall be valid, so far as itrelates to that person's claim, without the approval of the court)

(5) The permission of the court is required to amend or withdraw an admission.

(Rule 3.1(3) provides that the court may attach conditions when it makes an order)

14.1A Admissions Made before Commencement of Proceedings

r.14.1A **17.2, 17.4, 34.28, 34.30**
r.14.1A(1) **17.2, 17.4, 34.30, 49.9**
r.14.1A(2) **17.2, 17.4**
r.14.1A(2)(a) **34.28, 34.30**
r.14.1A(2)(b) **34.30**
r.14.1A(3) **17.2, 17.4**
r.14.1A(3)(a) **34.30**
r.14.1A(3)(b) **34.30, 34.31**
r.14.1A(4) **34.30**
r.14.1A(5) **34.30**

(1) A person may, by giving notice in writing, admit the truth of the whole or any part of another party's case before commencement of proceedings (a 'pre-action admission').

(2) Paragraphs (3) to (5) of this rule apply to a pre-action admission made in the types of proceedings listed at paragraph 1.1(2) of Practice Direction 14 if one of the following conditions is met—
(a) it is made after the party making it has received a letter before claim in accordance with the Practice Direction (Pre-action Conduct) or any relevant pre-action protocol; or
(b) it is made before such letter before claim has been received, but it is stated to be made under Part 14.
(3) A person may, by giving notice in writing, withdraw a pre-action admission—
(a) before commencement of proceedings, if the person to whom the admission was made agrees;
(b) after commencement of proceedings, if all parties to the proceedings consent or with the permission of the court.
(4) After commencement of proceedings—
(a) any party may apply for judgment on the pre-action admission; and
(b) the party who made the pre-action admission may apply to withdraw it.
(5) An application to withdraw a pre-action admission or to enter judgment on such an admission—
(a) must be made in accordance with Part 23;
(b) may be made as a cross-application.

[*Rule 14.1A will not apply to an admission made before 6 April 2007 (Civil Procedure (Amendment No. 3) Rules 2006 (SI 2006/3435), r. 5.*]

14.1B Admissions Made under the RTA Protocol

r.14.1B 17.4, 17.5
r.14.1B(2)(a) 8.43, 17.5
r.14.1B(2)(b) 8.52, 17.5
r.14.1B(3) 17.5
r.14.1B(4) 17.5

(1) This rule applies to a pre-action admission made in a case to which the Pre-Action Protocol for Low Value Personal Injury Claims in Road Traffic Accidents ('the RTA Protocol') applies.
(2) The defendant may, by giving notice in writing withdraw an admission of causation—
(a) before commencement of proceedings—
(i) during the initial consideration period (or any extension to that period) as defined in the RTA Protocol; or
(ii) at any time if the person to whom the admission was made agrees; or
(b) after commencement of proceedings—
(i) if all the parties to the proceedings consent; or
(ii) with the permission of the court.
(3) The defendant may, by giving notice in writing withdraw any other pre-action admission after commencement of proceedings—
(a) if all the parties to the proceedings consent; or
(b) with the permission of the court.
(4) An application under rule 14.1B(2)(b)(ii) or (3)(b) to withdraw a pre-action admission must be made in accordance with Part 23.

14.2 Period for Making an Admission

r.14.2 PC 12, PC 18, 12.10, 17.6
r.14.2(2)–(3) 17.6

(1) The period for returning an admission under rule 14.4 or for filing it under rules 14.5, 14.6 or 14.7 is—
(a) where the defendant is served with a claim form which states that particulars of claim will follow, 14 days after service of the particulars; and
(b) in any other case, 14 days after service of the claim form.
(2) Paragraph (1) is subject to the following rules—
(a) rule 6.35 (which specifies how the period for filing or returning an admission is calculated where the claim form is served out of the jurisdiction under rule 6.32 or 6.33); and
(b) rule 6.12(3) (which requires the court to specify the period for responding to the particulars of claim when it makes an order under that rule).
(3) A defendant may return an admission under rule 14.4 or file it under rules 14.5, 14.6 or 14.7 after the end of the period for returning or filing it specified in paragraph (1) if the claimant has not obtained default judgment under Part 12.
(4) If he does so, this Part shall apply as if he had made the admission within that period.

14.3 Admission by Notice in Writing — Application for Judgment

r.14.3 17.8, 29.9 r.14.3(1)–(2) 17.3

(1) Where a party makes an admission under rule 14.1(2) (admission by notice in writing), any other party may apply for judgment on the admission.
(2) Judgment shall be such judgment as it appears to the court that the applicant is entitled to on the admission.

14.4 Admission of Whole of Claim for Specified Amount of Money

r.14.4 PC 12, 13.8, 17.6, 17.7, 17.11 r.14.4(4) PC 12, 17.7
r.14.4(2) PC 12, 17.7 r.14.4(5)–(6) 17.7
r.14.4(3) 17.7

(1) This rule applies where—
  (a) the only remedy which the claimant is seeking is the payment of a specified amount of money; and
  (b) the defendant admits the whole of the claim.
(2) The defendant may admit the claim by returning to the claimant an admission in the relevant practice form.
(3) The claimant may obtain judgment by filing a request in the relevant practice form and, if he does so—
  (a) if the defendant has not requested time to pay, the procedure in paragraphs (4) to (6) will apply;
  (b) if the defendant has requested time to pay, the procedure in rule 14.9 will apply.
(4) The claimant may specify in his request for judgment—
  (a) the date by which the whole of the judgment debt is to be paid; or
  (b) the times and rate at which it is to be paid by instalments.
(5) On receipt of the request for judgment the court will enter judgment.
(6) Judgment will be for the amount of the claim (less any payments made) and costs—
  (a) to be paid by the date or at the rate specified in the request for judgment; or
  (b) if none is specified, immediately.

(Rule 14.14 deals with the circumstances in which judgment under this rule may include interest)

14.5 Admission of Part of a Claim for a Specified Amount of Money

r.14.5 PC 12, 13.8, 14.22, 17.6, 17.8, 42.12 r.14.5(4) 17.8
r.14.5(2) PC 12 r.14.5(5) PC 12, 17.8
r.14.5(3) PC 12, 17.8 r.14.5(7) PC 12

(1) This rule applies where—
  (a) the only remedy which the claimant is seeking is the payment of a specified amount of money; and
  (b) the defendant admits part of the claim.
(2) The defendant may admit part of the claim by filing an admission in the relevant practice form.
(3) On receipt of the admission, the court will serve a notice on the claimant requiring him to return the notice stating that—
  (a) he accepts the amount admitted in satisfaction of the claim;
  (b) he does not accept the amount admitted by the defendant and wishes the proceedings to continue; or
  (c) if the defendant has requested time to pay, he accepts the amount admitted in satisfaction of the claim, but not the defendant's proposals as to payment.
(4) The claimant must—
  (a) file the notice; and
  (b) serve a copy on the defendant,within 14 days after it is served on him.
(5) If the claimant does not file the notice within 14 days after it is served on him, the claim is stayed(GL) until he files the notice.
(6) If the claimant accepts the amount admitted in satisfaction of the claim, he may obtain judgment by filing a request in the relevant practice form and, if he does so—
  (a) if the defendant has not requested time to pay, the procedure in paragraphs (7) to (9) will apply;
  (b) if the defendant has requested time to pay, the procedure in rule 14.9 will apply.

(7) The claimant may specify in his request for judgment—
(a) the date by which the whole of the judgment debt is to be paid; or
(b) the time and rate at which it is to be paid by instalments.
(8) On receipt of the request for judgment, the court will enter judgment.
(9) Judgment will be for the amount admitted (less any payments made) and costs—
(a) to be paid by the date or at the rate specified in the request for judgment; or
(b) if none is specified, immediately.
(If the claimant files notice under paragraph (3) that he wishes the proceedings to continue, the procedure which then follows is set out in Part 26)

14.6 Admission of Liability to Pay Whole of Claim for Unspecified Amount of Money

r.14.6 PC 12, 11.9, 13.8, 17.6, 17.9, 42.8
r.14.6(2)–(3) PC 12
r.14.6(5) PC 12, 17.9
r.14.6(6) PC 12

(1) This rule applies where—
(a) the only remedy which the claimant is seeking is the payment of money;
(b) the amount of the claim is not specified; and
(c) the defendant admits liability but does not offer to pay a specified amount of money in satisfaction of the claim.
(2) The defendant may admit the claim by filing an admission in the relevant practice form.
(3) On receipt of the admission, the court will serve a copy on the claimant.
(4) The claimant may obtain judgment by filing a request in the relevant practice form.
(5) If the claimant does not file a request for judgment within 14 days after service of the admission on him, the claim is stayed(GL) until he files the request.
(6) On receipt of the request for judgment the court will enter judgment.
(7) Judgment will be for an amount to be decided by the court and costs.

14.7 Admission of Liability to Pay Claim for Unspecified Amount of Money Where Defendant Offers a Sum in Satisfaction of the Claim

r.14.7 PC 12, 11.9, 13.8, 14.22, 17.6, 45.8
r.14.7(2) PC 12
r.14.7(4) PC 12
r.14.7(6) PC 12
r.14.7(9) PC 12

(1) This rule applies where—
(a) the only remedy which the claimant is seeking is the payment of money;
(b) the amount of the claim is not specified; and
(c) the defendant—
(i) admits liability; and
(ii) offers to pay a specified amount of money in satisfaction of the claim.
(2) The defendant may admit the claim by filing an admission in the relevant practice form.
(3) On receipt of the admission, the court will serve a notice on the claimant requiring him to return the notice stating whether or not he accepts the amount in satisfaction of the claim.
(4) If the claimant does not file the notice within 14 days after it is served on him, the claim is stayed(GL) until he files the notice.
(5) If the claimant accepts the offer he may obtain judgment by filing a request in the relevant practice form and if he does so—
(a) if the defendant has not requested time to pay, the procedure in paragraphs (6) to (8) will apply;
(b) if the defendant has requested time to pay, the procedure in rule 14.9 will apply.
(6) The claimant may specify in his request for judgment—
(a) the date by which the whole of the judgment debt is to be paid; or
(b) the times and rate at which it is to be paid by instalments.
(7) On receipt of the request for judgment, the court will enter judgment.
(8) Judgment will be for the amount offered by the defendant (less any payments made) and costs—
(a) to be paid on the date or at the rate specified in the request for judgment; or
(b) if none is specified, immediately.

CPR 1–25 & PDs

(9) If the claimant does not accept the amount offered by the defendant, he may obtain judgment by filing a request in the relevant practice form.
(10) Judgment under paragraph (9) will be for an amount to be decided by the court and costs.

14.7A Automatic Transfer

r.14.7A **11.19, 17.9, 17.10, 42.8**

If—

(a) a claimant files a request for judgment for an amount of money to be decided by the court in accordance with rule 14.6 or 14.7; and
(b) the claim is a designated money claim,

the court will transfer the claim to the preferred court.

14.8 Allocation of Claims in Relation to Outstanding Matters

r.14.8 **PC 12, 17.9, 42.25**

Where the court enters judgment under rule 14.6 or 14.7 for an amount to be decided by the court it will—

(a) give any directions it considers appropriate; and
(b) if it considers it appropriate, allocate the case.

14.9 Request for Time to Pay

r.14.9 **PC 12, 17.7, 17.10, 17.11** r.14.9(4)–(5) **17.7**

(1) A defendant who makes an admission under rules 14.4, 14.5 or 14.7 (admission relating to a claim for a specified amount of money or offering to pay a specified amount of money) may make a request for time to pay.
(2) A request for time to pay is a proposal about the date of payment or a proposal to pay by instalments at the times and rate specified in the request.
(3) The defendant's request for time to pay must be served or filed (as the case may be) with his admission.
(4) If the claimant accepts the defendant's request, he may obtain judgment by filing a request in the relevant practice form.
(5) On receipt of the request for judgment, the court will enter judgment.
(6) Judgment will be—
  (a) where rule 14.4 applies, for the amount of the claim (less any payments made) and costs;
  (b) where rule 14.5 applies, for the amount admitted (less any payments made) and costs; or
  (c) where rule 14.7 applies, for the amount offered by the defendant (less any payments made) and costs; and

  (in all cases) will be for payment at the time and rate specified in the defendant's request for time to pay.

(Rule 14.10 sets out the procedure to be followed if the claimant does not accept the defendant's request for time to pay)

14.10 Determination of Rate of Payment

r.14.10 **PC 12, 17.11** r.14.10(4) **PC 12, 17.7**
r.14.10(2) **PC 12, 17.7**

(1) This rule applies where the defendant makes a request for time to pay under rule 14.9.
(2) If the claimant does not accept the defendant's proposals for payment, he must file a notice in the relevant practice form.
(3) Where the defendant's admission was served direct on the claimant, a copy of the admission and the request for time to pay must be filed with the claimant's notice.
(4) When the court receives the claimant's notice, it will enter judgment for the amount admitted (less any payments made) to be paid at the time and rate of payment determined by the court.

14.11 Determination of Rate of Payment by Court Officer

r.14.11 **PC 12, 11.9**

(1) A court officer may exercise the powers of the court under rule 14.10(4) where the amount outstanding (including costs) is not more than £50,000.
(2) Where a court officer is to determine the time and rate of payment, he must do so without a hearing.

14.12 Determination of Rate of Payment by Judge

r.14.12 PC 12, 11.9 r.14.12(2) 42.7
r.14.12(2A) 11.9, 42.8

(1) Where a judge is to determine the time and rate of payment, he may do so without a hearing.
(2) Where a judge is to determine the time and rate of payment at a hearing, the proceedings will be transferred automatically to the defendant's home court if—
(a) the only claim is for a specified amount of money;
(b) the defendant is an individual;
(c) the claim has not been transferred to another defendant's home court;
(d) the claim was not started in the defendant's home court; and
(e) the claim was not started in a specialist list.
(2A) Where the judge is to determine the time and rate of payment at a hearing, the proceedings will be transferred automatically to the preferred court if—
(a) the only claim is for a specified amount of money;
(b) the claim is a designated money claim;
(c) the defendant is not an individual; and
(d) the claim has not been transferred to another court.
(3) If there is to be a hearing to determine the time and rate of payment, the court will give each party at least 7 days' notice of the hearing.

14.13 Right of Redetermination

r.14.13 PC 12, 11.9 r.14.13(3) 42.7
r.14.13(3A) 11.9, 42.8

(1) Where—
(a) a court officer has determined the time and rate of payment under rule 14.11; or
(b) a judge has determined the time and rate of payment under rule 14.12 without a hearing, either party may apply for the decision to be redetermined by a judge.
(2) An application for redetermination must be made within 14 days after service of the determination on the applicant.
(3) Where an application for redetermination is made, the proceedings will be transferred to the defendant's home court if—
(a) the only claim (apart from a claim for interest or costs) is for a specified amount of money;
(b) the defendant is an individual;
(c) the claim has not been transferred to another defendant's home court;
(d) the claim was not started in the defendant's home court; and
(e) the claim was not started in a specialist list.
(3A) Where an application for re-determination is made, the proceedings will be transferred to the preferred court if—
(a) the only claim (apart from a claim for interest or costs) is for a specified amount of money;
(b) the claim is a designated money claim;
(c) the defendant is not an individual; and
(d) the claim has not been transferred to another court.

14.14 Interest

(1) Judgment under rule 14.4 (admission of whole of claim for specified amount of money) shall include the amount of interest claimed to the date of judgment if—
(a) the particulars of claim include the details required by rule 16.4;
(b) where interest is claimed under section 35A of the Senior Courts Act 1981 or section 69 of the County Courts Act 1984, the rate is no higher than the rate of interest payable on judgment debts at the date when the claim form was issued; and
(c) the claimant's request for judgment includes a calculation of the interest claimed for the period from the date up to which interest was stated to be calculated in the claim form to the date of the request for judgment.
(2) In any case where judgment is entered under rule 14.4 and the conditions in paragraph (1) are not satisfied judgment shall be for an amount of interest to be decided by the court.
(3) Where judgment is entered for an amount of interest to be decided by the court, the court will give directions for the management of the case.

PD 14 Practice Direction 14 — Admissions

This practice direction supplements CPR, Part 14.

[For commentary on a specific paragraph, please refer to the cross-references after the title of the paragraph.]

Admissions Generally

para.1.1 **8.16** para.1.1(2) **34.30**

1.1 (1) Rules 14.1, 14.1A and 14.2 deal with the manner in which a defendant may make an admission of a claim or part of a claim.

(2) Rule 14.1A makes provision about admissions made before commencement of a claim. It applies only to admissions made after 6 April 2007, and only in proceedings to which one of the following pre-action protocols apply:

(a) the Pre-action Protocol for Personal Injury Claims;

(b) the Pre-action Protocol for the Resolution of Clinical Disputes; or

(c) the Pre-action Protocol for Disease and Illness Claims.

(The Pre-action Protocol for Personal Injury Claims states that it is primarily designed for certain types of personal injury claim with a value of less than the fast track limit. But, para. 2.2 of the protocol indicates that it generally applies to all claims which include a claim for personal injury.)

1.2 Rules 14.3, 14.4, 14.5, 14.6 and 14.7 set out how judgment may be obtained on a written admission.

Forms

para.2.1 **17.6**

2.1 When particulars of claim are served on a defendant the forms for responding to the claim that will accompany them will include a form[1] for making an admission.

2.2 If the defendant is requesting time to pay he should complete as fully as possible the statement of means contained in the admission form, or otherwise give in writing the same details of his means as could have been given in the admission form.

Returning or Filing the Admission

3.1 If the defendant wishes to make an admission in respect of the whole of a claim for a specified amount of money, the admission form or other written notice of the admission should be completed and returned to the claimant within 14 days of service of the particulars of claim.[2]

3.2 If the defendant wishes to make an admission in respect of a part of a claim for a specified amount of money, or in respect of a claim for an unspecified amount of money, the admission form or other written notice of admission should be completed and filed with the court within 14 days of service of the particulars of claim.[3]

3.3 The defendant may also file a defence under rule 15.2.

Request for Time to Pay

4.1 A defendant who makes an admission in respect of a claim for a specified sum of money or offers to pay a sum of money in respect of a claim for an unspecified sum may, in the admission form, make a request for time to pay.[4]

4.2 If the claimant accepts the defendant's request, he may obtain judgment by filing a request for judgment contained in form N225A;[5] the court will then enter judgment for payment at the time and rate specified in the defendant's request.[6]

---

[1] Form N9A (specified amount) or N9C (unspecified amount).

[2] Rules 14.2 and 14.4.

[3] *Rules 14.2, 14.5, 14.6 and 14.7.*

[4] Rule 14.9.

[5] Rule 14.9(4).

[6] Rule 14.9(5) and (6).

4.3 If the claimant does not accept the request for time to pay, he should file notice to that effect by completing form N225A; the court will then enter judgment for the amount of the admission (less any payments made) at a time and rate of payment decided by the court (see rule 14.10).

Determining the Rate of Payment

5.1 In deciding the time and rate of payment the court will take into account:
- (1) the defendant's statement of means set out in the admission form or in any other written notice of the admission filed,
- (2) the claimant's objections to the defendant's request set out in the claimant's notice,[7] and
- (3) any other relevant factors.

5.2 The time and rate of payment may be decided:
- (1) by a judge with or without a hearing, or
- (2) by a court officer without a hearing provided that:
  - (a) the only claim is for a specified sum of money, and
  - (b) the amount outstanding is not more than £50,000 (including costs).

5.3 Where a decision has been made without a hearing whether by a court officer or by a judge, either party may apply for the decision to be redetermined by a judge.[8]

5.4 If the decision was made by a court officer the redetermination may take place without a hearing, unless a hearing is requested in the application notice.

5.5 If the decision was made by a judge the redetermination must be made at a hearing unless the parties otherwise agree.

5.6 Rule 14.13(2) describes how to apply for a redetermination.

Varying the Rate of Payment

6.1 Either party may, on account of a change in circumstances since the date of the decision (or redetermination as the case may be) apply to vary the time and rate of payment of instalments still remaining unpaid.

6.2 An application to vary under paragraph 6.1 above should be made in accordance with Part 23.

Withdrawing an Admission

para.7.2 17.4, 34.31

7.1 An admission made under Part 14 may be withdrawn with the court's permission.

7.2 In deciding whether to give permission for an admission to be withdrawn, the court will have regard to all the circumstances of the case, including:
- (a) the grounds upon which the applicant seeks to withdraw the admission including whether or not new evidence has come to light which was not available at the time the admission was made;
- (b) the conduct of the parties, including any conduct which led the party making the admission to do so;
- (c) the prejudice that may be caused to any person if the admission is withdrawn;
- (d) the prejudice that may be caused to any person if the application is refused;
- (e) the stage in the proceedings at which the application to withdraw is made, in particular in relation to the date or period fixed for trial;
- (f) the prospects of success (if the admission is withdrawn) of the claim or part of the claim in relation to which the offer was made; and
- (g) the interests of the administration of justice.

[7] Form N225A.
[8] Rule 14.13(1).

CPR Part 15 Defence and Reply

Part 15 **13.8, 28.5** [For commentary on a specific rule, please refer to the cross-references after the title of the rule.]

15.1 Part Not to Apply Where Claimant Uses Part 8 Procedure

r.15.1 **13.1, 18.4**

This Part does not apply where the claimant uses the procedure set out in Part 8 (alternative procedure for claims).

15.2 Filing a Defence

r.15.2 **18.4, 26.2, 35.8**

A defendant who wishes to defend all or part of a claim must file a defence.
(Part 14 contains further provisions which apply where the defendant admits a claim)

15.3 Consequence of Not Filing a Defence

r.15.3 **18.4, 18.6, 26.2**

If a defendant fails to file a defence, the claimant may obtain default judgment if Part 12 allows it.

15.4 The Period for Filing a Defence

r.15.4 **PC 15, PC 16, PC 18, PC 37, 19.3, 26.3, 87.16**
r.15.4(1) **PC 17**
r.15.4(1)(a)–(b) **PC 13, 18.5, 26.3**
r. 15.4(2) **28.7**
r.15.4(2)(a) **26.3**

(1) The general rule is that the period for filing a defence is—
  (a) 14 days after service of the particulars of claim; or
  (b) if the defendant files an acknowledgment of service under Part 10, 28 days after service of theparticulars of claim.

(Rule 7.4 provides for the particulars of claim to be contained in or served with the claim form or served within 14 days of service of the claim form)

(2) The general rule is subject to the following rules—
  (a) rule 6.35 (which specifies how the period for filing a defence is calculated where the claim form is served out of the jurisdiction under rule 6.32 or 6.33);
  (b) rule 11 (which provides that, where the defendant makes an application disputing the court's jurisdiction, the defendant need not file a defence before the hearing);
  (c) rule 24.4(2) (which provides that, if the claimant applies for summary judgment before the defendant has filed a defen ce, the defendant need not file a defence before the summary judgment hearing); and
  (d) rule 6.12(3) (which requires the court to specify the period for responding to the particulars of claim when it makes an order under that rule).

15.5 Agreement Extending the Period for Filing a Defence

r. 15.5 **PC 18, 18.6, 18.7, 26.4**
r.15.5(1) **3.7**
r.15.5(2) **18.7, 26.4**

(1) The defendant and the claimant may agree that the period for filing a defence specified in rule 15.4 shall be extended by up to 28 days.

(2) Where the defendant and the claimant agree to extend the period for filing a defence, the defendant must notify the court in writing.

15.6 Service of Copy of Defence

r.15.6 PC 18, 18.4, 26.2

A copy of the defence must be served on every other party.
(Part 16 sets out what a defence must contain)
(The Costs Practice Direction [PD 43–48] sets out the information about a funding arrangement to be provided with the defence where the defendant intends to seek to recover an additional liability)
('Funding arrangement' and 'additional liability' are defined in rule 43.2)

15.7 Making a Counterclaim

Part 20 applies to a defendant who wishes to make a counterclaim.

15.8 Reply to Defence

r.15.8 27.1

If a claimant files a reply to the defence, he must—
(a) file his reply when he files his allocation questionnaire; and
(b) serve his reply on the other parties at the same time as he files it.
(Rule 26.3(6) requires the parties to file allocation questionnaires and specifies the period for doing so)
(Part 22 requires a reply to be verified by a statement of truth)

15.9 No Statement of Case after a Reply to be Filed without Court's Permission

r.15.9 27.3

A party may not file or serve any statement of case after a reply without the permission of the court.

15.10 Claimant's Notice Where Defence Is That Money Claimed Has Been Paid

r.15.10 26.10, 42.12

(1) Where—
(a) the only claim (apart from a claim for costs and interest) is for a specified amount of money; and
(b) the defendant states in his defence that he has paid to the claimant the amount claimed,
the court will send notice to the claimant requiring him to state in writing whether he wishes the proceedings to continue.
(2) When the claimant responds, he must serve a copy of his response on the defendant
(3) If the claimant fails to respond under this rule within 28 days after service of the court's notice on him the claim shall be stayed(GL).
(4) Where a claim is stayed under this rule any party may apply for the stay(GL) to be lifted.
(If the claimant files notice under this rule that he wishes the proceedings to continue, the procedure which then follows is set out in Part 26)

15.11 Claim Stayed If It Is Not Defended or Admitted

r. 15.11 26.5

(1) Where—
(a) at least 6 months have expired since the end of the period for filing a defence specified in rule 15.4;
(b) no defendant has served or filed an admission or filed a defence or counterclaim; and
(c) the claimant has not entered or applied for judgment under Part 12 (default judgment), or part 24 (summary judgment),
the claim shall be stayed(GL).
(2) Where a claim is stayed(GL) under this rule any party may apply for the stay to be lifted.

CPR 1–25 & PDs

PD 15 Practice Direction 15 — Defence and Reply

This practice direction supplements CPR, Part 15.

[For commentary on a specific paragraph, please refer to the cross-references after the title of the paragraph.]

Defending the Claim

para.1.3 26.1

1.1 The provisions of Part 15 do not apply to claims in respect of which the Part 8 procedure is being used.

1.2 In relation to specialist proceedings (see Part 49) in respect of which special provisions for defence and reply are made by the rules and practice directions applicable to those claims, the provisions of Part 15 apply only to the extent that they are not inconsistent with those rules and practice directions.

1.3 Form N9B (specified amount) or N9D (unspecified amount or non-money claims) may be used for the purpose of defence and is included in the response pack served on the defendant with the particulars of claim.

1.4 Attention is drawn to r. 15.3 which sets out a possible consequence of not filing a defence.

(Part 16 (statements of case) and PD 16 contain rules and directions about the contents of a defence.)

(PD 43–48 contains details of the information required to be filed with a defence to comply with 44.15 (providing information about funding arrangements))

Statement of Truth

paras.2.1–2.2 PC 18

2.1 Part 22 requires a defence to be verified by a statement of truth.

2.2 The form of the statement of truth is as follows:
'[I believe] [the defendant believes] that the facts stated in this defence are true.'

2.3 Attention is drawn to r. 32.14 which sets out the consequences of verifying a statement of case containing a false statement without an honest belief in its truth.

(For information about statements of truth see Part 22 and PD 22.)

General

para.3.1 28.3 para.3.4 26.5

3.1 Where a defendant to a claim serves a counterclaim under Part 20, the defence and counterclaim should normally form one document with the counterclaim following on from the defence.

3.2 Where a claimant serves a reply and a defence to counterclaim, the reply and defence to counterclaim should normally form one document with the defence to counterclaim following on from the reply.

3.2A Rule 15.8(a) provides that a claimant must file any reply with his directions questionnaire. Where the date by which he must file his directions questionnaire is later than the date by which he must file his defence to counterclaim (because the time for filing the directions questionnaire under rule 26.3(6) is more than 14 days after the date on which it is deemed to be served), the court will normally order that the defence to counterclaim must be filed by the same date as the reply. Where the court does not make such an order the reply and defence to counterclaim may form separate documents.

3.3 Where a claim has been stayed under r. 15.10(3) or 15.11(1) any party may apply for the stay to be lifted.[1]

3.4 The application should be made in accordance with Part 23 and should give the reason for the applicant's delay in proceeding with or responding to the claim.

(PD 6A, para. 8.2, contains provisions about service by the court on the claimant of any notice of *funding filed with a defence.*)

---

[1] Rules 15.10(4) and 15.11(2).

CPR Part 16 Statements of Case

Part 16 13.7, 24.17, 77.60 [For commentary on a specific rule, please refer to the cross-references after the title of the rule.]

16.1 Part Not to Apply Where Claimant Uses Part 8 Procedure

r.16.1 13.1

This Part does not apply where the claimant uses the procedure set out in Part 8 (alternative procedure for claims).

16.2 Contents of the Claim Form

r. 16.2(1) 23.6, 24.19, 33.13
r.16.2(1A) 14.46, 23.18
r.16.2(1)(a) 23.6, 24.16, 24.19, 31.27
r.16.2(1)(b) 4.1, 23.7, 63.6
r.16.2(1)(c) 23.18
r.16.2(1)(d) 23.18
r.16.2(3) 14.43, 23.5
r.16.2(4) 23.5
r16.2(5) 4.1, 23.7

(1) The claim form must—
(a) contain a concise statement of the nature of the claim;
(b) specify the remedy which the claimant seeks;
(c) where the claimant is making a claim for money, contain a statement of value in accordance with rule 16.3;
(cc) where the claimant's only claim is for a specified sum, contain a statement of the interest accrued on that sum; and
(d) contain such other matters as may be set out in a practice direction.

(1A) In civil proceedings against the Crown, as defined in rule 66.1(2), the claim form must also contain—
(a) the names of the government departments and officers of the Crown concerned; and
(b) brief details of the circumstances in which it is alleged that the liability of the Crown arose.

(2) If the particulars of claim specified in rule 16.4 are not contained in, or are not served with the claim form, the claimant must state on the claim form that the particulars of claim will follow.

(3) If the claimant is claiming in a representative capacity, the claim form must state what that capacity is.

(4) If the defendant is sued in a representative capacity, the claim form must state what that capacity is.

(5) The court may grant any remedy to which the claimant is entitled even if that remedy is not specified in the claim form.

(Part 22 requires a claim form to be verified by a statement of truth)
(The Costs Practice Direction [PD 43–48] sets out the information about a funding arrangement to be provided with the statement of case where the defendant intends to seek to recover an additional liability)
('Funding arrangement' and 'additional liability' are defined in rule 43.2)

16.3 Statement of Value to Be Included in the Claim Form

r.16.3 23.8, 24.14, 26.9
r.16.3(2)–(4) 23.8
r.16.3(5) 23.9
r.16.3(6) 11.4, 23.10
r. 16.3(7) 23.8

(1) This rule applies where the claimant is making a claim for money.

(2) The claimant must, in the claim form, state—
(a) the amount of money claimed;
(b) that the claimant expects to recover—
(i) not more than £10,000;
(ii) more than £10,000 but not more than £25,000; or
(iii) more than £25,000; or
(c) that the claimant cannot say how much is likely to be recovered.

(3) In a claim for personal injuries, the claimant must also state in the claim form whether the amount which the claimant expects to recover as general damages for pain, suffering and loss of amenity is—
(a) not more than £1,000; or
(b) more than £1,000.

(4) In a claim which includes a claim by a tenant of residential premises against a landlord where the tenant is seeking an order requiring the landlord to carry out repairs or other work to the premises, the claimant must also state in the claim form—
(a) whether the estimated costs of those repairs or other work is—
(i) not more than £1,000; or
(ii) more than £1,000; and
(b) whether the value of any other claim for damages is—
(i) not more than £1,000; or
(ii) more than £1,000.

(5) If the claim form is to be issued in the High Court it must, where this rule applies—
(a) state that the claimant expects to recover more than £25,000;
(b) state that some other enactment provides that the claim may be commenced only in the High Court and specify that enactment;
(c) if the claim is a claim for personal injuries state that the claimant expects to recover £50,000 or more; or
(d) state that the claim is to be in one of the specialist High Court lists and state which list.

(6) When calculating how much the claimant expects to recover, the claimant must disregard any possibility—
(a) that the court may make an award of—
(i) interest;
(ii) costs;
(b) that the court may make a finding of contributory negligence;
(c) that the defendant may make a counterclaim or that the defence may include a set-off; or
(d) that the defendant may be liable to pay an amount of money which the court awards to the claimant to the Secretary of State for Social Security under section 6 of the Social Security (Recovery of Benefits) Act 1997.

(7) The statement of value in the claim form does not limit the power of the court to give judgment for the amount which it finds the claimant is entitled to.

16.4 Contents of the Particulars of Claim

r.16.4 **24.1, 89.24**
r.16.4(1) **49.2**
r.16.4(1)(a) **24.3, 24.17, 24.19, 33.1**
r.16.4(1)(b) **24.3**
r.16.4(1)(c) **4.9, 4.10, 24.3, 24.14**
r.16.4(1)(d)–(e) **24.3**
r.16.4(2) **24.3, 24.14, 64.21**
r.16.4(2)(a)–(b) **24.3**

(1) Particulars of claim must include—
(a) a concise statement of the facts on which the claimant relies;
(b) if the claimant is seeking interest, a statement to that effect and the details set out in paragraph (2);
(c) if the claimant is seeking aggravated damages(GL) or exemplary damages(GL), a statement to that effect and his grounds for claiming them;
(d) if the claimant is seeking provisional damages, a statement to that effect and his grounds for claiming them; and
(e) such other matters as may be set out in a practice direction.

(2) If the claimant is seeking interest he must—
(a) state whether he is doing so—

(i) under the terms of a contract;
(ii) under an enactment and if so which; or
(iii) on some other basis and if so what that basis is; and
(b) if the claim is for a specified amount of money, state—
(i) the percentage rate at which interest is claimed;
(ii) the date from which it is claimed;
(iii) the date to which it is calculated, which must not be later than the date on which the claim form is issued;
(iv) the total amount of interest claimed to the date of calculation; and
(v) the daily rate at which interest accrues after that date.

(Part 22 requires particulars of claim to be verified by a statement of truth)

16.5 Contents of Defence

r.16.5 **26.13, 89.24**
r. 16.5(1) **26.6, 26.7, 49.2**
r.16.5(1)(b) **26.6**
r.16.5(1)(c) **49.9**
r. 16.5(2) **26.6, 26.22**
r.16.5(2)(a) **33.1**
r.16.5(2)(b) **89.23**
r.16.5(3)–(4) **26.6, 49.2**
r.16.5(5) **26.6, 49.2, 49.9**
r. 16.5(6) **26.9**
r.16.5(7) **26.11**
r.16.5(8) **26.12**

(1) In his defence, the defendant must state—
(a) which of the allegations in the particulars of claim he denies;
(b) which allegations he is unable to admit or deny, but which he requires the claimant to prove; and
(c) which allegations he admits.
(2) Where the defendant denies an allegation—
(a) he must state his reasons for doing so; and
(b) if he intends to put forward a different version of events from that given by the claimant, he must state his own version.
(3) A defendant who—
(a) fails to deal with an allegation; but
(b) has set out in his defence the nature of his case in relation to the issue to which that allegation is relevant, shall be taken to require that allegation to be proved.
(4) Where the claim includes a money claim, a defendant shall be taken to require that any allegation relating to the amount of money claimed be proved unless he expressly admits the allegation.
(5) Subject to paragraphs (3) and (4), a defendant who fails to deal with an allegation shall be taken to admit that allegation.
(6) If the defendant disputes the claimant's statement of value under rule 16.3 he must—
(a) state why he disputes it; and
(b) if he is able, give his own statement of the value of the claim.
(7) If the defendant is defending in a representative capacity, he must state what that capacity is.
(8) If the defendant has not filed an acknowledgment of service under Part 10, the defendant must give an address for service.

(Part 22 requires a defence to be verified by a statement of truth)
(Rule 6.23 makes provision in relation to addresses for service.)

16.6 Defence of Set-off

r.16.6 **4.6, 26.20**

Where a defendant—
(a) contends he is entitled to money from the claimant; and
(b) relies on this as a defence to the whole or part of the claim,
the contention may be included in the defence and set off against the claim, whether or not it is also a Part 20 claim.

16.7 Reply to Defence

r. 16.7(1) **27.1**

(1) A claimant who does not file a reply to the defence shall not be taken to admit the matters raised in the defence.

(2) A claimant who—
(a) files a reply to a defence; but
(b) fails to deal with a matter raised in the defence,
shall be taken to require that matter to be proved.

(Part 22 requires a reply to be verified by a statement of truth)

16.8 Court's Power to Dispense with Statements of Case

r.16.8 24.2

If a claim form has been—
(a) issued in accordance with rule 7.2; and
(b) served in accordance with rule 7.5,
the court may make an order that the claim will continue without any other statement of case.

PD 16 Practice Direction 16 — Statements of Case

This practice direction supplements CPR, Part 16.

[For commentary on a specific paragraph, please refer to the cross-references after the title of the paragraph.]

General

para.1.4 23.3, 24.20

1.1 The provisions of Part 16 do not apply to claims in respect of which the Part 8 procedure is being used.

1.2 Where special provisions about statements of case are made by the rules and practice directions applying to particular types of proceedings, the provisions of Part 16 and of this practice direction apply only to the extent that they are not inconsistent with those rules and practice directions.

1.3 Examples of types of proceedings with special provisions about statements of case include:
(1) defamation claims (Part 53);
(2) possession claims (Part 55); and
(3) probate claims (Part 57).

1.4 If exceptionally a statement of case exceeds 25 pages (excluding schedules) an appropriate short summary must also be filed and served.

The Claim Form

para.2.2 23.5
para.2.3 23.5
para.2.5 23.5
para.2.6 14.1, 14.10, 14.31, 23.5, 24.9
para.2.6(a) 14.1
para.2.6(b) 14.34

2.1 Rule 16.2 refers to matters which the claim form must contain. Where the claim is for money, the claim form must also contain the statement of value referred to in r. 16.3.

2.2 The claim form must include an address at which the claimant resides or carries on business. This paragraph applies even though the claimant's address for service is the business address of his solicitor.

2.3 Where the defendant is an individual, the claimant should (if he is able to do so) include in the claim form an address at which the defendant resides or carries on business. This paragraph applies even though the defendant's solicitor have agreed to accept service on the defendant's behalf.

2.4 Any address which is provided for the purpose of these provisions must include a postcode or its equivalent in any EEA State (if applicable), unless the court orders otherwise. Postcode information for the United Kingdom may be obtained from www.royalmail.com or the Royal Mail Address Management Guide.

2.5 If the claim form does not show a full address, including postcode, at which the claimant(s) and defendant(s) reside or carry on business, the claim form will be issued but will be retained by the court and will not be served until the claimant has supplied a full address, including postcode, or the court has dispensed with the requirement to do so. The court will notify the claimant.

2.6 The claim form must be headed with the title of the proceedings, including the full name of each party. The full name means, in each case where it is known:
(a) in the case of an individual, his full unabbreviated name and title by which he is known;
(b) in the case of an individual carrying on business in a name other than his own name, the full unabbreviated name of the individual, together with the title by which he is known, and the full trading name (for example, John Smith 'trading as' or 'T/as' 'JS Autos');
(c) in the case of a partnership (other than a limited liability partnership (LLP)):
(i) where partners are being sued in the name of the partnership, the full name by which the partnership is known, together with the words '(A Firm)'; or
(ii) where partners are being sued as individuals, the full unabbreviated name of each partner and the title by which he is known;
(d) in the case of a company or limited liability partnership registered in England and Wales, the full registered name, including suffix (plc, limited, LLP, etc.), if any;

CPR 1–25 & PDs

(e) in the case of any other company or corporation, the full name by which it is known, including suffix where appropriate.

(For information about how and where a claim may be started see Part 7 and PD 7A.)

Particulars of Claim

para.3.1 15.4, 23.6, 24.1
para.3.3 15.4
para.3.6(2) 24.3
para.3.8 24.3

3.1 If practicable, the particulars of claim should be set out in the claim form.

3.2 Where the claimant does not include the particulars of claim in the claim form, particulars of claim may be served separately:

(1) either at the same time as the claim form, or

(2) within 14 days after service of the claim form[1] provided that the service of the particulars of claim is not later than four months from the date of issue of the claim form[2] (or six months where the claim form is to be served out of the jurisdiction[3]).

3.3 If the particulars of claim are not included in or have not been served with the claim form, the claim form must also contain a statement that particulars of claim will follow.[4]

3.4 Particulars of claim which are not included in the claim form must be verified by a statement of truth, the form of which is as follows:

[I believe] [the claimant believes] that the facts stated in these particulars of claim are true.

3.5 Attention is drawn to r. 32.14 which sets out the consequences of verifying a statement of case containing a false statement without an honest belief in its truth.

3.6 The full particulars of claim must include:

(1) the matters set out in r. 16.4, and

(2) where appropriate, the matters set out in practice directions relating to specific types of claims.

3.7 Attention is drawn to the provisions of r. 16.4(2) in respect of a claim for interest.

3.8 Particulars of claim served separately from the claim form must also contain:

(1) the name of the court in which the claim is proceeding,

(2) the claim number,

(3) the title of the proceedings, and

(4) the claimant's address for service.

Matters Which Must Be Included in the Particulars of Claim in Certain Types of Claim

para.4 24.6
para.4.2 4.12, 15.40, 24.13
para.4.3 15.38, 24.13

Personal injury claims

4.1 The particulars of claim must contain:

(1) the claimant's date of birth, and

(2) brief details of the claimant's personal injuries.

4.2 The claimant must attach to his particulars of claim a schedule of details of any past and future expenses and losses which he claims.

4.3 Where the claimant is relying on the evidence of a medical practitioner the claimant must attach to or serve with his particulars of claim a report from a medical practitioner about the personal injuries which he alleges in his claim.

4.4 In a provisional damages claim the claimant must state in his particulars of claim:

(1) that he is seeking an award of provisional damages under either the Senior Courts Act 1981, s. 32A or the County Courts Act 1984, s. 51,

(2) that there is a chance that at some future time the claimant will develop some serious disease or suffer some serious deterioration in his physical or mental condition, and

(3) specify the disease or type of deterioration in respect of which an application may be made at a future date.

(Part 41 and PD 41A contain information about awards for provisional damages.)

[1] *See rr.* 7.4(2) and 7.5(1).
[2] See r. 7.4(2) and 7.5(2).
[3] See r. 7.5(2).
[4] See r. 16.2(2).

Fatal accident claims

para.5 24.6

5.1 In a fatal accident claim the claimant must state in his particulars of claim:
(1) that it is brought under the Fatal Accidents Act 1976,
(2) the dependants on whose behalf the claim is made,
(3) the date of birth of each dependant, and
(4) details of the nature of the dependency claim.

5.2 A fatal accident claim may include a claim for damages for bereavement.

5.3 In a fatal accident claim the claimant may also bring a claim under the Law Reform (Miscellaneous Provisions) Act 1934 on behalf of the estate of the deceased.

(For information on apportionment under the Law Reform (Miscellaneous Provisions) Act 1934 and the Fatal Accidents Act 1976 or between dependants see Part 37 and PD 37.)

Hire-purchase claims

para.6 24.6

6.1 Where the claim is for the delivery of goods let under a hire-purchase agreement or conditional sale agreement to a person other than a company or other corporation, the claimant must state in the particulars of claim:
(1) the date of the agreement,
(2) the parties to the agreement,
(3) the number or other identification of the agreement,
(4) where the claimant was not one of the original parties to the agreement, the means by which the rights and duties of the creditor passed to him,
(5) whether the agreement is a regulated agreement, and if it is not a regulated agreement, the reason why,
(6) the place where the agreement was signed by the defendant,
(7) the goods claimed,
(8) the total price of the goods,
(9) the paid-up sum,
(10) the unpaid balance of the total price,
(11) whether a default notice or a notice under s. 76(1) or 98(1) of the Consumer Credit Act 1974 has been served on the defendant, and if it has, the date and method of service,
(12) the date when the right to demand delivery of the goods accrued,
(13) the amount (if any) claimed as an alternative to the delivery of goods, and
(14) the amount (if any) claimed in addition to:
(a) the delivery of the goods, or
(b) any claim under (13) above, with the grounds of each claim.

(If the agreement is a regulated agreement the procedure set out in PD 7B should be used.)

6.2 Where the claim is not for the delivery of goods, the claimant must state in his particulars of claim:
(1) the matters set out in para. 6.1(1) to (6) above,
(2) the goods let under the agreement,
(3) the amount of the total price,
(4) the paid-up sum,
(5) the amount (if any) claimed as being due and unpaid in respect of any instalment or instalments of the total price, and
(6) the nature and amount of any other claim and how it arises.

Other Matters to Be Included in Particulars of Claim

para.7.1 24.6
para.7.2 24.3, 24.6
para.7.3 PC 37, 12.8, 12.10, 15.38, 24.3, 87.8
para.7.4–7.6 24.3

7.1 Where a claim is made for an injunction or declaration in respect of or relating to any land or the possession, occupation, use or enjoyment of any land the particulars of claim must:
(1) state whether or not the injunction or declaration relates to residential premises, and
(2) identify the land (by reference to a plan where necessary).

7.2 Where a claim is brought to enforce a right to recover possession of goods the particulars of claim must contain a statement showing the value of the goods.

7.3 Where a claim is based upon a written agreement:
(1) a copy of the contract or documents constituting the agreement should be attached to or served with the particulars of claim and the original(s) should be available at the hearing, and
(2) any general conditions of sale incorporated in the contract should also be attached (but where the contract is or the documents constituting the agreement are bulky this practice direction is complied with by attaching or serving only the relevant parts of the contract or documents).

7.4 Where a claim is based upon an oral agreement, the particulars of claim should set out the contractual words used and state by whom, to whom, when and where they were spoken.

7.5 Where a claim is based upon an agreement by conduct, the particulars of claim must specify the conduct relied on and state by whom, when and where the acts constituting the conduct were done.

7.6 In a claim issued in the High Court relating to a consumer credit agreement, the particulars of claim must contain a statement that the action is not one to which the Consumer Credit Act 1974, s. 141, applies.

Matters Which Must Be Specifically Set Out In the Particulars of Claim If Relied On

para.8.1 **24.6, 49.96, 49.98** para.8.2 **24.3**

8.1 A claimant who wishes to rely on evidence:
(1) under the Civil Evidence Act 1968, s. 11 of a conviction of an offence, or
(2) under s. 12 of the above mentioned Act of a finding or adjudication of adultery or paternity,
must include in his particulars of claim a statement to that effect and give the following details:
(1) the type of conviction, finding or adjudication and its date,
(2) the court or court martial which made the conviction, finding or adjudication, and
(3) the issue in the claim to which it relates.

8.2 The claimant must specifically set out the following matters in his particulars of claim where he wishes to rely on them in support of his claim:
(1) any allegation of fraud,
(2) the fact of any illegality,
(3) details of any misrepresentation,
(4) details of all breaches of trust,
(5) notice or knowledge of a fact,
(6) details of unsoundness of mind or undue influence,
(7) details of wilful default, and
(8) any facts relating to mitigation of loss or damage.

General

para.9.1 **23.11, 63.18** para.9.3 **23.5**
para.9.2 **27.2**

9.1 Where a claim is for a sum of money expressed in a foreign currency it must expressly state:
(1) that the claim is for payment in a specified foreign currency,
(2) why it is for payment in that currency,
(3) the sterling equivalent of the sum at the date of the claim, and
(4) the source of the exchange rate relied on to calculate the sterling equivalent.

9.2 A subsequent statement of case must not contradict or be inconsistent with an earlier one; for example a reply to a defence must not bring in a new claim. Where new matters have come to light the appropriate course may be to seek the court's permission to amend the statement of case.

9.3 In clinical negligence claims, the words 'clinical negligence' should be inserted at the top of every statement of case.

The Defence

para.10.2 **26.6** para.10.7 **18.3, 26.6**
paras.10.4–10.6 **26.6**

General

10.1 Rule 16.5 deals with the contents of the defence.

10.2 A defendant should deal with every allegation in accordance with r. 16.5(1) and (2).

10.3 Rule 16.5(3), (4) and (5) sets out the consequences of not dealing with an allegation.

10.4 Where the defendant is an individual, and the claim form does not contain an address at which he resides or carries on business, or contains an incorrect address, the defendant must provide such an address in the defence.

10.5 Where the defendant's address for service is not where he resides or carries on business, he must still provide the address required by para. 10.4.

10.6 Any address which is provided for the purpose of these provisions must include a postcode, unless the court orders otherwise. Postcode information may be obtained from www.royalmail.com or the Royal Mail Address Management Guide.

10.7 Where a defendant to a claim or counterclaim is an individual, he must provide his date of birth (if known) in the acknowledgment of service, admission, defence, defence and counterclaim, reply or other response.

Statement of truth

para.11.2 **26.21**

11.1 Part 22 requires a defence to Be verified by a statement of truth.

11.2 The form of the statement of truth is as follows:

[I believe] [the defendant believes] that the facts stated in the defence are true.

11.3 Attention is drawn to r. 32.14 which sets out the consequences of verifying a statement of case containing a false statement without an honest belief in its truth.

Matters Which Must Be Included in the Defence

para.12.1 **26.13**
para.12.1(1)(c) **26.13**
para.12.1(2)–(3) **26.13**
para.12.2(1)–(2) **26.13**

Personal injury claims

12.1 Where the claim is for personal injuries and the claimant has attached a medical report in respect of his alleged injuries, the defendant should:

(1) state in his defence whether he:

(a) agrees,

(b) disputes, or

(c) neither agrees nor disputes but has no knowledge of,

the matters contained in the medical report,

(2) where he disputes any part of the medical report, give in his defence his reasons for doing so, and

(3) where he has obtained his own medical report on which he intends to rely, attach it to his defence.

12.2 Where the claim is for personal injuries and the claimant has included a schedule of past and future expenses and losses, the defendant should include in or attach to his defence a counter-schedule stating:

(1) which of those items he:

(a) agrees,

(b) disputes, or

(c) neither agrees nor disputes but has no knowledge of, and

(2) where any items are disputed, supplying alternative figures where appropriate.

(PD 43–48 contains details of the information required to be filed with certain statements of case to comply with r. 44.15 (providing information about funding arrangements).)

Other matters

para.13.1 **10.1, 26.15**
para.13.2 **26.18**
para.13.3 **24.7**

13.1 The defendant must give details of the expiry of any relevant limitation period relied on.

13.2 Rule 37.3 and PD 37, para. 2, contain information about a defence of tender.

13.3 A party may:

(1) refer in his statement of case to any point of law on which his claim or defence, as the case may be, is based,
(2) give in his statement of case the name of any witness he proposes to call, and
(3) attach to or serve with this statement of case a copy of any document which he considers is necessary to his claim or defence, as the case may be (including any expert's report to befiled in accordance with Part 35).

Competition Act 1998

para.14 **23.18, 24.6, 26.19**

14 Aparty who wishes to rely on a finding of the Office of Fair Trading as provided by the Competition Act 1998, s. 58, must include in his statement of case a statement to that effect and identify the Office's finding on which he seeks to rely.

Human Rights

para.15 **23.18, 24.6, 77.33** para.15.1 **24.3, 26.16, 74.23**

15.1 A party who seeks to rely on any provision of or right arising under the Human Rights Act 1998 or seeks a remedy available under that Act:
(1) must state that fact in his statement of case; and
(2) must in his statement of case:
(a) give precise details of the Convention right which it is alleged has been infringed and details of the alleged infringement;
(b) specify the relief sought;
(c) state if the relief sought includes:
(i) a declaration of incompatibility in accordance with s. 4 of that Act, or
(ii) damages in respect of a judicial act to which s. 9(3) of that Act applies;
(d) where the relief sought includes a declaration of incompatibility in accordance with s. 4 of that Act, give precise details of the legislative provision alleged to be incompatible and details of the alleged incompatibility;
(e) where the claim is founded on a finding of unlawfulness by another court or tribunal, give details of the finding; and
(f) where the claim is founded on a judicial act which is alleged to have infringed a Convention right of the party as provided by the Human Rights Act 1998, s. 9, the judicial act complained of and the court or tribunal which is alleged to have made it.

(PD 19A provides for notice to be given and parties joined in the circumstances referred to in (c), (d) and (f).)

15.2 A party who seeks to amend his statement of case to include the matters referred to in para. 15.1 must, unless the court orders otherwise, do so as soon as possible.
(Part 17 provides for the amendment of a statement of case.)

CPR Part 17 Amendments to Statements of Case

Part 17 **31.22, 77.39** [For commentary on a specific rule, please refer to the cross-references after the title of the rule.]

17.1 Amendments to Statements of Case

r.17.1 **16.37, 31.4**
r. 17.1(1) **31.2, 31.20**
r.17.1(2)(a) **31.2, 31.22, 34.31**
r.17.1(2)(b) **17.4, 31.3**

(1) A party may amend his statement of case at any time before it has been served on any other party.
(2) If his statement of case has been served, a party may amend it only—
 (a) with the written consent of all the other parties; or
 (b) with the permission of the court.
(3) If a statement of case has been served, an application to amend it by removing, adding or substituting a party must be made in accordance with rule 19.4.

(Part 22 requires amendments to a statement of case to be verified by a statement of truth unless the court orders otherwise)

17.2 Power of Court to Disallow Amendments Made without Permission

r.17.2 **31.22**
r.17.2(1)–(2) **31.2**

(1) If a party has amended his statement of case where permission of the court was not required, the court may disallow the amendment.
(2) A party may apply to the court for an order under paragraph (1) within 14 days of service of a copy of the amended statement of case on him.

17.3 Amendments to Statements of Case with the Permission of the Court

r.17.3 **31.4, 34.31**
r.17.3(1)–(2) **31.3**

(1) Where the court gives permission for a party to amend his statement of case, it may give directions as to—
 (a) amendments to be made to any other statement of case; and
 (b) service of any amended statement of case.
(2) The power of the court to give permission under this rule is subject to—
 (a) rule 19.1 (change of parties — general);
 (b) rule 19.4 (special provisions about adding or substituting parties after the end of a relevant limitation period[(GL)]); and
 (c) rule 17.4 (amendments of statement of case after the end of a relevant limitation period).

17.4 Amendments to Statements of Case after the End of a Relevant Limitation Period

r.17.4 **1.19, 14.91, 14.92, 14.94, 31.3, 31.22, 91.40**
r. 17.4(1) **31.22**
r.17.4(2) **31.25, 31.26**
r. 17.4(3) **14.91**
r. 17.4(4) **14.94**

(1) This rule applies where—
 (a) a party applies to amend his statement of case in one of the ways mentioned in this rule; and
 (b) a period of limitation has expired under—
  (i) the Limitation Act 1980;
  (ii) the Foreign Limitation Periods Act 1984; or

CPR 1–25 & PDs

(iii) any other enactment which allows such an amendment, or under which such an amendment is allowed.

(2) The court may allow an amendment whose effect will be to add or substitute a new claim, but only if the new claim arises out of the same facts or substantially the same facts as a claim in respect of which the party applying for permission has already claimed a remedy in the proceedings.

(3) The court may allow an amendment to correct a mistake as to the name of a party, but only wherethe mistake was genuine and not one which would cause reasonable doubt as to the identity of the party in question.

(4) The court may allow an amendment to alter the capacity in which a party claims if the new capacity is one which that party had when the proceedings started or has since acquired.

(Rule 19.5 specifies the circumstances in which the court may allow a new party to be added or substituted after the end of a relevant limitation period(GL))

PD 17 Practice Direction 17 — Amendments to Statements of Case

This practice direction supplements CPR, Part 17.

31.5, 31.18

[For commentary on a specific paragraph, please refer to the cross-references after the title of the paragraph.]

A party applying for an amendment will usually be responsible for the costs of and arising from the amendment.

Applications to Amend Where the Permission of the Court Is Required

paras.1.1–1.3 **31.3**
para.1.4 **30.10, 31.20**
para.1.5 **31.3**

1.1 The application may be dealt with at a hearing or, if rule 23.8 applies, without a hearing.

1.2 When making an application to amend a statement of case, the applicant should file with the court:
(1) the application notice, and
(2) a copy of the statement of case with the proposed amendments.

1.3 Where permission to amend has been given, the applicant should within 14 days of the date of the order, or within such other period as the court may direct, file with the court the amended statement of case.

1.4 If the substance of the statement of case is changed by reason of the amendment, the statement of case should be re-verified by a statement of truth.[1]

1.5 A copy of the order and the amended statement of case should be served on every party to the proceedings, unless the court orders otherwise.

General

para.2 **14.89**
para.2.1(1) **31.3**
para.2.1(2) **31.2**
para.2.2 **31.3, 31.20**
paras.2.3–2.4 **31.20**

2.1 The amended statement of case and the court copy of it should be endorsed as follows:
(1) where the court's permission was required:
'Amended [Particulars of Claim *or as may be*] by Order of [Master.............] [District Judge.............*or as may be*] dated............
(2) Where the court's permission was not required:
'Amended [Particulars of Claim *or as may be*] under CPR [rule 17.1(1) or (2)(a)] dated............'

2.2 The statement of case in its amended form need not show the original text. However, where the court thinks it desirable for both the original text and the amendments to be shown, the court may direct that the amendments should be shown either:
(1) by coloured amendments, either manuscript or computer generated, or
(2) by use of a numerical code in a monochrome computer generated document.

2.3 Where colour is used, the text to be deleted should be struck through in colour and any text replacing it should be inserted or underlined in the same colour.

2.4 The order of colours to be used for successive amendments is: (1) red, (2) green, (3) violet and (4) yellow.

(For information about changes to parties see Part 19 and PD 19A.)

[1] See Part 22 for information about the statement of truth.

CPR Part 18 Further Information

Part 18 **14.79, 24.20, 26.6, 30.1, 30.3, 31.23, 45.6, 45.16, 50.39, 71.33, 82.62** [For commentary on a specific rule, please refer to the cross-references after the title of the rule.]

18.1 Obtaining Further Information

r.18.1 **15.56, 23.2, 30.1, 30.2, 49.9**
r.18.1(1) **30.6**
r.18.1(2) **30.6**
r.18.1(3) **30.6**

(1) The court may at any time order a party to—
  (a) clarify any matter which is in dispute in the proceedings; or
  (b) give additional information in relation to any such matter, whether or not the matter is contained or referred to in a statement of case.
(2) Paragraph (1) is subject to any rule of law to the contrary.
(3) Where the court makes an order under paragraph (1), the party against whom it is made must—
  (a) file his response; and
  (b) serve it on the other parties,within the time specified by the court.

(Part 22 requires a response to be verified by a statement of truth)

(Part 53 (defamation) restricts requirements for providing further information about sources of information in defamation claims)

18.2 Restriction on the Use of Further Information

r.18.2 **30.7**

The court may direct that information provided by a party to another party (whether given voluntarily or following an order made under rule 18.1) must not be used for any purpose except for that of the proceedings in which it is given.

PD 18 Practice Direction 18 — Further Information

This practice direction supplements CPR, Part 18.

PD 18 30.1, 49.9 [For commentary on a specific paragraph, please refer to the cross-references after the title of the paragraph.]

Attention is also drawn to Part 22 (statements of truth).

Preliminary Request for Further Information or Clarification

para.1.1 **30.2, 77.44**
para.1.2 **26.8, 30.1, 30.2**
para.1.3 **30.2**
paras.1.4–1.5 **30.3**
para.1.6 **30.3**
para.1.6(1) **30.3**
para.1.6(2) **30.3, 30.4**
para.1(7) **30.3**

1.1 Before making an application to the court for an order under Part 18, the party seeking clarification or information (the first party) should first serve on the party from whom it is sought (the second party) a written request for that clarification or information (a Request) stating a date by which the response to the Request should be served. The date must allow the second party a reasonable time to respond.

1.2 A Request should be concise and strictly confined to matters which are reasonably necessary and proportionate to enable the first party to prepare his own case or to understand the case he has to meet.

1.3 Requests must be made as far as possible in a single comprehensive document and not piecemeal.

1.4 A Request may be made by letter if the text of the Request is brief and the reply is likely to be brief; otherwise the Request should be made in a separate document.

1.5 If a Request is made in a letter, the letter should, in order to distinguish it from any other that might routinely be written in the course of a case,
(1) state that it contains a Request made under Part 18, and
(2) deal with no matters other than the Request.

1.6 (1) A Request (whether made by letter or in a separate document) must—
(a) be headed with the name of the court and the title and number of the claim,
(b) in its heading state that it is a Request made under Part 18, identify the first party and the second party and state the date on which it is made,
(c) set out in a separate numbered paragraph each request for information or clarification,
(d) where a Request relates to a document, identify that document and (if relevant) the paragraph or words to which it relates,
(e) state the date by which the first party expects a response to the Request,
(2) (a) A Request which is not in the form of a letter may, if convenient, be prepared in such a way that the response may be given on the same document.
(b) To do this the numbered paragraphs of the Request should appear on the left hand half of each sheet so that the paragraphs of the response may then appear on the right.
(c) Where a Request is prepared in this form an extra copy should be served for the use of the second party.

1.7 Subject to the provisions of r. 6.23(5) and (6) and PD 6A, paras 4.1 to 4.3, a request should be served by email if reasonably practicable.

Responding to a Request

para.2.1 **30.4**
para.2.2(1)–(2) **30.4**
para.2.3(1) **30.4**
para.2.3(1)(c) **30.3**
para.2.3(2) **30.4**
para.2.4 **30.4**

2.1 A response to a Request must be in writing, dated and signed by the second party or his legal representative.

CPR 1–25 & PDs

2.2 (1) Where the Request is made in a letter the second party may give his response in a letter or in a formal reply.

(2) Such a letter should identify itself as a response to the Request and deal with no other matters than the response.

2.3 (1) Unless the Request is in the format described in paragraph 1.6(2) and the second party uses the document supplied for the purpose, a response must:

(a) be headed with the name of the court and the title and number of the claim,

(b) in its heading identify itself as a response to that Request,

(c) repeat the text of each separate paragraph of the Request and set out under each paragraph the response to it,

(d) refer to and have attached to it a copy of any document not already in the possession of the first party which forms part of the response.

(2) A second or supplementary response to a Request must identify itself as such in its heading.

2.4 The second party must when he serves his response on the first party serve on every other party and file with the court a copy of the Request and of his response.

Statements of Truth

para.3 **30.3, 30.4**

3 Attention is drawn to Part 22 and to the definition of a statement of case in Part 2 of the rules; a response should be verified by a statement of truth.

General Matters

para.4.1(1)–(2) **30.5** para.4.2(1)–(2) **30.5**

4.1 (1) If the second party objects to complying with the Request or part of it or is unable to do so at all or within the time stated in the Request he must inform the first party promptly and in any event within that time.

(2) He may do so in a letter or in a separate document (a formal response), but in either case he must give reasons and, where relevant, give a date by which he expects to be able to comply.

4.2 (1) There is no need for a second party to apply to the court if he objects to a Request or is unable to comply with it at all or within the stated time. He need only comply with paragraph 4.1(1) above.

(2) Where a second party considers that a Request can only be complied with at disproportionate expense and objects to comply for that reason he should say so in his reply and explain briefly why he has taken that view.

Applications for Orders under Part 18

paras.5.2–5.7 **30.6** para.5.8(2) **30.6**
para.5.8 **30.6**

5.1 Attention is drawn to Part 23 (applications) and to PD 23A.

5.2 An application notice for an order under Part 18 should set out or have attached to it the text of the order sought and in particular should specify the matter or matters in respect of which the clarification or information is sought.

5.3 (1) If a Request under paragraph 1 for the information or clarification has not been made, the application notice should, in addition, explain why not.

(2) If a Request for clarification or information has been made, the application notice or the evidence in support should describe the response, if any.

5.4 Both the first party and the second party should consider whether evidence in support of or in opposition to the application is required.

5.5 (1) Where the second party has made no response to a Request served on him, the first party need not serve the application notice on the second party, and the court may deal with the application without a hearing.

(2) Sub-paragraph (1) above only applies if at least 14 days have passed since the Request was served and the time stated in it for a response has expired.

5.6 *Unless paragraph 5.5 applies the application notice must be served on the second party and on all other parties to the claim.*

5.7 An order made under Part 18 must be served on all parties to the claim.

5.8 Costs:

(1) Attention is drawn to PD 43–48 and in particular the court's power to make a summary assessment of costs.

(2) Attention is also drawn to rule 44.13(1) which provides that the general rule is that if an order does not mention costs no party is entitled to costs relating to that order.

CPR Part 19 Parties and Group Litigation

Part 19 **14.70, 14.83, 14.93, 67.6, 67.13, 87.26, 88.25** [For commentary on a specific rule, please refer to the cross-references after the title of the rule.]

19.1 Parties — General

r.19.1 **14.2**

Any number of claimants or defendants may be joined as parties to a claim.

I ADDITION AND SUBSTITUTION OF PARTIES

19.2 Change of Parties — General

r.19.2 **14.83, 14.84, 16.34, 16.47, 31.3, 88.25**
r. 19.2(2) **14.83, 14.84, 38.31**
r.19.2(2)(a) **9.6, 14.65, 76.13**
r.19.2(2)(b) **14.65, 14.84, 29.12**
r.19.2(3) **14.84, 14.85**
r.19.2(4) **14.13, 14.84, 14.85, 14.93, 14.96, 84.39**

(1) This rule applies where a party is to be added or substituted except where the case falls within rule 19.5 (special provisions about changing parties after the end of a relevant limitation period(GL)).
(2) The court may order a person to be added as a new party if—
  (a) it is desirable to add the new party so that the court can resolve all the matters in dispute in the proceedings; or
  (b) there is an issue involving the new party and an existing party which is connected to the matters in dispute in the proceedings, and it is desirable to add the new party so that the court can resolve that issue.
(3) The court may order any person to cease to be a party if it is not desirable for that person to be a party to the proceedings.
(4) The court may order a new party to be substituted for an existing one if—
  (a) the existing party's interest or liability has passed to the new party; and
  (b) it is desirable to substitute the new party so that the court can resolve the matters in dispute in the proceedings.

19.3 Provisions Applicable Where Two or More Persons Are Jointly Entitled to a Remedy

(1) Where a claimant claims a remedy to which some other person is jointly entitled with him, all persons jointly entitled to the remedy must be parties unless the court orders otherwise.
(2) If any person does not agree to be a claimant, he must be made a defendant, unless the court orders otherwise.
(3) This rule does not apply in probate proceedings.

19.4 Procedure for Adding and Substituting Parties

(1) The court's permission is required to remove, add or substitute a party, unless the claim form has not been served.
(2) An application for permission under paragraph (1) may be made by—
(a) an existing party; or
(b) a person who wishes to become a party.
(3) An application for an order under rule 19.2(4) (substitution of a new party where existing party's interest or liability has passed)—
(a) may be made without notice; and
(b) must be supported by evidence.
(4) Nobody may be added or substituted as a claimant unless—
(a) he has given his consent in writing; and
(b) that consent has been filed with the court.
(4A) The Commissioners for HM Revenue and Customs may be added as a party to proceedings only if they consent in writing.
(5) An order for the removal, addition or substitution of a party must be served on—
(a) all parties to the proceedings; and
(b) any other person affected by the order.
(6) When the court makes an order for the removal, addition or substitution of a party, it may give consequential directions about—
(a) filing and serving the claim form on any new defendant;
(b) serving relevant documents on the new party; and
(c) the management of the proceedings.

19.4A Human Rights

Section 4 of the Human Rights Act 1998

(1) The court may not make a declaration of incompatibility in accordance with section 4 of the Human Rights Act 1998 unless 21 days' notice, or such other period of notice as the court directs, has been given to the Crown.
(2) Where notice has been given to the Crown a Minister, or other person permitted by that Act, shall be joined as a party on giving notice to the court.

(Only courts specified in section 4 of the Human Rights Act 1998 can make a declaration of incompatibility)

Section 9 of the Human Rights Act 1998

(3) Where a claim is made under that Act for damages in respect of a judicial act—
(a) that claim must be set out in the statement of case or the appeal notice; and
(b) notice must be given to the Crown.
(4) Where paragraph (3) applies and the appropriate person has not applied to be joined as a party within 21days, or such other period as the court directs, after the notice is served, the court may join the appropriate person as a party.

(Practice Direction 19A makes provision for these notices)

CPR 1–25 & PDs

19.5 Special Provisions about Adding or Substituting Parties after the End of a Relevant Limitation Period

r.19.5 14.90, 31.3, 31.9
r.19.5(2) 14.91, 14.92
r.19.5(3) 14.91, 14.94
r.19.5(3)(a) 1.23, 14.91, 14.92
r.19.5(3)(b) 14.91, 14.92, 84.39
r.19.5(3)(c) 14.13, 14.93
r.19.5(4) 14.95

(1) This rule applies to a change of parties after the end of a period of limitation under—
 (a) the Limitation Act 1980;
 (b) the Foreign Limitation Periods Act 1984; or
 (c) any other enactment which allows such a change, or under which such a change is allowed.
(2) The court may add or substitute a party only if—
 (a) the relevant limitation period(GL) was current when the proceedings were started; and
 (b) the addition or substitution is necessary.
(3) The addition or substitution of a party is necessary only if the court is satisfied that—
 (a) the new party is to be substituted for a party who was named in the claim form in mistake for the new party;
 (b) the claim cannot properly be carried on by or against the original party unless the new party is added or substituted as claimant or defendant; or
 (c) the original party has died or had a bankruptcy order made against him and his interest or liability has passed to the new party.
(4) In addition, in a claim for personal injuries the court may add or substitute a party where it directs that—
 (a) (i) section 11 (special time limit for claims for personal injuries); or
  (ii) section 12 (special time limit for claims under fatal accidents legislation),
 of the Limitation Act 1980 shall not apply to the claim by or against the new party; or
 (b) the issue of whether those sections apply shall be determined at trial.

(Rule 17.4 deals with other changes after the end of a relevant limitation period(GL))

19.5A Special Rules about Parties in Claims for Wrongful Interference with Goods

r.19.5A 14.5
r.19.5A(1) 24.3

(1) A claimant in a claim for wrongful interference with goods must, in the particulars of claim, state the name and address of every person who, to his knowledge, has or claims an interest in the goods and who is not a party to the claim.
(2) A defendant to a claim for wrongful interference with goods may apply for a direction that another person be made a party to the claim to establish whether the other person—
 (a) has a better right to the goods than the claimant; or
 (b) has a claim which might render the defendant doubly liable under section 7 of the Torts (Interference with Goods) Act 1977.
(3) Where the person referred to in paragraph (2) fails to attend the hearing of the application, or comply with any directions, the court may order that he is deprived of any claim against the defendant in respect of the goods.

(Rule 3.1(3) provides that the court may make an order subject to conditions)

(4) The application notice must be served on all parties and on the person referred to in paragraph (2).

II REPRESENTATIVE PARTIES

19.6 Representative Parties with Same Interest

r.19.6 14.41, 14.62, 14.63, 14.67, 88.37
r.19.6(1) 14.62, 79.39
r.19.6(2) 14.63
r.19.6(4) 79.39
r.19.6(4)(b) 14.62, 14.63, 88.37

(1) Where more than one person has the same interest in a claim—
 (a) the claim may be begun; or
 (b) the court may order that the claim be continued,

by or against one or more of the persons who have the same interest as representatives of any other persons who have that interest.

(2) The court may direct that a person may not act as a representative.
(3) Any party may apply to the court for an order under paragraph (2).
(4) Unless the court otherwise directs any judgment or order given in a claim in which a party is acting as a representative under this rule—
  (a) is binding on all persons represented in the claim; but
  (b) may only be enforced by or against a person who is not a party to the claim with the permission of the court.
(5) This rule does not apply to a claim to which rule 19.7 applies.

19.7 Representation of Interested Persons Who Cannot Be Ascertained etc.

r.19.7 14.62, 14.64, 14.66, 14.67
r.19.7(1) 14.62
r.19.7(2) 79.39
r.19.7(3)–(6) 14.64
r.19.7(7) 14.64, 79.39

(1) This rule applies to claims about—
  (a) the estate of a deceased person;
  (b) property subject to a trust; or
  (c) the meaning of a document, including a statute.
(2) The court may make an order appointing a person to represent any other person or persons in the claim where the person or persons to be represented—
  (a) are unborn;
  (b) cannot be found;
  (c) cannot easily be ascertained; or
  (d) are a class of persons who have the same interest in a claim and—
    (i) one or more members of that class are within sub-paragraphs (a), (b) or (c); or
    (ii) to appoint a representative would further the overriding objective.
(3) An application for an order under paragraph (2)—
  (a) may be made by—
    (i) any person who seeks to be appointed under the order; or
    (ii) any party to the claim; and
  (b) may be made at any time before or after the claim has started.
(4) An application notice for an order under paragraph (2) must be served on—
  (a) all parties to the claim, if the claim has started;
  (b) the person sought to be appointed, if that person is not the applicant or a party to the claim; and
  (c) any other person as directed by the court.
(5) The court's approval is required to settle a claim in which a party is acting as a representative under this rule.
(6) The court may approve a settlement where it is satisfied that the settlement is for the benefit of all the represented persons.
(7) Unless the court otherwise directs, any judgment or order given in a claim in which a party is acting as a representative under this rule—
  (a) is binding on all persons represented in the claim; but
  (b) may only be enforced by or against a person who is not a party to the claim with the permission of the court.

19.7A Representation of Beneficiaries by Trustees etc.

r.19.7A 14.42

(1) A claim may be brought by or against trustees, executors or administrators in that capacity without adding as parties any persons who have a beneficial interest in the trust or estate ('the beneficiaries').
(2) Any judgment or order given or made in the claim is binding on the beneficiaries unless the court orders otherwise in the same or other proceedings.

19.7B Postal Services Act 2000 (c. 26)

(1) An application under section 92 of the Postal Services Act 2000 for permission to bring proceedings in the name of the sender or addressee of a postal packet or his personal representative is made in accordance with Part 8.
(2) A copy of the application notice must be served on the universal service provider and on the person in whose name the applicant seeks to bring the proceedings.

19.8 Death

r.19.8 14.67
r. 19.8(1) 14.13
r.19.8(1)(b) 14.13
r.19.8(2)(a) 14.12
r.19.8(2)(b)(i)–(ii) 14.12
r.19.8(3)(a)–(b) 14.12
r. 19.8(4) 14.12, 14.13
r.19.8(5) 14.12, 14.13

(1) Where a person who had an interest in a claim has died and that person has no personal representative the court may order—
 (a) the claim to proceed in the absence of a person representing the estate of the deceased; or
 (b) a person to be appointed to represent the estate of the deceased.
(2) Where a defendant against whom a claim could have been brought has died and
 (a) a grant of probate or administration has been made, the claim must be brought against the persons who are the personal representatives of the deceased;
 (b) a grant of probate or administration has not been made—
  (i) the claim must be brought against 'the estate of' the deceased; and
  (ii) the claimant must apply to the court for an order appointing a person to represent the estate of the deceased in the claim.
(3) A claim shall be treated as having been brought against 'the estate of' the deceased in accordance with paragraph (2)(b)(i) where—
 (a) the claim is brought against the 'personal representatives' of the deceased but a grant of probate or administration has not been made; or
 (b) the person against whom the claim was brought was dead when the claim was started.
(4) Before making an order under this rule, the court may direct notice of the application to be given to any other person with an interest in the claim.
(5) Where an order has been made under paragraphs (1) or (2)(b)(ii) any judgment or order made or given in the claim is binding on the estate of the deceased.

19.8A Power to Make Judgments Binding on Non-parties

r.19.8A 14.14, 14.42
r.19.8A(7)–(8) 14.14

(1) This rule applies to any claim relating to—
 (a) the estate of a deceased person;
 (b) property subject to a trust; or
 (c) the sale of any property.
(2) The court may at any time direct that notice of—
 (a) the claim; or
 (b) any judgment or order given in the claim,
 be served on any person who is not a party but who is or may be affected by it.
(3) An application under this rule—
 (a) may be made without notice; and
 (b) must be supported by written evidence which includes the reasons why the person to be served should be bound by the judgment in the claim.
(4) Unless the court orders otherwise—
 (a) a notice of a claim or of a judgment or order under this rule must be—
  (i) in the form required by the practice direction;
  (ii) issued by the court; and
  (iii) accompanied by a form of acknowledgment of service with any necessary modifications;
 (b) a notice of a claim must also be accompanied by—
  (i) a copy of the claim form; and
  (ii) such other statements of case, witness statements or affidavits as the court may direct; and
 (c) a notice of a judgment or order must also be accompanied by a copy of the judgment or order.
(5) If a person served with notice of a claim files an acknowledgment of service of the notice within 14 days he will become a party to the claim.
(6) *If a person served with notice* of a claim does not acknowledge service of the notice he will be bound by any judgment given in the claim as if he were a party.

(7) If, after service of a notice of a claim on a person, the claim form is amended so as substantially to alter the remedy claimed, the court may direct that a judgment shall not bind that person unless a further notice, together with a copy of the amended claim form, is served on him.
(8) Any person served with a notice of a judgment or order under this rule—
(a) shall be bound by the judgment or order as if he had been a party to the claim; but
(b) may, provided he acknowledges service—
(i) within 28 days after the notice is served on him, apply to the court to set aside or vary the judgment or order; and
(ii) take part in any proceedings relating to the judgment or order.
(9) The following rules of Part 10 (acknowledgment of service) apply—
(a) rule 10.4; and
(b) rule 10.5, subject to the modification that references to the defendant are to be read as references to the person served with the notice.
(10) A notice under this rule is issued on the date entered on the notice by the court.

19.9 Derivative Claims — How Started

r.19.9 14.27, 14.43, 14.67
r.19.9(1) 14.27
r.19.9(2)–(4) 14.27

(1) This rule—
(a) applies to a derivative claim (where a company, other body corporate or trade union is alleged to be entitled to claim a remedy, and a claim is made by a member of it for it to be given that remedy), whether under Chapter 1 of Part 11 of the Companies Act 2006 or otherwise; but
(b) does not apply to a claim made pursuant to an order under section 996 of that Act.
(2) A derivative claim must be started by a claim form.
(3) The company, body corporate or trade union for the benefit of which a remedy is sought must be made a defendant to the claim.
(4) After the issue of the claim form, the claimant must not take any further step in the proceedings without the permission of the court, other than—
(a) a step permitted or required by rule 19.9A or 19.9C; or
(b) making an urgent application for interim relief.

19.9A Derivative Claims under Chapter 1 of Part 11 of the Companies Act 2006 — Application for Permission

r.19.9A 14.27, 14.28, 14.43
r.19.9A(2)–(10) 14.27
r.19.9A(12) 14.27

(1) In this rule—
'the Act' means the Companies Act 2006;
'derivative claim' means a derivative claim under Chapter 1 of Part 11 of the Act;
'permission application' means an application referred to in section 261(1), 262(2) or 264(2) of the Act;
'the company' means the company for the benefit of which the derivative claim is brought.
(2) When the claim form for a derivative claim is issued, the claimant must file—
(a) an application notice under Part 23 for permission to continue the claim; and
(b) the written evidence on which the claimant relies in support of the permission application.
(3) The claimant must not make the company a respondent to the permission application.
(4) Subject to paragraph (7), the claimant must notify the company of the claim and permission application by sending to the company as soon as reasonably practicable after the claim form is issued—
(a) a notice in the form set out in Practice Direction 19C, and to which is attached a copy of the provisions of the Act required by that form;
(b) copies of the claim form and the particulars of claim;
(c) the application notice; and
(d) a copy of the evidence filed by the claimant in support of the permission application.
(5) The claimant may send the notice and documents required by paragraph (4) to the company by any method permitted by Part 6 as if the notice and documents were being served on the company.
(6) The claimant must file a witness statement confirming that the claimant has notified the company in accordance with paragraph (4).

CPR 1–25 & PDs

(7) Where notifying the company of the permission application would be likely to frustrate some party* of the remedy sought, the court may, on application by the claimant, order that the company need not be notified for such period after the issue of the claim form as the court directs.
(8) An application under paragraph (7) may be made without notice.
(9) Where the court dismisses the claimant's permission application without a hearing, the court will notify the claimant and (unless the court orders otherwise) the company of that decision.
(10) The claimant may ask for an oral hearing to reconsider the decision to dismiss the permission application, but the claimant—
  (a) must make the request to the court in writing within seven days of being notified of the decision; and
  (b) must notify the company in writing, as soon as reasonably practicable, of that request unless the court orders otherwise.
(11) Where the court dismisses the permission application at a hearing pursuant to paragraph (10), it will notify the claimant and the company of its decision.
(12) Where the court does not dismiss the application under section 261(2) of the Act, the court will—
  (a) order that the company and any other appropriate party must be made respondents to the permission application; and
  (b) give directions for the service on the company and any other appropriate party of the application notice and the claim form.

19.9B Derivative Claims under Chapter 1 of Part 11 of the Companies Act 2006 — Members of Companies Taking over Claims by Companies or Other Members

r.19.9(B) 14.27, 14.28, 14.43

(1) This rule applies to proceedings under section 262(1) or 264(1) of the Companies Act 2006.
(2) The application for permission must be made by an application notice in accordance with Part 23.
(3) Rule 19.9A (except for paragraphs (1), (2) and (4)(b) of that rule, and paragraph (12)(b) so far as it applies to the claim form) applies to an application under this rule and references to the claimant in rule 19.9A are to be read as references to the person who seeks to take over the claim.

19.9C Derivative Claims — Other Bodies Corporate and Trade Unions

r.19.9C 14.27, 14.43

(1) This rule sets out the procedure where—
  (a) either—
    (i) a body corporate to which Chapter 1 of Part 11 of the Companies Act 2006 does not apply; or
    (ii) a trade union, is alleged to be entitled to a remedy; and
  (b) either—
    (i) a claim is made by a member for it to be given that remedy; or
    (ii) a member of the body corporate or trade union seeks to take over a claim already started, by the body corporate or trade union or one or more of its members, for it to be given that remedy.
(2) The member who starts, or seeks to take over, the claim must apply to the court for permission to continue the claim.
(3) The application for permission must be made by an application notice in accordance with Part 23.
(4) The procedure for applications in relation to companies under section 261, 262 or 264 (as the case requires) of the Companies Act 2006 applies to the permission application as if the body corporate or trade union were a company.
(5) Rules 19.9A (except for paragraph (1) of that rule) and 19.9B apply to the permission application as if the body corporate or trade union were a company.

[* Perhaps 'party' should be 'part'.]

19.9D Derivative Claims Arising in the Course of Other Proceedings

r.19.9D 14.27, 14.43

If a derivative claim (except such a claim in pursuance of an order under section 996 of the Companies Act 2006) arises in the course of other proceedings—

(a) in the case of a derivative claim under Chapter 1 of Part 11 of that Act, rule 19.9A or 19.9B applies, as the case requires; and
(b) in any other case, rule 19.9C applies.

19.9E Derivative Claims — Costs

r.19.9E 14.27, 14.43, 44.7

The court may order the company, body corporate or trade union for the benefit of which a derivative claim is brought to indemnify the claimant against liability for costs incurred in the permission application or in the derivative claim or both.

19.9F Derivative Claims — Discontinuance and Settlement

r.19.9F 14.27, 14.28, 14.43

Where the court has given permission to continue a derivative claim, the court may order that the claim may not be discontinued, settled or compromised without the permission of the court.

III GROUP LITIGATION

19.10 Definition

r.19.10 14.27

A Group Litigation Order ('GLO') means an order made under rule 19.11 to provide for the case management of claims which give rise to common or related issues of fact or law (the 'GLO issues').

19.11 Group Litigation Order

r.19.11 14.27, 14.66
r.19.11(2) 14.69
r.19.11(3) 14.71

(1) The court may make a GLO where there are or are likely to be a number of claims giving rise to the GLO issues.

(Practice Direction 19B provides the procedure for applying for a GLO)

(2) A GLO must—
  (a) contain directions about the establishment of a register (the 'group register') on which the claims managed under the GLO will be entered;
  (b) specify the GLO issues which will identify the claims to be managed as a group under the GLO; and
  (c) specify the court (the 'management court') which will manage the claims on the group register.
(3) A GLO may—
  (a) in relation to claims which raise one or more of the GLO issues—
    (i) direct their transfer to the management court;
    (ii) order their stay(GL) until further order; and
    (iii) direct their entry on the group register;
  (b) direct that from a specified date claims which raise one or more of the GLO issues should be started in the management court and entered on the group register; and
  (c) give directions for publicising the GLO.

19.12 Effect of the GLO

r.19.12 14.27
r.19.12(1)(a)–(b) 14.73
r.19.12(2) 14.73
r.19.12(3) 14.73
r.19.12(4) 14.73

(1) Where a judgment or order is given or made in a claim on the group register in relation to one or more GLO issues—
   (a) that judgment or order is binding on the parties to all other claims that are on the group register at the time the judgment is given or the order is made unless the court orders otherwise; and
   (b) the court may give directions as to the extent to which that judgment or order is binding on the parties to any claim which is subsequently entered on the group register.

(2) Unless paragraph (3) applies, any party who is adversely affected by a judgment or order which is binding on him may seek permission to appeal the order.

(3) A party to a claim which was entered on the group register after a judgment or order which is binding on him was given or made may not—
   (a) apply for the judgment or order to be set aside[(GL)], varied or stayed[(GL)]; or
   (b) appeal the judgment or order,

   but may apply to the court for an order that the judgment or order is not binding on him.

(4) Unless the court orders otherwise, disclosure of any document relating to the GLO issues by a party to a claim on the group register is disclosure of that document to all parties to claims—
   (a) on the group register; and
   (b) which are subsequently entered on the group register.

19.13 Case Management

r.19.13 **14.27, 14.70, 14.71**

Directions given by the management court may include directions—
(a) varying the GLO issues;
(b) providing for one or more claims on the group register to proceed as test claims;
(c) appointing the solicitor of one or more parties to be the lead solicitor for the claimants or defendants;
(d) specifying the details to be included in a statement of case in order to show that the criteria for entry of the claim on the group register have been met;
(e) specifying a date after which no claim may be added to the group register unless the court gives permission; and
(f) for the entry of any particular claim which meets one or more of the GLO issues on the group register.

(Part 3 contains general provisions about the case management powers of the court)

19.14 Removal from the Register

r.19.14 **14.27, 14.70**

(1) A party to a claim entered on the group register may apply to the management.
(2) If the management court orders the claim to be removed from the register it may give directions about the future management of the claim.

19.15 Test Claims

r.19,15 **14.72**

(1) Where a direction has been given for a claim on the group register to proceed as a test claim and that claim is settled, the management court may order that another claim on the group register be substituted as the test claim.
(2) Where an order is made under paragraph (1), any order made in the test claim before the date of substitution is binding on the substituted claim unless the court orders otherwise.

PD 19A Practice Direction 19A — Addition and Substitution of Parties

This practice direction supplements CPR, Part 19.

PD 19A **14.13, 31.5, 31.18, 68.7, 68.31** [For commentary on a specific paragraph, please refer to the cross-references after the title of the paragraph.]

A party applying for an amendment will usually be responsible for the costs of and arising from the amendment.

Changes of Parties

para.1.1 **14.83**
para.1.2 **14.88**
para.1.3 **PC 9, 14.87**
para. 1.4 **14.86, 14.87, 35.9**
para. 1.5 **14.89**

General

1.1 Parties may be removed, added or substituted in existing proceedings either on the court's own initiative or on the application of either an existing party or a person who wishes to become a party.

1.2 The application may be dealt with without a hearing where all the existing parties and the proposed new party are in agreement.

1.3 The application to add or substitute a new party should be supported by evidence setting out the proposed new party's interest in or connection with the claim.

1.4 The application notice should be filed in accordance with rule 23.3 and, unless the application is made under rule 19.2(4),[1] be served in accordance with rule 23.4.

1.5 An order giving permission to amend will, unless the court orders otherwise, be drawn up. It will be served by the court unless the parties wish to serve it or the court orders them to do so.

Addition or substitution of claimant

para.2.1 **PC 9, 14.87**
para.2.2 **14.83**
para.2.3(1)–(3) **14.89**

2.1 Where an application is made to the court to add or to substitute a new party to the proceedings as claimant, the party applying must file:
(1) the application notice,
(2) the proposed amended claim form and particulars of claim, and
(3) the signed, written consent of the new claimant to be so added or substituted.

2.2 Where the court makes an order adding or substituting a party as claimant but the signed, written consent of the new claimant has not been filed:
(1) the order, and
(2) the addition or substitution of the new party as claimant,
will not take effect until the signed, written consent of the new claimant is filed.

2.3 Where the court has made an order adding or substituting a new claimant, the court may direct:
(1) a copy of the order to be served on every party to the proceedings and any other person affected by the order,
(2) copies of the statements of case and of documents referred to in any statement of case to be served on the new party,
(3) the party who made the application to file within 14 days an amended claim form and particulars of claim.

Addition or substitution of defendant

para.3.2(1)–(3) **14.89**
para.3.3 **PC 9, 14.89**

3.1 The Civil Procedure Rules apply to a new defendant who has been added or substituted as they apply to any other defendant (see in particular the provisions of Parts 9, 10, 11 and 15).

[1] See rule 19.4(3)(a).

CPR 1–25 & PDs

3.2 Where the court has made an order adding or substituting a defendant whether on its own initiative or on an application, the court may direct:

(1) the claimant to file with the court within 14 days (or as ordered) an amended claim form and particulars of claim for the court file,

(2) a copy of the order to be served on all parties to the proceedings and any other person affected by it,

(3) the amended claim form and particulars of claim, forms for admitting, defending and acknowledging the claim and copies of the statements of case and any other documents referred to in any statement of case to be served on the new defendant.

(4) unless the court orders otherwise, the amended claim form and particulars of claim to be served on any other defendants.

3.3 A new defendant does not become a party to the proceedings until the amended claim form has been served on him.[2]

Removal of party

para.4 **14.89**

4 Where the court makes an order for the removal of a party from the proceedings:

(1) the claimant must file with the court an amended claim form and particulars of claim, and

(2) a copy of the order must be served on every party to the proceedings and on any other person affected by the order.

Transfer of interest or liability

para.5.2 **14.87, 14.96**

5.1 Where the interest or liability of an existing party has passed to some other person, application should be made to the court to add or substitute that person.[3]

5.2 The application must be supported by evidence showing the stage the proceedings have reached and what change has occurred to cause the transfer of interest or liability.

(For information about making amendments generally, see PD 17.)

Human Rights, Joining the Crown

para.6.2 **14.48, 14.80**
para.6.4(1) **14.48, 14.80**
para.6.6 **14.48, 14.80**

Section 4 of the Human Rights Act 1998

6.1 Where a party has included in his statement of case:

(1) a claim for a declaration of incompatibility in accordance with s. 4 of the Human Rights Act 1998, or

(2) an issue for the court to decide which may lead to the court considering making a declaration,

then the court may at any time consider whether notice should be given to the Crown as required by that Act and give directions for the content and service of the notice. The rule [i.e., r. 19.4A] allows a period of 21 days before the court will make the declaration but the court may vary this period of time.

6.2 The court will normally consider the issues and give the directions referred to in para. 6.1 at the case management conference.

6.3 Where a party amends his statement of case to include any matter referred to in para. 6.1, then the court will consider whether notice should be given to the Crown and give directions for the content and service of the notice.

(PD 16 requires a party to include issues under the Human Rights Act 1998 in his statement of case.)

6.4 (1) The notice given under r. 19.4A must be served on the person named in the list published under s. 17 of the Crown Proceedings Act 1947.

(The list, made by the Minister for the Civil Service, is annexed to PD 66.)

---

[2] *Ketteman v Hansel Properties Ltd* [1987] AC 189, HL.

[3] See rule 19.2(4).

(2) The notice will be in the form directed by the court but will normally include the directions given by the court and all the statements of case in the claim. The notice will also be served on all the parties.

(3) The court may require the parties to assist in the preparation of the notice.

(4) In the circumstances described in the National Assembly for Wales (Transfer of Functions) (No. 2) Order 2000 the notice must also be served on the National Assembly for Wales.

(Section 5(3) of the Human Rights Act 1998 provides that the Crown may give notice that it intends to become a party at any stage in the proceedings once notice has been given.)

6.5 Unless the court orders otherwise, the minister or other person permitted by the Human Rights Act 1998 to be joined as a party must, if he wishes to be joined, give notice of his intention to be joined as a party to the court and every other party. Where the minister has nominated a person to be joined as a party the notice must be accompanied by the written nomination.

(Section 5(2)(a) of the Human Rights Act 1998 permits a person nominated by a minister of the Crown to be joined as a party. The nomination may be signed on behalf of the minister.)

Section 9 of the Human Rights Act 1998

6.6 (1) The procedure in paras 6.1 to 6.5 also applies where a claim is made under ss. 7(1)(a) and 9(3) of the Human Rights Act 1998 for damages in respect of a judicial act.

(2) Notice must be given to the Lord Chancellor and should be served on the Treasury Solicitor on his behalf, except where the judicial act is of a court martial when the appropriate person is the Secretary of State for Defence and the notice must be served on the Treasury Solicitor on his behalf.

(3) The notice will also give details of the judicial act, which is the subject of the claim for damages, and of the court or tribunal that made it.

(Section 9(4) of the Human Rights Act 1998 provides that no award of damages may be made against the Crown as provided for in s. 9(3) unless the appropriate person is joined in the proceedings. The appropriate person is the minister responsible for the court concerned or a person or department nominated by him (s. 9(5) of the Act))

PD 19B Practice Direction 19B — Group Litigation

This practice direction supplements Section III of CPR, Part 19.

PD 19B **14.66** [For commentary on a specific paragraph, please refer to the cross-references after the title of the paragraph.]

Introduction

1 This practice direction deals with group litigation where the multiple parties are claimants. Section III of Part 19 (group litigation orders) also applies where the multiple parties are defendants. The court will give such directions in such a case as are appropriate.

Preliminary Steps

paras 2.1–2.3 **14.67**

2.1 Before applying for a group litigation order ('GLO') the solicitor acting for the proposed applicant should consult the Law Society's Multi-Party Actions Information Service in order to obtain information about other cases giving rise to the proposed GLO issues.

2.2 It will often be convenient for the claimants' solicitors to form a solicitors' group and to choose one of their number to take the lead in applying for the GLO and in litigating the GLO issues. The lead solicitor's role and relationship with the other members of the solicitors' group should be carefully defined in writing and will be subject to any directions given by the court under 19.13(c).

2.3 In considering whether to apply for a GLO, the applicant should consider whether any other order would be more appropriate. In particular he should consider whether, in the circumstances of the case, it would be more appropriate for:

(1) the claims to be consolidated; or

(2) the rules in Section II of Part 19 (representative parties) to be used.

Application for a GLO

para.3.1 **14.66, 14.68** paras 3.2–3.8 **14.68**

3.1 An application for a GLO must be made in accordance with CPR, Part 23, may be made at any time before or after any relevant claims have been issued and may be made either by a claimant or by a defendant.

3.2 The following information should be included in the application notice or in written evidence filed in support of the application:

(1) a summary of the nature of the litigation;

(2) the number, and nature of claims already issued;

(3) the number of parties likely to be involved;

(4) the common issues of fact or law (the 'GLO issues') that are likely to arise in the litigation; and

(5) whether there are any matters that distinguish smaller groups of claims within the wider group.

3.3 A GLO may not be made:

(1) in the Queen's Bench Division, without the consent of the Lord Chief Justice;

(2) in the Chancery Division, without the consent of the Vice-Chancellor; or

(3) in a county court, without the consent of the Head of Civil Justice.

3.4 The court to which the application for a GLO is made will, if minded to make the GLO, send to the Lord Chief Justice, the Vice-Chancellor, or the Head of Civil Justice, as appropriate:

(1) a copy of the application notice;

(2) a copy of any relevant written evidence; and

(3) a written statement as to why a GLO is considered to be desirable.

These steps may be taken either before or after a hearing of the application.

High Court in London

3.5 The application for the GLO should be made to the Senior Master in the Queen's Bench Division or the Chief Chancery Master in the Chancery Division. For claims that are proceeding or are likely to proceed in a specialist list, the application should be made to the senior judge of that list.

High Court outside London

3.6 Outside London, the application should be made to a presiding judge or a Chancery supervising judge of the circuit in which the district registry which has issued the application notice is situated.

County courts

3.7 The application should be made to the designated civil judge for the area in which the county court which has issued the application notice is situated.

3.8 The applicant for a GLO should request the relevant court to refer the application notice to the judge by whom the application will be heard as soon as possible after the application notice has been issued. This is to enable the judge to consider whether to follow the practice set out in para. 3.4 above prior to the hearing of the application.

3.9 The directions under paras 3.5, 3.6 and 3.7 above do not prevent the judges referred to from making arrangements for other judges to hear applications for GLOs when they themselves are unavailable.

GLO Made by Court of Its Own Initiative

para.4 **14.66, 14.68**

4 Subject to obtaining the appropriate consent referred to in para. 3.3 and the procedure set out in para. 3.4, the court may make a GLO of its own initiative.

(Rule 3.3 deals with the procedure that applies when a court proposes to make an order of its own initiative.)

The GLO

5 Paragraphs 2 and (3) of r. 19.11 set out rules relating to the contents of GLOs.

The Group Register

paras 6.1A **14.70**
paras 6.2–6.5 **14.70**
para.6.6(2) **14.70**

6.1 Once a GLO has been made a group register will be established on which will be entered such details as the court may direct of the cases which are to be subject to the GLO.

6.1A A claim must be issued before it can be entered on a group register.

6.2 An application for details of a case to be entered on a group register may be made by any party to the case.

6.3 An order for details of the case to be entered on the group register will not be made unless the case gives rise to at least one of the GLO issues.

(Rule 19.10 defines GLO issues.)

6.4 The court, if it is not satisfied that a case can be conveniently case managed with the other case son the group register, or if it is satisfied that the entry of the case on the group register would adversely affect the case management of the other cases, may refuse to allow details of the case to be entered on the group register, or order their removal from the register if already entered, although the case gives rise to one or more of the Group issues.

6.5 The group register will normally be maintained by and kept at the court but the court may direct this to be done by the solicitor for one of the parties to a case entered on the register.

6.6 (1) Rules 5.4 (register of claims), 5.4B (supply of documents to a party from court records) and 5.4C (supply of documents to a non-party from court records apply where the register is maintained by the court. A party to a claim on the group register may request documents relating to any other claim on the group register in accordance with r. 5.4 as if he were a party to those proceedings.

(2) Where the register is maintained by a solicitor, any person may inspect the group register during normal business hours and upon giving reasonable notice to the solicitor; the solicitor may charge a fee not exceeding the fee prescribed for a search at the court office.

6.7 In this paragraph, 'the court' means the management court specified in the GLO.

Allocation to Track

paras.7–9 **14.71**

7 Once a GLO has been made and unless the management court directs otherwise:
(1) every claim in a case entered on the group register will be automatically allocated, or reallocated (as the case may be), to the multi-track;
(2) any case management directions that have already been given in any such case otherwise than by the management court will be set aside; and
(3) any hearing date already fixed otherwise than for the purposes of the group litigation will be vacated.

Managing Judge

8 A judge ('the managing judge') will be appointed for the purpose of the GLO as soon as possible. He will assume overall responsibility for the management of the claims and will generally hear the GLO issues. A master or a district judge may be appointed to deal with procedural matters, which he will do in accordance with any directions given by the managing judge. A costs judge may be appointed and may be invited to attend case management hearings.

Claims to Be Started in Management Court

para.9.2 **14.70**

9.1 The management court may order that as from a specified date all claims that raise one or more of the GLO issues shall be started in the management court.
9.2 Failure to comply with an order made under para. 9.1 will not invalidate the commencement of the claim but the claim should be transferred to the management court and details entered on the group register as soon as possible. Any party to the claim may apply to the management court for an order under r. 19.14 removing the case from the register or, as the case may be, for an order that details of the case be not entered on the register.

Transfer

10 Where the management court is a county court and a claim raising one or more of the GLO issues is proceeding in the High Court, an order transferring the case to the management court and directing the details of the case to be entered on the group register can only be made in the High Court.

Publicising the GLO

para.11 **14.69**

11 After a GLO has been made, a copy of the GLO should be supplied:
(1) to the Law Society, 113 Chancery Lane, London WC2A 1PL; and
(2) to the Senior Master, Queen's Bench Division, Royal Courts of Justice, Strand, London WC2A 2LL.

Case Management

para.12 **14.71** para.12.2 **14.69**

12.1 The management court may give case management directions at the time the GLO is made or subsequently. Directions given at a case management hearing will generally be binding on all claims that are subsequently entered on the group register (see r. 19.12(1)).
12.2 Any application to vary the terms of the GLO must be made to the management court.
12.3 The management court may direct that one or more of the claims are to proceed as test claims.
12.4 The management court may give directions about how the costs of resolving common issues or the costs of claims proceeding as test claims are to be borne or shared as between the claimants on the group register.

Cut-off Dates

para.13 **14.70, 14.71**

13 The management court may specify a date after which no claim may be added to the group register unless the court gives permission. An early cut-off date may be appropriate in the case of

'instant disasters' (such as transport accidents). In the case of consumer claims, and particularly pharmaceutical claims, it may be necessary to delay the ordering of a cut-off date.

Statements of Case

para.14 14.71
para.14.1 14.71
para.14.3 14.71

14.1 The management court may direct that the GLO claimants serve 'group particulars of claim' which set out the various claims of all the claimants on the group register at the time the particulars are filed. Such particulars of claim will usually contain:
(1) general allegations relating to all claims; and
(2) a schedule containing entries relating to each individual claim specifying which of the general allegations are relied on and any specific facts relevant to the claimant.

14.2 The directions given under para. 14.1 should include directions as to whether the group particulars should be verified by a statement or statements of truth and, if so, by whom.

14.3 The specific facts relating to each claimant on the group register may be obtained by the use of a questionnaire. Where this is proposed, the management court should be asked to approve the questionnaire. The management court may direct that the questionnaires completed by individual claimants take the place of the schedule referred to in para. 14.1(2).

14.4 The management court may also give directions about the form that particulars of claim relating to claims which are to be entered on the group register should take.

The Trial

paras 15.1–15.2 14.71

15.1 The management court may give directions:
(1) for the trial of common issues; and
(2) for the trial of individual issues.

15.2 Common issues and test claims will normally be tried at the management court. Individual issues may be directed to be tried at other courts whose locality is convenient for the parties.

Costs

16.1 Part 48 contains rules about costs where a GLO has been made.

16.2 Where the court has made an order about costs in relation to any application or hearing which involved both:
(1) one or more of the GLO issues; and
(2) an issue or issues relevant only to individual claims;
and the court has not directed the proportion of the costs that is to relate to common costs and the proportion that is to relate to individual costs in accordance with r. 48.6A(5), the costs judge will make a decision as to the relevant proportions at or before the commencement of the detailed assessment of costs.

PD 19C Practice Direction 19C — Derivative Claims

This practice direction supplements CPR, Part 19.

Application of This Practice Direction

1 This practice direction:
(a) applies to:
(i) derivative claims, whether under the Companies Act 2006, part 11, ch. 1, or otherwise; and
(ii) applications for permission to continue or take over such claims; but
(b) does not apply to claims in pursuance of an order under s. 996 of that Act.

Claim Form

para.2(1) **14.27** para.2(2) **44.7**

2 (1) A claim form must be headed 'Derivative claim'.
(2) If the claimant seeks an order that the defendant company or other body concerned indemnify the claimant against liability for costs incurred in the permission application or the claim, this should be stated in the permission application or claim form or both, as the case requires.

Application for Order Delaying Notice

paras.3–6 **14.27**

3 If the applicant seeks an order under r. 19.9A(7) delaying notice to the defendant company or other body concerned, the applicant must also:
(a) state in the application notice the reasons for the application; and
(b) file with it any written evidence in support of the application.

Form to Be Sent to Defendant Company or Other Body

4 The form required by r. 19.9A(4)(a) to be sent to the defendant company or other body is set out at the end of this practice direction. There are separate versions of the form for claims involving a company, and claims involving a body corporate of another kind or a trade union.

Early Intervention by the Company

5 The decision whether the claimant's evidence discloses a prima facie case will normally be made without submissions from or (in the case of an oral hearing to reconsider such a decision reached pursuant to r. 19.9A(9)) attendance by the company. If without invitation from the court the company volunteers a submission or attendance, the company will not normally be allowed any costs of that submission or attendance.
(The Companies Act 2006, ss. 261, 262 and 264, contain provisions about disclosing a prima facie case in applications to continue a derivative claim.)

Hearing of Applications etc.

6 (1) Where a permission application to which this practice direction applies is made in the High Court it will be assigned to the Chancery Division and decided by a High Court judge.
(2) Where such an application is made in a county court it will be decided by a circuit judge.

Discontinuance of Derivative Claim

para.7 **14.28**

7 As a condition of granting permission to continue or take over a derivative claim, the court may order that the claim is not to be discontinued, settled or compromised without the court's permission. Such a condition may be appropriate where any future proposal to discontinue or settle might not come to the attention of members who might have an interest in taking over the claim.

Transitional Provisions

8 (1) From 1 October 2007 new rules came into force about procedures for derivative claims. The new rules are set out in CPR, rr. 19.9 to 19.9F.

(2) The rules of court in force immediately before 1 October 2007 apply to derivative claims begun before 1 October 2007. These (former r. 19.9) are set out below:

Derivative Claims

19.9 (1) This rule applies where a company, other incorporated body or trade union is alleged to be entitled to claim a remedy and a claim is made by one or more members of the company, body or trade union for it to be given that remedy (a 'derivative claim').

(2) The company, body or trade union for whose benefit a remedy is sought must be a defendant to the claim.

(3) After the claim form has been issued the claimant must apply to the court for permission to continue the claim and may not take any other step in the proceedings except—

(a) as provided by paragraph (5); or

(b) where the court gives permission.

(4) An application in accordance with paragraph (3) must be supported by written evidence.

(5) The—

(a) claim form;

(b) application notice; and

(c) written evidence in support of the application,

must be served on the defendant within the period within which the claim form must be served and, in any event, at least 14 days before the court is to deal with the application.

(6) If the court gives the claimant permission to continue the claim, the time within which the defence must be filed is 14 days after the date on which the permission is given or such period as the court may specify.

(7) The court may order the company, body or trade union to indemnify the claimant against any liability in respect of costs incurred in the claim.

THE FORMS

For Claims Involving a Company

Companies Act 2006, section 261 *or* 262 *or* 264
Civil Procedure Rules 1998, rule 19.9A(4)(a)
Notice in relation to derivative claim
To [*name of company etc.*] ('the company') in relation to a claim by [*claimant*]
Attached to this notice are:

- a copy of the claim form to which this notice relates;
- an application under rule 19.9A of the Civil Procedure Rules 1998 for permission to continue the claim; and
- copies of the evidence to be relied on by the claimant in obtaining permission to continue the claim.

The claim is a derivative claim. The claimant must obtain the permission of the court under section 261 of the Companies Act 2006 to continue the claim. A brief summary of the procedure follows.

The court will make its initial decision on the basis of the evidence filed by the claimant (copies are attached to this notice) and at present the company does not need to acknowledge service, file a defence or become involved in any other way. Initially the court may make its decision on the documents only, without a hearing; if it dismisses the application, the claimant may request reconsideration of that decision at a hearing but even at that hearing no additional evidence will be taken into account. If the court considers that the evidence filed by the claimant does not disclose a prima facie case, it must dismiss the application. It may then make consequential orders. If it does not dismiss the application at that stage, the court will adjourn the application to allow the company to obtain and file evidence and be heard on the application, and will make any necessary orders.
The court will notify the company of the outcome of each stage of the process.

The factors that the court must take into account are set out in section 263 of the Act. A copy of sections 263(1) to (4) of the Act is attached.

For Claims Involving a Body Corporate That Is Not a Company, or a Trade Union

Civil Procedure Rules 1998, rule 19.9A(4)(a)

Notice in relation to derivative claim

To [*name of body corporate etc.*] ('the corporation') [*or as appropriate*] in relation to a claim by [*claimant*]

Attached to this notice are:

- a copy of the claim form to which this notice relates;
- an application under rule 19.9A of the Civil Procedure Rules 1998 for permission to continue the claim; and
- copies of the evidence to be relied on by the claimant in obtaining permission to continue the claim.

The claim is a derivative claim. Under the Civil Procedure Rules 1998, the claimant must obtain the permission of the court to continue the claim. A brief summary of the procedure follows.

The court will make its initial decision on the basis of the evidence filed by the claimant (copies are attached to this notice) and at present the [*corporation*] does not need to acknowledge service, file a defence or become involved in any other way. Initially the court may make its decision on the documents only, without a hearing; if it dismisses the application, the claimant may request reconsideration of that decision at a hearing but even at that hearing no additional evidence will be taken into account. If the court considers that the evidence filed by the claimant does not disclose a prima facie case, it will dismiss the application. It may then make consequential orders. If it does not dismiss the application at that stage, the court will adjourn the application to allow the corporation to obtain and file evidence and be heard on the application, and will make any necessary orders. The court will notify the [*corporation*] of the outcome of each stage of the process.

CPR Part 20 Counterclaims and Other Additional Claims

Part 20 **PC.17, 8.2, 8.86, 10.6, 12.1, 14.1, 15.56, 16.35, 16.47, 21.18, 23.2, 23.4, 26.20, 28.1, 28.2, 28.5, 28.7, 29.1, 31.24, 36.4, 67.3, 68.45** [For commentary on the a specific rule, please refer to the cross-references after the title of rule.]

20.1 Purpose of This Part

The purpose of this Part is to enable counterclaims and other additional claims to be managed in the most convenient and effective manner.

20.2 Scope and Interpretation

r.20.2(2) **28.1**

(1) This Part applies to—
  (a) a counterclaim by a defendant against the claimant or against the claimant and some other person;
  (b) an additional claim by a defendant against any person (whether or not already a party) for contribution or indemnity or some other remedy; and
  (c) where an additional claim has been made against a person who is not already a party, any additional claim made by that person against any other person (whether or not already a party).

(2) In these Rules—
  (a) 'additional claim' means any claim other than the claim by the claimant against the defendant; and
  (b) unless the context requires otherwise, references to a claimant or defendant include a party bringing or defending an additional claim.

20.3 Application of These Rules to Additional Claims

r.20.3 **18.4, 67.3**
r.20.3(1) **PC 17, PC 18, 28.5**
r.20.3(2) **28.5**
r.20.3(2)(c) **PC 17**
r.20.3(3) **PC 18, 29.9**
r.20.3(4) **29.9**

(1) An additional claim shall be treated as if it were a claim for the purposes of these Rules, except as provided by this Part.

(2) The following rules do not apply to additional claims—
  (a) rules 7.5 and 7.6 (time within which a claim form may be served);
  (b) rule 16.3(5) (statement of value where claim to be issued in the High Court); and
  (c) Part 26 (case management—preliminary stage).

(3) Part 12 (default judgment) applies to a counterclaim but not to other additional claims.

(4) Part 14 (admissions) applies to a counterclaim, but only—
  (a) rules 14.1(1) and 14.1(2) (which provide that a party may admit the truth of another party's case in writing); and

(b) rule 14.3 (admission by notice in writing — application for judgment),
apply to other additional claims.

(Rule 12.3(2) sets out how to obtain judgment in default of defence for a counterclaim against the claimant, and rule 20.11 makes special provision for default judgment for some additional claims)

20.4 Defendant's Counterclaim against the Claimant

r.20.4(1) **28.3**
r.20.4(2) **PC 17**
r.20.4(2)(a) **28.2**
r.20.4(2)(b) **28.2, 29.4**
r.20.4(3) **PC 17, 28.5**

(1) A defendant may make a counterclaim against a claimant by filing particulars of the counterclaim.

(2) A defendant may make a counterclaim against a claimant—
(a) without the court's permission if he files it with his defence; or
(b) at any other time with the court's permission.

(Part 15 makes provision for a defence to a claim and applies to a defence to a counterclaim by virtue of rule 20.3)

(3) Part 10 (acknowledgment of service) does not apply to a claimant who wishes to defend a counterclaim.

20.5 Counterclaim against a Person Other Than the Claimant

r.20.5 **PC 17**
r.20.5(1) **PC 17, 28.2, 29.4**
r.20.5(3) **28.2**

(1) A defendant who wishes to counterclaim against a person other than the claimant must apply to the court for an order that that person be added as an additional party.

(2) An application for an order under paragraph (1) may be made without notice unless the court directs otherwise.

(3) Where the court makes an order under paragraph (1), it will give directions as to the management of the case.

20.6 Defendant's Additional Claim for Contribution or Indemnity from Another Party

r.20.6 **16.35, 29.4, 29.11**

(1) A defendant who has filed an acknowledgment of service or a defence may make an additional claim for contribution or indemnity against a person who is already a party to the proceedings by—
(a) filing a notice containing a statement of the nature and grounds of his additional claim; and
(b) serving the notice on that party.

(2) A defendant may file and serve a notice under this rule—
(a) without the court's permission, if he files and serves it—
(i) with his defence; or
(ii) if his additional claim for contribution or indemnity is against a party added to the claim later, within 28 days after that party files his defence; or
(b) at any other time with the court's permission.

20.7 Procedure for Making Any Other Additional Claim

r.20.7 **29.8, 29.11**
r.20.7(1) **29.4, 29.8**
r.20.7(2) **PC 18**
r.20.7(3) **PC 18, 29.4, 29.9**
r.20.7(3)(a) **29.4**
r.20.7(4) **PC 18, 29.8**
r.20.7(5) **PC 17, PC 18, 29.6, 32.7**

(1) This rule applies to any additional claim except—
(a) a counterclaim only against an existing party; and
(b) a claim for contribution or indemnity made in accordance with rule 20.6.

(2) An additional claim is made when the court issues the appropriate claim form.

(Rule 7.2(2) provides that a claim form is issued on the date entered on the form by the court)

(3) A defendant may make an additional claim—
(a) without the court's permission if the additional claim is issued before or at the same time as he files his defence;
(b) at any other time with the court's permission.

(Rule 15.4 sets out the period for filing a defence)

(4) Particulars of an additional claim must be contained in or served with the additional claim.
(5) An application for permission to make an additional claim may be made without notice, unless the court directs otherwise.

20.8 Service of Claim Form

(1) Where an additional claim may be made without the court's permission, any claim form must—
  (a) in the case of a counterclaim against an additional party only, be served on every other party when a copy of the defence is served;
  (b) in the case of any other additional claim, be served on the person against whom it is made within 14 days after the date on which the additional claim is issued by the court.
(2) Paragraph (1) does not apply to a claim for contribution or indemnity made in accordance rule 20.6.
(3) Where the court gives permission to make an additional claim it will at the same time give directions as to its service.

20.9 Matters Relevant to Question of Whether an Additional Claim Should Be Separate from the Claim

(1) This rule applies where the court is considering whether to—
  (a) permit an additional claim to be made;
  (b) dismiss an additional claim; or
  (c) require an additional claim to be dealt with separately from the claim by the claimant against the defendant.

(Rule 3.1(2)(e) and (j) deal respectively with the court's power to order that part of proceedings be dealt with as separate proceedings and to decide the order in which issues are to be tried)

(2) The matters to which the court may have regard include—
  (a) the connection between the additional claim and the claim made by the claimant against the defendant;
  (b) whether the additional claimant is seeking substantially the same remedy which some other party is claiming from him; and
  (c) whether the additional claimant wants the court to decide any question connected with the subject matter of the proceedings—
    (i) not only between existing parties but also between existing parties and a person not already a party; or
    (ii) against an existing party not only in a capacity in which he is already a party but also in some further capacity.

20.10 Effect of Service of an Additional Claim

(1) A person on whom an additional claim is served becomes a party to the proceedings if he is not a party already.
(2) When an additional claim is served on an existing party for the purpose of requiring the court to decide a question against that party in a further capacity, that party also becomes a party in the further capacity specified in the additional claim.

20.11 Special Provisions Relating to Default Judgment on an Additional Claim Other Than a Counterclaim or a Contribution or Indemnity Notice

CPR 1–25 & PDs

(1) This rule applies if—
  (a) the additional claim is not—
    (i) a counterclaim; or
    (ii) a claim by a defendant for contribution or indemnity against another defendant under rule 20.6; and
  (b) the party against whom an additional claim is made fails to file an acknowledgment of service or defence in respect of the additional claim.

(2) The party against whom the additional claim is made—
  (a) is deemed to admit the additional claim, and is bound by any judgment or decision in the proceedings in so far as it is relevant to any matter arising in the additional claim;
  (b) subject to paragraph (3), if default judgment under Part 12 is given against the additional claimant, the additional claimant may obtain judgment in respect of the additional claim by filling a request in the relevant practice form.

(3) An additional claimant may not enter judgment under paragraph (2)(b) without the court's permission if—
  (a) he has not satisfied the default judgment which has been given against him; or
  (b) he wishes to obtain judgment for any remedy other than a contribution or indemnity.

(4) An application for the court's permission under paragraph (3) may be made without notice unless the court directs otherwise.

(5) The court may at any time set aside or vary a judgment entered under paragraph (2)(b).

20.12 Procedural Steps on Service of an Additional Claim Form on a Non-party

r.20.12 **29.8, 29.11**
r.20.12(1) **PC 18, 28.3, 29.5, 29.9**
r.20.12(1)(d)(i)–(ii) **PC 18**
r.20.12(2) **PC 18, 28.3, 29.5, 29.9**

(1) Where an additional claim form is served on a person who is not already a party it must be accompanied by—
  (a) a form for defending the claim;
  (b) a form for admitting the claim;
  (c) a form for acknowledging service; and
  (d) a copy of—
    (i) every statement of case which has already been served in the proceedings; and
    (ii) such other documents as the court may direct.

(2) A copy of the additional claim form must be served on every existing party.

20.13 Case Management Where a Defence to an Additional Claim Is Filed

r.20.13 **PC 17, 28.7**
r.20.13(1)–(2) **PC 18, 29.9**

(1) Where a defence is filed to an additional claim the court must consider the future conduct of the proceedings and give appropriate directions.

(2) In giving directionss under paragraph (1) the court must ensure that, so far as practicable, the original claim and all additional claims are managed together.

(Part 66 contains provisions about counterclaims and other Part 20 claims in relation to proceedings by or against the Crown)

PD 20 Practice Direction 20 — Counterclaims and Other Additional Claims

This practice direction supplements CPR, Part 20.

PD20 **28.1, 28.2, 28.4** [For commentary on a specific paragraph, please refer to the cross-references after the title of the paragraph.]

An additional claim is any claim other than the claim by the claimant against the defendant.

Claims under this Part were formerly known as 'Part 20 claims'. As a result of the amendments to Part 20, introduced by Civil Procedure (Amendment No. 4) Rules 2005 (SI 2005/3515), they are now called 'additional claims'.

However, they are described as 'Part 20 claims' on a number of court forms. For the present, some of those forms will continue to refer to Part 20 claims. These references should be construed as being additional claims under this Part. Any reference to a Part 20 claimant or a Part 20 defendant means a claimant or defendant in an additional claim under this Part.

Cases Where Court's Permission to Make an Additional Claim Is Required

para.1.2 **28.2, 29.6**

1.1 Rules 20.4(2)(b), 20.5(1) and 20.7(3)(b) set out the circumstances in which the court's permission will be needed for making an additional claim.

1.2 Where an application is made for permission to make an additional claim the application notice should be filed together with a copy of the proposed additional claim.

Applications for Permission to Issue an Additional Claim

para.2.1 **28.2, 29.6** para.2.2 **29.6**
para.2.3 **28.2, 29.6**

2.1 An application for permission to make an additional claim must be supported by evidence:
(1) the stage which the proceedings have reached,
(2) the nature of the additional claim to be made or details of the question or issue which needs to be decided,
(3) a summary of the facts on which the additional claim is based, and
(4) the name and address of any proposed additional party.
(For further information regarding evidence see PD 32).

2.2 Where delay has been a factor contributing to the need to apply for permission to make an additional claim an explanation of the delay should be given in evidence.

2.3 Where possible the applicant should provide a timetable of the proceedings to date.

2.4 Rules 20.5(2) and 20.7(5) allow applications to be made to the court without notice unless the court directs otherwise.

General

para.3 **PC17, 28.5**

3. The CPR apply generally to additional claims as if they were claims. Parties should be aware that the provisions relating to failure to respond to a claim will apply.

Statement of Truth

para.4.1 **28.6, 29.8** para.4(2) **PC 18, 28.6, 29.8**

4.1 The contents of an additional claim should be verified by a statement of truth. Part 22 requires a statement of case to be verified by a statement of truth.

4.2 The form of the statement of truth should be as required by PD 22, para. 2.1.

4.3 Attention is drawn to r. 32.14 which sets out the consequences of verifying a statement of case containing a false statement without an honest belief in its truth.

Case Management Where There Is a Defence to an Additional Claim

para.5.1 **PC 17, PC 18, 28.7, 29.6**
para.5.2 **29.9**
para.5.3 **PC 18, 29.9**
para.5.4 **29.9**

5.1 Where the defendant to an additional claim files a defence, other than to a counterclaim, the court will arrange a hearing to consider case management of the additional claim. This will normally be at the same time as a case management hearing for the original claim and any other additional claims.

5.2 The court will give notice of the hearing to each party likely to be affected by any order made at the hearing.

5.3 At the hearing the court may:
(1) treat the hearing as a summary judgment hearing,
(2) order that the additional claim be dismissed,
(3) give directions about the way any claim, question or issue set out in or arising from the additional claim should be dealt with,
(4) give directions as to the part, if any, the additional defendant will take at the trial of the claim,
(5) give directions about the extent to which the additional defendant is to be bound by any judgment or decision to be made in the claim.

5.4 The court may make any of the orders in para. 5.3(1) to (5) either before or after any judgment in the claim has been entered by the claimant against the defendant.

Form of Counterclaim

para.6.1 **PC 17, 28.3**
para.6.2 **28.7**

6.1 Where a defendant to a claim serves a counterclaim, the defence and counterclaim should normally form one document with the counterclaim following on from the defence.

6.2 Where a claimant serves a reply and a defence to counterclaim, the reply and the defence to counterclaim should normally form one document with the defence to counterclaim following on from the reply.

Titles of Proceedings Where There Are Additional Claims

paras.7.1–7.11 **PC 17, PC 18**
para.7.2 **29.8**
paras.7.3 **14.1, 28.4, 29.4, 29.8**
paras.7.4 **14.1, 28.4, 29.4, 29.8**
para.7.4(c) **28.4**
para.7.5 **29.8**
para.7.9 **29.8**
para.7.10 **28.4**
para.7.11 **29.8**

7.1 PD 7A, para. 4, contains directions regarding the title to proceedings.

7.2 Where there are additional claims which add parties, the title to the proceedings should comprise a list of all parties describing each by giving them a single identification. Subject to para. 7.11, this identification should be used throughout.

7.3 Claimants and defendants in the original claim should always be referred to as such in the title to the proceedings, even if they subsequently acquire an additional procedural status.

7.4 Additional parties should be referred to in the title to the proceedings in accordance with the order in which they are joined to the proceedings, for example 'Third Party' or 'Fourth Party', whatever their actual procedural status.
Examples:
(a) If the defendant makes an additional claim against a single additional party, the additional party should be referred to in the title as 'Third Party'.
(b) If the defendant makes separate additional claims against two additional parties, the additional parties should be referred to in the title as 'Third Party' and 'Fourth Party'.
(c) If the defendant makes a counterclaim against the claimant and an additional party, the claimant should remain as 'Claimant' and the additional party should be referred to in the title as 'Third Party'.
(d) If the Third Party in example (b) makes an additional claim against a further additional party, that additional party should be referred to in the title as 'Fifth Party'.

7.5 *If an additional claim is* brought against more than one party jointly, they should be referred to in the title to the proceedings as, for example, 'First Named Third Party' and 'Second Named Third Party'.

7.6 In group litigation, the court should give directions about the designation of parties.

7.7 All parties should cooperate to ensure that two parties each making additional claims do not attribute the same nominal status to more than one party.

7.8 In proceedings with numerous parties, the court will if necessary give directions as to the preparation and updating of a list of parties giving their roles in the claim and each additional claim.

7.9 If an additional party ceases to be a party to the proceedings, for example because the claim against that party is discontinued or dismissed, all other additional parties should retain their existing nominal status.

7.10 In proceedings where there are additional parties, the description of all statements of case or other similar documents should clearly identify the nature of the document with reference to each relevant party.

Examples:

(e) In example (a), the defendant's additional claim should be headed 'Defendant's Additional Claim against Third Party' and the Third Party's defence to it should be headed 'Third Party's Defence to Defendant's Additional Claim'.

(f) In example (c), the defendant's counterclaim should be headed 'Defendanst's Counterclaim against Claimant and Third Party' and the Third Party's defence to it should be headed 'Third Party's Defence to Defendant's Counterclaim'.

7.11 In proceedings where there are fourth or subsequent parties, additional parties should be referred to in the text of statements of case or other similar documents by name, suitably abbreviated if appropriate. If parties have similar names, suitable distinguishing abbreviations should be used.

CPR Part 21 Children and Protected Parties

Part 21 **6.21, 14.15, 14.18, 14.22, 63.29**

21.1 Scope of This Part

r.2.1(2) **14.15, 14.16** r.21.1(2)(e) **14.23**

(1) This Part—
- (a) contains special provisions which apply in proceedings involving children and protected parties;
- (b) sets out how a person becomes a litigation friend; and
- (c) does not apply to proceedings under Part 75 where one of the parties to the proceedings is a child.

(2) In this Part—
- (a) 'the 2005 Act' means the Mental Capacity Act 2005;
- (b) 'child' means a person under 18;
- (c) 'lacks capacity' means lacks capacity within the meaning of the 2005 Act;
- (d) 'protected party' means a party, or an intended party, who lacks capacity to conduct the proceedings;
- (e) 'protected beneficiary' means a protected party who lacks capacity to manage and control any money recovered by him or on his behalf or for his benefit in the proceedings.

(Rules 6.13 and 6.25 contain provisions about the service of documents on children and protected parties)

(Rule 48.5 deals with costs where money is payable by or to a child or protected party)

21.2 Requirement for a Litigation Friend in Proceedings by or against Children and Protected Parties

r.21.2 **14.17** r.21.2(3)–(5) **14.20**

(1) A protected party must have a litigation friend to conduct proceedings on his behalf.

(2) A child must have a litigation friend to conduct proceedings on his behalf unless the court makes an order under paragraph

(3) The court may make an order permitting the child to conduct proceedings without a litigation friend.

(4) An application for an order under paragraph (3)—
- (a) may be made by the child;
- (b) if the child already has a litigation friend, must be made on notice to the litigation friend; and
- (c) if the child has no litigation friend, may be made without notice.

(5) Where—
- (a) the court has made an order under paragraph (3); and

(b) it subsequently appears to the court that it is desirable for a litigation friend to conduct the proceedings on behalf of the child,

the court may appoint a person to be the child's litigation friend.

21.3 Stage of Proceedings at Which a Litigation Friend Becomes Necessary

r.21.3(2) **14.17, 20.8** r.21.3(3)–(4) **14.17**

(1) This rule does not apply where the court has made an order under rule 21.2(3).
(2) A person may not, without the permission of the court—
 (a) make an application against a child or protected party before proceedings have started; or
 (b) take any step in proceedings except—
  (i) issuing and serving a claim form; or
  (ii) applying for the appointment of a litigation friend under rule 21.6,

 until the child or protected party has a litigation friend.
(3) If during proceedings a party lacks capacity to continue to conduct proceedings, no party may take any further step in the proceedings without the permission of the court until the protected party has a litigation friend.
(4) Any step taken before a child or protected party has a litigation friend has no effect unless the court orders otherwise.

21.4 Who May Be a Litigation Friend without a Court Order

r.21.4(3) **14.18, 14.19, 14.21** r.21.4(3)(c) **68.47**

(1) This rule does not apply if the court has appointed a person to be a litigation friend.
(2) A deputy appointed by the Court of Protection under the 2005 Act with power to conduct proceedings on the protected party's behalf is entitled to be the litigation friend of the protected party in any proceedings to which his power extends.
(3) If nobody has been appointed by the court or, in the case of a protected party, has been appointed as a deputy as set out in paragraph (2), a person may act as a litigation friend if he—
 (a) can fairly and competently conduct proceedings on behalf of the child or protected party;
 (b) has no interest adverse to that of the child or protected party; and
 (c) where the child or protected party is a claimant, undertakes to pay any costs which the child or protected party may be ordered to pay in relation to the proceedings, subject to any right he may have to be repaid from the assets of the child or protected party.

21.5 How a Person Becomes a Litigation Friend without a Court Order

r.21.5 **14.17, 14.19** r.21.5(4) **14.19**

(1) If the court has not appointed a litigation friend, a person who wishes to act as a litigation friend must follow the procedure set out in this rule.
(2) A deputy appointed by the Court of Protection under the 2005 Act with power to conduct proceedings on the protected party's behalf must file an official copy[(GL)] of the order of the Court of Protection which confers his power to act either—
 (a) where the deputy is to act as a litigation friend for a claimant, at the time the claim is made; or
 (b) where the deputy is to act as a litigation friend for a defendant, at the time when he first takes a step in the proceedings on behalf of the defendant.
(3) Any other person must file a certificate of suitability stating that he satisfies the conditions specified in rule 21.4(3) either—
 (a) where the person is to act as a litigation friend for a claimant, at the time when the claim is made; or
 (b) where the person is to act as a litigation friend for a defendant, at the time when he first takes a step in the proceedings on behalf of the defendant.
(4) The litigation friend must—
 (a) serve the certificate of suitability on every person on whom, in accordance with rule 6.13 (service on a parent, guardian etc.), the claim form should be served; and
 (b) file a certificate of service when filing the certificate of suitability.

(Rules 6.17 and 6.29 set out the details to be contained in a certificate of service)

21.6 How a Person Becomes a Litigation Friend by Court Order

r.21.6 PC 16, 14.18, 14.19, 20.8
r.21.6(2) 14.19
r.21.6(4) 32.15

(1) The court may make an order appointing a litigation friend.
(2) An application for an order appointing a litigation friend may be made by—
  (a) a person who wishes to be the litigation friend; or
  (b) a party.
(3) Where—
  (a) a person makes a claim against a child or protected party;
  (b) the child or protected party has no litigation friend;
  (c) the court has not made an order under rule 21.2(3) (order that a child can conduct proceedings without a litigation friend); and
  (d) either—
    (i) someone who is not entitled to be a litigation friend files a defence; or
    (ii) the claimant wishes to take some step in the proceedings,

  the claimant must apply to the court for an order appointing a litigation friend for the child or protected party.
(4) An application for an order appointing a litigation friend must be supported by evidence.
(5) The court may not appoint a litigation friend under this rule unless it is satisfied that the person to be appointed satisfies the conditions in rule 21.4(3).

21.7 Court's Power to Change a Litigation Friend and to Prevent a Person Acting as a Litigation Friend

r.21.7 14.21
r.21.7(2) 14.21
r.21.7(3) 14.21

(1) The court may—
  (a) direct that a person may not act as a litigation friend;
  (b) terminate a litigation friend's appointment; or
  (c) appoint a new litigation friend in substitution for an existing one.
(2) An application for an order under paragraph (1) must be supported by evidence.
(3) The court may not appoint a litigation friend under this rule unless it is satisfied that the person to be appointed satisfies the conditions in rule 21.4(3).

21.8 Appointment of a Litigation Friend by Court Order — Supplementary

r.21.8 15.45
r.21.8(1) 14.19, 14.21, 15.45
r.21.8(2) 14.19
r.21.8(3) 14.21
r.21.8(4) 14.19, 14.21

(1) An application for an order under rule 21.6 or rule 21.7 must be served on every person on whom, in accordance with rule 6.13 (service on parent, guardian etc.), the claim form must be served.
(2) Where an application for an order under rule 21.6 is in respect of a protected party, the application must also be served on the protected party unless the court orders otherwise.
(3) An application for an order under rule 21.7 must also be served on—
  (a) the person who is the litigation friend, or who is purporting to act as the litigation friend, when the application is made; and
  (b) the person who it is proposed should be the litigation friend, if he is not the applicant.
(4) On an application for an order under rule 21.6 or 21.7, the court may appoint the person proposed or any other person who satisfies the conditions specified in rule 21.4(3).

21.9 Procedure Where Appointment of a Litigation Friend Ceases

r.21.9(1)–(6) 14.21

(1) When a child who is not a protected party reaches the age of 18, the litigation friend's appointment ceases.
(2) Where a protected party regains or acquires capacity to conduct the proceedings, the litigation friend's appointment continues until it is ended by court order.

(3) An application for an order under paragraph (2) may be made by—
(a) the former protected party;
(b) the litigation friend; or
(c) a party.

(4) The child or protected party in respect of whom the appointment to act has ceased must serve notice on the other parties—
(a) stating that the appointment of his litigation friend to act has ceased;
(b) giving his address for service; and
(c) stating whether or not he intends to carry on the proceedings.

(5) If the child or protected party does not serve the notice required by paragraph (4) within 28 days after the day on which the appointment of the litigation friend ceases the court may, on application, strike out(GL) any claim brought by or defence raised by the child or protected party.

(6) The liability of a litigation friend for costs continues until—
(a) the person in respect of whom his appointment to act has ceased serves the notice referred to in paragraph (4); or
(b) the litigation friend serves notice on the parties that his appointment to act has ceased.

21.10 Compromise etc. by or on Behalf of a Child or Protected Party

r.21.10 **55.4, 66.30, 66.31, 66.54** r.21.(10)(2) **8.54, 13.2, 14.22, 70.8**
r.21.10(1) **14.22, 66.31**

(1) Where a claim is made—
(a) by or on behalf of a child or protected party; or
(b) against a child or protected party,
no settlement, compromise or payment (including any voluntary interim payment) and no acceptance of money paid into court shall be valid, so far as it relates to the claim by, on behalf of or against the child or protected party, without the approval of the court.

(2) Where—
(a) before proceedings in which a claim is made by or on behalf of, or against, a child or protected party (whether alone or with any other person) are begun, an agreement is reached for the settlement of the claim; and
(b) the sole purpose of proceedings is to obtain the approval of the court to a settlement or compromise of the claim, the claim must—
(i) be made using the procedure set out in Part 8 (alternative procedure for claims); and
(ii) include a request to the court for approval of the settlement or compromise.

(3) In proceedings to which Section II or Section III of Part 45 applies, the court will not make an order for detailed assessment of the costs payable to the child or protected party but will assess the costs in the manner set out in that Section.

(Rule 46.4 contains provisions about costs where money is payable to a child or protected party)

21.11 Control of Money Recovered by or on Behalf of a Child or Protected Party

r.21.11 **14.22** r.21.11(2) **14.23**

(1) Where in any proceedings—
(a) money is recovered by or on behalf of or for the benefit of a child or protected party; or
(b) money paid into court is accepted by or on behalf of a child or protected party,
the money will be dealt with in accordance with directions given by the court under this rule and not otherwise.

(2) Directions given under this rule may provide that the money shall be wholly or partly paid into court and invested or otherwise dealt with.

(3) Where money is recovered by or on behalf of a protected party or money paid into court is accepted by or on behalf of a protected party, before giving directions in accordance with this rule, the court will first consider whether the protected party is a protected beneficiary.

21.12 Expenses Incurred by a Litigation Friend

r.21.12 **14.18** r.21.12(6) **14.18**

(1) In proceedings to which rule 21.11 applies, a litigation friend who incurs expenses on behalf of a child or protected party in any proceedings is entitled on application to recover the amount paid or payable out of any money recovered or paid into court to the extent that it—
   (a) has been reasonably incurred; and
   (b) is reasonable in amount.
(2) Expenses may include all or part of—
   (a) a premium in respect of a costs insurance policy (as defined by section 58C(5) of the Courts and Legal Services Act 1990); or
   (b) interest on a loan taken out to pay an insurance premium in respect of a costs insurance policy or other recoverable disbursement.
(3) No application may be made under the rule for expenses that—
   (a) are of a type that may be recoverable on an assessment of costs payable by or out of money belonging to a child or protected party; but
   (b) are disallowed in whole or in part on such an assessment.

(Expenses which are also 'costs' as defined in rule 44.1(1)(a) are dealt with under rule 46.4(2))

(4) In deciding whether the expenses were reasonably incurred and reasonable in amount, the court will have regard to all the circumstances of the case including the factors set out in rule 44.4(3).
(5) When the court is considering the factors to be taken into account in assessing the reasonableness of the expenses, it will have regard to the facts and circumstances as they reasonably appeared to the litigation friend or to the child's or protected party's legal representative when the expense was incurred.
(6) Where the claim is settled or compromised, or judgment is given, on terms that an amount not exceeding £5,000 is paid to the child or protected party, the total amount the litigation friend may recover under paragraph (1) must not exceed 25% of the sum so agreed or awarded, unless the court directs otherwise. Such total amount must not exceed 50% of the sum so agreed or awarded.

21.13 Appointment of a Guardian of a Child's Estate

r.21.13 14.23

(1) The court may appoint the Official Solicitor to be a guardian of a child's estate where—
   (a) money is paid into court on behalf of the child in accordance with directions given under rule 21.11 (control of money received by a child or protected party);
   (b) the Criminal Injuries Compensation Authority notifies the court that it has made or intends to make an award to the child;
   (c) a court or tribunal outside England and Wales notifies the court that it has ordered or intends to order that money be paid to the child;
   (d) the child is absolutely entitled to the proceeds of a pension fund; or
   (e) in any other case, such an appointment seems desirable to the court.
(2) The court may not appoint the Official Solicitor under this rule unless—
   (a) the persons with parental responsibility (within the meaning of section 3 of the Children Act 1989) agree; or
   (b) the court considers that their agreement can be dispensed with.
(3) The Official Solicitor's appointment may continue only until the child reaches 18.

PD 21 Practice Direction 21— Children and Protected Parties

This practice direction supplements CPR, Part 21.

PD 21 14.15

General

paras.1.1–1.2 14.17 para.1.2(2) 14.20

1.1 In proceedings where one of the parties is a protected party, the protected party should be referred to in the title to the proceedings as 'A.B. (a protected party by C.D. his litigation friend)'.

1.2 In proceedings where one of the parties is a child, where:
(1) the child has a litigation friend, the child should be referred to in the title to the proceedings as 'A.B. (a child by C.D. his litigation friend)'; or
(2) the child is conducting the proceedings on his own behalf, the child should be referred to in the title as 'A.B. (a child)'.

1.3 A settlement of a claim by a child includes an agreement on a sum to be apportioned to a dependent child under the Fatal Accidents Act 1976.

The Litigation Friend

para.2.2 14.19

2.1 A person may become a litigation friend:
(a) without a court order under r. 21.5, or
(b) by a court order under r. 21.6.

2.2 A person who wishes to become a litigation friend without a court order pursuant to r. 21.5(3) must file a certificate of suitability in form N235:
(a) stating that he consents to act,
(b) stating that he knows or believes that the [claimant] [defendant] [is a child] [lacks capacity to conduct the proceedings],
(c) in the case of a protected party, stating the grounds of his belief and, if his belief is based upon medical opinion or the opinion of another suitably qualified expert, attaching any relevant document to the certificate,
(d) stating that he can fairly and competently conduct proceedings on behalf of the child or protected party and has no interest adverse to that of the child or protected party, and
(e) where the child or protected party is a claimant, undertaking to pay any costs which the child or protected party may be ordered to pay in relation to the proceedings, subject to any right he may have to be repaid from the assets of the child or protected party.

2.3 The certificate of suitability must be verified by a statement of truth.
(Part 22 contains provisions about statements of truth.)

2.4 The litigation friend is not required to serve the document referred to in para. 2.2(c) when he serves a certificate of suitability on the person to be served under r. 21.5(4)(a).

Application for a Court Order Appointing a Litigation Friend

para.3.3 14.19
para.3.4 14.19

3.1 Rule 21.6 sets out who may apply for an order appointing a litigation friend.

3.2 An application must be made in accordance with Part 23 and must be supported by evidence.

3.3 The evidence in support must satisfy the court that the proposed litigation friend:
(1) consents to act,
(2) can fairly and competently conduct proceedings on behalf of the child or protected party,
(3) has no interest adverse to that of the child or protected party, and
(4) where the child or protected party is a claimant, undertakes to pay any costs which the child or protected party may be ordered to pay in relation to the proceedings, subject to any right he may have to be repaid from the assets of the child or protected party.

CPR 1–25 & PDs

3.4 Where it is sought to appoint the Official Solicitor as the litigation friend, provision must be made for payment of his charges.

Procedure Where the Need for a Litigation Friend Has Come to an End

paras.4.2–4.4 **14.21** para.4.6 **14.21**

4.1 Rule 21.9 deals with the situation where the need for a litigation friend comes to an end during the proceedings because either:
(1) a child who is not also a protected party reaches the age of 18 (full age) during the proceedings, or
(2) a protected party regains or acquires capacity to conduct the proceedings.

4.2 A child on reaching full age must serve on the other parties to the proceedings and file with the court a notice:
(1) stating that he has reached full age,
(2) stating that his litigation friend's appointment has ceased,
(3) giving an address for service, and
(4) stating whether or not he intends to carry on with or continue to defend the proceedings.

4.3 If the notice states that the child intends to carry on with or continue to defend the proceedings he must subsequently be described in the proceedings as 'A.B. (formerly a child but now of full age)'.

4.4 Whether or not a child having reached full age serves a notice in accordance with r. 21.9(4) and para. 4.2 above, a litigation friend may, at any time after the child has reached full age, serve a notice on the other parties that his appointment has ceased.

4.5 Where a protected party regains or acquires capacity to conduct the proceedings, an application under r. 21.9(3) must be made for an order under r. 21.9(2) that the litigation friend's appointment has ceased.

4.6 The application must be supported by the following evidence:
(1) a medical report or other suitably qualified expert's report indicating that the protected party has regained or acquired capacity to conduct the proceedings,
(2) a copy of any relevant order or declaration of the Court of Protection, and
(3) if the application is made by the protected party, a statement whether or not he intends to carry on with or continue to defend the proceedings.

4.7 An order under r. 21.9(2) must be served on the other parties to the proceedings. The former protected party must file with the court a notice:
(1) stating that his litigation friend's appointment has ceased,
(2) giving an address for service, and
(3) stating whether or not he intends to carry on with or continue to defend the proceedings.

Settlement or Compromise by or on Behalf of a Child or Protected Party before the Issue of Proceedings

para.5.1 **PC 6** paras.5.4–5.5 **14.22**
para.5.1(1) **14.22** para.5.6(1)–(2) **PC 6**
para.5.2 **PC 6, 14.22**

5.1 Where a claim by or on behalf of a child or protected party has been dealt with by agreement before the issue of proceedings and only the approval of the court to the agreement is sought, the claim must, in addition to containing the details of the claim and satisfying the requirements of r. 21.10(2), include the following:
(1) subject to para. 5.3, the terms of the settlement or compromise or have attached to it a draft consent order in form N292;
(2) details of whether and to what extent the defendant admits liability;
(3) the age and occupation (if any) of the child or protected party;
(4) the litigation friend's approval of the proposed settlement or compromise;
(5) a copy of any financial advice relating to the proposed settlement; and
(6) in a personal injury case arising from an accident:
(a) details of the circumstances of the accident,
(b) any medical reports,

(c) where appropriate, a schedule of any past and future expenses and losses claimed and any other relevant information relating to the personal injury as set out in PD 16 (statements of case), and

(d) where considerations of liability are raised:

(i) any evidence or reports in any criminal proceedings or in an inquest, and

(ii) details of any prosecution brought.

5.2 (1) An opinion on the merits of the settlement or compromise given by counsel or solicitor acting for the child or protected party must, except in very clear cases, be obtained.

(2) A copy of the opinion and, unless the instructions on which it was given are sufficiently set out in it, a copy of the instructions, must be supplied to the court.

5.3 Where in any personal injury case a claim for damages for future pecuniary loss is settled, the provisions in paras 5.4 and 5.5 must in addition be complied with.

5.4 The court must be satisfied that the parties have considered whether the damages should wholly or partly take the form of periodical payments.

5.5 Where the settlement includes provision for periodical payments, the claim must:

(1) set out the terms of the settlement or compromise; or

(2) have attached to it a draft consent order,

which must satisfy the requirements of rr. 41.8 and 41.9 as appropriate.

5.6 Applications for the approval of a settlement or compromise will normally be heard by:

(1) a master or a district judge in proceedings involving a child; and

(2) a master, designated civil judge or his nominee in proceedings involving a protected party.

(For information about provisional damages claims see Part 41 and PD 41A.)

Settlement or Compromise by or on Behalf of a Child or Protected Party after Proceedings Have Been Issued

para.6.2 14.22, 63.29
para.6.3 14.22, 63.29
para.6.4 63.29

6.1 Where in any personal injury case a claim for damages for future pecuniary loss, by or on behalf of a child or protected party, is dealt with by agreement after proceedings have been issued, an application must be made for the court's approval of the agreement.

6.2 The court must be satisfied that the parties have considered whether the damages should wholly or partly take the form of periodical payments.

6.3 Where the settlement includes provision for periodical payments, an application under para. 6.1 must:

(1) set out the terms of the settlement or compromise; or

(2) have attached to it a draft consent order,

which must satisfy the requirements of rr. 41.8 and 41.9 as appropriate.

6.4 The court must be supplied with:

(1) an opinion on the merits of the settlement or compromise given by counsel or solicitor acting for the child or protected party, except in very clear cases; and

(2) a copy of any financial advice.

6.5 Applications for the approval of a settlement or compromise, except at the trial, will normally be heard by:

(1) a master or a district judge in proceedings involving a child; and

(2) a master, designated civil judge or his nominee in proceedings involving a protected party.

Apportionment under the Fatal Accidents Act 1976

para.7.4 14.22

7.1 A *judgment on* or *settlement* in respect of a claim under the Fatal Accidents Act 1976 must be apportioned between the persons by or on whose behalf the claim has been brought.

7.2 Where a claim is brought on behalf of a dependent child or children, any settlement (including an agreement on a sum to be apportioned to a dependent child under the Fatal Accidents Act 1976) must be approved by the court.

7.3 The money apportioned to any dependent child must be invested on the child's behalf in accordance with rr. 21.10 and 21.11 and paras 8 and 9 below.

7.4 In order to approve an apportionment of money to a dependent child, the court will require the following information:
(1) the matters set out in paras 5.1(2) and (3), and
(2) in respect of the deceased:
(a) where death was caused by an accident, the matters set out in paras 5.1(6)(a), (b) and (c), and
(b) his future loss of earnings, and
(3) the extent and nature of the dependency.

Control of Money Recovered by or on Behalf of a Child or Protected Party

para.8 14.23

8.1 When giving directions under r. 21.11, the court:
(1) may direct the money to be paid into court for investment,
(2) may direct that certain sums be paid direct to the child or protected beneficiary, his litigation friend or his legal representative for the immediate benefit of the child or protected beneficiary or for expenses incurred on his behalf, and
(3) may direct that the application in respect of the investment of the money be transferred to a local district registry.

8.2 The court will consider the general aims to be achieved for the money in court (the fund) by investment and will give directions as to the type of investment.

8.3 Where a child also lacks capacity to manage and control any money recovered by him or on his behalf in the proceedings, and is likely to remain so on reaching full age, his fund should be administered as a protected beneficiary's fund.

8.4 Where a child or protected beneficiary is in receipt of publicly funded legal services the fund will be subject to a first charge under the Access to Justice Act 1999, s. 10 (statutory charge), and an order for the investment of money on the child's or protected beneficiary's behalf must contain a direction to that effect.

Investment on Behalf of a Child

para.9 14.23

9.1 At the hearing of an application for the approval of a settlement or compromise the litigation friend or his legal representative must provide, in addition to the information required by paras 5 and 6:
(1) a CFO form 320 (initial application for investment of damages) for completion by the judge hearing the application; and
(2) any evidence or information which the litigation friend wishes the court to consider in relation to the investment of the award for damages.

9.2 Following the hearing in para. 9.1, the court will forward to the Court Funds Office a request for investment decision (form 212) and the Public Trustee's investment managers will make the appropriate investment.

9.3 Where an award for damages for a child is made at trial, unless para. 9.7 applies, the trial judge will:
(1) direct the money to be paid into court and placed into the special investment account until further investment directions have been given by the court;
(2) direct the litigation friend to make an application to a master or district judge for further investment directions; and
(3) give such other directions as the trial judge thinks fit, including a direction that the hearing of the application for further investment directions will be fixed for a date within 28 days from the date of the trial.

9.4 The application under para. 9.3(2) must be made by filing with the court:
(1) a completed CFO form 320; and
(2) any evidence or information which the litigation friend wishes the court to consider in relation to the investment of the award for damages.

9.5 The application must be sent in proceedings in the Royal Courts of Justice to the Masters' Support Unit (Room E16) at the Royal Courts of Justice.

9.6 If the application required by para. 9.3(2) is not made to the court, the money paid into court in accordance with para. 9.3(1) will remain in the special investment account subject to any further order of the court or para. 9.8.
9.7 If the money to be invested is very small the court may order it to be paid direct to the litigation friend to be put into a building society account (or similar) for the child's use.
9.8 If the money is invested in court, it must be paid out to the child on application when he reaches full age.

Investment on Behalf of a Protected Beneficiary

para.10 **14.23**

10.1 The Court of Protection has jurisdiction to make decisions in the best interests of a protected beneficiary. Fees may be charged for the administration of funds and these must be provided for in any settlement.
10.2 Where the sum to be administered for the benefit of the protected beneficiary is:
(1) £30,000 or more, unless a person with authority as:
(a) the attorney under a registered enduring power of attorney;
(b) the donee of a lasting power of attorney; or
(c) the deputy appointed by the Court of Protection,
to administer or manage the protected beneficiary's financial affairs has been appointed, the order approving the settlement will contain a direction to the litigation friend to apply to the Court of Protection for the appointment of a deputy, after which the fund will be dealt with as directed by the Court of Protection; or
(2) under £30,000, it may be retained in court and invested in the same way as the fund of a child.
10.3 A form of order transferring the fund to the Court of Protection is set out in form N292.
10.4 In order for the Court Funds Office to release a fund which is subject to the statutory charge, the litigation friend or his legal representative or the person with authority referred to in para. 10.2(1) must provide the appropriate regional office of the Legal Services Commission with an undertaking in respect of a sum to cover their costs, following which the regional office will advise the Court Funds Office in writing of that sum, enabling them to transfer the balance to the Court of Protection on receipt of a CFO form 200 payment schedule authorised by the court.
10.5 The CFO form 200 should be completed and presented to the court where the settlement or trial took place for authorisation, subject to paras 10.6 and 10.7.
10.6 Where the settlement took place in the Royal Courts of Justice the CFO form 200 must be completed and presented for authorisation:
(1) on behalf of a child, in the Masters' Support Unit, Room E105, and
(2) on behalf of a protected beneficiary, in the Judgment and Orders Section in the Action Department, Room E17.
10.7 Where the trial took place in the Royal Courts of Justice, the CFO form 200 is completed and authorised by the court officer.

Expenses Incurred by a Litigation Friend

para.11 **14.23** para.11.2 **14.18**

11.1 A litigation friend may make a claim for expenses under r. 21.12(1):
(1) where the court has ordered an assessment of costs under r. 46.4(2), at the detailed assessment hearing;
(2) where the litigation friend's expenses are not of a type which would be recoverable as costs on an assessment of costs between the parties, to the master or district judge at the hearing to approve the settlement or compromise under Part 21 (the master or district judge may adjourn the matter to the costs judge); or
(3) where an assessment of costs under r. 46.4(2) is not required, and no approval under Part 21 is necessary, by a Part 23 application supported by a witness statement to a costs judge or district judge as appropriate.

11.2 In all circumstances, the litigation friend must support a claim for expenses by filing a witness statement setting out:
(1) the nature and amount of the expense; and
(2) the reason the expense was incurred.

Guardian's Accounts

para.12 14.23

12. PD 40A, para. 8, deals with the approval of the accounts of a guardian of assets of a child.

Payment Out of Funds in Court

para.13 14.23

13.1 Applications to a master or district judge:
(1) for payment out of money from the fund for the benefit of the child, or
(2) to vary an investment strategy,
may be dealt with without a hearing unless the court directs otherwise.

13.2 When the child reaches full age:
(1) where his fund in court is a sum of money, it will be paid out to him on application; or
(2) where his fund is in the form of investments other than money (for example shares or unit trusts), the investments will on application be:
(a) sold and the proceeds of sale paid out to him; or
(b) transferred into his name.

13.3 Where the fund is administered by the Court of Protection, any payment out of money from that fund must be in accordance with any decision or order of the Court of Protection.

13.4 If an application is required for the payment out of money from a fund administered by the Court of Protection, that application must be made to the Court of Protection.
(For further information on payments out of court, see PD 37.)

CPR Part 22 Statements of Truth

Part 22 13.7, 82.25, 82.39, 82.110, 87.37 [For commentary on a specific rule, please refer to the cross-references after the title of the rule.]

22.1 Documents to Be Verified by a Statement of Truth

r.22.1 84.31
r.22.1(1)(a) 23.12, 24.5, 27.2, 28.6, 29.8, 30.3, 30.4
r.22.1(d) PC 5, 13.8, 18.3
r.22.1(2) 30.10, 31.20
r.22.1(3) 32.15
r.22.1(4) 23.12, 32.15
r.22.1(5) 23.15
r.22.1(6) 23.12, 23.14
r.22.1(6)(a)(i)–(ii) 23.13

(1) The following documents must be verified by a statement of truth—
  (a) a statement of case;
  (b) a response complying with an order under rule 18.1 to provide further information;
  (c) a witness statement;
  (d) an acknowledgment of service in a claim begun by way of the Part 8 procedure;
  (e) a certificate stating the reasons for bringing a possession claim or a landlord and tenant claim in the High Court in accordance with rules 55.3(2) and 56.2(2);
  (f) a certificate of service; and
  (g) any other document where a rule or practice direction requires.

(2) Where a statement of case is amended, the amendments must be verified by a statement of truth unless the court orders otherwise.

(Part 17 provides for amendments to statements of case)

(3) If an applicant wishes to rely on matters set out in his application notice as evidence, the application notice must be verified by a statement of truth.

(4) Subject to paragraph (5), a statement of truth is a statement that—
  (a) the party putting forward the document;
  (b) in the case of a witness statement, the maker of the witness statement; or
  (c) in the case of a certificate of service, the person who signs the certificate,

believes the facts stated in the document are true.

(5) If a party is conducting proceedings with a litigation friend, the statement of truth in—
  (a) a statement of case;
  (b) a response; or
  (c) an application notice,

is a statement that the litigation friend believes the facts stated in the document being verified are true.

(6) The statement of truth must be signed by—
  (a) in the case of a statement of case, a response or an application—
    (i) the party or litigation friend; or
    (ii) the legal representative on behalf of the party or litigation friend; and
  (b) in the case of a witness statement, the maker of the statement.

(7) A statement of truth which is not contained in the document which it verifies, must clearly identify that document.

(8) A statement of truth in a statement of case may be made by—
  (a) a person who is not a party; or

(b) by two parties jointly,
where this is permitted by a relevant practice direction.

22.2 Failure to Verify a Statement of Case

r.22.2(1) 23.14, 23.17 r.22.2(2) 23.17

(1) If a party fails to verify his statement of case by a statement of truth—
  (a) the statement of case shall remain effective unless struck out; but
  (b) the party may not rely on the statement of case as evidence of any of the matters set out in it.
(2) The court may strike out(GL) a statement of case which is not verified by a statement of truth.
(3) Any party may apply for an order under paragraph (2).

22.3 Failure to Verify a Witness Statement

If the maker of a witness statement fails to verify the witness statement by a statement of truth the court may direct that it shall not be admissible as evidence.

22.4 Power of the Court to Require a Document to Be Verified

r.22.4 23.17

(1) The court may order a person who has failed to verify a document in accordance with rule 22.1 to verify the document.
(2) Any party may apply for an order under paragraph (1).

PD 22 Practice Direction 22 — Statements of Truth

This practice direction supplements CPR, Part 22.

[For commentary on a specific paragraph, please refer to the cross-references after the title of the paragraph.]

Documents to Be Verified by a Statement of Truth

para.1.4(3) 25.2, 26.13 para.1.5 23.12

1.1 Rule 22.1(1) sets out the documents which must be verified by a statement of truth. The documents include:
(1) a statement of case,
(2) a response complying with an order under r. 18.1 to provide further information,
(3) a witness statement,
(4) an acknowledgment of service in a claim begun by the Part 8 procedure,
(5) a certificate stating the reasons for bringing a possession claim or a landlord and tenant claim in the High Court in accordance with rr. 55.3(2) and 56.2(2),
(6) a certificate of service.

1.2 If an applicant wishes to rely on matters set out in his application notice as evidence, the application notice must be verified by a statement of truth.[1]

1.3 An expert's report should also be verified by a statement of truth. For the form of the statement of truth verifying an expert's report (which differs from that set out below) see PD 35.

1.4 In addition, the following documents must be verified by a statement of truth:
(1) an application notice for:
(a) a third party debt order (r. 72.3),
(b) a hardship payment order (r. 72.7), or
(c) a charging order (r. 73.3);
(2) a notice of objections to an account being taken by the court, unless verified by an affidavit or witness statement;
(3) a schedule or counter-schedule of expenses and losses in a personal injury claim, and any amendments to such a schedule or counter-schedule, whether or not they are contained in a statement of case.

1.5 The statement of truth may be contained in the document it verifies or it may be in a separate document served subsequently, in which case it must identify the document to which it relates.

1.6 Where the form to be used includes a jurat for the content to be verified by an affidavit then a statement of truth is not required in addition.

Form of the Statement of Truth

para.2.1 23.12, 28.6, 29.8, 32.15 para.2.3 23.12
para.2.2A 43.7, 71.30

2.1 The form of the statement of truth verifying a statement of case, a response, an application notice or a notice of objections should be as follows:
'[I believe] [the (claimant or as may be) believes] that the facts stated in this [*name document being verified*] are true.'

2.2 The form of the statement of truth verifying a witness statement should be as follows:
'I believe that the facts stated in this witness statement are true.'

2.2A The form of the statement of truth verifying a costs budget should be as follows:
'The costs stated to have been incurred do not exceed the costs which my client is liable to pay in respect of such work. The future costs stated in this budget are a proper estimate of the reasonable and proportionate costs which my client will incur in this litigation.'

2.3 Where the statement of truth is contained in a separate document, the document containing the statement of truth must be headed with the title of the proceedings and the claim number. The document being verified should be identified in the statement of truth as follows:
(1) claim form: 'the claim form issued on [*date*]',

[1] See r. 22.1(3).

CPR 1–25 & PDs

(2) particulars of claim: 'the particulars of claim issued on [*date*]',
(3) statement of case: 'the [*defence or as may be*] served on the [*name of party*] on [*date*]',
(4) application notice: 'the application notice issued on [*date*] for [*set out the remedy sought*]',
(5) witness statement: 'the witness statement filed on [*date*] or served on [*party*] on [*date*]'.

Who May Sign the Statement of Truth

paras.3.4–3.5 23.13
para.3.6 23.13
para.3.6A 23.13, 23.15
para.3.6B 23.13, 23.15
para.3.7 23.13
para.3.8 23.15
para.3.9 23.13
para.3.10 23.13
para.3.11 23.13

3.1 In a statement of case, a response or an application notice, the statement of truth must be signed by:
(1) the party or his litigation friend,[2] or
(2) the legal representative[3] of the party or litigation friend.

3.2 A statement of truth verifying a witness statement must be signed by the witness.

3.3 A statement of truth verifying a notice of objections to an account must be signed by the objecting party or his legal representative.

3.4 Where a document is to be verified on behalf of a company or other corporation, subject to para. 3.7 below, the statement of truth must be signed by a person holding a senior position[4] in the company or corporation. That person must state the office or position held.

3.5 Each of the following persons is a person holding a senior position:
(1) in respect of a registered company or corporation, a director, the treasurer, secretary, chief executive, manager or other officer of the company or corporation, and
(2) in respect of a corporation which is not a registered company, in addition to those persons set out in (1), the mayor, chairman, president or town clerk or other similar officer of the corporation.

3.6 Where the document is to be verified on behalf of a partnership, those who may sign the statement of truth are:
(1) any of the partners, or
(2) a person having the control or management of the partnership business.

3.6A An insurer or the Motor Insurers' Bureau may sign a statement of truth in a statement of case on behalf of a party where the insurer or the Motor Insurers' Bureau has a financial interest in the result of proceedings brought wholly or partially by or against that party.

3.6B If insurers are conducting proceedings on behalf of many claimants or defendants a statement of truth in a statement of case may be signed by a senior person responsible for the case at a lead insurer, but:
(1) the person signing must specify the capacity in which he signs;
(2) the statement of truth must be a statement that the lead insurer believes that the facts stated in the document are true; and
(3) the court may order that a statement of truth also be signed by one or more of the parties.

3.7 Where a party is legally represented, the legal representative may sign the statement of truth on his behalf. The statement signed by the legal representative will refer to the client's belief, not his own. In signing he must state the capacity in which he signs and the name of his firm where appropriate.

3.8 Where a legal representative has signed a statement of truth, his signature will be taken by the court as his statement:
(1) that the client on whose behalf he has signed had authorised him to do so,
(2) that before signing he had explained to the client that in signing the statement of truth he would be confirming the client's belief that the facts stated in the document were true, and
(3) that before signing he had informed the client of the possible consequences to the client if it should subsequently appear that the client did not have an honest belief in the truth of those facts (see r. 32.14).

3.9 The individual who signs a statement of truth must print his full name clearly beneath his signature.

[2] See Part 21 (children and protected parties).
[3] See r. 2.3 for the definition of legal representative.
[4] PD 6A, para. 6.2, sets out the meaning of 'senior position'.

3.10 A legal representative who signs a statement of truth must sign in his own name and not that of his firm or employer.

3.11 The following are examples of the possible application of this practice direction describing who may sign a statement of truth verifying statements in documents other than a witness statement. These are only examples and not an indication of how a court might apply the practice direction to a specific situation.

Managing agent	An agent who manages property or investments for the party cannot sign a statement of truth. It must be signed by the party or by the legal representative of the party.
Trusts	Where some or all of the trustees comprise a single party one, some or all of the trustees comprising the party may sign a statement of truth. The legal representative of the trustees may sign it.
Insurers and the Motor Insurers' Bureau	If an insurer has a financial interest in a claim involving its insured then, if the insured is the party, the insurer may sign a statement of truth in a statement of case for the insured party. Paragraphs 3.4 and 3.5 apply to the insurer if it is a company. The claims manager employed by the insurer responsible for handling the insurance claim or managing the staff handling the claim may sign the statement of truth for the insurer (see next example). The position for the Motor Insurers' Bureau is similar.
Companies	Paragraphs 3.4 and 3.5 apply. The word manager will be construed in the context of the phrase 'a person holding a senior position' which it is used to define. The court will consider the size of the company and the size and nature of the claim. It would expect the manager signing the statement of truth to have personal knowledge of the content of the document or to be responsible for managing those who have that knowledge of the content. A small company may not have a manager, apart from the directors, who holds a senior position. A large company will have many such managers. In a larger company with specialist claims, insurance or legal departments the statement may be signed by the manager of such a department if he or she is responsible for handling the claim or managing the staff handling it.
In-house legal representatives	Legal representative is defined in r. 2.3(1). A legal representative employed by a party may sign a statement of truth. However a person who is not a solicitor, barrister or other authorised litigator, but who is employed by the company and is managed by such a person, is not employed by that person and so cannot sign a statement of truth. (This is unlike the employee of a solicitor in private practice who would come within the definition of legal representative.) However such a person may be a manager and able to sign the statement on behalf of the company in that capacity.

Inability of Persons to Read or Sign Documents to Be Verified by a Statement of Truth

para.3A.1 51.11

3A.1 Where a document containing a statement of truth is to be signed by a person who is unable to read or sign the document, it must contain a certificate made by an authorised person.

3A.2 An authorised person is a person able to administer oaths and take affidavits but need not be independent of the parties or their representatives.

3A.3 The authorised person must certify:

(1) that the document has been read to the person signing it;
(2) that that person appeared to understand it and approved its content as accurate;
(3) that the declaration of truth has been read to that person;
(4) that that person appeared to understand the declaration and the consequences of making a false declaration; and
(5) that that person signed or made his mark in the presence of the authorised person.

3A.4 The form of the certificate is set out at annex 1 to this practice direction.

Consequences of Failure to Verify

para.4.2 23.17 para.4.3 23.17

4.1 If a statement of case is not verified by a statement of truth, the statement of case will remain effective unless it is struck out,[5] but a party may not rely on the contents of a statement of case as evidence until it has been verified by a statement of truth.

4.2 Any party may apply to the court for an order that unless within such period as the court may specify the statement of case is verified by the service of a statement of truth, the statement of case will be struck out.

4.3 The usual order for the costs of an application referred to in para. 4.2 will be that the costs be paid by the party who had failed to verify in any event and forthwith.

Penalty

5. Attention is drawn to r. 32.14 which sets out the consequences of verifying a statement of case containing a false statement without an honest belief in its truth, and to the procedures set out in r. 81.18 and PD 81, paras 5.1 to 5.7.

ANNEX 1

annex 1 51.11

CERTIFICATE TO BE USED WHERE A PERSON IS UNABLE TO READ OR SIGN A DOCUMENT TO BE VERIFIED BY A STATEMENT OF TRUTH

I certify that I [*name and address of authorised person*] have read over the contents of this document and the declaration of truth to the person signing the document [*if there are exhibits, add* and explained the nature and effect of the exhibits referred to in it] who appeared to understand (a) the document and approved its content as accurate and (b) the declaration of truth and the consequences of making a false declaration, and made his mark in my presence.

[5] See r. 22.2(1).

CPR Part 23 General Rules about Applications for Court Orders

Part 23 **PC 14, PC 16, PC 26, PC 27, PC 28, PC 37, PC 38, 14.18, 14.19, 14.22, 14.27, 14.32, 14.77, 14.78, 14.86, 15.21, 15.30, 15.53, 15.58, 16.43, 17.5, 18.7, 19.3, 20.1, 20.2, 20.8, 20.9, 22.6, 30.6, 33.3, 35.9, 38.31, 40.3, 42.21, 43.8, 44.3, 44.6, 48.32, 50.68, 50.90, 54.27, 58.10, 66.4, 66.17, 66.21, 67.2, 68.65, 71.17, 71.20, 71.27, 72.9, 72.12, 73.14, 74.44, 77.43, 78.14, 79.3, 79.5, 79.34, 79.36, 79.39, 80.24, 81.9, 81.25, 81.29, 84.17, 84.20, 84.23, 84.24, 86.5, 86.8, 86.38, 87.57, 88.10, 88.12, 88.45, 88.47, 88.51**

[For commentary on a specific rule, please refer to the cross-references after the title of the rule.]

23.1 Meaning of 'Application Notice' and 'Respondent'

r.23.1 **14.1**

In this Part—

'application notice' means a document in which the applicant states his intention to seek a court order; and

'respondent' means—

(a) the person against whom the order is sought; and

(b) such other person as the court may direct.

23.2 Where to Make an Application

r.23.2(1)–(3) **32.2, 37.10**
r.23.2(4) **11.8, 32.2, 37.5**
r.23.2(4A) **11.8, 32.2**
r.23.2(5) **32.2, 37.10**

(1) The general rule is that an application must be made to the court where the claim was started.

(2) If a claim has been transferred to another court since it was started, an application must be made to the court to which the claim has been transferred.

(3) If the parties have been notified of a fixed date for the trial, an application must be made to the court where the trial is to take place.

(4) Subject to paragraph (4A), if an application is made before a claim has been started, it must be made to the court where it is likely that the claim to which the application relates will be started unless there is good reason to make the application to a different court.

(4A) If—

(a) an application is made before a claim has been started; and

(b) the claim is a designated money claim,

the application may be made in any county court.

(5) If an application is made after proceedings to enforce judgment have begun, it must be made to any court which is dealing with the enforcement of the judgment unless any rule or practice direction provides otherwise.

23.3 Application Notice to Be Filed

r.23.3 **PC 20, 14.87**
r.23.3(1) **32.8, 32.13, 37.5, 77.43**
r.23.3(2)(a) **32.13**
r.23.3(2)(b) **32.13, 37.5**

(1) The general rule is that an applicant must file an application notice.
(2) An applicant may make an application without filing an application notice if—
  (a) this is permitted by a rule or practice direction; or
  (b) the court dispenses with the requirement for an application notice.

23.4 Notice of an Application

r.23.4 **14.87**
r.23.4(1) **32.7, 32.12, 50.9**
r.23.4(2) **32.7**

(1) The general rule is that a copy of the application notice must be served on each respondent.
(2) An application may be made without serving a copy of the application notice if this is permitted by—
  (a) a rule;
  (b) a practice direction; or
  (c) a court order.

(Rule 23.7 deals with service of a copy of the application notice)

23.5 Time When an Application Is Made

r.23.5 **15.32**

Where an application must be made within a specified time, it is so made if the application notice is received by the court within that time.

23.6 What an Application Notice Must Include

r.23.6 **PC 19, PC 20, 32.8, 32.13, 37.5**

An application notice must state—
(a) what order the applicant is seeking; and
(b) briefly, why the applicant is seeking the order.

(Part 22 requires an application notice to be verified by a statement of truth if the applicant wishes to rely on matters set out in his application notice as evidence)

23.7 Service of a Copy of an Application Notice

r.23.7 **PC 9, 37.5, 68.65**
r.23.7(1) PC 14, **PC 16, PC 20, PC 26, PC 27, 32.12, 32.13, 32.22**
r.23.7(1)(b) **67.2**
r.23.7(2) **36.6**
r.23.7(3) **32.15, 36.6**
r.23.7(5) **32.15, 32.22**

(1) A copy of the application notice—
  (a) must be served as soon as practicable after it is filed; and
  (b) except where another time limit is specified in these Rules or a practice direction, must in any event be served at least 3 days before the court is to deal with the application.
(2) If a copy of the application notice is to be served by the court, the applicant must, when he files the application notice, file a copy of any written evidence in support.
(3) When a copy of an application notice is served it must be accompanied by—
  (a) a copy of any written evidence in support; and
  (b) a copy of any draft order which the applicant has attached to his application.
(4) If—
  (a) an application notice is served; but
  (b) the period of notice is shorter than the period required by these Rules or a practice direction,

  the court may direct that, in the circumstances of the case, sufficient notice has been given and hear the application.
(5) This rule does not require written evidence—
  (a) to be filed if it has already been filed; or
  (b) to be served on a party on whom it has already been served.

(*Part 6 contains the* general rules about service of documents including who must serve a copy of the application notice)

23.8 Applications Which May Be Dealt with without a Hearing

r.23.8 **1.30, 32.23, 37.5, 48.33, 77.43, 87.53** r.23.8(b) **32.44**
r.23.8(a) **32.35, 32.44** r.23.8(c) **15.28, 32.13, 32.44**

The court may deal with an application without a hearing if—
(a) the parties agree as to the terms of the order sought;
(b) the parties agree that the court should dispose of the application without a hearing, or
(c) the court does not consider that a hearing would be appropriate.

23.9 Service of Application Where Application Made without Notice

r.23.9 **PC 10, 15.31, 32.10, 33.5, 37.8, 37.12** r.23.9(3) **PC 19, 15.29, 32.10**
r.23.9(2) **32.10**

(1) This rule applies where the court has disposed of an application which it permitted to be made without service of a copy of the application notice.
(2) Where the court makes an order, whether granting or dismissing the application, a copy of the application notice and any evidence in support must, unless the court orders otherwise, be served with the order on any party or other person—
(a) against whom the order was made; and
(b) against whom the order was sought.
(3) The order must contain a statement of the right to make an application to set aside[(GL)] or vary the order under rule 23.10.

23.10 Application to Set Aside or Vary Order Made without Notice

r.23.10 **15.30, 15.31, 32.10, 32.44, 33.5, 35.13, 37.8, 37.12, 61.1, 81.25**

(1) A person who was not served with a copy of the application notice before an order was made under rule 23.9, may apply to have the order set aside[(GL)] or varied.
(2) An application under this rule must be made within 7 days after the date on which the order was served on the person making the application.

23.11 Power of the Court to Proceed in the Absence of a Party

r.23.11(1) **32.32, 62.1** r.23.11(2) **62.1**

(1) Where the applicant or any respondent fails to attend the hearing of an application, the court may proceed in his absence.
(2) Where—
(a) the applicant or any respondent fails to attend the hearing of an application; and
(b) the court makes an order at the hearing,
the court may, on application or of its own initiative, relist the application.

(Part 40 deals with service of orders)

23.12 Dismissal of Totally without Merit Applications

r.23.12 **14.55, 63.7**

If the court dismisses an application (including an application for permission to appeal or for permission to apply for judicial review) and it considers that the application is totally without merit—
(a) the court's order must record that fact; and
(b) the court must at the same time consider whether it is appropriate to make a civil restraint order.

PD 23A Practice Direction 23A — Applications

This practice direction supplements CPR, Part 23.

PD 23A **32.21, 77.43** [For commentary on a specific paragraph, please refer to the cross-references after the title of the paragraph.]

Reference to a Judge

para.1 **32.3**

1 A master or district judge may refer to a judge any matter which he thinks should properly be decided by a judge, and the judge may either dispose of the matter or refer it back to the master or district judge.

Application Notices

para.2.1 **32.8, 32.13, 37.5**
para.2.1(4) **32.13**
para.2.1(5) **15.30**
para.2.3 **32.13**
para.2.7 **PC 20, 32.1, 32.4, 33.3, 34.2, 37.9**
para.2.8 **PC 20, 32.1, 37.9, 37.10**
para.2.9 **PC 20, PC 24, 32.27, 37.11**
para.2.10 **32.7, 47.13**

2.1 An application notice must, in addition to the matters set out in r. 23.6, be signed and include:
(1) the title of the claim,
(2) the reference number of the claim,
(3) the full name of the applicant,
(4) where the applicant is not already a party, his address for service, including a postcode (postcode information may be obtained from www.royalmail.com or the Royal Mail Address Management Guide), and
(5) either a request for a hearing or a request that the application be dealt with without a hearing.
(Form N244 may be used.)

2.2 On receipt of an application notice containing a request for a hearing the court will notify the applicant of the time and date for the hearing of the application.

2.3 On receipt of an application notice containing a request that the application be dealt with without a hearing, the application notice will be sent to a master or district judge so that he may decide whether the application is suitable for consideration without a hearing.

2.4 Where the master or district judge agrees that the application is suitable for consideration without a hearing, the court will so inform the applicant and the respondent and may give directions for the filing of evidence. (Rules 23.9 and 23.10 enable a party to apply for an order made with out a hearing to be set aside or varied.)

2.5 Where the master or district judge does not agree that the application is suitable for consideration without a hearing, the court will notify the applicant and the respondent of the time, date and place for the hearing of the application and may at the same time give directions as to the filing of evidence.

2.6 If the application is intended to be made to a judge, the application notice should so state. In that case, paragraphs 2.3, 2.4 and 2.5 will apply as though references to the master or district judge were references to a judge.

2.7 Every application should be made as soon as it becomes apparent that it is necessary or desirable to make it.

2.8 Applications should wherever possible be made so that they can be considered at any other hearing for which a date has already been fixed or for which a date is about to be fixed. This is particularly so in relation to case management conferences, allocation and listing hearings and pre-trial reviews fixed by the court.

2.9 The parties must anticipate that at any hearing the court may wish to review the conduct of the case as a whole and give any necessary case management directions. They should be ready to assist the court in doing so and to answer questions the court may ask for this purpose.

2.10 Where a date for a hearing has been fixed and a party wishes to make an application at that hearing but he does not have sufficient time to serve an application notice he should inform the other party and the court (if possible in writing) as soon as he can of the nature of the application and the reason for it. He should then make the application orally at the hearing.

Applications without Service of Application Notice

3 An application may be made without serving an application notice only:
(1) where there is exceptional urgency,
(2) where the overriding objective is best furthered by doing so,
(3) by consent of all parties,
(4) with the permission of the court,
(5) where para. 2.10 above applies, or
(6) where a court order, rule or practice direction permits.

Giving Notice of an Application

para.4.1A 32.24 para.4.2 32.7

4.1 Unless the court otherwise directs or para. 3 or para. 4.1A of this practice direction applies the application notice must be served as soon as practicable after it has been issued and, if there is to be a hearing, at least three days before the hearing date (r. 23.7(1)(b)).

4.1A Where there is to be a telephone hearing the application notice must be served as soon as practicable after it has been issued and in any event at least five days before the date of the hearing.

4.2 Where an application notice should be served but there is not sufficient time to do so, informal notification of the application should be given unless the circumstances of the application require secrecy.

(Rule 2.8 explains how to calculate periods of time expressed in terms of days.)

Pre-action Applications

para.5 37.3

5 All applications made before a claim is commenced should be made under Part 23. Attention is drawn in particular to r. 23.2(4).

Telephone Hearings

para.6 32.24
paras.6.2–6.9 32.24
para.6.1 32.24, 37.11
para.6.1A 32.13
para.6.10(4)–(5) 32.24
paras.6.11–6.13 32.24

Interpretation

6.1 In this paragraph:
(a) 'designated legal representative' means the applicant's legal representative (if any), or the legal representative of such other party as the court directs to arrange the telephone hearing; and
(b) 'telephone conference enabled court' means:
(i) district registry of the High Court; or
(ii) a county court, in which telephone conferencing facilities are available.

When a hearing is to be conducted by telephone

6.2 Subject to para. 6.3, at a telephone conference enabled court the following hearings will be conducted by telephone unless the court otherwise orders:
(a) allocation hearings;
(b) listing hearings; and
(c) interim applications, case management conferences and pre-trial reviews with a time estimate of no more than one hour.

6.3 Paragraph 6.2 does not apply where:
(a) the hearing is of an application made without notice to the other party;
(b) all the parties are unrepresented; or
(c) more than four parties wish to make representations at the hearing (for this purpose where two or more parties are represented by the same person, they are to be treated as one party).

CPR 1–25 & PDs

6.4 A request for a direction that a hearing under para. 6.2 should not be conducted by telephone:
(a) must be made at least seven days before the hearing or such shorter time as the court may permit; and
(b) may be made by letter,
and the court shall determine such request without requiring the attendance of the parties.

6.5 The court may order that an application, or part of an application, to which para. 6.2 does not apply be dealt with by a telephone hearing. The court may make such order:
(a) of its own initiative; or
(b) at the request of the parties.

6.6 The applicant should indicate on his application notice if he seeks a court order under para. 6.5. Where he has not done so but nevertheless wishes to seek an order, the request should be made as early as possible.

6.7 An order under para. 6.5 will not normally be made unless every party entitled to be given notice of the application and to be heard at the hearing has consented to the order.

6.8 If the court makes an order under para. 6.5 it will give any directions necessary for the telephone hearing.

Conduct of the telephone hearing

6.9 No party, or representative of a party, to an application being heard by telephone may attend the judge in person while the application is being heard unless every other party to the application has agreed that he may do so.

6.10 If an application is to be heard by telephone the following directions will apply, subject to any direction to the contrary:
(1) The designated legal representative is responsible for arranging the telephone conference for precisely the time fixed by the court. The telecommunications provider used must be one on the approved panel of service providers (see Her Majesty's Courts and Tribunals Service website).
(2) The designated legal representative must tell the operator the telephone numbers of all those participating in the conference call and the sequence in which they are to be called.
(3) It is the responsibility of the designated legal representative to ascertain from all the other parties whether they have instructed counsel and, if so, the identity of counsel, and whether the legal representative and counsel will be on the same or different telephone numbers.
(4) The sequence in which they are to be called will be:
(a) the designated legal representative and (if on a different number) his counsel;
(b) the legal representative (and counsel) for all other parties; and
(c) the judge.
(5) Each speaker is to remain on the line after being called by the operator setting up the conference call. The call shall be connected at least 10 minutes before the time fixed for the hearing.
(6) When the judge has been connected the designated legal representative (or his counsel) will introduce the parties in the usual way.
(7) If the use of a 'speakerphone' by any party causes the judge or any other party any difficulty in hearing what is said the judge may require that party to use a hand-held telephone.
(8) The telephone charges debited to the account of the party initiating the conference call will be treated as part of the costs of the application.

Documents

6.11 Where a document is required to be filed and served the party or the designated legal representative must do so no later than 4 p.m. at least two days before the hearing.

6.12 A case summary and draft order must be filed and served in—
(a) multi-track cases; and
(b) small and fast track cases if the court so directs.

6.13 Any other document upon which a party seeks to rely must be filed and served in accordance with the period specified in para. 6.11.

(Rule 2.8 explains how to calculate periods of time expressed in terms of days.)

Videoconferencing

para.7 37.11

7 Where the parties to a matter wish to use videoconferencing facilities, and those facilities are available in the relevant court, they should apply to the master or district judge for directions. (PD 32, para. 29.1 and annex 3, provide guidance on the use of videoconferencing in the civil courts.)

Note of Proceedings

para.8 32.27

8 The procedural judge should keep, either by way of a note or a tape recording, brief details of all proceedings before him, including the dates of the proceedings and a short statement of the decision taken at each hearing.

Evidence

para.9.1 32.15
para.9.2 PC 20
para.9.4 PC 20, 32.15, 37.13
para.9.5 PC 20
para.9.6 32.15

9.1 The requirement for evidence in certain types of applications is set out in some of the rules and practice directions. Where there is no specific requirement to provide evidence it should be borne in mind that, as a practical matter, the court will often need to be satisfied by evidence of the facts that are relied on in support of or for opposing the application.

9.2 The court may give directions for the filing of evidence in support of or opposing a particular application. The court may also give directions for the filing of evidence in relation to any hearing that it fixes on its own initiative. The directions may specify the form that evidence is to take and when it is to be served.

9.3 Where it is intended to rely on evidence which is not contained in the application itself, the evidence, if it has not already been served, should be served with the application.

9.4 Where a respondent to an application wishes to rely on evidence which has not yet been served he should serve it as soon as possible and in any event in accordance with any directions the court may have given.

9.5 If it is necessary for the applicant to serve any evidence in reply it should be served as soon as possible and in any event in accordance with any directions the court may have given.

9.6 Evidence must be filed with the court as well as served on the parties. Exhibits should not be filed unless the court otherwise directs.

9.7 The contents of an application notice may be used as evidence (otherwise than at trial) provided the contents have been verified by a statement of truth.[1]

Consent Orders

para.10.2 32.39, 63.39
para.10.3 63.39

10.1 Rule 40.6 sets out the circumstances where an agreed judgment or order may be entered and sealed.

10.2 Where all parties affected by an order have written to the court consenting to the making of the order a draft of which has been filed with the court, the court will treat the draft as having been signed in accordance with r. 40.6(7).

10.3 Where a consent order must be made by a judge (i.e. r. 40.6(2) does not apply) the order must be drawn so that the judge's name and judicial title can be inserted.

10.4 The parties to an application for a consent order must ensure that they provide the court with any material it needs to be satisfied that it is appropriate to make the order. Subject to any rule or practice direction a letter will generally be acceptable for this purpose.

10.5 Where a judgment or order has been agreed in respect of an application or claim where a hearing date has been fixed, the parties must inform the court immediately. (Note that parties are reminded that under rr. 28.4 and 29.5 the case management timetable cannot be varied by written agreement of the parties.)

[1] See Part 22.

Other Applications Considered without a Hearing

para.11.2 **32.44**

11.1 Where r. 23.8(b) applies the parties should so inform the court in writing and each should confirm that all evidence and other material on which he relies has been disclosed to the other parties to the application.

11.2 Where r. 23.8(c) applies the court will treat the application as if it were proposing to make an order on its own initiative.

Applications to Stay Claim Where Related Criminal Proceedings

para.11A. 1 **56.5** para.11A.3 **56.5**

11A.1 An application for the stay of civil proceedings pending the determination of related criminal proceedings may be made by any party to the civil proceedings or by the prosecutor or any defendant in the criminal proceedings.

11A.2 Every party to the civil proceedings must, unless he is the applicant, be made a respondent to the application.

11A.3 The evidence in support of the application must contain an estimate of the expected duration of the stay and must identify the respects in which the continuance of the civil proceedings may prejudice the criminal trial.

11A.4 In order to make an application under para. 11A.1, it is not necessary for the prosecutor or defendant in the criminal proceedings to be joined as a party to the civil proceedings.

Miscellaneous

para.12.1 **PC 20, 32.21**

12.1 Except in the most simple application the applicant should bring to any hearing a draft of the order sought. If the case is proceeding in the Royal Courts of Justice and the order is unusually long or complex it should also be supplied on disk for use by the court office.

12.2 Where r. 23.11 applies, the power to relist the application in r. 23.11(2) is in addition to any other powers of the court with regard to the order (for example, to set aside, vary, discharge or suspend the order).

Costs

para.13.2 **68.29**

13.1 Attention is drawn to PD 43–48 and, in particular, to the court's power to make a summary assessment of costs.

13.2 Attention is also drawn to r. 44.13(1) which provides that if an order makes no mention of costs, none are payable in respect of the proceedings to which it relates.

PD 23B Practice Direction 23B — Applications under Particular Statutes

Applications under the Family Law Reform Act 1969, Part 3, for Use of Scientific Tests to Determine Parentage

1.1 In this section:
- (1) 'the Act' means the Family Law Reform Act 1969;
- (2) 'direction' means a direction under s. 20(1) of the Act made in any proceedings in which a person's parentage falls to be determined;
- (3) 'responsible adult' means:
  - (a) in relation to a person under 16 to whom sub-paragraph (b) does not apply the person having care and control of him;
  - (b) in relation to a person who lacks capacity (within the meaning of the Mental Capacity Act 2005) to give his consent to tests:
    - (i) a person having power under that Act to give consent on his behalf; or
    - (ii) if there is no such person, the person with whom he resides or in whose care he is.
- (4) 'samples' means bodily samples within the meaning of s. 25 of the Act; and
- (5) 'tests' means scientific tests within the meaning of s. 25 of the Act.

1.2 Where an application is made for a direction in respect of a person who either:
- (a) is under 16; or
- (b) lacks capacity (within the meaning of the Mental Capacity Act 2005) to give his consent to the tests,

the application notice must state the name and address of the responsible adult.

1.3 Unless the court orders otherwise:
- (1) the court will serve a copy of the application notice on every party to the proceedings other than the applicant; and
- (2) the applicant must serve a copy of the application notice personally on any other person who would be directed to give samples and, where para. 1.2 applies, on the responsible adult.

1.4 Unless the court orders otherwise, where the court gives a direction:
- (1) the court will serve a copy of the direction on every party to the proceedings;
- (2) the applicant must serve a copy of the direction personally on any other person directed to give samples and, where para. 1.2 applies, on the responsible adult; and
- (3) further consideration of the proceedings shall be adjourned until the court receives a report of the tests carried out or samples taken.

1.5 When the court receives the report of the tests carried out or samples taken, the court officer shall send a copy of the report to:
- (1) every party to the proceedings;
- (2) the responsible adult where para. 1.2 applies; and
- (3) every other person directed to give samples.

Applications in Proceedings under the National Debt Act 1870, s. 55

2.1 Where a claim is brought under the National Debt Act 1870, s. 55, the claimant must apply to the court for directions about giving notice of the claim.

2.2 The court may:
- (a) direct that notice of the proceedings shall be given by advertisement or by such other method as appropriate; or
- (b) dispense with notice.

CPR 1–25 & PDs

CPR Part 24 Summary Judgment

Part 24 **PC 22, 26.3, 26.5, 31.13, 33.1, 36.13, 42.19, 91.41** [For commentary on a specific rule, please refer to the cross-references after the title of the rule.]

24.1 Scope of This Part

This Part sets out a procedure by which the court may decide a claim or a particular issue without a trial.

(Part 53 makes special provision about summary disposal of defamation claims in accordance with the Defamation Act 1996)

24.2 Grounds for Summary Judgment

r.24.2 **33.1, 34.1, 34.9, 34.10, 61.37, 90.17** r.24.2(a) **32.29** r.24.2(b) **34.46**

The court may give summary judgment against a claimant or defendant on the whole of a claim or on a particular issue if—

(a) it considers that—
 (i) that claimant has no real prospect of succeeding on the claim or issue; or
 (ii) that defendant has no real prospect of successfully defending the claim or issue; and
(b) there is no other compelling reason why the case or issue should be disposed of at a trial.

(Rule 3.4 makes provision for the court to strike out(GL) a statement of case or part of a statement of case if it appears that it discloses no reasonable grounds for bringing or defending a claim)

24.3 Types of Proceedings in Which Summary Judgment Is Available

r.24.3(1)–(2) **34.7**

(1) The court may give summary judgment against a claimant in any type of proceedings.
(2) The court may give summary judgment against a defendant in any type of proceedings except—
 (a) proceedings for possession of residential premises against—
  (i) a mortgagor; or
  (ii) a tenant or person holding over after the end of his tenancy, whose occupancy is protected within the meaning of the Rent Act 1977, or the Housing Act 1988; and
 (b) proceedings for an admiralty claim *in rem*.

24.4 Procedure

r.24.4(1) **1.17, 32.6, 34.2**
r.24.4(1A) **14.47**
r.24.4(2) **PC 22, 18.5, 26.3, 34.3**
r.24.4(3) **PC 22, 34.5, 34.8, 61.37**
r.24.4(3)(b) **PC 22**
r.24.4(4) **34.8**

(1) A claimant may not apply for summary judgment until the defendant against whom the application is made has filed—
 (a) an acknowledgment of service; or
 (b) a defence,unless—
  (i) the court gives permission; or
  (ii) a practice direction provides otherwise.

(Rule 10.3 sets out the period for filing an acknowledgment of service and rule 15.4 the period for filing a defence)

(1A) In civil proceedings against the Crown, as defined in rule 66.1(2), a claimant may not apply for summary judgment until after expiry of the period for filing a defence specified in rule 15.4.
(2) If a claimant applies for summary judgment before a defendant against whom the application is made has filed a defence, that defendant need not file a defence before the hearing.
(3) Where a summary judgment hearing is fixed, the respondent (or the parties where the hearing is fixed of the court's own initiative) must be given at least 14 days' notice of—
(a) the date fixed for the hearing; and
(b) the issues which it is proposed that the court will decide at the hearing.
(4) A practice direction may provide for a different period of notice to be given.
(Part 23 contains the general rules about how to make an application)
(Rule 3.3 applies where the court exercises its powers of its own initiative)

24.5 Evidence for the Purposes of a Summary Judgment Hearing

r.24.5(1) **34.8**
r.24.5(2) **PC 22, 34.8**
r.24.5(3) **34.8**
r.24.5(3)(a)–(b) **PC 23**

(1) If the respondent to an application for summary judgment wishes to rely on written evidence at the hearing, he must—
(a) file the written evidence; and
(b) serve copies on every other party to the application,
at least 7 days before the summary judgment hearing.
(2) If the applicant wishes to rely on written evidence in reply, he must—
(a) file the written evidence; and
(b) serve a copy on the respondent,
at least 3 days before the summary judgment hearing.
(3) Where a summary judgment hearing is fixed by the court of its own initiative—
(a) any party who wishes to rely on written evidence at the hearing must—
(i) file the written evidence; and
(ii) unless the court orders otherwise, serve copies on every other party to the proceedings,
at least 7 days before the date of the hearing;
(b) any party who wishes to rely on written evidence at the hearing in reply to any other party's written evidence must—
(i) file the written evidence in reply; and
(ii) unless the court orders otherwise serve copies on every other party to the proceedings,
at least 3 days before the date of the hearing.
(4) This rule does not require written evidence—
(a) to be filed if it has already been filed; or
(b) to be served on a party on whom it has already been served.

24.6 Court's Powers When It Determines a Summary Judgment Application

r.24.6 **PC 22, 34.47, 67.7**

When the court determines a summary judgment application it may—
(a) give directions as to the filing and service of a defence;
(b) give further directions about the management of the case.
(Rule 3.1(3) provides that the court may attach conditions when it makes an order)

CPR 1–25 & PDs

PD 24 Practice Direction 24 — The Summary Disposal of Claims

This practice direction supplements CPR, Part 24.

[For commentary on a specific paragraph, please refer to the cross-references after the title of the paragraph.]

Applications for Summary Judgment under Part 24

1.1 Attention is drawn to Part 24 itself and to:
Part 3, in particular rule 3.1(3) and (5),
Part 22,
Part 23, in particular rule 23.6,
Part 32, in particular rule 32.6(2).

1.2 In this paragraph, where the context so admits, the word 'claim' includes:
(1) a part of a claim, and
(2) an issue on which the claim in whole or part depends.

1.3 An application for summary judgment under rule 24.2 may be based on:
(1) a point of law (including a question of construction of a document),
(2) the evidence which can reasonably be expected to be available at trial or the lack of it, or
(3) a combination of these.

1.4 Rule 24.4(1) deals with the stage in the proceedings at which an application under Part 24 can be made (but see paragraph 7.1 below).

Procedure for Making an Application

para.2(3) PC 22
para.2(5) PC 22, 34.8
para.2(6) 34.2

2 (1) Attention is drawn to rules 24.4(3) and 23.6.
(2) The application notice must include a statement that it is an application for summary judgment made under Part 24.
(3) The application notice or the evidence contained or referred to in it or served with it must:
(a) identify concisely any point of law or provision in a document on which the applicant relies, and/or
(b) state that it is made because the applicant believes that on the evidence the respondent has no real prospect of succeeding on the claim or issue or (as the case may be) of successfully defending the claim or issue to which the application relates,

and in either case state that the applicant knows of no other reason why the disposal of the claim or issue should await trial.
(4) Unless the application notice itself contains all the evidence (if any) on which the applicant relies, the application notice should identify the written evidence on which the applicant relies. This does not affect the applicant's right to file further evidence under rule 24.5(2).
(5) The application notice should draw the attention of the respondent to rule 24.5(1).
(6) Where the claimant has failed to comply with Practice Direction (Pre-action Conduct) or any relevant pre-action protocol, an application for summary judgment will not normally be entertained before the defence has been filed or, alternatively, the time for doing so has expired.

The Hearing

para.3(1) PC 22, PC 24

3 (1) The hearing of the application will normally take place before a master or a district judge.
(2) The master or district judge may direct that the application be heard by a High Court judge (if the case is in the High Court) or a circuit judge (if the case is in a county court).

The Court's Approach

para.4 34.34

4 Where it appears to the court possible that a claim or defence may succeed but improbable that it will do so, the court may make a conditional order, as described below.

Orders the Court May Make

para.5.1 34.9 para.5.2 34.34

5.1 The orders the court may make on an application under Part 24 include:
(1) judgment on the claim,
(2) the striking out or dismissal of the claim,
(3) the dismissal of the application,
(4) a conditional order.

5.2 A conditional order is an order which requires a party:
(1) to pay a sum of money into court, or
(2) to take a specified step in relation to his claim or defence, as the case may be,
and provides that that party's claim will be dismissed or his statement of case will be struck out if he does not comply.
(Note — the court will not follow its former practice of granting leave to a defendant to defend a claim, whether conditionally or unconditionally.)

Accounts and Inquiries

6 If a remedy sought by a claimant in his claim form includes, or necessarily involves, taking an account or making an inquiry, an application can be made under Part 24 by any party to the proceedings for an order directing any necessary accounts or inquiries to be taken or made.
(PD 40A contains further provisions as to orders for accounts and inquiries.)

Specific Performance

para.7 34.48

7.1 (1) If a remedy sought by a claimant in his claim form includes a claim—
(a) for specific performance of an agreement (whether in writing or not) for the sale, purchase, exchange, mortgage or charge of any property, or for the grant or assignment of a lease or tenancy of any property, with or without an alternative claim for damages, or
(b) for rescission of such an agreement, or
(c) for the forfeiture or return of any deposit made under such an agreement,
the claimant may apply under Part 24 for judgment.
(2) The claimant may do so at any time after the claim form has been served, whether or not the defendant has acknowledged service of the claim form, whether or not the time for acknowledging service has expired and whether or not any particulars of claim have been served.

7.2 The application notice by which an application under paragraph 7.1 is made must have attached to it the text of the order sought by the claimant.

7.3 The application notice and a copy of every affidavit or witness statement in support and of any exhibit referred to therein must be served on the defendant not less than 4 days before the hearing of the application. (Note — the 4 days replaces for these applications the 14 days specified in rule 24.4(3). Rule 24.5 cannot, therefore, apply.)
(This paragraph replaces RSC, ord. 86, rr. 1 and 2, but applies to county court proceedings as well as to High Court proceedings.)

Setting Aside Order for Summary Judgment

8.1 If an order for summary judgment is made against a respondent who does not appear at the hearing of the application, the respondent may apply for the order to be set aside or varied (see also rule 23.11).

8.2 On the hearing of an application under paragraph 8.1 the court may make such order as it thinks just.

Costs

9.1 Attention is drawn to Part 45 (fixed costs).

9.2 Attention is drawn to PD 43–48 and in particular to the court's power to make a summary assessment of costs.

9.3 Attention is also drawn to rule 44.13(1) which provides that if an order does not mention costs no party is entitled to costs relating to that order.

Case Management

para.10 34.47

10 Where the court dismisses the application or makes an order that does not completely dispose of the claim, the court will give case management directions as to the future conduct of the case.

CPR Part 25 Interim Remedies and Security for Costs

Part 25 **24.19, 45.6, 67.2, 77.42, 85.15, 88.20, 88.30** [For commentary on a specific rule, please refer to the cross-references after the title of the rule.]

I INTERIM REMEDIES

25.1 Orders for Interim Remedies

r.25.1 **36.3, 40.3, 77.42**
r.25.1(1) **32.33, 42.45**
r.25.1(1)(a) **77.42**
r.25.1(1)(b) **4.19, 4.20, 77.42**
r.25.1(1)(c) **40.3, 41.1, 41.2, 41.3, 77.42**
r.25.1(1)(c)(v)(vi) **41.10**
r.25.1(1)(d) **41.1, 41.2**
r.25.1(1)(e) **40.2**
r.25.1(1)(f) **38.1, 77.42**
r.25.1(1)(g) **38.25**
r.25.1(1)(h) **39.1, 77.42**
r.25.1(1)(k) **36.1, 36.4**
r.25.1(1)(l) **41.4**
r.25.1(1)(m) **40.3, 40.5, 40.6**
r.25.1(1)(n) **32.33**
r.25.1(1)(o) **32.33, 34.49, 63.36**
r.25.1(1)(p) **32.33**
r.25.1(2) **41.3, 41.10**
r.25.1(4) **37.1**

(1) The court may grant the following interim remedies—
 (a) an interim injunction(GL);
 (b) an interim declaration;
 (c) an order—
  (i) for the detention, custody or preservation of relevant property;
  (ii) for the inspection of relevant property;
  (iii) for the taking of a sample of relevant property;
  (iv) for the carrying out of an experiment on or with relevant property;
  (v) for the sale of relevant property which is of a perishable nature or which for any other good reason it is desirable to sell quickly; and
  (vi) for the payment of income from relevant property until a claim is decided;
 (d) an order authorising a person to enter any land or building in the possession of a party to the proceedings for the purposes of carrying out an order under sub-paragraph (c);
 (e) an order under section 4 of the Torts (Interference with Goods) Act 1977 to deliver up goods;
 (f) an order (referred to as a 'freezing injunction(GL)')—
  (i) restraining a party from removing from the jurisdiction assets located there; or
  (ii) restraining a party from dealing with any assets whether located within the jurisdiction or not;
 (g) an order directing a party to provide information about the location of relevant property or assets or to provide information about relevant property or assets which are or may be the subject of an application for a freezing injunction(GL);

CPR 1–25 & PDs

(h) an order (referred to as a 'search order') under section 7 of the Civil Procedure Act 1997 (order requiring a party to admit another party to premises for the purpose of preserving evidence etc.);
(i) an order under section 33 of the Senior Courts Act 1981 or section 52 of the County Courts Act 1984 (order for disclosure of documents or inspection of property before a claim has been made);
(j) an order under section 34 of the Senior Courts Act 1981 or section 53 of the County Courts Act 1984 (order in certain proceedings for disclosure of documents or inspection of property against a non-party);
(k) an order (referred to as an order for interim payment) under rule 25.6 for payment by a defendant on account of any damages, debt or other sum (except costs) which the court may hold the defendant liable to pay;
(l) an order for a specified fund to be paid into court or otherwise secured, where there is a dispute over a party's right to the fund;
(m) an order permitting a party seeking to recover personal property to pay money into court pending the outcome of the proceedings and directing that, if he does so, the property shall be given up to him;
(n) an order directing a party to prepare and file accounts relating to the dispute;
(o) an order directing any account to be taken or inquiry to be made by the court; and
(p) an order under Article 9 of Council Directive (EC) 2004/48 on the enforcement of intellectual property rights (order in intellectual property proceedings making the continuation of an alleged infringement subject to the lodging of guarantees).

(Rule 34.2 provides for the court to issue a witness summons requiring a witness to produce documents to the court at the hearing or on such date as the court may direct)

(2) In paragraph (1)(c) and (g), 'relevant property' means property (including land) which is the subject of a claim or as to which any question may arise on a claim.
(3) The fact that a particular kind of interim remedy is not listed in paragraph (1) does not affect any power that the court may have to grant that remedy.
(4) The court may grant an interim remedy whether or not there has been a claim for a final remedy of that kind.

25.2 Time When an Order for an Interim Remedy May Be Made

r.25.2 **PC 20, 44.8**
r.25.2(1) **37.3**
r.25.2(1)(b) **32.6**
r.25.2(2) **32.4, 37.3, 37.9**
r.25.2(2)(b) **32.5, 37.13**
r.25.2(2)(c) **34.2, 37.9, 67.2**
r.25.2(3) **PC 19, 32.5, 37.7, 41.7, 55.9**
r.25.2(4) **32.5, 41.7**

(1) An order for an interim remedy may be made at any time, including—
(a) before proceedings are started; and
(b) after judgment has been given.

(Rule 7.2 provides that proceedings are started when the court issues a claim form)

(2) However—
(a) paragraph (1) is subject to any rule, practice direction or other enactment which provides otherwise;
(b) the court may grant an interim remedy before a claim has been made only if—
(i) the matter is urgent; or
(ii) it is otherwise desirable to do so in the interests of justice; and
(c) unless the court otherwise orders, a defendant may not apply for any of the orders listed in rule 25.1(1) before he has filed either an acknowledgment of service or a defence.

(Part 10 provides for filing an acknowledgment of service and Part 15 for filing a defence)

(3) Where it grants an interim remedy before a claim has been commenced, the court should give directions requiring a claim to be commenced.
(4) In particular, the court need not direct that a claim be commenced where the application is made under section 33 of the Senior Courts Act 1981 or section 52 of the County Courts Act 1984 (order for disclosure, inspection etc. before commencement of a claim).

25.3 How to Apply for an Interim Remedy

r.25.3(1) 37.5, 77.42
r.25.3(2) 32.1, 32.13, 32.15, 33.7, 34.8, 37.5, 37.13, 40.3, 41.5, 48.32
r.25.3(3) PC 10, PC 19, 32.8, 37.13

(1) The court may grant an interim remedy on an application made without notice if it appears to the court that there are good reasons for not giving notice.
(2) An application for an interim remedy must be supported by evidence, unless the court orders otherwise.
(3) If the applicant makes an application without giving notice, the evidence in support of the application must state the reasons why notice has not been given.
(Part 3 lists general powers of the court)
(Part 23 contains general rules about making an application)

25.4 Application for an Interim Remedy Where There Is No Related Claim

(1) This rule applies where a party wishes to apply for an interim remedy but—
 (a) the remedy is sought in relation to proceedings which are taking place, or will take place, outside the jurisdiction; or
 (b) the application is made under section 33 of the Senior Courts Act 1981 or section 52 of the County Courts Act 1984 (order for disclosure, inspection etc. before commencement) before a claim has been commenced.
(2) An application under this rule must be made in accordance with the general rules about application contained in Part 23.
(The following provisions are also relevant—
- Rule 25.5 (inspection of property before commencement or against a non-party)
- Rule 31.16 (orders for disclosure of documents before proceedings start)
- Rule 31.17 (orders for disclosure of documents against a person not a party))

25.5 Inspection of Property before Commencement or against a Non-party

r.25.5(2) 41.7, 41.9
r.25.5(3) 41.7, 41.9

(1) This rule applies where a person makes an application under—
 (a) section 33(1) of the Senior Courts Act 1981 or section 52(1) of the County Courts Act 1984 (inspection etc. of property before commencement);
 (b) section 34(3) of the Senior Courts Act 1981 or section 53(3) of the County Courts Act 1984 (inspection etc. of property against a non-party).
(2) The evidence in support of such an application must show, if practicable by reference to any statement of case prepared in relation to the proceedings or anticipated proceedings, that the property—
 (a) is or may become the subject matter of such proceedings; or
 (b) is relevant to the issues that will arise in relation to such proceedings.
(3) A copy of the application notice and a copy of the evidence in support must be served on—
 (a) the person against whom the order is sought; and
 (b) in relation to an application under section 34(3) of the Senior Courts Act 1981 or section 53(3) of the County Courts Act 1984, every party to the proceedings other than the applicant.

25.6 Interim Payments — General Procedure

r.25.6 61.60
r.25.6(1) PC 24, 32.6, 36.4, 36.5
r.25.6(2) PC 24, 36.5, 36.17
r.25.6(3) PC 24, 36.6
r.25.6(4)–(5) PC 24, 36.6
r.25.6(7) 36.15

(1) The claimant may not apply for an order for an interim payment before the end of the period for filing an acknowledgment of service applicable to the defendant against whom the application is made.
(Rule 10.3 sets out the period for filing an acknowledgment of service)
(Rule 25.1(1)(k) defines an interim payment)
(2) The claimant may make more than one application for an order for an interim payment.

CPR 1–25 & PDs

(3) A copy of an application notice for an order for an interim payment must—
(a) be served at least 14 days before the hearing of the application; and
(b) be supported by evidence.
(4) If the respondent to an application for an order for an interim payment wishes to rely on written evidence at the hearing, he must—
(a) file the written evidence; and
(b) serve copies on every other party to the application,
at least 7 days before the hearing of the application.
(5) If the applicant wishes to rely on written evidence in reply, he must—
(a) file the written evidence; and
(b) serve a copy on the respondent,
at least 3 days before the hearing of the application.
(6) This rule does not require written evidence—
(a) to be filed if it has already been filed; or
(b) to be served on a party on whom it has already been served.
(7) The court may order an interim payment in one sum or in instalments.
(Part 23 contains general rules about applications)

25.7 Interim Payments — Conditions to Be Satisfied and Matters to Be Taken into Account

r.25.7 **PC 22, PC 24, 36.3, 36.7, 36.14, 61.60**
r.25.7(1) **36.7**
r.25.7(1)(a) **36.7**
r.25.7(1)(b) **36.7, 36.11**
r.25.7(1)(c) **32.29, 36.7, 36.8, 36.9, 36.10, 36.11, 36.12**
r.25.7(1)(d) **36.7, 36.8**
r.25.7(1)(e) **36.7, 36.8, 36.10, 36.11**
r.25.7(1)(e)(ii)(b) **36.11**
r.25.7(4) **36.15**
r.25.7(5) **36.12, 36.15**

(1) The court may only make an order for an interim payment where any of the following conditions are satisfied—
(a) the defendant against whom the order is sought has admitted liability to pay damages or some other sum of money to the claimant;
(b) the claimant has obtained judgment against that defendant for damages to be assessed or for a sum of money (other than costs) to be assessed;
(c) it is satisfied that, if the claim went to trial, the claimant would obtain judgment for a substantial amount of money (other than costs) against the defendant from whom he is seeking an order for an interim payment whether or not that defendant is the only defendant or one of a number of defendants to the claim;
(d) the following conditions are satisfied—
(i) the claimant is seeking an order for possession of land (whether or not any other order is also sought); and
(ii) the court is satisfied that, if the case went to trial, the defendant would be held liable (even if the claim for possession fails) to pay the claimant a sum of money for the defendant's occupation and use of the land while the claim for possession was pending; or
(e) in a claim in which there are two or more defendants and the order is sought against any one or more of those defendants, the following conditions are satisfied—
(i) the court is satisfied that, if the claim went to trial, the claimant would obtain judgment for a substantial amount of money (other than costs) against at least one of the defendants (but the court cannot determine which); and
(ii) all the defendants are either—
(a) a defendant that is insured in respect of the claim;
(b) a defendant whose liability will be met by an insurer under section 151 of the Road Traffic Act 1988 or an insurer acting under the Motor Insurers Bureau Agreement, or the Motor Insurers Bureau where it is acting itself; or
(c) a defendant that is a public body.
(2) [*revoked*]
(3) [*revoked*]

(4) The court must not order an interim payment of more than a reasonable proportion of the likely amount of the final judgment.
(5) The court must take into account—
(a) contributory negligence; and
(b) any relevant set-off or counterclaim.

25.8 Powers of Court Where It Has Made an Order for Interim Payment

r.25.8 **36.19, 61.60** r.25.8(5) **36.19**
r.25.8(2) **63.22**

(1) Where a defendant has been ordered to make an interim payment, or has in fact made an interim payment (whether voluntarily or under an order), the court may make an order to adjust the interim payment.
(2) The court may in particular—
(a) order all or part of the interim payment to be repaid;
(b) vary or discharge the order for the interim payment;
(c) order a defendant to reimburse, either wholly or partly, another defendant who has made an interim payment.
(3) The court may make an order under paragraph (2)(c) only if—
(a) the defendant to be reimbursed made the interim payment in relation to a claim in respect of which he has made a claim against the other defendant for a contribution(GL), indemnity(GL) or other remedy; and
(b) where the claim or part to which the interim payment relates has not been discontinued or disposed of, the circumstances are such that the court could make an order for interim payment under rule 25.7.
(4) The court may make an order under this rule without an application by any party if it makes the order when it disposes of the claim or any part of it.
(5) Where—
(a) a defendant has made an interim payment; and
(b) the amount of the payment is more than his total liability under the final judgment or order,the court may award him interest on the overpaid amount from the date when he made the interim payment.

25.9 Restriction on Disclosure of an Interim Payment

r.25.9 **PC 24, 36.18, 61.60**

The fact that a defendant has made an interim payment, whether voluntarily or by court order, shall not be disclosed to the trial judge until all questions of liability and the amount of money to be awarded have been decided unless the defendant agrees.

25.10 Interim Injunction to Cease If Claim Is Stayed

r.25.10 **37.71**

If—
(a) the court has granted an interim injunction(GL) other than a freezing injunction; and
(b) the claim is stayed(GL) other than by agreement between the parties,
the interim injunction(GL) shall be set aside(GL) unless the court orders that it should continue to have effect even though the claim is stayed.

25.11 Interim Injunction to Cease after 14 Days If Claim Struck Out

r.25.11 **37.71, 42.18**

(1) If—
(a) the court has granted an interim injunction(GL); and
(b) the claim is struck out under rule 3.7 (sanction for non-payment of certain fees),
the interim injunction shall cease to have effect 14 days after the date that the claim is struck out unless paragraph (2) applies.
(2) If the claimant applies to reinstate the claim before the interim injunction ceases to have effect under paragraph (1), the injunction shall continue until the hearing of the application unless the court orders otherwise.

II SECURITY FOR COSTS

25.12 Security for Costs

r.25.12 48.20, 67.2, 67.3, 67.29
r.25.12(1) 67.3
r.25.12(2) 67.2

(1) A defendant to any claim may apply under this Section of this Part for security for his costs of the proceedings.

(Part 3 provides for the court to order payment of sums into court in other circumstances. Rule 20.3 provides for this Section of this Part to apply to Part 20 claims)

(2) An application for security for costs must be supported by written evidence.

(3) Where the court makes an order for security for costs, it will—

(a) determine the amount of security; and

(b) direct—

(i) the manner in which; and

(ii) the time within which

the security must be given.

25.13 Conditions to Be Satisfied

r.25.13 20.21, 48.20, 67.2, 67.3, 67.29
r.25.13(1)(a) 67.6, 67.16
r.25.13(2) 67.6, 67.8
r.25.13(2)(a) 67.11, 67.14, 67.21, 67.22, 67.25
r.25.13(2)(a)(i)–(ii) 67.22
r.25.13(2)(c) 61.21, 67.2, 67.10, 67.12, 67.24
r.25.13(2)(d) 67.14, 67.15
r.25.13(2)(f) 67.13
r.25.13(2)(g) 67.15

(1) The court may make an order for security for costs under rule 25.12 if—

(a) it is satisfied, having regard to all the circumstances of the case, that it is just to make such an order; and

(b) (i) one or more of the conditions in paragraph (2) applies, or

(ii) an enactment permits the court to require security for costs.

(2) The conditions are—

(a) The claimant is—

(i) resident out of the jurisdiction; but

(ii) not resident in a Brussels Contracting State, a State bound by the Lugano Convention or a Regulation State, as defined in section 1(3) of the Civil Jurisdiction and Judgments Act 1982;

[*(b) revoked*]

(c) the claimant is a company or other body (whether incorporated inside or outside Great Britain) and there is reason to believe that it will be unable to pay the defendant's costs if ordered to do so;

(d) the claimant has changed his address since the claim was commenced with a view to evading the consequences of the litigation;

(e) the claimant failed to give his address in the claim form, or gave an incorrect address in that form;

(f) the claimant is acting as a nominal claimant, other than as a representative claimant under Part 19, and there is reason to believe that he will be unable to pay the defendant's costs if ordered to do so;

(g) the claimant has taken steps in relation to his assets that would make it difficult to enforce an order for costs against him.

(Rule 3.4 allows the court to strike out a statement of case and Part 24 for it to give summary judgment)

25.14 Security for Costs Other than from the Claimant

r.25.14 67.2, 67.3, 67.4, 67.13
r.25.14(1)(a) 67.16

(1) The defendant may seek an order against someone other than the claimant, and the court may make an order for security for costs against that person if—

(a) it is satisfied, having regard to all the circumstances of the case, that it is just to make such an order; and

(b) one or more of the conditions in paragraph (2) applies.

(2) The conditions are that the person—
(a) has assigned the right to the claim to the claimant with a view to avoiding the possibility of a costs order being made against him; or
(b) has contributed or agreed to contribute to the claimant's costs in return for a share of any money or property which the claimant may recover in the proceedings; and
is a person against whom a costs order may be made.
(Rule 48.2 makes provision for costs orders against non-parties)

25.15 Security for Costs of an Appeal

r.25.15 67.1, 67.2, 67.3, 67.4, 67.29

(1) The court may order security for costs of an appeal against—
(a) an appellant;
(b) a respondent who also appeals,
on the same grounds as it may order security for costs against a claimant under this Part.
(2) The court may also make an order under paragraph (1) where the appellant, or the respondent who also appeals, is a limited company and there is reason to believe it will be unable to pay the costs of the other parties to the appeal should its appeal be unsuccessful.

PD 25A Practice Direction 25A — Interim Injunctions

This practice direction supplements CPR, Part 25.

PD25A PC 19, 32.15, 38.3, 38.10, 38.17, 38.23, 38.25, 38.28, 38.29, 52.7, 63.7 [For commentary on a specific paragraph, please refer to the cross-references after the title of the paragraph.]

Jurisdiction

para.1.1–1.4 37.2   para.1.3 32.3

1.1 High Court judges and any other judge duly authorised may grant 'search orders'[1] and 'freezing injunctions'.[2]

1.2 In a case in the High Court, masters and district judges have the power to grant injunctions:
(1) by consent,
(2) in connection with charging orders and appointments of receivers,
(3) in aid of execution of judgments.

1.3 In any other case any judge who has jurisdiction to conduct the trial of the action has the power to grant an injunction in that action.

1.4 A master or district judge has the power to vary or discharge an injunction granted by any judge with the consent of all the parties.

Making an Application

para.2.1 37.5   para.2.4 37.5, 38.29
para.2.3 37.10

2.1 The application notice must state:
(1) the order sought, and
(2) the date, time and place of the hearing.

2.2 The application notice and evidence in support must be served as soon as practicable after issue and in any event not less than three days before the court is due to hear the application.[3]

2.3 Where the court is to serve, sufficient copies of the application notice and evidence in support for the court and for each respondent should be filed for issue and service.

2.4 Whenever possible a draft of the order sought should be filed with the application notice and a disk containing the draft should also be available to the court in a format compatible with the word processing software used by the court. This will enable the court officer to arrange for any amendments to be incorporated and for the speedy preparation and sealing of the order.

Evidence

para.3.1 PC 19, 38.3, 39.3   para.3.3 PC 19, 37.13, 37.72
para.3.2 37.13   para.3.4 37.13

3.1 Applications for search orders and freezing injunctions must be supported by affidavit evidence.

3.2 Applications for other interim injunctions must be supported by evidence set out in either:
(1) a witness statement, or
(2) a statement of case provided that it is verified by a statement of truth,[4] or
(3) the application provided that it is verified by a statement of truth,
unless the court, an Act, a rule or a practice direction requires evidence by affidavit.

3.3 The evidence must set out the facts on which the applicant relies for the claim being made against the respondent, including all material facts of which the court should be made aware.

3.4 Where an application is made without notice to the respondent, the evidence must also set out why notice was not given.
(See Part 32 and PD 32 for information about evidence.)

---

[1] *Rule 25.2(3).*
[2] Rule 25.1(1)(f).
[3] Rule 23.7(1) and (2) and see rule 23.7(4) (short service).
[4] See Part 22.

Urgent Applications and Applications without Notice

para.4.2 32.9, 37.6
para.4.3(1) 37.11, 38.3
para.4.3(2) 37.11
para.4.3(3) PC 19, 37.11
para.4.4(2) 37.8
para.4.5 PC 19
para.4.5(1) 37.6
para.4.5(5) 37.6

4.1 These fall into two categories:
(1) applications where a claim form has already been issued, and
(2) applications where a claim form has not yet been issued,
and, in both cases, where notice of the application has not been given to the respondent.

4.2 These applications are normally dealt with at a court hearing but cases of extreme urgency may be dealt with by telephone.

4.3 Applications dealt with at a court hearing after issue of a claim form:
(1) the application notice, evidence in support and a draft order (as in para. 2.4 above) should be filed with the court two hours before the hearing wherever possible,
(2) if an application is made before the application notice has been issued, a draft order (as in para. 2.4 above) should be provided at the hearing, and the application notice and evidence in support must be filed with the court on the same or next working day or as ordered by the court, and
(3) except in cases where secrecy is essential, the applicant should take steps to notify the respondent informally of the application.

4.4 Applications made before the issue of a claim form:
(1) in addition to the provisions set out at para. 4.3 above, unless the court orders otherwise, either the applicant must undertake to the court to issue a claim form immediately or the court will give directions for the commencement of the claim,[5]
(2) where possible the claim form should be served with the order for the injunction,
(3) an order made before the issue of a claim form should state in the title after the names of the applicant and respondent 'the Claimant and Defendant in an Intended Action'.

4.5 Applications made by telephone:
(1) where it is not possible to arrange a hearing, application can be made between 10.00 a.m. and 5.00 p.m. weekdays by telephoning the Royal Courts of Justice on (020) 7947 6000 and asking to be put in contact with a High Court judge of the appropriate Division available to deal with an emergency application in a High Court matter. The appropriate district registry may also be contacted by telephone. In county court proceedings, the appropriate county court should be contacted,
(2) where an application is made outside those hours the applicant should either:
(a) telephone the Royal Courts of Justice on (020) 7947 6000 where he will be put in contact with the clerk to the appropriate duty judge in the High Court (or the appropriate area circuit judge where known), or
(b) the Urgent Court Business Officer of the appropriate circuit who will contact the local duty judge,
(3) where the facility is available it is likely that the judge will require a draft order to be faxed to him,
(4) the application notice and evidence in support must be filed with the court on the same or next working day or as ordered, together with two copies of the order for sealing,
(5) injunctions will be heard by telephone only where the applicant is acting by counsel or solicitors.

Orders for Injunctions

para.5.1 40.6, 41.1
para.5.1(1) 77.42
para.5.1(2)–(3) 37.7
para.5.1(4) 37.5
para.5.1(5) 37.7
para.5.1A 37.64
para.5.2–5.3 37.65, 40.6

5.1 Any order for an injunction, unless the court orders otherwise, must contain:
(1) subject to para. 5.1B, an undertaking by the applicant to the court to pay any damages which the respondent sustains which the court considers the applicant should pay,
(2) if made without notice to any other party, an undertaking by the applicant to the court to serve on the respondent the application notice, evidence in support and any order made as soon as practicable,

[5] Rule 25.2(3).

CPR 1–25 & PDs

(3) if made without notice to any other party, a return date for a further hearing at which the other party can be present,
(4) if made before filing the application notice, an undertaking to file and pay the appropriate fee on the same or next working day, and
(5) if made before issue of a claim form:
  (a) an undertaking to issue and pay the appropriate fee on the same or next working day, or
  (b) directions for the commencement of the claim.

5.1 A When the court makes an order for an injunction, it should consider whether to require an undertaking by the applicant to pay any damages sustained by a person other than the respondent, including another party to the proceedings or any other person who may suffer loss as a consequence of the order.

5.1A Subject to para. 5.1B, when the court makes an order for an injunction, it should consider whether to require an undertaking by the applicant to pay any damages sustained by a person other than the respondent, including another party to the proceedings or any other person who may suffer loss as a consequence of the order.

5.1B (1) If in an Aarhus Convention claim the court is satisfied that an injunction is necessary to prevent significant environmental damage and to preserve the factual basis of the proceedings, the court will, in considering whether to require an undertaking by the applicant to pay any damages which the respondent or any other person may sustain as a result and the terms of any such undertaking—
  (a) have particular regard to the need for the terms of the order overall not to be such as would make continuing with the claim prohibitively expensive for the applicant; and
  (b) make such directions as are necessary to ensure that the case is heard promptly.
(2) 'Aarhus Convention claim' has the same meaning as in r. 45.41(2).

5.2 An order for an injunction made in the presence of all parties to be bound by it or made at a hearing of which they have had notice, may state that it is effective until trial or further order.

5.3 Any order for an injunction must set out clearly what the respondent must do or not do.

Freezing Injunctions

Orders to restrain disposal of assets worldwide and within England and Wales

6.1 An example of a freezing injunction is annexed to this practice direction.

6.2 This example may be modified as appropriate in any particular case. In particular, the court may if it considers it appropriate, require the applicant's solicitors, as well as the applicant, to give undertakings.

Search Orders

para.7.1 **40.6, 41.1**
para.7.2 **39.5, 40.6, 41.1**
para.7.3 **39.4, 40.6, 41.1**
para.7.3(2) **39.9**
para.7.4 **40.6, 41.1**
para.7.4(1) **15.41, 39.11**
para.7.4(2) **39.11**
para.7.4(4) **39.12**
para.7.4(5)–(6) **39.11**
para.7.5 **40.6, 41.1**
para.7.5(2)–(10) **39.13**
para.7.5(11)–(13) **39.14**
paras.7.6–7.7 **39.5, 40.6, 41.1**
para.7.8 **39.12, 40.6, 41.1**
para.7.9 **39.10, 39.12, 39.16, 40.6, 41.1**
para.7.10 **40.6, 41.1**
para.7.11 **39.10, 40.6, 41.1**

7.1 The following provisions apply to search orders in addition to those listed above.

The Supervising Solicitor

7.2 The Supervising Solicitor must be experienced in the operation of search orders. A SupervisingSolicitor may be contacted either through the Law Society or, for the London area, through the London Solicitors Litigation Association.

7.3 Evidence:
(1) the affidavit must state the name, firm and its address, and experience of the Supervising Solicitor, also the address of the premises and whether it is a private or business address, and
(2) the affidavit must disclose very fully the reason the order is sought, including the probability that relevant material would disappear if the order were not made.

7.4 Service:
(1) the order must be served personally by the Supervising Solicitor, unless the court otherwise orders, and must be accompanied by the evidence in support and any documents capable of being copied,

(2) confidential exhibits need not be served but they must be made available for inspection by the respondent in the presence of the applicant's solicitors while the order is carried out and after wards be retained by the respondent's solicitors on their undertaking not to permit the respondent:
   (a) to see them or copies of them except in their presence, and
   (b) to make or take away any note or record of them,
(3) the Supervising Solicitor may be accompanied only by the persons mentioned in the order,
(4) the Supervising Solicitor must explain the terms and effect of the order to the respondent in everyday language and advise him:
   (a) of his right to take legal advice and to apply to vary or discharge the order; and
   (b) that he may be entitled to avail himself of:
      (i) legal professional privilege; and
      (ii) the privilege against self-incrimination,
(5) where the Supervising Solicitor is a man and the respondent is likely to be an unaccompanied woman, at least one other person named in the order must be a woman and must accompany the Supervising Solicitor, and
(6) the order may only be served between 9.30 a.m. and 5.30 p.m. Monday to Friday unless the court otherwise orders.

7.5 Search and custody of materials:
(1) no material shall be removed unless clearly covered by the terms of the order,
(2) the premises must not be searched and no items shall be removed from them except in the presence of the respondent or a person who appears to be a responsible employee of the respondent,
(3) where copies of documents are sought, the documents should be retained for no more than two days before return to the owner,
(4) where material in dispute is removed pending trial, the applicant's solicitors should place it in the custody of the respondent's solicitors on their undertaking to retain it in safekeeping and to produce it to the court when required,
(5) in appropriate cases the applicant should insure the material retained in the respondent's solicitors' custody,
(6) the Supervising Solicitor must make a list of all material removed from the premises and supply a copy of the list to the respondent,
(7) no material shall be removed from the premises until the respondent has had reasonable time to check the list,
(8) if any of the listed items exists only in computer-readable form, the respondent must immediately give the applicant's solicitors effective access to the computers, with all necessary pass words, to enable them to be searched, and cause the listed items to be printed out,
(9) the applicant must take all reasonable steps to ensure that no damage is done to any computer or data,
(10) the applicant and his representatives may not themselves search the respondent's computers unless they have sufficient expertise to do so without damaging the respondent's system,
(11) the Supervising Solicitor shall provide a report on the carrying out of the order to the applicant's solicitors,
(12) as soon as the report is received the applicant's solicitors shall:
   (a) serve a copy of it on the respondent, and
   (b) file a copy of it with the court, and
(13) where the Supervising Solicitor is satisfied that full compliance with para. 7.5(7) and (8) above is impracticable, he may permit the search to proceed and items to be removed without compliance with the impracticable requirements.

7.6 General:
The Supervising Solicitor must not be an employee or member of the applicant's firm of solicitors.

7.7 If the court orders that the order need not be served by the Supervising Solicitor, the reason for so ordering must be set out in the order.

7.8 The search order must not be carried out at the same time as a police search warrant.

7.9 There is no privilege against self incrimination in:
(1) intellectual property cases in respect of a 'related offence' or for the recovery of a 'related penalty' as defined in the Senior Courts Act 1981, s. 72;
(2) proceedings for the recovery or administration of any property, for the execution of any trust or for an account of any property or dealings with property, in relation to—
(a) an offence under the Theft Act 1968 (see section 31 of the Theft Act 1968); or
(b) an offence under the Fraud Act 2006 (see section 13 of the Fraud Act 2006) or a related offence within the meaning given by section 13(4) of that Act—that is, conspiracy to defraud or any other offence involving any form of fraudulent conduct or purpose; or
(3) proceedings in which a court is hearing an application for an order under part IV or part V of the Children Act 1989 (see the Children Act 1989, s. 98).

However, the privilege may still be claimed in relation to material or information required to be disclosed by an order, as regards potential criminal proceedings outside those statutory provisions.

7.10 Applications in intellectual property cases should be made in the Chancery Division.

7.11 An example of a search order is annexed to this practice direction. This example may be modified as appropriate in any particular case.

Delivery-up Orders

para.8.2 40.6, 41.1

8.1 The following provisions apply to orders, other than search orders, for delivery up or preservation of evidence or property where it is likely that such an order will be executed at the premises of the respondent or a third party.

8.2 In such cases the court shall consider whether to include in the order for the benefit or protection of the parties similar provisions to those specified above in relation to injunctions and search orders.

Injunctions against Third Parties

para.9.2 37.66, 38.3, 39.6

9.1 The following provisions apply to orders which will affect a person other than the applicant or respondent, who:
(1) did not attend the hearing at which the order was made; and
(2) is served with the order.

9.2 Where such a person served with the order requests:
(1) a copy of any materials read by the judge, including material prepared after the hearing at the direction of the judge or in compliance with the order; or
(2) a note of the hearing,

the applicant, or his legal representative, must comply promptly with the request, unless the court orders otherwise.

ANNEX

annex 1.10, 37.63, 38.3, 38.10, 91.44

Freezing injunction

IN THE HIGH COURT OF JUSTICE
[ ] DIVISION

Before The Honourable Mr Justice [ ]

Claim No.
Dated

Applicant

Seal

Respondent

Name, address and reference of Respondent

PENAL NOTICE

IF YOU [ ][6] DISOBEY THIS ORDER YOU MAY BE HELD TO BE IN CONTEMPT OF COURT AND MAY BE IMPRISONED, FINED OR HAVE YOUR ASSETS SEIZED

ANY OTHER PERSON WHO KNOWS OF THIS ORDER AND DOES ANYTHING WHICH HELPS OR PERMITS THE RESPONDENT TO BREACH THE TERMS OF THIS ORDER MAY ALSO BE HELD TO BE IN CONTEMPT OF COURT AND MAY BE IMPRISONED, FINED OR HAVE THEIR ASSETS SEIZED.

THIS ORDER

1. This is a Freezing Injunction made against [ ] ('the Respondent') on [ ] by Mr Justice [ ] on the application of [ ] ('the Applicant'). The Judge read the Affidavits listed in Schedule A and accepted the undertakings set out in Schedule B at the end of this Order.
2. This order was made at a hearing without notice to the Respondent. The Respondent has a right to apply to the court to vary or discharge the order — see paragraph 13 below.
3. There will be a further hearing in respect of this order on [ ] ('the return date').
4. If there is more than one Respondent:
   (a) unless otherwise stated, references in this order to 'the Respondent' mean both or all of them; and
   (b) this order is effective against any Respondent on whom it is served or who is given notice it.

FREEZING INJUNCTION

[For injunction limited to assets in England and Wales]

5. Until the return date or further order of the court, the Respondent must not remove from England and Wales or in any way dispose of, deal with or diminish the value of any of his assets which are in England and Wales up to the value of £.

[For worldwide injunction]

5. Until the return date or further order of the court, the Respondent must not:
   (1) remove from England and Wales any of his assets which are in England and Wales up to the value of £ ; or
   (2) in any way dispose of, deal with or diminish the value of any of his assets whether they are in or outside England and Wales up to the same value.

[For either form of injunction]

6. Paragraph 5 applies to all the Respondent's assets whether or not they are in his own name and whether they are solely or jointly owned. For the purpose of this order the Respondent's assets include any asset which he has the power, directly or indirectly, to dispose of or deal with as if it were his own. The Respondent is to be regarded as having such power if a third party holds or controls the asset in accordance with his direct or indirect instructions.
7. This prohibition includes the following assets in particular:
   (a) the property known as [title/address] or the net sale money after payment of any mortgages if it has been sold;
   (b) the property and assets of the Respondent's business [known as [name]] [carried on at [address]] or the sale money if any of them have been sold; and
   (c) any money standing to the credit of any bank account including the amount of any cheque drawn on such account which has not been cleared.

[For injunction limited to assets in England and Wales]

8. If the total value free of charges or other securities ('unencumbered value') of the Respondent's assets in England and Wales exceeds £ , the Respondent may remove any of those assets from England and Wales or may dispose of or deal with them so long as the total unencumbered value of his assets still in England and Wales remains above £ .

[For worldwide injunction]

8. (1) If the total value free of charges or other securities ('unencumbered value') of the Respondent's assets in England and Wales exceeds £ , the Respondent may remove any of assets from England and Wales or may dispose of or deal with them so long as the unencumbered value of the Respondent's assets still in England and Wales remains above £ .

[6] Insert name of Respondent.

(2) If the total unencumbered value of the Respondent's assets in England and Wales does not exceed £ , the Respondent must not remove any of those assets from England and Wales and must not dispose of or deal with any of them. If the Respondent has other assets outside England and Wales, he may dispose of or deal with those assets outside England and Wales so long as the total unencumbered value of all his assets whether in or outside England and Wales remains above £ .

PROVISION OF INFORMATION

9. (1) Unless paragraph (2) applies, the Respondent must [immediately] [within hours of service of this order] and to the best of his ability inform the Applicant's solicitors of all his assets [in England and Wales] [worldwide] [exceeding £ in value] whether in his own name or not and whether solely or jointly owned, giving the value, location and details of all such assets.

(2) If the provision of any of this information is likely to incriminate the Respondent, he may be entitled to refuse to provide it, but is recommended to take legal advice before refusing to provide the information. Wrongful refusal to provide the information is contempt of court and may render the Respondent liable to be imprisoned, fined or have his assets seized.

10. Within [ ] working days after being served with this order, the Respondent must swear and serve on the Applicant's solicitors an affidavit setting out the above information.

EXCEPTIONS TO THIS ORDER

11. (1) This order does not prohibit the Respondent from spending £ a week towards his ordinary living expenses and also £ [or a reasonable sum] on legal advice and representation. [But before spending any money the Respondent must tell the Applicant's legal representatives where the money is to come from.]

[(2) This order does not prohibit the Respondent from dealing with or disposing of any of his assets in the ordinary and proper course of business.]

(3) The Respondent may agree with the Applicant's legal representatives that the above spending limits should be increased or that this order should be varied in any other respect, but any agreement must be in writing.

(4) The order will cease to have effect if the Respondent:

(a) provides security by paying the sum of £ into court, to be held to the order of the court; or

(b) makes provision for security in that sum by another method agreed with the Applicant's legal representatives.

COSTS

12. The costs of this application are reserved to the judge hearing the application on the return date.

VARIATION OR DISCHARGE OF THIS ORDER

13. Anyone served with or notified of this order may apply to the court at any time to vary or discharge this order (or so much of it as affects that person), but they must first inform the Applicant's solicitors. If any evidence is to be relied upon in support of the application, the substance of it must be communicated in writing to the Applicant's solicitors in advance.

INTERPRETATION OF THIS ORDER

14. A Respondent who is an individual who is ordered not to do something must not do it himself or in any other way. He must not do it through others acting on his behalf or on his instructions or with his encouragement.

15. A Respondent which is not an individual which is ordered not to do something must not do it itself or by its directors, officers, partners, employees or agents or in any other way.

PARTIES OTHER THAN THE APPLICANT AND RESPONDENT EFFECT OF THIS ORDER

16. It is a contempt of court for any person notified of this order knowingly to assist in or permit a breach of this order. Any person doing so may be imprisoned, fined or have their assets seized.

SET-OFF BY BANKS

17. This injunction does not prevent any bank from exercising any right of set-off it may have in respect of any facility which it gave to the respondent before it was notified of this order.

WITHDRAWALS BY THE RESPONDENT

18. No bank need enquire as to the application or proposed application of any money withdrawn by the Respondent if the withdrawal appears to be permitted by this order.

[For worldwide injunction]

PERSONS OUTSIDE ENGLAND AND WALES

19. (1) Except as provided in paragraph (2) below, the terms of this order do not affect or concern anyone outside the jurisdiction of this court.
 (2) The terms of this order will affect the following persons in a country or State outside the jurisdiction of this court:
  (a) the Respondent or his officer or agent appointed by power of attorney;
  (b) any person who:
   (i) is subject to the jurisdiction of this court;
   (ii) has been given written notice of this order at his residence or place of business within the jurisdiction of this court; and
   (iii) is able to prevent acts or omissions outside the jurisdiction of this court which constitute or assist in a breach of the terms of this order; and
  (c) any other person, only to the extent that this order is declared enforceable by or is enforced by a court in that country or State.

[For worldwide injunction]

ASSETS LOCATED OUTSIDE ENGLAND AND WALES

20. Nothing in this order shall, in respect of assets located outside England and Wales, prevent any third party from complying with:
 (1) what it reasonably believes to be its obligations, contractual or otherwise, under the laws and obligations of the country or State in which those assets are situated or under the proper law of any contract between itself and the Respondent; and
 (2) any orders of the courts of that country or State, provided that reasonable notice of any application for such an order is given to the Applicant's solicitors.

COMMUNICATIONS WITH THE COURT

All communications to the court about this order should be sent to:

[Insert the address and telephone number of the appropriate court office]

If the order is made at the Royal Courts of Justice, communications should be addressed as follows:

Where the order is made in the Chancery Division:

Room TM 5.07, Royal Courts of Justice, Strand, London WC2A 2LL quoting the case number.
The telephone number is (020) 7947 6322.

Where the order is made in the Queen's Bench Division:

Room WG08, Royal Courts of Justice, Strand, London WC2A 2LL quoting the case number. The telephone number is (020) 7947 6010.

Where the order is made in the Commercial Court

Room EB09, Royal Courts of Justice, Strand, London WC2A 2LL quoting the case number. The telephone number is (020) 7947 6826.

The offices are open between 10 a.m. and 4.30 p.m. Monday to Friday.

SCHEDULE A AFFIDAVITS

The Applicant relied on the following affidavits:
[name] [number of affidavit] [date sworn]
[filed on behalf of]
(1)
(2)

SCHEDULE B UNDERTAKINGS GIVEN TO THE COURT BY THE APPLICANT

Sch.B **38.15**

(1) If the court later finds that this order has caused loss to the Respondent, and decides that the Respondent should be compensated for that loss, the Applicant will comply with any order the court may make.

[(2) The Applicant will:

(a) on or before [date] cause a written guarantee in the sum of £ to be issued from a bank with a place of business within England or Wales, in respect of any order the court may make pursuant to paragraph (1) above; and

(b) immediately upon issue of the guarantee, cause a copy of it to be served on the Respondent.]

(3) As soon as practicable the Applicant will issue and serve a claim form [in the form of the draft produced to the court] [claiming the appropriate relief].

(4) The Applicant will [swear and file an affidavit] [cause an affidavit to be sworn and filed] [substantially in the terms of the draft affidavit produced to the court] [confirming the substance of what was said to the court by the Applicant's counsel/solicitors].

(5) The Applicant will serve upon the Respondent [together with this order] [as soon as practicable]:

(i) copies of the affidavits and exhibits containing the evidence relied upon by the Applicant, and any other documents provided to the court on the making of the application;

(ii) the claim form; and

(iii) an application notice for continuation of the order.

[(6) Anyone notified of this order will be given a copy of it by the Applicant's legal representatives.]

(7) The Applicant will pay the reasonable costs of anyone other than the Respondent which have been incurred as a result of this order including the costs of finding out whether that person holds any of the Respondent's assets and if the court later finds that this order has caused such person loss, and decides that such person should be compensated for that loss, the Applicant will comply with any order the court may make.

(8) If this order ceases to have effect (for example, if the Respondent provides security or the Applicant does not provide a bank guarantee as provided for above) the Applicant will immediately take all reasonable steps to inform in writing anyone to whom he has given notice of this order, or who he has reasonable grounds for supposing may act upon this order, that it has ceased to have effect.

[(9) The Applicant will not without the permission of the court use any information obtained as a result of this order for the purpose of any civil or criminal proceedings, either in England and Wales or in any other jurisdiction, other than this claim.]

[(10) The Applicant will not without the permission of the court seek to enforce this order in any country outside England and Wales [or seek an order of a similar nature including orders conferring a charge or other security against the Respondent or the Respondent's assets].]

NAME AND ADDRESS OF APPLICANT'S LEGAL REPRESENTATIVES

The Applicant's legal representatives are:

[Name, address, reference, fax and telephone numbers both in and out of office hours and email]

Search order

IN THE HIGH COURT OF JUSTICE

] **DIVISION**

Before The Honourable Mr Justice [ ]

Claim No.

Dated

Applicant

Seal

Respondent

Name, address and reference of Respondent

PENAL NOTICE

IF YOU [ ][7] DISOBEY THIS ORDER YOU MAY BE HELD TO BE IN CONTEMPT OF COURT AND LIABLE TO IMPRISONMENT OR FINED OR HAVE OR YOUR ASSETS SEIZED

ANY OTHER PERSON WHO KNOWS OF THIS ORDER AND DOES ANYTHING WHICH HELPS OR PERMITS THE RESPONDENT TO BREACH THE TERMS OF THIS ORDER MAY ALSO BE HELD TO BE IN CONTEMPT OF COURT AND MAY BE IMPRISONED, FINED OR HAVE THEIR ASSETS SEIZED.

THIS ORDER

1. This is a Search Order made against [ ] ('the Respondent') on [ ] by Mr Justice [ ] on the application of [ ] ('the Applicant'). The Judge read the Affidavits listed in Schedule F and accepted the undertakings set out in Schedules C, D and E at the end of this order.
2. This order was made at a hearing without notice to the Respondent. The Respondent has a right to apply to the court to vary or discharge the order — see paragraph 27 below.
3. There will be a further hearing in respect of this order on [ ] ('the return date').
4. If there is more than one Respondent:
(a) unless otherwise stated, references in this order to 'the Respondent' mean both or all of them; and
(b) this order is effective against any Respondent on whom it is served or who is given notice of it.
5. This order must be complied with by:
(a) the Respondent;
(b) any director, officer, partner or responsible employee of the Respondent; and
(c) if the Respondent is an individual, any other person having responsible control of the premises to be searched.

THE SEARCH

6. The Respondent must permit the following persons:[8]
(a) [ ] ('the Supervising Solicitor');
(b) [ ], a solicitor in the firm of [ ], the Applicant's solicitors; and
(c) up to [ ] other persons[9] being [their identity or capacity] accompanying them, (together 'the search party'), to enter the premises mentioned in Schedule A to this order and any other premises of the Respondent disclosed under paragraph 18 below and any vehicles under the Respondent's control on or around the premises ('the premises') so that they can search for, inspect, photograph or photocopy, and deliver into the safe keeping of the Applicant's solicitors all the documents and articles which are listed in Schedule B to this order ('the listed items').
7. Having permitted the search party to enter the premises, the Respondent must allow the search party to remain on the premises until the search is complete. In the event that it becomes necessary for any of those persons to leave the premises before the search is complete, the Respondent must allow them to re-enter the premises immediately upon their seeking re-entry on the same or the following day in order to complete the search.

RESTRICTIONS ON SEARCH

8. This order may not be carried out at the same time as a police search warrant.
9. Before the Respondent allows anybody on to the premises to carry out this order, he is entitled to have the Supervising Solicitor explain to him what it means in everyday language.
10. The Respondent is entitled to seek legal advice and to ask the court to vary or discharge this order. Whilst doing so, he may ask the Supervising Solicitor to delay starting the search for up to 2 hours or such other longer period as the Supervising Solicitor may permit. However, the Respondent must:
(a) *comply with* the terms of paragraph 27 below;
(b) not disturb or remove any listed items; and
(c) permit the Supervising Solicitor to enter, but not start to search.

[7] Insert name of Respondent.
[8] Where the premises are likely to be occupied by an unaccompanied woman and the Supervising Solicitor is a man, at least one of the persons accompanying him should be a woman.
[9] None of these persons should be people who could gain personally or commercially from anything they might read or see on the premises, unless their presence is essential.

11. (1) Before permitting entry to the premises by any person other than the Supervising Solicitor, the Respondent may, for a short time (not to exceed two hours, unless the Supervising Solicitor agrees to a longer period):
(a) gather together any documents he believes may be incriminating or privileged; and
(b) hand them to the Supervising Solicitor for him to assess whether they are incriminating or privileged as claimed.
(2) If the Supervising Solicitor decides that the Respondent is entitled to withhold production of any of the documents on the ground that they are privileged or incriminating, he will exclude them from the search, record them in a list for inclusion in his report and return them to the Respondent.
(3) If the Supervising Solicitor believes that the Respondent may be entitled to withhold production of the whole or any part of a document on the ground that it or part of it may be privileged or incriminating, or if the Respondent claims to be entitled to withhold production on those grounds, the Supervising Solicitor will exclude it from the search and retain it in his possession pending further order of the court.
12. If the Respondent wishes to take legal advice and gather documents as permitted, he must first inform the Supervising Solicitor and keep him informed of the steps being taken.
13. No item may be removed from the premises until a list of the items to be removed has been prepared, and a copy of the list has been supplied to the Respondent, and he has been given a reasonable opportunity to check the list.
14. The premises must not be searched, and items must not be removed from them, except in the presence of the Respondent.
15. If the Supervising Solicitor is satisfied that full compliance with paragraphs 13 or 14 is not practicable, he may permit the search to proceed and items to be removed without fully complying with them.

DELIVERY UP OF ARTICLES/DOCUMENTS

16. The Respondent must immediately hand over to the Applicant's solicitors any of the listed items,which are in his possession or under his control, save for any computer or hard disk integral to any computer. Any items the subject of a dispute as to whether they are listed items must immediately be handed over to the Supervising Solicitor for safe keeping pending resolution of the dispute or further order of the court.
17. The Respondent must immediately give the search party effective access to the computers on the premises, with all necessary passwords, to enable the computers to be searched. If they contain any listed items the Respondent must cause the listed items to be displayed so that they can be read and copied.[10] The Respondent must provide the Applicant's Solicitors with copies of all listed items contained in the computers. All reasonable steps shall be taken by the Applicant and the Applicant's solicitors to ensure that no damage is done to any computer or data. The Applicant and his representatives may not themselves search the Respondent's computers unless they have sufficient expertise to do so without damaging the Respondent's system.

PROVISION OF INFORMATION

18. The Respondent must immediately inform the Applicant's Solicitors (in the presence of the Supervising Solicitor) so far as he is aware:
(a) where all the listed items are;
(b) the name and address of everyone who has supplied him, or offered to supply him, with listed items;
(c) the name and address of everyone to whom he has supplied, or offered to supply, listed items; and
(d) full details of the dates and quantities of every such supply and offer.
19. Within [ ] working days after being served with this order the Respondent must swear and serve an affidavit setting out the above information.[11]

---

[10] If it is envisaged that the Respondent's computers are to be imaged (i.e. the hard drives are to be copied wholesale, thereby reproducing listed items and other items indiscriminately), special provision needs to be made and independent computer specialists need to be appointed, who should be required to give undertakings to the court.

[11] The period should ordinarily be longer than the period in paragraph (2) of Schedule D, if any of the information is likely to be included in listed items taken away of which the Respondent does not have copies.

PROHIBITED ACTS

20. Except for the purpose of obtaining legal advice, the Respondent must not directly or indirectly inform anyone of these proceedings or of the contents of this order, or warn anyone that proceedings have been or may be brought against him by the Applicant until 4.30 p.m. on the return date or further order of the court.

21. Until 4.30 p.m. on the return date the Respondent must not destroy, tamper with, cancel or part with possession, power, custody or control of the listed items otherwise than in accordance with the terms of this order.

22. [Insert any negative injunctions.]

23. [Insert any further order]

COSTS

24. The costs of this application are reserved to the judge hearing the application on the return date.

RESTRICTIONS ON SERVICE

25. This order may only be served between [ ] a.m./ p.m. and [ ] a.m./ p.m. [and on a weekday].[12]

26. This order must be served by the Supervising Solicitor, and paragraph 6 of the order must be carried out in his presence and under his supervision.

VARIATION AND DISCHARGE OF THIS ORDER

27. Anyone served with or notified of this order may apply to the court at any time to vary or discharge this order (or so much of it as affects that person), but they must first inform the Applicant's solicitors. If any evidence is to be relied upon in support of the application, the substance of it must be communicated in writing to the Applicant's solicitors in advance.

INTERPRETATION OF THIS ORDER

28. Any requirement that something shall be done to or in the presence of the Respondent means:
   (a) if there is more than one Respondent, to or in the presence of any one of them; and
   (b) if a Respondent is not an individual, to or in the presence of a director, officer partner or responsible employee.

29. A Respondent who is an individual who is ordered not to do something must not do it himself orin any other way. He must not do it through others acting on his behalf or on his instructions or with his encouragement.

30. A Respondent which is not an individual which is ordered not to do something must not do it itself or by its directors, officers, partners, employees or agents or in any other way.

COMMUNICATIONS WITH THE COURT

All communications to the court about this order should be sent to:

[Insert the address and telephone number of the appropriate court office]

If the order is made at the Royal Courts of Justice, communications should be addressed as follows:

Where the order is made in the Chancery Division:
Room TM 5.07, Royal Courts of Justice, Strand, London WC2A 2LL quoting the case number. The telephone number is (020) 7947 6322.

Where the order is made in the Queen's Bench Division:
Room WG08, Royal Courts of Justice, Strand, London WC2A 2LL quoting the case number. The telephone number is (020) 7947 6010.

Where the order is made in the Commercial Court:
Room EB09, Royal Courts of Justice, Strand, London WC2A 2LL quoting the case number. The telephone number is (020) 7947 6826.

The offices are open between 10 a.m. and 4.30 p.m. Monday to Friday.

[12] Normally, the order should be served in the morning (not before 9.30 a.m.) and on a weekday to enable the Respondent more readily to obtain legal advice.

SCHEDULE A THE PREMISES

SCHEDULE B THE LISTED ITEMS

SCHEDULE C UNDERTAKINGS GIVEN TO THE COURT BY THE APPLICANT

(1) If the court later finds that this order or carrying it out has caused loss to the Respondent, and decides that the Respondent should be compensated for that loss, the Applicant will comply with any order the court may make. Further if the carrying out of this order has been in breach of the terms of this order or otherwise in a manner inconsistent with the Applicant's solicitors' duties as officers of the court, the Applicant will comply with any order for damages the court may make.

[(2) As soon as practicable the Applicant will issue a claim form [in the form of the draft produced to the court] [claiming the appropriate relief].]

(3) The Applicant will [swear and file an affidavit] [cause an affidavit to be sworn and filed] [substantially in the terms of the draft affidavit produced to the court] [confirming the substance of what was said to the court by the Applicant's counsel/solicitors].

(4) The Applicant will not, without the permission of the court, use any information or documents obtained as a result of carrying out this order nor inform anyone else of these proceedings except for the purposes of these proceedings (including adding further Respondents) or commencing civil proceedings in relation to the same or related subject matter to these proceedings until after the return date.

[(5) The Applicant will maintain pending further order the sum of £ in an account controlled by the Applicant's solicitors.]

[(6) The Applicant will insure the items removed from the premises.]

SCHEDULE D UNDERTAKINGS GIVEN BY THE APPLICANT'S SOLICITORS

(1) The Applicant's solicitors will provide to the Supervising Solicitor for service on the Respondent:
- (i) a service copy of this order;
- (ii) the claim form (with defendant's response pack) or, if not issued, the draft produced to the court;
- (iii) an application for hearing on the return date;
- (iv) copies of the affidavits [or draft affidavits] and exhibits capable of being copied containing the evidence relied upon by the applicant;
- (v) a note of any allegation of fact made orally to the court where such allegation is not contained in the affidavits or draft affidavits read by the judge; and
- (vi) a copy of the skeleton argument produced to the court by the Applicant's [counsel/solicitors].

(2) The Applicant's solicitors will answer at once to the best of their ability any question whether a particular item is a listed item.

(3) Subject as provided below the Applicant's solicitors will retain in their own safe keeping all items obtained as a result of this order until the court directs otherwise.

(4) The Applicant's solicitors will return the originals of all documents obtained as a result of this order (except original documents which belong to the Applicant) as soon as possible and in any event within [2] working days of their removal.

SCHEDULE E UNDERTAKINGS GIVEN BY THE SUPERVISING SOLICITOR

Sch. E 39.5

(1) The Supervising Solicitor will use his best endeavours to serve this order upon the Respondent and at the same time to serve upon the Respondent the other documents required to be served and referred to in paragraph (1) of Schedule D.

(2) The Supervising Solicitor will offer to explain to the person served with the order its meaning and effect fairly and in everyday language, and to inform him of his right to take legal advice (including an explanation that the Respondent may be entitled to avail himself of the privilege against self-incrimination and legal professional privilege) and to apply to vary or discharge this order as mentioned in paragraph 27 above.

(3) The Supervising Solicitor will retain in the safe keeping of his firm all items retained by him as a result of this order until the court directs otherwise.

(4) Unless and until the court otherwise orders, or unless otherwise necessary to comply with any duty to the court pursuant to this order, the Supervising Solicitor shall not disclose to any person any information relating to those items, and shall keep the existence of such items confidential.

(4) Within [48] hours of completion of the search the Supervising Solicitor will make and provide to the Applicant's solicitors, the Respondent or his solicitors and to the judge who made this order (for the purposes of the court file) a written report on the carrying out of the order.

SCHEDULE F AFFIDAVITS

The Applicant relied on the following affidavits:
[name] [number of affidavit] [date sworn] [filed on behalf of]
(1)
(2)
NAME AND ADDRESS OF APPLICANT'S SOLICITORS
The Applicant's solicitors are:
[Name, address, reference, fax and telephone numbers both in and out of office hours.]

PD 25B Practice Direction 25B — Interim Payments

This practice direction supplements CPR, Part 25.

PD 25B **63.22** [For commentary on a specific paragraph, please refer to the cross-references after the title of the paragraph.]

General

para.1.2 **36.2**

1.1 Rule 25.7 sets out the conditions to be satisfied and matters to be taken into account before the court will make an order for an interim payment.

1.2 The permission of the court must be obtained before making a voluntary interim payment in respect of a claim by a child or protected party.
('Child' and 'protected party' have the same meaning as in r. 21.1(2).)

Evidence

para.2.1 **PC 24, 36.6**
para.2.1(2) **36.15**
para.2.2 **PC 24**

2.1 An application for an interim payment of damages must be supported by evidence dealing with the following:
(1) the sum of money sought by way of an interim payment,
(2) the items or matters in respect of which the interim payment is sought,
(3) the sum of money for which final judgment is likely to be given,
(4) the reasons for believing that the conditions set out in r. 25.7 are satisfied,
(5) any other relevant matters,
(6) in claims for personal injuries, details of special damages and past and future loss, and
(7) in a claim under the Fatal Accidents Act 1976, details of the person(s) on whose behalf the claim is made and the nature of the claim.

2.2 Any documents in support of the application should be exhibited, including, in personal in juries claims, the medical report(s).

2.3 If a respondent to an application for an interim payment wishes to rely on written evidence at the hearing he must comply with the provisions of r. 25.6(4).

2.4 If the applicant wishes to rely on written evidence in reply he must comply with the provisions of r. 25.6(5).

Interim Payment Where Account to Be Taken

2A.1 This section of this practice direction applies if a party seeks an interim payment under [r. 25.7(1)(b)*] where the court has ordered an account to be taken.

2A.2 If the evidence on the application for interim payment shows that the account is bound to result in a payment to the applicant the court will, before making an order for interim payment, order that the liable party pay to the applicant 'the amount shown by the account to be due'.

Instalments

para.3 **PC 24, 36.15**

3 Where an interim payment is to be paid in instalments the order should set out:
(1) the total amount of the payment,
(2) the amount of each instalment,
(3) the number of instalments and the date on which each is to be paid, and
(4) to whom the payment should be made.

[* The text issued by the Ministry of Justice mistakenly refers to r. 25.7(b).]

Compensation Recovery Payments

paras.4.1–4.4 36.15

4.1 Where in a claim for personal injuries there is an application for an interim payment of damages:

(1) which is other than by consent,

(2) which either:

(i) falls under the heads of damage set out in the Social Security (Recovery of Benefits) Act 1997 ('the 1997 Act'), sch. 2, col. 1, in respect of recoverable benefits received by the claimant set out in col. 2 of that schedule; or

(ii) includes damages in respect of a disease for which a lump sum payment within the definition in s. 1A(2) of the 1997 Act has been, or is likely to be made; and

(3) where the defendant is liable to pay a recoverable amount (as defined in r. 36.15(1)(c)) to the Secretary of State,

the defendant should obtain from the Secretary of State a certificate (as defined in r. 36.15(1)(e)).

4.2 A copy of the certificate must be filed at the hearing of the application for an interim payment.

4.3 The order will set out the deductible amount (as defined in r. 36.15(1)(d)).

4.4 The payment made to the claimant will be the net amount but the interim payment for the purposes of para. 5 below will be the gross amount.

Adjustment of Final Judgment Figure

para.5 PC 24, 36.19

5.1 In this paragraph 'judgment' means:

(1) any order to pay a sum of money,

(2) a final award of damages,

(3) an assessment of damages.

5.2 In a final judgment where an interim payment has previously been made which is less than the total amount awarded by the judge, the order should set out in a preamble:

(1) the total amount awarded by the judge, and

(2) the amounts and dates of the interim payment(s).

5.3 The total amount awarded by the judge should then be reduced by the total amount of any interim payments, and an order made for entry of judgment and payment of the balance.

5.4 In a final judgment where an interim payment has previously been made which is more than the total amount awarded by the judge, the order should set out in a preamble:

(1) the total amount awarded by the judge, and

(2) the amounts and dates of the interim payment(s).

5.5 An order should then be made for repayment, reimbursement, variation or discharge under r. 25.8(2) and for interest on an overpayment under r. 25.8(5).

5.6 PD 40B provides further information concerning adjustment of the final judgment sum.

CPR Part 26 Case Management — Preliminary Stage

Part 26 **PC 37, 28.5, 91.41** [For commentary on a specific rule, please refer to the cross-references after the title of the rule.]

26.1 Scope of This Part

(1) This Part provides for—
  (a) the automatic transfer of some defended cases between courts; and
  (b) the allocation of defended cases to case management tracks.
(2) There are three tracks—
  (a) the small claims track;
  (b) the fast track; and
  (c) the multi-track.

(Rule 26.6 sets out the normal scope of each track. Part 27 makes provision for the small claims track. Part 28 makes provision for the fast track. Part 29 makes provision for the multi-track)

26.2 Automatic Transfer — Generally

r.26.2 **12.10, 42.7**

(1) This rule applies where rule 26.2A does not apply. This rule applies to proceedings where—
  (a) the claim is for a specified amount of money;
  (b) the claim was commenced in a court which is not the defendant's home court;
  (c) the claim has not been transferred to another defendant's home court; and
  (d) the defendant is an individual.
(2) This rule does not apply where the claim was commenced in a specialist list[(GL)].
(3) Where this rule applies, the court will transfer the proceedings to the defendant's home court when a defence is filed, unless paragraph (4) applies.

(Rule 2.3 defines 'defendant's home court')

(4) Where the claimant notifies the court under rule 15.10 or rule 14.5 that he wishes the proceedings to continue, the court will transfer the proceedings to the defendant's home court when it receives that notification from the claimant.

(Rule 15.10 deals with a claimant's notice where the defence is that money claimed has been paid)
(Rule 14.5 sets out the procedure where the defendant admits part of a claim for a specified amount of money)

(5) Where—
  (a) the claim is against two or more defendants with different home courts; and
  (b) the defendant whose defence is filed first is an individual,
  proceedings are to be transferred under this rule to the home court of that defendant.
(6) The time when a claim is automatically transferred under this rule may be varied by a practice direction in respect of claims issued by the Production Centre.

(Rule 7.10 makes provision for the Production Centre)

26.2A Automatic Transfer of Designated Money Claims

r.26.2A **42.7**
r.26.2A(3) **42.7**
r.26.2A(4) **42.7, 42.8**
r.26.2A(5) **42.7, 42.8**
r.26.2A(6) **11.9, 42.7, 42.8**

(1) This rule applies where the claim is a designated money claim.
(2) If at any time a proper officer considers that the claim should be referred to a judge for directions, the proper officer may transfer the proceedings to the preferred court or the defendant's home court as appropriate.
(3) Subject to paragraph (5), if the defendant is an individual and the claim is for a specified sum of money, the court will, at the relevant time, transfer the claim to the defendant's home court (save that where there are two or more defendants, one or more of whom are individuals, the court will transfer the claim to the home court of the defendant who first files his defence).
(4) Subject to paragraph (5), in any other claim to which this rule applies, the court will, at the relevant time, transfer the claim to the preferred court.
(5) If a defendant under paragraph (3) or a claimant under paragraph (4) has specified a court other than the preferred court on their directions questionnaire, the court will transfer the claim to that court.
(6) The relevant time for the purposes of this rule is when—
  (a) all parties have filed their directions questionnaires;
  (b) any stay ordered by the court or period to attempt settlement through mediation has expired; or
  (c) if the claim falls within Practice Direction 7D—
    (i) the defence is filed; or
    (ii) enforcement of a default judgment other than by a warrant of execution is requested,
  whichever occurs first.

26.3 Directions Questionnaire

r.26.3(1) 42.12, 42.16, 42.21, 42.22
r.26.3(1B) 42.13
r.26.3(2) 42.12
r.26.3(4) 42.12
r.26.3(6) 27.1, 42.16
r.26.3(6A) 3.7, 42.16, 46.16, 48.1
r.26.3(7) 42.13
r.26.3(7A) 42.21
r.26.3 (7A)(b) 42.21, 43.8
r.26.3(8) 42.22, 42.25
r.26.3(10) 42.21, 42.22

(1) If a defendant files a defence—
  (a) a court officer will—
    (i) provisionally decide the track which appears to be most suitable for the claim; and
    (ii) serve on each party a notice of proposed allocation; and
  (b) the notice of proposed allocation will—
    (i) specify any matter to be complied with by the date specified in the notice;
    (ii) require the parties to file a completed directions questionnaire and serve copies on all other parties;
    (iii) state the address of the court or the court office to which the directions questionnaire must be returned;
    (iv) inform the parties how to obtain the directions questionnaire; and
    (v) if a case appears suitable for allocation to the fast track or multi-track, require the parties to file proposed directions by the date specified in the notice.';

(1A) [*Revoked*]
(1B) The court will always serve on any unrepresented party the appropriate directions questionnaire.
(2) Where there are two or more defendants and at least one of them files a defence, the court will serve the* a notice under paragraph (1)—
  (a) when all the defendants have filed a defence; or
  (b) when the period for the filing of the last defence has expired, whichever is the sooner.

(Rule 15.4 specifies the period for filing a defence)

(3) If proceedings are automatically transferred under rule 26.2 or rule 26.2A the court in which the proceedings have been commenced—
  (a) will serve the notice of proposed allocation before the proceedings are transferred; and
  (b) will not transfer the proceedings until all parties have complied with the notice or the time for doing so has expired.

[* The word 'the' was mistakenly not deleted by the amendment to this paragraph made by SI 2011/3103, r. 9(d)(iii).]

(4) If rule 15.10 or rule 14.5 applies, the court will not serve a notice under rule 26.3(1) until the claimant has filed a notice requiring the proceedings to continue.
(5) [*Revoked*]
(6) If a notice is served under rule 26.3(1)—
  (a) each party must file at court, and serve on all other parties, the documents required by the notice by no later than the date specified in it; and
  (b) the date specified will be—
    (i) if the notice relates to the small claims track, at least 14 days; or
    (ii) if the notice relates to the fast track or multi-track, at least 28 days,
  after the date when it is deemed to be served on the party in question.
(6A) The date for complying with a notice served under rule 26.3(1) may not be varied by agreement between the parties.
(7) The time when the court serves a directions questionnaire under this rule may be varied by a practice direction in respect of claims issued by the Production Centre.
(7A) If a claim is a designated money claim and a party does not comply with the notice served under rule 26.3(1) by the date specified—
  (a) the court will serve a further notice on that party, requiring them to comply within 7 days; and
  (b) if that party fails to comply with the notice served under subparagraph (a), the party's statement of case will be struck out without further order of the court.
(8) If a claim is not a designated money claim and a party does not comply with the notice served under rule 26.3(1) by the date specified, the court will make such order as it considers appropriate, including—
  (a) an order for directions;
  (b) an order striking out the claim;
  (c) an order striking out the defence and entering judgment; or
  (d) listing the case for a case management conference.
(9) [*Revoked*]
(10) Where an order has been made under rule 26.3(7A)(b) or 26.3(8), a party who was in default will not normally be entitled to an order for the costs of any application to set aside or vary that order nor of attending any case management conference and will, unless the court thinks it unjust to do so, be ordered to pay the costs that the default caused to any other party.

(Rule 7.10 makes provision for the Production Centre)
(Rules 6.14 and 6.26 specify when a document is deemed to be served)

26.4 Stay to Allow for Settlement of the Case

r.26.4 48.37, 56.3
r.26.4(1) 73.21
r.26.4(2) 42.42, 73.21
r.26.4(2A) 42.42, 73.21
r.26.4(3) 42.42
r.26.4(4)–(5) 42.42

(1) A party may, when filing the completed directions questionnaire, make a written request for the proceedings to be stayed(GL) while the parties try to settle the case by alternative dispute resolution(GL) or other means.
(2) If all parties request a stay the proceedings will be stayed for one month and the court will notify the parties accordingly.
(2A) If the court otherwise considers that such a stay would be appropriate, the court will direct that the proceedings, either in whole or in part, be stayed for one month, or for such other period as it considers appropriate.
(3) The court may extend the stay(GL) until such date or for such specified period as it considers appropriate.
(4) Where the court stays(GL) the proceedings under this rule, the claimant must tell the court if a settlement is reached.
(5) If the claimant does not tell the court by the end of the period of the stay(GL) that a settlement has been reached, the court will give such directions as to the management of the case as it considers appropriate.

26.5 Allocation

(1) The court will allocate the claim to a track—
   (a) when all parties have filed their directions questionnaires; or
   (b) when giving directions pursuant to rule 26.3(8),
   unless it has stayed the proceedings under rule 26.4.

(Rules 12.7 and 14.8 provide for the court to allocate a claim to a track where the claimant obtains default judgment on request or judgment on admission for an amount to be decided by the court)

(2) If the court has stayed(GL) the proceedings under rule 26.4, it will allocate the claim to a track at the end of the period of the stay.
(3) Before deciding the track to which to allocate proceedings or deciding whether to give directions for an allocation hearing to be fixed, the court may order a party to provide further information about his case.
(4) The court may hold an allocation hearing if it thinks it is necessary.
(5) [*Revoked*]

26.6 Scope of Each Track

(1) The small claims track is the normal track for—
   (a) any claim for personal injuries where—
      (i) the value of the claim is not more than £10,000; and
      (ii) the value of any claim for damages for personal injuries is not more than £1,000;
   (b) any claim which includes a claim by a tenant of residential premises against a landlord where—
      (i) the tenant is seeking an order requiring the landlord to carry out repairs or other work to the premises (whether or not the tenant is also seeking some other remedy);
      (ii) the cost of the repairs or other work to the premises is estimated to be not more than £1,000; and
      (iii) the value of any other claim for damages is not more than £1,000.

(Rule 2.3 defines 'claim for personal injuries' as proceedings in which there is a claim for damages in respect of personal injuries to the claimant or any other person or in respect of a person's death)

(2) For the purposes of paragraph (1) 'damages for personal injuries' means damages claimed as compensation for pain, suffering and loss of amenity and does not include any other damages which are claimed.
(3) Subject to paragraph (1), the small claims track is the normal track for any claim which has a value of not more than £10,000.

(Rule 26.7(4) provides that the court will not allocate to the small claims track certain claims in respect of harassment or unlawful eviction)

(4) Subject to paragraph (5), the fast track is the normal track for any claim—
   (a) for which the small claims track is not the normal track; and
   (b) which has a value—
      (i) for proceedings issued on or after 6th April 2009, of not more than £25,000; and
      (ii) for proceedings issued before 6th April 2009, of not more than £15,000.
(5) The fast track is the normal track for the claims referred to in paragraph (4) only if the court considers that—
   (a) the trial is likely to last for no longer than one day; and
   (b) oral expert evidence at trial will be limited to—
      (i) one expert per party in relation to any expert field; and
      (ii) expert evidence in two expert fields.
(6) The multi-track is the normal track for any claim for which the small claims track or the fast track is not the normal track.

26.7 General Rule for Allocation

r.26.7 **13.14**
r.26.7(2) **42.30**
r.26.7(3) **42.26, 42.27**
r.26.7(4) **42.27**

(1) In considering whether to allocate a claim to the normal track for that claim under rule 26.6, the court will have regard to the matters mentioned in rule 26.8(1).
(2) The court will allocate a claim which has no financial value to the track which it considers most suitable having regard to the matters mentioned in rule 26.8(1).
(3) [*Revoked*]
(4) The court will not allocate a claim to the small claims track, if it includes a claim by a tenant of residential premises against his landlord for a remedy in respect of harassment or unlawful eviction.

26.8 Matters Relevant to Allocation to a Track

r.26.8 **13.14, 42.26, 42.31, 42.41, 87.34**
r.26.8(2) **42.26**

(1) When deciding the track for a claim, the matters to which the court shall have regard include—
(a) the financial value, if any, of the claim;
(b) the nature of the remedy sought;
(c) the likely complexity of the facts, law or evidence;
(d) the number of parties or likely parties;
(e) the value of any counterclaim or other Part 20 claim and the complexity of any matters relating to it;
(f) the amount of oral evidence which may be required;
(g) the importance of the claim to persons who are not parties to the proceedings;
(h) the views expressed by the parties; and
(i) the circumstances of the parties.
(2) It is for the court to assess the financial value of a claim and in doing so it will disregard—
(a) any amount not in dispute;
(b) any claim for interest;
(c) costs; and
(d) any contributory negligence.
(3) Where—
(a) two or more claimants have started a claim against the same defendant using the same claim form; and
(b) each claimant has a claim against the defendant separate from the other claimants,
the court will consider the claim of each claimant separately when it assesses financial value under paragraph (1).

26.9 Notice of Allocation

r.26.9 **13.14, 42.33**

(1) When it has allocated a clwaim to a track, the court will serve notice of allocation on every party.
(2) [*Revoked*]
(Rule 26.5 provides that the court may, before allocating proceedings, order a party to provide further information about their case)

26.10 Reallocation

r.26.10 **13.14, 42.41**

The court may subsequently reallocate a claim to a different track.

26.11 Trial with a Jury

r.26.11 **60.3**

An application for a claim to be tried with a jury must be made within 28 days of service of the defence.
(Section 69 of the Senior Courts Act 1981 and section 66 of the County Courts Act 1984 specify when a claim may be tried with a jury)

PD 26 Practice Direction 26 — Case Management — Preliminary Stage: Allocation and Reallocation

This practice direction supplements CPR, Part 26.

[For commentary on a specific paragraph, please refer to the cross-references after the title of the paragraph.]

Reminders of Important Rule Provisions Other than Parts 26–29

Attention is drawn in particular to the following provisions of the Civil Procedure Rules:

Part 1 The Overriding Objective (defined in Rule 1.1).

The duty of the court to further that objective by actively managing cases (set out in Rule 1.4).

The requirement that the parties help the court to further that objective (set out in Rule 1.3).

Part 3 The court's case management powers (which may be exercised on application or on its own initiative) and the sanctions which it may impose.

Part 24 The court's power to grant summary judgment.

Parts 32–35 Evidence, especially the court's power to control evidence.

Attention is also drawn to the practice directions which supplement those Parts and Parts 27–29, and to those which relate to the various specialist jurisdictions.

The Directions Questionnaire

Form

2.1 (1) The notice of proposed allocation referred to in r. 26.3(1) will be—
in the small claims track, in form N149A (SCT);
in the fast track, in form N149B (FT); and
in the multi-track, in form N149C (MT),
and the directions questionnaire referred to in Part 26 will be in forms N180 and N181.

(2) Attention is drawn to Part 3 of the Civil Procedure Rules which requires costs budgets in all multi-track cases.

Provision of extra information

para.2.2 32.6
para.2.2(1) 42.15
para.2.2(2) 42.15, 47.4
para.2.2(3)(a) 33.4
para.2.2(3)(d) 41.5

2.2 (1) If a party wishes to give the court further information which is believed to be relevant to allocation or case management it shall be given when the party files the directions questionnaire and copied to all other parties.

(2) The general rule is that the court will not take such information into account unless the document containing it either:

(a) confirms that all parties have agreed that the information is correct and that it should be put before the court, or

(b) confirms that the party who has sent the document to the court has delivered a copy to all the other parties.

(3) The following are examples of information which will be likely to help the court:

(a) a party's intention to apply for summary judgment or some other order that may dispose of the case or reduce the amount in dispute or the number of issues remaining to be decided,

(b) a party's intention to issue a Part 20 claim or to add another party,

(c) the steps the parties have taken in the preparation of evidence (in particular expert evidence), the steps they intend to take and whether those steps are to be taken in cooperation with any other party,

(d) the directions the party believes will be appropriate to be given for the management of the case,

CPR 26–50 & PDs

(e) about any particular facts that may affect the timetable the court will set,
(f) any facts which may make it desirable for the court to fix an allocation hearing or a hearing at which case management directions will be given.

Consultation

para.2.3 **42.14**
para.2.3(1) **42.15**
para.2.3(2) **42.15**
para.2.3(3) **42.15**

2.3 (1) The parties must consult one another and cooperate in completing the allocation questionnaires and giving other information to the court.
(2) They must try to agree the case management directions which they will invite the court to make. Further details appear in the PD 28 and PD 29.
(Specimen directions for a case which is allocated to the multi-track are available on the Justice website at: www.justice.gov.uk/courts/procedure-rules/civil.)
(3) The process of consultation must not delay the filing of the directions questionnaire or, where required, the proposed directions (whether or not agreed).

Hearings before allocation

para.2.4 **33.4, 33.25, 37.11**
para.2.4(a) **42.19**
para.2.4(b) **42.12**

2.4 Where a court hearing takes place (for example on an application for an interim injunction or for summary judgment under Part 24) before the claim is allocated to a track, the court may at that hearing:
(1) dispense with the need for the parties to file directions questionnaires, treat the hearing as a directions hearing, make an order for directions and give directions for case management, or
(2) fix a date for directions questionnaires to be filed and give other directions.

Consequences of failure to file a directions questionnaire

2.5 (1) Parties must comply with the notice served under r. 26.3(1) by the date specified in it. Rules 26.3(7A), which concerns designated money claims, and 26.3(8), which concerns claims other than designated money claims, apply where a party is in default.
(2) A party's statement of case may be struck out under r. 26.3(7A)(b).
(3) Under r. 26.3(8) the court may give directions of its own initiative or list the case for a case management conference. Alternatively, if it appears appropriate to do so, the claim may be struck out or, where a defendant is in default, judgment may be entered against that defendant.
(4) Rule 26.3(10) provides for a costs sanction if an order is made under either rr. 26.3(7A)(b) or 26.3(8).

Stay to Allow for Settlement of the Case

para.3.1(1) **42.42**

Procedure for the parties to apply to extend the stay

3.1 (1) (a) The court will generally accept a letter from any party or from the solicitor for any party as an application to extend the stay under rule 26.4.
(b) The letter should—
(i) confirm that the application is made with the agreement of all parties, and
(ii) explain the steps being taken and identify any mediator or expert assisting with the process.
(2) (a) An order extending the stay must be made by a judge.
(b) The extension will generally be for no more than 4 weeks unless clear reasons are given to justify a longer time.
(3) More than one extension of the stay may be granted.

Position at the end of the stay if no settlement is reached

3.2 (1) At the end of the stay the file will be referred to a judge for his directions.
(2) He will consider whether to allocate the claim to a track and what other directions to give, or may require any party to give further information or fix an allocation hearing.

3.3 Any party may apply for a stay to be lifted.

Position where settlement is reached during a stay

3.4 Where the whole of the proceedings are settled during a stay, the taking of any of the following steps will be treated as an application for the stay to be lifted:

(1) an application for a consent order (in any form) to give effect to the settlement,
(2) an application for the approval of a settlement where a party is a person under a disability,
(3) giving notice of acceptance of money paid into court in satisfaction of the claim or applying for money in court to be paid out.

Allocation, Reallocation and Case Management

The court's general approach

4.1 The Civil Procedure Rules lay down the overriding objective, the powers and duties of the court and the factors to which it must have regard in exercising them. The court will expect to exercise its powers as far as possible in cooperation with the parties and their legal representatives so as to deal with the case justly in accordance with that objective.

Allocation to track

4.2 (1) In most cases the court will expect to have enough information from the statements of case and directions questionnaires to be able to allocate the claim to a track and to give case management directions.
(2) If the court does not have enough information to allocate the claim it will generally make an order under rule 26.5(3) requiring one or more parties to provide further information within 14 days.
(3) Where there has been no allocation hearing the notice of allocation will be in forms N154 (fast track), N155 (multi-track) or N157, N158, N159 or N160 (small claims).
(4) (a) The general rule is that the court will give brief reasons for its allocation decision, and these will be set out in the notice of allocation.
(b) The general rule does not apply where all the directions questionnaires which have been filed have expressed the wish for the claim to be allocated to the track to which the court has allocated it.
(5) Paragraph 6 of this practice direction deals with allocation hearings and paragraph 7 deals with allocation principles.
(6) Paragraph 11 of this practice direction deals with reallocation.

4.3 PD 27, PD 28 and PD 29 contain further information about the giving of case management directions at the allocation stage.

Summary Judgment or Other Early Termination

para.5.2 33.1
para.5.3(1) PC 22, 32.6, 33.3, 34.2, 45.2
para.5.3(2) PC 22, 33.4, 34.4
para.5.3(3)–(4) 33.4, 34.4
para.5.4 34.5

5.1 Part of the court's duty of active case management is the summary disposal of issues which do not need full investigation and trial (rule 1.4(2)(c)).

5.2 The court's powers to make orders to dispose of issues in that way include:
(a) under rule 3.4, striking out a statement of case, or part of a statement of case, and
(b) under Part 24, giving summary judgment where a claimant or a defendant has no reasonable prospect of success.

The court may use these powers on an application or on its own initiative. PD 24 contains further information.

5.3 (1) A party intending to make such an application should do so before or when filing his directions questionnaire.
(2) Where a party makes an application for such an order before a claim has been allocated to a track the court will not normally allocate the claim before the hearing of the application.
(3) Where a party files a directions questionnaire stating that he intends to make such an application but has not done so, the judge will usually direct that an allocation hearing is listed.
(4) The application may be heard at that allocation hearing if the application notice has been issued and served in sufficient time.

5.4 (1) This paragraph applies where the court proposes to make such an order of its own initiative.
(2) The court will not allocate the claim to a track but instead it will either:
(a) fix a hearing, giving the parties at least 14 days notice of the date of the hearing and of the issues which it is proposed that the court will decide, or

(b) make an order directing a party to take the steps described in the order within a stated time and specifying the consequence of not taking those steps.

5.5 Where the court decides at the hearing of an application or a hearing fixed under paragraph 5.4(2) (a) that the claim (or part of the claim) is to continue it may:

(1) treat that hearing as an allocation hearing, allocate the claim and give case management directions, or

(2) give other directions.

Allocation Hearings

General principle

para.6.1 42.23

6.1 The court will only hold an allocation hearing on its own initiative if it considers that it is necessary to do so.

Procedure

6.2 Where the court orders an allocation hearing to take place:

(1) it will give the parties at least seven days' notice of the hearing in form N153, and

(2) form N153 will give a brief explanation of the decision to order the hearing.

6.3 Power to treat another hearing as an allocation hearing

Where the court may treat another hearing as an allocation hearing it does not need to give notice to any party that it proposes to do so.

6.4 The notice of allocation after an allocation hearing will be in forms N154, N155 or N157.

Representation

para.6.5 42.23

6.5 A legal representative who attends an allocation hearing should, if possible, be the person responsible for the case and must in any event be familiar with the case, be able to provide the court with the information it is likely to need to take its decisions about allocation and case management, and have sufficient authority to deal with any issues that are likely to arise.

Sanctions

para.6.6(2) 42.22 para.6.6(3) 42.23

6.6 (1) This paragraph sets out the sanctions that the court will usually impose for default in connection with the allocation procedure, but the court may make a different order.

(2) (a) Where a directions hearing takes place because a party has failed to file a directions questionnaire or to provide further information which the court has ordered, the court will usually order that party to pay on the indemnity basis the costs of any other party who has attended the hearing, summarily assess the amount of those costs, and order them to be paid forthwith or within a stated period.

(b) The court may order that if the party does not pay those costs within the time stated his statement of case will be struck out.

(3) Where a party whose default has led to a fixing of an allocation hearing is still in default and does not attend the hearing the court will usually make an order specifying the steps he is required to take and providing that unless he takes them within a stated time his statement of case will be struck out.

Allocation Principles

Rules 26.6, 26.7 and 26.8

7.1 (1) Rule 26.6 sets out the scope of each track,

(2) Rule 26.7 states the general rule for allocation, and

(3) Rule 26.8 sets out the matters relevant to allocation to a track.

Objective of this paragraph

7.2 The object of this paragraph is to explain what will be the court's general approach to some of the matters set out in rule 26.8.

'the financial value of the claim'

7.3 (1) Rule 26.8(2) provides that it is for the court to assess the financial value of a claim.

(2) Where the court believes that the amount the claimant is seeking exceeds what he may reasonably be expected to recover it may make an order under rule 26.5(3) directing the claimant to justify the amount.

'any amount not in dispute'
para.7.4 42.26

7.4 In deciding, for the purposes of rule 26.8(2), whether an amount is in dispute the court will apply the following general principles:
(1) Any amount for which the defendant does not admit liability is in dispute,
(2) Any sum in respect of an item forming part of the claim for which judgment has been entered (for example a summary judgment) is not in dispute,
(3) Any specific sum claimed as a distinct item and which the defendant admits he is liable to pay is not in dispute,
(4) Any sum offered by the defendant which has been accepted by the claimant in satisfaction of any item which forms a distinct part of the claim is not in dispute.

It follows from these provisions that if, in relation to a claim the value of which is above the small claims track limit of £10,000, the defendant makes, before allocation, an admission that reduces the amount in dispute to a figure below £10,000 (see CPR Part 14), the normal track for the claim will be the small claims track. As to recovery of pre-allocation costs, the claimant can, before allocation, apply for judgment with costs on the amount of the claim that has been admitted (see CPR rule 14.3 but see also **PD 43–48, para. 15.1(3)**, under which the court has a discretion to allow pre-allocation costs).

'the views expressed by the parties'
para.7.5 **42.31**

7.5 The court will treat these views as an important factor, but the allocation decision is one for the court, to be taken in the light of all the circumstances, and the court will not be bound by any agreement or common view of the parties.

'the circumstances of the parties'
7.6 See paragraph 8.

'the value of any counterclaim or other Part 20 claim'
para.7.7 42.31

7.7 Where the case involves more than one money claim (for example where there is a Part 20 claim or there is more than one claimant each making separate claims) the court will not generally aggregate the claims. Instead it will generally regard the largest of them as determining the financial value of the claims.

The Small Claims Track — Allocation and Case Management

para.8.1(1)(c) 42.27
para.8.1(1)(d) 42.27
para.8.1(2) 42.26
para.8.1(2)(b) 42.27
para.8.1(2)(c) 42.27

Allocation

8.1 (1) (a) The small claims track is intended to provide a proportionate procedure by which most straightforward claims with a financial value of not more than £10,000 can be decided, without the need for substantial pre-hearing preparation and the formalities of a traditional trial, and without incurring large legal costs. (Rule 26.6 provides for a lower financial value in certain types of case.)
(b) The procedure laid down in Part 27 for the preparation of the case and the conduct of the hearing are designed to make it possible for a litigant to conduct his own case without legal representation if he wishes.
(c) Cases generally suitable for the small claims track will include consumer disputes, accident claims, disputes about the ownership of goods and most disputes between a landlord and tenant other than opposed claims under Part 56, disputed claims for possession under Part 55 and demotion claims whether in the alternative to possession claims or under Part 65.
(d) A case involving a disputed allegation of dishonesty will not usually be suitable for the small claims track.

(2) The court may allocate to the small claims track a claim, the value of which is above the limits mentioned in r. 26.6(2). The court will not normally allow more than one day for the hearing of such a claim.

Case management

8.2 (1) Directions for case management of claims allocated to the small claims track will generally be given by the court on allocation.

(2) Rule 27.4 contains further provisions about directions and PD 27 sets out the standard directions which the court will usually give.

The Fast Track

para.9.1(3)(b) 42.43

Allocation

9.1 (1) Where the court is to decide whether to allocate to the fast track or the multi-track a claim for which the normal track is the fast track, it will allocate the claim to the fast track unless it believes that it cannot be dealt with justly on that track.

(2) The court will, in particular, take into account the limits likely to be placed on disclosure, the extent to which expert evidence may be necessary and whether the trial is likely to last more than a day.

(3) (a) When it is considering the likely length of the trial the court will regard a day as being a period of 5 hours, and will consider whether that is likely to be sufficient time for the case to be heard.

(b) The court will also take into account the case management directions (including the fixing of a trial timetable) that are likely to be given and the court's powers to control evidence and to limit cross-examination.

(c) The possibility that a trial might last longer than one day is not necessarily a conclusive reason for the court to allocate or to reallocate a claim to the multi-track.

(d) A claim may be allocated to the fast track or ordered to remain on that track although there is to be a split trial.

(e) Where the case involves a counterclaim or other Part 20 claim that will be tried with the claim and as a result the trial will last more than a day, the court may not allocate it to the fast track.

Case management

9.2 (1) Directions for the case management of claims which have been allocated to the fast track will be given at the allocation stage or at the listing stage (in either case with or without a hearing) or at both, and if necessary at other times. The trial judge may, at or before the trial, give directions for its conduct.

(2) PD 28 contains further provisions and contains standard directions which the court may give.

The Multi-track

para.10.2(5) 42.10
para.10.2(6) 42.10
para.10.2(8) 42.10
para.10.2(9) 42.10
para.10.2(10) 42.10

10.1 paragraph 10.2 does not apply to:

(1) a claim for possession of land in the county court or a demotion claim whether in the alternative to a possession claim or under Part 65;

(2) any claim which is being dealt with at the Royal Courts of Justice. *Venue for allocation and case management*

Case management

10.2 (1) The case management of a claim which is allocated to the multi-track will normally be dealt with at a civil trial centre.

(2) In the case of a claim to which any of Parts 49 or 58 to 62 apply, case management must be dealt with at a civil trial centre. Sub-paragraphs (4) to (10) do not apply to such a claim. The claim will be allocated to the multi-track irrespective of its value, and must be transferred to a civil trial centre for allocation and case management if not already there.

(3) Where a claim is issued in or automatically transferred to a civil trial centre it will be allocated and managed at that court.

(4) The following sub-paragraphs apply to a claim which is issued in or automatically transferred to a court which is not a civil trial centre. Such a court is referred to as a 'feeder court'.

(5) Where a judge sitting at a feeder court decides, on the basis of the directions questionnaires and any other documents filed by the parties, that the claim should be dealt with on the multi-track he will normally make an order:

(a) allocating the claim to that track,

(b) giving case management directions, and

(c) transferring the claim to a civil trial centre.

(6) If he decides that an allocation hearing or some pre-allocation hearing is to take place (for example to strike out a statement of case under Part 3 of the Rules) that hearing will take place at the feeder court.

(7) If, before allocation, a hearing takes place at a feeder court and in exercising his powers under paragraph 2.4(1) above the judge allocates the claim to the multi-track, he will also normally make an order transferring the claim to a civil trial centre.

(8) A judge sitting at a feeder court may, rather than making an allocation order himself, transfer the claim to a civil trial centre for the decision about allocation to be taken there.

(9) When, following an order for transfer, the file is received at the civil trial centre, a judge sitting at that centre will consider it and give any further directions that appear necessary or desirable.

(10) Where there is reason to believe that more than one case management conference may be needed and the parties or their legal advisers are located inconveniently far from the civil trial centre, a judge sitting at a feeder court may, with the agreement of the designated civil judge and notwithstanding the allocation of the case to the multi-track, decide that in the particular circumstances of the case it should not be transferred to a civil trial centre, but should be case managed for the time being at the feeder court.

(11) A designated civil judge may at any time make an order transferring a claim from a feeder court to a civil trial centre and he may do so irrespective of the track, if any, to which it has been allocated. He may also permit a feeder court to keep for trial a claim or (subject to review from time to time) a category of claims. Any such permission should take into account the ability of the feeder court in relation to the civil trial centre to provide suitable and effective trial within an appropriate trial period.

(12) No order will be made by a feeder court fixing a date for a hearing at a civil trial centre unless that date has been given or confirmed by a judge or listing officer of that centre.

Case management

10.3 Part 29 of the Rules and PD 29 set out the procedure to be adopted.

Reallocation of Claims and the Variation of Directions

para.11.1 **42.41**
para.11.1(1) **42.41**
para.11.2 **42.41**

11.1 (1) Where a party is dissatisfied with an order made allocating the claim to a track he may appeal or apply to the court to reallocate the claim.

(2) He should appeal if the order was made at a hearing at which he was present or represented, or of which he was given due notice.

(3) In any other case he should apply to the court to reallocate the claim.

11.2 Where there has been a change in the circumstances since an order was made allocating the claim to a track the court may reallocate the claim. It may do so on application or on its own initiative.

PD 28 and PD 29 contain provisions about the variation of case management directions.

Determining the Amount to Be Paid under a Judgment or Order

para.12 **20.6**
para.12.1 **36.13**
para.12.1(1) **42.46**
para.12.1(2) **42.46**

Scope

12.1 (1) In the following paragraphs:

(a) a 'relevant order' means a judgment or order of the court which requires the amount of money to be paid by one party to another to be decided by the court; and

(b) a 'disposal hearing' means a hearing in accordance with para. 12.4.

(2) A relevant order may have been obtained:

(a) by a judgment in default under Part 12;

(b) by a judgment on an admission under Part 14;

(c) on the striking out of a statement of case under Part 3;

(d) on a summary judgment application under Part 24;

(e) on the determination of a preliminary issue or on a trial as to liability; or

(f) at trial.

(3) A relevant order includes any order for the amount of a debt, damages or interest to be decided by the court (including an order for the taking of an account or the making of an inquiry as to any sum due, and any similar order), but does not include an order for the assessment of costs.

Directions

para.12.2 **20.6**
para.12.2(1) **42.46, 42.48**
para.12.2(2) **42.49**
para.12.2(3) **42.46, 42.48**

12.2 (1) When the court makes a relevant order it will give directions, which may include:

(a) listing the claim for a disposal hearing;

(b) allocating or reallocating the claim (but see para. 12.3);

(c) directing the parties to file directions questionnaires by a specified date; and

(d) staying the claim while the parties try to settle the case by alternative dispute resolution or other means.

(2) Directions may specify the level or type of judge before whom a hearing or a further hearing will take place and the nature and purpose of that hearing.

(3) Where the parties apply for a relevant order by consent, they should if possible file with their draft consent order agreed directions for the court's approval.

Allocation

para.12.3 **20.6, 42.48**

12.3 (1) If, when the court makes a relevant order:

(a) the claim has not previously been allocated to a track; and

(b) the financial value of the claim (determined in accordance with Part 26) is such that the claim would, if defended be allocated to the small claims track,

the court will normally allocate it to that track.

(2) Where para. (1)(b) does not apply, the court will not normally allocate the claim to a track (other than the small claims track) unless:

(a) the amount payable appears to be genuinely disputed on substantial grounds; or

(b) the dispute is not suitable to be dealt with at a disposal hearing.

Disposal hearings

para.12.4(1) **42.47**
para.12.4(1)(b) **42.47**
para.12.4(2) **42.47**
para.12.4(3) **20.6, 42.47**
para.12.4(4) **42.47**

12.4 (1) A disposal hearing is a hearing:

(a) which will not normally last longer than 30 minutes, and

(b) at which the court will not normally hear oral evidence.

(2) At a disposal hearing the court may:

(a) decide the amount payable under or in consequence of the relevant order and give judgment for that amount; or

(b) give directions as to the future conduct of the proceedings.

(3) If the claim has been allocated to the small claims track, or the court decides at the disposal hearing to allocate it to that track, the court may treat the disposal hearing as a final hearing in accordance with Part 27.

(4) Rule 32.6 applies to evidence at a disposal hearing unless the court directs otherwise.

(5) Except where the claim has been allocated to the small claims track, the court will not exercise its power under sub-paragraph (2)(a) unless any written evidence on which the claimant relies has been served on the defendant at least three days before the disposal hearing.

Costs

12.5 (1) Attention is drawn to:

(a) PD 43–48 and in particular to the court's power to make a summary assessment of costs;

(b) r. 44.13(1) which provides that if an order makes no mention of costs, none are payable in respect of the proceedings to which it relates; and

(c) r. 27.14 (special rules about costs in cases allocated to the small claims track).

(2) Part 46 (fast track trial costs) will not apply to a case dealt with at a disposal hearing whatever the financial value of the claim. So the costs of a disposal hearing will be in the discretion of the court.

Jurisdiction of masters and district judges

para.12.6 **42.49**

12.6 Unless the court otherwise directs, a master or a district judge may decide the amount payable under a relevant order irrespective of the financial value of the claim and of the track to which the claim may have been allocated.

CPR Part 27 The Small Claims Track

Part 27 **45.33, 68.34, 68.35** [For commentary on a specific rule, please refer to the cross-references after the title of the rule.]

27.1 Scope of This Part

(1) This Part—

(a) sets out the special procedure for dealing with claims which have been allocated to the small claims track under Part 26; and

(b) limits the amount of costs that can be recovered in respect of a claim which has been allocated to the small claims track.

(Rule 27.14 deals with costs on the small claims track)

(2) A claim being dealt with under this Part is called a small claim.

(Rule 26.6 provides for the scope of the small claims track. A claim for a remedy for harassment or unlawful eviction relating, in either case, to residential premises shall not be allocated to the small claims track whatever the financial value of the claim. Otherwise, the small claims track will be the normal track for—

- any claim which has a financial value of not more than £10,000 subject to the special provisions about claims for personal injuries and housing disrepair claims;
- any claim for personal injuries which has a financial value of not more than £10,000 where the claim for damages for personal injuries is not more than £1,000; and
- any claim which includes a claim by a tenant of residential premises against his landlord for repairs or other work to the premises where the estimated cost of the repairs or other work is not more than £1,000 and the financial value of any other claim for damages in respect of those repairs or other work is not more than £1,000)

27.2 Extent to Which Other Parts Apply

r.27.2 **45.6**
r.27.2(1) **37.1, 49.8**
r.27.2(1)(b) **45.17, 50.2**
r.27.2(1)(c) **45.18, 51.18**
r.27.2(1)(e) **45.19, 54.13**
r.27.2(1)(f) **45.16**
r.27.2(1)(g) **45.29**
r.27.2(1)(h) **45.26**
r.27.2(3) **45.16**

(1) The following Parts of these Rules do not apply to small claims—

(a) Part 25 (interim remedies) except as it relates to interim injunctions(GL);

(b) Part 31 (disclosure and inspection);

(c) Part 32 (evidence) except rule 32.1 (power of court to control evidence);

(d) Part 33 (miscellaneous rules about evidence);

(e) Part 35 (experts and assessors) except rules 35.1 (duty to restrict expert evidence), 35.3 (experts — overriding duty to the court), 35.7 (court's power to direct that evidence is to be given by single joint expert) and 35.8 (instructions to a single joint expert);

(f) subject to paragraph (3), Part 18 (further information);

(g) Part 36 (offers to settle); and

(h) Part 39 (hearings) except rule 39.2 (general rule — hearing to be in public).

(2) The other Parts of these Rules apply to small claims except to the extent that a rule limits such application.
(3) The court of its own initiative may order a party to provide further information if it considers it appropriate to do so.

27.3 Court's Power to Grant a Final Remedy

r.27.3 45.4

The court may grant any final remedy in relation to a small claim which it could grant if the proceedings were on the fast track or the multi-track.

27.4 Preparation for the Hearing

r.27.4 45.7, 45.11
r.27.4(1)(a) 45.8
r.27.4(1)(b) 45.10
r.27.4(1)(c) 45.9
r.27.4(1)(d) 45.11
r.27.4(3)(a) 45.8, 45.17, 50.2
r.27.4(3)(b) 45.10

(1) After allocation the court will—
 (a) give standard directions and fix a date for the final hearing;
 (b) give special directions and fix a date for the final hearing;
 (c) give special directions and direct that the court will consider what further directions are to be given no later than 28 days after the date the special directions were given;
 (d) fix a date for a preliminary hearing under rule 27.6; or
 (e) give notice that it proposes to deal with the claim without a hearing under rule 27.10 and invite the parties to notify the court by a specified date if they agree the proposal.
(2) The court will—
 (a) give the parties at least 21 days' notice of the date fixed for the final hearing, unless the parties agree to accept less notice; and
 (b) inform them of the amount of time allowed for the final hearing.
(3) In this rule—
 (a) 'standard directions' means—
  (i) a direction that each party shall, at least 14 days before the date fixed for the final hearing, file and serve on every other party copies of all documents (including any expert's report) on which he intends to rely at the hearing; and
  (ii) any other standard directions set out in Practice Direction 27; and
 (b) 'special directions' means directions given in addition to or instead of the standard directions.

27.5 Experts

r.27.5 42.27, 45.19, 45.20, 54.13

No expert may give evidence, whether written or oral, at a hearing without the permission of the court.

27.6 Preliminary Hearing

r.27.6 45.11
r.27.6(4)–(5) 45.11

(1) The court may hold a preliminary hearing for the consideration of the claim, but only—
 (a) where—
  (i) it considers that special directions, as defined in rule 27.4, are needed to ensure a fair hearing; and
  (ii) it appears necessary for a party to attend at court to ensure that he understands what he must do to comply with the special directions; or
 (b) to enable it to dispose of the claim on the basis that one or other of the parties has no real prospect of success at a final hearing; or
 (c) to enable it to strike out(GL) a statement of case or part of a statement of case on the basis that the statement of case, or the part to be struck out, discloses no reasonable grounds for bringing or defending the claim.
(2) When considering whether or not to hold a preliminary hearing, the court must have regard to the desirability of limiting the expense to the parties of attending court.

CPR 26–50 & PDs

(3) Where the court decides to hold a preliminary hearing, it will give the parties at least 14 days' notice of the date of the hearing.
(4) The court may treat the preliminary hearing as the final hearing of the claim if all the parties agree.
(5) At or after the preliminary hearing the court will—
 (a) fix the date of the final hearing (if it has not been fixed already) and give the parties at least 21 days' notice of the date fixed unless the parties agree to accept less notice;
 (b) inform them of the amount of time allowed for the final hearing; and
 (c) give any appropriate directions.

27.7 Power of Court to Add to, Vary or Revoke Directions

r.27.7 45.7

The court may add to, vary or revoke directions.

27.8 Conduct of the Hearing

r.27.8 45.20, 45.23
r.27.8(4) 49.50
r.27.8(6) 45.25

(1) The court may adopt any method of proceeding at a hearing that it considers to be fair.
(2) Hearings will be informal.
(3) The strict rules of evidence do not apply.
(4) The court need not take evidence on oath.
(5) The court may limit cross-examination(GL).
(6) The court must give reasons for its decision.

27.9 Non-attendance of Parties at a Final Hearing

r.27.9 45.27
r.27.9(1) 45.24, 45.25, 45.26
r.27.9(1)(b) 45.24
r.27.9(2)–(4) 45.24

(1) If a party who does not attend a final hearing—
 (a) has given written notice to the court and the other party at least 7 days before the hearing date that he will not attend;
 (b) has served on the other party at least 7 days before the hearing date any other documents which he has filed with the court; and
 (c) has, in his written notice, requested the court to decide the claim in his absence and has confirmed his compliance with paragraphs (a) and (b) above,

 the court will take into account that party's statement of case and any other documents he has filed and served when it decides the claim.
(2) If a claimant does not—
 (a) attend the hearing; and
 (b) give the notice referred to in paragraph (1),

 the court may strike out (GL) the claim.
(3) If—
 (a) a defendant does not—
  (i) attend the hearing; or
  (ii) give the notice referred to in paragraph (1); and
 (b) the claimant either—
  (i) does attend the hearing; or
  (ii) gives the notice referred to in paragraph (1),

 the court may decide the claim on the basis of the evidence of the claimant alone.
(4) If neither party attends or gives the notice referred to in paragraph (1), the court may strike out(GL) the claim and any defence and counterclaim.

27.10 Disposal without a Hearing

r.27.10 43.12, 45.25, 45.26, 45.27

The court may, if all parties agree, deal with the claim without a hearing.

27.11 Setting Judgment Aside and Rehearing

r.27.11 45.26
r.27.11(1)–(4) 45.26
r.27.11(4)(a)–(b) 45.26
r.27.11(5) 45.26

(1) A party—
(a) who was neither present nor represented at the hearing of the claim; and
(b) who has not given written notice to the court under rule 27.9(1),
may apply for an order that a judgment under this Part shall be set aside(GL) and the claim reheard.

(2) A party who applies for an order setting aside a judgment under this rule must make the application not more than 14 days after the day on which notice of the judgment was served on him.

(3) The court may grant an application under paragraph (2) only if the applicant—
(a) had a good reason for not attending or being represented at the hearing or giving written notice to the court under rule 27.9(1); and
(b) has a reasonable prospect of success at the hearing.

(4) If a judgment is set aside(GL)—
(a) the court must fix a new hearing for the claim; and
(b) the hearing may take place immediately after the hearing of the application to set the judgment aside and may be dealt with by the judge who set aside(GL) the judgment.

(5) A party may not apply to set aside(GL) a judgment under this rule if the court dealt with the claim without a hearing under rule 27.10.

27.12 [*Revoked*]

27.13 [*Revoked*]

27.14 Costs on the Small Claims Track

r.27.14 8.32, 45.33, 68.35
r.27.14(2) 45.28
r.27.14(2)(a) 45.28, 70.2, 70.3, 70.7
r.27.14(2)(a)(ii) 70.7
r.27.14(2)(b)–(c) 45.28
r.27.14(2)(d) 45.28
r.27.14(2)(e) 45.28
r.27.14(2)(f) 45.28
r.27.14(2)(g) 45.29, 70.3
r.27.14(3) 45.29
r.27.14(5) 42.27, 43.32
r.27.14(6) 42.27, 43.32

(1) This rule applies to any case which has been allocated to the small claims track.

(Rules 44.9 and 44.11 make provision in relation to orders for costs made before a claim has been allocated to the small claims track)

(2) The court may not order a party to pay a sum to another party in respect of that other party's costs, fees and expenses, including those relating to an appeal, except—
(a) the fixed costs attributable to issuing the claim which—
(i) are payable under Part 45; or
(ii) would be payable under Part 45 if that Part applied to the claim;
(b) in proceedings which included a claim for an injunction or an order for specific performance a sum not exceeding the amount specified in Practice Direction 27 for legal advice and assistance relating to that claim;
(c) any court fees paid by that other party;
(d) expenses which a party or witness has reasonably incurred in travelling to and from a hearing or in staying away from home for the purposes of attending a hearing;
(e) a sum not exceeding the amount specified in Practice Direction 27 for any loss of earnings or loss of leave by a party or witness due to attending a hearing or to staying away from home for the purposes of attending a hearing;
(f) a sum not exceeding the amount specified in Practice Direction 27 for an expert's fees;
(g) such further costs as the court may assess by the summary procedure and order to be paid by a party who has behaved unreasonably;
(h) the Stage 1 and, where relevant, the Stage 2 fixed costs in rule 45.29 where—
(i) the claim was within the scope of the Pre-Action Protocol for Low Value Personal Injury Claims in Road Traffic Accidents ('the RTA Protocol');
(ii) the claimant reasonably believed that the claim was valued at more than the small claims track limit in accordance with paragraph 4.1(4) of the RTA Protocol; and

(iii) the defendant admitted liability under the process set out in the RTA Protocol; but
(iv) the defendant did not pay those Stage 1 and, where relevant, Stage 2 fixed costs; and
(i) in an appeal, the cost of any approved transcript reasonably incurred.

(3) A party's rejection of an offer in settlement will not of itself constitute unreasonable behaviour under paragraph (2)(g) but the court may take it into consideration when it is applying the unreasonableness test.

(4) The limits on costs imposed by this rule also apply to any fee or reward for acting on behalf of a party to the proceedings charged by a person exercising a right of audience by virtue of an order under section 11 of the Courts and Legal Services Act 1990 (a lay representative).

(5) [*Revoked*]

(6) [*Revoked*]

27.15 Claim Reallocated from the Small Claims Track to Another Track

r.27.15 **42.41, 45.30, 68.35**

Where a claim is allocated to the small claims track and subsequently reallocated to another track, rule 27.14 (costs on the small claims track) will cease to apply after the claim has been reallocated and the fast track or multi-track costs rules will apply from the date of reallocation.

PD 27 Practice Direction 27 — Small Claims Track

This practice direction supplements CPR, Part 27.

[For commentary on a specific paragraph, please refer to the cross-references after the title of the paragraph.]

Judges

para.1 45.20

1 The functions of the court described in Part 27 which are to be carried out by a judge will generally be carried out by a district judge but may be carried out by a circuit judge.

Case Management Directions

para.2.2 45.8
para.2.3 45.18
para.2.4 45.7
para.2.5 45.18

2.1 Rule 27.4 explains how directions will be given, and r. 27.6 contains provisions about the holding of a preliminary hearing and the court's powers at such a hearing.

2.2 Appendix A sets out details of the case that the court usually needs in the type of case described. Appendix B sets out the standard directions that the court may give. Appendix C sets out special directions that the court may give.

2.3 Before allocating the claim to the small claims track and giving directions for a hearing the court may require a party to give further information about that party's case.

2.4 A party may ask the court to give particular directions about the conduct of the case.

2.5 In deciding whether to make an order for exchange of witness statements the court will have regard to the following:
(a) whether either or both the parties are represented;
(b) the amount in dispute in the proceedings;
(c) the nature of the matters in dispute;
(d) whether the need for any party to clarify his case can better be dealt with by an order under para. 2.3;
(e) the need for the parties to have access to justice without undue formality, cost or delay.

Representation at a Hearing

para.3.1(1) 45.21
para.3.1(2) 45.21
para.3.2(1) 45.21
para.3.2(2) 45.21
para.3.2(3) 45.21
para.3.2(4) 45.21

3.1 In this paragraph:
(1) a lawyer means a barrister, a solicitor or a legal executive employed by a solicitor, and
(2) a lay representative means any other person.

3.2 (1) A party may present his own case at a hearing or a lawyer or lay representative may present it for him.
(2) The Lay Representatives (Rights of Audience) Order 1999 (SI 1999/1225) provides that a lay representative may not exercise any right of audience:
(a) where his client does not attend the hearing,
(b) at any stage after judgment, or
(c) on any appeal brought against any decision made by the district judge in the proceedings.
(3) However the court, exercising its general discretion to hear anybody, may hear a lay representative even in circumstances excluded by the Order.
(4) Any of its officers or employees may represent a corporate party.

Small Claim Hearing

paras.4.1 45.22
paras.4.2 45.22
para.4.3 45.23

4.1 (1) The general rule is that a small claim hearing will be in public.

CPR 26–50 & PDs

(2) The judge may decide to hold it in private if:
(a) the parties agree, or
(b) a ground mentioned in r. 39.2(3) applies.
(3) A hearing or part of a hearing which takes place other than at the court, for example at the home or business premises of a party, will not be in public.

4.2 A hearing that takes place at the court will generally be in the judge's room but it may take place in a courtroom.

4.3 Rule 27.8 allows the court to adopt any method of proceeding that it considers to be fair and to limit cross-examination. The judge may in particular:
(1) ask questions of any witness himself before allowing any other person to do so,
(2) ask questions of all or any of the witnesses himself before allowing any other person to ask questions of any witnesses,
(3) refuse to allow cross-examination of any witness until all the witnesses have given evidence-in-chief,
(4) limit cross-examination of a witness to a fixed time or to a particular subject or issue, or both.

Recording Evidence and the Giving of Reasons

para.5.1 45.25
para.5.3(1) 45.25
para.5.3(2) 45.25
para.5.4 45.25

5.1 A hearing that takes place at the court will be tape-recorded by the court. A party may obtain a transcript of such a recording on payment of the proper transcriber's charges.

5.2 Attention is drawn to the Contempt of Court Act 1981, s. 9 (which deals with the unauthorised use of tape recorders in court), and to Practice Direction (Tape Recorders) [1981] 1 WLR 1526 which relates to it.

5.3 (1) The judge may give reasons for his judgment as briefly and simply as the nature of the case allows.
(2) He will normally do so orally at the hearing, but he may give them later at a hearing either orally or in writing.

5.4 Where the judge decides the case without a hearing under r. 27.10 or a party who has given notice under r. 27.9(1) does not attend the hearing, the judge will prepare a note of his reasons and the court will send a copy to each party.

5.5 Nothing in this practice direction affects the duty of a judge at the request of a party to make a note of the matters referred to in the County Courts Act 1984, s. 80.

Non-attendance of a Party at a Hearing

6.1 Attention is drawn to r. 27.9 (which enables a party to give notice that he will not attend a final hearing and sets out the effect of his giving such notice and of not doing so), and to para. 3 above.

6.2 Nothing in those provisions affects the general power of the court to adjourn a hearing, for example where a party who wishes to attend a hearing on the date fixed cannot do so for a good reason.

Costs

para.7.2 45.28
para.7.3 45.28
para.7.3(2) 42.27, 45.19

7.1 Attention is drawn to r. 27.14 which contains provisions about the costs which may be ordered to be paid by one party to another.

7.2 The amount which a party may be ordered to pay under r. 27.14(2)(b) (for legal advice and assistance in claims including an injunction or specific performance) is a sum not exceeding £260.

7.3 The amounts which a party may be ordered to pay under r. 27.14(3)(c) (loss of earnings) and (d) (experts' fees) are:
(1) for the loss of earnings or loss of leave of each party or witness due to attending a hearing or staying away from home for the purpose of attending a hearing, a sum not exceeding £90 per day for each person, and
(2) for experts' fees, a sum not exceeding £750 for each expert.

(As to recovery of pre-allocation costs in a case in which an admission by the defendant has reduced the amount in dispute to a figure below £10,000, reference should be made to PD 26, para. 7.4, and to PD 43–48, para. 15.1(3).)

Appeals

para.8A 45.27
para.8.2 45.27
para.8.3 45.27

8.1 Part 52 deals with appeals and attention is drawn to that Part and PD 52.
8A An appellant's notice in small claims must be filed and served in form N164.
8.2 Where the court dealt with the claim to which the appellant is a party:
(1) under r. 27.10 without a hearing; or
(2) in his absence because he gave notice under r. 27.9 requesting the court to decide the claim in his absence,
an application for permission to appeal must be made to the appeal court.
8.3 Where an appeal is allowed the court will, if possible, dispose of the case at the same time without referring the claim to the lower court or ordering a new hearing. It may do so without hearing further evidence.

APPENDIX A INFORMATION AND DOCUMENTATION THE COURT USUALLY NEEDS IN PARTICULAR TYPES OF CASE

appendix A 42.4, 45.10, 45.14, 45.17, 45.18

Road Accident Cases (Where the Information or Documentation Is Available)

- witness statements (including statements from the parties themselves);
- invoices and estimates for repairs;
- agreements and invoices for any car hire costs;
- the Police accident report;
- sketch plan which should wherever possible be agreed;
- photographs of the scene of the accident and of the damage.

Building Disputes, Repairs, Goods Sold and Similar Contractual Claims (Where the Information or Documentation Is Available)

- any written contract;
- photographs;
- any plans;
- a list of works complained of;
- a list of any outstanding works;
- any relevant estimate, invoice or receipt including any relating to repairs to each of the defects;
- invoices for work done or goods supplied;
- estimates for work to be completed;
- a valuation of work done to date.

Landlord and Tenant Claims (Where the Information or Documentation Is Available)

- a calculation of the amount of any rent alleged to be owing, showing amounts received;
- details of breaches of an agreement which are said to justify withholding any deposit itemised showing how the total is made up and with invoices and estimates to support them.

Breach of Duty Cases (Negligence, Deficient Professional Services and the Like)

Details of the following:

- what it is said by the claimant was done negligently by the defendant;
- why it is said that the negligence is the fault of the defendant;
- what damage is said to have been caused;

- what injury or losses have been suffered and how any (and each) sum claimed has been calculated;
- the response of the defendant to each of the above.

APPENDIX B STANDARD DIRECTIONS

appendix B 45.8, 45.9

(*For use where the district judge specifies no other directions*)

THE COURT DIRECTS:

1 Each party must deliver to every other party and to the court office copies of all documents on which he intends to rely at the hearing no later than [ ] [14 days before the hearing]. (These should include the letter making the claim and the reply.)

2 The original documents must be brought to the hearing.

3 [Notice of hearing date and time allowed.]

4 The parties are encouraged to contact each other with a view to trying to settle the case or narrow the issues. However the court must be informed immediately if the case is settled by agreement before the hearing date.

5 No party may rely at the hearing on any report from an expert unless express permission has been granted by the court beforehand. Anyone wishing to rely on an expert must write to the court immediately on receipt of this Order and seek permission, giving an explanation why the assistance of an expert is necessary.

NOTE: Failure to comply with the directions may result in the case being adjourned and in the party at fault having to pay costs. The parties are encouraged always to try to settle the case by negotiating with each other. The court must be informed immediately if the case is settled before the hearing.

APPENDIX C SPECIAL DIRECTIONS

appendix C 45.15, 45.19

The must clarify his case.

He must do this by delivering to the court office and to the no later than [a list of [details of]

The must allow the to inspect by appointment within days of receiving a request to do so.

The hearing will not take place at the court but at .

The must bring to court at the hearing the .

Signed statements setting out the evidence of all witnesses on whom each party intends to rely must be prepared and copies included in the documents mentioned in paragraph 1. This includes the evidence of the parties themselves and of any other witness, whether or not he is going to come to court to give evidence.

The court may decide not to take into account a document [or video] or the evidence of a witness if these directions have not been complied with.

If he does not [do so] [ ] his [Claim] [Defence] [and Counterclaim] will be struck out and (*specify consequence*).

It appears to the court that expert evidence is necessary on the issue of and that that evidence should be given by a single expert to be instructed by the parties jointly. If the parties cannot agree about who to choose and what arrangements to make about paying his fee, either party MUST apply to the court for further directions. The evidence is to be given in the form of a written report. Either party may ask the expert questions and must then send copies of the questions and replies to the other party and to the court. Oral expert evidence may be allowed in exceptional circumstances but only after a further order of the court. Attention is drawn to the limit of £200 on expert's fees that may be recovered.

If either party intends to show a video as evidence he must:

(a) contact the court at once to make arrangements for him to do so, because the court may not have the necessary equipment, and

(b) provide the other party with a copy of the video or the opportunity to see it at least days before the hearing.

CPR Part 28 The Fast Track

[For commentary on a specific rule, please refer to the cross-references after the title of the rule.]

28.1 Scope of This Part

This Part contains general provisions about management of cases allocated to the fast track and applies only to cases allocated to that track.
(Part 27 sets out the procedure for claims allocated to the small claims track)
(Part 29 sets out the procedure for claims allocated to the multi-track)

28.2 General Provisions

r.28.2(1) **PC 25, 46.3, 50.1**
rr.28.2(2)–(4) **46.13**
r.28.2(2) **46.3**
r.28.2(4) **46.13, 61.1**
r.28.2(5) **46.23**

(1) When it allocates a case to the fast track, the court will give directions for the management of the case and set a timetable for the steps to be taken between the giving of the directions and the trial.
(2) When it gives directions, the court will—
   (a) fix the trial date; or
   (b) fix a period, not exceeding 3 weeks, within which the trial is to take place.
(3) The trial date or trial period will be specified in the notice of allocation.
(4) The standard period between the giving of directions and the trial will be not more than 30 weeks.
(5) The court's power to award trial costs is limited in accordance with Part 46.

28.3 Directions

r.28.3 **PC 25, 46.3, 50.1**
r.28.3(2) **46.4, 50.37**

(1) The matters to be dealt with by directions under rule 28.2(1) include—
   (a) disclosure of documents;
   (b) service of witness statements; and
   (c) expert evidence.
(2) If the court decides not to direct standard disclosure, it may—
   (a) direct that no disclosure take place; or
   (b) specify the documents or the classes of documents which the parties must disclose.
(Rule 31.6 explains what is meant by standard disclosure)
(Rule 26.6(5) deals with limitations in relation to expert evidence and the likely length of trial in fast track cases)

28.4 Variation of Case Management Timetable

r.28.4 **3.7, 48.1**
r.28.4(1) **46.16**
r.28.5(2) **46.16**

(1) A party must apply to the court if he wishes to vary the date which the court has fixed for—
   (a) the return of a pre-trial checklist under rule 28.5;
   (b) the trial; or
   (c) the trial period.
(2) Any date set by the court or these Rules for doing any act may not be varied by the parties if the variation would make it necessary to vary any of the dates mentioned in paragraph (1).
(Rule 2.11 allows the parties to vary a date by written agreement except where the rules provide otherwise or the court orders otherwise)

28.5 Pre-trial Checklist (Listing Questionnaire)

r.28.5(2) **46.3, 46.10**
r.28.5(3)–(5) **46.3**
r.28.5(3) **46.11**
r.28.5(4) **42.4, 46.11**
r.28.5(5) **42.4, 46.11**

(1) The court will send the parties a pre-trial checklist (listing questionnaire) for completion and return by the date specified in the notice of allocation unless it considers that the claim can proceed to trial without the need for a pre-trial checklist.
(2) The date specified for filing a pre-trial checklist will not be more than 8 weeks before the trial date or the beginning of the trial period.
(3) If no party files the completed pre-trial checklist by the date specified, the court will order that unless a completed pre-trial checklist is filed within 7 days from service of that order, the claim, defence and any counterclaim will be struck out without further order of the court.
(4) If—
 (a) a party files a completed pre-trial checklist but another party does not;
 (b) a party has failed to give all the information requested by the pre-trial checklist; or
 (c) the court considers that a hearing is necessary to enable it to decide what directions to give in order to complete preparation of the case for trial,

the court may give such directions as it thinks appropriate.

28.6 Fixing or Confirming the Trial Date and Giving Directions

r.28.6 **61.16**
r.28.6(1) **46.3, 46.17, 61.16**
r.28.6(1)(b) **46.19**
r.28.6(2) **46.13**

(1) As soon as practicable after the date specified for filing a completed pre-trial checklist the court will—
 (a) fix the date for the trial (or, if it has already done so, confirm that date);
 (b) give any directions for the trial, including a trial timetable, which it considers appropriate; and
 (c) specify any further steps that need to be taken before trial.
(2) The court will give the parties at least 3 weeks' notice of the date of the trial unless, in exceptional circumstances, the court directs that shorter notice will be given.

28.7 Conduct of Trial

r.28.7 **61.16**

Unless the trial judge otherwise directs, the trial will be conducted in accordance with any order previously made.

PD 28 Practice Direction 28 — The Fast Track

This practice direction supplements CPR, Part 28.

PD 28 42.34 [For commentary on a specific paragraph, please refer to the cross-references after the title of the paragraph.]

General

1.1 Attention is drawn in particular to the following Parts of the Civil Procedure Rules:

Part 1	The overriding objective
Part 3	The court's case management powers
Part 26	Case management — preliminary stage
Part 31	Disclosure and inspection of documents
Parts 32–34	Evidence
Part 35	Experts and assessors

and to the practice directions which relate to those Parts.

1.2 Attention is also drawn to:

Rule 26.6(5) — which makes provision about limitations on expert evidence and the length of trial in fast track cases.

Part 46 — Fast Track Trial Costs

Rule 19.4A and PD 19A, para. 6, on joining the Crown in certain cases raising Convention rights issues.

Case Management

para.2.3 41.5, 46.3 para.2.8 46.3
para.2.5 32.1, 46.3, 67.2

2.1 Case management of cases allocated to the fast track will generally be by directions given at two stages in the case:

(1) at allocation to the track, and

(2) on the filing of pre-trial checklists (listing questionnaires).

2.2 The court will seek whenever possible to give directions at those stages only and to do so without the need for a hearing to take place. It will expect to do so with the cooperation of the parties.

2.3 The court will however hold a hearing to give directions whenever it appears necessary or desirable to do so, and where this happens because of the default of a party or his legal repre sentative it will usually impose a sanction.

2.4 The court may give directions at any hearing on the application of a party or on its own initiative.

2.5 When any hearing has been fixed it is the duty of the parties to consider what directions the court should be asked to give and to make any application that may be appropriate to be dealt with at that hearing.

2.6 When the court fixes a hearing to give directions it will give the parties at least 3 days' notice of the hearing.

2.7 Appendix A contains forms of directions. When making an order the court will as far as possible base its order on those forms. Agreed directions which the parties file and invite the court to make should also be based on those forms.

2.8 Where a party needs to apply for a direction of a kind not included in the case management timetable which has been set (for example to amend his statement of case or for further information to be given by another party) he must do so as soon as possible so as to minimise the need to change that timetable.

2.9 Courts will make arrangements to ensure that applications and other hearings are listed promptly to avoid delay in the conduct of cases.

Directions on Allocation

3.1 Attention is drawn to the court's duty under rule 28.2(2) to set a case management timetable and to fix a trial date or a trial period, and to the matters which are to be dealt with by directions under Rule 28.3(1).

3.2 The court will seek to tailor its directions to the needs of the case and the steps of which it is aware that the parties have already taken to prepare the case. In particular it will have regard to the extent to which PD Pre-action Conduct or any pre-action protocol has or (as the case may be) has not been complied with.

3.3 At this stage the court's first concern will be to ensure that the issues between the parties be identified and that the necessary evidence is prepared and disclosed.

3.4 The court may have regard to any document filed by a party with their directions questionnaire containing further information provided that the document states either that its contents have been agreed with every other party or that it has been served on every other party and when it was served.

3.5 If:
(1) the parties have filed agreed directions for the management of the case, and
(2) the court considers that the proposals are suitable,
it may approve them and give directions in the terms proposed.

3.6 (1) To obtain the court's approval the agreed directions must:
(a) set out a timetable by reference to calendar dates for the taking of steps for the preparation of the case,
(b) include a date or a period (the trial period) when it is proposed that the trial will take place,
(c) include provision about disclosure of documents, and
(d) include provision about both factual and expert evidence.
(2) The latest proposed date for the trial or the end of the trial period must be not later than 30 weeks from the date the directions order is made.
(3) The trial period must not be longer than 3 weeks.
(4) The provision in (1)(c) above may:
(a) limit disclosure to standard disclosure between all parties or to less than that, and/or
(b) direct that disclosure will take place by the supply of copy documents without a list, but it must in that case either direct that the parties must serve a disclosure statement with the copies or record that they have agreed to disclose in that way without such a statement.
(5) The provision in (1)(d) may be to the effect that no expert evidence is required.

3.7 Directions agreed by the parties should also where appropriate contain provisions about:
(1) the filing of any reply or amended statement of case that may be required,
(2) dates for the service of requests for further information under PD 18 and questions to experts under rule 35.6 and when they are to be dealt with,
(3) the disclosure of evidence,
(4) the use of a single joint expert, or in cases where the use of a single expert has not been agreed the exchange and agreement of expert evidence (including whether exchange is to be simultaneous or sequential) and without-prejudice discussions of the experts.

3.8 If the court does not approve the agreed directions filed by the parties but decides that it will give directions on its own initiative without a hearing, it will take them into account in deciding what directions to give.

3.9 Where the court is to give directions on its own initiative and it is not aware of any steps taken by the parties other than the service of statements of case, its general approach will be:
(1) to give directions for the filing and service of any further information required to clarify either party's case,

(2) to direct standard disclosure between the parties,
(3) to direct the disclosure of witness statements by way of simultaneous exchange.
(4) to give directions for a single joint expert unless there is good reason not to do so,
(5) in cases where directions for a single expert are not given:
(a) to direct disclosure of experts' reports byway of simultaneous exchange, and
(b) if experts' reports are not agreed, to direct a discussion between the experts for the purpose set out in rule 35.12(1) and the preparation of a report under rule 35.12(3).

3.10 (1) If it appears to the court that the claim is one which will be allocated to the fast track but that it cannot properly give directions on its own initiative or approve agreed directions that have been filed, the court may either:
(a) allocate the claim to the fast track, fix a trial date or trial period and direct that a case management hearing is to be listed and give directions at that hearing, or
(b) direct that an allocation hearing is to be listed and give directions at that hearing.
(2) In either case the hearing will be listed as promptly as possible.

3.11 Where the court is proposing on its own initiative to make an order under rule 35.15 (which gives the court power to appoint an assessor), the court must, unless the parties have consented in writing to the order, list a directions hearing.

3.12 The table set out below contains a typical timetable the court may give for the preparation of the case.

Disclosure	4 weeks
Exchange of witness statements	10 weeks
Exchange of experts'reports	14 weeks
Sending of pre-trial checklists (listing questionnaires) by the court	20 weeks
Filing of completed pre-trial checklists	22 weeks
Hearing	30 weeks

These periods will run from the date of the notice of allocation.

3.13 (1) Where it considers that some or all of the steps in that timetable are not necessary the court may omit them and direct an earlier trial.
(2) This may happen where the court is informed that PD Pre-action Conduct or any pre-action protocol has been complied with or that steps which it would otherwise order to be taken have already been taken.
(3) It may also happen where an application (for example for summary judgment or for an injunction) has been heard before allocation and little or no further preparation is required. In such a case the court may dispense with the need for a pre-trial checklist.

Variation of Directions

para.4.2(1) **46.16**
para.4.2(2) **32.25, 46.16, 48.2**
para.4.3(1) **46.16**
para.4.3(2) **46.16**
para.4.3(3) **46.16**
para.4.5 **3.7**
para.4.5(1) **46.16**

4.1 This paragraph deals with the procedure to be adopted:
(1) where a party is dissatisfied with a direction given by the court,
(2) where the parties agree about changes they wish made to the directions given, or
(3) where a party wishes to apply to vary a direction.

4.2 (1) It is essential that any party who wishes to have a direction varied takes steps to do so as soon as possible.
(2) The court will assume for the purposes of any later application that a party who did not appeal and who made no application to vary within 14 days of service of the order containing the directions was content that they were correct in the circumstances then existing.

4.3 (1) Where a party is dissatisfied with a direction given or other order made by the court he may appeal or apply to the court for it to reconsider its decision.
(2) He should appeal if the direction was given or the order was made at a hearing at which he was present or represented, or of which he had due notice.
(3) In any other case he should apply to the court to reconsider its decision.
(4) If an application is made for the court to reconsider its decision:
(a) it will usually be heard by the judge who gave the directions or another judge of the same level,

(b) the court will give all parties at least 3 days' notice of the hearing, and
(c) the court may confirm its decision or make a different order.

4.4 Where there has been a change in the circumstances since the order was made the court may set aside or vary any direction it has given. It may do so on application or on its own initiative.

4.5 Where the parties agree about changes to be made to the directions given:
(1) If r. 2.11 (variation by agreement of a date set by the court for doing any act other than those stated in the note to that rule) or r. 31.5, 31.10(8) or 31.13 (agreements about disclosure) applied the parties need not file the written agreement.
(2) (a) In any other case the parties must apply for an order by consent.
(b) The parties must file a draft of the order sought and an agreed statement of the reasons why the variation is sought.
(c) The court may make an order in the agreed terms or in other terms without a hearing, but it may direct that a hearing is to be listed.

Failure to Comply with Case Management Directions

paras.5.1–5.3 **48.4**
para.5.4 **48.6, 61.11**
para.5.4(1) **42.36**
para.5.4(4) **46.16**
para.5.4(6) **46.16, 58.1**

5.1 Where a party has failed to comply with a direction given by the court any other party may apply for an order to enforce compliance or for a sanction to be imposed or both of these.

5.2 The party entitled to apply for such an order must do so without delay but should first warn the other party of his intention to do so.

5.3 The court may take any such delay into account when it decides whether to make an order imposing a sanction or whether to grant relief from a sanction imposed by the rules or any practice direction.

5.4 (1) The court will not allow a failure to comply with directions to lead to the postponement of the trial unless the circumstances of the case are exceptional.
(2) If it is practicable to do so the court will exercise its powers in a manner that enables the case to come on for trial on the date or within the period previously set.
(3) In particular the court will assess what steps each party should take to prepare the case for trial, direct that those steps are taken in the shortest possible time and impose a sanction for non-compliance. Such a sanction may, for example, deprive a party of the right to raise or contest an issue or to rely on evidence to which the direction relates.
(4) Where it appears that one or more issues are or can be made ready for trial at the time fixed while others cannot, the court may direct that the trial will proceed on the issues which are or will then be ready, and order that no costs will be allowed for any later trial of the remaining issues or that those costs will be paid by the party in default.
(5) Where the court has no option but to postpone the trial it will do so for the shortest possible time and will give directions for the taking of the necessary steps in the meantime as rapidly as possible.
(6) Litigants and lawyers must be in no doubt that the court will regard the postponement of a trial as an order of last resort. The court may exercise its power to require a party as well as his legal representative to attend court at a hearing where such an order is to be sought.

Pre-trial Checklists (Listing Questionnaires)

para.6.3 **46.11, 46.17**

6.1 (1) The pre-trial checklist (listing questionnaire) will be in form N170.
(2) Unless it has dispensed with listing questionnaires, the court will send forms N170 and N171 (notice of date for return of the listing questionnaire) to each party no later than two weeks before the date specified in the notice of allocation or in any later direction of the court for the return of the completed questionnaires.
(3) When all the pre-trial checklists have been filed or when the time for filing them has expired *and where a party has filed* a pre-trial checklist but another party has not done so, the file will be placed before a judge for his directions.

(4) Although the CPR do not require the parties to exchange copies of the checklists before they are filed they are encouraged to do so to avoid the court being given conflicting or incomplete information.

Attention is drawn to PD 43–48, Section 6, which requires a costs estimate to be filed and served at the same time as the pre-trial checklist is filed.

6.2 Attention is drawn to r. 28.6(1) (which sets out the court's duty at the pre-trial checklist stage) and to r. 28.5(4) (which sets out circumstances in which the court may decide to hold a hearing).

6.3 Where the judge decides to hold a hearing under r. 28.5(4) the court will fix a date which is as early as possible and the parties will be given at least three days' notice of the date.
The notice of such a hearing will be in form N153.

6.4 The court's general approach will be as set out in the following paragraphs. The court may however decide to make other orders, and in particular the court will take into account the steps, if any, which the parties have taken to prepare the case for trial.

6.5 (1) Where no party files a pre-trial checklist the court will order that unless a completed pre-trial checklist is filed within seven days from service of that order, the claim, defence and any counterclaim will be struck out.

(2) Where a party files a pre-trial checklist but another party does not do so, the court normally will give directions. These will usually fix or confirm the trial date and provide for steps to be taken to prepare the case for trial.

Directions the Court Will Give on Listing

para.7.2(1) **46.17** para.7.2(4) **46.18**

7.1 Directions the court must give:

(1) The court must confirm or fix the trial date, specify the place of trial and give a time estimate. The trial date must be fixed and the case listed on the footing that the hearing will end on the same calendar day as that on which it commenced.

(2) The court will serve a notice of hearing on the parties at least three weeks before the hearing unless they agree to accept shorter notice or the court authorises shorter service under r. 28.6(2), and

(3) The notice of hearing will be in form N172.

7.2 Other directions:

(1) The parties should seek to agree directions and may file the proposed order. The court may make an order in those terms or it may make a different order.

(2) Agreed directions should include provision about:
(a) evidence,
(b) a trial timetable and time estimate,
(c) the preparation of a trial bundle,
(d) any other matter needed to prepare the case for trial.

(3) The court will include such of these provisions as are appropriate in any order that it may make, whether or not the parties have filed agreed directions.

(4) (a) A direction giving permission to use expert evidence will say whether it gives permission for oral evidence or reports or both and will name the experts concerned.
(b) The court will not make a direction giving permission for an expert to give oral evidence unless it believes it is necessary in the interests of justice to do so.
(c) Where no 'without prejudice' meeting or other discussion between experts has taken place the court may grant that permission conditionally on such a discussion taking place and a report being filed before the trial.

7.3 The principles set out in para. 4 of this practice direction about the variation of directions apply also to directions given at this stage.

The Trial

para.8.1 **61.25** para.8.3 **46.22, 61.16**
para.8.2 **61.41** para.8.6 **46.22**

CPR 26–50 & PDs

8.1 The trial will normally take place at the court where the case is being managed, but it may be at another court if it is appropriate having regard to the needs of the parties and the availability of court resources.

8.2 The judge will generally have read the papers in the trial bundle and may dispense with an opening address.

8.3 The judge may confirm or vary any timetable given previously, or if none has been given set his own.

8.4 Attention is drawn to the provisions in Part 32 and the following parts of the Rules about evidence, and in particular—
(1) to rule 32.1 (court's power to control evidence and to restrict cross-examination), and
(2) to rule 32.5(2) (witness statements to stand as evidence-in-chief).

8.5 At the conclusion of the trial the judge will normally summarily assess the costs of the claim in accordance with rule 44.7 and Part 46 (fast track trial costs). Attention is drawn to the steps the practice directions about costs require the parties to take.

8.6 Where a trial is not finished on the day for which it is listed the judge will normally sit on the next court day to complete it.

APPENDIX FAST TRACK STANDARD DIRECTIONS

app. 42.4, 46.3, 46.17, 46.20

Further Statements of Case

The must file a and serve a copy on no later than .

Requests for Further Information

Any request for clarification or further information based on another party's statement of case shall be served no later than .
[Any such request shall be dealt with no later than].

Disclosure of Documents

[No disclosure of documents is required].
[[Each party] [The]
shall give [to the]
[to every other party] standard disclosure of documents
[relating to]
by serving copies together with a disclosure statement no later than].
[Disclosure shall take place as follows:
[Each party shall give standard discovery to every other party by list]
[Disclosure is limited to [standard] [disclosure by the to the]
[of documents relating to damage]
[the following documents].
[The latest date for delivery of the lists is]
[The latest date for service of any request to inspect or for a copy of a document is]].

Witnesses of Fact

Each party shall serve on every other party the witness statements of all witnesses of fact on whom he intends to rely.
There shall be simultaneous exchange of such statements no later than .

Expert Evidence

[No expert evidence being necessary, no party has permission to call or rely on expert evidence].
[On it appearing to the court that expert evidence is necessary on the issue of
[ ]

and that that evidence should be given by the report of a single expert instructed jointly by the parties, the shall no later than inform the court whether or not such an expert has been instructed].

[The expert evidence on the issue of
shall be limited to a single expert
jointly instructed by the parties.
If the parties cannot agree by who that expert is to be and about the payment of his fees either party may apply for further directions.
Unless the parties agree in writing or the court orders otherwise, the fees and expenses of such an expert shall be paid to him [by the parties equally]
[ ] and be limited to £ .
[The report of the expert shall be filed at the court no later than].
[No party shall be entitled to recover by way of costs from any other party more than £ for the fees or expenses of an expert].
The parties shall exchange reports setting out the substance of any expert evidence on which they intend to rely.
[The exchange shall take place simultaneously no later than].
[The shall serve his report(s) no later than the and the shall serve his reports no later than the].
[The exchange of reports relating to [causation] [ ]
shall take place simultaneously no later than .
The shall serve his report(s) relating to [damage] [ ] no later than
and the shall serve his reports relating to it no later than].
Reports shall be agreed if possible no later than [days after service] [ ].
[If the reports are not agreed within that time there shall be a without prejudice discussion between the relevant experts no later than
to identify the issues between them and to reach agreement if possible.
The experts shall prepare for the court a statement of the issues on which they agree and on which they disagree with a summary of their reasons, and that statement shall be filed with the court [no later than] [with] [no later than the date for filing] [the listing questionnaire].
[Each party has permission to use [ ] as expert witness(es) to give [oral] evidence [in the form of a report] at the trial in the field of provided that the substance of the evidence to be given has been disclosed as above and has not been agreed].
[Each party has permission to use in evidence experts' report(s) [and the court will consider when the claim is listed for trial whether expert oral evidence will be allowed].]
(See PD 35, paras 6, 7 and 9.)

Questions to Experts

The time for service on another party of any question addressed to an expert instructed by that party is not later than days after service of that expert's report.
Any such question shall be answered within days of service.

Requests for Information etc.

Each party shall serve any request for clarification or further information based on any document disclosed or statement served by another party no later than days after disclosure or service.
Any such request shall be dealt with within days of service.

Documents to be Filed with Pre-trial Checklists

The parties must file with their listing questionnaires* copies of [their experts' reports] [witness statements] [replies to requests for further information]

Dates for Filing Pre-trial Checklists and the Trial

Each party must file a completed pre-trial checklist no later than .
The trial of this case will take place [on] [on a date to be fixed between and].

Directions Following Filing of Pre-trial Checklist

Expert evidence

The parties have permission to rely at the trial on expert evidence as follows:

The claimant: Oral evidence—
Written evidence—

The defendant: Oral evidence—
Written evidence—

Trial timetable

The time allowed for the trial is
[The timetable for the trial may be agreed by the parties, subject to the approval of the trial judge].
[The timetable for the trial (subject to the approval of the trial judge) will be that].
[The evidence-in-chief for each party will be contained in witness statements and reports, the time allowed for cross-examination by the defendant is limited to
and the time allowed for cross-examination by the claimant is limited to].
[The time allowed for the claimant's evidence is . The time allowed for the defendant's evidence is].
The time allowed for the submissions on behalf of each party is .
The remainder of the time allowed for the trial (being) is reserved for the judge to consider and give the judgment and to deal with costs].

Trial bundle etc.

The claimant shall lodge an indexed bundle of documents contained in a ring binder and with each page clearly numbered at the court not more than 7 days and not less than 3 days before the start of the trial.
[A case summary (which should not exceed 250 words) outlining the matters still in issue, and referring where appropriate to the relevant documents shall be included in the bundle for the assistance of the judge in reading the papers before the trial].
[The parties shall seek to agree the contents of the trial bundle and the case summary].

Settlement

Each party must inform the court immediately if the claim is settled whether or not it is then possible to file a draft consent order to give effect to their agreement.

[* In the text issued by the Ministry of Justice the old term 'listing questionnaires' has not been changed to 'pre-trial checklists'.]

CPR Part 29 The Multi-track

Part 29 **13.14, 72.9, 86.18** [For commentary on a specific rule, please refer to the cross-references after the title of the rule.]

29.1 Scope of This Part

r.29.1(2) **42.4, 42.15, 47.6, 47.8, 52.15, 54.15**

(1) This Part contains general provisions about management of cases allocated to the multi-track and applies only to cases allocated to that track.
(Part 27 sets out the procedure for claims allocated to the small claims track)
(Part 28 sets out the procedure for claims allocated to the fast track)
(2) When drafting case management directions both the parties and the court should take as their starting point any relevant model directions and standard directions which can be found online at www.justice.gov.uk/courts/procedure-rules/civil and adapt them as appropriate to the circumstances of the particular case.

29.2 Case Management

r.29.2 **50.37**
r.29.2(1) **47.3**
r.29.2(1)(a)–(b) **PC 25, 50.1**
r.29.2(2) **47.12, 47.16, 61.1, 61.4, 61.5**
r.29.2(3) **47.16**

(1) When it allocates a case to the multi-track, the court will—
(a) give directions for the management of the case and set a timetable for the steps to be taken between the giving of directions and the trial; or may
(b) fix—
(i) a case management conference; or
(ii) a pre-trial review,
or both, and give such other directions relating to the management of the case as it sees fit.
(2) The court will fix the trial date or the period in which the trial is to take place as soon as practicable.
(3) When the court fixes the trial date or the trial period under paragraph (2), it will—
(a) give notice to the parties of the date or period; and
(b) specify the date by which the parties must file a pre-trial checklist.

29.3 Case Management Conference and Pre-trial Review

r.29.3(2) **1.40, 47.9, 61.8**

(1) The court may fix—
(a) a case management conference; or
(b) a pre-trial review,
at any time after the claim has been allocated.
(2) If a party has a legal representative, a representative—
(a) familiar with the case; and
(b) with sufficient authority to deal with any issues that are likely to arise,
must attend case management conferences and pre-trial reviews.
(Rule 3.1(2)(c) provides that the court may require a party to attend the court)

29.4 Steps Taken by the Parties

r.29.4 **47.6**

The parties must endeavour to agree appropriate directions for the management of the proceedings and submit agreed directions, or their respective proposals to the court at least seven days before any case management conference. Where the court approves agreed directions, or issues its own directions, the parties will be so notified by the court and the case management conference will be vacated.

29.5 Variation of Case Management Timetable

r.29.5 3.7, 48.1, 86.14 r.29.5(1) 47.30

(1) A party must apply to the court if he wishes to vary the date which the court has fixed for—
 (a) a case management conference;
 (b) a pre-trial review;
 (c) the return of a pre-trial checklist under rule 29.6;
 (d) the trial; or
 (e) the trial period.
(2) Any date set by the court or these Rules for doing any act may not be varied by the parties if the variation would make it necessary to vary any of the dates mentioned in paragraph (1).

(Rule 2.11 allows the parties to vary a date by written agreement except where the rules provide otherwise or the court orders otherwise)

29.6 Pre-trial Checklist (Listing Questionnaire)

r.29.6 47.17 r.29.6(3) 47.20
r.29.6(1) 47.16 r.29.6(4) 42.4, 47.20

(1) The court will send the parties a pre-trial checklist (listing questionnaire) for completion and return by the date specified in directions given under rule 29.2(3) unless it considers that the claim can proceed to trial without the need for a pre-trial checklist.
(2) Each party must file the completed pre-trial checklist by the date specified by the court.
(3) If no party files the completed pre-trial checklist by the date specified, the court will order that unless a completed pre-trial checklist is filed within 7 days from service of that order, the claim, defence and any counterclaim will be struck out without further order of the court.
(4) If—
 (a) a party files a completed pre-trial checklist but another party does not;
 (b) a party has failed to give all the information requested by the pre-trial checklist; or
 (c) the court considers that a hearing is necessary to enable it to decide what directions to give in order to complete preparation of the case for trial,

 the court may give such directions as it thinks appropriate.

29.7 Pre-trial Review

r.29.7 47.24

If, on receipt of the parties' pre-trial checklists, the court decides—
(a) to hold a pre-trial review; or
(b) to cancel a pre-trial review which has already been fixed,

it will serve notice of its decision at least 7 days before the date fixed for the hearing or, as the case may be, the cancelled hearing.

29.8 Setting a Trial Timetable and Fixing or Confirming the Trial Date or Week

r.29.8 61.16 r.29.8(ii) 44.13, 61.4
r.29.8(i) 61.16

As soon as practicable after—
 (a) each party has filed a completed pre-trial checklist;
 (b) the court has held a listing hearing under rule 29.6(3); or
 (c) the court has held a pre-trial review under rule 29.7,

the court will—
 (i) set a timetable for the trial unless a timetable has already been fixed, or the court considers that it would be inappropriate to do so;
 (ii) confirm the date for trial or the week within which the trial is to begin; and

(iii) notify the parties of the trial timetable (where one is fixed under this rule) and the date or trial period.

29.9 Conduct of Trial

r.29.9 61.16

Unless the trial judge otherwise directs, the trial will be conducted in accordance with any order previously made.

PD 29 Practice Direction 29 — The Multi-track

This practice direction supplements CPR, Part 29.

[For commentary on a specific paragraph, please refer to the cross-references after the title of the paragraph.]

General

1.1 Attention is drawn in particular to the following Parts of the Civil Procedure Rules:

Part 1	The overriding objective
Part 3	The court's case management powers
Part 26	Case management — preliminary stage
Part 31	Disclosure and inspection of documents
Parts 32 to 34	Evidence
Part 35	Experts and assessors

and to the practice directions which relate to those Parts.

Case Management in the Royal Courts of Justice

para.2 47.1
para.2.2 11.4, 42.32
para.2.6 11.4

2.1 This part of the practice direction applies to claims begun by claim form issued in the Central Office or Chancery Chambers in the Royal Courts of Justice.

2.2 A claim with an estimated value of less than £50,000 will generally, unless:
(a) it is required by an enactment to be tried in the High Court,
(b) it falls within a specialist list, or
(c) it falls within one of the categories specified in 2.6 below or is otherwise within the criteria of article 7(5) of the High Court and County Courts Jurisdiction Order 1991,
be transferred to a county court.

2.3 Paragraph 2.2 is without prejudice to the power of the court in accordance with Part 30 to transfer to a county court a claim with an estimated value that exceeds £50,000.

2.4 The decision to transfer may be made at any stage in the proceedings but should, subject to paragraph 2.5, be made as soon as possible and in any event not later than the date for the filing of pre-trial checklists (listing questionnaires).

2.5 If an application is made under rule 3.4 (striking out) or under Part 24 (summary judgment) or under Part 25 (interim remedies), it will usually be convenient for the application to be dealt with before a decision to transfer is taken.

2.6 Each party should state in his directions questionnaire whether he considers the claim should be managed and tried at the Royal Courts of Justice and, if so, why. Claims suitable for trial in the Royal Courts of Justice include:
(1) professional negligence claims,
(2) Fatal Accident Act claims,
(3) fraud or undue influence claims,
(4) defamation claims,
(5) claims for malicious prosecution or false imprisonment,
(6) claims against the police,
(7) contentious probate claims.
Such claims may fall within the criteria of article 7(5) of the High Court and County Courts Jurisdiction Order 1991.

2.7 Attention is drawn to PD 30.

Case Management — General Provisions

para.3.1 **47.1**
para.3.2(2) **47.1**
para.3.4 **47.28, 47.32**
para.3.5 **32.1, 47.1, 47.28, 67.2**
para.3.6 **47.28, 48.12**
para.3.7 **47.8**
para.3.8 **32.6, 47.28**
para.3.10 **2.6, 2.13, 42.5**

3.1 (1) Case management of a claim which is proceeding at the Royal Courts of Justice will be undertaken there.
(2) (a) Case management of any other claim which has been allocated to the multi-track will normally be undertaken at a civil trial centre,
(b) PD 26 provides for what will happen in the case of a claim which is issued in or transferred to a court which is not a civil trial centre.

3.2 The hallmarks of the multi-track are:
(1) the ability of the court to deal with cases of widely differing values and complexity, and
(2) the flexibility given to the court in the way it will manage a case in a way appropriate to its particular needs.

3.3 (1) On allocating a claim to the multi-track the court may give directions without a hearing, including fixing a trial date or a period in which the trial will take place,
(2) Alternatively, whether or not it fixes a trial date or period, it may either—
(a) give directions for certain steps to be taken and fix a date for a case management conference or a pre-trial review to take place after they have been taken, or
(b) fix a date for a case management conference.
(3) Attention is drawn to rule 29.2(2) which requires the court to fix a trial date or period as soon as practicable.

3.4 The court may give or vary directions at any hearing which may take place on the application of a party or of its own initiative.

3.5 When any hearing has been fixed it is the duty of the parties to consider what directions the court should be asked to give and to make any application that may be appropriate to be dealt with then.

3.6 The court will hold a hearing to give directions whenever it appears necessary or desirable to do so, and where this happens because of the default of a party or his legal representative it will usually impose a sanction.

3.7 When the court fixes a hearing to give directions it will give the parties at least 3 days' notice of the hearing unless rule 29.7 applies (7 days' notice to be given in the case of a pre-trial review).

3.8 Where a party needs to apply for a direction of a kind not included in the case management timetable which has been set (for example to amend his statement of case or for further information to be given by another party) he must do so as soon as possible so as to minimise the need to change that timetable.

3.9 Courts will make arrangements to ensure that applications and other hearings are listed promptly to avoid delay in the conduct of cases.

3.10 (1) Case management will generally be dealt with by:
(a) a master in cases proceeding in the Royal Courts of Justice,
(b) a district judge in cases proceeding in a district registry of the High Court, and
(c) a district judge or a circuit judge in cases proceeding in a county court.
(2) A master or a district judge may consult and seek the directions of a judge of a higher level about any aspect of case management.
(3) A member of the court staff who is dealing with the listing of a hearing may seek the directions of any judge about any aspect of that listing.

Case Management: Consideration of Periodical Payments

3A Attention is drawn to PD 41B and in particular to the direction that in a personal injury claim the court should consider and indicate to the parties as soon as practicable whether periodical payments or a lump sum is likely to be the more appropriate form for all or part of an award of damages for future pecuniary loss.

Directions on Allocation

4.1 Attention is drawn to the court's duties under Rule 29.2.

4.2 The court will seek to tailor its directions to the needs of the case and the steps which the parties have already taken to prepare the case of which it is aware. In particular it will have regard to the extent to which PD Pre-action Conduct or any pre-action protocol has or (as the case may be) has not been complied with.

4.3 At this stage the court's first concern will be to ensure that the issues between the parties are identified and that the necessary evidence is prepared and disclosed.

4.4 The court may have regard to any document filed by a party with his directions questionnaire containing further information, provided that the document states either that its contents has been agreed with every other party or that it has been served on every other party, and when it was served.

4.5 On the allocation of a claim to the multi-track the court will consider whether it is desirable or necessary to hold a case management conference straight away, or whether it is appropriate instead to give directions on its own initiative.

4.6 The parties and their advisers are encouraged to try to agree directions and to take advantage of rule 29.4 which provides that if:

(1) the parties agree proposals for the management of the proceedings (including a proposed trial date or period in which the trial is to take place), and

(2) the court considers that the proposals are suitable,

it may approve them without a hearing and give directions in the terms proposed.

4.7 (1) To obtain the court's approval the agreed directions must:

(a) set out a timetable by reference to calendar dates for the taking of steps for the preparation of the case,

(b) include a date or a period (the trial period) when it is proposed that the trial will take place,

(c) include provision about disclosure of documents, and

(d) include provision about both factual and expert evidence.

(2) The court will scrutinise the timetable carefully and in particular will be concerned to see that any proposed date or period for the trial and (if provided for) for a case management conference is no later than is reasonably necessary.

(3) The provision in (1)(c) above may:

(a) limit disclosure to standard disclosure or less than that, and/or

(b) direct that disclosure will take place by the supply of copy documents without a list, but it must in that case say either that the parties must serve a disclosure statement with the copies or that they have agreed to disclose in that way without such a statement.

(4) The provision in (1)(d) about expert evidence may be to the effect that none is required.

4.8 Directions agreed by the parties should also where appropriate contain provisions about:

(1) the filing of any reply or amended statement of case that may be required,

(2) dates for the service of requests for further information under PD 18 and of questions to experts under rule 35.6 and by when they are to be dealt with,

(3) the disclosure of evidence,

(4) the use of a single joint expert, or in cases where it is not agreed, the exchange of expert evidence (including whether exchange is to be simultaneous or sequential) and without prejudice discussions between experts.

(See PD 35, paras 6, 7 and 9.)

4.9 If the court does not approve the agreed directions filed by the parties but decides that it will give directions of its own initiative without fixing a case management conference, it will take them into account in deciding what directions to give.

4.10 Where the court is to give directions on its own initiative without holding a case management conference and it is not aware of any steps taken by the parties other than the exchange of statements of case, its general approach will be:

(1) to give directions for the filing and service of any further information required to clarify either party's case,
(2) to direct standard disclosure between the parties,
(3) to direct the disclosure of witness statements by way of simultaneous exchange,
(4) to give directions for a single joint expert on any appropriate issue unless there is a good reason not to do so,
(5) unless para. 4.11 (below) applies, to direct disclosure of experts' reports by way of simultaneous exchange on those issues where a single joint expert is not directed,
(6) if experts' reports are not agreed, to direct a discussion between experts for the purpose set out in r. 35.12(1) and the preparation of a statement under r. 35.12(3),
(7) to list a case management conference to take place after the date for compliance with those directions,
(8) to specify a trial period, and
(9) in such cases as the court thinks appropriate, the court may give directions requiring the parties to consider ADR. Such directions may be, for example, in the following terms:

'The parties shall by [date] consider whether the case is capable of resolution by ADR. If any party considers that the case is unsuitable for resolution by ADR, that party shall be prepared to justify that decision at the conclusion of the trial, should the judge consider that such means of resolution were appropriate, when he is considering the appropriate costs order to make.

The party considering the case unsuitable for ADR shall, not less than 28 days before the commencement of the trial, file with the court a witness statement without prejudice save as to costs, giving reasons upon which they rely for saying that the case was unsuitable.'

4.11 If it appears that expert evidence will be required both on issues of liability and on the amount of damages, the court may direct that the exchange of those reports that relate to liability will be exchanged simultaneously but that those relating to the amount of damages will be exchanged sequentially.

4.12 (1) If it appears to the court that it cannot properly give directions on its own initiative and no agreed directions have been filed which it can approve, the court will direct a case management conference to be listed.
(2) The conference will be listed as promptly as possible.

4.13 Where the court is proposing on its own initiative to make an order under r. 35.7 (which gives the court power to direct that evidence on a particular issue is to be given by a single expert) or under r. 35.15 (which gives the court power to appoint an assessor), the court must, unless the parties have consented in writing to the order, list a case management conference.

Case Management Conferences

para.5.1 47.10
para.5.2(3) 47.9
para.5.3 47.12
para.5.4 47.12
para.5.6 47.10, 47.11, 61.5, 61.17
para.5.7 47.11, 61.5, 61.17
para.5.8 32.6, 47.13
para.5.9 47.12

5.1 The court will at any case management conference:

(1) review the steps which the parties have taken in the preparation of the case, and in particular their compliance with any directions that the court may have given,
(2) decide and give directions about the steps which are to be taken to secure the progress of the claim in accordance with the overriding objective, and
(3) ensure as far as it can that all agreements that can be reached between the parties about the matters in issue and the conduct of the claim are made and recorded.

5.2 (1) Rule 29.3(2) provides that where a party has a legal representative, a representative familiar with the case and with sufficient authority to deal with any issues that are likely to arise must attend case management conferences and pre-trial reviews.
(2) That person should be someone who is personally involved in the conduct of the case, and who has the authority and information to deal with any matter which may reasonably be

expected to be dealt with at such a hearing, including the fixing of the timetable, the identification of issues and matters of evidence.

(3) Where the inadequacy of the person attending or of his instructions leads to the adjournment of a hearing, the court will expect to make a wasted costs order.

5.3 The topics the court will consider at a case management conference are likely to include:

(1) whether the claimant has made clear the claim he is bringing, in particular the amount he is claiming, so that the other party can understand the case he has to meet,

(2) whether any amendments are required to the claim, a statement of case or any other document,

(3) what disclosure of documents, if any, is necessary,

(4) what expert evidence is reasonably required in accordance with rule 35.1 and how and when that evidence should be obtained and disclosed,

(5) what factual evidence should be disclosed,

(6) what arrangements should be made about the giving of clarification or further information and the putting of questions to experts, and

(7) whether it will be just and will save costs to order a split trial or the trial of one or more preliminary issues.

5.4 In all cases the court will set a timetable for the steps it decides are necessary to be taken. These steps may include the holding of a case management conference or a pre-trial review, and the court will be alert to perform its duty to fix a trial date or period as soon as it can.

5.5 (1) The court will not at this stage give permission to use expert evidence unless it can identify each expert by name or field in its order and say whether his evidence is to be given orally or by the use of his report.

(2) A party who obtains expert evidence before obtaining a direction about it does so at his own risk as to costs, except where he obtained the evidence in compliance with a pre-action protocol.

5.6 To assist the court, the parties and their legal advisers should:

(1) ensure that all documents that the court is likely to ask to see (including witness statements and experts' reports) are brought to the hearing,

(2) consider whether the parties should attend,

(3) consider whether a case summary will be useful, and

(4) consider what orders each wishes to be made and give notice of them to the other parties.

5.7 (1) A case summary:

(a) should be designed to assist the court to understand and deal with the questions before it,

(b) should set out a brief chronology of the claim, the issues of fact which are agreed or in dispute and the evidence needed to decide them,

(c) should not normally exceed 500 words in length, and

(d) should be prepared by the claimant and agreed with the other parties if possible.

5.8 (1) Where a party wishes to obtain an order not routinely made at a case management conference and believes that his application will be opposed, he should issue and serve the application in time for it to be heard at the case management conference.

(2) If the time allowed for the case management conference is likely to be insufficient for the application to be heard he should inform the court at once so that a fresh date can be fixed.

(3) A costs sanction may be imposed on a party who fails to comply with sub-paragraph (1) or (2).

5.9 At a case management conference the court may also consider whether the case ought to be tried by a High Court judge or by a judge who specialises in that type of claim and how that question will be decided. In that case the claim may need to be transferred to another court.

Variation of Directions

para.6 47.26
para.6.2 32.6, 47.29
para.6.2(2) 32.25, 47.5, 48.2
para.6.3 47.33
para.6.3(2) 47.34
para.6.4 45.32
para.6.5 3.7
para.6.5(1) 47.30
para.6.5(2) 47.31

6.1 This paragraph deals with the procedure to be adopted:

(1) where a party is dissatisfied with a direction given by the court,

(2) where the parties have agreed about changes they wish made to the directions given, or
(3) where a party wishes to apply to vary a direction.

6.2 (1) It is essential that any party who wishes to have a direction varied takes steps to do so as soon as possible.
(2) The court will assume for the purposes of any later application that a party who did not appeal, and who made no application to vary within 14 days of service of the order containing the directions, was content that they were correct in the circumstances then existing.

6.3 (1) Where a party is dissatisfied with a direction given or other order made by the court he may appeal or apply to the court for it to reconsider its decision.
(2) Unless paragraph 6.4 applies, a party should appeal if the direction was given or the order was made at a hearing at which he was present, or of which he had due notice.
(3) In any other case he should apply to the court to reconsider its decision.
(4) If an application is made for the court to reconsider its decision:
(a) it will usually be heard by the judge who gave the directions or another judge of the same level,
(b) the court will give all parties at least 3 days' notice of the hearing, and
(c) the court may confirm its directions or make a different order.

6.4 Where there has been a change in the circumstances since the order was made the court may set aside or vary a direction it has given. It may do so on application or on its own initiative.

6.5 Where the parties agree about changes they wish made to the directions given:
(1) If rule 2.11 (variation by agreement of a date set by the court for doing any act other than those stated in the note to that rule) or rule 31.5, 31.10(8) or 31.13 (agreements about disclosure) applies the parties need not file the written agreement.
(2) (a) In any other case the parties must apply for an order by consent.
(b) The parties must file a draft of the order sought and an agreed statement of the reasons why the variation is sought.
(c) The court may make an order in the agreed terms or in other terms without a hearing, but it may direct that a hearing is to be listed.

Failure to Comply with Case Management Directions

para.7 **48.6**
paras.7.1–7.3 **48.4**
para.7.4 **48.6, 61.11**
para.7.4.(1) **42.36**
para.7.4(6) **58.1**

7.1 Where a party fails to comply with a direction given by the court any other party may apply for an order that he must do so or for a sanction to be imposed or both of these.

7.2 The party entitled to apply for such an order must do so without delay but should first warn the other party of his intention to do so.

7.3 The court may take any such delay into account when it decides whether to make an order imposing a sanction or to grant relief from a sanction imposed by the rules or any other practice direction.

7.4 (1) The court will not allow a failure to comply with directions to lead to the postponement of the trial unless the circumstances are exceptional.
(2) If it is practical to do so the court will exercise its powers in a manner that enables the case to come on for trial on the date or within the period previously set.
(3) In particular the court will assess what steps each party should take to prepare the case for trial, direct that those steps are taken in the shortest possible time and impose a sanction for non-compliance. Such a sanction may, for example, deprive a party of the right to raise or contest an issue or to rely on evidence to which the direction relates.
(4) Where it appears that one or more issues are or can be made ready for trial at the time fixed while others cannot, the court may direct that the trial will proceed on the issues which are then ready, and direct that no costs will be allowed for any later trial of the remaining issues or that those costs will be paid by the party in default.
(5) Where the court has no option but to postpone the trial it will do so for the shortest possible time and will give directions for the taking of the necessary steps in the meantime as rapidly as possible.
(6) Litigants and lawyers must be in no doubt that the court will regard the postponement of a trial as an order of last resort. Where it appears inevitable the court may exercise its power to

require a party as well as his legal representative to attend court at the hearing where such an order is to be sought.

(7) The court will not postpone any other hearing without a very good reason, and for that purpose the failure of a party to comply on time with directions previously given will not be treated as a good reason.

Pre-trial Checklists (Listing Questionnaires)

para.8.1(2) 47.16
para.8.1(5) 47.19
para.8.3(1) 47.20
para.8.3(2) 47.22
para.8.5 47.20

8.1 (1) The pre-trial checklist (listing questionnaire) will be in form N170.

(2) Unless it dispenses with pre-trial checklist and orders an early trial on a fixed date, the court will specify the date for filing completed pre-trial checklist when it fixes the trial date or trial period under r. 29.2(2).

(3) The date for filing the completed pre-trial checklist will be not later than eight weeks before the trial date or the start of the trial period.

(4) The court will serve the pre-trial checklist on the parties at least 14 days before that date.

(5) Although the rules do not require the parties to exchange copies of the checklists before they are filed they are encouraged to do so to avoid the court being given conflicting or incomplete information.

(6) The file will be placed before a judge for his directions when all the checklists have been filed or when the time for filing them has expired and where a party has filed a checklist but another party has not done so.

8.2 The court's general approach will be as set out in the following paragraphs. The court may however decide to make other orders, and in particular the court will take into account the steps, if any, of which it is aware which the parties have taken to prepare the case for trial.

8.3 (1) Where no party files a pre-trial checklist the court will order that unless a completed pre-trial checklist is filed within seven days from service of that order, the claim, defence and any counterclaim will be struck out without further order of the court.

(2) Where a party files a pre-trial checklist but another party (the defaulting party) does not do so, the court will fix a hearing under r. 29.6(4). Whether or not the defaulting party attends the hearing, the court will normally fix or confirm the trial date and make other orders about the steps to be taken to prepare the case for trial.

8.4 Where the court decides to hold a hearing under r. 29.6(4) the court will fix a date which is as early as possible and the parties will be given at least three days' notice of the date.

8.5 Where the court decides to hold a pre-trial review (whether or not this is in addition to a hearing under r. 29.6(4)) the court will give the parties at least seven days' notice of the date.

Directions the Court Will Give on Listing

Directions the court must give

9.1 The court must fix the trial date or week, give a time estimate and fix the place of trial.

Other directions

para.9.2 47.27
para.9.3 47.26

9.2 (1) The parties should seek to agree directions and may file an agreed order. The court may make an order in those terms or it may make a different order.

(2) Agreed directions should include provision about:

(a) evidence especially expert evidence,
(b) a trial timetable and time estimate,
(c) the preparation of a trial bundle, and
(d) any other matter needed to prepare the case for trial.

(3) The court will include such of these provisions as are appropriate in any order that it may make, whether or not the parties have filed agreed directions.

(4) Unless a direction doing so has been given before, a direction giving permission to use expert evidence will say whether it gives permission to use oral evidence or reports or both and will name the experts concerned.

9.3 The principles set out in para. 6 of this practice direction about variation of directions applies equally to directions given at this stage.

The Trial

para.10.1 **47.26, 61.25** para.10.3 **61.16**
para.10.2 **61.41**

10.1 The trial will normally take place at a civil trial centre but it may be at another court if it is appropriate having regard to the needs of the parties and the availability of court resources.

10.2 The judge will generally have read the papers in the trial bundle and may dispense with an opening address.

10.3 The judge may confirm or vary any timetable given previously, or if none has been given set his own.

10.4 Attention is drawn to the provisions in Part 32 and the following parts of the Rules about evidence, and in particular:
(1) to rule 32.1 (court's power to control evidence and to restrict cross-examination), and
(2) to rule 32.5(2) statements and reports to stand as evidence-in-chief.

10.5 In an appropriate case the judge may summarily assess costs in accordance with rule 44.7. Attention is drawn to the practice directions about costs and the steps the parties are required to take.

10.6 Once the trial of a multi-track claim has begun, the judge will normally sit on consecutive court days until it has been concluded.

CPR Part 30 Transfer

Part 30 **42.9, 77.51** [For commentary on a specific rule, please refer to the cross-references after the title of the rule.]

30.1 Scope of This Part

(1) This Part deals with the transfer of proceedings between county courts, between the High Court and the county courts and within the High Court.

(2) Practice Direction 30 makes provision about the transfer of proceedings between the court and a tribunal.

30.2 Transfer between County Courts and within the High Court

r.30.2 **11.10** r.30.2(6) **11.10**

(1) A county court may order proceedings before that court, or any part of them (such as a counter-claim or an application made in the proceedings), to be transferred to another county court if it is satisfied that—
  (a) an order should be made having regard to the criteria in rule 30.3; or
  (b) proceedings for—
    (i) the detailed assessment of costs; or
    (ii) the enforcement of a judgment or order, could be more conveniently or fairly taken in that other county court.

(2) If proceedings have been started in the wrong county court, a judge of the county court may order that the proceedings—
  (a) be transferred to the county court in which they ought to have been started;
  (b) continue in the county court in which they have been started; or
  (c) be struck out.

(3) An application for an order under paragraph (1) or (2) must be made to the county court where the claim is proceeding.

(4) The High Court may, having regard to the criteria in rule 30.3, order proceedings in the Royal Courts of Justice or a district registry, or any part of such proceedings (such as a counterclaim or an application made in the proceedings), to be transferred—
  (a) from the Royal Courts of Justice to a district registry; or
  (b) from a district registry to the Royal Courts of Justice or to another district registry.

(5) A district registry may order proceedings before it for the detailed assessment of costs to be transferred to another district registry if it is satisfied that the proceedings could be more conveniently or fairly taken in that other district registry.

(6) An application for an order under paragraph (4) or (5) must, if the claim is proceeding in a district registry, be made to that registry.

(7) Where some enactment, other than these Rules, requires proceedings to be started in a particular county court, neither paragraphs (1) nor (2) give the court power to order proceedings to be transferred to a county court which is not the court in which they should have been started or to order them to continue in the wrong court.

(8) Probate proceedings may only be transferred under paragraph (4) to the Chancery Division at the Royal Courts of Justice or to one of the Chancery district registries.

30.3 Criteria for a Transfer Order

r.30.3 **11.10**
r.30.3(2)(h) **14.45**
r.30.3(2) **42.9**

(1) Paragraph (2) sets out the matters to which the court must have regard when considering whether to make an order under—
 (a) section 40(2), 41(1) or 42(2) of the County Courts Act 1984 (transfer between the High Court and a county court);
 (b) rule 30.2(1) (transfer between county courts); or
 (c) rule 30.2(4) (transfer between the Royal Courts of Justice and the district registries).

(2) The matters to which the court must have regard include—
 (a) the financial value of the claim and the amount in dispute, if different;
 (b) whether it would be more convenient or fair for hearings (including the trial) to be held in some other court;
 (c) the availability of a judge specialising in the type of claim in question;
 (d) whether the facts, legal issues, remedies or procedures involved are simple or complex;
 (e) the importance of the outcome of the claim to the public in general;
 (f) the facilities available to the court at which the claim is being dealt with, particularly in relation to—
  (i) any disabilities of a party or potential witness;
  (ii) any special measures needed for potential witnesses; or
  (iii) security;
 (g) whether the making of a declaration of incompatibility under section 4 of the Human Rights Act 1998 has arisen or may arise;
 (h) in the case of civil proceedings by or against the Crown, as defined in rule 66.1(2), the location of the relevant government department or officers of the Crown and, where appropriate, any relevant public interest that the matter should be tried in London.

30.4 Procedure

(1) Where the court orders proceedings to be transferred, the court from which they are to be transferred must give notice of the transfer to all the parties.

(2) An order made before the transfer of the proceedings shall not be affected by the order to transfer.

30.5 Transfer between Divisions and to and from a Specialist List

r.30.5 **11.4, 42.6, 77.51**
r.30.5(1) **11.10**
r.30.5(2) **42.6**
r.30.5(3) **11.9, 11.10, 42.6, 72.2, 77.51**

(1) The High Court may order proceedings in any Division of the High Court to be transferred to another Division.

(2) A judge dealing with claims in a specialist list may order proceedings to be transferred to or from that list.

(3) An application for the transfer of proceedings to or from a specialist list must be made to a judge dealing with claims in that list.

30.6 Power to Specify Place Where Hearings Are to Be Held

The court may specify the place (for instance, a particular county court) where the trial or some other hearing in any proceedings is to be held and may do so without ordering the proceedings to be transferred.

(Practice Direction 54D contains provisions about where hearings may be held in proceedings in the Administrative Court)

30.7 Transfer of Control of Money in Court

The court may order that control of any money held by it under rule 21.11 (control of money recovered by or on behalf of a child or protected party) be transferred to another court if that court would be more convenient.

30.8 Transfer of Competition Law Claims

r.30.8 **2.14, 11.6** r.30.8(4) **11.6**

(1) This rule applies if, in any proceedings in the Queen's Bench Division (other than proceedings in the Commercial or Admiralty Courts), a district registry of the High Court or a county court, a party's statement of case raises an issue relating to the application of—
 (a) Article 101 or Article 102 of the Treaty on the Functioning of the European Union; or
 (b) Chapter I or II of Part I of the Competition Act 1998.
(2) Rules 30.2 and 30.3 do not apply.
(3) The court must transfer the proceedings to the Chancery Division of the High Court at the Royal Courts of Justice.
(4) If any such proceedings which have been commenced in the Queen's Bench Division or a Mercantile Court fall within the scope of rule 58.1(2), any party to those proceedings may apply for the transfer of the proceedings to the Commercial Court, in accordance with rule 58.4(2) and rule 30.5(3). If the application is refused, the proceedings must be transferred to the Chancery Division of the High Court at the Royal Courts of Justice.

PD 30 Practice Direction 30 — Transfer

This practice direction supplements CPR, Part 30.

Value of a Case and Transfer

1 In addition to the criteria set out in r. 30.3(2) attention is drawn to the financial limits set out in the High Court and County Courts Jurisdiction Order 1991, as amended.

2 Attention is also drawn to PD 29, para. 2.

Date of Transfer

3 Where the court orders proceedings to be transferred, the order will take effect from the date it is made by the court.

Procedure on Transfer

4.1 Where an order for transfer has been made the transferring court will immediately send notice of the transfer to the receiving court. The notice will contain:
(1) the name of the case, and
(2) the number of the case.

4.2 At the same time as the transferring court notifies the receiving court it will also notify the parties of the transfer under r. 30.4(1).

Procedure for an Appeal against Order of Transfer

5.1 Where a district judge orders proceedings to be transferred and both the transferring and receiving courts are county courts, any appeal against that order should be made in the receiving court.

5.2 The receiving court may, if it is more convenient for the parties, remit the appeal to the transferring court to be dealt with there.

Applications to Set Aside

6.1 Where a party may apply to set aside an order for transfer (e.g. under r. 23.10) the application should be made to the court which made the order.

6.2 Such application should be made in accordance with Part 23 of the Rules and PD 23A.

Transfer on the Criterion in Rule 30.3(2)(g)

7 A transfer should only be made on the basis of the criterion in r. 30.3(2)(g) where there is a real prospect that a declaration of incompatibility will be made.

Enterprise Act 2002

8.1 In this paragraph:
(1) 'the 1998 Act' means the Competition Act 1998;
(2) 'the 2002 Act' means the Enterprise Act 2002; and
(3) 'the CAT' means the Competition Appeal Tribunal.

8.2 Rules 30.1, 30.4 and 30.5 and paras 3 and 6 apply.

Transfer from the High Court or a county court to the Competition Appeal Tribunal under the Enterprise Act 2002, s. 16(4)

8.3 The High Court or a county court may pursuant to s. 16(4) of the 2002 Act, on its own initiative or on application by the claimant or defendant, order the transfer of any part of the proceedings before it, which relates to a claim to which s. 47A of the 1998 Act applies, to the CAT.

8.4 When considering whether to make an order under para. 8.3 the court shall take into account whether:
(1) there is a similar claim under s. 47A of the 1998 Act based on the same infringement currently before the CAT;
(2) the CAT has previously made a decision on a similar claim under s. 47A of the 1998 Act based on the same infringement; or

(3) the CAT has developed considerable expertise by previously dealing with a significant number of cases arising from the same or similar infringements.

8.5 Where the court orders a transfer under para. 8.3 it will immediately:
(1) send to the CAT:
(a) a notice of the transfer containing the name of the case; and
(b) all papers relating to the case; and
(2) notify the parties of the transfer.

8.6 An appeal against a transfer order made under para. 8.3 must be brought in the court which made the transfer order.

Transfer from the Competition Appeal Tribunal to the High Court under the Enterprise Act 2002, s. 16(5)

8.7 Where the CAT pursuant to s. 16(5) of the 2002 Act directs transfer of a claim made in proceedings under s. 47A of the 1998 Act to the High Court, the claim should be transferred to the Chancery Division of the High Court at the Royal Courts of Justice.

8.8 As soon as a claim has been transferred under para. 8.7, the High Court must:
(1) allocate a case number; and
(2) list the case for a case management hearing before a judge.

8.9 A party to a claim which has been transferred under para. 8.7 may apply to transfer it to the Commercial Court if it otherwise falls within the scope of r. 58.2(1), in accordance with the procedure set out in rr. 58.4(2) and 30.5(3).

Transfer to or from a Patents County Court (Rule 63.18)

para.9 **11.10**

9.1 When deciding whether to order a transfer of proceedings to or from a patents county court the court will consider whether—
(1) a party can only afford to bring or defend the claim in a patents county court; and
(2) the claim is appropriate to be determined by a patents county court having regard in particular to—
(a) the value of the claim (including the value of an injunction);
(b) the complexity of the issues; and
(c) the estimated length of the trial.

9.2 Where the court orders proceedings to be transferred to or from a patents county court it may—
(1) specify terms for such a transfer; and
(2) award reduced or no costs where it allows the claimant to withdraw the claim.

CPR Part 31 Disclosure and Inspection of Documents

Part 31 **14.79, 45.6, 47.14, 49.11, 49.86, 50.1, 50.2, 50.17, 50.23, 50.43, 50.46, 50.96, 82.62** [For commentary on a specific rule, please refer to the cross-references after the title of the rule.]

31.1 Scope of This Part

(1) This Part sets out rules about the disclosure and inspection of documents.
(2) This Part applies to all claims except a claim on the small claims track.

31.2 Meaning of Disclosure

r.31.2 **50.21** r.31.2(2) **50.33**

A party discloses a document by stating that the document exists or has existed.

31.3 Right of Inspection of a Disclosed Document

r.31.3 **50.6, 50.33, 50.34** r.31.3(2) **50.23, 50.35, 50.36**
r.31.3(1)(b) **50.50**

(1) A party to whom a document has been disclosed has a right to inspect that document except where—
 (a) the document is no longer in the control of the party who disclosed it;
 (b) the party disclosing the document has a right or a duty to withhold inspection of it;
 (c) paragraph (2) applies; or
 (d) rule 78.26 applies.
(Rule 31.8 sets out when a document is in the control of a party)
(Rule 31.19 sets out the procedure for claiming a right or duty to withhold inspection)
(Rule 78.26 contains rules in relation to the disclosure and inspection of evidence arising out of mediation of certain cross-border disputes.)
(2) Where a party considers that it would be disproportionate to the issues in the case to permit inspection of documents within a category or class of document disclosed under rule 31.6(b)—
 (a) he is not required to permit inspection of documents within that category or class; but
 (b) he must state in his disclosure statement that inspection of those documents will not be permitted on the grounds that to do so would be disproportionate.
(Rule 31.6 provides for standard disclosure)
(Rule 31.10 makes provision for a disclosure statement)
(Rule 31.12 provides for a party to apply for an order for specific inspection of documents)

CPR 26–50 & PDs

31.4 Meaning of Document

r.31.4 PC 25, 50.17

In this Part—

'document' means anything in which information of any description is recorded; and

'copy', in relation to a document, means anything onto which information recorded in the document has been copied, by whatever means and whether directly or indirectly.

31.5 Disclosure Limited to Standard Disclosure

r.31.5 50.37
r.31.5(1) 50.3
r.31.5(1)(a) 50.4
r.31.5(1)(b) 50.4, 50.37
r.31.5(1)(c) 50.4, 50.37
r.31.5(2) 50.10
rr.31.5(3)–(8) 50.3
r.31.5(3) 47.8, 50.11
r.31.5(4) 50.11
r.31.5(5) 47.8, 50.12
r.31.5(6) 50.11, 50.12, 50.13
r.31.5(7) 50.11, 50.13
r.31.5(7)(a) 50.37
r.31.5(7)(d) 50.14
r.31.5(7)(f) 50.15, 50.37
r.31.5(8) 50.16
r.31.5(9) 50.10
r.31.5(10) 50.11, 50.13

(1) In all claims to which rule 31.5(2) does not apply—
 (a) an order to give disclosure is an order to give standard disclosure unless the court directs otherwise;
 (b) the court may dispense with or limit standard disclosure; and
 (c) the parties may agree in writing to dispense with or to limit standard disclosure.

(2) Unless the court otherwise orders, paragraphs (3) to (8) apply to all multi-track claims, other than those which include a claim for personal injuries.

(3) Not less than 14 days before the first case management conference each party must file and serve a report verified by a statement of truth, which—
 (a) describes briefly what documents exist or may exist that are or may be relevant to the matters in issue in the case;
 (b) describes where and with whom those documents are or may be located;
 (c) in the case of electronic documents, describes how those documents are stored;
 (d) estimates the broad range of costs that could be involved in giving standard disclosure in the case, including the costs of searching for and disclosing any electronically stored documents; and
 (e) states which of the directions under paragraphs (7) or (8) are to be sought.

(4) In cases where the Electronic Documents Questionnaire has been exchanged, the Questionnaire should be filed with the report required by paragraph (3).

(5) Not less than seven days before the first case management conference, and on any other occasion as the court may direct, the parties must, at a meeting or by telephone, discuss and seek to agree a proposal in relation to disclosure that meets the overriding objective.

(6) If—
 (a) the parties agree proposals for the scope of disclosure; and
 (b) the court considers that the proposals are appropriate in all the circumstances,
 the court may approve them without a hearing and give directions in the terms proposed.

(7) At the first or any subsequent case management conference, the court will decide, having regard to the overriding objective and the need to limit disclosure to that which is necessary to deal with the case justly, which of the following orders to make in relation to disclosure—
 (a) an order dispensing with disclosure;
 (b) an order that a party disclose the documents on which it relies, and at the same time request any specific disclosure it requires from any other party;
 (c) an order that directs, where practicable, the disclosure to be given by each party on an issue by issue basis;
 (d) an order that each party disclose any documents which it is reasonable to suppose may contain information which enables that party to advance its own case or to damage that of any other party, or which leads to an enquiry which has either of those consequences;
 (e) an order that a party give standard disclosure;
 (f) any other order in relation to disclosure that the court considers appropriate.

(8) The court may at any point give directions as to how disclosure is to be given, and in particular—
 (a) what searches are to be undertaken, of where, for what, in respect of which time periods and by whom and the extent of any search for electronically stored documents;

(b) whether lists of documents are required;
(c) how and when the disclosure statement is to be given;
(d) in what format documents are to be disclosed (and whether any identification is required);
(e) what is required in relation to documents that once existed but no longer exist; and
(f) whether disclosure shall take place in stages.

(9) To the extent that the documents to be disclosed are electronic, the provisions of Practice Direction 31B — Disclosure of Electronic Documents will apply in addition to paragraphs (3) to (8).

31.6 Standard Disclosure — What Documents Are to Be Disclosed

r.31.6 PC 25, 50.5, 50.6, 50.8, 50.20, 50.29, 50.30, 50.42, 50.85
r.31.6(a) 50.5
r.31.6(b) 50.5, 50.20, 50.23, 50.33
r.31.6(b)(i) 50.5
r.31.6(b)(ii) 50.5
r.31.6(b)(iii) 50.5
r.31.6(c) 50.20, 50.23

Standard disclosure requires a party to disclose only—
(a) the documents on which he relies; and
(b) the documents which—
(i) adversely affect his own case;
(ii) adversely affect another party's case; or
(iii) support another party's case; and
(c) the documents which he is required to disclose by a relevant practice direction.

31.7 Duty of Search

r.31.7 PC 25, 50.20, 50.27
r.31.7(2) 50.20, 50.42
r.31.7(3) 50.20, 50.23

(1) When giving standard disclosure, a party is required to make a reasonable search for documents falling within rule 31.6(b) or (c).

(2) The factors relevant in deciding the reasonableness of a search include the following—
(a) the number of documents involved;
(b) the nature and complexity of the proceedings;
(c) the ease and expense of retrieval of any particular document; and
(d) the significance of any document which is likely to be located during the search.

(3) Where a party has not searched for a category or class of document on the grounds that to do so would be unreasonable, he must state this in his disclosure statement and identify the category or class of document.

(Rule 31.10 makes provision for a disclosure statement)

31.8 Duty of Disclosure Limited to Documents Which Are or Have Been in a Party's Control

r.31.8 PC 25, 50.6
r.31.8(1) 50.18
r.31.8(2) 50.6
r.31.8(3) 50.18

(1) A party's duty to disclose documents is limited to documents which are or have been in his control.

(2) For this purpose a party has or has had a document in his control if—
(a) it is or was in his physical possession;
(b) he has or has had a right to possession of it; or
(c) he has or has had a right to inspect or take copies of it.

31.9 Disclosure of Copies

r.31.9 50.19
r.31.9(1) 50.19

(1) A party need not disclose more than one copy of a document.

(2) A copy of a document that contains a modification, obliteration or other marking or feature—
(a) on which a party intends to rely; or
(b) which adversely affects his own case or another party's case or supports another party's case;
shall be treated as a separate document.

(Rule 31.4 sets out the meaning of a copy of a document)

CPR 26–50 & PDs

31.10 Procedure for Standard Disclosure

r.31.10 PC25, 50.22
r.31.10(2) PC 25, 50.21
r.31.10(3) 50.21
r.31.10(4) 50.21
r.31.10(5) 50.22, 50.30
r.31.10(6) PC25, 1.37, 50.22, 50.23, 50.30
r.31.10(6)(b)–(c) 50.30
r.31.10(7) PC25, 50.22
r.31.10(8) PC 25, 50.24
r.31.10(9) PC25, 50.22

(1) The procedure for standard disclosure is as follows.
(2) Each party must make and serve on every other party, a list of documents in the relevant practice form.
(3) The list must identify the documents in a convenient order and manner and as concisely as possible.
(4) The list must indicate—
(a) those documents in respect of which the party claims a right or duty to withhold inspection; and
(b) (i) those documents which are no longer in the party's control; and
(ii) what has happened to those documents.

(Rule 31.19(3) and (4) require a statement in the list of documents relating to any documents inspection of which a person claims he has a right or duty to withhold)

(5) The list must include a disclosure statement.
(6) A disclosure statement is a statement made by the party disclosing the documents—
(a) setting out the extent of the search that has been made to locate documents which he is required to disclose;
(b) certifying that he understands the duty to disclose documents; and
(c) certifying that to the best of his knowledge he has carried out that duty.
(7) Where the party making the disclosure statement is a company, firm, association or other organisation, the statement must also—
(a) identify the person making the statement; and
(b) explain why he is considered an appropriate person to make the statement.
(8) The parties may agree in writing—
(a) to disclose documents without making a list; and
(b) to disclose documents without the disclosing party making a disclosure statement.
(9) A disclosure statement may be made by a person who is not a party where this is permitted by a relevant practice direction.

31.11 Duty of Disclosure Continues during Proceedings

r.31.11 PC 25
r.31.11(2) 50.44

(1) Any duty of disclosure continues until the proceedings are concluded.
(2) If documents to which that duty extends come to a party's notice at any time during the proceedings, he must immediately notify every other party.

31.12 Specific Disclosure or Inspection

r.31.12 50.33, 50.41, 48.31
r.31.12(2)(b) 50.42
r.31.12(3) 50.6

(1) The court may make an order for specific disclosure or specific inspection.
(2) An order for specific disclosure is an order that a party must do one or more of the following things—
(a) disclose documents or classes of documents specified in the order;
(b) carry out a search to the extent stated in the order;
(c) disclose any documents located as a result of that search.
(3) An order for specific inspection is an order that a party permit inspection of a document referred to in rule 31.3(2).

(Rule 31.3(2) allows a party to state in his disclosure statement that he will not permit inspection of a document on the grounds that it would be disproportionate to do so.)
(Rule 78.26 contains rules in relation to the disclosure and inspection of evidence arising out of mediation of certain cross-border disputes.)

31.13 Disclosure in Stages

r. 31.13 PC 25, 50.38

The parties may agree in writing, or the court may direct, that disclosure or inspection or both shall take place in stages.

31.14 Documents Referred to in Statements of Case etc.

r.31.14 50.34
r.31.14(1) 50.34
r.31.14(2) 50.34

(1) A party may inspect a document mentioned in—
 (a) a statement of case;
 (b) a witness statement;
 (c) a witness summary; or
 (d) an affidavit[(GL)].
(2) Subject to rule 35.10(4), a party may apply for an order for inspection of any document mentioned in an expert's report which has not already been disclosed in the proceedings.

(Rule 35.10(4) makes provision in relation to instructions referred to in an expert's report)

31.15 Inspection and Copying of Documents

r.31.15(a)–(b) PC25, 50.33
r.31.15(c) PC 25, 50.33, 59.3

Where a party has a right to inspect a document—
(a) that party must give the party who disclosed the document written notice of his wish to inspect it;
(b) the party who disclosed the document must permit inspection not more than 7 days after the date on which he received the notice; and
(c) that party may request a copy of the document and, if he also undertakes to pay reasonable copying costs, the party who disclosed the document must supply him with a copy not more than 7 days after the date on which he received the request.

(Rule[s] 31.3 and 31.14 deal with the right of a party to inspect a document)

31.16 Disclosure before Proceedings Start

r.31.16 15.3, 50.84, 50.87, 50.95, 69.4
r.31.16(2) 50.88
r.31.16(3)(a)–(d) 50.85
r.31.16(4)(a)–(b) 50.88
r.31.16(5) 50.88

(1) This rule applies where an application is made to the court under any Act for disclosure before proceedings have started.
(2) The application must be supported by evidence.
(3) The court may make an order under this rule only where—
 (a) the respondent is likely to be a party to subsequent proceedings;
 (b) the applicant is also likely to be a party to those proceedings;
 (c) if proceedings had started, the respondent's duty by way of standard disclosure, set out in rule 31.6, would extend to the documents or classes of documents of which the applicant seeks disclosure; and
 (d) disclosure before proceedings have started is desirable in order to—
  (i) dispose fairly of the anticipated proceedings;
  (ii) assist the dispute to be resolved without proceedings; or
  (iii) save costs.
(4) An order under this rule must—
 (a) specify the documents or the classes of documents which the respondent must disclose; and
 (b) require him, when making disclosure, to specify any of those documents—
  (i) which are no longer in his control; or
  (ii) in respect of which he claims a right or duty to withhold inspection.
(5) Such an order may—
 (a) require the respondent to indicate what has happened to any documents which are no longer in his control; and
 (b) specify the time and place for disclosure and inspection.

(Rule 78.26 contains rules in relation to the disclosure and inspection of evidence arising out of mediation of certain cross-border disputes.)

31.17 Orders for Disclosure against a Person Not a Party

r.31.17 **50.34, 50.48, 50.84, 50.92, 50.95, 50.103, 57.6**
r.31.17(1) **PC 27**
r.31.17(2) **PC 27, 50.90**
r.31.17(3) **50.91**
r.31.17(3)(a)–(b) **PC 27**
r.31.17(4) **50.93**
r.31.17(5) **50.93**

(1) This rule applies where an application is made to the court under any Act for disclosure by a person who is not a party to the proceedings.
(2) The application must be supported by evidence.
(3) The court may make an order under this rule only where—
  (a) the documents of which disclosure is sought are likely to support the case of the applicant or adversely affect the case of one of the other parties to the proceedings; and
  (b) disclosure is necessary in order to dispose fairly of the claim or to save costs.
(4) An order under this rule must—
  (a) specify the documents or the classes of documents which the respondent must disclose; and
  (b) require the respondent, when making disclosure, to specify any of those documents—
    (i) which are no longer in his control; or
    (ii) in respect of which he claims a right or duty to withhold inspection.
(5) Such an order may—
  (a) require the respondent to indicate what has happened to any documents which are no longer in his control; and
  (b) specify the time and place for disclosure and inspection.

(Rule 78.26 contains rules in relation to the disclosure and inspection of evidence arising out of mediation of certain cross-border disputes.)

31.18 Rules Not to Limit Other Powers of the Court to Order Disclosure

r.31.18 **50.95**

Rules 31.16 and 31.17 do not limit any other power which the court may have to order—
(a) disclosure before proceedings have started; and
(b) disclosure against a person who is not a party to proceedings.

31.19 Claim to Withhold Inspection or Disclosure of a Document

r.31.19 **50.32, 50.34, 50.35, 50.82, 50.97**
r.31.19(1) **50.35, 50.82**
r.31.19(2) **50.82**
r.31.19(3) **PC 25, 50.35, 50.50**
r.31.19(4) **50.21, 50.35, 50.50, 50.82**
r.31.19(5) **50.35**
r.31.19(6) **50.35, 50.81**

(1) A person may apply, without notice, for an order permitting him to withhold disclosure of a document on the ground that disclosure would damage the public interest.
(2) Unless the court orders otherwise, an order of the court under paragraph (1)—
  (a) must not be served on any other person; and
  (b) must not be open to inspection by any person.
(3) A person who wishes to claim that he has a right or a duty to withhold inspection of a document, or part of a document, must state in writing—
  (a) that he has such a right or duty; and
  (b) the grounds on which he claims that right or duty.
(4) The statement referred to in paragraph (3) must be made—
  (a) in the list in which the document is disclosed; or
  (b) if there is no list, to the person wishing to inspect the document.
(5) A party may apply to the court to decide whether a claim made under paragraph (3) should be upheld.
(6) For the purpose of deciding an application under paragraph (1) (application to withhold disclosure) or paragraph (3) (claim to withhold inspection) the court may—
  (a) require the person seeking to withhold disclosure or inspection of a document to produce that document to the court; and
  (b) invite any person, whether or not a party, to make representations.
(7) An application under paragraph (1) or paragraph (5) must be supported by evidence.

(8) This Part does not affect any rule of law which permits or requires a document to be withheld from disclosure or inspection on the ground that its disclosure or inspection would damage the public interest.

31.20 Restriction on Use of a Privileged Document Inspection of Which Has Been Inadvertently Allowed

r. 31.20 50.77

Where a party inadvertently allows a privileged document to be inspected, the party who has inspected the document may use it or its contents only with the permission of the court.

31.21 Consequence of Failure to Disclose Documents or Permit Inspection

r. 31.21 50.40

A party may not rely on any document which he fails to disclose or in respect of which he fails to permit inspection unless the court gives permission.

31.22 Subsequent Use of Disclosed Documents and Completed Electronic Documents Questionnaires

r.31.22 38.25, 50.26, 50.45, 50.46, 50.48, 54.34
r.31.22(1) 50.45, 50.47
r.31.22(1)(a) 50.47
r.31.22(1)(b) 50.48
r.31.22(2) 50.45
r.31.22(3) 50.45
r.31.22(4) 50.45

(1) A party to whom a document has been disclosed may use the document only for the purpose of the proceedings in which it is disclosed, except where—
  (a) the document has been read to or by the court, or referred to, at a hearing which has been held in public;
  (b) the court gives permission; or
  (c) the party who disclosed the document and the person to whom the document belongs agree.

(2) The court may make an order restricting or prohibiting the use of a document which has been disclosed, even where the document has been read to or by the court, or referred to, at a hearing which has been held in public.

(3) An application for such an order may be made—
  (a) by a party; or
  (b) by any person to whom the document belongs.

(4) For the purpose of this rule, an Electronic Documents Questionnaire which has been completed and served by another party pursuant to Practice Direction 31B is to be treated as if it is a document which has been disclosed.

31.23 False Disclosure Statements

(1) Proceedings for contempt of court may be brought against a person if he makes, or causes to be made, a false disclosure statement, without an honest belief in its truth.
(Section 6 of Part 81 contains provisions in relation to committal for making a false disclosure statement.)

(2) [*Revoked*]

PD 31A Practice Direction 31A — Disclosure and Inspection

This practice direction supplements CPR, Part 31.

[For commentary on a specific paragraph, please refer to the cross-references after the title of the paragraph.]

General

para.1.4 50.24, 50.37

1.1 The normal order for disclosure will be an order that the parties give standard disclosure.

1.2 In order to give standard disclosure the disclosing party must make a reasonable search for documents falling within the paragraphs of rule 31.6.

1.3 Having made the search the disclosing party must (unless rule 31.10(8) applies) make a list of the documents of whose existence the party is aware that fall within those paragraphs and which are or have been in the party's control (see rule 31.8).

1.4 The obligations imposed by an order for standard disclosure may be dispensed with or limited either by the court or by written agreement between the parties. Any such written agreement should be lodged with the court.

The Search

para.2 50.20

2 The extent of the search which must be made will depend upon the circumstances of the case including, in particular, the factors referred to in rule 31.7(2). The parties should bear in mind the overriding principle of proportionality (see rule 1.1(2)(c)). It may, for example, be reasonable to decide not to search for documents coming into existence before some particular date, or to limit the search to documents in some particular place or places, or to documents falling into particular categories.

Electronic Disclosure

para.2A.1 50.17
para.2A.2 50.25
para.2A.3 50.33

2A.1 Rule 31.4 contains a broad definition of a document. This extends to electronic documents, including email and other electronic communications, word-processed documents and databases. In addition to documents that are readily accessible from computer systems and other electronic devices and media, the definition covers those documents that are stored on servers and back-up systems and electronic documents that have been 'deleted'. It also extends to additional information stored and associated with electronic documents known as metadata.

2A.2 PD 31B contains additional provisions in relation to the disclosure of electronic documents in cases that are likely to be allocated to the multi-track.

The List

para.3.1 50.21
para.3.2 50.21
para.3.3 PC 25, 50.44

3.1 The list should be in form N265.

3.2 In order to comply with rule 31.10(3) it will normally be necessary to list the documents in date order, to number them consecutively and to give each a concise description (e.g. letter, claimant to defendant). Where there is a large number of documents all falling into a particular category the disclosing party may list those documents as a category rather than individually e.g. 50 bank statements relating to account number _ at _ Bank, _ 20 _ to _ 20 _; or, 35 letters passing between _ and _ between _ 20 _ and _ 20 _.

3.3 The obligations imposed by an order for disclosure will continue until the proceedings come to an end. If, after a list of documents has been prepared and served, the existence of further documents to which the order applies comes to the attention of the disclosing party, the party must prepare and serve a supplemental list.

Disclosure Statement

para.4.1 PC 25
para.4.2 50.23
para.4.2(2) 50.23
para.4.3 PC 25, 50.22
para.4.4 PC 25, 50.23, 50.30
paras.4.5 50.21
paras.4.6 50.21
para.4.7 PC 25, 50.22

4.1 A list of documents must (unless rule 31.10(8)(b) applies) contain a disclosure statement complying with rule 31.10. The form of disclosure statement is set out in the Annex to this practice direction.

4.2 The disclosure statement should:

(1) expressly state that the disclosing party believes the extent of the search to have been reasonable in all the circumstances, and

(2) in setting out the extent of the search (see rule 31.10(6)) draw attention to any particular limitations on the extent of the search which were adopted for proportionality reasons and give the reasons why the limitations were adopted, e.g. the difficulty or expense that a search not subject to those limitations would have entailed or the marginal relevance of categories of documents omitted from the search.

4.3 Where rule 31.10(7) applies, the details given in the disclosure statement about the person making the statement must include his name and address and the office or position he holds in the disclosing party or the basis upon which he makes the statement on behalf of the party.

4.4 If the disclosing party has a legal representative acting for him, the legal representative must endeavour to ensure that the person making the disclosure statement (whether the disclosing party or, in a case to which rule 31.10(7) applies, some other person) understands the duty of disclosure under Part 31.

4.5 If the disclosing party wishes to claim that he has a right or duty to withhold a document, or part of a document, in his list of documents from inspection (see rule 31.19(3)), he must state in writing:

(1) that he has such a right or duty, and

(2) the grounds on which he claims that right or duty.

4.6 The statement referred to in paragraph 4.5 above should normally be included in the disclosure statement and must identify the document, or part of a document, to which the claim relates.

4.7 An insurer or the Motor Insurers' Bureau may sign a disclosure statement on behalf of a party where the insurer or the Motor Insurers' Bureau has a financial interest in the result of proceedings brought wholly or partially by or against that party. Rule 31.10(7) and paragraph 4.3 above shall apply to the insurer or the Motor Insurers' Bureau making such a statement.

Specific Disclosure

paras.5.1 50.41
para.5.2 PC 26, 50.41
para.5.3 50.41
para.5.4 50.14, 50.42

5.1 If a party believes that the disclosure of documents given by a disclosing party is inadequate he may make an application for an order for specific disclosure (see rule 31.12).

5.2 The application notice must specify the order that the applicant intends to ask the court to make and must be supported by evidence (see rule 31.12(2) which describes the orders the court may make).

5.3 The grounds on which the order is sought may be set out in the application notice itself but if not there set out must be set out in the evidence filed in support of the application.

5.4 In deciding whether or not to make an order for specific disclosure the court will take into account all the circumstances of the case and, in particular, the overriding objective described in Part 1. But if the court concludes that the party from whom specific disclosure is sought has failed adequately to comply with the obligations imposed by an order for disclosure (whether by failing to make a sufficient search for documents or otherwise) the court will usually make such order as is necessary to ensure that those obligations are properly complied with.

5.5 An order for specific disclosure may in an appropriate case direct a party to:

(1) carry out a search for any documents which it is reasonable to suppose may contain information which may:

(a) enable the party applying for disclosure either to advance his own case or to damage that of the party giving disclosure; or

(b) lead to a train of enquiry which has either of those consequences; and

(2) disclose any documents found as a result of that search.

Claims to Withhold Disclosure or Inspection of a Document

para.6.1 50.35

6.1 A claim to withhold inspection of a document, or part of a document, disclosed in a list of documents does not require an application to the court. Where such a claim has been made, a party who wishes to challenge it must apply to the court (see rule 31.19(5)).

6.2 Rule 31.19(1) and (6) provide a procedure enabling a party to apply for an order permitting disclosure of the existence of a document to be withheld.

Inspection of Documents Mentioned in Expert's Report (Rule 31.14(2))

7.1 If a party wishes to inspect documents referred to in the expert report of another party, before issuing an application he should request inspection of the documents informally, and inspection should be provided by agreement unless the request is unreasonable.

7.2 Where an expert report refers to a large number or volume of documents and it would be burdensome to copy or collate them, the court will only order inspection of such documents if it is satisfied that it is necessary for the just disposal of the proceedings and the party cannot reasonably obtain the documents from another source.

8 Attention is drawn to r. 31.23 which sets out the consequences of making a false disclosure statement without an honest belief in its truth, and to the procedures set out in r. 81.18 and PD 81, paras 5.1 to 5.7.

ANNEX DISCLOSURE STATEMENT

annex PC 25, 50.22, 50.23

I, the above-named claimant [or defendant] [*if party making disclosure is a company, firm or other organisation identify here who the person making the disclosure statement is and why he is the appropriate person to make it*] state that I have carried out a reasonable and proportionate search to locate all the documents which I am required to disclose under the order made by the court on day of. I did not search:

(1) for documents predating ,
(2) for documents located elsewhere than ,
(3) for documents in categories other than .
(4) for electronic documents.]

[*I carried out a search for electronic documents contained on or created by the following:* [*list what was searched and extent of search*] *I did not search for the following:*

(1) documents created before,
(2) documents contained on or created by the [Claimant's] [Defendant's] PCs/portable data storage media/databases/servers/back-up tapes/off-site storage/mobile phones/laptops/notebooks/handheld devices/PDA devices (*delete as appropriate*),
(3) documents contained on or created by the [Claimant's] [Defendant's] mail files/document files/calendar files/spreadsheet files/graphic and presentation files/web-based applications (*delete as appropriate*),
(4) documents other than by reference to the following keyword(s)/concept(s): (*delete if your search was not confined to specific keywords or concepts*).]

I certify that I understand the duty of disclosure and to the best of my knowledge I have carried out that duty. I certify that the list above is a complete list of all documents which are or have been in my control and which I am obliged under the said order to disclose.

PD 31B Practice Direction 31B — Disclosure of Electronic Documents

This practice direction supplements CPR, Part 31.

PD 31B 50.1, 50.10, 50.11, 50.25

Purpose, Scope and Interpretation

1. Rule 31.4 contains a broad definition of 'document'. This extends to Electronic Documents.
2. The purpose of this practice direction is to encourage and assist the parties to reach agreement in relation to the disclosure of Electronic Documents in a proportionate and cost-effective manner.
3. Unless the court orders otherwise, this practice direction only applies to proceedings that are (or are likely to be) allocated to the multi-track.
4. Unless the court orders otherwise, this practice direction only applies to proceedings started on or after 1 October 2010. PD 31A, paras 2A.2 to 2A.5, in force immediately before that date continues to apply to proceedings started before that date.
5. In this practice direction—
   (1) 'Data Sampling' means the process of checking data by identifying and checking representative individual documents;
   (2) 'Disclosure Data' means data relating to disclosed documents, including for example the type of document, the date of the document, the names of the author or sender and the recipient, and the party disclosing the document;
   (3) 'Electronic Document' means any document held in electronic form. It includes, for example, email and other electronic communications such as text messages and voicemail, word-processed documents and databases, and documents stored on portable devices such as memory sticks and mobile phones. In addition to documents that are readily accessible from computer systems and other electronic devices and media, it includes documents that are stored on servers and backup systems and documents that have been deleted. It also includes Metadata and other embedded data which is not typically visible on screen or a printout;
   (4) 'Electronic Image' means an electronic representation of a paper document;
   (5) 'Electronic Documents Questionnaire' means the questionnaire in the schedule to this practice direction;
   (6) 'Keyword Search' means a software-aided search for words across the text of an Electronic Document;
   (7) 'Metadata' is data about data. In the case of an Electronic Document, Metadata is typically embedded information about the document which is not readily accessible once the Native Electronic Document has been converted into an Electronic Image or paper document. It may include (for example) the date and time of creation or modification of a word-processing file, or the author and the date and time of sending an email. Metadata may be created automatically by a computer system or manually by a user;
   (8) 'Native Electronic Document' or 'Native Format' means an Electronic Document stored in the original form in which it was created by a computer software program; and
   (9) 'Optical Character Recognition (OCR)' means the computer-facilitated recognition of printed or written text characters in an Electronic Image in which the text-based contents cannot be searched electronically.

General Principles

para.6 50.25

6. When considering disclosure of Electronic Documents, the parties and their legal representatives should bear in mind the following general principles—
   (1) Electronic Documents should be managed efficiently in order to minimise the cost incurred;
   (2) technology should be used in order to ensure that document management activities are undertaken efficiently and effectively;

CPR 26–50 & PDs

(3) disclosure should be given in a manner which gives effect to the overriding objective;
(4) Electronic Documents should generally be made available for inspection in a form which allows the party receiving the documents the same ability to access, search, review and display the documents as the party giving disclosure; and
(5) disclosure of Electronic Documents which are of no relevance to the proceedings may place an excessive burden in time and cost on the party to whom disclosure is given.

Preservation of Documents

para.7 PC 25, 50.31

7. As soon as litigation is contemplated, the parties' legal representatives must notify their clients of the need to preserve disclosable documents. The documents to be preserved include Electronic Documents which would otherwise be deleted in accordance with a document retention policy or otherwise deleted in the ordinary course of business.

Discussions between the Parties before the First Case Management Conference in Relation to the Use of Technology and Disclosure

para.8 PC25, 50.25 para.9 PC25, 50.25

8. The parties and their legal representatives must, before the first case management conference, discuss the use of technology in the management of Electronic Documents and the conduct of proceedings, in particular for the purpose of—
(1) creating lists of documents to be disclosed;
(2) giving disclosure by providing documents and information regarding documents in electronic format; and
(3) presenting documents and other material to the court at the trial.
9. The parties and their legal representatives must also, before the first case management conference, discuss the disclosure of Electronic Documents. In some cases (for example heavy and complex cases) it may be appropriate to begin discussions before proceedings are commenced. The discussions should include (where appropriate) the following matters—
(1) the categories of Electronic Documents within the parties' control, the computer systems, electronic devices and media on which any relevant documents may be held, storage systems and document retention policies;
(2) the scope of the reasonable search for Electronic Documents required by r. 31.7;
(3) the tools and techniques (if any) which should be considered to reduce the burden and cost of disclosure of Electronic Documents, including—
(a) limiting disclosure of documents or certain categories of documents to particular date ranges, to particular custodians of documents, or to particular types of documents;
(b) the use of agreed Keyword Searches;
(c) the use of agreed software tools;
(d) the methods to be used to identify duplicate documents;
(e) the use of Data Sampling;
(f) the methods to be used to identify privileged documents and other non-disclosable documents, to redact documents (where redaction is appropriate), and for dealing with privileged or other documents which have been inadvertently disclosed; and
(g) the use of a staged approach to the disclosure of Electronic Documents;
(4) the preservation of Electronic Documents, with a view to preventing loss of such documents before the trial;
(5) the exchange of data relating to Electronic Documents in an agreed electronic format using agreed fields;
(6) the formats in which Electronic Documents are to be provided on inspection and the methods to be used;
(7) the basis of charging for or sharing the cost of the provision of Electronic Documents, and whether any arrangements for charging or sharing of costs are final or are subject to reallocation in accordance with any order for costs subsequently made; and
(8) whether it would be appropriate to use the services of a neutral electronic repository for storage of Electronic Documents.

The Electronic Documents Questionnaire

paras.10–13 PC25 para.11 PC25, 50.26

10. In some cases the parties may find it helpful to exchange the Electronic Documents Questionnaire in order to provide information to each other in relation to the scope, extent and most suitable format for disclosure of Electronic Documents in the proceedings.
11. The answers to the Electronic Documents Questionnaire must be verified by a statement of truth.
12. Answers to the Electronic Documents Questionnaire will only be available for inspection by non-parties if permission is given under r. 5.4C(2).
13. Rule 31.22 makes provision regulating the use of answers to the Electronic Documents Questionnaire.

Preparation for the First Case Management Conference

paras.14–16 50.27

14. The documents submitted to the court in advance of the first case management conference should include a summary of the matters on which the parties agree in relation to the disclosure of Electronic Documents and a summary of the matters on which they disagree.
15. If the parties indicate that they have been unable to reach agreement in relation to the disclosure of Electronic Documents and that no agreement is likely, the court will give written directions in relation to disclosure or order a separate hearing in relation to disclosure. When doing so, the court will consider making an order that the parties must complete and exchange all or any part of the Electronic Documents Questionnaire within 14 days or such other period as the court may direct.
16. The person signing the Electronic Documents Questionnaire should attend the first case management conference, and any subsequent hearing at which disclosure is likely to be considered.

Where the Parties Are Unable to Reach an Appropriate Agreement in Relation to the Disclosure of Electronic Documents

paras.17–19 50.27

17. If at any time it becomes apparent that the parties are unable to reach agreement in relation to the disclosure of Electronic Documents, the parties should seek directions from the court at the earliest practical date.
18. If the court considers that the parties' agreement in relation to the disclosure of Electronic Documents is inappropriate or insufficient, the court will give directions in relation to disclosure. When doing so, the court will consider making an order that the parties must complete and exchange all or any part of the Electronic Documents Questionnaire within 14 days or such other period as the court may direct.
19. If a party gives disclosure of Electronic Documents without first discussing with other parties how to plan and manage such disclosure, the court may require that party to carry out further searches for documents or to repeat other steps which that party has already carried out.

The Reasonable Search

paras.20–24 50.27 para.21 50.27

20. The extent of the reasonable search required by r. 31.7 for the purposes of standard disclosure is affected by the existence of Electronic Documents. The extent of the search which must be made will depend on the circumstances of the case including, in particular, the factors referred to in r. 31.7(2). The parties should bear in mind that the overriding objective includes dealing with the case in ways which are proportionate.
21. The factors that may be relevant in deciding the reasonableness of a search for Electronic Documents include (but are not limited to) the following—
    (1) the number of documents involved;
    (2) the nature and complexity of the proceedings;

CPR 26–50 & PDs

(3) the ease and expense of retrieval of any particular document. This includes:
   (a) the accessibility of Electronic Documents including email communications on computer systems, servers, backup systems and other electronic devices or media that may contain such documents taking into account alterations or developments in hardware or software systems used by the disclosing party and/or available to enable access to such documents;
   (b) the location of relevant Electronic Documents, data, computer systems, servers, backup systems and other electronic devices or media that may contain such documents;
   (c) the likelihood of locating relevant data;
   (d) the cost of recovering any Electronic Documents;
   (e) the cost of disclosing and providing inspection of any relevant Electronic Documents; and
   (f) the likelihood that Electronic Documents will be materially altered in the course of recovery, disclosure or inspection;

(4) the availability of documents or contents of documents from other sources; and
(5) the significance of any document which is likely to be located during the search.

22. Depending on the circumstances, it may be reasonable to search all of the parties' electronic storage systems, or to search only some part of those systems. For example, it may be reasonable to decide not to search for documents coming into existence before a particular date, or to limit the search to documents in a particular place or places, or to documents falling into particular categories.

23. In some cases a staged approach may be appropriate, with disclosure initially being given of limited categories of documents. Those categories may subsequently be extended or limited depending on the results initially obtained.

24. The primary source of disclosure of Electronic Documents is normally reasonably accessible data. A party requesting under r. 31.12 specific disclosure of Electronic Documents which are not reasonably accessible must demonstrate that the relevance and materiality justify the cost and burden of retrieving and producing [them].

Keyword and Other Automated Searches

paras.25–27 **50.27**

25. It may be reasonable to search for Electronic Documents by means of Keyword Searches or other automated methods of searching if a full review of each and every document would be unreasonable.

26. However, it will often be insufficient to use simple Keyword Searches or other automated methods of searching alone. The injudicious use of Keyword Searches and other automated search techniques—
   (1) may result in failure to find important documents which ought to be disclosed, and/or
   (2) may find excessive quantities of irrelevant documents, which if disclosed would place an excessive burden in time and cost on the party to whom disclosure is given.

27. The parties should consider supplementing Keyword Searches and other automated searches with additional techniques such as individually reviewing certain documents or categories of documents (for example important documents generated by key personnel) and taking such other steps as may be required in order to justify the selection to the court.

Disclosure of Metadata

28. Where copies of disclosed documents are provided in Native Format in accordance with para. 33 below, some Metadata will be disclosed with each document. A party requesting disclosure of additional Metadata or forensic image copies of disclosed documents (for example in relation to a dispute concerning authenticity) must demonstrate that the relevance and materiality of the requested Metadata justify the cost and burden of producing that Metadata.

29. Parties using document management or litigation support systems should be alert to the possibility that Metadata or other useful information relating to documents may not be stored with the documents.

Lists of Documents

para.30(2) 50.28 para.30(7) 50.28

30. If a party is giving disclosure of Electronic Documents, PD 31A, para. 3, is to be read subject to the following—
(1) form N265 may be amended to accommodate the sub-paragraphs which follow:
(2) a list of documents may by agreement between the parties be an electronic file in csv (comma-separated values) or other agreed format;
(3) documents may be listed otherwise than in date order where a different order would be more convenient;
(4) save where otherwise agreed or ordered, documents should be listed individually if a party already possesses data relating to the document (for example, type of document and date of creation) which make this possible (so that as far as possible each document may be given a unique reference number);
(5) a party should be consistent in the way in which documents are listed;
(6) consistent column headings should be repeated on each page of the list on which documents are listed, where the software used for preparing the list enables this to be carried out automatically; and
(7) the disclosure list number used in any supplemental list of documents should be unique and should run sequentially from the last number used in the previous list.

Provision of Disclosure Data in Electronic Form

para.31 50.28

31. Where a party provides another party with Disclosure Data in electronic form, the following provisions will apply unless the parties agree or the court directs otherwise—
(1) Disclosure Data should be set out in a single, continuous table or spreadsheet, each separate column containing exclusively one of the following types of Disclosure Data—
(a) disclosure list number (sequential)
(b) date
(c) document type
(d) author/sender
(e) recipient
(f) disclosure list number of any parent or covering document;
(2) other than for disclosure list numbers, blank entries are permissible and preferred if there is no relevant Disclosure Data (that is, the field should be left blank rather than state 'Undated');
(3) dates should be set out in the alphanumeric form '01 Jan 2010'; and
(4) Disclosure Data should be set out in a consistent manner.

Provision of Electronic Copies of Disclosed Documents

para.32 50.28 para.33 PC25, 50.28

32. The parties should cooperate at an early stage about the format in which Electronic Documents are to be provided on inspection. In the case of difficulty or disagreement, the matter should be referred to the court for directions at the earliest practical date, if possible at the first case management conference.

33. Save where otherwise agreed or ordered, electronic copies of disclosed documents should be provided in their Native Format, in a manner which preserves Metadata relating to the date of creation of each document.

34. A party should provide any available searchable OCR versions of Electronic Documents with the original. A party may however choose not to provide OCR versions of documents which have been redacted. If OCR versions are provided, they are provided on an 'as is' basis, with no assurance to the other party that the OCR versions are complete or accurate.

35. (1) Subject to sub-para. (2) below, if a party is providing in electronic form copies of disclosed documents and wishes to redact or otherwise make alterations to a document or documents, then—
(a) the party redacting or altering the document must inform the other party in accordance with r. 31.19 that redacted or altered versions are being supplied; and

(b) the party redacting or altering the document must ensure that the original unredacted and unaltered version is preserved, so that it remains available to be inspected if required.

(2) Sub-paragraph (1) above does not apply where the only alteration made to the document is an alteration to the Metadata as a result of the ordinary process of copying and/or accessing the document. Sub-paragraph (1) does apply to the alteration or suppression of Metadata in other situations.

Specialised Technology

para.36 50.28

36. If Electronic Documents are best accessed using technology which is not readily available to the party entitled to disclosure, and that party reasonably requires additional inspection facilities, the party making disclosure shall cooperate in making available to the other party such reasonable additional inspection facilities as may be appropriate in order to afford inspection in accordance with r. 31.3.

SCHEDULE
ELECTRONIC DOCUMENTS QUESTIONNAIRE

PART 1 — YOUR DISCLOSURE

Extent of a Reasonable Search

Date range and custodians

1. What date range do you consider that your searches for Electronic Documents should cover ('the date range')?
2. Identify the custodians or creators of your Electronic Documents whose repositories of documents you consider should be searched.[1]

Communications

3. Which forms of electronic communication were in use during the date range (so far as is relevant to these proceedings)?

A Communication	B In use during the date range? (yes/no)	C Are you searching for relevant documents in this category? (yes/no)	D Where and on what type of software/ equipment/ media is this communication stored?[2]	E (a) Are backups or archives of this communication available, and (b) if so, are you searching the backups or archives?
i) Email[3]				
ii) Other (provide details for each type[4])				
……				

[1] Include names of all those who may have or have had custody of disclosable documents, including secretaries, personal assistants, former employees and/or former participants. It may be helpful to identify different dates for particular custodians.

[2] State the geographical location (if known). Consider (at least) servers, desktop PCs, laptops, notebooks, hand-held devices, PDA devices, off-site storage, removable storage media (for example, CD-ROMs, DVDs, USB drives, memory sticks) and databases.

[3] Consider all types of email system (for example, Outlook, Lotus Notes, web-based accounts), whether stored on personal computers, portable devices or in web-based accounts (for example, Yahoo, Hotmail, Gmail).

[4] *For example, instant messaging,* voicemail, VOIP (Voice Over Internet Protocol), recorded telephone lines, text messaging, audio files, video files.

Electronic Documents

4. Apart from attachments to emails, which forms of Electronic Documents were created or stored by you during the date range?

A Communication	B In use during the date range? (yes/no)	C Are you searching for relevant documents in this category? (yes/no)	D Where and on what type of software/ equipment/media is this communication stored?[5]	E (a) Are backups or archives of this communication available, and (b) if so, are you searching the backups or archives?
i) Word (or equivalent — state which)				
ii) Excel (or equivalent — state which)				
iii) Electronic Images[6]				
iv) Other[7]				

Databases of Electronic Documents

5. In the following table identify database systems, including document management systems, used by you during the date range and which may contain disclosable Electronic Documents.

A Name	B Brief description	C Nature of data held	D Are you disclosing documents held in this database?(yes/no)	E Proposals for provision of relevant documents to or access by other parties to this litigation
1.				
2. (etc.)				

Method of Search

Keywords

6. Do you consider that Keyword Searches should be used as part of the process of determining which Electronic Documents you should disclose?
If yes, provide details of—
(1) the keywords used or to be used (by reference, if applicable, to individual custodians, creators, repositories, file types and/or date ranges);[8] and
(2) the extent to which the Keyword Searches have been or will be supplemented by a review of individual documents.

Other types of automated searches

7. Do you consider that automated searches or automated techniques other than Keyword Searches (for example, concept searches or clustering) should be used as part of the process of determining which Electronic Documents you should disclose?
If yes, provide details of—
(1) the process(es) used or to be used (by reference, if applicable, to individual custodians, creators, repositories, file types and/or date ranges);
(2) the extent to which the processes have been or will be supplemented by a review of individual documents; and
(3) how the methodology of automated searches will be made available for consideration by other parties.

[5] State the geographical location (if known). Consider (at least) servers, desktops and laptops.
[6] For example, pdf, tif, jpg.
[7] For example, Powerpoint or equivalent, specialist documents (such as CAD Drawings).
[8] Where Keyword Searches are used in order to identify irrelevant documents which are to be excluded from disclosure (for example a confidential name of a client or customer), a general description of the type of search may be given.

CPR 26–50 & PDs

8. If the answer to Question 6 or 7 is yes, state whether attachments to (a) emails (b) compressed files (c) embedded files and (d) imaged text will respond to your Keyword Searches or other automated search.
9. Are you using or intending to use computer software for other purposes in relation to disclosure? If so, provide details of the software, processes and methods to be used.

Potential Problems with the Extent of Search and Accessibility of Electronic Documents

10. Do any of the sources and/or documents identified in this Electronic Documents Questionnaire raise questions about the reasonableness of the search which ought to be taken into account?[9] If so, give details.
11. Are any documents which may be disclosable encrypted, password-protected or for other reasons difficult to access, or do you have any reason to believe that they may be?[10] If so, state which of the categories identified at Questions 3, 4 and 5 above are affected, and your proposals for making them accessible.
12. Are you aware of any other points in relation to disclosure of your Electronic Documents which require discussion between the parties? If so, give details.

Preservation of Electronic Documents

13. Do you have a document retention policy?
14. Have you given an instruction to preserve Electronic Documents, and if so, when?

Inspection

15. Subject to reconsideration after receiving the responses of other parties to this Electronic Documents Questionnaire, (a) in what format and (b) on what media do you intend to provide to other parties copies of disclosed documents which are or will be available in electronic form?
16. Subject to reconsideration after receiving the responses of other parties to this Electronic Documents Questionnaire, do you intend to provide other parties with Disclosure Data electronically, and if so, (a) in what format and (b) on what media?
17. Insofar as you have available or will have available searchable OCR versions of Electronic Documents, do you intend to provide the searchable OCR version to other parties?[11] If not, why not?

PART 2 — THE DISCLOSURE OF OTHER PARTIES

The Extent and Content of Their Search

18. Do you at this stage have any proposals about the date ranges which should be searched by other parties to the proceedings? If so, provide details.
19. Do you at this stage have any proposals about the custodians or creators whose repositories of documents should be searched for disclosable documents by other parties to the proceedings? If so, provide details.[12]
20. Do you consider that the other party(ies) should disclose all available Metadata[13] attaching to any documents? If yes, provide details of the documents or categories of documents.

[9] See PD 31B, which refers to the following matters which may be relevant: (a) the number of documents involved; (b) the nature and complexity of the proceedings; (c) the ease and expense of retrieval of any particular document; (d) the availability of documents or contents of documents from other sources; and (e) the significance of any document which is likely to be located during the search.

[10] For example, backups, archives, off-site or outsourced document storage, documents created by former employees, documents stored in other jurisdictions, documents in foreign languages.

[11] There is no requirement that you should obtain OCR versions of documents, and this question is directed only to OCR versions which you have available or expect to have available to you. If you do provide OCR versions to another party, they will be provided by you on an 'as is' basis, with no assurance to the other party that the OCR versions are complete or accurate. You may wish to exclude provision of OCR versions of documents which have been redacted.

[12] Include names of all those who may have or have had custody of disclosable documents, including secretaries, personal assistants, former employees and/or former participants. It may be helpful to identify different dates for particular custodians.

[13] 'Metadata' is information about the document or file which is recorded in the computer, such as the date and time of creation or modification of a word-processing file, or the author and the date and time of sending of an email. The question is directed to the more extensive Metadata which may be relevant where for example authenticity is disputed.

Proposals for the Method to Be Adopted for Their Searches

21. Do you at this stage have any proposals about the Keyword Searches, or other automated searches, which should be applied by other parties to their document sets? If so, provide details.

Inspection

22. Subject to reconsideration after receiving the responses of other parties to this Electronic Documents Questionnaire, (a) in what format and (b) on what media do you wish to receive copies of disclosed documents which are or will be available in electronic form?
23. Subject to reconsideration after receiving the responses of other parties to this Electronic Documents Questionnaire, do you wish to receive Disclosure Data electronically, and if so, (a) in what format and (b) on what media?

STATEMENT OF TRUTH

*[I believe][The [claimant][defendant] believes] that the facts stated in the answers to this Electronic Documents Questionnaire are true.

*I am duly authorised by the [claimant][defendant] to sign this statement.

Full name..

Name of legal representative's firm..

Signed..

Position or office held (if signing on behalf of firm or company)..............

Date..

* *delete as appropriate*

WARNING: Unless the court makes some other order, the answers given in this document may only be used for the purposes of the proceedings in which the document is produced unless it has been read to or by the court or referred to at a hearing which has been held in public or the court gives permission or the party who has completed this questionnaire agrees.

Guidance Notes

1. Technical expressions are defined in PD 31B.
2. The questions in the Electronic Documents Questionnaire are not intended to give rise to any implication about how disclosure should or should not be carried out. They are intended only to provide information to other parties and to the court.
3. Further facts and matters may come to parties' attention over the course of the proceedings which affect the answers to the Electronic Documents Questionnaire. Where detailed information is not yet available at the time the Electronic Documents Questionnaire is first answered, parties should give such information as they can, and supplement or amend their answers when further information is available. Answers should be updated by notifying other parties and the court without undue delay, and in any event before each case management conference at which disclosure is likely to be considered.
4. Some of the questions in the Electronic Documents Questionnaire require only a brief answer which may need to be elaborated after Electronic Documents Questionnaires have been exchanged. The purpose of such questions is to assist the parties in identifying the points which may require elaboration in order for meaningful discussions to take place between them.
5. Questions which refer to sources of Electronic Documents that are not considered to be relevant may be answered with a statement to that effect.
6. Questions about 'your' documents and about software, hardware or systems used by 'you' are directed, in the case of solicitors, to the solicitor's lay client's documents or to documents prepared on the lay client's behalf.

CPR Part 32 Evidence

Part 32 **45.6, 48.12, 51.18, 87.34, 87.37** [For commentary on a specific rule, please refer to the cross-references after the title of the rule.]

32.1 Power of Court to Control Evidence

r.32.1 **39.19, 42.36, 42.43, 45.6, 49.2, 49.73, 49.74, 51.14, 77.48, 91.43**
r.32.1(1) **49.8, 49.52**
r.32.1(1)(a)–(c) **61.17**
r.32.1 (2) **42.36, 49.8, 49.52, 50.75**
r.32.1(3) **49.8, 49.73**

(1) The court may control the evidence by giving directions as to—
(a) the issues on which it requires evidence;
(b) the nature of the evidence which it requires to decide those issues; and
(c) the way in which the evidence is to be placed before the court.

(2) The court may use its power under this rule to exclude evidence that would otherwise be admissible.

(3) The court may limit cross-examination[(GL)].

32.2 Evidence of Witnesses — General Rule

rr.32.2–32.19 **45.18**
r.32.2 **49.51**
r.32.2(1) **32.15**
r.32.2(2) **49.51**
r.32.2(2)(b) **51.14**
r.32.2(3)(b) **51.21**

(1) The general rule is that any fact which needs to be proved by the evidence of witnesses is to be proved—
(a) at trial, by their oral evidence given in public; and
(b) at any other hearing, by their evidence in writing.

(2) This is subject—
(a) to any provision to the contrary contained in these Rules or elsewhere; or
(b) to any order of the court.

(3) The court may give directions—
(a) identifying or limiting the issues to which factual evidence may be directed;
(b) identifying the witnesses who may be called or whose evidence may be read; or
(c) limiting the length or format of witness statements.

32.3 Evidence by Video Link or Other Means

r.32.3 **45.18, 49.51, 51.18, 58.11**

The court may allow a witness to give evidence through a video link or by other means.

32.4 Requirement to Serve Witness Statements for Use at Trial

r.32.4 **45.18**
r.32.4(1) **51.1**
r.32.4(2) **51.18**
r.32.4(3) **51.18**

(1) A witness statement is a written statement signed by a person which contains the evidence which that person would be allowed to give orally.
(2) The court will order a party to serve on the other parties any witness statement of the oral evidence which the party serving the statement intends to rely on in relation to any issues of fact to be decided at the trial.
(3) The court may give directions as to—
  (a) the order in which witness statements are to be served; and
  (b) whether or not the witness statements are to be filed.

32.5 Use at Trial of Witness Statements Which Have Been Served

r.32.5 **45.18**
r.32.5(1) **51.21**
r.32.5(2) **51.21, 53.7, 61.43**
r.32.5(3) **51.21, 61.43**
r.32.5(4) **46.5, 51.21, 61.43**
r.32.5(5) **1.17, 51.23, 53.12**

(1) If—
  (a) a party has served a witness statement; and
  (b) he wishes to rely at trial on the evidence of the witness who made the statement,
  he must call the witness to give oral evidence unless the court orders otherwise or he puts the statement in as hearsay evidence.

(Part 33 contains provisions about hearsay evidence)
(2) Where a witness is called to give oral evidence under paragraph (1), his witness statement shall stand as his evidence-in-chief(GL) unless the court orders otherwise.
(3) A witness giving oral evidence at trial may with the permission of the court—
  (a) amplify his witness statement; and
  (b) give evidence in relation to new matters which have arisen since the witness statement was served on the other parties.
(4) The court will give permission under paragraph (3) only if it considers that there is good reason not to confine the evidence of the witness to the contents of his witness statement.
(5) If a party who has served a witness statement does not—
  (a) call the witness to give evidence at trial; or
  (b) put the witness statement in as hearsay evidence,
  any other party may put the witness statement in as hearsay evidence.

32.6 Evidence in Proceedings Other than at Trial

r.32.6 **14.78, 15.30, 42.32, 42.47, 45.18**
r.32.6(1) **32.15**
r.32.6(2) **23.16, 23.17, 26.3**
r.32.6(2)(a)–(b) **32.15**

(1) Subject to paragraph (2), the general rule is that evidence at hearings other than the trial is to be by witness statement unless the court, a practice direction or any other enactment requires otherwise.
(2) At hearings other than the trial, a party may rely on the matters set out in—
  (a) his statement of case; or
  (b) his application notice,
  if the statement of case or application notice is verified by a statement of truth.

32.7 Order for Cross-examination

r.32.7 **32.30, 45.18, 50.32**

(1) Where, at a hearing other than the trial, evidence is given in writing, any party may apply to the court for permission to cross-examine the person giving the evidence.
(2) If the court gives permission under paragraph (1) but the person in question does not attend as required by the order, his evidence may not be used unless the court gives permission.

(Rules 78.26 to 78.28 contain rules in relation to evidence arising out of mediation of certain cross-border disputes. Rule 78.27(1)(b) relates specifically to this rule.)

32.8 Form of Witness Statement

r.32.8 **45.18**

A witness statement must comply with the requirements set out in Practice Direction 32. (Part 22 requires a witness statement to be verified by a statement of truth)

32.9 Witness Summaries

r.32.9 45.18, 49.64, 51.19 r.32.9(1) 46.5

(1) A party who—
 (a) is required to serve a witness statement for use at trial; but
 (b) is unable to obtain one,
may apply, without notice, for permission to serve a witness summary instead.
(2) A witness summary is a summary of—
 (a) the evidence, if known, which would otherwise be included in a witness statement; or
 (b) if the evidence is not known, the matters about which the party serving the witness summary proposes to question the witness.
(3) Unless the court orders otherwise, a witness summary must include the name and address of the intended witness.
(4) Unless the court orders otherwise, a witness summary must be served within the period in which a witness statement would have had to be served.
(5) Where a party serves a witness summary, so far as practicable rules 32.4 (requirement to serve witness statements for use at trial), 32.5(3) (amplifying witness statements), and 32.8 (form of witness statement) shall apply to the summary.

32.10 Consequence of Failure to Serve Witness Statement or Summary

r.32.10 43.27, 45.18, 48.28, 51.20

If a witness statement or a witness summary for use at trial is not served in respect of an intended witness within the time specified by the court, then the witness may not be called to give oral evidence unless the court gives permission.

32.11 Cross-examination on a Witness Statement

r.32.11 45.18, 51.22, 61.44

Where a witness is called to give evidence at trial, he may be cross-examined on his witness statement whether or not the statement or any part of it was referred to during the witness's evidence-in-chief(GL).

32.12 Use of Witness Statements for Other Purposes

r.32.12 45.18 r.32.12(1) 51.25

(1) Except as provided by this rule, a witness statement may be used only for the purpose of the proceedings in which it is served.
(2) Paragraph (1) does not apply if and to the extent that—
 (a) the witness gives consent in writing to some other use of it;
 (b) the court gives permission for some other use; or
 (c) the witness statement has been put in evidence at a hearing held in public.

32.13 Availability of Witness Statements for Inspection

r.32.13 15.56, 45.18, 51.24, 58.6 r.32.13(4) 51.24

(1) A witness statement which stands as evidence-in-chief(GL) is open to inspection during the course of the trial unless the court otherwise directs.
(2) Any person may ask for a direction that a witness statement is not open to inspection.
(3) The court will not make a direction under paragraph (2) unless it is satisfied that a witness statement should not be open to inspection because of—
 (a) the interests of justice;
 (b) the public interest;
 (c) the nature of any expert medical evidence in the statement;
 (d) the nature of any confidential information (including information relating to personal financial matters) in the statement; or
 (e) the need to protect the interests of any child or protected party.
(4) The court may exclude from inspection words or passages in the statement.

32.14 False Statements

r.32.14 23.15, 45.18, 51.10, 52.8, 87.14 r.32.14(1) 23.2

(1) Proceedings for contempt of court may be brought against a person if he makes, or causes to be made, a false statement in a document verified by a statement of truth without an honest belief in its truth.

(Part 22 makes provision for a statement of truth)

(Section 6 of Part 81 contains provisions in relation to committal for making a false statement of truth.)

(2) [*Revoked*]

32.15 Affidavit Evidence

r.32.15 14.78, 45.18 r.32.15(2) 15.30, 32.15

(1) Evidence must be given by affidavit(GL) instead of or in addition to a witness statement if this is required by the court, a provision contained in any other rule, a practice direction or any other enactment.

(2) Nothing in these Rules prevents a witness giving evidence by affidavit(GL) at a hearing other than the trial if he chooses to do so in a case where paragraph (1) does not apply, but the party putting forward the affidavit(GL) may not recover the additional cost of making it from any other party unless the court orders otherwise.

32.16 Form of Affidavit

r.32.16 45.18, 52.2

An affidavit(GL) must comply with the requirements set out in Practice Direction 32.

32.17 Affidavit Made outside the Jurisdiction

r.32.17 45.18

A person may make an affidavit(GL) outside the jurisdiction in accordance with—

(a) this Part; or

(b) the law of the place where he makes the affidavit(GL).

32.18 Notice to Admit Facts

r.32.18 45.18, 49.9

(1) A party may serve notice on another party requiring him to admit the facts, or the part of the case of the serving party, specified in the notice.

(2) A notice to admit facts must be served no later than 21 days before the trial.

(3) Where the other party makes any admission in response to the notice, the admission may be used against him only—

(a) in the proceedings in which the notice to admit is served; and

(b) by the party who served the notice.

(4) The court may allow a party to amend or withdraw any admission made by him on such terms as it thinks just.

32.19 Notice to Admit or Produce Documents

r.32.19 32.17, 45.18, 50.43 r.32.19(2) 50.43
r.32.19(1) 49.86

(1) A party shall be deemed to admit the authenticity of a document disclosed to him under Part 31 (disclosure and inspection of documents) unless he serves notice that he wishes the document to be proved at trial.

(2) A notice to prove a document must be served—

(a) by the latest date for serving witness statements; or

(b) within 7 days of disclosure of the document,

whichever is later.

32.20 Notarial Acts and Instruments

r.32.20 53.18

A notarial act or instrument may be received in evidence without further proof as duly authenticated in accordance with the requirements of law unless the contrary is proved.

PD 32 Practice Direction 32 — Evidence

This practice direction supplements CPR, Part 32.

PD 32 **32.15, 48.12, 49.51, 52.7** [For commentary on a specific paragraph, please refer to the cross-references after the title of the paragraph.]

Evidence in General

para.1.4 **52.7** para.1.7 **32.15**

1.1 Rule 32.2 sets out how evidence is to be given and facts are to be proved.

1.2 Evidence at a hearing other than the trial should normally be given by witness statement[1] (see para. 17 onwards). However, a witness may give evidence by affidavit if he wishes to do so[2] (and see para. 1.4 below).

1.3 Statements of case (see para. 26 onwards) and application notices[3] may also be used as evidence provided that their contents have been verified by a statement of truth.[4]

(For information regarding evidence by deposition see Part 34 and PD 34A.)

1.4 Affidavits must be used as evidence in the following instances:

(1) where sworn evidence is required by an enactment,[5] rule, order or practice direction, and

(2) in any application for a search order, a freezing injunction, or an order requiring an occupier to permit another to enter his land.

(Part 81 and PD 81 contain provisions about evidence in relation to contempt of court. Particular attention is drawn to rr. 81.10, 81.11, 81.14, 81.15, 81.26 and PD 81, paras 4.5 and 14.1.)

1.5 If a party believes that sworn evidence is required by a court in another jurisdiction for any purpose connected with the proceedings, he may apply to the court for a direction that evidence shall be given only by affidavit on any pre-trial applications.

1.6 The court may give a direction under r. 32.15 that evidence shall be given by affidavit instead of or in addition to a witness statement or statement of case:

(1) on its own initiative, or

(2) after any party has applied to the court for such a direction.

1.7 An affidavit, where referred to in the Civil Procedure Rules or a practice direction, also means an affirmation unless the context requires otherwise.

Affidavits

paras.2–16 **52.2**

Deponent

2 A deponent is a person who gives evidence by affidavit or affirmation.

Heading

para.3.2 **52.2**

3.1 The affidavit should be headed with the title of the proceedings (see PD 7A, para. 4, and PD 20, para. 7); where the proceedings are between several parties with the same status it is sufficient to identify the parties as follows:

	Number:
A.B. (and others)	Claimants/Applicants
C.D. (and others)	Defendants/Respondents
	(as appropriate)

3.2 At the top right-hand corner of the first page (and on the backsheet) there should be clearly written:

(1) the party on whose behalf it is made,

(2) the initials and surname of the deponent,

---

1 See rule 32.6(1).

2 *See rule 32.15(2).*

3 See Part 23 for information about making an application.

4 Rule 32.6(2) and see Part 22 for information about the statement of truth.

5 See, e.g., s. 3(5)(a) of the Protection from Harassment Act 1997.

(3) the number of the affidavit in relation to that deponent,
(4) the identifying initials and number of each exhibit referred to, and
(5) the date sworn.

Body of affidavit

paras.4.1–4.2 52.2

4.1 The affidavit must, if practicable, be in the deponent's own words, the affidavit should be expressed in the first person and the deponent should:
(1) commence 'I (*full name*) *of* (*address*) state on oath…',
(2) if giving evidence in his professional, business or other occupational capacity, give the address at which he works in (1) above, the position he holds and the name of his firm or employer,
(3) give his occupation or, if he has none, his description, and
(4) state if he is a party to the proceedings or employed by a party to the proceedings, if it be the case.

4.2 An affidavit must indicate:
(1) which of the statements in it are made from the deponent's own knowledge and which are matters of information or belief, and
(2) the source for any matters of information or belief.

4.3 Where a deponent:
(1) refers to an exhibit or exhibits, he should state 'there is now shown to me marked '…' the (*description of exhibit*)', and
(2) makes more than one affidavit (to which there are exhibits) in the same proceedings, the numbering of the exhibits should run consecutively throughout and not start again with each affidavit.

Jurat

para.5 52.2

5.1 The jurat of an affidavit is a statement set out at the end of the document which authenticates the affidavit.

5.2 It must:
(1) be signed by all deponents,
(2) be completed and signed by the person before whom the affidavit was sworn whose name and qualification must be printed beneath his signature,
(3) contain the full address of the person before whom the affidavit was sworn, and
(4) follow immediately on from the text and not be put on a separate page.

Format of affidavits

para.6.1(1)–(2) 52.2
para.6.1(4) 52.2
para.6.1(7) 52.2

6.1 An affidavit should:
(1) be produced on durable quality A4 paper with a 3.5 cm margin,
(2) be fully legible and should normally be typed on one side of the paper only,
(3) where possible, be bound securely in a manner which would not hamper filing, or otherwise each page should be endorsed with the case number and should bear the initials of the deponent and of the person before whom it was sworn,
(4) have the pages numbered consecutively as a separate document (or as one of several documents contained in a file),
(5) be divided into numbered paragraphs,
(6) have all numbers, including dates, expressed in figures, and
(7) give the reference to any document or documents mentioned either in the margin or in bold text in the body of the affidavit.

6.2 It is usually convenient for an affidavit to follow the chronological sequence of events or matters dealt with; each paragraph of an affidavit should as far as possible be confined to a distinct portion of the subject.

Inability of deponent to read or sign affidavit
para.7.1(1)–(3) 52.5

7.1 Where an affidavit is sworn by a person who is unable to read or sign it, the person before whom the affidavit is sworn must certify in the jurat that:
(1) he read the affidavit to the deponent,
(2) the deponent appeared to understand it, and
(3) the deponent signed or made his mark, in his presence.

7.2 If that certificate is not included in the jurat, the affidavit may not be used in evidence unless the court is satisfied that it was read to the deponent and that he appeared to understand it. Two versions of the form of jurat with the certificate are set out at Annex 1 to this practice direction.

Alterations to affidavits
para.8.1 52.2

8.1 Any alteration to an affidavit must be initialled by both the deponent and the person before whom the affidavit was sworn.

8.2 An affidavit which contains an alteration that has not been initialled may be filed or used in evidence only with the permission of the court.

Who may administer oaths and take affidavit
para.9 52.3

9.1 Only the following may administer oaths and take affidavits—
(1) a commissioner for oaths;[6]
(2) [*deleted*]
(3) other persons specified by statute;[7]
(4) certain officials of the Supreme Court;[8]
(5) a circuit judge or district judge;[9]
(6) any justice of the peace;[10] and
(7) certain officials of any county court appointed by the judge of that court for the purpose.[11]

9.2 An affidavit must be sworn before a person independent of the parties or their representatives.

Filing of affidavits
para.10 52.6 para.10.2 52.7

10.1 If the court directs that an affidavit is to be filed,[12] it must be filed in the court or Division, or office or registry of the court or Division where the action in which it was or is to be used, is proceeding or will proceed.

10.2 Where an affidavit is in a foreign language:
(1) the party wishing to rely on it:
(a) must have it translated, and
(b) must file the foreign-language affidavit with the court, and
(2) the translator must make and file with the court an affidavit verifying the translation and exhibiting both the translation and a copy of the foreign-language affidavit.

Exhibits

paras.11.3–11.4 51.7

Manner of exhibiting documents

11.1 A document used in conjunction with an affidavit should be:
(1) produced to and verified by the deponent, and remain separate from the affidavit, and

6 Commissioners for Oaths Acts 1889 and 1891.
7 Legal Services Act 2007, ss. 12 and 18, sch. 2 and sch. 4.
8 Section 2 of the Commissioners for Oaths Act 1889.
9 *Section 58 of the County Courts Act 1984.*
10 Section 58 as above.
11 Section 58 as above.
12 Rules 32.1(3) and 32.4(3)(b).

(2) identified by a declaration of the person before whom the affidavit was sworn.

11.2 The declaration should be headed with the name of the proceedings in the same way as the affidavit.

11.3 The first page of each exhibit should be marked:
(1) as in para. 3.2 above, and
(2) with the exhibit mark referred to in the affidavit.

Letters

12.1 Copies of individual letters should be collected together and exhibited in a bundle or bundles. They should be arranged in chronological order with the earliest at the top, and firmly secured.

12.2 When a bundle of correspondence is exhibited, the exhibit should have a front page attached stating that the bundle consists of original letters and copies. They should be arranged and secured as above and numbered consecutively.

Other documents

paras.13.1 51.7 para.13.2 51.7, 63.50

13.1 Photocopies instead of original documents may be exhibited provided the originals are made available for inspection by the other parties before the hearing and by the judge at the hearing.

13.2 Court documents must not be exhibited (official copies of such documents prove themselves).

13.3 Where an exhibit contains more than one document, a front page should be attached setting out a list of the documents contained in the exhibit; the list should contain the dates of the documents.

Exhibits other than documents

para.14 51.7

14.1 Items other than documents should be clearly marked with an exhibit number or letter in such a manner that the mark cannot become detached from the exhibit.

14.2 Small items may be placed in a container and the container appropriately marked.

General provisions

para.15.1(1) 51.7 para.15.4 51.8
para.15.3 51.17, 52.6

15.1 Where an exhibit contains more than one document:
(1) the bundle should not be stapled but should be securely fastened in a way that does not hinder the reading of the documents, and
(2) the pages should be numbered consecutively at bottom centre.

15.2 Every page of an exhibit should be clearly legible; typed copies of illegible documents should be included, paginated with 'a' numbers.

15.3 Where affidavits and exhibits have become numerous, they should be put into separate bundles and the pages numbered consecutively throughout.

15.4 Where on account of their bulk the service of exhibits or copies of exhibits on the other parties would be difficult or impracticable, the directions of the court should be sought as to arrangements for bringing the exhibits to the attention of the other parties and as to their custody pending trial.

Affirmations

para.16 52.4

16 All provisions in this or any other practice direction relating to affidavits apply to affirmations with the following exceptions:
(1) the deponent should commence 'I (*name*) of (*address*) do solemnly and sincerely affirm...', and
(2) in the jurat the word 'sworn' is replaced by the word 'affirmed'.

Witness Statements

para.17.1 51.4 para.17.2 51.3

Heading

17.1 The witness statement should be headed with the title of the proceedings (see PD 7A, para. 4, and PD 20, para. 7); where the proceedings are between several parties with the same status it is sufficient to identify the parties as follows:

CPR 26–50 & PDs

Number:
A.B. (and others) Claimants/Applicants
C.D. (and others) Defendants/Respondents
(as appropriate)

17.2 At the top right-hand corner of the first page there should be clearly written:
(1) the party on whose behalf it is made,
(2) the initials and surname of the witness,
(3) the number of the statement in relation to that witness,
(4) the identifying initials and number of each exhibit referred to, and
(5) the date the statement was made.

Body of witness statement

para.18.1 51.1, 51.5
para.18.2 51.6
para.18.5 51.7, 51.17
para.18.6 51.3

18.1 The witness statement must, if practicable, be in the intended witness's own words, the statement should be expressed in the first person and should also state:
(1) the full name of the witness,
(2) his place of residence or, if he is making the statement in his professional, business or other occupational capacity, the address at which he works, the position he holds and the name of his firm or employer,
(3) his occupation, or if he has none, his description, and
(4) the fact that he is a party to the proceedings or is the employee of such a party if it be the case.

18.2 A witness statement must indicate:
(1) which of the statements in it are made from the witness's own knowledge and which are matters of information or belief, and
(2) the source for any matters of information or belief.

18.3 An exhibit used in conjunction with a witness statement should be verified and identified by the witness and remain separate from the witness statement.

18.4 Where a witness refers to an exhibit or exhibits, he should state 'I refer to the (*description of exhibit*) marked "…"'.

18.5 The provisions of paras 11.3 to 15.4 (exhibits) apply similarly to witness statements as they do to affidavits.

18.6 Where a witness makes more than one witness statement to which there are exhibits, in the same proceedings, the numbering of the exhibits should run consecutively throughout and not start again with each witness statement.

Format of witness statement

para.19.1(1)–(4) 51.2
para.19.1(5)–(6) 51.5
para.19.1(7) 51.9
para.19.2 51.5

19.1 A witness statement should:
(1) be produced on durable quality A4 paper with a 3.5 cm margin,
(2) be fully legible and should normally be typed on one side of the paper only,
(3) where possible, be bound securely in a manner which would not hamper filing, or otherwise each page should be endorsed with the case number and should bear the initials of the witness,
(4) have the pages numbered consecutively as a separate statement (or as one of several statements contained in a file),
(5) be divided into numbered paragraphs,
(6) have all numbers, including dates, expressed in figures, and
(7) give the reference to any document or documents mentioned either in the margin or in bold text in the body of the statement.

19.2 It is usually convenient for a witness statement to follow the chronological sequence of the events or matters dealt with, each paragraph of a witness statement should as far as possible be confined to a distinct portion of the subject.

Statement of truth

para.20.1 58.11 para.20.2 51.10

20.1 A witness statement is the equivalent of the oral evidence which that witness would, if called, give in evidence; it must include a statement by the intended witness that he believes the facts in it are true.[13]

20.2 To verify a witness statement the statement of truth is as follows:
'I believe that the facts stated in this witness statement are true'

20.3 Attention is drawn to r. 32.14 which sets out the consequences of verifying a witness statement containing a false statement without an honest belief in its truth.

(PD 22, para. 3A, sets out the procedure to be followed where the person who should sign a document which is verified by a statement of truth is unable to read or sign the document.)

21 [*deleted*]

Alterations to witness statements

paras.22.1–22.2 51.12

22.1 Any alteration to a witness statement must be initialled by the person making the statement or by the authorised person where appropriate (see para. 21).

22.2 A witness statement which contains an alteration that has not been initialled may be used in evidence only with the permission of the court.

Filing of witness statements

para.23.1 51.15 para.23.2 51.16, 52.7

23.1 If the court directs that a witness statement is to be filed,[14] it must be filed in the court or Division, or office or registry of the court or Division where the action in which it was or is to be used, is proceeding or will proceed.

23.2 Where the court has directed that a witness statement in a foreign language is to be filed:
(1) the party wishing to rely on it must:
(a) have it translated, and
(b) file the foreign-language witness statement with the court, and
(2) the translator must make and file with the court an affidavit verifying the translation and exhibiting both the translation and a copy of the foreign-language witness statement.

Certificate of court officer

24.1 Where the court has ordered that a witness statement is not to be open to inspection by the public[15] or that words or passages in the statement are not to be open to inspection[16] the court officer will so certify on the statement and make any deletions directed by the court under r. 32.13(4).

Defects in affidavits, witness statements and exhibits

para.25 48.12, 52.6 para.25.1 51.13

25.1 Where:
(1) an affidavit,
(2) a witness statement, or
(3) an exhibit to either an affidavit or a witness statement
does not comply with Part 32 or this practice direction in relation to its form, the court may refuse to admit it as evidence and may refuse to allow the costs arising from its preparation.

25.2 Permission to file a defective affidavit or witness statement or to use a defective exhibit may be obtained from a judge[17] in the court where the case is proceeding.

13 See Part 22 for information about the statement of truth.
14 Rule 32.4(3)(b).
15 Rule 32.13(2).
16 Rule 32.13(4).
17 Rule 2.3(1); definition of judge.

Statements of Case

26.1 A statement of case may be used as evidence in an interim application provided it is verified by a statement of truth.[18]

26.2 To verify a statement of case the statement of truth should be set out as follows:
'[I believe] [the (*party on whose behalf the statement of case is being signed*) believes] that the facts stated in the statement of case are true'.

26.3 Attention is drawn to rule 32.14 which sets out the consequences of verifying a witness statement containing a false statement without an honest belief in its truth.

(For information regarding statements of truth see Part 22 and PD 22.)
(PD 7A and PD 17 provide further information concerning statements of case.)

Agreed Bundles for Hearings

para.27 53.11 para.27.2 59.7

27.1 The court may give directions requiring the parties to use their best endeavours to agree a bundle or bundles of documents for use at any hearing.

27.2 All documents contained in bundles which have been agreed for use at a hearing shall be admissible at that hearing as evidence of their contents, unless:
(1) the court orders otherwise; or
(2) a party gives written notice of objection to the admissibility of particular documents.

Videoconferencing

29.1 Guidance on the use of videoconferencing in the civil courts is set out at Annex 3 to this practice direction. A list of the sites which are available for videoconferencing can be found on Her Majesty's Courts and Tribunals Service website.

ANNEX 1

annex 1 52.5

Certificate to Be Used Where a Deponent to an Affidavit is Unable to Read or Sign it

Sworn at...... this....... day of.......... Before me, I having first read over the contents of this affidavit to the deponent [*if there are exhibits, add* 'and explained the nature and effect of the exhibits referred to in it'] who appeared to understand it and approved its content as accurate, and made his mark on the affidavit in my presence.

Or, (after, *Before me*) the witness to the mark of the deponent having been first sworn that he had read over etc. (*as above*) and that he saw him make his mark on the affidavit. (*Witness must sign*).

Certificate to Be Used Where a Deponent to an Affirmation is Unable to Read or Sign it

Affirmed at...... this....... day of......... Before me, I having first read over the contents of this affirmation to the deponent [*if there are exhibits, add* 'and explained the nature and effect of the exhibits referred to in it'] who appeared to understand it and approved its content as accurate, and made his mark on the affirmation in my presence.

Or, (after, *Before me*) the witness to the mark of the deponent having been first sworn that he had read over etc. (*as above*) and that he saw him make his mark on the affirmation. (*Witness must sign*).

ANNEX 2

[*deleted*]

ANNEX 3

annex 3 58.11

Videoconferencing Guidance

This guidance is for the use of videoconferencing (VCF) in civil proceedings. It is in part based, with permission, upon the protocol of the Federal Court of Australia. It is intended to provide a guide to

[18] See r. 32.6(2)(a).

all persons involved in the use of VCF, although it does not attempt to cover all the practical questions which might arise.

Videoconferencing Generally

1. The guidance covers the use of VCF equipment both (a) in a courtroom, whether via equipment which is permanently placed there or via a mobile unit, and (b) in a separate studio or conference room. In either case, the location at which the judge sits is referred to as the 'local site'. The other site or sites to and from which transmission is made are referred to as the 'remote site' and in any particular case any such site may be another courtroom. The guidance applies to cases where VCF is used for the taking of evidence and also to its use for other parts of any legal proceedings (for example, interim applications, case management conferences, pre-trial reviews).
2. VCF may be a convenient way of dealing with any part of proceedings: it can involve considerable savings in time and cost. Its use for the taking of evidence from overseas witnesses will, in particular, be likely to achieve a material saving of costs, and such savings may also be achieved by its use for taking domestic evidence. It is, however, inevitably not as ideal as having the witness physically present in court. Its convenience should not therefore be allowed to dictate its use. A judgment must be made in every case in which the use of VCF is being considered not only as to whether it will achieve an overall cost saving but as to whether its use will be likely to be beneficial to the efficient, fair and economic disposal of the litigation. In particular, it needs to be recognised that the degree of control a court can exercise over a witness at the remote site is or may be more limited than it can exercise over a witness physically before it.
3. When used for the taking of evidence, the objective should be to make the VCF session as close as possible to the usual practice in a trial court where evidence is taken in open court. To gain the maximum benefit, several differences have to be taken into account. Some matters, which are taken for granted when evidence is taken in the conventional way, take on a different dimension when it is taken by VCF: for example, the administration of the oath, ensuring that the witness understands who is at the local site and what their various roles are, the raising of any objections to the evidence and the use of documents.
4. It should not be presumed that all foreign governments are willing to allow their nationals or others within their jurisdiction to be examined before a court in England or Wales by means of VCF. If there is any doubt about this, enquiries should be directed to the Foreign and Commonwealth Office (International Legal Matters Unit, Consular Division) with a view to ensuring that the country from which the evidence is to be taken raises no objection to it at diplomatic level. The party who is directed to be responsible for arranging the VCF (see para. 8 below) will be required to make all necessary inquiries about this well in advance of the VCF and must be able to inform the court what those inquiries were and of their outcome.
5. Time zone differences need to be considered when a witness abroad is to be examined in England or Wales by VCF. The convenience of the witness, the parties, their representatives and the court must all be taken into account. The cost of the use of a commercial studio is usually greater outside normal business hours.
6. Those involved with VCF need to be aware that, even with the most advanced systems currently available, there are the briefest of delays between the receipt of the picture and that of the accompanying sound. If due allowance is not made for this, there will be a tendency to 'speak over' the witness, whose voice will continue to be heard for a millisecond or so after he or she appears on the screen to have finished speaking.
7. With current technology, picture quality is good, but not as good as a television picture. The quality of the picture is enhanced if those appearing on VCF monitors keep their movements to a minimum.

Preliminary Arrangements

8. The court's permission is required for any part of any proceedings to be dealt with by means of VCF. Before seeking a direction, the applicant should notify the listing officer, diary manager or other appropriate court officer of the intention to seek it, and should enquire as to the availability of court VCF equipment for the day or days of the proposed VCF. The application for a direction should be made to the master, district judge or judge, as may be appropriate. If all parties consent to a direction, permission can be sought by letter, fax or email, although the court may still

require an oral hearing. All parties are entitled to be heard on whether or not such a direction should be given and as to its terms. If a witness at a remote site is to give evidence by an interpreter, consideration should be given at this stage as to whether the interpreter should be at the local site or the remote site. If a VCF direction is given, arrangements for the transmission will then need to be made. The court will ordinarily direct that the party seeking permission to use VCF is to be responsible for this. That party is hereafter referred to as the 'VCF arranging party'.

9. Subject to any order to the contrary, all costs of the transmission, including the costs of hiring equipment and technical personnel to operate it, will initially be the responsibility of, and must be met by, the VCF arranging party. All reasonable efforts should be made to keep the transmission to a minimum and so keep the costs down. All such costs will be considered to be part of the costs of the proceedings and the court will determine at such subsequent time as is convenient or appropriate who, as between the parties, should be responsible for them and (if appropriate) in what proportions.

10. The local site will, if practicable, be a courtroom but it may instead be an appropriate studio or conference room. The VCF arranging party must contact the listing officer, diary manager or other appropriate officer of the court which made the VCF direction and make arrangements for the VCF transmission. Details of the remote site, and of the equipment to be used both at the local site (if not being supplied by the court) and the remote site (including the number of ISDN lines and connection speed), together with all necessary contact names and telephone numbers, will have to be provided to the listing officer, diary manager or other court officer. The court will need to be satisfied that any equipment provided by the parties for use at the local site and also that at the remote site is of sufficient quality for a satisfactory transmission. The VCF arranging party must ensure that an appropriate person will be present at the local site to supervise the operation of the VCF throughout the transmission in order to deal with any technical problems. That party must also arrange for a technical assistant to be similarly present at the remote site for like purposes.

11. It is recommended that the judge, practitioners and witness should arrive at their respective VCF sites about 20 minutes prior to the scheduled commencement of the transmission.

12. If the local site is not a courtroom, but a conference room or studio, the judge will need to determine who is to sit where. The VCF arranging party must take care to ensure that the number of microphones is adequate for the speakers and that the panning of the camera for the practitioners' table encompasses all legal representatives so that the viewer can see everyone seated there.

13. The proceedings, wherever they may take place, form part of a trial to which the public is entitled to have access (unless the court has determined that they should be heard in private). If the local site is to be a studio or conference room, the VCF arranging party must ensure that it provides sufficient accommodation to enable a reasonable number of members of the public to attend.

14. In cases where the local site is a studio or conference room, the VCF arranging party should make arrangements, if practicable, for the royal coat of arms to be placed above the judge's seat.

15. In cases in which the VCF is to be used for the taking of evidence, the VCF arranging party must arrange for recording equipment to be provided by the court which made the VCF direction so that the evidence can be recorded. An associate will normally be present to operate the recording equipment when the local site is a courtroom. The VCF arranging party should take steps to ensure that an associate is present to do likewise when it is a studio or conference room. The equipment should be set up and tested before the VCF transmission. It will often be a valuable safeguard for the VCF arranging party also to arrange for the provision of recording equipment at the remote site. This will provide a useful back-up if there is any reduction in sound quality during the transmission. A direction from the court for the making of such a back-up recording must, however, be obtained first. This is because the proceedings are court proceedings and, save as directed by the court, no other recording of them must be made. The court will direct what is to happen to the back-up recording.

16. Some countries may require that any oath or affirmation to be taken by a witness accord with local custom rather than the usual form of oath or affirmation used in England and Wales. The VCF arranging party must make all appropriate prior inquiries and put in place all arrangements necessary to enable the oath or affirmation to be taken in accordance with any local custom. That party must be in a position to inform the court what those inquiries were, what their outcome was and what arrangements have been made. If the oath or affirmation can be administered in the manner normal in England and Wales, the VCF arranging party must arrange in advance to

have the appropriate holy book at the remote site. The associate will normally administer the oath.

17. Consideration will need to be given in advance to the documents to which the witness is likely to be referred. The parties should endeavour to agree on this. It will usually be most convenient for a bundle of the copy documents to be prepared in advance, which the VCF arranging party should then send to the remote site.
18. Additional documents are sometimes quite properly introduced during the course of a witness's evidence. To cater for this, the VCF arranging party should ensure that equipment is available to enable documents to be transmitted between sites during the course of the VCF transmission. Consideration should be given to whether to use a document camera. If it is decided to use one, arrangements for its use will need to be established in advance. The panel operator will need to know the number and size of documents or objects if their images are to be sent by document camera. In many cases, a simpler and sufficient alternative will be to ensure that there are fax transmission and reception facilities at the participating sites.

The Hearing

19. The procedure for conducting the transmission will be determined by the judge. He will determine who is to control the cameras. In cases where the VCF is being used for an application in the course of the proceedings, the judge will ordinarily not enter the local site until both sites are on line. Similarly, at the conclusion of the hearing, he will ordinarily leave the local site while both sites are still on line. The following paragraphs apply primarily to cases where the VCF is being used for the taking of the evidence of a witness at a remote site. In all cases, the judge will need to decide whether court dress is appropriate when using VCF facilities. It might be appropriate when transmitting from courtroom to courtroom. It might not be when a commercial facility is being used.
20. At the beginning of the transmission, the judge will probably wish to introduce himself and the advocates to the witness. He will probably want to know who is at the remote site and will invite the witness to introduce himself and anyone else who is with him. He may wish to give directions as to the seating arrangements at the remote site so that those present are visible at the local site during the taking of the evidence. He will probably wish to explain to the witness the method of taking the oath or of affirming, the manner in which the evidence will be taken, and who will be conducting the examination and cross-examination. He will probably also wish to inform the witness of the matters referred to in paras 6 and 7 above (coordination of picture with sound, and picture quality).
21. The examination of the witness at the remote site should follow as closely as possible the practice adopted when a witness is in the courtroom. During examination, cross-examination and re-examination, the witness must be able to see the legal representative asking the question and also any other person (whether another legal representative or the judge) making any statements in regard to the witness's evidence. It will in practice be most convenient if everyone remains seated throughout the transmission.

CPR Part 33 Miscellaneous Rules about Evidence

Part 33 45.6, 53.9 [For commentary on a specific rule, please refer to the cross-references after the title of the rule.]

33.1 Introductory

In this Part—

(a) 'hearsay' means a statement made, otherwise than by a person while giving oral evidence in proceedings, which is tendered as evidence of the matters stated; and
(b) references to hearsay include hearsay of whatever degree.

33.2 Notice of Intention to Rely on Hearsay Evidence

r.33.2 49.94 r.33.2(3)–(4) 53.9
r.33.2(1)–(2) 51.6, 53.9

(1) Where a party intends to rely on hearsay evidence at trial and either—
  (a) that evidence is to be given by a witness giving oral evidence; or
  (b) that evidence is contained in a witness statement of a person who is not being called to give oral evidence;

  that party complies with section 2(1)(a) of the Civil Evidence Act 1995 by serving a witness statement on the other parties in accordance with the court's order.
(2) Where paragraph (1)(b) applies, the party intending to rely on the hearsay evidence must, when he serves the witness statement—
  (a) inform the other parties that the witness is not being called to give oral evidence; and
  (b) give the reason why the witness will not be called.
(3) In all other cases where a party intends to rely on hearsay evidence at trial, that party complies with section 2(1)(a) of the Civil Evidence Act 1995 by serving a notice on the other parties which—
  (a) identifies the hearsay evidence;
  (b) states that the party serving the notice proposes to rely on the hearsay evidence at trial; and
  (c) gives the reason why the witness will not be called.
(4) The party proposing to rely on the hearsay evidence must—
  (a) serve the notice no later than the latest date for serving witness statements; and
  (b) if the hearsay evidence is to be in a document, supply a copy to any party who requests him to do so.

33.3 Circumstances in Which Notice of Intention to Rely on Hearsay Evidence is Not Required

r.33.3 53.11 r.33.3(a) 51.6

Section 2(1) of the Civil Evidence Act 1995 (duty to give notice of intention to rely on hearsay evidence) does not apply—

(a) to evidence at hearings other than trials;
(aa) to an affidavit or witness statement which is to be used at trial but which does not contain *hearsay evidence*;

(b) to a statement which a party to a probate action wishes to put in evidence and which is alleged to have been made by the person whose estate is the subject of the proceedings; or
(c) where the requirement is excluded by a practice direction.

33.4 Power to Call Witness for Cross-examination on Hearsay Evidence

r.33.4 53.12 r.33.4(2) 53.12

(1) Where a party—
(a) proposes to rely on hearsay evidence; and
(b) does not propose to call the person who made the original statement to give oral evidence,
the court may, on the application of any other party, permit that party to call the maker of the statement to be cross-examined on the contents of the statement.
(2) An application for permission to cross-examine under this rule must be made not more than 14 days after the day on which a notice of intention to rely on the hearsay evidence was served on the applicant.

33.5 Credibility

r.33.5 53.14

(1) Where a party—
(a) proposes to rely on hearsay evidence; but
(b) does not propose to call the person who made the original statement to give oral evidence; and
(c) another party wishes to call evidence to attack the credibility of the person who made the statement,
the party who so wishes must give notice of his intention to the party who proposes to give the hearsay statement in evidence.
(2) A party must give notice under paragraph (1) not more than 14 days after the day on which a hearsay notice relating to the hearsay evidence was served on him.

33.6 Use of Plans, Photographs and Models as Evidence

r.33.6 49.90, 49.94, 59.2
r.33.6(2)–(3) 53.16
r.33.6(4) 47.14, 53.16
r.33.6(5) 49.94
r.33.6(6) 49.94, 53.16
r.33.6(7) 49.94
r.33.6(8) 53.16

(1) This rule applies to evidence (such as a plan, photograph or model) which is not—
(a) contained in a witness statement, affidavit[(GL)] or expert's report;
(b) to be given orally at trial; or
(c) evidence of which prior notice must be given under rule 33.2.
(2) This rule includes documents which may be received in evidence without further proof under section 9 of the Civil Evidence Act 1995.
(3) Unless the court orders otherwise the evidence shall not be receivable at a trial unless the party intending to put it in evidence has given notice to the other parties in accordance with this rule.
(4) Where the party intends to use the evidence as evidence of any fact then, except where paragraph (6) applies, he must give notice not later than the latest date for serving witness statements.
(5) He must give notice at least 21 days before the hearing at which he proposes to put in the evidence, if—
(a) there are not to be witness statements; or
(b) he intends to put in the evidence solely in order to disprove an allegation made in a witness statement.
(6) Where the evidence forms part of expert evidence, he must give notice when the expert's report is served on the other party.
(7) Where the evidence is being produced to the court for any reason other than as part of factual or expert evidence, he must give notice at least 21 days before the hearing at which he proposes to put in the evidence.
(8) Where a party has given notice that he intends to put in the evidence, he must give every other party an opportunity to inspect it and to agree to its admission without further proof.

33.7 Evidence of Finding on Question of Foreign Law

r.33.7 49.101

(1) This rule sets out the procedure which must be followed by a party who intends to put in evidence a finding on a question of foreign law by virtue of section 4(2) of the Civil Evidence Act 1972.
(2) He must give any other party notice of his intention.
(3) He must give the notice—
 (a) if there are to be witness statements, not later than the latest date for serving them; or
 (b) otherwise, not less than 21 days before the hearing at which he proposes to put the finding in evidence.
(4) The notice must—
 (a) specify the question on which the finding was made; and
 (b) enclose a copy of a document where it is reported or recorded.

33.8 Evidence of Consent of Trustee to Act

r.33.8 49.102

A document purporting to contain the written consent of a person to act as trustee and to bear his signature verified by some other person is evidence of such consent.

33.9 Human Rights

r.33.9 91.10

(1) This rule applies where a claim is—
 (a) for a remedy under section 7 of the Human Rights Act 1998 in respect of a judicial act which is alleged to have infringed the claimant's Article 5 Convention rights; and
 (b) based on a finding by a court or tribunal that the claimant's Convention rights have been infringed.
(2) The court hearing the claim—
 (a) may proceed on the basis of the finding of that other court or tribunal that there has been an infringement but it is not required to do so; and
 (b) may reach its own conclusion in the light of that finding and of the evidence heard by that other court or tribunal.

PD 33 Practice Direction 33 — Civil Evidence Act 1995

This practice direction supplements CPR, Part 33.

[For commentary on a specific paragraph, please refer to the cross-references after the title of the paragraph.]

1. Section 16(3A) of the Civil Evidence Act 1995 (as amended) provides that transitional provisions for the application of the provisions of the Civil Evidence Act 1995 to proceedings begun before 31 January 1997 may be made by practice direction.
2. Except as provided for by para. 3, the provisions of the Civil Evidence Act 1995 apply to claims commenced before 31 January 1997.
3. The provisions of the Civil Evidence Act 1995 do not apply to claims commenced before 31 January 1997 if, before 26 April 1999:
   (a) directions were given, or orders were made, as to the evidence to be given at the trial or hearing; or
   (b) the trial or hearing had begun.

CPR 26–50 & PDs

CPR Part 34 Witnesses, Depositions and Evidence for Foreign Courts

Part 34 **57.1, 57.2, 58.14, 72.11** [For commentary on a specific rule, please refer to the cross-references after the title of the rule.]

I WITNESSES AND DEPOSITIONS

34.1 Scope of This Section

(1) This Section of this Part provides—
 (a) for the circumstances in which a person may be required to attend court to give evidence or to produce a document; and
 (b) for a party to obtain evidence before a hearing to be used at the hearing.
(2) In this Section, reference to a hearing includes a reference to the trial.

34.2 Witness Summonses

r.34.2 **49.81**
r.34.2(1)–(3) **57.1**
r.34.2(4) **50.34, 57.1**
r.34.2(5) **50.34, 55.1, 57.1**

(1) A witness summons is a document issued by the court requiring a witness to—
 (a) attend court to give evidence; or
 (b) produce documents to the court.
(2) A witness summons must be in the relevant practice form.
(3) There must be a separate witness summons for each witness.
(4) A witness summons may require a witness to produce documents to the court either—
 (a) on the date fixed for a hearing; or
 (b) on such date as the court may direct.
(5) The only documents that a summons under this rule can require a person to produce before a hearing are documents which that person could be required to produce at the hearing.

34.3 Issue of a Witness Summons

r.34.3(1) 57.2
r.34.3(2) **57.2**
r.34.3(3) **57.2**
r.34.3(4) **57.9**

(1) A witness summons is issued on the date entered on the summons by the court.

(2) A party must obtain permission from the court where he wishes to—
(a) have a summons issued less than 7 days before the date of the trial;
(b) have a summons issued for a witness to attend court to give evidence or to produce documents on any date except the date fixed for the trial; or
(c) have a summons issued for a witness to attend court to give evidence or to produce documents at any hearing except the trial.
(3) A witness summons must be issued by—
(a) the court where the case is proceeding; or
(b) the court where the hearing in question will be held.
(4) The court may set aside(GL) or vary a witness summons issued under this rule.

34.4 Witness Summons in Aid of Inferior Court or of Tribunal

r.34.4(1)–(2) 57.3

(1) The court may issue a witness summons in aid of an inferior court or of a tribunal.
(2) The court which issued the witness summons under this rule may set it aside.
(3) In this rule, 'inferior court or tribunal' means any court or tribunal that does not have power to issue a witness summons in relation to proceedings before it.

34.5 Time for Serving a Witness Summons

r.34.5 57.4 r.34.5(2)–(3) 57.4
r.34.5(1) PC 28, 57.4

(1) The general rule is that a witness summons is binding if it is served at least 7 days before the date on which the witness is required to attend before the court or tribunal.
(2) The court may direct that a witness summons shall be binding although it will be served less than 7 days before the date on which the witness is required to attend before the court or tribunal.
(3) A witness summons which is—
(a) served in accordance with this rule; and
(b) requires the witness to attend court to give evidence,
is binding until the conclusion of the hearing at which the attendance of the witness is required.

34.6 Who is to Serve a Witness Summons

r.34.6(2) 57.6

(1) A witness summons is to be served by the court unless the party on whose behalf it is issued indicates in writing, when he asks the court to issue the summons, that he wishes to serve it himself.
(2) Where the court is to serve the witness summons, the party on whose behalf it is issued must deposit, in the court office, the money to be paid or offered to the witness under rule 34.7.

34.7 Right of Witness to Travelling Expenses and Compensation for Loss of Time

r.34.7 57.6

At the time of service of a witness summons the witness must be offered or paid—
(a) a sum reasonably sufficient to cover his expenses in travelling to and from the court; and
(b) such sum by way of compensation for loss of time as may be specified in Practice Direction 34A.

34.8 Evidence by Deposition

r.34.8 50.34, 58.2, 58.6 r.34.8(6)–(7) 58.2
r.34.8(3)–(4) 58.2

(1) A party may apply for an order for a person to be examined before the hearing takes place.
(2) A person from whom evidence is to be obtained following an order under this rule is referred to as a 'deponent' and the evidence is referred to as a 'deposition'.
(3) An order under this rule shall be for a deponent to be examined on oath before—
(a) a judge;
(b) an examiner of the court; or
(c) such other person as the court appoints.
(Rule 34.15 makes provision for the appointment of examiners of the court)
(4) The order may require the production of any document which the court considers is necessary for the purposes of the examination.

(5) The order must state the date, time and place of the examination.
(6) At the time of service of the order the deponent must be offered or paid—
 (a) a sum reasonably sufficient to cover his expenses in travelling to and from the place of examination; and
 (b) such sum by way of compensation for loss of time as may be specified in Practice Direction 34A.
(7) Where the court makes an order for a deposition to be taken, it may also order the party who obtained the order to serve a witness statement or witness summary in relation to the evidence to be given by the person to be examined.
(Part 32 contains the general rules about witness statements and witness summaries)

34.9 Conduct of Examination

r.34.9 58.3, 58.12, 58.13 r.34.9(1)–(6) 58.3

(1) Subject to any directions contained in the order for examination, the examination must be conducted in the same way as if the witness were giving evidence at a trial.
(2) If all the parties are present, the examiner may conduct the examination of a person not named in the order for examination if all the parties and the person to be examined consent.
(3) The examiner may conduct the examination in private if he considers it appropriate to do so.
(4) The examiner must ensure that the evidence given by the witness is recorded in full.
(5) The examiner must send a copy of the deposition—
 (a) to the person who obtained the order for the examination of the witness; and
 (b) to the court where the case is proceeding.
(6) The party who obtained the order must send each of the other parties a copy of the deposition which he receives from the examiner.

34.10 Enforcing Attendance of Witness

r.34.10 58.12, 58.13 r.34.10(1)–(2) 58.4

(1) If a person served with an order to attend before an examiner—
 (a) fails to attend; or
 (b) refuses to be sworn for the purpose of the examination or to answer any lawful question or produce any document at the examination,
 a certificate of his failure or refusal, signed by the examiner, must be filed by the party requiring the deposition.
(2) On the certificate being filed, the party requiring the deposition may apply to the court for an order requiring that person to attend or to be sworn or to answer any question or produce any document, as the case may be.
(3) An application for an order under this rule may be made without notice.
(4) The court may order the person against whom an order is made under this rule to pay any costs resulting from his failure or refusal.

34.11 Use of Deposition at a Hearing

r.34.11(1)–(4) 58.6

(1) A deposition ordered under rule 34.8 may be given in evidence at a hearing unless the court orders otherwise.
(2) A party intending to put in evidence a deposition at a hearing must serve notice of his intention to do so on every other party.
(3) He must serve the notice at least 21 days before the day fixed for the hearing.
(4) The court may require a deponent to attend the hearing and give evidence orally.
(5) Where a deposition is given in evidence at trial, it shall be treated as if it were a witness statement for the purposes of rule 32.13 (availability of witness statements for inspection).

34.12 Restrictions on Subsequent Use of Deposition Taken for the Purpose of Any Hearing Except the Trial

r.34.12 58.7

(1) Where the court orders a party to be examined about his or any other assets for the purpose of any hearing except the trial, the deposition may be used only for the purpose of the proceedings in which the order was made.

(2) However, it may be used for some other purpose—
(a) by the party who was examined;
(b) if the party who was examined agrees; or
(c) if the court gives permission.

34.13 Where a Person to Be Examined Is out of the Jurisdiction — Letter of Request

r.34.13 49.80, 58.10 r.34.13(2)–(6) 58.10

(1) This rule applies where a party wishes to take a deposition from a person who is—
(a) out of the jurisdiction; and
(b) not in a Regulation State within the meaning of Section III of this Part.

(1A) The High Court may order the issue of a letter of request to the judicial authorities of the country in which the proposed deponent is.

(2) A letter of request is a request to a judicial authority to take the evidence of that person, or arrange for it to be taken.

(3) The High Court may make an order under this rule in relation to county court proceedings.

(4) If the government of a country allows a person appointed by the High Court to examine a person in that country, the High Court may make an order appointing a special examiner for that purpose.

(5) A person may be examined under this rule on oath or affirmation or in accordance with any procedure permitted in the country in which the examination is to take place.

(6) If the High Court makes an order for the issue of a letter of request, the party who sought the order must file—
(a) the following documents and, except where paragraph (7) applies, a translation of them—
(i) a draft letter of request;
(ii) a statement of the issues relevant to the proceedings;
(iii) a list of questions or the subject matter of questions to be put to the person to be examined; and
(b) an undertaking to be responsible for the Secretary of State's expenses.

(7) There is no need to file a translation if—
(a) English is one of the official languages of the country where the examination is to take place; or
(b) a practice direction has specified that country as a country where no translation is necessary.

34.13A Letter of Request — Proceeds of Crime Act 2002

(1) This rule applies where a party to existing or contemplated proceedings in—
(a) the High Court; or
(b) a magistrates' court,
under Part 5 of the Proceeds of Crime Act 2002 (civil recovery of the proceeds etc. of unlawful conduct) wishes to take a deposition from a person who is out of the jurisdiction.

(2) The High Court may, on the application of such a party, order the issue of a letter of request to the judicial authorities of the country in which the proposed deponent is.

(3) Paragraphs (4) to (7) of rule 34.13 shall apply irrespective of where the proposed deponent is, and rule 34.23 shall not apply in cases where the proposed deponent is in a Regulation State within the meaning of Section III of this Part.

34.14 Fees and Expenses of Examiner of the Court

r.34.14(1)–(5) 58.5

(1) An examiner of the court may charge a fee for the examination.
(2) He need not send the deposition to the court unless the fee is paid.
(3) The examiner's fees and expenses must be paid by the party who obtained the order for examination.
(4) If the fees and expenses due to an examiner are not paid within a reasonable time, he may report that fact to the court.
(5) The court may order the party who obtained the order for examination to deposit in the court office a specified sum in respect of the examiner's fees and, where it does so, the examiner will not be asked to act until the sum has been deposited.
(6) An order under this rule does not affect any decision as to the party who is ultimately to bear the costs of the examination.

34.15 Examiners of the Court

r.34.15 58.2

(1) The Lord Chancellor shall appoint persons to be examiners of the court.
(2) The persons appointed shall be barristers or solicitor-advocates who have been practising for a period of not less than three years.
(3) The Lord Chancellor may revoke an appointment at any time.

II EVIDENCE FOR FOREIGN COURTS

34.16 Scope and Interpretation

r.34.16 58.12

(1) This Section applies to an application for an order under the 1975 Act for evidence to be obtained, other than an application made as a result of a request by a court in another Regulation State.
(2) In this Section—
  (a) 'the 1975 Act' means the Evidence (Proceedings in Other Jurisdictions) Act 1975; and
  (b) 'Regulation State' has the same meaning as in Section III of this Part.

34.17 Application for Order

r.34.17 58.12 r.34.17(b) 58.12

An application for an order under the 1975 Act for evidence to be obtained—
(a) must be—
  (i) made to the High Court;
  (ii) supported by written evidence; and
  (iii) accompanied by the request as a result of which the application is made, and where appropriate, a translation of the request into English; and
(b) may be made without notice.

34.18 Examination

r.34.18 58.12, 58.13

(1) The court may order an examination to be taken before—
  (a) any fit and proper person nominated by the person applying for the order;
  (b) an examiner of the court; or
  (c) any other person whom the court considers suitable.
(2) Unless the court orders otherwise—
  (a) the examination will be taken as provided by rule 34.9; and
  (b) rule 34.10 applies.
(3) The court may make an order under rule 34.14 for payment of the fees and expenses of the examination.

34.19 Dealing with Deposition

r.34.19 58.12

(1) The examiner must send the deposition of the witness to the Senior Master unless the court orders otherwise.
(2) The Senior Master will—
 (a) give a certificate sealed with the seal of the Senior Courts for use out of the jurisdiction identifying the following documents—
  (i) the request;
  (ii) the order of the court for examination; and
  (iii) the deposition of the witness; and
 (b) send the certificate and the documents referred to in paragraph (a) to—
  (i) the Secretary of State; or
  (ii) where the request was sent to the Senior Master by another person in accordance with a Civil Procedure Convention, to that other person,
 for transmission to the court or tribunal requesting the examination.

34.20 Claim to Privilege

r.34.20 58.12

(1) This rule applies where—
 (a) a witness claims to be exempt from giving evidence on the ground specified in section 3(1)(b) of the 1975 Act; and
 (b) that claim is not supported or conceded as referred to in section 3(2) of that Act.
(2) The examiner may require the witness to give the evidence which he claims to be exempt from giving.
(3) Where the examiner does not require the witness to give that evidence, the court may order the witness to do so.
(4) An application for an order under paragraph (3) may be made by the person who obtained the order under section 2 of the 1975 Act.
(5) Where such evidence is taken—
 (a) it must be contained in a document separate from the remainder of the deposition;
 (b) the examiner will send to the Senior Master—
  (i) the deposition; and
  (ii) a signed statement setting out the claim to be exempt and the ground on which it was made.
(6) On receipt of the statement referred to in paragraph (5)(b)(ii), the Senior Master will—
 (a) retain the document containing the part of the witness's evidence to which the claim to be exempt relates; and
 (b) send the statement and a request to determine that claim to the foreign court or tribunal together with the documents referred to in rule 34.17.
(7) The Senior Master will—
 (a) if the claim to be exempt is rejected by the foreign court or tribunal, send the document referred to in paragraph (5)(a) to that court or tribunal;
 (b) if the claim is upheld, send the document to the witness; and
 (c) in either case, notify the witness and person who obtained the order under section 2 of the foreign court or tribunal's decision.

34.21 Order under 1975 Act as Applied by Patents Act 1977

r.34.21 58.12

Where an order is made for the examination of witnesses under section 1 of the 1975 Act as applied by section 92 of the Patents Act 1977 the court may permit an officer of the European Patent Office to—
(a) attend the examination and examine the witnesses; or
(b) request the court or the examiner before whom the examination takes place to put specified questions to them.

III TAKING OF EVIDENCE — MEMBER STATES OF THE EUROPEAN UNION

34.22 Interpretation

In this Section—

(a) 'designated court' has the meaning given in Practice Direction 34A;
(b) 'Regulation State' has the same meaning as 'Member State' in the Taking of Evidence Regulation, that is all Member States except Denmark;
(c) 'the Taking of Evidence Regulation' means Council Regulation (EC) No. 1206/2001 of 28 May 2001 on cooperation between the courts of the Member States in the taking of evidence in civil and commercial matters.

(The Taking of Evidence Regulation is annexed to the relevant practice direction)

34.23 Where a Person to Be Examined Is in Another Regulation State

r.34.23(2)–(3) **58.8**
r.34.23(5) **58.9**
r.34.23(6)(b) **58.9**
r.34.23(6)(c) **58.9**

(1) Subject to rule 34.13A, this rule applies where a party wishes to take a deposition from a person who is in another Regulation State.
(2) The court may order the issue of a request to a designated court ('the requested court') in the Regulation State in which the proposed deponent is.
(3) If the court makes an order for the issue of a request, the party who sought the order must file—
 (a) a draft Form A as set out in the annex to the Taking of Evidence Regulation (request for the taking of evidence);
 (b) except where paragraph (4) applies, a translation of the form;
 (c) an undertaking to be responsible for costs sought by the requested court in relation to—
  (i) fees paid to experts and interpreters; and
  (ii) where requested by that party, the use of special procedures or communications technology; and
 (d) an undertaking to be responsible for the court's expenses.
(4) There is no need to file a translation if—
 (a) English is one of the official languages of the Regulation State where the examination is to take place; or
 (b) the Regulation State has indicated, in accordance with the Taking of Evidence Regulation, that English is a language which it will accept.
(5) Where article 17 of the Taking of Evidence Regulation (direct taking of evidence by the requested court) allows evidence to be taken directly in another Regulation State, the court may make an order for the submission of a request in accordance with that article.
(6) If the court makes an order for the submission of a request under paragraph (5), the party who sought the order must file—
 (a) a draft Form I as set out in the annex to the Taking of Evidence Regulation (request for direct taking of evidence);
 (b) except where paragraph (4) applies, a translation of the form; and
 (c) an undertaking to be responsible for the court's expenses.

34.24 Evidence for Courts of Other Regulation States

r.34.24(2) **58.13**
r.34.24(2)(c) **58.13**
r.34.24(3)–(4) **58.13**

(1) This rule applies where a court in another Regulation State ('the requesting court') issues a request for evidence to be taken from a person who is in the jurisdiction.
(2) An application for an order for evidence to be taken—
 (a) must be made to a designated court;

(b) must be accompanied by—
   (i) the form of request for the taking of evidence as a result of which the application is made; and
   (ii) where appropriate, a translation of the form of request; and
(c) may be made without notice.

(3) Rule 34.18(1) and (2) apply.

(4) The examiner must send—
(a) the deposition to the court for transmission to the requesting court; and
(b) a copy of the deposition to the person who obtained the order for evidence to be taken.

PD 34A Practice Direction 34A — Depositions and Court Attendance by Witnesses

This practice direction supplements CPR, Part 34.

[For commentary on a specific paragraph, please refer to the cross-references after the title of the paragraph.]

WITNESS SUMMONSES

para.1.2 57.1

Issue of Witness Summons

1.1 A witness summons may require a witness to:
(1) attend court to give evidence,
(2) produce documents to the court, or
(3) both,
on either a date fixed for the hearing or such date as the court may direct.[1]

1.2 Two copies of the witness summons[2] should be filed with the court for sealing, one of which will be retained on the court file.

1.3 A mistake in the name or address of a person named in a witness summons may be corrected if the summons has not been served.

1.4 The corrected summons must be re-sealed by the court and marked 'Amended and Re-sealed'.

Witness Summons Issued in Aid of an Inferior Court or Tribunal

paras.2.3–2.4 57.3

2.1 A witness summons may be issued in the High Court or a county court in aid of a court or tribunal which does not have the power to issue a witness summons in relation to the proceedings before it.[3]

2.2 A witness summons referred to in paragraph 2.1 may be set aside by the court which issued it.[4]

2.3 An application to set aside a witness summons referred to in paragraph 2.1 will be heard:
(1) in the High Court by a master at the Royal Courts of Justice or by a district judge in a District Registry, and
(2) in a county court by a district judge.

2.4 Unless the court otherwise directs, the applicant must give at least 2 days' notice to the party who issued the witness summons of the application, which will normally be dealt with at a hearing.

Travelling Expenses and Compensation for Loss of Time

paras.3.1–3.4 57.6

3.1 When a witness is served with a witness summons he must be offered a sum to cover his travelling expenses to and from the court and compensation for his loss of time.[5]

3.2 If the witness summons is to be served by the court, the party issuing the summons must deposit with the court:
(1) a sum sufficient to pay for the witness's expenses in travelling to the court and in returning to his home or place of work, and
(2) a sum in respect of the period during which earnings or benefit are lost, or such lesser sum as it may be proved that the witness will lose as a result of his attendance at court in answer to the witness summons.

---

[1] Rule 34.2(4).
[2] In form N20.
[3] Rule 34.4(1).
[4] Rule 34.4(2).
[5] Rule 34.7.

3.3 The sum referred to in 3.2(2) is to be based on the sums payable to witnesses attending the Crown Court.[6]

3.4 Where the party issuing the witness summons wishes to serve it himself,[7] he must:
(1) notify the court in writing that he wishes to do so, and
(2) at the time of service offer the witness the sums mentioned in paragraph 3.2 above.

DEPOSITIONS

para.4.1 58.10
paras.4.6–4.11 58.10, 58.12
paras.4.2 58.2, 58.10, 58.12
paras.4.12 58.3, 58.10, 58.12
paras.4.3–4.4 58.3, 58.10, 58.12
paras.4.12(4) 58.3
para.4.5 58.4, 58.10, 58.12

To Be Taken in England and Wales for Use as Evidence in Proceedings in Courts in England and Wales

4.1 A party may apply for an order for a person to be examined on oath before:
(1) a judge,
(2) an examiner of the court, or
(3) such other person as the court may appoint.[8]

4.2 The party who obtains an order for the examination of a deponent[9] before an examiner of the court[10] must:
(1) apply to the Foreign Process Section of the Masters' Secretary's Department at the Royal Courts of Justice for the allocation of an examiner,
(2) when allocated, provide the examiner with copies of all documents in the proceedings necessary to inform the examiner of the issues, and
(3) pay the deponent a sum to cover his travelling expenses to and from the examination and compensation for his loss of time.[11]

4.3 In ensuring that the deponent's evidence is recorded in full, the court or the examiner may permit it to be recorded on audiotape or videotape, but the deposition[12] must always be recorded in writing by him or by a competent shorthand writer or stenographer.

4.4 If the deposition is not recorded word for word, it must contain, as nearly as may be, the statement of the deponent; the examiner may record word for word any particular questions and answers which appear to him to have special importance.

4.5 If a deponent objects to answering any question or where any objection is taken to any question, the examiner must:
(1) record in the deposition or a document attached to it:
(a) the question,
(b) the nature of and grounds for the objection, and
(c) any answer given, and
(2) give his opinion as to the validity of the objection and must record it in the deposition or a document attached to it.

The court will decide as to the validity of the objection and any question of costs arising from it.

4.6 Documents and exhibits must:
(1) have an identifying number or letter marked on them by the examiner, and
(2) be preserved by the party or his legal representative[13] who obtained the order for the examination, or as the court or the examiner may direct.

[6] Fixed pursuant to the Prosecution of Offences Act 1985 and the Costs in Criminal Cases (General) Regulations 1986 (SI 1986/1335).
[7] Rule 34.6(1).
[8] Rule 34.8(3).
[9] See rule 34.8(2) for explanation of 'deponent' and 'deposition'.
[10] For the appointment of examiners of the court see rule 34.15.
[11] Rule 34.8(6).
[12] See rule 34.8(2) for explanation of 'deponent' and 'deposition'.
[13] For the definition of legal representative see rule 2.3.

4.7 The examiner may put any question to the deponent as to:
(1) the meaning of any of his answers, or
(2) any matter arising in the course of the examination.

4.8 Where a deponent:
(1) fails to attend the examination, or
(2) refuses to:
(a) be sworn, or
(b) answer any lawful question, or
(c) produce any document,
the examiner will sign a certificate[14] of such failure or refusal and may include in his certificate any comment as to the conduct of the deponent or of any person attending the examination.

4.9 The party who obtained the order for the examination must file the certificate with the court and may apply for an order that the deponent attend for examination or as may be.[15] The application may be made without notice.[16]

4.10 The court will make such order on the application as it thinks fit including an order for the deponent to pay any costs resulting from his failure or refusal.[17]

4.11 A deponent who wilfully refuses to obey an order made against him under Part 34 may be proceeded against for contempt of court.

4.12 A deposition must:
(1) be signed by the examiner,
(2) have any amendments to it initialled by the examiner and the deponent,
(3) be endorsed by the examiner with:
(a) a statement of the time occupied by the examination, and
(b) a record of any refusal by the deponent to sign the deposition and of his reasons for not doing so, and
(4) be sent by the examiner to the court where the proceedings are taking place for filing on the court file.

4.13 Rule 34.14 deals with the fees and expenses of an examiner.

Depositions to Be Taken Abroad for Use as Evidence in Proceedings before Courts in England and Wales Where the Taking of Evidence Regulation Does Not Apply

paras.5.2–5.3 **58.10** paras.5.8–5.9 **58.10**

5.1 Where a party wishes to take a deposition from a person outside the jurisdiction, the High Court may order the issue of a letter of request to the judicial authorities of the country in which the proposed deponent is.[18]

5.2 An application for an order referred to in paragraph 5.1 should be made by application notice in accordance with Part 23.

5.3 The documents which a party applying for an order for the issue of a letter of request must file with his application notice are set out in rule 34.13(6). They are as follows:
(1) a draft letter of request is set out in Annex A to this practice direction,
(2) a statement of the issues relevant to the proceedings,
(3) a list of questions or the subject matter of questions to be put to the proposed deponent,
(4) a translation of the documents in (1), (2) and (3) above unless the proposed deponent is in a country of which English is an official language, and
(5) an undertaking to be responsible for the expenses of the Secretary of State.
In addition to the documents listed above the party applying for the order must file a draft order.

5.4 The above documents should be filed with the Masters' Secretary in Room E214, Royal Courts of Justice, Strand, London WC2A 2LL.

[14] Rule 34.10.
[15] *Rule 34.10(2) and (3).*
[16] Rule 34.10(3).
[17] Rule 34.10(4).
[18] Rule 34.13(1).

5.5 The application will be dealt with by the Senior Master of the Queen's Bench Division of the High Court who will, if appropriate, sign the letter of request.
5.6 Attention is drawn to the provisions of rule 23.10 (application to vary or discharge an order made without notice).
5.7 If parties are in doubt as to whether a translation under paragraph 5.3(4) above is required, they should seek guidance from the Foreign Process Section of the Masters' Secretary's Department.
5.8 A special examiner appointed under rule 34.13(4) may be the British consul or the consul-general or his deputy in the country where the evidence is to be taken if:
(1) there is in respect of that country a Civil Procedure Convention providing for the taking of evidence in that country for the assistance of proceedings in the High Court or other court in this country, or
(2) with the consent of the Secretary of State.
5.9 The provisions of Paragraphs 4.1 to 4.12 above apply to the depositions referred to in this paragraph.

Depositions to Be Taken in England and Wales for Use as Evidence in Proceedings before Courts Abroad Pursuant to Letters of Request Where the Taking of Evidence Regulation Does Not Apply

paras.6.1–6.8 58.12

6.1 Section II of Part 34 relating to obtaining evidence for foreign courts and should be read in conjunction with this part of the practice direction.
6.2 The Evidence (Proceedings in Other Jurisdictions) Act 1975 applies to these depositions.
6.3 The written evidence supporting an application under r. 34.17 (which should be made by application notice: see Part 23) must include or exhibit:
(1) a statement of the issues relevant to the proceedings;
(2) a list of questions or the subject matter of questions to be put to the proposed deponent;
(3) a draft order; and
(4) a translation of the documents in (1) and (2) into English, if necessary.
6.4 (1) The Senior Master will send to the Treasury Solicitor any request:
(a) forwarded by the Secretary of State with a recommendation that effect should be given to the request without requiring an application to be made; or
(b) received by him in pursuance of a civil procedure convention providing for the taking of evidence of any person in England and Wales to assist a court or tribunal in a foreign country where no person is named in the document as the applicant.
(2) In relation to such a request, the Treasury Solicitor may, with the consent of the Treasury:
(a) apply for an order under the 1975 Act; and
(b) take such other steps as are necessary to give effect to the request.
6.5 The order for the deponent to attend and be examined together with the evidence upon which the order was made must be served on the deponent.
6.6 Attention is drawn to the provisions of r. 23.10 (application to vary or discharge an order made without notice).
6.7 Arrangements for the examination to take place at a specified time and place before an examiner of the court or such other person as the court may appoint shall be made by the applicant for the order and approved by the Senior Master.
6.8 The provisions of Paragraphs 4.2 to 4.12 apply to the depositions referred to in this paragraph, except that the examiner must send the deposition to the Senior Master.
(For further information about evidence see Part 32 and PD 32.)

TAKING OF EVIDENCE BETWEEN EU MEMBER STATES

Taking of Evidence Regulation

7.1 Where evidence is to be taken:
(a) from a person in another Member State of the European Union for use as evidence in proceedings before courts in England and Wales; or
(b) from a person in England and Wales for use as evidence in proceedings before a court in another Member State,

Council Regulation (EC) No. 1206/2001 of 28 May 2001 on cooperation between the courts of the Member States in the taking of evidence in civil or commercial matters ('the Taking of Evidence Regulation') applies.

7.2 The Taking of Evidence Regulation is annexed to this practice direction as annex B.

7.3 The Taking of Evidence Regulation does not apply to Denmark. In relation to Denmark, therefore, r. 34.13 and Section II of Part 34 will continue to apply.

(Article 21(1) of the Taking of Evidence Regulation provides that the Regulation prevails over other provisions contained in bilateral or multilateral agreements or arrangements concluded by the Member States and in particular the Hague Convention of 1 March 1954 on Civil Procedure and the Hague Convention of 18 March 1970 on the Taking of Evidence Abroad in Civil or Commercial Matters.)

Meaning of 'Designated Court'

8.1 In accordance with the Taking of Evidence Regulation, each Regulation State has prepared a list of courts competent to take evidence in accordance with the Regulation indicating the territorial and, where appropriate, special jurisdiction of those courts.

8.2 Where Part 34, Section III, refers to a 'designated court' in relation to another Regulation State, the reference is to the court, referred to in the list of competent courts of that State, which is appropriate to the application in hand.

8.3 Where the reference is to the 'designated court' in England and Wales, the reference is to the appropriate competent court in the jurisdiction. The designated courts for England and Wales are listed in Annex C to this practice direction.

Central Body

para.9.2 58.8

9.1 The Taking of Evidence Regulation stipulates that each Regulation State must nominate a Central Body responsible for:

(a) supplying information to courts;
(b) seeking solutions to any difficulties which may arise in respect of a request; and
(c) forwarding, in exceptional cases, at the request of a requesting court, a request to the competent court.

9.2 The United Kingdom has nominated the Senior Master, Queen's Bench Division, to be the Central Body for England and Wales.

9.3 The Senior Master, as Central Body, has been designated responsible for taking decisions on requests pursuant to art. 17 of the Regulation. Article 17 allows a court to submit a request to the Central Body or a designated competent authority in another Regulation State to take evidence directly in that State.

Evidence to Be Taken in Another Regulation State for Use in England and Wales

10.1 Where a person wishes to take a deposition from a person in another Regulation State, the court where the proceedings are taking place may order the issue of a request to the designated court in the Regulation State (r. 34.23(2)). The form of request is prescribed as form A in the Taking of Evidence Regulation.

10.2 An application to the court for an order under r. 34.23(2) should be made by application notice in accordance with Part 23.

10.3 Rule 34.23(3) provides that the party applying for the order must file a draft form of request in the prescribed form. Where completion of the form requires attachments or documents to accompany the form, these must also be filed.

10.4 If the court grants an order under r. 34.23(2), it will send the form of request directly to the designated court.

10.5 Where the taking of evidence requires the use of an expert, the designated court may require a deposit in advance towards the costs of that expert. The party who obtained the order is responsible for the payment of any such deposit which should be deposited with the court for onward transmission. Under the provisions of the Taking of Evidence Regulation, the designated court is not required to execute the request until such payment is received.

10.6 Article 17 permits the court where proceedings are taking place to take evidence directly from a deponent in another Regulation State if the conditions of the article are satisfied. Direct taking of evidence can only take place if evidence is given voluntarily without the need for coercive measures. Rule 34.23(5) provides for the court to make an order for the submission of a request to take evidence directly. The form of request is form I annexed to the Taking of Evidence Regulation and r. 34.23(6) makes provision for a draft of this form to be filed by the party seeking the order. An application for an order under r. 34.23(5) should be by application notice in accordance with Part 23.

10.7 Attention is drawn to the provisions of r. 23.10 (application to vary or discharge an order made without notice).

Evidence to Be Taken in England and Wales for Use in Another Regulation State

para. 11.2 58.13 paras. 11.4–11.7 58.13

11.1 Where a designated court in England and Wales receives a request to take evidence from a court in a Regulation State, the court will send the request to the Treasury Solicitor.

11.2 On receipt of the request, the Treasury Solicitor may, with the consent of the Treasury, apply for an order under r. 34.24.

11.3 An application to the court for an order must be accompanied by the form of request to take evidence and any accompanying documents, translated if required under para. 11.4.

11.4 The United Kingdom has indicated that, in addition to English, it will accept French as a language in which documents may be submitted. Where the form or request and any accompanying documents are received in French they will be translated into English by the Treasury Solicitor.

11.5 The order for the deponent to attend and be examined together with the evidence on which the order was made must be served on the deponent.

11.6 Arrangements for the examination to take place at a specified time and place shall be made by the Treasury Solicitor and approved by the court.

11.7 The court shall send details of the arrangements for the examination to such of:
(a) the parties and, if any, their representatives; or
(b) the representatives of the foreign court,
who have indicated, in accordance with the Taking of Evidence Regulation, that they wish to be present at the examination.

11.8 The provisions of para. 4.3 to 4.12 apply to the depositions referred to in this paragraph.

ANNEX A

Draft Letter of Request (Where the Taking of Evidence Regulation Does Not Apply)

To the Competent Judicial Authority of
in the of
I [name] Senior Master of the Queen's Bench Division of the Senior Courts of England and Wales respectfully request the assistance of your court with regard to the following matters.

1. A claim is now pending in the Division of the High Court of Justice in England and Wales entitled as follows
[*set out full title and claim number*]
in which [*name*] of [*address*] is the claimant and [*name*] of [*address*] is the defendant.
2. The names and addresses of the representatives or agents of [*set out names and addresses of representatives of the parties*].
3. The claim by the claimant is for:—
(a) [*set out the nature of the claim*]
(b) [*the relief sought, and*]
(c) [*a summary of the facts.*]
4. It is necessary for the purposes of justice and for the due determination of the matters in dispute between the parties that you cause the following witnesses, who are resident within your jurisdiction, to be examined. The names and addresses of the witnesses are as follows:—

5. The witnesses should be examined on oath or if that is not possible within your laws or is impossible of performance by reason of the internal practice and procedure of your court or by reason of practical difficulties, they should be examined in accordance with whatever procedure your laws provide for in these matters.
6. Either/
The witnesses should be examined in accordance with the list of questions annexed hereto.
Or/
The witnesses should be examined regarding [*set out full details of evidence sought*]
N.B. Where the witness is required to produce documents, these should be clearly identified.
7. I would ask that you cause me, or the agents of the parties (if appointed), to be informed of the date and place where the examination is to take place.
8. Finally, I request that you will cause the evidence of the said witnesses to be reduced into writing and all documents produced on such examinations to be duly marked for identification and that you will further be pleased to authenticate such examinations by the seal of your court or in such other way as is in accordance with your procedure and return the written evidence and documents produced to me addressed as follows:—

Senior Master of the Queen's Bench Division
Royal Courts of Justice
Strand
London WC2A 2LL
England

ANNEX B
COUNCIL REGULATION (EC) NO. 1206/2001

[The text of Regulation (EC) No. 1206/2001 may be downloaded from the EUR-Lex site: <http://eur-lex.europa.eu>.]

ANNEX C

annex C **58.8, 58.13**

Designated courts in England and Wales under the Taking of Evidence Regulation (see para. 8 above)

Area	Designated court
London and South Eastern Circuit	Royal Courts of Justice (Queen's Bench Division)
Midland Circuit	Birmingham Civil Justice Centre
Western Circuit	Bristol County Court
Wales Circuit	Cardiff Civil Justice Centre
Northern Circuit	Manchester County Court
North Eastern Circuit	Leeds County Court

PD 34B Practice Direction 34B — Fees for Examiners of the Court

This practice direction supplements CPR, Part 34.

Scope

1.1 This practice direction sets out:
(1) how to calculate the fees an examiner of the court ('an examiner') may charge; and
(2) the expenses he may recover.
(Rule 34.8(3)(b) provides that the court may make an order for evidence to be obtained by the examination of a witness before an examiner of the court.)

1.2 The party who obtained the order for the examination must pay the fees and expenses of the examiner.
(Rule 34.14 permits an examiner to charge a fee for the examination and contains other provisions about his fees and expenses, and r. 34.15 provides who may be appointed as an examiner of the court.)

The Examination Fee

2.1 An examiner may charge an hourly rate for each hour (or part of an hour) that he is engaged in examining the witness.

2.2 The hourly rate is to be calculated by reference to the formula set out in para. 3.

2.3 The examination fee will be the hourly rate multiplied by the number of hours the examination has taken. For example:

Examination fee = hourly rate × number of hours.

How to Calculate the Hourly Rate — The Formula

3.1 Divide the amount of the minimum annual salary of a post within Group 7 of the judicial salary structure as designated by the Review Body on Senior Salaries,[1] by 220 to give 'x'; and then divide 'x' by 6 to give **the hourly rate.**

For example:

$$\frac{\text{minimum annual salary}}{220} = \text{x}$$

$$\frac{\text{x}}{6} = \text{x}$$

Single Fee Chargeable on Making the Appointment for Examination

4.1 An examiner of court is also entitled to charge a single fee of twice the hourly rate (calculated in accordance with para. 3 above) as 'the appointment fee' when the appointment for the examination is made.

4.2 The examiner is entitled to retain the appointment fee where the witness fails to attend on the date and time arranged.

4.3 Where the examiner fails to attend on the date and time arranged he may not charge a further appointment fee for arranging a subsequent appointment.
(The examiner need not send the deposition to the court until his fees are paid — see r. 34.14(2).)

[1] The Report of the Review Body on Senior Salaries is published annually by the Stationery Office.

Examiners' Expenses

5.1 The examiner of court is also entitled to recover the following expenses:

(1) all reasonable travelling expenses;

(2) any other expenses reasonably incurred; and

(3) subject to para. 5.2, any reasonable charge for the room where the examination takes place.

5.2 No expenses may be recovered under para. 5.1(3) above if the examination takes place at the examiner's usual business address.

(If the examiner's fees and expenses are not paid within a reasonable time he may report the fact to the court, see r. 34.14(4) and (5).)

CPR Part 35 Experts and Assessors

Part 35 24.7, 45.6, 45.19, 46.7, 54.1, 54.3, 54.8, 54.10, 54.12, 54.13, 54.25 [For commentary on a specific rule, please refer to the cross-references after the title of the rule.]

35.1 Duty to Restrict Expert Evidence

r.35.1 45.6, 45.19, 54.1, 54.13, 54.28, 91.43

Expert evidence shall be restricted to that which is reasonably required to resolve the proceedings.

35.2 Interpretation and Definitions

r.35.2 8.23, 54.18
r.35.2(1) 54.1, 54.12

(1) A reference to an 'expert' in this Part is a reference to a person who has been instructed to give or prepare expert evidence for the purpose of proceedings.

(2) 'Single joint expert' means an expert instructed to prepare a report for the court on behalf of two or more of the parties (including the claimant) to the proceedings.

35.3 Experts — Overriding Duty to the Court

r.35.3 45.6, 45.19, 54.1, 54.7, 54.10, 54.13, 54.33

(1) It is the duty of experts to help the court on matters within their expertise.

(2) This duty overrides any obligation to the person from whom experts have received instructions or by whom they are paid.

35.4 Court's Power to Restrict Expert Evidence

r.35.4 54.12, 54.27
r.35.4(1) 54.1, 54.3, 54.12, 54.13
r.35.4(2) 47.6, 54.12, 54.13
r.35.4(3) 54.12, 54.13
r.35.4(3A) 42.27, 45.6, 45.19, 46.6, 54.13
r.35.4(4) 8.23, 42.27, 54.12

(1) No party may call an expert or put in evidence an expert's report without the court's permission.

(2) When parties apply for permission they must provide an estimate of the costs of the proposed expert evidence and identify—
  (a) the field in which expert evidence is required and the issues which the expert evidence will address; and
  (b) where practicable, the name of the proposed expert.

(3) If permission is granted it shall be in relation only to the expert named or the field identified under paragraph (2). The order granting permission may specify the issues which the expert evidence should address.

(3A) Where a claim has been allocated to the small claims track or the fast track, if permission is given for expert evidence, it will normally be given for evidence from only one expert on a particular issue.

(Paragraph 6 of Practice Direction 35 sets out some of the circumstances the court will consider when deciding whether expert evidence should be given by a single joint expert.)

(4) The court may limit the amount of a party's expert's fees and expenses that may be recovered from any other party.

CPR 26–50 & PDs

35.5 General Requirement for Expert Evidence to Be Given in a Written Report

r.35.5 54.27
r.35.5(1) 54.27
r.35.5(2) 45.6, 45.19, 46.6, 54.13, 54.14, 54.27

(1) Expert evidence is to be given in a written report unless the court directs otherwise.
(2) If a claim is on the small claims track or the fast track, the court will not direct an expert to attend a hearing unless it is necessary to do so in the interests of justice.

35.6 Written Questions to Experts

r.35.6 46.7, 54.18, 54.23, 54.32
r.35.6(1) 54.32
r.35.6(2)(a) 54.32
r.35.6(2)(b) 46.7, 54.32
r.35.6(2)(c) 54.32
r.35.6(3)–(4) 54.32

(1) A party may put written questions about an expert's report (which must be proportionate) to—
 (a) an expert instructed by another party; or
 (b) a single joint expert appointed under r. 35.7.
(2) Written questions under paragraph (1)—
 (a) may be put once only;
 (b) must be put within 28 days of service of the expert's report; and
 (c) must be for the purpose only of clarification of the report,
 unless in any case—
  (i) the court gives permission; or
  (ii) the other party agrees.
(3) An expert's answers to questions put in accordance with paragraph (1) shall be treated as part of the expert's report.
(4) Where—
 (a) a party has put a written question to an expert instructed by another party; and
 (b) the expert does not answer that question,
 the court may make one or both of the following orders in relation to the party who instructed the expert—
  (i) that the party may not rely on the evidence of that expert; or
  (ii) that the party may not recover the fees and expenses of that expert from any other party.

35.7 Court's Power to Direct that Evidence Is to Be Given by a Single Joint Expert

r.35.7 8.23, 45.6, 45.19, 46.6, 54.1, 54.13, 54.18, 54.26, 54.28, 81.16, 91.43

(1) Where two or more parties wish to submit expert evidence on a particular issue, the court may direct that the evidence on that issue is to be given by a single joint expert.
(2) Where the parties who wish to submit the evidence ('the relevant parties') cannot agree who should be the single joint expert, the court may—
 (a) select the expert from a list prepared or identified by the relevant parties; or
 (b) direct that the expert be selected in such other manner as the court may direct.

35.8 Instructions to a Single Joint Expert

r.35.8 45.6, 45.19, 54.13, 81.16
r.35.8(1)–(2) 54.26
r.35.8(3) 54.18
r.35.8(3)(b) 91.43
r.35.8(4) 54.18
r.35.8(4)(a) 91.43
r.35.8(5) 54.18

(1) Where the court gives a direction under rule 35.7 for a single joint expert to be used, any relevant party may give instructions to the expert.
(2) When a party gives instructions to the expert that party must, at the same time, send a copy to the other relevant parties.
(3) The court may give directions about—
 (a) the payment of the expert's fees and expenses; and
 (b) any inspection, examination or experiments which the expert wishes to carry out.
(4) The court may, before an expert is instructed—
 (a) limit the amount that can be paid by way of fees and expenses to the expert; and
 (b) direct that some or all of the relevant parties pay that amount into court.

(5) Unless the court otherwise directs, the relevant parties are jointly and severally liable(GL) for the payment of the expert's fees and expenses.

35.9 Power of Court to Direct a Party to Provide Information

r.35.9 54.25, 81.16

Where a party has access to information which is not reasonably available to another party, the court may direct the party who has access to the information to—
(a) prepare and file a document recording the information; and
(b) serve a copy of that document on the other party.

35.10 Contents of Report

r.35.10 91.52
r.35.10(2) 54.29
r.35.10(3) 50.34, 54.30, 54.38
r.35.10(4) 50.34, 54.30, 54.38

(1) An expert's report must comply with the requirements set out in Practice Direction 35.
(2) At the end of an expert's report there must be a statement that the expert understands and has complied with their duty to the court.
(3) The expert's report must state the substance of all material instructions, whether written or oral, on the basis of which the report was written.
(4) The instructions referred to in paragraph (3) shall not be privileged(GL) against disclosure but the court will not, in relation to those instructions—
(a) order disclosure of any specific document; or
(b) permit any questioning in court, other than by the party who instructed the expert,
unless it is satisfied that there are reasonable grounds to consider the statement of instructions given under paragraph (3) to be inaccurate or incomplete.

35.11 Use by One Party of Expert's Report Disclosed by Another

r.35.11 54.28

Where a party has disclosed an expert's report, any party may use that expert's report as evidence at the trial.

35.12 Discussions between Experts

r.35.12 46.6, 54.31, 54.39
r.35.12(1) 54.14
r.35.12(2) 54.31
r.35.12(3) 54.14, 54.31
r.35.12(4)–(5) 54.31

(1) The court may, at any stage, direct a discussion between experts for the purpose of requiring the experts to—
(a) identify and discuss the expert issues in the proceedings; and
(b) where possible, reach an agreed opinion on those issues.
(2) The court may specify the issues which the experts must discuss.
(3) The court may direct that following a discussion between the experts they must prepare a statement for the court setting out those issues on which—
(a) they agree; and
(b) they disagree, with a summary of their reasons for disagreeing.
(4) The content of the discussion between the experts shall not be referred to at the trial unless the parties agree.
(5) Where experts reach agreement on an issue during their discussions, the agreement shall not bind the parties unless the parties expressly agree to be bound by the agreement.

35.13 Consequence of Failure to Disclose Expert's Report

r.35.13 48.12, 54.27

A party who fails to disclose an expert's report may not use the report at the trial or call the expert to give evidence orally unless the court gives permission.

35.14 Expert's Right to Ask Court for Directions

r.35.14 46.7, 54.25, 54.33
r.35.14(1) 54.10
r.35.14(2)–(3) 54.33

(1) Experts may file written requests for directions for the purpose of assisting them in carrying out their functions.
(2) Experts must, unless the court orders otherwise, provide copies of the proposed requests for directions under paragraph (1)—
(a) to the party instructing them, at least 7 days before they file the requests; and
(b) to all other parties, at least 4 days before they file them.
(3) The court, when it gives directions, may also direct that a party be served with a copy of the directions.

35.15 Assessors

r.35.15 54.40
r.35.15(3) 54.40
r.35.15(5)–(7) 54.40

(1) This rule applies where the court appoints one or more persons under section 70 of the Senior Courts Act 1981 or section 63 of the County Courts Act 1984 as an assessor.
(2) An assessor will assist the court in dealing with a matter in which the assessor has skill and experience.
(3) An assessor will take such part in the proceedings as the court may direct and in particular the court may direct an assessor to—
(a) prepare a report for the court on any matter at issue in the proceedings; and
(b) attend the whole or any part of the trial to advise the court on any such matter.
(4) If an assessor prepares a report for the court before the trial has begun—
(a) the court will send a copy to each of the parties; and
(b) the parties may use it at trial.
(5) The remuneration to be paid to an assessor is to be determined by the court and will form part of the costs of the proceedings.
(6) The court may order any party to deposit in the court office a specified sum in respect of an assessor's fees and, where it does so, the assessor will not be asked to act until the sum has been deposited.
(7) Paragraphs (5) and (6) do not apply where the remuneration of the assessor is to be paid out of money provided by Parliament.

PD 35 Practice Direction 35 — Experts and Assessors

This practice direction supplements CPR, Part 35.

PD 35 **8.10, 46.26, 49.8, 54.10, 54.25** [For commentary on a specific paragraph, please refer to the cross-references after the title of the paragraph.]

Introduction

para.1 **54.13**

1. Part 35 is intended to limit the use of oral expert evidence to that which is reasonably required. In addition, where possible, matters requiring expert evidence should be dealt with by only one expert. Experts and those instructing them are expected to have regard to the guidance contained in the Protocol for the Instruction of Experts to Give Evidence in Civil Claims annexed to this practice direction.

(Further guidance on experts is contained in PD Pre-Action Conduct, annex C.)

Expert Evidence — General Requirements

2.1 Expert evidence should be the independent product of the expert uninfluenced by the pressures of litigation.

2.2 Experts should assist the court by providing objective, unbiased opinions on matters within their expertise, and should not assume the role of an advocate.

2.3 Experts should consider all material facts, including those which might detract from their opinions.

2.4 Experts should make it clear—

(a) when a question or issue falls outside their expertise; and

(b) when they are not able to reach a definite opinion, for example because they have insufficient information.

2.5 If, after producing a report, an expert's view changes on any material matter, such change of view should be communicated to all the parties without delay, and when appropriate to the court.

Form and Content of an Expert's Report

para.3 **54.29**
para.3.1 **54.29**
para.3.2 **54.6, 54.29**
para.3.2(5) **54.34**
para.3.3 **54.29**

3.1 An expert's report should be addressed to the court and not to the party from whom the expert has received instructions.

3.2 An expert's report must:

(1) give details of the expert's qualifications;

(2) give details of any literature or other material which has been relied on in making the report;

(3) contain a statement setting out the substance of all facts and instructions which are material to the opinions expressed in the report or upon which those opinions are based;

(4) make clear which of the facts stated in the report are within the expert's own knowledge;

(5) say who carried out any examination, measurement, test or experiment which the expert has used for the report, give the qualifications of that person, and say whether or not the test or experiment has been carried out under the expert's supervision;

(6) where there is a range of opinion on the matters dealt with in the report—

(a) summarise the range of opinions; and

(b) give reasons for the expert's own opinion;

(7) contain a summary of the conclusions reached;

(8) if the expert is not able to give an opinion without qualification, state the qualification; and

(9) contain a statement that the expert—

(a) understands their duty to the court, and has complied with that duty; and

(b) is aware of the requirements of Part 35, this practice direction and the Protocol for Instruction of Experts to Give Evidence in Civil Claims.

3.3 An expert's report must be verified by a statement of truth in the following form—
'I confirm that I have made clear which facts and matters referred to in this report are within my own knowledge and which are not. Those that are within my own knowledge I confirm to be true. The opinions I have expressed represent my true and complete professional opinions on the matters to which they refer.'
(Part 22 deals with statements of truth. Rule 32.14 sets out the consequences of verifying a document containing a false statement without an honest belief in its truth.)

Information

para.4 54.25

4. Under r. 35.9 the court may direct a party with access to information, which is not reasonably available to another party to serve on that other party a document, which records the information. The document served must include sufficient details of all the facts, tests, experiments and assumptions which underlie any part of the information to enable the party on whom it is served to make, or to obtain, a proper interpretation of the information and an assessment of its significance.

Instructions

para.5 54.38

5. Cross-examination of experts on the contents of their instructions will not be allowed unless the court permits it (or unless the party who gave the instructions consents). Before it gives permission the court must be satisfied that there are reasonable grounds to consider that the statement in the report of the substance of the instructions is inaccurate or incomplete. If the court is so satisfied, it will allow the cross-examination where it appears to be in the interests of justice.

Questions to Experts

para.6.1 54.32 para.6.2 54.32

6.1 Where a party sends a written question or questions under r. 35.6 direct to an expert, a copy of the questions must, at the same time, be sent to the other party or parties.

6.2 The party or parties instructing the expert must pay any fees charged by that expert for answering questions put under r. 35.6. This does not affect any decision of the court as to the party who is ultimately to bear the expert's fees.

Single Joint Expert

para.7 54.18

7. When considering whether to give permission for the parties to rely on expert evidence and whether that evidence should be from a single joint expert the court will take into account all the circumstances in particular, whether—
   (a) it is proportionate to have separate experts for each party on a particular issue with reference to—
      (i) the amount in dispute;
      (ii) the importance to the parties; and
      (iii) the complexity of the issue;
   (b) the instruction of a single joint expert is likely to assist the parties and the court to resolve the issue more speedily and in a more cost-effective way than separately instructed experts;
   (c) expert evidence is to be given on the issue of liability, causation or quantum;
   (d) the expert evidence falls within a substantially established area of knowledge which is unlikely to be in dispute or there is likely to be a range of expert opinion;
   (e) a party has already instructed an expert on the issue in question and whether or not that was done in compliance with any practice direction or relevant pre-action protocol;
   (f) questions put in accordance with r. 35.6 are likely to remove the need for the other party to instruct an expert if one party has already instructed an expert;
   (g) questions put to a single joint expert may not conclusively deal with all issues that may require testing prior to trial;

(h) a conference may be required with the legal representatives, experts and other witnesses which may make instruction of a single joint expert impractical; and
(i) a claim to privilege(GL) makes the instruction of any expert as a single joint expert inappropriate.

Orders

para.8 46.7, 54.10, 54.13, 54.33

8. Where an order requires an act to be done by an expert, or otherwise affects an expert, the party instructing that expert must serve a copy of the order on the expert. The claimant must serve the order on a single joint expert.

Discussions between Experts

para.9.1 54.31
para.9.2 54.31
para.9.3 54.31
para.9.4 54.31
para.9.6 54.31
para.9.7 54.31
para.9.8 54.31

9.1 Unless directed by the court discussions between experts are not mandatory. Parties must consider, with their experts, at an early stage, whether there is likely to be any useful purpose in holding an experts' discussion and if so when.

9.2 The purpose of discussions between experts is not for experts to settle cases but to agree and narrow issues and in particular to identify—
(i) the extent of the agreement between them;
(ii) the points of and short reasons for any disagreement;
(iii) action, if any, which may be taken to resolve any outstanding points of disagreement; and
(iv) any further material issues not raised and the extent to which these issues are agreed.

9.3 Where the experts are to meet, the parties must discuss and if possible agree whether an agenda is necessary, and if so attempt to agree one that helps the experts to focus on the issues which need to be discussed. The agenda must not be in the form of leading questions or hostile in tone.

9.4 Unless ordered by the court, or agreed by all parties, and the experts, neither the parties nor their legal representatives may attend experts' discussions.

9.5 If the legal representatives do attend—
(i) they should not normally intervene in the discussion, except to answer questions put to them by the experts or to advise on the law; and
(ii) the experts may if they so wish hold part of their discussions in the absence of the legal representatives.

9.6 A statement must be prepared by the experts dealing with para. 9.2(i)–(iv) above. Individual copies of the statements must be signed by the experts at the conclusion of the discussion, or as soon thereafter as practicable, and in any event within seven days. Copies of the statements must be provided to the parties no later than 14 days after signing.

9.7 Experts must give their own opinions to assist the court and do not require the authority of the parties to sign a joint statement.

9.8 If an expert significantly alters an opinion, the joint statement must include a note or addendum by that expert explaining the change of opinion.

Assessors

para.10.1 54.40
para.10.2 54.40
para.10.3 54.40
para.10.4 54.40

10.1 An assessor may be appointed to assist the court under r. 35.15. Not less than 21 days before making any such appointment, the court will notify each party in writing of the name of the proposed assessor, of the matter in respect of which the assistance of the assessor will be sought and of the qualifications of the assessor to give that assistance.

10.2 Where any person has been proposed for appointment as an assessor, any party may object to that person either personally or in respect of that person's qualification.

10.3 Any such objection must be made in writing and filed with the court within 7 days of receipt of the notification referred to in paragraph 10.1 and will be taken into account by the court in deciding whether or not to make the appointment.

10.4 Copies of any report prepared by the assessor will be sent to each of the parties but the assessor will not give oral evidence or be open to cross-examination or questioning.

Concurrent Expert Evidence

para.11.1 54.39
para.11.2 54.39
para.11.3 54.39
para.11.4(1) 54.39
para.11.4(2) 54.39
para.11.4(3) 54.39

11.1 At any stage in the proceedings the court may direct that some or all of the experts from like disciplines shall give their evidence concurrently. The following procedure shall then apply.

11.2 The court may direct that the parties agree an agenda for the taking of concurrent evidence, based upon the areas of disagreement identified in the experts' joint statements made pursuant to r. 35.12.

11.3 At the appropriate time the relevant experts will each take the oath or affirm. Unless the court orders otherwise, the experts will then address the items on the agenda in the manner set out in para. 11.4.

11.4 In relation to each issue on the agenda, and subject to the judge's discretion to modify the procedure—

(1) the judge may initiate the discussion by asking the experts, in turn, for their views. Once an expert has expressed a view the judge may ask questions about it. At one or more appropriate stages when questioning a particular expert, the judge may invite the other expert to comment or to ask that expert's own questions of the first expert;

(2) after the process set out in (1) has been completed for all the experts, the parties' representatives may ask questions of them. While such questioning may be designed to test the correctness of an expert's view, or seek clarification of it, it should not cover ground which has been fully explored already. In general a full cross-examination or re-examination is neither necessary nor appropriate; and

(3) after the process set out in (2) has been completed, the judge may summarise the experts' different positions on the issue and ask them to confirm or correct that summary.

ANNEX
PROTOCOL FOR THE INSTRUCTION OF EXPERTS TO GIVE EVIDENCE IN CIVIL CLAIMS

June 2005

annex 45.19, 54.7, 54.10, 54.25

1 Introduction

Expert witnesses perform a vital role in civil litigation. It is essential that both those who instruct experts and experts themselves are given clear guidance as to what they are expected to do in civil proceedings. The purpose of this protocol is to provide such guidance. It has been drafted by the Civil Justice Council and reflects the rules and practice directions current in June 2005, replacing the Code of Guidance on Expert Evidence. The authors of the protocol wish to acknowledge the valuable assistance they obtained by drawing on earlier documents produced by the Academy of Experts and the Expert Witness Institute, as well as suggestions made by the Clinical Dispute Forum. The protocol has been approved by the Master of the Rolls.

2 Aims of Protocol

para.2.2 54.1

2.1 This protocol offers guidance to experts and to those instructing them in the interpretation of and compliance with Part 35 and PD 35 and to further the objectives of the CPR in general. It is intended to assist in the interpretation of those provisions in the interests of good practice but it does not replace them. It sets out standards for the use of experts and the conduct of experts and those who instruct them. The existence of this protocol does not remove the need for experts and those who instruct them to be familiar with Part 35 and PD 35.

2.2 Experts and those who instruct them should also bear in mind Practice Direction Protocols, para. 1.4, which contains the following objectives, namely to:

(a) *encourage the exchange of early* and full information about the expert issues involved in a prospective legal claim;

(b) enable the parties to avoid or reduce the scope of litigation by agreeing the whole or part of an expert issue before commencement of proceedings; and
(c) support the efficient management of proceedings where litigation cannot be avoided.*

3 Application

3.1 This protocol applies to any steps taken for the purpose of civil proceedings by experts or those who instruct them on or after 5 September 2005.

3.2 It applies to all experts who are, or who may be, governed by Part 35 and to those who instruct them. Experts are governed by Part 35 if they are or have been instructed to give or prepare evidence for the purpose of civil proceedings in a court in England and Wales (r. 35.2).

3.3 Experts, and those instructing them, should be aware that some cases may be 'specialist proceedings' (Part 49) where there are modifications to the CPR. Proceedings may also be governed by other protocols. Further, some courts have published their own guides which supplement the CPR for proceedings in those courts. They contain provisions affecting expert evidence. Expert witnesses and those instructing them should be familiar with them when they are relevant.

3.4 Courts may take into account any failure to comply with this protocol when making orders in relation to costs, interest, time limits, the stay of proceedings and whether to order a party to pay a sum of money into court.

Limitation

3.5 If, as a result of complying with any part of this protocol, claims would or might be time barred under any provision in the Limitation Act 1980, or any other legislation that imposes a time limit for bringing an action, claimants may commence proceedings without complying with this protocol. In such circumstances, claimants who commence proceedings without complying with all, or any part, of this protocol must apply, giving notice to all other parties, to the court for directions as to the timetable and form of procedure to be adopted, at the same time as they request the court to issue proceedings. The court may consider whether to order a stay of the whole or part of the proceedings pending compliance with this protocol and may make orders in relation to costs.

4 Duties of Experts

para.4.1–4.2 54.10
para.4.3 54.1, 54.7, 54.10
para.4.4–4.6 54.10

4.1 Experts always owe a duty to exercise reasonable skill and care to those instructing them, and to comply with any relevant professional code of ethics. However when they are instructed to give or prepare evidence for the purpose of civil proceedings in England and Wales they have an overriding duty to help the court on matters within their expertise (r. 35.3). This duty overrides any obligation to the person instructing or paying them. Experts must not serve the exclusive interest of those who retain them.

4.2 Experts should be aware of the overriding objective that courts deal with cases justly. This includes dealing with cases proportionately, expeditiously and fairly (r. 1.1). Experts are under an obligation to assist the court so as to enable them to deal with cases in accordance with the overriding objective. However, the overriding objective does not impose on experts any duty to act as mediators between the parties or require them to trespass on the role of the court in deciding facts.

4.3 Experts should provide opinions which are independent, regardless of the pressures of litigation. In this context, a useful test of 'independence' is that the expert would express the same opinion if given the same instructions by an opposing party. Experts should not take it upon themselves to promote the point of view of the party instructing them or engage in the role of advocates.

4.4 Experts should confine their opinions to matters which are material to the disputes between the parties and provide opinions only in relation to matters which lie within their expertise. Experts should indicate without delay where particular questions or issues fall outside their expertise.

4.5 Experts should take into account all material facts before them at the time that they give their opinion. Their reports should set out those facts and any literature or any other material on which they have relied in forming their opinions. They should indicate if an opinion is provisional, or qualified, or where they consider that further information is required or if, for any other reason, they are not satisfied that an opinion can be expressed finally and without qualification.

[* The aims set out in PD 35, annex, para. 2.2, derive from the former PD Protocols which was replaced by PD Pre-action Conduct in 2009. The aims of the protocols can now be found in PD Pre-action Conduct, paras 1.1 and 1.2.]

4.6 Experts should inform those instructing them without delay of any change in their opinions on any material matter and the reason for it.

4.7 Experts should be aware that any failure by them to comply with the CPR or court orders or any excessive delay for which they are responsible may result in the parties who instructed them being penalised in costs and even, in extreme cases, being debarred from placing the experts' evidence before the court. In *Phillips v Symes* [2004] EWHC 2330 (Ch), [2005] 1 WLR 2043, Peter Smith J held that courts may also make orders for costs (under the Senior Courts Act 1981, s. 51) directly against expert witnesses who by their evidence cause significant expense to be incurred, and do so in flagrant and reckless disregard of their duties to the court.

5 Conduct of Experts Instructed Only to Advise

para.5.1 54.1, 54.22 para.5.2 54.22

5.1 Part 35 only applies where experts are instructed to give opinions which are relied on for the purposes of court proceedings. Advice which the parties do not intend to adduce in litigation is likely to be confidential; the protocol does not apply in these circumstances (*Carlson v Townsend* [2001] EWCA Civ 511, [2001] 1 WLR 2415; *Jackson v Marley Davenport Ltd* [2004] EWCA Civ 1225, [2004] 1 WLR 2926).

5.2 The same applies where, after the commencement of proceedings, experts are instructed only to advise (e.g. to comment upon a single joint expert's report) and not to give or prepare evidence for use in the proceedings.

5.3 However, this protocol does apply if experts who were formerly instructed only to advise are later instructed to give or prepare evidence for the purpose of civil proceedings.

6 The Need for Experts

6.1 Those intending to instruct experts to give or prepare evidence for the purpose of civil proceedings should consider whether expert evidence is appropriate, taking account of the principles set out in Parts 1 and 35, and in particular whether:
(a) it is relevant to a matter which is in dispute between the parties;
(b) it is reasonably required to resolve the proceedings (r. 35.1);
(c) the expert has expertise relevant to the issue on which an opinion is sought;
(d) the expert has the experience, expertise and training appropriate to the value, complexity and importance of the case; and whether
(e) these objects can be achieved by the appointment of a single joint expert (see section 17 below).

6.2 Although the court's permission is not generally required to instruct an expert, the court's permission is required before experts can be called to give evidence or their evidence can be put in (r. 35.4).

7 The Appointment of Experts

paras. 7.1–7.2 54.24 paras.7.6–7.7 54.24

7.1 Before experts are formally instructed or the court's permission to appoint named experts is sought, the following should be established:
(a) that they have the appropriate expertise and experience;
(b) that they are familiar with the general duties of an expert;
(c) that they can produce a report, deal with questions and have discussions with other experts within a reasonable time and at a cost proportionate to the matters in issue;
(d) a description of the work required;
(e) whether they are available to attend the trial, if attendance is required; and
(f) there is no potential conflict of interest.

7.2 Terms of appointment should be agreed at the outset and should normally include:
(a) the capacity in which the expert is to be appointed (e.g. party appointed expert, single joint expert or expert advisor);
(b) the services required of the expert (e.g. provision of expert's report, answering questions in writing, attendance at meetings and attendance at court);
(c) time for delivery of the report;
(d) the basis of the expert's charges (either daily or hourly rates and an estimate of the time likely to be required, or a total fee for the services);
(e) travelling expenses and disbursements;

(f) cancellation charges;
(g) any fees for attending court;
(h) time for making the payment;
(i) whether fees are to be paid by a third party; and
(j) if a party is publicly funded, whether or not the expert's charges will be subject to assessment by a costs officer.

7.3 As to the appointment of single joint experts, see section 17 below.

7.4 When necessary, arrangements should be made for dealing with questions to experts and discussions between experts, including any directions given by the court, and provision should be made for the cost of this work.

7.5 Experts should be informed regularly about deadlines for all matters concerning them. Those instructing experts should promptly send them copies of all court orders and directions which may affect the preparation of their reports or any other matters concerning their obligations.

Conditional and contingency fees

7.6 Payments contingent upon the nature of the expert evidence given in legal proceedings, or upon the outcome of a case, must not be offered or accepted. To do so would contravene experts' overriding duty to the court and compromise their duty of independence.

7.7 Agreement to delay payment of experts' fees until after the conclusion of cases is permissible as long as the amount of the fee does not depend on the outcome of the case.

8 Instructions

para.8.1 54.25

8.1 Those instructing experts should ensure that they give clear instructions, including the following:
(a) basic information, such as names, addresses, telephone numbers, dates of birth and dates of incidents;
(b) the nature and extent of the expertise which is called for;
(c) the purpose of requesting the advice or report, a description of the matter(s) to be investigated, the principal known issues and the identity of all parties;
(d) the statement(s) of case (if any), those documents which form part of standard disclosure and witness statements which are relevant to the advice or report;
(e) where proceedings have not been started, whether proceedings are being contemplated and, if so, whether the expert is asked only for advice;
(f) an outline programme, consistent with good case management and the expert's availability, for the completion and delivery of each stage of the expert's work; and
(g) where proceedings have been started, the dates of any hearings (including any case management conferences and/or pre-trial reviews), the name of the court, the claim number and the track to which the claim has been allocated.

8.2 Experts who do not receive clear instructions should request clarification and may indicate that they are not prepared to act unless and until such clear instructions are received.

8.3 As to the instruction of single joint experts, see section 17 below.

9 Experts' Acceptance of Instructions

para.9.1 54.25

9.1 Experts should confirm without delay whether or not they accept instructions. They should also inform those instructing them (whether on initial instruction or at any later stage) without delay if:
(a) instructions are not acceptable because, for example, they require work that falls outside their expertise, impose unrealistic deadlines, or are insufficiently clear;
(b) they consider that instructions are or have become insufficient to complete the work;
(c) they become aware that they may not be able to fulfil any of the terms of appointment;
(d) the instructions and/or work have, for any reason, placed them in conflict with their duties as an expert; or
(e) they are not satisfied that they can comply with any orders that have been made.

9.2 Experts must neither express an opinion outside the scope of their field of expertise, nor accept any instructions to do so.

10 Withdrawal

para.10.1 54.25

10.1 Where experts' instructions remain incompatible with their duties, whether through incompleteness, a conflict between their duty to the court and their instructions, or for any other substantial and significant reason, they may consider withdrawing from the case. However, experts should not withdraw without first discussing the position fully with those who instruct them and considering carefully whether it would be more appropriate to make a written request for directions from the court. If experts do withdraw, they must give formal written notice to those instructing them.

11 Experts' Right to Ask Court for Directions

11.1 Experts may request directions from the court to assist them in carrying out their functions as experts. Experts should normally discuss such matters with those who instruct them before making any such request. Unless the court otherwise orders, any proposed request for directions should be copied to the party instructing the expert at least seven days before filing any request to the court, and to all other parties at least four days before filing it (r. 35.14).

11.2 Requests to the court for directions should be made by letter, containing:

(a) the title of the claim;
(b) the claim number of the case;
(c) the name of the expert;
(d) full details of why directions are sought; and
(e) copies of any relevant documentation.

12 Power of the Court to Direct a Party to Provide Information

12.1 If experts consider that those instructing them have not provided information which they require, they may, after discussion with those instructing them and giving notice, write to the court to seek directions (r. 35.14).

12.2 Experts and those who instruct them should also be aware of r. 35.9. This provides that where one party has access to information which is not readily available to the other party, the court may direct the party who has access to the information to prepare, file and copy to the other party a document recording the information. If experts require such information which has not been disclosed, they should discuss the position with those instructing them without delay, so that a request for the information can be made, and, if not forthcoming, an application can be made to the court. Unless a document appears to be essential, experts should assess the cost and time involved in the production of a document and whether its provision would be proportionate in the context of the case.

13 Contents of Experts' Reports

paras.13.1–13.15 54.29

13.1 The content and extent of experts' reports should be governed by the scope of their instructions and general obligations, the contents of Part 35 and PD 35 and their overriding duty to the court.

13.2 In preparing reports, experts should maintain professional objectivity and impartiality at all times.

13.3 PD 35, para. 2, provides that experts' reports should be addressed to the court and gives detailed directions about the form and content of such reports. All experts and those who instruct them should ensure that they are familiar with these requirements.

13.4 Model forms of experts' reports are available from bodies such as the Academy of Experts or the Expert Witness Institute.

13.5 Experts' reports must contain statements that they—

(i) understand their duty to the court and have complied and will continue to comply with it; and
(ii) are aware of the requirements of Part 35 and PD 35, this protocol and PD Pre-action Conduct.

Experts' reports must also be verified by a statement of truth. The form of the statement of truth is as follows—

I confirm that I have made clear which facts and matters referred to in this report are within my own knowledge and which are not. Those that are within my own knowledge I confirm to be true. The opinions I have expressed represent my true and complete professional opinions on the matters to which they refer.

This wording is mandatory and must not be modified.

Qualifications

13.6 The details of experts' qualifications to be given in reports should be commensurate with the nature and complexity of the case. It may be sufficient merely to state academic and professional qualifications. However, where highly specialised expertise is called for, experts should include the detail of particular training and/or experience that qualifies them to provide that highly specialised evidence.

Tests

13.7 Where tests of a scientific or technical nature have been carried out, experts should state:

(a) the methodology used; and

(b) by whom the tests were undertaken and under whose supervision, summarising their respective qualifications and experience.

Reliance on the work of others

13.8 Where experts rely in their reports on literature or other material and cite the opinions of others without having verified them, they must give details of those opinions relied on. It is likely to assist the court if the qualifications of the originator(s) are also stated.

Facts

13.9 When addressing questions of fact and opinion, experts should keep the two separate and discrete.

13.10 Experts must state those facts (whether assumed or otherwise) upon which their opinions are based. They must distinguish clearly between those facts which experts know to be true and those facts which they assume.

13.11 Where there are material facts in dispute experts should express separate opinions on each hypothesis put forward. They should not express a view in favour of one or other disputed version of the facts unless, as a result of particular expertise and experience, they consider one set of facts as being improbable or less probable, in which case they may express that view, and should give reasons for holding it.

Range of opinion

13.12 If the mandatory summary of the range of opinion is based on published sources, experts should explain those sources and, where appropriate, state the qualifications of the originator(s) of the opinions from which they differ, particularly if such opinions represent a well-established school of thought.

13.13 Where there is no available source for the range of opinion, experts may need to express opinions on what they believe to be the range which other experts would arrive at if asked. In those circumstances, experts should make it clear that the range that they summarise is based on their own judgment and explain the basis of that judgment.

Conclusions

13.14 A summary of conclusions is mandatory. The summary should be at the end of the report after all the reasoning. There may be cases, however, where the benefit to the court is heightened by placing a short summary at the beginning of the report whilst giving the full conclusions at the end. For example, it can assist with the comprehension of the analysis and with the absorption of the detailed facts if the court is told at the outset of the direction in which the report's logic will flow in cases involving highly complex matters which fall outside the general knowledge of the court.

Basis of report: material instructions

13.15 The mandatory statement of the substance of all material instructions should not be incomplete or otherwise tend to mislead. The imperative is transparency. The term 'instructions' includes all material which solicitors place in front of experts in order to gain advice.

The omission from the statement of 'off-the-record' oral instructions is not permitted. Courts may allow cross-examination about the instructions if there are reasonable grounds to consider that the statement may be inaccurate or incomplete.

14 After Receipt of Experts' Reports

14.1 Following the receipt of experts' reports, those instructing them should advise the experts as soon as reasonably practicable whether, and if so when, the report will be disclosed to other parties; and, if so disclosed, the date of actual disclosure.

14.2 If experts' reports are to be relied upon, and if experts are to give oral evidence, those instructing them should give the experts the opportunity to consider and comment upon other reports within their area of expertise and which deal with relevant issues at the earliest opportunity.

14.3 Those instructing experts should keep experts informed of the progress of cases, including amendments to statements of case relevant to experts' opinion.

14.4 If those instructing experts become aware of material changes in circumstances or that relevant information within their control was not previously provided to experts, they should without delay instruct experts to review, and if necessary, update the contents of their reports.

15 Amendment of Reports

para.15.2 **54.29**

15.1 It may become necessary for experts to amend their reports:
(a) as a result of an exchange of questions and answers;
(b) following agreements reached at meetings between experts; or
(c) where further evidence or documentation is disclosed.

15.2 Experts should not be asked to, and should not, amend, expand or alter any parts of reports in a manner which distorts their true opinion, but may be invited to amend or expand reports to ensure accuracy, internal consistency, completeness and relevance to the issues and clarity. Although experts should generally follow the recommendations of solicitors with regard to the form of reports, they should form their own independent views as to the opinions and contents expressed in their reports and exclude any suggestions which do not accord with their views.

15.3 Where experts change their opinion following a meeting of experts, a simple signed and dated addendum or memorandum to that effect is generally sufficient. In some cases, however, the benefit to the court of having an amended report may justify the cost of making the amendment.

15.4 Where experts significantly alter their opinion, as a result of new evidence or because evidence on which they relied has become unreliable, or for any other reason, they should amend their reports to reflect that fact. Amended reports should include reasons for amendments. In such circumstances those instructing experts should inform other parties as soon as possible of any change of opinion.

15.5 When experts intend to amend their reports, they should inform those instructing them without delay and give reasons. They should provide the amended version (or an addendum or memorandum) clearly marked as such as quickly as possible.

16 Written Questions to Experts

para.16.1 **48.26**

16.1 The procedure for putting written questions to experts (r. 35.6) is intended to facilitate the clarification of opinions and issues after experts' reports have been served. Experts have a duty to provide answers to questions properly put. Where they fail to do so, the court may impose sanctions against the party instructing the expert, and, if, there is continued non-compliance, debar a party from relying on the report. Experts should copy their answers to those instructing them.

16.2 Experts' answers to questions automatically become part of their reports. They are covered by the statement of truth and form part of the expert evidence.

16.3 Where experts believe that questions put are not properly directed to the clarification of the report, or are disproportionate, or have been asked out of time, they should discuss the questions with those instructing them and, if appropriate, those asking the questions. Attempts should be made to resolve such problems without the need for an application to the court for directions.

Written requests for directions in relation to questions

16.4 If those instructing experts do not apply to the court in respect of questions, but experts still believe that questions are improper or out of time, experts may file written requests with the court for directions to assist in carrying out their functions as experts (r. 35.14). See Section 11 above.

17 Single Joint Experts

paras.17.2 **45.19**	para.17.3 **10.57**
paras.17.4–17.5 **54.22**	paras. 17.10–17.11 **54.26**
paras. 17.6–17.7 **54.26**	

17.1 Part 35 and PD 35 deal extensively with the instruction and use of joint experts by the parties and the powers of the court to order their use (see rr. 35.7 and 35.8; PD 35, para. 5).

17.2 The CPR encourage the use of joint experts. Wherever possible a joint report should be obtained. Consideration should therefore be given by all parties to the appointment of single joint experts in all cases where a court might direct such an appointment. Single joint experts are the norm in cases allocated to the small claims track and the fast track.

17.3 Where, in the early stages of a dispute, examinations, investigations, tests, site inspections, experiments, preparation of photographs, plans or other similar preliminary expert tasks are necessary, consideration should be given to the instruction of a single joint expert, especially where such matters are not, at that stage, expected to be contentious as between the parties. The objective of such an appointment should be to agree or to narrow issues.

17.4 Experts who have previously advised a party (whether in the same case or otherwise) should only be proposed as single joint experts if other parties are given all relevant information about the previous involvement.

17.5 The appointment of a single joint expert does not prevent parties from instructing their own experts to advise (but the costs of such expert advisers may not be recoverable in the case).

Joint instructions

17.6 The parties should try to agree joint instructions to single joint experts, but, in default of agreement, each party may give instructions. In particular, all parties should try to agree what documents should be included with instructions and what assumptions single joint experts should make.

17.7 Where the parties fail to agree joint instructions, they should try to agree where the areas of disagreement lie and their instructions should make this clear. If separate instructions are given, they should be copied at the same time to the other instructing parties.

17.8 Where experts are instructed by two or more parties, the terms of appointment should, unless the court has directed otherwise, or the parties have agreed otherwise, include:

(a) a statement that all the instructing parties are jointly and severally liable to pay the experts' fees and, accordingly, that experts' invoices should be sent simultaneously to all instructing parties or their solicitors (as appropriate); and

(b) a statement as to whether any order has been made limiting the amount of experts' fees and expenses (r. 35.8(4)(a)).

17.9 Where instructions have not been received by the expert from one or more of the instructing parties the expert should give notice (normally at least seven days) of a deadline to all instructing parties for the receipt by the expert of such instructions. Unless the instructions are received within the deadline the expert may begin work. In the event that instructions are received after the deadline but before the signing off of the report the expert should consider whether it is practicable to comply with those instructions without adversely affecting the timetable set for delivery of the report and in such a manner as to comply with the proportionality principle. An expert who decides to issue a report without taking into account instructions received after the deadline should inform the parties who may apply to the court for directions. In either event the report must show clearly that the expert did not receive instructions within the deadline, or, as the case may be, at all.

Conduct of the single joint expert

17.10 Single joint experts should keep all instructing parties informed of any material steps that they may be taking by, for example, copying all correspondence to those instructing them.

17.11 Single joint experts are Part 35 experts and so have an overriding duty to the court. They are the parties' appointed experts and therefore owe an equal duty to all parties. They should maintain independence, impartiality and transparency at all times.

17.12 Single joint experts should not attend any meeting or conference which is not a joint one, unless all the parties have agreed in writing or the court has directed that such a meeting may be held (*Peet v Mid Kent Area Healthcare Trust* [2001] EWCA Civ 1703, [2002] 1 WLR 2104) and who is to pay the experts' fees for the meeting.

17.13 Single joint experts may request directions from the court—see Section 11 above.

17.14 Single joint experts should serve their reports simultaneously on all instructing parties. They should provide a single report even though they may have received instructions which contain areas of conflicting fact or allegation. If conflicting instructions lead to different opinions (for example, because the instructions require experts to make different assumptions of fact), reports may need to contain more than one set of opinions on any issue. It is for the court to determine the facts.

Cross-examination

17.15 Single joint experts do not normally give oral evidence at trial but if they do, all parties may cross-examine them. In general written questions (r. 35.6) should be put to single joint experts before requests are made for them to attend court for the purpose of cross-examination (*Daniels v Walker* [2000] 1 WLR 1382).

18 Discussions between Experts

para.18.4 45.19, 54.31 para.18.5–18.6 54.31

18.1 The court has powers to direct discussions between experts for the purposes set out in the CPR (r. 35.12). Parties may also agree that discussions take place between their experts.

18.2 Where single joint experts have been instructed but parties have, with the permission of the court, instructed their own additional Part 35 experts, there may, if the court so orders or the parties agree, be discussions between the single joint experts and the additional Part 35 experts. Such discussions should be confined to those matters within the remit of the additional Part 35 experts or as ordered by the court.

18.3 The purpose of discussions between experts should be, wherever possible, to:

(a) identify and discuss the expert issues in the proceedings;

(b) reach agreed opinions on those issues, and, if that is not possible, to narrow the issues in the case;

(c) identify those issues on which they agree and disagree and summarise their reasons for disagreement on any issue; and

(d) identify what action, if any, may be taken to resolve any of the outstanding issues between the parties.

Arrangements for discussions between experts

18.4 Arrangements for discussions between experts should be proportionate to the value of cases. In small claims and fast-track cases there should not normally be meetings between experts. Where discussion is justified in such cases, telephone discussion or an exchange of letters should, in the interests of proportionality, usually suffice. In multi-track cases, discussion may be face to face, but the practicalities or the proportionality principle may require discussions to be by telephone or videoconference.

18.5 The parties, their lawyers and experts should cooperate to produce the agenda for any discussion between experts, although primary responsibility for preparation of the agenda should normally lie with the parties' solicitors.

18.6 The agenda should indicate what matters have been agreed and summarise concisely those which are in issue. It is often helpful for it to include questions to be answered by the experts. If agreement cannot be reached promptly or a party is unrepresented, the court may give directions for the drawing up of the agenda. The agenda should be circulated to experts and those instructing them to allow sufficient time for the experts to prepare for the discussion.

18.7 Those instructing experts must not instruct experts to avoid reaching agreement (or to defer doing so) on any matter within the experts' competence. Experts are not permitted to accept such instructions.

18.8 The parties' lawyers may only be present at discussions between experts if all the parties agree or the court so orders. If lawyers do attend, they should not normally intervene except to answer questions put to them by the experts or to advise about the law (*Hubbard v Lambeth, Southwark and Lewisham Health Authority* [2001] EWCA Civ 1455, [2002] Lloyd's Rep Med 8).

18.9 The content of discussions between experts should not be referred to at trial unless the parties agree (r. 35.12(4)). It is good practice for any such agreement to be in writing.

18.10 At the conclusion of any discussion between experts, a statement should be prepared setting out:

(a) a list of issues that have been agreed, including, in each instance, the basis of agreement;
(b) a list of issues that have not been agreed, including, in each instance, the basis of disagreement;
(c) a list of any further issues that have arisen that were not included in the original agenda for discussion;
(d) a record of further action, if any, to be taken or recommended, including as appropriate the holding of further discussions between experts.

18.11 The statement should be agreed and signed by all the parties to the discussion as soon as may be practicable.

18.12 Agreements between experts during discussions do not bind the parties unless the parties expressly agree to be bound by the agreement (r. 35.12(5)). However, in view of the overriding objective, parties should give careful consideration before refusing to be bound by such an agreement and be able to explain their refusal should it become relevant to the issue of costs.

19 Attendance of Experts at Court

para.19.2(a) 58.11

19.1 Experts instructed in cases have an obligation to attend court if called upon to do so and accordingly should ensure that those instructing them are always aware of their dates to be avoided and take all reasonable steps to be available.

19.2 Those instructing experts should:

(a) ascertain the availability of experts before trial dates are fixed;
(b) keep experts updated with timetables (including the dates and times experts are to attend) and the location of the court;
(c) give consideration, where appropriate, to experts giving evidence via a video-link;
(d) inform experts immediately if trial dates are vacated.

19.3 Experts should normally attend court without the need for the service of witness summonses, but on occasion they may be served to require attendance (Part 34). The use of witness summonses does not affect the contractual or other obligations of the parties to pay experts' fees.

CPR Part 36 Offers to Settle

Part 36 **PC 29, 1.21, 45.6, 45.29, 47.7, 47.11, 48.29, 56.2, 61.15, 63.29, 65.4, 66.1, 66.2, 66.3, 66.4, 66.5, 66.6, 66.21, 66.36, 66.38, 66.39, 66.40, 66.42, 66.44, 66.47, 68.19, 68.21, 68.31, 68.46, 68.54, 68.57, 69.9, 69.10, 70.3, 70.15, 71.12, 71.18, 71.23, 71.37**

36.A1 Scope of This Part

(1) This Part contains rules about—
  (a) offers to settle; and
  (b) the consequences where an offer to settle is made in accordance with this Part.
(2) Section I of this Part contains rules about offers to settle other than where Section II applies.
(3) Section II of this Part contains rules about offers to settle where the parties have followed the Pre-Action Protocol for Low Value Personal Injury Claims in Road Traffic Accidents ('the RTA Protocol') and have started proceedings under Part 8 in accordance with Practice Direction 8B.

I PART 36 OFFERS TO SETTLE

36.1 Scope of This Section

r.36.1(1) **66.47**
r.36.1(2) **66.6, 66.16, 66.44, 66.47**

(1) This Section does not apply to an offer to settle to which Section II of this Part applies.
(2) Nothing in this Section prevents a party making an offer to settle in whatever way he chooses, but if the offer is not made in accordance with rule 36.2, it will not have the consequences specified in rules 36.10, 36.11 and 36.14.

(Rule 44.3 requires the court to consider an offer to settle that does not have the costs consequences set out in this Section in deciding what order to make about costs)

36.2 Form and Content of a Part 36 Offer

r.36.2 **66.7, 66.16, 66.47**
r.36.2(2)(a) **PC 29, 66.7, 66.18**
r.36.2(2)(b) **PC 29, 66.7**
r.36.2(2)(c) **PC 29, 66.7, 66.8, 66.15, 66.16**
r.36.2(2)(d)–(e) **PC 29, 66.7**
r.36.2(3) **66.7**
r.36.2(5) **66.7**

(1) An offer to settle which is made in accordance with this rule is called a Part 36 offer.
(2) A Part 36 offer must—
  (a) be in writing;
  (b) state on its face that it is intended to have the consequences of Section I of Part 36;
  (c) specify a period of not less than 21 days within which the defendant will be liable for the claimant's costs in accordance with rule 36.10 if the offer is accepted;

(d) state whether it relates to the whole of the claim or to part of it or to an issue that arises in it and if so to which part or issue; and
(e) state whether it takes into account any counterclaim.

(Rule 36.7 makes provision for when a Part 36 offer is made)

(3) Rule 36.2(2)(c) does not apply if the offer is made less than 21 days before the start of the trial.
(4) In appropriate cases, a Part 36 offer must contain such further information as is required by rule 36.5 (Personal injury claims for future pecuniary loss), rule 36.6 (Offer to settle a claim for provisional damages), and rule 36.15 (Deduction of benefits).
(5) An offeror may make a Part 36 offer solely in relation to liability.

36.3 Part 36 Offers — General Provisions

r.36.3(1)(a)–(b) **66.6**
r.36.3(1)(c) **PC 29, 66.15, 69.9**
r.36.3(2)(a) **66.6**
r.36.3(2)(b) **66.6, 66.49**
r.36.3(3) **PC 29, 66.9**
r.36.3(4) **PC 29, 66.6, 66.49**
r.36.3(5) **PC 29, 66.17**
r.36.3(6) **PC 29, 66.6, 66.18, 66.44**
r.36.3(7) **PC 29, 66.1, 66.16, 66.17, 66.18, 66.20, 66.22**

(1) In this Part—
(a) the party who makes an offer is the 'offeror';
(b) the party to whom an offer is made is the 'offeree'; and
(c) 'the relevant period' means—
(i) in the case of an offer made not less than 21 days before trial, the period stated under rule 36.2(2)(c) or such longer period as the parties agree;
(ii) otherwise, the period up to end of the trial or such other period as the court has determined.

(2) A Part 36 offer—
(a) may be made at any time, including before the commencement of proceedings; and
(b) may be made in appeal proceedings.

(3) A Part 36 offer which offers to pay or offers to accept a sum of money will be treated as inclusive of all interest until—
(a) the date on which the period stated under rule 36.2(2) (c) expires; or
(b) if rule 36.2(3) applies, a date 21 days after the date the offer was made.

(4) A Part 36 offer shall have the consequences set out in this Section only in relation to the costs of the proceedings in respect of which it is made, and not in relation to the costs of any appeal from the final decision in those proceedings.
(5) Before expiry of the relevant period, a Part 36 offer may be withdrawn or its terms changed to be less advantageous to the offeree, only if the court gives permission.
(6) After expiry of the relevant period and provided that the offeree has not previously served notice of acceptance, the offeror may withdraw the offer or change its terms to be less advantageous to the offeree without the permission of the court.
(7) The offeror does so by serving written notice of the withdrawal or change of terms on the offeree.

(Rule 36.14(6) deals with the costs consequences following judgment of an offer that is withdrawn)

36.4 Part 36 Offers — Defendants' Offers

r.36.4 **66.11, 66.12**
r.36.4(1) **PC 29, 66.9, 66.21**
r.36.4(2) **66.9**

(1) Subject to rule 36.5(3) and rule 36.6(1), a Part 36 offer by a defendant to pay a sum of money in settlement of a claim must be an offer to pay a single sum of money.
(2) But, an offer that includes an offer to pay all or part of the sum, if accepted, at a date later than 14 days following the date of acceptance will not be treated as a Part 36 offer unless the offeree accepts the offer.

36.5 Personal Injury Claims for Future Pecuniary Loss

r.36.5 **PC 29, 63.28, 66.16, 66.38**
r.36.5(2) **66.44**
r.36.5(3) **66.11**
r.36.5(4) **66.11**
r.36.5(4)(a)–(c) **66.11**
r.36.5(4)(d) **66.11, 66.16**
r.36.5(5)–(7) **66.11**

(1) This rule applies to a claim for damages for personal injury which is or includes a claim for future pecuniary loss.
(2) An offer to settle such a claim will not have the consequences set out in rules 36.10, 36.11 and 36.14 unless it is made by way of a Part 36 offer under this rule.
(3) A Part 36 offer to which this rule applies may contain an offer to pay, or an offer to accept—
 (a) the whole or part of the damages for future pecuniary loss in the form of—
  (i) a lump sum; or
  (ii) periodical payments; or
  (iii) both a lump sum and periodical payments;
 (b) the whole or part of any other damages in the form of a lump sum.
(4) A Part 36 offer to which this rule applies—
 (a) must state the amount of any offer to pay the whole or part of any damages in the form of a lump sum;
 (b) may state—
  (i) what part of the lump sum, if any, relates to damages for future pecuniary loss; and
  (ii) what part relates to other damages to be accepted in the form of a lump sum;
 (c) must state what part of the offer relates to damages for future pecuniary loss to be paid or accepted in the form of periodical payments and must specify—
  (i) the amount and duration of the periodical payments;
  (ii) the amount of any payments for substantial capital purchases and when they are to be made; and
  (iii) that each amount is to vary by reference to the retail prices index (or to some other named index, or that it is not to vary by reference to any index); and
 (d) must state either that any damages which take the form of periodical payments will be funded in a way which ensures that the continuity of payment is reasonably secure in accordance with section 2(4) of the Damages Act 1996 or how such damages are to be paid and how the continuity of their payment is to be secured.
(5) Rule 36.4 applies to the extent that a Part 36 offer by a defendant under this rule includes an offer to pay all or part of any damages in the form of a lump sum.
(6) Where the offeror makes a Part 36 offer to which this rule applies and which offers to pay or to accept damages in the form of both a lump sum and periodical payments, the offeree may only give notice of acceptance of the offer as a whole.
(7) If the offeree accepts a Part 36 offer which includes payment of any part of the damages in the form of periodical payments, the claimant must, within 7 days of the date of acceptance, apply to the court for an order for an award of damages in the form of periodical payments under rule 41.8.

(Practice Direction 41B contains information about periodical payments under the Damages Act 1996)

36.6 Offer to Settle a Claim for Provisional Damages

r.36.6 **PC 29, 66.16** r.36.6(2)–(5) **66.12**

(1) An offeror may make a Part 36 offer in respect of a claim which includes a claim for provisional damages.
(2) Where he does so, the Part 36 offer must specify whether or not the offeror is proposing that the settlement shall include an award of provisional damages.
(3) Where the offeror is offering to agree to the making of an award of provisional damages the Part 36 offer must also state—
 (a) that the sum offered is in satisfaction of the claim for damages on the assumption that the injured person will not develop the disease or suffer the type of deterioration specified in the offer;
 (b) that the offer is subject to the condition that the claimant must make any claim for further damages within a limited period; and
 (c) what that period is.
(4) Rule 36.4 applies to the extent that a Part 36 offer by a defendant includes an offer to agree to the making of an award of provisional damages.

(5) If the offeree accepts the Part 36 offer, the claimant must, within 7 days of the date of acceptance, apply to the court for an order for an award of provisional damages under rule 41.2.

36.7 Time When a Part 36 Offer Is Made

r.36.7 **66.16**
r.36.7(1) **PC 29, 66.14, 66.21**
r.36.7(2) **66.18**

(1) A Part 36 offer is made when it is served on the offeree.
(2) A change in the terms of a Part 36 offer will be effective when notice of the change is served on the offeree.

(Rule 36.3 makes provision about when permission is required to change the terms of an offer to make it less advantageous to the offeree)

36.8 Clarification of a Part 36 Offer

r.36.8 **66.21**
r.36.8(1) **66.21**
r.36.8(2) **66.21**
r.36.8(3) **66.21**

(1) The offeree may, within 7 days of a Part 36 offer being made, request the offeror to clarify the offer.
(2) If the offeror does not give the clarification requested under paragraph (1) within 7 days of receiving the request, the offeree may, unless the trial has started, apply for an order that he does so.

(Part 23 contains provisions about making an application to the court)

(3) If the court makes an order under paragraph (2), it must specify the date when the Part 36 offer is to be treated as having been made.

36.9 Acceptance of a Part 36 Offer

r.36.9 **66.50**
r.36.9(1) **66.16, 66.22**
r.36.9(2) **PC 29, 66.1, 66.6, 66.16, 66.18, 66.20, 66.22**
r.36.9(3)(a)–(c) **66.30**
r.36.9(3)(d) **66.22, 66.29**
r.36.9(5) **66.22**

(1) A Part 36 offer is accepted by serving written notice of the acceptance on the offeror.
(2) Subject to rule 36.9(3), a Part 36 offer may be accepted at any time (whether or not the offeree has subsequently made a different offer) unless the offeror serves notice of withdrawal on the offeree.

(Rule 21.10 deals with compromise etc. by or on behalf of a child or protected party)

(3) The court's permission is required to accept a Part 36 offer where—
 (a) rule 36.12(4) applies;
 (b) rule 36.15(3)(b) applies, the relevant period has expired and further deductible amounts have been paid to the claimant since the date of the offer;
 (c) an apportionment is required under rule 41.3A; or
 (d) the trial has started.

(Rule 36.12 deals with offers by some but not all of multiple defendants)
(Rule 36.15 defines 'deductible amounts')
(Rule 41.3A requires an apportionment in proceedings under the Fatal Accidents Act 1976 and Law Reform (Miscellaneous Provisions) Act 1934)

(4) Where the court gives permission under paragraph (3), unless all the parties have agreed costs, the court will make an order dealing with costs, and may order that the costs consequences set out in rule 36.10 will apply.
(5) Unless the parties agree, a Part 36 offer may not be accepted after the end of the trial but before judgment is handed down.

36.10 Costs Consequences of Acceptance of a Part 36 Offer

r.36.10 **PC 29, 36.16, 66.6, 66.7, 66.8, 68.15, 66.16, 66.23, 66.24, 66.27, 66.55**
r.36.10(1) **PC 29, 66.23**
r.36.10(2) **66.7, 66.24, 66.33**
r.36.10(3) **PC 29, 66.23**
r.36.10(3)(a) **48.23**
r.36.10(4)(a) **66.25**
r.36.10(4)(b) **PC 29, 66.26**
r.36.10(5) **66.26**
r.36.10(6) **66.23**

(1) Subject to paragraph (2) and paragraph (4)(a), where a Part 36 offer is accepted within the relevant period the claimant will be entitled to the costs of the proceedings up to the date on which notice of acceptance was served on the offeror.
(2) Where—
(a) a defendant's Part 36 offer relates to part only of the claim; and
(b) at the time of serving notice of acceptance within the relevant period the claimant abandons the balance of the claim,
the claimant will be entitled to the costs of the proceedings up to the date of serving notice of acceptance unless the court orders otherwise.
(3) Costs under paragraphs (1) and (2) of this rule will be assessed on the standard basis if the amount of costs is not agreed.
(Rule 44.4(2) explains the standard basis for assessment of costs)
(Rule 44.12 contains provisions about when a costs order is deemed to have been made and applying for an order under section 194(3) of the Legal Services Act 2007)
(4) Where—
(a) a Part 36 offer that was made less than 21 days before the start of trial is accepted; or
(b) a Part 36 offer is accepted after expiry of the relevant period,
if the parties do not agree the liability for costs, the court will make an order as to costs.
(5) Where paragraph (4)(b) applies, unless the court orders otherwise—
(a) the claimant will be entitled to the costs of the proceedings up to the date on which the relevant period expired; and
(b) the offeree will be liable for the offeror's costs for the period from the date of expiry of the relevant period to the date of acceptance.
(6) The claimant's costs include any costs incurred in dealing with the defendant's counterclaim if the Part 36 offer states that it takes into account the counterclaim.

36.11 The Effect of Acceptance of a Part 36 Offer

r.36.11 **66.3, 66.6, 66.16, 66.24, 66.35, 66.55**
r.36.11(1) **PC 29, 66.33**
r.36.11(2) **66.33**
r.36.11(3) **66.7, 66.33**
r.36.11(5) **66.35**
r.36.11(6)(a)–(b) **66.34**
r.36.11(7) **66.34**
r.36.11(8) **66.35**

(1) If a Part 36 offer is accepted, the claim will be stayed.(GL)
(2) In the case of acceptance of a Part 36 offer which relates to the whole claim the stay(GL) will be upon the terms of the offer.
(3) If a Part 36 offer which relates to part only of the claim is accepted—
(a) the claim will be stayed(GL) as to that part upon the terms of the offer; and
(b) subject to rule 36.10(2), unless the parties have agreed costs, the liability for costs shall be decided by the court.
(4) If the approval of the court is required before a settlement can be binding, any stay(GL) which would otherwise arise on the acceptance of a Part 36 offer will take effect only when that approval has been given.
(5) Any stay(GL) arising under this rule will not affect the power of the court—
(a) to enforce the terms of a Part 36 offer;
(b) to deal with any question of costs (including interest on costs) relating to the proceedings.
(6) Unless the parties agree otherwise in writing, where a Part 36 offer by a defendant that is or that includes an offer to pay a single sum of money is accepted, that sum must be paid to the offeree within 14 days of the date of—
(a) acceptance; or
(b) the order when the court makes an order under rule 41.2 (order for an award of provisional damages) or rule 41.8 (order for an award of periodical payments), unless the court orders otherwise.
(7) If the accepted sum is not paid within 14 days or such other period as has been agreed the offeree may enter judgment for the unpaid sum.
(8) Where—
(a) a Part 36 offer (or part of a Part 36 offer) which is not an offer to which paragraph (6) applies is accepted; and
(b) a party alleges that the other party has not honoured the terms of the offer,
that party may apply to enforce the terms of the offer without the need for a new claim.

36.12 Acceptance of a Part 36 Offer Made by One or More, but Not All, Defendants

r.36.12(2)–(3) **66.32**
r.36.12(4) **66.30, 66.32**

(1) This rule applies where the claimant wishes to accept a Part 36 offer made by one or more, but not all, of a number of defendants.
(2) If the defendants are sued jointly or in the alternative, the claimant may accept the offer if—
 (a) he discontinues his claim against those defendants who have not made the offer; and
 (b) those defendants give written consent to the acceptance of the offer.
(3) If the claimant alleges that the defendants have a several liability(GL) to him, the claimant may—
 (a) accept the offer; and
 (b) continue with his claims against the other defendants if he is entitled to do so.
(4) In all other cases the claimant must apply to the court for an order permitting him to accept the Part 36 offer.

36.13 Restriction on Disclosure of a Part 36 Offer

r.36.13 **47.7, 66.3, 75.4**
r.36.13(1) **PC 29, 48.23, 66.3**
r.36.13(2) **PC 29, 66.3, 66.5**
r.36.13(3)(a) **66.13**

(1) A Part 36 offer will be treated as 'without prejudice(GL) except as to costs'.
(2) The fact that a Part 36 offer has been made must not be communicated to the trial judge or to the judge (if any) allocated in advance to conduct the trial until the case has been decided.
(3) Paragraph (2) does not apply—
 (a) where the defence of tender before claim(GL) has been raised;
 (b) where the proceedings have been stayed(GL) under rule 36.11 following acceptance of a Part 36 offer; or
 (c) where the offeror and the offeree agree in writing that it should not apply.

36.14 Costs Consequences Following Judgment

r.36.14 **PC 29, 66.6, 66.15, 66.16, 66.19, 66.36, 66.37, 66.43, 66.44, 66.55**
r.36.14(1) **66.36**
r.36.14(1)(a) **66.38**
r.36.14(1A) **66.36**
r.36.14(2)–(4) **66.37**
r.36.14(2) **PC 29, 66.19, 66.43, 69.9**
r.36.14(2)(a) **66.39**
r.36.14(2)(b) **66.39**
r.36.14(3) **PC 29, 64.26, 66.1, 66.8, 66.16, 66.19, 66.40, 66.42, 66.49**
r.36.14(3)(a) **66.41**
r.36.14(3)(d) **66.8, 66.40, 66.42**
r.36.14(5) **66.40**
r.36.14(6) **66.16**
r.36.14(6)(a) **66.6, 66.19, 66.37, 66.44**
r.36.14(6)(b) **66.37**
r.36.14(6)(c) **66.15, 66.37**

(1) This rule applies where upon judgment being entered—
 (a) a claimant fails to obtain a judgment more advantageous than a defendant's Part 36 offer; or
 (b) judgment against the defendant is at least as advantageous to the claimant as the proposals contained in a claimant's Part 36 offer.
(1A) For the purposes of paragraph (1), in relation to any money claim or money element of a claim, 'more advantageous' means better in money terms by any amount, however small, and 'at least as advantageous' shall be construed accordingly.*
(2) Subject to paragraph (6), where rule 36.14(1)(a) applies, the court will, unless it considers it unjust to do so, order that the defendant is entitled to—
 (a) his costs from the date on which the relevant period expired; and
 (b) interest on those costs.
(3) Subject to paragraph (6), where rule 36.14(1)(b) applies, the court will, unless it considers it unjust to do so, order that the claimant is entitled to—
 (a) interest on the whole or part of any sum of money (excluding interest) awarded at a rate not exceeding 10% above base rate(GL) for some or all of the period starting with the date on which the relevant period expired;
 (b) costs on the indemnity basis from the date on which the relevant period expired;
 (c) interest on those costs at a rate not exceeding 10% above base rate;(GL) and
 (d) an additional amount, which shall not exceed £75,000, calculated by applying the prescribed percentage set out below to an amount which is—
  (i) where the claim is or includes a money claim, the sum awarded to the claimant by the court; or

[* Rule 36.14(1A) applies to offers to settle made in accordance with r. 36.2 on or after 1 October 2011 (SI 2011/1979, r. 1(4)).]

(ii) where the claim is only a non-monetary claim, the sum awarded to the claimant by the court in respect of costs—

Amount awarded by the court	Prescribed percentage
up to £500,000	10% of the amount awarded;
above £500,000 up to £1,000,000	10% of the first £500,000 and 5% of any amount above that figure

(4) In considering whether it would be unjust to make the orders referred to in paragraphs (2) and (3) above, the court will take into account all the circumstances of the case including—
(a) the terms of any Part 36 offer;
(b) the stage in the proceedings when any Part 36 offer was made, including in particular how long before the trial started the offer was made;
(c) the information available to the parties at the time when the Part 36 offer was made; and
(d) the conduct of the parties with regard to the giving or refusing to give information for the purposes of enabling the offer to be made or evaluated.

(5) Where the court awards interest under this rule and also awards interest on the same sum and for the same period under any other power, the total rate of interest may not exceed 10% above base rate.(GL)

(6) Paragraphs (2) and (3) of this rule do not apply to a Part 36 offer—
(a) that has been withdrawn;
(b) that has been changed so that its terms are less advantageous to the offeree, and the offeree has beaten the less advantageous offer;
(c) made less than 21 days before trial, unless the court has abridged the relevant period.

(Rule 44.3 requires the court to consider an offer to settle that does not have the costs consequences set out in this Section in deciding what order to make about costs)

36.15 Deduction of Benefits and Lump Sum Payments

r.36.15 **PC 29, 66.16**
r.36.15(3) **66.10**
r.36.15(5) **66.10**
r.36.15(6) **66.10**
r.36.15(6)(c) **66.38**
r.36.15(7) **PC 29, 66.10**
r.36.15(8) **8.59, 66.52**
r.36.15(9) **66.30**

(1) In this rule and rule 36.9—
(a) 'the 1997 Act' means the Social Security (Recovery of Benefits) Act 1997;
(b) 'the 2008 Regulations' means the Social Security (Recovery of Benefits) (Lump Sum Payments) Regulations 2008;
(c) 'recoverable amount' means—
(i) 'recoverable benefits' as defined in section 1(4)(c) of the 1997 Act; and
(ii) 'recoverable lump sum payments' as defined in regulation 4 of the 2008 Regulations;
(d) 'deductible amount' means—
(i) any benefits by the amount of which damages are to be reduced in accordance with section 8 of, and Schedule 2 to the 1997 Act ('deductible benefits'); and
(ii) any lump sum payment by the amount of which damages are to be reduced in accordance with regulation 12 of the 2008 Regulations ('deductible lump sum payments'); and
(e) 'certificate'—
(i) in relation to recoverable benefits is construed in accordance with the provisions of the 1997 Act; and
(ii) in relation to recoverable lump sum payments has the meaning given in section 29 of the 1997 Act as applied by regulation 2 of, and modified by Schedule 1 to the 2008 Regulations.

(2) This rule applies where a payment to a claimant following acceptance of a Part 36 offer would be a compensation payment as defined in section 1(4)(b) or 1A(5)(b) of the 1997 Act.

(3) A defendant who makes a Part 36 offer should state either—
(a) that the offer is made without regard to any liability for recoverable amounts; or
(b) that it is intended to include any deductible amounts.

(4) Where paragraph (3)(b) applies, paragraphs (5) to (9) of this rule will apply to the Part 36 offer.

(5) Before making the Part 36 offer, the offeror must apply for a certificate.

(6) Subject to paragraph (7), the Part 36 offer must state—
 (a) the amount of gross compensation;
 (b) the name and amount of any deductible amount by which the gross amount is reduced; and
 (c) the net amount of compensation.
(7) If at the time the offeror makes the Part 36 offer, the offeror has applied for, but has not received a certificate, the offeror must clarify the offer by stating the matters referred to in paragraphs (6)(b) and (6)(c) not more than 7 days after receipt of the certificate.
(8) For the purposes of rule 36.14(1)(a), a claimant fails to recover more than any sum offered (including a lump sum offered under rule 36.5) if the claimant fails upon judgment being entered to recover a sum, once deductible amounts identified in the judgment have been deducted, greater than the net amount stated under paragraph (6)(c).

(Section 15(2) of the 1997 Act provides that the court must specify the compensation payment attributable to each head of damage. Schedule 1 to the 2008 Regulations modifies section 15 of the 1997 Act in relation to lump sum payments and provides that the court must specify the compensation payment attributable to each or any dependant who has received a lump sum payment.)

(9) Where—
 (a) further deductible amounts have accrued since the Part 36 offer was made; and
 (b) the court gives permission to accept the Part 36 offer,
 the court may direct that the amount of the offer payable to the offeree shall be reduced by a sum equivalent to the deductible amounts paid to the claimant since the date of the offer.

(Rule 36.9(3)(b) states that permission is required to accept an offer where the relevant period has expired and further deductible amounts have been paid to the claimant)

II RTA PROTOCOL OFFERS TO SETTLE

36.16 Scope of This Section

rr.36.16–36.22 **66.52** r.36.16 **8.57**

(1) Where this Section applies Section I does not apply.
(2) This Section applies to an offer to settle where the parties have followed the RTA Protocol and started proceedings under Part 8 in accordance with Practice Direction 8B ('the Stage 3 Procedure').
(3) A reference to the 'Court Proceeding Pack Form'* is a reference to the form used in the RTA Protocol.
(4) Nothing in this Section prevents a party making an offer to settle in whatever way that party chooses, but if the offer is not made in accordance with this Section, it will not have any costs consequences.

36.17 Form and Content of an RTA Protocol Offer

r.36.17 **8.57, 66.52** r.36.17(2)(a) **8.57, 66.52**

(1) An offer to settle which is made in accordance with this rule is called an RTA Protocol offer.
(2) An RTA Protocol offer must—
 (a) be set out in the Court Proceedings Pack (Part B) Form; and
 (b) contain the final total amount of the offer from both parties.

36.18 Time When an RTA Protocol Offer Is Made

r.36.18 **8.57, 66.52**

The RTA Protocol offer is deemed to be made on the first business day after the Court Proceedings Pack (Part A and Part B) Form is sent to the defendant.

36.19 General Provisions

r.36.19 **8.57, 66.52** r.36.19(a) **8.57, 66.52**

An RTA Protocol offer—
 (a) is treated as exclusive of all interest; and

[* 'Court Proceeding Pack Form' should be 'Court Proceedings Pack Form'.]

(b) has the consequences set out in this Section only in relation to the fixed costs of the Stage 3 Procedure as provided for in rule 45.29, and not in relation to the costs of any appeal from the final decision of those proceedings.

36.20 Restrictions on Disclosure of an RTA Protocol Offer

r.36.20 **8.57, 66.52** r.36.20(1) **8.49**

(1) The amount of the RTA Protocol offer must not be communicated to the court until the claim is determined.
(2) Any other offer to settle must not be communicated to the court at all.
(3) Once the claim is determined, the court will examine the RTA Protocol offer.

36.21 Costs Consequences Following Judgment

r.36.21 **8.57, 66.52** r.36.21(2)–(3) **8.58, 66.52**
r.36.21(1) **8.58, 66.52** r.36.21(1)(a)–(c) **66.52**

(1) This rule applies where, on the determination by the court, the claimant obtains judgment against the defendant for an amount of damages that is—
(a) less than or equal to the amount of the defendant's RTA Protocol offer;
(b) more than the defendant's RTA Protocol offer but less than the claimant's RTA Protocol offer; or
(c) equal to or more than the claimant's RTA Protocol offer.
(2) Where paragraph (1)(a) applies, the court will order the claimant to pay—
(a) the fixed costs in rule 45.38; and
(b) interest on those fixed costs from the first business day after the deemed date of the RTA Protocol offer under rule 36.18.
(3) Where paragraph (1)(b) applies, the court will order the defendant to pay the fixed costs in rule 45.32.
(4) Where paragraph (1)(c) applies, the court will order the defendant to pay—
(a) interest on the whole of the damages awarded at a rate not exceeding 10% above base rate for some or all of the period starting with the date specified in rule 36.18;
(b) the fixed costs in rule 45.32; and
(c) interest on those costs at a rate not exceeding 10% above base rate.

36.22 Deduction of Benefits

r.36.22 **8.57, 8.59, 66.52**

For the purposes of rule 36.21(1)(a) the amount of the judgment is less than the RTA Protocol offer where the judgment is less than that offer once deductible amounts identified in the judgment are deducted.
('Deductible amount' is defined in rule 36.15(1)(d).)

PD 36A Practice Direction 36A — Offers to Settle

This practice direction supplements CPR, Part 36.

Formalities of Part 36 Offers and Other Notices under This Part

para.1.1 **66.7** para.1.2 **PC29, 66.14**

1.1 A Part 36 offer may be made using form N242A.

1.2 Where a Part 36 offer, notice of acceptance or notice of withdrawal or change of terms is to be served on a party who is legally represented, the document to be served must be served on the legal representative.

Application for Permission to Withdraw a Part 36 Offer

para.2.2 **66.4** para.2.2(1) **66.17**

2.1 Rule 36.3(4) provides that before expiry of the relevant period a Part 36 offer may only be withdrawn or its terms changed to be less advantageous to the offeree with the permission of the court.

2.2 The permission of the court must be sought:

(1) by making an application under Part 23, which must be dealt with by a judge other than the judge (if any) allocated in advance to conduct the trial, unless the parties agree that such judge may hear the application;

(2) at a trial or other hearing, provided that it is not to the trial judge or to the judge (if any) allocated in advance to conduct the trial, unless the parties agree that such judge may hear the application.

Acceptance of a Part 36 Offer

para.3.1 **PC 29, 66.22** para.3.3 **66.30**
para.3.2 **66.4**

3.1 Where a Part 36 offer is accepted in accordance with r. 36.9(1) the notice of acceptance must be served on the offeror and filed with the court where the case is proceeding.

3.2 Where the court's permission is required to accept a Part 36 offer, the permission of the court must be sought:

(1) by making an application under Part 23, which must be dealt with by a judge other than the judge (if any) allocated in advance to conduct the trial, unless the parties agree that such judge may hear the application;

(2) at a trial or other hearing, provided that it is not to the trial judge or to the judge (if any) allocated in advance to conduct the trial, unless the parties agree that such judge may hear the application.

3.3 Where r. 36.9(3)(b) applies, the application for permission to accept the offer must:

(1) state:

(a) the net amount offered in the Part 36 offer;

(b) the deductible amounts that had accrued at the date the offer was made;

(c) the deductible amounts that have subsequently accrued; and

(2) be accompanied by a copy of the current certificate.

PD 36B Practice Direction 36B

This practice direction supplements CPR, Part 36.

PD 36B **66.53**

From 6 April 2007, new rules came into force concerning offers to settle, and Part 36, as it was in force immediately before 6 April 2007, was substituted by a new Part 36.

Rule 7 of the Civil Procedure (Amendment No. 3) Rules 2006 (SI 2006/3435) that brought those new rules into force and replaced the previous rules contained some provisions that dealt with how the rules are to apply to offers and payments into court made before 6 April 2007.

This Practice Direction explains how those provisions will operate.

Offers and Payments Made before 6 April 2007

para.1.2 **66.53**

1.1 SI 2006/3435, r. 7(2), provides that where a Part 36 offer or Part 36 payment was made before 6 April 2007, if it would have had the consequences set out in the rules of court contained in Part 36 as it was in force immediately before 6 April 2007, it will have the consequences set out in rr. 36.10, 36.11 and 36.14 after that date.

1.2 This provision makes clear that a Part 36 offer or Part 36 payment that was valid before 6 April 2007, will continue to be a valid Part 36 offer under the rules in force from 6 April 2007, and will have the consequences set out in those rules, specifically in relation to costs and the effect of acceptance.

Permission of the Court

para.2.1–2.2 **66.54**

2.1 SI 2006/3435, r. 7(3), provides that where a Part 36 offer or Part 36 payment was made before 6 April 2007, the permission of the court is required to accept that offer or payment, if permission would have been required under the rules of court contained in Part 36 as it was in force immediately before 6 April 2007.

2.2 This provision preserves the requirement to obtain the permission of the court to accept an offer as it existed under the rules in force immediately before 6 April 2007. Therefore, if permission would have been required before 6 April 2007, it will be required after that date. But, if permission would not have been required because the parties have been able to agree liability for costs, or if a further offer has been made triggering a new period for acceptance, permission will not be required after 6 April 2007.

Payments into Court Made before 6 April 2007

para.3.3 **66.56**

3.1 SI 2006/3435, r. 7(4), provides that r. 37.3 will apply to a Part 36 payment made before 6 April 2007 as if that payment into court had been made under a court order.

3.2 Rule 37.3 applies to all payments under Part 37, including payments into court under order, and permission is required to take the money out of court.

3.3 By applying r. 37.3 to payments into court made before 6 April 2007, this provision preserves in particular the requirement that permission be obtained to withdraw such payment.

3.4 But, r. 37.3 also provides that money may be taken out of court without the court's permission where a Part 36 offer (including an offer underlying a Part 36 payment) is accepted without needing the permission of the court and the defendant agrees that the sum may be paid out in satisfaction of the offer. PD 37, para. 3.4, makes provision about how to take money out of court.

3.5 This exception to the permission requirement preserves the right under r. 37.2, as it was in force immediately before 6 April 2007, to treat a payment into court made under order or by way of a *defence of tender before claim* as a Part 36 payment.

3.6 This provision has the effect that a Part 36 payment made before 6 April 2007 may be taken out of court simply by filing a request for payment if the offer underlying the Part 36 payment is accepted without needing permission. In those circumstances, it may be assumed that the defendant agrees to the money being used in satisfaction of the sum offered, and the requirement in PD 37, para. 3.4, to file a form 202 will not apply.

Offers Remaining Open for Acceptance

para.4.4 **66.57**

4.1 SI 2006/3435, r. 7(5), provides that the rules of court contained in Part 36 as it was in force immediately before 6 April 2007 shall continue to apply to a Part 36 offer or Part 36 payment made less than 21 days before 6 April 2007.

4.2 This provision preserves those rules in their entirety in relation to offers and payments made less than 21 days before 6 April 2007 for the period that they are expressed to remain open for acceptance.

4.3 SI 2006/3435, r. 7(6), provides that r. 7(5) ceases to apply at the expiry of 21 days from the date that the offer or payment was made, unless the trial has started within that period.

4.4 This provision has the effect that once the 21-day period has expired, the new regime (including the modifications at paragraphs (2), (3) and (4) of r. 7) will apply to the offer or payment.

4.5 If the trial has started within the 21-day period, the rules that were in force before 6 April 2007 will continue to apply to the offer or payment.

Offers Made before Commencement of Proceedings

para.5.4 **66.58**

5.1 SI 2006/3435, r. 7(7), deals with the position where, before 6 April 2007, a person made an offer to settle before commencement of proceedings which complied with the provisions of r. 36.10 as it was in force immediately before 6 April 2007.

5.2 The court will take that offer into account when making any order as to costs. This preserves the discretion of the court to take into account an offer made before commencement of proceedings as it existed before 6 April 2007.

5.3 The permission of the court will be required to accept such an offer after proceedings have been commenced. This preserves the position under r. 36.10(4) as it was in force immediately before 6 April 2007.

5.4 If proceedings are commenced after 6 April 2007, the requirement to pay money into court in respect of a defendant's money offer under r. 36.10(3)(a) (as it was in force before 6 April 2007) will not apply to a defendant's money offer made before the proceedings were commenced.

CPR Part 37 Miscellaneous Provisions about Payments into Court

37.1 Money Paid into Court under a Court Order

r.37.1 66.13, 66.50

A party who makes a payment into court under a court order must—

(a) serve notice of the payment on every other party; and
(b) in relation to each such notice, file a certificate of service.

37.2 Money Paid into Court Where Defendant Wishes to Rely on a Defence of Tender before Claim

r.37.2 26.18, 66.13 r.37.2(2) 66.13

(1) Where a defendant wishes to rely on a defence of tender before claim[(GL)] he must make a payment into court of the amount he says was tendered.
(2) If the defendant does not make a payment in accordance with paragraph (1), the defence of tender before claim will not be available to him until he does so.

37.3 Payment Out of Money Paid into Court

r.37.3 66.50, 66.56, 89.12

(1) Money paid into court under a court order or in support of a defence of tender before claim[(GL)] may not be paid out without the court's permission except where—
    (a) a Part 36 offer is accepted without needing the permission of the court; and
    (b) the defendant agrees that a sum paid into court by him should be used to satisfy the offer (in whole or in part).

(Rule 36.9 sets out when the court's permission is required to accept a Part 36 offer)

37.4 Payment into Court under Enactments

r.37.4 66.51

A practice direction may set out special provisions with regard to payments into court under various enactments.

PD 37 Practice Direction 37 — Miscellaneous Provisions about Payments into Court

This practice direction supplements CPR, Part 37.

Payment into Court under an Order, etc.

para.1.1(1)(a) **66.13, 66.50** para.1.2 **66.13, 66.50**

1.1 Except where para. 1.2 applies, a party paying money into court under an order or in support of a defence of tender before claim must:
(1) send to the Court Funds Office:
(a) the payment, usually a cheque made payable to the Accountant General of the Senior Courts;
(b) a sealed copy of the order or a copy of the defence; and
(c) a completed Court Funds Office form 100;
(2) serve a copy of the form 100 on each other party; and
(3) file at the court:
(a) a copy of the form 100; and
(b) a certificate of service confirming service of a copy of that form on each party served.

1.2 Instead of complying with para. 1.1(1), a litigant in person without a current account may, in a claim proceeding in a county court or district registry, make a payment into court by:
(1) lodging the payment in cash with the court; and
(2) giving the court a completed Court Funds Office form 100.

Applications Relating to Funds in Court

para.2 **26.18**

2.1 This paragraph applies to an application relating to money or securities which have been paid into court other than an application for the payment out of the money or securities (for example, an application for money to be invested, or for payment of interest to any person).

2.2 An application:
(1) must be made in accordance with Part 23; and
(2) may be made without notice, but the court may direct notice to be served on any person.

(Where money paid into court is accepted by or on behalf of a child or protected party, r. 21.11(1)(b) provides that the money shall be dealt with in accordance with directions given by the court under that rule and not otherwise. PD 21, paras 8 to 13, make further provision about how the money may be dealt with.)

Payment Out of Court

para.3.2–3.7 **66.50** para.3.8(1)–(2) **66.50**

3.1 Rule 37.3 provides that the court's permission is required to take money out of court except where the defendant agrees that the money which has been paid into court should be used to satisfy a Part 36 offer.

3.2 Permission may be obtained by making an application in accordance with Part 23. The application notice must state the grounds on which the order for payment out is sought. Evidence of any facts on which the applicant relies may also be necessary.

3.3 Where the court gives permission under r. 37.3, it will include a direction for the payment out of any money in court, including any interest accrued.

3.4 Where permission is not required to take money out of court, the requesting party should file a request for payment in Court Funds Office form 201 with the Court Funds Office, accompanied by a statement that the defendant agrees that the money should be used to satisfy the Part 36 offer in Court Funds Office form 202.

(PD 36B, para. 3.6, provides that a defendant who made a Part 36 payment before 6 April 2007, and whose Part 36 offer underlying the payment is accepted without requiring the permission of the court, is not required to file form 202.)

3.5 The request for payment should contain the following details:
(1) where the party receiving the payment is legally represented:
(a) the name, business address and reference of the legal representative; and
(b) the name of the bank and the sort code number, the title of the account and the account number where the payment is to be transmitted;
(2) where the party is acting in person:
(a) his name and address; and
(b) his bank account details as in sub-para. (1)(b) above; and
(3) whether the party receiving the payment is, or has been, in receipt of services funded by the Legal Services Commission as part of the Community Legal Service.

3.6 Where para. 3.4 applies, interest accruing up to the date of acceptance will be paid to the defendant.

(Rule 20.2 provides that in these Rules references to a claimant or defendant include a party bringing or defending an additional claim.)

3.7 Subject to para. 3.8, if a party does not wish the payment to be transmitted into his bank account or if he does not have a bank account, he may send a written request to the Accountant-General for the payment to be made to him by cheque.

3.8 Where a party seeking payment out of court has provided the necessary information, the payment:
(1) where a party is legally represented, must be made to the legal representative;
(2) if the party is not legally represented but has given notice under para. 3.5(3), must be made to the Legal Services Commission

Payment into Court by Life Assurance Company

para.4 66.51

4.1 A company wishing to make a payment into court under the Life Assurance Companies (Payment into Court) Act 1896 ('the 1896 Act') must file a witness statement or an affidavit setting out:
(1) a short description of the policy under which money is payable;
(2) a statement of the persons entitled under the policy, including their names and addresses so far as known to the company;
(3) a short statement of:
(a) the notices received by the company making any claim to the money assured, or withdrawing any such claim;
(b) the dates of receipt of such notices; and
(c) the names and addresses of the persons by whom they were given;
(4) a statement that, in the opinion of the board of directors of the company, no sufficient discharge can be obtained for the money which is payable, other than by paying it into court under the 1896 Act;
(5) a statement that the company agrees to comply with any order or direction the court may make:
(a) to pay any further sum into court; or
(b) to pay any costs;
(6) an undertaking by the company to immediately send to the Accountant General at the Court Funds Office any notice of claim received by the company after the witness statement or affidavit has been filed, together with a letter referring to the Court Funds Office reference number; and
(7) the company's address for service.

4.2 The witness statement or affidavit must be filed at:
(1) Chancery Chambers at the Royal Courts of Justice; or
(2) a Chancery district registry of the High Court.

4.3 The company must not deduct from the money payable by it under the policy any costs of the payment into court, except for any court fee.

4.4 If the company is a party to any proceedings issued in relation to the policy or the money assured by it, it may not make a payment into court under the 1896 Act without the permission of the court in those proceedings.

4.5 If a company pays money into court under the 1896 Act, unless the court orders otherwise it must immediately serve notice of the payment on every person who is entitled under the policy or has made a claim to the money assured.

Application for Payment Out of Money Paid into Court by Life Assurance Company

para.5.1–5.2 **66.51**

5.1 Any application for the payment out of money which has been paid into court under the 1896 Act must be made in accordance with para. 3 of this practice direction.

5.2 The application must be served on:
  (1) every person stated in the written evidence of the company which made the payment to be entitled to or to have an interest in the money;
  (2) any other person who has given notice of a claim to the money; and
  (3) the company which made the payment, if an application is being made for costs against it, but not otherwise.

Payment into Court under Trustee Act 1925

para.6.1–6.3 **66.51**

6.1 A trustee wishing to make a payment into court under the Trustee Act 1925, s. 63, must file a witness statement or an affidavit setting out:
  (1) a short description of:
    (a) the trust; and
    (b) the instrument creating the trust, or the circumstances in which the trust arose;
  (2) the names of the persons interested in or entitled to the money or securities to be paid into court, with their address so far as known to him;
  (3) a statement that he agrees to answer any inquiries which the court may make or direct relating to the application of the money or securities; and
  (4) his address for service.

6.2 The witness statement or affidavit must be filed at:
  (1) Chancery Chambers at the Royal Courts of Justice;
  (2) a Chancery district registry of the High Court; or
  (3) a county court.

6.3 If a trustee pays money or securities into court, unless the court orders otherwise he must immediately serve notice of the payment into court on every person interested in or entitled to the money or securities.

Application for Payment out of Funds Paid into Court by Trustee

para.7.1–7.2 **66.51**

7.1 An application for the payment out of any money or securities paid into court under the Trustee Act 1925, s. 63, must be made in accordance with para. 3 of this practice direction.

7.2 The application may be made without notice, but the court may direct notice to be served on any person.

Payment into Court under Vehicular Access across Common and Other Land (England) Regulations 2002

para.8.1–8.5 **66.51**

8.1 In this section of this practice direction:
  (1) expressions used have the meanings given by the Vehicular Access across Common and Other Land (England) Regulations 2002 (SI 2002/1711); and
  (2) a regulation referred to by number alone means the regulation so numbered in those Regulations.

8.2 Where the applicant wishes to pay money into a county court under reg. 14 he must file a witness statement or an affidavit when he lodges the money.

8.3 The witness statement or affidavit must:
  (1) state briefly why the applicant is making the payment into court; and
  (2) be accompanied by copies of:
    (a) the notice served under reg. 6;

(b) any counter-notice served under reg. 8;
(c) any amended notice or counter-notice served under reg. 9;
(d) any determination of the Lands Tribunal of a matter referred to it under reg. 10; and
(e) any determination of the value of the premises by a chartered surveyor following the service of a valuation notice under reg. 12.

8.4 If an applicant pays money into court under reg. 14, he must immediately serve notice of the payment and a copy of the witness statement or affidavit on the land owner.

8.5 An application for payment out of the money must be made in accordance with para. 3 of this practice direction.

CPR Part 38 Discontinuance

Part 38 55.3, 77.52 [For commentary on a specific rule, please refer to the cross-references after the title of the rule.]

38.1 Scope of This Part

r.38.1(1) 55.3 r.38.1(2) 55.2

(1) The rules in this Part set out the procedure by which a claimant may discontinue all or part of a claim.

(2) A claimant who—
  (a) claims more than one remedy; and
  (b) subsequently abandons his claim to one or more of the remedies but continues with his claim for the other remedies,

is not treated as discontinuing all or part of a claim for the purposes of this Part.

(The procedure for amending a statement of case, set out in Part 17, applies where a claimant abandons a claim for a particular remedy but wishes to continue with his claim for other remedies)

38.2 Right to Discontinue Claim

r.38.2(1) 55.4 r.38.2(3) 55.3
r.38.2(2)(a)–(c) 55.4

(1) A claimant may discontinue all or part of a claim at any time.

(2) However—
  (a) a claimant must obtain the permission of the court if he wishes to discontinue all or part of a claim in relation to which—
    (i) the court has granted an interim injunction(GL); or
    (ii) any party has given an undertaking to the court;
  (b) where the claimant has received an interim payment in relation to a claim (whether voluntarily or pursuant to an order under Part 25), he may discontinue that claim only if—
    (i) the defendant who made the interim payment consents in writing; or
    (ii) the court gives permission;
  (c) where there is more than one claimant, a claimant may not discontinue unless—
    (i) every other claimant consents in writing; or
    (ii) the court gives permission.

(3) Where there is more than one defendant, the claimant may discontinue all or part of a claim against all or any of the defendants.

38.3 Procedure for Discontinuing

r.38.3(2)–(4) 55.5

(1) To discontinue a claim or part of a claim, a claimant must—
  (a) file a notice of discontinuance; and
  (b) serve a copy of it on every other party to the proceedings.

(2) The claimant must state in the notice of discontinuance which he files that he has served notice of discontinuance on every other party to the proceedings.

(3) Where the claimant needs the consent of some other party, a copy of the necessary consent must be attached to the notice of discontinuance.

CPR 26–50 & PDs

(4) Where there is more than one defendant, the notice of discontinuance must specify against which defendants the claim is discontinued.

38.4 Right to Apply to Have Notice of Discontinuance Set Aside

r.38.4 55.6

(1) Where the claimant discontinues under rule 38.2(1) the defendant may apply to have the notice of discontinuance set aside(GL).
(2) The defendant may not make an application under this rule more than 28 days after the date when the notice of discontinuance was served on him.

38.5 When Discontinuance Takes Effect Where Permission of the Court Is Not Needed

r.38.5 55.7

(1) Discontinuance against any defendant takes effect on the date when notice of discontinuance is served on him under rule 38.3(1).
(2) Subject to rule 38.4, the proceedings are brought to an end as against him on that date.
(3) However, this does not affect proceedings to deal with any question of costs.

38.6 Liability for Costs

r.38.6 55.8 r.38.6(2)–(3) 55.8
r.38.6(1) 53.8, 55.8, 69.16

(1) Unless the court orders otherwise, a claimant who discontinues is liable for the costs which a defendant against whom the claimant discontinues incurred on or before the date on which notice of discontinuance was served on the defendant.
(2) If proceedings are only partly discontinued—
 (a) the claimant is liable under paragraph (1) for costs relating only to the part of the proceedings which he is discontinuing; and
 (b) unless the court orders otherwise, the costs which the claimant is liable to pay must not be assessed until the conclusion of the rest of the proceedings.
(3) This rule does not apply to claims allocated to the small claims track.

(Rule 44.12 provides for the basis of assessment where the right to costs arises on discontinuance and contains provisions about when a costs order is deemed to have been made and applying for an order under section 194(3) of the Legal Services Act 2007)

38.7 Discontinuance and Subsequent Proceedings

r.38.7 55.9

A claimant who discontinues a claim needs the permission of the court to make another claim against the same defendant if—
(a) he discontinued the claim after the defendant filed a defence; and
(b) the other claim arises out of facts which are the same or substantially the same as those relating to the discontinued claim.

38.8 Stay of Remainder of Partly Discontinued Proceedings Where Costs Not Paid

r.38.8 55.8

(1) This rule applies where—
 (a) proceedings are partly discontinued;
 (b) a claimant is liable to—
  (i) pay costs under rule 38.6; or
  (ii) make a payment pursuant to an order under section 194(3) of the Legal Services Act 2007; and
 (c) the claimant fails to pay those costs or make the payment within 14 days of—
  (i) the date on which the parties agreed the sum payable by the claimant; or
  (ii) the date on which the court ordered the costs to be paid or the payment to be made.
(2) Where this rule applies, the court may stay(GL) the remainder of the proceedings until the claimant pays the whole of the costs which the claimant is liable to pay under rule 38.6 or makes the payment pursuant to an order under section 194(3) of the Legal Services Act 2007.

(Rules 44.3C and 44.12 contain provisions about applying for an order under section 194(3) of the Legal Services Act 2007)

CPR Part 39 Miscellaneous Provisions Relating to Hearings

Part 39 **14.79, 45.6** [For commentary on a specific rule, please refer to the cross-references after the title of the rule.]

39.1 Interpretation

In this Part, reference to a hearing includes a reference to the trial.

39.2 General Rule — Hearing to Be in Public

r.39.2 **32.8, 32.27, 37.11, 45.6, 84.4**
r.39.2(1) **37.43, 61.20, 72.16, 91.47**
r.39.2(3) **37.43, 45.22, 50.66, 61.20, 61.21**
r.39.2(3)(a) **32.8, 77.50**
r.39.2(3)(c) **77.50**
r.39.2(3)(d) **PC 6, 61.21**
r.39.2(3)(e) **32.8**
r.39.2(4) **61.20, 63.35**

(1) The general rule is that a hearing is to be in public.
(2) The requirement for a hearing to be in public does not require the court to make special arrangements for accommodating members of the public.
(3) A hearing, or any part of it, may be in private if—
(a) publicity would defeat the object of the hearing;
(b) it involves matters relating to national security;
(c) it involves confidential information (including information relating to personal financial matters) and publicity would damage that confidentiality;
(d) a private hearing is necessary to protect the interests of any child or protected party;
(e) it is a hearing of an application made without notice and it would be unjust to any respondent for there to be a public hearing;
(f) it involves uncontentious matters arising in the administration of trusts or in the administration of a deceased person's estate; or
(g) the court considers this to be necessary, in the interests of justice.
(4) The court may order that the identity of any party or witness must not be disclosed if it considers non-disclosure necessary in order to protect the interests of that party or witness.

39.3 Failure to Attend the Trial

r.39.3 **8.3, 62.2, 62.4**
r.39.3(1)–(2) **62.2**
r.39.3(3) **62.2**
r.39.3(4) **62.2**
r.39.3(5) **20.22, 45.26, 62.2, 62.3, 87.54**
r.39.3(5)(b) **62.2**

(1) The court may proceed with a trial in the absence of a party but—
(a) if no party attends the trial, it may strike out(GL) the whole of the proceedings;
(b) if the claimant does not attend, it may strike out his claim and any defence to counterclaim; and
(c) if a defendant does not attend, it may strike out his defence or counterclaim (or both).
(2) Where the court strikes out proceedings, or any part of them, under this rule, it may subsequently restore the proceedings, or that part.
(3) Where a party does not attend and the court gives judgment or makes an order against him, the party who failed to attend may apply for the judgment or order to be set aside.(GL)
(4) An application under paragraph (2) or paragraph (3) must be supported by evidence.
(5) Where an application is made under paragraph (2) or (3) by a party who failed to attend the trial, the court may grant the application only if the applicant—
(a) acted promptly when he found out that the court had exercised its power to strike out(GL) or to enter judgment or make an order against him;

(b) had a good reason for not attending the trial; and
(c) has a reasonable prospect of success at the trial.

39.4 Timetable for Trial

r.39.4 46.19, 61.16

When the court sets a timetable for a trial in accordance with rule 28.6 (fixing or confirming the trial date and giving directions — fast track) or rule 29.8 (setting a trial timetable and fixing or confirming the trial date or week — multi-track) it will do so in consultation with the parties.

39.5 Trial Bundles

r.39.5(1) 59.3 r.39.5(2) 59.1

(1) Unless the court orders otherwise, the claimant must file a trial bundle containing documents required by—
(a) a relevant practice direction; and
(b) any court order.
(2) The claimant must file the trial bundle not more than 7 days and not less than 3 days before the start of the trial.

39.6 Representation at Trial of Companies or Other Corporations

r.39.6 61.35

A company or other corporation may be represented at trial by an employee if—
(a) the employee has been authorised by the company or corporation to appear at trial on its behalf; and
(b) the court gives permission.

39.7 Impounded Documents

(1) Documents impounded by order of the court must not be released from the custody of the court except in compliance—
(a) with a court order; or
(b) with a written request made by a Law Officer or the Director of Public Prosecutions.
(2) A document released from the custody of the court under paragraph (1)(b) must be released into the custody of the person who requested it.
(3) Documents impounded by order of the court, while in the custody of the court, may not be inspected except by a person authorised to do so by a court order.

PD 39A Practice Direction 39A—Miscellaneous Provisions Relating to Hearings

This practice direction supplements CPR, Part 39.

[For commentary on a specific paragraph, please refer to the cross-references after the title of the paragraph.]
PD 39A PC 28

Hearings

para.1 15.56
para.1.1–1.15 84.4
para.1.4A 61.20
para.1.5 61.20, 61.21, 87.23
para.1.5(8) 67.2
para.1.6 PC 6, 61.21
para.1.10 32.27, 84.4
para.1.11 84.4, 91.47
para.1.12 61.21, 84.4, 91.47
para.1.15 61.23, 84.4

1.1 In Part 39, reference to a hearing includes reference to the trial.[1]

1.2 The general rule is that a hearing is to be in public.[2]

1.3 Rule 39.2(3) sets out the type of proceedings which may be dealt with in private.

1.4 The decision as to whether to hold a hearing in public or in private must be made by the judge conducting the hearing having regard to any representations which may have been made to him.

1.4A The judge should also have regard to Article 6(1) of the European Convention on Human Rights. This requires that, in general, court hearings are to be held in public, but the press and public may be excluded in the circumstances specified in that Article. Article 6(1) will usually be relevant, for example, where a party applies for a hearing which would normally be held in public to be held in private as well as where a hearing would normally be held in private. The judge may need to consider whether the case is within any of the exceptions permitted by Article 6(1).

1.5 The hearings set out below shall in the first instance be listed by the court as hearings in private under rule 39.2(3)(c), namely:

(1) a claim by a mortgagee against one or more individuals for an order for possession of land,
(2) a claim by a landlord against one or more tenants or former tenants for the repossession of a dwelling house based on the non-payment of rent,
(3) an application to suspend a warrant of execution or a warrant of possession or to stay execution where the court is being invited to consider the ability of a party to make payments to another party,
(4) a redetermination under rule 14.13 or an application to vary or suspend the payment of a judgment debt by instalments,
(5) an application for a charging order (including an application to enforce a charging order), third party debt order, attachment of earnings order, administration order, or the appointment of a receiver,
(6) an order to attend court for questioning,
(7) the determination of an LSC funded client under regulations 9 and 10 of the Community Legal Service (Costs) Regulations 2000, or of an assisted person's liability for costs under regulation 127 of the Civil Legal Aid (General) Regulations 1989,
(8) an application for security for costs to be provided by a claimant who is a company or a limited liability partnership in the circumstances set out in r. 25.13(2)(c), and
(9) proceedings brought under the Consumer Credit Act 1974, the Inheritance (Provision for Family and Dependants) Act 1975 or the Protection from Harassment Act 1997,
(10) an application by a trustee or personal representative for directions as to bringing or defending legal proceedings.

1.6 Rule 39.2(3)(d) states that a hearing may be in private where it involves the interests of a child or patient. This includes the approval of a compromise or settlement on behalf of a child or patient or an application for the payment of money out of court to such a person.

[1] Rule 39.1.
[2] Rule 39.2(1).

1.7 Attention is drawn to PD 27, para. [4.1*] (relating to the hearing of claims in the small claims track), which provides that the judge may decide to hold a small claim hearing in private if the parties agree or if a ground mentioned in rule 39.2(3) applies. A hearing of a small claim in premises other than the court will not be a hearing in public.

1.7A Attention is drawn to PD 52D, para. 31.2(8), which provides that an appeal to a county court against certain decisions under the Representation of the People Act 1983 is to be heard in private unless the court orders otherwise. Attention is also drawn to PD 52D, para. 31.2(9), which provides that an appeal to the Court of Appeal against such a decision of a county court may be heard in private if the Court of Appeal so orders.

1.8 Nothing in this practice direction prevents a judge ordering that a hearing taking place in public shall continue in private, or vice versa.

1.9 If the court or judge's room in which the proceedings are taking place has a sign on the door indicating that the proceedings are private, members of the public who are not parties to the proceedings will not be admitted unless the court permits.

1.10 Where there is no such sign on the door of the court or judge's room, members of the public will be admitted where practicable. The judge may, if he thinks it appropriate, adjourn the proceedings to a larger room or court.

1.11 When a hearing takes place in public, members of the public may obtain a transcript of any judgment given or a copy of any order made, subject to payment of the appropriate fee.

1.12 When a judgment is given or an order is made in private, if any member of the public who is not a party to the proceedings seeks a transcript of the judgment or a copy of the order, he must seek the leave of the judge who gave the judgment or made the order.

1.13 A judgment or order given or made in private, when drawn up, must have clearly marked in the title:

'Before [*title and name of judge*] sitting in Private'

1.14 References to hearings being in public or private or in a judge's room contained in the Civil Procedure Rules (including the Rules of the Supreme Court and the County Court Rules scheduled to Part 50) and the practice directions which supplement them do not restrict any existing rights of audience or confer any new rights of audience in respect of applications or proceedings which under the rules previously in force would have been heard in court or in chambers respectively.

1.15 Where the court lists a hearing of a claim by a mortgagee for an order for possession of land under para. 1.5(1) above to be in private, any fact which needs to be proved by the evidence of witnesses may be proved by evidence in writing.

(CPR, r. 32.2, sets out the general rule as to how evidence is to be given and facts are to be proved.)

Failure to Attend the Trial

2.1 Rule 39.3 sets out the consequences of a party's failure to attend the trial.

2.2 The court may proceed with a trial in the absence of a party.[3] In the absence of:

(1) the defendant, the claimant may:
  (a) prove his claim at trial and obtain judgment on his claim and for costs, and
  (b) seek the striking out of any counterclaim,

(2) the claimant, the defendant may:
  (a) prove any counterclaim at trial and obtain judgment on his counterclaim and for costs, and
  (b) seek the striking out of the claim, or

(3) both parties, the court may strike out the whole of the proceedings.

2.3 Where the court has struck out proceedings, or any part of them, on the failure of a party to attend, that party may apply in accordance with Part 23 for the proceedings, or that part of them, to be restored and for any judgment given against that party to be set aside.[4]

[* *The text issued by the Ministry of Justice mistakenly refers to para. 5.1.*]

3 Rule 39.3(1).

4 Rule 39.3(2) and (3).

2.4 The application referred to in paragraph 2.3 above must be supported by evidence giving reasons for the failure to attend court and stating when the applicant found out about the order against him.

Bundles of Documents for Hearings or Trial

para.3 59.2
para.3.3 59.3
para.3.8 59.4
para.3.9 59.2
para.3.10 59.3, 59.5

3.1 Unless the court orders otherwise, the claimant must file the trial bundle not more than seven days and not less than three days before the start of the trial.

3.2 Unless the court orders otherwise, the trial bundle should include a copy of:
(1) the claim form and all statements of case,
(2) a case summary and/or chronology where appropriate,
(3) requests for further information and responses to the requests,
(4) all witness statements to be relied on as evidence,
(5) any witness summaries,
(6) any notices of intention to rely on hearsay evidence under rule [33.2*],
(7) any notices of intention to rely on evidence (such as a plan, photograph etc.) under rule 33.6 which is not:
(a) contained in a witness statement, affidavit or expert's report,
(b) being given orally at trial,
(c) hearsay evidence under rule 33.2,
(8) any medical reports and responses to them,
(9) any experts' reports and responses to them,
(10) any order giving directions as to the conduct of the trial, and
(11) any other necessary documents.

3.3 The originals of the documents contained in the trial bundle, together with copies of any other court orders should be available at the trial.

3.4 The preparation and production of the trial bundle, even where it is delegated to another person, is the responsibility of the legal representative[5] who has conduct of the claim on behalf of the claimant.

3.5 The trial bundle should be paginated (continuously) throughout, and indexed with a description of each document and the page number. Where the total number of pages is more than 100, numbered dividers should be placed at intervals between groups of documents.

3.6 The bundle should normally be contained in a ring binder or lever arch file. Where more than one bundle is supplied, they should be clearly distinguishable, for example, by different colours or letters. If there are numerous bundles, a core bundle should be prepared containing the core documents essential to the proceedings, with references to the supplementary documents in the other bundles.

3.7 For convenience, experts' reports may be contained in a separate bundle and cross referenced in the main bundle.

3.8 If a document to be included in the trial bundle is illegible, a typed copy should be included in the bundle next to it, suitably cross-referenced.

3.9 The contents of the trial bundle should be agreed where possible. The parties should also agree where possible:
(1) that the documents contained in the bundle are authentic even if not disclosed under Part 31, and
(2) that documents in the bundle may be treated as evidence of the facts stated in them even if a notice under the Civil Evidence Act 1995 has not been served.

Where it is not possible to agree the contents of the bundle, a summary of the points on which the parties are unable to agree should be included.

3.10 The party filing the trial bundle should supply identical bundles to all the parties to the proceedings and for the use of the witnesses.

[* The text issued by the Ministry of Justice refers, mistakenly, to rule 32.2.]
[5] For the definition of legal representative see rule 2.3.

Settlement or Discontinuance after the Trial Date Is Fixed

para.4.1 **61.15** para.4.12 **61.15**

4.1 Where:
(1) an offer to settle a claim is accepted,
(2) or a settlement is reached, or
(3) a claim is discontinued,
which disposes of the whole of a claim for which a date or 'window' has been fixed for the trial, the parties must ensure that the listing officer for the trial court is notified immediately.

4.2 If an order is drawn up giving effect to the settlement or discontinuance, a copy of the sealed order should be filed with the listing officer.

Representation at Hearings

para.5.1 **61.35, 61.36** paras.5.2–5.6 **61.35**

5.1 At any hearing, a written statement containing the following information should be provided for the court:
(1) the name and address of each advocate,
(2) his qualification or entitlement to act as an advocate, and
(3) the party for whom he so acts.

5.2 Where a party is a company or other corporation and is to be represented at a hearing by an employee the written statement should contain the following additional information:
(1) The full name of the company or corporation as stated in its certificate of registration.
(2) The registered number of the company or corporation.
(3) The position or office in the company or corporation held by the representative.
(4) The date on which and manner in which the representative was authorised to act for the company or corporation, e.g. —— 20 —— : written authority from managing director; or —— 20 —— : Board resolution dated —— 20 ——.

5.3 Rule 39.6 is intended to enable a company or other corporation to represent itself as a litigant in person. Permission under rule 39.6(b) should therefore be given by the court unless there is some particular and sufficient reason why it should be withheld. In considering whether to grant permission the matters to be taken into account include the complexity of the issues and the experience and position in the company or corporation of the proposed representative.

5.4 Permission under rule 39.6(b) should be obtained in advance of the hearing from, preferably, the judge who is to hear the case, but may, if it is for any reason impracticable or inconvenient to do so, be obtained from any judge by whom the case could be heard.

5.5 The permission may be obtained informally and without notice to the other parties. The judge who gives the permission should record in writing that he has done so and supply a copy to the company or corporation in question and to any other party who asks for one.

5.6 Permission should not normally be granted under Rule 39.6:
(a) in jury trials;
(b) in contempt proceedings.

Recording of Proceedings

para.6.1 **61.55** paras.6.3–6.5 **61.55**

6.1 At any hearing, whether in the High Court or a county court, the proceedings will be taperecorded unless the judge directs otherwise.

6.2 No party or member of the public may use unofficial recording equipment in any court or judge's room without the permission of the court. To do so without permission constitutes a contempt of court.[6]

6.3 Any party or person may require a transcript or transcripts of the recording of any hearing to be supplied to him, upon payment of the charges authorised by any scheme in force for the making of the recording or the transcript.

---

[6] Section 9 of the Contempt of Court Act 1981.

6.4 Where the person requiring the transcript or transcripts is not a party to the proceedings and the hearing or any part of it was held in private under CPR rule 39.2, paragraph 6.3 does not apply unless the court so orders.

6.5 Attention is drawn to [PD 52, paras 5.17 and 5.18* which deal] with the provision of transcripts for use in the Court of Appeal at public expense.

Exhibits at Trial

para.7 61.42

7 Exhibits which are handed in and proved during the course of the trial should be recorded on an exhibit list and kept in the custody of the court until the conclusion of the trial, unless the judge directs otherwise. At the conclusion of the trial it is the parties' responsibility to obtain the return of those exhibits which they handed in and to preserve them for the period in which any appeal may take place.

Citation of Authorities Human Rights

para.8 91.37

8.1 If it is necessary for a party to give evidence at a hearing of an authority referred to in s. 2 of the Human Rights Act 1998:

(1) the authority to be cited should be an authoritative and complete report; and
(2) the party must give to the court and any other party a list of the authorities he intends to cite and copies of the reports not less than three days before the hearing. (Section 2(1) of the Human Rights Act 1998 requires the court to take into account the authorities listed there.)
(3) Copies of the complete original texts issued by the European Court and Commission either paper based or from the Court's judgment database (HUDOC), which is available on the Internet, may be used.

[* The next issued by the Ministry of Justice refers to an earlier direction.]

PD 39B Practice Direction 39B — Court Sittings

This practice direction supplements CPR, Part 39.

PD 39B **61.24** [For commentary on a specific paragraph, please refer to the cross-references after the title of the paragraph.]

Court Sittings

1.1 (1) The sittings of the Court of Appeal and of the High Court shall be four in every year, that is to say:

(a) the Michaelmas sittings which shall begin on 1 October and end on 21 December;

(b) the Hilary sittings which shall begin on 11 January and end on the Wednesday before Easter Sunday;

(c) the Easter sittings which, subject to sub-para. (3), shall begin on the second Tuesday after Easter Sunday and end on the Friday before the spring holiday; and

(d) the Trinity sittings which shall begin on the second Tuesday after the spring holiday and end on 31 July.

(1A) (a) in sub-para. (1)(a) and (b) the sittings shall begin on the first Monday after the specified date if the latter falls on a weekend; and

(b) in sub-para. (1)(a) and (d) the sittings shall end on the Friday immediately preceding the specified date if the latter falls on a weekend.

(2) In the above paragraph 'spring holiday' means the bank holiday falling on the last Monday in May or any day appointed instead of that day under the Banking and Financial Dealings Act 1971, s. 1(2).

(3) The Easter sitting in 2011 shall begin on Wednesday, 4th May.

Vacations: The High Court

para.2.1(1)–(2) **61.24**
para.2.2 **61.24**
para.2.3(2)–(3) **61.24**
para.2.4–2.5 **61.24**

2.1 (1) One or more judges of each Division of the High Court shall sit in vacation on such days as the senior judge of that Division may from time to time direct, to hear such cases, claims, matters or applications as require to be immediately or promptly heard and to hear other cases, claims, matters or applications if the senior judge of that Division determines that sittings are necessary for that purpose.

(2) Any party to a claim or matter may at any time apply to the court for an order that such claim or matter be heard in vacation and, if the court is satisfied that the claim or matter requires to be immediately or promptly heard, it may make an order accordingly and fix a date for the hearing.

(3) Any judge of the High Court may hear such other cases, claims, matters or applications in vacation as the court may direct.

2.2 The directions in para. [2.1*] shall not apply in relation to the trial or hearing of cases, claims, matters or applications outside the Royal Courts of Justice but the senior presiding judge of each circuit, with the concurrence of the senior presiding judge, and the Vice-Chancellor of the County Palatine of Lancaster and the Chancery supervising judge for Birmingham, Bristol and Cardiff, with the concurrence of the Vice-Chancellor, may make such arrangements for vacation sittings in the courts for which they are respectively responsible as they think desirable.

2.3 (1) Subject to the discretion of the judge, any appeal and any application normally made to a judge may be made in the month of September.

(2) In the month of August, save with the permission of a judge or under arrangements for vacation sittings in courts outside the Royal Courts of Justice, appeals to a judge will be limited to the matters set out in para. [2.5†] below, and only applications of real urgency will be dealt

[* The text issued by the Ministry of Justice mistakenly refers to para. 3.1.]
[† The text issued by the Ministry of Justice mistakenly refers to para. 3.5.]

with, for example, urgent applications in respect of injunctions or for possession under RSC, ord. 113 in CPR, sch. 1.

(3) It is desirable, where this is practical, that applications or appeals are submitted to a master, district judge or judge prior to the hearing of the application or appeal so that they can be marked 'fit for August' or 'fit for vacation'. If they are so marked, then normally the judge will be prepared to hear the application or appeal in August, if marked 'fit for August' or in September if marked 'fit for vacation'. A request to have the papers so marked should normally be made in writing, shortly setting out the nature of the application or appeal and the reasons why it should be dealt with in August or in September, as the case may be.

Chancery masters

2.4 There is no distinction between term time and vacation so far as business before the Chancery masters is concerned. The masters will deal with all types of business throughout the year, and when a master is on holiday his list will normally be taken by a deputy master.

Queen's Bench masters

2.5 (1) An application notice may, without permission, be issued returnable before a master in the month of August for any of the following purposes:
to set aside a claim form or particulars of claim, or service of a claim form or particulars of claim;
to set aside judgment; for stay of execution;
for any order by consent;
for judgment or permission to enter judgment;
for approval of settlements or for interim payment;
for relief from forfeiture; for charging order; for garnishee order;
for appointment or discharge of a receiver;
for relief by way of interpleader by a sheriff or High Court enforcement officer;
for transfer to a county court or for trial by master;
for time where time is running in the month of August;

(2) In any case of urgency any other type of application notice (that is, other than those for the purposes in (1) above), may, with the permission of a master be issued returnable before a master during the month of August.

CPR Part 40 Judgments, Orders, Sale of Land etc.

[For commentary on a specific rule, please refer to the cross-references after the title of the rule.]

I JUDGMENTS AND ORDERS

40.1 Scope of This Section

This Section sets out rules about judgments and orders which apply except where any other of these Rules or a practice direction makes a different provision in relation to the judgment or order in question.

40.2 Standard Requirements

r.40.2(1)–(2) **32.40, 63.7, 63.37**
r.40.2(3) **63.37, 74.6**
r.40.2(4) **63.7, 63.37, 74.6**

(1) Every judgment or order must state the name and judicial title of the person who made it, unless it is—
 (a) default judgment entered under rule 12.4(1) (entry of default judgment where judgment is entered by a court officer) or a default costs certificate obtained under rule 47.11;
 (b) judgment entered under rule 14.4, 14.5, 14.6, 14.7 and 14.9 (entry of judgment on admission where judgment is entered by a court officer);
 (c) a consent order under rule 40.6(2) (consent orders made by court officers);
 (d) an order made by a court officer under rule 70.5 (orders to enforce awards as if payable under a court order); or
 (e) an order made by a court officer under rule 71.2 (orders to obtain information from judgment debtors).
(2) Every judgment or order must—
 (a) bear the date on which it is given or made; and
 (b) be sealed(GL) by the court.
(3) Paragraph (4) applies where a party applies for permission to appeal against a judgment or order at the hearing at which the judgment or order was made.
(4) Where this paragraph applies, the judgment or order shall state—
 (a) whether or not the judgment or order is final;
 (b) whether an appeal lies from the judgment or order and, if so, to which appeal court;
 (c) whether the court gives permission to appeal; and
 (d) *if not, the appropriate* appeal court to which any further application for permission may be made.

40.3 Drawing up and Filing of Judgments and Orders

r.40.3(1) 63.37
r.40.3(1)(c) 32.40
r.40.3(3) 32.40, 63.37

(1) Except as is provided at paragraph (4) below or by any Practice Direction, every judgment or order will be drawn up by the court unless—
(a) the court orders a party to draw it up;
(b) a party, with the permission of the court, agrees to draw it up;
(c) the court dispenses with the need to draw it up; or
(d) it is a consent order under rule 40.6.
(2) The court may direct that—
(a) a judgment or an order drawn up by a party must be checked by the court before it is sealed(GL); or
(b) before a judgment or an order is drawn up by the court, the parties must file an agreed statement of its terms.
(3) Where a judgment or an order is to be drawn up by a party—
(a) he must file it no later than 7 days after the date on which the court ordered or permitted him to draw it up so that it can be sealed(GL) by the court; and
(b) if he fails to file it within that period, any other party may draw it up and file it.
(4) Except for orders made by the court of its own initiative and unless the court otherwise orders, every judgment or order made in claims proceeding in the Queen's Bench Division at the Royal Courts of Justice, other than in the Administrative Court, will be drawn up by the parties, and rule 40.3 is modified accordingly.

40.4 Service of Judgments and Orders

r.40.4(1)–(2) 32.40, 63.37

(1) Where a judgment or an order has been drawn up by a party and is to be served by the court—
(a) the party who drew it up must file a copy to be retained at court and sufficient copies for service on him and on the other parties; and
(b) once it has been sealed(GL), the court must serve a copy of it on each party to the proceedings.
(2) Unless the court directs otherwise, any order made otherwise than at trial must be served on—
(a) the applicant and the respondent; and
(b) any other person on whom the court orders it to be served.
(Rule 6.21 sets out who is to serve a document other than the claim form)

40.5 Power to Require Judgment or Order to Be Served on a Party as Well as His Solicitor

r.40.5 1.37, 32.40, 63.37

Where the party on whom a judgment or order is to be served is acting by a solicitor, the court may order the judgment or order to be served on the party as well as on his solicitor.

40.6 Consent Judgments and Orders

r.40.6 63.38, 71.3
r.40.6(2)(b) 32.36, 63.38
r.40.6(3) 32.36
r.40.6(5)–(6) 63.39
r.40.6(7) 32.39
r.40.6(7)(b) 63.13

(1) This rule applies where all the parties agree the terms in which a judgment should be given or an order should be made.
(2) A court officer may enter and seal(GL) an agreed judgment or order if—
(a) the judgment or order is listed in paragraph (3);
(b) none of the parties is a litigant in person; and
(c) the approval of the court is not required by these Rules, a practice direction or any enactment before an agreed order can be made.
(3) The judgments and orders referred to in paragraph (2) are—
(a) a judgment or order for—
(i) the payment of an amount of money (including a judgment or order for damages or the value of goods to be decided by the court); or

(ii) the delivery up of goods with or without the option of paying the value of the goods or the agreed value.

(b) an order for—

(i) the dismissal of any proceedings, wholly or in part;

(ii) the stay(GL) of proceedings on agreed terms, disposing of the proceedings, whether those terms are recorded in a schedule to the order or elsewhere;

(iii) the stay(GL) of enforcement of a judgment, either unconditionally or on condition that the money due under the judgment is paid by instalments specified in the order;

(iv) the setting aside under Part 13 of a default judgment which has not been satisfied;

(v) the payment out of money which has been paid into court;

(vi) the discharge from liability of any party;

(vii) the payment, assessment or waiver of costs, or such other provision for costs as may be agreed.

(4) Rule 40.3 (drawing up and filing of judgments and orders) applies to judgments and orders entered and sealed(GL) by a court officer under paragraph (2) as it applies to other judgments and orders.

(5) Where paragraph (2) does not apply, any party may apply for a judgment or order in the terms agreed.

(6) The court may deal with an application under paragraph (5) without a hearing.

(7) Where this rule applies—

(a) the order which is agreed by the parties must be drawn up in the terms agreed;

(b) it must be expressed as being 'By Consent';

(c) it must be signed by the legal representative acting for each of the parties to whom the order relates or, where paragraph (5) applies, by the party if he is a litigant in person.

40.7 When Judgment or Order Takes Effect

r.40.7 32.40, 50.44, 63.1, 63.42 r.40.7(1) 4.2, 48.31, 63.1, 74.20

(1) A judgment or order takes effect from the day when it is given or made, or such later date as the court may specify.

(2) This rule applies to all judgments and orders except those to which rule 40.10 (judgment against a State) applies.

40.8 Time from Which Interest Begins to Run

r.40.8 64.31, 71.24 r.40.8(1)(b) 64.30
r.40.8(1) 71.24

(1) Where interest is payable on a judgment pursuant to section 17 of the judgments Act 1838 or section 74 of the County Courts Act 1984, the interest shall begin to run from the date that judgment is given unless—

(a) a rule in another Part or a practice direction makes different provision; or

(b) the court orders otherwise.

(2) The court may order that interest shall begin to run from a date before the date that judgment is given.

40.9 Who May Apply to Set Aside or Vary a Judgment or Order

r.40.9 4.2

A person who is not a party but who is directly affected by a judgment or order may apply to have the judgment or order set aside or varied.

40.10 Judgment against a State in Default of Acknowledgment of Service

r.40.10 4.2

(1) Where the claimant obtains default judgment under Part 12 on a claim against a State where the defendant has failed to file an acknowledgment of service, the judgment does not take effect until 2 months after service on the State of—

(a) a copy of the judgment; and

(b) a copy of the evidence in support of the application for permission to enter default judgment *(unless the evidence* has already been served on the State in accordance with an order made under Part 12).

(2) In this rule, 'State' has the meaning given by section 14 of the State Immunity Act 1978.

40.11 Time for Complying with a Judgment or Order

r. 40.11 17.11, 63.17

A party must comply with a judgment or order for the payment of an amount of money (including costs) within 14 days of the date of the judgment or order, unless—
(a) the judgment or order specifies a different date for compliance (including specifying payment by instalments);
(b) any of these Rules specifies a different date for compliance; or
(c) the court has stayed the proceedings or judgment.
(Parts 12 and 14 specify different dates for complying with certain default judgments and judgments on admissions)

40.12 Correction of Errors in Judgments and Orders

r.40.12 4.2, 37.64, 81.24, 82.100 r.40.12(1) 42.45, 63.42

(1) The court may at any time correct an accidental slip or omission in a judgment or order.
(2) A party may apply for a correction without notice.

40.13 Cases Where Court Gives Judgment Both on Claim and Counterclaim

r.40.13 63.19 r.40.13(2)–(3) 63.19

(1) This rule applies where the court gives judgment for specified amounts both for the claimant on his claim and against the claimant on a counterclaim.
(2) If there is a balance in favour of one of the parties, it may order the party whose judgment is for the lesser amount to pay the balance.
(3) In a case to which this rule applies, the court may make a separate order as to costs against each party.

40.14 Judgment in Favour of Certain Part Owners Relating to the Detention of Goods

r.40.14 63.31

(1) In this rule 'part owner' means one of two or more persons who have an interest in the same goods.
(2) Where—
  (a) a part owner makes a claim relating to the detention of the goods; and
  (b) the claim is not based on a right to possession,
  any judgment or order given or made in respect of the claim is to be for the payment of damages only, unless the claimant had the written authority of every other part owner of the goods to make the claim on his behalf as well as for himself.
(3) This rule applies notwithstanding anything in subsection (3) of section 3 of the Torts (Interference with Goods) Act 1977, but does not affect the remedies and jurisdiction mentioned in subsection (8) of that section.

II SALE OF LAND ETC. AND CONVEYANCING COUNSEL

40.15 Scope of This Section

(1) This Section—
  (a) deals with the court's power to order the sale, mortgage, partition or exchange of land; and
  (b) contains provisions about conveyancing counsel.
(Section 131 of the Senior Courts Act 1981 provides for the appointment of the conveyancing counsel of the Supreme Court)
(2) In this Section 'land' includes any interest in, or right over, land.

40.16 Power to Order Sale etc.

In any proceedings relating to land, the court may order the land, or part of it, to be—
(a) sold;
(b) mortgaged;

(c) exchanged; or
(d) partitioned.

40.17 Power to Order Delivery Up of Possession etc.

Where the court has made an order under rule 40.16, it may order any party to deliver up to the purchaser or any other person—

(a) possession of the land;
(b) receipt of rents or profits relating to it; or
(c) both.

40.18 Reference to Conveyancing Counsel

(1) The court may direct conveyancing counsel to investigate and prepare a report on the title of any land or to draft any document.
(2) The court may take the report on title into account when it decides the issue in question. (Provisions dealing with the fees payable to conveyancing counsel are set out in the Costs Practice Direction [PD 43–48, para. 8.8])

40.19 Party May Object to Report

(1) Any party to the proceedings may object to the report on title prepared by conveyancing counsel.
(2) Where there is an objection, the issue will be referred to a judge for determination.
(Part 23 contains general rules about making an application)

III DECLARATORY JUDGMENTS

40.20

r.40.20 4.1, 4.19

The court may make binding declarations whether or not any other remedy is claimed.

PD 40A Practice Direction 40A — Accounts, Inquiries etc.

This practice direction supplements CPR, Part 40.

PD 40 34.49, 63.36 [For commentary on a specific paragraph, please refer to the cross-references after the title of the paragraph.]

Accounts and Inquiries: General

para.1.1 34.49, 63.36 para.1.2 34.49, 63.36

1.1 Where the court orders any account to be taken or any inquiry to be made, it may, by the same or a subsequent order, give directions as to the manner in which the account is to be taken and verified or the inquiry is to be conducted.

1.2 In particular, the court may direct that in taking an account, the relevant books of account shall be evidence of their contents but that any party may take such objections to the contents as he may think fit.

1.3 Any party may apply to the court in accordance with CPR Part 23 for directions as to the taking of an account or the conduct of an inquiry or for the variation of directions already made.

1.4 Every direction for the taking of an account or the making of an inquiry shall be numbered in the order so that, as far as possible, each distinct account and inquiry is given its own separate number.

Verifying the Account

para.2(1) 34.49, 63.36

2. Subject to any order to the contrary:
   (1) the accounting party must make out his account and verify it by an affidavit or witness statement to which the account is exhibited,
   (2) the accounting party must file the account with the court and at the same time notify the other parties that he has done so and of the filing of any affidavit or witness statement verifying or supporting the account.

Objections

para.3.1 34.49, 63.36

3.1 Any party who wishes to contend:
   (a) that an accounting party has received more than the amount shown by the account to have been received, or
   (b) that the accounting party should be treated as having received more than he has actually received, or
   (c) that any item in the account is erroneous in respect of amount, or
   (d) that in any other respect the account is inaccurate,

   must, unless the court directs otherwise, give written notice to the accounting party of his objections.

3.2 The written notice referred to in paragraph 3.1 must, so far as the objecting party is able to do so:
   (a) state the amount by which it is contended that the account understates the amount received by the accounting party,
   (b) state the amount which it is contended that the accounting party should be treated as having received in addition to the amount he actually received,
   (c) specify the respects in which it is contended that the account is inaccurate, and
   (d) in each case, give the grounds on which the contention is made.

3.3 The contents of the written notice must, unless the notice contains a statement of truth, be verified by either an affidavit or a witness statement to which the notice is an exhibit.

(Part 22 and PD 22 contain provisions about statements of truth.)

Allowances

4. In taking any account all just allowances shall be made without any express direction to that effect.

Management of Proceedings

para.5 34.49, 63.36

5. The court may at any stage in the taking of an account or in the course of an inquiry direct a hearing in order to resolve an issue that has arisen and for that purpose may order that points of claim and points of defence be served and give any necessary directions.

Delay

6.1 If it appears to the court that there is undue delay in the taking of any account or the progress of any inquiry the court may require the accounting party or the party with the conduct of the inquiry, as the case may be, to explain the delay and may then make such order for the management of the proceedings (including a stay) and for costs as the circumstances may require.

6.2 The directions the court may give under para. 6.1 include a direction that the Official Solicitor take over the conduct of the proceedings and directions providing for the payment of the Official Solicitor's costs.

Distribution

7. Where some of the persons entitled to share in a fund are known but there is, or is likely to be, difficulty or delay in ascertaining other persons so entitled, the court may direct, or allow, immediate payment of their shares to the known persons without reserving any part of those shares to meet the subsequent costs of ascertaining the other persons.

Guardian's Accounts

8. The accounts of a person appointed guardian of the property of a child (defined in CPR, r. 21.1(2)) must be verified and approved in such manner as the court may direct.

Accounts and Inquiries to be Conducted before Master or District Judge

para.9 34.49, 63.36

9. Unless the court orders otherwise, an account or inquiry will be taken or made:
(1) by a master or district judge, if the proceedings are in the High Court; and
(2) by a district judge, if the proceedings are in a county court.

Advertisements

para.10 34.49, 63.36

10. The court may:
(1) direct any necessary advertisement; and
(2) fix the time within which the advertisement should require a reply.

Examination of Claims

para.11 34.49
para.11.1(1) 63.36
para.11.1(3) 63.36

11.1 Where the court orders an account of debts or other liabilities to be taken, it may direct any party, within a specified time, to:
(1) examine the claims of persons claiming to be owed money out of the estate or fund in question.
(2) determine, so far as he is able, which of them are valid; and
(3) file written evidence:
(a) stating his findings and his reasons for them; and
(b) listing any other debts which are or may be owed out of the estate or fund.

11.2 Where the court orders an inquiry for next of kin or other unascertained claimants to an estate or fund, it may direct any party, within a specified time, to:
(1) examine the claims that are made;
(2) determine, so far as he is able, which of them are valid; and
(3) file written evidence stating his findings and his reasons for them.

11.3 If the personal representatives or trustees concerned are not the parties directed by the court to examine claims, the court may direct them to join with the party directed to examine claims in producing the written evidence required by this rule.

Consideration of Claims by the Court

para.12 34.49, 63.36

12. For the purpose of considering a claim the court may:
(1) direct it to be investigated in any manner;
(2) direct the person making the claim to give further details of it; and
(3) direct that person to:
(a) file written evidence; or
(b) attend court to give evidence, to support his claim.

Notice of Decision

para.13 34.49

13. If:
(1) the court has allowed or disallowed any claim or part of a claim; and
(2) the person making the claim was not present when the decision was made, the court will serve on that person a notice informing him of its decision.

Interest on Debts

para.14 34.49

14. (1) Where an account of the debts of a deceased person is directed by any judgment, unless the deceased's estate is insolvent or the court orders otherwise, interest shall be allowed:
(a) on any debt which carries interest, at the rate it carries, and
(b) on any other debt, from the date of the judgment, at the rate payable on judgment debts at that date.
(2) Where interest on a debt is allowed under para. (1)(b), it shall be paid out of any assets of the estate which remain after payment of:
(a) any costs of the proceedings directed to be paid out of the estate;
(b) all the debts which have been established; and
(c) the interest on such of those debts as by law carry interest.
(3) For the purpose of this rule:
(a) 'debt' includes funeral, testamentary or administration expenses; and
(b) in relation to any expenses incurred after the judgment, para. (1)(b) applies as if, instead of the date of the judgment, it referred to the date when the expenses became payable.

Interest on Legacies

para.15 34.49

15. Where an account of legacies is directed by any judgment, then, subject to:
(a) any directions contained in the will or codicil in question; and
(b) any order made by the court,
interest shall be allowed on each legacy at the basic rate payable for the time being on funds in court or at such other rate as the court shall direct, beginning one year after the testator's death.

PD 40B Practice Direction 40B — Judgments and Orders

This practice direction supplements CPR, Part 40.

[For commentary on a specific paragraph, please refer to the cross-references after the title of the paragraph.]

Drawing Up and Filing of Judgments and Orders

1.1 Rule 40.2 sets out the standard requirements for judgments and orders and rule 40.3 deals with how judgments and orders should be drawn up.

1.2 A party who has been ordered or given permission to draw up an order must file it for sealing within seven days of being ordered or permitted to do so.[1] If he falls to do so, any other party may draw it up and file it.[2]

1.3 If the court directs that a judgment or order which is being drawn up by a party must be checked by the court before it is sealed, the party responsible must file the draft within seven days of the date the order was made with a request that the draft be checked before it is sealed.

1.4 If the court directs the parties to file an agreed statement of terms of an order which the court is to draw up,[3] the parties must do so no later than seven days from the date the order was made, unless the court directs otherwise.

1.5 If the court requires the terms of an order which is being drawn up by the court to be agreed by the parties the court may direct that a copy of the draft order is to be sent to all the parties:
(1) for their agreement to be endorsed on it and returned to the court before the order is sealed, or
(2) with notice of an appointment to attend before the court to agree the terms of the order.

Preparation of Deeds or Documents under an Order

2.1 Where a judgment or order directs any deed or document to be prepared, executed or signed, the order will state:
(1) the person who is to prepare the deed or document, and
(2) if the deed or document is to be approved, the person who is to approve it.

2.2 If the parties are unable to agree the form of the deed or document, any party may apply in accordance with Part 23 for the form of the deed or document to be settled.

2.3 In such case the judge may:
(1) settle the deed or document himself, or
(2) refer it to
(a) a master, or
(b) a district judge, or
(c) a conveyancing counsel of the Senior Courts to settle.

(See also PD 40D.)

Consent Orders

para.3.4 63.13 para.3.5 63.16, 63.38

3.1 Rule 40.6(3) sets out the types of consent judgments and orders which may be entered and sealed by a court officer. The court officer may do so in those cases provided that:
(1) none of the parties is a litigant in person, and
(2) the approval of the court is not required by the Rules, a practice direction or any enactment.[4]

3.2 If a consent order filed for sealing appears to be unclear or incorrect the court officer may refer it to a judge for consideration.[5]

---

[1] Rule 40.3(3)(a).
[2] Rule 40.3(3)(b).
[3] Rule 40.3(2)(b).
[4] Rule 40.6(2).
[5] Rule 3.2.

3.3 Where a consent judgment or order does not come within the provisions of rule 40.6(2):
(1) an application notice requesting a judgment or order in the agreed terms should be filed with the draft judgment or order to be entered or sealed, and
(2) the draft judgment or order must be drawn so that the judge's name and judicial title can be inserted.

3.4 A consent judgment or order must:
(1) be drawn up in the terms agreed,
(2) bear on it the words 'By Consent', and
(3) be signed by
(a) solicitors or counsel acting for each of the parties to the order, or
(b) where a party is a litigant in person, the litigant.[6]

3.5 Where the parties draw up a consent order in the form of a stay of proceedings on agreed terms, disposing of the proceedings,[7] and where the terms are recorded in a schedule to the order, any direction for:
(1) payment of money out of court, or
(2) payment and assessment of costs
should be contained in the body of the order and not in the schedule.

Correction of Errors in Judgments and Orders

paras.4.1–4.5 63.42

4.1 Where a judgment or order contains an accidental slip or omission a party may apply for it to be corrected.[8]

4.2 The application notice (which may be an informal document such as a letter) should describe the error and set out the correction required. An application may be dealt with without a hearing:
(1) where the applicant so requests,
(2) with the consent of the parties, or
(3) where the court does not consider that a hearing would be appropriate.

4.3 The judge may deal with the application without notice if the slip or omission is obvious or may direct notice of the application to be given to the other party or parties.

4.4 If the application is opposed it should, if practicable, be listed for hearing before the judge who gave the judgment or made the order.

4.5 The court has an inherent power to vary its own orders to make the meaning and intention of the court clear.

Adjustment of Final Judgment Figure in Respect of Compensation Recovery Payments

para.5.1 36.15, 63.21, 63.22 para.5.1A 36.15, 63.22

5.1 In a final judgment[9] where some or all of the damages awarded:
(1) fall under the heads of damage set out in the Social Security (Recovery of Benefits) Act 1997 ('the 1997 Act'), sch. 2, col. 1, in respect of recoverable benefits received by the claimant set out in col. 2 of that schedule; and
(2) where the defendant has paid to the Secretary of State the recoverable benefits in accordance with the certificate (as defined in r. 36.15(1)(e)),
there will be stated in the preamble to the judgment or order the amount awarded under each head of damage and the amount by which it has been reduced in accordance with s. 8 of and sch. 2 to the 1997 Act.

5.1A Where damages are awarded in a case where a lump sum payment (to be construed in accordance with s. 1A of the 1997 Act) has been made to a dependant, then s. 15 of the 1997 Act (as modified by the Social Security (Recovery of Benefits) (Lump Sum Payments) Regulations 2008 (SI 2008/1596), sch. 1) sets out what the court order must contain.

[6] Rule 40.6(7).
[7] Rule 40.6(3)(b)(ii).
[8] Rule [40.12]. [The text issued by the Ministry of Justice mistakenly refers to r. 40.10.]
[9] In this paragraph final 'judgment' includes any order to pay a sum of money, a final award of damages and an assessment of damages. [The text issued by the Ministry of Justice omits this footnote, but still refers to it in the next footnote.]

5.2 The judgment or order should then provide for entry of judgment and payment of the balance.

Adjustment of Final Judgment Figure in Respect of an Interim Payment

para.6 PC 24, 36.19 paras.6.1–6.4 36.19

6.1 In a final judgment[10] where an interim payment has previously been made which is less than the total amount awarded by the judge, the judgment or order should set out in a preamble:
(1) the total amount awarded by the judge, and
(2) the amount and date of the interim payment(s).

6.2 The total amount awarded by the judge should then be reduced by the total amount of any interim payments, and the judgment or order should then provide for entry of judgment and payment of the balance.

6.3 In a final judgment where an interim payment has previously been made which is more than the total amount awarded by the judge, the judgment or order should set out in a preamble:
(1) the total amount awarded by the judge, and
(2) the amount and date of the interim payment(s).

6.4 An order should then be made for repayment, reimbursement, variation or discharge under rule 25.8(2) and for interest on an overpayment under rule 25.8(5).

Statement as to Service of a Claim Form

7.1 Where a party to proceedings which have gone to trial requires a statement to be included in the judgment as to where, and by what means the claim form issued in those proceedings was served, application should made to the trial judge when judgment is given.

7.2 If the judge so orders, the statement will be included in a preamble to the judgment as entered.

Orders Requiring an Act to be Done

para.8.1 63.9 para.8.2 48.30, 63.9

8.1 An order which requires an act to be done (other than a judgment or order for the payment of an amount of money) must specify the time within which the act should be done.

8.2 The consequences of failure to do an act within the time specified may be set out in the order. In this case the wording of the following examples suitably adapted must be used:
(1) Unless the [claimant] [defendant] serves his list of documents by 4.00 p.m. on Friday, January 22, 1999 his [claim] [defence] will be struck out and judgment entered for the [defendant] [claimant], or
(2) Unless the [claimant] [defendant] serves his list of documents within 14 days of service of this order his [claim] [defence] will be struck out and judgment entered for the [defendant] [claimant].

Example (1) should be used wherever possible.

Non-compliance with an Injunction or Undertaking

para.9.1 37.49

9. PD 81, para. 1, contains provisions about penal notices on judgments and orders and paras 2.1 to 2.4 contain provisions about penal notices in relation to undertakings.

Foreign Currency

para.10 63.18, 63.31

10. Where judgment is ordered to be entered in a foreign currency, the order should be in the following form:

'It is ordered that the defendant pay the claimant (*state the sum in the foreign currency*) or the sterling equivalent at the time of payment.'

[10] As in note 9 above.

Costs

11.1 Attention is drawn to the Costs Practice Direction [PD 43–48] and, in particular, to the court's power to make a summary assessment of costs and the provisions relating to interest in detailed assessment proceedings.

11.2 Attention is also drawn to r. 44.13(1) which provides that if an order makes no mention of costs, none are payable in respect of the proceedings to which it relates.

Judgments Paid by Instalments

para.12 63.17

12. Where a judgment is to be paid by instalments, the judgment should set out:
(1) the total amount of the judgment,
(2) the amount of each instalment,
(3) the number of instalments and the date on which each is to be paid, and
(4) to whom the instalments should be paid.

Order to Make an Order of the Supreme Court an Order of the High Court

para.13.1–13.3 79.3

13.1 Application may be made in accordance with Part 23 for an order to make an order of the Supreme Court an order of the High Court. The application should be made to the procedural judge of the Division, District Registry or court in which the proceedings are taking place and may be made without notice unless the court directs otherwise.

13.2 The application must be supported by the following evidence:
(1) details of the order which was the subject of the appeal to the Supreme Court,
(2) details of the order of the Supreme Court, with a copy annexed, and
(3) a copy annexed of the certificate of the Registrar of the Supreme Court of the assessment of the costs of the appeal to the Supreme Court in the sum of £.......

13.3 The order to make an order of the Supreme Court an order of the High Court should be in form PF 68.

Examples of Forms of Trial Judgment

para.14 63.32

14.1 The following general forms may be used:
(1) judgment after trial before judge without jury — form No. 45,
(2) judgment after trial before judge with jury — form No. 46,
(3) judgment after trial before a Master or district judge — form No. 47,
(4) judgment after trial before a judge of the Technology and Construction court — form No. 47 but with any necessary modifications.

14.2 A trial judgment should, in addition to the matters set out in paragraphs 5, 6 and 7 above, have the following matters set out in a preamble:
(1) the questions put to a jury and their answers to those questions,
(2) the findings of a jury and whether unanimous or by a majority,
(3) any order made during the course of the trial concerning the use of evidence,
(4) any matters that were agreed between the parties prior to or during the course of the trial in respect of
(a) liability,
(b) contribution,
(c) the amount of the damages or part of the damages, and
(5) the findings of the judge in respect of each head of damage in a personal injury case.

14.3 Form No. 49 should be used for a trial judgment against an estate.
The forms referred to in this practice direction are listed in PD 4.

14.4 On any application or appeal concerning:
(i) a committal order;
(ii) a refusal to grant habeas corpus; or
(iii) a secure accommodation order made under s. 25 of the Children Act 1998,
if the court ordering the release of the person concludes that his Convention rights have been infringed by the making of the order to which the application or appeal relates, the judgment

or order should so state. If the court does not do so, that failure will not prevent another court from deciding the matter.

For Information About

(1) Orders for provisional damages: see Part 41 and PD 41A.
(2) Orders in respect of children and protected parties: see Part 21 and PD 21.
(3) Orders containing directions for payment of money out of court: see Parts 36 and 37 and PD 36 and 37.
(4) Taking accounts and conducting inquiries under a judgment or order: see PD 40A.

PD 40D Practice Direction 40D — 1 Court's Powers in Relation to Land 2 Conveyancing Counsel of the Court

This practice direction supplements CPR, Part 40.

PART 1 COURT'S POWERS IN RELATION TO LAND

Application to the Court Where Land Subject to an Encumbrance

1.1 In this paragraph 'encumbrance' has the same meaning as it has in s. 205(1) of the Law of Property Act 1925.

1.2 Where land subject to any encumbrance is sold or exchanged any party to the sale or exchange may apply to the court for a direction under s. 50 of the Law of Property Act 1925 (discharge of encumbrances by the court on sales or exchanges).

1.3 The directions a court may give on such an application include a direction for the payment into court of a sum of money that the court considers sufficient to meet:

(1) the value of the encumbrance; and

(2) further costs, expenses and interest that may become due on or in respect of the encumbrance.

(Section 50(1) of the Law of Property Act 1925 contains provisions relating to the calculation of these amounts.)

1.4 Where a payment into court has been made in accordance with a direction under s. 50(1) the court may:

(1) declare the land to be freed from the encumbrance; and

(2) make any order it considers appropriate for giving effect to an order made under r. 40.16 or relating to the money in court and the income thereof.

1.5 An application under s. 50 should:

(1) if made in existing proceedings, be made in accordance with CPR, Part 23;

(2) otherwise, be made by claim form under CPR, Part 8.

Directions about the Sale etc.

2 Where the court has made an order under r. 40.16 it may give any other directions it considers appropriate for giving effect to the order. In particular the court may give directions:

(1) appointing a party or other person to conduct the sale;

(2) for obtaining evidence of the value of the land;

(3) as to the manner of sale;

(4) settling the particulars and conditions of the sale;

(5) fixing a minimum or reserve price;

(6) as to the fees and expenses to be allowed to an auctioneer or estate agent;

(7) for the purchase money to be paid

(a) into court;

(b) to trustees; or

(c) to any other person;

(8) for the result of a sale to be certified;

(9) under r. 40.18.

Application for Permission to Bid

3.1 Where:

(1) the court has made an order under r. 40.16 for land to be sold; and

(2) a party wishes to bid for land,

he should apply to the court for permission to do so.

3.2 An application for permission to bid must be made before the sale takes place.

3.3 If the court gives permission to all the parties to bid, it may appoint an independent person to conduct the sale.

3.4 'Bid' in this paragraph includes submitting a tender or other offer to buy.

Certifying Sale Result

4.1 If:
(1) the court has directed the purchase money to be paid into court; or
(2) the court has directed that the result of the sale be certified,
the result of the sale must be certified by the person having conduct of the sale.

4.2 Unless the court directs otherwise, the certificate must give details of:
(1) the amount of the purchase price;
(2) the amount of the fees and expenses payable to any auctioneer or estate agent;
(3) the amount of any other expenses of the sale;
(4) the net amount received in respect of the sale; and must be verified by a statement of truth.
(Part 22 sets out requirements about statements of truth.)

4.3 The certificate must be filed:
(1) if the proceedings are being dealt with in the Royal Courts of Justice, in Chancery Chambers;
(2) if the proceedings are being dealt with anywhere else, in the court where the proceedings are being dealt with.

Fees and Expenses of Auctioneers and Estate Agents

5.1 (1) Where the court has ordered the sale of land under r. 40.16, auctioneer's and estate agent's charges may, unless the court orders otherwise, include:
(a) commission;
(b) fees for valuation of the land;
(c) charges for advertising the land;
(2) The court's authorisation is required for charges relating to surveys.

5.2 If the total amount of the auctioneer's and estate agent's charges authorised under para. 5.1(1):
(1) does not exceed 2.5 per cent of the sale price; and
(2) does not exceed the rate of commission that that agent would normally charge on a sole agency basis,
the charges may, unless the court orders otherwise and subject to para. 5.3(3) and (4), be met by deduction of the amount of the charges from the proceeds of sale without the need for any further authorisation from the court.

5.3 If:
(1) a charge made by an auctioneer or estate agent (whether in respect of fees or expenses or both) is not authorised under para. 5.1(1);
(2) the total amount of the charges so authorised exceeds the limits set out in para. 5.2;
(3) the land is sold in lots or by valuation; or
(4) the sale is of investment property, business property or farm property,
an application must be made to the court for approval of the fees and expenses to be allowed.

5.4 An application under para. 5.3 may be made by any party or, if he is not a party, by the person having conduct of the sale, and may be made either before or after the sale has taken place.

PART 2 CONVEYANCING COUNSEL OF THE COURT

Reference to Conveyancing Counsel

6.1 When the court refers a matter under r. 40.18, the court may specify a particular conveyancing counsel.

6.2 If the court does not specify a particular conveyancing counsel, references will be distributed among conveyancing counsel in accordance with arrangements made by the Chief Chancery Master.

6.3 Notice of every reference under r. 40.18 must be given to the Chief Chancery Master.

6.4 The court will send a copy of the order, together with all other necessary documents, to conveyancing counsel.

6.5 A court order sent to conveyancing counsel under para. 6.4 will be sufficient authority for him to prepare his report or draft the document.

6.6 (1) An objection under r. 40.19 to a report on title prepared by conveyancing counsel must be made by application notice.

(2) The application notice must state:

(a) the matters the applicant objects to; and

(b) the reason for the objection.

PD 40E Practice Direction 40E — Reserved Judgments

This practice direction supplements CPR, Part 40.

PD 40E 63.33, 75.20

Scope and Interpretation

para.1.1 63.33

1.1 This practice direction applies to all reserved judgments which the court intends to hand down in writing.

1.2 In this practice direction:

(a) 'relevant court office' means the office of the court in which judgment is to be given; and

(b) 'working day' means any day on which the relevant court office is open.

Availability of Reserved Judgments before Handing Down

paras.2.3–2.4 63.33 para.2.7 63.33

2.1 Where judgment is to be reserved the judge (or presiding judge) may, at the conclusion of the hearing, invite the views of the parties' legal representatives as to the arrangements made for the handing down of the judgment.

2.2 Unless the court directs otherwise, the following provisions of this paragraph apply where the judge or presiding judge is satisfied that the judgment will attract no special degree of confidentiality or sensitivity.

2.3 The court will provide a copy of the draft judgment to the parties' legal representatives by 4 p.m. on the second working day before handing down, or at such other time as the court may direct.

2.4 A copy of the draft judgment may be supplied, in confidence, to the parties provided that:

(a) neither the draft judgment nor its substance is disclosed to any other person or used in the public domain; and

(b) no action is taken (other than internally) in response to the draft judgment, before the judgment is handed down.

2.5 Where a copy of the draft judgment is supplied to a party's legal representatives in electronic form, they may supply a copy to that party in the same form.

2.6 If a party to whom a copy of the draft judgment is supplied under para. 2.4 is a partnership, company, government department, local authority or other organisation of a similar nature, additional copies may be distributed in confidence within the organisation, provided that all reasonable steps are taken to preserve its confidential nature and the requirements of para. 2.4 are adhered to.

2.7 If the parties or their legal representatives are in any doubt about the persons to whom copies of the draft judgment may be distributed they should enquire of the judge or presiding judge.

2.8 Any breach of the obligations or restrictions under para. 2.4 or failure to take all reasonable steps under para. 2.6 may be treated as contempt of court.

2.9 The case will be listed for judgment, and judgment handed down at the appropriate time.

Corrections to the Draft Judgment

para.3.1 63.33

3.1 Unless the parties or their legal representatives are told otherwise when the draft judgment is circulated, any proposed corrections to the draft judgment should be sent to the clerk of the judge who prepared the draft with a copy to any other party.

Orders Consequential on Judgment

para.4.2 63.33 para.4.5(a) 75.20
paras.4.4–4.5 63.33

4.1 Following the circulation of the draft judgment the parties or their legal representatives must seek to agree orders consequential upon the judgment.

4.2 In respect of any draft agreed order the parties must:

(a) fax or email a copy to the clerk to the judge or presiding judge (together with any proposed corrections or amendments to the draft judgment); and

(b) file four copies (with completed backsheets) in the relevant court office, by 12 noon on the working day before handing down.

4.3 A copy of a draft order must bear the case reference, the date of handing down and the name of the judge or presiding judge.

4.4 Where a party wishes to apply for an order consequential on the judgment the application must be made by filing written submissions with the clerk to the judge or presiding judge by 12 noon on the working day before handing down.

4.5 Unless the court orders otherwise:

(a) where judgment is to be given by an appeal court (which has the same meaning as in r. 52.1(3)(b)), the application will be determined without a hearing; and

(b) where judgment is to be given by any other court, the application will be determined at a hearing.

Attendance at Handing Down

paras.5.1–5.2 63.33

5.1 If there is not to be an oral hearing of an application for an order consequential on judgment:

(a) the parties' advocates need not attend on the handing down of judgment; and

(b) the judgment may be handed down by a judge sitting alone.

5.2 Where para. 5.1 (a) applies but an advocate does attend the handing down of judgment, the court may if it considers such attendance unnecessary, disallow the costs of the attendance.

CPR 26–50 & PDs

PD 40F Practice Direction 40F — Non-Disclosure Injunctions Information Collection Scheme

PD 40F **37.43**

1 This practice direction provides for a scheme for the recording, and transmission to the Ministry of Justice for analysis, of certain data in relation to injunctions(GL) prohibiting publication of private or confidential information. The purpose of the scheme is to enable the Ministry of Justice to collate and publish, in anonymised form, information about applications for injunctions where the Human Rights Act 1998, s. 12, is engaged.

2 The scheme applies in any civil proceedings in the High Court or Court of Appeal in which the court considers an application for an injunction prohibiting the publication of private or confidential information, the continuation of such an injunction, or an appeal against the grant or refusal of such an injunction. The scheme does not apply to proceedings to which the Family Procedure Rules 2010 apply, to immigration or asylum proceedings, to proceedings which raise issues of national security or to proceedings to which Part 21 applies.

3 An injunction to which this practice direction applies is called a 'Non-disclosure injunction'.

4 Except where a direction under para. 6 is made, following the hearing of an application for a non-disclosure injunction(GL) or any appeal against the grant or refusal of any such injunction the judge will record the following information in the form attached in the Annex (the information)—
(a) the claim or application number;
(b) whether the hearing was of—
(i) an application for an interim injunction;
(ii) an application for an extension or variation of an interim injunction;
(iii) an application for a final injunction; or
(iv) an appeal against the grant or refusal of an interim or final injunction.
(c) whether the hearing was on notice, or without notice to—
(i) the defendant; or
(ii) any third party liable to be affected by the order.
(d) whether the parties consented to the order;
(e) whether any derogations from the principle of open justice were sought, and if so—
(i) what they were;
(ii) whether they were granted;
(iii) if granted, whether with the parties' consent.

5 Derogations from the principle of open justice include, but are not limited to—
(a) an order that the hearing be held wholly or partly in private;
(b) an order that the names of one or more of the parties not be disclosed;
(c) an order that access to documents on the court file be restricted (under r. 5.4C or the inherent jurisdiction);
(d) an order that the provision of documents to third parties be restricted (under PD 25A, para. 9.2); and
(e) an order prohibiting disclosure of the existence of the proceedings or the order.

6 Subject to any express direction to the contrary in the order, any order made by the court on an application for a non-disclosure injunction(GL) or appeal from the grant or refusal of such an injunction shall be deemed to include a provision giving permission to a court officer to transmit the information to the Chief Statistician in the Ministry of Justice in order for it to be analysed and published in such form as does not enable the public identification of the parties to any proceedings.

7 If, in exceptional circumstances, the judge makes any direction under para. 6, the judge shall report that fact, and the nature of any derogation from open justice contained in the non-disclosure injunction to the Master of the Rolls. The Master of the Rolls is, following consultation with the judge, entitled to transmit such information as he sees fit to the Chief Statistician to enable publication by the Ministry of Justice of the bare fact that an injunction of that type had been made.

8 Once completed the form in the Annex will be sent by a court officer to the Chief Statistician in the Ministry of Justice.

ANNEX

[The High Court and Court of Appeal privacy injunctions statistics form is available at <http://www.justice.gov.uk/courts/procedure-rules/civil>.]

CPR Part 41 Damages

[For commentary on a specific rule, please refer to the cross-references after the title of the rule.]

I PROCEEDINGS TO WHICH SECTION 32A OF THE SENIOR COURTS ACT 1981 OR SECTION 51 OF THE COUNTY COURTS ACT 1984 APPLIES

41.1 Application and Definitions

(1) This Part applies to proceedings to which SCA s. 32A or CCA s. 51 applies.
(2) In this Part—
  (a) 'SCA s. 32A' means section 32A of the Senior Courts Act 1981;
  (b) 'CCA s. 51' means section 51 ofthe County Courts Act 1984; and
  (c) 'award of provisional damages' means an award of damages for personal injuries under which
    (i) damages are assessed on the assumption referred to in SCA s. 32A or CCA s. 51 that the injured person will not develop the disease or suffer the deterioration; and
    (ii) the injured person is entitled to apply for further damages at a future date if he develops the disease or suffers the deterioration.

41.2 Order for an Award of Provisional Damages

r.41.2 **66.12** r.41.2(1)(a) **63.24**

(1) The court may make an order for an award of provisional damages if—
  (a) the particulars of claim include a claim for provisional damages; and
  (b) the court is satisfied that SCA s. 32A or CCA s. 51 applies.

(Rule 16.4(1)(d) sets out what must be included in the particulars of claim where the claimant is claiming provisional damages)

(2) An order for an award of provisional damages—
  (a) must specify the disease or type of deterioration in respect of which an application may be made at a future date;
  (b) must specify the period within which such an application may be made; and
  (c) may be made in respect of more than one disease or type of deterioration and may, in respect of each disease or type of deterioration, specify a different period within which a subsequent application may be made.
(3) The claimant may make more than one application to extend the period specified under paragraph (2)(b) or (2)(c).

41.3 Application for Further Damages

(1) The claimant may not make an application for further damages after the end of the period specified under rule 41.2(2), or such period as extended by the court.
(2) Only one application for further damages may be made in respect of each disease or type of deterioration specified in the award of provisional damages.
(3) The claimant must give at least 28 days' written notice to the defendant of his intention to apply for further damages.
(4) If the claimant knows—
  (a) that the defendant is insured in respect of the claim; and

(b) the identity of the defendant's insurers,
he must also give at least 28 days' written notice to the insurers.

(5) Within 21 days after the end of the 28 day notice period referred to in paragraphs (3) and (4), the claimant must apply for directions.

41.3A

r.41.3A 63.29, 66.30

(1) Where—
(a) a claim includes claims arising under—
(i) the Fatal Accidents Act 1976; and
(ii) the Law Reform (Miscellaneous Provisions) Act 1934; and
(b) (a single sum of money is ordered or agreed to be paid in satisfaction of the claims, the court will apportion the money between the different claims.

(2) Where, in an action in which a claim under the Fatal Accidents Act 1976 is made by or on behalf of more than one person, a single sum of money is ordered or agreed to be paid in satisfaction of the claim, the court will apportion it between the persons entitled to it.

(3) Unless it has already been apportioned by the court, a jury or agreement between the parties, the court will apportion money under paragraphs (1) and (2)—
(a) when it gives directions under rule 21.11 (control of money received by a child or patient); or
(b) if rule 21.11 does not apply, on application by one of the parties in accordance with Part 23.

II PERIODICAL PAYMENTS UNDER THE DAMAGES ACT 1996

41.4 Scope and Interpretation

r.41.4 63.29, 66.11

(1) This Section of this Part contains rules about the exercise of the court's powers under section 2(1) of the 1996 Act to order that all or part of an award of damages in respect of personal injury is to take the form of periodical payments.

(2) In this Section—
(a) 'the 1996 Act' means the Damages Act 1996;
(b) 'damages' means damages for future pecuniary loss; and
(c) 'periodical payments' means periodical payments under section 2(1) of the 1996 Act.

41.5 Statement of Case

r.41.5 63.29, 66.11

(1) In a claim for damages for personal injury, each party in its statement of case may state whether it considers periodical payments or a lump sum is the more appropriate form for all or part of an award of damages and where such statement is given must provide relevant particulars of the circumstances which are relied on.

(2) Where a statement under paragraph (1) is not given, the court may order a party to make such a statement.

(3) Where the court considers that a statement of case contains insufficient particulars under paragraph (1), the court may order a party to provide such further particulars as it considers appropriate.

41.6 Court's Indication to Parties

r.41.6 63.29, 66.11

The court shall consider and indicate to the parties as soon as practicable whether periodical payments or a lump sum is likely to be the more appropriate form for all or part of an award of damages.

41.7 Factors to Be Taken into Account

r.41.7 63.29, 66.11

When considering—

(a) its indication as to whether periodical payments or a lump sum is likely to be the more appropriate form for all or part of an award of damages under rule 41.6; or

(b) whether to make an order under section 2(1)(a) of the 1996 Act,
the court shall have regard to all the circumstances of the case and in particular the form of award which best meets the claimant's needs, having regard to the factors set out in Practice Direction 41B.

41.8 The Award

r.41.8 63.29, 66.11
r.41.8(1) 63.29
r.41.8(2)–(4) 63.29

(1) Where the court awards damages in the form of periodical payments, the order must specify—
  (a) the annual amount awarded, how each payment is to be made during the year and at what intervals;
  (b) the amount awarded for future—
    (i) loss of earnings and other income; and
    (ii) care and medical costs and other recurring or capital costs;
  (c) that the claimant's annual future pecuniary losses, as assessed by the court, are to be paid for the duration of the claimant's life, or such other period as the court orders; and
  (d) that the amount of the payments shall vary annually by reference to the retail prices index, unless the court orders otherwise under section 2(9) of the 1996 Act.

(2) Where the court orders that any part of the award shall continue after the claimant's death, for the benefit of the claimant's dependants, the order must also specify the relevant amount and duration of the payments and how each payment is to be made during the year and at what intervals.

(3) Where an amount awarded under paragraph (1)(b) is to increase or decrease on a certain date, the order must also specify—
  (a) the date on which the increase or decrease will take effect; and
  (b) the amount of the increase or decrease at current value.

(4) Where damages for substantial capital purchases are awarded under paragraph (1)(b)(ii), the order must also specify—
  (a) the amount of the payments at current value;
  (b) when the payments are to be made; and
  (c) that the amount of the payments shall be adjusted by reference to the retail prices index, unless the court orders otherwise under section 2(9) of the 1996 Act.

41.9 Continuity of Payment

r.41.9 63.29, 66.11

(1) An order for periodical payments shall specify that the payments must be funded in accordance with section 2(4) of the 1996 Act, unless the court orders an alternative method of funding.

(2) Before ordering an alternative method of funding, the court must be satisfied that—
  (a) the continuity of payment under the order is reasonably secure; and
  (b) the criteria set out in Practice Direction 41B are met.

(3) An order under paragraph (2) must specify the alternative method of funding.

41.10 Assignment or Charge

r.41.10 63.29, 66.11

Where the court under section 2(6) (a) of the 1996 Act is satisfied that special circumstances make an assignment or charge of periodical payments necessary, it shall, in deciding whether or not to approve the assignment or charge, also have regard to the factors set out in Practice Direction 41B.

PD 41A Practice Direction 41A — Provisional Damages

This practice direction supplements CPR, Part 41.

PD 41 63.26, 66.12 [For commentary on a specific paragraph, please refer to the cross-references after the title of the paragraph.]

Claims for Provisional Damages

1.1 Part 16 and PD 16 set out information which must be included in the particulars of claim if a claim for provisional damages is made.

Judgment for an Award of Provisional Damages

2.1 When giving judgment at trial the judge will:
- (1) specify the disease or type of deterioration, or diseases or types of deterioration, which
  - (a) for the purpose of the award of immediate damages it has been assumed will not occur, and
  - (b) will entitle the claimant to further damages if it or they do occur at a future date,
- (2) give an award of immediate damages,
- (3) specify the period or periods within which an application for further damages may be made in respect of each disease or type of deterioration, and
- (4) direct what documents are to be filed and preserved as the case file in support of any application for further damages.

2.2 The claimant may make an application or applications to extend the periods referred to in para. 2.1(3) above.[1]

2.3 A period specified under para. 2.1(3) may be expressed as being for the duration of the life of the claimant.

2.4 The documents to be preserved as the case file ('the case file documents') referred to in para. 2.1(4) will be set out in a schedule to the judgment as entered.

2.5 Causation of any further damages within the scope of the order shall be determined when any application for further damages is made.

2.6 A form for a provisional damages judgment is set out in the Annex to this practice direction.

The Case File

para.3.2 63.26

3.1 The case file documents must be preserved until the expiry of the period or periods specified or of any extension of them.

3.2 The case file documents will normally include:
- (1) the judgment as entered,
- (2) the statements of case,
- (3) a transcript of the judge's oral judgment,
- (4) all medical reports relied on, and
- (5) a transcript of any parts of the claimant's own evidence which the judge considers necessary.

3.3 The associate/court clerk will:
- (1) ensure that the case file documents are provided by the parties where necessary and filed on the court file,
- (2) endorse the court file
  - (a) to the effect that it contains the case file documents, and
  - (b) with the period during which the case file documents must be preserved, and
- (3) preserve the case file documents in the court office where the proceedings took place.

3.4 Any subsequent order:
- (1) extending the period within which an application for further damages may be made, or
- (2) of the Court of Appeal discharging or varying the provisions of the original judgment or of any subsequent order under sub-paragraph (1) above,

---

[1] See r. 41.2(3).

CPR 26–50 & PDs

will become one of the case file documents and must be preserved accordingly and any variation of the period within which an application for further damages may be made should be endorsed on the court file containing the case file documents.

3.5 On an application to extend the periods referred to in paragraph 2.1(3) above a current medical report should be filed.

3.6 Legal representatives are reminded that it is their duty to preserve their own case file.

Consent Orders

paras.4–5 **63.26**

4.1 An application to give effect to a consent order for provisional damages should be made in accordance with Part 23. If the claimant is a child or protected party[2] the approval of the court must also be sought and the application for approval will normally be dealt with at a hearing.

4.2 The order should be in the form of a consent judgment and should contain:

(1) the matters set out in para. 2.1(1) to (3) above, and

(2) a direction as to the documents to be preserved as the case file documents, which will normally be

(a) the consent judgment,

(b) any statements of case,

(c) an agreed statement of facts, and

(d) any agreed medical report(s).

4.3 The claimant or his legal representative must lodge the case file documents in the court office where the proceedings are taking place for inclusion in the court file. The court file should be endorsed as in para. 3.3(2) above, and the case file documents preserved as in para. 13(3) above.

Default Judgment

para.5.1 **20.2**

5.1 Where a defendant:

(1) fails to file an acknowledgment of service in accordance with Part 10, and

(2) fails to file a defence in accordance with Part 15,

within the time specified for doing so, the claimant may not, unless he abandons his claim for provisional damages, enter judgment in default but should make an application in accordance with Part 23 for directions.

5.2 The master or district judge will normally direct the following issues to be decided:

(1) whether the claim is an appropriate one for an award of provisional damages and if so, on what terms, and

(2) the amount of immediate damages.

5.3 If the judge makes an award of provisional damages, the provisions of para. 3 above apply.

ANNEX

Example of an Award of Provisional Damages after Trial

Title of proceedings

THIS CLAIM having been tried before [*title and name of judge*] without a jury at [the Royal Courts of Justice *or as may be*] and [*title and name of judge*] having ordered that judgment as set out below be entered for the claimant

IT IS ORDERED:

(1) that the defendant pay the claimant by way of immediate damages the sum of £............ (being (i) £............. for special damages and £................ [agreed interest] [interest at the rate of............ from............ to.................. (ii) £................ for general damages and £........... [agreed interest] [interest at the rate of 2% from............ to..............] and (iii) £............ for loss of future earnings and/or earning capacity) on the assumption that the claimant would not at a future date as a result of the act or omission giving rise to the claim develop the following disease/type of deterioration namely [set out disease or type of deterioration]
[*set out disease or type of deterioration*]

[2] See Part 21 for the meaning of 'child' and 'protected party'.

(2) that if the claimant at a further date does develop that [disease] [type of deterioration] he should be entitled to apply for further damages provided that the application is made on or before [*set out period*]
(3) that the documents set out in the schedule to this order be filed on the court file and preserved as the case file until the expiry of the period set out in paragraph (2) above or of any extension of that period which has been ordered
(4) (costs)

Schedule

[*list documents referred to in paragraph (3)*]

CPR 26–50 & PDs

PD 41B Practice Direction 41B — Periodical Payments under the Damages Act 1996

This practice direction supplements CPR, Part 41.

Part 41B 63.29, 66.11

Factors to Be Taken into Account (Rule 41.7)

para.1 61.29

1. The factors which the court shall have regard to under r. 41.7 include:
   (1) the scale of the annual payments taking into account any deduction for contributory negligence;
   (2) the form of award preferred by the claimant including:
      (a) the reasons for the claimant's preference; and
      (b) the nature of any financial advice received by the claimant when considering the form of award; and
   (3) the form of award preferred by the defendant including the reasons for the defendant's preference.

The Award (Rule 41.8)

para.2 63.29

2.1 An order may be made under r. 41.8(2) where a dependant would have had a claim under the Fatal Accidents Act 1976, s. 1, if the claimant had died at the time of the accident.

2.2 Examples of circumstances which might lead the court to order an increase or decrease under r. 41.8(3) are where the court determines that:
   (1) the claimant's condition will change leading to an increase or reduction in his or her need to incur care, medical or other recurring or capital costs;
   (2) gratuitous carers will no longer continue to provide care;
   (3) the claimant's educational circumstances will change;
   (4) the claimant would have received a promotional increase in pay;
   (5) the claimant will cease earning.

Continuity of Payment (Rule 41.9)

para.3 63.29

3. Before ordering an alternative method of funding under r. 41.9(1), the court must be satisfied that the following criteria are met:
   (1) that a method of funding provided for under s. 2(4) of the 1996 Act is not possible or there are good reasons to justify an alternative method of funding;
   (2) that the proposed method of funding can be maintained for the duration of the award or for the proposed duration of the method of funding; and
   (3) that the proposed method of funding will meet the level of payment ordered by the court.

Assignment or Charge (Rule 41.10)

para.4 63.29

4. The factors which the court shall have regard to under r. 41.10 include:
   (1) whether the capitalised value of the assignment or charge represents value for money;
   (2) whether the assignment or charge is in the claimant's best interests, taking into account whether these interests can be met in some other way; and
   (3) how the claimant will be financially supported following the assignment or charge.

Variation

5. *The Damages (Variation of Periodical Payments) Order 2005 (SI 2005/841)* sets out provisions which enable the court in certain circumstances to provide in an order for periodical payments that it may be varied.

Settlement

6. Where the parties settle a claim to which r. 36.5 applies, any consent order, whether made under r. 40.6 or on an application under Part 23, must satisfy the requirements of rr. 41.8 and 41.9.

Settlement or Compromise on Behalf of Child or Protected Party

7. Where a claim for damages for personal injury is made by or on behalf of a child or protected party and is settled prior to the start of proceedings or before trial, the provisions of PD 21 must be complied with.

CPR Part 42 Change of Solicitor

Part 42 21.3, 22.2 [For commentary on a specific rule, please refer to the cross-references after the title of the rule.]

42.1 Solicitor Acting for a Party

r.42.1 21.3, 22.3

Where the address for service of a party is the business address of his solicitor, the solicitor will be considered to be acting for that party until the provisions of this Part have been complied with.

(Part 6 contains provisions about the address for service)

42.2 Change of Solicitor — Duty to Give Notice

r.42.2 22.4
r.42.2(5) 21.3, 22.3
r.42.2(6)(a) 22.5
r.42.2(6)(b) 22.5
r.42.2(6)(b)(i) 22.5

(1) This rule applies where—
  (a) a party for whom a solicitor is acting wants to change his solicitor;
  (b) a party, after having conducted the claim in person, appoints a solicitor to act on his behalf (except where the solicitor is appointed only to act as an advocate for a hearing); or
  (c) a party, after having conducted the claim by a solicitor, intends to act in person.

(2) Where this rule applies, the party or his solicitor (where one is acting) must—
  (a) file notice of the change; and
  (b) serve notice of the change on every other party and, where paragraph (1)(a) or (c) applies, on the former solicitor.

(3) The notice must state the party's new address for service.

(4) The notice filed at court must state that notice has been served as required by paragraph (2)(b).

(5) Subject to paragraph (6), where a party has changed his solicitor or intends to act in person, the former solicitor will be considered to be the party's solicitor unless and until—
  (a) notice is filed and served in accordance with paragraph (2); or
  (b) the court makes an order under rule 42.3 and the order is served as required by paragraph (3) of that rule.

(6) Where the certificate of a person to whom legal aid is provided is revoked or withdrawn—
  (a) the solicitor who acted for that person will cease to be a solicitor acting in the case as soon as the solicitor's retainer is determined under regulation 24 or 41 of the Civil Legal Aid (Procedure) Regulations 2012; and
  (b) if that person wishes to continue—
    (i) where he appoints a solicitor to act on his behalf, paragraph (2) will apply as if he had previously conducted the claim in person; and
    (ii) where he wants to act in person, he must give an address for service.

(Rules 6.23 and 6.24 contain provisions about a party's address for service)

('LSC funded client' and 'assisted person' are defined in rule 43.2)

(7) 'Certificate' in paragraph (6) means a certificate issued under the Civil Legal Aid (Procedure) Regulations 2012.

42.3 Order That a Solicitor Has Ceased to Act

r.42.3 22.6
r.42.3(2)–(3) 22.6

(1) A solicitor may apply for an order declaring that he has ceased to be the solicitor acting for a party.

(2) Where an application is made under this rule—
(a) notice of the application must be given to the party for whom the solicitor is acting, unless the court directs otherwise; and
(b) the application must be supported by evidence.
(3) Where the court makes an order that a solicitor has ceased to act—
(a) a copy of the order must be served on every party to the proceedings; and
(b) if it is served by a party or the solicitor, the party or the solicitor (as the case may be) must file a certificate of service.

42.4 Removal of Solicitor Who Has Ceased to Act on Application of Another Party

r.42.4 22.7
r.42.4(1) 22.7
r.42.4(3) 22.7

(1) Where—
(a) a solicitor who has acted for a party—
(i) has died;
(ii) has become bankrupt;
(iii) has ceased to practise; or
(iv) cannot be found; and
(b) the party has not given notice of a change of solicitor or notice of intention to act in person as required by rule 42.2(2),
any other party may apply for an order declaring that the solicitor has ceased to be the solicitor acting for the other party in the case.
(2) Where an application is made under this rule, notice of the application must be given to the party to whose solicitor the application relates unless the court directs otherwise.
(3) Where the court makes an order made under this rule—
(a) a copy of the order must be served on every other party to the proceedings; and
(b) where it is served by a party, that party must file a certificate of service.

CPR 26–50 & PDs

PD 42 Practice Direction 42 — Change of Solicitor

This practice direction supplements CPR, Part 42.

[For commentary on a specific paragraph, please refer to the cross-references after the title of the paragraph.]

Solicitor Acting for a Party

para.1.2 22.4 para.1.3 22.3

1.1 Rule 42.1 states that where the address for service of a party is the business address[1] of that party's solicitor, the solicitor will be considered to be acting for that party until the provisions of Part 42 have been complied with.

1.2 Subject to r. 42.2(6) (where the certificate of a LSC funded client or assisted person is revoked or discharged), where a party has changed his solicitor or intends to act in person, the former solicitor will be considered to be the party's solicitor unless or until:
   (1) a notice of the change is
      (a) filed with the court,[2] and
      (b) served on every other party,[3] or
   (2) the court makes an order under r. 42.3 and the order is served on every other party.[4]
   The notice should not be filed until every other party has been served.

1.3 A solicitor appointed to represent a party only as an advocate at a hearing will not be considered to be acting for that party within the meaning of Part 42.

Notice of Change of Solicitor

para.2.2 22.5 para.2.7 22.4
para.2.5 22.4

2.1 Rule 42.2(1) sets out the circumstances following which a notice of the change must be filed and served.

2.2 A notice of the change giving the last known address of the former assisted person must also be filed and served on every party where, under r. 42.2(6):
   (1) the certificate of a LSC funded client or assisted person is revoked or discharged,
   (2) the solicitor who acted for that person has ceased to act on determination of his retainer under reg. 83 of [the Civil Legal Aid (General) Regulations 1989], and
   (3) the assisted person wishes either to act in person or appoint another solicitor to act on his behalf.

2.3 In addition, where a party or solicitor changes his address for service, a notice of that change should be filed and served on every party.

2.4 A party who, having conducted a claim by a solicitor, intends to act in person must give in the notice an address for service that is within the United Kingdom.[5]

2.5 Form N434 should be used to give notice of any change. The notice should be filed in the court office in which the claim is proceeding.

2.6 Where the claim is proceeding in the High Court the notice should be filed either in the appropriate district registry or if the claim is proceeding in the Royal Courts of Justice, as follows:
   (1) a claim proceeding in the Queen's Bench Division — in the Action Department of the Central Office,
   (2) a claim proceeding in the Chancery Division — in Chancery Chambers,
   (3) a claim proceeding in the Administrative Court — in the Administrative Court Office,
   (4) a claim proceeding in the Admiralty and Commercial Registry — in the Admiralty and Commercial Registry, and

---

1 Rules 6.7 and 6.23 contain provisions about service on the business address of a solicitor.
2 Rule 42.2(2)(a).
3 Rule 42.2(2)(b).
4 Rule 42.2(5).
5 See r. 6.23.

(5) a claim proceeding in the Technology and Construction Court — in the Registry of the Technology and Construction Court.

2.7 Where the claim is the subject of an appeal to the Court of Appeal, the notice should also be filed in the Civil Appeals Office.

(PD 43–48 contains details of the information required to be included when the funding arrangements for the claim change.)

Application for an Order That a Solicitor Has Ceased to Act

3.1 A solicitor may apply under r. 42.3 for an order declaring that he has ceased to be the solicitor acting for a party.

3.2 The application should be made in accordance with Part 23[6] and must be supported by evidence.[7] Unless the court directs otherwise the application notice must be served on the party.[8]

3.3 An order made under r. 42.3 must be served on every party and takes effect when it is served. Where the order is not served by the court, the person serving must file a certificate of service in form N215.

Application by Another Party to Remove a Solicitor

para.4.2 22.7

4.1 Rule 42.4 sets out circumstances in which any other party may apply for an order declaring that a solicitor has ceased to be the solicitor acting for another party in the proceedings.

4.2 The application should be made in accordance with Part 23 and must be supported by evidence. Unless the court directs otherwise the application notice must be served on the party to whose solicitor the application relates.

4.3 An order made under r. 42.4 must be served on every other party to the proceedings. Where the order is not served by the court, the person serving must file a certificate of service in form N215.

New Address for Service Where Order Made under Rules 42.3 or 42.4

5.1 Where the court has made an order under r. 42.3 that a solicitor has ceased to act or under r. 42.4 declaring that a solicitor has ceased to be the solicitor for a party, the party for whom the solicitor was acting must give a new address for service to comply with rr. 6.23(1) and 6.24.

(Rule 6.23(2)(a) provides that a party must give an address for service within the United Kingdom or where a solicitor is acting for a party, an address for service either in the United Kingdom or any other EEA State.)

(Until such time as a new address for service is given r. 6.9 will apply.)

[Part 43 has been revoked with effect from 1 April 2013.]

CPR 26–50 & PDs

[6] See Part 23 and PD 23A.
[7] See Part 32 and PD 32 for information about evidence.
[8] Rule 42.3(2).

CPR Part 44 General Rules about Costs

Part 44 **43.19, 54.12, 68.28** [For commentary on a specific rule, please refer to the cross-references after the title of the rule.]

I GENERAL

44.1 Interpretation and Application

r.44.1 **70.2, 71.2** r.44.1(1) **71.1**

(1) In Parts 44 to 47, unless the context otherwise requires—
'authorised court officer' means any officer of—
(i) a county court;
(ii) a district registry;
(iii) the Principal Registry of the Family Division; or
(iv) the Costs Office,
whom the Lord Chancellor has authorised to assess costs;
'conditional fee agreement' means an agreement enforceable under section 58 of the Courts and Legal Services Act 1990;
'costs' includes fees, charges, disbursements, expenses, remuneration, reimbursement allowed to a litigant in person under rule 46.5 and any fee or reward charged by a lay representative for acting on behalf of a party in proceedings allocated to the small claims track;
'costs judge' means a taxing master of the Senior Courts;
'Costs Office' means the Senior Courts Costs Office;
'costs officer' means—
(i) a costs judge;
(ii) a district judge; or
(iii) an authorised court officer;
'detailed assessment' means the procedure by which the amount of costs is decided by a costs officer in accordance with Part 47;
'the Director (legal aid)' means the person designated as the Director of Legal Aid Casework pursuant to section 4 of the Legal Aid, Sentencing and Punishment of Offenders Act 2012, or a person entitled to exercise the functions of the Director;
'fixed costs' means costs the amounts of which are fixed by these rules whether or not the court has a discretion to allow some other or no amount, and include—
(i) the amounts which are to be allowed in respect of legal representatives' charges in the circumstances set out in Section I of Part 45;
(ii) fixed recoverable costs calculated in accordance with rule 45.11;
(iii) the additional costs allowed by rule 45.18;

(iv) fixed costs determined under rule 45.21;
(v) costs fixed by rules 45.37 and 45.38;
'free of charge' has the same meaning as in section 194(10) of the 2007 Act;
'fund' includes any estate or property held for the benefit of any person or class of person and any fund to which a trustee or personal representative is entitled in that capacity;
'HMRC' means HM Revenue and Customs;
'legal aid' means civil legal services made available under arrangements made for the purposes of Part 1of the Legal Aid, Sentencing and Punishment of Offenders Act 2012;
'paying party' means a party liable to pay costs;
'the prescribed charity' has the same meaning as in section 194(8) of the 2007 Act;
'pro bono representation' means legal representation provided free of charge;
'receiving party' means a party entitled to be paid costs;
'summary assessment' means the procedure whereby costs are assessed by the judge who has heard the case or application;
'VAT' means Value Added Tax;
'the 2007 Act' means the Legal Services Act 2007.
('Legal representative' has the meaning given in rule 2.3).
(2) The costs to which Parts 44 to 47 apply include—
(a) the following costs where those costs may be assessed by the court—
(i) costs of proceedings before an arbitrator or umpire;
(ii) costs of proceedings before a tribunal or other statutory body; and
(iii) costs payable by a client to their legal representative; and
(b) costs which are payable by one party to another party under the terms of a contract, where the court makes an order for an assessment of those costs.
(3) Where advocacy or litigation services are provided to a client under a conditional fee agreement, costs are recoverable under Parts 44 to 47 notwithstanding that the client is liable to pay the legal representative's fees and expenses only to the extent that sums are recovered in respect of the proceedings, whether by way of costs or otherwise.

44.2 Court's Discretion as to Costs

r.44.2 **1.37, 55.8, 66.29, 66.36, 66.45, 66.47, 68.4, 68.6, 69.8, 71.6**
r.44.2(1) **68.3, 82.87**
r.44.2(1)(c) **68.20, 68.27**
r.44.2(2) **5.5, 68.3, 68.6, 82.87**
r.44.2(2)(a) **66.39, 68.18, 68.45, 69.2**
r.44.2(4) **8.4, 66.16, 68.4, 68.5, 73.23**
r.44.2(4)(a) **68.16, 82.90**
r.44.2(4)(b) **68.11**
r.44.2(4)(c) **66.19, 66.37, 68.5**
r.44.2(5) **8.4, 68.4, 68.5, 68.6**
r.44.2(5)(b) **66.45, 68.11**
r.44.2(5)(c) **73.23**
r.44.2(5)(d) **66.45, 68.16, 71.43**
r.44.2(6) **68.4**
r.44.2(6)(f) **68.44**
r.44.2(6)(g) **64.31, 68.20, 71.24, 73.23**
r.44.2(7) **68.4, 68.13, 68.44**
r.44.2(8) **64.31, 71.9, 71.27**

(1) The court has discretion as to—
(a) whether costs are payable by one party to another;
(b) the amount of those costs; and
(c) when they are to be paid.
(2) If the court decides to make an order about costs—
(a) the general rule is that the unsuccessful party will be ordered to pay the costs of the successful party; but
(b) the court may make a different order.
(3) The general rule does not apply to the following proceedings—
(a) proceedings in the Court of Appeal on an application or appeal made in connection with proceedings in the Family Division; or
(b) proceedings in the Court of Appeal from a judgment, direction, decision or order given or made in probate proceedings or family proceedings.
(4) In deciding what order (if any) to make about costs, the court will have regard to all the circumstances, including—
(a) the conduct of all the parties;
(b) whether a party has succeeded on part of its case, even if that party has not been wholly successful; and

(c) any admissible offer to settle made by a party which is drawn to the court's attention, and which is not an offer to which costs consequences under Part 36 apply.

(5) The conduct of the parties includes—

(a) conduct before, as well as during, the proceedings and in particular the extent to which the parties followed the Practice Direction — Pre-Action Conduct or any relevant pre-action protocol;

(b) whether it was reasonable for a party to raise, pursue or contest a particular allegation or issue;

(c) the manner in which a party has pursued or defended its case or a particular allegation or issue; and

(d) whether a claimant who has succeeded in the claim, in whole or in part, exaggerated its claim.

(6) The orders which the court may make under this rule include an order that a party must pay—

(a) a proportion of another party's costs;

(b) a stated amount in respect of another party's costs;

(c) costs from or until a certain date only;

(d) costs incurred before proceedings have begun;

(e) costs relating to particular steps taken in the proceedings;

(f) costs relating only to a distinct part of the proceedings; and

(g) interest on costs from or until a certain date, including a date before judgment.

(7) Before the court considers making an order under paragraph (6)(f), it will consider whether it is practicable to make an order under paragraph (6)(a) or (c) instead.

(8) Where the court orders a party to pay costs subject to detailed assessment, it will order that party to pay a reasonable sum on account of costs, unless there is good reason not to do so.

44.3 Basis of Assessment

r.44.3 **1.29, 5.16, 43.3, 66.16, 66.19, 66.26, 66.44, 68.4, 68.6, 68.27**
r.44.3(1) **68.3, 71.36, 71.38, 71.40, 71.41, 71.42**
r.44.3(1)(c) **68.20**
r.44.3(2) **68.3, 68.6, 71.40, 86.33**
r.44.3(2)(a) **68.18, 68.45, 71.40**
r.44.3(2)(b) **71.40**
r.44.3(4) **1.37, 66.6, 68.4, 68.5, 71.45**
r.44.3(4)(a) **68.16**
r.44.3(4)(b) **68.11**
r.44.3(4)(c) **68.5**
r.44.3(5) **1.37, 43.9, 68.4, 68.5, 68.16, 71.40**
r.44.3(5)(a) **1.8, 8.3, 82.90**
r.44.3(5)(b) **68.11**
r.44.3(5)(d) **1.28, 68.11**
r.44.3(5)(e) **1.28**
r.44.3(6) **68.4**
r.44.3(6)(f) **68.44**
r.44.3(6)(g) **68.20**
r.44.3(7) **68.1, 68.4, 68.13, 68.44**

(1) Where the court is to assess the amount of costs (whether by summary or detailed assessment) it will assess those costs—

(a) on the standard basis; or

(b) on the indemnity basis,

but the court will not in either case allow costs which have been unreasonably incurred or are unreasonable in amount.

(Rule 44.5 sets out how the court decides the amount of costs payable under a contract.)

(2) Where the amount of costs is to be assessed on the standard basis, the court will—

(a) only allow costs which are proportionate to the matters in issue. Costs which are disproportionate in amount may be disallowed or reduced even if they were reasonably or necessarily incurred; and

(b) resolve any doubt which it may have as to whether costs were reasonably and proportionately incurred or were reasonable and proportionate in amount in favour of the paying party.

(Factors which the court may take into account are set out in rule 44.4.)

(3) Where the amount of costs is to be assessed on the indemnity basis, the court will resolve any doubt which it may have as to whether costs were reasonably incurred or were reasonable in amount in favour of the receiving party.

(4) Where—

(a) the court makes an order about costs without indicating the basis on which the costs are to be assessed; or

(b) the court makes an order for costs to be assessed on a basis other than the standard basis or the indemnity basis,

the costs will be assessed on the standard basis.

(5) Costs incurred are proportionate if they bear a reasonable relationship to—
(a) the sums in issue in the proceedings;
(b) the value of any non-monetary relief in issue in the proceedings;
(c) the complexity of the litigation;
(d) any additional work generated by the conduct of the paying party; and
(e) any wider factors involved in the proceedings, such as reputation or public importance.

(6) Where the amount of a solicitor's remuneration in respect of non-contentious business is regulated by any general orders made under the Solicitors Act 1974, the amount of the costs to be allowed in respect of any such business which falls to be assessed by the court will be decided in accordance with those general orders rather than this rule and rule 44.4.

(7) Paragraphs (2)(a) and (5) do not apply in relation to—
(a) cases commenced before 1st April 2013; or
(b) costs incurred in respect of work done before 1st April 2013,
and in relation to such cases or costs, rule 44.4.(2)(a) as it was in force immediately before1st April 2013 will apply instead.

44.4 Factors to be Taken into Account in Deciding the Amount of Costs

r.44.4 5.16, 68.4, 70.3, 71.38
r.44.4(1) 43.18, 71.43
r.44.4(2) 71.36, 71.39
r.44.4(3) 42.27, 68.4, 71.37, 71.48
r.44.4(3)(h) 43.18, 71.37

(1) The court will have regard to all the circumstances in deciding whether costs were—
(a) if it is assessing costs on the standard basis—
(i) proportionately and reasonably incurred; or
(ii) proportionate and reasonable in amount, or
(b) if it is assessing costs on the indemnity basis—
(i) unreasonably incurred; or
(ii) unreasonable in amount.

(2) In particular, the court will give effect to any orders which have already been made.

(3) The court will also have regard to—
(a) the conduct of all the parties, including in particular—
(i) conduct before, as well as during, the proceedings; and
(ii) the efforts made, if any, before and during the proceedings in order to try to resolve the dispute;
(b) the amount or value of any money or property involved;
(c) the importance of the matter to all the parties;
(d) the particular complexity of the matter or the difficulty or novelty of the questions raised;
(e) the skill, effort, specialised knowledge and responsibility involved;
(f) the time spent on the case;
(g) the place where and the circumstances in which work or any part of it was done; and
(h) the receiving party's last approved or agreed budget.
(Rule 35.4(4) gives the court power to limit the amount that a party may recover with regard to the fees and expenses of an expert.)

44.5 Amount of Costs where Costs are Payable under a Contract

r.44.5 68.4, 71.62
r.44.5(3) 68.4, 71.37, 71.39

(1) Subject to paragraphs (2) to (4), where the court assesses (whether by summary or detailed assessment) costs which are payable by the paying party to the receiving party under the terms of a contract, the costs payable under those terms are, unless the contract expressly provides otherwise, to be presumed to be costs which—
(a) have been reasonably incurred; and
(b) are reasonable in amount,
and the court will assess them accordingly.

(2) The presumptions in paragraph (1) are rebuttable. Practice Direction 44 — General rules about costs sets out circumstances where the court may order otherwise.

(3) Paragraph (1) does not apply where the contract is between a solicitor and client.

44.6 Procedure for Assessing Costs

r.44.6 **71.2**

(1) Where the court orders a party to pay costs to another party (other than fixed costs) it may either—
 (a) make a summary assessment of the costs; or
 (b) order detailed assessment of the costs by a costs officer,
 unless any rule, practice direction or other enactment provides otherwise.
 (Practice Direction 44 — General rules about costs sets out the factors which will affect the court's decision under paragraph (1).)
(2) A party may recover the fixed costs specified in Part 45 in accordance with that Part.

44.7 Time for Complying with an Order for Costs

r.44.7 **32.31, 68.20, 68.27**

(1) A party must comply with an order for the payment of costs within 14 days of—
 (a) the date of the judgment or order if it states the amount of those costs;
 (b) if the amount of those costs (or part of them) is decided later in accordance with Part 47, the date of the certificate which states the amount; or
 (c) in either case, such other date as the court may specify.
 (Part 47 sets out the procedure for detailed assessment of costs.)

44.8 Legal Representative's Duty to Notify the Party

r.44.8 **68.20, 68.25, 68.27**

Where—

(a) the court makes a costs order against a legally represented party; and
(b) the party is not present when the order is made,

the party's legal representative must notify that party in writing of the costs order no later than 7 days after the legal representative receives notice of the order.
(Paragraph 10.1 of Practice Direction 44 defines 'party' for the purposes of this rule.)

44.9 Cases where Costs Orders Deemed to have been Made

r.44.9 **64.31** r.44.9(1)–(2) **68.34**

(1) Subject to paragraph (2), where a right to costs arises under—
 (a) rule 3.7 (defendant's right to costs where claim is struck out for non-payment of fees);
 (b) rule 36.10(1) or (2) (claimant's entitlement to costs where a Part 36 offer is accepted); or
 (c) rule 38.6 (defendant's right to costs where claimant discontinues),
 a costs order will be deemed to have been made on the standard basis.
(2) Paragraph 1(b) does not apply where a Part 36 offer is accepted before the commencement of proceedings.
(3) Where such an order is deemed to be made in favour of a party with pro bono representation, that party may apply for an order under section 194(3) of the 2007 Act.
(4) Interest payable under section 17 of the Judgments Act 1838 or section 74 of the County Courts Act 1984 on the costs deemed to have been ordered under paragraph (1) will begin to run from the date on which the event which gave rise to the entitlement to costs occurred.

44.10 Where the Court Makes no Order for Costs

r.44.10(1)(a) **68.29** r.44.10(3) **68.29**
r.44.10(1)(b) **68.29** r.44.10(4) **68.36**
r.44.10(2) **68.29** r.44.10(5) **68.33**

(1) Where the court makes an order which does not mention costs—
 (a) subject to paragraphs (2) and (3), the general rule is that no party is entitled—
  (i) to costs; or
  (ii) to seek an order under section 194(3) of the 2007 Act,
  in relation to that order; but
 (b) *this does not affect* any entitlement of a party to recover costs out of a fund held by that party as trustee or personal representative, or under any lease, mortgage or other security.

(2) Where the court makes—
  (a) an order granting permission to appeal;
  (b) an order granting permission to apply for judicial review; or
  (c) any other order or direction sought by a party on an application without notice,
 and its order does not mention costs, it will be deemed to include an order for applicant's costs in the case.
(3) Any party affected by a deemed order for costs under paragraph (2) may apply at any time to vary the order.
(4) The court hearing an appeal may, unless it dismisses the appeal, make orders about the costs of the proceedings giving rise to the appeal as well as the costs of the appeal.
(5) Subject to any order made by the transferring court, where proceedings are transferred from one court to another, the court to which they are transferred may deal with all the costs, including the costs before the transfer.

44.11 Court's Powers in relation to Misconduct

r.44.11 71.26 r.44.11(1)(b) 71.26

(1) The court may make an order under this rule where—
  (a) a party or that party's legal representative, in connection with a summary or detailed assessment, fails to comply with a rule, practice direction or court order; or
  (b) it appears to the court that the conduct of a party or that party's legal representative, before or during the proceedings or in the assessment proceedings, was unreasonable or improper.
(2) Where paragraph (1) applies, the court may—
  (a) disallow all or part of the costs which are being assessed; or
  (b) order the party at fault or that party's legal representative to pay costs which that party or legal representative has caused any other party to incur.
(3) Where—
  (a) the court makes an order under paragraph (2) against a legally represented party; and
  (b) the party is not present when the order is made,
 the party's legal representative must notify that party in writing of the order no later than 7 days after the legal representative receives notice of the order.

44.12 Set Off

r.44.12 63.20, 69.9, 69.11

(1)* Where a party entitled to costs is also liable to pay costs, the court may assess the costs which that party is liable to pay and either—
  (a) set off the amount assessed against the amount the party is entitled to be paid and direct that party to pay any balance; or
  (b) delay the issue of a certificate for the costs to which the party is entitled until the party has paid the amount which that party is liable to pay.

II QUALIFIED ONE-WAY COSTS SHIFTING

44.13 Qualified One-way Costs Shifting: Scope and Interpretation

r.44.13 69.3, 69.4, 77.40 r.44.13(1)(a)–(b) 68.29
r.44.13(1) 68.29, 69.4 r.44.13(2) 68.36, 69.4

(1) This Section applies to proceedings which include a claim for damages—
  (a) for personal injuries;
  (b) under the Fatal Accidents Act 1976; or
  (c) which arises out of death or personal injury and survives for the benefit of an estate by virtue of section 1(1) of the Law Reform (Miscellaneous Provisions) Act 1934,
 but does not apply to applications pursuant to section 33 of the Senior Courts Act 1981 or section 52 of the County Courts Act 1984 (applications for pre-action disclosure), or where rule 44.17 applies.

[* There is no other paragraph in r 44.12.]

(2) In this Section, 'claimant' means a person bringing a claim to which this Section applies or an estate on behalf of which such a claim is brought, and includes a person making a counterclaim or an additional claim.

44.14 Effect of Qualified One-way Costs Shifting

rr.44.14–44.16 **69.4**
r.44.14 **69.8**
r.44.14(1) **69.6, 69.7, 69.9, 69.9, 69.10, 69.11, 69.12, 69.16**
r.44.14(2) **69.10, 69.11**
r.44.13(2) **69.12**

(1) Subject to rules 44.15 and 44.16, orders for costs made against a claimant may be enforced without the permission of the court but only to the extent that the aggregate amount in money terms of such orders does not exceed the aggregate amount in money terms of any orders for damages and interest made in favour of the claimant.
(2) Orders for costs made against a claimant may only be enforced after the proceedings have been concluded and the costs have been assessed or agreed.
(3) An order for costs which is enforced only to the extent permitted by paragraph (1) shall not be treated as an unsatisfied or outstanding judgment for the purposes of any court record.

44.15 Exceptions to Qualified One-way Costs Shifting where Permission not Required

r.44.15 **5.17, 33.26, 69.6, 69.13, 69.14, 69.15, 71.58**

Orders for costs made against the claimant may be enforced to the full extent of such orders without the permission of the court where the proceedings have been struck out on the grounds that—
(a) the claimant has disclosed no reasonable grounds for bringing the proceedings;
(b) the proceedings are an abuse of the court's process; or
(c) the conduct of—
(i) the claimant; or
(ii) a person acting on the claimant's behalf and with the claimant's knowledge of such conduct,
is likely to obstruct the just disposal of the proceedings.

44.16 Exceptions to Qualified One-way Costs Shifting where Permission Required

r.44.16 **33.26, 69.6**
r.44.16(1) **69.15, 69.16**
r.44.16(2) **69.17**
r.44.16(3) **69.17**

(1) Orders for costs made against the claimant may be enforced to the full extent of such orders with the permission of the court where the claim is found on the balance of probabilities to be fundamentally dishonest.
(2) Orders for costs made against the claimant may be enforced up to the full extent of such orders with the permission of the court, and to the extent that it considers just, where—
(a) the proceedings include a claim which is made for the financial benefit of a person other than the claimant or a dependant within the meaning of section 1(3) of the Fatal Accidents Act 1976 (other than a claim in respect of the gratuitous provision of care, earnings paid by an employer or medical expenses); or
(b) a claim is made for the benefit of the claimant other than a claim to which this Section applies.
(3) Where paragraph (2)(a) applies, the court may, subject to rule 46.2, make an order for costs against a person, other than the claimant, for whose financial benefit the whole or part of the claim was made.

44.17 Transitional Provision

r.44.17 **69.3**

This Section does not apply to proceedings where the claimant has entered into a pre-commencement funding arrangement (as defined in rule 48.2).

III DAMAGES-BASED AGREEMENTS

44.18 Award of Costs where there is a Damages-based Agreement

r.44.17 **69.3**

(1) The fact that a party has entered into a damages-based agreement will not affect the making of any order for costs which otherwise would be made in favour of that party.

(2) Where costs are to be assessed in favour of a party who has entered into a damages-based agreement—

(a) the party's recoverable costs will be assessed in accordance with rule 44.3; and

(b) the party may not recover by way of costs more than the total amount payable by that party under the damages-based agreement for legal services provided under that agreement.

PD 44 Practice Direction 44 — General Rules about Costs

This practice direction supplements Part 44.

SECTION I — GENERAL

Documents and Forms

1.1 In respect of any document which is required by PD 44 to PD 47 to be signed by a party or that party's legal representative, the provisions of PD 22 relating to who may sign apply as if the document in question was a statement of truth. Statements of truth are not required in assessment proceedings unless a rule or practice direction so requires or the court so orders.
(PD 22 makes provision for cases in which a party is a child, a protected party or a company or other corporation and cases in which a document is signed on behalf of a partnership.)

1.2 Form N260 is a model form of statement of costs to be used for summary assessments.
(Further details about statements of costs are given in para. 9.5 below.)
Precedents A, B and C in the Schedule of Costs Precedents annexed to this practice direction are model forms of bills of costs to be used for detailed assessments. A party wishing to rely upon a bill which departs from the model forms should include in the background information of the bill an explanation for that departure.
(Further details about bills of costs are given in PD 47.)

Special Provisions relating to VAT

para.2.2 71.54
para.2.3 71.5, 71.54
para.2.4 71.5
para.2.5 71.54
para.2.6 71.54
para.2.7 71.54
para.2.8 71.54
para.2.9 71.54
para.2.11 71.53, 71.54
para.2.13 71.54
para.2.14 71.32

Scope of this subsection

2.1 This subsection deals with claims for VAT which are made in respect of costs being dealt with by way of summary assessment or detailed assessment.

VAT registration number

2.2 The number allocated by HMRC to every person registered under the Value Added Tax Act 1994 (except a Government Department) must appear in a prominent place at the head of every statement, bill of costs, fee sheet, account or voucher on which VAT is being included as part of a claim for costs.

Entitlement to VAT on costs

2.3 VAT should not be included in a claim for costs if the receiving party is able to recover the VAT as input tax. Where the receiving party is able to obtain credit from HMRC for a proportion of the VAT as input tax, only that proportion which is not eligible for credit should be included in the claim for costs.

2.4 The receiving party has responsibility for ensuring that VAT is claimed only when the receiving party is unable to recover the VAT or a proportion thereof as input tax.

2.5 Where there is a dispute as to whether VAT is properly claimed the receiving party must provide a certificate signed by the legal representatives or the auditors of the receiving party substantially in the form illustrated in Precedent F in the Schedule of Costs Precedents annexed to PD 47. Where the receiving party is a litigant in person who is claiming VAT, evidence to support the claim (such as a letter from HMRC) must be produced at the hearing at which the costs are assessed.

2.6 Where there is a dispute as to whether any service in respect of which a charge is proposed to be made in the bill is zero rated or exempt from VAT, reference should be made to HMRC and its view obtained and made known at the hearing at which the costs are assessed. Such enquiry should be made by the receiving party. In the case of a bill from a solicitor to the solicitor's legal representative's own client, such enquiry should be made by the client.

Form of bill of costs where VAT rate changes

2.7 Where there is a change in the rate of VAT, suppliers of goods and services are entitled by the Value Added Tax Act 1994, s. 88(1) and (2), in most circumstances to elect whether the new or the old rate of VAT should apply to a supply where the basic and actual tax points span a period during which the rate changed.

2.8 It will be assumed, unless a contrary indication is given in writing, that an election to take advantage of the provisions mentioned in para. 2.7 and to charge VAT at the lower rate has been made. In any case in which an election to charge at the lower rate is not made, such a decision must be justified to the court assessing the costs.

Apportionment

2.9 Subject to 2.7 and 2.8, all bills of costs, fees and disbursements on which VAT is included must be divided into separate parts so as to show work done before, on and after the date or dates from which any change in the rate of VAT takes effect. Where, however, a lump sum charge is made for work which spans a period during which there has been a change in VAT rates, and paras 2.7 and 2.8 above do not apply, reference should be made to paragraphs 30.7 or 30.8 of the VAT Guide (Notice 700) (or any revised edition of that notice) published by HMRC. If necessary, the lump sum should be apportioned. The totals of profit costs and disbursements in each part must be carried separately to the summary.

Change in VAT rate between the conclusion of a detailed settlement and the issue of a final certificate

2.10 Should there be a change in the rate between the conclusion of a detailed assessment and the issue of the final costs certificate, any interested party may apply for the detailed assessment to be varied so as to take account of any increase or reduction in the amount of tax payable. Once the final costs certificate has been issued, no variation under this paragraph will be permitted.

Disbursements not classified as such for VAT purposes

2.11 (1) Legal representatives often make payments to third parties for the supply of goods or services where no VAT was chargeable on the supply by the third party: for example, the cost of meals taken and travel costs. The question whether legal representatives should include VAT in respect of these payments when invoicing their clients or in claims for costs between litigants should be decided in accordance with this practice direction and with the criteria set out in the VAT Guide (Notice 700).

(2) Payments to third parties which are normally treated as part of the legal representative's overheads (for example, postage costs and telephone costs) will not be treated as disbursements. The third party supply should be included as part of the costs of the legal representatives' legal services and VAT must be added to the total bill charged to the client.

(3) Disputes may arise in respect of payments made to a third party which the legal representative shows as disbursements in the invoice delivered to the receiving party. Some payments, although correctly described as disbursements for some purposes, are not classified as disbursements for VAT purposes. Items not classified as disbursements for VAT purposes must be shown as part of the services provided by the legal representative and, therefore, VAT must be added in respect of them whether or not VAT was chargeable on the supply by the third party.

(4) Guidance as to the circumstances in which disbursements may or may not be classified as disbursements for VAT purposes is given in the VAT Guide (Notice 700, paragraph 25.1). One of the key issues is whether the third party supply—

(a) was made to the legal representative (and therefore subsumed in the onward supply of legal services); or

(b) was made direct to the receiving party (the third party having no right to demand payment from the legal representative, who makes the payment only as agent for the receiving party).

(5) Examples of payments under subpara. (4)(a) are: travelling expenses, such as an airline ticket, and subsistence expenses, such as the cost of meals, where the person travelling and receiving the meals is the legal representative. The supplies by the airline and the restaurant are supplies to the legal representative, not to the client.

(6) Payments under subpara. (4)(b) are classified as disbursements for VAT purposes and, therefore, the legal representative need not add VAT in respect of them. Simple examples are payments by a legal representative of court fees and payment of fees to an expert witness.

Litigants in person

2.12 Where a litigant acts in person, that litigant is not treated for the purposes of VAT as having supplied services and therefore no VAT is chargeable in respect of work done by that litigant (even where, for example, that litigant is a solicitor or other legal representative). Consequently in such circumstances a bill of costs should not claim any VAT.

Government departments

2.13 On an assessment between parties, where costs are being paid to a government department in respect of services rendered by its legal staff, VAT should not be added.

Payment pursuant to an order under s. 194(3) of the 2007 Act

2.14 Where an order is made under s. 194(3) of the 2007 Act, any bill presented for agreement or assessment pursuant to that order must not include a claim for VAT.

Costs Budgets

para.3.2 **43.18, 43.19**
para.3.3 **43.19**
para.3.4 **43.18**
para.3.6 **43.19**
para.3.7 **43.18, 43.19**

3.1 In any case where the parties have filed budgets in accordance with PD 3E but the court has not made a costs management order under r. 3.15, the provisions of this subsection shall apply.

3.2 If there is a difference of 20 per cent or more between the costs claimed by a receiving party on detailed assessment and the costs shown in a budget filed by that party, the receiving party must provide a statement of the reasons for the difference with the bill of costs.

3.3 If a paying party—

(a) claims to have reasonably relied on a budget filed by a receiving party; or

(b) wishes to rely upon the costs shown in the budget in order to dispute the reasonableness or proportionality of the costs claimed,

the paying party must serve a statement setting out the case in this regard in that party's points of dispute.

3.4 On an assessment of the costs of a party, the court will have regard to the last approved or agreed budget, and may have regard to any other budget previously filed by that party, or by any other party in the same proceedings. Such other budgets may be taken into account when assessing the reasonableness and proportionality of any costs claimed.

3.5 Subject to para. 3.4, paras 3.6 and 3.7 apply where there is a difference of 20 per cent or more between the costs claimed by a receiving party and the costs shown in a budget filed by that party.

3.6 Where it appears to the court that the paying party reasonably relied on the budget, the court may restrict the recoverable costs to such sum as is reasonable for the paying party to pay in the light of that reliance, notwithstanding that such sum is less than the amount of costs reasonably and proportionately incurred by the receiving party.

3.7 Where it appears to the court that the receiving party has not provided a satisfactory explanation for that difference, the court may regard the difference between the costs claimed and the costs shown in the budget as evidence that the costs claimed are unreasonable or disproportionate.

Court's Discretion as to Costs: Rule 44.2

para.4.1 **68.26**
para.4.2 **68.29**

4.1 The court may make an order about costs at any stage in a case.

4.2 There are certain costs orders which the court will commonly make in proceedings before trial. The following table sets out the general effect of these orders. The table is not an exhaustive list of the orders which the court may make.

Term	Effect
Costs Costs in any event	The party in whose favour the order is made is entitled to that party's costs in respect of the part of the proceedings to which the order relates, whatever other costs orders are made in the proceedings.
Costs in the case Costs in the application	The party in whose favour the court makes an order for costs at the end of the proceedings is entitled to that party's costs of the part of the proceedings to which the order relates.
Costs reserved	The decision about costs is deferred to a later occasion, but if no later order is made the costs will be costs in the case.
Claimant's/Defendant's costs in case/application	If the party in whose favour the costs order is made is awarded costs at the end the proceedings, that party is entitled to that party's costs of the part of the proceedings to which the order relates. If any other party is awarded costs at the end of the proceedings, the party in whose favour the final costs order is made is not liable to pay the costs of any other party in respect of the part of the proceedings to which the order relates.
Costs thrown away	Where, for example, a judgment or order is set aside, the party in whose favour the costs order is made is entitled to the costs which have been incurred as a consequence. This includes the costs of— • preparing for and attending any hearing at which the judgment or order which has been set aside was made; • preparing for and attending any hearing to set aside the judgment or order in question; • preparing for and attending any hearing at which the court orders the proceedings or the part in question to be adjourned; • any steps taken to enforce a judgment or order which has subsequently been set aside.
Costs of and caused by	Where, for example, the court makes this order on an application to amend a statement of case, the party in whose favour the costs order is made is entitled to the costs of preparing for and attending the application and the costs of any consequential amendment to his own statement of case.
Costs here and below	The party in whose favour the costs order is made is entitled not only to that party's costs in respect of the proceedings in which the court makes the order but also to that party's costs of the proceedings in any lower court. In the case of an appeal from a Divisional Court the party is not entitled to any costs incurred in any court below the Divisional Court.
No order as to costs Each party to pay own costs	Each party is to bear that party's own costs of the part of the proceedings to which the order relates whatever costs order the court makes at the end of the proceedings.

Fees of Counsel

para.5.1 **68.30** para.5.1(2) **68.30**

5.1 (1) When making an order for costs the court may state an opinion as to whether or not the hearing was fit for the attendance of one or more counsel, and, if it does so, the court conducting a detailed assessment of those costs will have regard to the opinion stated.

(2) The court will generally express an opinion only where—

(a) the paying party asks it to do so;

(b) more than one counsel appeared for a party; or

(c) the court wishes to record its opinion that the case was not fit for the attendance of counsel.

5.2 (1) Where the court refers any matter to the conveyancing counsel of the court the fees payable to counsel in respect of the work done or to be done will be assessed by the court in accordance with r. 44.2.

(2) An appeal from a decision of the court in respect of the fees of such counsel will be dealt with under the general rules as to appeals set out in Part 52. If the appeal is against the decision of an authorised court officer, it will be dealt with in accordance with rr. 47.22 to 47.24.

Basis of Assessment: Rule 44.3

Costs on the indemnity basis

6.1 If costs are awarded on the indemnity basis, the court assessing costs will disallow any costs—
(a) which it finds to have been unreasonably incurred; or
(b) which it considers to be unreasonable in amount.

Costs on the standard basis

6.2 If costs are awarded on the standard basis, the court assessing costs will disallow any costs—
(a) which it finds to have been unreasonably incurred;
(b) which it considers to be unreasonable in amount;
(c) which it considers to have been disproportionately incurred or to be disproportionate in amount; or
(d) about which it has doubts as to whether they were reasonably or proportionately incurred, or whether they are reasonable and proportionate in amount.

Amount of Costs where Costs are Payable Pursuant to a Contract: Rule 44.5

paras.7.1–7.3 **68.49, 87.44**

Application of rule 44.5

7.1 Rule 44.5 only applies if the court is assessing costs payable under a contract. It does not—
(a) require the court to make an assessment of such costs; or
(b) require a mortgagee to apply for an order for those costs where there is a contractual right to recover out of the mortgage funds.

Costs relating to a mortgage

7.2 (1) The following principles apply to costs relating to a mortgage.
(2) An order for the payment of costs of proceedings by one party to another is always a discretionary order: Senior Courts Act 1981, s. 51 ('the s. 51 discretion').
(3) Where there is a contractual right to the costs, the discretion should ordinarily be exercised so as to reflect that contractual right.
(4) The power of the court to disallow a mortgagee's costs sought to be added to the mortgage security is a power that does not derive from s. 51, but from the power of the courts of equity to fix the terms on which redemption will be allowed.
(5) A decision by a court to refuse costs in whole or in part to a mortgagee may be—
(a) a decision in the exercise of the s. 51 discretion;
(b) a decision in the exercise of the power to fix the terms on which redemption will be allowed;
(c) a decision as to the extent of a mortgagee's contractual right to add the mortgagee's costs to the security; or
(d) a combination of two or more of these things.
(6) A mortgagee is not to be deprived of a contractual or equitable right to add costs to the security merely by reason of an order for payment of costs made without reference to the mortgagee's contractual or equitable rights, and without any adjudication as to whether or not the mortgagee should be deprived of those costs.

7.3 (1) Where the contract entitles a mortgagee to—
(a) add the costs of litigation relating to the mortgage to the sum secured by it; or
(b) require a mortgagor to pay those costs,
the mortgagor may make an application for the court to direct that an account of the mortgagee's costs be taken.
(Rule 25.1(1)(n) provides that the court may direct that a party file an account.)
(2) The mortgagor may then dispute an amount in the mortgagee's account on the basis that it has been unreasonably incurred or is unreasonable in amount.
(3) Where a mortgagor disputes an amount, the court may make an order that the disputed costs are assessed under r. 44.5.

Procedure for Assessing Costs: Rule 44.6

para.8.2 **68.28**

8.1 *Subject to para. 8.3*, where the court does not order fixed costs (or no fixed costs are provided for) the amount of costs payable will be assessed by the court. Rule 44.6 allows the court making an order about costs either—

(a) to make a summary assessment of the amount of the costs; or
(b) to order the amount to be decided in accordance with Part 47 (a detailed assessment).

8.2 An order for costs will be treated as an order for the amount of costs to be decided by a detailed assessment unless the order otherwise provides.

8.3 Where a party is entitled to costs some of which are fixed costs and some of which are not, the court will assess those costs which are not fixed. For example, the court will assess the disbursements payable in accordance with rr. 45.12 or 45.19. The decision whether such assessment should be summary or detailed will be made in accordance with paras 9.1 to 9.10 of this practice direction.

Summary Assessment: General Provisions

para.9.2 PC 21, PC 28, PC 30, 32.31, 46.23, 68.27, 71.32
para.9.2(b) PC 33, 75.21
para.9.3 68.27
para.9.4 32.31, 32.38
para.9.5 PC 9, PC 14, PC 16, PC 21, PC 22, PC 23, PC 24, 32.31
para.9.5(2) 46.23, 71.32
para.9.5(3) 71.5
para.9.5(4) PC 30, PC 33
para.9.6 32.31, 46.23
para.9.7 32.31
para.9.8 PC 21, 32.31, 46.23, 68.27
para.9.9 PC 21, 46.23, 68.27
para.9.9(1) PC 16, 32.31
para.9.9(2) 32.31
para.9.10 46.23, 71.3, 71.38

When the court should consider whether to make a summary assessment

9.1 Whenever a court makes an order about costs which does not provide only for fixed costs to be paid the court should consider whether to make a summary assessment of costs.

Timing of summary assessment

9.2 The general rule is that the court should make a summary assessment of the costs—
(a) at the conclusion of the trial of a case which has been dealt with on the fast track, in which case the order will deal with the costs of the whole claim; and
(b) at the conclusion of any other hearing, which has lasted not more than one day, in which case the order will deal with the costs of the application or matter to which the hearing related. If this hearing disposes of the claim, the order may deal with the costs of the whole claim,

unless there is good reason not to do so, for example where the paying party shows substantial grounds for disputing the sum claimed for costs that cannot be dealt with summarily.

Summary assessment of mortgagee's costs

9.3 The general rule in para. 9.2 does not apply to a mortgagee's costs incurred in mortgage possession proceedings or other proceedings relating to a mortgage unless the mortgagee asks the court to make an order for the mortgagee's costs to be paid by another party.

(Paragraphs 7.2 and 7.3 deal in more detail with costs relating to mortgages.)

Consent orders

9.4 Where an application has been made and the parties to the application agree an order by consent without any party attending, the parties should seek to agree a figure for costs to be inserted in the consent order or agree that there should be no order for costs.

Duty of parties and legal representatives

9.5 (1) It is the duty of the parties and their legal representatives to assist the judge in making a summary assessment of costs in any case to which para. 9.2 above applies, in accordance with the following subparagraphs.
(2) Each party who intends to claim costs must prepare a written statement of those costs showing separately in the form of a schedule—
(a) the number of hours to be claimed;
(b) the hourly rate to be claimed;
(c) the grade of fee earner;
(d) the amount and nature of any disbursement to be claimed, other than counsel's fee for appearing at the hearing;
(e) the amount of legal representative's costs to be claimed for attending or appearing at the hearing;
(f) counsel's fees; and
(g) any VAT to be claimed on these amounts.

(3) The statement of costs should follow as closely as possible Form N260 and must be signed by the party or the party's legal representative. Where a party is—
(a) an assisted person;
(b) a LSC funded client;
(c) a person for whom civil legal services (within the meaning of Part 1 of the Legal Aid, Sentencing and Punishment of Offenders Act 2012) are provided under arrangements made for the purposes of that Part of that Act; or
(d) represented by a person in the party's employment,
the statement of costs need not include the certificate appended at the end of Form N260.
(4) The statement of costs must be filed at court and copies of it must be served on any party against whom an order for payment of those costs is intended to be sought as soon as possible and in any event—
(a) for a fast track trial, not less than 2 days before the trial; and
(b) for all other hearings, not less than 24 hours before the time fixed for the hearing.

9.6 The failure by a party, without reasonable excuse, to comply with para. 9.5 will be taken into account by the court in deciding what order to make about the costs of the claim, hearing or application, and about the costs of any further hearing or detailed assessment hearing that may be necessary as a result of that failure.

No summary assessment by a costs officer

9.7 The court awarding costs cannot make an order for a summary assessment of costs by a costs officer. If a summary assessment of costs is appropriate but the court awarding costs is unable to do so on the day, the court may give directions as to a further hearing before the same judge.

Assisted persons etc.

9.8 The court will not make a summary assessment of the costs of a receiving party who is an assisted person or LSC funded client or who is a person for whom civil legal services (within the meaning of Part 1 of the Legal Aid, Sentencing and Punishment of Offenders Act 2012) are provided under arrangements made for the purposes of that Part of that Act.

Children or protected parties

9.9 (1) The court will not make a summary assessment of the costs of a receiving party who is a child or protected party within the meaning of Part 21 unless the legal representative acting for the child or protected party has waived the right to further costs (see PD 46, para. 2.1).
(2) The court may make a summary assessment of costs payable by a child or protected party.

Disproportionate or unreasonable costs

9.10 The court will not give its approval to disproportionate or unreasonable costs. When the amount of the costs to be paid has been agreed between the parties the order for costs must state that the order is by consent.

Legal Representative's Duty to Notify Party: Rule 44.8

para.10.1 68.25 para.10.3 68.25

10.1 For the purposes of r. 44.8 and para. 10.2, 'party' includes any person (for example, an insurer, a trade union or the LSC or Lord Chancellor) who has instructed the legal representative to act for the party or who is liable to pay the legal representative's fees.

10.2A legal representative who notifies a party of an order under r. 44.8 must also explain why the order came to be made.

10.3 Although r. 44.8 does not specify any sanction for breach of the rule the court may, either in the order for costs itself or in a subsequent order, require the legal representative to produce to the court evidence showing that the legal representative took reasonable steps to comply with the rule.

Court's Powers in relation to Misconduct: Rule 44.11

para.11.1 71.26 para.11.2 71.26

11.1 Before making an order under r. 44.11, the court must give the party or legal representative in question a reasonable opportunity to make written submissions or, if the legal representative so desires, to attend a hearing.

11.2 Conduct which is unreasonable or improper includes steps which are calculated to prevent or inhibit the court from furthering the overriding objective.

11.3 Although r. 44.11(3) does not specify any sanction for breach of the obligation imposed by the rule the court may, either in the order under r. 44.11(2) or in a subsequent order, require the legal representative to produce to the court evidence that the legal representative took reasonable steps to comply with the obligation.

SECTION II — QUALIFIED ONE-WAY COSTS SHIFTING

Qualified One-way Costs Shifting

para.12.2 **69.17**
para.12.3 **69.17**
para.12.4(a) **69.15**
para.12.4(b) **69.16**
para.12.4(c) **69.16**
para.12.5 **69.17**

12.1 This subsection applies to proceedings to which Section II of Part 44 applies.

12.2 Examples of claims made for the financial benefit of a person other than the claimant or a dependant within the meaning of the Fatal Accidents Act 1976, s. 1(3), within the meaning of r. 44.16(2) are subrogated claims and claims for credit hire.

12.3 'Gratuitous provision of care' within the meaning of r. 44.16(2)(a) includes the provision of personal services rendered gratuitously by persons such as relatives and friends for things such as personal care, domestic assistance, child-minding, home maintenance and decorating, gardening and chauffeuring.

12.4 In a case to which r. 44.16(1) applies (fundamentally dishonest claims)—

(a) the court will normally direct that issues arising out of an allegation that the claim is fundamentally dishonest be determined at the trial;

(b) where the proceedings have been settled, the court will not, save in exceptional circumstances, order that issues arising out of an allegation that the claim was fundamentally dishonest be determined in those proceedings;

(c) where the claimant has served a notice of discontinuance, the court may direct that issues arising out of an allegation that the claim was fundamentally dishonest be determined notwithstanding that the notice has not been set aside pursuant to r. 38.4;

(d) the court may, as it thinks fair and just, determine the costs attributable to the claim having been found to be fundamentally dishonest.

12.5 The court has power to make an order for costs against a person other than the claimant under the Senior Courts Act 1981, s. 51(3), and r. 46.2. In a case to which r. 44.16(2)(a) applies (claims for the benefit of others)—

(a) the court will usually order any person other than the claimant for whose financial benefit such a claim was made to pay all the costs of the proceedings or the costs attributable to the issues to which r. 44.16(2)(a) applies, or may exceptionally make such an order permitting the enforcement of such an order for costs against the claimant.

(b) the court may, as it thinks fair and just, determine the costs attributable to claims for the financial benefit of persons other than the claimant.

12.6 In proceedings to which r. 44.16 applies, the court will normally order the claimant or, as the case may be, the person for whose benefit a claim was made to pay costs notwithstanding that the aggregate amount in money terms of such orders exceeds the aggregate amount in money terms of any orders for damages, interest and costs made in favour of the claimant.

12.7 Assessments of costs may be on a standard or indemnity basis and may be subject to a summary or detailed assessment.

CPR Part 45 Fixed Costs

Part 45 **43.5, 43.28, 66.23, 68.34, 68.47, 70.1, 70.3, 70.7, 70.16, 71.32** [For commentary on a specific rule, please refer to the cross-references after the title of the rule.]

I FIXED COSTS

section I 70.3, 70.4

45.1 Scope of this Section

rr.45.1–45.8 70.2, 70.3
r.45(1)(1) 70.3
r.45.1(2)(a) 70.3
r.45.1(2)(b) 70.3
r.45.1(2)(c) 70.3
r.45.1(2)(d) 70.3, 70.5
r.45.1(3) 70.3
r.45.1(4) 70.4
r.45.1(2)(e) 70.3, 70.5
r.45.1(2)(f) 70.3
r.45.1(2)(g) 70.3

(1) This Section sets out the amounts which, unless the court orders otherwise, are to be allowed in respect of legal representatives' charges.
(2) This Section applies where—
  (a) the only claim is a claim for a specified sum of money where the value of the claim exceeds £25 and—
    (i) judgment in default is obtained under rule 12.4(1);
    (ii) judgment on admission is obtained under rule 14.4(3);
    (iii) judgment on admission on part of the claim is obtained under rule 14.5(6);
    (iv) summary judgment is given under Part 24;
    (v) the court has made an order to strike out a defence under rule 3.4(2)(a) as disclosing no reasonable grounds for defending the claim; or
    (vi) rule 45.4 applies;
  (b) the only claim is a claim where the court gave a fixed date for the hearing when it issued the claim and judgment is given for the delivery of goods, and the value of the claim exceeds £25;
  (c) the claim is for the recovery of land, including a possession claim under Part 55, whether or not the claim includes a claim for a sum of money and the defendant gives up possession, pays the amount claimed, if any, and the fixed commencement costs stated in the claim form;
  (d) the claim is for the recovery of land, including a possession claim under Part 55, where one of the grounds for possession is arrears of rent, for which the court gave a fixed date for the hearing when it issued the claim and judgment is given for the possession of land (whether or not the order for possession is suspended on terms) and the defendant—
    (i) has neither delivered a defence, or counterclaim, nor otherwise denied liability; or
    (ii) has delivered a defence which is limited to specifying his proposals for the payment of arrears of rent;
  (e) the claim is a possession claim under Section II of Part 55 (accelerated possession claims of land let on an assured shorthold tenancy) and a possession order is made where the defendant has neither delivered a defence, or counterclaim, nor otherwise denied liability;
  (f) the claim is a demotion claim under Section III of Part 65 or a demotion claim is made in the same claim form in which a claim for possession is made under Part 55 and that demotion claim is successful; or
  (g) a judgment creditor has taken steps under Parts 70 to 73 to enforce a judgment or order.
  (Practice Direction 7B sets out the types of case where a court will give a fixed date for a hearing when it issues a claim.)
(3) No sum in respect of legal representatives' charges will be allowed where the only claim is for a sum of money or goods not exceeding £25.
(4) Any appropriate court fee will be allowed in addition to the costs set out in this Section.
(5) The claim form may include a claim for fixed commencement costs.

45.2 Amount of Fixed Commencement Costs in a Claim for the Recovery of Money or Goods

r.45.2 70.5, 70.7

(1) The amount of fixed commencement costs in a claim to which rule 45.1(2)(a) or (b) applies—
  (a) will be calculated by reference to Table 1; and
  (b) the amount claimed, or the value of the goods claimed if specified, in the claim form is to be used for determining the band in Table 1 that applies to the claim.
(2) The amounts shown in Table 4 are to be allowed in addition, if applicable.

Table 1 Fixed costs on commencement of a claim for the recovery of money or goods

Relevant band	Where the claim form is served by the court or by any method other than personal service by the claimant	Where— • the claim form is served personally by the claimant; and • there is only one defendant	Where there is more than one defendant, for each additional defendant personally served at separate addresses by the claimant
Where— the value of the claim exceeds £25 but does not exceed £500	£50	£60	£15
Where— the value of the claim exceeds £500 but does not exceed £1,000	£70	£80	£15
Where— the value of the claim exceeds £1,000 but does not exceed £5,000; or the only claim is for delivery of goods and no value is specified or stated on the claim form	£80	£90	£15
Where— the value of the claim exceeds £5,000	£100	£110	£15

45.3 When Defendant only Liable for Fixed Commencement Costs

r.45.3 70.3

Where—

(a) the only claim is for a specified sum of money; and
(b) the defendant pays the money claimed within 14 days after being served with the particulars of claim, together with the fixed commencement costs stated in the claim form,

the defendant is not liable for any further costs unless the court orders otherwise.

45.4 Costs on Entry of Judgment in a Claim for the Recovery of Money or Goods

r.45.4 20.5, 70.3, 70.5

Where—

(a) the claimant has claimed fixed commencement costs under rule 45.2; and
(b) judgment is entered in a claim to which rule 45.1(2)(a) or (b) applies in the circumstances specified in Table 2, the amount to be included in the judgment for the claimant's legal representative's charges is the total of—
    (i) the fixed commencement costs; and
    (ii) the relevant amount shown in Table 2.

Table 2 Fixed Costs on Entry of Judgment in a claim for the recovery of money or goods

	Where the amount of the judgment exceeds £25 but does not exceed £5,000	Where the amount of the judgment exceeds £5,000
Where judgment in default of an acknowledgment of service is entered under rule 12.4(1) (entry of judgment by request on claim for money only)	£22	£30
Where judgment in default of a defence is entered under rule 12.4(1) (entry of judgment by request on claim for money only)	£25	£35
Where judgment is entered under rule 14.4 (judgment on admission), or rule 14.5 (judgment on admission of part of claim) and claimant accepts the defendant's proposal as to the manner of payment	£40	£55
Where judgment is entered under rule 14.4 (judgment on admission), or rule 14.5 (judgment on admission of part of claim) and court decides the date or time of payment	£55	£70
Where summary judgment is given under Part 24 or the court strikes out a defence under rule 3.4(2)(a), in either case, on application by a party	£175	£210
Where judgment is given on a claim for delivery of goods under a regulated agreement within the meaning of the Consumer Credit Act 1974 and no other entry in this table applies	£60	£85

45.5 Amount of Fixed Commencement Costs in a Claim for the Recovery of Land or a Demotion Claim

r.45.5 70.3, 70.5

(1) The amount of fixed commencement costs in a claim to which rule 45.1(2)(c), (d) or (f) applies will be calculated by reference to Table 3.
(2) The amounts shown in Table 4 are to be allowed in addition, if applicable.

Table 3 Fixed costs on commencement of a claim for the recovery of land or a demotion claim

Where the claim form is served by the court or by any method other than personal service by the claimant	Where— • the claim form is served personally by the claimant; and • there is only one defendant	Where there is more than one defendant, for each additional defendant personally served at separate addresses by the claimant
£69.50	£77.00	£15.00

45.6 Costs on Entry of Judgment in a Claim for the Recovery of Land or a Demotion Claim

r.45.6(1) 70.5 r.45.6(2) 70.5

(1) Where—
(a) the claimant has claimed fixed commencement costs under rule 45.5; and
(b) judgment is entered in a claim to which rule 45.1(2)(d) or (f) applies, the amount to be included in the judgment for the claimant's legal representative's charges is the total of—
(i) the fixed commencement costs; and
(ii) the sum of £57.25.

(2) Where an order for possession is made in a claim to which rule 45.1(2)(e) applies, the amount allowed for the claimant's legal representative's charges for preparing and filing—
(a) the claim form;
(b) the documents that accompany the claim form; and
(c) the request for possession,
is £79.50.

45.7 Miscellaneous Fixed Costs

r.45.7 70.5

Table 4 shows the amount to be allowed in respect of legal representative's charges in the circumstances mentioned.

Table 4 Miscellaneous Fixed Costs

For service by a party of any document other than the claim form required to be served personally including preparing and copying a certificate of service for each individual served	£15.00
Where service by an alternative method or at an alternative place is permitted by an order under rule 6.15 for each individual served	£53.25
Where a document is served out of the jurisdiction—	
(a) in Scotland, Northern Ireland, the Isle of Man or the Channel Islands;	£68.25
(b) in any other place	£77.00

45.8 Fixed Enforcement Costs

r.45.8 70.3, 70.5

Table 5 shows the amount to be allowed in respect of legal representatives' costs in the circumstances mentioned. The amounts shown in Table 4 are to be allowed in addition, if applicable.

Table 5 Fixed Enforcement Costs

For an application under rule 70.5(4) that an award may be enforced as if payable under a court order, where the amount outstanding under the award:	
exceeds £25 but does not exceed £250	£30.75
exceeds £250 but does not exceed £600	£41.00
exceeds £600 but does not exceed £2,000	£69.50
exceeds £2,000	£75.50
On attendance to question a judgment debtor (or officer of a company or other corporation) who has been ordered to attend court under rule 71.2 where the questioning takes place before a court officer, including attendance by a responsible representative of the legal representative	for each half hour or part, £15.00
On the making of a final third party debt order under rule 72.8(6)(a) or an order for the payment to the judgment creditor of money in court under rule 72.10(1)(b):	
if the amount recovered is less than £150	one-half of the amount recovered
otherwise	£98.50
On the making of a final charging order under rule 73.8(2)(a):	£110.00 The court may also allow reasonable disbursements in respect of search fees and the registration of the order.
Where a certificate is issued and registered under Schedule 6 to the Civil Jurisdiction and Judgments Act 1982, the costs of registration	£39.00

Where permission is given under RSC Order 45, rule 3 to enforce a judgment or order giving possession of land and costs are allowed on the judgment or order, the amount to be added to the judgment or order for costs—	
(a) basic costs	£42.50
(b) where notice of the proceedings is to be to more than one person, for each additional person	£2.75
Where a writ of execution as defined in the RSC Order 46, rule 1, is issued against any party	£51.75
Where a request is filed for the issue of a warrant of execution under CCR Order 26, rule 1, for a sum exceeding £25	£2.25
Where an application for an attachment of earnings order is made and costs are allowed under CCR Order 27, rule 9 or CCR Order 28, rule 10, for each attendance on the hearing of the application	£8.50

II ROAD TRAFFIC ACCIDENTS — FIXED RECOVERABLE COSTS

section II, rr.45.9–45.15 **5.8, 68.2, 70.8, 70.9, 70.10, 70.15, 71.30, 71.60**

45.9 Scope and Interpretation

r.45.9(2)(b) **70.8**
r.45.9(2)(c) **70.8**
r.45.9(2)(d) **70.8**
r.45.9(4) **70.8**

(1) Subject to paragraph (3), this Section sets out the costs which are to be allowed in—
(a) proceedings to which rule 46.14(1) applies (costs-only proceedings); or
(b) proceedings for approval of a settlement or compromise under rule 21.10(2),
in cases to which this Section applies.
(2) This Section applies where—
(a) the dispute arises from a road traffic accident occurring on or after 6 October 2003;
(b) the agreed damages include damages in respect of personal injury, damage to property, or both;
(c) the total value of the agreed damages does not exceed £10,000; and
(d) if a claim had been issued for the amount of the agreed damages, the small claims track would not have been the normal track for that claim.
(3) This Section does not apply where—
(a) the claimant is a litigant in person; or
(b) Section III of this Part applies.
(4) In this Section—
(a) 'road traffic accident' means an accident resulting in bodily injury to any person or damage to property caused by, or arising out of, the use of a motor vehicle on a road or other public place in England and Wales;
(b) 'motor vehicle' means a mechanically propelled vehicle intended for use on roads; and
(c) 'road' means any highway and any other road to which the public has access and includes bridges over which a road passes.

45.10 Application of Fixed Recoverable Costs

r.45.10 **70.9, 70.15**

Subject to rule 45.13, the only costs which are to be allowed are-
(a) fixed recoverable costs calculated in accordance with rule 45.11; and
(b) disbursements allowed in accordance with rule 45.12.
(Rule 45.13 provides for where a party issues a claim for more than the fixed recoverable costs.)

45.11 Amount of Fixed Recoverable Costs

r.45.11 **70.2, 70.15**
r.45.11(1) **70.9, 70.10**
r.45.11(2) **70.10, 70.12**
r.45.11(3) **70.9, 70.10**

(1) Subject to paragraphs (2) and (3), the amount of fixed recoverable costs is the total of—
  (a) £800;
  (b) 20% of the damages agreed up to £5,000; and
  (c) 15% of the damages agreed between £5,000 and £10,000.
(2) Where the claimant—
  (a) lives or works in an area set out in Practice Direction 45; and
  (b) instructs a legal representative who practises in that area,
  the fixed recoverable costs will include, in addition to the costs specified in paragraph (1), an amount equal to 12.5% of the costs allowable under that paragraph.
(3) Where appropriate, VAT may be recovered in addition to the amount of fixed recoverable costs and any reference in this Section to fixed recoverable costs is a reference to those costs net of any such VAT.

45.12 Disbursements

r.45.12 **70.13, 70.15**
r.45.12(1) **70.9**
r.45.12(2) **70.9**

(1) The court—
  (a) may allow a claim for a disbursement of a type mentioned in paragraph (2); but
  (b) will not allow a claim for any other type of disbursement.
(2) The disbursements referred to in paragraph (1) are—
  (a) the cost of obtaining—
    (i) medical records;
    (ii) a medical report;
    (iii) a police report;
    (iv) an engineer's report; or
    (v) a search of the records of the Driver Vehicle Licensing Authority;*
  (b) where they are necessarily incurred by reason of one or more of the claimants being a child or protected party as defined in Part 21—
    (i) fees payable for instructing counsel; or
    (ii) court fees payable on an application to the court; or
  (c) any other disbursement that has arisen due to a particular feature of the dispute.

45.13 Claims for an Amount of Costs Exceeding Fixed Recoverable Costs

r.45.13(1) **70.10, 70.14**
r.45.13(2) **70.14**

(1) The court will entertain a claim for an amount of costs (excluding any success fee or disbursements) greater than the fixed recoverable costs but only if it considers that there are exceptional circumstances making it appropriate to do so.
(2) If the court considers such a claim appropriate, it may—
  (a) summarily assess the costs; or
  (b) make an order for the costs to be subject to detailed assessment.
(3) If the court does not consider the claim appropriate, it will make an order for fixed recoverable costs (and any permitted disbursements) only.

45.14 Failure to Achieve Costs Greater than Fixed Recoverable Costs

r.45.14 **70.14, 70.15**

(1) This rule applies where—
  (a) costs are assessed in accordance with rule 45.13(2); and
  (b) the court assesses the costs (excluding any VAT) as being an amount which is less than 20% greater than the amount of the fixed recoverable costs.

[* *Sic.* The correct title is the Driver and Vehicle Licensing Agency.]

(2) The court must order the defendant to pay to the claimant the lesser of—
(a) the fixed recoverable costs; and
(b) the assessed costs.

45.15 Costs of the Costs-only Proceedings or the Detailed Assessment

r.45.15 **8.44, 70.14, 70.15** r.45.15(7) **71.18**

Where—

(a) the court makes an order for fixed recoverable costs in accordance with rule 45.13(3); or
(b) rule 45.14 applies, the court may—
(i) decide not to make an award of the payment of the claimant's costs in bringing the proceedings under rule 46.14; and
(ii) make orders in relation to costs that may include an order that the claimant pay the defendant's costs of defending those proceedings.

III PRE-ACTION PROTOCOL FOR LOW VALUE PERSONAL INJURY CLAIMS IN ROAD TRAFFIC ACCIDENTS

section III, rr.45.16–45.27 **8.56, 13.4, 71.60** rr.45.16–45.28 **5.8, 70.16**

45.16 Scope and Interpretation

(1) This Section applies to claims that have been or should have been started under Part 8 in accordance with Practice Direction 8B ('the Stage 3 Procedure').
(2) Where a party has not complied with the RTA Protocol rule 45.24 will apply.
'RTA Protocol' means the Pre-Action Protocol for Low Value Personal Injury Claims in Road Traffic Accidents.
(3) A reference to 'Claim Notification Form' is a reference to the form used in the RTA Protocol.

45.17 Application of Fixed Costs, and Disbursements

r.45.17 **70.16**

The only costs allowed are-
(a) fixed costs in rule 45.18; and
(b) disbursements in accordance with rule 45.19.

45.18 Amount of Fixed Costs

r.45.18 **70.2, 70.5, 70.16**

(1) Subject to paragraph (4), the amount of fixed costs is set out in Table 6.
(2) In Table 6—
'Type A fixed costs' means the legal representative's costs;
'Type B fixed costs' means the advocate's costs; and
'Type C fixed costs' means the costs for the advice on the amount of damages where the claimant is a child.
(3) 'Advocate' has the same meaning as in rule 45.37(2)(a).
(4) Subject to rule 45.24(2) the court will not award more or less than the amounts shown in Table 1.*
(5) Where the claimant—
(a) lives or works in an area set out in Practice Direction 45; and
(b) instructs a legal representative who practises in that area,
the fixed costs will include, in addition to the costs set out in Table 6, an amount equal to 12.5% of the Stage 1 and 2 and Stage 3 Type A fixed costs.

[* *Sic.* The reference should be to Table 6.]

Table 6 Fixed costs in relation to the RTA Protocol

Stage 1 fixed costs		£200
Stage 2 fixed costs		£300
Stage 3—		
	Type A fixed costs	£250
	Type B fixed costs	£250
	Type C fixed costs	£150

(6) Where appropriate, value added tax (VAT) may be recovered in addition to the amount of fixed costs and any reference in this Section to fixed costs is a reference to those costs net of any such VAT.

45.19 Disbursements

r.45.19 **70.16** r.45.19(2)(a) **8.45**

(1) The court—
  (a) may allow a claim for a disbursement of a type mentioned in paragraph (2); but
  (b) will not allow a claim for any other type of disbursement.
(2) The disbursements referred to in paragraph (1) are—
  (a) the cost of obtaining—
    (i) medical records;
    (ii) a medical report or reports as provided for in the RTA Protocol;
    (iii) an engineer's report;
    (iv) a search of the records of the—
      (aa) Driver Vehicle Licensing Authority;*
      (bb) Motor Insurance Database;
  (b) court fees as a result of Part 21 being applicable;
  (c) court fees payable where proceedings are started as a result of a limitation period that is about to expire;
  (d) court fees in respect of the Stage 3 Procedure;
  (e) any other disbursement that has arisen due to a particular feature of the dispute.

45.20 Where the Claimant Obtains Judgment for an Amount more than the Defendant's RTA Protocol Offer

rr.45.20–45.22 **6.13** r.45.20(2)(a)(i) **6.12**
r.45.20 **8.58, 66.52** r.45.20(2)(a)(iii) **6.12**

Where rule 36.21(1)(b) or (c) applies, the court will order the defendant to pay—
(a) where not already paid by the defendant, the Stage 1 and 2 fixed costs;
(b) where the claim is determined—
  (i) on the papers, Stage 3 Type A fixed costs;
  (ii) at a Stage 3 hearing, Stage 3 Type A and B fixed costs; or
  (iii) at a Stage 3 hearing and the claimant is a child, Type A, B and C fixed costs; and
(c) disbursements allowed in accordance with rule 45.19.

45.21 Settlement at Stage 2 where the Claimant is a Child

r.45.21 **70.2**

(1) This rule applies where—
  (a) the claimant is a child;
  (b) there is a settlement at Stage 2 of the RTA Protocol; and
  (c) an application is made to the court to approve the settlement.
(2) Where the court approves the settlement at a settlement hearing it will order the defendant to pay—
  (a) the Stage 1 and 2 fixed costs;
  (b) the Stage 3 Type A, B and C fixed costs; and
  (c) disbursements allowed in accordance with rule 45.19.

[* *Sic.* The correct title is the Driver and Vehicle Licensing Agency.]

(3) Where the court does not approve the settlement at a settlement hearing it will order the defendant to pay the Stage 1 and 2 fixed costs.
(4) Paragraphs (5) and (6) apply where the court does not approve the settlement at the first settlement hearing but does approve the settlement at a second settlement hearing.
(5) At the second settlement hearing the court will order the defendant to pay—
 (a) the Stage 3 Type A and C fixed costs for the first settlement hearing;
 (b) disbursements allowed in accordance with rule 45.19; and
 (c) the Stage 3 Type B fixed costs for one of the hearings.
(6) The court in its discretion may also order—
 (a) the defendant to pay an additional amount of either or both the Stage 3—
  (i) Type A fixed costs;
  (ii) Type B fixed costs; or
 (b) the claimant to pay an amount equivalent to either or both the Stage 3—
  (i) Type A fixed costs;
  (ii) Type B fixed costs.

45.22 Settlement at Stage 3 where the Claimant is a Child

r.45.23B 70.16

(1) This rule applies where—
 (a) the claimant is a child;
 (b) there is a settlement after proceedings are started under the Stage 3 Procedure;
 (c) the settlement is more than the defendant's RTA Protocol offer; and
 (d) an application is made to the court to approve the settlement.
(2) Where the court approves the settlement at the settlement hearing it will order the defendant to pay—
 (a) the Stage 1 and 2 fixed costs;
 (b) the Stage 3 Type A, B and C fixed costs; and
 (c) disbursements allowed in accordance with rule 45.19.
(3) Where the court does not approve the settlement at the settlement hearing it will order the defendant to pay the Stage 1 and 2 fixed costs.
(4) Paragraphs (5) and (6) apply where the court does not approve the settlement at the first settlement hearing but does approve the settlement at the Stage 3 hearing.
(5) At the Stage 3 hearing the court will order the defendant to pay—
 (a) the Stage 3 Type A and C fixed costs for the settlement hearing;
 (b) disbursements allowed in accordance with rule 45.19; and
 (c) the Stage 3 Type B fixed costs for one of the hearings.
(6) The court in its discretion may also order—
 (a) he* defendant to pay an additional amount of either or both the Stage 3—
  (i) Type A fixed costs;
  (ii) Type B fixed costs; or
 (b) the claimant to pay an amount equivalent to either or both of the Stage 3—
  (i) Type A fixed costs;
  (ii) Type B fixed costs.
(7) Where the settlement is not approved at the Stage 3 hearing the court will order the defendant to pay the Stage 3 Type A fixed costs.

45.23 Where the Court Orders that the Claim is not Suitable to be Determined under the Stage 3 Procedure and the Claimant is a Child

r.45.23B 70.16

Where—
(a) the claimant is a child; and
(b) at a settlement hearing or the Stage 3 hearing the court orders that the claim is not suitable to be determined under the Stage 3 Procedure,

[* *Sic.* 'he' should be 'the'.]

the court will order the defendant to pay—
(i) the Stage 1 and 2 fixed costs; and
(ii) the Stage 3 Type A, B and C fixed costs.

45.24 Failure to Comply or Electing not to Continue with the RTA Protocol — Costs Consequences

(1) This rule applies where the claimant—
(a) does not comply with the process set out in the RTA Protocol; or
(b) elects not to continue with that process,
and starts proceedings under Part 7.
(2) Where a judgment is given in favour of the claimant but—
(a) the court determines that the defendant did not proceed with the process set out in the RTA Protocol because the claimant provided insufficient information on the Claim Notification Form;
(b) the court considers that the claimant acted unreasonably—
(i) by discontinuing the process set out in the RTA Protocol and starting proceedings under Part 7;
(ii) by valuing the claim at more than £10,000, so that the claimant did not need to comply with the RTA Protocol; or
(iii) except for paragraph (2)(a), in any other way that caused the process in the RTA Protocol to be discontinued; or
(c) the claimant did not comply with the RTA Protocol at all despite the claim falling within the scope of the RTA Protocol,
the court may order the defendant to pay no more than the fixed costs in rule 45.18 together with the disbursements allowed in accordance with rule 45.19.
(3) Where the claimant starts proceedings under paragraph 7.22 of the RTA Protocol and the court orders the defendant to make an interim payment of no more than the interim payment made under paragraph 7.14(2) or (3) of that Protocol the court will, on the final determination of the proceedings, order the defendant to pay no more than—
(a) the Stage 1 and 2 fixed costs; and
(b) the disbursements allowed in accordance with rule 45.19.

45.25 Where the Parties have Settled after Proceedings have Started

(1) This rule applies where an application is made under rule 45.29 (costs-only application after a claim is started under Part 8 in accordance with Practice Direction 8B).
(2) Where the settlement is more than the defendant's RTA Protocol offer the court will order the defendant to pay—
(a) the Stage 1 and 2 fixed costs where not already paid by the defendant;
(b) the Stage 3 Type A fixed costs; and
(c) disbursements allowed in accordance with rule 45.19.
(3) Where the settlement is less than or equal to the defendant's RTA Protocol offer the court will order the defendant to pay—
(a) the Stage 1 and 2 fixed costs where not already paid by the defendant; and
(b) disbursements allowed in accordance with rule 45.19.
(4) The court may, in its discretion, order either party to pay the costs of the application.

45.26 Where the Claimant Obtains Judgment for an Amount equal to or less than the Defendant's RTA Protocol Offer

r.45.26 **8.58, 66.52**

Where rule 36.21(1)(a) applies, the court will order the claimant to pay-
(a) where the claim is determined—
(i) on the papers, Stage 3 Type A fixed costs; or
(ii) at a hearing, Stage 3 Type A and B fixed costs;
(b) any Stage 3 disbursements allowed in accordance with rule 45.19.

45.27 Adjournment

Where the court adjourns a settlement hearing or a Stage 3 hearing it may, in its discretion, order a party to pay—
(a) an additional amount of the Stage 3 Type B fixed costs; and
(b) any court fee for that adjournment.

45.28 Account of Payment of Stage 1 Fixed Costs

Where a claim no longer continues under the RTA Protocol the court will, when making any order as to costs including an order for fixed recoverable costs under Section II of this Part, take into account the Stage 1 fixed costs that have been paid by the defendant.

45.29 Costs-only Application after a Claim is Started under Part 8 in accordance with Practice Direction 8B

r.45.29 45.28 rr.45.29A–L 70.16

(1) This rule sets out the procedure where—
(a) the parties to a dispute have reached an agreement on all issues (including which party is to pay the costs) which is made or confirmed in writing; but
(b) they have failed to agree the amount of those costs; and
(c) proceedings have been started under Part 8 in accordance with Practice Direction 8B.
(2) Either party may make an application for the court to determine the costs.
(3) Where an application is made under this rule the court will assess the costs in accordance with rule 45.22 or rule 45.25.
(4) Rule 44.5 (amount of costs where costs are payable pursuant to a contract) does not apply to an application under this rule.

IV SCALE COSTS FOR CLAIMS IN A PATENTS COUNTY COURT

section IV 71.60

45.30 Scope and Interpretation

rr.45.30–45.32 70.17 r.45.30(2) 70.17
rr.45.30–45.36 43.5

(1) Subject to paragraph (2), this Section applies to proceedings in a patents county court.
(2) This Section does not apply where—
(a) the court considers that a party has behaved in a manner which amounts to an abuse of the court's process; or
(b) the claim concerns the infringement or revocation of a patent or registered design the validity of which has been certified by a court in earlier proceedings.
(3) The court will make a summary assessment of the costs of the party in whose favour any order for costs is made. Rules 44.2(8), 44.7(b) and Part 47 do not apply to this Section.
(4) 'Scale costs' means the costs set out in Table A and Table B of the Practice Direction supplementing this Part.

45.31 Amount of Scale Costs

r.45.31 6.12 r.45.31(5) 70.17
r.45.31(1) 70.17

(1) Subject to rule 45.32, the court will not order a party to pay total costs of more than—
(a) £50,000 on the final determination of a claim in relation to liability; and
(b) £25,000 on an inquiry as to damages or account of profits.
(2) The amounts in paragraph (1) apply after the court has applied the provision on set off in accordance with rule 44.12(a).
(3) The maximum amount of scale costs that the court will award for each stage of the claim is set out in Practice Direction 45.
(4) The amount of the scale costs awarded by the court in accordance with paragraph (3) will depend on the nature and complexity of the claim.
(5) Where appropriate, value added tax (VAT) may be recovered in addition to the amount of the scale costs and any reference in this Section to scale costs is a reference to those costs net of any such VAT.

45.32 Summary Assessment of the Costs of an Application where a Party has Behaved Unreasonably

Costs awarded to a party under rule 63.26(2) are in addition to the total costs that may be awarded to that party under rule 45.31.

V FIXED COSTS: HM REVENUE AND CUSTOMS

rr.45.33–45.36 70.17

45.33 Scope, Interpretation and Application

(1) This Section sets out the amounts which, unless the court orders otherwise, are to be allowed in respect of HM Revenue and Customs charges in the cases to which this Section applies.
(2) For the purpose of this Section—
 (a) 'HMRC Officer' means a person appointed by the Commissioners under section 2 of the Commissioners for Revenue and Customs Act 2005 and authorised to conduct county court proceedings for recovery of debt under section 25(1A) of that Act;
 (b) 'Commissioners' means commissioners for HMRC appointed under section 1 of the Commissioners for Revenue and Customs Act 2005;
 (c) 'debt' means any sum payable to the Commissioners under or by virtue of an enactment or under a contract settlement; and
 (d) 'HMRC charges' means the fixed costs set out in Tables 7 and 8 in this Section.
(3) HMRC charges must, for the purpose of this Section, be claimed as 'legal representative's costs' on relevant court forms.
(4) This Section applies where the only claim is a claim conducted by an HMRC Officer in the county court for recovery of a debt and the Commissioners obtain judgment on the claim.
(5) Any appropriate court fee will be allowed in addition to the costs set out in this Section.
(6) The claim form may include a claim for fixed commencement costs.

45.34 Amount of Fixed Commencement Costs in a County Court Claim for the Recovery of Money

r.45.34 70.5

The amount of fixed commencement costs in a claim to which rule 45.33 applies—
(a) will be calculated by reference to Table 7; and

Table 7 Fixed costs on commencement of a County Court claim conducted by an HMRC Officer

Where the value of the claim does not exceed £25	Nil
Where the value of the claim exceeds £25 but does not exceed £500	£33
Where the value of the claim exceeds £500 but does not exceed £1,000	£47
Where the value of the claim exceeds £1,000 but does not exceed £5,000	£53
Where the value of the claim exceeds £5,000 but does not exceed £15,000	£67
Where the value of the claim exceeds £15,000 but does not exceed £50,000	£90
Where the value of the claim exceeds £50,000 but does not exceed £100,000	£113
Where the value of the claim exceeds £100,000 but does not exceed £150,000	£127
Where the value of the claim exceeds £150,000 but does not exceed £200,000	£140
Where the value of the claim exceeds £200,000 but does not exceed £250,000	£153
Where the value of the claim exceeds £250,000 but does not exceed £300,000	£167
Where the value of the claim exceeds £300,000	£180

(b) the amount claimed in the claim form is to be used for determining which claim band in Table 7 applies.

45.35 Costs on Entry of Judgment in a County Court Claim for Recovery of Money

r.45.35 70.5

Where—
(a) an HMRC Officer has claimed fixed commencement costs under Rule 45.34; and
(b) judgment is entered in a claim to which rule 45.33 applies,
the amount to be included in the judgment for HMRC charges is the total of—
(i) the fixed commencement costs; and
(ii) the amount in Table 8 relevant to the value of the claim.

Table 8 Fixed costs on entry of judgment in a County Court claim conducted by an HMRC Officer

Where the value of the claim does not exceed £5,000	£15
Where the value of the claim exceeds £5,000	£20

45.36 When the Defendant is only Liable for Fixed Commencement Costs

r.45.36 43.5

Where—
(a) the only claim is for a specified sum of money; and
(b) the defendant pays the money claimed within 14 days after service of the particulars of claim, together with the fixed commencement costs stated in the claim form,
the defendant is not liable for any further costs unless the court orders otherwise.

VI FAST TRACK TRIAL COSTS

45.37 Scope of this Section

r.45.37 70.2

(1) This Section deals with the amount of costs which the court may award as the costs of an advocate for preparing for and appearing at the trial of a claim in the fast track (referred to in this rule as 'fast track trial costs').
(2) For the purposes of this Section—
(a) 'advocate' means a person exercising a right of audience as a representative of, or on behalf of, a party;
(b) 'fast track trial costs' means the costs of a party's advocate for preparing for and appearing at the trial, but does not include—
(i) any other disbursements; or
(ii) any value added tax payable on the fees of a party's advocate; and
(c) 'trial' includes a hearing where the court decides an amount of money or the value of goods following a judgment under Part 12 (default judgment) or Part 14 (admissions) but does not include—
(i) the hearing of an application for summary judgment under Part 24; or
(ii) the court's approval of a settlement or other compromise under rule 21.10.

45.38 Amount of Fast Track Trial Costs

r.45.38 42.27, 46.23, 70.2, 70.5, 71.7
r.45.38(2) 71.7
r.45.38(3) 71.7
r.45.38(4) 71.7
r.45.38(6) 71.7

(1) Table 9 shows the amount of fast track trial costs which the court may award (whether by summary or detailed assessment).

Table 9

Value of the claim	Amount of fast track trial costs which the court may award
No more than £3,000	£485
More than £3,000 but not more than £10,000	£690
More than £10,000 but not more than £15,000	£1,035
For proceedings issued on or after 6th April 2009, more than £15,000	£1,650

(2) The court may not award more or less than the amount shown in the table except where—
(a) it decides not to award any fast track trial costs; or
(b) rule 45.39 applies,
but the court may apportion the amount awarded between the parties to reflect their respective degrees of success on the issues at trial.
(3) Where the only claim is for the payment of money—
(a) for the purpose of quantifying fast track trial costs awarded to a claimant, the value of the claim is the total amount of the judgment excluding—
(i) interest and costs; and
(ii) any reduction made for contributory negligence.
(b) for the purpose of quantifying fast track trial costs awarded to a defendant, the value of the claim is—
(i) the amount specified in the claim form (excluding interest and costs);
(ii) if no amount is specified, the maximum amount which the claimant reasonably expected to recover according to the statement of value included in the claim form under rule 16.3; or
(iii) more than £15,000, if the claim form states that the claimant cannot reasonably say how much is likely to be recovered.
(4) Where the claim is only for a remedy other than the payment of money, the value of the claim is deemed to be more than £3,000 but not more than £10,000, unless the court orders otherwise.
(5) Where the claim includes both a claim for the payment of money and for a remedy other than the payment of money, the value of the claim is deemed to be the higher of—
(a) the value of the money claim decided in accordance with paragraph (3); or
(b) the deemed value of the other remedy decided in accordance with paragraph (4),
unless the court orders otherwise.
(6) Where—
(a) a defendant has made a counterclaim against the claimant;
(b) the counterclaim has a higher value than the claim; and
(c) the claimant succeeds at trial both on the claim and the counterclaim,
for the purpose of quantifying fast track trial costs awarded to the claimant, the value of the claim is the value of the defendant's counterclaim calculated in accordance with this rule.

45.39 Power to Award More or Less than the Amount of Fast Track Trial Costs

r.45.39 71.7
r.45.39(2) 71.7
r.45.39(3) 71.8
r.45.39(4) 71.8
r.45.39(6) 71.7
r.45.39(7) 71.8
r.45.39(8) 71.8

(1) This rule sets out when a court may award—
(a) an additional amount to the amount of fast track trial costs shown in Table 9 in rule 45.38(1); or
(b) less than those amounts.
(2) If—
(a) in addition to the advocate, a party's legal representative attends the trial;
(b) the court considers that it was necessary for a legal representative to attend to assist the advocate; and
(c) the court awards fast track trial costs to that party,
the court may award an additional £345 in respect of the legal representative's attendance at the trial.
(3) If the court considers that it is necessary to direct a separate trial of an issue then the court may award an additional amount in respect of the separate trial but that amount is limited in accordance with paragraph (4) of this rule.
(4) The additional amount the court may award under paragraph (3) will not exceed two-thirds of the amount payable for that claim, subject to a minimum award of £485.
(5) Where the party to whom fast track trial costs are to be awarded is a litigant in person, the court will award—
(a) if the litigant in person can prove financial loss, two-thirds of the amount that would otherwise be awarded; or

(b) if the litigant in person fails to prove financial loss, an amount in respect of the time spent reasonably doing the work at the rate specified in Practice Direction 46.

(6) Where a defendant has made a counterclaim against the claimant, and—

(a) the claimant has succeeded on his claim; and

(b) the defendant has succeeded on his counterclaim,

the court will quantify the amount of the award of fast track trial costs to which—

(i) but for the counterclaim, the claimant would be entitled for succeeding on his claim; and

(ii) but for the claim, the defendant would be entitled for succeeding on his counterclaim,

and make one award of the difference, if any, to the party entitled to the higher award of costs.

(7) Where the court considers that the party to whom fast track trial costs are to be awarded has behaved unreasonably or improperly during the trial, it may award that party an amount less than would otherwise be payable for that claim, as it considers appropriate.

(8) Where the court considers that the party who is to pay the fast track trial costs has behaved improperly during the trial the court may award such additional amount to the other party as it considers appropriate.

45.40 Fast Track Trial Costs where there is More than One Claimant or Defendant

r.45.40 71.7

(1) Where the same advocate is acting for more than one party—

(a) the court may make only one award in respect of fast track trial costs payable to that advocate; and

(b) the parties for whom the advocate is acting are jointly entitled to any fast track trial costs awarded by the court.

(2) Where—

(a) the same advocate is acting for more than one claimant; and

(b) each claimant has a separate claim against the defendant,

the value of the claim, for the purpose of quantifying the award in respect of fast track trial costs is to be ascertained in accordance with paragraph (3).

(3) The value of the claim in the circumstances mentioned in paragraph (2) or (5) is—

(a) where the only claim of each claimant is for the payment of money—

(i) if the award of fast track trial costs is in favour of the claimants, the total amount of the judgment made in favour of all the claimants jointly represented; or

(ii) if the award is in favour of the defendant, the total amount claimed by the claimants,

and in either case, quantified in accordance with rule 45.38(3);

(b) where the only claim of each claimant is for a remedy other than the payment of money, deemed to be more than £3,000 but not more than £10,000; and

(c) where claims of the claimants include both a claim for the payment of money and for a remedy other than the payment of money, deemed to be—

(i) more than £3,000 but not more than £10,000; or

(ii) if greater, the value of the money claims calculated in accordance with subparagraph (a) above.

(4) Where—

(a) there is more than one defendant; and

(b) any or all of the defendants are separately represented,

the court may award fast track trial costs to each party who is separately represented.

(5) Where—

(a) there is more than one claimant; and

(b) a single defendant,

the court may make only one award to the defendant of fast track trial costs, for which the claimants are jointly and severally liable.

(6) For the purpose of quantifying the fast track trial costs awarded to the single defendant under paragraph (5), the value of the claim is to be calculated in accordance with paragraph (3) of this rule.

VII COSTS LIMITS IN AARHUS CONVENTION CLAIMS

rr.45.41–45.44 **70.19**

45.41 Scope and Interpretation

r.45.41 **44.13**

(1) This Section provides for the costs which are to be recoverable between the parties in Aarhus Convention claims.
(2) In this Section, 'Aarhus Convention claim' means a claim for judicial review of a decision, act or omission all or part of which is subject to the provisions of the UNECE Convention on Access to Information, Public Participation in Decision-Making and Access to Justice in Environmental Matters done at Aarhus, Denmark on 25 June 1998, including a claim which proceeds on the basis that the decision, act or omission, or part of it, is so subject.

(Rule 52.9A makes provision in relation to costs of an appeal.)

[Rules 45.41 to 45.44 do not apply in relation to a claim commenced before 1 April 2013 (SI 2013/262, r. 22(8)).]

45.42 Opting Out

r.45.42 **44.13** r.45.42(a) **70.19**

Rules 45.43 to 45.44 do not apply where the claimant—

(a) has not stated in the claim form that the claim is an Aarhus Convention claim; or
(b) has stated in the claim form that—
 (i) the claim is not an Aarhus Convention claim, or
 (ii) although the claim is an Aarhus Convention claim, the claimant does not wish those rules to apply.

45.43 Limit on Costs Recoverable from a Party in an Aarhus Convention Claim

r.45.43 **44.13**

(1) Subject to rule 45.44, a party to an Aarhus Convention claim may not be ordered to pay costs exceeding the amount prescribed in Practice Direction 45.
(2) Practice Direction 45 may prescribe a different amount for the purpose of paragraph (1) according to the nature of the claimant.

45.44 Challenging whether the Claim is an Aarhus Convention Claim

r.45.44(1) **44.13, 70.19** r.45.44(2) **44.13**

(1) If the claimant has stated in the claim form that the claim is an Aarhus Convention claim, rule 45.43 will apply unless—
 (a) the defendant has in the acknowledgment of service filed in accordance with rule 54.8—
  (i) denied that the claim is an Aarhus Convention claim; and
  (ii) set out the defendant's grounds for such denial; and
 (b) the court has determined that the claim is not an Aarhus Convention claim.
(2) Where the defendant argues that the claim is not an Aarhus Convention claim, the court will determine that issue at the earliest opportunity.
(3) In any proceedings to determine whether the claim is an Aarhus Convention claim—
 (a) if the court holds that the claim is not an Aarhus Convention claim, it will normally make no order for costs in relation to those proceedings;
 (b) if the court holds that the claim is an Aarhus Convention claim, it will normally order the defendant to pay the claimant's costs of those proceedings on the indemnity basis, and that order may be enforced notwithstanding that this would increase the costs payable by the defendant beyond the amount prescribed in Practice Direction 45.

PD 45 Practice Direction 45 — Fixed Costs

This practice direction supplements CPR, Part 45.

SECTION I — FIXED COSTS

Fixed Costs in Small Claims

para.1.2 70.5, 70.7 para.1.3 70.6

1.1 Under r. 27.14 the costs which can be awarded to a claimant in a small claim include the fixed costs payable under Part 45 attributable to issuing the claim.

1.2 Those fixed costs are the sum of—
   (a) the fixed commencement costs calculated in accordance with Table 1 of r. 45.2;
   (b) the appropriate court fee or fees paid by the claimant.

Claims to which Part 45 does not apply

1.3 In a claim to which Part 45 does not apply, no amount shall be entered on the claim form for the charges of the claimant's legal representative, but the words 'to be assessed' shall be inserted.

SECTION II — ROAD TRAFFIC ACCIDENTS: FIXED RECOVERABLE COSTS IN COSTS-ONLY PROCEEDINGS

Scope

paras.2.1–2.10 70.8 para.2.6 70.8
para.2.1 70.8 para.2.7 70.8
para.2.3 70.8

2.1 Section II of Part 45 ('the Section') provides for certain fixed costs to be recoverable between parties in respect of costs incurred in disputes which are settled prior to proceedings being issued. The Section applies to road traffic accident disputes as defined in r. 45.9(4)(a), where the accident which gave rise to the dispute occurred on or after 6 October 2003.

2.2 The Section does not apply to disputes where the total agreed value of the damages is within the small claims limit or exceeds £10,000. Rule 26.8(2) sets out how the financial value of a claim is assessed for the purposes of allocation to track.

2.3 Fixed recoverable costs are to be calculated by reference to the amount of agreed damages which are payable to the receiving party. In calculating the amount of these damages—
   (a) account must be taken of both general and special damages and interest;
   (b) any interim payments made must be included;
   (c) where the parties have agreed an element of contributory negligence, the amount of damages attributed to that negligence must be deducted;
   (d) any amount required by statute to be paid by the compensating party directly to a third party (such as sums paid by way of compensation recovery payments and National Health Service expenses) must not be included.

2.4 The Section applies to cases which fall within the scope of the Uninsured Drivers Agreement dated 13 August 1999. The section does not apply to cases which fall within the scope of the Untraced Drivers Agreement dated 14 February 2003.

Fixed recoverable costs formula

2.5 The amount of fixed costs recoverable is the sum of—
   (a) £800;
   (b) 20% of the agreed damages up to £5,000; and
   (c) 15% of the agreed damages between £5,000 and £10,000.

   For example, agreed damages of £7,523 would result in recoverable costs of £2,178.45 i.e. £800 + (20% of £5,000) + (15% of £2,523).

Additional costs for work in specified areas

2.6 The area referred to in rr. 45.11(2) and 45.18(5) consists of (within London) the county court districts of Barnet, Bow, Brentford, Central London, Clerkenwell and Shoreditch, Edmonton, Ilford, Lambeth,

Mayor's and City of London, Romford, Wandsworth, West London, Willesden and Woolwich and (outside London) the county court districts of Bromley, Croydon, Dartford, Gravesend and Uxbridge.

Multiple claimants

2.7 Where two or more potential claimants instruct the same legal representative, the provisions of the section apply in respect of each claimant.

Information to be included in the claim form

2.8 Costs-only proceedings are commenced using the procedure set out in r. 46.14. A claim form should be issued in accordance with Part 8. Where the claimant is claiming an amount of costs which exceed the amount of the fixed recoverable costs the claim form must give details of the exceptional circumstances to justify the additional costs.

2.9 The claimant must also include on the claim form details of any disbursements. The disbursements that may be claimed are set out in r. 45.12(1). If the disbursement falls within r. 45.12(2)(c) (disbursements that have arisen due to a particular feature of the dispute) the claimant must give details of the particular feature of the dispute that made the disbursement necessary.

Disbursements

2.10 If the parties agree the amount of the fixed recoverable costs and the only dispute is as to the payment of, or amount of, a disbursement, then proceedings should be issued under r. 46.14.

SECTION IV — SCALE COSTS FOR PROCEEDINGS IN A PATENTS COUNTY COURT

Tables A and B

para.3.3 70.17

3.1 Tables A and B set out the maximum amount of scale costs which the court will award for each stage of a claim in a patents county court.

3.2 Table A sets out the scale costs for each stage of a claim up to determination of liability.

3.3 Table B sets out the scale costs for each stage of an inquiry as to damages or account of profits.

Table A

Stage of a claim	*Maximum amount of costs*
Particulars of claim	£6,125
Defence and counterclaim	£6,125
Reply and defence to counterclaim	£6,125
Reply to defence to counterclaim	£3,000
Attendance at a case management conference	£2,500
Making or responding to an application	£2,500
Providing or inspecting disclosure or product/process description	£5,000
Performing or inspecting experiments	£2,500
Preparing witness statements	£5,000
Preparing experts' report	£7,500
Preparing for and attending trial and judgment	£15,000
Preparing for determination on the papers	£5,000

Table B

Stage of a claim	*Maximum amount of costs*
Points of claim	£2,500
Points of defence	£2,500
Attendance at a case management conference	£2,500
Making or responding to an application	£2,500
Providing or inspecting disclosure	£2,500

Stage of a claim	*Maximum amount of costs*
Preparing witness statements	£5,000
Preparing experts' report	£5,000
Preparing for and attending trial and judgment	£7,500
Preparing for determination on the papers	£2,500

SECTION VI — FAST TRACK TRIAL COSTS

Scope

4.1 Section VI of Part 45 applies to the costs of an advocate for preparing for and appearing at the trial of a claim in the fast track.

4.2 It applies only where, at the date of the trial, the claim is allocated to the fast track. It does not apply in any other case, irrespective of the final value of the claim.

4.3 In particular it does not apply to a disposal hearing at which the amount to be paid under a judgment or order is decided by the court (see PD 26, para. 12.4).

SECTION VII — COSTS LIMITS IN AARHUS CONVENTION CLAIMS

Limit on Costs Recoverable from a Party in an Aarhus Convention Claim: Rule 45.43

para.5.1 **44.13, 70.19** para.5.2 **44.13, 70.19**

5.1 Where a claimant is ordered to pay costs, the amount specified for the purpose of r. 45.43(1) is—

(a) £5,000 where the claimant is claiming only as an individual and not as, or on behalf of, a business or other legal person;

(b) in all other cases, £10,000.

5.2 Where a defendant is ordered to pay costs, the amount specified for the purpose of r. 45.43(1) is £35,000.

CPR Part 46 Costs — Special Cases

Part 46 **46.23, 50.89, 68.28** [For commentary on a specific rule, please refer to the cross-references after the title of the rule.]

I COSTS PAYABLE BY OR TO PARTICULAR PERSONS

46.1 Pre-commencement Disclosure and Orders for Disclosure against a Person who is not a Party

r.46.1 **50.94, 68.32**
r.46.1(2) **50.89, 50.94**
r.46.1(3) **50.89, 50.94, 68.32**

(1) This paragraph applies where a person applies—
(a) for an order under—
(i) section 33 of the Senior Courts Act 1981; or
(ii) section 52 of the County Courts Act 1984,
(which give the court powers exercisable before commencement of proceedings); or
(b) for an order under—
(i) section 34 of the Senior Courts Act 1981; or
(ii) section 53 of the County Courts Act 1984,
(which give the court power to make an order against a non-party for disclosure of documents, inspection of property etc.).
(2) The general rule is that the court will award the person against whom the order is sought that person's costs—
(a) of the application; and
(b) of complying with any order made on the application.
(3) The court may however make a different order, having regard to all the circumstances, including—
(a) the extent to which it was reasonable for the person against whom the order was sought to oppose the application; and
(b) whether the parties to the application have complied with any relevant pre-action protocol.

46.2 Costs Orders in favour of or against Non-parties

r.46.2 **44.23, 68.61, 69.17**

(1) Where the court is considering whether to exercise its power under section 51 of the Senior Courts Act 1981 (costs are in the discretion of the court) to make a costs order in favour of or against a person who is not a party to proceedings, that person must—
(a) be added as a party to the proceedings for the purposes of costs only; and
(b) be given a reasonable opportunity to attend a hearing at which the court will consider the matter further.

(2) This rule does not apply—
(a) where the court is considering whether to—
(i) make an order against the Lord Chancellor in proceedings in which the Lord Chancellor has provided legal aid to a party to the proceedings;
(ii) make a wasted costs order (as defined in rule 46.8); and
(b) in proceedings to which rule 46.1 applies (pre-commencement disclosure and orders for disclosure against a person who is not a party).

46.3 Limitations on Court's Power to Award Costs in favour of Trustee or Personal Representative

r.46.3 44.8, 71.45

(1) This rule applies where—
(a) a person is or has been a party to any proceedings in the capacity of trustee or personal representative; and
(b) rule 44.5 does not apply.
(2) The general rule is that that person is entitled to be paid the costs of those proceedings, insofar as they are not recovered from or paid by any other person, out of the relevant trust fund or estate.
(3) Where that person is entitled to be paid any of those costs out of the fund or estate, those costs will be assessed on the indemnity basis.

46.4 Costs where Money is Payable by or to a Child or Protected Party

r.46.4(1) 68.47
r.46.4(2) 68.47
r.46.4(2)(b) 68.47

(1) This rule applies to any proceedings where a party is a child or protected party and—
(a) money is ordered or agreed to be paid to, or for the benefit of, that party; or
(b) money is ordered to be paid by that party or on that party's behalf.
('Child' and 'protected party' have the same meaning as in rule 21.1(2).)
(2) The general rule is that—
(a) the court must order a detailed assessment of the costs payable by, or out of money belonging to, any party who is a child or protected party; and
(b) on an assessment under paragraph (a), the court must also assess any costs payable to that party in the proceedings, unless—
(i) the court has issued a default costs certificate in relation to those costs under rule 47.11; or
(ii) the costs are payable in proceedings to which Section II or Section III of Part 45 applies.
(3) The court need not order detailed assessment of costs in the circumstances set out in Practice Direction 46.
(4) Where—
(a) a claimant is a child or protected party; and
(b) a detailed assessment has taken place under paragraph (2)(a),
the only amount payable by the child or protected party is the amount which the court certifies as payable.
(This rule applies to a counterclaim by or on behalf of a child or protected party by virtue of rule 20.3.)

46.5 Litigants in Person

r.46.5 71.1
r.46.5(2) 71.64
r.46.5(6) 71.64, 71.65

(1) This rule applies where the court orders (whether by summary assessment or detailed assessment) that the costs of a litigant in person are to be paid by any other person.
(2) The costs allowed under this rule will not exceed, except in the case of a disbursement, two-thirds of the amount which would have been allowed if the litigant in person had been represented by a legal representative.

(3) The litigant in person shall be allowed—
(a) costs for the same categories of—
(i) work; and
(ii) disbursements,
which would have been allowed if the work had been done or the disbursements had been made by a legal representative on the litigant in person's behalf;
(b) the payments reasonably made by the litigant in person for legal services relating to the conduct of the proceedings; and
(c) the costs of obtaining expert assistance in assessing the costs claim.
(4) The amount of costs to be allowed to the litigant in person for any item of work claimed will be—
(a) where the litigant can prove financial loss, the amount that the litigant can prove to have been lost for time reasonably spent on doing the work; or
(b) where the litigant cannot prove financial loss, an amount for the time reasonably spent on doing the work at the rate set out in Practice Direction 46.
(5) A litigant who is allowed costs for attending at court to conduct the case is not entitled to a witness allowance in respect of such attendance in addition to those costs.
(6) For the purposes of this rule, a litigant in person includes—
(a) a company or other corporation which is acting without a legal representative; and
(b) any of the following who acts in person (except where any such person is represented by a firm in which that person is a partner)—
(i) a barrister;
(ii) a solicitor;
(iii) a solicitor's employee;
(iv) a manager of a body recognised under section 9 of the Administration of Justice Act 1985; or
(v) a person who, for the purposes of the 2007 Act, is an authorised person in relation to an activity which constitutes the conduct of litigation (within the meaning of that Act).

46.6 Costs where the Court has Made a Group Litigation Order

r.46.6 14.74
r.46.6(2) **68.51**
r.46.6(3) **68.51**
r.46.6(4) **68.51**
r.46.6(5) **68.51**
r.46.6(6) **68.51**
r.46.6(7) **68.51**

(1) This rule applies where the court has made a Group Litigation Order ('GLO').
(2) In this rule—
'individual costs' means costs incurred in relation to an individual claim on the group register;
'common costs' means—
(i) costs incurred in relation to the GLO issues;
(ii) individual costs incurred in a claim while it is proceeding as a test claim, and
(iii) costs incurred by the lead legal representative in administering the group litigation; and
'group litigant' means a claimant or defendant, as the case may be, whose claim is entered on the group register.
(3) Unless the court orders otherwise, any order for common costs against group litigants imposes on each group litigant several liability for an equal proportion of those common costs.
(4) The general rule is that where a group litigant is the paying party, he will, in addition to any costs he is liable to pay to the receiving party, be liable for—
(a) the individual costs of his claim; and
(b) an equal proportion, together with all the other group litigants, of the common costs.
(5) Where the court makes an order about costs in relation to any application or hearing which involved—
(a) one or more GLO issues; and
(b) issues relevant only to individual claims,
the court will direct the proportion of the costs that is to relate to common costs and the proportion that is to relate to individual costs.
(6) Where common costs have been incurred before a claim is entered on the group register, the court may order the group litigant to be liable for a proportion of those costs.

(7) Where a claim is removed from the group register, the court may make an order for costs in that claim which includes a proportion of the common costs incurred up to the date on which the claim is removed from the group register.

(Part 19 sets out rules about group litigation.)

46.7 Orders in respect of Pro Bono Representation

r.46.7 **71.32**
r.46.7(1)(a) **71.32**
r.46.7(1)(b) **71.32**
r.46.7(3) **71.32**

(1) Where the court makes an order under section 194(3) of the 2007 Act—
(a) the court may order the payment to the prescribed charity of a sum no greater than the costs specified in Part 45 to which the party with pro bono representation would have been entitled in accordance with that Part and in respect of that representation had it not been provided free of charge; or
(b) where Part 45 does not apply, the court may determine the amount of the payment (other than a sum equivalent to fixed costs) to be made by the paying party to the prescribed charity by—
(i) making a summary assessment; or
(ii) making an order for detailed assessment,
of a sum equivalent to all or part of the costs the paying party would have been ordered to pay to the party with pro bono representation in respect of that representation had it not been provided free of charge.

(2) Where the court makes an order under section 194(3) of the 2007 Act, the order must direct that the payment by the paying party be made to the prescribed charity.

(3) The receiving party must send a copy of the order to the prescribed charity within 7 days of receipt of the order.

(4) Where the court considers making or makes an order under section 194(3) of the 2007 Act, Parts 44 to 47 apply, where appropriate, with the following modifications—
(a) references to 'costs orders', 'orders about costs' or 'orders for the payment of costs' are to be read, unless otherwise stated, as if they refer to an order under section 194(3);
(b) references to 'costs' are to be read as if they referred to a sum equivalent to the costs that would have been claimed by, incurred by or awarded to the party with pro bono representation in respect of that representation had it not been provided free of charge; and
(c) references to 'receiving party' are to be read, as meaning a party who has pro bono representation and who would have been entitled to be paid costs in respect of that representation had it not been provided free of charge.

II COSTS RELATING TO LEGAL REPRESENTATIVES

46.8 Personal Liability of Legal Representative for Costs — Wasted Costs Orders

r.46.8(2) **68.64**
r.46.8(3)(b) **68.65**

(1) This rule applies where the court is considering whether to make an order under section 51(6) of the Senior Courts Act 1981 (court's power to disallow or (as the case may be) order a legal representative to meet, 'wasted costs').

(2) The court will give the legal representative a reasonable opportunity to make written submissions or, if the legal representative prefers, to attend a hearing before it makes such an order.

(3) When the court makes a wasted costs order, it will—
(a) specify the amount to be disallowed or paid; or
(b) direct a costs judge or a district judge to decide the amount of costs to be disallowed or paid.

(4) The court may direct that notice must be given to the legal representative's client, in such manner as the court may direct—
(a) of any proceedings under this rule; or
(b) of any order made under it against his legal representative.

46.9 Basis of Detailed Assessment of Solicitor and Client Costs

r.46.9 6.17, 65.18, 71.45
r.46.9(3) 6.17, 65.18
r.46.9(4) 6.19, 6.21

(1) This rule applies to every assessment of a solicitor's bill to a client except a bill which is to be paid out of the Community Legal Service Fund under the Legal Aid Act 1988 or the Access to Justice Act 1999 or by the Lord Chancellor under Part 1 of the Legal Aid, Sentencing and Punishment of Offenders Act 2012.
(2) Section 74(3) of the Solicitors Act 1974 applies unless the solicitor and client have entered into a written agreement which expressly permits payment to the solicitor of an amount of costs greater than that which the client could have recovered from another party to the proceedings.
(3) Subject to paragraph (2), costs are to be assessed on the indemnity basis but are to be presumed—
 (a) to have been reasonably incurred if they were incurred with the express or implied approval of the client;
 (b) to be reasonable in amount if their amount was expressly or impliedly approved by the client;
 (c) to have been unreasonably incurred if—
  (i) they are of an unusual nature or amount; and
  (ii) the solicitor did not tell the client that as a result the costs might not be recovered from the other party.
(4) Where the court is considering a percentage increase on the application of the client, the court will have regard to all the relevant factors as they reasonably appeared to the solicitor or counsel when the conditional fee agreement was entered into or varied.

46.10 Assessment Procedure

r.46.10 65.9, 65.18
r.46.10(2) 71.20
r.46.10(3) 71.20
r.46.10(4) 71.20

(1) This rule sets out the procedure to be followed where the court has made an order under Part III of the Solicitors Act 1974 for the assessment of costs payable to a solicitor by the solicitor's client.
(2) The solicitor must serve a breakdown of costs within 28 days of the order for costs to be assessed.
(3) The client must serve points of dispute within 14 days after service on the client of the breakdown of costs.
(4) The solicitor must serve any reply within 14 days of service on the solicitor of the points of dispute.
(5) Either party may file a request for a hearing date—
 (a) after points of dispute have been served; but
 (b) no later than 3 months after the date of the order for the costs to be assessed.
(6) This procedure applies subject to any contrary order made by the court.

III COSTS ON ALLOCATION AND RE-ALLOCATION

46.11 Costs on the Small Claims Track and Fast Track

r.46.11(1) 68.34
r.46.11(2) 68.34

(1) Part 27 (small claims) and Part 45 Section VI (fast track trial costs) contain special rules about—
 (a) liability for costs;
 (b) the amount of costs which the court may award; and
 (c) the procedure for assessing costs.
(2) Once a claim is allocated to a particular track, those special rules shall apply to the period before, as well as after, allocation except where the court or a practice direction provides otherwise.

46.12 Limitation on Amount Court may Allow where a Claim Allocated to the Fast Track Settles before Trial

r.46.12 71.8

(1) Where the court—
 (a) assesses costs in relation to a claim which—
  (i) has been allocated to the fast track; and
  (ii) settles before the start of the trial; and

(b) is considering the amount of costs to be allowed in respect of a party's advocate for preparing for the trial,

it may not allow, in respect of those advocate's costs, an amount that exceeds the amount of fast track trial costs which would have been payable in relation to the claim had the trial taken place.

(2) When deciding the amount to be allowed in respect of the advocate's costs, the court will have regard to—

(a) when the claim was settled; and

(b) when the court was notified that the claim had settled.

(3) In this rule, 'advocate' and 'fast track trial costs' have the meanings given to them by Part 45 Section VI.

46.13 Costs following Allocation, Re-allocation and Non-allocation

r.46.13(2) 45.31 r.46.13(3) 68.34, 71.43

(1) Any costs orders made before a claim is allocated will not be affected by allocation.

(2) Where—

(a) claim is allocated to a track; and

(b) the court subsequently re-allocates that claim to a different track,then unless the court orders otherwise, any special rules about costs applying—

(i) to the first track, will apply to the claim up to the date of re-allocation; and

(ii) to the second track, will apply from the date of re-allocation.

(3) Where the court is assessing costs on the standard basis of a claim which concluded without being allocated to a track, it may restrict those costs to costs that would have been allowed on the track to which the claim would have been allocated if allocation had taken place.

IV COSTS-ONLY PROCEEDINGS

46.14 Costs-only Proceedings

r.46.14 68.2, 68.51, 71.23, 71.68 r.46.14(5) 71.68
r.46.14(4) 71.68

(1) This rule applies where—

(a) the parties to a dispute have reached an agreement on all issues (including which party is to pay the costs) which is made or confirmed in writing; but

(b) they have failed to agree the amount of those costs; and

(c) no proceedings have been started.

(2) Where this rule applies, the procedure set out in this rule must be followed.

(3) Proceedings under this rule are commenced by issuing a claim form in accordance with Part 8.

(4) The claim form must contain or be accompanied by the agreement or confirmation.

(5) In proceedings to which this rule applies the court may make an order for the payment of costs the amount of which is to be determined by assessment and/or, where appropriate, for the payment of fixed costs.

(6) Where this rule applies but the procedure set out in this rule has not been followed by a party—

(a) that party will not be allowed costs greater than those that would have been allowed to that party had the procedure been followed; and

(b) the court may award the other party the costs of the proceedings up to the point where an order for the payment of costs is made.

(7) Rule 44.5 (amount of costs where costs are payable pursuant to a contract) does not apply to claims started under the procedure in this rule.

PD 46 Practice Direction 46 — Costs Special Cases

This practice direction supplements CPR, Part 46.

Awards of Costs in favour of a Trustee or Personal Representative: Rule 46.3

1.1 A trustee or personal representative is entitled to an indemnity out of the relevant trust fund or estate for costs properly incurred. Whether costs were properly incurred depends on all the circumstances of the case including whether the trustee or personal representative ('the trustee')—
- (a) obtained directions from the court before bringing or defending the proceedings;
- (b) acted in the interests of the fund or estate or in substance for a benefit other than that of the estate, including the trustee's own; and
- (c) acted in some way unreasonably in bringing or defending, or in the conduct of, the proceedings.

1.2 The trustee is not to be taken to have acted for a benefit other than that of the fund by reason only that the trustee has defended a claim in which relief is sought against the trustee personally.

Costs where Money is Payable by or to a Child or Protected Party: Rule 46.4

para.2.1 68.47 para.2.1(b) 68.47

2.1 The circumstances in which the court need not order the assessment of costs under r. 46.4(3) are as follows—
- (a) where there is no need to do so to protect the interests of the child or protected party or their estate;
- (b) where another party has agreed to pay a specified sum in respect of the costs of the child or protected party and the legal representative acting for the child or protected party has waived the right to claim further costs;
- (c) where the court has decided the costs payable to the child or protected party by way of summary assessment and the legal representative acting for the child or protected party has waived the right to claim further costs; and
- (d) where an insurer or other person is liable to discharge the costs which the child or protected party would otherwise be liable to pay to the legal representative and the court is satisfied that the insurer or other person is financially able to discharge those costs.

Litigants in Person: Rule 46.5

para.3.2 71.64 para.3.4 71.64

3.1 In order to qualify as an expert for the purpose of r. 46.5(3)(c) (expert assistance in connection with assessing the claim for costs), the person in question must be a—
- (a) barrister;
- (b) solicitor;
- (c) Fellow of the Institute of Legal Executives;
- (d) Fellow of the Association of Costs Lawyers;
- (e) law costs draftsman who is a member of the Academy of Experts;
- (f) law costs draftsman who is a member of the Expert Witness Institute.

3.2 Where a self-represented litigant wishes to prove that the litigant has suffered financial loss, the litigant should produce to the court any written evidence relied on to support that claim, and serve a copy of that evidence on any party against whom the litigant seeks costs at least 24 hours before the hearing at which the question may be decided.

3.3 A self-represented litigant who commences detailed assessment proceedings under r. 47.5 should serve copies of that written evidence with the notice of commencement.

3.4 The amount, which may be allowed to a self-represented litigant under r. 45.39(5)(b) and *r. 46.5(4)(b), is £18 per hour.*

Orders in respect of Pro Bono Representation: Rule 46.7

para.4.1 71.32

4.1 Where an order is sought under the Legal Services Act 2007, s. 194(3), the party who has pro bono representation must prepare, file and serve a written statement of the sum equivalent to the costs that party would have claimed for that legal representation had it not been provided free of charge.

Personal Liability of Legal Representative for Costs — Wasted Costs Orders: Rule 46.8

para.5.2 68.65
para.5.5 68.65
para.5.5(b) 68.64
para.5.5(c) 68.64
para.5.7 68.65
para.5.9 68.65

5.1 A wasted costs order is an order—
(a) that the legal representative pay a sum (either specified or to be assessed) in respect of costs to a party; or
(b) for costs relating to a specified sum or items of work to be disallowed.

5.2 Rule 46.8 deals with wasted costs orders against legal representatives. Such orders can be made at any stage in the proceedings up to and including the detailed assessment proceedings. In general, applications for wasted costs are best left until after the end of the trial.

5.3 The court may make a wasted costs order against a legal representative on its own initiative.

5.4 A party may apply for a wasted costs order—
(a) by filing an application notice in accordance with Part 23; or
(b) by making an application orally in the course of any hearing.

5.5 It is appropriate for the court to make a wasted costs order against a legal representative, only if—
(a) the legal representative has acted improperly, unreasonably or negligently;
(b) the legal representative's conduct has caused a party to incur unnecessary costs, or has meant that costs incurred by a party prior to the improper, unreasonable or negligent act or omission have been wasted;
(c) it is just in all the circumstances to order the legal representative to compensate that party for the whole or part of those costs.

5.6 The court will give directions about the procedure to be followed in each case in order to ensure that the issues are dealt with in a way which is fair and as simple and summary as the circumstances permit.

5.7 As a general rule the court will consider whether to make a wasted costs order in two stages—
(a) at the first stage the court must be satisfied—
(i) that it has before it evidence or other material which, if unanswered, would be likely to lead to a wasted costs order being made; and
(ii) the wasted costs proceedings are justified notwithstanding the likely costs involved;
(b) at the second stage, the court will consider, after giving the legal representative an opportunity to make representations in writing or at a hearing, whether it is appropriate to make a wasted costs order in accordance with para. 5.5 above.

5.8 The court may proceed to the second stage described in paragraph 5.7 without first adjourning the hearing if it is satisfied that the legal representative has already had a reasonable opportunity to make representations.

5.9 On an application for a wasted costs order under Part 23 the application notice and any evidence in support must identify—
(a) what the legal representative is alleged to have done or failed to do; and
(b) the costs that the legal representative may be ordered to pay or which are sought against the legal representative.

Assessment of Solicitor and Client Costs: Rules 46.9 and 46.10

paras.6.4–6.19 65.9
para.6.4 6.16
para.6.5 6.16
para.6.6 71.20
para.6.8 71.20

6.1 A client and solicitor may agree whatever terms they consider appropriate about the payment of the solicitor's charges. If however, the costs are of an unusual nature, either in amount or the type of costs incurred, those costs will be presumed to have been unreasonably incurred unless the solicitor satisfies the court that the client was informed that they were unusual and that they might not be allowed on an assessment of costs between the parties. That information must have been given to the client before the costs were incurred.

6.2 Costs as between a solicitor and client are assessed on the indemnity basis. The presumptions in r. 46.9(3) are rebuttable.

6.3 If a party fails to comply with the requirements of r. 46.10 concerning the service of a breakdown of costs or points of dispute, any other party may apply to the court in which the detailed assessment hearing should take place for an order requiring compliance. If the court makes such an order, it may—
(a) make it subject to conditions including a condition to pay a sum of money into court; and
(b) specify the consequence of failure to comply with the order or a condition.

6.4 The procedure for obtaining an order under Part III of the Solicitors Act 1974 is by a Part 8 claim, as modified by r. 67.3 and PD 67. Precedent J of the Schedule of Costs Precedents is a model form of claim form. The application must be accompanied by the bill or bills in respect of which assessment is sought, and, if the claim concerns a conditional fee agreement, a copy of that agreement. If the original bill is not available a copy will suffice.

6.5 Model forms of order, which the court may make, are set out in Precedents K, L and M of the Schedule of Costs Precedents.

6.6 The breakdown of costs referred to in r. 46.10 is a document which contains the following information—
(a) details of the work done under each of the bills sent for assessment; and
(b) in applications under the Solicitors Act 1974, s. 70, a cash account showing money received by the solicitor to the credit of the client and sums paid out of that money on behalf of the client but not payments out which were made in satisfaction of the bill or of any items which are claimed in the bill.

6.7 Precedent P of the Schedule of Costs Precedents is a model form of breakdown of costs. A party who is required to serve a breakdown of costs must also serve—
(a) copies of the fee notes of counsel and of any expert in respect of fees claimed in the breakdown, and
(b) written evidence as to any other disbursement which is claimed in the breakdown and which exceeds £250.

6.8 The provisions relating to default costs certificates (r. 47.11) do not apply to cases to which rule 46.10 applies.

6.9 The time for requesting a detailed assessment hearing is within three months after the date of the order for the costs to be assessed.

6.10 The form of request for a hearing date must be in form N258C. The request must be accompanied by copies of—
(a) the order sending the bill or bills for assessment;
(b) the bill or bills sent for assessment;
(c) the solicitor's breakdown of costs and any invoices or accounts served with that breakdown;
(d) a copy of the points of dispute;
(e) a copy of any replies served;
(f) a statement signed by the party filing the request or that party's legal representative giving the names and addresses for service of all parties to the proceedings.

6.11 The request must include the estimated length of hearing.

6.12 On receipt of the request the court will fix a date for the hearing, or will give directions.

6.13 The court will give at least 14 days' notice of the time and place of the detailed assessment hearing.

6.14 Unless the court gives permission, only the solicitor whose bill it is and parties who have served points of dispute may be heard and only items specified in the points of dispute may be raised.

6.15 If a party wishes to vary that party's breakdown of costs, points of dispute or reply, an amended *or supplementary document* must be filed with the court and copies of it must be served on all other relevant parties. Permission is not required to vary a breakdown of costs, points of dispute or a reply but the court may disallow the variation or permit it only upon conditions, including conditions as to the payment of any costs caused or wasted by the variation.

6.16 Unless the court directs otherwise the solicitor must file with the court the papers in support of the bill not less than seven days before the date for the detailed assessment hearing and not more than 14 days before that date.

6.17 Once the detailed assessment hearing has ended it is the responsibility of the legal representative appearing for the solicitor or, as the case may be, the solicitor in person to remove the papers filed in support of the bill.

6.18 If, in the course of a detailed assessment hearing of a solicitor's bill to that solicitor's client, it appears to the court that in any event the solicitor will be liable in connection with that bill to pay money to the client, it may issue an interim certificate specifying an amount which in its opinion is payable by the solicitor to the client.

6.19 After the detailed assessment hearing is concluded the court will—

(a) complete the court copy of the bill so as to show the amount allowed;

(b) determine the result of the cash account;

(c) award the costs of the detailed assessment hearing in accordance with the Solicitors Act 1974, s. 70(8); and

(d) issue a final costs certificate.

Costs on the Small Claims and Fast Tracks: Rule 46.11

para.7.1(1) **68.34** para.7.1(2) **68.34**

7.1 (1) Before a claim is allocated to either the small claims track or the fast track the court is not restricted by any of the special rules that apply to that track but see para. 8.2 below.

(2) Where a claim has been so allocated, the special rules which relate to that track will apply to work done before as well as after allocation save to the extent (if any) that an order for costs in respect of that work was made before allocation.

(3) Where a claim, issued for a sum in excess of the normal financial scope of the small claims track, is allocated to that track only because an admission of part of the claim by the defendant reduces the amount in dispute to a sum within the normal scope of that track; on entering judgment for the admitted part before allocation of the balance of the claim the court may allow costs in respect of the proceedings down to that date.

Costs following Allocation, Reallocation and Non-allocation: Rule 46.13

para.8.1 **68.35**

8.1 Before reallocating a claim from the small claims track to another track, the court must decide whether any party is to pay costs to the date of the order to reallocate in accordance with the rules about costs contained in Part 27 If it decides to make such an order the court will make a summary assessment of those costs in accordance with that Part.

8.2 Where a settlement is reached or a Part 36 offer accepted in a case which has not been allocated but would, if allocated, have been suitable for allocation to the small claims track, r. 46.13 enables the court to allow only small claims track costs in accordance with r. 27.14. This power is not exercisable if the costs are to be paid on the indemnity basis.

Costs-only Proceedings: Rule 46.14

para.9.3 **71.68**
para.9.4 **68.2**
para.9.5 **71.68**
para.9.7 **71.68**
para.9.9 **71.68**
para.9.10 **71.68**
para.9.11 **71.68**
para.9.12 **71.67**

9.1 A claim form under r. 46.14 should not be issued in the High Court unless the dispute to which the agreement relates was of such a value or type that proceedings would have been commenced in the High Court.

9.2 A claim form which is to be issued in the High Court at the Royal Courts of Justice will be issued in the Costs Office.

9.3 Attention is drawn to r. 8.2 (in particular to paragraph (b)(ii)) and to r. 46.14(3). The claim form must—

(a) identify the claim or dispute to which the agreement relates;

(b) state the date and terms of the agreement on which the claimant relies;

(c) set out or attach a draft of the order which the claimant seeks;

(d) state the amount of the costs claimed.

9.4 Unless the court orders otherwise or Section II of Part 45 applies the costs will be treated as being claimed on the standard basis.

9.5 The evidence required under r. 8.5 includes copies of the documents on which the claimant relies to prove the defendant's agreement to pay costs.

9.6 A costs judge or a district judge has jurisdiction to hear and decide any issue which may arise in a claim issued under this rule irrespective of the amount of the costs claimed or of the value of the claim to which the agreement to pay costs relates. The court may make an order by consent under para. 9.8, or an order dismissing a claim under para. 9.10 below.

9.7 When the time for filing the defendant's acknowledgment of service has expired, the claimant may request in writing that the court to make an order in the terms of the claim, unless the defendant has filed an acknowledgment of service stating the intention to contest the claim or to seek a different order.

9.8 Rule 40.6 applies where an order is to be made by consent. An order may be made by consent in terms which differ from those set out in the claim form.

9.9 Where costs are ordered to be assessed, the general rule is that this should be by detailed assessment. However when an order is made under this rule following a hearing and the court is in a position to summarily assess costs it should generally do so.

9.10 If the defendant opposes the claim the defendant must file a witness statement in accordance with r. 8.5(3). The court will then give directions including, if appropriate, a direction that the claim shall continue as if it were a Part 7 claim. A claim is not treated as opposed merely because the defendant disputes the amount of the claim for costs.

9.11 A claim issued under this rule may be dealt with without being allocated to a track. Rule 8.9 does not apply to claims issued under this rule.

9.12 Where there are other issues nothing in r. 46.14 prevents a person from issuing a claim form under Part 7 or Part 8 to sue on an agreement made in settlement of a dispute where that agreement makes provision for costs, nor from claiming in that case an order for costs or a specified sum in respect of costs but the 'costs-only' procedure in r. 46.14 must be used where the sole issue is the amount of costs.

CPR Part 47 Procedure for Detailed Assessment of Costs and Default Provisions

Part 47 **67.2, 71.18** [For commentary on a specific rule, please refer to the cross-references after the title of the rule.]

I GENERAL RULES ABOUT DETAILED ASSESSMENT

47.1 Time when Detailed Assessment may be Carried Out

r.47.1 **68.28, 71.10**

The general rule is that the costs of any proceedings or any part of the proceedings are not to be assessed by the detailed procedure until the conclusion of the proceedings, but the court may order them to be assessed immediately.

(Practice Direction 47 gives further guidance about when proceedings are concluded for the purpose of this rule.)

47.2 No Stay of Detailed Assessment where there is an Appeal

Detailed assessment is not stayed pending an appeal unless the court so orders.

47.3 Powers of an Authorised Court Officer

(1) An authorised court officer has all the powers of the court when making a detailed assessment, except—
   (a) power to make a wasted costs order as defined in rule 46.8;
   (b) power to make an order under—
      (i) rule 44.11 (powers in relation to misconduct);
      (ii) rule 47.8 (sanction for delay in commencing detailed assessment proceedings);
      (iii) paragraph (2) (objection to detailed assessment by authorised court officer); and

CPR 26–50 & PDs

(c) power to make a detailed assessment of costs payable to a solicitor by that solicitor's client, unless the costs are being assessed under rule 46.4 (costs where money is payable to a child or protected party).

(2) Where a party objects to the detailed assessment of costs being made by an authorised court officer, the court may order it to be made by a costs judge or a district judge.

(Practice Direction 47 sets out the relevant procedure.)

47.4 Venue for Detailed Assessment Proceedings

r.47.4 71.11 r.47.4(3) 71.11
r.47.4(2) 71.11

(1) All applications and requests in detailed assessment proceedings must be made to or filed at the appropriate office.

(Practice Direction 47 sets out the meaning of 'appropriate office' in any particular case)

(2) The court may direct that the appropriate office is to be the Costs Office.

(3) A county court may direct that another county court is to be the appropriate office.

(4) A direction under paragraph (3) may be made without proceedings being transferred to that court.

(Rule 30.2 makes provision for any county court to transfer the proceedings to another county court for detailed assessment of costs.)

II COSTS PAYABLE BY ONE PARTY TO ANOTHER — COMMENCEMENT OF DETAILED ASSESSMENT PROCEEDINGS

47.5 Application of this Section

This Section of Part 47 applies where a cost officer is to make a detailed assessment of—

(a) costs which are payable by one party to another; or

(b) the sum which is payable by one party to the prescribed charity pursuant to an order under section 194(3) of the 2007 Act.

47.6 Commencement of Detailed Assessment Proceedings

r.47.6(1) 71.12 r.47.6(2) 71.12

(1) Detailed assessment proceedings are commenced by the receiving party serving on the paying party—

(a) notice of commencement in the relevant practice form; and

(b) a copy of the bill of costs.

(Rule 47.7 sets out the period for commencing detailed assessment proceedings.)

(2) The receiving party must also serve a copy of the notice of commencement and the bill on any other relevant persons specified in Practice Direction 47.

(3) A person on whom a copy of the notice of commencement is served under paragraph (2) is a party to the detailed assessment proceedings (in addition to the paying party and the receiving party).

(Practice Direction 47 deals with—

other documents which the party must file when requesting detailed assessment;

the court's powers where it considers that a hearing may be necessary;

the form of a bill; and

the length of notice which will be given if a hearing date is fixed.)

47.7 Period for Commencing Detailed Assessment Proceedings

r.47.7 71.12

The following table shows the period for commencing detailed assessment proceedings.

Source of right to detailed assessment	*Time by which detailed assessment proceedings must be commenced*
Judgment, direction, order, award or other determination	3 months after the date of the judgment etc. Where detailed assessment is stayed pending an appeal, 3 months after the date of the order lifting the stay
Discontinuance under Part 38	3 months after the date of service of notice of discontinuance under rule 38.3; or 3 months after the date of the dismissal of application to set the notice of discontinuance aside under rule 38.4
Acceptance of an offer to settle under Part 36	3 months after the date when the right to costs arose

47.8 Sanction for Delay in Commencing Detailed Assessment Proceedings

r.47.8 71.26
r.47.8(2) 71.25
r.47.8(3) 71.25

(1) Where the receiving party fails to commence detailed assessment proceedings within the period specified—
 (a) in rule 47.7; or
 (b) by any direction of the court,
the paying party may apply for an order requiring the receiving party to commence detailed assessment proceedings within such time as the court may specify.
(2) On an application under paragraph (1), the court may direct that, unless the receiving party commences detailed assessment proceedings within the time specified by the court, all or part of the costs to which the receiving party would otherwise be entitled will be disallowed.
(3) If—
 (a) the paying party has not made an application in accordance with paragraph (1); and
 (b) the receiving party commences the proceedings later than the period specified in rule 47.7,
the court may disallow all or part of the interest otherwise payable to the receiving party under—
 (i) section 17 of the Judgments Act 1838; or
 (ii) section 74 of the County Courts Act 1984,
but will not impose any other sanction except in accordance with rule 44.11 (powers in relation to misconduct).
(4) Where the costs to be assessed in a detailed assessment are payable out of the Community Legal Service Fund, this rule applies as if the receiving party were the solicitor to whom the costs are payable and the paying party were the Legal Services Commission.
(5) Where the costs to be assessed in a detailed assessment are payable by the Lord Chancellor under Part 1 of the Legal Aid, Sentencing and Punishment of Offenders Act 2012, this rule applies as if the receiving party were the solicitor to whom the costs are payable and the paying party were the Lord Chancellor.

47.9 Points of Dispute and Consequence of not Serving

r.47.9(2) 71.14
r.47.9(3) 71.15
r.47.9(4) 71.15

(1) The paying party and any other party to the detailed assessment proceedings may dispute any item in the bill of costs by serving points of dispute on—
 (a) the receiving party; and
 (b) every other party to the detailed assessment proceedings.
(2) The period for serving points of dispute is 21 days after the date of service of the notice of commencement.
(3) If a party serves points of dispute after the period set out in paragraph (2), that party may not be heard further in the detailed assessment proceedings unless the court gives permission.
(Practice Direction 47 sets out requirements about the form of points of dispute.)
(4) The receiving party may file a request for a default costs certificate if—
 (a) the period set out in paragraph (2) for serving points of dispute has expired; and
 (b) the receiving party has not been served with any points of dispute.

(5) If any party (including the paying party) serves points of dispute before the issue of a default costs certificate the court may not issue the default costs certificate.

(Section IV of this Part sets out the procedure to be followed after points of dispute have been served.)

47.10 Procedure where Costs are Agreed

r.47.10(1) 71.3

(1) If the paying party and the receiving party agree the amount of costs, either party may apply for a costs certificate (either interim or final) in the amount agreed.

(Rule 47.16 and rule 47.17 contain further provisions about interim and final costs certificates respectively)

(2) An application for a certificate under paragraph (1) must be made to the court which would be the venue for detailed assessment proceedings under rule 47.4.

III COSTS PAYABLE BY ONE PARTY TO ANOTHER — DEFAULT PROVISIONS

47.11 Default Costs Certificate

r.47.11 71.15
r.47.11(2) 71.15
r.47.11(4) 71.32

(1) Where the receiving party is permitted by rule 47.9 to obtain a default costs certificate, that party does so by filing a request in the relevant practice form.

(Practice Direction 47 deals with the procedure by which the receiving party may obtain a default costs certificate.)

(2) A default costs certificate will include an order to pay the costs to which it relates.

(3) Where a receiving party obtains a default costs certificate, the costs payable to that party for the commencement of detailed assessment proceedings will be the sum set out in Practice Direction 47.

(4) A receiving party who obtains a default costs certificate in detailed assessment proceedings pursuant to an order under section 194(3) of the 2007 Act must send a copy of the default costs certificate to the prescribed charity.

47.12 Setting Aside a Default Costs Certificate

r.47.12 71.15
r.47.12(3) 71.32

(1) The court will set aside a default costs certificate if the receiving party was not entitled to it.

(2) In any other case, the court may set aside or vary a default costs certificate if it appears to the court that there is some good reason why the detailed assessment proceedings should continue.

(Practice Direction 47 contains further details about the procedure for setting aside a default costs certificate and the matters which the court must take into account)

(3) Where the court sets aside or varies a default costs certificate in detailed assessment proceedings pursuant to an order under section 194(3) of the Legal Services Act 2007, the receiving party must send a copy of the order setting aside or varying the default costs certificate to the prescribed charity.

IV COSTS PAYABLE BY ONE PARTY TO ANOTHER — PROCEDURE WHERE POINTS OF DISPUTE ARE SERVED

47.13 Optional Reply

r.47.13 71.16

(1) Where any party to the detailed assessment proceedings serves points of dispute, the receiving party may serve a reply on the other parties to the assessment proceedings.

(2) The receiving party may do so within 21 days after being served with the points of dispute to which the reply relates.

(Practice Direction 47 sets out the meaning of 'reply'.)

47.14 Detailed Assessment Hearing

(1) Where points of dispute are served in accordance with this Part, the receiving party must file a request for a detailed assessment hearing within 3 months of the expiry of the period for commencing detailed assessment proceedings as specified—
  (a) in rule 47.7; or
  (b) by any direction of the court.
(2) Where the receiving party fails to file a request in accordance with paragraph (1), the paying party may apply for an order requiring the receiving party to file the request within such time as the court may specify.
(3) On an application under paragraph (2), the court may direct that, unless the receiving party requests a detailed assessment hearing within the time specified by the court, all or part of the costs to which the receiving party would otherwise be entitled will be disallowed.
(4) If—
  (a) the paying party has not made an application in accordance with paragraph (2); and
  (b) the receiving party files a request for a detailed assessment hearing later than the period specified in paragraph (1),

  the court may disallow all or part of the interest otherwise payable to the receiving party under—
    (i) section 17 of the Judgments Act 1838; or
    (ii) section 74 of the County Courts Act 1984,

  but will not impose any other sanction except in accordance with rule 44.11 (powers in relation to misconduct).
(5) No party other than—
  (a) the receiving party;
  (b) the paying party; and
  (c) any party who has served points of dispute under rule 47.9,

  may be heard at the detailed assessment hearing unless the court gives permission.
(6) Only items specified in the points of dispute may be raised at the hearing, unless the court gives permission.
(7) If an assessment is carried out at more than one hearing, then for the purposes of rule 52.4 time for appealing shall not start to run until the conclusion of the final hearing, unless the court orders otherwise.

(Practice Direction 47 specifies other documents which must be filed with the request for hearing and the length of notice which the court will give when it fixes a hearing date.)

[Rule 47.14(7) does not apply where the final hearing was concluded before 1 April 2013 (SI 2013/262, r. 22(9)).]

47.15 Provisional Assessment

(1) This rule applies to any detailed assessment proceedings commenced in the High Court or a county court on or after 1 April 2013 in which the costs claimed are the amount set out in paragraph 14.1 of the practice direction supplementing this Part, or less.
(2) In proceedings to which this rule applies, the parties must comply with the procedure set out in Part 47 as modified by paragraph 14 Practice Direction 47.
(3) The court will undertake a provisional assessment of the receiving party's costs on receipt of Form N258 and the relevant supporting documents specified in Practice Direction 47.
(4) The provisional assessment will be based on the information contained in the bill and supporting papers and the contentions set out in Precedent G (the points of dispute and any reply).
(5) The court will not award more than £1,500 to any party in respect of the costs of the provisional assessment.

(6) The court may at any time decide that the matter is unsuitable for a provisional assessment and may give directions for the matter to be listed for hearing. The matter will then proceed under rule 47.14 without modification.

(7) When a provisional assessment has been carried out, the court will send a copy of the bill, as provisionally assessed, to each party with a notice stating that any party who wishes to challenge any aspect of the provisional assessment must, within 21 days of the receipt of the notice, file and serve on all other parties a written request for an oral hearing. If no such request is filed and served within that period, the provisional assessment shall be binding upon the parties, save in exceptional circumstances.

(8) The written request referred to in paragraph (7) must—

(a) identify the item or items in the court's provisional assessment which are sought to be reviewed at the hearing; and

(b) provide a time estimate for the hearing.

(9) The court then will fix a date for the hearing and give at least 14 days' notice of the time and place of the hearing to all parties.

(10) Any party which has requested an oral hearing, will pay the costs of and incidental to that hearing unless—

(a) it achieves an adjustment in its own favour by 20% or more of the sum provisionally assessed; or

(b) the court otherwise orders.

V INTERIM COSTS CERTIFICATE AND FINAL COSTS CERTIFICATE

47.16 Power to Issue an Interim Certificate

r.47.16 **71.9, 71.27** r.47.16(6) **68.30**

(1) The court may at any time after the receiving party has filed a request for a detailed assessment hearing—

(a) issue an interim costs certificate for such sum as it considers appropriate; or

(b) amend or cancel an interim certificate.

(2) An interim certificate will include an order to pay the costs to which it relates, unless the court orders otherwise.

(3) The court may order the costs certified in an interim certificate to be paid into court.

(4) Where the court—

(a) issues an interim costs certificate; or

(b) amends or cancels an interim certificate,

in detailed assessment proceedings pursuant to an order under section 194(3) of the 2007 Act, the receiving party must send a copy of the interim costs certificate or the order amending or cancelling the interim costs certificate to the prescribed charity.

47.17 Final Costs Certificate

r.47.17 **71.32** r.47.17(3) **71.28**
r.47.17(2) **71.28** r.47.17(5) **71.28**

(1) In this rule a 'completed bill' means a bill calculated to show the amount due following the detailed assessment of the costs.

(2) The period for filing the completed bill is 14 days after the end of the detailed assessment hearing.

(3) When a completed bill is filed the court will issue a final costs certificate and serve it on the parties to the detailed assessment proceedings.

(4) Paragraph (3) is subject to any order made by the court that a certificate is not to be issued until other costs have been paid.

(5) A final costs certificate will include an order to pay the costs to which it relates, unless the court orders otherwise.

(Practice Direction 47 deals with the form of a final costs certificate.)

(6) Where the court issues a final costs certificate in detailed assessment proceedings pursuant to an order under section 194(3) of the 2007 Act, the receiving party must send a copy of the final costs certificate to the prescribed charity.

VI DETAILED ASSESSMENT PROCEDURE FOR COSTS OF A LSC FUNDED CLIENT, AN ASSISTED PERSON OR PERSON TO WHOM LEGAL AID IS MADE AVAILABLE WHERE COSTS ARE PAYABLE OUT OF THE COMMUNITY LEGAL SERVICE FUND OR BY THE LORD CHANCELLOR UNDER PART 1 OF THE LEGAL AID, SENTENCING AND PUNISHMENT OF OFFENDERS ACT 2012

47.18 Detailed Assessment Procedure where Costs are Payable out of the Community Legal Services Fund or by the Lord Chancellor under Part 1 of the Legal Aid, Sentencing and Punishment of Offenders Act 2012

r.47.18(1) 71.21
r.47.18(2) 71.12
r.47.18(3) 71.12
r.47.18(5) 71.18
r.47.18(7) 71.18

(1) Where the court is to assess costs of a LSC funded client, an assisted person or a person to whom legal aid is provided which are payable out of the Community Legal Services Fundor by the Lord Chancellor under Part 1 of the Legal Aid, Sentencing and Punishment of Offenders Act 2012, that person's solicitor may commence detailed assessment proceedings by filing a request in the relevant practice form.
(2) A request under paragraph (1) must be filed within 3 months after the date when the right to detailed assessment arose.
(3) The solicitor must also serve a copy of the request for detailed assessment on the LSC funded client, the assisted personor the person to whom legal aid is provided, if notice of that person's interest has been given to the court in accordance with community legal service or legal aid regulations.
(4) Where the solicitor has certified that the LSC funded client or that person wishes to attend an assessment hearing, the court will, on receipt of the request for assessment, fix a date for the assessment hearing.
(5) Where paragraph (3) does not apply, the court will, on receipt of the request for assessment provisionally assess the costs without the attendance of the solicitor, unless it considers that a hearing is necessary.
(6) After the court has provisionally assessed the bill, it will return the bill to the solicitor.
(7) The court will fix a date for an assessment hearing if the solicitor informs the court, within 14 days after receiving the provisionally assessed bill, that the solicitor wants the court to hold such a hearing.

47.19 Detailed Assessment Procedure where Costs are Payable out of a Fund other than the Community Legal Service Fund

r.47.19 68.2

(1) Where the court is to assess costs which are payable out of a fund other than the Community Legal Service Fund, the receiving party may commence detailed assessment proceedings by filing a request in the relevant practice form.
(2) A request under paragraph (1) must be filed within 3 months after the date when the right to detailed assessment arose.
(3) The court may direct that the party seeking assessment serve a copy of the request on any person who has a financial interest in the outcome of the assessment.
(4) The court will, on receipt of the request for assessment, provisionally assess the costs without the attendance of the receiving party, unless the court considers that a hearing is necessary.
(5) After the court has provisionally assessed the bill, it will return the bill to the receiving party.
(6) The court will fix a date for an assessment hearing if the receiving party informs the court, within 14 days after receiving the provisionally assessed bill, that the receiving party wants the court to hold such a hearing.

VII COSTS OF DETAILED ASSESSMENT PROCEEDINGS

47.20 Liability for Costs of Detailed Assessment Proceedings

(1) The receiving party is entitled to the costs of the detailed assessment proceedings except where—
  (a) the provisions of any Act, any of these Rules or any relevant practice direction provide otherwise; or
  (b) the court makes some other order in relation to all or part of the costs of the detailed assessment proceedings.

(2) Paragraph (1) does not apply where the receiving party has pro bono representation in the detailed assessment proceedings but that party may apply for an order in respect of that representation under section 194(3) of the 2007 Act.

(3) In deciding whether to make some other order, the court must have regard to all the circumstances, including—
  (a) the conduct of all the parties;
  (b) the amount, if any, by which the bill of costs has been reduced; and
  (c) whether it was reasonable for a party to claim the costs of a particular item or to dispute that item.

(4) The provisions of Part 36 apply to the costs of detailed assessment proceedings with the following modifications—
  (a) 'claimant' refers to 'receiving party' and 'defendant' refers to 'paying party';
  (b) 'trial' refers to 'detailed assessment hearing';
  (c) in rule 36.9(5), at the end insert 'or, where the Part 36 offer is made in respect of the detailed assessment proceedings, after the commencement of the detailed assessment hearing.';
  (d) for rule 36.11(7) substitute 'If the accepted sum is not paid within 14 days or such other period as has been agreed the offeree may apply for a final costs certificate for the unpaid sum.';
  (e) a reference to 'judgment being entered' is to the completion of the detailed assessment, and references to a 'judgment' being advantageous or otherwise are to the outcome of the detailed assessment.

(5) The court will usually summarily assess the costs of detailed assessment proceedings at the conclusion of those proceedings.

(6) Unless the court otherwise orders, interest on the costs of detailed assessment proceedings will run from the date of default, interim or final costs certificate, as the case may be.

(7) For the purposes of rule 36.14, detailed assessment proceedings are to be regarded as an independent claim.

[Rule 47.20(1) to (5) and (7) do not apply to detailed assessments commenced before 1 April 2013 and in relation to such detailed assessments, rr. 47.18 and 47.19 as they were in force immediately before 1 April 2013 apply instead (SI 2013/262, r. 22(10)). Rule 47.20(6) does not apply where the date of the default, interim or final costs certificate (as the case may be) is before 1 April 2013 (SI 2013/262, r. 22(11)).]

VIII APPEALS FROM AUTHORISED COURT OFFICERS IN DETAILED ASSESSMENT PROCEEDINGS

47.21 Right to Appeal

Any party to detailed assessment proceedings may appeal against a decision of an authorised court officer in those proceedings.

47.22 Court to Hear Appeal

An appeal against a decision of an authorised court officer lies to a costs judge or a district judge of the High Court.

47.23 Appeal Procedure

r.47.23(1) 71.29 r.47.23(2) 71.29

(1) The appellant must file an appeal notice within 21 days after the date of the decision against which it is sought to appeal.
(2) On receipt of the appeal notice, the court will—
  (a) serve a copy of the notice on the parties to the detailed assessment proceedings; and
  (b) give notice of the appeal hearing to those parties.

47.24 Powers of the Court on Appeal

r.47.24 71.29

On an appeal from an authorised court officer the court will—

(a) re-hear the proceedings which gave rise to the decision appealed against; and
(b) make any order and give any directions as it considers appropriate.

PD 47 Practice Direction 47 — Procedure for Detailed Assessment of Costs and Default Provisions

Time when Assessment may be Carried Out: Rule 47.1

para.1.1 **71.10**
para.1.2 **68.28**
para.1.4 **68.28**

1.1 For the purposes of r. 47.1, proceedings are concluded when the court has finally determined the matters in issue in the claim, whether or not there is an appeal, or made an award of provisional damages under Part 41.

1.2 The court may order or the parties may agree in writing that, although the proceedings are continuing, they will nevertheless be treated as concluded.

1.3 A party who is served with a notice of commencement (see para. 5.2 below) may apply to a costs judge or a district judge to determine whether the party who served it is entitled to commence detailed assessment proceedings. On hearing such an application the orders which the court may make include: an order allowing the detailed assessment proceedings to continue, or an order setting aside the notice of commencement.

1.4 A costs judge or a district judge may make an order allowing detailed assessment proceedings to be commenced where there is no realistic prospect of the claim continuing.

No Stay of Detailed Assessment where there is an Appeal: Rule 47.2

2. An application to stay the detailed assessment of costs pending an appeal may be made to the court whose order is being appealed or to the court which will hear the appeal.

Powers of an Authorised Court Officer: Rule 47.3

3.1 The court officers authorised by the Lord Chancellor to assess costs in the Costs Office and the Principal Registry of the Family Division are authorised to deal with claims where the base costs excluding VAT do not exceed £35,000 in the case of senior executive officers, or their equivalent, and £110,000 in the case of principal officers.

3.2 Where the receiving party, paying party and any other party to the detailed assessment proceedings who has served points of dispute are agreed that the assessment should not be made by an authorised court officer, the receiving party should so inform the court when requesting a hearing date. The court will then list the hearing before a costs judge or a district judge.

3.3 In any other case a party who objects to the assessment being made by an authorised court officer must make an application to the costs judge or district judge under Part 23 setting out the reasons for the objection.

Venue for Detailed Assessment Proceedings: Rule 47.4

para.4.1 **71.11**
para.4.1(b) **71.11**
para.4.2 **71.11**
para.4.2(2)(b) **71.11**
para.4.2(2)(c) **71.11**
para.4.3(2) **71.11**

4.1 For the purposes of r. 47.4(1) the 'appropriate office' means—

(a) the district registry or county court in which the case was being dealt with when the judgment or order was made or the event occurred which gave rise to the right to assessment, or to which it has subsequently been transferred;

(b) where a tribunal, person or other body makes an order for the detailed assessment of costs, a county court (subject to para. 4.2); or

(c) in all other cases, including Court of Appeal cases, the Costs Office.

4.2 (1) This paragraph applies where the appropriate office is any of the following county courts: Barnet, Bow, Brentford, Bromley, Central London, Clerkenwell and Shoreditch, Croydon, Edmonton, Ilford, Kingston, Lambeth, Mayors and City of London, Romford, Uxbridge, Wandsworth, West London, Willesden and Woolwich.

(2) Where this paragraph applies—
(a) the receiving party must file any request for a detailed assessment hearing in the Costs Office and, for all purposes relating to that detailed assessment (other than the issue of default costs certificates and applications to set aside default costs certificates), the Costs Office will be treated as the appropriate office in that case;
(b) default costs certificates should be issued and applications to set aside default costs certificates should be issued and heard in the relevant county court; and
(c) unless an order is made under r. 47.4(2) directing that the Costs Office as part of the High Court shall be the appropriate office, an appeal from any decision made by a costs judge shall lie to the Designated Civil Judge for the London Group of County Courts or such judge as the Designated Civil Judge shall nominate. The appeal notice and any other relevant papers should be lodged at the Central London Civil Justice Centre.

4.3 (1) A direction under r. 47.4(2) or (3) specifying a particular court, registry or office as the appropriate office may be given on application or on the court's own initiative.
(2) Unless the Costs Office is the appropriate office for the purposes of r. 47.4(1) an order directing that an assessment is to take place at the Costs Office will be made only if it is appropriate to do so having regard to the size of the bill of costs, the difficulty of the issues involved, the likely length of the hearing, the cost to the parties and any other relevant matter.

Commencement of Detailed Assessment Proceedings: Rule 47.6

5.1 Precedents A, B, C and D in the Schedule of Costs Precedents annexed to this practice direction are model forms of bills of costs for detailed assessment.

5.2 The receiving party must serve on the paying party and all the other relevant persons the following documents—
(a) a notice of commencement in form N252;
(b) a copy of the bill of costs;
(c) copies of the fee notes of counsel and of any expert in respect of fees claimed in the bill;
(d) written evidence as to any other disbursement which is claimed and which exceeds £500;
(e) a statement giving the name and address for service of any person upon whom the receiving party intends to serve the notice of commencement.

5.3 The notice of commencement must be completed to show as separate items—
(a) the total amount of the costs claimed in the bill;
(b) the extra sum which will be payable by way of fixed costs and court fees if a default costs certificate is obtained.

5.4 Where the notice of commencement is to be served outside England and Wales the date to be inserted in the notice of commencement for the paying party to send points of dispute is a date (not less than 21 days from the date of service of the notice) which must be calculated by reference to Section IV of Part 6 as if the notice were a claim form and as if the date to be inserted was the date for the filing of a defence.

5.5 (1) For the purposes of r. 47.6(2) a 'relevant person' means—
(a) any person who has taken part in the proceedings which gave rise to the assessment and who is directly liable under an order for costs made against that person;
(b) any person who has given to the receiving party notice in writing that that person has a financial interest in the outcome of the assessment and wishes to be a party accordingly;
(c) any other person whom the court orders to be treated as such.
(2) Where a party is unsure whether a person is or is not a relevant person, that party may apply to the appropriate office for directions.
(3) The court will generally not make an order that the person in respect of whom the application is made will be treated as a relevant person, unless within a specified time that person

applies to the court to be joined as a party to the assessment proceedings in accordance with Part 19 (Parties and Group Litigation).

5.6 Where—
(a) the bill of costs is capable of being copied electronically; and
(b) before the detailed assessment hearing,
a paying party requests an electronic copy of the bill, the receiving party must supply the paying party with a copy in its native format (for example, in Excel or an equivalent) free of charge not more than seven days after receipt of the request.

Form and contents of bills of costs — general

5.7 A bill of costs may consist of such of the following sections as may be appropriate—
(1) title page;
(2) background information;
(3) items of costs claimed under the headings specified in para. 5.12;
(4) summary showing the total costs claimed on each page of the bill;
(5) schedules of time spent on non-routine attendances; and
(6) the certificates referred to in para. 5.21.
If the only dispute between the parties concerns disbursements, the bill of costs shall be limited to items (1) and (2) above, a list of the disbursements in issue and brief written submissions in respect of those disbursements.

5.8 Where it is necessary or convenient to do so, a bill of costs may be divided into two or more parts, each part containing sections (2), (3) and (4) above. Circumstances in which it will be necessary or convenient to divide a bill into parts include the following—
(1) Where the receiving party acted in person during the course of the proceedings (whether or not that party also had a legal representative at that time) the bill must be divided into different parts so as to distinguish between;
(a) the costs claimed for work done by the legal representative; and
(b) the costs claimed for work done by the receiving party in person.
(2) Where the receiving party had pro bono representation for part of the proceedings and an order under the Legal Services Act 2007, s. 194(3), has been made, the bill must be divided into different parts so as to distinguish between—
(a) the sum equivalent to the costs claimed for work done by the legal representative acting free of charge; and
(b) the costs claimed for work not done by the legal representative acting free of charge.
(3) Where the receiving party was represented by different legal representatives during the course of the proceedings, the bill must be divided into different parts so as to distinguish between the costs payable in respect of each legal representative.
(4) Where the receiving party obtained legal aid or LSC funding or is a person for whom civil legal services (within the meaning of Part 1 of the Legal Aid, Sentencing and Punishment of Offenders Act 2012) were provided under arrangements made for the purposes of that Part of that Act in respect of all or part of the proceedings, the bill must be divided into separate parts so as to distinguish between—
(a) costs claimed before legal aid or LSC funding was granted or before civil legal services were provided;
(b) costs claimed after legal aid or LSC funding was granted or after civil legal services were provided; and
(c) any costs claimed after legal aid or LSC funding ceased or after civil legal services ceased to be provided.
(5) Where the bill covers costs payable under an order or orders under which there are different paying parties the bill must be divided into parts so as to deal separately with the costs payable by each paying party.
(6) Where the bill covers costs payable under an order or orders, in respect of which the receiving party wishes to claim interest from different dates, the bill must be divided to enable such interest to be calculated.

5.9 Where a party claims costs against another party and also claims costs against the LSC or Lord Chancellor only for work done in the same period, the costs claimed against the LSC or Lord

Chancellor only can be claimed either in a separate part of the bill or in additional columns in the same part of the bill. Precedents B and C in the Schedule of Costs Precedents annexed to this practice direction show how bills should be drafted when costs are claimed against the LSC only.

Form and content of bills of costs: title page

5.10 The title page of the bill of costs must set out—

(1) the full title of the proceedings;

(2) the name of the party whose bill it is and a description of the document showing the right to assessment (as to which see para. 13.3 of this practice direction);

(3) if VAT is included as part of the claim for costs, the VAT number of the legal representative or other person in respect of whom VAT is claimed;

(4) details of all legal aid certificates, LSC certificates, certificates recording the determinations of the Director of Legal Aid Casework and relevant amendment certificates in respect of which claims for costs are included in the bill.

Form and content of bills of costs: background information

5.11 The background information included in the bill of costs should set out—

(1) a brief description of the proceedings up to the date of the notice of commencement;

(2) a statement of the status of the legal representatives' employee in respect of whom costs are claimed and (if those costs are calculated on the basis of hourly rates) the hourly rates claimed for each such person.

(3) a brief explanation of any agreement or arrangement between the receiving party and his legal representatives, which affects the costs claimed in the bill.

Form and content of bills of costs: heads of costs

5.12 The bill of costs may consist of items under such of the following heads as may be appropriate—

(1) attendances at court and upon counsel up to the date of the notice of commencement;

(2) attendances on and communications with the receiving party;

(3) attendances on and communications with witnesses including any expert witness;

(4) attendances to inspect any property or place for the purposes of the proceedings;

(5) attendances on and communications with other persons, including offices of public records;

(6) communications with the court and with counsel;

(7) work done on documents:

(8) work done in connection with negotiations with a view to settlement if not already covered in the heads listed above;

(9) attendances on and communications with London and other agents and work done by them;

(10) other work done which was of or incidental to the proceedings and which is not already covered in the heads listed above.

5.13 In respect of each of the heads of costs—

(1) 'communications' means letters out emails out and telephone calls;

(2) communications, which are not routine communications, must be set out in chronological order;

(3) routine communications must be set out as a single item at the end of each head;

5.14 Routine communications are letters out, emails out and telephone calls which because of their simplicity should not be regarded as letters or emails of substance or telephone calls which properly amount to an attendance.

5.15 Each item claimed in the bill of costs must be consecutively numbered.

5.16 In each part of the bill of costs which claims items under head (1) in para. 5.12 (attendances at court and upon counsel) a note should be made of—

(1) all relevant events, including events which do not constitute chargeable items;

(2) any orders for costs which the court made (whether or not a claim is made in respect of those costs in this bill of costs).

5.17 The numbered items of costs may be set out on paper divided into columns. Precedents A, B and C in the Schedule of Costs Precedents annexed to this practice direction illustrate various model forms of bills of costs.

5.18 In respect of heads (2) to (10) in para. 5.12 above, if the number of attendances and communications other than routine communications is twenty or more, the claim for the costs of those items in that section of the bill of costs should be for the total only and should refer to a schedule in which the full record of dates and details is set out. If the bill of costs contains more than one schedule each schedule should be numbered consecutively.

5.19 The bill of costs must not contain any claims in respect of costs or court fees which relate solely to the detailed assessment proceedings other than costs claimed for preparing and checking the bill.

5.20 The summary must show the total profit costs and disbursements claimed separately from the total VAT claimed. Where the bill of costs is divided into parts the summary must also give totals for each part. If each page of the bill gives a page total the summary must also set out the page totals for each page.

5.21 The bill of costs must contain such of the certificates, the texts of which are set out in Precedent F of the Schedule of Costs Precedents annexed to this practice direction, as are appropriate.

5.22 The following provisions relate to work done by legal representatives—

(1) Routine letters out, routine emails out and routine telephone calls will in general be allowed on a unit basis of 6 minutes each, the charge being calculated by reference to the appropriate hourly rate. The unit charge for letters out and emails out will include perusing and considering the routine letters in or emails in.

(2) The court may, in its discretion, allow an actual time charge for preparation of electronic communications sent by legal representatives, which properly amount to attendances provided that the time taken has been recorded.

(3) Local travelling expenses incurred by legal representatives will not be allowed. The definition of 'local' is a matter for the discretion of the court. As a matter of guidance, 'local' will, in general, be taken to mean within a radius of 10 miles from the court dealing with the case at the relevant time. Where travelling and waiting time is claimed, this should be allowed at the rate agreed with the client unless this is more than the hourly rate on the assessment.

(4) The cost of postage, couriers, out-going telephone calls, fax and telex messages will in general not be allowed but the court may exceptionally in its discretion allow such expenses in unusual circumstances or where the cost is unusually heavy.

(5) The cost of making copies of documents will not in general be allowed but the court may exceptionally in its discretion make an allowance for copying in unusual circumstances or where the documents copied are unusually numerous in relation to the nature of the case. Where this discretion is invoked the number of copies made, their purpose and the costs claimed for them must be set out in the bill.

(6) Agency charges as between principal legal representatives and their agents will be dealt with on the principle that such charges, where appropriate, form part of the principal legal representative's charges. Where these charges relate to head (1) in para. 5.12 (attendances at court and on counsel) they must be included in their chronological order in that head. In other cases they must be included in head (9) (attendances on London and other agents).

Period for Commencing Detailed Assessment Proceedings: Rule 47.7

para.6.1 71.12

6.1 The time for commencing the detailed assessment proceedings may be extended or shortened either by agreement (r. 2.11) or by the court (r. 3.1(2)(a)). Any application is to the appropriate office.

6.2 The detailed assessment proceedings are commenced by service of the documents referred to. Permission to commence assessment proceedings out of time is not required.

Sanction for Delay in Commencing Detailed Assessment Proceedings: Rule 47.8

7 An application for an order under r. 47.8 must be made in writing and be issued in the appropriate office. The application notice must be served at least seven days before the hearing.

Points of Dispute and Consequences of not Serving: Rule 47.9

para.8.2 71.14 para.8.3 71.18

8.1 Time for service of points of dispute may be extended or shortened either by agreement (r. 2.11) or by the court (r. 3.1(2)(a)). Any application is to the appropriate office.

8.2 Points of dispute must be short and to the point. They must follow Precedent G in the Schedule of Costs Precedents annexed to this practice direction, so far as practicable. They must:
(a) identify any general points or matters of principle which require decision before the individual items in the bill are addressed; and
(b) identify specific points, stating concisely the nature and grounds of dispute.
Once a point has been made it should not be repeated but the item numbers where the point arises should be inserted in the left hand box as shown in Precedent G.

8.3 The paying party must state in an open letter accompanying the points of dispute what sum, if any, that party offers to pay in settlement of the total costs claimed. The paying party may also make an offer under Part 36.

Procedure where Costs are Agreed and on Discontinuance: Rule 47.10

para.9.1 71.3 para.9.3 71.3

9.1 Where the parties have agreed terms as to the issue of a costs certificate (either interim or final) they should apply under r. 40.6 (Consent judgments and orders) for an order that a certificate be issued in the terms set out in the application. Such an application may be dealt with by a court officer, who may issue the certificate.

9.2 Where in the course of proceedings the receiving party claims that the paying party has agreed to pay costs but that the paying party will neither pay those costs nor join in a consent application under para. 9.1, the receiving party may apply under Part 23 for a certificate either interim or final to be issued.

9.3 Nothing in r. 47.10 prevents parties who seek a judgment or order by consent from including in the draft a term that a party shall pay to another party a specified sum in respect of costs.

9.4 (1) The receiving party may discontinue the detailed assessment proceedings in accordance with Part 38 (Discontinuance).
(2) Where the receiving party discontinues the detailed assessment proceedings before a detailed assessment hearing has been requested, the paying party may apply to the appropriate office for an order about the costs of the detailed assessment proceedings.
(3) Where a detailed assessment hearing has been requested the receiving party may not discontinue unless the court gives permission.
(4) A bill of costs may be withdrawn by consent whether or not a detailed assessment hearing has been requested.

Default Costs Certificate: Rule 47.11

para.10.7 70.3, 70.5 para.10 8 70.3

10.1 (1) A request for the issue of a default costs certificate must be made in form N254 and must be signed by the receiving party or his legal representative.
(2) The request must be accompanied by a copy of the document giving the right to detailed assessment and must be filed at the appropriate office. (Paragraph 13.3 below identifies the appropriate documents.)

10.2 A default costs certificate will be in form N255.

10.3 Attention is drawn to rr. 40.3 (Drawing up and Filing of Judgments and Orders) and 40.4 (Service of Judgments and Orders) which apply to the preparation and service of a default costs certificate. The receiving party will be treated as having permission to draw up a default costs certificate by virtue of this practice direction.

10.4 The issue of a default costs certificate does not prohibit, govern or affect any detailed assessment of the same costs which are payable out of the Community Legal Service Fund or by the Lord Chancellor under Part 1 of the Legal Aid, Sentencing and Punishment of Offenders Act 2012.

10.5 An application for an order staying enforcement of a default costs certificate may be made either—

(a) to a costs judge or district judge of the court office which issued the certificate; or

(b) to the court (if different) which has general jurisdiction to enforce the certificate.

10.6 Proceedings for enforcement of default costs certificates may not be issued in the Costs Office.

Default costs certificate: fixed costs on the issue of a default costs certificate

10.7 Unless PD 45, para. 1.2 (Fixed Costs in Small Claims), applies or unless the court orders otherwise, the fixed costs to be included in a default costs certificate are £80 plus a sum equal to any appropriate court fee payable on the issue of the certificate.

10.8 The fixed costs included in a certificate must not exceed the maximum sum specified for costs and court fee in the notice of commencement.

Setting aside Default Costs Certificate: Rule 47.12

para.11.1–11.3 71.15

11.1 A court officer may set aside a default costs certificate at the request of the receiving party under r. 47.12. A costs judge or a district judge will make any other order or give any directions under this rule.

11.2 (1) An application for an order under r. 47.12(2) to set aside or vary a default costs certificate must be supported by evidence.

(2) In deciding whether to set aside or vary a certificate under r. 47.12(2) the matters to which the court must have regard include whether the party seeking the order made the application promptly.

(3) As a general rule a default costs certificate will be set aside under r. 47.12 only if the applicant shows a good reason for the court to do so and if the applicant files with the application a copy of the bill, a copy of the default costs certificate and a draft of the points of dispute the applicant proposes to serve if the application is granted.

11.3 Attention is drawn to r. 3.1(3) (which enables the court when making an order to make it subject to conditions) and to r. 44.2(8) (which enables the court to order a party whom it has ordered to pay costs to pay an amount on account before the costs are assessed). A costs judge or a district judge may exercise the power of the court to make an order under r. 44.2(8) although he did not make the order about costs which led to the issue of the default costs certificate.

Optional Reply: Rule 47.13

12.1 A reply served by the receiving party under R. 47.13 must be limited to points of principle and concessions only. It must not contain general denials, specific denials or standard form responses.

12.2 Whenever practicable, the reply must be set out in the form of Precedent G.

Detailed Assessment Hearing: Rule 47.14

para.13.2 71.18
para.13.2(d) 71.16
para.13.2(i) 65.6, 71.30
para.13.12 71.12
para.13.13 71.31, 71.33

13.1 The time for requesting a detailed assessment hearing is within three months of the expiry of the period for commencing detailed assessment proceedings.

13.2 The request for a detailed assessment hearing must be in form N258. The request must be accompanied by—

(a) a copy of the notice of commencement of detailed assessment proceedings;

(b) a copy of the bill of costs,

(c) the document giving the right to detailed assessment (see para. 13.3 below);

(d) a copy of the points of dispute, annotated as necessary in order to show which items have been agreed and their value and to show which items remain in dispute and their value;

(e) as many copies of the points of dispute so annotated as there are persons who have served points of dispute;

(f) a copy of any replies served;

(g) copies of all orders made by the court relating to the costs which are to be assessed;

(h) copies of the fee notes and other written evidence as served on the paying party in accordance with para. 5.2 above;
(i) where there is a dispute as to the receiving party's liability to pay costs to the legal representatives who acted for the receiving party, any agreement, letter or other written information provided by the legal representative to the client explaining how the legal representative's charges are to be calculated;
(j) a statement signed by the receiving party or the legal representative giving the name, address for service, reference and telephone number and fax number, if any, of—
  (i) the receiving party;
  (ii) the paying party;
  (iii) any other person who has served points of dispute or who has given notice to the receiving party under para. 5.5(1)(b) above;

and giving an estimate of the length of time the detailed assessment hearing will take;
(k) where the application for a detailed assessment hearing is made by a party other than the receiving party, such of the documents set out in this paragraph as are in the possession of that party;
(l) where the court is to assess the costs of an assisted person or LSC funded client or person to whom civil legal services (within the meaning of Part 1 of the Legal Aid, Sentencing and Punishment of Offenders Act 2012) are provided under arrangement made for the purposes of that Part of that Act—
  (i) the legal aid certificate, LSC certificate, the certificate recording the determination of the Director of Legal Aid Casework and relevant amendment certificates, any authorities and any certificates of discharge or revocation or withdrawal;
  (ii) a certificate, in Precedent F(3) of the Schedule of Costs Precedents;
  (iii) if that person has a financial interest in the detailed assessment hearing and wishes to attend, the postal address of that person to which the court will send notice of any hearing;
  (iv) if the rates payable out of the LSC fund or by the Lord Chancellor under Part 1 of the Legal Aid, Sentencing and Punishment of Offenders Act 2012 are prescribed rates, a schedule to the bill of costs setting out all the items in the bill which are claimed against other parties calculated at the legal aid prescribed rates with or without any claim for enhancement: (further information as to this schedule is set out in para. 17 of this practice direction);
  (v) a copy of any default costs certificate in respect of costs claimed in the bill of costs.

13.3 'The document giving the right to detailed assessment' means such one or more of the following documents as are appropriate to the detailed assessment proceedings—
(a) a copy of the judgment or order of the court or tribunal giving the right to detailed assessment;
(b) a copy of the notice served under r. 3.7 (sanctions for non-payment of certain fees) where a claim is struck out under that rule;
(c) a copy of the notice of acceptance where an offer to settle is accepted under Part 36 (Offers to settle);
(d) a copy of the notice of discontinuance in a case which is discontinued under Part 38 (Discontinuance);
(e) a copy of the award made on an arbitration under any Act or pursuant to an agreement, where no court has made an order for the enforcement of the award;
(f) a copy of the order, award or determination of a statutorily constituted tribunal or body.

13.4 On receipt of the request for a detailed assessment hearing the court will fix a date for the hearing, or, if the costs officer so decides, will give directions or fix a date for a preliminary appointment.

13.5 Unless the court otherwise orders, if the only dispute between the parties concerns disbursements, the hearing shall take place in the absence of the parties on the basis of the documents and the court will issue its decision in writing.

13.6 The court will give at least 14 days' notice of the time and place of the detailed assessment hearing to every person named in the statement referred to in para. 13.2(j) above.

13.7 If either party wishes to make an application in the detailed assessment proceedings the provisions of Part 23 apply.

13.8 (1) This paragraph deals with the procedure to be adopted where a date has been given by the court for a detailed assessment hearing and—
(a) the detailed assessment proceedings are settled; or
(b) a party to the detailed assessment proceedings wishes to apply to vary the date which the court has fixed; or
(c) the parties to the detailed assessment proceedings agree about changes they wish to make to any direction given for the management of the detailed assessment proceedings.

(2) If detailed assessment proceedings are settled, the receiving party must give notice of that fact to the court immediately, preferably by fax.

(3) A party who wishes to apply to vary a direction must do so in accordance with Part 23.

(4) If the parties agree about changes they wish to make to any direction given for the management of the detailed assessment proceedings—
(a) they must apply to the court for an order by consent; and
(b) they must file a draft of the directions sought and an agreed statement of the reasons why the variation is sought; and
(c) the court may make an order in the agreed terms or in other terms without a hearing, but it may direct that a hearing is to be listed.

13.10 (1) If a party wishes to vary that party's bill of costs, points of dispute or a reply, an amended or supplementary document must be filed with the court and copies of it must be served on all other relevant parties.

(2) Permission is not required to vary a bill of costs, points of dispute or a reply but the court may disallow the variation or permit it only upon conditions, including conditions as to the payment of any costs caused or wasted by the variation.

13.11 Unless the court directs otherwise the receiving party must file with the court the papers in support of the bill not less than seven days before the date for the detailed assessment hearing and not more than 14 days before that date.

13.12 The papers to be filed in support of the bill and the order in which they are to be arranged are as follows—
(i) instructions and briefs to counsel arranged in chronological order together with all advices, opinions and drafts received and response to such instructions;
(ii) reports and opinions of medical and other experts;
(iii) any other relevant papers;
(iv) a full set of any relevant statements of case
(v) correspondence, file notes and attendance notes;

13.13 The court may direct the receiving party to produce any document which in the opinion of the court is necessary to enable it to reach its decision. These documents will in the first instance be produced to the court, but the court may ask the receiving party to elect whether to disclose the particular document to the paying party in order to rely on the contents of the document, or whether to decline disclosure and instead rely on other evidence.

13.14 Once the detailed assessment hearing has ended it is the responsibility of the receiving party to remove the papers filed in support of the bill.

Provisional Assessment: Rule 47.15

para.14.1 71.18
para.14.2 71.18
para.14.4(1) 71.18
para.14.4(2) 71.18

14.1 The amount of costs referred to in r. 47.15(1) is £75,000.

14.2 The following provisions of Part 47 and this practice direction will apply to cases falling within r. 47.15—
(1) rr. 47.1, 47.2, 47.4 to 47.13, 47.14 (except paras (6) and (7)), 47.16, 47.17, 47.20 and 47.21; and
(2) paras 1, 2, 4 to 12, 13 (with the exception of paras 13.4 to 13.7, 13.9, 13.11 and 13.14), 15, and 16, of this practice direction.

14.3 In cases falling within r. 47.15, when the receiving party files a request for a detailed assessment hearing, that party must file—

(a) the request in form N258;
(b) the documents set out at paras 8.3 and 13.2 of this practice direction;
(c) an additional copy of the bill, including a statement of the costs claimed in respect of the detailed assessment drawn on the assumption that there will not be an oral hearing following the provisional assessment;
(d) the offers made (those marked 'without prejudice save as to costs' or made under Part 36 must be contained in a sealed envelope, marked 'Part 36 or similar offers', but not indicating which party or parties have made them);
(e) completed Precedent G (points of dispute and any reply).

14.4 (1) On receipt of the request for detailed assessment and the supporting papers, the court will use its best endeavours to undertake a provisional assessment within 6 weeks. No party will be permitted to attend the provisional assessment.
(2) Once the provisional assessment has been carried out the court will return Precedent G (the points of dispute and any reply) with the court's decisions noted upon it. Within 14 days of receipt of Precedent G the parties must agree the total sum due to the receiving party on the basis of the court's decisions. If the parties are unable to agree the arithmetic, they must refer the dispute back to the court for a decision on the basis of written submissions.

14.5 When considering whether to depart from the order indicated by r 47.15(10) the court will take into account the conduct of the parties and any offers made.

14.6 If a party wishes to be heard only as to the order made in respect of the costs of the initial provisional assessment, the court will invite each side to make written submissions and the matter will be finally determined without a hearing. The court will decide what if any order for costs to make in respect of this procedure.

Power to Issue an Interim Certificate: Rule 47.16

15 A party wishing to apply for an interim certificate may do so by making an application in accordance with Part 23.

Final Costs Certificate: Rule 47.17

para.16.4 71.28

16.1 At the detailed assessment hearing the court will indicate any disallowance or reduction in the sums claimed in the bill of costs by making an appropriate note on the bill.

16.2 The receiving party must, in order to complete the bill after the detailed assessment hearing make clear the correct figures agreed or allowed in respect of each item and must re-calculate the summary of the bill appropriately.

16.3 The completed bill of costs must be filed with the court no later than 14 days after the detailed assessment hearing.

16.4 At the same time as filing the completed bill of costs, the party whose bill it is must also produce receipted fee notes and receipted accounts in respect of all disbursements except those covered by a certificate in Precedent F(5) in the Schedule of Costs Precedents annexed to this practice direction.

16.5 No final costs certificate will be issued until all relevant court fees payable on the assessment of costs have been paid.

16.6 If the receiving party fails to file a completed bill in accordance with r. 47.17 the paying party may make an application under Part 23 seeking an appropriate order under r. 3.1.

16.7 A final costs certificate will show—
(a) the amount of any costs which have been agreed between the parties or which have been allowed on detailed assessment;
(b) where applicable the amount agreed or allowed in respect of VAT on such costs.

This provision is subject to any contrary statutory provision relating to costs payable out of the Community Legal Service Fund or by the Lord Chancellor under Part 1 of the Legal Aid, Sentencing and Punishment of Offenders Act 2012.

16.8 A final costs certificate will include disbursements in respect of the fees of counsel only if receipted fee notes or accounts in respect of those disbursements have been produced to the court and only to the extent indicated by those receipts.

16.9 Where the certificate relates to costs payable between parties a separate certificate will be issued for each party entitled to costs.

16.10 Form N257 is a model form of interim costs certificate and form N256 is a model form of final costs certificate.

16.11 An application for an order staying enforcement of an interim costs certificate or final costs certificate may be made either—

(a) to a costs judge or district judge of the court office which issued the certificate; or

(b) to the court (if different) which has general jurisdiction to enforce the certificate.

16.12 An interim or final costs certificate may be enforced as if it were a judgment for the payment of an amount of money. However, proceedings for the enforcement of interim costs certificates or final costs certificates may not be issued in the Costs Office.

Detailed Assessment Procedure where Costs are Payable out of the Community Legal Service Fund or by the Lord Chancellor under Part 1 of the Legal Aid, Sentencing and Punishment of Offenders Act 2012: Rule 47.18

para.17 71.25
para.17.2 71.12, 71.21
para.17.2(1)(f) 71.21
para.17.2(2) 71.12

17.1 The time for requesting a detailed assessment under r. 47.18 is within three months after the date when the right to detailed assessment arose.

17.2 (1) The request for a detailed assessment of costs must be in form N258A. The request must be accompanied by—

(a) a copy of the bill of costs;

(b) the document giving the right to detailed assessment (see para. 13.3 above);

(c) copies of all orders made by the court relating to the costs which are to be assessed;

(d) copies of any fee notes of counsel and any expert in respect of fees claimed in the bill;

(e) written evidence as to any other disbursement which is claimed and which exceeds £500;

(f) the legal aid certificates, LSC certificates, certificates recording the determinations of the Director of Legal Aid Casework, any relevant amendment certificates, any authorities and any certificates of discharge, revocation or withdrawal; and

(g) a statement signed by the legal representative giving the representative's name, address for service, reference, telephone number, fax number, email address where available and, if the assisted person has a financial interest in the detailed assessment and wishes to attend, giving the postal address of that person, to which the court will send notice of any hearing.

(2) The relevant papers in support of the bill as described in para. 13.12 must only be lodged if requested by the costs officer.

17.3 Where the court has provisionally assessed a bill of costs it will send to the legal representative a notice, in form N253 annexed to this practice direction, of the amount of costs which the court proposes to allow together with the bill itself. The legal representative should, if the provisional assessment is to be accepted, then complete the bill.

17.4 If the solicitor whose bill it is, or any other party wishes to make an application in the detailed assessment proceedings, the provisions of Part 23 applies.

17.5 It is the responsibility of the legal representative to complete the bill by entering in the bill the correct figures allowed in respect of each item, recalculating the summary of the bill appropriately and completing the Community Legal Service assessment certificate (form EX80A).

Costs payable by the Legal Services Commission or Lord Chancellor at prescribed rates

17.6 Where the costs of an assisted person or LSC funded client or person to whom civil legal services (within the meaning of Part 1 of the Legal Aid, Sentencing and Punishment of Offenders Act 2012) are provided under arrangements made for the purposes of that Part of that Act are payable by another person but costs can be claimed against the LSC or Lord Chancellor at prescribed rates (with or without enhancement), the solicitor of the assisted person or LSC funded client or person to whom civil legal services are provided must file a legal aid/ LSC schedule in accordance with para. 13.2(l) above. The schedule should follow as closely as possible Precedent E of the Schedule of Costs Precedents annexed to this practice direction.

17.7 The schedule must set out by reference to the item numbers in the bill of costs, all the costs claimed as payable by another person, but the arithmetic in the schedule should claim those items at prescribed rates only (with or without any claim for enhancement).

17.8 Where there has been a change in the prescribed rates during the period covered by the bill of costs, the schedule (as opposed to the bill) should be divided into separate parts, so as to deal separately with each change of rate. The schedule must also be divided so as to correspond with any divisions in the bill of costs.

17.9 If the bill of costs contains additional columns setting out costs claimed against the LSC or Lord Chancellor only, the schedule may be set out in a separate document or, alternatively, may be included in the additional columns of the bill.

17.10 The detailed assessment of the legal aid/ LSC schedule will take place immediately after the detailed assessment of the bill of costs but on occasions, the court may decide to conduct the detailed assessment of the legal aid/ LSC schedule separately from any detailed assessment of the bill of costs. This will occur, for example, where a default costs certificate is obtained as between the parties but that certificate is not set aside at the time of the detailed assessment of the legal aid costs.

17.11 Where costs have been assessed at prescribed rates it is the responsibility of the legal representative to enter the correct figures allowed in respect of each item and to recalculate the summary of the legal aid/ LSC schedule.

Detailed Assessment Procedure where Costs are Payable out of a Fund other than the Community Legal Service Fund or by the Lord Chancellor under Part 1 of the Legal Aid, Sentencing and Punishment of Offenders Act 2012: Rule 47.19

18.1 Rule 47.19 enables the court to direct under r. 47.19(3) that the receiving party must serve a copy of the request for assessment and copies of the documents which accompany it, on any person who has a financial interest in the outcome of the assessment.

18.2 A person has a financial interest in the outcome of the assessment if the assessment will or may affect the amount of money or property to which that person is or may become entitled out of the fund. Where an interest in the fund is itself held by a trustee for the benefit of some other person, that trustee will be treated as the person having such a financial interest unless it is not appropriate to do so. 'Trustee' includes a personal representative, receiver or any other person acting in a fiduciary capacity.

18.3 The request for a detailed assessment of costs out of the fund should be in form N258B, be accompanied by the documents set out at para. 17.2(1) (a) to (e) and the following—

(a) a statement signed by the receiving party giving his name, address for service, reference, telephone number,

(b) a statement of the postal address of any person who has a financial interest in the outcome of the assessment; and

(c) if a person having a financial interest is a child or protected party, a statement to that effect.

18.4 The court will decide, having regard to the amount of the bill, the size of the fund and the number of persons who have a financial interest, which of those persons should be served and may give directions about service and about the hearing. The court may dispense with service on all or some of those persons.

18.5 Where the court makes an order dispensing with service on all such persons it may proceed at once to make a provisional assessment, or, if it decides that a hearing is necessary, give appropriate directions. Before deciding whether a hearing is necessary, the court may require the receiving party to provide further information relating to the bill.

18.6 (1) The court will send the provisionally assessed bill to the receiving party with a notice in form N253. If the receiving party is legally represented the legal representative should, if the provisional assessment is to be accepted, then complete the bill.

(2) The court will fix a date for a detailed assessment hearing, if the receiving party informs the court within 14 days after receiving the notice in form N253, that the receiving party wants the court to hold such a hearing.

18.7 The court will give at least 14 days' notice of the time and place of the hearing to the receiving party and to any person who has a financial and who has been served with a copy of the request for assessment.

18.8 If any party or any person who has a financial interest wishes to make an application in the detailed assessment proceedings, the provisions of Part 23 (General Rules about Applications for Court Orders) apply.

18.9 If the receiving party is legally represented the legal representative must complete the bill by inserting the correct figures in respect of each item and must recalculate the summary of the bill.

Costs of Detailed Assessment Proceedings — Rule 47.20: Offers to Settle under Part 36 or Otherwise

para.19 71.23

19. Where an offer to settle is made, whether under Part 36 or otherwise, it should specify whether or not it is intended to be inclusive of the cost of preparation of the bill, interest and VAT. Unless the offer states otherwise it will be treated as being inclusive of these.

Appeals from Authorised Court Officers in Detailed Assessment Proceedings: Rules 47.22 to 47.25

paras.20.1–20.6 71.29
para.20.2 71.29
para.20.5 71.29

20.1 This Section relates only to appeals from authorised court officers in detailed assessment proceedings. All other appeals arising out of detailed assessment proceedings (and arising out of summary assessments) are dealt with in accordance with Part 52 and Practice Directions 52A to 52E. The destination of appeals is dealt with in accordance with the Access to Justice Act 1999 (Destination of Appeals) Order 2000.

20.2 In respect of appeals from authorised court officers, there is no requirement to obtain permission, or to seek written reasons.

20.3 The appellant must file a notice which should be in form N161 (an appellant's notice).

20.4 The appeal will be heard by a costs judge or a district judge of the High Court, and is a re-hearing.

20.5 The appellant's notice should, if possible, be accompanied by a suitable record of the judgment appealed against. Where reasons given for the decision have been officially recorded by the court an approved transcript of that record should accompany the notice. Where there is no official record the following documents will be acceptable—

(a) the officer's comments written on the bill;
(b) advocates' notes of the reasons agreed by the respondent if possible and approved by the authorised court officer.

When the appellant was unrepresented before the authorised court officer, it is the duty of any advocate for the respondent to make a note of the reasons promptly available, free of charge to the appellant where there is no official record or if the court so directs. Where the appellant was represented before the authorised court officer, it is the duty of the appellant's own former advocate to make a note available. The appellant should submit the note of the reasons to the costs judge or district judge hearing the appeal.

20.6 Where the appellant is not able to obtain a suitable record of the authorised court officer's decision within the time in which the appellant's notice must be filed, the appellant's notice must still be completed to the best of the appellant's ability. It may however be amended subsequently with the permission of the costs judge or district judge hearing the appeal.

SCHEDULE OF COSTS PRECEDENTS

precedents A–D 71.13
precedent C 71.21
precedent D 71.21
precedent F 71.54
precedent G 71.14, 71.18

[The following precedents, in the schedule to PD 47, may be viewed at <http://www.justice.gov.uk/courts/procedure-rules/civil>:

A: Model form of bill of costs
B: Model form of bill of costs (detailed assessment of additional liability only)
C: Model form of bill of costs (payable by defendant and the LSC)
D: Model form of bill of costs (alternative form, single column for amounts claimed, separate parts for costs payable by the LSC only)
E: Legal Aid/LSC schedule of costs
F: Certificates for inclusion in bill of costs
G: Points of dispute and reply
H: Costs budget
J: Solicitors Act 1974: Part 8 claim form under Part III of the Act
K: Solicitors Act 1974: order for delivery of bill
L: Solicitors Act 1974: order for detailed assessment (client)
M: Solicitors Act 1974: order for detailed assessment (solicitors)
P: Solicitors Act 1974: breakdown of costs

Form N253 is online at <http://hmctsformfinder.justice.gov.uk>.]

CPR Part 48 Part 2 of the Legal Aid, Sentencing and Punishment of Offenders Act 2012 relating to Civil Litigation Funding and Costs: Transitional Provision in Relation to Pre-Commencement Funding Arrangements

Part 48 **71.56** [For commentary on a specific rule, please refer to the cross-references after the title of the rule.]

r.48.1 **68.32**
r.48.1(2) **57.6**
r.48.1(3) **68.32**

48.1

(1) The provisions of CPR Parts 43 to 48 relating to funding arrangements, and the attendant provisions of the Costs Practice Direction, will apply in relation to a pre-commencement funding arrangement as they were in force immediately before 1 April 2013, with such modifications (if any) as may be made by a practice direction on or after that date.
(2) A reference in rule 48.2 to a rule is to that rule as it was in force immediately before 1 April 2013.

r.48.2 **6.11, 69.3**
r.48.2(1)(a)(i) **69.3**
r.48.2(1)(b) **6.3**

48.2

(1) A pre-commencement funding arrangement is—
  (a) in relation to proceedings other than insolvency-related proceedings, publication and privacy proceedings or a mesothelioma claim—
    (i) a funding arrangement as defined by rule 43.2(1)(k)(i) where—
      (aa) the agreement was entered into before 1 April 2013 specifically for the purposes of the provision to the person by whom the success fee is payable of advocacy or litigation services in relation to the matter that is the subject of the proceedings in which the costs order is to be made; or
      (bb) the agreement was entered into before 1 April 2013 and advocacy or litigation services were provided to that person under the agreement in connection with that matter before 1 April 2013;
    (ii) a funding arrangement as defined by rule 43.2(1)(k)(ii) where the party seeking to recover the insurance premium took out the insurance policy in relation to the proceedings before 1 April 2013;
    (iii) a funding arrangement as defined by rule 43.2(1)(k)(iii) where the agreement with the membership organisation to meet the costs was made before 1 April 2013 specifically in respect of the costs of other parties to proceedings relating to the matter which is the subject of the proceedings in which the costs order is to be made;
  (b) in relation to insolvency-related proceedings, publication and privacy proceedings or a mesothelioma claim—
    (i) a funding arrangement as defined by rule 43.2(1)(k)(i) where—
      (aa) the agreement was entered into before the relevant date specifically for the purposes of the provision to the person by whom the success fee is payable of advocacy or litigation services in relation to the matter that is the subject of the proceedings in which the costs order is to be made; or
      (bb) the agreement was entered into before the relevant date and advocacy or litigation services were provided to that person under the agreement in connection with that matter before the relevant date;
    (ii) a funding arrangement as defined by rule 43.2(1)(k)(ii) where the party seeking to recover the insurance premium took out the insurance policy in relation to the proceedings before the relevant date.

(2) In paragraph (1)—
(a) 'insolvency-related proceedings' means any proceedings—
(i) in England and Wales brought by a person acting in the capacity of—
(aa) a liquidator of a company which is being wound up in England and Wales or Scotland under Parts IV or V of the Insolvency Act 1986; or
(bb) a trustee of a bankrupt's estate under Part IX of the Insolvency Act 1986;
(ii) brought by a person acting in the capacity of an administrator appointed pursuant to the provisions of Part II of the Insolvency Act 1986;
(iii) in England and Wales brought by a company which is being wound up in England and Wales or Scotland under Parts IV or V of the Insolvency Act 1986; or
(iv) brought by a company which has entered administration under Part II of the Insolvency Act 1986;
(b) 'news publisher' means a person who publishes a newspaper, magazine or website containing news or information about or comment on current affairs;
(c) 'publication and privacy proceedings' means proceedings for—
(i) defamation;
(ii) malicious falsehood;
(iii) breach of confidence involving publication to the general public;
(iv) misuse of private information; or
(v) harassment, where the defendant is a news publisher.
(d) 'a mesothelioma claim' is a claim for damages in respect of diffuse mesothelioma (within the meaning of the Pneumoconiosis etc. (Workers' Compensation) Act 1979; and
(e) 'the relevant date' is the date on which sections 44 and 46 of the Legal Aid, Sentencing and Punishment of Offenders Act 2012 came into force in relation to proceedings of the sort in question.

PD 48 Practice Direction 48 — Part 2 of the Legal Aid, Sentencing and Punishment of Offenders Act 2012 relating to Civil Litigation Funding and Costs: Transitional Provision and Exceptions

This practice direction supplements CPR, Part 48.

PD 48 71.56

Transitional Provisions: General

1.1 Sections 44 and 46 of the Legal Aid, Sentencing and Punishment of Offenders Act 2012 ('the 2012 Act') make changes to the effect that a costs order may not include, respectively, provision requiring the payment by one party of all or part of a success fee payable by another party under a conditional fee agreement or of an amount in respect of all or part of the premium of a costs insurance policy taken out by another party. These changes come into force on 1 April 2013.

1.2 Sections 44(6) and 46(3) of the 2012 Act make saving provisions to the effect, respectively, that these changes do not apply so as to prevent a costs order including such provision where the conditional fee agreement in relation to the proceedings was entered into (or, in relation to a collective conditional fee agreement, services were provided to the party under the agreement), or the costs insurance policy in relation to the proceedings taken out, before the date on which the changes come into force.

1.3 The provisions in the CPR relating to funding arrangements have accordingly been revoked (either in whole or in part as they relate to funding arrangements) with effect from 1 April 2013; but they will remain relevant, and will continue to have effect notwithstanding the revocations, after that date for those cases covered by the saving provisions.

1.4 The provisions in the CPR in force prior to 1 April 2012 relating to funding arrangements include—

(a) CPR, rr. 43.2(1)(a), (k), (l), (m), (n), (o), 43.2(3) and 43.2(4);
(b) CPR, rr. 44.3A, 44.3B, 44.12B, 44.15 and 44.16;
(c) CPR, rr. 45.8, 45.10, 45.12, 45.13, Sections III to V (45.15 to 45.19, 45.20 to 22 and 45.23 to 26), 45.28 and 45.31 to 45.40;
(d) CPR, r. 46.3;
(e) CPR, r. 48.8.

Mesothelioma Claims

2.1 By virtue of s. 48 of the 2012 Act, the changes relating to recoverable success fees and insurance premiums which are made by ss. 44 and 46 of the Act may not be commenced, and accordingly will not apply, in relation to mesothelioma claims (defined by s. 48(2) of the Act as having the same meaning as in the Pneumoconiosis etc. (Workers' Compensation) Act 1979) until such time as a review has been carried out and the conclusions of that review published. It will accordingly remain possible for a costs order in favour of a party to such proceedings to include provision requiring the payment of success fees and premiums under after-the-event costs insurance policies, and so the provisions of the CPR relating to funding arrangements as in force immediately prior to 1 April 2013 will continue to apply in relation to such proceedings, whether commenced before or after 1 April 2013. This will include the provision for fixed recoverable success fees in respect of employers' liability disease claims in Section V of Part 45 (CPR, rr. 45.23 to 45.26), which will otherwise cease to apply other than to claims in which a CFA was entered into or a costs insurance policy taken out before 1 April 2013.

2.2 On the later date when ss. 44 and 46 are brought into force in relation to mesothelioma claims, *the saving provisions* of sections 44(6) and 46(3) will have effect in relation to funding arrangements in such claims as they do more generally, save that the operative date for the saving provisions will not be 1 April 2013 but the later date.

Insolvency-related Proceedings and Publication and Privacy Proceedings

3.1 Sections 44 and 46 of the 2012 Act are not being commenced immediately in relation to certain proceedings related to insolvency. Until such time as those sections are commenced in relation to those proceedings, therefore, they are in a similar position as regards funding arrangements to mesothelioma claims.

3.2 Similarly, ss. 44 and 46 of the 2012 Act are not being commenced immediately in respect of publication and privacy proceedings, which will accordingly be in a similar position as regards funding arrangements to mesothelioma claims and insolvency-related proceedings until such time as those sections are commenced in relation to them.

New Provision in relation to Clinical Negligence Claims

4.1 Section 46 of the 2012 Act enables the Lord Chancellor by regulations to provide that a costs order may include provision requiring the payment of an amount in respect of all or part of the premium of a costs insurance policy, where—

(a) the order is made in favour of a party to clinical negligence proceedings of a prescribed description;

(b) the party has taken out a costs insurance policy insuring against the risk of incurring a liability to pay for one or more expert reports in respect of clinical negligence in connection with the proceedings (or against that risk and other risks);

(c) the policy is of a prescribed description;

(d) the policy states how much of the premium relates to the liability to pay for such an expert report or reports, and the amount to be paid is in respect of that part of the premium.

4.2 The regulations made under the power are the Recovery of Costs Insurance Premiums in Clinical Negligence Proceedings Regulations 2013 (SI 2013/92). The regulations relate only to clinical negligence cases where a costs insurance policy is taken out on or after 1 April 2013, so the provisions in force in the CPR prior to 1 April 2013 relating to funding arrangements will not apply.

CPR Part 49 Specialist Proceedings

49

These Rules apply to proceedings under—

(a) the Companies Act 1985;
(b) the Companies Act 2006; and
(c) other legislation relating to companies and limited liability partnerships,

subject to the provision of the relevant practice direction which applies to those proceedings.

PD 49A Practice Direction 49A — Applications under the Companies Acts and Related Legislation

PD 49A 11.7, 13.7, 42.25, 85.3, 85.4, 85.5, 85.7

This practice direction supplements CPR, Part 49.

I GENERAL

Definitions

1 In this practice direction:
'the 1985 Act' means the Companies Act 1985;
'the 2006 Act' means the Companies Act 2006;
'the CJPA' means the Criminal Justice and Police Act 2001;
'the EC Regulation' means Council Regulation (EC) No. 2157/2001 of 8 October 2001 on the Statute for a European Company (SE);
'Part VII FSMA' means Part VII of the Financial Services and Markets Act 2000;
'the Cross-Border Mergers Regulations' means the Companies (Cross-Border Mergers) Regulations 2007 (SI 2007/2974).

Application of This Practice Direction

para.2 85.3

2 This practice direction applies to proceedings under:
(a) the 1985 Act;
(b) the 2006 Act (except proceedings under part 11, ch. 1, or part 30 of that Act);
(c) the CJPA, s. 59;
(d) the EC Regulation, arts 22, 25 and 26;
(e) Part VII FSMA; and
(f) the Cross-Border Mergers Regulations.

(CPR, Part 19, and PD 19C contain provisions about proceedings under the 2006 Act, part 11, ch. 1 (derivative claims).)

Application of This Practice Direction to Certain Proceedings in Relation to Limited Liability Partnerships

para.3 85.3

3 This practice direction applies to proceedings under the 1985 Act and 2006 Act as applied to limited liability partnerships by regulations made under the Limited Liability Partnerships Act 2000.

Title of Documents

para.4(1)–(2) 85.5

4 (1) The claim form in proceedings under the 1985 Act, the 2006 Act, Part VII FSMA, the EC Regulation or the Cross-Border Mergers Regulations, and any application, affidavit, witness statement, notice or other document in such proceedings, must be entitled 'In the matter of [the name of the company in question] and in the matter of [the relevant law]', where '[the relevant law]' means 'the Companies Act 1985', 'the Companies Act 2006', 'Part VII of the Financial Services and Markets Act 2000', 'Council Regulation (EC) No 2157/2001 of 8 October 2001 on the Statute for a European Company (SE)' or 'the Companies (Cross-Border Merger) Regulations 2007', as the case may be.

(2) Where a company changes its name in the course of proceedings, the title must be altered by—
(a) substituting the new name for the old; and
(b) inserting the old name in brackets at the end of the title.

CPR 26–50 & PDs

Starting Proceedings and Notification of Application Made

para.5 42.25
para.5(1) 85.4
para.5(1)(b) 85.4
para.5(2) 85.4
para.5(3) 85.7

5 (1) Proceedings to which this practice direction applies must be started by a Part 8 claim form—
(a) unless a provision of this or another practice direction provides otherwise, but
(b) subject to any modification of that procedure by this or any other practice direction.
(2) The claim form—
(a) will, where issued in the High Court, be issued out of the Companies Court or a Chancery district registry; or
(b) will, where issued in a county court, be issued out of a county court office.
(3) Where this practice direction requires a party to proceedings to notify another person of an application, such notification must, unless the court orders otherwise, be given by sending to that other person a copy of the claim form as soon as reasonably practicable after the claim form has been issued.

SECTION II PARTICULAR APPLICATIONS UNDER THE 2006 ACT

References to Provisions of the 2006 Act in This Section

6 In this Section, a reference to a section by number, not otherwise identified, is to the section so numbered in the 2006 Act.

Company Generally to Be Made a Party to a Claim under the 2006 Act

para.7 85.6
para.7(1)–(2) 85.6

7 (1) Where in a claim under the 2006 Act the company concerned is not the claimant, the company is to be made a defendant to the claim unless—
(a) any other enactment, the CPR or this or another practice direction makes a different provision; or
(b) the court orders otherwise.
(2) Where an application is made in the course of proceedings to which the company is or is required to be a defendant, the company must be made a respondent to the application unless—
(a) any other enactment, the CPR or this or another practice direction makes a different provision; or
(b) the court orders otherwise.

Applications under Section 169 (Director's Right to Protest against Removal)

para.8 85.7

8 (1) This paragraph applies to an application for an order under s. 169(5).
(2) The claimant must notify the director concerned of the application.

Applications under Section 244 (Disclosure under Court Order of Protected Information)

9 (1) This paragraph applies to an application for an order under s. 244.
(2) The claimant must notify the director concerned of the application.

Applications under Section 295 (Application not to Circulate Members' Statement) or Section 317 (Application not to Circulate Members' Statement)

para.10 85.7

10 (1) This paragraph applies to an application for an order under s. 295 or 317.
(2) The claimant must notify each member who requested the circulation of the relevant statement of the application.

Proceedings under Section 370 (Unauthorised Donations — Enforcement of Directors' Liabilities by Shareholder Action)

para.11 85.4

11 Proceedings to enforce a director's liability under s. 370 must be started by a Part 7 claim form.

Proceedings under Section 456 (Application in Respect of Defective Accounts or Directors' Report)

para.12 85.7

12 (1) This paragraph applies to an application for a declaration under s. 456(1).
(2) The claimant must notify any former director who was a director at the time of the approval of the annual accounts or directors' report of the application.

Proceedings under Section 511, 514, 515 or 518 (Representations or Statements Made by the Auditor)

para.13 85.7

13 (1) This paragraph applies to an application for an order under s. 511(6), 514(7), 515(7) or 518(9).
(2) The claimant must notify the auditor of the application.

Proceedings under Section 527 (Members' Powers to Require Website Publication of Audit Concerns)

para.14 85.7

14 (1) This paragraph applies to an application for an order under s. 527(5).
(2) The claimant must, unless the court orders otherwise, notify each member who requested a statement to be placed on the website of the application.

Proceedings under Parts 26 and 27 of the 2006 Act (Applications to Sanction a Compromise or Arrangement)

para.15 85.6, 85.8

15 (1) This paragraph applies to an application for an order under parts 26 and 27 of the 2006 Act to sanction a compromise or arrangement.
(2) Where the application is made by the company concerned, or by a liquidator or administrator of the company, there need be no defendant to the claim unless the court so orders.
(3) The claim form must be supported by written evidence, including—
(a) statutory information about the company; and
(b) the terms of the proposed compromise or arrangement.
(4) The claim form must seek—
(a) directions for convening a meeting of creditors or members or both, as the case requires;
(b) the sanction of the court to the compromise or arrangement, if it is approved at the meeting or meetings, and a direction for a further hearing for that purpose; and
(c) a direction that the claimant files a copy of a report to the court by the chairman of the meeting or of each meeting.

Proceedings under Section 955 (Takeovers — Enforcement by the Court)

para.16 85.4

16 Proceedings for an order under s. 955 must be started by a Part 7 claim form.

Proceedings under Section 968 (Takeovers — Effect on Contractual Restrictions)

para.17 85.4

17 Proceedings to recover compensation under s. 968(6) must be started by a Part 7 claim form.

Applications under Section 1132 (Production and Inspection of Documents Where Offence Suspected)

para.18 85.7

18 (1) This paragraph applies to an application for an order under s. 1132.
(2) No notice need be given to any person against whom the order is sought.

SECTION III OTHER APPLICATIONS

Applications under the EC Regulation — Article 25

para.19 85.3 para.19(4) 85.6

19 (1) In this paragraph and paras 20 and 21—
(a) a reference to an article by number is a reference to the article so numbered in the EC Regulation; and
(b) 'SE' means a European public limited-liability company (Societas Europaea) within the meaning of the EC Regulation.
(1A) Any document that is filed with the court must, if not in English, be accompanied by a translation of that document into English—
(a) certified by a notary public or other qualified person; or
(b) accompanied by written evidence confirming that the translation is accurate.
(2) An application for a certificate under art. 25(2)—
(a) must set out the pre-merger acts and formalities applicable to the applicant company;
(b) must be accompanied by evidence that those acts and formalities have been completed; and
(c) must be accompanied by copies of—
(i) the draft terms of merger, as provided for in art. 20;
(ii) the entry in the *London Gazette* containing the particulars specified in art. 21;
(iii) a directors' report;
(iv) an expert's report; and
(v) the resolution of the applicant company approving the draft terms of merger in accordance with art. 23.
(3) In para. (2)(c)—
'directors' report' in relation to a company means a report by the directors of the company containing the information required by s. 908 of the 2006 Act;
'expert's report' in relation to a company means a report to the members of the company drawn up in accordance with—
(a) s. 909 of the 2006 Act; or
(b) art. 22.
(4) There need be no defendant to the application.

Applications under the EC Regulation — Article 22 (Appointment of an Independent Expert)

para.20 15.5, 85.3

20
(1) An application under art. 22 for the appointment of an independent expert must be made—
(a) where the application is made at the same time as or after the application under art. 25(2) for the approval of the pre-merger acts and formalities has been filed with the court, by application notice pursuant to Part 23; or
(b) where no application under art. 25(2) has been made, by a Part 8 claim form.
(2) The application (whether by a claim form or application notice, as the case may be) must be accompanied by evidence in support of the application.

Applications under the EC Regulation — Article 26

para.21 85.3
para.21(2) 85.6

21 (1) Where under art. 26(2) a merging company is required to submit a certificate to the High Court, that company must, if no other merging company has begun proceedings under art. 26, start such proceedings by way of a Part 8 claim form.
(2) There need be no defendant to the claim.
(3) The claim form—
(a) must name the SE and all of the merging companies;
(b) must be accompanied by the documents referred to in sub-para. (5); and
(c) must be served on each of the other merging companies.
(4) Where under art. 26(2) a merging company is required to submit a certificate to the High Court, and proceedings under art. 26 have already been begun, the company—
(a) must, not more than 14 days after service on it of the claim form, file an acknowledgment of service and serve it on each of the other merging companies; and
(b) must file the documents, in relation to each merging company, referred to in sub-para. (5) within the time limit specified in art. 26(2), and serve copies of them on each of the other merging companies.
(5) The documents in relation to each merging company are—
(a) the certificate issued under art. 25(2) in respect of the company;
(b) a copy of the draft terms of merger approved by the company;
(c) evidence that arrangements for employee involvement have been determined by the company pursuant to Council Directive 2001/86/EC of 8 October 2001 supplementing the Statute for a European company with regard to the involvement of employees; and
(d) evidence that the SE has been formed in accordance with art. 26(4).

Applications under the Cross-Border Mergers Regulations

para.22 85.3

22 (1) In this paragraph and paras 23 to 25 a reference to a regulation by number is a reference to the regulation so numbered in the Cross-Border Mergers Regulations.
(2) Any document that is filed with the court must, if not in English, be accompanied by a translation of that document into English—
(a) certified by a notary public or other qualified person; or
(b) accompanied by written evidence confirming that the translation is accurate.

Application for Approval of Pre-merger Requirements

para.23 85.3 para.23(2) 85.6

23 (1) This paragraph applies to an application under reg. 6.
(2) There need be no defendant to the application.
(3) The application must—
(a) set out the pre-merger acts and formalities required by regs 7 to 10 and 12 to 15 applicable to the applicant company; and
(b) be accompanied by evidence that those acts and formalities have been completed properly.
(4) Where an application under reg. 11 to summon a meeting of creditors has been made, the court will not determine the application under reg. 6 to approve the pre-merger requirements until the result of the meeting is known.
(5) Where the court makes an order certifying that all pre-merger acts and formalities have been completed properly, the applicant must draw up the order and file it no later than seven days after the date on which the order was made so that it can be sealed(GL) by the court. The court will seal(GL) and return the order to the applicant within 15 days of receipt.

Application for Appointment of Independent Expert or to Summon a Meeting of Members or Creditors

para.24 85.3

24 (1) This paragraph applies to—
(a) an application for the appointment of an independent expert under reg. 9;
(b) an application under reg. 11 for an order to summon a meeting of members or creditors or both.

(2) The application must be made—
(a) where the application is made at the same time as or after the application for approval of the pre-merger acts and formalities under reg. 6 has been filed with the court, by application notice pursuant to Part 23; or
(b) where no application under reg. 6 has been made, by a Part 8 claim form.
(3) The application (whether by claim form or application notice, as the case may be) must be accompanied by evidence in support of the application.

Application for the Approval of the Completion of the Merger

para.25 85.3 para.25(3) 85.6

25 (1) This paragraph applies to an application under reg. 16.
(2) The application must be made by a Part 8 claim form.
(3) There need be no defendant to the application.
(4) The claim form must be accompanied by—
(a) the documents referred to in reg. 16(1)(b), (c) and (e);
(b) where appropriate, evidence that reg. 16(1)(f) has been complied with; and
(c) such other evidence as may be required to enable the court to decide the application.
(5) Where the court makes an order under reg. 16 approving the merger, it will fix a date on which the consequences of the merger are to take effect.

Applications under Section 59 of the CJPA

para.26 85.3

26 (1) In sub-paras (2) to (8)—
(a) a reference to a section by number, not otherwise identified, is a reference to the section so numbered in the CJPA; and
(b) references to a relevant interest in property have the same meaning as in s. 59 of the CJPA.
(2) This paragraph applies to applications under s. 59 in respect of property seized in exercise of the power conferred by s. 448(3) of the 1985 Act (including any additional powers of seizure conferred by s. 50 that are exercisable by reference to that power).
(3) The application must be supported by evidence—
(a) that the claimant has a relevant interest in the property to which the application relates; and
(b) in the case of an application under s. 59(2), that one or more of the grounds set out in s. 59(3) is satisfied in relation to the property.
(4) Where the claimant has a relevant interest in the property, the defendants to the claim are to be—
(a) the person in possession of the property; and
(b) any other person who appears to have a relevant interest in the property.
(5) Where the claimant is in possession of the property, the defendants are to be—
(a) the person from whom the property was seized; and
(b) any other person who appears to have a relevant interest in the property.
(6) In the case of an application for the return of seized property, the claimant must serve a copy of the claim form and the claimant's evidence in support of it on the person specified, by the notice given under s. 52 when the property was seized, as the person to whom notice of such an application should be given.
(7) If the claimant knows the identity of the person who seized the property, the claimant must also notify that person of the application.
(8) When the court issues the claim form it will fix a date for the hearing.

SECTION IV CONDUCT OF PROCEEDINGS

Reduction of Capital — Evidence

para.27 85.8

27 In the case of an application to confirm a reduction in capital, if any shares were issued otherwise than for cash—

(a) for any shares so issued on or after 1 January 1901, it is sufficient to set out in the application the extent to which the shares are, or are treated as being, paid up; and
(b) for any shares so issued between 1 September 1867 and 31 December 1900, the application must also show that the requirement as to the filing of the relevant contract with the Registrar of Joint Stock Companies in the Companies Act 1867, s. 25, was complied with.

SECTION V MISCELLANEOUS

Service of Documents

para.28 85.7

28 The parties are responsible for service of documents in proceedings to which this practice direction applies.

Transitional Provisions

29 A claim started, or an application made, before 1 October 2007 may be continued in accordance with the practice direction in force on 30 September 2007 as if it had not been revoked.

PD 49B Practice Direction 49B — Order under Section 127 Insolvency Act 1986

This practice direction supplements CPR, Part 49.

PD 49B **85.11** paras.2–7 **82.67**
para.1 **85.10**

1 Attention is drawn to the undesirability of asking as a matter of course for a winding-up order as an alternative to an order under the Companies Act 2006, s. 994. The petition should not ask for a winding-up order unless that is the remedy which the petitioner prefers or it is thought that it may be the only remedy to which the petitioner is entitled.

2 Whenever a winding-up order is asked for in a contributory's petition, the petition must state whether the petitioner consents or objects to an order under the Insolvency Act 1986, s. 127 ('a s.127 order'), in the standard form. If he objects, the written evidence in support must contain a short statement of his reasons.

3 If the petitioner objects to a s.127 order in the standard form but consents to such an order in a modified form, the petition must set out in the form of order to which he consents, and the written evidence in support must contain a short statement of his reasons for seeking the modification.

4 If the petition contains a statement that the petitioner consents to a s.127 order, whether in the standard or a modified form, but the petitioner changes his mind before the first hearing of the petition, he must notify the respondents and may apply on notice to a judge for an order directing that no s.127 order or a modified order only (as the case may be) shall be made by the registrar, but validating dispositions made without notice of the order made by the judge.

5 If the petition contains a statement that the petitioner consents to a s.127 order, whether in the standard or a modified form, the registrar shall without further enquiry make an order in such form at the first hearing unless an order to the contrary has been made by the judge in the meantime.

6 If the petition contains a statement that the petitioner objects to a s.127 order in the standard form, the company may apply (in the case of urgency, without notice) to the judge for an order.

7 Section 127 Order — Standard Form:

Title etc.

ORDER that notwithstanding the presentation of the said Petition

(1) payments made into or out of the bank accounts of the Company in the ordinary course of business of the Company and

(2) dispositions of the property of the Company made in the ordinary course of its business for proper value between the date of presentation of the Petition and the date of judgment on the Petition or further order in the meantime

shall not be void by virtue of the provisions of section 127 of the Insolvency Act 1986 in the event of an Order for the winding up of the Company being made on the said Petition provided that [*the relevant bank*] shall be under no obligation to verify for itself whether any transaction through the company's bank accounts is in the ordinary course of business, or that it represents full market value for the relevant transaction.

This form of Order may be departed from where the circumstances of the case require.

CPR Part 50 Application of the Schedules

[For commentary on a specific rule, please refer to the cross-references after the title of the rule.]
r.50(2) **1.6**

50 (1) The Schedules to these Rules set out, with modifications, certain provisions previously contained in the Rules of the Supreme Court 1965 and the County Court Rules 1981.

(2) These Rules apply in relation to the proceedings to which the Schedules apply subject to the provisions in the Schedules and the relevant practice directions.

(3) A provision previously contained in the Rules of the Supreme Court 1965—
(a) is headed 'RSC';
(b) is numbered with the Order and rule numbers it bore as part of the RSC; and
(c) unless otherwise stated in the Schedules or the relevant practice direction, applies only to proceedings in the High Court.

(4) A provision previously contained in the County Court Rules 1981—
(a) is headed 'CCR';
(b) is numbered with the Order and rule numbers it bore as part of the CCR; and
(c) unless otherwise stated in the Schedules or the relevant practice direction, applies only to proceedings in the county court.

(5) A reference in a Schedule to a rule by number alone is a reference to the rule so numbered in the Order in which the reference occurs.

(6) A reference in a Schedule to a rule by number prefixed by 'CPR' is a reference to the rule with that number in these Rules.

(7) In the Schedules, unless otherwise stated, 'the Act' means—
(a) in a provision headed 'RSC', the Senior Courts Act 1981; and
(b) in a provision headed 'CCR', the County Courts Act 1984.

CPR Part 51 Transitional Arrangements and Pilot Schemes

51.1

Practice Direction 51A makes provision for the extent to which these Rules shall apply to proceedings issued before 26 April 1999.

51.2

Practice directions may modify or disapply any provision of these Rules—
(a) for specified periods; and
(b) in relation to proceedings in specified courts,
during the operation of pilot schemes for assessing the use of new practices and procedures in connection with proceedings.

PD 51A Practice Direction 51A — Transitional Arrangements

This practice direction supplements CPR, Part 51.

[For commentary on a specific paragraph, please refer to the cross-references after the title of the paragraph.]

Contents of This Practice Direction

1 (1) This Practice Direction deals with the application of the Civil Procedure Rules ('CPR') to proceedings issued before 26 April 1999 ('existing proceedings').

(2) In this Practice Direction 'the previous rules' means, as appropriate the Rules of the Supreme Court 1965 ('RSC') or County Court Rules 1981 ('CCR') in force immediately before 26 April 1999.

General Scheme of Transitional Arrangements

2 The general scheme is:

(a) to apply the previous rules to undefended cases, allowing them to progress to their disposal, but

(b) to apply the CPR to defended cases so far as is practicable.

Where the Previous Rules Will Normally Apply

General principle

3 Where an initiating step has been taken in a case before 26 April 1999, in particular one that uses forms or other documentation required by the previous rules, the case will proceed in the first instance under the previous rules. Any step which a party must take in response to something done by another party in accordance with the previous rules must also be in accordance with those rules.

Responding to old process

4 A party who is served with an old type of originating process (writ, summons etc.) on or after 26 April 1999 is required to respond in accordance with the previous rules and the instructions on any forms received with the originating process.

Filing and service of pleadings where old process served

5 Where a case has been begun by an old type of originating process (whether served before or after 26 April 1999), filing and service of pleadings will continue according to the previous rules.

Automatic Directions/Discovery

High Court

6 (1) Where the timetable for automatic directions under RSC Order 25, rule 8 or automatic discovery under RSC Order 24 has begun to apply to proceedings before 26 April 1999, those directions will continue to have effect on or after 26 April 1999.

County court

(2) Where automatic directions under CCR Order 17, rule 11 have begun to apply to existing proceedings before 26 April 1999 or the court has sent out notice that automatic directions under CCR Order 17, rule 11 (Form N. 450) will apply (even if the timetable will not begin until 26 April 1999 or after), those directions will continue to have effect on or after 26 April 1999.

(3) However CCR Order 17, rule 11(9) will not apply and therefore proceedings will not be struck out where there has been no request for a hearing to be fixed within 15 months of the date when pleadings were deemed to close. (But see paragraph 19.)

High Court and county court

(4) However, if the case comes before the court on or after 26 April 1999, the new rules may apply. (See paragraph 15.)

Default judgment

7 (1) If a party wishes default judgment to be entered in existing proceedings, he must do so in accordance with the previous rules.

(2) Where default judgment has been entered and there are outstanding issues to be resolved (e.g. damages to be assessed), the court officer may refer the proceedings to the judge, so that case management decisions about the proceedings and the conduct of the hearing can be made in accordance with the practice set out in paragraph 15.

(3) If a party needs to apply for permission to enter default judgment, he must make that application under CPR Part 23 (general rules about applications for court orders).

(4) An application to set aside judgment entered in default must be made under CPR Part 23 (general rules about applications for court orders) and CPR Part 13 (setting aside or varying default judgment) will apply to the proceedings as it would apply to default judgment entered under the CPR.

(5) CPR rule 15.11 (claims stayed if it is not defended or admitted) applies to these proceedings.

Judgment on admission in the county court

8 (1) If a party to existing proceedings in the county court wishes to request judgment to be entered on an admission, he must do so in accordance with the previous rules.

(2) Where judgment has been entered and there are outstanding issues to be resolved (e.g. damages to be assessed), the court officer may refer the proceedings to the judge, so that case management decisions about the proceedings and the conduct of the hearing can be made in accordance with the practice set out in paragraph 15.

(3) If a party needs to apply for permission to enter judgment, he must make that application under CPR Part 23 (general rules about applications for court orders).

Order inconsistent with CPR

9 Where a court order has been made before 26 April 1999, that order must still be complied with on or after 26 April 1999.

Steps taken before 26 April 1999

10 (1) Where a party has taken any step in the proceedings in accordance with the previous rules that step will remain valid on or after 26 April 1999.

(2) A party will not normally be required to take any action that would amount to taking that step again under the CPR. For example if discovery has been given, a party will not normally be required to provide disclosure under CPR Part 31.

Where the CPR Will Normally Apply

General principle

11 Where a new step is to be taken in any existing proceedings on or after 26 April 1999, it is to be taken under the CPR.

Part 1 (overriding objective) to apply

12 Part 1 (overriding objective) will apply to all existing proceedings from 26 April 1999 onwards.

Originating process

13 (1) Only claim forms under the CPR will be issued by the court on or after 26 April 1999.

(2) If a request to issue an old type of originating process (writ, summons etc.) is received at the court on or after 26 April 1999 it will be returned unissued.

(3) An application made on or after 26 April 1999 to extend the validity of originating process issued before 26 April 1999 must be made in accordance with CPR Part 23 (general rules about applications for court orders), but the court will decide whether to allow the application in accordance with the previous law.

Application to the court

14 (1) Any application to the court made on or after 26 April 1999 must be made in accordance with CPR Part 23 (general rules about applications for court orders).

(2) Any other relevant CPR will apply to the substance of the application, unless this practice direction provides otherwise. (See paragraphs 13(3) (application to extend the validity of originating process) and 18(2) (costs)).

(3) For example, a party wishing to apply for summary judgment must do so having regard to the test in CPR Part 24. A party wishing to apply for an interim remedy must do so under CPR Part 25 etc.

(4) Any other CPR will apply as necessary. For example, CPR Part 4 will apply as to forms and CPR Part 6 will apply to service of documents.

(5) If the pleadings have not been filed at court, the applicant must file all pleadings served when he files his application notice.

First time before a judge on or after 26 April 1999

15 (1) When proceedings come before a judge (whether at a hearing or on paper) for the first time on or after 26 April 1999, he may direct how the CPR are to apply to the proceedings and may disapply certain provisions of the CPR. He may also give case management directions (which may include allocating the proceedings to a case management track).

(2) The general presumption will be that the CPR will apply to the proceedings from then on unless the judge directs or this practice direction provides otherwise. (See paragraphs 13(3) (application to extend the validity of originating process) and 18(2) (costs).)

(3) If an application has been issued before 26 April 1999 and the hearing of the application has been set for a date on or after 26 April 1999, the general presumption is that the application will be decided having regard to the CPR. (For example an application for summary judgment issued before 26 April 1999, with a hearing date set for 1 May 1999, will be decided having regard to the test in CPR Part 24 (summary judgment).)

(4) When the first occasion on which existing proceedings are before a judge on or after 26 April 1999 is a trial or hearing of a substantive issue, the general presumption is that the trial or hearing will be conducted having regard to the CPR.

Where pleadings deemed to close on or after 26 April 1999

16 (1) This paragraph applies to existing proceedings where pleadings are deemed to close on or after 26 April 1999. However, this paragraph does not apply to those county court proceedings where notice that automatic directions apply (Form N. 450) has been sent (in which case the automatic directions will apply—see paragraph 6).

(2) CPR Part 26 (case management—preliminary stage) applies to these proceedings.

(3) If a defence is filed at court on or after 26 April 1999, the court will serve an allocation questionnaire where CPR rule 26.3 would apply, unless it dispenses with the need for one.

(4) If pleadings have not been filed at court (this will normally be the case in the Queen's Bench Division) the claimant must file copies of all the pleadings served within 14 days of the date that pleadings are deemed to close.

(5) Unless it dispenses with the need for one, the court will then serve an allocation questionnaire.

(6) In the previous rules pleadings are deemed to close:

(a) High court:

(i) 14 days after service of any reply, or

(ii) if there is no reply, 14 days after service of the defence to counterclaim, or

(iii) if there is no reply or defence to counterclaim, 14 days after the service of the defence.

(b) County court:

14 days after the delivery of a defence or, where a counterclaim is served with the defence, 28 days after the delivery of the defence.

(7) Where there are 2 or more defendants the court will normally wait until the claimant has filed copies of all the pleadings before serving an allocation questionnaire. However, the court may (in cases where there is a delay) serve allocation questionnaires despite the fact that pleadings have not closed in respect of any other defendant.

(8) The court will then allocate the proceedings in accordance with CPR rule 26.5.

(9) The CPR will then apply generally to the proceedings.

Agreement to apply the CPR

17 The parties may agree in writing that the CPR will apply to any proceedings from the date of the agreement. When they do so:

(a) all those who are parties at that time must agree,

(b) the CPR must apply in their entirety,

(c) the agreement is irrevocable,

(d) the claimant must file a copy of the agreement at court.

Costs

18 (1) Any assessment of costs that takes place on or after 26 April 1999 will be in accordance with CPR Parts 43 to 48.

(2) However, the general presumption is that no costs for work undertaken before 26 April 1999 will be disallowed if those costs would have been allowed in a costs taxation before 26 April 1999.

(3) The decision as to whether to allow costs for work undertaken on or after 26 April will generally be taken in accordance with CPR Parts 43 to 48.

(PD 43–48 contains more information on the operation of the transitional arrangements in relation to costs.)

Existing proceedings after one year

para.19(3)(b) 56.3

19 (1) If any existing proceedings have not come before a judge, at a hearing or on paper, between 26 April 1999 and 25 April 2000, those proceedings shall be stayed.

(2) Any party to those proceedings may apply for the stay to be lifted.

(3) Proceedings of the following types will not be stayed as a result of this provision:

(a) where the case has been given a fixed trial date which is after 25 April 2000,

(b) personal injury cases where there is no issue on liability but the proceedings have been adjourned by court order to determine the prognosis,

(c) where the court is dealing with the continuing administration of an estate or a trust or a receivership,

(d) applications relating to funds in court.

(4) For the purposes of this paragraph proceedings will not be 'existing proceedings' once final judgment has been given.

[PD 51B withdrawn as from 1 October 2012.
PD 51C withdrawn as from 1 April 2010 and replaced by PD 5C.
PD 51D withdrawn as from 1 April 2013.
PD 51E withdrawn as from 1 April 2013.
PD 51F withdrawn as from 1 October 2012 and replaced by PD 40F.
PD 51G withdrawn as from 1 April 2013.
PD 51H withdrawn as from 1 April 2013 and replaced by PD 51I.]

PD 51I Practice Direction 51I — The Second Mediation Service Pilot Scheme

This practice direction supplements CPR, Part 26.

Scope and Interpretation

1.1 In this practice direction—
   (a) 'the CCMCC' means the County Court Money Claims Centre;
   (b) 'MCOL' means Money Claim Online; and
   (c) 'the Mediation Service' means the Small Claims Mediation Service operated by Her Majesty's Courts and Tribunals Service.

1.2 This practice direction is made under r. 51.2. It provides for a pilot scheme ('the Second Mediation Service Pilot Scheme') to operate in the CCMCC, the Production Centre and MCOL for a period of six months from 1 April to 30 September 2013.

1.3 The Second Mediation Service Pilot Scheme will apply to claims issued at the CCMCC, the Production Centre or MCOL if—
   (a) the claim is one which would normally be allocated to the small claims track pursuant to r. 26.6; and
   (b) the directions questionnaires are filed, as appropriate, at the CCMCC, the Production Centre or MCOL, within the six-month period of the pilot.

1.4 This pilot scheme will not apply to—
   (a) road traffic accident, personal injury or housing disrepair claims; or
   (b) any claim in which any party to the proceedings does not agree to referral to the Mediation Service.

Referral to the Mediation Service

2.1 Where all parties indicate on their directions questionnaire that they agree to mediation, the claim will be referred to the Mediation Service.

Modifications of Relevant Rules and Practice Directions

3.1 The following modifications will apply during the operation of the Mediation Service Pilot Scheme.

Production Centre

3.2 In PD 7C—
   (a) para. 1.3(2) is modified to provide that the functions of the Production Centre will include—
      (i) the handling of directions questionnaires; and
      (ii) provisionally deciding the track which appears to be most suitable for the claim; and
   (b) para. 1.3(2)(e) is modified by substituting for the words'following the filing of a defence', the words 'if all parties have filed their directions questionnaires'.

Money Claim Online

3.3 In PD 7E, para. 12.1(3) is modified by substituting the following—
   '(3) if a defence is filed to all or part of the claim, when all parties have filed their directions questionnaires;'

Allocation to track where the Second Mediation Service Pilot Scheme applies

3.4 Rule 26.5(1) is modified to provide that if—
   (a) a claim is referred to the Mediation Service under this pilot scheme; and
   (b) the CCMCC, the Production Centre or MCOL has not been notified in writing that a settlement has been agreed,

the claim will be allocated to a track in accordance with r. 26.5 no later than four weeks from the date on which the last directions questionnaire is filed.

Stay of Claims Following Settlement under the Second Mediation Service Pilot Scheme

4.1 If a claim to which this pilot scheme applies is settled, the proceedings will automatically be stayed with liberty to apply for the purpose of carrying into effect the settlement agreement, unless the parties have agreed that the claim is to be dismissed or discontinued.

CPR Part 52 Appeals

Part 52 **14.36, 45.33, 62.2, 74.56, 74.57, 74.62, 77.22, 84.11** [For commentary on a specific rule, please refer to the cross-references after the title of the rule.]

I GENERAL RULES ABOUT APPEALS

52.1 Scope and Interpretation

r.52.1(2) **74.12** r.52.1(3)(d) **74.3**

(1) The rules in this Part apply to appeals to—
(a) the civil division of the Court of Appeal;
(b) the High Court; and
(c) a county court.

(2) This Part does not apply to an appeal in detailed assessment proceedings against a decision of an authorised court officer.

(Rules 47.20 to 47.23 deal with appeals against a decision of an authorised court officer in detailed assessment proceedings)

(3) In this Part—
(a) 'appeal' includes an appeal by way of case stated;
(b) 'appeal court' means the court to which an appeal is made;
(c) 'lower court' means the court, tribunal or other person or body from whose decision an appeal is brought;
(d) 'appellant' means a person who brings or seeks to bring an appeal;
(e) 'respondent' means—
(i) a person other than the appellant who was a party to the proceedings in the lower court and who is affected by the appeal; and
(ii) a person who is permitted by the appeal court to be a party to the appeal; and
(f) 'appeal notice' means an appellant's or respondent's notice.

(4) This Part is subject to any rule, enactment or practice direction which sets out special provisions with regard to any particular category of appeal.

52.2 Parties to Comply with Practice Directions 52A to 52E

All parties to an appeal must comply with Practice Directions 52A to 52E.

52.3 Permission

r.52.3 PC 32, PC 33, 45.27, 63.7, 74.12
r.52.3(1) 74.37
r.52.3(1)(a)(i)–(iii) 74.12
r.52.3(1)(f) 74.38
r.52.3(2) PC 32, PC 33, 74.13
r.52.3(2)(b) 74.13
r.52.3(3) PC 32, PC 33, 74.13, 74.48
r.52.3(4) PC 32, PC 33, 74.17
r.52.3(4A) 74.17
r.52.3(5) 74.17
r.52.3(6) 74.14
r.52.3(6)(a) 32.29
r.52.3(7) 74.19

(1) An appellant or respondent requires permission to appeal—
(a) where the appeal is from a decision of a judge in a county court or the High Court, except where the appeal is against—
(i) a committal order;
(ii) a refusal to grant habeas corpus; or
(iii) a secure accommodation order made under section 25 of the Children Act 1989; or
(b) as provided by Practice Direction 52.

(Other enactments may provide that permission is required for particular appeals)

(2) An application for permission to appeal may be made—
(a) to the lower court at the hearing at which the decision to be appealed was made; or
(b) to the appeal court in an appeal notice.

(Rule 52.4 sets out the time limits for filing an appellant's notice at the appeal court. Rule 52.5 sets out the time limits for filing a respondent's notice at the appeal court. Any application for permission to appeal to the appeal court must be made in the appeal notice (see rules 52.4(1) and 52.5(3)) (Rule 52.13(1) provides that permission is required from the Court of Appeal for all appeals to that court from a decision of a county court or the High Court which was itself made on appeal)

(3) Where the lower court refuses an application for permission to appeal, a further application for permission to appeal may be made to the appeal court.

(4) Subject to paragraph (4A), where the appeal court, without a hearing, refuses permission to appeal, the person seeking permission may request the decision to be reconsidered at a hearing.

(4A) (a) Where a judge of the Court of Appeal or of the High Court, a Designated Civil Judge or a Specialist Circuit Judge refuses permission to appeal without a hearing and considers that the application is totally without merit, the judge may make an order that the person seeking permission may not request the decision to be reconsidered at a hearing.
(b) For the purposes of subparagraph (a) 'Specialist Circuit Judge' means a Patents County Court judge and any circuit judge in any county court nominated to hear cases in the Mercantile, Chancery or Technology and Construction Court lists.

(4B) Rule 3.3(5) will not apply to an order that the person seeking permission may not request the decision to be reconsidered at a hearing made under paragraph (4A).

(5) A request under paragraph (4) must be filed within 7 days after service of the notice that permission has been refused.

(6) Permission to appeal may be given only where—
(a) the court considers that the appeal would have a real prospect of success; or
(b) there is some other compelling reason why the appeal should be heard.

(7) An order giving permission may—
(a) limit the issues to be heard; and
(b) be made subject to conditions.

(Rule 3.1(3) also provides that the court may make an order subject to conditions)
(Rule 25.15 provides for the court to order security for costs of an appeal)

52.4 Appellant's Notice

r.52.4(1) 45.27
r.52.4(2) 74.23
r.52.4(2)(a) PC 32, PC 33, 74.20, 80.22
r.52.4(2)(b) PC 32, PC 33, 63.43, 74.13, 74.20, 80.22
r.52.4(3) PC 32, PC 33, 74.31, 77.40

(1) Where the appellant seeks permission from the appeal court it must be requested in the appellant's notice.

(2) *The appellant must file* the appellant's notice at the appeal court within—
(a) such period as may be directed by the lower court (which may be longer or shorter than the period referred to in sub-paragraph (b)); or

(b) where the court makes no such direction, 21 days after the date of the decision of the lower court that the appellant wishes to appeal.

(3) Subject to paragraph (4) and unless the appeal court orders otherwise, an appellant's notice must be served on each respondent—
(a) as soon as practicable; and
(b) in any event not later than 7 days,
after it is filed.

(4) Where an appellant seeks permission to appeal against a decision to refuse to grant an interim injunction under section 41 of the Policing and Crime Act 2009 the appellant is not required to serve the appellant's notice on the respondent.

52.5 Respondent's Notice

(1) A respondent may file and serve a respondent's notice.

(2) A respondent who—
(a) is seeking permission to appeal from the appeal court; or
(b) wishes to ask the appeal court to uphold the order of the lower court for reasons different from or additional to those given by the lower court,
must file a respondent's notice.

(3) Where the respondent seeks permission from the appeal court it must be requested in the respondent's notice.

(4) A respondent's notice must be filed within—
(a) such period as may be directed by the lower court; or
(b) where the court makes no such direction, 14 days, after the date in paragraph (5).

(5) The date referred to in paragraph (4) is—
(a) the date the respondent is served with the appellant's notice where—
(i) permission to appeal was given by the lower court; or
(ii) permission to appeal is not required;
(b) the date the respondent is served with notification that the appeal court has given the appellant permission to appeal; or
(c) the date the respondent is served with notification that the application for permission to appeal and the appeal itself are to be heard together.

(6) Unless the appeal court orders otherwise a respondent's notice must be served on the appellant and any other respondent—
(a) as soon as practicable; and
(b) in any event not later than 7 days,
after it is filed.

(7) This rule does not apply where rule 52.4(4) applies.

52.6 Variation of Time

(1) An application to vary the time limit for filing an appeal notice must be made to the appeal court.

(2) The parties may not agree to extend any date or time limit set by—
(a) these Rules;
(b) Practice Direction 52; or
(c) an order of the appeal court or the lower court.

(Rule 3.1(2)(a) provides that the court may extend or shorten the time for compliance with any rule, practice direction or court order (even if an application for extension is made after the time for compliance has expired))

(Rule 3.1(2)(b) provides that the court may adjourn or bring forward a hearing)

52.7 Stay(GL)

Unless—
(a) the appeal court or the lower court orders otherwise; or
(b) the appeal is from the Immigration and Asylum Chamber of the Upper Tribunal,
an appeal shall not operate as a stay of any order or decision of the lower court.

52.8 Amendment of Appeal Notice

r.52.8 74.23, 74.45

An appeal notice may not be amended without the permission of the appeal court.

52.9 Striking Out(GL) Appeal Notices and Setting Aside or Imposing Conditions on Permission to Appeal

r.52.9 74.47, 74.57
r.52.9(1) 74.47
r.52.9(1)(c) 33.27, 74.48
r.52.9(2) 74.47
r.52.9(3) 74.47

(1) The appeal court may—
 (a) strike out the whole or part of an appeal notice;
 (b) set aside(GL) permission to appeal in whole or in part;
 (c) impose or vary conditions upon which an appeal may be brought.
(2) The court will only exercise its powers under paragraph (1) where there is a compelling reason for doing so.
(3) Where a party was present at the hearing at which permission was given he may not subsequently apply for an order that the court exercise its powers under sub-paragraphs (1)(b) or (1)(c).

52.9A Orders to Limit the Recoverable Costs of an Appeal

r.52.9A 75.22
r.52.9A(4) 75.22

(1) In any proceedings in which costs recovery is normally limited or excluded at first instance, an appeal court may make an order that the recoverable costs of an appeal will be limited to the extent which the court specifies.
(2) In making such an order the court will have regard to—
 (a) the means of both parties;
 (b) all the circumstances of the case; and
 (c) the need to facilitate access to justice.
(3) If the appeal raises an issue of principle or practice upon which substantial sums may turn, it may not be appropriate to make an order under paragraph (1).
(4) An application for such an order must be made as soon as practicable and will be determined without a hearing unless the court orders otherwise.

52.10 Appeal Court's Powers

r.52.10 67.29
r.52.10(1)–(2) 75.19
r.52.10(2)(b) 75.18
r.52.10(2)(e) 75.21
r.52.10(3) 75.19
r.52.10(5) 69.14, 75.19
r.52.10(6) 14.55, 63.7, 69.14

(1) In relation to an appeal the appeal court has all the powers of the lower court.
(Rule 52.1(4) provides that this Part is subject to any enactment that sets out special provisions with regard to any particular category of appeal—where such an enactment gives a statutory power to a tribunal, person or other body it may be the case that the appeal court may not exercise that power on an appeal)
(2) The appeal court has power to—
 (a) affirm, set aside or vary any order or judgment made or given by the lower court;
 (b) refer any claim or issue for determination by the lower court;
 (c) order a new trial or hearing;
 (d) make orders for the payment of interest;
 (e) make a costs order.
(3) In an appeal from a claim tried with a jury the Court of Appeal may, instead of ordering a new trial—
 (a) make an order for damages(GL); or
 (b) vary an award of damages made by the jury.

(4) The appeal court may exercise its powers in relation to the whole or part of an order of the lower court. (Part 3 contains general rules about the court's case management powers)
(5) If the appeal court—
 (a) refuses an application for permission to appeal;
 (b) strikes out an appellant's notice; or
 (c) dismisses an appeal,
 and it considers that the application, the appellant's notice or the appeal is totally without merit, the provisions of paragraph (6) must be complied with.
(6) Where paragraph (5) applies—
 (a) the court's order must record the fact that it considers the application, the appellant's notice or the appeal to be totally without merit; and
 (b) the court must at the same time consider whether it is appropriate to make a civil restraint order.

52.11 Hearing of Appeals

r.52.11 75.5
r.52.11(1) 75.5
r.52.11(2) 75.16
r.52.11(3) 1.31, 75.6, 75.14, 84.8
r.52.11(3)(a) 74.63, 75.8
r.52.11(3)(b) 74.18
r.52.11(4) 75.12

(1) Every appeal will be limited to a review of the decision of the lower court unless—
 (a) a practice direction makes different provision for a particular category of appeal; or
 (b) the court considers that in the circumstances of an individual appeal it would be in the interests of justice to hold a rehearing.
(2) Unless it orders otherwise, the appeal court will not receive—
 (a) oral evidence; or
 (b) evidence which was not before the lower court.
(3) The appeal court will allow an appeal where the decision of the lower court was—
 (a) wrong; or
 (b) unjust because of a serious procedural or other irregularity in the proceedings in the lower court.
(4) The appeal court may draw any inference of fact which it considers justified on the evidence.
(5) At the hearing of the appeal a party may not rely on a matter not contained in his appeal notice unless the appeal court gives permission.

52.12 Non-disclosure of Part 36 Offers and Payments

r.52.12(1) 66.3, 75.4
r.52.12(2)–(3) 75.4

(1) The fact that a Part 36 offer or payment into court has been made must not be disclosed to any judge of the appeal court who is to hear or determine—
 (a) an application for permission to appeal; or
 (b) an appeal,
 until all questions (other than costs) have been determined.
(2) Paragraph (1) does not apply if the Part 36 offer or payment into court is relevant to the substance of the appeal.
(3) Paragraph (1) does not prevent disclosure in any application in the appeal proceedings if disclosure of the fact that a Part 36 offer or payment into court has been made is properly relevant to the matter to be decided.

(Rule 36.3 has the effect that a Part 36 offer made in proceedings at first instance will not have consequences in any appeal proceedings. Therefore, a fresh Part 36 offer needs to be made in appeal proceedings. However, rule 52.12 applies to a Part 36 offer whether made in the original proceedings or in the appeal.)

52.12A Statutory Appeals—Court's Power to Hear Any Person

r.52.12A 74.57
r.52.12A(2) 74.57

(1) In a statutory appeal, any person may apply for permission—
 (a) to file evidence; or
 (b) to make representations at the appeal hearing.
(2) An application under paragraph (1) must be made promptly.

II SPECIAL PROVISIONS APPLYING TO THE COURT OF APPEAL

52.13 Second Appeals to the Court

r.52.13 74.12, 84.13
r.52.13(1) PC 33, 74.13, 74.15
r.52.13(2) 74.15
r.52.13(2)(a)–(b) 74.15

(1) Permission is required from the Court of Appeal for any appeal to that court from a decision of a county court or the High Court which was itself made on appeal.
(2) The Court of Appeal will not give permission unless it considers that—
(a) the appeal would raise an important point of principle or practice; or
(b) there is some other compelling reason for the Court of Appeal to hear it.

52.14 Assignment of Appeals to the Court of Appeal

r.52.14 74.7, 74.10
r.52.14(1) 74.10

(1) Where the court from or to which an appeal is made or from which permission to appeal is sought ('the relevant court') considers that—
(a) an appeal which is to be heard by a county court or the High Court would raise an important point of principle or practice; or
(b) there is some other compelling reason for the Court of Appeal to hear it, the relevant court may order the appeal to be transferred to the Court of Appeal.

(The Master of the Rolls has the power to direct that an appeal which would be heard by a county court or the High Court should be heard instead by the Court of Appeal—see section 57 of the Access to Justice Act 1999)

(2) The Master of the Rolls or the Court of Appeal may remit an appeal to the court in which the original appeal was or would have been brought.

52.15 Judicial Review Appeals

r.52.15(1)–(4) 77.40

(1) Where permission to apply for judicial review has been refused at a hearing in the High Court, the person seeking that permission may apply to the Court of Appeal for permission to appeal.
(1A) Where permission to apply for judicial review of a decision of the Upper Tribunal has been refused by the High Court or where permission to apply for judicial review has been refused and recorded as totally without merit in accordance with rule 23.12—
(a) the applicant may apply to the Court of Appeal for permission to appeal;
(b) the application will be determined on paper without an oral hearing.
(2) An application in accordance with paragraphs (1) or (1A) must be made within 7 days of the decision of the High Court to refuse to give permission to apply for judicial review.
(3) On an application under paragraph (1), the Court of Appeal may, instead of giving permission to appeal, give permission to apply for judicial review.
(4) Where the Court of Appeal gives permission to apply for judicial review in accordance with paragraph (3), the case will proceed in the High Court unless the Court of Appeal orders otherwise.

52.16 Who May Exercise the Powers of the Court of Appeal

r.52.16 74.44
r.52.16(3) 74.44
r.52.16(3)(d) 84.17
r.52.16(5) 74.44
r.52.16(6) 74.44
r.52.16(6A) 74.44
r.52.16(7) 74.44

(1) A court officer assigned to the Civil Appeals Office who is—
(a) a barrister; or
(b) a solicitor

may exercise the jurisdiction of the Court of Appeal with regard to the matters set out in paragraph (2) with the consent of the Master of the Rolls.

(2) The matters referred to in paragraph (1) are—
(a) any matter incidental to any proceedings in the Court of Appeal;
(b) any other matter where there is no substantial dispute between the parties; and
(c) the dismissal of an appeal or application where a party has failed to comply with any order, rule or practice direction.

(3) A court officer may not decide an application for—
   (a) permission to appeal;
   (b) bail pending an appeal;
   (c) an injunction(GL);
   (d) a stay(GL) of any proceedings, other than a temporary stay of any order or decision of the lower court over a period when the Court of Appeal is not sitting or cannot conveniently be convened.
(4) Decisions of a court officer may be made without a hearing.
(5) A party may request any decision of a court officer to be reviewed by the Court of Appeal.
(6) At the request of a party, a hearing will be held to reconsider a decision of—
   (a) a single judge; or
   (b) a court officer,
   made without a hearing.
(6A) A request under paragraph (5) or (6) must be filed within 7 days after the party is served with notice of the decision.
(7) A single judge may refer any matter for a decision by a court consisting of two or more judges.

(Section 54(6) of the Senior Courts Act 1981 provides that there is no appeal from the decision of a single judge on an application for permission to appeal)
(Section 58(2) of the Senior Courts Act 1981 provides that there is no appeal to the Supreme Court from decisions of the Court of Appeal that—
(a) are taken by a single judge or any officer or member of staff of that court in proceedings incidental to any cause or matter pending before the civil division of that court; and
(b) do not involve the determination of an appeal or of an application for permission to appeal, and which may be called into question by rules of court. Rules 52.16(5) and (6) provide the procedure for the calling into question of such decisions)

III PROVISIONS ABOUT REOPENING APPEALS

52.17 Reopening of Final Appeals

r.52.17 63.43, 74.54
r.52.17(1) 74.54
r.52.17(3) 63.46, 74.54
r.52.17(4)–(6) 74.55
r.52.17(7) 63.46, 74.55

(1) The Court of Appeal or the High Court will not reopen a final determination of any appeal unless—
   (a) it is necessary to do so in order to avoid real injustice;
   (b) the circumstances are exceptional and make it appropriate to reopen the appeal; and
   (c) there is no alternative effective remedy.
(2) In paragraphs (1), (3), (4) and (6), 'appeal' includes an application for permission to appeal.
(3) This rule does not apply to appeals to a county court.
(4) Permission is needed to make an application under this rule to reopen a final determination of an appeal even in cases where under rule 52.3(1) permission was not needed for the original appeal.
(5) There is no right to an oral hearing of an application for permission unless, exceptionally, the judge so directs.
(6) The judge will not grant permission without directing the application to be served on the other party to the original appeal and giving him an opportunity to make representations.
(7) There is no right of appeal or review from the decision of the judge on the application for permission, which is final.
(8) The procedure for making an application for permission is set out in Practice Direction 52.

IV STATUTORY RIGHTS OF APPEAL

52.18 Appeals under the Law of Property Act 1922

r.52.18 74.57, 74.61

An appeal lies to the High Court against a decision of the Secretary of State under paragraph 16 of Schedule 15 to the Law of Property Act 1922.

52.19 Appeals from Certain Tribunals

r.52.19 74.57, 74.66

(1) A person who was a party to proceedings before a tribunal referred to in section 11(1) of the Tribunals and Inquiries Act 1992 and is dissatisfied in point of law with the decision of the tribunal may appeal to the High Court.
(2) The tribunal may, of its own initiative or at the request of a party to the proceedings before it, state, in the form of a special case for the decision of the High Court, a question of law arising in the course of the proceedings.

52.20 Appeals under Certain Planning Legislation

r.52.20 74.57, 74.64

(1) Where the Secretary of State has given a decision in proceedings on an appeal under Part VII of the Town and Country Planning Act 1990 against an enforcement notice—
(a) the appellant;
(b) the local planning authority; or
(c) another person having an interest in the land to which the notice relates,
may appeal to the High Court against the decision on a point of law.
(2) Where the Secretary of State has given a decision in proceedings on an appeal under Part VIII of that Act against a notice under section 207 of that Act—
(a) the appellant;
(b) the local planning authority; or
(c) any person (other than the appellant) on whom the notice was served,
may appeal to the High Court against the decision on a point of law.
(3) Where the Secretary of State has given a decision in proceedings on an appeal under section 39 of the Planning (Listed Buildings and Conservation Areas) Act 1990 against a listed building enforcement notice—
(a) the appellant;
(b) the local planning authority; or
(c) any other person having an interest in the land to which the notice relates,
may appeal to the High Court against the decision on a point of law.

PD 52A Practice Direction 52A — Appeals: General Provisions

This practice direction supplements CPR, Part 52.

PD 52A 74.4, 84.11

Contents of this Practice Direction

This practice direction is divided into the following sections—

SECTION I — PRACTICE DIRECTIONS SUPPLEMENTING PART 52

1.1 There are five Practice Directions supplementing Part 52—
- PD 52A — Appeals: general provisions
- PD 52B — Appeals in the county courts and the High Court
- PD 52C — Appeals to the Court of Appeal
- PD 52D — Statutory appeals and appeals subject to special provision
- PD 52E — Appeals by way of case stated

SECTION II — INTRODUCTION

2.1 These Practice Directions apply to all appeals to which Part 52 applies.

2.2 Part 52 complements the provisions of sections 54 to 57 of the Access to Justice Act 1999 and provides a uniform procedure for appeals in the county courts and the High Court and a modified procedure for the Civil Division of the Court of Appeal. Part 52 does not apply to—
(a) family proceedings in the High Court or county courts but does apply to appeals to the Court of Appeal from decisions made in family proceedings with such modifications as may be required;
(b) appeals in detailed assessment proceedings against the decision of an authorised court officer.

SECTION III — DESTINATIONS OF APPEAL

para.3.5 45.27, 74.4
para.3.6 74.6
para.3.8(1) 74.6
para.3.8(2) 74.6

3.1 Section 56 of the Access to Justice Act 1999 enables the Lord Chancellor by Order to specify the destinations of appeal in different cases. The Access to Justice Act 1999 (Destination of Appeals) Order 2000 (SI 2000/1071) made under section 56, specifies the general destinations of appeal which apply subject to any statutory provision to the contrary. The destinations of appeal provided by that Order are explained in the following paragraphs of this section of this practice direction.

3.2 'Statutory appeals' and 'Appeals by way of case stated' are dealt with in PD52D — refer to those provisions for the appropriate court to which such an appeal may lie.

3.3 The court or judge to which an appeal is to be made (subject to obtaining any necessary permission) is set out in the tables below—
Table 1 deals with appeals in proceedings other than family and insolvency proceedings;
Table 2 deals with appeals in insolvency proceedings; and
Table 3 deals with appeals in family proceedings which may be heard in the Family Division and to which the CPR may apply.

3.4 Definitions of terms and abbreviations used in Tables 1, 2 and 3—
'Destination': the court to which the appeal lies.
'Pt 7 Claim (not MT)': Part 7 Claim, other than a claim allocated to the multi-track.

'Pt 7 Claim (MT)': Part 7 Claim, allocated to the multi-track.
'Pt 8 Claim (not MT)': Part 8 Claim, other than a claim allocated to the multi-track.
'Pt 8 Claim (MT)': Part 8 Claim, allocated to the multi-track.
'DJ': district judge.
'CJ': circuit judge including a recorder or a district judge who is exercising the jurisdiction of a circuit judge with the permission of the designated civil judge in respect of the case.
'CJ (CC)': circuit judge in the county court.
'Master': master, district judge sitting in a district registry or any other judge referred to in article 2 of the Destination of Appeals Order.
'Final': A final decision within the meaning of paragraphs 3.6 to 3.8 of this practice direction.
'Interim': A decision that is not a final decision within the meaning of paragraphs 3.6 to 3.8 of this practice direction.
'HCJ': single judge of the High Court.
'HCJ(FD)': single judge of the family Division of the High Court.
'CA': Court of Appeal.
'Other': claims or originating or pre-action applications started otherwise than by a Part 7 or Part 8 claim (for example an application under Part 23).
'Specialist': specialist proceedings (under the Companies Act 1985 or the Companies Act 1989 or to which Sections I, II or III of Part 57 or any of Parts 58,59,60, 62 or 63 apply).

(Note: Tables 1, 2 and 3 do not include so-called 'leapfrog' appeals either to the Court of Appeal pursuant to section 57 of the Access to Justice Act 1999 or to the Supreme Court pursuant to section 13 of the Administration of Justice Act 1969.)

3.5 The destinations in the tables set out below apply whether the decision is interim or final. For the meaning of 'final decision' for the purposes of this table see paragraphs 3.6 to 3.8 below.

Table 1 — Proceedings other than family or insolvency proceedings

Court	Deciding judge	Nature of claim	Interim / final	Destination
County	DJ	Pt 7 Claim	Interim	CJ (CC)
		Pt 7 Claim (not MT)	Final	
		Pt 7 Claim (MT)	Final	CA
		Pt 8 Claim	Interim / final	CJ (CC)
		Other	Interim / final	
		Specialist	Interim	
			Final	CA
	CJ	Pt 7 Claim	Interim	HCJ
		Pt 7 Claim (not MT)	Final	
		Pt 7 Claim (MT)	Final	CA
		Pt 8 Claim	Interim / final	HCJ
		Other	Interim / final	
		Specialist	Interim	
			Final	CA
High	Master	Pt 7 Claim	Interim	HCJ
		Pt 7 Claim (not MT)	Final	
		Pt 7 Claim (MT)	Final	CA
		Pt 8 Claim	Interim / final	HCJ
		Other	Interim / final	
		Specialist	Interim	
			Final	CA
	HCJ	Any	Interim / final	CA

Table 2 — Insolvency proceedings

Court	Deciding judge	Destination
County	DJ or CJ	HCJ
High	Registrar	
	HCJ	CA

Table 3 — Family proceedings in the Principal Registry of the Family Division and to which the CPR will apply

The proceedings to which this table applies include proceedings under the Inheritance (Provision for Family and Dependants) Act 1975 and proceedings under the Trusts of Land and Appointment of Trustees Act 1996.

Deciding judge	Nature of claim	Decision under appeal	Destination
DJ	Part 7 Claim (not MT)	Any decision other than a final decision	HCJ(FD)
	Pt 7 Claim (MT)	Final decision	CA
	Part 8 Claim (not MT)	Any decision	HCJ(FD)
	Part 8 Claim (MT)		
HCJ(FD)	Any	Any decision	CA

3.6 A 'final decision' is a decision of a court that would finally determine (subject to any possible appeal or detailed assessment of costs) the entire proceedings whichever way the court decided the issues before it.

3.7 A decision is to be treated as a final decision for destination of appeal purposes where it—
(a) is made at the conclusion of part of a hearing or trial which has been split into parts; and
(b) would, if it had been made at the conclusion of that hearing or trial, have been a final decision.

3.8 (1) The following are examples of final decisions—
- a judgment on liability at the end of a split trial;
- a judgment at the conclusion of an assessment of damages following a judgment on liability.

(2) The following are examples of decisions that are not final—
- a case management decision (within the meaning of paragraph 4.6);
- a grant or refusal of interim relief;
- summary judgment;
- striking out a claim or statement of case;
- a summary or detailed assessment of costs;
- an order for the enforcement of a final decision.

Filing appellant's notice in wrong court

3.9 (1) Where a party attempts to file an appellant's notice in a court which does not have jurisdiction to issue the notice, a court officer may notify that party in writing that the appeal court does not have jurisdiction in respect of the notice.
(2) Before notifying a person under paragraph (1) the court officer must confer—
(a) with a judge of the appeal court; or
(b) where the Court of Appeal is the appeal court, with a court officer who exercises the jurisdiction of that Court under rule 52.16.
(3) Where a court officer, in the Court of Appeal, notifies a person under paragraph (1), rule 52.16(5) and (6) shall not apply.

SECTION IV — OBTAINING PERMISSION TO APPEAL

Where to apply for permission

4.1 An application for permission to appeal may be made—

(a) to the lower court at the hearing at which the decision to be appealed against is given (in which case the lower court may adjourn the hearing to give a party an opportunity to apply for permission to appeal); or

(b) where the lower court refuses permission to appeal or where no application is made to the lower court, to the appeal court in accordance with rule 52.4.

Form

para.4.2 **PC 32, 74.13, 74.23**

4.2 An application for permission to appeal to the appeal court must be made using an appellant's notice (form N161 or N164 (small claims track)).

Appeals from masters and district judges of High Court

para.4.3 **84.11**

4.3 In relation to appeals from masters or district judges of the High Court: appeals, applications for permission and any other applications in the appeal may be heard and directions in the appeal may be given by a High Court Judge or by any person authorised under section 9 of the Senior Courts Act 1981 to act as a judge of the High Court.

Where the lower court is a county court

para.4.4 **84.11**

para.4.4(b) **84.11**

para.4.5 **84.11**

4.4 Where the lower court is a county court—

(a) subject to sub-paragraph (b), appeals and applications for permission to appeal will be heard by a High Court judge or by a person authorised under paragraphs (1), (2) or (4) of the Table in section 9(1) of the Senior Courts Act 1981 to act as a judge of the High Court;

(b) an appeal or application for permission to appeal from the decision of a recorder may be heard by a designated civil judge who is authorised under paragraph (5) of the Table in section 9(1) of the Senior Courts Act 1981 to act as a judge of the High Court; and

(c) other applications in the appeal may be heard and directions in the appeal may be given either by a High Court judge or by any person authorised under section 9 of the Senior Courts Act 1981 to act as a judge of the High Court.

4.5 The designated civil judge in consultation with the presiding judge has responsibility for allocating appeals from decisions of district judges to circuit judges.

Appeal in relation to case management decision

para.4.6 **74.6**

4.6 Where the application is for permission to appeal from a case management decision, the court dealing with the application may take into account whether—

(a) the issue is of sufficient significance to justify the costs of an appeal;

(b) the procedural consequences of an appeal (e.g. loss of trial date) outweigh the significance of the case management decision;

(c) it would be more convenient to determine the issue at or after trial.

Case management decisions include decisions made under rule 3.1(2) and decisions about disclosure, filing of witness statements or experts' reports, directions about the timetable of the claim, adding a party to a claim and security for costs.

Second appeal

4.7 An application for permission to appeal from a decision of the High Court or a county court which was itself made on appeal is a second appeal and must be made to the Court of Appeal. If permission to appeal is granted the appeal will be heard by the Court of Appeal.

SECTION V — SKELETON ARGUMENTS

5.1 (1) The purpose of a skeleton argument is to assist the court by setting out as concisely as practicable the arguments upon which a party intends to rely.

(2) A skeleton argument must—
- be concise;
- both define and confine the areas of controversy;
- be set out in numbered paragraphs;
- be cross-referenced to any relevant document in the bundle;
- be self-contained and not incorporate by reference material from previous skeleton arguments;
- not include extensive quotations from documents or authorities.

(3) Documents to be relied on must be identified.

(4) Where it is necessary to refer to an authority, a skeleton argument must—
(a) state the proposition of law the authority demonstrates; and
(b) identify the parts of the authority that support the proposition.
If more than one authority is cited in support of a given proposition, the skeleton argument must briefly state why.

(5) The cost of preparing a skeleton argument which—
(a) does not comply with the requirements set out in this paragraph; or
(b) was not filed within the time limits provided by this practice direction (or any further time granted by the court),
will not be allowed on assessment except as directed by the court.

5.2 The appellant should consider what other information the appeal court will need. This may include a list of persons who feature in the case or glossaries of technical terms. A chronology of relevant events will be necessary in most appeals.

5.3 Any statement of costs must show the amount claimed for the skeleton argument separately.

SECTION VI — DISPOSING OF APPLICATIONS AND APPEALS BY CONSENT

Dismissal of applications or appeals by consent
para.6.3 74.50

6.1 An appellant who does not wish to pursue an application or appeal may request the appeal court to dismiss the application or the appeal. If such a request is granted it will usually be subject to an order that the appellant pays the costs of the application or appeal.

6.2 If the appellant wishes to have the application or appeal dismissed without costs, his request must be accompanied by a letter signed by the respondent stating that the respondent so consents.

6.3 Where a settlement has been reached disposing of the application or appeal, the parties may make a joint request to the court for the application or appeal to be dismissed by consent. If the request is granted the application or appeal will be dismissed.

Allowing unopposed appeals or applications on paper

6.4 The appeal court will not normally make an order allowing an appeal unless satisfied that the decision of the lower court was wrong or unjust because of a serious procedural or other irregularity. The appeal court may, however, set aside or vary the order of the lower court by consent and without determining the merits of the appeal if it is satisfied that there are good and sufficient reasons for so doing. Where the appeal court is requested by all parties to allow an application or an appeal the court may consider the request on the papers. The request should set out the relevant history of the proceedings and the matters relied on as justifying the order and be accompanied by a draft order.

Disposal of applications and appeals involving children or protected parties
para.6.5 74.50

6.5 Where one of the parties is a child or protected party, any disposal of an application or the appeal requires the court's approval. A draft order signed by the parties' solicitors should be sent to the appeal court, together with an opinion from the advocate acting on behalf of the child or protected party and, in the case of a protected party, any relevant documents prepared for the Court of Protection.

SECTION VII — REOPENING APPEALS (RULE 52.17)

7.1 A party applying for permission to reopen an appeal or an application for permission to appeal must apply for such permission from the court whose decision the party wishes to reopen.
7.2 The application for permission must be made by application notice and be supported by written evidence, verified by a statement of truth. A copy of the application for permission must not be served on any other party to the original appeal unless the court so directs.
7.3 Where the court directs that the application for permission is to be served on another party, that party may, within 14 days of the service on him of the copy of the application, file and serve a written statement either supporting or opposing the application.
7.4 The application for permission will be considered on paper by a single judge.

SECTION VIII — TRANSITIONAL PROVISIONS

8.1 This practice direction and PD 52B, PD 52C, PD 52D and PD 52E shall come into force on 1 October 2012 and shall apply to all appeals where—
(a) the appeal notice was filed; or
(b) permission to appeal was given
on or after that date.
8.2 The appeal court may at any time direct that, in relation to any appeal, one or more of PD 52A, PD 52B, PD 52C, PD 52D or PD 52E shall apply irrespective of the date on which the appeal notice was filed or permission to appeal was given.

PD 52B Practice Direction 52B — Appeals in the County Courts and High Court

This Practice Direction supplements CPR, Part 52.

Contents of this Practice Direction

This practice direction is divided into the following sections—

SECTION I — APPLICATION

1.1 This practice direction applies to—
(a) appeals within a county court (from a district judge to a circuit judge);
(b) appeals from a county court to the High Court; and
(c) appeals within the High Court (from a master, a district judge sitting in a district registry, a registrar in bankruptcy, a registrar of the Companies Court, a costs judge or an officer of the High Court to a judge of the High Court).

SECTION II — VENUE FOR APPEALS AND FILLING OF NOTICES AND APPLICATIONS

section II 84.11 para.2.1 74.9

2.1 Appeals within a county court, appeals from a county court and appeals within the High Court to a judge of the High Court must be brought in the appropriate appeal centre and all other notices (including any respondent's notice) and applications must be filed at that appeal centre. The venue for an appeal within a county court will be determined by the designated civil judge and may be different from the appeal centre.

2.2 The tables at the end of this practice direction set out the appeal centres for each circuit.

SECTION III — EXTENDING TIME IN WHICH TO APPEAL

para.3.2 PC 32, 74.21, 74.23

3.1 A party may apply to the lower court for an extension of time in which to file an appellant's notice. The application must be made at the same time as the appellant applies to the lower court for permission to appeal.

3.2 Where the time for filing an appellant's notice has expired, the appellant must include an application for an extension of time within the appellant's notice (form N161 or, in respect of a small claim, form N164) stating the reason for the delay and the steps taken prior to making the application.

3.3 The court may make an order granting or refusing an extension of time and may do so with or without a hearing. If an order is made without a hearing, any party seeking to set aside or vary the order may apply, within 14 days of service of the order, for a hearing.

SECTION IV — INITIATING AN APPEAL

para.4.1 45.27
para.4.2 PC 32, 45.27, 74.24
para.4.2(d) PC 32, 74.23
para.4.3 PC 32, 74.23, 74.44

4.1 An appellant's notice (form N161 or, in respect of a small claim, form N164) must be filed and served in all cases. The appellant's notice must be accompanied by the appropriate fee or, if appropriate, a fee remission application or certificate.

Documents to be filed with the appellant's notice

4.2 The appellant must file with the appellant's notice—
(a) three copies of the appellant's notice and one additional copy for each respondent;
(b) a copy of the sealed order under appeal;
(c) where an application was made to the lower court for permission to appeal, a copy of any order granting or refusing permission to appeal together with a copy of the reasons, if any, for allowing or refusing permission to appeal; and
(d) grounds of appeal, which must be set out on a separate sheet attached to the appellant's notice and must set out, in simple language, clearly and concisely, why the order of the lower court was wrong or unjust because of a serious procedural or other irregularity (rule 52.11(3)).

Applications in the appeal

4.3 Any application to be made in the appeal (for example, for a stay of the order of the lower court, or for an extension of time) should be included within the appellant's notice. Where the applicant qualifies for fee remission, any application for a transcript of the judgment of the lower court at public expense should be made within the appellant's notice.

SECTION V — CASE MANAGING THE APPEAL; ORDERS OF THE COURT

para.5.1 74.29

5.1 The appeal court may make orders for the case management of an appeal.
5.2 When making a case management order, the court may dispense with any requirements of or directions made in this practice direction.

SECTION VI — CONDUCT OF THE APPEAL

Service of appellant's notice on the respondent

para.6 74.30
para.6.1 PC 33, 74.31, 74.32, 74.50

6.1 The appellant must file a certificate of service of the appellant's notice with the court as soon as practicable after service.

Transcript of the judgment of the lower court or other record of reasons

para.6.2 PC 32, 45.27, 74.30, 74.50

6.2 Except where the claim has been allocated to the small claims track, the appellant must obtain a transcript or other record of reasons of the lower court as follows—
(a) where the judgment has been officially recorded, the appellant must apply for an approved transcript as soon as possible and, in any event, within 7 days of the filing of the appellant's notice;
(b) where the judgment under appeal has been handed down in writing, the appellant must obtain and retain a copy of the written judgment;
(c) in any other case, the appellant must cause a note of the judgment under appeal to be made and typed. The parties to the appeal should agree the note, which should then be sent to the judge of the lower court for approval. The parties and their advocates have a duty to make, and to cooperate in agreeing, a note of the judgment.

Appeal bundle

para.6.3 PC 32, 45.27, 74.25, 74.26

6.3 As soon as practicable, but in any event within 35 days of the filing of the appellant's notice, the *appellant must file* an appeal bundle which must contain only those documents relevant to the appeal. The appeal bundle must be paginated and indexed.

Documents relevant to the appeal

para.6.4 45.27, 74.50
para.6.4(1) 74.25
para.6.4(2) 74.25

6.4 (1) Subject to any order made by the court, the following documents must be included in the appeal bundle—
(a) a copy of the appellant's notice;
(b) a copy of any respondent's notice;
(c) a copy of any appellant's or respondent's skeleton argument;
(d) a copy of the order under appeal;
(e) a copy of the order of the lower court granting or refusing permission to appeal together with a copy of the judge's reasons, if any, for granting or refusing permission;
(f) a copy of any order allocating the case to a track;
(g) a transcript of the judgment of the lower court or other record of reasons (except in appeals in cases which were allocated to the small claims track and subject to any order of the court).

(2) The following documents should also be considered for inclusion in the appeal bundle but should be included only where relevant to the appeal—
(a) statements of case;
(b) application notices;
(c) other orders made in the case;
(d) a chronology of relevant events;
(e) witness statements made in support of any application made in the appellant's notice;
(f) other witness statements;
(g) any other documents which any party considers would assist the appeal court.

Service of the appeal bundle

para.6.5(a) PC 32, 74.31
para.6.5(b) PC 32, 74.31
para.6.5(c) 74.31

6.5 A copy of the appeal bundle must be served on each respondent—
(a) where permission to appeal was granted by the lower court, at the same time as filing the appeal bundle;
(b) where the appeal court has granted permission to appeal, as soon as practicable after notification and in any event within 14 days of the grant of permission;
(c) where the appeal court directs that the application for permission to appeal is to be heard on the same occasion as the appeal, as soon as practicable and in any event within 14 days after notification of the hearing date.

Late documents

para.6.6 74.26

6.6 Any relevant document which is obtained or created after the appeal bundle has been filed (for example a respondent's notice or a skeleton argument) should be added to the appeal bundle as soon as practicable and, in any event, no less than seven days before the hearing of the appeal or any application.

SECTION VII — DETERMINATION OF APPLICATIONS

para.7.1 74.13
para.7.4(a) 74.18

7.1 Applications made in the appeal, including applications for permission to appeal under rule 52.3(2)(a) or rule 52.5(3), may be determined with or without a hearing.

7.2 Where the court refuses an application for permission to appeal without a hearing, the appellant (or, where appropriate, the respondent) may request the application to be reconsidered at a hearing.

7.3 Where the court determines any other application without hearing the respondent (including an application for permission to bring the appeal out of time) any party affected by the determination may apply to have the order set aside or varied.

7.4 Any request or application made under this section must be made within seven days of service of notification of the determination upon the person making the application. Where any such request or application is made—
(a) a copy of the request or application must be served on all other parties at the same time; and
(b) the court will give directions for the determination of the application.

SECTION VIII — HEARINGS

Attendance at permission hearings

para.8.1(a) 74.18

8.1 Where a respondent to an appeal or cross-appeal attends the hearing of an application for permission to appeal, costs will not be awarded to the respondent unless—

(a) the court has ordered or requested attendance by the respondent;

(b) the court has ordered that the appeal be listed at the same time as the determination of other applications;

(c) the court has ordered that the hearing of the appeal will follow the hearing of the application if permission is granted; or

(d) the court considers it just, in all the circumstances, to award costs to the respondent.

Respondent's documents

para.8.2 74.25

8.2 A respondent who has been served with an appeal bundle and who considers that relevant documents have been omitted may file and serve on all parties a respondent's supplemental appeal bundle containing copies of other relevant documents. The supplemental appeal bundle must be filed and served as soon as practicable after service of the appeal bundle, but in any event not less than seven days before the hearing.

Skeleton arguments

para.8.3 PC.32, 74.28

8.3 Subject to any order of the court, the parties to the appeal should file and serve skeleton arguments only where—

(a) the complexity of the issues of fact or law in the appeal justify them; or

(b) skeleton arguments would assist the court in respects not readily apparent from the papers in the appeal.

Table A — Table of appeal centres for each circuit

Circuit	Court	Appeal Centre
Midland		
	Birmingham CJC	Birmingham CJC
	Boston	Lincoln
	Burton -upon-Trent	Nottingham
	Buxton	Nottingham
	Chesterfield	Nottingham
	Coventry	Coventry
	Derby	Nottingham
	Dudley	Walsall
	Hereford	Worcester
	Kettering	Northampton
	Kidderminster	Worcester
	Leicester	Leicester
	Lincoln	Lincoln
	Mansfield	Nottingham
	Northampton	Northampton
	Nottingham	Nottingham
	Nuneaton	Coventry
	Redditch	Worcester
	Stafford	Stoke-on-Trent
	Stoke-on-Trent	Stoke-on-Trent
	Telford	Telford
	Walsall	Walsall
	Warwick	Coventry
	Wolverhampton	Walsall

Circuit	Court	Appeal Centre
	Worcester	Worcester
North East		
	Barnsley	Sheffield
	Bradford	Bradford
	Darlington	Teesside
	Doncaster	Sheffield
	Durham	Newcastle-upon-Tyne
	Gateshead	Newcastle-upon-Tyne
	Grimsby	Kingston-upon-Hull
	Halifax	Halifax
	Harrogate	Leeds
	Hartlepool	Teesside
	Huddersfield	Huddersfield
	Kingston-upon-Hull	Kingston-upon-Hull
	Leeds	Leeds
	Morpeth	Newcastle-upon-Tyne
	Newcastle-upon-Tyne	Newcastle-upon-Tyne
	North Shields	Newcastle-upon-Tyne
	Rotherham	Sheffield
	Scarborough	Leeds
	Scunthorpe	Kingston-upon-Hull
	Sheffield	Sheffield
	Skipton	Skipton
	South Shields	Newcastle-upon-Tyne
	Sunderland	Newcastle-upon-Tyne
	Teesside	Teesside
	Wakefield	Leeds
	York	Leeds
Northern		
	Accrington	Preston
	Altrincham	Manchester CJC
	Barrow-in-Furness	Carlisle
	Birkenhead	Liverpool
	Blackburn	Preston
	Blackpool	Preston
	Bolton	Manchester CJC
	Burnley	Preston
	Bury	Manchester CJC
	Carlisle	Carlisle
	Chester CJC	Chester CJC
	Crewe	Chester CJC
	Kendal	Carlisle
	Lancaster	Preston
	Liverpool	Liverpool
	Macclesfield	Chester CJC
	Manchester CJC	Manchester CJC
	Oldham	Manchester CJC
	Preston	Preston
	St Helens	Liverpool
	Stockport	Manchester CJC
	Tameside	Manchester CJC
	Warrington	Chester CJC
	West Cumbria	Carlisle
	Wigan	Liverpool
Wales		
	Aberystwyth	Swansea
	Blackwood	Cardiff CJC
	Brecknock	Swansea

Circuit	Court	Appeal Centre
	Bridgend	Cardiff CJC
	Caernarfon	Wrexham
	Cardiff	Cardiff CJC
	Carmarthen	Swansea
	Conwy & Colwyn	Wrexham
	Haverfordwest	Swansea
	Llanelli	Swansea
	Llangefni	Wrexham
	Merthyr Tydfil	Cardiff CJC
	Mold	Wrexham
	Neath & Port Talbot	Swansea
	Newport (Gwent)	Cardiff CJC
	Pontypridd	Cardiff CJC
	Rhyl	Wrexham
	Swansea	Swansea
	Welshpool & Newtown	Wrexham
Western		
	Aldershot & Farnham	Aldershot & Farnham
	Barnstaple	Barnstaple
	Basingstoke	Basingstoke
	Bath	Bristol CJC
	Bodmin	Bodmin
	Bournemouth	Bournemouth
	Bristol	Bristol CJC
	Cheltenham	Bristol CJC
	Exeter	Exeter
	Gloucester	Bristol CJC
	Newport (Isle of Wight)	Newport (Isle of Wight)
	Plymouth	Plymouth
	Portsmouth	Portsmouth
	Salisbury	Salisbury
	Southampton	Southampton
	Swindon	Swindon
	Taunton	Bristol CJC
	Torquay & Newton Abbot	Torquay & Newton Abbot
	Trowbridge	Trowbridge
	Truro	Truro
	Weston-Super-Mare	Bristol CJC
	Weymouth & Dorchester	Weymouth & Dorchester
	Winchester	Winchester
	Yeovil	Bristol
South East		
	Aylesbury	Oxford
	Banbury	Oxford
	Barnet	Barnet
	Basildon	Southend
	Bedford	Luton
	Bow	Bow
	Brentford	Brentford
	Brighton	Brighton
	Bromley	Bromley
	Bury St Edmunds	Cambridge
	Cambridge	Cambridge
	Canterbury	Canterbury
	Central London CJC	Central London CJC
	Chelmsford	Southend
	Chichester	Chichester

Circuit	Court	Appeal Centre
	Clerkenwell & Shoreditch	Clerkenwell & Shoreditch
	Colchester	Southend
	Croydon	Croydon
	Dartford	Dartford
	Eastbourne	Eastbourne
	Edmonton	Edmonton
	Guildford	Guildford
	Hastings	Hastings
	Hertford	Luton
	High Wycombe	Oxford
	Horsham	Horsham
	Hove	Hove
	Ipswich	Norwich
	Kingston-upon-Thames	Kingston-upon-Thames
	King's Lynn	Norwich
	Lambeth	Lambeth
	Lewes	Lewes
	Luton	Luton
	Maidstone	Maidstone
	Mayor's and City	Mayor's and City
	Medway	Medway
	Milton Keynes	Oxford
	Norwich	Norwich
	Oxford	Oxford
	Peterborough	Cambridge
	Reading	Oxford
	Reigate	Reigate
	Romford	Romford
	Slough	Oxford
	Southend	Southend
	St Albans	Luton
	Staines	Staines
	Thanet	Thanet
	Tunbridge Wells	Tunbridge Wells
	Uxbridge	Uxbridge
	Wandsworth	Wandsworth
	Watford	Watford
	Willesden	Willesden
	West London	West London
	Woolwich	Woolwich
	Worthing	Worthing

Table B — Appeals from a county court or within the High Court: appeal centres for each circuit

Circuit	Appeal centres
Midland Circuit	Birmingham Nottingham
North Eastern Circuit	Leeds Newcastle Sheffield
Northern Circuit	Manchester Liverpool Preston Chester

Circuit	Appeal centres
Wales Circuit	Cardiff
	Swansea
	Mold
Western Circuit	Bristol
	Exeter
	Winchester
South Eastern Circuit	Royal Courts of Justice
	Lewes
	Luton
	Norwich
	Reading
	Chelmsford
	St Albans
	Maidstone
	Oxford

PD 52C Practice Direction 52C — Appeals to the Court of Appeal

This practice direction supplements CPR, Part 52.

PD 52C 74.25, 84.11

Contents of this Practice Direction

This practice direction is divided into the following sections—

SECTION I — INTRODUCTION AND INTERPRETATION

para.1 74.28

1 In this practice direction—

'appeal notice' means either an appellant's notice in form N161 or a respondent's notice in form N162;

'appellant's notice' means an appeal notice filed by an appellant and a 'respondent's notice' means an appeal notice filed by a respondent;

'hearing date' means the date on which the appeal is listed to be heard, including a 'floating' date over two or more days;

'listing window notification' means the letter sent by the Civil Appeals Office in accordance with Section 5: Timetable Part 1 notifying the parties of the window within which the appeal is likely to be heard; and 'date of the listing window notification' means the date of such letter;

'replacement skeleton argument' means a skeleton argument which has been amended in order to include cross-references to the appeal bundle and is lodged and served in accordance with the timetable at Section 5 Part 2.

2 The court may make such directions as the case may require and such directions will prevail over any provision of this practice direction.

SECTION II — STARTING AN APPEAL TO THE COURT OF APPEAL

Filing the Appellant's Notice and Accompanying Documents

para.3.3 PC 32, PC 33, 74.24 para.3.3(g) 74.28

3 (1) An appellant's notice (form N161) must be filed and served in all cases. The appellant's notice must be accompanied by the appropriate fee or, if appropriate, a fee remission certificate.

(2) The appellant's notice and accompanying documents must be filed in the Civil Appeals Office Registry, Room E307, Royal Courts of Justice, Strand, London, WC2A 2LL.

(3) At the same time as filing an appellant's notice, the appellant must provide for the use of the court three copies of the appellant's notice and one copy of each of the following—

(a) the sealed order or tribunal determination being appealed;

(b) any order granting or refusing permission to appeal, together with a copy of the judge's or tribunal's reasons for granting or refusing permission to appeal;

(c) any witness statements or affidavits relied on in support of any application included in the appellant's notice;

(d) in cases where the decision of the lower court was itself made on appeal, the first order, the reasons given by the judge who made it, and the appellant's notice of appeal against that order;

(e) in a claim for judicial review or a statutory appeal, the original decision which was the subject of the application to the lower court;
(f) the order allocating the case to a track (if any);
(g) the appellant's skeleton argument in support of the appeal;
(h) the approved transcript of the judgment.

(4) The appellant must also provide to the court one copy of the appellant's notice for each respondent for sealing by the court and return to the appellant for service.

(5) Where the appellant applies for permission to appeal, additional documents are required: see Section 4 of this practice direction.

(5) Provisions in relation to the skeleton argument are set out in paragraph 31.

Extension of Time for Filing Appellant's Notice

para.4.1(b) PC 33

4 (1) Where the time for filing an appellant's notice has expired, the appellant must—
(a) file the appellant's notice; and
(b) include in that appellant's notice an application for an extension of time.

(2) The appellant's notice must state the reason for the delay and the steps taken prior to the application being made.

(3) Where the appellant's notice includes an application for an extension of time and permission to appeal has been given or is not required, the respondent has the right to oppose that application and to be heard at any hearing of that application. In respect of any application to extend time—
(a) The respondent must–
(i) be served with a copy of any evidence filed in support of the application; and
(ii) inform the court in writing of any objections to the grant of the extension of time within seven days of being served with the appellant's notice.
(b) A respondent who unreasonably opposes an application for an extension of time may be ordered to pay the costs of the application.
(c) An application for an extension of time will normally be determined without a hearing unless the court directs otherwise.

Grounds of Appeal

para.5.1 PC 32, 74.23 para.5.2 74.23

5 (1) The grounds of appeal must identify as concisely as possible the respects in which the judgment of the court below is—
(a) wrong; or
(b) unjust because of a serious procedural or other irregularity,
as required by rule 52.11(3).

(2) The reasons why the decision under appeal is wrong or unjust must not be included in the grounds of appeal and must be confined to the skeleton argument.

Second Appeals

para.5A 74.23

5A An application to make a second appeal must identify in the grounds of appeal—
(a) the important point of principle or practice, or
(b) the compelling reason
which is said to justify the grant of permission to appeal.

Non-availability of Documents

para.6 PC 33, 74.24

6 If the appellant is unable to provide any of the necessary documents in time, the appellant must complete the appeal notice on the basis of the available documents. The notice may be amended *subsequently with the permission* of the court (see paragraph 30).

Service of Appellant's Notice on the Respondent

para.7.1 PC 33, 15.5, 74.32

7.1 The Civil Appeals Office will not serve documents. Where service is required by the Rules or this practice direction, it must be effected by the parties.

7.2 The evidence in support of any application made in an appellant's notice must be filed and served with the appellant's notice.

7.3 An application for an order to dispense with service of the appellant's notice under rule 6.28 must be made in the appeal notice or, thereafter, by application notice under Part 23.

SECTION III — RESPONDENT'S NOTICE (RULE 52.5) AND RESPONDENT'S SKELETON ARGUMENT

Respondent's Notice

para.8.2 PC 32 para.8(3) PC 32, 74.37

8 (1) A respondent who seeks to appeal against any part of the order made by the court below must file an appeal notice.

(2) A respondent who seeks a variation of the order of the lower court must file an appeal notice and must obtain permission to appeal.

(3) A respondent who seeks to contend that the order of the court below should be upheld for reasons other than those given by that court must file a respondent's notice.

(4) The notice may be amended subsequently with the permission of the court (see paragraph 30).

Skeleton Argument to be Lodged with the Respondent's Notice

para.9 PC 33, 74.40

9A respondent who files a respondent's notice must, within 14 days of filing the notice, lodge a skeleton argument with the court and serve a copy of the skeleton argument on every other party to the appeal.

(Provisions in relation to the skeleton argument are set out in paragraph 31.)

Documents to be Filed with Respondent's Notice

para.10 PC 32, 74.41

10 The respondent must file the following documents with the respondent's notice—

(a) two additional copies of the respondent's notice for the court; and

(b) one copy each for the appellant and any other respondents.

Applications within Respondent's Notice

11 (1) A respondent may include an application within a respondent's notice.

(2) The parties must consider whether it would be more convenient for any application to be listed with the appeal or whether the application needs to be considered in advance.

(3) Where parties consider that the time estimate for the appeal will be affected by listing the application with the appeal, they must inform the court without delay.

Time Limits: Rule 52.5(4) and (5)

12 Where an extension of time is required, the respondent must apply in the respondent's notice and explain the delay.

Respondent's Skeleton Argument (where no Respondent's Notice Filed)

para.13 PC 33 para.13(1) 74.40

13 (1) In all cases where the respondent is legally represented and proposes to address the court, the respondent must lodge and serve a skeleton argument.

(2) A respondent's skeleton argument must be lodged and served in accordance with Part 1 of the Timetable in Section 5.

(Provisions in relation to the skeleton argument are set out in paragraph 31.)

SECTION IV — PROCEDURE WHERE PERMISSION TO APPEAL IS SOUGHT FROM THE COURT OF APPEAL

Documents for Use on an Application for Permission

para.14 PC 33, 74.15

14 (1) Within 14 days of filing the appeal notice the appellant must lodge a bundle containing only those documents which are necessary for the court to determine that application.

(2) The bundle of documents must—

(a) be paginated and in chronological order;

(b) contain an index at the front.

Determination of Applications for Permission to Appeal

para.15 PC 33, 74.13 para.15(1) PC 32

15 (1) Applications for permission to appeal will generally be considered by the court without a hearing in the first instance. The court will notify the parties of the decision and the reasons for it.

(2) If permission is refused the appellant is entitled to have the decision reconsidered at an oral hearing, except where rule 52.3(4A) (applications totally without merit) applies. The hearing may be before the same judge.

(3) A request for the decision to be reconsidered at an oral hearing must be filed within seven days after service of the letter giving notice that permission has been refused. A copy of the request must be served by the appellant on the respondent at the same time.

Permission Hearing

para.16 74.15 para.16(3) 74.18
para.16(2) 74.18

16 (1) Where an appellant who is represented makes a request for a decision to be reconsidered at an oral hearing, the appellant's advocate must at least four days before the hearing file a brief written statement—

(a) informing the court and the respondent of the points which are to be raised at the hearing; and

(b) setting out the reasons why permission should be granted notwithstanding the reasons given for the refusal of permission.

(2) The court will notify the respondent of the hearing but the respondent is not expected to attend unless the court so directs.

(3) If the court directs the respondent to attend the permission hearing, the appellant must supply the respondent with a copy of the skeleton argument and any documents to which the appellant intends to refer.

Appellant in Receipt of Services Funded by the Legal Services Commission Applying for Permission to Appeal

para.17 74.15

17 Where the appellant is in receipt of services funded by the Legal Services Commission and permission to appeal has been refused by the court without a hearing, the appellant must send a copy of the court's reasons for refusing permission to the Legal Services Commission as soon as it has been received. The court will require confirmation that this has been done if a hearing is requested to reconsider the application.

Limited Permission: Rule 52.3

18 (1) If, under rule 52.3(7), the court grants permission to appeal on some issues only, it will—

(a) refuse permission on any remaining issues; or

(b) adjourn the application in respect of those issues to the hearing of the appeal.

(2) If the court adjourns the application under sub-paragraph (1)(b), the appellant must inform the court and the respondent in writing, within 14 days after the date of the court's order,

whether the appellant intends to pursue the application. If the appellant intends to pursue the application, the parties must include in any time estimate for the appeal hearing an allowance for the adjourned application.

(3) If the court refuses permission to appeal on the remaining issues without a hearing and the applicant wishes to have that decision reconsidered at an oral hearing, the time limit in rule 52.3(5) applies. Any application for an extension of this time should be made promptly. When hearing the appeal on the issues for which permission has been given the court will not normally grant an application to extend time in relation to the remaining issues.

Respondent Need Not Take any Action when Served with an Appellant's Notice

para.19 **74.18**

19 Unless the court directs otherwise, a respondent need not take any action when served with an appellant's notice until notified that permission to appeal has been granted.

Respondent's Costs of Permission Applications

para.20 **74.18**
para.20(1) **68.24**
para.20(2) **74.18**

20 (1) In most cases an application for permission to appeal will be determined without the need for the respondent to file submissions or attend a hearing. In such circumstances an order for costs will not normally be made in favour of a respondent who voluntarily makes submissions or attends a hearing.

(2) If the court directs the respondent to file submissions or attend a hearing, it will normally award costs to the respondent if permission is refused.

SECTION V — TIMETABLE

para.21 **PC 33, 74.25, 74.28, 74.40, 74.42, 74.51**

21 The timetable for the conduct of an appeal after the date of the listing window notification is set out below:

Timetable Part 1 — Listing window notification to lodging bundle

Period within which step is to be taken	Action	Cross-reference to relevant provisions in this practice direction
Within 14 days of service of: 1. the appellant's notice if permission has been given by the lower court or is not needed; 2. notification that permission has been granted by the Court of Appeal; or 3. notification that the permission application will be listed with the appeal to follow	**Respondent's notice** (if any) must be filed and served	Paragraph 8 (respondent's notice)
Within 14 days of filing a respondent's notice	**If respondent has filed a respondent's notice,** respondent must lodge and serve a skeleton argument on every other party	Paragraph 9 (skeleton argument to be lodged with the respondent's notice or within 14 days of filing respondent's notice)
7 days after date of listing window notification	Appellant must serve **proposed bundle index** on every respondent	Paragraph 27 (bundle of documents)
14 days after date of listing window notification	**Appeal questionnaire** must be filed and served on every respondent	Paragraph 1 (listing window notification defined) Paragraph 23 (appeal questionnaire)

Period within which step is to be taken	Action	Cross-reference to relevant provisions in this practice direction
7 days after service of appellant's appealquestionnaire	**If a respondent disagrees with appellant's time estimate**, that respondent must file and serve on every other party its own time estimate	Paragraph 24 (time estimate)
21 days after listing window notification	**Appeal skeleton**: appellant must serve on every respondent an appeal skeleton (without bundle cross references)	Paragraph 31 (skeleton argument)
21 days after date of the listing window notification	**Agree bundle**: the respondent must either agree the contents of the appeal bundle or notify the appellant of the documents that the respondent considers should be included in, or removed from, the appeal bundle by sending a revised index. If there is no agreement in relation to inclusion of a particular document, it must be placed in a supplemental bundle prepared by the party who has proposed its inclusion.	Paragraph 27 (bundle of documents) Paragraph 28 (bundle: appeals from Upper Tribunal Immigration and Asylum Chamber)
42 days after date of listing window notification	**Where respondent has not filed a respondent's notice**, respondent must lodge skeleton argument and serve on every other party	Paragraph 13 (respondent's skeleton argument (where no respondent's notice filed)) Paragraph 31 (skeleton argument)

Timetable Part 2 — Steps to be taken once hearing date fixed: lodging bundles, supplemental skeletons and bundles of authorities

Time before hearing date when step is to be taken	Action	Cross-reference to relevant provisions in this practice direction
No later than 42 days before the appeal hearing	Lodge, as directed by the court, the appropriate number of appeal bundles and serve a copy on all other parties to the appeal	Paragraph 27 (bundle of documents) Paragraph 28 (bundle: appeals from Upper Tribunal Immigration and Asylum Chamber)
No later than14 days before date of appeal hearing	Appellant must lodge and serve replacement skeleton argument	Paragraph 1 (replacement skeleton argument defined) Paragraph 31 (skeleton argument content, length and format) Paragraph 32 (supplementary skeleton argument)
No later than 7 days before the date of the hearing	Respondent must lodge and serve replacement skeleton argument	Paragraph 1 (replacement skeleton argument defined) Paragraph 32 (supplementary skeleton argument)

Time before hearing date when step is to be taken	Action	Cross-reference to relevant provisions in this practice direction
No later than 7 days before date of appeal hearing	Bundles of authorities must be lodged	Paragraph 29 (bundle of authorities)
No later than 7 days before the date of the hearing	Every document needed for the appeal hearing (if not already lodged or filed) must be lodged or filed	

SECTION VI — MANAGEMENT OF THE APPEAL

Listing and Hear-by Dates

para.22 74.32

22 The hear-by date is the last day of the listing window.

Appeal Questionnaire

para.23 PC 33, 74.34

23 The appellant must complete and file the appeal questionnaire and serve it on the respondent within 14 days after the date of the listing window notification.

Time Estimates

para.24 PC 33, 74.34

24 If the respondent disagrees with the appellant's time estimate, the respondent must inform the court within 7 days of service of the appeal questionnaire. In the absence of such notification the respondent will be deemed to have accepted the appellant's time estimate.

Multiple Appeals

25 (1) If two or more appeals are pending in the same or related proceedings, the parties must seek directions as to whether they should be heard together or consecutively by the same judges.

(2) Whether appeals are heard together or consecutively, the parties must attempt to agree a single appeal bundle or set of bundles for all the appeals and seek directions if they are unable to do so.

Expedition

26 (1) The court may direct that the hearing of an appeal be expedited.

(2) The court will deal with requests for expedition without a hearing. Requests for expedition must be made by letter setting out succinctly the grounds on which expedition is sought. The letter (or, if time is particularly short, email) must be marked for the immediate attention of the court and copied to the other parties to the appeal.

(3) If an expedited appeal hearing is required as a matter of extreme urgency, the Civil Appeals Office must be informed as soon as possible. If necessary, parties or their legal representatives should call the Royal Courts of Justice switchboard on (020) 7947 6000 and ask a member of the security staff to contact the duty judge.

(4) An expedited hearing will be listed at the convenience of the court and not according to the availability of counsel.

SECTION VII — BUNDLES, AMENDMENT AND SKELETON ARGUMENTS

para.27 PC 33
para.27(1) 74.25, 74.26
para.27(2) 74.25
para 27(3) 74.25

Bundle of Documents

27 (1) The appellant must lodge an appeal bundle which must contain only those documents relevant to the appeal. The bundle must—

(a) be paginated and in chronological order;
(b) contain an index at the front.

Documents relevant to the appeal

(2) Subject to any order made by the court, the following documents must be included in the appeal bundle—
(a) a copy of the appellant's notice;
(b) a copy of any respondent's notice;
(c) a copy of any appellant's or respondent's skeleton argument;
(d) a copy of the order under appeal;
(e) a copy of the order of the lower court granting or refusing permission to appeal together with a copy of the judge's reasons, if any, for granting or refusing permission;
(f) a copy of any order allocating the case to a track;
(g) the approved transcript of the judgment of the lower court (except in appeals in cases which were allocated to the small claims track but subject to any order of the court).

Documents which may be included

(3) The following documents should also be considered for inclusion in the appeal bundle but should be included only where relevant to the appeal—
(a) statements of case;
(b) application notices;
(c) other orders made in the case;
(d) a chronology of relevant events;
(e) witness statements made in support of any application made in the appellant's notice;
(f) other witness statements;
(g) other documents which the appellant or respondent consider relevant to the appeal.

Bundles not to include originals

(4) Unless otherwise directed, the appeal bundle should not include original material such as original documents, photographs and recorded media. Such material should be provided to the court, if necessary, at the hearing.

Destruction of bundles

(5) Bundles lodged with the court will not be returned to the parties but will be destroyed in the confidential waste system at the conclusion of the proceedings and without further notification.

Appeals from the Upper Tribunal Immigration and Asylum Chamber

28 (1) In an appeal from the Immigration and Asylum Chamber of the Upper Tribunal (other than an appeal relating to a claim for judicial review)—
(a) the Immigration and Asylum Chamber of the Upper Tribunal, upon request, shall send to the Civil Appeals Office copies of the documents which were before the relevant Tribunal when it considered the appeal;
(b) the appellant is not required to file an appeal bundle;
(c) the appellant must file with the appellant's notice the documents specified in paragraph 4(3)(a) to (e) and (g) of this practice direction.

Bundle of Authorities

para.29 PC 33, 74.51 para.29(4)(b) 74.51

29 (1) After consultation with any opposing advocate, the appellant's advocate must file a bundle containing photocopies of the authorities upon which each party will rely at the hearing.
(2) The most authoritative report of each authority must be used in accordance with the Practice Direction on Citation of Authorities (2012) and must have the relevant passages marked by a vertical line in the margin.
(3) Photocopies of authorities should not be in landscape format and the type should not be reduced in size.
(4) *The bundle should not*—
(a) include authorities for propositions not in dispute; or
(b) contain more than 10 authorities unless the issues in the appeal justify more extensive citation.

(5) A bundle of authorities must bear a certificate by the advocates responsible for arguing the case that the requirements of sub-paragraphs (2) to (4) of this paragraph have been complied with in respect of each authority included.

Amendment of Appeal Notice: Rule 52.8

para.30 74.23 para.30(3) 74.45

30 (1) An appeal notice may not be amended without the permission of the court.
(2) An application for permission to amend made before permission to appeal has been considered will normally be determined without a hearing.
(3) An application for permission to amend (after permission to appeal has been granted) and any submissions in opposition will normally be dealt with at the hearing unless that would cause unnecessary expense or delay, in which case a request should be made for the application to amend to be heard in advance.
(4) Legal representatives must—
(a) inform the court at the time they make the application if the existing time estimate is affected by the proposed amendment; and
(b) attempt to agree any revised time estimate no later than seven days after service of the application.

Skeleton Argument

para.31 PC 33 para.31(4) 74.29
para.31(1) 74.29

31 (1) Any skeleton argument must comply with the provisions of Section 5 of Practice Direction 52A and must—
(a) not normally exceed 25 pages (excluding front sheets and back sheets);
(b) be printed on A4 paper in not less than 12 point font and 1.5 line spacing.
(2) Where an appellant has filed a skeleton argument in support of an application for permission to appeal, the same skeleton argument may be relied upon in the appeal or the appellant may file an appeal skeleton argument (Timetable Section 5, Part 1).
(3) At the hearing the court may refuse to hear argument on a point not included in a skeleton argument filed within the prescribed time.
(4) The court may disallow the cost of preparing an appeal skeleton argument which does not comply with these requirements or was not filed within the prescribed time.

Supplementary Skeleton Arguments

para.32 74.23, 74.42

32 (1) A party may file a supplementary skeleton argument only where strictly necessary and only with the permission of the court.
(2) If a party wishes to rely on a supplementary skeleton argument, it must be lodged and served as soon as practicable. It must be accompanied by a request for permission setting out the reasons why a supplementary skeleton argument is necessary and why it could not reasonably have been lodged earlier.
(3) Only exceptionally will the court allow the use of a supplementary skeleton argument if lodged later than seven days before the hearing.

PD 52D Practice Direction 52D —Statutory Appeals and Appeals Subject to Special Provision

This practice direction supplements CPR, Part 52.

PD 52D **3.8, 74.57**

Contents of this Practice Direction

This practice direction is divided into the following sections:

SECTION I — INTRODUCTION

1.1 This practice direction applies to all statutory appeals, and to other appeals which are subject to special provision, but not to appeals by way of case stated (to which Practice Direction 52E applies).

SECTION II — ROUTES OF APPEAL

2.1 In this practice direction, the court to which an appeal lies is prescribed by statute.

SECTION III — GENERAL PROVISIONS ABOUT STATUTORY APPEALS

para.3.3(1) 74.57 para.3.3(2) 74.57

3.1 This Section contains general provisions about statutory appeals (paragraphs 3.2–3.8). For where this practice direction or a statute makes additional special provision see also Section 4.

3.2 Where any of the provisions in this Section provide for documents to be filed at the appeal court, those documents are in addition to any documents required under Part 52 or Practice Direction 52B or 52C.

3.3 (1) Where the appellant wishes to appeal against a decision of the Administrative Appeals Chamber of the Upper Tribunal, the appellant's notice must be filed within 21 days of the date on which the Upper Tribunal's decision on permission to appeal to the Court of Appeal is given.

(2) Where the appellant wishes to appeal against a decision of any other Chamber of the Upper Tribunal, the appellant's notice must be filed within 28 days of the date on which the Upper Tribunal's decision on permission to appeal to the Court of Appeal is given.

Service of appellant's notice: rule 52.4(3)

para.3.4(1) 74.57

3.4 (1) The appellant must serve the appellant's notice on the respondent and on the chairman of the tribunal, Minister of State, government department or other person from whose decision the appeal is brought.

(2) In the case of an appeal from the decision of a tribunal that has no chairman or member who acts as a chairman, the appellant's notice must be served on the member (or members if more than one) of the tribunal.

Variation of time: rule 52.6

para.3.5 74.57

3.5 Where any statute prescribes a period within which an appeal must be filed then, unless the statute otherwise provides, the appeal court may not extend that period.

Applications by third parties (rule 52.12A)

para.3.7 74.57

3.6 Where all the parties consent, the court may deal with an application under rule 52.12A without a hearing.

3.7 An application for permission must be made by letter to the relevant court office, identifying the appeal, explaining who the applicant is and indicating why and in what form the applicant wants to participate in the hearing.

3.8 If the applicant is seeking a prospective order as to costs, the letter must say what kind of order and on what grounds.

SECTION IV — SPECIFIC APPEALS

section IV 74.59

Provisions about Specific Appeals

4.1 This Section sets out special provisions about the appeals listed in the Table below. This Section is not exhaustive and does not create, amend or remove any right of appeal.

4.2 Part 52 applies to all appeals to which this Section applies subject to any special provisions set out in this Section.

4.3 Where any of the provisions in this Section provide for documents to be filed at the appeal court, these documents are in addition to any documents required under Part 52 or Practice Direction 52B or 52C.

Certain Appeals to the High Court to be Heard in Chancery Division

5.1 Any appeal to the High Court, and any case stated or question referred for the opinion of that court under any of the following enactments shall be heard in the Chancery Division—

(1) section 38(3) of the Clergy Pensions Measure 1961;
(2) regulation 74 of the European Public Limited-Liability Company Regulations 2004 (SI 2004/2326).
(3) the Industrial and Provident Societies Act 1965;
(4) section 222(3) of the Inheritance Tax Act 1984;
(5) the Land Registration Act 2002;
(6) paragraph 16 of Schedule 15 to the Law of Property Act 1922;
(7) section 215 or 217 of the Pensions Act 2003;
(8) section 151 of the Pension Schemes Act 1993;
(9) section 13 and 13B of the Stamp Act 1891;
(10) regulation 8(3) of the Stamp Duty Reserve Tax Regulations 1986 (SI 1086/1711).

Table

Statute (or description of appeal)	Appropriate court	Relevant paragraph in this practice direction
Agricultural Land Tribunal	High Court	18.1
Architects Act 1997, s. 22	High Court	19.1
Chiropractors Act 1994, s. 31	High Court	19.1
Civil partnership — conditional order for dissolution or nullity	CA	6.1
Clergy Pensions Measure 1961, s. 38(3)	High Court	5.1
Competition: Articles 101 and 102 of the Treaty on the Functioning of the European Union and Chapters I and II of Part I of the Competition Act 1998	CA	7.1
Competition Appeal Tribunal	CA	8.1
Contempt of court	CA	9.1
Court of Protection	CA	10.1
Decree nisi of divorce or nullity of marriage	CA	6.1
Dentists Act 1984, ss. 29 and 44	High Court	19.1
Employment Appeal Tribunal	CA	11.1

Statute (or description of appeal)	Appropriate court	Relevant paragraph in this practice direction
European Public Limited-Liability Company Regulations 2004 (SI 2004/2326), reg. 74	High Court	20.1
Extradition Act 2003	High Court	21.1
Friendly Societies Act 1974	High Court	5.1 and 22.1
Friendly Societies Act 1992	High Court	5.1 and 22.1
Health Professions Order 2001 (SI 2002/254), art. 38	High Court	19.1
Housing Act 1996, ss.204 and 204A	County Court	28.1
Immigration and Asylum Act 1999, Part II	County Court	29.1
Immigration and Asylum Appeals	CA	12.1
Inheritance Tax Act 1984, s. 222	High Court	5.1 and 23.1
Land Registration Act 2002	High Court	5.1 and 24.1
Law of Property Act 1922, para. 16 of Sch. 15	High Court	5.1
Local Government (Miscellaneous Provisions) Act 1976	County Court	30.1
Medical Act 1983, s. 40	High Court	19.1
Medicines Act 1968, ss. 82(3) and 83	High Court	19.1
Merchant Shipping Act 1995	High Court	25.1
Nurses, Midwives and Health Visitors Act 1997, s.12	High Court	19.1
Nursing and Midwifery Order 2001 (SI 2002/253), art. 38	High Court	19.1
Opticians Act 1989, s. 23	High Court	19.1
Osteopaths Act 1993, s. 31	High Court	19.1
Patents Court: on appeal from Comptroller	CA	13.1
Patents: revocation of patent	CA	14.1
Pensions Act 2004, ss. 215 and 217	High Court	5.1
Pension Schemes Act 1993, s. 151	High Court	5.1
Pharmacy Act 1954	High Court	19.1
Pharmacy Order 2010 (SI 2010/231), art. 58	High Court	19.1
Planning (Listed Buildings and Conservation Areas) Act 1990, s. 65	High Court	26.1
Proscribed Organisations Appeal Commission	CA	15.1
Representation of the People Act 1983, s. 56	County Court	31.1-31.3
Serious Crime Prevention Orders	CA	16.1
Solicitors Disciplinary Tribunal	High Court	27.1
Special Immigration Appeals Commission	CA	17.1
Stamp Duty Reserve Tax Regulations 1986 (SI 1986/1711), reg. 8	High Court	5.1 and 23.1
Town and Country Planning Act 1990, s. 289	High Court	26.1
UK Borders Act 2007, s. 11	County Court	32.1

Appeals to the Court of Appeal

Appeal against decree nisi of divorce or nullity of marriage or conditional dissolution *or nullity order in relation to civil partnership*

6.1 (1) The appellant must file the appellant's notice at the Court of Appeal within 28 days after the date on which the decree was pronounced or conditional order made.

(2) The appellant must file the following documents with the appellant's notice—
  (a) the decree or conditional order; and
  (b) a certificate of service of the appellant's notice.
(3) The appellant's notice must be served on the appropriate district judge (see sub-paragraph (6)) in addition to the persons to be served under rule 52.4(3) and in accordance with that rule.
(4) The lower court may not alter the time limits for filing of the appeal notices.
(5) Where an appellant intends to apply to the Court of Appeal for an extension of time for serving or filing the appellant's notice the appellant must give notice of that intention to the appropriate district judge (see sub-paragraph 6) before the application is made.
(6) In this paragraph 'the appropriate district judge' means, where the lower court is—
  (a) a county court, the district judge of that court;
  (b) a district registry, the district judge of that registry;
  (c) the Principal Registry of the Family Division, the senior district judge of that division.

Appeals relating to the application of Articles 101 and 102 of the Treaty on the Functioning of the European Union and Chapters I and II of Part I of the Competition Act 1998

7.1 (1) This paragraph applies to any appeal to the Court of Appeal relating to the application of—
  (a) Article 101 or Article 102 of the Treaty on the Functioning of the European Union; or
  (b) Chapter I or Chapter II of Part I of the Competition Act 1998.
(2) In this paragraph—
  (a) 'the Act' means the Competition Act 1998;
  (b) 'the Commission'means the European Commission;
  (c) 'the Competition Regulation' means Council Regulation (EC) No. 1/2003 of 16 December 2002 on the implementation of the rules on competition laid down in Articles 81 and 82 of the Treaty establishing the European Community (as amended in consequence of the Treaty on the Functioning of the European Union);
  (d) 'national competition authority' means—
    (i) the Office of Fair Trading; and
    (ii) any other person or body designated pursuant to Article 35 of the Competition Regulation as a national competition authority of the United Kingdom;
  (e) 'the Treaty' means the Treaty on the Functioning of the European Union.
(3) Any party whose appeal notice raises an issue relating to the application of Article 101 or 102 of the Treaty, or Chapter I or II of Part I of the Act, must—
  (a) state that fact in the appeal notice; and
  (b) serve a copy of the appeal notice on the Office of Fair Trading at the same time as it is served on the other party to the appeal (addressed to the Director of Competition Policy Coordination, Office of Fair Trading, Fleetbank House, 2–6 Salisbury Square, London EC4Y 8JX).
(4) Attention is drawn to the provisions of article 15.3 of the Competition Regulation, which entitles competition authorities and the Commission to submit written observations to national courts on issues relating to the application of Article 101 or 102 and, with the permission of the court in question, to submit oral observations to the court.
(5) A national competition authority may also make written observations to the Court of Appeal, or apply for permission to make oral observations, on issues relating to the application of Chapter I or II.
(6) If a national competition authority or the Commission intends to make written observations to the Court of Appeal, it must give notice of its intention to do so by letter to the Civil Appeals Office at the earliest opportunity.
(7) An application by a national competition authority or the Commission for permission to make oral representations at the hearing of an appeal must be made by letter to the Civil Appeals Office at the earliest opportunity, identifying the appeal and indicating why the applicant wishes to make oral representations.

(8) If a national competition authority or the Commission files a notice under sub-paragraph (6) or an application under sub-paragraph (7), it must at the same time serve a copy of the notice or application on every party to the appeal.

(9) Any request by a national competition authority or the Commission for the court to send it any documents relating to an appeal should be made at the same time as filing a notice under sub-paragraph (6) or an application under sub-paragraph (7).

(10) When the Court of Appeal receives a notice under sub-paragraph (6) it may give case management directions to the national competition authority or the Commission, including directions about the date by which any written observations are to be filed.

(11) The Court of Appeal will serve on every party to the appeal a copy of any directions given or order made—
(a) on an application under sub-paragraph (7); or
(b) under sub-paragraph (10).

(12) Every party to an appeal which raises an issue relating to the application of Article 101 or 102, and any national competition authority which has been served with a copy of a party's appeal notice, is under a duty to notify the Court of Appeal at any stage of the appeal if they are aware that—
(a) the Commission has adopted, or is contemplating adopting, a decision in relation to proceedings which it has initiated; and
(b) the decision referred to in (a) above has or would have legal effects in relation to the particular agreement, decision or practice in issue before the court.

(13) Where the Court of Appeal is aware that the Commission is contemplating adopting a decision as mentioned in sub-paragraph (12)(a), it shall consider whether to stay the appeal pending the Commission's decision.

(14) Where any judgment is given which decides on the application of Article 101 or 102, the court shall direct that a copy of the transcript of the judgment shall be sent to the Commission. Judgments may be sent to the Commission electronically to comp-amicus@cec.eu.int or by post to the European Commission DG Competition, B-1049, Brussels.

Appeal from Competition Appeal Tribunal

8.1 (1) Where the appellant applies for permission to appeal at the hearing at which the decision is delivered by the tribunal and—
(a) permission is given; or
(b) permission is refused and the appellant wishes to make an application to the Court of Appeal for permission to appeal,
the appellant's notice must be filed at the Court of Appeal within 14 days after the date of that hearing.

(2) Where the appellant applies in writing to the Registrar of the tribunal for permission to appeal and—
(a) permission is given; or
(b) permission is refused and the appellant wishes to make an application to the Court of Appeal for permission to appeal,
the appellant's notice must be filed at the Court of Appeal within 14 days after the date of receipt of the tribunal's decision on permission.

(3) Where the appellant does not make an application to the tribunal for permission to appeal, but wishes to make an application to the Court of Appeal for permission, the appellant's notice must be filed at the Court of Appeal within 14 days after the end of the period within which the appellant may make a written application to the Registrar of the tribunal.

Appeals in cases of contempt of court (section 13 Administration of Justice Act 1960)

9.1 In an appeal under section 13 of the Administration of Justice Act 1960 (appeals in cases of contempt of court), the appellant must serve the appellant's notice on the court or the Upper Tribunal from whose order or decision the appeal is brought in addition to the persons to be served under rule 52.4(3) and in accordance with that rule.

Appeal from the Court of Protection

10.1 (1) In this paragraph—
(a) 'P' means a person who lacks, or who is alleged to lack, capacity within the meaning of the Mental Capacity Act 2005 to make a decision or decisions in relation to any matter that is subject to an order of the Court of Protection;
(b) 'the person effecting notification' means—
(i) the appellant;
(ii) an agent duly appointed by the appellant; or
(iii) such other person as the Court of Protection may direct, who is required to notify P in accordance with this paragraph; and
(c) 'final order' means a decision of the Court of Appeal that finally determines the appeal proceedings before it.

(2) Where P is not a party to the proceedings, unless the Court of Appeal directs otherwise, the person effecting notification must notify P—
(a) that an appellant's notice has been filed with the Court of Appeal and—
(i) who the appellant is;
(ii) what final order the appellant is seeking;
(iii) what will happen if the Court of Appeal makes the final order sought by the appellant; and
(iv) that P may apply under rule 52.12A (Statutory appeals: court's power to hear any person) by letter for permission to file evidence or make representations at the appeal hearing;
(b) of the final order, the effect of the final order and what steps P can take in relation to it; and
(c) of such other events and documents as the Court of Appeal may direct.
(Paragraphs 3.6 to 3.8 of this practice direction(PD 52D) contain provisions on how a third party can apply for permission to file evidence or make representations at an appeal hearing.)

(3) The person effecting notification must provide P with the information specified in sub-paragraph (2)—
(a) within 14 days of the date on which the appellant's notice was filed with the Court of Appeal;
(b) within 14 days of the date on which the final order was made; or
(c) within such time as the Court of Appeal may direct,
as the case may be.

(4) The person effecting notification must provide P in person with the information specified in sub-paragraph (2) in a way that is appropriate to P's circumstances (for example, using simple language, visual aids or any other appropriate means).

(5) Where P is to be notified as to—
(a) the existence or effect of a document other than the appellant's notice or final order; or
(b) the taking place of an event,
the person effecting notification must explain to P—
(i) in the case of a document, what the document is and what effect, if any, it has; or
(ii) in the case of an event, what the event is and its relevance to P.

(6) The person effecting notification must, within seven days of notifying P, file a certificate of notification (form N165) which certifies—
(a) the date on which P was notified; and
(b) that P was notified in accordance with this paragraph.

(7) Where the person effecting notification has not notified P in accordance with this paragraph, a certificate of non-notification (form N165) must be filed with the Court of Appeal stating the reason why notification has not been effected.

(8) Where the person effecting notification must file a certificate of non-notification with the Court of Appeal, the certificate must be filed within the following time limits—
(a) where P is to be notified in accordance with sub-paragraph (2)(a) (appellant's notice), within 21 days of the appellant's notice being filed with the Court of Appeal;
(b) where P is to be notified in accordance with sub-paragraph (2)(b) (final order), within 21 days of the final order being made by the Court of Appeal; or
(c) where P is to be notified of such other events and documents as may be directed by the Court of Appeal, within such time as the Court of Appeal directs.

(9) The appellant or such other person as the Court of Appeal may direct may apply to the Court of Appeal seeking an order—
(a) dispensing with the requirement to comply with the provisions of this paragraph; or
(b) requiring some other person to comply with the provisions of this paragraph.
(10) An application made under sub-paragraph (9) may be made in the appellant's notice or by Part 23 application notice.

(Paragraphs 6.1 to 6.3 of Practice Direction 52A contain provisions about the dismissal of applications or appeals by consent. Paragraph 6.5 of Practice Direction 52A contains provisions about allowing unopposed appeals or applications involving a child or protected party.)

Appeal from Employment Appeal Tribunal

11.1 (1) This paragraph applies to an appeal to the Court of Appeal from the Employment Appeal Tribunal (EAT) under section 37 of the Employment Tribunals Act 1996.
(2) If an application for permission to appeal to the Court of Appeal is refused by the EAT or is not made, then such an application must be made to the Court of Appeal within 21 days of the date of the sealed order of the EAT.
(3) An application for extension of time for filing an appellant's notice may be entertained by the EAT but such applications should normally be made to the Court of Appeal.

Immigration and asylum appeals

12.1 The provisions of paragraph 28 of Practice Direction 52C (bundle of documents in immigration appeals and asylum appeals) apply to appeals from the Upper Tribunal Immigration and Asylum Chamber.

Appeal from Patents Court on appeal from Comptroller

13.1 Where the appeal is from a decision of the Patents Court which was itself made on an appeal from a decision of the Comptroller-General of Patents, Designs and Trade Marks, the appellant must serve the appellant's notice on the Comptroller in addition to the persons to be served under rule 52.4(3) and in accordance with that rule.

Appeal against order for revocation of patent

14.1 (1) This paragraph applies where an appeal lies to the Court of Appeal from an order for the revocation of a patent.
(2) The appellant must serve the appellant's notice on the Comptroller-General of Patents, Designs and Trade Marks (the 'Comptroller') in addition to the persons to be served under rule 52.4(3) and in accordance with that rule.
(3) Where, before the appeal hearing, the respondent decides not to oppose the appeal or not to attend the appeal hearing, the respondent must immediately serve notice of that decision on—
(a) the Comptroller; and
(b) the appellant.
(4) Where the respondent serves a notice in accordance with sub-paragraph (3), copies of the following documents must also be served on the Comptroller with that notice—
(a) the petition;
(b) any statements of claim;
(c) any written evidence filed in the claim.
(5) Within 14 days after receiving the notice in accordance with sub-paragraph (3), the Comptroller must serve on the appellant a notice stating an intention to attend the appeal hearing or otherwise.
(6) The Comptroller may attend the appeal hearing and oppose the appeal—
(a) in any case where notice has been given under paragraph (5) of the intention to attend; and
(b) in any other case (including, in particular, a case where the respondent withdraws his opposition to the appeal during the hearing) if the Court of Appeal so directs or permits.

Appeal from Proscribed Organisations Appeal Commission

15.1 The appellant's notice must be filed at the Court of Appeal within 14 days after the date when the Proscribed Organisations Appeal Commission—

(a) granted; or
(b) where section 6(2)(b) of the Terrorism Act 2000 applies, refused permission to appeal.

Appeals in relation to serious crime prevention orders

16.1 (1) This paragraph applies to an appeal under section 23(1) of the Serious Crime Act 2007 or section 16 of the Senior Courts Act 1981 in relation to a serious crime prevention order and is made.
(2) The appellant must serve the appellant's notice on any person who made representations in the proceedings by virtue of section 9(1), (2) or (3) of the Serious Crime Act 2007 in addition to the persons to be served under rule 52.4(3) and in accordance with that rule.

Appeal from Special Immigration Appeals Commission

17.1 (1) An application for permission to appeal to the Court of Appeal must first be made to the Special Immigration Appeals Commission pursuant section 7(2) of the Special Immigration Appeals Commission Act 1997 and paragraph 27 of the Special Immigration Appeals Commission (Procedure) Rules 2003(SI 2003/1034) (as amended).
(2) The appellant's notice must be filed at the Court of Appeal within 21 days of the date on which the Special Immigration Appeals Commission's decision granting or refusing permission to appeal to the Court of Appeal is given.

Appeals to the High Court

Reference of question of law by Agricultural Land Tribunal

18.1 (1) A question of law referred to the High Court by an Agricultural Land Tribunal under section 6 of the Agriculture (Miscellaneous Provisions) Act 1954 shall be referred by way of case stated by the Tribunal.
(2) Where the proceedings before the tribunal arose on an application under section 11 of the Agricultural Holdings Act 1986, an—
(a) application notice for an order under section 6 that the tribunal refers a question of law to the court; and
(b) appellant's notice by which an appellant seeks the court's determination on a question of law,
must be served on the authority having power to enforce the statutory requirement specified in the notice in addition to every other party to those proceedings and on the secretary of the tribunal.
(3) Where, in accordance with sub-paragraph (2), a notice is served on the authority mentioned in that paragraph, that authority may attend the appeal hearing and make representations to the court.

Appeals against decisions affecting the registration of architects and health care professionals

19.1 (1) This paragraph applies to an appeal to the High Court under—
(a) section 22 of the Architects Act 1997;
(b) section 31 of the Chiropractors Act 1994;
(c) section 29 or section 44 of the Dentists Act 1984;
(d) article 38 of the Health Professions Order 2001 (SI 2002/254);
(e) section 40 of the Medical Act 1983;
(f) section 82(3) and 83(2) of the Medicines Act 1968;
(g) section 12 of the Nurses, Midwives and Health Visitors Act 1997;
(h) article 38 of the Nursing and Midwifery Order 2001 (SI 2002/253);
(i) section 23 of the Opticians Act 1989;
(j) section 31 of the Osteopaths Act 1993;
(k) section 10 of the Pharmacy Act 1954;
(l) article 58 of the Pharmacy Order 2010 (SI 2010/231).
(2) Every appeal to which this paragraph applies must be supported by written evidence and, if the court so orders, oral evidence and will be by way of rehearing.
(3) The appellant must file the appellant's notice within 28 days after the decision that the appellant wishes to appeal.
(4) In the case of an appeal under an enactment specified in column 1 of the following table, the persons to be made respondents are the persons specified in relation to that enactment

in column 2 of the table and the person to be served with the appellant's notice is the Registrar of the relevant Council.

Appeals under regulation 74 of the European Public Limited-Liability Company Regulations 2004

20.1 (1) In this paragraph—

(a) 'the 2004 Regulations' means the European Public Limited-Liability Company Regulations 2004 (SI 2004/2326);

(b) 'the EC Regulation'means Council Regulation (EC) No 2157/2001 of 8 October 2001 on the Statute for a European company (SE);

(c) 'SE' means a European public limited-liability company (Societas Europaea) within the meaning of Article 1 of the EC Regulation.

1	2
Enactment	*Respondent*
Architects Act 1997, s. 22	The Architects'Registration Council of the United Kingdom*
Chiropractors Act 1994, s. 31	The General Chiropractic Council
Dentists Act 1984, ss. 29 and 44	The General Dental Council
Health Professions Order 2001 (SI 2002/254), art. 38	The Health Professions Council
Medical Act 1983, s. 40	The General Medical Council
Medicines Act 1968, ss. 82(3) and 83(2)	The Pharmaceutical Society of Great Britain**
Nurses, Midwives and Health Visitors Act 1997, s.12; Nursing and Midwifery Order 2001 (SI 2002/253), art. 38	The Nursing and Midwifery Council
Opticians Act 1989, s.23	The General Optical Council
Osteopaths Act 1993, s. 31	The General Osteopathic Council
Pharmacy Act 1954, s.10	The Royal Pharmaceutical Society of Great Britain
Pharmacy Order 2010 (SI 2010/231), art. 58	The General Pharmaceutical Council

[* Now the Architects Registration Board.]
[** Now the Royal Pharmaceutical Society of Great Britain.]

(2) This paragraph applies to appeals under regulation 74 of the 2004 Regulations against the opposition—

(a) of the Secretary of State or national financial supervisory authority to the transfer of the registered office of an SE under Article 8(14) of the EC Regulation; and

(b) of the Secretary of State to the participation by a company in the formation of an SE by merger under Article 19 of the EC Regulation.

(3) Where an SE seeks to appeal against the opposition of the national financial supervisory authority to the transfer of its registered office under Article 8(14) of the EC Regulation, it must serve the appellant's notice on both the national financial supervisory authority and the Secretary of State.

(4) The appellant's notice must contain an application for permission to appeal.

(5) The appeal will be a review of the decision of the Secretary of State and not a rehearing. The grounds of review are set out in regulation 74(2) of the 2004 Regulations.

(6) The appeal will be heard by a High Court judge.

Appeals under the Extradition Act 2003

para.21.1 74.60 para.21.1(2) 74.60

21.1 (1) In this paragraph, 'the Act' means the Extradition Act 2003.

(2) Appeals to the High Court under the Act must be started in the Administrative Court of the Queen's Bench Division at the Royal Courts of Justice in London.

(3) Where an appeal is brought under section 26 or 28 of the Act—

(a) the appellant's notice must be filed and served before the expiry of seven days, starting with the day on which the order is made;
(b) the appellant must endorse the appellant's notice with the date of the person's arrest;
(c) the High Court must begin to hear the substantive appeal within 40 days of the person's arrest; and
(d) the appellant must serve a copy of the appellant's notice on the Crown Prosecution Service, if they are not a party to the appeal, in addition to the persons to be served under rule 52.4(3) and in accordance with that rule.

(4) The High Court may extend the period of 40 days under sub-paragraph (3)(c) if it believes it to be in the interests of justice to do so.

(5) Where an appeal is brought under section 103 of the Act, the appellant's notice must be filed and served before the expiry of 14 days, starting with the day on which the Secretary of State informs the person under section 100(1) or (4) of the Act that an order has made in respect of the person.

(6) Where an appeal is brought under section 105 of the Act, the appellant's notice must be filed and served before the expiry of 14 days, starting with the day on which the order for discharge is made.

(7) Where an appeal is brought under section 108 of the Act the appellant's notice must be filed and served before the expiry of 14 days, starting with the day on which the Secretary of State informs the person that an order for extradition has been made.

(8) Where an appeal is brought under section 110 of the Act the appellant's notice must be filed and served before the expiry of 14 days, starting with the day on which the Secretary of State informs the person acting on behalf of a category 2 territory, as defined in section 69 of the Act, of the order for discharge.

(Section 69 of the Act provides that a category 2 territory is that designated for the purposes of Part 2 of the Act.)

(9) Subject to sub-paragraph (10), where an appeal is brought under section 103, 105, 108 or 110 of the Act, the High Court must begin to hear the substantive appeal within 76 days of the appellant's notice being filed.

(10) Where an appeal is brought under section 103 of the Act before the Secretary of State has decided whether the person is to be extradited—
(a) the period of 76 days does not start until the day on which the Secretary of State informs the person of the decision; and
(b) the Secretary of State must, as soon as practicable after the person has been informed of the decision, inform the High Court—
(i) of the decision; and
(ii) of the date on which the person was informed of the decision.

(11) The High Court may extend the period of 76 days if it believes it to be in the interests of justice to do so.

(12) Where an appeal is brought under section 103, 105, 108 or 110 of the Act, the appellant must serve a copy of the appellant's notice on—
(a) the Crown Prosecution Service; and
(b) the Home Office,
if they are not a party to the appeal, in addition to the persons to be served under rule 52.4(3) and in accordance with that rule.

Appeals affecting industrial and provident societies etc.

22.1 (1) This paragraph applies to all appeals under—
(a) the Friendly Societies Act 1974;
(b) the Friendly Societies Act 1992; and
(c) the Industrial and Provident Societies Act 1965.

(2) At any stage on an appeal, the court may—
(a) direct that the appellant's notice be served on any person;
(b) direct that notice be given by advertisement or otherwise of—
(i) the bringing of the appeal;
(ii) the nature of the appeal; and
(iii) the time when the appeal will or is likely to be heard; or

(c) give such other directions as it thinks proper to enable any person interested in—
(i) the society, trade union, alleged trade union or industrial assurance company; or
(ii) the subject matter of the appeal,
to appear and be heard at the appeal hearing.

Appeals under section 222 of the Inheritance Tax Act 1984 and regulation 8(3) of the Stamp Duty Reserve Tax Regulations 1986

23.1 (1) This paragraph applies to appeals to the High Court under section 222(3) of the Inheritance Tax Act 1984 (the '1984 Act') and regulation 8(3) of the Stamp Duty Reserve Tax Regulations 1986 (SI 1986/1711, the '1986 Regulations').
(2) The appellant's notice must—
(a) state the date on which the Commissioners for Her Majesty's Revenue and Customs (the 'Board') gave notice to the appellant under section 221 of the 1984 Act or regulation 6 of the 1986 Regulations of the determination that is the subject of the appeal;
(b) state the date on which the appellant gave to the Board notice of appeal under section 222(1) of the 1984 Act or regulation 8(1) of the 1986 Regulations and, if notice was not given within the time permitted, whether Her Majesty's Revenue and Customs (HMRC) have given their consent or the tribunal has given permission for notice to be given after the time permitted, and where applicable, the date of such consent or permission; and
(c) either state that the appellant and the Board have agreed that the appeal may be to the High Court or contain an application for permission to appeal to the High Court.
(3) The appellant must file the following documents with the appellant's notice—
(a) two copies of the notice referred to in sub-paragraph 2(a);
(b) two copies of the notice of appeal (under section 222(1) of the 1984 Act or regulation 8(1) of the 1986 Regulations) referred to in paragraph 2(b); and
(c) where the appellant's notice contains an application for permission to appeal, written evidence setting out the grounds on which it is alleged that the matters to be decided on the appeal are likely to be substantially confined to questions of law.
(4) The appellant must—
(a) file the appellant's notice at the court; and
(b) serve the appellant's notice on the Board,
within 30 days of the date on which the appellant gave to the Board notice of appeal under section 222(1) of the 1984 Act or regulation 8(1) of the 1986 Regulations or, if HMRC have given consent or the tribunal has given permission for notice to be given after the time permitted, within 30 days of the date on which such consent or permission was given.
(5) The court will set a date for the hearing of not less than 40 days from the date that the appellant's notice was filed.
(6) Where the appellant's notice contains an application for permission to appeal—
(a) a copy of the written evidence filed in accordance with sub-paragraph (3)(c) must be served on the Board with the appellant's notice; and
(b) the Board—
(i) may file written evidence; and
(ii) if it does so, must serve a copy of that evidence on the appellant, within 30 days after service of the written evidence under sub-paragraph (6)(a).
(7) The appellant may not rely on any grounds of appeal not specified in the notice referred to in sub-paragraph (2)(b) on the hearing of the appeal without the permission of the court.

Appeal against a decision of the adjudicator under section 111 of the Land Registration Act 2002

24.1 (1) A person who is aggrieved by a decision of the adjudicator and who wishes to appeal that decision must obtain permission to appeal.
(2) The appellant must serve on the adjudicator a copy of the appeal court's decision on a request for permission to appeal as soon as reasonably practicable and in any event within 14 days of receipt by the appellant of the decision on permission.
(3) The appellant must serve on the adjudicator and the Chief Land Registrar a copy of any order by the appeal court to stay a decision of the adjudicator pending the outcome of the appeal as soon as reasonably practicable and in any event within 14 days of receipt by the appellant of the appeal court's order to stay.

(4) The appellant must serve on the adjudicator and the Chief Land Registrar a copy of the appeal court's decision on the appeal as soon as reasonably practicable and in any event within 14 days of receipt by the appellant of the appeal court's decision.

Appeals under the Merchant Shipping Act 1995

25.1 (1) This paragraph applies to appeals under the Merchant Shipping Act 1995 and for this purpose a rehearing and an application under section 61 of the Merchant Shipping Act 1995 are treated as appeals.

(2) The appellant must file any report to the Secretary of State containing the decision from which the appeal is brought with the appellant's notice.

(3) Where a rehearing by the High Court is ordered under sections 64 or 269 of the Merchant Shipping Act 1995, the Secretary of State must give reasonable notice to the parties whom he considers to be affected by the rehearing.

Appeals under s 289(6) of the Town and Country Planning Act 1990 and s 65(5) of the Planning (Listed Buildings and Conservation Areas) Act 1990

26.1 (1) An application for permission to appeal to the High Court under section 289 of the Town and Country Planning Act 1990 ('the TCP Act') or section 65 of the Planning (Listed Buildings and Conservation Areas) Act 1990 ('the PLBCA Act') must be made within 28 days after notice of the decision is given to the applicant.

(2) The application—

(a) must be in writing and must set out the reasons why permission should be granted; and

(b) if the time for applying has expired, must include an application to extend the time for applying, and must set out the reasons why the application was not made within that time.

(3) The applicant must, before filing the application, serve a copy of it on the persons referred to in sub-paragraph (12) with the draft appellant's notice and a copy of the witness statement or affidavit to be filed with the application.

(4) The applicant must file the application in the Administrative Court Office with—

(a) a copy of the decision being appealed;

(b) a draft appellant's notice;

(c) a witness statement or affidavit verifying any facts relied on; and

(d) a witness statement or affidavit giving the name and address of, and the place and date of service on, each person who has been served with the application. If any person who ought to be served has not been served, the witness statement or affidavit must state that fact and the reason why the person was not served.

(5) An application will be heard–

(a) by a single judge; and

(b) unless the court otherwise orders, not less than 21 days after it was filed at the Administrative Court Office.

(6) Practice Direction 54D applies to applications and appeals under this paragraph.

(7) Any person served with the application is entitled to appear and be heard.

(8) Any respondent who intends to use a witness statement or affidavit at the hearing—

(a) must file it in the Administrative Court Office; and

(b) must serve a copy on the applicant as soon as is practicable and in any event, unless the court otherwise allows, at least two days before the hearing.

(9) The court may allow the applicant to use a further witness statement or affidavit.

(10) Where on the hearing of an application the court is of the opinion that a person who ought to have been served has not been served, the court may adjourn the hearing, on such terms as it directs, in order that the application may be served on that person.

(11) Where the court grants permission—

(a) it may impose terms as to costs and as to giving security;

(b) it may give directions; and

(c) the relevant appellant's notice must be served and filed within seven days of the grant.

(12) The persons to be served with the appellant's notice are—

(a) the Secretary of State;

(b) the local planning authority who served the notice or gave the decision, as the case may be, or, where the appeal is brought by that authority, the appellant or applicant in the proceedings in which the decision appealed against was given;
(c) in the case of an appeal brought by virtue of section 289(1) of the TCP Act or section 65(1) of the PLBCA Act, any other person having an interest in the land to which the notice relates; and
(d) in the case of an appeal brought by virtue of section 289(2) of the TCP Act, any other person on whom the notice to which those proceedings related was served.

(13) The appeal will be heard and determined by a single judge unless the court directs that the matter be heard and determined by a Divisional Court.

(14) The court may remit the matter to the Secretary of State to the extent necessary to enable the Secretary of State to provide the court with such further information in connection with the matter as the court may direct.

(15) Where the court is of the opinion that the decision appealed against was erroneous in point of law, it will not set aside or vary that decision but will remit the matter to the Secretary of State for rehearing and determination in accordance with the opinion of the court.

(16) The court may give directions as to the exercise, until an appeal brought by virtue of section 289(1) of the TCP Act is finally concluded and any rehearing and determination by the Secretary of State has taken place, of the power to serve, and institute proceedings (including criminal proceedings) concerning—
(a) a stop notice under section 183 of that Act; and
(b) a breach of condition notice under section 187A of that Act.

Appeals from decisions of the Law Society or the Solicitors Disciplinary Tribunal to the High Court

27.1 (1) This paragraph applies to appeals from the Law Society or the Solicitors Disciplinary Tribunal ('the Tribunal') to the High Court under the Solicitors Act 1974, Administration of Justice Act 1985, the Courts and Legal Services Act 1990, the European Communities (Lawyer's Practice) Regulations 2000 (SI 2000/1119) or the European Communities (Recognition of Professional Qualifications) Regulations 2007 (SI 2007/2781).

(2) The appellant must file the appellant's notice in the Administrative Court.

(3) Unless the court otherwise orders the appellant must serve the appellant's notice on—
(a) every party to the proceedings before the Tribunal; and
(b) the Law Society.

Appeals to the County Court

Appeals under sections 204 and 204A of the Housing Act 1996

para.28.1(2) 74.61

28.1 (1) An appellant should include appeals under section 204 and section 204A of the Housing Act 1996 in one appellant's notice.

(2) If it is not possible to do so (for example because an urgent application under section 204A is required) the appeals may be included in separate appellant's notices.

(3) An appeal under section 204A may include an application for an order under section 204A(4)(a) requiring the authority to secure that accommodation is available for the applicant's occupation.

(4) If, exceptionally, the court makes an order under section 204A(4)(a) without notice, the appellant's notice must be served on the authority together with the order. Such an order will normally require the authority to secure that accommodation is available until a hearing date when the authority can make representations as to whether the order under section 204A(4)(a) should be continued.

(5) Unless the court orders otherwise—
(a) the appellant shall file and serve its proposed case management directions for the appeal together with the appellant's notice;
(b) the respondent shall within 14 days thereafter either agree those directions or file and serve alternative proposed directions;
(c) within 14 days after service of the appellant's notice the respondent must disclose any documents relevant to the decision under appeal, in so far as not previously disclosed;

(d) within 14 days after receipt of any documents disclosed under sub-paragraph (c) the appellant may make any amendments to its grounds of appeal which arise out of those documents.

Appeal under Part II of the Immigration and Asylum Act 1999 (carriers' liability)

29.1 (1) A person appealing to a county court under section 35A or section 40B of the Immigration and Asylum Act 1999 ('the Act') against a decision by the Secretary of State to impose a penalty under section 32 or a charge under section 40 of the Act must, subject to sub-paragraph (2), file the appellant's notice within 28 days after receiving the penalty notice or charge notice.

(2) Where the appellant has given notice of objection to the Secretary of State under section 35(4) or section 40A(3) of the Act within the time prescribed for doing so, the appellant must file the appellant's notice within 28 days after receiving notice of the Secretary of State's decision in response to the notice of objection.

(3) Sections 35A and 40B of the Act provide that any appeal under those sections shall be a rehearing of the Secretary of State's decision to impose a penalty or charge, and therefore rule 52.11(1) does not apply.

Local Government (Miscellaneous Provisions) Act 1976

30.1 Where one of the grounds upon which an appeal against a notice under sections 21, 23 or 35 of the Local Government (Miscellaneous Provisions) Act 1976 is brought is that—

(a) it would have been fairer to serve the notice on another person; or

(b) that it would be reasonable for the whole or part of the expenses to which the appeal relates to be paid by some other person,

that person must be made a respondent to the appeal, unless the court, on application of the appellant made without notice, otherwise directs.

Representation of the People Act 1983 — appeals against decisions of registration officers

31.1 (1) This paragraph applies in relation to an appeal against a decision of a registration officer, being a decision referred to in section 56(1) of the Representation of the People Act 1983 ('the Act').

(2) Where a person ('the appellant') has given notice of such an appeal in accordance with the relevant requirements of section 56, and of the regulations made under section 53 ('the Regulations'), of the Act, the registration officer must, within seven days after the appellant receives the notice, forward—

(a) the notice; and

(b) the statement required by the Regulations,

by post to the county court.

(3) The respondents to the appeal will be—

(a) the registration officer; and

(b) if the decision of the registration officer was given in favour of any other person than the appellant, that other person.

(4) On the hearing of the appeal—

(a) the statement forwarded to the court by the registration officer, and any document containing information submitted to the court by the registration officer pursuant to the Regulations, are admissible as evidence of the facts stated in them; and

(b) the court—

(i) may draw any inference of fact that the registration officer might have drawn; and

(ii) may give any decision and make any order that the registration officer ought to have given or made.

(5) A respondent to an appeal (other than the registration officer) is not liable for nor entitled to costs, unless he appears before the court in support of the registration officer's decision.

(6) Rule 52.4 (appellant's notice) does not apply to an appeal to which this paragraph applies.

Representation of the People Act 1983 — special provision in relation to anonymous entries in the register

31.2 (1) In this paragraph—

(a) 'anonymous entry' has the meaning given by section 9B(4) of the Representation of the People Act 1983;

(b) 'appeal notice' means the notice required by regulation 32 of the Representation of the People (England and Wales) Regulations 2001.

(2) This paragraph applies to an appeal to a county court to which paragraph 31.1 (Representation of the People Act 1983 — appeals against decisions of registration officers) applies if a party to the appeal is a person—

(a) whose entry in the register is an anonymous entry; or

(b) who has applied for such an entry.

(3) This paragraph also applies to an appeal to the Court of Appeal from a decision of a county court in an appeal to which paragraph 31.1 applies.

(4) The appellant may indicate in the appeal notice that an application for an anonymous entry has been applied for, or that the entry in the register is an anonymous entry.

(5) The respondent or any other person who applies to become a party to the proceedings may indicate in a respondent's notice or an application to join the proceedings that the entry in the register is an anonymous entry, or that an application has been made for an anonymous entry.

(6) Where the appellant gives such an indication in the appeal notice, the court will refer the matter to a district judge for directions about the further conduct of the proceedings, and, in particular, directions about how the matter should be listed in the court list.

(7) Where the court otherwise becomes aware that a party to the appeal is a person referred to in sub-paragraph (2), the court will give notice to the parties that no further step is to be taken until the court has given any necessary directions for the further conduct of the matter.

Representation of the People Act 1983 — appeals selected as test cases

31.3 (1) Where two or more appeals to which paragraph 31.1 (Representation of the People Act 1983 — appeals against decisions of registration officers) applies involve the same point of law, the court may direct that one appeal ('the test-case appeal') is to be heard first as a test case.

(2) The court will send a notice of the direction to each party to all of those appeals.

(3) Where a notice under sub-paragraph (2) is served on any party to an appeal (other than the test-case appeal), that party may (within seven days after the notice is served on that party) give notice to the court requesting the appeal to be heard and—

(a) the court will hear that appeal after the test-case appeal is disposed of;

(b) the court will give the parties to that appeal notice of the day on which it will be heard; and

(c) the party who gave the notice is not entitled to receive any costs of the separate hearing of that appeal unless the judge otherwise orders.

(4) Where no notice is given under sub-paragraph (3) within the period limited by that paragraph—

(a) the decision on the test-case appeal binds the parties to each of the other appeals;

(b) without further hearing, the court will make, in each other appeal, an order similar to the order in the test-case appeal; and

(c) the party to each other appeal who is in the same interest as the unsuccessful party to the selected appeal is liable for the costs of the test-case appeal in the same manner and to the same extent as the unsuccessful party to that appeal and an order directing the party to pay such costs may be made and enforced accordingly.

(5) Sub-paragraph (4)(a) does not affect the right to appeal to the Court of Appeal of any party to an appeal other than the test-case appeal.

Appeals under section 11 of the UK Borders Act 2007

32.1 (1) A person appealing to a county court under section 11 of the UK Borders Act 2007 ('the Act') against a decision by the Secretary of State to impose a penalty under section 9(1) of the Act, must, subject to sub-paragraph (2), file the appellant's notice within 28 days after receiving the penalty notice.

(2) Where the appellant has given notice of objection to the Secretary of State under section 10 of the Act within the time prescribed for doing so, the appellant's notice must be filed within 28 days after receiving notice of the Secretary of State's decision in response to the notice of objection.

PD 52E Practice Direction 52E —Appeals by way of Case Stated

This practice direction supplements CPR, Part 52.

Contents of this Practice Direction

This practice direction is divided into the following sections:

SECTION I — INTRODUCTION: APPEALS BY WAY OF CASE STATED

1.1 An appeal by case stated is an appeal to a superior court on the basis of a set of facts specified by the inferior court for the superior court to make a decision on the application of the law to those facts.

1.2 (1) This Section applies where, under any enactment—
(a) an appeal lies to the court by way of case stated; or
(b) a question of law may be referred to the court by way of case stated.
(2) This Section is subject to any provision governing a specific category of appeal in any enactment or Practice Direction 52A, 52B or 52D.

SECTION II — CASE STATED BY CROWN COURT OR MAGISTRATES' COURT

Application to state a case

paras.2.1–2.4 74.56 para.2.2 74.56

2.1 The procedure for applying to the Crown Court or a magistrates'court to have a case stated for the opinion of the High Court is set out in the Criminal Procedure Rules.

Filing of appellant's notice

2.2 An appellant must file the appellant's notice at the appeal court within 10 days of the date of the case stated by the court.

Documents to be lodged

2.3 The appellant must lodge the following documents with the appellant's notice—
(a) the stated case;
(b) a copy of the judgment, order or decision in respect of which the case has been stated; and
(c) where the judgment, order or decision in respect of which the case has been stated was itself given or made on appeal, a copy of the judgment, order or decision appealed from.

Service of appellant's notice

2.4 The appellant must serve the appellant's notice and accompanying documents on all respondents within 4 days after they are filed or lodged at the appeal court.

SECTION III — CASE STATED BY MINISTER, GOVERNMENT DEPARTMENT, TRIBUNAL OR OTHER PERSON

Application to state a case

paras.3.1–3.14 74.56

3.1 The procedure for applying to a Minister, government department, tribunal or other person ('Minister or tribunal etc.') to have a case stated for the opinion of the court may be set out in—
(a) the enactment which provides for the right of appeal; or
(b) any rules of procedure relating to the Minister or tribunal etc.

Signing of stated case by Minister or tribunal etc.

3.2 (1) A case stated by a tribunal must be signed by—

(a) the chairman or president (where there is one); or
(b) in any other instance, by the member or members, of the tribunal.
(2) A case stated by any other person must be signed by that person or by a person authorised to do so.

Service of stated case by Minister or tribunal etc.

3.3 The Minister or tribunal etc. must serve the stated case on—
(a) the party who requested it; or
(b) the party as a result of whose application to the court the case was stated.

3.4 Where an enactment provides that a Minister or tribunal etc. may state a case or refer a question of law to the court by way of case stated without a request being made, the Minister or tribunal etc. must—
(a) serve the stated case on those parties that the Minister or tribunal etc. considers appropriate and on any other party who may be affected by the decision of the court; and
(b) give notice to every other party to the proceedings that the stated case has been served on the party named and on the date specified in the notice.

Filing and service of appellant's notice

para.3.6 74.56

3.5 The party on whom the stated case was served must file the appellant's notice and the stated case at the appeal court and serve copies of the notice and stated case on—
(a) the Minister or tribunal etc. who stated the case; and
(b) every party to the proceedings to which the stated case relates, within four days after the stated case was served on that party.

3.6 Where paragraph 3.4 applies the Minister or tribunal etc. must—
(a) file an appellant's notice and the stated case at the appeal court; and
(b) serve copies of those documents on the persons served under paragraph 3.4 within 14 days after stating the case.

3.7 Where—
(a) a stated case has been served by the Minister or tribunal etc. in accordance with paragraph 3.3; and
(b) the party on whom the stated case was served does not file an appellant's notice in accordance with paragraph 3.5,

any other party may file an appellant's notice with the stated case at the appeal court and serve a copy of the notice and the case on the persons listed in paragraph 3.5 within the period of time set out in paragraph 3.8.

3.8 The period of time referred to in paragraph 3.7 is 14 days from the last day on which the party on whom the stated case was served may file an appellant's notice in accordance with paragraph 3.5.

Amendment of stated case

para.3.10 74.56

3.9 The court may amend the stated case or order it to be returned to the Minister or tribunal etc. for amendment and may draw inferences of fact from the facts stated in the case.
Right of Minister or government department to be heard on the appeal

3.10 Where the case is stated by a Minister or government department, that Minister or department, as the case may be, is entitled to appear on the appeal and to make representations to the court.

Application for order to state a case

3.11 An application to the court for an order requiring a Minister or tribunal etc. to state a case for the decision of the court, or to refer a question of law to the court by way of case stated must be made to the court, which would be the appeal court if the case were stated.

3.12 An application to the court for an order directing a Minister or tribunal etc. to—
(a) state a case for determination by the court; or
(b) refer a question of law to the court by way of case stated, must be made in accordance with Part 23.

3.13 The *application notice must contain*—
(a) the grounds of the application;
(b) the question of law on which it is sought to have the case stated; and

(c) any reasons given by the Minister or tribunal etc. for the refusal to state a case

3.14 The application notice must be filed at the appeal court and served on—

(a) the Minister, department, secretary of the tribunal or other person as the case may be; and

(b) every party to the proceedings to which the application relates, within 14 days after the appellant receives notice of the refusal of his request to state a case.

CPR Part 53 Defamation Claims

53.1 Scope of This Part

This Part contains rules about defamation claims.

53.2 Summary Disposal under the Defamation Act 1996

(1) This rule provides for summary disposal in accordance with the Defamation Act 1996 ('the Act').

(2) In proceedings for summary disposal under sections 8 and 9 of the Act, rules 24.4 (procedure), 24.5 (evidence) and 24.6 (directions) apply.

(3) An application for summary judgment under Part 24 may not be made if—
   (a) an application has been made for summary disposal in accordance with the Act, and that application has not been disposed of; or
   (b) summary relief has been granted on an application for summary disposal under the Act.

(4) The court may on any application for summary disposal direct the defendant to elect whether or not to make an offer to make amends under section 2 of the Act.

(5) When it makes a direction under paragraph (4), the court will specify the time by which and the manner in which—
   (a) the election is to be made; and
   (b) notification of it is to be given to the court and the other parties.

53.3 Sources of Information

Unless the court orders otherwise, a party will not be required to provide further information about the identity of the defendant's sources of information.

(Part 18 provides for requests for further information)

PD 53 Practice Direction 53 — Defamation Claims

This practice direction supplements CPR, Part 53.
[For commentary on a specific paragraph, please refer to the cross-references after the title of the paragraph.]

General

1 This practice direction applies to defamation claims.

Statements of Case

para.2 24.6, 26.17

2.1 Statements of case should be confined to the information necessary to inform the other party of the nature of the case he has to meet. Such information should be set out concisely and in a manner proportionate to the subject matter of the claim.

2.2 (1) In a claim for libel the publication the subject of the claim must be identified in the claim form.
(2) In a claim for slander the claim form must so far as possible contain the words complained of, and identify the person to whom they were spoken and when.

2.3 (1) The claimant must specify in the particulars of claim the defamatory meaning which he alleges that the words or matters complained of conveyed, both:
(a) as to their natural and ordinary meaning; and
(b) as to any innuendo meaning (that is a meaning alleged to be conveyed to some person by reason of knowing facts extraneous to the words complained of).
(2) In the case of an innuendo meaning, the claimant must also identify the relevant extraneous facts.

2.4 In a claim for slander the precise words used and the names of the persons to whom they were spoken and when must, so far as possible, be set out in the particulars of claim, if not already contained in the claim form.

2.5 Where a defendant alleges that the words complained of are true he must:
(1) specify the defamatory meanings he seeks to justify; and
(2) give details of the matters on which he relies in support of that allegation.

2.6 Where a defendant alleges that the words complained of are fair comment on a matter of public interest he must:
(1) specify the defamatory meaning he seeks to defend as fair comment on a matter of public interest; and
(2) give details of the matters on which he relies in support of that allegation.

2.7 Where a defendant alleges that the words complained of were published on a privileged occasion he must specify the circumstances he relies on in support of that contention.

2.8 Where a defendant alleges that the words complained of are true, or are fair comment on a matter of public interest, the claimant must serve a reply specifically admitting or denying the allegation and giving the facts on which he relies.

2.9 If the defendant contends that any of the words or matters are fair comment on a matter of public interest, or were published on a privileged occasion, and the claimant intends to allege that the defendant acted with malice, the claimant must serve a reply giving details of the facts or matters relied on.

2.10 (1) A claimant must give full details of the facts and matters on which he relies in support of his claim for damages.
(2) Where a claimant seeks aggravated or exemplary damages he must provide the information specified in r. 16.4(1)(c).

2.11 A defendant who relies on an offer to make amends under s. 2 of the Defamation Act 1996, as his defence must:
(1) state in his defence:
(a) that he is relying on the offer in accordance with s. 4(2) of the Defamation Act 1996; and

(b) that it has not been withdrawn by him or been accepted, and

(2) attach a copy of the offer he made with his defence.

Court's Powers in Connection with an Offer of Amends

3.1 Sections 2 to 4 of the Defamation Act 1996 make provision for a person who has made a statement which is alleged to be defamatory to make an offer to make amends. Section 3 provides for the court to assist in the process of making amends.

3.2 A claim under s. 3 of the Defamation Act 1996 made other than in existing proceedings may be made under CPR Part 8:

(1) where the parties agree on the steps to make amends, and the sole purpose of the claim is for the court to make an order under s. 3(3) for an order that the offer be fulfilled; or

(2) where the parties do not agree:

(a) on the steps to be taken by way of correction, apology and publication (see s. 3(4));

(b) on the amount to be paid by way of compensation (see s. 3(5)); or

(c) on the amount to be paid by way of costs (see s. 3(6)).

(Applications in existing proceedings made under s. 3 of the Defamation Act 1996 must be made in accordance with CPR Part 23.)

3.3 (1) A claim or application under s. 3 of the Defamation Act 1996 must be supported by written evidence.

(2) The evidence referred to in para. (1) must include:

(a) a copy of the offer of amends;

(b) details of the steps taken to fulfil the offer of amends;

(c) a copy of the text of any correction and apology;

(d) details of the publication of the correction and apology;

(e) a statement of the amount of any sum paid as compensation;

(f) a statement of the amount of any sum paid for costs;

(g) why the offer is unsatisfactory.

(3) Where any step specified in s. 2(4) of the Defamation Act 1996 has not been taken, then the evidence referred to in sub-para. (2)(c) to (f) must state what steps are proposed by the party to fulfil the offer of amends and the date or dates on which each step will be fulfilled and, if none, that no proposal has been made to take that step.

Ruling on Meaning

4.1 At any time the court may decide:

(1) whether a statement complained of is capable of having any meaning attributed to it in a statement of case;

(2) whether the statement is capable of being defamatory of the claimant;

(3) whether the statement is capable of bearing any other meaning defamatory of the claimant.

4.2 An application for a ruling on meaning may be made at any time after the service of particulars of claim. Such an application should be made promptly.

(This provision disapplies for these applications the usual time restriction on making applications in r. 24.4(1).)

4.3 Where an application is made for a ruling on meaning, the application notice must state that it is an application for a ruling on meaning made in accordance with this practice direction.

4.4 The application notice or the evidence contained or referred to in it, or served with it, must identify precisely the statement, and the meaning attributed to it, that the court is being asked to consider.

(Rule 3.3 applies where the court exercises its powers of its own initiative.)

(Following a ruling on meaning the court may exercise its power under r. 3.4.)

(Section 7 of the Defamation Act 1996 applies to rulings on meaning.)

Summary Disposal

5.1 Where an application is made for summary disposal, the application notice must state:

(1) that it is an application for summary disposal made in accordance with s. 8 of the Defamation Act 1996.

(2) the matters set out in para. 2(3) of PD 24; and

(3) whether or not the defendant has made an offer to make amends under s. 2 of the Act and whether or not it has been withdrawn.

5.2 An application for summary disposal may be made at any time after the service of particulars of claim.

(This provision disapplies for these applications the usual time restriction on making applications in r. 24.4(1).)

5.3 (1) This paragraph applies where:

(a) the court has ordered the defendant in defamation proceedings to agree and publish a correction and apology as summary relief under s. 8(2) of the Defamation Act 1996; and

(b) the parties are unable to agree its content within the time specified in the order.

(2) Where the court grants this type of summary relief under the Act, the order will specify the date by which the parties should reach agreement about the content, time, manner, form and place of publication of the correction and apology.

(3) Where the parties cannot agree the content of the correction and apology by the date specified in the order, then the claimant must prepare a summary of the judgment given by the court and serve it on all the other parties within three days following the date specified in the order.

(4) Where the parties cannot agree the summary of the judgment prepared by the claimant they must within three days of receiving the summary:

(a) file with the court and serve on all the other parties a copy of the summary showing the revisions they wish to make to it; and

(b) apply to the court for the court to settle the summary.

(5) The court will then itself settle the summary and the judge who delivered the judgment being summarised will normally do this.

Statements in Open Court

6.1 This paragraph only applies where a party wishes to accept a Part 36 offer or other offer of settlement in relation to a claim for:

(1) libel;
(2) slander;
(3) malicious falsehood;
(4) misuse of private or confidential information.

6.2 A party may apply for permission to make a statement in open court before or after he accepts the Part 36 offer in accordance with r. 36.9(1) or other offer to settle the claim.

6.3 The statement that the applicant wishes to make must be submitted for the approval of the court and must accompany the notice of application.

6.4 The court may postpone the time for making the statement if other claims relating to the subject matter of the statement are still proceeding.

(Applications must be made in accordance with Part 23.)

Transitional Provision Relating to Section 4 of the Defamation Act 1952

7 Paragraph 3 of this practice direction applies, with any necessary modifications to an application to the court to determine any question as to the steps to be taken to fulfil an offer made under s. 4 of the Defamation Act 1952.

(Section 4 of the Defamation Act 1952 is repealed by the Defamation Act 1996. The commencement order bringing in the repeal makes transitional provision for offers which have been made at the date the repeal came into force.)

CPR Part 54 Judicial Review and Statutory Review

Part 54 2.22, 77.1, 77.36, 77.51, 77.53 [For commentary on a specific rule, please refer to the cross-references after the title of the rule.]

I JUDICIAL REVIEW

54.1 Scope and Interpretation

r.54.1(2)(a) 77.1 r.54.1(2)(f) 77.45

(1) This Section of this Part contains rules about judicial review.
(2) In this Section—
  (a) a 'claim for judicial review' means a claim to review the lawfulness of—
    (i) an enactment; or
    (ii) a decision, action or failure to act in relation to the exercise of a public function.
  (e) 'the judicial review procedure' means the Part 8 procedure as modified by this Section;
  (f) 'interested party' means any person (other than the claimant and defendant) who is directly affected by the claim; and
  (g) 'court' means the High Court, unless otherwise stated.
  (Rule 8.1(6)(b) provides that a rule or practice direction may, in relation to a specified type of proceedings, disapply or modify any of the rules set out in Part 8 as they apply to those proceedings)

54.1A Who May Exercise the Powers of the High Court

(1) A court officer assigned to the Administrative Court office who is—
  (a) a barrister; or
  (b) a solicitor,
  may exercise the jurisdiction of the High Court with regard to the matters set out in paragraph (2) with the consent of the President of the Queen's Bench Division.
(2) The matters referred to in paragraph (1) are—
  (a) any matter incidental to any proceedings in the High Court;
  (b) any other matter where there is no substantial dispute between the parties; and
  (c) the dismissal of an appeal or application where a party has failed to comply with any order, rule or practice direction.
(3) A court officer may not decide an application for—
  (a) permission to bring judicial review proceedings;
  (b) *an injunction;*
  (c) a stay of any proceedings, other than a temporary stay of any order or decision of the lower court over a period when the High Court is not sitting or cannot conveniently be convened, unless the parties seek a stay by consent.

(4) Decisions of a court officer may be made without a hearing.
(5) A party may request any decision of a court officer to be reviewed by a judge of the High Court.
(6) At the request of a party, a hearing will be held to reconsider a decision of a court officer, made without a hearing.
(7) A request under paragraph (5) or (6) must be filed within 7 days after the party is served with notice of the decision.

54.2 When This Section Must Be Used

r.54.2 77.53

The judicial review procedure must be used in a claim for judicial review where the claimant is seeking—

(a) a mandatory order;
(b) a prohibiting order;
(c) a quashing order; or
(d) an injunction under section 30 of the Senior Courts Act 1981 (restraining a person from acting in any office in which he is not entitled to act).

54.3 When This Section May Be Used

r.54.3(1)–(2) 77.53

(1) The judicial review procedure may be used in a claim for judicial review where the claimant is seeking—
(a) a declaration; or
(b) an injunction[(GL)].
(Section 31(2) of the Senior Courts Act 1981 sets out the circumstances in which the court may grant a declaration or injunction in a claim for judicial review)
(Where the claimant is seeking a declaration or injunction in addition to one of the remedies listed in rule 54.2, the judicial review procedure must be used)
(2) A claim for judicial review may include a claim for damages, restitution or the recovery of a sum due but may not seek such a remedy alone.
(Section 31(2) of the Senior Courts Act 1981 sets out the circumstances in which the court may award damages, restitution or the recovery of a sum due on a claim for judicial review)

54.4 Permission Required

r.54.4 PC 34, 77.32

The court's permission to proceed is required in a claim for judicial review whether started under this Section or transferred to the Administrative Court.

54.5 Time Limit for Filing Claim Form

r.54.5 10.5
r.54.5(1) PC 34, 77.36, 77.38, 77.54
r.54.5(2) PC 34, 77.36
r.54.5(3) 77.36

(A1) In this rule—
'the planning acts' has the same meaning as in section 336 of the Town and Country Planning Act 1990;
'decision governed by the Public Contracts Regulations 2006' means any decision the legality of which is or may be affected by a duty owed to an economic operator by virtue of regulation 47A of those Regulations (and for this purpose it does not matter that the claimant is not an economic operator); and
'economic operator' has the same meaning as in regulation 4 of the Public Contracts Regulations 2006.

(1) The claim form must be filed—
(a) promptly; and
(b) in any event not later than 3 months after the grounds to make the claim first arose.
(2) The time limits in this rule may not be extended by agreement between the parties.
(3) This rule does not apply when any other enactment specifies a shorter time limit for making the claim for judicial review.
(4) Paragraph (1) does not apply in the cases specified in paragraphs (5) and (6).

(5) Where the application for judicial review relates to a decision made by the Secretary of State or local planning authority under the planning acts, the claim form must be filed not later than six weeks after the grounds to make the claim first arose.

(6) Where the application for judicial review relates to a decision governed by the Public Contracts Regulations 2006, the claim form must be filed within the time within which an economic operator would have been required by regulation 47D(2) of those Regulations (and disregarding the rest of that regulation) to start any proceedings under those Regulations in respect of that decision.

54.6 Claim Form

r.54.6(1) 77.33

(1) In addition to the matters set out in rule 8.2 (contents of the claim form) the claimant must also state—
   (a) the name and address of any person he considers to be an interested party;
   (b) that he is requesting permission to proceed with a claim for judicial review;
   (c) any remedy (including any interim remedy) he is claiming; and
   (d) where appropriate, the grounds on which it is contended that the claim is an Aarhus Convention claim.

   (Rules 45.41 to 45.44 make provision about costs in Aarhus Convention claims.)
   (Part 25 sets out how to apply for an interim remedy)

(2) The claim form must be accompanied by the documents required by Practice Direction 54A.

54.7 Service of Claim Form

r.54.7 PC 34, 77.36, 77.45

The claim form must be served on—
(a) the defendant; and
(b) unless the court otherwise directs, any person the claimant considers to be an interested party,
within 7 days after the date of issue.

54.7A Judicial Review of Decisions of the Upper Tribunal

(1) This rule applies where an application is made, following refusal by the Upper Tribunal of permission to appeal against a decision of the First Tier Tribunal, for judicial review—
   (a) of the decision of the Upper Tribunal refusing permission to appeal; or
   (b) which relates to the decision of the First Tier Tribunal which was the subject of the application for permission to appeal.

(2) Where this rule applies—
   (a) the application may not include any other claim, whether against the Upper Tribunal or not; and
   (b) any such other claim must be the subject of a separate application.

(3) The claim form and the supporting documents required by paragraph (4) must be filed no later than 16 days after the date on which notice of the Upper Tribunal's decision was sent to the applicant.

(4) The supporting documents are—
   (a) the decision of the Upper Tribunal to which the application relates, and any document giving reasons for the decision;
   (b) the grounds of appeal to the Upper Tribunal and any documents which were sent with them;
   (c) the decision of the First Tier Tribunal, the application to that Tribunal for permission to appeal and its reasons for refusing permission; and
   (d) any other documents essential to the claim.

(5) The claim form and supporting documents must be served on the Upper Tribunal and any other interested party no later than 7 days after the date of issue.

(6) The Upper Tribunal and any person served with the claim form who wishes to take part in the proceedings for judicial review must, no later than 21 days after service of the claim form, file and serve on the applicant and any other party an acknowledgment of service in the relevant practice form.

(7) The court will give permission to proceed only if it considers—
 (a) that there is an arguable case, which has a reasonable prospect of success, that both the decision of the Upper Tribunal refusing permission to appeal and the decision of the First Tier Tribunal against which permission to appeal was sought are wrong in law; and
 (b) that either—
  (i) the claim raises an important point of principle or practice; or
  (ii) there is some other compelling reason to hear it.
(8) If the application for permission is refused on paper without an oral hearing, rule 54.12(3) (request for reconsideration at a hearing) does not apply.
(9) If permission to apply for judicial review is granted—
 (a) if the Upper Tribunal or any interested party wishes there to be a hearing of the substantive application, it must make its request for such a hearing no later than 14 days after service of the order granting permission; and
 (b) if no request for a hearing is made within that period, the court will make a final order quashing the refusal of permission without a further hearing.
(10) The power to make a final order under paragraph (9)(b) may be exercised by the Master of the Crown Office or a Master of the Administrative Court.

54.8 Acknowledgment of Service

r.54.8 PC 34, 44.11, 77.45 r.54.8(2) 18.2, 77.37
r.54.8(1) 77.37 r.54.8(3)–(4) 77.37

(1) Any person served with the claim form who wishes to take part in the judicial review must file an acknowledgment of service in the relevant practice form in accordance with the following provisions of this rule.
(2) Any acknowledgment of service must be—
 (a) filed not more than 21 days after service of the claim form; and
 (b) served on—
  (i) the claimant; and
  (ii) subject to any direction under rule 54.7(b), any other person named in the claim form,
 as soon as practicable and, in any event, not later than 7 days after it is filed.
(3) The time limits under this rule may not be extended by agreement between the parties.
(4) The acknowledgment of service—
 (a) must—
  (i) where the person filing it intends to contest the claim, set out a summary of his grounds for doing so; and
  (ii) state the name and address of any person the person filing it considers to be an interested party; and
 (b) may include or be accompanied by an application for directions.
(5) Rule 10.3(2) does not apply.

54.9 Failure to File Acknowledgment of Service

r.54.9(1)(a)–(b) 77.37, 77.45 r.54.9(2) 77.37

(1) Where a person served with the claim form has failed to file an acknowledgment of service in accordance with rule 54.8, he—
 (a) may not take part in a hearing to decide whether permission should be given unless the court allows him to do so; but
 (b) provided he complies with rule 54.14 or any other direction of the court regarding the filing and service of—
  (i) detailed grounds for contesting the claim or supporting it on additional grounds; and
  (ii) any written evidence,
 may take part in the hearing of the judicial review.
(2) Where that person takes part in the hearing of the judicial review, the court may take his failure to file an acknowledgment of service into account when deciding what order to make about costs.
(3) Rule 8.4 does not apply.

54.10 Permission Given

r.54.10 PC 34 r.54.10(2) 77.40, 77.42
r.54.10(1) 77.40

(1) Where permission to proceed is given the court may also give directions.
(2) Directions under paragraph (1) may include—
(a) a stay(GL) of proceedings to which the claim relates;
(b) directions requiring the proceedings to be heard by a Divisional Court.
(Rule 3.7 provides a sanction for the non-payment of the fee payable when permission to proceed has been given)

54.11 Service of Order Giving or Refusing Permission

r.54.11 PC 34, 77.40, 77.41, 77.45

The court will serve—
(a) the order giving or refusing permission; and
(b) any directions,
on—
(i) the claimant;
(ii) the defendant; and
(iii) any other person who filed an acknowledgment of service.

54.12 Permission Decision without a Hearing

r.54.12(1)–(4) 77.40 r.54.12(7) 77.40
r.54.12(5) 77.40, 77.45

(1) This rule applies where the court, without a hearing—
(a) refuses permission to proceed; or
(b) gives permission to proceed—
(i) subject to conditions; or
(ii) on certain grounds only.
(2) The court will serve its reasons for making the decision when it serves the order giving or refusing permission in accordance with rule 54.11.
(3) Subject to paragraph (7), the claimant may not appeal but may request the decision to be reconsidered at a hearing.
(4) A request under paragraph (3) must be filed within 7 days after service of the reasons under paragraph (2).
(5) The claimant, defendant and any other person who has filed an acknowledgment of service will be given at least 2 days' notice of the hearing date.
(6) The court may give directions requiring the proceedings to be heard by a Divisional Court.
(7) Where the court refuses permission to proceed and records the fact that the application is totally without merit in accordance with rule 23.12, the claimant may not request that decision to be reconsidered at a hearing.

54.13 Defendant etc. May Not Apply to Set Aside(GL)

r.54.13 77.40, 77.45

Neither the defendant nor any other person served with the claim form may apply to set aside(GL) an order giving permission to proceed.

54.14 Response

r.54.14 PC 34, 77.37 r.54.14(2) 77.41
r.54.14(1) 77.41, 77.45

(1) A defendant and any other person served with the claim form who wishes to contest the claim or support it on additional grounds must file and serve—
(a) detailed grounds for contesting the claim or supporting it on additional grounds; and
(b) any written evidence,
within 35 days after service of the order giving permission.
(2) The following rules do not apply—

(a) rule 8.5(3) and 8.5(4) (defendant to file and serve written evidence at the same time as acknowledgment of service); and
(b) rule 8.5(5) and 8.5(6) (claimant to file and serve any reply within 14 days).

54.15 Where Claimant Seeks to Rely on Additional Grounds

r.54.15 77.41

The court's permission is required if a claimant seeks to rely on grounds other than those for which he has been given permission to proceed.

54.16 Evidence

(1) Rule 8.6(1) does not apply.
(2) No written evidence may be relied on unless—
  (a) it has been served in accordance with any—
    (i) rule under this Section; or
    (ii) direction of the court; or
  (b) the court gives permission.

54.17 Court's Powers to Hear Any Person

r.54.17(1)–(2) 77.45

(1) Any person may apply for permission—
  (a) to file evidence; or
  (b) make representations at the hearing of the judicial review.
(2) An application under paragraph (1) should be made promptly.

54.18 Judicial Review May Be Decided Without a Hearing

r.54.18 PC 34, 77.46

The court may decide the claim for judicial review without a hearing where all the parties agree.

54.19 Court's Powers in Respect of Quashing Orders

r.54.19(2)(a)–(b) 77.55

(1) This rule applies where the court makes a quashing order in respect of the decision to which the claim relates.
(2) The court may—
  (a) (i) remit the matter to the decision-maker; and
    (ii) direct it to reconsider the matter and reach a decision in accordance with the judgment of the court; or
  (b) in so far as any enactment permits, substitute its own decision for the decision to which the claim relates.

(Section 31 of the Senior Courts Act 1981 enables the High Court, subject to certain conditions, to substitute its own decision for the decision in question)

54.20 Transfer

r.54.20 77.51

The court may—

(a) order a claim to continue as if it had not been started under this Section; and
(b) where it does so, give directions about the future management of the claim.

(Part 30 (transfer) applies to transfers to and from the Administrative Court)

PD 54A Practice Direction 54A — Judicial Review

This practice direction supplements CPR, Part 54.

PD 54A 2.22, 77.1, 77.41 [For commentary on a specific paragraph, please refer to the cross-references after the title of the paragraph.]

I General Provisions Relating to Judicial Review

1.1 In addition to Part 54 and this practice direction attention is drawn to:
- s. 31 of the Senior Courts Act 1981; and
- the Human Rights Act 1998

The Court

para.2.1 11.2

2.1 Part 54 claims for judicial review are dealt with in the Administrative Court.
(PD 54D contains provisions about where a claim for judicial review may be started, administered and heard.)

Time Limit for Filing Claim Form: Rule 54.5

4.1 Where the claim is for a quashing order in respect of a judgment, order or conviction, the date when the grounds to make the claim first arise, for the purposes of r. 54.5(1)(b), is the date of that judgment, order or conviction.

Claim Form: Rule 54.6

Interested parties

para.5.1 77.36

5.1 Where the claim for judicial review relates to proceedings in a court or tribunal, any other parties to those proceedings must be named in the claim form as interested parties under r. 54.6(1)(a) (and therefore served with the claim form under r. 54.7(b)).

5.2 For example, in a claim by a defendant in a criminal case in the magistrates' or Crown Court for judicial review of a decision in that case, the prosecution must always be named as an interested party.

Human rights

paras.5.3–5.4 77.33

5.3 Where the claimant is seeking to raise any issue under the Human Rights Act 1998, or seeks a remedy available under that Act, the claim form must include the information required by PD 16, para. 15.

Devolution issues

5.4 Where the claimant intends to raise a devolution issue, the claim form must:
(1) specify that the applicant wishes to raise a devolution issue and identify the relevant provisions of the Government of Wales Act 2006, the Northern Ireland Act 1998 or the Scotland Act 1998; and
(2) contain a summary of the facts, circumstances and points of law on the basis of which it is alleged that a devolution issue arises.

5.5 In this practice direction 'devolution issue' has the same meaning as in the Government of Wales Act 2006, sch. 9, para. 1; the Northern Ireland Act 1998, sch. 10, para. 1; and the Scotland Act 1998, sch. 6, para. 1.

Claim form

para.5.6 PC 34, 59.6, 77.33, 77.36
para.5.7 PC 34, 59.6, 77.33
para.5.8 PC 34, 59.6, 77.33

5.6 The claim form must include or be accompanied by:
(1) a detailed statement of the claimant's grounds for bringing the claim for judicial review;
(2) a statement of the facts relied on;

(3) any application to extend the time limit for filing the claim form;
(4) any application for directions.

5.7 In addition, the claim form must be accompanied by:
(1) any written evidence in support of the claim or application to extend time;
(2) a copy of any order that the claimant seeks to have quashed;
(3) where the claim for judicial review relates to a decision of a court or tribunal, an approved copy of the reasons for reaching that decision;
(4) copies of any documents on which the claimant proposes to rely;
(5) copies of any relevant statutory material;
(6) a list of essential documents for advance reading by the court (with page references to the passages relied on); and

5.8 Where it is not possible to file all the above documents, the claimant must indicate which documents have not been filed and the reasons why they are not currently available.

Bundle of documents
para.5.9 59.6, 77.33

5.9 The claimant must file two copies of a paginated and indexed bundle containing all the documents referred to in paras 5.6 and 5.7.

5.10 Attention is drawn to r. 8.5(1) and (7).

Service of Claim Form: Rule 54.7

6.1 Except as required by r. 54.11 or 54.12(2), the Administrative Court will not serve documents and service must be effected by the parties.

6.2 Where the defendant or interested party to the claim for judicial review is—
(a) the Immigration and Asylum Chamber of the First-tier Tribunal, the address for service of the claim form is Official Correspondence Unit, PO Box 6987, Leicester, LE1 6ZX or fax number (0116) 249 4240;
(b) the Crown, service of the claim form must be effected on the solicitor acting for the relevant government department as if the proceedings were civil proceedings as defined in the Crown Proceedings Act 1947.

(PD 66 gives the list published under the Crown Proceedings Act 1947, s. 17, of the solicitors acting in civil proceedings (as defined in that Act) for the different government departments on whom service is to be effected, and of their addresses.)

(Part 6 contains provisions about the service of claim forms.)

Acknowledgment of Service: Rule 54.8

7.1 Attention is drawn to r. 8.3(2) and PD 8 and to r. 10.5.

Permission Given: Rule 54.10

Directions

8.1 Case management directions under r. 54.10(1) may include directions about serving the claim form and any evidence on other persons.

8.2 Where a claim is made under the Human Rights Act 1998, a direction may be made for giving notice to the Crown or joining the Crown as a party. Attention is drawn to r. 19.4A and PD 19A, para. 6.

Permission without a hearing
para.8.4 77.32, 77.40

8.4 The court will generally, in the first instance, consider the question of permission without a hearing.

Permission hearing
para.8.5 77.32, 77.40, 77.45 para.8.6 77.40, 77.45

8.5 Neither the defendant nor any other interested party need attend a hearing on the question of permission unless the court directs otherwise.

8.6 Where the defendant or any party does attend a hearing, the court will not generally make an order for costs against the claimant.

Service of Order Giving or Refusing Permission: Rule 54.11

9.1 An order refusing permission or giving it subject to conditions or on certain grounds only must set out or be accompanied by the court's reasons for coming to that decision.

Response: Rule 54.14

para. 10.1 77.41

10.1 Where the party filing the detailed grounds intends to rely on documents not already filed, he must file a paginated bundle of those documents when he files the detailed grounds.

Where Claimant Seeks to Rely on Additional Grounds: Rule 54.15

para. 11.1 77.41

11.1 Where the claimant intends to apply to rely on additional grounds at the hearing of the claim for judicial review, he must give notice to the court and to any other person served with the claim form no later than seven clear days before the hearing (or the warned date where appropriate).

Evidence: Rule 54.16

para. 12.1 77.44

12.1 Disclosure is not required unless the court orders otherwise.

Court's Powers to Hear Any Person: Rule 54.17

paras. 13.1–13.5 77.45

13.1 Where all the parties consent, the court may deal with an application under r. 54.17 without a hearing.

13.2 Where the court gives permission for a person to file evidence or make representations at the hearing of the claim for judicial review, it may do so on conditions and may give case management directions.

13.3 An application for permission should be made by letter to the Administrative Court office, identifying the claim, explaining who the applicant is and indicating why and in what form the applicant wants to participate in the hearing.

13.4 If the applicant is seeking a prospective order as to costs, the letter should say what kind of order and on what grounds.

13.5 Applications to intervene must be made at the earliest reasonable opportunity, since it will usually be essential not to delay the hearing.

Transfer: Rule 54.20

paras. 14.1–14.2 77.51

14.1 Attention is drawn to r. 30.5.

14.2 In deciding whether a claim is suitable for transfer to the Administrative Court, the court will consider whether it raises issues of public law to which Part 54 should apply.

Skeleton arguments

para.15.1 PC 34, 77.47
para.15.2 PC 34
para.15.3 77.47

15.1 The claimant must file and serve a skeleton argument not less than 21 working days before the date of the hearing of the judicial review (or the warned date).

15.2 The defendant and any other party wishing to make representations at the hearing of the judicial review must file and serve a skeleton argument not less than 14 working days before the date of the hearing of the judicial review (or the warned date).

15.3 Skeleton arguments must contain:

(1) a time estimate for the complete hearing, including delivery of judgment;
(2) a list of issues;
(3) a list of the legal points to be taken (together with any relevant authorities with page references to the passages relied on);
(4) a chronology of events (with page references to the bundle of documents (see para. 16.1);

(5) a list of essential documents for the advance reading of the court (with page references to the passages relied on) (if different from that filed with the claim form) and a time estimate for that reading; and
(6) a list of persons referred to.

Bundle of Documents to Be Filed

para. 16.1 77.47 para. 16.2 77.47

16.1 The claimant must file a paginated and indexed bundle of all relevant documents required for the hearing of the judicial review when he files his skeleton argument.
16.2 The bundle must also include those documents required by the defendant and any other party who is to make representations at the hearing.

Agreed Final Order

para. 17.1–17.4 77.46

17.1 If the parties agree about the final order to be made in a claim for judicial review, the claimant must file at the court a document (with two copies) signed by all the parties setting out the terms of the proposed agreed order together with a short statement of the matters relied on as justifying the proposed agreed order and copies of any authorities or statutory provisions relied on.
17.2 The court will consider the documents referred to in para. 17.1 and will make the order if satisfied that the order should be made.
17.3 If the court is not satisfied that the order should be made, a hearing date will be set.
17.4 Where the agreement relates to an order for costs only, the parties need only file a document signed by all the parties setting out the terms of the proposed order.

II APPLICATIONS FOR PERMISSION TO APPLY FOR JUDICIAL REVIEW IN IMMIGRATION AND ASYLUM CASES — CHALLENGING REMOVAL

18.1 (1) This section applies where:
(a) a person has been served with a copy of directions for his removal from the United Kingdom by the Immigration and Nationality Directorate of the Home Office and notified that this section applies; and
(b) that person makes an application for permission to apply for judicial review before his removal takes effect.
(2) This section does not prevent a person from applying for judicial review after he has been removed.
(3) The requirements contained in this section of this practice direction are additional to those contained elsewhere in the practice direction.

18.2 (1) A person who makes an application for permission to apply for judicial review must file a claim form and a copy at court, and the claim form must:
(a) indicate on its face that this section of the practice direction applies; and
(b) be accompanied by:
(i) a copy of the removal directions and the decision to which the application relates; and
(ii) any document served with the removal directions including any document which contains the Immigration and Nationality Directorate's factual summary of the case; and
(c) contain or be accompanied by the detailed statement of the claimant's grounds for bringing the claim for judicial review; or
(d) if the claimant is unable to comply with paragraph (b) or (c), contain or be accompanied by a statement of the reasons why.
(2) The claimant must, immediately upon issue of the claim, send copies of the issued claim form and accompanying documents to the address specified by the Immigration and Nationality Directorate.
(Rule 54.7 also requires the defendant to be served with the claim form within seven days of the date of issue. Rule 6.5(8) provides that service on a government department must be effected on the solicitor acting for that department, which in the case of the Immigration and Nationality Directorate is the Treasury Solicitor. The address for the Treasury Solicitor may be found in annex 2 to PD 66.)

18.3 Where the claimant has not complied with para. 18.2(1)(b) or (c) and has provided reasons why he is unable to comply, and the court has issued the claim form, the Administrative Court:
(a) will refer the matter to a judge for consideration as soon as practicable; and
(b) will notify the parties that it has done so.

18.4 If, upon a refusal to grant permission to apply for judicial review, the court indicates that the application is clearly without merit, that indication will be included in the order refusing permission.

SECTION III APPLICATIONS FOR PERMISSION TO APPLY FOR JUDICIAL REVIEW OF DECISIONS OF THE UPPER TRIBUNAL

19.1 A person who makes an application for permission to apply for judicial review of the decision of the Upper Tribunal refusing permission to appeal must file a claim form which must—
(a) state on its face that the application is made under r. 54.7A;
(b) set out succinctly the grounds on which it is argued that the criteria in r. 54.7A(7) are met; and
(c) be accompanied by the supporting documents required under r. 54.7A(4).

19.2 If the Upper Tribunal or any interested party wishes there to be a hearing of the substantive application under r. 54.7A(9), it must make its request in writing (by letter copied to the claimant) for such a hearing no later than 14 days after service of the order granting permission.

PD 54C Practice Direction 54C — References by the Legal Services Commission

PD 54C 2.22

1.1 This practice direction applies where the Legal Services Commission ('the Commission') refers to the High Court a question that arises on a review of a decision about an individual's financial eligibility for a representation order in criminal proceedings under the Criminal Defence Service (Financial Eligibility) Regulations 2006 (SI 2006/2492).

1.2 A reference of a question by the Legal Services Commission must be made to the Administrative Court.

1.3 Part 52 does not apply to a review under this paragraph.

1.4 The Commission must:

(a) file at the court:

(i) the individual's applications for a representation order and for a review, and any supporting documents;

(ii) a copy of the question on which the court's decision is sought; and

(iii) a statement of the Commission's observations on the question; and

(b) serve a copy of the question and the statement on the individual.

1.5 The individual may file representations on the question at the court within seven days after service on him of the copy of the question and the statement.

1.6 The question will be decided without a hearing unless the court directs otherwise.

PD 54D Practice Direction 54D — Administrative Court (Venue)

This Practice Direction supplements CPR, Part 54.

PD 54D 2.22, 77.33

Scope and Purpose

1.1 This practice direction concerns the place in which a claim before the Administrative Court should be started and administered and the venue at which it will be determined.

1.2 This practice direction is intended to facilitate access to justice by enabling cases to be administered and determined in the most appropriate location. To achieve this purpose it provides flexibility in relation to where claims are to be administered and enables claims to be transferred to different venues.

Venue — General Provisions

para.2.1 11.2

2.1 The claim form in proceedings in the Administrative Court may be issued at the Administrative Court Office of the High Court at—

(1) the Royal Courts of Justice in London; or

(2) at the District Registry of the High Court at Birmingham, Cardiff, Leeds, or Manchester unless the claim is one of the excepted classes of claim set out in para. 3 which may only be started and determined at the Royal Courts of Justice in London.

2.2 Any claim started in Birmingham will normally be determined at a court in the Midland region (geographically covering the area of the Midland Circuit); in Cardiff in Wales; in Leeds in the North-Eastern Region (geographically covering the area of the North Eastern Circuit); in London at the Royal Courts of Justice; and in Manchester, in the North-Western Region (geographically covering the Northern Circuit).

Excepted Classes of Claim

para.3 77.33

3.1 The excepted classes of claim referred to in para. 2.1(2) are—

(1) proceedings to which Part 76 or Part 79 applies, and for the avoidance of doubt—

(a) proceedings relating to control orders (within the meaning of Part 76);

(b) financial restrictions proceedings (within the meaning of Part 79);

(c) proceedings relating to terrorism or alleged terrorists (where that is a relevant feature of the claim); and

(d) proceedings in which a special advocate is or is to be instructed;

(2) proceedings to which RSC, ord. 115, applies;

(3) proceedings under the Proceeds of Crime Act 2002;

(4) appeals to the Administrative Court under the Extradition Act 2003;

(5) proceedings which must be heard by a Divisional Court; and

(6) proceedings relating to the discipline of solicitors.

3.2 If a claim form is issued at an Administrative Court office other than in London and includes one of the excepted classes of claim, the proceedings will be transferred to London.

Urgent Applications

4.1 During the hours when the court is open, where an urgent application needs to be made to the Administrative Court outside London, the application must be made to the judge designated to deal with such applications in the relevant district registry.

4.2 Any urgent application to the Administrative Court during the hours when the court is closed, must be made to the duty out of hours High Court judge by telephoning (020) 7947 6000.

Assignment to Another Venue

5.1 The proceedings may be transferred from the office at which the claim form was issued to another office. Such transfer is a judicial act.

5.2 The general expectation is that proceedings will be administered and determined in the region with which the claimant has the closest connection, subject to the following considerations as applicable—

(1) any reason expressed by any party for preferring a particular venue;
(2) the region in which the defendant, or any relevant office or department of the defendant, is based;
(3) the region in which the claimant's legal representatives are based;
(4) the ease and cost of travel to a hearing;
(5) the availability and suitability of alternative means of attending a hearing (for example, by video link);
(6) the extent and nature of media interest in the proceedings in any particular locality;
(7) the time within which it is appropriate for the proceedings to be determined;
(8) whether it is desirable to administer or determine the claim in another region in the light of the volume of claims issued at, and the capacity, resources and workload of, the court at which it is issued;
(9) whether the claim raises issues sufficiently similar to those in another outstanding claim to make it desirable that it should be determined together with, or immediately following, that other claim; and
(10) whether the claim raises devolution issues and for that reason whether it should more appropriately be determined in London or Cardiff.

5.3 (1) When an urgent application is made under para. 4.1 or 4.2, this will not by itself decide the venue for the further administration or determination of the claim.
(2) The court dealing with the urgent application may direct that the case be assigned to a particular venue.
(3) When an urgent application is made under para. 4.2, and the court does not make a direction under sub-para. (2), the claim will be assigned in the first place to London but may be reassigned to another venue at a later date.

5.4 The court may on an application by a party or of its own initiative direct that the claim be determined in a region other than that of the venue in which the claim is currently assigned. The considerations in para. 5.2 apply.

5.5 Once assigned to a venue, the proceedings will be both administered from that venue and determined by a judge of the Administrative Court at a suitable court within that region, or, if the venue is in London, at the Royal Courts of Justice. The choice of which court (of those within the region which are identified by the presiding judge of the circuit suitable for such hearing) will be decided, subject to availability, by the considerations in para. 5.2.

5.6 When giving directions under r. 54.10, the court may direct that proceedings be reassigned to another region for hearing (applying the considerations in para. 5.2) If no such direction is given, the claim will be heard in the same region as that in which the permission application was determined (whether on paper or at a hearing).

CPR Part 55 Possession Claims

Part 55 **15.10, 20.2, 35.1, 35.15, 42.27, 62.3, 67.3, 70.3, 79.2, 87.4, 87.5, 87.54** [For commentary on a specific rule, please refer to the cross-references after the title of the rule.]

55.1 Interpretation

r.55.1(b) 35.3, 35.4

In this Part—

(a) 'a possession claim' means a claim for the recovery of possession of land (including buildings or parts of buildings);
(b) 'a possession claim against trespassers' means a claim for the recovery of land which the claimant alleges is occupied only by a person or persons who entered or remained on the land without the consent of a person entitled to possession of that land but does not include a claim against a tenant or sub-tenant whether his tenancy has been terminated or not;
(c) 'mortgage' includes a legal or equitable mortgage and a legal or equitable charge and 'mortgagee' is to be interpreted accordingly;
(d) 'the 1985 Act' means the Housing Act 1985;
(e) 'the 1988 Act' means the Housing Act 1988;
(f) 'a demotion claim' means a claim made by a landlord for an order under section 82A of the 1985 Act or section 6A of the 1988 Act ('a demotion order');
(g) 'a demoted tenancy' means a tenancy created by virtue of a demotion order; and
(h) 'a suspension claim' means a claim made by a landlord for an order under section 121A of the 1985 Act.

I GENERAL RULES

55.2 Scope

(1) The procedure set out in this Section of this Part must be used where the claim includes—
  (a) a possession claim brought by a—
    (i) landlord (or former landlord);
    (ii) mortgagee; or
    (iii) licensor (or former licensor);
  (b) a possession claim against trespassers; or
  (c) a claim by a tenant seeking relief from forfeiture.

(Where a demotion claim or a suspension claim (or both) is made in the same claim form in which a possession claim is started, this Section of this Part applies as modified by rule 65.12. Where the claim is a demotion claim or a suspension claim only, or a suspension claim made in addition to a demotion claim, Section III of Part 65 applies)

(2) This Section of this Part—
 (a) is subject to any enactment or practice direction which sets out special provisions with regard to any particular category of claim;
 (b) does not apply where the claimant uses the procedure set out in Section II of this Part; and
 (c) does not apply where the claimant seeks an interim possession order under Section III of this Part except where the court orders otherwise or that Section so provides.

55.3 Starting the Claim

r.55.3 PC 37, 11.3
r.55.3(1) PC 37, 35.5
r.55.3(2) PC 37, 87.7

(1) The claim must be started in the county court for the district in which the land is situated unless paragraph (2) applies or an enactment provides otherwise.
(2) The claim may be started in the High Court if the claimant files with his claim form a certificate stating the reasons for bringing the claim in that court verified by a statement of truth in accordance with rule 22.1(1).
(3) Practice Direction 55A refers to circumstances which may justify starting the claim in the High Court.
(4) Where, in a possession claim against trespassers, the claimant does not know the name of a person in occupation or possession of the land, the claim must be brought against 'persons unknown' in addition to any named defendants.
(5) The claim form and form of defence sent with it must be in the forms set out in Practice Direction 55A.

55.4 Particulars of Claim

r.55.4 PC 37, 15.4, 35.6, 87.8

The particulars of claim must be filed and served with the claim form.

(Part 16 and Practice Direction 55A provide details about the contents of the particulars of claim)

55.5 Hearing Date

r.55.5 PC 37, 87.15
r.55.5(2) 35.7
r.55.5(3) 87.15

(1) The court will fix a date for the hearing when it issues the claim form.
(2) In a possession claim against trespassers the defendant must be served with the claim form, particulars of claim and any witness statements—
 (a) in the case of residential property, not less than 5 days; and
 (b) in the case of other land, not less than 2 days,
 before the hearing date.
(3) In all other possession claims—
 (a) the hearing date will be not less than 28 days from the date of issue of the claim form;
 (b) the standard period between the issue of the claim form and the hearing will be not more than 8 weeks; and
 (c) the defendant must be served with the claim form and particulars of claim not less than 21 days before the hearing date.

(Rule 3.1(2)(a) provides that the court may extend or shorten the time for compliance with any rule)

55.6 Service of Claims against Trespassers

r.55.6 15.19, 35.7

Where, in a possession claim against trespassers, the claim has been issued against 'persons unknown', the claim form, particulars of claim and any witness statements must be served on those persons by—

(a) (i) attaching copies of the claim form, particulars of claim and any witness statements to the main door or some other part of the land so that they are clearly visible; and

(ii) if practicable, inserting copies of those documents in a sealed transparent envelope addressed to 'the occupiers' through the letter box; or

(b) placing stakes in the land in places where they are clearly visible and attaching to each stake copies of the claim form, particulars of claim and any witness statements in a sealed transparent envelope addressed to 'the occupiers'.

55.7 Defendant's Response

r.55.7(1) 35.7, 87.16
r.55.7(2) 35.8
r.55.7(3) PC 37
r.55.7(4) 20.2, 35.8

(1) An acknowledgment of service is not required and Part 10 does not apply.
(2) In a possession claim against trespassers rule 15.2 does not apply and the defendant need not file a defence.
(3) Where, in any other possession claim, the defendant does not file a defence within the time specified in rule 15.4, he may take part in any hearing but the court may take his failure to do so into account when deciding what order to make about costs.
(4) Part 12 (default judgment) does not apply in a claim to which this Part applies.

55.8 The Hearing

r.55.8(1) 62.2
r.55.8(1)(b) 87.34
r.55.8(2) PC 37, 35.15
r.55.8(3) 35.10
r.55.8(4) PC 37, 87.18
r.55.8(5) 35.6
r.55.8(6) 35.10

(1) At the hearing fixed in accordance with rule 55.5(1) or at any adjournment of that hearing, the court may—
 (a) decide the claim; or
 (b) give case management directions.
(2) Where the claim is genuinely disputed on grounds which appear to be substantial, case management directions given under paragraph (1)(b) will include the allocation of the claim to a track or directions to enable it to be allocated.
(3) Except where—
 (a) the claim is allocated to the fast track or the multi-track; or
 (b) the court orders otherwise,
 any fact that needs to be proved by the evidence of witnesses at a hearing referred to in paragraph (1) may be proved by evidence in writing.
 (Rule 32.2(1) sets out the general rule about evidence. Rule 32.2(2) provides that rule 32.2(1) is subject to any provision to the contrary)
(4) Subject to paragraph (5), all witness statements must be filed and served at least 2 days before the hearing.
(5) In a possession claim against trespassers all witness statements on which the claimant intends to rely must be filed and served with the claim form.
(6) Where the claimant serves the claim form and particulars of claim, the claimant must produce at the hearing a certificate of service of those documents and rule 6.17(2)(a) does not apply.

55.9 Allocation

r.55.9 PC 37, 87.34

(1) When the court decides the track for a possession claim, the matters to which it shall have regard include—
 (a) the matters set out in rule 26.8 as modified by the relevant practice direction;
 (b) the amount of any arrears of rent or mortgage instalments;
 (c) the importance to the defendant of retaining possession of the land;
 (d) the importance of vacant possession to the claimant; and
 (e) if applicable, the alleged conduct of the defendant.
(2) The court will only allocate possession claims to the small claims track if all the parties agree.
(3) Where a possession claim has been allocated to the small claims track the claim shall be treated, for the purposes of costs, as if it were proceeding on the fast track except that trial costs shall be in the discretion of the court and shall not exceed the amount that would be recoverable under rule 46.2 (amount of fast track costs) if the value of the claim were up to £3,000.

(4) Where all the parties agree the court may, when it allocates the claim, order that rule 27.14 (costs on the small claims track) applies and, where it does so, paragraph (3) does not apply.

55.10 Possession Claims Relating to Mortgaged Residential Property

r.55.10 PC 37, 87.17, 87.18, 87.19, 87.25, 87.26
r.55.10(2) PC 37, 87.6
r.55.10(4A) 87.26

(1) This rule applies where a mortgagee seeks possession of land which consists of or includes residential property.
(2) Within 5 days of receiving notification of the date of the hearing by the court, the claimant must send a notice to—
(a) the property, addressed to 'the tenant or the occupier';
(b) the housing department of the local authority within which the property is located; and
(c) any registered proprietor (other than the claimant) of a registered charge over the property.
(3) The notice referred to in paragraph (2)(a) must—
(a) state that a possession claim for the property has started;
(b) show the name and address of the claimant, the defendant and the court which issued the claim form; and
(c) give details of the hearing.
(3A) The notice referred to in paragraph 2(b) must contain the information in paragraph (3) and must state the full address of the property.
(4) The claimant must produce at the hearing—
(a) a copy of the notices; and
(b) evidence that they have been sent.
(4A) An unauthorised tenant of residential property may apply to the court for the order for possession to be suspended.

55.10A Electronic Issue of Certain Possession Claims

r.55.10A PC 37, 87.11

(1) A practice direction may make provision for a claimant to start certain types of possession claim in certain courts by requesting the issue of a claim form electronically.
(2) The practice direction may, in particular—
(a) provide that only particular provisions apply in specific courts;
(b) specify—
(i) the type of possession claim which may be issued electronically;
(ii) the conditions that a claim must meet before it may be issued electronically;
(c) specify the court where the claim may be issued;
(d) enable the parties to make certain applications or take further steps in relation to the claim electronically;
(e) specify the requirements that must be fulfilled in relation to such applications or steps;
(f) enable the parties to correspond electronically with the court about the claim;
(g) specify the requirements that must be fulfilled in relation to electronic correspondence;
(h) provide how any fee payable on the filing of any document is to be paid where the document is filed electronically.
(3) The Practice Direction may disapply or modify these Rules as appropriate in relation to possession claims started electronically.

II ACCELERATED POSSESSION CLAIMS OF PROPERTY LET ON AN ASSURED SHORTHOLD TENANCY

section II 70.3

55.11 When This Section May Be Used

r.55.11 35.16

(1) The claimant may bring a possession claim under this Section of this Part where—
(a) the claim is brought under section 21 of the 1988 Act to recover possession of residential property let under an assured shorthold tenancy; and
(b) subject to rule 55.12(2), all the conditions listed in rule 55.12(1) are satisfied.

(2) The claim must be started in the county court for the district in which the property is situated.
(3) In this Section of this Part, a 'demoted assured shorthold tenancy' means a demoted tenancy where the landlord is a registered social landlord or a private registered provider of social housing.
(By virtue of section 20B of the 1988 Act, a demoted assured shorthold tenancy is an assured shorthold tenancy)

55.12 Conditions

r.55.12 35.16

(1) The conditions referred to in rule 55.11(1)(b) are that—
- (a) the tenancy and any agreement for the tenancy were entered into on or after 15 January 1989;
- (b) the only purpose of the claim is to recover possession of the property and no other claim is made;
- (c) the tenancy did not immediately follow an assured tenancy which was not an assured shorthold tenancy;
- (d) the tenancy fulfilled the conditions provided by section 19A or 20(1)(a) to (c) of the 1988 Act;
- (e) the tenancy—
  - (i) was the subject of a written agreement;
  - (ii) arises by virtue of section 5 of the 1988 Act but follows a tenancy that was the subject of a written agreement; or
  - (iii) relates to the same or substantially the same property let to the same tenant and on the same terms (though not necessarily as to rent or duration) as a tenancy which was the subject of a written agreement; and
- (f) a notice in accordance with sections 21(1) or 21(4) of the 1988 Act was given to the tenant in writing.

(2) If the tenancy is a demoted assured shorthold tenancy, only the conditions in paragraph (1)(b) and (f) need be satisfied.

55.13 Claim Form

r.55.13 35.16

(1) The claim form must—
- (a) be in the form set out in Practice Direction 55A; and
- (b) (i) contain such information; and
  - (ii) be accompanied by such documents, as are required by that form.

(2) All relevant sections of the form must be completed.
(3) The court will serve the claim form by first class post (or an alternative service which provides for delivery on the next working day).

55.14 Defence

r.55.14 35.16

(1) A defendant who wishes to—
- (a) oppose the claim; or
- (b) seek a postponement of possession in accordance with rule 55.18,

must file his defence within 14 days after service of the claim form.
(2) The defence should be in the form set out in Practice Direction 55A.

55.15 Claim Referred to Judge

r.55.15 35.16

(1) On receipt of the defence the court will—
- (a) send a copy to the claimant; and
- (b) refer the claim and defence to a judge.

(2) Where the period set out in rule 55.14 has expired without the defendant filing a defence—
- (a) the claimant may file a written request for an order for possession; and
- (b) the court will refer that request to a judge.

(3) Where the defence is received after the period set out in rule 55.14 has expired but before a request is filed in accordance with paragraph (2), paragraph (1) will still apply.
(4) Where—
- (a) the period set out in rule 55.14 has expired without the defendant filing a defence; and

(b) the claimant has not made a request for an order for possession under paragraph (2) within 3 months after the expiry of the period set out in rule 55.14,

the claim will be stayed.

55.16 Consideration of the Claim

r.55.16 35.16 r.55.16(1)(c) 35.16

(1) After considering the claim and any defence, the judge will—
   (a) make an order for possession under rule 55.17;
   (b) where he is not satisfied as to any of the matters set out in paragraph (2)—
      (i) direct that a date be fixed for a hearing; and
      (ii) give any appropriate case management directions; or
   (c) strike out the claim if the claim form discloses no reasonable grounds for bringing the claim.
(2) The matters referred to in paragraph (1)(b) are that—
   (a) the claim form was served; and
   (b) the claimant has established that he is entitled to recover possession under section 21 of the 1988 Act against the defendant.
(3) The court will give all parties not less than 14 days' notice of a hearing fixed under paragraph (1)(b)(i).
(4) Where a claim is struck out under paragraph 1(c)—
   (a) the court will serve its reasons for striking out the claim with the order; and
   (b) the claimant may apply to restore the claim within 28 days after the date the order was served on him.

55.17 Possession Order

r.55.17 35.16

Except where rules 55.16(1)(b) or (c) apply, the judge will make an order for possession without requiring the attendance of the parties.

55.18 Postponement of Possession

r.55.18 35.16

(1) Where the defendant seeks postponement of possession on the ground of exceptional hardship under section 89 of the Housing Act 1980, the judge may direct a hearing of that issue.
(2) Where the judge directs a hearing under paragraph (1)—
   (a) the hearing must be held before the date on which possession is to be given up; and
   (b) the judge will direct how many days' notice the parties must be given of that hearing.
(3) Where the judge is satisfied, on a hearing directed under paragraph (1), that exceptional hardship would be caused by requiring possession to be given up by the date in the order of possession, he may vary the date on which possession must be given up.

55.19 Application to Set Aside or Vary

r.55.19 35.16

The court may—
(a) on application by a party within 14 days of service of the order; or
(b) of its own initiative,

set aside or vary any order made under rule 55.17.

III INTERIM POSSESSION ORDERS

55.20 When This Section May Be Used

r.55.20 35.14

(1) This Section of this Part applies where the claimant seeks an Interim Possession Order.
(2) In this Section—
   (a) 'IPO' means Interim Possession Order; and
   (b) 'premises' has the same meaning as in section 12 of the Criminal Law Act 1977.

(3) Where this Section requires an act to be done within a specified number of hours, rule 2.8(4) does not apply.

55.21 Conditions for IPO Application

r.55.21 35.14

(1) An application for an IPO may be made where the following conditions are satisfied—
  (a) the only claim made is a possession claim against trespassers for the recovery of premises;
  (b) the claimant—
    (i) has an immediate right to possession of the premises; and
    (ii) has had such a right throughout the period of alleged unlawful occupation; and
  (c) the claim is made within 28 days of the date on which the claimant first knew, or ought reasonably to have known, that the defendant (or any of the defendants), was in occupation.

(2) An application for an IPO may not be made against a defendant who entered or remained on the premises with the consent of a person who, at the time consent was given, had an immediate right to possession of the premises.

55.22 The Application

r.55.22 35.14

(1) Rules 55.3(1) and (4) apply to the claim.

(2) The claim form and the defendant's form of witness statement must be in the form set out in Practice Direction 55A.

(3) When he files his claim form, the claimant must also file—
  (a) an application notice in the form set out in Practice Direction 55A; and
  (b) written evidence.

(4) The written evidence must be given—
  (a) by the claimant personally; or
  (b) where the claimant is a body corporate, by a duly authorised officer.
  (Rule 22.1(6)(b) provides that the statement of truth must be signed by the maker of the witness statement)

(5) The court will—
  (a) issue—
    (i) the claim form; and
    (ii) the application for the IPO; and
  (b) set a date for the hearing of the application.

(6) The hearing of the application will be as soon as practicable but not less than 3 days after the date of issue.

55.23 Service

r.55.23 35.14

(1) Within 24 hours of the issue of the application, the claimant must serve on the defendant—
  (a) the claim form;
  (b) the application notice together with the written evidence in support; and
  (c) a blank form for the defendant's witness statement (as set out in Practice Direction 55A) which must be attached to the application notice.

(2) The claimant must serve the documents listed in paragraph (1) in accordance with rule 55.6(a).

(3) At or before the hearing the claimant must file a certificate of service in relation to the documents listed in paragraph (1) and rule 6.17(2)(a) does not apply.

55.24 Defendant's Response

r.55.24 35.14

(1) At any time before the hearing the defendant may file a witness statement in response to the application.

(2) The witness statement should be in the form set out in Practice Direction 55A.

55.25 Hearing of the Application

r.55.25 35.14 r.55.25(1) 35.14

r.55.25(3) 35.14

(1) In deciding whether to grant an IPO, the court will have regard to whether the claimant has given, or is prepared to give, the following undertakings in support of his application—
 (a) if, after an IPO is made, the court decides that the claimant was not entitled to the order to—
  (i) reinstate the defendant if so ordered by the court; and
  (ii) pay such damages as the court may order; and
 (b) before the claim for possession is finally decided, not to—
  (i) damage the premises;
  (ii) grant a right of occupation to any other person; and
  (iii) damage or dispose of any of the defendant's property.
(2) The court will make an IPO if—
 (a) the claimant has—
  (i) filed a certificate of service of the documents referred to in rule 55.23(1); or
  (ii) proved service of those documents to the satisfaction of the court; and
 (b) the court considers that—
  (i) the conditions set out in rule 55.21(1) are satisfied; and
  (ii) any undertakings given by the claimant as a condition of making the order are adequate.
(3) An IPO will be in the form set out in Practice Direction 55A and will require the defendant to vacate the premises specified in the claim form within 24 hours of the service of the order.
(4) On making an IPO the court will set a date for the hearing of the claim for possession which will be not less than 7 days after the date on which the IPO is made.
(5) Where the court does not make an IPO—
 (a) the court will set a date for the hearing of the claim;
 (b) the court may give directions for the future conduct of the claim; and
 (c) subject to such directions, the claim shall proceed in accordance with Section I of this Part.

55.26 Service and Enforcement of the IPO

r.55.26 35.14

(1) An IPO must be served within 48 hours after it is sealed.
(2) The claimant must serve the IPO on the defendant together with copies of—
 (a) the claim form; and
 (b) the written evidence in support,
 in accordance with rule 55.6(a).
(3) CCR Order 26, rule 17 does not apply to the enforcement of an IPO.
(4) If an IPO is not served within the time limit specified by this rule, the claimant may apply to the court for directions for the claim for possession to continue under Section I of this Part.

55.27 After IPO Made

r.55.27 35.14

(1) Before the date for the hearing of the claim, the claimant must file a certificate of service in relation to the documents specified in rule 55.26(2).
(2) The IPO will expire on the date of the hearing of the claim.
(3) At the hearing the court may make any order it considers appropriate and may, in particular—
 (a) make a final order for possession;
 (b) dismiss the claim for possession;
 (c) give directions for the claim for possession to continue under Section I of this Part; or
 (d) enforce any of the claimant's undertakings.
(4) Unless the court directs otherwise, the claimant must serve any order or directions in accordance with rule 55.6(a).
(5) CCR Order 24, rule 6 applies to the enforcement of a final order for possession.

55.28 Application to Set Aside IPO

r.55.28 35.14

(1) If the defendant has left the premises, he may apply on grounds of urgency for the IPO to be set aside before the date of the hearing of the claim.
(2) An application under paragraph (1) must be supported by a witness statement.

(3) On receipt of the application, the court will give directions as to—
   (a) the date for the hearing; and
   (b) the period of notice, if any, to be given to the claimant and the method of service of any such notice.
(4) No application to set aside an IPO may be made under rule 39.3.
(5) Where no notice is required under paragraph (3)(b), the only matters to be dealt with at the hearing of the application to set aside are whether—
   (a) the IPO should be set aside; and
   (b) any undertaking to reinstate the defendant should be enforced,
   and all other matters will be dealt with at the hearing of the claim.
(6) The court will serve on all the parties—
   (a) a copy of the order made under paragraph (5); and
   (b) where no notice was required under paragraph (3)(b), a copy of the defendant's application to set aside and the witness statement in support.
(7) Where notice is required under paragraph (3)(b), the court may treat the hearing of the application to set aside as the hearing of the claim.

PD 55A Practice Direction 55A — Possession Claims

This practice direction supplements CPR, Part 55.
PD 5A 8.85, 35.15, 87.4 [For commentary on a specific paragraph, please refer to the cross-references after the title of the paragraph.]

SECTION I GENERAL RULES

Starting the Claim: Rule 55.3

para.1 11.3
para.1.2 35.5
para.1.3 PC 37, 35.5, 87.7
para.1.4 PC 37, 87.7
para.1.6 PC 37

1.1 Except where the county court does not have jurisdiction, possession claims should normally be brought in the county court. Only exceptional circumstances justify starting a claim in the High Court.

1.2 If a claimant starts a claim in the High Court and the court decides that it should have been started in the county court, the court will normally either strike the claim out or transfer it to the county court on its own initiative. This is likely to result in delay and the court will normally disallow the costs of starting the claim in the High Court and of any transfer.

1.3 Circumstances which may, in an appropriate case, justify starting a claim in the High Court are if:

(1) there are complicated disputes of fact;
(2) there are points of law of general importance; or
(3) the claim is against trespassers and there is a substantial risk of public disturbance or of serious harm to persons or property which properly require immediate determination.

1.4 The value of the property and the amount of any financial claim may be relevant circumstances, but these factors alone will not normally justify starting the claim in the High Court.

1.5 The claimant must use the appropriate claim form and particulars of claim form set out in Table 1 to PD 4. The defence must be in form N11, N11B, N11M or N11R, as appropriate.

1.6 High Court claims for the possession of land subject to a mortgage will be assigned to the Chancery Division.

1.7 A claim which is not a possession claim may be brought under the procedure set out in Section I of Part 55 if it is started in the same claim form as a possession claim which, by virtue of r. 55.2(1) must be brought in accordance with that Section.

(Rule 7.3 provides that a claimant may use a single claim form to start all claims which can be conveniently disposed of in the same proceedings.)

1.8 For example a claim under the Mobile Homes Act 1983, sch. 1, part 1, paras 4, 5 or 6, may be brought using the procedure set out in Section I of CPR, Part 55, if the claim is started in the same claim form as a claim enforcing the rights referred to in the Caravan Sites Act 1968, s. 3(1)(b) (which, by virtue of CPR, r. 55.2(1), must be brought under Section I of Part 55).

1.9 Where the claim form includes a demotion claim, the claim must be started in the county court for the district in which the land is situated.

Particulars of Claim: Rule 55.4

para.2 24.14
para.2.1 PC 37, 24.6, 35.6, 87.8

2.1 In a possession claim the particulars of claim must:

(1) identify the land to which the claim relates;
(2) state whether the claim relates to residential property;
(3) state the ground on which possession is claimed;
(4) give full details about any mortgage or tenancy agreement; and
(5) give details of every person who, to the best of the claimant's knowledge, is in possession of the property.

Residential property let on a tenancy

para.2.2 **24.6**
para.2.3 **24.6**
para.2.4 **24.6**

2.2 Paragraphs 2.3 to 2.4B apply if the claim relates to residential property let on a tenancy.

2.3 If the claim includes a claim for non-payment of rent the particulars of claim must set out:

(1) the amount due at the start of the proceedings;
(2) in schedule form, the dates and amounts of all payments due and payments made under the tenancy agreement for a period of two years immediately preceding the date of issue, or if the first date of default occurred less than two years before the date of issue from the first date of default and a running total of the arrears;
(3) the daily rate of any rent and interest;
(4) any previous steps taken to recover the arrears of rent with full details of any court proceedings; and
(5) any relevant information about the defendant's circumstances, in particular:
(a) whether the defendant is in receipt of social security benefits; and
(b) whether any payments are made on his behalf directly to the claimant under the Social Security Contributions and Benefits Act 1992.

2.3A If the claimant wishes to rely on a history of arrears which is longer than two years, he should state this in his particulars and exhibit a full (or longer) schedule to a witness statement.

2.4 If the claimant knows of any person (including a mortgagee) entitled to claim relief against forfeiture as underlessee under s. 146(4) of the Law of Property Act 1925 (or in accordance with s. 38 of the Senior Courts Act 1981, or s. 138(9C) of the County Courts Act 1984):

(1) the particulars of claim must state the name and address of that person; and
(2) the claimant must file a copy of the particulars of claim for service on him.

2.4A If the claim for possession relates to the conduct of the tenant, the particulars of claim must state details of the conduct alleged.

2.4B If the possession claim relies on a statutory ground or grounds for possession, the particulars of claim must specify the ground or grounds relied on.

Land subject to a mortgage

para.2.5 **PC 37, 24.6, 87.9**
para.2.5(1) **87.6, 87.9**
para.2.5(2)(a)–(c) **87.9**
para.2.5(3) **87.9, 87.33**
para.2.5(4)–(5) **87.9, 87.46**
para.2.5(6) **87.9**
para.2.5(8) **87.9**
para.2.5A **PC 37, 87.9**

2.5 If the claim is a possession claim by a mortgagee, the particulars of claim must also set out:

(1) if the claim relates to residential property whether:
(a) a land charge of Class F has been registered under s. 2(7) of the Matrimonial Homes Act 1967;
(b) a notice registered under s. 2(8) or 8(3) of the Matrimonial Homes Act 1983 has been entered and on whose behalf; or
(c) a notice under s. 31(10) of the Family Law Act 1996 has been registered and on whose behalf; and

if so, that the claimant will serve notice of the claim on the persons on whose behalf the land charge is registered or the notice or caution entered;

(2) the state of the mortgage account by including:
(a) the amount of:
(i) the advance;
(ii) any periodic repayment; and
(iii) any payment of interest required to be made;
(b) the amount which would have to be paid (after taking into account any adjustment for early settlement) in order to redeem the mortgage at a stated date not more than 14 days after the claim started specifying the amount of solicitor's costs and administration charges which would be payable;
(c) if the loan which is secured by the mortgage is a regulated consumer credit agreement, *the total amount outstanding* under the terms of the mortgage; and
(d) the rate of interest payable:
(i) at the commencement of the mortgage;

(ii) immediately before any arrears referred to in sub-paragraph (3) accrued;
(iii) at the commencement of the proceedings;

(3) if the claim is brought because of failure to pay the periodic payments when due:
(a) in schedule form, the dates and amounts of all payments due and payments made under the mortgage agreement or mortgage deed for a period of two years immediately preceding the date of issue, or if the first date of default occurred less than two years before the date of issue from the first date of default and a running total of the arrears;
(b) give details of:
(i) any other payments required to be made as a term of the mortgage (such as for insurance premiums, legal costs, default interest, penalties, administrative or other charges);
(ii) any other sums claimed and stating the nature and amount of each such charge; and
(iii) whether any of these payments is in arrears and whether or not it is included in the amount of any periodic payment;

(4) whether or not the loan which is secured by the mortgage is a regulated consumer credit agreement and, if so, specify the date on which any notice required by ss. 76 or 87 of the Consumer Credit Act 1974 was given;

(5) if appropriate details that show the property is not one to which s. 141 of the Consumer Credit Act 1974 applies;

(6) any relevant information about the defendant's circumstances, in particular:
(a) whether the defendant is in receipt of social security benefits; and
(b) whether any payments are made on his behalf directly to the claimant under the Social Security Contributions and Benefits Act 1992;

(7) give details of any tenancy entered into between the mortgagor and mortgagee (including any notices served); and

(8) state any previous steps which the claimant has taken to recover the money secured by the mortgage or the mortgaged property and, in the case of court proceedings, state:
(a) the dates when the claim started and concluded; and
(b) the dates and terms of any orders made.

2.5A If the claimant wishes to rely on a history of arrears which is longer than two years, he should state this in his particulars and exhibit a full (or longer) schedule to a witness statement.

Possession claim against trespassers

para.2.6 24.6, 35.6

2.6 If the claim is a possession claim against trespassers, the particulars of claim must state the claimant's interest in the land or the basis of his right to claim possession and the circumstances in which it has been occupied without licence or consent.

Possession claim in relation to a demoted tenancy by a housing action trust or a local housing authority

para.2.7 24.6

2.7 If the claim is a possession claim under the Housing Act 1996, s. 143D (possession claim in relation to a demoted tenancy where the landlord is a housing action trust or a local housing authority), the particulars of claim must have attached to them a copy of the notice to the tenant served under s. 143E of the 1996 Act.

Hearing Date: Rule 55.5

para.3.2 35.7

3.1 The court may exercise its powers under r. 3.1(2)(a) and (b) to shorten the time periods set out in r. 55.5(2) and (3).

3.2 Particular consideration should be given to the exercise of this power if:
(1) the defendant, or a person for whom the defendant is responsible, has assaulted or threatened to assault:
(a) the claimant;
(b) a member of the claimant's staff; or
(c) another resident in the locality;

(2) there are reasonable grounds for fearing such an assault; or
(3) the defendant, or a person for whom the defendant is responsible, has caused serious damage or threatened to cause serious damage to the property or to the home or property of another resident in the locality.

3.3 Where para. 3.2 applies but the case cannot be determined at the first hearing fixed under r. 55.5, the court will consider what steps are needed to finally determine the case as quickly as reasonably practicable.

Service in Claims against Trespassers: Rule 55.6

para.4.1 35.7

4.1 If the claim form is to be served by the court and in accordance with r. 55.6(b) the claimant must provide sufficient stakes and transparent envelopes.

The Hearing: Rule 55.8

para.5.1 87.18
para.5.4 35.10, 87.18
para.5.5 8.82

5.1 Attention is drawn to r. 55.8(3). Each party should wherever possible include all the evidence he wishes to present in his statement of case, verified by a statement of truth.

5.2 If relevant the claimant's evidence should include the amount of any rent or mortgage arrears and interest on those arrears. These amounts should, if possible, be up to date to the date of the hearing (if necessary by specifying a daily rate of arrears and interest). However, r. 55.8(4) does not prevent such evidence being brought up to date orally or in writing on the day of the hearing if necessary.

5.3 If relevant the defendant should give evidence of:
(1) the amount of any outstanding social security or housing benefit payments relevant to rent or mortgage arrears; and
(2) the status of:
(a) any claims for social security or housing benefit about which a decision has not yet been made; and
(b) any applications to appeal or review a social security or housing benefit decision where that appeal or review has not yet concluded.

5.4 If:
(1) the maker of a witness statement does not attend a hearing; and
(2) the other party disputes material evidence contained in his statement, the court will normally adjourn the hearing so that oral evidence can be given.

5.5 The claimant must bring two completed copies of form N123 to the hearing.

Consumer Credit Act Claims Relating to the Recovery of Land

para.7.1 87.48

7.1 Any application by the defendant for a time order under s. 129 of the Consumer Credit Act 1974 may be made:
(1) in his defence; or
(2) by application notice in the proceedings.

Enforcement of Charging Order by Sale

7.2 A party seeking to enforce a charging order by sale should follow the procedure set out in r. 73.10 and the Part 55 procedure should not be used.

SECTION II ACCELERATED POSSESSION CLAIMS OF PROPERTY LET ON AN ASSURED SHORTHOLD TENANCY

Postponement of Possession: Rule 55.18

8.1 If the judge is satisfied as to the matters set out in r. 55.16(2), he will make an order for possession in accordance with r. 55.17, whether or not the defendant seeks a postponement of possession on the ground of exceptional hardship under s. 89 of the Housing Act 1980.

8.2 In a claim in which the judge is satisfied that the defendant has shown exceptional hardship, he will only postpone possession without directing a hearing under r. 55.18(1) if:

(1) he considers that possession should be given up six weeks after the date of the order or, if the defendant has requested postponement to an earlier date, on that date; and

(2) the claimant indicated on his claim form that he would be content for the court to make such an order without a hearing.

8.3 In all other cases if the defendant seeks a postponement of possession under s. 89 of the Housing Act 1980, the judge will direct a hearing under r. 55.18(1).

8.4 If, at that hearing, the judge is satisfied that exceptional hardship would be caused by requiring possession to be given up by the date in the order of possession, he may vary that order under r. 55.18(3) so that possession is to be given up at a later date. That later date may be no later than six weeks after the making of the order for possession on the papers (see s. 89 of the Housing Act 1980).

SECTION III INTERIM POSSESSION ORDERS

9.1 The claim form must be in form N5, the application notice seeking the interim possession order must be in form N130 and the defendant's witness statement must be in form N133.

9.2 The IPO will be in form N134.

SECTION IV ORDERS FIXING A DATE FOR POSSESSION

10.1 This paragraph applies where the court has made an order postponing the date for possession under the Housing Act 1985, s. 85(2)(b) (secure tenancies) or under the Housing Act 1988, s. 9(2)(b) (assured tenancies).

10.2 If the defendant fails to comply with any of the terms of the order which relate to payment, the claimant, after following the procedure set out in para. 10.3, may apply for an order fixing the date upon which the defendant has to give up possession of the property. Unless the court further postpones the date for possession, the defendant will be required to give up possession on that date.

10.3 At least 14 days and not more than three months before applying for an order under para. 10.2, the claimant must give written notice to the defendant in accordance with para. 10.4.

10.4 The notice referred to in para. 10.3 must:

(1) state that the claimant intends to apply for an order fixing the date upon which the defendant is to give up possession of the property;

(2) record the current arrears and state how the defendant has failed to comply with the order referred to in para. 10.1 (by reference to a statement of the rent account enclosed with the notice);

(3) request that the defendant reply to the claimant within seven days, agreeing or disputing the stated arrears; and

(4) inform the defendant of his right to apply to the court:

(a) for a further postponement of the date for possession; or

(b) to stay or suspend enforcement.

10.5 In his reply to the notice, the defendant must:

(1) where he disputes the stated arrears, provide details of payments or credits made;

(2) where he agrees the stated arrears, explain why payments have not been made.

10.6 An application for an order under para. 10.2 must be made by filing an application notice in accordance with Part 23. The application notice must state whether or not there is any outstanding claim by the defendant for housing benefit.

10.7 The claimant must file the following documents with the application notice:

(1) a copy of the notice referred to in para. 10.3;

(2) a copy of the defendant's reply, if any, to the notice and any relevant subsequent correspondence between the claimant and the defendant;

(3) a statement of the rent account showing:

(a) the arrears that have accrued since the first failure to pay in accordance with the order referred to in para. 10.2; or

(b) the arrears that have accrued during the period of two years immediately preceding the date of the application notice, where the first such failure to pay occurs more than two years before that date.

10.8 Rules 23.7 (service of a copy of an application notice) and 23.10 (right to set aside or vary an order made without service of the application notice) and PD 23A, paras 2.3, 2.4 and 2.5 (dealing with applications without a hearing), do not apply to an application under this Section.

10.9 On being filed, the application will be referred to the district judge who:
(1) will normally determine the application without a hearing by fixing the date for possession as the next working day; but
(2) if he considers that a hearing is necessary:
(a) will fix a date for the application to be heard; and
(b) direct service of the application notice and supporting evidence on the defendant.

10.10 The court does not have jurisdiction to review a decision that it was reasonable to make an order for possession.

PD 55B Practice Direction 55B — Possession Claims Online

This practice direction supplements r. 55.10A.
PD 55B PC 37, 87.7, 87.11, 87.13

Scope of This Practice Direction

1.1 This practice direction provides for a scheme ('Possession Claims Online') to operate in specified county courts:
(1) enabling claimants and their representatives to start certain possession claims under Part 55 by requesting the issue of a claim form electronically via the PCOL website; and
(2) where a claim has been started electronically, enabling the claimant or defendant and their representatives to take further steps in the claim electronically as specified below.

1.2 In this practice direction:
(1) 'PCOL website' means the website which may be accessed via the Business Link website and through which Possession Claims Online will operate; and
(2) 'specified court' means a county court specified on the PCOL website as one in which Possession Claims Online is available.

Information on the PCOL Website

2.1 The PCOL website contains further details and guidance about the operation of Possession Claims Online.

2.2 In particular the PCOL website sets out:
(1) the specified courts; and
(2) the dates from which Possession Claims Online will be available in each specified court.

2.3 The operation of Possession Claims Online in any specified court may be restricted to taking certain of the steps specified in this practice direction, and in such cases the PCOL website will set out the steps which may be taken using Possession Claims Online in that specified court.

Security

3.1 Her Majesty's Courts and Tribunals Service will take such measures as it thinks fit to ensure the security of steps taken or information stored electronically. These may include requiring users of Possession Claims Online:
(1) to enter a customer identification number or password;
(2) to provide personal information for identification purposes; and
(3) to comply with any other security measures,
before taking any step online.

Fees

para.4.2 87.13

4.1 A step may only be taken using Possession Claims Online on payment of the prescribed fee where a fee is payable. Where this practice direction provides for a fee to be paid electronically, it may be paid by:
(1) credit card;
(2) debit card; or
(3) any other method which Her Majesty's Courts and Tribunals Service may permit.

4.2 A defendant who wishes to claim exemption from payment of fees must do so through an organisation approved by Her Majesty's Courts and Tribunals Service before taking any step using PCOL which attracts a fee. If satisfied that the defendant is entitled to fee exemption, the organisation will submit the fee exemption form through the PCOL website to Her Majesty's Courts Service. The defendant may then use PCOL to take such a step.
(Her Majesty's Courts Service website contains guidance as to when the entitlement to claim an exemption from payment of fees arises. The PCOL website will contain a list of organisations through which the defendant may claim an exemption from fees.)

Claims Which May Be Started Using Possession Claims Online

para.5.1(1)–(5) 87.12 para.5.2 87.12

5.1 A claim may be started online if:
(1) it is brought under Section I of Part 55;
(2) it includes a possession claim for residential property by:
(a) a landlord against a tenant, solely on the ground of arrears of rent (but not a claim for forfeiture of a lease); or
(b) a mortgagee against a mortgagor, solely on the ground of default in the payment of sums due under a mortgage,
relating to land within the district of a specified court;
(3) it does not include a claim for any other remedy except for payment of arrears of rent or money due under a mortgage, interest and costs;
(3A) the claimant has an address for service in the United Kingdom;
(4) the defendant has an address for service in England and Wales; and
(5) the claimant is able to provide a postcode for the property.

5.2 A claim must not be started online if a defendant is known to be a child or protected party.

Starting a Claim

para.6.1 87.14
para.6.2 PC 37, 87.14
para.6.3 PC 37, 87.14
paras.6.3A–6.3B PC 37, 87.14
para.6.3C PC 37
paras.6.5–6.11 87.14

6.1 A claimant may request the issue of a claim form by:
(1) completing an online claim form at the PCOL website;
(2) paying the appropriate issue fee electronically at the PCOL website or by some other means approved by Her Majesty's Courts and Tribunals Service.

6.2 The particulars of claim must be included in the online claim form and may not be filed separately. It is not necessary to file a copy of the tenancy agreement, mortgage deed or mortgage agreement with the particulars of claim.

6.2A In the case of a possession claim for residential property that relies on a statutory ground or grounds for possession, the claimant must specify, in section 4(a) of the online claim form, the ground or grounds relied on.

6.3 Subject to paras. 6.3A and 6.3B, the particulars of claim must include a history of the rent or mortgage account, in schedule form setting out:
(1) the dates and amounts of all payments due and payments made under the tenancy agreement, mortgage deed or mortgage agreement either from the first date of default if that date occurred less than two years before the date of issue or for a period of two years immediately preceding the date of issue; and
(2) a running total of the arrears.

6.3A Paragraph 6.3B applies where the claimant has, before commencing proceedings, provided the defendant in schedule form with:
(1) details of the dates and amounts of all payments due and payments made under the tenancy agreement, mortgage deed or mortgage account:
(a) for a period of two years immediately preceding the date of commencing proceedings; or
(b) if the first date of default occurred less than two years before that date, from the first date of default; and
(2) a running total of the arrears.

6.3B Where this paragraph applies the claimant may, in place of the information required by para. 6.3, include in his particulars of claim a summary only of the arrears containing at least the following information:
(1) The amount of arrears as stated in the notice of seeking possession served under either the Housing Act 1985, s. 83, or the Housing Act 1988, s. 8, or at the date of the claimant's letter before action, as appropriate;
(2) the dates and amounts of the last three payments in cleared funds made by the defendant or, if less than three payments have been made, the dates and amounts of all payments made;

(3) the arrears at the date of issue, assuming that no further payments are made by the defendant.

6.3C Where the particulars of claim include a summary only of the arrears the claimant must:
(1) serve on the defendant not more than seven days after the date of issue, a full, up-to-date arrears history containing at least the information required by para. 6.3; and
(2) either:
(a) make a witness statement confirming that he has complied with sub-para. (1) or (2) of para. 6.3A as appropriate, and including or exhibiting the full arrears history; or
(b) verify by way of oral evidence at the hearing that he has complied with sub-para. (1) or (2) of para. 6.3A as appropriate and also produce and verify the full arrears history.

(Rule 55.8(4) requires all witness statements to be filed and served at least two days before the hearing.)

6.4 If the claimant wishes to rely on a history of arrears which is longer than two years, he should state this in his particulars and exhibit a full (or longer) schedule to a witness statement.

6.5 When an online claim form is received, an acknowledgment of receipt will automatically be sent to the claimant. The acknowledgment does not constitute notice that the claim form has been issued or served.

6.6 When the court issues a claim form following the submission of an online claim form, the claim is 'brought' for the purposes of the Limitation Act 1980 and any other enactment on the date on which the online claim form is received by the court's computer system. The court will keep a record, by electronic or other means, of when online claim forms are received.

6.7 When the court issues a claim form it will:
(1) serve a printed version of the claim form and a defence form on the defendant; and
(2) send the claimant notice of issue by post or, where the claimant has supplied an email address, by electronic means.

6.8 The claim shall be deemed to be served on the fifth day after the claim was issued irrespective of whether that day is a business day or not.

6.9 Where the period of time within which a defence must be filed ends on a day when the court is closed, the defendant may file his defence on the next day that the court is open.

6.10 The claim form shall have printed on it a unique customer identification number or a password by which the defendant may access the claim on the PCOL website.

6.11 PCOL will issue the proceedings in the appropriate county court by reference to the postcode provided by the claimant and that court shall have jurisdiction to hear and determine the claim and to carry out enforcement of any judgment irrespective of whether the property is within or outside the jurisdiction of that court.

(Rule 30.2(1) authorises proceedings to be transferred from one county court to another.)

Defence

para.7.1 PC 37

7.1 A defendant wishing to file:
(1) a defence; or
(2) a counterclaim (to be filed together with a defence) to a claim which has been issued through the PCOL system, may, instead of filing a written form, do so by:
(a) completing the relevant online form at the PCOL website; and
(b) if the defendant is making a counterclaim, paying the appropriate fee electronically at the PCOL website or by some other means approved by Her Majesty's Courts and Tribunals Service.

7.2 Where a defendant files a defence by completing the relevant online form, he must not send the court a hard copy.

7.3 When an online defence form is received, an acknowledgment of receipt will automatically be sent to the defendant. The acknowledgment does not constitute notice that the defence has been served.

7.4 The online defence form will be treated as being filed:
(1) on the day the court receives it, if it receives it before 4 p.m. on a working day; and
(2) otherwise, on the next working day after the court receives the online defence form.

7.5 A defence is filed when the online defence form is received by the court's computer system. The court will keep a record, by electronic or other means, of when online defence forms are received.

Statement of Truth

8.1 Part 22 requires any statement of case to be verified by a statement of truth. This applies to any online claims and defences and application notices.

8.2 Part 22 also requires that if an applicant wishes to rely on matters set out in his application notice as evidence, the application notice must be verified by a statement of truth. This applies to any application notice completed online that contains matters on which the applicant wishes to rely as evidence.

8.3 Attention is drawn to:

(1) PD 22, para. 2, which stipulates the form of the statement of truth; and
(2) PD 22, para. 3, which provides who may sign a statement of truth; and
(3) r. 32.14, which sets out the consequences of making, or causing to be made, a false statement in a document verified by a statement of truth, without an honest belief in its truth.

Signature

9.1 Any provision of the CPR which requires a document to be signed by any person is satisfied by that person entering his name on an online form.

Communication with the Court Electronically by the Messaging Service

10.1 If the PCOL website specifies that a court accepts electronic communications relating to claims brought using Possession Claims Online the parties may communicate with the court using the messaging service facility, available on the PCOL website ('the messaging service').

10.2 The messaging service is for brief and straightforward communications only. The PCOL website contains a list of examples of when it will not be appropriate to use the messaging service.

10.3 Parties must not send to the court forms or attachments via the messaging service.

10.4 The court shall treat any forms or attachments sent via the messaging service as not having been filed or received.

10.5 The court will normally reply via the messaging service where:

(1) the response is to a message transmitted via the messaging service; and
(2) the sender has provided an email address.

Electronic Applications

11.1 Certain applications in relation to a possession claim started online may be made electronically ('online applications'). An online application may be made if a form for that application is published on the PCOL website ('online application form') and the application is made at least five clear days before the hearing.

11.2 If a claim for possession has been started online and a party wishes to make an online application, he may do so by:

(1) completing the appropriate online application form at the PCOL website; and
(2) paying the appropriate fee electronically at the PCOL website or by some other means approved by Her Majesty's Courts and Tribunals Service.

11.3 When an online application form is received, an acknowledgment of receipt will automatically be sent to the applicant. The acknowledgment does not constitute a notice that the online application form has been issued or served.

11.4 Where an application must be made within a specified time, it is so made if the online application form is received by the court's computer system within that time. The court will keep a record, by electronic or other means, of when online application forms are received.

11.5 When the court receives an online application form it shall:

(1) serve a copy of the online application endorsed with the date of the hearing by post on the claimant at least two clear days before the hearing; and
(2) send the defendant notice of service and confirmation of the date of the hearing by post; provided that

(3) where either party has provided the court with an email address for service, service of the application and/or the notice of service and confirmation of the hearing date may be effected by electronic means.

Request for Issue of Warrant

12.1 Where:

(1) the court has made an order for possession in a claim started online; and

(2) the claimant is entitled to the issue of a warrant of possession without requiring the permission of the court,

the claimant may request the issue of a warrant by completing an online request form at the PCOL website and paying the appropriate fee electronically at the PCOL website or by some other means approved by Her Majesty's Courts and Tribunals Service.

12.2 A request under para. 12.1 will be treated as being filed:

(1) on the day the court receives the request, if it receives it before 4 p.m. on a working day; and

(2) otherwise, on the next working day after the court receives the request.

(**CCR, ord. 26, r.** 5, sets out certain circumstances in which a warrant of execution may not be issued without the permission of the court. CCR, ord. 26, r. 17(6), applies r. 5 of that Order with necessary modifications to a warrant of possession.)

Application to Suspend Warrant of Possession

13.1 Where the court has issued a warrant of possession, the defendant may apply electronically for the suspension of the warrant, provided that:

(1) the application is made at least five clear days before the appointment for possession; and

(2) the defendant is not prevented from making such an application without the permission of the court.

13.2 The defendant may apply electronically for the suspension of the warrant, by:

(1) completing an online application for suspension at the PCOL website; and

(2) paying the appropriate fee electronically at the PCOL website or by some other means approved by Her Majesty's Courts and Tribunals Service.

13.3 When an online application for suspension is received, an acknowledgment of receipt will automatically be sent to the defendant. The acknowledgment does not constitute a notice that the online application for suspension has been served.

13.4 Where an application must be made within a specified time, it is so made if the online application for suspension is received by the court's computer system within that time. The court will keep a record, by electronic or other means, of when online applications for suspension are received.

13.5 When the court receives an online application for suspension it shall:

(1) serve a copy of the online application for suspension endorsed with the date of the hearing by post on the claimant at least two clear days before the hearing; and

(2) send the defendant notice of service and confirmation of the date of the hearing by post; provided that

(3) where either party has provided the court with an email address for service, service of the application and/or the notice of service and confirmation of the hearing date may be effected by electronic means.

Viewing the Case Record

14.1 A facility will be provided on the PCOL website for parties or their representatives to view:

(1) an electronic record of the status of claims started online, which will be reviewed and, if necessary, updated at least once each day; and

(2) all information relating to the case that has been filed by the parties electronically.

14.2 In addition, where the PCOL website specifies that the court has the facility to provide viewing of such information by electronic means, the parties or their representatives may view the following information electronically:

(1) court orders made in relation to the case; and

(2) details of progress on enforcement and subsequent orders made.

CPR Part 56 Landlord and Tenant Claims and Miscellaneous Provisions about Land

Part 56 **13.2, 42.27** [For commentary on a specific rule, please refer to the cross-references after the title of the rule.]

I LANDLORD AND TENANT CLAIMS

56.1 Scope and Interpretation

(1) In this Section of this Part 'landlord and tenant claim' means a claim under—
(a) the Landlord and Tenant Act 1927;
(b) the Leasehold Property (Repairs) Act 1938;
(c) the Landlord and Tenant Act 1954;
(d) the Landlord and Tenant Act 1985;
(e) the Landlord and Tenant Act 1987; or
(f) section 214 of the Housing Act 2004.

(2) A practice direction may set out special provisions with regard to any particular category of landlord and tenant claim.

56.2 Starting the Claim

(1) The claim must be started in the county court for the district in which the land is situated unless paragraph (2) applies or an enactment provides otherwise.

(2) Unless an enactment provides otherwise, the claim may be started in the High Court if the claimant files with the claim form a certificate stating the reasons for bringing the claim in that court verified by a statement of truth in accordance with rule 22.1(1).

(3) Practice Direction 56 refers to circumstances which may justify starting the claim in the High Court.

56.3 Claims for a New Tenancy under Section 24 and for the Termination of a Tenancy under Section 29(2) of the Landlord and Tenant Act 1954

(1) This rule applies to a claim for a new tenancy under section 24 and to a claim for the termination of a tenancy under section 29(2) of the 1954 Act.

(2) In this rule—
(a) 'the 1954 Act' means the Landlord and Tenant Act 1954;
(b) 'an unopposed claim' means a claim for a new tenancy under section 24 of the 1954 Act in circumstances where the grant of a new tenancy is not opposed;
(c) 'an opposed claim' means a claim for—
(i) a new tenancy under section 24 of the 1954 Act in circumstances where the grant of a new tenancy is opposed; or
(ii) the termination of a tenancy under section 29(2) of the 1954 Act.

(3) Where the claim is an unopposed claim—
(a) the claimant must use the Part 8 procedure, but the following rules do not apply—
(i) rule 8.5; and
(ii) rule 8.6; and
(b) [*revoked*]
(c) the court will give directions about the future management of the claim following receipt of the acknowledgment of service.

(4) Where the claim is an opposed claim the claimant must use the Part 7 procedure.
(Practice Direction 56 contains provisions about evidence, including expert evidence in opposed claims)

II MISCELLANEOUS PROVISIONS ABOUT LAND

56.4 Scope

A practice direction may set out special provisions with regard to claims under the following enactments—

(a) the Chancel Repairs Act 1932;
(b) the Leasehold Reform Act 1967;
(c) the Access to Neighbouring Land Act 1992;
(d) the Leasehold Reform, Housing and Urban Development Act 1993; and
(e) the Commonhold and Leasehold Reform Act 2002.

PD 56 Practice Direction 56 — Landlord and Tenant Claims and Miscellaneous Provisions about Land

This practice direction supplements CPR, Part 56.

PD 56 13.2 [For commentary on a specific paragraph, please refer to the cross-references after the title of the paragraph.]

SECTION I LANDLORD AND TENANT CLAIMS

1.1 In this section of this practice direction:
'the 1927 Act' means the Landlord and Tenant Act 1927;
'the 1954 Act' means the Landlord and Tenant Act 1954;
'the 1985 Act' means the Landlord and Tenant Act 1985; and
'the 1987 Act' means the Landlord and Tenant Act 1987.

Starting the Claim: Rule 56.2

para.2.1 13.2

2.1 Subject to para. 2.1A, the claimant in a landlord and tenant claim must use the Part 8 procedure as modified by Part 56 and this practice direction.

2.1A Where the landlord and tenant claim is a claim for:
(1) a new tenancy under s. 24 of the 1954 Act in circumstances where the grant of a new tenancy is opposed; or
(2) the termination of a tenancy under s. 29(2) of the 1954 Act,
the claimant must use the Part 7 procedure as modified by Part 56 and this practice direction.

2.2 Except where the county court does not have jurisdiction, landlord and tenant claims should normally be brought in the county court. Only exceptional circumstances justify starting a claim in the High Court.

2.3 If a claimant starts a claim in the High Court and the court decides that it should have been started in the county court, the court will normally either strike the claim out or transfer it to the county court on its own initiative. This is likely to result in delay and the court will normally disallow the costs of starting the claim in the High Court and of any transfer.

2.4 Circumstances which may, in an appropriate case, justify starting a claim in the High Court are if:
(1) there are complicated disputes of fact; or
(2) there are points of law of general importance.

2.5 The value of the property and the amount of any financial claim may be relevant circumstances, but these factors alone will not normally justify starting the claim in the High Court.

2.6 A landlord and tenant claim started in the High Court must be brought in the Chancery Division.

Claims for a New Tenancy under Section 24 and Termination of a Tenancy under Section 29(2) of the 1954 Act

3.1 This paragraph applies to a claim for a new tenancy under s. 24 and termination of a tenancy under s. 29(2) of the 1954 Act where r. 56.3 applies and in this paragraph:
(1) 'an unopposed claim' means a claim for a new tenancy under s. 24 of the 1954 Act in circumstances where the grant of a new tenancy is not opposed;
(2) 'an opposed claim' means a claim for:
  (a) a new tenancy under s. 24 of the 1954 Act in circumstances where the grant of a new tenancy is opposed; or
  (b) the termination of a tenancy under s. 29(2) of the 1954 Act; and
(3) 'grounds of opposition' means:
  (a) the grounds specified in s. 30(1) of the 1954 Act on which a landlord may oppose an application for a new tenancy under s. 24(1) of the 1954 Act or make an application under s. 29(2) of the 1954 Act; or

(b) any other basis on which the landlord asserts that a new tenancy ought not to be granted.

Precedence of claim forms where there is more than one application to the court under s. 24(1) or s. 29(2) of the 1954 Act

3.2 Where more than one application to the court under s. 24(1) or s. 29(2) of the 1954 Act is made, the following provisions shall apply:

(1) once an application to the court under s. 24(1) of the 1954 Act has been served on a defendant, no further application to the court in respect of the same tenancy whether under s. 24(1) or s. 29(2) of the 1954 Act may be served by that defendant without the permission of the court;

(2) if more than one application to the court under s. 24(1) of the 1954 Act in respect of the same tenancy is served on the same day, any landlord's application shall stand stayed until further order of the court;

(3) if applications to the court under both s. 24(1) and s. 29(2) of the 1954 Act in respect of the same tenancy are served on the same day, any tenant's application shall stand stayed until further order of the court; and

(4) if a defendant is served with an application under s. 29(2) of the 1954 Act ('the s. 29(2) application') which was issued at a time when an application to the court had already been made by that defendant in respect of the same tenancy under s. 24(1) of the 1954 Act ('the s. 24(1) application'), the service of the s. 29(2) application shall be deemed to be a notice under r. 7.7 requiring service or discontinuance of the s. 24(1) application within a period of 14 days after the service of the s. 29(2) application.

Defendant where the claimant is the tenant making a claim for a new tenancy under s. 24 of the 1954 Act

3.3 Where a claim for a new tenancy under s. 24 of the 1954 Act is made by a tenant, the person who, in relation to the claimant's current tenancy, is the landlord as defined in s. 44 of the 1954 Act must be a defendant.

Contents of the claim form in all cases

3.4 The claim form must contain details of:

(1) the property to which the claim relates;

(2) the particulars of the current tenancy (including date, parties and duration), the current rent (if not the original rent) and the date and method of termination;

(3) every notice or request given or made under ss. 25 or 26 of the 1954 Act; and

(4) the expiry date of:

(a) the statutory period under s. 29A(2) of the 1954 Act; or

(b) any agreed extended period made under s. 29B(1) or 29B(2) of the 1954 Act.

Claim form where the claimant is the tenant making a claim for a new tenancy under s. 24 of the 1954 Act

3.5 Where the claimant is the tenant making a claim for a new tenancy under s. 24 of the 1954 Act, in addition to the details specified in para. 3.4, the claim form must contain details of:

(1) the nature of the business carried on at the property;

(2) whether the claimant relies on s. 23(1A), 41 or 42 of the 1954 Act and, if so, the basis on which he does so;

(3) whether the claimant relies on s. 31A of the 1954 Act and, if so, the basis on which he does so;

(4) whether any, and if so what part, of the property comprised in the tenancy is occupied neither by the claimant nor by a person employed by the claimant for the purpose of the claimant's business;

(5) the claimant's proposed terms of the new tenancy; and

(6) the name and address of:

(a) anyone known to the claimant who has an interest in the reversion in the property (whether immediate or in not more than 15 years) on the termination of the claimant's current tenancy and who is likely to be affected by the grant of a new tenancy; or

(b) if the claimant does not know of anyone specified by sub-paragraph (6)(a), anyone who has a freehold interest in the property.

3.6 The claim form must be served on the persons referred to in para. 3.5(6)(a) or (b) as appropriate.

Claim form where the claimant is the landlord making a claim for a new tenancy under s. 24 of the 1954 Act

3.7 Where the claimant is the landlord making a claim for a new tenancy under s. 24 of the 1954 Act, in addition to the details specified in para. 3.4, the claim form must contain details of:

(1) the claimant's proposed terms of the new tenancy;

(2) whether the claimant is aware that the defendant's tenancy is one to which s. 32(2) of the 1954 Act applies and, if so, whether the claimant requires that any new tenancy shall be a tenancy of the whole of the property comprised in the defendant's current tenancy or just of the holding as defined by s. 23(3) of the 1954 Act; and

(3) the name and address of:

(a) anyone known to the claimant who has an interest in the reversion in the property (whether immediate or in not more than 15 years) on the termination of the claimant's current tenancy and who is likely to be affected by the grant of a new tenancy; or

(b) if the claimant does not know of anyone specified by sub-paragraph (3)(a), anyone who has a freehold interest in the property.

3.8 The claim form must be served on the persons referred to in para. 3.7(3)(a) or (b) as appropriate.

Claim form where the claimant is the landlord making an application for the termination of a tenancy under s. 29(2) of the 1954 Act

3.9 Where the claimant is the landlord making an application for the termination of a tenancy under s. 29(2) of the 1954 Act, in addition to the details specified in para. 3.4, the claim form must contain:

(1) the claimant's grounds of opposition;

(2) full details of those grounds of opposition; and

(3) the terms of a new tenancy that the claimant proposes in the event that his claim fails.

Acknowledgment of service where the claim is an unopposed claim and where the claimant is the tenant

3.10 Where the claim is an unopposed claim and the claimant is the tenant, the acknowledgment of service is to be in form N210 and must state with particulars:

(1) whether, if a new tenancy is granted, the defendant objects to any of the terms proposed by the claimant and if so:

(a) the terms to which he objects; and

(b) the terms that he proposes in so far as they differ from those proposed by the claimant;

(2) whether the defendant is a tenant under a lease having less than 15 years unexpired at the date of the termination of the claimant's current tenancy and, if so, the name and address of any person who, to the knowledge of the defendant, has an interest in the reversion in the property expectant (whether immediate or in not more than 15 years from that date) on the termination of the defendant's tenancy;

(3) the name and address of any person having an interest in the property who is likely to be affected by the grant of a new tenancy; and

(4) if the claimant's current tenancy is one to which s. 32(2) of the 1954 Act applies, whether the defendant requires that any new tenancy shall be a tenancy of the whole of the property comprised in the claimant's current tenancy.

Acknowledgment of service where the claim is an unopposed claim and the claimant is the landlord

3.11 Where the claim is an unopposed claim and the claimant is the landlord, the acknowledgment of service is to be in form N210 and must state with particulars:

(1) the nature of the business carried on at the property;

(2) if the defendant relies on s. 23(1A), 41 or 42 of the 1954 Act, the basis on which he does so;

(3) whether any, and if so what part, of the property comprised in the tenancy is occupied neither by the defendant nor by a person employed by the defendant for the purpose of the defendant's business;

(4) the name and address of:

(a) anyone known to the defendant who has an interest in the reversion in the property (whether immediate or in not more than 15 years) on the termination of the defendant's current tenancy and who is likely to be affected by the grant of a new tenancy; or

(b) if the defendant does not know of anyone specified by sub-paragraph (4)(a), anyone who has a freehold interest in the property; and

(5) whether, if a new tenancy is granted, the defendant objects to any of the terms proposed by the claimant and, if so:

(a) the terms to which he objects; and

(b) the terms that he proposes in so far as they differ from those proposed by the claimant.

Acknowledgment of service and defence where the claim is an opposed claim and where the claimant is the tenant

3.12 Where the claim is an opposed claim and the claimant is the tenant:

(1) the acknowledgment of service is to be in form N9; and

(2) in his defence the defendant must state with particulars:

(a) the defendant's grounds of opposition;

(b) full details of those grounds of opposition;

(c) whether, if a new tenancy is granted, the defendant objects to any of the terms proposed by the claimant and if so:

(i) the terms to which he objects; and

(ii) the terms that he proposes in so far as they differ from those proposed by the claimant;

(d) whether the defendant is a tenant under a lease having less than 15 years unexpired at the date of the termination of the claimant's current tenancy and, if so, the name and address of any person who, to the knowledge of the defendant, has an interest in the reversion in the property expectant (whether immediately or in not more than 15 years from that date) on the termination of the defendant's tenancy;

(e) the name and address of any person having an interest in the property who is likely to be affected by the grant of a new tenancy; and

(f) if the claimant's current tenancy is one to which s. 32(2) of the 1954 Act applies, whether the defendant requires that any new tenancy shall be a tenancy of the whole of the property comprised in the claimant's current tenancy.

Acknowledgment of service and defence where the claimant is the landlord making an application for the termination of a tenancy under s. 29(2) of the 1954 Act

3.13 Where the claim is an opposed claim and the claimant is the landlord:

(1) the acknowledgment of service is to be in form N9; and

(2) in his defence the defendant must state with particulars:

(a) whether the defendant relies on s. 23(1A), 41 or 42 of the 1954 Act and, if so, the basis on which he does so;

(b) whether the defendant relies on s. 31A of the 1954 Act and, if so, the basis on which he does so; and

(c) the terms of the new tenancy that the defendant would propose in the event that the claimant's claim to terminate the current tenancy fails.

Evidence in an unopposed claim

3.14 Where the claim is an unopposed claim, no evidence need be filed unless and until the court directs it to be filed.

Evidence in an opposed claim

3.15 Where the claim is an opposed claim, evidence (including expert evidence) must be filed by the parties as the court directs and the landlord shall be required to file his evidence first.

Grounds of opposition to be tried as a preliminary issue

3.16 Unless in the circumstances of the case it is unreasonable to do so, any grounds of opposition shall be tried as a preliminary issue.

Applications for interim rent under s. 24A to 24D of the 1954 Act

3.17 Where proceedings have already been commenced for the grant of a new tenancy or the termination of an existing tenancy, the claim for interim rent under s. 24A of the 1954 Act shall be made in those proceedings by:

(1) the claim form;

(2) the acknowledgment of service or defence; or

(3) an application on notice under Part 23.

3.18 Any application under s. 24D(3) of the 1954 Act shall be made by an application on notice under Part 23 in the original proceedings.

3.19 Where no other proceedings have been commenced for the grant of a new tenancy or termination of an existing tenancy or where such proceedings have been disposed of, an application for interim rent under s. 24A of the 1954 Act shall be made under the procedure in Part 8 and the claim form shall include details of:

(1) the property to which the claim relates;
(2) the particulars of the relevant tenancy (including date, parties and duration) and the current rent (if not the original rent);
(3) every notice or request given or made under ss. 25 or 26 of the 1954 Act;
(4) if the relevant tenancy has terminated, the date and mode of termination; and
(5) if the relevant tenancy has been terminated and the landlord has granted a new tenancy of the property to the tenant:
(a) particulars of the new tenancy (including date, parties and duration) and the rent; and
(b) in a case where s. 24C(2) of the 1954 Act applies but the claimant seeks a different rent under s. 24C(3) of that Act, particulars and matters on which the claimant relies as satisfying s. 24C(3).

Other Claims under Part II of the 1954 Act

4.1 The mesne landlord to whose consent a claim for the determination of any question arising under para. 4(3) of sch. 6 to the 1954 Act shall be made a defendant to the claim.

4.2 If any dispute as to the rateable value of any holding has been referred under s. 37(5) of the 1954 Act to the Commissioners for HM Revenue and Customs for decision by a valuation officer, any document purporting to be a statement of the valuation officer of his decision is admissible as evidence of the matters contained in it.

Claim for Compensation for Improvements under Part I of the 1927 Act

5.1 This paragraph applies to a claim under Part I of the 1927 Act.

The claim form

5.2 The claim form must include details of:

(1) the nature of the claim or the matter to be determined;
(2) the property to which the claim relates;
(3) the nature of the business carried on at the property;
(4) particulars of the lease or agreement for the tenancy including:
(a) the names and addresses of the parties to the lease or agreement;
(b) its duration;
(c) the rent payable;
(d) details of any assignment or other devolution of the lease or agreement;
(5) the date and mode of termination of the tenancy;
(6) if the claimant has left the property, the date on which he did so;
(7) particulars of the improvement or proposed improvement to which the claim relates; and
(8) if the claim is for payment of compensation, the amount claimed;

5.3 The court will fix a date for a hearing when it issues the claim form.

Defendant

5.4 The claimant's immediate landlord must be a defendant to the claim.

5.5 The defendant must immediately serve a copy of the claim form and any document served with it and of his acknowledgment of service on his immediate landlord. If the person so served is not the freeholder, he must serve a copy of these documents on his landlord and so on from landlord to landlord.

Evidence

5.6 Evidence need not be filed—with the claim form or acknowledgment of service.

Certification under section 3 of the 1927 Act

5.7 If the court intends to certify under s. 3 of the 1927 Act that an improvement is a proper improvement or has been duly executed, it shall do so by way of an order.

Compensation under section 1 or 8 of the 1927 Act

para.5.8 **93.63** para.5.9 **93.63**

5.8 A claim under s. 1(1) or 8(1) of the 1927 Act must be in writing, signed by the claimant, his solicitor or agent and include details of:

(1) the name and address of the claimant and of the landlord against whom the claim is made;
(2) the property to which the claim relates;
(3) the nature of the business carried on at the property;
(4) a concise statement of the nature of the claim;
(5) particulars of the improvement, including the date when it was completed and costs; and
(6) the amount claimed.

5.9 A mesne landlord must immediately serve a copy of the claim on his immediate superior landlord. If the person so served is not the freeholder, he must serve a copy of the document on his landlord and so on from landlord to landlord.

(Paragraphs 5.8 and 5.9 provide the procedure for making claims under s. 1(1) and 8(1) of the 1927 Act—these 'claims' do not, at this stage, relate to proceedings before the court.)

Transfer to Leasehold Valuation Tribunal under 1985 Act

6.1 If a question is ordered to be transferred to a leasehold valuation tribunal for determination under s. 31C of the 1985 Act the court will:

(1) send notice of the transfer to all parties to the claim; and
(2) send to the leasehold valuation tribunal:
  (a) copies certified by the district judge of all entries in the records of the court relating to the question;
  (b) the order of transfer; and
  (c) all documents filed in the claim relating to the question.

(paragraph 6.1 no longer applies to proceedings in England but continues to apply to proceedings in Wales.)

Claim to Enforce Obligation under Part I of the 1987 Act

7.1 A copy of the notice served under s. 19(2)(a) of the 1987 Act must accompany the claim form seeking an order under s. 19(1) of that Act.

Claim for Acquisition Order under Section 28 of the 1987 Act

8.1 This paragraph applies to a claim for an acquisition order under s. 28 of the 1987 Act.

Claim form

8.2 The claim form must:

(1) identify the property to which the claim relates and give details to show that s. 25 of the 1987 Act applies;
(2) give details of the claimants to show that they constitute the requisite majority of qualifying tenants;
(3) state the names and addresses of the claimants and of the landlord of the property, or, if the landlord cannot be found or his identity ascertained, the steps taken to find him or ascertain his identity;
(4) state the name and address of:
  (a) the person nominated by the claimants for the purposes of part III of the 1987 Act; and
  (b) every person known to the claimants who is likely to be affected by the application, including (but not limited to), the other tenants of flats contained in the property (whether or not they could have made a claim), any mortgagee or superior landlord of the landlord, and any tenants' association (within the meaning of s. 29 of the 1985 Act); and
(5) state the grounds of the claim.

Notice under section 27

8.3 A copy of the notice served on the landlord under s. 27 of the 1987 Act must accompany the claim form unless the court has dispensed with the requirement to serve a notice under s. 27(3) of the 1987 Act.

Defendants

8.4 The landlord of the property (and the nominated person, if he is not a claimant) must be defendants.

Service

8.5 A copy of the claim form must be served on each of the persons named by the claimant under para. 8.2(4)(b) together with a notice that he may apply to be made a party.

Payment into court by nominated person

8.6 If the nominated person pays money into court in accordance with an order under s. 33(1) of the 1987 Act, he must file a copy of the certificate of the surveyor selected under s. 33(2)(a) of that Act.

Claim for an Order Varying Leases under the 1987 Act

9.1 This paragraph applies to a claim for an order under s. 38 or s. 40 of the 1987 Act.

Claim form

9.2 The claim form must state:

(1) the name and address of the claimant and of the other current parties to the lease or leases to which the claim relates;

(2) the date of the lease or leases, the property to which they relate, any relevant terms and the variation sought;

(3) the name and address of every person known to the claimant who is likely to be affected by the claim, including (but not limited to), the other tenants of flats contained in premises of which the relevant property forms a part, any previous parties to the lease, any mortgagee or superior landlord of the landlord, any mortgagee of the claimant and any tenants' association (within the meaning of s. 29 of the 1985 Act); and

(4) the grounds of the claim.

Defendants

9.3 The other current parties to the lease must be defendants.

Service

9.4 A copy of the claim form must be served on each of the persons named under para. 9.2(3).

9.5 If the defendant knows of or has reason to believe that another person or persons are likely to be affected by the variation, he must serve a copy of the claim form on those persons, together with a notice that they may apply to be made a party.

Defendant's application to vary other leases

9.6 If a defendant wishes to apply to vary other leases under s. 36 of the 1987 Act:

(1) he must make the application in his acknowledgment of service;

(2) paras 9.2 to 9.5 apply as if the defendant were the claimant; and

(3) Part 20 does not apply.

(Paragraphs 9.1 to 9.6 no longer apply to proceedings in England but continue to apply to proceedings in Wales.)

Service of Documents in Claims under the 1987 Act

10.1 All documents must be served by the parties.

10.2 If a notice is to be served in or before a claim under the 1987 Act, it must be served:

(1) in accordance with s. 54, and

(2) in the case of service on a landlord, at the address given under s. 48(1).

SECTION II MISCELLANEOUS PROVISIONS ABOUT LAND

Access to Neighbouring Land Act 1992

11.1 The claimant must use the Part 8 procedure.

11.2 The claim form must set out:
(1) details of the dominant and servient land involved and whether the dominant land includes or consists of residential property;
(2) the work required;
(3) why entry to the servient land is required with plans (if applicable);
(4) the names and addresses of the persons who will carry out the work;
(5) the proposed date when the work will be carried out; and
(6) what (if any) provision has been made by way of insurance in the event of possible injury to persons or damage to property arising out of the proposed work.

11.3 The owner and occupier of the servient land must be defendants to the claim.

Chancel Repairs Act 1932

12.1 The claimant in a claim to recover the sum required to put a chancel in proper repair must use the Part 8 procedure.

12.2 A notice to repair under s. 2 of the Chancel Repairs Act 1932 must:
(1) state:
(a) the responsible authority by whom the notice is given;
(b) the chancel alleged to be in need of repair;
(c) the repairs alleged to be necessary; and
(d) the grounds on which the person to whom the notice is addressed is alleged to be liable to repair the chancel; and
(2) call upon the person to whom the notice is addressed to put the chancel in proper repair.

12.3 The notice must be served in accordance with Part 6.

Leasehold Reform Act 1967

13.1 In this paragraph a section or schedule referred to by number means the section or schedule so numbered in the Leasehold Reform Act 1967.

13.2 If a tenant of a house and premises wishes to pay money into court under ss. 11(4), 13(1) or 13(3):
(1) he must file in the office of the appropriate court an application notice containing or accompanied by evidence stating:
(a) the reasons for the payment into court,
(b) the house and premises to which the payment relates;
(c) the name and address of the landlord; and
(d) so far as they are known to the tenant, the name and address of every person who is or may be interested in or entitled to the money;
(2) on the filing of the witness statement the tenant must pay the money into court and the court will send notice of the payment to the landlord and every person whose name and address are given in the witness statement;
(3) any subsequent payment into court by the landlord under s. 11(4) must be made to the credit of the same account as the payment into court by the tenant and sub-paras (1) and (2) will apply to the landlord as if he were a tenant;
(4) the appropriate court for the purposes of sub-para. (1)(a) is the county court for the district in which the property is situated or, if the payment into court is made by reason of a notice under s. 13(3), any other county court as specified in the notice.

13.3 If an order is made transferring an application to a leasehold valuation tribunal under s. 21(3), the court will:
(1) send notice of the transfer to all parties to the application; and
(2) send to the tribunal copies of the order of transfer and all documents filed in the proceedings.
(paragraph 13.3 no longer applies to proceedings in England but continues to apply to proceedings in Wales.)

13.4 A claim under s. 17 or 18 for an order for possession of a house and premises must be made in accordance with Part 55.

13.5 In a claim under s. 17 or 18, the defendant must:
(1) immediately after being served with the claim form, serve on every person in occupation of the property or part of it under an immediate or derivative subtenancy, a notice

informing him of the claim and of his right under para. 3(4) of sch. 2 [to] take part in the hearing of the claim with the permission of the court; and

(2) within 14 days after being served with the claim form, file a defence stating the ground, if any, on which he intends to oppose the claim and giving particulars of every such subtenancy.

13.6 An application made to the High Court under s. 19 or 27 shall be assigned to the Chancery Division.

Leasehold Reform, Housing and Urban Development Act 1993

14.1 In this paragraph:

(1) 'the 1993 Act' means the Leasehold Reform, Housing and Urban Development Act 1993; and

(2) a section or schedule referred to by number means the section or schedule so numbered in the 1993 Act.

14.2 If a claim is made under s. 23(1) by a person other than the reversioner:

(1) on the issue of the claim form in accordance with Part 8, the claimant must send a copy to the reversioner; and

(2) the claimant must promptly inform the reversioner either:

(a) of the court's decision; or

(b) that the claim has been withdrawn.

14.3 Where an application is made under s. 26(1) or (2) or s. 50(1) or (2):

(1) it must be made by the issue of a claim form in accordance with the Part 8 procedure which need not be served on any other party; and

(2) the court may grant or refuse the application or give directions for its future conduct, including the addition as defendants of such persons as appear to have an interest in it.

14.4 An application under s. 26(3) must be made by the issue of a claim form in accordance with the Part 8 procedure and:

(1) the claimants must serve the claim form on any person who they know or have reason to believe is a relevant landlord, giving particulars of the claim and the hearing date and informing that person of his right to be joined as a party to the claim;

(2) the landlord whom it is sought to appoint as the reversioner must be a defendant, and must file an acknowledgment of service;

(3) a person on whom notice is served under sub-para. (1) must be joined as a defendant to the claim if he gives notice in writing to the court of his wish to be added as a party, and the court will notify all other parties of the addition.

14.5 If a person wishes to pay money into court under s. 27(3), s. 51(3) or para. 4 of sch. 8:

(1) he must file in the office of the appropriate court an application notice containing or accompanied by evidence stating:

(a) the reasons for the payment into court,

(b) the interest or interests in the property to which the payment relates or where the payment into court is made under s. 51(3), the flat to which it relates;

(c) details of any vesting order;

(d) the name and address of the landlord; and

(e) so far as they are known to the tenant, the name and address of every person who is or may be interested in or entitled to the money;

(2) on the filing of the witness statement the money must be paid into court and the court will send notice of the payment to the landlord and every person whose name and address are given in the witness statement;

(3) any subsequent payment into court by the landlord must be made to the credit of the same account as the earlier payment into court;

(4) the appropriate court for the purposes of sub-para. (1) is:

(a) where a vesting order has been made, the county court that made the order; or

(b) where no such order has been made, the county court in whose district the property is situated.

14.6 If an order is made transferring an application to a leasehold valuation tribunal under s. 91(4), the court will:

(1) send notice of the transfer to all parties to the application; and

(2) send to the tribunal copies of the order of transfer and all documents filed in the proceedings.

(paragraph 14.6 no longer applies to proceedings in England but continues to apply to proceedings in Wales.)

14.7 If a relevant landlord acts independently under sch. 1, para. 7, he is entitled to require any party to claims under the 1993 Act (as described in para. 7(1)(b) of sch. 1) to supply him, on payment of the reasonable costs of copying, with copies of all documents which that party has served on the other parties to the claim.

Transfer to Leasehold Valuation Tribunal under the Commonhold and Leasehold Reform Act 2002

15.1 If a question is ordered to be transferred to a leasehold valuation tribunal for determination under the Commonhold and Leasehold Reform Act 2002, sch. 12, para. 3, the court will:

(1) send notice of the transfer to all parties to the claim; and

(2) send to the leasehold valuation tribunal:

(a) the order of transfer; and

(b) all documents filed in the claim relating to the question.

(paragraph 15.1 applies to proceedings in England but does not apply to proceedings in Wales.)

CPR Part 57 Probate and Inheritance

Part 57 **11.7, 74.5** [For commentary on a specific rule, please refer to the cross-references after the title of the rule.]

57.1 Scope of This Part and Definitions

(1) This Part contains rules about—
- (a) probate claims;
- (b) claims for the rectification of wills;
- (c) claims and applications to—
  - (i) substitute another person for a personal representative; or
  - (ii) remove a personal representative; and
- (d) claims under the Inheritance (Provision for Family and Dependants) Act 1975.

(2) In this Part:
- (a) 'probate claim' means a claim for—
  - (i) the grant of probate of the will, or letters of administration of the estate, of a deceased person;
  - (ii) the revocation of such a grant; or
  - (iii) a decree pronouncing for or against the validity of an alleged will;

  not being a claim which is non-contentious (or common form) probate business;
  (Section 128 of the Senior Courts Act 1981 defines non-contentious (or common form) probate business.)
- (b) 'relevant office' means—
  - (i) in the case of High Court proceedings in a Chancery district registry, that registry;
  - (ii) in the case of any other High Court proceedings, Chancery Chambers at the Royal Courts of Justice, Strand, London, WC2A 2LL; and
  - (iii) in the case of county court proceedings, the office of the county court in question;
- (c) 'testamentary document' means a will, a draft of a will, written instructions for a will made by or at the request of, or under the instructions of, the testator, and any document purporting to be evidence of the contents, or to be a copy, of a will which is alleged to have been lost or destroyed;
- (d) 'will' includes a codicil.

I PROBATE CLAIMS

57.2 General

r.57.2(3) **11.6, 11.7**

(1) This Section contains rules about probate claims.
(2) Probate claims in the High Court are assigned to the Chancery Division.
(3) Probate claims in the county court must only be brought in—

(a) a county court where there is also a Chancery district registry; or
(b) the Central London County Court.

(4) All probate claims are allocated to the multi-track.

57.3 How to Start a Probate Claim

A probate claim must be commenced—

(a) in the relevant office; and
(b) using the procedure in Part 7.

57.4 Acknowledgment of Service and Defence

r.57.4 **18.2** r.57.4(3) **18.2**

(1) A defendant who is served with a claim form must file an acknowledgment of service.

(2) Subject to paragraph (3), the period for filing an acknowledgment of service is—
(a) if the defendant is served with a claim form which states that particulars of claim are to follow, 28 days after service of the particulars of claim; and
(b) in any other case, 28 days after service of the claim form.

(3) If the claim form is served out of the jurisdiction under rule 6.32 or 6.33 the period for filing an acknowledgment of service is 14 days longer than the relevant period specified in rule 6.35 or Practice Direction 6B.

(4) Rule 15.4 (which provides the period for filing a defence) applies as if the words 'under Part 10' were omitted from rule 15.4(1)(b).

57.5 Lodging of Testamentary Documents and Filing of Evidence about Testamentary Documents

r.57.5(5) **15.58**

(1) Any testamentary document of the deceased person in the possession or control of any party must be lodged with the court.

(2) Unless the court directs otherwise, the testamentary documents must be lodged in the relevant office—
(a) by the claimant when the claim form is issued; and
(b) by a defendant when he acknowledges service.

(3) The claimant and every defendant who acknowledges service of the claim form must in written evidence—
(a) describe any testamentary document of the deceased of which he has any knowledge or, if he does not know of any such testamentary document, state that fact, and
(b) if any testamentary document of which he has knowledge is not in his possession or under his control, give the name and address of the person in whose possession or under whose control it is or, if he does not know the name or address of that person, state that fact.

(A specimen form for the written evidence about testamentary documents is annexed to Practice Direction 57.)

(4) Unless the court directs otherwise, the written evidence required by paragraph (3) must be filed in the relevant office—
(a) by the claimant, when the claim form is issued; and
(b) by a defendant when he acknowledges service.

(5) Except with the permission of the court, a party shall not be allowed to inspect the testamentary documents or written evidence lodged or filed by any other party until he himself has lodged his testamentary documents and filed his evidence.

(6) The provisions of paragraphs (2) and (4) may be modified by a practice direction under this Part.

57.6 Revocation of Existing Grant

(1) In a probate claim which seeks the revocation of a grant of probate or letters of administration every person who is entitled, or claims to be entitled, to administer the estate under that grant must be made a party to the claim.

(2) If the claimant is the person to whom the grant was made, he must lodge the probate or letters of administration in the relevant office when the claim form is issued.

(3) If a defendant has the probate or letters of administration under his control, he must lodge it in the relevant office when he acknowledges service.
(4) Paragraphs (2) and (3) do not apply where the grant has already been lodged at the court, which in this paragraph includes the Principal Registry of the Family Division or a district probate registry.

57.7 Contents of Statements of Case

r.57.7(1) **23.6** r.57.7(5) **68.37**

(1) The claim form must contain a statement of the nature of the interest of the claimant and of each defendant in the estate.
(2) If a party disputes another party's interest in the estate he must state this in his statement of case and set out his reasons.
(3) Any party who contends that at the time when a will was executed the testator did not know of and approve its contents must give particulars of the facts and matters relied on.
(4) Any party who wishes to contend that—
(a) a will was not duly executed;
(b) at the time of the execution of a will the testator lacked testamentary capacity; or
(c) the execution of a will was obtained by undue influence or fraud,
must set out the contention specifically and give particulars of the facts and matters relied on.
(5) (a) A defendant may give notice in his defence that he does not raise any positive case, but insists on the will being proved in solemn form and, for that purpose, will cross-examine the witnesses who attested the will.
(b) If a defendant gives such a notice, the court will not make an order for costs against him unless it considers that there was no reasonable ground for opposing the will.

57.8 Counterclaim

(1) A defendant who contends that he has any claim or is entitled to any remedy relating to the grant of probate of the will, or letters of administration of the estate, of the deceased person must serve a counterclaim making that contention.
(2) If the claimant fails to serve particulars of claim within the time allowed, the defendant may, with the permission of the court, serve a counterclaim and the probate claim shall then proceed as if the counterclaim were the particulars of claim.

57.9 Probate Counterclaim in Other Proceedings

(1) In this rule 'probate counterclaim' means a counterclaim in any claim other than a probate claim by which the defendant claims any such remedy as is mentioned in rule 57.1(2)(a).
(2) Subject to the following paragraphs of this rule, this Part shall apply with the necessary modifications to a probate counterclaim as it applies to a probate claim.
(3) A probate counterclaim must contain a statement of the nature of the interest of each of the parties in the estate of the deceased to which the probate counterclaim relates.
(4) Unless an application notice is issued within 7 days after the service of a probate counterclaim for an order under rule 3.1(2)(e) or 3.4 for the probate counterclaim to be dealt with in separate proceedings or to be struck out, and the application is granted, the court shall order the transfer of the proceedings to either—
(a) the Chancery Division (if it is not already assigned to that Division) and to either the Royal Courts of Justice or a Chancery district registry (if it is not already proceeding in one of those places); or
(b) if the county court has jurisdiction, to a county court where there is also a Chancery district registry or the Central London County Court.
(5) If an order is made that a probate counterclaim be dealt with in separate proceedings, the order shall order the transfer of the probate counterclaim as required under paragraph (4).

57.10 Failure to Acknowledge Service or to File a Defence

r.57.10(1) **20.2**

(1) A default judgment cannot be obtained in a probate claim and rule 10.2 and Part 12 do not apply.
(2) If any of several defendants fails to acknowledge service the claimant may—

(a) after the time for acknowledging service has expired; and
(b) upon filing written evidence of service of the claim form and (if no particulars of claim were contained in or served with the claim form) the particulars of claim on that defendant;

proceed with the probate claim as if that defendant had acknowledged service.

(3) If no defendant acknowledges service or files a defence then, unless on the application of the claimant the court orders the claim to be discontinued, the claimant may, after the time for acknowledging service or for filing a defence (as the case may be) has expired, apply to the court for an order that the claim is to proceed to trial.

(4) When making an application under paragraph (3) the claimant must file written evidence of service of the claim form and (if no particulars of claim were contained in or served with the claim form) the particulars of claim on each of the defendants.

(5) Where the court makes an order under paragraph (3), it may direct that the claim be tried on written evidence.

57.11 Discontinuance and Dismissal

(1) Part 38 does not apply to probate claims.

(2) At any stage of a probate claim the court, on the application of the claimant or of any defendant who has acknowledged service, may order that—
(a) the claim be discontinued or dismissed on such terms as to costs or otherwise as it thinks just; and
(b) a grant of probate of the will, or letters of administration of the estate, of the deceased person be made to the person entitled to the grant.

II RECTIFICATION OF WILLS

57.12

(1) This Section contains rules about claims for the rectification of a will.

(Section 20 of the Administration of Justice Act 1982 provides for rectification of a will. Additional provisions are contained in rule 55 of the Non-Contentious Probate Rules 1987.)

(2) Every personal representative of the estate shall be joined as a party.

(3) Practice Direction 57 makes provision for lodging the grant of probate or letters of administration with the will annexed in a claim under this Section.

III SUBSTITUTION AND REMOVAL OF PERSONAL REPRESENTATIVES

57.13

r.57.13 74.5

(1) This Section contains rules about claims and applications for substitution or removal of a personal representative.

(2) Claims under this Section must be brought in the High Court and are assigned to the Chancery Division.

(Section 50 of the Administration of Justice Act 1985 gives the High Court power to appoint a substitute for, or to remove, a personal representative.)

(3) Every personal representative of the estate shall be joined as a party.

(4) Practice Direction 57 makes provision for lodging the grant of probate or letters of administration in a claim under this Section.

(5) If substitution or removal of a personal representative is sought by application in existing proceedings, this rule shall apply with references to claims being read as if they referred to applications.

IV CLAIMS UNDER THE INHERITANCE (PROVISION FOR FAMILY AND DEPENDANTS) ACT 1975

57.14 Scope of This Section

This Section contains rules about claims under the Inheritance (Provision for Family and Dependants) Act 1975 ('the Act').

57.15 Proceedings in the High Court

(1) Proceedings in the High Court under the Act shall be issued in either—
 (a) the Chancery Division; or
 (b) the Family Division.

(2) The Civil Procedure Rules apply to proceedings under the Act which are brought in the Family Division, except that the provisions of the Family Proceedings Rules 1991 relating to the drawing up and service of orders apply instead of the provisions in Part 40 and Practice Direction 40B.

57.16 Procedure for Claims under Section 1 of the Act

(1) A claim under section 1 of the Act must be made by issuing a claim form in accordance with Part 8.

(2) Rule 8.3 (acknowledgment of service) and rule 8.5 (filing and serving written evidence) apply as modified by paragraphs (3) to (5) of this rule.

(3) The written evidence filed and served by the claimant with the claim form must have exhibited to it an official copy of—
 (a) the grant of probate or letters of administration in respect of the deceased's estate; and
 (b) every testamentary document in respect of which probate or letters of administration were granted.

(4) Subject to paragraph (4A), the time within which a defendant must file and serve—
 (a) an acknowledgment of service; and
 (b) any written evidence,
 is not more than 21 days after service of the claim form on him.

(4A) If the claim form is served out of the jurisdiction under rule 6.32 or 6.33, the period for filing an acknowledgment of service and any written evidence is 7 days longer than the relevant period specified in rule 6.35 or Practice Direction 6B.

(5) A defendant who is a personal representative of the deceased must file and serve written evidence, which must include the information required by Practice Direction 57.

PD 57 Practice Direction 57 — Probate

This practice direction supplements CPR, Part 57.
PD 57 11.7

I PROBATE CLAIMS

General

1.1 This Section of this practice direction applies to contentious probate claims.
1.2 The rules and procedure relating to non-contentious probate proceedings (also known as 'common form') are the Non-Contentious Probate Rules 1987 (SI 1987/2024) as amended.

How to Start a Probate Claim

2.1 A claim form and all subsequent court documents relating to a probate claim must be marked at the top 'In the estate of [name] deceased (Probate)'.
2.2 The claim form must be issued out of:
(1) Chancery Chambers at the Royal Courts of Justice; or
(2) one of the Chancery district registries; or
(3) if the claim is suitable to be heard in the county court:
(a) a county court in a place where there is also a Chancery district registry; or
(b) the Central London County Court.
There are Chancery district registries at Birmingham, Bristol, Caernarfon, Cardiff, Leeds, Liverpool, Manchester, Mold, Newcastle upon Tyne and Preston.
(Section 32 of the County Courts Act 1984 identifies which probate claims may be heard in a county court.)
2.3 When the claim form is issued, the relevant office will send a notice to Leeds District Probate Registry, Coronet House, Queen Street, Leeds LS1 2BA, DX 26451 Leeds (Park Square), telephone (0113)2431505, requesting that all testamentary documents, grants of representation and other relevant documents currently held at any probate registry are sent to the relevant office.
2.4 The commencement of a probate claim will, unless a court otherwise directs, prevent any grant of probate or letters of administration being made until the probate claim has been disposed of. (Rule 45 of the Non-Contentious Probate Rules 1987 makes provision for notice of the probate claim to be given, and s. 117 of the Senior Courts Act 1981 for the grant of letters of administration pending the determination of a probate claim. Paragraph 8 of this practice direction makes provision about an application for such a grant.)

Testamentary Documents and Evidence about Testamentary Documents

3.1 Unless the court orders otherwise, if a testamentary document is held by the court (whether it was lodged by a party or it was previously held at a probate registry) when the claim has been disposed of the court will send it to the Leeds District Probate Registry.
3.2 The written evidence about testamentary documents required by this Part:
(1) should be in the form annexed to this practice direction; and
(2) must be signed by the party personally and not by his solicitor or other representative (except that if the party is a child or protected party the written evidence must be signed by his litigation friend).
3.3 In a case in which there is urgent need to commence a probate claim (for example, in order to be able to apply immediately for the appointment of an administrator pending the determination of the claim) and it is not possible for the claimant to lodge the testamentary documents or to file the evidence about testamentary documents in the relevant office at the same time as the claim form is to be issued, the court may direct that the claimant shall be allowed to issue the claim form upon his giving an undertaking to the court to lodge the documents and file the evidence within such time as the court shall specify.

Case Management

4 In giving case management directions in a probate claim the court will give consideration to the questions:
(1) whether any person who may be affected by the claim and who is not joined as a party should be joined as a party or given notice of the claim, whether under r. 19.8A or otherwise; and
(2) whether to make a representation order under r. 19.6 or r. 19.7.

Summary Judgment

5.1 If an order pronouncing for a will in solemn form is sought on an application for summary judgment, the evidence in support of the application must include written evidence proving due execution of the will.
5.2 If a defendant has given notice in his defence under r. 57.7(5) that he raises no positive case but:
(1) he insists that the will be proved in solemn form; and
(2) for that purpose he will cross-examine the witnesses who attested the will,
any application by the claimant for summary judgment is subject to the right of that defendant to require those witnesses to attend court for cross-examination.

Settlement of a Probate Claim

6.1 If at any time the parties agree to settle a probate claim, the court may:
(1) order the trial of the claim on written evidence, which will lead to a grant in solemn form;
(2) order that the claim be discontinued or dismissed under r. 57.11, which will lead to a grant in common form; or
(3) pronounce for or against the validity of one or more wills under s. 49 of the Administration of Justice Act 1985.
(For a form of order which is also applicable to discontinuance and which may be adapted as appropriate, see PF 38 CH.)
(Section 49 of the Administration of Justice Act 1985 permits a probate claim to be compromised without a trial if every 'relevant beneficiary', as defined in that section, has consented to the proposed order. It is only available in the High Court.)
6.2 Applications under s. 49 of the Administration of Justice Act 1985 may be heard by a master or district judge and must be supported by written evidence identifying the relevant beneficiaries and exhibiting the written consent of each of them. The written evidence of testamentary documents required by r. 57.5 will still be necessary.

Application for an Order to Bring in a Will, etc.

7.1 Any party applying for an order under s. 122 of the Senior Courts Act 1981 ('the 1981 Act') must serve the application notice on the person against whom the order is sought. (Section 122 of the 1981 Act empowers the court to order a person to attend court for examination, and to answer questions and bring in documents, if there are reasonable grounds for believing that such person has knowledge of a testamentary document. Rule 50(1) of the Non-Contentious Probate Rules 1987 makes similar provision where a probate claim has not been commenced.)
7.2 An application for the issue of a witness summons under s. 123 of the 1981 Act:
(1) may be made without notice; and
(2) must be supported by written evidence setting out the grounds of the application.
(Section 123 of the 1981 Act empowers the court, where it appears that any person has in his possession, custody or power a testamentary document, to issue a witness summons ordering such person to bring in that document. Rule 50(2) of the Non-Contentious Probate Rules makes similar provision where a probate claim has not been commenced.)
7.3 An application under s. 122 or 123 of the 1981 Act should be made to a master or district judge.
7.4 A person against whom a witness summons is issued under s. 123 of the 1981 Act who denies that the testamentary document referred to in the witness summons is in his possession or under his control may file written evidence to that effect.

Administration Pending the Determination of a Probate Claim

8.1 An application under s. 117 of the Senior Courts Act 1981 for an order for the grant of administration pending the determination of a probate claim should be made by application notice in the probate claim.

8.2 If an order for a grant of administration is made under s. 117 of the 1981 Act:

(1) Rules 69.4 to 69.7 shall apply as if the administrator were a receiver appointed by the court;

(2) if the court allows the administrator remuneration under r. 69.7, it may make an order under s. 117(3) of the 1981 Act assigning the remuneration out of the estate of the deceased; and

(3) every application relating to the conduct of the administration shall be made by application notice in the probate claim.

8.3 An order under s. 117 may be made by a master or district judge.

8.4 If an order is made under s. 117 an application for the grant of letters of administration should be made to the Principal Registry of the Family Division, First Avenue House, 42–49 High Holborn, London WC1V 6NP.

8.5 The appointment of an administrator to whom letters of administration are granted following an order under s. 117 will cease automatically when a final order in the probate claim is made but will continue pending any appeal.

II RECTIFICATION OF WILLS

Scope of This Section

9 This Section of this practice direction applies to claims for the rectification of a will.

Lodging the Grant

10.1 If the claimant is the person to whom the grant was made in respect of the will of which rectification is sought, he must, unless the court orders otherwise, lodge the probate or letters of administration with the will annexed with the court when the claim form is issued.

10.2 If a defendant has the probate or letters of administration in his possession or under his control, he must, unless the court orders otherwise, lodge it in the relevant office within 14 days after the service of the claim form on him.

Orders

11 A copy of every order made for the rectification of a will shall be sent to the Principal Registry of the Family Division for filing, and a memorandum of the order shall be endorsed on, or permanently annexed to, the grant under which the estate is administered.

III SUBSTITUTION AND REMOVAL OF PERSONAL REPRESENTATIVES

Scope of This Section

12 This Section of this practice direction applies to claims and applications for substitution or removal of a personal representative. If substitution or removal of a personal representative is sought by application in existing proceedings, this Section shall apply with references to the claim, claim form and claimant being read as if they referred to the application, application notice and applicant respectively.

Starting the Claim

13.1 The claim form must be accompanied by:

(1) either—

(a) a sealed or certified copy of the grant of probate or letters of administration, or

(b) where the claim is to substitute or remove an executor and is made before a grant of probate has been issued, the original or, if the original is not available, a copy of the will; and

(2) written evidence containing the grounds of the claim and the following information so far as it is known to the claimant:

(a) brief details of the property comprised in the estate, with an approximate estimate of its capital value and any income that is received from it;

(b) brief details of the liabilities of the estate;
(c) the names and addresses of the persons who are in possession of the documents relating to the estate;
(d) the names of the beneficiaries and their respective interests in the estate; and
(e) the name, address and occupation of any proposed substituted personal representative;

13.2 If the claim is for the appointment of a substituted personal representative, the claim form must be accompanied by:
(1) a signed or (in the case of the Public Trustee or a corporation) sealed consent to act; and
(2) written evidence as to the fitness of the proposed substituted personal representative, if an individual, to act.

Production of the Grant

14.1 On the hearing of the claim the personal representative must produce to the court the grant of representation to the deceased's estate.

14.2 If an order is made substituting or removing the personal representative, the grant (together with a sealed copy of the order) must be sent to and remain in the custody of the Principal Registry of the Family Division until a memorandum of the order has been endorsed on or permanently annexed to the grant.

14.3 Where the claim is to substitute or remove an executor and the claim is made before a grant of probate has been issued, paras 14.1 and 14.2 do not apply. Where in such a case an order is made substituting or removing an executor a sealed copy of the order must be sent to the Principal Registry of the Family Division where it will be recorded and retained pending any application for a grant. An order sent to the Principal Registry in accordance with this paragraph must be accompanied by a note of the full name and date of death of the deceased, if it is not apparent on the face of the order.

IV CLAIMS UNDER THE INHERITANCE (PROVISION FOR FAMILY AND DEPENDANTS) ACT 1975

Acknowledgment of Service by Personal Representatives: Rule 57.16(4)

15 Where a defendant who is a personal representative wishes to remain neutral in relation to the claim, and agrees to abide by any decision which the court may make, he should state this in Section A of the acknowledgment of service form.

Written Evidence of Personal Representative: Rule 57.16(5)

16 The written evidence filed by a defendant who is a personal representative must state to the best of that person's ability:
(1) full details of the value of the deceased's net estate, as defined in s. 25(1) of the Act;
(2) the person or classes of persons beneficially interested in the estate, and:
(a) the names and (unless they are parties to the claim) addresses of all living beneficiaries; and
(b) the value of their interests in the estate so far as they are known.
(3) whether any living beneficiary (and if so, naming him) is a child or a person who lacks capacity (within the meaning of the Mental Capacity Act 2005); and
(4) any facts which might affect the exercise of the court's powers under the Act.

Separate Representation of Claimants

17 If a claim is made jointly by two or more claimants, and it later appears that any of the claimants have a conflict of interests:
(1) any claimant may choose to be represented at any hearing by separate solicitors or counsel, or may appear in person; and
(2) if the court considers that claimants who are represented by the same solicitors or counsel *ought to be separately represented*, it may adjourn the application until they are.

Production of the Grant

18.1 On the hearing of a claim the personal representative must produce to the court the original grant of representation to the deceased's estate.

18.2 If the court makes an order under the Act, the original grant (together with a sealed copy of the order) must be sent to the Principal Registry of the Family Division for a memorandum of the order to be endorsed on or permanently annexed to the grant in accordance with s. 19(3) of the Act.

18.3 Every final order embodying terms of compromise made in proceedings under the Act, whether made with or without a hearing, must contain a direction that a memorandum of the order shall be endorsed on or permanently annexed to the probate or letters of administration and a copy of the order shall be sent to the Principal Registry of the Family Division with the relevant grant of probate or letters of administration for endorsement.

ANNEX A
FORM OF WITNESS STATEMENT OR AFFIDAVIT ABOUT TESTAMENTARY DOCUMENTS (CPR, RULE 57.5)

[*Title of the claim*]

I [*name and address*] the claimant/defendant in this claim state [on oath] that I have no knowledge of any document:

(1) being or purported to be or having the form or effect of a will or codicil of [*name of deceased*] whose estate is the subject of this claim;

(2) being or purporting to be a draft or written instructions for any such will or codicil made by or at the request of or under the instructions of the deceased;

(3) being or purporting to be evidence of the contents or a copy of any such will or codicil which is alleged to have been lost or destroyed, except [*describe any testamentary document of the deceased, and if any such document is not in your control, give the name and address of the person who you believe has possession or control of it, or state that you do not know the name and address of that person*].

[I believe that the facts stated in this witness statement are true] [*or jurat for affidavit*]

[*NOTE: 'testamentary document' is defined in CPR, r. 57.1.*]

CPR Part 58 Commercial Court

Part 58 2.17, 2.18, 11.7, 74.5 [For commentary on a specific rule, please refer to the cross-references after the title of the rule.]

58.1 Scope of This Part and Interpretation

r.58.1 2.17 r.58.1(2) 11.6, 11.7

(1) This Part applies to claims in the Commercial Court of the Queen's Bench Division.
(2) In this Part and Practice Direction 58, 'commercial claim' means any claim arising out of the transaction of trade and commerce and includes any claim relating to—
  (a) a business document or contract;
  (b) the export or import of goods;
  (c) the carriage of goods by land, sea, air or pipeline;
  (d) the exploitation of oil and gas reserves or other natural resources;
  (e) insurance and re-insurance;
  (f) banking and financial services;
  (g) the operation of markets and exchanges;
  (h) the purchase and sale of commodities;
  (i) the construction of ships;
  (j) business agency; and
  (k) arbitration.

58.2 Specialist List

r.58.2(1) 11.4

(1) The commercial list is a specialist list for claims proceeding in the Commercial Court.
(2) One of the judges of the Commercial Court shall be in charge of the commercial list.

58.3 Application of the Civil Procedure Rules

These Rules and their practice directions apply to claims in the commercial list unless this Part or a practice direction provides otherwise.

58.4 Proceedings in the Commercial List

(1) A commercial claim may be started in the commercial list.
(2) Rule 30.5 applies to claims in the commercial list, except that a Commercial Court judge may order a claim to be transferred to any other specialist list.

(Rule 30.5(3) provides that an application for the transfer of proceedings to or from a specialist list must be made to a judge dealing with claims in that list)

58.5 Claim Form and Particulars of Claim

r.58.5(1)(b) 15.4

(1) If, in a Part 7 claim, particulars of claim are not contained in or served with the claim form—
  (a) the claim form must state that, if an acknowledgment of service is filed which indicates an intention to defend the claim, particulars of claim will follow;

(b) when the claim form is served, it must be accompanied by the documents specified in rule 7.8(1);
(c) the claimant must serve particulars of claim within 28 days of the filing of an acknowledgment of service which indicates an intention to defend; and
(d) rule 7.4(2) does not apply.

(2) A statement of value is not required to be included in the claim form.
(3) If the claimant is claiming interest, he must—
(a) include a statement to that effect; and
(b) give the details set out in rule 16.4(2),
in both the claim form and the particulars of claim.

58.6 Acknowledgment of Service

r.58.6(1)–(3) **18.1** r.58.6(3) **15.53**

(1) A defendant must file an acknowledgment of service in every case.
(2) Unless paragraph (3) applies, the period for filing an acknowledgment of service is 14 days after service of the claim form.
(3) Where the claim form is served out of the jurisdiction, or on the agent of a defendant who is overseas, the time periods provided by rules 6.12(3), 6.35 and 6.37(5) apply after service of the claim form.

58.7 Disputing the Court's Jurisdiction

r.58.7 **19.3, 19.5**

(1) Part 11 applies to claims in the commercial list with the modifications set out in this rule.
(2) An application under rule 11 (1) must be made within 28 days after filing an acknowledgment of service.
(3) If the defendant files an acknowledgment of service indicating an intention to dispute the court's jurisdiction, the claimant need not serve particulars of claim before the hearing of the application.

58.8 Default Judgment

r.58.8 **20.2, 20.3**

(1) If, in a Part 7 claim in the commercial list, a defendant fails to file an acknowledgment of service, the claimant need not serve particulars of claim before he may obtain or apply for default judgment in accordance with Part 12.
(2) Rule 12.6(1) applies with the modification that paragraph (a) shall be read as if it referred to the claim form instead of the particulars of claim.

58.9 Admissions

r.58.9(1) **17.8**

(1) Rule 14.5 does not apply to claims in the commercial list.
(2) If the defendant admits part of a claim for a specified amount of money, the claimant may apply under rule 14.3 for judgment on the admission.
(3) Rule 14.14(1) applies with the modification that paragraph (a) shall be read as if it referred to the claim form instead of the particulars of claim.

58.10 Defence and Reply

(1) Part 15 (defence and reply) applies to claims in the commercial list with the modification to rule 15.8 that the claimant must—
(a) file any reply to a defence; and
(b) serve it on all other parties,
within 21 days after service of the defence.
(2) Rule 6.35 (in relation to the period for filing a defence where the claim form is served out of the jurisdiction) applies to claims in the commercial list, except that if the particulars of claim are served after the defendant has filed an acknowledgment of service the period for filing a defence is 28 days from service of the particulars of claim.

58.11 Statements of Case

The court may at any time before or after the issue of the claim form order a claim in the commercial list to proceed without the filing or service of statements of case.

58.12 Part 8 Claims

r.58.12 13.10

Part 8 applies to claims in the commercial list, with the modification that a defendant to a Part 8 claim who wishes to rely on written evidence must file and serve it within 28 days after filing an acknowledgment of service.

58.13 Case Management

r.58.13(1) 2.17, 42.25

(1) All proceedings in the commercial list are treated as being allocated to the multi-track and Part 26 does not apply.
(2) The following parts only of Part 29 apply—
 (a) rule 29.3(2) (legal representative to attend case management conferences and pre-trial reviews);
 (b) rule 29.5 (variation of case management timetable) with the exception of rule 29.5(1)(c).
(3) As soon as practicable the court will hold a case management conference which must be fixed in accordance with Practice Direction 58.
(4) At the case management conference or at any hearing at which the parties are represented the court may give such directions for the management of the case as it considers appropriate.

58.14 Disclosure—Ships Papers

(1) If, in proceedings relating to a marine insurance policy, the underwriters apply for specific disclosure under rule 31.12, the court may—
 (a) order a party to produce all the ships papers; and
 (b) require that party to use his best endeavours to obtain and disclose documents which are not or have not been in his control.
(2) An order under this rule may be made at any stage of the proceedings and on such terms, if any, as to staying the proceedings or otherwise, as the court thinks fit.

58.15 Judgments and Orders

(1) Except for orders made by the court on its own initiative and unless the court orders otherwise, every judgment or order will be drawn up by the parties, and rule 40.3 is modified accordingly.
(2) An application for a consent order must include a draft of the proposed order signed on behalf of all the parties to whom it relates.
(3) Rule 40.6 (consent judgments and orders) does not apply.

PD 58 Practice Direction 58 — Commercial Court

This practice direction supplements CPR, Part 58.

PD 58 2.17, 11.7 [For commentary on a specific paragraph, please refer to the cross-references after the title of the paragraph.]

General

para.1.3 2.17

1.1 This practice direction applies to commercial claims proceeding in the commercial list of the Queen's Bench Division. It supersedes all previous practice directions and practice statements in the Commercial Court.

1.2 All proceedings in the commercial list, including any appeal from a judgment, order or decision of a master or district judge before the proceedings were transferred to the Commercial Court, will be heard or determined by a Commercial Court judge, except that:

(1) another judge of the Queen's Bench Division or Chancery Division may hear urgent applications if no Commercial Court judge is available; and

(2) unless the court otherwise orders, any application relating to the enforcement of a Commercial Court judgment or order for the payment of money will be dealt with by a master of the Queen's Bench Division or a district judge.

1.3 Provisions in other practice directions which refer to a master or district judge are to be read, in relation to claims in the commercial list, as if they referred to a Commercial Court judge.

1.4 The Admiralty and Commercial Registry in the Royal Courts of Justice is the administrative office of the court for all proceedings in the commercial list.

Starting Proceedings in the Commercial Court

para.2.1 11.7
para.2.3 2.17, 23.5
para.2.4 13.6

2.1 Claims in the Commercial Court must be issued in the Admiralty and Commercial Registry.

2.2 When the Registry is closed, a request to issue a claim form may be made by fax, using the procedure set out in Appendix A to this practice direction. If a request is made which complies with that procedure, the claim form is issued when the fax is received by the Registry.

2.3 The claim form must be marked in the top right hand corner 'Queen's Bench Division, Commercial Court'.

2.4 A claimant starting proceedings in the commercial list, other than an arbitration claim, must use form N1(CC) for Part 7 claims or form N208(CC) for Part 8 claims.

Applications before Proceedings Are Issued

3.1 A party who intends to bring a claim in the commercial list must make any application before the claim form is issued to a Commercial Court judge.

3.2 The written evidence in support of such an application must state that the claimant intends to bring proceedings in the commercial list.

3.3 If the Commercial Court judge hearing the application considers that the proceedings should not be brought in the commercial list, he may adjourn the application to be heard by a master or by a judge who is not a Commercial Court judge.

Transferring Proceedings to or from the Commercial Court

4.1 If an application is made to a court other than the Commercial Court to transfer proceedings to the commercial list, the other court may:

(1) adjourn the application to be heard by a Commercial Court judge; or

(2) dismiss the application.

4.2 If the Commercial Court orders proceedings to be transferred to the commercial list:

(1) it will order them to be transferred to the Royal Courts of Justice; and

(2) it may give case management directions.

4.3 An application by a defendant, including a Part 20 defendant, for an order transferring proceedings from the commercial list should be made promptly and normally not later than the first case management conference.

4.4 A party applying to the Commercial Court to transfer a claim to the commercial list must give notice of the application to the court in which the claim is proceeding, and the Commercial Court will not make an order for transfer until it is satisfied that such notice has been given.

Acknowledgment of Service

para.5.2 13.6

5.1 For Part 7 claims, a defendant must file an acknowledgment of service using form N9(CC).

5.2 For Part 8 claims, a defendant must file an acknowledgment of service using form N210(CC).

Default Judgment and Admissions

para.6 20.2

6. PD 12 and PD 14 apply with the following modifications:
   (1) PD 12, para. 4.1(1), is to be read as referring to the service of the claim form; and
   (2) the references to 'particulars of claim' in PD 14, paras 2.1, 3.1 and 3.2, are to be read as referring to the claim form.

Variation of Time Limits

7.1 If the parties, in accordance with r. 2.11, agree in writing to vary a time limit, the claimant must notify the court in writing, giving brief written reasons for the agreed variation.

7.2 The court may make an order overriding an agreement by the parties varying a time limit.

Amendments

8. PD 17, para. 2.2, is modified so that amendments to a statement of case must show the original text, unless the court orders otherwise.

Service of Documents

para.9 15.5

9. Unless the court orders otherwise, the Commercial Court will not serve documents or orders and service must be effected by the parties.

Case Management

para.10.2 42.20
para.10.7 42.20
para.10.8 42.20, 59.6
para.10.9 47.24

10.1 The following parts only of PD 29 apply:
   (1) para. 5 (case management conferences), excluding para. 5.9 and modified so far as is made necessary by other specific provisions of this practice direction; and
   (2) para. 7 (failure to comply with case management directions).

10.2 If the proceedings are started in the commercial list, the claimant must apply for a case management conference:
   (a) for a Part 7 claim, within 14 days of the date when all defendants who intend to file and serve a defence have done so; and
   (b) for a Part 8 claim, within 14 days of the date when all defendants who intend to serve evidence have done so.

10.3 If the proceedings are transferred to the commercial list, the claimant must apply for a case management conference within 14 days of the date of the order transferring them, unless the judge held, or gave directions for, a case management conference when he made the order transferring the proceedings.

10.4 Any party may, at a time earlier than that provided in paras 10.2 or 10.3, apply in writing to the court to fix a case management conference.

10.5 If the claimant does not make an application in accordance with paras 10.2 or 10.3, any other party may apply for a case management conference.

10.6 The court may fix a case management conference at any time on its own initiative. If it does so, the court will give at least seven days' notice to the parties, unless there are compelling reasons for a shorter period of notice.

10.7 Not less than seven days before a case management conference, each party must file and serve:
(1) a completed case management information sheet; and
(2) an application notice for any order which that party intends to seek at the case management conference, other than directions referred to in the case management information sheet.

10.8 Unless the court orders otherwise, the claimant, in consultation with the other parties, must prepare:
(1) a case memorandum, containing a short and uncontroversial summary of what the case is about and of its material case history;
(2) a list of issues, with a section listing important matters which are not in dispute; and
(3) a case management bundle containing:
(a) the claim form;
(b) all statements of case (excluding schedules), except that, if a summary of a statement of case has been filed, the bundle should contain the summary, and not the full statement of case;
(c) the case memorandum;
(d) the list of issues;
(e) the case management information sheets and, if a pre-trial timetable has been agreed or ordered, that timetable;
(f) the principal orders of the court; and
(g) any agreement in writing made by the parties as to disclosure,
and provide copies of the case management bundle for the court and the other parties at least seven days before the first case management conference or any earlier hearing at which the court may give case management directions.

10.9 The claimant, in consultation with the other parties, must revise and update the documents referred to in para. 10.8 appropriately as the case proceeds. This must include making all necessary revisions and additions at least seven days before any subsequent hearing at which the court may give case management directions.

Pre-trial Review

para.11.3 47.24

11.1 At any pre-trial review or case management hearing, the court will ensure that case management directions have been complied with and give any further directions for the trial that are necessary.

11.2 Advocates who are to represent the parties at the trial should represent them at the pre-trial review and any case management hearing at which arrangements for the trial are to be discussed.

11.3 Before the pre-trial review, the parties must discuss and, if possible, agree a draft written timetable for the trial.

11.4 The claimant must file a copy of the draft timetable for the trial at least two days before the hearing of the pre-trial review. Any parts of the timetable which are not agreed must be identified and short explanations of the disagreement must be given.

11.5 At the pre-trial review, the court will set a timetable for the trial, unless a timetable has already been fixed or the court considers that it would be inappropriate to do so or appropriate to do so at a later time.

Case Management Where There Is a Part 20 Claim

12. PD 20, para. 5, applies, except that, unless the court otherwise orders, the court will give case management directions for Part 20 claims at the same case management conferences as it gives directions for the main claim.

Evidence for Applications

13.1 The general requirement is that, unless the court orders otherwise:

(1) evidence in support of an application must be filed and served with the application (see r. 23.7(3));

(2) evidence in answer must be filed and served within 14 days after the application is served; and

(3) evidence in reply must be filed and served within seven days of the service of evidence in answer.

13.2 In any case in which the application is likely to require an oral hearing of more than half a day the periods set out in paras 13.1(2) and (3) will be 28 days and 14 days respectively.

13.3 If the date fixed for the hearing of an application means that the times in paras 13.1(2) and (3) cannot both be achieved, the evidence must be filed and served:

(1) as soon as possible; and

(2) in sufficient time to ensure that the application may fairly proceed on the date fixed.

13.4 The parties may, in accordance with r. 2.11, agree different periods from those in paras 13.1(2) and (3) provided that the agreement does not affect the date fixed for the hearing of the application.

Judgments and Orders

14.1 An application for a consent order must include a draft of the proposed order signed on behalf of all parties to whom it relates (see PD 23A, para. 10.4).

14.2 Judgments and orders are generally drawn up by the parties (see r. 58.15). The parties are not therefore required to supply draft orders on disk (see PD 23A, para. 12.1).

APPENDIX A PROCEDURE FOR ISSUE OF CLAIM FORM WHEN REGISTRY IS CLOSED — PARAGRAPH 2.2

appendix A 12.7

1. A request to issue a claim form may be made by fax when the Registry is closed, provided that:
   (a) the claim form is signed by a solicitor acting on behalf of the claimant; and
   (b) it does not require the permission of the court for its issue (unless such permission has already been given).
2. The solicitor requesting the issue of the claim form ('the issuing solicitor') must:
   (a) endorse on the claim form and sign the endorsement set out below;
   (b) send a copy of the claim form so endorsed to the Registry by fax for issue under para. 2.2 of this practice direction; and
   (c) complete and sign a certificate in the form set out below, certifying that he has received a transmission report confirming that the fax has been transmitted in full, and stating the time and date of transmission.
3. When the Registry is next open to the public after the issue of a claim form in accordance with this procedure, the issuing solicitor or his agent must attend and deliver to the Registry:
   (a) the original of the claim form which was sent by fax (including the endorsement and the certificate) or, if the claim form has been served, a true and certified copy of it;
   (b) as many copies of the claim form as the Registry requires; and
   (c) the transmission report.
4. When a court officer at the Registry has checked that:
   (a) the claim form delivered under para. 3 matches the claim form received by fax; and
   (b) the correct issue fee has been paid,

   he will allocate a number to the case, and seal, mark as 'original' and date the claim form with the date of issue (being the date when the fax is recorded at the Registry as having been received).
5. If the issuing solicitor has served the unsealed claim form on any person, that solicitor must as soon as practicable:
   (a) inform that person of the case number; and
   (b) if requested, serve him with a copy of the sealed and dated claim form at any address in the United Kingdom, unless the court orders otherwise.

6. Any person served with a claim form issued under this procedure may, without paying a fee, inspect and take copies of the documents lodged at the Registry under paras 2 and 3 above.
7. The issue of a claim form in accordance with this procedure takes place when the fax is recorded at the Registry as having been received, and the claim form has the same effect for all purposes as a claim form issued under Part 7 or 8. Unless the court otherwise orders, the sealed version of the claim form retained by the Registry is conclusive proof that the claim form was issued at the time and on the date stated.
8. If the procedure set out in this Appendix is not complied with, the court may declare that a claim form shall be treated as not having been issued.

Endorsement

A claim form issued pursuant to a request by fax must be endorsed as follows:

(1) This claim form is issued under paragraph 2.2 of Practice Direction 58 and may be served notwithstanding that it does not bear the seal of the Court.

(2) A true copy of this claim form and endorsement has been sent to the Admiralty and Commercial Registry, Royal Courts of Justice, Strand, London WC2A 2LL, at the time and date certified below by the solicitor whose name appears below ('the issuing solicitor').

(3) It is the duty of the issuing solicitor or his agent to attend at the Registry when it is next open to the public for the claim form to be sealed.

(4) Any person served with this unsealed claim form:
 (a) will be notified by the issuing solicitor of the case number;
 (b) may require the issuing solicitor to serve that person with a copy of the sealed claim form at an address in the United Kingdom, unless the court orders otherwise; and
 (c) may inspect without charge the documents lodged at the Registry by the issuing solicitor.

(5) I, the issuing solicitor, undertake [to the Court, to the defendants named in this claim form, and to any other person served with this claim form]:
 (a) that the statement in paragraph 2 above is correct;
 (b) that the time and date given in the certificate with this endorsement are correct;
 (c) that this claim form is a claim form which may be issued under paragraph 2.2 of and Appendix A to Practice Direction 58;
 (d) that I will comply in all respects with the requirements of Appendix A of Practice Direction 58; and
 (e) that I will indemnify any person served with the claim form before it is sealed against any loss suffered as a result of the claim form being or becoming invalid as a result of any failure to comply with Appendix A of Practice Direction 58.

(Signed)

Solicitor for the claimant

Note: the endorsement may be signed in the name of the firm of solicitors rather than an individual solicitor, or by solicitors' agents in their capacity as agents acting on behalf of their professional clients.

Certificate

The issuing solicitor must sign a certificate in the following form:

I certify that I have received a transmission report confirming that the transmission of a copy of this claim form to the Registry by fax was fully completed and that the time and date of transmission to the Registry were [*enter the time and date shown on the transmission report*].

Dated

(Signed)

Solicitor for the claimant

Note: the certificate must be signed in the name of the firm of solicitors rather than an individual solicitor, or by solicitors' agents in their capacity as agents acting on behalf of their professional clients.

[The following forms are annexed to PD 58:

N1(CC)	Claim form (CPR, Part 7)
N1C(CC)	Notes for defendant on replying to the Part 7 claim form (Commercial Court)
N9(CC)	Acknowledgment of service
N208(CC)	Claim form (CPR, Part 8)
N208C(CC)	Notes for defendant on replying to the Part 8 claim form
N210(CC)	Acknowledgment of service (Part 8) claim
N211(CC)	Claim form (additional claims—CPR, Part 20)
N211C(CC)	Notes for Part 20 defendant on replying to the Part 20 claim form (Commercial Court)
N213(CC)	Acknowledgment of service (Part 20 claim)

These forms are online at http://hmctsformfinder.justice.gov.uk>.]

CPR Part 59 Mercantile Courts

Part 59 2.19, 11.7, 74.5 [For commentary on a specific rule, please refer to the cross-references after the title of the rule.]

59.1 Scope of This Part and Interpretation

r.59.1(2) 2.19, 11.7
r.59.1(3) 2.19
r.59.1(3)(a) 11.4

(1) This Part applies to claims in Mercantile Courts.
(2) A claim may only be started in a Mercantile Court if it—
(a) relates to a commercial or business matter in a broad sense; and
(b) is not required to proceed in the Chancery Division or in another specialist list.
(3) In this Part and Practice Direction 59—
(a) 'Mercantile Court' means a specialist list established within the courts listed in Practice Direction 59;
(b) 'mercantile claim' means a claim proceeding in a Mercantile Court; and
(c) 'Mercantile judge' means a judge authorised to sit in a Mercantile Court.

59.2 Application of the Civil Procedure Rules

These Rules and their practice directions apply to mercantile claims unless this Part or a practice direction provides otherwise.

59.3 Transfer of Proceedings

Rule 30.5 applies with the modifications that—
(a) a Mercantile judge may transfer a mercantile claim to another Mercantile Court; and
(b) a Commercial Court judge may transfer a claim from the Commercial Court to a Mercantile Court.
(Rule 30.5(3) provides that an application for the transfer of proceedings to or from a specialist list must be made to a judge dealing with claims in that list)

59.4 Claim Form and Particulars of Claim

(1) If particulars of claim are not contained in or served with the claim form—
(a) the claim form must state that, if an acknowledgment of service is filed which indicates an intention to defend the claim, particulars of claim will follow;
(b) when the claim form is served, it must be accompanied by the documents specified in rule 7.8(1);
(c) the claimant must serve particulars of claim within 28 days of the filing of an acknowledgment of service which indicates an intention to defend; and
(d) rule 7.4(2) does not apply.
(2) If the claimant is claiming interest, he must—
(a) include a statement to that effect; and
(b) give the details set out in rule 16.4(2),
in both the claim form and the particulars of claim.
(3) Rules 12.6(1)(a) and 14.14(1)(a) apply with the modification that references to the particulars of claim shall be read as if they referred to the claim form.

59.5 Acknowledgment of Service

r.59.5(1)–(3) 18.1 r.59.5(3) 15.53

(1) A defendant must file an acknowledgment of service in every case.
(2) Unless paragraph (3) applies, the period for filing an acknowledgment of service is 14 days after service of the claim form.
(3) Where the claim form is served out of the jurisdiction, or on the agent of a defendant who is overseas, the time periods provided by rules 6.12(3), 6.35 and 6.37(5) apply after service of the claim form.

59.6 Disputing the Court's Jurisdiction

r.59.6 19.3, 19.5

(1) Part 11 applies to mercantile claims with the modifications set out in this rule.
(2) An application under rule 11(1) must be made within 28 days after filing an acknowledgment of service.
(3) If the defendant files an acknowledgment of service indicating an intention to dispute the court's jurisdiction, the claimant need not serve particulars of claim before the hearing of the application.

59.7 Default Judgment

r.59.7 20.3

(1) Part 12 applies to mercantile claims, except that rules 12.10 and 12.11 apply as modified by paragraphs (2) and (3) of this rule.
(2) If, in a Part 7 claim—
 (a) the claim form has been served but no particulars of claim have been served; and
 (b) the defendant has failed to file an acknowledgment of service,
 the claimant must make an application if he wishes to obtain a default judgment.
(3) The application may be made without notice, but the court may direct it to be served on the defendant.

59.8 Admissions

(1) Rule 14.5 does not apply to mercantile claims.
(2) If the defendant admits part of a claim for a specified amount of money, the claimant may apply under rule 14.3 for judgment on the admission.

59.9 Defence and Reply

(1) Part 15 (defence and reply) applies to mercantile claims with the modification to rule 15.8 that the claimant must—
 (a) file any reply to a defence; and
 (b) serve it on all other parties,
 within 21 days after service of the defence.
(2) Rule 6.35 (in relation to the period for filing a defence where the claim form is served out of the jurisdiction) applies to mercantile claims, except that if the particulars of claim are served after the defendant has filed an acknowledgment of service the period for filing a defence is 28 days from service of the particulars of claim.

59.10 Statements of Case

The court may at any time before or after issue of the claim form order a mercantile claim to proceed without the filing or service of statements of case.

59.11 Case Management

r.59.11(1) 42.25

(1) All mercantile claims are treated as being allocated to the multi-track, and Part 26 does not apply.
(2) The following parts only of Part 29 apply—
 (a) rule 29.3(2) (appropriate legal representative to attend case management conferences and pre-trial reviews); and

(b) rule 29.5 (variation of case management timetable) with the exception of rule 29.5(1)(c).

(3) As soon as practicable the court will hold a case management conference which must be fixed in accordance with Practice Direction 59.

(4) At the case management conference or at any hearing at which the parties are represented the court may give such directions for the management of the case as it considers appropriate.

59.12 Judgments and Orders

(1) Except for orders made by the court of its own initiative and unless the court otherwise orders every judgment or order will be drawn up by the parties, and rule 40.3 is modified accordingly.

(2) An application for a consent order must include a draft of the proposed order signed on behalf of all the parties to whom it relates.

(3) Rule 40.6 (consent judgments and orders) does not apply.

PD 59 Practice Direction 59 — Mercantile Courts

This practice direction supplements CPR, Part 59.
PD 59 **2.19, 11.7** [For commentary on a specific paragraph, please refer to the cross-references after the title of the paragraph.]

General

1.1 This practice direction applies to mercantile claims.
1.2 Mercantile Courts are established in:
(1) the following district registries of the High Court: Birmingham, Bristol, Cardiff, Chester, Leeds, Liverpool, Manchester, Mold and Newcastle upon Tyne; and
(2) the Commercial Court of the Queen's Bench Division at the Royal Courts of Justice (called 'The London Mercantile Court').
1.3 All mercantile claims will be heard or determined by a mercantile judge, except that:
(1) an application may be heard and determined by any other judge who, if the claim were not a mercantile claim, would have jurisdiction to determine it, if:
(a) the application is urgent and no mercantile judge is available to hear it; or
(b) a mercantile judge directs it to be heard by another judge; and
(2) unless the court otherwise orders, all proceedings for the enforcement of a Mercantile Court judgment or order for the payment of money will be dealt with by a district judge.
1.4 Provisions in other practice directions which refer to a master or district judge are to be read, in relation to mercantile claims, as if they referred to a mercantile judge.

Starting Proceedings in a Mercantile Court

para.2.1 **2.19, 11.7** para.2.2 **23.5**

2.1 A claim should only be started in a Mercantile Court if it will benefit from the expertise of a mercantile judge.
2.2 The claim form must be marked in the top right hand corner 'Queen's Bench Division, ________ District Registry, Mercantile Court' or 'Queen's Bench Division, The London Mercantile Court'.

Applications before Proceedings Are Issued

3.1 A party who intends to bring a claim in a Mercantile Court must make any application before the claim form is issued to a judge of that court.
3.2 The written evidence in support of such an application should show why the claim is suitable to proceed as a mercantile claim.

Transfer of Proceedings to or from a Mercantile Court

4.1 If a claim which has not been issued in a Mercantile Court is suitable to continue as a mercantile claim:
(1) any party wishing the claim to be transferred to a Mercantile Court may make an application for transfer to the court to which transfer is sought;
(2) if all parties consent to the transfer, the application may be made by letter to the mercantile listing officer of the court to which transfer is sought, stating why the case is suitable to be transferred to that court and enclosing the written consents of the parties, the claim form and statements of case.
4.2 If an application for transfer is made to a court which does not have power to make the order, that court may:
(1) adjourn the application to be heard by a mercantile judge; or
(2) dismiss the application.
4.3 A mercantile judge may make an order under r. 59.3 of his own initiative.

Default Judgment and Admissions

5. PD 12 and PD 14 apply with the following modifications:
(1) PD 12, para. 4.1(1), is to be read as referring to the service of the claim form; and

(2) the references to 'particulars of claim' in PD 14, paras 2.1, 3.1 and 3.2, are to be read as referring to the claim form.

Variation of Time Limits by Agreement

6.1 If the parties, in accordance with r. 2.11, agree in writing to vary a time limit, the claimant must notify the court in writing, giving brief written reasons for the agreed variation.
6.2 The court may make an order overriding an agreement by the parties varying a time limit.

Case Management

7.1 The following parts only of PD 29 apply:
(1) para. 5 (case management conferences), excluding para. 5.9 and modified so far as is made necessary by other specific provisions of this practice direction; and
(2) para. 7 (failure to comply with case management directions).
7.2 If proceedings are started in a Mercantile Court, the claimant must apply for a case management conference:
(1) for a Part 7 claim, within 14 days of the date when all defendants who intend to file and serve a defence have done so; and
(2) for a Part 8 claim, within 14 days of the date when all defendants who intend to serve evidence have done so.
7.3 If proceedings are transferred to a Mercantile Court, the claimant must apply for a case management conference within 14 days of receiving an acknowledgment of the transfer from the receiving court, unless the judge held, or gave directions for, a case management conference when he made the order transferring the proceedings.
7.4 Any party may, at a time earlier than that provided in paras 7.2 or 7.3, apply in writing to the court to fix a case management conference.
7.5 If the claimant does not make an application in accordance with paras 7.2 or 7.3, any other party may apply for a case management conference.
7.6 The court may fix a case management conference at any time on its own initiative. If it does so, the court will give at least seven days' notice to the parties, unless there are compelling reasons for a shorter period of notice.
7.7 Not less than seven days before a case management conference:
(1) each party shall file and serve:
(a) a case management information sheet substantially in the form set out at Appendix A to this practice direction; and
(b) an application notice for any order which that party intends to seek at the case management conference, other than directions referred to in the case management information sheet; and
(2) the claimant (or other party applying for the conference) shall in addition file and serve:
(a) a case management file containing:
—the claim form;
—the statements of case (excluding schedules of more than 15 pages);
—any orders already made;
—the case management information sheets; and
—a short list of the principal issues to be prepared by the claimant; and
(b) a draft order substantially in the form set out at Appendix B to this practice direction, setting out the directions which that party thinks appropriate.
7.8 In appropriate cases:
(1) the parties may, not less than seven days before the date fixed for the case management conference, submit agreed directions for the approval of the judge;
(2) the judge will then either:
(a) make the directions proposed; or
(b) make them with alterations; or
(c) require the case management conference to proceed; but
(3) the parties must assume that the conference will proceed until informed to the contrary.

7.9 If the parties submit agreed directions and the judge makes them with alterations, any party objecting to the alterations may, within seven days of receiving the order containing the directions, apply to the court for the directions to be varied.

7.10 The directions given at the case management conference:
(1) will normally cover all steps in the case through to trial, including the fixing of a trial date or window, or directions for the taking of steps to fix the trial date or window; and
(2) may include the fixing of a progress monitoring date or dates, and make provision for the court to be informed as to the progress of the case at the date or dates fixed.

7.11 If the court fixes a progress monitoring date, it may after that date fix a further case management conference or a pre-trial review on its own initiative if:
(1) no or insufficient information is provided by the parties; or
(2) it is appropriate in view of the information provided.

Pre-trial Review and Questionnaire

8.1 The court may order a pre-trial review at any time.

8.2 Each party must file and serve a completed pre-trial checklist substantially in the form set out in Appendix C to this practice direction:
(1) if a pre-trial review has been ordered, not less than seven days before the date of the review; or
(2) if no pre-trial review has been ordered, not less than six weeks before the trial date.

8.3 When pre-trial checklists are filed under para. 8.2(2):
(1) the judge will consider them and decide whether to order a pre-trial review; and
(2) if he does not order a pre-trial review, he may on his own initiative give directions for the further preparation of the case or as to the conduct of the trial.

8.4 At a pre-trial review:
(1) the parties should if possible be represented by the advocates who will be appearing at the trial;
(2) any representatives appearing must be fully informed and authorised for the purposes of the review; and
(3) the court will give such directions for the conduct of the trial as it sees fit.

Evidence for Applications

9.1 The general requirement is that, unless the court orders otherwise:
(1) evidence in support of an application must be filed and served with the application: see r. 23.7(3);
(2) evidence in answer must be filed and served within 14 days after the application is served;
(3) evidence in reply must be filed and served within seven days of the service of the evidence in answer.

9.2 In any case in which the application is likely to require an oral hearing of more than half a day the periods set out in paras 9.1(2) and (3) will be 28 days and 14 days respectively.

9.3 If the date fixed for the hearing of the application means that the times in paras 9.1(2) and (3) cannot both be achieved, the evidence must be filed and served:
(1) as soon as possible; and
(2) in sufficient time to ensure that the application may fairly proceed on the date fixed.

9.4 The parties may, in accordance with r. 2.11, agree different periods from those provided above, provided that the agreement does not affect the ability to proceed on the date fixed for the hearing of the application.

Files for Applications

10. Before the hearing of any application, the applicant must:
(1) provide to the court and each other party an appropriate indexed file for the application with consecutively numbered pages; and
(2) attach to the file an estimate of the reading time required by the judge.

Judgments and Orders

11.1 After any hearing the claimant must draw up a draft order, unless the decision was made on the application of another party in which case that party must do so.

11.2 A draft order must be submitted by the party responsible for drawing it up within three clear days of the decision, with sufficient copies for each party and for one to be retained by the court.

11.3 The sealed orders will be returned to the party submitting them, who will be responsible for serving the order on the other parties.

11.4 Orders must be dated with the date of the decision, except for consent orders submitted for approval, which must be left undated.

ANNEX A CASE MANAGEMENT INFORMATION SHEET MERCANTILE COURTS

[Title of case]

This information sheet must be filed with Mercantile Listing at least seven days before the case management conference, and copies served on all other parties: see PD 59, para. 7.7.

Party filing:

Solicitors:

Advocate(s) for trial:

Date:

Substance of case

1. What in about 20 words maximum is the case about? Please provide a separate concise list of issues in a complex case.

Parties

2. Are all parties still effective?
3. Do you intend to add any further party?

Statements of case

4. Do you intend to amend your statement of case?
5. Do you require any 'further information' see CPR, Part 18?

Disclosure

6. By what date can you give standard disclosure?
7. Do you contend that to search for any type of document falling within r. 31.6(b) would be unreasonable within r. 31.7(2); if so, what type and on what grounds?
8. Is any specific disclosure required (r. 31.12)?
9. Is a full disclosure order appropriate?
10. By what dates could you give:
    (i) any specific disclosure referred to at 8; and
    (ii) full disclosure?

Admissions

11. Can you make any additional admissions?

Preliminary issues

12. Are any issues suitable for trial as preliminary issues? If yes, which?

Witnesses of fact

13. On how many witnesses of fact do you intend to rely at the trial (subject to the court's direction)?
14. Please name them, or explain why you do not.
15. Which of them will be called to give oral evidence?
16. When can you serve their witness statements?
17. Will any require an interpreter?

Expert evidence

18. Are there issues requiring expert evidence?
19. If yes, what issues?
20. Might a single joint expert be suitable on any issues (see r. 35.7)?

21. What experts do you intend (subject to the court's direction) to call? Please give the number, their names and expertise.
22. By what date can you serve signed expert reports?
23. Should there be meetings of experts of like disciplines, of all disciplines? By when?
24. Which experts, if any, do you intend not to call at the trial?
25. Will any require an interpreter?

Trial

26. What are the advocates' present estimates of the length of the trial?
27. What is the earliest date that you think the case can be ready for trial?
28. Where should the trial be held?
29. Is a pre-trial review advisable?

ADR

30. Might some form of alternative dispute resolution assist to resolve the dispute or some part of it?
31. Has this been considered with the client?
32. Has this been considered with the other parties?
33. Do you want the case to be stayed pending ADR or other means of settlement (r. 26.4); or any other directions relating to ADR?

Other applications

34. What applications, if any, not covered above, will you be making at the conference? Costs
35. What, do you estimate, are your costs to date?
36. What, do you estimate, will be your costs to end of trial?

[Signature of party/solicitor]

ANNEX B STANDARD DIRECTIONS IN MERCANTILE COURTS

[Title of case with judge's name]
Order for directions
made on [ ]

1. Standard disclosure is to be made by [ ]. Inspection on 48 hours' notice to be completed by [ ].
2. Signed statements of witnesses of fact, and hearsay notices when required by r. 33.2, are to be exchanged not later than [ ]. Unless otherwise ordered, the witness statements are to stand as the evidence-in-chief of the witnesses at trial.
3. Each party has permission to call at the trial expert witnesses as follows:

Number *Expertise* *Issue(s) to be covered*

whose reports are to be exchanged by [ ].

4. Experts of like disciplines are to:
   (i) meet without prejudice by [ ] to identify the issues between them and to attempt to reach agreement on such issues, and
   (ii) prepare a joint statement pursuant to r. 35.12(3), by [ ].

or

3. Expert evidence in the following field(s) of expertise is limited to a written report by a single expert jointly instructed by the parties:

Expertise *Issue(s) to be covered*

4. (i) The report of the single joint expert is to be produced by [ ].
   (ii) Any questions to the expert are to be presented to him by [ ] and answered by [ ].
   (iii) Any party may apply not later than [ ] for an order that the expert witness shall give oral evidence at the trial.
5. The case will be tried in [ ] by judge alone, estimated length of trial [ ] days, [commencing on] [not before]. [The claimant is to apply to the mercantile listing officer to fix a date for the trial, not later than [ ], specifying dates which any party wishes to avoid.]
6. [The progress monitoring date is [ ]. Each party is to notify the court in writing by that date (*with a copy to all other parties*) of the progress of the case, including:
   (i) whether the directions have been complied with in all respects;
   (ii) if any directions are outstanding, which of them and why; and

(iii) whether a further case management conference or a pre-trial review is required.]
7. There will be a pre-trial review on [ ]. [In the event of both parties notifying the court in writing not less than [ ] days before the pre-trial review that it is not required, then it will be vacated.]
8. Signed pre-trial checklists are to be filed and served by [ ] [not less than seven days before the pre-trial review] [not less than six weeks before the trial date].
9. Trial bundles must be agreed, prepared and delivered to counsel not less than [ ] days before the trial date, and to the court not less than [ ] days before the trial date.
10. Costs in the case.
DATED

ANNEX C PRE-TRIAL CHECKLIST MERCANTILE COURTS

[Title of case]

Where a pre-trial review has been ordered, this checklist must be filed with Mercantile Listing not less than seven days before the pre-trial review, and copies served on all other parties. Where a pre-trial review has not been ordered, it must be filed and served not less than six weeks before the trial date. See PD 59, para. 8.2.

a. Trial date:
b. Whether pre-trial review ordered:
c. Date of review:
d. Party lodging:
e. Solicitors:
f. Advocate(s) for trial:
g. Date lodged:

[Note: this checklist should normally be completed with the involvement of the advocate(s) instructed for trial.]

1. Have all the directions made to date been carried out?
2. If not, what remains to be carried out? When will it be carried out?
3. Do you intend to take any further steps regarding:
   (i) statements of case?
   (ii) disclosure?
   (iii) witnesses and witness statements?
   (iv) experts and expert reports?
   If yes in any case, what and by when?
4. Will the preparation of trial bundles be completed not later than three weeks before the date fixed for trial? If not, what is the position?
5. What witnesses of fact do you intend to call?
6. (Where directions for expert evidence have been given) what experts do you intend to call?
7. Is any interpreter needed: for whom?
8. If a pre-trial review has not been ordered, do you think one would be useful?
9. What are the advocate(s)' confirmed estimates of the minimum and maximum lengths of the trial? A confirmed estimate signed by the advocate(s) and dated must be attached.
10. (i) Might some form of alternative dispute resolution now assist?
    (ii) Has the question been considered with the client?
    (iii) Has the question been explored with the other parties to the case?

[Signature of party/solicitor]

CPR Part 60 Technology and Construction Court Claims

Part 60 **2.16, 11.7, 74.5** [For commentary on a specific rule, please refer to the cross-references after the title of the rule.]

60.1 General

r.60.1 **2.16**

(1) This Part applies to Technology and Construction Court claims ('TCC claims').
(2) In this Part and Practice Direction 60—
  (a) 'TCC claim' means a claim which—
    (i) satisfies the requirements of paragraph (3); and
    (ii) has been issued in or transferred into the specialist list for such claims;
  (b) 'Technology and Construction Court' means any court in which TCC claims are dealt with in accordance with this Part or Practice Direction 60; and
  (c) 'TCC judge' means any judge authorised to hear TCC claims.
(3) A claim may be brought as a TCC claim if—
  (a) it involves issues or questions which are technically complex; or
  (b) a trial by a TCC judge is desirable.

(Practice Direction 60 gives examples of types of claims which it may be appropriate to bring as TCC claims.)

(4) TCC claims include all official referees' business referred to in section 68(1)(a) of the Senior Courts Act 1981.
(5) TCC claims will be dealt with—
  (a) in a Technology and Construction Court; and
  (b) by a TCC judge, unless—
    (i) this Part or Practice Direction 60 permits otherwise; or
    (ii) a TCC judge directs otherwise.

60.2 Specialist List

r.60.2(1) **11.4**

(1) TCC claims form a specialist list.
(2) A judge will be appointed to be the judge in charge of the TCC specialist list.

60.3 Application of the Civil Procedure Rules

These Rules and their practice directions apply to TCC claims unless this Part or a practice direction provides otherwise.

60.4 Issuing a TCC Claim

A TCC claim must be issued in—

(a) the High Court in London;
(b) a district registry of the High Court; or
(c) a county court specified in Practice Direction 60.

60.5 Reply

Part 15 (defence and reply) applies to TCC claims with the modification to rule 15.8 that the claimant must—

(a) file any reply to a defence; and
(b) serve it on all other parties,
within 21 days after service of the defence.

60.6 Case Management

r.60.6 42.20 r.60.6(1) 42.25

(1) All TCC claims are treated as being allocated to the multi-track and Part 26 does not apply.
(2) Part 29 and Practice Direction 29 apply to the case management of TCC claims, except where they are varied by or inconsistent with Practice Direction 60.

60.7 Judgments and Orders

r.60.7 63.37

(1) Except for orders made by the court of its own initiative and unless the court otherwise orders, every judgment or order made in claims proceeding in the Technology and Construction Court will be drawn up by the parties, and rule 40.3 is modified accordingly.
(2) An application for a consent order must include a draft of the proposed order signed on behalf of all the parties to whom it relates.
(3) Rule 40.6 (consent judgments and orders) does not apply.

PD 60 Practice Direction 60 — Technology and Construction Court Claims

This practice direction supplements CPR, Part 60.
PD 60 **2.16, 11.7** [For commentary on a specific paragraph, please refer to the cross-references after the title of the paragraph.]

General

1 This practice direction applies to Technology and Construction Court claims ('TCC claims').

TCC Claims

para.2.1 **42.9**

2.1 The following are examples of the types of claim which it may be appropriate to bring as TCC claims:
- (a) building or other construction disputes, including claims for the enforcement of the decisions of adjudicators under the Housing Grants, Construction and Regeneration Act 1996;
- (b) engineering disputes;
- (c) claims by and against engineers, architects, surveyors, accountants and other specialised advisers relating to the services they provide;
- (d) claims by and against local authorities relating to their statutory duties concerning the development of land or the construction of buildings;
- (e) claims relating to the design, supply and installation of computers, computer software and related network systems;
- (f) claims relating to the quality of goods sold or hired, and work done, materials supplied or services rendered;
- (g) claims between landlord and tenant for breach of a repairing covenant;
- (h) claims between neighbours, owners and occupiers of land in trespass, nuisance etc.;
- (i) claims relating to the environment (for example, pollution cases);
- (j) claims arising out of fires;
- (k) claims involving taking of accounts where these are complicated; and
- (l) challenges to decisions of arbitrators in construction and engineering disputes including applications for permission to appeal and appeals.

2.2 A claim given as an example in para. 2.1 will not be suitable for this specialist list unless it demonstrates the characteristics in r. 60.1(3). Similarly, the examples are not exhaustive and other types of claim may be appropriate to this specialist list.

How to Start a TCC Claim

para.3.2 **23.5** para.3.3–3.4 **2.16, 11.7**

3.1 TCC claims must be issued in the High Court or in a county court specified in this practice direction.

3.2 The claim form must be marked in the top right-hand corner 'Technology and Construction Court' below the words 'The High Court, Queen's Bench Division' or 'The ____ County Court'.

3.3 TCC claims brought in the High Court outside London may be issued in any District Registry, but it is preferable that wherever possible they should be issued in one of the following district registries, in which a TCC judge will usually be available: Birmingham, Bristol, Cardiff, Chester, Exeter, Leeds, Liverpool, Manchester, Mold, Newcastle upon Tyne and Nottingham.

3.4 The county courts in which a TCC claim may be issued are the following: Birmingham, Bristol, Cardiff, Central London, Chester, Exeter, Leeds, Liverpool, Newcastle, Nottingham and Salford.

Applications before Proceedings Are Issued

4.1 A party who intends to issue a TCC claim must make any application before the claim form is issued to a TCC judge.

4.2 The written evidence in support of such an application must state that the proposed claim is a TCC claim.

Transfer of Proceedings

para.5 11.10

5.1 Where no TCC judge is available to deal with a claim which has been issued in a High Court District Registry or one of the county courts listed in para. 3.4 above, the claim may be transferred:

(1) if it has been issued in a district registry, to another district registry or to the High Court in London; or

(2) if it has been issued in a county court, to another county court where a TCC judge would be available.

5.2 paragraph 5.1 is without prejudice to the court's general powers to transfer proceedings under Part 30.

(Rule 30.5(3) provides that an application for the transfer of proceedings to or from a specialist list must be made to a judge dealing with claims in that list.)

5.3 A party applying to a TCC judge to transfer a claim to the TCC specialist list must give notice of the application to the court in which the claim is proceeding, and a TCC judge will not make an order for transfer until he is satisfied that such notice has been given.

Assignment of Claim to a TCC Judge

para.6.1 2.16

6.1 When a TCC claim is issued or an order is made transferring a claim to the TCC specialist list, the court will assign the claim to a named TCC judge ('the assigned TCC judge') who will have the primary responsibility for the case management of that claim.

6.2 All documents relating to the claim must be marked in similar manner to the claim form with the words 'Technology and Construction Court' and the name of the assigned TCC judge.

Applications

7.1 An application should normally be made to the assigned TCC judge. If the assigned TCC judge is not available, or the court gives permission, the application may be made to another TCC judge.

7.2 If an application is urgent and there is no TCC judge available to deal with it, the application may be made to any judge who, if the claim were not a TCC claim, would be authorised to deal with the application.

Case Management Conference

para.8.1 47.11
para.8.2 42.20, 47.11
para.8.3 47.11
para.8.6 47.16

8.1 The court will fix a case management conference within 14 days of the earliest of these events:

(1) the filing of an acknowledgment of service;

(2) the filing of a defence; or

(3) the date of an order transferring the claim to a TCC.

8.2 When the court notifies the parties of the date and time of the case management conference, it will at the same time send each party a case management information sheet and a case management directions form.

(The case management information sheet and the case management directions form are in the form set out in Appendices A and B to this practice direction.)

8.3 Not less than two days before the case management conference, each party must file and serve on all other parties:

(1) completed copies of the case management information sheet and case management directions form; and

(2) an application notice for any order which that party intends to seek at the case management conference, other than directions referred to in the case management directions form.

8.4 The parties are encouraged to agree directions to propose to the court by reference to the case management directions form.

8.5 If any party fails to file or serve the case management information sheet and the case management directions form by the date specified, the court may:

(1) impose such sanction as it sees fit; and

(2) either proceed with or adjourn the case management conference.

8.6 The directions given at the case management conference will normally include the fixing of dates for:

(1) any further case management conferences;

(2) a pre-trial review;

(3) the trial of any preliminary issues that it orders to be tried; and

(4) the trial.

Pre-trial Review

9.1 When the court fixes the date for a pre-trial review it will send each party a pre-trial review questionnaire and a pre-trial review directions form.

(The pre-trial review questionnaire is in the form set out in Appendix C to this practice direction.)

9.2 Each party must file and serve on all other parties completed copies of the questionnaire not less than two days before the date fixed for the pre-trial review.

9.3 The parties are encouraged to agree directions to propose to the court.

9.4 If any party fails to return or exchange the questionnaire by the date specified the court may:

(1) impose such sanction as it sees fit; and

(2) either proceed with or adjourn the pre-trial review.

9.5 At the pre-trial review, the court will give such directions for the conduct of the trial as it sees fit.

Listing

10 The provisions about listing questionnaires and listing in Part 29 and PD 29 do not apply to TCC claims.

Trial

para.11.1 2.16

11.1 Whenever possible the trial of a claim will be heard by the assigned TCC judge.

11.2 A TCC claim may be tried at any place where there is a TCC judge available to try the claim.

[The following forms are appended to PD 60:

app.A 42.20

Appendix A TCC/CM1 Case management information sheet

app.B 42.20

Appendix B TCC/CMD Case management directions form

Appendix C TCC/PTR1 Pre-trial review questionnaire

These forms are online at <http://hmctsformfinder.justice.gov.uk>.]

CPR Part 61 Admiralty Claims

Part 61 2.18, 11.7, 74.5 [For commentary on a specific rule, please refer to the cross-references after the title of the rule.]

61.1 Scope and Interpretation

r.61.1(3) 42.25

(1) This Part applies to admiralty claims.
(2) In this Part—
(a) 'admiralty claim' means a claim within the Admiralty jurisdiction of the High Court as set out in section 20 of the Senior Courts Act 1981;
(b) 'the Admiralty Court' means the Admiralty Court of the Queen's Bench Division of the High Court of Justice;
(c) 'claim *in rem*' means a claim in an admiralty action *in rem*;
(d) 'collision claim' means a claim within section 20(3)(b) of the Senior Courts Act 1981;
(e) 'limitation claim' means a claim under the Merchant Shipping Act 1995 for the limitation of liability in connection with a ship or other property;
(f) 'salvage claim' means a claim—
(i) for or in the nature of salvage;
(ii) for special compensation under Article 14 of Schedule 11 to the Merchant Shipping Act 1995;
(iii) for the apportionment of salvage; and
(iv) arising out of or connected with any contract for salvage services;
(g) 'caution against arrest' means a caution entered in the Register under rule 61.7;
(h) 'caution against release' means a caution entered in the Register under rule 61.8;
(i) 'the Register' means the Register of cautions against arrest and release which is open to inspection as provided by Practice Direction 61;
(j) 'the Marshal' means the Admiralty Marshal;
(k) 'ship' includes any vessel used in navigation; and
(l) 'the Registrar' means the Queen's Bench Master with responsibility for Admiralty claims.
(3) Part 58 (Commercial Court) applies to claims in the Admiralty Court except where this Part provides otherwise.
(4) The Registrar has all the powers of the Admiralty judge except where a rule or practice direction provides otherwise.

61.2 Admiralty Claims

r.61.2 11.2
r.61.2(1) 11.7
r.61.2(3) 2.18

(1) The following claims must be started in the Admiralty Court—
(a) a claim—
(i) *in rem*;
(ii) for damage done by a ship;
(iii) concerning the ownership of a ship;
(iv) under the Merchant Shipping Act 1995;

(v) for loss of life or personal injury specified in section 20(2)(f) of the Senior Courts Act 1981;
(vi) by a master or member of a crew for wages;
(vii) in the nature of towage; or
(viii) in the nature of pilotage;
(b) a collision claim;
(c) a limitation claim; or
(d) a salvage claim.

(2) Any other admiralty claim may be started in the Admiralty Court.

(3) Rule 30.5 applies to claims in the Admiralty Court except that the Admiralty Court may order the transfer of a claim to—
(a) the Commercial list;
(b) a Mercantile Court;
(c) the Mercantile list at the Central London County Court; or
(d) any other appropriate court.

61.3 Claims *in Rem*

r.61.3 18.1

(1) This rule applies to claims *in rem*.

(2) A claim *in rem* is started by the issue of an *in rem* claim form as set out in Practice Direction 61.

(3) Subject to rule 61.4, the particulars of claim must—
(a) be contained in or served with the claim form; or
(b) be served on the defendant by the claimant within 75 days after service of the claim form.

(4) An acknowledgment of service must be filed within 14 days after service of the claim form.

(5) The claim form must be served—
(a) in accordance with Practice Direction 61; and
(b) within 12 months after the date of issue and rules 7.5 and 7.6 are modified accordingly.

(6) If a claim form has been issued (whether served or not), any person who wishes to defend the claim may file an acknowledgment of service.

61.4 Special Provisions Relating to Collision Claims

r.61.4 18.1

(1) This rule applies to collision claims.

(2) A claim form need not contain or be followed by particulars of claim and rule 7.4 does not apply.

(3) An acknowledgment of service must be filed.

(4) A party who wishes to dispute the court's jurisdiction must make an application under Part 11 within 2 months after filing his acknowledgment of service.

(5) Every party must—
(a) within 2 months after the defendant files the acknowledgment of service; or
(b) where the defendant applies under Part 11, within 2 months after the defendant files the further acknowledgment of service,

file at the court a completed collision statement of case in the form specified in Practice Direction 61.

(6) A collision statement of case must be—
(a) in the form set out in Practice Direction 61; and
(b) verified by a statement of truth.

(7) A claim form in a collision claim may not be served out of the jurisdiction unless—
(a) the case falls within section 22(2)(a), (b) or (c) of the Senior Courts Act 1981; or
(b) the defendant has submitted to or agreed to submit to the jurisdiction; and the court gives permission in accordance with Section IV of Part 6.

(8) Where permission to serve a claim form out of the jurisdiction is given, the court will specify the period within which the defendant may file an acknowledgment of service and, where appropriate, a collision statement of case.

(9) Where, in a collision claim *in rem* ('the original claim')—
(a) (i) a Part 20 claim; or
(ii) a cross-claim *in rem*

arising out of the same collision or occurrence is made; and

(b) (i) the party bringing the original claim has caused the arrest of a ship or has obtained security in order to prevent such arrest; and

(ii) the party bringing the Part 20 claim or cross-claim is unable to arrest a ship or otherwise obtain security,

the party bringing the Part 20 claim or cross-claim may apply to the court to stay the original claim until sufficient security is given to satisfy any judgment that may be given in favour of that party.

(10) The consequences set out in paragraph (11) apply where a party to a claim to establish liability for a collision claim (other than a claim for loss of life or personal injury)—

(a) makes an offer to settle in the form set out in paragraph (12) not less than 21 days before the start of the trial;

(b) that offer is not accepted; and

(c) the maker of the offer obtains at trial an apportionment equal to or more favourable than his offer.

(11) Where paragraph (10) applies the parties will, unless the court considers it unjust, be entitled to the following costs—

(a) the maker of the offer will be entitled to—

(i) all his costs from 21 days after the offer was made; and

(ii) his costs before then in the percentage to which he would have been entitled had the offer been accepted; and

(b) all other parties to whom the offer was made—

(i) will be entitled to their costs up to 21 days after the offer was made in the percentage to which they would have been entitled had the offer been accepted; but

(ii) will not be entitled to their costs thereafter.

(12) An offer under paragraph (10) must be in writing and must contain—

(a) an offer to settle liability at stated percentages;

(b) an offer to pay costs in accordance with the same percentages;

(c) a term that the offer remain open for 21 days after the date it is made; and

(d) a term that, unless the court orders otherwise, on expiry of that period the offer remains open on the same terms except that the offeree should pay all the costs from that date until acceptance.

61.5 Arrest

(1) In a claim *in rem*—

(a) a claimant; and

(b) a judgment creditor

may apply to have the property proceeded against arrested.

(2) Practice Direction 61 sets out the procedure for applying for arrest.

(3) A party making an application for arrest must—

(a) request a search to be made in the Register before the warrant is issued to determine whether there is a caution against arrest in force with respect to that property; and

(b) file a declaration in the form set out in Practice Direction 61.

(4) A warrant of arrest may not be issued as of right in the case of property in respect of which the beneficial ownership, as a result of a sale or disposal by any court in any jurisdiction exercising admiralty jurisdiction *in rem*, has changed since the claim form was issued.

(5) A warrant of arrest may not be issued against a ship owned by a State where by any convention or treaty, the United Kingdom has undertaken to minimise the possibility of arrest of ships of that State until—

(a) notice in the form set out in Practice Direction 61 has been served on a consular officer at the consular office of that State in London or the port at which it is intended to arrest the ship; and

(b) a copy of that notice is attached to any declaration under paragraph (3)(b).

(6) Except—

(a) with the permission of the court; or

(b) where notice has been given under paragraph (5),

a warrant of arrest may not be issued in a claim *in rem* against a foreign ship belonging to a port of a State in respect of which an order in council has been made under section 4 of the Consular Relations Act 1968, until the expiration of 2 weeks from appropriate notice to the consul.

(7) A warrant of arrest is valid for 12 months but may only be executed if the claim form—
  (a) has been served; or
  (b) remains valid for service at the date of execution.

(8) Property may only be arrested by the Marshal or his substitute.

(9) Property under arrest—
  (a) may not be moved unless the court orders otherwise; and
  (b) may be immobilised or prevented from sailing in such manner as the Marshal may consider appropriate.

(10) Where an *in rem* claim form has been issued and security sought, any person who has filed an acknowledgment of service may apply for an order specifying the amount and form of security to be provided.

61.6 Security in Claim *in Rem*

(1) This rule applies if, in a claim *in rem*, security has been given to—
  (a) obtain the release of property under arrest; or
  (b) prevent the arrest of property.

(2) The court may order that the—
  (a) amount of security be reduced and may stay the claim until the order is complied with; or
  (b) claimant may arrest or re-arrest the property proceeded against to obtain further security.

(3) The court may not make an order under paragraph (2)(b) if the total security to be provided would exceed the value of the property at the time—
  (a) of the original arrest; or
  (b) security was first given (if the property was not arrested).

61.7 Cautions against Arrest

(1) Any person may file a request for a caution against arrest.

(2) When a request under paragraph (1) is filed the court will enter the caution in the Register if the request is in the form set out in Practice Direction 61 and—
  (a) the person filing the request undertakes—
    (i) to file an acknowledgment of service; and
    (ii) to give sufficient security to satisfy the claim with interest and costs; or
  (b) where the person filing the request has constituted a limitation fund in accordance with Article 11 of the Convention on Limitation of Liability for Maritime Claims 1976 he—
    (i) states that such a fund has been constituted; and
    (ii) undertakes that the claimant will acknowledge service of the claim form by which any claim may be begun against the property described in the request.

(3) A caution against arrest—
  (a) is valid for 12 months after the date it is entered in the Register; but
  (b) may be renewed for a further 12 months by filing a further request.

(4) Paragraphs (1) and (2) apply to a further request under paragraph (3)(b).

(5) Property may be arrested if a caution against arrest has been entered in the Register but the court may order that—
  (a) the arrest be discharged; and
  (b) the party procuring the arrest pays compensation to the owner of or other persons interested in the arrested property.

61.8 Release and Cautions against Release

(1) Where property is under arrest—
  (a) an *in rem* claim form may be served upon it; and
  (b) it may be arrested by any other person claiming to have an *in rem* claim against it.

(2) Any person who—
  (a) claims to have an *in rem* right against any property under arrest; and

(b) wishes to be given notice of any application in respect of that property or its proceeds of sale,

may file a request for a caution against release in the form set out in Practice Direction 61.

(3) When a request under paragraph (2) is filed, a caution against release will be entered in the Register.

(4) Property will be released from arrest if—

(a) it is sold by the court;

(b) the court orders release on an application made by any party;

(c) (i) the arresting party; and

(ii) all persons who have entered cautions against release

file a request for release in the form set out in Practice Direction 61; or

(d) any party files—

(i) a request for release in the form set out in Practice Direction 61 (containing an undertaking); and

(ii) consents to the release of the arresting party and all persons who have entered cautions against release.

(5) Where the release of any property is delayed by the entry of a caution against release under this rule any person who has an interest in the property may apply for an order that the person who entered the caution pay damages for losses suffered by the applicant because of the delay.

(6) The court may not make an order under paragraph (5) if satisfied that there was good reason to—

(a) request the entry of; and

(b) maintain the caution.

(7) Any person—

(a) interested in property under arrest or in the proceeds of sale of such property; or

(b) whose interests are affected by any order sought or made,

may be made a party to any claim *in rem* against the property or proceeds of sale.

(8) Where—

(a) (i) a ship is not under arrest but cargo on board her is; or

(ii) a ship is under arrest but cargo on board her is not; and

(b) persons interested in the ship or cargo wish to discharge the cargo,

they may, without being made parties, request the Marshal to authorise steps to discharge the cargo.

(9) If—

(a) the Marshal considers a request under paragraph (8) reasonable; and

(b) the applicant gives an undertaking in writing acceptable to the Marshal to pay—

(i) his fees; and

(ii) all expenses to be incurred by him or on his behalf

on demand,

the Marshal will apply to the court for an order to permit the discharge of the cargo.

(10) Where persons interested in the ship or cargo are unable or unwilling to give an undertaking as referred to in paragraph (9)(b), they may—

(a) be made parties to the claim; and

(b) apply to the court for an order for—

(i) discharge of the cargo; and

(ii) directions as to the fees and expenses of the Marshal with regard to the discharge and storage of the cargo.

61.9 Judgment in Default

r.61.9 20.2

(1) In a claim *in rem* (other than a collision claim) the claimant may obtain judgment in default of—

(a) an acknowledgment of service only if—

(i) the defendant has not filed an acknowledgment of service; and

(ii) the time for doing so set out in rule 61.3(4) has expired; and

(b) defence only if—
(i) a defence has not been filed; and
(ii) the relevant time limit for doing so has expired.

(2) In a collision claim, a party who has filed a collision statement of case within the time specified by rule 61.4(5) may obtain judgment in default of a collision statement of case only if—
(a) the party against whom judgment is sought has not filed a collision statement of case; and
(b) the time for doing so set out in rule 61.4(5) has expired.

(3) An application for judgment in default—
(a) under paragraph (1) or paragraph (2) in an *in rem* claim must be made by filing—
(i) an application notice as set out in Practice Direction 61;
(ii) a certificate proving service of the claim form; and
(iii) evidence proving the claim to the satisfaction of the court; and
(b) under paragraph (2) in any other claim must be made in accordance with Part 12 with any necessary modifications.

(4) An application notice seeking judgment in default and, unless the court orders otherwise, all evidence in support, must be served on all persons who have entered cautions against release on the Register.

(5) The court may set aside or vary any judgment in default entered under this rule.

(6) The claimant may apply to the court for judgment against a party at whose instance a notice against arrest was entered where—
(a) the claim form has been served on that party;
(b) the sum claimed in the claim form does not exceed the amount specified in the undertaking given by that party in accordance with rule 61.7(2)(a)(ii); and
(c) that party has not fulfilled that undertaking within 14 days after service on him of the claim form.

61.10 Sale by the Court, Priorities and Payment Out

(1) An application for an order for the survey, appraisement or sale of a ship may be made in a claim *in rem* at any stage by any party.

(2) If the court makes an order for sale, it may—
(a) set a time within which notice of claims against the proceeds of sale must be filed; and
(b) the time and manner in which such notice must be advertised.

(3) Any party with a judgment against the property or proceeds of sale may at any time after the time referred to in paragraph (2) apply to the court for the determination of priorities.

(4) An application notice under paragraph (3) must be served on all persons who have filed a claim against the property.

(5) Payment out of the proceeds of sale will be made only to judgment creditors and—
(a) in accordance with the determination of priorities; or
(b) as the court orders.

61.11 Limitation Claims

(1) This rule applies to limitation claims.

(2) A claim is started by the issue of a limitation claim form as set out in Practice Direction 61.

(3) The—
(a) claimant; and
(b) at least one defendant
must be named in the claim form, but all other defendants may be described.

(4) The claim form—
(a) must be served on all named defendants and any other defendant who requests service upon him; and
(b) may be served on any other defendant.

(5) The claim form may not be served out of the jurisdiction unless—
(a) the claim falls within section 22(2)(a), (b) or (c) of the Senior Courts Act 1981;
(b) *the defendant has* submitted to or agreed to submit to the jurisdiction of the court; or
(c) the Admiralty Court has jurisdiction over the claim under any applicable Convention; and
the court grants permission in accordance with Section IV of Part 6.

(6) An acknowledgment of service is not required.
(7) Every defendant upon whom a claim form is served must—
(a) within 28 days of service file—
(i) a defence; or
(ii) a notice that the defendant admits the right of the claimant to limit liability; or
(b) if the defendant wishes to—
(i) dispute the jurisdiction of the court; or
(ii) argue that the court should not exercise its jurisdiction,
file within 14 days of service (or where the claim form is served out of the jurisdiction, within the time specified in rule 6.35) an acknowledgment of service as set out in Practice Direction 61.
(8) If a defendant files an acknowledgment of service under paragraph (7)(b) he will be treated as having accepted that the court has jurisdiction to hear the claim unless he applies under Part 11 within 14 days after filing the acknowledgment of service.
(9) Where one or more named defendants admits the right to limit—
(a) the claimant may apply for a restricted limitation decree in the form set out in Practice Direction 61; and
(b) the court will issue a decree in the form set out in Practice Direction 61 limiting liability only against those named defendants who have admitted the claimant's right to limit liability.
(10) A restricted limitation decree—
(a) may be obtained against any named defendant who fails to file a defence within the time specified for doing so; and
(b) need not be advertised, but a copy must be served on the defendants to whom it applies.
(11) Where all the defendants upon whom the claim form has been served admit the claimant's right to limit liability—
(a) the claimant may apply to the Admiralty Registrar for a general limitation decree in the form set out in Practice Direction 61; and
(b) the court will issue a limitation decree.
(12) Where one or more of the defendants upon whom the claim form has been served do not admit the claimant's right to limit, the claimant may apply for a general limitation decree in the form set out in Practice Direction 61.
(13) When a limitation decree is granted the court—
(a) may—
(i) order that any proceedings relating to any claim arising out of the occurrence be stayed;
(ii) order the claimant to establish a limitation fund if one has not been established or make such other arrangements for payment of claims against which liability is limited; or
(iii) if the decree is a restricted limitation decree, distribute the limitation fund; and
(b) will, if the decree is a general limitation decree, give directions as to advertisement of the decree and set a time within which notice of claims against the fund must be filed or an application made to set aside the decree.
(14) When the court grants a general limitation decree the claimant must—
(a) advertise it in such manner and within such time as the court directs; and
(b) file—
(i) a declaration that the decree has been advertised in accordance with paragraph (a); and
(ii) copies of the advertisements.
(15) No later than the time set in the decree for filing claims, each of the defendants who wishes to assert a claim must file and serve his statement of case on—
(a) the limiting party; and
(b) all other defendants except where the court orders otherwise.
(16) Any person other than a defendant upon whom the claim form has been served may apply to the court within the time fixed in the decree to have a general limitation decree set aside.
(17) An application under paragraph (16) must be supported by a declaration—
(a) stating that the applicant has a claim against the claimant arising out of the occurrence; and

(b) setting out grounds for contending that the claimant is not entitled to the decree, either in the amount of limitation or at all.

(18) The claimant may constitute a limitation fund by making a payment into court.

(19) A limitation fund may be established before or after a limitation claim has been started.

(20) If a limitation claim is not commenced within 75 days after the date the fund was established—

(a) the fund will lapse; and

(b) all money in court (including interest) will be repaid to the person who made the payment into court.

(21) Money paid into court under paragraph (18) will not be paid out except under an order of the court.

(22) A limitation claim for—

(a) a restricted decree may be brought by counterclaim; and

(b) a general decree may only be brought by counterclaim with the permission of the court.

61.12 Stay of Proceedings

Where the court orders a stay of any claim *in rem*—

(a) any property under arrest in the claim remains under arrest; and

(b) any security representing the property remains in force,

unless the court orders otherwise.

61.13 Assessors

The court may sit with assessors when hearing—

(a) collision claims; or

(b) other claims involving issues of navigation or seamanship, and

the parties will not be permitted to call expert witnesses unless the court orders otherwise.

PD 61 Practice Direction 61—Admiralty Claims

This practice direction supplements CPR, Part 61.

PD 61 2.18, 11.7 [For commentary on a specific paragraph, please refer to the cross-references after the title of the paragraph.]

Scope: Rule 61.1

1.1 PD 58 also applies to Admiralty claims except where it is inconsistent with Part 61 or this practice direction.

Case Management

2.1 After a claim form is issued the Registrar will issue a direction in writing stating:
- (1) whether the claim will remain in the Admiralty Court or be transferred to another court; and
- (2) if the claim remains in the Admiralty Court:
  - (a) whether it will be dealt with by:
    - (i) the Admiralty judge; or
    - (ii) the Registrar; and
  - (b) whether the trial will be in London or elsewhere.

2.2 In making these directions the Registrar will have regard to:
- (1) the nature of the issues and the sums in dispute; and
- (2) the criteria set in r. 26.8 so far as they are applicable.

2.3 Where the Registrar directs that the claim will be dealt with by the Admiralty judge, case management directions will be given and any case management conference or pre-trial review will be heard by the Admiralty judge.

Claims *In Rem:* Rule 61.3

3.1 A claim form *in rem* must be in form ADM1.

3.2 The claimant in a claim *in rem* may be named or may be described, but if not named in the claim form must identify himself by name if requested to do so by any other party.

3.3 The defendant must be described in the claim form.

3.4 The acknowledgment of service must be in form ADM2. The person who acknowledges service must identify himself by name.

3.5 The period for acknowledging service under r. 61.3(4) applies irrespective of whether the claim form contains particulars of claim.

3.6 A claim form *in rem* may be served in the following ways:
- (1) on the property against which the claim is brought by fixing a copy of the claim form:
  - (a) on the outside of the property in a position which may reasonably be expected to be seen; or
  - (b) where the property is freight, either:
    - (i) on the cargo in respect of which the freight was earned; or
    - (ii) on the ship on which the cargo was carried;
- (2) if the property to be served is in the custody of a person who will not permit access to it, by leaving a copy of the claim form with that person;
- (3) where the property has been sold by the Marshal, by filing the claim form at the court;
- (4) where there is a notice against arrest, on the person named in the notice as being authorised to accept service;
- (5) on any solicitor authorised to accept service;
- (6) in accordance with any agreement providing for service of proceedings; or
- (7) in any other manner as the court may direct under r. 6.15 provided that the property against which the claim is brought or part of it is within the jurisdiction of the court.

3.7 In claims where the property:
- (1) is to be arrested; or
- (2) is already under arrest in current proceedings,

the Marshal will serve the *in rem* claim form if the claimant requests the court to do so.

3.8 In all other cases *in rem* claim forms must be served by the claimant.

3.9 Where the defendants are described and not named on the claim form (for example as 'the Owners of the Ship X'), any acknowledgment of service in addition to stating that description must also state the full names of the persons acknowledging service and the nature of their ownership.

3.10 After the acknowledgment of service has been filed, the claim will follow the procedure applicable to a claim proceeding in the Commercial list except that the claimant is allowed 75 days to serve the particulars of claim.

3.11 A defendant who files an acknowledgment of service to an *in rem* claim does not lose any right he may have to dispute the jurisdiction of the court (see r. 10.1(3)(b) and Part 11).

3.12 Any person who pays the prescribed fee may, during office hours, search for, inspect and take a copy of any claim form *in rem* whether or not it has been served.

Collision Claims: Rule 61.4

4.1 A collision statement of case must be in form ADM3.

4.2 A collision statement of case must contain:
- (1) in part 1 of the form, answers to the questions set out in that part; and
- (2) in part 2 of the form, a statement:
  - (a) of any other facts and matters on which the party filing the collision statement of case relies;
  - (b) of all allegations of negligence or other fault which the party filing the collision statement of case makes; and
  - (c) of the remedy which the party filing the collision statement of case claims.

4.3 When he files his collision statement of case each party must give notice to every other party that he has done so.

4.4 Within 14 days after the last collision statement of case is filed each party must serve a copy of his collision statement of case on every other party.

4.5 Before the coming into force of Part 61, a collision statement of case was known as a preliminary act and the law relating to preliminary acts will continue to apply to collision statements of case.

Arrest: Rule 61.5

5.1 An application for arrest must be:
- (1) in form ADM4 (which must also contain an undertaking); and
- (2) accompanied by a declaration in form ADM5.

5.2 When it receives an application for arrest that complies with the rules and the practice direction the court will issue an arrest warrant.

5.3 The declaration required by r. 61.5(3)(b) must be verified by a statement of truth and must state:
- (1) in every claim:
  - (a) the nature of the claim or counterclaim and that it has not been satisfied and if it arises in connection with a ship, the name of that ship;
  - (b) the nature of the property to be arrested and, if the property is a ship, the name of the ship and her port of registry; and
  - (c) the amount of the security sought, if any;
- (2) in a claim against a ship by virtue of the Senior Courts Act 1981, s. 21(4):
  - (a) the name of the person who would be liable on the claim if it were not commenced *in rem*;
  - (b) that the person referred to in sub-paragraph (a) was, when the right to bring the claim arose:
    - (i) the owner or charterer of; or
    - (ii) in possession or in control of,

    the ship in connection with which the claim arose; and
  - (c) that at the time the claim form was issued the person referred to in sub-paragraph (a) was either:
    - (i) the beneficial owner of all the shares in the ship in respect of which the warrant is required; or
    - (ii) the charterer of it under a charter by demise;

(3) in the cases set out in rr. 61.5(5) and (6) that the relevant notice has been sent or served, as appropriate; and
(4) in the case of a claim in respect of liability incurred under the Merchant Shipping Act 1995, s. 153, the facts relied on as establishing that the court is not prevented from considering the claim by reason of s. 166(2) of that Act.

5.4 The notice required by r. 61.5(5)(a) must be in form ADM6.

5.5 Property is arrested:
(1) by service on it of an arrest warrant in form ADM9 in the manner set out at para. 3.6(1); or
(2) where it is not reasonably practicable to serve the warrant, by service of a notice of the issue of the warrant:
(a) in the manner set out in para. 3.6(1) on the property; or
(b) by giving notice to those in charge of the property.

5.6 When property is arrested the Registrar will issue standard directions in form ADM10.

5.7 The Marshal does not insure property under arrest.

Cautions against Arrest: Rule 61.7

6.1 The entry of a caution against arrest is not treated as a submission to the jurisdiction of the court.

6.2 The request for a caution against arrest must be in form ADM7.

6.3 On the filing of such a request, a caution against arrest will be entered in the Register.

6.4 The Register is open for inspection when the Admiralty and Commercial Registry is open.

Release and Cautions against Release: Rule 61.8

7.1 The request for a caution against release must be in form ADM11.

7.2 On the filing of such a request, a caution against release will be entered in the Register.

7.3 The Register is open for inspection when the Admiralty and Commercial Registry is open.

7.4 A request for release under r. 61.8(4)(c) and (d) must be in form ADM12.

7.5 A withdrawal of a caution against release must be in form ADM12A.

Judgment in Default: Rule 61.9

para.8.1 20.2

8.1 An application notice for judgment in default must be in form ADM13.

Sale by the Court and Priorities: Rule 61.10

9.1 Any application to the court concerning:
(1) the sale of the property under arrest; or
(2) the proceeds of sale of property sold by the court
will be heard in public and the application notice served on:
(a) all parties to the claim;
(b) all persons who have requested cautions against release with regard to the property or the proceeds of sale; and
(c) the Marshal.

9.2 Unless the court orders otherwise an order for sale will be in form ADM14.

9.3 An order for sale before judgment may only be made by the Admiralty judge.

9.4 Unless the Admiralty judge orders otherwise, a determination of priorities may only be made by the Admiralty judge.

9.5 When:
(1) proceeds of sale are paid into court by the Marshal; and
(2) such proceeds are in a foreign currency,
the funds will be placed on one-day-call interest-bearing account unless the court orders otherwise.

9.6 Unless made at the same time as an application for sale, or other prior application, an application to place foreign currency on longer-term deposit may be made to the Registrar.

9.7 Notice of the placement of foreign currency in an interest-bearing account must be given to all parties interested in the fund by the party who made the application under para. 9.6.

9.8 Any interested party who wishes to object to the mode of investment of foreign currency paid into court may apply to the Registrar for directions.

Limitation Claims: Rule 61.11

10.1 The claim form in a limitation claim must be:
(1) in form ADM15; and
(2) accompanied by a declaration:
(a) setting out the facts upon which the claimant relies; and
(b) stating the names and addresses (if known) of all persons who, to the knowledge of the claimant, have claims against him in respect of the occurrence to which the claim relates (other than named defendants),
verified by a statement of truth.

10.2 A defence to a limitation claim must be in form ADM16A.

10.3 A notice admitting the right of the claimant to limit liability in a limitation claim must be in form ADM16.

10.4 An acknowledgment of service in a limitation claim must be in form ADM16B.

10.5 An application for a restricted limitation decree must be in form ADM17 and the decree issued by the court on such an application must be in form ADM18.

10.6 An application for a general limitation decree must be in form ADM17A.

10.7 Where:
(1) the right to limit is not admitted; and
(2) the claimant seeks a general limitation decree in form ADM17A,
the claimant must, within seven days after the date of the filing of the defence of the defendant last served or the expiry of the time for doing so, apply for an appointment before the Registrar for a case management conference.

10.8 On an application under r. 61.11(12) the Registrar may:
(1) grant a general limitation decree; or
(2) if he does not grant a decree:
(a) order service of a defence;
(b) order disclosure by the claimant; or
(c) make such other case management directions as may be appropriate.

10.9 The fact that a limitation fund has lapsed under r. 61.11(20)(a) does not prevent the establishment of a new fund.

10.10 Where a limitation fund is established, it must be:
(1) the sterling equivalent of the number of special drawing rights to which the claimant claims to be entitled to limit his liability under the Merchant Shipping Act 1995; together with
(2) interest from the date of the occurrence giving rise to his liability to the date of payment into court.

10.11 Where the claimant does not know the sterling equivalent referred to in para. 10.10(1) on the date of payment into court he may:
(1) calculate it on the basis of the latest available published sterling equivalent of a special drawing right as fixed by the International Monetary Fund; and
(2) in the event of the sterling equivalent of a special drawing right on the date of payment into court being different from that used for calculating the amount of that payment into court the claimant may:
(a) make up any deficiency by making a further payment into court which, if made within 14 days after the payment into court, will be treated, except for the purpose of the rules relating to the accrual of interest on money paid into court, as if made on the date of that payment into court; or
(b) apply to the court for payment out of any excess amount (together with any interest accrued) paid into court.

10.12 An application under para. 10.11(2)(b):
(1) *may be made without notice to any* party; and
(2) must be supported by evidence proving, to the satisfaction of the court, the sterling equivalent of the appropriate number of special drawing rights on the date of payment into court.

10.13 The claimant must give notice in writing to every named defendant of:
(1) any payment into court specifying:
(a) the date of the payment in;
(b) the amount paid in;
(c) the amount and rate of interest included; and
(d) the period to which it relates; and
(2) any excess amount (and interest) paid out to him under para. 10.11(2)(b).

10.14 A claim against the fund must be in form ADM20.

10.15 A defendant's statement of case filed and served in accordance with r. 61.11(15) must contain particulars of the defendant's claim.

10.16 Any defendant who is unable to file and serve a statement of case in accordance with r. 61.11(15) and para. 10.15 must file a declaration, verified by a statement of truth, in form ADM21 stating the reason for his inability.

10.17 No later than seven days after the time for filing claims or declarations, the Registrar will fix a date for a case management conference at which directions will be given for the further conduct of the proceedings.

10.18 Nothing in r. 61.11 prevents limitation being relied on by way of defence.

Proceedings against or Concerning the International Oil Pollution Compensation Fund 1992 and the International Oil Pollution Supplementary Fund

11.1 For the purposes of the Merchant Shipping Act 1995 ('the Act'), s. 177, the Fund may be given notice of proceedings by any party to a claim against an owner or guarantor in respect of liability under s. 153 of the Act by that person serving a notice in writing on the Fund together with copies of the claim form and any statements of case served in the claim.

11.2 Notice given to the Fund under para. 11.1 shall be deemed to have been given to the Supplementary Fund.

11.3 The Fund or the Supplementary Fund may intervene in any claim to which para. 11.1 applies, (whether or not served with the notice), by serving notice of intervention on the:
(1) owner;
(2) guarantor; and
(3) court.

11.4 Where a judgment is given against:
(1) the Fund in any claim under s. 175 of the Act;
(2) the Supplementary Fund in any claim under s. 176A of the Act,
the Registrar will arrange for a stamped copy of the judgment to be sent by post to:
(a) the Fund (where sub-paragraph (1) applies);
(b) the Supplementary Fund (where sub-paragraph (2) applies).

11.5 Notice to the Registrar of the matters set out in:
(1) s. 176(3)(b) of the Act in proceedings under s. 175; or
(2) s. 176B(2)(b) of the Act in proceedings under s. 176A,
must be given in writing and sent to the court by:
(a) the Fund (where sub-paragraph (1) applies);
(b) the Supplementary Fund (where sub-paragraph (2) applies).

Other Claims

12.1 This section applies to Admiralty claims which, before the coming into force of Part 61, would have been called claims *in personam*. Subject to the provisions of Part 61 and this practice direction relating to limitation claims and to collision claims, the following provisions apply to such claims.

12.2 All such claims will proceed in accordance with Part 58 (Commercial Court).

12.3 The claim form must be in form ADM1A and must be served by the claimant.

12.4 The claimant may be named or may be described, but if not named in the claim form must identify himself by name if requested to do so by any other party.

12.5 The defendant must be named in the claim form.

12.6 Any person who files a defence must identify himself by name in the defence.

References to the Registrar

13.1 The court may at any stage in the claim refer any question or issue for determination by the Registrar (a 'reference').

13.2 Unless the court orders otherwise, where a reference has been ordered:

(1) if particulars of claim have not already been served, the claimant must file and serve particulars of claim on all other parties within 14 days after the date of the order; and

(2) any party opposing the claim must file a defence to the claim within 14 days after service of the particulars of claim on him.

13.3 Within seven days after the defence is filed, the claimant must apply for an appointment before the Registrar for a case management conference.

Undertakings

14.1 Where, in Part 61 or this practice direction, any undertaking to the Marshal is required it must be given:

(1) in writing and to his satisfaction; or

(2) in accordance with such other arrangements as he may require.

14.2 Where any party is dissatisfied with a direction given by the Marshal in this respect he may apply to the Registrar for a ruling.

[The following forms are annexed to PD 61:

ADM1	Claim form (Admiralty claim *in rem*)
ADM1A	Claim form (Admiralty claim)
ADM1C	Notes for defendant
ADM2	Acknowledgment of service
ADM3	Collision statement of case
ADM4	Application and undertaking for arrest and custody
ADM5	Declaration in support of application for warrant of arrest
ADM6	Notice to consular officer of intention to apply for warrant of arrest
ADM7	Request for caution against arrest
ADM9	Warrant of arrest
ADM10	Standard directions to the Admiralty Marshal
ADM11	Request for caution against release
ADM12	Request and undertaking for release
ADM12A	Request for withdrawal of caution against release
ADM13	Application for judgment in default of filing an acknowledgment of service and/or defence or collision statement of case
ADM14	Order for sale of a ship
ADM15	Claim form (Admiralty limitation claim)
ADM15B	Notes for defendant (Admiralty limitation claim)
ADM16	Notice of admission of right of claimant to limit liability
ADM16A	Defence to Admiralty limitation claim
ADM16B	Acknowledgment of service (Admiralty limitation claim)
ADM17	Application for restricted limitation decree
ADM17A	Application for general limitation decree
ADM18	Restricted limitation decree
ADM19	General limitation decree
ADM20	Defendant's claim in a limitation claim
ADM21	Declaration as to inability of a defendant to file and serve statement of case under a decree of limitation

These forms are online at <http://hmctsformfinder.justice.gov.uk>.]

CPR Part 62 Arbitration Claims

Part 62 PC 31, 20.2, 53.3, 72.1, 72.10, 72.18 [For commentary on a specific rule, please refer to the cross-references after the title of the rule.]

62.1 Scope of This Part and Interpretation

(1) This Part contains rules about arbitration claims.
(2) In this Part—
  (a) 'the 1950 Act' means the Arbitration Act 1950;
  (b) 'the 1975 Act' means the Arbitration Act 1975;
  (c) 'the 1979 Act' means the Arbitration Act 1979;
  (d) 'the 1996 Act' means the Arbitration Act 1996;
  (e) references to—
    (i) the 1996 Act; or
    (ii) any particular section of that Act
  include references to that Act or to the particular section of that Act as applied with modifications by the ACAS Arbitration Scheme (England and Wales) Order 2001; and
  (f) 'arbitration claim form' means a claim form in the form set out in Practice Direction 62.
(3) Part 58 (Commercial Court) applies to arbitration claims in the Commercial Court, Part 59 (Mercantile Court) applies to arbitration claims in the Mercantile Court and Part 60 (Technology and Construction Court claims) applies to arbitration claims in the Technology and Construction Court, except where this Part provides otherwise.

I CLAIMS UNDER THE 1996 ACT

62.2 Interpretation

(1) In this Section of this Part 'arbitration claim' means—
  (a) any application to the court under the 1996 Act;
  (b) a claim to determine—
    (i) whether there is a valid arbitration agreement;
    (ii) whether an arbitration tribunal is properly constituted; or
  what matters have been submitted to arbitration in accordance with an arbitration agreement;
  (c) a claim to declare that an award by an arbitral tribunal is not binding on a party; and
  (d) any other application affecting—
    (i) arbitration proceedings (whether started or not); or
    (ii) an arbitration agreement.

(2) This Section of this Part does not apply to an arbitration claim to which Sections II or III of this Part apply.

62.3 Starting the Claim

r.62.3(1) 20.2, 72.2
r.62.3(2) 72.2
r.62.3(4) 72.2

(1) Except where paragraph (2) applies an arbitration claim must be started by the issue of an arbitration claim form in accordance with the Part 8 procedure.
(2) An application under section 9 of the 1996 Act to stay legal proceedings must be made by application notice to the court dealing with those proceedings.
(3) The courts in which an arbitration claim may be started are set out in Practice Direction 62.
(4) Rule 30.5 applies with the modification that a judge of the Technology and Construction Court may transfer the claim to any other court or specialist list.

62.4 Arbitration Claim Form

r.62.4(1) PC 31
r.62.4(1)(a)–(f) 72.3
r.62.4(2) PC 31, 72.4

(1) An arbitration claim form must—
 (a) include a concise statement of—
  (i) the remedy claimed; and
  (ii) any questions on which the claimant seeks the decision of the court;
 (b) give details of any arbitration award challenged by the claimant, identifying which part or parts of the award are challenged and specifying the grounds for the challenge;
 (c) show that any statutory requirements have been met;
 (d) specify under which section of the 1996 Act the claim is made;
 (e) identify against which (if any) defendants a costs order is sought; and
 (f) specify either—
  (i) the persons on whom the arbitration claim form is to be served, stating their role in the arbitration and whether they are defendants; or
  (ii) that the claim is made without notice under section 44(3) of the 1996 Act and the grounds relied on.
(2) Unless the court orders otherwise an arbitration claim form must be served on the defendant within 1 month from the date of issue and rules 7.5 and 7.6 are modified accordingly.
(3) Where the claimant applies for an order under section 12 of the 1996 Act (extension of time for beginning arbitral proceedings or other dispute resolution procedures), he may include in his arbitration claim form an alternative application for a declaration that such an order is not needed.

62.5 Service Out of the Jurisdiction

r.62.5(1) PC 31, 72.1, 72.5, 72.8
r.62.5(1)(c) 37.55, 72.5
r.62.5(2)–(3) PC 31, 72.5
r.62.5(4) PC 31, 72.8

(1) The court may give permission to serve an arbitration claim form out of the jurisdiction if—
 (a) the claimant seeks to—
  (i) challenge; or
  (ii) appeal on a question of law arising out of,
 an arbitration award made within the jurisdiction;
(The place where an award is treated as made is determined by section 53 of the 1996 Act.)
 (b) the claim is for an order under section 44 of the 1996 Act; or
 (c) the claimant—
  (i) seeks some other remedy or requires a question to be decided by the court affecting an arbitration (whether started or not), an arbitration agreement or an arbitration award; and
  (ii) the seat of the arbitration is or will be within the jurisdiction or the conditions in section 2(4) of the 1996 Act are satisfied.
(2) *An application for permission* under paragraph (1) must be supported by written evidence—
 (a) stating the grounds on which the application is made; and
 (b) showing in what place or country the person to be served is, or probably may be found.
(3) Rules 6.40 to 6.46 apply to the service of an arbitration claim form under paragraph (1).

(4) An order giving permission to serve an arbitration claim form out of the jurisdiction must specify the period within which the defendant may file an acknowledgment of service.

62.6 Notice

r.62.6(1)–(3) **72.6**

(1) Where an arbitration claim is made under section 24, 28 or 56 of the 1996 Act, each arbitrator must be a defendant.
(2) Where notice must be given to an arbitrator or any other person it may be given by sending him a copy of—
  (a) the arbitration claim form; and
  (b) any written evidence in support.
(3) Where the 1996 Act requires an application to the court to be made on notice to any other party to the arbitration, that notice must be given by making that party a defendant.

62.7 Case Management

r.62.7(1)–(3) **72.9**
r.62.7(2) **42.25**
r.62.7(4) **72.9**

(1) Part 26 and any other rule that requires a party to file an allocation questionnaire does not apply.
(2) Arbitration claims are allocated to the multi-track.
(3) Part 29 does not apply.
(4) The automatic directions set out in Practice Direction 62 apply unless the court orders otherwise.

62.8 Stay of Legal Proceedings

r.62.8(1)–(3) **72.10**

(1) An application notice seeking a stay of legal proceedings under section 9 of the 1996 Act must be served on all parties to those proceedings who have given an address for service.
(2) A copy of an application notice under paragraph (1) must be served on any other party to the legal proceedings (whether or not he is within the jurisdiction) who has not given an address for service, at—
  (a) his last known address; or
  (b) a place where it is likely to come to his attention.
(3) Where a question arises as to whether—
  (a) an arbitration agreement has been concluded; or
  (b) the dispute which is the subject-matter of the proceedings falls within the terms of such an agreement,

the court may decide that question or give directions to enable it to be decided and may order the proceedings to be stayed pending its decision.

62.9 Variation of Time

r.62.9(1)–(2) **72.12**
r.62.9(3)(a)–(c) **72.12**

(1) The court may vary the period of 28 days fixed by section 70(3) of the 1996 Act for—
  (a) challenging the award under section 67 or 68 of the Act; and
  (b) appealing against an award under section 69 of the Act.
(2) An application for an order under paragraph (1) may be made without notice being served on any other party before the period of 28 days expires.
(3) After the period of 28 days has expired—
  (a) an application for an order extending time under paragraph (1) must—
    (i) be made in the arbitration claim form; and
    (ii) state the grounds on which the application is made;
  (b) any defendant may file written evidence opposing the extension of time within 7 days after service of the arbitration claim form; and
  (c) if the court extends the period of 28 days, each defendant's time for acknowledging service and serving evidence shall start to run as if the arbitration claim form had been served on the date when the court's order is served on that defendant.

62.10 Hearings

r.62.10 61.21, 72.16 r.62.10(3) PC 31, 72.16
r.62.10(1)–(2) 72.16 r.62.10(4)(a)–(b) 72.16

(1) The court may order that an arbitration claim be heard either in public or in private.
(2) Rule 39.2 does not apply.
(3) Subject to any order made under paragraph (1)—
 (a) the determination of—
  (i) a preliminary point of law under section 45 of the 1996 Act; or
  (ii) an appeal under section 69 of the 1996 Act on a question of law arising out of an award,
 will be heard in public; and
 (b) all other arbitration claims will be heard in private.
(4) Paragraph (3)(a) does not apply to—
 (a) the preliminary question of whether the court is satisfied of the matters set out in section 45(2)(b); or
 (b) an application for permission to appeal under section 69(2)(b).

II OTHER ARBITRATION CLAIMS

r.62.11–62.16 72.17

62.11 Scope of This Section

rr.62.11 72.17

(1) This Section of this Part contains rules about arbitration claims to which the old law applies.
(2) In this Section—
 (a) 'the old law' means the enactments specified in Schedules 3 and 4 of the 1996 Act as they were in force before their amendment or repeal by that Act; and
 (b) 'arbitration claim' means any application to the court under the old law and includes an appeal (or application for permission to appeal) to the High Court under section 1(2) of the 1979 Act.
(3) This Section does not apply to—
 (a) a claim to which Section III of this Part applies; or
 (b) a claim on the award.

62.12 Applications to Judge

r.62.12 72.17

A claim—
(a) seeking permission to appeal under section 1(2) of the 1979 Act;
(b) under section 1(5) of that Act (including any claim seeking permission); or
(c) under section 5 of that Act,
must be made in the High Court and will be heard by a judge of the Commercial Court unless any such judge directs otherwise.

62.13 Starting the Claim

r.62.13 72.17 r.62.13(1) 20.2

(1) Except where paragraph (2) applies an arbitration claim must be started by the issue of an arbitration claim form in accordance with the Part 8 procedure.
(2) Where an arbitration claim is to be made in existing proceedings—
 (a) it must be made by way of application notice; and
 (b) any reference in this Section of this Part to an arbitration claim form includes a reference to an application notice.
(3) The arbitration claim form in an arbitration claim under section 1(5) of the 1979 Act (including any claim seeking permission) must be served on—
 (a) the arbitrator or umpire; and
 (b) any other party to the reference.

62.14 Claims in District Registries

r.62.14 72.17

If—

(a) a claim is to be made under section 12(4) of the 1950 Act for an order for the issue of a witness summons to compel the attendance of the witness before an arbitrator or umpire; and
(b) the attendance of the witness is required within the district of a District Registry,

the claim may be started in that Registry.

62.15 Time Limits and Other Special Provisions about Arbitration Claims

r.62.15 72.17

(1) An arbitration claim to—
  (a) remit an award under section 22 of the 1950 Act;
  (b) set aside an award under section 23(2) of that Act or otherwise; or
  (c) direct an arbitrator or umpire to state the reasons for an award under section 1(5) of the 1979 Act,

  must be made, and the arbitration claim form served, within 21 days after the award has been made and published to the parties.
(2) An arbitration claim to determine any question of law arising in the course of a reference under section 2(1) of the Arbitration Act 1979 must be made, and the arbitration claim form served, within 14 days after—
  (a) the arbitrator or umpire gave his consent in writing to the claim being made; or
  (b) the other parties so consented.
(3) An appeal under section 1(2) of the 1979 Act must be filed, and the arbitration claim form served, within 21 days after the award has been made and published to the parties.
(4) Where reasons material to an appeal under section 1(2) of the 1979 Act are given on a date subsequent to the publication of the award, the period of 21 days referred to in paragraph (3) will run from the date on which reasons are given.
(5) In every arbitration claim to which this rule applies—
  (a) the arbitration claim form must state the grounds of the claim or appeal;
  (b) where the claim or appeal is based on written evidence, a copy of that evidence must be served with the arbitration claim form; and
  (c) where the claim or appeal is made with the consent of the arbitrator, the umpire or the other parties, a copy of every written consent must be served with the arbitration claim form.
(6) In an appeal under section 1(2) of the 1979 Act—
  (a) a statement of the grounds for the appeal specifying the relevant parts of the award and reasons; and
  (b) where permission is required, any written evidence in support of the contention that the question of law concerns—
    (i) a term of a contract; or
    (ii) an event,

    which is not a 'one-off' term or event,

  must be filed and served with the arbitration claim form.
(7) Any written evidence in reply to written evidence under paragraph (6)(b) must be filed and served on the claimant not less than 2 days before the hearing.
(8) A party to a claim seeking permission to appeal under section 1(2) of the 1979 Act who wishes to contend that the award should be upheld for reasons not expressed or fully expressed in the award and reasons must file and serve on the claimant, a notice specifying the grounds of his contention not less than 2 days before the hearing.

62.16 Service Out of the Jurisdiction

r.62.16 72.17

(1) Subject to paragraph (2)—
  (a) any arbitration claim form in an arbitration claim under the 1950 Act or the 1979 Act; or
  (b) any order made in such a claim,

  may be served out of the jurisdiction with the permission of the court if the arbitration to which the claim relates—

(i) is governed by the law of England and Wales; or
(ii) has been, is being, or will be, held within the jurisdiction.

(2) An arbitration claim form seeking permission to enforce an award may be served out of the jurisdiction with the permission of the court whether or not the arbitration is governed by the law of England and Wales.

(3) An application for permission to serve an arbitration claim form out of the jurisdiction must be supported by written evidence—
(a) stating the grounds on which the application is made; and
(b) showing in what place or country the person to be served is, or probably may be found.

(4) Rules 6.40 to 6.46 apply to the service of an arbitration claim form under paragraph (1).

(5) An order giving permission to serve an arbitration claim form out of the jurisdiction must specify the period within which the defendant may file an acknowledgment of service.

III ENFORCEMENT

62.17 Scope of This Section

r.62.17 **72.18**

This Section of this Part applies to all arbitration enforcement proceedings other than by a claim on the award.

62.18 Enforcement of Awards

r.62.18(1) **72.19, 73.7**
r.62.18(2) **72.19**
r.62.18(3) **72.19**
r.62.18(4) **72.19**
r.62.18(5) **72.19**
r.62.18(6)(a)–(c) **72.19**
r.62.18(7)–(11) **72.19**

(1) An application for permission under—
(a) section 66 of the 1996 Act;
(b) section 101 of the 1996 Act;
(c) section 26 of the 1950 Act; or
(d) section 3(1)(a) of the 1975 Act,
to enforce an award in the same manner as a judgment or order may be made without notice in an arbitration claim form.

(2) The court may specify parties to the arbitration on whom the arbitration claim form must be served.

(3) The parties on whom the arbitration claim form is served must acknowledge service and the enforcement proceedings will continue as if they were an arbitration claim under Section I of this Part.

(4) With the permission of the court the arbitration claim form may be served out of the jurisdiction irrespective of where the award is, or is treated as, made.

(5) Where the applicant applies to enforce an agreed award within the meaning of section 51(2) of the 1996 Act—
(a) the arbitration claim form must state that the award is an agreed award; and
(b) any order made by the court must also contain such a statement.

(6) An application for permission must be supported by written evidence—
(a) exhibiting—
(i) where the application is made under section 66 of the 1996 Act or under section 26 of the 1950 Act, the arbitration agreement and the original award (or copies);
(ii) where the application is under section 101 of the 1996 Act, the documents required to be produced by section 102 of that Act; or
(iii) where the application is under section 3(1)(a) of the 1975 Act, the documents required to be produced by section 4 of that Act;
(b) stating the name and the usual or last known place of residence or business of the claimant and of the person against whom it is sought to enforce the award; and
(c) *stating either*—
(i) that the award has not been complied with; or
(ii) the extent to which it has not been complied with at the date of the application.

(7) An order giving permission must—
(a) be drawn up by the claimant; and
(b) be served on the defendant by—
(i) delivering a copy to him personally; or
(ii) sending a copy to him at his usual or last known place of residence or business.

(8) An order giving permission may be served out of the jurisdiction—
(a) without permission; and
(b) in accordance with rules 6.40 to 6.46 as if the order were an arbitration claim form.

(9) Within 14 days after service of the order or, if the order is to be served out of the jurisdiction, within such other period as the court may set—
(a) the defendant may apply to set aside the order; and
(b) the award must not be enforced until after—
(i) the end of that period; or
(ii) any application made by the defendant within that period has been finally disposed of.

(10) The order must contain a statement of—
(a) the right to make an application to set the order aside; and
(b) the restrictions on enforcement under rule 62.18(9)(b).

(11) Where a body corporate is a party any reference in this rule to place of residence or business shall have effect as if the reference were to the registered or principal address of the body corporate.

62.19 Interest on Awards

r.62.19(1) 72.20 r.62.19(2) 72.20

(1) Where an applicant seeks to enforce an award of interest the whole or any part of which relates to a period after the date of the award, he must file a statement giving the following particulars—
(a) whether simple or compound interest was awarded;
(b) the date from which interest was awarded;
(c) where rests were provided for, specifying them;
(d) the rate of interest awarded; and
(e) a calculation showing—
(i) the total amount claimed up to the date of the statement; and
(ii) any sum which will become due on a daily basis.

(2) A statement under paragraph (1) must be filed whenever the amount of interest has to be quantified for the purpose of—
(a) obtaining a judgment or order under section 66 of the 1996 Act (enforcement of the award); or
(b) enforcing such a judgment or order.

62.20 Registration in High Court of Foreign Awards

(1) Where—
(a) an award is made in proceedings on an arbitration in any part of a British overseas territory or other territory to which Part I of the Foreign Judgments (Reciprocal Enforcement) Act 1933 ('the 1933 Act') extends;
(b) Part II of the Administration of Justice Act 1920 extended to that part immediately before Part I of the 1933 Act was extended to that part; and
(c) an award has, under the law in force in the place where it was made, become enforceable in the same manner as a judgment given by a court in that place, rules 74.1 to 74.7 and 74.9 apply in relation to the award as they apply in relation to a judgment given by the court subject to the modifications in paragraph (2).

(2) The modifications referred to in paragraph (1) are as follows—
(a) for references to the State of origin are substituted references to the place where the award was made; and
(b) the written evidence required by rule 74.4 must state (in addition to the matters required by that rule) that to the best of the information or belief of the maker of the statement the award has, under the law in force in the place where it was made, become enforceable in the same manner as a judgment given by a court in that place.

62.21 Registration of Awards under the Arbitration (International Investment Disputes) Act 1966

(1) In this rule—
   (a) 'the 1966 Act' means the Arbitration (International Investment Disputes) Act 1966;
   (b) 'award' means an award under the Convention;
   (c) 'the Convention' means the Convention on the settlement of investment disputes between States and nationals of other States which was opened for signature in Washington on 18th March 1965;
   (d) 'judgment creditor' means the person seeking recognition or enforcement of an award; and
   (e) 'judgment debtor' means the other party to the award.

(2) Subject to the provisions of this rule, the following provisions of RSC Order 71 apply with such modifications as may be necessary in relation to an award as they apply in relation to a judgment to which Part II of the Foreign Judgments (Reciprocal Enforcement) Act 1933 applies—
   (a) rule 74.1;
   (b) rule 74.3;
   (c) rule 74.4(1), (2)(a) to (d), and (4)
   (d) rule 74.6 (except paragraph (3)(c) to (e)); and
   (e) rule 74.9(2).

(3) An application to have an award registered in the High Court under section 1 of the 1966 Act must be made in accordance with the Part 8 procedure.

(4) The written evidence required by rule 74.4 in support of an application for registration must—
   (a) exhibit the award certified under the Convention instead of the judgment (or a copy of it); and
   (b) in addition to stating the matters referred to in rule 74.4(2)(a) to (d), state whether—
      (i) at the date of the application the enforcement of the award has been stayed (provisionally or otherwise) under the Convention; and
      (ii) any, and if so what, application has been made under the Convention, which, if granted, might result in a stay of the enforcement of the award.

(5) Where, on granting permission to register an award or an application made by the judgment debtor after an award has been registered, the court considers—
   (a) that the enforcement of the award has been stayed (whether provisionally or otherwise) under the Convention; or
   (b) that an application has been made under the Convention which, if granted, might result in a stay of the enforcement of the award,

the court may stay the enforcement of the award for such time as it considers appropriate.

PD 62 Practice Direction 62 — Arbitration

This practice direction supplements CPR, Part 62.

PD 62 72.1 [For commentary on a specific paragraph, please refer to the cross-references after the title of the paragraph.]

SECTION I

1.1 This Section of this practice direction applies to arbitration claims to which Section I of Part 62 applies.

1.2 In this Section 'the 1996 Act' means the Arbitration Act 1996.

1.3 Where a rule provides for a document to be sent, it may be sent:
(1) by first-class post;
(2) through a document exchange; or
(3) by fax, electronic mail or other means of electronic communication.

Starting the Claim: Rule 62.3

paras.2.1–2.2 72.2 para.2.3(1)–(2) PC 31, 72.2

2.1 An arbitration claim under the 1996 Act (other than under s. 9) must be started in accordance with the High Court and County Courts (Allocation of Arbitration Proceedings) Order 1996 (SI 1996/3215) by the issue of an arbitration claim form.

2.2 An arbitration claim form must be substantially in [form N8].

2.3 Subject to para. 2.1, an arbitration claim form:
(1) may be issued at the courts set out in column 1 of the table below and will be entered in the list set out against that court in column 2;
(2) relating to a landlord and tenant or partnership dispute must be issued in the Chancery Division of the High Court.

Court	List
Admiralty and Commercial Registry at the Royal Courts of Justice, London	Commercial list
Technology and Construction Court Registry, St Dunstan's House, London	TCC list
District Registry of the High Court (where mercantile court established)	Mercantile list
District Registry of the High Court (where arbitration claim form marked 'Technology and Construction Court' in top right-hand corner)	TCC list

2.3A An arbitration claim form must, in the case of an appeal, or application for permission to appeal, from a judge-arbitrator, be issued in the Civil Division of the Court of Appeal. The judge hearing the application may adjourn the matter for oral argument beforef two judges of that court.

Arbitration Claim Form: Rule 62.4

para.3.1 72.4 para.3.2 PC 31, 72.4

Service

3.1 The court may exercise its powers under r. 6.15 to permit service of an arbitration claim form at the address of a party's solicitor or representative acting for that party in the arbitration.

3.2 Where the arbitration claim form is served by the claimant he must file a certificate of service within seven days of service of the arbitration claim form.

(Rule 6.17 specifies what a certificate of service must show.)

Acknowledgment of Service or Making Representations by Arbitrator or ACAS

paras.4.1–4.3 72.8

4.1 Where:
(1) an arbitrator; or

(2) ACAS (in a claim under the 1996 Act as applied with modifications by the ACAS Arbitration Scheme (England and Wales) Order 2001 (SI 2001/1185)), is sent a copy of an arbitration claim form (including an arbitration claim form sent under r. 62.6(2)), that arbitrator or ACAS (as the case may be) may:
(a) apply to be made a defendant; or
(b) make representations to the court under para. 4.3.

4.2 An application under para. 4.1(2)(a) to be made a defendant:
(1) must be served on the claimant; but
(2) need not be served on any other party.

4.3 An arbitrator or ACAS may make representations by filing written evidence or in writing to the court.

Supply of Documents from Court Records

para.5.1 15.58, 72.7

5.1 An arbitration claim form may only be inspected with the permission of the court.

Case Management: Rule 62.7

para.6.1 72.9 paras.6.2–6.7 PC 31, 72.9

6.1 The following directions apply unless the court orders otherwise.

6.2 A defendant who wishes to rely on evidence before the court must file and serve his written evidence:
(1) within 21 days after the date by which he was required to acknowledge service; or,
(2) where a defendant is not required to file an acknowledgment of service, within 21 days after service of the arbitration claim form.

6.3 A claimant who wishes to rely on evidence in reply to written evidence filed under para. 6.2 must file and serve his written evidence within seven days after service of the defendant's evidence.

6.4 Agreed indexed and paginated bundles of all the evidence and other documents to be used at the hearing must be prepared by the claimant.

6.5 Not later than five days before the hearing date estimates for the length of the hearing must be filed together with a complete set of the documents to be used.

6.6 Not later than two days before the hearing date the claimant must file and serve:
(1) a chronology of the relevant events cross-referenced to the bundle of documents;
(2) (where necessary) a list of the persons involved; and
(3) a skeleton argument which lists succinctly:
(a) the issues which arise for decision;
(b) the grounds of relief (or opposing relief) to be relied upon;
(c) the submissions of fact to be made with the references to the evidence; and
(d) the submissions of law with references to the relevant authorities.

6.7 Not later than the day before the hearing date the defendant must file and serve a skeleton argument which lists succinctly:
(1) the issues which arise for decision;
(2) the grounds of relief (or opposing relief) to be relied upon;
(3) the submissions of fact to be made with the references to the evidence; and
(4) the submissions of law with references to the relevant authorities.

Securing the Attendance of Witnesses

paras.7.1–7.3 72.11

7.1 A party to arbitral proceedings being conducted in England or Wales who wishes to rely on s. 43 of the 1996 Act to secure the attendance of a witness must apply for a witness summons in accordance with Part 34.

7.2 If the attendance of the witness is required within the district of a district registry, the application may be made at that registry.

7.3 A witness summons will not be issued until the applicant files written evidence showing that the application is made with:
(1) the permission of the tribunal; or
(2) the agreement of the other parties.

Interim Remedies

para.8.1 72.2

8.1 An application for an interim remedy under s. 44 of the 1996 Act must be made in an arbitraion claim form.

Applications under Sections 32 and 45 of the 1996 Act

9.1 This paragraph applies to arbitration claims for the determination of:
(1) a question as to the substantive jurisdiction of the arbitral tribunal under s. 32 of the 1996 Act; and
(2) a preliminary point of law under s. 45 of the 1996 Act.

9.2 Where an arbitration claim is made without the agreement in writing of all the other parties to the arbitral proceedings but with the permission of the arbitral tribunal, the written evidence or witness statements filed by the parties must set out any evidence relied on by the parties in support of their contention that the court should, or should not, consider the claim.

9.3 As soon as practicable after the written evidence is filed, the court will decide whether or not it should consider the claim and, unless the court otherwise directs, will so decide without a hearing.

Decisions without a Hearing

para.10.2 72.12

10.1 Having regard to the overriding objective the court may decide particular issues without a hearing. For example, as set out in para. 9.3, the question whether the court is satisfied as to the matters set out in s. 32(2)(b) or s. 45(2)(b) of the 1996 Act.

10.2 The court will generally decide whether to extend the time limit under s. 70(3) of the 1996 Act without a hearing. Where the court makes an order extending the time limit, the defendant must file his written evidence within 21 days from service of the order.

Variation of Time: Rule 62.9

para.11.1(1)–(2) 72.12

11.1 An application for an order under r. 62.9(1):
(1) before the period of 28 days has expired, must be made in a Part 23 application notice; and
(2) after the period of 28 days has expired, must be set out in a separately identified part in the arbitration claim form.

Applications for Permission to Appeal

paras.12.1–12.9 72.15
para.12.1 72.15
para.12.4 72.15
para.12.5 72.15
para.12.6(1) 72.15
para.12.6(2) 72.15
para.12.7 72.15
para.12.8 72.15
para.12.9 72.15
para.12.11 72.15
para.12.12 72.15
para.12.14 72.15

12.1 Where a party seeks permission to appeal to the court on a question of law arising out of an arbitration award, the arbitration claim form must, in addition to complying with r. 62.4(1)—
(1) identify the question of law;
(2) state the grounds (but not the argument) on which the party challenges the award and contends that permission should be given;
(3) be accompanied by a skeleton argument in support of the application in accordance with para. 12.2; and
(4) append the award.

12.2 Subject to para. 12.3, the skeleton argument—
(1) must be printed in 12 point font, with 1½ line spacing;
(2) should not exceed 15 pages in length; and
(3) must contain an estimate of how long the court is likely to need to deal with the application on the papers.

12.3 If the skeleton argument exceeds 15 pages in length the author must write to the court explaining why that is necessary.

12.4 Written evidence may be filed in support of the application only if it is necessary to show (insofar as that is not apparent from the award itself)—
(1) that the determination of the question raised by the appeal will substantially affect the rights of one or more of the parties;
(2) that the question is one which the tribunal was asked to determine;
(3) that the question is one of general public importance;
(4) that it is just and proper in all the circumstances for the court to determine the question raised by the appeal.
Any such evidence must be filed and served with the arbitration claim form.

12.5 Unless there is a dispute whether the question raised by the appeal is one which the tribunal was asked to determine, no arbitration documents may be put before the court other than—
(1) the award; and
(2) any document (such as the contract or the relevant parts thereof) which is referred to in the award and which the court needs to read to determine a question of law arising out of the award.
In this practice direction 'arbitration documents' means documents adduced in or produced for the purposes of the arbitration.

12.6 A respondent who wishes to oppose an application for permission to appeal must file a respondent's notice which—
(1) sets out the grounds (but not the argument) on which the respondent opposes the application; and
(2) states whether the respondent wishes to contend that the award should be upheld for reasons not expressed (or not fully expressed) in the award and, if so, states those reasons (but not the argument).

12.7 The respondent's notice must be filed and served within 21 days after the date on which the respondent was required to acknowledge service and must be accompanied by a skeleton argument in support which complies with para. 12.2 above.

12.8 Written evidence in opposition to the application should be filed only if it complies with the requirements of para. 12.4 above. Any such evidence must be filed and served with the respondent's notice.

12.9 The applicant may file and serve evidence or argument in reply only if it is necessary to do so. Any such evidence or argument must be as brief as possible and must be filed and served within seven days after service of the respondent's notice.

12.10 If either party wishes to invite the court to consider arbitration documents other than those specified in para. 12.5 above the counsel or solicitor responsible for settling the application documents must write to the court explaining why that is necessary.

12.11 If a party or its representative fails to comply with the requirements of paras 12.1 to 12.9 the court may penalise that party or representative in costs.

12.12 The court will normally determine applications for permission to appeal without an oral hearing but may direct otherwise, particularly with a view to saving time (including court time) or costs.

12.13 Where the court considers that an oral hearing is required, it may give such further directions as are necessary.

12.14 Where the court refuses an application for permission to appeal without an oral hearing, it will provide brief reasons.

12.15 The bundle for the hearing of any appeal should contain only the claim form, the respondent's notice, the arbitration documents referred to in para. 12.5, the order granting permission to appeal and the skeleton arguments.

SECTION II

13.1 This Section of this practice direction applies to arbitration claims to which Section II of Part 62 applies.

Starting the Claim: Rule 62.13

14.1 An arbitration claim must be started in the Commercial Court and, where required to be heard by a judge, be heard by a judge of that court unless he otherwise directs.

SECTION III

15.1 This Section of this practice direction applies to enforcement proceedings to which Section III of Part 62 applies.

Registration of Awards under the Arbitration (International Investment Disputes) Act 1966: Rule 62.21

16.1 Awards ordered to be registered under the 1966 Act and particulars will be entered in the Register kept for that purpose at the Admiralty and Commercial Registry.

[The following forms are annexed to PD 62:

N8	Claim form (arbitration)
N8A	Arbitration claim—notes for the claimant
N8B	Arbitration claim—notes for the defendant
N15	Acknowledgment of service (arbitration claim)

These forms are online at <http://hmctsformfinder.justice.gov.uk>.]

CPR Part 63 Intellectual Property Claims

Part 63 **2.21, 11.4, 11.7, 11.10, 42.25, 74.5** [For commentary on a specific rule, please refer to the cross-references after the title of the rule.]

63.1 Scope of This Part and Interpretation

r.63.1(3) **42.25**

(1) This Part applies to all intellectual property claims including—
  (a) registered intellectual property rights such as—
    (i) patents;
    (ii) registered designs; and
    (iii) registered trade marks; and
  (b) unregistered intellectual property rights such as—
    (i) copyright;
    (ii) design right;
    (iii) the right to prevent passing off; and
    (iv) the other rights set out in Practice Direction 63.

(2) In this Part—
  (a) 'the 1977 Act' means the Patents Act 1977;
  (b) 'the 1988 Act' means the Copyright, Designs and Patents Act 1988;
  (c) 'the 1994 Act' means the Trade Marks Act 1994;
  (d) 'the Comptroller' means the Comptroller General of Patents, Designs and Trade Marks;
  (e) 'patent' means a patent under the 1977 Act or a supplementary protection certificate granted by the Patent Office under Article 10(1) of Council Regulation (EEC) No. 1768/92 or of Regulation (EC) No. 1610/96 of the European Parliament and the Council and includes any application for a patent or supplementary protection certificate;
  (f) 'Patents Court' means the Patents Court of the High Court constituted as part of the Chancery Division by section 6(1) of the Senior Courts Act 1981;
  (g) 'patents county court' means a county court designated as a patents county court under section 287(1) of the 1988 Act;
  (h) 'patents judge' means a person nominated under section 291(1) of the 1988 Act as the patents judge of a patents county court;

(i) [*revoked*]
(j) 'the register' means whichever of the following registers is appropriate—
  (i) patents maintained by the Comptroller under section 32 of the 1977 Act;
  (ii) designs maintained by the registrar under section 17 of the Registered Designs Act 1949;
  (iii) trade marks maintained by the registrar under section 63 of the 1994 Act;
  (iv) Community trade marks maintained by the Office for Harmonisation in the Internal Market under Article 83 of Council Regulation (EC) No. 40/94;
  (v) Community designs maintained by the Office for Harmonisation in the Internal Market under Article 72 of Council Regulation (EC) No. 6/2002; and
  (vi) plant varieties maintained by the Controller under regulation 12 of the Plant Breeders' Rights Regulations 1998; and
(k) 'the registrar' means—
  (i) the registrar of trade marks; or
  (ii) the registrar of registered designs,
whichever is appropriate.

(3) Save as provided in rule 63.27, claims to which this Part applies are allocated to the multi-track.

I PATENTS AND REGISTERED DESIGNS

section I 11.10

63.2 Scope of Section I and Allocation

r.63.2(1) 11.4, 11.6 r.63.2(2) 2.21, 11.4, 11.6

(1) This Section applies to—
  (a) any claim under—
    (i) the 1977 Act;
    (ii) the Registered Designs Act 1949;
    (iii) the Defence Contracts Act 1958; and
  (b) any claim relating to—
    (i) Community registered designs;
    (ii) semiconductor topography rights; or
    (iii) plant varieties.
(2) Claims to which this Section applies must be started in—
  (a) the Patents Court; or
  (b) a patents county court.

63.3 Specialist List

r.63.3 11.4

Claims in the Patents Court and a patents county court form specialist lists for the purpose of rule 30.5.

63.4 *[Revoked]*

63.5 Starting the Claim

Claims to which this Section applies must be started—
  (a) by a Part 7 claim form; or
  (b) in existing proceedings under Part 20.

63.6 Claim for Infringement or Challenge to Validity of a Patent or Registered Design

r.63.6 24.6

A statement of case in a claim for infringement or a claim in which the validity of a patent or registered design is challenged must contain particulars as set out in Practice Direction 63.

63.7 Defence and Reply

Part 15 applies with the modification—
  (a) to rule 15.4(1)(b) that in a claim for infringement under rule 63.6, the period for filing a defence where the defendant files an acknowledgment of service under Part 10 is 42 days after service of the particulars of claim;

(b) that where rule 15.4(2) provides for a longer period to file a defence than in rule 63.7(a), then the period of time in rule 15.4(2) will apply; and
(c) to rule 15.8 that the claimant must—
(i) file any reply to a defence; and
(ii) serve it on all other parties,
within 21 days of service of the defence.

63.8 Case Management

(1) Parties do not need to file an allocation questionnaire.
(2) The following provisions only of Part 29 apply—
(a) rule 29.3(2) (legal representatives to attend case management conferences);
(b) rule 29.4 (the court's approval of agreed proposals for the management of proceedings); and
(c) rule 29.5 (variation of case management timetable) with the exception of paragraph (1)(b) and (c).
(3) As soon as practicable the court will hold a case management conference which must be fixed in accordance with Practice Direction 63.

63.9 Disclosure and Inspection

Part 31 is modified to the extent set out in Practice Direction 63.

63.10 Application to Amend a Patent Specification in Existing Proceedings

(1) An application under section 75 of the 1977 Act for permission to amend the specification of a patent by the proprietor of the patent must be made by application notice.
(2) The application notice must—
(a) give particulars of—
(i) the proposed amendment sought; and
(ii) the grounds upon which the amendment is sought;
(b) state whether the applicant will contend that the claims prior to the amendment are valid; and
(c) be served by the applicant on all parties and the Comptroller within 7 days of it being filed.
(3) The application notice must, if it is reasonably possible, be served on the Comptroller electronically.
(4) Unless the court otherwise orders, the Comptroller will, as soon as practicable, advertise the application to amend in the journal.
(5) The advertisement will state that any person may apply to the Comptroller for a copy of the application notice.
(6) Within 14 days of the first appearance of the advertisement any person who wishes to oppose the application must file and serve on all parties and the Comptroller a notice opposing the application which must include the grounds relied on.
(7) Within 28 days of the first appearance of the advertisement the applicant must apply to the court for directions.
(8) Unless the court otherwise orders, the applicant must within 7 days serve on the Comptroller any order of the court on the application.
(9) In this rule 'the journal' means the journal published pursuant to rules under section 123(6) of the 1977 Act.

63.11 Court's Determination of Question or Application

(1) This rule applies where the Comptroller—
(a) declines to deal with a question under section 8(7), 12(2), 37(8) or 61(5) of the 1977 Act;
(b) declines to deal with an application under section 40(5) of the 1977 Act; or
(c) certifies under section 72(7)(b) of the 1977 Act that the court should determine the question whether a patent should be revoked.
(2) Any person seeking the court's determination of that question or application must start a claim for that purpose within 14 days of receiving notification of the Comptroller's decision.
(3) A person who fails to start a claim within the time prescribed by rule 63.11(2) will be deemed to have abandoned the reference or application.

(4) A party may apply to the Comptroller or the court to extend the period for starting a claim prescribed by rule 63.11(2) even where the application is made after expiration of that period.

63.12 Application by Employee for Compensation

(1) An application by an employee for compensation under section 40(1) or (2) of the 1977 Act must be made—
  (a) in a claim form; and
  (b) within the period prescribed by paras (2), (3) and (4).
(2) The prescribed period begins on the date of the grant of the patent and ends 1 year after the patent has ceased to have effect.
(3) Where the patent has ceased to have effect as a result of failure to pay renewal fees, the prescribed period continues as if the patent has remained continuously in effect provided that—
  (a) the renewal fee and any additional fee are paid in accordance with section 25(4) of the 1977 Act; or
  (b) restoration is ordered by the Comptroller following an application under section 28 of the 1977 Act.
(4) Where restoration is refused by the Comptroller following an application under section 28 of the 1977 Act, the prescribed period will end 1 year after the patent has ceased to have effect or 6 months after the date of refusal, whichever is the later.

II REGISTERED TRADE MARKS AND OTHER INTELLECTUAL PROPERTY RIGHTS

section II 11.10, 23.5

63.13 Allocation

r.63.13 11.6

Claims relating to matters arising out of the 1994 Act and other intellectual property rights set out in Practice Direction 63 must be started in—

(a) the Chancery Division;
(b) a patents county court; or
(c) save as set out in Practice Direction 63, a county court where there is also a Chancery District Registry.

III SERVICE OF DOCUMENTS AND PARTICIPATION BY THE COMPTROLLER

63.14 Service of Documents

(1) Subject to paragraph (2), Part 6 applies to service of a claim form and any document in any proceedings under this Part.
(2) A claim form relating to a registered right may be served—
  (a) on a party who has registered the right at the address for service given for that right in the United Kingdom Patent Office register, provided the address is within the United Kingdom; or
  (b) in accordance with rule 6.32(1), 6.33(1) or 6.33(2) on a party who has registered the right at the address for service given for that right in the appropriate register at—
    (i) the United Kingdom Patent Office; or
    (ii) the Office for Harmonisation in the Internal Market.
(3) Where a party seeks any remedy (whether by claim form, counterclaim or application notice), which would if granted affect an entry in any United Kingdom Patent Office register, that party must serve on the Comptroller or registrar—
  (a) the claim form, counterclaim or application notice;
  (b) any other statement of case where relevant (including any amended statement of case); and
  (c) any accompanying documents.

63.15 Participation by the Comptroller

Where the documents set out in rule 63.14(3) are served, the Comptroller or registrar—

(a) may take part in proceedings; and
(b) need not serve a defence or other statement of case unless the court orders otherwise.

IV APPEALS

63.16 Appeals from Decisions of the Comptroller or the Registrar

(1) Part 52 applies to appeals from decisions of the Comptroller and the registrar.
(2) Appeals about patents must be made to the Patents Court, and other appeals to the Chancery Division.
(3) Where Part 52 requires a document to be served, it must also be served on the Comptroller or registrar, as appropriate.

V PATENTS COUNTY COURT

63.17 Scope of This Section

This Part, as modified by this Section, applies to claims started in or transferred to a patents county court.

63.18 Transfer of Proceedings

When considering whether to transfer proceedings to or from a patents county court, the court will have regard to the provisions of Practice Direction 30.

63.19 Patents Judge

(1) Subject to paragraph (2), proceedings in a patents county court will be dealt with by the patents judge of that court.
(2) When a matter needs to be dealt with urgently and it is not practicable or appropriate for the patents judge to deal with it, the matter may be dealt with by another judge with appropriate specialist experience nominated by the Chancellor of the High Court.

63.20 Statements of Case

(1) Part 16 applies with the modification that a statement of case must set out concisely all the facts and arguments upon which the party serving it relies.
(2) The particulars of claim must state whether the claimant has complied with paragraph 7.1(1) and Annex A (paragraph 2) of the Practice Direction (Pre-action Conduct).

63.21 Statement of Truth

Part 22 applies with the modification that the statement of truth verifying a statement of case must be signed by a person with knowledge of the facts alleged, or if no one person has knowledge of all the facts, by persons who between them have knowledge of all the facts alleged.

63.22 Defence and Reply

(1) Rule 63.7 does not apply and Part 15 applies with the following modifications.
(2) Where the particulars of claim contain a confirmation in accordance with rule 63.20(2), the period for filing a defence is 42 days after service of the particulars of claim unless rule 15.4(2) provides for a longer period to do so.
(3) Where the particulars of claim do not contain a confirmation in accordance with rule 63.20(2), the period for filing a defence is 70 days after service of the particulars of claim.
(4) Where the claimant files a reply to a defence it must be filed and served on all other parties within 28 days of service of the defence.
(5) Where the defendant files a reply to a defence to a counterclaim it must be filed and served on all other parties within 14 days of service of the defence to the counterclaim.
(6) The periods in this rule may only be extended by order of the court and for good reason.

63.23 Case Management

(1) At the first case management conference after those defendants who intend to file and serve a defence have done so, the court will identify the issues and decide whether to make an order in accordance with paragraph 29.1 of Practice Direction 63.
(2) Save in exceptional circumstances the court will not consider an application by a party to submit material in addition to that ordered under paragraph (1).

(3) The court may determine the claim on the papers where all parties consent.

63.24 Disclosure and Inspection

(1) Rule 63.9 does not apply.
(2) Part 31 applies save that the provisions on standard disclosure do not apply.

63.25 Applications

(1) Part 23 applies with the modifications set out in this rule.
(2) Except at the case management conference provided for in rule 63.23(1), a respondent to an application must file and serve on all relevant parties a response within 5 days of the service of the application notice.
(3) The court will deal with an application without a hearing unless the court considers it necessary to hold a hearing.
(4) An application to transfer the claim to the High Court or to stay proceedings must be made before or at the case management conference provided for in rule 63.23(1).
(5) The court will consider an application to transfer the claim later in the proceedings only where there are exceptional circumstances.

63.26 Costs

(1) Subject to paragraph (2), the court will reserve the costs of an application to the conclusion of the trial when they will be subject to summary assessment.
(2) Where a party has behaved unreasonably the court will make an order for costs at the conclusion of the hearing.
(3) Where the court makes a summary assessment of costs, it will do so in accordance with Section VII of Part 45.

63.27 Allocation to the Small Claims Track

(1) A claim started in or transferred to a patents county court will be allocated to the small claims track if—
    (a) rule 63.13, but not rule 63.2, applies to the claim;
    (b) the value of the claim is not more than £10,000;
    (c) it is stated in the particulars of claim that the claimant wishes the claim to be allocated to the small claims track; and
    (d) no objection to the claim being allocated to the small claims track is raised by the defendant in the defence.
(2) Where rule 63.27(1) applies, the parties do not need to file an allocation questionnaire.
(3) If either—
    (a) the requirements of rule 63.27(1)(a), (b) and (c) are satisfied, but in the defence the defendant objects to the claim being allocated to the small claims track; or
    (b) the requirements of rule 63.27(1)(a) and (b) are satisfied, but not (c), and in the defence the defendant requests that the claim be allocated to the small claims track, the court will allocate the claim to the small claims track or the multi-track in accordance with Part 26 (case management — preliminary stage).
(4) Part 27 (small claims track) shall apply to claims allocated to the small claims track in a patents county court with the modification to rule 27.2(1)(a) that Part 25 (interim remedies) shall not apply to such claims at all. Section VII of Part 45 (scale costs for claims in a patents county court) shall not apply to claims allocated to the small claims track in a patents county court.

63.28 Extent to which Rules in this Part Apply to Small Claims

(1) To the extent provided by this rule, this Part shall apply to a claim allocated to, or requested to be allocated to, the small claims track in a patents county court.
(2) Rules 63.1, 63.13, 63.18, 63.20, 63.21, 63.22, 63.25, 63.26(1) and (2), and 63.27 shall apply to the claim.
(3) No other rules in this Part shall apply.

PD 63 Practice Direction 63 — Intellectual Property Claims

This practice direction supplements CPR, Part 63.

PD 63 2.21, 11.7, 24.20

Contents of This Practice Direction

1.1 This practice direction is divided into four sections—

SECTION I PROVISIONS ABOUT PATENTS AND THOSE OTHER RIGHTS WITHIN THE SCOPE OF SECTION I OF PART 63

Scope of Section I

2.1 This Section applies to claims within the scope of Section 1 of Part 63.

Starting the Claim (Rule 63.5)

para.3.1(a) 23.5

3.1 A claim form to which this Section applies must—

(a) be marked 'Chancery Division Patents Court' or 'Patents County Court' as the case may be, in the top right-hand corner below the title of the court, and

(b) state the number of any patent or registered design to which the claim relates.

Claim for Infringement or Challenge to Validity (Rule 63.6)

para.4 24.6

4.1 In a claim for infringement of a patent—

(1) the statement of case must—

(a) show which of the claims in the specification of the patent are alleged to be infringed; and

(b) give at least one example of each type of infringement alleged; and

(2) a copy of each document referred to in the statement of case, and where necessary a translation of the document, must be served with the statement of case.

4.2 Where the validity of a patent or registered design is challenged—

(1) the statement of case must contain particulars of—

(a) the remedy sought; and

(b) the issues except those relating to validity of the patent or registered design;

(2) the statement of case must have a separate document attached to and forming part of it headed 'Grounds of Invalidity' which must—

(a) specify the grounds on which validity of the patent or registered design is challenged; and

(b) include particulars that will clearly define every issue (including any challenge to any claimed priority date) which it is intended to raise; and

(3) a copy of each document referred to in the Grounds of Invalidity, and where necessary a translation of the document, must be served with the Grounds of Invalidity.

4.3 Where in an application in which the validity of a patent or a registered design is challenged, the Grounds of Invalidity include an allegation—

(1) that the invention is not a patentable invention because it is not new or does not include an *inventive step, the* particulars must specify details of the matter in the state of the art relied on, as set out in para. 4.4;

(2) that the specification of the patent does not disclose the invention clearly enough and completely enough for it to be performed by a person skilled in the art, the particulars must state,

if appropriate, which examples of the invention cannot be made to work and in which respects they do not work or do not work as described in the specification; or

(3) that the registered design is not new or lacks individual character, the particulars must specify details of any prior design relied on, as set out in para. 4.4.

4.4 The details required under para. 4.3(1) and (3) are—

(1) in the case of matter or a design made available to the public by written description, the date on which and the means by which it was so made available, unless this is clear from the fact of the matter; and

(2) in the case of matter or a design made available to the public by use—

(a) the date or dates of such use;

(b) the name of all persons making such use;

(c) the place of such use;

(d) any written material which identifies such use;

(e) the existence and location of any apparatus employed in such use; and

(f) all facts and matters relied on to establish that such matter was made available to the public.

4.5 In any proceedings in which the validity of a patent is challenged, where a party alleges that machinery or apparatus was used before the priority date of the claim the court may order inspection of that machinery or apparatus.

4.6 If the validity of a patent is challenged on the ground that the invention did not involve an inventive step, a party who wishes to rely on the commercial success of the patent must state in the statement of case the grounds on which that party so relies.

Case Management (Rule 63.8)

5.1 The following paragraphs only of PD 29 apply—

(1) para. 5 (case management conferences)—

(a) excluding para. 5.9; and

(b) modified so far as is made necessary by other specific provisions of this practice direction; and

(2) para. 7 (failure to comply with case management directions).

5.2 Case management will be dealt with by—

(1) a judge of the Patents Court, a patents judge or a master, but

(2) a master may only deal with the following matters—

(a) orders by way of settlement, except settlement of procedural disputes;

(b) applications for extension of time;

(c) applications for permission to serve out of the jurisdiction;

(d) applications for security for costs;

(e) other matters as directed by a judge of the court; and

(f) enforcement of money judgments.

5.3 The claimant must apply for a case management conference within 14 days of the date when all defendants who intend to file and serve a defence have done so.

5.4 Where the claim has been transferred, the claimant must apply for a case management conference within 14 days of the date of the order transferring the claim, unless the court held or gave directions for a case management conference when it made the order transferring the claim.

5.5 Any party may, at a time earlier than that provided in paras 5.3 and 5.4, apply in writing to the court to fix a case management conference.

5.6 If the claimant does not make an application in accordance with paras 5.3 and 5.4, any other party may apply for a case management conference.

5.7 The court may fix a case management conference at any time on its own initiative.

5.8 Not less than four days before a case management conference, each party must file and serve an application notice for any order which that party intends to seek at the case management conference.

5.9 Unless the court orders otherwise, the claimant, or the party who makes an application under para. 5.6, in consultation with the other parties, must prepare a case management bundle containing—

(1) the claim form;

(2) all other statements of case (excluding schedules), except that, if a summary of a statement of case has been filed, the bundle must contain the summary, and not the full statement of case;

(3) a pre-trial timetable, if one has been agreed or ordered;
(4) the principal orders of the court; and
(5) any agreement in writing made by the parties as to disclosure,

and provide copies of the case management bundle for the court and the other parties at least four days before the first case management conference or any earlier hearing at which the court may give case management directions.

5.10 At the case management conference the court may direct that—
(1) a scientific adviser under the Senior Courts Act 1981, s. 70(3), or under the County Courts Act 1984, s. 63(1), be appointed; and
(2) a document setting out basic undisputed technology should be prepared.

(Rule 35.15 applies to scientific advisers.)

5.11 Where a trial date has not been fixed by the court, a party may apply for a trial date by filing a certificate which must—
(1) state the estimated length of the trial, agreed if possible by all parties;
(2) detail the time required for the judge to consider the documents;
(3) identify the area of technology; and
(4) assess the complexity of the technical issues involved by indicating the complexity on a scale of 1 to 5 (with 1 being the least and 5 the most complex).

5.12 The claimant, in consultation with the other parties, must revise and update the documents, referred to in para. 5.9 appropriately as the case proceeds. This must include making all necessary revisions and additions at least seven days before any subsequent hearing at which the court may give case management directions.

Disclosure and Inspection (Rule 63.9)

6.1 Standard disclosure does not require the disclosure of documents that relate to—
(1) the infringement of a patent by a product or process where—
(a) not less than 21 days before the date for service of a list of documents the defendant notifies the claimant and any other party of the defendant's intention to serve—
(i) full particulars of the product or process alleged to infringe; and
(ii) any necessary drawings or other illustrations; and
(b) on or before the date for service the defendant serves on the claimant and any other party the documents referred to in para. 6.1(1)(a);
(2) any ground on which the validity of a patent is put in issue, except documents which came into existence within the period—
(a) beginning two years before the earliest claimed priority date; and
(b) ending two years after that date; and
(3) the issue of commercial success.

6.2 The particulars served under para. 6.1(1)(b) must be accompanied by a signed written statement which must state that the person making the statement—
(1) is personally acquainted with the facts to which the particulars relate;
(2) verifies that the particulars are a true and complete description of the product or process alleged to infringe; and
(3) understands that he or she may be required to attend court in order to be cross-examined on the contents of the particulars.

6.3 Where the issue of commercial success arises, the patentee must, within such time limit as the court may direct, serve a schedule containing—
(1) where the commercial success relates to an article or product—
(a) an identification of the article or product (for example by product code number) which the patentee asserts has been made in accordance with the claims of the patent;
(b) a summary by convenient periods of sales of any such article or product;
(c) a summary for the equivalent periods of sales, if any, of any equivalent prior article or product marketed before the article or product in sub-para. (a); and
(d) a summary by convenient periods of any expenditure on advertising and promotion which supported the marketing of the articles or products in sub-paras (a) and (c); or
(2) where the commercial success relates to the use of a process—
(a) an identification of the process which the patentee asserts has been used in accordance with the claims of the patent;

(b) a summary by convenient periods of the revenue received from the use of such process;
(c) a summary for the equivalent periods of the revenues, if any, received from the use of any equivalent prior art process; and
(d) a summary by convenient periods of any expenditure which supported the use of the process in sub-paras (a) and (c).

Experiments

7.1 A party seeking to establish any fact by experimental proof conducted for the purpose of litigation must, at least 21 days before service of the application notice for directions under para. 7.3, or within such other time as the court may direct, serve on all parties a notice—
(1) stating the facts which the party seeks to establish; and
(2) giving full particulars of the experiments proposed to establish them.

7.2 A party served with a notice under para. 7.1—
(1) must within 21 days after such service, serve on the other party a notice stating whether or not each fact is admitted; and
(2) may request the opportunity to inspect a repetition of all or a number of the experiments identified in the notice served under para. 7.1.

7.3 Where any fact which a party seeks to establish by experimental proof is not admitted, that party must apply to the court for permission and directions by application notice.

Use of Models or Apparatus

8.1 A party that intends to rely on any model or apparatus must apply to the court for directions at the first case management conference.

Time Estimates for Trial, Trial Bundle, Reading Guide and Detailed Trial Timetable

9.1 Not less than one week before the beginning of the trial, each party must inform the court in writing of the estimated length of its—
(1) oral submissions;
(2) examination in chief, if any, of its own witnesses; and
(3) cross-examination of witnesses of any other party.

9.2 At least four days before the date fixed for the trial, the claimant must file—
(1) the trial bundle;
(2) a reading guide for the judge; and
(3) a detailed trial timetable which should be agreed, if possible.

9.3 The reading guide filed under para. 9.2 must—
(1) be short and, if possible, agreed;
(2) set out the issues, the parts of the documents that need to be read on each issue and the most convenient order in which they should be read;
(3) identify the relevant passages in text books and cases, if appropriate; and
(4) not contain argument.

Application to Amend a Patent Specification in Existing Proceedings (Rule 63.10)

10.1 Where the application notice is served on the Comptroller electronically under r. 63.10(3), the applicant must comply with any requirements for the sending of electronic communications to the Comptroller.

10.2 Not later than two days before the first hearing date the applicant, the Comptroller if wishing to be heard, the parties to the proceedings and any other opponent, must file and serve a document stating the directions sought.

Request to Limit a European Patent (UK) under the European Patent Convention

11.1 Paragraphs 11.2 to 11.4 apply where there are proceedings before the court in which the validity of a European patent (UK) may be put in issue.

11.2 Where the proprietor of the European patent (UK) intends to file a request under the European Patent Convention, art. 105a, to limit the European patent (UK) by amendment of the claims, the proprietor must serve on all the parties to the proceedings a copy of the intended request (including a copy of the intended complete version of the amended claims and, as the case may be, of the amended description and drawings) at least 28 days prior to filing the request with the European Patent Office.

11.3 Where a copy of an intended request is served on the party in accordance with para. 11.2, any party may apply to the court for such directions or other order as may be appropriate.

11.4 Reference to 'European Patent Convention' means the Convention on the Grant of European Patents of 5th October 1973 as amended from time to time.

Application by Employee for Compensation (Rule 63.12)

12.1 Where an employee applies for compensation under s. 40(1) or (2) of the 1977 Act, the court will at the case management conference give directions as to—

(1) the manner in which the evidence, including any accounts of expenditure and receipts relating to the claim, is to be given at the hearing of the claim and if written evidence is to be given, specify the period within which witness statements must be filed; and

(2) the provision to the claimant by the defendant or a person deputed by the defendant, of reasonable facilities for inspecting and taking extracts from the accounts by which the defendant proposes to verify the accounts in sub-para. (1) or from which those accounts have been derived.

Communication of Information to the European Patent Office

13.1 The court may authorise the communication of any such information in the court files as the court thinks fit to—

(1) the European Patent Office; or

(2) the competent authority of any country which is a party to the European Patent Convention.

13.2 Before authorising the communication of information under para. 13.1, the court will permit any party who may be affected by the disclosure to make representations, in writing or otherwise, on the question of whether the information should be disclosed.

Order Affecting Entry in the Register of Patents or Designs

14.1 Where any order of the court affects the validity of an entry in the register, the party in whose favour the order is made, must serve a copy of such order on the Comptroller within 14 days.

14.2 Where the order is in favour of more than one party, a copy of the order must be served by such party as the court directs.

European Community Designs

15.1 The Patents Court and the patents county court at the Central London County Court are the designated Community design courts under Council Regulation (EC) 6/2002, art. 80(5).

15.2 Where a counterclaim is filed at the Community design court, for a declaration of invalidity of a registered Community design, the Community design court will inform the Office for Harmonisation in the Internal Market of the date on which the counterclaim was filed, in accordance with Council Regulation (EC) 6/2002, art. 86(2).

15.3 On filing a counterclaim under para. 15.2, the party filing it must inform the Community design court in writing that it is a counterclaim to which para. 15.2 applies and that the Office for Harmonisation in the Internal Market needs to be informed of the date on which the counterclaim was filed.

15.4 Where a Community design court has given a judgment which has become final on a counterclaim for a declaration of invalidity of a registered Community design, the Community design court will send a copy of the judgment to the Office for Harmonisation in the Internal Market, in accordance with Council Regulation (EC) 6/2002, art. 86(4).

15.5 The party in whose favour judgment is given under para. 15.4 must inform the Community design court at the time of judgment that para. 15.4 applies and that the Office for Harmonisation in the Internal Market needs to be sent a copy of the judgment.

SECTION II PROVISIONS ABOUT REGISTERED TRADE MARKS AND OTHER INTELLECTUAL PROPERTY RIGHTS

Allocation (Rule 63.13)

para.16.1 2.21 para.16.2 11.6

16.1 The other intellectual property rights referred to in r. 63.13 are—
(1) copyright;
(2) rights in performances;
(3) rights conferred under part VII of the 1988 Act;
(4) design right;
(5) Community design right;
(6) association rights;
(7) moral rights;
(8) database rights;
(9) unauthorised decryption rights;
(10) hallmarks;
(11) technical trade secrets litigation;
(12) passing off;
(13) protected designations of origin, protected geographical indications and traditional speciality guarantees;
(14) registered trade marks; and
(15) Community trade marks.

16.2 There are Chancery district registries at Birmingham, Bristol, Caernarfon, Cardiff, Leeds, Liverpool, Manchester, Mold, Newcastle upon Tyne and Preston.

16.3 The county courts at Caernarfon, Mold and Preston do not have jurisdiction in relation to registered trade marks and Community trade marks.

Starting the Claim

para.17.1 23.5

17.1 A claim form to which Section II of Part 63 applies must be marked in the top right-hand corner 'Intellectual Property' below the title of the court in which it is issued.

17.2 In the case of claims concerning registered trade marks and Community trade marks, the claim form must state the registration number of any trade mark to which the claim relates.

Reference to the Court by the Registrar or the Comptroller

18.1 This paragraph applies where—
(1) an application is made to the registrar under the 1994 Act and the registrar refers the application to the court; or
(2) a reference is made to the Comptroller under s. 246 of the 1988 Act and the Comptroller refers the whole proceedings or a particular question or issue to the court under s. 251(1) of that Act.

18.2 Where para. 18.1 applies, the applicant under the 1994 Act or the person making the reference under s. 246 of the 1988 Act, as the case may be, must start a claim seeking the court's determination of the reference within 14 days of receiving notification of the decision to refer.

18.3 If the person referred to in para. 18.2 does not start a claim within the period prescribed by that paragraph, that person will be deemed to have abandoned the reference.

18.4 The period prescribed under para. 18.2 may be extended by—
(1) the registrar or the Comptroller as the case may be; or
(2) the court
where a party so applies, even if the application is not made until after the expiration of that period.

Application to the Court under Section 19 of the 1994 Act

19.1 Where an application is made under s. 19 of the 1994 Act, the applicant must serve the claim form or application notice on all identifiable persons having an interest in the goods, materials or articles within the meaning of s. 19 of the 1994 Act.

Order Affecting Entry in the Register of Trade Marks

20.1 Where any order of the court affects the validity of an entry in the register, the provisions of paras 14.1 and 14.2 apply.

European Community Trade Marks

21.1 The Chancery Division, the patents county court at the Central London County Court and the county courts where there is also a Chancery district registry, except Caernarfon, Mold and Preston, are designated Community trade mark courts for the purposes of Council Regulation (EC) 40/94, art. 91(1).

21.2 Where a counterclaim is filed at the Community trade mark court, for revocation or for a declaration of invalidity of a Community trade mark, the Community trade mark court will inform the Office for Harmonisation in the Internal Market of the date on which the counterclaim was filed, in accordance with Council Regulation (EC) 40/94, art. 96(4).

21.3 On filing a counterclaim under para. 21.2, the party filing it must inform the Community trade mark court in writing that it is a counterclaim to which para. 21.2 applies and that the Office for Harmonisation in the Internal Market needs to be informed of the date on which the counterclaim was filed.

21.4 Where the Community trade mark court has given a judgment which has become final on a counterclaim for revocation or for a declaration of invalidity of a Community trade mark, the Community trade mark court will send a copy of the judgment to the Office for Harmonisation in the Internal Market, in accordance with Council Regulation (EC) 40/94, art. 96(6).

21.5 The party in whose favour judgment is given under para. 21.4 must inform the Community trade mark court at the time of judgment that para. 21.4 applies and that the Office for Harmonisation in the Internal Market needs to be sent a copy of the judgment.

Claim for Additional Damages under Section 97(2), Section 191J(2) or Section 229(3) of the 1988 Act

22.1 Where a claimant seeks to recover additional damages under s. 97(2), s. 191J(2) or s. 229(3) of the 1988 Act, the particulars of claim must include—
(1) a statement to that effect; and
(2) the grounds for claiming them.

Application for Delivery Up or Forfeiture under the 1988 Act

23.1 An applicant who applies under s. 99, 114, 195, 204, 230 or 231 of the 1988 Act for delivery up or forfeiture must serve—
(1) the claim form; or
(2) application notice, where appropriate,
on all identifiable persons who have an interest in the goods, material or articles within the meaning of s. 114, 204 or 231 of the 1988 Act.

Association Rights

24.1 Where an application is made under regulations made under the Olympic Symbol etc (Protection) Act 1995, s. 7, the applicant must serve the claim form or application notice on all identifiable persons having an interest in the goods, materials or articles within the meaning of the regulations.

SECTION III PROVISIONS ABOUT APPEALS

Reference to the Court by an Appointed Person

25.1 This paragraph applies where a person appointed by the Lord Chancellor to hear and decide appeals under s. 77 of the 1994 Act, refers an appeal to the Chancery Division under s. 76(3) of the 1994 Act.

25.2 The appellant must file a claim form seeking the court's determination of the appeal within *14 days* of receiving notification of the decision to refer.

25.3 The appeal will be deemed to have been abandoned if the appellant does not file a claim form within the period prescribed by para. 25.2.

25.4 The period prescribed under para. 25.2 may be extended by—
(1) the person appointed by the Lord Chancellor; or
(2) the court
where the appellant so applies, even if such application is not made until after the expiration of that period.

SECTION IV PROVISIONS ABOUT FINAL ORDERS

Costs

26.1 Where the court makes an order for delivery up or destruction of infringing goods, or articles designed or adapted to make such goods, the person against whom the order is made must pay the costs of complying with that order unless the court orders otherwise.
26.2 Where the court finds that an intellectual property right has been infringed, the court may, at the request of the applicant, order appropriate measures for the dissemination and publication of the judgment to be taken at the expense of the infringer.

SECTION V PROVISIONS ABOUT PROCEEDINGS IN A PATENTS COUNTY COURT

Scope of Section V

27.1 Except as provided for in para. 27.2 this practice direction, as modified by this Section, applies to claims in a patents county court.
27.2 Paragraphs 5.10 to 9.1 and para. 9.2(3) do not apply to a claim in a patents county court.

Claims for Infringement or Challenge to Validity

28.1 Paragraph 4.2(2) is modified so that the grounds for invalidity must be included in the statement of case and not in a separate document.

Case Management (Rule 63.23)

29.1 At the case management conference referred to in r. 63.23 the court may order any of the following—
(1) specific disclosure;
(2) a product or process description (or a supplementary product or process description where one has already been provided);
(3) experiments;
(4) witness statements;
(5) experts' reports;
(6) cross examination at trial;
(7) written submissions or skeleton arguments.
29.2 The court will make an order under paragraph 29.1 only—
(1) in relation to specific and identified issues; and
(2) if the court is satisfied that the benefit of the further material in terms of its value in resolving those issues appears likely to justify the cost of producing and dealing with it.

Applications (Rule 63.25)

30.1 Where the court considers that a hearing is necessary under r. 63.25(3) the court will conduct a hearing by telephone or videoconference in accordance with PD 23A, paras 6.2 to 7, unless it considers that a hearing in person would be more cost-effective for the parties or is otherwise necessary in the interests of justice.

Determination of the Claim

31.1 Where possible, the court will determine the claim solely on the basis of the parties' statements of case and oral submissions.
31.2 The court will set the timetable for the trial and will, so far as appropriate, allocate equal time to the parties. Cross-examination will be strictly controlled by the court. The court will endeavour to ensure that the trial lasts no more than two days.

Small Claims

32.1 This practice direction shall apply to a claim allocated to the small claims track in a patents county court to the extent provided by paras 32.2 and 32.3.

32.2 The following paragraphs shall apply—

(1) in Section II, 16.1, 17.1, 17.2, 19.1, 20.1, 21.1 to 21.5, 22.1, 23.1, 24.1;

(2) in Section IV, 26.1, 26.2;

(3) in Section V, 30.1, 31.1.

32.3 No other provision in this practice direction shall apply.

CPR Part 64 Estates, Trusts and Charities

para.64 14.36

64.1 General

(1) This Part contains rules—
  (a) in Section I, about claims relating to—
    (i) the administration of estates of deceased persons, and
    (ii) trusts; and
  (b) in Section II, about charity proceedings.
(2) In this Part Practice Directions 64A and 64B, where appropriate, references to trustees include executors and administrators.
(3) All proceedings in the High Court to which this Part applies must be brought in the Chancery Division.

I CLAIMS RELATING TO THE ADMINISTRATION OF ESTATES AND TRUSTS

64.2 Scope of This Section

This Section of this Part applies to claims—
  (a) for the court to determine any question arising in—
    (i) the administration of the estate of a deceased person; or
    (ii) the execution of a trust;
  (b) for an order for the administration of the estate of a deceased person, or the execution of a trust, to be carried out under the direction of the court ('an administration order');
  (c) under the Variation of Trusts Act 1958; or
  (d) under section 48 of the Administration of Justice Act 1985.

64.3 Claim Form

A claim to which this Section applies must be made by issuing a Part 8 claim form.

64.4 Parties

(1) In a claim to which this Section applies, other than an application under section 48 of the Administration of Justice Act 1985—
  (a) all the trustees must be parties;
  (b) if the claim is made by trustees, any of them who does not consent to being a claimant must be made a defendant; and
  (c) the claimant may make parties to the claim any persons with an interest in or claim against the estate, or an interest under the trust, who it is appropriate to make parties having regard to the nature of the order sought.
(2) In addition, in a claim under the Variation of Trusts Act 1958, unless the court directs otherwise any person who—
  (a) created the trust; or
  (b) provided property for the purposes of the trust,
  must, if still alive, be made a party to the claim.
(The court may, under rule 19.2, order additional persons to be made parties to a claim)

II CHARITY PROCEEDINGS

64.5 Scope of This Section and Interpretation

(1) This Section applies to charity proceedings.
(2) In this Section—
(a) 'the Act' means the Charities Act 1993;
(b) 'charity proceedings' has the same meaning as in section 33(8) of the Act; and
(c) 'the Commissioners' means the Charity Commissioners for England and Wales.

64.6 Application for Permission to Take Charity Proceedings

r.64.6 **14.36** r.64.6(6) **14.36**

(1) An application to the High Court under section 33(5) of the Act for permission to start charity proceedings must be made within 21 days after the refusal by the Commissioners of an order authorising proceedings.
(2) The application must be made by issuing a Part 8 claim form, which must contain the information specified in Practice Direction 64A.
(3) The Commissioners must be made defendants to the claim, but the claim form need not be served on them or on any other person.
(4) The judge considering the application may direct the Commissioners to file a written statement of their reasons for their decision.
(5) The court will serve on the applicant a copy of any statement filed under paragraph (4).
(6) The judge may either—
(a) give permission without a hearing; or
(b) fix a hearing.

PD 64A Practice Direction 64A — Estates, Trusts and Charities

This practice direction supplements CPR, Part 64.
PD 64A 13.7

I CLAIMS RELATING TO THE ADMINISTRATION OF ESTATES AND TRUSTS

Examples of Claims under Rule 64.2(a)

para.1(2)(b) 34.50

1 The following are examples of the types of claims which may be made under r. 64.2(a):
(1) a claim for the determination of any of the following questions:
(a) any question as to who is included in any class of persons having:
(i) a claim against the estate of a deceased person;
(ii) a beneficial interest in the estate of such a person; or
(iii) a beneficial interest in any property subject to a trust;
(b) any question as to the rights or interests of any person claiming:
(i) to be a creditor of the estate of a deceased person;
(ii) to be entitled under a will or on the intestacy of a deceased person; or
(iii) to be beneficially entitled under a trust;
(2) a claim for any of the following remedies:
(a) an order requiring a trustee (whether administrative or dispositive):
(i) to provide and, if necessary, verify accounts;
(ii) to pay into court money which he holds in that capacity; or
(iii) to do or not to do any particular act;
(b) an order approving any sale, purchase, compromise or other transaction by a trustee; or
(c) an order directing any act to be done which the court could order to be done if the estate or trust in question were being administered or executed under the direction of the court.

Determining Certain Claims under Rule 64.2(a) without a Hearing

para.1A.1 34.50 para.1A.3 34.50

1A.1 Where a claim is made by a trustee for a remedy within para. 1(2)(b) (including a case where the remedy sought is approval of a transaction affected by conflict of interests or duties), the court may be requested to determine the claim without a hearing.
1A.2 The claim form in such a case may be issued in accordance with r. 8.2A (issue of claim form without naming defendants), and no separate application for permission under r. 8.2A need be made.
1A.3 The claim form must be accompanied by—
(a) a witness statement setting out the material facts justifying determination without a hearing and in particular—
(i) identifying those affected by the remedy sought and
(ii) detailing any consultation of those so affected and the result of that consultation;
(b) the advice of a lawyer having a 10-year High Court qualification within the meaning of the Courts and Legal Services Act 1990, s. 71, on the merits of the claim;
(c) a draft order for the remedy sought;
(d) a statement of costs.
1A.4 If the court considers that the case does not require an oral hearing, it will proceed to consider the claim on the papers.
1A.5 If the court considers that an oral hearing is required, it will give appropriate directions.
1A.6 If the court considers it appropriate, it will make the order sought and may direct that the claimant must—
(a) serve notice of the order on the interested parties in accordance with r. 19.8A, and
(b) file a certificate of service within 7 days of doing so.

Applications by Trustees for Directions

2 A separate practice direction (PD 64B) contains guidance about applications by trustees for directions.

Administration Orders: Rule 64.2(b)

3.1 The court will only make an administration order if it considers that the issues between the parties cannot properly be resolved in any other way.

3.2 If, in a claim for an administration order, the claimant alleges that the trustees have not provided proper accounts, the court may:

(1) stay the proceedings for a specified period, and order them to file and serve proper accounts within that period; or

(2) if necessary to prevent proceedings by other creditors or persons claiming to be entitled to the estate or fund, make an administration order and include in it an order that no such proceedings are to be taken without the court's permission.

3.3 Where an administration order has been made in relation to the estate of a deceased person, and a claim is made against the estate by any person who is not a party to the proceedings:

(1) no party other than the executors or administrators of the estate may take part in any proceedings relating to the claim without the permission of the court; and

(2) the court may direct or permit any other party to take part in the proceedings, on such terms as to costs or otherwise as it thinks fit.

3.4 Where an order is made for the sale of any property vested in trustees, those persons shall have the conduct of the sale unless the court directs otherwise.

Applications under the Variation of Trusts Act 1958: Rule 64.2(c)

4.1 Where children or unborn beneficiaries will be affected by a proposed arrangement under the Act, the evidence filed in support of the application must:

(1) show that their litigation friends or the trustees support the arrangements as being in the interests of the children or unborn beneficiaries; and

(2) unless para. 4.3 applies or the court orders otherwise, be accompanied by a written opinion to this effect by the advocate who will appear on the hearing of the application.

4.2 A written opinion filed under para. 4.1(2) must:

(1) if it is given on formal instructions, be accompanied by a copy of those instructions; or

(2) otherwise, state fully the basis on which it is given.

4.3 No written opinion needs to be filed in support of an application to approve an arrangement under s. 1(1)(d) of the Act (discretionary interests under protective trusts).

4.4 Where the interests of two or more children, or two or more of the children and unborn beneficiaries, are similar, only a single written opinion needs to be filed.

Applications under Section 48 of the Administration of Justice Act 1985: Rule 64.2(d)

5 A Part 8 claim form for an application by trustees under s. 48 of the Administration of Justice Act 1985 (power of High Court to authorise action to be taken in reliance on legal opinion) may be issued without naming a defendant, under r. 8.2A. No separate application for permission under r. 8.2A need be made.

Prospective Costs Orders

6.1 These paragraphs are about the costs of applications under r. 64.2(a).

6.2 Where trustees have power to agree to pay the costs of a party to such an application, and exercise such a power, r. 48.3 applies. In such a case, an order is not required and the trustees are entitled to recover out of the trust fund any costs which they pay pursuant to the agreement made in the exercise of such power.

6.3 Where the trustees do not have, or decide not to exercise, a power to make such an agreement, the trustees or the party concerned may apply to the court at any stage of proceedings for an order that the costs of any party (including the costs of the trustees) shall be paid out of the fund (a '*prospective costs order*').

6.4 The court, on an application for a prospective costs order, may:

(a) in the case of the trustees' costs, authorise the trustees to raise and meet such costs out of the fund;

(b) in the case of the costs of any other party, authorise or direct the trustees to pay such costs (or any part of them, or the costs incurred up to a particular time) out of the trust fund to be assessed, if not agreed by the trustees, on the indemnity basis or, if the court directs, on the standard basis, and to make payments from time to time on account of such costs. A model form of order is annexed to this practice direction.

6.5 The court will always consider whether it is possible to deal with the application for a prospective costs order on paper without a hearing and in an ordinary case would expect to be able to do so. The trustees must consider whether a hearing is needed for any reason. If they consider that it is they should say so and explain why in their evidence. If any party to the application referred to in para. 6.1 above (or any other person interested in the trust fund) considers that a hearing is necessary (for instance because he wishes to oppose the making of a prospective costs order) this should be stated, and the reasons explained, in his evidence, if any, or otherwise in a letter to the court.

6.6 If the court would be minded to refuse the application on a consideration of the papers alone, the parties will be notified and given the opportunity, within a stated time, to ask for a hearing.

6.7 The evidence in support of an application for a prospective costs order should be given by witness statement. The trustees and the applicant (if different) must ensure full disclosure of the relevant matters to show that the case is one which falls within the category of case where a prospective costs order can properly be made.

6.8 The model form of order is designed for use in the more straightforward cases, where a question needs to be determined which has arisen in the administration of the trust, whether the claimants are the trustees or a beneficiary. The form may be adapted for use in less straightforward cases, in particular where the proceedings are hostile, but special factors may also have to be reflected in the terms of the order in such a case.

II CHARITY PROCEEDINGS

Role of Attorney-General

para.7 14.36

7 The Attorney-General is a necessary party to all charity proceedings, other than any commenced by the Charity Commissioners, and must be joined as a defendant if he is not a claimant.

Service on Charity Commissioners or Attorney-General

8 Any document required or authorised to be served on the Commissioners or the Attorney-General must be served on the Treasury Solicitor in accordance with PD 66, para. 2.1.

Applications for Permission to Take Charity Proceedings: Rule 64.6

para.9.1 14.36 para.9.2 14.36

9.1 The claim form for an application under s. 33(5) of the Act must state:

(1) the name, address and description of the applicant;
(2) details of the proceedings which he wishes to take;
(3) the date of the Commissioners' refusal to grant an order authorising the taking of proceedings;
(4) the grounds on which the applicant alleges that it is a proper case for taking proceedings; and
(5) if the application is made with the consent of any other party to the proposed proceedings, that fact.

9.2 If the Commissioners have given reasons for refusing to grant an order, a copy of their reasons must be filed with the claim form.

Appeals against Orders of the Charity Commissioners

para.10 14.36

10 Part 52 applies to any appeal against an order of the Charity Commissioners. Section III of PD 52 contains special provisions about such appeals.

APPENDIX

Model form of prospective costs order

UPON THE APPLICATION etc.

AND UPON HEARING etc.

AND UPON READING etc.

AND UPON the Solicitors for the............ Defendant undertaking to make the repayments mentioned in paragraph 2 below in the circumstances there mentioned

IT IS [BY CONSENT] ORDERED THAT:

1. The Claimants as trustees of........... ('the [Settlement/Scheme]') do—
   (a) pay from the assets of the [Settlement/Scheme] the costs of and incidental to these proceedings incurred by the............ Defendant such costs to be subject to a detailed assessment on the indemnity basis if not agreed and (for the avoidance of doubt) to—
      (i) include costs incurred by the..... Defendant from and after [*date*] in anticipation of being appointed to represent any class of persons presently or formerly beneficially interested under the trusts of the [Settlement/Scheme] irrespective of whether [he/she] is in fact so appointed; and
      (ii) exclude (in the absence of any further order) costs incurred in prosecuting any Part 20 claim or any appeal;
   (b) indemnify the........... Defendant in respect of any costs which he may be ordered to pay to any other party to these proceedings in connection therewith.
2. Until the outcome of the detailed assessment (or the agreement regarding costs) contemplated in paragraph 1 above, the Claimants as trustees do pay from the assets of the [Settlement/Scheme] to the Solicitors for the............ Defendant monthly (or at such other intervals as may be agreed) such sums on account of the costs referred to in paragraph 1(a) of this Order as the Solicitors for the........Defendant shall certify—
      (i) to have been reasonably and property incurred and not to exceed such amount as is likely in their opinion to be allowed on a detailed assessment on the indemnity basis; and
      (ii) to have accrued on account of the present proceedings in the period prior to the date of such certificate and not to have been previously provided for under this Order.

   PROVIDED ALWAYS that the Solicitors for the............ Defendant shall repay such sums (if any) as, having been paid to them on account, are disallowed on a detailed assessment or are otherwise agreed to be repaid and any such sums shall be repaid together with interest at 1% above the base rate for the time being of [Barclays] Bank plc from and including the date of payment to those Solicitors up to and including the date of repayment, such interest to accrue daily.
3. Any party may apply to vary or discharge paragraphs 1 and 2 of this Order but only in respect of costs to be incurred after the date of such application.

Note: this form of order assumes that the trustees are the claimants. If the claimant is a beneficiary and the trustees are defendants, references to the parties need to be adapted accordingly.

PD 64B Practice Direction 64B — Applications to the Court for Directions by Trustees in Relation to the Administration of the Trust

This practice direction supplements Section I of CPR, Part 64.

1 This practice direction is about applications to the court for directions by trustees in relation to the administration of the trust.

Contents of the Claim Form

2 If confidentiality of the directions sought is important (for example, where the directions relate to actual or proposed litigation with a third party who could find out what directions the trustees are seeking through access to the claim form under r. 5.4) the statement of the remedy sought, for the purposes of r. 8.2(b), may be expressed in general terms. The trustees must, in that case, state specifically in the evidence what it is that they seek to be allowed to do.

Proceedings in Private

3 The proceedings will in the first instance be listed in private (see PD 39A, para. 1.5, and r. 39.2(3)(f)). Accordingly the order made, as well as the other documents among the court records (apart from a claim form which has been served), will not be open to inspection by third parties without the court's permission (r. 5.4(2)). If the matter is disposed of without a hearing, the order made will be expressed to have been made in private.

Joining Defendants or Giving Notice to Those Interested

4.1 Rule 64.4(1)(c) deals with the joining of beneficiaries as defendants. Often, especially in the case of a private trust, it will be clear that some, and which, beneficiaries need to be joined as defendants. Sometimes, if there are only two views of the appropriate course, and one is advocated by one beneficiary who will be joined, it may not be necessary for other beneficiaries to be joined since the trustees may be able to present the other arguments. Equally, in the case of a pension trust, it may not be necessary for a member of every possible different class of beneficiaries to be joined.

4.2 In some cases the court may be able to assess whether or not to give the directions sought, or what directions to give, without hearing from any party other than the trustees. If the trustees consider that their case is in that category they may apply to the court to issue the claim form without naming any defendants under r. 8.2A. They must apply to the court before the claim form is issued (r. 8.2A(2)) and include a copy of the claim form that they propose to issue (r. 8.2A(3)(b)).

4.3 In other cases the trustees may know that beneficiaries need to be joined as defendants, or to be given notice, but may be in doubt as to which. Examples could include a case concerning a pension scheme with many beneficiaries and a number of different categories of interest, especially if they may be differently affected by the action for which directions are sought, or a private trust with a large class of discretionary beneficiaries. In those cases the trustees may apply to issue the claim form without naming any defendants under r. 8.2A. The application may be combined with an application to the court for directions as to which persons to join as parties or to give notice to under r. 19.8A.

4.4 In the case of a charitable trust the Attorney-General is always the appropriate defendant, and almost always the only one.

Case Management Directions

5.1 The claim will be referred to the master or district judge once a defendant has acknowledged service, or otherwise on expiry of the period for acknowledgment of service (or, if no defendant is named, as soon as the claimants' evidence has been filed), to consider directions for the management of the case. Such directions may be given without a hearing in some cases; these might include directions as to parties or as to notice of proceedings, as mentioned in para. 4 above.

Proceeding without a Hearing

6.1 (1) The court will dispose of the application without a hearing if it considers that to do so will save time or expense, and that a hearing is not necessary. The trustees must therefore consider whether a hearing is necessary and, if so, explain why in their evidence.
(2) When considering whether to hold a hearing, the court will take into account any dispute between the parties as to directions, but will not necessarily direct a hearing for that reason alone.
(3) If a defendant considers that a hearing is needed, and that the need is not sufficiently explained in the trustees' evidence, that defendant should so state in evidence, giving reasons why.

6.2 Where the court deals with an application without a hearing, it will in any order give the parties an opportunity, within a stated time, to apply to vary or discharge the order at an oral hearing.

6.3 In charity cases, the master or district judge may deal with the case without a hearing on the basis of a letter by or on behalf of the Attorney-General that sets out his attitude to the application.

Evidence

7.1 The trustees' evidence should be given by witness statement. In order to ensure that, if directions are given, the trustees are properly protected by the order, they must ensure full disclosure of relevant matters, even if the case is to proceed with the participation of beneficiaries as defendants.

7.2 Applications for directions whether or not to take or defend or pursue litigation should be supported by evidence of the following matters—
(1) the advice of an appropriately qualified lawyer as to the prospects of success;
(2) an estimate in summary form of—
(a) the value or other significance to the trust estate of the issues in the proceedings;
(b) the costs likely to be incurred by the trustees in the proceedings, by reference to the principal stages in the proceedings; and
(c) the costs of other parties to the proceedings for which, if unsuccessful, the trustees may be exposed to liability;
(3) any known facts concerning the means of other parties to the proceedings; and
(4) any other factors relevant to the court's decision whether to give the directions sought.

7.3 References in this practice direction to an appropriately qualified lawyer mean one whose qualifications and experience are appropriate to the circumstances of the case. The qualifications should be stated. If the advice is given on formal instructions, the instructions should always be put in evidence as well, so that the court can see the basis on which the advice was given. If it is not, the advice must state fully the basis on which it is given.

7.4 In the case of a pension trust the evidence should include the latest actuarial valuation, and should describe the membership profile and, if a deficit on winding up is likely, the priority provisions and their likely effect.

7.5 On an application for directions about actual or possible litigation the evidence should also state whether (i) PD Pre-action Conduct or any relevant pre-action protocol has been complied with; and (ii) the trustees have proposed or undertaken, or intend to propose, mediation by ADR, and (in each case) if not why not.

7.6 If a beneficiary of the trust is a party to the litigation about which directions are sought, with an interest opposed to that of the trustees, that beneficiary should be a defendant to the trustees' application, but any material which would be privileged as regards that beneficiary in the litigation should be put in evidence as exhibits to the trustees' witness statement, and should not be served on the beneficiary. However if the trustees' representatives consider that no harm would be done by the disclosure of all or some part of the material, then that material should be served on that defendant. That defendant may also be excluded from part of the hearing, including that which is devoted to discussion of the material withheld.

Consultation with beneficiaries

7.7 The evidence must explain what, if any, consultation there has been with beneficiaries, and with what result. In preparation for an application for directions in respect of litigation, the following guidance is to be followed:
(1) If the trust is a private trust where the beneficiaries principally concerned are not numerous and are all or mainly adult, identified and traceable, the trustees will be expected to have

canvassed with all the adult beneficiaries the proposed or possible courses of action before applying for directions.

(2) If it is a private trust with a larger number of beneficiaries, including those not yet born or identified, or children, it is likely that there will nevertheless be some adult beneficiaries principally concerned, with whom the trustees must consult.

(3) In relation to a charitable trust the trustees must have consulted the Attorney-General, through the Treasury Solicitor, as well as the Charity Commissioners whose consent to the application will have been needed under the Charities Act 1993, s. 33.

(4) In relation to a pension trust, unless the members are very few in number, no particular steps by way of consultation with beneficiaries (including, where relevant, employers) or their representatives are required in preparation for the application, though the trustees' evidence should describe any consultation that has in fact taken place. If no consultation has taken place, the court could in some cases direct that meetings of one or more classes of beneficiaries be held to consider the subject matter of the application, possibly as a preliminary to deciding whether a member of a particular class ought to be joined as a defendant, though in a case concerning actual or proposed litigation, steps would need to be considered to protect privileged material from too wide disclosure.

7.8 (1) If the court gives directions allowing the trustees to take, defend or pursue litigation it may do so up to a particular stage in the litigation, requiring the trustees, before they carry on beyond that point, to renew their application to the court. What stage that should be will depend on the likely management of the litigation under the CPR. If the application is to be renewed after disclosure of documents, and disclosed documents need to be shown to the court, it may be necessary to obtain permission to do this from the court in which the other litigation is proceeding.

(2) In such a case the court will if possible deal with the matter without a hearing, and in deciding whether to do so will take into account the advice of an appropriately qualified lawyer supporting the continuation by the trustees of the pursuit or defence (as the case may be) of the proceedings.

7.9 In a case of urgency, such as where a limitation period or period for service of proceedings is about to expire, the court may be able to give directions on a summary consideration of the evidence to cover the steps which need to be taken urgently, but limiting those directions so that the application needs to be renewed on fuller consideration at an early stage.

7.10 In any application for directions where a child is a defendant, the court will expect to have put before it the instructions to and advice of an appropriately qualified lawyer as to the benefits and disadvantages of the proposed, and any other relevant, course of action from the point of view of the child beneficiary.

7.11 The master or district judge may give the directions sought though, if the directions relate to actual or proposed litigation, only if it is a plain case, and therefore the master or district judge may think it appropriate to give the directions without a hearing: see PD 2B, paras 4.1 and 5.1(e), and see also para. 6 above. Otherwise the case will be referred to the judge.

7.12 Where a hearing takes place, if the advice of a lawyer has been put in evidence in accordance with para. 7.2 or 7.10, that lawyer should if possible appear on the hearing.

CPR Part 65 Proceedings Relating to Anti-social Behaviour and Harassment

65.1 Scope of This Part

This Part contains rules—

(a) in Section I, about injunctions under the Housing Act 1996;
(b) in Section II, about applications by local authorities under section 91(3) of the Anti-social Behaviour Act 2003 for a power of arrest to be attached to an injunction;
(c) in Section III, about claims for demotion orders under the Housing Act 1985 and Housing Act 1988 and proceedings relating to demoted tenancies;

(d) in Section IV, about anti-social behaviour orders under the Crime and Disorder Act 1998;
(e) in Section V, about claims under section 3 of the Protection from Harassment Act 1997;
(f) in Section VI, about applications for drinking banning orders and interim drinking banning orders under sections 4 and 9 of the Violent Crime Reduction Act 2006;
(g) in Section VII, about parenting orders under sections 26A and 26B of the Anti-social Behaviour Act 2003; and
(h) in Section VIII, about injunctions under the Policing and Crime Act 2009.

I HOUSING ACT 1996 INJUNCTIONS

65.2 Scope of This Section and Interpretation

(1) This Section applies to applications for an injunction and other related proceedings under Chapter III of Part V of the Housing Act 1996 (injunctions against anti-social behaviour).
(2) In this Section 'the 1996 Act' means the Housing Act 1996.

65.3 Applications for an Injunction

r.65.3(1) **88.7**
r.65.3(2)(b)–(c) **88.7**
r.65.3(3) **88.7**
r.65.3(4)(b) **88.7**
r.65.3(4)(e) **88.7**
r.65.3(5)–(6) **88.7**

(1) An application for an injunction under Chapter III of Part V of the 1996 Act shall be subject to the Part 8 procedure as modified by this rule and Practice Direction 65.
(2) The application must be—
 (a) made by a claim form in accordance with Practice Direction 65;
 (b) commenced in the court for the district in which the defendant resides or the conduct complained of occurred; and
 (c) supported by a witness statement which must be filed with the claim form.
(3) The claim form must state—
 (a) the matters required by rule 8.2; and
 (b) the terms of the injunction applied for.
(4) An application under this rule may be made without notice and where such an application without notice is made—
 (a) the witness statement in support of the application must state the reasons why notice has not been given; and
 (b) the following rules do not apply—
  (i) 8.3;
  (ii) 8.4;
  (iii) 8.5(2) to (6);
  (iv) 8.6(1);
  (v) 8.7; and
  (vi) 8.8.
(5) In every application made on notice, the application notice must be served, together with a copy of the witness statement, by the claimant on the defendant personally.
(6) An application made on notice may be listed for hearing before the expiry of the time for the defendant to file an acknowledgment of service under rule 8.3, and in such a case—
 (a) the claimant must serve the application notice and witness statement on the defendant not less than two days before the hearing; and
 (b) the defendant may take part in the hearing whether or not he has filed an acknowledgment of service.

65.4 *Injunction Containing Provisions to Which a Power of Arrest Is Attached*

r.65.4 **88.12**
r.65.4(1) **88.7, 88.9**
r.65.4(2) **88.9**
r.65.4(2)(a) **88.7**
r.65.4(3)–(4) **88.9**

(1) In this rule 'relevant provision' means a provision of an injunction to which a power of arrest is attached.
(Sections 153C(3) and 153D(4) of the 1996 Act confer powers to attach a power of arrest to an injunction)

(2) Where an injunction contains one or more relevant provisions—
(a) each relevant provision must be set out in a separate paragraph of the injunction; and
(b) subject to paragraph (3), the claimant must deliver a copy of the relevant provisions to any police station for the area where the conduct occurred.
(3) Where the injunction has been granted without notice, the claimant must not deliver a copy of the relevant provisions to any police station for the area where the conduct occurred before the defendant has been served with the injunction containing the relevant provisions.
(4) Where an order is made varying or discharging any relevant provision, the claimant must—
(a) immediately inform the police station to which a copy of the relevant provisions was delivered under paragraph (2)(b); and
(b) deliver a copy of the order to any police station so informed.

65.5 Application for Warrant of Arrest under Section 155(3) of the 1996 Act

r.65.5(1)–(2) **88.10**

(1) An application for a warrant of arrest under section 155(3) of the 1996 Act must be made in accordance with Part 23 and may be made without notice.
(2) An applicant for a warrant of arrest under section 155(3) of the 1996 Act must—
(a) file an affidavit setting out grounds for the application with the application notice; or
(b) give oral evidence as to the grounds for the application at the hearing.

65.6 Proceedings following Arrest

r.65.6(2) **88.11, 88.12**
r.65.6(4) **88.12**
r.65.6(4)(a)–(b) **88.11**
r.65.6(5) **88.11, 88.12**
r.65.6(6) **88.11**

(1) This rule applies where a person is arrested pursuant to—
(a) a power of arrest attached to a provision of an injunction; or
(b) a warrant of arrest.
(2) The judge before whom a person is brought following his arrest may—
(a) deal with the matter; or
(b) adjourn the proceedings.
(3) Where the proceedings are adjourned the judge may remand the arrested person in accordance with section 155(2)(b) or (5) of the 1996 Act.
(4) Where the proceedings are adjourned and the arrested person is released—
(a) the matter must be dealt with (whether by the same or another judge) within 28 days of the date on which the arrested person appears in court; and
(b) the arrested person must be given not less than 2 days' notice of the hearing.
(5) An application notice seeking the committal for contempt of court of the arrested person may be issued even if the arrested person is not dealt with within the period mentioned in paragraph (4)(a).
(6) Sections 2 and 8 of Part 81 apply where an application is made in a county court to commit a person for breach of an injunction, as if references in those Sections to the judge included references to a district judge.

(For applications for the discharge of a person committed to prison for contempt of court see rules 81.31 and 81.32.)

65.7 Recognisance

r.65.7 **88.11, 88.12**

(1) Where, in accordance with paragraph 2(2)(b) of Schedule 15 to the 1996 Act, the court fixes the amount of any recognisance with a view to it being taken subsequently, the recognisance may be taken by—
(a) a judge;
(b) a justice of the peace;
(c) a justices' clerk;
(d) a police officer of the rank of inspector or above or in charge of a police station; or
(e) where the arrested person is in his custody, the governor or keeper of a prison, with the same consequences as if it had been entered into before the court.
(2) The person having custody of an applicant for bail must release him if satisfied that the required recognisances have been taken.

II APPLICATIONS BY LOCAL AUTHORITIES FOR POWER OF ARREST TO BE ATTACHED TO AN INJUNCTION

65.8 Scope of This Section and Interpretation

(1) This Section applies to applications by local authorities under section 91(3) of the Anti-social Behaviour Act 2003 or under section 27(3) of the Police and Justice Act 2006 for a power of arrest to be attached to an injunction.

(Section 91 of the 2003 Act and section 27 of the 2006 Act apply to proceedings in which a local authority is a party by virtue of section 222 of the Local Government Act 1972 (power of local authority to bring, defend or appear in proceedings for the promotion or protection of the interests of inhabitants in their area))

(2) In this Section 'the 2003 Act' means the Anti-social Behaviour Act 2003.

(3) In this Section 'the 2006 Act' means the Police and Justice Act 2006.

65.9 Applications under Section 91(3) of the 2003 Act or Section 27(3) of the 2006 Act for a Power of Arrest to Be Attached to Any Provision of an Injunction

r.65.9(1)–(3) 88.12

(1) An application under section 91(3) of the 2003 Act or section 27(3) of the 2006 Act for a power of arrest to be attached to any provision of an injunction must be made in the proceedings seeking the injunction by—
- (a) the claim form;
- (b) the acknowledgment of service;
- (c) the defence or counterclaim in a Part 7 claim; or
- (d) application under Part 23.

(2) Every application must be supported by written evidence.

(3) Every application made on notice must be served personally, together with a copy of the written evidence, by the local authority on the person against whom the injunction is sought not less than 2 days before the hearing.

(Attention is drawn to rule 25.3(3)—applications without notice)

65.10 Injunction Containing Provisions to Which a Power of Arrest Is Attached

r.65.10(1A)(a)–(b) 88.12

(1) Where a power of arrest is attached to a provision of an injunction on the application of a local authority under section 91(3) of the 2003 Act, the following rules in Section I of this Part shall apply—
- (a) rule 65.4; and
- (b) paragraphs (1), (2), (4) and (5) of rule 65.6.

(1A) Where a power of arrest is attached to a provision of an injunction on the application of a local authority under section 27(3) of the 2006 Act, the following rules in Section I of this Part apply—
- (a) rule 65.4;
- (b) paragraphs (1), (2), (4) and (5) of rule 65.6;
- (c) paragraph (1) of rule 65.7, as if the reference to paragraph 2(2)(b) of Schedule 15 to the Housing Act 1996 was a reference to paragraph 2(2)(b) of Schedule 10 to the 2006 Act; and
- (d) paragraph (2) of rule 65.7.

(2) CCR Order 29, rule 1 shall apply where an application is made in a county court to commit a person for breach of an injunction.

III DEMOTION CLAIMS, PROCEEDINGS RELATING TO DEMOTED TENANCIES AND APPLICATIONS TO SUSPEND THE RIGHT TO BUY

section III 70.3, 70.5

65.11 Scope of This Section and Interpretation

(1) This Section applies to—
- (a) claims by a landlord for an order under section 82A of the Housing Act 1985 or under section 6A of the Housing Act 1988 ('a demotion order');

(aa) claims by a landlord for an order under section 121A of the Housing Act 1985 ('a suspension order'); and
(b) proceedings relating to a tenancy created by virtue of a demotion order.
(2) In this Section—
(a) 'a demotion claim' means a claim made by a landlord for a demotion order;
(b) 'a demoted tenancy' means a tenancy created by virtue of a demotion order;
(c) 'suspension claim' means a claim made by a landlord for a suspension order; and
(d) 'suspension period' means the period during which the suspension order suspends the right to buy in relation to the dwelling house.

65.12 Demotion Claims or Suspension Claims Made in the Alternative to Possession Claims

Where a demotion order or suspension order (or both) is claimed in the alternative to a possession order, the claimant must use the Part 55 procedure and Section I of Part 55 applies, except that the claim must be made in the county court for the district in which the property to which the claim relates is situated.

65.13 Other Demotion or Suspension Claims

Where a demotion claim or suspension claim (or both) is made other than in a possession claim, rules 65.14 to 65.19 apply.

65.14 Starting a Demotion or Suspension Claim

(1) The claim must be made in the county court for the district in which the property to which the claim relates is situated.
(2) The claim form and form of defence sent with it must be in the forms set out in Practice Direction 65.
(Part 16 and Practice Direction 65 provide details about the contents of the particulars of claim)

65.15 Particulars of Claim

The particulars of claim must be filed and served with the claim form.

65.16 Hearing Date

(1) The court will fix a date for the hearing when it issues the claim form.
(2) The hearing date will be not less than 28 days from the date of issue of the claim form.
(3) The standard period between the issue of the claim form and the hearing will be not more than 8 weeks.
(4) The defendant must be served with the claim form and the particulars of claim not less than 21 days before the hearing date.
(Rule 3.1(2)(a) provides that the court may extend or shorten the time for compliance with any rule and rule 3.1(2)(b) provides that the court may adjourn or bring forward a hearing)

65.17 Defendant's Response

(1) An acknowledgment of service is not required and Part 10 does not apply.
(2) Where the defendant does not file a defence within the time specified in rule 15.4 he may take part in any hearing but the court may take his failure to do so into account when deciding what order to make about costs.
(3) Part 12 (default judgment) does not apply.

65.18 The Hearing

(1) At the hearing fixed in accordance with rule 65.16(1) or at any adjournment of that hearing the court may—
(a) decide the claim; or
(b) give case management directions.
(2) Where the claim is genuinely disputed on grounds which appear to be substantial, case management directions given under paragraph (1)(b) will include the allocation of the claim to a track or directions to enable it to be allocated.

(3) Except where—
(a) the claim is allocated to the fast track or the multi-track; or
(b) the court directs otherwise,
any fact that needs to be proved by the evidence of witnesses at a hearing referred to in paragraph (1) may be proved by evidence in writing.

(Rule 32.2(1) sets out the general rule about evidence. Rule 32.2(2) provides that rule 32.2(1) is subject to any provision to the contrary)

(4) All witness statements must be filed and served at least two days before the hearing.
(5) Where the claimant serves the claim form and particulars of claim, the claimant must produce at the hearing a certificate of service of those documents and rule 6.17(2)(a) does not apply.

65.19 Allocation

When the court decides the track for the claim, the matters to which it shall have regard include—
(a) the matters set out in rule 26.8; and
(b) the nature and extent of the conduct alleged.

65.20 Proceedings Relating to Demoted Tenancies

A practice direction may make provision about proceedings relating to demoted tenancies.

IV ANTI-SOCIAL BEHAVIOUR ORDERS UNDER THE CRIME AND DISORDER ACT 1998

65.21 Scope of This Section and Interpretation

(1) This Section applies to applications in proceedings in a county court under sub-sections (2), (3) or (3B) of section 1B of the Crime and Disorder Act 1998 by a relevant authority, and to applications for interim orders under section 1D of that Act.
(2) In this Section—
(a) 'the 1998 Act' means the Crime and Disorder Act 1998;
(b) 'relevant authority' has the same meaning as in section 1(1A) of the 1998 Act; and
(c) 'the principal proceedings' means any proceedings in a county court.

65.22 Application Where the Relevant Authority is a Party in Principal Proceedings

r.65.22(1)–(3) 88.19

(1) Subject to paragraph (2)—
(a) where the relevant authority is the claimant in the principal proceedings, an application under section 1B(2) of the 1998 Act for an order under section 1B(4) of the 1998 Act must be made in the claim form; and
(b) where the relevant authority is a defendant in the principal proceedings, an application for an order must be made by application notice which must be filed with the defence.
(2) Where the relevant authority becomes aware of the circumstances that lead it to apply for an order after its claim is issued or its defence filed, the application must be made by application notice as soon as possible thereafter.
(3) Where the application is made by application notice, it should normally be made on notice to the person against whom the order is sought.

65.23 Application by a Relevant Authority to Join a Person to the Principal Proceedings

r.65.23(1)(a)–(c) 88.19 r.65.23(2)–(3) 88.19

(1) An application under section 1B(3B) of the 1998 Act by a relevant authority which is a party to the principal proceedings to join a person to the principal proceedings must be made—
(a) in accordance with Section I of Part 19;
(b) in the same application notice as the application for an order under section 1B(4) of the 1998 Act against the person; and
(c) as soon as possible after the relevant authority considers that the criteria in section 1B(3A) of the 1998 Act are met.

(2) The application notice must contain—
 (a) the relevant authority's reasons for claiming that the person's anti-social acts are material in relation to the principal proceedings; and
 (b) details of the anti-social acts alleged.
(3) The application should normally be made on notice to the person against whom the order is sought.

65.24 Application Where the Relevant Authority is Not Party in Principal Proceedings

r.65.24(1)(a)–(b) **88.19** r.65.24(2)(a)–(b) **88.19**

(1) Where the relevant authority is not a party to the principal proceedings—
 (a) an application under section 1B(3) of the 1998 Act to be made a party must be made in accordance with Section I of Part 19; and
 (b) the application to be made a party and the application for an order under section 1B(4) of the 1998 Act must be made in the same application notice.
(2) The applications—
 (a) must be made as soon as possible after the authority becomes aware of the principal proceedings; and
 (b) should normally be made on notice to the person against whom the order is sought.

65.25 Evidence

r.65.25 **88.19**

An application for an order under section 1B(4) of the 1998 Act must be accompanied by written evidence, which must include evidence that section 1E of the 1998 Act has been complied with.

65.26 Application for an Interim Order

r.65.26(1)–(2) **88.20**

(1) An application for an interim order under section 1D of the 1998 Act must be made in accordance with Part 25.
(2) The application should normally be made—
 (a) in the claim form or application notice seeking the order; and
 (b) on notice to the person against whom the order is sought.

V PROCEEDINGS UNDER THE PROTECTION FROM HARASSMENT ACT 1997

65.27 Scope of This Section

This Section applies to proceedings under section 3 of the Protection from Harassment Act 1997 ('the 1997 Act').

65.28 Claims under Section 3 of the 1997 Act

r.65.28(a)–(b) **88.37**

A claim under section 3 of the 1997 Act—

 (a) shall be subject to the Part 8 procedure; and
 (b) must be commenced—
  (i) if in the High Court, in the Queen's Bench Division;
  (ii) if in the county court, in the court for the district in which the defendant resides or carries on business or the court for the district in which the claimant resides or carries on business.

65.29 Applications for Issue of a Warrant of Arrest under Section 3(3) of the 1997 Act

r.65.29(2) **88.38**

(1) An application for a warrant of arrest under section 3(3) of the 1997 Act—
 (a) must be made in accordance with Part 23; and
 (b) may be made without notice.
(2) The application notice must be supported by affidavit evidence which must—
 (a) set out the grounds for the application;
 (b) state whether the claimant has informed the police of the conduct of the defendant as described in the affidavit; and

(c) state whether, to the claimant's knowledge, criminal proceedings are being pursued.

65.30 Proceedings Following Arrest

r.65.30(1) **88.39** r.65.30(2)(a)–(b) **88.39**

(1) The judge before whom a person is brought following his arrest may—
(a) deal with the matter; or
(b) adjourn the proceedings.
(2) Where the proceedings are adjourned and the arrested person is released—
(a) the matter must be dealt with (whether by the same or another judge) within 28 days of the date on which the arrested person appears in court; and
(b) the arrested person must be given not less than 2 days' notice of the hearing.

VI DRINKING BANNING ORDERS UNDER THE VIOLENT CRIME REDUCTION ACT 2006

65.31 Scope of This Section and Interpretation

(1) This Section applies to applications in proceedings in a county court under sub-sections (2), (3) or (5) of section 4 of the Violent Crime Reduction Act 2006 by a relevant authority, and to applications for interim orders under section 9 of that Act.
(2) In this Section—
(a) 'the 2006 Act' means the Violent Crime Reduction Act 2006;
(b) 'relevant authority' has the same meaning as in section 14(1) of the 2006 Act; and
(c) 'the principal proceedings' means any proceedings in a county court.

65.32 Application Where the Relevant Authority Is a Party in Principal Proceedings

r.65.32(1)–(3) **88.29**

(1) Subject to paragraph (2)—
(a) where the relevant authority is the claimant in the principal hproceedings, an application under section 4(2) of the 2006 Act for an order under section 4(7) of the 2006 Act must be made in the claim form; and
(b) where the relevant authority is a defendant in the principal proceedings, an application for an order must be made by application notice which must be filed with the defence.
(2) Where the relevant authority becomes aware of the circumstances that lead it to apply for an order after its claim is issued or its defence filed, the application must be made by application notice as soon as possible thereafter.
(3) Where the application is made by application notice, it should normally be made on notice to the person against whom the order is sought.

65.33 Application Where the Relevant Authority Is Not a Party in Principal Proceedings

r.65.33(1)(a)–(b) **88.29** r.65.33(2) **88.29**

(1) Where the relevant authority is not a party to the principal proceedings—
(a) an application under section 4(3) of the 2006 Act to be made a party must be made in accordance with Section I of Part 19; and
(b) the application to be made a party and the application for an order under section 4(7) of the 2006 Act must be made in the same application notice.
(2) The applications—
(a) must be made as soon as possible after the relevant authority becomes aware of the principal proceedings; and
(b) should normally be made on notice to the person against whom the order is sought.

65.34 Application by a Relevant Authority to Join a Person to the Principal Proceedings

r.65.34(1)(a)–(c) **88.29** r.65.34(2)–(3) **88.29**

(1) An application under section 4(5) of the 2006 Act by a relevant authority which is a party to the principal proceedings to join a person to the principal proceedings must be made—
(a) in accordance with Section I of Part 19;

(b) in the same application notice as the application for an order under section 4(7) of the 2006 Act against the person; and
(c) as soon as possible after the relevant authority considers that the criteria in section 4(4) of the 2006 Act are met.

(2) The application notice must contain—
(a) the relevant authority's reasons for claiming that the person's conduct is material in relation to the principal proceedings; and
(b) details of the conduct alleged.

(3) The application should normally be made on notice to the person against whom the order is sought.

65.35 Evidence

r.65.35 **88.29**

An application for an order under section 4(7) of the 2006 Act must be accompanied by written evidence, which must include evidence that section 4(6) of the 2006 Act has been complied with.

65.36 Application for an Interim Order

r.65.35(1)–(3) **88.30**

(1) An application for an interim order under section 9 of the 2006 Act must be made in accordance with Part 25.

(2) The application should normally be made—
(a) in the claim form or application notice seeking the order; and
(b) on notice to the person against whom the order is sought.

(3) An application for an interim order may be—
(a) made without a copy of the application notice being served on the person against whom the order is sought;
(b) heard in the absence of the person against whom the order is sought,
with the permission of the court.

VII PARENTING ORDERS UNDER THE ANTI-SOCIAL BEHAVIOUR ACT 2003

65.37 Scope of This Section and Interpretation

(1) This Section of this Part applies in relation to applications for parenting orders under sections 26A and 26B of the Anti-social Behaviour Act 2003 by a relevant authority.

(2) In this Section—
(a) 'the 2003 Act' means the Anti-social Behaviour Act 2003; and
(b) 'relevant authority' has the same meaning as in section 26C of the 2003 Act.

65.38 Applications for Parenting Orders

r.65.38(1) **88.25** r.65.38(2)(a) **88.25**
r.65.38(2) **88.25** r.65.38(3) **88.25**

(1) Subject to paragraph (2)—
(a) where the relevant authority is the claimant in the proceedings, an application for an order under section 26A or 26B of the 2003 Act must be made in the claim form; and
(b) where the relevant authority is a defendant in the proceedings, an application for such an order must be made by application notice which must be filed with the defence.

(2) Where the relevant authority becomes aware of the circumstances that lead it to apply for an order after its claim is issued or its defence filed, the application must be made by application notice as soon as possible thereafter.

(3) Where the application is made by application notice, it must normally be made on notice to the person against whom the order is sought.

65.39 Applications by the Relevant Authority to Be Joined to Proceedings

r.65.39(1)(a)–(b) **88.25** r.65.39(2)(b) **88.25**

(1) Where the relevant authority is not a party to the proceedings—
(a) an application under section 26C(2) of the 2003 Act to be made a party must be made in accordance with Section I of Part 19; and

(b) the application to be made a party and the application for an order under section 26A or 26B of the 2003 Act must be made in the same application notice.

(2) The applications—

(a) must be made as soon as possible after the relevant authority becomes aware of the proceedings; and

(b) must normally be made on notice to the person against whom the order is sought.

65.40 Applications by the Relevant Authority to Join a Parent to Proceedings

r.65.40(1)(a)–(b) 88.25 r.65.40(2)–(4) 88.25

(1) An application under section 26C(3) of the 2003 Act by a relevant authority which is a party to the proceedings to join a parent to those proceedings must be made—

(a) in the same application notice as the application for an order under section 26A or 26B of the 2003 Act; and

(b) as soon as possible after the relevant authority considers that the grounds for the application are met.

(2) Rule 19.2 does not apply in relation to an application made by a relevant authority under section 26C(3) of the 2003 Act to join a parent to the proceedings.

(3) The application notice must contain—

(a) the relevant authority's reasons for claiming the anti-social behaviour of the child or young person is material in relation to the proceedings; and

(b) details of the behaviour alleged.

(4) The application must normally be made on notice to the person against whom the order is sought.

65.41 Evidence

r.65.41 88.25

An application under section 26A, 26B or 26C of the 2003 Act must be accompanied by written evidence.

VIII INJUNCTIONS UNDER THE POLICING AND CRIME ACT 2009

65.42 Scope of This Section and Interpretation

(1) This Section applies to applications for an injunction and other related proceedings under Part 4 of the Policing and Crime Act 2009 (Injunctions: gang-related violence).

(2) In this Section 'the 2009 Act' means the Policing and Crime Act 2009.

65.43 Applications for an Injunction

r.65.43 88.43 r.65.43(4) 88.44
r.65.43(2)(a)–(c) 88.43 r.65.43(5)–(6) 88.43

(1) An application for an injunction under Part 4 of the 2009 Act is subject to the Part 8 procedure as modified by this rule and Practice Direction 65.

(2) The application must be—

(a) made by a claim form in accordance with Practice Direction 65;

(b) commenced in the court for the district in which the defendant resides or the conduct complained of occurred; and

(c) supported by a witness statement which must be filed with the claim form.

(3) The claim form must state—

(a) the matters required by rule 8.2; and

(b) the terms of the injunction applied for.

(4) An application under this rule may be made without notice and where such an application without notice is made—

(a) the witness statement in support of the application must state the reasons why notice has not been given; and

(b) the following rules do not apply—

(i) 8.3;

(ii) 8.4;

(iii) 8.5(2) to (6);

(iv) 8.6(1);
(v) 8.7; and
(vi) 8.8.

(5) In every application made on notice, the application notice must be served, together with a copy of the witness statement, by the claimant on the defendant personally.

(6) An application made on notice may be listed for hearing before the expiry of the time for the defendant to file an acknowledgment of service under rule 8.3, and in such a case—
(a) the claimant must serve the application notice and witness statement on the defendant not less than 2 days before the hearing; and
(b) the defendant may take part in the hearing whether or not the defendant has filed an acknowledgment of service.

65.44 Injunction Containing Provisions to Which a Power of Arrest Is Attached

r.65.44(1)–(3) **88.47** r.65.44(4) **88.51**

(1) In this rule 'relevant provision' means a provision of an injunction to which a power of arrest is attached.

(Section 36(6) and (7) and section 40(3) and 41(4) of the 2009 Act confer powers to attach a power of arrest to an injunction.)

(2) Where an injunction contains one or more relevant provisions—
(a) each relevant provision must be set out in a separate paragraph of the injunction; and
(b) subject to paragraph (3), the claimant must deliver a copy of the relevant provisions to any police station for the area where the conduct occurred.

(3) Where the injunction has been granted without notice, the claimant must not deliver a copy of the relevant provisions to any police station for the area where the conduct occurred before the defendant has been served with the injunction containing the relevant provisions.

(4) Where an order is made varying or discharging any relevant provision, the claimant must—
(a) immediately inform the police station to which a copy of the relevant provisions was delivered under paragraph (2)(b); and
(b) deliver a copy of the order to any police station so informed.

65.45 Application to Vary or Discharge an Injunction

r.65.45(1)–(3) **88.51**

(1) An application to vary or discharge an injunction under section 42(1)(b) of the 2009 Act must be made in accordance with Part 23.

(2) An application by the claimant to vary or discharge the injunction under section 42(1)(b) of the 2009 Act may be made without notice.

(3) If an application under this rule is made without giving notice, the application notice must state the reasons why notice has not been given.

65.46 Application for Warrant of Arrest under Section 44(2) of the 2009 Act

r.65.46(2) **88.47**

(1) An application for a warrant of arrest under section 44(2) of the 2009 Act must be made in accordance with Part 23 and may be made without notice.

(2) An applicant for a warrant of arrest under section 44(2) of the 2009 Act must—
(a) file an affidavit setting out grounds for the application with the application notice; or
(b) give oral evidence of the grounds for the application at the hearing.

(3) Where in accordance with sub-paragraph (2)(b), oral evidence is given, the applicant must produce a written record of that evidence which must be served on the person arrested at the time of the arrest.

65.47 Proceedings following Arrest under the 2009 Act

r.65.47(1)–(4) **88.47**

(1) This rule applies where a person is arrested pursuant to—
(a) a power of arrest attached to a provision of an injunction; or
(b) a warrant of arrest.

(2) The judge before whom a person is brought following his arrest may—

(a) deal with the matter; or
(b) adjourn the proceedings.

(3) If proceedings under section 43 or 44 of the 2009 Act are adjourned and the arrested person is released—
(a) the matter must be dealt with (whether by the same or another judge) within 28 days of the date on which the arrested person appears in court; and
(b) the arrested person must be given not less than 2 days' notice of the hearing.

(4) An application notice seeking the committal for contempt of court of the arrested person may be issued even if the arrested person is not dealt with within the period in sub-paragraph (3)(a).

(5) Sections 2 and 8 of Part 81 apply where an application is made in a county court to commit a person for breach of an injunction as if references in those Sections to the judge include references to a district judge.

(For applications for the discharge of a person committed to prison for contempt of court see rules 81.31 and 81.32.)

65.48 Recognisance

r.65.48(1)–(2) **88.48**

(1) Where, in accordance with paragraph 2(2)(b) of Schedule 5 to the 2009 Act, the court fixes the amount of any recognisance with a view to it being taken subsequently, the recognisance may be taken by—
(a) a judge;
(b) a justice of the peace;
(c) a justices' clerk;
(d) a police officer of the rank of inspector or above, or in charge of a police station; or
(e) where the arrested person is in custody, the governor or keeper of a prison,
with the same consequences as if it had been entered into before the court.

(2) The person having custody of an applicant for bail must release that person if satisfied that the required recognisances have been taken.

65.49 Applications for a Power of Arrest to be Attached to Any Provision of an Injunction

r.65.49(1) **88.45** r.65.49(3) **88.45**

(1) An application under section 34 or 39 of the 2009 Act which includes an application for a power of arrest to be attached to any provision of an injunction must be made in the proceedings seeking the injunction by—
(a) the claim form; or
(b) an application under Part 23.

(2) Every application must be supported by written evidence.

(3) Every application made on notice must be served personally, together with a copy of the written evidence, by the applicant on the person against whom the injunction is sought not less than 2 days before the hearing.

(Attention is drawn to rule 25.3(3) — applications without notice.)

PD 65 Practice Direction 65 — Anti-social Behaviour and Harassment

This practice direction supplements CPR, Part 65.

I HOUSING ACT 1996 AND POLICING AND CRIME ACT 2009 INJUNCTIONS

Issuing the Claim

para.1 **88.7** para.1.1 **88.43**

1.1 An application for an injunction under chapter III of part V of the 1996 Act or part 4 of the 2009 Act must be made by form N16A and for the purposes of applying PD 8A to applications under Section I or Section VIII of Part 65, form N16A shall be treated as the Part 8 claim form.

Application for an injunction against a child

1A.1 (1) Attention is drawn to the provisions of Part 21 and PD 21: in particular to the requirement for a child to have a litigation friend unless the court makes an order under r. 21.2(3), and the procedure for appointment of a litigation friend. The Official Solicitor may be invited to act as litigation friend where there is no other willing and suitable person.

(2) When an application for an injunction is made without notice in accordance with r. 65.43(4) and the court grants permission for the application to be heard without the child having a litigation friend, the court will consider whether to direct the applicant to—

(a) make an application for a litigation friend at the earliest opportunity after the child is served with the injunction;

(b) ensure that the terms of the injunction and the consequences resulting from any breach of those terms are explained to the child at the time the injunction is served;

(c) ensure that an appropriate and responsible adult is present at the time the injunction is served;

(d) file a witness statement confirming compliance with any such directions.

Hearings

para.1.2 **88.43**

1.2 Unless the court otherwise orders, an application on notice for an injunction under r. 65.43 or any other hearing requiring the respondent's attendance must be heard at one of the following county courts—

(a) Birmingham
(b) Bradford
(c) Bristol
(d) Cardiff
(e) Croydon
(f) Leicester
(g) Liverpool
(h) Manchester
(i) Newcastle
(j) Nottingham
(k) Peterborough
(l) Portsmouth
(m) Preston
(n) Sheffield
(o) West London.

(Attention is drawn to the statutory guidance on listing for hearings. These hearings will take place in courts which have been identified as having suitable facilities if special measures are needed for potential witnesses or security.)

Warrant of Arrest on an Application under Section 155(3) of the 1996 Act or Section 44(2) of the 2009 Act

para.2.1 **88.10, 88.47** para.2.1(2) **88.47**

2.1 In accordance with s. 155(4) of the 1996 Act, and s. 44(3) of the 2009 Act, a warrant of arrest on an application under s. 155(3) of the 1996 Act or s. 44(2) of the 2009 Act shall not be issued unless:
(1) the application is substantiated on oath; and
(2) in any proceedings under the 1996 Act the judge has reasonable grounds for believing that the defendant has failed to comply with the injunction.

Application for Bail

paras.3.1 **88.11, 88.12, 88.47** para.3.3 **88.11, 88.12**
paras.3.2 **88.11, 88.12, 88.47**

3.1 An application for bail by a person arrested under:
(1) a power of arrest attached to an injunction under chapter III of part V of the 1996 Act or part 4 of the 2009 Act; or
(2) a warrant of arrest issued on an application under s. 155(3) of the 1996 Act or part 4 of the 2009 Act,

may be made either orally or in an application notice.

3.2 An application notice seeking bail must contain:
(1) the full name of the person making the application;
(2) the address of the place where the person making the application is detained at the time when the application is made;
(3) the address where the person making the application would reside if that person were to be granted bail;
(4) the amount of the recognisance in which that person would agree to be bound; and
(5) the grounds on which the application is made and, where previous application has been refused, full details of any change in circumstances which has occurred since that refusal.

3.3 A copy of the application notice must be served on the person who obtained the injunction.

Remand for Medical Examination and Report

para.4.1 **88.11, 88.12**

4.1 Section 156(4) of the 1996 Act and s. 45(5) of the 2009 Act provides that the judge has power to make an order under the Mental Health Act 1983, s. 35, in certain circumstances. If he does so attention is drawn to s. 35(8) of that Act, which provides that a person remanded to hospital under that section may obtain at his own expense an independent report on his mental condition from a registered medical practitioner chosen by him and apply to the court on the basis of it for his remand to be terminated under s. 35(7).

Applications by Local Authorities for Power of Arrest to Be Attached to an Injunction

Application for bail under the 2006 Act

para.4A.1 **88.12**

4A.1 The following paragraphs of Section I of this practice direction apply in relation to an application for bail by a person arrested under a power of arrest attached to an injunction under s. 27 of the 2006 Act:
(1) para. 3.1(1), as if a reference to the Housing Act 1996, part V, ch. III, was a reference to s. 27of the 2006 Act;
(2) para. 3.2; and
(3) para. 3.3.

Remand for medical examination and report

4A.2 Paragraph 4.1 of Section I of this practice direction applies in relation to s. 27 of the 2006 Act, as if a reference in para. 4.1 to the Housing Act 1996, s. 156(4), was a reference to s. 27(11) of the 2006 Act.

II DEMOTION OR SUSPENSION CLAIMS

(Suspension claims may be made in England, but may not be made in Wales.)

paras.5.1–9.3 **88.29, 88.30**

Demotion Claims Made in the Alternative to Possession Claims

5.1 If the claim relates to residential property let on a tenancy and if the claim includes a demotion claim, the particulars of claim must:
(1) state whether the demotion claim is a claim under s. 82A(2) of the 1985 Act or under s. 6A(2)of the 1988 Act;
(2) state whether the claimant is a local housing authority, a housing action trust, a registered social landlord or a private registered provider of social housing;
(3) provide details of any statement of express terms of the tenancy served on the tenant under s. 82A(7) of the 1985 Act or under s. 6A(10) of the 1988 Act, as applicable; and
(4) state details of the conduct alleged.

Suspension Claims Made in the Alternative to Possession Claims

5A.1 If the claim relates to a residential property let on a tenancy and if the claim includes a suspension claim, the particulars of claim must:
(1) state that the suspension claim is a claim under s. 121A of the 1985 Act;
(2) state which of the bodies the claimant's interest belongs to in order to comply with the landlord condition under s. 80 of the 1985 Act;
(3) state details of the conduct alleged; and
(4) explain why it is reasonable to make the suspension order, having regard in particular to the factors set out in s. 121A(4) of the 1985 Act.

Other Demotion or Suspension Claims

6.1 Demotion claims, other than those made in the alternative to possession claims, must be made in the county court for the district in which the property to which the claim relates is situated.
6.2 The claimant must use the appropriate claim form and particulars of claim form set out in Table 1 of PD 4. The defence must be in form N11D as appropriate.
6.3 The claimant's evidence should include details of the conduct alleged, and any other matters relied upon.

Particulars of Claim

7.1 In a demotion claim the particulars of claim must:
(1) state whether the demotion claim is a claim under s. 82A(2) of the 1985 Act or under s. 6A(2)of the 1988 Act;
(2) state whether the claimant is a local housing authority, a housing action trust, a registered social landlord or a private registered provider of social housing;
(3) identify the property to which the claim relates;
(4) provide the following details about the tenancy to which the demotion claim relates:
(a) the parties to the tenancy;
(b) the period of the tenancy;
(c) the amount of the rent;
(d) the dates on which the rent is payable; and
(e) any statement of express terms of the tenancy served on the tenant under s. 82A(7) of the 1985 Act or under s. 6A(10) of the 1988 Act, as applicable; and
(5) state details of the conduct alleged.

Hearing Date

8.1 The court may use its powers under r. 3.1(2)(a) and (b) to shorten the time periods set out in r. 65.16(2), (3) and (4).
8.2 Particular consideration should be given to the exercise of this power if:
(1) the defendant, or a person for whom the defendant is responsible, has assaulted or threatened to assault:
(a) the claimant;
(b) a member of the claimant's staff; or
(c) another resident in the locality;
(2) there are reasonable grounds for fearing such an assault; or

(3) the defendant, or a person for whom the defendant is responsible, has caused serious damage or threatened to cause serious damage to the property or to the home or property of another resident in the locality.

8.3 Where para. 8.2 applies but the case cannot be determined at the first hearing fixed under r. 65.16, the court will consider what steps are needed to finally determine the case as quickly as reasonably practicable.

The Hearing

9.1 Attention is drawn to r. 65.18(3). Each party should wherever possible include all the evidence he wishes to present in his statement of case, verified by a statement of truth.

9.2 The claimant's evidence should include details of the conduct to which s. 153A or 153B of the 1996 Act applies and in respect of which the demotion claim is made.

9.3 If:

(1) the maker of a witness statement does not attend a hearing; and

(2) the other party disputes material evidence contained in the statement,

the court will normally adjourn the hearing so that oral evidence can be given.

III PROCEEDINGS RELATING TO DEMOTED TENANCIES

Proceedings for the Possession of a Demoted Tenancy

10.1 Proceedings against a tenant of a demoted tenancy for possession must be brought under the procedure in Part 55 (possession claims).

Proceedings in Relation to a Written Statement of Demoted Tenancy Terms

11.1 Proceedings as to whether a statement supplied in pursuance to s. 143M(4)(b) of the 1996 Act (written statement of certain terms of tenancy) is accurate must be brought under the procedure in Part 8.

Recovery of Costs

12.1 Attention is drawn to s. 143N(4) of the 1996 Act which provides that if a person takes proceedings under chapter 1A of the 1996 Act in the High Court which he could have taken in the county court, he is not entitled to recover any costs.

IV ANTI-SOCIAL BEHAVIOUR ORDERS UNDER THE CRIME AND DISORDER ACT 1998

Service of an Order under Sections 1B(4) or 1D of the 1998 Act

para.13 88.14

13.1 An order under s. 1B(4) or an interim order under s. 1D of the 1998 Act must be served personally on the defendant.

Application to join a person to the principal proceedings

13.2 An application by a relevant authority under s. 1B(3B) of the 1998 Act to join a person to the principal proceedings may only be made against a person aged 18 or over.

V PROCEEDINGS UNDER THE PROTECTION FROM HARASSMENT ACT 1997

Warrant of Arrest on Application under Section 3(3) of the 1997 Act

14.1 In accordance with s. 3(5) of the 1997 Act, a warrant of arrest on an application under s. 3(3) of that Act may only be issued if:

(1) the application is substantiated on oath; and

(2) the judge has reasonable grounds for believing that the defendant has done anything which he is prohibited from doing by the injunction.

SECTION VI DRINKING BANNING ORDERS UNDER THE VIOLENT CRIME REDUCTION ACT 2006

Service of an Order under Section 4(7) or 9 of the 2006 Act

para.15.1 **88.31**

15.1 An order under s. 4(7) or an interim order under s. 9 of the 2006 Act must be served personally on the defendant.

Application to Join a Person to the Principal Proceedings

para.15.2 **88.28**

15.2 An application by a relevant authority under s. 4(5) of the 2006 Act to join a person to the principal proceedings may only be made against a person aged 18 or over.

VII PARENTING ORDERS UNDER THE ANTI-SOCIAL BEHAVIOUR ACT 2003

Applications for Parenting Orders

para.16.1 **88.25**
para.16.2 **88.26**
para.16.3 **88.24**

16.1 Where the applicant is a registered social landlord or a private registered provider of social housing, the application must be supported by evidence that the relevant local authority has been consulted in accordance with s. 26B(8) of the 2003 Act.

16.2 An order under s. 26A or 26B of the 2003 Act must be served personally on the defendant.

16.3 An application by a relevant authority under s. 26C(3) of the 2003 Act to join a person to the proceedings may only be made against a person aged 18 or over.

CPR Part 66 Crown Proceedings

Part 66 14.44

66.1 Scope of This Part and Interpretation

(1) This Part contains rules for civil proceedings by or against the Crown, and other civil proceedings to which the Crown is a party.

(2) In this Part—

(a) 'the Act' means the Crown Proceedings Act 1947;

(b) 'civil proceedings by the Crown' means the civil proceedings described in section 23(1) of the Act, but excluding the proceedings described in section 23(3);

(c) 'civil proceedings against the Crown' means the civil proceedings described in section 23(2) of the Act, but excluding the proceedings described in section 23(3);

(d) 'civil proceedings to which the Crown is a party' has the same meaning as it has for the purposes of Parts III and IV of the Act by virtue of section 38(4).

66.2 Application of the Civil Procedure Rules

These Rules and their practice directions apply to civil proceedings by or against the Crown and to other civil proceedings to which the Crown is a party unless this Part, a practice direction or any other enactment provides otherwise.

66.3 Action on Behalf of the Crown

(1) Where by reason of a rule, practice direction or court order the Crown is permitted or required—

(a) to make a witness statement,

(b) to swear an affidavit,

(c) to verify a document by a statement of truth;

(d) to make a disclosure statement; or

(e) to discharge any other procedural obligation,

that function shall be performed by an appropriate officer acting on behalf of the Crown.

(2) The court may if necessary nominate an appropriate officer.

66.4 Counterclaims, Other Part 20 Claims, and Set-off

r.66.4(1)–(2) 28.3 r.66.4(3)–(4) 28.2

(1) In a claim by the Crown for taxes, duties or penalties, the defendant cannot make a counterclaim or other Part 20 claim or raise a defence of set-off.

(2) In any other claim by the Crown, the defendant cannot make a counterclaim or other Part 20 claim or raise a defence of set-off which is based on a claim for repayment of taxes, duties or penalties.

(3) In proceedings by or against the Crown in the name of the Attorney-General, no counterclaim or other Part 20 claim can be made or defence of set-off raised without the permission of the court.

(4) In proceedings by or against the Crown in the name of a government department, no counterclaim or other Part 20 claim can be made or defence of set-off raised without the permission of the court unless the subject-matter relates to that government department.

66.5 Applications in Revenue Matters

(1) This rule sets out the procedure under section 14 of the Act, which allows the Crown to make summary applications in the High Court in certain revenue matters.
(2) The application must be made in the High Court using the Part 8 procedure.
(3) The title of the claim form must clearly identify the matters which give rise to the application.

66.6 Enforcement against the Crown

r.66.6 79.40

(1) The following rules do not apply to any order against the Crown—
  (a) Parts 69 to 73;
  (b) RSC Orders 45 to 47 and 52; and
  (c) CCR Orders 25 to 29.
(2) In paragraph (1), 'order against the Crown' means any judgment or order against the Crown, a government department, or an officer of the Crown as such, made—
  (a) in civil proceedings by or against the Crown;
  (b) in proceedings in the Administrative Court;
  (c) in connection with an arbitration to which the Crown is a party; or
  (d) in other civil proceedings to which the Crown is a party.
(3) An application under section 25(1) of the Act for a separate certificate of costs payable to the applicant may be made without notice.

66.7 Money Due from the Crown

r.66.7 2.4, 79.41 r.66.7(3) 2.10

(1) None of the following orders—
  (a) a third party debt order under Part 72;
  (b) an order for the appointment of a receiver under Part 69; or
  (c) an order for the appointment of a sequestrator under RSC Order 45,
  may be made or have effect in respect of any money due from the Crown.
(2) In paragraph (1), 'money due from the Crown' includes money accruing due, and money alleged to be due or accruing due.
(3) An application for an order under section 27 of the Act—
  (a) restraining a person from receiving money payable to him by the Crown; and
  (b) directing payment of the money to the applicant or another person,
  may be made under Part 23.
(4) The application must be supported by written evidence setting out the facts on which it is based, and in particular identifying the debt from the Crown.
(5) Where the debt from the Crown is money in a National Savings Bank account, the witness must if possible identify the number of the account and the name and address of the branch where it is held.
(6) Notice of the application, with a copy of the written evidence, must be served—
  (a) on the Crown, and
  (b) on the person to be restrained,
  at least 7 days before the hearing.
(7) Rule 72.8 applies to an application under this rule as it applies to an application under rule 72.2 for a third party debt order, except that the court will not have the power to order enforcement to issue against the Crown.

PD 66 Practice Direction 66 — Crown Proceedings

This practice direction supplements CPR, Part 66.

PD 66 14.45, 15.50, 42.9

Transfer

1.1 Rule 30.3(2) sets out the circumstances to which the court must have regard when considering whether to make an order under the County Courts Act 1984, s. 40(2), 41(1) or 42(2) (transfer between the High Court and County Court), CPR, r. 30.2(1) (transfer between county courts) or r. 30.2(4) (transfer between the Royal Courts of Justice and the district registries).

1.2 From time to time the Attorney-General will publish a note concerning the organisation of the Government Legal Service and matters relevant to the venue of Crown proceedings, for the assistance of practitioners and judges. When considering questions of venue under r. 30.3(2), the court should have regard to the Attorney-General's note in addition to all the other circumstances of the case.

Service of Documents

2.1 In civil proceedings by or against the Crown, documents required to be served on the Crown must be served in accordance with r. 6.10 or 6.23(7).

(The list published under the Crown Proceedings Act 1947, s. 17, of the solicitors acting for the different government departments on whom service is to be effected, and of their addresses is in annex 2 to this practice direction.)

ANNEX 1
DISPUTES AS TO VENUE—FACTORS TO BE TAKEN INTO CONSIDERATION

Attorney-General's note to supplement PD 66.

annex 14.46, 15.52

Introduction

Until the recent rule changes, the Crown was entitled in High Court matters to insist that venue was the Royal Courts of Justice in London (RCJ) (RSC, ord. 77, r. 2). This rule has now been revoked. A new r. 30.3(2)(h) of the CPR provides that in cases involving civil proceedings by or against the Crown, when considering whether to order a transfer of those proceedings, the court must have regard to, 'the location of the relevant government department or officers of the Crown and, where appropriate, any relevant public interest that the matter should be tried in London'.

PD 66, para. 2, provides that the Attorney-General will publish a note concerning the organisation of the Government Legal Service and matters relevant to the venue of Crown proceedings, for the assistance of practitioners and judges. When considering questions of venue under CPR, r. 30.3(2), the court should have regard to the Attorney-General's note in addition to all the other circumstances of the case.

This note sets out the further factors to be taken into consideration where there is a dispute as to venue between a claimant and a government department. Where there is such a dispute, it should be dealt with at a case management conference.

Organisation of the Government Legal Service

The Government Legal Service (GLS) has the responsibility for advising the Government about its legal affairs and has the conduct of civil litigation on its behalf. The Treasury Solicitor conducts this litigation for the majority of Government Departments but lawyers in HM Revenue and Customs, the Department for the Environment, Food and Rural Affairs and the Department for Work and Pensions (which also acts for the Department of Health and the Food Standards Agency) have the conduct of litigation for their Departments. All Government litigation lawyers are based in the London [*sic*] with the exception of HM Revenue and Customs, whose personal injury lawyers are in Manchester. A full list of addresses for service is [in annex 2 to PD 66].

Factors to Be Taken into Account Generally

Location
Whilst a number of government departments have offices outside London, central government bodies are based in London and the GLS is geared towards processing claims in the RCJ (see above). Where there is a High Court claim, many witnesses as well as lawyers and officials are London based and there may be a disproportionate cost in transferring them to a venue outside London. That is not to say, bearing in mind the overriding objective, that the Crown would oppose transfer away from the RCJ where it was appropriate, for example in personal injury disputes.

Precedent value
Some cases have important precedent value or are of general importance to the public, which may make them more suitable for being heard in the RCJ.

Special Considerations in Relation to HM Revenue and Customs
HM Revenue and Customs has no lawyers outside London, except for those personal injury lawyers based in Manchester.

The work of HM Revenue and Customs is very specialised, needing in many cases to be dealt with by specialist judges in the Chancery Division familiar, for example, with tax work.

There is also the public interest to consider. All revenue cases (including those of HM Revenue and Customs) have important precedent value that applies across the entire tax system, with implications for the Exchequer.

ANNEX 2

LIST OF AUTHORISED GOVERNMENT DEPARTMENTS

26 October 2012

List of authorised government departments and the names and addresses for service of the person who is, or is acting for the purposes of the Act as, solicitor for such departments, published by the Minister for the Civil Service in pursuance of section 17 of the Crown Proceedings Act 1947.

Authorised government departments	**Solicitors and addresses for service**
Departments whose solicitor is the Treasury Solicitor	
Advisory, Conciliation and Arbitration Service	The Treasury Solicitor
Board of Trade	One Kemble Street
Cabinet Office	London WC2B 4TS
Commissioners for the Reduction of National Debt[1]	
Crown Prosecution Service	
Department for Business, Innovation and Skills	
Department for Communities and Local Government	
Department for Culture, Media and Sport	
Department for Education	
Department for Environment, Food and Rural Affairs	
Department for International Development	
Department for Transport	
Department of Energy and Climate Change	
Foreign and Commonwealth Office	
Forestry Commissioners	
Government Actuary's Department	
Government Equalities Office	
Health and Safety Executive	
Her Majesty's Chief Inspector of Education and Training in Wales	
Her Majesty's Treasury	
Home Office	
Ministry of Defence	

[1] The functions of the Commissioners for the Reduction of National Debt and the Public Works Loan Board are carried out within the UK Debt Management Office.

Authorised government departments	Solicitors and addresses for service
Ministry of Justice The National Archives National Savings and Investments Northern Ireland Office Office for Standards in Education, Children's Services and Skills Ordnance Survey Privy Council Office Public Works Loan Board[2] Revenue and Customs Prosecutions Office Royal Mint Serious Fraud Office Statistics Board (UK Statistics Authority) Wales Office (Office of the Secretary of State for Wales)	
Other departments	
Department of Health Department for Work and Pensions	The Solicitor to the Department for Work and Pensions and the Department of Health Caxton House 2nd Floor Tothill Street London SW1H 9NA
Crown Estate Commissioners	Legal Director The Crown Estate 16 New Burlington Place London W1S 2HX
Export Credits Guarantee Department	The General Counsel Export Credits Guarantee Department PO Box 2200 2 Exchange Tower Harbour Exchange Square London E14 9GS
Gas and Electricity Markets Authority	Senior Legal Director Office of Gas and Electricity Markets 9 Millbank London SW1P 3GE
Her Majesty's Revenue and Customs	General Counsel and Solicitor to Her Majesty's Revenue and Customs HM Revenue and Customs South West Wing Bush House Strand London WC2B 4RD
Office of Fair Trading	General Counsel Fleetbank House 2–6 Salisbury Square London EC4Y 8JX

[2] The functions of the Commissioners for the Reduction of National Debt and the Public Works Loan Board are carried out within the UK Debt Management Office.

Authorised government departments	Solicitors and addresses for service
Office of Qualifications and Examinations Regulation (Ofqual)	Head of Legal Ofqual 1410 Spring Place Herald Avenue Coventry Business Park Coventry West Midlands CV5 6UB
Office of Rail Regulation	Director of Legal Services ORR One Kemble Street London WC2B 4AN
Water Services Regulation Authority (OFWAT)	Director of Legal Services and Board Secretary Water Services Regulation Authority (OFWAT) Centre City Tower 7 Hill Street Birmingham B5 4UA
Welsh Assembly Government	The Director of Legal Services to the Welsh Assembly Government Cathays Park Cardiff CF10 3NQ

CPR Part 67 Proceedings Relating to Solicitors

Part 67 65.9

67.1 Scope and Interpretation

(1) This Part contains rules about the following types of proceedings relating to solicitors—
  (a) proceedings to obtain an order for a solicitor to deliver a bill or cash account and proceedings in relation to money or papers received by a solicitor (rule 67.2);
  (b) proceedings under Part III of the Solicitors Act 1974 relating to the remuneration of solicitors (rule 67.3); and
  (c) proceedings under Schedule 1 to the Solicitors Act 1974 arising out of the Law Society's intervention in a solicitor's practice (rule 67.4).
(2) In this Part—
  'the Act' means the Solicitors Act 1974; and
  'LLP' means limited liability partnership.

(Part 48 and Section 56 of the Costs Practice Direction [PD 43–48] contain provisions about the procedure and basis for the detailed assessment of solicitor and client costs under Part III of the Act)
Practice Direction 52 contains provisions about appeals to the High Court from the Solicitors Disciplinary Tribunal under section 49 of the Act)

67.2 Power to Order Solicitor to Deliver Cash Account etc.

(1) Where the relationship of solicitor and client exists or has existed, the orders which the court may make against the solicitor, on the application of the client or his personal representatives, include any of the following—
  (a) to deliver a bill or cash account;
  (b) to pay or deliver up any money or securities;
  (c) to deliver a list of the moneys or securities which the solicitor has in his possession or control on behalf of the applicant;
  (d) to pay into or lodge in court any such money or securities.
(2) An application for an order under this rule must be made—
  (a) by Part 8 claim form; or
  (b) if the application is made in existing proceedings, by application notice in accordance with Part 23.
(3) If the solicitor alleges that he has a claim for costs against the applicant, the court may make an order for—
  (a) the detailed assessment and payment of those costs; and
  (b) securing the payment of the costs, or protecting any solicitor's lien.

67.3 Proceedings under Part III of the Act

r.67.3(1)(a)–(b) 71.20 r.67.3(2)–(3) 71.20

(1) A claim for an order under Part III of the Act for the assessment of costs payable to a solicitor by his client—
  (a) which—
    (i) relates to contentious business done in a county court; and
    (ii) is within the financial limit of the county court's jurisdiction specified in section 69(3) of the Act,
  may be made in that county court;
  (b) in every other case, must be made in the High Court.

(Rule 30.2 makes provision for any county court to transfer the proceedings to another county court for detailed assessment of costs)

(Provisions about the venue for detailed assessment proceedings are contained in rule 47.4 and Section 31 of the Costs Practice Direction [PD 43–48])

(2) A claim for an order under Part III of the Act must be made—
  (a) by Part 8 claim form; or
  (b) if the claim is made in existing proceedings, by application notice in accordance with Part 23.

(A model form of claim form is annexed to the Costs Practice Direction)

(3) A claim in the High Court under Part III of the Act may be determined by—
  (a) a High Court judge;
  (b) a Master, a costs judge or a district judge of the Principal Registry of the Family Division; or
  (c) a district judge, if the costs are for—
    (i) contentious business done in proceedings in the district registry of which he is the district judge;
    (ii) contentious business done in proceedings in a county court within the district of that district registry; or
    (iii) non-contentious business.

67.4 Proceedings under Schedule 1 to the Act

(1) Proceedings in the High Court under Schedule 1 to the Act must be brought—
  (a) in the Chancery Division; and
  (b) by Part 8 claim form, unless paragraph (4) below applies.

(2) The heading of the claim form must state that the claim relates to a solicitor and is made under Schedule 1 to the Act.

(3) Where proceedings are brought under paragraph 6(4) or 9(8) of Schedule 1 to the Act, the court will give directions and fix a date for the hearing immediately upon issuing the claim form.

(4) If the court has made an order under Schedule 1 to the Act, any subsequent application for an order under that Schedule which has the same parties may be made by a Part 23 application in the same proceedings.

(5) The table below sets out who must be made a defendant to each type of application under Schedule 1.

Defendants to applications under Schedule 1 to the Act

Paragraph of Schedule 1 under which the application is made	Defendant to application
Paragraph 5	if the application relates to money held on behalf of an individual solicitor, the solicitor if the application relates to money held on behalf of a firm, every partner in the firm if the application relates to money held on behalf of a LLP or other corporation, the LLP or other corporation
Paragraph 6(4) or 9(8)	the Law Society
Paragraph 8, 9(4), 9(5) or 9(6)	the person against whom the Law Society is seeking an order
Paragraph 9(10)	the person from whom the Law Society took possession of the documents which it wishes to dispose of or destroy
Paragraph 10	if the application relates to postal packets addressed to an individual solicitor, the solicitor if the application relates to postal packets addressed to a firm, every partner in the firm if the application relates to postal packets addressed to a LLP or other corporation, the LLP or other corporation
Paragraph 11	the trustee whom the Law Society is seeking to replace and, if he is a co-trustee, the other trustees of the trust

(6) At any time after the Law Society has issued an application for an order under paragraph 5 of Schedule 1 to the Act, the court may, on an application by the Society—
  (a) make an interim order under that paragraph to have effect until the hearing of the application; and
  (b) order the defendant, if he objects to the order being continued at the hearing, to file and serve written evidence showing cause why the order should not be continued.

PD 67 Practice Direction 67 — Proceedings Relating to Solicitors

This practice direction supplements CPR, part 67.

General

1 This practice direction applies to proceedings under r. 67.2 and to the following types of claim under r. 67.3 and part III of the Solicitors Act 1974 ('the Act'):

(1) an application under s. 57(5) of the Act for a costs officer to enquire into the facts and certify whether a non-contentious business agreement should be set aside or the amount payable under it reduced;
(2) a claim under s. 61(1) of the Act for the court to enforce or set aside a contentious business agreement and determine questions as to its validity and effect;
(3) a claim by a client under s. 61(3) of the Act for a costs officer to examine a contentious business agreement as to its fairness and reasonableness;
(4) where the amount agreed under a contentious business agreement has been paid, a claim under s. 61(5) of the Act for the agreement to be reopened and the costs assessed;
(5) proceedings under s. 62 of the Act for the examination of a contentious business agreement, where the client makes the agreement as a representative of a person whose property will be chargeable with the amount payable;
(6) proceedings under s. 63 of the Act where, after some business has been done under a contentious business agreement, but before the solicitor has wholly performed it:
   (a) the solicitor dies or becomes incapable of acting; or
   (b) the client changes solicitor;
(7) where an action is commenced on a gross sum bill, an application under s. 64(3) of the Act for an order that the bill be assessed;
(8) a claim under s. 68 of the Act for the delivery by a solicitor of a bill of costs and for the delivery up of, or otherwise in relation to, any documents;
(9) an application under s. 69 of the Act for an order that the solicitor be at liberty to commence an action to recover his costs within one month of delivery of the bill;
(10) a claim under s. 70(1) of the Act, by the party chargeable with the solicitor's bill, for an order that the bill be assessed and that no action be taken on the bill until the assessment is completed;
(11) a claim under s. 70(2) of the Act, by either party, for an order that the bill be assessed and that no action be commenced or continued on the bill until the assessment is completed;
(12) a claim under s. 70(3) of the Act, by the party chargeable with the bill, for detailed assessment showing special circumstances;
(13) a claim under s. 71(1) of the Act, by a person other than the party chargeable with the bill, for detailed assessment;
(14) a claim under s. 71(3) of the Act, by any person interested in any property out of which a trustee, executor or administrator has paid or is entitled to pay a solicitor's bill, for detailed assessment; and
(15) a claim by a solicitor under s. 73 of the Act for a charging order.

Proceedings in the Costs Office

para.2.1(1)–(2) **71.20** para.2.2A **71.20**

2.1 Where a claim to which this practice direction applies is made by Part 8 claim form in the High Court in London:
(1) if the claim is of a type referred to in para. 1(1) to (5), it must be issued in the Costs Office;
(2) in any other case, the claim may be issued in the Costs Office.

2.2 A claim which is made by Part 8 claim form in a district registry or by Part 23 application notice in existing High Court proceedings may be referred to the Costs Office.

2.2A Where a claim under s. 70 or 71 of the Act is made by Part 8 claim form in the Costs Office, the court will fix a date for the hearing of the claim when the claim form is issued.

2.3 'Costs Office' has the same meaning as set out in [r. 43.2(1)(ba)*].

Jurisdiction and Allocation of Claims between Judiciary

para.3.2 71.20

3.1 Rule 67.3(3) makes provision about jurisdiction to determine claims under part III of the Act.

3.2 Claims for any of the orders listed in para. 1 should normally be made to a master, costs judge or district judge. Only exceptional circumstances will justify making the claim directly to a High Court judge.

3.3 PD 23A, para. 1, sets out the circumstances in which a matter may be referred to a judge.

Evidence in Proceedings for Order for Detailed Assessment

para.4 71.20

4 Where a Part 8 claim is brought for an order for the detailed assessment of a solicitor's bill of costs, the parties are not required to comply with r. 8.5 unless:

(1) the claim will be contested; or

(2) the court directs that the parties should comply with r. 8.5.

Drawing Up and Service of Orders

5 Unless the court orders otherwise, an order in proceedings in the Costs Office to which this practice direction applies shall be drawn up and served by the party who made the relevant claim or application.

[* The text issued by the Ministry of Justice mistakenly refers to r. 43.1(2)(b).]

CPR Part 68 References to the European Court

[For commentary on a specific rule, please refer to the cross-references after the title of the rule.]

68.1 Interpretation

r.68.1(d) 78.14

In this Part—

(a) 'the court' means the court making the order;
(b) 'the European Court' means the Court of Justice of the European Communities;
(c) 'order' means an order referring a question to the European Court for a preliminary ruling under—
  (i) article 234 of the Treaty establishing the European Community;
  (ii) article 150 of the Euratom Treaty;
  (iii) article 41 of the ECSC Treaty;
  (iv) the Protocol of 3 June 1971 on the interpretation by the European Court of the Convention of 27 September 1968 on Jurisdiction and the Enforcement of Judgments in Civil and Commercial Matters; or
  (v) the Protocol of 19 December 1988 on the interpretation by the European Court of the Convention of 19 June 1980 on the Law applicable to Contractual Obligations; and
(d) 'reference' means a request to the European Court for a preliminary ruling.

68.2 Making Order

r.68.2(1)–(3) 78.14

(1) An order may be made at any stage of the proceedings—
  (a) by the court of its own initiative; or
  (b) on an application by a party in accordance with Part 23.
(2) An order may not be made—
  (a) in the High Court, by a Master or district judge;
  (b) in a county court, by a district judge.
(3) The reference, which must contain the information required by Practice Direction 68, must be set out in a schedule to the order, and the court may give directions on the preparation of the schedule.

68.2A Request to Apply the Urgent Preliminary Ruling Procedure

r.68.2A 78.15

Any request by the court to the European Court that the preliminary ruling be dealt with under its urgent preliminary ruling procedure must be made in a document separate from the order or in a covering letter.

68.3 Transmission to the European Court

r.68.3(1)–(3) 78.14

(1) The Senior Master will send a copy of—
  (a) the order; and
  (b) where relevant, any request to apply the urgent preliminary ruling procedure to the Registrar of the European Court.
(2) Where an order is made by a county court, a court officer will send a copy of it to the Senior Master for onward transmission to the European Court.

(3) Unless the court orders otherwise, the Senior Master will not send a copy of the order to the European Court until—
(a) the time for appealing against the order has expired; or
(b) any application for permission to appeal has been refused, or any appeal has been determined.

68.4 Stay of Proceedings

r.68.4 78.14

Where an order is made, unless the court orders otherwise the proceedings will be stayed until the European Court has given a preliminary ruling on the question referred to it.

PD 68 Practice Direction 68 — References to the European Court

This practice direction supplements CPR, Part 68.

[For commentary on a specific paragraph, please refer to the cross-references after the title of the paragraph.]

Wording of References

paras.1.1–1.3 78.14

1.1 Where the court intends to refer a question to the European Court it may direct the parties to produce a draft of the reference but responsibility for the terms of the reference lies with the court making the reference and not with the parties.

1.2 The reference should identify as clearly and succinctly as possible the question on which the court seeks the ruling of the European Court. In choosing the wording of the reference, it should be remembered that it will need to be translated into many other languages.

1.3 The court will incorporate the reference as a schedule to its order. The schedule must—

(1) give the full name of the referring court;
(2) identify the parties;
(3) summarise the nature and history of the proceedings, including the salient facts, indicating whether these are proved or admitted or assumed;
(4) set out the relevant rules of national law;
(5) summarise the relevant contentions of the parties;
(6) explain why a ruling of the European Court is sought;
(7) identify the provisions of Community law which the European Court is being requested to interpret;
(8) state the question on which a ruling of the European Court is sought; and
(9) state any opinion on the answer to the question that may have been expressed by the court in the course of delivering judgment.

1.4 If some of these matters are conveniently set out in a judgment, the relevant passages should be summarised succinctly. If it is not possible to produce such a summary, only those passages that contain information of the kind referred to in para. 1.3 should be cited.

1.5 The reference should not exceed 20 pages in length.

Request to Apply the Urgent Preliminary Ruling Procedure

para.1A.1 78.15

1A.1 The request to the European Court to apply its urgent preliminary ruling procedure must set out—

(1) the matters of fact and law which establish the urgency;
(2) the reasons why the urgent preliminary ruling procedure applies; and
(3) in so far as possible, the court's view on the answer to the question referred to the European Court for a preliminary ruling.

Transmission to the European Court

para.2.2 78.14

2.1 The order containing the reference, and where relevant any request to the European Court to apply its urgent preliminary ruling procedure, must be sent to the Senior Master, Room E101, Queen's Bench Division, Royal Courts of Justice, Strand, London, WC2A 2LL, for onward transmission to the European Court.

2.2 The relevant court file must also be sent to the Senior Master at the above address.

European Court Information Note

3 There are annexed to this practice direction—

(1) an Information Note issued by the European Court; and

(2) a supplement to the Information Note following the implementation of the urgent ruling procedure applicable to references concerning the area of freedom, security and justice.*

ANNEX

COURT OF JUSTICE OF THE EUROPEAN UNION INFORMATION NOTE ON REFERENCES FROM NATIONAL COURTS FOR A PRELIMINARY RULING

I GENERAL

1. The preliminary ruling system is a fundamental mechanism of European Union law aimed at enabling national courts to ensure uniform interpretation and application of that law in all the member States.
2. The Court of Justice of the European Union has jurisdiction to give preliminary rulings on the interpretation of European Union law and on the validity of acts of the institutions, bodies, offices or agencies of the Union. That general jurisdiction is conferred on it by art. 19(3)(b) of the Treaty on European Union (OJEU 2008 C 115, p. 13) ('the TEU') and art. 267 of the Treaty on the Functioning of the European Union (OJEU 2008 C 115, p. 47) ('the TFEU').
3. Article 256(3) TFEU provides that the General Court is to have jurisdiction to hear and determine questions referred for a preliminary ruling under art. 267, in specific areas laid down by the Statute. Since no provisions have been introduced into the Statute in that regard, the Court of Justice alone has jurisdiction to give preliminary rulings.
4. While art. 267 TFEU confers on the Court of Justice a general jurisdiction, a number of provisions exist which lay down exceptions to or restrictions on that jurisdiction. This is true in particular of arts 275 and 276 TFEU and art. 10 of Protocol (No. 36) on Transitional Provisions of the Treaty of Lisbon (OJEU 2008 C 115, p. 322).
5. The preliminary ruling procedure being based on cooperation between the Court of Justice and national courts, it may be helpful, in order to ensure that that cooperation is effective, to provide the national courts with the following information.
6. This practical information, which is in no way binding, is intended to provide guidance to national courts as to whether it is appropriate to make a reference for a preliminary ruling and, should they proceed, to help them formulate and submit questions to the Court.

The Role of the Court of Justice in the Preliminary Ruling Procedure

7. Under the preliminary ruling procedure, the Court's role is to give an interpretation of European Union law or to rule on its validity, not to apply that law to the factual situation underlying the main proceedings, which is the task of the national court. It is not for the Court either to decide issues of fact raised in the main proceedings or to resolve differences of opinion on the interpretation or application of rules of national law.
8. In ruling on the interpretation or validity of European Union law, the Court makes every effort to give a reply which will be of assistance in resolving the dispute, but it is for the referring court to draw the appropriate conclusions from that reply, if necessary by disapplying the rule of national law in question.

The Decision to Submit a Question to the Court

The originator of the question

9. Under art. 267 TFEU, any court or tribunal of a member State, in so far as it is called upon to give a ruling in proceedings intended to arrive at a decision of a judicial nature, may as a rule refer

[* In this edition of *Blackstone's Civil Practice*, these documents have been replaced by the revised information note published in OJEU 2011, C160, p. 1.]

a question to the Court of Justice for a preliminary ruling.[1] Status as a court or tribunal is interpreted by the Court of Justice as a self-standing concept of European Union law.

10. It is for the national court alone to decide whether to refer a question to the Court of Justice for a preliminary ruling, whether or not the parties to the main proceedings have requested it to do so.

References on interpretation

11. Any court or tribunal *may* refer a question to the Court of Justice on the interpretation of a rule of European Union law if it considers it necessary to do so in order to resolve a dispute brought before it.

12. However, courts or tribunals against whose decisions there is no judicial remedy under national law *must, as a rule,* refer such a question to the Court, unless the Court has already ruled on the point (and there is no new context that raises any serious doubt as to whether that case-law may be applied), or unless the correct interpretation of the rule of law in question is obvious.

13. Thus, a court or tribunal against whose decisions there is a judicial remedy may, in particular when it considers that sufficient guidance is given by the case-law of the Court of Justice, itself decide on the correct interpretation of European Union law and its application to the factual situation before it. However, a reference for a preliminary ruling may prove particularly useful, at an appropriate stage of the proceedings, when there is a new question of interpretation of general interest for the uniform application of European Union law in all the member States, or where the existing case-law does not appear to be applicable to a new set of facts.

14. It is for the national court to explain why the interpretation sought is necessary to enable it to give judgment.

References on determination of validity

15. Although national courts may reject pleas raised before them challenging the validity of acts of an institution, body, office or agency of the Union, the Court of Justice has exclusive jurisdiction to declare such an act invalid.

16. All national courts *must* therefore refer a question to the Court when they have doubts about the validity of such an act, stating the reasons for which they consider that that act may be invalid.

17. However, if a national court has serious doubts about the validity of an act of an institution, body, office or agency of the Union on which a national measure is based, it may exceptionally suspend application of that measure temporarily or grant other interim relief with respect to it. It must then refer the question of validity to the Court of Justice, stating the reasons for which it considers the act to be invalid.

The Stage at Which to Submit a Question for a Preliminary Ruling

18. A national court or tribunal may refer a question to the Court for a preliminary ruling as soon as it finds that a ruling on the point or points of interpretation or validity is necessary to enable it to give judgment; it is the national court which is in the best position to decide at what stage of the proceedings such a question should be referred.

19. It is, however, desirable that a decision to seek a preliminary ruling should be taken when the national proceedings have reached a stage at which the national court is able to define the factual and legal context of the question, so that the Court of Justice has available to it all the information necessary to check, where appropriate, that European Union law applies to the main proceedings. It may also be in the interests of justice to refer a question for a preliminary ruling only after both sides have been heard.

The Form of the Reference for a Preliminary Ruling

20. The decision by which a national court or tribunal refers a question to the Court of Justice for a preliminary ruling may be in any form allowed by national law as regards procedural steps.

[1] Article 10(1) to (3) of Protocol No. 36 provides that the powers of the Court of Justice in relation to acts adopted before the entry into force of the Treaty of Lisbon (OJ 2007 C 306, p. 1) under Title VI of the TEU, in the field of police cooperation and judicial cooperation in criminal matters, and which have not since been amended, are, however, to remain the same for a maximum period of five years from the date of entry into force of the Treaty of Lisbon (1 December 2009). During that period, such acts may, therefore, form the subject matter of a reference for a preliminary ruling only where the order for reference is made by a court of a member State which has accepted the jurisdiction of the Court of Justice, it being a matter for each State to determine whether the right to refer a question to the Court is to be available to all of its national courts or is to be reserved to the courts of last instance.

It must however be borne in mind that it is that document which serves as the basis of the proceedings before the Court and that it must therefore contain such information as will enable the latter to give a reply which is of assistance to the national court. Moreover, it is only the actual reference for a preliminary ruling which is notified to the interested persons entitled to submit observations to the Court, in particular the member States and the institutions, and which is translated.

21. Owing to the need to translate the reference, it should be drafted simply, clearly and precisely, avoiding superfluous detail.
22. A maximum of about 10 pages is often sufficient to set out in a proper manner the context of a reference for a preliminary ruling. The order for reference must be succinct but sufficiently complete and must contain all the relevant information to give the Court and the interested persons entitled to submit observations a clear understanding of the factual and legal context of the main proceedings. In particular, the order for reference must:
    - include a brief account of the subject-matter of the dispute and the relevant findings of fact, or, at least, set out the factual situation on which the question referred is based;
    - set out the tenor of any applicable national provisions and identify, where necessary, the relevant national case-law, giving in each case precise references (for example, a page of an official journal or specific law report, with any internet reference);
    - identify the European Union law provisions relevant to the case as accurately as possible;
    - explain the reasons which prompted the national court to raise the question of the interpretation or validity of the European Union law provisions, and the relationship between those provisions and the national provisions applicable to the main proceedings;
    - include, if need be, a summary of the main relevant arguments of the parties to the main proceedings.

    In order to make it easier to read and refer to the document, it is helpful if the different points or paragraphs of the order for reference are numbered.
23. Finally, the referring court may, if it considers itself able, briefly state its view on the answer to be given to the questions referred for a preliminary ruling.
24. The question or questions themselves should appear in a separate and clearly identified section of the order for reference, generally at the beginning or the end. It must be possible to understand them without referring to the statement of the grounds for the reference, which will however provide the necessary background for a proper assessment.
25. Under the preliminary ruling procedure, the Court will, as a rule, use the information contained in the order for reference, including nominative or personal data. It is therefore for the referring court itself, if it considers it necessary, to render anonymous, in the order for reference, one or more persons concerned by the dispute in the main proceedings.

The Effects of the Reference for a Preliminary Ruling on the National Proceedings

26. A reference for a preliminary ruling calls for the national proceedings to be stayed until the Court of Justice has given its ruling.
27. However, the national court may still order protective measures, particularly in connection with a reference on determination of validity (see point 17 above).

Costs and Legal Aid

28. Preliminary ruling proceedings before the Court of Justice are free of charge and the Court does not rule on the costs of the parties to the main proceedings; it is for the national court to rule on those costs.
29. If a party has insufficient means and where it is possible under national rules, the national court may grant that party legal aid to cover the costs, including those of lawyers' fees, which it incurs before the Court. The Court itself may also grant legal aid where the party in question is not already in receipt of legal aid under national rules or to the extent to which that aid does not cover, or covers only partly, costs incurred before the Court.

Communication between the National Court and the Court of Justice

30. The order for reference and the relevant documents (including, where applicable, the case file or a copy of the case file) are to be sent by the national court directly to the Court of Justice, by

registered post (addressed to the Registry of the Court of Justice, L-2925 Luxembourg, telephone +352-4303-1).

31. The Court Registry will stay in contact with the national court until a ruling is given, and will send it copies of the procedural documents.
32. The Court of Justice will send its ruling to the national court. It would welcome information from the national court on the action taken upon its ruling in the national proceedings and, where appropriate, a copy of the national court's final decision.

II THE URGENT PRELIMINARY RULING PROCEDURE (PPU)

33. This part of the note provides practical information on the urgent preliminary ruling procedure applicable to references relating to the area of freedom, security and justice. The procedure is governed by art. 23a of Protocol (No. 3) on the Statute of the Court of Justice of the European Union (OJEU 2008 C 115, p. 210) and art. 104b of the Rules of Procedure of the Court of Justice. National courts may request that this procedure be applied or request the application of the accelerated procedure under the conditions laid down in art. 23a of the Protocol and art. 104a of the Rules of Procedure.

Conditions for the Application of the Urgent Preliminary Ruling Procedure

34. The urgent preliminary ruling procedure is applicable only in the areas covered by Title V of Part Three of the TFEU, which relates to the area of freedom, security and justice.
35. The Court of Justice decides whether this procedure is to be applied. Such a decision is generally taken only on a reasoned request from the referring court. Exceptionally, the Court may decide of its own motion to deal with a reference under the urgent preliminary ruling procedure, where that appears to be required.
36. The urgent preliminary ruling procedure simplifies the various stages of the proceedings before the Court, but its application entails significant constraints for the Court and for the parties and other interested persons participating in the procedure, particularly the member States.
37. It should therefore be requested only where it is absolutely necessary for the Court to give its ruling on the reference as quickly as possible. Although it is not possible to provide an exhaustive list of such situations, particularly because of the varied and evolving nature of the rules of European Union law governing the area of freedom, security and justice, a national court or tribunal might, for example, consider submitting a request for the urgent preliminary ruling procedure to be applied in the following situations: in the case, referred to in the fourth paragraph of art. 267 TFEU, of a person in custody or deprived of his liberty, where the answer to the question raised is decisive as to the assessment of that person's legal situation or, in proceedings concerning parental authority or custody of children, where the identity of the court having jurisdiction under European Union law depends on the answer to the question referred for a preliminary ruling.

The Request for Application of the Urgent Preliminary Ruling Procedure

38. To enable the Court to decide quickly whether the urgent preliminary ruling procedure should be applied, the request must set out the matters of fact and law which establish the urgency and, in particular, the risks involved in following the normal preliminary ruling procedure.
39. In so far as it is able to do so, the referring court should briefly state its view on the answer to be given to the question(s) referred. Such a statement makes it easier for the parties and other interested persons participating in the procedure to define their positions and facilitates the Court's decision, thereby contributing to the rapidity of the procedure.
40. The request for the urgent preliminary ruling procedure must be submitted in an unambiguous form that enables the Court Registry to establish immediately that the file must be dealt with in a particular way. Accordingly, the referring court is asked to couple its request with a mention of art. 104b of the Rules of Procedure and to include that mention in a clearly identifiable place in its reference (for example at the head of the page or in a separate judicial document). Where appropriate, a covering letter from the referring court can usefully refer to that request.
41. As regards the order for reference itself, it is particularly important that it should be succinct where the matter is urgent, as this will help to ensure the rapidity of the procedure.

Communication between the Court of Justice, the National Court and the Parties

42. As regards communication with the national court or tribunal and the parties before it, national courts or tribunals which submit a request for an urgent preliminary ruling procedure are requested to state the email address or any fax number which may be used by the Court of Justice, together with the email addresses or any fax numbers of the representatives of the parties to the proceedings.
43. A copy of the signed order for reference together with a request for the urgent preliminary ruling procedure can initially be sent to the Court by email (ECJ-Registry@curia.europa.eu) or by fax (+352 43 37 66). Processing of the reference and of the request can then begin upon receipt of the emailed or faxed copy. The originals of those documents must, however, be sent to the Court Registry as soon as possible.

CPR Part 69 Court's Power to Appoint a Receiver

Part 69 79.1, 79.40 [For commentary on a specific rule, please refer to the cross-references after the title of the rule.]

69.1 Scope of This Part

(1) This Part contains provisions about the court's power to appoint a receiver.
(2) In this Part 'receiver' includes a manager.

69.2 Court's Power to Appoint Receiver

(1) The court may appoint a receiver—
  (a) before proceedings have started;
  (b) in existing proceedings; or
  (c) on or after judgment.
(2) A receiver must be an individual.
(3) The court may at any time—
  (a) terminate the appointment of a receiver; and
  (b) appoint another receiver in his place.

(Practice Direction 69 describes the powers for the court to appoint a receiver)

69.3 How to Apply for the Appointment of a Receiver

An application for the appointment of a receiver—

(a) may be made without notice; and
(b) must be supported by written evidence.

69.4 Service of Order Appointing Receiver

An order appointing a receiver must be served by the party who applied for it on—

(a) the person appointed as receiver;
(b) unless the court orders otherwise, every other party to the proceedings; and
(c) such other persons as the court may direct.

69.5 Security

r.69.5 79.37

(1) The court may direct that before a receiver begins to act or within a specified time he must either—
  (a) give such security as the court may determine; or
  (b) file and serve on all parties to the proceedings evidence that he already has in force sufficient security,

  to cover his liability for his acts and omissions as a receiver.
(2) The court may terminate the appointment of the receiver if he fails to—
  (a) give the security; or
  (b) satisfy the court as to the security he has in force, by the date specified.

69.6 Receiver's Application for Directions

(1) The receiver may apply to the court at any time for directions to assist him in carrying out his function as a receiver.
(2) The court, when it gives directions, may also direct the receiver to serve on any person—
(a) the directions; and
(b) the application for directions.
(Practice Direction 69 makes provision for the form of applications by, and directions to, a receiver)

69.7 Receiver's Remuneration

r.69.7 79.37

(1) A receiver may only charge for his services if the court—
(a) so directs; and
(b) specifies the basis on which the receiver is to be remunerated.
(2) The court may specify—
(a) who is to be responsible for paying the receiver; and
(b) the fund or property from which the receiver is to recover his remuneration.
(3) If the court directs that the amount of a receiver's remuneration is to be determined by the court—
(a) the receiver may not recover any remuneration for his services without a determination by the court; and
(b) the receiver or any party may apply at any time for such a determination to take place.
(4) Unless the court orders otherwise, in determining the remuneration of a receiver the court shall award such sum as is reasonable and proportionate in all the circumstances and which takes into account—
(a) the time properly given by him and his staff to the receivership;
(b) the complexity of the receivership;
(c) any responsibility of an exceptional kind or degree which falls on the receiver in consequence of the receivership;
(d) the effectiveness with which the receiver appears to be carrying out, or to have carried out, his duties; and
(e) the value and nature of the subject matter of the receivership.
(5) The court may refer the determination of a receiver's remuneration to a costs judge.

69.8 Accounts

r.69.8 79.37

(1) The court may order a receiver to prepare and serve accounts.
(Practice Direction 69 contains provisions about directions for the preparation and service of accounts)
(2) A party served with such accounts may apply for an order permitting him to inspect any document in the possession of the receiver relevant to those accounts.
(3) Any party may, within 14 days of being served with the accounts, serve notice on the receiver—
(a) specifying any item in the accounts to which he objects;
(b) giving the reason for such objection; and
(c) requiring the receiver, within 14 days of receipt of the notice, either—
(i) to notify all the parties who were served with the accounts that he accepts the objection; or
(ii) if he does not accept the objection, to apply for an examination of the accounts in relation to the contested item.
(4) When the receiver applies for the examination of the accounts he must at the same time file—
(a) the accounts; and
(b) a copy of the notice served on him under this rule.
(5) If the receiver fails to comply with paragraph (3)(c) of this rule, any party may apply to the court for an examination of the accounts in relation to the contested item.
(6) At the conclusion of its examination of the accounts the court will certify the result.
(Practice Direction 40A provides for inquiries into accounts)

69.9 Non-compliance by Receiver

(1) If a receiver fails to comply with any rule, practice direction or direction of the court the court may order him to attend a hearing to explain his non-compliance.
(2) At the hearing the court may make any order it considers appropriate, including—
  (a) terminating the appointment of the receiver;
  (b) reducing the receiver's remuneration or disallowing it altogether; and
  (c) ordering the receiver to pay the costs of any party.
(3) Where—
  (a) the court has ordered a receiver to pay a sum of money into court; and
  (b) the receiver has failed to do so,
  the court may order him to pay interest on that sum for the time he is in default at such rate as it considers appropriate.

69.10 Application for Discharge of Receiver

(1) A receiver or any party may apply for the receiver to be discharged on completion of his duties.
(2) The application notice must be served on the persons who were required under rule 69.4 to be served with the order appointing the receiver.

69.11 Order Discharging or Terminating Appointment of Receiver

(1) An order discharging or terminating the appointment of a receiver may—
  (a) require him to pay into court any money held by him; or
  (b) specify the person to whom he must pay any money or transfer any assets still in his possession; and
  (c) make provision for the discharge or cancellation of any guarantee given by the receiver as security.
(2) The order must be served on the persons who were required under rule 69.4 to be served with the order appointing the receiver.

PD 69 Practice Direction 69 — Court's Power to Appoint a Receiver

This practice direction supplements CPR, Part 69.

[For commentary on a specific paragraph, please refer to the cross-references after the title of the paragraph.]

Court's Power to Appoint Receiver

1.1 The court's powers to appoint a receiver are set out in:
- (1) the Senior Courts Act 1981, s. 37 (powers of the High Court with respect to injunctions and receivers);
- (2) the County Courts Act 1984, s. 38 (remedies available in county courts); and
- (3) the County Courts Act 1984, s. 107 (receivers by way of equitable execution).

Applications before Proceedings Are Started—Rule 69.2(1)(a)

2.1 The court will normally only consider an application for the appointment of a receiver before proceedings are started after notice of the application has been served.

2.2 Rule 25.2(2) contains provisions about the grant of an order before proceedings are started.

Related Injunctions

3.1 If a person applies at the same time for:
- (1) the appointment of a receiver; and
- (2) a related injunction,

he must use the same claim form or application notice for both applications.

3.2 PD 2B sets out who may grant injunctions. Among other things, it provides that a master or a district judge may grant an injunction related to an order appointing a receiver by way of equitable execution.

Evidence in Support of an Application: Rule 69.3

para.4.1 **79.36** para.4.2(1)–(3) **79.36**

4.1 The written evidence in support of an application for the appointment of a receiver must:
- (1) explain the reasons why the appointment is required;
- (2) give details of the property which it is proposed that the receiver should get in or manage, including estimates of:
  - (a) the value of the property; and
  - (b) the amount of income it is likely to produce;
- (3) if the application is to appoint a receiver by way of equitable execution, give details of:
  - (a) the judgment which the applicant is seeking to enforce;
  - (b) the extent to which the debtor has failed to comply with the judgment;
  - (c) the result of any steps already taken to enforce the judgment; and
  - (d) why the judgment cannot be enforced by any other method; and
- (4) if the applicant is asking the court to allow the receiver to act:
  - (a) without giving security; or
  - (b) before he has given security or satisfied the court that he has security in place,

  explain the reasons why that is necessary.

4.2 In addition, the written evidence should normally identify an individual whom the court is to be asked to appoint as receiver ('the nominee'), and should:
- (1) state the name, address and position of the nominee;
- (2) include written evidence by a person who knows the nominee, stating that he believes the nominee is a suitable person to be appointed as receiver, and the basis of that belief; and
- (3) be accompanied by written consent, signed by the nominee, to act as receiver if appointed.

4.3 *If the applicant does not* nominate a person to be appointed as receiver, or if the court decides not to appoint the nominee, the court may:
- (1) order that a suitable person be appointed as receiver; and

(2) direct any party to nominate a suitable individual to be appointed.

4.4 A party directed to nominate a person to be appointed as receiver must file written evidence containing the information required by para. 4.2 and accompanied by the written consent of the nominee.

Appointment of Receiver to Enforce a Judgment

para.5 79.35

5 Where a judgment creditor applies for the appointment of a receiver as a method of enforcing a judgment, in considering whether to make the appointment the court will have regard to:
(1) the amount claimed by the judgment creditor;
(2) the amount likely to be obtained by the receiver; and
(3) the probable costs of his appointment.

Court's Directions

para.6.3(3)–(4) 79.37

6.1 The court may give directions to the receiver when it appoints him or at any time afterwards.

6.2 The court will normally, when it appoints a receiver, give directions in relation to security—see para. 7 below.

6.3 Other matters about which the court may give directions include:
(1) whether, and on what basis, the receiver is to be remunerated for carrying out his functions;
(2) the preparation and service of accounts—see r. 69.8(1) and para. 10 below;
(3) the payment of money into court; and
(4) authorising the receiver to carry on an activity or incur an expense.

Directions Relating to Security: Rule 69.5

para.7.2 79.37

7.1 An order appointing a receiver will normally specify the date by which the receiver must:
(1) give security; or
(2) file and serve evidence to satisfy the court that he already has security in force.

7.2 Unless the court directs otherwise, security will be given:
(1) if the receiver is an authorised insolvency practitioner, by the bond provided by him under the Insolvency Practitioners Regulations 1990 (SI 1990/439) or the Insolvency Practitioners Regulations 2005 (SI 2005/524) extended to cover appointment as a court-appointed receiver; or
(2) in any other case, by a guarantee.

7.3 Where the court has given directions about giving security, then either:
(1) written evidence of the bond, the sufficiency of its cover and that it includes appointment as a court-appointed receiver must be filed at court; or
(2) a guarantee should be prepared in a form, and entered into with a clearing bank or insurance company, approved by the court.

Receiver's Application for Directions: Rule 69.6

8.1 An application by a receiver for directions may be made by filing an application notice in accordance with Part 23.

8.2 If the directions sought by the receiver are unlikely to be contentious or important to the parties, he may make the application by letter, and the court may reply by letter. In such cases the receiver need not serve his letter or the court's reply on the parties, unless the court orders him to do so.

8.3 Where a receiver applies for directions by letter, the court may direct him to file and serve an application notice.

Receiver's Remuneration: Rule 69.7

para.9.1–9.6 79.37

9.1 A receiver may only charge for his services if the court gives directions permitting it and specifying how the remuneration is to be determined.

9.2 The court will normally determine the amount of the receiver's remuneration on the basis of the criteria in r. 69.7(4). Parts 43 to 48 (costs) do not apply to the determination of the remuneration of a receiver.

9.3 Unless the court orders otherwise, the receiver will only be paid or be able to recover his remuneration after the amount of it has been determined.

9.4 An application by a receiver for the amount of his remuneration to be determined must be supported by:

(1) written evidence showing:

(a) on what basis the remuneration is claimed; and

(b) that it is justified and in accordance with Part 69; and

(2) a certificate signed by the receiver that he considers that the remuneration he claims is reasonable and proportionate.

9.5 The court may, before determining the amount of a receiver's remuneration:

(1) require the receiver to provide further information in support of his claim; and

(2) appoint an assessor under r. 35.15 to assist the court.

9.6 Paragraphs 9.1 to 9.5 do not apply to expenses incurred by a receiver in carrying out his functions. These are accounted for as part of his account for the assets he has recovered, and not dealt with as part of the determination of his remuneration.

Accounts: Rule 69.8

para.10.1–10.3 79.37

10.1 When the court gives directions under r. 69.8(1) for the receiver to prepare and serve accounts, it may:

(1) direct the receiver to prepare and serve accounts either by a specified date or at specified intervals; and

(2) specify the persons on whom he must serve the accounts.

10.2 A party should not apply for an order under r. 69.8(2) permitting him to inspect documents in the possession of the receiver, without first asking the receiver to permit such inspection without an order.

10.3 Where the court makes an order under r. 69.8(2), it will normally direct that the receiver must:

(1) permit inspection within seven days after being served with the order; and

(2) provide a copy of any documents the subject of the order within seven days after receiving a request for a copy from the party permitted to inspect them, provided that party has undertaken to pay the reasonable cost of making and providing the copy.

CPR Part 70 General Rules about Enforcement of Judgments and Orders

Part 70 70.3, 79.1, 79.40 [For commentary on a specific rule, please refer to the cross-references after the title of the rule.]

70.1 Scope of This Part and Interpretation

(1) This Part contains general rules about enforcement of judgments and orders.
(Rules about specific methods of enforcement are contained in Parts 71 to 73, Schedule 1 RSC Orders 45 to 47 and 52 and Schedule 2 CCR Orders 25 to 29)
(2) In this Part and in Parts 71 to 73—
  (a) 'judgment creditor' means a person who has obtained or is entitled to enforce a judgment or order;
  (b) 'judgment debtor' means a person against whom a judgment or order was given or made;
  (c) 'judgment or order' includes an award which the court has—
    (i) registered for enforcement;
    (ii) ordered to be enforced; or
    (iii) given permission to enforce

  as if it were a judgment or order of the court, and in relation to such an award, 'the court which made the judgment or order' means the court which registered the award or made such an order; and
  (d) 'judgment or order for the payment of money' includes a judgment or order for the payment of costs, but does not include a judgment or order for the payment of money into court.

70.2 Methods of Enforcing Judgments or Orders

(1) Practice Direction 70 sets out methods of enforcing judgments or orders for the payment of money.
(2) A judgment creditor may, except where an enactment, rule or practice direction provides otherwise—
  (a) use any method of enforcement which is available; and
  (b) use more than one method of enforcement, either at the same time or one after another.

70.3 Transfer of Proceedings for Enforcement

r.70.3 79.2 r.70.3(2) 79.2

(1) A judgment creditor wishing to enforce a High Court judgment or order in a county court must apply to the High Court for an order transferring the proceedings to that county court.
(2) A practice direction may make provisions about the transfer of proceedings for enforcement.
(CCR Order 25 rule 13 contains provisions about the transfer of county court proceedings to the High Court for enforcement.)

70.4 Enforcement of Judgment or Order by or against Non-party

If a judgment or order is given or made in favour of or against a person who is not a party to proceedings, it may be enforced by or against that person by the same methods as if he were a party.

70.5 Enforcement of Decisions of Bodies Other Than the High Court and County Courts and Compromises Enforceable by Enactment

r.70.5 **63.37, 70.6, 79.3**
r.70.5(4A) **79.3**
r.70.5(1)–(2) **79.3**
r.70.5(6) **79.3**
r.70.5(2A) **79.3**
r.70.5(8) **79.3**
r.70.5(4) **70.3, 79.3**

(1) This rule applies, subject to paragraph (2), where an enactment provides that—
 (a) a decision of a court, tribunal, body or person other than the High Court or a county court; or
 (b) a compromise,
may be enforced as if it were a court order or that any sum of money payable under that decision or compromise may be recoverable as if payable under a court order.
(2) This rule does not apply to—
 (a) any judgment to which Part 74 applies;
 (b) arbitration awards;
 (c) any order to which RSC Order 115 applies; or
 (d) proceedings to which Part 75 (traffic enforcement) applies.
(2A) Unless paragraph (3) applies, a party may enforce the decision or compromise by applying for a specific method of enforcement under Parts 71 to 73, Schedule 1 RSC Orders 45 to 47 and 52 and Schedule 2 CCR Orders 25 to 29 and must—
 (a) file with the court a copy of the decision or compromise being enforced; and
 (b) provide the court with the information required by Practice Direction 70.
(3) If an enactment provides that a decision or compromise is enforceable or a sum of money is recoverable if a court so orders, an application for such an order must be made in accordance with paragraphs (4) to (7A) of this rule.
(4) The application—
 (a) may, unless paragraph (4A) applies, be made without notice; and
 (b) must be made to the court for the district where the person against whom the order is sought, resides or carries on business, unless the court otherwise orders.
(4A) Where a compromise requires a person to whom a sum of money is payable under the compromise to do anything in addition to discontinuing or not starting proceedings ('a conditional compromise'), an application under paragraph (4) must be made on notice.
(5) The application notice must—
 (a) be in the form; and
 (b) contain the information
required by Practice Direction 70.
(6) A copy of the decision or compromise must be filed with the application notice.
(7) An application other than in relation to a conditional compromise may be dealt with by a court officer without a hearing.
(7A) Where an application relates to a conditional compromise, the respondent may oppose it by filing a response within 14 days of service of the application notice and if the respondent—
 (a) does not file a response within the time allowed, the court will make the order; or
 (b) files a response within the time allowed, the court will make such order as appears appropriate.
(8) If an enactment provides that a decision or compromise may be enforced in the same manner as an order of the High Court if it is registered, any application to the High Court for registration must be made in accordance with Practice Direction 70.

70.6 Effect of Setting Aside Judgment or Order

If a judgment or order is set aside, any enforcement of the judgment or order shall cease to have effect unless the court otherwise orders.

PD 70 Practice Direction 70 — Enforcement of Judgments and Orders

This practice direction supplements CPR, Parts 70, 71, 72 and 73 and sch. 2, CCR, ord. 27.

[For commentary on a specific paragraph, please refer to the cross-references after the title of the paragraph.]

SECTION I GENERAL

Methods of Enforcing Money Judgments: Rule 70.2

1.1 A judgment creditor may enforce a judgment or order for the payment of money by any of the following methods:
  (1) a writ of fieri facias or warrant of execution (see RSC, ord. 46 and ord. 47 in CPR, sch. 1; CCR, ord. 26 in CPR, sch. 2);
  (2) a third party debt order (see Part 72);
  (3) a charging order, stop order or stop notice (see Part 73);
  (4) in a county court, an attachment of earnings order (see CCR, ord. 27 in CPR, sch. 2);
  (5) the appointment of a receiver (see Part 69).

1.2 In addition the court may make the following orders against a judgment debtor:
  (1) an order of committal, but only if permitted by:
    (a) a rule; and
    (b) the Debtors Acts 1869 and 1878;[1] and
  (2) in the High Court, a writ of sequestration, but only if permitted by r. 81.20

1.3 The enforcement of a judgment or order may be affected by:
  (1) the enactments relating to insolvency; and
  (2) county court administration orders.

Transfer of County Court Proceedings to Another County Court for Enforcement: Rule 70.3

para.2.1–2.4 79.2

2.1 Subject to Section 2 of this practice direction, if a judgment creditor is required by a rule or practice direction to enforce a judgment or order of one county court in a different county court, he must first make a request in writing to the court in which the case is proceeding to transfer the proceedings to that other court.

2.2 Subject to Section 2 of this practice direction, on receipt of such a request, a court officer will transfer the proceedings to the other court unless a judge orders otherwise.

2.3 The court will give notice of the transfer to all the parties.

2.4 When the proceedings have been transferred, the parties must take any further steps in the proceedings in the court to which they have been transferred, unless a rule or practice direction provides otherwise.

(Part 52 and PD 52A and PD 52B provide to which court or judge an appeal against the judgment or order, or an application for permission to appeal, must be made.)

Enforcement of High Court Judgment or Order in a County Court: Rule 70.3

para.3 79.2

3.1 If a judgment creditor wishes to enforce a High Court judgment or order in a county court, he must file the following documents in the county court with his application notice or request for enforcement:
  (1) a copy of the judgment or order;

[1] See Part 81, in particular Sections 2 and 8, and CCR, ord. 28 in CPR, sch. 2.

(2) a certificate verifying the amount due under the judgment or order;
(3) if a writ of execution has previously been issued in the High Court to enforce the judgment or order, a copy of the relevant enforcement officer's return to the writ; and
(4) a copy of the order transferring the proceedings to the county court.

3.2 In this paragraph and para. 7:
(1) 'enforcement officer' means an individual who is authorised to act as an enforcement officer under the Courts Act 2003; and
(2) 'relevant enforcement officer' means:
(a) in relation to a writ of execution which is directed to a single enforcement officer, that officer;
(b) in relation to a writ of execution which is directed to two or more enforcement officers, the officer to whom the writ is allocated.

Enforcement of Decisions of Bodies Other Than the High Court and County Courts and Compromises Enforceable by Enactment

para.4.1 79.3 para.4.3 79.3

4.1 The information referred to in r. 70.5(2A) must—
(a) be included in form N322B or, where para. 4.1A applies, in the form required by para. 4.1A(2);
(b) specify the statutory provision under which enforcement or the recovery of a sum of money is sought;
(c) state the name and address of the person against whom enforcement or recovery is sought;
(d) where the decision or compromise requires that person to pay a sum of money, state the amount which remains unpaid; and
(e) confirm that, where a sum of money is being recovered pursuant to a compromise, the compromise is not a conditional compromise.

4.1A (1) This paragraph applies where—
(a) either—
(i) the decision to be enforced is a decision of an employment tribunal in England and Wales; or
(ii) the application is for the recovery of a compromise sum under the Employment Tribunals Act 1996, s. 19A(3); and
(b) the party seeking to enforce the decision wishes to enforce by way of a writ of fieri facias.
(2) The form which is to be used is—
(a) where para. (1)(a)(i) applies, form N471;
(b) where para. (1)(a)(ii) applies, form N471A.

4.2 An application under r. 70.5(3) for an order to enforce a decision or compromise must be made by filing an application notice in form N322A.

4.3 The application notice must state—
(a) the name and address of the person against whom the order is sought;
(b) how much remains unpaid or what obligation remains to be performed; and
(c) where the application relates to a conditional compromise, details of what under the compromise the applicant is required to do and has done under the compromise in addition to discontinuing or not starting proceedings.

4.4 Where—
(a) the application relates to a conditional compromise; and
(b) the application notice is served by the applicant on the respondent,
the applicant must file a certificate of service with the court within seven days of service of the application notice.

Registration of Decisions in the High Court for Enforcement: Rule 70.5(8)

paras.5.1–5.2 79.3

5.1 An application to the High Court under an enactment to register a decision for enforcement must be made in writing to the head clerk of the Action Department at the Royal Courts of Justice, Strand, London WC2A 2LL.

5.2 The application must:
(1) specify the statutory provision under which the application is made;
(2) state the name and address of the person against whom it is sought to enforce the decision;
(3) if the decision requires that person to pay a sum of money, state the amount which remains unpaid.

Interest on Judgment Debts

6. If a judgment creditor is claiming interest on a judgment debt, he must include in his application or request to issue enforcement proceedings in relation to that judgment details of:
(1) the amount of interest claimed and the sum on which it is claimed;
(2) the dates from and to which interest has accrued; and
(3) the rate of interest which has been applied and, where more than one rate of interest has been applied, the relevant dates and rates.
(Interest may be claimed on High Court judgment debts under the Judgments Act 1838, s. 17. The County Courts (Interest on Judgment Debts) Order 1991 specifies when interest may be claimed on county court judgment debts.)

Enforcing a Judgment or Order against a Partnership

paras.6A.1–6A.4 79.38

6A.1 A judgment or order made against a partnership may be enforced against any property of the partnership within the jurisdiction.
6A.2 Subject to para. 6A.3, a judgment or order made against a partnership may be enforced against any person who is not a limited partner and who:
(1) acknowledged service of the claim form as a partner;
(2) having been served as a partner with the claim form, failed to acknowledge service of it;
(3) admitted in his statement of case that he is or was a partner at a material time; or
(4) was found by the court to have been a partner at a material time.
6A.3 A judgment or order made against a partnership may not be enforced against a limited partner or a member of the partnership who was ordinarily resident outside the jurisdiction when the claim form was issued unless that partner or member:
(1) acknowledged service of the claim form as a partner;
(2) was served within the jurisdiction with the claim form as a partner; or
(3) was served out of the jurisdiction with the claim form, as a partner, with the permission of the court given under Section IV of Part 6.
6A.4 A judgment creditor wishing to enforce a judgment or order against a person in circumstances not set out in paras 6A.2 or 6A.3 must apply to the court for permission to enforce the judgment or order.

Payment of Debt after Issue of Enforcement Proceedings

7.1 If a judgment debt or part of it is paid:
(1) after the judgment creditor has issued any application or request to enforce it; but
(2) before:
(a) any writ or warrant has been executed; or
(b) in any other case, the date fixed for the hearing of the application,
the judgment creditor must, unless para. 7.2 applies, immediately notify the court in writing.
7.2 If a judgment debt or part of it is paid after the judgment creditor has applied to the High Court for a writ of execution, para. 7.1 does not apply, and the judgment creditor must instead immediately notify the relevant enforcement officer in writing.

SECTION II AUTOMATIC TRANSFER OF PROCEEDINGS IN DESIGNATED MONEY CLAIMS

section II 42.7, 79.2

Scope

8.1 This Section applies to applications for orders to obtain information from judgment debtors and applications for enforcement of judgments made in Northampton Country Court in respect of designated money claims where the proceedings have not been transferred to another county court.

Applications under Parts 71, 72 and 73

9.1 Where an application is made to which r. 71.2(2)(b)(ii), 72.3(1)(b)(ii) or 73.3(2)(e) applies, it must be filed in the court for the district in which the judgment debtor resided or carries on business.

Applications under Order 27

10.1 Where an application is made under r. 3(2), the application must be filed in the court for the district in which the judgment creditor resides or carries on business.

10.2 Where an application is made under r. 3(3), the application must be filed in the court for the district in which one or more of the debtors resides or carries on business.

Automatic Transfer

11.1 Unless the court is satisfied that the application does not comply with the Rules, it will transfer the proceedings to the court in which the application was filed and a court officer will inform the Country Court Money Claims Centre of the transfer.

CPR Part 71 Orders to Obtain Information from Judgment Debtors

Part 71 **70.3, 79.1, 79.3, 79.6, 79.12, 79.40, 83.40** [For commentary on a specific rule, please refer to the cross-references after the title of the rule.]

71.1 Scope of This Part

This Part contains rules which provide for a judgment debtor to be required to attend court to provide information, for the purpose of enabling a judgment creditor to enforce a judgment or order against him.

71.2 Order to Attend Court

r.71.2 **63.37, 79.6**
r.71.2(1)(b) **79.6**
r.71.2(2)(b)(ii) **42.7, 79.2**
r.71.2(3)(b)(ii) **79.2**

(1) A judgment creditor may apply for an order requiring—
- (a) a judgment debtor; or
- (b) if a judgment debtor is a company or other corporation, an officer of that body, to attend court to provide information about—
  - (i) the judgment debtor's means; or
  - (ii) any other matter about which information is needed to enforce a judgment or order.

(2) An application under paragraph (1)—
- (a) may be made without notice; and
- (b) must be issued in the court which made the judgment or order which it is sought to enforce, except that—
  - (i) if the proceedings have since been transferred to a different court, it must be issued in that court; or
  - (ii) subject to subparagraph (b)(i), if it is to enforce a judgment made in Northampton County Court in respect of a designated money claim, it must be issued in accordance with section 2 of Practice Direction 70.

(3) The application notice must—
- (a) be in the form; and
- (b) contain the information

required by Practice Direction 71.

(4) An application under paragraph (1) may be dealt with by a court officer without a hearing.

(5) If the application notice complies with paragraph (3), an order to attend court will be issued in the terms of paragraph (6).

(6) A person served with an order issued under this rule must—
- (a) attend court at the time and place specified in the order;
- (b) when he does so, produce at court documents in his control which are described in the order; and
- (c) answer on oath such questions as the court may require.

(7) An order under this rule will contain a notice in the following terms, or in terms to substantially the same effect—

'If you the within-named [ ] do not comply with this order you may be held to be in contempt of court and imprisoned or fined, or your assets may be seized.'

71.3 Service of Order

r.71.3 79.6

(1) An order to attend court must, unless the court otherwise orders, be served personally on the person ordered to attend court not less than 14 days before the hearing.
(2) If the order is to be served by the judgment creditor, he must inform the court not less than 7 days before the date of the hearing if he has been unable to serve it.

71.4 Travelling Expenses

r.71.4 79.6

(1) A person ordered to attend court may, within 7 days of being served with the order, ask the judgment creditor to pay him a sum reasonably sufficient to cover his travelling expenses to and from court.
(2) The judgment creditor must pay such a sum if requested.

71.5 Judgment Creditor's Affidavit

r.71.5 79.6

(1) The judgment creditor must file an affidavit(GL) or affidavits—
  (a) by the person who served the order (unless it was served by the court) giving details of how and when it was served;
  (b) stating either that—
    (i) the person ordered to attend court has not requested payment of his travelling expenses; or
    (ii) the judgment creditor has paid a sum in accordance with such a request; and
  (c) stating how much of the judgment debt remains unpaid.
(2) The judgment creditor must either—
  (a) file the affidavit(GL) or affidavits not less than 2 days before the hearing; or
  (b) produce it or them at the hearing.

71.6 Conduct of the Hearing

r.71.6 79.6

(1) The person ordered to attend court will be questioned on oath.
(2) The questioning will be carried out by a court officer unless the court has ordered that the hearing shall be before a judge.
(3) The judgment creditor or his representative—
  (a) may attend and ask questions where the questioning takes place before a court officer; and
  (b) must attend and conduct the questioning if the hearing is before a judge.

71.7 Adjournment of the Hearing

If the hearing is adjourned, the court will give directions as to the manner in which notice of the new hearing is to be served on the judgment debtor.

71.8 Failure to Comply with Order

r.71.8 79.6

(1) If a person against whom an order has been made under rule 71.2—
  (a) fails to attend court;
  (b) refuses at the hearing to take the oath or to answer any question; or
  (c) otherwise fails to comply with the order,

  the court will refer the matter to a High Court judge or circuit judge.
(2) That judge may, subject to paragraphs (3) and (4), make a committal order against the person.
(3) A committal order for failing to attend court may not be made unless the judgment creditor has complied with rules 71.4 and 71.5.
(4) If a committal order is made, the judge will direct that—
  (a) the order shall be suspended provided that the person—
    (i) attends court at a time and place specified in the order; and

(ii) complies with all the terms of that order and the original order; and

(b) if the person fails to comply with any term on which the committal order is suspended, he shall be brought before a judge to consider whether the committal order should be discharged.

(Part 81 contains provisions in relation to committal.)

PD 71 Practice Direction 71 — Orders to Obtain Information from Judgment Debtors

This practice direction supplements CPR, Part 71.

[For commentary on a specific paragraph, please refer to the cross-references after the title of the paragraph.]

Application Notice: Rule 71.2

para.1.2 79.6

1.1 An application by a judgment creditor under r. 71.2(1) must be made by filing an application notice in form N316 if the application is to question an individual judgment debtor, or N316A if the application is to question an officer of a company or other corporation.

1.2 The application notice must:
- (1) state the name and address of the judgment debtor;
- (2) identify the judgment or order which the judgment creditor is seeking to enforce;
- (3) if the application is to enforce a judgment or order for the payment of money, state the amount presently owed by the judgment debtor under the judgment or order;
- (4) if the judgment debtor is a company or other corporation, state:
  - (a) the name and address of the officer of that body whom the judgment creditor wishes to be ordered to attend court; and
  - (b) his position in the company;
- (5) if the judgment creditor wishes the questioning to be conducted before a judge, state this and give his reasons;
- (6) if the judgment creditor wishes the judgment debtor (or other person to be questioned) to be ordered to produce specific documents at court, identify those documents; and
- (7) if the application is to enforce a judgment or order which is not for the payment of money, identify the matters about which the judgment creditor wishes the judgment debtor (or officer of the judgment debtor) to be questioned.

1.3 The court officer considering the application notice:
- (1) may, in any appropriate case, refer it to a judge (r. 3.2); and
- (2) will refer it to a judge for consideration, if the judgment creditor requests the judgment debtor (or officer of the judgment debtor) to be questioned before a judge.

Order to Attend Court: Rule 71.2

para.2.2 79.6

2.1 The order will provide for the judgment debtor (or other person to be questioned) to attend the county court for the district in which he resides or carries on business, unless a judge decides otherwise.

2.2 The order will provide for questioning to take place before a judge only if the judge considering the request decides that there are compelling reasons to make such an order.

Service of Order to Attend Court: Rule 71.3

para.3 79.6

3 Service of an order to attend court for questioning may be carried out by:
- (a) the judgment creditor (or someone acting on the judgment creditor's behalf);
- (b) a High Court enforcement officer; or
- (c) a county court bailiff.

Attendance at Court: Normal Procedure: Rule 71.6

para.4.2 79.6

4.1 The court officer will ask a standard series of questions, as set out in the forms in Appendices A and B to this practice direction. The form in Appendix A will be used if the person being questioned is the judgment debtor, and the form in Appendix B will be used if the person is an officer of a company or other corporation.

4.2 The judgment creditor or his representative may either:
(1) attend court and ask questions himself; or
(2) request the court officer to ask additional questions, by attaching a list of proposed additional questions to his application notice.

4.3 The court officer will:
(1) make a written record of the evidence given, unless the proceedings are tape-recorded;
(2) at the end of the questioning, read the record of evidence to the person being questioned and ask him to sign it; and
(3) if the person refuses to sign it, note that refusal on the record of evidence.

Attendance at Court: Procedure Where the Order is to Attend before a Judge: Rule 71.6

para.5.1 79.6

5.1 Where the hearing takes places before a judge, the questioning will be conducted by the judgment creditor or his representative, and the standard questions in the forms in Appendices A and B will not be used.

5.2 The proceedings will be tape-recorded and the court will not make a written record of the evidence.

Failure to Comply with Order: Reference to Judge: Rule 71.8(1)

6 If a judge or court officer refers to a High Court judge or circuit judge the failure of a judgment debtor to comply with an order under r. 71.2, he shall certify in writing the respect in which the judgment debtor failed to comply with the order.

Suspended Committal Order: Rule 71.8(2) and (4)(a)

para.7.1 79.6

7.1 A committal order will be suspended provided that the person attends court at a time and place specified in the order (r. 71.8(4)(a)(i)). The appointment specified will be:
(1) before a judge, if:
  (a) the original order under r. 71.2 was to attend before a judge; or
  (b) the judge making the suspended committal order so directs; and
(2) otherwise, before a court officer.

7.2 Rule 71.3 and para. 3 of this practice direction (service of order), and r. 71.5(1)(a) and (2) (affidavit of service), apply with the necessary changes to a suspended committal order as they do to an order to attend court.

Breach of Terms on Which Committal Order Is Suspended: Rule 71.8(4)(b)

8.1 If:
(1) the judgment debtor fails to attend court at the time and place specified in the suspended committal order; and
(2) it appears to the judge or court officer that the judgment debtor has been duly served with the order,

the judge or court officer will certify in writing the debtor's failure to attend.

8.2 If the judgment debtor fails to comply with any other term on which the committal order was suspended, the judge or court officer will certify in writing the non-compliance and set out details of it.

8.3 A warrant to bring the judgment debtor before a judge may be issued on the basis of a certificate under para. 8.1 or 8.2.

8.4 The hearing under r. 71.8(4)(b) may take place before a master or district judge.

8.5 At the hearing the judge will discharge the committal order unless he is satisfied beyond reasonable doubt that:
(1) the judgment debtor has failed to comply with:
  (a) the original order to attend court; and
  (b) the terms on which the committal order was suspended; and
(2) both orders have been duly served on the judgment debtor.

8.6 If the judge decides that the committal order should not be discharged, a warrant of committal shall be issued immediately.

[The following forms are appended to PD 71:

Appendix A EX140 Record of examination (individual)

Appendix B EX141 Record \of examination (officer of company or corporation)

These forms are online at http://hmctsformfinder.justice.gov.uk>.]

CPR Part 72 Third Party Debt Orders

Part 72 70.3, 79.1, 79.3, 79.40 [For commentary on a specific rule, please refer to the cross-references after the title of the rule.]

72.1 Scope of This Part and Interpretation

(1) This Part contains rules which provide for a judgment creditor to obtain an order for the payment to him of money which a third party who is within the jurisdiction owes to the judgment debtor.

(2) In this Part, 'bank or building society' includes any person carrying on a business in the course of which he lawfully accepts deposits in the United Kingdom.

72.2 Third Party Debt Order

r.72.2(1)(a) 79.13 r.72.2(3) 79.17

(1) Upon the application of a judgment creditor, the court may make an order (a 'final third party debt order') requiring a third party to pay to the judgment creditor—
  (a) the amount of any debt due or accruing due to the judgment debtor from the third party; or
  (b) so much of that debt as is sufficient to satisfy the judgment debt and the judgment creditor's costs of the application.

(2) The court will not make an order under paragraph 1 without first making an order (an 'interim third party debt order') as provided by rule 72.4(2).

(3) In deciding whether money standing to the credit of the judgment debtor in an account to which section 40 of the Senior Courts Act 1981 or section 108 of the County Courts Act 1984 relates may be made the subject of a third party debt order, any condition applying to the account that a receipt for money deposited in the account must be produced before any money is withdrawn will be disregarded.

(Section 40(3) of the Senior Courts Act 1981 and section 108(3) of the County Courts Act 1984 contain a list of other conditions applying to accounts that will also be disregarded.)

72.3 Application for Third Party Debt Order

r.72.3 79.14 r.72.3(b)(ii) 42.7

(1) An application for a third party debt order—
  (a) may be made without notice; and
  (b) must be issued in the court which made the judgment or order which it is sought to enforce, except that—
    (i) if the proceedings have since been transferred to a different court, it must be issued in that court; or
    (ii) subject to subparagraph (b)(i), if it is to enforce a judgment made in Northampton County Court in respect of a designated money claim, it must be issued in accordance with section 2 of Practice Direction 70.

(2) The application notice must—
  (a) (i) be in the form; and
    (ii) contain the information
  required by Practice Direction 72; and
  (b) be verified by a statement of truth.

72.4 Interim Third Party Debt Order

r.72.4(1) 79.14 r.72.4(4) 79.15
r.72.4(3) 79.14

(1) An application for a third party debt order will initially be dealt with by a judge without a hearing.
(2) The judge may make an interim third party debt order—
 (a) fixing a hearing to consider whether to make a final third party debt order; and
 (b) directing that until that hearing the third party must not make any payment which reduces the amount he owes the judgment debtor to less than the amount specified in the order.
(3) An interim third party debt order will specify the amount of money which the third party must retain, which will be the total of—
 (a) the amount of money remaining due to the judgment creditor under the judgment or order; and
 (b) an amount for the judgment creditor's fixed costs of the application, as specified in Practice Direction 72.
(4) An interim third party debt order becomes binding on a third party when it is served on him.
(5) The date of the hearing to consider the application shall be not less than 28 days after the interim third party debt order is made.

72.5 Service of Interim Order

r.72.5(1)(a)–(b) 79.15 r.72.5(2) 79.15

(1) Copies of an interim third party debt order, the application notice and any documents filed in support of it must be served—
 (a) on the third party, not less than 21 days before the date fixed for the hearing; and
 (b) on the judgment debtor not less than—
  (i) 7 days after a copy has been served on the third party; and
  (ii) 7 days before the date fixed for the hearing.
(2) If the judgment creditor serves the order, he must either—
 (a) file a certificate of service not less than 2 days before the hearing; or
 (b) produce a certificate of service at the hearing.

72.6 Obligations of Third Parties Served with Interim Order

r.72.6(1)–(2) 79.15 r.72.6(2)(c)(iii) 79.15
r.72.6(4) 79.15

(1) A bank or building society served with an interim third party debt order must carry out a search to identify all accounts held with it by the judgment debtor.
(2) The bank or building society must disclose to the court and the creditor within 7 days of being served with the order, in respect of each account held by the judgment debtor—
 (a) the number of the account;
 (b) whether the account is in credit; and
 (c) if the account is in credit—
  (i) whether the balance of the account is sufficient to cover the amount specified in the order;
  (ii) the amount of the balance at the date it was served with the order, if it is less than the amount specified in the order; and
  (iii) whether the bank or building society asserts any right to the money in the account, whether pursuant to a right of set-off or otherwise, and if so giving details of the grounds for that assertion.
(3) If—
 (a) the judgment debtor does not hold an account with the bank or building society; or
 (b) the bank or building society is unable to comply with the order for any other reason (for example, because it has more than one account holder whose details match the information contained in the order, and cannot identify which account the order applies to),

the bank or building society must inform the court and the judgment creditor of that fact within 7 days of being served with the order.

(4) Any third party other than a bank or building society served with an interim third party debt order must notify the court and the judgment creditor in writing within 7 days of being served with the order, if he claims—
(a) not to owe any money to the judgment debtor; or
(b) to owe less than the amount specified in the order.

72.7 Arrangements for Debtors in Hardship

r.72.7 79.15

(1) If—
(a) a judgment debtor is an individual;
(b) he is prevented from withdrawing money from his account with a bank or building society as a result of an interim third party debt order; and
(c) he or his family is suffering hardship in meeting ordinary living expenses as a result,
the court may, on an application by the judgment debtor, make an order permitting the bank or building society to make a payment or payments out of the account ('a hardship payment order').
(2) An application for a hardship payment order may be made—
(a) in High Court proceedings, at the Royal Courts of Justice or to any district registry; and
(b) in county court proceedings, to any county court.
(3) A judgment debtor may only apply to one court for a hardship payment order.
(4) An application notice seeking a hardship payment order must—
(a) include detailed evidence explaining why the judgment debtor needs a payment of the amount requested; and
(b) be verified by a statement of truth.
(5) Unless the court orders otherwise, the application notice—
(a) must be served on the judgment creditor at least 2 days before the hearing; but
(b) does not need to be served on the third party.
(6) A hardship payment order may—
(a) permit the third party to make one or more payments out of the account; and
(b) specify to whom the payments may be made.

72.8 Further Consideration of the Application

r.72.8 79.16 r.72.8(5)–(6) 79.16

(1) If the judgment debtor or the third party objects to the court making a final third party debt order, he must file and serve written evidence stating the grounds for his objections.
(2) If the judgment debtor or the third party knows or believes that a person other than the judgment debtor has any claim to the money specified in the interim order, he must file and serve written evidence stating his knowledge of that matter.
(3) If—
(a) the third party has given notice under rule 72.6 that he does not owe any money to the judgment debtor, or that the amount which he owes is less than the amount specified in the interim order; and
(b) the judgment creditor wishes to dispute this,
the judgment creditor must file and serve written evidence setting out the grounds on which he disputes the third party's case.
(4) Written evidence under paragraphs (1), (2) or (3) must be filed and served on each other party as soon as possible, and in any event not less than 3 days before the hearing.
(5) If the court is notified that some person other than the judgment debtor may have a claim to the money specified in the interim order, it will serve on that person notice of the application and the hearing.
(6) At the hearing the court may—
(a) make a final third party debt order;
(b) discharge the interim third party debt order and dismiss the application;
(c) decide any issues in dispute between the parties, or between any of the parties and any other person who has a claim to the money specified in the interim order; or
(d) direct a trial of any such issues, and if necessary give directions.

72.9 Effect of Final Third Party Debt* Order

r.72.9(2) **79.16**

(1) A final third party debt order shall be enforceable as an order to pay money.
(2) If—
 (a) the third party pays money to the judgment creditor in compliance with a third party debt order; or
 (b) the order is enforced against him,
 the third party shall, to the extent of the amount paid by him or realised by enforcement against him, be discharged from his debt to the judgment debtor.
(3) Paragraph (2) applies even if the third party debt order, or the original judgment or order against the judgment debtor, is later set aside.

72.10 Money in Court

(1) If money is standing to the credit of the judgment debtor in court—
 (a) the judgment creditor may not apply for a third party debt order in respect of that money; but
 (b) he may apply for an order that the money in court, or so much of it as is sufficient to satisfy the judgment or order and the costs of the application, be paid to him.
(2) An application notice seeking an order under this rule must be served on—
 (a) the judgment debtor; and
 (b) the Accountant General at the Court Funds Office.
(3) If an application notice has been issued under this rule, the money in court must not be paid out until the application has been disposed of.

72.11 Costs

If the judgment creditor is awarded costs on an application for an order under rule 72.2 or 72.10—
 (a) he shall, unless the court otherwise directs, retain those costs out of the money recovered by him under the order; and
 (b) the costs shall be deemed to be paid first out of the money he recovers, in priority to the judgment debt.

[* The word 'debt' is omitted from the heading in the Queen's Printer's copy.]

PD 72 Practice Direction 72 — Third Party Debt Orders

This practice direction supplements CPR, Part 72.

[For commentary on a specific paragraph, please refer to the cross-references after the title of the paragraph.]

Application Notice: Rule 72.3

paras.1.2–1.3 79.14

1.1 An application for a third party debt order must be made by filing an application notice in form N349.

1.2 The application notice must contain the following information:
(1) the name and address of the judgment debtor;
(2) details of the judgment or order sought to be enforced;
(3) the amount of money remaining due under the judgment or order;
(4) if the judgment debt is payable by instalments, the amount of any instalments which have fallen due and remain unpaid;
(5) the name and address of the third party;
(6) if the third party is a bank or building society:
(a) its name and the address of the branch at which the judgment debtor's account is believed to be held; and
(b) the account number;
or, if the judgment creditor does not know all or part of this information, that fact;
(7) confirmation that to the best of the judgment creditor's knowledge or belief the third party:
(a) is within the jurisdiction; and
(b) owes money to or holds money to the credit of the judgment debtor;
(8) if the judgment creditor knows or believes that any person other than the judgment debtor has any claim to the money owed by the third party:
(a) his name and (if known) his address; and
(b) such information as is known to the judgment creditor about his claim;
(9) details of any other applications for third party debt orders issued by the judgment creditor in respect of the same judgment debt; and
(10) the sources or grounds of the judgment creditor's knowledge or belief of the matters referred to in (7), (8) and (9).

1.3 The court will not grant speculative applications for third party debt orders, and will only make an interim third party debt order against a bank or building society if the judgment creditor's application notice contains evidence to substantiate his belief that the judgment debtor has an account with the bank or building society in question.

Interim Third Party Debt Order: Rule 72.4

2 An interim third party debt order will specify the amount of money which the third party must retain (r. 72.4(3)). This will include, in respect of the judgment creditor's fixed costs of the application, the amount which would be allowed to the judgment creditor under r. 45.8 if the whole balance of the judgment debt were recovered.

Interim Orders Relating to Bank or Building Society Accounts: Rule 72.6(1)–(3)

3.1 A bank or building society served with an interim third party debt order is only required by r. 72.6, unless the order states otherwise:
(1) to retain money in accounts held solely by the judgment debtor (or, if there are joint judgment debtors, accounts held jointly by them or solely by either or any of them); and
(2) to search for and disclose information about such accounts.

3.2 The bank or building society is not required, for example, to retain money in, or disclose information about:
(1) accounts in the joint names of the judgment debtor and another person; or
(2) if the interim order has been made against a firm, accounts in the names of individual members of that firm.

Attachment of Debts Owed by a Partnership

paras.3A.1–3A.3 79.38

3A.1 This paragraph relates to debts due or accruing due to a judgment creditor from a partnership.

3A.2 An interim third party debt order under r. 72.4(2) relating to such debts must be served on:
(1) a member of the partnership within the jurisdiction;
(2) a person authorised by a partner; or
(3) some other person having the control or management of the partnership business.

3A.3 Where an order made under r. 72.4(2) requires a partnership to appear before the court, it will be sufficient for a partner to appear before the court.

Transfer

4 The court may, on an application by a judgment debtor who wishes to oppose an application for a third party debt order, transfer it to the court for the district where the judgment debtor resides or carries on business, or to another court.

Applications for Hardship Payment Orders: Rule 72.7

paras.5.1–5.6 79.15

5.1 The court will treat an application for a hardship payment order as being made:
(1) in the proceedings in which the interim third party debt order was made; and
(2) under the same claim number,
regardless of where the judgment debtor makes the application.

5.2 An application for a hardship payment order will be dealt with by the court to which it is made.
(Rule 72.7(2) provides that an application may be made:
• in High Court proceedings, in the Royal Courts of Justice or to any district registry; and
• in county court proceedings, to any county court.)

5.3 If the application is made to a different court from that dealing with the application for a third party debt order:
(1) the application for a third party debt order will not be transferred; but
(2) the court dealing with that application will send copies of:
(a) the application notice; and
(b) the interim third party debt order
to the court hearing the application for a hardship payment order

5.4 Rule 72.7(3) requires an application for a hardship payment order to be served on the judgment creditor at least two days before the court is to deal with the application, unless the court orders otherwise. In cases of exceptional urgency the judgment debtor may apply for a hardship payment order without notice to the judgment creditor and a judge will decide whether to:
(1) deal with the application without it being served on the judgment creditor; or
(2) direct it to be served.

5.5 If the judge decides to deal with the application without it being served on the judgment creditor, where possible he will normally:
(1) direct that the judgment creditor be informed of the application; and
(2) give him the opportunity to make representations,
by telephone, fax or other appropriate method of communication.

5.6 The evidence filed by a judgment debtor in support of an application for a hardship payment order should include documentary evidence, for example (if appropriate) bank statements, wage slips and mortgage statements, to prove his financial position and need for the payment.

Final Orders Relating to Building Society Accounts

6. A final third party debt order will not require a payment which would reduce to less than £1 the amount in a judgment debtor's account with a building society or credit union.

CPR Part 73 Charging Orders, Stop Orders and Stop Notices

Part 73 **70.3, 79.1, 79.3, 79.25, 79.40** [For commentary on a specific rule, please refer to the cross-references after the title of the rule.]

73.1 Scope of This Part and Interpretation

(1) This Part contains rules which provide for a judgment creditor to enforce a judgment by obtaining—
  (a) a charging order (Section I);
  (b) a stop order (Section II); or
  (c) a stop notice (Section III),
over or against the judgment debtor's interest in an asset.

(2) In this Part—
  (a) 'the 1979 Act' means the Charging Orders Act 1979;
  (b) 'the 1992 Regulations' means the Council Tax (Administration & Enforcement) Regulations 1992;
  (c) 'funds in court' includes securities held in court;
  (d) 'securities' means securities of any of the kinds specified in section 2(2)(b) of the 1979 Act.

I CHARGING ORDERS

73.2 Scope of This Section

This Section applies to an application by a judgment creditor for a charging order under—
(a) section 1 of the 1979 Act; or
(b) regulation 50 of the 1992 Regulations.

73.3 Application for Charging Order

r.73.3(2)(e) **42.7, 79.2** r.73.3(4) **79.25**

(1) An application for a charging order may be made without notice.

(2) An application for a charging order must be issued in the court which made the judgment or order which it is sought to enforce, unless—
  (a) the proceedings have since been transferred to a different court, in which case the application must be issued in that court;
  (b) the application is made under the 1992 Regulations, in which event it must be issued in the county court for the district in which the relevant dwelling (as defined in regulation 50(3)(b) of those Regulations) is situated;
  (c) the application is for a charging order over an interest in a fund in court, in which event it must be issued in the court in which the claim relating to that fund is or was proceeding;

(d) the application is to enforce a judgment or order of the High Court and it is required by section 1(2) of the 1979 Act to be made to a county court; or
(e) the application is to enforce a judgment made in Northampton County Court in respect of a designated money claim, in which event the application must be issued in accordance with section 2 of Practice Direction 70.

(3) Subject to paragraph (2), a judgment creditor may apply for a single charging order in respect of more than one judgment or order against the same debtor.

(4) The application notice must—
(a) (i) be in the form; and
(ii) contain the information,
required by Practice Direction 73; and
(b) be verified by a statement of truth.

73.4 Interim Charging Order

r.73.4 79.25

(1) An application for a charging order will initially be dealt with by a judge without a hearing.

(2) The judge may make an order (an 'interim charging order')—
(a) imposing a charge over the judgment debtor's interest in the asset to which the application relates; and
(b) fixing a hearing to consider whether to make a final charging order as provided by rule 73.8(2)(a).

73.5 Service of Interim Order

r.73.5(1)–(2) 79.25

(1) Copies of the interim charging order, the application notice and any documents filed in support of it must, not less than 21 days before the hearing, be served on the following persons—
(a) the judgment debtor;
(b) such other creditors as the court directs;
(c) if the order relates to an interest under a trust, on such of the trustees as the court directs;
(d) if the interest charged is in securities other than securities held in court, then—
(i) in the case of stock for which the Bank of England keeps the register, the Bank of England;
(ii) in the case of government stock to which (i) does not apply, the keeper of the register;
(iii) in the case of stock of any body incorporated within England and Wales, that body;
(iv) in the case of stock of any body incorporated outside England and Wales or of any state or territory outside the United Kingdom, which is registered in a register kept in England and Wales, the keeper of that register;
(v) in the case of units of any unit trust in respect of which a register of the unit holders is kept in England and Wales, the keeper of that register; and
(e) if the interest charged is in funds in court, the Accountant General at the Court Funds Office.

(2) If the judgment creditor serves the order, he must either—
(a) file a certificate of service not less than 2 days before the hearing; or
(b) produce a certificate of service at the hearing.

73.6 Effect of Interim Order in Relation to Securities

r.73.6 79.25

(1) If a judgment debtor disposes of his interest in any securities, while they are subject to an interim charging order which has been served on him, that disposition shall not, so long as that order remains in force, be valid as against the judgment creditor.

(2) A person served under rule 73.5(1)(d) with an interim charging order relating to securities must not, unless the court gives permission—
(a) permit any transfer of any of the securities; or
(b) pay any dividend, interest or redemption payment relating to them.

(3) If a person acts in breach of paragraph (2), he will be liable to pay to the judgment creditor—
(a) the value of the securities transferred or the amount of the payment made (as the case may be); or

(b) if less, the amount necessary to satisfy the debt in relation to which the interim charging order was made.

73.7 Effect of Interim Order in Relation to Funds in Court

If a judgment debtor disposes of his interest in funds in court while they are subject to an interim charging order which has been served on him and on the Accountant General in accordance with rule 73.5(1), that disposition shall not, so long as that order remains in force, be valid as against the judgment creditor.

73.8 Further Consideration of the Application

r.73.8 79.25 r.73.8(2)(a) 79.25
r.73.8(2) 79.25

(1) If any person objects to the court making a final charging order, he must—
(a) file; and
(b) serve on the applicant;
written evidence stating the grounds of his objections, not less than 7 days before the hearing.
(2) At the hearing the court may—
(a) make a final charging order confirming that the charge imposed by the interim charging order shall continue, with or without modification;
(b) discharge the interim charging order and dismiss the application;
(c) decide any issues in dispute between the parties, or between any of the parties and any other person who objects to the court making a final charging order; or
(d) direct a trial of any such issues, and if necessary give directions.
(3) If the court makes a final charging order which charges securities other than securities held in court, the order will include a stop notice unless the court otherwise orders.
(Section III of this Part contains provisions about stop notices.)
(4) Any order made at the hearing must be served on all the persons on whom the interim charging order was required to be served.

73.9 Discharge or Variation of Order

(1) Any application to discharge or vary a charging order must be made to the court which made the charging order.
(Section 3(5) of the 1979 Act and regulation 51(4) of the 1992 Regulations provide that the court may at any time, on the application of the debtor, or of any person interested in any property to which the order relates, or (where the 1992 Regulations apply) of the authority, make an order discharging or varying the charging order.)
(2) The court may direct that—
(a) any interested person should be joined as a party to such an application; or
(b) the application should be served on any such person.
(3) An order discharging or varying a charging order must be served on all the persons on whom the charging order was required to be served.

73.10 Enforcement of Charging Order by Sale

r.73.10 79.27, 79.28, 87.4

(1) Subject to the provisions of any enactment, the court may, upon a claim by a person who has obtained a charging order over an interest in property, order the sale of the property to enforce the charging order.
(2) A claim for an order for sale under this rule should be made to the court which made the charging order, unless that court does not have jurisdiction to make an order for sale.
(A claim under this rule is a proceeding for the enforcement of a charge, and section 23(c) of the County Courts Act 1984 provides the extent of the county court's jurisdiction to hear and determine such proceedings.)
(3) The claimant must use the Part 8 procedure.
(4) A copy of the charging order must be filed with the claim form.
(5) The claimant's written evidence must include the information required by Practice Direction 73.

II STOP ORDERS

73.11 Interpretation

In this Section, 'stop order' means an order of the High Court not to take, in relation to funds in court or securities specified in the order, any of the steps listed in section 5(5) of the 1979 Act.

73.12 Application for Stop Order

(1) The High Court may make—
(a) a stop order relating to funds in court, on the application of any person—
(i) who has a mortgage or charge on the interest of any person in the funds; or
(ii) to whom that interest has been assigned; or
(iii) who is a judgment creditor of the person entitled to that interest; or
(b) a stop order relating to securities other than securities held in court, on the application of any person claiming to be beneficially entitled to an interest in the securities.
(2) An application for a stop order must be made—
(a) by application notice in existing proceedings; or
(b) by Part 8 claim form if there are no existing proceedings in the High Court.
(3) The application notice or claim form must be served on—
(a) every person whose interest may be affected by the order applied for; and
(b) either—
(i) the Accountant General at the Court Funds Office, if the application relates to funds in court; or
(ii) the person specified in rule 73.5(1)(d), if the application relates to securities other than securities held in court.

73.13 Stop Order Relating to Funds in Court

A stop order relating to funds in court shall prohibit the transfer, sale, delivery out, payment or other dealing with—
(a) the funds or any part of them; or
(b) any income on the funds.

73.14 Stop Order Relating to Securities

(1) A stop order relating to securities other than securities held in court may prohibit all or any of the following steps—
(a) the registration of any transfer of the securities;
(b) the making of any payment by way of dividend, interest or otherwise in respect of the securities; and
(c) in the case of units of a unit trust, any acquisition of or other dealing with the units by any person or body exercising functions under the trust.
(2) The order shall specify—
(a) the securities to which it relates;
(b) the name in which the securities stand;
(c) the steps which may not be taken; and
(d) whether the prohibition applies to the securities only or to the dividends or interest as well.

73.15 Variation or Discharge of Order

(1) The court may, on the application of any person claiming to have a beneficial interest in the funds or securities to which a stop order relates, make an order discharging or varying the order.
(2) An application notice seeking the variation or discharge of a stop order must be served on the person who obtained the order.

III STOP NOTICES

73.16 General

In this Section—

(a) 'stop notice' means a notice issued by the court which requires a person or body not to take, in relation to securities specified in the notice, any of the steps listed in section 5(5) of the 1979 Act, without first giving notice to the person who obtained the notice; and
(b) 'securities' does not include securities held in court.

73.17 Request for Stop Notice

(1) The High Court may, on the request of any person claiming to be beneficially entitled to an interest in securities, issue a stop notice.
(A stop notice may also be included in a final charging order, by either the High Court or a county court, under rule 73.8(3).)
(2) A request for a stop notice must be made by filing—
  (a) a draft stop notice; and
  (b) written evidence which—
    (i) identifies the securities in question;
    (ii) describes the applicant's interest in the securities; and
    (iii) gives an address for service for the applicant.
  (A sample form of stop notice is annexed to Practice Direction 73.)
(3) If a court officer considers that the request complies with paragraph (2), he will issue a stop notice.
(4) The applicant must serve copies of the stop notice and his written evidence on the person to whom the stop notice is addressed.

73.18 Effect of Stop Notice

(1) A stop notice—
  (a) takes effect when it is served in accordance with rule 73.17(4); and
  (b) remains in force unless it is withdrawn or discharged in accordance with rule 73.20 or 73.21.
(2) While a stop notice is in force, the person on whom it is served—
  (a) must not—
    (i) register a transfer of the securities described in the notice; or
    (ii) take any other step restrained by the notice,
  without first giving 14 days' notice to the person who obtained the stop notice; but
  (b) must not, by reason only of the notice, refuse to register a transfer or to take any other step, after he has given 14 days' notice under paragraph (2)(a) and that period has expired.

73.19 Amendment of Stop Notice

(1) If any securities are incorrectly described in a stop notice which has been obtained and served in accordance with rule 73.17, the applicant may request an amended stop notice in accordance with that rule.
(2) The amended stop notice takes effect when it is served.

73.20 Withdrawal of Stop Notice

(1) A person who has obtained a stop notice may withdraw it by serving a request for its withdrawal on—
  (a) the person or body on whom the stop notice was served; and
  (b) the court which issued the stop notice.
(2) The request must be signed by the person who obtained the stop notice, and his signature must be witnessed by a practising solicitor.

73.21 Discharge or Variation of Stop Notice

(1) The court may, on the application of any person claiming to be beneficially entitled to an interest in the securities to which a stop notice relates, make an order discharging or varying the notice.
(2) An application to discharge or vary a stop notice must be made to the court which issued the notice.
(3) The application notice must be served on the person who obtained the stop notice.

73.22

Practice Direction 73 makes provision for the procedure to be followed when applying for an order under section 23 of the Partnership Act 1890.

PD 73 Practice Direction 73 — Charging Orders, Stop Orders and Stop Notices

This practice direction supplements CPR, Part 73.

[For commentary on a specific paragraph, please refer to the cross-references after the title of the paragraph.]

I CHARGING ORDERS

Application Notice: Rule 73.3

para.1.2 79.25

1.1 An application for a charging order must be made by filing an application notice in form N379 if the application relates to land, or N380 if the application relates to securities.

1.2 The application notice must contain the following information:
(1) the name and address of the judgment debtor;
(2) details of the judgment or order sought to be enforced;
(3) the amount of money remaining due under the judgment or order;
(4) if the judgment debt is payable by instalments, the amount of any instalments which have fallen due and remain unpaid;
(5) if the judgment creditor knows of the existence of any other creditors of the judgment debtor, their names and (if known) their addresses;
(6) identification of the asset or assets which it is intended to charge;
(7) details of the judgment debtor's interest in the asset; and
(8) the names and addresses of the persons on whom an interim charging order must be served under r. 73.5(1).

1.3 A judgment creditor may apply in a single application notice for charging orders over more than one asset, but if the court makes interim charging orders over more than one asset, it will draw up a separate order relating to each asset.

High Court and County Court Jurisdiction

2. The jurisdiction of the High Court and the county court to make charging orders is set out in the Charging Orders Act 1979, s. 1(2).

Transfer

3. The court may, on an application by a judgment debtor who wishes to oppose an application for a charging order, transfer it to the court for the district where the judgment debtor resides or carries on business, or to another court.

Enforcement of Charging Orders by Sale: Rule 73.10

para.4.5 79.28 paras.4A.1–4A.3 79.38

4.1 A county court has jurisdiction to determine a claim under r. 73.10 for the enforcement of a charging order if the amount owing under the charge does not exceed the county court limit.

4.2 A claim in the High Court for an order for sale of land to enforce a charging order must be started in Chancery Chambers at the Royal Courts of Justice, or a Chancery district registry. (There are Chancery district registries at Birmingham, Bristol, Caernarfon, Cardiff, Leeds, Liverpool, Manchester, Mold, Newcastle upon Tyne and Preston.)

4.3 The written evidence in support of a claim under r. 73.10 must:
(1) identify the charging order and the property sought to be sold;
(2) state the amount in respect of which the charge was imposed and the amount due at the date of issue of the claim;
(3) verify, so far as known, the debtor's title to the property charged;
(4) state, so far as the claimant is able to identify:
(a) the names and addresses of any other creditors who have a prior charge or other security over the property; and

(b) the amount owed to each such creditor; and
(5) give an estimate of the price which would be obtained on sale of the property;
(6) if the claim relates to land, give details of every person who to the best of the claimant's knowledge is in possession of the property; and
(7) if the claim relates to residential property:
(a) state whether:
(i) a land charge of Class F; or
(ii) a notice under the Family Law Act 1996, s. 31(10), or under any provision of an Act which preceded that section,
has been registered; and
(b) if so, state:
(i) on whose behalf the land charge or notice has been registered; and
(ii) that the claimant will serve notice of the claim on that person.

4.4 The claimant must take all reasonable steps to obtain the information required by para. 4.3(4) before issuing the claim.

4.5 Sample forms of orders for sale are set out in Appendix A to this practice direction for guidance. These are not prescribed forms of order and they may be adapted or varied by the court to meet the requirements of individual cases.

4A.1 A charging order or interim charging order may be made against any property, within the jurisdiction, belonging to a judgment debtor that is a partnership.

4A.2 For the purposes of r. 73.5(1)(a) (service of the interim order), the specified documents must be served on:
(1) a master;
(2) a person authorised by a partner; or
(3) some other person having the control or management of the partnership business.

4A.3 Where an order requires a partnership to appear before the court, it will be sufficient for a partner to appear before the court.

II STOP NOTICES

5. A sample form of stop notice is set out in Appendix B to this practice direction.

III APPLICATIONS FOR ORDERS MADE UNDER SECTION 23 OF THE PARTNERSHIP ACT 1890

6.1 This paragraph relates to orders made under the Partnership Act 1890, s. 23 ('Section 23').

6.2 The following applications must be made in accordance with Part 23:
(1) an application for an order under Section 23 made by a judgment creditor of a partner;
(2) an application for any order by a partner of the judgment debtor in consequence of any application made by the judgment creditor under Section 23.

6.3 The powers conferred on a judge by Section 23 may be exercised by:
(1) a master;
(2) the Admiralty Registrar; or
(3) a district judge.

6.4 Every application notice filed under this paragraph by a judgment creditor, and every order made following such an application, must be served on the judgment debtor and on any of the other partners that are within the jurisdiction.

6.5 Every application notice filed under this paragraph by a partner of a judgment debtor, and every order made following such an application, must be served:
(1) on the judgment creditor and the judgment debtor; and
(2) on the other partners of the judgment debtor who are not joined in the application and who are within the jurisdiction.

6.6 An application notice or order served under this paragraph on one or more, but not all, of the partners of a partnership shall be deemed to have been served on all the partners of that partnership.

[PD 73 has the following appendices:

Appendix A Sample forms of order for sale following a charging order

Appendix B Sample form of stop notice

These appendices may be viewed at <http://www.justice.gov.uk/courts/procedure-rules/civil>.]

CPR Part 74 Enforcement of Judgments in Different Jurisdictions

[For commentary on a specific rule, please refer to the cross-references after the title of the rule.]

74.1 Scope of This Part and Interpretation

(1) Section I of this Part applies to the enforcement in England and Wales of judgments of foreign courts.

(2) Section II applies to the enforcement in foreign countries of judgments of the High Court and of county courts.

(3) Section III applies to the enforcement of United Kingdom judgments in other parts of the United Kingdom.

(4) Section IV applies to the enforcement in England and Wales of European Community judgments and Euratom inspection orders.

(4A) Section V applies to—

(a) the certification of judgments and court settlements in England and Wales as European Enforcement Orders; and

(b) the enforcement in England and Wales of judgments, court settlements and authentic instruments certified as European Enforcement Orders by other Member States.

(5) In this Part:

(a) 'the 1920 Act' means the Administration of Justice Act 1920;

(b) 'the 1933 Act' means the Foreign Judgments (Reciprocal Enforcement) Act 1933;

(c) 'the 1982 Act' means the Civil Jurisdiction and Judgments Act 1982;

(d) 'the Judgments Regulation' means Council Regulation (EC) No. 44/2001 of 22nd December 2000 on jurisdiction and the recognition and enforcement of judgments in civil and commercial matters, as amended from time to time and as applied by the Agreement made on 19th October 2005 between the European Community and the Kingdom of Denmark on jurisdiction and the recognition and enforcement of judgments in civil and commercial matters;
(e) 'the EEO Regulation' means Council Regulation (EC) No. 805/2004 creating a European Enforcement Order for uncontested claims;
(f) 'the Lugano Convention' means the Convention on jurisdiction and the recognition and enforcement of judgments in civil and commercial matters, between the European Community and the Republic of Iceland, the Kingdom of Norway, the Swiss Confederation and the Kingdom of Denmark and signed by the European Community on 30th October 2007.

(A copy of the EEO Regulation is annexed to Practice Direction 74B and can be found at http://europa.eu.int/eur-lex/pri/en/oj/dat/2004/l_143/l_14320040430en00150039.pdf)

I ENFORCEMENT IN ENGLAND AND WALES OF JUDGMENTS OF FOREIGN COURTS

r.74.2–74.11 **80.13**

74.2 Interpretation

r.74.2 **80.13** r.74.2(1)(c) **80.13**

(1) In this Section:
(a) 'Contracting State' has the meaning given in section 1(3) of the 1982 Act;
(b) 'Regulation State' means a Member State;
(c) 'judgment' means, subject to any other enactment, any judgment given by a foreign court or tribunal, whatever the judgment may be called, and includes—
(i) a decree;
(ii) an order;
(iii) a decision;
(iv) a writ of execution; and
(v) the determination of costs by an officer of the court;
(d) 'State of origin', in relation to any judgment, means the State in which that judgment was given.

(2) For the purposes of this Section, 'domicile' is to be determined—
(a) in an application under the 1982 Act or the Lugano Convention, in accordance with sections 41 to 46 that Act;
(b) in an application under the Judgments Regulation, in accordance with paragraphs 9 to 12 of Schedule 1 to the Civil Jurisdiction and Judgments Order 2001.

74.3 Applications for Registration

r.74(3) **80.13** r.74.3(2) **80.13**

(1) This Section provides rules about applications under—
(a) section 9 of the 1920 Act, in respect of judgments to which Part II of that Act applies;
(b) section 2 of the 1933 Act, in respect of judgments to which Part I of that Act applies;
(c) section 4 of the 1982 Act;
(d) the Judgments Regulation; and
(e) the Lugano Convention,
for the registration of foreign judgments for enforcement in England and Wales.

(2) Applications—
(a) must be made to the High Court; and
(b) may be made without notice.

74.4 Evidence in Support

r.74.4 **80.13**
r.74.4(1)–(2) **80.14**
r.74.4(2)(e) **80.18**
r.74.4(3) **80.15**
r.74.4(3)(a)–(b) **80.15**
r.74.4(4) **80.16**
r.74.4(5) **80.17**

(1) An application for registration of a judgment under the 1920, 1933 or 1982 Act must be supported by written evidence exhibiting—
(a) the judgment or a verified or certified or otherwise authenticated copy of it; and
(b) where the judgment is not in English, a translation of it into English—
(i) certified by a notary public or other qualified person; or
(ii) accompanied by written evidence confirming that the translation is accurate.
(2) The written evidence in support of the application must state—
(a) the name of the judgment creditor and his address for service within the jurisdiction;
(b) the name of the judgment debtor and his address or place of business, if known;
(c) the grounds on which the judgment creditor is entitled to enforce the judgment;
(d) in the case of a money judgment, the amount in respect of which it remains unsatisfied; and
(e) where interest is recoverable on the judgment under the law of the State of origin—
(i) the amount of interest which has accrued up to the date of the application, or
(ii) the rate of interest, the date from which it is recoverable, and the date on which it ceases to accrue.
(3) Written evidence in support of an application under the 1920 Act must also state that the judgment is not a judgment—
(a) which under section 9 of that Act may not be ordered to be registered; or
(b) to which section 5 of the Protection of Trading Interests Act 1980 applies.
(4) Written evidence in support of an application under the 1933 Act must also—
(a) state that the judgment is a money judgment;
(b) confirm that it can be enforced by execution in the State of origin;
(c) confirm that the registration could not be set aside under section 4 of that Act;
(d) confirm that the judgment is not a judgment to which section 5 of the Protection of Trading Interests Act 1980 applies;
(e) where the judgment contains different provisions, some but not all of which can be registered for enforcement, set out those provisions in respect of which it is sought to register the judgment; and
(f) be accompanied by any further evidence as to—
(i) the enforceability of the judgment in the State of origin, and
(ii) the law of that State under which any interest has become due under the judgment,
which may be required under the relevant Order in Council extending Part I of the 1933 Act to that State.
(5) Written evidence in support of an application under the 1982 Act must also exhibit—
(a) documents which show that, under the law of the State of origin, the judgment is enforceable on the judgment debtor and has been served;
(b) in the case of a judgment in default, a document which establishes that the party in default was served with the document instituting the proceedings or with an equivalent document; and
(c) where appropriate, a document showing that the judgment creditor is in receipt of legal aid in the State of origin.
(6) An application for registration under the Judgments Regulation or the Lugano Convention must, in addition to the evidence required by that Regulation or that Convention, be supported by the evidence required by paragraphs (1)(b) and (2)(e) of this rule.

74.5 Security for Costs

r.74.5 80.13

(1) Subject to paragraphs (2) and (3), section II of Part 25 applies to an application for security for the costs of—
(a) the application for registration;
(b) any proceedings brought to set aside the registration; and
(c) any appeal against the granting of the registration,
as if the judgment creditor were a claimant.
(2) A judgment creditor making an application under the 1982 Act, the Lugano Convention, or the Judgments Regulation may not be required to give security solely on the ground that he is resident out of the jurisdiction.

(3) Paragraph (1) does not apply to an application under the 1933 Act where the relevant Order in Council otherwise provides.

74.6 Registration Orders

r.74.6 80.13
r.74.6(1) 80.19, 80.20
r.74.6(2) 80.20
r.74.6(3) 80.19
r.74.6(3)(d) 80.22

(1) An order granting permission to register a judgment ('registration order') must be drawn up by the judgment creditor and served on the judgment debtor—
 (a) by delivering it to the judgment debtor personally;
 (b) by any of the methods of service permitted under the Companies Act 2006; or
 (c) in such other manner as the court may direct.
(2) Permission is not required to serve a registration order out of the jurisdiction, and rules 6.40, 6.42, 6.43 and 6.46 apply to such an order as they apply to a claim form.
(3) A registration order must state—
 (a) full particulars of the judgment registered;
 (b) the name of the judgment creditor and his address for service within the jurisdiction;
 (c) the right of the judgment debtor—
  (i) in the case of registration following an application under the 1920 or the 1933 Act, to apply to have the registration set aside;
  (ii) in the case of registration following an application under the 1982 Act, the Lugano Convention, or the Judgments Regulation, to appeal against the registration order;
 (d) the period within which such an application or appeal may be made; and
 (e) that no measures of enforcement will be taken before the end of that period, other than measures ordered by the court to preserve the property of the judgment debtor.

74.7 Applications to Set Aside Registration

r.74.7 80.13
r.74.7(1)–(3) 80.21

(1) An application to set aside registration under the 1920 or the 1933 Act must be made within the period set out in the registration order.
(2) The court may extend that period; but an application for such an extension must be made before the end of the period as originally fixed or as subsequently extended.
(3) The court hearing the application may order any issue between the judgment creditor and the judgment debtor to be tried.

74.8 Appeals

r.74.8 80.13, 91.40
r.74.8(1)–(2) 80.22
r.74.8(4) 80.22

(1) An appeal against the granting or the refusal of registration under the 1982 Act or the Lugano Convention or the Judgments Regulation must be made in accordance with Part 52, subject to the following provisions of this rule.
(2) Permission is not required—
 (a) to appeal; or
 (b) to put in evidence.
(3) If—
 (a) the judgment debtor is not domiciled within a Contracting State or a Regulation State, as the case may be, and
 (b) an application to extend the time for appealing is made within two months of service of the registration order,

the court may extend the period for filing an appellant's notice against the order granting registration, but not on grounds of distance.
(4) The appellant's notice must be served—
 (a) where the appeal is against the granting of registration, within—
  (i) one month; or
  (ii) where service is to be effected on a party not domiciled within the jurisdiction, two months, of service of the registration order;

(b) where the appeal is against the refusal of registration, within one month of the decision on the application for registration.

74.9 Enforcement

r.74.9 **80.13, 8.19** r.74.9(2) **80.20**

(1) No steps may be taken to enforce a judgment—
 (a) before the end of the period specified in accordance with rule 74.6(3)(d), or that period as extended by the court; or
 (b) where there is an application under rule 74.7 or an appeal under rule 74.8, until the application or appeal has been determined.
(2) Any party wishing to enforce a judgment must file evidence of the service on the judgment debtor of—
 (a) the registration order; and
 (b) any other relevant order of the court.
(3) Nothing in this rule prevents the court from making orders to preserve the property of the judgment debtor pending final determination of any issue relating to the enforcement of the judgment.

74.10 Recognition

r.74.10 **80.13, 80.19**

(1) Registration of a judgment serves as a decision that the judgment is recognised for the purposes of the 1982 Act, the Lugano Convention and the Judgments Regulation.
(2) An application for recognition of a judgment is governed by the same rules as an application for registration of a judgment under the 1982 Act, the Lugano Convention or the Judgments Regulation, except that rule 74.4(5)(a) and (c) does not apply.

74.11 Authentic Instruments and Court Settlements

r.74.11 **80.13**

The rules governing the registration of judgments under the 1982 Act, the Lugano Convention or the Judgments Regulation apply as appropriate and with any necessary modifications for the enforcement of—
(a) authentic instruments which are subject to—
 (i) article 50 of Schedule 3C to the 1982 Act;
 (ii) article 57 of the Lugano Convention; and
 (iii) article 57 of the Judgments Regulation; and
(b) court settlements which are subject to—
 (i) article 51 of Schedule 1 to the 1982 Act;
 (ii) article 58 of the Lugano Convention; and
 (iii) article 58 of the Judgments Regulation.

II ENFORCEMENT IN FOREIGN COUNTRIES OF JUDGMENTS OF THE HIGH COURT AND COUNTY COURTS

74.12 Application for a Certified Copy of a Judgment

(1) This Section applies to applications—
 (a) to the High Court under section 10 of the 1920 Act;
 (b) to the High Court or to a county court under section 10 of the 1933 Act;
 (c) to the High Court or to a county court under section 12 of the 1982 Act; or
 (d) to the High Court or to a county court under article 54 of the Judgments Regulation or under article 54 of the Lugano Convention.
(2) A judgment creditor who wishes to enforce in a foreign country a judgment obtained in the High Court or in a county court must apply for a certified copy of the judgment.
(3) The application may be made without notice.

74.13 Evidence in Support

(1) The application must be supported by written evidence exhibiting copies of—

(a) the claim form in the proceedings in which judgment was given;
(b) evidence that it was served on the defendant;
(c) the statements of case; and
(d) where relevant, a document showing that for those proceedings the applicant was a person to whom legal aid, as defined in rule 44.1, was provided

(2) The written evidence must—
(a) identify the grounds on which the judgment was obtained;
(b) state whether the defendant objected to the jurisdiction and, if he did, the grounds of his objection;
(c) show that the judgment—
(i) has been served in accordance with Part 6 and rule 40.4, and
(ii) is not subject to a stay of execution;
(d) state—
(i) the date on which the time for appealing expired or will expire;
(ii) whether an appeal notice has been filed;
(iii) the status of any application for permission to appeal; and
(iv) whether an appeal is pending;
(e) state whether the judgment provides for the payment of a sum of money, and if so, the amount in respect of which it remains unsatisfied;
(f) state whether interest is recoverable on the judgment, and if so, either—
(i) the amount of interest which has accrued up to the date of the application, or
(ii) the rate of interest, the date from which it is recoverable, and the date on which it ceases to accrue.

III ENFORCEMENT OF UNITED KINGDOM JUDGMENTS IN OTHER PARTS OF THE UNITED KINGDOM

74.14 Interpretation

r.74.14 **80.12**

In this Section—
(a) 'money provision' means a provision for the payment of one or more sums of money in a judgment whose enforcement is governed by section 18 of, and Schedule 6 to, the 1982 Act; and
(b) 'non-money provision' means a provision for any relief or remedy not requiring payment of a sum of money in a judgment whose enforcement is governed by section 18 of, and Schedule 7 to, the 1982 Act.

74.15 Registration of Money Judgments in the High Court

r.74.15 **80.12**

(1) This rule applies to applications to the High Court under paragraph 5 of Schedule 6 to the 1982 Act for the registration of a certificate for the enforcement of the money provisions of a judgment—
(a) which has been given by a court in another part of the United Kingdom, and
(b) to which section 18 of that Act applies.

(2) The certificate must within six months of the date of its issue be filed in the Central Office of the Senior Courts, together with a copy certified by written evidence to be a true copy.

74.16 Registration of Non-money Judgments in the High Court

r.74.16 **80.12**

(1) This rule applies to applications to the High Court under paragraph 5 of Schedule 7 to the 1982 Act for the registration for enforcement of the non-money provisions of a judgment—
(a) which has been given by a court in another part of the United Kingdom, and
(b) to which section 18 of that Act applies.

(2) An application under paragraph (1) may be made without notice.

(3) An application under paragraph (1) must be accompanied—
(a) by a certified copy of the judgment issued under Schedule 7 to the 1982 Act; and
(b) by a certificate, issued not more than six months before the date of the application, stating that the conditions set out in paragraph 3 of Schedule 7 are satisfied in relation to the judgment.

(4) Rule 74.6 applies to judgments registered under Schedule 7 to the 1982 Act as it applies to judgments registered under section 4 of that Act.
(5) Rule 74.7 applies to applications to set aside the registration of a judgment under paragraph 9 of Schedule 7 to the 1982 Act as it applies to applications to set aside registrations under the 1920 and 1933 Acts.

74.17 Certificates of High Court and County Court Money Judgments

r.74.17 **80.12**

(1) This rule applies to applications under paragraph 2 of Schedule 6 to the 1982 Act for a certificate to enable the money provisions of a judgment of the High Court or of a county court to be enforced in another part of the United Kingdom.
(2) The judgment creditor may apply for a certificate by filing at the court where the judgment was given or has been entered written evidence stating—
   (a) the name and address of the judgment creditor and, if known, of the judgment debtor;
   (b) the sums payable and unsatisfied under the money provisions of the judgment;
   (c) where interest is recoverable on the judgment, either—
      (i) the amount of interest which has accrued up to the date of the application, or
      (ii) the rate of interest, the date from which it is recoverable, and the date on which it ceases to accrue;
   (d) that the judgment is not stayed;
   (e) the date on which the time for appealing expired or will expire;
   (f) whether an appeal notice has been filed;
   (g) the status of any application for permission to appeal; and
   (h) whether an appeal is pending.

74.18 Certified Copies of High Court and County Court Non-money Judgments

r.74.18 **80.12**

(1) This rule applies to applications under paragraph 2 of Schedule 7 to the 1982 Act for a certified copy of a judgment of the High Court or of a county court to which section 18 of the Act applies and which contains non-money provisions for enforcement in another part of the United Kingdom.
(2) An application under paragraph (1) may be made without notice.
(3) The applicant may apply for a certified copy of a judgment by filing at the court where the judgment was given or has been entered written evidence stating—
   (a) full particulars of the judgment;
   (b) the name and address of the judgment creditor and, if known, of the judgment debtor;
   (c) that the judgment is not stayed;
   (d) the date on which the time for appealing expired or will expire;
   (e) whether an appeal notice has been filed;
   (f) the status of any application for permission to appeal; and
   (g) whether an appeal is pending.

IV ENFORCEMENT IN ENGLAND AND WALES OF EUROPEAN COMMUNITY JUDGMENTS

74.19 Interpretation

r.74.19 **80.23**

In this Section—
(a) 'Community judgment' means any judgment, decision or order which is enforceable under—
   (i) article 244 or 256 of the Treaty establishing the European Community;
   (ii) article 18,159 or 164 of the Euratom Treaty;
   (iii) article 44 or 92 of the ECSC Treaty;
   (iv) article 82 of Council Regulation (EC) 40/94 of 20 December 1993 on the Community trade mark; or
   (v) article 71 of Council Regulation (EC) 6/2002 of 12 December 2001 on Community designs;

(b) 'Euratom inspection order' means an order made by the President of the European Court, or a decision of the Commission of the European Communities, under article 81 of the Euratom Treaty;
(c) 'European Court' means the Court of Justice of the European Communities;
(d) 'order for enforcement' means an order under the authority of the Secretary of State that the Community judgment to which it is appended is to be registered for enforcement in the United Kingdom.

74.20 Application for Registration of a Community Judgment

r.74.20 **80.23**

An application to the High Court for the registration of a Community judgment may be made without notice.

74.21 Evidence in Support

r.74.21 **80.23**

(1) An application for registration must be supported by written evidence exhibiting—
(a) the Community judgment and the order for its enforcement, or an authenticated copy; and
(b) where the judgment is not in English, a translation of it into English—
(i) certified by a notary public or other qualified person; or
(ii) accompanied by written evidence confirming that the translation is accurate.
(2) Where the application is for registration of a Community judgment which is a money judgment, the evidence must state—
(a) the name of the judgment creditor and his address for service within the jurisdiction;
(b) the name of the judgment debtor and his address or place of business, if known;
(c) the amount in respect of which the judgment is unsatisfied; and
(d) that the European Court has not suspended enforcement of the judgment.

74.22 Registration Orders

r.74.22 **80.23**

(1) A copy of the order granting permission to register a Community judgment ('the registration order') must be served on every person against whom the judgment was given.
(2) The registration order must state the name and address for service of the person who applied for registration, and must exhibit—
(a) a copy of the registered Community judgment; and
(b) a copy of the order for its enforcement.
(3) In the case of a Community judgment which is a money judgment, the registration order must also state the right of the judgment debtor to apply within 28 days for the variation or cancellation of the registration under rule 74.23.

74.23 Application to Vary or Cancel Registration

(1) An application to vary or cancel the registration of a Community judgment which is a money judgment on the ground that at the date of registration the judgment had been partly or wholly satisfied must be made within 28 days of the date on which the registration order was served on the judgment debtor.
(2) The application must be supported by written evidence.

74.24 Enforcement

No steps may be taken to enforce a Community judgment which is a money judgment—
(a) before the end of the period specified in accordance with rule 74.23(1); or
(b) where an application is made under that rule, until it has been determined.

74.25 Application for Registration of Suspension Order

(1) Where the European Court has made an order that the enforcement of a registered Community judgment should be suspended, an application for the registration of that order in the High Court is made by filing a copy of the order in the Central Office of the Senior Courts.
(2) The application may be made without notice.

74.26 Registration and Enforcement of a Euratom Inspection Order

(1) Rules 74.20, 74.21(1), and 74.22(1) and (2), which apply to the registration of a Community judgment, also apply to the registration of a Euratom inspection order but with the necessary modifications.
(2) An application under article 6 of the European Communities (Enforcement of Community Judgments) Order 1972 to give effect to a Euratom inspection order may be made on written evidence, and—
(a) where the matter is urgent, without notice;
(b) otherwise, by claim form.

V EUROPEAN ENFORCEMENT ORDERS

74.27 Interpretation

r.74.27 **80.24**

In this Section—

(a) 'European Enforcement Order' has the meaning given in the EEO Regulation;
(b) 'EEO' means European Enforcement Order;
(c) 'judgment', 'authentic instrument', 'member state of origin', 'member state of enforcement', and 'court of origin' have the meanings given by Article 4 of the EEO Regulation; and
(d) 'Regulation State' has the same meaning as 'Member State' in the EEO Regulation, that is all Member States except Denmark.

74.28 Certification of Judgments of the Courts of England and Wales

An application for an EEO certificate must be made by filing the relevant practice form in accordance with Article 6 of the EEO Regulation.

74.29 Applications for a Certificate of Lack or Limitation of Enforceability

An application under Article 6(2) of the EEO Regulation for a certificate indicating the lack or limitation of enforceability of an EEO certificate must be made to the court of origin by application in accordance with Part 23.

74.30 Applications for Rectification or Withdrawal

An application under Article 10 of the EEO Regulation for rectification or withdrawal of an EEO certificate must be made to the court of origin and may be made by application in accordance with Part 23.

74.31 Enforcement of European Enforcement Orders in England and Wales

r.74.31 **80.24** r.74.31(2) **80.24**

(1) A person seeking to enforce an EEO in England and Wales must lodge at the court in which enforcement proceedings are to be brought the documents required by Article 20 of the EEO Regulation.
(2) Where a person applies to enforce an EEO expressed in a foreign currency, the application must contain a certificate of the sterling equivalent of the judgment sum at the close of business on the date nearest preceding the date of the application.

(Part 70 contains further rules about enforcement.)

74.32 Refusal of Enforcement

r.74.32 **80.24** r.74.32(3) **80.24**

(1) An application under Article 21 of the EEO Regulation that the court should refuse to enforce an EEO must be made by application in accordance with Part 23 to the court in which the EEO is being enforced.
(2) The judgment debtor must, as soon as practicable, serve copies of any order made under Article 21(1) on—
(a) all other parties to the proceedings and any other person affected by the order ('the affected persons'); and

(b) any court in which enforcement proceedings are pending in England and Wales ('the relevant courts').

(3) Upon service of the order on the affected persons, all enforcement proceedings under the EEO in the relevant courts will cease.

74.33 Stay of or Limitation on Enforcement

r.74.33 **80.24**

(1) Where an EEO certificate has been lodged and the judgment debtor applies to stay or limit the enforcement proceedings under Article 23 of the EEO Regulation, such application must be made in accordance with Part 23 to the court in which the EEO is being enforced.

(2) The judgment debtor shall, as soon as practicable, serve a copy of any order made under the Article on—

(a) all other parties to the proceedings and any other person affected by the order; and

(b) any court in which enforcement proceedings are pending in England and Wales;

and the order will not have effect on any person until it has been served in accordance with this rule and they have received it.

PD 74A Practice Direction 74A — Enforcement of Judgments in Different Jurisdictions

This practice direction supplements CPR, Part 74.

[For commentary on a specific paragraph, please refer to the cross-references after the title of the paragraph.]

1 This practice direction is divided into two sections:
(1) Section I—Provisions about the enforcement of judgments
(2) Section II—The Merchant Shipping (Liner Conferences) Act 1982

I ENFORCEMENT OF JUDGMENTS

Meaning of 'Judgment'

2 In r. 74.2(1)(c), the definition of 'judgment' is 'subject to any other enactment'. Such provisions include:
(1) s. 9(1) of the 1920 Act, which limits enforcement under that Act to judgments of superior courts;
(2) s. 1(1) of the 1933 Act, which limits enforcement under that Act to judgments of those courts specified in the relevant Order in Council;
(3) s. 1(2) of the 1933 Act, which limits enforcement under that Act to money judgments.

Registers

para.3.1 80.19

3 There will be kept in the Central Office of the Senior Courts at the Royal Courts of Justice, under the direction of the Senior Master:
(1) registers of foreign judgments ordered by the High Court to be enforced following applications under:
(a) s. 9 of the 1920 Act;
(b) s. 2 of the 1933 Act;
(c) s. 4 of the 1982 Act;
(d) the Judgments Regulation; or
(e) the Lugano Convention;
(2) registers of certificates issued for the enforcement in foreign countries of High Court judgments under the 1920,1933 and 1982 Acts, and under art. 54 of the Judgments Regulation and art. 54 of the Lugano Convention;
(3) a register of certificates filed in the Central Office of the High Court under r. 74.15(2) for the enforcement of money judgments given by the courts of Scotland or Northern Ireland;
(4) a register of certificates issued under r. 74.16(3) for the enforcement of non-money judgments given by the courts of Scotland or Northern Ireland;
(5) registers of certificates issued under rr. 74.17 and 74.18 for the enforcement of High Court judgments in Scotland or Northern Ireland under sch. 6 or sch. 7 to the 1982 Act; and
(6) a register of Community judgments and Euratom inspection orders ordered to be registered under art. 3 of the European Communities (Enforcement of Community Judgments) Order 1972 (SI 1972/1590).

Making an Application

para.4.1 80.13, 80.23 para.4.4 80.13

4.1 Applications for the registration for enforcement in England and Wales of:
(1) foreign judgments under r. 74.3;
(2) judgments of courts in Scotland or Northern Ireland under r. 74.15 or 74.16; and
(3) European Community judgments under r. 74.20,
are assigned to the Queen's Bench Division and may be heard by a master.

4.2 An application under r. 74.12 for a certified copy of a High Court or county court judgment for enforcement abroad must be made:
  (1) in the case of a judgment given in the Chancery Division or the Queen's Bench Division of the High Court, to a master, registrar or district judge;
  (2) in the case of a judgment given in the Family Division of the High Court, to a district judge of that Division;
  (3) in the case of a county court judgment, to a district judge.

4.3 An application under r. 74.17 or 74.18 for a certificate or a certified copy of a High Court or county court judgment for enforcement in Scotland or Northern Ireland must be made:
  (1) in the case of a judgment given in the Chancery Division or the Queen's Bench Division of the High Court, to a master, registrar or district judge;
  (2) in the case of a judgment given in the Family Division of the High Court, to a district judge of that Division;
  (3) in the case of a county court judgment, to a district judge.

4.4 The following applications must be made under Part 23:
  (1) applications under r. 74.3 for the registration of a judgment;
  (2) applications under r. 74.7 to set aside the registration of a judgment;
  (3) applications under r. 74.12 for a certified copy of a judgment;
  (4) applications under section III for a certificate for enforcement of a judgment;
  (5) applications under r. 74.20 for the registration of a Community judgment;
  (6) applications under r. 74.23 to vary or cancel the registration of a Community judgment; and
  (7) applications under r. 74.25 for the registration of an order of the European Court that the enforcement of a registered Community judgment should be suspended.

Applications under the 1933 Act

5 Foreign judgments are enforceable in England and Wales under the 1933 Act where there is an agreement on the reciprocal enforcement of judgments between the United Kingdom and the country in which the judgment was given. Such an agreement may contain particular provisions governing the enforcement of judgments (for example limiting the categories of judgments which are enforceable, or the courts whose judgments are enforceable). Any such specific limitations will be listed in the Order in Council giving effect in the United Kingdom to the agreement in question, and the rules in Section I of Part 74 will take effect subject to such limitations.

Evidence in Support of an Application under the Judgments Regulation: Rule 74.4(6)

para.6.1–6.5 **80.18**

6.1 Where a judgment is to be recognised or enforced in a Regulation State, the Judgments Regulation applies.

6.2 As a consequence of art. 38(2) of the Judgments Regulation, the provisions in Chapter III of that Regulation relating to declaring judgments enforceable are the equivalent, in the United Kingdom, of provisions relating to registering judgments for enforcement.

6.3 Chapter III of, and Annex V to, the Judgments Regulation are annexed to this practice direction. They were originally published in the official languages of the European Community in the *Official Journal of the European Communities* by the Office for Official Publications of the European Communities.

6.4 Sections 2 and 3 of Chapter III of the Judgments Regulation (in particular articles 40, 53, 54 and 55, and Annex V) set out the evidence needed in support of an application.

6.5 The Judgments Regulation is supplemented by the Civil Jurisdiction and Judgments Order 2001 (SI 2001/3929). The Order also makes amendments, in respect of that Regulation, to the Civil Jurisdiction and Judgments Act 1982.

Evidence in Support of an Application under the Lugano Convention: Rule 74(4)

paras.6A.1–6A.5 **80.18**

6A.1 Where a judgment is to be recognised or enforced in a Contracting State which is a State bound by the Lugano Convention, that Convention applies.

6A.2 As a consequence of art. 38(2) of the Lugano Convention the provisions of Title III of that Convention relating to declaring judgments enforceable are the equivalent, in the United Kingdom, of provisions relating to registering judgments for enforcement.

6A.3 Title III of, and annex V to, the Lugano Convention are annexed to this practice direction. They were originally published in the official languages of the European Community in the *Official Journal of the European Communities* by the Office for Official Publications of the European Communities.

6A.4 Sections 2 and 3 of Title III of the Lugano Convention (in particular articles 40, 53, 54 and annex V) set out the evidence needed in support of an application.

6A.5 The Civil Jurisdiction and Judgments Regulations 2009 (SI 2009/3131) make amendments to the Civil Jurisdiction and Judgments Act 1982 in respect of the Lugano Convention.

Certified Copies of Judgments Issued under Rule 74.12

7.1 In an application by a judgment creditor under r. 74.12 for the enforcement abroad of a High Court judgment, the certified copy of the judgment will be an office copy, and will be accompanied by a certificate signed by a judge. The judgment and certificate will be sealed with the seal of the Senior Courts.

7.2 In an application by a judgment creditor under r. 74.12 for the enforcement abroad of a county court judgment, the certified copy will be a sealed copy, and will be accompanied by a certificate signed by a judge.

7.3 In applications under the 1920,1933 or 1982 Acts, the certificate will be in form No. 110, and will have annexed to it a copy of the claim form by which the proceedings were begun.

7.4 In an application under the Judgments Regulation, the certificate will be in the form of Annex V to the Regulation.

7.5 In an application under the Lugano Convention, the certificate will be in the form of annex V to the Convention.

Certificates under Section III of Part 74

8.1 A certificate of a money judgment of a court in Scotland or Northern Ireland must be filed for enforcement under r. 74.15(2) in the Action Department of the Central Office of the Senior Courts, Royal Courts of Justice, Strand, London WC2A 2LL. The copy will be sealed by a court officer before being returned to the applicant.

8.2 A certificate issued under r. 74.17 for the enforcement in Scotland or Northern Ireland of a money judgment of the High Court or of a county court will be in form No. 111.

8.3 In an application by a judgment creditor under r. 74.18 for the enforcement in Scotland or Northern Ireland of a non-money judgment of the High Court or of a county court, the certified copy of the judgment will be a sealed copy to which will be annexed a certificate in form No. 112.

Material Additional to Section IV of Part 74

9.1 Enforcement of Community judgments and of Euratom inspection orders is governed by the European Communities (Enforcement of Community Judgments) Order 1972 (SI 1972/1590).

9.2 The Treaty establishing the European Community is the Treaty establishing the European Economic Community (Rome, 1957); relevant amendments are made by the Treaty of Amsterdam (1997, Cm 3780).

9.3 The text of the Protocol of 3 June 1971 on the interpretation by the European Court of the Convention of 27 September 1968 on Jurisdiction and the Enforcement of Judgments in Civil and Commercial Matters is set out in the Civil Jurisdiction and Judgments Act 1982, sch. 2.

9.4 The text of the Protocol of 19 December 1988 on the interpretation by the European Court of the Convention of 19 June 1980 on the Law applicable to Contractual Obligations is set out in the Contracts (Applicable Law) Act 1990, sch. 3. After the commencement on 17 December 2009 of EC Regulation 593/2008 ('the Rome I Regulation') this Convention and Protocol will only apply to contracts concluded before that date.

II THE MERCHANT SHIPPING (LINER CONFERENCES) ACT 1982

Content of This Section

10 The Merchant Shipping (Liner Conferences) Act 1982 ('the Act') contains provisions for the settlement of disputes between liner conferences, shipping lines and shippers. This Section of this practice direction deals with the enforcement by the High Court under s. 9 of the Act of recommendations of conciliators, and determinations and awards of costs.

Exercise of Powers under the Act

11 The powers of the High Court under the Act are exercised by the Commercial Court.

Applications for Registration

12.1 An application under s. 9 of the Act for the registration of a recommendation, determination or award is made under Part 23.

12.2 An application for the registration of a recommendation must be supported by written evidence exhibiting:
- (1) a verified or certified or otherwise authenticated copy of:
  - (a) the recommendation;
  - (b) the reasons for it; and
  - (c) the record of settlement;
- (2) where any of those documents is not in English, a translation of it into English:
  - (a) certified by a notary public or other qualified person; or
  - (b) accompanied by written evidence confirming that the translation is accurate; and
  - (3) copies of the acceptance of the recommendation by the parties on whom it is binding, or otherwise verifying the acceptance where it is not in writing.

12.3 The evidence in support of the application must:
- (1) give particulars of the failure to implement the recommendation; and
- (2) confirm that none of the grounds which would render it unenforceable is applicable.

12.4 An application for the registration of a determination of costs or an award of costs must be supported by written evidence:
- (1) exhibiting a verified or certified or otherwise authenticated copy of the recommendation or other document containing the determination or award; and
- (2) stating that the costs have not been paid.

Order for Registration

13.1 The applicant must draw up the order giving permission to register the recommendation, determination or award.

13.2 The order must include a provision that the reasonable costs of the registration should be assessed.

Register of Recommendations

14 There will be kept in the Admiralty and Commercial Registry at the Royal Courts of Justice, under the direction of the Senior Master, a register of the recommendations, determinations and awards ordered to be registered under s. 9 of the Act, with particulars of enforcement.

APPENDIX 1

[Appendix 1 is not printed here, because it consists of extracts from Regulation (EC) No. 44/2001, which is printed in **appendix** 4.]

APPENDIX 2

[Appendix 2 is Title III of, and Annex V to, the Lugano Convention 2007. The Convention was published in [2009] OJEU L147, p. 5, which may be downloaded from the EUR-Lex site: <http://eur-lex.europa.eu>.]

PD 74B Practice Direction 74B — European Enforcement Orders

This practice direction supplements Section V of Part 74.

Council Regulation

1.1 Certification and enforcement of European Enforcement Orders is governed by Council Regulation (EC) No. 805/2004 creating a European Enforcement Order for uncontested claims.

1.2 The EEO Regulation is annexed to this practice direction and can be found at http://europa.eu.int/eur-lex/pri/en/oj/dat/2004/l_143/l_14320040430en00150039.pdf. It was originally published in the official languages of the European Community in the *Official Journal of the European Communities* by the Office for Official Publications of the European Communities.

1.3 Section V of Part 74 sets out the procedure for enforcement under the EEO Regulation. A claim that does not meet the requirements of the EEO Regulation, or which the judgment creditor does not wish to enforce using the EEO Regulation, may be enforceable using another method of enforcement.

Certification of Judgments of the Courts of England and Wales (Rule 74.28)

2.1 An application under r. 74.28 for a certificate of a High Court or county court judgment for enforcement in another Regulation State must be made using form N219 or form N219A:

(1) in the case of a judgment given in the Chancery or Queen's Bench Division of the High Court, or in a district registry, to a master, registrar or district judge; or

(2) in the case of a county court judgment, to a district judge.

2.2 Where the application is granted, the court will send the EEO certificate and a sealed copy of the judgment to the person making the application. Where the court refuses the application, the court will give reasons for the refusal and may give further directions.

Applications for a Certificate of Lack of Enforceability (Rule 74.29)

3.1 An application must be supported by written evidence in support of the grounds on which the judgment has ceased to be enforceable or its enforceability has been suspended or limited.

Application for Rectification or Withdrawal (Rule 74.30)

4.1 An application must be supported by written evidence in support of the grounds on which it is contended that the EEO should be rectified or withdrawn.

Enforcement of European Enforcement Orders in England and Wales (Rule 74.31)

5.1 When an EEO is lodged at the court in which enforcement proceedings are to be brought, it will be assigned a case number.

5.2 A copy of a document will satisfy the conditions necessary to establish its authenticity if it is an official copy of the court.

5.3 If judgment is set aside in the court of origin, the judgment creditor must notify all courts in which enforcement proceedings are pending in England and Wales under the EEO as soon as reasonably practicable after the order is served on the judgment creditor. Notification may be by any means available including fax, email, post or telephone.

An Application for Refusal of Enforcement (Rule 74.32)

6.1 An application must be accompanied by an official copy of the earlier judgment, any other documents relied upon and any translations required by the EEO Regulation and supported by written evidence showing:

(1) why the earlier judgment is irreconcilable with the judgment which the judgment creditor is seeking to enforce; and

(2) why the irreconcilability was not, and could not have been, raised as an objection in the proceedings in the court of origin.

Stay or Limitation of Enforcement (Rule 74.33)

7.1 Unless the court orders otherwise, an application must be accompanied by evidence of the application in the court of origin, including:
(1) the application (or equivalent foreign process) or a copy of the application (or equivalent foreign process) certified by an appropriate officer of the court of origin; and
(2) where that document is not in English, a translation of it into English:
(a) certified by a notary public or person qualified to certify a translation in the member State of the court of origin under art. 20(2)(c) of the EEO Regulation; or
(b) accompanied by written evidence confirming that the translation is accurate.

7.2 The written evidence in support of the application must state:
(1) that an application has been brought in the member State of origin;
(2) the nature of that application; and
(3) the date on which the application was filed, the state of the proceedings and the date by which it is believed that the application will be determined.

ANNEX

[The annex is Regulation (EC) No. 805/2004, which may be downloaded from the EUR-Lex site: <http://eur-lex.europa.eu>.]

[The following are not included in *Blackstone's Civil Practice*:
CPR Part 75 Traffic Enforcement
PD 75 Practice Direction 75 — Traffic Enforcement
CPR Part 76 Proceedings under the Prevention of Terrorism Act 2005
CPR Part 77 Provisions in Support of Criminal Justice
PD 77 Practice Direction 77 — Applications for and Relating to Serious Crime Prevention Orders]

CPR Part 78 European Procedures

Part 78 12.11

78.1 Scope of This Part and Interpretation

(1) Section I contains rules about European orders for payment made under Regulation (EC) No 1896/2006 of the European Parliament and of the Council of 12 December 2006 creating a European order for payment procedure.

(2) Section II contains rules about the European small claims procedure under Regulation (EC) No 861/2007 of the European Parliament and of the Council of 11 July 2007 establishing a European small claims procedure.

(2A) Section III contains rules about mediated cross-border disputes that are subject to Directive 2008/52/EC of the European Parliament and of the Council of 21 May 2008 on certain aspects of mediation in civil and commercial matters.

(3) In this Part—

(a) unless otherwise stated, a reference to an Annex is to an Annex to Practice Direction 78; and

(b) 'Service Regulation' means Regulation (EC) 1393/2007 on service, within the same meaning as rule 6.31 (e).

(4) Except where—

(a) the EOP Regulation (which has the same meaning as in rule 78.2(2)(a));

(b) the ESCP Regulation (which has the same meaning as in rule 78.12(2)(a)); or

(c) the Service Regulation

makes different provisions about the certification or verification of translations, every translation required by this Part or such Regulation must be accompanied by a statement by the person making it that it is a correct translation. The statement must include that person's name, address and qualifications for making the translation.

I EUROPEAN ORDER FOR PAYMENT PROCEDURE

78.2 Scope of This Section and Interpretation

(1) This Section applies to applications for European orders for payment and other related proceedings under Regulation (EC) No 1896/2006 of the European Parliament and of the Council of 12 December 2006 creating a European order for payment procedure.

(2) In this Section—

(a) 'EOP Regulation' means Regulation (EC) No 1896/2006 of the European Parliament and of the Council of 12 December 2006 creating a European order for payment procedure. A copy of the EOP Regulation can be found at Annex 1;

(b) 'court of origin' has the meaning given by article 5(4) of the EOP Regulation;

(c) 'EOP' means a European order for payment;

(d) 'EOP application' means an application for an EOP;

(e) 'EOP application form A' means the Application for a European order for payment form A, annexed to the EOP Regulation at Annex I to that Regulation;

(f) 'European order for payment' means an order for payment made by a court under article 12(1) of the EOP Regulation;

(g) 'Member State' has the meaning given by article 2(3) of the EOP Regulation;

(h) 'Member State of origin' has the meaning given by article 5(1) of the EOP Regulation;

(i) 'statement of opposition' means a statement of opposition filed in accordance with article 16 of the EOP Regulation.

EOP Applications Made to a Court in England and Wales

78.3 Application for a European Order for Payment

Where a declaration provided by the claimant under article 7(3) of the EOP Regulation contains any deliberate false statement, rule 32.14 applies as if the EOP application form A were verified by a statement of truth.

(An EOP application is made in accordance with the EOP Regulation and in particular article 7 of that Regulation.)

78.4 Withdrawal of EOP Application

(1) At any stage before a statement of opposition is filed, the claimant may notify the court that the claimant no longer wishes to proceed with the claim.

(2) Where the claimant notifies the court in accordance with paragraph (1)—

(a) the court will notify the defendant that the application has been withdrawn; and

(b) no order as to costs will be made.

78.5 Transfer of Proceedings Where an EOP Application Has Been Opposed

(1) Where a statement of opposition is filed in accordance with article 16 of the EOP Regulation and the claimant has not opposed the transfer of the matter—

(a) the EOP application will be treated as if it had been started as a claim under Part 7 and the EOP application form A will be treated as a Part 7 claim form including particulars of claim; and

(b) thereafter, these Rules apply with necessary modifications and subject to this rule and rules 78.6 and 78.7.

(2) When the court notifies the claimant in accordance with article 17(3) of the EOP Regulation the court will also—

(a) notify the claimant—

(i) that the EOP application form A is now treated as a Part 7 claim form including particulars of claim; and

(ii) of the time within which the defendant must respond under rule 78.6; and

(b) *notify the defendant*—

(i) that a statement of opposition has been received;

(ii) that the application will not continue under Part 78;

(iii) that the application has been transferred under article 17 of the EOP Regulation;

(iv) that the EOP application form A is now treated as a Part 7 claim form including particulars of claim; and
(v) of the time within which the defendant must respond under rule 78.6.

78.6 Filing of Acknowledgment of Service and Defence Where an EOP Application Is Transferred under Article 17 of the EOP Regulation

(1) The defendant must file a defence within 30 days of the date of the notice issued by the court under rule 78.5(2)(b).
(2) If the defendant wishes to dispute the court's jurisdiction, the defendant must instead—
(a) file an acknowledgment of service within the period specified in paragraph (1); and
(b) make an application under Part 11 within the period specified in that Part.
(3) Where this rule applies, the following rules do not apply—
(a) rule 10.1(3);
(b) rule 10.3; and
(c) rule 15.4(1).

78.7 Default Judgment

(1) If—
(a) the defendant fails to file an acknowledgment of service within the period specified in rule 78.6(2)(a); and
(b) does not within that period—
(i) file a defence in accordance with Part 15 (except rule 15.4(1)) and rule 78.6(1); or
(ii) file an admission in accordance with Part 14,
the claimant may obtain default judgment if Part 12 allows it.
(2) Where this rule applies, rule 10.2 does not apply.

78.8 Review in Exceptional Cases

An application for a review under article 20 of the EOP Regulation must be made in accordance with Part 23.

Enforcement of EOPs in England and Wales

78.9 Enforcement of European Orders for Payment

(1) A person seeking to enforce an EOP in England and Wales must file at the court in which enforcement proceedings are to be brought the documents required by article 21 of the EOP Regulation.
(2) Where a person applies to enforce an EOP expressed in a foreign currency, the application must contain a certificate of the sterling equivalent of the judgment sum at the close of business on the date nearest preceding the date of the application.

(Parts 70 to 74 contain further rules about enforcement.)

78.10 Refusal of Enforcement

(1) An application under article 22 of the EOP Regulation that the court should refuse to enforce an EOP must be made in accordance with Part 23 to the court in which the EOP is being enforced.
(2) The judgment debtor must, as soon as practicable, serve copies of any order made under article 22 on—
(a) all other parties to the proceedings and any other person affected by the order ('the affected persons'); and
(b) any court in which enforcement proceedings of the EOP are pending in England and Wales ('the relevant courts').
(3) Upon service of the order on the affected persons, all enforcement proceedings of the EOP in the relevant courts will cease.

78.11 Stay of or Limitation on Enforcement

(1) Where the defendant has sought a review and also applies for a stay of or limitation on enforcement in accordance with article 23 of the EOP Regulation, such application must be made in accordance with Part 23 to the court in which the EOP is being enforced.

(2) The defendant must, as soon as practicable, serve a copy of any order made under article 23 on—
   (a) all other parties to the proceedings and any other person affected by the order; and
   (b) any court in which enforcement proceedings are pending in England and Wales, and the order will not have effect on any person until it has been served in accordance with this rule and they have received it.

II EUROPEAN SMALL CLAIMS PROCEDURE

78.12 Scope of This Section and Interpretation

(1) This Section applies to the European small claims procedure under Regulation (EC) No 861/2007 of the European Parliament and of the Council of 11 July 2007 establishing a European small claims procedure.
(2) In this Section—
   (a) 'ESCP Regulation' means Regulation (EC) No 861/2007 of the European Parliament and of the Council of 11 July 2007 establishing a European small claims procedure. A copy of the ESCP Regulation can be found at Annex 2;
   (b) 'defendant's response' means the response to the ESCP claim form;
   (c) 'ESCP' means the European small claims procedure established by the ESCP Regulation;
   (d) 'ESCP claim form' means the claim form completed and filed in the ESCP;
   (e) 'ESCP counterclaim' has the meaning given to counterclaim by recital 16 of the ESCP Regulation;
   (f) 'ESCP judgment' means a judgment given in the ESCP;
   (g) 'Member State' has the meaning given by article 2(3) of the ESCP Regulation;
   (h) 'Member State of enforcement' is the Member State in which the ESCP judgment is to be enforced;
   (i) 'Member State of judgment' is the Member State in which the ESCP judgment is given.

ESCP Claims Made in a Court in England and Wales

78.13 Filing an ESCP Claim Form

r.78.13 45.34

Where a declaration provided by the claimant in the ESCP claim form contains any deliberate false statement, rule 32.14 applies as if the ESCP claim form were verified by a statement of truth.

(An ESCP claim form is completed and filed in accordance with the ESCP Regulation, in particular article 4(1), and in accordance with this paragraph.)

78.14 Allocation of ESCP Claims

r.78.14(1) 45.34

(1) ESCP claims are treated as if they were allocated to the small claims track.
(2) Part 27 applies, except rule 27.14.

78.15 Transfer of Proceedings Where the Claim Is Outside the Scope of the ESCP Regulation—Article 4(3) of the ESCP Regulation

(1) Where the court identifies that the claim is outside the scope of the ESCP Regulation, the court will notify the claimant of this in a transfer of proceedings notice.
(2) If the claimant wishes to withdraw the claim, the claimant must notify the court of this within 21 days of the date of the transfer of proceedings notice.
(3) Where the claimant has notified the court in accordance with paragraph (2), the claim is automatically withdrawn.
(4) Where the claimant has not notified the court in accordance with paragraph (2) and the claim is instead to be transferred under article 4(3) of the ESCP Regulation—
   (a) the claim will be treated as if it had been started as a claim under Part 7 and the ESCP claim form will be treated as a Part 7 claim form including particulars of claim; and
   (b) thereafter, these Rules apply with necessary modifications and subject to this rule, and the court will notify the claimant of the transfer and its effect.

78.16 Defendant's Response

Where a declaration provided by the defendant in the defendant's response contains any deliberate false statement, rule 32.14 applies as if the defendant's response were verified by a statement of truth.

(The defendant's response is made in accordance with the ESCP Regulation and in particular article 5(3) of the ESCP Regulation.)

78.17 Transfer of Proceedings Where the Defendant Claims That the Non-monetary Claim Exceeds the Limit Set in Article 2(1) of the ESCP Regulation—Article 5(5) of the ESCP Regulation

(1) This rule applies where, under article 5(5) of the ESCP Regulation, the defendant claims that the value of a non-monetary claim exceeds the limit in article 2(1) of the ESCP Regulation.
(2) When the court dispatches the defendant's response to the claimant, it will—
 (a) notify the claimant that the court is considering whether the claim is outside the scope of the ESCP Regulation in a consideration of transfer notice; and
 (b) send a copy of the notice to the defendant.
(3) If the claimant wishes to withdraw the claim in the event that the court decides that the claim is outside the scope of the ESCP Regulation the claimant must notify the court and the defendant of this within 21 days of the date of the consideration of transfer notice.
(4) The court will notify the defendant as well as the claimant of its decision whether the claim is outside the scope of the ESCP Regulation.

(Article 5(5) of the ESCP Regulation provides that the court shall decide within 30 days of dispatching the defendant's response to the claimant, whether the claim is within the scope of the ESCP Regulation.)

(5) If the court decides that the claim is outside the scope of the ESCP Regulation and the claimant has notified the court and defendant in accordance with paragraph (3), the claim is automatically withdrawn.
(6) If the court decides that the claim is outside the scope of the ESCP Regulation and the claimant has not notified the court and defendant in accordance with paragraph (3)—
 (a) the claim will be treated as if it had been started as a claim under Part 7 and the ESCP claim form will be treated as a Part 7 claim form including particulars of claim;
 (b) the defendant's response will be treated as a defence; and
 (c) thereafter, these Rules apply with necessary modifications and subject to this rule, and the court will notify the parties.
(7) This rule applies to an ESCP counterclaim as if the counterclaim were an ESCP claim.

78.18 Transfer of Proceedings Where the ESCP Counterclaim Exceeds the Limit Set in Article 2(1) of the ESCP Regulation—Article 5(7) of the ESCP Regulation

(1) Where the ESCP counterclaim exceeds the limit set in article 2(1) of the ESCP Regulation, the court will—
 (a) notify the defendant of this in a transfer of proceedings notice; and
 (b) send a copy of the notice to the claimant,

when the court dispatches the defendant's response to the claimant.
(2) If the defendant wishes to withdraw the ESCP counterclaim, the defendant must notify the court and the claimant of this within 21 days of the date of the transfer of proceedings notice.
(3) If the defendant notifies the court and claimant under paragraph (2), the ESCP counterclaim is automatically withdrawn.
(4) If the defendant does not notify the court and claimant in accordance with paragraph (2)—
 (a) the claim will be treated as if it had been started as a claim under Part 7 and the ESCP claim form will be treated as a Part 7 claim form including particulars of claim;
 (b) the defendant's response and ESCP counterclaim are to be treated as the defence and counterclaim; and
 (c) thereafter, these Rules apply with necessary modifications and subject to this rule, and the court will notify the parties.

78.19 Review of Judgment

An application for a review under article 18 of the ESCP Regulation must be made in accordance with Part 23.

Enforcement of ESCP Judgments in England and Wales

78.20 Enforcement of an ESCP Judgment

(1) A person seeking to enforce an ESCP judgment in England and Wales must file at the court in which enforcement proceedings are to be brought the documents required by article 21 of the ESCP Regulation.

(2) Where a person applies to enforce an ESCP judgment expressed in a foreign currency, the application must contain a certificate of the sterling equivalent of the judgment sum at the close of business on the date nearest preceding the date of the application.

(Parts 70 to 74 contain further rules about enforcement.)

78.21 Refusal of Enforcement

(1) An application under article 22 of the ESCP Regulation that the court should refuse to enforce an ESCP judgment must be made in accordance with Part 23 to the court in which the ESCP judgment is being enforced.

(2) The judgment debtor must, as soon as practicable, serve copies of any order made under article 22 on—

(a) all other parties to the proceedings and any other person affected by the order ('the affected persons'); and

(b) any court in which enforcement proceedings are pending in England and Wales ('the relevant courts').

(3) Upon service of the order on the affected persons, all enforcement proceedings of the ESCP judgment in the relevant courts will cease.

78.22 Stay of or Limitation on Enforcement

(1) An application by the defendant under article 23 of the ESCP Regulation must be made in accordance with Part 23 to the court in which the ESCP judgment is being enforced.

(2) The defendant must, as soon as practicable, serve a copy of any order made under article 23 on—

(a) all other parties to the proceedings and any other person affected by the order; and

(b) any court in which enforcement proceedings are pending in England and Wales,

and the order will not have effect on any person until it has been served in accordance with this rule and they have received it.

III MEDIATION DIRECTIVE

78.23 Scope of This Section and Interpretation

r.78.23–78.28 **15.56, 73.14**

(1) This Section applies to mediated cross-border disputes that are subject to Directive 2008/52/EC of the European Parliament and of the Council of 21 May 2008 on certain aspects of mediation in civil and commercial matters.

(2) In this Section—

'Mediation Directive' means Directive 2008/52/EC of the European Parliament and of the Council of 21 May 2008 on certain aspects of mediation in civil and commercial matters. A copy of the Directive can be found at Annex 3;*

'cross-border dispute' has the meaning given by article 2 of the Mediation Directive;

'mediation' has the meaning given by article 3(a) of the Mediation Directive;

'mediation administrator' means a person involved in the administration of the mediation process;

'mediation evidence' means evidence arising out of or in connection with a mediation process;

'mediation settlement' means the content of a written agreement resulting from mediation of a relevant dispute;

[* I.e., annex 3 to PD 78.]

'mediation settlement agreement' means a written agreement resulting from mediation of a relevant dispute;
'mediation settlement enforcement order' means an order made under rule 78.24(5);
'mediator' has the meaning given by article 3(b) of the Mediation Directive; and
'relevant dispute' means a cross-border dispute that is subject to the Mediation Directive.

78.24 Making a Mediation Settlement Enforceable (Mediation Settlement Enforcement Orders)

r.78.24 **15.56, 73.14** r.78.24(1)(b) **13.2**

(1) Where the parties, or one of them with the explicit consent of the others, wish to apply for a mediation settlement to be made enforceable, the parties or party may apply—
  (a) where there are existing proceedings in England and Wales, by an application made in accordance with Part 23; or
  (b) where there are no existing proceedings in England and Wales, by the Part 8 procedure as modified by this rule and Practice Direction 78 — European Procedures.
(2) Where rule 78.24(1)(b) applies, rules 8.3 to 8.8 will not apply.
(3) The mediation settlement agreement must be annexed to the application notice or claim form when it is filed.
(4) Except to the extent that paragraph (7) applies, the parties must file any evidence of explicit consent to the application under paragraph (1) when the parties file the application or claim form.
(5) Subject to paragraph (6), where an application is made under paragraph (1), the court will make an order making the mediation settlement enforceable.
(6) The court will not make an order under paragraph (5) unless the court has evidence that each of the parties to the mediation settlement agreement has given explicit consent to the application for the order.
(7) Where a party to the mediation settlement agreement—
  (a) has agreed in the mediation settlement agreement that a mediation settlement enforcement order should be made in respect of that mediation settlement;
  (b) is a party to the application under paragraph (1); or
  (c) has written to the court consenting to the application for the mediation settlement enforcement order,

that party is deemed to have given explicit consent to the application for the mediation settlement enforcement order.
(8) An application under paragraph (1) will be dealt with without a hearing, unless the court otherwise directs.

78.25 Mediation Settlement Enforcement Orders: Foreign Currency

r.78.25 **15.56, 73.14**

(1) Where a person applies to enforce a mediation settlement enforcement order which is expressed in a foreign currency, the application must contain a certificate of the sterling equivalent of the sum remaining due under the order at the close of business on the day before the date of the application.

(Parts 70 to 74 contain further rules about enforcement.)

78.26 Mediation Evidence: Disclosure or Inspection

r.78.26 **15.56, 50.33, 73.14** r.78.26(3) **50.68**
r.78.26(1) **50.68**

(1) Where a person seeks disclosure or inspection of mediation evidence that is in the control of a mediator or mediation administrator, that person must apply—
  (a) where there are existing proceedings in England and Wales, by an application made in accordance with Part 23; and
  (b) where there are no existing proceedings in England and Wales, by the Part 8 procedure.
(2) Where the application is made—
  (a) under paragraph (1)(a), the mediator or mediation administrator who has control of the mediation evidence must be named as a respondent to the application and must be served with a copy of the application notice; and

(b) under paragraph (1)(b), the mediator or mediation administrator who has control of the mediation evidence must be made a party to the claim.

(3) Evidence in support of the application under paragraph (1)(a) or (1)(b) must include evidence that—

(a) all parties to the mediation agree to the disclosure or inspection of the mediation evidence;

(b) disclosure or inspection of the mediation evidence is necessary for overriding considerations of public policy, in accordance with article 7(1)(a) of the Mediation Directive; or

(c) disclosure or inspection of the mediation settlement is necessary to implement or enforce the mediation settlement agreement.

(4) This rule does not apply to proceedings in England and Wales that have been allocated to the small claims track.

(5) Where this rule applies, Parts 31 to 34 apply to the extent they are consistent with this rule.

78.27 Mediation Evidence: Witnesses and Depositions

r.78.27 15.56, 73.14

(1) This rule applies where a party wishes to obtain mediation evidence from a mediator or mediation administrator by—

(a) a witness summons;

(b) cross-examination with permission of the court under rule 32.7 or 33.4;

(c) an order under rule 34.8 (evidence by deposition);

(d) an order under rule 34.10 (enforcing attendance of witness);

(e) an order under rule 34.11(4) (deponent's evidence to be given orally); or

(f) an order under rule 34.13(1A) (order for the issue of a letter of request).

(2) When applying for a witness summons, permission under rule 32.7 or 33.4 or an order under rule 34.8, 34.10, 34.11(4) or 34.13(1A), the party must provide the court with evidence that—

(a) all parties to the mediation agree to the obtaining of the mediation evidence;

(b) obtaining the mediation evidence is necessary for overriding considerations of public policy, in accordance with article 7(1)(a) of the Mediation Directive; or

(c) the disclosure or inspection of the mediation settlement is necessary to implement or enforce the mediation settlement agreement.

(3) When considering a request for a witness summons, permission under rule 32.7 or 33.4 or an order under rule 34.8, 34.10, 34.11(4) or 34.13(1A), the court may invite any person, whether or not a party, to make representations.

(4) This rule does not apply to proceedings in England and Wales that have been allocated to the small claims track.

(5) Where this rule applies, Parts 31 to 34 apply to the extent they are consistent with this rule.

78.28 Mediation Evidence: Small Claims

r.78.28 15.56, 73.14

Where a party wishes to rely on mediation evidence in proceedings that are allocated to the small claims track, that party must inform the court immediately.

PD 78 Practice Direction 78 — European Procedures

PD 78 12.11

This practice direction supplements CPR, Part 78.

EOP Regulation and Application of the Civil Procedure Rules

para.1.1 12.11

1.1 EOP applications are primarily governed by the EOP Regulation. Where the EOP Regulation is silent, the Civil Procedure Rules apply with necessary modifications.

Rule 78.3 Application for a European Order for Payment

paras.2.1–2.2 12.11

2.1 An EOP application form A must be:
   (1) completed in English or accompanied by a translation into English; and
   (2) filed at court in person or by post.

2.2 An EOP application made to the High Court will be assigned to the Queen's Bench Division, but that will not prevent the application being transferred where appropriate.

Filing Documents at Court Other Than the EOP Application Form A

3 Documents other than the EOP application form A that are filed at or sent to the court in the EOP proceedings, including statements of opposition, may be filed, in addition to by post or in person, by:
   (1) fax; or
   (2) other electronic means where the facilities are available.

Service

para.4 12.11

4 Where the EOP Regulation is silent on service, the Service Regulation and the Civil Procedure Rules apply as appropriate.

Article 9 of the EOP Regulation—Completion or Rectification of the EOP Application Form A

5.1 Article 9 of the EOP Regulation makes provision for the completion or rectification of the EOP application form A within a specified time.

5.2 The time specified for the purposes of art. 9 will normally be within 30 days of the date of the request by the court to complete or rectify the EOP application form A (using form B annexed to the EOP Regulation).

Applications under Part 23

6.1 Where an application is made under Section I of Part 78, there will not normally be an oral hearing.

6.2 Where an oral hearing is to be held, it will normally take place by telephone or videoconference.

Rule 78.9 Enforcement of European Orders for Payment

7.1 When an EOP is filed at the High Court or county court in which enforcement proceedings are to be brought, it will be assigned a case number.

7.2 A copy of a document will satisfy the conditions necessary to establish its authenticity if it is an official copy of the court of origin.

7.3 If judgment is set aside in the court of origin, the judgment creditor must notify all courts in which enforcement proceedings are pending in England and Wales under the EOP as soon as reasonably practicable after the order is served on the judgment creditor. Notification may be by any means available including fax, email, post or telephone.

Rule 78.10 An Application for Refusal of Enforcement

8.1 An application must be accompanied by an official copy of the earlier judgment, any other documents relied upon and any translations required by the EOP Regulation.

8.2 Where the applicant relies on art. 22(1) of the EOP Regulation, the application must be supported by written evidence showing:

(1) why the earlier judgment is irreconcilable with the judgment which the claimant is seeking to enforce; and

(2) why the irreconcilability was not, and could not have been, raised as an objection in the proceedings in the court of origin.

8.3 Where the applicant relies on art. 22(2), the application must be supported by written evidence of the extent to which the defendant has paid the claimant the amount awarded in the EOP.

Rule 78.11 Stay of or Limitation on Enforcement

9.1 Unless the court orders otherwise, an application must be accompanied by evidence of the review application in the court of origin, including:

(1) the review application or a copy of the review application certified by an appropriate officer of the court of origin; and

(2) where that document is not in English, a translation of it into English.

9.2 The written evidence in support of the application must state:

(1) that a review application has been brought in the member State of origin;

(2) the nature of that review application; and

(3) the date on which the review application was filed, the stage the application has reached and the date by which it is believed that the application will be determined.

ESCP Regulation and Application of the Civil Procedure Rules

para.10 45.33

10 Claims under the ESCP are primarily governed by the ESCP Regulation. Where the ESCP Regulation is silent, the Civil Procedure Rules apply with necessary modifications. In particular, Part 52 applies to any appeals.

Rule 78.13 Filing an ESCP Claim Form

11 An ESCP claim form must be filed at court in person or by post.

Article 4(4) of the ESCP Regulation—Inadequate or Insufficient Information

12.2 Article 4(4) of the ESCP Regulation makes provision for:

(1) the completion or rectification of the claim form;

(2) the supply of supplementary information or documents; or

(3) the withdrawal of the claim,

within a specified time.

12.2 The time specified for the purposes of art. 4(4) is within 30 days of the date of the request by the court to complete or rectify the claim form (using Form B annexed to the ESCP Regulation).

Rule 78.14 Allocation of ESCP Claims

13.1 Rule 78.14(1) provides that ESCP claims are treated as if they were allocated to the small claims track. However, r. 78.14(2) disapplies r. 27.14 on costs because recital 29 to the ESCP Regulation contains different provisions on costs.

13.2 Rule 26.6(1) (scope of the small claims track) is also disapplied because art. 2(1) of the ESCP Regulation has a different financial limit.

Filing Documents at Court Other Than the ESCP Claim Form

14 Documents other than the ESCP claim form that are filed at or sent to the court in the ESCP proceedings, including the defendant's response, may be filed, in addition to by post or in person, by:

(1) fax; or

(2) other electronic means where the facilities are available.

Service

para.15 45.33

15 Where the ESCP Regulation is silent on service, the Service Regulation and the Civil Procedure Rules apply as appropriate.

Rule 78.17 Transfer of Proceedings Where the Defendant Claims That the Nonmonetary Claim Exceeds the Limit Set in Article 2(1) of the ESCP Regulation— Article 5(5) of the ESCP Regulation

16.1 Rule 78.17(7) applies to counterclaims as if the counterclaim were an ESCP claim because the second paragraph of art. 5(7) of the ESCP Regulation applies certain provisions about claims inthe ESCP Regulation, including art. 5(5), to ESCP counterclaims.

16.2 Attention is also drawn to the first paragraph of art. 5(7) of the ESCP Regulation (transfer of claim and counterclaim in certain circumstances).

Oral Hearing under Article 8 of the ESCP Regulation

17.1 Attention is drawn to art. 5(1) of the ESCP Regulation, which sets out limitations on when oral hearings may be held.

17.2 Where an oral hearing is to be held, it will normally take place by telephone or videoconference.

Applications under Part 23

18.1 Where an application is made under Section II of Part 78 there will not normally be an oral hearing.

18.2 Where an oral hearing is to be held, it will normally take place by telephone or videoconference.

Rule 78.20 Enforcement of an ESCP Judgment

19.1 When an ESCP judgment is filed at the High Court or county court in which enforcement proceedings are to be brought, it will be assigned a case number.

19.2 A copy of a document will satisfy the conditions necessary to establish its authenticity if it is an official copy of the courts of the member State of judgment.

19.3 If judgment is set aside in the member State of judgment, the judgment creditor must notify all courts in which proceedings are pending in England and Wales to enforce the ESCP judgment as soon as reasonably practicable after the order is served on the judgment creditor. Notification may be by any means available including fax, email, post or telephone.

Rule 78.21 Application for Refusal of Enforcement

20.1 An application must be accompanied by an official copy of the earlier judgment, any other documents relied upon and any translations required by the ESCP Regulation.

20.2 The application must be supported by written evidence showing:

(1) why the earlier judgment is irreconcilable with the judgment which the claimant is seeking to enforce; and

(2) why the irreconcilability was not, and could not have been, raised as an objection in the proceedings in the member State of judgment.

Rule 78.22 Stay of or Limitation on Enforcement—Application Following Application for Review or Where the Judgment Has Been Challenged

21.1 This paragraph applies where a defendant makes an application under art. 23 of the ESCP Regulation in circumstances where:

(1) an application for review has been made under art. 18 ('review application'); or

(2) the defendant has challenged the judgment.

21.2 Unless the court orders otherwise, the application under art. 23 must be accompanied by evidence of the review application or challenge in the member State of judgment. This must include a copy of the document initiating the review application or challenge or a copy of the review application or challenge, certified by an appropriate officer of the court in the member State of judgment.

21.3 Where a document is not in English, it must be accompanied by a translation of it into English.

21.4 The written evidence in support of the application must state:

(1) that a review application or challenge has been brought in the member State of judgment;

(2) the nature of that review application or challenge; and

(3) the date on which the review application or challenge was filed, the state of the proceedings and the date by which it is believed that the application or challenge will be determined.

Rule 78.24 Making a Mediation Settlement Enforceable (Mediation Settlement Enforcement Orders)

para.22.2 **13.2, 13.7**

22.1 Where an application for a mediation settlement enforcement order is made under r. 78.24(1)(a) in accordance with Part 23, a copy of the application notice, mediation settlement agreement and evidence of explicit consent must be served on all parties to the mediation settlement agreement who are not also parties to the application.

22.2 Where an application for a mediation settlement enforcement order is made under r. 78.24(1)(b) by the Part 8 procedure—

(1) the claim form may be issued without naming a defendant; and

(2) a copy of the claim form, mediation settlement agreement and evidence of explicit consent must be served on all parties to the mediation settlement agreement who are not also parties to the application.

22.3 No document relating to an application for a mediation settlement enforcement order may be inspected by a person who is not a party to the proceedings under rule 5.4C without the permission of the court.

22.4 Where the application is supported by evidence of explicit consent to the application by a party to the mediation settlement agreement, the evidence must be in English or accompanied by a translation into English.

22.5 Where a party to the mediation settlement agreement writes to the court consenting to the making of the mediation settlement enforcement order, the correspondence must be in English or accompanied by a translation into English.

22.6 Where the parties to pending proceedings agree to apply for a mediation settlement enforcement order, they must inform the court immediately.

ANNEX 1

The EOP Regulation

[Regulation (EC) No. 1896/2006 (the EOP Regulation) may be downloaded from the EUR-Lex site: <http://eur-lex.europa.eu>.]

ANNEX 2

The ESCP Regulation

[Regulation (EC) No. 861/2007 (the ESCP Regulation) may be downloaded from the EUR-Lex site: <http://eur-lex.europa.eu>.]

ANNEX 3

The Mediation Directive

[Directive 2008/52/EC (the Mediation Directive) may be downloaded from the EUR-Lex site: <http://eur-lex.europa.eu>.]

[The following are not included in *Blackstone's Civil Practice:*

CPR Part 79 Proceedings under the Counter-Terrorism Act 2008

CPR Part 80 Proceedings under the Terrorism Prevention and Investigation Measures Act 2011]

CPR Part 81 Applications and Proceedings in relation to Contempt of Court

I SCOPE AND INTERPRETATION

Part 81 79.1, 81.1, 81.9, 81.26, 81.29

81.1 Scope

r.81.1 81.16

(1) This Part sets out the procedure in respect of—
 (a) contempt of court; and
 (b) the penal, contempt and disciplinary provisions of the County Courts Act 1984.

(2) So far as applicable, and with the necessary modifications, this Part applies in relation to an order requiring a person—
  (a) guilty of contempt of court; or
  (b) punishable by virtue of any enactment as if that person had been guilty of contempt of the High Court,

  to pay a fine or to give security for good behaviour, as it applies in relation to an order of committal.

(3) Unless otherwise stated, this Part applies to procedure in the Court of Appeal, the High Court and county courts.

81.2 Saving for Other Powers

r.81.1(2) **81.18** r.81.1(3) **81.26**

(1) This Part is concerned only with procedure and does not itself confer upon the court the power to make an order for—
  (a) committal;
  (b) sequestration; or
  (c) the imposition of a fine in respect of contempt of court.

(2) Nothing in this Part affects the power of the court to make an order requiring a person—
  (a) guilty of contempt of court; or
  (b) punishable by virtue of any enactment as if that person had been guilty of contempt of the High Court,

  to pay a fine or to give security for good behaviour.

(3) Nothing in this Part affects any statutory or inherent power of the court to make a committal order of its own initiative against a person guilty of contempt of court.

81.3 Interpretation

In this Part—

'applicant' means a person making—
  (i) an application for permission to make a committal application;
  (ii) a committal application; or
  (iii) an application for a writ of sequestration;

'committal application' means any application for an order committing a person to prison;

'respondent' means a person—
  (i) against whom a committal application is made or is intended to be made; or
  (ii) against whose property it is sought to issue a writ of sequestration; and

'undertaking' means an undertaking to the court.

II COMMITTAL FOR BREACH OF A JUDGMENT, ORDER OR UNDERTAKING TO DO OR ABSTAIN FROM DOING AN ACT

Section 2 **88.11, 81.25, 81.28**

81.4 Enforcement of Judgment, Order or Undertaking to Do or Abstain from Doing an Act

r.81.4 **15.41, 37.63, 63.10, 81.28**
r.81.4(1) **81.4**
r.81.4(2) **81.4**
r.81.4(3) **81.4**
r.81.4(4) **81.25**
r.81.4(5)(a) **81.4**
r.81.4(5)(b) **81.4**
r.81.4(5)(c) **81.4**

(1) If a person—
  (a) required by a judgment or order to do an act does not do it within the time fixed by the judgment or order; or
  (b) disobeys a judgment or order not to do an act,

  then, subject to the Debtors Acts 1869 and 1878 and to the provisions of these Rules,the judgment or order may be enforced by an order for committal.

(2) If the time fixed by the judgment or order for doing an act has been varied by a subsequent order or agreement of the parties under rule 2.11, then references in paragraph (1)(a) to the time fixed are references to the time fixed by that subsequent order or agreement.

(3) If the person referred to in paragraph (1) is a company or other corporation, the committal order may be made against any director or other officer of that company or corporation.

(4) So far as applicable, and with the necessary modifications, this Section applies to undertakings given by a party as it applies to judgments or orders.

(Rules 81.17(3) and (4) make provision for cases in which both this Section and Section 6 (Committal for making a false statement of truth or disclosure statement) may be relevant.)

(5) If a judgment or order requires a person to deliver goods or pay their value—
(a) the judgment or order may not be enforced by a committal order under paragraph (1);
(b) the person entitled to enforce the judgment or order may apply to the court for an order requiring that the goods be delivered within a specified time; and
(c) where the court grants such an order, that order may be enforced under paragraph (1).

81.5 Requirement for Service of a Copy of the Judgment or Order and Time for Service

r.81.5 81.25, 81.28
r.81.5(1) 81.5
r.81.5(1)(a) 81.5
r.81.5(1)(b) 81.5
r.81.5(1)(c) 81.5
r.81.5(2) 81.5

(1) Unless the court dispenses with service under rule 81.8, a judgment or order may not be enforced under rule 81.4 unless a copy of it has been served on the person required to do or not do the act in question, and in the case of a judgment or order requiring a person to do an act—
(a) the copy has been served before the end of the time fixed for doing the act, together with a copy of any order fixing that time;
(b) where the time for doing the act has been varied by a subsequent order or agreement under rule 2.11, a copy of that subsequent order or agreement has also been served; and
(c) where the judgment or order was made under rule 81.4(5), or was made pursuant to an earlier judgment or order requiring the act to be done, a copy of the earlier judgment or order has also been served.

(2) Where the person referred to in paragraph (1) is a company or other corporation, a copy of the judgment or order must also be served on the respondent before the end of the time fixed for doing the act.

(3) Copies of the judgment or order and any orders or agreements fixing or varying the time for doing an act must be served in accordance with rule 81.6 or 81.7, or in accordance with an order for alternative service made under rule 81.8(2)(b).

81.6 Method of Service — Copies of Judgments or Orders

r. 81.6 81.5, 81.25, 81.28

Subject to rules 81.7 and 81.8, copies of judgments or orders and any orders or agreements fixing or varying the time for doing an act must be served personally.

81.7 Method of Service —Copies of Undertakings

r.81.7 63.10, 81.28
r.81.7(1) 81.25
r.81.7(2) 81.25
r.81.7(3) 81.25

(1) Subject to paragraph (2) and rule 81.8, a copy of any document recording an undertaking will be delivered by the court to the person who gave the undertaking—
(a) by handing to that person a copy of the document before that person leaves the court building;
(b) by posting a copy to that person at the residence or place of business of that person where this is known; or
(c) by posting a copy to that person's solicitor.

(2) If delivery cannot be effected in accordance with paragraph (1), the court officer will deliver a copy of the document to the party for whose benefit the undertaking was given and that party must serve it personally on the person who gave the undertaking as soon as practicable.

(3) Where the person referred to in paragraph (1) is a company or other corporation, a copy of the judgment or order must also be served on the respondent.

81.8 Dispensation with Personal Service

r.81.8 81.28
r.81.8(1) 81.5
r.81.8(2)(a) 81.5, 81.6
r.81.8(2)(b) 81.5

(1) In the case of a judgment or order requiring a person not to do an act, the court may dispense with service of a copy of the judgment or order in accordance with rules 81.5 to 81.7 if it is satisfied that the person has had notice of it—
(a) by being present when the judgment or order was given or made; or
(b) by being notified of its terms by telephone, email or otherwise.
(2) In the case of any judgment or order the court may—
(a) dispense with service under rules 81.5 to 81.7 if the court thinks it just to do so; or
(b) make an order in respect of service by an alternative method or at an alternative place.

81.9 Requirement for a Penal Notice on Judgments and Orders

r.81.9 **63.10, 81.6, 81.28**
r.81.9(1) **37.63, 81.6**
r.81.9(2) **63.10**

(1) Subject to paragraph (2), a judgment or order to do or not do an act may not be enforced under rule 81.4 unless there is prominently displayed, on the front of the copy of the judgment or order served in accordance with this Section, a warning to the person required to do or not do the act in question that disobedience to the order would be a contempt of court punishable by imprisonment, a fine or sequestration of assets.
(2) An undertaking to do or not do an act which is contained in a judgment or order may be enforced under rule 81.4 notwithstanding that the judgment or order does not contain the warning described in paragraph (1).
(Paragraphs 2.1 to 2.4 of the Practice Direction supplementing this Part and form N117 contain provisions about penal notices and warnings in relation to undertakings.)

81.10 How to Make the Committal Application

r.81.10 **52.7, 81.16**
r.81.10(1) **81.9**
r.81.10(3) **81.29**
r.81.10(3)(a) **81.9**
r.81.10(3)(b) **81.9**
r.81.10(4) **81.11, 81.29**
r.81.10(5) **81.29**
r.81.10(5)(a) **81.11**
r.81.10(5)(b) **81.11**

(1) A committal application is made by an application notice under Part 23 in the proceedings in which the judgment or order was made or the undertaking was given.
(2) Where the committal application is made against a person who is not an existing party to the proceedings, it is made against that person by an application notice under Part 23.
(3) The application notice must—
(a) set out in full the grounds on which the committal application is made and must identify, separately and numerically, each alleged act of contempt including, if known, the date of each of the alleged acts; and
(b) be supported by one or more affidavits containing all the evidence relied upon.
(4) Subject to paragraph (5), the application notice and the evidence in support must be served personally on the respondent.
(5) The court may—
(a) dispense with service under paragraph (4) if it considers it just to do so; or
(b) make an order in respect of service by an alternative method or at an alternative place.

81.11 Committal for Breach of a Solicitor's Undertaking

r.81.11 **52.7**
r.81.11(1) **81.25**
r.81.11(2) **81.25**
r.81.11(3) **81.25**
r.81.11(4) **81.25**
r.81.11(5) **81.25**
r.81.11(6) **81.25**

(1) The applicant must obtain permission from the court before making a committal application under this rule.
(2) The application for permission must be made by filing an application notice under Part 23.
(3) The application for permission must be supported by an affidavit setting out—
(a) the name, description and address of the respondent; and
(b) the grounds on which the committal order is sought.
(4) The application for permission may be made without notice.
(5) Rules 23.9 and 23.10 do not apply.

(6) Unless the applicant makes the committal application within 14 days after permissionhas been granted under this rule, the permission will lapse.

III COMMITTAL FOR INTERFERENCE WITH THE DUE ADMINISTRATION OF JUSTICE

81.12 Scope

(1) This Section regulates committal applications in relation to interference withthe due administration of justice in connection with proceedings—
 (a) in the High Court;
 (b) in a Divisional Court;
 (c) in the Court of Appeal;
 (d) in an inferior court (which includes a county court); or
 (e) which are criminal proceedings,
 except where the contempt is committed in the face of the court or consists of disobedience to an order of the court or a breach of an undertaking to the court.
(2) This Section also regulates committal applications otherwise than in connection with any proceedings.
(3) A committal application under this Section may not be made without the permission of the court.
(The procedure for applying for permission to make a committal application is set out in rule 81.14.)
(Rules 81.17(5) and (6) make provision for cases in which both this Section and Section 6 (Committal for making a false statement of truth or disclosure statement) may be relevant.)

81.13 Court to which Application for Permission under this Section is to be Made

(1) Where contempt of court is committed in connection with any proceedings—
 (a) in the High Court (other than proceedings in a Divisional Court), the application for permission may be made only to a single judge of the Division of the High Court in which the proceedings were commenced or to which they have subsequently been transferred;
 (b) in a Divisional Court, the application for permission may be made only to a single judge of the Queen's Bench Division;
 (c) in the Court of Appeal, the application for permission may be made only to a Divisional Court of the Queen's Bench Division;
 (d) in an inferior court, the application for permission may be made only to a single judge of the Queen's Bench Division; and
 (e) which are criminal proceedings, the application for permission may be made only to a Divisional Court of the Queen's Bench Division.
(2) Where contempt of court is committed otherwise than in connection with any proceedings, the application for permission may be made only to the Administrative Court.

81.14 Application for Permission (High Court, Divisional Court or Administrative Court)

r.81.14 52.7 r.81.14(2) 15.11

(1) The application for permission to make a committal application must bemade by a Part 8 claim form which must include or be accompanied by—
 (a) a detailed statement of the applicant's grounds for bringing the committal application; and
 (b) an affidavit setting out the facts and exhibiting all documents relied upon.
(2) The claim form and the documents referred to in paragraph (1) must be served personally on the respondent unless the court otherwise directs.
(3) Within 14 days of service on the respondent of the claim form, the respondent—
 (a) must file and serve an acknowledgment of service; and
 (b) may file and serve evidence.
(4) The court will consider the application for permission at an oral hearing, unless it considers that such a hearing is not appropriate.
(5) If the respondent intends to appear at the permission hearing referred to in paragraph (4), the respondent must give seven days' notice in writing of such intention to the court and any other party and at the same time provide a written summary of the submissions which the respondent proposes to make.
(6) Where permission to proceed is given, the court may give such directions as it thinks fit, and may—
 (a) transfer the proceedings to another court; or
 (b) direct that the application be listed for hearing before a single judge or a Divisional Court.

IV (1) CERTIFICATIONS BY ANY COURT, TRIBUNAL ETC. TO THE HIGH COURT UNDER ANY ENACTMENT; AND (2) APPLICATIONS TO THE HIGH COURT UNDER SECTION 336 OF THE CHARITIES ACT 2011

81.15 Certifications of Conduct, and Applications under Section 336 of the Charities Act 2011, to the High Court under this Section

r.81.15 81.32

(1) This Section applies where, by virtue of any enactment, the High Court has power to punish or take steps for the punishment of any person charged with having done oromitted to do anything in relation to a court, tribunal or person which, if it had been an actor omission in relation to the High Court, would have been a contempt of that court.
(2) Subject to paragraph (3), an order under this Section may be made by a single judge of the Administrative Court.
(3) An order made on an application under section 336 of the Charities Act 2011 ('a section 336 application') may be made only by a single judge of the Chancery Division.
(4) The certification or section 336 application, as appropriate, must be in the for mannexed to Practice Direction 81 at Annex A, and include or be accompanied by—
 (a) a detailed statement of the grounds for the certification or section 336 application;
 (b) any written evidence relied upon; and
 (c) any other documents required for the disposal of the certification or section 336 application.
(5) Subject to paragraph (6), the certification or section 336 application, accompanied by the other documents referred to in paragraph (4), must be served personally on the respondent.
(6) The court may—
 (a) dispense with service under paragraph (5) if it thinks it just to do so; or
 (b) make an order in respect of service by an alternative method or at an alternative place.
(7) Within 14 days of service on the respondent of the certification or section 336 application, the respondent—
 (a) must file and serve an acknowledgment of service in the form annexed to Practice Direction 81 at Annex B; and
 (b) may file and serve evidence.

V CONTEMPT IN THE FACE OF THE COURT

81.16 Committal for Contempt in the Face of the Court

(1) Where—
 (a) contempt has occurred in the face of the court; and
 (b) that court has power to commit for contempt,
 the court may deal with the matter of its own initiative and give such directions as it thinks fit for the disposal of the matter.

VI COMMITTAL FOR MAKING A FALSE STATEMENT OF TRUTH (RULE 32.14) OR DISCLOSURE STATEMENT (RULE 31.23)

81.17 Scope and Interaction with Other Sections of this Part

r.81.17 50.22, 51.10, 52.8

(1) This Section contains rules about committal applications in relation to making, or causing to be made—
 (a) a false statement in a document verified by a statement of truth; or
 (b) a false disclosure statement,
 without an honest belief in its truth.
(2) Where the committal application relates only to a false statement of truth or disclosure statement, this Section applies.
(3) Where the committal application relates to both—
 (a) a false statement of truth or disclosure statement; and
 (b) breach of a judgment, order or undertaking to do or abstain from doing an act,

Section 2 (Committal for breach of a judgment, order or undertaking to do or abstain from doing an act) applies, but subject to paragraph (4).

(4) To the extent that a committal application referred to in paragraph (3) relates to a false statement of truth or disclosure statement—
(a) the applicant must obtain the permission of the court in accordance with rule 81.18; or
(b) the court may direct that the matter be referred to the Attorney General with a request that the Attorney General consider whether to bring proceedings for contempt of court.

(5) Where the committal application relates to both—
(a) a false statement of truth or disclosure statement; and
(b) other interference with the due administration of justice,
Section 3 (Committal for interference with the due administration of justice) applies, but subject to paragraph (6).

(6) To the extent that a committal application referred to in paragraph (5) relates to a false statement of truth or disclosure statement, the court may direct that the matter be referred to the Attorney General with a request that the Attorney General consider whether to bring proceedings for contempt of court.

81.18 Committal Application in relation to a False Statement of Truth or Disclosure Statement

r.81.18 23.15, 50.22, 51.10, 52.8

(1) A committal application in relation to a false statement of truth or disclosure statement in connection with proceedings in the High Court, a Divisional Court or the Court of Appeal, may be made only—
(a) with the permission of the court dealing with the proceedings in which the false statement or disclosure statement was made; or
(b) by the Attorney General.

(2) Where permission is required under paragraph (1)(a), rule 81.14 applies as if the reference in that rule to a Part 8 claim form were a reference to a Part 23 application notice and the references to the claim form were references to the Part 23 application notice.

(3) A committal application in relation to a false statement of truth or disclosure statement in connection with proceedings in a county court may be made only—
(a) with the permission of a single judge of the Queen's Bench Division; or
(b) by the Attorney General.

(4) Where permission is required under paragraph (3)(a) rule 81.14 applies without the modifications referred to in paragraph (2).

(Under rule 81.14(6)(b), the court granting permission may direct that the application be listed for hearing before a single judge or a Divisional Court.)

(5) The court may direct that the matter be referred to the Attorney General with a request that the Attorney General consider whether to bring proceedings for contempt of court.

(6) Where the committal application is made by the Attorney General, the application may be made to a single judge or a Divisional Court of the Queen's Bench Division.

VII WRIT OF SEQUESTRATION TO ENFORCE A JUDGMENT, ORDER OR UNDERTAKING

section 7 81.28

81.19 Scope

r.81.19 81.27

This Section contains rules about applications to the High Court for a writ of sequestration to enforce a judgment, order or undertaking.

81.20 Writ of Sequestration to Enforce a Judgment, Order or Undertaking

r.81.20 81.28 r.81.20(1) 81.29

(1) If—
(a) a person required by a judgment or order to do an act does not do it within the time fixed by the judgment or order; or
(b) a person disobeys a judgment or order not to do an act,

then, subject to the provisions of these Rules and if the court permits, the judgment or order may be enforced by a writ of sequestration against the property of that person.

(2) If the time fixed by the judgment or order for doing an act has been varied by a subsequent order or agreement of the parties under rule 2.11, references in paragraph (1)(a) to the time fixed are references to the time fixed by that subsequent order or agreement.

(3) If the person referred to in paragraph (1) is a company or other corporation, the writ of sequestration may in addition be issued against the property of any director or other officer of that company or corporation.

(4) So far as applicable, and with the necessary modifications, this Section applies to undertakings given by a party as it applies to judgments or orders.

81.21 Requirement for Service of a Copy of the Judgment or Order and Time for Service

r.81.21 **81.28**

(1) Unless the court dispenses with service under rule 81.24, a judgment or order may not be enforced by writ of sequestration unless a copy of it has been served on the person required to do or not do the act in question, and in the case of a judgment or orderrequiring a person to do an act—

(a) the copy has been served before the end of the time fixed for doing the act, together with a copy of any order fixing that time;

(b) where the time for doing the act has been varied by a subsequent order or agreement under rule 2.11, a copy of that subsequent order or agreement has also been served; and

(c) where the judgment or order was made under rule 81.4(5), or was made pursuant to an earlier judgment or order requiring the act to be done, a copy of the earlier judgment or order has also been served.

(2) Where the person referred to in paragraph (1) is a company or other corporation, a copy of the judgment or order must also be served on the respondent before the end of the time fixed for doing the act.

(3) Copies of the judgment or order and any orders or agreements fixing or varying the time for doing an act must be served in accordance with rule 81.22 or 81.23, or in accordance with an order for alternative service made under rule 81.24(2)(b).

81.22 Method of Service — Copies of Judgments or Orders

r.81.22 **81.28**

Subject to rules 81.23 and 81.24, copies of judgments or orders and any orders or agreements fixing or varying the time for doing an act must be served personally.

81.23 Method of Service —Copies of Undertakings

r.81.23 **81.28**

(1) Subject to paragraph (2) and rule 81.24, a copy of any document recording an undertaking will be delivered by the court to the person who gave the undertaking—

(a) by handing to that person a copy of the document before that person leaves the court building;

(b) by posting a copy to that person at the residence or place of business of that person where this is known; or

(c) by posting a copy to that person's solicitor.

(2) If delivery cannot be effected in accordance with paragraph (1), the court officer will deliver a copy of the document to the party for whose benefit the undertaking was given and that party must serve it personally on the person who gave the undertaking as soon as practicable.

(3) Where the person referred to in paragraph (1) is a company or other corporation, a copy of the judgment or order must also be served on the respondent.

81.24 Dispensation with Personal Service

r.81.24 **81.28**

(1) In the case of a judgment or order requiring a person not to do an act, the court may dispense with service of a copy of the judgment or order in accordance with rules 81.21 to 81.23 if it is satisfied that the person has had notice of it—

(a) by being present when the judgment or order was given or made; or

(b) by being notified of its terms by telephone, email or otherwise.

(2) In the case of any judgment or order the court may—
(a) dispense with service under rules 81.21 to 81.23 if the court thinks it just to do so; or
(b) make an order in respect of service by an alternative method or at an alternative place.

81.25 Requirement for a Penal Notice on Judgments and Orders

r.81.25 **81.28**

(1) Subject to paragraph (2), a judgment or order to do or not do an act may not be enforced by a writ of sequestration unless there is prominently displayed, on the front of the copy of the judgment or order served in accordance with this Section, a warning to the person required to do or not do the act in question that disobedience to the order would be a contempt of court punishable by imprisonment, a fine or sequestration of assets.
(2) An undertaking to do or not do an act which is contained in a judgment or order may be enforced by a writ of sequestration notwithstanding that the judgment or order does not contain the warning described in paragraph (1).

(Paragraphs 2.1 to 2.4 of the Practice Direction supplementing this Part and form N117 contain provisions about penal notices and warnings in relation to undertakings.)

81.26 How to Make an Application for Permission to Issue a Writ of Sequestration

r.81.26 **52.7**
r.81.26(1) **81.27**
r.81.26(1)(a) **81.27**
r.81.26(2) **81.29**
r.81.26(3) **81.29**
r.81.26(4) **81.29**
r.81.26(5) **81.29**

(1) An application for permission to issue a writ of sequestration must be made—
(a) to a single judge of the Division of the High Court in which the proceedings were commenced or to which they have subsequently been transferred; or
(b) in any other case, to a single judge of the Queen's Bench Division.
(2) An application for permission to issue a writ of sequestration must be made by filing an application notice under Part 23.
(3) The application notice must—
(a) set out in full the grounds on which the application is made and must identify, separately and numerically, each alleged act of contempt including, if known, the date of each of the alleged acts; and
(b) be supported by one or more affidavits containing all the evidence relied upon.
(4) Subject to paragraph (5), the application notice must be served personally on the respondent.
(5) The court may—
(a) dispense with service under paragraph (4) if the court thinks it just to do so; or
(b) make an order in respect of service by an alternative method or at an alternative place.

81.27 Form of Writ of Sequestration

r.81.27 **81.27**

A writ of sequestration must be in Form No 67 as set out in Practice Direction 4.

VIII GENERAL RULES ABOUT COMMITTAL APPLICATIONS, ORDERS FOR COMMITTAL AND WRITS OF SEQUESTRATION

section 8 **88.11**

81.28 The Hearing

r.81.28(1) ***81.16***
r.81.28(2)(a) **81.16**
r.81.28(2)(b) **81.16**
r.81.28(3) **81.16**
r.81.28(4) **81.16**
r.81.28(5) **81.17**
r.81.28(6) **81.17**

(1) Unless the court hearing the committal application or application fo: sequestration otherwise permits, the applicant may not rely on—
(a) any grounds other than—
(i) those set out in the claim form or application notice; or

(ii) in relation to a committal application under Section 3 or 4, the statement of grounds required by rule 81.14(1)(a) (where not included in the claim form) or 81.15(4)(a); or

(b) any evidence unless it has been served in accordance with the relevant Section of this Part or the Practice Direction supplementing this Part.

(2) At the hearing, the respondent is entitled—

(a) to give oral evidence, whether or not the respondent has filed or served written evidence, and, if doing so, may be cross-examined; and

(b) with the permission of the court, to call a witness to give oral evidence whether or not the witness has made an affidavit or witness statement.

(3) The court may require or permit any party or other person (other than the respondent) to give oral evidence at the hearing.

(4) The court may give directions requiring the attendance for cross-examination of a witness who has given written evidence.

(5) If the court hearing an application in private decides to make a committal order against the respondent, it will in public state—

(a) the name of the respondent;

(b) in general terms, the nature of the contempt of court in respect of which the committal order is being made; and

(c) the length of the period of the committal order.

(Rule 39.2 contains provisions about hearings in private.)

(6) Where a committal order is made in the absence of the respondent, the court may onits own initiative fix a date and time when the respondent is to be brought before the court.

81.29 Power to Suspend Execution of a Committal Order

r.81.29(1) **81.20**
r.81.29(2) **81.20**

(1) The court making the committal order may also order that its execution will be suspended for such period or on such terms or conditions as it may specify.

(2) Unless the court otherwise directs, the applicant must serve on the respondent a copy of any order made under paragraph (1).

81.30 Warrant of Committal

r.81.30 **81.17**
r.81.30(2)(a) **81.17**
r.81.30(2)(b) **81.17**
r.81.30(3) **81.17**

(1) If a committal order is made, the order will be for the issue of a warrant of committal.

(2) Unless the court orders otherwise—

(a) a copy of the committal order must be served on the respondent either before or at the time of the execution of the warrant of committal; or

(b) where the warrant of committal has been signed by the judge, the committal order may be served on the respondent at any time within 36 hours after the execution of the warrant.

(3) Without further order of the court, a warrant of committal must not be enforced more than 2 years after the date on which the warrant is issued.

81.31 Discharge of a Person in Custody

r.81.31 **81.22**
r.81.31(2) **81.22**
r.81.31(3) **81.22**
r.81.31(4) **81.22**
r.81.31(5) **81.22**

(1) A person committed to prison for contempt of court may apply to the court to be discharged.

(2) The application must—

(a) be in writing and attested by the governor of the prison (or any other officer of the prison not below the rank of principal officer);

(b) show that the person committed to prison for contempt has purged, or wishes to purge, the contempt; and

(c) be served on the person (if any) at whose instance the warrant of committal was issued at least *one day before the* application is made.

(3) Paragraph (2) does not apply to—

(a) a warrant of committal to which CCR Order 27 rule 8, or CCR Order 28 rule 4 or 14 relates; or

(b) an application made by the Official Solicitor acting with official authority for the discharge of a person in custody.

(4) If the committal order is made in a county court and—
(a) does not direct that any application for discharge must be made to a judge; or
(b) was made by a district judge under section 118 of the County Courts Act 1984,
the application for discharge may be made to a district judge.

(5) If the committal order is made in the High Court, the application for discharge may be made to a single judge of the Division in which the committal order was made.

81.32 Discharge of a Person in Custody where a Writ of Sequestration has been Issued

r.81.32 81.22

(1) Where—
(a) a writ of sequestration has been issued to enforce a judgment or order;
(b) the property is in the custody or power of the respondent;
(c) the respondent has been committed for failing to deliver up any property or depositit in court or elsewhere; and
(d) the commissioners appointed by the writ of sequestration take possession of the property as if it belonged to the respondent,
then, without prejudice to rule 81.31(1), the court may discharge the respondent and give such directions for dealing with the property taken by the commissioners as it thinks fit.

IX PENAL, CONTEMPT AND DISCIPLINARY PROVISIONS UNDER THE COUNTY COURTS ACT 1984

81.33 Scope

(1) This Section applies to county courts only and contains rules in relation to the penal, contempt and disciplinary provisions of the County Courts Act 1984.

(2) In this Section, 'the Act' means the County Courts Act 1984.

81.34 Offences under Sections 14, 92 or 118 of the Act

r.81.34 12.1

(1) This rule applies where it is alleged that any person has committed anoffence–
(a) under section 14 of the Act, by assaulting an officer of the court acting in the execution of the officer's duties;
(b) under section 92 of the Act, by rescuing or attempting to rescue any goods seized in execution; or
(c) under section 118 of the Act, by wilfully insulting a judge, juror, witness or any officer of the court or by wilfully interrupting the proceedings of a county court orotherwise misbehaving in court,
and the alleged offender has not been taken into custody and brought before the court.

(2) The court will issue a summons, which must be served on the alleged offender personally not less than 7 days before the day of the hearing stated in the summons.

(3) Rule 81.30 applies, with the necessary modifications, where an order is made under section 14, 92 or 118 of the Act committing a person to prison.

81.35 Offences under Section 124 of the Act

Where a complaint is made against an officer of the court under section 124 of theAct for having lost the opportunity of levying execution, the court will issue a summons,which must be served on the alleged offender personally not less than 7 days before the day of the hearing stated in the summons.

81.36 Notice to Give Evidence before or after a Fine Is Imposed under Section 55 of the Act

(1) Before or after imposing a fine on any person under section 55 of the Act for disobeying a witness summons or refusing to be sworn or give evidence, the court may direct that notice be given to that person in accordance with paragraph (2).

(2) The notice must state that if the recipient of the notice can demonstrate any reason why a fine should not be or should not have been imposed, that person may giveevidence—
   (a) by witness statement, affidavit or otherwise; and
   (b) on a day named in the notice.

81.37 Non-payment of Fine

(1) If a fine is not paid in accordance with the order imposing it, the court officer will, as soon as reasonably possible, report the matter to a judge.
(2) Where by an order imposing a fine—
   (a) the amount of the fine is directed to be paid by instalments; and
   (b) default is made in the payment of any instalment,
   the same proceedings may be taken as if default had been made in payment of the whole of the fine.
(3) If the court makes an order for payment of a fine to be enforced by warrant of execution, the order will be treated as an application to the court for the issue of the warrant at the time when the order was made.

81.38 Repayment of Fine

If a person pays a fine and later gives evidence to satisfy the court that, if the evidence had been given earlier, no fine or a smaller fine would have been imposed, thecourt may order the whole or part of the fine to be repaid.

PD 81 Practice Direction 81 — Applications and Proceedings in relation to Contempt of Court

This practice direction supplements CPR, Part 81.

PD 81 **81.1, 81.9, 81.16, 81.29**

SECTION II OF PART 81 — COMMITTAL FOR BREACH OF A JUDGMENT, ORDER OR UNDERTAKING TO DO OR ABSTAIN FROM DOING AN ACT

Requirement for a Penal Notice on Judgments and Orders — Form of Penal Notice—Rule 81.9

para.1 **81.6, 81.28**

1 A judgment or order which restrains a party from doing an act or requires an act to be done must, if disobedience is to be dealt with by proceedings for contempt of court, have a penal notice endorsed on it as follows (or in words to substantially the same effect)—

'If you the within-named [ ] do not comply with this order you may be held to be in contempt of court and imprisoned or fined, or your assets may be seized.'

Requirement for a Penal Notice on Judgments and Orders — Undertakings — Rule 81.9

para.2.2 **63.10, 81.25**
para.2.3 **63.10, 81.25**
para.2.4 **81.25**

2.1 The provisions of PD 40B, para. 8.1, apply to an order which contains an undertaking by a party to do or not do an act, subject to para. 2.2 below.

(PD 40B, para. 8.1, contains provisions about specifying the time within which acts must be done.)

2.2 The court may decline to—

(1) accept an undertaking; and

(2) deal with disobedience in respect of an undertaking by contempt of court proceedings, unless the party giving the undertaking has made a signed statement to the effect that that party understands the terms of the undertaking and the consequences of failure to comply with it.

2.3 The statement may be endorsed on the order containing the undertaking or may be filed in a separate document such as a letter.

2.4 Where the order containing an undertaking is made in a county court, form N117 may be used.

SECTION IV OF PART 81 — (1) CERTIFICATIONS BY ANY COURT, TRIBUNAL ETC. TO THE HIGH COURT UNDER ANY ENACTMENT; (2) APPLICATIONS TO THE HIGH COURT UNDER SECTION 336 OF THE CHARITIES ACT 2011

Scope of Section 4 of Part 81

para.3 **81.32**

3 Section 4 of Part 81 contains rules in relation to statutory powers of the High Court to commit any person for contempt in respect of anything done or not done in relation to a court, tribunal or person. The statutory powers include—

(1) section 336 of the Charities Act 2011;
(2) *sections 436 and 453C of the Companies Act 1985;*
(3) paragraph 8 of Schedule 6 to the Data Protection Act 1998; and
(4) sections 18, 161 and 232 of the Financial Services and Markets Act 2000.

SECTION V OF PART 81 — CONTEMPT IN THE FACE OF THE COURT

Committal for Contempt in the Face of the Court — Rule 81.16

4.1 Where the committal proceedings relate to a contempt in the face of the court the matters referred to in para. 4.3 should be given particular attention. Normally, it will be appropriate to defer consideration of the respondent's actions and behaviour to allow the respondent time to reflect on what has occurred. The time needed for the following procedures should allow such a period of reflection.

4.2 A Part 8 claim form and an application notice are not required for contempt falling under Section 5 of Part 81, but other provisions of this practice direction should be applied, as necessary, or adapted to the circumstances.

4.3 The judge should—

(1) tell the respondent of the possible penalty that the respondent faces;

(2) inform the respondent in detail, and preferably in writing, of the actions and behaviour of the respondent which have given rise to the committal application;

(3) if the judge considers that an apology would remove the need for the committal application, tell the respondent;

(4) have regard to the need for the respondent to be—

(a) allowed a reasonable time for responding to the committal application, including, if necessary, preparing a defence;

(b) made aware of the availability of assistance from the Community Legal Service and how to contact the Service;

(c) given the opportunity, if unrepresented, to obtain legal advice;

(d) if unable to understand English, allowed to make arrangements, seeking the court's assistance if necessary, for an interpreter to attend the hearing; and

(e) brought back before the court for the committal application to be heard within a reasonable time;

(5) allow the respondent an opportunity to—

(a) apologise to the court;

(b) explain the respondent's actions and behaviour; and

(c) if the contempt is proved, to address the court on the penalty to be imposed on the respondent; and

(6) where appropriate, nominate a suitable person to give the respondent the information. (It is likely to be appropriate to nominate a person where the effective communication of information by the judge to the respondent was not possible when the incident occurred.)

4.4 If there is a risk of the appearance of bias, the judge should ask another judge to hear the committal application.

4.5 Where the committal application is to be heard by another judge, a written statement by the judge before whom the actions and behaviour of the respondent which have given rise to the committal application took place may be admitted as evidence of those actions and behaviour.

SECTION VI OF PART 81 — COMMITTAL FOR MAKING A FALSE STATEMENT OF TRUTH OR DISCLOSURE STATEMENT

Committal Application in relation to a False Statement of Truth or Disclosure Statement — Rule 81.18

para.5 23.15

5.1 Rules 81.18(1)(b) and 81.18(3)(b) provide that a committal application may be made by the Attorney General. However, the Attorney General prefers a request that comes from the court to one made direct by a party to the proceedings in which the alleged contempt occurred without prior consideration by the court. A request to the Attorney General is not a way of appealing against, or reviewing, the decision of the judge.

5.2 Where the permission of the court is sought under r. 81.18(1)(a) or 81.18(3)(a) so that r. 81.14 is applied by r. 81.18(2) or 81.18(4), the affidavit evidence in support of the application must—

(1) identify the statement said to be false;

(2) explain—

(a) why it is false; and

(b) why the maker knew the statement to be false at the time it was made; and

(3) explain why contempt proceedings would be appropriate in the light of the overriding objective in Part 1.

5.3 The court may—

(1) exercise any of its powers under the rules (including the power to give directions under r. 81.14(6));

(2) initiate steps to consider if there is a contempt of court and, where there is, to punish it; or
(3) as provided by r. 81.18(5), direct that the matter be referred to the Attorney General with a request to consider whether to bring proceedings for contempt of court.

5.4 A request to the Attorney General to consider whether to bring proceedings for contempt of court must be made in writing and sent to the Attorney General's Office at 20 Victoria Street, London, SW1H 0NF.

5.5 A request to the Attorney General must be accompanied by a copy of any order directing that the matter be referred to the Attorney General and must—
(1) identify the statement said to be false;
(2) explain—
(a) why it is false; and
(b) why the maker knew the statement to be false at the time it was made; and
(3) explain why contempt proceedings would be appropriate in the light of the overriding objective in Part 1.

5.6 Once the applicant receives the result of the request to the Attorney General, the applicant must send a copy of it to the court that will deal with the committal application, and the court will give such directions as it sees fit.

5.7 The rules do not change the law of contempt or introduce new categories of contempt. A person applying to commence such proceedings should consider whether the incident complained of does amount to contempt of court and whether such proceedings would further the overriding objective in Part 1.

SECTION VII OF PART 81 — WRIT OF SEQUESTRATION TO ENFORCE A JUDGMENT, ORDER OR UNDERTAKING

Requirement for a Penal Notice on Judgments and Orders — Form of Penal Notice — Rule 81.25

para.6 81.28

6 Paragraphs 1 and 2.1 to 2.4 apply to judgments and orders to be enforced by a writ of sequestration.

Levying Execution on Certain Days

para.7.1 81.30 para.7.2 81.30

7.1 Unless the court orders otherwise, a writ of sequestration to enforce a judgment, order or undertaking must not be executed on a Sunday, Good Friday or Christmas Day.

7.2 Paragraph 7.1 does not apply to an Admiralty claim *in rem*.

SECTION VIII OF PART 81 — GENERAL RULES ABOUT COMMITTAL APPLICATIONS, ORDERS FOR COMMITTAL AND WRITS OF SEQUESTRATION

General rules

8.1 Subject to para. 8.2, this Section of the practice direction applies in relation to all matters covered by Part 81.

8.2 Where there is a conflict between the provisions in this Section of the practice direction and specific provisions elsewhere in this practice direction or in Part 81, the specific provisions prevail.

Human Rights

para.9 81.15

9 In all cases the Convention rights of those involved should particularly be borne in mind. It should be noted that the standard of proof, having regard to the possibility that a person may be sent to prison, is that the allegation be proved beyond reasonable doubt.

(Section 1 of the Human Rights Act 1998 defines 'the Convention rights'.)

Court to which Applications Should be Made and Levels of Judiciary

para.10.2 81.28

10.1 A committal application or an application for permission to make a committal application—
(1) may be made in a county court if the alleged contempt is a contempt which a county court has power to punish; and
(2) must otherwise be made in the High Court.

10.2 Except where under an enactment a master or district judge has power to make a committal order, a committal order can only be made—

(1) in High Court proceedings, by a High Court judge or a person authorised to act as such; or

(2) in county court proceedings, by a circuit judge or a person authorised to act as such.

10.3 Paragraph 10.4 applies in relation to proceedings in any court (the first court) where the judge or judges exercising the jurisdiction of the first court are deemed to constitute a court of the High Court by virtue of an enactment.

10.4 The reference in para. 10.2(1) to a High Court judge will be construed as a reference to a judge of the first court.

General Rules about Applications: Applications which Cannot be Made without Permission

11 If the committal application is one which cannot be made without permission—

(1) the permission may only be granted by a judge who would have power to hear the committal application if permission were granted;

(2) the date on which and the name of the judge by whom the requisite permission was granted must be stated on the claim form or application notice by which the committal application is commenced;

(3) the claim form or application notice may not be issued or filed until the requisite permission has been granted; and

(4) rules 23.9 and 23.10 do not apply.

General Rules about Applications: Applications by Claim Form

12 If the application for permission to make a committal application or the committal application is commenced by the issue of a claim form—

(1) Part 8 will apply—

(a) subject to the provisions of Part 81 and this practice direction, in particular sub-paras (2) to (4);

(b) as though references to'claimant' were references to the applicant; and

(c) as though references to'defendant' were references to the respondent;

(2) an amendment to the claim form may be made with the permission of the court but not otherwise;

(3) r. 8.4 does not apply; and

(4) the claim form must contain a prominent notice stating the possible consequences of the court making a committal order and of the respondent not attending the hearing. A form of notice which may be used is annexed to this practice direction at annex 3.

General Rules about Applications: Applications by Application Notice

para.13.1 81.9, 81.29
para.13.2 81.29
para.13.2(1) 81.9
para.13.2(2) 81.9
para.13.2(4) 81.9

13.1 Where the application is made by application notice, the application notice must state that the application is made in the proceedings in question, and its title and reference number must correspond with the title and reference number of those proceedings.

13.2 If the application for permission to make a committal application or the committal application is commenced by the filing of an application notice—

(1) Part 23 will apply subject to the provisions of Part 81 and this practice direction, in particular sub-paras (2) to (4);

(2) an amendment to the application notice may be made with the permission of the court but not otherwise;

(3) the court may not dispose of the application without a hearing; and

(4) the application notice must contain a prominent notice stating the possible consequences of the court making a committal order and of the respondent not attending the hearing. A form of notice which may be used is annexed to this practice direction at annex 3.

Evidence and Information

para.14.1 81.16
para.14.2 81.16
para.14.3 81.16
para.14.4 81.16

14.1 Written evidence in support of or in opposition to a committal application must be given by affidavit.

14.2 Written evidence served in support of or in opposition to a committal application must, unless the court otherwise directs, be filed.

14.3 The following rules do not apply to committal applications—

(1) r. 35.7 (court's power to direct that evidence is to be given by a single joint expert);

(2) r. 35.8 (instructions to single joint expert); and

(3) r. 35.9 (power of court to direct a party to provide information).

14.4 An order under r. 18.1 (obtaining further information) may not be made against a respondent to a committal application.

The Hearing — Rule 81.28

para.15.1 **81.10, 81.29**
para.15.2 **81.10, 81.11, 81.29**
para.15.4 **81.13**
para.15.5 **81.13**
para.15.6(1) **81.13**
para.15.6(2) **81.13**
para.15.6(3) **81.13**
para.15.6(4) **81.13**

15.1 When issuing or filing the claim form or application notice for a committal application, the applicant must obtain from the court a date for the hearing of the committal application.

15.2 Unless the court otherwise directs, the hearing date of a committal application must not be less than 14 days after service of the claim form or application notice on the respondent. The hearing date must be specified in the claim form or application notice or in a notice of hearing attached to and served with the claim form or application notice.

15.3 Paragraphs 15.1 and 15.2 apply to certifications of conduct and applications under section 336 of the Charities Act 2011 ('section 336 application') referred to in Section 4 of Part 81 as if references to the claim form or application notice were references to the certification or section 336 application.

(The definition of'applicant' in r. 81.3 includes a person who makes a committal application by way of certification or section 336 application.)

15.4 The court may on the hearing date—

(1) give case management directions with a view to a hearing of the committal application on a future date; or

(2) if the committal application is ready to be heard, proceed to hear it.

15.5 In dealing with any committal application, the court will have regard to the need for the respondent to have details of the alleged acts of contempt and the opportunity to respond to the committal application.

15.6 The court will also have regard to the need for the respondent to be—

(1) allowed a reasonable time for responding to the committal application including, if necessary, preparing a defence;

(2) made aware of the availability of assistance from the Community Legal Service and how to contact the Service;

(3) given the opportunity, if unrepresented, to obtain legal advice; and

(4) if unable to understand English, allowed to make arrangements, seeking the assistance of the court if necessary, for an interpreter to attend the hearing.

Striking Out, Procedural Defects and Discontinuance

para.16.1 **81.14**
para.16.2 **81.14**
para.16.3 **81.14**

16.1 On application by the respondent or on its own initiative, the court may strike out a committal application if it appears to the court—

(1) that the application and the evidence served in support of it disclose no reasonable ground for alleging that the respondent is guilty of a contempt of court;

(2) that the application is an abuse of the court's process or, if made in existing proceedings, is otherwise likely to obstruct the just disposal of those proceedings; or

(3) that there has been a failure to comply with a rule, practice direction or court order.

16.2 The court may waive any procedural defect in the commencement or conduct of a committal application if satisfied that no injustice has been caused to the respondent by the defect.

16.3 A committal application may not be discontinued without the permission of the court.

ANNEX 1

Rule 81.15(4) — Certifications of Conduct, and Applications Under Section 336 of the Charities Act 2011, to the High Court Under Section 4 of Part 81

Form of Certification, or Section 336 Application

[The form, titled 'Certification, or application under section 336 of the Charities Act 2011, in relation to conduct alleged to constitute contempt of court (CPR Part 81, Section 4)', may be viewed at <http://www.justice.gov.uk/courts/procedure-rules/civil>.]

ANNEX 2

Rule 81.15(7) — Certifications of Conduct, and Applications Under Section 336 of the Charities Act 2011, to the High Court Under Section 4 of Part 81

Form of Acknowledgment of Service (N210C)

[Form N210C is online at <http://hmctsformfinder.justice.gov.uk>.]

ANNEX 3

annex 3 81.9

Paragraphs 12(4) and 13.2(4)

Form of Penal Notice to be Included on Committal Applications

Important Notice

The Court has power to send you to prison, to fine you or seize your assets if it finds that any of the allegations made against you are true and amount to a contempt of court. **You must attend court** on the date shown on the front of this form. It is in your own interest to do so. You should bring with you any witnesses and documents which you think will help you put your side of the case. If you consider the allegations are not true you must tell the court why. If it is established that they are true, you must tell the court of any good reason why they do not amount to a contempt of court, or, if they do, why you should not be punished. If you need advice, you should show this document at once to your solicitor or go to a Citizens' Advice Bureau or similar organisation.

Glossary

Scope

This glossary is a guide to the meaning of certain legal expressions as used in these Rules, but it does not give the expressions any meaning in the Rules which they do not otherwise have in the law.

Expression	Meaning
Affidavit	A written, sworn statement of evidence.
Alternative dispute resolution	Collective description of methods of resolving disputes otherwise than through the normal trial process.
Base rate	The interest rate set by the Bank of England which is used as the basis for other banks' rates.
Budget	An estimate of the reasonable and proportionate costs (including disbursements) which a party intends to incur in the proceedings.
Contribution	A right of someone to recover from a third person all or part of the amount which he himself is liable to pay.
Counterclaim	A claim brought by a defendant in response to the claimant's claim, which is included in the same proceedings as the claimant's claim.
Cross-examination (and see 'evidence-in-chief')	Questioning of a witness by a party other than the party who called the witness.
Damages	A sum of money awarded by the court as compensation to the claimant.
• aggravated damages	Additional damages which the court may award as compensation for the defendant's objectionable behaviour.
• exemplary damages	Damages which go beyond compensating for actual loss and are awarded to show the court's disapproval of the defendant's behaviour.
Damages-based agreement	A damages-based agreement is an agreement which complies with the provisions of the Damages-Based Agreements Regulations 2013.
Defence of tender before claim	A defence that, before the claimant started proceedings, the defendant unconditionally offered to the claimant the amount due or, if no specified amount is claimed, an amount sufficient to satisfy the claim.
Divisional Court	With or without capital letters, means a divisional court constituted under section 66 of the Senior Courts Act 1981.
Evidence-in-chief (and see 'cross-examination')	The evidence given by a witness for the party who called him.
Indemnity	A right of someone to recover from a third party the whole amount which he himself is liable to pay.
Injunction	A court order prohibiting a person from doing something or requiring a person to do something.
Joint liability (and see 'several liability')	Parties who are jointly liable share a single liability and each party can be held liable for the whole of it.
Limitation period	The period within which a person who has a right to claim against another person must start court proceedings to establish that right. The expiry of the period may be a defence to the claim.
List	Cases are allocated to different lists depending on the subject matter of the case. The lists are used for administrative purposes and may also have their own procedures and judges.
Official copy	A copy of an official document, supplied and marked as such by the office which issued the original.
Practice form	Form to be used for a particular purpose in proceedings, the form and purpose being specified by a practice direction.

Expression	Meaning
Pre-action protocol	Statements of best practice about pre-action conduct which have been approved by the Head of Civil Justice and are listed in Practice Direction (Pre-action Conduct).
Privilege	The right of a party to refuse to disclose a document or produce a document or to refuse to answer questions on the ground of some special interest recognised by law.
Seal	A seal is a mark which the court puts on a document to indicate that the document has been issued by the court.
Service	Steps required by rules of court to bring documents used in court proceedings to a person's attention.
Set aside	Cancelling a judgment or order or a step taken by a party in the proceedings.
Several liability (and see 'joint liability')	A person who is severally liable with others may remain liable for the whole claim even where judgment has been obtained against the others.
Stay	A stay imposes a halt on proceedings, apart from taking any steps allowed by the Rules or the terms of the stay. Proceedings can be continued if a stay is lifted.
Strike out	Striking out means the court ordering written material to be deleted so that it may no longer be relied upon.
Without prejudice	Negotiations with a view to a settlement are usually conducted 'without prejudice', which means that the circumstances in which the content of those negotiations may be revealed to the court are very restricted.

CPR Schedule 1

sch. 1 1.6, 12.1 [For commentary on a specific RSC order, please refer to the cross-references after the title of the RSC rule.]

RSC ORDER 17 — INTERPLEADER

ord. 17 14.75

Rule 1 Entitlement to Relief by Way of Interpleader

(1) Where—
 (a) a person is under a liability in respect of a debt or in respect of any money, goods or chattels and he is, or expects to be, sued for or in respect of that debt or money or those goods or chattels by two or more persons making adverse claims thereto; or
 (b) claim is made to any money, goods or chattels taken or intended to be taken by a sheriff in execution under any process, or to the proceeds or value of any such goods or chattels, by a person other than the person against whom the process is issued,

the person under liability as mentioned in sub-paragraph (a) or (subject to rule 2) the sheriff, may apply to the court for relief by way of interpleader.

(2) References in this Order to a sheriff shall be construed as including references to—
 (a) an individual authorised to act as an enforcement officer under the Courts Act 2003; and
 (b) any other officer charged with the execution of process by or under the authority of the High Court.

Rule 2 Claim to Goods, etc., Taken in Execution

r.2(1) PC 7, 14.76, 14.77 r.2(3) 14.76
r.2.2 PC 7, 14.76 r.2.4 14.76, 79.10

(1) Any person making a claim to or in respect of any money, goods or chattels taken or intended to be taken in execution under process of the court, or to the proceeds or value of any such goods or chattels, must give notice of his claim to the sheriff charged with the execution of the process and must include in his notice a statement of his address, and that address shall be his address for service.

(2) On receipt of a claim made under this rule the sheriff must forthwith give notice thereof to the execution creditor and the execution creditor must, within seven days after receiving the notice, give notice to the sheriff informing him whether he admits or disputes the claim. An execution creditor who gives notice in accordance with this paragraph admitting a claim shall only be liable to the sheriff for any fees and expenses incurred by the sheriff before receipt of that notice.

(3) Where—
 (a) the sheriff receives a notice from an execution creditor under paragraph (2) disputing a claim, or the execution creditor fails, within the period mentioned in that paragraph, to give the required notice; and
 (b) the claim made under this rule is not withdrawn,

the sheriff may apply to the court for relief under this order.

(4) A sheriff who receives a notice from an execution creditor under paragraph (2) admitting a claim made under this rule shall withdraw from possession of the money, goods or chattels claimed and may apply to the court for relief under this order of the following kind, that is to say, an order restraining the bringing of a claim against him for or in respect of his having taken possession of that money or those goods or chattels.

Rule 2A Claim in Respect of Goods Protected from Seizure

r.2A 14.77 r.2A(1)–(6) 14.77

(1) Where a judgment debtor whose goods have been seized, or are intended to be seized, by a sheriff under a writ of execution claims that such goods are not liable to execution by virtue of section 138(3A) of the Act, he must within 5 days of the seizure give notice in writing to the sheriff

identifying all those goods in respect of which he makes such a claim and the grounds of such claim in respect of each item.

(2) Upon receipt of a notice of claim under paragraph (1), the sheriff must forthwith give notice thereof to the execution creditor and to any person who has made a claim to, or in respect of, the goods under rule 2(1) and the execution creditor and any person who has made claim must, within 7 days of receipt of such notice, inform the sheriff in writing whether he admits or disputes the judgment debtor's claim in respect of each item.

(3) The sheriff shall withdraw from possession of any goods in respect of which the judgment debtor's claim is admitted or if the execution creditor or any person claiming under rule 2(1) fails to notify him in accordance with paragraph (2) and the sheriff shall so inform the parties in writing.

(4) Where the sheriff receives notice from—

(a) the execution creditor; or

(b) any such person to whom notice was given under paragraph (2),

that the claim or any part thereof is disputed, he must forthwith seek the directions of the court and may include therein an application for an order restraining the bringing of any claim against him for, or in respect of, his having seized any of those goods or his having failed so to do.

(5) The sheriff's application for directions under paragraph (4) shall be made by an application in accordance with CPR Part 23 and, on the hearing of the application, the court may—

(a) determine the judgment debtor's claim summarily; or

(b) give such directions for the determination of any issue raised by such claim as may be just.

(6) A Master and a district judge of a district registry shall have power to make an order of the kind referred to in paragraph (4) and the reference to Master shall be construed in accordance with rule 4.

Rule 3 Mode of Application

r.3(1) PC 7, 14.78
r.3(2) 14.78
r.3(4) PC 7, 14.78
r.3(6) PC 7, 14.78

(1) An application for relief under this order must be made by claim form unless made in an existing claim, in which case it must be made by accordance with CPR Part 23.

(2) Where the applicant is a sheriff who has withdrawn from possession of money, goods or chattels taken in execution and who is applying for relief under rule 2(4) the claim form must be served on any person who made a claim under that rule to or in respect of that money or those goods or chattels, and that person may attend the hearing of the application.

(4) Subject to paragraph (5) a claim form or application notice under this rule must be supported by evidence that the applicant—

(a) claims no interest in the subject-matter in dispute other than for charges or costs;

(b) does not collude with any of the claimants to that subject-matter; and

(c) is willing to pay or transfer that subject-matter into court or to dispose of it as the court may direct.

(5) Where the applicant is a sheriff, he shall not provide such evidence as is referred to in paragraph (4) unless directed by the court to do so.

(6) Any person who makes a claim under rule 2 and who is served with a claim form under this rule shall within 14 days serve on the execution creditor and the sheriff a witness statement or affidavit specifying any money and describing any goods and chattels claimed and setting out the grounds upon which such claim is based.

(7) Where the applicant is a sheriff a claim form under this rule must give notice of the requirement in paragraph (6).

Rule 4 To Whom Sheriff May Apply for Relief

r.4 14.76

An application to the court for relief under this order may, if the applicant is a sheriff, be made—

(a) where the claim in question is proceeding in the Royal Courts of Justice, to a Master or, if the execution to which the application relates has been or is to be levied in the district of a District Registry, either to a Master or to the district judge of that Registry;

(b) where the claim in question is proceeding in a District Registry, to the district judge of that Registry or, if such execution has been or is to be levied in the district of some other District Registry or outside the district of any District Registry, either to the said district judge or to the district judge of that other registry or to a Master as the case may be.

Where the claim in question is proceeding in the Admiralty Court or the Family Division, references in this rule to a Master shall be construed as references to the Admiralty Registrar or to a Registrar of that Division.

Rule 5 Powers of Court Hearing Claim

r.5(1)(a) 14.79 r.5(2)–(3) 14.79

(1) Where on the hearing of a claim under this order all the persons by whom adverse claims to the subject-matter in dispute (hereafter in this Order referred to as 'the interpleader claimants') appear, the court may order—
 (a) that any interpleader claimant be made a defendant in any claim pending with respect to the subject-matter in dispute in substitution for or in addition to the applicant for relief under this order; or
 (b) that an issue between the interpleader claimants be stated and tried and may direct which of the interpleader claimants is to be claimant and which defendant.

(2) Where—
 (a) the applicant under this order is a sheriff; or
 (b) all the interpleader claimants consent or any of them so requests; or
 (c) the question at issue between the interpleader claimants is a question of law and the facts are not in dispute,

 the court may summarily determine the question at issue between the interpleader claimants and make an order accordingly on such terms as may be just.

(3) Where an interpleader claimant, having been duly served with a claim form under this order, does not appear at the hearing or, having appeared, fails or refuses to comply with an order made in the proceedings, the court may make an order declaring the interpleader claimant, and all persons claiming under him, for ever barred from prosecuting his claim against the applicant for such relief and all persons claiming under him, but such an order shall not affect the rights of the interpleader claimants as between themselves.

Rule 6 Power to Order Sale of Goods Taken in Execution

r.6–r.10 14.79

Where an application for relief under this order is made by a sheriff who has taken possession of any goods or chattels in execution under any process, and an interpleader claimant alleges that he is entitled, under a bill of sale or otherwise. to the goods or chattels by way of security for debt, the court may order those goods or chattels or any part thereof to be sold and may direct that the proceeds of sale be applied in such manner and on such terms as may be just and as may be specified in the order.

Rule 7 Power to Stay Proceedings

Where a defendant to a claim applies for relief under this Order in the claim, the court may by order stay all further proceedings in the claim.

Rule 8 Other Powers

(1) Subject to the foregoing rules of this Order, the court may in or for the purposes of any interpleader proceedings make such order as to costs or any other matter as it thinks just.

(2) Where the interpleader claimant fails to appear at the hearing, the Court may direct that the sheriff's and execution creditor's costs shall be assessed by a master or, where the hearing was heard in a district registry, by a district judge of that registry and the following CPR rules shall apply—
 (a) 44.4 (basis of assessment);
 (b) 44.5 (factors to be taken into account in deciding the amount of costs);
 (c) 48.4 (limitations on court's power to award costs in favour of trustee or personal representative); and
 (d) 48.6 (litigants in person).

(3) Where the claim in question is proceeding in the Admiralty Court or the Family Division, references in this rule to a Master shall be construed as references to the Admiralty Registrar or to a Registrar of that Division.

Rule 9 One Order in Several Proceedings

Where the Court considers it necessary or expedient to make an order in any interpleader proceedings in several proceedings pending in several Divisions, or before different judges of the same Division, the court may make such an order; and the order shall be entitled in all those causes or matters and shall be binding on all the parties to them.

Rule 10 Disclosure

CPR Parts 31 and 18 shall, with the necessary modifications, apply in relation to an interpleader issue as they apply in relation to any other proceedings.

Rule 11 Trial of Interpleader Issue

r.11 14.79 r.11(1) 14.79

(1) CPR Part 39 shall, with the necessary modifications, apply to the trial of an interpleader issue as it applies to the trial of a claim.
(2) The court by whom an interpleader issue is tried may give such judgment or make such order as finally to dispose of all questions arising in the interpleader proceedings.

RSC ORDER 45 — ENFORCEMENT OF JUDGMENTS AND ORDERS: GENERAL

ord. 45 79.1, 79.40

Rule 1 Enforcement of Judgment, etc., for Payment of Money

(4) In this Order references to any writ shall be construed as including references to any further writ in aid of the first mentioned writ.

Rule 1A Interpretation

In this Order, and in RSC Orders 46 and 47—

(a) 'enforcement officer' means an individual who is authorised to act as an enforcement officer under the Courts Act 2003; and
(b) 'relevant enforcement officer' means—
  (i) in relation to a writ of execution which is directed to a single enforcement officer, that officer;
  (ii) in relation to a writ of execution which is directed to two or more enforcement officers, the officer to whom the writ is allocated.

Rule 2 Notice of Seizure

r.2 81.28

When first executing a writ of fieri facias, the Sheriff or his officer or the relevant enforcement officer shall deliver to the debtor or leave at each place where execution is levied a notice in Form No. 55 in Practice Direction 4 informing the debtor of the execution.

Rule 3 Enforcement of Judgment for Possession of Land

(1) Subject to the provisions of these rules, a judgment or order for the giving of possession of land may be enforced by one or more of the following means, that is to say—
  (a) writ of possession;
  (b) in a case in which rule 81.4 applies, an order of committal;
  (c) in a case in which rule 81.20 applies, writ of sequestration.
(2) A writ of possession to enforce a judgment or order for the giving of possession of any land shall not be issued without the permission of the court except where the judgment or order was given or made in proceedings by a mortgagee or mortgagor or by any person having the right to foreclose or redeem any mortgage, being proceedings in which there is a claim for—
  (a) payment of moneys secured by the mortgage;

(b) sale of the mortgaged property;
(c) foreclosure;
(d) delivery of possession (whether before or after foreclosure or without foreclosure) to the mortgagee by the mortgagor or by any other person who is alleged to be in possession of the property;
(e) redemption;
(f) reconveyance of the land or its release from the security; or
(g) delivery of possession by the mortgagee.

(2A) In paragraph (2) 'mortgage' includes a legal or equitable mortgage and a legal or equitable charge, and reference to a mortgagor, a mortgagee and mortgaged land is to be interpreted accordingly.

(3) Such permission as is referred to in paragraph (2) shall not be granted unless it is shown—
(a) that every person in actual possession of the whole or any part of the land has received such notice of the proceedings as appears to the court sufficient to enable him to apply to the court for any relief to which he may be entitled; and
(b) if the operation of the judgment or order is suspended by subsection (2) of section 16 of the Landlord and Tenant Act, 1954, that the applicant has not received notice in writing from the tenant that he desires that the provisions of paragraphs (a) and (b) of that subsection shall have effect.

(4) A writ of possession may include provision for enforcing the payment of any money adjudged or ordered to be paid by the judgment or order which is to be enforced by the writ.

Rule 4 Enforcement of Judgment for Delivery of Goods

r.4(2) 81.4

(1) Subject to the provisions of these rules, a judgment or order for the delivery of any goods which does not give a person against whom the judgment is given or order made the alternative of paying the assessed value of the goods may be enforced by one or more of the following means, that is to say—
(a) writ of delivery to recover the goods without alternative provision for recovery of the assessed value thereof (hereafter in this rule referred to as a 'writ of specific delivery');
(b) in a case in which rule 81.4 applies, an order of committal;
(c) in a case in which rule 81.20 applies, writ of sequestration.

(2) Subject to the provisions of these rules, a judgment or order for the delivery of any goods or payment of their assessed value may be enforced by one or more of the following means, that is to say—
(a) writ of delivery to recover the goods or their assessed value;
(b) by order of the court, writ of specific delivery;
(c) in a case in which rule 81.20 applies, writ of sequestration.

An application for an order under sub-paragraph (b) shall be made in accordance with CPR Part 23, which must be served on the defendant against whom the judgment or order sought to be enforced was given or made.

(3) A writ of specific delivery, and a writ of delivery to recover any goods or their assessed value, may include provision for enforcing the payment of any money adjudged or ordered to be paid by the judgment or order which is to be enforced by the writ.

(4) A judgment or order for the payment of the assessed value of any goods may be enforced by the same means as any other judgment or order for the payment of money.

Rule 8 Court May Order Act to Be Done at Expense of Disobedient Party

If a mandatory order, an injunction or a judgment or order for the specific performance of a contract is not complied with, then, without prejudice to its powers under section 39 of the Act and its powers to punish the disobedient party for contempt, the court may direct that the act required to be done may, so far as practicable, be done by the party by whom the order or judgment was obtained or some other person appointed by the court, at the cost of the disobedient party, and upon the act being done the expenses incurred may be ascertained in such manner as the court may direct and execution may issue against the disobedient party for the amount so ascertained and for costs.

Rule 11 Matters Occurring after Judgment: Stay of Execution, etc.

Without prejudice to Order 47, rule 1, a party against whom a judgment has been given or an order made may apply to the court for a stay of execution of the judgment or order or other relief on the ground of matters which have occurred since the date of the judgment or order, and the court may by order grant such relief, and on such terms, as it thinks just.

Rule 12 Forms of Writs

(1) A writ of fieri facias must be in such of the Forms Nos. 53 to 63 in Practice Direction 4 as is appropriate in the particular case.
(2) A writ of delivery must be in Form No. 64 or 65 in Practice Direction 4, whichever is appropriate.
(3) A writ of possession must be in Form No. 66 or 66A in Practice Direction 4, whichever is appropriate.

RSC ORDER 46 — WRITS OF EXECUTION: GENERAL

ord.46 79.1, 79.40, 81.28

Rule 1 Definition

r.1 81.28

In this Order, unless the context otherwise requires, 'writ of execution' includes a writ of fieri facias, a writ of possession, a writ of delivery, a writ of sequestration and any further writ in aid of any of the aforementioned writs.

Rule 2 When Permission to Issue Any Writ of Execution Is Necessary

r.2 10.50, 79.9

(1) A writ of execution to enforce a judgment or order may not issue without the permission of the court in the following cases, that is to say—
  (a) where 6 years or more have elapsed since the date of the judgment or order;
  (b) where any change has taken place, whether by death or otherwise, in the parties entitled or liable to execution under the judgment or order;
  (c) where the judgment or order is against the assets of a deceased person coming to the hands of his executors or administrators after the date of the judgment or order, and it is sought to issue execution against such assets;
  (d) where under the judgment or order any person is entitled to a remedy subject to the fulfilment of any condition which it is alleged has been fulfilled;
  (e) where any goods sought to be seized under a writ of execution are in the hands of a receiver appointed by the court or a sequestrator.
(2) Paragraph (1) is without prejudice to section 2 of the Reserve and Auxiliary Forces (Protection of Civil Interests) Act 1951, or any other enactment or rule by virtue of which a person is required to obtain the permission of the court for the issue of a writ of execution or to proceed to execution on or otherwise to the enforcement of a judgment or order.
(3) Where the court grants permission, whether under this rule or otherwise, for the issue of a writ of execution and the writ is not issued within one year after the date of the order granting such permission, the order shall cease to have effect, without prejudice, however, to the making of a fresh order.

Rule 3 Permission Required for Issue of Writ in Aid of Other Writ

r.3 79.34

A writ of execution in aid of any other writ of execution shall not issue without the permission of the court.

Rule 4 Application for Permission to Issue Writ

(1) An application for permission to issue a writ of execution may be made in accordance with CPR Part 23 but the application notice need not be served on the respondent unless the court directs.
(2) Such an application must be supported by a witness statement or affidavit—

(a) identifying the judgment or order to which the application relates and, if the judgment or order is for the payment of money, stating the amount originally due thereunder and the amount due thereunder at the date the application notice is filed;
(b) stating, where the case falls within rule 2(1)(a), the reasons for the delay in enforcing the judgment or order;
(c) stating, where the case falls within rule 2(1)(b), the change which has taken place in the parties entitled or liable to execution since the date of the judgment or order;
(d) stating, where the case falls within rule 2(1)(c) or (d), that a demand to satisfy the judgment or order was made on the person liable to satisfy it and that he has refused or failed to do so;
(e) giving such other information as is necessary to satisfy the court that the applicant is entitled to proceed to execution on the judgment or order in question and that the person against whom it is sought to issue execution is liable to execution on it.

(3) The court hearing such application may grant permission in accordance with the application or may order that any issue or question, a decision on which is necessary to determine the rights of the parties, be tried in any manner in which any question of fact or law arising in proceedings may be tried and, in either case, may impose such terms as to costs or otherwise as it thinks just.

Rule 5 Application for Permission to Issue Writ of Sequestration

Notwithstanding anything in rules 2 and 4, an application for permission to issue a writ of sequestration must be made in accordance with Part 81 and in particular Section 7 of that Part.

Rule 6 Issue of Writ of Execution

r.6 79.8

(1) Issue of a writ of execution takes place on its being sealed by a court officer of the appropriate office.
(2) Before such a writ is issued, a praecipe for its issue must be filed.
(3) The praecipe must be signed by or on behalf of the solicitor of the person entitled to execution or, if that person is acting in person, by him.
(4) No such writ shall be sealed unless at the time of the tender thereof for sealing—
(a) the person tendering it produces—
(i) the judgment or order on which the writ is to issue, or an office copy thereof,
(ii) where the writ may not issue without the permission of the court, the order granting such permission or evidence of the granting of it;
(iii) where judgment on failure to acknowledge service has been entered against a State, as defined in section 14 of the State Immunity Act 1978, evidence that the State has been served in accordance with CPR rule 40.10 and that the judgment has taken effect; and
(b) the court officer authorised to seal it is satisfied that the period, if any, specified in the judgment or order for the payment of any money or the doing of any other act thereunder has expired.
(5) Every writ of execution shall bear the date of the day on which it is issued.
(6) In this rule 'the appropriate office' means—
(a) where the proceedings in which execution is to issue are in a District Registry, that Registry;
(b) where the proceedings are in the Principal Registry of the Family Division, that Registry;
(c) where the proceedings are Admiralty proceedings or commercial proceedings which are not in a District Registry, the Admiralty and Commercial Registry;
(ca) where the proceedings are in the Chancery Division, Chancery Chambers;
(d) in any other case, the Central Office of the Senior Courts.

Rule 8 Duration and Renewal of Writ of Execution

r.8 79.7, 81.31

(1) For the purpose of execution, a writ of execution is valid in the first instance for 12 months beginning with the date of its issue.
(2) Where a writ has not been wholly executed the court may by order extend the validity of the writ from time to time for a period of 12 months at any one time beginning with the day on which the order is made, if an application for extension is made to the court before the day next

following that on which the writ would otherwise expire or such later day, if any, as the court may allow.

(3) Before a writ the validity of which had been extended under paragraph (2) is executed either the writ must be sealed with the seal of the office out of which it was issued showing the date on which the order extending its validity was made or the applicant for the order must serve a notice (in Form No. 71 in Practice Direction 4) sealed as aforesaid, on the sheriff to whom the writ is directed or the relevant enforcement officer informing him of the making of the order and the date thereof.

(4) The priority of a writ, the validity of which has been extended under this rule, shall be determined by reference to the date on which it was originally delivered to the sheriff or the relevant enforcement officer.

(5) The production of a writ of execution, or of such a notice as is mentioned in paragraph (3) purporting in either case to be sealed as mentioned in that paragraph, shall be evidence that the validity of that writ, or, as the case may be, of the writ referred to in that notice, has been extended under paragraph (2).

(6) If, during the validity of a writ of execution, an interpleader summons is issued in relation to an execution under that writ, the validity of the writ shall be extended until the expiry of 12 months from the conclusion of the interpleader proceedings.

Rule 9 Return to Writ of Execution

(1) Any party at whose instance or against whom a writ of execution was issued may serve a notice on the sheriff to whom the writ was directed or the relevant enforcement officer requiring him, within such time as may be specified in the notice, to indorse on the writ a statement of the manner in which he has executed it and to send to that party a copy of the statement.

(2) If a sheriff or enforcement officer on whom such a notice is served fails to comply with it the party by whom it was served may apply to the court for an order directing the sheriff or enforcement officer to comply with the notice.

RSC ORDER 47 — WRITS OF FIERI FACIAS

ord.47 79.1, 79.40

Rule 1 Power to Stay Execution by Writ of Fieri Facias

r.1 79.5

(1) Where a judgment is given or an order made for the payment by any person of money, and the court is satisfied, on an application made at the time of the judgment or order, or at any time thereafter, by the judgment debtor or other party liable to execution—

(a) that there are special circumstances which render it inexpedient to enforce the judgment or order; or

(b) that the applicant is unable from any cause to pay the money,

then, notwithstanding anything in rule 2 or 3, the court may by order stay the execution of the judgment or order by writ of fieri facias either absolutely or for such period and subject to such conditions as the court thinks fit.

(2) An application under this rule, if not made at the time the judgment is given or order made, must be made in accordance with CPR Part 23 and may be so made notwithstanding that the party liable to execution did not acknowledge service of the claim form or serve a defence or take any previous part in the proceedings.

(3) The grounds on which an application under this rule is made must be set out in the application notice and be supported by a witness statement or affidavit made by or on behalf of the applicant substantiating the said grounds and, in particular, where such application is made on the grounds of the applicant's inability to pay, disclosing his income, the nature and value of any property of his and the amount of any other liabilities of his.

(4) The application notice and a copy of the supporting witness statement or affidavit must, not less than 4 clear days before the hearing, be served on the party entitled to enforce the judgment or order.

(5) An order staying execution under this rule may be varied or revoked by a subsequent order.

Rule 3 Separate Writs to Enforce Payment of Costs, etc.

(1) Where only the payment of money, together with costs to be assessed in accordance with CPR Part 47 (detailed costs assessment), is adjudged or ordered, then, if when the money becomes payable under the judgment or order the costs have not been assessed, the party entitled to enforce that judgment or order may issue a writ of fieri facias to enforce payment of the sum (other than for costs) adjudged or ordered and, not less than 8 days after the issue of that writ, he may issue a second writ to enforce payment of the assessed costs.

(2) A party entitled to enforce a judgment or order for the delivery of possession of any property (other than money) may, if he so elects, issue a separate writ of fieri facias to enforce payment of any damages or costs awarded to him by that judgment or order.

Rule 4 No Expenses of Execution in Certain Cases

Where a judgment or order is for less than £600 and does not entitle the claimant to costs against the person against whom the writ of fieri facias to enforce the judgment or order is issued, the writ may not authorise the sheriff or enforcement officer to whom it is directed to levy any fees, poundage or other costs of execution.

Rule 5 Writ of Fieri Facias De Bonis Ecclesiasticis, etc.

(1) Where it appears upon the return of any writ of fieri facias that the person against whom the writ was issued has no goods or chattels in the county of the sheriffs to whom the writ was directed or the district of the relevant enforcement officer but that he is the incumbent of a benefice named in the return, then, after the writ and return have been filed, the party by whom the writ of fieri facias was issued may issue a writ of fieri facias de bonis ecclesiasticis or a writ of sequestrari de bonis ecclesiasticis directed to the bishop of the diocese within which that benefice is.

(2) Any such writ must be delivered to the bishop to be executed by him.

(3) Only such fees for the execution of any such writ shall be taken by or allowed to the bishop or any diocesan officer as are for the time being authorised by or under any enactment, including any measure of the General Synod.

Rule 6 Order for Sale Otherwise than by Auction

r.6 79.11

(1) An order of the court under paragraph 10 of Schedule 7 to the Courts Act 2003 that a sale of goods seized under an execution may be made otherwise than by public auction may be made on the application of—

  (a) the person at whose instance the writ of execution under which the sale is to be made was issued;
  (b) the person against whom that writ was issued (in this rule referred to as 'the judgment debtor');
  (c) if the writ was directed to a sheriff, that sheriff; and
  (d) if the writ was directed to one or more enforcement officers, the relevant enforcement officer.

(2) Such an application must be made in accordance with CPR Part 23 and the application notice must contain a short statement of the grounds of the application.

(3) Where the applicant for an order under this rule is not the sheriff or enforcement officer, the sheriff or enforcement officer must, on the demand of the applicant, send to the applicant a list stating—

  (a) whether he has notice of the issue of another writ or writs of execution against the goods of the judgment debtor; and
  (b) so far as is known to him, the name and address of every creditor who has obtained the issue of another such writ of execution,

and where the sheriff or enforcement officer is the applicant, he must prepare such a list.

(4) Not less than 4 clear days before the hearing the applicant must serve the application notice on each of the other persons by whom the application might have been made and on every person named in the list under paragraph (3).

(5) Service of the application notice on a person named in the list under paragraph (3) is notice to him for the purpose of paragraph 10(3) of Schedule 7 to the Courts Act 2003.

(Paragraph 10(3) provides that if the person who seized the goods has notice of another execution or other executions, the court must not consider an application for leave to sell privately until the notice prescribed by Civil Procedure Rules has been given to the other execution creditor or creditors)

(6) The applicant must produce the list under paragraph (3) to the court on the hearing of the application.

(7) Every person on whom the application notice was served may attend and be heard on the hearing of the application.

RSC ORDER 54 — APPLICATIONS FOR WRIT OF HABEAS CORPUS

Rule 1 Application for Writ of Habeas Corpus Ad Subjiciendum

(1) Subject to rule 11, an application for a writ of habeas corpus ad subjiciendum shall be made to a judge in court, except that—

(a) it shall be made to a Divisional Court of the Queen's Bench Division if the court so directs;

(b) it may be made to a judge otherwise than in court at any time when no judge is sitting in court; and

(c) any application on behalf of a child must be made in the first instance to a judge otherwise than in court.

(2) An application for such writ may be made without notice being served on any other party and, subject to paragraph (3) must be supported by a witness statement or affidavit by the person restrained showing that it is made at his instance and setting out the nature of the restraint.

(3) Where the person restrained is unable for any reason to make the witness statement or affidavit required by paragraph (2) the witness statement or affidavit may be made by some other person on his behalf and that witness statement or affidavit must state that the person restrained is unable to make the witness statement or affidavit himself and for what reason.

Rule 2 Power of Court to Whom Application Made without Notice Being Served on Any Other Party

(1) The court or judge to whom an application under rule 1 is made without notice being served on any other party may make an order forthwith for the writ to issue, or may—

(a) where the application is made to a judge otherwise than in court, direct the issue of a claim form seeking the writ, or that an application therefor be made by claim form to a Divisional Court or to a judge in court;

(b) where the application is made to a judge in court, adjourn the application so that notice thereof may be given, or direct that an application be made by claim form to a Divisional Court;

(c) where the application is made to a Divisional Court, adjourn the application so that notice thereof may be given.

(2) The claim form must be served on the person against whom the issue of the writ is sought and on such other persons as the court or judge may direct, and, unless the court or judge otherwise directs, there must be at least 8 clear days between the service of the claim form and the date named therein for the hearing of the application.

Rule 3 Copies of Witness Statements or Affidavits to Be Supplied

Every party to an application under rule 1 must supply to every other party on demand and on payment of the proper charges copies of the witness statements or affidavits which he proposes to use at the hearing of the application.

Rule 4 Power to Order Release of Person Restrained

(1) Without prejudice to rule 2(1), the court or judge hearing an application for a writ of habeas corpus ad subjiciendum may in its or his discretion order that the person restrained be released, and such order shall be a sufficient warrant to any governor of a prison, constable or other person for the release of the person under restraint.

(2) Where such an application in criminal proceedings is heard by a judge and the judge does not *order the release* of the person restrained, he shall direct that the application be made by claim form to a Divisional Court of the Queen's Bench Division.

Rule 5 Directions as to Return to Writ

Where a writ of habeas corpus ad subjiciendum is ordered to issue, the court or judge by whom the order is made shall give directions as to the court or judge before whom, and the date on which, the writ is returnable.

Rule 6 Service of Writ and Notice

(1) Subject to paragraphs (2) and (3), a writ of habeas corpus ad subjiciendum must be served personally on the person to whom it is directed.
(2) If it is not possible to serve such writ personally, or if it is directed to a governor of a prison or other public official, it must be served by leaving it with a servant or agent of the person to whom the writ is directed at the place where the person restrained is confined or restrained.
(3) If the writ is directed to more than one person, the writ must be served in manner provided by this rule on the person first named in the writ, and copies must be served on each of the other persons in the same manner as the writ.
(4) There must be served with the writ a notice (in Form No. 90 in Practice Direction 4) stating the court or judge before whom and the date on which the person restrained is to be brought and that in default of obedience proceedings for committal of the party disobeying will be taken.

Rule 7 Return to the Writ

(1) The return to a writ of habeas corpus ad subjiciendum must be indorsed on or annexed to the writ and must state all the causes of the detainer of the person restrained.
(2) The return may be amended, or another return substituted therefor, by permission of the court or judge before whom the writ is returnable.

Rule 8 Procedure at Hearing of Writ

When a return to a writ of habeas corpus ad subjiciendum is made, the return shall first be read, and motion then made for discharging or remanding the person restrained or amending or quashing the return, and where that person is brought up in accordance with the writ, his counsel shall be heard first, then the counsel for the Crown, and then one counsel for the person restrained in reply.

Rule 9 Bringing Up Prisoner to Give Evidence, etc.

(1) An application for a writ of habeas corpus ad testificandum or of habeas corpus ad respondendum must be made on witness statement or affidavit to a judge.
(2) An application for an order to bring up a prisoner, otherwise than by writ of habeas corpus, to give evidence in any proceedings, civil or criminal, before any court, tribunal or justice, must be made on witness statement or affidavit to a judge.

Rule 10 Form of Writ

A writ of habeas corpus must be in Form No. 89, 91 or 92 in Practice Direction 4, whichever is appropriate.

Rule 11 Applications Relative to the Custody, etc., of Child

r.11 11.2

An application by a parent or guardian of a child for a writ of habeas corpus ad subjiciendum relative to the custody, care or control of the child must be made in the Family Division, and this Order shall accordingly apply to such applications with the appropriate modifications.

[RSC Ord. 79 — Criminal Proceedings is not included in *Blackstone's Civil Practice*.]

RSC ORDER 109 — THE ADMINISTRATION OF JUSTICE ACT 1960

Rule 1 Applications under Act

(1) Any of the following applications, that is to say—
(a) an application under section 2 of the Administration of Justice Act 1960, or under that section as applied by section 13 of that Act, to extend the time within which an application may

be made to a Divisional Court for permission to appeal to the Supreme Court under section 1 of that Act, or section 13 thereof, from an order or decision of that court, and

(b) an application by a defendant under section 9(3) of that Act to a Divisional Court for permission to be present on the hearing of any proceedings preliminary or incidental to an appeal to the Supreme Court under section 1 of that Act from a decision of that court

must be made to a Divisional Court except in vacation when it may be made to a judge.

(2) Any such application to a Divisional Court, if not made in the proceedings before the Divisional Court from whose order or decision the appeal in question is brought, must be made by the issue of a claim form.

(3) Any such application to a judge must, in the case of such an application as is referred to in paragraph (1)(a) be made by the issue of a claim form and, in the case of such an application as is referred to in paragraph (1)(b) need not be served on any other person unless, in the latter case, the judge otherwise directs.

(4) No application notice or copy of the claim form (as the case may be) by which such an application as is referred to in paragraph (1)(b) is made, need be given to any party affected thereby unless the Divisional Court otherwise directs.

(5) Where any application to which this rule applies is made in vacation to a single judge and the judge refuses the application, the applicant shall be entitled to have the application determined by a Divisional Court.

Rule 2 Appeals under Section 13 of Act

(1) An appeal to a Divisional Court of the Supreme Court under section 13 of the Administration of Justice Act 1960, shall be heard and determined by a Divisional Court of the Queen's Bench Division.

(4) Unless the court gives permission, there shall be not more than 4 clear days between the date on which the order or decision appealed against was made and the day named in the notice of appeal for the hearing of the appeal.

(5) The notice must be served, and the appeal entered, not less than one clear day before the day named in the notice for the hearing of the appeal.

Rule 3 Release of Appellant on Bail

(1) Where, in the case of an appeal under section 13 of the Administration of justice Act 1960, to a Divisional Court or to the Supreme Court from a Divisional Court, the appellant is in custody, the High Court may order his release on his giving security (whether by recognisance, with or without sureties, or otherwise and for such reasonable sum as the court may fix) for his appearance, within 10 days after the judgment of the Divisional Court or, as the case may be, of the Supreme Court, on the appeal before the court from whose order or decision the appeal is brought unless the order or decision is reversed by that judgment.

(2) Order 79, rule 9(1) to (6) and (8) shall apply in relation to an application to the High Court for bail pending an appeal under the said section 13 to which this rule applies, and to the admission of a person to bail in pursuance of an order made on the application, as they apply in relation to an application to that court for bail in criminal proceedings, and to the admission of a person to bail in pursuance of an order made on the application, but with the substitution, for references to the defendant, of references to the appellant, and, for references to the prosecutor, of references to the court officer of the court from whose order or decision the appeal is brought and to the parties to the proceedings in that court who are directly affected by the appeal.

Rule 4 Release of Appellant on Bail by the Court of Appeal

(1) Where, in the case of an appeal under section 13 of the Administration of Justice Act 1960 to the Court of Appeal or to the Supreme Court from the Court of Appeal, the appellant is in custody, the Court of Appeal may order his release on his giving security (whether by recognisance, with or without sureties, or otherwise and for such reasonable sum as that court may fix) for his appearance within 10 days after the judgment of the Court of Appeal or, as the case may be, of the Supreme Court on the appeal shall have been given, before the court from whose order or decision the appeal is brought unless the order or decision is reversed by that judgment.

(2) An application for the release of a person under paragraph (1) pending an appeal to the Court of Appeal or the Supreme Court under the said section 13 must be made in accordance with CPR

Part 23, and the application notice must, at least 24 hours before the day named therein for the hearing, be served on the court from whose order or decision the appeal is brought and on all parties to the proceedings in that court who are directly affected by the appeal.

(3) Order 79, rules 9(6), (6A), (6B) and (8) shall apply in relation to the grant of bail under this rule by the Court of Appeal in a case of criminal contempt of court as they apply in relation to the grant of bail in criminal proceedings by the High Court, but with the substitution for references to a judge of references to the Court of Appeal and for references to the defendant of references to the appellant.

(4) When granting bail under this rule in a case of civil contempt of court, the Court of Appeal may order that the recognisance or other security to be given by the appellant or the recognisance of any surety shall be given before any person authorised by virtue of section 119(1) of the Magistrates' Courts Act 1980 to take a recognisance where a magistrates' court having power to take it has, instead of taking it, fixed the amount in which the principal and his sureties, if any, are to be bound. An order by the Court of Appeal granting bail as aforesaid must be in Form 98 in Practice Direction 4 with the necessary adaptations.

(5) Where in pursuance of an order of the Court of Appeal under paragraph (4) of this rule a recognisance is entered into or other security given before any person, it shall be the duty of that person to cause the recognisance of the appellant or any surety or, as the case may be, a statement of the other security given, to be transmitted forthwith to the designated officer for the court which committed the appellant; and a copy of such recognisance or statement shall at the same time be sent to the governor or keeper of the prison or other place of detention in which the appellant is detained, unless the recognisance or security was given before such governor or keeper.

(6) The powers conferred on the Court of Appeal by paragraphs (1), (3) and (4) of this rule may be exercised by a single judge.

RSC ORDER 113 — SUMMARY PROCEEDINGS FOR POSSESSION OF LAND

Rule 7 Writ of Possession

(1) Order 45, rule 3(2) shall not apply in relation to an order for possession in a possession claim against trespassers under Part 55 but no writ of possession to enforce such an order shall be issued after the expiry of three months from the date of the order without the permission of the court.

An application for permission may be made without notice being served on any other party unless the court otherwise directs.

(2) The writ of possession shall be in Form No. 66A.

[The following are not included in *Blackstone's Civil Practice*:

RSC Ord. 115 — Confiscation and Forfeiture in Connection with Criminal Proceedings

Practice Direction RSC 115 — Restraint Orders and Appointment of Receivers in Connection with Criminal Proceedings and Investigations]

PD RSC 46 & CCR 26
Practice Direction RSC 46 and CCR 26 — Execution

This practice direction supplements RSC, ord. 46 in CPR, sch. 1, and CCR, ord. 26 in CPR, sch. 2.

Levying Execution on Certain Days

1.1 Unless the Court orders otherwise, a writ of execution or a warrant of execution to enforce a judgment or order must not be executed on a Sunday, Good Friday or Christmas Day.

1.2 paragraph 1.1 does not apply to an Admiralty claim *in rem*.

PD RSC 54 Practice Direction RSC 54 — Application for Writ of Habeas Corpus

This practice direction supplements CPR, Part 50 and sch. 1.

Terminology

1.1 In this practice direction:

(1) 'Order 54' means those provisions contained in Schedule 1, RSC Order 54 which were previously contained in the Rules of the Supreme Court (1965);

(2) a reference to a rule or Part prefixed with CPR is a reference to a rule or Part contained in the CPR rules; and

(3) a reference to a rule number alone is a reference to the rule so numbered in Order 54.

Scope

2.1 This practice direction supplements Order 54 (which sets out how to apply for a writ of habeas corpus) by providing further detail about the application.

2.2 This practice direction must be read together with Order 54.

2.3 It also lists at paragraph 7 other practice directions which governed procedure relating to Order 54 before 26 April 1999 and which will continue to do so.

Form to Be Used Where Court Directs Claim Form to Be Used

3.1 Where the court directs that an application be made by claim form, under:

(1) rule 2 (on hearing application under rule 1); or

(2) rule 4(2) (application in criminal proceedings ordered to be made to Divisional Court of the Queen's Bench Division),

the claimant must use Form 87 modified in accordance with the guidance set out in the Forms practice direction.

Form to Be Used for Notice of Adjourned Application Directed by Court

4.1 Where the court directs under rule 2(1)(c) that an application made under rule 1 is adjourned to allow for service of notice of the application, such notice must be given in modified Form 88.

Service

5.1 The party seeking the writ must serve:

(1) the claim form in accordance with rule 2(2); and

(2) the writ of habeas corpus ad subjiciendum and notice in Form 90, as modified, in accordance with rule 6.

(CPR rule 6.3 provides that the court will normally serve a document which it has issued or prepared.)

The Administrative Court

6.1 When the court directs that an application is to be made by claim form under:

(1) rule 2(1) (powers of court to whom application made under rule 1); or

(2) rule 4(2) (power of court where application made in criminal proceedings)

the application must be entered in the Administrative Court List in accordance with Practice Direction (Crown Office List) [1987] 1 WLR 232, [1987] 1 All ER 368.

Practice Directions etc., Which Apply to Order 54

7.1 On and after 26 April 1999, the practice directions, statements and practice notes set out in Table 1 continue to apply to proceedings under Order 54.

Table 1

Practice Direction etc.	Content
Practice Direction (Crown Office List: Criminal Proceedings) [1983] 1 WLR 925, [1983] 2 All ER 1020.	Urgent matters outside London—consultation of Crown Office and continuation in London
Practice Note (Crown Office List: Estimated Length of Hearing) [1987] 1 All ER 1184.	Need for accuracy in time estimates
Practice Direction (Crown Office List) [1987] 1 WLR 232, [1987] 1 All ER 368.	Parts of the List
Practice Direction (Crown Office List: Preparation for Hearings) [1994] 1 WLR 1551, [1994] 4 All ER 671.	Preparation for hearings; documentation; time limits; skeleton arguments; amendment of grounds.
Practice Direction (Crown Office List: Consent Orders) [1997] 1 WLR 825, [1997] 2 All ER 799.	Consent orders
Practice Statement (Supreme Court: Judgments) [1998] 1 WLR 825, [1998] 2 All ER 667.	Judgments

CPR Schedule 2

[For commentary on a specific CCR order, please refer to the cross-references after the title of the CCR rule.]

CCR ORDER 1 — CITATION, APPLICATION AND INTERPRETATION

Rule 6 Application of RSC to County Court Proceedings

Where by virtue of these rules or section 76 of the Act or otherwise any provision of the RSC is applied in relation to proceedings in a county court, that provision shall have effect with the necessary modifications and in particular—

(b) any reference in that provision to a Master, district judge of the Principal Registry of the Family Division, the Admiralty registrar, or a district judge or taxing officer shall be construed as a reference to the district judge of the county court; and

(d) any reference in that provision to an office of the Senior Courts having the conduct of the business of a division or court or a district registry shall be construed as a reference to the county court office.

CCR ORDER 16 — TRANSFER OF PROCEEDINGS

Rule 7 Interpleader Proceedings under Execution

(1) This rule applies to interpleader proceedings under an execution which are ordered to be transferred from the High Court.

(1A) In this rule references to the sheriff shall be interpreted as including references to an individual authorised to act as an enforcement officer under the Courts Act 2003.

(2) Notice of the hearings or pre-trial review of the proceedings shall be given by the court officer to the sheriff as well as to every other party to the proceedings.

(3) The interpleader claimant shall, within 8 days of the receipt by him of the notice referred to in paragraph (2), file in triplicate particulars of any goods alleged to be his property and the grounds of his interpleader claim and the court officer shall send a copy to the execution creditor and to the sheriff, but the judge may hear the proceedings or, as the case may be, the district judge may proceed with the pre-trial review, if he thinks fit, notwithstanding that the particulars have not been filed.

(4) Subject to any directions in the order of the High Court, damages may be claimed against the execution creditor in the same manner as in interpleader proceedings commenced in a county court.

(5) On any day fixed for the pre-trial review of the proceedings or for the hearing of any application by the sheriff or other party for directions the court may order the sheriff—

(a) to postpone the sale of the goods seized;

(b) to remain in possession of such goods until the hearing of the proceedings; or

(c) to hand over possession of such goods to the district judge,

and, where a direction is given under sub-paragraph (c), the district judge shall be allowed reasonable charges for keeping possession of the goods, not exceeding those which might be allowed to the sheriff, and, if the district judge is directed to sell the goods, such charges for the sale as would be allowed under an execution issued by the county court.

(6) No order made in the proceedings shall prejudice or affect the rights of the sheriff to any proper charges and the judge may make such order with respect to them as may be just.

(7) The charges referred to in paragraphs (5) and (6) shall ultimately be borne in such manner as the judge shall direct.

(8) The order made at the hearing of the proceedings shall direct how any money in the hands of the sheriff is to be disposed of.

CCR ORDER 22 — JUDGMENTS AND ORDERS

Rule 8 Certificate of Judgment

r.8 63.48, 79.2

(1) Any person who wishes to have a certificate of any judgment or order given or made in a claim shall make a request in writing to the court stating—
 (a) if he is a party to the claim whether the certificate—
  (i) is required for the purpose of taking proceedings on the judgment or order in another court;
  (ii) is required for the purpose of enforcing the judgment or order in the High Court; or
  (iii) is for the purpose of evidence only;
 (b) if he is not a party to the claim, the purpose for which the certificate is required, the capacity in which he asks for it and any other facts showing that the certificate may properly be granted.

(1A) Where the certificate is required for the purpose of enforcing the judgment or order in the High Court, the applicant shall also either—
 (a) state that—
  (i) it is intended to enforce the judgment or order by execution against goods; or
  (ii) the judgment or order to be enforced is an order for possession of land made in a possession claim against trespassers; or
 (b) confirm that an application has been made for an order under section 42 of the Act (transfer to High Court by order of a county court) and attach a copy of the application to the request for a certificate.

(2) Where the request is made by a person who is not a party to the claim, the request shall be referred to the district judge, who may, if he thinks fit, refer it to the judge.

(3) Without prejudice to paragraph (2), for the purposes of section 12(2) of the Act a certificate under this rule may be signed by the court manager or any other officer of the court acting on his behalf.

Rule 10 Variation of Payment

r.10 63.48

(1) Where a judgment or order has been given or made for the payment of money, the person entitled to the benefit of the judgment or order or, as the case may be, the person liable to make the payment (in this rule referred to as 'the judgment creditor' and 'the debtor' respectively) may apply in accordance with the provisions of this rule for a variation in the date or rate of payment.

(2) The judgment creditor may apply in writing, without notice being served on any other party, for an order that the money, if payable in one sum, be paid at a later date than that by which it is due or by instalments or, if the money is already payable by instalments, that it be paid by the same or smaller instalments, and the court officer may make an order accordingly unless no payment has been made under the judgment or order for 6 years before the date of the application in which case he shall refer the application to the district judge.

(3) The judgment creditor may apply to the district judge on notice for an order that the money, if payable in one sum, be paid at an earlier date than that by which it is due or, if the money is payable by instalments, that it be paid in one sum or by larger instalments, and any such application shall be made in writing stating the proposed terms and the grounds on which it is made.

(4) Where an application is made under paragraph (3)—
 (a) the proceedings shall be automatically transferred to the debtor's home court if the judgment or order was not given or made in that court; and
 (b) the court officer shall fix a day for the hearing of the application before the district judge and give to the judgment creditor and the debtor not less than 8 days' notice of the day so fixed,

and at the hearing the district judge may make such order as seems just.

(5) The debtor may apply for an order that the money, if payable in one sum, be paid at a later date than that by which it is due or by instalments or, if the money is already payable by instalments, that it be paid by smaller instalments, and any such application shall be in the appropriate form stating the proposed terms, the grounds on which it is made and including a signed statement of the debtor's means.

(6) Where an application is made under paragraph (5), the court officer shall—
  (a) send the judgment creditor a copy of the debtor's application (and statement of means); and
  (b) require the judgment creditor to notify the court in writing, within 14 days of service of notification upon him, giving his reasons for any objection he may have to the granting of the application.

(7) If the judgment creditor does not notify the court of any objection within the time stated, the court officer shall make an order in the terms applied for.

(8) Upon receipt of a notice from the judgment creditor under paragraph (6), the court officer may determine the date and rate of payment and make an order accordingly.

(9) Any party affected by an order made under paragraph (8) may, within 14 days of service of the order on him and giving his reasons, apply on notice for the order to be reconsidered and, where such an application is made—
  (a) the proceedings shall be automatically transferred to the debtor's home court if the judgment or order was not given or made in that court; and
  (b) the court officer shall fix a day for the hearing of the application before the district judge and give to the judgment creditor and the debtor not less than 8 days' notice of the day so fixed.

(10) On hearing an application under paragraph (9), the district judge may confirm the order or set it aside and make such new order as he thinks fit and the order so made shall be entered in the records of the court.

(11) Any order made under any of the foregoing paragraphs may be varied from time to time by a subsequent order made under any of those paragraphs.

Rule 11 Set-off of Cross-judgments

r.11 63.48

(1) An application under section 72 of the Act for permission to set off any sums, including costs, payable under several judgments or orders each of which was obtained in a county court shall be made in accordance with this rule.

(2) Where the judgments or orders have been obtained in the same county court, the application may be made to that court on the day when the last judgment or order is obtained, if both parties are present, and in any other case shall be made on notice.

(3) Where the judgments or orders have been obtained in different county courts, the application may be made to either of them on notice, and notice shall be given to the other court.

(4) The district judge of the court to which the application is made and the district judge of any other court to which notice is given under paragraph (3) shall forthwith stay execution on any judgment or order in his court to which the application relates and any money paid into court under the judgment or order shall be retained until the application has been disposed of.

(5) The application may be heard and determined by the court and any order giving permission shall direct how any money paid into court is to be dealt with.

(6) Where the judgments or orders have been obtained in different courts, the court in which an order giving permission is made shall send a copy of the order to the other court, which shall deal with any money paid into that court in accordance with the order.

(7) The court officer or, as the case may be, each of the court officers affected shall enter satisfaction in the records of his court for any sums ordered to be set off, and execution or other process for the enforcement of any judgment or order not wholly satisfied shall issue only for the balance remaining payable.

(8) Where an order is made by the High Court giving permission to set off sums payable under several judgments and orders obtained respectively in the High Court and a county court, the court officer of the county court shall, on receipt of a copy of the order, proceed in accordance with paragraph (7).

Rule 13 Order of Appellate Court

r.13 63.48

Where the Court of Appeal or High Court has heard and determined an appeal from a county court, the party entitled to the benefit of the order of the Court of Appeal or High Court shall deposit the order or an office copy thereof in the office of the county court.

CCR ORDER 24 — SUMMARY PROCEEDINGS FOR THE RECOVERY OF LAND

Part I Land

Rule 6 Warrant of Possession

r.6 35.13

(1) Subject to paragraphs (2) and (3), a warrant of possession to enforce an order for possession in a possession claim against trespassers under Part 55 may be issued at any time after the making of the order and subject to the provisions of Order 26, rule 17, a warrant of restitution may be issued in aid of the warrant of possession.

(2) No warrant of possession shall be issued after the expiry of 3 months from the date of the Order without the permission of the court, and an application for such permission may be made without notice being served on any other party unless the court otherwise directs.

(3) Nothing in this rule shall authorise the issue of a warrant of possession before the date on which possession is ordered to be given.

CCR ORDER 25 — ENFORCEMENT OF JUDGMENTS AND ORDERS: GENERAL

ord.25 79.1, 79.40

Rule 1 Judgment Creditor and Debtor

In this Order and Orders 26 to 29 'judgment creditor' means the person who has obtained or is entitled to enforce a judgment or order and 'debtor' means the person against whom it was given or made.

Rule 6 Description of Parties

Where the name or address of the judgment creditor or the debtor as given in the request for the issue of a warrant of execution or delivery, judgment summons or warrant of committal differs from his name or address in the judgment or order sought to be enforced and the judgment creditor satisfies the court officer that the name or address as given in the request is applicable to the person concerned, the judgment creditor or the debtor, as the case may be, shall be described in the warrant or judgment summons as 'C.D. of [name and address as given in the request] suing [or sued] as A.D. of [name and address in the judgment or order]'.

Rule 7 Recording and Giving Information as to Warrants and Orders

(1) Subject to paragraph (1A), every district judge by whom a warrant or order is issued or received for execution shall from time to time state in the records of his court what has been done in the execution of the warrant or order.

(1A) Where a warrant of execution issued by a court ('the home court') is sent to another court for execution ('the foreign court'), paragraph (1) shall not apply to the district judge of the home court, but when such a warrant is returned to the home court under paragraph (7), the court officer of the home court shall state in the records of his court what has been done in the execution of the warrant or order.

(2) If the warrant or order has not been executed within one month from the date of its issue or receipt by him, the court officer of the court responsible for its execution shall, at the end of that month and every subsequent month during which the warrant remains outstanding, send notice of the reason for non-execution to the judgment creditor and, if the warrant or order was received from another court, to that court.

(3) The district judge responsible for executing a warrant or order shall give such information respecting it as may reasonably be required by the judgment creditor and, if the warrant or order was received by him from another court, by the district judge of that court.

(4) Where money is received in pursuance of a warrant of execution or committal sent by one court to another court, the foreign court shall, subject to paragraph (5) and to section 346 of Insolvency Act 1986 and section 326 of the Companies Act 1948 send the money to the judgment creditor in the manner prescribed by the Court Funds Rules 1987 and, where the money is received in pursuance of a warrant of committal, make a return to the home court.

(5) Where interpleader proceedings are pending, the court shall not proceed in accordance with paragraph (4) until the interpleader proceedings are determined and the district judge shall then make a return showing how the money is to be disposed of and, if any money is payable to the judgment creditor, the court shall proceed in accordance with paragraph (4).

(6) Where a warrant of committal has been received from another court, the foreign court shall, on the execution of the warrant, send notice thereof to the home court.

(7) Mere a warrant of execution has been received from another court, either—
 (a) on the execution of the warrant; or
 (b) if the warrant is not executed—
  (i) on the making of a final return to the warrant; or
  (ii) on suspension of the warrant under rule 8 (suspension of judgment or execution) or Order 26, rule 10 (withdrawal and suspension of warrant at creditor's request),

the foreign court shall return the warrant to the home court.

Rule 8 Suspension of Judgment or Execution

r.8 79.5

(1) The power of the court to suspend or stay a judgment or order or to stay execution of any warrant may be exercised by the district judge or, in the case of the power to stay execution of a warrant of execution and in accordance with the provisions of this rule, by the court officer.

(2) An application by the debtor to stay execution of a warrant of execution shall be in the appropriate form stating the proposed terms, the grounds on which it is made and including a signed statement of the debtor's means.

(3) Where the debtor makes an application under paragraph (2), the court shall—
 (a) send the judgment creditor a copy of the debtor's application (and statement of means); and
 (b) require the creditor to notify the court in writing, within 14 days of service of notification upon him, giving his reasons for any objection he may have to the granting of the application.

(4) If the judgment creditor does not notify the court of any objection within the time stated, the court officer may make an order suspending the warrant on terms of payment.

(5) Upon receipt of a notice by the judgment creditor under paragraph (3)(b), the court officer may, if the judgment creditor objects only to the terms offered, determine the date and rate of payment and make an order suspending the warrant on terms of payment.

(6) Any party affected by an order made under paragraph (5) may, within 14 days of service of the order on him and giving his reasons, apply on notice for the order to be reconsidered and the court shall fix a day for the hearing of the application before the district judge and give to the judgment creditor and the debtor not less than 8 days' notice of the day so fixed.

(7) On hearing an application under paragraph (6), the district judge may confirm the order or set it aside and make such new order as he thinks fit and the order so made shall be entered in the records of the court.

(8) Where the judgment creditor states in his notice under paragraph (3)(b) that he wishes the bailiff to proceed to execute the warrant, the court shall fix a day for a hearing before the district judge of the debtor's application and give to the judgment creditor and to the debtor not less than 2 days' notice of the day so fixed.

(9) Subject to any directions given by the district judge, where a warrant of execution has been suspended, it may be re-issued on the judgment creditor's filing a request showing that any condition subject to which the warrant was suspended has not been complied with.

(10) Where an order is made by the district judge suspending a warrant of execution, the debtor may be ordered to pay the costs of the warrant and any fees or expenses incurred before its suspension and the order may authorise the sale of a sufficient portion of any goods seized to cover such costs, fees and expenses and the expenses of sale.

Rule 13 Transfer to High Court for Enforcement

r.13 79.2

(1) Where the judgment creditor makes a request for a certificate of judgment under Order 22, rule 8(1) for the purpose of enforcing the judgment or order in the High Court—
 (a) by execution against goods; or

(b) where the judgment or order to be enforced is an order for possession of land made in a possession claim against trespassers,

the grant of a certificate by the court shall take effect as an order to transfer the proceedings to the High Court and the transfer shall have effect on the grant of that certificate.

(2) On the transfer of proceedings in accordance with paragraph (1), the court shall give notice to the debtor or the person against whom the possession order was made that the proceedings have been transferred and shall make an entry of that fact in the records of his court.

(3) In a case where a request for a certificate of judgment is made under Order 22, rule 8(1) for the purpose of enforcing a judgment or order in the High Court and—

(a) an application for a variation in the date or rate of payment of money due under a judgment or order;

(b) an application under either CPR rule 39.3(3) or CPR rule 13.4;

(c) a request for an administration order; or

(d) an application for a stay of execution under section 88 of the Act,

is pending, the request for the certificate shall not be dealt with until those proceedings are determined.

CCR ORDER 26 — WARRANTS OF EXECUTION, DELIVERY AND POSSESSION

ord.26 79.1, 79.40

Rule 1 Application for Warrant of Execution

(1) A judgment creditor desiring a warrant of execution to be issued shall file a request in that behalf certifying—

(a) the amount remaining due under the judgment or order; and

(b) where the order made is for payment of a sum of money by instalments—

(i) that the whole or part of any instalment due remains unpaid; and

(ii) the amount for which the warrant is to be issued.

(1A) The court officer shall discharge the functions—

(a) under section 85(2) of the Act of issuing a warrant of execution;

(b) under section 85(3) of the Act of entering in the record mentioned in that subsection and on the warrant the precise time of the making of the application to issue the warrant, and

(c) under section 103(1) of the Act of sending the warrant of execution to another county court.

(2) Where the court has made an order for payment of a sum of money by instalments and default has been made in payment of such an instalment, a warrant of execution may be issued for the whole of the said sum of money and costs then remaining unpaid or, subject to paragraph (3), for such part as the judgment creditor may request, not being in the latter case less than £50 or the amount of one monthly instalment or, as the case may be, 4 weekly instalments, whichever is the greater.

(3) In any case to which paragraph (2) applies no warrant shall be issued unless at the time when it is issued—

(a) the whole or part of an instalment which has already become due remains unpaid; and

(b) any warrant previously issued for part of the said sum of money and costs has expired or has been satisfied or abandoned.

(4) Where a warrant is issued for the whole or part of the said sum of money and costs, the court officer shall, unless the district judge responsible for execution of the warrant directs otherwise, send a warning notice to the person against whom the warrant is issued and, where such a notice is sent, the warrant shall not be levied until 7 days thereafter.

(5) Where judgment is given or an order made for payment otherwise than by instalments of a sum of money and costs to be assessed in accordance with CPR Part 47 (detailed assessment procedure) and default is made in payment of the sum of money before the costs have been assessed, a warrant of execution may issue for recovery of the sum of money and a separate warrant may issue subsequently for the recovery of the costs if default. is made in payment of them.

Rule 2 Execution of High Court Judgment

(1) Where it is desired to enforce by warrant of execution a judgment or order of the High Court, or a judgment, order, decree or award which is or has become enforceable as if it were a judgment

of the High Court, the request referred to in rule 1(1) may be filed in any court in the district of which execution is to be levied.

(2) Subject to Order 25, rule 9(5), any restriction imposed by these rules on the issue of execution shall apply as if the judgment, order, decree or award were a judgment or order of the county court, but permission to issue execution shall not be required if permission has already been given by the High Court.

(3) Notice of the issue of the warrant shall be sent by the county court to the High Court.

Rule 3 Execution against Farmer

If after the issue of a warrant of execution the district judge for the district in which the warrant is to be executed has reason to believe that the debtor is a farmer, the execution creditor shall, if so required by the district judge, furnish him with an official certificate, dated not more than three days beforehand, of the result of a search at the Land Registry as to the existence of any charge registered against the debtor under the Agricultural Credits Act 1928.

Rule 4 Concurrent Warrants

Two or more warrants of execution may be issued concurrently for execution in different districts, but—

(a) no more shall be levied under all the warrants together than is authorised to be levied under one of them; and

(b) the costs of more than one such warrant shall not be allowed against the debtor except by order of the court.

Rule 5 Permission to Issue Certain Warrants

r.5 79.9

(1) A warrant of execution shall not issue without the permission of the court where—

(a) six years or more have elapsed since the date of the judgment or order;

(b) any change has taken place, whether by death or otherwise in the parties entitled to enforce the judgment or order or liable to have it enforced against them;

(c) the judgment or order is against the assets of a deceased person coming into the hands of his executors or administrators after the date of the judgment or order and it is sought to issue execution against such assets; or

(d) any goods to be seized under a warrant of execution are in the hands of a receiver appointed by a court.

(2) An application for permission shall be supported by a witness statement or affidavit establishing the applicant's right to relief and may be made without notice being served on any other party in the first instance but the court may direct the application notice to be served on such persons as it thinks fit.

(3) Where, by reason of one and the same event, a person seeks permission under paragraph (1)(b) to enforce more judgments or orders than one, he may make one application only, specifying in a schedule all the judgments or orders in respect of which it is made, and if the application notice is directed to be served on any person, it need set out only such part of the application as affects him.

(4) Paragraph (1) is without prejudice to any enactment, rule or direction by virtue of which a person is required to obtain the permission of the court for the issue of a warrant or to proceed to execution or otherwise to the enforcement of a judgment or order.

Rule 6 Duration and Renewal of Warrant

(1) A warrant of execution shall, for the purpose of execution, be valid in the first instance for 12 months beginning with the date of its issue, but if not wholly executed, it may be renewed from time to time, by order of the court, for a period of 12 months at any one time, beginning with the day next following that on which it would otherwise expire, if an application for renewal is made before that day or such later day (if any) as the court may allow.

(2) A note of any such renewal shall be indorsed on the warrant and it shall be entitled to priority according to the time of its original issue or, where appropriate, its receipt by the district judge responsible for its execution.

Rule 7 Notice on Levy

Any bailiff upon levying execution shall deliver to the debtor or leave at the place where execution is levied a notice of the warrant.

Rule 8 Bankruptcy or Winding Up of Debtor

(1) Where the district judge responsible for the execution of a warrant is required by any provision of the Insolvency Act 1986 or any other enactment relating to insolvency to retain the proceeds of sale of goods sold under the warrant or money paid in order to avoid a sale, the court shall, as soon as practicable after the sale or the receipt of the money, send notice to the execution creditor and, if the warrant issued out of another court, to that court.

(2) Where the district judge responsible for the execution of a warrant—

(a) receives notice that a bankruptcy order has been made against the debtor or, if the debtor is a company, that a provisional liquidator has been appointed or that an order has been made or a resolution passed for the winding up of the company; and

(b) withdraws from possession of goods seized or pays over to the official receiver or trustee in bankruptcy or, if the debtor is a company, to the liquidator the proceeds of sale of goods sold under the warrant or money paid in order to avoid a sale or seized or received in part satisfaction of the warrant,

the court shall send notice to the execution creditor and, if the warrant issued out of another court, to that court.

(3) Where the court officer of a court to which a warrant issued out of another court has been sent for execution receives any such notice as is referred to in paragraph (2)(a) after he has sent to the home court any money seized or received in part satisfaction of the warrant, he shall forward the notice to that court.

Rule 10 Withdrawal and Suspension of Warrant at Creditor's Request

(1) Where an execution creditor requests the district judge responsible for executing a warrant to withdraw from possession, he shall, subject to the following paragraphs of this rule, be treated as having abandoned the execution, and the court shall mark the warrant as withdrawn by request of the execution creditor.

(2) Where the request is made in consequence of a claim having been made under Order 33, rule 1, to goods seized under the warrant, the execution shall be treated as being abandoned in respect only of the goods claimed.

(3) If the district judge responsible for executing a warrant is requested by the execution creditor to suspend it in pursuance of an arrangement between him and the debtor, the court shall mark the warrant as suspended by request of the execution creditor and the execution creditor may subsequently apply to the district judge holding the warrant for it to be re-issued and, if he does so, the application shall be deemed for the purpose of section 85(3) of the Act to be an application to issue the warrant.

(4) Nothing in this rule shall prejudice any right of the execution creditor to apply for the issue of a fresh warrant or shall authorise the re-issue of a warrant which has been withdrawn or has expired or has been superseded by the issue of a fresh warrant.

Rule 11 Suspension of Part Warrant

Where a warrant issued for part of a sum of money and costs payable under a judgment or order is suspended on payment of instalments, the judgment or order shall, unless the court otherwise directs, be treated as suspended on those terms as respects the whole of the sum of money and costs then remaining unpaid.

Rule 12 Inventory and Notice Where Goods Removed

(1) Where goods seized in execution are removed, the court shall forthwith deliver or send to the debtor a sufficient inventory of the goods removed and shall, not less than 4 days before the time fixed for the sale, give him notice of the time and place at which the goods will be sold.

(2) The inventory and notice shall be given to the debtor by delivering them to him personally or by sending them to him by post at his place of residence or, if his place of residence is not known,

by leaving them for him, or sending them to him by post, at the place from which the goods were removed.

Rule 13 Account of Sale

Where goods are sold under an execution, the court shall furnish the debtor with a detailed account in writing of the sale and of the application of the proceeds.

Rule 14 Notification to Foreign Court of Payment Made

Where, after a warrant has been sent to a foreign court for execution but before a final return has been made to the warrant, the home court is notified of a payment made in respect of the sum for which the warrant is issued, the home court shall send notice of the payment to the foreign court.

Rule 15 Order for Private Sale

(1) Subject to paragraph (6), an order of the court under section 97 of the Act that a sale under an execution may be made otherwise than by public auction may be made on the application of the execution creditor or the debtor or the district judge responsible for the execution of the warrant.
(2) Where he is not the applicant for an order under this rule, the district judge responsible for the execution of the warrant shall, on the demand of the applicant, furnish him with a list containing the name and address of every execution creditor under any other warrant or writ of execution against the goods of the debtor of which the district judge has notice, and where the district judge is the applicant, he shall prepare such a list.
(3) Not less than 4 days before the day fixed for the hearing of the application, the applicant shall give notice of the application to each of the other persons by whom the application might have been made and to every person named in the list referred to in paragraph (2).
(4) The applicant shall produce the list to the court on the hearing of the application.
(5) Every person to whom notice of the application was given may attend and be heard on the hearing of the application.
(6) Where the district judge responsible for the execution of the warrant is the district judge by whom it was issued and he has no notice of any other warrant or writ of execution against the goods of the debtor, an order under this rule may be made by the court of its own motion with the consent of the execution creditor and the debtor or after giving them an opportunity of being heard.

Rule 16 Warrant of Delivery

(1) Except where an Act or rule provides otherwise, a judgment or order for the delivery of any goods shall be enforceable by warrant of delivery in accordance with this rule.
(2) If the judgment or order does not give the person against whom it was given or made the alternative of paying the value of the goods, it may be enforced by a warrant of specific delivery, that is to say, a warrant to recover the goods without alternative provision for recovery of their value.
(3) If the judgment or order is for the delivery of the goods or payment of their value, it may be enforced by a warrant of delivery to recover the goods or their value.
(4) Where a warrant of delivery is issued, the judgment creditor shall be entitled, by the same or a separate warrant, to execution against the debtor's goods for any money payable under the judgment or order which is to be enforced by the warrant of delivery.
(4A) Where a judgment or order is given or made for the delivery of goods or payment of their value and a warrant is issued to recover the goods or their value, money paid into court under the warrant shall be appropriated first to any sum of money and costs awarded.
(5) The foregoing provisions of this Order, so far as applicable, shall have effect, with the necessary modifications, in relation to warrants of delivery as they have effect in relation to warrants of execution.

Rule 17 Warrant of Possession

r.17 PC 38
r.17(2A) PC 38, 87.53
r.17(4) PC 38, 79.34, 87.57
r.17(5) PC 38

(1) A judgment or order for the recovery of land shall be enforceable by warrant of possession.

(2) Without prejudice to paragraph (3A), the person applying for a warrant of possession must file a certificate that the land which is subject [*sic*] of the judgment or order has not been vacated.
(2A) When applying for a warrant of possession of a dwelling-house subject to a mortgage, the claimant must certify that notice has been given in accordance with the Dwelling Houses (Execution of Possession Orders by Mortgagees) Regulations 2010.
(3) Where a warrant of possession is issued, the judgment creditor shall be entitled, by the same or a separate warrant, to execution against the debtor's goods for any money payable under the judgment or order which is to be enforced by the warrant of possession.
(3A) In a case to which paragraph (3) applies or where an order for possession has been suspended on terms as to payment of a sum of money by instalments, the judgment creditor shall in his request certify—
   (a) the amount of money remaining due under the judgment or order; and
   (b) that the whole or part of any instalment due remains unpaid.
(4) A warrant of restitution may be issued, with the permission of the court, in aid of any warrant of possession.
(5) An application for permission under paragraph (4) may be made without notice being served on any other party and shall be, supported by evidence of wrongful re-entry into possession following the execution of the warrant of possession and of such further facts as would, in the High Court, enable the judgment creditor to have a writ of restitution issued.
(6) Rules 5 and 6 shall apply, with the necessary modifications, in relation to a warrant of possession and any further warrant in aid of such a warrant as they apply in relation to a warrant of execution.

Rule 18 Saving for Enforcement by Committal

Nothing in rule 16 or 17 shall prejudice any power to enforce a judgment or order for the delivery of goods or the recovery of land by an order of committal.

CCR ORDER 27 — ATTACHMENT OF EARNINGS

ord.27 79.1, 79.40

Part I General

Rule 1 Interpretation

(1) In this Order—
'the Act of 1971' means the Attachment of Earnings Act 1971 and, unless the context otherwise requires, expressions used in that Act have the same meanings as in that Act.

Rule 2 Index of Orders

(1) The court officer of every court shall keep a nominal index of the debtors residing within the district of his court in respect of whom there are in force attachment of earnings orders which have been made by that court or of which the court officer has received notice from another court.
(2) Where a debtor in respect of whom a court has made an attachment of earnings order resides within the district of another court, the court officer of the first-mentioned court shall send a copy of the order to the court officer of the other court for entry in his index.
(3) The court officer shall, on the request of any person having a judgment or order against a person believed to be residing within the district of the court, cause a search to be made in the index of the court and issue a certificate of the result of the search.

Rule 3 Appropriate Court

r.3 79.2, 79.5 r.3(4) 42.7, 79.2

(1) Subject to paragraphs (2), (3) and (4), an application for an attachment of earnings order may be made to the court for the district in which the debtor resides.
(2) Subject to paragraph (4), if the debtor does not reside within England or Wales, or the creditor does not know where the debtor resides, the application may be made to the court in which, or *for the district in which*, the judgment or order sought to be enforced was obtained.
(3) Subject to paragraph (4), where the creditor applies for attachment of earnings orders in respect of two or more debtors jointly liable under a judgment or order, the application may be made to

the court for the district in which any of the debtors resides, so however that if the judgment or order was given or made by any such court, the application shall be made to that court.

(4) Where the judgment was made in Northampton County Court in respect of a designated money claim and the proceedings have not since been transferred to a different court, the application must be made in accordance with section 2 of Practice Direction 70.

Rule 4 Mode of Applying

(1) A judgment creditor who desires to apply for an attachment of earnings order shall file his application certifying the amount of money remaining due under the judgment or order and that the whole or part of any instalment due remains unpaid and, where it is sought to enforce an order of a magistrates' court—

(a) a certified copy of the order; and

(b) a witness statement or affidavit verifying the amount due under the order or, if payments under the order are required to be made to the designated officer for the magistrates' court, a certificate by that designated officer to the same effect.

(2) On the filing of the documents mentioned in paragraph (1) the court officer shall, where the order to be enforced is a maintenance order, fix a day for the hearing of the application.

Rule 5 Service and Reply

(1) Notice of the application together with a form of reply in the appropriate form, shall be served on the debtor in the manner set out in CPR rule 6.20.

(2) The debtor shall, within 8 days after service on him of the documents mentioned in paragraph (1), file a reply in the form provided, and the instruction to that effect in the notice to the debtor shall constitute a requirement imposed by virtue of section 14(4) of the Act of 1971:

Provided that no proceedings shall be taken for an offence alleged to have been committed under section 23(2)(c) or (f) of the Act of 1971 in relation to the requirement unless the said documents have been served on the debtor personally or the court is satisfied that they came to his knowledge in sufficient time for him to comply with the requirement.

(2A) Nothing in paragraph (2) shall require a defendant to file a reply if, within the period of time mentioned in that paragraph, he pays to the judgment creditor the money remaining due under the judgment or order and, where such payment is made, the judgment creditor shall so inform the court officer.

(3) On receipt of a reply the court officer shall send a copy to the applicant.

Rule 6 Notice to Employer

Without prejudice to the powers conferred by section 14(1) of the Act of 1971, the court officer may, at any stage of the proceedings, send to any person appearing to have the debtor in his employment a notice requesting him to give to the court, within such period as may be specified in the notice, a statement of the debtor's earnings and anticipated earnings with such particulars as may be so specified.

Rule 7 Attachment of Earnings Order

r.7(1) 79.21

(1) On receipt of the debtor's reply, the court officer may, if he has sufficient information to do so, make an attachment of earnings order and a copy of the order shall be sent to the parties and to the debtor's employer.

(2) Where an order is made under paragraph (1), the judgment creditor or the debtor may, within 14 days of service of the order on him and giving his reasons, apply on notice for the order to be re-considered and the court officer shall fix a day for the hearing of the application and give to the judgment creditor and the debtor not less than 2 days' notice of the day so fixed.

(3) On hearing an application under paragraph (2), the district judge may confirm the order or set it aside and make such new order as he thinks fit and the order so made shall be entered in the records of the court.

(4) Where an order is not made under paragraph (1), the court officer shall refer the application to the district judge who shall, if he considers that he has sufficient information to do so without the attendance of the parties, determine the application.

(5) Where the district judge does not determine the application under paragraph (4), he shall direct that a day be fixed for the hearing of the application whereupon the court officer shall fix such a day and give to the judgment creditor and the debtor not less than 8 days' notice of the day so fixed.
(6) Where an order is made under paragraph (4), the judgment creditor or the debtor may, within 14 days of service of the order on him and giving his reasons, apply on notice for the order to be re-considered; and the court officer shall fix a day for the hearing of the application and give to the judgment creditor and the debtor not less than 2 days' notice of the day so fixed.
(7) On hearing an application under paragraph (6), the district judge may confirm the order or set it aside and make such new order as he thinks fit and the order so made shall be entered in the records of the court.
(8) If the creditor does not appear at the hearing of the application under paragraph (5) but—
  (a) the court has received a witness statement or affidavit of evidence from him; or
  (b) the creditor requests the court in writing to proceed in his absence,
the court may proceed to hear the application and to make an order thereon.
(9) An attachment of earnings order may be made to secure the payment of a judgment debt if the debt is—
  (a) of not less than £50; or
  (b) for the amount remaining payable under a judgment for a sum of not less than £50.

Rule 7A Failure by Debtor

(1) If the debtor has failed to comply with rule 5(2) or to make payment to the judgment creditor, the court officer may issue an order under section 14(1) of the Act of 1971 which shall—
  (a) be indorsed with or incorporate a notice warning the debtor of the consequences of disobedience to the order;
  (b) be served on the debtor personally; and
  (c) direct that any payments made thereafter shall be paid into the court and not direct to the judgment creditor.
(2) Without prejudice to rule 16, if the person served with an order made pursuant to paragraph (1) fails to obey it or to file a statement of his means or to make payment, the court officer shall issue a notice calling on that person to show good reason why he should not be imprisoned and any such notice shall be served on the debtor personally not less than 5 days before the hearing.
(3) [*Revoked*]
(4) In this rule 'statement of means' means a statement given under section 14(1) of the Act of 1971.

Rule 7B Suspended Committal Order

(1) If the debtor fails to attend at an adjourned hearing of an application for an attachment of earnings order and a committal order is made, the judge or district judge may direct that the committal order shall be suspended so long as the debtor attends at the time and place specified in the committal order and paragraphs (2), (4) and (5) of Order 28, rule 7 shall apply, with the necessary modifications, where such a direction is given as they apply where a direction is given under paragraph (1) of that rule.
(2) Where a committal order is suspended under paragraph (1) and the debtor fails to attend at the time and place specified under paragraph (1), a certificate to that effect given by the court officer shall be sufficient authority for the issue of a warrant of committal.

Rule 8 Failure by Debtor — Maintenance Orders

(1) An order made under section 23(1) of the Act of 1971 for the attendance of the debtor at an adjourned hearing of an application for an attachment of earnings order to secure payments under a maintenance order shall—
  (a) be served on the debtor personally not less than 5 days before the day fixed for the adjourned hearing; and
  (b) direct that any payments made thereafter shall be paid into the court and not direct to the judgment creditor.
(2) An application by a debtor for the revocation of an order committing him to prison and, if he is already in custody, for his discharge under subsection (7) of the said section 23 shall be made to the judge or district judge in writing without notice to any other party showing the reasons for

the debtor's failure to attend the court or his refusal to be sworn or to give evidence, as the case may be, and containing an undertaking by the debtor to attend the court or to be sworn or to give evidence when next ordered or required to do so.

(3) The application shall, if the debtor has already been lodged in prison, be attested by the governor of the prison (or any other officer of the prison not below the rank of principal officer) and in any other case be made on witness statement or affidavit.

(4) Before dealing with the application the judge or district judge may, if he thinks fit, cause notice to be given to the judgment creditor that the application has been made and of a day and hour when he may attend and be heard.

Rule 9 Costs

(1) Where costs are allowed to the judgment creditor on an application for an attachment of earnings order, there may be allowed—

(a) a charge of a solicitor for attending the hearing and, if the court so directs, for serving the application;

(b) if the court certifies that the case is fit for counsel, a fee to counsel; and

(c) the court fee on the issue of the application.

(2) For the purpose of paragraph (1)(a) a solicitor who has prepared on behalf of the judgment creditor a witness statement or affidavit or request under rule 7(3) shall be treated as having attended the hearing.

(3) The costs may be fixed and allowed without detailed assessment under CPR Part 47.

Rule 10 Contents and Service of Order

(1) An attachment of earnings order shall contain such of the following particulars relating to the debtor as are known to the court, namely—

(a) his full name and address;

(b) his place of work; and

(c) the nature of his work and his works number, if any, and those particulars shall be the prescribed particulars for the purposes of section 6(3) of the Act of 1971.

(2) An attachment of earnings order and any order varying or discharging such an order shall be served on the debtor and on the person to whom the order is directed, and CPR Part 6 and CPR rules 40.4 and 40.5 shall apply with the further modification that where the order is directed to a corporation which has requested the court that any communication relating to the debtor or to the class of persons to whom he belongs shall be directed to the corporation at a particular address, service may, if the district judge thinks fit, be effected on the corporation at that address.

(3) Where an attachment of earnings order is made to enforce a judgment or order of the High Court or a magistrates' court, a copy of the attachment of earnings order and of any order discharging it shall be sent by the court officer of the county court to the court officer of the High Court, or, as the case may be, the designated officer for the magistrates' court.

Rule 11 Application to Determine Whether Particular Payments Are Earnings

An application to the court under section 16 of the Act of 1971 to determine whether payments to the debtor of a particular class or description are earnings for the purpose of an attachment of earnings order may be made to the district judge in writing and the court officer shall there upon fix a date and time for the hearing of the application by the court and give notice thereof to the persons mentioned in the said section 16(2)(a), (b) and (c).

Rule 12 Notice of Cesser

Where an attachment of earnings order ceases to have effect under section 8(4) of the Act of 1971, the court officer of the court in which the matter is proceeding shall give notice of the cesser to the person to whom the order was directed.

Rule 13 Variation and Discharge by Court of Own Motion

(1) Subject to paragraph (9), the powers conferred by section 9(1) of the Act of 1971 may be exercised by the court of its own motion in the circumstances mentioned in the following paragraphs.

(2) Where it appears to the court that a person served with an attachment of earnings order directed to him has not the debtor in his employment, the court may discharge the order.

(3) Where an attachment of earnings order which has lapsed under section 9(4) of the Act of 1971 is again directed to a person who appears to the court to have the debtor in his employment, the court may make such consequential variations in the order as it thinks fit.

(4) Where, after making an attachment of earnings order, the court makes or is notified of the making of another such order in respect of the same debtor which is not to secure the payment of a judgment debt or payments under an administration order, the court may discharge or vary the first-mentioned order having regard to the priority accorded to the other order by paragraph 8 of Schedule 3 to the Act of 1971.

(5) Where, after making an attachment of earnings order, the court makes an order under section 4(1)(b) of the Act of 1971 or makes an administration order, the court may discharge the attachment of earnings order or, if it exercises the power conferred by section 5(3) of the said Act, may vary the order in such manner as it thinks fit.

(6) On making a consolidated attachment of earnings order the court may discharge any earlier attachment of earnings order made to secure the payment of a judgment debt by the same debtor.

(7) Where it appears to the court that a bankruptcy order has been made against a person in respect of whom an attachment of earnings order is in force to secure the payment of a judgment debt, the court may discharge the attachment of earnings order.

(8) Where an attachment of earnings order has been made to secure the payment of a judgment debt and the court grants permission to issue execution for the recovery of the debt, the court may discharge the order.

(9) Before varying or discharging an attachment of earnings order of its own motion under any of the foregoing paragraphs of this rule, the court shall, unless it thinks it unnecessary in the circumstances to do so, give the debtor and the person on whose application the order was made an opportunity of being heard on the question whether the order should be varied or discharged, and for that purpose the court officer may give them notice of a date, time and place at which the question will be considered.

Rule 14 Transfer of Attachment Order

(1) Where the court by which the question of making a consolidated attachment order falls to be considered is not the court by which any attachment of earnings order has been made to secure the payment of a judgment debt by the debtor, the district judge of the last-mentioned court shall, at the request of the district judge of the first-mentioned court, transfer to that court the matter in which the attachment of earnings order was made.

(2) Without prejudice to paragraph (1), if in the opinion of the judge or district judge of any court by which an attachment of earnings order has been made, the matter could more conveniently proceed in some other court, whether by reason of the debtor having become resident in the district of that court or otherwise, he may order the matter to be transferred to that court.

(3) The court to which proceedings arising out of an attachment of earnings are transferred under this rule shall have the same jurisdiction in relation to the order as if it has been made by that court.

Rule 15 Exercise of Power to Obtain Statement of Earnings etc.

(1) An order under section 14(1) of the Act of 1971 shall be indorsed with or incorporate a notice warning the person to whom it is directed of the consequences of disobedience to the order and shall be served on him personally.

(2) Order 34, rule 2, shall apply, with the necessary modifications, in relation to any penalty for failure to comply with an order under the said section 14(1) or, subject to the proviso to rule 5(2), any penalty for failure to comply with a requirement mentioned in that rule, as it applies in relation to a fine under section 55 of the County Courts Act 1984.

Rule 16 Offences

(1) *Where it is alleged that* a person has committed any offence mentioned in section 23(2)(a), (b), (d), (e) or (f) of the Act of 1971 in relation to proceedings in, or to an attachment of earnings order made by, a county court, the district judge shall, unless it is decided to proceed against the

alleged offender summarily, issue a summons calling upon him to show cause why he should not be punished for the alleged offence.

The summons shall be served on the alleged offender personally not less than 14 days before the return day.

(2) Order 34, rules 3 and 4, shall apply, with the necessary modifications, to proceedings for an offence under section 23(2) of the Act of 1971 as they apply to proceedings for offences under the County Courts Act 1984.

Rule 17 Maintenance Orders

(1) The foregoing rules of this Order shall apply in relation to maintenance payments as they apply in relation to a judgment debt, subject to the following paragraphs.

(2) An application for an attachment of earnings order to secure payments under a maintenance order made by a county court shall be made to that county court.

(3) Any application under section 32 of the Matrimonial Causes Act 1973 for permission to enforce the payment of arrears which became due more than 12 months before the application for an attachment of earnings order shall be made in that application.

(3A) Notice of the application together with a form of reply in the appropriate form, shall be served on the debtor in the manner set out in CPR rule 6.20.

(3B) Service of the notice shall be effected not less than 21 days before the hearing, but service may be effected at any time before the hearing on the applicant satisfying the court by witness statement or affidavit that the respondent is about to remove from his address for service.

(3C) Rule 5(2A) shall not apply.

(4) An application by the debtor for an attachment of earnings order to secure payments under a maintenance order may be made on the making of the maintenance order or an order varying the maintenance order, and rules 4 and 5 shall not apply.

(5) Rule 7 shall have effect as if for paragraphs (1) to (8) there were substituted the following paragraph—

'(1) An application for an attachment of earnings order may be heard and determined by the district judge, who shall hear the application in private.'

(6) Rule 9 shall apply as if for the reference to the amount payable under the relevant adjudication there were substituted a reference to the arrears due under the related maintenance order.

(7) Where an attachment of earnings order made by the High Court designates the court officer of a county court as the collecting officer, that officer shall, on receipt of a certified copy of the order from the court officer of the High Court, send to the person to whom the order is directed a notice as to the mode of payment.

(8) Where an attachment of earnings order made by a county court to secure payments under a maintenance order ceases to have effect and—

(a) the related maintenance order was made by that court; or

(b) the related maintenance order was an order of the High Court and—

(i) the court officer of the county court has received notice of the cessation from the court officer of the High Court; or

(ii) a committal order has been made in the county court for the enforcement of the related maintenance order,

the court officer of the county court shall give notice of the cessation to the person to whom the attachment of earnings order was directed.

(9) Where an attachment of earnings order has been made by a county court to secure payments under a maintenance order, notice under section 10(2) of the Act of 1971 to the debtor and to the person to whom the district judge is required to pay sums received under the order shall be in the form provided for that purpose, and if the debtor wishes to request the court to discharge the attachment of earnings order or to vary it otherwise than by making the appropriate variation, he shall apply to the court, within 14 days after the date of the notice, for the remedy desired.

(10) Rule 13 shall have effect as if for paragraphs (4) to (7) there were substituted the following paragraph—

'(4) Where it appears to the court by which an attachment of earnings order has been made that he related maintenance order has ceased to have effect, whether by virtue of the terms of the maintenance order or under section 28 of the Matrimonial Causes Act 1973 or otherwise, the court may discharge or vary the attachment of earnings order.'

Part II Consolidated Attachment of Earnings Orders

Rule 18 Cases in Which Consolidated Order May be Made

Subject to the provisions of rules 19 to 21, the court may make a consolidated attachment order where—

(a) two or more attachment of earnings orders are in force to secure the payment of judgment debts by the same debtor; or

(b) on an application for an attachment of earnings order to secure the payment of a judgment debt, or for a consolidated attachment order to secure the payment of two or more judgment debts, it appears to the court that an attachment of earnings order is already in force to secure the payment of a judgment debt by the same debtor.

Rule 19 Application for Consolidated Order

(1) An application for a consolidated attachment order may be made—

(a) by the debtor in respect of whom the order is sought; or

(b) by any person who has obtained or is entitled to apply for an attachment of earnings order to secure the payment of a judgment debt by that debtor.

(2) An application under paragraph (1) may be made in the proceedings in which any attachment of earnings order (other than a priority order) is in force and rules 3, 4 and 5 of this Order shall not apply.

(3) Where the judgment which it is sought to enforce was not given by the court which made the attachment of earnings order, the judgment shall be automatically transferred to the court which made the attachment of earnings order.

(3A) An application under paragraph (1)(b) shall certify the amount of money remaining due under the judgment or order and that the whole or part of any instalment due remains unpaid.

(3B) Where an application for a consolidated attachment of earnings order is made, the court officer shall—

(a) notify any party who may be affected by the application of its terms; and

(b) require him to notify the court in writing, within 14 days of service of notification upon him, giving his reasons for any objection he may have to the granting of the application.

(3C) If notice of any objection is not given within the time stated, the court officer shall make a consolidated attachment of earnings order.

(3D) If any party objects to the making of a consolidated attachment of earnings order, the court officer shall refer the application to the district judge who may grant the application after considering the objection made and the reasons given.

(3E) In the foregoing paragraphs of this rule, a party affected by the application means—

(a) where the application is made by the debtor, the creditor in the proceedings in which the application is made and any other creditor who has obtained an attachment of earnings order which is in force to secure the payment of a judgment debt by the debtor;

(b) where the application is made by the judgment creditor, the debtor and every person who, to the knowledge of the applicant, has obtained an attachment of earnings order which is in force to secure the payment of a judgment debt by the debtor.

(4) A person to whom two or more attachment of earnings orders are directed to secure the payment of judgment debts by the same debtor may request the court in writing to make a consolidated attachment order to secure the payment of those debts, and on receipt of such a request paragraphs (3B) to (3E) shall apply, with the necessary modifications, as if the request were an application by the judgment creditor.

Rule 20 Making of Consolidated Order by Court of Its Own Motion

Where an application is made for an attachment of earnings order to secure the payment of a judgment debt by a debtor in respect of whom an attachment of earnings order is already in force to secure the payment of another judgment debt and no application is made for a consolidated attachment order, the court officer may make such an order of his own motion after giving all persons concerned an opportunity of submitting written objections.

Rule 21 Extension of Consolidated Order

(1) Where a consolidated attachment order is in force to secure the payment of two or more judgment debts, any creditor to whom another judgment debt is owed by the same judgment debtor may apply to the court by which the order was made for it to be extended so as to secure the payment of that debt as well as the first-mentioned debts and, if the application is granted, the court may either vary the order accordingly or may discharge it and make a new consolidated attachment order to secure payment of all the aforesaid judgment debts.
(2) An application under this rule shall be treated for the purposes of rules 19 and 20 as an application for a consolidated attachment order.

Rule 22 Payments under Consolidated Order

Instead of complying with section 13 of the Act of 1971, a court officer who receives payments made to him in compliance with a consolidated attachment order shall, after deducting such court fees, if any, in respect of proceedings for or arising out of the order as are deductible from those payments, deal with the sums paid as he would if they had been paid by the debtor to satisfy the relevant adjudications in proportion to the amounts payable thereunder, and for that purpose dividends may from time to time be declared and distributed among the creditors entitled thereto.

CCR ORDER 28 — JUDGMENT SUMMONSES

ord.28 79.1, 79.30, 79.40

Rule 1 Application for Judgment Summons

r.1 79.2

(1) An application for the issue of a judgment summons may be made to the court for the district in which the debtor resides or carries on business or, if the summons is to issue against two or more persons jointly liable under the judgment or order sought to be enforced, in the court for the district in which any of the debtors resides or carries on business.
(2) The judgment creditor shall make his application by filing a request in that behalf certifying the amount of money remaining due under the judgment or order, the amount in respect of which the judgment summons is to issue and that the whole or part of any instalment due remains unpaid.
(3) The judgment creditor must file with the request all written evidence on which he intends to rely.

Rule 2 Mode of Service

(1) Subject to paragraph (2), a judgment summons shall be served personally on every debtor against whom it is issued.
(2) Where the judgment creditor or the judgment creditor's solicitor gives a certificate for postal service in respect of a debtor residing or carrying on business within the district of the court, the judgment summons will, unless the district judge otherwise directs, be served on that debtor by the court sending it to the debtor by first-class post at the address stated in the request for the judgment summons and, unless the contrary is shown, the date of service is deemed to be the seventh day after the date on which the judgment summons was sent to the debtor.
(3) Where a judgment summons has been served on a debtor in accordance with paragraph (2), no order of commitment shall be made against him unless—
  (a) he appears at the hearing; or
  (b) it is made under section 110(2) of the Act.
(4) The written evidence on which the judgment creditor intends to rely must be served with the judgment summons.

Rule 3 Time for Service

(1) The judgment summons and written evidence must be served not less than 14 days before the day fixed for the hearing.
(2) A notice of non-service will be sent pursuant to CPR rule 6.18 in respect of a judgment summons which has been sent by post under rule 2(2) and has been returned to the court undelivered.
(3) CPR rules 7.5 and 7.6 apply, with the necessary modifications, to a judgment summons as they apply to a claim form.

Rule 4 Enforcement of Debtor's Attendance

(1) Order 27, rules 711 and 8, shall apply, with the necessary modifications, to an order made under section 110(1) of the Act for the attendance of the debtor at an adjourned hearing of a judgment summons as they apply to an order made under section 23(1) of the Attachment of Earnings Act 1971 for the attendance of the debtor at an adjourned hearing of an application for an attachment of earnings order.

(1A) An order made under section 110(1) of the Act must be served personally on the judgment debtor.

(1B) Copies of—
 (a) the judgment summons; and
 (b) the written evidence,
must be served with the order.

(2) At the time of service of the order there shall be paid or tendered to the debtor a sum reasonably sufficient to cover his expenses in travelling to and from the court, unless such a sum was paid to him at the time of service of the judgment summons.

Rule 5 Evidence

(1) No person may be committed on an application for a judgment summons unless—
 (a) the order is made under section 110(2) of the Act; or
 (b) the judgment creditor proves that the debtor—
  (i) has or has had since the date of the judgment or order the means to pay the sum in respect of which he has made default; and
  (ii) has refused or neglected or refuses or neglects to pay that sum.

(2) The debtor may not be compelled to give evidence.

Rule 7 Suspension of Committal Order

(1) If on the hearing of a judgment summons a committal order is made, the judge may direct execution of the order to be suspended to enable the debtor to pay the amount due.

(2) A note of any direction given under paragraph (1) shall be entered in the records of the court and notice of the suspended committal order shall be sent to the debtor.

(3) Where a judgment summons is issued in respect of one or more but not all of the instalments payable under a judgment or order for payment by instalments and a committal order is made and suspended under paragraph (1), the judgment or order shall, unless the judge otherwise orders, be suspended for so long as the, execution of the committal order is suspended.

(4) Where execution of a committal order is suspended under paragraph (1) and the debtor subsequently desires to apply for a further suspension, the debtor shall attend at or write to the court office and apply for the suspension he desires, stating the reasons for his inability to comply with the terms of the original suspension, and the court shall fix a day for the hearing of the application by the judge and give at least 3 days' notice thereof to the judgment creditor and the debtor.

(5) The district judge may suspend execution of the committal order pending the hearing of an application under paragraph (4).

Rule 8 New Order on Judgment Summons

(1) Where on the hearing of a judgment summons, the judge makes a new order for payment of the amount of the judgment debt remaining unpaid, there shall be included in the amount payable under the order for the purpose of any enforcement proceedings, otherwise than by judgment summons, any amount in respect of which a committal order has already been made and the debtor imprisoned.

(2) No judgment summons under the new order shall include any amount in respect of which the debtor was imprisoned before the new order was made, and any amount subsequently paid shall be appropriated in the first instance to the amount due under the new order.

Rule 9 Notification of Order on Judgment of High Court

(1) Notice of the result of the hearing of a judgment summons on a judgment or order of the High Court shall be sent by the county court to the High Court.

(2) If a committal order or a new order for payment is made on the hearing, the office copy of the judgment or order filed in the county court shall be deemed to be a judgment or order of the court in which the judgment summons is heard.

Rule 10 Costs on Judgment Summons

(1) No costs shall be allowed to the judgment creditor on the hearing of a judgment summons unless—
  (a) a committal order is made; or
  (b) the sum in respect of which the judgment summons was issued is paid before the hearing.
(2) Where costs are allowed to the judgment creditor,
  (a) there may be allowed—
    (i) a charge of the judgment creditor's solicitor for attending the hearing and, if the judge so directs, for serving the judgment summons;
    (ii) a fee to counsel if the court certifies that the case is fit for counsel;
    (iii) any travelling expenses paid to the debtor, and
    (iv) the court fee on the issue of the judgment summons;
  (b) the costs may be fixed and allowed without detailed assessment under CPR Part 47.

Rule 11 Issue of Warrant of Committal

(1) A judgment creditor desiring a warrant to be issued pursuant to a committal order shall file a request in that behalf.
(2) Where two or more debtors are to be committed in respect of the same judgment or order, a separate warrant of committal shall be issued for each of them.
(3) Where a warrant of committal is sent to a foreign court for execution, that court shall indorse on it a notice as to the effect of section 122(3) of the Act addressed to the governor of the prison of that court.

Rule 12 Notification to Foreign Court of Part Payment before Debtor Lodged in Prison

Where, after a warrant of committal has been sent to a foreign court for execution but before the debtor is lodged in prison, the home court is notified that an amount which is less than the sum on payment of which the debtor is to be discharged has been paid, the home court shall send notice of the payment to the foreign court.

Rule 13 Payment after Debtor Lodged in Prison

(1) Where, after the debtor has been lodged in prison under a warrant of committal, payment is made of the sum on payment of which the debtor is to be discharged, then—
  (a) if the payment is made to the court responsible for the execution of the warrant, the court officer shall make and sign a certificate of payment and send it by post or otherwise to the gaoler;
  (b) if the payment is made to the court which issued the warrant of committal after the warrant has been sent to a foreign court for execution, the home court shall send notice of the payment to the foreign court, and the court officer at the foreign court shall make and sign a certificate of payment and send it by post or otherwise to the gaoler;
  (c) if the payment is made to the gaoler, he shall sign a certificate of payment and send the amount to the court which made the committal order.
(2) Where, after the debtor has been lodged in prison under a warrant of committal, payment is made of an amount less than the sum on payment of which the debtor is to be discharged, then subject to paragraph (3), paragraph (1)(a) and (b) shall apply with the substitution of references to a notice of payment for the references to a certificate of payment and paragraph (1)(c) shall apply with the omission of the requirement to make and sign a certificate of payment.
(3) Where, after the making of a payment to which paragraph (2) relates, the balance of the sum on payment of which the debtor is to be discharged is paid, paragraph (1) shall apply without the modifications mentioned in paragraph (2).

Rule 14 Discharge of Debtor Otherwise than on Payment

(1) Where the judgment creditor lodges with the district judge a request that a debtor lodged in prison under a warrant of committal may be discharged from custody, the district judge shall

CPR Glossary, Schs, Other PDs

make an order for the discharge of the debtor in respect of the warrant of committal and the court shall send the gaoler a certificate of discharge.

(2) Where a debtor who has been lodged in prison under a warrant of committal desires to apply for his discharge under section 121 of the Act, the application shall be made to the judge in writing and without notice showing the reasons why the debtor alleges that he is unable to pay the sum in respect of which he has been committed and ought to be discharged and stating any offer which he desires to make as to the terms on which his discharge is to be ordered, and Order 27, rule 8(3) and (4), shall apply, with the necessary modifications, as it applies to an application by a debtor for his discharge from custody under section 23(7) of the Attachment of Earnings Act 1971.

(3) If in a case to which paragraph (2) relates the debtor is ordered to be discharged from custody on terms which include liability to re-arrest if the terms are not complied with, the judge may, on the application of the judgment creditor if the terms are not complied with, order the debtor to be re-arrested and imprisoned for such part of the term of imprisonment as remained unserved at the time of discharge.

(4) Where an order is made under paragraph (3), a duplicate warrant of committal shall be issued, indorsed with a certificate signed by the court officer as to the order of the judge.

CCR ORDER 33 — INTERPLEADER PROCEEDINGS

ord.33 12.1, 14.75

Part I Under Execution

Rule 1 Notice of Claim

r.1(1) PC 8, 14.80 r.1(2)(a)–(b) PC 8, 14.80

(A1) In this Part of this Order 'the interpleader claimant' means any person making a claim to or in respect of goods seized in execution or the proceeds or value thereof and 'the interpleader claim' means that claim.

(1) The interpleader claimant shall deliver to the bailiff holding the warrant of execution, or file in the office of the court for the district in which the goods were seized, notice of his claim stating—

(a) the grounds of the interpleader claim or, in the case of a claim for rent, the particulars required by section 102(2) of the Act; and

(b) the interpleader claimant's full name and address.

(2) On receipt of an interpleader claim made under this rule, the court shall—

(a) send notice thereof to the execution creditor; and

(b) except where the interpleader claim is to the proceeds or value of the goods, send to the interpleader claimant a notice requiring him to make a deposit or give security in accordance with section 100 of the Act.

Rule 2 Reply to Interpleader Claim

r.2 PC 8, 14.80

(1) Within 4 days after receiving notice of an interpleader claim under rule 1(2) the execution creditor shall give notice to the court informing him whether he admits or disputes the interpleader claim or requests the district judge to withdraw from possession of the goods or money claimed.

(2) If, within the period aforesaid, the execution creditor gives notice to the court admitting the interpleader claim or requesting the district judge to withdraw from possession of the goods or money claimed, the execution creditor shall not be liable to the district judge for any fees or expenses incurred after receipt of the notice.

Rule 3 Order Protecting District Judge

r.3 14.80

Where the execution creditor gives the court such a notice as is mentioned in rule 2(2), the district judge shall withdraw from possession of the goods or money claimed and may apply to the judge, on *notice to the interpleader claimant*, for an order restraining the bringing of a claim against the district judge for or in respect of his having taken possession of the goods or money and on the hearing of the application the judge may make such order as may be just.

Rule 4 Issue of Interpleader Proceedings

r.4 PC 8

(1) Where the execution creditor gives notice under rule 2(1) disputing an interpleader claim made under rule 1 or fails, within the period mentioned in rule 2(1), to give the notice required by that rule, the district judge shall, unless the interpleader claim is withdrawn, issue an interpleader notice to the execution creditor and the interpleader claimant.
(2) On the issue of an interpleader notice under paragraph (1) the court officer shall enter the proceedings in the records of the court, fix a day for the hearing by the judge and prepare sufficient copies of the notice for service under this rule.
(3) Subject to paragraph (4) the notice shall be served on the execution creditor and the interpleader claimant in the manner set out in CPR rule 6.20.
(4) Service shall be effected not less than 14 days before the return day.

Rule 5 Claim for Damages

Where in interpleader proceedings under an execution the interpleader claimant claims from the execution creditor or the district judge, or the execution creditor claims from the district judge, damages arising or capable of arising out of the execution—
(a) the party claiming damages shall, within 8 days after service of the notice on him under rule 4(3), give notice of this claim to the court and to any other party against whom the claim is made, stating the amount and the grounds of the claim; and
(b) the party from whom damages are claimed may pay money into court in satisfaction of the claim as if the interpleader proceedings were a claim brought in accordance with CPR Part 7 by the person making the claim.

Part II Otherwise Than under Execution

Rule 6 Application for Relief

r.6(1) PC 8
r.6(2) 14.81
r.6(3) PC 8, 14.81

(1) Where a person (in this Part of this Order called 'the applicant') is under a liability in respect of a debt or any money or goods and he is, or expects to be, sued for or in respect of the debt, money or goods by two or more persons making adverse claims thereto ('the interpleader claimants'), he may apply to the court, in accordance with these rules, for relief by way of interpleader.
(2) The application shall be made to the court in which the claim is pending against the applicant or, if no claim is pending against him, to the court in which he might be sued.
(3) The application shall be made by filing a witness statement or affidavit showing that—
 (a) the applicant claims no interest in the subject-matter in dispute other than for charges or costs;
 (b) the applicant does not collude with any of the interpleader claimants; and
 (c) the applicant is willing to pay or transfer the subject-matter into court or to dispose of it as the court may direct,

together with as many copies of the witness statement or affidavit as there are interpleader claimants.

Rule 7 Relief in Pending Claim

r.7 14.81

Where the applicant is a defendant in a pending claim—
(a) the witness statement or affidavit and copies required by rule 6(3) shall be filed within 14 days after service on him of the claim form;
(b) the return day of the application shall be a day fixed for the pre-trial review of the claim including the interpleader proceedings and, if a day has already been fixed for the pre-trial review or hearing of the claim, the court shall, if necessary, postpone it;
(c) the interpleader claimant, the applicant and the claimant in the claim shall be given notice of the application, which shall be prepared by the court together with sufficient copies for service;

(d) the notice to the interpleader claimant shall be served on him, together with a copy of the witness statement or affidavit filed under rule 6(3) and of the claim form and particulars of claim in the claim, not less than 21 days before the return day in the same manner as an interpleader notice in accordance with rule 4(3);
(e) the notices to the applicant and the claimant shall be sent to them by the court and the notice to the claimant shall be accompanied by a copy of the said witness statement or affidavit.

Rule 8 Relief Otherwise Than in Pending Claim

r.8 **14.81**

Where the applicant is not a defendant in a pending claim—
(a) the court shall enter the proceedings in the records of the court;
(b) the court shall fix a day for the pre-trial review or, if the court so directs, a day for the hearing of the proceedings and shall prepare and issue an interpleader notice, together with sufficient copies for service;
(c) the notice together with a copy of the witness statement or affidavit filed under rule 6(3), shall be served on each of the claimants not less than 21 days before the return day in the same manner as an interpleader notice to be served under rule 4(3); and
(d) the court shall deliver or send a notice of issue to the applicant.

Rule 9 Payment into Court etc.

Before or after the court officer proceeds under rule 7 or 8 the district judge may direct the applicant to bring the subject-matter of the proceedings into court, or to dispose of it in such manner as the district judge thinks fit, to abide the order of the court.

Rule 10 Reply by Interpleader Claimant

r.10 **PC 8, 14.81**

(1) An interpleader claimant shall, within 14 days after service on him of the notice under rule 7(c) or the interpleader notice under rule 8(c), file—
 (a) a notice that he makes no interpleader claim; or
 (b) particulars stating the grounds of his interpleader claim to the subject matter,
together in either case with sufficient copies for service under paragraph (2).
(2) The court shall send to each of the other parties a copy of any notice or particulars filed under paragraph (1).
(3) The court may, if it thinks fit, hear the proceedings although no notice or particulars have been filed.

Rule 11 Order Barring Interpleader Claim etc.

r.11(1)–(3) **14.82**

(1) Where an interpleader claimant does not appear on any day fixed for a pre-trial review or the hearing of interpleader proceedings, or fails or refuses to comply with an order made in the proceedings, the court may make an order barring his interpleader claim.
(2) If, where the applicant is a defendant in a pending claim, the claimant does not appear on any day fixed for a pre-trial review or the hearing of the interpleader proceedings, the claim including the interpleader proceedings may be struck out.
(3) In any other case where a day is fixed for the hearing of interpleader proceedings, the court shall hear and determine the proceedings and give judgment finally determining the rights and claims of the parties.
(4) Where the court makes an order barring the interpleader claim of an interpleader claimant, the order shall declare the interpleader claimant, and all persons claiming under him, forever barred from prosecuting his interpleader claim against the applicant and all persons claiming under im, but unless the interpleader claimant has filed a notice under rule 10 that he makes no interpleader claim, such an order shall not affect the rights of the interpleader claimants as between *themselves*.

CCR ORDER 39 — ADMINISTRATION ORDERS

ord.39 79.1, 79.12

Rule 1 Exercise of Powers by District Judge

Any powers conferred on the court by Part VI of the Act, section 4 of the Attachment of Earnings Act 1971 or this Order may be exercised by the district judge or, in the circumstances mentioned in this Order, by the court officer.

Rule 2 Request and List of Creditors

(1) A debtor who desires to obtain an administration order under Part VI of the Act shall file a request in that behalf in the court for the district in which he resides or carries on business.

(2) Where on his examination under CPR Part 71, or otherwise, a debtor furnishes to the court on oath a list of his creditors and the amounts which he owes to them respectively and sufficient particulars of his resources and needs, the court may proceed as if the debtor had filed a request under paragraph (1).

(3) Where a debtor is ordered to furnish a list under section 4(1)(b) of the said Act of 1971, then, unless otherwise directed, the list shall be filed within 14 days after the making of the order.

Rule 3 Verification on Oath

The statements in the request mentioned in rule 2(1) and the list mentioned in rule 2(3) shall be verified by the debtor on oath.

Rule 5 Orders Made by the Court Officer

(1) The question whether an administration order should be made, and the terms of such an order, may be decided by the court officer in accordance with the provisions of this rule.

(2) On the filing of a request or list under rule 2, the court officer may, if he considers that the debtor's means are sufficient to discharge in full and within a reasonable period the total amount of the debts included in the list, determine the amount and frequency of the payments to be made under such an order ('the proposed rate') and—

(a) notify the debtor of the proposed rate requiring him to give written reasons for any objection he may have to the proposed rate within 14 days of service of notification upon him;

(b) send to each creditor mentioned in the list provided by the debtor a copy of the debtor's request or of the list together with the proposed rate;

(c) require any such creditor to give written reasons for any objection he may have to the making of an administration order within 14 days of service of the documents mentioned in sub-paragraph (b) upon him.

Objections under sub-paragraph (c) may be to the making of an order, to the proposed rate or to the inclusion of a particular debt in the order.

(3) Where no objection under paragraph (2)(a) or (c) is received within the time stated, the court officer may make an administration order providing for payment in full of the total amount of the debts included in the list.

(4) Where the debtor or a creditor notifies the court of any objection within the time stated, the court officer shall fix a day for a hearing at which the district judge will decide whether an administration order should be made and the court officer shall give not less than 14 days' notice of the day so fixed to the debtor and to each creditor mentioned in the list provided by the debtor.

(5) Where the court officer is unable to fix a rate under paragraph (2) (whether because he considers that the debtor's means are insufficient or otherwise), he shall refer the request to the district judge.

(6) Where the district judge considers that he is able to do so without the attendance of the parties, he may fix the proposed rate providing for payment of the debts included in the list in full or to such extent and within such a period as appears practicable in the circumstances of the case.

(7) Where the proposed rate is fixed under paragraph (6), paragraphs (2) to (4) shall apply with the necessary modifications as if the rate had been fixed by the court officer.

(8) Where the district judge does not fix the proposed rate under paragraph (6), he shall direct the court officer to fix a day for a hearing at which the district judge will decide whether an

administration order should be made and the court officer shall give not less than 14 days' notice of the day so fixed to the debtor and to each creditor mentioned in the list provided by the debtor.

(9) Where an administration order is made under paragraph (3), the court officer may exercise the power of the court under section 5 of the Attachment of Earnings Act 1971 to make an attachment of earnings order to secure the payments required by the administration order.

Rule 6 Notice of Objection by Creditor

(1) Any creditor to whom notice has been given under rule 5(8) and who objects to any debt included in the list furnished by the debtor shall, not less than 7 days before the day of hearing, give notice of his objection, stating the grounds thereof, to the court officer, to the debtor and to the creditor to whose debt he objects.

(2) Except with the permission of the court, no creditor may object to a debt unless he has given notice of his objection under paragraph (1).

Rule 7 Procedure on Day of Hearing

On the day of the hearing—

(a) any creditor, whether or not he is mentioned in the list furnished by the debtor, may attend and prove his debt or, subject to rule 6, object to any debt included in that list;

(b) every debt included in that list shall be taken to be proved unless it is objected to by a creditor or disallowed by the court or required by the court to be supported by evidence;

(c) any creditor whose debt is required by the court to be supported by evidence shall prove his debt;

(d) the court may adjourn proof of any debt and, if it does so, may either adjourn consideration of the question whether an administration order should be made or proceed to determine the question, in which case, if an administration order is made, the debt, when proved, shall be added to the debts scheduled to the order;

(e) any creditor whose debt is admitted or proved, and, with the permission of the court, any creditor the proof of whose debt has been adjourned, shall be entitled to be heard and to adduce evidence on the question whether an administration order should be made and, if so, in what terms.

Rule 8 Direction for Order to Be Subject to Review

(1) The court may, on making an administration order or at any subsequent time, direct that the order shall be subject to review at such time or at such intervals as the court may specify.

(2) Where the court has directed that an administration order shall be subject to review, the court officer shall give to the debtor and to every creditor who appeared when the order was made not less than 7 days' notice of any day appointed for such a review.

(3) Nothing in this rule shall require the court officer to fix a day for a review under rule 13A.

Rule 9 Service of Order

Where an administration order is made, the court officer shall send a copy to—

(a) the debtor;

(b) every creditor whose name was included in the list furnished by the debtor;

(c) any other creditor who has proved his debt; and

(d) every other court in which, to the knowledge of the district judge, judgment has been obtained against the debtor or proceedings are pending in respect of any debt scheduled to the order.

Rule 10 Subsequent Objection by Creditor

(1) After an administration order has been made, a creditor who has not received notice under rule 5 and who wishes to object to a debt scheduled to the order, or to the manner in which payment is directed to be made by instalments, shall give notice to the court officer of his objection and of the grounds thereof.

(2) On receipt of such notice the court shall consider the objection and may—

  (a) allow it;

  (b) dismiss it; or

  (c) adjourn it for hearing on notice being given to such persons and on such terms as to security for costs or otherwise as the court thinks fit.

(3) Without prejudice to the generality of paragraph (2), the court may dismiss an objection if it is not satisfied that the creditor gave notice of it within a reasonable time of his becoming aware of the administration order.

Rule 11 Subsequent Proof by Creditor

(1) Any creditor whose debt is not scheduled to an administration order, and any person who after the date of the order became a creditor of the debtor, shall, if he wishes to prove his debt, send particulars of his claim to the court officer, who shall give notice of it to the debtor and to every creditor whose debt is so scheduled.
(2) If neither the debtor nor any creditor gives notice to the court officer, within 7 days after receipt of notice under paragraph (1), that he objects to the claim, then, unless it is required by the court to be supported by evidence, the claim shall be taken to be proved.
(3) If the debtor or a creditor gives notice of objection within the said period of 7 days or the court requires the claim to be supported by evidence, the court officer shall fix a day for consideration of the claim and give notice of it to the debtor, the creditor by whom the claim was made and the creditor, if any, making the objection, and on the hearing the court may either disallow the claim or allow it in whole or in part.
(4) If a claim is taken to be proved under paragraph (2) or allowed under paragraph (3), the debt shall be added to the schedule to the order and a copy of the order shall then be sent to the creditor by whom the claim was made.

Rule 12 Permission to Present Bankruptcy Petition

An application by a creditor under section 112(4) of the Act for permission to present or join in a bankruptcy petition shall be made on notice to the debtor in accordance with CPR Part 23, but the court may, if it thinks fit, order that notice be given to any other creditor whose debt is scheduled to the administration order.

Rule 13 Conduct of Order

(1) The court manager or such other officer of the court as the court making an administration order shall from time to time appoint shall have the conduct of the order and shall take all proper steps to enforce the order (including exercising the power of the court under section 5 of the Attachment of Earnings Act 1971 to make an attachment of earnings order to secure payments required by the administration order) or to bring to the attention of the court any matter which may make it desirable to review the order.
(2) Without prejudice to section 115 of the Act, any creditor whose debt is scheduled to the order may, with the permission of the court, take proceedings to enforce the order.
(3) The debtor or, with the permission of the court, any such creditor may apply to the court to review the order.
(4) When on a matter being brought to its attention under paragraph (1) the court so directs or the debtor or a creditor applies for the review of an administration order, rule 8(2) shall apply as if the order were subject to review under that rule.
(5) Nothing in this rule shall require the court officer to fix a day for a review under rule 13A.

Rule 13A Review by Court Officer in Default of Payment

(1) Where it appears that the debtor is failing to make payments in accordance with the order, the court officer shall (either of his own initiative or on the application of a creditor whose debt is scheduled to the administration order) send a notice to the debtor—
 (a) informing him of the amounts which are outstanding; and
 (b) requiring him (within 14 days of service of the notice upon him) to—
  (i) make the payments as required by the order; or
  (ii) explain his reasons for failing to make the payments; and
  (iii) make a proposal for payment of the amounts outstanding; or
  (iv) make a request to vary the order.
(2) If the debtor does not comply with paragraph (1)(b) within the time stated, the court officer shall revoke the administration order.

(3) The court officer shall refer a notice given by a debtor under paragraph (1)(b)(ii), (iii) or (iv) to the district judge who may—
  (a) without requiring the attendance of the parties—
    (i) revoke the administration order or vary it so as to provide for payment of the debts included in the order in full or to such extent and within such a period as appears practicable in the circumstances of the case; or
    (ii) suspend the operation of the administration order for such time and on such terms as he thinks fit; or
  (b) require the court officer to fix a day for the review of the administration order and to give to the debtor and to every creditor whose debt is scheduled to the administration order not less than 8 days' notice of the day so fixed.

(4) Any party affected by an order made under paragraph (2) or (3)(a) may, within 14 days of service of the order on him and giving his reasons, apply on notice for the district judge to consider the matter afresh and the court officer shall fix a day for the hearing of the application before the district judge and give to the debtor and to every creditor whose debt is scheduled to the administration order not less than 8 days' notice of the day so fixed.

(5) On hearing an application under paragraph (4), the district judge may confirm the order or set it aside and make such new order as he thinks fit and the order so made shall be entered in the records of the court.

Rule 14 Review of Order

(1) On the review of an administration order the court may—
  (a) if satisfied that the debtor is unable from any cause to pay any instalment due under the order, suspend the operation of the order for such time and on such terms as it thinks fit;
  (b) if satisfied that there has been a material change in any relevant circumstances since the order was made, vary any provision of the order made by virtue of section 112(6) of the Act;
  (c) if satisfied that the debtor has failed without reasonable cause to comply with any provision of the order or that it is otherwise just and expedient to do so, revoke the order, either forthwith or on failure to comply with any condition specified by the court; or
  (d) make an attachment of earnings order to secure the payments required by the administration order or vary or discharge any such attachment of earnings order already made.

(2) The court officer shall send a copy of any order varying or revoking an administration order to the debtor, to every creditor whose debt is scheduled to the administration order and, if the administration order is revoked, to any other court to which a copy of the administration order was sent pursuant to rule 9.

Rule 16 Discharge of Attachment of Earnings Order

On the revocation of an administration order any attachment of earnings order made to secure the payments required by the administration order shall be discharged.

Rule 17 Declaration of Dividends

(1) The officer having the conduct of an administration order shall from time to time declare dividends and distribute them among the creditors entitled to them.

(2) When a dividend is declared, notice shall be sent by the officer to each of the creditors.

Rule 18 Creditors to Rank Equally

All creditors scheduled under section 113(d) of the Act before an administration order is superseded under section 117(2) of the Act shall rank equally in proportion to the amount of their debts subject to the priority given by the said paragraph (d) to those scheduled as having been creditors before the date of the order, but no payment made to any creditor by way of dividend or otherwise shall be disturbed by reason of any subsequent proof by any creditor under the said paragraph (d).

Rule 19 Change of Debtor's Address

(1) A debtor who changes his residence shall forthwith inform the court of his new address.

(2) Mere the debtor becomes resident in the district of another court, the court in which the administration order is being conducted may transfer the proceedings to that other court.

CCR ORDER 44 — THE AGRICULTURAL HOLDINGS ACT 1986

ord.44 1.6

Rule 4 Enforcement of Order Imposing Penalty

(1) When taking any proceedings for the enforcement in a county court of an order under section 27 of the Agricultural Holdings Act 1986, the party in whose favour the order was made shall file—
   (a) a certified copy of the order; and
   (b) a certificate specifying the amount due under the order and stating whether any previous proceedings have been taken for its enforcement and, if so, the nature of the proceedings and their result.

(2) Where it is desired to enforce the order by warrant of execution, the proceedings may be taken in any court in the district of which execution is to be levied.

CCR ORDER 49 — MISCELLANEOUS STATUTES

ord.49 1.6

Rule 18A Telecommunications Act 1984

CPR Rule 35.15 applies to proceedings under paragraph 5 of Schedule 2 to the Telecommunications Act 1984.

Rule 19 Trade Union and Labour Relations Consolidation Act 1992

(1) Where a complainant desires to have an order of the Certification Officer under section 82 of the Trade Union and Labour Relations Consolidation Act 1992 recorded in the county court, he shall produce the order and a copy thereof to the court for the district in which he resides or the head or main office of the trade union is situate.

(2) The order shall be recorded by filing it, and the copy shall be sealed and dated and returned to the complainant.

(3) The sealed copy shall be treated as if it were the notice of issue in a claim begun by the complainant.

(4) The costs, if any, allowed for recording the order shall be recoverable as if they were payable under the order.

(5) The order shall not be enforced until proof is given to the satisfaction of the court that the order has not been obeyed and, if the order is for payment of money, of the amount remaining unpaid.

Notes on Text of the CPR

The text of the CPR printed above incorporates the amendments in the following list. The date after an amendment is the date on which it came into force. The notes at the end set out transitional provisions. The list does not include amendments of contents lists and cross-references.

The titles of the statutory instruments referred to are:

SI 1999/1008: Civil Procedure (Amendment) Rules 1999
SI 2000/221: Civil Procedure (Amendment) Rules 2000
SI 2000/940: Civil Procedure (Amendment No. 2) Rules 2000
SI 2000/1317: Civil Procedure (Amendment No. 3) Rules 2000
SI 2000/2092: Civil Procedure (Amendment No. 4) Rules 2000
SI 2001/256: Civil Procedure (Amendment) Rules 2001
SI 2001/1388: Civil Procedure (Amendment No. 2) Rules 2001
SI 2001/1769: Civil Procedure (Amendment No. 3) Rules 2001
SI 2001/2792: Civil Procedure (Amendment No. 4) Rules 2001
SI 2001/4015: Civil Procedure (Amendment No. 5) Rules 2001
SI 2001/4016: Civil Procedure (Amendment No. 6) Rules 2001
SI 2002/2058: Civil Procedure (Amendment) Rules 2002
SI 2002/3219: Civil Procedure (Amendment No. 2) Rules 2002
SI 2003/364: Civil Procedure (Amendment) Rules 2003
SI 2003/1242: Civil Procedure (Amendment No. 2) Rules 2003
SI 2003/1329: Civil Procedure (Amendment No. 3) Rules 2003
SI 2003/2113: Civil Procedure (Amendment No. 4) Rules 2003
SI 2003/3361: Civil Procedure (Amendment No. 5) Rules 2003
SI 2004/1306: Civil Procedure (Amendment) Rules 2004
SI 2004/2072: Civil Procedure (Amendment No. 2) Rules 2004
SI 2004/3129: Civil Procedure (Amendment No. 3) Rules 2004
SI 2004/3419: Civil Procedure (Amendment No. 4) Rules 2004
SI 2005/352: Civil Procedure (Amendment) Rules 2005
SI 2005/656: Civil Procedure (Amendment No. 2) Rules 2005
SI 2005/2292: Civil Procedure (Amendment No. 3) Rules 2005
SI 2005/2292: Civil Procedure (Amendment No. 4) Rules 2005
SI 2006/1689: Civil Procedure (Amendment) Rules 2006
SI 2006/3132: Civil Procedure (Amendment No. 2) Rules 2006
SI 2006/3435: Civil Procedure (Amendment No. 3) Rules 2006
SI 2007/1655: Civil Jurisdiction and Judgments Regulations 2007
SI 2007/2204: Civil Procedure (Amendment) Rules 2007
SI 2007/3543: Civil Procedure (Amendment No. 2) Rules 2007
SI 2008/2178: Civil Procedure (Amendment) Rules 2008
SI 2008/3085: Civil Procedure (Amendment No. 2) Rules 2008
SI 2008/3327: Civil Procedure (Amendment No. 3) Rules 2008
SI 2009/2092: Civil Procedure (Amendment) Rules 2009
SI 2009/3131: Civil Jurisdiction and Judgments Regulations 2009
SI 2009/3390: Civil Procedure (Amendment No. 2) Rules 2009
SI 2010/621: Civil Procedure (Amendment) Rules 2010
SI 2010/1953: Civil Procedure (Amendment No. 2) Rules 2010
SI 2010/2577: Civil Procedure (Amendment No. 3) Rules 2010
SI 2011/88: Civil Procedure (Amendment) Rules 2011
SI 2011/1979: Civil Procedure (Amendment No. 2) Rules 2011
SI 2011/2970: Civil Procedure (Amendment No. 3) Rules 2011
SI 2011/3103: Civil Procedure (Amendment No. 4) Rules 2011
SI 2012/505: Civil Procedure (Amendment) Rules 2012
SI 2012/2208: Civil Procedure (Amendment No. 2) Rules 2012

SI 2013/262: Civil Procedure (Amendment) Rules 2013
SI 2013/515: Civil Procedure (Amendment No. 2) Rules 2013
SI 2013/534: Legal Aid, Sentencing and Punishment of Offenders Act 2012 (Consequential, Transitional and Saving Provisions) Regulations 2013
SI 2013/789: Civil Procedure (Amendment No. 3) Rules 2013
SI 2013/1412: Civil Procedure (Amendment No. 4) Rules 2013
r. 1.1 amended by SI 2013/262, r. 4 (1 April 2013);
r. 1.2 amended by: (a) SI 2005/656, r. 3 (14 March 2005); (b) SI 2008/3085, r. 3 (4 December 2008); (c) SI 2011/2970, r. 3 (15 December 2011);
r. 2.1 amended by: (a) SI 1999/1008, r. 3 (26 April 1999); (b) SI 2003/1242, r. 3 (2 June 2003); (c) SI 2005/3515, r. 3 (6 April 2006); (d) SI 2007/2204, r. 3(a) (1 October 2007); (e) SI 2008/2178, r. 3 (1 October 2008);
r. 2.3(1) amended by: (a) SI 2000/2092, r. 3 (2 October 2000); (b) SI 2004/2072, r. 3 (1 October 2004); (c) SI 2007/2204, r. 3(b) (1 October 2007); (d) SI 2009/3390, r. 3(a) (1 February 2010); (e) SI 2011/3103, r. 3 (19 March 2012);
r. 2.3(2) amended by SI 2001/4015, r. 3 (25 March 2002);
r. 2.8(5) amended by SI 2009/3390, r. 3(b) (1 April 2010);
r. 3.1(2) amended by SI 2005/2292, r. 3 (1 October 2005);
r. 3.1(4) amended by SI 2008/3327, r. 3 (6 April 2009);
r. 3.1(6A) inserted by SI 1999/1008, r. 4 (26 April 1999); amended by SI 2006/3435, r. 3 (6 April 2007);
r. 3.1(8) inserted by SI 2013/262, r. 5(d) (1 April 2013);
r. 3.3 amended by: (a) SI 2004/2072, r. 4 (1 October 2004); (b) SI 2005/2292, r. 4 (1 October 2005);
r. 3.4 amended by SI 2004/2072, r. 5 (1 October 2004);
r. 3.5 amended by SI 2000/221, r. 3 (2 May 2000);
r. 3.5A inserted by SI 2011/3103, r. 4 (19 March 2012);
r. 3.7(1) substituted by SI 2000/2092, r. 4 (2 October 2000); amended by SI 2002/2058, r. 3 (2 December 2002); amended by: (a) SI 2007/3543, r. 3(a)–(c) (6 April 2008); (b) SI 2013/262, r. 5(e) (1 April 2013) (see note 22);
r. 3.7(2) substituted by SI 2000/2092, r. 4 (2 October 2000); amended by SI 2007/3543, r. 3(d) (6 April 2008);
r. 3.7(4) amended by: (a) SI 2005/2292, r. 5 (1 October 2005); (b) SI 2007/3543, r. 3(e) (6 April 2008); (c) SI 2008/2178, r. 4(a) (1 October 2008);
r. 3.7(5) substituted by SI 2007/3543, r. 3(f) (6 April 2008);
r. 3.7(6) amended by: (a) SI 2005/2292, r. 5 (1 October 2005); (b) SI 2008/2178, r. 4(c) (1 October 2008);
r. 3.7(7) substituted by SI 2003/1242, r. 4 (2 June 2003); amended by: (a) SI 2007/3543, r. 3(g); (b) SI 2008/2178, r. 4(d) (1 October 2008);
r. 3.7(8) inserted by SI 2003/1242, r. 4 (2 June 2003);
r. 3.7A inserted by SI 2005/2292, r. 6 (1 October 2005); amended by: (a) SI 2007/3543, r. 4 (6 April 2008); (b) SI 2013/262, r. 5(e) (1 April 2013);
r. 3.7B inserted by SI 2005/2292, r. 7 (1 October 2005);
r. 3.8 amended by SI 2013/262, r. 5(f) (1 April 2013) (see note 23);
r. 3.9 amended by SI 2013/262, r. 5(g) (1 April 2013) (see note 23);
r. 3.12 inserted by SI 2013/262, r. 5(h) (1 April 2013); amended by SI 2013/515, r. 4 (1 April 2013);
rr. 3.13 to 3.21 inserted by SI 2013/262, r. 5(h) (1 April 2013);
r. 5.2 amended by SI 2001/2792, r. 3 (25 March 2002);
r. 5.4 substituted by SI 2004/2072, r. 7 (1 October 2004); amended by SI 2005/2292, r. 8 (1 October 2005); substituted by SI 2006/1689, r. 3(a) (2 October 2006);
r. 5.4A inserted by SI 2004/1306, r. 3 (1 June 2004);
r. 5.4B inserted by SI 2006/1689, r. 3(b) (2 October 2006); amended by SI 2009/3390, r. 4(b) (6 April 2010);
r. 5.4C inserted by SI 2006/1689, r. 3(b) (2 October 2006); amended by: (a) SI 2006/3132 (18 December 2006); (b) SI 2011/88, r. 3 (6 April 2011);
r. 5.4D inserted by SI 2006/1689, r. 3(b) (2 October 2006);
r. 5.5 inserted by SI 2002/2058, r. 4 (2 December 2002);
Part 6 substituted by SI 2008/2178, r. 5 and sch. 1 (1 October 2008);
r. 6.2 amended by: (a) SI 2009/3390, r. 5(a) (6 April 2010); (b) SI 2011/88, r. 4(b) (6 April 2011);

r. 6.3 amended by: (a) SI 2009/2092, r. 3(a) (1 October 2009); (b) SI 2009/3390, r. 5(b) (6 April 2010); (c) SI 2011/88, r. 4(d) (6 April 2011);
r. 6.4 amended by SI 2011/88, r. 4(e) (6 April 2011);
r. 6.6 amended by: (a) SI 2009/3390, r. 5(c) (6 April 2010); (b) SI 2011/88, r. 4(f) (6 April 2011);
r. 6.7 substituted by SI 2011/88, r. 4(g) (6 April 2011); amended by SI 2011/1979, r. 3(a) (1 September 2011);
r. 6.8 amended by: (a) SI 2011/88, r. 4(h) (6 April 2011); (b) SI 2011/1979, r. 3(b) (1 September 2011);
r. 6.9 amended by SI 2011/88, r. 4(i) (6 April 2011);
r. 6.14 amended by SI 2011/88, r. 4(j) (6 April 2011);
r. 6.20 amended by: (a) SI 2009/2092, r. 3(a) (1 October 2009); (b) SI 2009/3390, r. 5(b) (6 April 2010); (c) SI 2011/88, r. 4(l) (6 April 2011);
r. 6.21 amended by SI 2011/88, r. 4(m) (6 April 2011);
r. 6.22 amended by SI 2011/88, r. 4(n) (6 April 2011);
r. 6.23 amended by: (a) SI 2009/3390, r. 5(b) and (f) (6 April 2010); (b) SI 2011/88, r. 4(o) (6 April 2011); (c) SI 2011/1979, r. 3(c) (1 September 2011);
r. 6.26 amended by SI 2011/88, r. 4(p) (6 April 2011);
r. 6.31 amended by SI 2009/3131, reg 29 (1 January 2010) (see note 19);
r. 6.33 amended by SI 2009/3131, regs 30 and 31 (1 January 2010) (see note 19);
r. 6.40 amended by SI 2011/88, r. 4(q) (6 April 2011);
r. 6.41 amended by SI 2011/88, r. 4(r) (6 April 2011);
r. 6.42 amended by SI 2011/88, r. 4(s) (6 April 2011);
r. 6.43 amended by SI 2011/88, r. 4(t) (6 April 2011);
r. 6.44 amended by SI 2011/88, r. 4(u) (6 April 2011);
r. 6.45 amended by SI 2011/88, r. 4(v) (6 April 2011);
r. 7.1 amended by SI 2009/3390, r. 6(a) (6 April 2010);
r. 7.2A inserted by SI 2006/1689, r. 4 (2 October 2006); amended by SI 2009/3390, r. 6(c) (6 April 2010);
r. 7.4 substituted by SI 2008/3327, r. 4 (6 April 2009); amended by SI 2009/3390, r. 6(d) (6 April 2010);
r. 7.5 substituted by SI 2008/2178, r. 6(d) (1 October 2008);
r. 7.6 substituted by SI 2008/2178, r. 6(d) (1 October 2008);
r. 7.10 amended by SI 2009/3390, r. 6(e) (6 April 2010);
r. 7.11 inserted by SI 2000/2092, r. 6 (2 October 2000);
r. 7.12 inserted by SI 2003/3361, r. 3 (1 February 2004);
r. 8.2A inserted by SI 2000/221, r. 5 (2 May 2000); amended by SI 2001/256, r. 5 (26 March 2001);
r. 8.3(4) revoked by SI 2001/4015, r. 11 (25 March 2002);
r. 10.3 amended by: (a) SI 2000/940, r. 6 (2 May 2000); (b) SI 2005/2292, r. 17 (1 October 2005); (c) SI 2008/2178, r. 8(a) (1 October 2008); (d) SI 2009/3390, r. 9 (6 April 2010);
r. 10.5 amended by SI 2008/2178, r. 8(b) (1 October 2008);
r. 11 amended by: (a) SI 2001/4015, r. 12 (25 March 2002); (b) SI 2005/2292, r. 18 (1 October 2005);
r. 12.3 amended by SI 2000/221, r. 6 (2 May 2000);
r. 12.4(2) amended by SI 2005/2292, r. 19(a) (6 April 2006);
r. 12.4(4) inserted by SI 2005/2292, r. 19(b) (1 October 2005); amended by SI 2008/2178, r. 9(c) (1 October 2008);
r. 12.5A inserted by SI 2011/3103, r. 5 (19 March 2012);
r. 12.10 amended by: (a) SI 2000/940, r. 7 (2 May 2000); (b) SI 2001/4015, r. 13 (1 March 2002); (c) SI 2005/2292, r. 20 (1 October 2005); (d) SI 2007/2204, r. 5(a) (1 October 2007); (e) SI 2008/2178, r. 9(d) (1 October 2008);
r. 12.11 amended by: (a) SI 2000/940, r. 8 (2 May 2000); (b) SI 2001/4015, r. 14 (1 March 2002); (c) SI 2005/2292, r. 21 (1 October 2005); (d) SI 2007/1655, sch., paras 28 and 30 (1 July 2007); (e) SI 2007/2204, r. 5(b) (1 October 2007); (f) SI 2008/2178, r. 9(e) and (f) (1 October 2008); (g) SI 2009/3131, regs 32 and 33 (1 January 2010) (see note 19);
r. 13.4(1) amended by SI 2011/3103, r. 6(a) (19 March 2012);
r. 13.4(1A) inserted by SI 1999/1008, r. 5 (26 April 1999), and revoked by SI 2000/2092, r. 7 (2 October 2000);

r. 13.4(1B) inserted by SI 2011/3103, r. 6(b) (19 March 2012);
r. 13.5 revoked by SI 2004/1306, r. 21 (30 June 2004);
r. 14.1 amended by: (a) SI 2006/3435, r. 4(a) and (b) (6 April 2007); (b) SI 2007/2204, r. 6 (1 October 2007);
r. 14.1A inserted by SI 2006/3435, r. 4(c) (6 April 2007); amended by: (a) SI 2008/3327, r. 5 (6 April 2009); (b) SI 2009/3390, r. 10 (6 April 2010);
r. 14.1B inserted by SI 2010/621, r. 3 (30 April 2010);
r. 14.2 amended by: (a) SI 2000/940, r. 9 (2 May 2000); (b) SI 2008/2178, r. 11 (1 October 2008);
r. 14.7A inserted by SI 2011/3103, r. 7(b) (19 March 2012);
r. 14.12 amended by SI 2011/3103, r. 7(c) (19 March 2012);
r. 14.13 amended by SI 2011/3103, r. 7(d) (19 March 2012);
r. 15.4 amended by: (a) SI 2000/940, r. 10 (2 May 2000); (b) SI 2008/2178, r. 12 (1 October 2008);
r. 16.2(1) amended by SI 2005/3515, r. 5 (6 April 2006);
r. 16.2(1A) inserted by SI 2005/2292, r. 22 (1 October 2005);
r. 16.3 amended by: (a) SI 1999/1008, r. 6 (26 April 1999); (b) SI 2008/3327, r. 6 (6 April 2009); (c) SI 2013/262, r. 6 (1 April 2013) (see note 24);
r. 16.5 amended by SI 2008/2178, r. 13 (1 October 2008);
r. 17.1 amended by SI 2000/221, r. 7 (2 May 2000);
r. 17.4 amended by SI 2001/256, r. 7 (26 March 2001);
Part 19 substituted by SI 2000/221, r. 9 and sch. 2 (2 May 2000);
r. 19.4(4A) inserted by SI 2005/2292, r. 23 (1 October 2005);
r. 19.4A inserted by SI 2000/2092, r. 8 (2 October 2000);
r. 19.5 amended by SI 2001/256, r. 8 (26 March 2001);
r. 19.5A inserted by SI 2001/256, r. 9 (26 March 2001);
r. 19.7A inserted by SI 2002/2058, r. 6(a) (2 December 2002);
r. 19.7B inserted by SI 2005/2292, r. 24 (1 October 2005);
r. 19.8A inserted by SI 2001/256, r. 10 (26 March 2001); substituted by SI 2002/2058, r. 6(b) (2 December 2002);
r. 19.9 substituted by SI 2007/2204, r. 7 and sch. 1 (1 October 2007) (see note 15); amended by SI 2007/3543, r. 5(a);
r. 19.9A inserted by SI 2007/2204, r. 7 and sch. 1 (1 October 2007) (see note 15); amended by: (a) SI 2007/3543, r. 5(b) (6 April 2008); (b) SI 2009/3390, r. 13(b) (6 April 2010);
r. 19.9B inserted by SI 2007/2204, r. 7 and sch. 1 (1 October 2007) (see note 15);
r. 19.9C inserted by SI 2007/2204, r. 7 and sch. 1 (1 October 2007) (see note 15); amended by SI 2007/3543, r. 5(c) (6 April 2008);
r. 19.9D inserted by SI 2007/2204, r. 7 and sch. 1 (1 October 2007) (see note 15); amended by SI 2007/3543, r. 5(d) (6 April 2008);
r. 19.9E inserted by SI 2007/2204, r. 7 and sch. 1 (1 October 2007) (see note 15);
r. 19.9F inserted by SI 2007/2204, r. 7 and sch. 1 (1 October 2007) (see note 15); amended by SI 2007/3543, r. 5(e) (6 April 2008);
Part 20 substituted by SI 2005/3515, r. 6 and sch. (6 April 2006);
Part 21 substituted by SI 2007/2204, r. 8 and sch. 2 (1 October 2007);
r. 21.5 amended by SI 2008/2178, r. 15(b) (1 October 2008);
r. 21.8 amended by SI 2008/2178, r. 15(d) (1 October 2008);
r. 21.10(3) amended by: (a) SI 2010/621, r. 4 (30 April 2010); (b) SI 2013/262, r. 7(a) (1 April 2013);
r. 21.12 amended by SI 2013/262, r. 7(b) (1 April 2013);
r. 22.1 amended by: (a) SI 2001/1769, r. 3 (31 May 2001); (b) SI 2001/1769, r. 4 (15 October 2001); (c) SI 2001/4015, r. 16 (25 March 2002); (d) SI 2004/3419, r. 4 (1 April 2005);
r. 23.2 amended by SI 2011/3103, r. 8 (19 March 2012);
r. 23.10(1) substituted by SI 2000/221, r. 11 (2 May 2000);
r. 23.12 inserted by SI 2004/2072, r. 9 (1 October 2004); amended by SI 2005/2292, r. 26 (1 October 2005);
r. 24.2 amended by SI 2000/1317, r. 9 (3 July 2000); r. 24.3(2) amended by: (a) SI 1999/1008, r. 7 (26 April 1999); (b) SI 2000/2092, r. 9 (2 October 2000);
r. 24.4(1A) inserted by SI 2005/2292, r. 27 (1 October 2005);
r. 24.4(4) inserted by SI 2000/221, r. 12 (2 May 2000);
Part 25 title amended by SI 2000/221, r. 13(1) (2 May 2000);

r. 25.1 amended by: (a) SI 2002/2058, r. 7 (2 December 2002); (b) SI 2005/3515, r. 7(a) (6 April 2006);
r. 25.2(3) substituted by SI 2005/3515, r. 7(b) (6 April 2006);
r. 25.7 amended by SI 2004/3419, r. 5 (1 April 2005);
r. 25.10 amended by SI 2001/4015 (25 March 2002);
r. 25.11 inserted by SI 1999/1008, r. 8 (26 April 1999);
r. 25.12 inserted by SI 2000/221, r. 13(2) (2 May 2000);
r. 25.13 inserted by SI 2000/221, r. 13(2) (2 May 2000); amended by: (a) SI 2001/4015, r. 18 (1 March 2002); (b) SI 2002/3219, r. 3 (1 April 2003); (c) SI 2009/3131, reg. 34 (1 January 2010) (see note 19);
rr. 25.14 and 25.15 inserted by SI 2000/221, r. 13(2) (2 May 2000);
r. 26.2 amended by SI 2011/3103, r. 9(b) (19 March 2012);
r. 26.2A inserted by SI 2011/3103, r. 9(c) (19 March 2012); amended by SI 2013/262, r. 8(b) (1 April 2013) (see note 22);
r. 26.3 amended by: (a) SI 2001/4015, r. 19 (25 March 2002); (b) SI 2011/3103, r. 9(d) (19 March 2012); (c) SI 2012/2208, r. 3 (1 October 2012); (d) SI 2013/262, r. 8(c) (1 April 2013) (see note 22);
r. 26.4 amended by: (a) SI 2005/2292, r. 28 (1 October 2005); (b) SI 2013/262, r. 8(d) (1 April 2013) (see note 22);
r. 26.5 amended by SI 2013/262, r. 8(e) (1 April 2013) (see note 22);
r. 26.6 amended by: (a) SI 2008/3327, r. 7 (6 April 2009); (b) SI 2013/262, r. 8(f) (1 April 2013) (see note 24);
r. 26.7(3) revoked by SI 2013/262, r. 8(g) (1 April 2013) (see note 24);
r. 26.9 amended by SI 2013/262, r. 8(h) (1 April 2013) (see note 22);
r. 26.11 inserted by SI 2000/2092, r. 10 (2 October 2000);
r. 27.1 amended by SI 2013/262, r. 9(a) (1 April 2013) (see note 24);
r. 27.2(1) amended by: (a) SI 2000/221, r. 15 (2 May 2000); (b) SI 2005/2292, r. 29(a) (1 October 2005); amended by SI 2006/3435, r. 6(a) (6 April 2007);
r. 27.2(3) inserted by SI 2005/2292, r. 29(b) (1 October 2005);
r. 27.4 amended by SI 2009/3390, r. 14 (6 April 2010);
r. 27.5 amended by: (a) SI 2012/2208, r. 4(a) (1 October 2012); SI 2013/262, r. 9(b) (1 April 2013);
r. 27.9(1) substituted by SI 2005/2292, r. 30 (1 October 2005);
rr. 27.12 and 27.13 revoked by SI 2000/2092, r. 11 (2 October 2000) (see note 1);
r. 27.14(1) amended by SI 2013/262, r. 9(c)(i) (1 April 2013);
r. 27.14(2) substituted by SI 2006/1689, r. 5(a) (2 October 2006); amended by: (a) SI 2009/3390, r. 14 (6 April 2010); (b) SI 2010/621, r. 5 (30 April 2010); (c) SI 2012/2208, r. 4(b) (1 October 2012);
r. 27.14(2A) inserted by SI 2005/2292, r. 31 (a) (1 October 2005); renumbered as r. 27.14(3) and amended by SI 2006/1689, r. 5(c) and (d) (2 October 2006);
r. 27.14(3) amended by SI 2005/2292, r. 31(b) (1 October 2005); replaced by renumbered former r. 27.14(2A) by SI 2006/1689, r. 5(b) and (c) (2 October 2006);
r. 27.14(5) and (6) revoked by SI 2013/262, r. 9(c)(ii) (1 April 2013);
r. 28.4 amended by SI 2002/2058, r. 8 (2 December 2002);
r. 28.5 substituted by SI 2002/2058, r. 9 (2 December 2002); amended by SI 2005/2292, r. 32 (1 October 2005);
r. 28.6 amended by SI 2002/2058, r. 8 (2 December 2002);
r. 29.1 amended by SI 2013/262, r. 10(a) (1 April 2013);
r. 29.2 amended by: (a) SI 2002/2058, r. 8 (2 December 2002); (b) SI 2013/262, r. 10(b) (1 April 2013);
r. 29.4 substituted by SI 2013/262, r. 10(c) (1 April 2013) (see note 25);
r. 29.5 amended by SI 2002/2058, r. 8 (2 December 2002);
r. 29.6 substituted by SI 2002/2058, r. 10 (2 December 2002); amended by SI 2005/2292, r. 33 (1 October 2005);
r. 29.7 amended by SI 2002/2058, r. 11 (2 December 2002);
r. 29.8 amended by: (a) SI 2002/2058, r. 8 (2 December 2002); (b) SI 2013/262, r. 10(d) (1 April 2013);

r. 30.1 amended by: (a) SI 2003/2113, r. 5 (6 October 2003); (b) SI 2009/3390, r. 15(a) (6 April 2010);
r. 30.3(2) amended by: (a) SI 2000/2092, r. 13 (2 October 2000); (b) SI 2005/2292, r. 34 (1 October 2005); (c) SI 2010/1953, r. 3 (31 January 2011);
r. 30.5 amended by SI 2005/3515, r. 8 (6 April 2006);
r. 30.7 amended by SI 2007/2204, r. 9 (1 October 2007);
r. 30.8 revoked by SI 2000/2092, r. 14 (2 October 2000); new r. 30.8 inserted by: SI 2003/3361, r. 5 (1 May 2004); substituted by SI 2004/1306, r. 5 (1 June 2004); amended by: (a) SI 2005/2292, r. 35 (1 October 2005); (b) Treaty of Lisbon (Changes in Terminology or Numbering) Order 2012 (SI 2012/1809), art. 3(1) and sch., part 2 (1 August 2012);
r. 31.3 amended by SI 2011/88, r. 9(a) (6 April 2011);
r. 31.5 substituted by SI 2013/262, r. 11 (1 April 2013) (see note 26);
r. 31.14 amended by SI 2001/4015, r. 20 (25 March 2002);
r. 31.22 amended by SI 2010/1953, r. 4 (1 October 2010);
r. 31.23 inserted by SI 2000/221, r. 16 (2 May 2000); amended by SI 2012/2208, r. 5 (1 October 2012) (see note 21);
r. 32.1 amended by SI 2012/2208, r. 6 (1 October 2012) (see note 21);
r. 32.2 amended by SI 2013/262, r. 12 (1 April 2013);
r. 32.6 amended by SI 2000/221, r. 17 (2 May 2000);
r. 32.8 amended by SI 2009/3390, r. 16 (6 April 2010);
r. 32.13 amended by: (a) SI 2001/256, r. 12 (26 March 2001); (b) SI 2007/2204, r. 10 (1 October 2007);
r. 32.16 amended by SI 2009/3390, r. 16 (6 April 2010);
r. 32.20 inserted by SI 2005/2292, r. 36 (1 October 2005);
r. 33.3 amended by SI 1999/1008, r. 10 (26 April 1999);
r. 33.9 inserted by SI 2000/2092, r. 15 (2 October 2000);
Part 34 title amended by SI 2002/2058, r. 12(a) (2 December 2002);
r. 34.1 substituted by SI 2002/2058, r. 12(c) (2 December 2002);
r. 34.7 amended by SI 2009/3390, r. 17 (6 April 2010);
r. 34.8 amended by SI 2009/3390, r. 17 (6 April 2010);
r. 34.13 amended by: (a) SI 1999/1008, r. 11(a) (26 April 1999); (b) SI 2003/2113, r. 7 (1 January 2004);
r. 34.13A inserted by SI 2003/3361, r. 6 (1 February 2004);
r. 34.14 amended by SI 1999/1008, r. 11(b) (26 April 1999);
rr. 34.16 to 34.21 inserted by SI 2002/2058, r. 12(d) and sch. 2 (2 December 2002);
r. 34.16 amended by: (a) SI 2003/2113, r. 8 (1 January 2004); (b) SI 2004/1306, r. 6 (1 June 2004);
r. 34.19 amended by SI 2009/2092, r. 4 (1 October 2009);
r. 34.22 inserted by SI 2003/2113, r. 9 and sch. 1, part II (1 January 2004); amended by SI 2009/3390, r. 17 (6 April 2010);
r. 34.23 inserted by SI 2003/2113, r. 9 and sch. 1, part II (1 January 2004); amended by: (a) SI 2003/3361, r. 7 (1 February 2004); (b) SI 2004/1306, r. 7 (1 June 2004);
r. 34.24 inserted by SI 2003/2113, r. 9 and sch. 1, part II (1 January 2004);
r. 35.2 substituted by SI 2009/2092, r. 5(b) (1 October 2009);
r. 35.3 amended by SI 2009/2092, r. 5(c) and (d) (1 October 2009);
r. 35.4 amended by: (a) SI 2009/2092, r. 5(e), (f), (g) and (h) (1 October 2009); (b) SI 2013/262, r. 13 (1 April 2013) (see note 27);
r. 35.5 amended by SI 2009/2092, r. 5(i) (1 October 2009);
r. 35.6 amended by SI 2009/2092, r. 5(j) (1 October 2009);
r. 35.7 substituted by SI 2009/2092, r. 5(k) (1 October 2009);
r. 35.8 amended by SI 2009/2092, r. 5(l), (m), (n) and (o) (1 October 2009);
r. 35.9 amended by SI 2009/2092, r. 5(p) (1 October 2009);
r. 35.10 amended by: (a) SI 2009/2092, r. 5(q) (1 October 2009); SI 2009/3390, r. 18 (6 April 2010);
r. 35.12 amended by: (a) SI 2001/4015, r. 21 (25 March 2002); (b) SI 2009/2092, r. 5(r) (1 October 2009);
r. 35.14 amended by: (a) SI 2001/4015, r. 22 (25 March 2002); (b) SI 2009/2092, r. 5(s) (1 October 2009);
r. 35.15 substituted by SI 2009/2092, r. 5(t) (1 October 2009);

Part 36 substituted by SI 2006/3435, r. 7(1) and sch. 1 (6 April 2007) (see note 14);
r. 36.A1 inserted by SI 2010/621, r. 6(b) (30 April 2010);
r. 36.1 amended by SI 2010/621, r. 6(b)–(d) (30 April 2010);
r. 36.2 amended by SI 2010/621, r. 6(e) (30 April 2010);
r. 36.3 amended by SI 2010/621, r. 6(f) (30 April 2010);
r. 36.9 amended by SI 2008/2178, r. 17(b) (1 October 2008);
r. 36.10 amended by SI 2008/2178, r. 17(c) (1 October 2008);
r. 36.14 amended by: (a) SI 2010/621, r. 6(g) (30 April 2010); (b) SI 2011/1979, r. 3(a) (1 October 2011); (c) SI 2013/262, r. 14 (1 April 2013) (see note 28);
r. 36.15 amended by SI 2008/2178, r. 17(d) (1 October 2008);
rr. 36.16 to 36.22 inserted by SI 2010/621, r. 6(h) and sch. 1 (30 April 2010);
Part 37 substituted by SI 2006/3435, r. 8 and sch. 2 (6 April 2007) (see note 14);
r. 38.6 amended by SI 2008/2178, r. 18 (1 October 2008);
r. 38.8 amended by: (a) SI 2000/1317, r. 10 (3 July 2000); (b) SI 2008/2178, r. 19 (1 October 2008);
r. 39.2 amended by SI 2007/2204, r. 12 (1 October 2007);
r. 39.3(4) amended by SI 2000/2092, r. 18 (2 October 2000);
r. 39.8 inserted by SI 2001/1388, r. 12 (31 May 2001); revoked by SI 2006/1689, r. 6 (2 October 2006);
Part 40, title amended by SI 2000/221, r. 18(1) (2 May 2000);
r. 40.1 substituted by SI 2000/221, r. 18(3) (2 May 2000); amended by SI 2004/3419, r. 6 (1 April 2005);
r. 40.2 amended by: (a) SI 2001/2792, r. 4 (25 March 2002); (b) SI 2005/3515, r. 9 (6 April 2006); (c) SI 2012/2208, r. 7 (1 October 2012);
r. 40.3 amended by SI 2005/2292, r. 37 (1 October 2005);
rr. 40.15 to 40.19 inserted by SI 2000/221, r. 18(4) (2 May 2000);
r. 40.20 inserted by SI 2001/256, r. 13 (26 March 2001);
Part 41 title amended by SI 2004/3129, r. 10 (in force by SI 2005/547) (1 April 2005);
r. 41.3 amended by SI 2004/3419, r. 7 (1 April 2005);
r. 41.3A inserted by SI 2006/3435, r. 9 (6 April 2007);
rr. 41.4 to 41.10 inserted by SI 2004/3129, r. 11 and sch. 1 (in force by SI 2005/547) (1 April 2005);
rr. 41.7, 41.9 and 41.10 amended by SI 2009/3390, r. 21 (6 April 2010);
r. 42.2(1) amended by SI 1999/1008, r. 16 (26 April 1999);
r. 42.2(5) inserted by SI 2004/1306, r. 8 (1 June 2004);
r. 42.2(6) substituted and (7) inserted by SI 2000/1317, r. 11 (3 July 2000); amended by SI 2013/534, sch., para. 13(a) (1 April 2013 subject to reg. 14(2));
Part 43 revoked by SI 2013/262, r. 15 (1 April 2013);
Parts 44 to 48 substituted by SI 2013/262, r. 16 (1 April 2013);
r. 44.3 amended by SI 2013/505, r. 5 (1 April 2013);
r. 45.18 amended by SI 2013/789, r. 3 (30 April 2013) (see note 30);
r. 46.9 amended by SI 2013/534, sch., para. 2(a) (1 April 2013);
r. 47.8 amended by SI 2013/534, sch., para. 2(b) (1 April 2013);
heading to Part 47, Section VI, amended by SI 2013/534, sch., para. 2(c) (1 April 2013);
r. 47.18 amended by SI 2013/534, sch., para. 2(d), (e) and (f) (1 April 2013);
Part 49 amended by: (a) SI 2001/1388, r. 13 (15 October 2001); (b) SI 2001/4015, r. 28 (25 March 2002); (c) SI 2002/3219, r. 6 (1 April 2003); (d) SI 2007/2204, r. 17 (1 October 2007); substituted by SI 2009/2092, r. 9 (1 October 2009);
title of Part 51 substituted by SI 2001/2792, r. 5(a) (15 October 2001);
r. 51 renumbered r. 51.1 by SI 2001/2792, r. 5(b) (15 October 2001); amended by SI 2009/3390, r. 27 (6 April 2010);
r. 51.2 inserted by SI 2001/2792, r. 5(c) (15 October 2001);
Part 52 inserted by SI 2000/221, r. 19 (2 May 2000) (see note 3);
r. 52.1(2) substituted by SI 2000/2092, r. 21 (2 October 2000) (see note 1);
r. 52.2 amended by: (a) SI 2009/3390, r. 28(b) and (c) (6 April 2010); (b) SI 2012/2208, r. 8(a) (1 October 2012);
r. 52.3 amended by: (a) SI 2005/3515, r. 11(b) (6 April 2006); (b) SI 2006/1689, r. 7(1) (2 October 2006); (c) SI 2008/2178, r. 26 (1 October 2008) (see note 17); (d) SI 2009/3390, r. 28(c) (6 April 2010); (e) SI 2012/2208, r. 8(b) (1 October 2012);
r. 52.4 amended by: (a) SI 2005/3515, r. 11(c) (6 April 2006); (b) SI 2010/1953, r. 6(a) and (b) (31 January 2011);

r. 52.5 amended by SI 2010/1953, r. 6(c) (31 January 2011);
r. 52.6 amended by SI 2009/3390, r. 28(c) (6 April 2010);
r. 52.7 amended by: (a) SI 2006/1689, r. 7(2) (2 October 2006); (b) SI 2009/3390, r. 28(d) (15 February 2010);
r. 52.9A inserted by SI 2013/262, r. 17 (1 April 2013);
r. 52.10 amended by SI 2004/2072, r. 13 (1 October 2004);
r. 52.12 amended by: (a) SI 2003/3361, r. 10 (1 April 2004); (b) SI 2006/3435, r. 13 (6 April 2007);
r. 52.12A inserted by SI 2007/2204, r. 18(c) (1 October 2007);
r. 52.15 amended by: (a) SI 2012/2208, r. 8(c) (1 October 2012); (b) SI 2013/1412, r. 3 (1 July 2013) (see note 31);
r. 52.16 amended by SI 2003/3361, r. 11 (1 February 2004);
r. 52.17 inserted by SI 2003/2113, r. 14 (6 October 2003);
heading to sect. IV inserted by SI 2007/2204, r. 18(d) (1 October 2007); amended by SI 2007/3543, r. 6 (6 April 2008);
rr. 52.18 to 52.20 inserted by SI 2007/2204, r. 18(d) (1 October 2007);
Part 53 inserted by SI 2000/221, r. 20 (28 February 2000);
Part 54 inserted by SI 2000/2092, r. 22 (2 October 2000) (see note 4);
r. 54.1 amended by: (a) SI 2003/364, r. 5(a) and (b) (1 April 2003 by SI 2003/754); (b) SI 2003/3361, r. 12 (1 May 2004);
r. 54.1A inserted by SI 2012/2208, r. 9(b) (1 October 2012);
r. 54.2 amended by SI 2003/364, r. 5(c) (1 April 2003 by SI 2003/754);
r. 54.3 amended by: (a) SI 2003/364, r. 5(c) (1 April 2003 by SI 2003/754); (b) SI 2003/3361, r. 13 (1 May 2004);
r. 54.4 amended by SI 2003/364, r. 5(d) (1 April 2003 by SI 2003/754);
r. 54.5 amended by SI 2013/1412, r. 4(a) (1 July 2013) (see note 31);
r. 54.6 amended by: (a) SI 2009/3390, r. 29(b) (6 April 2010); (b) SI 2013/262, r. 18 (1 April 2013) (see note 29);
r. 54.7A inserted by SI 2012/2208, r. 9(c) (1 October 2012);
r. 54.10 amended by SI 2010/2577, r. 3 (20 October 2010);
r. 54.12 amended by: (a) SI 2010/2577, r. 4 (20 October 2010); (b) SI 2013/1412, r. 4(b) (1 July 2013) (see note 31);
r. 54.16 amended by: (a) SI 2002/2058, r. 21 (2 December 2002); (b) SI 2003/364, r. 5(d) (1 April 2003 by SI 2003/754);
r. 54.19 amended by SI 2007/3543, r. 7(b) and (c) (6 April 2008);
r. 54.20 amended by SI 2003/364, r. 5(e) (1 April 2003 by SI 2003/754);
rr. 54.21 to 54.27 inserted by SI 2003/364, r. 5(f) and sch. (1 April 2003 by SI 2003/ 754); revoked by SI 2007/3543, r. 7(d) (6 April 2008);
rr. 54.28 to 54.36 inserted by SI 2005/352, r. 7 and sch. 4 (4 April 2005), SI 2005/3515, r. 12(b) (6 April 2006) and SI 2006/1689, r. 8(3) (2 October 2006); revoked by SI 2009/3390, r. 29(c) (15 February 2010);
Part 55 inserted by SI 2001/256, r. 17 (15 October 2001) (see note 5);
r. 55.1 amended by: (a) SI 2004/1306, r. 10 (30 June 2004); (b) SI 2005/2292, r. 42 (1 October 2005);
r. 55.2 amended by SI 2002/2058, r. 22(b) (2 December 2002);
r. 55.3 amended by SI 2009/3390, r. 30(a) and (b) (6 April 2010);
r. 55.8 amended by SI 2008/2178, r. 28 (1 October 2008);
r. 55.9 amended by SI 2004/1306, r. 12 (30 June 2004);
r. 55.10 amended by: (a) SI 2008/3327, r. 11 (6 April 2009); (b) SI 2009/2092, r. 11 (1 October 2009); (c) SI 2010/621, r. 10(a) (30 April 2010); (d) SI 2010/1953, r. 7 (1 October 2010);
r. 55.10A inserted by SI 2005/2292, r. 44 (1 October 2005);
r. 55.11 amended by: (a) SI 2004/1306, r. 13 (30 June 2004); (b) SI 2010/621, r. 10(b) (1 April 2010);
r. 55.12 amended by SI 2004/1306, r. 14 (30 June 2004);
r. 55.13 amended by: (a) SI 2005/3515, r. 13 (6 April 2006); (b) SI 2009/3390, r. 30(b) (6 April 2010);
r. 55.14 amended by SI 2009/3390, r. 30(b) (6 April 2010);
rr. 55.20 to 55.28 inserted by SI 2002/2058, r. 22(c) and sch. 3 (2 December 2002);
rr. 55.22, 55.23, 55.24 and 55.25 amended by SI 2009/3390, r. 30(b) (6 April 2010);
Part 56 inserted by SI 2001/256, r. 18 (15 October 2001) (see note 5);
r. 56.1 amended by SI 2008/2178, r. 29(a) (1 October 2008);

CPR Glossary, Schs, Other PDs

r. 56.2 amended by: (a) SI 2004/1306, r. 15 (1 June 2004) (see note 12); (b) SI 2008/2178, r. 29(b) (1 October 2008); (c) SI 2009/3390, r. 31(a) (6 April 2010);
r. 56.3 substituted by SI 2004/1306, r. 16 (30 June 2004) (see note 12); amended by SI 2008/2178, r. 29(c) (1 October 2008);
r. 56.4 amended by SI 2002/3219, r. 7 (1 April 2003);
Part 57 inserted by SI 2001/1388, r. 14 (15 October 2001) (see note 6); title amended by SI 2002/2058, r. 23(a) (2 December 2002);
r. 57.1 amended by SI 2002/2058, r. 23(c) (2 December 2002);
r. 57.2 amended by SI 2003/2113, r. 15 (6 October 2003);
r. 57.4 amended by: (a) SI 2008/2178, r. 30(a) (1 October 2008); (b) SI 2009/3390, r. 32(a) (6 April 2010);
r. 57.7 amended by SI 2007/3543, r. 8 (6 April 2008);
r. 57.9 amended by SI 2003/3361, r. 14 (1 April 2004);
rr. 57.12 and 57.13 amended by SI 2009/3390, r. 32(c) (6 April 2010);
rr. 57.14 to 57.16 inserted by SI 2002/2058, r. 23(d) and sch. 4 (2 December 2002);
r. 57.15 amended by SI 2009/3390, r. 32(d) (6 April 2010);
r. 57.16 amended by: (a) SI 2004/1306, r. 17 (30 June 2004); (b) SI 2008/2178, r. 30(b) (1 October 2008); (c) SI 2009/3390, r. 32(b) and (e) (6 April 2010);
Part 58 inserted by SI 2001/4015, r. 29 (25 March 2002);
r. 58.1 amended by SI 2009/3390, r. 33(a) (6 April 2010);
r. 58.4 amended by SI 2005/3515, r. 14 (6 April 2006);
r. 58.6 amended by SI 2008/2178, r. 31(a) (1 October 2008);
r. 58.10 amended by SI 2008/2178, r. 31(b) (1 October 2008);
r. 58.13 amended by SI 2009/3390, r. 33(b) (6 April 2010);
Part 59 inserted by SI 2001/4015, r. 29 (25 March 2002);
r. 59.1 amended by: (a) SI 2006/1689, r. 9 (2 October 2006); (b) SI 2009/3390, r. 34(a) (6 April 2010);
r. 59.3 amended by SI 2005/3515, r. 15 (6 April 2006);
r. 59.5 amended by SI 2008/2178, r. 32(a) (1 October 2008);
r. 59.9 amended by SI 2008/2178, r. 32(b) (1 October 2008);
r. 59.11 amended by SI 2009/3390, r. 34(b) (6 April 2010);
Part 60 inserted by SI 2001/4015, r. 29 (25 March 2002);
r. 60.1 amended by SI 2009/3390, r. 35(a) (6 April 2010);
r. 60.4 amended by SI 2009/3390, r. 35(c) (6 April 2010);
r. 60.6 amended by SI 2009/3390, r. 35(d) (6 April 2010);
r. 60.7 inserted by SI 2005/2292, r. 45 (1 October 2005);
Part 61 inserted by SI 2001/4015, r. 29 (25 March 2002);
r. 61.1 amended by SI 2009/3390, r. 36(a) (6 April 2010);
r. 61.2 amended by SI 2005/3515, r. 16 (6 April 2006);
r. 61.3 amended by SI 2009/3390, r. 36(a) (6 April 2010);
r. 61.4 amended by SI 2009/3390, r. 36(a) (6 April 2010);
r. 61.5 amended by SI 2009/3390, r. 36(a) and (b) (6 April 2010);
rr. 61.7, 61.8, 61.9 and 61.11 amended by SI 2009/3390, r. 36(a) (6 April 2010);
Part 62 inserted by SI 2001/4015, r. 29 (25 March 2002);
r. 62.1 amended by SI 2009/3390, r. 37 (6 April 2010);
r. 62.3 amended by: (a) SI 2005/3515, r. 17 (6 April 2006); (b) SI 2009/3390, r. 37 (6 April 2010);
r. 62.5 amended by SI 2008/2178, r. 34(a) (1 October 2008);
r. 62.7 amended by SI 2009/3390, r. 37 (6 April 2010);
r. 62.16 amended by SI 2008/2178, r. 34(b) (1 October 2008);
r. 62.18 amended by SI 2008/2178, r. 34(c) (1 October 2008);
r. 62.20 amended by: (a) SI 2002/2058, r. 24 (2 December 2002); (b) SI 2008/2178, r. 34(d) (1 October 2008);
r. 62.21 amended by SI 2002/2058, r. 25 (2 December 2002);
Part 63 inserted by SI 2002/3219, r. 8 and sch. (1 April 2003); substituted by SI 2009/2092, r. 12 and sch. 1 (1 October 2009);
r. 63.1 amended by: (a) SI 2009/3390, r. 38(a) and (b) (6 April 2010); (b) SI 2012/2208, r. 10(b) (1 October 2012);

r. 63.4 revoked by SI 2010/1953, r. 8(b) (1 October 2010);
rr. 63.6, 63.8, 63.9 and 63.13 amended by SI 2009/3390, r. 38(a) (6 April 2010);
rr. 63.17 to 63.26 inserted by SI 2010/1953, r. 8(c) and sch. 2 (1 October 2010);
r. 63.27 inserted by SI 2012/2208, r. 10(c) (1 October 2012); amended by SI 2013/262, r. 19 (1 April 2013) (see note 24);
r. 63.28 inserted by SI 2012/2208, r. 10(c) (1 October 2012);
Part 64 inserted by SI 2002/2058, r. 26(a) and sch. 5 (2 December 2002);
r. 64.1 amended by SI 2009/3390, r. 39(a) (6 April 2010);
r. 64.2 amended by SI 2009/3390, r. 39(b) (6 April 2010);
Part 65 inserted by SI 2004/1306, r. 18 and sch. 2 (1 June 2004) (see note 13);
r. 65.1 amended by: (a) SI 2007/2204, r. 19(b) and (c) (1 October 2007); (b) SI 2008/2178, r. 36(b) (1 October 2008); (c) SI 2009/2092, r. 13(b) and (c) (31 August 2009); (d) SI 2010/1953, r. 9(b) (31 January 2011);
r. 65.3 amended by: (a) SI 2004/2072, r. 14 (1 September 2004); (b) SI 2009/3390, r. 40(a) (6 April 2010);
r. 65.6 amended by SI 2012/2208, r. 11(a) (1 October 2012) (see note 21);
r. 65.8 amended by SI 2007/2204, r. 19(d) (1 October 2007);
r. 65.9 amended by SI 2007/2204, r. 19(e) (1 October 2007);
r. 65.10 amended by SI 2007/2204, r. 19(f) (1 October 2007);
Part 65, Section III, heading amended by SI 2005/2292, r. 48(a) (1 October 2005);
r. 65.11 amended by SI 2005/2292, r. 48(b) and (c) (1 October 2005);
r. 65.12 amended by SI 2005/2292, r. 48(d) (1 October 2005);
r. 65.13 amended by SI 2005/2292, r. 48(e) (1 October 2005);
r. 65.14 amended by: (a) SI 2005/2292, r. 48(f) (1 October 2005); (b) SI 2009/3390, r. 40(a) (6 April 2010);
r. 65.17 amended by SI 2005/2292, r. 48(g) (1 October 2005);
r. 65.18 amended by: (a) SI 2005/2292, r. 48(h) (1 October 2005); (b) SI 2008/2178, r. 36(c) (1 October 2008);
r. 65.19 amended by SI 2005/2292, r. 48(i) (1 October 2005);
rr. 65.31 to 65.36 inserted by SI 2009/2092, r. 13(d) and sch. 2 (31 August 2009);
rr. 65.37 to 65.41 inserted by SI 2007/2204, r. 19(g) (1 October 2007);
rr. 65.42 to 65.49 inserted by SI 2010/1953, r. 9(c) and sch. 3 (31 January 2011);
r. 65.47 amended by SI 2012/2208, r. 11(b) (1 October 2012) (see note 21);
Part 66 inserted by SI 2005/2292, r. 49 and sch. 2 (1 October 2005);
Part 67 inserted by SI 2004/3419, r. 16 and sch. 2 (1 April 2005);
Part 68 inserted by SI 2002/2058, r. 26(b) and sch. 6 (2 December 2002);
r. 68.1 amended by SI 2009/2092, r. 14(b) (1 October 2009);
r. 68.2 amended by: (a) SI 2009/2092, r. 14(c) and (d) (1 October 2009); (b) SI 2009/3390, r. 42 (6 April 2010);
r. 68.2A inserted by SI 2009/2092, r. 14(e) (1 October 2009);
r. 68.3 amended by SI 2009/2092, r. 14(f) (1 October 2009);
Part 69 inserted by SI 2002/2058, r. 26(c) and sch. 7 (2 December 2002);
r. 69.10 amended by SI 2004/1306, r. 19 (30 June 2004);
Part 70 inserted by SI 2001/2792, r. 6 (25 March 2002) (see note 7);
r. 70.2 amended by SI 2009/3390, r. 44(a) (6 April 2010);
r. 70.5 substituted by SI 2008/3327, r. 12(b) (6 April 2009); amended by SI 2009/3390, r. 44(b) (6 April 2010);
Part 71 inserted by SI 2001/2792, r. 6 (25 March 2002) (see note 7);
r. 71.2 amended by: (a) SI 2009/3390, r. 45 (6 April 2010); (b) SI 2012/505, r. 3 (19 March 2012); (c) SI 2012/2208, r. 12(a) (1 October 2012) (see note 21);
r. 71.8 amended by: (a) SI 2001/4015, r. 31 (25 March 2002); (b) SI 2012/2208, r. 12(b) (1 October 2012) (see note 21);
Part 72 inserted by SI 2001/2792, r. 6 (25 March 2002) (see note 7);
r. 72.1 amended by SI 2001/4015, r. 32 (25 March 2002);
r. 72.3 amended by: (a) SI 2009/3390, r. 46 (6 April 2010); (b) SI 2012/505, r. 4 (19 March 2012);
r. 72.4 amended by SI 2009/3390, r. 46 (6 April 2010);
r. 72.6 amended by SI 2001/4015, r. 33 (25 March 2002);

Part 73 inserted by SI 2001/2792, r. 6 (25 March 2002) (see note 7);
r. 73.3 amended by: (a) SI 2009/3390, r. 47(a) (6 April 2010); (b) SI 2012/505, r. 5 (19 March 2012);
r. 73.10 amended by SI 2009/3390, r. 47(a) (6 April 2010);
r. 73.22 inserted by SI 2006/1689, r. 10 (2 October 2006); amended by SI 2009/3390, r. 47(b) (6 April 2010);
Part 74 inserted by SI 2002/2058, r. 29(a) and sch. 8 (2 December 2002);
r. 74.1 amended by: (a) SI 2005/2292, r. 50 (21 October 2005); (b) SI 2007/1655, sch., paras 28 and 31(a) (1 July 2007); (c) SI 2009/3131, reg. 35 (1 January 2010) (see note 19);
r. 74.2 amended by: (a) SI 2007/1655, sch., paras 28 and 31(b) (1 July 2007); (b) SI 2009/3131, reg. 36 (1 January 2010) (see note 19);
r. 74.3 amended by SI 2009/3131, reg. 37 (1 January 2010) (see note 19);
r. 74.4 amended by SI 2009/3131, reg. 38 (1 January 2010) (see note 19);
r. 74.5 amended by SI 2009/3131, reg. 39 (1 January 2010) (see note 19);
r. 74.6 amended by: (a) SI 2008/2178, r. 37(a) (1 October 2008); (b) SI 2009/2092, r. 15(a) (1 October 2009); (c) SI 2009/3131, reg. 40 (1 January 2010) (see note 19);
r. 74.8 amended by SI 2009/3131, reg. 41 (1 January 2010) (see note 19);
r. 74.10 amended by SI 2009/3131, reg. 42 (1 January 2010) (see note 19);
r. 74.11 substituted by SI 2009/3131, reg. 43 (1 January 2010) (see note 19);
r. 74.12 amended by SI 2009/3131, reg. 44 (1 January 2010) (see note 19);
r. 74.13 amended by SI 2013/534, sch., para. 13(b) (1 April 2013 subject to reg. 14(2));
r. 74.15 amended by SI 2009/2092, r. 15(b) (1 October 2009) (see note 19);
r. 74.19 amended by SI 2003/3361, r. 18 (1 April 2004);
r. 74.25 amended by SI 2009/2092, r. 15(c) (1 October 2009);
rr. 74.27 to 74.33 inserted by SI 2005/2292, r. 52 and sch. 3 (21 October 2005);
r. 74.31 amended by SI 2008/2178, r. 37(b) (12 December 2008);
r. 74.32 amended by SI 2008/2178, r. 37(c) (12 December 2008);
r. 74.33 amended by SI 2008/2178, r. 37(d) (12 December 2008);
Parts 75, 76 and 77 are omitted from appendix 1;
Part 78 inserted by SI 2008/2178, r. 38 and sch. 2 (12 December 2008 in so far as it relates to European orders for payment; 1 January 2009 in so far as it relates to the European small claims procedure); title of Part 74 amended by SI 2011/88, r. 12(a) (6 April 2011);
r. 78.1 amended by: (a) SI 2009/3390, r. 52 (6 April 2010); (b) SI 2011/88, r. 12(c) (6 April 2011);
rr. 78.23 to 78.28 inserted by SI 2011/88, r. 12(d) and sch. 2 (6 April 2011) (see note 20);
Parts 79 and 80 are omitted from appendix 1;
Part 81 inserted by SI 2012/2208, r. 16 and sch. (1 October 2012) (see note 21);
Glossary amended by: (a) 49th Update — Practice Direction Amendments; (b) SI 2012/2208, r. 17 (1 October 2012); (b) SI 2013/262, r. 21 (1 April 2013);
sch. 1, RSC, ord. 10, revoked by SI 2001/256, sch. 3 (15 October 2001);
sch. 1, RSC, ord. 11, revoked by SI 2000/221, sch. 8 (2 May 2000);
sch. 1, RSC, ord. 15, rr. 6A and 7, revoked by SI 2000/221, sch. 8 (2 May 2000);
sch. 1, RSC, ord. 15, r. 9, amended by SI 2000/940, r. 12 (2 May 2000); revoked by SI 2002/2058, r. 36 and sch. 10 (2 December 2002);
sch. 1, RSC, ord. 15, rr. 11, 12, 12A and 13, revoked by SI 2000/221, sch. 8 (2 May 2000);
sch. 1, RSC, ord. 15, r. 13A, revoked by SI 2001/256, r. 19 (26 March 2001);
sch. 1, RSC, ord. 15, r. 14, amended by SI 2001/2792, r. 7 (15 October 2001); revoked by SI 2002/2058, r. 36 and sch. 10 (2 December 2002);
sch. 1, RSC, ord. 15, r. 15, revoked by SI 2000/221, sch. 8 (2 May 2000);
sch. 1, RSC, ord. 15, r. 16, revoked by SI 2001/256, r. 19 (26 March 2001);
sch. 1, RSC, ord. 15, r. 17, revoked by SI 2000/221, sch. 8 (2 May 2000);
sch. 1, RSC, ord. 17, r. 1, amended by SI 2003/3361, r. 19 (1 April 2004);
sch. 1, RSC, ord. 17, r. 8, amended by SI 1999/1008, r. 27 (26 April 1999);
sch. 1, RSC, ord. 23, revoked by SI 2000/221, sch. 8 (2 May 2000);
sch. 1, RSC, ord. 30, amended by SI 1999/1008, r. 28 (26 April 1999); revoked by SI 2002/2058, r. 36 and sch. 10 (2 December 2002);
sch. 1, RSC, ord. 31, revoked by SI 2000/221, sch. 8 (2 May 2000);
sch. 1, RSC, ord. 44, rr. 1 to 11, revoked by SI 2002/2058, r. 36 and sch. 10 (2 December 2002);
sch. 1, RSC, ord. 44, r. 12, revoked by SI 2000/221, sch. 8 (2 May 2000);

sch. 1, RSC, ord. 45, r. 1A, inserted by SI 2003/3361, r. 20 (1 April 2004);
sch. 1, RSC, ord. 45, r. 1 (1), (2) and (3), revoked by SI 2001/2792, sch. 5 (25 March 2002);
sch. 1, RSC, ord. 45, r. 2, amended by: (a) SI 2003/3361, r. 21 (1 April 2004); (b) SI 2009/3390, r. 53 (6 April 2010);
sch. 1, RSC, ord. 45, r. 3, amended by: (a) SI 2001/256, r. 20 (15 October 2001); (b) SI 2012/2208, r. 18(1)(i) (1 October 2012) (see note 21);
sch. 1, RSC, ord. 45, r. 4, amended by SI 2012/2208, r. 18(a)(ii) and (iii) (1 October 2012) (see note 21);
sch. 1, RSC, ord. 45, rr. 5, 6 and 7 revoked by SI 2012/2208, r. 18(a)(iv) (1 October 2012) (see note 21);
sch. 1, RSC, ord. 45, r. 8, amended by SI 2003/3361, r. 22 (1 May 2004);
sch. 1, RSC, ord. 45, rr. 9 and 10, revoked by SI 2001/2792, sch. 5 (25 March 2002);
sch. 1, RSC, ord. 45, r. 12, amended by: (a) SI 2009/3390, r. 53 (6 April 2010); (b) SI 2012/2208, r. 18(a)(iv) (1 October 2012) (see note 21);
sch. 1, RSC, ord. 45, rr. 13 and 14, revoked by SI 2001/2792, sch. 5 (25 March 2002);
sch. 1, RSC, ord. 46, r. 5, substituted by SI 2012/2208, r. 18(b) (1 October 2012) (see note 21);
sch. 1, RSC, ord. 46, r. 6, amended by SI 2009/2092, r. 19 (1 October 2009);
sch. 1, RSC, ord. 46, r. 8, amended by: (a) SI 2003/3361, r. 23 (1 April 2004); (b) SI 2009/3390, r. 54 (6 April 2010);
sch. 1, RSC, ord. 46, r. 8, amended by SI 2003/3361, r. 23 (1 April 2004);
sch. 1, RSC, ord. 46, r. 9, amended by SI 2003/3361, r. 24 (1 April 2004);
sch. 1, RSC, ord. 47, r. 2, revoked by SI 2003/3361, r. 25 (1 April 2004);
sch. 1, RSC, ord. 47, r. 4, amended by SI 2003/3361, r. 26 (1 April 2004);
sch. 1, RSC, ord. 47, r. 5, amended by SI 2003/3361, r. 27 (1 April 2004);
sch. 1, RSC, ord. 47, r. 6, amended by SI 2003/3361, r. 28 (1 April 2004);
sch. 1, RSC, ord. 48, amended by SI 1999/1008, r. 31 (26 April 1999); revoked by SI 2001/2792, sch. 5 (25 March 2002);
sch. 1, RSC, ord. 49, revoked by SI 2001/2792, sch. 5 (25 March 2002);
sch. 1, RSC, ord. 50, revoked by SI 2001/2792, sch. 5 (25 March 2002);
sch. 1, RSC, ord. 51, amended by SI 2001/2792, r. 7 (15 October 2001); revoked by SI 2002/2058, r. 36 and sch. 10 (2 December 2002);
sch. 1, RSC, ord. 52, revoked by SI 2012/2208, r. 18(c) (1 October 2012) (see note 21);
sch. 1, RSC, ord. 53, revoked by SI 2000/2092, r. 23 (2 October 2000) (see note 4);
sch. 1, RSC. ord. 54, r. 9, amended by SI 1999/1008, r. 62 (26 April 1999);
sch. 1, RSC, ord. 55, revoked by SI 2000/221, sch. 8 (2 May 2000);
sch. 1, RSC, ord. 56, revoked by SI 2000/221, sch. 8 (2 May 2000);
sch. 1, RSC, ord. 57, revoked by SI 2000/2092, r. 24 (2 October 2000);
sch. 1, RSC, ord. 58, revoked by SI 2000/221, sch. 8 (2 May 2000);
sch. 1, RSC, ord. 59, revoked by SI 2000/221, sch. 8 (2 May 2000);
sch. 1, RSC, ord. 60, revoked by SI 2000/221, sch. 8 (2 May 2000);
sch. 1, RSC, ord. 61, revoked by SI 2000/221, sch. 8 (2 May 2000);
sch. 1, RSC, ord. 62, revoked by SI 2004/3419, r. 17 (1 April 2005);
sch. 1, RSC, ord. 64, revoked by SI 2012/2208, r. 18(d) (1 October 2012) (see note 21);
sch. 1, RSC, ord. 69, revoked by SI 2002/2058, r. 36 and sch. 10 (2 December 2002);
sch. 1, RSC, ord. 70, revoked by SI 2002/2058, r. 36 and sch. 10 (2 December 2002);
sch. 1, RSC, ord. 71, amended by: (a) SI 1999/1008, r. 62 (26 April 1999); (b) SI 2000/221, r. 22 (2 May 2000); (c) SI 2001/4015, r. 35 (1 March 2002); revoked by SI 2002/2058, r. 36 and sch. 10 (2 December 2002);
sch. 1, RSC, ord. 74, r. 1, revoked by SI 2001/4015, r. 37 (25 March 2002);
sch. 1, RSC, ord. 74, r. 2, revoked by SI 2000/221, sch. 8 (2 May 2000);
sch. 1, RSC, ord. 77, revoked by SI 2005/2292, r. 55(a) (1 October 2005);
sch. 1, RSC, ord. 79, is omitted from appendix 1;
sch. 1, RSC, ord. 81, revoked by SI 2006/1689, r. 12(a) (2 October 2006);
sch. 1, RSC, ord. 82, revoked by SI 2000/221, r. 40 (28 February 2000);
sch. 1, RSC, ord. 85, revoked by SI 2002/2058, r. 36 and sch. 10 (2 December 2002);
sch. 1, RSC, ord. 87, revoked by SI 2002/2058, r. 36 and sch. 10 (2 December 2002);
sch. 1, RSC, ord. 88, rr. 1 to 5, revoked by SI 2001/256, sch. 3 (15 October 2001);

sch. 1, RSC, ord. 88, r. 5A, revoked by SI 2001/2792, r. 3 (25 March 2002);
sch. 1, RSC, ord. 88, r. 7, revoked by SI 2001/256, sch. 3 (15 October 2001);
sch. 1, RSC, ord. 91, r. 1, revoked by SI 2003/2113, r. 19(a) (6 October 2003);
sch. 1, RSC, ord. 91, rr. 2, 3, 4, 5, 5A and 6, revoked by SI 2000/221, sch. 8 (2 May 2000);
sch. 1, RSC, ord. 92, rr. 1 and 2, revoked by SI 2002/2058, r. 36 and sch. 10 (2 December 2002);
sch. 1, RSC, ord. 92, r. 3A, revoked by SI 2001/4015, r. 37 (14 January 2002);
sch. 1, RSC, ord. 92, rr. 4 and 5, revoked by SI 2002/2058, r. 36 and sch. 10 (2 December 2002);
sch. 1, RSC, ord. 93, r. 1, revoked by SI 2006/1689, r. 12(b) (2 October 2006);
sch. 1, RSC, ord. 93, r. 2, revoked by SI 2006/3435, r. 15(a) (6 April 2007);
sch. 1, RSC, ord. 93, rr. 4 and 5, revoked by SI 2007/2204, r. 20 (1 October 2007);
sch. 1, RSC, ord. 93, r. 6, revoked by SI 2002/2058, r. 36 and sch. 10 (2 December 2002);
sch. 1, RSC, ord. 93, rr. 9 and 10, revoked by SI 2007/2204, r. 20 (1 October 2007);
sch. 1, RSC, ord. 93, rr. 11 and 12 revoked by SI 2000/221, sch. 8 (2 May 2000);
sch. 1, RSC, ord. 93, r. 15, revoked by SI 2001/256, sch. 3 (15 October 2001);
sch. 1, RSC, ord. 93, rr. 16 to 19, revoked by SI 2007/2204, r. 20 (1 October 2007);
sch. 1, RSC, ord. 93, r. 20, revoked by SI 2001/1388, r. 15 (15 October 2001);
sch. 1, RSC, ord. 93, r. 21, revoked by SI 2002/2058, r. 36 and sch. 10 (2 December 2002);
sch. 1, RSC, ord. 93, r. 22, revoked by SI 2006/3435, r. 15(a) (6 April 2007);
sch. 1, RSC, ord. 93, r. 23, revoked by SI 2001/4015, r. 38(b) (14 January 2002);
sch. 1, RSC, ord. 94, rr. 1 to 3, revoked by SI 2006/3435, r. 15(b) (6 April 2007);
sch. 1, RSC, ord. 94, rr. 4 and 5, revoked by SI 2007/2204, r. 20 (1 October 2007);
sch. 1, RSC, ord. 94, rr. 6 and 7, revoked by SI 2000/221, sch. 8 (2 May 2000);
sch. 1, RSC, ord. 93, rr. 8 and 9, revoked by SI 2007/2204, r. 20 (1 October 2007);
sch. 1, RSC, ord. 94, rr. 10, 10A and 11, revoked by SI 2000/221, sch. 8 (2 May 2000);
sch. 1, RSC, ord. 93, rr. 12 and 13, revoked by SI 2007/2204, r. 20 (1 October 2007);
sch. 1, RSC, ord. 94. rr. 14 and 15, revoked by SI 2006/3435, r. 15(b) (6 April 2007);
sch. 1, RSC, ord. 94, r. 16, inserted by SI 1999/1008, r. 48 (26 April 1999); revoked by SI 2004/1306, r. 21 (30 June 2004);
sch. 1, RSC, ord. 95, r. 1, revoked by SI 2007/2204, r. 20 (1 October 2007);
sch. 1, RSC, ord. 95, rr. 2 and 3, revoked by SI 2006/3435, r. 15(c) (6 April 2007);
sch. 1, RSC, ord. 95, rr. 4 to 6, revoked by SI 2007/2204, r. 20 (1 October 2007);
sch. 1, RSC, ord. 96, revoked by SI 2007/3543, r. 12 (6 April 2008);
sch. 1, RSC, ord. 97, amended by SI 1999/1008, r. 51 (26 April 1999); revoked by SI 2001/256, sch. 3 (15 October 2001);
sch. 1, RSC, ord. 98, revoked by SI 2004/1306, r. 21 (30 June 2004);
sch. 1, RSC, ord. 99, rr. A1 to 3, revoked by SI 2002/2058, r. 36 and sch. 10 (2 December 2002);
sch. 1, RSC, ord. 99, r. 4, amended by SI 2000/221, r. 26 (2 May 2000); revoked by SI 2002/2058, r. 36 and sch. 10 (2 December 2002);
sch. 1, RSC, ord. 99, rr. 5 to 7, revoked by SI 2002/2058, r. 36 and sch. 10 (2 December 2002);
sch. 1, RSC, ord. 99, r. 8, revoked by SI 1999/1008, r. 53 (26 April 1999);
sch. 1, RSC, ord. 99, rr. 9 and 10, revoked by SI 2002/2058, r. 36 and sch. 10 (2 December 2002);
sch. 1, RSC, ord. 101, revoked by SI 2000/221, sch. 8 (2 May 2000);
sch. 1, RSC, ord. 106, revoked by SI 2004/3419, r. 17 (1 April 2005);
sch. 1, RSC, ord. 108, amended by SI 2000/221, r. 28 (2 May 2000); revoked by SI 2002/2058, r. 36 and sch. 10 (2 December 2002);
sch. 1, RSC, ord. 109, r. 1, amended by: (a) SI 1999/1008, r. 55 (26 April 1999); (b) SI 2009/2092, r. 21(a) (1 October 2009);
sch. 1, RSC, ord. 109, r. 2, amended by SI 2000/221, r. 29(a) (2 May 2000);
sch. 1, RSC, ord. 109, r. 3, amended by: (a) SI 2000/221, r. 29(b) (2 May 2000); (b) SI 2009/2092, r. 21(b) (1 October 2009);
sch. 1, RSC, ord. 109, r. 4, amended by: (a) SI 2001/256, r. 23 (1 April 2001); (b) Courts Act 2003 (Consequential Provisions) (No. 2) Order 2005 (SI 2005/617), sch., para. 175 (1 April 2005); (c) SI 2009/2092, r. 21(c) (1 October 2009); (d) SI 2009/3390, r. 57 (6 April 2010);
sch. 1, RSC, ord. 110, revoked by SI 2006/3435, r. 15(e) (6 April 2007);
sch. 1, RSC, ord. 111, revoked by SI 2000/221, sch. 8 (2 May 2000);
sch. 1, RSC, ord. 112, revoked by SI 2006/1689, r. 12(c) (2 October 2006);

sch. 1, RSC, ord. 113, rr. 1 to 6, amended by SI 1999/1008, r. 58 (26 April 1999); revoked by SI 2001/256, sch. 3 (15 October 2001);
sch. 1, RSC, ord. 113, r. 7, amended by SI 2001/256, r. 25 (15 October 2001);
sch. 1, RSC, ord. 114, amended by: (a) SI 1999/1008, r. 59 (26 April 1999); (b) SI 2000/221, r. 30 (2 May 2000); revoked by SI 2002/2058, r. 36 and sch. 10 (2 December 2002);
sch. 1, RSC, ord. 115, is omitted from appendix 1;
sch. 1, RSC, ord. 116, revoked by SI 2010/1953, r. 12 (1 October 2010);
sch. 2, CCR, ord. 1, r. 6, amended by SI 2009/2092, r. 22 (1 October 2009);
sch. 2, CCR, ord. 3, revoked by SI 2000/221, sch. 8 (2 May 2000);
sch. 2, CCR, ord. 4, r. 3, revoked by SI 2003/2113, r. 19(b) (6 October 2003);
sch. 2, CCR, ord. 5, r. 3, revoked by SI 2006/1689, r. 12(d) (2 October 2006);
sch. 2, CCR, ord. 5, rr. 5 to 8, revoked by SI 2000/221, sch. 8 (2 May 2000);
sch. 2, CCR, ord. 5, r. 10, revoked by SI 2006/1689, r. 12(d) (2 October 2006);
sch. 2, CCR, ord. 5, rr. 12 to 14, revoked by SI 2002/2058, r. 36 and sch. 10 (2 December 2002);
sch. 2, CCR, ord. 6, rr. 3, 5 and 5A, revoked by SI 2001/256, sch. 3 (15 October 2001);
sch. 2, CCR, ord. 6, r. 6, revoked by SI 2003/1242, r. 3 (2 June 2003);
sch. 2, CCR, ord. 7, revoked by SI 2001/256, sch. 3 (15 October 2001);
sch. 2, CCR, ord. 13, revoked by SI 2000/221, sch. 8 (2 May 2000);
sch. 2, CCR, ord. 16, r. 7, amended by SI 2003/3361, r. 32 (1 April 2004);
sch. 2, CCR, ord. 19, revoked by SI 2002/2058, r. 36 and sch. 10 (2 December 2002);
sch. 2, CCR, ord. 22, r. 8, amended by; (a) SI 2001/2792, r. 13 (15 October 2001); (b) SI 2001/2792, r. 13 (25 March 2002);
sch. 2, CCR, ord. 24, rr. 1 to 5, amended by SI 1999/1008, r. 66 (26 April 1999); revoked by SI 2001/256, sch. 3 (15 October 2001); revoked by SI 2002/2058, r. 36 and sch. 10 (2 December 2002);
sch. 2, CCR, ord. 24, r. 6, amended by SI 2001/256, r. 27(a) (15 October 2001);
sch. 2, CCR, ord. 24, r. 7, revoked by SI 2001/256, sch. 3 (15 October 2001);
sch. 2, CCR, ord. 24, rr. 8 to 15, amended by SI 2001/256, r. 27(b) to (d) (15 October 2001); revoked by SI 2002/2058, r. 36 and sch. 10 (2 December 2002);
sch. 2, CCR, ord. 25, r. 2, revoked by SI 2001/2792, sch. 5 (25 March 2002);
sch. 2, CCR, ord. 25, r. 3, amended by SI 2000/221, r. 32 (2 May 2000); revoked by SI 2001/2792, sch. 5 (25 March 2002);
sch. 2, CCR, ord. 25, rr. 4, 5 and 5A, revoked by SI 2001/2792, sch. 5 (25 March 2002);
sch. 2, CCR, ord. 25, r. 8, amended by SI 2001/2792, r. 14 (25 March 2002);
sch. 2, CCR, ord. 25, rr. 9 and 10 revoked by SI 2006/1689, r. 12(e) (2 October 2006);
sch. 2, CCR, ord. 25, rr. 11 and 12, revoked by SI 2001/2792, sch. 5 (25 March 2002);
sch. 2, CCR, ord. 25, r. 13, amended by: (a) SI 2001/2792, r. 15 (15 October 2001); (b) SI 2001/2792, r. 15 (25 March 2002);
sch. 2, CCR, ord. 26, r. 17, amended by: (a) SI 2008/3327, r. 15 (6 April 2009); (b) SI 2010/1953, r. 13 (1 October 2010);
sch. 2, CCR, ord. 27, r. 3, amended by SI 2012/505, r. 6 (19 March 2012);
sch. 2, CCR, ord. 27, r. 4, amended by: (a) SI 2001/256, r. 28(a) (1 April 2001); (b) Courts Act 2003 (Consequential Provisions) (No. 2) Order 2005 (SI 2005/617), sch., para. 176 (1 April 2005);
sch. 2, CCR, ord. 27, r. 5, amended by: (a) SI 2000/221, r. 33 (2 May 2000); (b) SI 2001/2792, r. 16 (25 March 2002); (c) SI 2008/2178, r. 40(a) (1 October 2008);
sch. 2, CCR, ord. 27, r. 7A, amended by SI 2013/262, r. 20 (1 April 2013);
sch. 2, CCR, ord. 27, r. 10, amended by: (a) SI 2001/256, r. 28(b) (1 April 2001); (b) Courts Act 2003 (Consequential Provisions) (No. 2) Order 2005 (SI 2005/617), sch., para. 176 (1 April 2005);
sch. 2, CCR, ord. 27, r. 17, amended by: (a) SI 1999/1008, r. 67 (26 April 1999); (b) SI 2000/221, r. 33 (2 May 2000); (c) SI 2001/2792, r. 17 (25 March 2002); (d) SI 2008/2178, r. 40(b) (1 October 2008);
sch. 2, CCR, ord. 28, r. 1, amended by SI 2001/4015, r. 39(a) (25 March 2002);
sch. 2, CCR, ord. 28, r. 2, amended by: (a) SI 2001/4015, r. 39(b) (25 March 2002); (b) SI 2008/2178, r. 41(a) (1 October 2008);
sch. 2, CCR, ord. 28, r. 3, amended by: (a) SI 2001/4015, r. 39(c) (25 March 2002); (b) SI 2008/2178, r. 41(b) (1 October 2008);

sch. 2, CCR, ord. 28, r. 4, amended by SI 2001/4015, r. 39(d) (25 March 2002);
sch. 2, CCR, ord. 28, rr. 1 to 4, amended by SI 2001/4015, r. 39(a) to (d) (25 March 2002);
sch. 2, CCR, ord. 28, r. 5, substituted by SI 2001/4015, r. 39(e) (25 March 2002);
sch. 2, CCR, ord. 28, r. 9, amended by SI 2001/2792, r. 17 (25 March 2002);
sch. 2, CCR, ord. 28, r. 10(3), revoked by SI 2001/4015, r. 39(f) (25 March 2002);
sch. 2, CCR, ord. 28, r. 13, amended by SI 1999/1008, r. 68 (26 April 1999);
sch. 2, CCR, ord. 29, revoked by SI 2012/2208, r. 19(a) (1 October 2012) (see note 21);
sch. 2, CCR, ord. 30, amended by SI 2000/221, r. 34 (2 May 2000); revoked by SI 2001/2792, sch. 5 (25 March 2002);
sch. 1, CCR, ord. 31, revoked by SI 2001/2792, sch. 5 (25 March 2002);
sch. 2, CCR, ord. 33, r. 4, amended by: (a) SI 2000/221, r. 35 (2 May 2000); (b) SI 2001/2792, r. 18 (25 March 2002); (c) SI 2008/2178, r. 43 (1 October 2008);
sch. 2, CCR, ord. 34, revoked by SI 2012/2208, r. 19(b) (1 October 2012) (see note 21);
sch. 2, CCR, ord. 35, amended by SI 2001/4015, r. 41 (1 March 2002); revoked by SI 2002/2058, r. 36 and sch. 10 (2 December 2002);
sch. 2, CCR, ord. 37, r. 1, revoked by SI 2002/2058, r. 36 and sch. 10 (2 December 2002);
sch. 2, CCR, ord. 37, r. 6, revoked by SI 2000/221, sch. 8 (2 May 2000);
sch. 2, CCR, ord. 37, r. 8(1) and (2), revoked by SI 2002/2058, r. 36 and sch. 10 (2 December 2002);
sch. 2, CCR, ord. 37, r. 8(3), revoked by SI 2001/2792, sch. 5 (25 March 2002);
sch. 2, CCR, ord. 38, revoked by SI 2004/3419, r. 17 (1 April 2005);
sch. 2, CCR, ord. 39, r. 2, amended by SI 2001/2792, r. 19 (25 March 2002);
sch. 2, RSC, ord. 42, revoked by SI 2005/2292, r. 55(b) (1 October 2005);
sch. 2, CCR, ord. 43, revoked by SI 2001/256, sch. 3 (15 October 2001);
sch. 2, CCR, ord. 44, rr. 1 to 3, revoked by the Regulatory Reform (Agricultural Tenancies) (England and Wales) Order 2006 (SI 2006/2805) (19 October 2006);
sch. 2, CCR, ord. 45, r. 1, revoked by SI 2006/3435, r. 15(f) (6 April 2007);
sch. 2, CCR, ord. 46, revoked by SI 2006/3435, r. 15(g) (6 April 2007);
sch. 2, CCR, ord. 47, revoked by SI 2006/1689, r. 12(f) (2 October 2006);
sch. 2, CCR, ord. 48B, amended by: (a) SI 1999/1008, r. 71 (26 April 1999); (b) SI 2001/1388, r. 17 (1 June 2001); (c) SI 2001/2792, r. 22 (25 March 2002);
sch. 2, CCR, ord. 48D, inserted by SI 1999/1008, r. 72 (26 April 1999); revoked by SI 2003/2113, r. 19(c) (6 October 2003);
sch. 2, CCR, ord. 49, r. 1, amended by SI 1999/1008, r. 73 (26 April 1999); revoked by SI 2001/256, sch. 3 (15 October 2001);
sch. 2, CCR, ord. 49, rr. 1A, 2 and 4, revoked by SI 2001/256, sch. 3 (15 October 2001);
sch. 2, CPR, ord. 49, rr. 4A and 5, revoked by SI 2003/2113, r. 19(d) (6 October 2003);
sch. 2, CCR, ord. 49, r. 6, revoked by SI 2000/2092, r. 27 (2 October 2000);
sch. 2, CCR, ord. 49, r. 6A, amended by: (a) SI 1999/1008, r. 73 (26 April 1999); (b) SI 2000/221, r. 38 (2 May 2000); (c) SI 2000/2092, r. 28 (2 October 2000); revoked by SI 2001/256, sch. 3 (15 October 2001);
sch. 2, CCR, ord. 49, r. 6B, amended by: (a) SI 1999/1008, r. 73 (26 April 1999); (b) SI 2001/2792, r. 23 (in force by SI 2001/2792, r. 1(b), and SI 2001/3164) (15 October 2001); revoked by SI 2004/1306, r. 21 (30 June 2004);
sch. 2, CCR, ord. 49, r. 7, revoked by SI 2006/3435, r. 15(h) (6 April 2007);
sch. 2, CCR, ord. 49, rr. 8 and 9, revoked by SI 2001/256, sch. 3 (15 October 2001);
sch. 2, CCR, ord. 49, rr. 10 and 11, revoked by SI 2000/221, sch. 8 (2 May 2000);
sch. 2, CCR, ord. 49, r. 12, revoked by SI 2006/3435, r. 15(h) (6 April 2007);
sch. 2, CCR, ord. 49, r. 13, amended by SI 1999/1008, r. 73 (26 April 1999); revoked by SI 2001/256, sch. 3 (15 October 2001);
sch. 2, CCR, ord. 49, r. 15, revoked by SI 2005/2292, r. 55(c) (1 October 2005);
sch. 2, CCR, ord. 49, r. 16, revoked by SI 2001/256, sch. 3 (15 October 2001);
sch. 2, CCR, ord. 49, r. 17, revoked by SI 2006/1689, r. 12(g) (2 October 2006);
sch. 2, CCR, ord. 49, r. 18, revoked by SI 1999/1008, r. 73 (26 April 1999);
sch. 2, CCR, ord. 49, r. 18B, revoked by SI 2003/2113, r. 19(d) (6 October 2003);
sch. 2, CCR, ord. 49, r. 20, revoked by SI 2002/2058, r. 36 and sch. 10 (2 December 2002);

Note 1. The following transitional provision is made by SI 2000/2092, r. 29:
Where a person has, before 2nd October 2000, filed a notice of appeal in a claim allocated to the small claims track—
(a) Part 52 shall not apply to the appeal to which that notice relates; and
(b) rules 27.12 and 27.13 shall apply to that appeal as if they had not been revoked.

Note 3. The following transitional provision is made by SI 2000/221, r. 39, as substituted by SI 2000/940, r. 2:
Where a person has filed a notice of appeal or applied for permission to appeal before 2 May 2000—
(a) rule 19 of these Rules shall not apply to the appeal to which that notice or application relates; and
(b) the rules of court relating to appeals in force immediately before 2 May 2000 shall apply to that appeal as if they had not been revoked.

Note 4. The following transitional provision is made by SI 2000/2092, r. 30:
Where a person has, before 2nd October 2000, filed an application for permission to make an application for judicial review in accordance with RSC Order 53—
(a) Part 54 shall not apply to that application for permission or the application for judicial review to which it relates; and
(b) RSC Order 53 shall apply to those applications as if it had not been revoked.

Note 5. The following transitional provision is made by SI 2001/256, r. 31:
Where a claim form—
(a) relates to proceedings to which Part 55 or Part 56 would apply if it was issued on or after the date of entry into force of rules 17 and 18 of these Rules [i.e., 15 October 2001], but
(b) is issued before that date,
those rules shall not apply, and the rules of court in force immediately before that date shall apply as if they had not been amended or revoked.

Note 6. The following transitional provision is made by SI 2001/1388, r. 19:
Where a claim form—
(a) relates to proceedings to which Part 57 would apply if it was issued on or after 15th October 2001, but
(b) is issued before that date,
that Part shall not apply to the proceedings, and the rules of court in force immediately before that date shall apply as if they had not been amended or revoked.

Note 7. The following transitional provision is made by SI 2001/2792, r. 24:
(1) Parts 70 to 73 shall not apply to any enforcement proceedings specified in paragraph (2) which are issued before 25th March 2002, and the rules of court in force immediately before that date shall apply to those proceedings as if they had not been amended or revoked.
(2) The enforcement proceedings to which this rule applies are—
  (a) an application for an order for oral examination;
  (b) an application for a garnishee order;
  (c) an application by a judgment creditor for an order for the payment to him of money standing in court to the credit of a judgment debtor;
  (d) an application for a charging order;
  (e) a claim for the enforcement of a charging order by sale of the property charged; and
  (f) an application for a stop order.

Note 12. The following transitional provision is made by SI 2004/1306, r. 20(1):
(1) In the circumstances where article 29(1) or (4) of the Regulatory Reform (Business Tenancies) (England and Wales) Order 2003 applies—
  (a) the amendments to Part 56 made by rules 15 and 16 of these Rules shall not apply; and
  (b) Part 56 shall continue to apply on and after 1st June 2004 as if those amendments had not been made.

Note 13. The following transitional provision is made by SI 2004/1306, r. 20(2):
(2) Where an application for an injunction under Chapter III of Part V of the Housing Act 1996 has been issued before 30th June 2004—
  (a) Section I of Part 65 shall not apply in relation to that application; and

(b) CCR Order 49, rule 6B shall continue to apply on and after 30th June 2004 as if it had not been revoked.

Note 14. The following transitional provision is made by SI 2006/3435, r. 7:

(1) For Part 36, substitute Part 36 (Offers to settle) as set out at Schedule 1 to these Rules.
(2) Where a Part 36 offer or Part 36 payment was made before 6th April 2007, if it would have had the consequences set out in the rules of court contained in Part 36 as it was in force immediately before 6th April 2007, it will have the consequences set out in rules 36.10, 36.11 and 36.14 after that date.
(3) Where a Part 36 offer or Part 36 payment was made before 6th April 2007, the permission of the court is required to accept that offer or payment, if permission would have been required under the rules of court contained in Part 36 as it was in force immediately before 6th April 2007.
(4) Rule 37.3 will apply to a Part 36 payment made before 6th April 2007 as if that payment into court had been made under a court order.
(5) Subject to paragraph (6), where a person has made a Part 36 offer or Part 36 payment less than 21 days before 6th April 2007—
 (a) paragraphs (1) to (4) of this Rule shall not apply to the offer or payment; and
 (b) the rules of court contained in Part 36 as it was in force immediately before 6th April 2007 shall continue to apply to that offer or payment as if they had not been revoked.
(6) Paragraph (5) ceases to apply to a Part 36 offer or Part 36 payment made less than 21 days before 6th April 2007 at the expiry of 21 days from the date that offer or payment was made unless the trial has started within that period.
(7) Where, before 6th April 2007, a person has made an offer to settle before commencement of proceedings which complied with rule 36.10 as it was in force immediately before 6th April 2007—
 (a) the court will take that offer into account when making any order as to costs; and
 (b) the permission of the court will be required to accept the offer after proceedings have been commenced.

Note 15. The following transitional provision is made by SI 2007/2204, r. 21:

(1) The amendments to Part 19 made by rule 7 of these Rules apply as follows—
 (a) rule 19.9 and rule 19.9A apply only to a derivative claim issued on or after 1st October 2007;
 (b) rule 19.9B applies to the taking over of a derivative claim only where the relevant application for permission to take over the claim is filed on or after 1st October 2007;
 (c) rule 19.9C—
  (i) applies to a derivative claim issued on or after 1st October 2007; and
  (ii) applies to the taking over of a derivative claim only where the relevant application for permission to take over the claim is filed on or after 1st October 2007;
 (d) rule 19.9D applies to a derivative claim that arises in the course of other proceedings only if—
  (i) rule 19.9A would apply to the claim if it were brought; or
  (ii) rule 19.9B or 19.9C would apply to the taking over of the claim; and
 (e) rules 19.9E and 19.9F apply to a derivative claim only if rule 19.9A, 19.9B or 19.9C also applies to the claim.
(2) The rules of court relating to a derivative claim (within the meaning of those rules) in force immediately before 1st October 2007 apply as if they had not been amended to any derivative claim in respect of which the claim form was issued before 1st October 2007.

Note 17. The following transitional provision is made by SI 2008/2178, r. 44:

The amendments made by rule 26 of these Rules to rule 52.3 do not apply to proceedings where the notice of appeal was filed before 1st October 2008 and rule 52.3 in force immediately before that date will continue to apply to these proceedings as if that rule had not been amended.

Note 19. The following transitional provision is made by SI 2009/3131, reg. 48:

(1) Notwithstanding the amendments made by these Regulations, the relevant instruments continue to have effect as if the amendments had not been made, for the purposes of proceedings, judgments and authentic instruments to which the 1988 Convention continues to apply pursuant to article 63 of the 2007 Lugano Convention (transitional provision).
(2) In this regulation—
 (a) 'the 1988 Convention' means the Convention on jurisdiction and the enforcement of judgments in civil and commercial matters done at Lugano on 16th September 1988;

(b) 'the 2007 Lugano Convention' means the Convention on jurisdiction and the recognition and enforcement of judgments in civil and commercial matters, between the European Community and the Republic of Iceland, the Kingdom of Norway, the Swiss Confederation and the Kingdom of Denmark signed on behalf of the European Community on 30th October 2007;

(c) 'the relevant instruments' means—
   (i) the Civil Jurisdiction and Judgments Act 1982;
   (ii) the Civil Jurisdiction and Judgments Act 1982 (Interim Relief) Order 1997;
   (iii) the Civil Jurisdiction and Judgments Act (Provisional Measures) (Scotland) (Order) 1979;
   (iv) the Civil Procedure Rules 1998;
   (v) the Employment Tribunals (Enforcement of Orders in Other Jurisdictions) (Scotland) Regulations 2002; and
   (vi) the Civil Jurisdiction and Judgments (Authentic Instruments and Court Settlements) Order 1993.

Note 20. The following transitional provision is made by SI 2011/88, r. 13:

The amendments made by rule 12 of these Rules, which insert a new Section III in Part 78, apply only where the mediation of a cross-border dispute was commenced on or after 6th April 2011.

Note 21. The following transitional provision is made by SI 2012/2208, r. 20:

The amendments made by Rules 5, 6, 11, 12, 16, 18 and 19 and the Schedule to these Rules shall apply—

(a) to all applications in relation to contempt of court that are made on or after the date that these Rules come into force, subject to subparagraph (b); and
(b) in relation to contempt to which Section 5 of Part 81 of the Civil Procedure Rules 1998 applies (contempt in the face of the court), to all acts or omissions alleged to constitute contempt in the face of the court that are alleged to have occurred on or after that date.

Note 22. The following transitional provision is made by SI 2013/262, r. 22(1):

The following amendments do not apply where a defence is received before 1 April 2013—

(a) the amendments made by rules 5(e), 8(a) to (e) and (h) of these Rules; and
(b) the amendments made by paragraphs 3 and 9(a) to (j) and (m) and (n) of the 60th Update — Practice Direction amendments, that amends the Practice Directions supplementing the Civil Procedure Rules.

Note 23. The following transitional provision is made by SI 2013/262, r. 22(2):

The amendments made by rule 5(f) and (g) of these Rules do not apply to applications made before 1 April 2013 for relief from any sanction imposed for a failure to comply with any rule, practice direction or court order.

Note 24. The following transitional provision is made by SI 2013/262, r. 22(3):

The following amendments do not apply to claims issued before 1 April 2013—

(a) the amendments made by rules 6, 8(f) and (g), 9(a) and 19 of these Rules; and
(b) the amendments made by paragraphs 9(k) and (l)(i) and 10(c) of the 60th Update — Practice Direction amendments that amends the Practice Directions supplementing the Civil Procedure Rules.

Note 25. The following transitional provision is made by SI 2013/262, r. 22(4):

The amendment made by rule 10(c) of these Rules does not apply where any case management conference takes place or is due to take place before 9 April 2013.

Note 26. The following transitional provision is made by SI 2013/262, r. 22(5):

The amendment made by rule 11 of these Rules does not apply where the first case management conference takes place or is due to take place before 16 April 2013.

Note 27. The following transitional provision is made by SI 2013/262, r. 22(6):

The amendments made by rule 13 of these Rules do not apply in relation to an application for permission made before 1 April 2013.

Note 28. The following transitional provision is made by SI 2013/262, r. 22(7):

The amendments made by rule 14 of these Rules do not apply in relation to a claimant's Part 36 offer which was made before 1 April 2013.

Note 29. The following transitional provision is made by SI 2013/262, r. 22(8):

The amendments made by rule 18 and the provision made by rules 45.41 to 45.44... (costs limits in Aarhus Convention claims) do not apply in relation to a claim commenced before 1 April 2013.

Note 30. The following transitional provision is made by SI 2013/789, r. 4:

The amendments made by rule 3(b) apply only to a claim where the Claim Notification Form is sent in accordance with the Pre-Action Protocol for Low Value Personal Injury Claims in Road Traffic Accidents on or after 30th April 2013.

Note 31. The following transitional provisions are made by SI 2013/1412, r. 5:

(1) The amendments made to rules 52.15 and 54.12 do not apply to an application for judicial review where the claim form was filed before 1 July 2013.

(2) The amendments made to rule 54.5 do not apply to an application for judicial review where the grounds arose before 1 July 2013.

Practice Direction — Insolvency Proceedings

PART ONE GENERAL PROVISIONS

Definitions

1.1 In this practice direction:

(1) 'The Act' means the Insolvency Act 1986 and includes the Act as applied to limited liability partnerships by the Limited Liability Partnerships Regulations 2001 (SI 2001/1090) or to any other person or body by virtue of the Act or any other legislation;

(2) 'The Insolvency Rules' means the rules for the time being in force and made under s. 411 and s. 412 of the Act in relation to insolvency proceedings,* and, save where otherwise provided, any reference to a rule is to a rule in the Insolvency Rules;

(3) 'CPR' means the Civil Procedure Rules and 'CPR' followed by a Part or rule identified by number means the Part or rule with that number in those Rules;

(4) 'EC Regulation on Insolvency Proceedings' means Council Regulation (EC) No. 1346/2000 of 29 May 2000 on Insolvency Proceedings;

(5) 'Service Regulation' means Council Regulation (EC) No. 1393/2007 of 13 November 2007 on the service in the Member States of judicial and extrajudicial documents in civil and commercial matters (service of documents);

(6) 'Insolvency proceedings' means:

(a) any proceedings under the Act, the Insolvency Rules, the Administration of Insolvent Estates of Deceased Persons Order 1986 (SI 1986/1999), the Insolvent Partnerships Order 1994 (SI 1994/2421) or the Limited Liability Partnerships Regulations 2001;

(b) any proceedings under the EC Regulation on Insolvency Proceedings or the Cross-Border Insolvency Regulations 2006 (SI 2006/1030);

(7) References to a 'company' include a limited liability partnership and references to a 'contributory' include a member of a limited liability partnership;

(8) References to a 'registrar' are to a registrar in bankruptcy of the High Court and (save in cases where it is clear from the context that a particular provision applies only to the Royal Courts of Justice) include a district judge in a district registry of the High Court and in any county court having insolvency jurisdiction;

(9) 'Court' means any court having insolvency jurisdiction;

(10) 'Royal Courts of Justice' means the Royal Courts of Justice, Strand, London WC2A 2LL or such other place in London where the registrars sit;

(11) In Part Five of this practice direction: (a) 'appointee' means:

(i) a provisional liquidator appointed under s. 135 of the Act;

(ii) a special manager appointed under s. 177 or s. 370 of the Act;

(iii) a liquidator appointed by the members of a company or partnership or by the creditors of a company or partnership or by the Secretary of State pursuant to s. 137 of the Act, or by the court pursuant to s. 140 of the Act;

(iv) an administrator of a company appointed to manage the property, business and affairs of that company under the Act or other enactment and to which the provisions of the Act are applicable;

(v) a trustee in bankruptcy (other than the official receiver) appointed under the Act;

(vi) a nominee or supervisor of a voluntary arrangement under part 1 or part 8 of the Act;

(vii) a licensed insolvency practitioner appointed by the court pursuant to s. 273 of the Act;

(viii) an interim receiver appointed by the court pursuant to s. 286 of the Act;

(b) 'assessor' means a person appointed in accordance with CPR, r. 35.15;

(c) 'remuneration application' means any application to fix, approve or challenge the remuneration or expenses of an appointee or the basis of remuneration;

[* These are the Insolvency Rules 1986 (SI 1986/1925), abbreviated as IR 1986.]

(d) 'remuneration' includes expenses (where the Act or the Insolvency Rules give the court jurisdiction in relation thereto) and, in the case of an administrator, any pre-appointment administration costs or remuneration.

Coming into Force

2.1 This practice direction shall come into force on 23 February 2012 and shall replace all previous practice directions, practice statements and practice notes relating to insolvency proceedings.

Distribution of Business

3.1 As a general rule all petitions and applications (except those listed in paras 3.2 and 3.3 below) should be listed for initial hearing before a registrar in accordance with IR 1986, r. 7.6A(2) and (3).

3.2 The following applications relating to insolvent companies should always be listed before a judge:
(1) applications for committal for contempt;
(2) applications for an administration order;
(3) applications for an injunction;
(4) applications for the appointment of a provisional liquidator;
(5) interim applications and applications for directions or case management after any proceedings have been referred or adjourned to the judge (except where liberty to apply to the registrar has been given).

3.3 The following applications relating to insolvent individuals should always be listed before a judge:
(1) applications for committal for contempt;
(2) applications for an injunction;
(3) interim applications and applications for directions or case management after any proceedings have been referred or adjourned to the judge (except where liberty to apply to the registrar has been given).

3.4 When deciding whether to hear proceedings or to refer or adjourn them to the judge, the registrar should have regard to the following factors:
(1) the complexity of the proceedings;
(2) whether the proceedings raise new or controversial points of law;
(3) the likely date and length of the hearing;
(4) public interest in the proceedings.

Court Documents

4.1 All insolvency proceedings should be commenced and applications in proceedings should be made using the forms prescribed by the Act, the Insolvency Rules or other legislation under which the same is or are brought or made and/or should contain the information prescribed by the Act, the Insolvency Rules or other legislation.

4.2 Every court document in insolvency proceedings under parts 1 to 7 of the Act shall be headed:

IN THE HIGH COURT OF JUSTICE CHANCERY DIVISION
[DISTRICT REGISTRY] or in the Royal Courts of Justice [COMPANIES COURT]
or
IN THE [ ] COUNTY COURT
followed by
IN THE MATTER OF [name of company]
AND IN THE MATTER OF THE INSOLVENCY ACT 1986

4.3 Every court document in insolvency proceedings under parts 9 to 11 of the Act shall be headed:

IN THE [HIGH COURT OF JUSTICE] or [[ ] COUNTY COURT]
IN BANKRUPTCY
IN THE MATTER OF [name of bankrupt]
or
RE: [name of bankrupt].
Every application should also be headed:
AND IN THE MATTER OF THE INSOLVENCY ACT 1986

4.4 Every court document in proceedings to which the Act applies by virtue of other legislation should also be headed:

IN THE MATTER OF [THE FINANCIAL SERVICES AND MARKETS ACT 2000 or as the case may be]
AND IN THE MATTER OF THE INSOLVENCY ACT 1986

Evidence

5.1 Subject to the provisions of IR 1986, r. 7.9, or any other provisions or directions as to the form in which evidence should be given, written evidence in insolvency proceedings must be given by witness statement.

Service of Court Documents in Insolvency Proceedings

6.1 Except where the Insolvency Rules otherwise provide, CPR, Part 6, applies to the service of court documents both within and out of the jurisdiction as modified by this practice direction or as the court may otherwise direct.

6.2 Except where the Insolvency Rules otherwise provide or as may be required under the Service Regulation, service of documents in insolvency proceedings will be the responsibility of the parties and will not be undertaken by the court.

6.3 A document which, pursuant to IR 1986, r. 12A.16(3)(b), is treated as a claim form, is deemed to have been served on the date specified in CPR, r. 6.14, and any other document is deemed to have been served on the date specified in CPR, r. 6.26, unless the court otherwise directs.

6.4 Except as provided below, service out of the jurisdiction of an application which is to be treated as a claim form under IR 1986, r. 12A.16(3), requires the permission of the court.

6.5 An application which is to be treated as a claim form under IR 1986, r. 12A.16(3), may be served out of the jurisdiction without the permission of the court if:

(1) the application is by an office-holder appointed in insolvency proceedings in respect of a company with its centre of main interests within the jurisdiction exercising a statutory power under the Act, and the person to be served is to be served within the EU; or

(2) it is a copy of an application, being served on a member State liquidator.

6.6 An application for permission to serve out of the jurisdiction must be supported by a witness statement setting out:

(1) the nature of the claim or application and the relief sought;

(2) that the applicant believes that the claim has a reasonable prospect of success; and

(3) the address of the person to be served or, if not known, in what place or country that person is, or is likely, to be found.

6.7 CPR, rr. 6.36 and 6.37(1) and (2), do not apply in insolvency proceedings.

Jurisdiction

7.1 Where CPR, r. 2.4, provides for the court to perform any act, that act may be performed by a registrar.

Drawing Up of Orders

8.1 The court will draw up all orders except orders on the application of the official receiver or for which the Treasury Solicitor is responsible or where the court otherwise directs.

Urgent Applications

9.1 In the Royal Courts of Justice the registrars (and in other courts exercising insolvency jurisdiction the district judges) operate urgent applications lists for urgent and time-critical applications and may be available to hear urgent applications at other times. Parties asking for an application to be dealt with in the urgent applications lists or urgently at any other time must complete the certificate below:

No:
Heading of action
I estimate that this matter is likely to occupy the court for...........mins/hours. I certify that it is urgent for the following reasons:
....[name of representative]..
[telephone number]
Counsel/Solicitor for the............................
WARNING. If, in the opinion of the Registrar/District Judge, the application is not urgent then such sanction will be applied as is thought appropriate in all the circumstances.

PART TWO COMPANY INSOLVENCY

Administrations

10.1 In the absence of special circumstances, an application for the extension of an administration should be made not less than one month before the end of the administration. The evidence in support of any later application must explain why the application is being made late. The court will consider whether any part of the costs should be disallowed where an application is made less than one month before the end of the administration.

Winding-up Petitions

11.1 Before presenting a winding-up petition the creditor must conduct a search to ensure that no petition is already pending. Save in exceptional circumstances a second winding-up petition should not be presented whilst a prior petition is pending. A petitioner who presents his own petition while another petition is pending does so at risk as to costs.

11.2 Every creditor's winding-up petition must (in the case of a company) contain the following:
(1) the full name and address of the petitioner;
(2) the name and number of the company in respect of which a winding-up order is sought;
(3) the date of incorporation of the company and the Companies Act or Acts under which it was incorporated;
(4) the address of the company's registered office;
(5) a statement of the nominal capital of the company, the manner in which its shares are divided up and the amount of the capital paid up or credited as paid up;
(6) brief details of the principal objects for which the company was established followed, where appropriate, by the words 'and other objects stated in the memorandum of association of the company';
(7) details of the basis on which it is contended that the company is insolvent including, where a debt is relied on, sufficient particulars of the debt (the amount, nature and approximate date(s) on which it was incurred) to enable the company and the court to identify the debt;
(8) a statement that the company is insolvent and unable to pay its debts;
(9) a statement that for the reasons set out in the evidence verifying the petition the EC Regulation on Insolvency Proceedings either applies or does not and if the former whether the proceedings will be main, territorial or secondary proceedings;
(10) the statement that, 'In the circumstances it is just and equitable that the company be wound up under the provisions of the Insolvency Act 1986';
(11) a prayer that the company be wound up, for such other order as the court thinks fit and any other specific relief sought.

Similar information (so far as is appropriate) should be given where the petition is presented against a partnership.

11.3 The statement of truth verifying the petition in accordance with IR 1986, r. 4.12, should be made no more than 10 business days before the date of issue of the petition.

11.4 Where the company to be wound up has been struck off the register, the petition should state that fact and include as part of the relief sought an order that it be restored to the register. Save where the petition has been presented by a Minister of the Crown or a government department, evidence of service on the Treasury Solicitor or the Solicitor for the affairs of the Duchy of Lancaster (as appropriate) should be filed exhibiting the bona vacantia waiver letter.

Gazetting of the petition

11.5.1 IR 1986, r. 4.11, must be complied with (unless waived by the court): it is designed to ensure that the class remedy of winding up by the court is made available to all creditors, and is not used as a means of putting improper pressure on the company to pay the petitioner's debt or costs. Failure to comply with the rule, without good reason accepted by the court, may lead to the summary dismissal of the petition on the return date (IR 1986, r. 4.11(6)) or to the court depriving the petitioner of the costs of the hearing. If the court, in its discretion, grants an adjournment, this will usually be on terms that notice of the petition is gazetted or otherwise given in accordance with the rule in due time for the adjourned hearing. No further adjournment for the purpose of gazetting will normally be granted.

11.5.2 Copies of every notice gazetted in connection with a winding-up petition, or where this is not practicable a description of the form and content of the notice, must be lodged with the court as soon as possible after publication and in any event not later than five business days before the hearing of the petition. This direction applies even if the notice is defective in any way (e.g. is published on a date not in accordance with the Insolvency Rules, or omits or misprints some important words) or if the petitioner decides not to pursue the petition (e.g. on receiving payment).

Errors in petitions

11.6.1 Applications for permission to amend errors in petitions which are discovered after a winding up order has been made should be made to the member of court staff in charge of the winding-up list in the Royal Courts of Justice or to a district judge in any other court.

11.6.2 Where the error is an error in the name of the company, the member of court staff in charge of the winding-up list in the Royal Courts of Justice or a district judge in any other court may make any necessary amendments to ensure that the winding-up order is drawn up with the correct name of the company inserted. If there is any doubt, e.g. where there might be another company in existence which could be confused with the company to be wound up, the member of court staff in charge of the winding-up list will refer the application to a registrar at the Royal Courts of Justice and a district judge may refer it to a judge.

11.6.3 Where it is discovered that the company has been struck off the Register of Companies prior to the winding-up order being made, the matter must be restored to the list as soon as possible to enable an order for the restoration of the name to be made as well as the order to wind up.

Rescission of a winding-up order

11.7.1 An application to rescind a winding up order must be made by application.

11.7.2 The application should normally be made within five business days after the date on which the order was made (rule 7.47(4)) failing which it should include an application to extend time. Notice of any such application must be given to the petitioning creditor, any supporting or opposing creditor and the official receiver.

11.7.3 Applications will only be entertained if made (a) by a creditor, or (b) by a contributory, or (c) by the company jointly with a creditor or with a contributory. The application must be supported by a witness statement which should include details of assets and liabilities and (where appropriate) reasons for any failure to apply within five business days.

11.7.4 In the case of an unsuccessful application the costs of the petitioning creditor, any supporting creditors and of the official receiver will normally be ordered to be paid by the creditor or the contributory making or joining in the application. The reason for this is that if the costs of an unsuccessful application are made payable by the company, they fall unfairly on the general body of creditors.

Validation orders

11.8.1 A company against which a winding-up petition has been presented may apply to the court after presentation of the petition for relief from the effects of s. 127(1) of the Act by seeking an order that a disposition or dispositions of its property, including payments out of its bank account (whether such account is in credit or overdrawn), shall not be void in the event of a winding-up order being made on the hearing of the petition (a validation order).

11.8.2 An application for a validation order should generally be made to the registrar. An application should be made to the judge only if: (a) it is urgent and no registrar is available to hear it; or (b) it is complex or raises new or controversial points of law; or (c) it is estimated to last longer than 30 minutes.

11.8.3 Save in exceptional circumstances, notice of the making of the application should be given to: (a) the petitioning creditor; (b) any person entitled to receive a copy of the petition pursuant to IR 1986, r. 4.10; (c) any creditor who has given notice to the petitioner of his intention to appear on the hearing of the petition pursuant to IR 1986, r. 4.16; and (d) any creditor who has been substituted as petitioner pursuant to IR 1986, r. 4.19.

11.8.4 The application should be supported by a witness statement which, save in exceptional circumstances, should be made by a director or officer of the company who is intimately acquainted with the company's affairs and financial circumstances. If appropriate, supporting evidence in the form of a witness statement from the company's accountant should also be produced.

11.8.5 The extent and contents of the evidence will vary according to the circumstances and the nature of the relief sought, but in the majority of cases it should include, as a minimum, the following information:

(1) when and to whom notice has been given in accordance with para. 11.8.3. above;
(2) the company's registered office;
(3) the company's nominal and paid-up capital;
(4) brief details of the circumstances leading to presentation of the petition;
(5) how the company became aware of presentation of the petition;
(6) whether the petition debt is admitted or disputed and, if the latter, brief details of the basis on which the debt is disputed;
(7) full details of the company's financial position including details of its assets (including details of any security and the amount(s) secured) and liabilities, which should be supported, as far as possible, by documentary evidence, e.g. the latest filed accounts, any draft audited accounts, management accounts or estimated statement of affairs;
(8) a cash flow forecast and profit and loss projection for the period for which the order is sought;
(9) details of the dispositions or payments in respect of which an order is sought;
(10) the reasons relied on in support of the need for such dispositions or payments to be made;
(11) any other information relevant to the exercise of the court's discretion;
(12) details of any consents obtained from the persons mentioned in para. 11.8.3. above (supported by documentary evidence where appropriate);
(13) details of any relevant bank account, including its number and the address and sort code of the bank at which such account is held.

11.8.6 Where an application is made urgently to enable payments to be made which are essential to continued trading (e.g. wages) and it is not possible to assemble all the evidence listed above, the court may consider granting limited relief for a short period, but there should be sufficient evidence to satisfy the court that the interests of creditors are unlikely to be prejudiced.

11.8.7 Where the application involves a disposition of property the court will need details of the property (including its title number if the property is land) and to be satisfied that any proposed disposal will be at a proper value. Accordingly, an independent valuation should be obtained and exhibited to the evidence.

11.8.8 The court will need to be satisfied by credible evidence either that the company is solvent and able to pay its debts as they fall due or that a particular transaction or series of transactions in respect of which the order is sought will be beneficial to or will not prejudice the interests of all the unsecured creditors as a class (*Denney v John Hudson and Co. Ltd [1992] BCLC 901*; *Re Fairway Graphics Ltd [1991] BCLC 468*).

11.8.9 A draft of the order sought should be attached to the application.

11.8.10 Similar considerations to those set out above are likely to apply to applications seeking ratification of a transaction or payment after the making of a winding-up order.

Applications

12.1 In accordance with IR 1986, r. 13.2(2), in the Royal Courts of Justice the member of court staff in charge of the winding-up list has been authorised to deal with applications:

(1) to extend or abridge time prescribed by the Insolvency Rules in connection with winding up (rule 4.3);
(2) for permission to withdraw a winding-up petition (rule 4.15);

(3) for the substitution of a petitioner (rule 4.19);
(4) by the official receiver for limited disclosure of a statement of affairs (rule 4.35);
(5) by the official receiver for relief from duties imposed upon him by the Insolvency Rules (rule 4.47);
(6) by the official receiver for permission to give notice of a meeting by advertisement only (rule 4.59);
(7) to transfer proceedings from the High Court (Royal Courts of Justice) to a county court after the making of a winding-up order (rule 7.11).

12.2 In district registries or a county court such applications must be made to a district judge.

PART THREE PERSONAL INSOLVENCY

Statutory Demands

Deemed date of service

13.1.1 A statutory demand is deemed to be served on the date applicable to the method of service set out in CPR, r. 6.26, unless the statutory demand is advertised in which case it is deemed served on the date of the appearance of the advertisement pursuant to r. 6.3.

Service abroad of statutory demands

13.2.1 A statutory demand is not a document issued by the court. Permission to serve out of the jurisdiction is not, therefore, required.

13.2.2 CPR, r. 6.3(2) ('requirements as to service'), applies to service of the statutory demand whether within or out of the jurisdiction.

13.2.3 A creditor wishing to serve a statutory demand out of the jurisdiction in a foreign country with which a civil procedure convention has been made (including the Hague Convention) may and, if the assistance of a British consul is desired, must adopt the procedure prescribed by CPR, rr. 6.42 and 6.43. In the case of any doubt whether the country is a 'convention country', enquiries should be made of the Queen's Bench Masters' Secretary Department, Room E216, Royal Courts of Justice.

13.2.4 In all other cases, service of the demand must be effected by private arrangement in accordance with CPR, r. 6.3(2), and local foreign law.

13.2.5 When a statutory demand is to be served out of the jurisdiction, the time limits of 21 days and 18 days respectively referred to in the demand must be amended as provided in the next paragraph. For this purpose reference should be made to the table set out in PD 6B.

13.2.6 A creditor should amend the statutory demand as follows:
(1) for any reference to 18 days there must be substituted the appropriate number of days set out in the table plus 4 days;
(2) for any reference to 21 days there must be substituted the appropriate number of days in the table plus 7 days.

13.2.7 Attention is drawn to the fact that in all forms of the statutory demand the figure '18' and the figure '21' occur in more than one place.

Substituted service of statutory demands

13.3.1 The creditor is under an obligation to do all that is reasonable to bring the statutory demand to the debtor's attention and, if practicable, to cause personal service to be effected (IR 1986, r. 6.3(2)).

13.3.2 In the circumstances set out in IR 1986, r. 6.3(3), the demand may instead be advertised. As there is no statutory form of advertisement, the court will accept an advertisement in the following form:

STATUTORY DEMAND
(Debt for liquidated sum payable immediately following a judgment or order of the court) To (Block letters)
of
TAKE NOTICE that a statutory demand has been issued by:
Name of Creditor:
Address:

The creditor demands payment of £. . . . . .the amount now due on a judgment or order of the (High Court of Justice . . . . Division) (. . . . . County Court) dated the [day] of [month] 20[. . .].

The statutory demand is an important document and it is deemed to have been served on you on the date of the first appearance of this advertisement. You must deal with this demand within 21 days of the service upon you or you could be made bankrupt and your property and goods taken away from you. If you are in any doubt as to your position, you should seek advice immediately from a solicitor or your nearest Citizens' Advice Bureau. The statutory demand can be obtained or is available for inspection and collection from:

Name:

Address:

(Solicitor for) the Creditor

Tel. No. Reference:

You have only 21 days from the date of the first appearance of this advertisement before the creditor may present a bankruptcy petition. You have only 18 days from the date of the first appearance of this advertisement within which to apply to the court to set aside the demand.

13.3.3 Where personal service is not effected or the demand is not advertised in the limited circumstances permitted by IR 1986, r. 6.3(3), substituted service is permitted, but the creditor must have taken all those steps which would justify the court making an order for substituted service of a petition. The steps to be taken to obtain an order for substituted service of a petition are set out below. Failure to comply with these requirements may result in the court declining to issue the petition (IR 1986, r. 6.11(9)) or dismissing it.

13.3.4 In most cases, evidence of the following steps will suffice to justify acceptance for presentation of a petition where the statutory demand has been served by substituted service (or to justify making an order for substituted service of a petition):

(1) One personal call at the residence and place of business of the debtor where both are known or at either of such places as is known. Where it is known that the debtor has more than one residential or business address, personal calls should be made at all the addresses.

(2) Should the creditor fail to effect personal service, a first class prepaid letter should be written to the debtor referring to the call(s), the purpose of the same and the failure to meet the debtor, adding that a further call will be made for the same purpose on the [day] of [month] 20[...] at [...] hours at [place]. At least two business days' notice should be given of the appointment and copies of the letter sent to all known addresses of the debtor. The appointment letter should also state that:

(a) in the event of the time and place not being convenient, the debtor should propose some other time and place reasonably convenient for the purpose;

(b) (In the case of a statutory demand) if the debtor fails to keep the appointment the creditor proposes to serve the debtor by [advertisement] [post] [insertion through a letter box] or as the case may be, and that, in the event of a bankruptcy petition being presented, the court will be asked to treat such service as service of the demand on the debtor;

(c) (In the case of a petition) if the debtor fails to keep the appointment, application will be made to the Court for an order for substituted service either by advertisement, or in such other manner as the court may think fit.

(3) When attending any appointment made by letter, inquiry should be made as to whether the debtor has received all letters left for him. If the debtor is away, inquiry should also be made as to whether or not letters are being forwarded to an address within the jurisdiction (England and Wales) or elsewhere.

(4) If the debtor is represented by a solicitor, an attempt should be made to arrange an appointment for personal service through such solicitor. The Insolvency Rules enable a solicitor to accept service of a statutory demand on behalf of his client but there is no similar provision in respect of service of a bankruptcy petition.

(5) The certificate of service of a statutory demand filed pursuant to IR 1986, r. 6.11, should deal with all the above matters including all relevant facts as to the debtor's whereabouts and whether the appointment letter(s) have been returned. It should also set out the

reasons for the belief that the debtor resides at the relevant address or works at the relevant place of business and whether, so far as is known, the debtor is represented by a solicitor.

Setting aside a statutory demand

13.4.1 The application (form 6.4) and witness statement in support (form 6.5) exhibiting a copy of the statutory demand must be filed in court within 18 days of service of the statutory demand on the debtor. Where service is effected by advertisement the period of 18 days is calculated from the date of the first appearance of the advertisement. Three copies of each document must be lodged with the application to enable the court to serve notice of the hearing date on the applicant, the creditor and the person named in part B of the statutory demand.

13.4.2 Where copies of the documents are not lodged with the application, any order of the registrar fixing a venue is conditional upon copies of the documents being lodged on the next business day after the registrar's order otherwise the application will be deemed to have been dismissed.

13.4.3 Where the debt claimed in the statutory demand is based on a judgment, order, liability order, costs certificate, tax assessment or decision of a tribunal, the court will not at this stage inquire into the validity of the debt nor, as a general rule, will it adjourn the application to await the result of an application to set aside the judgment, order, decision, costs certificate or any appeal.

13.4.4 Where the debtor (a) claims to have a counterclaim, set-off or cross-demand (whether or not he could have raised it in the action in which the judgment or order was obtained) which equals or exceeds the amount of the debt or debts specified in the statutory demand or (b) disputes the debt (not being a debt subject to a judgment, order, liability order, costs certificate or tax assessment) the court will normally set aside the statutory demand if, in its opinion, on the evidence there is a genuine triable issue.

13.4.5 A debtor who wishes to apply to set aside a statutory demand after the expiration of 18 days from the date of service of the statutory demand must apply for an extension of time within which to apply. If the applicant wishes to apply for an injunction to restrain presentation of a petition the application must be made to the judge. Paragraphs 1 and 2 of form 6.5 (witness statement in support of application to set aside statutory demand) should be used in support of the application for an extension of time with the following additional paragraphs:

'(3) To the best of my knowledge and belief the creditor(s) named in the demand has/have not presented a petition against me.

(4) The reasons for my failure to apply to set aside the demand within 18 days after service are as follows:...'

If application is made to restrain presentation of a bankruptcy petition the following additional paragraph should be added:

'(5) Unless restrained by injunction the creditor(s) may present a bankruptcy petition against me'.

Bankruptcy Petitions

Listing of petitions

14.1.1 All petitions presented will be listed under the name of the debtor unless the court directs otherwise.

Content of petitions

14.2.1 The attention of practitioners is drawn to the following points:

(1) A creditor's petition does not require dating, signing or witnessing but must be verified in accordance with IR 1986, r. 6.12.

(2) In the heading it is only necessary to recite the debtor's name e.g. Re John William Smith or Re J W Smith (Male). Any alias or trading name will appear in the body of the petition.

14.2.2 Where the petition is based solely on a statutory demand, only the debt claimed in the demand may be included in the petition.

14.2.3 The attention of practitioners is also drawn to IR 1986, rr. 6.7 and 6.8, and in particular to r. 6.8(1) where the 'aggregate sum' is made up of a number of debts.

14.2.4 The date of service of the statutory demand should be recited as follows:

(1) In the case of personal service, the date of service as set out in the certificate of service should be recited and whether service is effected before/after 1700 hours on Monday to Friday or at any time on a Saturday or a Sunday.

(2) In the case of substituted service (other than by advertisement), the date alleged in the certificate of service should be recited.

(3) In the strictly limited case of service by advertisement under r. 6.3, the date to be alleged is the date of the advertisement's appearance or, as the case may be, its first appearance (see rr. 6.3(3) and 6.11(8)).

Searches

14.3.1 The petitioning creditor shall, before presenting a petition, conduct a search for petitions presented against the debtor in the previous 18 months (a) in the Royal Courts of Justice, (b) in the Central London County Court and (c) in any county court which he believes is or was within that period the debtor's own county court within the meaning of IR 1986, r. 6.9A(3), and shall include the following certificate at the end of the petition:

'I/we certify that I/we have conducted a search for petitions presented against the debtor in the period of 18 months ending today and that [no prior petitions have been presented in the said period which are still pending] [a prior petition (No [...]) has been presented and is pending in the [Court] and we are issuing this petition at risk as to costs].
Signed... Dated...'.

Deposit

14.4.1 The deposit will be taken by the court and forwarded to the official receiver. In the Royal Courts of Justice the petition fee and deposit should be paid in the Fee Room, which will record the receipt and will impress two entries on the original petition, one in respect of the court fee and the other in respect of the deposit. In a district registry or a county court, the petition fee and deposit should be handed to the duly authorised officer of the court's staff who will record its receipt.

14.4.2 In all cases cheque(s) for the whole amount should be made payable to 'HM Courts and Tribunals Service' or 'HMCTS'.

Certificates of continuing debt and of notice of adjournment

14.5.1 On the hearing of a petition where a bankruptcy order is sought, in order to satisfy the court that the debt on which the petition is founded has not been paid or secured or compounded for the court will normally accept as sufficient a certificate signed by the person representing the petitioning creditor in the following form:

'I certify that I have/my firm has made enquiries of the petitioning creditor(s) within the last business day prior to the hearing/adjourned hearing and to the best of my knowledge and belief the debt on which the petition is founded is still due and owing and has not been paid or secured or compounded for save as to . . .
Signed... Dated...'.

14.5.2 For convenience, in the Royal Courts of Justice this certificate is incorporated in the attendance sheet for the parties to complete when they come to court and which is filed after the hearing. A fresh certificate will be required on each adjourned hearing.

14.5.3 On any adjourned hearing of a petition where a bankruptcy order is sought, in order to satisfy the court that the petitioner has complied with IR 1986, r. 6.29, the petitioner will be required to file evidence of the date on which, manner in which and address to which notice of the making of the order of adjournment and of the venue for the adjourned hearing has been sent to:

(1) the debtor, and

(2) any creditor who has given notice under IR 1986, r. 6.23, but was not present at the hearing when the order for adjournment was made or was present at the hearing but the date of the adjourned hearing was not fixed at that hearing.

For convenience, in the Royal Courts of Justice this certificate is incorporated in the attendance sheet for the parties to complete when they come to court and which is filed after the hearing and is as follows:

'I certify that the petitioner has complied with rule 6.29 by sending notice of adjournment to the debtor [supporting/opposing creditor(s)] on [date] at [address]'.

A fresh certificate will be required on each adjourned hearing.

Extension of hearing date of petition

14.6.1 Late applications for extension of hearing dates under IR 1986, r. 6.28, and failure to attend on the listed hearing of a petition, will be dealt with as follows:

(1) If an application is submitted less than two clear working days before the hearing date (for example, later than Monday for Thursday, or Wednesday for Monday) the costs of the application will not be allowed under IR 1986, r. 6.28(3).

(2) If the petition has not been served and no extension has been granted by the time fixed for the hearing of the petition, and if no one attends for the hearing, the petition may be dismissed or relisted for hearing about 21 days later. The court will notify the petitioning creditor's solicitors (or the petitioning creditor in person), and any known supporting or opposing creditors or their solicitors, of the new date and times. Written evidence should then be filed on behalf of the petitioning creditor explaining fully the reasons for the failure to apply for an extension or to appear at the hearing, and (if appropriate) giving reasons why the petition should not be dismissed.

(3) On the relisted hearing the court may dismiss the petition if not satisfied it should be adjourned or a further extension granted.

14.6.2 All applications for an extension should include a statement of the date fixed for the hearing of the petition.

14.6.3 The petitioning creditor should contact the court (by solicitors or in person) on or before the hearing date to ascertain whether the application has reached the file and been dealt with. It should not be assumed that an extension will be granted.

Substituted service of bankruptcy petitions

14.7.1 In most cases evidence that the steps set out in para. 13.3.4. have been taken will suffice to justify an order for substituted service of a bankruptcy petition.

Validation orders

14.8.1 A person against whom a bankruptcy petition has been presented ('the debtor') may apply to the court after presentation of the petition for relief from the effects of s. 284(1)–(3) of the Act by seeking an order that any disposition of his assets or payment made out of his funds, including any bank account (whether it is in credit or overdrawn) shall not be void in the event of a bankruptcy order being made on the petition (a 'validation order').

14.8.2 Save in exceptional circumstances, notice of the making of the application should be given to (a) the petitioning creditor(s) or other petitioner, (b) any creditor who has given notice to the petitioner of his intention to appear on the hearing of the petition pursuant to IR 1986, r. 6.23, (c) any creditor who has been substituted as petitioner pursuant to IR 1986, r. 6.30, and (d) any creditor who has carriage of the petition pursuant to IR 1986, r. 6.31.

14.8.3 The application should be supported by a witness statement which, save in exceptional circumstances, should be made by the debtor. If appropriate, supporting evidence in the form of a witness statement from the debtor's accountant should also be produced.

14.8.4 The extent and contents of the evidence will vary according to the circumstances and the nature of the relief sought, but in a case where the debtor is trading or carrying on business it should include, as a minimum, the following information:

(1) when and to whom notice has been given in accordance with para. 14.8.2. above;

(2) brief details of the circumstances leading to presentation of the petition;

(3) how the debtor became aware of the presentation of the petition;

(4) whether the petition debt is admitted or disputed and, if the latter, brief details of the basis on which the debt is disputed;

(5) full details of the debtor's financial position including details of his assets (including details of any security and the amount(s) secured) and liabilities, which should be supported, as far as possible, by documentary evidence, e.g. accounts, draft accounts, management accounts or estimated statement of affairs;

(6) a cash flow forecast and profit and loss projection for the period for which the order is sought;

(7) details of the dispositions or payments in respect of which an order is sought;
(8) the reasons relied on in support of the need for such dispositions or payments to be made;
(9) any other information relevant to the exercise of the court's discretion;
(10) details of any consents obtained from the persons mentioned in para. 14.8.2. above (supported by documentary evidence where appropriate);
(11) details of any relevant bank account, including its number and the address and sort code of the bank at which such account is held.

14.8.5 Where an application is made urgently to enable payments to be made which are essential to continued trading (e.g. wages) and it is not possible to assemble all the evidence listed above, the court may consider granting limited relief for a short period, but there must be sufficient evidence to satisfy the court that the interests of creditors are unlikely to be prejudiced.

14.8.6 Where the debtor is not trading or carrying on business and the application relates only to a proposed sale, mortgage or remortgage of the debtor's home evidence of the following will generally suffice:
(1) when and to whom notice has been given in accordance with para. 14.8.2. above;
(2) whether the petition debt is admitted or disputed and, if the latter, brief details of the basis on which the debt is disputed;
(3) details of the property to be sold, mortgaged or remortgaged (including its title number);
(4) the value of the property and the proposed sale price, or details of the mortgage or remortgage;
(5) details of any existing mortgages or charges on the property and redemption figures;
(6) the costs of sale (e.g. solicitors' or agents' costs);
(7) how and by whom any net proceeds of sale (or sums coming into the debtor's hands as a result of any mortgage or remortgage) are to be held pending the final hearing of the petition;
(8) any other information relevant to the exercise of the court's discretion;
(9) details of any consents obtained from the persons mentioned in para. 14.8.2. above (supported by documentary evidence where appropriate).

14.8.7 Whether or not the debtor is trading or carrying on business, where the application involves a disposition of property the court will need to be satisfied that any proposed disposal will be at a proper value. Accordingly an independent valuation should be obtained and exhibited to the evidence.

14.8.8 The court will need to be satisfied by credible evidence that the debtor is solvent and able to pay his debts as they fall due or that a particular transaction or series of transactions in respect of which the order is sought will be beneficial to or will not prejudice the interests of all the unsecured creditors as a class (*Denney* v *John Hudson and Co. Ltd* [1992] BCLC 901, [1992] BCC 503, CA; *Re Fairway Graphics Ltd* [1991] BCLC 468).

14.8.9 A draft of the order sought should be attached to the application.

14.8.10 Similar considerations to those set out above are likely to apply to applications seeking ratification of a transaction or payment after the making of a bankruptcy order.

Applications

15.1 In accordance with IR 1986, r. 13.2(2), in the Royal Courts of Justice the member of court staff in charge of the winding-up list has been authorised to deal with applications:
(1) by petitioning creditors to extend the time for hearing petitions (rule 6.28);
(2) by the official receiver:
  (a) to transfer proceedings from the High Court to a county court (rule 7.13);
  (b) to amend the title of the proceedings (rules 6.35 and 6.47).

15.2 In district registries or a county court such applications must be made to the district judge.

Orders without Attendance

16.1 In suitable cases the court will normally be prepared to make orders under part 8 of the Act (individual voluntary arrangements), without the attendance of the parties, provided there is no bankruptcy order in existence and (so far as is known) no pending petition. The orders are:
(1) A 14-day interim order adjourning the application for 14 days for consideration of the nominee's report, where the papers are in order, and the nominee's signed consent to act

includes a waiver of notice of the application or the consent by the nominee to the making of an interim order without attendance.

(2) A standard order on consideration of the nominee's report, extending the interim order to a date seven weeks after the date of the proposed meeting, directing the meeting to be summoned and adjourning to a date about three weeks after the meeting. Such an order may be made without attendance if the nominee's report has been delivered to the court and complies with s. 256(1) of the Act and IR 1986, r. 5.11(2) and (3), and proposes a date for the meeting not less than 14 days from that on which the nominee's report is filed in court under r. 5.11 nor more than 28 days from that on which that report is considered by the court under r. 5.13.

(3) A 'concertina' order, combining orders as under (1) and (2) above. Such an order may be made without attendance if the initial application for an interim order is accompanied by a report of the nominee and the conditions set out in (1) and (2) above are satisfied.

(4) A final order on consideration of the chairman's report. Such an order may be made without attendance if the chairman's report has been filed and complies with r. 5.27(1). The order will record the effect of the chairman's report and may discharge the interim order.

16.2 Provided that the conditions under sub-paras (2) and (4) above are satisfied and that the appropriate report has been lodged with the court in due time the parties need not attend or be represented on the adjourned hearing for consideration of the nominee's report or of the chairman's report (as the case may be) unless they are notified by the court that attendance is required.

Sealed copies of the order made (in all four cases as above) will be posted by the court to the applicant or his solicitor and to the nominee.

16.3 In suitable cases the court may also make consent orders without attendance by the parties. The written consent of the parties will be required. Examples of such orders are as follows:

(1) on applications to set aside a statutory demand, orders:

(a) dismissing the application, with or without an order for costs as may be agreed (permission will be given to present a petition on or after the seventh day after the date of the order, unless a different date is agreed);

(b) setting aside the demand, with or without an order for costs as may be agreed; or

(2) On petitions where there is a negative list of supporting or opposing creditors in form 6.21, or a statement signed by or on behalf of the petitioning creditor that no notices have been received from supporting or opposing creditors, orders:

(a) dismissing the petition, with or without an order for costs as may be agreed; or

(b) if the petition has not been served, giving permission to withdraw the petition (with no order for costs).

(3) On other applications, orders:

(a) for sale of property, possession of property, disposal of proceeds of sale;

(b) giving interim directions;

(c) dismissing the application, with or without an order for costs as may be agreed;

(d) giving permission to withdraw the application, with or without an order for costs as may be agreed.

16.4 If, as may often be the case with orders under sub-paras (3)(a) or (b) above, an adjournment is required, whether generally with liberty to restore or to a fixed date, the order by consent may include an order for the adjournment. If adjournment to a date is requested, a time estimate should be given and the court will fix the first available date and time on or after the date requested.

16.5 The above lists should not be regarded as exhaustive, nor should it be assumed that an order will be made without attendance as requested.

16.6 Applications for consent orders without attendance should be lodged at least two clear working days (and preferably longer) before any hearing date.

16.7 Whenever a document is lodged or a letter sent, the correct case number should be quoted. A note should also be given of the date and time of the next hearing (if any).

Bankruptcy Restrictions Undertakings

17.1 Where a bankrupt has given a bankruptcy restrictions undertaking, the Secretary of State or official receiver must file a copy in court and send a copy to the bankrupt as soon as reasonably practicable

(IR 1986, r. 6.250). In addition the Secretary of State must notify the court immediately that the bankrupt has given such an undertaking in order that any hearing date can be vacated.

Persons at Risk of Violence

18.1 Where an application is made pursuant to IR 1986, r. 5.67, 5.68, 5A 18, or 6.235B, or otherwise to limit disclosure of information as to a person's current address by reason of the possibility of violence, the relevant application should be accompanied by a witness statement which includes the following:

(1) The grounds upon which it is contended that disclosure of the current address as defined by the Insolvency Rules might reasonably be expected to lead to violence against the debtor or a person who normally resides with him or her as a member of his or her family or where appropriate any other person.

(2) Where the application is made in respect of the address of the debtor, the debtor's proposals with regard to information which may safely be given to potential creditors in order that they can recognise that the debtor is a person who may be indebted to them, in particular the address at which the debtor previously resided or carried on business and the nature of such business.

(3) The terms of the order sought by the applicant by reference to the court's particular powers as set out in the rule under which the application is made and, unless impracticable, a draft of the order sought.

(4) Where the application is made by the debtor in respect of whom a nominee or supervisor has been appointed or against whom a bankruptcy order has been made, evidence of the consent of the nominee/supervisor, or, in the case of bankruptcy, the trustee in bankruptcy, if one has been appointed, and the official receiver if a trustee in bankruptcy has not been appointed. Where such consent is not available the statement must indicate whether such consent has been refused.

The application shall in any event make such person a respondent to the application.

18.2 The application shall be referred to the registrar who will consider it without a hearing in the first instance but without prejudice to the right of the court to list it for hearing if:

(1) the court is minded to refuse the application;

(2) the consent of any respondent is not attached;

(3) the court is of the view that there is another reason why listing is appropriate.

PART FOUR APPEALS

Appeals

19.1 An appeal from a decision of a county court (whether made by a district judge, a recorder or a circuit judge) or of a registrar in insolvency proceedings lies to a judge of the High Court.

19.2 An appeal from a decision of a judge of the High Court, whether at first instance or on appeal, lies to the Court of Appeal.

19.3 A first appeal, whether under para. 19.1 or 19.2 above, is subject to the permission requirements of CPR, r. 52.3.

19.4 An appeal from a decision of a judge of the High Court which was made on a first appeal requires the permission of the Court of Appeal.

Filing appeals

19.5.1 An appeal from a decision of a registrar must be filed at the Royal Courts of Justice in London.

19.5.2 An appeal from a decision of a district judge sitting in a district registry of the High Court may be filed:

(1) at the Royal Courts of Justice in London; or

(2) in that district registry.

19.6 The court centres at which appeals from decisions of county courts on any particular circuit must be filed, managed and heard (unless the appeal court otherwise orders) are as follows:

Midland Circuit: Birmingham

North Eastern Circuit: Leeds or Newcastle upon Tyne

Northern Circuit: Manchester or Liverpool

Wales Circuit: Cardiff, Caernarfon or Mold

Western Circuit: Bristol South Eastern Circuit: Royal Courts of Justice.

19.7 Where the lower court is a county court:

(1) an appeal or application for permission to appeal from a decision of a district judge will be heard or considered by a High Court judge or by any person authorised under the Senior Courts Act 1981, s. 9, to act as a judge of the High Court in the Chancery Division;

(2) an appeal or application for permission to appeal from a decision of a recorder or a circuit judge will be heard or considered by a High Court judge or by a person authorised under paras (1), (2) or (4) of the table in the Senior Courts Act 1981, s. 9(1), to act as a judge of the High Court in the Chancery Division;

(3) other applications in any appeal or application for permission to appeal may be heard or considered and directions may be given by a High Court judge or by any person authorised under the Senior Courts Act 1981, s. 9, to act as a judge of the High Court in the Chancery Division.

19.8 In the case of appeals from decisions of registrars or district judges in the High Court, appeals, applications for permission to appeal and other applications may be heard or considered and directions may be given by a High Court judge or by any person authorised under the Senior Courts Act 1981, s. 9, to act as a judge of the High Court in the Chancery Division.

19.9.1 CPR, Part 52, and Sections I and IV of PD 52 and its forms shall, as appropriate, apply to appeals in insolvency proceedings, save as provided below.

19.9.2 Paragraphs 8.2 to 8.8, 8.13, 8.14 and 8A.1 of PD 52 shall not apply, and para. 8.9 shall apply with the exclusion of the last sentence.

PART FIVE
APPLICATIONS RELATING TO THE REMUNERATION OF APPOINTEES

Remuneration of Appointees

Introduction

20.1.1 This Part of the practice direction applies to any remuneration application made under the Act or the Insolvency Rules.

The objective and guiding principles

20.2.1 The objective of this Part of the practice direction is to ensure that the remuneration of an appointee which is fixed and approved by the court is fair, reasonable and commensurate with the nature and extent of the work properly undertaken by the appointee in any given case and is fixed and approved by a process which is consistent and predictable.

20.2.2 Set out below are the guiding principles by reference to which remuneration applications are to be considered both by applicants, in the preparation and presentation of their application, and by the court determining such applications.

20.2.3 The guiding principles are as follows:

(1) *'Justification'* It is for the appointee who seeks to be remunerated at a particular level and/or in a particular manner to justify his claim and in order to do so the appointee should be prepared to provide full particulars of the basis for and the nature of his claim for remuneration.

(2) *'The benefit of the doubt'* The corollary of guiding principle (1) is that on any remuneration application, if after considering the evidence before it and after having regard to the guiding principles (in particular guiding principle (3)), the matters contained in para. 20.4.2 (in particular para. 20.4.2. (10)) and the matters referred to in para. 20.4.3. (as appropriate) there remains any element of doubt as to the appropriateness, fairness or reasonableness of the remuneration sought or to be fixed (whether arising from a lack of particularity as to the basis for and the nature of the appointee's claim to remuneration or otherwise) such element of doubt should be resolved by the court against the appointee.

(3) *'Professional integrity'* The court should (where this is the case) give weight to the fact that the appointee is a member of a regulated profession and as such is subject to rules

CPR Glossary, Schs, Other PDs

and guidance as to professional conduct and the fact that (where this is the case) the appointee is an officer of the court.

(4) *'The value of the service rendered'* The remuneration of an appointee should reflect the value of the service rendered by the appointee, not simply reimburse the appointee in respect of time expended and cost incurred.

(5) *'Fair and reasonable'* The amount of the appointee's remuneration should represent fair and reasonable remuneration for the work properly undertaken or to be undertaken.

(6) *'Proportionality'*

(a) *'Proportionality of information'* In considering the nature and extent of the information which should be provided by an appointee in respect of a remuneration application the court, the appointee and any other parties to the application shall have regard to what is proportionate by reference to the amount of remuneration to be fixed, the nature, complexity and extent of the work to be completed (where the application relates to future remuneration) or that has been completed by the appointee and the value and nature of the assets and liabilities with which the appointee will have to deal or has had to deal.

(b) *'Proportionality of remuneration'* The amount of remuneration to be fixed by the court should be proportionate to the nature, complexity and extent of the work to be completed (where the application relates to future remuneration) or that has been completed by the appointee and the value and nature of the assets and/or potential assets and the liabilities and/or potential liabilities with which the appointee will have to deal or has had to deal, the nature and degree of the responsibility to which the appointee has been subject in any given case, the nature and extent of the risk (if any) assumed by the appointee and the efficiency (in respect of both time and cost) with which the appointee has completed the work undertaken.

(7) *'Professional guidance'* In respect of an application for the fixing and approval of the remuneration of an appointee, the appointee may have regard to the relevant and current statements of practice promulgated by any relevant regulatory and professional bodies in relation to the fixing of the remuneration of an appointee. In considering a remuneration application, the court may also have regard to such statements of practice and the extent of compliance with such statements of practice by the appointee.

(8) *'Timing of application'* The court will take into account whether any application should have been made earlier and if so the reasons for any delay in making it.

Hearing of remuneration applications

20.3.1 On the hearing of the application the court shall consider the evidence then available to it and may either summarily determine the application or adjourn it giving such directions as it thinks appropriate.

20.3.2 Whilst the application will normally be determined summarily by a registrar sitting alone, where it is sufficiently complex, the court may direct that:

(1) an assessor or a costs judge prepare a report to the court in respect of the remuneration which is sought to be fixed and approved; and/or

(2) the application be heard by the registrar sitting with or without an assessor or a costs judge or by a judge sitting with or without an assessor or a costs judge.

Relevant criteria and procedure

20.4.1 When considering a remuneration application the court shall have regard to the objective, the guiding principles and all relevant circumstances including the matters referred to in para. 20.4.2. and where appropriate para. 20.4.3., each of which should be addressed in the evidence placed before the court.

20.4.2 On any remuneration application, the appointee should:

(1) Provide a narrative description and explanation of:

(a) the background to, the relevant circumstances of and the reasons for the appointment;

(b) the work undertaken or to be undertaken in respect of the appointment; the description should be divided, in so far as possible, into individual tasks or categories of task (general descriptions of work, tasks, or categories of task should (in so far as possible) be avoided);

(c) the reasons why it is or was considered reasonable and/or necessary and/or beneficial for such work to be done, giving details of why particular tasks or categories of task were undertaken and why such tasks or categories of task are to be undertaken or have been undertaken by particular individuals and in a particular manner;
(d) the amount of time to be spent or that has been spent in respect of work to be completed or that has been completed and why it is considered to be fair, reasonable and proportionate;
(e) what is likely to be and has been achieved, the benefits that are likely to and have accrued as a consequence of the work that is to be or has been completed, the manner in which the work required in respect of the appointment is progressing and what, in the opinion of the appointee, remains to be achieved.

(2) Provide details sufficient for the court to determine the application by reference to the criteria which are required to be taken into account by reference to the Insolvency Rules and any other applicable enactments or rules relevant to the fixing of the remuneration.

(3) Provide a statement of the total number of hours of work undertaken or to be undertaken in respect of which the remuneration is sought, together with a breakdown of such hours by individual member of staff and individual tasks or categories of tasks to be performed or that have been performed. Where appropriate, a proportionate level of detail should also be given of:
(a) the tasks or categories of tasks to be undertaken as a proportion of the total amount of work to be undertaken in respect of which the remuneration is sought and the tasks or categories of tasks that have been undertaken as a proportion of the total amount of work that has been undertaken in respect of which the remuneration is sought; and
(b) the tasks or categories of task to be completed by individual members of staff or grade of personnel including the appointee as a proportion of the total amount of work to be completed by all members of staff including the appointee in respect of which the remuneration is sought, or the tasks or categories of task that have been completed by individual members of staff or grade of personnel as a proportion of the total amount of work that has been completed by all members of staff including the appointee in respect of which the remuneration is sought.

(4) Provide a statement of the total amount to be charged for the work to be undertaken or that has been undertaken in respect of which the remuneration is sought which should include:
(a) a breakdown of such amounts by individual member of staff and individual task or categories of task performed or to be performed;
(b) details of the time expended or to be expended and the remuneration charged or to be charged in respect of each individual task or category of task as a proportion (respectively) of the total time expended or to be expended and the total remuneration charged or to be charged.

In respect of an application pursuant to which some or all of the amount of the appointee's remuneration is to be fixed on a basis other than time properly spent, the appointee shall provide (for the purposes of comparison) the same details as are required by sub-para. (4), but on the basis of what would have been charged had he been seeking remuneration on the basis of the time properly spent by him and his staff.

(5) Provide details of each individual to be engaged or who has been engaged in work in respect of the appointment and in respect of which the remuneration is sought, including details of their relevant experience, training, qualifications and the level of their seniority.

(6) Provide an explanation of:
(a) the steps, if any, to be taken or that have been taken by the appointee to avoid duplication of effort and cost in respect of the work to be completed or that has been completed in respect of which the remuneration is sought;
(b) the steps to be taken or that have been taken to ensure that the work to be completed or that has been completed is to be or was undertaken by individuals of appropriate experience and seniority relative to the nature of the work to be or that has been undertaken.

(7) Provide details of the individual rates charged by the appointee and members of his staff in respect of the work to be completed or that has been completed and in respect of which the remuneration is sought. Such details should include:
(a) a general explanation of the policy adopted in relation to the fixing or calculation of such rates and the recording of time spent;
(b) where, exceptionally, the appointee seeks remuneration in respect of time spent by secretaries, cashiers or other administrative staff whose work would otherwise be regarded as an overhead cost forming a component part of the rates charged by the appointee and members of his staff, a detailed explanation as to why such costs should be allowed should be provided.
(8) Where the remuneration application is in respect of a period of time during which the charge-out rates of the appointee and/or members of his staff engaged in work in respect of the appointment have increased, provide an explanation of the nature, extent and reason for such increase and the date when such increase took effect. This sub-para, does not apply to applications to which para. 20.4.3. applies.
(9) Provide details of any remuneration previously fixed or approved in relation to the appointment (whether by the court or otherwise) including in particular the amounts that were previously sought to be fixed or approved and the amounts that were in fact fixed or approved and the basis upon which such amounts were fixed or approved.
(10) In order that the court may be able to consider the views of any persons who the appointee considers have an interest in the assets that are under his control, provide details of:
(a) what (if any) consultation has taken place between the appointee and those persons and if no such consultation has taken place an explanation as to the reason why;
(b) the number and value of the interests of the persons consulted including details of the proportion (by number and by value) of the interests of such persons by reference to the entirety of those persons having an interest in the assets under the control of the appointee.
(11) Provide such other relevant information as the appointee considers, in the circumstances, ought to be provided to the court.

20.4.3 This paragraph applies to applications where some or all of the remuneration of the appointee is to be fixed and approved on a basis other than time properly spent. On such applications in addition to the matters referred to in para. 20.4.2. (as applicable) the appointee shall:
(1) Provide a full description of the reasons for remuneration being sought by reference to the basis contended for.
(2) Where the remuneration is sought to be fixed by reference to a percentage of the value of the assets which are realised or distributed, provide a full explanation of the basis upon which any percentage rates to be applied to the values of the assets realised and/or distributed have been chosen.
(3) Provide a statement that to the best of the appointee's belief the percentage rates or other bases by reference to which some or all of the remuneration is to be fixed are similar to the percentage rates or other bases that are applied or have been applied in respect of other appointments of a similar nature.
(4) Provide a comparison of the amount to be charged by reference to the basis contended for and the amount that would otherwise have been charged by reference to the other available bases of remuneration, including the scale of fees in IR 1986, sch. 6.

20.4.4 If and in so far as any of the matters referred to in para. 20.4.2. or 20.4.3 (as appropriate) are not addressed in the evidence, an explanation for why this is the case should be included in such evidence.

20.4.5 For the avoidance of doubt and where appropriate and proportionate, paras 20.4.2 to 20.4.4 (inclusive) are applicable to applications for the apportionment of remuneration as between a new appointee and a former appointee in circumstances where some or all of the former appointee's remuneration was based upon a set amount under the Insolvency Rules and the former appointee has ceased (for whatever reason) to hold office before the time has elapsed or the work has been completed in respect of which the set amount of remuneration was fixed.

20.4.6 The evidence placed before the court by the appointee in respect of any remuneration application should include the following documents:
(1) a copy of the most recent receipts and payments account;
(2) copies of any reports by the appointee to the persons having an interest in the assets under his control relevant to the period for which the remuneration sought to be fixed and approved relates;
(3) any schedules or such other documents providing the information referred to in paras 20.4.2 and 20.4.3 where these are likely to be of assistance to the court in considering the application;
(4) evidence of any consultation with those persons having an interest in the assets under the control of appointee in relation to the remuneration of the appointee.

20.4.7 On any remuneration application the court may make an order allowing payments of remuneration to be made on account subject to final approval whether by the court or otherwise.

20.4.8 Unless otherwise ordered by the court (or as may otherwise be provided for in any enactment or rules of procedure) the costs of and occasioned by an application for the fixing and/or approval of the remuneration of an appointee, including those of any assessor, shall be paid out of the assets under the control of the appointee.

Practice Direction — Directors Disqualification Proceedings

PART ONE

1. Application and Interpretation

1.1 In this practice direction:

(1) 'the Act' means the Company Directors Disqualification Act 1986;

(2) 'the Disqualification Rules' means the rules for the time being in force made under s. 411 of the Insolvency Act 1986 in relation to disqualification proceedings;[1]

(3) 'the Insolvency Rules' means the rules for the time being in force made under ss. 411 and 412 of the Insolvency Act 1986 in relation to insolvency proceedings;

(4) 'CPR' means the Civil Procedure Rules 1998 and 'CPR' followed by 'Part' or 'rule' and a number means the Part or rule with that number in those Rules;

(5) 'disqualification proceedings' has the meaning set out in para. 1.3 below;

(6) 'a disqualification application' is an application under the Act for the making of a disqualification order;

(7) 'registrar' means any judge of the High Court or the county court who is a registrar within the meaning of the Insolvency Rules;

(8) 'Companies Court registrar' means any judge of the High Court sitting in the Royal Courts of Justice in London who is a registrar within the meaning of the Insolvency Rules;

(9) except where the context otherwise requires references to:

(a) 'company' or 'companies' shall include references to 'partnership' or 'partnerships' and to 'limited liability partnership' and 'limited liability partnerships';

(b) 'director' shall include references to an 'officer' of a partnership and to a 'member' of a limited liability partnership;

(c) 'shadow director' shall include references to a 'shadow member' of a limited liability partnership

and, in appropriate cases, the forms annexed to this practice direction shall be varied accordingly;

(10) 'disqualification order' has the meaning set out in s. 1 of the Act and 'disqualification undertaking' has the meaning set out in s. 1A or s. 9B of the Act (as the context requires);

(11) a 'section 8A application' is an application under s. 8A of the Act to reduce the period for which a disqualification undertaking is in force or to provide for it to cease to be in force;

(12) 'specified regulator' has the meaning set out in s. 9E(2) of the Act.

1.2 This practice direction shall come into effect on 26 April 1999 and shall replace all previous practice directions relating to disqualification proceedings.

1.3 This practice direction applies to the following proceedings ('disqualification proceedings'):

(1) disqualification applications made:

(a) under s. 2(2)(a) of the Act (after the person's conviction of an indictable offence in connection with the affairs of a company);

(b) under s. 3 of the Act (on the ground of persistent breaches of provisions of companies legislation);

(c) under s. 4 of the Act (on the ground of fraud etc.);

(d) by the Secretary of State or the official receiver under s. 7(1) of the Act (on the ground that the person is or has been a director of a company which has at any time become

---

[1] The current rules are the Insolvent Companies (Disqualification of Unfit Directors) Proceedings Rules 1987 (SI 1987/2023). *For convenience relevant references to the* Insolvent Companies (Disqualification of Unfit Directors) Proceedings Rules 1987, which apply to disqualification applications under ss. 7, 8 and 9A of the Act (see r. 1(3)) are set out in footnotes to this practice direction. This practice direction applies certain provisions contained in the Insolvent Companies (Disqualification of Unfit Directors) Proceedings Rules 1987 to disqualification proceedings other than applications under ss. 7, 8 and 9A of the Act.

insolvent and his conduct makes him unfit to be concerned in the management of a company);

(e) by the Secretary of State under s. 8 of the Act (on it appearing to the Secretary of State from investigative material that it is expedient in the public interest that a disqualification order should be made); or

(f) by the Office of Fair Trading or a specified regulator under s. 9A of the Act (on the ground of breach of competition law by an undertaking and unfitness to be concerned in the management of a company);

(2) any application made under s. 7(2) or 7(4) of the Act;

(3) any application for permission to act made under s. 17 of the Act for the purposes of any of ss. 1(1)(a), 1A(1)(a) or 9B(4), or made under s. 12(2) of the Act;

(4) any application for a court order made under CPR Part 23 in the course of any of the proceedings set out in sub-paras (1) to (3) above;

(5) any application under the Act to the extent provided for by subordinate legislation;[2]

(6) any section 8A application.

2. Multi-track

2.1 All disqualification proceedings are allocated to the multi-track. The CPR relating to allocation questionnaires and track allocation shall not apply.

3. Rights of Audience

3.1 Official receivers and deputy official receivers have right of audience in any proceedings to which this practice direction applies, including cases where a disqualification application is made by the Secretary of State or by the official receiver at his direction, and whether made in the High Court or a county court.[3]

PART TWO DISQUALIFICATION APPLICATIONS

4. Commencement

4.1 Sections 2(2)(a), 3(4), 4(2), 6(3) and 8(3) of the Act identify the civil courts which have jurisdiction to deal with disqualification applications.

4.1A A disqualification application must be commenced by a claim form issued:

(1) in the case of a disqualification application under s. 9A of the Act, in the High Court out of the office of the Companies Court registrar at the Royal Courts of Justice;

(2) in any other case:

(a) in the High Court out of the office of the Companies Court registrar or a Chancery district registry; and

(b) in the county court, out of a county court office.

4.2 Disqualification applications shall be made by the issue of a claim form in the form annexed hereto and the use of the procedure set out in CPR, Part 8,[4] as modified by this practice direction and (where the application is made under ss. 7, 8 or 9A of the Act) the Disqualification Rules. Rule 8.1(3) of the CPR (power of the court to order the application to continue as if the claimant had not used the Part 8 procedure) shall not apply.

4.3 When the claim form is issued, the claimant will be given a date for the first hearing of the disqualification application. This date is to be not less than eight weeks from the date of issue of the claim form.[5] The first hearing will be before a registrar.

[2] Current subordinate legislation includes the Insolvent Partnerships Order 1994 (SI 1994/2421) and the Limited Liability Partnerships Regulations 2001 (SI 2001/1090).

[3] Rule 10 of the Insolvent Companies (Disqualification of Unfit Directors) Proceedings Rules 1987.

[4] Rule 2(2) of the Insolvent Companies (Disqualification of Unfit Directors) Proceedings Rules 1987 as amended.

[5] Rule 7(1) of the Insolvent Companies (Disqualification of Unfit Directors) Proceedings Rules 1987.

5. Headings

5.1 Every claim form by which an application under the Act is begun and all affidavits, notices and other documents in the proceedings must be entitled in the matter of the company or companies in question and in the matter of the Act. In the case of any disqualification application under ss. 7 or 9A of the Act it is not necessary to mention in the heading any company other than that referred to in s. 6(1)(a) or 9A(2) of the Act (as the case may be).

6. The Claim Form

6.1 Rule 8.2 of the CPR does not apply. The claim form must state:

(1) that CPR, Part 8 (as modified by this practice direction), applies, and (if the application is made under ss. 7, 8 or 9A of the Act) that the application is made in accordance with the Disqualification Rules;[6]

(2) that the claimant seeks a disqualification order, and the section of the Act pursuant to which the disqualification application is made;

(3) the period for which, in accordance with the Act, the court has power to impose a disqualification period.

The periods are as follows:

(a) where the application is under s. 2 of the Act, for a period of up to 15 years;

(b) where the application is under s. 3 of the Act, for a period of up to five years;

(c) where the application is under s. 4 of the Act, for a period of up to 15 years;

(d) where the application is under s. 7 of the Act, for a period of not less than two, and up to 15, years;[7]

(e) where the application is under ss. 8 or 9A of the Act, for a period of up to 15 years.[8]

(4) in cases where the application is made under ss. 7 or 8 of the Act, that on the first hearing of the application, the court may hear and determine it summarily, without further or other notice to the defendant, and that, if the application is so determined, the court may impose a period of disqualification of up to five years but that if at the hearing of the application the court, on the evidence then before it, is minded to impose, in the case of any defendant, disqualification for any period longer than five years, it will not make a disqualification order on that occasion but will adjourn the application to be heard (with further evidence, if any) at a later date that will be notified to the defendant;[9]

(5) that any evidence which the defendant wishes the court to take into consideration must be filed in court in accordance with the time limits set out in paragraph 9 below (which time limits shall be set out in the notes to the claim form).[10]

7. Service of the Claim Form*

7.1 Service of claim forms in disqualification proceedings will be the responsibility of the parties and will not be undertaken by the court.

7.2 The claim form shall be served by the claimant on the defendant. It may be served by sending it by first class post to his last known address; and the date of service shall, unless the contrary is shown, be deemed to be the seventh day following that on which the claim form was posted.[11] Rule 6.7(1) of the CPR shall be modified accordingly. Otherwise Sections I and II of Part 6 apply.[12]

7.3 Where any claim form or order of the court or other document is required under any disqualification proceedings to be served on any person who is not in England and Wales, the court may order service on him to be effected within such time and in such manner as it thinks fit, may require such proof of service as it thinks fit,[13] and may give such directions as to acknowledgment of service as it thinks fit. Section III of CPR, Part 6, shall not apply.

6 Rule 4(a) of the Insolvent Companies (Disqualification of Unfit Directors) Proceedings Rules 1987.

7 Rule 4(b)(i) of the Insolvent Companies (Disqualification of Unfit Directors) Proceedings Rules 1987.

8 Rule 4(b)(ii) of the Insolvent Companies (Disqualification of Unfit Directors) Proceedings Rules 1987.

9 Rule 4(c) and (d) of the Insolvent Companies (Disqualification of Unfit Directors) Proceedings Rules 1987.

10 Rule 4(e) of the Insolvent Companies (Disqualification of Unfit Directors) Proceedings Rules 1987.

[* *In paras 7.2 and 7.3*, references to CPR, Part 6, were not updated when it was amended on 1 October 2008.]

11 Rule 5(1) of the Insolvent Companies (Disqualification of Unfit Directors) Proceedings Rules 1987.

12 Attention is drawn to CPR, r. 6.14(2), regarding a certificate of service of the claim form.

13 Rule 5(2) of the Insolvent Companies (Disqualification of Unfit Directors) Proceedings Rules 1987.

7.4 The claim form served on the defendant shall be accompanied by an acknowledgment of service.

8. Acknowledgment of Service

8.1 The form of acknowledgment of service is annexed to this practice direction. CPR rules 8.3(2) and 8.3(3)(a) do not apply to disqualification applications.

8.2 In cases brought under ss. 7, 8 or 9A of the Act, the form of acknowledgment of service shall state that the defendant should indicate:[14]

(1) whether he contests the application on the grounds that, in the case of any particular company:

(a) he was not a director or shadow director of that company at a time when conduct of his, or of other persons, in relation to that company is in question; or

(b) his conduct as director or shadow director of that company was not as alleged in support of the application for a disqualification order;

(c) in the case of an application made under s. 7 of the Act, the company has at no time become insolvent within the meaning of s. 6; or

(d) in the case of an application under s. 9A of the Act, the undertaking which is a company did not commit a breach of competition law within the meaning of that section.

(2) whether, in the case of any conduct of his, he disputes the allegation that such conduct makes him unfit to be concerned in the management of a company; and

(3) whether he, while not resisting the application for a disqualification order, intends to adduce mitigating factors with a view to reducing the period of disqualification.

8.3 The defendant shall:

(1) (subject to any directions to the contrary given under para. 7.3 above) file an acknowledgment of service in the prescribed form not more than 14 days after service of the claim form; and

(2) serve the acknowledgment of service on the claimant and any other party.

8.4 Where the defendant has failed to file an acknowledgment of service and the time period for doing so has expired, the defendant may attend the hearing of the application but may not take part in the hearing unless the court gives permission.

9. Evidence

9.1 Evidence in disqualification applications shall be by affidavit, except where the official receiver is a party, in which case his evidence may be in the form of a written report (with or without affidavits by other persons) which shall be treated as if it had been verified by affidavit by him and shall be prima facie evidence of any matter contained in it.[15]

9.2 In the affidavits or (as the case may be) the official receiver's report in support of the application, there shall be included:

(1) a statement of the matters by reference to which it is alleged that a disqualification order should be made against the defendant;[16] and

(2) a statement of the steps taken to comply with any requirements imposed by ss. 16(1) and 9C(4) of the Act.

9.3 When the claim form is issued:

(1) the affidavit or report in support of the disqualification application must be filed in court;

(2) exhibits must be lodged with the court where they shall be retained until the conclusion of the proceedings; and

CPR Glossary, Schs, Other PDs

[14] Rule 5(4) of the Insolvent Companies (Disqualification of Unfit Directors) Proceedings Rules 1987. Note that the requirements of para. 8.2(1)(c) and (d) of this practice direction are additional to the provisions in the said r. 5(4). [In the text issued by the Ministry of Justice the last sentence of this footnote is erroneously located in the next footnote and erroneously refers to para. 8.1(2) instead of para. 8.2(1).]

[15] Rule 3(2) of the Insolvent Companies (Disqualification of Unfit Directors) Proceedings Rules 1987. Section 441 of the Companies Act 1985 makes provision for the admissibility in legal proceedings of a certified copy of a report of inspectors appointed under part XIV of the Companies Act 1985.

[16] Rule 3(3) of the Insolvent Companies (Disqualification of Unfit Directors) Proceedings Rules 1987.

(3) copies of the affidavit/report and exhibits shall be served with the claim form on the defendant.[17]

9.4 The defendant shall, within 28 days from the date of service of the claim form:[18]

(1) file in court any affidavit evidence in opposition to the disqualification application that he or she wishes the court to take into consideration; and

(2) lodge the exhibits with the court where they shall be retained until the conclusion of the proceedings; and

(3) at the same time, serve upon the claimant a copy of the affidavits and exhibits.

9.5 In cases where there is more than one defendant, each defendant is required to serve his evidence on the other defendants unless the court otherwise orders.

9.6 The claimant shall, within 14 days from receiving the copy of the defendant's evidence:[19]

(1) file in court any further affidavit or report in reply he wishes the court to take into consideration; and

(2) lodge the exhibits with the court where they shall be retained until the conclusion of the proceedings; and

(3) at the same time serve a copy of the affidavits/reports and exhibits upon the defendant.

9.7 Prior to the first hearing of the disqualification application, the time for serving evidence may be extended by written agreement between the parties. After the first hearing, the extension of time for serving evidence is governed by CPR rules 2.11 and 29.5.

9.8 So far as is possible all evidence should be filed before the first hearing of the disqualification application.

10. The First Hearing of the Disqualification Application

10.1 The date fixed for the hearing of the disqualification application shall be not less than eight weeks from the date of issue of the claim form.[20]

10.2 The hearing shall in the first instance be before the registrar.[21]

10.3 The registrar shall either determine the case on the date fixed or give directions and adjourn it.[22]

10.4 All interim directions should in so far as possible be sought at the first hearing of the disqualification application so that the disqualification application can be determined at the earliest possible date. The parties should take all such steps as they respectively can to avoid successive directions hearings.

10.5 In the case of a disqualification application made under ss. 7, 8 or 9A of the Act, the registrar shall adjourn the case for further consideration if:

(1) he forms the provisional opinion that a disqualification order ought to be made, and that a period of disqualification longer than five years is appropriate,[23]

or

(2) he is of opinion that questions of law or fact arise which are not suitable for summary determination.[24]

10.6 If the registrar adjourns the application for further consideration he shall:

(1) direct whether the application is to be heard by a registrar or by a judge.[25] This direction may at any time be varied by the court either on application or of its own initiative. If the court varies the direction in the absence of any of the parties, notice will be given to the parties;

(2) consider whether or not to adjourn the application to a judge so that the judge can give further directions;

[17] Rule 3(1) of the Insolvent Companies (Disqualification of Unfit Directors) Proceedings Rules 1987.

[18] Rule 6(1) of the Insolvent Companies (Disqualification of Unfit Directors) Proceedings Rules 1987.

[19] Rule 6(2) of the Insolvent Companies (Disqualification of Unfit Directors) Proceedings Rules 1987.

[20] Rule 7(1) of the Insolvent Companies (Disqualification of Unfit Directors) Proceedings Rules 1987.

[21] Rule 7(2) of the Insolvent Companies (Disqualification of Unfit Directors) Proceedings Rules 1987.

[22] Rule 7(3) of the Insolvent Companies (Disqualification of Unfit Directors) Proceedings Rules 1987.

[23] Rule 7(4)(a) of the Insolvent Companies (Disqualification of Unfit Directors) Proceedings Rules 1987.

[24] Rule 7(4)(b) of the Insolvent Companies (Disqualification of Unfit Directors) Proceedings Rules 1987.

[25] Rule 7(5)(a) of the Insolvent Companies (Disqualification of Unfit Directors) Proceedings Rules 1987.

(3) consider whether or not to make any direction with regard to fixing the trial date or a trial window;
(4) state the reasons for the adjournment.[26]

11. Case Management

11.1 On the first or any subsequent hearing of the disqualification application, the registrar may also give directions as to the following matters:
(1) the filing in court and the service of further evidence (if any) by the parties;[27]
(2) the timetable for the steps to be taken between the giving of directions and the hearing of the application;
(3) such other matters as the registrar thinks necessary or expedient with a view to an expeditious disposal of the application or the management of it generally;[28]
(4) the time and place of the adjourned hearing;[29] and
(5) the manner in which and the time within which notice of the adjournment and the reasons for it are to be given to the parties.[30]

11.2 Where a case is adjourned other than to a judge, it may be heard by the registrar who originally dealt with the case or by another registrar.[31]

11.3 If the Companies Court registrar adjourns the application to a judge, all directions having been complied with and the evidence being complete, the application will be referred to the Listing Office and any practice direction relating to listing shall apply accordingly.

11.4 In all disqualification applications, the court may direct a pre-trial review ('PTR'), a case management conference or pre-trial checklists (listing questionnaires) (in the form annexed to this practice direction) and will fix a trial date or trial period in accordance with the provisions of CPR, Part 29 (the multi-track), as modified by any relevant practice direction made there under.

11.5 At the hearing of the PTR, the registrar may give any further directions as appropriate and, where the application is to be heard in the Royal Courts of Justice in London, unless the trial date has already been fixed, may direct the parties (by counsel's clerks if applicable) to attend the registrar at a specified time and place in order solely to fix a trial date. The court will give notice of the date fixed for the trial to the parties.

11.6 In all cases, the parties must inform the court immediately of any material change to the information provided in a pre-trial checklist.

12. The Trial

12.1 Trial bundles containing copies of:
(1) the claim form;
(2) the acknowledgment of service;
(3) all evidence filed by or on behalf of each of the parties to the proceedings, together with the exhibits thereto;
(4) all relevant correspondence; and
(5) such other documents as the parties consider necessary;
shall be lodged with the court.

12.2 Skeleton arguments should be prepared by all the parties in all but the simplest cases whether the case is to be heard by a registrar or a judge. They should comply with all relevant guidelines.

12.3 The advocate for the claimant should also in all but the simplest cases provide: (a) a chronology; (b) a dramatis personae; (c) in respect of each defendant, a list of references to the relevant evidence.

[26] Rule 7(5)(b) of the Insolvent Companies (Disqualification of Unfit Directors) Proceedings Rules 1987.
[27] Rule 7(5)(c)(ii) of the Insolvent Companies (Disqualification of Unfit Directors) Proceedings Rules 1987.
[28] Rule 7(5)(c)(iii) of the Insolvent Companies (Disqualification of Unfit Directors) Proceedings Rules 1987.
[29] Rule 7(5)(c)(iv) of the Insolvent Companies (Disqualification of Unfit Directors) Proceedings Rules 1987.
[30] Rule 7(5)(c)(i) of the Insolvent Companies (Disqualification of Unfit Directors) Proceedings Rules 1987.
[31] Rule 7(6) of the Insolvent Companies (Disqualification of Unfit Directors) Proceedings Rules 1987.

12.4 The documents mentioned in paras 12.1–12.3 above must be delivered to the court in accordance with any order of the court and/or any relevant practice direction.[32]

(1) If the case is to be heard by a judge sitting in the Royal Courts of Justice, London, but the name of the judge is not known, or the judge is a deputy judge, these documents must be delivered to the Clerk of the Lists. If the name of the judge (other than a deputy judge) is known, these documents must be delivered to the judge's clerk.

(2) If the case is to be heard by a Companies Court registrar, these documents must be delivered to Room 409, Thomas More Building, Royal Courts of Justice. Copies must be provided to the other party so far as possible when they are delivered to the court.

(3) If the case is to be heard in the Chancery district registries in Birmingham, Bristol, Caernarfon, Cardiff, Leeds, Liverpool, Manchester, Mold, Newcastle upon Tyne or Preston, the addresses for delivery are set out in annex 1.

(4) If the case is to be heard in a county court, the documents should be delivered to the relevant county court office.

12.5 Copies of documents delivered to the court must, so far as possible, be provided to each of the other parties to the claim.

12.6 The provisions in paras 12.1 to 12.5 above are subject to any order of the court making different provision.

13. Summary Procedure

13.1 If the parties decide to invite the court to deal with the application under the procedure adopted in *Re Carecraft Construction Co. Ltd* [1994] 1 WLR 172, they should inform the court immediately and obtain a date for the hearing of the application.

13.2 Whenever the *Carecraft* procedure is adopted, the claimant must:

(1) except where the court otherwise directs, submit a written statement containing in respect of each defendant any material facts which (for the purposes of the application) are either agreed or not opposed (by either party); and

(2) specify in writing the period of disqualification which the parties accept that the agreed or unopposed facts justify or the band of years (e.g. 4 to 6 years) or bracket (i.e. 2 to 5 years; 6 to 10 years; 11 to 15 years) into which they will submit the case falls.

13.3 Paragraph 12.4 above applies to the documents mentioned in para. 13.2 above unless the court otherwise directs.

13.4 Unless the court otherwise orders, a hearing under the *Carecraft* procedure will be held in private.

13.5 If the court is minded to make a disqualification order having heard the parties' representations, it will usually give judgment and make the disqualification order in public. Unless the court otherwise orders, the written statement referred to in para. 13.2 shall be annexed to the disqualification order.

13.6 If the court refuses to make the disqualification order under the *Carecraft* procedure, the court shall give further directions for the hearing of the application.

14. Making and Setting Aside of Disqualification Order

14.1 The court may make a disqualification order against the defendant, whether or not the latter appears, and whether or not he has completed and returned the acknowledgment of service of the claim form, or filed evidence.[33]

14.2 Any disqualification order made in the absence of the defendant may be set aside or varied by the court on such terms as it thinks just.[34]

[32] Attention is drawn to the provisions of the Chancery Guide. chapter 7 of that Guide dated September 2000 provides guidance on the preparation of trial bundles and skeleton arguments. Unless the court otherwise orders, para. 7.16 of the Chancery Guide requires that trial bundles be delivered to the court seven days before trial and para. 7.21 requires that skeleton arguments be *delivered to the court not less than two clear days before trial*. [See now paras 7.15 and 7.20 of the 2009 edition of the Chancery Guide.]

[33] Rule 8(1) of the Insolvent Companies (Disqualification of Unfit Directors) Proceedings Rules 1987.

[34] Rule 8(2) of the Insolvent Companies (Disqualification of Unfit Directors) Proceedings Rules 1987.

15. Service of Disqualification Orders

15.1 Service of disqualification orders will be the responsibility of the claimant.

16. Commencement of Disqualification Order

16.1 Unless the court otherwise orders, the period of disqualification imposed by a disqualification order shall begin at the end of the period of 21 days beginning with the date of the order.[35]

PART THREE APPLICATIONS UNDER SECTIONS 7(2) AND 7(4) OF THE ACT

17. Applications for Permission to Make a Disqualification Application after the End of the Period of 2 Years Specified in Section 7(2) of the Act

17.1 Such applications shall be made by form N208 under CPR, Part 8, save where it is sought to join a director or former director to existing proceedings, in which case such application shall be made by application notice under CPR, Part 23, and PD 23A shall apply save as modified below.

18. Applications for Extra Information Made under Section 7(4) of the Act

18.1 Such applications may be made:
(1) by form N208 under CPR, Part 8;
(2) by application notice in existing disqualification proceedings; or
(3) by application under the Insolvency Rules 1986 in the relevant insolvency, if the insolvency practitioner against whom the application is made remains the office-holder.

19. Provisions Applicable to Applications under Sections 7(2) and 7(4) of the Act

19.1 *Headings:* Every claim form and notice by which such an application is begun and all affidavits, notices and other documents in relation thereto must be entitled in the matter of the company or companies in question and in the matter of the Act.

19.2 *Service:*
(1) Service of claim forms and application notices seeking orders under s. 7(2) or 7(4) of the Act will be the responsibility of the applicant and will not be undertaken by the court.
(2) Where any claim form, application notice or order of the court or other document is required in any application under s. 7(2) or (4) of the Act to be served on any person who is not in England and Wales, the court may order service on him to be effected within such time and in such manner as it thinks fit, may require such proof of service as it thinks fit, and may make such directions as to acknowledgment of service as it thinks fit. Section III of CPR, Part 6, does not apply.

PART FOUR APPLICATIONS FOR PERMISSION TO ACT

20. Commencing an Application for Permission to Act

20.1 This practice direction governs applications for permission made under:
(1) s. 17 of the Act for the purposes of any of ss. 1(1)(a), 1A(1)(a) or 9B(4); and
(2) s. 12(2) of the Act.

20.2 Sections 12 and 17 of the Act identify the courts which have jurisdiction to deal with applications for permission to act. Subject to these sections, such applications may be made:
(1) by form N208 under CPR, Part 8; or
(2) by application notice in an existing disqualification application.

20.3 In the case of a person subject to disqualification under s. 12A or 12B of the Act (by reason of being disqualified in Northern Ireland), permission to act notwithstanding disqualification can only be granted by the High Court of Northern Ireland.

[35] Section 1(2) of the Act (as amended).

21. Headings

21.1 Every claim form or application notice by which an application for permission to act is begun, and all affidavits, notices and other documents in the application must be entitled in the matter of the company or companies in question and in the matter of the Act.

21.2 Every application notice by which an application for permission to act is made and all affidavits, notices and other documents in the application shall be entitled in the same manner as the heading of the claim form in the existing disqualification application.

22. Evidence

22.1 Evidence in support of an application for permission to act shall be by affidavit.

23. Service[36]

23.1 Where a disqualification application has been made under s. 9A of the Act or a disqualification undertaking has been accepted under s. 9B of the Act, the claim form or application notice (as appropriate), together with the evidence in support thereof, must be served on the Office of Fair Trading or specified regulator which made the relevant disqualification application or accepted the disqualification undertaking (as the case may be).

23.2 In all other cases, the claim form or application notice (as appropriate), together with the evidence in support thereof, must be served on the Secretary of State.

PART FIVE APPLICATIONS

24. Form of Application

24.1 CPR, Part 23, and PD 23A (general rules about applications for court orders) shall apply in relation to applications governed by this practice direction (see para. 1.3(4) above) save as modified below.

25. Headings

25.1 Every notice and all affidavits in relation thereto must be entitled in the same manner as the claim form in the proceedings in which the application is made.

26. Service

26.1 Service of application notices in disqualification proceedings will be the responsibility of the parties and will not be undertaken by the court.

26.2 Where any application notice or order of the court or other document is required in any application to be served on any person who is not in England and Wales, the court may order service on him to be effected within such time and in such manner as it thinks fit, and may also require such proof of service as it thinks fit. Section III of CPR, Part 6, does not apply.

PART SIX DISQUALIFICATION PROCEEDINGS OTHER THAN IN THE ROYAL COURTS OF JUSTICE

27.1 Where a disqualification application or a section 8A application is made by a claim form issued other than in the Royal Courts of Justice this practice direction shall apply with the following modifications:

(1) Upon the issue of the claim form the court shall endorse it with the date and time for the first hearing before a district judge. The powers exercisable by a registrar under this practice direction shall be exercised by a district judge.

(2) If the district judge (either at the first hearing or at any adjourned hearing before him) directs that the disqualification claim or section 8A application is to be heard by a High

[36] Adresses for service on government departments are set out in the List of Authorised Governament Departments issued by the Cabinet Office under the Crown Proceedings Act 1947, s. 17, which is in annex 2 to PD 66.

Court judge or by an authorised circuit judge he will direct that the case be entered forthwith in the list for hearing by that judge and the court will allocate (i) a date for the hearing of the trial by that judge and (ii) unless the district judge directs otherwise a date for the hearing of a PTR by the trial judge.

PART SEVEN DISQUALIFICATION UNDERTAKINGS

28. Costs

28.1 The general rule is that the court will order the defendant to pay:
(1) the costs of the Secretary of State (and, in the case of a disqualification application made under s. 7(1)(b) of the Act, the costs of the official receiver) if:
(a) a disqualification application under s. 7 or 8 of the Act has been commenced; and
(b) that application is discontinued because the Secretary of State has accepted a disqualification undertaking under s. 1A of the Act;
(2) the costs of the Office of Fair Trading or a specified regulator if:
(a) a disqualification application under s. 9A of the Act has been commenced; and
(b) that application is discontinued because the Office of Fair Trading or specified regulator (as the case may be) has accepted a disqualification undertaking under s. 9B of the Act.

28.2 The general rule will not apply where the court considers that the circumstances are such that it should make another order.

APPLICATIONS UNDER SECTION 8A OF THE ACT TO REDUCE THE PERIOD FOR WHICH A DISQUALIFICATION UNDERTAKING IS IN FORCE OR TO PROVIDE FOR IT TO CEASE TO BE IN FORCE

29. Headings

29.1 Every claim form by which a section 8A application is begun and all affidavits, notices and other documents in the proceedings must be entitled in the matter of a disqualification undertaking and its date and in the matter of the Act.

30. Commencement: The Claim Form

30.1. Section 8A(3) of the Act identifies the courts which have jurisdiction to deal with section 8A applications.

30.1A. A section 8A application must be commenced by a claim form issued:
(1) in the case of a disqualification undertaking given under s. 9B of the Act, in the High Court out of the office of the Companies Court registrar at the Royal Courts of Justice;
(2) in any other case,
(a) in the High Court out of the office of the Companies Court registrar or a Chancery district registry; and
(b) in the county court, out of a county court office.

30.2. A section 8A application shall be made by the issue of a Part 8 claim form in the form annexed hereto and the use of the procedure set out in CPR, Part 8, as modified by this practice direction. Rule 8.1(3) of the CPR (power of the court to order the application to continue as if the claimant had not used the Part 8 procedure) shall not apply.

30.3. When the claim form is issued, the claimant will be given a date for the first hearing of the section 8A application. This date is to be not less than eight weeks from the date of issue of the claim form. The first hearing will be before [a] registrar.

30.4. Rule 8.2 of the CPR does not apply. The claim form must state:
(1) that CPR, Part 8 (as modified by this practice direction), applies;
(2) the form of order the claimant seeks.

30.5. In the case of a disqualification undertaking given under s. 9B of the Act, the defendant to the s. 8A application shall be the Office of Fair Trading or specified regulator which accepted the undertaking. In all other cases, the Secretary of State shall be made the defendant to the section 8A application.

30.6 Service of claim forms in section 8A applications will be the responsibility of the claimant and will not be undertaken by the court. The claim form may be served by sending it by first-class post and the date of service shall, unless the contrary is shown, be deemed to be the seventh day following that on which the claim form was posted. Rule 6.7(1) of the CPR shall be modified accordingly. Otherwise Sections I and II of CPR, Part 6, apply.[37] *

30.7 Where any order of the court or other document is required to be served on any person who is not in England and Wales, the court may order service on him to be effected within such time and in such manner as it thinks fit and may require such proof of service as it thinks fit. Part 6 of the CPR shall not apply.

30.8 The claim form served on the defendant shall be accompanied by an acknowledgment of service in the form annexed hereto.

31. Acknowledgment of Service

31.1 The defendant shall:

(1) file an acknowledgment of service in the relevant practice form not more than 14 days after service of the claim form; and

(2) serve a copy of the acknowledgment of service on the claimant and any other party.

31.2 Where the defendant has failed to file an acknowledgment of service and the time period for doing so has expired, the defendant may nevertheless attend the hearing of the application and take part in the hearing as provided for by s. 8A(2) or (2A) of the Act. However, this is without prejudice to the court's case management powers and its powers to make costs orders.

32. Evidence

32.1 Evidence in section 8A applications shall be by affidavit. The undertaking (or a copy) shall be exhibited to the affidavit.

32.2 When the claim form is issued:

(1) the affidavit in support of the section 8A application must be filed in court;

(2) exhibits must be lodged with the court where they shall be retained until the conclusion of the proceedings; and

(3) copies of the affidavit and exhibits shall be served with the claim form on the defendant.

32.3 The defendant shall, within 28 days from the date of service of the claim form:

(1) file in court any affidavit evidence that he wishes the court to take into consideration on the application; and

(2) lodge the exhibits with the court where they shall be retained until the conclusion of the proceedings; and

(3) at the same time, serve upon the claimant a copy of the affidavits and exhibits.

32.4 The claimant shall, within 14 days from receiving the copy of the defendant's evidence:

(1) file in court any further affidavit evidence in reply he wishes the court to take into consideration; and

(2) lodge the exhibits with the court where they shall be retained until the conclusion of the proceedings; and

(3) at the same time serve a copy of the affidavits and exhibits upon the defendant.

32.5 Prior to the first hearing of the section 8A application, the time for serving evidence may be extended by written agreement between the parties. After the first hearing, the extension of time for serving evidence is governed by CPR, rr. 2.11 and 29.5.

32.6 So far as is possible all evidence should be filed before the first hearing of the section 8A application.

33. Hearings and Case Management

33.1 The date fixed for the first hearing of the section 8A application shall be not less than eight weeks from the date of issue of the claim form.

33.2 The hearing shall in the first instance be before the registrar.

[37] Attention is drawn to CPR, r. 6.14(2), regarding a certificate of service of the claim form.

[* In para. 30.6, the reference to CPR, Part 6, was not updated when Part 6 was amended on 1 October 2008.]

33.3 The registrar shall either determine the case on the date fixed or give directions and adjourn it.

33.4 All interim directions should in so far as possible be sought at the first hearing of the section 8A application so that the section 8A application can be determined at the earliest possible date. The parties should take all such steps as they respectively can to avoid successive directions hearings.

33.5 If the registrar adjourns the application for further consideration he shall:

(1) direct whether the application is to be heard by a registrar or by a judge. This direction may at any time be varied by the court either on application or of its own initiative. If the court varies the direction in the absence of any of the parties, notice will be given to the parties;

(2) consider whether or not to adjourn the application to a judge so that the judge can give further directions;

(3) consider whether or not to make any direction with regard to fixing the trial date or a trial window.

33.6 On the first or any subsequent hearing of the section 8A application, the registrar may also give directions as to the following matters:

(1) the filing in court and the service of further evidence (if any) by the parties;

(2) the timetable for the steps to be taken between the giving of directions and the hearing of the section 8A application;

(3) such other matters as the registrar thinks necessary or expedient with a view to an expeditious disposal of the section 8A application or the management of it generally;

(4) the time and place of the adjourned hearing.

33.7 Where a case is adjourned other than to a judge, it may be heard by the registrar who originally dealt with the case or by another registrar.

33.8 If the Companies Court registrar adjourns the application to a judge, all directions having been complied with and the evidence being complete, the application will be referred to the Listing Office and any practice direction relating to listing shall apply accordingly.

33.9 In all section 8A applications, the court may direct a pre-trial review ('PTR'), a case management conference or pre-trial checklists (listing questionnaires) (in the form annexed to this practice direction) and will fix a trial date or trial period in accordance with the provisions of CPR, Part 29, as modified by any relevant practice direction made thereunder.

33.10 At the hearing of the PTR, the registrar may give any further directions as appropriate and, where the application is to be heard in the Royal Courts of Justice in London, unless the trial date has already been fixed, may direct the parties (by counsel's clerks, if applicable) to attend the registrar at a specified time and place in order solely to fix a trial date. The court will give notice of the date fixed for the trial to the parties.

33.11 In all cases, the parties must inform the court immediately of any material change to the information provided in a pre-trial checklist.

34. The Trial

34.1 Trial bundles containing copies of:

(1) the claim form;

(2) the acknowledgment of service;

(3) all evidence filed by or on behalf of each of the parties to the proceedings, together with the exhibits thereto;

(4) all relevant correspondence; and

(5) such other documents as the parties consider necessary;

shall be lodged with the court.

34.2 Skeleton arguments should be prepared by all the parties in all but the simplest cases whether the case is to be heard by a registrar or a judge. They should comply with all relevant guidelines.

34.3 The advocate for the claimant should also in all but the simplest cases provide: (a) chronology; (b) a dramatis personae.

CPR Glossary, Schs, Other PDs

34.4 The documents mentioned in paras 34.1 to 34.3 above must be delivered to the court in accordance with any order of the court and/or [any] relevant practice direction.[38]

(1) If the case is to be heard by a judge sitting in the Royal Courts of Justice, London, but the name of the judge is not known, or the judge is a deputy judge, these documents must be delivered to the Clerk of the Lists. If the name of the judge (other than a deputy judge) is known, these documents must be delivered to the judge's clerk.

(2) If the case is to be heard by a Companies Court registrar, these documents must be delivered to Room 409, Thomas More Building, Royal Courts of Justice. Copies must be provided to the other party so far as possible when they are delivered to the court.

(3) If the case is to be heard in the Chancery district registries in Birmingham, Bristol, Caernarfon, Cardiff, Leeds, Liverpool, Manchester, Mold, Newcastle upon Tyne, or Preston, the addresses for delivery are set out in Annex 1.

(4) If the case is to be heard in a county court, the documents should be delivered to the relevant county court office.

34.5 Copies of documents delivered to the court must, so far as possible, be provided to each of the other parties to the claim.

34.6 The provisions in paras 34.1 to 34.5 above are subject to any order of the court making different provision.

35. Appeals

35.1 Rules 7.47 and 7.49 of the Insolvency Rules, as supplemented by Part Four of PD Insolvency Proceedings, apply to an appeal from, or review of, a decision made by the court in the course of:

(1) disqualification proceedings under any of ss. 6 to 8A or 9A of the Act;

(2) an application made under s. 17 of the Act for the purposes of any of ss. 1(1)(a), 1A(1)(a) or 9B(4), for permission to act notwithstanding a disqualification order made, or a disqualification undertaking accepted, under any of ss. 6 to 10.

Any such decision, and any appeal from it, constitutes 'insolvency proceedings' for the purposes of PD Insolvency Proceedings.[39]

35.2 An appeal from a decision made by the court in the course of disqualification proceedings under any of ss. 2(2) (a), 3 or 4 of the Act or on an application for permission to act notwithstanding a disqualification order made under any of those sections is governed by CPR, Part 52, and PD 52.

ANNEX 1

Birmingham: The Chancery Listing Officer, The District Registry of the Chancery Division of the High Court, 33 Bull Street, Birmingham B4 6DS.

Bristol: The Chancery Listing Officer, The District Registry of the Chancery Division of the High Court, 3rd Floor, Greyfriars, Lewins Mead, Bristol BS1 2NR.

Caernarfon: The Chancery Listing Officer, The District Registry of the Chancery Division of the High Court, 1st Floor, Llanberis Road, Caernarfon, LL55 2DF.

Cardiff: The Chancery Listing Officer, The District Registry of the Chancery Division of the High Court, 1st Floor, 2 Park Street, Cardiff CF10 1EE.

[38] Attention is drawn to the provisions of the Chancery Guide. chapter 7 of that Guide dated September 2000 provides guidance on the preparation of trial bundles and skeleton arguments. Unless the court otherwise orders, para. 7.16 of the Chancery Guide requires that trial bundles be delivered to the court seven days before trial and para. 7.21 requires that skeleton arguments be delivered to the court not less than two clear days before trial. [See now paras 7.15 and 7.20 of the 2009 edition of the Chancery Guide.] Addresses for service on government departments are set out in the List of Authorised Government Departments issued by the Cabinet Office under the Crown Proceedings Act 1947, s. 17, which is in annex 2 to PD 66.

[39] *CPR, r. 2.1(2)*, and s. 21(2) of the Act. See also the Insolvent Companies (Disqualification of Unfit Directors) Proceedings Rules 1987, r. 2(4), and *Re Tasbian Ltd (No. 2)* [1991] BCLC 59; *Re Probe Data Systems Ltd (No. 3)* [1992] BCLC 405; and *Secretary of State for Trade and Industry v Paulin* [2005] EWHC 888 (Ch), *The Times*, 26 May 2005.

Leeds: The Chancery Listing Officer, The District Registry of the Chancery Division of the High Court, Leeds Combined Court Centre, The Court House, 1 Oxford Row, Leeds LS1 3BG.

Liverpool and Manchester: The Chancery Listing Officer, The District Registry of the Chancery Division of the High Court, Manchester Courts of Justice, Crown Square, Manchester M60 9DJ.

Mold: The Chancery Listing Officer, The District Registry of the Chancery Division of the High Court, Law Courts, Civic Centre, Mold, CH7 1AE.

Newcastle upon Tyne: The Chancery Listing Officer, The District Registry of the Chancery Division of the High Court, The Law Courts, Quayside, Newcastle upon Tyne NE1 3LA.

Preston: The Chancery Listing Officer, The District Registry of the Chancery Division of the High Court, The Combined Court Centre, Ringway, Preston PR1 2LL.

[FORMS

The forms annexed to this practice direction are online at <http://hmctsformfinder.justice.gov.uk>.

N500	Claim form: directors disqualification applications
N500A	Notes for claimant on completing claim form N500: directors disqualification application
N500B	Notes for defendant: directors disqualification application
N501	Claim form: directors disqualification: section 8A application
N501A	Notes for claimant on completing claim form N501: directors disqualification: section 8A application
N501B	Notes for defendant: directors disqualification: section 8A application
N502	Acknowledgment of service: directors disqualification application
N503	Acknowledgment of service: directors disqualification: section 8A application
N504	Pre-trial checklist: directors disqualification]

[The following are not included in *Blackstone's Civil Practice*:
Practice Direction Relating to the Use of the Welsh Language in Cases in the Civil Courts in Wales
Practice Direction — Devolution Issues
Practice Direction — Application for a Warrant under the Competition Act 1998
Practice Direction — Civil Recovery Proceedings
Practice Direction — Competition Law — Claims Relating to the Application of Articles 81 and 82 of the EC Treaty and Chapters I and II of Part I of the Competition Act 1998]

Practice Direction — Proceedings under Enactments Relating to Equality

Scope and Interpretation

1.1 This practice direction applies to certain county court proceedings under the enactments defined in para. 1.2.

1.2 In this practice direction—
(1) 'the 2006 Act' means the Equality Act 2006;
(2) 'the 2010 Act' means the Equality Act 2010;
(3) 'the Commission' means the Commission for Equality and Human Rights.

1.3 For proceedings which relate to conduct before 1 October 2010, the Practice Direction—Proceedings under Enactments Relating to Discrimination* applies.

Commission to Be Given Notice of Claims

2. When a claim under s. 114 of the 2010 Act is commenced, the claimant must give notice of the commencement of the proceedings to the Commission and file a copy of that notice.

Assessors

3. Rule 35.15 has effect in relation to an assessor who is to be appointed in proceedings under s. 114 (7) of the 2010 Act.

Exclusion of Persons from Certain Proceedings

4.1 In a claim brought under s. 114 of the 2010 Act the court may, where it considers it expedient in the interests of national security—
(a) exclude from all or part of the proceedings—
(i) the claimant;
(ii) a representative of the claimant;
(iii) an assessor;
(b) permit a claimant or representative who has been excluded to make a statement to the court before the commencement of the proceedings, or the part of the proceedings, to which the exclusion relates;
(c) take steps to keep secret all or part of the reasons for its decision in the claim.

4.2 In this paragraph, a 'special advocate' means a person appointed under s. 117(5) of the 2010 Act.

4.3 In proceedings to which this paragraph refers, where the claimant or a representative of the claimant has been excluded from all or part of the proceedings—
(a) the court will inform the Attorney General of the proceedings; and
(b) the Attorney General may appoint a special advocate to represent the interests of a claimant in, or in any part of, proceedings to which an exclusion under para. 4.1 relates.

4.4 In exercise of its powers under para. 4.1(c), the court may order the special advocate not to communicate (directly or indirectly) with any person (including the excluded claimant)—
(a) on any matter discussed or referred to; or
(b) with regard to any material disclosed,
during or with reference to any part of the proceedings to which an exclusion under para. 4.1 relates.

4.5 Where the court makes an order referred to in para. 4.4 (or any similar order), the special advocate may apply for permission to seek instructions from, or otherwise to communicate with an excluded person and the court may make directions for that purpose.

[* Practice Direction — Proceedings under Enactments Relating to Discrimination may be viewed at <http://www.justice.gov.uk/courts/procedure-rules/civil>.]

Expenses of Commission

5.1 This paragraph applies where the Commission has, in respect of a claim, provided a claimant with assistance under s. 28 of the 2006 Act.

5.2 If the Commission claims a charge for expenses incurred by it in providing such assistance, it must give notice of the claim to—
(a) the court; and
(b) the claimant,
within 14 days of determination of the proceedings.

5.3 If notice is given to the court under para. 5.2—
(a) money paid into court for the benefit of the claimant that relates to costs and expenses must not be paid out unless this is permitted by an order of the court; and
(b) the court may order the expenses incurred by the Commission to be assessed and paid as if they were costs payable by claimant to own solicitor.

5.4 The court may either—
(a) make a summary assessment of the expenses; or
(b) order detailed assessment of the expenses by a costs officer.

[Practice Direction — Application for a Warrant under the Enterprise Act 2002 is not included in *Blackstone's Civil Practice*.]

Practice Direction — County Court Closures

Scope and Interpretation

1.1 This practice direction prescribes the procedure for the transfer of work from a county court prior to its closure.

1.2 In this practice direction—

'closing court' means a court which is subject to closure; and

'recipient court' means a court or courts to which work from the closing court is to be transferred in accordance with paras 2.1–2.5.

Transfer of Work

2.1 If a court is to be closed, work shall be transferred to the recipient court which has been identified in directions made by the Lord Chancellor, under the County Courts Act 1984, s. 2, having consulted the Lord Chief Justice and, where necessary, following consultation between the Lord Chief Justice and the Master of the Rolls, Chancellor of the High Court or the President of the Family Division.

2.2 The transfer of work shall, so far as possible and subject to any direction of a judge in any particular case, be in accordance with the annexed schedules, namely: 'Schedule 1 — Civil Proceedings (generally)', 'Schedule 2 — Family Proceedings' and 'Schedule 3 — Insolvency Proceedings' ('the schedules').

2.3 Any case falling outside the categories of work listed in the schedules will be referred to a judge in the closing court for determination of the appropriate recipient court.

2.4 If a case is transferred from the closing court to a recipient court by an order made under CPR, r. 3.3(4), or the Family Procedure Rules 2010 (SI 2010/2955), r. 4.3(4), the closing court shall notify all parties that they may apply to the recipient court, on notice and within seven days of the date of service of the transfer order, to vary the court to which the case should be transferred.

2.5 On the date that a court closes, all work which has not previously been transferred from that court shall be transferred to the recipient court or courts in accordance with para. 2.1.

ANNEX

Schedule 1 — Civil Proceedings (Generally)

Key

Court A	**Closing court**
Court B	**Recipient court. There may be more than one recipient court.**

	Timing (period prior to closure)	*Procedure*	*Action (subject to any direction of a judge in accordance with para. 2.2 of the practice direction)*
1.1	3 months	Request to issue a Part 7 claim at Court A	Transfer to and issue in the name of Court B
1.2	3 months	Cases transferred to Court A on receipt of a defence from a defendant	Case to remain at Court A for directions under CPR Part 26
1.3	3 months	Requirement to list a case/ application for date post-closure	Transfer proceedings to Court B for that court to list for hearing
2	2 months	Request to issue Part 8 claim at Court A (including claim for possession under Part 55)	Issue the case at Court A but transfer proceedings to Court B for that court to list for hearing

3.1	6 weeks	Request to issue or re-issue warrant of execution (including possession warrants not issued through PCOL) where Court A is the home court	Transfer warrant to Court B for execution
3.2	6 weeks	Receipt of a foreign warrant (electronic)	Before printing — update executing field to 'Court B' (where it will then be executed as a foreign warrant)
3.3	6 weeks	Receipt of foreign warrant (paper)	Forward to Court B for manual input and execution
3.4	6 weeks	Receipt of possession warrants from PCOL	Update executing field to 'Court B'. This will create a final return — warrants should then be entered as a foreign warrant at Court B
4	2 months (or when lists become full, whichever is the sooner)	Receipt of enforcement process that requires a hearing, including applications for an order to obtain information from judgment debtors	Transfer proceedings to Court B for that court to list for hearing
5	2 months	Consolidated orders	Transfer to Court B following payment of dividend

Schedule 2 — Family Proceedings

Key

Court A **Closing court**

Court B **Recipient court. There may be more than one recipient court.**

	Timing (months period prior to closure)	*Procedure*	*Action (subject to any direction of a judge in accordance with para. 2.2 of the practice direction)*
1.1	3 months	Request to issue new family proceedings	To be forwarded to and issued in the name of Court B
1.2	3 months	Request to issue applications within existing family proceedings	Transfer proceedings to Court B for that court to list for hearing

Schedule 3 — Insolvency Proceedings

Key

Court A **Closing court**

Court B **Recipient court. There may be more than one recipient court.**

	Timing (months prior to closure)	*Procedure*	*Action (subject to any direction of a judge in accordance with para. 2.2 of the practice direction)*
1.1	2 months (or when lists become full whichever is the sooner)	Insolvency — creditors petitions	Transfer proceedings to Court B for that court to list for hearing

1.2	2 months (or when lists become full, whichever is the sooner)	Insolvency — winding-up petitions (High Court)	Transfer proceedings to Court B for that court to list for hearing
1.3	2 months (or when lists become full whichever is the sooner)	Insolvency — statutory demands	Transfer proceedings to Court B for that court to list for hearing (should judicial practice be to list for hearing)
1.4	2 months (or when lists become full whichever is the sooner)	Insolvency — company voluntary arrangements	Transfer proceedings to Court B for that court to list for hearing (should judicial practice be to list for hearing)
1.5	2 months (or when lists become full whichever is the sooner)	Insolvency — transfers in from other county courts	Transfer to Court B
1.6	2 months (or when lists become full whichever is the sooner)	Insolvency — applications	Transfer proceedings to Court B for that court to list for hearing (should a hearing be necessary)

Practice Direction — Citation of Authorities (2012)

Preamble

1. This practice direction is issued in order to clarify the practice and procedure governing the citation of authorities and applies throughout the Senior Courts of England and Wales, including the Crown Court, in county courts and in magistrates' courts.

Repeal

2. Practice Direction (Court of Appeal: Citation of Authority) [1995] 1 WLR 1096 of 22 June 1995, Practice Statement (Court of Appeal: Authorities) [1996] 1 WLR 854 of 15 May 1996, para. 8 of Practice Statement (Supreme Court: Judgments) [1998] 1 WLR 825 of 22 April 1998, para. 3 of Practice Direction (Judgments: Form and Citation) [2001] 1 WLR 194 of 11 January 2001, and, in so far as they remain in force, paras 10.1 and 10.2 of Practice Direction (Court of Appeal (Civil Division)) [1999] 1 WLR 1027 of 19 April 1999 are hereby revoked.

Variation

3. [*Amends Practice Direction (Criminal Proceedings: Consolidation) [2002] 1 WLR 2870 of 8 July 2002.*]
4. [*Amended PD 52.*]

Citation of Authority

5. When authority is cited, whether in written or oral submissions, the following practice should be followed.
6. Where a judgment is reported in the Official Law Reports (AC, QB, Ch, Fam) published by the Incorporated Council of Law Reporting for England and Wales, that report must be cited. These are the most authoritative reports; they contain a summary of the argument. Other series of reports and official transcripts of judgment may only be used when a case is not reported in the Official Law Reports.
7. If a judgment is not (or not yet) reported in the Official Law Reports but it is reported in the Weekly Law Reports (WLR) or the All England Law Reports (All ER) that report should be cited. If the case is reported in both the WLR and the All ER either report may properly be cited.
8. If a judgment is not reported in the Official Law Reports, the WLR, or the All ER, but it is reported in any of the authoritative specialist series of reports which contain a headnote and are made by individuals holding a Senior Courts qualification (for the purposes of the Courts and Legal Services Act 1990, s. 115), the specialist report should be cited.
9. Where a judgment is not reported in any of the reports referred to in paras 6 to 8 above, but is reported in other reports, they may be cited.
10. Where a judgment has not been reported, reference may be made to the official transcript if that is available, not the handed-down text of the judgment, as this may have been subject to late revision after the text was handed down. Official transcripts may be obtained from, for instance, BAILLI <http://www.bailii.org/>. An unreported case should not usually be cited unless it contains a relevant statement of legal principle not found in reported authority.
11. Occasions arise when one report is fuller than another, or when there are discrepancies between reports. On such occasions, the practice outlined above need not be followed, but the court should be given a brief explanation why this course is being taken, and the alternative references should be given.
12. If a judgment under appeal has been reported before the hearing but after skeleton arguments have been filed with the court, and counsel wish to argue from the published report rather than from the official transcript, the court should be provided with photocopies of the report for the use of the court.
13. Judgments reported in any series of reports, including those of the Incorporated Council of Law Reporting, should be provided either by way of a photocopy of the published report or by way of a copy of a reproduction of the judgment in electronic form that has been authorised by the

CPR Glossary, Schs, Other PDs

publisher of the relevant series, but in any event (1) the report must be presented to the court in an easily legible form (a 12-point font is preferred but a 10 or 11-point font is acceptable) and (2) the advocate presenting the report is satisfied that it has not been reproduced in a garbled form from the data source. In any case of doubt the court will rely on the printed text of the report (unless the editor of the report has certified that an electronic version is more accurate because it corrects an error contained in an earlier printed text of the report).

14. This direction is made by the Lord Chief Justice with the agreement of the Master of the Rolls and the President of the Family Division. It is issued in accordance with the procedure laid down in the Constitutional Reform Act 2005, sch. 2, part 1.

The Right Honourable The Lord Judge, the Lord Chief Justice of England and Wales

Queen's Bench Masters' Practice Direction (11) — Claims, Judgments and Enforcement of Judgments in Foreign Currency

[*This practice direction is still in force, to the extent that it has not been superseded by the CPR and practice directions (see 63.18). The passages in square brackets have been reworded editorially to reflect changes in terminology and procedure made by the CPR.*]

1 Subject to any order or direction which the court may make or give in any particular case, the following practice shall be followed in relation to the making of claims and the enforcement of judgments expressed in a foreign currency.

2 [*Deals with the statement of value to be endorsed on the claim form. Superseded by PD 16, para. 9.1.*]

Pleading Claims in Foreign Currency

3 Where the [claimant] seeks to obtain a judgment expressed in a foreign currency, he should expressly state in his [claim form], whether [it includes particulars] of [claim] or not, that he makes his claim for payment in a specified foreign currency and unless the facts themselves clearly show this, he should plead the facts relied on to support such a claim in his [particulars] of claim. (See Federal Commerce and Navigation Co. Ltd v Tradax Export SA [1977] QB 324.)

Default Judgment for Debts or [Claims for Specified Amounts] in Foreign Currency

4 [*Wording of the judgment is now to be found in PD 40B, para. 10.*]

[Summary] Judgment

5 [*Wording of the judgment is now to be found in PD 40B, para. 10.*] The amount of the fixed costs will be calculated on the sterling equivalent of the foreign currency claimed as [stated in the claim form], unless the court orders otherwise.

6 [*Revoked 26 June 1991.*]

Payment of Foreign Currency into Court in Satisfaction

7 [*Superseded by PD 36, paras 9.1 to 9.4, as in force until 5 April 2007.*]

Orders for Conditional Payment of Foreign Currency into Court

8 Where the court makes a conditional order for payment of money into court, e.g., when [making a conditional order] on an application for summary judgment under [Part 24], or when setting aside a default judgment or granting an adjournment of [a case management hearing] or the trial or hearing of [a claim] or making any other order conditional upon payment of money into court, the court may order that such monies be paid into court in a foreign currency, and the court may further order that such money should be placed in a foreign currency account and if practicable should be placed in such an account which is an interest-bearing account.

Entry of Judgment in Foreign Currency

9 [*Wording of the judgment is now to be found in PD 40B, para. 10.*]

Interest on Judgment Debt in Foreign Currency

10 A judgment entered in foreign currency will carry the statutory rate of interest on the amount of the judgment in foreign currency and such interest will be added to the amount of the judgment itself for the purposes of enforcement of the judgment.

Enforcement of Judgment Debt in Foreign Currency by Writ of Fi. Fa.

11 (a) Where the [judgment creditor] desires to proceed to enforce a judgment expressed in foreign currency by the issue of a writ of fieri facias, the praecipe for the issue of the writ must first be endorsed and signed by or on behalf of the solicitor for the [judgment creditor] or by the [judgment creditor] if he is acting in person with the following certificate:

CPR Glossary, Schs, Other PDs

Sterling equivalent of judgment
I/We certify that the rate current in London for the purpose of (*state the unit of foreign currency in which the judgment is expressed*) at the close of business on the day of 201 (*being the date nearest to or most nearly preceding the date of the issue of the writ of fi. fa.*) was to the £ sterling and at this rate the sum of (*state the amount of the judgment debt in foreign currency*) amounts to £ .
Dated the day of 201.
Signed
(Solicitor for the [judgment debtor]).

(b) The amount so certified will then be entered in the writ of fi. fa. by adapting [form No. 53, writ of fieri facias] to meet the circumstances of the case but substituting the following recital:

Whereas in the above-named [claim] it was the day of 201 adjudged (or ordered) that the defendant CD do pay the [claimant] AB (*state the sum of the foreign currency for which judgment was entered*) or the sterling equivalent at the time of payment, and whereas the sterling equivalent at the date of issue of this writ is £ as appears by the certificate endorsed and signed by or on behalf of the [judgment creditor] on the praecipe for the issue of this writ.

Enforcement of Judgment Debt in Foreign Currency by [Third Party Debt] Proceedings

12 (a) Where the [judgment creditor] desires to proceed to enforce a judgment in foreign currency by [third party debt] proceedings, the [written evidence] made in support of an application for an order under [CPR, r. 72.2] must contain words to the following effect:

The rate current in London for the purpose of (*state the amount of the judgment in foreign currency*) at the close of business on the day of 201 (*being the date nearest to or most nearly preceding the [signing of the written evidence]*) was to the £ sterling, and at this rate the sum of (*state the amount of the judgment debt in foreign currency*) amounts to £ sterling. I have ascertained the above information (*state the source of the information*) and [believe] the same to be true.

The master will then make an [interim order] for the sterling equivalent of the judgment debt as so verified.

(b) Where the [judgment creditor] desires to attach a debt due or accruing due to the defendant within the jurisdiction in the unit of foreign currency in which the judgment debt is itself expressed, the [written evidence] made in support of an application for an order under [r. 72.2] must state all the relevant facts relied on and in such event the master may make the order to attach such debt due or accruing due in that foreign currency.

[Third Party Debt] Proceedings Where the Judgment Debt Is in Sterling and the Debt to Be [Attached Is] in Foreign Currency

13 For the procedure to be followed see Choice Investments Ltd v Jeromnimon [1981] QB 149.

Enforcement of Judgment Debt in Foreign Currency by Other Modes of Enforcement

14 Where the [judgment creditor] desires to proceed to enforce a judgment expressed in a foreign currency by other means of enforcement, e.g. by obtaining an order imposing a charge on land or interest in land under [CPR, r. 73.2], or by obtaining an order imposing a charge on securities under [CPR, r. 73.6], or some other similar order or by obtaining an order for the appointment of a receiver by way of equitable execution, under [CPR, r. 69.2], the [written evidence] made in respect of any such application shall contain words similar to those set out in para. 12(a) above. The master will then make an order for the sterling equivalent of the judgment expressed in foreign currency as so verified by such [written evidence].

15 These directions are issued with the concurrence of the Chief Chancery Master acting on the authority of the Vice-Chancellor so far as they apply to the practice in the Chancery Division, and of the Senior District Judge of the Family Division so far as they apply to the practice in that Division.

16 [*Superseded by the Insolvency Rules 1986 (SI 1986/1925), r. 4.91.*]

Practice Guidance — McKenzie Friends (Civil and Family Courts)

1 This Guidance applies to civil and family proceedings in the Court of Appeal (Civil Division), the High Court of Justice, the county courts and the Family Proceedings Court in the magistrates' courts.[1] It is issued as guidance (not as a practice direction) by the Master of the Rolls, as Head of Civil Justice, and the President of the Family Division, as Head of Family Justice. It is intended to remind courts and litigants of the principles set out in the authorities and supersedes the guidance contained in Practice Note (Family Courts: McKenzie Friends) (No. 2) [2008] 1 WLR 2757, which is now withdrawn.[2] It is issued in light of the increase in litigants in person (litigants) in all levels of the civil and family courts.

The Right to Reasonable Assistance

2 Litigants have the right to have reasonable assistance from a layperson, sometimes called a McKenzie Friend (MF). Litigants assisted by MFs remain litigants in person. MFs have no independent right to provide assistance. They have no right to act as advocates or to carry out the conduct of litigation.

What McKenzie Friends May Do

3 MFs may:
(i) provide moral support for litigants;
(ii) take notes;
(iii) help with case papers;
(iv) quietly give advice on any aspect of the conduct of the case.

What McKenzie Friends May Not Do

4 MFs may not:
(i) act as the litigants' agent in relation to the proceedings;
(ii) manage litigants' cases outside court, for example by signing court documents; or
(iii) address the court, make oral submissions or examine witnesses.

Exercising the Right to Reasonable Assistance

5 While litigants ordinarily have a right to receive reasonable assistance from MFs the court retains the power to refuse to permit such assistance. The court may do so where it is satisfied that, in that case, the interests of justice and fairness do not require the litigant to receive such assistance.

6 A litigant who wishes to exercise this right should inform the judge as soon as possible indicating who the MF will be. The proposed MF should produce a short curriculum vitae or other statement setting out relevant experience, confirming that he or she has no interest in the case and understands the MF's role and the duty of confidentiality.

7 If the court considers that there might be grounds for circumscribing the right to receive such assistance, or a party objects to the presence of, or assistance given by a MF, it is not for the

[1] References to the judge or court should be read where proceedings are taking place under the Family Proceedings Courts (Matrimonial Proceedings etc) Rules 1991, as a reference to a justices' clerk or assistant justices' clerk who is specifically authorised by a justices' clerk to exercise the functions of the court at the relevant hearing. Where they are taking place under the Family Proceedings Courts (Children Act 1989) Rules 1991 they should be read consistently with the provisions of those Rules, specifically rule 16A(5A).

[2] *R v Leicester City Justices, ex parte Barrow* [1991] 2 QB 260; *Chauhan v Chauhan* [1997] FCR 206, *R v Bow County Court, ex parte Pelling* [1999] 1 WLR 1807; *Attorney-General v Purvis* [2003] EWHC 3190 (Admin), BAILII; *Clarkson v Gilbert* [2000] 2 FLR 839; *United Building and Plumbing Contractors v Kajla* [2002] EWCA Civ 628, [2002] CP Rep 53; *Re O (Children) (Hearing in Private: Assistance)* [2005] EWCA Civ 759, [2006] Fam 1; *Westland Helicopters Ltd v Sheikh Salah Al-Hejailan (No 2)* [2004] EWHC 1688 (Comm), [2004] 2 Lloyd's Rep 535; *Agassi v Robinson (No. 2)* [2005] EWCA Civ 1507, [2006] 1 WLR 2126; *Re N (A Child) (McKenzie Friend: Rights of Audience)* [2008] EWHC 2042 (Fam), [2008] 1 WLR 2743.

litigant to justify the exercise of the right. It is for the court or the objecting party to provide sufficient reasons why the litigant should not receive such assistance.

8 When considering whether to circumscribe the right to assistance or refuse a MF permission to attend the right to a fair trial is engaged. The matter should be considered carefully. The litigant should be given a reasonable opportunity to argue the point. The proposed MF should not be excluded from that hearing and should normally be allowed to help the litigant.

9 Where proceedings are in closed court, i.e. the hearing is in chambers, is in private, or the proceedings relate to a child, the litigant is required to justify the MF's presence in court. The presumption in favour of permitting a MF to attend such hearings, and thereby enable litigants to exercise the right to assistance, is a strong one.

10 The court may refuse to allow a litigant to exercise the right to receive assistance at the start of a hearing. The court can also circumscribe the right during the course of a hearing. It may be refused at the start of a hearing or later circumscribed where the court forms the view that a MF may give, has given, or is giving, assistance which impedes the efficient administration of justice. However, the court should also consider whether a firm and unequivocal warning to the litigant and/or MF might suffice in the first instance.

11 A decision by the court not to curtail assistance from a MF should be regarded as final, save on the ground of subsequent misconduct by the MF or on the ground that the MF's continuing presence will impede the efficient administration of justice. In such event the court should give a short judgment setting out the reasons why it has curtailed the right to assistance. Litigants may appeal such decisions. MFs have no standing to do so.

12 The following factors should not be taken to justify the court refusing to permit a litigant receiving such assistance:

(i) the case or application is simple or straightforward, or is, for instance, a directions or case management hearing;
(ii) the litigant appears capable of conducting the case without assistance;
(iii) the litigant is unrepresented through choice;
(iv) the other party is not represented;
(v) the proposed MF belongs to an organisation that promotes a particular cause;
(vi) the proceedings are confidential and the court papers contain sensitive information relating to a family's affairs.

13 A litigant may be denied the assistance of a MF because its provision might undermine or has undermined the efficient administration of justice. Examples of circumstances where this might arise are:

(i) the assistance is being provided for an improper purpose;
(ii) the assistance is unreasonable in nature or degree;
(iii) the MF is subject to a civil proceedings order or a civil restraint order;
(iv) the MF is using the litigant as a puppet;
(v) the MF is directly or indirectly conducting the litigation;
(vi) the court is not satisfied that the MF fully understands the duty of confidentiality.

14 Where a litigant is receiving assistance from a MF in care proceedings, the court should consider the MF's attendance at any advocates' meetings directed by the court, and, with regard to cases commenced after 1 April 2008, consider directions in accordance with para. 13.2 of the Practice Direction (Public Law Proceedings: Case Management) [2008] 1 WLR 1040.

15 Litigants are permitted to communicate any information, including filed evidence, relating to the proceedings to MFs for the purpose of obtaining advice or assistance in relation to the proceedings.

16 Legal representatives should ensure that documents are served on litigants in good time to enable them to seek assistance regarding their content from MFs in advance of any hearing or advocates' meeting.

17 The High Court can, under its inherent jurisdiction, impose a civil restraint order on MFs who repeatedly act in ways that undermine the efficient administration of justice.

Rights of Audience and Rights to Conduct Litigation

18 MFs do not have a right of audience or a right to conduct litigation. It is a criminal offence to exercise rights of audience or to conduct litigation unless properly qualified and authorised to do

so by an appropriate regulatory body or, in the case of an otherwise unqualified or unauthorised individual (i.e., a lay individual including a MF), the court grants such rights on a case-by-case basis.[3]

19 Courts should be slow to grant any application from a litigant for a right of audience or a right to conduct litigation to any layperson, including a MF. This is because a person exercising such rights must ordinarily be properly trained, be under professional discipline (including an obligation to insure against liability for negligence) and be subject to an overriding duty to the court. These requirements are necessary for the protection of all parties to litigation and are essential to the proper administration of justice.

20 Any application for a right of audience or a right to conduct litigation to be granted to any layperson should therefore be considered very carefully. The court should only be prepared to grant such rights where there is good reason to do so taking into account all the circumstances of the case, which are likely to vary greatly. Such grants should not be extended to laypersons automatically or without due consideration. They should not be granted for mere convenience.

21 Examples of the type of special circumstances which have been held to justify the grant of a right of audience to a lay person, including a MF, are:

(i) that person is a close relative of the litigant;

(ii) health problems preclude the litigant from addressing the court, or conducting litigation, and the litigant cannot afford to pay for a qualified legal representative;

(iii) the litigant is relatively inarticulate and prompting by that person may unnecessarily prolong the proceedings.

22 It is for the litigant to persuade the court that the circumstances of the case are such that it is in the interests of justice for the court to grant a lay person a right of audience or a right to conduct litigation.

23 The grant of a right of audience or a right to conduct litigation to laypersons who hold themselves out as professional advocates or professional MFs or who seek to exercise such rights on a regular basis, whether for reward or not, will however only be granted in exceptional circumstances. To do otherwise would tend to subvert the will of Parliament.

24 If a litigant wants a layperson to be granted a right of audience, an application must be made at the start of the hearing. If a right to conduct litigation is sought such an application must be made at the earliest possible time and must be made, in any event, before the layperson does anything which amounts to the conduct of litigation. It is for litigants to persuade the court, on a case-by-case basis, that the grant of such rights is justified.

25 Rights of audience and the right to conduct litigation are separate rights. The grant of one right to a layperson does not mean that a grant of the other right has been made. If both rights are sought their grant must be applied for individually and justified separately.

26 Having granted either a right of audience or a right to conduct litigation, the court has the power to remove either right. The grant of such rights in one set of proceedings cannot be relied on as a precedent supporting their grant in future proceedings.

Remuneration

27 Litigants can enter into lawful agreements to pay fees to MFs for the provision of reasonable assistance in court or out of court by, for instance, carrying out clerical or mechanical activities, such as photocopying documents, preparing bundles, delivering documents to opposing parties or the court, or the provision of legal advice in connection with court proceedings. Such fees cannot be lawfully recovered from the opposing party.

28 Fees said to be incurred by MFs for carrying out the conduct of litigation, where the court has not granted such a right, cannot lawfully be recovered from either the litigant for whom they carry out such work or the opposing party.

29 Fees said to be incurred by MFs for carrying out the conduct of litigation after the court has granted such a right are in principle recoverable from the litigant for whom the work is carried out. Such fees cannot be lawfully recovered from the opposing party.

30 Fees said to be incurred by MFs for exercising a right of audience following the grant of such a right by the court are in principle recoverable from the litigant on whose behalf the right is

[3] Legal Services Act 2007, ss. 12 to 19 and sch. 3.

exercised. Such fees are also recoverable, in principle, from the opposing party as a recoverable disbursement: **CPR, r. 48.6(2) and (3)(ii).**

Personal Support Unit and Citizens Advice Bureau

31 Litigants should also be aware of the services provided by local Personal Support Units and Citizens Advice Bureaux. The PSU at the Royal Courts of Justice in London can be contacted on (020) 7947 7701, by email at cbps@bello.co.uk or at the enquiry desk. The CAB at the Royal Courts of Justice in London can be contacted on (020) 7947 6564 or at the enquiry desk.

Lord Neuberger of Abbotsbury, Master of the Rolls
Sir Nicholas Wall, President of the Family Division
12 July 2010

Practice Guidance: The Use of Live Text-Based Forms of Communication (including Twitter) from Court for the Purposes of Fair and Accurate Reporting

1 This practice guidance (the Guidance) applies to court proceedings which are open to the public and to those parts of the proceedings which are not subject to reporting restrictions. It is issued (as guidance and not a practice direction) following a consultation relating to the use of live, text-based communications. Those consulted included the Judiciary, the Secretary of State for Justice, the Attorney General, the Director of Public Prosecutions, the Bar Council, the Law Society, the Press Complaints Commission, and the Society of Editors in addition to interested members of the public via the Judiciary website.

2 The Guidance clarifies the use which may be made of live text-based communications, such as mobile email, social media (including Twitter) and internet-enabled laptops in and from courts throughout England and Wales. For the purposes of this Guidance these means of communication are referred to, compendiously, as live, text-based communications. The Guidance is consistent with the legislative structure which:

(a) prohibits:

  (i) the taking of photographs in court (Criminal Justice Act 1925, s. 41); and

  (ii) the use of sound-recording equipment in court unless the leave of the judge has first been obtained (Contempt of Court Act 1981, s. 9); and

(b) requires compliance with the strict prohibition rules created by the Contempt of Court Act 1981, ss. 1, 2 and 4, in relation to the reporting of court proceedings.

3 The Guidance replaces the Interim Practice Guidance of 20 December 2010 and has immediate effect.

General Principles

4 The judge has an overriding responsibility to ensure that proceedings are conducted consistently with the proper administration of justice, and to avoid any improper interference with its pro-cesses.

5 A fundamental aspect of the proper administration of justice is the principle of open justice. Fair and accurate reporting of court proceedings forms part of that principle. The principle is however subject to well-known statutory and discretionary exceptions. Two such exceptions are the prohibitions, set out in para. 2, on photography in court and on making sound recordings of court proceedings.

6 The statutory prohibition on photography in court, by any means, is absolute. There is no judicial discretion to suspend or dispense with it. Any equipment which has photographic capability must not have that function activated.

7 Sound recordings are also prohibited unless, in the exercise of its discretion, the court permits such equipment to be used. In criminal proceedings, some of the factors relevant to the exercise of that discretion are contained in the Consolidated Criminal Practice Direction, para. I.2.2. The same factors are likely to be relevant when consideration is being given to the exercise of this discretion in civil or family proceedings.

Use of Live, Text-based Communications: General Considerations

8 The normal, indeed almost invariable, rule has been that mobile phones must be turned off in court. There is however no statutory prohibition on the use of live text-based communications in open court.

9 Where a member of the public, who is in court, wishes to use live text-based communications during court proceedings an application for permission to activate and use, in silent mode, a mobile phone, small laptop or similar piece of equipment, solely in order to make live, text-based communications of the proceedings will need to be made. The application may be made formally or informally (for instance by communicating a request to the judge through court staff).

10 It is presumed that a representative of the media or a legal commentator using live, text-based communications from court does not pose a danger of interference to the proper administration of justice in the individual case. This is because the most obvious purpose of permitting the use of live, text-based communications would be to enable the media to produce fair and accurate reports of the proceedings. As such, a representative of the media or a legal commentator who wishes to use live, text-based communications from court may do so without making an application to the court.

11 When considering, either generally on its own motion, or following a formal application or informal request by a member of the public, whether to permit live, text-based communications, and if so by whom, the paramount question for the judge will be whether the application may interfere with the proper administration of justice.

12 In considering the question of permission under para. 11, the factors identified in the Consolidated Criminal Practice Direction, para. I.2.2, are likely to be relevant.

13 Without being exhaustive, the danger to the administration of justice is likely to be at its most acute in the context of criminal trials e.g., where witnesses who are out of court may be informed of what has already happened in court and so coached or briefed before they then give evidence, or where information posted on, for instance, Twitter about inadmissible evidence may influence members of a jury. However, the danger is not confined to criminal proceedings; in civil and sometimes family proceedings, simultaneous reporting from the courtroom may create pressure on witnesses, distracting or worrying them.

14 It may be necessary for the judge to limit live, text-based communications to representatives of the media for journalistic purposes but to disallow its use by the wider public in court. That may arise if it is necessary, for example, to limit the number of mobile electronic devices in use at any given time because of the potential for electronic interference with the court's own sound recording equipment, or because the widespread use of such devices in court may cause a distraction in the proceedings.

15 Subject to these considerations, the use of an unobtrusive, hand-held, silent piece of modern equipment for the purposes of simultaneous reporting of proceedings to the outside world as they unfold in court is generally unlikely to interfere with the proper administration of justice.

16 Permission to use live, text-based communications from court may be withdrawn by the court at any time.

Lord Judge, the Lord Chief Justice of England and Wales

14 December 2011

Appendix 2 Pre-action Protocols

Each protocol begins with a list of its contents

Pre-action Protocols

Practice Direction — Pre-action Conduct

I INTRODUCTION

Aims

1.1 The aims of this practice direction are to—
  (1) enable parties to settle the issue between them without the need to start proceedings (that is, a court claim); and
  (2) support the efficient management by the court and the parties of proceedings that cannot be avoided.

1.2 These aims are to be achieved by encouraging the parties to—
  (1) exchange information about the issue, and
  (2) consider using a form of Alternative Dispute Resolution ('ADR').

Scope

2.1 This practice direction describes the conduct the court will normally expect of the prospective parties prior to the start of proceedings.

2.2 There are some types of application where the principles in this practice direction clearly cannot or should not apply. These include, but are not limited to, for example—
  (1) applications for an order where the parties have agreed between them the terms of the court order to be sought ('consent orders');
  (2) applications for an order where there is no other party for the applicant to engage with;
  (3) most applications for directions by a trustee or other fiduciary;
  (4) applications where telling the other potential party in advance would defeat the purpose of the application (for example, an application for an order to freeze assets).

2.3 Section II deals with the approach of the court in exercising its powers in relation to pre-action conduct. Subject to para. 2.2, it applies in relation to all types of proceedings including those governed by the pre-action protocols that have been approved by the Head of Civil Justice and which are listed in para. 5.2 of this practice direction.

2.4 Section III deals with principles governing the conduct of the parties in cases which are not subject to a pre-action protocol.

2.5 Section III of this practice direction is supplemented by two annexes aimed at different types of claimant.
  (1) Annex A sets out detailed guidance on a pre-action procedure that is likely to satisfy the court in most circumstances where no pre-action protocol or other formal pre-action procedure applies. It is intended as a guide for parties, particularly those without legal representation, in straightforward claims that are likely to be disputed. It is not intended to apply to debt claims where it is not disputed that the money is owed and where the claimant follows a statutory or other formal pre-action procedure.
  (2) Annex B sets out some specific requirements that apply where the claimant is a business and the defendant is an individual. The requirements may be complied with at any time between the claimant first intimating the possibility of court proceedings and the claimant's letter before claim.

2.6 Section IV contains requirements that apply to all cases including those subject to the pre-action protocols (unless a relevant pre-action protocol contains a different provision). It is supplemented by Annex C, which sets out guidance on instructing experts.

Definitions

3.1 In this practice direction together with the Annexes—
  (1) 'proceedings' means any proceedings started under Part 7 or Part 8 of the Civil Procedure Rules 1998 ('CPR');
  (2) 'claimant' and 'defendant' refer to the respective parties to potential proceedings;

(3) 'ADR' means alternative dispute resolution, and is the collective description of methods of resolving disputes otherwise than through the normal trial process; (see paragraph 8.2 for further information); and

(4) 'compliance' means acting in accordance with, as applicable, the principles set out in Section III of this practice direction, the requirements in Section IV and a relevant pre-action protocol. The words 'comply' and 'complied' should be construed accordingly.

II THE APPROACH OF THE COURTS

Compliance

4.1 The CPR enable the court to take into account the extent of the parties' compliance with this practice direction or a relevant pre-action protocol (see para. 5.2) when giving directions for the management of claims (see CPR, r. 3.1(4) and (5)) and when making orders about who should pay costs (see CPR, r. 44.3(5)(a)).

4.2 The court will expect the parties to have complied with this practice direction or any relevant pre-action protocol. The court may ask the parties to explain what steps were taken to comply prior to the start of the claim. Where there has been a failure of compliance by a party the court may ask that party to provide an explanation.

Assessment of compliance

4.3 When considering compliance the court will—

(1) be concerned about whether the parties have complied in substance with the relevant principles and requirements and is not likely to be concerned with minor or technical shortcomings;

(2) consider the proportionality of the steps taken compared to the size and importance of the matter;

(3) take account of the urgency of the matter. Where a matter is urgent (for example, an application for an injunction) the court will expect the parties to comply only to the extent that it is reasonable to do so. (paragraph 9.5 and 9.6 of this practice direction concern urgency caused by limitation periods.)

Examples of non-compliance

4.4 The court may decide that there has been a failure of compliance by a party because, for example, that party has—

(1) not provided sufficient information to enable the other party to understand the issues;

(2) not acted within a time limit set out in a relevant pre-action protocol, or, where no specific time limit applies, within a reasonable period;

(3) unreasonably refused to consider ADR (para. 8 in Section III of this practice direction and the pre-action protocols all contain similar provisions about ADR); or

(4) without good reason, not disclosed documents requested to be disclosed.

Sanctions for non-compliance

4.5 The court will look at the overall effect of non-compliance on the other party when deciding whether to impose sanctions.

4.6 If, in the opinion of the court, there has been non-compliance, the sanctions which the court may impose include—

(1) staying (that is suspending) the proceedings until steps which ought to have been taken have been taken;

(2) an order that the party at fault pays the costs, or part of the costs, of the other party or parties (this may include an order under r. 27.14(2)(g) in cases allocated to the small claims track);

(3) an order that the party at fault pays those costs on an indemnity basis (r. 44.4(3) sets out the definition of the assessment of costs on an indemnity basis);

(4) if the party at fault is the claimant in whose favour an order for the payment of a sum of money is subsequently made, an order that the claimant is deprived of interest on all or part of that sum, and/or that interest is awarded at a lower rate than would otherwise have been awarded;

(5) if the party at fault is a defendant, and an order for the payment of a sum of money is subsequently made in favour of the claimant, an order that the defendant pay interest on all or part of that sum at a higher rate, not exceeding 10 per cent above base rate, than would otherwise have been awarded.

COMMENCEMENT OF PRE-ACTION PROTOCOLS

5.1 When considering compliance, the court will take account of a relevant pre-action protocol if the proceedings were started after the relevant pre-action protocol came into force.

5.2 The following table sets out the pre-action protocols currently in force and the dates that they came into force—

Pre-action protocol	Came into force
Personal Injury	26 April 1999
Clinical Disputes	26 April 1999
Construction and Engineering	2 October 2000
Defamation	2 October 2000
Professional Negligence	16 July 2001
Judicial Review	4 March 2002
Disease and Illness	8 December 2003
Housing Disrepair	8 December 2003
Possession Claims Based on Rent Arrears	2 October 2006
Possession Claims Based on Mortgage Arrears etc.	19 November 2008
Dilapidations (commercial property)	1 January 2012

III THE PRINCIPLES GOVERNING THE CONDUCT OF THE PARTIES IN CASES NOT SUBJECT TO A PRE-ACTION PROTOCOL

Overview of Principles

6.1 The principles that should govern the conduct of the parties are that, unless the circumstances make it inappropriate, before starting proceedings the parties should—

(1) exchange sufficient information about the matter to allow them to understand each other's position and make informed decisions about settlement and how to proceed;

(2) make appropriate attempts to resolve the matter without starting proceedings, and in particular consider the use of an appropriate form of ADR in order to do so.

6.2 The parties should act in a reasonable and proportionate manner in all dealings with one another. In particular, the costs incurred in complying should be proportionate to the complexity of the matter and any money at stake. The parties must not use this practice direction as a tactical device to secure an unfair advantage for one party or to generate unnecessary costs.

Exchanging Information before Starting Proceedings

7.1 Before starting proceedings—

(1) the claimant should set out the details of the matter in writing by sending a letter before claim to the defendant. This letter before claim is not the start of proceedings; and

(2) the defendant should give a full written response within a reasonable period, preceded, if appropriate, by a written acknowledgment of the letter before claim.

7.2 A 'reasonable period of time' will vary depending on the matter. As a general guide—

(1) the defendant should send a letter of acknowledgment within 14 days of receipt of the letter before claim (if a full response has not been sent within that period);

(2) where the matter is straightforward, for example an undisputed debt, then a full response should normally be provided within 14 days;

(3) where a matter requires the involvement of an insurer or other third party or where there are issues about evidence, then a full response should normally be provided within 30 days;

(4) where the matter is particularly complex, for example requiring specialist advice, then a period of longer than 30 days may be appropriate;

(5) a period of longer than 90 days in which to provide a full response will only be considered reasonable in exceptional circumstances.

7.3 Annex A sets out detailed guidance on a pre-action procedure that is likely to satisfy the court in most circumstances where no pre-action protocol applies and where the claimant does not follow any statutory or other formal pre-action procedure.

7.4 Annex B sets out the specific information that should be provided in a debt claim by a claimant who is a business against a defendant who is an individual.

ALTERNATIVE DISPUTE RESOLUTION

8.1 Starting proceedings should usually be a step of last resort, and proceedings should not normally be started when a settlement is still actively being explored. Although ADR is not compulsory, the parties should consider whether some form of ADR procedure might enable them to settle the matter without starting proceedings. The court may require evidence that the parties considered some form of ADR (see para. 4.4(3)).

8.2 It is not practicable in this practice direction to address in detail how the parties might decide to resolve a matter. However, some of the options for resolving a matter without starting proceedings are—

(1) discussion and negotiation;
(2) mediation (a form of negotiation with the help of an independent person or body);
(3) early neutral evaluation (where an independent person or body, for example a lawyer or an expert in the subject, gives an opinion on the merits of a dispute); or
(4) arbitration (where an independent person or body makes a binding decision), many types of business are members of arbitration schemes for resolving disputes with consumers.

8.3 The Legal Services Commission has published a booklet on *Alternatives to Court*, CLS Direct Information Leaflet 23 (www.clsdirect.org.uk) which lists a number of organisations that provide alternative dispute resolution services. The National Mediation Helpline on 0845 603 0809 or at www.nationalmediationhelpline.com can provide information about mediation.

8.4 The parties should continue to consider the possibility of reaching a settlement at all times. This still applies after proceedings have been started, up to and during any trial or final hearing.

IV REQUIREMENTS THAT APPLY IN ALL CASES

Specific Provisions

9.1 The following requirements (including Annex C) apply in all cases except where a relevant pre-action protocol contains its own provisions about the topic.

Disclosure

9.2 Documents provided by one party to another in the course of complying with this practice direction or any relevant pre-action protocol must not be used for any purpose other than resolving the matter, unless the disclosing party agrees in writing.

Information about funding arrangements

[*Version of para. 9.3 applying to a funding arrangement entered into before 1 October 2009*]

9.3 Where a party enters into a funding arrangement within the meaning of r. 43.2(1)(k), that party should inform the other parties about this arrangement as soon as possible.

[*Version of para. 9.3 applying to a funding arrangement entered into on or after 1 October 2009*]

9.3 Where a party enters into a funding arrangement within the meaning of r. 43.2(1)(k), that party must inform the other parties about this arrangement as soon as possible and in any event either within seven days of entering into the funding arrangement concerned or, where a claimant enters into a funding arrangement before sending a letter before claim, in the letter before claim.

(CPR, r. 44.3B(1)(c), provides that a party may not recover certain additional costs where information about a funding arrangement was not provided.)

Experts

9.4 Where the evidence of an expert is necessary the parties should consider how best to minimise expense. Guidance on instructing experts can be found in Annex C.

Limitation periods

9.5 There are statutory time limits for starting proceedings ('the limitation period'). If a claimant starts a claim after the limitation period applicable to that type of claim has expired the defendant will be entitled to use that as a defence to the claim.

9.6 In certain instances compliance may not be possible before the expiry of the limitation period. If, for any reason, proceedings are started before the parties have complied, they should seek to agree to apply to the court for an order to stay (i.e. suspend) the proceedings while the parties take steps to comply.

Notifying the court

9.7 Where proceedings are started the claimant should state in the claim form or the particulars of claim whether they have complied with Sections III and IV of this practice direction or any relevant protocol.

Transitional provision

9.8 The amendments to para. 9.3 do not apply to a funding arrangement entered into before 1 October 2009 and para. 9.3 in force immediately before that date will continue to apply to that funding arrangement as if para. 9.3 had not been amended.

ANNEX A

Guidance on pre-action procedure where no pre-action protocol or other formal pre-action procedure applies.

General

1.1 This Annex sets out detailed guidance on a pre-action procedure that is likely to satisfy the court in most circumstances where no pre-action protocol or other formal pre-action procedure applies. It is intended as a guide for parties, particularly those without legal representation, in straightforward claims that are likely to be disputed. It is not intended to apply to debt claims where it is not disputed that the money is owed and where the claimant follows a statutory or other formal pre-action procedure.

Claimant's Letter before Claim

2.1 The claimant's letter should give concise details about the matter. This should enable the defendant to understand and investigate the issues without needing to request further information. The letter should include—

(1) the claimant's full name and address;
(2) the basis on which the claim is made (i.e. why the claimant says the defendant is liable);
(3) a clear summary of the facts on which the claim is based;
(4) what the claimant wants from the defendant;
(5) if financial loss is claimed, an explanation of how the amount has been calculated; and
(6) details of any funding arrangement (within the meaning of rule 43.2(1)(k) of the CPR) that has been entered into by the claimant.

2.2 The letter should also—

(1) list the essential documents on which the claimant intends to rely;
(2) set out the form of ADR (if any) that the claimant considers the most suitable and invite the defendant to agree to this;
(3) state the date by which the claimant considers it reasonable for a full response to be provided by the defendant; and
(4) identify and ask for copies of any relevant documents not in the claimant's possession and which the claimant wishes to see.

2.3 Unless the defendant is known to be legally represented the letter should—

(1) refer the defendant to this practice direction and in particular draw attention to para. 4 concerning the court's powers to impose sanctions for failure to comply with the practice direction; and
(2) inform the defendant that ignoring the letter before claim may lead to the claimant starting proceedings and may increase the defendant's liability for costs.

Defendant's Acknowledgment of the Letter before Claim

3.1 Where the defendant is unable to provide a full written response within 14 days of receipt of the letter before claim the defendant should, instead, provide a written acknowledgment within 14 days.

3.2 The acknowledgment—

(1) should state whether an insurer is or may be involved;
(2) should state the date by which the defendant (or insurer) will provide a full written response; and
(3) may request further information to enable the defendant to provide a full response.

3.3 If the date stated under para. 3.2(2) of this Annex is longer than the period stated in the letter before claim, the defendant should give reasons why a longer period is needed.
3.4 If the defendant (or insurer) does not provide either a letter of acknowledgment or full response within 14 days, and proceedings are subsequently started, then the court is likely to consider that the claimant has complied.
3.5 Where the defendant is unable to provide a full response within 14 days of receipt of the letter before claim because the defendant intends to seek advice then the written acknowledgment should state—
(1) that the defendant is seeking advice;
(2) from whom the defendant is seeking advice; and
(3) when the defendant expects to have received that advice and be in a position to provide a full response
3.6 A claimant should allow a reasonable period of time of up to 14 days for a defendant to obtain advice.

Defendant's Full Response

4.1 The defendant's full written response should—
(1) accept the claim in whole or in part; or
(2) state that the claim is not accepted.
4.2 Unless the defendant accepts the whole of the claim, the response should—
(1) give reasons why the claim is not accepted, identifying which facts and which parts of the claim (if any) are accepted and which are disputed, and the basis of that dispute;
(2) state whether the defendant intends to make a counterclaim against the claimant (and, if so, provide information equivalent to a claimant's letter before claim);
(3) state whether the defendant alleges that the claimant was wholly or partly to blame for the problem that led to the dispute and, if so, summarise the facts relied on;
(4) state whether the defendant agrees to the claimant's proposals for ADR and if not, state why not and suggest an alternative form of ADR (or state why none is considered appropriate);
(5) list the essential documents on which the defendant intends to rely;
(6) enclose copies of documents requested by the claimant, or explain why they will not be provided; and
(7) identify and ask for copies of any further relevant documents, not in the defendant's possession and which the defendant wishes to see.
4.3 If the defendant (or insurer) does not provide a full response within the period stated in the claimant's letter before claim (or any longer period stated in the defendant's letter of acknowledgment), and a claim is subsequently started, then the court is likely to consider that the claimant has complied.
4.4 If the claimant starts proceedings before any longer period stated in the defendant's letter of acknowledgment, the court will consider whether or not the longer period requested by the defendant was reasonable.

Claimant's Reply

5.1 The claimant should provide the documents requested by the defendant within as short a period of time as is practicable or explain in writing why the documents will not be provided.
5.2 If the defendant has made a counterclaim the claimant should provide information equivalent to the defendant's full response (see Paragraphs 4.1 to 4.3 above).

Taking Stock

6.1 In following the above procedure, the parties will have a genuine opportunity to resolve the matter without needing to start proceedings. At the very least, it should be possible to establish what issues remain outstanding so as to narrow the scope of the proceedings and therefore limit potential costs.
6.2 If having completed the procedure the matter has not been resolved then the parties should undertake a further review of their respective positions to see if proceedings can still be avoided.

ANNEX B

Information to be provided in a debt claim where the claimant is a business and the defendant is an individual

1. Where para. 7.4 of the practice direction applies the claimant should—
   (1) provide details of how the money can be paid (for example the method of payment and the address to which it can be sent);
   (2) state that the defendant can contact the claimant to discuss possible repayment options, and provide the relevant contact details; and
   (3) inform the defendant that free independent advice and assistance can be obtained from organisations including those listed in the table below.

Independent advice organisations

Organisation	Address	Telephone number	Email address
National Debtline	Tricorn House 51-53 Hagley Road Edgbaston Birmingham B16 8TP	Freephone 0808 808 4000	www.nationaldebtline.co.uk
Consumer Credit Counselling Service (CCCS)		Freephone 0800 138 1111	www.cccs.co.uk
Citizens Advice	Check your local Yellow Pages or Thomson local directory for address and telephone numbers		www.citizensadvice.org.uk
Community Legal Advice (formerly Community Legal Services Direct)		0845 345 4345	www.wclsdirect.org.uk

2. The information set out in para. 1 of this Annex may be provided at any time between the claimant first intimating the possibility of court proceedings and the claimant's letter before claim.
3. Where the defendant is unable to provide a full response within the time specified in the letter before claim because the defendant intends to seek debt advice then the written acknowledgment should state—
   (1) that the defendant is seeking debt advice;
   (2) who the defendant is seeking advice from; and
   (3) when the defendant expects to have received that advice and be in a position to provide a full response.
4. A claimant should allow a reasonable period of time of up to 14 days for a defendant to obtain debt advice.
5. But the claimant need not allow the defendant time to seek debt advice if the claimant knows that—
   (1) the defendant has already received relevant debt advice and the defendant's circumstances have not significantly changed; or
   (2) the defendant has previously asked for time to seek debt advice but has not done so.

ANNEX C GUIDANCE ON INSTRUCTING EXPERTS

1. The CPR contain extensive provisions which strictly control the use of experts both before and after proceedings are started. These provisions are contained in—
   (1) CPR, Part 35;
   (2) PD 35; and
   (3) the Protocol for the Instruction of Experts to give Evidence in Civil Claims which is annexed to PD 35.
2. *Parties should be* aware that once proceedings have been started—
   (1) expert evidence may not be used in court without the permission of the court;

(2) a party who instructs an expert will not necessarily be able to recover the cost from another party; and
(3) it is the duty of an expert to help the court on the matters within the expert's scope of expertise and this duty overrides any obligation to the person instructing or paying the expert.

3. Many matters can and should be resolved without the need for advice or evidence from an expert. If an expert is needed, the parties should consider how best to minimise the expense for example by agreeing to instruct—
(1) a single joint expert (i.e. engaged and paid jointly by the parties whether instructed jointly or separately); or
(2) an agreed expert (i.e. the parties agree the identity of the expert but only one party instructs the expert and pays the expert's costs).

4. If the parties do not agree that the nomination of a single joint expert is appropriate, then the party seeking the expert evidence (the first party) should give the other party (the second party) a list of one or more experts in the relevant field of expertise whom the first party would like to instruct.

5. Within 14 days of receipt of the list of experts, the second party may indicate in writing an objection to one or more of the experts listed. If there remains on the list one or more experts who are acceptable, then the first party should instruct an expert from the list.

6. If the second party objects to all the listed experts, the first party may then instruct an expert of the first party's own choice. Both parties should bear in mind that if proceedings are started the court will consider whether a party has acted reasonably when instructing (or rejecting) an expert.

Pre-action Protocol for Personal Injury Claims

1 INTRODUCTION

1.1 Lord Woolf in his final Access to Justice Report of July 1996 recommended the development of pre-action protocols:

> To build on and increase the benefits of early but well informed settlement which genuinely satisfy both parties to dispute.

1.2 The aims of pre-action protocols are:

- more pre-action contact between the parties
- better and earlier exchange of information
- better pre-action investigation by both sides
- to put the parties in a position where they may be able to settle cases fairly and early without litigation
- to enable proceedings to run to the court's timetable and efficiently, if litigation does become necessary
- to promote the provision of medical or rehabilitation treatment (not just in high-value cases) to address the needs of the claimant.

1.3 The concept of protocols is relevant to a range of initiatives for good litigation and pre-litigation practice, especially:

- predictability in the time needed for steps pre-proceedings
- standardisation of relevant information, including documents to be disclosed.

1.4 The courts will be able to treat the standards set in protocols as the normal reasonable approach to pre-action conduct. If proceedings are issued, it will be for the court to decide whether non-compliance with a protocol should merit adverse consequences. Guidance on the court's likely approach will be given from time to time in practice directions.

1.5 If the court has to consider the question of compliance after proceedings have begun, it will not be concerned with minor infringements, e.g. failure by a short period to provide relevant information. One minor breach will not exempt the 'innocent' party from following the protocol. The court will look at the effect of non-compliance on the other party when deciding whether to impose sanctions.

2 NOTES OF GUIDANCE

2.1 The protocol has been kept deliberately simple to promote ease of use and general acceptability. The notes of guidance which follow relate particularly to issues which arose during the piloting of the protocol.

Scope of the Protocol

2.2 This protocol is intended to apply to all claims which include a claim for personal injury (except those claims covered by the Pre-action Protocol for the Resolution of Clinical Disputes and the Pre-action Protocol for Disease and Illness Claims) and to the entirety of those claims: not only to the personal injury element of a claim which also includes, for instance, property damage.

2.3 This protocol is primarily designed for those road traffic, tripping and slipping and accident at work cases which include an element of personal injury with a value of less than the fast track limit and which are likely to be allocated to that track. This is because time will be of the essence, after proceedings are issued, especially for the defendant, if a case is to be ready for trial within 30 weeks of allocation. Also, proportionality of work and costs to the value of what is in dispute is particularly important in lower-value claims. For some claims within the value 'scope' of the fast track some flexibility in the timescale of the protocol may be necessary; see also para. 3.8.

2.4 However, the 'cards on the table' approach advocated by the protocol is equally appropriate to some higher-value claims. The spirit, if not the letter of the protocol, should still be followed for multi-track type claims. In accordance with the sense of the civil justice reforms, the court will expect to see the spirit of reasonable pre-action behaviour applied in all cases, regardless of the existence of a specific protocol. In particular with regard to personal injury cases with a value of more than the fast track limit, to avoid the necessity of proceedings parties are expected to comply with the protocol as far as possible, e.g. in respect of letters before action, exchanging information and documents and agreeing experts.

2.5 The timetable and the arrangements for disclosing documents and obtaining expert evidence may need to be varied to suit the circumstances of the case. Where one or both parties consider the detail of the protocol is not appropriate to the case, and proceedings are subsequently issued, the court will expect an explanation as to why the protocol has not been followed, or has been varied.

Early Notification

2.6 The claimant's legal representative may wish to notify the defendant and/or his insurer as soon as they know a claim is likely to be made, but before they are able to send a detailed letter of claim, particularly for instance, when the defendant has no or limited knowledge of the incident giving rise to the claim or where the claimant is incurring significant expenditure as a result of the accident which he hopes the defendant might pay for, in whole or in part. If the claimant's representative chooses to do this, it will not start the timetable for responding.

The Letter of Claim

2.7 The specimen letter of claim at Annex A will usually be sent to the individual defendant. In practice, he/she may have no personal financial interest in the financial outcome of the claim/dispute because he/she is insured. Court-imposed sanctions for non-compliance with the protocol may be ineffective against an insured. This is why the protocol emphasises the importance of passing the letter of claim to the insurer and the possibility that the insurance cover might be affected. If an insurer receives the letter of claim only after some delay by the insured, it would not be unreasonable for the insurer to ask the claimant for additional time to respond.

2.8 In road traffic cases, the letter of claim should always contain the name and address of the hospital where the claimant was treated and, where available, the claimant's hospital reference number.

2.9 The priority at letter-of-claim stage is for the claimant to provide sufficient information for the defendant to assess liability. Sufficient information should also be provided to enable the defendant to estimate the likely size of the claim.

2.10 Once the claimant has sent the letter of claim no further investigation on liability should normally be carried out until a response is received from the defendant indicating whether liability is disputed.

2.10A Where a claim no longer continues under the Pre-Action Protocol for Low Value Personal Injury Claims in Road Traffic Accidents the Claim Notification Form ('CNF') completed by the claimant under that protocol can be used as the letter of claim under this protocol unless the defendant has notified the claimant that there is inadequate information in the CNF.

Reasons for Early Issue

2.11 The protocol recommends that a defendant be given three months to investigate and respond to a claim before proceedings are issued. This may not always be possible, particularly where a claimant only consults a solicitor close to the end of any relevant limitation period. In these circumstances, the claimant's solicitor should give as much notice of the intention to issue proceedings as is practicable and the parties should consider whether the court might be invited to extend time for service of the claimant's supporting documents and for service of any defence, or alternatively, to stay the proceedings while the recommended steps in the protocol are followed.

Status of Letters of Claim and Response

2.12 Letters of claim and response are not intended to have the same status as a statement of case in proceedings. Matters may come to light as a result of investigation after the letter of claim has been sent, or after the defendant has responded, particularly if disclosure of documents takes place outside the recommended three-month period. These circumstances could mean that the 'pleaded' case of one or both parties is presented slightly differently than in the letter of claim and response. It would not be consistent with the spirit of the protocol for a party to 'take a point' on this in the proceedings, provided that there was no obvious intention by the party who changed their position to mislead the other party.

Disclosure of Documents

2.13 The aim of the early disclosure of documents by the defendant is not to encourage 'fishing expeditions' by the claimant, but to promote an early exchange of relevant information to help in clarifying or resolving issues in dispute. The claimant's solicitor can assist by identifying in the letter of claim or in a subsequent letter the particular categories of documents which they consider are relevant.

Experts

2.14 The protocol encourages joint selection of, and access to, experts. The report produced is not a joint report for the purposes of CPR, Part 35. Most frequently this will apply to the medical expert, but on occasions also to liability experts, e.g. engineers. The protocol promotes the practice of the claimant obtaining a medical report, disclosing it to the defendant who then asks questions and/or agrees it and does not obtain his own report. The protocol provides for nomination of the expert by the claimant in personal injury claims because of the early stage of the proceedings and the particular nature of such claims. If proceedings have to be issued, a medical report must be attached to these proceedings. However, if necessary after proceedings have commenced and with the permission of the court, the parties may obtain further expert reports. It would be for the court to decide whether the costs of more than one expert's report should be recoverable.

2.15 Some solicitors choose to obtain medical reports through medical agencies, rather than directly from a specific doctor or hospital. The defendant's prior consent to the action should be sought and, if the defendant so requests, the agency should be asked to provide in advance the names of the doctor(s) whom they are considering instructing.

Alternative Dispute Resolution

2.16 The parties should consider whether some form of alternative dispute resolution procedure would be more suitable than litigation, and if so, endeavour to agree which form to adopt. Both the claimant and defendant may be required by the court ro provide evidence that alternative means of resolving their dispute were considered. The courts take the view that litigation should be a last resort, and that claims should not be issued prematurely when a settlement is still actively being explored. Parties are warned that if the protocol is not followed (including this paragraph) then the court must have regard to such conduct when determining costs.

2.17 It is not practicable in this protocol to address in detail how the parties might decide which method to adopt to resolve their particular dispute. However, summarised below are some of the options for resolving disputes without litigation:

- Discussion and negotiation.
- Early neutral evaluation by an independent third party (for example, a lawyer experienced in the field of personal injury or an individual experienced in the subject matter of the claim).
- Mediation — a form of facilitated negotiation assisted by an independent neutral party.

2.18 The Legal Services Commission has published a booklet on *Alternatives to Court* (CLS Direct Information Leaflet 23) (www.clsdirect.org.uk/legalhelp/leaflet23.jsp), which lists a number of organisations that provide alternative dispute resolution services.

2.19 *It is expressly recognised that no party can or should be forced to mediate or enter into any form of ADR.*

Stocktake

2.20 Where a claim is not resolved when the protocol has been followed, the parties might wish to carry out a 'stocktake' of the issues in dispute, and the evidence that the court is likely to need to decide those issues, before proceedings are started. Where the defendant is insured and the pre-action steps have been conducted by the insurer, the insurer would normally be expected to nominate solicitors to act in the proceedings and the claimant's solicitor is recommended to invite the insurer to nominate solicitors to act in the proceedings and do so 7–14 days before the intended issue date.

3 THE PROTOCOL

Letter of Claim

3.1 Subject to para. 2.10A the claimant shall send to the proposed defendant two copies of a letter of claim, immediately sufficient information is available to substantiate a realistic claim and before issues of quantum are addressed in detail. One copy of the letter is for the defendants, the second for passing on to his insurers.

3.2 The letter shall contain a **clear summary of the facts** on which the claim is based together with an indication of the **nature of any injuries** suffered and of **any financial loss incurred**. In cases of road traffic accidents, the letter should provide the name and address of the hospital where treatment has been obtained and the claimant's hospital reference number. Where the case is funded by a conditional fee agreement (or collective conditional fee agreement), notification should be given of the existence of the agreement and where appropriate, that there is a success fee and/or insurance premium, although not the level of the success fee or premium.

3.3 Solicitors are recommended to use a **standard format** for such a letter — an example is at Annex A: this can be amended to suit the particular case.

3.4 The letter should ask for **details of the insurer** and that a copy should be sent by the proposed defendant to the insurer where appropriate. If the insurer is known, a copy shall be sent directly to the insurer. Details of the claimant's National Insurance number and date of birth should be supplied to the defendant's insurer once the defendant has responded to the letter of claim and confirmed the identity of the insurer. This information should not be supplied in the letter of claim.

3.5 **Sufficient information** should be given in order to enable the defendant's insurer/solicitor to commence investigations and at least put a broad valuation on the 'risk'.

3.6 The **defendant should reply within 21 calendar days** of the date of posting of the letter identifying the insurer (if any) and, if necessary, identifying specifically any significant omissions from the letter of claim. If there has been no reply by the defendant or insurer within 21 days, the claimant will be entitled to issue proceedings.

3.7 The **defendant**('s insurers) will have a **maximum of three months** from the date of acknowledgment of the claim **to investigate**. No later than the end of that period the defendant (insurer) shall reply, stating whether liability is denied and, if so, giving reasons for their denial of liability including any alternative version of events relied upon.

3.8 Where the accident occurred outside England and Wales and/or where the defendant is outside the jurisdiction, the time periods of 21 days and three months should normally be extended up to 42 days and six months.

3.9 Where the claimant's investigation indicates that the value of the claim has increased to more than the value of the fast track limit since the letter of claim, the claimant should notify the defendant as soon as possible.

Documents

3.10 If the **defendant denies liability**, he should enclose with the letter of reply, **documents** in his possession which are **material to the issues** between the parties, and which would be likely to be ordered to be disclosed by the court, either on an application for pre-action disclosure, or on disclosure during proceedings.

3.11 Attached at Annex B are **specimen**, but non-exhaustive, **lists** of documents likely to be material in different types of claim. Where the claimant's investigation of the case is well advanced, the letter of claim could indicate which classes of documents are considered relevant for early disclosure. Alternatively these could be identified at a later stage.

3.12 Where the defendant admits primary liability, but alleges contributory negligence by the claimant, the defendant should give reasons supporting those allegations and disclose those documents from Annex B which are relevant to the issues in dispute. The claimant should respond to the allegations of contributory negligence before proceedings are issued.

3.13 No charge will be made for providing copy documents under the protocol.

Special Damages

3.14 The claimant will send to the defendant as soon as practicable a schedule of special damages with supporting documents, particularly where the defendant has admitted liability.

Experts

3.15 Before any party instructs an expert he should give the other party a list of the **name**(s) of **one or more experts** in the relevant speciality whom he considers are suitable to instruct.

3.16 Where a medical expert is to be instructed the claimant's solicitor will organise access to relevant medical records — see specimen letter of instruction at Annex C.

3.17 **Within 14 days** the other party may indicate **an objection** to one or more of the named experts. The first party should then instruct a mutually acceptable expert (which is not the same as a joint expert). It must be emphasised that if the claimant nominates an expert in the original letter of claim, the defendant has 14 days to object to one or more of the named experts after expiration of the period of 21 days within which he has to reply to the letter of claim, as set out in para. 3.6.

3.18 If the second party objects to all the listed experts, the parties may then instruct **experts of their own choice. It** would be for the court to decide subsequently, if proceedings are issued, whether either party had acted unreasonably.

3.19 If the **second party does not object to an expert nominated**, he shall not be entitled to rely on his own expert evidence within that particular speciality unless:
(a) the first party agrees,
(b) the court so directs, or
(c) the first party's expert report has been amended and the first party is not prepared to disclose the original report.

3.20 **Either party may send to an agreed expert written questions** on the report, relevant to the issues, via the first party's solicitors. The expert should send answers to the questions separately and directly to each party.

3.21 The cost of a report from an agreed expert will usually be paid by the instructing first party: the costs of the expert replying to questions will usually be borne by the party which asks the questions.

4 REHABILITATION

4.1 The claimant or the defendant or both shall consider as early as possible whether the claimant has reasonable needs that could be met by rehabilitation treatment or other measures.

4.2 The parties shall consider, in such cases, how those needs might be addressed. The Rehabilitation Code (which is attached at Annex D) may be helpful in considering how to identify the claimant's needs and how to address the cost of providing for those needs.

4.3 The time limit set out in para. 3.7 of this protocol shall not be shortened, except by consent to allow these issues to be addressed.

4.4 The provision of any report obtained for the purposes of assessment of provision of a party's rehabilitation needs shall not be used in any litigation arising out of the accident, the subject of the claim, save by consent and shall in any event be exempt from the provisions of paras 3.15 to 3.21 inclusive of this protocol.

5 RESOLUTION OF ISSUES

5.1 Where the defendant admits liability in whole or in part, before proceedings are issued, any medical reports obtained under this protocol on which a party relies should be disclosed to the *other party. The claimant should* delay issuing proceedings for 21 days from disclosure of the report (unless such delay would cause his claim to become time-barred), to enable the parties to consider whether the claim is capable of settlement.

5.2 Part 36 of the CPR permits claimants and defendants to make offers to settle pre-proceedings. Parties should always consider before issuing if it is appropriate to make Part 36 offers. If such an offer is made, the party making the offer must always supply sufficient evidence and/or information to enable the offer to be properly considered.

5.3 Where the defendant has admitted liability, the claimant should send to the defendant schedules of special damages and loss at least 21 days before proceedings are issued (unless that would cause the claimant's claim to become time-barred).

ANNEX A LETTER OF CLAIM

To
Defendant

Dear Sirs
Re: **Claimant's full name**
Claimant's full address
Claimant's Clock or Works Number
Claimant's Employer (*name and address*)

We are instructed by the above named to claim damages in connection with *an accident at work/a road traffic accident/a tripping accident* on day of (*year*) at (*place of accident which must be sufficiently detailed to establish location*)

Please confirm the identity of your insurers. Please note that the insurers will need to see this letter as soon as possible and it may affect your insurance cover and/or the conduct of any subsequent legal proceedings if you do not send this letter to them.

The circumstances of the accident are:
(*brief outline*)

The reason why we are alleging fault is:
(*simple explanation e.g. defective machine, broken ground*)

A description of our client's injuries is as follows:
(*brief outline*)

(In cases of road traffic accidents)

Our client (*state hospital reference number*) received treatment for the injuries at (*name and address of hospital*).

Our client is still suffering from the effects of his/her injury. We invite you to participate with us in addressing his/her immediate needs by use of rehabilitation.

He is employed as (*occupation*) and has had the following time off work (*dates of absence*). His approximate weekly income is (*insert if known*).

If you are our client's employers, please provide us with the usual earnings details which will enable us to calculate his financial loss.

We are obtaining a police report and will let you have a copy of the same upon your undertaking to meet half the fee.

We have also sent a letter of claim to (*name and address*) and a copy of that letter is attached. We understand their insurers are (*name, address and claims number if known*).

At this stage of our enquiries we would expect the documents contained in parts (*insert appropriate parts of standard disclosure list*) to be relevant to this action.

Please note that we have entered into a conditional fee agreement with our client dated in relation to this claim which provides for a success fee within the meaning of section 58(2) of the Courts and Legal Services Act 1990. Our client has taken out an insurance policy with [name of insurance company] of [address of insurance company] to which section 29 of the Access to Justice Act 1999 applies. The policy number is the policy is dated . [Where the funding arrangement is an insurance policy, the party must state the name and address of the insurer, the policy number and the date of the policy, and must identify the claim or claims to which it relates (including Part 20 claims if any).]

A copy of this letter is attached for you to send to your insurers. Finally we expect an acknowledgment of this letter within 21 days by yourselves or your insurers.

Yours faithfully

ANNEX B PRE-ACTION PERSONAL INJURY PROTOCOL STANDARD DISCLOSURE LISTS FAST TRACK DISCLOSURE

Road Traffic Accident Cases

Section A

In all cases where liability is at issue—

(i) Documents identifying nature, extent and location of damage to defendant's vehicle where there is any dispute about point of impact.
(ii) MOT certificate where relevant.
(iii) Maintenance records where vehicle defect is alleged or it is alleged by defendant that there was an unforeseen defect which caused or contributed to the accident.

Section B

Accident involving commercial vehicle as potential defendant—

(i) Tachograph charts or entry from individual control book.
(ii) Maintenance and repair records required for operators' licence where vehicle defect is alleged or it is alleged by defendant that there was an unforeseen defect which caused or contributed to the accident.

Section C

Cases against local authorities where highway design defect is alleged—

(i) Documents produced to comply with the Road Traffic Act 1988, s. 39, in respect of the duty designed to promote road safety to include studies into road accidents in the relevant area and documents relating to measures recommended to prevent accidents in the relevant area.

Highway tripping claims

Documents from highway authority for a period of 12 months prior to the accident—

(i) Records of inspection for the relevant stretch of highway.
(ii) Maintenance records including records of independent contractors working in relevant area.
(iii) Records of the minutes of highway authority meetings where maintenance or repair policy has been discussed or decided.
(iv) Records of complaints about the state of highways.
(v) Records of other accidents which have occurred on the relevant stretch of highway.

Workplace claims

(i) Accident book entry.
(ii) First aider report.
(iii) Surgery record.
(iv) Foreman/supervisor accident report.
(v) Safety representatives accident report.
(vi) RIDDOR report to HSE.
(vii) Other communications between defendants and HSE.
(viii) Minutes of Health and Safety Committee meeting(s) where accident/matter considered.
(ix) Report to DSS.
(x) Documents listed above relative to any previous accident/matter identified by the claimant and relied upon as proof of negligence.
(xi) Earnings information where defendant is employer.

Documents produced to comply with requirements of the Management of Health and Safety at Work Regulations 1999 (SI 1999/3242):*

(i) Pre-accident risk assessment required by reg. 3.
(ii) Post-accident reassessment required by reg. 3.
(iii) Accident investigation report prepared in implementing the requirements of regs 5, 7 and 11.

[* The protocol refers to an earlier version of these regulations and has been updated editorially.]

(iv) Health surveillance records in appropriate cases required by reg. 6.
(v) Information provided to employees under reg. 10.
(vi) Documents relating to the employee's health and safety training required by reg. 13.

Workplace Claims — Disclosure Where Specific Regulations Apply

Section A — Workplace (Health, Safety and Welfare) Regulations 1992 (SI 1992/3004)

(i) Repair and maintenance records required by reg. 5.
(ii) Housekeeping records to comply with the requirements of reg. 9.
(iii) Hazard warning signs or notices to comply with reg. 17 (traffic routes).

Section B — Provision and Use of Work Equipment Regulations 1998 (SI 1998/2306)

(i) Manufacturers' specifications and instructions in respect of relevant work equipment establishing its suitability to comply with reg. 4.*
(ii) Maintenance log/maintenance records required to comply with reg. 5.*
(iii) Documents providing information and instructions to employees to comply with reg. 8.
(iv) Documents provided to the employee in respect of training for use to comply with reg. 9.
(v) Any notice, sign or document relied upon as a defence to alleged breaches of regs 14 to 18 dealing with controls and control systems.
(vi) Instruction/training documents issued to comply with the requirements of reg. 22 in so far as it deals with maintenance operations where the machinery is not shut down.
(vii) Copies of markings required to comply with reg. 23.
(viii) Copies of warnings required to comply with reg. 24.

Section C — Personal Protective Equipment at Work Regulations 1992 (SI 1992/2966)

(i) Documents relating to the assessment of the personal protective equipment to comply with reg. 6.
(ii) Documents relating to the maintenance and replacement of personal protective equipment to comply with reg. 7.
(iii) Record of maintenance procedures for personal protective equipment to comply with reg. 7.
(iv) Records of tests and examinations of personal protective equipment to comply with reg. 7.
(v) Documents providing information, instruction and training in relation to the personal protective equipment to comply with reg. 9.
(vi) Instructions for use of personal protective equipment to include the manufacturers' instructions to comply with reg. 10.

Section D — Manual Handling Operations Regulations 1992 (SI 1992/2793)

(i) Manual handling risk assessment carried out to comply with the requirements of reg. 4(1)(b)(i).
(ii) Reassessment carried out post-accident to comply with requirements of reg. 4(1)(b)(i).
(iii) Documents showing the information provided to the employee to give general indications related to the load and precise indications on the weight of the load and the heaviest side of the load if the centre of gravity was not positioned centrally to comply with reg. 4(1)(b)(iii).
(iv) Documents relating to training in respect of manual handling operations and training records.

Section E — Health and Safety (Display Screen Equipment) Regulations 1992 (SI 1992/2792)

(i) Analysis of work stations to assess and reduce risks carried out to comply with the requirements of reg. 2.
(ii) Reassessment of analysis of work stations to assess and reduce risks following development of symptoms by the claimant.
(iii) Documents detailing the provision of training including training records to comply with the requirements of reg. 6.
(iv) Documents providing information to employees to comply with the requirements of reg. 7.

[* Reference corrected editorially.]

Section F — Control of Substances Hazardous to Health Regulations 2002 (SI 2002/2677)*

(i) Risk assessment carried out to comply with the requirements of reg. 6.
(ii) Reviewed risk assessment carried out to comply with the requirements of reg. 6.
(iii) Copy labels from containers used for storage handling and disposal of carcinogens to comply with the requirements of reg. 7(5)(e).
(iv) Warning signs identifying designation of areas and installations which may be contaminated by carcinogens to comply with the requirements of reg. 7(5)(d).
(v) Documents relating to the assessment of the personal protective equipment to comply with reg. 7(3A).
(vi) Documents relating to the maintenance and replacement of personal protective equipment to comply with reg. 7(9).
(vii) Record of maintenance procedures for personal protective equipment to comply with reg. 7(9).
(viii) Records of tests and examinations of personal protective equipment to comply with reg. 7(9).
(ix) Documents providing information, instruction and training in relation to the personal protective equipment to comply with reg. 7(9).
(x) Instructions for use of personal protective equipment to include the manufacturers' instructions to comply with reg. 7(9).
(xi) Air monitoring records for substances assigned a maximum exposure limit or occupational exposure standard to comply with the requirements of reg. 7.
(xii) Maintenance examination and test of control measures records to comply with reg. 9.
(xiii) Monitoring records to comply with the requirements of reg. 10.
(xiv) Health surveillance records to comply with the requirements of reg. 11.
(xv) Documents detailing information, instruction and training including training records for employees to comply with the requirements of reg. 12.
(xvi) Labels and health and safety data sheets supplied to the employers to comply with the Chemicals (Hazard Information and Packaging for Supply) Regulations 1994 (SI 1994/3247).

Section G — Construction (Design and Management) Regulations 1994 (SI 1994/3140) as amended by the Construction (Design and Management) (Amendment) Regulations 2000 (SI 2000/2380)

(i) Notification of a project form (HSE F10) to comply with the requirements of reg. 7.
(ii) Health and safety plan to comply with requirements of reg. 15.
(iii) Health and safety file to comply with the requirements of regs 12 and 14.
(iv) Information and training records provided to comply with the requirements of reg. 17.
(v) Records of advice from and views of persons at work to comply with the requirements of reg. 18.

Section H — Pressure Systems and Transportable Gas Containers Regulations 1989 (SI 1989/2169)†

(i) Information and specimen markings provided to comply with the requirements of reg. 5.
(ii) Written statements specifying the safe operating limits of a system to comply with the requirements of reg. 7.
(iii) Copy of the written scheme of examination required to comply with the requirements of reg. 8.
(iv) Examination records required to comply with the requirements of reg. 9.
(v) Instructions provided for the use of operator to comply with reg. 11.
(vi) Records kept to comply with the requirements of reg. 13.
(vii) Records kept to comply with the requirements of reg. 22.

[* The protocol refers to an earlier version of these regulations and has been updated editorially.]
[† These regulations were revoked by the Pressure Systems Safety Regulations 2000 (SI 2000/128), reg. 18(2).]

Section I — Lifting Operations and Lifting Equipment Regulations 1998 (SI 1998/2307)

(i) Record kept to comply with the requirements of reg. 10.*

Section J — Noise at Work Regulations 1989 (SI 1989/1790)

(i) Any risk assessment records required to comply with the requirements of regs 4 and 5.
(ii) Manufacturers' literature in respect of all ear protection made available to claimant to comply with the requirements of reg. 8.
(iii) All documents provided to the employee for the provision of information to comply with reg. 11.

Section K — Construction (Head Protection) Regulations 1989 (SI 1989/2209)

(i) Pre-accident assessment of head protection required to comply with reg. 3(4).
(ii) Post-accident reassessment required to comply with reg. 3(5).

Section L — Construction (General Provisions) Regulations 1961 (SI 1961/1580)

(i) Report prepared following inspections and examinations of excavations etc. to comply with the requirements of reg. 9
(ii) Report prepared following inspections and examinations of work in cofferdams and caissons to comply with the requirements of regs 17 and 18.

Section M — Pressure Systems and Transportable Gas Containers Regulations 1989 (SI 1989/2169)†

(i) Information and specimen markings provided to comply with the requirements of reg. 5.
(ii) Written statements specifying the safe operating limits of a system to comply with the requirements of reg. 7.
(iii) Copy of the written scheme of examination required to comply with the requirements of reg. 8.
(iv) Examination records required to comply with the requirements of reg. 9.
(v) Instructions provided for the use of operator to comply with reg. 11.

ANNEX C LETTER OF INSTRUCTION TO MEDICAL EXPERT

Dear Sir,
Re: (*Name and Address*)
D.O.B. —
Telephone No. —
Date of Accident —

We are acting for the above named in connection with injuries received in an accident which occurred on the above date. The main injuries appear to have been (*main injuries*).

We should be obliged if you would examine our Client and let us have a full and detailed report dealing with any relevant pre-accident medical history, the injuries sustained, treatment received and present condition, dealing in particular with the capacity for work and giving a prognosis.

It is central to our assessment of the extent of our Client's injuries to establish the extent and duration of any continuing disability. Accordingly, in the prognosis section we would ask you to specifically comment on any areas of continuing complaint or disability or impact on daily living. If there is such continuing disability you should comment upon the level of suffering or inconvenience caused and, if you are able, give your view as to when or if the complaint or disability is likely to resolve.

[* Reference corrected editorially.]
[† These regulations were revoked by the Pressure Systems Safety Regulations 2000 (SI 2000/128), reg. 18(2). Section M of annex B repeats section H, omitting items (vi) and (vii).]

Please send our Client an appointment direct for this purpose. Should you be able to offer a cancellation appointment please contact our Client direct. We confirm we will be responsible for your reasonable fees.

We are obtaining the notes and records from our Client's GP and Hospitals attended and will forward them to you when they are to hand/or please request the GP and Hospital records direct and advise that any invoice for the provision of these records should be forwarded to us.

In order to comply with Court Rules we would be grateful if you would insert above your signature a statement that the contents are true to the best of your knowledge and belief.

In order to avoid further correspondence we can confirm that on the evidence we have there is no reason to suspect we may be pursuing a claim against the hospital or its staff.

We look forward to receiving your report within weeks. If you will not be able to prepare your report within this period please telephone us upon receipt of these instructions.

When acknowledging these instructions it would assist if you could give an estimate as to the likely time scale for the provision of your report and also an indication as to your fee.

Yours faithfully

ANNEX D THE 2007 REHABILITATION CODE

The aim of this code is to promote the use of rehabilitation and early intervention in the compensation process so that the injured person makes the best and quickest possible medical, social and psychological recovery. This objective applies whatever the severity of the injuries sustained by the claimant. The code is designed to ensure that the claimant's need for rehabilitation is assessed and addressed as a priority, and that the process of so doing is pursued on a collaborative basis by the claimant's lawyer and the compensator.

Therefore, in every case, where rehabilitation is likely to be of benefit, the earliest possible notification to the compensator of the claim and of the need for rehabilitation will be expected.

1. Introduction

1.1 The purpose of the personal injury claims process is to put the individual back into the same position as he or she would have been in, had the accident not occurred, in so far as money can achieve that objective. The purpose of the rehabilitation code is to provide a framework within which the claimant's health, quality of life and ability to work are restored as far as possible before, or simultaneously with, the process of assessing compensation.

1.2 Although the code is recognised by the Personal Injury Pre-Action Protocol, its provisions are not mandatory. It is recognised that the aims of the code can be achieved without strict adherence to the terms of the code, and therefore it is open to the parties to agree an alternative framework to achieve the early rehabilitation of the claimant.

1.3 However, the code provides a useful framework within which claimants' lawyers and the compensator can work together to ensure that the needs of injured claimants are assessed at an early stage.

1.4 In any case where agreement on liability is not reached it is open to the parties to agree that the code will in any event operate, and the question of delay pending resolution of liability should be balanced with the interests of the injured party. However, unless so agreed, the code does not apply in the absence of liability or prior to agreement on liability being reached.

1.5 In this code the expression 'the compensator' shall include any loss adjuster, solicitor or other person acting on behalf of the compensator.

2. The claimant's solicitor

2.1 It should be the duty of every claimant's solicitor to consider, from the earliest practicable stage, and in consultation with the claimant, the claimant's family, and where appropriate the claimant's treating physician(s), whether it is likely or possible that early intervention, rehabilitation or medical treatment would improve their present and/or long-term physical and mental well-being. This duty is ongoing throughout the life of the case but is of most importance in the early stages.

2.2 The claimant's solicitors will in any event be aware of their responsibilities under section 4 of the Pre-Action Protocol for Personal Injury Claims.

2.3 It shall be the duty of a claimant's solicitor to consider, with the claimant and/or the claimant's family, whether there is an immediate need for aids, adaptations, adjustments to employment to enable the claimant to keep his/her existing job, obtain suitable alternative employment with the same employer or retrain for new employment, or other matters that would seek to alleviate problems caused by disability, and then to communicate with the compensators as soon as practicable about any such rehabilitation needs, with a view to putting this code into effect.

2.4 It shall not be the responsibility of the solicitor to decide on the need for treatment or rehabilitation or to arrange such matters without appropriate medical or professional advice.

2.5 It is the intention of this code that the claimant's solicitor will work with the compensator to address these rehabilitation needs and that the assessment and delivery of rehabilitation needs shall be a collaborative process.

2.6 It must be recognised that the compensator will need to receive from the claimants' solicitors sufficient information for the compensator to make a proper decision about the need for intervention, rehabilitation or treatment. To this extent the claimant's solicitor must comply with the requirements of the Pre-Action Protocol to provide the compensator with full and adequate details of the injuries sustained by the claimant, the nature and extent of any or any likely continuing disability and any suggestions that may already have been made concerning rehabilitation and/or early intervention.

2.7 There is no requirement under the Pre-Action Protocol, or under this code, for the claimant's solicitor to have obtained a full medical report. It is recognised that many cases will be identified for consideration under this code before medical evidence has actually been commissioned or obtained.

3. The Compensator

3.1 It shall be the duty of the compensator, from the earliest practicable stage in any appropriate case, to consider whether it is likely that the claimant will benefit in the immediate, medium or longer term from further medical treatment, rehabilitation or early intervention. This duty is ongoing throughout the life of the case but is most important in the early stages.

3.2 If the compensator considers that a particular claim might be suitable for intervention, rehabilitation or treatment, the compensator will communicate this to the claimant's solicitor as soon as practicable.

3.3 On receipt of such communication, the claimant's solicitor will immediately discuss these issues with the claimant and/or the claimant's family pursuant to his duty set out above.

3.4 Where a request to consider rehabilitation has been communicated by the claimant's solicitor to the compensator, it will usually be expected that the compensator will respond to such request within 21 days.

3.5 Nothing in this or any other code of practice shall in any way modify the obligations of the compensator under the protocol to investigate claims rapidly and in any event within three months (except where time is extended by the claimant's solicitor) from the date of the formal claim letter. It is recognised that, although the rehabilitation assessment can be done even where liability investigations are outstanding, it is essential that such investigations proceed with the appropriate speed.

4. Assessment

4.1 Unless the need for intervention, rehabilitation or treatment has already been identified by medical reports obtained and disclosed by either side, the need for and extent of such intervention, rehabilitation or treatment will be considered by means of an assessment by an appropriately qualified person.

4.2 An assessment of rehabilitation needs may be carried out by any person or organisation suitably qualified, experienced and skilled to carry out the task. The claimant's solicitor and the compensator should endeavour to agree on the person or organisation to be chosen.

4.3 No solicitor or compensator may insist on the assessment being carried out by a particular person or organisation if (on reasonable grounds) the other party objects, such objection to be raised within 21 days from the date of notification of the suggested assessor.

4.4 The assessment may be carried out by a person or organisation which has a direct business connection with the solicitor or compensator, only if the other party agrees. The solicitor or compensator will be expected to reveal to the other party the existence of and nature of such a business connection.

5. The Assessment Process

5.1 Where possible, the agency to be instructed to provide the assessment should be agreed between the claimant's solicitor and the compensator. The method of providing instructions to that agency will be agreed between the solicitor and the compensator.

5.2 The assessment agency will be asked to carry out the assessment in a way that is appropriate to the needs of the case and, in a simple case, may include, by prior appointment, a telephone interview but in more serious cases will probably involve a face-to-face discussion with the claimant. The report will normally cover the following headings:

- The injuries sustained by the claimant.
- The current disability/incapacity arising from those injuries. Where relevant to the overall picture of the claimant's needs, any other medical conditions not arising from the accident should also be separately annotated.
- The claimant's domestic circumstances (including mobility accommodation and employment) where relevant.
- The injuries/disability in respect of which early intervention or early rehabilitation is suggested.
- The type of intervention or treatment envisaged.
- The likely cost.
- The likely outcome of such intervention or treatment.

5.3 The report should not deal with issues relating to legal liability and should therefore not contain a detailed account of the accident circumstances.

5.4 In most cases it will be expected that the assessment will take place within 14 days from the date of the letter of referral to the assessment agency.

5.5 It must be remembered that the compensator will usually only consider such rehabilitation to deal with the effects of the injuries that have been caused in the relevant accident and will normally not be expected to fund treatment for conditions which do not directly relate to the accident unless the effect of such conditions has been exacerbated by the injuries sustained in the accident.

6. The Assessment Report

6.1 The report agency will, on completion of the report, send copies on to both the claimant's solicitor and compensator simultaneously. Both parties will have the right to raise questions on the report, disclosing such correspondence to the other party.

6.2 It is recognised that for this assessment report to be of benefit to the parties, it should be prepared and used wholly outside the litigation process. Neither side can therefore, unless they agree in writing, rely on its contents in any subsequent litigation.

6.3 The report, any correspondence related to it and any notes created by the assessing agency to prepare it, will be covered by legal privilege and will not be disclosed in any legal proceedings unless the parties agree. Any notes or documents created in connection with the assessment process will not be disclosed in any litigation, and any person involved in the preparation of the report or involved in the assessment process, shall not be a compellable witness at court. This principle is also set out in para. 4.4 of the Pre-Action Protocol.

6.4 The provision in para. 6.3 above as to treating the report etc. as outside the litigation process is limited to the assessment report and any notes relating to it. Any notes and reports created during the subsequent case management process will be covered by the usual principle in relation to disclosure of documents and medical records relating to the claimant.

6.5 The compensator will pay for the report within 28 days of receipt.

6.6 This code intends that the parties will continue to work together to ensure that the rehabilitation which has been recommended proceeds smoothly and that any further rehabilitation needs are also assessed.

7. Recommendations

7.1 When the assessment report is disclosed to the compensator, the compensator will be under a duty to consider the recommendations made and the extent to which funds will be made available to implement all or some of the recommendations. The compensator will not be required to pay for intervention treatment that is unreasonable in nature, content or cost or where adequate and timely provision is otherwise available. The claimant will be under no obligation to undergo intervention, medical or investigation treatment that is unreasonable in all the circumstances of the case.

7.2 The compensator will normally be expected to respond to the claimant's solicitor within 21 days from the date upon which the assessment report is disclosed as to the extent to which the recommendations have been accepted and rehabilitation treatment would be funded and will be expected to justify, within that same timescale, any refusal to meet the cost of recommended rehabilitation.

7.3 If funds are provided by the compensator to the claimant to enable specific intervention, rehabilitation or treatment to occur, the compensator warrants that they will not, in any legal proceedings connected with the claim, dispute the reasonableness of that treatment, nor the agreed costs, provided of course that the claimant has had the recommended treatment. The compensator will not, should the claim fail or be later discontinued, or any element of contributory negligence be assessed or agreed, seek to recover from the claimant any funds that they have made available pursuant to this code.

Pre-action Protocol for the Resolution of Clinical Disputes

EXECUTIVE SUMMARY

1. The Clinical Disputes Forum is a multi-disciplinary body which was formed in 1997, as a result of Lord Woolf's 'Access to Justice' inquiry. One of the aims of the Forum is to find less adversarial and more cost-effective ways of resolving disputes about healthcare and medical treatment. The names and addresses of the Chairman and Secretary of the Forum can be found at Annex E.
2. This protocol is the Forum's first major initiative. It has been drawn up carefully, including extensive consultations with most of the key stakeholders in the medico-legal system.
3. The protocol—
   - encourages a climate of openness when something has 'gone wrong' with a patient's treatment or the patient is dissatisfied with that treatment and/or the outcome. This reflects the new and developing requirements for clinical governance within healthcare;
   - provides **general guidance** on how this more open culture might be achieved when disputes arise;
   - recommends a **timed sequence** of steps for patients and healthcare providers, and their advisers, to follow when a dispute arises. This should facilitate and speed up exchanging relevant information and increase the prospects that disputes can be resolved without resort to legal action.
4. This protocol has been prepared by a working party of the Clinical Disputes Forum. It has the support of the Lord Chancellor's Department, the Department of Health and NHS Executive, the Law Society, the Legal Aid Board and many other key organisations.

1 WHY THIS PROTOCOL?

Mistrust in Healthcare Disputes

1.1 The number of complaints and claims against hospitals, GPs, dentists and private healthcare providers is growing as patients become more prepared to question the treatment they are given, to seek explanations of what happened, and to seek appropriate redress. Patients may require further treatment, an apology, assurances about future action, or compensation. These trends are unlikely to change. The Patients' Charter encourages patients to have high expectations, and a revised NHS Complaints Procedure was implemented in 1996. The civil justice reforms and new Rules of Court should make litigation quicker, more user friendly and less expensive.

1.2 It is clearly in the interests of patients, healthcare professionals and providers that patients' concerns, complaints and claims arising from their treatment are resolved as quickly, efficiently and professionally as possible. A climate of mistrust and lack of openness can seriously damage the patient/clinician relationship, unnecessarily prolong disputes (especially litigation), and reduce the resources available for treating patients. It may also cause additional work for, and lower the morale of, healthcare professionals.

1.3 At present there is often mistrust by both sides. This can mean that patients fail to raise their concerns with the healthcare provider as early as possible. Sometimes patients may pursue a complaint or claim which has little merit, due to a lack of sufficient information and understanding. It can also mean that patients become reluctant, once advice has been taken on a potential claim, to disclose sufficient information to enable the provider to investigate that claim efficiently and, where appropriate, resolve it.

1.4 On the side of the healthcare provider this mistrust can be shown in a reluctance to be honest with patients, a failure to provide prompt clear explanations, especially of adverse outcomes (whether or not there may have been negligence) and a tendency to 'close ranks' once a claim is made.

What Needs to Change

1.5 If that mistrust is to be removed, and a more cooperative culture is to develop—
- healthcare professionals and providers need to adopt a constructive approach to complaints and claims. They should accept that concerned patients are entitled to an explanation and an apology, if warranted, and to appropriate redress in the event of negligence. An overly defensive approach is not in the long-term interest of their main goal: patient care;
- patients should recognise that unintended and/or unfortunate consequences of medical treatment can only be rectified if they are brought to the attention of the healthcare provider as soon as possible.

1.6 A protocol which sets out 'ground rules' for the handling of disputes at their early stages should, if it is to be subscribed to, and followed—
- encourage greater openness between the parties;
- encourage parties to find the most appropriate way of resolving the particular dispute;
- reduce delay and costs;
- reduce the need for litigation.

Why This Protocol Now?

1.7 Lord Woolf in his Access to Justice Report in July 1996, concluded that major causes of costs and delay in medical negligence litigation occur at the pre-action stage. He recommended that patients and their advisers, and healthcare providers, should work more closely together to try to resolve disputes cooperatively, rather than proceed to litigation. He specifically recommended a pre-action protocol for medical negligence cases.

1.8 A fuller summary of Lord Woolf's recommendations is at Annex D.

Where the Protocol Fits In

1.9 Protocols serve the needs of litigation and pre-litigation practice, especially—
- predictability in the time needed for steps pre-proceedings;
- standardisation of relevant information, including records and documents to be disclosed.

1.10 Building upon Lord Woolf's recommendations, the Lord Chancellor's Department is now promoting the adoption of protocols in specific areas, including medical negligence.

1.11 It is recognised that contexts differ significantly. For example: patients tend to have an ongoing relationship with a GP, more so than with a hospital; clinical staff in the National Health Service are often employees, while those in the private sector may be contractors; providing records quickly may be relatively easy for GPs and dentists, but can be a complicated procedure in a large multi-department hospital. The protocol which follows is intended to be sufficiently broadly based, and flexible, to apply to all aspects of the health service: primary and secondary; public and private sectors.

Enforcement of the Protocol and Sanctions

1.12 The civil justice reforms will be implemented in April 1999. One new set of Court Rules and procedures is replacing the existing rules for both the High Court and county courts. This and the personal injury protocol are being published with the Rules, practice directions and key court forms. The courts will be able to treat the standards set in protocols as the normal reasonable approach to pre-action conduct.

1.13 If proceedings are issued it will be for the court to decide whether non-compliance with a protocol should merit sanctions. Guidance on the court's likely approach will be given from time to time in practice directions.

1.14 If the court has to consider the question of compliance after proceedings have begun it will not be concerned with minor infringements, e.g. failure by a short period to provide relevant information. One minor breach will not entitle the 'innocent' party to abandon following the protocol. The court will look at the effect of non-compliance on the other party when deciding whether to impose sanctions.

2 THE AIMS OF THE PROTOCOL

2.1 The *general* aims of the protocol are—
- to maintain/restore the patient/healthcare provider relationship;
- to resolve as many disputes as possible without litigation.

2.2 The *specific* objectives are—

Openness

- to encourage early communication of the perceived problem between patients and healthcare providers;
- to encourage patients to voice any concerns or dissatisfaction with their treatment as soon as practicable;
- to encourage healthcare providers to develop systems of early reporting and investigation for serious adverse treatment outcomes and to provide full and prompt explanations to dissatisfied patients;
- to ensure that sufficient information is disclosed by both parties to enable each to understand the other's perspective and case, and to encourage early resolution.

Timeliness

- to provide an early opportunity for healthcare providers to identify cases where an investigation is required and to carry out that investigation promptly;
- to encourage primary and private healthcare providers to involve their defence organisations or insurers at an early stage;
- to ensure that all relevant medical records are provided to patients or their appointed representatives on request, to a realistic timetable by any healthcare provider;
- to ensure that relevant records which are not in healthcare providers' possession are made available to them by patients and their advisers at an appropriate stage;
- where a resolution is not achievable to lay the ground to enable litigation to proceed on a reasonable timetable, at a reasonable and proportionate cost and to limit the matters in contention;
- to discourage the prolonged pursuit of unmeritorious claims and the prolonged defence of meritorious claims.

Awareness of Options

- to ensure that patients and healthcare providers are made aware of the available options to pursue and resolve disputes and what each might involve.

2.3 This protocol does not attempt to be prescriptive about a number of related clinical governance issues which will have a bearing on healthcare providers' ability to meet the standards within the protocol. Good clinical governance requires the following to be considered—

(a) **Clinical risk management:** the protocol does not provide any detailed guidance to healthcare providers on clinical risk management or the adoption of risk management systems and procedures. This must be a matter for the NHS Executive,* the National Health Service Litigation Authority, individual trusts and providers, including GPs, dentists and the private sector. However, effective co-ordinated, focused clinical risk management strategies and procedures can help in managing risk and in the early identification and investigation of adverse outcomes.

(b) **Adverse outcome reporting:** the protocol does not provide any detailed guidance on which adverse outcomes should trigger an investigation. However, healthcare providers should have in place procedures for such investigations, including recording of statements of key witnesses. These procedures should also cover when and how to inform patients that an adverse outcome has occurred.

(c) **The professional's duty to report:** the protocol does not recommend changes to the codes of conduct of professionals in healthcare, or attempt to impose a specific duty on those

[* The NHS Executive ceased to exist in April 2002.]

professionals to report known adverse outcomes or untoward incidents. Lord Woolf in his final report suggested that the professional bodies might consider this. The General Medical Council is preparing guidance to doctors about their duty to report adverse incidents and to cooperate with inquiries.

3 THE PROTOCOL

3.1 This protocol is not a comprehensive code governing all the steps in clinical disputes. Rather it attempts to set out **a code of good practice** which parties should follow when litigation might be a possibility.

3.2 The **commitments** section of the protocol summarises the guiding principles which healthcare providers and patients and their advisers are invited to endorse when dealing with patient dissatisfaction with treatment and its outcome, and with potential complaints and claims.

3.3 The **steps** section sets out in a more prescriptive form, a recommended sequence of actions to be followed if litigation is a prospect.

Good Practice Commitments

3.4 **Healthcare providers** should—

(i) ensure that **key staff**, including claims and litigation managers, are appropriately trained and have some knowledge of healthcare law, and of complaints procedures and civil litigation practice and procedure;

(ii) develop an approach to **clinical governance** that ensures that clinical practice is delivered to commonly accepted standards and that this is routinely monitored through a system of clinical audit and clinical risk management (particularly adverse outcome investigation);

(iii) set up **adverse outcome reporting systems** in all specialties to record and investigate unexpected serious adverse outcomes as soon as possible. Such systems can enable evidence to be gathered quickly, which makes it easier to provide an accurate explanation of what happened and to defend or settle any subsequent claims;

(iv) use the results of **adverse incidents and complaints positively** as a guide to how to improve services to patients in the future;

(v) ensure **that patients receive clear and comprehensible information** in an accessible form about how to raise their concerns or complaints;

(vi) establish **efficient and effective systems of recording and storing patient records,** notes, diagnostic reports and X-rays, and to retain these in accordance with Department of Health guidance (currently for a minimum of eight years in the case of adults, and all obstetric and paediatric notes for children until they reach the age of 25);

(vii) **advise patients** of a serious adverse outcome and provide on request to the patient or the patient's representative an oral or written explanation of what happened, information on further steps open to the patient, including where appropriate an offer of future treatment to rectify the problem, an apology, changes in procedure which will benefit patients and/or compensation.

3.5 **Patients and their advisers** should—

(i) **report any concerns and dissatisfaction** to the healthcare provider as soon as is reasonable to enable that provider to offer clinical advice where possible, to advise the patient if anything has gone wrong and take appropriate action;

(ii) consider the **full range of options** available following an adverse outcome with which a patient is dissatisfied, including a request for an explanation, a meeting, a complaint, and other appropriate dispute resolution methods (including mediation) and negotiation, not only litigation;

(iii) **inform the healthcare provider when the patient is satisfied** that the matter has been concluded: legal advisers should notify the provider when they are no longer acting for the patient, particularly if proceedings have not started.

Protocol Steps

3.6 The steps of this protocol which follow have been kept deliberately simple. An illustration of the likely sequence of events in a number of healthcare situations is at Annex A.

Obtaining the Health Records

3.7 Any request for records by the **patient** or their adviser should—
- **provide sufficient information** to alert the healthcare provider where an adverse outcome has been serious or had serious consequences;
- be as **specific as possible** about the records which are required.

3.8 Requests for copies of the patient's clinical records should be made using the Law Society and Department of Health approved **standard forms** (enclosed at Annex B), adapted as necessary.

3.9 The copy records should be provided **within 40 days** of the request and for a cost not exceeding the charges permissible under the Access to Health Records Act 1990 (currently a maximum of £10 plus photocopying and postage).

3.10 In the rare circumstances that the healthcare provider is in difficulty in complying with the request within 40 days, the **problem should be explained** quickly and details given of what is being done to resolve it.

3.11 It will not be practicable for healthcare providers to investigate in detail each case when records are requested. But healthcare providers should **adopt a policy on which cases will be investigated** (see paragraph 3.5 on clinical governance and adverse outcome reporting).

3.12 If the healthcare provider fails to provide the health records within 40 days, the patient or their adviser can then apply to the court for an **order for pre-action disclosure.** The new Civil Procedure Rules should make pre-action applications to the court easier. The court will also have the power to impose costs sanctions for unreasonable delay in providing records.

3.13 If either the patient or the healthcare provider considers **additional health records are required from a third party,** in the first instance these should be requested by or through the patient. Third party healthcare providers are expected to cooperate. The Civil Procedure Rules will enable patients and healthcare providers to apply to the court for pre-action disclosure by third parties.

Letter of Claim

3.14 Annex C1 to this protocol provides **a template for the recommended contents of a letter of claim:** the level of detail will need to be varied to suit the particular circumstances.

3.15 If, following the receipt and analysis of the records, and the receipt of any further advice (including from experts if necessary—see Section 4), the patient/adviser decides that there are grounds for a claim, they should then send, as soon as practicable, to the healthcare provider/potential defendant, a **letter of claim.** Any letter of claim sent to an NHS trust or independent sector treatment centre should be copied to the National Health Service Litigation Authority.

3.16 This letter should contain a **clear summary of the facts** on which the claim is based, including the alleged adverse outcome, and the **main allegations of negligence.** It should also describe the **patient's injuries,** and present condition and prognosis. The **financial loss** incurred by the plaintiff should be outlined with an indication of the heads of damage to be claimed and the scale of the loss, unless this is impracticable.

3.17 In more complex cases a **chronology** of the relevant events should be provided, particularly if the patient has been treated by a number of different healthcare providers.

3.18 The letter of claim **should refer to any relevant documents,** including health records, and if possible enclose copies of any of those which will not already be in the potential defendant's possession, e.g. any relevant general practitioner records if the plaintiff 's claim is against a hospital.

3.19 **Sufficient information** must be given to enable the healthcare provider defendant to **commence investigations** and to put an initial valuation on the claim.

3.20 Letters of claim are **not** intended to have the same formal status as a **pleading,** nor should any sanctions necessarily apply if the letter of claim and any subsequent statement of claim in the proceedings differ.

3.21 **Proceedings should not be issued until after four months from the letter of claim,** unless there is a limitation problem and/or the patient's position needs to be protected by early issue.

3.22 The patient or their adviser may want to make an **offer to settle** the claim at this early stage by *putting forward an amount* of compensation which would be satisfactory (possibly including any costs incurred to date). If an offer to settle is made, generally this should be supported by a medical report which deals with the injuries, condition and prognosis, and by a schedule of loss and supporting documentation. The level of detail necessary will depend on the value of the claim. Medical reports may not be necessary where there is no significant continuing injury, and a detailed schedule may not be necessary in a low value case. The Civil Procedure Rules are expected to set out the legal and procedural requirements for making offers to settle.

The Response

3.23 Attached at Annex C2 is a template for the suggested contents of the **letter of response**.

3.24 The healthcare provider should **acknowledge** the letter of claim **within 14 days of receipt** and should identify who will be dealing with the matter.

3.25 The healthcare provider should, **within four months** of the letter of claim, provide **a reasoned answer**—

- if the **claim is admitted** the healthcare provider should say so in clear terms;
- if only **part of the claim is admitted** the healthcare provider should make clear which issues of breach of duty and/or causation are admitted and which are denied and why;
- if it is intended that any **admissions will be binding;**
- if the claim is denied, this should include specific comments on the allegations of negligence, and if a synopsis or chronology of relevant events has been provided and is disputed, the healthcare provider's version of those events;
- where additional documents are relied upon, e.g. an internal protocol, copies should be provided.

3.26 If the patient has made an offer to settle, the healthcare provider should **respond to that offer** in the response letter, preferably with reasons. The provider may make its own offer to settle at this stage, either as a counter-offer to the patient's, or of its own accord, but should accompany any offer by any supporting medical evidence, and/or by any other evidence in relation to the value of the claim which is in the healthcare provider's possession.

3.27 If the parties reach agreement on liability, but time is needed to resolve the value of the claim, they should aim to agree a reasonable period.

4 EXPERTS

4.1 In clinical negligence disputes **expert opinions** may be needed—

- on breach of duty and causation;
- on the patient's condition and prognosis;
- to assist in valuing aspects of the claim.

4.2 The civil justice reforms and the new **Civil Procedure Rules** will encourage economy in the use of experts and a **less adversarial expert culture.** It is recognised that in clinical negligence disputes, the parties and their advisers will require flexibility in their approach to expert evidence. Decisions on whether experts might be instructed jointly, and on whether reports might be disclosed sequentially or by exchange, should rest with the parties and their advisers. Sharing expert evidence may be appropriate on issues relating to the value of the claim. However, this protocol does not attempt to be prescriptive on issues in relation to expert evidence.

4.3 Obtaining expert evidence will often be an expensive step and may take time, especially in specialised areas of medicine where there are limited numbers of suitable experts. Patients and healthcare providers, and their advisers, will therefore need to consider carefully how best to obtain any necessary expert help quickly and cost-effectively. Assistance with locating a suitable expert is available from a number of sources.

5 ALTERNATIVE DISPUTE RESOLUTION

5.1 The parties should consider whether some form of alternative dispute resolution procedure would be more suitable than litigation, and if so, endeavour to agree which form to adopt. Both the claimant and defendant may be required by the court to provide evidence that alternative means of resolving their dispute were considered. The courts take the view that litigation should be a last resort, and that claims should not be issued prematurely when a settlement is still actively being explored. Parties are warned that if the protocol is not followed (including this paragraph) then the court must have regard to such conduct when determining costs.

5.2 It is not practicable in this protocol to address in detail how the parties might decide which method to adopt to resolve their particular dispute. However, summarised below are some of the options for resolving disputes without litigation:

- Discussion and negotiation. Parties should bear in mind that carefully planned face-to-face meetings may be particularly helpful in exploring further treatment for the patient, in reaching understandings about what happened, and on both parties' positions, in narrowing the issues in dispute and, if the timing is right, in helping to settle the whole matter especially if the patient wants an apology, explanation, or assurances about how other patients will be affected.
- Early neutral evaluation by an independent third party (for example, a lawyer experienced in the field of clinical negligence or an individual experienced in the subject matter of the claim).
- Mediation — a form of facilitated negotiation assisted by an independent neutral party. The Clinical Disputes Forum has published a *Guide to Mediation* which will assist — available on the Clinical Disputes Forum website at www.clinicaldisputesforum.org.uk.
- The **NHS Complaints Procedure** is designed to provide patients with an explanation of what happened and an apology if appropriate. It is not designed to provide compensation for cases of negligence. However, patients might choose to use the procedure if their only, or main, goal is to obtain an explanation, or to obtain more information to help them decide what other action might be appropriate.

5.3 The Legal Services Commission has published a booklet on *Alternatives to Court* (CLS Direct Information Leaflet 23) (www.clsdirect.org.uk/legalhelp/leaflet23.jsp), which lists a number of organisations that provide alternative dispute resolution services.

5.4 *It is expressly recognised that no party can or should be forced to mediate or enter into any form of ADR.*

ANNEX A ILLUSTRATIVE FLOWCHART

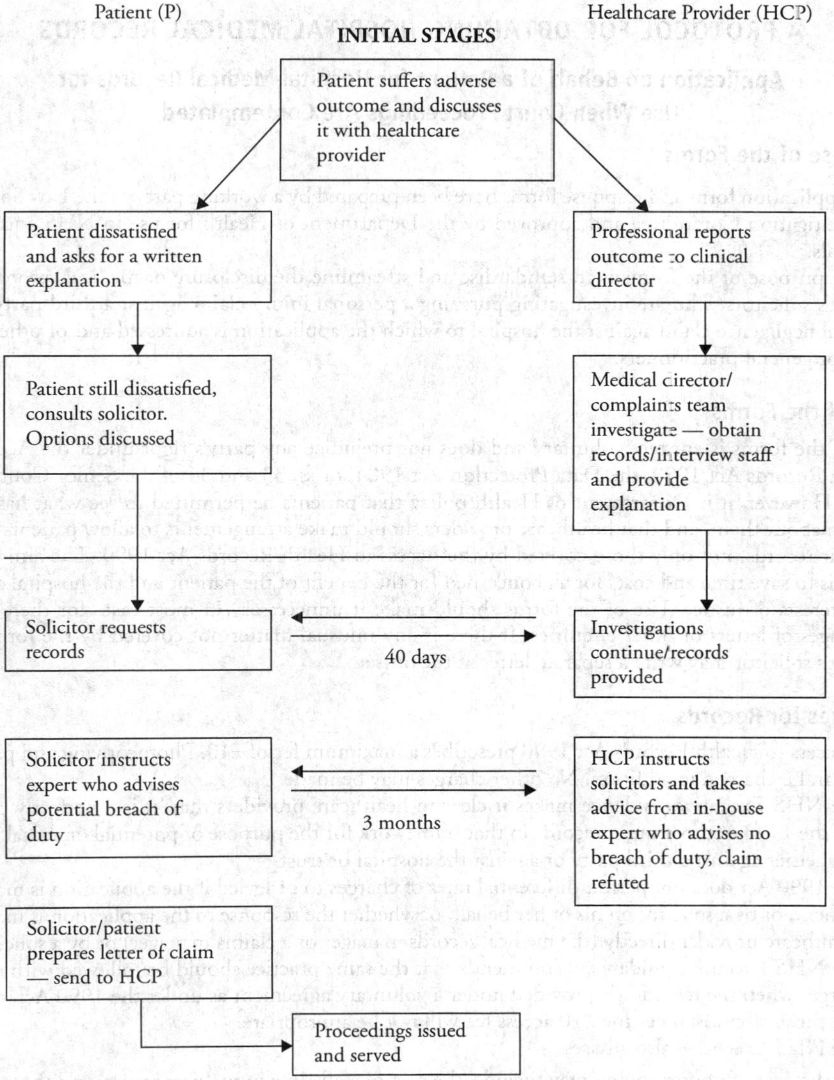

ANNEX B MEDICAL NEGLIGENCE AND PERSONAL INJURY CLAIMS

A PROTOCOL FOR OBTAINING HOSPITAL MEDICAL RECORDS

Application on Behalf of a Patient for Hospital Medical Records for Use When Court Proceedings Are Contemplated

Purpose of the Forms

This application form and response forms have been prepared by a working party of the Law Society's Civil Litigation Committee and approved by the Department of Health for use in NHS and Trust hospitals.

The purpose of the forms is to standardise and streamline the disclosure of medical records to a patient's solicitors, who are investigating pursuing a personal injury claim against a third party, or a medical negligence claim against the hospital to which the application is addressed and/or other hospitals or general practitioners.

Use of the Forms

Use of the forms is entirely voluntary and does not prejudice any party's right under the Access to Health Records Act 1990, the Data Protection Act 1984, or ss. 33 and 34 of the Senior Courts Act 1981. However, it is Department of Health policy that patients be permitted to see what has been written about them, and that healthcare providers should make arrangements to allow patients to see all their records, not only those covered by the Access to Health Records Act 1990. The aim of the forms is to save time and costs for all concerned for the benefit of the patient and the hospital and in the interests of justice. Use of the forms should make it unnecessary in most cases for there to be exchanges of letters or other enquiries. If there is any unusual matter not covered by the form, the patient's solicitor may write a separate letter at the outset.

Charges for Records

The Access to Health Records Act 1990 prescribes a maximum fee of £10. Photocopying and postage costs can be charged in addition. No other charges may be made.

The NHS Executive guidance makes it clear to healthcare providers that 'it is a perfectly proper use' of the 1990 Act to request records in that framework for the purpose of potential or actual litigation, whether against a third party or against the hospital or trust.

The 1990 Act does not permit differential rates of charges to be levied if the application is made by the patient, or by a solicitor on his or her behalf, or whether the response to the application is made by the healthcare provider directly (the medical records manager or a claims manager) or by a solicitor.

The NHS Executive guidance recommends that the same practice should be followed with regard to charges when the records are provided under a voluntary agreement as under the 1990 Act, except that in those circumstances the £10 access fee will not be appropriate.

The NHS Executive also advises—

- that the cost of photocopying may include 'the cost of staff time in making copies' and the costs of running the copier (but not costs of locating and sifting records);
- that the common practice of setting a standard rate for an application or charging an administration fee is not acceptable because there will be cases when this fails to comply with the 1990 Act.

Records: What Might Be Included

X-rays and test results form part of the patient's records. Additional charges for copying X-rays are permissible. If there are large numbers of X-rays, the records officer should check with the patient/solicitor before arranging copying.

Reports on an 'adverse incident' and reports on the patient made for risk management and audit purposes may form part of the records and be disclosable: the exception will be any specific record or *report made solely or mainly in connection* with an actual or potential claim.

Records: Quality Standards

When copying records healthcare providers should ensure—

1. All documents are legible, and complete, if necessary by photocopying at less than 100% size.
2. Documents larger than A4 in the original, e.g. ITU charts, should be reproduced in A3, or reduced to A4 where this retains readability.
3. Documents are only copied on one side of paper, unless the original is two sided.
4. Documents should not be unnecessarily shuffled or bound and holes should not be made in the copied papers.

Enquiries/Further Information

Any enquiries about the forms should be made initially to the solicitors making the request. Comments on the use and content of the forms should be made to the Secretary, Civil Litigation Committee, The Law Society, 113 Chancery Lane, London WC2A 1 PL, telephone (020) 7320 5739, or to the NHS Management Executive, Quarry House, Quarry Hill, Leeds LS2 7UE.

The Law Society

May 1998

Application on Behalf of a Patient for Hospital Medical Records for Use When Court Proceedings Are Contemplated

This should be completed as fully as possible

Insert Hospital Name and Address	TO: Medical Records Officer Hospital

1(a)	Full name of patient (including previous surnames)	
(b)	Address now	
(c)	Address at start of treatment	
(d)	Date of birth (and death, if applicable)	
(e)	Hospital ref. number, if available	
(f)	N.I. number, if available	
2	This application is made because the patient is considering	
	(a) a claim against your hospital as detailed in para. 7 overleaf	YES/NO
	(b) pursuing an action against someone else	YES/NO
3	Department(s) where treatment was received	
4	Name(s) of consultant(s) at your hospital in charge of the treatment	
5	Whether treatment at your hospital was private or NHS, wholly or in part	
6	A description of the treatment received, with approximate dates	
7	If the answer to Q2(a) is 'Yes' details of	
	(a) the likely nature of the claim	
	(b) grounds for the claim	
	(c) approximate dates of the events involved	
8	If the answer to Q2(b) is 'Yes' insert	
	(a) the names of the proposed defendants	
	(b) whether legal proceedings yet begun	YES/NO
	(c) if appropriate, details of the claim and action number	

Pre-action Protocols

9	We confirm we will pay reasonable copying charges	
10	We request prior details of	YES/NO
	(a) photocopying and administration charges for medical records	
	(b) number of and cost of copying X-ray and scan films	YES/NO
11	Any other relevant information, particular requirements, or any particular documents *not* required (e.g. copies of computerised records)	
	Signature of Solicitor	
	Name	
	Address	
	Ref.	
	Telephone Number	
	Fax number	

Please print name beneath each signature. Signature by child over 12 but under 18 years also requires signature by parent

Signature of patient

Signature of parent or next friend if appropriate

Signature of personal representative where patient has died

First Response to Application for Hospital Records

NAME OF PATIENT Our ref. Your ref.		
1	Date of receipt of patient's application	
2	We intend that copy medical records will be dispatched within 6 weeks of that date	YES/NO
3	We require prepayment of photocopying charges	YES/NO
4	If estimate of photocopying charges requested or prepayment required the amount will be	£ / notified to you
5	The cost of X-ray and scan films will be	£ / notified to you
6	If there is any problem, we shall write to you within those 6 weeks	YES/NO
7	Any other information	
	Please address further correspondence to	
	Signed	
	Direct telephone number	
	Direct fax number	
	Dated	

Second Response Enclosing Patient's Hospital Medical Records

Address | Our Ref.
Your Ref.

1	NAME OF PATIENT: We confirm that the enclosed copy medical records are all those within the control of the hospital, relevant to the application which you have made to the best of our knowledge and belief, subject to paras 2–5 below	YES/NO
2	Details of any other documents which have not yet been located	
3	Date by when it is expected that these will be supplied	
4	Details of any records which we are not producing	
5	The reasons for not doing so	
6	An invoice for copying and administration charges is attached	YES/NO
	Signed	
	Date	

ANNEX C TEMPLATES FOR LETTERS OF CLAIM AND RESPONSE

C1 Letter of Claim

Essential Contents

1. **Client's name, address, date of birth, etc.**
2. **Dates of allegedly negligent treatment**
3. **Events giving rise to the claim:**
   - an outline of what happened, including details of other relevant treatments to the client by other healthcare providers.
4. **Allegation of negligence and causal link with injuries:**
   - an outline of the allegations or a more detailed list in a complex case;
   - an outline of the causal link between allegations and the injuries complained of.
5. **The Client's injuries, condition and future prognosis**
6. **Request for clinical records (if not previously provided)**
   - use the Law Society form if appropriate or adapt;
   - specify the records required;
   - if other records are held by other providers, and may be relevant, say so;
   - state what investigations have been carried out to date, e.g. information from client and witnesses, any complaint and the outcome, if any clinical records have been seen or experts advice obtained.
7. **The likely value of the claim**
   - an outline of the main heads of damage, or, in straightforward cases, the details of loss.

Optional information
What investigations have been carried out
An offer to settle without supporting evidence
Suggestions for obtaining expert evidence
Suggestions for meetings, negotiations, discussion or mediation
Possible enclosures
Chronology
Clinical records request form and client's authorisation
Expert report(s)
Schedules of loss and supporting evidence

C2 Letter of Response

Essential Contents

1. Provide **requested records** and invoice for copying:
   - explain if records are incomplete or extensive records are held and ask for further instructions;
   - request additional records from third parties.
2. **Comments on events and/or chronology:**
   - if events are disputed or the healthcare provider has further information or documents on which they wish to rely, these should be provided, e.g. internal protocol;
   - details of any further information needed from the patient or a third party should be provided.
3. **If breach of duty and causation are accepted:**
   - suggestions might be made for resolving the claim and/or requests for further information;
   - a response should be made to any offer to settle.
4. **If breach of duty and/or causation are denied:**
   - a bare denial will not be sufficient. If the healthcare provider has other explanations for what happened, these should be given at least in outline;
   - suggestions might be made for the next steps, e.g. further investigations, obtaining expert evidence, meetings/negotiations or mediation, or an invitation to issue proceedings.

Optional Matters

An offer to settle if the patient has not made one, or a counter offer to the patient's with supporting evidence

Possible enclosures:

Clinical records
Annotated chronology
Expert reports

ANNEX D LORD WOOLF'S RECOMMENDATIONS

1. Lord Woolf in his Access to Justice Report in July 1996, following a detailed review of the problems of medical negligence claims, identified that one of the major sources of **costs and delay** is at **the pre-litigation** stage because—
   (a) Inadequate incident reporting and record keeping in hospitals, and mobility of staff, make it difficult to establish facts, often several years after the event.
   (b) Claimants must incur the cost of an expert in order to establish whether they have a viable claim.
   (c) There is often a long delay before a claim is made.
   (d) Defendants do not have sufficient resources to carry out a full investigation of every incident, and do not consider it worthwhile to start an investigation as soon as they receive a request for records, because many cases do not proceed beyond that stage.
   (e) Patients often give the defendant little or no notice of a firm intention to pursue a claim. Consequently, many incidents are not investigated by the defendants until after proceedings have started.
   (f) Doctors and other clinical staff are traditionally reluctant to admit negligence or apologise to, or negotiate with, claimants for fear of damage to their professional reputations or career prospects.
2. Lord Woolf acknowledged that under the present arrangements **healthcare providers**, faced with possible medical negligence claims, have a number of **practical problems** to contend with—
   (a) Difficulties of finding patients' records and tracing former staff, which can be exacerbated by late notification and by the health care provider's own failure to identify adverse incidents.
   (b) The healthcare provider may have only treated the patient for a limited time or for a specific complaint: the patient's previous history may be relevant but the records may be in the possession of one of several other healthcare providers.
   (c) The large number of potential claims which do not proceed beyond the stage of a request for medical records, or an explanation; and that it is difficult for healthcare providers to investigate *fully every* case whenever a patient asks to see the records.

ANNEX E HOW TO CONTACT THE FORUM

The Clinical Disputes Forum

Chairman
Dr Alastair Scotland
Medical Director and Chief Officer
National Clinical Assessment Authority
9th Floor, Market Towers
London
SW8 5NQ
Telephone: (020) 7273 0850

Secretary
Sarah Leigh
c/o Margaret Dangoor
3 Clydesdale Gardens
Richmond
Surrey
TW10 5EG
Telephone: (020) 8408 1012

Pre-action Protocol for Construction and Engineering Disputes

1 INTRODUCTION

1.1 This pre-action protocol applies to all construction and engineering disputes (including professional negligence claims against architects, engineers and quantity surveyors).

Exceptions

1.2 A claimant shall not be required to comply with this protocol before commencing proceedings to the extent that the proposed proceedings (i) are for the enforcement of the decision of an adjudicator to whom a dispute has been referred pursuant to s. 108 of the Housing Grants, Construction and Regeneration Act 1996 ('the 1996 Act'), (ii) include a claim for interim injunctive relief, (iii) will be the subject of a claim for summary judgment pursuant to CPR, Part 24, or (iv) relate to the same or substantially the same issues as have been the subject of recent adjudication under the 1996 Act, or some other formal alternative dispute resolution procedure.

Objectives

1.3 The objectives of this protocol are as set out in PD Protocols, namely:
- (i) to encourage the exchange of early and full information about the prospective legal claim;
- (ii) to enable parties to avoid litigation by agreeing a settlement of the claim before commencement of proceedings; and
- (iii) to support the efficient management of proceedings where litigation cannot be avoided.

Compliance

1.4 If proceedings are commenced, the court will be able to treat the standards set in this protocol as the normal reasonable approach to pre-action conduct. If the court has to consider the question of compliance after proceedings have begun, it will be concerned with substantial compliance and not minor departures, e.g. failure by a short period to provide relevant information. Minor departures will not exempt the 'innocent' party from following the protocol. The court will look at the effect of non-compliance on the other party when deciding whether to impose sanctions. For sanctions generally, see PD Protocols, para. 2 'Compliance with Protocols'.

Proportionality

1.5 The overriding objective (CPR, r. 1.1) applies to the pre-action period. The protocol must not be used as a tactical device to secure advantage for one party or to generate unnecessary costs. In lower-value claims (such as those likely to proceed in the county court), the letter of claim and the response should be simple and the costs of both sides should be kept to a modest level. In all cases the costs incurred at the protocol stage should be proportionate to the complexity of the case and the amount of money which is at stake. The protocol does not impose a requirement on the parties to marshal and disclose all the supporting details and evidence that may ultimately be required if the case proceeds to litigation.

2 OVERVIEW OF THE PROTOCOL

General Aim

2 The general aim of this protocol is to ensure that before court proceedings commence:

(i) the claimant and the defendant have provided sufficient information for each party to know the nature of the other's case;

(ii) each party has had an opportunity to consider the other's case, and to accept or reject all or any part of the case made against him at the earliest possible stage;

(iii) there is more pre-action contact between the parties;

(iv) better and earlier exchange of information occurs;

(v) there is better pre-action investigation by the parties;

(vi) the parties have met formally on at least one occasion with a view to
- defining and agreeing the issues between them; and
- exploring possible ways by which the claim may be resolved;

(vii) the parties are in a position where they may be able to settle cases early and fairly without recourse to litigation; and

(viii) proceedings will be conducted efficiently if litigation does become necessary.

3 THE LETTER OF CLAIM

3 Prior to commencing proceedings, the claimant or his solicitor shall send to each proposed defendant (if appropriate to his registered address) a copy of a letter of claim which shall contain the following information:

(i) the claimant's full name and address;

(ii) the full name and address of each proposed defendant;

(iii) a clear summary of the facts on which each claim is based;

(iv) the basis on which each claim is made, identifying the principal contractual terms and statutory provisions relied on;

(v) the nature of the relief claimed: if damages are claimed, a breakdown showing how the damages have been quantified; if a sum is claimed pursuant to a contract, how it has been calculated; if an extension of time is claimed, the period claimed;

(vi) where a claim has been made previously and rejected by a defendant, and the claimant is able to identify the reason(s) for such rejection, the claimant's grounds of belief as to why the claim was wrongly rejected;

(vii) the names of any experts already instructed by the claimant on whose evidence he intends to rely, identifying the issues to which that evidence will be directed.

4 THE DEFENDANT'S RESPONSE

The Defendant's Acknowledgment

4.1 Within 14 calendar days of receipt of the letter of claim, the defendant should acknowledge its receipt in writing and may give the name and address of his insurer (if any). If there has been no acknowledgment by or on behalf of the defendant within 14 days, the claimant will be entitled to commence proceedings without further compliance with this protocol.

Objections to the Court's Jurisdiction or the Named Defendant

4.2.1 If the defendant intends to take any objection to all or any part of the claimant's claim on the grounds that (i) the court lacks jurisdiction, (ii) the matter should be referred to arbitration, or (iii) the defendant named in the letter of claim is the wrong defendant, that objection should be raised by the defendant within 28 days after receipt of the letter of claim. The letter of objection *shall specify* the parts of the claim to which the objection relates, setting out the grounds relied on, and, where appropriate, shall identify the correct defendant (if known). Any failure to take such objection shall not prejudice the defendant's rights to do so in any subsequent proceedings, but the court may take such failure into account when considering the question of costs.

Pre-action Protocols

4.2.2 Where such notice of objection is given, the defendant is not required to send a letter of response in accordance with para. 4.3.1. in relation to the claim or those parts of it to which the objection relates (as the case may be).

4.2.3 If at any stage before the claimant commences proceedings, the defendant withdraws his objection, then para. 4.3 and the remaining part of this protocol will apply to the claim or those parts of it to which the objection related as if the letter of claim had been received on the date on which notice of withdrawal of the objection had been given.

The Defendant's Response

4.3.1 Within 28 days from the date of receipt of the letter of claim, or such other period as the parties may reasonably agree (up to a maximum of three months), the defendant shall send a letter of response to the claimant which shall contain the following information:

(i) the facts set out in the letter of claim which are agreed or not agreed, and if not agreed, the basis of the disagreement;

(ii) which claims are accepted and which are rejected, and if rejected, the basis of the rejection;

(iii) if a claim is accepted in whole or in part, whether the damages, sums or extensions of time claimed are accepted or rejected, and if rejected, the basis of the rejection;

(iv) if contributory negligence is alleged against the claimant, a summary of the facts relied on;

(v) whether the defendant intends to make a counterclaim, and if so, giving the information which is required to be given in a letter of claim by para. 3(iii) to (vi) above;

(vi) the names of any experts already instructed on whose evidence it is intended to rely, identifying the issues to which that evidence will be directed.

4.3.2 If no response is received by the claimant within the period of 28 days (or such other period as has been agreed between the parties), the claimant shall be entitled to commence proceedings without further compliance with this protocol.

Claimant's Response to Counterclaim

4.4 The claimant shall provide a response to any counterclaim within the equivalent period allowed to the defendant to respond to the letter of claim under para. 4.3.1. above.

5 PRE-ACTION MEETING

5.1 Within 28 days after receipt by the claimant of the defendant's letter of response, or (if the claimant intends to respond to the counterclaim) after receipt by the defendant of the claimant's letter of response to the counterclaim, the parties should normally meet.

5.2 The aim of the meeting is for the parties to agree what are the main issues in the case, to identify the root cause of disagreement in respect of each issue, and to consider (i) whether, and if so how, the issues might be resolved without recourse to litigation, and (ii) if litigation is unavoidable, what steps should be taken to ensure that it is conducted in accordance with the overriding objective as defined in CPR, r. 1.1.

5.3 In some circumstances, it may be necessary to convene more than one meeting. It is not intended by this protocol to prescribe in detail the manner in which the meetings should be conducted. But the court will normally expect that those attending will include:

(i) where the party is an individual, that individual, and where the party is a corporate body, a representative of that body who has authority to settle or recommend settlement of the dispute;

(ii) a legal representative of each party (if one has been instructed);

(iii) where the involvement of insurers has been disclosed, a representative of the insurer (who may be its legal representative); and

(iv) where a claim is made or defended on behalf of some other party (such as, for example, a claim made by a main contractor pursuant to a contractual obligation to pass on subcontractor claims), the party on whose behalf the claim is made or defended and/or his legal representatives.

5.4 In respect of each agreed issue or the dispute as a whole, the parties should consider whether some form of alternative dispute resolution procedure would be more suitable than litigation, and if so, endeavour to agree which form to adopt. It is expressly recognised that no party can or should be forced to mediate or enter into any form of alternative dispute resolution.

5.5 If the parties are unable to agree on a means of resolving the dispute other than by litigation they should use their best endeavours to agree:

(i) if there is any area where expert evidence is likely to be required, how the relevant issues are to be defined and how expert evidence is to be dealt with including whether a joint expert may be appointed, and if so, who that should be; and (so far as is practicable)

(ii) the extent of disclosure of documents with a view to saving costs; and

(iii) the conduct of the litigation with the aim of minimising cost and delay.

5.6 Any party who attended any pre-action meeting shall be at liberty to disclose to the court:

(i) that the meeting took place, when and who attended;

(ii) the identity of any party who refused to attend, and the grounds for such refusal;

(iii) if the meeting did not take place, why not;

(iv) any agreements concluded between the parties; and

(v) the fact of whether alternative means of resolving the dispute were considered or agreed.

5.7 Except as provided in para. 5.6, everything said at a pre-action meeting shall be treated as 'without prejudice'.

6 LIMITATION OF ACTION

6.1 If by reason of complying with any part of this protocol a claimant's claim may be time-barred under any provision of the Limitation Act 1980, or any other legislation which imposes a time limit for bringing an action, the claimant may commence proceedings without complying with this protocol. In such circumstances, a claimant who commences proceedings without complying with all, or any part, of this protocol must apply to the court on notice for directions as to the timetable and form of procedure to be adopted, at the same time as he requests the court to issue proceedings. The court will consider whether to order a stay of the whole or part of the proceedings pending compliance with this protocol.

Pre-action Protocol for Defamation

1 INTRODUCTION

1.1 Lord Irvine of Lairg, in his foreword to the Pre-action Protocol for Personal Injury Claims identified the value of creating pre-action protocols as a key part of the civil justice reforms. He hoped that pre-action protocols would set effective and enforceable standards for the efficient conduct of pre-action litigation.

1.2 Lord Irvine went on to state that:

The protocol aims to improve pre-action communication between the parties by establishing a timetable for the exchange of information relevant to the dispute and by setting standards for the content of correspondence. Compliance with the protocol will enable parties to make an informed judgement on the merits of their cases earlier than tends to happen today, because they will have earlier access to the information they need. This will provide every opportunity for improved communications between the parties designed to lead to an increase in the number of pre-action settlements.

1.3 It is against this background that a Pre-action Protocol for Claims in Defamation is submitted. This protocol is intended to encourage exchange of information between parties at an early, stage and to provide a clear framework within which parties to a claim in defamation, acting in good faith, can explore the early and appropriate resolution of that claim.

1.4 There are important features which distinguish defamation claims from other areas of civil litigation, and these must be borne in mind when both applying, and reviewing the application of, the pre-action protocol. In particular, time is always 'of the essence' in defamation claims; the limitation period is (uniquely) only one year, and almost invariably, a claimant will be seeking an immediate correction and/or apology as part of the process of restoring his/her reputation.

1.5 This pre-action protocol embraces the spirit of the reforms to the civil justice system envisaged by Lord Woolf, and now enacted in the Civil Procedure Rules. It aims to incorporate the concept of the overriding objective, as provided by the Rules at Part 1, before the commencement of any court proceedings, namely: dealing with a case justly includes, so far as is practicable:

- ensuring that the parties are on an equal footing;
- saving expense;

dealing with the case in ways which are proportionate:

- to the amount of money involved;
- to the importance of the case;
- to the complexity of the issues; and
- to the financial position of each party;
- ensuring that it is dealt with expeditiously and fairly; and
- allotting to it an appropriate share of the court's resources, while taking into account the need to allot resources to other cases.

2 AIMS OF THE PROTOCOL

- This protocol aims to set out a code of good practice which parties should follow when litigation is being considered.
- It encourages early communication of a claim.
- It aims to encourage both parties to disclose sufficient information to enable each to understand the other's case and to promote the prospect of early resolution.
- It sets a timetable for the exchange of information relevant to the dispute.
- It sets standards for the content of correspondence.
- It identifies options which either party might adopt to encourage settlement of the claim.

- Should a claim proceed to litigation, the extent to which the protocol has been followed both in practice and in spirit by the parties will assist the court in dealing with liability for costs and making other orders.
- Letters of claim and responses sent pursuant to this protocol are not intended to have the same status as a statement of case in proceedings.
- It aims to keep the costs of resolving disputes subject to this protocol proportionate.

3 PRE-ACTION PROTOCOL

Letter of Claim

3.1 The claimant should notify the defendant of his/her claim in writing at the earliest reasonable opportunity.

3.2 The letter of claim should include the following information:
- name of claimant;
- sufficient details to identify the publication or broadcast which contained the words complained of;
- the words complained of and, if known, the date of publication; where possible, a copy or transcript of the words complained of should be enclosed;
- factual inaccuracies or unsupportable comment within the words complained of; the claimant should give a sufficient explanation to enable the defendant to appreciate why the words are inaccurate or unsupportable;
- the nature of the remedies sought by the claimant.
- Where relevant, the letter of claim should also include:
- any facts or matters which make the claimant identifiable from the words complained of;
- details of any special facts relevant to the interpretation of the words complained of and/or any particular damage caused by the words complained of.

3.3 It is desirable for the claimant to identify in the letter of claim the meaning(s) he/she attributes to the words complained of.

Defendant's Response to Letter of Claim

3.4 The defendant should provide a full response to the letter of claim as soon as reasonably possible. If the defendant believes that he/she will be unable to respond within 14 days (or such shorter time limit as specified in the letter of claim), then he/she should specify the date by which he/she intends to respond.

3.5 The response should include the following:
- whether or to what extent the claimant's claim is accepted, whether more information is required or whether it is rejected;
- if the claim is accepted in whole or in part, the defendant should indicate which remedies it is willing to offer;
- if more information is required, then the defendant should specify precisely what information is needed to enable the claim to be dealt with and why;
- if the claim is rejected, then the defendant should explain the reasons why it is rejected, including a sufficient indication of any facts on which the defendant is likely to rely in support of any substantive defence;
- It is desirable for the defendant to include in the response to the letter of claim the meaning(s) he/she attributes to the words complained of.

Proportionality of Costs

3.6 In formulating both the letter of claim and response and in taking any subsequent steps, the parties should act reasonably to keep costs proportionate to the nature and gravity of the case and the stage the complaint has reached.

Alternative Dispute Resolution

3.7 The parties should consider whether some form of alternative dispute resolution procedure would be more suitable than litigation, and if so, endeavour to agree which form to adopt. Both the claimant and defendant may be required by the court to provide evidence that alternative means of resolving their dispute were considered. The courts take the view that litigation should be a last resort, and that claims should not be issued prematurely when a settlement is still actively being explored. Parties are warned that if the protocol is not followed (including this paragraph) then the court must have regard to such conduct when determining costs.

3.8 It is not practicable in this protocol to address in detail how the parties might decide which method to adopt to resolve their particular dispute. However, summarised below are some of the options for resolving disputes without litigation:

- Discussion and negotiation.
- Early neutral evaluation by an independent third party (for example, a lawyer experienced in the field of defamation or an individual experienced in the subject matter of the claim).
- Mediation — a form of facilitated negotiation assisted by an independent neutral party.
- The Reference to the Press Complaints Commission (an independent body which deals with complaints from members of the public about the editorial content of newspapers and magazines).

3.9 The Legal Services Commission has published a booklet on *Alternatives to Court* (CLS Direct Information Leaflet 23) (www.clsdirect.org.uk/legalhelp/leaflet23.jsp), which lists a number of organisations that provide alternative dispute resolution services.

3.10 *It is expressly recognised that no party can or should be forced to mediate or enter into any form of ADR.*

Professional Negligence Pre-action Protocol

This protocol merges the two protocols previously produced by the Solicitors Indemnity Fund (SIF) and Claims against Professionals (CAP).

A INTRODUCTION

A1 This protocol is designed to apply when a claimant wishes to claim against a professional (other than construction professionals and healthcare providers) as a result of that professional's alleged negligence or equivalent breach of contract or breach of fiduciary duty. Although these claims will be the usual situation in which the protocol will be used, there may be other claims for which the protocol could be appropriate. For a more detailed explanation of the scope of the protocol see Guidance Note C2.

A2 The aim of this protocol is to establish a framework in which there is an early exchange of information so that the claim can be fully investigated and, if possible, resolved without the need for litigation. This includes:
- (a) ensuring that the parties are on an equal footing;
- (b) saving expense;
- (c) dealing with the dispute in ways which are proportionate:
  - (i) to the amount of money involved;
  - (ii) to the importance of the case;
  - (iii) to the complexity of the issues;
  - (iv) to the financial position of each party;
- (d) ensuring that it is dealt with expeditiously and fairly.

A3 This protocol is not intended to replace other forms of pre-action dispute resolution (such as internal complaints procedures, the Surveyors and Valuers Arbitration Scheme, etc.). Where such procedures are available, parties are encouraged to consider whether they should be used. If, however, these other procedures are used and fail to resolve the dispute, the protocol should be used before litigation is started, adapting it where appropriate. See also Guidance Note C3.

A4 The courts will be able to treat the standards set in this protocol as the normal reasonable approach. If litigation is started, it will be for the court to decide whether sanctions should be imposed as a result of substantial non-compliance with a protocol. Guidance on the courts' likely approach is given in PD Protocols. The court is likely to disregard minor departures from this protocol and so should the parties as between themselves.

A5 Both in operating the timetable and in requesting and providing information during the protocol period, the parties are expected to act reasonably, in line with the court's expectations of them. See also Guidance Note C1.2.

B THE PROTOCOL

B1 Preliminary Notice

(See also Guidance Note C3.1)

B1.1 As soon as the claimant decides there is a reasonable chance that he will bring a claim against a professional, the claimant is encouraged to notify the professional in writing.

B1.2 This letter should contain the following information:
- (a) the identity of the claimant and any other parties;
- (b) a brief outline of the claimant's grievance against the professional;
- (c) if possible, a general indication of the financial value of the potential claim.

B1.3 This letter should be addressed to the professional and should ask the professional to inform his professional indemnity insurers, if any, immediately.

Pre-action Protocols

B1.4 The professional should acknowledge receipt of the claimant's letter within 21 days of receiving it. Other than this acknowledgment, the protocol places no obligation upon either party to take any further action.

B2 Letter of Claim

B2.1 As soon as the claimant decides there are grounds for a claim against the professional, the claimant should write a detailed letter of claim to the professional.

B2.2 The letter of claim will normally be an open letter (as opposed to being 'without prejudice') and should include the following:

(a) The identity of any other parties involved in the dispute or a related dispute.

(b) A clear chronological summary (including key dates) of the facts on which the claim is based. Key documents should be identified, copied and enclosed.

(c) The allegations against the professional. What has he done wrong? What has he failed to do?

(d) An explanation of how the alleged error has caused the loss claimed.

(e) An estimate of the financial loss suffered by the claimant and how it is calculated. Supporting documents should be identified, copied and enclosed. If details of the financial loss cannot be supplied, the claimant should explain why and should state when he will be in a position to provide the details. This information should be sent to the professional as soon as reasonably possible.

If the claimant is seeking some form of non-financial redress, this should be made clear.

(f) Confirmation whether or not an expert has been appointed. If so, providing the identity and discipline of the expert, together with the date upon which the expert was appointed.

(g) A request that a copy of the letter of claim be forwarded immediately to the professional's insurers, if any.

B2.3 The letter of claim is not intended to have the same formal status as a statement of case. If, however, the letter of claim differs materially from the statement of case in subsequent proceedings, the court may decide, in its discretion, to impose sanctions.

B2.4 If the claimant has sent other letters of claim (or equivalent) to any other party in relation to this dispute or related dispute, those letters should be copied to the professional. (If the claimant is claiming against someone else to whom this protocol does not apply, please see Guidance Note C4.)

B3 The Letter of Acknowledgment

B3.1 The professional should acknowledge receipt of the letter of claim within 21 days of receiving it.

B4 Investigations

B4.1 The professional will have three months from the date of the letter of acknowledgment to investigate.

B4.2 If the professional is in difficulty in complying with the three-month time period, the problem should be explained to the claimant as soon as possible. The professional should explain what is being done to resolve the problem and when the professional expects to complete the investigations. The claimant should agree to any reasonable request for an extension of the three-month period.

B4.3 The parties should supply promptly, at this stage and throughout, whatever relevant information or documentation is reasonably requested. (Please see Guidance Note C5). (If the professional intends to claim against someone who is not currently a party to the dispute, please see Guidance Note C4.)

B5 Letter of Response and Letter of Settlement

B5.1 As soon as the professional has completed his investigations, the professional should send to the claimant:

(a) a letter of response; or

(b) a letter of settlement; or

(c) *both.*

The letters of response and settlement can be contained within a single letter.

The letter of response

B5.2 The letter of response will normally be an open letter (as opposed to being 'without prejudice') and should be a reasoned answer to the claimant's allegations:

(a) If the claim is admitted the professional should say so in clear terms.
(b) If only part of the claim is admitted the professional should make clear which parts of the claim are admitted and which are denied.
(c) If the claim is denied in whole or in part, the letter of response should include specific comments on the allegations against the professional and, if the claimant's version of events is disputed, the professional should provide his version of events.
(d) If the professional is unable to admit or deny the claim, the professional should identify any further information which is required.
(e) If the professional disputes the estimate of the claimant's financial loss, the letter of response should set out the professional's estimate. If an estimate cannot be provided, the professional should explain why and should state when he will be in a position to provide an estimate. This information should be sent to the claimant as soon as reasonably possible.
(f) Where additional documents are relied upon, copies should be provided.

B5.3 The letter of response is not intended to have the same formal status as a defence. If, however, the letter of response differs materially from the defence in subsequent proceedings, the court may decide, in its discretion, to impose sanctions.

The letter of settlement

B5.4 The letter of settlement will normally be a without prejudice letter and should be sent if the professional intends to make proposals for settlement. It should:

(a) Set out the professional's views to date on the claim identifying those issues which the professional believes are likely to remain in dispute and those which are not. (The letter of settlement does not need to include this information if the professional has sent a letter of response.)
(b) Make a settlement proposal or identify any further information which is required before the professional can formulate its proposals.
(c) Where additional documents are relied upon, copies should be provided.

Effect of letter of response and/or letter of settlement

B5.5 If the letter of response denies the claim in its entirety and there is no letter of settlement, it is open to the claimant to commence proceedings.

B5.6 In any other circumstance, the professional and the claimant should commence negotiations with the aim of concluding those negotiations within six months of the date of the letter of acknowledgment (*not* from the date of the letter of response).

B5.7 If the claim cannot be resolved within this period:

(a) The parties should agree within 14 days of the end of the period whether the period should be extended and, if so, by how long.
(b) The parties should seek to identify those issues which are still in dispute and those which can be agreed.
(c) If an extension of time is not agreed it will then be open to the claimant to commence proceedings.

B6 Alternative Dispute Resolution

B6.1 The parties should consider whether some form of alternative dispute resolution procedure would be more suitable than litigation, and if so, endeavour to agree which form to adopt. Both the claimant and defendant may be required by the court to provide evidence that alternative means of resolving their dispute were considered. The courts take the view that litigation should be a last resort, and that claims should not be issued prematurely when a settlement is still actively being explored. Parties are warned that if the protocol is not followed (including this paragraph) then the court must have regard to such conduct when determining costs.

B6.2 It is not practicable in this protocol to address in detail how the parties might decide which method to adopt to resolve their particular dispute. However, summarised below are some of the options for resolving disputes without litigation:

- Discussion and negotiation.

Pre-action Protocols

- Early neutral evaluation by an independent third party (for example, a lawyer experienced in the field of professional negligence or an individual experienced in the subject matter of the claim).
- Mediation – a form of facilitated negotiation assisted by an independent neutral party.

B6.3 The Legal Services Commission has published a booklet on *Alternatives to Court* (CLS Direct Information Leaflet 23) (www.clsdirect.org.uk/legalhelp/leaflet23.jsp), which lists a number of organisations that provide alternative dispute resolution services.

B6.4 *It is expressly recognised that no party can or should be forced to mediate or enter into any form of ADR.*

B7 Experts

(The following provisions apply where the claim raises an issue of professional expertise whose resolution requires expert evidence.)

B7.1 If the claimant has obtained expert evidence prior to sending the letter of claim, the professional will have equal right to obtain expert evidence prior to sending the letter of response/letter of settlement.

B7.2 If the claimant has not obtained expert evidence prior to sending the letter of claim, the parties are encouraged to appoint a joint expert. If they agree to do so, they should seek to agree the identity of the expert and the terms of the expert's appointment.

B7.3 If agreement about a joint expert cannot be reached, all parties are free to appoint their own experts. (For further details on experts see Guidance Note C6.)

B8 Proceedings

B8.1 Unless it is necessary (for example, to obtain protection against the expiry of a relevant limitation period) the claimant should not start court proceedings until:

(a) the letter of response denies the claim in its entirety and there is no letter of settlement (see para. B5.5 above); or

(b) the end of the negotiation period (see paras B5.6 and B5.7 above).

(For further discussion of statutory time limits for the commencement of litigation, please see Guidance Note C7.)

B8.2 Where possible 14 days' written notice should be given to the professional before proceedings are started, indicating the court within which the claimant is intending to commence litigation.

B8.3 Proceedings should be served on the professional, unless the professional's solicitor has notified the claimant in writing that he is authorised to accept service on behalf of the professional.

C GUIDANCE NOTES

C1 Introduction

C1.1 The protocol has been kept simple to promote ease of use and general acceptability. The guidance notes which follow relate particularly to issues on which further guidance may be required.

C1.2 The Woolf reforms envisages that parties will act reasonably in the pre-action period. Accordingly, in the event that the protocol and the guidelines do not specifically address a problem, the parties should comply with the spirit of the protocol by acting reasonably.

C2 Scope of Protocol

C2.1 The protocol is specifically designated for claims of negligence against professionals. This will include claims in which the allegation against a professional is that they have breached a contractual term to take reasonable skill and care. The protocol is also appropriate for claims of breach of fiduciary duty against professionals.

C2.2 The protocol is not intended to apply to claims:

(a) against architects, engineers and quantity surveyors — parties should use the Construction and Engineering Disputes (CED) protocol;

(b) *against healthcare providers* — parties should use the Pre-action Protocol for the Resolution of Clinical Disputes;

(c) concerning defamation — parties should use the Pre-action Protocol for Defamation.

C2.3 'Professional' is deliberately left undefined in the protocol. If it becomes an issue as to whether a defendant is or is not a professional, parties are reminded of the overriding need to act reasonably (see paras A4 and C1.2 above). Rather than argue about the definition of 'professional', therefore, the parties are invited to use this protocol, adapting it where appropriate.

C2.4 The protocol may not be suitable for disputes with professionals concerning intellectual property claims, etc. Until specific protocols are created for those claims, however, parties are invited to use this protocol, adapting it where necessary.

C2.5 Allegations of professional negligence are sometimes made in response to an attempt by the professional to recover outstanding fees. Where possible these allegations should be raised before litigation has commenced, in which case the parties should comply with the protocol before either party commences litigation. If litigation has already commenced it will be a matter for the court whether sanctions should be imposed against either party. In any event, the parties are encouraged to consider applying to the court for a stay to allow the protocol to be followed.

C3 Interaction with Other Pre-action Methods of Dispute Resolution

C3.1 There are a growing number of methods by which disputes can be resolved without the need for litigation, e.g., internal complaints procedures, the Surveyors and Valuers Arbitration Scheme, and so on. The preliminary notice procedure of the protocol (see para. B1) is designed to enable both parties to take stock at an early stage and to decide before work starts on preparing a letter of claim whether the grievance should be referred to one of these other dispute resolution procedures. (For the avoidance of doubt, however, there is no obligation on either party under the protocol to take any action at this stage other than giving the acknowledgment provided for in para. B1.4.)

C3.2 Accordingly, parties are free to use (and are encouraged to use) any of the available pre-action procedures in an attempt to resolve their dispute. If appropriate, the parties can agree to suspend the protocol timetable whilst the other method of dispute resolution is used.

C3.3 If these methods fail to resolve the dispute, however, the protocol should be used before litigation is commenced. Because there has already been an attempt to resolve the dispute, it may be appropriate to adjust the protocol's requirements. In particular, unless the parties agree otherwise, there is unlikely to be any benefit in duplicating a stage which has in effect already been undertaken. However, if the protocol adds anything to the earlier method of dispute resolution, it should be used, adapting it where appropriate. Once again, the parties are expected to act reasonably.

C4 Multi-party Disputes

C4.1 Paragraph B2.2(a) of the protocol requires a claimant to identify any other parties involved in the dispute or a related dispute. This is intended to ensure that all relevant parties are identified as soon as possible.

C4.2 If the dispute involves more than two parties, there are a number of potential problems. It is possible that different protocols will apply to different defendants. It is possible that defendants will claim against each other. It is possible that other parties will be drawn into the dispute. It is possible that the protocol timetable against one party will not be synchronised with the protocol timetable against a different party. How will these problems be resolved?

C4.3 As stated in para. C1.2 above, the parties are expected to act reasonably. What is 'reasonable' will, of course, depend upon the specific facts of each case. Accordingly, it would be inappropriate for the protocol to set down generalised rules. Whenever a problem arises, the parties are encouraged to discuss how it can be overcome. In doing so, parties are reminded of the protocol's aims which include the aim to resolve the dispute without the need for litigation (para. A2 above).

C5 Investigations

C5.1 Paragraph B4.3 is intended to encourage the early exchange of relevant information, so that issues in the dispute can be clarified or resolved. It should not be used as a 'fishing expedition' by either party. No party is obliged under para. B4.3 to disclose any document which a court could not order them to disclose in the pre-action period.

C5.2 This protocol does not alter the parties' duties to disclose documents under any professional regulation or under general law.

C6 Experts

C6.1 Expert evidence is not always needed, although the use and role of experts in professional negligence claims is often crucial. However, the way in which expert evidence is used in, say, an insurance brokers' negligence case, is not necessarily the same as in, say, an accountants' case. Similarly, the approach to be adopted in a £10,000 case does not necessarily compare with the approach in a £10 million case. The protocol therefore is designed to be flexible and does not dictate a standard approach. On the contrary it envisages that the parties will bear the responsibility for agreeing how best to use experts.

C6.2 If a joint expert is used, therefore, the parties are left to decide issues such as: the payment of the expert, whether joint or separate instructions are used, how and to whom the expert is to report, how questions may be addressed to the expert and how the expert should respond, whether an agreed statement of facts is required, and so on.

C6.3 If separate experts are used, the parties are left to decide issues such as: whether the experts' reports should be exchanged, whether there should be an experts' meeting, and so on.

C6.4 Even if a joint expert is appointed, it is possible that parties will still want to instruct their own experts. The protocol does not prohibit this.

C7 Proceedings

C7.1 This protocol does not alter the statutory time limits for starting court proceedings. A claimant is required to start proceedings within those time limits.

C7.2 If proceedings are for any reason started before the parties have followed the procedures in this protocol, the parties are encouraged to agree to apply to the court for a stay whilst the protocol is followed.

Pre-action Protocol for Judicial Review

INTRODUCTION

This protocol applies to proceedings within England and Wales only. It does not affect the time limit specified by CPR, r. 54.5(1), which requires that any claim form in an application for judicial review must be filed promptly and in any event not later than three months after the grounds to make the claim first arose or the shorter time limits specified by r. 54.5(5) and (6) which set out that a claim form for certain planning judicial reviews must be filed within six weeks and a claim form for certain procurement judicial reviews must be filed within 30 days.[1]

1. Judicial review allows people with a sufficient interest in a decision or action by a public body to ask a judge to review the lawfulness of:
   - an enactment; or
   - a decision, action or failure to act in relation to the exercise of a public function.[2]
2. Judicial review may be used where there is no right of appeal or where all avenues of appeal have been exhausted.

Alternative Dispute Resolution

3.1 The parties should consider whether some form of alternative dispute resolution procedure would be more suitable than litigation, and if so, endeavour to agree which form to adopt. Both the claimant and defendant may be required by the court to provide evidence that alternative means of resolving their dispute were considered. The courts take the view that litigation should be a last resort, and that claims should not be issued prematurely when a settlement is still actively being explored. Parties are warned that if the protocol is not followed (including this paragraph) then the court must have regard to such conduct when determining costs. However, parties should also note that a claim for judicial review must be filed promptly and in any event not later than three months after the grounds to make the claim first arose.

3.2 It is not practicable in this protocol to address in detail how the parties might decide which method to adopt to resolve their particular dispute. However, summarised below are some of the options for resolving disputes without litigation:
- Discussion and negotiation.
- Ombudsmen — the Parliamentary and Health Service and the Local Government Ombudsmen have discretion to deal with complaints relating to maladministration. The British and Irish Ombudsman Association provide information about Ombudsman schemes and other complaint handling bodies and this is available from their website at www.bioa.org.uk. Parties may wish to note that the ombudsmen are not able to look into a complaint once court action has been commenced.
- Early neutral evaluation by an independent third party (for example, a lawyer experienced in the field of administrative law or an individual experienced in the subject matter of the claim).
- Mediation — a form of facilitated negotiation assisted by an independent neutral party.

3.3 The Legal Services Commission has published a booklet on *Alternatives to Court* (CLS Direct *Information Leaflet* 23) (www.clsdirect.org.uk), which lists a number of organisations that provide alternative dispute resolution services.

3.4 *It is expressly recognised that no party can or should be forced to mediate or enter into any form of ADR.*

[1] While the court does have the discretion under r. 3.1(2)(a) to allow a late claim, this is only used in exceptional circumstances. Compliance with the protocol alone is unlikely to be sufficient to persuade the court to allow a late claim.
[2] Rule 54.1(2).

Pre-action Protocols

4. Judicial review may not be appropriate in every instance.
Claimants are strongly advised to seek appropriate legal advice when considering such proceedings and, in particular, before adopting this protocol or making a claim. Although the Legal Services Commission will not normally grant Full Representation before a letter before claim has been sent and the proposed defendant given a reasonable time to respond, initial funding may be available, for eligible claimants, to cover the work necessary to write this. (See Annex C for more information.)
5. This protocol sets out a code of good practice and contains the steps which parties should generally follow before making a claim for judicial review.
6. This protocol does not impose a greater obligation on a public body to disclose documents or give reasons for its decision than that already provided for in statute or common law. How ever, where the court considers that a public body should have provided *relevant* documents and/or information, particularly where this failure is a breach of a statutory or common law requirement, it may impose sanctions.

This protocol *will not be appropriate* where the defendant does not have the legal power to change the decision being challenged, for example decisions issued by tribunals such as the Asylum and Immigration Tribunal.

This protocol *will not be appropriate* in urgent cases, for example, when directions have been set, or are in force, for the claimant's removal from the UK, or where there is an urgent need for an interim order to compel a public body to act where it has unlawfully refused to do so (for example, the failure of a local housing authority to secure interim accommodation for a homeless claimant) a claim should be made immediately. A letter before claim will not stop the implementation of a disputed decision in all instances.

This protocol may not be appropriate in cases where one of the shorter time limits in r. 54.5(5) or (6) applies. In those cases, the parties should still attempt to comply with this protocol but the court will not apply normal cost sanctions where the court is satisfied that it has not been possible to comply because of the shorter time limits.
7. All claimants will need to satisfy themselves whether they should follow the protocol, depending upon the circumstances of his or her case. Where the use of the protocol is appropriate, the court will normally expect all parties to have complied with it and will take into account compliance or non-compliance when giving directions for case management of proceedings or when making orders for costs.[3] However, even in emergency cases, it is good practice to fax to the defendant the draft claim form which the claimant intends to issue. A claimant is also normally required to notify a defendant when an interim mandatory order is being sought.

THE LETTER BEFORE CLAIM

8. Before making a claim, the claimant should send a letter to the defendant. The purpose of this letter is to identify the issues in dispute and establish whether litigation can be avoided.
9. Claimants should normally use the suggested standard format for the letter outlined at Annex A.
10. The letter should contain the date and details of the decision, act or omission being challenged and a clear summary of the facts on which the claim is based. It should also contain the details of any relevant information that the claimant is seeking and an explanation of why this is considered relevant. If the claim is considered to be an Aarhus Convention claim, the letter should state this clearly and explain the reasons, since specific rules as to costs apply to such claims.
11. The letter should normally contain the details of any interested parties[4] known to the claimant. They should be sent a copy of the letter before claim for information. Claimants are strongly advised to seek appropriate legal advice when considering such proceedings and, in particular, before sending the letter before claim to other interested parties or making a claim.
12. A claim should not normally be made until the proposed reply date given in the letter before claim has passed, unless the circumstances of the case require more immediate action to be taken.

[3] PD 43–48.
[4] See CPR, r. 54.1(2)(f).

THE LETTER OF RESPONSE

13. Defendants should normally respond within 14 days using the standard format at Annex B. Failure to do so will be taken into account by the court and sanctions may be imposed unless there are good reasons.[5]
14. Where it is not possible to reply within the proposed time limit the defendant should send an interim reply and propose a reasonable extension. Where an extension is sought, reasons should be given and, where required, additional information requested. This will not affect the time limit for making a claim for judicial review[6] nor will it bind the claimant where he or she considers this to be unreasonable. However, where the court considers that a subsequent claim is made prematurely it may impose sanctions.
15. If the claim is being conceded in full, the reply should say so in clear and unambiguous terms.
16. If the claim is being conceded in part or not being conceded at all, the reply should say so in clear and unambiguous terms, and:
    (a) where appropriate, contain a new decision, clearly identifying what aspects of the claim are being conceded and what are not, or, give a clear timescale within which the new decision will be issued;
    (b) provide a fuller explanation for the decision, if considered appropriate to do so;
    (c) address any points of dispute, or explain why they cannot be addressed;
    (d) enclose any relevant documentation requested by the claimant, or explain why the documents are not being enclosed; and
    (e) where appropriate, confirm whether or not they will oppose any application for an interim remedy.

    If the letter before claim has stated that the claim is an Aarhus Convention claim but the defendant does not accept this, the reply should state this clearly and explain the reasons.
17. The response should be sent to all interested parties[7] identified by the claimant and contain details of any other parties who the defendant considers also have an interest.

ANNEX A LETTER BEFORE CLAIM

Section 1 Information Required in a Letter before Claim

Proposed Claim for Judicial Review

1. To (Insert the name and address of the proposed defendant — see details in section 2)
2. The claimant (Insert the title, first and last name and the address of the claimant)
3. Reference details (When dealing with large organisations it is important to understand that the information relating to any particular individual's previous dealings with it may not be immediately available, therefore it is important to set out the relevant reference numbers for the matter in dispute and/or the identity of those within the public body who have been handling the particular matter in dispute – see details in section 3)
4. The details of the matter being challenged (Set out clearly the matter being challenged, particularly if there has been more than one decision)
5. The issue (Set out the date and details of the decision, or act or omission being challenged, a brief summary of the facts and why it is contended to be wrong)
6. The details of the action that the defendant is expected to take (Set out the details of the remedy sought, including whether a review or any interim remedy is being requested)
7. The details of the legal advisers, if any, dealing with this claim (Set out the name, address and reference details of any legal advisers dealing with the claim)
8. The details of any interested parties (Set out the details of any interested parties and confirm that they have been sent a copy of this letter)
9. The details of any information sought (Set out the details of any information that is sought. This may include a request for a fuller explanation of the reasons for the decision that is being challenged)

[5] See PD Protocols, paras 2 and 3.
[6] See CPR, r. 54.5(1).
[7] See CPR, r. 54.1(2)(f).

Pre-action Protocols

10. The details of any documents that are considered relevant and necessary (Set out the details of any documentation or policy in respect of which the disclosure is sought and explain why these are relevant. If you rely on a statutory duty to disclose, this should be specified)
11. The address for reply and service of court documents (Insert the address for the reply)
12. Proposed reply date (The precise time will depend upon the circumstances of the individual case. However, although a shorter or longer time may be appropriate in a particular case, 14 days is a reasonable time to allow in most circumstances)

Section 2 Address for Sending the Letter before Claim

Public bodies have requested that, for certain types of cases, in order to ensure a prompt response, letters before claim should be sent to specific addresses.

Where the claim concerns a decision in an immigration, asylum or nationality case the claim may be sent electronically to the following UK Border Agency email address: UKBAPAP@UKBA.gsi.gov.uk. Alternatively the claim may be sent by post to the following UK Border Agency postal address:

Judicial Review Unit
UK Border Agency
Lunar House
40 Wellesley Rd
Croydon
CR9 2BY

Where the claim concerns a decision by the Legal Services Commission:

The address on the decision letter/notification; and
Legal Director
Corporate Legal Team
Legal Services Commission
102 Petty France
London SW1H 9AJ

Where the claim concerns a decision by a local authority:

The address on the decision letter/notification; and
Their legal department[8]

Where the claim concerns a decision by a department or body for whom Treasury Solicitor acts *and the Treasury Solicitor has already been involved in the case* a copy should also be sent, quoting the Treasury Solicitor's reference, to:

Treasury Solicitor
One Kemble Street
London WC2B 4TS

In all other circumstances, the letter should be sent to the address on the letter notifying the decision.

Section 3 Specific Reference Details Required

Public bodies have requested that the following information should be provided in order to ensure prompt response.

Where the claim concerns an immigration, asylum or nationality case, dependent upon the nature of the case:

The Home Office reference number
The port reference number
The Asylum and Immigration Tribunal reference number
The National Asylum Support Service reference number

Or, if these are unavailable:

The full name, nationality and date of birth of the claimant.

Where the claim concerns a decision by the Legal Services Commission:

The certificate reference number.

[8] The relevant address should be available from a range of sources such as the *Phone Book, Business and Services Directory, Thomson Local*, CAB, etc.

ANNEX B RESPONSE TO A LETTER BEFORE CLAIM

Information Required in a Response to a Letter before Claim

Proposed Claim for Judicial Review

1. The claimant (Insert the title, first and last names and the address to which any reply should be sent)
2. From (Insert the name and address of the defendant)
3. Reference details (Set out the relevant reference numbers for the matter in dispute and the identity of those within the public body who have been handling the issue)
4. The details of the matter being challenged (Set out details of the matter being challenged, providing a fuller explanation of the decision, where this is considered appropriate)
5. Response to the proposed claim (Set out whether the issue in question is conceded in part, or in full, or will be contested. Where it is not proposed to disclose any information that has been requested, explain the reason for this. Where an interim reply is being sent and there is a realistic prospect of settlement, details should be included)
6. Details of any other interested parties (Identify any other parties who you consider have an interest who have not already been sent a letter by the claimant)
7. Address for further correspondence and service of court documents (Set out the address for any future correspondence on this matter)

ANNEX C NOTES ON PUBLIC FUNDING FOR LEGAL COSTS IN JUDICIAL REVIEW

Public funding for legal costs in judicial review is available from legal professionals and advice agencies which have contracts with the Legal Services Commission as part of the Community Legal Service. Funding may be provided for:

- Legal Help to provide initial advice and assistance with any legal problem; or
- Legal Representation to allow you to be represented in court if you are taking or defending court proceedings. This is available in two forms:
  — Investigative Help is limited to funding to investigate the strength of the proposed claim. It includes the issue and conduct of proceedings only so far as is necessary to obtain disclosure of relevant information or to protect the client's position in relation to any urgent hearing or time limit for the issue of proceedings. This includes the work necessary to write a letter before claim to the body potentially under challenge, setting out the grounds of challenge, and giving that body a reasonable opportunity, typically 14 days, in which to respond.
  — Full Representation is provided to represent you in legal proceedings and includes litigation services, advocacy services, and all such help as is usually given by a person providing representation in proceedings, including steps preliminary or incidental to proceedings, and/or arriving at or giving affect to a compromise to avoid or bring to an end any proceedings. Except in emergency cases, a proper letter before claim must be sent and the other side must be given an opportunity to respond before Full Representation is granted.

Further information on the type(s) of help available and the criteria for receiving that help may be found in the *Legal Service Manual*, vol. 3, *The Funding Code*. This may be found on the Legal Services Commission website at: <http://www.legalservices.gov.uk/>.

A list of contracted firms and advice agencies may be found on the Community Legal Service website at: <http://www.justask.org.uk/>.*

[* Now www.communitylegaladvice.org.uk.]

Pre-action Protocol for Disease and Illness Claims

1 INTRODUCTION

1.1 Lord Woolf in his *Final Report* of July 1996 recommended the development of protocols: 'to build on and increase the benefits of early but well-informed settlements which genuinely satisfy both parties to a dispute'.

1.2 The aims of these protocols are:
- more contact between the parties;
- better and earlier exchange of information;
- better investigation by both sides;
- to put the parties in a position where they may be able to settle cases fairly and early without litigation;
- to enable proceedings to run to the court's timetable and efficiently, if litigation does become necessary.

1.3 The concept of protocols is relevant to a range of initiatives for good claims practice, especially:
- predictability in the time needed for steps to be taken;
- standardisation of relevant information, including documents to be disclosed.

1.4 The courts will be able to treat the standards set in protocols as the normal reasonable approach. If proceedings are issued, it will be for the court to decide whether non-compliance with a protocol should merit adverse consequences. Guidance on the court's likely approach will be given from time to time in practice directions.

1.5 If the court has to consider the question of compliance after proceedings have begun, it will not be concerned with minor infringements, e.g., failure by a short period to provide relevant information. One minor breach will not exempt the 'innocent' party from following the protocol. The court will look at the effect of non-compliance on the other party when deciding whether to impose sanctions.

2 NOTES OF GUIDANCE

Scope of the Protocol

2.1 This protocol is intended to apply to all personal injury claims where the injury is not as the result of an accident but takes the form of an illness or disease.

2.2 This protocol covers disease claims which are likely to be complex and frequently not suitable for fast track procedures even though they may fall within fast track limits. Disease for the purpose of this protocol primarily covers any illness physical or psychological, any disorder, ailment, affliction, complaint, malady, or derangement other than a physical or psychological injury solely caused by an accident or other similar single event.

2.3 In appropriate cases it may be agreed between the parties that this protocol can be applied rather than the Pre-action Protocol for Personal Injury Claims where a single event occurs but causes a disease or illness.

2.4 This protocol is not limited to diseases occurring in the workplace but will embrace diseases occurring in other situations for example through occupation of premises or the use of products. It is not intended to cover those cases, which are dealt with as a 'group' or 'class' action.

2.5 The 'cards on the table' approach advocated by the Pre-action Protocol for Personal Injury Claims is equally appropriate to disease claims. The spirit of that protocol, and of the clinical negligence protocol is followed here, in accordance with the sense of the civil justice reforms.

2.6 The timetable and the arrangements for disclosing documents and obtaining expert evidence may need to be varied to suit the circumstances of the case. If a party considers the detail of the protocol to be inappropriate they should communicate their reasons to all of the parties at that stage. If proceedings are subsequently issued, the court will expect an explanation as to why the protocol has not been followed, or has been varied.

2.7 In a terminal disease claim with short life expectancy, for instance where a claimant has a disease such as mesothelioma, the timescale of the protocol is likely to be too long. In such a claim, the claimant may not be able to follow the protocol and the defendant would be expected to treat the claim with urgency including any request for an interim payment.

2.8 In a claim for mesothelioma, additional provisions apply, which are set out in annex C of this protocol.

2A ALTERNATIVE DISPUTE RESOLUTION

2A.1 The parties should consider whether some form of alternative dispute resolution procedure would be more suitable than litigation, and if so, endeavour to agree which form to adopt. Both the claimant and defendant may be required by the court to provide evidence that alternative means of resolving their dispute were considered. The courts take the view that litigation should be a last resort, and that claims should not be issued prematurely when a settlement is still actively being explored. Parties are warned that if the protocol is not followed (including this paragraph) then the court must have regard to such conduct when determining costs.

2A.2 It is not practicable in this protocol to address in detail how the parties might decide which method to adopt to resolve their particular dispute. However, summarised below are some of the options for resolving disputes without litigation:

- Discussion and negotiation.
- Early neutral evaluation by an independent third party (for example, a lawyer experienced in the field of disease or illness, or an individual experienced in the subject matter of the claim).
- Mediation – a form of facilitated negotiation assisted by an independent neutral party.
- Arbitration (where an independent person or body makes a binding decision).

2A.3 The Legal Services Commission has published a booklet on *Alternatives to Court* (CLS Direct Information Leaflet 23) <http://www.communitylegaladvice.org.uk/media/808/FD/leaflet23e.pdf>, which lists a number of organisations that provide alternative dispute resolution services.

2A.4 *It is expressly recognised that no party can or should be forced to mediate or enter into any form of ADR, but the parties should continue to consider the possibility of reaching a settlement at all times.*

3 THE AIMS OF THE PROTOCOL

3.1 The *general* aims of the protocol are:

- to resolve as many disputes as possible without litigation;
- where a claim cannot be resolved to identify the relevant issues which remain in dispute.

3.2 The *specific* objectives are:

Openness

- to encourage early communication of the perceived problem between the parties or their insurers;
- to encourage employees to voice any concerns or worries about possible work-related illness as soon as practicable;
- to encourage employers to develop systems of early reporting and investigation of suspected occupational health problems and to provide full and prompt explanations to concerned employees or former employees;
- to apply such principles to perceived problems outside the employer/employee relationship, for example occupiers of premises or land and producers of products;
- to ensure that sufficient information is disclosed by both parties to enable each to understand the other's perspective and case, and to encourage early resolution;

Timeliness

- to provide an early opportunity for employers (past or present) or their insurers to identify cases where an investigation is required and to carry out that investigation promptly;

Pre-action Protocols

- to encourage employers (past or present) or other defendants to involve and identify their insurers at an early stage;
- to ensure that all relevant records including health and personnel records are provided to employees (past or present) or their appointed representatives promptly on request, by any employer (past or present) or their insurers. This should be complied with to a realistic timetable;
- to ensure that relevant records which are in the claimant's possession including where appropriate GP and hospital records are made available to the defendant or to the nominated insurance manager or solicitor representing the defendant by claimants or their advisers at an appropriate stage;
- to proceed on a reasonable timetable where a resolution is not achievable to lay the ground to enable litigation to proceed at a reasonable and proportionate cost, and to limit the matters in contention;
- to communicate promptly where any of the requested information is not available or does not exist;
- to discourage the prolonged pursuit of unmeritorious claims and the prolonged defence of meritorious claims;
- to encourage all parties, at the earliest possible stage, to disclose voluntarily any additional documents which will assist in resolving any issue;
- to promote the provision of medical or rehabilitation treatment in appropriate cases to address the needs of the claimant.

4 THE PROTOCOL

This protocol is not a comprehensive code governing all the steps in disease claims. Rather it attempts to set out *a code of good practice which* parties should follow.

This protocol must be read in conjunction with the Practice Direction on Pre-action Conduct.

Obtaining Occupational Records Including Health Records

4.1 In appropriate cases, a *potential claimant* may request occupational records including health records and personnel records before sending a letter of claim.

4.2 Any request for records by the *potential claimant* or his adviser should *provide sufficient information* to alert the *potential defendant* or his insurer where a possible disease claim is being investigated. Annex A1 provides a suggested form for this purpose for use in cases arising from employment. Similar forms can be prepared and used in other situations.

4.3 The copy records should be provided *within a maximum of 40 days* of the request at no cost. Although these will primarily be occupational records, it will be good practice for a *potential defendant* to disclose product data documents identified by a *potential claimant* at this stage which may resolve a causation issue.

4.4 Where the potential defendant or his insurer has difficulty in providing information quickly (in particular where the information is, or may be, held by someone else such as the Health and Safety Executive) details should be provided of steps being taken to resolve this problem together with a reasonable time estimate for doing so.

4.5 If the *potential defendant* or his insurer fails to provide the records including health records within 40 days and fails to comply with para. 4.4 above, the *potential claimant* or his adviser may then apply to the court for an *order for pre-action disclosure.* The CPR make pre-action applications to the court easier. The court also has the power to impose costs sanctions for unreasonable delay in providing records.

5 COMMUNICATION

5.1 If either the *potential claimant* or his adviser considers *additional records are required from a third party,* such as records from previous employers or GP and hospital records, in the first instance these should be requested by the *potential claimant* or their advisers. Third party record holders would be expected to cooperate. The CPR enable parties to apply to the court for pre-action disclosure by third parties.

5.2 As soon as the records have been received and analysed, the *potential claimant* or his adviser should consider whether a claim should be made. GP and hospital records will normally be obtained before a decision is reached.

5.3 If a decision is made not to proceed further at this stage against a party identified as a *potential defendant,* the *potential claimant* or his adviser should notify that *potential defendant* in writing as soon as practicable.

6 LETTER OF CLAIM

6.1 Where a decision is made to make a claim, the claimant shall send to the proposed defendant two copies of a letter of claim, as soon as sufficient information is available to substantiate a realistic claim and before issues of quantum are addressed in detail. One copy is for the defendants, the second for passing on to his insurers.

6.2 This letter shall contain a *clear summary of the facts* on which the claim is based, including details of the illness or disease alleged, and the *main allegations of fault*. It shall also give details of present condition and prognosis. The *financial loss* incurred by the claimant should be outlined. Where the case is funded by a conditional fee agreement, notification should be given of the existence of the agreement and where appropriate, that there is a success fee and insurance premium, although not the level of the success fee or premium.

6.3 Where the funding arrangement is an insurance policy the party must state—

(1) the name and address of the insurer;
(2) the policy number;
(3) the date of the policy;
(4) the claim or claims to which it relates (including Part 20 claims if any);
(5) the level of cover; and
(6) whether the premiums are staged and if so the points at which the increased premiums are payable.

6.4 Solicitors are recommended to use *a standard format* for such a letter — an example is at annex B: this can be amended to suit the particular case, for example, if the client has rehabilitation needs these can also be detailed in the letter.

6.5 A *chronology* of the relevant events (e.g. dates or periods of exposure) should be provided. In the case of alleged occupational disease an appropriate employment history should also be provided (with a work history from HM Revenue and Customs), particularly if the claimant has been employed by a number of different employers and the illness in question has a long latency period. Where there is more than one employer the chronology should state if there was any relevant exposure during each of those different periods of employment. Details should also be given about any periods of self-employment during which there was any relevant exposure and whether any claims have been made and payments received under the Pneumoconiosis etc. (Workers' Compensation) Act 1979.

6.6 The letter of claim should identify any *relevant documents*, including health records not already in the defendant's possession e.g. any relevant GP and hospital records. These will need to be disclosed in confidence to the nominated insurance manager or solicitor representing the defendant following receipt of their letter of acknowledgment. Where the action is brought under the Law Reform (Miscellaneous Provisions) Act 1934 or the Fatal Accidents Act 1976 then *relevant documents* will normally include copies of the death certificate, the post mortem report, the inquest depositions and if obtained by that date the grant of probate or letters of administration.

6.7 The letter of claim should indicate whether a claim is also being made against any *other potential defendant* and identify any known insurer involved. Copies of any relevant result from the Association of British Insurers Employers' Liability Tracing Service, both positive and negative, should be attached to the letter of claim. If the claimant receives any insurance database results after sending the letter of claim those results should be forwarded to the defendant as soon as is reasonably practicable.

6.8 Sufficient information should be given to enable the defendant's insurer/solicitor to commence *investigations* and at least to put a broad valuation on the 'risk'.

6.9 It is not a requirement for the claimant to provide *medical evidence* with the letter of claim, but the claimant may choose to do so in very many cases.

6.10 *Letters of claim and response* are not intended to have the same *status* as a statement of case in proceedings. Matters may come to light as a result of investigation after the letter of claim has been sent, or after the defendant has responded, particularly if disclosure of documents takes place outside the recommended 90-day period. These circumstances could mean that the 'pleaded' case of one or both parties is presented slightly differently than in the letter of claim or response. It would not be consistent with the spirit of the protocol for a party to 'take a point' on this in the proceedings, provided that there was no obvious intention by the party who changed their position to mislead the other party.

6.11 *Proceedings should not be issued until after 90 days from the date of acknowledgment* (see para. 7), unless there is a limitation problem and/or the claimant's position needs to be protected by early issue (see paras 2.6 and 2.7).

7 THE RESPONSE

7.1 The defendant should *send an acknowledgment within 21 days* of the date of posting of the letter of claim, identifying the liability insurer (if any) who will be dealing with the matter and, if necessary, identifying specifically any significant omissions from the letter of claim. If there has been no acknowledgment by the defendant or insurer within 21 days, the claimant will be entitled to issue proceedings.

7.2 The identity of all relevant insurers, if more than one, should be notified to the claimant by the insurer identified in the acknowledgment letter, within 30 days of the date of that acknowledgment. For claims with a long latency period it is recognised that it may not be possible to identify the full insurance history within 30 days. In these circumstances the insurer or defendant should notify the claimant in writing as soon as possible. In any event, within 30 days the insurer or the defendant should state which other insurers have been identified. Where insurers have not been identified the defendant or insurer should state what steps have been taken to determine this information.

7.3 The defendant or his representative should, *within 90 days of the date of the acknowledgment letter*, provide a *reasoned answer:*

- if the *claim is admitted*, they should say so in clear terms;
- if only *part of the claim is admitted* they should make clear which issues of fault and/or causation and/or limitation are admitted and which remain in issue and why;
- if the *claim is not admitted in full*, they should explain why and should, for example, include comments on the employment status of the claimant (including job description(s) and details of the department(s) where the claimant worked), the allegations of fault, causation and of limitation, and if a synopsis or chronology of relevant events has been provided and is disputed, their version of those events;
- if the *claim is not admitted in full*, the defendant should enclose with his letter of reply *documents* in his possession which are *material to the issues* between the parties and which would be likely to be ordered to be disclosed by the court, either on an application for pre-action disclosure, or on disclosure during proceedings. Reference can be made to the documents annexed to the personal injury protocol.
- where more than one defendant receives a letter of claim, the timetable will be activated for each defendant by the date on the letter of claim addressed to them. If any defendant wishes to extend the timetable because the number of defendants will cause complications, they should seek agreement to a different timetable as soon as possible.

7.4 If the parties reach agreement on liability and/or causation, but time is needed to resolve other issues including the value of the claim, they should aim to agree a reasonable period.

7.5 Where it is not practicable for the defendant to complete his investigations within 90 days, the defendant should indicate the difficulties and outline the further time needed. Any request for an extension of time should be made, with reasons, as soon as the defendant becomes aware that an extension is needed and normally before the 90-day period has expired. Such an extension of time should be agreed in circumstances where reasonable justification has been shown. Lapse of many years since the circumstances giving rise to the claim does not, by itself, constitute reasonable justification for further time.

7.6 Where the relevant negligence occurred outside England and Wales and/or where the defendant is outside the jurisdiction, the time periods of 21 days and 90 days should normally be extended up to 42 days and 180 days.

8 SPECIAL DAMAGES

8.1 The claimant will send to the defendant as soon as practicable a schedule of special damages with supporting documents, particularly where the defendant has admitted liability.

9 EXPERTS

9.1 In disease claims expert opinions may be needed on one or more of the following—

- knowledge, fault, causation and apportionment;

- condition and prognosis;
- valuing aspects of the claim.

9.2 The civil justice reforms and the CPR encourage economy in the use of experts and a less adversarial expert culture. It is recognised that in disease claims, the parties and their advisers will require flexibility in their approach to expert evidence. Decisions on whether experts might be instructed jointly, and on whether reports might be disclosed sequentially or by exchange, should rest with the parties and their advisers. Sharing expert evidence may be appropriate on various issues including those relating to the value of the claim. However, this protocol does not attempt to be prescriptive on issues in relation to expert evidence.

9.3 Obtaining expert evidence will often be an expensive step and may take time, especially in specialised areas where there are limited numbers of suitable experts. Claimants, defendants and their advisers, will therefore need to consider carefully how best to obtain any necessary expert help quickly and cost-effectively.

9.4 The protocol recognises that a flexible approach must be adopted in the obtaining of medical reports in claims of this type. There will be very many occasions where the claimant will need to obtain a medical report before writing the letter of claim. In such cases the defendant will be entitled to obtain their own medical report. In some other instances it may be more appropriate to send the letter of claim before the medical report is obtained. Defendants will usually need to see a medical report before they can reach a view on causation.

9.5 Where the parties agree the nomination of a single expert is appropriate, before any party instructs an expert he should give the other party a list of the *name(s) of one or more experts* in the relevant speciality whom he considers are suitable to instruct. The parties are encouraged to agree the instruction of a single expert to deal with discrete areas such as cost of care.

9.6 *Within 14 days* the other party may indicate an objection to one or more of the named experts. The first party should then instruct a mutually acceptable expert. If the Claimant nominates an expert in the original letter of claim, the 14 days is in addition to the 21 days in para. 7.1.

9.7 If the second party objects to all the listed experts, the parties may then instruct *experts of their own choice.* It would be for the court to decide subsequently, if proceedings are issued, whether either party had acted unreasonably.

9.8 If the *second party does not object to an expert nominated,* he shall not be entitled to rely on his own expert evidence within that particular speciality unless:

(a) the first party agrees,

(b) the court so directs, or

(c) the first party's expert report has been amended and the first party is not prepared to disclose the original report.

9.9 *Either party may send to an agreed expert written questions* on the report, relevant to the issues, via the first party's solicitors. The expert should send answers to the questions separately and directly to each party.

9.10 The cost of a report from an agreed expert will usually be paid by the instructing first party: the costs of the expert replying to questions will usually be borne by the party which asks the questions.

9.11 Where the defendant admits liability in whole or in part, before proceedings are issued, any medical report obtained under this protocol which *the claimant* relies upon, should be disclosed to the other party.

9.12 Where the defendant obtains a medical report on which he seeks to rely this should be disclosed to the claimant.

9.13 For further guidance see CPR, Part 35, PD 35 and the Protocol for the Instruction of Experts to Give Evidence in Civil Claims which is annexed to that practice direction.

10 RESOLUTION OF ISSUES

10.1 Part 36 of the CPR enables claimants and defendants to make formal offers to settle before proceedings are started. Parties should consider making such an offer, since to do so often leads to settlement. If such an offer is made, the party making the offer must always supply sufficient evidence and/or information to enable the offer to be properly considered.

10.2 Where a claim is not resolved when the protocol has been followed, the parties might wish to carry out a 'stocktake' of the issues in dispute, and the evidence that the court is likely to need to decide those issues, before proceedings are started.

10.3 Prior to proceedings it will be usual for all parties to disclose those expert reports relating to liability and causation upon which they propose to rely.

10.4 The claimant should delay issuing proceedings for 21 days from disclosure of reports to enable the parties to consider whether the claim is capable of settlement.

10.5 Where the defendant is insured and the pre-action steps have been conducted by the insurer, the insurer would normally be expected to nominate solicitors to accept service of the proceedings and the claimant's solicitor is recommended to invite the insurer to nominate solicitors to accept service of the proceedings and to do so seven to 14 days before the intended issue date.

11 LIMITATION

11.1 If by reason of complying with any part of this protocol a claimant's claim may be time-barred under any provision of the Limitation Act 1980, or any other legislation which imposes a time limit for bringing an action, the claimant may commence proceedings without complying with this protocol. In such circumstances, a claimant who commences proceedings without complying with all, or any part, of this protocol may apply to the court on notice for directions as to the timetable and form of procedure to be adopted, at the same time as he requests the court to issue proceedings. The court will consider whether to order a stay of the whole or part of the proceedings pending compliance with this protocol.

ANNEX A LETTER REQUESTING OCCUPATIONAL RECORDS INCLUDING HEALTH RECORDS

Dear Sirs,

We are acting on behalf of the above-named who has developed the following *(disease)*. We are investigating whether this disease may have been caused:

- during the course of his employment with [you] [*(name of employer if different)*;
- whilst at your premises at *(address)*;
- as a result of your product *(name)*.

We are writing this in accordance with the Pre-action Protocol for Disease and Illness Claims.

We seek the following records:

(details, e.g., personnel, occupational health)

Please note your insurers may require you to advise them of this request.

We enclose a request form and expect to receive the records within 40 days.

If you are not able to comply with this request within this time, please advise us of the reason.

Yours faithfully

ANNEX A1 APPLICATION ON BEHALF OF A POTENTIAL CLAIMANT FOR USE WHERE A DISEASE CLAIM IS BEING INVESTIGATED

This should be completed as fully as possible.

Company

Name

Address

1 (a) Full name of claimant (including previous surnames)
  (b) Address now
  (c) Address at date of termination of employment, if different
  (d) Date of birth (and death, if applicable)
  (e) National Insurance number, if available
2 Department(s) where claimant worked
3 This application is made because the claimant is considering:
  (a) a claim against you as detailed in point 4 YES/NO
  (b) pursuing an action against someone else YES/NO
4 If the answer to point 3(a) is 'Yes' details of:
  (a) the likely nature of the claim, e.g., dermatitis

(b) grounds for the claim, e.g., exposure to chemical
(c) approximate dates of the events involved

5 If the answer to point 3(b) is 'Yes' insert:
(a) the names of the proposed defendants
(b) have legal proceedings been started? YES/NO
(c) if appropriate, details of the claim and action number

6 Any other relevant information or documents requested

Signature of solicitor

Name

Address

Ref.

Telephone number

Fax number

I authorise you to disclose all of your records relating to me/the claimant to my solicitor and to your legal and insurance representatives.

Signature of claimant

Signature of personal representative where claimant has died

ANNEX B TEMPLATE FOR LETTER OF CLAIM

To Defendant

Dear Sirs

Re: *(Claimant's full name)*

(Claimant's full address)
National Insurance number:

Date of birth:

Clock or works number:

Employer: *(name and address)*

We are instructed by the above named to claim damages in connection with a claim for:
(specify occupational disease)

We are writing this letter in accordance with the Pre-action Protocol for Disease and Illness Claims.

Please confirm the identity of your insurers. Please note that your insurers will need to see this letter as soon as possible and it may affect your insurance cover if you do not send this to them.

The Claimant was employed by you *(if the claim arises out of public or occupiers' liability give appropriate details)* as *(job description)* from *(date)* to *(date)*. During the relevant period of his employment he worked:

(description of precisely where the claimant worked and what he did to include a description of any machines used and details of any exposure to noise or substances)

The circumstances leading to the development of this condition are as follows:

(give chronology of events and in appropriate cases attach a work history from HM Revenue and Customs)

The reason why we are alleging fault is:

(details should be given of contemporary and comparable employees who have suffered from similar problems if known; any protective equipment provided; complaints; the supervisors concerned, if known)

Our client's employment history is attached.

[We have also made a claim against:
(insert details)

Their insurers' details are:

(insert if known)]

We have the following documents in support of our client's claim and will disclose these in confidence to your nominated insurance manager or solicitor when we receive their acknowledgment letter:

(e.g., occupational health notes; GP notes)

[We have obtained a medical report from *(name)* and will disclose this when we receive your acknowledgment of this letter.

(This is optional at this stage.)]

From the information we presently have:

(i) the Claimant first became aware of symptoms on *(insert approximate date);*
(ii) the Claimant first received medical advice about those symptoms on *(insert date) (give details of advice given if appropriate).*
(iii) the Claimant first believed that those symptoms might be due to exposure leading to this claim on *(insert approximate date).*

A description of our client's condition is as follows:

(this should be sufficiently detailed to allow the defendant to put a broad value on the claim)

(For appropriate cases) Our client is still suffering from the effect of his/her condition. We invite you to participate with us in addressing his/her immediate needs by use of rehabilitation.

He has the following time off work:

(insert dates)

He is presently employed as a *(job description)* and his average net weekly income is £ ______.

If you are our client's employers, please provide us with the usual earnings details, which will enable us to calculate his financial loss.

[Please note that we have entered into a conditional fee agreement with our client dated ______ in relation to this claim which provides for a success fee within the meaning of section 58(2) of the Courts and Legal Services Act 1990. Our client has taken out an insurance policy dated with *(name and address of insurance company)* to which section 29 of the Access to Justice Act 1999 applies in respect of this claim.] The policy number is [*insert*], the policy is dated [*insert*] and the level of cover is [*insert*]. The premiums payable under the insurance policy [are not] [are] staged [and the points at which the increased premiums are payable are as follows:].

A copy of this letter is attached for you to send to your insurers. Finally we expect an acknowledgment of this letter within 21 days by yourselves or your insurers.

Yours faithfully

ANNEX C GUIDANCE FOR CASES INVOLVING MESOTHELIOMA — EARLY NOTIFICATION LETTER

Purpose

1. The purpose of the early notification letter is twofold. First, the intention is to give defendants and their insurers as much advance warning as possible about the possibility of a claim so that they can begin to investigate the matter. This is particularly so where relevant information may be decades old and may take time to locate and retrieve. Second, where the claimant has severely limited life expectancy it gives advance warning to defendants of the need for urgency in locating relevant information.
2. It is intended that the early notification letter will be sent before the letter of claim and will not start the timetable for response as set out in para. 7 of this protocol.
3. As soon as sufficient information is available to identify a proposed defendant, the claimant should send to the proposed defendant two copies of the early notification letter. One copy is for the defendant, the second for passing on to the defendant's insurers. The claimant should also send a further copy of the same letter directly to the defendant's insurer, where known. In the case of a defunct company the further copy of the letter should be sent to the relevant insurer or handler of that defunct company.

Content of Early Notification Letter

4. All copies of the early notification letter should be clearly marked 'MESOTHELIOMA CLAIM'.
5. The early notification letter should contain basic information sufficient to identify the claimant, the periods of relevant exposure and the potential defendants. As a minimum, the early notification letter should contain the following information:
   (a) name and address of the claimant/deceased;
   (b) national insurance number of the claimant/deceased (if known);
   (c) claimant/deceased's date of birth;
   (e) employers, where known, of relevant employment and/or exposure;
   (f) occupiers of premises, where known, of relevant employment and/or exposure;
   (g) date or approximate dates, where known, of relevant employment and/or exposure;
   (h) direct contact details, including email address, for the claimant's legal representative;
   (i) marital status;
   (j) details of dependants; and
   (k) date of diagnosis.
6. Solicitors are recommended to use a standard format for the early notification letter. An example is set out in annex D. This can be amended to suit the particular case.
7. The early notification letter should indicate whether a claim is also being made against any other potential defendant and identify any known insurer involved.
8. The early notification letter is not intended to have the same status as a statement of case in proceedings. Matters may come to light as a result of investigation after the letter of claim has been sent.

Employment and Exposure History

9. In view of the joint and several liability provided for in the Compensation Act 2006 in mesothelioma cases the information set out in para. 6.5 of this protocol is particularly relevant.

Defendant's response

10. The defendant should respond within 14 days of the date of the letter confirming that the matter is receiving urgent attention.

Compliance with This Protocol

11. Attention is drawn to PD 3D, para. 9.1, which provides that in living mesothelioma claims (normally where the claimant has severely limited life expectancy) strict adherence to this protocol may not be required. The issue of compliance with this protocol in relation to certain mesothelioma claims is also recognised at para. 2.7 of this protocol.

ANNEX D EARLY NOTIFICATION LETTER FOR USE IN CASES INVOLVING MESOTHELIOMA

URGENT – MESOTHELIOMA CLAIM
YOU MUST DEAL WITH THIS LETTER IMMEDIATELY

Dear Sirs,

We are acting on behalf of the above-named who has developed mesothelioma. We are investigating whether this disease may have been caused:

during the course of his employment with you / *name of employer if different* whilst at your premises at (*address*)

between the approximate dates of: (*insert relevant dates of employment/at the premises*)

as a result of your product (*name*)

Please note your insurers will require you to advise them of this letter. You must pass a copy of this letter to your insurer immediately.

We are writing this letter in accordance with the Pre-action Protocol for Disease and Illness Claims.

Our client's details are as follows:
Name:
Address:
National insurance number (*if known*):
Date of birth:
Marital status:
Details of dependants:
Date of diagnosis:

We require a response from you confirming this matter is receiving urgent attention with 14 days of the date of this letter.

The direct email address, which you may use for urgent communications and which should be followed up with paper copies, is: (*insert email address*)

Yours faithfully

Pre-action Protocol for Housing Disrepair Cases

1 INTRODUCTION

Following a review of the problems of civil housing disrepair claims, Lord Woolf recommended in his *Final Report* in July 1996 that there should be a pre-action protocol.

The protocol, which covers claims in England and Wales, is intended to encourage the exchange of information between parties at an early stage and to provide a clear framework within which parties in a housing disrepair claim can attempt to achieve an early and appropriate resolution of the issues. An attempt has been made to draft the protocol in plain English and to keep the contents straightforward in order to make the protocol accessible and easy to use by all, including those representing themselves.

The protocol embraces the spirit of the Woolf reforms to the civil justice system. As Lord Woolf noted, landlords and tenants have a common interest in maintaining housing stock in good condition. It is generally common ground that in principle court action should be treated as a last resort, and it is hoped that the protocol will lead to the avoidance of unnecessary litigation. Before using the protocol tenants should therefore ensure that the landlord is aware of the disrepair. Tenants should also consider whether other options for having repairs carried out and/or obtaining compensation are more appropriate. Examples of other options are set out in para. 4.1(b).

Should a claim proceed to litigation, the court will expect all parties to have complied with the protocol as far as possible. The court has the power to order parties who have unreasonably failed to comply with the protocol to pay costs or be subject to other sanctions.

2 AIMS OF THE PROTOCOL

PD Protocols provides that the objectives of pre-action protocols are:

(1) to encourage the exchange of early and full information about the prospective legal claim,
(2) to enable parties to avoid litigation by agreeing a settlement of the claim before the commencement of proceedings,
(3) to support the efficient management of proceedings where litigation cannot be avoided. The specific aims of this protocol are:
- To avoid unnecessary litigation.
- To promote the speedy and appropriate carrying out of any repairs which are the landlord's responsibility.
- To ensure that tenants receive any compensation to which they are entitled as speedily as possible.
- To promote good pre-litigation practice, including the early exchange of information and to give guidance about the instruction of experts.
- To keep the costs of resolving disputes down.

3 PROTOCOL

When using this protocol, please refer to the guidance notes in para. 4.

3.1 Definitions

For the purposes of this protocol:

(a) A disrepair claim is a civil claim arising from the condition of residential premises and may include a related personal injury claim. (See para. 4.4 (c), (d) and (e) of the guidance notes.)

Pre-action Protocols

It does not include disrepair claims which originate as counterclaims or set-offs in other proceedings.

(b) The types of claim which this protocol is intended to cover include those brought under the Landlord and Tenant Act 1985, s. 11, the Defective Premises Act 1972, s. 4, common law nuisance and negligence, and those brought under the express terms of a tenancy agreement or lease. It does not cover claims brought under the Environmental Protection Act 1990, s. 82 (which are heard in the magistrates' court).

(c) This protocol covers claims by any person with a disrepair claim as referred to in paragraphs (a) and (b) above, including tenants, lessees and members of the tenant's family. The use of the term 'tenant' in this protocol is intended to cover all such people. (See also paragraph 4.4(e).)

3.2 Early Notification Letter

(a) Notice of the claim should be given to the landlord as soon as possible. In order to avoid delay in notifying the landlord it may be appropriate to send a letter notifying the landlord of the claim (early notification letter) before sending a letter setting out the full details of the claim (letter of claim). An early notification letter is intended to be a helpful tool, but it will not be necessary in every case. It might be appropriate where, for example, a repair is urgent or there is likely to be some delay before enough details are available to make a claim. The early notification letter to the landlord should give the following information:
   (i) tenant's name, the address of the property, tenant's address if different, tenant's telephone number and when access is available;
   (ii) details of the defects, including any defects outstanding, in the form of a schedule, if appropriate. Attached at annex G is a specimen schedule which can be used to inform the landlord of the disrepair;
   (iii) details of any notification previously given to the landlord of the need for repair or information as to why the tenant believes that the landlord has knowledge of the need for repair;
   (iv) proposed expert (see para. 3.6);
   (v) proposed letter of instruction to expert (see annex C);
   (vi) tenant's disclosure of such relevant documents as are readily available.

(b) The early notification letter should also request the following disclosure from the landlord: All relevant records or documents including:
   (i) copy of tenancy agreement including tenancy conditions;
   (ii) documents or computerised records relating to notice given, disrepair reported, inspection reports or repair works to the property.

(c) The early notification letter should include the authorisation for release of the information (except in a case where the tenant is acting in person).

(d) Specimen early notification letters are attached at annex A. They may be suitably adapted as appropriate.

3.3 Letter of Claim

(a) The tenant should send to the landlord a letter of claim at the earliest reasonable opportunity. The letter of claim should contain the following details *(if they have not already been provided in an early notification letter):*
   (i) tenant's name, the address of the property, tenant's address if different, the tenant's telephone number and when access is available;
   (ii) details of the defects, including any defects outstanding, in the form of a schedule, if appropriate. Attached at annex G is a specimen schedule which can be used to inform the landlord of the disrepair;
   (iii) history of the defects, including attempts to rectify them;
   (iv) details of any notification previously given to the landlord of the need for repair or information as to why the tenant believes that the landlord has knowledge of the need for repair;
   (v) the effect of the defects on the tenant (see para. 4.4(c), (d) and (e) regarding personal injury claims);
   (vi) details of any special damages (see form attached at annex E and definition of 'special damages' at para. 4.10);
   (vii) proposed expert (see para. 3.6);

(viii) proposed letter of instruction to the expert (see annex C);
(ix) tenant's disclosure of relevant documents.

(b) If not already requested in an early notification letter, the letter of claim should also request the following disclosure from the landlord:
All relevant records or documents including:
(i) copy of tenancy agreement including tenancy conditions;
(ii) tenancy file;
(iii) documents relating to notice given, disrepair reported, inspection reports or requirements to the property;
(iv) computerised records.

(c) If not requested in an early notification letter, the letter of claim should also include the authorisation for release of the information (except in a case where the tenant is acting in person).

(d) Specimen letters of claim are attached at annex B. It will be seen that there are different versions depending on whether or not an early notification letter has been sent. The letters may be suitably adapted as appropriate.

3.4 Limitation Period

The procedures in this protocol do not extend statutory limitation periods. If a limitation period is about to expire, the tenant may need to issue proceedings immediately unless the landlord confirms that they will not rely on limitation as a defence in subsequent proceedings. (See para. 4.8 for guidance about the limitation period, and para. 4.10 for a definition of 'limitation period'.) Alternatively the tenant can ask the landlord to agree to extend the limitation period.

3.5 Landlord's Response

3.5.1 Response to first letter

The landlord should normally reply within 20 working days of the date of receipt of the first letter from the tenant, i.e., the early notification letter or the letter of claim if no early notification letter is sent. (See para. 4.10 for a definition of 'working days'.) The landlord's response to the first letter, whether an early notification letter or a letter of claim, should include the following:

Disclosure

(a) All relevant records or documents including:
(i) copy of tenancy agreement including tenancy conditions;
(ii) documents or computerised records relating to notice given, disrepair reported, inspection reports or requirements to the property.

Expert

(b) A response to the tenant's proposals for instructing an expert including:
(i) whether or not the proposed single joint expert is agreed;
(ii) whether the letter of instruction is agreed;
(iii) if the single joint expert is agreed but with separate instructions, a copy of the letter of instruction;
(iv) if the appointment of a single joint expert is not agreed, whether the landlord agrees to a joint inspection.

3.5.2 Response to letter of claim

(a) The landlord's response to the tenant's letter of claim should include:
(i) whether liability is admitted and if so, in respect of which defects. If liability is disputed in respect of some or all of the defects, the reasons for this;
(ii) any point which the landlord wishes to make regarding lack of notice of the repair or regarding any difficulty in gaining access;
(iii) a full schedule of intended works including anticipated start and completion dates and a timetable for the works;
(iv) any offer of compensation;
(v) any offer in respect of costs;
(vi) the information set out at para. 3.5.1.(a) and (b), if it has not already been provided.

Pre-action Protocols

(b) On receipt of the letter of claim (whether or not an early notification letter was sent), the landlord may provide a response to the issues set out at paragraph (a) above either:
  (i) within 20 working days of the date of receipt of the letter of claim (see para. 4.10 for a definition of 'working days'); or
  (ii) within 20 working days of the date of receipt of the report of the single joint expert (see para. 3.6(h)) or date of receipt of the experts' agreed schedule following a joint inspection (see para. 3.6(g)).

3.5.3 If landlord does not respond

(a) If no response is received from the landlord to the early notification letter within 20 working days, the tenant should send a letter of claim giving as many of the details outlined at para. 3.3 as possible, on the basis of the information the tenant has to hand.
(b) Failure to respond within the time limits set out in paras 3.5.1 and 3.5.2, or at all, to the early notification letter or the letter of claim will be a breach of the protocol. (See para. 4.7(a) and (b) regarding time limits and the power of the court if the protocol is breached.)

3.6 Experts

General

See para. 4.6 for guidance regarding the use of experts.

(a) Tenants should remember that in some cases it might not be necessary to instruct an expert to provide evidence of disrepair, for example, if the only issue relates to the level of any damages claimed. It may be advisable to take photographs of any defects before and after works, and consideration should be given to the use of video footage, particularly if an expert has not been instructed.
(b) The expert should be instructed to report on all items of disrepair which the landlord ought reasonably to know about, or which the expert ought reasonably to report on. The expert should be asked to provide a schedule of works, an estimate of the costs of repair, and to list any urgent works.
(c) Information is given at para. 4.6(a) about obtaining lists of independent experts who can be instructed in disrepair cases.

Single joint expert

(d) If the landlord does not raise an objection to the proposed expert or letter of instruction within 20 working days of the date of receipt of the early notification letter or letter of claim, the expert should be instructed as a single joint expert, using the tenant's proposed letter of instruction. Attached at annex C are specimen letters of instruction to an expert. Alternatively, if the parties cannot agree joint instructions, the landlord and tenant should send their own separate instructions to the single joint expert. If sending separate instructions, the landlord should send the tenant a copy of the landlord's letter of instruction with their response to the first letter. (The tenant has already forwarded the proposed letter of instruction to the landlord.)

Joint inspection

(e) If it is not possible to reach agreement to instruct a single joint expert, even with separate instructions, the parties should attempt to arrange a joint inspection, i.e., an inspection by different experts instructed by each party to take place at the same time. If the landlord wishes to send their own expert to a joint inspection, they should inform both the tenant's expert and the tenant's solicitor. If the landlord instructs their own expert to inspect then the tenant can also instruct their own expert. It will be for the court to decide subsequently, if proceedings are issued, whether or not either party has acted reasonably.

Time limits

(f) Whether a single joint expert or a joint inspection is used, the property should be inspected within 20 working days of the date that the landlord responds to the tenant's first letter.
(g) If there is a joint inspection, the experts should produce an agreed schedule of works detailing:
  (i) the defects and required works which are agreed and a timetable for the agreed works;
  (ii) the areas of disagreement and the reasons for disagreement.

  The agreed schedule should be sent to both the landlord and the tenant within 10 working days of the joint inspection.

(h) If there is a single joint expert, a copy of the report should be sent to both the landlord and the tenant within 10 working days of the inspection. Either party can ask relevant questions of the expert.

(i) At annex D are flowcharts showing the time limits in the protocol.

Urgent cases

(j) The protocol does not prevent a tenant from instructing an expert at an earlier stage if this is considered necessary for reasons of urgency, and the landlord should give access in such cases. Appropriate cases may include:
   (i) where the tenant reasonably considers that there is a significant risk to health and safety;
   (ii) where the tenant is seeking an interim injunction;
   (iii) where it is necessary to preserve evidence.

Access

(k) Tenants must give reasonable access to the landlord for inspection and repair in line with the tenancy agreement. The landlord should give reasonable notice of the need for access, except in the case of an emergency. The landlord must give access to common parts as appropriate, e.g., for the inspection of a shared heating system.

Costs

(l) Terms of appointment should be agreed at the outset and should include:
   (i) the basis of the expert's charges (either daily or hourly rates and an estimate of the time likely to be required, or a fee for the services);
   (ii) any travelling expenses and other relevant expenses;
   (iii) rates for attendance at court should this become necessary, and provisions for payment on late notice of cancellation of a court hearing;
   (iv) time for delivery of report;
   (v) time for making payment;
   (vi) whether fees are to be paid by a third party; and
   (vii) arrangements for dealing with questions for experts and discussions between experts and for providing for the cost involved.

(m) If a single joint expert is instructed, each party will pay one half of the cost of the report. If a joint inspection is carried out, each party will pay the full cost of the report from their own expert. (See para. 3.7.)

(n) The expert should send separately and directly to both parties answers to any questions asked.

3.7 Costs

(a) If the tenant's claim is settled without litigation on terms which justify bringing it, the landlord will pay the tenant's reasonable costs or out-of-pocket expenses. (See para. 4.10 for a definition of 'costs' and 'out-of-pocket expenses'.)

(b) Attached at annex F is a statement of costs form which can be used to inform the landlord of the costs of the claim.

4 GUIDANCE NOTES

4.1 Alternative Dispute Resolution

(a) The parties should consider whether some form of alternative dispute resolution procedure (see para. 4.10 for a definition of alternative dispute resolution) would be more suitable than litigation, and if so, endeavour to agree which form to adopt. Both the claimant and defendant may be required by the court to provide evidence that alternative means of resolving their dispute were considered. The courts take the view that litigation should be a last resort, and that claims should not be issued prematurely when a settlement is still actively being explored. Parties are warned that if the protocol is not followed (including this paragraph) then the court must have regard to such conduct when determining costs.

(b) It is not practicable in this protocol to address in detail how the parties might decide which method to adopt to resolve their particular dispute. However, summarised below are some of the options for resolving disputes without litigation:
   - Discussion and negotiation.

- Early neutral evaluation by an independent third party (for example, a lawyer experienced in the field of housing disrepair or an individual experienced in the subject matter of the claim).
- Mediation — a form of facilitated negotiation assisted by an independent neutral party.
- Other options in respect of the following specific categories:
  (i) For council tenants:
  - Local authority repairs, complaints and/or arbitration procedures.
  - The Right to Repair Scheme. The scheme is only suitable for small, urgent repairs of less than £250 in value.
    Information and leaflets about the scheme in England can be obtained from the Department for Communities and Local Government, Eland House, Bressenden Place, London SW1E 5DU. Tel: (020) 7944 3672. www.communities.gov.uk/index.asp?id=1152130. Information about the scheme in Wales can be obtained from the National Assembly for Wales, Cathays Park, Cardiff, CF10 3NQ. Tel: (029) 2082 5111.
  - Commission for Local Administration in England. Tel: 0845 602 1983.
  - The Local Government Ombudsman for Wales. Tel: (01656) 661325.

  (ii) For tenants of social landlords who are not council tenants, and for tenants of qualifying private landlords:
  - In England, the Independent Housing Ombudsman, 3rd Floor, Norman House, 105–109 Strand, London WC2R 0AA. Tel: (020) 7836 3630.
  - In Wales, the National Assembly for Wales, Cathays Park, Cardiff CF10 3NQ. Tel: (029) 2082 5111.
  - Local authority environmental health officers.

  (iii) For private tenants:
  - Local authority environmental health officers.

(c) The Legal Services Commission has published a booklet on *Alternatives to Court* (CLS Direct Information Leaflet 23) (www.clsdirect.org.uk/legalhelp/leaflet23.jsp), which lists a number of organisations that provide alternative dispute resolution services.

(d) *It is expressly recognised that no party can or should be forced to mediate or enter into any form of ADR.*

(e) Information about repair rights generally is available free of charge from the following web pages: www.shelter.org.uk/housingadvice/index.asp and www.legalservices.gov.uk/leaflets/cls/index.htm.

(f) The former Department for Transport, Local Government and the Regions issued *Good Practice Guidance on Housing Disrepair Legal Obligations* in January 2002. Copies of the Guidance (ISBN 185112 523X) can be obtained from Communities and Local Government Publications, PO Box 236, Wetherby LS23 7NB. Tel: 0870 1226 236. Fax: 0870 1226 237. Textphone: 0870 1207 405. Email: communities@twoten.com. Free to download from the Communities and Local Government website at www.communities.gov.uk/index.asp?id=1502470. A summary, Housing Research Summary No. 154, is available free on the Communities and Local Government website at the following link www.communities.gov.uk/index.asp?id=1155697. Hard copies are no longer available. The Communities and Local Government website www.communities.gov.uk/index.asp?id=1150232 is a general source of information for landlords and tenants.

4.2 Scope of the Protocol

(a) This protocol is intended to apply to all civil law claims which include a claim for disrepair, but not to counterclaims or set-offs in disrepair claims which originate as other proceedings. (See para. 4.10 for an explanation of 'counterclaim' and 'set-off'.) In cases which involve a counterclaim or set-off, the landlord and tenant will still be expected to act reasonably in exchanging information and trying to settle the case at an early stage.

(b) In practice, most disrepair cases will have a value of more than £1,000 but less than £15,000 and so are likely to be allocated to the fast track if they come to court. (See para. 4.10 for an explanation of 'the fast track'.) The protocol is aimed at this type of case. The need to keep costs down is especially important in claims of lower value. The approach of the protocol is however, equally *appropriate to all claims* and the protocol should also be followed in small claims track and multi-track claims. (See para. 4.10 for an explanation of 'small claims track' and 'multi-track'.) The court will expect to see reasonable pre-action behaviour applied in all cases.

4.3 Early Notification Letter

(a) The early notification letter is not intended to replace the direct reporting of defects to the landlord at an early stage, using any procedure the landlord may have established. The protocol is for use in those cases where, despite the landlord's knowledge of the disrepair, the matter remains unresolved.

(b) It is recognised that disrepair cases can range from straightforward to highly complex, and that it is not always possible to obtain detailed information at an early stage. In order to avoid unnecessary delay and to ensure that notice of the claim is given to the landlord at the earliest possible opportunity, the protocol suggests the use of two letters in some cases; an early notification letter and a later letter of claim. (See para. 3.2(a) and annexes A and B.)

(c) A copy of the protocol need only be sent to the landlord if the tenant has reason to believe that the landlord will not have access to the protocol, e.g., because the landlord is an individual or small organisation. If in doubt, a copy should be sent.

4.4 Letters of Claim and Landlord's Response

(a) Letters of claim and a landlord's response are not intended to have the same status as a statement of case in court proceedings. Matters may come to light after the letter of claim has been sent, or after the landlord has responded, which could mean that the case of one or both parties is presented slightly differently than in the letters of claim or in the landlord's response. It would be inconsistent with the spirit of the protocol to seek to capitalise on this in the proceedings, provided that there was no intention to mislead. In particular, advantage should not be taken regarding discrepancies relating to the general details of notice given in the early notification letter.

(b) See para. 4.3(c) regarding the sending of a copy of the protocol by the tenant to the landlord.

Cases with a personal injury element

(c) Housing disrepair claims may contain a personal injury element. This should be set out in the letter of claim, as should a clear indication of the identities of all persons who plan to make a personal injury claim.

(d) There is also a Pre-action Protocol for Personal Injury Claims. This protocol should be followed for that part of the disrepair claim which forms a personal injury claim, unless it is insufficient to warrant separate procedures and would therefore be dealt with only as part of the disrepair claim and evidenced by a general practitioner's letter. The Pre-action Protocol for Personal Injury Claims should be followed for any claim which requires expert evidence other than a general practitioner's letter. If the disrepair claim is urgent, it would be reasonable to pursue separate disrepair and personal injury claims, which could then be case-managed or consolidated at a later date.

(e) Paragraph 3.3(a)(v) refers to the effect of the defects on 'the tenant'. This should be taken to include all persons who have a personal injury claim. The details of any such claim and of all likely claimants should be set out in the letter of claim.

4.5 Disclosure of Documents

(a) When giving disclosure, the landlord should copy all relevant documents. In housing disrepair claims, this includes any and all documents relating in particular to the disrepair and to notice given by the tenant to the landlord of the disrepair. Notice is often given by personal attendance at the landlord's office, and copies of any notes of meetings and oral discussions should also be copied, along with other relevant documents. Documents regarding rent arrears or tenants' disputes will not normally be relevant.

(b) The aim of the early disclosure of documents by the landlord is not to encourage 'fishing expeditions' by the tenant, but to promote an early exchange of relevant information to help in clarifying or resolving issues in dispute. The tenant should assist by identifying the particular categories of documents which they consider relevant.

(c) The 20 working days time limit specified in para. 3.5 runs from the date of receipt of either letter. Receipt of the letter is deemed to have taken place two days after the date of the letter. If necessary, a written request for extra time should be made by the landlord to the tenant. Should a case come to court, the court will decide whether the parties have acted reasonably, and whether any sanctions, including costs orders, are appropriate. The principles regarding time limits are referred to again at para. 4.7.

(d) Nothing in the protocol restricts the right of the tenant to look personally at their file or to request a copy of the whole file. Neither is the landlord prevented from sending to the tenant a copy of the whole file, should the landlord wish.

4.6 Experts

(a) Information about independent experts can be obtained from:
   (i) The Chartered Institute of Environmental Health, Chadwick Court, 15 Hatfields, London SE1 8DJ. Tel: (020) 7928 6006. Ask for a copy of the Consultants and Trainers Directory.
   (ii) The Law Society, 113 Chancery Lane, London WC2A 1PL, Tel: (020) 7831 0344. Refer to the Society's Expert Witness Directory.
   (iii) The Royal Institution of Chartered Surveyors, 12 Great George Street, Parliament Square, London SW1P 3AD, Tel: 0845 304 4111. Ask for a copy of the relevant regional directory.
(b) The protocol encourages the use of a single joint expert. In order to make it less likely that a second expert will be necessary, the protocol provides for the landlord to forward their own instructions directly to the single joint expert if they cannot agree joint instructions. Both parties can ask relevant questions of the expert. If the parties cannot agree on a single joint expert, either with joint or separate instructions, the protocol suggests a joint inspection by each party's expert.
(c) The specimen letters at annexes A and B ask for reasons to be given as to why the landlord objects to the expert proposed by the tenant. Should a case come to court, it will be for the court to decide whether the parties have acted reasonably and whether the costs of more than one expert should be recoverable.
(d) Parties should bear in mind that it may not always be necessary to obtain expert evidence of disrepair, and in view of this, the protocol encourages the use of photos before and after works, and if appropriate, video evidence.
(e) Parties are reminded that the CPR provide that expert evidence should be restricted to that which is necessary and that the court's permission is required to use an expert's report. The court may limit the amount of experts' fees and expenses recoverable from another party.
(f) When instructing an expert, regard should be had to any approved Code of Guidance for Experts and whether a copy of the protocol should be sent to the expert.

4.7 Time Limits

(a) The timescales given in the protocol are longstops and every attempt should be made to comply with the protocol as soon as possible. If parties are able to comply earlier than the timescales provided, they should do so.
(b) Time limits in the protocol may be changed by agreement. However, it should always be borne in mind that the court will expect an explanation as to why the protocol has not been followed or has been varied and breaches of the protocol may lead to costs or other orders being made by the court.

4.8 Limitation Period

(a) In cases where the limitation period will shortly expire, the tenant should ask in the first letter for an extension of the limitation period. The extension requested should be only so long as is necessary to avoid the cost of starting court proceedings.
(b) It will be for the court to decide whether refusal to grant the request is reasonable and whether any sanctions, including costs orders, are appropriate.

4.9 Contact Point

Where a landlord is not an individual, a person should be designated to act as a point of contact for the tenant as soon as possible after the landlord receives the first letter from the tenant and (if one is involved) their solicitor. The appointee's name and contact details should be sent to the tenant and their solicitor as soon as possible after the appointment is made.

4.10 Glossary

alternative dispute resolution. Mediation, or other dispute resolution method, which seeks to settle disputes without the need for court proceedings.

counterclaim. A claim that either party makes in response to an initial claim by the other.

costs. Legal fees or, in a small track claim, out-of-pocket expenses incurred as a result of a claim. (See **out-of-pocket expenses** below.)

damages. Money obtained as the result of a claim to compensate for inconvenience and/or distress suffered because of the condition of the property. (See also **special damages** below.)

defect/disrepair. A fault or problem with a property, for which the landlord is responsible.

disclosure. The making available by one party to the other of documentation relevant to the claim.

fast track/multi-track/small claims track. Cases which proceed to court will be allocated to separate tracks depending on their value. The separate tracks have different rules and procedures. Housing cases worth between £1,000 and £15,000 where there is a claim for works to be done will usually be allocated to the **fast track.** Housing cases where the costs of the repairs and/or the damages do not exceed £1,000 will usually be dealt with on the **small claims track.** Cases over £15,000 will usually be allocated to the **multi-track.**

joint inspection. An inspection of a property carried out at the same time by one expert instructed by the tenant and by one expert instructed by the landlord.

limitation period. The time limit after which a legal action cannot be started. In most housing cases it is six years. In personal injury cases it is three years.

litigation. A court case or court proceedings. The taking of legal action by someone.

notice. Notification of a disrepair, either directly by the tenant in writing or orally to the landlord or his employee, or indirectly, by inspection of the property by the landlord or his employee.

out-of-pocket expenses. Expenses incurred in a small track claim as a result of the claim, such as loss of earnings and experts' fees.

protocol. A code or procedure — in this case for dealing with housing disrepair.

set-off. Where one party agrees with the other's claim or part of it, but sets up one which counterbalances it.

single joint expert. An expert who is instructed by both the tenant and the landlord, either with joint or separate instructions.

special damages. Compensation for loss of or damage to specific items, e.g., clothes, carpets, curtains, wallpaper, bedding or extra electricity costs.

tenant. Someone who rents land (including property) owned by another. (See also the definition at para. 3.1(c).)

third party. Someone other than the landlord or tenant.

working days. All days other than Saturdays, Sundays and bank holidays.

5 ANNEXES

Specimen Letters

It will be noted that the attached specimen letters are in pairs for use by solicitors and by tenants acting in person respectively.

It is emphasised that they may be suitably adapted as appropriate.

The letters, with the paragraph of the protocol to which each one relates, are as follows:

Annex A early notification letter (see para. 3.2).

Annex B letter of claim (see para. 3.3).

Note: There are two versions of this:

(a) for use where an early notification letter has been sent;

(b) for other cases.

Annex C letter of instruction to expert (see para. 3.6).

Annex D early notification letter flowchart.

Annex E special damages form.

Annex F statement of costs.

Annex G schedule.

ANNEX A EARLY NOTIFICATION LETTER

(i) Letter from Solicitor

To Landlord

Dear Sirs,

Re: *(tenant's name and address of property)*

We are instructed by your above-named tenant. *(Include a sentence stating how the case is being funded.)* We are using the Housing Disrepair Protocol. [We enclose a copy of the protocol for your information.*]

REPAIRS

Your tenant complains of the following defects at the property *(set out nature of defects)*.

[We enclose a schedule, which sets out the disrepair in each room.*]

You received notice of the defects as follows: *(list details of notice relied on)*.

Please arrange to inspect the property as soon as possible. Access will be available on the following dates and times: *(list dates and times as appropriate)*

Please let us know what repairs you propose to carry out and the anticipated date for completion of the works.

DISCLOSURE

Please also provide within 20 working days of receipt of this letter, the following:

All relevant records or documents including:

(i) copy of tenancy agreement including tenancy conditions;

(ii) documents or computerised records relating to notice given, disrepair, reported, inspection reports or repair works to the property.

We enclose a signed authority from our clients for you to release this information to ourselves.

We also enclose copies of the following relevant documents from our client: *(list documents enclosed)*

EXPERT

If agreement is not reached about the carrying out of repairs within 20 working days of this letter, we propose to jointly instruct a single joint expert *(insert expert's name and address)* to carry out an inspection of the property and provide a report. We enclose a copy of their CV, plus a draft letter of instruction. Please let us know if you agree to his/her appointment. If you object, please let us know your reasons within 20 working days.

If you do not object to the expert being instructed as a single joint expert, but wish to provide your own instructions, you should send those directly to *(insert expert's name)* within 20 working days of this letter. Please send to ourselves a copy of your letter of instruction. If you do not agree to a single joint expert, we will instruct *(insert expert's name)* to inspect the property in any event. In those circumstances, if you wish to instruct your expert to attend at the same time, please let ourselves and *(insert expert's name)* know within 20 working days of this letter.

CLAIM

Our client's disrepair claim requires further investigation. We will write to you as soon as possible with further details of the history of the defects and of notice relied on, along with details of our client's claim for general and special damages.

Yours faithfully,

* Delete as appropriate

(ii) Letter from Tenant

To Landlord

Dear

Re: *(your name and address of property)*

I write regarding disrepair at the above address. I am using the Housing Disrepair Protocol. [I enclose a copy of the protocol for your information.*]

REPAIRS

The following defects exist at the property *(set out nature of defects)*.

[I enclose a schedule which sets out the disrepair in each room.*]

Please arrange to inspect the property as soon as possible. Access will be available on the following dates and times: *(list dates and time as appropriate)*

You received notice of the defects as follows: *(list details of notice relied on)*.

Please let me know what repairs you propose to carry out and the anticipated date for completion of the works.

DISCLOSURE

Please also provide within 20 working days of receipt of this letter, the following:

All relevant records or documents including:

(i) copy of tenancy agreement including tenancy conditions;
(ii) documents or computerised records relating to notice given, disrepair reported, inspection reports or repair works to the property.

I also enclose copies of the following relevant documents: *(list documents enclosed)*

EXPERT

If agreement is not reached about the carrying out of repairs within 20 working days, I propose that we jointly instruct a single joint expert *(insert expert's name and address)* to carry out an inspection of the property and provide a report. I enclose a copy of their CV, plus a draft letter of instruction. Please let me know if you agree to his/her appointment. If you object, please let me know your reasons within 20 working days.

If you do not object to the expert being appointed as a single joint expert but wish to provide your own instructions, you should send those directly to *(insert expert's name)* within 20 working days. Please send a copy of your letter of instruction to me. If you do not agree to a single joint expert I will instruct *(insert expert's name)* to inspect the property in any event. In those circumstances if you wish your expert to attend at the same time, please let me and *(insert expert's name)* know within 20 working days.

CLAIM

I will write to you as soon as possible with further details of the history of the defects and of notice relied on, along with details of my claim for general and special damages.

Yours sincerely

ANNEX B LETTER OF CLAIM

(a) For Use Where an Early Notification Letter Has Been Sent (As Set Out in Annex A)

(i) Letter from Solicitor

To Landlord

Dear Sirs,

Re: *(tenant's name and address of property)*

We write further to our letter of *(insert date)* regarding our client's housing disrepair claim. We have now taken full instructions from our client.

* Delete as appropriate

Pre-action Protocols

REPAIRS

The history of the disrepair is as follows: *(set out history of defects).*

[I enclose a schedule which sets out the disrepair in each room.*]

You received notice of the defects as follows: *(list details of notice relied on).*

The defects at the property are causing *(set out the effects of the disrepair on the client and their family, including any personal injury element; specify if there will be any additional claimant).*

Please forward to us within 20 working days of receipt of this letter a full schedule of works together with the anticipated date for completion of the works proposed.

CLAIM

We take the view that you are in breach of your repairing obligations. Please provide us with your proposals for compensation. *(Alternatively, set out suggestions for general damages, e.g., £x for x years).* [Our client also requires compensation for special damages, and we attach a schedule of the special damages claimed.*]

Yours faithfully,

(ii) Letter from Tenant

To Landlord

Dear

Re: *(your name and address of property)*

I write further to my letter of (insert date) regarding my housing disrepair claim. I am now able to provide you with further details.

REPAIRS

The history of the disrepair is as follows: *(set out history of defects).*

You received notice of the defects as follows: *(list details of notice relied on).*

The defects at the property are causing *(set out the effects of the disrepair on you and your family, including any personal injury element; specify if there will be any additional claimant).*

Please forward to me within 20 working days of receipt of this letter a full schedule of works together with the anticipated date for completion of the works proposed.

CLAIM

I take the view that you are in breach of your repairing obligations. Please provide me with your proposals for compensation. *(Alternatively, set out suggestions for general damages, e.g., £x for x years).* [I also require compensation for special damages, and I attach a schedule of the special damages claimed.*]

Yours sincerely,

(b) For Use Where an Early Notification Letter Has Not Been Sent

(i) Letter from Solicitor

To Landlord

Dear Sirs,

Re: *(tenant's name and address of property)*

We are instructed by your above-named tenant. *(Insert a sentence stating how the case is being funded.)* We are using the Housing Disrepair Protocol. [We enclose a copy of the protocol for your information.*]

* Delete as appropriate

REPAIRS

Your tenant complains of the following defects at the property: *(set out nature and history of defects).*

[We enclose a schedule which sets out the disrepair in each room.*]

You received notice of the defects as follows: *(list details of notice relied on).*

The defects at the property are causing *(set out the effects of the disrepair on the client and their family, including any personal injury element, specifying if there are any additional claimants).*

Please provide within 20 working days of receipt of this letter a full schedule of the works you propose to carry out to remedy the above defects and the anticipated date for completion of the works.

DISCLOSURE

Please also provide within 20 working days of this letter the following:

All relevant records or documents including:

(i) copy of tenancy agreement including tenancy conditions;
(ii) tenancy file;
(iii) documents relating to notice given, disrepair reported, inspection reports or repair works to the property;
(iv) computerised records.

We enclose a signed authority from our clients for you to release this information to ourselves.

We also enclose copies of the following relevant documents: *(list documents enclosed)*

EXPERT

If agreement is not reached about the carrying out of repairs within 20 working days of receipt of this letter, we propose to jointly instruct a single joint expert *(insert expert's name and address)* to carry out an inspection of the property and provide a report. We enclose a copy of their *CV,* plus a draft letter of instruction. Please let me know if you agree to his/her appointment. If you object, please let me know your reasons within 20 working days.

If you do not object to the expert being instructed a single joint expert, but wish to provide your own instructions, you should send those directly to *(insert expert's name)* within 20 working days. Please send a copy of your letter of instruction to ourselves. If you do not agree to a single joint expert, we will instruct *(insert expert's name)* to inspect the property in any event. In those circumstances, if you wish to instruct your expert to attend at the same time please let ourselves and *(insert expert's name)* know within 20 working days.

CLAIM

We take the view that you are in breach of your repairing obligations. Please provide us with your proposals for compensation. *(Alternatively, set out suggestions for general damages, e.g., £x for x years.)* [Our client also requires compensation for the special damages, and we attach a schedule of the special damages claimed.*]

Yours faithfully,

(ii) Letter from Tenant

To Landlord

Dear

Re: (your name and address of property)

I write regarding the disrepair at the above address. I am using the Housing Disrepair Protocol. [I enclose a copy of the protocol for your information.*]

REPAIRS

The property has the following defects: *(set out nature and history of defects).*

[I enclose a schedule which sets out the disrepair in each room.*]

You received notice of the defects as follows: *(list details of notice relied on).*

* Delete as appropriate

Pre-action Protocols

The defects at the property are causing (*set out the effects of the disrepair on you and your family, including any personal injury element, specifying if there are any additional claimants*).

Please provide within 20 working days of receipt of this letter a full schedule of the works you propose to carry out to remedy the above defects and the anticipated date for completion of the works.

DISCLOSURE

Please also provide within 20 working days of receipt of this letter the following:

All relevant records or documents including:

(i) copy of tenancy agreement including tenancy conditions;
(ii) tenancy file;
(iii) documents relating to notice given, disrepair reported, inspection reports or repair works to the property;
(iv) computerised records.

I also enclose copies of the following relevant documents: *(list documents enclosed).*

EXPERT

If agreement is not reached about the carrying out of repairs within 20 working days of receipt of this letter, I propose that we jointly instruct a single joint expert *(insert expert's name and address)* to carry out an inspection of the property and provide a report. I enclose a copy of their CV, plus a draft letter of instruction. Please let me know if you agree to his/her appointment. If you object, please let me know your reasons within 20 working days.

If you do not object to the expert being instructed as a single joint expert, but wish to provide your own instructions, you should send those directly to *(insert expert's name)* within 20 working days. Please also send a copy of the letter of instruction to me. If you do not agree to a single joint expert, I will instruct *(insert expert's name)* to inspect the property in any event. In those circumstances, if you wish to instruct your expert to attend at the same time please let me and *(insert expert's name)* know within 20 working days.

CLAIM

I take the view that you are in breach of your repairing obligations. Please provide me with your proposals for compensation. *(Alternatively, set out suggestions for general damages, e.g. £x for x years.)* [I also require compensation for special damages, and I attach a schedule of the special damages claimed.*]

Yours sincerely

ANNEX C LETTER OF INSTRUCTION TO EXPERT

(i) Letter from Solicitor

Dear

Re: *(tenant's name and address of property)*

We act for the above-named in connection with a housing disrepair claim at the above property. We are using the Housing Disrepair Protocol. [We enclose a copy of the Protocol for your information.*]

Please carry out an inspection of the above property by *(datexs†)* and provide a report covering the following points:

(a) whether you agree that the defects are as claimed;
(b) whether any of the defects is structural;
(c) the cause of the defect(s);
(d) the age, character and prospective life of the property.

Access will be available on the following dates and times: *(list dates and times as appropriate)*

[You are instructed as a single joint expert.] [The landlord is *(landlord's name and details)*.] [The landlord will be providing you with their own instructions direct.] [The landlord will contact you to confirm that their expert will attend at the same time as you to carry out a joint inspection.]*

* Delete as appropriate

† The date to be inserted should be 20 working days from the date of the letter, in accordance with para. 3.6(f) of the protocol.

Please provide the report within 10 working days of the inspection. Please contact us immediately if there are any works which require an interim injunction.

If the case proceeds to court, the report may be used in evidence. In order to comply with court rules we would be grateful if you would insert above your signature a statement that the contents are true to the best of your knowledge and belief. We refer you to Part 35 of the Civil Procedure Rules which specifies experts' responsibilities, the contents of any report, and the statements experts must sign.

(Insert details as to cost and payment.)

Yours sincerely

(ii) Letter from Tenant

Dear

Re: *(your name and address of property)*

I am currently in dispute with my landlord about disrepair at the above property. I am using the Housing Disrepair Protocol. [I enclose a copy of the protocol for your information.*]

Please carry out an inspection of the above property by *(date †)* and provide a report covering the following points:

(a) whether you agree that the defects are as claimed;
(b) whether any of the defects is structural;
(c) the cause of the defect(s);
(d) the age, character and prospective life of the property.

Access will be available on the following dates and times: *(list dates and times as appropriate).*

[You are instructed as a single joint expert.] [The landlord is *(landlord's name and details).*] [The landlord will be providing you with their own instructions direct.] [The landlord will contact you to confirm that their expert will attend at the same time as you to carry out a joint inspection.]*

Please provide the report within 10 working days of the inspection. Please contact me immediately if there are any works which require an interim injunction.

If the case proceeds to court, the report may be used in evidence. In order to comply with court rules I would be grateful if you would insert above your signature a statement that the contents are true to the best of your knowledge and belief. I refer you to Part 35 of the Civil Procedure Rules which specifies experts' responsibilities, the contents of any report, and the statements experts must sign.

(Insert details as to cost and payment.)

Yours sincerely

* Delete as appropriate

ANNEX D EARLY NOTIFICATION LETTER FLOWCHART

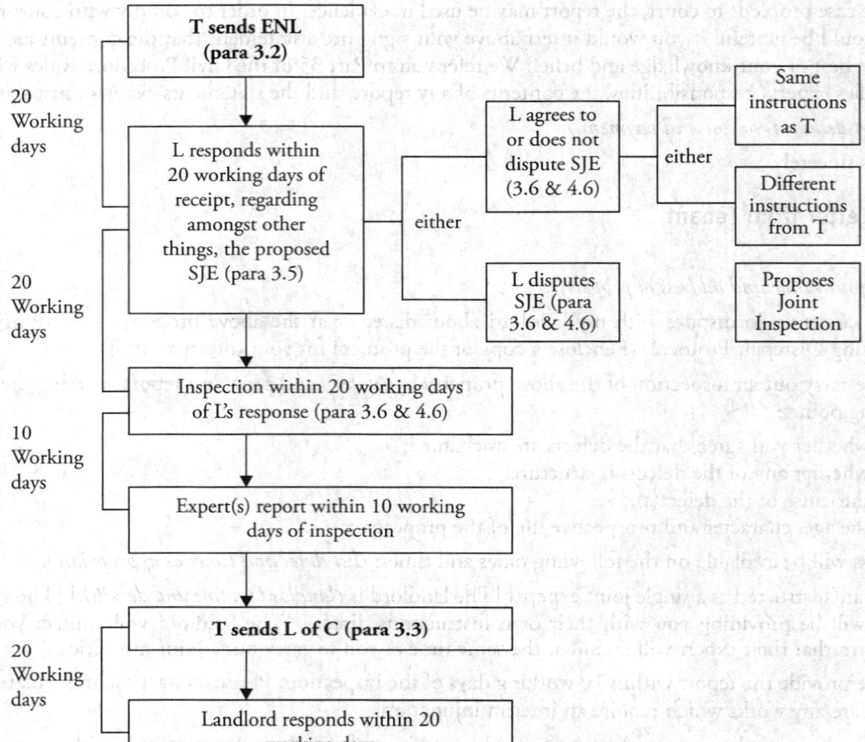

ANNEX E SPECIAL DAMAGES FORM

SPECIAL DAMAGES FORM

	ITEM	DATE PURCHASED	WHERE PURCHASED	PRICE	RECEIPTS – YES/NO	HOW DAMAGED
1						
2						
3						
4						
5						
6						
7						
8						
9						
10						

[ANNEX F STATEMENT OF COSTS

Annex F is form N260, which is online at <http://hmctscourtfinder.justice.gov.uk/HMCTS/FormFinder.do>.]

ANNEX G SCHEDULE

Schedule
Disrepair Protocol
TENANT

	Item Number	Room (tick where appropriate)	Disrepair (identify briefly)	Notice given (How was the landlord made aware of the problem)	Inconvenience suffered (How has the disrepair affected you)
Exterior of premises, roof and access Comment:					
Entrance, hall and storage Comment:					
Living room (s) Comment:					
Kitchen Comment:					
Bathroom Comment:					
Bedroom 1 Comment:					
Bedroom 2 Comment:					
Bedroom 3 Comment:					
Other Comment:					

Pre-action Protocols

Pre-action Protocol for Possession Claims Based on Rent Arrears

AIMS AND SCOPE OF THE PROTOCOL

This protocol applies to residential possession claims by social landlords (such as local authorities, registered social landlords and housing action trusts) and private registered providers of social housing which are based solely on claims for rent arrears. The protocol does not apply to claims in respect of long leases or to claims for possession where there is no security of tenure.

The protocol reflects the guidance on good practice given to social landlords and private registered providers in the collection of rent arrears. It recognises that it is in the interests of both landlords and tenants to ensure that rent is paid promptly and to ensure that difficulties are resolved wherever possible without court proceedings.

Its aim is to encourage more pre-action contact between landlords and tenants and to enable court time to be used more effectively.

Courts should take into account whether this protocol has been followed when considering what orders to make. Registered social landlords, private registered providers of social housing and local authorities should also comply with guidance issued from time to time by the Housing Corporation and the Department for Communities and Local Government.

INITIAL CONTACT

1. The landlord should contact the tenant as soon as reasonably possible if the tenant falls into arrears to discuss the cause of the arrears, the tenant's financial circumstances, the tenant's entitlement to benefits and repayment of the arrears. Where contact is by letter, the landlord should write separately to each named tenant.
2. The landlord and tenant should try to agree affordable sums for the tenant to pay towards arrears, based upon the tenant's income and expenditure (where such information has been supplied in response to the landlord's enquiries). The landlord should clearly set out in pre-action correspondence any time limits with which the tenant should comply.
3. The landlord should provide, on a quarterly basis, rent statements in a comprehensible format showing rent due and sums received for the past 13 weeks. The landlord should, upon request, provide the tenant with copies of rent statements in a comprehensible format from the date when arrears first arose showing all amounts of rent due, the dates and amounts of all payments made, whether through housing benefit or by the tenant, and a running total of the arrears.
4. (a) If the landlord is aware that the tenant has difficulty in reading or understanding information given, the landlord should take reasonable steps to ensure that the tenant understands any information given. The landlord should be able to demonstrate that reasonable steps have been taken to ensure that the information has been appropriately communicated in ways that the tenant can understand.
   (b) If the landlord is aware that the tenant is under 18 or is particularly vulnerable, the landlord should consider at an early stage:
      (i) whether or not the tenant has the mental capacity to defend possession proceedings and, if not, make an application for the appointment of a litigation friend in accordance with CPR, Part 21;
      (ii) whether or not any issues arise under the Disability Discrimination Act 1995; and
      (iii) in the case of a local authority landlord, whether or not there is a need for a community care assessment in accordance with the National Health Service and Community Care Act 1990.
5. If the tenant meets the appropriate criteria, the landlord should arrange for arrears to be paid by the Department for Work and Pensions from the tenant's benefit.

6. The landlord should offer to assist the tenant in any claim the tenant may have for housing benefit.
7. Possession proceedings for rent arrears should not be started against a tenant who can demonstrate that he has:
   (a) provided the local authority with all the evidence required to process a housing benefit claim;
   (b) a reasonable expectation of eligibility for housing benefit; and
   (c) paid other sums due not covered by housing benefit.
   The landlord should make every effort to establish effective ongoing liaison with housing benefit departments and, with the tenant's consent, make direct contact with the relevant housing benefit department before taking enforcement action.
   The landlord and tenant should work together to resolve any housing benefit problems.
8. Bearing in mind that rent arrears may be part of a general debt problem, the landlord should advise the tenant to seek assistance from CAB, debt advice agencies or other appropriate agencies as soon as possible.

AFTER SERVICE OF STATUTORY NOTICES

9. After service of a statutory notice but before the issue of proceedings, the landlord should make reasonable attempts to contact the tenant, to discuss the amount of the arrears, the cause of the arrears, repayment of the arrears and the housing benefit position.
10. If the tenant complies with an agreement to pay the current rent and a reasonable amount towards arrears, the landlord should agree to postpone court proceedings so long as the tenant keeps to such agreement. If the tenant ceases to comply with such agreement, the landlord should warn the tenant of the intention to bring proceedings and give the tenant clear time limits within which to comply.

ALTERNATIVE DISPUTE RESOLUTION

11. The parties should consider whether it is possible to resolve the issues between them by discussion and negotiation without recourse to litigation. The parties may be required by the court to provide evidence that alternative means of resolving the dispute were considered. Courts take the view that litigation should be a last resort, and that claims should not be issued prematurely when a settlement is still actively being explored.
    The Legal Services Commission has published a booklet on *Alternatives to Court* (CLS Direct Information Leaflet 23) (www.clsdirect.org.uk/legalhelp/leaflet23.jsp), which lists a number of organisations that provide alternative dispute resolution services.

COURT PROCEEDINGS

12. Not later than ten days before the date set for the hearing, the landlord should:
    (a) provide the tenant with up-to-date rent statements;
    (b) disclose what knowledge he possesses of the tenant's housing benefit position to the tenant.
13.
    (a) The landlord should inform the tenant of the date and time of any court hearing and the order applied for. The landlord should advise the tenant to attend the hearing as the tenant's home is at risk. Records of such advice should be kept.
    (b) If the tenant complies with an agreement made after the issue of proceedings to pay the current rent and a reasonable amount towards arrears, the landlord should agree to postpone court proceedings so long as the tenant keeps to such agreement.
    (c) If the tenant ceases to comply with such agreement, the landlord should warn the tenant of the intention to restore the proceedings and give the tenant clear time limits within which to comply.
14. If the landlord unreasonably fails to comply with the terms of the protocol, the court may impose one or more of the following sanctions:
    (a) an order for costs;
    (b) in cases other than those brought solely on mandatory grounds, adjourn, strike out or dismiss claims.
15. If the tenant unreasonably fails to comply with the terms of the protocol, the court may take such failure into account when considering whether it is reasonable to make possession orders.

Pre-Action Protocol for Possession Claims Based on Mortgage or Home Purchase Plan Arrears in Respect of Residential Property

I INTRODUCTION

1 Preamble

1.1 This protocol describes the behaviour the court will normally expect of the parties prior to the start of a possession claim within the scope of para. 3.1 below.

1.2 This protocol does not alter the parties' rights and obligations.

1.3 It is in the interests of the parties that mortgage payments or payments under home purchase plans are made promptly and that difficulties are resolved wherever possible without court proceedings. However in some cases an order for possession may be in the interest of both the lender and the borrower.

2 Aims

2.1 The aims of this protocol are to—

(1) ensure that a lender or home purchase plan provider (in this protocol collectively referred to as 'the lender') and a borrower or home purchase plan customer (in this protocol collectively referred to as 'the borrower') act fairly and reasonably with each other in resolving any matter concerning mortgage or home purchase plan arrears; and

(2) encourage more pre-action contact between the lender and the borrower in an effort to seek agreement between the parties, and where this cannot be reached, to enable efficient use of the court's time and resources.

2.2 Where either party is required to communicate and provide information to the other, reasonable steps should be taken to do so in a way that is clear, fair and not misleading. If the lender is aware that the borrower may have difficulties in reading or understanding the information provided, the lender should take reasonable steps to ensure that information is communicated in a way that the borrower can understand.

3 Scope

3.1 This protocol applies to arrears on—

(1) first charge residential mortgages and home purchase plans regulated by the Financial Services Authority under the Financial Services and Markets Act 2000;

(2) second charge mortgages over residential property and other secured loans regulated under the Consumer Credit Act 1974 on residential property; and

(3) unregulated residential mortgages.

3.2 Where a potential claim includes a money claim and a claim for possession this protocol applies to both.

4 Definitions

4.1 *In this protocol*—

(1) 'possession claim' means a claim for the recovery of possession of property under Part 55 of the Civil Procedure Rules 1998 ('CPR');

(2) 'home purchase plan' means a method of purchasing a property by way of a sale and lease arrangement that does not require the payment of interest;
(3) 'bank holiday' means a bank holiday under the Banking and Financial Dealings Act 1971;
(4) 'business day' means any day except Saturday, Sunday, a bank holiday, Good Friday or Christmas day; and
(5) 'Mortgage Rescue Scheme' means the shared equity and mortgage to rent scheme established either—
(a) by the UK Government to help certain categories of vulnerable borrowers avoid repossession of their property in England, announced in September 2008 and opened in January 2009; or
(b) by the Welsh Assembly Government to help certain categories of vulnerable borrowers avoid repossession of their property in Wales, first announced in June 2008.

II ACTIONS PRIOR TO THE START OF A POSSESSION CLAIM

5 Initial Contact and Provision of Information

5.1 Where the borrower falls into arrears the lender should provide the borrower with—
(1) where appropriate, the required regulatory information sheet or the National Homelessness Advice Service booklet on mortgage arrears; and
(2) information concerning the amount of arrears which should include—
(a) the total amount of the arrears;
(b) the total outstanding of the mortgage or the home purchase plan; and
(c) whether interest or charges will be added, and if so and where appropriate, details or an estimate of the interest or charges that may be payable.

5.2 The parties should take all reasonable steps to discuss with each other, or their representatives, the cause of the arrears, the borrower's financial circumstances and proposals for repayment of the arrears (see 7.1). For example, parties should consider whether the causes of the arrears are temporary or long term and whether the borrower may be able to pay the arrears in a reasonable time.

5.3 The lender should advise the borrower to make early contact with the housing department of the borrower's local authority and, should, where necessary, refer the borrower to appropriate sources of independent debt advice.

5.4 The lender should consider a reasonable request from the borrower to change the date of regular payment (within the same payment period) or the method by which payment is made. The lender should either agree to such a request or, where it refuses such a request, it should, within a reasonable period of time, give the borrower a written explanation of its reasons for the refusal.

5.5 The lender should respond promptly to any proposal for payment made by the borrower. If the lender does not agree to such a proposal it should give reasons in writing to the borrower within 10 business days of the proposal.

5.6 If the lender submits a proposal for payment, the borrower should be given a reasonable period of time in which to consider such proposals. The lender should set out the proposal in sufficient detail to enable the borrower to understand the implications of the proposal.

5.7 If the borrower fails to comply with an agreement, the lender should warn the borrower, by giving the borrower 15 business days' notice in writing, of its intention to start a possession claim unless the borrower remedies the breach in the agreement.

6 Postponing the Start of a Possession Claim

6.1 A lender should consider not starting a possession claim for mortgage arrears where the borrower can demonstrate to the lender that the borrower has—
(1) submitted a claim to—
(a) the Department for Work and Pensions (DWP) for Support for Mortgage Interest (SMI); or
(b) an insurer under a mortgage payment protection policy; or
(c) a participating local authority for support under a Mortgage Rescue Scheme, and has provided all the evidence required to process a claim;
(2) a reasonable expectation of eligibility for payment from the DWP or from the insurer or support from the local authority; and

(3) an ability to pay a mortgage instalment not covered by a claim to the DWP or the insurer in relation to a claim under para. 6.1(1)(a) or (b).

6.2 If a borrower can demonstrate that reasonable steps have been or will be taken to market the property at an appropriate price in accordance with reasonable professional advice, the lender should consider postponing starting a possession claim. The borrower must continue to take all reasonable steps actively to market the property where the lender has agreed to postpone starting a possession claim.

6.3 Where the lender has agreed to postpone starting a possession claim the borrower should provide the lender with a copy of the particulars of sale, the home information pack and (where relevant) details of purchase offers received within a reasonable period of time specified by the lender. The borrower should give the lender details of the estate agent and the conveyancer instructed to deal with the sale. The borrower should also authorise the estate agent and the conveyancer to communicate with the lender about the progress of the sale and the borrower's conduct during the process.

6.4 Where the lender decides not to postpone the start of a possession claim it should inform the borrower of the reasons for this decision at least five business days before starting proceedings.

7 Alternative Dispute Resolution

7.1 The court takes the view that starting a possession claim is usually a last resort and that such a claim should not normally be started when a settlement is still actively being explored. Discussion between the parties may include options such as—

(1) extending the term of the mortgage;
(2) changing the type of a mortgage;
(3) deferring payment of interest due under the mortgage; or
(4) capitalising the arrears.

8 Complaints to the Financial Ombudsman Service

8.1 The lender should consider whether to postpone the start of a possession claim where the borrower has made a genuine complaint to the Financial Ombudsman Service (FOS) about the potential possession claim.

8.2 Where a lender does not intend to await the decision of the FOS it should give notice to the borrower with reasons that it intends to start a possession claim at least five business days before doing so.

9 Compliance

9.1 Parties should be able, if requested by the court, to explain the actions that they have taken to comply with this protocol.

Pre-action Protocol for Low Value Personal Injury Claims in Road Traffic Accidents

I INTRODUCTION

Definitions

1.1 In this protocol—

(1) 'claim' means a claim, prior to the start of proceedings, for payment of damages under the process set out in this protocol;

(2) 'claimant' means a person starting a claim under this protocol;

(3) 'defendant' means the insurer of the person who is subject to the claim under this protocol, unless the context indicates that it means—

(a) the person who is subject to the claim;

(b) the defendant's legal representative; or

(c) the Motor Insurers' Bureau ('MIB');

(4) 'legal representative' has the same meaning as in CPR, r. 2.3(1);

(5) 'pecuniary losses' means past and future expenses and losses;

(6) 'vehicle-related damages' means damages for—

(a) the pre-accident value of the vehicle;

(b) vehicle repair;

(c) vehicle insurance excess;
(d) vehicle hire;
(7) 'child' means a person under 18;
(8) 'business day' means any day except Saturday, Sunday, a bank holiday, Good Friday or Christmas Day;
(9) 'bank holiday' means a bank holiday under the Banking and Financial Dealings Act 1971;
(10) 'road traffic accident' means an accident resulting in bodily injury to any person caused by, or arising out of, the use of a motor vehicle on a road or other public place in England and Wales unless the injury was caused wholly or in part by a breach by the defendant of one or more of the relevant statutory provisions[1] as defined by the Health and Safety at Work etc. Act 1974, s. 53;
(11) 'motor vehicle' means a mechanically propelled vehicle intended for use on roads;
(12) 'road' means any highway and any other road to which the public has access and includes bridges over which a road passes;
(13) 'medical expert' means a person who is—
(a) registered with the General Medical Council;
(b) registered with the General Dental Council; or
(c) a psychologist or physiotherapist registered with the Health Professions Council;
(14) 'admission of liability' means the defendant admits that—
(a) the accident occurred;
(b) the accident was caused by the defendant's breach of duty; and
(c) the defendant caused some loss to the claimant, the nature and extent of which is not admitted;
(15) 'deductible amount' has the same meaning as in CPR, r. 36.15(1)(d); and
(16) 'certificate of recoverable benefits' has the same meaning as in CPR, r. 36.15(1)(e)(i).

1.2 A reference to a rule or practice direction, unless otherwise defined, is a reference to a rule in the Civil Procedure Rules 1998 ('CPR') or a practice direction supplementing them.

1.3 Subject to para. 1.4 the standard forms used in the process set out in this protocol are available from Her Majesty's Courts and Tribunals Service website at—
(1) Claim Notification Form ('Form RTA 1');
(2) Defendant Only Claim Notification Form ('Form RTA 2');
(3) Medical Report Form ('Form RTA 3');
(4) Interim Settlement Pack Form ('Form RTA 4');
(5) Stage 2 Settlement Pack Form ('Form RTA 5');
(6) Court Proceedings Pack (Part A) Form ('Form RTA 6'); and
(7) Court Proceedings Pack (Part B) Form ('Form RTA 7').

1.4 The information required in Form RTA 3 may be provided in a different format to that set out in that Form.

Preamble

2.1 This protocol describes the behaviour the court will normally expect of the parties prior to the start of proceedings where a claimant claims damages valued at no more than £10,000 as a result of a personal injury sustained by that person in a road traffic accident.

Aims

3.1 The aim of this protocol is to ensure that—
(1) the defendant pays damages and costs using the process set out in the protocol without the need for the claimant to start proceedings;
(2) damages are paid within a reasonable time; and
(3) the claimant's legal representative receives the fixed costs at the end of each stage in this protocol.

[1] See— Control of Substances Hazardous to Health Regulations 2002 (SI 2002/2677); Lifting Operations and Lifting Equipment Regulations 1998 (SI 1998/2307); Management of Health and Safety at Work Regulations 1999 (SI 1999/3242); Manual Handling Operations Regulations 1992 (SI 1992/2793); Personal Protective Equipment at Work Regulations 1992 (SI 1992/2966); Provision and Use of Work Equipment Regulations 1998 (SI 1998/2306); Work at Height Regulations 2005 (SI 2005/735); Workplace (Health, Safety and Welfare) Regulations 1992 (SI 1992/3004).

Scope

4.1 This protocol applies where—
(1) a claim for damages arises from a road traffic accident occurring on or after 30 April 2010;
(2) the claim includes damages in respect of personal injury;
(3) the claimant values the claim at not more than £10,000 on a full liability basis including pecuniary losses but excluding interest ('the upper limit'); and
(4) if proceedings were started the small claims track would not be the normal track for that claim.

(Paragraphs 1.1(6) and 4.3 state the damages that are excluded for the purposes of valuing the claim under para. 4.1)

(Rule 26.6 provides that the small claims track is not the normal track where the value of any claim for damages for personal injuries (defined as compensation for pain, suffering and loss of amenity) is more than £1,000)

4.2 This protocol ceases to apply to a claim where, at any stage, the claimant notifies the defendant that the claim has now been revalued at more than the upper limit.
4.3 A claim may include vehicle-related damages but these are excluded for the purposes of valuing the claim under para. 4.1.
4.4 This protocol does not apply to a claim—
(1) in respect of a breach of duty owed to a road user by a person who is not a road user;
(2) made to the MIB pursuant to the Untraced Drivers' Agreement 2003 or any subsequent or supplementary Untraced Drivers' Agreements;
(3) where the claimant or defendant is—
(a) deceased; or
(b) a protected party as defined in r. 21.1(2)(d);
(4) where the claimant is bankrupt; or
(5) where the defendant's vehicle is registered outside the United Kingdom.
4.5 The fixed costs in r. 45.18 apply in relation to a claimant only where a claimant has a legal representative.

II GENERAL PROVISIONS

Communication between the parties

5.1 The address for electronic communication with the defendant can be found at www.rtapiclaimsprocess.org.uk. The claimant will give an address for contact in the Claim Notification Form ('CNF'). Subject to para. 6.1(2) where the protocol requires information to be sent to a party it must be sent electronically.
5.2 Where the claimant has sent the CNF electronically to the wrong defendant the claimant may, in this circumstance only, resubmit the CNF to the correct defendant. The period in para. 6.11 or 6.13 starts from the date the CNF was sent to the correct defendant.

Time periods

5.3 A reference to a fixed number of days is a reference to business days as defined in para. 1.1(8).
5.4 Where a party should respond within a fixed number of days, the period for response starts the first business day after the information was sent to that party.
5.5 All time periods, except those stated in—
(1) para. 6.11 (the insurer's response);
(2) para. 6.13 (MIB's response); and
(3) para. 7.30 (the further consideration period)
may be varied by agreement between the parties.
5.6 Where this protocol requires the defendant to pay an amount within a fixed number of days the claimant must receive the cheque or the transfer of the amount from the defendant before the end of the period specified in the relevant provision.

Limitation period

5.7 Where compliance with this protocol is not possible before the expiry of the limitation period the claimant may start proceedings and apply to the court for an order to stay (i.e. suspend) the proceedings while the parties take steps to follow this protocol. Where proceedings are started in a case to which this paragraph applies the claimant should use the procedure set out under Part 8 in accordance with PD 8B ('the Stage 3 Procedure').

5.8 Where the parties are then unable to reach a settlement at the end of Stage 2 of this protocol the claimant must, in order to proceed to Stage 3, apply to lift the stay and request directions in the existing proceedings.

Claimant's reasonable belief of the value of the claim

5.9 Where the claimant reasonably believes that the claim is valued at between £1,000 and £10,000 but it subsequently becomes apparent that the value of the claim is less than £1,000, the claimant is entitled to the Stage 1 and (where relevant) the Stage 2 fixed costs.

Claimants without a legal representative

5.10 Where the claimant does not have a legal representative, on receipt of the CNF the defendant must explain—

(1) the period within which a response is required; and

(2) that the claimant may obtain independent legal advice, for example from a legal representative, a Citizens Advice Bureau, a local law centre or a trade union.

Discontinuing the protocol process

5.11 Claims which no longer continue under this protocol cannot subsequently re-enter the process.

III THE STAGES OF THE PROCESS

Stage 1

Completion of the Claim Notification Form

6.1 The claimant must complete and send—

(1) the CNF to the defendant's insurer; and

(2) the 'Defendant Only CNF' to the defendant by first class post.

6.2 The 'Defendant Only CNF' must be sent at the same time or as soon as practicable after the CNF is sent.

6.3 All boxes in the CNF that are marked as mandatory must be completed before it is sent. The claimant must make a reasonable attempt to complete those boxes that are not marked as mandatory.

6.4 A claim for vehicle-related damages will ordinarily be dealt with outside the provisions of this protocol under industry agreements between relevant organisations and insurers. Where there is a claim for vehicle-related damages the claimant must—

(1) state in the CNF that the claim is being dealt with by a third party; or

(2)

(a) explain in the CNF that the legal representative is dealing with the recovery of these additional amounts; and

(b) attach any relevant invoices and receipts to the CNF or explain when they are likely to be sent to the defendant.

6.5 Where the claimant is a child, this must be noted in the relevant section of the CNF.

6.6 The statement of truth in the CNF must be signed by the claimant or the claimant's legal representative. Where the claimant is a child the statement of truth may be signed by the parent or guardian. On the electronically completed CNF the person may enter their name in the signature box to satisfy this requirement.

Rehabilitation

6.7 The claimant must set out details of rehabilitation in the CNF. The parties should at all stages consider the Rehabilitation Code which is set out in Annex D of the Pre-Action Protocol for Personal Injury Claims.

Failure to complete the Claim Notification Form

6.8 Where the defendant considers that inadequate mandatory information has been provided in the CNF, that shall be a valid reason for the defendant to decide that the claim should no longer continue under this protocol.

6.9 Rule 45.24(2) sets out the sanctions available to the court where it considers that the claimant provided inadequate information in the CNF.

Response from insurer

6.10 The defendant must send to the claimant an electronic acknowledgment the next day after receipt of the CNF.

6.11 The defendant must complete the 'Insurer Response' section of the CNF ('the CNF response') and send it to the claimant within 15 days.

Application for a certificate of recoverable benefits

6.12 The defendant must, before the end of Stage 1, apply to the Compensation Recovery Unit (CRU) for a certificate of recoverable benefits.

Motor Insurers' Bureau

6.13 Where no insurer is identified and the claim falls to be dealt with by the MIB or its agents the CNF response must be completed and sent to the claimant within 30 days.

6.14 Where the MIB passes the claim to an insurer to act on its behalf, that insurer must notify the claimant of that fact. There is no extension to the time period in para. 6.13.

Contributory negligence, liability not admitted or failure to respond

6.15 The claim will no longer continue under this protocol where the defendant, within the period in para. 6.11 or 6.13—

(1) makes an admission of liability but alleges contributory negligence (other than in relation to the claimant's admitted failure to wear a seat belt);
(2) does not complete and send the CNF response;
(3) does not admit liability; or
(4) notifies the claimant that the defendant considers that—
 (a) there is inadequate mandatory information in the CNF; or
 (b) if proceedings were issued, the small claims track would be the normal track for that claim.

6.16 Where the defendant does not admit liability under para. 6.15(3), the defendant must give brief reasons in the CNF response.

6.17 Where para. 6.15 applies the claim will proceed under the Pre-Action Protocol for Personal Injury Claims starting at para. 3.7 of that protocol (which allows a maximum of three months for the defendant to investigate the claim) except that where para. 6.15(4)(a) applies the claim will proceed under para. 3.1 of that protocol.

(Paragraph 2.10A of the Pre-Action Protocol on Personal Injury provides that the CNF can be used as the letter of claim except where the claim no longer continues under this protocol because the CNF contained inadequate information)

Stage 1 fixed costs

6.18 Except where the claimant is a child, the defendant must pay the Stage 1 fixed costs in r. 45.18 where—

(1) liability is admitted; or
(2) liability is admitted and contributory negligence is alleged only in relation to the claimant's admitted failure to wear a seat belt, within 10 days after sending the CNF response to the claimant as provided in para. 6.11 or 6.13.

6.19 Where the defendant fails to pay the Stage 1 fixed costs within the period specified in para. 6.18 the claimant may give written notice that the claim will no longer continue under this protocol. Unless the claimant's notice is sent to the defendant within 10 days after the expiry of the period in para. 6.18 the claim will continue under this protocol.

Stage 2

The medical report

7.1 The claimant should obtain a medical report, if one has not already been obtained.

7.2 The claimant must check the factual accuracy of any medical report before it is sent to the defendant. There will be no further opportunity for the claimant to challenge the factual accuracy of a medical report after it has been sent to the defendant.

7.3 Where the claimant was not wearing a seat belt the medical report must contain sufficient information to enable the defendant to calculate the appropriate reduction of damages in accordance with principles set out in existing case law.

Initial medical reports

7.4 It is expected that most claimants will obtain a medical report from one expert. Where it is clear that one expert cannot deal with all elements of the injury the claimant may obtain a report from a second medical expert in a different discipline.

Further initial medical report on recommendation

7.5 Those two medical experts may each separately recommend that the claimant obtain a further initial medical report from a medical expert in a different discipline. Therefore the claimant may obtain a maximum of one initial medical report from four different disciplines, two of which are only on the recommendation of one or both of the first two medical experts.

Subsequent medical reports

7.6 On the recommendation of the medical expert who provided the initial medical report, a subsequent medical report may be obtained from that same medical expert. A subsequent medical report may be necessary—

(1) where the first medical report recommends that further time is required before a prognosis of the claimant's injuries can be determined; or

(2) where the claimant is receiving continuing treatment.

Stay of process

7.7 Where subsequent medical reports need to be obtained the parties should agree to stay the process in this protocol for a suitable period. The claimant may then request an interim payment in accordance with paras 7.8 to 7.11.

Request for an interim payment

7.8 Where the claimant requests an interim payment of £1,000, the defendant should make an interim payment to the claimant in accordance with para. 7.13.

7.9 The claimant must send to the defendant the Interim Settlement Pack and initial medical reports (containing the recommendation that a subsequent medical report is required) in order to request the interim payment.

7.10 The claimant must also send evidence of pecuniary losses and disbursements. This will assist the defendant in considering whether to make an offer to settle the claim.

7.11 Where an interim payment of more than £1,000 is requested the claimant must specify in the Interim Settlement Pack the amount requested, the heads of damage which are the subject of the request and the reasons for the request.

7.12 The interim payment of £1,000 is only in relation to general damages. Where more than £1,000 is requested by the claimant, the amount in excess of £1,000 is only in relation to pecuniary losses.

Interim payment of £1,000

7.13 Where para. 7.8 applies the defendant must pay £1,000 within 10 days of receiving the Interim Settlement Pack.

Interim payment of more than £1,000

7.14 Subject to paras 7.17 and 7.18, where the claimant has requested an interim payment of more than £1,000 the defendant must pay—

(1) the full amount requested less any deductible amount which is payable to the CRU;

(2) the amount of £1,000; or

(3) some other amount of more than £1,000 but less than the amount requested by the claimant, within 15 days of receiving the Interim Settlement Pack.

7.15 Where a payment is made under para. 7.14(2) or (3) the defendant must briefly explain in the Interim Settlement Pack why the full amount requested by the claimant is not agreed.

Vehicle-related damages — interim payments

7.16 Claims for vehicle-related damages will ordinarily be dealt with outside the provisions of this protocol under industry agreements between relevant organisations and insurers. However, where the claimant has paid for the vehicle-related damages, the sum may be included in a request for an interim payment under para. 7.11.

Application for a certificate of recoverable benefits

7.17 Paragraph 7.18 applies where the defendant agrees to make a payment in accordance with para. 7.14(1) or (3) but does not yet have a certificate of recoverable benefits or does not have one that will remain in force for at least 10 days from the date of receiving the Interim Settlement Pack.

7.18 The defendant should apply for a certificate of recoverable benefits as soon as possible, notify the claimant that it has done so and must make the interim payment under para. 7.14(1) or (3) no more than 30 days from the date of receiving the Interim Settlement Pack.

Request for an interim payment where the claimant is a child

7.19 The interim payment provisions in this protocol do not apply where the claimant is a child. Where the claimant is a child and an interim payment is reasonably required proceedings must be started under CPR, Part 7, and an application for an interim payment can be made within those proceedings.

(Rule 21.10 provides that no payment, which relates to a claim by a child, is valid without the approval of the court)

7.20 Paragraph 7.19 does not prevent a defendant from making a payment direct to a treatment provider.

Interim payment — supplementary provisions

7.21 Where the defendant does not comply with para. 7.13 or 7.14 the claimant may start proceedings under CPR, Part 7, and apply to the court for an interim payment in those proceedings.

7.22 Where the defendant does comply with para. 7.14(2) or (3) but the claimant is not content with the amount paid, the claimant may still start proceedings. However, the court will order the defendant to pay no more than the Stage 2 fixed costs where the court awards an interim payment of no more than the amount offered by the defendant or the court makes no award.

7.23 Where para. 7.21 or 7.22 applies the claimant must give notice to the defendant that the claim will no longer continue under this protocol. Unless the claimant's notice is sent to the defendant within 10 days after the expiry of the period in para. 7.13, 7.14 or 7.18 as appropriate, the claim will continue under this protocol.

Medical reports obtained without recommendation

7.24 Where a further initial medical report or a subsequent medical report is obtained without recommendation from a medical expert—
(1) the defendant at the end of Stage 2 may refuse to pay; or
(2) the court at Stage 3 may refuse to allow, the costs of this medical report.

7.25 Brief details should be provided in the Stage 2 Settlement Pack Form—
(a) by the claimant explaining why they obtained a further initial report or a subsequent medical report without recommendation; and
(b) if relevant, by the defendant explaining why they will not pay for the report.

Submitting the Stage 2 Settlement Pack to the defendant

7.26 The Stage 2 Settlement Pack which must comprise—
(1) the Stage 2 Settlement Pack Form;
(2) a medical report or reports;
(3) evidence of pecuniary losses; and
(4) evidence of disbursements (for example the cost of any medical report),
should be sent to the defendant within 15 days of the claimant approving the final medical report and agreeing to rely on the prognosis in that report.

7.27 Where the defendant alleges contributory negligence because of the claimant's failure to wear a seat belt, the Stage 2 Settlement Pack Form must also suggest a percentage reduction (which may be 0 per cent) in the amount of damages.

Consideration of claim

7.28 There is a 35-day period for consideration of the Stage 2 Settlement Pack by the defendant ('the total consideration period'). This comprises a period of up to 15 days for the defendant to consider the Stage 2 Settlement Pack ('the initial consideration period') and make an offer. The remainder of the total consideration period ('the negotiation period') is for any further negotiation between the parties.

7.29 The total consideration period can be extended by the parties agreeing to extend either the initial consideration period or the negotiation period or both.

7.30 Where a party makes an offer five days or less before the end of the total consideration period (including any extension to this period under para. 7.29), there will be a further period of five days after the end of the total consideration period for the relevant party to consider that offer. During this period ('the further consideration period') no further offers can be made by either party.

Defendant accepts offer or makes counter-offer

7.31 Within the initial consideration period (or any extension agreed under para. 7.29) the defendant must either accept the offer made by the claimant on the Stage 2 Settlement Pack Form or make a counter-offer using that form.

7.32 The claim will no longer continue under this protocol where the defendant gives notice to the claimant within the initial consideration period (or any extension agreed under para. 7.29) that the defendant—

(a) considers that, if proceedings were started, the small claims track would be the normal track for that claim; or

(b) withdraws the admission of causation.

7.33 Where the defendant does not respond within the initial consideration period (or any extension agreed under para. 7.29), the claim will no longer continue under this protocol and the claimant may start proceedings under CPR, Part 7.

7.34 When making a counter-offer the defendant must propose an amount for each head of damage and may, in addition, make an offer that is higher than the total of the amounts proposed for all heads of damage. The defendant must also explain in the counter-offer why a particular head of damage has been reduced. The explanation will assist the claimant when negotiating a settlement and will allow both parties to focus on those areas of the claim that remain in dispute.

7.35 Where the defendant has obtained a certificate of recoverable benefits from the CRU the counter-offer must state the name and amount of any deductible amount.

7.36 On receipt of a counter-offer from the defendant the claimant has until the end of the total consideration period or the further consideration period to accept or decline the counter-offer.

7.37 Any offer to settle made at any stage by either party will automatically include, and cannot exclude—

(1) the Stage 2 fixed costs in r. 45.18;

(2) an agreement in principle to pay disbursements.

7.38 Where there is a dispute about the amount or validity of any disbursement the parties may use the procedure set out in r. 46.14.

(Rule 46.14 provides that where the parties to a dispute have a written agreement on all issues but have failed to agree the amount of the costs, they may start proceedings under that rule so that the court can determine the amount of those costs.)

Withdrawal of offer after the consideration period

7.39 Where a party withdraws an offer made in the Stage 2 Settlement Pack Form after the total consideration period or further consideration period, the claim will no longer continue under this protocol and the claimant may start proceedings under CPR, Part 7.

Settlement

7.40 Except where the claimant is a child or paras 7.41 and 7.42 apply, the defendant must pay—

(1) the agreed damages less any—

(a) deductible amount which is payable to the CRU; and

(b) previous interim payment;

(2) any unpaid Stage 1 fixed costs in r. 45.18;

(3) the Stage 2 fixed costs in r. 45.18;

(4) the relevant disbursements allowed in accordance with r. 45.19,

within 10 days of the end of the relevant period in paras 7.28 to 7.30 during which the parties agreed a settlement.

(Rule 21.10 provides that the approval of the court is required where, before proceedings are started, a claim is made by a child and a settlement is reached. The provisions in PD 8B, para. 6.1, set out what must be filed with the court when an application is made to approve a settlement)

Application for certificate of recoverable benefits

7.41 paragraph 7.42 applies where, at the date of the acceptance of an offer in the Stage 2 Settlement Pack, the defendant does not have a certificate of recoverable benefits that will remain in force for at least 10 days.

7.42 The defendant should apply for a fresh certificate of recoverable benefits as soon as possible, notify the claimant that it has done so and must pay the amounts set out in para. 7.40 within 30 days of the end of the relevant period in paras 7.28 to 7.30.

Vehicle-related damages — additional damages

7.43 paragraph 7.44 applies where at the end of the relevant period in paras 7.28 to 7.30 the claim ('the original damages') has not settled and there remain vehicle-related damages ('the additional damages') being dealt with by a third party separate from the claim. The original damages include all elements of the claim in the existing Stage 2 Settlement Pack.

7.44 Where para. 7.43 applies the claimant must, in relation to the additional damages—
(1) notify the defendant that this separate claim is being considered;
(2) obtain all relevant information from the third party; and
(3) make a separate offer by amending the Stage 2 Settlement Pack Form.

7.45 Within 15 days of the claimant sending the offer under para. 7.44(3), the defendant must either agree the offer made by the claimant or make a counter-offer.

7.46 The counter-offer must explain why a particular head of damage has been reduced to assist the claimant when negotiating a settlement and to allow both parties to focus on those areas of the claim that remain in dispute.

Original damages and additional damages are agreed

7.47 Where the original damages and additional damages are agreed within the period in para. 7.45 the defendant must pay the claimant in accordance with para. 7.53.

Original damages are not agreed, additional damages are agreed

7.48 paragraph 7.49 applies where—
(1) the original damages are not agreed; but
(2) the additional damages are agreed.

7.49 Where para. 7.48 applies—
(1) the defendant must pay the agreed amount of the additional damages within 10 days of agreeing those damages, and
(2) the claimant must continue with the provisions in paras 7.55 to 7.66 of this protocol.

Original damages are agreed, additional damages are not agreed

7.50 Paragraph 7.51 applies where—
(1) the original damages are agreed; but
(2) the additional damages are not agreed.

7.51 Where para. 7.50 applies—
(1) the defendant must, in relation to the original damages, pay the claimant in accordance with para. 7.53; and
(2) the claimant may start proceedings under CPR, Part 7, in relation to the additional damages.

Original damages and additional damages are not agreed

7.52 Paragraphs 7.55 to 7.66 apply where the original and additional damages are not agreed.

Settlement after claim for additional damages

7.53 Except where the claimant is a child or para. 7.54 applies, the defendant must pay—
(1) the agreed damages less any—
(a) deductible amount which is payable to the CRU; and
(b) previous interim payment;
(2) any unpaid Stage 1 fixed costs in r. 45.18;
(3) the Stage 2 fixed costs in r. 45.18;
(4) the relevant disbursements allowed in accordance with r. 45.19,
within 10 days of agreeing to pay the damages.

(Rule 21.10 provides that the approval of the court is required where, before proceedings are started, a claim is made by a child and a settlement is reached. The provisions in PD 8B, para. 6.1, set out what must be filed with the court when an application is made to approve a settlement)

Application for certificate of recoverable benefits

7.54 Where at the date on which damages are agreed the defendant does not have a certificate of recoverable benefits that remains in force for at least 10 days the defendant should apply for a fresh certificate as soon as possible, notify the claimant that it has done so and must pay the amounts set out in para. 7.53 within 30 days of the date on which damages are agreed.

Failure to reach agreement — general

7.55 Where the parties do not reach an agreement on—
(1) the original damages within the periods specified in paras 7.28 to 7.30; or
(2) the original damages and, where relevant, the additional damages under para. 7.45,

the claimant must send to the defendant the Court Proceedings Pack (Part A and Part B) Form which must contain—

(a) in Part A, the schedule of the claimant's losses and the defendant's responses comprising only the figures specified in sub-paras (1) and (2) above, together with supporting comments and evidence from both parties on any disputed heads of damage; and

(b) in Part B, the final offer and counter-offer from the Stage 2 Settlement Pack Form and, where relevant, the offer and any final counter-offer made under para. 7.45.

7.56 The deductible amount should only be deducted from the personal injury damages.

7.57 Comments in the Court Proceedings Pack (Part A) Form must not raise anything that has not been raised in the Stage 2 Settlement Pack Form.

7.58 The defendant should then check that the Court Proceedings Pack (Part A and Part B) Form complies with paras 7.55 to 7.57. If the defendant considers that the Court Proceedings Pack (Part A and Part B) Form does not comply it must be returned to the claimant within five days with an explanation as to why it does not comply.

7.59 Where the defendant intends to nominate a legal representative to accept service the name and address of the legal representative should be provided in the Court Proceedings Pack (Part A) Form.

7.60 Where the defendant fails to return the Court Proceedings Pack (Part A and Part B) Form within the period in para. 7.58, the claimant should assume that the defendant has no further comment to make.

Non-settlement payment by the defendant at the end of Stage 2

7.61 Except where the claimant is a child the defendant must pay to the claimant—

(1) the final offer of damages made by the defendant in the Court Proceedings Pack (Part A and Part B) Form less any—

(a) deductible amount which is payable to the CRU; and

(b) previous interim payment;

(2) any unpaid Stage 1 fixed costs in r. 45.18;

(3) the Stage 2 fixed costs in r. 45.18; and

(4) the disbursements in r. 45.19(2) that have been agreed.

7.62 Where the amount of a disbursement is not agreed the defendant must pay such amount for the disbursement as the defendant considers reasonable.

7.63 Subject to paras 7.64 and 7.65 the defendant must pay the amounts in paras 7.61 and 7.62 within 15 days of receiving the Court Proceedings Pack (Part A and Part B) Form from the claimant.

7.64 Paragraph 7.65 applies where the defendant is required to make the payments in para. 7.61 but does not have a certificate of recoverable benefits that remains in force for at least 10 days.

7.65 The defendant should apply for a fresh certificate of recoverable benefits as soon as possible, notify the claimant that it has done so and must pay the amounts set out in para. 7.61 within 30 days of receiving the Court Proceedings Pack (Part A and Part B) Form from the claimant.

7.66 Where the defendant does not comply with para. 7.63 or 7.65 the claimant may give written notice that the claim will no longer continue under this protocol and start proceedings under CPR, Part 7.

General provisions

7.67 Where the claimant gives notice to the defendant that the claim is unsuitable for this protocol (for example, because there are complex issues of fact or law in relation to the vehicle-related damages) then the claim will no longer continue under this protocol. However, where the court considers that the claimant acted unreasonably in giving such notice it will award no more than the fixed costs in r. 45.18.

Stage 3

Stage 3 Procedure

8.1 The Stage 3 Procedure is set out in PD 8B.

Pre-action Protocol for Claims for Damages in Relation to the Physical State of Commercial Property at Termination of a Tenancy (The 'Dilapidations Protocol')

1 Introduction

1.1 This protocol applies to commercial property situated in England and Wales. It relates to claims for damages for dilapidations against tenants at the termination of a tenancy. These are generally referred to as terminal dilapidations claims. There is a separate Pre-action Protocol for Housing Disrepair Cases.

1.2 This protocol sets out conduct that the court would normally expect prospective parties to follow prior to the commencement of proceedings. It establishes a reasonable process and timetable for the exchange of information relevant to a dispute, sets standards for the content and quality of schedules and quantified demands and, in particular, the conduct of pre-action negotiations.

1.3 If the landlord or tenant does not seek professional advice from a surveyor they should still, in so far as reasonably possible, fully comply with the terms of this protocol. In this protocol 'surveyor' is intended to encompass reference to any other suitably qualified person.

1.4 This protocol does not define 'dilapidations', 'repair', 'reinstatement' or 'redecoration'. Work to property which may be required will depend on the contractual terms of the lease and any other relevant documents.

1.5 Where the court considers non-compliance, and the sanctions to impose where it has occurred, it will, amongst other things, be concerned about whether the parties have complied in substance with the relevant principles and requirements and is not likely to be concerned with minor or technical shortcomings (see PD Pre-action Conduct, paras 4.3 to 4.5).

2 Overview of Protocol — General Aim

2.1 The protocol's objectives are:

2.1.1 to encourage the exchange of early and full information about the dispute;

2.1.2 to enable the parties to avoid litigation by agreeing a settlement of the dispute before proceedings are commenced; and

2.1.3 to support the efficient management of proceedings where litigation cannot be avoided.

2.2 A flowchart is attached at Annex A, which shows each of the stages that the parties are expected to undertake before the commencement of proceedings.

THE PROTOCOL

3 The Schedule of Dilapidations (Schedule)

3.1 The landlord should send the tenant a schedule in the form attached at either Annex B or Annex C. It should set out what the landlord considers to be the breaches, the works required to be done to remedy those breaches and, if relevant, the landlord's costings.

Pre-action Protocols

3.2 Breaches should be separated into relevant categories e.g. repair, reinstatement, redecoration etc. They should be listed separately in the schedule and should (where appropriate) identify any notices served by the landlord requiring reinstatement works to be undertaken.

3.3 Schedules should be sent within a reasonable time. What is a reasonable time will vary from case to case, but will generally be within 56 days after the termination of the tenancy.

3.4 The landlord may send a schedule before termination of the tenancy. However, if it does so, at the termination of the tenancy the landlord should:

3.4.1 confirm that the situation remains as stated in the schedule; or

3.4.2 send a further schedule within a reasonable time.

3.5 The schedule should be endorsed either by the landlord, or where it is prepared by a surveyor, by the landlord's surveyor. If the schedule has been prepared by the landlord's surveyor, then in endorsing the schedule, the surveyor should have regard to the principles laid down in the Royal Institution of Chartered Surveyors' Guidance Note on Dilapidations.

3.6 The endorsement should confirm that in the landlord's or the landlord's surveyor's opinion:

3.6.1 all the works set out in the schedule are reasonably required to remedy breaches referred to in para. 3.1 above;

3.6.2 where endorsed by the landlord, full account has been taken of its intentions for the property;

3.6.3 where endorsed by the landlord's surveyor, full account has been taken of the landlord's intentions for the property, as advised by the landlord; and

3.6.4 the costings, if any, are reasonable.

3.7 Wherever possible the schedule should be sent electronically to enable the tenant's comments to be incorporated in one document.

4 Quantified Demand

4.1 The quantified demand is not intended to have the same status as a statement of case in proceedings.

4.2 The quantified demand should:

4.2.1 set out clearly all aspects of the dispute, and set out and substantiate the monetary sum sought as damages in respect of the breaches detailed in the schedule as well as any other items of loss for which damages are sought. It should also set out whether VAT applies;

4.2.2 confirm that the landlord and/or its surveyor will attend a meeting or meetings as proposed under Section 7 below;

4.2.3 be sent within the same timescale for sending the tenant a schedule (see para. 3.3 above); and

4.2.4 specify a date (being a reasonable time) by which the tenant should respond. This will usually be within 56 days after sending the quantified demand.

4.3 Where the monetary sum sought is based on the cost of works, it should be fully quantified and substantiated by either an invoice or a detailed estimate.

4.4 If the quantified demand includes any other losses, they must be set out in detail, substantiated and fully quantified. The landlord should explain the legal basis for the recovery of losses, e.g. whether they are sought as part of the damages claim or under some express or implied provision of the lease.

4.5 The figures set out in the quantified demand should be restricted to the landlord's likely loss. This is not necessarily the same as the cost of works to remedy the breaches.

4.6 The quantified demand should not include items of work that are likely to be superseded by the landlord's intentions for the property.

4.7 If the landlord's surveyor prepares the quantified demand, the surveyor should have regard to the principles laid down in the Royal Institution of Chartered Surveyors' Guidance Note on Dilapidations.

5 The Response

5.1 The response is not intended to have the same status as a defence in proceedings.

5.2 The tenant should respond to the quantified demand within a reasonable time. This will usually be within 56 days after the landlord sends the quantified demand.

5.3 Where appropriate, the tenant should respond using the schedule provided by the landlord. The response should be set out in sufficient detail to enable the landlord to understand clearly the tenant's views on each item.

5.4 The response should be endorsed either by the tenant or, where it is prepared by a surveyor, by the tenant's surveyor. In endorsing the schedule, the tenant's surveyor should have regard to the principles laid down in the Royal Institution of Chartered Surveyors' Guidance Note on Dilapidations.

5.5 The endorsement should confirm that in the tenant's or tenant's surveyor's opinion:

5.5.1 the works detailed in the response are all that were reasonably required for the tenant to remedy the alleged breaches of its covenants or obligations;

5.5.2 any costs set out in the response are reasonably payable for such works; and

5.5.3 account has been taken of what the tenant, or tenant's surveyor, reasonably believes to be the landlord's intentions for the property.

5.6 If the tenant or tenant's surveyor considers that any items in the schedule or quantified demand are likely to be superseded by works to be carried out by the landlord or are likely to be superseded by the landlord's intentions for the property then:

5.6.1 this should be stated in the response;

5.6.2 particulars should be given of the material on which the tenant or tenant's surveyor relies; and

5.6.3 the items to which this view is relevant should be identified.

6 Disclosure of Documents

6.1 Disclosure will generally be limited to the documents required to be enclosed with the quantified demand and the tenant's response. The parties can agree that further disclosure may be given. If either or both of the parties consider that further disclosure should be given but there is disagreement about some aspect of that process, they may be able to make an application for pre-action disclosure under CPR, Part 31. Parties should assist each other and avoid the necessity for such an application.

7 Negotiations

7.1 The landlord and tenant and/or their respective surveyors are encouraged to meet before the tenant is required to respond to the quantified demand and should generally meet within 28 days after the tenant sends the response. The meetings will be without prejudice and the parties should seek to agree as many of the items in dispute as possible.

8 Alternative Dispute Resolution

8.1 The parties should consider whether some form of alternative dispute resolution procedure would be more suitable than litigation, and if so, endeavour to agree which form to adopt. Both the landlord and the tenant may be required by the court to provide evidence that alternative means of resolving their dispute were considered. The courts take the view that litigation should be a last resort, and that claims should not be issued prematurely when a settlement is still actively being explored. Parties are warned that the court will take into account the extent of the parties' compliance with this protocol when making orders about who should pay costs (see CPR, r. 44.3(4) and (5)(a)).

8.2 Information on mediation and other forms of alternative dispute resolution may be found through the following: <http://www.justice.gov.uk/guidance/mediation/index.htm>. The Royal Institute of Chartered Surveyors (www.rics.org/) and Property Litigation Association (www.pla.org.uk) websites also list a number of experienced mediators.

8.3 It is expressly recognised that no party can or should be forced to mediate or enter into any form of alternative dispute resolution.

9 Quantification of Loss

9.1 Prior to issuing proceedings, the landlord should quantify its loss by providing to the tenant a detailed breakdown of the issues and consequential losses based on either a formal diminution valuation or an account of the actual expenditure or, where it has carried out some but not all remedial action, a combination of both; unless, in all the circumstances, it would be unreasonable to do so.

9.2 If a formal diminution valuation is produced, it should be prepared by a valuer.

9.3 If the landlord has not carried out all the works specified in the schedule but intends to carry out some or all of them, the landlord must:

9.3.1 identify which works it intends to carry out;

9.3.2 state when it intends to do such proposed works;

9.3.3 state what steps it has taken towards getting such proposed works done, e.g. preparing a specification or bills of quantities or inviting tenders; and

9.3.4 clearly show the scope of such proposed works to enable any effect on the dilapidations claim to be identified.

9.4 In a case falling within para. 9.3, or in a case where the landlord has not carried out all the works specified in the schedule, and does not intend to carry out some or all of the works so specified, then it should provide a formal diminution valuation unless, in all the circumstances, it would be reasonable not to.

9.5 If the tenant relies on a defence on the basis of diminution, it must state its case for so doing and provide a diminution valuation to the landlord.

9.6 The tenant's diminution valuation shall be sent to the landlord within a reasonable time. A 'reasonable time' will vary from case to case but generally will be within 56 days after the landlord sends the tenant a detailed breakdown of issues and losses under para. 9.1.

10 Stocktake

10 Where the procedure set out in this protocol has not resolved the dispute between the landlord and tenant, they should undertake a further review of their respective positions. The parties should consider the state of the papers and the evidence in order to see if proceedings can be avoided and, at the least, narrow the issues between them.

ANNEX A

Send schedule
(normally within 56 days after the termination of the tenancy)

↓

Send Quantified Demand
(normally within 56 days after the termination of the tenancy)

↓

Send tenant's Response
(normally within 56 days after landlord sending the Quantified Demand)

↓

Negotiations

↓

Quantification of Loss

↓

Stocktake

↓

Court Proceedings

NB:

1 The provisions of this protocol should be adopted in respect of each of the stages detailed in this flowchart.

2 The parties should consider throughout this process whether alternative dispute resolution would assist in settling the dispute.

ANNEX B
SCHEDULE OF DILAPIDATIONS WHERE PREPARED BY A SURVEYOR

[Annex B may be viewed at <http://www.justice.gov.uk/courts/procedure-rules/civil>.]

ANNEX C
SCHEDULE OF DILAPIDATIONS WHERE PREPARED BY THE LANDLORD

[Annex C may be viewed at <http://www.justice.gov.uk/courts/procedure-rules/civil>.]

Appendix 3 Court Fees Orders

Civil Proceedings Fees Order 2008

(SI 2008/1053)

The Lord Chancellor, with the consent and sanction of the Treasury, makes the following Order in exercise of the powers conferred by section 92 of the Courts Act 2003 and sections 414 and 415 of the Insolvency Act 1986. In accordance with section 92(5) and (6) of that Act the Lord Chancellor has consulted the Lord Chief Justice, the Master of the Rolls, the President of the Queen's Bench Division, the President of the Family Division, the Chancellor of the High Court, the Head of Civil Justice, the Deputy Head of Civil Justice and the Civil Justice Council.

1 Citation and Commencement

(1) This Order may be cited as the Civil Proceedings Fees Order 2008 and shall come into force on 1st May 2008.

(2) In this Order—

- (a) 'CCBC' means County Court Bulk Centre;
- (b) 'the CPR' means the Civil Procedure Rules 1998;
- (c) 'LSC' means the Legal Services Commission established under section 1 of the Access to Justice Act 1999;
- (d) expressions also used in the CPR have the same meaning as in those Rules.

2 Fees Payable

The fees set out in column 2 of Schedule 1 are payable in the Supreme Court and in county courts in respect of the items described in column 1 in accordance with and subject to the directions specified in that column.

3

No fee is payable in respect of—

- (a) non-contentious probate business;
- (b) the enrolment of documents;
- (c) criminal proceedings (except proceedings on the Crown side of the Queen's Bench Division to which the fees in Schedule 1 are applicable);
- (d) proceedings by sheriffs, under-sheriffs, deputy-sheriffs or other officers of the sheriff; or
- (e) family proceedings in the High Court or in a county court.

4

Where by any convention entered into by Her Majesty with any foreign power it is provided that no fee is required to be paid in respect of any proceedings, the fees specified in this Order are not payable in respect of those proceedings.

5 Remissions and Part Remissions

Schedule 2 applies for the purpose of ascertaining whether a party is entitled to a remission or part remission of a fee prescribed by this Order.

6 Revocations

The instruments listed in column 1 of the table in Schedule 3 (which have the references listed in column 2) are revoked.

SCHEDULE 1 FEES TO BE TAKEN

[Schedule introduced by art. 2]

Column 1 *Number and description of fee*	*Column 2* *Amount of fee*
1 Starting proceedings (High Court and county court)	
1.1 On starting proceedings (including proceedings issued after permission to issue is granted but excluding Claim Production Centre cases brought by Centre users or cases brought by Money Claim OnLine users) to recover a sum of money where the sum claimed—	
(a) does not exceed £300;	£35
(b) exceeds £300 but does not exceed £500;	£50
(c) exceeds £500 but does not exceed £1,000;	£70
(d) exceeds £1,000 but does not exceed £1,500;	£80
(e) exceeds £1,500 but does not exceed £3,000;	£95
(f) exceeds £3,000 but does not exceed £5,000;	£120
(g) exceeds £5,000 but does not exceed £15,000;	£245
(h) exceeds £15,000 but does not exceed £50,000;	£395
(i) exceeds £50,000 but does not exceed £100,000;	£685
(j) exceeds £100,000 but does not exceed £150,000;	£885
(k) exceeds £150,000 but does not exceed £200,000;	£1,080
(l) exceeds £200,000 but does not exceed £250,000;	£1,275
(m) exceeds £250,000 but does not exceed £300,000;	£1,475
(n) exceeds £300,000 or is not limited.	£1,670
1.2 On starting proceedings to recover a sum of money in Claim Production Centre cases brought by Centre users, where the sum claimed:	
(a) does not exceed £300;	£15
(b) exceeds £300 but does not exceed £500;	£30
(c) exceeds £500 but does not exceed £1,000;	£55
(d) exceeds £1,000 but does not exceed £1,500;	£65
(e) exceeds £1,500 but does not exceed £3,000;	£75
(f) exceeds £3,000 but does not exceed £5,000;	£85
(g) exceeds £5,000 but does not exceed £15,000;	£190
(h) exceeds £15,000 but does not exceed £50,000;	£310
(i) exceeds £50,000 but does not exceed £100,000.	£550
1.3 On starting proceedings to recover a sum of money brought by Money Claim OnLine users where the sum claimed:	
(a) does not exceed £300;	£25
(b) exceeds £300 but does not exceed £500;	£35
(c) exceeds £500 but does not exceed £1,000;	£60
(d) exceeds £1,000 but does not exceed £1,500;	£70
(e) exceeds £1,500 but does not exceed £3,000;	£80
(f) exceeds £3,000 but does not exceed £5,000;	£100
(g) exceeds £5,000 but does not exceed £15,000;	£210
(h) exceeds £15,000 but does not exceed £50,000;	£340
(i) exceeds £50,000 but does not exceed £100,000.	£595
Fees 1.1, 1.2 and 1.3. Where the claimant is making a claim for interest on a specified sum of money, the amount on which the fee is calculated is the total amount of the claim and the interest.	
1.4 On starting proceedings for the recovery of land:	
(a) in the High Court;	£465
(b) in the county court, other than where fee 1.4(c) applies;	£175
(c) using the Possession Claims Online website.	£100

Column 1 *Number and description of fee*	*Column 2* *Amount of fee*
1.5 On starting proceedings for any other remedy (including proceedings issued after permission to issue is granted):	
in the High Court;	£465
in the county court.	£175
Fees 1.1, 1.4 and 1.5. Recovery of land or goods. Where a claim for money is additional or alternative to a claim for recovery of land or goods, only fee 1.4 or 1.5 is payable.	
Fees 1.1and 1.5. Claims other than recovery of land or goods. Where a claim for money is additional to a non money claim (other than a claim for recovery of land or goods), then fee 1.1 is payable in addition to fee 1.5. Where a claim for money is alternative to a non money claim (other than a claim for recovery of land or goods), only fee 1.1 is payable in the High Court, and, in the county court, whichever is greater of fee 1.1 or fee 1.5 is payable.	
Fees 1.1 and 1.5. Where more than one non money claim is made in the same proceedings, fee 1.5 is payable once only, in addition to any fee which may be payable under fee 1.1.	
Fees 1.1 and 1.5 are not payable where fee 1.8(b), fee 1.9(a), fee 3 or fee 10.1 applies.	
Fees 1.1 and fee 1.5. Amendment of claim or counterclaim. Where the claim or counterclaim is amended, and the fee paid before amendment is less than that which would have been payable if the document, as amended, had been so drawn in the first instance, the party amending the document must pay the difference.	
1.6 On the filing of proceedings against a party or parties not named in the proceedings. Fee 1.6 is payable by a defendant who adds or substitutes a party or parties to the proceedings or by a claimant who adds or substitutes a defendant or defendants.	£45
1.7 On the filing of a counterclaim.	The same fee as if the remedy sought were the subject of separate proceedings
No fee is payable on a counterclaim which a defendant is required to make under rule 57.8 of the CPR (requirement to serve a counterclaim if a defendant makes a claim or seeks a remedy in relation to a grant of probate of a will, or letters of administration of an estate, of a deceased person).	
1.8 (a) On an application for permission to issue proceedings.	£45
(b) On an application for an order under Part 3 of the Solicitors Act 1974 for the assessment of costs payable to a solicitor by a client or on starting costs-only proceedings.	£45
1.9 (a) For permission to apply for judicial review.	£60
Where the court has made an order giving permission to proceed with a claim for judicial review, there is payable by the claimant within 7 days of service on the claimant of that order:	
1.9 (b) if the judicial review procedure has been started.	£215
1.9 (c) if the claim for judicial review was started otherwise than by using the judicial review procedure.	£60
2 General Fees (High Court and county courts)	
2.1 On the claimant filing a directions questionnaire; or where the court dispenses with the need for a directions questionnaire, within 14 days of the date of despatch of the notice of allocation to track; or where the CPR or a Practice Direction provide for automatic allocation or provide that the rules on allocation do not apply, within 28 days of the filing of the defence (or the filing of the last defence if there is more than one defendant), or within 28 days of the expiry of the time permitted for filing all defences if sooner:	

Column 1 *Number and description of fee*	*Column 2* *Amount of fee*
(a) if the case is on the small claims track or a directions questionnaire (small claims track) has been filed and the claim exceeds £1,500;	£40
(b) if the case is on the fast track or multi-track or a directions questionnaire (fast track and multi-track) has been filed.	£220
Fee 2.1 is payable by the claimant except where the action is proceeding on the counterclaim alone, when it is payable by the defendant: on the defendant filing a directions questionnaire; or where the court dispenses with the need for a directions questionnaire, within 14 days of the date of despatch of the notice of allocation to track; or where the CPR or a Practice Direction provide for automatic allocation or provide that the rules on allocation do not apply, within 28 days of the filing of the defence to the counterclaim (or the filing of the last defence to the counterclaim if there is more than one party entitled to file a defence to the counterclaim), or within 28 days of the expiry of the time permitted for filing all defences to the counterclaim if sooner.	
Where fee 2.1 is payable on the filing of a directions questionnaire, by the claimant or the defendant as the case may be, the fee payable is based on the track for the case specified in the directions questionnaire. If the case is subsequently allocated to a track which attracts a higher fee then the difference in fee is payable, by the party liable to pay the fee, within 14 days of the date of despatch of notice of allocation to track. If the case is allocated to a track which attracts a lower fee the difference in fee will be refunded.	
2.2 On the claimant filing a pre-trial check list (listing questionnaire); or where the court fixes the trial date or trial week without the need for a pre-trial check list, within 14 days of the date of despatch of the notice (or the date when oral notice is given if no written notice is given) of the trial week or the trial date if no trial week is fixed.	£110
Fee 2.2 is payable by the claimant except where the action is proceeding on the counterclaim alone, when it is payable by the defendant: on the defendant filing a pre-trial check list; or where the court fixes the trial date or trial week without the need for a pre-trial check list, within 14 days of the date of despatch of the notice (or the date when oral notice is given if no written notice is given) of the trial week or the trial date if no trial week is fixed.	
Fees 2.1 and 2.2 in the High Court and the county court.	
Fees 2.1 and 2.2 are payable as appropriate where the court allocates a case to track for a trial of the assessment of damages.	
Fees 2.1 and 2.2 are not payable in relation to claims managed under a Group Litigation Order after that Order is made.	
Fees 2.1 and 2.2 are payable once only in the same proceedings.	
Fee 2.1 is not payable where the procedure in Part 8 of the CPR is used.	
Fee 2.2 is not payable where the court fixed the hearing date on the issue of the claim.	
Fees 2.1 and 2.2 in the county court	
Fee 2.1 is not payable in proceedings where the only claim is a claim to recover a sum of money and the sum claimed does not exceed £1,500.	
Fee 2.2 is not payable in respect of a case on the small claims track.	
2.3 On the occasion of fee 2.2 becoming payable; or where the claim is on the small claims track, within 14 days of the date of despatch of the notice (or the date when oral notice is given if no written notice is given) of the trial week or the trial date if no trial week is fixed a fee payable for the hearing of:	
(a) a case on the multi-track;	£1,090
(b) a case on the fast track;	£545
(c) a case on the small claims track where the sum claimed:	
(i) does not exceed £300;	£25
(ii) exceeds £300 but does not exceed £500;	£55
(iii) exceeds £500 but does not exceed £1,000;	£80
(iv) exceeds £1,000 but does not exceed £1,500;	£110
(v) exceeds £1,500 but does not exceed £3,000;	£165
(vi) exceeds £3,000.	£325

Column 1 *Number and description of fee*	*Column 2* *Amount of fee*
Fee 2.3 is payable by the claimant except where the action is proceeding on the counterclaim alone, when it is payable by the defendant: on the defendant filing a pre-trial check list; or where the claim is on the small claims track or the court fixes the trial date or trial week without the need for a pre-trial check list, within 14 days of the date of despatch of the notice (or the date when oral notice is given if no written notice is given) of the trial week or the trial date if no trial week is fixed. Where a case is on the multi-track or fast track and, after a hearing date has been fixed, the court receives notice in writing from the party who paid the hearing fee that the case has been settled or discontinued then the following percentages of the hearing fee will be refunded: (i) 100% if the court is notified more than 28 days before the hearing; (ii) 75% if the court is notified between 15 and 28 days before the hearing; (iii) 50% if the court is notified between 7 and 14 days before the hearing. Where a case is on the small claims track and, after a hearing date has been fixed, the court receives notice in writing from the party who paid the hearing fee, at least 7 days before the date set for the hearing, that the case has been settled or discontinued the hearing fee will be refunded in full. Fee 2.3 is not payable in respect of a case where the court fixed the hearing date on the issue of the claim.	
2.4 In the High Court on filing: an appellant's notice: or a respondent's notice where the respondent is appealing or wishes to ask the appeal court to uphold the order of the lower court for reasons different from or additional to those given by the lower court.	£235
2.5 In the county court on filing: an appellant's notice, or a respondent's notice where the respondent is appealing or wishes to ask the appeal court to uphold the order of the lower court for reasons different from or additional to those given by the lower court:	
(a) in a claim allocated to the small claims track;	£115
(b) in all other claims.	£135
Fees 2.4 and 2.5 do not apply on appeals against a decision made in detailed assessment proceedings.	
2.6 On an application on notice where no other fee is specified.	£80
2.7 On an application by consent or without notice where no other fee is specified. For the purpose of fee 2.7 a request for a judgment or order on admission or in default does not constitute an application and no fee is payable. Fee 2.7 is not payable in relation to an application by consent for an adjournment of a hearing where the application is received by the court at least 14 days before the date set for that hearing. Fees 2.6 and 2.7 are not payable when an application is made in an appeal notice or is filed at the same time as an appeal notice.	£45
2.8 On an application for a summons or order for a witness to attend court to be examined on oath or an order for evidence to be taken by deposition, other than an application for which fee 7.2 or 8.3 is payable.	£40
2.9 On an application to vary a judgment or suspend enforcement, including an application to suspend a warrant of possession. Where more than one remedy is sought in the same application only one fee is payable.	£40
2.10 Register of judgments, orders and fines kept under section 98 of the Courts Act 2003: On a request for the issue of a certificate of satisfaction.	£15

Column 1 *Number and description of fee*	*Column 2* *Amount of fee*
3 Companies Act 1985, Companies Act 2006 and Insolvency Act 1986 (High Court and county court)	
3.1 On entering a bankruptcy petition:	
(a) if presented by a debtor or the personal representative of a deceased debtor;	£175
(b) if presented by a creditor or other person.	£220
3.2 On entering a petition for an administration order.	£175
3.3 On entering any other petition. One fee only is payable where more than one petition is presented in relation to a partnership.	£220
3.4(a) On a request for a certificate of discharge from bankruptcy;	£70
(b) after the first certificate, for each copy.	£5
3.5 On an application under the Companies Act 1985, the Companies Act 2006 or the Insolvency Act 1986 other than one brought by petition and where no other fee is specified. Fee 3.5 is not payable where the application is made in existing proceedings.	£155
3.6 On an application for the conversion of a voluntary arrangement into a winding up or bankruptcy under Article 37 of Council Regulation (EC) No 1346/2000.	£155
3.7 On an application, for the purposes of Council Regulation (EC) No 1346/2000, for an order confirming creditors' voluntary winding up (where the company has passed a resolution for voluntary winding up, and no declaration under section 89 of the Insolvency Act 1986 has been made).	£35
3.8 On filing: a notice of intention to appoint an administrator under paragraph 14 of Schedule B1 to the Insolvency Act 1986 or in accordance with paragraph 27 of that Schedule; or a notice of appointment of an administrator in accordance with paragraphs 18 or 29 of that Schedule. Where a person pays fee 3.8 on filing a notice of intention to appoint an administrator, no fee is payable on that same person filing a notice of appointment of that administrator.	£35
3.9 On submitting a nominee's report under section 2(2) of the Insolvency Act 1986.	£35
3.10 On filing documents in accordance with paragraph 7(1) of Schedule A1 to the Insolvency Act 1986.	£35
3.11 On an application by consent or without notice within existing proceedings where no other fee is specified.	£35
3.12 On an application with notice within existing proceedings where no other fee is specified.	£70
3.13 On a search in person of the bankruptcy and companies records, in a county court.	£45
Requests and applications with no fee: No fee is payable on a request or on an application to the Court by the Official Receiver when applying only in the capacity of Official Receiver to the case (and not as trustee or liquidator), or on an application to set aside a statutory demand.	
4 Copy Documents (Court of Appeal, High Court and county court)	
4.1 On a request for a copy of a document (other than where fee 4.2 applies):	
(a) for ten pages or less;	£5
(b) for each subsequent page. Note: The fee payable under fee 4.1 includes: where the court allows a party to fax to the court for the use of that party a document that has not been requested by the court and is not intended to be placed on the court file; where a party requests that the court fax a copy of a document from the court file; the court provides a subsequent copy of a document which it has previously provided.	50p
4.2 On a request for a copy of a document on a computer disk or in other electronic form, for each such copy.	£5

Column 1 *Number and description of fee*	*Column 2* *Amount of fee*
5 Determination of costs (Senior Court and county court) Fee 5 does not apply to the determination in the Senior Courts of costs incurred in the Court of Protection.	
5.1 On filing a request for detailed assessment where the party filing the request is legally aided, is funded by the Legal Services Commission or is a person for whom civil legal services have been made available under arrangements made by the Lord Chancellor under Part 1 of the Legal Aid, Sentencing and Punishment of Offenders Act 2012 and no other party is ordered to pay the costs of the proceedings.	£195
5.2 On the filing of a request for detailed assessment in any case where fee 5.1 does not apply; or on the filing of a request for a hearing date for the assessment of costs payable to a solicitor by a client pursuant to an order under Part 3 of the Solicitors Act 1974 where the amount of the costs claimed:	
(a) does not exceed £15,000;	£325
(b) exceeds £15,000 but does not exceed £50,000;	£655
(c) exceeds £50,000 but does not exceed £100,000;	£980
(d) exceeds £100,000 but does not exceed £150,000;	£1,310
(e) exceeds £150,000 but does not exceed £200,000;	£1,635
(f) exceeds £200,000 but does not exceed £300,000;	£2,455
(g) exceeds £300,000 but does not exceed £500,000;	£4,090
(h) exceeds £500,000.	£5,455
Where there is a combined party and party and legal aid, or a combined party and party and Legal Services Commission, or a combined party and party and Lord Chancellor, or a combined party and party and one or more of legal aid, Legal Services Commission or Lord Chancellor determination of costs, fee 5.2 will be attributed proportionately to the party and party, legal aid, Legal Services Commission or Lord Chancellor (as the case may be) portions of the bill on the basis of the amount allowed.	
5.3 On a request for the issue of a default costs certificate.	£60
5.4 On commencing an appeal against a decision made in detailed assessment proceedings.	£205
5.5 On a request or application to set aside a default costs certificate.	£105
6 Determination in the Senior Court of costs incurred in the Court of Protection	
6.1 On the filing of a request for detailed assessment:	
(a) where the amount of the costs to be assessed (excluding VAT and disbursements) does not exceed £3,000;	£110
(b) in all other cases.	£220
6.2 On an appeal against a decision made in detailed assessment proceedings.	£65
6.3 On a request or application to set aside a default costs certificate.	£65
7 Enforcement in the High Court	
7.1 On sealing a writ of execution/possession/delivery. Where the recovery of a sum of money is sought in addition to a writ of possession and delivery, no further fee is payable.	£60
7.2 On an application for an order requiring a judgment debtor or other person to attend court to provide information in connection with enforcement of a judgment or order.	£50
7.3 (a) On an application for a third party debt order or the appointment of a receiver by way of equitable execution.	£100
(b) On an application for a charging order. Fee 7.3(a) is payable in respect of each third party against whom the order is sought. Fee 7.3(b) is payable in respect of each charging order applied for.	£100
7.4 On an application for a judgment summons.	£100
7.5 On a request or application to register a judgment or order, or for permission to enforce an arbitration award, or for a certificate or a certified copy of a judgment or order for use abroad.	£60

Column 1 *Number and description of fee*	*Column 2* *Amount of fee*
8 Enforcement in the county court	
8.1 On an application for or in relation to enforcement of a judgment or order of a county court or through a county court, by the issue of a warrant of execution against goods except a warrant to enforce payment of a fine:	
(a) in cases other than CCBC cases;	£100
(b) in CCBC cases.	£70
8.2 On a request for a further attempt at execution of a warrant at a new address following a notice of the reason for non-execution (except a further attempt following suspension and CCBC cases brought by Centre users).	£30
8.3 On an application for an order requiring a judgment debtor or other person to attend court to provide information in connection with enforcement of a judgment or order.	£50
8.4(a) On an application for a third party debt order or the appointment of a receiver by way of equitable execution.	£100
(b) On an application for a charging order.	£100
Fee 8.4(a) is payable in respect of each third party against whom the order is sought. Fee 8.4(b) is payable in respect of each charging order applied for.	
8.5 On an application for a judgment summons.	£100
8.6 On the issue of a warrant of possession or a warrant of delivery. Where the recovery of a sum of money is sought in addition, no further fee is payable.	£110
8.7 On an application for an attachment of earnings order (other than a consolidated attachment of earnings order) to secure payment of a judgment debt. Fee 8.7 is payable for each defendant against whom an order is sought. Fee 8.7 is not payable where the attachment of earnings order is made on the hearing of a judgment summons.	£100
8.8 On a consolidated attachment of earnings order or on an administration order.	For every £1 or part of a £1 of the money paid into court in respect of debts due to creditors - 10p
Fee 8.8 is calculated on any money paid into court under any order at the rate in force at the time when the order was made (or, where the order has been amended, at the time of the last amendment before the date of payment).	
8.9 On an application for the enforcement of an award for a sum of money or other decision made by any court, tribunal, body or person other than the High Court or a county court.	£40
8.10 On a request for an order to recover a sum that is: a specified debt within the meaning of the Enforcement of Road Traffic Debts Order 1993; or pursuant to an enactment, treated as a specified debt for the purposes of that Order. No fee is payable on: an application for an extension of time to serve a statutory declaration or a witness statement in connection with any such order; or a request to issue a warrant of execution to enforce any such order.	£7
8A Service in the county court	
8A.1 On a request for service by a bailiff of an order to attend court for questioning.	£100
9 Sale (county court only)	
9.1 For removing or taking steps to remove goods to a place of deposit.	The reasonable expenses incurred

Court Fees Orders

Column 1 *Number and description of fee*	Column 2 *Amount of fee*
Fee 9.1 is to include the reasonable expenses of feeding and caring for any animals.	
9.2 For advertising a sale by public auction pursuant to section 97 of the County Courts Act 1984.	The reasonable expenses incurred
9.3 For the appraisement of goods.	5p in the £1 or part of a £1 of the appraised value
9.4 For the sale of goods (including advertisements, catalogues, sale and commission and delivery of goods).	15p in the £1 or part of a £1 on the amount realised by the sale or such other sum as the district judge may consider to be justified in the circumstances
9.5 Where no sale takes place by reason of an execution being withdrawn, satisfied or stopped.	(a) 10p in the £1 or part of a £1 on the value of the goods seized, the value to be the appraised value where the goods have been appraised or such other sum as the district judge may consider to be justified in the circumstances; and in addition (b) any sum payable under fee 9.1, 9.2 or 9.3

FEES PAYABLE IN HIGH COURT ONLY

10 Miscellaneous proceedings or matters

Bills of Sale

10.1 On filing any document under the Bills of Sale Acts [*sic*] 1878 and the Bills of Sale Act (1878) Amendment Act 1882 or on an application under section 15 of the Bills of Sale Act 1878 for an order that a memorandum of satisfaction be written on a registered copy of the bill.	£25
Searches	
10.2 For an official certificate of the result of a search for each name, in any register or index held by the court; or in the Court Funds Office, for an official certificate of the result of a search of unclaimed balances for a specified period of up to 50 years.	£45
10.3 On a search in person of the court's records, including inspection, for each 15 minutes or part of 15 minutes.	£7

Column 1 *Number and description of fee*	*Column 2* *Amount of fee*
Judge sitting as arbitrator	
10.4 On the appointment of:	
(a) a judge of the Commercial Court as an arbitrator or umpire under section 93 of the Arbitration Act 1996; or	£2,390
(b) a judge of the Technology and Construction Court as an arbitrator or umpire under section 93 of the Arbitration Act 1996.	£1,860
10.5 For every day or part of a day (after the first day) of the hearing before:	
(a) a judge of the Commercial Court; or	£2,390
(b) a judge of the Technology and Construction Court, so appointed as arbitrator or umpire.	£1,860
Where fee 10.4 has been paid on the appointment of a judge of the Commercial Court or a judge of the Technology and Construction Court as an arbitrator or umpire but the arbitration does not proceed to a hearing or an award, the fee will be refunded.	
11 Fees payable in Admiralty matters	
In the Admiralty Registrar and Marshal's Office:	
11.1 On the issue of a warrant for the arrest of a ship or goods.	£220
11.2 On the sale of a ship or goods	
Subject to a minimum fee of £200:	
(a) for every £100 or fraction of £100 of the price up to £100,000;	£1
(b) for every £100 or fraction of £100 of the price exceeding £100,000.	50p
Where there is sufficient proceeds of sale in court, fee 11.2 will be payable by transfer from the proceeds of sale in court.	
11.3 On entering a reference for hearing by the Registrar.	£70
FEES PAYABLE IN HIGH COURT AND COURT OF APPEAL ONLY	
12 Affidavits	
12.1 On taking an affidavit or an affirmation or attestation upon honour in lieu of an affidavit or a declaration except for the purpose of receipt of dividends from the Accountant General and for a declaration by a shorthand writer appointed in insolvency proceedings: for each person making any of the above.	£11
12.2 For each exhibit referred to in an affidavit, affirmation, attestation or declaration for which fee 12.1 is payable.	£2
FEES PAYABLE IN COURT OF APPEAL ONLY	
13 Fees payable in appeals to the Court of Appeal	
13.1(a) Where in an appeal notice, permission to appeal or an extension of time for appealing is applied for (or both are applied for): on filing an appellant's notice; or where the respondent is appealing, on filing a respondent's notice.	£235
13.1(b) Where permission to appeal is not required or has been granted by the lower court: on filing an appellant's notice, or on filing a respondent's notice where the respondent is appealing.	£465
13.1(c) On the appellant filing an appeal questionnaire (unless the appellant has paid fee 13.1(b)), or on the respondent filing an appeal questionnaire (unless the respondent has paid fee 13.1(b)).	£465
13.2 On filing a respondent's notice where the respondent wishes to ask the appeal court to uphold the order of the lower court for reasons different from or additional to those given by the lower court.	£235
13.3 On filing an application notice.	£235
Fee 13.3 is not payable for an application made in an appeal notice.	

SCHEDULE 2 REMISSIONS AND PART REMISSIONS

[Schedule introduced by art. 4]

Interpretation

1.—(1) In this Schedule—

'child' means a child or young person in respect of whom a party is entitled to receive child benefit in accordance with section 141, and regulations made under section 142, of the Social Security Contributions and Benefits Act 1992;

'child care costs' has the meaning given in Part 3 of the Criminal Legal Aid (Financial Resources) Regulations 2013;

'couple' has the meaning given in section 3(5A) of the Tax Credits Act 2002;

'disposable monthly income' has the meaning given in paragraph 5;

'excluded benefits' means—

(a) any of the following benefits payable under the Social Security Contributions and Benefits Act 1992—

(i) attendance allowance paid under section 64;

(ii) severe disablement allowance;

(iii) carer's allowance;

(iv) disability living allowance;

(v) constant attendance allowance paid under section 104 or paragraph 4 or 7(2) of Schedule 8 as an increase to a disablement pension;

(vi) council tax benefit;

(vii) any payment made out of the social fund;

(viii) housing benefit;

(b) any direct payment made under the Community Care, Services for Carers and Children's Services (Direct Payments) (England) Regulations 2003 or the Community Care, Services for Carers and Children's Services (Direct Payments) (Wales) Regulations 2004;

(c) a back to work bonus payable under section 26 of the Jobseekers Act 1995;

(d) any exceptionally severe disablement allowance paid under the Personal Injuries (Civil-ians) Scheme 1983;

(e) any pension paid under the Naval, Military and Air Forces etc (Disablement and Death) Service Pension Order 2006;

(f) any payment made from the Independent Living Funds;

(g) any financial support paid under an agreement for the care of a foster child;

(h) personal independence payment under Part 4 of the Welfare Reform Act 2012; and

(i) armed forces independence payment under the Armed Forces and Reserve Forces (Compensation Scheme) Order 2011;

'gross annual income' means total annual income, for the 12 months preceding the application for remission or part remission, from all sources other than receipt of any of the excluded benefits;

'gross monthly income' means total monthly income, for the month in which the application for remission or part remission is made, from all sources other than receipt of any of the excluded benefits;

'the Independent Living Funds' means any payment made from the funds listed at regulation 20(2)(b) of the Criminal Legal Aid (Financial Resources) Regulations 2013;

'partner' means a person with whom the party lives as a couple and includes a person with whom the party is not currently living but from whom the party is not living separate and apart;

'party' means the individual who would, but for this Schedule, be liable to pay the fee required under this Order;

'restraint order' means—

(h) an order under section 42(1A) of the Senior Courts Act 1981; or

(i) a civil restraint order under rule 3.11 of the Civil Procedure Rules 1998 or a practice direction made under that rule.

(2) Paragraphs 2, 3 and 4—
(a) do not apply to a party for whom civil legal services, for which a certificate has been issued under the Civil Legal Aid (Procedure) Regulations 2012, have been made available under arrangements made for the purposes of Part 1 of that Act for the purposes of the proceedings; and
(b) are subject to the provisions of paragraphs 10 (vexatious litigants) and 11 (exception).

Full Remission of Fees — Qualifying Benefits

2.—(1) No fee is payable under this Order if, at the time when a fee would otherwise be payable, the party is in receipt of a qualifying benefit.
(2) The following are qualifying benefits for the purposes of sub-paragraph (1)—
(a) income support under the Social Security Contributions and Benefits Act 1992;
(b) working tax credit, provided that no child tax credit is being paid to the party;
(c) income-based jobseeker's allowance under the Jobseekers Act 1995; and
(d) guarantee credit under the State Pension Credit Act 2002; and
(e) income-related employment and support allowance under the Welfare Reform Act 2007.

Full Remission of Fees — Gross Annual Income

3.—(1) No fee is payable under this Order if, at the time when the fee would otherwise be payable, the party has the number of children specified in column 1 of the following table and—
(a) if the party is single, the gross annual income of the party does not exceed the amount set out in the appropriate row of column 2; or
(b) if the party is one of a couple, the gross annual income of the couple does not exceed the amount set out in the appropriate row of column 3.

Column 1 *Number of children of party paying fee*	*Column 2* *Single*	*Column 3* *Couple*
no children	£13,000	£18,000
1 child	£15,930	£20,930
2 children	£18,860	£23,860
3 children	£21,790	£26,790
4 children	£24,720	£29,720

(2) If the party paying the fee has more than 4 children then the relevant amount of gross annual income is the amount specified in the table for 4 children plus the sum of £2,930 for each additional child.

Full and Part Remission of Fees — Disposable Monthly Income

4.—(1) No fee is payable under this Order if, at the time when the fee would otherwise be payable, the disposable monthly income of the party is £50 or less.
(2) The maximum amount of fee payable is—
(a) if the disposable monthly income of the party is more than £50 but does not exceed £210, an amount equal to one-quarter of every £10 of the party's disposable monthly income up to a maximum of £50; and
(b) if the disposable monthly income is more than £210, an amount equal to £50 plus one-half of every £10 over £200 of the party's disposable monthly income.
(3) Where the fee that would otherwise be payable under this Order is greater than the maximum fee which a party is required to pay as calculated in sub-paragraph (2), the fee will be remitted to the amount payable under that sub-paragraph.

Disposable Monthly Income

5.—(1) A party's disposable monthly income is the gross monthly income of the party for the month in which the fee becomes payable ('the period') less the deductions referred to in sub-paragraphs (2) and (3).
(2) There are to be deducted from the gross monthly income—
(a) income tax paid or payable in respect of the period;

(b) any contributions estimated to have been paid under Part 1 of the Social Security Contributions and Benefits Act 1992 in respect of the period;
(c) either—
(i) monthly rent or monthly payment in respect of a mortgage debt or hereditable security, payable in respect of the only or main dwelling of the party, less any housing benefit paid under the Social Security Contributions and Benefits Act 1992; or
(ii) the monthly cost of the living accommodation of the party;
(d) any child care costs paid or payable in respect of the period;
(e) if the party is making bona fide payments for the maintenance of a child who is not a member of the household of the party, the amount of such payments paid or payable in respect of the period; and
(f) any amount paid or payable by the party, in respect of the period, in pursuance of a court order.
(3) There will be deducted from the gross monthly income an amount representing the cost of living expenses in respect of the period being—
(a) £315; plus
(b) £244 for each child of the party; plus
(c) £159, if the party has a partner.

Resources of Partners

6.—(1) For the purpose of determining whether a party is entitled to the remission or part remission of a fee in accordance with this Schedule, the income of a partner, if any, is to be included as income of the party.
(2) The receipt by a partner of a qualifying benefit does not entitle a party to remission of a fee.

Application for Remission or Part Remission of Fees

7.—(1) An application for remission or part remission of a fee must be made to the court officer at the time when the fee would otherwise be payable.
(2) Where a claim for full remission of fees is made, the party must provide documentary evidence of, as the case may be—
(a) entitlement to a qualifying benefit; or
(b) gross annual income and, if applicable, the children included for the purposes of paragraph 3.
(3) Where a claim for full or part remission of fees under paragraph 4 is made, the party must provide documentary evidence of—
(a) such of the party's gross monthly income as is derived from—
(i) employment;
(ii) rental or other income received from persons living with the party by reason of their residence in the party's home;
(iii) a pension; or
(iv) a state benefit, not being an excluded benefit; and
(b) any expenditure being deducted from the gross monthly income in accordance with paragraph 5(2).

Remission in Exceptional Circumstances

8. Where it appears to the Lord Chancellor that the payment of any fee prescribed by this Order would, owing to the exceptional circumstances of the particular case, involve undue financial hardship, the Lord Chancellor may reduce or remit the fee in that case.

Refunds

9.—(1) Subject to sub-paragraph (3), where a party has not provided the documentary evidence required by paragraph 7 and a fee has been paid at a time when, under paragraphs 2, 3 or 4, it was not payable, the fee will be refunded if documentary evidence relating to the time when the fee became payable is provided at a later date.
(2) Subject to sub-paragraph (3), where a fee has been paid at a time where the Lord Chancellor, if all the circumstances had been known, would have reduced or remitted the fee under paragraph 8, the fee or the amount by which the fee would have been reduced, as the case may be, will be refunded.

(3) No refund will be made under this paragraph unless the party who paid the fee applies within 6 months of paying the fee.

(4) The Lord Chancellor may extend the period of 6 months mentioned in sub-paragraph (3) if the Lord Chancellor considers that there is a good reason for an application being made after the end of the period of 6 months.

Vexatious Litigants

10.—(1) This paragraph applies where—

(a) a restraint order is in force against a party; and

(b) the party makes an application for permission to—

(i) issue proceedings or take a step in proceedings as required by the restraint order;

(ii) apply for amendment or discharge of the order; or

(iii) appeal the order.

(2) The fee prescribed for the application by Schedule 1 is payable in full.

(3) If the court grants the permission requested the applicant will be refunded the difference between—

(a) the fee paid; and

(b) the fee that would have been payable if this Schedule had been applied without reference to this paragraph.

Exception

11. This Schedule does not apply to fee 8.8 (fee payable on a consolidated attachment of earnings order or an administration order).

SCHEDULE 3 REVOCATIONS

[Schedule introduced by art. 6]

Column Title	*Column 2 Reference*
The Civil Proceedings Fees Order 2004	S.I. 2004/3121
The Civil Proceedings Fees (Amendment) Order 2005	S.I. 2005/473
The Civil Proceedings Fees (Amendment No. 2) Order 2005	S.I. 2005/3445
The Civil Proceedings Fees (Amendment) Order 2006	S.I. 2006/719
The Civil Proceedings Fees (Amendment) Order 2007	S.I. 2007/680
The Civil Proceedings Fees (Amendment) (No. 2) Order 2007	S.I. 2007/2176
The Civil Proceedings Fees (Amendment) (No. 2) (Amendment) Order 2007	S.I. 2007/2801

NOTES ON TEXT

The text printed above incorporates the following amendments:

sch. 1 substituted by the Civil Proceedings Fees (Amendment No. 2) Order 2013 (SI 2013/1410), art. 3;

in fee 13.1(c) a closing parenthesis has been added editorially after 'fee 13.1(b)' the first time it occurs;

sch. 2, para. 1, amended by: (a) SI 2013/534, sch., para. 18 (1 April 2013 subject to reg. 14(2)); (b) Personal Independence Payment (Supplementary Provisions and Consequential Amendments) Regulations 2013 (SI 2013/388), sch., para. 42 (8 April 2013); (c) Armed Forces and Reserve Forces Compensation Scheme (Consequential Provisions: Subordinate Legislation) Order 2013 (SI 2013/591), sch., para. 39 (8 April 2013).

The title of SI 2013/534 is The Legal Aid, Sentencing and Punishment of Offenders Act 2012 (Consequential, Transitional and Saving Provisions) Regulations 2013.

Non-Contentious Probate Fees (Indian Ocean Tsunami) Order 2005

(SI 2005/266)

The Lord Chancellor, in exercise of the powers conferred upon him by sections 92 and 108(6) of the Courts Act 2003 and section 128 of the Finance Act 1990, with the consent of the Treasury under section 92(1) of the Courts Act 2003 and after consultation with the Lord Chief Justice, the Master of the Rolls, the President of the Family Division, the Vice-Chancellor, the Head of Civil Justice and the Deputy Head of Civil Justice and the Civil Justice Council under section 92(5) and (6) of the Courts Act 2003, hereby makes the following Order:

1 Citation, Commencement and Interpretation

(1) This Order may be cited as the Non-Contentious Probate Fees (Indian Ocean Tsunami) Order 2005 and shall come into force on the 4th March 2005.

(2) In this Order 'the 2004 Order' means the Non-Contentious Probate Fees Order 2004.

2 Remission of Fees

Notwithstanding the provisions of Article 4 of the 2004 Order, where it appears to the Lord Chancellor that an application for a grant is in respect of a death occurring as a result of the earthquake and tsunami in the Indian Ocean on 26th December 2004, he shall remit any fee prescribed by that Order in that case.

3 Transitional Provision

Where—

(a) a fee has been paid under the 2004 Order after 26th December 2004 but before 4th March 2005 and

(b) if this Order had been in force when the fee was paid, the Lord Chancellor would have remitted the fee,

the fee shall be refunded.

Non-Contentious Probate Fees (London Terrorist Bombings) Order 2005

(SI 2005/3359)

The Lord Chancellor makes the following Order in exercise of the powers conferred upon him by sections 92 and 108(6) of the Courts Act 2003 and section 128 of the Finance Act 1990. In accordance with section 92 of the Courts Act 2003, he has consulted the Lord Chief Justice, the Master of the Rolls, the President of the Queen's Bench Division, the President of the Family Division, the Chancellor of the High Court, the Head of Civil Justice, the Deputy Head of Civil Justice, and the Civil Justice Council.

1 Citation, Commencement and Interpretation

(1) This order may be cited as the Non-Contentious Probate Fees (London Terrorist Bombings) Order 2005 and shall come into force on 29th December 2005.

(2) In this Order 'the 2004 Order' means the Non-Contentious Probate Fees Order 2004.

2 Remission of Fees

Notwithstanding the provisions of Article 4 of the 2004 Order, where it appears to the Lord Chancellor that an application for a grant is in respect of—

(a) a death occurring as a result of another person's detonation of a bomb in London on 7th July 2005, or

(b) a death occurring as a result of action taken in a police operation following another person's attempted detonation of a bomb in London on 21st July 2005,

he shall remit any fee prescribed by the 2004 Order.

3 Transitional Provision

Where—

(a) a fee has been paid under the 2004 Order after 7th July 2005 but before 29th December 2005 and

(b) if this Order had been in force when the fee was paid, the Lord Chancellor would have remitted the fee,

the fee shall be refunded.

Non-Contentious Probate Fees Order 2004

(SI 2004/3120)

The Lord Chancellor, in exercise of the powers conferred upon him by sections 92 and 108(6) of the Courts Act 2003, and section 128 of the Finance Act 1990 with the consent of the Treasury under section 92(1) of the Courts Act 2003 and after consultation with the Lord Chief Justice, the Master of the Rolls, the President of the Family Division, the Vice-Chancellor, the Head of Civil Justice and the Deputy Head of Civil Justice and the Civil Justice Council under section 92(5) and (6) of the Courts Act 2003, hereby makes the following Order:

1 Citation, Commencement and Interpretation

(1) This Order may be cited as the Non-Contentious Probate Fees Order 2004 and shall come into force on the 4th January 2005.

(2) In this Order—

(a) a fee referred to by number means the fee so numbered in Schedule 1 to this Order;

(b) 'assessed value' means the value of the net real and personal estate (excluding settled land if any) passing under the grant as shown—

(i) in the Inland Revenue affidavit (for a death occurring before 13th March 1975), or

(ii) in the Inland Revenue account (for a death occurring on or after 13th March 1975), or

(iii) in the case in which, in accordance with arrangements made between the President of the Family Division and the Commissioners of the Inland Revenue, or regulations made under section 256(1)(a) of the Inheritance Tax Act 1984 and from time to time in force, no such affidavit or account is required to be delivered, in the oath which is sworn to lead to the grant, and in the case of an application to reseal means the value, as shown, passing under the grant upon its being resealed;

(c) 'authorised place of deposit' means any place in which, by virtue of a direction given under section 124 of the Senior Courts Act 1981 original wills and other documents under the control of the High Court (either in the principal registry or in any district registry) are deposited and preserved;

(d) 'grant' means a grant of probate or letters of administration;

(e) 'district registry' includes the probate registry of Wales, any district probate registry and any sub-registry attached to it;

(f) 'the principal registry' means the Principal Registry of the Family Division and any sub-registry attached to it.

2 Fees to Be Taken

The fees set out in column 2 of Schedule 1 to this Order shall be taken in the principal registry and in each district registry in respect of the items described in column 1 in accordance with and subject to any directions specified in column 1.

3 Exclusion of Certain Death Gratuities

In determining the value of any personal estate for the purposes of this Order there shall be excluded the value of a death gratuity payable under section 17(2) of the Judicial Pensions Act 1981 or section 4(3) of the Judicial Pensions and Retirement Act 1993, or payable to the personal representatives of a deceased civil servant by virtue of a scheme made under section 1 of the Superannuation Act 1972.

4 Remission of Fees

Schedule 1A applies for the purpose of ascertaining whether a party is entitled to a remission or part remission of a fee prescribed by this Order.

5

The Lord Chancellor may, on the ground of financial hardship or for other reasonable cause, remit in whole or in part any fee prescribed by this Order.

6

(1) Where by any convention entered into by Her Majesty with any foreign power it is provided that no fee shall be required to be paid in respect of any proceedings, the fees specified in this Order shall not be taken in respect of those proceedings.
(2) Where any application for a grant is withdrawn before the issue of a grant, a registrar may reduce or remit a fee.
(3) Fee 7 shall not be taken where a search is made for research or similar purposes by permission of the President of the Family Division for a document over 100 years old filed in the principal registry or a district registry or another authorised place of deposit.

7 Special Exemption — Armed Forces

Where a fee has been paid or fees have been paid for the application of a grant (other than fee 3.2) and at the time of payment of that fee or those fees—
(a) the application for the grant was in respect of an estate exempt from Inheritance Tax by virtue of section 154 of the Inheritance Tax Act 1984 (exemption for members of the armed forces etc); and
(b) was in respect of a death occurring before 20th March 2003;
the Lord Chancellor shall upon receiving a written application refund the difference between any fee or fees paid and fee 3.2.

8 Revocation

The Order specified in Schedule 2 in so far as it was made under section 128 of the Finance Act 1990 shall be revoked.

SCHEDULE 1 FEES TO BE TAKEN

[Schedule introduced by article 2]

Column 1 *Number and description of fee*	*Column 2* *Amount of fee*
1 Application for a grant On an application for a grant (or for resealing a grant) other than on an application to which fee 3 applies, where the assessed value of the estate exceeds £5,000.	£45
2 Personal application fee Where the application under fee 1 is made by a personal applicant (not being an application to which fee 3 applies) fee 2 is payable in addition to fee 1 where the assessed value of the estate exceeds £5,000.	£60
3 Special applications 3.1 For a duplicate or second or subsequent grant (including one following a revoked grant) in respect of the same deceased person, other than a grant preceded only by a grant limited to settled land, to trust property, or to part of the estate.	£20
3.2 On an application for a grant relating to a death occurring on or after 20th March 2003 in respect of an estate exempt from inheritance tax by virtue of section 154 of the Inheritance Tax Act 1984 (exemption for members of the armed forces etc).	£10
4 Caveats For the entry or the extension of a caveat.	£20

Column 1 *Number and description of fee*	*Column 2* *Amount of fee*
5 Search On an application for a standing search to be carried out in an estate, for each period of six months including the issue of a copy grant and will, if any (irrespective of the number of pages).	£6
6 Deposit of wills On depositing a will for safe custody in the principal registry or a district registry.	£20
7 Inspection On inspection of any will or other document retained by the registry (in the presence of an officer of the registry).	£20
8 Copy documents On a request for a copy of any document whether or not provided as a certified copy:	
(a) for the first copy;	£6
(b) for every subsequent copy of the same document if supplied at the same time;	£1
(c) where copies of any document are made available on a computer disk or in other electronic form, for each such copy;	£6
(d) where a search of the index is required, in addition to fee 8(a), (b) or (c) as appropriate, for each period of 4 years searched after the first 4 years.	£4
9 Oaths Except on a personal application for a grant, for administering an oath:	
9.1 for each deponent to each affidavit;	£6
9.2 for marking each exhibit.	£2
10 Determination of costs For determining costs.	The same fees as are payable from time to time for determining costs under the Civil Proceedings Fees Order 2008, (the relevant fees are set out in fee 5 in Schedule 1 to that Order)
11 Settling documents For perusing and settling citations, advertisements, oaths, affidavits, or other documents, for each document settled.	£12

SCHEDULE 1A REMISSIONS AND PART REMISSIONS

[Schedule introduced by article 4]

1 Interpretation

(1) In this Schedule—

'child' means a child or young person in respect of whom a party is entitled to receive child benefit in accordance with section 141, and regulations made under section 142, of the Social Security Contributions and Benefits Act 1992;

'child care costs' has the meaning given in Part 3 of the Criminal Legal Aid (Financial Resources) Regulations 2013;

'couple' has the meaning given in section 3(5A) of the Tax Credits Act 2002;

'disposable monthly income' has the meaning given in paragraph 5;

'excluded benefits' means—

(a) any of the following benefits payable under the Social Security Contributions and Benefits Act 1992—

(i) attendance allowance paid under section 64;

(ii) severe disablement allowance;

(iii) carer's allowance;
(iv) disability living allowance;
(v) constant attendance allowance paid under section 104 or paragraph 4 or 7(2) of Schedule 8 as an increase to a disablement pension;
(vi) council tax benefit;
(vii) any payment made out of the social fund;
(viii) housing benefit;

(b) any direct payment made under the Community Care, Services for Carers and Children's Services (Direct Payments) (England) Regulations 2003 or the Community Care, Services for Carers and Children's Services (Direct Payments) (Wales) Regulations 2004;
(c) a back to work bonus payable under section 26 of the Jobseekers Act 1995;
(d) any exceptionally severe disablement allowance paid under the Personal Injuries (Civilians) Scheme 1983;
(e) any pension paid under the Naval, Military and Air Forces etc. (Disablement and Death) Service Pensions Order 2006;
(f) any payment made from the Independent Living Funds;
(g) any financial support paid under an agreement for the care of a foster child;
(h) personal independence payment under Part 4 of the Welfare Reform Act 2012; and
(i) armed forces independence payment under the Armed Forces and Reserve Forces (Compensation Scheme) Order 2011;

'gross annual income' means total annual income, for the 12 months preceding the application for remission or part remission, from all sources other than receipt of any of the excluded benefits;

'gross monthly income' means total monthly income, for the month in which the application for remission or part remission is made, from all sources other than receipt of any of the excluded benefits;

'the Independent Living Funds' means any payment made from the funds listed at regulation 20(2)(b) of the Criminal Legal Aid (Financial Resources) Regulations 2013;

'partner' means a person with whom the party lives as a couple and includes a person with whom the party is not currently living but from whom the party is not living separate and apart;

'party' means the individual who would, but for this Schedule, be liable to pay the fee required under this Order;

(2) Paragraphs 2, 3 and 4 do not apply to a party for whom civil legal services, for which a certificate has been issued under the Civil Legal Aid (Procedure) Regulations 2012, have been made available under arrangements made for the purposes of Part 1 of that Act for the purposes of the proceedings.

2 Full Remission of Fees — Qualifying Benefits

(1) No fee is payable under this Order if, at the time when a fee would otherwise be payable, the party is in receipt of a qualifying benefit.

(2) The following are qualifying benefits for the purpose of sub-paragraph (1)—
(a) income support under the Social Security Contributions and Benefits Act 1992;
(b) working tax credit, provided that no child tax credit is being paid to the party;
(c) income-based jobseeker's allowance under the Jobseekers Act 1995;
(d) guarantee credit under the State Pension Credit Act 2002; and
(e) income-related employment and support allowance under the Welfare Reform Act 2007.

3 Full Remission of Fees — Gross Annual Income

(1) No fee is payable under this Order if, at the time when the fee would otherwise be payable, the party has the number of children specified in column 1 of the following table and—
(a) if the party is single, the gross annual income of the party does not exceed the amount set out in the appropriate row of column 2; or
(b) if the party is one of a couple, the gross annual income of the couple does not exceed the amount set out in the appropriate row of column 3.

Column 1 *Number of children of fee-paying party*	*Column 2* *Single*	*Column 3* *Couple*
no children	£13,000	£18,000
1 child	£15,930	£20,930
2 children	£18,860	£23,860
3 children	£21,790	£26,790
4 children	£24,720	£29,720

(2) If the party paying the fee has more than 4 children then the relevant amount of gross annual income is the amount specified in the table for 4 children plus the sum of £2,930 for each additional child.

4 Full and Part Remission of Fees — Disposable Monthly Income

(1) No fee is payable under this Order if, at the time when the fee would otherwise be payable, the disposable monthly income of the party is £50 or less.

(2) The maximum amount of fee payable is—

(a) if the disposable monthly income of the party is more than £50 but does not exceed £210, an amount equal to one-quarter of every £10 of the party's disposable monthly income up to a maximum of £50; and

(b) if the disposable monthly income is more than £210, an amount equal to £50 plus one-half of every £10 over £200 of the party's disposable monthly income.

(3) Where the fee that would otherwise be payable under this Order is greater than the maximum fee which a party is required to pay as calculated in sub-paragraph (2), the fee will be remitted to the amount payable under that sub-paragraph.

5 Disposable Monthly Income

(1) A party's disposable monthly income is the gross monthly income of the party for the month in which the fee becomes payable ('the period') less the deductions referred to in sub-paragraphs (2) and (3).

(2) There is to be deducted from the gross monthly income—

(a) income tax paid or payable in respect of the period;

(b) any contributions estimated to have been paid under Part 1 of the Social Security Contributions and Benefits Act 1992 in respect of the period;

(c) either—

(i) monthly rent or monthly payment in respect of a mortgage debt or hereditable security, payable in respect of the only or main dwelling of the party, less any housing benefit paid under the Social Security Contributions and Benefits Act 1992; or

(ii) the monthly cost of the living accommodation of the party;

(d) any child care costs paid or payable in respect of the period;

(e) if the party is making bona fide payments for the maintenance of a child who is not a member of the household of the party, the amount of such payments paid or payable in respect of the period; and

(f) any amount paid or payable by the party, in respect of the period, in pursuance of a court order.

(3) There will be deducted from the gross monthly income an amount representing the cost of living expenses in respect of the period being—

(a) £315; plus

(b) £244 for each child of the party; plus

(c) £159, if the party has a partner.

6 Resources of Partners

(1) For the purpose of determining whether a party is entitled to the remission or part remission of a fee in accordance with this Schedule, the income of a partner, if any, is to be included as income of the party.

(2) The receipt by a partner of a qualifying benefit does not entitle a party to remission of a fee.

7 Application for Remission or Part Remission of Fees

(1) An application for remission or part remission of a fee must be made to the court officer at the time when the fee would otherwise be payable.
(2) Where a claim for full remission of fees is made, the party must provide documentary evidence of, as the case may be—
   (a) entitlement to a qualifying benefit; or
   (b) gross annual income and, if applicable, the children included for the purposes of paragraph 3.
(3) Where a claim for full or part remission of fees under paragraph 4 is made, the party must provide documentary evidence of—
   (a) such of the party's gross monthly income as is derived from—
      (i) employment;
      (ii) rental or other income received from persons living with the party by reason of their residence in the party's home;
      (iii) a pension; or
      (iv) a state benefit, not being an excluded benefit; and
   (b) any expenditure being deducted from the gross monthly income in accordance with paragraph 5(2).

8. Remission in Exceptional Circumstances

Where it appears to the Lord Chancellor that the payment of any fee prescribed by this Order would, owing to the exceptional circumstances of the particular case, involve undue financial hardship, the Lord Chancellor may reduce or remit the fee in that case.

9. Refunds

(1) Subject to sub-paragraph (3), where a party has not provided the documentary evidence required by paragraph 7 and a fee has been paid at a time when, under paragraphs 2, 3 or 4, it was not payable, the fee will be refunded if documentary evidence relating to the time when the fee became payable is provided at a later date.
(2) Subject to sub-paragraph (3), when a fee has been paid at a time where the Lord Chancellor, if all the circumstances had been known, would have reduced or remitted the fee under paragraph 8, the fee or the amount by which the fee would have been reduced, as the case may be, will be refunded.
(3) No refund will be made under this paragraph unless the party who paid the fee applies within 6 months of paying the fee.
(4) The Lord Chancellor may extend the period of 6 months mentioned in sub-paragraph (3) if the Lord Chancellor considers that there is a good reason for an application being made after the end of the period of 6 months.

SCHEDULE 2 ORDER REVOKED

[Schedule introduced by article 8]

Title	*Reference*
The Non-Contentious Probate Fees (Amendment) Order 2000	S.I. 2000/642

NOTES ON TEXT

The text printed above incorporates the following amendments:

arts 4 and 5 amended by Non-Contentious Probate Fees (Amendment) Order 2007 (SI 2007/2174), art. 3;

sch. 1 substituted by Non-Contentious Probate Fees (Amendment) Order 2011 (SI 2011/588); amended by Non-Contentious Probate Fees (Amendment) Order 2013 (SI 2013/1408);

sch. 1A inserted by Non-Contentious Probate Fees (Amendment) Order 2007 (SI 2007/2174), art. 4 and sch.; substituted by Non-Contentious Probate Fees (Amendment) Order 2009 (SI 2009/1497);

sch. 1A, para. 1, amended by: (a) Legal Aid, Sentencing and Punishment of Offenders Act 2012 (Consequential, Transitional and Saving Provisions) Regulations 2013 (SI 2013/534), sch., para. 14 (1 April 2013 subject to reg. 14(2)); (b) Personal Independence Payment (Supplementary Provisions and Consequential Amendments) Regulations 2013 (SI 2013/388), sch., para. 35 (8 April 2013); (c) Armed Forces and Reserve Forces Compensation Scheme (Consequential Provisions: Subordinate Legislation) Order 2013 (SI 2013/591), sch., para. 31 (8 April 2013).

Appendix 4 Selected Legislation

Access to Justice Act 1999

(1999 CHAPTER 22)

An Act to establish the Legal Services Commission, the Community Legal Service and the Criminal Defence Service; to amend the law of legal aid in Scotland; to make further provision about legal services; to make provision about appeals, courts, judges and court proceedings; to amend the law about magistrates and magistrates' courts; and to make provision about immunity from action and costs and indemnities for certain officials exercising judicial functions. [27th July 1999]

PART II OTHER FUNDING OF LEGAL SERVICES

Conditional Fee and Litigation Funding Agreements

27. Conditional Fee Agreements

[(1) *Substitutes s. 58 of, and inserts s. 58A into, the Courts and Legal Services Act 1990.*]

(2) In section 120(4) of the Courts and Legal Services Act 1990 (orders and regulations subject to affirmative procedure), for '58,' substitute '58(4),'.

28. Litigation Funding Agreements

In the Courts and Legal Services Act 1990, after section 58A (inserted by section 27 above) insert—

'**58B Litigation Funding Agreements**

(1) A litigation funding agreement which satisfies all of the conditions applicable to it by virtue of this section shall not be unenforceable by reason only of its being a litigation funding agreement.

(2) For the purposes of this section a litigation funding agreement is an agreement under which
- (a) a person ("the funder") agrees to fund (in whole or in part) the provision of advocacy or litigation services (by someone other than the funder) to another person ("the litigant"); and
- (b) the litigant agrees to pay a sum to the funder in specified circumstances.

(3) The following conditions are applicable to a litigation funding agreement—
- (a) the funder must be a person, or person of a description, prescribed by the Lord Chancellor;
- (b) the agreement must be in writing;
- (c) the agreement must not relate to proceedings which by virtue of section 58A(1) and (2) cannot be the subject of an enforceable conditional fee agreement or to proceedings of any such description as may be prescribed by the Lord Chancellor;
- (d) the agreement must comply with such requirements (if any) as may be so prescribed;
- (e) the sum to be paid by the litigant must consist of any costs payable to him in respect of the proceedings to which the agreement relates together with an amount calculated by reference to the funder's anticipated expenditure in funding the provision of the services; and
- (f) that amount must not exceed such percentage of that anticipated expenditure as may be prescribed by the Lord Chancellor in relation to proceedings of the description to which the agreement relates.

(4) Regulations under subsection (3)(a) may require a person to be approved by the Lord Chancellor or by a prescribed person.

(5) The requirements which the Lord Chancellor may prescribe under subsection (3)(d)—
- (a) include requirements for the funder to have provided prescribed information to the litigant before the agreement is made; and
- (b) may be different for different descriptions of litigation funding agreements.

(6) In this section (and in the definitions of "advocacy services" and "litigation services" as they apply for its purposes) "proceedings" includes any sort of proceedings for resolving disputes (and not just proceedings in a court), whether commenced or contemplated.

(7) Before making regulations under this section, the Lord Chancellor shall consult—
- (a) the designated judges;
- (b) the General Council of the Bar;

(c) the Law Society; and
(d) such other bodies as he considers appropriate.

(8) A costs order made in any proceedings may, subject in the case of court proceedings to rules of court, include provision requiring the payment of any amount payable under a litigation funding agreement.

(9) Rules of court may make provision with respect to the assessment of any costs which include fees payable under a litigation funding agreement.'

Costs

29. Recovery of Insurance Premiums by Way of Costs

Where in any proceedings a costs order is made in favour of any party who has taken out an insurance policy against the risk of incurring a liability in those proceedings, the costs payable to him may, subject in the case of court proceedings to rules of court, include costs in respect of the premium of the policy.

[Section 29 has been repealed by the Legal Aid, Sentencing and Punishment of Offenders Act 2012, s. 46(2), with effect from 1 April 2013 (Legal Aid, Sentencing and Punishment of Offenders Act 2012 (Commencement No. 5 and Saving Provision) Order 2013 (SI 2013/77), art. 3). This repeal does not apply in relation to a costs order made in favour of a party to proceedings who took out a costs insurance policy in relation to the proceedings before 1 April 2013 (2012 Act, s. 46(3)). By art. 4 of the Commencement Order, the repeal also does not apply to the following saved proceedings:

(a) proceedings relating to a claim for damages in respect of diffuse mesothelioma;
(b) publication and privacy proceedings;
(c) proceedings in England and Wales brought by a person acting in the capacity of—
  (i) a liquidator of a company which is being wound up in England and Wales or Scotland under Parts IV or V of the 1986 Act; or
  (ii) a trustee of a bankrupt's estate under Part IX of the 1986 Act;
(d) proceedings brought by a person acting in the capacity of an administrator appointed pursuant to the provisions of Part II of the 1986 Act;
(e) proceedings in England and Wales brought by a company which is being wound up in England and Wales or Scotland under Parts IV or V of the 1986 Act; or
(f) proceedings brought by a company which has entered administration under Part II of the 1986 Act.

By art. 1(2) of the Commencement Order:

'company' means a company within the meaning of section 1 of the Companies Act 2006 or a company which may be wound up under Part V of the 1986 Act;

'news publisher' means a person who publishes a newspaper, magazine or website containing news or information about or comment on current affairs;

'proceedings' has the same meaning as in the Courts and Legal Services Act 1990, s. 58A(4);

'publication and privacy proceedings' means proceedings for—
  (a) defamation;
  (b) malicious falsehood;
  (c) breach of confidence involving publication to the general public;
  (d) misuse of private information; or
  (e) harassment, where the defendant is a news publisher.]

30. Recovery Where Body Undertakes to Meet Costs Liabilities

(1) This section applies where a body of a prescribed description undertakes to meet (in accordance with arrangements satisfying prescribed conditions) liabilities which members of the body or other persons who are parties to proceedings may incur to pay the costs of other parties to the proceedings.

(2) If in any of the proceedings a costs order is made in favour of any of the members or other persons, the costs payable to him may, subject to subsection (3) and (in the case of court proceedings) to rules of court, include an additional amount in respect of any provision made by or on behalf of the body in connection with the proceedings against the risk of having to meet such liabilities.

(3) But the additional amount shall not exceed a sum determined in a prescribed manner; and there may, in particular, be prescribed as a manner of determination one which takes into account the likely cost to the member or other person of the premium of an insurance policy against the risk of incurring a liability to pay the costs of other parties to the proceedings.
(4) In this section 'prescribed' means prescribed by regulations made by the Lord Chancellor by statutory instrument; and a statutory instrument containing such regulations shall be subject to annulment in pursuance of a resolution of either House of Parliament.
(5) Regulations under subsection (1) may, in particular, prescribe as a description of body one which is for the time being approved by the Lord Chancellor or by a prescribed person.

[Section 30 has been repealed by the Legal Aid, Sentencing and Punishment of Offenders Act 2012, s. 47(1), with effect from 1 April 2013 (Legal Aid, Sentencing and Punishment of Offenders Act 2012 (Commencement No. 5 and Saving Provision) Order 2013 (SI 2013/77), art. 3). This repeal does not apply in relation to a costs order made in favour of a person to whom a body gave an undertaking before 1 April 2013 if the undertaking was given specifically in respect of the costs of other parties to proceedings relating to the matter which is the subject of the proceedings in which the costs order is made (2012 Act, s. 47(2)).]

31. Rules as to Costs

In section 51 of the Senior Courts Act 1981 (costs), in subsection (2) (rules regulating matters relating to costs), insert at the end 'or for securing that the amount awarded to a party in respect of the costs to be paid by him to such representatives is not limited to what would have been payable by him to them if he had not been awarded costs.'

PART IV APPEALS, COURTS, JUDGES AND COURT PROCEEDINGS

Appeals

54. Permission to Appeal

(1) Rules of court may provide that any right of appeal to —
 (a) a county court,
 (b) the High Court, or
 (c) the Court of Appeal, may be exercised only with permission.
(2) This section does not apply to a right of appeal in a criminal cause or matter.
(3) For the purposes of subsection (1) rules of court may make provision as to —
 (a) the classes of case in which a right of appeal may be exercised only with permission,
 (b) the court or courts which may give permission for the purposes of this section,
 (c) any considerations to be taken into account in deciding whether permission should be given, and
 (d) any requirements to be satisfied before permission may be given, and may make different provision for different circumstances.
(4) No appeal may be made against a decision of a court under this section to give or refuse permission (but this subsection does not affect any right under rules of court to make a further application for permission to the same or another court).
(5) For the purposes of this section a right to make an application to have a case stated for the opinion of the High Court constitutes a right of appeal.
(6) For the purposes of this section a right of appeal to the Court of Appeal includes—
 (a) the right to make an application for a new trial, and
 (b) the right to make an application to set aside a verdict, finding or judgment in any cause or matter in the High Court which has been tried, or in which any issue has been tried, by a jury.

55. Second Appeals

(1) Where an appeal is made to a county court or the High Court in relation to any matter, and on hearing the appeal the court makes a decision in relation to that matter, no appeal may be made to the Court of Appeal from that decision unless the Court of Appeal considers that—
 (a) the appeal would raise an important point of principle or practice, or
 (b) there is some other compelling reason for the Court of Appeal to hear it.
(2) This section does not apply in relation to an appeal in a criminal cause or matter.

56. Power to Prescribe Alternative Destination of Appeals

(1) The Lord Chancellor may by order provide that appeals which would otherwise lie to—
(a) a county court,
(b) the High Court, or
(c) the Court of Appeal,
shall lie instead to another of those courts, as specified in the order.
(2) This section does not apply to an appeal in a criminal cause or matter.
(3) An order under subsection (1)—
(a) may make different provision for different classes of proceedings or appeals, and
(b) may contain consequential amendments or repeals of enactments.
(4) Before making an order under subsection (1) the Lord Chancellor shall consult—
(a) the Lord Chief Justice,
(b) the Master of the Rolls,
(c) the President of the Queen's Bench Division,
(d) the President of the Family Division, and
(e) the Chancellor of the High Court.
(5) An order under subsection (1) shall be made by statutory instrument.
(6) No such order may be made unless a draft of it has been laid before and approved by resolution of each House of Parliament.
(7) For the purposes of this section an application to have a case stated for the opinion of the High Court constitutes an appeal.
(8) The Lord Chief Justice may nominate a judicial office holder (as defined in section 109(4) of the Constitutional Reform Act 2005) to exercise his functions under this section.

57. Assignment of Appeals to Court of Appeal

(1) Where in any proceedings in a county court or the High Court a person appeals, or seeks permission to appeal, to a court other than the Court of Appeal or the Supreme Court—
(a) the Master of the Rolls, or
(b) the court from which or to which the appeal is made, or from which permission to appeal is sought,
may direct that the appeal shall be heard instead by the Court of Appeal.
(2) The power conferred by subsection (l)(b) shall be subject to rules of court.

PART VII SUPPLEMENTARY

110. Short Title

This Act may be cited as the Access to Justice Act 1999.

COMMENCEMENT

The commencement dates of the provisions printed above are:

s. 27 (see note 1): 1 April 2000, by SI 2000/774, art. 2;
s. 28: to be brought into force by order of the Lord Chancellor under s. 108(1);
ss. 29 (see note 1) and 30 (see note 1): 1 April 2000, by SI 2000/774, art. 2;
s. 31: to be brought into force by order of the Lord Chancellor under s. 108(1);
ss. 54–7: 27 September 1999, by s. 108(3);
s. 110: 27 July 1999.

Note 1. SI 2000/900 makes the following transitional provisions:

1. This Order may be cited as the Access to Justice Act 1999 (Transitional Provisions) Order 2000 and shall come into force on 1st April 2000.
(2) In this Order a reference to a section by number alone means the section so numbered in the Access to Justice Act 1999.

2. —(1) Section 58A(6) and (7) of the Courts and Legal Services Act 1990 shall not apply, as regards a party to proceedings, to:
(a) any proceedings in relation to which that party entered into a conditional fee agreement before 1st April 2000; or

(b) any proceedings arising out of the same cause of action as any proceedings to which sub-paragraph (a) refers.

(2) The coming into force of section 27 (Conditional fee agreements) shall not affect the validity of any conditional fee agreement entered into before 1st April 2000, and any such agreement shall continue to have effect after that date as if section 27 had not come into force.

(3) In paragraphs 1(a) and (2) 'conditional fee agreement' has the same meaning as in section 58 of the Courts and Legal Services Act 1990 as that section stands immediately before the coming into force of section 27 of the Access to Justice Act 1999.

3. Section 29 (Recovery of insurance premiums by way of costs) shall not apply, as regards a party to proceedings, to:

(a) any proceedings in relation to which that party took out an insurance policy of the sort referred to in section 29 before 1st April 2000; or

(b) any proceedings arising out of the same cause of action as any proceedings to which sub-paragraph (a) refers.

4. Section 30 (Recovery where body undertakes to meet costs liabilities) shall not apply, as regards a party to proceedings, to:

(a) any proceedings in relation to which that party gave an undertaking before 1st April 2000 which, if it had been given after that date, would have been an undertaking to which section 30(1) applied; or

(b) any proceedings arising out of the same cause of action as any proceedings to which sub-paragraph (a) refers.

NOTES ON TEXT

Only selected provisions of the Act are printed above, incorporating the following amendments:

s. 28 (prospectively inserted s. 58B of Courts and Legal Services Act 1990) amended by: (a) Secretary of State for Constitutional Affairs Order 2003 (SI 2003/1887), sch. 2, para. 11(1)(b); (b) Transfer of Functions (Lord Chancellor and Secretary of State) Order 2005 (SI 2005/3429), sch., para. 4(b);

s. 30 amended by: (a) Secretary of State for Constitutional Affairs Order 2003 (SI 2003/1887), sch. 2, para. 11(1)(c); (b) Transfer of Functions (Lord Chancellor and Secretary of State) Order 2005 (SI 2005/3429), sch., para. 4(c);

s. 31 amended by Constitutional Reform Act 2005, sch. 11, para. 1(2);

s. 56 amended by Constitutional Reform Act 2005, sch. 4, para. 280 (in force by SI 2005/2505 and by SI 2006/2014);

s. 57 amended by Constitutional Reform Act 2005, sch. 9, para. 68(1) and (2) (in force by SI 2009/1604).

Access to Justice Act 1999 (Destination of Appeals) Order 2000

(SI 2000/1071)

The Lord Chancellor, in exercise of the powers conferred on him by section 56(1) and (3) of the Access to Justice Act 1999, having consulted as required by section 56(4), makes the following Order of which a draft has, in accordance with section 56(6), been laid before and approved by resolution of each House of Parliament:

1. Citation, Commencement and Interpretation

(1) This Order maybe cited as the Access to Justice Act 1999 (Destination of Appeals) Order 2000 and shall come into force on 2nd May 2000.

(2) In this Order—

(a) 'decision' includes any judgment, order or direction of the High Court or a county court;

(b) 'family proceedings' means proceedings which are business of any description which in the High Court is for the time being assigned to the Family Division and to no other Division by or under section 61 of (and Schedule 1 to) the Senior Courts Act 1981; and

(c) 'final decision' means a decision of a court that would finally determine (subject to any possible appeal or detailed assessment of costs) the entire proceedings whichever way the court decided the issues before it.

(3) A decision of a court shall be treated as a final decision where it—

(a) is made at the conclusion of part of a hearing or trial which has been split into parts: and

(b) would, if made at the conclusion of that hearing or trial, be a final decision under paragraph (2)(c).

(4) Articles 2 to 6—

(a) do not apply to an appeal in family proceedings: and

(b) are subject to —

(i) any enactment that provides a different route of appeal (other than section 16(1) of the Senior Courts Act 1981 or section 77(1) of the County Courts Act 1984); and

(ii) any requirement to obtain permission to appeal.

2. Appeals from the High Court

Subject to articles 4 and 5, an appeal shall lie to a judge of the High Court where the decision to be appealed is made by—

(a) a person holding an office referred to in Part II of Schedule 2 to the Senior Courts Act 1981;

(b) a district judge of the High Court; or

(c) a person appointed to act as a deputy for any person holding such an office as is referred to in sub-paragraphs (a) and (b) or to act as a temporary additional officer in any such office.

3. Appeals from a County Court

(1) Subject to articles 4 and 5 and to paragraph (2), an appeal shall lie from a decision of a county court to the High Court.

(2) Subject to articles 4 and 5, where the decision to be appealed is made by a district judge or deputy district judge of a county court, an appeal shall lie to a judge of a county court.

4. Appeals in a Claim Allocated to the Multi-track or in Specialist Proceedings

An appeal shall lie to the Court of Appeal where the decision to be appealed is a final decision—

(a) in a claim made under Part 7 of the Civil Procedure Rules 1998 and allocated to the multi-track under those Rules; or

(b) made in proceedings under the Companies Act 1985 or the Companies Act 1989* or to which Sections I, II or III of Part 57 or any of Parts 58 to 63 of the Civil Procedure Rules 1998 apply.

5. Appeals Where Decision Was Itself Made on Appeal

Where—

(a) an appeal is made to a county court or the High Court (other than from the decision of an officer of the court authorised to assess costs by the Lord Chancellor); and
(b) on hearing the appeal the court makes a decision,

an appeal shall lie from that decision to the Court of Appeal and not to any other court.

6. Transitional Provisions

Where a person has filed a notice of appeal or applied for permission to appeal before 2nd May 2000—

(a) this Order shall not apply to the appeal to which that notice or application relates; and
(b) that appeal shall lie to the court to which it would have lain before 2nd May 2000.

NOTES ON TEXT

The text printed above incorporates the following amendments:

arts 1 and 2 amended by Constitutional Reform Act 2005, sch. 11, para. 1(2);
art. 4 amended by: (a) Civil Procedure (Modification of Enactments) Order 2002 (SI 2002/439), art. 12; (b) Civil Procedure (Modification of Enactments) Order 2003 (SI 2003/490), art. 2
The following provisions are omitted: arts 7 and 8 (consequential amendments).

[* The references to the Companies Act 1985 and the Companies Act 1989 are to be construed as including references to the provisions of the Companies Act 2006 corresponding to repealed provisions of the Companies Acts 1985 and 1989 (Companies Act 2006, s. 1297(5)).]

Civil Jurisdiction and Judgments Act 1982

(1982 CHAPTER 27)

An Act to make further provision about the jurisdiction of courts and tribunals in the United Kingdom and certain other territories and about the recognition and enforcement of judgments given in the United Kingdom or elsewhere; to provide for the modification of certain provisions relating to legal aid; and for connected purposes. [13th July 1982]

PART I IMPLEMENTATION OF THE CONVENTIONS

Main Implementing Provisions

1. Interpretation of References to the Conventions and Contracting States

(1) In this Act—

'the 1968 Convention' means the Convention on jurisdiction and the enforcement of judgments in civil and commercial matters (including the Protocol annexed to that Convention), signed at Brussels on 27th September 1968;

'the 1971 Protocol' means the Protocol on the interpretation of the 1968 Convention by the European Court, signed at Luxembourg on 3rd June 1971;

'the Accession Convention' means the Convention on the accession to the 1968 Convention and the 1971 Protocol of Denmark, the Republic of Ireland and the United Kingdom, signed at Luxembourg on 9th October 1978;

'the 1982 Accession Convention' means the Convention on the accession of the Hellenic Republic to the 1968 Convention and the 1971 Protocol, with the adjustments made to them by the Accession Convention, signed at Luxembourg on 25th October 1982;

'the 1989 Accession Convention' means the Convention on the accession of the Kingdom of Spain and the Portuguese Republic to the 1968 Convention and the 1971 Protocol, with the adjustments made to them by the Accession Convention and the 1982 Accession Convention, signed at Donostia—San Sebastián on 26th May 1989;

'the 1996 Accession Convention' means the Convention on the accession of the Republic of Austria, the Republic of Finland and the Kingdom of Sweden to the 1968 Convention and the 1971 Protocol, with the adjustments made to them by the Accession Convention, the 1982 Accession Convention and the 1989 Accession Convention, signed at Brussels on 29th November 1996;

'the Brussels Conventions' means the 1968 Convention, the 1971 Protocol, the Accession Convention, the 1982 Accession Convention, the 1989 Accession Convention and the 1996 Accession Convention;

'the Lugano Convention' means the Convention on jurisdiction and the recognition and enforcement of judgments in civil and commercial matters, between the European Community and the Republic of Iceland, the Kingdom of Norway, the Swiss Confederation and the Kingdom of Denmark signed on behalf of the European Community on 30th October 2007;

'the Maintenance Regulation' means Council Regulation (EC) No. 4/2009 including as applied in relation to Denmark by virtue of the Agreement made on 19th October 2005 between the European Community and the Kingdom of Denmark;

'the Regulation' means Council Regulation (EC) No. 44/2001 of 22nd December 2000 on jurisdiction and the recognition and enforcement of judgments in civil and commercial matters, as amended from time to time and as applied by the Agreement made on 19th October 2005 between the European Community and the Kingdom of Denmark on jurisdiction and the recognition and enforcement of judgments in civil and commercial matters.

(2) In this Act, unless the context otherwise requires—

(a) references to, or to any provision of, the 1968 Convention or the 1971 Protocol are references to that Convention, Protocol or provision as amended by the Accession Convention, the 1982 Accession Convention, the 1989 Accession Convention and the 1996 Accession Convention; and

(b) any reference in any provision to a numbered Article without more is a reference—
(i) to the Article so numbered of the 1968 Convention, in so far as the provision applies in relation to that Convention, and
(ii) to the Article so numbered of the Lugano Convention, in so far as the provision applies in relation to that Convention,

and any reference to a sub-division of a numbered Article shall be construed accordingly.

(3) In this Act—

'Contracting State', without more, in any provision means—
(a) in the application of the provision in relation to the Brussels Conventions, a Brussels Contracting State; and
(b) in the application of the provision in relation to the Lugano Convention, a State bound by the Lugano Convention;

'Brussels Contracting State' means a state which is one of the original parties to the 1968 Convention or one of the parties acceding to that Convention under the Accession Convention, or under the 1982 Accession Convention, or under the 1989 Accession Convention, but only with respect to any territory—
(a) to which the Brussels Conventions apply; and
(b) which is excluded from the scope of the Regulation pursuant to Articles 349 and 355 of the Treaty on the Functioning of the European Union;

'Maintenance Regulation State', in any provision, in the application of that provision in relation to the Maintenance Regulation means a Member State;

'Regulation State' in any provision, in the application of that provision in relation to the Regulation, means a Member State;

'State bound by the Lugano Convention' in any provision, in the application of that provision in relation to the Lugano Convention has the same meaning as in Article 1(3) of that Convention.

(4) Any question arising as to whether it is the Regulation, any of the Brussels Conventions, or the Lugano Convention which applies in the circumstances of a particular case shall be determined as follows—
(a) in accordance with Article 64 of the Lugano Convention (which determines the relationship between the Brussels Conventions and the Lugano Convention); and
(b) in accordance with Article 68 of the Regulation (which determines the relationship between the Brussels Conventions and the Regulation).

PART IV MISCELLANEOUS PROVISIONS

Provisions Relating to Jurisdiction

24. Interim Relief and Protective Measures in Cases of Doubtful Jurisdiction

(1) Any power of a court in England and Wales or Northern Ireland to grant interim relief pending trial or pending the determination of an appeal shall extend to a case where—
(a) the issue to be tried, or which is the subject of the appeal, relates to the jurisdiction of the court to entertain the proceedings; or
(b) the proceedings involve the reference of any matter to the European Court under the 1971 Protocol; or
(c) the proceedings involve a reference of any matter relating to the Regulation or the Lugano Convention to the European Court under Article 68 of the Treaty establishing the European Community.

(2) Any power of a court in Scotland to grant protective measures pending the decision of any hearing shall apply to a case where—
(a) the subject of the proceedings includes a question as to the jurisdiction of the court to entertain them; or
(b) the proceedings involve the reference of a matter to the European Court under the 1971 Protocol; or
(c) the proceedings involve a reference of any matter relating to the Regulation or the Lugano Convention to the European Court under Article 68 of the Treaty establishing the European Community.

(3) Subsections (1) and (2) shall not be construed as restricting any power to grant interim relief or protective measures which a court may have apart from this section.

25 Interim Relief in England and Wales and Northern Ireland in the Absence of Substantive Proceedings

(1) The High Court in England and Wales or Northern Ireland shall have power to grant interim relief where—

(a) proceedings have been or are to be commenced in a Brussels Contracting State or a State bound by the Lugano Convention other than the United Kingdom or in a part of the United Kingdom other than that in which the High Court in question exercises jurisdiction; and

(b) they are or will be proceedings whose subject-matter is either within the scope of the Regulation as determined by Article 1 of the Regulation or within the scope of the Lugano Convention as determined by Article 1 of the Lugano Convention (whether or not the Regulation or the Lugano Convention has effect in relation to the proceedings).

(2) On an application for any interim relief under subsection (1) the court may refuse to grant that relief if, in the opinion of the court, the fact that the court has no jurisdiction apart from this section in relation to the subject-matter of the proceedings in question makes it inexpedient for the court to grant it.

(3) Her Majesty may by Order in Council extend the power to grant interim relief conferred by subsection (1) so as to make it exercisable in relation to proceedings of any of the following descriptions, namely—

(a) proceedings commenced or to be commenced otherwise than in a Brussels Contracting State or a State bound by the Lugano Convention;

(b) proceedings whose subject-matter is not within the scope either of the Regulation as determined by Article 1 of the Regulation or the Lugano Convention as determined by Article 1 of the Lugano Convention;

(c) arbitration proceedings.

(4) An Order in Council under subsection (3) —

(a) may confer power to grant only specified descriptions of interim relief;

(b) may make different provision for different classes of proceedings, for proceedings pending in different countries or courts outside the United Kingdom or in different parts of the United Kingdom, and for other different circumstances; and

(c) may impose conditions or restrictions on the exercise of any power conferred by the Order.

(5) An Order in Council under subsection (3) which confers power to grant interim relief in relation to arbitration proceedings may provide for the repeal of any provision of section 12(6) of the Arbitration Act 1950 or section 21(1) of the Arbitration Act (Northern Ireland) 1937 to the extent that it is superseded by the provisions of the Order.

(6) Any Order in Council under subsection (3) shall be subject to annulment in pursuance of a resolution of either House of Parliament.

(7) In this section 'interim relief', in relation to the High Court in England and Wales or Northern Ireland, means interim relief of any kind which that court has power to grant in proceedings relating to matters within its jurisdiction, other than—

(a) a warrant for the arrest of property; or

(b) provision for obtaining evidence.

PART V SUPPLEMENTARY AND GENERAL PROVISIONS

Domicile

41. Domicile of Individuals

(1) Subject to Article 52 (which contains provisions for determining whether a party is domiciled in a Contracting State), the following provisions of this section determine, for the purposes of the 1968 Convention or, as the case may be, and* this Act, whether an individual is domiciled in the United Kingdom or in a particular part of, or place in, the United Kingdom or in a state other than a Contracting State.

(2) An individual is domiciled in the United Kingdom if and only if—

(a) he is resident in the United Kingdom; and

[* The word 'and' should have been repealed when the preceding words, 'the Lugano Convention', were repealed.]

(b) the nature and circumstances of his residence indicate that he has a substantial connection with the United Kingdom.

(3) Subject to subsection (5), an individual is domiciled in a particular part of the United Kingdom if and only if—

(a) he is resident in that part; and

(b) the nature and circumstances of his residence indicate that he has a substantial connection with that part.

(4) An individual is domiciled in a particular place in the United Kingdom if and only if he—

(a) is domiciled in the part of the United Kingdom in which that place is situated; and

(b) is resident in that place.

(5) An individual who is domiciled in the United Kingdom but in whose case the requirements of subsection (3)(b) are not satisfied in relation to any particular part of the United Kingdom shall be treated as domiciled in the part of the United Kingdom in which he is resident.

(6) In the case of an individual who—

(a) is resident in the United Kingdom, or in a particular part of the United Kingdom; and

(b) has been so resident for the last three months or more,

the requirements of subsection (2)(b) or, as the case may be, subsection (3)(b) shall be presumed to be fulfilled unless the contrary is proved.

(7) An individual is domiciled in a state other than a Contracting State if and only if—

(a) he is resident in that state; and

(b) the nature and circumstances of his residence indicate that he has a substantial connection with that state.

41A. Domicile of Individuals for the Purposes of the Lugano Convention

(1) Subject to Article 59 of the Lugano Convention (which contains provisions for determining whether a party is domiciled in a State bound by the Lugano Convention), the following provisions of this section determine, for the purposes of the Lugano Convention, whether an individual is domiciled in the United Kingdom or in a particular part of, or place in, the United Kingdom or in a state other than a State bound by the Lugano Convention.

(2) An individual is domiciled in the United Kingdom if and only if—

(a) he is resident in the United Kingdom; and

(b) the nature and circumstances of his residence indicate that he has a substantial connection with the United Kingdom.

(3) Subject to subsection (5), an individual is domiciled in a particular part of the United Kingdom if and only if—

(a) he is resident in that part; and

(b) the nature and circumstances of his residence indicate that he has a substantial connection with that part.

(4) An individual is domiciled in a particular place in the United Kingdom if and only if he—

(a) is domiciled in the part of the United Kingdom in which that place is situated; and

(b) is resident in that place.

(5) An individual who is domiciled in the United Kingdom but in whose case the requirements of subsection (3)(b) are not satisfied in relation to any particular part of the United Kingdom shall be treated as domiciled in the part of the United Kingdom in which he is resident.

(6) In the case of an individual who—

(a) is resident in the United Kingdom, or in a particular part of the United Kingdom; and

(b) has been so resident for the last three months or more,

the requirements of subsection (2)(b) or, as the case may be, subsection (3)(b) shall be presumed to be fulfilled unless the contrary is proved.

(7) An individual is domiciled in a state other than a State bound by the Lugano Convention if and only if—

(a) he is resident in that state; and

(b) the nature and circumstances of his residence indicate that he has a substantial connection *with that state*.

42. Domicile and Seat of Corporation or Association

(1) For the purposes of this Act the seat of a corporation or association (as determined by this section) shall be treated as its domicile.

(2) The following provisions of this section determine where a corporation or association has its seat—

(a) for the purpose of Article 53 (which for the purposes of the 1968 Convention equates the domicile of such a body with its seat); and

(b) for the purposes of this Act other than the provisions mentioned in section 43(1)(b) and (c).

(3) A corporation or association has its seat in the United Kingdom if and only if—

(a) it was incorporated or formed under the law of a part of the United Kingdom and has its registered office or some other official address in the United Kingdom; or

(b) its central management and control is exercised in the United Kingdom.

(4) A corporation or association has its seat in a particular part of the United Kingdom if and only if it has its seat in the United Kingdom and—

(a) it has its registered office or some other official address in that part; or

(b) its central management and control is exercised in that part; or

(c) it has a place of business in that part.

(5) A corporation or association has its seat in a particular place in the United Kingdom if and only if it has its seat in the part of the United Kingdom in which that place is situated and—

(a) it has its registered office or some other official address in that place; or

(b) its central management and control is exercised in that place; or

(c) it has a place of business in that place.

(6) Subject to subsection (7), a corporation or association has its seat in a state other than the United Kingdom if and only if—

(a) it was incorporated or formed under the law of that state and has its registered office or some other official address there; or

(b) its central management and control is exercised in that state.

(7) A corporation or association shall not be regarded as having its seat in a Contracting State other than the United Kingdom if it is shown that the courts of that state would not regard it as having its seat there.

(8) In this section—

'business' includes any activity carried on by a corporation or association, and 'place of business' shall be construed accordingly;

'official address', in relation to a corporation or association, means an address which it is required by law to register, notify or maintain for the purpose of receiving notices or other communications.

General

50. Interpretation: General

In this Act, unless the context otherwise requires—

'the Accession Convention', 'the 1982 Accession Convention', 'the 1989 Accession Convention' and 'the 1996 Accession Convention' have the meaning given by section 1(1);

'Article' and references to sub-divisions of numbered Articles are to be construed in accordance with section 1(2)(b);

'association' means an unincorporated body of persons;

'Brussels Contracting State' has the meaning given by section 1(3);

'the Brussels Conventions' has the meaning given by section 1(1);

'Contracting State' has the meaning given by section 1(3);

'the 1968 Convention' has the meaning given by section 1(1), and references to that Convention and to provisions of it are to be construed in accordance with section 1(2)(a);

'corporation' means a body corporate, and includes a partnership subsisting under the law of Scotland;

'court', without more, includes a tribunal;

'court of law', in relation to the United Kingdom, means any of the following courts, namely—

(a) the Supreme Court,

(b) in England and Wales or Northern Ireland, the Court of Appeal, the High Court, the Crown Court, a county court and a magistrates' court,

(c) in Scotland, the Court of Session and a sheriff court;

'the Crown' is to be construed in accordance with section 51(2);
'enactment' includes an enactment comprised in Northern Ireland legislation;
'judgment', subject to sections 15(1) and 18(2) and to paragraph 1 of Schedules 6 and 7, means any judgment or order (by whatever name called) given or made by a court in any civil proceedings;
'the Lugano Convention' has the meaning given by section 1(1);
'magistrates' court', in relation to Northern Ireland, means a court of summary jurisdiction;
'the Maintenance Regulation' has the meaning given by section 1(1);
'Maintenance Regulation State' has the meaning given by section 1(3);
'modifications' includes additions, omissions and alterations;
'overseas country' means any country or territory outside the United Kingdom;
'part of the United Kingdom' means England and Wales, Scotland or Northern Ireland;
'the 1971 Protocol' has the meaning given by section 1(1), and references to that Protocol and to provisions of it are to be construed in accordance with section 1(2)(a);
'the Regulation' has the meaning given by section 1(1);
'Regulation State' has the meaning given by section 1(3);
'rules of court', in relation to any court, means rules, orders or regulations made by the authority having power to make rules, orders or regulations regulating the procedure of that court, and includes—
(a) in Scotland, Acts of Sederunt;
(b) in Northern Ireland, Judgment Enforcement Rules;
'State bound by the Lugano Convention' has the meaning given by section 1(3);
'statutory provision' means any provision contained in an Act, or in any Northern Ireland legislation, or in—
(a) subordinate legislation (as defined in section 21(1) of the Interpretation Act 1978); or
(b) any instrument of a legislative character made under any Northern Ireland legislation;
'tribunal'—
(a) means a tribunal of any description other than a court of law;
(b) in relation to an overseas country, includes, as regards matters relating to maintenance within the meaning of the 1968 Convention, any authority having power to give, enforce, vary or revoke a maintenance order.

51. Application to Crown

(1) This Act binds the Crown.
(2) In this section and elsewhere in this Act references to the Crown do not include references to Her Majesty in Her private capacity or to Her Majesty in right of Her Duchy of Lancaster or to the Duke of Cornwall.

55. Short Title

This Act may be cited as the Civil Jurisdiction and Judgments Act 1982.

NOTES ON TEXT

Only selected provisions of the Act are printed above, incorporating the following amendments:
s. 1(1) amended by: (a) SI 1989/1346, art. 3; (b) SI 1990/2591, arts 3 and 4; (c) Civil Jurisdiction and Judgments Act 1991, s. 2(1) to (3); (d) SI 2000/1824, art. 3; (e) SI 2001/3929, sch. 2, para. 1(a); (f) SI 2007/1655, reg. 2(1) and (2); (g) SI 2009/3131, reg. 3(1) and (2); (h) SI 2011/1215, regs 3 and 4(1) and (2);
s. 1(2) amended by: (a) SI 1990/2591, art. 5; (b) Civil Jurisdiction and Judgments Act 1991, s. 2(1) and (4); (c) SI 2000/1824, arts 4 and 9; (d) SI 2009/3131, reg. 3(1) and (3);
s. 1(3) amended by: (a) SI 1990/2591, art. 6; (b) Civil Jurisdiction and Judgments Act 1991, s. 2(1), (5) and (6); (c) SI 2000/1824, arts 5 and 10; (d) SI 2001/3929, sch. 2, para. 1(b); (e) SI 2007/1655, reg. 2(1) and (3); (f) SI 2009/3131, reg. 3(1) and (4); (g) SI 2011/1215, regs 3 and 4(1) and (3); (h) SI 2012/1809, sch., part 1;
s. 1(4) inserted by SI 2001/3929, sch. 2, para. 1(c); amended by SI 2009/3131, reg. 3(1) and (5);
s. 24 amended by: (a) SI 2001/3929, sch. 2, para. 9; (b) SI 2009/3131, reg. 16;
s. 25 amended by: (a) Civil Jurisdiction and Judgments Act 1991, sch. 2, para. 12; (b) SI 2009/3131, reg. 17;

s. 41 amended by: (a) Civil Jurisdiction and Judgments Act 1991, sch. 2, para. 16; (b) SI 2009/3131, reg. 18(1);
s. 41A inserted by SI 2009/3131, reg. 18(2);
s. 42 amended by: (a) Civil Jurisdiction and Judgments Act 1991, sch. 2, para. 17; (b) SI 2009/3131, reg. 19;
s. 50 amended by: (a) SI 1990/2591, art. 9; (b) Civil Jurisdiction and Judgments Act 1991, sch. 2, para. 25; (c) SI 2000/1824, art. 7; (d) SI 2001/3929, sch. 2, para. 18; (e) Constitutional Reform Act 2005, sch. 17, para. 23 (in force by SI 2009/1604); (f) SI 2009/3131, reg. 24; (g) SI 2011/1215, regs 3 and 5.

The titles of the statutory instruments referred to above (apart from commencement orders) are: Civil Jurisdiction and Judgments Act 1982 (Amendment) Order 1989 (SI 1989/1346); Civil Jurisdiction and Judgments Act 1982 (Amendment) Order 1990 (SI 1990/2591) (which came into force on 1 December 1991); Civil Jurisdiction and Judgments Act 1982 (Amendment) Order 2000 (SI 2000/1824) (part of which came into force on 1 August 2000 and the remainder on 1 January 2001); Civil Jurisdiction and Judgments Order 2001 (SI 2001/3929); Civil Jurisdiction and Judgments Regulations 2007 (SI 2007/1655); Civil Jurisdiction and Judgments Regulations 2009 (SI 2009/3131); Civil Jurisdiction and Judgments (Maintenance) (Rules of Court) Regulations 2011 (SI 2011/1215); Treaty of Lisbon (Changes in Terminology or Numbering) Order 2012 (SI 2012/1809).

The Civil Jurisdiction and Judgments Act 1991 was brought into force by SI 1992/745.

Civil Liability (Contribution) Act 1978

(1978 CHAPTER 47)

1. Entitlement to Contribution

(1) Subject to the following provisions of this section, any person liable in respect of any damage suffered by another person may recover contribution from any other person liable in respect of the same damage (whether jointly with him or otherwise).

(2) A person shall be entitled to recover contribution by virtue of subsection (1) above notwithstanding that he has ceased to be liable in respect of the damage in question since the time when the damage occurred, provided that he was so liable immediately before he made or was ordered or agreed to make the payment in respect of which the contribution is sought.

(3) A person shall be liable to make contribution by virtue of subsection (1) above notwithstanding that he has ceased to be liable in respect of the damage in question since the time when the damage occurred, unless he ceased to be liable by virtue of the expiry of a period of limitation or prescription which extinguished the right on which the claim against him in respect of the damage was based.

(4) A person who has made or agreed to make any payment in bona fide settlement or compromise of any claim made against him in respect of any damage (including a payment into court which has been accepted) shall be entitled to recover contribution in accordance with this section without regard to whether or not he himself is or ever was liable in respect of the damage, provided, however, that he would have been liable assuming that the factual basis of the claim against him could be established.

(5) A judgment given in any action brought in any part of the United Kingdom by or on behalf of the person who suffered the damage in question against any person from whom contribution is sought under this section shall be conclusive in the proceedings for contribution as to any issue determined by that judgment in favour of the person from whom the contribution is sought.

(6) References in this section to a person's liability in respect of any damage are references to any such liability which has been or could be established in an action brought against him in England and Wales by or on behalf of the person who suffered the damage; but it is immaterial whether any issue arising in any such action was or would be determined (in accordance with the rules of private international law) by reference to the law of a country outside England and Wales.

2. Assessment of Contribution

(1) Subject to subsection (3) below, in any proceedings for contribution under section 1 above the amount of the contribution recoverable from any person shall be such as may be found by the court to be just and equitable having regard to the extent of that person's responsibility for the damage in question.

(2) Subject to subsection (3) below, the court shall have power in any such proceedings to exempt any person from liability to make contribution or to direct that the contribution to be recovered from any person shall amount to a complete indemnity.

(3) Where the amount of the damages which have or might have been awarded in respect of the damage in question in any action brought in England and Wales by or on behalf of the person who suffered it against the person from whom the contribution is sought was or would have been subject to—

(a) any limit imposed by or under any enactment or by any agreement made before the damage occurred;

(b) any reduction by virtue of section 1 of the Law Reform (Contributory Negligence) Act 1945 or section 5 of the Fatal Accidents Act 1976; or

(c) any corresponding limit or reduction under the law of a country outside England and Wales;

the person from whom the contribution is sought shall not by virtue of any contribution awarded *under section 1 above* be required to pay in respect of the damage a greater amount than the amount of those damages as so limited or reduced.

3. Proceedings against Persons Jointly Liable for the Same Debt or Damage

Judgment recovered against any person liable in respect of any debt or damage shall not be a bar to an action, or to the continuance of an action, against any person who is (apart from any such bar) jointly liable with him in respect of the same debt or damage.

4. Successive Actions against Persons Liable (Jointly or Otherwise) for the Same Damage

If more than one action is bought in respect of any damage by or on behalf of the person by whom it was suffered against persons liable in respect of the damage (whether jointly or otherwise) the plaintiff shall not be entitled to costs in any of those actions, other than that in which judgment is first given, unless the court is of the opinion that there was reasonable ground for bringing the action.

5. Application to the Crown

Without prejudice to section 4(1) of the Crown Proceedings Act 1947 (indemnity and contribution), this Act shall bind the Crown, but nothing in this Act shall be construed as in any way affecting Her Majesty in Her private capacity (including in right of Her Duchy of Lancaster) or the Duchy of Cornwall.

6. Interpretation

(1) A person is liable in respect of any damage for the purposes of this Act if the person who suffered it (or anyone representing his estate or dependants) is entitled to recover compensation from him in respect of that damage (whatever the legal basis of his liability, whether tort, breach of contract, breach of trust or otherwise).

(2) References in this Act to an action brought by or on behalf of the person who suffered any damage include references to an action brought for the benefit of his estate or dependants.

(3) In this Act 'dependants' has the same meaning as in the Fatal Accidents Act 1976.

(4) In this Act, except in section 1(5) above, 'action' means an action brought in England and Wales.

7. Savings

(3) The right to recover contribution in accordance with section 1 above supersedes any right, other than an express contractual right, to recover contribution (as distinct from indemnity) otherwise than under this Act in corresponding circumstances; but nothing in this Act shall affect—

(a) any express or implied contractual or other right to indemnity; or

(b) any express contractual provision regulating or excluding contribution;

which would be enforceable apart from this Act (or render enforceable any agreement for indemnity or contribution which would not be enforceable apart from this Act).

Courts and Legal Services Act 1990

(1990 CHAPTER 41)

An Act to make provision with respect to the procedure in, and allocation of business between, the High Court and other courts; to make provision with respect to legal services;. . . and for connected purposes. [1st November 1990]

PART II LEGAL SERVICES

Miscellaneous

58. Conditional fee agreements

[This version of s. 58 does not apply to the 'saved proceedings' listed in the note to the Access to Justice Act 1999, s. 29, in this appendix (Legal Aid, Sentencing and Punishment of Offenders Act 2012 (Commencement No. 5 and Saving Provision) Order 2013 (SI 2013/77), arts 2(1)(a), 3(a) and 4).]

(1) A conditional fee agreement which satisfies all of the conditions applicable to it by virtue of this section shall not be unenforceable by reason only of its being a conditional fee agreement; but (subject to subsection (5)) any other conditional fee agreement shall be unenforceable.

(2) For the purposes of this section and section 58A—
  (a) a conditional fee agreement is an agreement with a person providing advocacy or litigation services which provides for his fees and expenses, or any part of them, to be payable only in specified circumstances;
  (b) a conditional fee agreement provides for a success fee if it provides for the amount of any fees to which it applies to be increased, in specified circumstances, above the amount which would be payable if it were not payable only in specified circumstances; and
  (c) references to a success fee, in relation to a conditional fee agreement, are to the amount of the increase.

(3) The following conditions are applicable to every conditional fee agreement—
  (a) it must be in writing;
  (b) it must not relate to proceedings which cannot be the subject of an enforceable conditional fee agreement; and
  (c) it must comply with such requirements (if any) as may be prescribed by the Lord Chancellor.

(4) The following further conditions are applicable to a conditional fee agreement which provides for a success fee—
  (a) it must relate to proceedings of a description specified by order made by the Lord Chancellor;
  (b) it must state the percentage by which the amount of the fees which would be payable if it were not a conditional fee agreement is to be increased; and
  (c) that percentage must not exceed the percentage specified in relation to the description of proceedings to which the agreement relates by order made by the Lord Chancellor.

(4A) The additional conditions are applicable to a conditional fee agreement which—
  (a) provides for a success fee, and
  (b) relates to proceedings of a description specified by order made by the Lord Chancellor for the purposes of this subsection.

(4B) The additional conditions are that—
  (a) the agreement must provide that the success fee is subject to a maximum limit,
  (b) the maximum limit must be expressed as a percentage of the descriptions of damages awarded in the proceedings that are specified in the agreement,
  (c) that percentage must not exceed the percentage specified by order made by the Lord Chancellor in relation to the proceedings or calculated in a manner so specified, and
  (d) those descriptions of damages may only include descriptions of damages specified by order made by the Lord Chancellor in relation to the proceedings.

(5) If a conditional fee agreement is an agreement to which section 57 of the Solicitors Act 1974 (non-contentious business agreements between solicitor and client) applies, subsection (1) shall not make it unenforceable.

[For the purposes of s. 58(4)(a), the relevant order is the Conditional Fee Agreements Order 2013 (SI 2013/689), art. 2. For the purposes of s. 58(4)(c), the relevant order is SI 2013/689, art. 3. For the purposes of s. 58(4B)(c), the relevant order is SI 2013/689, art. 5(1). For the purposes of s. 58(4)(d), the relevant order is SI 2013/689, art. 5(2).]

58. Conditional Fee Agreements

[This version of s. 58 applies to the 'saved proceedings' listed in the note to the Access to Justice Act 1999, s. 29, in this appendix.]

(1) A conditional fee agreement which satisfies all of the conditions applicable to it by virtue of this section shall not be unenforceable by reason only of its being a conditional fee agreement; but (subject to subsection (5)) any other conditional fee agreement shall be unenforceable.

(2) For the purposes of this section and section 58A—
  (a) a conditional fee agreement is an agreement with a person providing advocacy or litigation services which provides for his fees and expenses, or any part of them, to be payable only in specified circumstances; and
  (b) a conditional fee agreement provides for a success fee if it provides for the amount of any fees to which it applies to be increased, in specified circumstances, above the amount which would be payable if it were not payable only in specified circumstances.

(3) The following conditions are applicable to every conditional fee agreement—
  (a) it must be in writing;
  (b) it must not relate to proceedings which cannot be the subject of an enforceable conditional fee agreement; and
  (c) it must comply with such requirements (if any) as may be prescribed by the Lord Chancellor.

(4) The following further conditions are applicable to a conditional fee agreement which provides for a success fee—
  (a) it must relate to proceedings of a description specified by order made by the Lord Chancellor;
  (b) it must state the percentage by which the amount of the fees which would be payable if it were not a conditional fee agreement is to be increased; and
  (c) that percentage must not exceed the percentage specified in relation to the description of proceedings to which the agreement relates by order made by the Lord Chancellor.

(5) If a conditional fee agreement is an agreement to which section 57 of the Solicitors Act 1974 (non-contentious business agreements between solicitor and client) applies, subsection (1) shall not make it unenforceable.

58A. Conditional fee agreements: supplementary

[This version of s. 58A does not apply to the 'saved proceedings' listed in the note to the Access to Justice Act 1999, s. 29, in this appendix (Legal Aid, Sentencing and Punishment of Offenders Act 2012 (Commencement No. 5 and Saving Provision) Order 2013 (SI 2013/77), arts 2(1)(a), 3(a) and 4).]

(1) The proceedings which cannot be the subject of an enforceable conditional fee agreement are—
  (a) criminal proceedings, apart from proceedings under section 82 of the Environmental Protection Act 1990; and
  (b) family proceedings.

(2) In subsection (1) 'family proceedings' means proceedings under any one or more of the following—
  (a) the Matrimonial Causes Act 1973;
  (b) the Adoption and Children Act 2002;
  (c) the Domestic Proceedings and Magistrates' Courts Act 1978;
  (d) Part III of the Matrimonial and Family Proceedings Act 1984;
  (e) Parts I, II and IV of the Children Act 1989;
  (f) Parts 4 and 4A of the Family Law Act 1996;
  (fa) Chapter 2 of Part 2 of the Civil Partnership Act 2004 (proceedings for dissolution etc. of civil partnership);
  (fb) Schedule 5 to the 2004 Act (financial relief in the High Court or a county court etc.);
  (fc) Schedule 6 to the 2004 Act (financial relief in magistrates' courts etc.);
  (fd) Schedule 7 to the 2004 Act (financial relief in England and Wales after overseas dissolution etc. of a civil partnership); and
  (g) the inherent jurisdiction of the High Court in relation to children.

(3) The requirements which the Lord Chancellor may prescribe under section 58(3)(c)—
  (a) include requirements for the person providing advocacy or litigation services to have provided prescribed information before the agreement is made; and
  (b) may be different for different descriptions of conditional fee agreements (and, in particular, may be different for those which provide for a success fee and those which do not).

(4) In section 58 and this section (and in the definitions of 'advocacy services' and 'litigation services' as they apply for their purposes) 'proceedings' includes any sort of proceedings for resolving disputes (and not just proceedings in a court), whether commenced or contemplated.

(5) Before making an order under section 58(4), (4A) or (4B), the Lord Chancellor shall consult—
  (a) the designated judges;
  (b) the General Council of the Bar;
  (c) the Law Society; and
  (d) such other bodies as he considers appropriate.

(6) A costs order made in proceedings may not include provision requiring the payment by one party of all or part of a success fee payable by another party under a conditional fee agreement.

(7) Rules of court may make provision with respect to the assessment of any costs which include fees payable under a conditional fee agreement (including one which provides for a success fee).

The following transitional provision is made by the Legal Aid, Sentencing and Punishment of Offenders Act 2012, s. 44(6):

The [substitution of a new subsection (6) in the Courts and Legal Services Act 1990, s. 58A] does not prevent a costs order including provision in relation to a success fee payable by a person ('P') under a conditional fee agreement entered into before [1 April 2013] if—

(a) the agreement was entered into specifically for the purposes of the provision to P of advocacy or litigation services in connection with the matter that is the subject of the proceedings in which the costs order is made, or

(b) advocacy or litigation services were provided to P under the agreement in connection with that matter before the commencement day.

58A. Conditional Fee Agreements: Supplementary

[This version of s. 58A applies to the 'saved proceedings' listed in the note to the Access to Justice Act 1999, s. 29, in this appendix.]

(1) The proceedings which cannot be the subject of an enforceable conditional fee agreement are—
  (a) criminal proceedings, apart from proceedings under section 82 of the Environmental Protection Act 1990 and
  (b) family proceedings.

(2) In subsection (1) 'family proceedings' means proceedings under any one or more of the following—
  (a) the Matrimonial Causes Act 1973;
  (b) the Adoption and Children Act 2002;
  (c) the Domestic Proceedings and Magistrates' Courts Act 1978;
  (d) Part III of the Matrimonial and Family Proceedings Act 1984;
  (e) Parts I, II and IV of the Children Act 1989;
  (f) Parts 4 and 4A of the Family Law Act 1996;
  (fa) chapter 2 of Part 2 of the Civil Partnership Act 2004 (proceedings for dissolution etc. of civil partnership);
  (fb) Schedule 5 to the 2004 Act (financial relief in the High Court or a county court etc.);
  (fc) Schedule 6 to the 2004 Act (financial relief in magistrates' courts etc.);
  (fd) Schedule 7 to the 2004 Act (financial relief in England and Wales after overseas dissolution etc. of a civil partnership); and
  (g) the inherent jurisdiction of the High Court in relation to children.

(3) The requirements which the Lord Chancellor may prescribe under section 58(3)(c) —
  (a) include requirements for the person providing advocacy or litigation services to have provided prescribed information before the agreement is made; and
  (b) may be different for different descriptions of conditional fee agreements (and, in particular, may be different for those which provide for a success fee and those which do not).

(4) In section 58 and this section (and in the definitions of 'advocacy services' and 'litigation services' as they apply for their purposes) 'proceedings' includes any sort of proceedings for resolving disputes (and not just proceedings in a court), whether commenced or contemplated.

(5) Before making an order under section 58(4), the Lord Chancellor shall consult—
(a) the designated judges;
(b) the General Council of the Bar;
(c) the Law Society; and
(d) such other bodies as he considers appropriate.

(6) A costs order made in any proceedings may, subject in the case of court proceedings to rules of court, include provision requiring the payment of any fees payable under a conditional fee agreement which provides for a success fee.

(7) Rules of court may make provision with respect to the assessment of any costs which include fees payable under a conditional fee agreement (including one which provides for a success fee).

58AA. Damages-based Agreements

(1) A damages-based agreement which satisfies the conditions in subsection (4) is not unenforceable by reason only of its being a damages-based agreement.

(2) But (subject to subsection (9)) a damages-based agreement which does not satisfy those conditions is unenforceable.

(3) For the purposes of this section—
(a) a damages-based agreement is an agreement between a person providing advocacy services, litigation services or claims management services and the recipient of those services which provides that—
(i) the recipient is to make a payment to the person providing the services if the recipient obtains a specified financial benefit in connection with the matter in relation to which the services are provided, and
(ii) the amount of that payment is to be determined by reference to the amount of the financial benefit obtained;
(b) [*repealed*].

(4) The agreement—
(a) must be in writing;
(aa) must not relate to proceedings which by virtue of section 58A(1) and (2) cannot be the subject of an enforceable conditional fee agreement or to proceedings of a description prescribed by the Lord Chancellor;
(b) if regulations so provide, must not provide for a payment above a prescribed amount or for a payment above an amount calculated in a prescribed manner;
(c) must comply with such other requirements as to its terms and conditions as are prescribed; and
(d) must be made only after the person providing services under the agreement has complied with such requirements (if any) as may be prescribed as to the provision of information.

(5) Regulations under subsection (4) are to be made by the Lord Chancellor and may make different provision in relation to different descriptions of agreements.

(6) Before making regulations under subsection (4) the Lord Chancellor must consult—
(a) the designated judges,
(b) the General Council of the Bar,
(c) the Law Society, and
(d) such other bodies as the Lord Chancellor considers appropriate.

(6A) Rules of court may make provision with respect to the assessment of costs in proceedings where a party in whose favour a costs order is made has entered into a damages-based agreement in connection with the proceedings.

(7) In this section—
'payment' includes a transfer of assets and any other transfer of money's worth (and the reference in subsection (4)(b) to a payment above a prescribed amount, or above an amount calculated in a prescribed manner, is to be construed accordingly);
'claims management services' has the same meaning as in Part 2 of the Compensation Act 2006 (see section 4(2) of that Act).

(7A) In this section (and in the definitions of 'advocacy services' and 'litigation services' as they apply for the purposes of this section) 'proceedings' includes any sort of proceedings for resolving disputes (and not just proceedings in a court), whether commenced or contemplated.

(8) Nothing in this section applies to an agreement entered into before the coming into force of the first regulations made under subsection (4).

(9) Where section 57 of the Solicitors Act 1974 (non-contentious business agreements between solicitor and client) applies to a damages-based agreement other than one relating to an employment matter, subsections (1) and (2) of this section do not make it unenforceable.

(10) For the purposes of subsection (9) a damages-based agreement relates to an employment matter if the matter in relation to which the services are provided is a matter that is, or could become, the subject of proceedings before an employment tribunal.

[For the purposes of s. 58AA(4)(b), the relevant regulations are the Damages-based Agreements Regulations 2013 (SI 2013/609), regs 4 and 7. For the purposes of s. 58AA(4)(c), the requirements are prescribed by SI 2013/609, reg 8. For the purposes of s. 58AA(4)(d), the requirements are prescribed by SI 2013/609, reg 5. The version of s. 58AA printed here does not apply in relation to an agreement entered into before 1 April 2013 (Legal Aid, Sentencing and Punishment of Offenders Act 2012, s. 45(13).]

58B Litigation Funding Agreements

[For the text of this section, which has not yet been brought into force, see the Access to Justice Act 1999, s. 28, in this appendix.]

58C Recovery of Insurance Premiums by way of Costs

(1) A costs order made in favour of a party to proceedings who has taken out a costs insurance policy may not include provision requiring the payment of an amount in respect of all or part of the premium of the policy, unless such provision is permitted by regulations under subsection (2).

(2) The Lord Chancellor may by regulations provide that a costs order may include provision requiring the payment of such an amount where—
- (a) the order is made in favour of a party to clinical negligence proceedings of a prescribed description,
- (b) the party has taken out a costs insurance policy insuring against the risk of incurring a liability to pay for one or more expert reports in respect of clinical negligence in connection with the proceedings (or against that risk and other risks),
- (c) the policy is of a prescribed description,
- (d) the policy states how much of the premium relates to the liability to pay for an expert report or reports in respect of clinical negligence ('the relevant part of the premium'), and
- (e) the amount is to be paid in respect of the relevant part of the premium.

(3) Regulations under subsection (2) may include provision about the amount that may be required to be paid by the costs order, including provision that the amount must not exceed a prescribed maximum amount.

(4) The regulations may prescribe a maximum amount, in particular, by specifying—
- (a) a percentage of the relevant part of the premium;
- (b) an amount calculated in a prescribed manner.

(5) In this section—

'clinical negligence' means breach of a duty of care or trespass to the person committed in the course of the provision of clinical or medical services (including dental or nursing services);

'clinical negligence proceedings' means proceedings which include a claim for damages in respect of clinical negligence;

'costs insurance policy', in relation to a party to proceedings, means a policy insuring against the risk of the party incurring a liability in those proceedings;

'expert report' means a report by a person qualified to give expert advice on all or most of the matters that are the subject of the report;

'proceedings' includes any sort of proceedings for resolving disputes (and not just proceedings in court), whether commenced or contemplated.

[Section 58C does not apply in relation to a costs order made in favour of a party to proceedings who took out a costs insurance policy in relation to the proceedings before 1 April 2013 (Legal Aid, Sentencing and Punishment of Offenders Act 2012, s. 46(3)). It also does not apply to the 'saved proceedings' listed in the note to the Access to Justice Act 1999, s. 29, in this appendix (Legal Aid, Sentencing and Punishment of Offenders Act 2012 (Commencement No. 5 and Saving Provision) Order 2013 (SI 2013/77), arts 2(1)(c), 3(c) and 4).

The regulations made under s. 58C(2) are the Recovery of Costs Insurance Premiums in Clinical Negligence Proceedings (No. 2) Regulations 2013 (SI 2013/739).]

61. Right of Barrister to Enter into Contract for the Provision of His Services

(1) Any rule of law which prevents a barrister from entering into a contract for the provision of his services as a barrister is hereby abolished.

(2) Nothing in subsection (1) prevents the General Council of the Bar from making rules (however described) which prohibit barristers from entering into contracts or restrict their right to do so.

PART VI MISCELLANEOUS AND SUPPLEMENTAL

Supplemental

119. Interpretation

(1) In this Act—

...

'advocacy services' means any services which it would be reasonable to expect a person who is exercising, or contemplating exercising, a right of audience in relation to any proceedings, or contemplated proceedings, to provide;

'authorised advocate' means any person (including a barrister or solicitor) who has a right of audience granted by an authorised body in accordance with the provisions of this Act;

'authorised body' and 'appropriate authorised body'—

(a) in relation to any right of audience or proposed right of audience, have the meanings given in section 27; and

(b) in relation to any right to conduct litigation or proposed right to conduct litigation, have the meanings given in section 28;

'authorised litigator' means any person (including a solicitor) who has a right to conduct litigation granted by an authorised body in accordance with the provisions of this Act;...

'court' includes—

(a) any tribunal which the Council on Tribunals is under a duty to keep under review;

(b) any court-martial; and

(c) a statutory inquiry within the meaning of section 19(1) of the Tribunals and Inquiries Act 1971;

'designated judge' means the Lord Chief Justice, the Master of the Rolls, the President of the Queen's Bench Division, the President of the Family Division or the Chancellor of the High Court;...

'litigation services' means any services which it would be reasonable to expect a person who is exercising, or contemplating exercising, a right to conduct litigation in relation to any proceedings, or contemplated proceedings, to provide;

'member', in relation to any professional or other body (other than any body established by this Act), includes any person who is not a member of that body but who may be subject to disciplinary sanctions for failure to comply with any of that body's rules;

'multi-national partnership' has the meaning given by section 89(9);

'probate services' means the drawing or preparation of any papers on which to found or oppose a grant of probate or a grant of letters of administration and the administration of the estate of a deceased person;

'prescribed' means prescribed by regulations under this Act;

'proceedings' means proceedings in any court;...

'right of audience' means the right to appear before and address a court including the right to call and examine witnesses;

'right to conduct litigation' means the right—
(a) to issue proceedings before any court; and
(b) to perform any ancillary functions in relation to proceedings (such as entering appearances to actions);
'solicitor' means solicitor of the Senior Courts; and
'the statutory objective' has the meaning given in section 17(2)....

124. Commencement

(1) The following provisions come into force on the passing of this Act—
(a) sections 1, 5, 119 to 123, this section and section 125(1); and
(b) paragraphs 2 and 3 of Schedule 17.
(2) The following provisions come into force at the end of the period of two months beginning on the day on which this Act is passed—
(a) sections 6, 8, 11, 16, 64, 65, 72, 73, 85, 87 and 88, 90 to 92, 94 to 97, 98 and 108 to 110;
(b) paragraphs 1, 11, 12, 16 and 20 of Schedule 17;
(c) paragraphs 7, 8, 14 to 16, 55 and 57 of Schedule 18; and
(d) paragraph 1 of Schedule 19.
(3) The other provisions of this Act shall come into force on such date as may be appointed by order made by the Lord Chancellor or by the Secretary of State or by both, acting jointly.
(4) Different dates may be appointed for different provisions of this Act and for different purposes.
[*Section 58 was brought into force by SI 1993/2132, ss. 61 and 62 by SI 1990/2484, ss. 63(1)(a) and (2) and 113 by SI 1991/608.*]

125. Short Title, Minor and Consequential Amendments, Transitional and Repeals

(1) This Act may be cited as the Courts and Legal Services Act 1990.

NOTES ON TEXT

Only selected provisions of the Act are printed above, incorporating the following amendments:

'Senior Courts' substituted for 'Supreme Court' (Constitutional Reform Act 2005, sch. 11, paras 1(2) and 4);

s. 58 substituted by Access to Justice Act 1999, s. 27(1) (in force by SI 2000/774, art. 2); for a transitional provision see the notes on commencement at the end of the Access to Justice Act 1999 in this appendix; s. 58 amended by: (a) Secretary of State for Constitutional Affairs Order 2003 (SI 2003/1887), sch. 2, para. 8(1); (b) Transfer of Functions (Lord Chancellor and Secretary of State) Order 2005 (SI 2005/3429), sch., para. 2; (c) Legal Aid, Sentencing and Punishment of Offenders Act 2012, s. 44(1) and (2) (in force by SI 2013/77, arts 2(1)(a) and 3(a), not applying, by art. 4, to 'saved proceedings');

s. 58A inserted by Access to Justice Act 1999, s. 27(1) (in force by SI 2000/774, art. 2); for a transitional provision see the notes on commencement at the end of the Access to Justice Act 1999 in this appendix; s. 58A amended by: (a) Secretary of State for Constitutional Affairs Order 2003 (SI 2003/1887), sch. 2, para. 8(1); (b) Adoption and Children Act 2002, sch. 3, para. 80 (in force by SI 2005/2213); (c) Civil Partnership Act 2004, sch. 27, para. 138, and sch. 30 (in force by SI 2005/3175); (d) Transfer of Functions (Lord Chancellor and Secretary of State) Order 2005 (SI 2005/3429), sch., para. 2; (e) Forced Marriage (Civil Protection) Act 2007, s. 3 and sch. 2; (f) Legal Aid, Sentencing and Punishment of Offenders Act 2012, s. 44(3) and (4) (in force by SI 2013/77, arts 2(1)(a) and 3(a), not applying, by art. 4, to 'saved proceedings');

s. 58AA inserted by the Coroners and Justice Act 2009, s. 154(1) and (2) (in force by s. 182(1)(e)); amended by Legal Aid, Sentencing and Punishment of Offenders Act 2012, s. 45 (in force by SI 2013/77, arts 2(1)(b) and 3(b), subject to s. 45(13) of the 2012 Act);

s. 58C inserted by Legal Aid, Sentencing and Punishment of Offenders Act 2012, s. 46(1) (in force by SI 2013/77, arts 2(1)(c) and 3(c), not applying, by art. 4, to 'saved proceedings');

s. 119 amended by: (a) Access to Justice Act 1999, sch. 6, para. 10 (in force by SI 1999/2657, art. 2(a)); (b) Constitutional Reform Act 2005, sch. 4, para. 216 (in force by SI 2005/2505).

Damages-based Agreements Regulations 2013

(SI 2013/609)

The Lord Chancellor in exercise of the powers conferred by sections 58AA(4) and (5) and 120(3) of the Courts and Legal Services Act 1990, having consulted in accordance with section 58AA(6) of that Act, makes the following Regulations, a draft of which has been laid before and approved by resolution of each House of Parliament in accordance with section 120(4) of that Act.

1. Citation, Commencement, Interpretation and Application

(1) These Regulations may be cited as the Damages-based Agreements Regulations 2013 and come into force on 1st April 2013.

(2) In these Regulations—

'the Act' means the Courts and Legal Services Act 1990;

'claim for personal injuries' has the same meaning as in Rule 2.3 of the Civil Procedure Rules 1998;

'client' means the person who has instructed the representative to provide advocacy services, litigation services (within section 119 of the Act) or claims management services (within the meaning of section 4(2)(b) of the Compensation Act 2006) and is liable to make a payment for those services;

'costs' means the total of the representative's time reasonably spent, in respect of the claim or proceedings, multiplied by the reasonable hourly rate of remuneration of the representative;

'employment matter' means a matter that is, or could become, the subject of proceedings before an employment tribunal;

'expenses' means disbursements incurred by the representative, including the expense of obtaining an expert's report and, in an employment matter only, counsel's fees;

'payment' means that part of the sum recovered in respect of the claim or damages awarded that the client agrees to pay the representative, and excludes expenses but includes, in respect of any claim or proceedings to which these regulations apply other than an employment matter, any disbursements incurred by the representative in respect of counsel's fees;

'representative' means the person providing the advocacy services, litigation services or claims management services to which the damages-based agreement relates.

(3) Subject to paragraphs (4), (5) and (6), these Regulations shall apply to all damages-based agreements entered into on or after the date on which these Regulations come into force.

(4) Subject to paragraph (6), these Regulations shall not apply to any damages-based agreement to which section 57 of the Solicitors Act 1974 (non-contentious business agreements between solicitor and client) applies.

(5) In these Regulations—

(a) regulation 4 does not apply; and

(b) regulations 5, 6, 7 and 8 only apply,

to any damages-based agreement in respect of an employment matter.

(6) Where these Regulations relate to an employment matter, they apply to all damages-based agreements signed on or after the date on which these Regulations come into force.

2. Revocation of 2010 Regulations and Transitional Provision

(1) Subject to paragraph (2), the Damages-based Agreements Regulations 2010 ('the 2010 Regulations') are revoked.

(2) The 2010 Regulations shall continue to have effect in respect of any damages-based agreement to which those Regulations applied and which was signed before the date on which these Regulations come into force.

3. Requirements of an Agreement in respect of All Damages-based Agreements

The requirements prescribed for the purposes of section 58AA(4)(c) of the Act are that the terms and conditions of a damages-based agreement must specify—

(a) the claim or proceedings or parts of them to which the agreement relates;
(b) the circumstances in which the representative's payment, expenses and costs, or part of them, are payable; and
(c) the reason for setting the amount of the payment at the level agreed, which, in an employment matter, shall include having regard to, where appropriate, whether the claim or proceedings is one of several similar claims or proceedings.

4. Payment in respect of Claims or Proceedings other than an Employment Matter

(1) In respect of any claim or proceedings, other than an employment matter, to which these Regulations apply, a damages-based agreement must not require an amount to be paid by the client other than—
 (a) the payment, net of—
  (i) any costs (including fixed costs under Part 45 of the Civil Procedure Rules 1998); and
  (ii) where relevant, any sum in respect of disbursements incurred by the representative in respect of counsel's fees,
 that have been paid or are payable by another party to the proceedings by agreement or order; and
 (b) any expenses incurred by the representative, net of any amount which has been paid or is payable by another party to the proceedings by agreement or order.
(2) In a claim for personal injuries—
 (a) the only sums recovered by the client from which the payment shall be met are—
  (i) general damages for pain, suffering and loss of amenity; and
  (ii) damages for pecuniary loss other than future pecuniary loss,
  net of any sums recoverable by the Compensation Recovery Unit of the Department for Work and Pensions; and
 (b) subject to paragraph (4), a damages-based agreement must not provide for a payment above an amount which, including VAT, is equal to 25% of the combined sums in paragraph (2)(a)(i) and (ii) which are ultimately recovered by the client.
(3) Subject to paragraph (4), in any other claim or proceedings to which this regulation applies, a damages-based agreement must not provide for a payment above an amount which, including VAT, is equal to 50% of the sums ultimately recovered by the client.
(4) The amounts prescribed in paragraphs (2)(b) and (3) shall only apply to claims or proceedings at first instance.

NOTES ON TEXT

Regulations 5–8 (employment matters) have been omitted.

Fatal Accidents Act 1976

(1976 CHAPTER 30)

1. Right of Action for Wrongful Act Causing Death

(1) If death is caused by any wrongful act, neglect or default which is such as would (if death had not ensued) have entitled the person injured to maintain an action and recover damages in respect thereof, the person who would have been liable if death had not ensued shall be liable to an action for damages, notwithstanding the death of the person injured.

(2) Subject to section 1A(2) below, every such action shall be for the benefit of the dependants of the person ('the deceased') whose death has been so caused.

(3) In this Act 'dependant' means—

(a) the wife or husband or former wife or husband of the deceased;

(b) any person who—

(i) was living with the deceased in the same household immediately before the date of the death; and

(ii) had been living with the deceased in the same household for at least two years before that date; and

(iii) was living during the whole of that period as the husband or wife of the deceased;

(c) any parent or other ascendant of the deceased;

(d) any person who was treated by the deceased as his parent;

(e) any child or other descendant of the deceased;

(f) any person (not being a child of the deceased) who, in the case of any marriage to which the deceased was at any time a party, was treated by the deceased as a child of the family in relation to that marriage;

(g) any person who is, or is the issue of, a brother, sister, uncle or aunt of the deceased.

(4) The reference to the former wife or husband of the deceased in subsection (3)(a) above includes a reference to a person whose marriage to the deceased has been annulled or declared void as well as a person whose marriage to the deceased has been dissolved.

(5) In deducing any relationship for the purposes of subsection (3) above—

(a) any relationship by affinity shall be treated as a relationship of consanguinity, any relationship of the half blood as a relationship of the whole blood, and the stepchild of any person as his child, and

(b) an illegitimate person shall be treated as the legitimate child of his mother and reputed father.

(6) Any reference in this Act to injury includes any disease and any impairment of a person's physical or mental condition.

1A. Bereavement

(1) An action under this Act may consist of or include a claim for damages for bereavement.

(2) A claim for damages for bereavement shall only be for the benefit—

(a) of the wife or husband of the deceased; and

(b) where the deceased was a minor who was never married—

(i) of his parents, if he was legitimate; and

(ii) of his mother, if he was illegitimate.

(3) Subject to subsection (5) below, the sum to be awarded as damages under this section shall be £7,500.

(4) Where there is a claim for damages under this section for the benefit of both the parents of the deceased, the sum awarded shall be divided equally between them (subject to any deduction falling to be made in respect of costs not recovered from the defendant).

(5) The Lord Chancellor may by order made by statutory instrument, subject to annulment in pursuance of a resolution of either House of Parliament, amend this section by varying the sum for the time being specified in subsection (3) above.

2. Persons Entitled to Bring the Action

(1) The action shall be brought by and in the name of the executor or administrator of the deceased.

(2) If—

(a) there is no executor or administrator of the deceased, or

(b) no action is brought within six months after the death by and in the name of an executor or administrator of the deceased,

the action may be brought by and in the name of all or any of the persons for whose benefit an executor or administrator could have brought it.

(3) Not more than one action shall lie for and in respect of the same subject matter of complaint.

(4) The plaintiff in the action shall be required to deliver to the defendant or his solicitor full particulars of the persons for whom and on whose behalf the action is brought and of the nature of the claim in respect of which damages are sought to be recovered.

3. Assessment of Damages

(1) In the action such damages, other than damages for bereavement, may be awarded as are proportioned to the injury resulting from the death to the dependants respectively.

(2) After deducting the costs not recovered from the defendant any amount recovered otherwise than as damages for bereavement shall be divided among the dependants in such shares as may be directed.

(3) In an action under this Act where there fall to be assessed damages payable to a widow in respect of the death of her husband there shall not be taken into account the re-marriage of the widow or her prospects of re-marriage.

(4) In an action under this Act where there fall to be assessed damages payable to a person who is a dependant by virtue of section 1(3)(b) above in respect of the death of the person with whom the dependant was living as husband or wife there shall be taken into account (together with any other matter that appears to the court to be relevant to the action) the fact that the dependant had no enforceable right to financial support by the deceased as a result of their living together.

(5) If the dependants have incurred funeral expenses in respect of the deceased, damages may be awarded in respect of those expenses.

(6) Money paid into court in satisfaction of a cause of action under this Act may be in one sum without specifying any person's share.

4. Assessment of Damages; Disregard of Benefits

In assessing damages in respect of a person's death in an action under this Act, benefits which have accrued or will or may accrue to any person from his estate or otherwise as a result of his death shall be disregarded.

5. Contributory Negligence

Where any person dies as the result partly of his own fault and partly of the fault of any other person or persons, and accordingly if an action were brought for the benefit of the estate under the Law Reform (Miscellaneous Provisions) Act 1934 the damages recoverable would be reduced under section 1(1) of the Law Reform (Contributory Negligence) Act 1945, any damages recoverable in an action under this Act shall be reduced to a proportionate extent.

High Court and County Courts Jurisdiction Order 1991

(SI 1991/724)

The Lord Chancellor, in exercise of the powers conferred upon him by sections 1 and 120 of the Courts and Legal Services Act 1990, having consulted as required by section 1(9) of that Act, hereby makes the following Order a draft of which has, in accordance with section 120(4) of that Act, been laid before and approved by resolution of each House of Parliament—

1. Title and Commencement

This Order may be cited as the High Court and County Courts Jurisdiction Order 1991 and shall come into force on 1st July 1991.

1A. Interpretation

In this Order—

(a) 'the EOP Regulation' means Regulation (EC) No 1896/2006 of the European Parliament and of the Council of 12 December 2006 creating a European order for payment procedure; and
(b) 'the ESCP Regulation' means Regulation (EC) No 861/2007 of the European Parliament and of the Council of 11 July 2007 establishing a European small claims procedure.

2. Jurisdiction

(1) A county court shall have jurisdiction under—
 (a) sections 146 and 147 of the Law of Property Act 1925,
 (b) [*Revoked*]
 (c) section 26 of the Arbitration Act 1950,
 (d) section 63(2) of the Landlord and Tenant Act 1954,
 (e) section 28(3) of the Mines and Quarries (Tips) Act 1969,
 (f) section *66* of the Taxes Management Act 1970,
 (g) section 41 of the Administration of Justice Act 1970,
 (h) [*Revoked*]
 (i) section 13 of the Torts (Interference with Goods) Act 1977,
 (j) section 87 of the Magistrates' Courts Act 1980,
 (k) sections 19 and 20 of the Local Government Finance Act 1982,
 (l) sections 15, 16, 21, 25 and 139 of the County Courts Act 1984,
 (m) section 39(4) of, and paragraph 3(1) of Schedule 3 to, the Legal Aid Act 1988,
 (n) sections 99, 102(5), 114, 195, 204, 230, 231 and 235(5) of the Copyright, Designs and Patents Act 1988,
 (o) section 40 of the Housing Act 1988, and
 (p) sections 13 and 14 of the Trusts of Land and Appointment of Trustees Act 1996.
 (q) the EOP Regulation,
 (r) the ESCP Regulation,
 whatever the amount involved in the proceedings and whatever the value of any fund or asset connected with the proceedings.

(2) A county court shall have jurisdiction under—
 (a) section 10 of the Local Land Charges Act 1975, and
 (b) section 10(4) of the Rentcharges Act 1977,
 where the sum concerned or amount claimed does not exceed £5,000.

(3) A county court shall have jurisdiction under the following provisions of the Law of Property Act 1925 where the capital value of the land or interest in land which is to be dealt with does not exceed £30,000;
 (a) sections 3, 49, 66, 181, and 188;
 (b) proviso (iii) to paragraph 3 of Part III of Schedule 1;
 (c) proviso (v) to paragraph 1(3) of Part IV of Schedule 1.
 (d) provisos (iii) and (iv) to paragraph 1(4) of Part IV of Schedule 1.

(4) A county court shall have jurisdiction under sections 89, 90, 91 and 92 of the Law of Property Act 1925 where the amount owing in respect of the mortgage or charge at the commencement of the proceedings does not exceed £30,000.
(5) A county court shall have jurisdiction under the proviso to section 136(1) of the Law of Property Act 1925 where the amount or value of the debt or thing in action does not exceed £30,000.
(6) A county court shall have jurisdiction under section 1(6) of the Land Charges Act 1972—
(a) in the case of a land charge of Class C(i), C(ii) or D(i), if the amount does not exceed £30,000;
(b) in the case of a land charge of Class C(iii), if it is for a specified capital sum of money not exceeding £30,000 or, where it is not for a specified capital sum, if the capital value of the land affected does not exceed £30,000;
(c) in the case of a land charge of Class A, Class B, Class C(iv), Class D(ii), Class D(iii) or Class E, if the capital value of the land affected does not exceed £30,000;
(d) in the case of a land charge of Class F, if the land affected by it is the subject of an order made by the court under section 1 of the Matrimonial Homes Act 1983 or an application for an order under that section relating to that land has been made to the court;
(e) in a case where an application under section 23 of the Deeds of Arrangement Act 1914 could be entertained by the court.
(7) A county court shall have jurisdiction under sections 69, 70 and 71 of the Solicitors Act 1974 where a bill of costs relates wholly or partly to contentious business done in a county court and the amount of the bill does not exceed £5,000.
(7A) A patents county court and the county courts listed in paragraph (7B) shall have jurisdiction under the following provisions of the Trade Marks Act 1994—
(a) sections 15, 16, 19, 23(5), 25(4)(b), 30, 31, 46, 47, 64, 73 and 74;
(b) paragraph 12 of Schedule 1; and
(c) paragraph 14 of Schedule 2,
to include jurisdiction to hear and determine any claims or matters ancillary to, or arising from proceedings brought under such provisions.
(7B) For the purposes of paragraph (7A), the county courts at—
(a) Birmingham;
(b) Bristol;
(c) Cardiff;
(d) Leeds;
(e) Liverpool;
(f) Manchester; and
(e) Newcastle upon Tyne,
shall have jurisdiction.

3. Injunctions

The High Court shall have jurisdiction to hear an application for an injunction made in the court of or in anticipation of proceedings in a county court where a county court may not, by virtue of regulations under section 38(3)(b) of the County Courts Act 1984 or otherwise, grant such an injunction.

4. Allocation — Commencement of Proceedings

Subject to articles 4A, 5, 6, 6A and 6B, proceedings in which both the county courts and the High Court have jurisdiction may be commenced either in a county court or in the High Court.

4A.

Except for proceedings to which article 5 applies, a claim for money in which the county courts have jurisdiction may only be commenced in the High Court if the value of the claim is more than £25,000.

5.

(1) Proceedings which include a claim for damages in respect of personal injuries may only be commenced in the High Court if the value of the claim is £50,000 or more.
(2) In this article 'personal injuries' means personal injuries to the claimant or any other person, and includes disease, impairment of physical or mental condition, and death.
(3) This article does not apply to proceedings which include a claim for damages in respect of an alleged breach of duty of care committed in the course of the provision of clinical or medical services (including dental or nursing services).

6.

Applications and appeals under section 19 of the Local Government Finance Act 1982 and appeals under section 20 of that Act shall be commenced in the High Court.

6A.

Applications under section 1 of the Access to Neighbouring Land Act 1992 shall be commenced in a county court.

6B.

Applications under article 4 of the ESCP Regulation must be commenced in a county court.

8. Enforcement

(1) Subject to paragraph (1A) a judgment or order of a county court for the payment of a sum of money which it is sought to enforce wholly or partially by execution against goods—
  (a) shall be enforced only in the High Court where the sum which it is sought to enforce is £5,000 or more;
  (b) shall be enforced only in a county court where the sum which it is sought to enforce is less than £600;
  (c) in any other case may be enforced in either the High Court or a county court.

(1A) A judgment or order of a county court for the payment of a sum of money in proceedings arising out of an agreement regulated by the Consumer Credit Act 1974 shall be enforced only in a county court.

(2) Section 85(1) of the County Courts Act 1984 is amended by the insertion, at the beginning of the subsection, of the words 'Subject to article 8 of the High Court and County Courts Jurisdiction Order 1991'.

(2) Subject to paragraph (3), where—
  (a) an enactment provides that a sum of money shall be or may be recoverable as if it were payable under a county court order; and
  (b) the recovery of that sum is sought wholly or partially by execution against goods, payment of that sum shall be enforced in accordance with paragraphs (1)(a) to (c).

(3) Paragraph (1)(b) does not apply to the enforcement of—
  (a) a sum of money recoverable under section 15(1) of the Employment Tribunals Act 1996; or
  (b) a compromise sum which is recoverable under section 19A(3) of that Act.

8A. Enforcement of Traffic Penalties*

(1) Proceedings for the recovery of—
  (a) increased penalty charges provided for in charge certificates issued under—
    (i) paragraph 6 of Schedule 6 to the 1991 Act;
    (ii) paragraph 8 of Schedule 1 to the London Local Authorities Act 1996;
    (iii) regulation 17 of the Road User Charging (Enforcement and Adjudication) (London) Regulations 2001;
    (iv) regulation 21 of the Civil Enforcement of Parking Contraventions (England) General Regulations 2007; and
    (v) regulation 13 of the Civil Enforcement of Parking Contraventions (Penalty Charge Notices, Enforcement and Adjudication) (Wales) Regulations 2008;
  (b) amounts payable by a person other than a local authority under an adjudication of a parking adjudicator pursuant to section 73 of the 1991 Act;
  (c) amounts payable by a person other than a local authority under an adjudication pursuant to—
    (i) the Road User Charging (Enforcement and Adjudication) (London) Regulations 2001;
    (ii) the Civil Enforcement of Parking Contraventions (England) Representations and Appeals Regulations 2007; and
    (iii) the Civil Enforcement of Parking Contraventions (Representations and Appeals) (Wales) Regulations 2008; and

[* This para. (2) was inserted by SI 2009/577 despite the presence of the preceding para. (2).]

(d) increased fixed penalties referred to in—
(i) regulation 17(6) of the Road Traffic (Vehicle Emissions) (Fixed Penalty) (England) Regulations 2002; and
(ii) regulation 17(6) of the Road Traffic (Vehicle Emissions) (Fixed Penalty) (Wales) Regulations 2003,
shall be taken in Northampton County Court.

(2) In this article, 'the 1991 Act' means the Road Traffic Act 1991.

(3) In this article, 'a local authority' means:—
(a) in England, a London borough council, the Common Council of the City of London, Transport for London, a county or district council or the Council of the Isles of Scilly; and
(b) in Wales, a county or county borough council.

8B. Enforcement of Possession Orders against Trespassers

(1) A judgment or order of a county court for possession of land made in a possession claim against trespassers may be enforced in the High Court or a county court.

(2) In this article 'a possession claim against trespassers' has the same meaning as in Part 55 of the Civil Procedure Rules 1998.

9. Value of Claim

For the purposes of Articles 4A and 5, the value of the claim shall be calculated in accordance with rule 16.3(6) of the Civil Procedure Rules 1998.

11. Crown Proceedings — Transitional Provisions

For a period of two years from the date upon which this Order comes into force no order shall be made transferring proceedings in the High Court to which the Crown is a party to a county court, except—

(a) when the proceedings are set down to be tried or heard; or
(b) with the consent of the Crown.

12. Savings

This Order shall not apply to:

(a) family proceedings within the meaning of Part V of the Matrimonial and Family Proceedings Act 1984.

NOTES ON TEXT

The text printed above incorporates the following amendments:

art. 1A inserted by High Court and County Courts Jurisdiction (Amendment) Order 2008 (SI 2008/2934), art. 3;

art. 2 amended by: (a) High Court and County Courts Jurisdiction (Amendment) Order 1996 (SI 1996/3141), art. 2; (b) High Court and County Courts Jurisdiction (Amendment) Order 2005 (SI 2005/587), art. 3; (c) High Court and County Courts Jurisdiction (Amendment) Order 2008 (SI 2008/2934), arts 4 and 5;

art. 4 amended by: (a) Access to Neighbouring Land Act 1992, s. 7 (in force by SI 1992/3349); (b) High Court and County Courts Jurisdiction (Amendment) Order 1999 (SI 1999/1014), art. 4; (c) High Court and County Courts Jurisdiction (Amendment) Order 2008 (SI 2008/2934), art. 6;

art. 4A inserted by High Court and County Courts Jurisdiction (Amendment) Order 1999 (SI 1999/1014), art. 5; substituted by High Court and County Courts Jurisdiction (Amendment) Order 2009 (SI 2009/577), art. 2;

art. 5 amended by: (a) High Court and County Courts Jurisdiction (Amendment) Order 1999 (SI 1999/1014), arts 3 and 6; (b) High Court and County Courts Jurisdiction (Amendment) Order 2009 (SI 2009/577), art. 3;

art. 6 amended by High Court and County Courts Jurisdiction (Amendment) Order 1993 (SI 1993/1407), art. 3;

art. 6A inserted by Access to Neighbouring Land Act 1992, s. 7 (in force by SI 1992/3349);

art. 6B inserted by High Court and County Courts Jurisdiction (Amendment) Order 2008 (SI 2008/2934), art. 7;

art. 7 revoked by High Court and County Courts Jurisdiction (Amendment) Order 1999 (SI 1999/1014), art. 7;

art. 8 amended by: (a) High Court and County Courts Jurisdiction (Amendment) Order 1993 (SI 1993/1407), art. 4; (b) High Court and County Courts Jurisdiction (Amendment) Order 1995 (SI 1995/205), art. 5; (c) High Court and County Courts Jurisdiction (Amendment) Order 1996 (SI 1996/3141), art. 3; (d) High Court and County Courts Jurisdiction (Amendment) Order1999 (SI 1999/1014), art. 8; (e) High Court and County Courts Jurisdiction (Amendment) Order 2009 (SI 2009/577), art. 4;

art. 8A inserted by High Court and County Courts Jurisdiction (Amendment) Order 1993 (SI 1993/1407), art. 5, and amended by: (a) High Court and County Courts Jurisdiction (Amendment) Order 1996 (SI 1996/3141), art. 4; (b) High Court and County Courts Jurisdiction (Amendment) Order 2001 (SI 2001/1387); (c) High Court and County Courts Jurisdiction (Amendment) Order 2009 (SI 2009/577), art. 5;

art. 8B inserted by High Court and County Courts Jurisdiction (Amendment No. 2) Order 2001 (SI 2001/2685);

art. 9 substituted by High Court and County Courts Jurisdiction (Amendment) Order 1999 (SI 1999/1014), art. 9; amended by High Court and County Courts Jurisdiction (Amendment) Order 2009 (SI 2009/577), arts 6 and 7;

art. 10 revoked by High Court and County Courts Jurisdiction (Amendment) Order 1999 (SI 1999/1014), art. 10;

art. 12(b) revoked by High Court and County Courts Jurisdiction (Amendment) Order 1999 (SI 1999/1014), art. 11;

Article 2(8) and the schedule (amendments of other legislation) have been omitted.

Human Rights Act 1998

(1998 CHAPTER 42)

An Act to give further effect to rights and freedoms guaranteed under the European Convention on Human Rights; to make provision with respect to holders of certain judicial offices who become judges of the European Court of Human Rights; and for connected purposes.

[9th November 1998]

Introduction

1. The Convention Rights

(1) In this Act 'the Convention rights' means the rights and fundamental freedoms set out in—

(a) Articles 2 to 12 and 14 of the Convention,

(b) Articles 1 to 3 of the First Protocol, and

(c) Article 1 of the Thirteenth Protocol,

as read with Articles 16 to 18 of the Convention.

(2) Those Articles are to have effect for the purposes of this Act subject to any designated derogation or reservation (as to which see sections 14 and 15).

(3) The Articles are set out in Schedule 1.

(4) The Secretary of State may by order make such amendments to this Act as he considers appropriate to reflect the effect, in relation to the United Kingdom, of a protocol.

(5) In subsection (4) 'protocol' means a protocol to the Convention—

(a) which the United Kingdom has ratified; or

(b) which the United Kingdom has signed with a view to ratification.

(6) No amendment may be made by an order under subsection (4) so as to come into force before the protocol concerned is in force in relation to the United Kingdom.

2. Interpretation of Convention Rights

(1) A court or tribunal determining a question which has arisen in connection with a Convention right must take into account any—

(a) judgment, decision, declaration or advisory opinion of the European Court of Human Rights,

(b) opinion of the Commission given in a report adopted under Article 31 of the Convention,

(c) decision of the Commission in connection with Article 26 or 27(2) of the Convention, or

(d) decision of the Committee of Ministers taken under Article 46 of the Convention,

whenever made or given, so far as, in the opinion of the court or tribunal, it is relevant to the proceedings in which that question has arisen.

(2) Evidence of any judgment, decision, declaration or opinion of which account may have to be taken under this section is to be given in proceedings before any court or tribunal in such manner as may be provided by rules.

(3) In this section 'rules' means rules of court or, in the case of proceedings before a tribunal, rules made for the purposes of this section—

(a) by the Lord Chancellor or the Secretary of State, in relation to any proceedings outside Scotland;

(b) by the Secretary of State, in relation to proceedings in Scotland; or

(c) by a Northern Ireland department, in relation to proceedings before a tribunal in Northern Ireland—

(i) which deals with transferred matters; and

(ii) for which no rules made under paragraph (a) are in force.

Legislation

3. Interpretation of Legislation

(1) So far as it is possible to do so, primary legislation and subordinate legislation must be read and given effect in a way which is compatible with the Convention rights.

(2) This section—
  (a) applies to primary legislation and subordinate legislation whenever enacted;
  (b) does not affect the validity, continuing operation or enforcement of any incompatible primary legislation; and
  (c) does not affect the validity, continuing operation or enforcement of any incompatible subordinate legislation if (disregarding any possibility of revocation) primary legislation prevents removal of the incompatibility.

4. Declaration of Incompatibility

(1) Subsection (2) applies in any proceedings in which a court determines whether a provision of primary legislation is compatible with a Convention right.
(2) If the court is satisfied that the provision is incompatible with a Convention right, it may make a declaration of that incompatibility.
(3) Subsection (4) applies in any proceedings in which a court determines whether a provision of subordinate legislation, made in the exercise of a power conferred by primary legislation, is compatible with a Convention right.
(4) If the court is satisfied—
  (a) that the provision is incompatible with a Convention right, and
  (b) that (disregarding any possibility of revocation) the primary legislation concerned prevents removal of the incompatibility,

  it may make a declaration of that incompatibility.
(5) In this section 'court' means—
  (a) the Supreme Court;
  (b) the Judicial Committee of the Privy Council;
  (c) the Courts-Martial Appeal Court;
  (d) in Scotland, the High Court of Justiciary sitting otherwise than as a trial court or the Court of Session;
  (e) in England and Wales or Northern Ireland, the High Court or the Court of Appeal;
  (f) the Court of Protection, in any matter being dealt with by the President of the Family Division, the Vice-Chancellor or a puisne judge of the High Court.
(6) A declaration under this section ('a declaration of incompatibility')—
  (a) does not affect the validity, continuing operation or enforcement of the provision in respect of which it is given; and
  (b) is not binding on the parties to the proceedings in which it is made.

5. Right of Crown to Intervene

(1) Where a court is considering whether to make a declaration of incompatibility, the Crown is entitled to notice in accordance with rules of court.
(2) In any case to which subsection (1) applies—
  (a) a Minister of the Crown (or a person nominated by him),
  (b) a member of the Scottish Executive,
  (c) a Northern Ireland Minister,
  (d) a Northern Ireland department,

  is entitled, on giving notice in accordance with rules of court, to be joined as a party to the proceedings.
(3) Notice under subsection (2) may be given at any time during the proceedings.
(4) A person who has been made a party to criminal proceedings (other than in Scotland) as the result of a notice under subsection (2) may, with leave, appeal to the Supreme Court against any declaration of incompatibility made in the proceedings.
(5) In subsection (4) —

  'criminal proceedings' includes all proceedings before the Courts-Martial Appeal Court; and

  'leave' means leave granted by the court making the declaration of incompatibility or by the Supreme Court.

Public Authorities

6. Acts of Public Authorities

(1) It is unlawful for a public authority to act in a way which is incompatible with a Convention right.
(2) Subsection (1) does not apply to an act if—
(a) as the result of one or more provisions of primary legislation, the authority could not have acted differently; or
(b) in the case of one or more provisions of, or made under, primary legislation which cannot be read or given effect in a way which is compatible with the Convention rights, the authority was acting so as to give effect to or enforce those provisions.
(3) In this section 'public authority' includes—
(a) a court or tribunal, and
(b) any person certain of whose functions are functions of a public nature,
but does not include either House of Parliament or a person exercising functions in connection with proceedings in Parliament.
(4) [*repealed*]
(5) In relation to a particular act, a person is not a public authority by virtue only of subsection (3) (b) if the nature of the act is private.
(6) 'An act' includes a failure to act but does not include a failure to —
(a) introduce in, or lay before, Parliament a proposal for legislation; or
(b) make any primary legislation or remedial order.

7. Proceedings

(1) A person who claims that a public authority has acted (or proposes to act) in a way which is made unlawful by section 6(1) may—
(a) bring proceedings against the authority under this Act in the appropriate court or tribunal, or
(b) rely on the Convention right or rights concerned in any legal proceedings,
but only if he is (or would be) a victim of the unlawful act.
(2) In subsection (1)(a) 'appropriate court or tribunal' means such court or tribunal as may be determined in accordance with rules; and proceedings against an authority include a counter-claim or similar proceeding.
(3) If the proceedings are brought on an application for judicial review, the applicant is to be taken to have a sufficient interest in relation to the unlawful act only if he is, or would be, a victim of that act.
(4) If the proceedings are made by way of a petition for judicial review in Scotland, the applicant shall be taken to have title and interest to sue in relation to the unlawful act only if he is, or would be, a victim of that act.
(5) Proceedings under subsection (1)(a) must be brought before the end of—
(a) the period of one year beginning with the date on which the act complained of took place; or
(b) such longer period as the court or tribunal considers equitable having regard to all the circumstances,
but that is subject to any rule imposing a stricter time limit in relation to the procedure in question.
(6) In subsection (1)(b) 'legal proceedings' includes—
(a) proceedings brought by or at the instigation of a public authority; and
(b) an appeal against the decision of a court or tribunal.
(7) For the purposes of this section, a person is a victim of an unlawful act only if he would be a victim for the purposes of Article 34 of the Convention if proceedings were brought in the European Court of Human Rights in respect of that act.
(8) Nothing in this Act creates a criminal offence.
(9) In this section 'rules' means—
(a) in relation to proceedings before a court or tribunal outside Scotland, rules made by the Lord Chancellor or the Secretary of State for the purposes of this section or rules of court,
(b) in relation to proceedings before a court or tribunal in Scotland, rules made by the Secretary of State for those purposes,

(c) in relation to proceedings before a tribunal in Northern Ireland—
(i) which deals with transferred matters; and
(ii) for which no rules made under paragraph (a) are in force,
rules made by a Northern Ireland department for those purposes,
and includes provision made by order under section 1 of the Courts and Legal Services Act 1990.

(10) In making rules, regard must be had to section 9.

(11) The Minister who has power to make rules in relation to a particular tribunal may, to the extent he considers it necessary to ensure that the tribunal can provide an appropriate remedy in relation to an act (or proposed act) of a public authority which is (or would be) unlawful as a result of section 6(1), by order add to—
(a) the relief or remedies which the tribunal may grant; or
(b) the grounds on which it may grant any of them.

(12) An order made under subsection (11) may contain such incidental, supplemental, consequential or transitional provision as the Minister making it considers appropriate.

(13) 'The Minister' includes the Northern Ireland department concerned.

8. Judicial Remedies

(1) In relation to any act (or proposed act) of a public authority which the court finds is (or would be) unlawful, it may grant such relief or remedy, or make such order, within its powers as it considers just and appropriate.

(2) But damages may be awarded only by a court which has power to award damages, or to order the payment of compensation, in civil proceedings.

(3) No award of damages is to be made unless, taking account of all the circumstances of the case, including—
(a) any other relief or remedy granted, or order made, in relation to the act in question (by that or any other court), and
(b) the consequences of any decision (of that or any other court) in respect of that act,
the court is satisfied that the award is necessary to afford just satisfaction to the person in whose favour it is made.

(4) In determining—
(a) whether to award damages, or
(b) the amount of an award,
the court must take into account the principles applied by the European Court of Human Rights in relation to the award of compensation under Article 41 of the Convention.

(5) A public authority against which damages are awarded is to be treated—
(a) in Scotland, for the purposes of section 3 of the Law Reform (Miscellaneous Provisions) (Scotland) Act 1940 as if the award were made in an action of damages in which the authority has been found liable in respect of loss or damage to the person to whom the award is made;
(b) for the purposes of the Civil Liability (Contribution) Act 1978 as liable in respect of damage suffered by the person to whom the award is made.

(6) In this section—
'court' includes a tribunal;
'damages' means damages for an unlawful act of a public authority; and
'unlawful' means unlawful under section 6(1).

9. Judicial Acts

(1) Proceedings under section 7(1)(a) in respect of a judicial act may be brought only—
(a) by exercising a right of appeal;
(b) on an application (in Scotland a petition) for judicial review; or
(c) in such other forum as may be prescribed by rules.

(2) That does not affect any rule of law which prevents a court from being the subject of judicial review.

(3) In proceedings under this Act in respect of a judicial act done in good faith, damages may not be awarded otherwise than to compensate a person to the extent required by Article 5(5) of the Convention.

(4) An award of damages permitted by subsection (3) is to be made against the Crown; but no award may be made unless the appropriate person, if not a party to the proceedings, is joined.

(5) In this section—

'appropriate person' means the Minister responsible for the court concerned, or a person or government department nominated by him;

'court' includes a tribunal;

'judge' includes a member of a tribunal, a justice of the peace and a clerk or other officer entitled to exercise the jurisdiction of a court;

'judicial act' means a judicial act of a court and includes an act done on the instructions, or on behalf, of a judge; and

'rules' has the same meaning as in section 7(9).

Remedial Action

10. Power to Take Remedial Action

(1) This section applies if—

(a) a provision of legislation has been declared under section 4 to be incompatible with a Convention right and, if an appeal lies—

(i) all persons who may appeal have stated in writing that they do not intend to do so;

(ii) the time for bringing an appeal has expired and no appeal has been brought within that time; or

(iii) an appeal brought within that time has been determined or abandoned; or

(b) it appears to a Minister of the Crown or Her Majesty in Council that, having regard to a finding of the European Court of Human Rights made after the coming into force of this section in proceedings against the United Kingdom, a provision of legislation is incompatible with an obligation of the United Kingdom arising from the Convention.

(2) If a Minister of the Crown considers that there are compelling reasons for proceeding under this section, he may by order make such amendments to the legislation as he considers necessary to remove the incompatibility.

(3) If, in the case of subordinate legislation, a Minister of the Crown considers—

(a) that it is necessary to amend the primary legislation under which the subordinate legislation in question was made, in order to enable the incompatibility to be removed, and

(b) that there are compelling reasons for proceeding under this section,

he may by order make such amendments to the primary legislation as he considers necessary.

(4) This section also applies where the provision in question is in subordinate legislation and has been quashed, or declared invalid, by reason of incompatibility with a Convention right and the Minister proposes to proceed under paragraph 2(b) of Schedule 2.

(5) If the legislation is an Order in Council, the power conferred by subsection (2) or (3) is exercisable by Her Majesty in Council.

(6) In this section 'legislation' does not include a Measure of the Church Assembly or of the General Synod of the Church of England.

(7) Schedule 2 makes further provision about remedial orders.

Other Rights and Proceedings

11. Safeguard for Existing Human Rights

A person's reliance on a Convention right does not restrict—

(a) any other right or freedom conferred on him by or under any law having effect in any part of the United Kingdom; or

(b) his right to make any claim or bring any proceedings which he could make or bring apart from sections 7 to 9.

12. Freedom of Expression

(1) This section applies if a court is considering whether to grant any relief which, if granted, might affect the exercise of the Convention right to freedom of expression.

(2) If the person against whom the application for relief is made ('the respondent') is neither present nor represented, no such relief is to be granted unless the court is satisfied—

(a) that the applicant has taken all practicable steps to notify the respondent; or
(b) that there are compelling reasons why the respondent should not be notified.

(3) No such relief is to be granted so as to restrain publication before trial unless the court is satisfied that the applicant is likely to establish that publication should not be allowed.

(4) The court must have particular regard to the importance of the Convention right to freedom of expression and, where the proceedings relate to material which the respondent claims, or which appears to the court, to be journalistic, literary or artistic material (or to conduct connected with such material), to—
(a) the extent to which—
(i) the material has, or is about to, become available to the public; or
(ii) it is, or would be, in the public interest for the material to be published;
(b) any relevant privacy code.

(5) In this section—
'court' includes a tribunal; and
'relief includes any remedy or order (other than in criminal proceedings).

13. Freedom of Thought, Conscience and Religion

(1) If a court's determination of any question arising under this Act might affect the exercise by a religious organisation (itself or its members collectively) of the Convention right to freedom of thought, conscience and religion, it must have particular regard to the importance of that right.

(2) In this section 'court' includes a tribunal.

Derogations and Reservations

14. Derogations

(1) In this Act 'designated derogation' means any derogation by the United Kingdom from an Article of the Convention, or of any protocol to the Convention, which is designated for the purposes of this Act in an order made by the Secretary of State.

(3) If a designated derogation is amended or replaced it ceases to be a designated derogation.

(4) But subsection (3) does not prevent the Secretary of State from exercising his power under subsection (1) to make a fresh designation order in respect of the Article concerned.

(5) The Secretary of State must by order make such amendments to Schedule 3 as he considers appropriate to reflect—
(a) any designation order; or
(b) the effect of subsection (3).

(6) A designation order may be made in anticipation of the making by the United Kingdom of a proposed derogation.

15. Reservations

(1) In this Act 'designated reservation' means—
(a) the United Kingdom's reservation to Article 2 of the First Protocol to the Convention; and
(b) any other reservation by the United Kingdom to an Article of the Convention, or of any protocol to the Convention, which is designated for the purposes of this Act in an order made by the Secretary of State.

(2) The text of the reservation referred to in subsection (1)(a) is set out in Part II of Schedule 3.

(3) If a designated reservation is withdrawn wholly or in part it ceases to be a designated reservation.

(4) But subsection (3) does not prevent the Secretary of State from exercising his power under subsection (1)(b) to make a fresh designation order in respect of the Article concerned.

(5) The Secretary of State must by order make such amendments to this Act as he considers appropriate to reflect—
(a) any designation order; or
(b) the effect of subsection (3).

16. Period for Which Designated Derogations Have Effect

(1) If it has not already been withdrawn by the United Kingdom, a designated derogation ceases to have effect for the purposes of this Act at the end of the period of five years beginning with the date on which the order designating it was made.

(2) At any time before the period—
 (a) fixed by subsection (1), or
 (b) extended by an order under this subsection,
 comes to an end, the Secretary of State may by order extend it by a further period of five years.
(3) An order under section 14(1) ceases to have effect at the end of the period for consideration, unless a resolution has been passed by each House approving the order.
(4) Subsection (3) does not affect—
 (a) anything done in reliance on the order; or
 (b) the power to make a fresh order under section 14(1).
(5) In subsection (3) 'period for consideration' means the period of forty days beginning with the day on which the order was made.
(6) In calculating the period for consideration, no account is to be taken of any time during which—
 (a) Parliament is dissolved or prorogued; or
 (b) both Houses are adjourned for more than four days.
(7) If a designated derogation is withdrawn by the United Kingdom, the Secretary of State must by order make such amendments to this Act as he considers are required to reflect that withdrawal.

17. Periodic Review of Designated Reservations

(1) The appropriate Minister must review the designated reservation referred to in section 15(1)(a)—
 (a) before the end of the period of five years beginning with the date on which section 1(2) came into force; and
 (b) if that designation is still in force, before the end of the period of five years beginning with the date on which the last report relating to it was laid under subsection (3).
(2) The appropriate Minister must review each of the other designated reservations (if any)—
 (a) before the end of the period of five years beginning with the date on which the order designating the reservation first came into force; and
 (b) if the designation is still in force, before the end of the period of five years beginning with the date on which the last report relating to it was laid under subsection (3).
(3) The Minister conducting a review under this section must prepare a report on the result of the review and lay a copy of it before each House of Parliament.

Parliamentary Procedure

19. Statements of Compatibility

(1) A Minister of the Crown in charge of a Bill in either House of Parliament must, before Second Reading of the Bill—
 (a) make a statement to the effect that in his view the provisions of the Bill are compatible with the Convention rights ('a statement of compatibility'); or
 (b) make a statement to the effect that although he is unable to make a statement of compatibility the government nevertheless wishes the House to proceed with the Bill.
(2) The statement must be in writing and be published in such manner as the Minister making it considers appropriate.

Supplemental

20. Orders etc. under This Act

(1) Any power of a Minister of the Crown to make an order under this Act is exercisable by statutory instrument.
(2) The power of the Lord Chancellor or the Secretary of State to make rules (other than rules of court) under section 2(3) or 7(9) is exercisable by statutory instrument.
(3) Any statutory instrument made under section 14, 15 or 16(7) must be laid before Parliament.
(4) No order may be made by the Lord Chancellor or the Secretary of State under section 1(4), 7(11) or 16(2) unless a draft of the order has been laid before, and approved by, each House of Parliament.
(5) *Any statutory instrument* made under section 18(7) or Schedule 4, or to which subsection (2) applies, shall be subject to annulment in pursuance of a resolution of either House of Parliament.
(6) The power of a Northern Ireland department to make—
 (a) rules under section 2(3)(c) or 7(9)(c), or

(b) an order under section 7(11),

is exercisable by statutory rule for the purposes of the Statutory Rules (Northern Ireland) Order 1979.

(7) Any rules made under section 2(3)(c) or 7(9)(c) shall be subject to negative resolution; and section 41(6) of the Interpretation Act (Northern Ireland) 1954 (meaning of 'subject to negative resolution') shall apply as if the power to make the rules were conferred by an Act of the Northern Ireland Assembly.

(8) No order may be made by a Northern Ireland department under section 7(11) unless a draft of the order has been laid before, and approved by, the Northern Ireland Assembly.

21. Interpretation etc.

(1) In this Act—

'amend' includes repeal and apply (with or without modifications);

'the appropriate Minister' means the Minister of the Crown having charge of the appropriate authorised government department (within the meaning of the Crown Proceedings Act 1947);

'the Commission' means the European Commission of Human Rights;

'the Convention' means the Convention for the Protection of Human Rights and Fundamental Freedoms, agreed by the Council of Europe at Rome on 4th November 1950 as it has effect for the time being in relation to the United Kingdom;

'declaration of incompatibility' means a declaration under section 4;

'Minister of the Crown' has the same meaning as in the Ministers of the Crown Act 1975;

'Northern Ireland Minister' includes the First Minister and the deputy First Minister in Northern Ireland;

'primary legislation' means any—

(a) public general Act;
(b) local and personal Act;
(c) private Act;
(d) Measure of the Church Assembly;
(e) Measure of the General Synod of the Church of England;
(f) Order in Council—
  (i) made in exercise of Her Majesty's Royal Prerogative;
  (ii) made under section 38(1)(a) of the Northern Ireland Constitution Act 1973 or the corresponding provision of the Northern Ireland Act 1998; or
  (iii) amending an Act of a kind mentioned in paragraph (a), (b) or (c);

and includes an order or other instrument made under primary legislation (otherwise than by the National Assembly for Wales, a member of the Scottish Executive, a Northern Ireland Minister or a Northern Ireland department) to the extent to which it operates to bring one or more provisions of that legislation into force or amends any primary legislation;

'the First Protocol' means the protocol to the Convention agreed at Paris on 20th March 1952;

'the Eleventh Protocol' means the protocol to the Convention (restructuring the control machinery established by the Convention) agreed at Strasbourg on 11th May 1994;

'the Thirteenth Protocol' means the protocol to the Convention (concerning the abolition of the death penalty in all circumstances) agreed at Vilnius on 3rd May 2002;

'remedial order' means an order under section 10;

'subordinate legislation' means any—

(a) Order in Council other than one—
  (i) made in exercise of Her Majesty's Royal Prerogative;
  (ii) made under section 38(1)(a) of the Northern Ireland Constitution Act 1973 or the corresponding provision of the Northern Ireland Act 1998; or
  (iii) amending an Act of a kind mentioned in the definition of primary legislation;
(b) Act of the Scottish Parliament;
(c) Act of the Parliament of Northern Ireland;
(d) Measure of the Assembly established under section 1 of the Northern Ireland Assembly Act 1973;
(e) Act of the Northern Ireland Assembly;

(f) order, rules, regulations, scheme, warrant, byelaw or other instrument made under primary legislation (except to the extent to which it operates to bring one or more provisions of that legislation into force or amends any primary legislation);
(g) order, rules, regulations, scheme, warrant, byelaw or other instrument made under legislation mentioned in paragraph (b), (c), (d) or (e) or made under an Order in Council applying only to Northern Ireland;
(h) order, rules, regulations, scheme, warrant, byelaw or other instrument made by a member of the Scottish Executive, a Northern Ireland Minister or a Northern Ireland department in exercise of prerogative or other executive functions of Her Majesty which are exercisable by such a person on behalf of Her Majesty;

'transferred matters' has the same meaning as in the Northern Ireland Act 1998; and
'tribunal' means any tribunal in which legal proceedings may be brought.

(2) The references in paragraphs (b) and (c) of section 2(1) to Articles are to Articles of the Convention as they had effect immediately before the coming into force of the Eleventh Protocol.
(3) The reference in paragraph (d) of section 2(1) to Article 46 includes a reference to Articles 32 and 54 of the Convention as they had effect immediately before the coming into force of the Eleventh Protocol.
(4) The references in section 2(1) to a report or decision of the Commission or a decision of the Committee of Ministers include references to a report or decision made as provided by paragraphs 3, 4 and 6 of Article 5 of the Eleventh Protocol (transitional provisions).
(5) Any liability under the Army Act 1955, the Air Force Act 1955 or the Naval Discipline Act 1957 to suffer death for an offence is replaced by a liability to imprisonment for life or any less punishment authorised by those Acts; and those Acts shall accordingly have effect with the necessary modifications.

22. Short Title, Commencement, Application and Extent

(1) This Act may be cited as the Human Rights Act 1998.
(2) Sections 18, 20 and 21(5) and this section come into force on the passing of this Act.
(3) The other provisions of this Act come into force on such day as the Secretary of State may by order appoint; and different days may be appointed for different purposes.
(4) Paragraph (b) of subsection (1) of section 7 applies to proceedings brought by or at the instigation of a public authority whenever the act in question took place; but otherwise that subsection does not apply to an act taking place before the coming into force of that section.
(5) This Act binds the Crown.
(6) This Act extends to Northern Ireland.
(7) Section 21(5), so far as it relates to any provision contained in the Army Act 1955, the Air Force Act 1955 or the Naval Discipline Act 1957, extends to any place to which that provision extends.

[*Section 19 was brought into force on 24 November 1998 by the Human Rights Act 1998 (Commencement) Order 1998 (SI 1998/2882). All remaining provisions were brought into force on 2 October 2000 by the Human Rights Act 1998 (Commencement No. 2) Order 2000 (SI 2000/1851).*]

Section 1(3)

SCHEDULE 1 THE ARTICLES

PART I THE CONVENTION

Rights and Freedoms

Article 2 Right to Life

1. Everyone's right to life shall be protected by law. No one shall be deprived of his life intentionally save in the execution of a sentence of a court following his conviction of a crime for which this penalty is provided by law.
2. Deprivation of life shall not be regarded as inflicted in contravention of this Article when it results from the use of force which is no more than absolutely necessary:
   (a) in defence of any person from unlawful violence;
   (b) in order to effect a lawful arrest or to prevent the escape of a person lawfully detained;
   (c) in action lawfully taken for the purpose of quelling a riot or insurrection.

Article 3 Prohibition of Torture

No one shall be subjected to torture or to inhuman or degrading treatment or punishment.

Article 4 Prohibition of Slavery and Forced Labour

1. No one shall be held in slavery or servitude.
2. No one shall be required to perform forced or compulsory labour.
3. For the purpose of this Article the term 'forced or compulsory labour' shall not include:
   (a) any work required to be done in the ordinary course of detention imposed according to the provisions of Article 5 of this Convention or during conditional release from such detention;
   (b) any service of a military character or, in case of conscientious objectors in countries where they are recognised, service exacted instead of compulsory military service;
   (c) any service exacted in case of an emergency or calamity threatening the life or well-being of the community;
   (d) any work or service which forms part of normal civic obligations.

Article 5 Right to Liberty and Security

1. Everyone has the right to liberty and security of person. No one shall be deprived of his liberty save in the following cases and in accordance with a procedure prescribed by law:
   (a) the lawful detention of a person after conviction by a competent court;
   (b) the lawful arrest or detention of a person for non-compliance with the lawful order of a court or in order to secure the fulfilment of any obligation prescribed by law;
   (c) the lawful arrest or detention of a person effected for the purpose of bringing him before the competent legal authority on reasonable suspicion of having committed an offence or when it is reasonably considered necessary to prevent his committing an offence or fleeing after having done so;
   (d) the detention of a minor by lawful order for the purpose of educational supervision or his lawful detention for the purpose of bringing him before the competent legal authority;
   (e) the lawful detention of persons for the prevention of the spreading of infectious diseases, of persons of unsound mind, alcoholics or drug addicts or vagrants;
   (f) the lawful arrest or detention of a person to prevent his effecting an unauthorised entry into the country or of a person against whom action is being taken with a view to deportation or extradition.
2. Everyone who is arrested shall be informed promptly, in a language which he understands, of the reasons for his arrest and of any charge against him.
3. Everyone arrested or detained in accordance with the provisions of paragraph 1(c) of this Article shall be brought promptly before a judge or other officer authorised by law to exercise judicial power and shall be entitled to trial within a reasonable time or to release pending trial. Release may be conditioned by guarantees to appear for trial.
4. Everyone who is deprived of his liberty by arrest or detention shall be entitled to take proceedings by which the lawfulness of his detention shall be decided speedily by a court and his release ordered if the detention is not lawful.
5. Everyone who has been the victim of arrest or detention in contravention of the provisions of this Article shall have an enforceable right to compensation.

Article 6 Right to a Fair Trial

1. In the determination of his civil rights and obligations or of any criminal charge against him, everyone is entitled to a fair and public hearing within a reasonable time by an independent and impartial tribunal established by law. Judgment shall be pronounced publicly but the press and public may be excluded from all or part of the trial in the interest of morals, public order or national security in a democratic society, where the interests of juveniles or the protection of the private life of the parties so require, or to the extent strictly necessary in the opinion of the court in special circumstances where publicity would prejudice the interests of justice.
2. Everyone charged with a criminal offence shall be presumed innocent until proved guilty according to law.
3. Everyone charged with a criminal offence has the following minimum rights:

(a) to be informed promptly, in a language which he understands and in detail, of the nature and cause of the accusation against him;
(b) to have adequate time and facilities for the preparation of his defence;
(c) to defend himself in person or through legal assistance of his own choosing or, if he has not sufficient means to pay for legal assistance, to be given it free when the interests of justice so require;
(d) to examine or have examined witnesses against him and to obtain the attendance and examination of witnesses on his behalf under the same conditions as witnesses against him;
(e) to have the free assistance of an interpreter if he cannot understand or speak the language used in court.

Article 7 No Punishment without Law

1. No one shall be held guilty of any criminal offence on account of any act or omission which did not constitute a criminal offence under national or international law at the time when it was committed. Nor shall a heavier penalty be imposed than the one that was applicable at the time the criminal offence was committed.
2. This Article shall not prejudice the trial and punishment of any person for any act or omission which, at the time when it was committed, was criminal according to the general principles of law recognised by civilised nations.

Article 8 Right to Respect for Private and Family Life

1. Everyone has the right to respect for his private and family life, his home and his correspondence.
2. There shall be no interference by a public authority with the exercise of this right except such as is in accordance with the law and is necessary in a democratic society in the interests of national security, public safety or the economic well being of the country, for the prevention of disorder or crime, for the protection of health or morals, or for the protection of the rights and freedoms of others.

Article 9 Freedom of Thought, Conscience and Religion

1. Everyone has the right to freedom of thought, conscience and religion; this right includes freedom to change his religion or belief and freedom, either alone or in community with others and in public or private, to manifest his religion or belief, in worship, teaching, practice and observance.
2. Freedom to manifest one's religion or beliefs shall be subject only to such limitations as are prescribed by law and are necessary in a democratic society in the interests of public safety, for the protection of public order, health or morals, or for the protection of the rights and freedoms of others.

Article 10 Freedom of Expression

1. Everyone has the right to freedom of expression. This right shall include freedom to hold opinions and to receive and impart information and ideas without interference by public authority and regardless of frontiers. This Article shall not prevent States from requiring the licensing of broadcasting, television or cinema enterprises.
2. The exercise of these freedoms, since it carries with it duties and responsibilities, may be subject to such formalities, conditions, restrictions or penalties as are prescribed by law and are necessary in a democratic society, in the interests of national security, territorial integrity or public safety, for the prevention of disorder or crime, for the protection of health or morals, for the protection of the reputation or rights of others, for preventing the disclosure of information received in confidence, or for maintaining the authority and impartiality of the judiciary.

Article 11 Freedom of Assembly and Association

1. Everyone has the right to freedom of peaceful assembly and to freedom of association with others, including the right to form and to join trade unions for the protection of his interests.
2. No restrictions shall be placed on the exercise of these rights other than such as are prescribed by law and are necessary in a democratic society in the interests of national security or public safety, for the prevention of disorder or crime, for the protection of health or morals or for the protection of the rights and freedoms of others. This Article shall not prevent the imposition of lawful

restrictions on the exercise of these rights by members of the armed forces, of the police or of the administration of the State.

Article 12 Right to Marry

Men and women of marriageable age have the right to marry and to found a family, according to the national laws governing the exercise of this right.

Article 14 Prohibition of Discrimination

The enjoyment of the rights and freedoms set forth in this Convention shall be secured without discrimination on any ground such as sex, race, colour, language, religion, political or other opinion, national or social origin, association with a national minority, property, birth or other status.

Article 16 Restrictions on Political Activity of Aliens

Nothing in Articles 10, 11 and 14 shall be regarded as preventing the High Contracting Parties from imposing restrictions on the political activity of aliens.

Article 17 Prohibition of Abuse of Rights

Nothing in this Convention may be interpreted as implying for any State, group or person any right to engage in any activity or perform any act aimed at the destruction of any of the rights and freedoms set forth herein or at their limitation to a greater extent than is provided for in the Convention.

Article 18 Limitation on Use of Restrictions on Rights

The restrictions permitted under this Convention to the said rights and freedoms shall not be applied for any purpose other than those for which they have been prescribed.

PART II THE FIRST PROTOCOL

Article 1 Protection of Property

Every natural or legal person is entitled to the peaceful enjoyment of his possessions. No one shall be deprived of his possessions except in the public interest and subject to the conditions provided for by law and by the general principles of international law.

The preceding provisions shall not, however, in any way impair the right of a State to enforce such laws as it deems necessary to control the use of property in accordance with the general interest or to secure the payment of taxes or other contributions or penalties.

Article 2 Right to Education

No person shall be denied the right to education. In the exercise of any functions which it assumes in relation to education and to teaching, the State shall respect the right of parents to ensure such education and teaching in conformity with their own religious and philosophical convictions.

Article 3 Right to Free Elections

The High Contracting Parties undertake to hold free elections at reasonable intervals by secret ballot, under conditions which will ensure the free expression of the opinion of the people in the choice of the legislature.

PART III ARTICLE 1 OF THE THIRTEENTH PROTOCOL

Abolition of the Death Penalty

The death penalty shall be abolished. No one shall be condemned to such penalty or executed.

SCHEDULE 2 REMEDIAL ORDERS

Orders

1.—(1) A remedial order may—

(a) contain such incidental, supplemental, consequential or transitional provision as the person making it considers appropriate;

(b) be made so as to have effect from a date earlier than that on which it is made;
(c) make provision for the delegation of specific functions;
(d) make different provision for different cases.

(2) The power conferred by sub-paragraph (1)(a) includes—
(a) power to amend primary legislation (including primary legislation other than that which contains the incompatible provision); and
(b) power to amend or revoke subordinate legislation (including subordinate legislation other than that which contains the incompatible provision).

(3) A remedial order may be made so as to have the same extent as the legislation which it affects.

(4) No person is to be guilty of an offence solely as a result of the retrospective effect of a remedial order.

Procedure

2. No remedial order may be made unless—
(a) a draft of the order has been approved by a resolution of each House of Parliament made after the end of the period of 60 days beginning with the day on which the draft was laid; or
(b) it is declared in the order that it appears to the person making it that, because of the urgency of the matter, it is necessary to make the order without a draft being so approved.

Orders Laid in Draft

3.—(1) No draft may be laid under paragraph 2(a) unless—
(a) the person proposing to make the order has laid before Parliament a document which contains a draft of the proposed order and the required information; and
(b) the period of 60 days, beginning with the day on which the document required by this sub-paragraph was laid, has ended.

(2) If representations have been made during that period, the draft laid under paragraph 2(a) must be accompanied by a statement containing—
(a) a summary of the representations; and
(b) if, as a result of the representations, the proposed order has been changed, details of the changes.

Urgent Cases

4.—(1) If a remedial order ('the original order') is made without being approved in draft, the person making it must lay it before Parliament, accompanied by the required information, after it is made.

(2) If representations have been made during the period of 60 days beginning with the day on which the original order was made, the person making it must (after the end of that period) lay before Parliament a statement containing—
(a) a summary of the representations; and
(b) if, as a result of the representations, he considers it appropriate to make changes to the original order, details of the changes.

(3) If sub-paragraph (2)(b) applies, the person making the statement must—
(a) make a further remedial order replacing the original order; and
(b) lay the replacement order before Parliament.

(4) If, at the end of the period of 120 days beginning with the day on which the original order was made, a resolution has not been passed by each House approving the original or replacement order, the order ceases to have effect (but without that affecting anything previously done under either order or the power to make a fresh remedial order).

Definitions

5. In this Schedule—
'representations' means representations about a remedial order (or proposed remedial order) made to the person making (or proposing to make) it and includes any relevant Parliamentary report or resolution; and

'required information' means

(a) an explanation of the incompatibility which the order (or proposed order) seeks to remove, including particulars of the relevant declaration, finding or order; and

(b) a statement of the reasons for proceeding under section 10 and for making an order in those terms.

Calculating Periods

6. In calculating any period for the purposes of this Schedule, no account is to be taken of any time during which—

(a) Parliament is dissolved or prorogued; or

(b) both Houses are adjourned for more than four days.

7.—(1) This paragraph applies in relation to—

(a) any remedial order made, and any draft of such an order proposed to be made,—

(i) by the Scottish Ministers; or

(ii) within devolved competence (within the meaning of the Scotland Act 1998) by Her Majesty in Council; and

(b) any document or statement to be laid in connection with such an order (or proposed order).

(2) This Schedule has effect in relation to any such order (or proposed order), document or statement subject to the following modifications.

(3) Any reference to Parliament, each House of Parliament or both Houses of Parliament shall be construed as a reference to the Scottish Parliament.

(4) Paragraph 6 does not apply and instead, in calculating any period for the purposes of this Schedule, no account is to be taken of any time during which the Scottish Parliament is dissolved or is in recess for more than four days.

SCHEDULE 3 DEROGATION AND RESERVATION

PART II RESERVATION

At the time of signing the present (First) Protocol, I declare that, in view of certain provisions of the Education Acts in the United Kingdom, the principle affirmed in the second sentence of Article 2 is accepted by the United Kingdom only so far as it is compatible with the provision of efficient instruction and training, and the avoidance of unreasonable public expenditure.

Dated 20 March 1952. Made by the United Kingdom Permanent Representative to the Council of Europe.

NOTES ON TEXT

The text printed above incorporates the following amendments:

s. 1 amended by: (a) Transfer of Functions (Miscellaneous) Order 2001 (SI 2001/3500), sch. 2, para. 7; (b) Secretary of State for Constitutional Affairs Order 2003 (SI 2003/1887), sch. 2, para. 10(1); (c) Human Rights Act 1998 (Amendment) Order 2004 (SI 2004/1574), art. 2(1);

s. 2 amended by: (a) Secretary of State for Constitutional Affairs Order 2003 (SI 2003/1887), sch. 2, para. 10(2); (b) Transfer of Functions (Lord Chancellor and Secretary of State) Order 2005 (SI 2005/3429), sch., para. 3;

s. 4 amended by: (a) Mental Capacity Act 2005, sch. 6, para. 43 (in force by SI 2007/1897); (b) Constitutional Reform Act 2005, sch. 9, para. 66(1) and (2) (in force by SI 2009/1604);

s. 5 amended by Constitutional Reform Act 2005, sch. 9, para. 66(1) and (3) (in force by SI 2009/1604);

s. 6 amended by Constitutional Reform Act 2005, sch. 9, para. 66(1) and (4), and sch. 18, part 5 (in force by SI 2009/1604);

s. 7 amended by: (a) Secretary of State for Constitutional Affairs Order 2003 (SI 2003/1887), sch. 2, para. 10(2); (b) Transfer of Functions (Lord Chancellor and Secretary of State) Order 2005 (SI 2005/3429), sch., para. 3;

s. 14 amended by: (a) Human Rights Act (Amendment) Order 2001 (SI 2001/1216), art. 2; (b) Transfer of Functions (Miscellaneous) Order 2001 (SI 2001/3500), sch. 2, para. 7; (c) Secretary of State for Constitutional Affairs Order 2003 (SI 2003/1887), sch. 2, para. 10(1);

s. 15 amended by Transfer of Functions (Miscellaneous) Order 2001 (SI 2001/3500), sch. 2, para. 7; (c) Secretary of State for Constitutional Affairs Order 2003 (SI 2003/1887), sch. 2, para. 10(1);

s. 16 amended by: (a) Human Rights Act (Amendment) Order 2001 (SI 2001/1216), art. 3; (b) Transfer of Functions (Miscellaneous) Order 2001 (SI 2001/3500), sch. 2, para. 7; (c) Secretary of State for Constitutional Affairs Order 2003 (SI 2003/1887), sch. 2, para. 10(1);

s. 20 amended by: (a) Secretary of State for Constitutional Affairs Order 2003 (SI 2003/1887), sch. 2, para. 10(2); (b) Transfer of Functions (Lord Chancellor and Secretary of State) Order 2005 (SI 2005/3429), sch., para. 3;

s. 21 amended by Human Rights Act 1998 (Amendment) Order 2004 (SI 2004/1574), art. 2(2);

sch. 2, para. 7, inserted by Scotland Act 1998 (Consequential Modifications) Order 2000 (SI 2000/2040), sch., para. 21;

sch. 3, part I, repealed by Human Rights Act (Amendment) Order 2001 (SI 2001/1216), art. 4; new part I inserted by Human Rights Act 1998 (Amendment No. 2) Order 2001 (SI 2001/4032); repealed by Human Rights Act 1998 (Amendment) Order 2005 (SI 2005/1071);

sch. 3, part III, substituted by Human Rights Act 1998 (Amendment) Order 2004 (SI 2004/1574), art. 2(3).

The following provisions are omitted:

s. 18 (appointment of judges to the European Court of Human Rights); sch. 4 (judicial pensions).

Law Reform (Contributory Negligence) Act 1945

(8 & 9 GEO. 6 CHAPTER 28)

1. Apportionment of Liability in Case of Contributory Negligence

(1) Where any person suffers damage as the result partly of his own fault and partly of the fault of any other person or persons, a claim in respect of that damage shall not be defeated by reason of the fault of the person suffering the damage, but the damages recoverable in respect thereof shall be reduced to such extent as the court thinks just and equitable having regard to the claimant's share in the responsibility of the damage: Provided that—

(a) this subsection shall not operate to defeat any defence arising under a contract;

(b) where any contract or enactment providing for the limitation of liability is applicable to the claim, the amount of damages recoverable by the claimant by virtue of this subsection shall not exceed the maximum limit so applicable.

(2) Where damages are recoverable by any person by virtue of the foregoing subsection subject to such reduction as is therein mentioned, the court shall find and record the total damages which would have been recoverable if the claimant had not been at fault.

(5) Where, in any case to which subsection (1) of this section applies, one of the persons at fault avoids liability to any other such person or his personal representative by pleading the Limitation Act 1939, or any other enactment limiting the time within which proceedings may be taken, he shall not be entitled to recover any damages from that other person or representative by virtue of the said subsection.

(6) Where any case to which subsection (1) of this section applies is tried with a jury, the jury shall determine the total damages which would have been recoverable if the claimant had not been at fault and the extent to which those damages are to be reduced.

4. Interpretation

The following expressions have the meanings hereby respectively assigned to them, that is to say—

'court' means, in relation to any claim, the court or arbitrator by or before whom the claim falls to be determined;

'damage' includes loss of life and personal injury;

'fault' means negligence, breach of statutory duty or other act or omission which gives rise to liability in tort or would, apart from this Act, give rise to the defence of contributory negligence.

Law Reform (Miscellaneous Provisions) Act 1934

(24 & 25 GEO. 5 CHAPTER 41)

1. Effect of Death on Certain Causes of Action

(1) Subject to the provisions of this section, on the death of any person after the commencement of this Act all causes of action subsisting against or vested in him shall survive against, or, as the case may be, for the benefit of, his estate. Provided that this subsection shall not apply to causes of action for defamation.

(1A) The right of a person to claim under section 1A of the Fatal Accidents Act 1976 (bereavement) shall not survive for the benefit of his estate on his death.

(2) Where a cause of action survives as aforesaid for the benefit of the estate of a deceased person, the damages recoverable for the benefit of the estate of that person:—

(a) shall not include—

(i) any exemplary damages;

(ii) any damages for loss of income in respect of any period after that person's death;

(c) where the death of that person has been caused by the act or omission which gives rise to the cause of action, shall be calculated without reference to any loss or gain to his estate consequent on his death, except that a sum in respect of funeral expenses may be included.

(4) Where damage has been suffered by reason of any act or omission in respect of which a cause of action would have subsisted against any person if that person had not died before or at the same time as the damage was suffered, there shall be deemed, for the purposes of this Act, to have been subsisting against him before his death such cause of action in respect of that act or omission as would have subsisted if he had died after the damage was suffered.

(5) The rights conferred by this Act for the benefit of the estates of deceased persons shall be in addition to and not in derogation of any rights conferred on the dependants of deceased persons by the Fatal Accidents Acts 1846 to 1908* and so much of this Act as relates to causes of action against the estates of deceased persons shall apply in relation to causes of action under the said Act as it applies in relation to other causes of action not expressly excepted from the operation of subsection (1) of this section.

(6) In the event of the insolvency of an estate against which proceedings are maintainable by virtue of this section, any liability in respect of the cause of action in respect of which the proceedings are maintainable shall be deemed to be a debt provable in the administration of the estate, notwithstanding that it is a demand in the nature of unliquidated damages arising otherwise than by a contract, promise or breach of trust.

[* Includes a reference to the Fatal Accidents Act 1976.]

Misrepresentation Act 1967

(1967 CHAPTER 7)

1. Removal of Certain Bars to Rescission for Innocent Misrepresentation

Where a person has entered into a contract after a misrepresentation has been made to him, and—
(a) the misrepresentation has become a term of the contract, or
(b) the contract has been performed;
or both, then, if otherwise he would be entitled to rescind the contract without alleging fraud, he shall be so entitled, subject to the provisions of this Act, notwithstanding the matters mentioned in paragraphs (a) and (b) of this section.

2. Damages for Misrepresentation

(1) Where a person has entered into a contract after a misrepresentation has been made to him by another party thereto and as a result thereof he has suffered loss, then, if the person making the misrepresentation would be liable to damages in respect thereof had the misrepresentation been made fraudulently, that person shall be so liable notwithstanding that the misrepresentation was not made fraudulently, unless he proves that he had reasonable ground to believe and did believe up to the time the contract was made that the facts represented were true.
(2) Where a person has entered into a contract after a misrepresentation has been made to him otherwise than fraudulently, and he would be entitled, by reason of the misrepresentation, to rescind the contract, then, if it is claimed, in any proceedings arising out of the contract, that the contract ought to be or has been rescinded, the court or arbitrator may declare the contract subsisting and award damages in lieu of rescission, if of opinion that it would be equitable to do so having regard to the nature of the misrepresentation and the loss that would be caused by it if the contract were upheld, as well as to the loss that rescission would cause to the other party.
(3) Damages may be awarded against a person under subsection (2) of this section whether or no the is liable to damages under subsection (1) thereof, but where he is so liable any award under the said subsection (2) shall be taken into account in assessing his liability under the said subsection (1).

3. Avoidance of Provision Excluding Liability for Misrepresentation

If a contract contains a term which would exclude or restrict—
(a) any liability to which a party to a contract may be subject by reason of any misrepresentation made by him before the contract was made; or
(b) any remedy available to another party to the contract by reason of such a misrepresentation,
that term shall be of no effect except in so far as it satisfies the requirement of reasonableness as stated in section II (1) of the Unfair Contract Terms Act 1977; and it is for those claiming that the term satisfies that requirement to show that it does.

5. Saving for Past Transactions

Nothing in this Act shall apply in relation to any misrepresentation or contract of sale which is made before the commencement of this Act.
[*The Act came into force on 22 April 1967.*]

Regulation (EC) No. 44/2001

of 22 December 2000 on jurisdiction and the recognition and enforcement of judgments in civil and commercial matters (OJ L 012, 16.01.2001, pp. 0001–0023)

THE COUNCIL OF THE EUROPEAN UNION,

Having regard to the Treaty establishing the European Community, and in particular Article 61(c) and Article 67(1) thereof,

Having regard to the proposal from the Commission,[1]

Having regard to the opinion of the European Parliament,[2]

Having regard to the opinion of the Economic and Social Committee,[3]

Whereas:

(1) The Community has set itself the objective of maintaining and developing an area of freedom security and justice, in which the free movement of persons is ensured. In order to establish progressively such an area, the Community should adopt, amongst other things, the measures relating to judicial cooperation in civil matters which are necessary for the sound operation of the internal market.

(2) Certain differences between national rules governing jurisdiction and recognition of judgments hamper the sound operation of the internal market. Provisions to unify the rules of conflict of jurisdiction in civil and commercial matters and to simplify the formalities with a view to rapid and simple recognition and enforcement of judgments from Member States bound by this Regulation are essential.

(3) This area is within the field of judicial cooperation in civil matters within the meaning of Article 65 of the Treaty.

(4) In accordance with the principles of subsidiarity and proportionality as set out in Article 5 of the Treaty, the objectives of this Regulation cannot be sufficiently achieved by the Member States and can therefore be better achieved by the Community. This Regulation confines itself to the minimum required in order to achieve those objectives and does not go beyond what is necessary for that purpose.

(5) On 27 September 1968 the Member States, acting under Article 293, fourth indent, of the Treaty, concluded the Brussels Convention on Jurisdiction and the Enforcement of Judgments in Civil and Commercial Matters, as amended by Conventions on the Accession of the New Member States to that Convention (hereinafter referred to as the 'Brussels Convention').[4] On 16 September 1988 Member States and EFTA States concluded the Lugano Convention on Jurisdiction and the Enforcement of Judgments in Civil and Commercial Matters, which is a parallel Convention to the 1968 Brussels Convention. Work has been undertaken for the revision of those Conventions, and the Council has approved the content of the revised texts. Continuity in the results achieved in that revision should be ensured.

(6) In order to attain the objective of free movement of judgments in civil and commercial matters, it is necessary and appropriate that the rules governing jurisdiction and the recognition and enforcement of judgments be governed by a Community legal instrument which is binding and directly applicable.

(7) The scope of this Regulation must cover all the main civil and commercial matters apart from certain well-defined matters.

(8) There must be a link between proceedings to which this Regulation applies and the territory of the Member States bound by this Regulation. Accordingly common rules on jurisdiction should, in principle, apply when the defendant is domiciled in one of those Member States.

(9) A defendant not domiciled in a Member State is in general subject to national rules of jurisdiction applicable in the territory of the Member State of the court seised, and a defendant

---

[1] OJC 376, 28.12.1999, p. 1.

[2] *OJC 146, 17.5.2001, p. 101.*

[3] OJC 117, 26.4.2000, p. 6.

[4] OJ L 299, 31.12.1972, p. 32. OJ L 304, 30.10.1978, p. 1. OJ L 388, 31.12.1982, p. 1. OJ L 285, 3.10.1989, p. 1. OJ C15, 15.1.1997, p. 1. For a consolidated text, see OJC 27, 26.1.1998, p. 1.

domiciled in a Member State not bound by this Regulation must remain subject to the Brussels Convention.

(10) For the purposes of the free movement of judgments, judgments given in a Member State bound by this Regulation should be recognised and enforced in another Member State bound by this Regulation, even if the judgment debtor is domiciled in a third State.

(11) The rules of jurisdiction must be highly predictable and founded on the principle that jurisdiction is generally based on the defendant's domicile and jurisdiction must always be available on this ground save in a few well-defined situations in which the subject-matter of the litigation or the autonomy of the parties warrants a different linking factor. The domicile of a legal person must be defined autonomously so as to make the common rules more transparent and avoid conflicts of jurisdiction.

(12) In addition to the defendant's domicile, there should be alternative grounds of jurisdiction based on a close link between the court and the action or in order to facilitate the sound administration of justice.

(13) In relation to insurance, consumer contracts and employment, the weaker party should be protected by rules of jurisdiction more favourable to his interests than the general rules provide for.

(14) The autonomy of the parties to a contract, other than an insurance, consumer or employment contract, where only limited autonomy to determine the courts having jurisdiction is allowed, must be respected subject to the exclusive grounds of jurisdiction laid down in this Regulation.

(15) In the interests of the harmonious administration of justice it is necessary to minimise the possibility of concurrent proceedings and to ensure that irreconcilable judgments will not be given in two Member States. There must be a clear and effective mechanism for resolving cases of *lis pendens* and related actions and for obviating problems flowing from national differencesas to the determination of the time when a case is regarded as pending. For the purposes of this Regulation that time should be defined autonomously.

(16) Mutual trust in the administration of justice in the Community justifies judgments given in a Member State being recognised automatically without the need for any procedure except in cases of dispute.

(17) By virtue of the same principle of mutual trust, the procedure for making enforceable in one Member State a judgment given in another must be efficient and rapid. To that end, the declaration that a judgment is enforceable should be issued virtually automatically after purely formal checks of the documents supplied, without there being any possibility for the court to raise of its own motion any of the grounds for non-enforcement provided for by this Regulation.

(18) However, respect for the rights of the defence means that the defendant should be able to appeal in an adversarial procedure, against the declaration of enforceability, if he considers one of the grounds for non-enforcement to be present. Redress procedures should also be available to the claimant where his application for a declaration of enforceability has been rejected.

(19) Continuity between the Brussels Convention and this Regulation should be ensured, and transitional provisions should be laid down to that end. The same need for continuity applies as regards the interpretation of the Brussels Convention by the Court of Justice of the European Communities and the 1971 Protocol[5] should remain applicable also to cases already pending when this Regulation enters into force.

(20) The United Kingdom and Ireland, in accordance with Article 3 of the Protocol on the position of the United Kingdom and Ireland annexed to the Treaty on European Union and to the Treaty establishing the European Community, have given notice of their wish to take part in the adoption and application of this Regulation.

(21) Denmark, in accordance with Articles 1 and 2 of the Protocol on the position of Denmark annexed to the Treaty on European Union and to the Treaty establishing the European Community, is not participating in the adoption of this Regulation, and is therefore not bound by it nor subject to its application.*

[5] OJ L 204, 2.8.1975, p. 28. OJ L 304, 30.10.1978, p. 1. OJ L 388, 31.12.1982, p. 1. OJ L 285, 3.10.1989, p. 1. OJ C 15, 15.1.1997, p. 1. For a consolidated text see OJC 27, 26.1.1998, p. 28.

[* The Regulation applies to Denmark as from 1 July 2007 under an agreement between the European Community and Denmark, OJ L 299, 16.11.2005, p. 62 (referred to as the 'EC–Denmark Agreement' in the following editorial notes). Council Decision 2006/325/EC, OJ L 120, 5.5.2006, p. 22; information concerning date of entry into force, OJ L 94, 4.4.2007, p. 70.]

(22) Since the Brussels Convention remains in force in relations between Denmark and the Member States that are bound by this Regulation, both the Convention and the 1971 Protocol continue to apply between Denmark and the Member States bound by this Regulation.
(23) The Brussels Convention also continues to apply to the territories of the Member States which fall within the territorial scope of that Convention and which are excluded from this Regulation pursuant to Article 299 of the Treaty.
(24) Likewise for the sake of consistency, this Regulation should not affect rules governing jurisdiction and the recognition of judgments contained in specific Community instruments.
(25) Respect for international commitments entered into by the Member States means that this Regulation should not affect conventions relating to specific matters to which the Member States are parties.
(26) The necessary flexibility should be provided for in the basic rules of this Regulation in order to take account of the specific procedural rules of certain Member States. Certain provisions of the Protocol annexed to the Brussels Convention should accordingly be incorporated in this Regulation.
(27) In order to allow a harmonious transition in certain areas which were the subject of special provisions in the Protocol annexed to the Brussels Convention, this Regulation lays down, for a transitional period, provisions taking into consideration the specific situation in certain Member States.
(28) No later than five years after entry into force of this Regulation the Commission will present are port on its application and, if need be, submit proposals for adaptations.
(29) The Commission will have to adjust Annexes I to IV on the rules of national jurisdiction, the courts or competent authorities and redress procedures available on the basis of the amendments forwarded by the Member State concerned; amendments made to Annexes V and VI should be adopted in accordance with Council Decision 1999/468/EC of 28 June 1999 laying down the procedures for the exercise of implementing powers conferred on the Commission,[6]

HAS ADOPTED THIS REGULATION:

CHAPTER I SCOPE

Article 1

1. This Regulation shall apply in civil and commercial matters whatever the nature of the court or tribunal. It shall not extend, in particular, to revenue, customs or administrative matters.
2. The Regulation shall not apply to:
   (a) the status or legal capacity of natural persons, rights in property arising out of a matrimonial relationship, wills and succession;
   (b) bankruptcy, proceedings relating to the winding-up of insolvent companies or other legal persons, judicial arrangements, compositions and analogous proceedings;
   (c) social security;
   (d) arbitration.
3. In this Regulation, the term 'Member State' shall mean Member States with the exception of Denmark.[*]

CHAPTER II JURISDICTION

Section 1 General Provisions

Article 2

1. Subject to this Regulation, persons domiciled in a Member State shall, whatever their nationality, be sued in the courts of that Member State.
2. Persons who are not nationals of the Member State in which they are domiciled shall be governed by the rules of jurisdiction applicable to nationals of that State.

[6] OJL 184, 17.7.1999, p. 23.
[[*] Article 1(3) does not apply in relation to Denmark (EC–Denmark Agreement (see footnote to recital (21)), art. 2(a)).]

Article 3

1. Persons domiciled in a Member State may be sued in the courts of another Member State only by virtue of the rules set out in Sections 2 to 7 of this Chapter.
2. In particular the rules of national jurisdiction set out in Annex I shall not be applicable as against them.

Article 4

1. If the defendant is not domiciled in a Member State, the jurisdiction of the courts of each Member State shall, subject to Articles 22 and 23, be determined by the law of that Member State.
2. As against such a defendant, any person domiciled in a Member State may, whatever his nationality, avail himself in that State of the rules of jurisdiction there in force, and in particular those specified in Annex I, in the same way as the nationals of that State.

Section 2 Special Jurisdiction

Article 5

A person domiciled in a Member State may, in another Member State, be sued:

1. (a) in matters relating to a contract, in the courts for the place of performance of the obligation in question;
   (b) for the purpose of this provision and unless otherwise agreed, the place of performance of the obligation in question shall be:
   — in the case of the sale of goods, the place in a Member State where, under the contract, the goods were delivered or should have been delivered,
   — in the case of the provision of services, the place in a Member State where, under the contract, the services were provided or should have been provided,
   (c) if sub-paragraph (b) does not apply then sub-paragraph (a) applies;
2. in matters relating to maintenance, in the courts for the place where the maintenance creditor is domiciled or habitually resident or, if the matter is ancillary to proceedings concerning the status of a person, in the court which, according to its own law, has jurisdiction to entertain those proceedings, unless that jurisdiction is based solely on the nationality of one of the parties;
3. in matters relating to tort, delict or quasi-delict, in the courts for the place where the harmful event occurred or may occur;
4. as regards a civil claim for damages or restitution which is based on an act giving rise to criminal proceedings, in the court seised of those proceedings, to the extent that that court has jurisdiction under its own law to entertain civil proceedings;
5. as regards a dispute arising out of the operations of a branch, agency or other establishment, in the courts for the place in which the branch, agency or other establishment is situated;
6. as settlor, trustee or beneficiary of a trust created by the operation of a statute, or by a written instrument, or created orally and evidenced in writing, in the courts of the Member State in which the trust is domiciled;
7. as regards a dispute concerning the payment of remuneration claimed in respect of the salvage of a cargo or freight, in the court under the authority of which the cargo or freight in question:
   (a) has been arrested to secure such payment, or
   (b) could have been so arrested, but bail or other security has been given;
   provided that this provision shall apply only if it is claimed that the defendant has an interest in the cargo or freight or had such an interest at the time of salvage.

Article 6

A person domiciled in a Member State may also be sued:

1. where he is one of a number of defendants, in the courts for the place where any one of them is domiciled, provided the claims are so closely connected that it is expedient to hear and determine them together to avoid the risk of irreconcilable judgments resulting from separate proceedings;
2. as a third party in an action on a warranty or guarantee or in any other third party proceedings, in the court seised of the original proceedings, unless these were instituted solely with the object of removing him from the jurisdiction of the court which would be competent in his case;

3. on a counterclaim arising from the same contract or facts on which the original claim was based, in the court in which the original claim is pending;
4. in matters relating to a contract, if the action may be combined with an action against the same defendant in matters relating to rights *in rem* in immovable property, in the court of the Member State in which the property is situated.

Article 7

Where by virtue of this Regulation a court of a Member State has jurisdiction in actions relating to liability from the use or operation of a ship, that court, or any other court substituted for this purpose by the internal law of that Member State, shall also have jurisdiction over claims for limitation of such liability.

Section 3 Jurisdiction in Matters Relating to Insurance

Article 8

In matters relating to insurance, jurisdiction shall be determined by this Section, without prejudice to Article 4 and point 5 of Article 5.

Article 9

1. An insurer domiciled in a Member State may be sued:
   (a) in the courts of the Member State where he is domiciled, or
   (b) in another Member State, in the case of actions brought by the policyholder, the insured or a beneficiary, in the courts for the place where the plaintiff is domiciled,
   (c) if he is a co-insurer, in the courts of a Member State in which proceedings are brought against the leading insurer.
2. An insurer who is not domiciled in a Member State but has a branch, agency or other establishment in one of the Member States shall, in disputes arising out of the operations of the branch, agency or establishment, be deemed to be domiciled in that Member State.

Article 10

In respect of liability insurance or insurance of immovable property, the insurer may in addition be sued in the courts for the place where the harmful event occurred. The same applies if movable and immovable property are covered by the same insurance policy and both are adversely affected by the same contingency.

Article 11

1. In respect of liability insurance, the insurer may also, if the law of the court permits it, be joined in proceedings which the injured party has brought against the insured.
2. Articles 8, 9 and 10 shall apply to actions brought by the injured party directly against the insurer, where such direct actions are permitted.
3. If the law governing such direct actions provides that the policy holder or the insured may be joined as a party to the action, the same court shall have jurisdiction over them.

Article 12

1. Without prejudice to Article 11(3), an insurer may bring proceedings only in the courts of the Member State in which the defendant is domiciled, irrespective of whether he is the policy-holder, the insured or a beneficiary.
2. The provisions of this Section shall not affect the right to bring a counterclaim in the court in which, in accordance with this Section, the original claim is pending.

Article 13

The provisions of this Section may be departed from only by an agreement:
1. which is entered into after the dispute has arisen, or
2. which allows the policyholder, the insured or a beneficiary to bring proceedings in courts other than those indicated in this Section, or

3. which is concluded between a policyholder and an insurer, both of whom are at the time of conclusion of the contract domiciled or habitually resident in the same Member State, and which has the effect of conferring jurisdiction on the courts of that State even if the harmful event were to occur abroad, provided that such an agreement is not contrary to the law of that State, or
4. which is concluded with a policyholder who is not domiciled in a Member State, except in so far as the insurance is compulsory or relates to immovable property in a Member State,or
5. which relates to a contract of insurance in so far as it covers one or more of the risks set out in Article 14.

Article 14

The following are the risks referred to in Article 13(5):
1. any loss of or damage to:
   (a) seagoing ships, installations situated offshore or on the high seas, or aircraft, arising from perils which relate to their use for commercial purposes;
   (b) goods in transit other than passengers' baggage where the transit consists of or includes carriage by such ships or aircraft;
2. any liability, other than for bodily injury to passengers or loss of or damage to their baggage:
   (a) arising out of the use or operation of ships, installations or aircraft as referred to in point 1(a) in so far as, in respect of the latter, the law of the Member State in which such aircraft are registered does not prohibit agreements on jurisdiction regarding insurance of such risks;
   (b) for loss or damage caused by goods in transit as described in point 1(b);
3. any financial loss connected with the use or operation of ships, installations or aircraft as referred to in point 1(a), in particular loss of freight or charter-hire;
4. any risk or interest connected with any of those referred to in points 1 to 3;
5. notwithstanding points 1 to 4, all 'large risks' as defined in Council Directive 73/239/EEC,[7] as amended by Council Directives 88/357/EEC[8] and 90/618/EEC,[9] as they may be amended.

Section 4 Jurisdiction over Consumer Contracts

Article 15

1. In matters relating to a contract concluded by a person, the consumer, for a purpose which can be regarded as being outside his trade or profession, jurisdiction shall be determined by this Section, without prejudice to Article 4 and point 5 of Article 5, if:
   (a) it is a contract for the sale of goods on instalment credit terms; or
   (b) it is a contract for a loan repayable by instalments, or for any other form of credit, made to finance the sale of goods; or
   (c) in all other cases, the contract has been concluded with a person who pursues commercial or professional activities in the Member State of the consumer's domicile or, by any means, directs such activities to that Member State or to several States including that Member State, and the contract falls within the scope of such activities.
2. Where a consumer enters into a contract with a party who is not domiciled in the Member State but has a branch, agency or other establishment in one of the Member States, that party shall, in disputes arising out of the operations of the branch, agency or establishment, be deemed to be domiciled in that State.
3. This Section shall not apply to a contract of transport other than a contract which, for an inclusive price, provides for a combination of travel and accommodation.

Article 16

1. A consumer may bring proceedings against the other party to a contract either in the courts of the Member State in which that party is domiciled or in the courts for the place where the consumer is domiciled.

[7] OJ L 228, 16.8.1973, p. 3. Directive as last amended by Directive 2000/26/EC of the European Parliament and of the Council (OJ L 181, 20.7.2000, p. 65). OJ L 330, 29.11.1990, p. 44.
[8] OJ L 172, 4.7.1988, p. 1. Directive as last amended by Directive 2000/26/EC.
[9] OJ L 160, 30.6.2000, p. 37.

2. Proceedings may be brought against a consumer by the other party to the contract only in the courts of the Member State in which the consumer is domiciled.
3. This Article shall not affect the right to bring a counterclaim in the court in which, in accordance with this Section, the original claim is pending.

Article 17

The provisions of this Section may be departed from only by an agreement:
1. which is entered into after the dispute has arisen; or
2. which allows the consumer to bring proceedings in courts other than those indicated in this Section; or
3. which is entered into by the consumer and the other party to the contract, both of whom are at the time of conclusion of the contract domiciled or habitually resident in the same Member State, and which confers jurisdiction on the courts of that Member State, provided that such an agreement is not contrary to the law of that Member State.

Section 5 Jurisdiction over Individual Contracts of Employment

Article 18

1. In matters relating to individual contracts of employment, jurisdiction shall be determined by this Section, without prejudice to Article 4 and point 5 of Article 5.
2. Where an employee enters into an individual contract of employment with an employer who is not domiciled in a Member State but has a branch, agency or other establishment in one of the Member States, the employer shall, in disputes arising out of the operations of the branch, agency or establishment, be deemed to be domiciled in that Member State.

Article 19

An employer domiciled in a Member State may be sued:
1. in the courts of the Member State where he is domiciled; or
2. in another Member State:
   (a) in the courts for the place where the employee habitually carries out his work or in the courts for the last place where he did so, or
   (b) if the employee does not or did not habitually carry out his work in any one country, in the courts for the place where the business which engaged the employee is or was situated.

Article 20

1. An employer may bring proceedings only in the courts of the Member State in which the employee is domiciled.
2. The provisions of this Section shall not affect the right to bring a counterclaim in the court in which, in accordance with this Section, the original claim is pending.

Article 21

The provisions of this Section may be departed from only by an agreement on jurisdiction:
1. which is entered into after the dispute has arisen; or
2. which allows the employee to bring proceedings in courts other than those indicated in this Section.

Section 6 Exclusive Jurisdiction

Article 22

The following courts shall have exclusive jurisdiction, regardless of domicile:
1. in proceedings which have as their object rights *in rem* in immovable property or tenancies of immovable property, the courts of the Member State in which the property is situated.

   However, in proceedings which have as their object tenancies of immovable property concluded for temporary private use for a maximum period of six consecutive months, the courts of the Member State in which the defendant is domiciled shall also have jurisdiction, provided that the tenant is a natural person and that the landlord and the tenant are domiciled in the same Member State;

2. in proceedings which have as their object the validity of the constitution, the nullity or the dissolution of companies or other legal persons or associations of natural or legal persons, or of the validity of the decisions of their organs, the courts of the Member State in which the company, legal person or association has its seat. In order to determine that seat, the court shall apply its rules of private international law;
3. in proceedings which have as their object the validity of entries in public registers, the courts of the Member State in which the register is kept;
4. in proceedings concerned with the registration or validity of patents, trade marks, designs, or other similar rights required to be deposited or registered, the courts of the Member State in which the deposit or registration has been applied for, has taken place or is under the terms of a Community instrument or an international convention deemed to have taken place.
   Without prejudice to the jurisdiction of the European Patent Office under the Convention on the Grant of European Patents, signed at Munich on 5 October 1973, the courts of each Member State shall have exclusive jurisdiction, regardless of domicile, in proceedings concerned with the registration or validity of any European patent granted for that State;
5. in proceedings concerned with the enforcement of judgments, the courts of the Member State in which the judgment has been or is to be enforced.

Section 7 Prorogation of Jurisdiction

Article 23

1. If the parties, one or more of whom is domiciled in a Member State, have agreed that a court or the courts of a Member State are to have jurisdiction to settle any disputes which have arisen or which may arise in connection with a particular legal relationship, that court or those courts shall have jurisdiction. Such jurisdiction shall be exclusive unless the parties have agreed otherwise. Such an agreement conferring jurisdiction shall be either:
   (a) in writing or evidenced in writing; or
   (b) in a form which accords with practices which the parties have established between themselves; or
   (c) in international trade or commerce, in a form which accords with a usage of which the parties are or ought to have been aware and which in such trade or commerce is widely known to, and regularly observed by, parties to contracts of the type involved in the particular trade or commerce concerned.
2. Any communication by electronic means which provides a durable record of the agreement shall be equivalent to 'writing'.
3. Where such an agreement is concluded by parties, none of whom is domiciled in a Member State, the courts of other Member States shall have no jurisdiction over their disputes unless the court or courts chosen have declined jurisdiction.
4. The court or courts of a Member State on which a trust instrument has conferred jurisdiction shall have exclusive jurisdiction in any proceedings brought against a settlor, trustee or beneficiary, if relations between these persons or their rights or obligations under the trust are involved.
5. Agreements or provisions of a trust instrument conferring jurisdiction shall have no legal force if they are contrary to Articles 13, 17 or 21, or if the courts whose jurisdiction they purport to exclude have exclusive jurisdiction by virtue of Article 22.

Article 24

Apart from jurisdiction derived from other provisions of this Regulation, a court of a Member State before which a defendant enters an appearance shall have jurisdiction. This rule shall not apply where appearance was entered to contest the jurisdiction, or where another court has exclusive jurisdiction by virtue of Article 22.

Section 8 Examination as to Jurisdiction and Admissibility

Article 25

Where a court of a Member State is seised of a claim which is principally concerned with a matter over which the courts of another Member State have exclusive jurisdiction by virtue of Article 22, it shall declare of its own motion that it has no jurisdiction.

Article 26

1. Where a defendant domiciled in one Member State is sued in a court of another Member Stateand does not enter an appearance, the court shall declare of its own motion that it has no jurisdiction unless its jurisdiction is derived from the provisions of this Regulation.
2. The court shall stay the proceedings so long as it is not shown that the defendant has been able to receive the document instituting the proceedings or an equivalent document in sufficient time to enable him to arrange for his defence, or that all necessary steps have been taken to this end.
3. Article 19 of Council Regulation (EC) No. 1348/2000 of 29 May 2000 on the service in the Member States of judicial and extra judicial documents in civil or commercial matters[10] shall apply instead of the provisions of paragraph 2 if the document instituting the proceedings or an equivalent document had to be transmitted from one Member State to another pursuant to this Regulation.
4. Where the provisions of Regulation (EC) No. 1348/2000 are not applicable, Article 15 of the Hague Convention of 15 November 1965 on the Service Abroad of Judicial and Extrajudicial Documents in Civil or Commercial Matters shall apply if the document instituting the proceedings or an equivalent document had to be transmitted pursuant to that Convention.

Section 9 Lis Pendens — Related Actions

Article 27

1. Where proceedings involving the same cause of action and between the same parties are brought in the courts of different Member States, any court other than the court first seised shall of its own motion stay its proceedings until such time as the jurisdiction of the court first seised is established.
2. Where the jurisdiction of the court first seised is established, any court other than the court first seised shall decline jurisdiction in favour of that court.

Article 28

1. Where related actions are pending in the courts of different Member States, any court other than the court first seised may stay its proceedings.
2. Where these actions are pending at first instance, any court other than the court first seised may also, on the application of one of the parties, decline jurisdiction if the court first seised has jurisdiction over the actions in question and its law permits the consolidation thereof.
3. For the purposes of this Article, actions are deemed to be related where they are so closely connected that it is expedient to hear and determine them together to avoid the risk of irreconcilable judgments resulting from separate proceedings.

Article 29

Where actions come within the exclusive jurisdiction of several courts, any court other than the court first seised shall decline jurisdiction in favour of that court.

Article 30

For the purposes of this Section, a court shall be deemed to be seised:

1. at the time when the document instituting the proceedings or an equivalent document is lodged with the court, provided that the plaintiff has not subsequently failed to take the steps he was required to take to have service effected on the defendant, or
2. if the document has to be served before being lodged with the court, at the time when it is received by the authority responsible for service, provided that the plaintiff has not subsequently failed to take the steps he was required to take to have the document lodged with the court.

[10] OJ L 160, 30.6.2000, p. 37.

Section 10 Provisional, Including Protective, Measures

Article 31

Application may be made to the courts of a Member State for such provisional, including protective, measures as may be available under the law of that State, even if, under this Regulation, the courts of another Member State have jurisdiction as to the substance of the matter.

CHAPTER III RECOGNITION AND ENFORCEMENT

Article 32

For the purposes of this Regulation, 'judgment' means any judgment given by a court or tribunal of a Member State, whatever the judgment may be called, including a decree, order, decision or writ of execution, as well as the determination of costs or expenses by an officer of the court.

Section 1 Recognition

Article 33

1. A judgment given in a Member State shall be recognised in the other Member States without any special procedure being required.
2. Any interested party who raises the recognition of a judgment as the principal issue in a dispute may, in accordance with the procedures provided for in Sections 2 and 3 of this Chapter, apply for a decision that the judgment be recognised.
3. If the outcome of proceedings in a court of a Member State depends on the determination of an incidental question of recognition that court shall have jurisdiction over that question.

Article 34

A judgment shall not be recognised:
1. if such recognition is manifestly contrary to public policy in the Member State in which recognition is sought;
2. where it was given in default of appearance, if the defendant was not served with the document which instituted the proceedings or with an equivalent document in sufficient time and in such a way as to enable him to arrange for his defence, unless the defendant failed to commence proceedings to challenge the judgment when it was possible for him to do so;
3. if it is irreconcilable with a judgment given in a dispute between the same parties in the Member State in which recognition is sought;
4. if it is irreconcilable with an earlier judgment given in another Member State or in a third State involving the same cause of action and between the same parties, provided that the earlier judgment fulfils the conditions necessary for its recognition in the Member State addressed.

Article 35

1. Moreover, a judgment shall not be recognised if it conflicts with Sections 3,4 or 6 of Chapter II, or in a case provided for in Article 72.
2. In its examination of the grounds of jurisdiction referred to in the foregoing paragraph, the court or authority applied to shall be bound by the findings of fact on which the court of the Member State of origin based its jurisdiction.
3. Subject to the paragraph 1, the jurisdiction of the court of the Member State of origin may not be reviewed. The test of public policy referred to in point 1 of Article 34 may not be applied to the rules relating to jurisdiction.

Article 36

Under no circumstances may a foreign judgment be reviewed as to its substance.

Article 37

1. A court of a Member State in which recognition is sought of a judgment given in another Member State may stay the proceedings if an ordinary appeal against the judgment has been lodged.
2. A court of a Member State in which recognition is sought of a judgment given in Ireland or the United Kingdom may stay the proceedings if enforcement is suspended in the State of origin, by reason of an appeal.

Section 2 Enforcement

Article 38

1. A judgment given in a Member State and enforceable in that State shall be enforced in another Member State when, on the application of any interested party, it has been declared enforceable there.
2. However, in the United Kingdom, such a judgment shall be enforced in England and Wales, in Scotland, or in Northern Ireland when, on the application of any interested party, it has been registered for enforcement in that part of the United Kingdom.

Article 39

1. The application shall be submitted to the court or competent authority indicated in the list in Annex II.
2. The local jurisdiction shall be determined by reference to the place of domicile of the party against whom enforcement is sought, or to the place of enforcement.

Article 40

1. The procedure for making the application shall be governed by the law of the Member State in which enforcement is sought.
2. The applicant must give an address for service of process within the area of jurisdiction of the court applied to. However, if the law of the Member State in which enforcement is sought does not provide for the furnishing of such an address, the applicant shall appoint a representative *ad litem*.
3. The documents referred to in Article 53 shall be attached to the application.

Article 41

The judgment shall be declared enforceable immediately on completion of the formalities in Article 53 without any review under Articles 34 and 35. The party against whom enforcement is sought shall not at this stage of the proceedings be entitled to make any submissions on the application.

Article 42

1. The decision on the application for a declaration of enforceability shall forth with be brought to the notice of the applicant in accordance with the procedure laid down by the law of the Member State in which enforcement is sought.
2. The declaration of enforceability shall be served on the party against whom enforcement is sought, accompanied by the judgment, if not already served on that party.

Article 43

1. The decision on the application for a declaration of enforceability may be appealed against by either party.
2. The appeal is to be lodged with the court indicated in the list in Annex III.
3. The appeal shall be dealt with in accordance with the rules governing procedure in contradictory matters.
4. If the party against whom enforcement is sought fails to appear before the appellate court in proceedings concerning an appeal brought by the applicant, Article 26(2) to (4) shall apply even where the party against whom enforcement is sought is not domiciled in any of the Member States.
5. An appeal against the declaration of enforceability is to be lodged within one month of service thereof. If the party against whom enforcement is sought is domiciled in a Member State other than that in which the declaration of enforceability was given, the time for appealing shall be two months and shall run from the date of service, either on him in person or at his residence. No extension of time may be granted on account of distance.

Article 44

The judgment given on the appeal may be contested only by the appeal referred to in Annex IV.

Article 45

1. The court with which an appeal is lodged under Article 43 or Article 44 shall refuse or revoke a declaration of enforceability only on one of the grounds specified in Articles 34 and 35. It shall give its decision without delay.
2. Under no circumstances may the foreign judgment be reviewed as to its substance.

Article 46

1. The court with which an appeal is lodged under Article 43 or Article 44 may, on the application of the party against whom enforcement is sought, stay the proceedings if an ordinary appeal has been lodged against the judgment in the Member State of origin or if the time for such an appeal has not yet expired; in the latter case, the court may specify the time within which such an appeal is to be lodged.
2. Where the judgment was given in Ireland or the United Kingdom, any form of appeal available in the Member State of origin shall be treated as an ordinary appeal for the purposes of paragraph 1.
3. The court may also make enforcement conditional on the provision of such security as it shall determine.

Article 47

1. When a judgment must be recognised in accordance with this Regulation, nothing shall prevent the applicant from availing himself of provisional, including protective, measures in accordance with the law of the Member State requested without a declaration of enforceability under Article 41 being required.
2. The declaration of enforceability shall carry with it the power to proceed to any protective measures.
3. During the time specified for an appeal pursuant to Article 43(5) against the declaration of enforceability and until any such appeal has been determined, no measures of enforcement may be taken other than protective measures against the property of the party against whom enforcement is sought.

Article 48

1. Where a foreign judgment has been given in respect of several matters and the declaration of enforceability cannot be given for all of them, the court or competent authority shall give it for one or more of them.
2. An applicant may request a declaration of enforceability limited to parts of a judgment.

Article 49

A foreign judgment which orders a periodic payment by way of a penalty shall be enforceable in the Member State in which enforcement is sought only if the amount of the payment has been finally determined by the courts of the Member State of origin.

Article 50

1. An applicant who, in the Member State of origin has benefited from complete or partial legal aid or exemption from costs or expenses, shall be entitled, in the procedure provided for in this Section, to benefit from the most favourable legal aid or the most extensive exemption from costs or expenses provided for by the law of the Member State addressed.
2. However, an applicant who requests the enforcement of a decision given by an administrative authority in Denmark in respect of a maintenance order may, in the Member State addressed, claim the benefits referred to in the first paragraph if he presents a statement from the Danish Ministry of Justice to the effect that he fulfils the financial requirements to qualify for the grant of complete or partial legal aid or exemption from costs or expenses.

Article 51

No security, bond or deposit, however described, shall be required of a party who in one Member State applies for enforcement of a judgment given in another Member State on the ground that he is a foreign national or that he is not domiciled or resident in the State in which enforcement is sought.

Article 52

In proceedings for the issue of a declaration of enforceability, no charge, duty or fee calculated by reference to the value of the matter at issue may be levied in the Member State in which enforcement is sought.

Section 3 Common Provisions

Article 53

1. A party seeking recognition or applying for a declaration of enforceability shall produce a copy of the judgment which satisfies the conditions necessary to establish its authenticity.
2. A party applying for a declaration of enforceability shall also produce the certificate referred to in Article 54, without prejudice to Article 55.

Article 54

The court or competent authority of a Member State where a judgment was given shall issue, at the request of any interested party, a certificate using the standard form in Annex V to this Regulation.

Article 55

1. If the certificate referred to in Article 54 is not produced, the court or competent authority may specify a time for its production or accept an equivalent document or, if it considers that it has sufficient information before it, dispense with its production.
2. If the court or competent authority so requires, a translation of the documents shall be produced. The translation shall be certified by a person qualified to do so in one of the Member States.

Article 56

No legalisation or other similar formality shall be required in respect of the documents referred to in Article 53 or Article 55(2), or in respect of a document appointing a representative *ad litem*.

CHAPTER IV AUTHENTIC INSTRUMENTS AND COURT SETTLEMENTS

Article 57

1. A document which has been formally drawn up or registered as an authentic instrument and is enforceable in one Member State shall, in another Member State, be declared enforceable there, on application made in accordance with the procedures provided for in Articles 38, et seq. The court with which an appeal is lodged under Article 43 or Article 44 shall refuse or revoke a declaration of enforceability only if enforcement of the instrument is manifestly contrary to public policy in the Member State addressed.
2. Arrangements relating to maintenance obligations concluded with administrative authorities or authenticated by them shall also be regarded as authentic instruments within the meaning of paragraph 1.
3. The instrument produced must satisfy the conditions necessary to establish its authenticity in the Member State of origin.
4. Section 3 of Chapter III shall apply as appropriate. The competent authority of a Member State where an authentic instrument was drawn up or registered shall issue, at the request of any interested party, a certificate using the standard form in Annex VI to this Regulation.

Article 58

A settlement which has been approved by a court in the course of proceedings and is enforceable in the Member State in which it was concluded shall be enforceable in the State addressed under the same conditions as authentic instruments. The court or competent authority of a Member State where a court settlement was approved shall issue, at the request of any interested party, a certificate using the standard form in Annex V to this Regulation.

CHAPTER V GENERAL PROVISIONS

Article 59

1. In order to determine whether a party is domiciled in the Member State whose courts are seised of a matter, the court shall apply its internal law.
2. If a party is not domiciled in the Member State whose courts are seised of the matter, then, in order to determine whether the party is domiciled in another Member State, the court shall apply the law of that Member State.

Article 60

1. For the purposes of this Regulation, a company or other legal person or association of natural or legal persons is domiciled at the place where it has its:
   (a) statutory seat, or
   (b) central administration, or
   (c) principal place of business.
2. For the purposes of the United Kingdom and Ireland 'statutory seat' means the registered office or, where there is no such office anywhere, the place of incorporation or, where there is no such place anywhere, the place under the law of which the formation took place.
3. In order to determine whether a trust is domiciled in the Member State whose courts are seised of the matter, the court shall apply its rules of private international law.

Article 61

Without prejudice to any more favourable provisions of national laws, persons domiciled in a Member State who are being prosecuted in the criminal courts of another Member State of which they are not nationals for an offence which was not intentionally committed may be defended by persons qualified to do so, even if they do not appear in person. However, the court seised of the matter may order appearance in person; in the case of failure to appear, a judgment given in the civil action without the person concerned having had the opportunity to arrange for his defence need not be recognised or enforced in the other Member States.

Article 62

1. In Sweden, in summary proceedings concerning orders to pay (betalningsföreläggande) and assistance (handräckning), the expression 'court' includes the 'Swedish enforcement service' (kronofogdemyndighet).
2. In matters relating to maintenance, the expression 'court' includes the Danish administrative authorities.

Article 63

1. A person domiciled in the territory of the Grand Duchy of Luxembourg and sued in the court of another Member State pursuant to Article 5(1) may refuse to submit to the jurisdiction of that court if the final place of delivery of the goods or provision of the services is in Luxembourg.
2. Where, under paragraph 1, the final place of delivery of the goods or provision of the services is in Luxembourg, any agreement conferring jurisdiction must, in order to be valid, be accepted in writing or evidenced in writing within the meaning of Article 23(1)(a).
3. The provisions of this Article shall not apply to contracts for the provision of financial services.
4. The provisions of this Article shall apply for a period of six years from entry into force of this Regulation.

Article 64

1. In proceedings involving a dispute between the master and a member of the crew of a seagoing ship registered in Greece or in Portugal,* concerning remuneration of other conditions of service, a court in a Member State shall establish whether the diplomatic or consular officer responsible for the ship has been notified of the dispute. It may act as soon as that officer has been notified.
2. The provisions of this Article shall apply for a period of six years from entry into force of this Regulation.

[* Article 64 applies to seagoing ships registered in Denmark (EC–Denmark Agreement (see footnote to recital (21)), art. 2(d)).]

Article 65

1. The jurisdiction specified in Article 6(2), and Article 11 in actions on a warranty [or*] guarantee or in any other third party proceedings may not be resorted to [in†] Germany, Austria and Hungary. Any person domiciled in another Member State may be sued in the courts:
   (a) of Germany, pursuant to Articles 68 and 72 to 74 of the Code of Civil Procedure (Zivilproz-essordnung) concerning third-party notices,
   (b) of Austria, pursuant to Article 21 of the Code of Civil Procedure (Zivilprozessordnung) concerning third-party notices;
   (c) of Hungary, pursuant to Articles 58 to 60 of the Code of Civil Procedure (Polgári perrendtartás) concerning third-party notices;
2. Judgments given in other Member States by virtue of Article 6(2), or Article 11 shall be recognised and enforced in Germany, Austria and Hungary in accordance with Chapter III. Any effects which judgments given in these States may have on third parties by application of the provisions in paragraph 1 shall also be recognised in the other Member States.

CHAPTER VIII FINAL PROVISIONS

Article 76

This Regulation shall enter into force on 1 March 2002.‡

This Regulation is binding in its entirety and directly applicable in the Member States in accordance with the Treaty establishing the European Community.

Done at Brussels, 22 December 2000.
For the Council
The President
C. Pierret

NOTES ON TEXT

Articles 66–75 and annexes 1–6 have been omitted.
The text printed above incorporates the corrigendum published in [2001] OJ L 307 28 and the following amendments:
art. 50 supplemented by EC–Denmark Agreement (see footnote to recital (21)), art. 2(b);
art. 62 supplemented by EC–Denmark Agreement (see footnote to recital (21)), art. 2(c);
art. 65 amended by Act of Accession, annex II, point 18.A.3(a).

The Act of Accession referred to above is the Act concerning the conditions of accession of the Czech Republic, the Republic of Estonia, the Republic of Cyprus, the Republic of Latvia, the Republic of Lithuania, the Republic of Hungary, the Republic of Malta, the Republic of Poland, the Republic of Slovenia and the Slovak Republic and the adjustments to the Treaties on which the European Union is founded [2003] OJ L 236 33.

[* *In the Official Journal this word is 'of'.*]
[† This word is omitted in the Official Journal.]
[‡ In relation to Denmark, the Regulation entered into force 1 July 2007 (EC–Denmark Agreement (see footnote to recital (21)), art. 2(e); information concerning date of entry into force, OJ L 94, 4.4.2007, p. 70).]

Sale of Goods Act 1979

(1979 CHAPTER 54)

PART I CONTRACTS TO WHICH ACT APPLIES

1. Contracts to Which Act Applies

(1) This Act applies to contracts of sale of goods made on or after (but not to those made before) 1 January 1894.
(2) In relation to contracts made on certain dates, this Act applies subject to the modification of certain of its sections as mentioned in Schedule 1 below.
(3) Any such modification is indicated in the section concerned by a reference to Schedule 1 below.
(4) Accordingly, where a section does not contain such a reference, this Act applies in relation to the contract concerned without such modification of the section.

PART II FORMATION OF THE CONTRACT

Contract of Sale

2. Contract of Sale

(1) A contract of sale of goods is a contract by which the seller transfers or agrees to transfer the property in goods to the buyer for a money consideration, called the price.
(2) There may a contract of sale between one part owner and another.
(3) A contract of sale may be absolute or conditional.
(4) Where under a contract of sale the property in the goods is transferred from the seller to the buyer the contact is called a sale.
(5) Where under a contract of sale the transfer of the property in the goods is to take place at a future time or subject to some condition later to be fulfilled the contract is called an agreement to sell.
(6) An agreement to sell becomes a sale when the time elapses or the conditions are fulfilled subject to which the property in the goods is to be transferred.

3. Capacity to Buy and Sell

(1) Capacity to buy and sell is regulated by the general law concerning capacity to contract and to transfer and acquire property.
(2) Where necessaries are sold and delivered to a minor or to a person who by reason of drunkenness is incompetent to contract, he must pay a reasonable price for them.
(3) In subsection (2) above 'necessaries' means goods suitable to the condition in life of the minor or other person concerned and to his actual requirements at the time of the sale and delivery.

[*The words 'to a minor or' in s. 3(2) and 'minor or other' in s. 3(3) were repealed, for Scotland only, by the Age of Legal Capacity (Scotland) Act 1991, s. 10 and sch. 2.*]

Formalities of Contract

4. How Contract of Sale Is Made

(1) Subject to this and any other Act, a contract of sale may be made in writing (either with or without seal), or by word of mouth, or partly in writing and partly by word of mouth, or may be implied from the conduct of the parties.
(2) Nothing in this section affects the law relating to corporations.

Subject Matter of Contract

5. Existing or Future Goods

(1) The goods which form the subject of a contract of sale may be either existing goods, owned or possessed by the seller, or goods to be manufactured or acquired by him after the making of the contract of sale, in this Act called future goods.

(2) There may be a contract for the sale of goods the acquisition of which by the seller depends on a contingency which may or may not happen.

(3) Where by a contract of sale the seller purports to effect a present sale of future goods, the contract operates as an agreement to sell the goods.

6. Goods Which Have Perished

Where there is a contract for the sale of specific goods, and the goods without the knowledge of the seller have perished at the time when a contract is made, the contract is void.

7. Goods Perishing before Sale but after Agreement to Sell

Where there is an agreement to sell specific goods and subsequently the goods, without any fault on the part of the seller or buyer, perish before the risk passes to the buyer, the agreement is avoided.

The Price

8. Ascertainment of Price

(1) The price in a contract of sale may be fixed by the contract, or may be left to be fixed in a manner agreed by the contract, or may be determined by the course of dealing between the parties.

(2) Where the price is not determined as mentioned in subsection (1) above the buyer must pay a reasonable price.

(3) What is a reasonable price is a question of fact dependent on the circumstances of each particular case.

9. Agreement to Sell at Valuation

(1) Where there is an agreement to sell goods on the terms that the price is to be fixed by the valuation of a third party, and he cannot or does not make the valuation, the agreement is avoided; but if the goods or any part of them have been delivered to and appropriated by the buyer he must pay a reasonable price for them.

(2) Where the third party is prevented from making the valuation by the fault of the seller or buyer, the party not at fault may maintain an action for damages against the party at fault.

Implied Terms etc.

10. Stipulations about Time

(1) Unless a different intention appears from the terms of the contract, stipulations as to time of payment are not of the essence of a contract of sale.

(2) Whether any other stipulation as to time is or is not of the essence of the contract depends on the terms of the contract.

(3) In a contract of sale 'month' prima facie means calendar month.

11. When Condition to Be Treated as Warranty

(1) This section does not apply to Scotland.

(2) Where a contract of sale is subject to a condition to be fulfilled by the seller, the buyer may waive the condition, or may elect to treat the breach of the condition as a breach of warranty and not as a ground for treating the contract as repudiated.

(3) Whether a stipulation in a contract of sale is a condition, the breach of which may give rise to a right to treat the contract as repudiated, or a warranty, the breach of which may give rise to a claim for damages but not to a right to reject the goods and treat the contract as repudiated, depends in each case on the construction of the contract; and a stipulation may be a condition, though called a warranty in the contract.

(4) Subject to section 35A below where a contract of sale is not severable and the buyer has accepted the goods or part of them, the breach of a condition to be fulfilled by the seller can only be treated as a breach of warranty, and not as a ground for rejecting the goods and treating the contract as repudiated, unless there is an express or implied term of the contract to that effect.

(6) Nothing in this section affects a condition or warranty whose fulfilment is excused by law by reason of impossibility or otherwise.

(7) Paragraph 2 of Schedule 1 below applies in relation to a contract made before 22 April 1967 or (in the application of this Act to Northern Ireland) 28 July 1967.

12. Implied Terms about Title, etc.

(1) In a contract of sale, other than one to which subsection (3) below applies, there is an implied term on the part of the seller that in the case of a sale he has a right to sell the goods, and in the case of an agreement to sell he will have such a right at the time when the property is to pass.

(2) In a contract of sale, other than one to which subsection (3) below applies, there is also an implied term that—
  (a) the goods are free, and will remain free until the time when the property is to pass, from any charge or encumbrance not disclosed or known to the buyer before the contract is made, and
  (b) the buyer will enjoy quiet possession of the goods except so far as it may be disturbed by the owner or other person entitled to the benefit of any charge or encumbrance so disclosed or known.

(3) This subsection applies to a contract of sale in the case of which there appears from the contract or is to be inferred from its circumstances an intention that the seller should transfer only such title as he or a third person may have.

(4) In a contract to which subsection (3) above applies there is an implied term that all charges or encumbrances known to the seller and not known to the buyer have been disclosed to the buyer before the contract is made.

(5) In a contract to which subsection (3) above applies there is also an implied term that none of the following will disturb the buyer's quiet possession of the goods, namely—
  (a) the seller;
  (b) in a case where the parties to the contract intend that the seller should transfer only such title as a third person may have, that person;
  (c) anyone claiming through or under the seller or that third person otherwise than under a charge or encumbrance disclosed or known to the buyer before the contract is made.

(5A) As regards England and Wales and Northern Ireland, the term implied by subsection (1) above is a condition and the terms implied by subsections (2), (4) and (5) above are warranties.

(6) Paragraph 3 of Schedule 1 below applies in relation to a contract made before 18 May 1973.

13. Sale by Description

(1) Where there is a contract for the sale of goods by description, there is an implied term that the goods will correspond with the description.

(1A) As regards England and Wales and Northern Ireland, the term implied by subsection (1) above is a condition.

(2) If the sale is by sample as well as by description it is not sufficient that the bulk of the goods corresponds with the sample if the goods do not also correspond with the description.

(3) A sale of goods is not prevented from being a sale by description by reason only that, being exposed for sale or hire, they are selected by the buyer.

(4) Paragraph 4 of Schedule 1 below applies in relation to a contract made before 18 May 1973.

14. Implied Terms about Quality or Fitness

(1) Except as provided by this section and section 15 below and subject to any other enactment, there is no implied term about the quality or fitness for any particular purpose of goods supplied under a contract of sale.

(2) Where the seller sells goods in the course of a business, there is an implied term that the goods supplied under the contract are of satisfactory quality.

(2A) For the purposes of this Act, goods are of satisfactory quality if they meet the standard that a reasonable person would regard as satisfactory, taking account of any description of the goods, the price (if relevant) and all the other relevant circumstances.

(2B) For the purposes of this Act, the quality of goods includes their state and condition and the following (among others) are in appropriate cases aspects of the quality of goods—
  (a) fitness for all the purposes for which goods of the kind in question are commonly supplied,
  (b) appearance and finish,

(c) freedom from minor defects,
(d) safety, and
(e) durability.

(2C) The term implied by subsection (2) above does not extend to any matter making the quality of goods unsatisfactory—
(a) which is specifically drawn to the buyer's attention before the contract is made,
(b) where the buyer examines the goods before the contract is made, which that examination ought to reveal, or
(c) in the case of a contract for sale by sample, which would have been apparent on a reasonable examination of the sample.

(2D) If the buyer deals as consumer or, in Scotland, if a contract of sale is a consumer contract, the relevant circumstances mentioned in subsection (2A) above include any public statements on the specific characteristics of the goods made about them by the seller, the producer or his representative, particularly in advertising or on labelling.

(2E) A public statement is not by virtue of subsection (2D) above a relevant circumstance for the purposes of subsection (2A) above in the case of a contract of sale, if the seller shows that—
(a) at the time the contract was made, he was not, and could not reasonably have been, aware of the statement,
(b) before the contract was made, the statement had been withdrawn in public or, to the extent that it contained anything which was incorrect or misleading, it had been corrected in public, or
(c) the decision to buy the goods could not have been influenced by the statement.

(2F) Subsections (2D) and (2E) above do not prevent any public statement from being a relevant circumstance for the purposes of subsection (2A) above (whether or not the buyer deals as consumer or, in Scotland, whether or not the contract of sale is a consumer contract) if the statement would have been such a circumstance apart from those subsections.

(3) Where the seller sells goods in the course of a business and the buyer, expressly or by implication, makes known—
(a) to the seller, or
(b) where the purchase price of part of it is payable by instalments and the goods were previously sold by a credit-broker to the seller, to that credit-broker, any particular purpose for which the goods are being bought,

there is an implied term that the goods supplied under the contract are reasonably fit for that purpose, whether or not that is a purpose for which such goods are commonly supplied, except where the circumstances show that the buyer does not rely, or that it is unreasonable for him to rely, on the skill or judgment of the seller or credit-broker.

(4) An implied term about quality or fitness for a particular purpose may be annexed to a contract of sale by usage.

(5) The preceding provisions of this section apply to a sale by a person who in the course of a business is acting as agent for another as they apply to a sale by a principal in the course of a business, except where that other is not selling in the course of a business and either the buyer knows that fact or reasonable steps are taken to bring it to the notice of the buyer before the contract is made.

(6) As regards England and Wales and Northern Ireland, the terms implied by subsections (2) and (3) above are conditions.

(7) Paragraph 5 of Schedule 1 below applies in relation to a contract made on or after 18 May 1973 and before the appointed day, and paragraph 6 in relation to one made before 18 May 1973.

(8) In subsection (7) above and paragraph 5 of Schedule 1 below references to the appointed day are to the day appointed for the purposes of those provisions by an order of the Secretary of State made by statutory instrument.

Sale by Sample

15. Sale by Sample

(1) A contract of sale is a contract for sale by sample where there is an express or implied term to that effect in the contract.

(2) In the case of a contract for sale by sample there is an implied term—
(a) that the bulk will correspond with the sample in quality;

(c) that the goods will be free from any defect, making their quality unsatisfactory, which would not be apparent on reasonable examination of the sample.

(3) As regards England and Wales and Northern Ireland, the term implied by subsection (2) above is a condition.

(4) Paragraph 7 of Schedule 1 below applies in relation to a contract made before 18 May 1973.

Miscellaneous

15A. Modification of Remedies for Breach of Condition in Non-consumer Cases

(1) Where in the case of a contract of sale—

(a) the buyer would, apart from this subsection, have the right to reject goods by reason of a breach on the part of the seller of a term implied by section 13, 14 or 15 above, but

(b) the breach is so slight that it would be unreasonable for him to reject them,

then, if the buyer does not deal as consumer, the breach is not to be treated as a breach of condition but may be treated as a breach of warranty.

(2) This section applies unless a contrary intention appears in, or is to be implied from, the contract.

(3) It is for the seller to show that a breach fell within subsection (1)(b) above.

(4) This section does not apply to Scotland.

PART III EFFECTS OF THE CONTRACT

Transfer of Property as Between Seller and Buyer

16. Goods Must Be Ascertained

Subject to section 20A below where there is a contract for the sale of unascertained goods no property in the goods is transferred to the buyer unless and until the goods are ascertained.

17. Property Passes When Intended to Pass

(1) Where there is a contract for the sale of specific or ascertained goods the property in them is transferred to the buyer at such time as the parties to the contract intend it to be transferred.

(2) For the purpose of ascertaining the intention of the parties regard shall be had to the terms of the contract, the conduct of the parties and the circumstances of the case.

18. Rules for Ascertaining Intention

Unless a different intention appears, the following are rules for ascertaining the intention of the parties as to the time at which the property in the goods is to pass to the buyer.

Rule 1.— Where there is an unconditional contract for the sale of specific goods in a deliverable state the property in the goods passes to the buyer when the contract is made, and it is immaterial whether the time of payment or the time of delivery, or both, be postponed.

Rule 2.— Where there is a contract for the sale of specific goods and the seller is bound to do something to the goods for the purpose of putting them into a deliverable state, the property does not pass until the thing is done and the buyer has notice that it has been done.

Rule 3.— Where there is a contract for the sale of specific goods in a deliverable state but the seller is bound to weigh, measure, test, or do some other act or thing with reference to the goods for the purpose of ascertaining the price, the property does not pass until the act or thing is done and the buyer has notice that it has been done.

Rule 4.— When goods are delivered to the buyer on approval or on sale or return or other similar terms the property in the goods passes to the buyer: —

(a) when he signifies his approval or acceptance to the seller or does any other act adopting the transaction;

(b) if he does not signify his approval or acceptance to the seller but retains the goods without giving notice of rejection, then, if a time has been fixed for the return of the goods, on the expiration of that time, and, if no time has been fixed, on the expiration of a reasonable time.

Rule 5.—(1) Where there is a contract for the sale of unascertained or future goods by description, and goods of that description and in a deliverable state are unconditionally appropriated to the contract, either by the seller with the assent of the buyer or by the buyer with the assent of the seller, the property in the goods then passes to the buyer; and the assent may be express or implied, and may be given either before of after the appropriation is made.

(2) Where, in pursuance of the contract, the seller delivers the goods to the buyer or to a carrier or other bailee or custodier (whether named by the buyer or not) for the purpose of transmission to the buyer, and does not reserve the right of disposal, he is to be taken to have unconditionally appropriated the goods to the contract.

(3) Where there is a contract for the sale of a specified quantity of unascertained goods in a deliverable state forming part of a bulk which is identified either in the contract or by subsequent agreement between the parties and the bulk is reduced to (or to less than) that quantity, then, if the buyer under that contract is the only buyer to whom goods are then due out of the bulk—

(a) the remaining goods are to be taken as appropriated to that contract at the time when the bulk is so reduced; and

(b) the property in those goods then passes to that buyer.

(4) Paragraph (3) above applies also (with the necessary modifications) where a bulk is reduced to (or to less than) the aggregate of the quantities due to a single buyer under separate contracts relating to that bulk and he is the only buyer to whom goods are then due out of that bulk.

19. Reservation of Right of Disposal

(1) Where there is a contract for the sale of specific goods or where goods are subsequently appropriated to the contract, the seller may, by the terms of the contract or appropriation, reserve the right of disposal of the goods until certain conditions are fulfilled; and in such a case, notwithstanding the delivery of the goods to the buyer, or to a carrier or other bailee or custodier for the purpose of transmission to the buyer, the property in the goods does not pass to the buyer until the conditions imposed by the seller are fulfilled.

(2) Where goods are shipped, and by the bill of lading the goods are deliverable to the order of the seller or his agent, the seller is prima facie to be taken to reserve the right of disposal.

(3) Where the seller of goods draws on the buyer for the price, and transmits the bill of exchange and bill of lading to the buyer together to secure acceptance or payment of the bill of exchange, the buyer is bound to return the bill of lading if he does not honour the bill of exchange, and if he wrongfully retains the bill of lading the property in the goods does not pass to him.

20. Passing of Risk

(1) Unless otherwise agreed, the goods remain at the seller's risk until the property in them is transferred to the buyer, but when the property in them is transferred to the buyer the goods are at the buyer's risk whether delivery has been made or not.

(2) But where delivery has been delayed through the fault of either buyer or seller the goods are at the risk of the party at fault as regards any loss which might not have occurred but for such fault.

(3) Nothing in this section affects the duties or liabilities of either seller or buyer as a bailee or custodier of the goods of the other party.

(4) In a case where the buyer deals as consumer or, in Scotland, where there is a consumer contract in which the buyer is a consumer, subsections (1) to (3) above must be ignored and the goods remain at the seller's risk until they are delivered to the consumer.

20A. Undivided Shares in Goods Forming Part of a Bulk

(1) This section applies to a contract for the sale of a specified quantity of unascertained goods if the following conditions are met—

(a) the goods or some of them form part of a bulk which is identified either in the contract or by subsequent agreement between the parties; and

(b) the buyer has paid the price for some or all of the goods which are the subject of the contract and which form part of the bulk.

(2) Where this section applies, then (unless the parties agree otherwise), as soon as the conditions *specified in paragraphs* (a) and (b) of subsection (1) above are met or at such later time as the parties may agree—

(a) property in an undivided share in the bulk is transferred to the buyer, and

(b) the buyer becomes an owner in common of the bulk.

(3) Subject to subsection (4) below, for the purposes of this section, the undivided share of a buyer in a bulk at any time shall be such share as the quantity of goods paid for and due to the buyer out of the bulk bears to the quantity of goods in the bulk at that time.
(4) Where the aggregate of the undivided shares of buyers in a bulk determined under subsection (3) above would at any time exceed the whole of the bulk at that time, the undivided share in the bulk of each buyer shall be reduced proportionately so that the aggregate of the undivided shares is equal to the whole bulk.
(5) Where a buyer has paid the price for only some of the goods due to him out of a bulk, any delivery to the buyer out of the bulk shall, for the purposes of this section, be ascribed in the first place to the goods in respect of which payment has been made.
(6) For the purposes of this section payment of part of the price for any goods shall be treated as payment for a corresponding part of the goods.

20B. Deemed Consent by Co-owner to Dealings in Bulk Goods

(1) A person who has become an owner in common of a bulk by virtue of section 20A above shall be deemed to have consented to—
  (a) any delivery of goods out of the bulk to any other owner in common of the bulk, being goods which are due to him under his contract;
  (b) any dealing with or removal, delivery or disposal of goods in the bulk by any other person who is an owner in common of the bulk in so far as the goods fall within that co-owner's undivided share in the bulk at the time of the dealing, removal, delivery or disposal.
(2) No cause of action shall accrue to anyone against a person by reason of that person having acted in accordance with paragraph (a) or (b) of subsection (1) above in reliance on any consent deemed to have been given under that subsection.
(3) Nothing in this section or section 20A above shall—
  (a) impose an obligation on a buyer of goods out of a bulk to compensate any other buyer of goods out of that bulk for any shortfall in the goods received by that other buyer;
  (b) affect any contractual arrangement between buyers of goods out of a bulk for adjustments between themselves; or
  (c) affect the rights of any buyer under his contract.

Transfer of Title

21. Sale by Person Not the Owner

(1) Subject to this Act, where goods are sold by a person who is not their owner, and who does not sell them under the authority or with the consent of the owner, the buyer acquires no better title to the goods than the seller had, unless the owner of the goods is by his conduct precluded from denying the seller's authority to sell.
(2) Nothing in this Act affects—
  (a) the provisions of the Factors Acts or any enactment enabling the apparent owner of goods to dispose of them as if he were their true owner;
  (b) the validity of any contract of sale under any special common law or statutory power of sale or under the order of a court of competent jurisdiction.

22. Market Overt

(2) This section does not apply to Scotland.
(3) Paragraph 8 of Schedule 1 below applies in relation to a contract under which goods were sold before 1 January 1968 or (in the application of this Act to Northern Ireland) 29 August 1967.

23. Sale under Voidable Title

When the seller of goods has a voidable title to them, but his title has not been avoided at the time of the sale, the buyer acquires a good title to the goods, provided he buys them in good faith and without notice of the seller's defect of title.

24. Seller in Possession after Sale

Where a person having sold goods continues or is in possession of the goods, or of the documents of title to the goods, the delivery or transfer by that person, or by a mercantile agent acting for him, of the goods or documents of title under any sale, pledge, or other disposition thereof, to any person receiving the same in good faith and without notice of the previous sale, has the same effect as if the person making the delivery or transfer were expressly authorised by the owner of the goods to make the same.

25. Buyer in Possession after Sale

(1) Where a person having bought or agreed to buy goods obtains, with the consent of the seller, possession of the goods or the documents of title to the goods, the delivery or transfer by that person, or by a mercantile agent acting for him, of the goods or documents of title, under any sale, pledge, or other disposition thereof, to any person receiving the same in good faith and without notice of any lien or other right of the original seller in respect of the goods, has the same effect as if the person making the delivery or transfer were a mercantile agent in possession of the goods or documents of title with the consent of the owner.

(2) For the purposes of subsection (1) above—

(a) the buyer under a conditional sale agreement is to be taken not to be a person who has bought or agreed to buy goods, and

(b) 'conditional sale agreement' means an agreement for the sale of goods which is a consumer credit agreement within the meaning of the Consumer Credit Act 1974 under which the purchase price or part of it is payable by instalments, and the property in the goods is to remain in the seller (notwithstanding that the buyer is to be in possession of the goods) until such conditions as to the payment of instalments or otherwise as may be specified in the agreement are fulfilled.

(3) Paragraph 9 of Schedule 1 below applies in relation to a contract under which a person buys or agrees to buy goods and which is made before the appointed day.

(4) In subsection (3) above and paragraph 9 of Schedule 1 below references to the appointed day are to the day appointed for the purposes of those provisions by an order of the Secretary of State made by statutory instrument.

26. Supplementary to Sections 24 and 25

In sections 24 and 25 above 'mercantile agent' means a mercantile agent having in the customary course of his business as such agent authority either—

(a) to sell goods, or

(b) to consign goods for the purpose of sale, or

(c) to buy goods, or

(d) to raise money on the security of goods.

PART IV PERFORMANCE OF THE CONTRACT

27. Duties of Seller and Buyer

It is the duty of the seller to deliver the goods, and of the buyer to accept and pay for them, in accordance with the terms of the contract of sale.

28. Payment and Delivery Are Concurrent Conditions

Unless otherwise agreed, delivery of the goods and payment of the price are concurrent conditions, that is to say, the seller must be ready and willing to give possession of the goods to the buyer in exchange for the price and the buyer must be ready and willing to pay the price in exchange for possession of the goods.

29. Rules about Delivery

(1) Whether it is for the buyer to take possession of the goods or for the seller to send them to the buyer is a question depending in each case on the contract, express or implied, between the parties.

(2) Apart from any such contract, express or implied, the place of delivery is the seller's place of business if he has one, and if not, his residence; except that, if the contract is for the sale of specific goods, which to the knowledge of the parties when the contract is made are in some other place, then that place is the place of delivery.

(3) Where under the contract of sale the seller is bound to send the goods to the buyer, but no time for sending them is fixed, the seller is bound to send them within a reasonable time.

(4) Where the goods at the time of sale are in the possession of a third person, there is no delivery by seller to buyer unless and until the third person acknowledges to the buyer that he holds the goods on his behalf; but nothing in this section affects the operation of the issue or transfer of any document of title to goods.

(5) Demand or tender of delivery may be treated as ineffectual unless made at a reasonable hour; and what is a reasonable hour is a question of fact.

(6) Unless otherwise agreed, the expenses of and incidental to putting the goods into a deliverable state must be borne by the seller.

30. Delivery of Wrong Quantity

(1) Where the seller delivers to the buyer a quantity of goods less than he contracted to sell, the buyer may reject them, but if the buyer accepts the goods so delivered he must pay for them at the contract rate.

(2) Where the seller delivers to the buyer a quantity of goods larger than he contracted to sell, the buyer may accept the goods included in the contract and reject the rest, or he may reject the whole.

(2A) A buyer who does not deal as consumer may not—

(a) where the seller delivers a quantity of goods less than he contracted to sell, reject the good sunder subsection (1) above, or

(b) where the seller delivers a quantity of goods larger than he contracted to sell, reject the whole under subsection (2) above,

if the shortfall or, as the case may be, excess is so slight that it would be unreasonable for him to do so.

(2B) It is for the seller to show that a shortfall or excess fell within subsection (2A) above.

(2C) Subsections (2A) and (2B) above do not apply to Scotland.

(2D) Where the seller delivers a quantity of goods—

(a) less than he contracted to sell, the buyer shall not be entitled to reject the goods under subsection (1) above,

(b) larger than he contracted to sell, the buyer shall not be entitled to reject the whole under subsection (2) above,

unless the shortfall or excess is material.

(2E) Subsection (2D) above applies to Scotland only.

(3) Where the seller delivers to the buyer a quantity of goods larger than he contracted to sell and the buyer accepts the whole of the goods so delivered he must pay for them at the contract rate.

(5) This section is subject to any usage of trade, special agreement, or course of dealing between the parties.

31. Instalment Deliveries

(1) Unless otherwise agreed, the buyer of goods is not bound to accept delivery of them by instalments.

(2) Where there is a contract for the sale of goods to be delivered by stated instalments, which are to be separately paid for, and the seller makes defective deliveries in respect of one or more instalments, or the buyer neglects or refuses to take delivery of or pay for one or more instalments, it is a question in each case depending on the terms of the contract and the circumstances of the case whether the breach of contract is a repudiation of the whole contract or whether it is a severable breach giving rise to a claim for compensation but not to a right to treat the whole contract as repudiated.

32. Delivery to Carrier

(1) Where, in pursuance of a contract of sale, the seller is authorised or required to send the goods to the buyer, delivery of the goods to a carrier (whether named by the buyer or not) for the purpose of transmission to the buyer is prima facie deemed to be delivery of the goods to the buyer.

(2) Unless otherwise authorised by the buyer, the seller must make such contact with the carrier on behalf of the buyer as may be reasonable having regard to the nature of the goods and the other circumstances of the case; and if the seller omits to do so, and the goods are lost or damaged in course of transit, the buyer may decline to treat the delivery to the carrier as a delivery to himself or may hold the seller responsible in damages.

(3) Unless otherwise agreed, where goods are sent by the seller to the buyer by a route involving sea transit, under circumstances in which it is usual to insure, the seller must give such notice to the

buyer as may enable him to insure them during their sea transit, and if the seller fails to do so, the goods are at his risk during such sea transit.

(4) In a case where the buyer deals as consumer or, in Scotland, where there is a consumer contract in which the buyer is a consumer, subsections (1) to (3) above must be ignored, but if in pursuance of a contract of sale the seller is authorised or required to send the goods to the buyer, delivery of the goods to the carrier is not delivery of the goods to the buyer.

33. Risk Where Goods Are Delivered at Distant Place

Where the seller of goods agrees to deliver them at his own risk at a place other than that where they are when sold, the buyer must nevertheless (unless otherwise agreed) take any risk of deterioration in the goods necessarily incident to the course of transit.

34. Buyer's Right of Examining the Goods

Unless otherwise agreed, when the seller tenders delivery of goods to the buyer, he is bound on request to afford the buyer a reasonable opportunity of examining the goods for the purpose of ascertaining whether they are in conformity with the contract and, in the case of a contract for sale by sample, of comparing the bulk with the sample.

35. Acceptance

(1) The buyer is deemed to have accepted the goods subject to subsection (2) below—
- (a) when he intimates to the seller that he has accepted them, or
- (b) when the goods have been delivered to him and he does any act in relation to them which is inconsistent with the ownership of the seller.

(2) Where goods are delivered to the buyer, and he has not previously examined them, he is not deemed to have accepted them under subsection (1) above until he has had a reasonable opportunity of examining them for the purpose—
- (a) of ascertaining whether they are in conformity with the contract, and
- (b) in the case of a contract for sale by sample, of comparing the bulk with the sample.

(3) Where the buyer deals as consumer or (in Scotland) the contract of sale is a consumer contract, the buyer cannot lose his right to rely on subsection (2) above by agreement, waiver or otherwise.

(4) The buyer is also deemed to have accepted the goods when after the lapse of a reasonable time he retains the goods without intimating to the seller that he has rejected them.

(5) The questions that are material in determining for the purposes of subsection (4) above whether a reasonable time has elapsed include whether the buyer has had a reasonable opportunity of examining the goods for the purpose mentioned in subsection (2) above.

(6) The buyer is not by virtue of this section deemed to have accepted the goods merely because—
- (a) he asks for, or agrees to, their repair by or under an arrangement with the seller, or
- (b) the goods are delivered to another under a sub-sale or other disposition.

(7) Where the contract is for the sale of goods making one or more commercial units, a buyer accepting any goods included in a unit is deemed to have accepted all the goods making the unit; and in this subsection 'commercial unit' means a unit division of which would materially impair the value of the goods or the character of the unit.

(8) Paragraph 10 of Schedule 1 below applies in relation to a contract made before 22 April 1967 or (in the application of this Act to Northern Ireland) 28 July 1967.

35A. Right of Partial Rejection

(1) If the buyer—
- (a) has the right to reject the goods by reason of a breach on the part of the seller that affects some or all of them, but
- (b) accepts some of the goods, including, where there are any goods unaffected by the breach, all such goods,

he does not by accepting them lose his right to reject the rest.

(2) In the case of a buyer having the right to reject an instalment of goods, subsection (1) above applies as if references to the goods were references to the goods comprised in the instalment.

(3) For the purposes of subsection (1) above, goods are affected by a breach if by reason of the breach they are not in conformity with the contract.

(4) This section applies unless a contrary intention appears in, or is to be implied from, the contract.

36. Buyer Not Bound to Return Rejected Goods

Unless otherwise agreed, where goods are delivered to the buyer, and he refuses to accept them, having the right to do so, he is not bound to return them to the seller, but it is sufficient if he intimates to the seller that he refuses to accept them.

37. Buyer's Liability for Not Taking Delivery of Goods

(1) When the seller is ready and willing to deliver the goods, and requests the buyer to take delivery,and the buyer does not within a reasonable time after such request take delivery of the goods, he is liable to the seller for any loss occasioned by his neglect or refusal to take delivery, and also for a reasonable charge for the care and custody of the goods.

(2) Nothing in this section affects the rights of the seller where the neglect or refusal of the buyer to take delivery amounts to a repudiation of the contract.

PART V RIGHTS OF UNPAID SELLER AGAINST THE GOODS

Preliminary

38. Unpaid Seller Defined

(1) The seller of goods is an unpaid seller within the meaning of this Act—
 (a) when the whole of the price has not been paid or tendered;
 (b) when a bill of exchange or other negotiable instrument has been received as conditional payment, and the condition on which it was received has not been fulfilled by reason of the dishonour of the instrument or otherwise.

(2) In this Part of this Act 'seller' includes any person who is in the position of a seller, as, for instance, an agent of the seller to whom the bill of lading has been indorsed, or a consignor or agent who has himself paid (or is directly responsible for) the price.

39. Unpaid Seller's Rights

(1) Subject to this and any other Act, notwithstanding that the property in the goods may have passed to the buyer, the unpaid seller of goods, as such, has by implication of law—
 (a) a lien on the goods or right to retain them for the price while he is in possession of them;
 (b) in the case of the insolvency of the buyer, a right of stopping the goods in transit after he has parted with the possession of them;
 (c) a right of re-sale as limited by this Act.

(2) Where the property in goods has not passed to the buyer, the unpaid seller has (in addition to his other remedies) a right of withholding delivery similar to and coextensive with his rights of lien or retention and stoppage in transit where the property has passed to the buyer.

PART 5A ADDITIONAL RIGHTS OF BUYER IN CONSUMER CASES

48A. Introductory

(1) This section applies if—
 (a) the buyer deals as consumer or, in Scotland, there is a consumer contract in which the buyer is a consumer, and
 (b) the goods do not conform to the contract of sale at the time of delivery.

(2) If this section applies, the buyer has the right—
 (a) under and in accordance with section 48B below, to require the seller to repair or replace the goods, or
 (b) under and in accordance with section 48C below—
  (i) to require the seller to reduce the purchase price of the goods to the buyer by an appropriate amount, or
  (ii) to rescind the contract with regard to the goods in question.

(3) For the purposes of subsection (1)(b) above goods which do not conform to the contract of sale at any time within the period of six months starting with the date on which the goods were delivered to the buyer must be taken not to have so conformed at that date.

(4) Subsection (3) above does not apply if—
 (a) it is established that the goods did so conform at that date;

(b) its application is incompatible with the nature of the goods or the nature of the lack of conformity.

48B. Repair or Replacement of the Goods

(1) If section 48A above applies, the buyer may require the seller—
(a) to repair the goods, or
(b) to replace the goods.
(2) If the buyer requires the seller to repair or replace the goods, the seller must—
(a) repair or, as the case may be, replace the goods within a reasonable time but without causing significant inconvenience to the buyer;
(b) bear any necessary costs incurred in doing so (including in particular the cost of any labour, materials or postage).
(3) The buyer must not require the seller to repair or, as the case may be, replace the goods if that remedy is—
(a) impossible, or
(b) disproportionate in comparison to the other of those remedies, or
(c) disproportionate in comparison to an appropriate reduction in the purchase price under paragraph (a), or rescission under paragraph (b), of section 48C(1) below.
(4) One remedy is disproportionate in comparison to the other if the one imposes costs on the seller which, in comparison to those imposed on him by the other, are unreasonable, taking into account—
(a) the value which the goods would have if they conformed to the contract of sale,
(b) the significance of the lack of conformity, and
(c) whether the other remedy could be effected without significant inconvenience to the buyer.
(5) Any question as to what is a reasonable time or significant inconvenience is to be determined by reference to—
(a) the nature of the goods, and
(b) the purpose for which the goods were acquired.

48C. Reduction of Purchase Price or Rescission of Contract

(1) If section 48A above applies, the buyer may—
(a) require the seller to reduce the purchase price of the goods in question to the buyer by an appropriate amount, or
(b) rescind the contract with regard to those goods,
if the condition in subsection (2) below is satisfied.
(2) The condition is that—
(a) by virtue of section 48B(3) above the buyer may require neither repair nor replacement of the goods; or
(b) the buyer has required the seller to repair or replace the goods, but the seller is in breach of the requirement of section 48B(2)(a) above to do so within a reasonable time and without significant inconvenience to the buyer.
(3) For the purposes of this Part, if the buyer rescinds the contract, any reimbursement to the buyer may be reduced to take account of the use he has had of the goods since they were delivered to him.

48D. Relation to Other Remedies etc.

(1) If the buyer requires the seller to repair or replace the goods the buyer must not act under subsection (2) until he has given the seller a reasonable time in which to repair or replace (as the case may be) the goods.
(2) The buyer acts under this subsection if—
(a) in England and Wales or Northern Ireland he rejects the goods and terminates the contract for breach of condition;
(b) in Scotland he rejects any goods delivered under the contract and treats it as repudiated;
(c) he requires the goods to be replaced or repaired (as the case may be).

48E. Powers of the Court

(1) In any proceedings in which a remedy is sought by virtue of this Part the court, in addition to any other power it has, may act under this section.

(2) On the application of the buyer the court may make an order requiring specific performance or,in Scotland, specific implement by the seller of any obligation imposed on him by virtue of section 48B above.

(3) Subsection (4) applies if—

(a) the buyer requires the seller to give effect to a remedy under section 48B or 48C above or has claims to rescind under section 48C, but

(b) the court decides that another remedy under section 48B or 48C is appropriate.

(4) The court may proceed—

(a) as if the buyer had required the seller to give effect to the other remedy, or if the other remedy is rescission under section 48C

(b) as if the buyer had claimed to rescind the contract under that section.

(5) If the buyer has claimed to rescind the contract the court may order that any reimbursement to the buyer is reduced to take account of the use he has had of the goods since they were delivered to him.

(6) The court may make an order under this section unconditionally or on such terms and conditions as to damages, payment of the price and otherwise as it thinks just.

48F. Conformity with the Contract

For the purposes of this Part, goods do not conform to a contract of sale if there is, in relation to the goods, a breach of an express term of the contract or a term implied by section 13, 14 or 15 above.

PART VI ACTIONS FOR BREACH OF THE CONTRACT

Seller's Remedies

49. Action for Price

(1) Where, under a contract of sale, the property in the goods has passed to the buyer and he wrongfully neglects or refuses to pay for the goods according to the terms of the contract, the seller may maintain an action against him for the price of the goods.

(2) Where, under a contract of sale, the price is payable on a day certain irrespective of delivery and the buyer wrongfully neglects or refuses to pay such price, the seller may maintain an action for the price, although the property in goods has not passed and the goods have not been appropriated to the contract.

(3) Nothing in this section prejudices the right of the seller in Scotland to recover interest on the price from the date of tender of the goods, or from the date on which the price was payable, as the case may be.

50. Damages for Non-acceptance

(1) Where the buyer wrongfully neglects or refuses to accept and pay for the goods, the seller may maintain an action against him for damages for non-acceptance.

(2) The measure of damages is the estimated loss directly and naturally resulting in the ordinary course of events, from the buyer's breach of contract.

(3) Where there is an available market for the goods in question the measure of damages is prima facie to be ascertained by the difference between the contract price and the market or current price at the time or times when the goods ought to have been accepted or (if no time was fixed for acceptance) at the time of the refusal to accept.

Buyer's Remedies

51. Damages for Non-delivery

(1) Where the seller wrongfully neglects or refuses to deliver the goods to the buyer, the buyer may maintain an action against the seller for damages for non-delivery.

(2) The measure of damages is the estimated loss directly and naturally resulting, in the ordinary course of events, from the seller's breach of contract.

(3) Where there is an available market for the goods in question the measure of damages is prima facie to be ascertained by the difference between the contract price and the market or current price of the goods at the time or times when they ought to have been delivered or (if no time wasfixed) at the time of the refusal to deliver.

52. Specific Performance

(1) If any action for breach of contract to deliver specific or ascertained goods the court may, if it thinks fit, on the plaintiff's application, by its judgment or decree direct that the contract shall be performed specifically, without giving the defendant the option of retaining the goods on payment of damages.
(2) The plaintiff's application may be made at any time before judgment or decree.
(3) The judgment or decree may be unconditional, or on such terms and conditions as to damages, payment of the price and otherwise as seem just to the court.
(4) The provisions of this section shall be deemed to be supplementary to, and not in derogation of, the right of specific implement in Scotland.

53. Remedy for Breach of Warranty

(1) Where there is a breach of warranty by the seller, or where the buyer elects (or is compelled) to treat any breach of a condition on the part of the seller as a breach of warranty, the buyer is not by reason only of such breach of warranty entitled to reject the goods; but he may—
   (a) set up against the seller the breach of warranty in diminution or extinction of the price, or
   (b) maintain an action against the seller for damages for the breach of warranty.
(2) The measure of damages for breach of warranty is the estimated loss directly and naturally resulting, in the ordinary course of events, from the breach of warranty.
(3) In the case of breach of warranty of quality such loss is prima facie the difference between the value of the goods at the time of delivery to the buyer and the value they would have had if they had fulfilled the warranty.
(4) The fact that the buyer has set up the breach of warranty in diminution or extinction of the price does not prevent him from maintaining an action for the same breach of warranty if he has suffered further damage.
(5) This section does not apply to Scotland.

Interest, etc.

54. Interest, etc.

Nothing in this Act affects the right of the buyer or the seller to recover interest or special damages in any case where by law interest or special damages may be recoverable, or to recover money paid where the consideration for the payment of it has failed.

PART VII SUPPLEMENTARY

55. Exclusion of Implied Terms

(1) Where a right duty or liability would arise under a contract of sale of goods by implication of law, it may (subject to the Unfair Contract Terms Act 1977) be negatived or varied by express agreement, or by the course of dealing between the parties, or by such usage as binds both parties to the contract.
(2) An express term does not negative a term implied by this Act unless inconsistent with it.
(3) Paragraph 11 of Schedule 1 below applies in relation to a contract made on or after 18 May 1973 and before 1 February 1978, and paragraph 12 in relation to one made before 18 May 1973.

56. Conflict of Laws

Paragraph 13 of Schedule 1 below applies in relation to a contract made on or after 18 May 1973 and before 1 February 1978, so as to make provision about conflict of laws in relation to such a contract.

57. Auction Sales

(1) Where goods are put up for sale by auction in lots, each lot is prima facie deemed to be the subject of a separate contract of sale.
(2) *A sale by auction is complete* when the auctioneer announces its completion by the fall of the hammer, or in other customary manner; and until the announcement is made any bidder may retract his bid.

(3) A sale by auction may be notified to be subject to a reserve or upset price, and a right to bid may also be reserved expressly by or on behalf of the seller.
(4) Where a sale by auction is not notified to be subject to a right to bid by or on behalf of the seller,it is not lawful for the seller to bid himself or to employ any person to bid at the sale, or for the auctioneer knowingly to take any bid from the seller or any such person.
(5) A sale contravening subsection (4) above may be treated as fraudulent by the buyer.
(6) Where, in respect of a sale by auction, a right to bid is expressly reserved (but not otherwise) the seller or any one person on his behalf may bid at the auction.

59. Reasonable Time a Question of Fact

Where a reference is made in this Act to a reasonable time the question what is a reasonable time is a question of fact.

60. Rights etc. Enforceable by Action

Where a right, duty or liability is declared by this Act, it may (unless otherwise provided by this Act) be enforced by action.

61. Interpretation

(1) In this Act, unless the context or subject matter otherwise requires,—

'action' includes counterclaim and set-off, and in Scotland condescendence and claim and compensation;

'bulk' means a mass or collection of goods of the same kind which—
(a) is contained in a defined space or area; and
(b) is such that any goods in the bulk are interchangeable with any other goods therein of the same number or quantity;

'business' includes a profession and the activities of any government department (including a Northern Ireland department) or local or public authority;

'buyer' means a person who buys or agrees to buy goods;

'consumer contract' has the same meaning as in section 25(1) of the Unfair Contract Terms Act 1977; and for the purposes of this Act the onus of proving that a contract is not to be regarded as a consumer contract shall lie on the seller

'contract of sale' includes an agreement to sell as well as a sale,

'credit-broker' means a person acting in the course of a business of credit brokerage carried on by him, that is a business of effecting introductions of individuals desiring to obtain credit—
(a) to persons carrying on any business so far as it relates to the provision of credit, or
(b) to other persons engaged in credit brokerage;

'defendant' includes in Scotland defender, respondent, and claimant in a multiple-poinding;

'delivery' means voluntary transfer of possession from one person to another; except that in relation to sections 20A and 20B above it includes such appropriation of goods to the contract as results in property in the goods being transferred to the buyer;

'document of title to goods' has the same meaning as it has in the Factors Acts;

'Factors Acts' means the Factors Act 1889, the Factors (Scotland) Act 1890, and any enactment amending or substituted for the same;

'fault' means wrongful act or default;

'future goods' means goods to be manufactured or acquired by the seller after the making of the contract of sale;

'goods' includes all personal chattels other than things in action and money, and in Scotland all corporeal moveables except money; and in particular 'goods' includes emblements, industrial growing crops, and things attached to or forming part of the land which are agreed to be severed before sale or under the contract of sale; and includes an undivided share in goods;

'plaintiff' includes pursuer, complainer, claimant in a multiplepoinding and defendant or defender counter-claiming;

'producer' means the manufacturer of goods, the importer of goods into the European Economic Area or any person purporting to be a producer by placing his name, trade mark or other distinctive sign on the goods;

'property' means the general property in goods, and not merely a special property;
'repair' means, in cases where there is a lack of conformity in goods for the purposes of section 48F of this Act, to bring the goods into conformity with the contract;
'sale' includes a bargain and sale as well as a sale and delivery;
'seller' means a person who sells or agrees to sell goods;
'specific goods' means goods identified and agreed on at the time a contract of sale is made; and includes an undivided share, specified as a fraction or percentage, of goods identified and agreed on as aforesaid;
'warranty' (as regards England and Wales and Northern Ireland) means an agreement with reference to goods which are the subject of a contract of sale, but collateral to the main purpose of such contract, the breach of which gives rise to a claim for damages, but not to a right to reject the goods and treat the contract as repudiated.

(3) A thing is deemed to be done in good faith within the meaning of this Act when it is in fact done honestly, whether it is done negligently or not.
(4) A person is deemed to be insolvent within the meaning of this Act if he has either ceased to pay his debts in the ordinary course of business or he cannot pay his debts as they become due.
(5) Goods are in a deliverable state within the meaning of this Act when they are in such a state that the buyer would under the contract be bound to take delivery of them.
(5A) References in this Act to dealing as consumer are to be construed in accordance with Part I of the Unfair Contract Terms Act 1977; and, for the purposes of this Act, it is for a seller claiming that the buyer does not deal as consumer to show that he does not.
(6) As regards the definition of 'business' in subsection (1) above, paragraph 14 of Schedule 1 below applies in relation to a contract made on or after 18 May 1973 and before 1 February 1978, and paragraph 15 in relation to one made before 18 May 1973.

62. Savings: rules of law etc.

(1) The rules in bankruptcy relating to contracts of sale apply to those contracts, notwithstanding anything in this Act.
(2) The rules of the common law, including the law merchant, except in so far as they are inconsistent with the provisions of this Act, and in particular the rules relating to the law of principal and agent and the effect of fraud, misrepresentation, duress or coercion, mistake, or other invalidating cause, apply to contracts for the sale of goods.
(3) Nothing in this Act or the Sale of Goods 1893 affects the enactments relating to bills of sale, or any enactment relating to the sale of goods which is not expressly repealed or amended by this Act or that.
(4) The provisions of this Act about contracts of sale do not apply to a transaction in the form of a contract of sale which is intended to operate by way of mortgage, pledge, charge, or other security.
(5) Nothing in this Act prejudices or affects the landlord's right of hypothec in Scotland.

64. Short title and commencement

(1) This Act may be cited as the Sale of Goods Act 1979.
(2) This Act comes into force on 1 January 1980.

Unfair Contract Terms Act 1977

(1977 CHAPTER 50)

PART I

1. Scope of Part I

(1) For the purposes of this Part of this Act, 'negligence' means the breach—
  (a) of any obligation, arising from the express or implied terms of a contract, to take reasonable care or exercise reasonable skill in the performance of the contract;
  (b) of any common law duty to take reasonable care or exercise reasonable skill (but not any stricter duty);
  (c) of the common duty of care imposed by the Occupiers' Liability Act 1957 or the Occupier's Liability Act (Northern Ireland) 1957.

(2) This Part of the Act is subject to Part III; and in relation to contracts, the operation of sections 2 to 4 and 7 is subject to the exceptions made by Schedule I.

(3) In the case of both contract and tort, sections 2 to 7 apply (except where the contrary is stated in section 6(4)) only to business liability, that is liability to breach of obligations or duties arising—
  (a) from things done or to be done by a person in the course of a business (whether his own business or another's); or
  (b) from the occupation of premises used for business purposes of the occupier; and references to liability are to be read accordingly but liability of an occupier of premises for breach of an obligation or duty towards a person obtaining access to the premises for recreational or educational purposes, being liability for loss or damage suffered by reason of the dangerous state of the premises, is not a business liability of the occupier unless granting that person such access for the purposes concerned falls within the business purposes of the occupier.

(4) In relation to any breach of duty or obligation, it is immaterial for any purpose of this Part of this Act whether the breach was inadvertent or intentional, or whether liability for it arises directly or vicariously.

2. Negligence Liability

(1) A person cannot by reference to any contract term or to a notice given to persons generally or to particular persons exclude or restrict his liability for death or personal injury resulting from negligence.

(2) In the case of other loss or damage, a person cannot so exclude or restrict his liability for negligence except in so far as the term or notice satisfies the requirement of reasonableness

(3) Where a contract term or notice purports to exclude or restrict liability for negligence a person's agreement to or awareness of it is not of itself to be taken as indicating his voluntary acceptance of any risk.

3. Liability Arising in Contract

(1) This section applies as between contracting parties where one of them deals as consumer or on the other's written standard terms of business.

(2) As against that party, the other cannot by reference to any contract term—
  (a) when himself in breach of contract, exclude or restrict any liability of his in respect of the breach; or
  (b) claim to be entitled—
    (i) to render a contractual performance substantially different from that which was reasonably expected of him, or
    (ii) in respect of the whole of any part of his contractual obligation, to render no performance at all,

except in so far as (in any of the cases mentioned above in this subsection) the contract term satisfies the requirement of reasonableness.

6. Sale and Hire-purchase

(1) Liability for breach of the obligations arising from—
  (a) section 12 of the Sale of Goods Act 1979 (seller's implied undertakings as to title, etc.);
  (b) section 8 of the Supply of Goods (Implied Terms) Act 1973 (the corresponding thing in relation to hire-purchase),

cannot be excluded or restricted by reference to any contract term.

(2) As against a person dealing as consumer, liability for breach of the obligations arising from—
  (a) section 13, 14 or 15 of the 1979 Act (seller's implied undertakings as to conformity of goods with description or sample, or as to their quality of fitness for a particular purpose);
  (b) section 9, 10 or 11 of the 1973 Act (the corresponding things in relation to hire-purchase),

cannot be excluded or restricted by reference to any contract term.

(3) As against a person dealing otherwise than as consumer, the liability specified in subsection (2) above can be excluded or restricted by reference to a contract term, but only in so far as the term satisfies the requirement of reasonableness.

(4) The liabilities referred to in this section are not only the business liabilities defined by section 1(3), but include those arising under any contract of sale of goods or hire-purchase agreement.

11. The 'Reasonableness' Test

(1) In relation to a contract term, the requirement of reasonableness for the purposes of this Part of this Act, section 3 of the Misrepresentation Act 1967 and section 3 of the Misrepresentation Act (Northern Ireland) 1967 is that the term shall have been a fair and reasonable one to be included having regard to the circumstances which were, or ought reasonably to have been, known to or in the contemplation of the parties when the contract was made.

(2) In determining for the purposes of section 6 or 7 above whether a contract term satisfies the requirement of reasonableness, regard shall be had in particular to the matters specified in Schedule 2 to this Act; but this subsection does not prevent the court or arbitrator from holding, in accordance with any rule of law, that a term which purports to exclude or restrict any relevant liability is not a term of the contract.

(3) In relation to a notice (not being a notice having contractual effect), the requirement of reasonableness under this Act is that it should be fair and reasonable to allow reliance on it, having regard to all the circumstances obtaining when the liability arose or (but for the notice) would have arisen.

(4) Where by reference to a contract term or notice a person seeks to restrict liability to a specified sum of money, and the question arises (under this or any other Act) whether the term or notice satisfies the requirement of reasonableness, regard shall be had in particular (but without prejudice to subsection (2) above in the case of contract terms) to —
  (a) the resources which he could expect to be available to him for the purpose of meeting the liability should it arise; and
  (b) how far it was open to him to cover himself by insurance.

(5) It is for those claiming that a contract term or notice satisfies the requirement of reasonableness to show that it does.

12. 'Dealing as Consumer'

(1) A party to contract 'deals as consumer' in relation to another party if—
  (a) he neither makes the contract in the course of a business nor holds himself out as doing so; and
  (b) the other party does make the contract in the course of a business; and
  (c) in the case of a contract governed by the law of sale of goods or hire-purchase, or by section 7 of this Act, the goods passing under or in pursuance of the contract are of a type ordinarily supplied for private use or consumption.

(1A) But if the first party mentioned in subsection (1) is an individual paragraph (c) of that subsection must be ignored.

(2) But the buyer is not in any circumstances to be regarded as dealing as consumer—
  (a) if he is an individual and the goods are second hand goods sold at public auction at which *individuals have* the opportunity of attending the sale in person;
  (b) if he is not an individual and the goods are sold by auction or by competitive tender.

(3) Subject to this, it is for those claiming that a party does not deal as consumer to show that he does not.

13. Varieties of Exemption Clause

(1) To the extent that this Part of this Act prevents the exclusion or restriction of any liability it also prevents—
(a) making the liability or its enforcement subject to restrictive or onerous conditions;
(b) excluding or restricting any right or remedy in respect of the liability, or subjecting a person to any prejudice in consequence of his pursuing any such right or remedy;
(c) excluding or restricting rules of evidence or procedure;
and (to that extent) sections 2 and 5 to 7 also prevent excluding or restricting liability by reference to terms and notices which exclude or restrict the relevant obligation or duty.
(2) But an agreement in writing to submit present or future differences to arbitration is not to betreated under this Part of this Act as excluding or restricting any liability.

14. Interpretation of Part I

In this Part of the Act—
'business' includes a profession and the activities of any government department or local or public authority;
'goods' has the same meaning as in the Sale of Goods Act 1979;
'hire-purchase agreement' has the same meaning as in the Consumer Credit Act 1974;
'negligence' has the meaning given by section 1(1);
'notice' includes an announcement, whether or not in writing, and any other communication or pretended communication; and
'personal injury' includes any disease and any impairment of physical or mental condition.

Section 1(2)

SCHEDULE 1 SCOPE OF SECTIONS 2 TO 4 AND 7

1. Sections 2 to 4 of this Act do not extend to—
(a) any contract of insurance (including a contract to pay an annuity on human life);
(b) any contract so far as it relates to the creation or transfer of an interest in land, or to the termination of such an interest, whether by extinction, merger, surrender, forfeiture or otherwise;
(c) any contract so far as it relates to the creation or transfer of a right or interest in any patent, trade mark, copyright, registered design, technical or commercial information or other intellectual property, or relates to the termination of any such right or interest;
(d) any contract so far as it relates—
(i) to the formation or dissolution of a company (which means any body corporate or unincorporated association and includes a partnership), or
(ii) to its constitution or the rights or obligations of its corporators or members;
(e) any contract so far as it relates to the creation or transfer of securities or of any right or interest in securities.
2. Section 2(1) extends to—
(a) any contract of marine salvage or towage;
(b) any charterparty of a ship or hovercraft; and
(c) any contract for the carriage of goods by ship or hovercraft;
but subject to this sections 2 to 4 and 7 do not extend to any such contract except in favour of a person dealing as a consumer.
3. Where goods are carried by ship or hovercraft in pursuance of a contract which either—
(a) specifies that as the means of carriage over part of the journey to be covered, or
(b) makes no provision as to the means of carriage and does not exclude that means, then sections 2(2), 3 and 4 do not, except in favour of a person dealing as consumer, extend to the contract as it operates for and in relation to the carriage of the goods by that means.
4. Section 2(1) and (2) do not extend to a contract of employment, except in favour of the employee.
5. Section 2(1) does not affect the validity of any discharge and indemnity given by a person, on or in connection with an award to him of compensation for pneumoconiosis attributable to employment in the coal industry, in respect of any further claim arising from his contracting the disease.

Sections 11(2) and 24(2)

SCHEDULE 2

'GUIDELINES' FOR APPLICATION OF REASONABLENESS TEST

The matters to which regard is to be had in particular for the purposes of sections 6(3), 7(3) and (4), 20 and 21 are any of the following which appear to be relevant—

(a) the strength of the bargaining positions of the parties relative to each other, taking into account (among other things) alternative means by which the customer's requirements could have been met;

(b) whether the customer received an inducement to agree to the term, or in accepting it had an opportunity of entering into a similar contract with other persons, but without having to accept a similar term;

(c) whether the customer knew or ought reasonably to have known of the existence and extent of the term (having regard, among other things, to any custom of the trade and any previous course of dealing between the parties);

(d) where the term excludes or restricts any relevant liability if some condition is not complied with, whether it was reasonable at the time of the contract to expect that compliance with that condition would be practicable;

(e) whether the goods were manufactured, processed or adapted to the special order of the customer.

Index

This is a subject index to the contents of the **procedural checklists** (FC), **chapters 1** to **92** and **appendix 1** of *Blackstone's Civil Practice*.

Each heading in **chapters 1** to **92** is numbered. The first heading in **chapter 2** is **2.1**, the second is **2.2**, and so on. This index refers to headings by their numbers.

Appendix 1 consists of the Civil Procedure Rules (CPR) and supplementing practice directions (PDs). The Civil Procedure Rules are divided into numbered Parts. The Parts are divided into rules.

In this index, **CPR** followed by a number is a reference to a rule in the Civil Procedure Rules in **appendix 1**. For example, **CPR 55.7** is a reference to rule 55.7 in **appendix 1**.

A Part of the Civil Procedure Rules may have one or more supplementing practice directions. A practice direction is given the same number as the Part which it supplements. For example, the first practice direction supplementing Part 6 is **PD 6A**, the second is **PD 6B**, and so on. Those numbers are used in this index to identify practice directions supplementing Parts of the Civil Procedure Rules. The other practice directions in **appendix 1** are identified as follows:

PD Directors Disqualification	Practice Direction — Directors Disqualification Proceedings
PD Equality	Practice Direction — Proceedings under Enactments Relating to Equality
PD Insolvency	Practice Direction — Insolvency Proceedings
PG McKenzie Friends	Practice Guidance: McKenzie Friends (Civil and Family Courts)
PG Twitter	Interim Practice Guidance: The Use of Live Text-based Forms of Communication (including Twitter) from Court for the Purposes of Fair and Accurate Reporting
QB Masters' PD(11)	Queen's Bench Masters Practice Direction (11) — Claims Judgments and Enforcement of Judgments in Foreign Currency

2014

January

M		6	13	20	27
T		7	14	21	28
W	1	8	15	22	29
T	2	9	16	23	30
F	3	10	17	24	31
S	4	11	18	25	
S	5	12	19	26	

February

M		3	10	17	24
T		4	11	18	25
W		5	12	19	26
T		6	13	20	27
F		7	14	21	28
S	1	8	15	22	
S	2	9	16	23	

March

M		3	10	17	24	31
T		4	11	18	25	
W		5	12	19	26	
T		6	13	20	27	
F		7	14	21	28	
S	1	8	15	22	29	
S	2	9	16	23	30	

April

M		7	14	21	28
T	1	8	15	22	29
W	2	9	16	23	30
T	3	10	17	24	
F	4	11	18	25	
S	5	12	19	26	
S	6	13	20	27	

May

M		5	12	19	26
T		6	13	20	27
W		7	14	21	28
T	1	8	15	22	29
F	2	9	16	23	30
S	3	10	17	24	31
S	4	11	18	25	

June

M		2	9	16	23	30
T		3	10	17	24	
W		4	11	18	25	
T		5	12	19	26	
F		6	13	20	27	
S		7	14	21	28	
S	1	8	15	22	29	

July

M		7	14	21	28
T	1	8	15	22	29
W	2	9	16	23	30
T	3	10	17	24	31
F	4	11	18	25	
S	5	12	19	26	
S	6	13	20	27	

August

M		4	11	18	25
T		5	12	19	26
W		6	13	20	27
T		7	14	21	28
F	1	8	15	22	29
S	2	9	16	23	30
S	3	10	17	24	31

September

M	1	8	15	22	29
T	2	9	16	23	30
W	3	10	17	24	
T	4	11	18	25	
F	5	12	19	26	
S	6	13	20	27	
S	7	14	21	28	

October

M		6	13	20	27
T		7	14	21	28
W	1	8	15	22	29
T	2	9	16	23	30
F	3	10	17	24	31
S	4	11	18	25	
S	5	12	19	26	

November

M		3	10	17	24
T		4	11	18	25
W		5	12	19	26
T		6	13	20	27
F		7	14	21	28
S	1	8	15	22	29
S	2	9	16	23	30

December

M	1	8	15	22	29
T	2	9	16	23	30
W	3	10	17	24	31
T	4	11	18	25	
F	5	12	19	26	
S	6	13	20	27	
S	7	14	21	28	